NAVE'S *complete* WORD STUDY TOPICAL BIBLE

ORVILLE J. NAVE

Edited by Warren Baker

NAVE'S *complete* WORD STUDY TOPICAL BIBLE

God's Word to you is our highest calling.

Nave's Complete Word Study Topical Bible
By Orville James Nave
Edited by Warren Baker

Published by AMG Publishers
6815 Shallowford Rd.
Chattanooga, TN 37421

ISBN 0-89957-679-6

First printing—June 2005

Cover designed by ImageWright, Chattanooga, Tennessee
Interior design and typesetting by Warren Baker
Proofreading by Doris Barnes, Lisa Bluford, Melissa Jenks, Charlyne Kirkendoll, Claire Lickert, Cheri Mullins, Gayle Pearson, Betty Stone, and Ray Whittaker
Database provided by Randy Beck, president of WORDsearch® Corp.
For more information see www.wordsearchbible.com.
Database processing by Karen Bishop of WORDsearch® Corp.

Library of Congress Cataloging-in-Publication Data

Nave, Orville J. (Orville James), 1841-1917.
Nave's complete word study topical Bible / by Orville James Nave ; edited by Warren Baker.
p. cm.
Rev. ed. of: Nave's topical Bible.
Summary: "Arrangement of Scripture quotes and references under more than 22,000 topics and subtopics, with an index of Strong's numbers for every word in the text of the KJV Bible"--Provided by publisher.
Includes index.
ISBN-13: 978-0-89957-679-4 (hardcover : alk. paper)
ISBN-10: 0-89957-679-6 (hardcover : alk. paper)
1. Bible--Indexes. I. Title: Complete word study topical Bible. II. Baker, Warren, 1961- III. Nave, Orville J. (Orville James), 1841-1917. Topical Bible. IV. Title.

BS432.N3 2005
220.3--dc22

2005013074

Printed in Canada
10 09 08 07 06 05 –T– 10 9 8 7 6 5 4 3 2 1

To my sons,
Ben, Joey, and Tim Baker

Preface to the Original Edition

The object of this book is to bring together in cyclopedic form and under familiar headings all that the Bible contains on particular subjects. The subjects formulated are of practical value to every profession and to all who desire to consult the Bible.

The method pursued in preparing this Digest has been, first, to analyze topically each verse of the Bible, each series of verses, and each chapter and series of chapters; and, second, to group under suitable headings all the Scriptures related to the subjects found in the analysis. The first verse in the Bible may serve to illustrate: "In the beginning God created the heaven and the earth." "In the beginning." Some authorities interpret this phrase as meaning the beginning of time; therefore the author noted, "Time, Beginning of, Gen. 1:1." Other authorities interpret it as referring to the beginning of the creation; therefore the author noted, "Creation, Beginning of, Gen. 1:1." "In the beginning God created." The author noted, "God, Creator, Gen. 1:1." "In the beginning God created the heaven." Note, "Heaven, Creation of, Gen. 1:1." "In the beginning God created the heaven and the earth." "Earth, Creation of, Gen. 1:1." This process was faithfully adhered to throughout the work.

Three classifications of Scripture verses have been published in America, two of which are erroneously styled "a complete analysis" of the Scriptures. Each author followed, with slight and unimportant modifications in arrangement, Mr. Matthew Talbot's classification of verses made in England one hundred years ago. Mr. Talbot's mode of treatment was to arrange all verses of the Bible, as best he might, under thirty general headings. When each verse had been assigned under the heading to which it seemed best adapted the work he undertook was complete. He used no verse more than once, regardless of the many different and distinct subjects it might contain. It was consequently a classification of verses rather than a topical analysis of matter. American publishers have followed this erroneous mode of treatment, and as a result the so-called analyses of the Scriptures hitherto offered to Bible students and Christian teachers have been unsatisfactory. This Digest is an analysis of the matter without regard to verse divisions except for convenience of reference. Verses, parts of verses, series of verses, and chapters are cited or quoted as often as they contain distinct subjects. Numerous verses are repeated from one to thirty times each, according to the number of subjects they contain and their position in extensive citations or extracts. The verse before referred to has been quoted or cited under five different and equally important headings, while other analyses quote it only once. The familiar verse, Rom. 5:1, "Therefore being justified by faith, we have peace with God through our Lord Jesus Christ," is cited under nine headings; namely, Justification, Faith, Peace, Salvation by Faith, Jesus the Saviour, Atonement, Mediation, Propitiation, and Reconciliation, while in other analyses it is used but once, under Justification.

Passages variously interpreted by different religious schools or accepted authorities are cited under the subjects they are claimed to support, without reference to the personal views of the author.

To provide against doubt that this Digest would be complete in its classification of matter respecting the principles and practice of law, I secured the assistance of the Honorable John Welch, Judge of the Supreme Court of the State of Ohio, U.S.A., and author of *Welch's Index-Digest of Ohio Decisions.* Judge Welch made a consecutive and analytical study of the Bible for this work, from the standpoint of a learned jurist and successful author, and his notes have been incorporated with the author's. Lawyers, judges, legislators, and statesmen may, therefore, rely on this work as a complete and valuable handbook of the Bible for the purposes of their professions. All subjects relating to the principles and practice of law are classified under headings in common use.

Some subjects abound in the Scriptures to such an extent, and are used so frequently by religious teachers and others, that, were references only given in this work to the books, chapters, and verses containing them, the student would stagger at the thought of developing the topics. In order to make this class of subjects quickly and easily available the verses, or parts of verses, themselves are printed. This method of treatment might have been extended, but the size of a convenient volume had to be taken into consideration. Minor topics are made almost equally available by brief sub-topical divisions followed by references.

One of the most important, and it is believed valuable, features of this book is its elaborate system of cross references to kindred and antithetical subjects. Wide scope is thus given each subject by connecting it with those to which it is related.

Under the sub-topic, INSTANCES OF, are grouped all the illustrative facts that occur in the Scriptures relating to each subject. As a book of illustrations this work should prove valuable. It also contains numerous and elaborate Bible readings, with a wide range of subjects.

An Index contains a handy reference to the pages and columns in which each verse of the Bible is quoted or referred to throughout the work, to enable anyone who may be studying any particular verse to find what topics the author noted in it, and with what Scriptures it is grouped.

It was not the object of the author in preparing this Digest to develop religious subjects only, but to note and classify everything found in the Scriptures. It is believed that it is approximately exhaustive. It is the result of fourteen years of delightful and untiring study of the word of God, aided by my wife, Anna Semans Nave, who has been an indefatigable assistant from the inception of the work. All pioneer works of an analytic character, as well as all noteworthy commentaries, have been consulted, in order to bring into it all useful materials to be found. Its preparation was inspired by the obvious deficiency of such helps in the use of the Scriptures. This deficiency was felt by the author in preparing sermons, lectures, and other forms of religious instruction. The quiet of army garrisons, apart from the rush and distraction of dense communities, has been favorable to its careful preparation. With the belief that it will contribute to make the Scriptures more quickly, easily, and fully available where particular subjects are under consideration, I offer it to the public.

ORVILLE J. NAVE

Fort McPherson, GA

Preface to the Complete Word Study Edition

Orville J. Nave originally published his topical Bible in 1896, while he was serving as an army chaplain. Eleven years later, it was revised and published as Nave's Topical Bible. With Bible references organized under more than 22,000 topics and subtopics, his work has become a classic reference tool for every Christian's library. Unlike a concordance, which lists references under the words of Scripture, Nave listed them under topics, allowing the reader quick access to what the Bible says about people, topics, and places.

Nave's Complete Word Study Topical Bible represents a new and revised edition of Nave's wonderful reference tool. The text has been completely reset in a layout that is easy to read and easy to follow. The Scripture text that accompanies each topic has been restructured as well. In previous editions, long passages of Scripture were cited, but many references to single verses of Scripture were not cited. This meant that Scripture citations for some topics were very complete, but many others required the reader to look up verse after verse to study the topic. In an effort to make this tool more useful overall, the Nave's Complete Word Study Topical Bible cites the KJV text of Scripture for almost every single-verse reference under every topic. This gives the reader a quicker review of what the Bible says about each topic. The references for longer passages are merely listed in the work, so that the user can do an in-depth study of any topic.

In addition, the words of Christ are underlined for easy identification. This way you can quickly discern what the Lord Jesus had to say on each topic. There is also the Complete Word Study Translation Guide. This index lists every English word found in the KJV Bible and lists the Strongs number for the original language words (Hebrew, Aramaic, and Greek) that were translated by they English word in the text of the KJV Bible.

Nave's Complete Word Study Topical Bible brings the awesome research and work of Orville Nave into the twenty-first century. Not only have the Scripture passages been restructured and the type reset, but also the entire text of the topical Bible is provided for you in a popular Bible software program on a CD found at the back of the book.

WARREN BAKER

Chattanooga, TN

Table of Contents

How to Use the Topical Bible

JESUS, Humility of
Lk 5:27–28; Ac 8:32–33; Php 2:7–8
Zec 9:9 — Rejoice greatly, O daughter of Zion; shout, O daughter of Jerusalem: behold, thy King cometh unto thee: he *is* just, and having salvation; lowly, and riding upon an ass, and upon a colt the foal of an ass.
Mt 9:10 — And it came to pass, as Jesus sat at meat in the house, behold, many publicans and sinners came and sat down with him and his disciples.
Mt 21:5 — Tell ye the daughter of Sion, Behold, thy King cometh unto thee, meek, and sitting upon an ass, and a colt the foal of an ass.
Mk 2:14 — And as he passed by, he saw Levi the *son* of Alphaeus sitting at the receipt of custom, and said unto him, Follow me. And he arose and followed him.
Lk 22:27 — For whether *is* greater, he that sitteth at meat, or he that serveth? *is* not he that sitteth at meat? but I am among you as he that serveth.
Jn 13:5 — After that he poureth water into a bason, and began to wash the disciples' feet, and to wipe *them* with the towel wherewith he was girded.
Jn 13:14 — If I then, *your* Lord and Master, have washed your feet; ye also ought to wash one another's feet.
2Co 8:9 — For ye know the grace of our Lord Jesus Christ, that, though he was rich, yet for your sakes he became poor, that ye through his poverty might be rich.
2Co 10:1 — Now I Paul myself beseech you by the meekness and gentleness of Christ, who in presence *am* base among you, but being absent am bold toward you:

See: Jesus, Meekness of
See: Meekness

The Topical Bible includes more than 22,000 topics and subtopics.

Longer scripture passages are conveniently listed under each topic.

Scripture text is underlined to indicate the Words of Christ.

The text is given for almost every single-verse reference.

Cross references to other entries in the Topical Bible are listed throughout.

How to Use the Translation Index

mind, ed, ful, ing, s — 2142, 3336, 3824, 5315, 5973/3820, 6310, 7307 ✉ ***363, 1011, 1014, 1106, 1271, 1374, 1771, 1878, 3195, 3403, 3421, 3540, 3563, 3661, 3675, 4288, 4290, 4993, 4995, 5012, 5279, 5426, 5427, 5590***: Ne 4:6; Hab 1:11; Ac 20:13

mingle, d — 1101, 3610, 3947, 4537, 6148, 6151, 6154 ✉ **3396**: Ex 6:51; Da 2:43; Mt 27:34

Miniamin — 4509: *2Ch 31:15; Ne 12:17, 41*

MINISTER, ed, eth, ing, s; ministration; ministry — 1777, 3027, 5656, 6399, 8120, 8334, 8335 ✉ ***1247, 1248, 1249, 1325, 2023, 2038, 2418, 3008, 3009, 3010, 3011, 3930, 5256, 5257, 5524***: Nu 4:12; 1Sa 2:18; Lk 1:23; Gal 3:5

God's ministers:
- commissioned by God: Ex 3:10; Isa 6:8; Mt 28:19
- requirements of:
  - receiving God's words: Eze 3:10
  - living a godly lifestyle: 1Ti 3:2-4, 6, 7
- objectives of:
  - being ambassadors for Christ: 2Co 5:20
  - testifying to the gospel: Ac 20:24
- responsibilities of:
  - being an example to the flock: 1Ti 4:12
  - being responsible for the flock: Heb 13:17
  - exercising spiritual gifts: 1Ti 4:14

Minni — 4508: *Jer 51:27*

Minnith — 4511: *Jgs 11:33; Eze 27:17*

When a word is in all caps, there is additional information at the end of the entry.

OT Strong's numbers are listed in plain type.

The symbol ✉ is used to separate OT Strong's numbers from NT Strong's numbers.

NT Strong's numbers are listed in bold italic type.

Verse references in italics indicate that all occurrences of the word are listed.

Books of the Bible

Genesis	Ge	Nahum	Na
Exodus	Ex	Habakkuk	Hab
Leviticus	Le	Zephaniah	Zep
Numbers	Nu	Haggai	Hag
Deuteronomy	Dt	Zechariah	Zec
Joshua	Jos	Malachi	Mal
Judges	Jgs	Matthew	Mt
Ruth	Ru	Mark	Mk
1 Samuel	1Sa	Luke	Lk
2 Samuel	2Sa	John	Jn
1 Kings	1Ki	Acts	Ac
2 Kings	2Ki	Romans	Ro
1 Chronicles	1Ch	1 Corinthians	1Co
2 Chronicles	2Ch	2 Corinthians	2Co
Ezra	Ezr	Galatians	Gal
Nehemiah	Ne	Ephesians	Eph
Esther	Est	Philippians	Php
Job	Job	Colossians	Col
Psalms	Ps	1 Thessalonians	1Th
Proverbs	Pr	2 Thessalonians	2Th
Ecclesiastes	Ecc	1 Timothy	1Ti
Song of Songs	SS	2 Timothy	2Ti
Isaiah	Isa	Titus	Tit
Jeremiah	Jer	Philemon	Phm
Lamentations	La	Hebrews	Heb
Ezekiel	Eze	James	Jas
Daniel	Da	1 Peter	1Pe
Hosea	Hos	2 Peter	2Pe
Joel	Joel	1 John	1Jn
Amos	Am	2 John	2Jn
Obadiah	Ob	3 John	3Jn
Jonah	Jnh	Jude	Jude
Micah	Mic	Revelation	Rev

Topical Bible

A

AARON

• Lineage of.

Ex 6:16–20; 1Ch 6:2–3

Jos 21:4 — And the lot came out for the families of the Kohathites: and the children of Aaron the priest, *which were* of the Levites, had by lot out of the tribe of Judah, and out of the tribe of Simeon, and out of the tribe of Benjamin, thirteen cities.

Jos 21:10 — Which the children of Aaron, *being* of the families of the Kohathites, *who were* of the children of Levi, had: for theirs was the first lot.

1Ch 23:13 — The sons of Amram; Aaron and Moses: and Aaron was separated, that he should sanctify the most holy things, he and his sons for ever, to burn incense before the LORD, to minister unto him, and to bless in his name for ever.

• Marriage of.

Ex 6:23 — And Aaron took him Elisheba, daughter of Amminadab, sister of Naashon, to wife; and she bare him Nadab, and Abihu, Eleazar, and Ithamar.

• Children of.

1Ch 24:1–2

Ex 6:23 — And Aaron took him Elisheba, daughter of Amminadab, sister of Naashon, to wife; and she bare him Nadab, and Abihu, Eleazar, and Ithamar.

Ex 6:25 — And Eleazar Aaron's son took him *one* of the daughters of Putiel to wife; and she bare him Phinehas: these *are* the heads of the fathers of the Levites according to their families.

1Ch 6:3 — And the children of Amram; Aaron, and Moses, and Miriam. The sons also of Aaron; Nadab, and Abihu, Eleazar, and Ithamar.

• Descendants of.

1Ch 6:3–15; 6:50–53; 24:1–31

Ex 6:23 — And Aaron took him Elisheba, daughter of Amminadab, sister of Naashon, to wife; and she bare him Nadab, and Abihu, Eleazar, and Ithamar.

Ex 6:25 — And Eleazar Aaron's son took him *one* of the daughters of Putiel to wife; and she bare him Phinehas: these *are* the heads of the fathers of the Levites according to their families.

• Meets Moses in the wilderness and is made spokesman for Moses.

Ex 4:14–16; 4:27–31; 7:1–2

• Inspiration of.

Ex 12:1 — And the LORD spake unto Moses and Aaron in the land of Egypt, saying,

Le 10:8 — And the LORD spake unto Aaron, saying,

Le 11:1 — And the LORD spake unto Moses and to Aaron, saying unto them,

Le 13:1 — And the LORD spake unto Moses and Aaron, saying,

Le 15:1 — And the LORD spake unto Moses and to Aaron, saying,

Nu 2:1 — And the LORD spake unto Moses and unto Aaron, saying,

Nu 4:1 — And the LORD spake unto Moses and unto Aaron, saying,

Nu 4:17 — And the LORD spake unto Moses and unto Aaron, saying,

Nu 18:1 — And the LORD said unto Aaron, Thou and thy sons and thy father's house with thee shall bear the iniquity of the sanctuary: and thou and thy sons with thee shall bear the iniquity of your priesthood.

Nu 19:1 — And the LORD spake unto Moses and unto Aaron, saying,

Nu 20:12 — And the LORD spake unto Moses and Aaron, Because ye believed me not, to sanctify me in the eyes of the children of Israel, therefore ye shall not bring this congregation into the land which I have given them.

• Commissioned as a deliverer of Israel.

Ex 6:26–27

Ex 6:13 — And the LORD spake unto Moses and unto Aaron, and gave them a charge unto the children of Israel, and unto Pharaoh king of Egypt, to bring the children of Israel out of the land of Egypt.

Jos 24:5 — I sent Moses also and Aaron, and I plagued Egypt, according to that which I did among them: and afterward I brought you out.

1Sa 12:8 — When Jacob was come into Egypt, and your fathers cried unto the LORD, then the LORD sent Moses and Aaron, which brought forth your fathers out of Egypt, and made them dwell in this place.

Ps 77:20 — Thou leddest thy people like a flock by the hand of Moses and Aaron.

Ps 105:26 — He sent Moses his servant; *and* Aaron whom he had chosen.

Mic 6:4 — For I brought thee up out of the land of Egypt, and redeemed thee out of the house of servants; and I sent before thee Moses, Aaron, and Miriam.

• Summoned to Sinai with Nadab, Abihu, and seventy elders.

Ex 24:9–10

Ex 19:24 — And the LORD said unto him, Away, get thee down, and thou shalt come up, thou, and Aaron with thee: but let not the priests and the people break through to come up unto the LORD, lest he break forth upon them.

Ex 24:1 — And he said unto Moses, Come up unto the LORD, thou, and Aaron, Nadab, and Abihu, and seventy of the elders of Israel; and worship ye afar off.

• Priesthood of.

Nu 17:1–18:1

Ex 28:1 — And take thou unto thee Aaron thy brother, and his sons with him, from among the children of Israel, that he may minister unto me in the priest's office, *even* Aaron, Nadab and Abihu, Eleazar and Ithamar, Aaron's sons.

Ex 29:9 — And thou shalt gird them with girdles, Aaron and his sons, and put the bonnets on them: and the priest's office shall be theirs for a perpetual statute: and thou shalt consecrate Aaron and his sons.

Ps 99:6 — Moses and Aaron among his priests, and Samuel among them that call upon his name; they called upon the LORD, and he answered them.

Heb 5:4 — And no man taketh this honour unto himself, but he that is called of God, as *was* Aaron.

• Consecration of, to the priesthood.

Ex 28:1–29:46; Le 8:1–36

• Enters upon the priestly office.

Le 9:1–24

See: Priest, High

• Descendants of, ordained priests forever.

Ex 28:40–43

Ex 29:9 — And thou shalt gird them with girdles, Aaron and his sons, and put the bonnets on them: and the priest's office shall be theirs for a perpetual statute: and thou shalt consecrate Aaron and his sons.

Nu 3:3 — These *are* the names of the sons of Aaron, the priests which were anointed, whom he consecrated to minister in the priest's office.

Nu 18:1 — And the LORD said unto Aaron, Thou and thy sons and thy father's house with thee shall bear the iniquity of the sanctuary: and thou and thy sons with thee shall bear the iniquity of your priesthood.

1Ch 23:13 — The sons of Amram; Aaron and Moses: and Aaron was separated, that he should sanctify the most holy things, he and his sons for ever, to burn incense before the LORD, to minister unto him, and to bless in his name for ever.

2Ch 26:18 — And they withstood Uzziah the king, and said unto him, *It appertaineth* not unto thee, Uzziah, to burn incense unto the LORD, but to the priests the sons of Aaron, that are consecrated to burn incense: go out of the sanctuary; for thou hast trespassed; neither *shall it be* for thine honour from the LORD God.

• Judges Israel in the absence of Moses.

Ex 24:14 — And he said unto the elders, Tarry ye here for us, until we come again unto you: and, behold, Aaron and Hur *are* with you: if any man have any matters to do, let him come unto them.

• Makes the golden calf.

Ex 32:1–35; Dt 9:20–21

Ac 7:40 — Saying unto Aaron, Make us gods to go before us: for *as for* this Moses, which brought us out of the land of Egypt, we wot not what is become of him.

• Rod of, buds.

Nu 17:1–13

Heb 9:4 — Which had the golden censer, and the ark of the covenant overlaid round about with gold, wherein *was* the golden pot that had manna, and Aaron's rod that budded, and the tables of the covenant;

• Rod of, preserved.

Nu 17:1–13

Heb 9:4 — Which had the golden censer, and the ark of the covenant overlaid round about with gold, wherein *was* the golden pot that had manna, and Aaron's rod that budded, and the tables of the covenant;

• Murmured against, by the people.

Ex 5:20–21; 16:2–10; Nu 14:2–5; 16:3–11

Nu 14:10 — But all the congregation bade stone them with stones. And the glory of the LORD appeared in the tabernacle of the congregation before all the children of Israel.

Nu 16:41 — But on the morrow all the congregation of the children of Israel murmured against Moses and against Aaron, saying, Ye have killed the people of the LORD.

Nu 20:2 — And there was no water for the congregation: and they gathered themselves together against Moses and against Aaron.

Ps 106:16 — They envied Moses also in the camp, *and* Aaron the saint of the LORD.

• Places pot of manna in the ark.

Ex 16:34 — As the LORD commanded Moses, so Aaron laid it up before the Testimony, to be kept.

• With Hur supports the hands of Moses during battle.

Ex 17:12 — But Moses' hands *were* heavy; and they took a stone, and put *it* under him, and he sat thereon; and Aaron and Hur stayed up his hands, the one on the one side, and the other on the other side; and his hands were steady until the going down of the sun.

• His benedictions upon the people.

Le 9:22 — And Aaron lifted up his hand toward the people, and blessed them, and came down from offering of the sin offering, and the burnt offering, and peace offerings.

Nu 6:23 — Speak unto Aaron and unto his sons, saying, On this wise ye shall bless the children of Israel, saying unto them,

• Forbidden to mourn the death of his sons, Nadab and Abihu.

Le 10:6 — And Moses said unto Aaron, and unto Eleazar and unto Ithamar, his sons, Uncover not your heads, neither rend your clothes; lest ye die, and lest wrath come upon all the people: but let your brethren, the whole house of Israel, bewail the burning which the LORD hath kindled.

Le 10:19 — And Aaron said unto Moses, Behold, this day have they offered their sin offering and their burnt offering before the LORD; and such things have befallen me: and *if* I had eaten the sin offering to day, should it have been accepted in the sight of the LORD?

• Intercedes for Miriam.

Nu 12:11–12

- **Stays the plague by priestly intercession.**
  Nu 16:46–48
- **Jealous of Moses.**
  Nu 12:1 — And Miriam and Aaron spake against Moses because of the Ethiopian woman whom he had married: for he had married an Ethiopian woman.
- **His presumption, when the rock is smitten.**
  Nu 20:10–12
- **Not permitted to enter Canaan.**
  Nu 20:23–29
  Nu 20:12 — And the LORD spake unto Moses and Aaron, Because ye believed me not, to sanctify me in the eyes of the children of Israel, therefore ye shall not bring this congregation into the land which I have given them.
- **Age of, at death.**
  Nu 33:38–39
  Ex 7:7 — And Moses *was* fourscore years old, and Aaron fourscore and three years old, when they spake unto Pharaoh.
- **Death and burial of.**
  Nu 20:27–28
  Dt 10:6 — And the children of Israel took their journey from Beeroth of the children of Jaakan to Mosera: there Aaron died, and there he was buried; and Eleazar his son ministered in the priest's office in his stead.
  Dt 32:50 — And die in the mount whither thou goest up, and be gathered unto thy people; as Aaron thy brother died in mount Hor, and was gathered unto his people:
- **Character of.**
  Ps 106:16 — They envied Moses also in the camp, *and* Aaron the saint of the LORD.

ABADDON • Angel of the bottomless pit.

Rev 9:11 — And they had a king over them, *which is* the angel of the bottomless pit, whose name in the Hebrew tongue *is* Abaddon, but in the Greek tongue hath *his* name Apollyon.

ABAGTHA • A Persian chamberlain.

Est 1:10 — On the seventh day, when the heart of the king was merry with wine, he commanded Mehuman, Biztha, Harbona, Bigtha, and Abagtha, Zethar, and Carcas, the seven chamberlains that served in the presence of Ahasuerus the king,

ABANA • River of Damascus.

2Ki 5:12 — *Are* not Abana and Pharpar, rivers of Damascus, better than all the waters of Israel? may I not wash in them, and be clean? So he turned and went away in a rage.

ABARIM ◈See: Nebo

ABBA • Father.

Mk 14:36 — And he said, Abba, Father, all things *are* possible unto thee; take away this cup from me: nevertheless not what I will, but what thou wilt.

Ro 8:15 — For ye have not received the spirit of bondage again to fear; but ye have received the Spirit of adoption, whereby we cry, Abba, Father.

Gal 4:6 — And because ye are sons, God hath sent forth the Spirit of his Son into your hearts, crying, Abba, Father.

ABDA • Father of Adoniram.

1Ki 4:6 — And Ahishar *was* over the household: and Adoniram the son of Abda *was* over the tribute.

ABDEEL • Father of Shelemiah.

Jer 36:26 — But the king commanded Jerahmeel the son of Hammelech, and Seraiah the son of Azriel, and Shelemiah the son of Abdeel, to take Baruch the scribe and Jeremiah the prophet: but the LORD hid them.

ABDI • Father of Kish.

2Ch 29:12 — Then the Levites arose, Mahath the son of Amasai, and Joel the son of Azariah, of the sons of the Kohathites: and of the sons of Merari, Kish the son of Abdi, and Azariah the son of Jehalelel: and of the Gershonites; Joah the son of Zimmah, and Eden the son of Joah:

ABDIEL • A Gadite.

1Ch 5:15 — Ahi the son of Abdiel, the son of Guni, chief of the house of their fathers.

ABDON

- **A judge of Israel, in the time of the judges.**
  Jgs 12:13–15
- **A Levitical city.**
  Jos 21:30 — And out of the tribe of Asher, Mishal with her suburbs, Abdon with her suburbs,
  1Ch 6:74 — And out of the tribe of Asher; Mashal with her suburbs, and Abdon with her suburbs,
- **A Benjamite chief.**
  1Ch 8:23 — And Abdon, and Zichri, and Hanan,
- **Son of Gibeon.**
  1Ch 8:30 — And his firstborn son Abdon, and Zur, and Kish, and Baal, and Nadab,
  1Ch 9:36 — And his firstborn son Abdon, then Zur, and Kish, and Baal, and Ner, and Nadab,
- **Son of Micah, called also Achbor.**
  2Ki 22:12 — And the king commanded Hilkiah the priest, and Ahikam the son of Shaphan, and Achbor the son of Michaiah, and Shaphan the scribe, and Asahiah a servant of the king's, saying,
  2Ch 34:20 — And the king commanded Hilkiah, and Ahikam the son of Shaphan, and Abdon the son of Micah, and Shaphan the scribe, and Asaiah a servant of the king's, saying,

ABED-NEGO

- **Called also Azariah.**
- **A Jewish captive in Babylon.**
  Da 1:6–20; 3:12–30

Da 2:17 — Then Daniel went to his house, and made the thing known to Hananiah, Mishael, and Azariah, his companions:

Da 2:49 — Then Daniel requested of the king, and he set Shadrach, Meshach, and Abed-nego, over the affairs of the province of Babylon: but Daniel *sat* in the gate of the king.

Heb 11:34 — Quenched the violence of fire, escaped the edge of the sword, out of weakness were made strong, waxed valiant in fight, turned to flight the armies of the aliens.

ABEL

• Son of Adam.

• History of.

Ge 4:1–15

Ge 4:25 — And Adam knew his wife again; and she bare a son, and called his name Seth: For God, *said she,* hath appointed me another seed instead of Abel, whom Cain slew.

• References to the death of.

Mt 23:35 — That upon you may come all the righteous blood shed upon the earth, from the blood of righteous Abel unto the blood of Zacharias son of Barachias, whom ye slew between the temple and the altar.

Lk 11:51 — From the blood of Abel unto the blood of Zacharias, which perished between the altar and the temple: verily I say unto you, It shall be required of this generation.

Heb 11:4 — By faith Abel offered unto God a more excellent sacrifice than Cain, by which he obtained witness that he was righteous, God testifying of his gifts: and by it he being dead yet speaketh.

Heb 12:24 — And to Jesus the mediator of the new covenant, and to the blood of sprinkling, that speaketh better things than *that of* Abel.

1Jn 3:12 — Not as Cain, *who* was of that wicked one, and slew his brother. And wherefore slew he him? Because his own works were evil, and his brother's righteous.

• A stone.

1Sa 6:18 — And the golden mice, *according to* the number of all the cities of the Philistines *belonging* to the five lords, *both* of fenced cities, and of country villages, even unto the great *stone* of Abel, whereon they set down the ark of the LORD: *which stone remaineth* unto this day in the field of Joshua, the Beth-shemite.

ABEL-BETH-MAACHAH

• Called also Abel-Maim.

• A city in the north of Palestine.

• Sheba slain in.

2Sa 20:14–22

• Taken by Benhadad.

1Ki 15:20 — So Ben-hadad hearkened unto king Asa, and sent the captains of the hosts which he had against the cities of Israel, and smote Ijon, and Dan, and Abel-beth-maachah, and all Cinneroth, with all the land of Naphtali.

2Ch 16:4 — And Ben-hadad hearkened unto king Asa, and sent the captains of his armies against the cities of Israel; and they smote Ijon, and Dan, and Abel-maim, and all the store cities of Naphtali.

• Taken by Tiglath.

2Ki 15:29 — In the days of Pekah king of Israel came Tiglath-pileser king of Assyria, and took Ijon, and Abel-beth-maachah, and Janoah, and Kedesh, and Hazor, and Gilead, and Galilee, all the land of Naphtali, and carried them captive to Assyria.

ABEL-MEHOLAH

• A city near the Jordan.

Jgs 7:22 — And the three hundred blew the trumpets, and the LORD set every man's sword against his fellow, even throughout all the host: and the host fled to Beth-shittah in Zererath, *and* to the border of Abel-meholah, unto Tabbath.

1Ki 4:12 — Baana the son of Ahilud; *to him pertained* Taanach and Megiddo, and all Beth-shean, which is by Zartanah beneath Jezreel, from Beth-shean to Abel-meholah, *even* unto *the place that is* beyond Jokneam:

• Elisha's birthplace.

1Ki 19:16 — And Jehu the son of Nimshi shalt thou anoint *to be* king over Israel: and Elisha the son of Shaphat of Abel-meholah shalt thou anoint *to be* prophet in thy room.

ABEL-MIZRAIM • Place where the Israelites mourned for Jacob.

Ge 50:11 — And when the inhabitants of the land, the Canaanites, saw the mourning in the floor of Atad, they said, This *is* a grievous mourning to the Egyptians: wherefore the name of it was called Abel-mizraim, which *is* beyond Jordan.

ABEL-SHITTIM ➜See: Shittim

ABETTING ➜See: Complicity

ABEZ • A city of Issachar.

Jos 19:20 — And Rabbith, and Kishion, and Abez,

ABI

• Mother of Hezekiah.

2Ki 18:2 — Twenty and five years old was he when he began to reign; and he reigned twenty and nine years in Jerusalem. His mother's name also *was* Abi, the daughter of Zachariah.

• Called Abijah.

2Ch 29:1 — Hezekiah began to reign *when he was* five and twenty years old, and he reigned nine and twenty years in Jerusalem. And his mother's name *was* Abijah, the daughter of Zechariah.

ABI-ALBON

• Called also Abiel.

• One of David's heroes.

2Sa 23:31 — Abi-albon the Arbathite, Azmaveth the Barhumite,

1Ch 11:32 — Hurai of the brooks of Gaash, Abiel the Arbathite,

ABIA

• Called also Abijah. Chief of the twenty-four courses of priests.

1Ch 24:10 — The seventh to Hakkoz, the eighth to Abijah,

Ne 12:4 — Iddo, Ginnetho, Abijah,

Lk 1:5 — There was in the days of Herod, the king of Judaea, a certain priest named Zacharias, of the course of Abia: and his wife *was* of the daughters of Aaron, and her name *was* Elisabeth.

• King of Judah.

*See: Abijam

ABIAH

• Wife of Hezron.

1Ch 2:24 — And after that Hezron was dead in Caleb-ephratah, then Abiah Hezron's wife bare him Ashur the father of Tekoa.

• Son of Samuel.

1Sa 8:1–5

1Ch 6:28 — And the sons of Samuel; the firstborn Vashni, and Abiah.

ABIASAPH • Son of Korah.

Ex 6:24 — And the sons of Korah; Assir, and Elkanah, and Abiasaph: these *are* the families of the Korhites.

ABIATHAR, high priest

• Called Ahimelech.

2Sa 8:17 — And Zadok the son of Ahitub, and Ahimelech the son of Abiathar, *were* the priests; and Seraiah *was* the scribe;

1Ch 24:3 — And David distributed them, both Zadok of the sons of Eleazar, and Ahimelech of the sons of Ithamar, according to their offices in their service.

1Ch 24:6 — And Shemaiah the son of Nethaneel the scribe, *one* of the Levites, wrote them before the king, and the princes, and Zadok the priest, and Ahimelech the son of Abiathar, and *before* the chief of the fathers of the priests and Levites: one principal household being taken for Eleazar, and *one* taken for Ithamar.

1Ch 24:31 — These likewise cast lots over against their brethren the sons of Aaron in the presence of David the king, and Zadok, and Ahimelech, and the chief of the fathers of the priests and Levites, even the principal fathers over against their younger brethren.

• Called Abimelech.

1Ch 18:16 — And Zadok the son of Ahitub, and Abimelech the son of Abiathar, *were* the priests; and Shavsha was scribe;

• Son of Ahimelech.

1Sa 22:20 — And one of the sons of Ahimelech the son of Ahitub, named Abiathar, escaped, and fled after David.

• Escapes to David from the vengeance of Saul, who slew the priests in the city of Nob.

1Sa 6:1–19:24; 22:20–23

• Consults the ephod for David.

1Sa 22:10 — And he enquired of the LORD for him, and gave him victuals, and gave him the sword of Goliath the Philistine.

1Sa 23:9 — And David knew that Saul secretly practised mischief against him; and he said to Abiathar the priest, Bring hither the ephod.

1Sa 30:7 — And David said to Abiathar the priest, Ahimelech's son, I pray thee, bring me hither the ephod. And Abiathar brought thither the ephod to David.

• Associate high priest with Zadok in the reign of David.

2Sa 15:35 — And *hast thou* not there with thee Zadok and Abiathar the priests? therefore it shall be, *that* what thing soever thou shalt hear out of the king's house, thou shalt tell *it* to Zadok and Abiathar the priests.

2Sa 20:25 — And Sheva *was* scribe: and Zadok and Abiathar *were* the priests:

1Ki 4:4 — And Benaiah the son of Jehoiada *was* over the host: and Zadok and Abiathar *were* the priests:

1Ch 15:11 — And David called for Zadok and Abiathar the priests, and for the Levites, for Uriel, Asaiah, and Joel, Shemaiah, and Eliel, and Amminadab,

• But called Ahimelech and father of Abiathar.

2Sa 8:17 — And Zadok the son of Ahitub, and Ahimelech the son of Abiathar, *were* the priests; and Seraiah *was* the scribe;

1Ch 18:16 — And Zadok the son of Ahitub, and Abimelech the son of Abiathar, *were* the priests; and Shavsha was scribe;

• Loyal to David when Absalom rebelled; leaves Jerusalem with the ark of the covenant, but is directed by David to return with the ark.

2Sa 15:24–29

• Aids David by sending his son from Jerusalem to David with secret information concerning the counsel of Ahithophel.

2Sa 15:35–36; 17:15–22

1Ki 2:26 — And unto Abiathar the priest said the king, Get thee to Anathoth, unto thine own fields; for thou *art* worthy of death: but I will not at this time put thee to death, because thou barest the ark of the Lord GOD before David my father, and because thou hast been afflicted in all wherein my father was afflicted.

• Supports Adonijah's pretensions to the throne.

1Ki 1:7 — And he conferred with Joab the son of Zeruiah, and with Abiathar the priest: and they following Adonijah helped *him*.

• **Thrust out of office by Solomon.**
1Sa 2:31–35; 1Ki 2:26–27
See: Ahimelech

ABIB
• **Called also Nisan.**
• **First month in the Jewish calendar.**
Ex 12:2 — This month *shall be* unto you the beginning of months: it *shall be* the first month of the year to you.
• **Passover instituted, and Israelites depart from Egypt in.**
Ex 23:15 — Thou shalt keep the feast of unleavened bread: (thou shalt eat unleavened bread seven days, as I commanded thee, in the time appointed of the month Abib; for in it thou camest out from Egypt: and none shall appear before me empty:)
Dt 16:1 — Observe the month of Abib, and keep the passover unto the LORD thy God: for in the month of Abib the LORD thy God brought thee forth out of Egypt by night.
• **Tabernacle set up in.**
Ex 40:2 — On the first day of the first month shalt thou set up the tabernacle of the tent of the congregation.
Ex 40:17 — And it came to pass in the first month in the second year, on the first *day* of the month, *that* the tabernacle was reared up.
• **Israelites arrive at the wilderness of Zin in.**
Nu 20:1 — Then came the children of Israel, *even* the whole congregation, into the desert of Zin in the first month: and the people abode in Kadesh; and Miriam died there, and was buried there.
• **Enter Canaan in.**
Jos 4:19 — And the people came up out of Jordan on the tenth *day* of the first month, and encamped in Gilgal, in the east border of Jericho.
• **Jordan's overflow in.**
1Ch 12:15 — These *are* they that went over Jordan in the first month, when it had overflown all his banks; and they put to flight all *them* of the valleys, *both* toward the east, and toward the west.

ABIDA • Son of Midian.
1Ch 1:33 — And the sons of Midian; Ephah, and Epher, and Henoch, and Abida, and Eldaah. All these *are* the sons of Keturah.

ABIDAH • A descendant of Abraham.
Ge 25:4 — And the sons of Midian; Ephah, and Epher, and Hanoch, and Abidah, and Eldaah. All these *were* the children of Keturah.

ABIEL
• **Saul's grandfather.**
1Sa 14:51 — And Kish *was* the father of Saul; and Ner the father of Abner *was* the son of Abiel.
• **A Benjamite.**
1Sa 9:1 — Now there was a man of Benjamin, whose name *was* Kish, the son of Abiel, the son of Zeror, the son of Bechorath, the son of Aphiah, a Benjamite, a mighty man of power.
See: Abi-Albon

ABIEZER
• **Called also Jeezer. Progenitor of Abiezrites.**
Nu 26:30 — These *are* the sons of Gilead: *of* Jeezer, the family of the Jeezerites: of Helek, the family of the Helekites:
Jos 17:2 — There was also *a lot* for the rest of the children of Manasseh by their families; for the children of Abiezer, and for the children of Helek, and for the children of Asriel, and for the children of Shechem, and for the children of Hepher, and for the children of Shemida: these *were* the male children of Manasseh the son of Joseph by their families.
Jgs 6:34 — But the Spirit of the LORD came upon Gideon, and he blew a trumpet; and Abi-ezer was gathered after him.
Jgs 8:2 — And he said unto them, What have I done now in comparison of you? *Is* not the gleaning of the grapes of Ephraim better than the vintage of Abi-ezer?
• **One of David's heroes.**
2Sa 23:27 — Abiezer the Anethothite, Mebunnai the Hushathite,
1Ch 27:12 — The ninth *captain* for the ninth month *was* Abiezer the Anetothite, of the Benjamites: and in his course *were* twenty and four thousand.

ABIGAIL
• **Nabal's wife.**
• **Her wisdom and tact, and marriage to David.**
1Sa 25:1–44
1Sa 27:3 — And David dwelt with Achish at Gath, he and his men, every man with his household, *even* David with his two wives, Ahinoam the Jezreelitess, and Abigail the Carmelitess, Nabal's wife.
2Sa 2:2 — So David went up thither, and his two wives also, Ahinoam the Jezreelitess, and Abigail Nabal's wife the Carmelite.
• **Mother of Chileab by David.**
2Sa 3:3 — And his second, Chileab, of Abigail the wife of Nabal the Carmelite; and the third, Absalom the son of Maacah the daughter of Talmai king of Geshur;
1Ch 3:1 — Now these were the sons of David, which were born unto him in Hebron; the firstborn Amnon, of Ahinoam the Jezreelitess; the second Daniel, of Abigail the Carmelitess:
• **Taken captive and rescued by David.**
1Sa 30:1–18
• **Sister of David, and mother of Amasa.**
1Ch 2:16–17
2Sa 17:25 — And Absalom made Amasa captain of the host instead of Joab: which Amasa was a man's son, whose name *was* Ithra an Israelite, that went in

to Abigail the daughter of Nahash, sister to Zeruiah Joab's mother.

ABIHAIL

• Father of Esther.

Est 2:15 — Now when the turn of Esther, the daughter of Abihail the uncle of Mordecai, who had taken her for his daughter, was come to go in unto the king, she required nothing but what Hegai the king's chamberlain, the keeper of the women, appointed. And Esther obtained favour in the sight of all them that looked upon her.

• The second wife of Rehoboam.

2Ch 11:18–19

• Father of Zuriel.

Nu 3:35 — And the chief of the house of the father of the families of Merari *was* Zuriel the son of Abihail: *these* shall pitch on the side of the tabernacle northward.

• Wife of Abishur.

1Ch 2:29 — And the name of the wife of Abishur *was* Abihail, and she bare him Ahban, and Molid.

ABIHU

• Son of Aaron.

Ex 6:23 — And Aaron took him Elisheba, daughter of Amminadab, sister of Naashon, to wife; and she bare him Nadab, and Abihu, Eleazar, and Ithamar.

Nu 3:2 — And these *are* the names of the sons of Aaron; Nadab the firstborn, and Abihu, Eleazar, and Ithamar.

• Summoned by God to Sinai.

Ex 24:9 — Then went up Moses, and Aaron, Nadab, and Abihu, and seventy of the elders of Israel:

• Called to the priesthood.

Ex 28:1 — And take thou unto thee Aaron thy brother, and his sons with him, from among the children of Israel, that he may minister unto me in the priest's office, *even* Aaron, Nadab and Abihu, Eleazar and Ithamar, Aaron's sons.

• Death of.

Le 10:1–2

Nu 26:61 — And Nadab and Abihu died, when they offered strange fire before the LORD.

• Died childless.

Nu 3:4 — And Nadab and Abihu died before the LORD, when they offered strange fire before the LORD, in the wilderness of Sinai, and they had no children: and Eleazar and Ithamar ministered in the priest's office in the sight of Aaron their father.

ABIHUD

• Called also Ahihud.

• Son of Bela.

1Ch 8:3 — And the sons of Bela were, Addar, and Gera, and Abihud,

ABIJAH

• Son of Jeroboam.

1Ki 14:1–18

→See: Abia

→See: Abijam

ABIJAM

• Abijah and Abia.

• King of Judah.

1Ki 14:31–15:1

2Ch 12:16 — And Rehoboam slept with his fathers, and was buried in the city of David: and Abijah his son reigned in his stead.

• History of.

1Ki 15:1–8; 2Ch 13:1–22

2Ch 11:22 — And Rehoboam made Abijah the son of Maachah the chief, to be ruler among his brethren: for *he thought* to make him king.

• Succeeded by Asa.

1Ki 15:8 — And Abijam slept with his fathers; and they buried him in the city of David: and Asa his son reigned in his stead.

2Ch 14:1 — So Abijah slept with his fathers, and they buried him in the city of David: and Asa his son reigned in his stead. In his days the land was quiet ten years.

ABILENE • A Roman province in Palestine.

Lk 3:1 — Now in the fifteenth year of the reign of Tiberius Caesar, Pontius Pilate being governor of Judaea, and Herod being tetrarch of Galilee, and his brother Philip tetrarch of Ituraea and of the region of Trachonitis, and Lysanias the tetrarch of Abilene,

ABIMAEL • Son of Joktan.

Ge 10:28 — And Obal, and Abimael, and Sheba,

1Ch 1:22 — And Ebal, and Abimael, and Sheba,

ABIMELECH

• King of Gerar.

Ge 20:1–18; 21:22–32; 26:1–35

• Son of Gideon.

Jgs 9:1–57

Jgs 8:31 — And his concubine that *was* in Shechem, she also bare him a son, whose name he called Abimelech.

2Sa 11:21 — Who smote Abimelech the son of Jerubbesheth? did not a woman cast a piece of a millstone upon him from the wall, that he died in Thebez? why went ye nigh the wall? then say thou, Thy servant Uriah the Hittite is dead also.

→See: Achish

→See: Ahimelech

ABINADAB

• A Levite, in whose house the ark of God rested twenty years.

1Sa 7:1–2; 2Sa 6:3–4

1Ch 13:7 — And they carried the ark of God in a new cart out of the house of Abinadab: and Uzza and Ahio drave the cart.

• **Son of Jesse.**

1Sa 16:8 — Then Jesse called Abinadab, and made him pass before Samuel. And he said, Neither hath the LORD chosen this.

1Sa 17:13 — And the three eldest sons of Jesse went *and* followed Saul to the battle: and the names of his three sons that went to the battle *were* Eliab the first born, and next unto him Abinadab, and the third Shammah.

• **Son of Saul.**

1Sa 31:2 — And the Philistines followed hard upon Saul and upon his sons; and the Philistines slew Jonathan, and Abinadab, and Melchi-shua, Saul's sons.

• **Called also Ishui.**

1Sa 14:49 — Now the sons of Saul were Jonathan, and Ishui, and Melchi-shua: and the names of his two daughters *were these;* the name of the first-born Merab, and the name of the younger Michal:

• **Father of one of Solomon's purveyors.**

1Ki 4:11 — The son of Abinadab, in all the region of Dor; which had Taphath the daughter of Solomon to wife:

ABINOAM • Father of Barak.

Jgs 4:6 — And she sent and called Barak the son of Abinoam out of Kedesh-naphtali, and said unto him, Hath not the LORD God of Israel commanded, *saying,* Go and draw toward mount Tabor, and take with thee ten thousand men of the children of Naphtali and of the children of Zebulun?

ABIRAM

• **An Israelite who conspired with Dathan against Moses and Aaron.**

Nu 16:1–50; 26:9–10

Dt 11:6 — And what he did unto Dathan and Abiram, the sons of Eliab, the son of Reuben: how the earth opened her mouth, and swallowed them up, and their households, and their tents, and all the substance that *was* in their possession, in the midst of all Israel:

Ps 106:17 — The earth opened and swallowed up Dathan, and covered the company of Abiram.

• **Son of Hiel.**

1Ki 16:34 — In his days did Hiel the Bethelite build Jericho: he laid the foundation thereof in Abiram his firstborn, and set up the gates thereof in his youngest *son* Segub, according to the word of the LORD, which he spake by Joshua the son of Nun.

ABISHAG • Wife of David.

1Ki 1:1–4; 2:13–25

ABISHAI

• **Son of Zeruiah, David's sister.**

1Ch 2:16 — Whose sisters *were* Zeruiah, and Abigail. And the sons of Zeruiah; Abishai, and Joab, and Asahel, three.

• **One of David's chief men.**

2Sa 23:18 — And Abishai, the brother of Joab, the son of Zeruiah, was chief among three. And he lifted up his spear against three hundred, *and* slew *them,* and had the name among three.

• **Seeks Saul's life.**

1Sa 26:6–8

• **Pursues and slays Abner.**

2Sa 2:24 — Joab also and Abishai pursued after Abner: and the sun went down when they were come to the hill of Ammah, that *lieth* before Giah by the way of the wilderness of Gibeon.

2Sa 3:30 — So Joab and Abishai his brother slew Abner, because he had slain their brother Asahel at Gibeon in the battle.

• **Defeats the Edomites.**

1Ch 18:12 — Moreover Abishai the son of Zeruiah slew of the Edomites in the valley of salt eighteen thousand.

• **Defeats the Ammonites.**

2Sa 10:10 — And the rest of the people he delivered into the hand of Abishai his brother, that he might put *them* in array against the children of Ammon.

2Sa 10:14 — And when the children of Ammon saw that the Syrians were fled, then fled they also before Abishai, and entered into the city. So Joab returned from the children of Ammon, and came to Jerusalem.

• **Seeks the life of Shimei.**

2Sa 16:9 — Then said Abishai the son of Zeruiah unto the king, Why should this dead dog curse my lord the king? let me go over, I pray thee, and take off his head.

2Sa 19:21 — But Abishai the son of Zeruiah answered and said, Shall not Shimei be put to death for this, because he cursed the LORD's anointed?

• **Leads a division of David's army against Absalom.**

2Sa 18:2 — And David sent forth a third part of the people under the hand of Joab, and a third part under the hand of Abishai the son of Zeruiah, Joab's brother, and a third part under the hand of Ittai the Gittite. And the king said unto the people, I will surely go forth with you myself also.

2Sa 18:5 — And the king commanded Joab and Abishai and Ittai, saying, *Deal* gently for my sake with the young man, *even* with Absalom. And all the people heard when the king gave all the captains charge concerning Absalom.

• **Overthrows Sheba.**

2Sa 20:1–22

• **Saves David from being slain by a Philistine.**

2Sa 21:17 — But Abishai the son of Zeruiah succoured him, and smote the Philistine, and killed him. Then the men of David sware unto him, saying, Thou shalt go no more out with us to battle, that thou quench not the light of Israel.

• **Obtains water from the well of Bethlehem for David.**

1Ch 11:15–20

ABISHALOM ⇾See: Absalom

1Ki 15:2 — Three years reigned he in Jerusalem. And his mother's name *was* Maachah, the daughter of Abishalom.

1Ki 15:10 — And forty and one years reigned he in Jerusalem. And his mother's name *was* Maachah, the daughter of Abishalom.

ABISHUA

• A high priest.

1Ch 6:4–5

1Ch 6:50 — And these *are* the sons of Aaron; Eleazar his son, Phinehas his son, Abishua his son,

• A son of Bela.

1Ch 8:4 — And Abishua, and Naaman, and Ahoah,

ABISHUR • Son of Shammai.

1Ch 2:28–29

ABITAL • Wife of David.

2Sa 3:4 — And the fourth, Adonijah the son of Haggith; and the fifth, Shephatiah the son of Abital;

1Ch 3:3 — The fifth, Shephatiah of Abital: the sixth, Ithream by Eglah his wife.

ABITUB • A Benjamite.

1Ch 8:11 — And of Hushim he begat Abitub, and Elpaal.

ABIUD • Ancestor of Jesus.

Mt 1:13 — And Zorobabel begat Abiud; and Abiud begat Eliakim; and Eliakim begat Azor;

ABLUTION

Mk 7:2–5; 7:8–9

Ex 19:10 — And the LORD said unto Moses, Go unto the people, and sanctify them to day and to morrow, and let them wash their clothes,

Ex 19:14 — And Moses went down from the mount unto the people, and sanctified the people; and they washed their clothes.

Mt 15:2 — Why do thy disciples transgress the tradition of the elders? for they wash not their hands when they eat bread.

Lk 11:38 — And when the Pharisee saw *it,* he marvelled that he had not first washed before dinner.

Heb 9:10 — *Which stood* only in meats and drinks, and divers washings, and carnal ordinances, imposed *on them* until the time of reformation.

• Of priests.

Ex 30:18–21; 40:31–32; Nu 19:1–22

Ex 29:4 — And Aaron and his sons thou shalt bring unto the door of the tabernacle of the congregation, and shalt wash them with water.

Ex 40:12 — And thou shalt bring Aaron and his sons unto the door of the tabernacle of the congregation, and wash them with water.

Le 8:6 — And Moses brought Aaron and his sons, and washed them with water.

Le 16:4 — He shall put on the holy linen coat, and he shall have the linen breeches upon his flesh, and shall be girded with a linen girdle, and with the linen mitre shall he be attired: these *are* holy garments; therefore shall he wash his flesh in water, and *so* put them on.

Le 16:24 — And he shall wash his flesh with water in the holy place, and put on his garments, and come forth, and offer his burnt offering, and the burnt offering of the people, and make an atonement for himself, and for the people.

Le 16:26 — And he that let go the goat for the scapegoat shall wash his clothes, and bathe his flesh in water, and afterward come into the camp.

Le 16:28 — And he that burneth them shall wash his clothes, and bathe his flesh in water, and afterward he shall come into the camp.

2Ch 4:6 — He made also ten lavers, and put five on the right hand, and five on the left, to wash in them: such things as they offered for the burnt offering they washed in them; but the sea *was* for the priests to wash in.

• Of burnt offerings.

Le 1:9 — But his inwards and his legs shall he wash in water: and the priest shall burn all on the altar, *to be* a burnt sacrifice, an offering made by fire, of a sweet savour unto the LORD.

Le 1:13 — But he shall wash the inwards and the legs with water: and the priest shall bring *it* all, and burn *it* upon the altar: it *is* a burnt sacrifice, an offering made by fire, of a sweet savour unto the LORD.

Le 9:14 — And he did wash the inwards and the legs, and burnt *them* upon the burnt offering on the altar.

2Ch 4:6 — He made also ten lavers, and put five on the right hand, and five on the left, to wash in them: such things as they offered for the burnt offering they washed in them; but the sea *was* for the priests to wash in.

• Of the dead.

Ac 9:37 — And it came to pass in those days, that she was sick, and died: whom when they had washed, they laid *her* in an upper chamber.

• Of infants.

Eze 16:4 — And *as for* thy nativity, in the day thou wast born thy navel was not cut, neither wast thou washed in water to supple *thee;* thou wast not salted at all, nor swaddled at all.

• Of the face.

Mt 6:17 — But thou, when thou fastest, anoint thine head, and wash thy face;

• Of the feet.

Ge 18:4 — Let a little water, I pray you, be fetched, and wash your feet, and rest yourselves under the tree:

Ge 19:2 — And he said, Behold now, my lords, turn in, I pray you, into your servant's house, and tarry all night, and wash your feet, and ye shall rise up early, and go on your ways. And they said, Nay; but we will abide in the street all night.

Ge 24:32 — And the man came into the house: and he ungirded his camels, and gave straw and provender for the camels, and water to wash his feet, and the men's feet that *were* with him.

Ge 43:24 — And the man brought the men into Joseph's house, and gave *them* water, and they washed their feet; and he gave their asses provender.

Ex 30:19 — For Aaron and his sons shall wash their hands and their feet thereat:

Ex 30:21 — So they shall wash their hands and their feet, that they die not: and it shall be a statute for ever to them, *even* to him and to his seed throughout their generations.

Ex 40:31 — And Moses and Aaron and his sons washed their hands and their feet thereat:

Jgs 19:21 — So he brought him into his house, and gave provender unto the asses: and they washed their feet, and did eat and drink.

2Sa 11:8 — And David said to Uriah, Go down to thy house, and wash thy feet. And Uriah departed out of the king's house, and there followed him a mess *of meat* from the king.

SS 5:3 — I have put off my coat; how shall I put it on? I have washed my feet; how shall I defile them?

Lk 7:38 — And stood at his feet behind *him* weeping, and began to wash his feet with tears, and did wipe *them* with the hairs of her head, and kissed his feet, and anointed *them* with the ointment.

Lk 7:44 — And he turned to the woman, and said unto Simon, Seest thou this woman? I entered into thine house, thou gavest me no water for my feet: but she hath washed my feet with tears, and wiped *them* with the hairs of her head.

Jn 13:5 — After that he poureth water into a bason, and began to wash the disciples' feet, and to wipe *them* with the towel wherewith he was girded.

1Ti 5:10 — Well reported of for good works; if she have brought up children, if she have lodged strangers, if she have washed the saints' feet, if she have relieved the afflicted, if she have diligently followed every good work.

• Of the hands.

Ex 30:18–21; 40:30–32

• Of the hands, as a token of innocency.

Dt 21:6 — And all the elders of that city, *that are* next unto the slain *man,* shall wash their hands over the heifer that is beheaded in the valley:

Ps 26:6 — I will wash mine hands in innocency: so will I compass thine altar, O LORD:

Mt 27:24 — When Pilate saw that he could prevail nothing, but *that* rather a tumult was made, he took water, and washed *his* hands before the multitude, saying, I am innocent of the blood of this just person: see ye *to it.*

• For defilement.

• Of lepers.

Le 14:8–9

• Of those having bloody issue.

Le 15:5–13

• Of those having eaten that which died.

Le 17:15–16

• Traditional forms of, not observed by Jesus.

Lk 11:38–39

→See: Purification

→See: Defilement

• Figurative.

Isa 4:3–4; Tit 3:5–6

Ps 51:2 — Wash me throughly from mine iniquity, and cleanse me from my sin.

Ps 51:7 — Purge me with hyssop, and I shall be clean: wash me, and I shall be whiter than snow.

Ps 65:3 — Iniquities prevail against me: *as for* our transgressions, thou shalt purge them away.

Ps 73:13 — Verily I have cleansed my heart *in* vain, and washed my hands in innocency.

Ps 79:9 — Help us, O God of our salvation, for the glory of thy name: and deliver us, and purge away our sins, for thy name's sake.

Pr 16:6 — By mercy and truth iniquity is purged: and by the fear of the LORD *men* depart from evil.

Pr 20:9 — Who can say, I have made my heart clean, I am pure from my sin?

Isa 1:16 — Wash you, make you clean; put away the evil of your doings from before mine eyes; cease to do evil;

Isa 1:18 — Come now, and let us reason together, saith the LORD: though your sins be as scarlet, they shall be as white as snow; though they be red like crimson, they shall be as wool.

Da 12:10 — Many shall be purified, and made white, and tried; but the wicked shall do wickedly: and none of the wicked shall understand; but the wise shall understand.

Zec 13:1 — In that day there shall be a fountain opened to the house of David and to the inhabitants of Jerusalem for sin and for uncleanness.

Jn 13:8 — Peter saith unto him, Thou shalt never wash my feet. Jesus answered him, If I wash thee not, thou hast no part with me.

Ac 22:16 — And now why tarriest thou? arise, and be baptized, and wash away thy sins, calling on the name of the Lord.

1Co 5:7 — Purge out therefore the old leaven, that ye may be a new lump, as ye are unleavened. For even Christ our passover is sacrificed for us:

1Co 6:11 — And such were some of you: but ye are washed, but ye are sanctified, but ye are justified in the name of the Lord Jesus, and by the Spirit of our God.

2Co 7:1 — Having therefore these promises, dearly beloved, let us cleanse ourselves from all filthiness of the flesh and spirit, perfecting holiness in the fear of God.

Eph 5:26 — That he might sanctify and cleanse it with the washing of water by the word,

Heb 1:3 — Who being the brightness of *his* glory, and the express image of his person, and upholding all things by the word of his power, when he had by himself purged our sins, sat down on the right hand of the Majesty on high;

Heb 9:14 — How much more shall the blood of Christ, who through the eternal Spirit offered himself without spot to God, purge your conscience from dead works to serve the living God?

Heb 10:22 — Let us draw near with a true heart in full assurance of faith, having our hearts sprinkled from an evil conscience, and our bodies washed with pure water.

Jas 4:8 — Draw nigh to God, and he will draw nigh to you. Cleanse *your* hands, *ye* sinners; and purify *your* hearts, *ye* double minded.

2Pe 1:9 — But he that lacketh these things is blind, and cannot see afar off, and hath forgotten that he was purged from his old sins.

1Jn 1:7 — But if we walk in the light, as he is in the light, we have fellowship one with another, and the blood of Jesus Christ his Son cleanseth us from all sin.

1Jn 1:9 — If we confess our sins, he is faithful and just to forgive us *our* sins, and to cleanse us from all unrighteousness.

Rev 1:5 — And from Jesus Christ, *who is* the faithful witness, *and* the first begotten of the dead, and the prince of the kings of the earth. Unto him that loved us, and washed us from our sins in his own blood,

Rev 7:14 — And I said unto him, Sir, thou knowest. And he said to me, These are they which came out of great tribulation, and have washed their robes, and made them white in the blood of the Lamb.

Rev 22:14 — Blessed *are* they that do his commandments, that they may have right to the tree of life, and may enter in through the gates into the city.

→See: Regeneration

ABNER

- **Son of Ner.**
- **Cousin of Saul.**

1Sa 14:50–51

1Sa 9:1 — Now there was a man of Benjamin, whose name *was* Kish, the son of Abiel, the son of Zeror, the son of Bechorath, the son of Aphiah, a Benjamite, a mighty man of power.

- **Captain of the host.**

1Sa 14:50 — And the name of Saul's wife *was* Ahinoam, the daughter of Ahimaaz: and the name of the captain of his host *was* Abner, the son of Ner, Saul's uncle.

1Sa 17:55 — And when Saul saw David go forth against the Philistine, he said unto Abner, the captain of the host, Abner, whose son *is* this youth? And Abner said, *As* thy soul liveth, O king, I cannot tell.

1Sa 26:5 — And David arose, and came to the place where Saul had pitched: and David beheld the place where Saul lay, and Abner the son of Ner, the captain of his host: and Saul lay in the trench, and the people pitched round about him.

1Sa 26:14 — And David cried to the people, and to Abner the son of Ner, saying, Answerest thou not, Abner? Then Abner answered and said, Who *art* thou *that* criest to the king?

- **Dedicated spoils of war to the tabernacle.**

1Ch 26:27–28

- **Loyalty of, to the house of Saul.**

2Sa 2:8–32

- **Alienation of, from the house of Saul.**

2Sa 3:6–21

- **Murdered by Joab; David's sorrow for.**

2Sa 3:27–39

ABOMINATION

- **Things that are, to God.**
  - **Idolatry.**

Dt 7:25— The graven images of their gods shall ye burn with fire: thou shalt not desire the silver or gold *that is* on them, nor take *it* unto thee, lest thou be snared therein: for it *is* an abomination to the LORD thy God.

Dt 27:15 — Cursed *be* the man that maketh *any* graven or molten image, an abomination unto the LORD, the work of the hands of the craftsman, and putteth *it* in *a* secret *place.* And all the people shall answer and say, Amen.

Dt 32:16 — They provoked him to jealousy with strange *gods,* with abominations provoked they him to anger.

- **Unjust weights and measures.**

Dt 25:13–16

Pr 11:1 — A false balance *is* abomination to the LORD: but a just weight *is* his delight.

Pr 20:10 — Divers weights, *and* divers measures, both of them *are* alike abomination to the LORD.

Pr 20:23 — Divers weights *are* an abomination unto the LORD; and a false balance *is* not good.

- **Uncleanness.**

Le 18:22 — Thou shalt not lie with mankind, as with womankind: it *is* abomination.

Le 20:13 — If a man also lie with mankind, as he lieth with a woman, both of them have committed an abomination: they shall surely be put to death; their blood *shall be* upon them.

Dt 24:4 — Her former husband, which sent her away, may not take her again to be his wife, after that she is defiled; for that *is* abomination before the LORD: and thou shalt not cause the land to sin, which the LORD thy God giveth thee *for* an inheritance.

- **Incest.**

Le 18:6–18

- **Lying with a woman in her menses.**

Le 18:19 — Also thou shalt not approach unto a woman to uncover her nakedness, as long as she is put apart for her uncleanness.

- **Adultery.**

Le 18:20 — Moreover thou shalt not lie carnally with thy neighbour's wife, to defile thyself with her.

- **Sodomy.**

Le 18:22–23

- **Offering seed to Molech.**

Le 18:21 — And thou shalt not let any of thy seed pass through *the fire* to Molech, neither shalt thou profane the name of thy God: I *am* the LORD.

- **Or children in sacrifice.**

Dt 18:10 — There shall not be found among you *any one* that maketh his son or his daughter to pass through the fire, or that useth divination, *or* an observer of times, or an enchanter, or a witch,

- **Sorcery and necromancy.**

Dt 18:10–11

- **The hire of a whore and price of a dog, as a consecrated gift.**

Dt 23:18 — Thou shalt not bring the hire of a whore, or the price of a dog, into the house of the LORD thy God for any vow: for even both these *are* abomination unto the LORD thy God.

- **Unclassified scripture relating to.**

Pr 6:16–19; 15:8–9

Dt 22:5 — The woman shall not wear that which pertaineth unto a man, neither shall a man put on a woman's garment: for all that do so *are* abomination unto the LORD thy God.

Pr 3:32 — For the froward *is* abomination to the LORD: but his secret *is* with the righteous.

Pr 8:7 — For my mouth shall speak truth; and wickedness *is* an abomination to my lips.

Pr 11:20 — They that are of a froward heart *are* abomination to the LORD: but *such as are* upright in *their* way *are* his delight.

Pr 12:22 — Lying lips *are* abomination to the LORD: but they that deal truly *are* his delight.

Pr 15:26 — The thoughts of the wicked *are* an abomination to the LORD: but *the words* of the pure *are* pleasant words.

Pr 16:5 — Every one *that is* proud in heart *is* an abomination to the LORD: *though* hand *join* in hand, he shall not be unpunished.

Pr 17:15 — He that justifieth the wicked, and he that condemneth the just, even they both *are* abomination to the LORD.

Pr 20:10 — Divers weights, *and* divers measures, both of them *are* alike abomination to the LORD.

Pr 20:23 — Divers weights *are* an abomination unto the LORD; and a false balance *is* not good.

Pr 21:27 — The sacrifice of the wicked *is* abomination: how much more, *when* he bringeth it with a wicked mind?

Pr 24:9 — The thought of foolishness *is* sin: and the scorner *is* an abomination to men.

Pr 28:9 — He that turneth away his ear from hearing the law, even his prayer *shall be* abomination.

Pr 29:27 — An unjust man *is* an abomination to the just: and *he that is* upright in the way *is* abomination to the wicked.

ABORTION

Ex 21:22–25; Ps 82:3–4; 139:13–16; Jer 7:30–34

Ps 127:3 — Lo, children *are* an heritage of the LORD: *and* the fruit of the womb *is his* reward.

Jer 1:5 — Before I formed thee in the belly I knew thee; and before thou camest forth out of the womb I sanctified thee, *and* I ordained thee a prophet unto the nations.

- **As a judgment.**

Hos 9:14 — Give them, O LORD: what wilt thou give? give them a miscarrying womb and dry breasts.

- **Of animals, caused by thunder.**

Ps 29:9 — The voice of the LORD maketh the hinds to calve, and discovereth the forests: and in his temple doth every one speak of *his* glory.

ABRAHAM

- **Called also Abram.**
- **Son of Terah.**

Ge 11:26–27

- **Marries Sarah.**

Ge 11:29 — And Abram and Nahor took them wives: the name of Abram's wife *was* Sarai; and the name of Nahor's wife, Milcah, the daughter of Haran, the father of Milcah, and the father of Iscah.

- **Dwells in Ur, but removes to Haran.**

Ge 11:31 — And Terah took Abram his son, and Lot the son of Haran his son's son, and Sarai his daughter in law, his son Abram's wife; and they went forth with them from Ur of the Chaldees, to go into the land of Canaan; and they came unto Haran, and dwelt there.

Ne 9:7 — Thou *art* the LORD the God, who didst choose Abram, and broughtest him forth out of Ur of the Chaldees, and gavest him the name of Abraham;

Ac 7:4 — Then came he out of the land of the Chaldaeans, and dwelt in Charran: and from thence, when his father was dead, he removed him into this land, wherein ye now dwell.

- **Removes to Canaan.**

Ge 12:4–6

Ac 7:4 — Then came he out of the land of the Chaldaeans, and dwelt in Charran: and from thence, when his father was dead, he removed him into this land, wherein ye now dwell.

- **Divine call of.**

Ge 12:1–3; Ac 7:2–3

Jos 24:3 — And I took your father Abraham from the other side of the flood, and led him throughout all the land of Canaan, and multiplied his seed, and gave him Isaac.

Ne 9:7 — Thou *art* the LORD the God, who didst choose Abram, and broughtest him forth out of Ur of the Chaldees, and gavest him the name of Abraham;

Isa 51:2 — Look unto Abraham your father, and unto Sarah *that* bare you: for I called him alone, and blessed him, and increased him.

Heb 11:8 — By faith Abraham, when he was called to go out into a place which he should after receive for an inheritance, obeyed; and he went out, not knowing whither he went.

- **Canaan given to.**

Ge 15:7–21

Ge 12:1 — Now the LORD had said unto Abram, Get thee out of thy country, and from thy kindred, and from thy father's house, unto a land that I will shew thee:

Ge 12:7 — And the LORD appeared unto Abram, and said, Unto thy seed will I give this land: and there builded he an altar unto the LORD, who appeared unto him.

Eze 33:24 — Son of man, they that inhabit those wastes of the land of Israel speak, saying, Abraham was one, and he inherited the land: but we *are* many; the land is given us for inheritance.

• Dwells in Bethel.

Ge 12:8 — And he removed from thence unto a mountain on the east of Bethel, and pitched his tent, *having* Bethel on the west, and Hai on the east: and there he builded an altar unto the LORD, and called upon the name of the LORD.

• Sojourns in Egypt.

Ge 12:10–20

Ge 26:1 — And there was a famine in the land, beside the first famine that was in the days of Abraham. And Isaac went unto Abimelech king of the Philistines unto Gerar.

• Deferring to Lot, chooses Hebron.

Ge 13:1–18

Ge 14:13 — And there came one that had escaped, and told Abram the Hebrew; for he dwelt in the plain of Mamre the Amorite, brother of Eshcol, and brother of Aner: and these *were* confederate with Abram.

Ge 35:27 — And Jacob came unto Isaac his father unto Mamre, unto the city of Arbah, which *is* Hebron, where Abraham and Isaac sojourned.

• Dwells in Gerar.

Ge 20:1–18; 21:22–34

• Defeats Chedorlaomer.

Ge 14:5–24

Heb 7:1 — For this Melchisedec, king of Salem, priest of the most high God, who met Abraham returning from the slaughter of the kings, and blessed him;

• Is blessed by Melchizedek.

Ge 14:18–20; Heb 7:1–10

• God's covenant with.

Ge 15:1–21; 17:1–22; Gal 3:6–18; 4:22–31; Heb 6:13–14

Mic 7:20 — Thou wilt perform the truth to Jacob, *and* the mercy to Abraham, which thou hast sworn unto our fathers from the days of old.

Lk 1:73 — The oath which he sware to our father Abraham,

Ro 4:13 — For the promise, that he should be the heir of the world, *was* not to Abraham, or to his seed, through the law, but through the righteousness of faith.

Ro 15:8 — Now I say that Jesus Christ was a minister of the circumcision for the truth of God, to confirm the promises *made* unto the fathers:

Gal 3:29 — And if ye *be* Christ's, then are ye Abraham's seed, and heirs according to the promise.

• Called Abraham.

Ge 17:5 — Neither shall thy name any more be called Abram, but thy name shall be Abraham; for a father of many nations have I made thee.

Ne 9:7 — Thou *art* the LORD the God, who didst choose Abram, and broughtest him forth out of Ur of the Chaldees, and gavest him the name of Abraham;

• Circumcision of.

Ge 17:10–14; 17:23–27

• Angels appear to.

Ge 18:1–16

Ge 22:11 — And the angel of the LORD called unto him out of heaven, and said, Abraham, Abraham: and he said, Here *am* I.

Ge 22:15 — And the angel of the LORD called unto Abraham out of heaven the second time,

Ge 24:7 — The LORD God of heaven, which took me from my father's house, and from the land of my kindred, and which spake unto me, and that sware unto me, saying, Unto thy seed will I give this land; he shall send his angel before thee, and thou shalt take a wife unto my son from thence.

• His questions about the destruction of the righteous and wicked in Sodom.

Ge 18:23–32

• Witnesses the destruction of Sodom.

Ge 19:27–28

• Ishmael born to.

Ge 16:3 — And Sarai Abram's wife took Hagar her maid the Egyptian, after Abram had dwelt ten years in the land of Canaan, and gave her to her husband Abram to be his wife.

Ge 16:15 — And Hagar bare Abram a son: and Abram called his son's name, which Hagar bare, Ishmael.

• Dwells in Gerar; deceives Abimelech concerning Sarah, his wife.

Ge 20:1–18

• Isaac born to.

Ge 21:2–3; Gal 4:22–30

• Sends Hagar and Ishmael away.

Ge 21:10–14; Gal 4:22–30

• Trial of his faith in the offering of Isaac.

Ge 22:1–19

Heb 11:17 — By faith Abraham, when he was tried, offered up Isaac: and he that had received the promises offered up his only begotten *son,*

Jas 2:21 — Was not Abraham our father justified by works, when he had offered Isaac his son upon the altar?

• Sarah, his wife, dies.

Ge 23:1–2

• He purchases a place for her burial, and buries her in a cave.

Ge 23:3–20

• Marries Keturah.

Ge 25:1 — Then again Abraham took a wife, and her name *was* Keturah.

• Provides a wife for Isaac.

Ge 24:1–67

• Children of.

Ge 21:2–3; 25:1–4; 1Ch 1:32–34

Ge 16:15 — And Hagar bare Abram a son: and Abram called his son's name, which Hagar bare, Ishmael.

• Testament of.

Ge 25:5–6

• Wealth of.

Ge 13:2 — And Abram *was* very rich in cattle, in silver, and in gold.

Ge 24:35 — And the LORD hath blessed my master greatly; and he is become great: and he hath given him flocks, and herds, and silver, and gold, and menservants, and maidservants, and camels, and asses.

Isa 51:2 — Look unto Abraham your father, and unto Sarah *that* bare you: for I called him alone, and blessed him, and increased him.

• Age of, at different periods.

Ge 12:4 — So Abram departed, as the LORD had spoken unto him; and Lot went with him: and Abram *was* seventy and five years old when he departed out of Haran.

Ge 16:16 — And Abram *was* fourscore and six years old, when Hagar bare Ishmael to Abram.

Ge 21:5 — And Abraham was an hundred years old, when his son Isaac was born unto him.

Ge 25:7 — And these *are* the days of the years of Abraham's life which he lived, an hundred threescore and fifteen years.

• Death.

Ge 25:8–10

Ge 15:15 — And thou shalt go to thy fathers in peace; thou shalt be buried in a good old age.

• In paradise.

Lk 16:22–31

Mt 8:11 — And I say unto you, That many shall come from the east and west, and shall sit down with Abraham, and Isaac, and Jacob, in the kingdom of heaven.

Lk 13:28 — There shall be weeping and gnashing of teeth, when ye shall see Abraham, and Isaac, and Jacob, and all the prophets, in the kingdom of God, and you *yourselves* thrust out.

• Friend of God.

2Ch 20:7 — *Art* not thou our God, *who* didst drive out the inhabitants of this land before thy people Israel, and gavest it to the seed of Abraham thy friend for ever?

Isa 41:8 — But thou, Israel, *art* my servant, Jacob whom I have chosen, the seed of Abraham my friend.

Jas 2:23 — And the scripture was fulfilled which saith, Abraham believed God, and it was imputed unto him for righteousness: and he was called the Friend of God.

• Piety of.

Ge 12:7–8; 22:3–13; Ne 9:7–8; Ro 4:16–18

Ge 13:4 — Unto the place of the altar, which he had made there at the first: and there Abram called on the name of the LORD.

Ge 13:18 — Then Abram removed *his* tent, and came and dwelt in the plain of Mamre, which *is* in Hebron, and built there an altar unto the LORD.

Ge 18:19 — For I know him, that he will command his children and his household after him, and they shall keep the way of the LORD, to do justice and judgment; that the LORD may bring upon Abraham that which he hath spoken of him.

Ge 20:7 — Now therefore restore the man *his* wife; for he *is* a prophet, and he shall pray for thee, and thou shalt live: and if thou restore *her* not, know thou that thou shalt surely die, thou, and all that *are* thine.

Ge 21:33 — And *Abraham* planted a grove in Beersheba, and called there on the name of the LORD, the everlasting God.

Ge 26:5 — Because that Abraham obeyed my voice, and kept my charge, my commandments, my statutes, and my laws.

2Ch 20:7 — *Art* not thou our God, *who* didst drive out the inhabitants of this land before thy people Israel, and gavest it to the seed of Abraham thy friend for ever?

Isa 41:8 — But thou, Israel, *art* my servant, Jacob whom I have chosen, the seed of Abraham my friend.

Jas 2:23 — And the scripture was fulfilled which saith, Abraham believed God, and it was imputed unto him for righteousness: and he was called the Friend of God.

• A prophet.

Ge 20:7 — Now therefore restore the man *his* wife; for he *is* a prophet, and he shall pray for thee, and thou shalt live: and if thou restore *her* not, know thou that thou shalt surely die, thou, and all that *are* thine.

• Faith of.

Ro 4:1–22; Gal 3:6–9; Heb 11:8–10; 11:17–19; Jas 2:21–24

Ge 15:6 — And he believed in the LORD; and he counted it to him for righteousness.

• Unselfishness of.

Ge 21:25–30

Ge 13:9 — *Is* not the whole land before thee? separate thyself, I pray thee, from me: if *thou wilt take* the left hand, then I will go to the right; or if *thou depart* to the right hand, then I will go to the left.

• Independence of, in character.

Ge 23:6–16

Ge 14:23 — That I will not *take* from a thread even to a shoelatchet, and that I will not take any thing that *is* thine, lest thou shouldest say, I have made Abram rich:

• Ancestors of, idolatrous.

Jos 24:2 — And Joshua said unto all the people, Thus saith the LORD God of Israel, Your fathers dwelt on the other side of the flood in old time, *even* Terah, the father of Abraham, and the father of Nachor: and they served other gods.

• How regarded by his descendants.

Jn 8:33–40; 8:52–59

Mt 3:9 — And think not to say within yourselves, We have Abraham to *our* father: for I say unto you, that God is able of these stones to raise up children unto Abraham.

Lk 13:16 — And ought not this woman, being a daughter of Abraham, whom Satan hath bound, lo, these eighteen years, be loosed from this bond on the sabbath day?

Lk 13:28 — There shall be weeping and gnashing of teeth, when ye shall see Abraham, and Isaac, and Jacob, and all the prophets, in the kingdom of God, and you *yourselves* thrust out.

Lk 19:9 — And Jesus said unto him, This day is salvation come to this house, forsomuch as he also is a son of Abraham.

ABSALOM

- **Called also Abishalom.**
- **Son of David by Maacah.**

2Sa 3:3 — And his second, Chileab, of Abigail the wife of Nabal the Carmelite; and the third, Absalom the son of Maacah the daughter of Talmai king of Geshur;

1Ch 3:2 — The third, Absalom the son of Maachah the daughter of Talmai king of Geshur: the fourth, Adonijah the son of Haggith:

- **Beauty of.**

2Sa 14:25 — But in all Israel there was none to be so much praised as Absalom for his beauty: from the sole of his foot even to the crown of his head there was no blemish in him.

- **Slays Amnon.**

2Sa 13:22–29

- **Flees to Geshur.**

2Sa 13:37–38

- **Is permitted by David to return to Jerusalem.**

2Sa 14:1–24

- **His demagogism.**

2Sa 15:2–6

2Sa 15:13 — And there came a messenger to David, saying, The hearts of the men of Israel are after Absalom.

- **His conspiracy.**

2Sa 15:1–17:29

- **His death and burial.**

2Sa 18:9–17

- **David's mourning for.**

2Sa 18:33–19:8

- **Children of.**

2Sa 14:27 — And unto Absalom there were born three sons, and one daughter, whose name *was* Tamar: she was a woman of a fair countenance.

2Sa 18:18 — Now Absalom in his lifetime had taken and reared up for himself a pillar, which *is* in the king's dale: for he said, I have no son to keep my name in remembrance: and he called the pillar after his own name: and it is called unto this day, Absalom's place.

1Ki 15:2 — Three years reigned he in Jerusalem. And his mother's name *was* Maachah, the daughter of Abishalom.

2Ch 11:20 — And after her he took Maachah the daughter of Absalom; which bare him Abijah, and Attai, and Ziza, and Shelomith.

- **Pillar of.**

2Sa 18:18 — Now Absalom in his lifetime had taken and reared up for himself a pillar, which *is* in the king's dale: for he said, I have no son to keep my name in remembrance: and he called the pillar after his own name: and it is called unto this day, Absalom's place.

ABSTEMIOUSNESS

Pr 23:1–3

- **Instances of.**
  - **Daniel and his Hebrew companions.**

    Da 1:8–16
  - **John the Baptist.**

    Mt 11:18

⇾See: Abstinence, Total

⇾See: Temperance

ABSTINENCE, Total

- **From intoxicating beverages.**

Le 10:8–10; Nu 6:3–4; Jgs 13:13–14; Pr 23:31–32; Jer 35:6–8

Jgs 13:4 — Now therefore beware, I pray thee, and drink not wine nor strong drink, and eat not any unclean *thing:*

Est 1:8 — And the drinking *was* according to the law; none did compel: for so the king had appointed to all the officers of his house, that they should do according to every man's pleasure.

Pr 23:20 — Be not among winebibbers; among riotous eaters of flesh:

Pr 31:4 — *It is* not for kings, O Lemuel, *it is* not for kings to drink wine; nor for princes strong drink:

Jer 35:14 — The words of Jonadab the son of Rechab, that he commanded his sons not to drink wine, are performed; for unto this day they drink none, but obey their father's commandment: notwithstanding I have spoken unto you, rising early and speaking; but ye hearkened not unto me.

Lk 1:15 — For he shall be great in the sight of the Lord, and shall drink neither wine nor strong drink; and he shall be filled with the Holy Ghost, even from his mother's womb.

⇾See: Temperance

- **Instances of.**
  - **Israelites in the wilderness.**

    Dt 29:6
  - **Samson.**

    Nu 6:3–4; Jgs 13:3–5; 13:13–14; 16:17
  - **Daniel.**

    Da 1:8; 1:12
  - **Rechabites.**

    Jer 35:6–14
  - **John the Baptist.**

    Mt 11:18; Lk 1:15; 7:33

ABUNDANT LIFE

Jn 10:10 — The thief cometh not, but for to steal, and to kill, and to destroy: I am come that they might have life, and that they might have *it* more abundantly.

ABUSE

Eph 6:1–4

Ge 2:18 — And the LORD God said, *It is* not good that the man should be alone; I will make him an help meet for him.

Ge 2:20 — And Adam gave names to all cattle, and to the fowl of the air, and to every beast of the field; but for Adam there was not found an help meet for him.

Ps 127:3 — Lo, children *are* an heritage of the LORD: *and* the fruit of the womb *is his* reward.

Pr 12:10 — A righteous *man* regardeth the life of his beast: but the tender mercies of the wicked *are* cruel.

Eph 5:25 — Husbands, love your wives, even as Christ also loved the church, and gave himself for it;

1Pe 3:7 — Likewise, ye husbands, dwell with *them* according to knowledge, giving honour unto the wife, as unto the weaker vessel, and as being heirs together of the grace of life; that your prayers be not hindered.

ACCAD • A city conquered by Nimrod.

Ge 10:10 — And the beginning of his kingdom was Babel, and Erech, and Accad, and Calneh, in the land of Shinar.

ACCESSORY ✦See: Complicity

ACCHO

• Called also Ptolemais.

• A town of Phenicia.

Jgs 1:31 — Neither did Asher drive out the inhabitants of Accho, nor the inhabitants of Zidon, nor of Ahlab, nor of Achzib, nor of Helbah, nor of Aphik, nor of Rehob:

Ac 21:7 — And when we had finished *our* course from Tyre, we came to Ptolemais, and saluted the brethren, and abode with them one day.

ACCOMPLICE ✦See: Complicity

ACCOUNTABILITY ✦See: Responsibility

ACCURSED

• What so called.

Dt 21:23 — His body shall not remain all night upon the tree, but thou shalt in any wise bury him that day; (for he that is hanged *is* accursed of God;) that thy land be not defiled, which the LORD thy God giveth thee *for* an inheritance.

Jos 6:17 — And the city shall be accursed, *even* it, and all that *are* therein, to the LORD: only Rahab the harlot shall live, she and all that *are* with her in the house, because she hid the messengers that we sent.

Jos 7:1 — But the children of Israel committed a trespass in the accursed thing: for Achan, the son of Carmi, the son of Zabdi, the son of Zerah, of the tribe of Judah, took of the accursed thing: and the anger of the LORD was kindled against the children of Israel.

1Ch 2:7 — And the sons of Carmi; Achar, the troubler of Israel, who transgressed in the thing accursed.

Isa 65:20 — There shall be no more thence an infant of days, nor an old man that hath not filled his days: for the child shall die an hundred years old; but the sinner *being* an hundred years old shall be accursed.

Gal 1:8 — But though we, or an angel from heaven, preach any other gospel unto you than that which we have preached unto you, let him be accursed.

ACCUSATION, False

Ps 41:5–9

Ex 23:1 — Thou shalt not raise a false report: put not thine hand with the wicked to be an unrighteous witness.

Ex 23:7 — Keep thee far from a false matter; and the innocent and righteous slay thou not: for I will not justify the wicked.

Le 19:16 — Thou shalt not go up and down *as* a talebearer among thy people: neither shalt thou stand against the blood of thy neighbour: I *am* the LORD.

Mt 5:11 — Blessed are ye, when *men* shall revile you, and persecute *you*, and shall say all manner of evil against you falsely, for my sake.

Lk 3:14 — And the soldiers likewise demanded of him, saying, And what shall we do? And he said unto them, Do violence to no man, neither accuse *any* falsely; and be content with your wages.

2Ti 3:3 — Without natural affection, trucebreakers, false accusers, incontinent, fierce, despisers of those that are good,

1Pe 4:14 — If ye be reproached for the name of Christ, happy *are ye;* for the spirit of glory and of God resteth upon you: on their part he is evil spoken of, but on your part he is glorified.

✦See: Conspiracy

✦See: Evidence

✦See: Falsehood, False Witness

✦See: Persecution

✦See: Speaking; evil

✦See: Talebearer

• Incidents illustrative of.

• Against Joseph by Potiphar's wife.

Ge 39:7–20

• Against Joseph's brethren by Joseph.

Ge 42:9–14

• Against Moses by Korah.

Nu 16:3 — And they gathered themselves together against Moses and against Aaron, and said unto them, *Ye take* too much upon you, seeing all the congregation *are* holy, every one of them, and the LORD *is* among them: wherefore then lift ye up yourselves above the congregation of the LORD?

Nu 16:13 — *Is it* a small thing that thou hast brought us up out of a land that floweth with milk and honey, to kill us in the wilderness, except thou make thyself altogether a prince over us?

• Against the prophet Ahimelech by Saul.

1Sa 22:11–16

• Against Abner by Joab.

2Sa 3:24–27

• Against David by the princes of Ammon.

2Sa 10:3 — And the princes of the children of Ammon said unto Hanun their lord, Thinkest thou that David doth honour thy father, that he hath sent comforters unto thee? hath not David *rather* sent his servants unto thee, to search the city, and to spy it out, and to overthrow it?

- **Against Elijah by Ahab.**
  1Ki 18:17–18
- **Against Naboth by Jezebel.**
  1Ki 21:10 — And set two men, sons of Belial, before him, to bear witness against him, saying, Thou didst blaspheme God and the king. And *then* carry him out, and stone him, that he may die.
  1Ki 21:13 — And there came in two men, children of Belial, and sat before him: and the men of Belial witnessed against him, *even* against Naboth, in the presence of the people, saying, Naboth did blaspheme God and the king. Then they carried him forth out of the city, and stoned him with stones, that he died.
- **Against Jews, returned under Ezra.**
  Ezr 4:6–16; Ne 6:6–8
- **Against Jeremiah.**
  Jer 37:13–14; 43:2–3
  Jer 26:8 — Now it came to pass, when Jeremiah had made an end of speaking all that the LORD had commanded *him* to speak unto all the people, that the priests and the prophets and all the people took him, saying, Thou shalt surely die.
  Jer 26:11 — Then spake the priests and the prophets unto the princes and to all the people, saying, This man *is* worthy to die; for he hath prophesied against this city, as ye have heard with your ears.
- **Against Amos.**
  Am 7:10–11
- **Against Mary.**
  Mt 1:19 — Then Joseph her husband, being a just *man,* and not willing to make her a publick example, was minded to put her away privily.
- **Against Jesus.**
  Mt 12:2–14; 26:59–61; Mk 14:53–65
  Mt 9:34 — But the Pharisees said, He casteth out devils through the prince of the devils.
  Mt 10:25 — It is enough for the disciple that he be as his master, and the servant as his lord. If they have called the master of the house Beelzebub, how much more *shall they call* them of his household?
  Mk 3:22 — And the scribes which came down from Jerusalem said, He hath Beelzebub, and by the prince of the devils casteth he out devils.
  Lk 23:2 — And they began to accuse him, saying, We found this *fellow* perverting the nation, and forbidding to give tribute to Caesar, saying that he himself is Christ a King.
  Jn 18:30 — They answered and said unto him, If he were not a malefactor, we would not have delivered him up unto thee.
- **Against Stephen.**
  Ac 6:11 — Then they suborned men, which said, We have heard him speak blasphemous words against Moses, and *against* God.
  Ac 6:13 — And set up false witnesses, which said, This man ceaseth not to speak blasphemous words against this holy place, and the law:
- **Against Paul.**
  Ac 24:5–6
  Ac 17:7 — Whom Jason hath received: and these all do contrary to the decrees of Caesar, saying that there is another king, *one* Jesus.
  Ac 21:28 — Crying out, Men of Israel, help: This is the man, that teacheth all *men* every where against the people, and the law, and this place: and further brought Greeks also into the temple, and hath polluted this holy place.
  Ac 24:13 — Neither can they prove the things whereof they now accuse me.
  Ac 25:2 — Then the high priest and the chief of the Jews informed him against Paul, and besought him,
  Ac 25:7 — And when he was come, the Jews which came down from Jerusalem stood round about, and laid many and grievous complaints against Paul, which they could not prove.
  Ro 3:8 — And not *rather,* (as we be slanderously reported, and as some affirm that we say,) Let us do evil, that good may come? whose damnation is just.
- **Against Paul and Silas.**
  Ac 16:20–21
- **Satan falsely accuses Job.**
  Job 1:9–10; Job 2:4–5

ACELDAMA • The field of blood.

Mt 27:8 — Wherefore that field was called, The field of blood, unto this day.
Ac 1:19 — And it was known unto all the dwellers at Jerusalem; insomuch as that field is called in their proper tongue, Aceldama, that is to say, The field of blood.

ACHAIA

- **A region of Greece.**
- **Paul visits.**
  Ac 18:1–28
  Ac 19:21 — After these things were ended, Paul purposed in the spirit, when he had passed through Macedonia and Achaia, to go to Jerusalem, saying, After I have been there, I must also see Rome.
  Ro 16:5 — Likewise *greet* the church that is in their house. Salute my wellbeloved Epaenetus, who is the firstfruits of Achaia unto Christ.
  1Co 16:15 — I beseech you, brethren, (ye know the house of Stephanas, that it is the firstfruits of Achaia, and *that* they have addicted themselves to the ministry of the saints,)
  2Co 1:1 — Paul, an apostle of Jesus Christ by the will of God, and Timothy *our* brother, unto the church of God which is at Corinth, with all the saints which are in all Achaia:
- **Benevolence of the Christians in.**
  Ro 15:26 — For it hath pleased them of Macedonia and Achaia to make a certain contribution for the poor saints which are at Jerusalem.

2Co 9:2 — For I know the forwardness of your mind, for which I boast of you to them of Macedonia, that Achaia was ready a year ago; and your zeal hath provoked very many.

2Co 11:10 — As the truth of Christ is in me, no man shall stop me of this boasting in the regions of Achaia.

ACHAICUS • A citizen of Corinth.

1Co 16:17–18

ACHAN • Sin and punishment of.

Jos 7:1–26

Jos 22:20 — Did not Achan the son of Zerah commit a trespass in the accursed thing, and wrath fell on all the congregation of Israel? and that man perished not alone in his iniquity.

1Ch 2:7 — And the sons of Carmi; Achar, the troubler of Israel, who transgressed in the thing accursed.

ACHAZ ➜See: Ahaz

ACHBOR

• Father of King Baal-hanan.

Ge 36:39 — And Baal-hanan the son of Achbor died, and Hadar reigned in his stead: and the name of his city *was* Pau; and his wife's name *was* Mehetabel, the daughter of Matred, the daughter of Mezahab.

1Ch 1:49 — And when Shaul was dead, Baal-hanan the son of Achbor reigned in his stead.

• Or Abdon, one of Josiah's courtiers.

2Ki 22:14 — So Hilkiah the priest, and Ahikam, and Achbor, and Shaphan, and Asahiah, went unto Huldah the prophetess, the wife of Shallum the son of Tikvah, the son of Harhas, keeper of the wardrobe; (now she dwelt in Jerusalem in the college;) and they communed with her.

2Ch 34:20 — And the king commanded Hilkiah, and Ahikam the son of Shaphan, and Abdon the son of Micah, and Shaphan the scribe, and Asaiah a servant of the king's, saying,

• Father of Elnathan.

Jer 26:22 — And Jehoiakim the king sent men into Egypt, *namely,* Elnathan the son of Achbor, and *certain* men with him into Egypt.

Jer 36:12 — Then he went down into the king's house, into the scribe's chamber: and, lo, all the princes sat there, *even* Elishama the scribe, and Delaiah the son of Shemaiah, and Elnathan the son of Achbor, and Gemariah the son of Shaphan, and Zedekiah the son of Hananiah, and all the princes.

Jer 36:25 — Nevertheless Elnathan and Delaiah and Gemariah had made intercession to the king that he would not burn the roll: but he would not hear them.

ACHIM • Ancestor of Jesus.

Mt 1:14 — And Azor begat Sadoc; and Sadoc begat Achim; and Achim begat Eliud;

ACHISH

• Called also Abimelech.

• King of the Philistines.

• David escapes to.

1Sa 21:10–15; 27:1–28:2; 29:1–11; 1Ki 2:39–40

ACHMETHA • A Persian city.

Ezr 6:2 — And there was found at Achmetha, in the palace that is in the province of the Medes, a roll, and therein *was* a record thus written:

ACHOR • A valley near Jericho.

Jos 7:26 — And they raised over him a great heap of stones unto this day. So the LORD turned from the fierceness of his anger. Wherefore the name of that place was called, The valley of Achor, unto this day.

Jos 15:7 — And the border went up toward Debir from the valley of Achor, and so northward, looking toward Gilgal, *that is* before the going up to Adummim, which *is* on the south side of the river: and the border passed toward the waters of En-shemesh, and the goings out thereof were at En-rogel:

Isa 65:10 — And Sharon shall be a fold of flocks, and the valley of Achor a place for the herds to lie down in, for my people that have sought me.

Hos 2:15 — And I will give her her vineyards from thence, and the valley of Achor for a door of hope: and she shall sing there, as in the days of her youth, and as in the day when she came up out of the land of Egypt.

ACHSAH

• Caleb's daughter.

Jos 15:16–19; Jgs 1:9–13

• Called Achsa.

1Ch 2:49 — She bare also Shaaph the father of Madmannah, Sheva the father of Machbenah, and the father of Gibea: and the daughter of Caleb *was* Achsa.

ACHSHAPH • An ancient city in North Palestine.

Jos 11:1 — And it came to pass, when Jabin king of Hazor had heard *those things,* that he sent to Jobab king of Madon, and to the king of Shimron, and to the king of Achshaph,

Jos 12:20 — The king of Shimron-meron, one; the king of Achshaph, one;

Jos 19:25 — And their border was Helkath, and Hali, and Beten, and Achshaph,

ACHZIB

• A city of Asher.

Jos 19:29 — And *then* the coast turneth to Ramah, and to the strong city Tyre; and the coast turneth to Hosah; and the outgoings thereof are at the sea from the coast to Achzib:

Jgs 1:31 — Neither did Asher drive out the inhabitants of Accho, nor the inhabitants of Zidon, nor of Ahlab, nor of Achzib, nor of Helbah, nor of Aphik, nor of Rehob:

• **A city of Judah.**

Jos 15:44 — And Keilah, and Achzib, and Mareshah; nine cities with their villages:

• **Called also Chezib.**

Ge 38:5 — And she yet again conceived, and bare a son; and called his name Shelah: and he was at Chezib, when she bare him.

ACRE

• **The indefinite quantity of land a yoke of oxen could plow in a day.**

1Sa 14:14 — And that first slaughter, which Jonathan and his armourbearer made, was about twenty men, within as it were an half acre of land, *which* a yoke *of oxen might plow.*

Isa 5:10 — Yea, ten acres of vineyard shall yield one bath, and the seed of an homer shall yield an ephah.

ACROSTIC POETRY ↞See: Poetry

ACTIONS AT LAW

• **Duty of defendant.**

Mt 5:40 — And if any man will sue thee at the law, and take away thy coat, let him have *thy* cloke also.

↞**See: Adjudication at Law**

↞**See: Arbitration**

ADADAH • A city of Judah.

Jos 15:22 — And Kinah, and Dimonah, and Adadah,

ADAH

• **Wife of Lamech.**

Ge 4:19–23

• **Wife of Esau.**

Ge 36:10–12

ADAIAH

• **Grandfather of Josiah.**

2Ki 22:1 — Josiah *was* eight years old when he began to reign, and he reigned thirty and one years in Jerusalem. And his mother's name *was* Jedidah, the daughter of Adaiah of Boscath.

• **A musician.**

1Ch 6:41 — The son of Ethni, the son of Zerah, the son of Adaiah,

• **A priest.**

1Ch 9:12 — And Adaiah the son of Jeroham, the son of Pashur, the son of Malchijah, and Maasiai the son of Adiel, the son of Jahzerah, the son of Meshullam, the son of Meshillemith, the son of Immer;

Ne 11:12 — And their brethren that did the work of the house *were* eight hundred twenty and two: and Adaiah the son of Jeroham, the son of Pelaliah, the son of Amzi, the son of Zechariah, the son of Pashur, the son of Malchiah,

• **A Benjamite.**

1Ch 8:21 — And Adaiah, and Beraiah, and Shimrath, the sons of Shimhi;

• **Father of Maaseiah.**

2Ch 23:1 — And in the seventh year Jehoiada strengthened himself, and took the captains of hundreds, Azariah the son of Jeroham, and Ishmael the son of Jehohanan, and Azariah the son of Obed, and Maaseiah the son of Adaiah, and Elishaphat the son of Zichri, into covenant with him.

• **Two sons of Bani.**

Ezr 10:29 — And of the sons of Bani; Meshullam, Malluch, and Adaiah, Jashub, and Sheal, and Ramoth.

Ezr 10:39 — And Shelemiah, and Nathan, and Adaiah,

• **Son of Joiarib.**

Ne 11:5 — And Maaseiah the son of Baruch, the son of Col-hozeh, the son of Hazaiah, the son of Adaiah, the son of Joiarib, the son of Zechariah, the son of Shiloni.

ADALIA • Son of Haman.

Est 9:8 — And Poratha, and Adalia, and Aridatha,

ADAM

• **The first man.**

• **Creation of.**

Ge 1:26–28

Ge 2:7 — And the LORD God formed man *of* the dust of the ground, and breathed into his nostrils the breath of life; and man became a living soul.

1Co 15:45 — And so it is written, The first man Adam was made a living soul; the last Adam *was made* a quickening spirit.

1Ti 2:13 — For Adam was first formed, then Eve.

• **History of, before he sinned.**

Ge 1:26–30; 2:16–25

• **Temptation and sin of.**

Ge 3:1–24; Ro 5:14–21

Job 31:33 — If I covered my transgressions as Adam, by hiding mine iniquity in my bosom:

Isa 43:27 — Thy first father hath sinned, and thy teachers have transgressed against me.

Hos 6:7 — But they like men have transgressed the covenant: there have they dealt treacherously against me.

1Ti 2:14 — And Adam was not deceived, but the woman being deceived was in the transgression.

• **Subsequent history of.**

Ge 3:20–4:2; 5:1–5

Ge 4:25 — And Adam knew his wife again; and she bare a son, and called his name Seth: For God, *said she,* hath appointed me another seed instead of Abel, whom Cain slew.

• **His death.**

Ge 5:5 — And all the days that Adam lived were nine hundred and thirty years: and he died.

• **Progenitor of the human race.**

Dt 32:8 — When the most High divided to the nations their inheritance, when he separated the sons of Adam, he set the bounds of the people according to the number of the children of Israel.

Mal 2:10 — Have we not all one father? hath not one God created us? why do we deal treacherously every man against his brother, by profaning the covenant of our fathers?

• Brought sin into the world.

1Co 15:22 — For as in Adam all die, even so in Christ shall all be made alive.

1Co 15:45 — And so it is written, The first man Adam was made a living soul; the last Adam *was made* a quickening spirit.

• Type of Christ.

Ro 5:14 — Nevertheless death reigned from Adam to Moses, even over them that had not sinned after the similitude of Adam's transgression, who is the figure of him that was to come.

• A name of Christ.

1Co 15:45 — And so it is written, The first man Adam was made a living soul; the last Adam *was made* a quickening spirit.

1Co 15:47 — The first man *is* of the earth, earthy: the second man *is* the Lord from heaven.

• A city near the Jordan.

Jos 3:16 — That the waters which came down from above stood *and* rose up upon an heap very far from the city Adam, that *is* beside Zaretan: and those that came down toward the sea of the plain, *even* the salt sea, failed, *and* were cut off: and the people passed over right against Jericho.

ADAMAH

• Called also Adami.

• A city of Naphtali.

Jos 19:33 — And their coast was from Heleph, from Allon to Zaanannim, and Adami, Nekeb, and Jabneel, unto Lakum; and the outgoings thereof were at Jordan:

Jos 19:36 — And Adamah, and Ramah, and Hazor,

ADAMANT

• A flint.

Eze 3:9 — As an adamant harder than flint have I made thy forehead: fear them not, neither be dismayed at their looks, though they *be* a rebellious house.

Zec 7:12 — Yea, they made their hearts *as* an adamant stone, lest they should hear the law, and the words which the LORD of hosts hath sent in his spirit by the former prophets: therefore came a great wrath from the LORD of hosts.

→See: Diamond

ADAMI →See: Adamah

ADAR

• Twelfth month in Jewish calendar.

Ezr 6:15 — And this house was finished on the third day of the month Adar, which was in the sixth year of the reign of Darius the king.

Est 3:7 — In the first month, that *is,* the month Nisan, in the twelfth year of king Ahasuerus, they cast Pur, that *is,* the lot, before Haman from day to day, and from month to month, *to* the twelfth *month,* that *is,* the month Adar.

Est 8:12 — Upon one day in all the provinces of king Ahasuerus, *namely,* upon the thirteenth *day* of the twelfth month, which *is* the month Adar.

Est 9:1 — Now in the twelfth month, that *is,* the month Adar, on the thirteenth day of the same, when the king's commandment and his decree drew near to be put in execution, in the day that the enemies of the Jews hoped to have power over them, (though it was turned to the contrary, that the Jews had rule over them that hated them;)

• Son of Bela.

1Ch 8:3 — And the sons of Bela were, Addar, and Gera, and Abihud,

→See: Hazar-Addar

ADBEEL • Son of Ishmael.

Ge 25:13 — And these *are* the names of the sons of Ishmael, by their names, according to their generations: the firstborn of Ishmael, Nebajoth; and Kedar, and Adbeel, and Mibsam,

1Ch 1:29 — These *are* their generations: The firstborn of Ishmael, Nebaioth; then Kedar, and Adbeel, and Mibsam,

ADDAN

• Called also Addon.

• Uncertain whether person or town.

Ezr 2:59 — And these *were* they which went up from Tel-melah, Tel-harsa, Cherub, Addan, *and* Immer: but they could not shew their father's house, and their seed, whether they *were* of Israel:

Ne 7:61 — And these *were* they which went up *also* from Telmelah, Telharesha, Cherub, Addon, and Immer: but they could not shew their father's house, nor their seed, whether they *were* of Israel.

ADDER • A venomous serpent.

Ge 49:17 — Dan shall be a serpent by the way, an adder in the path, that biteth the horse heels, so that his rider shall fall backward.

Ps 58:4 — Their poison *is* like the poison of a serpent: *they are* like the deaf adder *that* stoppeth her ear;

Ps 91:13 — Thou shalt tread upon the lion and adder: the young lion and the dragon shalt thou trample under feet.

Ps 140:3 — They have sharpened their tongues like a serpent; adders' poison *is* under their lips. Selah.

Pr 23:32 — At the last it biteth like a serpent, and stingeth like an adder.

ADDON →See: Addan

ADER • A Benjamite.

1Ch 8:15 — And Zebadiah, and Arad, and Ader,

ADIEL

• A man of the tribe of Simeon.

1Ch 4:36 — And Elioenai, and Jaakobah, and Jeshohaiah, and Asaiah, and Adiel, and Jesimiel, and Benaiah,

• **A priest.**

1Ch 9:12 — And Adaiah the son of Jeroham, the son of Pashur, the son of Malchijah, and Maasiai the son of Adiel, the son of Jahzerah, the son of Meshullam, the son of Meshillemith, the son of Immer;

• **Father of Azmaveth.**

1Ch 27:25 — And over the king's treasures *was* Azmaveth the son of Adiel: and over the storehouses in the fields, in the cities, and in the villages, and in the castles, *was* Jehonathan the son of Uzziah:

ADIN • A Jewish captive.

Ezr 2:15 — The children of Adin, four hundred fifty and four.

Ezr 8:6 — Of the sons also of Adin; Ebed the son of Jonathan, and with him fifty males.

Ne 7:20 — The children of Adin, six hundred fifty and five.

ADINA • One of David's heroes.

1Ch 11:42 — Adina the son of Shiza the Reubenite, a captain of the Reubenites, and thirty with him,

ADINO • One of David's valiant men.

2Sa 23:8 — These *be* the names of the mighty men whom David had: The Tachmonite that sat in the seat, chief among the captains; the same *was* Adino the Eznite: *he lift up his spear* against eight hundred, whom he slew at one time.

ADITHAIM • A city of Judah.

Jos 15:36 — And Sharaim, and Adithaim, and Gederah, and Gederothaim; fourteen cities with their villages:

ADJUDICATION AT LAW

• **To be avoided.**

Pr 25:8–10

Pr 17:14 — The beginning of strife *is as* when one letteth out water: therefore leave off contention, before it be meddled with.

Pr 20:3 — *It is* an honour for a man to cease from strife: but every fool will be meddling.

Mt 5:25 — Agree with thine adversary quickly, whiles thou art in the way with him; lest at any time the adversary deliver thee to the judge, and the judge deliver thee to the officer, and thou be cast into prison.

→See: Actions at Law

→See: Arbitration

→See: Compromise

→See: Court

→See: Justice

ADLAI • Father of Shaphat.

1Ch 27:29 — And over the herds that fed in Sharon *was* Shitrai the Sharonite: and over the herds *that were* in the valleys *was* Shaphat the son of Adlai:

ADMAH • A city in the vale of Siddim.

Ge 10:19 — And the border of the Canaanites was from Sidon, as thou comest to Gerar, unto Gaza; as thou goest, unto Sodom, and Gomorrah, and Admah, and Zeboim, even unto Lasha.

Ge 14:2 — *That these* made war with Bera king of Sodom, and with Birsha king of Gomorrah, Shinab king of Admah, and Shemeber king of Zeboiim, and the king of Bela, which is Zoar.

Dt 29:23 — *And that* the whole land thereof *is* brimstone, and salt, *and* burning, *that* it is not sown, nor beareth, nor any grass groweth therein, like the overthrow of Sodom, and Gomorrah, Admah, and Zeboim, which the LORD overthrew in his anger, and in his wrath:

Hos 11:8 — How shall I give thee up, Ephraim? *how* shall I deliver thee, Israel? how shall I make thee as Admah? *how* shall I set thee as Zeboim? mine heart is turned within me, my repentings are kindled together.

ADMATHA • A Persian prince.

Est 1:14 — And the next unto him *was* Carshena, Shethar, Admatha, Tarshish, Meres, Marsena, *and* Memucan, the seven princes of Persia and Media, which saw the king's face, *and* which sat the first in the kingdom;)

ADMONITION →See: Wicked; warned

ADNA

• **A son of Pahath-Moab.**

Ezr 10:30 — And of the sons of Pahath-moab; Adna, and Chelal, Benaiah, Maaseiah, Mattaniah, Bezaleel, and Binnui, and Manasseh.

• **A priest.**

Ne 12:15 — Of Harim, Adna; of Meraioth, Helkai;

ADNAH

• **One of David's captains.**

1Ch 12:20 — As he went to Ziklag, there fell to him of Manasseh, Adnah, and Jozabad, and Jediael, and Michael, and Jozabad, and Elihu, and Zilthai, captains of the thousands that *were* of Manasseh.

• **A military chief.**

2Ch 17:14 — And these *are* the numbers of them according to the house of their fathers: Of Judah, the captains of thousands; Adnah the chief, and with him mighty men of valour three hundred thousand.

ADONI-BEZEK • King of Bezek.

Jgs 1:4–7

ADONI-ZEDEK • A king of Jerusalem.

Jos 10:1–27

ADONIJAH

• **Son of David and Haggith.**

1Ki 1:5–6

2Sa 3:4 — And the fourth, Adonijah the son of Haggith; and the fifth, Shephatiah the son of Abital;

1Ch 3:2 — The third, Absalom the son of Maachah the daughter of Talmai king of Geshur: the fourth, Adonijah the son of Haggith:

- **Usurpation of, and downfall.**
  1Ki 1:1–53
- **Executed by Solomon.**
  1Ki 2:13 — And Adonijah the son of Haggith came to Bath-sheba the mother of Solomon. And she said, Comest thou peaceably? And he said, Peaceably.
  1Ki 2:25 — And king Solomon sent by the hand of Benaiah the son of Jehoiada; and he fell upon him that he died.

- **A Levite.**
  2Ch 17:8 — And with them *he sent* Levites, *even* Shemaiah, and Nethaniah, and Zebadiah, and Asahel, and Shemiramoth, and Jehonathan, and Adonijah, and Tobijah, and Tob-adonijah, Levites; and with them Elishama and Jehoram, priests.

  →**See: Adonikam**

ADONIKAM

- **Called also Adonijah.**
- **A Jew who returned with Ezra from Babylon.**
  Ezr 2:13 — The children of Adonikam, six hundred sixty and six.
  Ne 7:18 — The children of Adonikam, six hundred threescore and seven.
  Ne 10:16 — Adonijah, Bigvai, Adin,

ADONIRAM

- **Called also Adoram.**
- **A taxgatherer.**
  2Sa 20:24 — And Adoram *was* over the tribute: and Jehoshaphat the son of Ahilud *was* recorder:
  1Ki 4:6 — And Ahishar *was* over the household: and Adoniram the son of Abda *was* over the tribute.
  1Ki 5:14 — And he sent them to Lebanon ten thousand a month by courses: a month they were in Lebanon, *and* two months at home: and Adoniram *was* over the levy.
  1Ki 12:18 — Then king Rehoboam sent Adoram, who *was* over the tribute; and all Israel stoned him with stones, that he died. Therefore king Rehoboam made speed to get him up to his chariot, to flee to Jerusalem.

ADOPTION

Ge 15:3 — And Abram said, Behold, to me thou hast given no seed: and, lo, one born in my house is mine heir.

- **Of children.**
  - **Joseph's sons.**
    Ge 48:5 — And now thy two sons, Ephraim and Manasseh, which were born unto thee in the land of Egypt before I came unto thee into Egypt, *are* mine; as Reuben and Simeon, they shall be mine.
    Ge 48:14 — And Israel stretched out his right hand, and laid it upon Ephraim's head, who *was* the younger, and his left hand upon Manasseh's head, guiding his hands wittingly; for Manasseh *was* the firstborn.
    Ge 48:16 — The Angel which redeemed me from all evil, bless the lads; and let my name be named on them, and the name of my fathers Abraham and Isaac; and let them grow into a multitude in the midst of the earth.
    Ge 48:22 — Moreover I have given to thee one portion above thy brethren, which I took out of the hand of the Amorite with my sword and with my bow.
  - **Moses.**
    Ex 2:5–10
    Ac 7:21 — And when he was cast out, Pharaoh's daughter took him up, and nourished him for her own son.
    Heb 11:24 — By faith Moses, when he was come to years, refused to be called the son of Pharaoh's daughter;
  - **Esther.**
    Est 2:7 — And he brought up Hadassah, that *is,* Esther, his uncle's daughter: for she had neither father nor mother, and the maid *was* fair and beautiful; whom Mordecai, when her father and mother were dead, took for his own daughter.
- **Spiritual.**
  Ex 4:22–23; Dt 32:5–6; Isa 43:6–7; Jn 1:12–13; Ro 8:14–17; 9:1–33; 2Co 6:17–18; Gal 4:5–7; Heb 2:10–11; 12:6–7; 1Jn 3:1–2
  Nu 6:27 — And they shall put my name upon the children of Israel; and I will bless them.
  Dt 14:1 — Ye *are* the children of the LORD your God: ye shall not cut yourselves, nor make any baldness between your eyes for the dead.
  Dt 26:18 — And the LORD hath avouched thee this day to be his peculiar people, as he hath promised thee, and that *thou* shouldest keep all his commandments;
  Dt 27:9 — And Moses and the priests the Levites spake unto all Israel, saying, Take heed, and hearken, O Israel; this day thou art become the people of the LORD thy God.
  Dt 28:10 — And all people of the earth shall see that thou art called by the name of the LORD; and they shall be afraid of thee.
  2Sa 7:14 — I will be his father, and he shall be my son. If he commit iniquity, I will chasten him with the rod of men, and with the stripes of the children of men:
  1Ch 22:10 — He shall build an house for my name; and he shall be my son, and I *will be* his father; and I will establish the throne of his kingdom over Israel for ever.
  1Ch 28:6 — And he said unto me, Solomon thy son, he shall build my house and my courts: for I have chosen him *to be* my son, and I will be his father.
  2Ch 7:14 — If my people, which are called by my name, shall humble themselves, and pray, and seek my face, and turn from their wicked ways; then will I hear from heaven, and will forgive their sin, and will heal their land.

Pr 14:26 — In the fear of the LORD *is* strong confidence: and his children shall have a place of refuge.

Isa 8:18 — Behold, I and the children whom the LORD hath given me *are* for signs and for wonders in Israel from the LORD of hosts, which dwelleth in mount Zion.

Isa 63:8 — For he said, Surely they *are* my people, children *that* will not lie: so he was their Saviour.

Isa 63:16 — Doubtless thou *art* our father, though Abraham be ignorant of us, and Israel acknowledge us not: thou, O LORD, *art* our father, our redeemer; thy name *is* from everlasting.

Jer 3:19 — But I said, How shall I put thee among the children, and give thee a pleasant land, a goodly heritage of the hosts of nations? and I said, Thou shalt call me, My father; and shalt not turn away from me.

Jer 31:9 — They shall come with weeping, and with supplications will I lead them: I will cause them to walk by the rivers of waters in a straight way, wherein they shall not stumble: for I am a father to Israel, and Ephraim *is* my firstborn.

Jer 31:20 — *Is* Ephraim my dear son? *is he* a pleasant child? for since I spake against him, I do earnestly remember him still: therefore my bowels are troubled for him; I will surely have mercy upon him, saith the LORD.

Hos 1:9 — Then said *God,* Call his name Lo-ammi: for ye *are* not my people, and I will not be your *God.*

Hos 11:1 — When Israel *was* a child, then I loved him, and called my son out of Egypt.

Mt 5:9 — Blessed *are* the peacemakers: for they shall be called the children of God.

Mt 13:43 — Then shall the righteous shine forth as the sun in the kingdom of their Father. Who hath ears to hear, let him hear.

Lk 6:35 — But love ye your enemies, and do good, and lend, hoping for nothing again; and your reward shall be great, and ye shall be the children of the Highest: for he is kind unto the unthankful and *to* the evil.

Jn 11:52 — And not for that nation only, but that also he should gather together in one the children of God that were scattered abroad.

Ac 15:17 — That the residue of men might seek after the Lord, and all the Gentiles, upon whom my name is called, saith the Lord, who doeth all these things.

Ro 8:19 — For the earnest expectation of the creature waiteth for the manifestation of the sons of God.

Ro 8:21 — Because the creature itself also shall be delivered from the bondage of corruption into the glorious liberty of the children of God.

Ro 8:29 — For whom he did foreknow, he also did predestinate *to be* conformed to the image of his Son, that he might be the firstborn among many brethren.

Gal 3:26 — For ye are all the children of God by faith in Christ Jesus.

Gal 3:29 — And if ye *be* Christ's, then are ye Abraham's seed, and heirs according to the promise.

Eph 1:5 — Having predestinated us unto the adoption of children by Jesus Christ to himself, according to the good pleasure of his will,

Eph 2:19 — Now therefore ye are no more strangers and foreigners, but fellowcitizens with the saints, and of the household of God;

Eph 3:6 — That the Gentiles should be fellowheirs, and of the same body, and partakers of his promise in Christ by the gospel:

Eph 3:15 — Of whom the whole family in heaven and earth is named,

Php 2:15 — That ye may be blameless and harmless, the sons of God, without rebuke, in the midst of a crooked and perverse nation, among whom ye shine as lights in the world;

Heb 1:5 — For unto which of the angels said he at any time, Thou art my Son, this day have I begotten thee? And again, I will be to him a Father, and he shall be to me a Son?

Heb 2:13 — And again, I will put my trust in him. And again, Behold I and the children which God hath given me.

Heb 12:9 — Furthermore we have had fathers of our flesh which corrected *us,* and we gave *them* reverence: shall we not much rather be in subjection unto the Father of spirits, and live?

1Jn 3:10 — In this the children of God are manifest, and the children of the devil: whosoever doeth not righteousness is not of God, neither he that loveth not his brother.

1Jn 4:4 — Ye are of God, little children, and have overcome them: because greater is he that is in you, than he that is in the world.

Rev 21:7 — He that overcometh shall inherit all things; and I will be his God, and he shall be my son.

• Typified.

• In Israel.

Ex 4:22 — And thou shalt say unto Pharaoh, Thus saith the LORD, Israel *is* my son, *even* my firstborn:

Hos 11:1 — When Israel *was* a child, then I loved him, and called my son out of Egypt.

Ro 9:4 — Who are Israelites; to whom *pertaineth* the adoption, and the glory, and the covenants, and the giving of the law, and the service *of God,* and the promises;

See: God, Fatherhood of

See: Righteous; promises to, expressed or implied; unity of, with Christ

ADORAIM • A city of Judah.

2Ch 11:9 — And Adoraim, and Lachish, and Azekah,

ADORAM • Officer over the tribute.

2Sa 20:24 — And Adoram *was* over the tribute: and Jehoshaphat the son of Ahilud *was* recorder:

See: Adoniram

ADRAMMELECH

• An Assyrian idol.

2Ki 17:31 — And the Avites made Nibhaz and Tartak, and the Sepharvites burnt their children in fire to Adrammelech and Anammelech, the gods of Sepharvaim.

- **Son of Sennacherib.**

2Ki 19:37 — And it came to pass, as he was worshipping in the house of Nisroch his god, that Adrammelech and Sharezer his sons smote him with the sword: and they escaped into the land of Armenia. And Esar-haddon his son reigned in his stead.

Isa 37:38 — And it came to pass, as he was worshipping in the house of Nisroch his god, that Adrammelech and Sharezer his sons smote him with the sword; and they escaped into the land of Armenia: and Esar-haddon his son reigned in his stead.

ADRAMYTTIUM • A city of Mysia.

Ac 27:2 — And entering into a ship of Adramyttium, we launched, meaning to sail by the coasts of Asia; *one* Aristarchus, a Macedonian of Thessalonica, being with us.

ADRIA • Sea of.

Ac 27:27 — But when the fourteenth night was come, as we were driven up and down in Adria, about midnight the shipmen deemed that they drew near to some country;

ADRIEL • Saul's son-in-law.

2Sa 21:8–9

1Sa 18:19 — But it came to pass at the time when Merab Saul's daughter should have been given to David, that she was given unto Adriel the Meholathite to wife.

ADULLAM

- **A cave near the Dead Sea.**
  - **David takes refuge in.**

1Sa 22:1 — David therefore departed thence, and escaped to the cave Adullam: and when his brethren and all his father's house heard it, they went down thither to him.

2Sa 23:13 — And three of the thirty chief went down, and came to David in the harvest time unto the cave of Adullam: and the troop of the Philistines pitched in the valley of Rephaim.

1Ch 11:15 — Now three of the thirty captains went down to the rock to David, into the cave of Adullam; and the host of the Philistines encamped in the valley of Rephaim.

Ps 57:1 — [To the chief Musician, Altaschith, Michtam of David, when he fled from Saul in the cave.] Be merciful unto me, O God, be merciful unto me: for my soul trusteth in thee: yea, in the shadow of thy wings will I make my refuge, until *these* calamities be overpast.

Ps 142:1 — [Maschil of David; A Prayer when he was in the cave.] I cried unto the LORD with my voice; with my voice unto the LORD did I make my supplication.

- **An ancient city of Canaan.**

Ge 38:1 — And it came to pass at that time, that Judah went down from his brethren, and turned in to a certain Adullamite, whose name *was* Hirah.

Jos 12:15 — The king of Libnah, one; the king of Adullam, one;

Jos 15:35 — Jarmuth, and Adullam, Socoh, and Azekah,

2Ch 11:7 — And Beth-zur, and Shoco, and Adullam,

Ne 11:30 — Zanoah, Adullam, and *in* their villages, at Lachish, and the fields thereof, at Azekah, and *in* the villages thereof. And they dwelt from Beer-sheba unto the valley of Hinnom.

Mic 1:15 — Yet will I bring an heir unto thee, O inhabitant of Mareshah: he shall come unto Adullam the glory of Israel.

ADULTERY

Job 24:15–18; 31:9–12; Pr 2:16–19; 5:3–22; 6:24–29; 6:32–33; 7:5–23; 9:13–18; 23:27–28; 30:18–20; Isa 57:3–4; Jer 5:7–8; 7:9–10; Eze 18:5–6; Hos 4:1–2; Mk 10:11–12; Ro 1:28–29; 1Co 5:9–10; 6:15–16; 1Ti 1:9–10; 1Pe 4:3–4; 2Pe 2:9–10; Rev 2:20–22

Ge 20:3 — But God came to Abimelech in a dream by night, and said to him, Behold, thou *art but* a dead man, for the woman which thou hast taken; for she *is* a man's wife.

2Sa 12:14 — Howbeit, because by this deed thou hast given great occasion to the enemies of the LORD to blaspheme, the child also *that is* born unto thee shall surely die.

Job 31:1 — I made a covenant with mine eyes; why then should I think upon a maid?

Pr 22:14 — The mouth of strange women *is* a deep pit: he that is abhorred of the LORD shall fall therein.

Pr 29:3 — Whoso loveth wisdom rejoiceth his father: but he that keepeth company with harlots spendeth *his* substance.

Pr 31:3 — Give not thy strength unto women, nor thy ways to that which destroyeth kings.

Jer 3:1 — They say, If a man put away his wife, and she go from him, and become another man's, shall he return unto her again? shall not that land be greatly polluted? but thou hast played the harlot with many lovers; yet return again to me, saith the LORD.

Jer 23:10 — For the land is full of adulterers; for because of swearing the land mourneth; the pleasant places of the wilderness are dried up, and their course is evil, and their force *is* not right.

Hos 4:11 — Whoredom and wine and new wine take away the heart.

Mt 5:28 — But I say unto you, That whosoever looketh on a woman to lust after her hath committed adultery with her already in his heart.

Mt 5:32 — But I say unto you, That whosoever shall put away his wife, saving for the cause of fornication, causeth her to commit adultery: and whosoever shall marry her that is divorced committeth adultery.

Mt 15:19 — For out of the heart proceed evil thoughts, murders, adulteries, fornications, thefts, false witness, blasphemies:

Mt 19:9 — And I say unto you, Whosoever shall put away his wife, except *it be* for fornication, and shall marry another, committeth adultery: and whoso marrieth her which is put away doth commit adultery.

Mk 7:21 — For from within, out of the heart of men, proceed evil thoughts, adulteries, fornications, murders,

Mk 10:19 — Thou knowest the commandments, Do not commit adultery, Do not kill, Do not steal, Do not bear false witness, Defraud not, Honour thy father and mother.

Lk 16:18 — Whosoever putteth away his wife, and marrieth another, committeth adultery: and whosoever marrieth her that is put away from *her* husband committeth adultery.

Ac 15:20 — But that we write unto them, that they abstain from pollutions of idols, and *from* fornication, and *from* things strangled, and *from* blood.

Ac 15:29 — That ye abstain from meats offered to idols, and from blood, and from things strangled, and from fornication: from which if ye keep yourselves, ye shall do well. Fare ye well.

Ro 7:3 — So then if, while *her* husband liveth, she be married to another man, she shall be called an adulteress: but if her husband be dead, she is free from that law; so that she is no adulteress, though she be married to another man.

1Co 6:18 — Flee fornication. Every sin that a man doeth is without the body; but he that committeth fornication sinneth against his own body.

1Co 10:8 — Neither let us commit fornication, as some of them committed, and fell in one day three and twenty thousand.

2Co 12:21 — *And* lest, when I come again, my God will humble me among you, and *that* I shall bewail many which have sinned already, and have not repented of the uncleanness and fornication and lasciviousness which they have committed.

Gal 5:19 — Now the works of the flesh are manifest, which are *these;* Adultery, fornication, uncleanness, lasciviousness,

Gal 5:21 — Envyings, murders, drunkenness, revellings, and such like: of the which I tell you before, as I have also told *you* in time past, that they which do such things shall not inherit the kingdom of God.

2Ti 3:6 — For of this sort are they which creep into houses, and lead captive silly women laden with sins, led away with divers lusts,

Jas 2:11 — For he that said, Do not commit adultery, said also, Do not kill. Now if thou commit no adultery, yet if thou kill, thou art become a transgressor of the law.

2Pe 2:14 — Having eyes full of adultery, and that cannot cease from sin; beguiling unstable souls: an heart they have exercised with covetous practices; cursed children:

Jude 1:7 — Even as Sodom and Gomorrha, and the cities about them in like manner, giving themselves over to fornication, and going after strange flesh, are set forth for an example, suffering the vengeance of eternal fire.

Rev 9:21 — Neither repented they of their murders, nor of their sorceries, nor of their fornication, nor of their thefts.

See: Lasciviousness

See: Rape

See: Sensuality

See: Sodomy

See: Whore

See: Whoredom

• Forbidden.

1Co 5:9–11; Eph 4:19–20; 5:11–12; 1Th 4:3–5

Ex 20:14 — Thou shalt not commit adultery.

Le 18:20 — Moreover thou shalt not lie carnally with thy neighbour's wife, to defile thyself with her.

Le 19:29 — Do not prostitute thy daughter, to cause her to be a whore; lest the land fall to whoredom, and the land become full of wickedness.

Dt 5:18 — Neither shalt thou commit adultery.

Dt 23:17 — There shall be no whore of the daughters of Israel, nor a sodomite of the sons of Israel.

Mt 5:27 — Ye have heard that it was said by them of old time, Thou shalt not commit adultery:

Mt 19:18 — He saith unto him, Which? Jesus said, Thou shalt do no murder, Thou shalt not commit adultery, Thou shalt not steal, Thou shalt not bear false witness,

Lk 18:20 — Thou knowest the commandments, Do not commit adultery, Do not kill, Do not steal, Do not bear false witness, Honour thy father and thy mother.

Ac 15:20 — But that we write unto them, that they abstain from pollutions of idols, and *from* fornication, and *from* things strangled, and *from* blood.

Ro 13:9 — For this, Thou shalt not commit adultery, Thou shalt not kill, Thou shalt not steal, Thou shalt not bear false witness, Thou shalt not covet; and if *there be* any other commandment, it is briefly comprehended in this saying, namely, Thou shalt love thy neighbour as thyself.

Ro 13:13 — Let us walk honestly, as in the day; not in rioting and drunkenness, not in chambering and wantonness, not in strife and envying.

1Co 6:13 — Meats for the belly, and the belly for meats: but God shall destroy both it and them. Now the body *is* not for fornication, but for the Lord; and the Lord for the body.

1Co 6:15 — Know ye not that your bodies are the members of Christ? shall I then take the members of Christ, and make *them* the members of an harlot? God forbid.

1Co 6:18 — Flee fornication. Every sin that a man doeth is without the body; but he that committeth fornication sinneth against his own body.

1Co 10:8 — Neither let us commit fornication, as some of them committed, and fell in one day three and twenty thousand.

Eph 5:3 — But fornication, and all uncleanness, or covetousness, let it not be once named among you, as becometh saints;

Col 3:5 — Mortify therefore your members which are upon the earth; fornication, uncleanness, inordinate affection, evil concupiscence, and covetousness, which is idolatry:

1Th 4:7 — For God hath not called us unto uncleanness, but unto holiness.

Jas 2:11 — For he that said, Do not commit adultery, said also, Do not kill. Now if thou commit no adultery, yet if thou kill, thou art become a transgressor of the law.

- **Forgiveness of.**
  - **Instances of.**
    Jgs 19:1–4; Jn 8:10–11
- **Penalties for.**
  Ex 22:16–17; Le 19:20–22; 20:10–12; Nu 5:11–30; Dt 22:13–29; 27:22–23; 2Sa 12:10–12; Jer 29:22–23; Eze 16:40–41; 23:47–48; Jn 8:4–5; 1Co 5:1–13; 6:9–10; Eph 5:5–6; Rev 18:9–10

  Ge 20:7 — Now therefore restore the man *his* wife; for he *is* a prophet, and he shall pray for thee, and thou shalt live: and if thou restore *her* not, know thou that thou shalt surely die, thou, and all that *are* thine.

  Ge 26:11 — And Abimelech charged all *his* people, saying, He that toucheth this man or his wife shall surely be put to death.

  Ge 38:24 — And it came to pass about three months after, that it was told Judah, saying, Tamar thy daughter in law hath played the harlot; and also, behold, she *is* with child by whoredom. And Judah said, Bring her forth, and let her be burnt.

  Le 21:9 — And the daughter of any priest, if she profane herself by playing the whore, she profaneth her father: she shall be burnt with fire.

  Dt 27:20 — Cursed *be* he that lieth with his father's wife; because he uncovereth his father's skirt. And all the people shall say, Amen.

  Eze 16:38 — And I will judge thee, as women that break wedlock and shed blood are judged; and I will give thee blood in fury and jealousy.

  Eze 23:45 — And the righteous men, they shall judge them after the manner of adulteresses, and after the manner of women that shed blood; because they *are* adulteresses, and blood *is* in their hands.

  Mal 3:5 — And I will come near to you to judgment; and I will be a swift witness against the sorcerers, and against the adulterers, and against false swearers, and against those that oppress the hireling in *his* wages, the widow, and the fatherless, and that turn aside the stranger *from his right,* and fear not me, saith the LORD of hosts.

  1Co 10:8 — Neither let us commit fornication, as some of them committed, and fell in one day three and twenty thousand.

  Gal 5:19 — Now the works of the flesh are manifest, which are *these;* Adultery, fornication, uncleanness, lasciviousness,

  Gal 5:21 — Envyings, murders, drunkenness, revellings, and such like: of the which I tell you before, as I have also told *you* in time past, that they which do such things shall not inherit the kingdom of God.

  Heb 13:4 — Marriage *is* honourable in all, and the bed undefiled: but whoremongers and adulterers God will judge.

  Rev 21:8 — But the fearful, and unbelieving, and the abominable, and murderers, and whoremongers, and sorcerers, and idolaters, and all liars, shall have their part in the lake which burneth with fire and brimstone: which is the second death.

  Rev 22:15 — For without *are* dogs, and sorcerers, and whoremongers, and murderers, and idolaters, and whosoever loveth and maketh a lie.
- **Figurative.**
  Eze 16:15–16; Hos 1:1–11

  Jer 3:2 — Lift up thine eyes unto the high places, and see where thou hast not been lien with. In the ways hast thou sat for them, as the Arabian in the wilderness; and thou hast polluted the land with thy whoredoms and with thy wickedness.

  See: Whoredom

  See: Idolatry
- **Instances of.**
  - **Sodomites.**
    Ge 19:5–8
  - **Lot.**
    Ge 19:31–38
  - **Shechem.**
    Ge 34:2
  - **Reuben.**
    Ge 35:22
  - **Judah.**
    Ge 38:1–24
  - **Potiphar's wife.**
    Ge 39:7–12
  - **The Levite's concubine.**
    Jgs 19:2
  - **The Gibeahites.**
    Jgs 19:22–25
  - **Gilead.**
    Jgs 11:1
  - **Samson.**
    Jgs 16:1
  - **Sons of Eli.**
    1Sa 2:22
  - **David.**
    2Sa 11:1–5
  - **Amnon.**
    2Sa 13:1–20
  - **Absalom.**
    2Sa 16:22
  - **Israelites.**
    Ex 32:6; 32:25; Jer 29:23; Eze 22:9–11; 33:26; Hos 7:4
  - **Herod.**
    Mt 14:3–4; Mk 6:17–18; Lk 3:19
  - **Samaritan woman.**
    Jn 4:17–18
  - **The woman brought to Jesus in the temple.**
    Jn 8:4–11
  - **Corinthians.**
    1Co 5:1–5
  - **Heathen.**
    Eph 4:17–19; 1Pe 4:3

ADUMMIM • Place between the fords of the Jordan and Jerusalem.

Jos 15:7 — And the border went up toward Debir from the valley of Achor, and so northward, looking toward Gilgal, *that is* before the going up to Adummim, which *is* on the south side of the river: and the border passed toward the waters of En-shemesh, and the goings out thereof were at En-rogel:

Jos 18:17 — And was drawn from the north, and went forth to En-shemesh, and went forth toward Geliloth, which *is* over against the going up of Adummim, and descended to the stone of Bohan the son of Reuben,

ADVENT

See: Jesus, Second Coming of
See: Millennium

ADVERSITY *See: Afflictions*

ADVICE *See: Counsel*

ADVOCATE

• Tertullus.

Ac 24:1–9

• Figurative.

1Jn 2:1 — My little children, these things write I unto you, that ye sin not. And if any man sin, we have an advocate with the Father, Jesus Christ the righteous:

AENEAS • Healed.

Ac 9:33–34

AENON *See: Enon*

AFFECTIONS

• Should be supremely set upon God.

Dt 6:5 — And thou shalt love the LORD thy God with all thine heart, and with all thy soul, and with all thy might.

Mk 12:30 — And thou shalt love the Lord thy God with all thy heart, and with all thy soul, and with all thy mind, and with all thy strength: this is the first commandment.

• Should be set upon the commandments of God.

Ps 19:8–10

Ps 119:20 — My soul breaketh for the longing *that it hath* unto thy judgments at all times.

Ps 119:97 — O how love I thy law! it *is* my meditation all the day.

Ps 119:103 — How sweet are thy words unto my taste! *yea, sweeter* than honey to my mouth!

Ps 119:167 — My soul hath kept thy testimonies; and I love them exceedingly.

• Upon the house and worship of God.

Ps 84:1–2

1Ch 29:3 — Moreover, because I have set my affection to the house of my God, I have of mine own proper good, of gold and silver, *which* I have given to the house of my God, over and above all that I have prepared for the holy house,

Ps 26:8 — LORD, I have loved the habitation of thy house, and the place where thine honour dwelleth.

Ps 27:4 — One *thing* have I desired of the LORD, that will I seek after; that I may dwell in the house of the LORD all the days of my life, to behold the beauty of the LORD, and to enquire in his temple.

• Upon the people of God.

2Co 7:13–16

Ps 16:3 — *But* to the saints that *are* in the earth, and *to* the excellent, in whom *is* all my delight.

Ro 12:10 — *Be* kindly affectioned one to another with brotherly love; in honour preferring one another;

1Th 2:8 — So being affectionately desirous of you, we were willing to have imparted unto you, not the gospel of God only, but also our own souls, because ye were dear unto us.

• Upon heavenly things.

Col 3:1–2

• Should be zealously engaged for God.

Ps 69:9 — For the zeal of thine house hath eaten me up; and the reproaches of them that reproached thee are fallen upon me.

Ps 119:139 — My zeal hath consumed me, because mine enemies have forgotten thy words.

Gal 4:18 — But *it is* good to be zealously affected always in *a* good *thing,* and not only when I am present with you.

• Christ claims the first place in.

Mt 10:37 — He that loveth father or mother more than me is not worthy of me: and he that loveth son or daughter more than me is not worthy of me.

Lk 14:26 — If any *man* come to me, and hate not his father, and mother, and wife, and children, and brethren, and sisters, yea, and his own life also, he cannot be my disciple.

• Enkindled by communion with Christ.

Lk 24:32 — And they said one to another, Did not our heart burn within us, while he talked with us by the way, and while he opened to us the scriptures?

• Blessedness of making God the object of.

Ps 91:14 — Because he hath set his love upon me, therefore will I deliver him: I will set him on high, because he hath known my name.

• Should not grow cold.

Ps 106:12–13

Mt 24:12 — And because iniquity shall abound, the love of many shall wax cold.

Gal 4:15 — Where is then the blessedness ye spake of? for I bear you record, that, if *it had been* possible, ye would have plucked out your own eyes, and have given them to me.

Rev 2:4 — Nevertheless I have *somewhat* against thee, because thou hast left thy first love.

• Of saints, supremely set on God.

Ps 42:1 — As the hart panteth after the water brooks, so panteth my soul after thee, O God.

Ps 73:25 — Whom have I in heaven *but thee?* and *there is* none upon earth *that* I desire beside thee.

Ps 119:10 — With my whole heart have I sought thee: O let me not wander from thy commandments.

• Of the wicked, not sincerely set on God.

Isa 58:1–2; Eze 33:31–32

Lk 8:13 — They on the rock *are they,* which, when they hear, receive the word with joy; and these have no root, which for a while believe, and in time of temptation fall away.

• Carnal, should be mortified.

Ro 8:13 — For if ye live after the flesh, ye shall die: but if ye through the Spirit do mortify the deeds of the body, ye shall live.

Ro 13:14 — But put ye on the Lord Jesus Christ, and make not provision for the flesh, to *fulfil* the lusts *thereof.*

1Co 9:27 — But I keep under my body, and bring *it* into subjection: lest that by any means, when I have preached to others, I myself should be a castaway.

Col 3:5 — Mortify therefore your members which are upon the earth; fornication, uncleanness, inordinate affection, evil concupiscence, and covetousness, which is idolatry:

1Th 4:5 — Not in the lust of concupiscence, even as the Gentiles which know not God:

• Carnal affections crucified in saints.

Ro 6:6 — Knowing this, that our old man is crucified with *him,* that the body of sin might be destroyed, that henceforth we should not serve sin.

Gal 5:24 — And they that are Christ's have crucified the flesh with the affections and lusts.

• False teachers seek to captivate.

Gal 1:10 — For do I now persuade men, or God? or do I seek to please men? for if I yet pleased men, I should not be the servant of Christ.

Gal 4:17 — They zealously affect you, *but* not well; yea, they would exclude you, that ye might affect them.

2Ti 3:6 — For of this sort are they which creep into houses, and lead captive silly women laden with sins, led away with divers lusts,

2Pe 2:3 — And through covetousness shall they with feigned words make merchandise of you: whose judgment now of a long time lingereth not, and their damnation slumbereth not.

2Pe 2:18 — For when they speak great swelling *words* of vanity, they allure through the lusts of the flesh, *through much* wantonness, those that were clean escaped from them who live in error.

Rev 2:14 — But I have a few things against thee, because thou hast there them that hold the doctrine of Balaam, who taught Balac to cast a stumbling-block before the children of Israel, to eat things sacrificed unto idols, and to commit fornication.

Rev 2:20 — Notwithstanding I have a few things against thee, because thou sufferest that woman Jezebel, which calleth herself a prophetess, to teach and to seduce my servants to commit fornication, and to eat things sacrificed unto idols.

• Of the wicked, are unnatural and perverted.

Ro 1:31 — Without understanding, covenantbreakers, without natural affection, implacable, unmerciful:

2Ti 3:3 — Without natural affection, trucebreakers, false accusers, incontinent, fierce, despisers of those that are good,

2Pe 2:10 — But chiefly them that walk after the flesh in the lust of uncleanness, and despise government. Presumptuous *are they,* selfwilled, they are not afraid to speak evil of dignities.

AFFLICTED, Duty to the

Isa 58:6–7; Mt 25:34–45; Lk 10:30–37; Php 2:1–2; Jas 5:13–15

Job 6:14 — To him that is afflicted pity *should be shewed* from his friend; but he forsaketh the fear of the Almighty.

Job 22:29 — When *men* are cast down, then thou shalt say, *There is* lifting up; and he shall save the humble person.

Isa 58:10 — And *if* thou draw out thy soul to the hungry, and satisfy the afflicted soul; then shall thy light rise in obscurity, and thy darkness *be* as the noonday:

1Ti 5:10 — Well reported of for good works; if she have brought up children, if she have lodged strangers, if she have washed the saints' feet, if she have relieved the afflicted, if she have diligently followed every good work.

AFFLICTIONS

• Consolation in.

Ge 16:7–13; 21:12–21; 26:17–33; Ex 3:7–8; 3:16–17; 14:13–14; Job 5:6–27; 11:16–19; 31:19–22; Ps 9:9–10; 27:5–6; 34:19–20; 37:23–24; 37:32–33; 56:8–10; 62:1–2; 62:5–8; 62:11–12; 94:17–19; 103:13–14; 138:7–8; Isa 14:31–32; 30:19–20; 40:1–2; 41:13–14; 50:7–10; 51:3–13; 61:1–3; 66:13–14; Jer 39:17–18; La 3:31–33; Hos 2:14–15; 6:1–3; Mt 5:10–12; 10:29–31; 25:34–36; 28:9–10; Lk 6:21–23; 12:6–7; Ro 8:35–39; 2Co 1:3–5; 4:8–10; 4:16–17; 1Th 4:16–18; 2Th 2:16–17; Heb 2:14–15; 4:15–16; 12:1–4; 13:5–6; 1Pe 2:21–24; 4:12–14; Rev 2:9–10; 7:1–17

Ge 31:42 — Except the God of my father, the God of Abraham, and the fear of Isaac, had been with me, surely thou hadst sent me away now empty. God hath seen mine affliction and the labour of my hands, and rebuked *thee* yesternight.

Dt 33:27 — The eternal God *is thy* refuge, and underneath *are* the everlasting arms: and he shall thrust out the enemy from before thee; and shall say, Destroy *them.*

2Sa 22:28 — And the afflicted people thou wilt save: but thine eyes *are* upon the haughty, *that* thou mayest bring *them* down.

Job 16:5 — *But* I would strengthen you with my mouth, and the moving of my lips should asswage *your grief.*

Job 29:25 — I chose out their way, and sat chief, and dwelt as a king in the army, as one *that* comforteth the mourners.

Job 35:10 — But none saith, Where *is* God my maker, who giveth songs in the night;

Ps 23:4 — Yea, though I walk through the valley of the shadow of death, I will fear no evil: for thou *art* with me; thy rod and thy staff they comfort me.

Ps 30:5 — For his anger *endureth but* a moment; in his favour is life: weeping may endure for a night, but joy *cometh* in the morning.

Ps 31:7 — I will be glad and rejoice in thy mercy: for thou hast considered my trouble; thou hast known my soul in adversities;

Ps 34:4 — I sought the LORD, and he heard me, and delivered me from all my fears.

Ps 41:3 — The LORD will strengthen him upon the bed of languishing: thou wilt make all his bed in his sickness.

Ps 42:5 — Why art thou cast down, O my soul? and why *art* thou disquieted in me? hope thou in God: for I shall yet praise him *for* the help of his countenance.

Ps 46:1 — God *is* our refuge and strength, a very present help in trouble.

Ps 50:15 — And call upon me in the day of trouble: I will deliver thee, and thou shalt glorify me.

Ps 55:22 — Cast thy burden upon the LORD, and he shall sustain thee: he shall never suffer the righteous to be moved.

Ps 68:6 — God setteth the solitary in families: he bringeth out those which are bound with chains: but the rebellious dwell in a dry *land*.

Ps 69:20 — Reproach hath broken my heart; and I am full of heaviness: and I looked *for some* to take pity, but *there was* none; and for comforters, but I found none.

Ps 69:33 — For the LORD heareth the poor, and despiseth not his prisoners.

Ps 71:20 — *Thou,* which hast shewed me great and sore troubles, shalt quicken me again, and shalt bring me up again from the depths of the earth.

Ps 73:26 — My flesh and my heart faileth: *but* God *is* the strength of my heart, and my portion for ever.

Ps 112:4 — Unto the upright there ariseth light in the darkness: *he is* gracious, and full of compassion, and righteous.

Ps 119:50 — This *is* my comfort in my affliction: for thy word hath quickened me.

Ps 119:52 — I remembered thy judgments of old, O LORD; and have comforted myself.

Ps 119:54 — Thy statutes have been my songs in the house of my pilgrimage.

Ps 119:92 — Unless thy law *had been* my delights, I should then have perished in mine affliction.

Ps 119:143 — Trouble and anguish have taken hold on me: *yet* thy commandments *are* my delights.

Ps 138:3 — In the day when I cried thou answeredst me, *and* strengthenedst me *with* strength in my soul.

Ps 140:12 — I know that the LORD will maintain the cause of the afflicted, *and* the right of the poor.

Ps 145:14 — The LORD upholdeth all that fall, and raiseth up all *those that be* bowed down.

Ps 147:3 — He healeth the broken in heart, and bindeth up their wounds.

Pr 12:13 — The wicked is snared by the transgression of *his* lips: but the just shall come out of trouble.

Ecc 4:1 — So I returned, and considered all the oppressions that are done under the sun: and behold the tears of *such as were* oppressed, and they had no comforter; and on the side of their oppressors *there was* power; but they had no comforter.

Isa 4:6 — And there shall be a tabernacle for a shadow in the daytime from the heat, and for a place of refuge, and for a covert from storm and from rain.

Isa 25:4 — For thou hast been a strength to the poor, a strength to the needy in his distress, a refuge from the storm, a shadow from the heat, when the blast of the terrible ones *is* as a storm *against* the wall.

Isa 40:29 — He giveth power to the faint; and to *them that have* no might he increaseth strength.

Isa 41:10 — Fear thou not; for I *am* with thee: be not dismayed; for I *am* thy God: I will strengthen thee; yea, I will help thee; yea, I will uphold thee with the right hand of my righteousness.

Isa 41:17 — *When* the poor and needy seek water, and *there is* none, *and* their tongue faileth for thirst, I the LORD will hear them, *I* the God of Israel will not forsake them.

Isa 42:3 — A bruised reed shall he not break, and the smoking flax shall he not quench: he shall bring forth judgment unto truth.

Isa 43:2 — When thou passest through the waters, I *will be* with thee; and through the rivers, they shall not overflow thee: when thou walkest through the fire, thou shalt not be burned; neither shall the flame kindle upon thee.

Isa 49:13 — Sing, O heavens; and be joyful, O earth; and break forth into singing, O mountains: for the LORD hath comforted his people, and will have mercy upon his afflicted.

Isa 50:4 — The Lord GOD hath given me the tongue of the learned, that I should know how to speak a word in season to *him that is* weary: he wakeneth morning by morning, he wakeneth mine ear to hear as the learned.

Isa 54:4 — Fear not; for thou shalt not be ashamed: neither be thou confounded; for thou shalt not be put to shame: for thou shalt forget the shame of thy youth, and shalt not remember the reproach of thy widowhood any more.

Isa 54:11 — O thou afflicted, tossed with tempest, *and* not comforted, behold, I will lay thy stones with fair colors, and lay thy foundations with sapphires.

Isa 58:10 — And *if* thou draw out thy soul to the hungry, and satisfy the afflicted soul; then shall thy light rise in obscurity, and thy darkness *be* as the noonday:

Isa 63:9 — In all their affliction he was afflicted, and the angel of his presence saved them: in his love and in his pity he redeemed them; and he bare them, and carried them all the days of old.

Isa 66:5 — Hear the word of the LORD, ye that tremble at his word; your brethren that hated you, that cast you out for my name's sake, said, Let the LORD be glorified: but he shall appear to your joy, and they shall be ashamed.

Jer 31:13 — Then shall the virgin rejoice in the dance, both young men and old together: for I will turn their mourning into joy, and will comfort them, and make them rejoice from their sorrow.

Jer 31:25 — For I have satiated the weary soul, and I have replenished every sorrowful soul.

La 3:57 — Thou drewest near in the day *that* I called upon thee: thou saidst, Fear not.

Eze 11:16 — Therefore say, Thus saith the Lord GOD; Although I have cast them far off among the heathen, and although I have scattered them among the countries, yet will I be to them as a little sanctuary in the countries where they shall come.

Na 1:7 — The LORD *is* good, a strong hold in the day of trouble; and he knoweth them that trust in him.

Zep 3:18 — I will gather *them that are* sorrowful for the solemn assembly, *who* are of thee, *to whom* the reproach of it *was* a burden.

Mt 5:4 — Blessed *are* they that mourn: for they shall be comforted.

Mt 11:28 — Come unto me, all *ye* that labour and are heavy laden, and I will give you rest.

Mt 14:27 — But straightway Jesus spake unto them, saying, Be of good cheer; it is I; be not afraid.

Mt 25:40 — And the King shall answer and say unto them, Verily I say unto you, Inasmuch as ye have done *it* unto one of the least of these my brethren, ye have done *it* unto me.

Mt 28:5 — And the angel answered and said unto the women, Fear not ye: for I know that ye seek Jesus, which was crucified.

Mk 6:50 — For they all saw him, and were troubled. And immediately he talked with them, and saith unto them, Be of good cheer: it is I; be not afraid.

Lk 7:13 — And when the Lord saw her, he had compassion on her, and said unto her, Weep not.

Lk 21:18 — But there shall not an hair of your head perish.

Jn 14:1 — Let not your heart be troubled: ye believe in God, believe also in me.

Jn 14:16 — And I will pray the Father, and he shall give you another Comforter, that he may abide with you for ever;

Jn 14:18 — I will not leave you comfortless: I will come to you.

Jn 14:27 — Peace I leave with you, my peace I give unto you: not as the world giveth, give I unto you. Let not your heart be troubled, neither let it be afraid.

Jn 15:18 — If the world hate you, ye know that *it hated* me before it hated you.

Jn 15:20 — Remember the word that I said unto you, The servant is not greater than his lord. If they have persecuted me, they will also persecute you; if they have kept my saying, they will keep yours also.

Jn 16:20 — Verily, verily, I say unto you, That ye shall weep and lament, but the world shall rejoice: and ye shall be sorrowful, but your sorrow shall be turned into joy.

Jn 16:22 — And ye now therefore have sorrow: but I will see you again, and your heart shall rejoice, and your joy no man taketh from you.

Jn 16:33 — These things I have spoken unto you, that in me ye might have peace. In the world ye shall have tribulation: but be of good cheer; I have overcome the world.

Ac 12:5 — Peter therefore was kept in prison: but prayer was made without ceasing of the church unto God for him.

Ac 23:11 — And the night following the Lord stood by him, and said, Be of good cheer, Paul: for as thou hast testified of me in Jerusalem, so must thou bear witness also at Rome.

Ro 8:28 — And we know that all things work together for good to them that love God, to them who are the called according to *his* purpose.

Ro 12:12 — Rejoicing in hope; patient in tribulation; continuing instant in prayer;

Ro 12:15 — Rejoice with them that do rejoice, and weep with them that weep.

Ro 15:4 — For whatsoever things were written aforetime were written for our learning, that we through patience and comfort of the scriptures might have hope.

2Co 1:7 — And our hope of you *is* stedfast, knowing, that as ye are partakers of the sufferings, so *shall ye be* also of the consolation.

2Co 7:6 — Nevertheless God, that comforteth those that are cast down, comforted us by the coming of Titus;

2Co 12:9 — And he said unto me, My grace is sufficient for thee: for my strength is made perfect in weakness. Most gladly therefore will I rather glory in my infirmities, that the power of Christ may rest upon me.

Gal 6:2 — Bear ye one another's burdens, and so fulfil the law of Christ.

Php 1:19 — For I know that this shall turn to my salvation through your prayer, and the supply of the Spirit of Jesus Christ,

1Th 4:13 — But I would not have you to be ignorant, brethren, concerning them which are asleep, that ye sorrow not, even as others which have no hope.

2Th 1:7 — And to you who are troubled rest with us, when the Lord Jesus shall be revealed from heaven with his mighty angels,

2Ti 2:12 — If we suffer, we shall also reign with *him:* if we deny *him,* he also will deny us:

2Ti 4:17 — Notwithstanding the Lord stood with me, and strengthened me; that by me the preaching might be fully known, and *that* all the Gentiles might hear: and I was delivered out of the mouth of the lion.

Heb 2:18 — For in that he himself hath suffered being tempted, he is able to succour them that are tempted.

Heb 6:18 — That by two immutable things, in which *it was* impossible for God to lie, we might have a strong consolation, who have fled for refuge to lay hold upon the hope set before us:

Heb 13:3 — Remember them that are in bonds, as bound with them; *and* them which suffer adversity, as being yourselves also in the body.

Jas 1:12 — Blessed *is* the man that endureth temptation: for when he is tried, he shall receive the crown of life, which the Lord hath promised to them that love him.

Jas 1:27 — Pure religion and undefiled before God and the Father is this, To visit the fatherless and widows in their affliction, *and* to keep himself unspotted from the world.

Jas 5:8 — Be ye also patient; stablish your hearts: for the coming of the Lord draweth nigh.

Jas 5:10 — Take, my brethren, the prophets, who have spoken in the name of the Lord, for an example of suffering affliction, and of patience.

1Pe 5:7 — Casting all your care upon him; for he careth for you.

1Pe 5:9 — Whom resist stedfast in the faith, knowing that the same afflictions are accomplished in your brethren that are in the world.

Rev 3:2 — Be watchful, and strengthen the things which remain, that are ready to die: for I have not found thy works perfect before God.

Rev 3:10 — Because thou hast kept the word of my patience, I also will keep thee from the hour of temptation, which shall come upon all the world, to try them that dwell upon the earth.

• Deliverance From.

See: Prayer; answered

• Design of.

Dt 30:1–3; Jgs 2:21–22; 1Ki 8:33–48; 2Ch 6:24–31; 7:13–14; Job 33:16–30; 36:8–10; Ps 106:43–44; 107:10–14; 107:17–21; 107:23–31; Isa 1:25–27; 4:3–4; 9:13–14; 52:5–6; Eze 14:10–11; Da 4:25–27; Jn 9:2–3; 2Co 1:4–6; Php 1:29–30; 2Th 1:4–5; Heb 2:10–18; 5:8–9; 12:5–11; 1Pe 1:6–7

Dt 8:2 — And thou shalt remember all the way which the LORD thy God led thee these forty years in the wilderness, to humble thee, *and* to prove thee, to know what *was* in thine heart, whether thou wouldest keep his commandments, or no.

Dt 8:16 — Who fed thee in the wilderness with manna, which thy fathers knew not, that he might humble thee, and that he might prove thee, to do thee good at thy latter end;

Dt 31:17 — Then my anger shall be kindled against them in that day, and I will forsake them, and I will hide my face from them, and they shall be devoured, and many evils and troubles shall befall them; so that they will say in that day. Are not these evils come upon us, because our God *is* not among us?

Job 33:11 — He putteth my feet in the stocks, he marketh all my paths.

Ps 66:10 — For thou, O God, hast proved us: thou hast tried us, as silver is tried.

Ps 119:71 — *It is* good for me that I have been afflicted; that I might learn thy statutes.

Ecc 7:14 — In the day of prosperity be joyful, but in the day of adversity consider: God also hath set the one over against the other, to the end that man should find nothing after him.

Jer 24:5 — Thus saith the LORD, the God of Israel; Like these good figs, so will I acknowledge them that are carried away captive of Judah, whom I have sent out of this place into the land of the Chaldeans for *their* good.

La 1:5 — Her adversaries are the chief, her enemies prosper; for the LORD hath afflicted her for the multitude of her transgressions: her children are gone into captivity before the enemy.

Eze 6:10 — And they shall know that I *am* the LORD, *and that* I have not said in vain that I would do this evil unto them.

Da 4:34 — And at the end of the days I Nebuchadnezzar lifted up mine eyes unto heaven, and mine understanding returned unto me, and I blessed the most High, and I praised and honoured him that liveth for ever, whose dominion *is* an everlasting dominion, and his kingdom *is* from generation to generation:

Hos 5:15 — I will go *and* return to my place, till they acknowledge their offence, and seek my face: in their affliction they will seek me early.

Am 4:6 — And I also have given you cleanness of teeth in all your cities, and want of bread in all your places: yet have ye not returned unto me, saith the LORD.

Mic 6:9 — The LORD'S voice crieth unto the city, and *the man of* wisdom shall see thy name: hear ye the rod, and who hath appointed it.

Mal 3:3 — And he shall sit *as* a refiner and purifier of silver: and he shall purify the sons of Levi, and purge them as gold and silver, that they may offer unto the LORD an offering in righteousness.

Jn 11:4 — When Jesus heard *that*, he said, This sickness is not unto death, but for the glory of God, that the Son of God might be glorified thereby.

Jn 15:2 — Every branch in me that beareth not fruit he taketh away: and every *branch* that beareth fruit, he purgeth it, that it may bring forth more fruit.

Jn 21:19 — This spake he, signifying by what death he should glorify God. And when he had spoken this, he saith unto him, Follow me.

1Co 11:32 — But when we are judged, we are chastened of the Lord, that we should not be condemned with the world.

2Co 4:11 — For we which live are alway delivered unto death for Jesus' sake, that the life also of Jesus might be made manifest in our mortal flesh.

2Co 4:17 — For our light affliction, which is but for a moment, worketh for us a far more exceeding *and* eternal weight of glory;

2Co 12:7 — And lest I should be exalted above measure through the abundance of the revelations, there was given to me a thorn in the flesh, the messenger of Satan to buffet me, lest I should be exalted above measure.

1Pe 5:10 — But the God of all grace, who hath called us unto his eternal glory by Christ Jesus, after that ye have suffered a while, make you perfect, stablish, strengthen, settle *you*.

Rev 2:10 — Fear none of those things which thou shalt suffer: behold, the devil shall cast *some* of you into prison, that ye may be tried; and ye shall have tribulation ten days: be thou faithful unto death, and I will give thee a crown of life.

See: Afflictions, Benefits of

• Despondency in.

Job 9:16–35; Ps 22:1–2

Job 4:5 — But now it is come upon thee, and thou faintest; it toucheth thee, and thou art troubled.

Pr 24:10 — *If* thou faint in the day of adversity, thy strength *is* small.

La 3:39 — Wherefore doth a living man complain, a man for the punishment of his sins?

Mt 27:46 — And about the ninth hour Jesus cried with a loud voice, saying, Eli, Eli, lama sabachthani? that is to say, My God, my God, why hast thou forsaken me?

Mk 15:34 — And at the ninth hour Jesus cried with a loud voice, saying, Eloi, Eloi, lama sabachthani? which is, being interpreted, My God, my God, why hast thou forsaken me?

Lk 18:1 — And he spake a parable unto them *to this end,* that men ought always to pray, and not to faint;

• Dispensation of God.

Dt 28:15–68; Ru 1:20–21; 1Sa 2:6–7; 2Ch 7:12–22; Job 5:17–18; 12:14–25; Ps 78:31–34; 88:6–7; 89:38–45; Da 4:24–26

Ex 4:11 — And the LORD said unto him, Who hath made man's mouth? or who maketh the dumb, or deaf, or the seeing, or the blind? have not I the LORD?

Dt 32:39 — See now that I, *even* I, *am* he, and *there is* no god with me: I kill, and I make alive; I wound, and I heal: neither *is there any* that can deliver out of my hand.

2Sa 16:10 — And the king said, What have I to do with you, ye sons of Zeruiah? so let him curse, because the LORD hath said unto him, Curse David. Who shall then say, Wherefore hast thou done so?

2Ki 6:33 — And while he yet talked with them, behold, the messenger came down unto him: and he said, Behold, this evil *is* of the LORD; what should I wait for the LORD any longer?

2Ki 15:5 — And the LORD smote the king, so that he was a leper unto the day of his death, and dwelt in a several house. And Jotham the king's son *was* over the house, judging the people of the land.

Job 1:21 — And said, Naked came I out of my mother's womb, and naked shall I return thither: the LORD gave, and the LORD hath taken away; blessed be the name of the LORD.

Job 5:6 — Although affliction cometh not forth of the dust, neither doth trouble spring out of the ground;

Job 6:4 — For the arrows of the Almighty *are* within me, the poison whereof drinketh up my spirit: the terrors of God do set themselves in array against me.

Job 9:12 — Behold, he taketh away, who can hinder him? who will say unto him, What doest thou?

Job 9:22 — This *is* one *thing,* therefore I said *it,* He destroyeth the perfect and the wicked.

Job 10:8 — Thine hands have made me and fashioned me together round about; yet thou dost destroy me.

Job 11:10 — If he cut off, and shut up, or gather together, then who can hinder him?

Job 19:6 — Know now that God hath overthrown me, and hath compassed me with his net.

Job 19:21 — Have pity upon me, have pity upon me, O ye my friends; for the hand of God hath touched me.

Job 21:17 — How oft is the candle of the wicked put out! and *how oft* cometh their destruction upon them! *God* distributeth sorrows in his anger.

Job 23:16 — For God maketh my heart soft, and the Almighty troubleth me:

Job 27:2 — *As* God liveth, *who* hath taken away my judgment; and the Almighty, *who* hath vexed my soul;

Job 30:11 — Because he hath loosed my cord, and afflicted me, they have also let loose the bridle before me.

Job 34:29 — When he giveth quietness, who then can make trouble? and when he hideth *his* face, who then can behold him? whether *it be done* against a nation, or against a man only:

Ps 38:3 — *There is* no soundness in my flesh because of thine anger; neither *is there any* rest in my bones because of my sin.

Ps 66:11 — Thou broughtest us into the net; thou laidst affliction upon our loins.

Ps 71:20 — *Thou,* which hast shewed me great and sore troubles, shalt quicken me again, and shalt bring me up again from the depths of the earth.

Ps 88:16 — Thy fierce wrath goeth over me; thy terrors have cut me off.

Ps 90:7 — For we are consumed by thine anger, and by thy wrath are we troubled.

Ps 90:15 — Make us glad according to the days *wherein* thou hast afflicted us, *and* the years *wherein* we have seen evil.

Ps 102:10 — Because of thine indignation and thy wrath: for thou hast lifted me up, and cast me down.

Ps 102:23 — He weakened my strength in the way; he shortened my days.

Isa 30:20 — And *though* the Lord give you the bread of adversity, and the water of affliction, yet shall not thy teachers be removed into a corner any more, but thine eyes shall see thy teachers:

Isa 45:7 — I form the light, and create darkness: I make peace, and create evil: I the LORD do all these *things.*

Jer 45:3 — Thou didst say, Woe is me now! for the LORD hath added grief to my sorrow; I fainted in my sighing, and I find no rest.

La 1:5 — Her adversaries are the chief, her enemies prosper; for the LORD hath afflicted her for the multitude of her transgressions: her children are gone into captivity before the enemy.

La 3:1 — I *am* the man *that* hath seen affliction by the rod of his wrath.

Am 3:6 — Shall a trumpet be blown in the city, and the people not be afraid? shall there be evil in a city, and the LORD hath not done *it?*

Jnh 2:3 — For thou hadst cast me into the deep, in the midst of the seas; and the floods compassed me about: all thy billows and thy waves passed over me.

Mic 1:12 — For the inhabitant of Maroth waited carefully for good: but evil came down from the LORD unto the gate of Jerusalem.

Ro 8:20 — For the creature was made subject to vanity, not willingly, but by reason of him who hath subjected *the same* in hope,

1Co 11:32 — But when we are judged, we are chastened of the Lord, that we should not be condemned with the world.

Heb 12:10 — For they verily for a few days chastened *us* after their own pleasure; but he for *our* profit, that *we* might be partakers of his holiness.

Rev 3:19 — As many as I love, I rebuke and chasten: be zealous therefore, and repent.

- **From Satan.**

Job 1:1–2:13

2Co 12:7 — And lest I should be exalted above measure through the abundance of the revelations, there was given to me a thorn in the flesh, the messenger of Satan to buffet me, lest I should be exalted above measure.

See: Temptation

- **Impenitence in.**

See: Afflictions; obduracy in

- **Mocking at.**

Job 12:5 — He that is ready to slip with *his* feet *is as* a lamp despised in the thought of him that is at ease.

Pr 17:5 — Whoso mocketh the poor reproacheth his Maker: *and* he that is glad at calamities shall not be unpunished.

- **Murmuring in.**

See: Murmuring

- **Obduracy in.**

Le 26:23–24; 26:27–28; Job 36:12–13; Ps 78:31–32; Isa 22:12–13; Hos 7:9–10; Am 4:6–11; Rev 9:20–21; 16:1–21

Isa 8:21 — And they shall pass through it, hardly bestead and hungry: and it shall come to pass, that when they shall be hungry, they shall fret themselves, and curse their king and their God, and look upward.

Isa 9:13 — For the people turneth not unto him that smiteth them, neither do they seek the LORD of hosts.

Isa 26:11 — LORD, *when* thy hand is lifted up, they will not see: *but* they shall see, and be ashamed for *their* envy at the people; yea, the fire of thine enemies shall devour them.

Isa 42:25 — Therefore he hath poured upon him the fury of his anger, and the strength of battle: and it hath set him on fire round about, yet he knew not; and it burned him, yet he laid *it* not to heart.

Isa 57:17 — For the iniquity of his covetousness was I wroth, and smote him: I hid me, and was wroth, and he went on frowardly in the way of his heart.

Jer 2:30 — In vain have I smitten your children; they received no correction: your own sword hath devoured your prophets, like a destroying lion.

Jer 2:35 — Yet thou sayest, Because I am innocent, surely his anger shall turn from me. Behold, I will plead with thee, because thou sayest, I have not sinned.

Jer 3:3 — Therefore the showers have been withholden, and there hath been no latter rain; and thou hadst a whore's forehead, thou refusedst to be ashamed.

Jer 5:3 — O LORD, *are* not thine eyes upon the truth? thou hast stricken them, but they have not grieved; thou hast consumed them, *but* they have refused to receive correction: they have made their faces harder than a rock; they have refused to return.

Jer 7:28 — But thou shalt say unto them, This *is* a nation that obeyeth not the voice of the LORD their God, nor receiveth correction: truth is perished, and is cut off from their mouth.

Da 9:13 — As *it is* written in the law of Moses, all this evil is come upon us: yet made we not our prayer before the LORD our God, that we might turn from our iniquities, and understand thy truth.

Hos 7:14 — And they have not cried unto me with their heart, when they howled upon their beds: they assemble themselves for corn and wine, *and* they rebel against me.

Hos 9:17 — My God will cast them away, because they did not hearken unto him: and they shall be wanderers among the nations.

Zep 3:2 — She obeyed not the voice; she received not correction; she trusted not in the LORD; she drew not near to her God.

Zep 3:7 — I said, Surely thou wilt fear me, thou wilt receive instruction; so their dwelling should not be cut off, howsoever I punished them: but they rose early, *and* corrupted all their doings.

Hag 2:17 — I smote you with blasting and with mildew and with hail in all the labours of your hands; yet ye *turned* not to me, saith the LORD.

- **As a judgment.**

See: Judgment

See: Impenitence

- **Instances of.**
  - **Pharaoh.**

    Ex 9:30–34; 14:5–9

    Ex 8:19 — Then the magicians said unto Pharaoh, This *is* the finger of God: and Pharaoh's heart was hardened, and he hearkened not unto them; as the LORD had said.
  - **Asa.**

    2Ch 16:12 — And Asa in the thirty and ninth year of his reign was diseased in his feet, until his disease *was* exceeding *great:* yet in his disease he sought not to the LORD, but to the physicians.
  - **Ahaz.**

    2Ch 28:22–23

- **Penitence in.**
  - **Instances of.**
    - **Pharaoh.**

      Ex 9:27–30; 12:30–31; 14:5–9

      Ex 8:8 — Then Pharaoh called for Moses and Aaron, and said, Intreat the LORD, that he may take away the frogs from me, and from my people; and I will let the people go, that they may do sacrifice unto the LORD.
    - **David.**

      2Sa 12:15–16

2Sa 12:23 — But now he is dead, wherefore should I fast? can I bring him back again? I shall go to him, but he shall not return to me.

• **Nebuchadnezzar.**

Da 4:28–37

• **Levites.**

Ne 9:33 — Howbeit thou *art* just in all that is brought upon us; for thou hast done right, but we have done wickedly:

• **Prayer in.**

1Sa 1:10–11; 1Ki 8:35–50; 2Ch 6:24–39; 20:4–13; 33:12–13; Ne 4:4–5; Ps 3:1–2; 6:1–7; 7:1–2; 7:6–7; 9:13–14; 10:12–15; 13:1–4; 17:1–2; 17:6–9; 17:13–14; 20:1–2; 22:1–21; 25:16–19; 27:11–12; 30:9–10; 31:1–4, 14–18; 35:1–3, 22–23; 38:1–22; 39:12–13; 43:1–5; 44:23–26; 54:1–3; 55:1–17; 56:1–57:2; 59:1–60:3; 61:1–2; 64:1–2; 69:1–71:24; 74:1–23; 77:1–20; 79:1–80:16; 83:1–18; 85:5–7; 86:1–17; 88:9–12; 89:39–51; 94:1–23; 109:1–31; 119:41–42, 76–77, 121–123, 145–149, 153–154; 123:3–4; 130:1–8; 140:1–142:2; 142:5–143:12; Isa 38:2–3, 14–19; 63:15–17; 64:9–12; Jer 14:8–9, 19–21; 17:17–18; 20:7–8; 32:16–25; La 1:1–5:22; Jnh 2:1–10; Hab 1:12–13; Mt 15:22–28; Ac 4:29–30; 7:59–60; Jas 5:13–16

Ge 32:11 — Deliver me, I pray thee, from the hand of my brother, from the hand of Esau: for I fear him, lest he will come and smite me, *and* the mother with the children.

Ge 43:14 — And God Almighty give you mercy before the man, that he may send away your other brother, and Benjamin. If I be bereaved *of my children,* I am bereaved.

Ex 17:4 — And Moses cried unto the LORD, saying, What shall I do unto this people? they be almost ready to stone me.

Nu 20:16 — And when we cried unto the LORD, he heard our voice, and sent an angel, and hath brought us forth out of Egypt: and, behold, we *are* in Kadesh, a city in the uttermost of thy border:

2Sa 12:22 — And he said, While the child was yet alive, I fasted and wept: for I said, Who can tell *whether* GOD will be gracious to me, that the child may live?

2Sa 15:31 — And *one* told David, saying, Ahithophel *is* among the conspirators with Absalom. And David said, O LORD, I pray thee, turn the counsel of Ahithophel into foolishness.

2Sa 22:7 — In my distress I called upon the LORD, and cried to my God: and he did hear my voice out of his temple, and my cry *did enter* into his ears.

2Ki 19:16 — LORD, bow down thine ear, and hear: open, LORD, thine eyes, and see: and hear the words of Sennacherib, which hath sent him to reproach the living God.

2Ki 19:19 — Now therefore, O LORD our God, I beseech thee, save thou us out of his hand, that all the kingdoms of the earth may know that thou *art* the LORD God, *even* thou only.

2Ki 20:3 — I beseech thee, O LORD, remember now how I have walked before thee in truth and with a perfect heart, and have done *that which is* good in thy sight. And Hezekiah wept sore.

1Ch 5:20 — And they were helped against them, and the Hagarites were delivered into their hand, and all that *were* with them: for they cried to God in the battle, and he was intreated of them; because they put their trust in him.

2Ch 14:11 — And Asa cried unto the LORD his God, and said, LORD, *it is* nothing with thee to help, whether with many, or with them that have no power: help us, O LORD our God; for we rest on thee, and in thy name we go against this multitude. O LORD, thou *art* our God; let not man prevail against thee.

Ne 4:9 — Nevertheless we made our prayer unto our God, and set a watch against them day and night, because of them.

Ne 6:9 — For they all made us afraid, saying, Their hands shall be weakened from the work, that it be not done. Now therefore, *O God,* strengthen my hands.

Ne 6:14 — My God, think thou upon Tobiah and Sanballat according to these their works, and on the prophetess Noadiah, and the rest of the prophets, that would have put me in fear.

Ne 9:32 — Now therefore, our God, the great, the mighty, and the terrible God, who keepest covenant and mercy, let not all the trouble seem little before thee, that hath come upon us, on our kings, on our princes, and on our priests, and on our prophets, and on our fathers, and on all thy people, since the time of the kings of Assyria unto this day.

Job 10:2 — I will say unto God, Do not condemn me; shew me wherefore thou contendest with me.

Job 10:9 — Remember, I beseech thee, that thou hast made me as the clay; and wilt thou bring me into dust again?

Job 10:15 — If I be wicked, woe unto me; and *if* I be righteous, *yet* will I not lift up my head. *I am* full of confusion; therefore see thou mine affliction;

Job 13:21 — Withdraw thine hand far from me: and let not thy dread make me afraid.

Job 16:20 — My friends scorn me: *but* mine eye poureth out *tears* unto God.

Ps 3:7 — Arise, O LORD; save me, O my God: for thou hast smitten all mine enemies *upon* the cheek bone; thou hast broken the teeth of the ungodly.

Ps 4:1 — Hear me when I call, O God of my righteousness: thou hast enlarged me *when I was* in distress; have mercy upon me, and hear my prayer.

Ps 5:8 — Lead me, O LORD, in thy righteousness because of mine enemies; make thy way straight before my face.

Ps 10:1 — Why standest thou afar off, O LORD? *why* hidest thou *thyself* in times of trouble?

Ps 16:1 — Preserve me, O God: for in thee do I put my trust.

Ps 25:2 — O my God, I trust in thee: let me not be ashamed, let not mine enemies triumph over me.

Ps 25:22 — Redeem Israel, O God, out of all his troubles.

Ps 28:1 — Unto thee will I cry, O LORD my rock; be not silent to me: lest, *if* thou be silent to me, I become like them that go down into the pit.

Ps 31:9 — Have mercy upon me, O LORD, for I am in trouble: mine eye is consumed with grief, *yea,* my soul and my belly.

Ps 35:17 — Lord, how long wilt thou look on? rescue my soul from their destructions, my darling from the lions.

Ps 35:19 — Let not them that are mine enemies wrongfully rejoice over me: *neither* let them wink with the eye that hate me without a cause.

Ps 35:25 — Let them not say in their hearts, Ah, so would we have it: let them not say, We have swallowed him up.

Ps 39:10 — Remove thy stroke away from me: I am consumed by the blow of thine hand.

Ps 40:13 — Be pleased, O LORD, to deliver me: O LORD, make haste to help me.

Ps 40:17 — But I *am* poor and needy; *yet* the Lord thinketh upon me: thou *art* my help and my deliverer; make no tarrying, O my God.

Ps 42:9 — I will say unto God my rock, Why hast thou forgotten me? why go I mourning because of the oppression of the enemy?

Ps 44:4 — Thou art my King, O God: command deliverances for Jacob.

Ps 50:15 — And call upon me in the day of trouble: I will deliver thee, and thou shalt glorify me.

Ps 60:11 — Give us help from trouble: for vain *is* the help of man.

Ps 90:15 — Make us glad according to the days *wherein* thou hast afflicted us, *and* the years *wherein* we have seen evil.

Ps 102:2 — Hide not thy face from me in the day *when* I am in trouble; incline thine ear unto me: in the day *when* I call answer me speedily.

Ps 102:24 — I said, O my God, take me not away in the midst of my days: thy years *are* throughout all generations.

Ps 106:47 — Save us, O LORD our God, and gather us from among the heathen, to give thanks unto thy holy name, *and* to triumph in thy praise.

Ps 108:6 — That thy beloved may be delivered: save *with* thy right hand, and answer me.

Ps 108:12 — Give us help from trouble: for vain *is* the help of man.

Ps 116:4 — Then called I upon the name of the LORD; O LORD, I beseech thee, deliver my soul.

Ps 119:22 — Remove from me reproach and contempt; for I have kept thy testimonies.

Ps 119:28 — My soul melteth for heaviness: strengthen thou me according unto thy word.

Ps 119:39 — Turn away my reproach which I fear: for thy judgments *are* good.

Ps 119:82 — Mine eyes fail for thy word, saying, When wilt thou comfort me?

Ps 119:84 — How many *are* the days of thy servant? when wilt thou execute judgment on them that persecute me?

Ps 119:107 — I am afflicted very much: quicken me, O LORD, according unto thy word.

Ps 119:134 — Deliver me from the oppression of man: so will I keep thy precepts.

Ps 119:170 — Let my supplication come before thee: deliver me according to thy word.

Ps 119:173 — Let thine hand help me; for I have chosen thy precepts.

Ps 120:2 — Deliver my soul, O LORD, from lying lips, *and* from a deceitful tongue.

Ps 126:4 — Turn again our captivity, O LORD, as the streams in the south.

Isa 33:22 — For the LORD *is* our judge, the LORD *is* our lawgiver, the LORD *is* our king; he will save us.

Isa 51:9 — Awake, awake, put on strength, O arm of the LORD; awake, as in the ancient days, in the generations of old. *Art* thou not it that hath cut Rahab, *and* wounded the dragon?

Isa 64:1 — Oh that thou wouldest rend the heavens, that thou wouldest come down, that the mountains might flow down at thy presence,

Jer 10:24 — O LORD, correct me, but with judgment; not in thine anger, lest thou bring me to nothing.

Jer 15:15 — O LORD, thou knowest: remember me, and visit me, and revenge me of my persecutors; take me not away in thy longsuffering: know that for thy sake I have suffered rebuke.

Jer 16:19 — O LORD, my strength, and my fortress, and my refuge in the day of affliction, the Gentiles shall come unto thee from the ends of the earth, and shall say, Surely our fathers have inherited lies, vanity, and *things* wherein *there is* no profit.

Jer 18:19 — Give heed to me, O LORD, and hearken to the voice of them that contend with me.

Da 6:10 — Now when Daniel knew that the writing was signed, he went into his house; and his windows being open in his chamber toward Jerusalem, he kneeled upon his knees three times a day, and prayed, and gave thanks before his God, as he did aforetime.

Joel 1:19 — O LORD, to thee will I cry: for the fire hath devoured the pastures of the wilderness, and the flame hath burned all the trees of the field.

Jnh 1:14 — Wherefore they cried unto the LORD, and said, We beseech thee, O LORD, we beseech thee, let us not perish for this man's life, and lay not upon us innocent blood: for thou, O LORD, hast done as it pleased thee.

Mt 8:25 — And his disciples came to *him,* and awoke him, saying, Lord, save us: we perish.

Mt 14:30 — But when he saw the wind boisterous, he was afraid; and beginning to sink, he cried, saying, Lord, save me.

Mt 26:39 — And he went a little farther, and fell on his face, and prayed, saying, O my Father, if it be possible, let this cup pass from me: nevertheless not as I will, but as thou *wilt.*

Mt 26:42 — He went away again the second time, and prayed, saying, O my Father, if this cup may not pass away from me, except I drink it, thy will be done.

Mt 26:44 — And he left them, and went away again, and prayed the third time, saying the same words.

Mt 27:46 — And about the ninth hour Jesus cried with a loud voice, saying, Eli, Eli, lama sabachthani? that is to say, My God, my God, why hast thou forsaken me?

Mk 14:36 — And he said, Abba, Father, *all* things are possible unto thee; take away this cup from me: nevertheless not what I will, but what thou wilt.

Mk 15:34 — And at the ninth hour Jesus cried with a loud voice, saying, Eloi, Eloi, lama sabachthani? which is, being interpreted, My God, my God, why hast thou forsaken me?

Lk 18:1 — And he spake a parable unto them *to this end,* that men ought always to pray, and not to faint;

Lk 22:42 — Saying, Father, if thou be willing, remove this cup from me: nevertheless not my will, but thine, be done.

Lk 23:46 — And when Jesus had cried with a loud voice, he said, Father, into thy hands I commend my spirit: and having said thus, he gave up the ghost.

Jn 11:3 — Therefore his sisters sent unto him, saying, Lord, behold, he whom thou lovest is sick.

2Co 12:8 — For this thing I besought the Lord thrice, that it might depart from me.

✢See: Prayer

- **Prayer in, answered.**

✢See: Prayer; answered

- **Prayer for the afflicted.**

✢See: Intercession

- **Resignation in.**

Job 34:31–32; La 3:22–36; 1Th 3:3–4; Heb 12:3–12; 1Pe 4:12–13; 5:6–7

Job 5:17 — Behold, happy *is* the man whom God correcteth: therefore despise not thou the chastening of the Almighty:

Job 13:15 — Though he slay me, yet will I trust in him: but I will maintain mine own ways before him.

Job 34:34 — Let men of understanding tell me, and let a wise man hearken unto me.

Ps 4:4 — Stand in awe, and sin not: commune with your own heart upon your bed, and be still. Selah.

Ps 37:1 — Fret not thyself because of evildoers, neither be thou envious against the workers of iniquity.

Ps 46:10 — Be still, and know that I *am* God: I will be exalted among the heathen, I will be exalted in the earth.

Pr 3:11— My son, despise not the chastening of the LORD; neither be weary of his correction:

La 3:39 — Wherefore doth a living man complain, a man for the punishment of his sins?

Mic 6:9 — The LORD'S voice crieth unto the city, and *the man of* wisdom shall see thy name: hear ye the rod, and who hath appointed it.

Mt 26:39 — And he went a little farther, and fell on his face, and prayed, saying, O my Father, if it be possible, let this cup pass from me: nevertheless not as I will, but as thou *wilt.*

Mk 14:36 — And he said, Abba, Father, all things *are* possible unto thee; take away this cup from me: nevertheless not what I will, but what thou wilt.

Lk 21:19 — In your patience possess ye your souls.

Lk 22:42 — Saying, Father, if thou be willing, remove this cup from me: nevertheless not my will, but thine, be done.

Jn 18:11 — Then said Jesus unto Peter, Put up thy sword into the sheath: the cup which my Father hath given me, shall I not drink it?

Ro 5:3 — And not only *so,* but we glory in tribulations also: knowing that tribulation worketh patience;

Ro 12:12 — Rejoicing in hope; patient in tribulation; continuing instant in prayer;

2Co 12:9 — And he said unto me, My grace is sufficient for thee: for my strength is made perfect in weakness. Most gladly therefore will I rather glory in my infirmities, that the power of Christ may rest upon me.

Php 2:14 — Do all things without murmurings and disputings:

Col 1:11 — Strengthened with all might, according to his glorious power, unto all patience and longsuffering with joyfulness;

2Th 1:4 — So that we ourselves glory in you in the churches of God for your patience and faith in all your persecutions and tribulations that ye endure:

2Ti 2:3 — Thou therefore endure hardness, as a good soldier of Jesus Christ.

2Ti 4:5 — But watch thou in all things, endure afflictions, do the work of an evangelist, make full proof of thy ministry.

Heb 10:34 — For ye had compassion of me in my bonds, and took joyfully the spoiling of your goods, knowing in yourselves that ye have in heaven a better and an enduring substance.

Jas 1:10 — But the rich, in that he is made low: because as the flower of the grass he shall pass away.

Jas 4:7 — Submit yourselves therefore to God. Resist the devil, and he will flee from you.

1Pe 1:6 — Wherein ye greatly rejoice, though now for a season, if need be, ye are in heaviness through manifold temptations:

1Pe 2:20 — For what glory *is it,* if, when ye be buffeted for your faults, ye shall take it patiently? but if, when ye do well, and suffer *for it,* ye take it patiently, this *is* acceptable with God.

1Pe 4:19 — Wherefore let them that suffer according to the will of God commit the keeping of their souls *to him* in well doing, as unto a faithful Creator.

✢See: Resignation

- **Resignation in, exemplified.**

Job 1:21–22; Lk 23:40–41; Ro 5:3–4; 2Co 6:4–10

Jgs 10:15 — And the children of Israel said unto the LORD, We have sinned: do thou unto us whatsoever seemeth good unto thee; deliver us only, we pray thee, this day.

1Sa 3:18 — And Samuel told him every whit, and hid nothing from him. And he said, It *is* the LORD: let him do what seemeth him good.

2Sa 12:23 — But now he is dead, wherefore should I fast? can I bring him back again? I shall go to him, but he shall not return to me.

2Sa 15:26 — But if he thus say, I have no delight in thee; behold, *here am* I, let him do to me as seemeth good unto him.

2Sa 16:10 — And the king said, What have I to do with you, ye sons of Zeruiah? so let him curse, because the LORD hath said unto him, Curse David. Who shall then say, Wherefore hast thou done so?

2Sa 16:12 — It may be that the LORD will look on mine affliction, and that the LORD will requite me good for his cursing this day.

2Sa 24:14 — And David said unto Gad, I am in a great strait: let us fall now into the hand of the LORD; for his mercies *are* great: and let me not fall into the hand of man.

2Ki 4:26 — Run now, I pray thee, to meet her, and say unto her, *Is it* well with thee? *is it* well with thy husband? *is it* well with the child? And she answered, *It is* well.

2Ki 20:19 — Then said Hezekiah unto Isaiah, Good is the word of the LORD which thou hast spoken. And he said, *Is it* not *good,* if peace and truth be in my days?

Ne 9:33 — Howbeit thou *art* just in all that is brought upon us; for thou hast done right, but we have done wickedly:

Est 4:16 — Go, gather together all the Jews that are present in Shushan, and fast ye for me, and neither eat nor drink three days, night or day: I also and my maidens will fast likewise; and so will I go in unto the king, which *is* not according to the law: and if I perish, I perish.

Job 2:10 — But he said unto her, Thou speakest as one of the foolish women speaketh. What? shall we receive good at the hand of God, and shall we not receive evil? In all this did not Job sin with his lips.

Job 13:15 — Though he slay me, yet will I trust in him: but I will maintain mine own ways before him.

Job 14:14 — If a man die, shall he live *again?* all the days of my appointed time will I wait, till my change come.

Ps 39:9 — I was dumb, I opened not my mouth; because thou didst *it.*

Ps 71:20 — *Thou,* which hast shewed me great and sore troubles, shalt quicken me again, and shalt bring me up again from the depths of the earth.

Ps 119:75 — I know, O LORD, that thy judgments *are* right, and that *thou* in faithfulness hast afflicted me.

Isa 39:8 — Then said Hezekiah to Isaiah, Good *is* the word of the LORD which thou hast spoken. He said moreover, For there shall be peace and truth in my days.

Jer 10:19 — Woe is me for my hurt! my wound is grievous: but I said, Truly this *is* a grief, and I must bear it.

La 1:18 — The LORD is righteous; for I have rebelled against his commandment: hear, I pray you, all people, and behold my sorrow: my virgins and my young men are gone into captivity.

La 3:39 — Wherefore doth a living man complain, a man for the punishment of his sins?

Da 9:14 — Therefore hath the LORD watched upon the evil, and brought it upon us: for the LORD our God *is* righteous in all his works which he doeth: for we obeyed not his voice.

Mic 7:9 — I will bear the indignation of the LORD, because I have sinned against him, until he plead my cause, and execute judgment for me: he will bring me forth to the light, *and* I shall behold his righteousness.

Ac 21:14 — And when he would not be persuaded, we ceased, saying, The will of the Lord be done.

2Co 7:4 — Great *is* my boldness of speech toward you, great *is* my glorying of you: I am filled with comfort, I am exceeding joyful in all our tribulation.

2Th 1:4 — So that we ourselves glory in you in the churches of God for your patience and faith in all your persecutions and tribulations that ye endure:

Jas 5:11 — Behold, we count them happy which endure. Ye have heard of the patience of Job, and have seen the end of the Lord; that the Lord is very pitiful, and of tender mercy.

See: Resignation

- **Instances of resignation in.**
  - **Aaron, at the death of Nadab and Abihu.**
    Le 10:1–3
  - **Eli, when judgments against his house were foretold.**
    1Sa 3:15–18
  - **David, at the death of his child.**
    2Sa 12:23
  - **The Shunammite.**
    2Ki 4:18–37
  - **Jesus, in Gethsemane.**
    Mt 26:39; Mk 14:36; Lk 22:42; Jn 18:11
  - **Paul and Silas in prison.**
    Ac 16:23–25

AFFLICTIONS of Saints

- **To be expected.**

Jn 16:33 — These things I have spoken unto you, that in me ye might have peace. In the world ye shall have tribulation: but be of good cheer; I have overcome the world.

Ac 14:22 — Confirming the souls of the disciples, *and* exhorting them to continue in the faith, and that we must through much tribulation enter into the kingdom of God.

- **Comparatively light.**

Ac 20:23–24

Ro 8:18 — For I reckon that the sufferings of this present time *are* not worthy *to be compared* with the glory which shall be revealed in us.

2Co 4:17 — For our light affliction, which is but for a moment, worketh for us a far more exceeding *and* eternal weight of glory;

- **Temporary.**

Isa 54:7–8

Ps 30:5 — For his anger *endureth but* a moment; in his favour is life: weeping may endure for a night, but joy *cometh* in the morning.

Ps 103:9 — He will not always chide: neither will he keep *his anger* for ever.

Jn 16:20 — Verily, verily, I say unto you, That ye shall weep and lament, but the world shall rejoice: and ye shall be sorrowful, but your sorrow shall be turned into joy.

1Pe 1:6 — Wherein ye greatly rejoice, though now for a season, if need be, ye are in heaviness through manifold temptations:

1Pe 5:10 — But the God of all grace, who hath called us unto his eternal glory by Christ Jesus, after that ye have suffered a while, make you perfect, stablish, strengthen, settle *you.*

• Joy under.

Job 5:17 — Behold, happy *is* the man whom God correcteth: therefore despise not thou the chastening of the Almighty:

Jas 5:11 — Behold, we count them happy which endure. Ye have heard of the patience of Job, and have seen the end of the Lord; that the Lord is very pitiful, and of tender mercy.

• End in joy and blessedness.

Ps 126:5–6; Isa 61:2–3; 1Pe 4:13–14

Mt 5:4 — Blessed *are* they that mourn: for they shall be comforted.

• Often arise from the profession of the gospel.

2Ti 3:11–12

Mt 24:9 — Then shall they deliver you up to be afflicted, and shall kill you: and ye shall be hated of all nations for my name's sake.

Jn 15:21 — But all these things will they do unto you for my name's sake, because they know not him that sent me.

• Exhibit the love and faithfulness of God.

Heb 12:6–7

Dt 8:5 — Thou shalt also consider in thine heart, that, as a man chasteneth his son, *so* the LORD thy God chasteneth thee.

Ps 119:75 — I know, O LORD, that thy judgments *are* right, and that *thou* in faithfulness hast afflicted me.

Pr 3:12 — For whom the LORD loveth he correcteth; even as a father the son *in whom* he delighteth.

1Co 11:32 — But when we are judged, we are chastened of the Lord, that we should not be condemned with the world.

Rev 3:19 — As many as I love, I rebuke and chasten: be zealous therefore, and repent.

AFFLICTIONS of the Wicked

• God is glorified in.

Eze 38:22–23

Ex 14:4 — And I will harden Pharaoh's heart, that he shall follow after them; and I will be honoured upon Pharaoh, and upon all his host; that the Egyptians may know that I *am* the LORD. And they did so.

• God holds in derision.

Pr 1:26–27

Ps 37:13 — The Lord shall laugh at him: for he seeth that his day is coming.

• Are multiplied.

Dt 31:17 — Then my anger shall be kindled against them in that day, and I will forsake them, and I will hide my face from them, and they shall be devoured, and many evils and troubles shall befall them; so that they will say in that day. Are not these evils come upon us, because our God *is* not among us?

Job 20:5 — That the triumphing of the wicked *is* short, and the joy of the hypocrite *but* for a moment?

Job 21:17 — How oft is the candle of the wicked put out! and *how oft* cometh their destruction upon them! *God* distributeth sorrows in his anger.

Ps 32:10 — Many sorrows *shall be* to the wicked: but he that trusteth in the LORD, mercy shall compass him about.

• Continual.

Job 15:20 — The wicked man travaileth with pain all *his* days, and the number of years is hidden to the oppressor.

Ecc 2:23— For all his days *are* sorrows, and his travail grief; yea, his heart taketh not rest in the night. This is also vanity.

Isa 32:10 — Many days and years shall ye be troubled, ye careless women: for the vintage shall fail, the gathering shall not come.

• Often sudden.

Ps 73:19 — How are they *brought* into desolation, as in a moment! they are utterly consumed with terrors.

Pr 6:15 — Therefore shall his calamity come suddenly; suddenly shall he be broken without remedy.

Isa 30:13 — Therefore this iniquity shall be to you as a breach ready to fall, swelling out in a high wall, whose breaking cometh suddenly at an instant.

Rev 18:10 — Standing afar off for the fear of her torment, saying, Alas, alas, that great city Babylon, that mighty city! for in one hour is thy judgment come.

• Are often judicially sent.

Job 21:17 — How oft is the candle of the wicked put out! and *how oft* cometh their destruction upon them! *God* distributeth sorrows in his anger.

Ps 107:17 — Fools because of their transgression, and because of their iniquities, are afflicted.

Jer 30:15 — Why criest thou for thine affliction? thy sorrow *is* incurable for the multitude of thine iniquity: *because* thy sins were increased, I have done these things unto thee.

• Are for examples to others.

Ps 64:7–9; Zep 3:6–7

1Co 10:5 — But with many of them God was not well pleased: for they were overthrown in the wilderness.

1Co 10:11 — Now all these things happened unto them for ensamples: and they are written for our admonition, upon whom the ends of the world are come.

2Pe 2:6 — And turning the cities of Sodom and Gomorrah into ashes condemned *them* with an overthrow, making *them* an ensample unto those that after should live ungodly;

• Are ineffectual for their conversion.

Ex 9:30 — But as for thee and thy servants, I know that ye will not yet fear the LORD God.

Isa 9:13 — For the people turneth not unto him that smiteth them, neither do they seek the LORD of hosts.

Jer 2:30 — In vain have I smitten your children; they received no correction: your own sword hath devoured your prophets, like a destroying lion.

Hag 2:17 — I smote you with blasting and with mildew and with hail in all the labours of your hands; yet ye *turned* not to me, saith the LORD.

• **Their persecution of saints, a cause of.**

Dt 30:7 — And the LORD thy God will put all these curses upon thine enemies, and on them that hate thee, which persecuted thee.

Ps 55:19 — God shall hear, and afflict them, even he that abideth of old. Selah. Because they have no changes, therefore they fear not God.

Zec 2:9 — For, behold, I will shake mine hand upon them, and they shall be a spoil to their servants: and ye shall know that the LORD of hosts hath sent me.

2Th 1:6 — Seeing *it is* a righteous thing with God to recompense tribulation to them that trouble you;

• **Impenitence is a cause of.**

Pr 1:30–31; Am 4:6–12; Zec 7:11–12; Rev 2:21–22

Eze 24:13 — In thy filthiness *is* lewdness: because I have purged thee, and thou wast not purged, thou shalt not be purged from thy filthiness any more, till I have caused my fury to rest upon thee.

• **Sometimes humble them.**

1Ki 21:27 — And it came to pass, when Ahab heard those words, that he rent his clothes, and put sackcloth upon his flesh, and fasted, and lay in sackcloth, and went softly.

• **Frequently harden.**

Ne 9:28–29

Jer 5:3 — O LORD, *are* not thine eyes upon the truth? thou hast stricken them, but they have not grieved; thou hast consumed them, *but* they have refused to receive correction: they have made their faces harder than a rock; they have refused to return.

• **Produce slavish fear.**

Job 15:24 — Trouble and anguish shall make him afraid; they shall prevail against him, as a king ready to the battle.

Ps 73:19 — How are they *brought* into desolation, as in a moment! they are utterly consumed with terrors.

Jer 49:3 — Howl, O Heshbon, for Ai is spoiled: cry, ye daughters of Rabbah, gird you with sackcloth; lament, and run to and fro by the hedges; for their king shall go into captivity, *and* his priests and his princes together.

Jer 49:5 — Behold, I will bring a fear upon thee, saith the Lord GOD of hosts, from all those that be about thee; and ye shall be driven out every man right forth; and none shall gather up him that wandereth.

• **Saints should not be alarmed at.**

Pr 3:25–26

AFFLICTIONS, Benefits of

• **Benefits of, described.**

Dt 4:30–31; 30:1–2; 1Ki 8:47–53; 2Ch 6:28–31; Job 5:6–11; Ps 94:12–13; Pr 3:11–12; Ecc 7:2–3; Jer 22:22–23; La 3:27–28; Hos 2:6–7; Ro 5:3–4; Php 1:12–14; Jas 1:2–4

1Ki 8:33 — When thy people Israel be smitten down before the enemy, because they have sinned against thee, and shall turn again to thee, and confess thy name, and pray, and make supplication unto thee in this house:

1Ki 8:35 — When heaven is shut up, and there is no rain, because they have sinned against thee; if they pray toward this place, and confess thy name, and turn from their sin, when thou afflictest them:

Job 5:17 — Behold, happy *is* the man whom God correcteth: therefore despise not thou the chastening of the Almighty:

Job 23:10 — But he knoweth the way that I take: *when* he hath tried me, I shall come forth as gold.

Isa 19:20 — And it shall be for a sign and for a witness unto the LORD of hosts in the land of Egypt: for they shall cry unto the LORD because of the oppressors, and he shall send them a saviour, and a great one, and he shall deliver them.

Isa 19:22 — And the LORD shall smite Egypt: he shall smite and heal *it:* and they shall return *even* to the LORD, and he shall be intreated of them, and shall heal them.

Isa 26:9 — With my soul have I desired thee in the night; yea, with my spirit within me will I seek thee early: for when thy judgments *are* in the earth, the inhabitants of the world will learn righteousness.

Isa 27:9 — By this therefore shall the iniquity of Jacob be purged; and this is all the fruit to take away his sin; when he maketh all the stones of the altar as chalkstones that are beaten in sunder, the groves and images shall not stand up.

Jer 2:27 — Saying to a stock, Thou *art* my father; and to a stone, Thou hast brought me forth: for they have turned *their* back unto me, and not *their* face: but in the time of their trouble they will say, Arise, and save us.

Jer 31:19 — Surely after that I was turned, I repented; and after that I was instructed, I smote upon *my* thigh: I was ashamed, yea, even confounded, because I did bear the reproach of my youth.

Eze 6:9 — And they that escape of you shall remember me among the nations whither they shall be carried captives, because I am broken with their whorish heart, which hath departed from me, and with their eyes, which go a whoring after their idols: and they shall lothe themselves for the evils which they have committed in all their abominations.

Eze 20:37 — And I will cause you to pass under the rod, and I will bring you into the bond of the covenant:

Eze 20:43 — And there shall ye remember your ways, and all your doings, wherein ye have been defiled; and ye shall lothe yourselves in your own sight for all your evils that ye have committed.

Hos 5:15 — I will go *and* return to my place, till they acknowledge their offence, and seek my face: in their affliction they will seek me early.

Ro 8:17 — And if children, then heirs; heirs of God, and joint-heirs with Christ; if so be that we suffer with *him,* that we may be also glorified together.

Ro 8:28 — And we know that all things work together for good to them that love God, to them who are the called according to *his* purpose.

2Co 4:17 — For our light affliction, which is but for a moment, worketh for us a far more exceeding *and* eternal weight of glory;

Php 1:19 — For I know that this shall turn to my salvation through your prayer, and the supply of the Spirit of Jesus Christ,

Heb 12:5 — And ye have forgotten the exhortation which speaketh unto you as unto children, My son, despise not thou the chastening of the Lord, nor faint when thou art rebuked of him:

Jas 1:12 — Blessed *is* the man that endureth temptation: for when he is tried, he shall receive the crown of life, which the Lord hath promised to them that love him.

1Pe 1:7 — That the trial of your faith, being much more precious than of gold that perisheth, though it be tried with fire, might be found unto praise and honour and glory at the appearing of Jesus Christ:

1Pe 4:14 — If ye be reproached for the name of Christ, happy *are ye;* for the spirit of glory and of God resteth upon you: on their part he is evil spoken of, but on your part he is glorified.

• Benefits of, illustrated.

Ge 22:16–18; 32:9–31; Ex 9:27–28; 10:16–17; 12:31–33; Jgs 10:6–8; 1Sa 12:9–10; 1Ki 13:1–10; 2Ch 33:12–13; Ezr 9:5–15; Ne 9:4–38; Job 34:31–32; Job 40:1–5; Ps 18:4–6; 66:10–12; 78:34–35; Jer 31:18–19; La 3:19–20; Jnh 2:1–10; Lk 15:11–24

Ge 22:12 — And he said, Lay not thine hand upon the lad, neither do thou any thing unto him: for now I know that thou fearest God, seeing thou hast not withheld thy son, thine only *son* from me.

Ge 42:21 — And they said one to another, We *are* verily guilty concerning our brother, in that we saw the anguish of his soul, when he besought us, and we would not hear; therefore is this distress come upon us.

Ex 10:7 — And Pharaoh's servants said unto him, How long shall this man be a snare unto us? let the men go, that they may serve the LORD their God: knowest thou not yet that Egypt is destroyed?

Nu 21:7 — Therefore the people came to Moses, and said, We have sinned, for we have spoken against the LORD, and against thee; pray unto the LORD, that he take away the serpents from us. And Moses prayed for the people.

Jgs 10:10 — And the children of Israel cried unto the LORD, saying, We have sinned against thee, both because we have forsaken our God, and also served Baalim.

2Ch 15:4 — But when they in their trouble did turn unto the LORD God of Israel, and sought him, he was found of them.

Ps 119:67 — Before I was afflicted I went astray: but now have I kept thy word.

Ps 119:71 — *It is* good for me that I have been afflicted; that I might learn thy statutes.

Isa 26:16 — LORD, in trouble have they visited thee, they poured out a prayer *when* thy chastening *was* upon them.

Hos 6:1 — Come, and let us return unto the LORD: for he hath torn, and he will heal us; he hath smitten, and he will bind us up.

Ac 8:24 — Then answered Simon, and said, Pray ye to the Lord for me, that none of these things which ye have spoken come upon me.

• Exemplified Joseph's brethren.

Ge 42:21 — And they said one to another, We *are* verily guilty concerning our brother, in that we saw the anguish of his soul, when he besought us, and we would not hear; therefore is this distress come upon us.

• Exemplified Joseph.

Ge 45:7–8

Ge 45:5 — Now therefore be not grieved, nor angry with yourselves, that ye sold me hither: for God did send me before you to preserve life.

• Exemplified Israel.

Dt 8:3 — And he humbled thee, and suffered thee to hunger, and fed thee with manna, which thou knewest not, neither did thy fathers know; that he might make thee know that man doth not live by bread only, but by every *word* that proceedeth out of the mouth of the LORD doth man live.

Dt 8:5 — Thou shalt also consider in thine heart, that, as a man chasteneth his son, *so* the LORD thy God chasteneth thee.

• Exemplified Josiah.

2Ki 22:19 — Because thine heart was tender, and thou hast humbled thyself before the LORD, when thou heardest what I spake against this place, and against the inhabitants thereof, that they should become a desolation and a curse, and hast rent thy clothes, and wept before me; I also have heard *thee,* saith the LORD.

• Exemplified Hezekiah.

2Ch 32:25–26

• Exemplified Manasseh.

2Ch 33:12 — And when he was in affliction, he besought the LORD his God, and humbled himself greatly before the God of his fathers,

• Exemplified Jonah.

Jnh 2:7 — When my soul fainted within me I remembered the LORD: and my prayer came in unto thee, into thine holy temple.

• Exemplified prodigal son.

Lk 15:21 — And the son said unto him, Father, I have sinned against heaven, and in thy sight, and am no more worthy to be called thy son.

AFFLICTIONS, Exemplified

• In Pharaoh and the Egyptians.

Ex 9:14–15; 14:24–25

• Ahaziah.

2Ki 1:1–4

• Gehazi.

2Ki 5:27 — The leprosy therefore of Naaman shall cleave unto thee, and unto thy seed for ever. And he went out from his presence a leper *as white* as snow.

- **Jehoram.**
  2Ch 21:12–19
- **Uzziah.**
  2Ch 26:19–21
- **Ahaz, etc..**
  2Ch 28:5–8
  2Ch 28:22 — And in the time of his distress did he trespass yet more against the LORD: this *is that* king Ahaz.

AFFLICTIONS, Forsaken by Friends in

Job 19:13–19
Job 2:9 — Then said his wife unto him, Dost thou still retain thine integrity? curse God, and die.

- **Instances of.**
  - **David.**
    Ps 31:11–12; 41:9; 88:8; 88:18
  - **Jesus.**
    Mt 26:56
  - **Paul.**
    2Ti 4:16
  - **National lessons from.**
    Joel 1:1–2:32

AFFLICTIONS, Miscellany of Minor Sub-Topics

- **God regulates the measure of afflictions.**
  Ps 80:5 — Thou feedest them with the bread of tears; and givest them tears to drink in great measure.
  Isa 9:1 — Nevertheless the dimness *shall* not *be* such as *was* in her vexation, when at the first he lightly afflicted the land of Zebulun and the land of Naphtali, and afterward did more grievously afflict *her by* the way of the sea, beyond Jordan, in Galilee of the nations.
  Jer 46:28 — Fear thou not, O Jacob my servant, saith the LORD: for I *am* with thee; for I will make a full end of all the nations whither I have driven thee: but I will not make a full end of thee, but correct thee in measure; yet will I not leave thee wholly unpunished.
- **Determines the continuance of.**
  Ge 15:13–14
  Nu 14:33 — And your children shall wander in the wilderness forty years, and bear your whoredoms, until your carcases be wasted in the wilderness.
  Isa 10:25 — For yet a very little while, and the indignation shall cease, and mine anger in their destruction.
  Jer 29:10 — For thus saith the LORD, That after seventy years be accomplished at Babylon I will visit you, and perform my good word toward you, in causing you to return to this place.
- **Does not willingly send.**
  La 3:33 — For he doth not afflict willingly nor grieve the children of men.
- **Man is born to.**
  Job 5:6–7
  Job 14:1 — Man *that is* born of a woman *is* of few days, and full of trouble.
- **Saints appointed to.**
  1Th 3:3 — That no man should be moved by these afflictions: for yourselves know that we are appointed thereunto.
- **Consequent upon the fall.**
  Ge 3:16–19
- **Sin produces.**
  Job 4:8 — Even as I have seen, they that plow iniquity, and sow wickedness, reap the same.
  Pr 1:31 — Therefore shall they eat of the fruit of their own way, and be filled with their own devices.
- **Sinners corrected by.**
  Ps 89:30–32; Ac 13:10–11
  2Sa 12:14 — Howbeit, because by this deed thou hast given great occasion to the enemies of the LORD to blaspheme, the child also *that is* born unto thee shall surely die.
  Isa 57:17 — For the iniquity of his covetousness was I wroth, and smote him: I hid me, and was wroth, and he went on frowardly in the way of his heart.
- **Often severe.**
  Job 16:7–16
  Ps 42:7 — Deep calleth unto deep at the noise of thy waterspouts: all thy waves and thy billows are gone over me.
  Ps 66:12 — Thou hast caused men to ride over our heads; we went through fire and through water: but thou broughtest us out into a wealthy *place.*
  Jnh 2:3 — For thou hadst cast me into the deep, in the midst of the seas; and the floods compassed me about: all thy billows and thy waves passed over me.
  Rev 7:14 — And I said unto him, Sir, thou knowest. And he said to me, These are they which came out of great tribulation, and have washed their robes, and made them white in the blood of the Lamb.
- **Always less than deserved.**
  Ezr 9:13 — And after all that is come upon us for our evil deeds, and for our great trespass, seeing that thou our God hast punished us less than our iniquities *deserve,* and hast given us *such* deliverance as this;
  Ps 103:10 — He hath not dealt with us after our sins; nor rewarded us according to our iniquities.
- **Results of, good.**
  Ex 1:11–12; Dt 8:15–16; Jer 24:5–6
  Ge 50:20 — But as for you, ye thought evil against me; *but* God meant it unto good, to bring to pass, as *it is* this day, to save much people alive.
  Eze 20:37 — And I will cause you to pass under the rod, and I will bring you into the bond of the covenant:
- **Tempered with mercy.**
  Ps 78:38–39; 106:43–46; Isa 30:18–21; Mic 7:7–9
  La 3:32 — But though he cause grief, yet will he have compassion according to the multitude of his mercies.
  Na 1:12 — Thus saith the LORD: Though *they be* quiet, and likewise many, yet thus shall they be cut down, when he shall pass through. Though I have afflicted thee, I will afflict thee no more.

AFFLICTIONS, Unclassified Scripture Relating

• Unclassified.

Ge 3:16–17; Job 3:1–26; 5:6–7, 17–18; 6:1–30; 7:2–6; 16:6–14; 17:7–16; 19:7–20; 30:15–19; 33:19–22; 36:8–12; Ps 6:6–7; 18:4–6; 31:9–13; 32:3–4; 39:1–4; 42:6–7; 55:4–8; 66:10–12; 69:1–3; 77:2–4; 80:5–6; 88:3–18; 102:3–11; 107:4–5, 17–19; 109:22–24; 143:3–4; Pr 3:11–12; Ecc 2:22–23; 7:2–4; Isa 24:1–16; 26:16–17; La 3:1–36; 2Co 1:8–9; 4:7–12; 4:16–17; 6:4–10; 11:23–30; Heb 12:6–7

Dt 8:5 — Thou shalt also consider in thine heart, that, as a man chasteneth his son, *so* the LORD thy God chasteneth thee.

2Sa 7:14 — I will be his father, and he shall be my son. If he commit iniquity, I will chasten him with the rod of men, and with the stripes of the children of men:

Job 9:18 — He will not suffer me to take my breath, but filleth me with bitterness.

Job 12:5 — He that is ready to slip with *his* feet *is as* a lamp despised in the thought of him that is at ease.

Job 14:1 — Man *that is* born of a woman *is* of few days, and full of trouble.

Job 14:22 — But his flesh upon him shall have pain, and his soul within him shall mourn.

Job 23:10 — But he knoweth the way that I take: *when* he hath tried me, I shall come forth as gold.

Job 36:15 — He delivereth the poor in his affliction, and openeth their ears in oppression.

Ps 69:20 — Reproach hath broken my heart; and I am full of heaviness: and I looked *for some* to take pity, but *there was* none; and for comforters, but I found none.

Ps 73:10 — Therefore his people return hither: and waters of a full *cup* are wrung out to them.

Ps 89:32 — Then will I visit their transgression with the rod, and their iniquity with stripes.

Ps 90:10 — The days of our years *are* threescore years and ten; and if by reason of strength *they be* fourscore years, yet *is* their strength labour and sorrow; for it is soon cut off, and we fly away.

Ps 107:10 — Such as sit in darkness and in the shadow of death, *being* bound in affliction and iron;

Ps 116:3 — The sorrows of death compassed me, and the pains of hell gat hold upon me: I found trouble and sorrow.

Ps 141:7 — Our bones are scattered at the grave's mouth, as when one cutteth and cleaveth *wood* upon the earth.

Pr 12:25 — Heaviness in the heart of man maketh it stoop: but a good word maketh it glad.

Pr 13:12 — Hope deferred maketh the heart sick: but *when* the desire cometh, *it is* a tree of life.

Pr 14:10 — The heart knoweth his own bitterness; and a stranger doth not intermeddle with his joy.

Pr 14:13 — Even in laughter the heart is sorrowful; and the end of that mirth *is* heaviness.

Pr 15:13 — A merry heart maketh a cheerful countenance: but by sorrow of the heart the spirit is broken.

Pr 15:15 — All the days of the afflicted *are* evil: but he that is of a merry heart *hath* a continual feast.

Pr 17:3 — The fining pot *is* for silver, and the furnace for gold: but the LORD trieth the hearts.

Pr 17:22 — A merry heart doeth good *like* a medicine: but a broken spirit drieth the bones.

Pr 18:14 — The spirit of a man will sustain his infirmity; but a wounded spirit who can bear?

Isa 1:6 — From the sole of the foot even unto the head *there is* no soundness in it; *but* wounds, and bruises, and putrifying sores: they have not been closed, neither bound up, neither mollified with ointment.

Isa 48:10 — Behold, I have refined thee, but not with silver; I have chosen thee in the furnace of affliction.

La 1:7 — Jerusalem remembered in the days of her affliction and of her miseries all her pleasant things that she had in the days of old, when her people fell into the hand of the enemy, and none did help her: the adversaries saw her, *and* did mock at her sabbaths.

La 1:12 — *Is it* nothing to you, all ye that pass by? behold, and see if there be any sorrow like unto my sorrow, which is done unto me, wherewith the LORD hath afflicted *me* in the day of his fierce anger.

Zec 13:9 — And I will bring the third part through the fire, and will refine them as silver is refined, and will try them as gold is tried: they shall call on my name, and I will hear them: I will say, It *is* my people: and they shall say, The LORD *is* my God.

Mk 9:49 — For every one shall be salted with fire, and every sacrifice shall be salted with salt.

Jn 15:2 — Every branch in me that beareth not fruit he taketh away: and every *branch* that beareth fruit, he purgeth it, that it may bring forth more fruit.

Jn 16:33 — These things I have spoken unto you, that in me ye might have peace. In the world ye shall have tribulation: but be of good cheer; I have overcome the world.

Heb 12:9 — Furthermore we have had fathers of our flesh which corrected *us*, and we gave *them* reverence: shall we not much rather be in subjection unto the Father of spirits, and live?

1Pe 5:9 — Whom resist stedfast in the faith, knowing that the same afflictions are accomplished in your brethren that are in the world.

Rev 3:19 — As many as I love, I rebuke and chasten: be zealous therefore, and repent.

✦See: Penitent

✦See: Persecution

✦See: Poor

✦See: Sorrow

✦See: Temptation

AFFLUENCE

Mt 6:19–20; 1Co 4:1–21

Lk 12:48 — But he that knew not, and did commit things worthy of stripes, shall be beaten with few *stripes.* For unto whomsoever much is given, of him shall be much required: and to whom men have committed much, of him they will ask the more.

Jas 5:1 — Go to now, *ye* rich men, weep and howl for your miseries that shall come upon *you.*

AGABUS • A prophet.

Ac 11:28 — And there stood up one of them named Agabus, and signified by the spirit that there should be great dearth throughout all the world: which came to pass in the days of Claudius Caesar.

Ac 21:10 — And as we tarried *there* many days, there came down from Judaea a certain prophet, named Agabus.

AGAG

• A king of the Amalekites.

Nu 24:7 — He shall pour the water out of his buckets, and his seed *shall be* in many waters, and his king shall be higher than Agag, and his kingdom shall be exalted.

• A king of the Amalekites. Taken prisoner by Saul, and slain by Samuel.

1Sa 15:8 — And he took Agag the king of the Amalekites alive, and utterly destroyed all the people with the edge of the sword.

1Sa 15:33 — And Samuel said, As thy sword hath made women childless, so shall thy mother be childless among women. And Samuel hewed Agag in pieces before the LORD in Gilgal.

AGAPE

Mt 5:44 — <u>But I say unto you, Love your enemies, bless them that curse you, do good to them that hate you, and pray for them which despitefully use you, and persecute you;</u>

1Pe 2:23 — Who, when he was reviled, reviled not again; when he suffered, he threatened not; but committed *himself* to him that judgeth righteously:

AGAR ⇜See: Hagar

AGATE • A precious stone.

Ex 28:19 — And the third row a ligure, an agate, and an amethyst.

Isa 54:12 — And I will make thy windows of agates, and thy gates of carbuncles, and all thy borders of pleasant stones.

Eze 27:16 — Syria *was* thy merchant by reason of the multitude of the wares of thy making: they occupied in thy fairs with emeralds, purple, and broidered work, and fine linen, and coral, and agate.

AGE

1Ti 5:1–16

Pr 16:31 — The hoary head *is* a crown of glory, *if* it be found in the way of righteousness.

Phm 1:9 — Yet for love's sake I rather beseech *thee*, being such an one as Paul the aged, and now also a prisoner of Jesus Christ.

AGE, Old ⇜See: Old Age

AGED

• Gospel invitation to.

Mt 20:5–6

⇜**See: Old Age**

AGEE • Father of Shammah.

2Sa 23:11 — And after him *was* Shammah the son of Agee the Hararite. And the Philistines were gathered together into a troop, where was a piece of ground full of lentiles: and the people fled from the Philistines.

AGENCY

• In salvation of men.

Job 33:14–30; Mt 5:13–16; 1Co 1:26–29

Ps 8:2 — Out of the mouth of babes and sucklings hast thou ordained strength because of thine enemies, that thou mightest still the enemy and the avenger.

Mt 4:19 — And he saith unto them, <u>Follow me, and I will make you fishers of men.</u>

Lk 1:17 — And he shall go before him in the spirit and power of Elias, to turn the hearts of the fathers to the children, and the disobedient to the wisdom of the just; to make ready a people prepared for the Lord.

Lk 5:10 — And so *was* also James, and John, the sons of Zebedee, which were partners with Simon. And Jesus said unto Simon, <u>Fear not; from henceforth thou shalt catch men.</u>

Lk 10:17 — And the seventy returned again with joy, saying, Lord, even the devils are subject unto us through thy name.

Lk 10:21 — In that hour Jesus rejoiced in spirit, and said, <u>I thank thee, O Father, Lord of heaven and earth, that thou hast hid these things from the wise and prudent, and hast revealed them unto babes: even so, Father; for so it seemed good in thy sight.</u>

Jn 15:16 — <u>Ye have not chosen me, but I have chosen you, and ordained you, that ye should go and bring forth fruit, and *that* your fruit should remain: that whatsoever ye shall ask of the Father in my name, he may give it you.</u>

1Th 2:4 — But as we were allowed of God to be put in trust with the gospel, even so we speak; not as pleasing men, but God, which trieth our hearts.

1Ti 1:11 — According to the glorious gospel of the blessed God, which was committed to my trust.

1Ti 6:20 — O Timothy, keep that which is committed to thy trust, avoiding profane *and* vain babblings, and oppositions of science falsely so called:

Jas 5:20 — Let him know, that he which converteth the sinner from the error of his way shall save a soul from death, and shall hide a multitude of sins.

⇜**See: Preaching**

• In executing judgments.

1Sa 15:1–19; 2Ki 9:6–7; 19:25–26; Ps 17:13–14; Isa 10:5–6; Jer 51:20–23

Ge 3:15 — And I will put enmity between thee and the woman, and between thy seed and her seed; it shall bruise thy head, and thou shalt bruise his heel.

2Sa 7:14 — I will be his father, and he shall be my son. If he commit iniquity, I will chasten him with the rod of men, and with the stripes of the children of men:

2Ch 22:7 — And the destruction of Ahaziah was of God by coming to Joram: for when he was come, he went out with Jehoram against Jehu the son of Nimshi, whom the LORD had anointed to cut off the house of Ahab.

Isa 13:5 — They come from a far country, from the end of heaven, *even* the LORD, and the weapons of his indignation, to destroy the whole land.

Isa 41:15 — Behold, I will make thee a new sharp threshing instrument having teeth: thou shalt thresh the mountains, and beat *them* small, and shalt make the hills as chaff.

Jer 27:8 — And it shall come to pass, *that* the nation and kingdom which will not serve the same Nebuchadnezzar the king of Babylon, and that will not put their neck under the yoke of the king of Babylon, that nation will I punish, saith the LORD, with the sword, and with the famine, and with the pestilence, until I have consumed them by his hand.

- **Free moral.**

See: Contingencies

AGRICULTURE

- **Divine institution of.**

Ge 2:15 — And the LORD God took the man, and put him into the garden of Eden to dress it and to keep it.

Ge 3:19 — In the sweat of thy face shalt thou eat bread, till thou return unto the ground; for out of it wast thou taken: for dust thou *art,* and unto dust shalt thou return.

Ge 3:23 — Therefore the LORD God sent him forth from the garden of Eden, to till the ground from whence he was taken.

- **Practiced by Cain.**

Ge 4:2 — And she again bare his brother Abel. And Abel was a keeper of sheep, but Cain was a tiller of the ground.

- **Practiced by Noah.**

Ge 9:20 — And Noah began *to be* an husbandman, and he planted a vineyard:

- **Practiced by Elisha.**

1Ki 19:19 — So he departed thence, and found Elisha the son of Shaphat, who *was* plowing *with* twelve yoke *of oxen* before him, and he with the twelfth: and Elijah passed by him, and cast his mantle upon him.

- **Practiced by David.**

1Ch 27:26–31

- **Practiced by Uzziah.**

2Ch 26:10 — Also he built towers in the desert, and digged many wells: for he had much cattle, both in the low country, and in the plains: husbandmen *also,* and vine dressers in the mountains, and in Carmel: for he loved husbandry.

- **Practiced by Solomon.**

Ecc 2:4–6

- **God to be acknowledged in.**

Jer 5:24 — Neither say they in their heart, Let us now fear the LORD our God, that giveth rain, both the former and the latter, in his season: he reserveth unto us the appointed weeks of the harvest.

Hos 2:8 — For she did not know that I gave her corn, and wine, and oil, and multiplied her silver and gold, *which* they prepared for Baal.

- **Requires wisdom.**

Isa 28:26 — For his God doth instruct him to discretion, *and* doth teach him.

- **Requires diligence.**

Pr 27:23 — Be thou diligent to know the state of thy flocks, *and* look well to thy herds.

Pr 27:27 — And *thou shalt have* goats' milk enough for thy food, for the food of thy household, and *for* the maintenance for thy maidens.

Ecc 11:6 — In the morning sow thy seed, and in the evening withhold not thine hand: for thou knowest not whether shall prosper, either this or that, or whether they both *shall be* alike good.

- **Requires patience.**

Jas 5:7 — Be patient therefore, brethren, unto the coming of the Lord. Behold, the husbandman waiteth for the precious fruit of the earth, and hath long patience for it, until he receive the early and latter rain.

- **Requires toil.**

2Ti 2:6 — The husbandman that laboureth must be first partaker of the fruits.

- **Persons engaged in.**

- **Called husbandmen.**

2Ch 26:10 — Also he built towers in the desert, and digged many wells: for he had much cattle, both in the low country, and in the plains: husbandmen *also,* and vine dressers in the mountains, and in Carmel: for he loved husbandry.

- **Called laborers.**

Mt 9:37 — Then saith he unto his disciples, The harvest truly *is* plenteous, but the labourers *are* few;

Mt 20:1 — For the kingdom of heaven is like unto a man *that is* an householder, which went out early in the morning to hire labourers into his vineyard.

- **Called tillers of the ground.**

Ge 4:2 — And she again bare his brother Abel. And Abel was a keeper of sheep, but Cain was a tiller of the ground.

- **Planters of vineyards exempted from military service.**

Dt 20:6 — And what man *is he* that hath planted a vineyard, and hath not *yet* eaten of it? let him *also* go and return unto his house, lest he die in the battle, and another man eat of it.

- **Fruits blasted because of sin.**

Joel 1:10–11

Isa 5:10 — Yea, ten acres of vineyard shall yield one bath, and the seed of an homer shall yield an ephah.

Isa 7:23 — And it shall come to pass in that day, *that* every place shall be, where there were a thousand vines at a thousand silverlings, it shall *even* be for briers and thorns.

Jer 12:13 — They have sown wheat, but shall reap thorns: they have put themselves to pain, *but* shall not profit: and they shall be ashamed of your revenues because of the fierce anger of the LORD.

- **Laws concerning.**

Ex 22:5–6; 23:10–12; Le 19:9–10, 23–25; 25:2–12, 15–16; 25:19–28; Dt 5:13–14; 22:9–10; 23:24–25; 24:19–21; Pr 3:9–10; 27:23–27

Ex 20:9 — Six days shalt thou labour, and do all thy work:

Ex 34:21 — Six days thou shalt work, but on the seventh day thou shalt rest: in earing time and in harvest thou shalt rest.

Le 19:19 — Ye shall keep my statutes. Thou shalt not let thy cattle gender with a diverse kind: thou shalt not sow thy field with mingled seed: neither shall a garment mingled of linen and woollen come upon thee.

Dt 5:22 — These words the LORD spake unto all your assembly in the mount out of the midst of the fire, of the cloud, and of the thick darkness, with a great voice: and he added no more. And he wrote them in two tables of stone, and delivered them unto me.

Ecc 5:9 — Moreover the profit of the earth is for all: the king *himself* is served by the field.

Mt 12:1 — At that time Jesus went on the sabbath day through the corn; and his disciples were an hungred, and began to pluck the ears of corn, and to eat.

- **Facts about.**

1Sa 13:19–21; Isa 28:24–28; Mt 13:3–8

Ge 8:22 — While the earth remaineth, seedtime and harvest, and cold and heat, and summer and winter, and day and night shall not cease.

2Co 9:6 — But this *I say,* He which soweth sparingly shall reap also sparingly; and he which soweth bountifully shall reap also bountifully.

Gal 6:7 — Be not deceived; God is not mocked: for whatsoever a man soweth, that shall he also reap.

See: Husbandman

- **Figurative.**
  - **Fallow ground.**

Jer 4:3 — For thus saith the LORD to the men of Judah and Jerusalem, Break up your fallow ground, and sow not among thorns.

  - **Sowing wheat, but reaping thorns.**

Jer 12:13 — They have sown wheat, but shall reap thorns: they have put themselves to pain, *but* shall not profit: and they shall be ashamed of your revenues because of the fierce anger of the LORD.

  - **Parable of the sower.**

Mt 13:3–8; 13:19–23; Lk 8:5–15

  - **Parable of the tares.**

Mt 13:24–30; 13:36–43

- **Operations in.**

See: Churning
See: Gleaning
See: Grafting
See: Irrigation
See: Manure
See: Mowing
See: Pruning
See: Reaping
See: Sower
See: Threshing

- **Implements of.**

See: Ax
See: Cart
See: Fan
See: Fork
See: Goad
See: Harrow
See: Mattock
See: Mill
See: Plow
See: Pruning; Pruning-Hook
See: Shovel
See: Sickle
See: Sieve

- **Products of.**

See: Apple
See: Barley
See: Butter
See: Chaff
See: Corn
See: Cucumber
See: Date
See: Fig
See: Fitch
See: Garlic
See: Gourd
See: Grape
See: Honey
See: Leek
See: Melon
See: Milk
See: Oil
See: Onion
See: Pomegranate
See: Rye
See: Stubble
See: Wheat
See: Wine

- **Animals of.**

See: Ass
See: Barn
See: Camel
See: Fence
See: Garner
See: Goat

→See: Horse

→See: Kine

→See: Mule

→See: Sheep

→See: Swine

→See: Vineyard

AGRIPPA • King.

Ac 25:26 — Of whom I have no certain thing to write unto my lord. Wherefore I have brought him forth before you, and specially before thee, O king Agrippa, that, after examination had, I might have somewhat to write.

AGUE

Le 26:16 — I also will do this unto you; I will even appoint over you terror, consumption, and the burning ague, that shall consume the eyes, and cause sorrow of heart: and ye shall sow your seed in vain, for your enemies shall eat it.

AGUR • Son of Jakeh.

Pr 30:1 — The words of Agur the son of Jakeh, *even* the prophecy: the man spake unto Ithiel, even unto Ithiel and Ucal,

AHAB

• King of Israel.

1Ki 16:29 — And in the thirty and eighth year of Asa king of Judah began Ahab the son of Omri to reign over Israel: and Ahab the son of Omri reigned over Israel in Samaria twenty and two years.

• Marries Jezebel.

1Ki 16:31 — And it came to pass, as if it had been a light thing for him to walk in the sins of Jeroboam the son of Nebat, that he took to wife Jezebel the daughter of Ethbaal king of the Zidonians, and went and served Baal, and worshipped him.

• Idolatry of.

1Ki 16:30–33; 18:18–19; 21:25–26

• Other wickedness of.

2Ch 22:3–4

2Ki 3:2 — And he wrought evil in the sight of the LORD; but not like his father, and like his mother: for he put away the image of Baal that his father had made.

2Ch 21:6 — And he walked in the way of the kings of Israel, like as did the house of Ahab: for he had the daughter of Ahab to wife: and he wrought *that which was* evil in the eyes of the LORD.

Mic 6:16 — For the statutes of Omri are kept, and all the works of the house of Ahab, and ye walk in their counsels; that I should make thee a desolation, and the inhabitants thereof an hissing: therefore ye shall bear the reproach of my people.

• Reproved by Elijah; assembles the prophets of Baal.

1Ki 18:17–46

• Fraudulently confiscates Naboth's vineyard.

1Ki 21:1–29

• Defeats Ben-hadad.

1Ki 20:1–43

• Closing history and death of.

1Ki 22:1–53; 2Ch 18:1–34

• Succeeded by his son, Ahaziah.

1Ki 22:40 — So Ahab slept with his fathers; and Ahaziah his son reigned in his stead.

• Prophecies against.

1Ki 21:19–24; 22:19–28; 2Ki 9:25–26

1Ki 20:42 — And he said unto him, Thus saith the LORD, Because thou hast let go out of *thy* hand a man whom I appointed to utter destruction, therefore thy life shall go for his life, and thy people for his people.

2Ki 9:8 — For the whole house of Ahab shall perish: and I will cut off from Ahab him that pisseth against the wall, and him that is shut up and left in Israel:

• Sons of, murdered.

2Ki 10:1–8

• A false prophet.

Jer 29:21–22

AHARAH

• Called also Ehi and Ahiram and Aher.

• Son of Benjamin.

Ge 46:21 — And the sons of Benjamin were Belah, and Becher, and Ashbel, Gera, and Naaman, Ehi, and Rosh, Muppim, and Huppim, and Ard.

Nu 26:38 — The sons of Benjamin after their families: of Bela, the family of the Belaites: of Ashbel, the family of the Ashbelites: of Ahiram, the family of the Ahiramites:

1Ch 7:12 — Shuppim also, and Huppim, the children of Ir, *and* Hushim, the sons of Aher.

1Ch 8:1 — Now Benjamin begat Bela his firstborn, Ashbel the second, and Aharah the third,

AHARHEL • Son of Harum.

1Ch 4:8 — And Coz begat Anub, and Zobebah, and the families of Aharhel the son of Harum.

AHASAI • A grandson of Immer.

Ne 11:13 — And his brethren, chief of the fathers, two hundred forty and two: and Amashai the son of Azareel, the son of Ahasai, the son of Meshillemoth, the son of Immer,

AHASBAI

• Father of Eliphelet.

2Sa 23:34 — Eliphelet the son of Ahasbai, the son of the Maachathite, Eliam the son of Ahithophel the Gilonite,

1Ch 11:35 — Ahiam the son of Sacar the Hararite, Eliphal the son of Ur,

→See: Ur

AHASUERUS

- **King of Persia, history of.**
  Est 1–10
  - **See: Artaxerxes**
- **Father of Darius.**
  Da 9:1

AHAVA • A river of Babylon.

Ezr 8:15 — And I gathered them together to the river than runneth to Ahava; and there abode we in tents three days: and I viewed the people, and the priests, and found there none of the sons of Levi.

Ezr 8:21 — Then I proclaimed a fast there, at the river of Ahava, that we might afflict ourselves before our God, to seek of him a right way for us, and for our little ones, and for all our substance.

Ezr 8:31 — Then we departed from the river of Ahava on the twelfth *day* of the first month, to go unto Jerusalem: and the hand of our God was upon us, and he delivered us from the hand of the enemy, and of such as lay in wait by the way.

AHAZ

- **King of Judah, son and successor of Jotham.**
  2Ki 15:38–16:1; 2Ch 27:9–28:1
  - **Idolatrous abominations of.**
    2Ki 16:3–4; 2Ch 28:2–4, 22–25
  - **Kingdom of, invaded by the kings of Syria and Samaria.**
    2Ki 16:5–6; 2Ch 28:5–8
  - **Robs the temple to purchase aid from the king of Assyria.**
    2Ki 16:7–9, 17–18
    2Ch 28:21 — For Ahaz took away a portion *out* of the house of the LORD, and *out* of the house of the king, and of the princes, and gave *it* unto the king of Assyria: but he helped him not.
  - **Visits Damascus; changes the pattern for the altar.**
    2Ki 16:10–13
  - **Perverts the forms of worship.**
    2Ki 16:14–16
  - **Sundial of.**
    2Ki 20:11 — And Isaiah the prophet cried unto the LORD: and he brought the shadow ten degrees backward, by which it had gone down in the dial of Ahaz.
    Isa 38:8 — Behold, I will bring again the shadow of the degrees, which is gone down in the sun dial of Ahaz, ten degrees backward. So the sun returned ten degrees, by which degrees it was gone down.
  - **Prophets in the reign of.**
    Isa 1:1 — The vision of Isaiah the son of Amoz, which he saw concerning Judah and Jerusalem in the days of Uzziah, Jotham, Ahaz, *and* Hezekiah, kings of Judah.
    Hos 1:1 — The word of the LORD that came unto Hosea, the son of Beeri, in the days of Uzziah, Jotham, Ahaz, *and* Hezekiah, kings of Judah, and in the days of Jeroboam the son of Joash, king of Israel.
    Mic 1:1 — The word of the LORD that came to Micah the Morasthite in the days of Jotham, Ahaz, *and* Hezekiah, kings of Judah, which he saw concerning Samaria and Jerusalem.
  - **Prophecies concerning.**
    Isa 7:13–25
  - **Succeeded by Hezekiah.**
    2Ki 16:20 — And Ahaz slept with his fathers, and was buried with his fathers in the city of David: and Hezekiah his son reigned in his stead.
- **Son of Micah.**
  1Ch 9:41–42
  1Ch 8:35 — And the sons of Micah *were,* Pithon, and Melech, and Tarea, and Ahaz.

AHAZIAH

- **King of Judah.**
  - **Called Azariah and Jehoahaz.**
    2Ch 21:17 — And they came up into Judah, and brake into it, and carried away all the substance that was found in the king's house, and his sons also, and his wives; so that there was never a son left him, save Jehoahaz, the youngest of his sons.
    2Ch 25:23 — And Joash the king of Israel took Amaziah king of Judah, the son of Joash, the son of Jehoahaz, at Beth-shemesh, and brought him to Jerusalem, and brake down the wall of Jerusalem from the gate of Ephraim to the corner gate, four hundred cubits.
  - **History of.**
    2Ki 8:25–29; 9:16–29
  - **Gifts of, to the temple.**
    2Ki 12:18 — And Jehoash king of Judah took all the hallowed things that Jehoshaphat, and Jehoram, and Ahaziah, his fathers, kings of Judah, had dedicated, and his own hallowed things, and all the gold *that was* found in the treasures of the house of the LORD, and in the king's house, and sent *it* to Hazael king of Syria: and he went away from Jerusalem.
  - **Brethren of, slain.**
    2Ki 10:13–14
  - **Succeeded by Athaliah.**
    2Ch 22:10–12
- **King of Israel.**
  - **History of.**
    1Ki 22:51–53; 2Ki 1:1–18; 2Ch 20:35–37
    1Ki 22:40 — So Ahab slept with his fathers; and Ahaziah his son reigned in his stead.
    1Ki 22:49 — Then said Ahaziah the son of Ahab unto Jehoshaphat, Let my servants go with thy servants in the ships. But Jehoshaphat would not.
  - **Succeeded by Jehoram.**
    2Ki 3:1 — Now Jehoram the son of Ahab began to reign over Israel in Samaria the eighteenth year of Jehoshaphat king of Judah, and reigned twelve years.

AHBAN • Son of Abishur.

1Ch 2:29 — And the name of the wife of Abishur *was* Abihail, and she bare him Ahban, and Molid.

AHER ➜See: Aharah

AHI

• Son of Shamer.

1Ch 7:34 — And the sons of Shamer; Ahi, and Rohgah, Jehubbah, and Aram.

• Son of Abdiel.

1Ch 5:15 — Ahi the son of Abdiel, the son of Guni, chief of the house of their fathers.

AHIA ➜See: Ahimelech

AHIAH

• Grandson of Phinehas.

1Sa 14:3 — And Ahiah, the son of Ahitub, I-chabod's brother, the son of Phinehas, the son of Eli, the LORD'S priest in Shiloh, wearing an ephod. And the people knew not that Jonathan was gone.

1Sa 14:18 — And Saul said unto Ahiah, Bring hither the ark of God. For the ark of God was at that time with the children of Israel.

• One of Solomon's scribes.

1Ki 4:3 — Elihoreph and Ahiah, the sons of Shisha, scribes; Jehoshaphat the son of Ahilud, the recorder.

• A Benjamite.

1Ch 8:7 — And Naaman, and Ahiah, and Gera, he removed them, and begat Uzza, and Ahihud.

AHIAM

• One of David's heroes.

2Sa 23:33 — Shammah the Hararite, Ahiam the son of Sharar the Hararite,

• Called also Sacar.

1Ch 11:35 — Ahiam the son of Sacar the Hararite, Eliphal the son of Ur,

AHIAN • Son of Shemidah.

1Ch 7:19 — And the sons of Shemidah were, Ahian, and Shechem, and Likhi, and Aniam.

AHIEZER

• Captain of the tribe of Dan.

Nu 2:25–26

Nu 1:12 — Of Dan; Ahiezer the son of Ammishaddai.

• Contributes to the tabernacle.

Nu 7:66–71

• One of David's valiant men.

1Ch 12:3 — The chief *was* Ahiezer, then Joash, the sons of Shemaah the Gibeathite; and Jeziel, and Pelet, the sons of Azmaveth; and Berachah, and Jehu the Antothite,

AHIHUD

• A prince of Asher. Assists in allotting the land of Canaan among the tribes.

Nu 34:27 — And the prince of the tribe of the children of Asher, Ahihud the son of Shelomi.

• A son of Bela.

1Ch 8:7 — And Naaman, and Ahiah, and Gera, he removed them, and begat Uzza, and Ahihud.

AHIJAH

• Called also Ahiah.

• Son of Bela.

1Ch 8:7 — And Naaman, and Ahiah, and Gera, he removed them, and begat Uzza, and Ahihud.

• Son of Jerahmeel.

1Ch 2:25 — And the sons of Jerahmeel the firstborn of Hezron were, Ram the firstborn, and Bunah, and Oren, and Ozem, *and* Ahijah.

• A priest in Shiloh. Probably identical with Ahimelech, mentioned in 1Sa 22:11.

1Sa 22:11 — Then the king sent to call Ahimelech the priest, the son of Ahitub, and all his father's house, the priests that *were* in Nob: and they came all of them to the king.

• Was priest in Saul's reign.

1Sa 14:3 — And Ahiah, the son of Ahitub, I-chabod's brother, the son of Phinehas, the son of Eli, the LORD'S priest in Shiloh, wearing an ephod. And the people knew not that Jonathan was gone.

1Sa 14:18 — And Saul said unto Ahiah, Bring hither the ark of God. For the ark of God was at that time with the children of Israel.

• Slain.

1Sa 22:11–19

• One of David's heroes.

1Ch 11:36 — Hepher the Mecherathite, Ahijah the Pelonite,

• Called also Eliam.

2Sa 23:34 — Eliphelet the son of Ahasbai, the son of the Maachathite, Eliam the son of Ahithophel the Gilonite,

• A Levite who was treasurer in the tabernacle.

1Ch 26:20 — And of the Levites, Ahijah *was* over the treasures of the house of God, and over the treasures of the dedicated things.

• Son of Shisha.

1Ki 4:3 — Elihoreph and Ahiah, the sons of Shisha, scribes; Jehoshaphat the son of Ahilud, the recorder.

• A prophet in Shiloh.

1Ki 11:29–39

• Father of Baasha.

1Ki 15:27 — And Baasha the son of Ahijah, of the house of Issachar, conspired against him; and Baasha smote him at Gibbethon, which *belonged* to the Philistines; for Nadab and all Israel laid siege to Gibbethon.

1Ki 15:33 — In the third year of Asa king of Judah began Baasha the son of Ahijah to reign over all Israel in Tirzah, twenty and four years.

2Ki 9:9 — And I will make the house of Ahab like the house of Jeroboam the son of Nebat, and like the house of Baasha the son of Ahijah:

• An Israelite, who subscribed to the covenant of Nehemiah

Ne 10:26 — And Ahijah, Hanan, Anan,

AHIKAM • Son of Shaphan.

2Ki 22:12–14; Jer 40:5–41:18

2Ki 25:22 — And *as for* the people that remained in the land of Judah, whom Nebuchadnezzar king of Babylon had left, even over them he made Gedaliah the son of Ahikam, the son of Shaphan, ruler.

2Ch 34:20 — And the king commanded Hilkiah, and Ahikam the son of Shaphan, and Abdon the son of Micah, and Shaphan the scribe, and Asaiah a servant of the king's, saying,

Jer 26:24 — Nevertheless the hand of Ahikam the son of Shaphan was with Jeremiah, that they should not give him into the hand of the people to put him to death.

Jer 39:14 — Even they sent, and took Jeremiah out of the court of the prison, and committed him unto Gedaliah the son of Ahikam the son of Shaphan, that he should carry him home: so he dwelt among the people.

Jer 43:6 — *Even* men, and women, and children, and the king's daughters, and every person that Nebuzar-adan the captain of the guard had left with Gedaliah the son of Ahikam the son of Shaphan, and Jeremiah the prophet, and Baruch the son of Neriah.

AHILUD

• Father of Baana.

1Ki 4:12 — Baana the son of Ahilud; *to him pertained* Taanach and Megiddo, and all Beth-shean, which is by Zartanah beneath Jezreel, from Beth-shean to Abel-meholah, *even* unto *the place that is* beyond Jokneam:

• Father of Jehoshaphat.

2Sa 8:16 — And Joab the son of Zeruiah *was* over the host; and Jehoshaphat the son of Ahilud *was* recorder;

2Sa 20:24 — And Adoram *was* over the tribute: and Jehoshaphat the son of Ahilud *was* recorder:

1Ki 4:3 — Elihoreph and Ahiah, the sons of Shisha, scribes; Jehoshaphat the son of Ahilud, the recorder.

1Ch 18:15 — And Joab the son Zeruiah was over the host; and Jehoshaphat the son of Ahilud, recorder.

AHIMAAZ

• Father-in-law of King Saul.

1Sa 14:50 — And the name of Saul's wife *was* Ahinoam, the daughter of Ahimaaz: and the name of the captain of his host *was* Abner, the son of Ner, Saul's uncle.

• Son of Zadok, the high priest.

• Loyal to David.

2Sa 17:17–20; 18:1–33; 1Ch 6:8–9

2Sa 15:36 — Behold, *they have* there with them their two sons, Ahimaaz Zadok's *son,* and Jonathan Abiathar's *son;* and by them ye shall send unto me every thing that ye can hear.

1Ch 6:53 — Zadok his son, Ahimaaz his son.

• Solomon's son-in-law.

1Ki 4:15 — Ahimaaz *was* in Naphtali; he also took Basmath the daughter of Solomon to wife:

AHIMAN

• A giant of Hebron.

Nu 13:22 — And they ascended by the south, and came unto Hebron; where Ahiman, Sheshai, and Talmai, the children of Anak, *were.* (Now Hebron was built seven years before Zoan in Egypt.)

Jos 15:14 — And Caleb drove thence the three sons of Anak, Sheshai, and Ahiman, and Talmai, the children of Anak.

• A Levite.

1Ch 9:17 — And the porters *were,* Shallum, and Akkub, and Talmon, and Ahiman, and their brethren: Shallum *was* the chief;

AHIMELECH

• A high priest, during the reign of David. Gives shewbread and the sword of Goliath to David.

1Sa 21:1–15

Mk 2:26 — How he went into the house of God in the days of Abiathar the high priest, and did eat the shewbread, which is not lawful to eat but for the priests, and gave also to them which were with him?

• Slain by command of Saul.

1Sa 22:9–22

• Called also Ahia.

• A Hittite, and friend of David.

1Sa 26:6 — Then answered David and said to Ahi-melech the Hittite, and to Abishai the son of Zeruiah, brother to Joab, saying, Who will go down with me to Saul to the camp? And Abishai said, I will go down with thee.

AHIMOTH • A Levite.

1Ch 6:25 — And the sons of Elkanah; Amasai, and Ahimoth.

AHINADAB • Son of Iddo.

1Ki 4:14 — Ahinadab the son of Iddo *had* Mahanaim:

AHINOAM

• Wife of King Saul.

1Sa 14:50 — And the name of Saul's wife *was* Ahinoam, the daughter of Ahimaaz: and the name of the captain of his host *was* Abner, the son of Ner, Saul's uncle.

• Wife of King David.

1Sa 18:1–30

1Sa 25:43 — David also took Ahinoam of Jezreel; and they were also both of them his wives.

1Sa 27:3 — And David dwelt with Achish at Gath, he and his men, every man with his household, *even* David with his two wives, Ahinoam the Jezreelitess, and Abigail the Carmelitess, Nabal's wife.

1Sa 30:5 — And David's two wives were taken captives, Ahinoam the Jezreelitess, and Abigail the wife of Nabal the Carmelite.

2Sa 3:2 — And unto David were sons born in Hebron: and his firstborn was Amnon, of Ahinoam the Jezreelitess;

AHIO

• A Levite, who drove the cart bearing the ark.

2Sa 6:3–4

1Ch 13:7 — And they carried the ark of God in a new cart out of the house of Abinadab: and Uzza and Ahio drave the cart.

• A Benjamite.

1Ch 8:14 — And Ahio, Shashak, and Jeremoth,

• Son of Jehiel.

1Ch 8:31 — And Gedor, and Ahio, and Zacher.

1Ch 9:37 — And Gedor, and Ahio, and Zechariah, and Mikloth.

AHIRA • Captain of the tribe of Naphtali.

Nu 7:78–83

Nu 1:15 — Of Naphtali; Ahira the son of Enan.

Nu 2:29 — Then the tribe of Naphtali: and the captain of the children of Naphtali *shall be* Ahira the son of Enan.

Nu 10:27 — And over the host of the tribe of the children of Naphtali *was* Ahira the son of Enan.

AHIRAM •See: Aharah

AHISAMACH • Father of Aholiab.

Ex 31:6 — And I, behold, I have given with him Aholiab, the son of Ahisamach, of the tribe of Dan: and in the hearts of all that are wise hearted I have put wisdom, that they may make all that I have commanded thee;

Ex 35:34 — And he hath put in his heart that he may teach, *both* he, and Aholiab, the son of Ahisamach, of the tribe of Dan.

Ex 38:23 — And with him *was* Aholiab, son of Ahisamach, of the tribe of Dan, an engraver, and a cunning workman, and an embroiderer in blue, and in purple, and in scarlet, and fine linen.

AHISHAHAR • Son of Bilhan.

1Ch 7:10 — The sons also of Jediael; Bilhan: and the sons of Bilhan; Jeush, and Benjamin, and Ehud, and Chenaanah, and Zethan, and Tharshish, and Ahishahar.

AHISHAR • One of Solomon's household officers.

1Ki 4:6 — And Ahishar *was* over the household: and Adoniram the son of Abda *was* over the tribute.

AHITHOPHEL

• One of David's counsellors.

2Sa 15:12 — And Absalom sent for Ahithophel the Gilonite, David's counsellor, from his city, *even* from Giloh, while he offered sacrifices. And the conspiracy was strong; for the people increased continually with Absalom.

1Ch 27:33 — And Ahithophel *was* the king's counsellor: and Hushai the Archite *was* the king's companion:

• Joins Absalom.

2Sa 16:20–17:23

2Sa 15:31 — And *one* told David, saying, Ahithophel *is* among the conspirators with Absalom. And David said, O LORD, I pray thee, turn the counsel of Ahithophel into foolishness.

2Sa 15:34 — But if thou return to the city, and say unto Absalom, I will be thy servant, O king; *as* I *have been* thy father's servant hitherto, so *will* I now also *be* thy servant: then mayest thou for me defeat the counsel of Ahithophel.

2Sa 16:15 — And Absalom, and all the people the men of Israel, came to Jerusalem, and Ahithophel with him.

• Probably referred to by David in.

Ps 55:12–14

• Suicide of.

2Sa 17:1–14

2Sa 17:23 — And when Ahithophel saw that his counsel was not followed, he saddled *his* ass, and arose, and gat him home to his house, to his city, and put his household in order, and hanged himself, and died, and was buried in the sepulchre of his father.

AHITUB

• High priest, father of Ahiah.

1Sa 22:11–12

1Sa 14:3 — And Ahiah, the son of Ahitub, I-chabod's brother, the son of Phinehas, the son of Eli, the LORD's priest in Shiloh, wearing an ephod. And the people knew not that Jonathan was gone.

1Sa 22:9 — Then answered Doeg the Edomite, which was set over the servants of Saul, and said, I saw the son of Jesse coming to Nob, to Ahimelech the son of Ahitub.

1Sa 22:20 — And one of the sons of Ahimelech the son of Ahitub, named Abiathar, escaped, and fled after David.

• Father of Zadok.

2Sa 8:17 — And Zadok the son of Ahitub, and Ahimelech the son of Abiathar, *were* the priests; and Seraiah *was* the scribe;

1Ch 18:16 — And Zadok the son of Ahitub, and Abimelech the son of Abiathar, *were* the priests; and Shavsha was scribe;

• Ruler of the house of God.

1Ch 9:11 — And Azariah the son of Hilkiah, the son of Meshullam, the son of Zadok, the son of Meraioth, the son of Ahitub, the ruler of the house of God;

Ne 11:11 — Seraiah the son of Hilkiah, the son of Meshullam, the son of Zadok, the son of Meraioth, the son of Ahitub, *was* the ruler of the house of God.

• Probably identical with "Ruler of the House of God" or confused with Azariah.

1Ch 6:11–12

1Ch 6:8 — And Ahitub begat Zadok, and Zadok begat Ahimaaz,

2Ch 31:10 — And Azariah the chief priest of the house of Zadok answered him, and said, Since *the people* began to bring the offerings into the house of the LORD, we have had enough to eat, and have left plenty: for the LORD hath blessed his people; and that which is left *is* this great store.

AHLAB • A city of Asher, the original inhabitants of which were not expelled.

Jgs 1:31 — Neither did Asher drive out the inhabitants of Accho, nor the inhabitants of Zidon, nor of Ahlab, nor of Achzib, nor of Helbah, nor of Aphik, nor of Rehob:

AHLAI

• Daughter of Sheshan.

1Ch 2:34–35

1Ch 2:31 — And the sons of Appaim; Ishi. And the sons of Ishi; Sheshan. And the children of Sheshan; Ahlai.

• Father of Zabad.

1Ch 11:41 — Uriah the Hittite, Zabad the son of Ahlai,

AHOAH

• Son of Bela.

1Ch 8:4 — And Abishua, and Naaman, and Ahoah,

• Called also Ahiah.

1Ch 8:7 — And Naaman, and Ahiah, and Gera, he removed them, and begat Uzza, and Ahihud.

• Called also Ira.

1Ch 7:7 — And the sons of Bela; Ezbon, and Uzzi, and Uzziel, and Jerimoth, and Iri, five; heads of the house of *their* fathers, mighty men of valour; and were reckoned by their genealogies twenty and two thousand and thirty and four.

AHOLAH • Name of an imaginary woman; typical of idolatry.

Eze 23:4–5

Eze 23:36 — The LORD said moreover unto me; Son of man, wilt thou judge Aholah and Aholibah? yea, declare unto them their abominations;

Eze 23:44 — Yet they went in unto her, as they go in unto a woman that playeth the harlot: so went they in unto Aholah and unto Aholibah, the lewd women.

AHOLIAB • An artificer of the tabernacle.

Ex 36:1–2

Ex 31:6 — And I, behold, I have given with him Aholiab, the son of Ahisamach, of the tribe of Dan: and in the hearts of all that are wise hearted I have put wisdom, that they may make all that I have commanded thee;

Ex 35:34 — And he hath put in his heart that he may teach, *both* he, and Aholiab, the son of Ahisamach, of the tribe of Dan.

Ex 38:23 — And with him *was* Aholiab, son of Ahisamach, of the tribe of Dan, an engraver, and a cunning workman, and an embroiderer in blue, and in purple, and in scarlet, and fine linen.

AHOLIBAH • An imaginary character; typical of idolatry.

Eze 23:4–5

Eze 23:36 — The LORD said moreover unto me; Son of man, wilt thou judge Aholah and Aholibah? yea, declare unto them their abominations;

Eze 23:44 — Yet they went in unto her, as they go in unto a woman that playeth the harlot: so went they in unto Aholah and unto Aholibah, the lewd women.

AHOLIBAMAH

• Wife of Esau.

Ge 36:2 — Esau took his wives of the daughters of Canaan; Adah the daughter of Elon the Hittite, and Aholibamah the daughter of Anah the daughter of Zibeon the Hivite;

Ge 36:14 — And these were the sons of Aholibamah, the daughter of Anah the daughter of Zibeon, Esau's wife: and she bare to Esau Jeush, and Jaalam, and Korah.

Ge 36:25 — And the children of Anah *were* these; Dishon, and Aholibamah the daughter of Anah.

• She is probably identical with Judith.

Ge 26:34 — And Esau was forty years old when he took to wife Judith the daughter of Beeri the Hittite, and Bashemath the daughter of Elon the Hittite:

• An Edomitish prince.

Ge 36:41 — Duke Aholibamah, duke Elah, duke Pinon,

AHUMAI • Son of Jahath.

1Ch 4:2 — And Reaiah the son of Shobal begat Jahath; and Jahath begat Ahumai and Lahad. These *are* the families of the Zorathites.

AHUZAM • Son of Ashur.

1Ch 4:6 — And Naarah bare him Ahuzam, and Hepher, and Temeni, and Haahashtari. These *were* the sons of Naarah.

AHUZZATH • A friend of Abimelech.

Ge 26:26 — Then Abimelech went to him from Gerar, and Ahuzzath one of his friends, and Phichol the chief captain of his army.

AI

• A royal city of the Canaanites.

• Conquest and destruction of.

Jos 7:1–8:35

• Rebuilt.

Ezr 2:28 — The men of Bethel and Ai, two hundred twenty and three.

• Called also Aija.

Ne 11:31 — The children also of Benjamin from Geba *dwelt* at Michmash, and Aija, and Bethel, and *in* their villages,

• Called also Aiath.

Isa 10:28 — He is come to Aiath, he is passed to Migron; at Michmash he hath laid up his carriages:

• **Population of.**

Jos 8:25 — And *so* it was, *that* all that fell that day, both of men and women, *were* twelve thousand, *even* all the men of Ai.

• **A city of the Ammonites.**

Jer 49:3 — Howl, O Heshbon, for Ai is spoiled: cry, ye daughters of Rabbah, gird you with sackcloth; lament, and run to and fro by the hedges; for their king shall go into captivity, *and* his priests and his princes together.

AIAH ➜See: Ajah

AIATH ➜See: Ai

AIDS

Le 18:22–24; 20:13–16; Ro 1:24–32

AIJA ➜See: Ai

AIJALON ➜See: Ajalon

AIJELETH SHAHAR

• **A musical term which probably indicated the sprightly movement of the music set to.**

Ps 22:1–31

➜**See: Title**

AIN • A city of Simeon.

Jos 15:32 — And Lebaoth, and Shilhim, and Ain, and Rimmon: all the cities *are* twenty and nine, with their villages:

Jos 19:7 — Ain, Remmon, and Ether, and Ashan; four cities and their villages:

Jos 21:16 — And Ain with her suburbs, and Juttah with her suburbs, *and* Beth-shemesh with her suburbs; nine cities out of those two tribes.

1Ch 4:32 — And their villages *were*, Etam, and Ain, Rimmon, and Tochen, and Ashan, five cities:

• **Called also Ashan.**

1Ch 6:59 — And Ashan with her suburbs, and Beth-shemesh with her suburbs:

• **Possibly identical with En-Rimmon.**

Ne 11:29 — And at En-rimmon, and at Zareah, and at Jarmuth,

• **A landmark on the northern boundary of Palestine.**

Nu 34:11 — And the coast shall go down from Shepham to Riblah, on the east side of Ain; and the border shall descend, and shall reach unto the side of the sea of Chinnereth eastward:

AJAH

• **Called also Aiah.**

• **A Horite.**

Ge 36:24 — And these *are* the children of Zibeon; both Ajah, and Anah: this *was that* Anah that found the mules in the wilderness, as he fed the asses of Zibeon his father.

1Ch 1:40 — The sons of Shobal; Alian, and Manahath, and Ebal, Shephi, and Onam. And the sons of Zibeon; Aiah, and Anah.

• **Father of Rizpah.**

2Sa 21:8–11

2Sa 3:7 — And Saul had a concubine, whose name *was* Rizpah, the daughter of Aiah: and *Ish-bosheth* said to Abner, Wherefore hast thou gone in unto my father's concubine?

AJALON

• **A city of Dan.**

Jos 19:42 — And Shaalabbin, and Ajalon, and Jethlah,

• **Assigned to the Levites.**

Jos 21:24 — Aijalon with her suburbs, Gath-rimmon with her suburbs; four cities.

1Sa 14:31 — And they smote the Philistines that day from Michmash to Aijalon: and the people were very faint.

1Ch 6:69 — And Aijalon with her suburbs, and Gath-rimmon with her suburbs:

• **Amorites of, not exterminated.**

Jgs 1:35 — But the Amorites would dwell in mount Heres in Aijalon, and in Shaalbim: yet the hand of the house of Joseph prevailed, so that they became tributaries.

• **A city of Zebulun.**

Jgs 12:12 — And Elon the Zebulonite died, and was buried in Aijalon in the country of Zebulun.

• **A city of Judah.**

2Ch 11:10 — And Zorah, and Aijalon, and Hebron, which *are* in Judah and in Benjamin fenced cities.

2Ch 28:18 — The Philistines also had invaded the cities of the low country, and of the south of Judah, and had taken Beth-shemesh, and Ajalon, and Gederoth, and Shocho with the villages thereof, and Timnah with the villages thereof, Gimzo also and the villages thereof: and they dwelt there.

• **A valley.**

Jos 10:12 — Then spake Joshua to the LORD in the day when the LORD delivered up the Amorites before the children of Israel, and he said in the sight of Israel, Sun, stand thou still upon Gibeon; and thou, Moon, in the valley of Ajalon.

AKAN

• **A Horite.**

Ge 36:27 — The children of Ezer *are* these; Bilhan, and Zaavan, and Akan.

• **Called also Jaakan.**

Dt 10:6 — And the children of Israel took their journey from Beeroth of the children of Jaakan to Mosera: there Aaron died, and there he was buried; and Eleazar his son ministered in the priest's office in his stead.

• **Called also Jakan.**

1Ch 1:42 — The sons of Ezer; Bilhan, and Zavan, *and* Jakan. The sons of Dishan; Uz, and Aran.

AKKUB

• One of the Nethinim.

Ezr 2:45 — The children of Lebanah, the children of Hagabah, the children of Akkub,

• A returned exile.

1Ch 9:17 — And the porters *were,* Shallum, and Akkub, and Talmon, and Ahiman, and their brethren: Shallum *was* the chief;

Ezr 2:42 — The children of the porters: the children of Shallum, the children of Ater, the children of Talmon, the children of Akkub, the children of Hatita, the children of Shobai, *in* all an hundred thirty and nine.

Ne 7:45 — The porters: the children of Shallum, the children of Ater, the children of Talmon, the children of Akkub, the children of Hatita, the children of Shobai, an hundred thirty and eight.

Ne 8:7 — Also Jeshua, and Bani, and Sherebiah, Jamin, Akkub, Shabbethai, Hodijah, Maaseiah, Kelita, Azariah, Jozabad, Hanan, Pelaiah, and the Levites, caused the people to understand the law: and the people *stood* in their place.

Ne 12:25 — Mattaniah, and Bakbukiah, Obadiah, Meshullam, Talmon, Akkub, *were* porters keeping the ward at the thresholds of the gates.

• A son of Elioenai.

1Ch 3:24 — And the sons of Elioenai *were,* Hodaiah, and Eliashib, and Pelaiah, and Akkub, and Johanan, and Dalaiah, and Anani, seven.

AKRABBIM • A chain of hills in the south of Palestine.

Nu 34:4 — And your border shall turn from the south to the ascent of Akrabbim, and pass on to Zin: and the going forth thereof shall be from the south to Kadesh-barnea, and shall go on to Hazar-addar, and pass on to Azmon:

Jos 15:3 — And it went out to the south side to Maaleh-acrabbim, and passed along to Zin, and ascended up on the south side unto Kadesh-barnea, and passed along to Hezron, and went up to Adar, and fetched a compass to Karkaa:

Jgs 1:36 — And the coast of the Amorites *was* from the going up to Akrabbim, from the rock, and upward.

AL-TASCHITH • Title of.

Ps 57:1–59:17; 75:1–10

✣See: Music

ALABASTER • A white stone; vessels made of.

Mt 26:7 — There came unto him a woman having an alabaster box of very precious ointment, and poured it on his head, as he sat *at meat.*

Mk 14:3 — And being in Bethany in the house of Simon the leper, as he sat at meat, there came a woman having an alabaster box of ointment of spikenard very precious; and she brake the box, and poured *it* on his head.

Lk 7:37 — And, behold, a woman in the city, which was a sinner, when she knew that *Jesus* sat at meat in the Pharisee's house, brought an alabaster box of ointment,

ALAMETH • Son of Becher.

1Ch 7:8 — And the sons of Becher; Zemira, and Joash, and Eliezer, and Elioenai, and Omri, and Jerimoth, and Abiah, and Anathoth, and Alameth. All these *are* the sons of Becher.

ALAMMELECH • A town of Asher.

Jos 19:26 — And Alammelech, and Amad, and Misheal; and reacheth to Carmel westward, and to Shihor-libnath;

ALAMOTH

• A musical term.

1Ch 15:20 — And Zechariah, and Aziel, and Shemiramoth, and Jehiel, and Unni, and Eliab, and Maaseiah, and Benaiah, with psalteries on Alamoth;

• Inscription to.

Ps 46:1–11

✣See: Music

ALCOHOL

Isa 28:1–29

Le 10:9 — Do not drink wine nor strong drink, thou, nor thy sons with thee, when ye go into the tabernacle of the congregation, lest ye die: *it shall be* a statute for ever throughout your generations:

Nu 6:3 — He shall separate *himself* from wine and strong drink, and shall drink no vinegar of wine, or vinegar of strong drink, neither shall he drink any liquor of grapes, nor eat moist grapes, or dried.

Nu 28:7 — And the drink offering thereof *shall be* the fourth *part* of an hin for the one lamb: in the holy *place* shalt thou cause the strong wine to be poured unto the LORD *for* a drink offering.

Dt 14:26 — And thou shalt bestow that money for whatsoever thy soul lusteth after, for oxen, or for sheep, or for wine, or for strong drink, or for whatsoever thy soul desireth: and thou shalt eat there before the LORD thy God, and thou shalt rejoice, thou, and thine household,

Dt 29:6 — Ye have not eaten bread, neither have ye drunk wine or strong drink: that ye might know that I *am* the LORD your God.

Jgs 13:4 — Now therefore beware, I pray thee, and drink not wine nor strong drink, and eat not any unclean *thing:*

Jgs 13:7 — But he said unto me, Behold, thou shalt conceive, and bear a son; and now drink no wine nor strong drink, neither eat any unclean *thing:* for the child shall be a Nazarite to God from the womb to the day of his death.

Jgs 13:14 — She may not eat of any *thing* that cometh of the vine, neither let her drink wine or strong drink, nor eat any unclean *thing:* all that I commanded her let her observe.

Pr 20:1 — Wine *is* a mocker, strong drink *is* raging: and whosoever is deceived thereby is not wise.

Pr 31:4 — *It is* not for kings, O Lemuel, *it is* not for kings to drink wine; nor for princes strong drink:
Pr 31:6 — Give strong drink unto him that is ready to perish, and wine unto those that be of heavy hearts.
Isa 5:11 — Woe unto them that rise up early in the morning, *that* they may follow strong drink; that continue until night, *till* wine inflame them!
Isa 5:22 — Woe unto *them that are* mighty to drink wine, and men of strength to mingle strong drink:
Isa 24:9 — They shall not drink wine with a song; strong drink shall be bitter to them that drink it.

ALEMETH

• A Levitical city.

1Ch 6:60 — And out of the tribe of Benjamin; Geba with her suburbs, and Alemeth with her suburbs, and Anathoth with her suburbs. All their cities throughout their families *were* thirteen cities.

See: Almon

• Son of Jehoadah.

1Ch 8:36 — And Ahaz begat Jehoadah; and Jehoadah begat Alemeth, and Azmaveth, and Zimri; and Zimri begat Moza,

• Son of Jarah.

1Ch 9:42 — And Ahaz begat Jarah; and Jarah begat Alemeth, and Azmaveth, and Zimri; and Zimri begat Moza;

ALEXANDER

• Son of Simon who bore the cross of Jesus.

Mk 15:21 — And they compel one Simon a Cyrenian, who passed by, coming out of the country, the father of Alexander and Rufus, to bear his cross.

• A relative of the high priest.

• Present at the defense of Peter and John.

Ac 4:6 — And Annas the high priest, and Caiaphas, and John, and Alexander, and as many as were of the kindred of the high priest, were gathered together at Jerusalem.

• A Jew of Ephesus.

Ac 19:33 — And they drew Alexander out of the multitude, the Jews putting him forward. And Alexander beckoned with the hand, and would have made his defence unto the people.

• A copper-smith.

1Ti 1:20 — Of whom is Hymenaeus and Alexander; whom I have delivered unto Satan, that they may learn not to blaspheme.
2Ti 4:14 — Alexander the coppersmith did me much evil: the Lord reward him according to his works:

ALEXANDRIA

• A city of Egypt.

Ac 6:9 — Then there arose certain of *the synagogue,* which is called the synagogue of the Libertines, and Cyrenians, and Alexandrians, and of them of Cilicia and of Asia, disputing with Stephen.

• Ships of.

Ac 27:6 — And there the centurion found a ship of Alexandria sailing into Italy; and he put us therein.
Ac 28:11 — And after three months we departed in a ship of Alexandria, which had wintered in the isle, whose sign was Castor and Pollux.

• Apollos born in.

Ac 18:24 — And a certain Jew named Apollos, born at Alexandria, an eloquent man, *and* mighty in the scriptures, came to Ephesus.

ALGUM

• Called also Almug.

• Trees of Ophir and Lebanon.

1Ki 10:11–12; 2Ch 9:10–11
2Ch 2:8 — Send me also cedar trees, fir trees, and algum trees, out of Lebanon: for I know that thy servants can skill to cut timber in Lebanon; and, behold, my servants *shall be* with thy servants,

ALIAH See: Alvah

ALIAN See: Alvan

ALIENS

• Strangers, heathen.

• To be treated with justice.

Le 19:33–34
Ex 22:21 — Thou shalt neither vex a stranger, nor oppress him: for ye were strangers in the land of Egypt.
Ex 23:9 — Also thou shalt not oppress a stranger: for ye know the heart of a stranger, seeing ye were strangers in the land of Egypt.
Dt 1:16 — And I charged your judges at that time, saying, Hear *the causes* between your brethren, and judge righteously between *every* man and his brother, and the stranger *that is* with him.
Dt 10:19 — Love ye therefore the stranger: for ye were strangers in the land of Egypt.
Dt 24:14 — Thou shalt not oppress an hired servant *that is* poor and needy, *whether he be* of thy brethren, or of thy strangers that *are* in thy land within thy gates:
Dt 24:17 — Thou shalt not pervert the judgment of the stranger, *nor* of the fatherless; nor take a widow's raiment to pledge:
Dt 27:19 — Cursed *be* he that perverteth the judgment of the stranger, fatherless, and widow. And all the people shall say, Amen.
Jer 7:6 — *If* ye oppress not the stranger, the fatherless, and the widow, and shed not innocent blood in this place, neither walk after other gods to your hurt:
Jer 22:3 — Thus saith the LORD; Execute ye judgment and righteousness, and deliver the spoiled out of the hand of the oppressor: and do no wrong, do no violence to the stranger, the fatherless, nor the widow, neither shed innocent blood in this place.
Eze 22:29 — The people of the land have used oppression, and exercised robbery, and have vexed the poor and needy: yea, they have oppressed the stranger wrongfully.
Mal 3:5 — And I will come near to you to judgment; and I will be a swift witness against the sorcerers,

and against the adulterers, and against false swearers, and against those that oppress the hireling in *his* wages, the widow, and the fatherless, and that turn aside the stranger *from his right,* and fear not me, saith the LORD of hosts.

- **Religious privileges of.**
  Ex 12:48–49; Nu 15:14–15
  Nu 9:14 — And if a stranger shall sojourn among you, and will keep the passover unto the LORD; according to the ordinance of the passover, and according to the manner thereof, so shall he do: ye shall have one ordinance, both for the stranger, and for him that was born in the land.
- **Kindness to Edomites, enjoined.**
  Dt 23:7 — Thou shalt not abhor an Edomite; for he *is* thy brother: thou shalt not abhor an Egyptian; because thou wast a stranger in his land.
- **Jews authorized to purchase, as slaves.**
  Le 25:44–45
- **Jews to take usury from.**
  Dt 15:3 — Of a foreigner thou mayest exact *it again:* but *that* which is thine with thy brother thine hand shall release;
  Dt 23:20 — Unto a stranger thou mayest lend upon usury; but unto thy brother thou shalt not lend upon usury: that the LORD thy God may bless thee in all that thou settest thine hand to in the land whither thou goest to possess it.
- **Jews not permitted to make kings of.**
  Dt 17:15 — Thou shalt in any wise set *him* king over thee, whom the LORD thy God shall choose: *one* from among thy brethren shalt thou set king over thee: thou mayest not set a stranger over thee, which *is* not thy brother.
- **Forbidden to eat the passover.**
  Ex 12:45 — A foreigner and an hired servant shall not eat thereof.
- **Partially exempt from Jewish law.**
  Dt 14:21 — Ye shall not eat *of* any thing that dieth of itself: thou shalt give it unto the stranger that *is* in thy gates, that he may eat it; or thou mayest sell it unto an alien: for thou *art* an holy people unto the LORD thy God. Thou shalt not seethe a kid in his mother's milk.
- **Numerous in times of David and Solomon.**
  2Sa 22:45–46
  2Ch 2:17 — And Solomon numbered all the strangers that *were* in the land of Israel, after the numbering wherewith David his father had numbered them; and they were found an hundred and fifty thousand and three thousand and six hundred.
  2Ch 15:9 — And he gathered all Judah and Benjamin, and the strangers with them out of Ephraim and Manasseh, and out of Simeon: for they fell to him out of Israel in abundance, when they saw that the LORD his God *was* with him.
- **Oppressed.**
  Eze 22:29 — The people of the land have used oppression, and exercised robbery, and have vexed the poor and needy: yea, they have oppressed the stranger wrongfully.
- **Rights of.**
  Eze 47:22–23
  Nu 35:15 — These six cities shall be a refuge, *both* for the children of Israel, and for the stranger, and for the sojourner among them: that every one that killeth any person unawares may flee thither.
  Jos 20:9 — These were the cities appointed for all the children of Israel, and for the stranger that sojourneth among them, that whosoever killeth *any* person at unawares might flee thither, and not die by the hand of the avenger of blood, until he stood before the congregation.
- **David's kindness to.**
  2Sa 15:19–20
- **Hospitality to, required by Jesus.**
  Mt 25:35 — For I was an hungred, and ye gave me meat: I was thirsty, and ye gave me drink: I was a stranger, and ye took me in:
  Mt 25:38 — When saw we thee a stranger, and took *thee* in? or naked, and clothed *thee?*
  Mt 25:43 — I was a stranger, and ye took me not in: naked, and ye clothed me not: sick, and in prison, and ye visited me not.

See: Gleaning
See: Heathen
See: Hospitality
See: Inhospitableness
See: Proselyte
See: Strangers

ALLEGORY

- **Of the trees seeking a king.**
  Jgs 9:8–15
- **Messiah's kingdom represented under, of the wolf and the lamb dwelling together.**
  Isa 11:6–8
- **Wilderness to blossom as the rose.**
  Isa 35:1–10
- **The two covenants.**
  Gal 4:24 — Which things are an allegory: for these are the two covenants; the one from the mount Sinai, which gendereth to bondage, which is Agar.

See: Parables
See: Symbols and Similitudes

ALLIANCES

- **Political.**
  - **With idolaters forbidden.**
    Ex 23:32–33; 34:12–15; Isa 31:1–9
    Dt 7:2 — And when the LORD thy God shall deliver them before thee; thou shalt smite them, *and* utterly destroy them; thou shalt make no covenant with them, nor shew mercy unto them:
    Jgs 2:2 — And ye shall make no league with the inhabitants of this land; ye shall throw down

their altars: but ye have not obeyed my voice: why have ye done this?

2Ch 19:2 — And Jehu the son of Hanani the seer went out to meet him, and said to king Jehoshaphat, Shouldest thou help the ungodly, and love them that hate the LORD? therefore is wrath upon thee from before the LORD.

2Ch 20:37 — Then Eliezer the son of Dodavah of Mareshah prophesied against Jehoshaphat, saying, Because thou hast joined thyself with Ahaziah, the LORD hath broken thy works. And the ships were broken, that they were not able to go to Tarshish.

Isa 30:2 — That walk to go down into Egypt, and have not asked at my mouth; to strengthen themselves in the strength of Pharaoh, and to trust in the shadow of Egypt!

Eze 17:15 — But he rebelled against him in sending his ambassadors into Egypt, that they might give him horses and much people. Shall he prosper? shall he escape that doeth such *things?* or shall he break the covenant, and be delivered?

Hos 4:17 — Ephraim *is* joined to idols: let him alone.

Hos 5:13 — When Ephraim saw his sickness, and Judah *saw* his wound, then went Ephraim to the Assyrian, and sent to king Jareb: yet could he not heal you, nor cure you of your wound.

Hos 12:1 — Ephraim feedeth on wind, and followeth after the east wind: he daily increaseth lies and desolation; and they do make a covenant with the Assyrians, and oil is carried into Egypt.

- **Ratification of, by oaths.**

Ge 26:28–31; Jos 9:15–20; 1Sa 20:16–17

Ge 21:23 — Now therefore swear unto me here by God that thou wilt not deal falsely with me, nor with my son, nor with my son's son: *but* according to the kindness that I have done unto thee, thou shalt do unto me, and to the land wherein thou hast sojourned.

- **Ratification of, by giving the hand.**

La 5:6 — We have given the hand *to* the Egyptians, *and to* the Assyrians, to be satisfied with bread.

See: Covenant

See: Treaty

- **Instances of.**
  - **Between Abraham and Mamre, Eshcol, and Aner.**

Ge 14:13

  - **Abraham and Abimelech.**

Ge 21:22–32

  - **Isaac and Abimelech.**

Ge 26:26–31

  - **Canaanitish nations against Israel.**

Jos 9:1–2

  - **Joshua and the Gibeonites.**

Jos 9:1–27

  - **Moabites, Amalekites, and Ammonites.**

Jgs 3:12–13

  - **Solomon and Hiram.**

1Ki 5:12; Am 1:9

  - **Asa and Benhadad.**

1Ki 15:18–19; 2Ch 16:3

  - **Jehoshaphat and Ahab.**

1Ki 22:1–53; 2Ch 18:1

  - **Jehoshaphat and Ahaziah.**

2Ch 20:35

  - **Ahaz and Tiglath.**

2Ki 16:7–8; 2Ch 28:16, 21

  - **Rezin and Pekah.**

2Ki 16:5

  - **Zedekiah and Pharaoh.**

Jer 37:1–8; Eze 17:15–17

ALLON

- **Son of Jedaiah.**

1Ch 4:37 — And Ziza the son of Shiphi, the son of Allon, the son of Jedaiah, the son of Shimri, the son of Shemaiah;

- **A city of Naphtali.**

Jos 19:33 — And their coast was from Heleph, from Allon to Zaanannim, and Adami, Nekeb, and Jabneel, unto Lakum; and the outgoings thereof were at Jordan:

ALLON-BACHUTH • Place where Rebekah was buried.

Ge 35:8 — But Deborah Rebekah's nurse died, and she was buried beneath Bethel under an oak: and the name of it was called Allon-bachuth.

ALLOY, of metals

Isa 1:25 — And I will turn my hand upon thee, and purely purge away thy dross, and take away all thy tin:

ALMODAD • Son of Joktan.

Ge 10:26 — And Joktan begat Almodad, and Sheleph, and Hazar-maveth, and Jerah,

1Ch 1:20 — And Joktan begat Almodad, and Sheleph, and Hazarmaveth, and Jerah,

ALMON

- **Levitical city of Benjamin.**

Jos 21:18 — Anathoth with her suburbs, and Almon with her suburbs; four cities.

- **Called Alemeth.**

1Ch 6:60 — And out of the tribe of Benjamin; Geba with her suburbs, and Alemeth with her suburbs, and Anathoth with her suburbs. All their cities throughout their families *were* thirteen cities.

ALMON-DIBLATHAIM

- **Camping place of Israelites.**

Nu 33:46–47

- **Probably identical with Beth-diblathaim.**

Jer 48:22 — And upon Dibon, and upon Nebo, and upon Beth-diblathaim,

• **Probably identical with Diblath.**

Eze 6:14 — So will I stretch out my hand upon them, and make the land desolate, yea, more desolate than the wilderness toward Diblath, in all their habitations: and they shall know that I *am* the LORD.

ALMOND

• **A tree.**

• **Fruit of.**

Ge 43:11 — And their father Israel said unto them, If *it must be* so now, do this; take of the best fruits in the land in your vessels, and carry down the man a present, a little balm, and a little honey, spices, and myrrh, nuts, and almonds:

• **Aaron's rod of the.**

Nu 17:8 — And it came to pass, that on the morrow Moses went into the tabernacle of witness; and, behold, the rod of Aaron for the house of Levi was budded, and brought forth buds, and bloomed blossoms, and yielded almonds.

• **Bowls of candlestick in the tabernacle fashioned after the nuts of the.**

Ex 25:33–34; 37:19–20

• **Figurative use of.**

Ecc 12:5 — Also *when* they shall be afraid of *that which is* high, and fears *shall be* in the way, and the almond tree shall flourish, and the grasshopper shall be a burden, and desire shall fail: because man goeth to his long home, and the mourners go about the streets:

Jer 1:11 — Moreover the word of the LORD came unto me, saying, Jeremiah, what seest thou? And I said, I see a rod of an almond tree.

ALMS

• **Enjoined.**

Dt 15:7–11; 2Co 9:5–7

Mt 5:42 — Give to him that asketh thee, and from him that would borrow of thee turn not thou away.

Mt 19:21 — Jesus said unto him, If thou wilt be perfect, go *and* sell that thou hast, and give to the poor, and thou shalt have treasure in heaven: and come *and* follow me.

Lk 12:33 — Sell that ye have, and give alms; provide yourselves bags which wax not old, a treasure in the heavens that faileth not, where no thief approacheth, neither moth corrupteth.

Gal 2:10 — Only *they would* that we should remember the poor; the same which I also was forward to do.

1Ti 6:18 — That they do good, that they be rich in good works, ready to distribute, willing to communicate;

Heb 13:16 — But to do good and to communicate forget not: for with such sacrifices God is well pleased.

• **To be given without ostentation.**

Mt 6:1–4

Ro 12:8 — Or he that exhorteth, on exhortation: he that giveth, *let him do it* with simplicity; he that ruleth, with diligence; he that sheweth mercy, with cheerfulness.

• **To be given freely.**

2Co 9:6–7

• **Withholding, not of love.**

1Jn 3:17 — But whoso hath this world's good, and seeth his brother have need, and shutteth up his bowels *of compassion* from him, how dwelleth the love of God in him?

• **Solicited by the unfortunate.**

Jn 9:8 — The neighbours therefore, and they which before had seen him that he was blind, said, Is not this he that sat and begged?

Ac 3:2 — And a certain man lame from his mother's womb was carried, whom they laid daily at the gate of the temple which is called Beautiful, to ask alms of them that entered into the temple;

See: Beneficence

See: Gifts from God

See: Giving

See: Liberality

See: Poor

• **Instances of giving.**

• **Zaccheus.**

Lk 19:8

• **Dorcas.**

Ac 9:36

• **Cornelius.**

Ac 10:2

• **The early Christians.**

Ac 2:44–45; 4:34–37; 6:1–3; 11:29–30; 24:17; Ro 15:25–28; 1Co 16:1–4; 2Co 8:1–4; 9:1; Heb 6:10

ALOES

• **Used as perfume.**

Ps 45:8 — All thy garments *smell* of myrrh, and aloes, *and* cassia, out of the ivory palaces, whereby they have made thee glad.

Pr 7:17 — I have perfumed my bed with myrrh, aloes, and cinnamon.

SS 4:14 — Spikenard and saffron; calamus and cinnamon, with all trees of frankincense; myrrh and aloes, with all the chief spices:

• **In embalming the dead.**

Jn 19:39 — And there came also Nicodemus, which at the first came to Jesus by night, and brought a mixture of myrrh and aloes, about an hundred pound *weight.*

• **Lign-aloes.**

Nu 24:6 — As the valleys are they spread forth, as gardens by the river's side, as the trees of lign aloes which the LORD hath planted, *and* as cedar trees beside the waters.

ALPHA

• **A title of Christ.**

Rev 1:8 — I am Alpha and Omega, the beginning and the ending, saith the Lord, which is, and which was, and which is to come, the Almighty.

Rev 1:11 — Saying, I am Alpha and Omega, the first and the last: and, What thou seest, write in a book, and send *it* unto the seven churches which are in Asia; unto Ephesus, and unto Smyrna, and unto Pergamos, and unto Thyatira, and unto Sardis, and unto Philadelphia, and unto Laodicea.

Rev 21:6 — And he said unto me, It is done. I am Alpha and Omega, the beginning and the end. I will give unto him that is athirst of the fountain of the water of life freely.

Rev 22:13 — I am Alpha and Omega, the beginning and the end, the first and the last.

- **Compare.**

Isa 41:4 — Who hath wrought and done *it,* calling the generations from the beginning? I the LORD, the first, and with the last; I *am* he.

Isa 44:6 — Thus saith the LORD the King of Israel, and his redeemer the LORD of hosts; I *am* the first, and I *am* the last; and beside me *there is* no God.

Isa 48:12 — Hearken unto me, O Jacob and Israel, my called; I *am* he; I *am* the first, I also *am* the last.

- **And Omega.**

Rev 1:8 — I am Alpha and Omega, the beginning and the ending, saith the Lord, which is, and which was, and which is to come, the Almighty.

Rev 1:11 — Saying, I am Alpha and Omega, the first and the last: and, What thou seest, write in a book, and send *it* unto the seven churches which are in Asia; unto Ephesus, and unto Smyrna, and unto Pergamos, and unto Thyatira, and unto Sardis, and unto Philadelphia, and unto Laodicea.

Rev 21:6 — And he said unto me, It is done. I am Alpha and Omega, the beginning and the end. I will give unto him that is athirst of the fountain of the water of life freely.

Rev 22:13 — I am Alpha and Omega, the beginning and the end, the first and the last.

ALPHEUS

- **Father of James.**

Mt 10:3 — Philip, and Bartholomew; Thomas, and Matthew the publican; James *the son* of Alphaeus, and Lebbaeus, whose surname was Thaddaeus;

Mk 3:18 — And Andrew, and Philip, and Bartholomew, and Matthew, and Thomas, and James the *son* of Alphaeus, and Thaddaeus, and Simon the Canaanite,

- **Father of Levi.**

Mk 2:14 — And as he passed by, he saw Levi the *son* of Alphaeus sitting at the receipt of custom, and said unto him, Follow me. And he arose and followed him.

ALTAR

- **Built by Noah.**

Ge 8:20 — And Noah builded an altar unto the LORD; and took of every clean beast, and of every clean fowl, and offered burnt offerings on the altar.

- **Built by Abraham.**

Ge 12:7–8

Ge 13:18 — Then Abram removed *his* tent, and came and dwelt in the plain of Mamre, which *is* in Hebron, and built there an altar unto the LORD.

Ge 22:9 — And they came to the place which God had told him of; and Abraham built an altar there, and laid the wood in order, and bound Isaac his son, and laid him on the altar upon the wood.

- **Built by Isaac.**

Ge 26:25 — And he builded an altar there, and called upon the name of the LORD and pitched his tent there: and there Isaac's servants digged a well.

- **Built by Jacob.**

Ge 35:1–7

Ge 33:20 — And he erected there an altar, and called it El-elohe-Israel.

- **Built by Moses.**

Ex 17:15 — And Moses built an altar, and called the name of it Jehovah-nissi:

Ex 24:4 — And Moses wrote all the words of the LORD, and rose up early in the morning, and builded an altar under the hill, and twelve pillars, according to the twelve tribes of Israel.

- **Built by Balaam.**

Nu 23:1 — And Balaam said unto Balak, Build me here seven altars, and prepare me here seven oxen and seven rams.

Nu 23:14 — And he brought him into the field of Zophim, to the top of Pisgah, and built seven altars, and offered a bullock and a ram on *every* altar.

Nu 23:29 — And Balaam said unto Balak, Build me here seven altars, and prepare me here seven bullocks and seven rams.

- **Built by Joshua.**

Dt 27:4–7; Jos 8:30–32

- **Built by Reubenites and Gadites.**

Jos 22:10 — And when they came unto the borders of Jordan, that *are* in the land of Canaan, the children of Reuben and the children of Gad and the half tribe of Manasseh built there an altar by Jordan, a great altar to see to.

Jos 22:34 — And the children of Reuben and the children of Gad called the altar *Ed:* for it *shall be* a witness between us that the LORD *is* God.

- **Built by Gideon.**

Jgs 6:26–27

- **Built by Samuel.**

1Sa 7:17 — And his return *was* to Ramah; for there *was* his house; and there he judged Israel; and there he built an altar unto the LORD.

- **Built by Saul.**

1Sa 14:35 — And Saul built an altar unto the LORD: the same was the first altar that he built unto the LORD.

- **Built by David.**

2Sa 24:18–19

- **Built by Elijah.**

1Ki 18:31–32

- **Mosaic commandments prescribing the construction of.**

Ex 20:24–26; Dt 27:5–7; Jos 8:30–31

Eze 43:13 — And these *are* the measures of the altar after the cubits: The cubit *is* a cubit and an hand breadth; even the bottom *shall be* a cubit, and the breadth a cubit, and the border thereof by the edge thereof round about *shall be* a span: and this *shall be* the higher place of the altar.

- **Used in idolatrous worship.**

Jgs 6:25 — And it came to pass the same night, that the LORD said unto him, Take thy father's young bullock, even the second bullock of seven years old, and throw down the altar of Baal that thy father hath, and cut down the grove that *is* by it:

1Ki 12:32 — And Jeroboam ordained a feast in the eighth month, on the fifteenth day of the month, like unto the feast that *is* in Judah, and he offered upon the altar. So did he in Bethel, sacrificing unto the calves that he had made: and he placed in Bethel the priests of the high places which he had made.

1Ki 16:32 — And he reared up an altar for Baal in the house of Baal, which he had built in Samaria.

1Ki 18:26 — And they took the bullock which was given them, and they dressed *it,* and called on the name of Baal from morning even until noon, saying, O Baal, hear us. But *there was* no voice, nor any that answered. And they leaped upon the altar which was made.

2Ki 16:10 — And king Ahaz went to Damascus to meet Tiglath-pileser king of Assyria, and saw an altar that *was* at Damascus: and king Ahaz sent to Urijah the priest the fashion of the altar, and the pattern of it, according to all the workmanship thereof.

2Ki 23:12 — And the altars that *were* on the top of the upper chamber of Ahaz, which the kings of Judah had made, and the altars which Manasseh had made in the two courts of the house of the LORD, did the king beat down, and brake *them* down from thence, and cast the dust of them into the brook Kidron.

2Ki 23:15 — Moreover the altar that *was* at Bethel, *and* the high place which Jeroboam the son of Nebat, who made Israel to sin, had made, both that altar and the high place he brake down, and burned the high place, *and* stamped *it* small to powder, and burned the grove.

Isa 27:9 — By this therefore shall the iniquity of Jacob be purged; and this is all the fruit to take away his sin; when he maketh all the stones of the altar as chalkstones that are beaten in sunder, the groves and images shall not stand up.

Isa 65:3 — A people that provoketh me to anger continually to my face; that sacrificeth in gardens, and burneth incense upon altars of brick;

Hos 8:11 — Because Ephraim hath made many altars to sin, altars shall be unto him to sin.

Ac 17:23 — For as I passed by, and beheld your devotions, I found an altar with this inscription, TO THE UNKNOWN GOD. Whom therefore ye ignorantly worship, him declare I unto you.

- **Of burnt offerings.**
  - **Called Brazen Altar.**

Ex 39:39 — The brasen altar, and his grate of brass, his staves, and all his vessels, the laver and his foot,

1Ki 8:64 — The same day did the king hallow the middle of the court that *was* before the house of the LORD: for there he offered burnt offerings, and meat offerings, and the fat of the peace offerings: because the brasen altar that *was* before the LORD *was* too little to receive the burnt offerings, and meat offerings, and the fat of the peace offerings.

  - **Called Altar of God.**

Ps 43:4 — Then will I go unto the altar of God, unto God my exceeding joy: yea, upon the harp will I praise thee, O God my God.

  - **Called Altar of the Lord.**

Mal 2:13 — And this have ye done again, covering the altar of the LORD with tears, with weeping, and with crying out, insomuch that he regardeth not the offering any more, or receiveth *it* with good will at your hand.

- **In the tabernacle.**
  - **Pattern of.**

Ex 27:1–8

  - **Constructed by Bezaleel.**

Ex 38:1–7

Ex 37:1 — And Bezaleel made the ark *of* shittim wood: two cubits and a half *was* the length of it, and a cubit and a half the breadth of it, and a cubit and a half the height of it:

  - **Location of.**

Ex 40:6 — And thou shalt set the altar of the burnt offering before the door of the tabernacle of the tent of the congregation.

Ex 40:29 — And he put the altar of burnt offering *by* the door of the tabernacle of the tent of the congregation, and offered upon it the burnt offering and the meat offering; as the LORD commanded Moses.

Eze 8:16 — And he brought me into the inner court of the LORD's house, and, behold, at the door of the temple of the LORD, between the porch and the altar, *were* about five and twenty men, with their backs toward the temple of the LORD, and their faces toward the east; and they worshipped the sun toward the east.

Mt 23:35 — That upon you may come all the righteous blood shed upon the earth, from the blood of righteous Abel unto the blood of Zacharias son of Barachias, whom ye slew between the temple and the altar.

  - **Furniture of.**

Ex 27:3–7; 38:3–7; 1Sa 2:13–14

  - **Horns of.**

Ex 27:2 — And thou shalt make the horns of it upon the four corners thereof: his horns shall be of the same: and thou shalt overlay it with brass.

- **How sanctified.**

Ex 29:36–37; 30:26–28; Le 8:10–11; Nu 7:1–89; Eze 43:18–27

Ex 29:44 — And I will sanctify the tabernacle of the congregation, and the altar: I will sanctify also both Aaron and his sons, to minister to me in the priest's office.

Ex 40:10 — And thou shalt anoint the altar of the burnt offering, and all his vessels, and sanctify the altar: and it shall be an altar most holy.

See: Blood

- **Sanctified everything that touched it.**
  Mt 23:18–19
  Ex 29:37 — Seven days thou shalt make an atonement for the altar, and sanctify it; and it shall be an altar most holy: whatsoever toucheth the altar shall be holy.
  Ex 30:29 — And thou shalt sanctify them, that they may be most holy: whatsoever toucheth them shall be holy.
- **A place of refuge.**
  Ex 21:14 — But if a man come presumptuously upon his neighbour, to slay him with guile; thou shalt take him from mine altar, that he may die.
  1Ki 1:50 — And Adonijah feared because of Solomon, and arose, and went, and caught hold on the horns of the altar.
  1Ki 2:28 — Then tidings came to Joab: for Joab had turned after Adonijah, though he turned not after Absalom. And Joab fled unto the tabernacle of the LORD, and caught hold on the horns of the altar.
- **In Solomon's temple.**
  - **Description of.**
    2Ch 4:1 — Moreover he made an altar of brass, twenty cubits the length thereof, and twenty cubits the breadth thereof, and ten cubits the height thereof.
  - **Renewed by Asa.**
    2Ch 15:8 — And when Asa heard these words, and the prophecy of Oded the prophet, he took courage, and put away the abominable idols out of all the land of Judah and Benjamin, and out of the cities which he had taken from mount Ephraim, and renewed the altar of the LORD, that *was* before the porch of the LORD.
  - **Removed by Ahaz, and one of idolatrous fashion substituted.**
    2Ki 16:14–17
  - **Cleansed by Hezekiah.**
    2Ch 28:18–24
  - **Repaired by Manasseh.**
    2Ch 33:16 — And he repaired the altar of the LORD, and sacrificed thereon peace offerings and thank offerings, and commanded Judah to serve the LORD God of Israel.
  - **Furniture of, taken to Babylon.**
    2Ki 25:14 — And the pots, and the shovels, and the snuffers, and the spoons, and all the vessels of brass wherewith they ministered, took they away.
- **In second temple.**
  Ezr 3:1–6
- **Ezekiel's vision of.**
  Eze 43:13–27
  ✣See: Tabernacle
  ✣See: Temple
- **Of incense.**
  - **Called the Golden Altar.**
    Ex 39:38 — And the golden altar, and the anointing oil, and the sweet incense, and the hanging for the tabernacle door,
    Nu 4:11 — And upon the golden altar they shall spread a cloth of blue, and cover it with a covering of badgers' skins, and shall put to the staves thereof:
  - **Called Altar of Sweet Incense.**
    Le 4:7 — And the priest shall put *some* of the blood upon the horns of the altar of sweet incense before the LORD, which *is* in the tabernacle of the congregation: and shall pour all the blood of the bullock at the bottom of the altar of the burnt offering, which *is at* the door of the tabernacle of the congregation.
  - **Called Altar before the Lord.**
    Le 16:18 — And he shall go out unto the altar that *is* before the LORD, and make an atonement for it; and shall take of the blood of the bullock, and of the blood of the goat, and put *it* upon the horns of the altar round about.
- **Pattern of.**
  Ex 30:1–5
- **Constructed.**
  Ex 37:25–28
- **Location of.**
  Ex 30:6 — And thou shalt put it before the vail that *is* by the ark of the testimony, before the mercy seat that *is* over the testimony, where I will meet with thee.
  Ex 40:5 — And thou shalt set the altar of gold for the incense before the ark of the testimony, and put the hanging of the door to the tabernacle.
  Ex 40:26 — And he put the golden altar in the tent of the congregation before the vail:
- **A cover made for, of the censers of Korah.**
  Nu 16:36–40
- **Uses of.**
  Ex 30:7–10, 26–27
  Ex 40:27 — And he burnt sweet incense thereon; as the LORD commanded Moses.
  Le 4:7 — And the priest shall put *some* of the blood upon the horns of the altar of sweet incense before the LORD, which *is* in the tabernacle of the congregation: and shall pour all the blood of the bullock at the bottom of the altar of the burnt offering, which *is at* the door of the tabernacle of the congregation.
  Le 4:18 — And he shall put *some* of the blood upon the horns of the altar which *is* before the LORD, that *is* in the tabernacle of the congregation, and shall pour out all the blood at the bottom of the altar of the burnt offering, which *is at* the door of the tabernacle of the congregation.
  Le 8:15 — And he slew *it;* and Moses took the blood, and put *it* upon the horns of the altar round about with his finger, and purified the altar, and poured the blood at the bottom of the altar, and sanctified it, to make reconciliation upon it.
  Le 9:9 — And the sons of Aaron brought the blood unto him: and he dipped his finger in the blood, and put *it* upon the horns of the altar, and poured out the blood at the bottom of the altar:

Le 16:12 — And he shall take a censer full of burning coals of fire from off the altar before the LORD, and his hands full of sweet incense beaten small, and bring *it* within the vail:

Le 16:18 — And he shall go out unto the altar that *is* before the LORD, and make an atonement for it; and shall take of the blood of the bullock, and of the blood of the goat, and put *it* upon the horns of the altar round about.

• How prepared for carrying.

Nu 4:14–15

• Carried by the Kohathites.

Nu 3:27–31

• In Solomon's temple.

1Ki 6:19–20

1Ki 7:48 — And Solomon made all the vessels that *pertained* unto the house of the LORD: the altar of gold, and the table of gold, whereupon the shewbread *was,*

1Ch 28:18 — And for the altar of incense refined gold by weight; and gold for the pattern of the chariot of the cherubims, that spread out *their wings,* and covered the ark of the covenant of the LORD.

• Seen in John's vision.

Rev 8:3 — And another angel came and stood at the altar, having a golden censer; and there was given unto him much incense, that he should offer *it* with the prayers of all saints upon the golden altar which was before the throne.

Rev 9:13 — And the sixth angel sounded, and I heard a voice from the four horns of the golden altar which is before God,

ALTRUISM

• Disinterested benevolence.

Mt 20:26–28; Mk 10:43–45; Lk 22:26–27; Jn 13:4–17; Ac 20:33–35; Ro 15:1–3; 1Co 9:18–22; 10:31–33; Php 2:3–8

Mt 23:11 — But he that is greatest among you shall be your servant.

Mk 9:35 — And he sat down, and called the twelve, and saith unto them, If any man desire to be first, *the same* shall be last of all, and servant of all.

1Co 10:24 — Let no man seek his own, but every man another's *wealth.*

2Co 4:5 — For we preach not ourselves, but Christ Jesus the Lord; and ourselves your servants for Jesus' sake.

2Co 6:10 — As sorrowful, yet alway rejoicing; as poor, yet making many rich; as having nothing, and *yet* possessing all things.

2Co 8:9 — For ye know the grace of our Lord Jesus Christ, that, though he was rich, yet for your sakes he became poor, that ye through his poverty might be rich.

Gal 6:10 — As we have therefore opportunity, let us do good unto all *men,* especially unto them who are of the household of faith.

See: Alms

See: Beneficence

See: Charitableness

See: Duty; of man to man

See: Liberality

See: Love

ALUSH • Camping place of the Israelites.

Nu 33:13 — And they departed from Dophkah, and encamped in Alush.

ALVAH

• Duke of Edom.

Ge 36:40 — And these *are* the names of the dukes *that came* of Esau, according to their families, after their places, by their names; duke Timnah, duke Alvah, duke Jetheth,

• Called Aliah.

1Ch 1:51 — Hadad died also. And the dukes of Edom were; duke Timnah, duke Aliah, duke Jetheth,

ALVAN

• Son of Shobal.

Ge 36:23 — And the children of Shobal *were* these; Alvan, and Manahath, and Ebal, Shepho, and Onam.

• Called Alian.

1Ch 1:40 — The sons of Shobal; Alian, and Manahath, and Ebal, Shephi, and Onam. And the sons of Zibeon; Aiah, and Anah.

AMAD • A town of Asher.

Jos 19:26 — And Alammelech, and Amad, and Misheal; and reacheth to Carmel westward, and to Shihor-libnath;

AMAL • Son of Helem.

1Ch 7:35 — And the sons of his brother Helem; Zophah, and Imna, and Shelesh, and Amal.

AMALEK

• Son of Eliphaz.

Ge 36:12 — And Timna was concubine to Eliphaz Esau's son; and she bare to Eliphaz Amalek: these *were* the sons of Adah Esau's wife.

1Ch 1:36 — The sons of Eliphaz; Teman, and Omar, Zephi, and Gatam, Kenaz, and Timna, and Amalek.

• Probably not the ancestor of the Amalekites mentioned in time of Abraham.

Ge 14:7 — And they returned, and came to En-mishpat, which *is* Kadesh, and smote all the country of the Amalekites, and also the Amorites that dwelt in Hazezon-tamar.

AMALEKITES

• A people inhabiting the country south of Idumea and east of the Red Sea.

Nu 13:29 — The Amalekites dwell in the land of the south: and the Hittites, and the Jebusites, and the Amorites, dwell in the mountains: and the Canaanites dwell by the sea, and by the coast of Jordan.

Nu 14:25 — (Now the Amalekites and the Canaanites dwelt in the valley.) To morrow turn you, and get you into the wilderness by the way of the Red sea.

1Sa 15:7 — And Saul smote the Amalekites from Havilah *until* thou comest to Shur, that *is* over against Egypt.

1Sa 27:8 — And David and his men went up, and invaded the Geshurites, and the Gezrites, and the Amalekites: for those *nations were* of old the inhabitants of the land, as thou goest to Shur, even unto the land of Egypt.

- **Defeated by Chedorlaomer.**

Ge 14:7 — And they returned, and came to En-mishpat, which *is* Kadesh, and smote all the country of the Amalekites, and also the Amorites that dwelt in Hazezon-tamar.

- **Defeated by Joshua.**

Ex 17:8 — Then came Amalek, and fought with Israel in Rephidim.

Ex 17:13 — And Joshua discomfited Amalek and his people with the edge of the sword.

- **Defeated by Gideon.**

Jgs 7:1–25

- **Defeated by Saul.**

1Sa 14:47–48; 15:1–33

- **Defeated by David.**

1Sa 27:8–9; 30:1–20

- **Defeated by the Simeonites.**

1Ch 4:42–43

- **Defeat the Israelites.**

Nu 14:45 — Then the Amalekites came down, and the Canaanites which dwelt in that hill, and smote them, and discomfited them, *even* unto Hormah.

Jgs 3:13 — And he gathered unto him the children of Ammon and Amalek, and went and smote Israel, and possessed the city of palm trees.

- **Israel commanded to destroy.**

Dt 25:17–19

1Sa 28:18 — Because thou obeyedst not the voice of the LORD, nor executedst his fierce wrath upon Amalek, therefore hath the LORD done this thing unto thee this day.

- **Prophecies against.**

Ex 17:14 — And the LORD said unto Moses, Write this *for* a memorial in a book, and rehearse *it* in the ears of Joshua: for I will utterly put out the remembrance of Amalek from under heaven.

Ex 17:16 — For he said, Because the LORD hath sworn *that* the LORD *will have* war with Amalek from generation to generation.

Nu 24:20 — And when he looked on Amalek, he took up his parable, and said, Amalek *was* the first of the nations; but his latter end *shall be* that he perish for ever.

AMAM

- **A city of Judah.**

Jos 15:26 — Amam, and Shema, and Moladah,

- **Probably situated within the district assigned afterward to Simeon.**

Jos 19:1–9

AMANA • A mountain mentioned in SS.

SS 4:8 — Come with me from Lebanon, *my* spouse, with me from Lebanon: look from the top of Amana, from the top of Shenir and Hermon, from the lions' dens, from the mountains of the leopards.

AMANUENSIS

Jer 36:4 — Then Jeremiah called Baruch the son of Neriah: and Baruch wrote from the mouth of Jeremiah all the words of the LORD, which he had spoken unto him, upon a roll of a book.

Jer 45:1 — The word that Jeremiah the prophet spake unto Baruch the son of Neriah, when he had written these words in a book at the mouth of Jeremiah, in the fourth year of Jehoiakim the son of Josiah king of Judah, saying,

AMARIAH

- **Two Levites.**

1Ch 6:7 — Meraioth begat Amariah, and Amariah begat Ahitub,

1Ch 6:52 — Meraioth his son, Amariah his son, Ahitub his son,

1Ch 23:19 — Of the sons of Hebron; Jeriah the first, Amariah the second, Jahaziel the third, and Jekameam the fourth.

1Ch 24:23 — And the sons *of Hebron;* Jeriah *the first,* Amariah the second, Jahaziel the third, Jekameam the fourth.

- **Chief priest in the reign of Jehoshaphat.**

2Ch 19:11 — And, behold, Amariah the chief priest is over you in all matters of the LORD; and Zebadiah the son of Ishmael, the ruler of the house of Judah, for all the king's matters: also the Levites *shall be* officers before you. Deal courageously, and the LORD shall be with the good.

- **A high priest and father of Ahitub.**

1Ch 6:11 — And Azariah begat Amariah, and Amariah begat Ahitub,

Ezr 7:3 — The son of Amariah, the son of Azariah, the son of Meraioth,

- **A Levite, who assisted in distributing temple gifts.**

2Ch 31:15–19

- **Son of Hizkiah.**

Zep 1:1 — The word of the LORD which came unto Zephaniah the son of Cushi, the son of Gedaliah, the son of Amariah, the son of Hizkiah, in the days of Josiah the son of Amon, king of Judah.

- **Father of Zechariah.**

Ne 11:4 — And at Jerusalem dwelt *certain* of the children of Judah, and of the children of Benjamin. Of the children of Judah; Athaiah the son of Uzziah, the son of Zechariah, the son of Amariah, the son of Shephatiah, the son of Mahalaleel, of the children of Perez;

• **A priest that returned from exile.**
Ne 10:3 — Pashur, Amariah, Malchijah,
Ne 12:2 — Amariah, Malluch, Hattush,

• **Probably identical with one mentioned in Ne 12:13.**
Ne 12:13 — Of Ezra, Meshullam; of Amariah, Jehohanan;

• **A returned exile that divorces his idolatrous wife.**
Ezr 10:42 — Shallum, Amariah, *and* Joseph.

AMASA

• **Nephew of David.**
2Sa 17:25 — And Absalom made Amasa captain of the host instead of Joab: which Amasa was a man's son, whose name *was* Ithra an Israelite, that went in to Abigail the daughter of Nahash, sister to Zeruiah Joab's mother.
1Ch 2:17 — And Abigail bare Amasa: and the father of Amasa *was* Jether the Ishmeelite.

• **Joins Absalom.**
2Sa 17:25 — And Absalom made Amasa captain of the host instead of Joab: which Amasa was a man's son, whose name *was* Ithra an Israelite, that went in to Abigail the daughter of Nahash, sister to Zeruiah Joab's mother.

• **Returns to David, and is made captain of the host.**
2Sa 19:13 — And say ye to Amasa, *Art* thou not of my bone, and of my flesh? God do so to me, and more also, if thou be not captain of the host before me continually in the room of Joab.

• **Slain.**
2Sa 20:8–12
1Ki 2:5 — Moreover thou knowest also what Joab the son of Zeruiah did to me, *and* what he did to the two captains of the hosts of Israel, unto Abner the son of Ner, and unto Amasa the son of Jether, whom he slew, and shed the blood of war in peace, and put the blood of war upon his girdle that *was* about his loins, and in his shoes that *were* on his feet.
1Ki 2:32 — And the LORD shall return his blood upon his own head, who fell upon two men more righteous and better than he, and slew them with the sword, my father David not knowing *thereof, to wit,* Abner the son of Ner, captain of the host of Israel, and Amasa the son of Jether, captain of the host of Judah.

• **Son of Hadlai.**
2Ch 28:12 — Then certain of the heads of the children of Ephraim, Azariah the son of Johanan, Berechiah the son of Meshillemoth, and Jehizkiah the son of Shallum, and Amasa the son of Hadlai, stood up against them that came from the war,

AMASAI

• **A Levite and ancestor of Samuel.**
1Ch 6:25 — And the sons of Elkanah; Amasai, and Ahimoth.
1Ch 6:35 — The son of Zuph, the son of Elkanah, the son of Mahath, the son of Amasai,

• **Leader of a body of men disaffected toward Saul, who joined David.**
1Ch 12:18 — Then the spirit came upon Amasai, *who was* chief of the captains, *and he said,* Thine *are we,* David, and on thy side, thou son of Jesse: peace, peace *be* unto thee, and peace *be* to thine helpers; for thy God helpeth thee. Then David received them, and made them captains of the band.

• **A priest and trumpeter.**
1Ch 15:24 — And Shebaniah, and Jehoshaphat, and Nethaneel, and Amasai, and Zechariah, and Benaiah, and Eliezer, the priests, did blow with the trumpets before the ark of God: and Obed-edom and Jehiah *were* doorkeepers for the ark.

• **A Levite of the Kohathites.**
2Ch 29:12 — Then the Levites arose, Mahath the son of Amasai, and Joel the son of Azariah, of the sons of the Kohathites: and of the sons of Merari, Kish the son of Abdi, and Azariah the son of Jehalelel: and of the Gershonites; Joah the son of Zimmah, and Eden the son of Joah:

AMASHAI • A chieftain of Judah.

Ne 11:13 — And his brethren, chief of the fathers, two hundred forty and two: and Amashai the son of Azareel, the son of Ahasai, the son of Meshillemoth, the son of Immer,

AMASIAH • A chief of the tribe of Judah.

2Ch 17:16 — And next him *was* Amasiah the son of Zichri, who willingly offered himself unto the LORD; and with him two hundred thousand mighty men of valour.

AMAZIAH

• **A Levite.**
1Ch 6:45 — The son of Hashabiah, the son of Amaziah, the son of Hilkiah,

• **King of Judah.**

• **History of.**
2Ki 14:1–29; 2Ch 25:1–28

• **An idolatrous priest at Bethel.**
Am 7:10–17

• **Father of Joshah.**
1Ch 4:34 — And Meshobab, and Jamlech, and Joshah the son of Amaziah,

AMBASSADORS

• **Sent by Moses to Edom.**
Nu 20:14 — And Moses sent messengers from Kadesh unto the king of Edom, Thus saith thy brother Israel, Thou knowest all the travail that hath befallen us:

• **Sent by Moses to the Amorites.**
Nu 21:21 — And Israel sent messengers unto Sihon king of the Amorites, saying,

• **Sent by Gibeonites to the Israelites.**
Jos 9:4 — They did work wilily, and went and made as if they had been ambassadors, and took old sacks

upon their asses, and wine bottles, old, and rent, and bound up;

- **Sent by Israelites to various nations.**

Jgs 11:12–28

- **Sent by Hiram to David.**

2Sa 5:11 — And Hiram king of Tyre sent messengers to David, and cedar trees, and carpenters, and masons: and they built David an house.

- **Sent by Hiram to Solomon.**

1Ki 5:1 — And Hiram king of Tyre sent his servants unto Solomon; for he had heard that they had anointed him king in the room of his father: for Hiram was ever a lover of David.

- **Sent by Benhadad to Ahab.**

1Ki 20:2–6

- **Sent by Amaziah to Jehoash.**

2Ki 14:8 — Then Amaziah sent messengers to Jehoash, the son of Jehoahaz son of Jehu, king of Israel, saying, Come, let us look one another in the face.

- **Sent by Ahaz to Tiglath.**

2Ki 16:7 — So Ahaz sent messengers to Tiglath-pileser king of Assyria, saying, I *am* thy servant and thy son: come up, and save me out of the hand of the king of Syria, and out of the hand of the king of Israel, which rise up against me.

- **Sent by Hoshea to So.**

2Ki 17:4 — And the king of Assyria found conspiracy in Hoshea: for he had sent messengers to So king of Egypt, and brought no present to the king of Assyria, as *he had done* year by year: therefore the king of Assyria shut him up, and bound him in prison.

- **Sent by Sennacherib through Rabshakeh to Hezekiah.**

2Ki 19:9 — And when he heard say of Tirhakah king of Ethiopia, Behold, he is come out to fight against thee: he sent messengers again unto Hezekiah, saying,

- **Sent by Berodach to Hezekiah.**

2Ki 20:12 — At that time Berodach-baladan, the son of Baladan, king of Babylon, sent letters and a present unto Hezekiah: for he had heard that Hezekiah had been sick.

2Ch 32:31 — Howbeit in *the business of* the ambassadors of the princes of Babylon, who sent unto him to enquire of the wonder that was *done* in the land, God left him, to try him, that he might know all *that was* in his heart.

- **Sent by Zedekiah to Egypt.**

Eze 17:15 — But he rebelled against him in sending his ambassadors into Egypt, that they might give him horses and much people. Shall he prosper? shall he escape that doeth such *things?* or shall he break the covenant, and be delivered?

- **Other references to.**

Isa 39:1–2

Pr 13:17 — A wicked messenger falleth into mischief: but a faithful ambassador *is* health.

Isa 18:2 — That sendeth ambassadors by the sea, even in vessels of bulrushes upon the waters, *saying,* Go, ye swift messengers, to a nation scattered and peeled, to a people terrible from their beginning hitherto; a nation meted out and trodden down, whose land the rivers have spoiled!

Isa 30:4 — For his princes were at Zoan, and his ambassadors came to Hanes.

Isa 33:7 — Behold, their valiant ones shall cry without: the ambassadors of peace shall weep bitterly.

Isa 36:11 — Then said Eliakim and Shebna and Joah unto Rabshakeh, Speak, I pray thee, unto thy servants in the Syrian language; for we understand *it:* and speak not to us in the Jews' language, in the ears of the people that *are* on the wall.

Lk 14:32 — Or else, while the other is yet a great way off, he sendeth an ambassage, and desireth conditions of peace.

- **Figurative.**

Ob 1:1–21

Job 33:23 — If there be a messenger with him, an interpreter, one among a thousand, to shew unto man his uprightness:

2Co 5:20 — Now then we are ambassadors for Christ, as though God did beseech *you* by us: we pray *you* in Christ's stead, be ye reconciled to God.

Eph 6:20 — For which I am an ambassador in bonds: that therein I may speak boldly, as I ought to speak.

AMBER • A vegetable fossil.

Eze 1:4 — And I looked, and, behold, a whirlwind came out of the north, a great cloud, and a fire infolding itself, and a brightness *was* about it, and out of the midst thereof as the colour of amber, out of the midst of the fire.

Eze 1:27 — And I saw as the colour of amber, as the appearance of fire round about within it, from the appearance of his loins even upward, and from the appearance of his loins even downward, I saw as it were the appearance of fire, and it had brightness round about.

Eze 8:2 — Then I beheld, and lo a likeness as the appearance of fire: from the appearance of his loins even downward, fire; and from his loins even upward, as the appearance of brightness, as the colour of amber.

AMBITION

- **Falsely charged against Moses.**

Nu 16:13 — *Is it* a small thing that thou hast brought us up out of a land that floweth with milk and honey, to kill us in the wilderness, except thou make thyself altogether a prince over us?

- **Parable of the thistle, illustrating.**

2Ki 14:9 — And Jehoash the king of Israel sent to Amaziah king of Judah, saying, The thistle that *was* in Lebanon sent to the cedar that *was* in Lebanon, saying, Give thy daughter to my son to wife: and there passed by a wild beast that *was* in Lebanon, and trode down the thistle.

- **Unclassified scripture relating to.**

Job 20:6–7; Ps 49:11–13; Hab 2:5–6; Mt 4:8–10; 23:5–7; Mk 9:33–37; 10:35–45; 12:38–39; Lk 4:5–8; Php 3:4–17; Jas 4:1–2

Isa 5:8 — Woe unto them that join house to house, *that* lay field to field, till *there be* no place, that they may be placed alone in the midst of the earth!

Hab 2:9 — Woe to him that coveteth an evil covetousness to his house, that he may set his nest on high, that he may be delivered from the power of evil!

Mt 16:26 — For what is a man profited, if he shall gain the whole world, and lose his own soul? or what shall a man give in exchange for his soul?

Mt 18:1 — At the same time came the disciples unto Jesus, saying, Who is the greatest in the kingdom of heaven?

Mt 20:20 — Then came to him the mother of Zebedee's children with her sons, worshipping *him,* and desiring a certain thing of him.

Mt 23:12 — And whosoever shall exalt himself shall be abased; and he that shall humble himself shall be exalted.

Lk 9:25 — For what is a man advantaged, if he gain the whole world, and lose himself, or be cast away?

Lk 9:46 — Then there arose a reasoning among them, which of them should be greatest.

Lk 11:43 — Woe unto you, Pharisees! for ye love the uppermost seats in the synagogues, and greetings in the markets.

Lk 22:24 — And there was also a strife among them, which of them should be accounted the greatest.

Lk 22:26 — But *ye* shall not *be* so: but he that is greatest among you, let him be as the younger; and he that is chief, as he that doth serve.

Jn 5:44 — How can ye believe, which receive honour one of another, and seek not the honour that *cometh* from God only?

1Ti 3:1 — This *is* a true saying, If a man desire the office of a bishop, he desireth a good work.

1Jn 2:16 — For all that *is* in the world, the lust of the flesh, and the lust of the eyes, and the pride of life, is not of the Father, but is of the world.

See: Pride

- **Instances of.**
  - **Lucifer.**
    Isa 14:12–15
  - **Eve.**
    Ge 3:5–6
  - **The builders of Babel.**
    Ge 11:4
  - **Aaron and Miriam.**
    Nu 12:2–10
  - **Korah and his co-conspirators.**
    Nu 16:3–35
  - **Abimelech.**
    Jgs 9:1–6
  - **Absalom.**
    2Sa 15:1–13; 18:18
  - **Ahithophel.**
    2Sa 17:23
  - **Adonijah.**
    1Ki 1:5
  - **Sennacherib.**
    2Ki 19:23
  - **Haman.**
    Est 5:9–13; 6:6–9
  - **Diotrephes.**
    3Jn 1:9–10

AMBUSH

- **Instances of.**
  - **At Ai.**
    Jos 8:2–22
  - **At Shechem.**
    Jgs 9:25, 34
  - **At Gibeah.**
    Jgs 20:29–41
  - **Near Zemaraim.**
    2Ch 13:13
  - **By Jehoshaphat.**
    2Ch 20:22

  See: Armies

- **Figurative.**

Jer 51:12 — Set up the standard upon the walls of Babylon, make the watch strong, set up the watchmen, prepare the ambushes: for the LORD hath both devised and done that which he spake against the inhabitants of Babylon.

AMEN

- **A word used to reenforce a statement.**

Dt 27:12–26

Nu 5:22 — And this water that causeth the curse shall go into thy bowels, to make *thy* belly to swell, and *thy* thigh to rot: And the woman shall say, Amen, amen.

Ne 5:13 — Also I shook my lap, and said, So God shake out every man from his house, and from his labour, that performeth not this promise, even thus be he shaken out, and emptied. And all the congregation said, Amen, and praised the LORD. And the people did according to this promise.

2Co 1:20 — For all the promises of God in him *are* yea, and in him Amen, unto the glory of God by us.

Rev 1:18 — I *am* he that liveth, and was dead; and, behold, I am alive for evermore, Amen; and have the keys of hell and of death.

Rev 22:20 — He which testifieth these things saith, Surely I come quickly. Amen. Even so, come, Lord Jesus.

- **Used in prayer.**

1Ki 1:36 — And Benaiah the son of Jehoiada answered the king, and said, Amen: the LORD God of my lord the king say so *too.*

1Ch 16:36 — Blessed *be* the LORD God of Israel for ever and ever. And all the people said, Amen, and praised the LORD.

Ne 8:6 — And Ezra blessed the LORD, the great God. And all the people answered, Amen, Amen, with lifting up their hands: and they bowed their heads, and worshipped the LORD with *their* faces to the ground.

Ps 41:13 — Blessed *be* the LORD God of Israel from everlasting, and to everlasting. Amen, and Amen.

Ps 72:19 — And blessed *be* his glorious name for ever: and let the whole earth be filled *with* his glory; Amen, and Amen.

Ps 89:52 — Blessed *be* the LORD for evermore. Amen, and Amen.

Ps 106:48 — Blessed *be* the LORD God of Israel from everlasting to everlasting: and let all the people say, Amen. Praise ye the LORD.

Jer 28:6 — Even the prophet Jeremiah said, Amen: the LORD do so: the LORD perform thy words which thou hast prophesied, to bring again the vessels of the LORD's house, and all that is carried away captive, from Babylon into this place.

Mt 6:13 — And lead us not into temptation, but deliver us from evil: For thine is the kingdom, and the power, and the glory, for ever. Amen.

1Co 14:16 — Else when thou shalt bless with the spirit, how shall he that occupieth the room of the unlearned say Amen at thy giving of thanks, seeing he understandeth not what thou sayest?

Rev 5:14 — And the four beasts said, Amen. And the four *and* twenty elders fell down and worshipped him that liveth for ever and ever.

Rev 19:4 — And the four and twenty elders and the four beasts fell down and worshipped God that sat on the throne, saying, Amen; Alleluia.

• A title of Christ.

Rev 3:14 — And unto the angel of the church of the Laodiceans write; These things saith the Amen, the faithful and true witness, the beginning of the creation of God;

AMENS

Rev 22:1–21

Dt 27:15 — Cursed *be* the man that maketh *any* graven or molten image, an abomination unto the LORD, the work of the hands of the craftsman, and putteth *it* in *a* secret *place*. And all the people shall answer and say, Amen.

Ne 5:13 — Also I shook my lap, and said, So God shake out every man from his house, and from his labour, that performeth not this promise, even thus be he shaken out, and emptied. And all the congregation said, Amen, and praised the LORD. And the people did according to this promise.

2Co 1:20 — For all the promises of God in him *are* yea, and in him Amen, unto the glory of God by us.

AMETHYST • A precious stone.

Ex 28:19 — And the third row a ligure, an agate, and an amethyst.

Ex 39:12 — And the third row, a ligure, an agate, and an amethyst.

Rev 21:20 — The fifth, sardonyx; the sixth, sardius; the seventh, chrysolite; the eighth, beryl; the ninth, a topaz; the tenth, a chrysoprasus; the eleventh, a jacinth; the twelfth, an amethyst.

AMI

• Ancestor of one of the families of the Nethinim.

✦See: Amon.

AMINADAB ✦See: Amminadab

AMMAH • A mountain.

2Sa 2:24 — Joab also and Abishai pursued after Abner: and the sun went down when they were come to the hill of Ammah, that *lieth* before Giah by the way of the wilderness of Gibeon.

AMMI • A figurative name given to Israel.

Hos 2:1 — Say ye unto your brethren, Ammi; and to your sisters, Ru-hamah.

AMMIEL

• One of the twelve spies.

Nu 13:12 — Of the tribe of Dan, Ammiel the son of Gemalli.

• Father of Machir.

2Sa 9:4–5

2Sa 17:27 — And it came to pass, when David was come to Mahanaim, that Shobi the son of Nahash of Rabbah of the children of Ammon, and Machir the son of Ammiel of Lo-debar, and Barzillai the Gileadite of Rogelim,

• Father of Bath-sheba.

1Ch 3:5 — And these were born unto him in Jerusalem; Shimea, and Shobab, and Nathan, and Solomon, four, of Bath-shua the daughter of Ammiel:

• Called also Eliam.

2Sa 11:3 — And David sent and enquired after the woman. And *one* said, *Is* not this Bath-sheba, the daughter of Eliam, the wife of Uriah the Hittite?

• Son of Obed-edom.

1Ch 26:5 — Ammiel the sixth, Issachar the seventh, Peulthai the eighth: for God blessed him.

AMMIHUD

• Son of Laadan.

1Ch 7:26 — Laadan his son, Ammihud his son, Elishama his son,

• Father of Elishama.

Nu 1:10 — Of the children of Joseph: of Ephraim; Elishama the son of Ammihud: of Manasseh; Gamaliel the son of Pedahzur.

Nu 2:18 — On the west side *shall be* the standard of the camp of Ephraim according to their armies: and the captain of the sons of Ephraim *shall be* Elishama the son of Ammihud.

• Father of Shemuel.

Nu 34:20 — And of the tribe of the children of Simeon, Shemuel the son of Ammihud.

• Father of Pedahel.

Nu 34:28 — And the prince of the tribe of the children of Naphtali, Pedahel the son of Ammihud.

• Father of the king of Gesher.

2Sa 13:37 — But Absalom fled, and went to Talmai, the son of Ammihud, king of Geshur. And *David* mourned for his son every day.

• **Son of Omri.**
1Ch 9:4 — Uthai the son of Ammihud, the son of Omri, the son of Imri, the son of Bani, of the children of Pharez the son of Judah.

AMMIHUR ✦See: Ammihud

AMMINADAB

• **Father-in-law of Aaron.**
Ex 6:23 — And Aaron took him Elisheba, daughter of Amminadab, sister of Naashon, to wife; and she bare him Nadab, and Abihu, Eleazar, and Ithamar.

• **Father of Nashon.**
Nu 1:7 — Of Judah; Nahshon the son of Amminadab.
Nu 2:3 — And on the east side toward the rising of the sun shall they of the standard of the camp of Judah pitch throughout their armies: and Nahshon the son of Amminadab *shall be* captain of the children of Judah.

• **Lineage of.**
Ru 4:18–20
1Ch 2:10 — And Ram begat Amminadab; and Amminadab begat Nahshon, prince of the children of Judah;
Mt 1:4 — And Aram begat Aminadab; and Aminadab begat Naasson; and Naasson begat Salmon;
Lk 3:33 — Which was *the son* of Aminadab, which was *the son* of Aram, which was *the son* of Esrom, which was *the son* of Phares, which was *the son* of Juda,

• **A son of Kohath.**
1Ch 6:22 — The sons of Kohath; Amminadab his son, Korah his son, Assir his son,

• **A son of Uzziel.**
1Ch 15:10–11

AMMINADIB ✦See: Amminadab

AMMISHADDAI • Father of Ahiezer.
Nu 1:12 — Of Dan; Ahiezer the son of Ammishaddai.

AMMITTAI • Father of Jonah.
2Ki 14:25 — He restored the coast of Israel from the entering of Hamath unto the sea of the plain, according to the word of the LORD God of Israel, which he spake by the hand of his servant Jonah, the son of Amittai, the prophet, which *was* of Gath-hepher.
Jnh 1:1 — Now the word of the LORD came unto Jonah the son of Amittai, saying,

AMMIZABAD • Son of Benaiah.
1Ch 27:6 — This *is that* Benaiah, *who was* mighty *among* the thirty, and above the thirty: and in his course *was* Ammizabad his son.

AMMON ✦See: Ben-Ammi

AMMONITES

• **Descendants of Ben-ammi. One of the sons of Lot.**
Ge 19:38 — And the younger, she also bare a son, and called his name Benammi: the same *is* the father of the children of Ammon unto this day.

• **Character of.**
Jgs 10:6 — And the children of Israel did evil again in the sight of the LORD, and served Baalim, and Ashtaroth, and the gods of Syria, and the gods of Zidon, and the gods of Moab, and the gods of the children of Ammon, and the gods of the Philistines, and forsook the LORD, and served not him.
2Ki 23:13 — And the high places that *were* before Jerusalem, which *were* on the right hand of the mount of corruption, which Solomon the king of Israel had builded for Ashtoreth the abomination of the Zidonians, and for Chemosh the abomination of the Moabites, and for Milcom the abomination of the children of Ammon, did the king defile.
2Ch 20:25 — And when Jehoshaphat and his people came to take away the spoil of them, they found among them in abundance both riches with the dead bodies, and precious jewels, which they stripped off for themselves, more than they could carry away: and they were three days in gathering of the spoil, it was so much.
Jer 27:3 — And send them to the king of Edom, and to the king of Moab, and to the king of the Ammonites, and to the king of Tyrus, and to the king of Zidon, by the hand of the messengers which come to Jerusalem unto Zedekiah king of Judah;
Jer 27:9 — Therefore hearken not ye to your prophets, nor to your diviners, nor to your dreamers, nor to your enchanters, nor to your sorcerers, which speak unto you, saying, Ye shall not serve the king of Babylon:
Eze 25:3 — And say unto the Ammonites, Hear the word of the Lord GOD; Thus saith the Lord GOD; Because thou saidst, Aha, against my sanctuary, when it was profaned; and against the land of Israel, when it was desolate; and against the house of Judah, when they went into captivity;
Eze 25:6 — For thus saith the Lord GOD; Because thou hast clapped *thine* hands, and stamped with the feet, and rejoiced in heart with all thy despite against the land of Israel;
Am 1:13 — Thus saith the LORD; For three transgressions of the children of Ammon, and for four, I will not turn away *the punishment* thereof; because they have ripped up the women with child of Gilead, that they might enlarge their border:
Zep 2:10 — This shall they have for their pride, because they have reproached and magnified *themselves* against the people of the LORD of hosts.

• **Territory of.**
Nu 21:24 — And Israel smote him with the edge of the sword, and possessed his land from Arnon unto Jabbok, even unto the children of Ammon: for the border of the children of Ammon *was* strong.
Dt 2:19 — And *when* thou comest nigh over against the children of Ammon, distress them not, nor meddle with them: for I will not give thee of the land of the children of Ammon *any* possession; because I have given it unto the children of Lot *for* a possession.
Jos 12:2 — Sihon king of the Amorites, who dwelt in Heshbon, *and* ruled from Aroer, which *is* upon the bank of the river Arnon, and from the middle of the

river, and from half Gilead, even unto the river Jabbok, *which is* the border of the children of Ammon;

Jos 13:10 — And all the cities of Sihon king of the Amorites, which reigned in Heshbon, unto the border of the children of Ammon;

Jos 13:25 — And their coast was Jazer, and all the cities of Gilead, and half the land of the children of Ammon, unto Aroer that *is* before Rabbah;

Jgs 11:13 — And the king of the children of Ammon answered unto the messengers of Jephthah, Because Israel took away my land, when they came up out of Egypt, from Arnon even unto Jabbok, and unto Jordan: now therefore restore those *lands* again peaceably.

• Israelites forbidden to disturb.

Dt 2:19 — And *when* thou comest nigh over against the children of Ammon, distress them not, nor meddle with them: for I will not give thee of the land of the children of Ammon *any* possession; because I have given it unto the children of Lot *for* a possession.

Dt 2:37 — Only unto the land of the children of Ammon thou camest not, nor unto any place of the river Jabbok, *nor* unto the cities in the mountains, nor unto whatsoever the LORD our God forbad us.

• Excluded from the congregation of Israel.

Dt 23:3–6

• Confederate with Moabites and Amalekites against Israel.

Jgs 3:12–13

• Defeated by the Israelites.

Jgs 10:7–18; 11:32–33; 12:1–3; 1Sa 11:1–15; 2Sa 10:1–11:1; 12:26–31; 1Ch 20:1–3; 2Ch 20:1–37; 26:7–8

2Sa 8:12 — Of Syria, and of Moab, and of the children of Ammon, and of the Philistines, and of Amalek, and of the spoil of Hadadezer, son of Rehob, king of Zobah.

2Sa 17:27 — And it came to pass, when David was come to Mahanaim, that Shobi the son of Nahash of Rabbah of the children of Ammon, and Machir the son of Ammiel of Lo-debar, and Barzillai the Gileadite of Rogelim,

1Ch 18:11 — Them also king David dedicated unto the LORD, with the silver and the gold that he brought from all *these* nations; from Edom, and from Moab, and from the children of Ammon, and from the Philistines, and from Amalek.

2Ch 27:5 — He fought also with the king of the Ammonites, and prevailed against them. And the children of Ammon gave him the same year an hundred talents of silver, and ten thousand measures of wheat, and ten thousand of barley. So much did the children of Ammon pay unto him, both the second year, and the third.

• Conspire against the Jews.

Ne 4:7–8

• Solomon takes wives from.

1Ki 11:1 — But king Solomon loved many strange women, together with the daughter of Pharaoh, women of the Moabites, Ammonites, Edomites, Zidonians, *and* Hittites;

2Ch 12:13 — So king Rehoboam strengthened himself in Jerusalem, and reigned: for Rehoboam *was* one and forty years old when he began to reign, and he reigned seventeen years in Jerusalem, the city which the LORD had chosen out of all the tribes of Israel, to put his name there. And his mother's name *was* Naamah an Ammonitess.

Ne 13:26 — Did not Solomon king of Israel sin by these things? yet among many nations was there no king like him, who was beloved of his God, and God made him king over all Israel: nevertheless even him did outlandish women cause to sin.

• Jews intermarry with.

Ezr 10:10–44

Ezr 9:12 — Now therefore give not your daughters unto their sons, neither take their daughters unto your sons, nor seek their peace or their wealth for ever: that ye may be strong, and eat the good of the land, and leave *it* for an inheritance to your children for ever.

Ne 13:23 — In those days also saw I Jews *that* had married wives of Ashdod, of Ammon, *and* of Moab:

• Kings of Baalis.

Jer 40:14 — And said unto him, Dost thou certainly know that Baalis the king of the Ammonites hath sent Ishmael the son of Nethaniah to slay thee? But Gedaliah the son of Ahikam believed them not.

Jer 41:10 — Then Ishmael carried away captive all the residue of the people that *were* in Mizpah, *even* the king's daughters, and all the people that remained in Mizpah, whom Nebuzar-adan the captain of the guard had committed to Gedaliah the son of Ahikam: and Ishmael the son of Nethaniah carried them away captive, and departed to go over to the Ammonites.

• Kings of Hanun.

2Sa 10:1–19; 1Ch 19:1–19

• Kings of Nahash.

1Sa 11:1–15; 2Sa 10:1–2; 1Ch 19:1–2

• Idols of Milcom.

2Ki 23:13 — And the high places that *were* before Jerusalem, which *were* on the right hand of the mount of corruption, which Solomon the king of Israel had builded for Ashtoreth the abomination of the Zidonians, and for Chemosh the abomination of the Moabites, and for Milcom the abomination of the children of Ammon, did the king defile.

• Idols of Molech.

→See: Molech

• Prophecies concerning.

Jer 9:25–26; 25:15–21; 27:1–11; 49:1–6; Eze 21:28–32; 25:1–11; Am 1:13–15; Zep 2:8–11

Isa 11:14 — But they shall fly upon the shoulders of the Philistines toward the west; they shall spoil them of the east together: they shall lay their hand upon Edom and Moab; and the children of Ammon shall obey them.

Eze 21:20 — Appoint a way, that the sword may come to Rabbath of the Ammonites, and to Judah in Jerusalem the defenced.

Da 11:41 — He shall enter also into the glorious land, and many *countries* shall be overthrown: but these shall escape out of his hand, *even* Edom, and Moab, and the chief of the children of Ammon.

AMNESTY

• For political offenses to Shimei.

2Sa 19:16–23

• For political offenses to Amasa.

2Sa 17:25 — And Absalom made Amasa captain of the host instead of Joab: which Amasa was a man's son, whose name *was* Ithra an Israelite, that went in to Abigail the daughter of Nahash, sister to Zeruiah Joab's mother.

2Sa 19:13 — And say ye to Amasa, *Art* thou not of my bone, and of my flesh? God do so to me, and more also, if thou be not captain of the host before me continually in the room of Joab.

AMNON

• Son of David.

2Sa 3:2 — And unto David were sons born in Hebron: and his firstborn was Amnon, of Ahinoam the Jezreelitess;

1Ch 3:1 — Now these were the sons of David, which were born unto him in Hebron; the firstborn Amnon, of Ahinoam the Jezreelitess; the second Daniel, of Abigail the Carmelitess:

• Incest of, and death.

2Sa 13:1–39

• Son of Shimon.

1Ch 4:20 — And the sons of Shimon *were,* Amnon, and Rinnah, Ben-hanan, and Tilon. And the sons of Ishi *were,* Zoheth, and Ben-zoheth.

AMOK • A priest.

Ne 12:7 — Sallu, Amok, Hilkiah, Jedaiah. These *were* the chief of the priests and of their brethren in the days of Jeshua.

Ne 12:20 — Of Sallai, Kallai; of Amok, Eber;

AMON

• Governor of the city of Samaria.

1Ki 22:26 — And the king of Israel said, Take Micaiah, and carry him back unto Amon the governor of the city, and to Joash the king's son;

2Ch 18:25 — Then the king of Israel said, Take ye Micaiah, and carry him back to Amon the governor of the city, and to Joash the king's son;

• King of Judah.

2Ki 21:18–26; 2Ch 33:21–25

Zep 1:1 — The word of the LORD which came unto Zephaniah the son of Cushi, the son of Gedaliah, the son of Amariah, the son of Hizkiah, in the days of Josiah the son of Amon, king of Judah.

Mt 1:10 — And Ezekias begat Manasses; and Manasses begat Amon; and Amon begat Josias;

• Ancestor of one of the families of the Nethinim.

Ne 7:59 — The children of Shephatiah, the children of Hattil, the children of Pochereth of Zebaim, the children of Amon.

• Called Ami.

Ezr 2:57 — The children of Shephatiah, the children of Hattil, the children of Pochereth of Zebaim, the children of Ami.

AMORITES

• Descendants of Canaan.

Ge 10:15–16; 1Ch 1:13–14

• Were giants.

Am 2:9 — Yet destroyed I the Amorite before them, whose height *was* like the height of the cedars, and he *was* strong as the oaks; yet I destroyed his fruit from above, and his roots from beneath.

• Smitten by Chedorlaomer and rescued by Abraham.

Ge 14:1–24

• Territory of.

Dt 3:8–9; Jos 12:2–3; Jgs 1:35–36

Ge 14:7 — And they returned, and came to En-mishpat, which *is* Kadesh, and smote all the country of the Amalekites, and also the Amorites that dwelt in Hazezon-tamar.

Nu 13:29 — The Amalekites dwell in the land of the south: and the Hittites, and the Jebusites, and the Amorites, dwell in the mountains: and the Canaanites dwell by the sea, and by the coast of Jordan.

Nu 21:13 — From thence they removed, and pitched on the other side of Arnon, which *is* in the wilderness that cometh out of the coasts of the Amorites: for Arnon *is* the border of Moab, between Moab and the Amorites.

Dt 1:4 — After he had slain Sihon the king of the Amorites, which dwelt in Heshbon, and Og the king of Bashan, which dwelt at Astaroth in Edrei:

Dt 1:7 — Turn you, and take your journey, and go to the mount of the Amorites, and unto all *the places* nigh thereunto, in the plain, in the hills, and in the vale, and in the south, and by the sea side, to the land of the Canaanites, and unto Lebanon, unto the great river, the river Euphrates.

Dt 1:19 — And when we departed from Horeb, we went through all that great and terrible wilderness, which ye saw by the way of the mountain of the Amorites, as the LORD our God commanded us; and we came to Kadesh-barnea.

Jos 5:1 — And it came to pass, when all the kings of the Amorites, which *were* on the side of Jordan westward, and all the kings of the Canaanites, which *were* by the sea, heard that the LORD had dried up the waters of Jordan from before the children of Israel, until we were passed over, that their heart melted, neither was there spirit in them any more, because of the children of Israel.

Jos 10:5 — Therefore the five kings of the Amorites, the king of Jerusalem, the king of Hebron, the king of Jarmuth, the king of Lachish, the king of Eglon, gathered themselves together, and went up, they and all their hosts, and encamped before Gibeon, and made war against it.

Jgs 11:22 — And they possessed all the coasts of the Amorites, from Arnon even unto Jabbok, and from the wilderness even unto Jordan.

• Given to descendants of Abraham.

Dt 2:26–36

Ge 15:21 — And the Amorites, and the Canaanites, and the Girgashites, and the Jebusites.

Ge 48:22 — Moreover I have given to thee one portion above thy brethren, which I took out of the hand of the Amorite with my sword and with my bow.

Dt 1:20 — And I said unto you, Ye are come unto the mountain of the Amorites, which the LORD our God doth give unto us.

Dt 7:1 — When the LORD thy God shall bring thee into the land whither thou goest to possess it, and hath cast out many nations before thee, the Hittites, and the Girgashites, and the Amorites, and the Canaanites, and the Perizzites, and the Hivites, and the Jebusites, seven nations greater and mightier than thou;

Jos 3:10 — And Joshua said, Hereby ye shall know that the living God *is* among you, and *that* he will without fail drive out from before you the Canaanites, and the Hittites, and the Hivites, and the Perizzites, and the Girgashites, and the Amorites, and the Jebusites.

Jgs 11:23 — So now the LORD God of Israel hath dispossessed the Amorites from before his people Israel, and shouldest thou possess it?

Am 2:10 — Also I brought you up from the land of Egypt, and led you forty years through the wilderness, to possess the land of the Amorite.

• Allotted to Reuben, Gad, and Manasseh.

Nu 32:33–42; Jos 13:15–21

• Conquest of.

Nu 21:21–30; Jgs 1:34–36

Jos 10:11 — And it came to pass, as they fled from before Israel, *and* were in the going down to Bethhoron, that the LORD cast down great stones from heaven upon them unto Azekah, and they died: *they were* more which died with hailstones than they whom the children of Israel slew with the sword.

• Chiefs of.

Jos 13:21 — And all the cities of the plain, and all the kingdom of Sihon king of the Amorites, which reigned in Heshbon, whom Moses smote with the princes of Midian, Evi, and Rekem, and Zur, and Hur, and Reba, *which were* dukes of Sihon, dwelling in the country.

• Wickedness of.

Ge 15:16 — But in the fourth generation they shall come hither again: for the iniquity of the Amorites *is* not yet full.

2Ki 21:11 — Because Manasseh king of Judah hath done these abominations, *and* hath done wickedly above all that the Amorites did, which *were* before him, and hath made Judah also to sin with his idols:

Ezr 9:1 — Now when these things were done, the princes came to me, saying, The people of Israel, and the priests, and the Levites, have not separated themselves from the people of the lands, *doing* according to their abominations, *even* of the Canaanites, the Hittites, the Perizzites, the Jebusites, the Ammonites, the Moabites, the Egyptians, and the Amorites.

• Idolatry of.

Jgs 6:10 — And I said unto you, I *am* the LORD your God; fear not the gods of the Amorites, in whose land ye dwell: but ye have not obeyed my voice.

1Ki 21:26 — And he did very abominably in following idols, according to all *things* as did the Amorites, whom the LORD cast out before the children of Israel.

• Judgments denounced against.

Ex 34:10–11; Dt 20:17–18

Ex 23:24 — Thou shalt not bow down to their gods, nor serve them, nor do after their works: but thou shalt utterly overthrow them, and quite break down their images.

Ex 33:2 — And I will send an angel before thee; and I will drive out the Canaanite, the Amorite, and the Hittite, and the Perizzite, the Hivite, and the Jebusite:

• Hornets sent among.

Jos 24:12 — And I sent the hornet before you, which drave them out from before you, *even* the two kings of the Amorites; *but* not with thy sword, nor with thy bow.

• Not exterminated.

Jgs 1:34–36; 3:1–3, 5–8; 1Ki 9:20–21

1Sa 7:14 — And the cities which the Philistines had taken from Israel were restored to Israel, from Ekron even unto Gath; and the coasts thereof did Israel deliver out of the hands of the Philistines. And there was peace between Israel and the Amorites.

2Sa 21:2 — And the king called the Gibeonites, and said unto them; (now the Gibeonites *were* not of the children of Israel, but of the remnant of the Amorites; and the children of Israel had sworn unto them: and Saul sought to slay them in his zeal to the children of Israel and Judah.)

2Ch 8:7 — *As for* all the people *that were* left of the Hittites, and the Amorites, and the Perizzites, and the Hivites, and the Jebusites, which *were* not of Israel,

• Intermarry with Jews.

Ezr 9:1–2; 10:18–44

• Kings of.

Jos 10:3–26

AMOS

• A prophet.

Am 1:1 — The words of Amos, who was among the herdmen of Tekoa, which he saw concerning Israel in the days of Uzziah king of Judah, and in the days of Jeroboam the son of Joash king of Israel, two years before the earthquake.

• Forbidden to prophesy in Israel.

Am 7:10–17

• Vision of.

Am 8:2 — And he said, Amos, what seest thou? And I said, A basket of summer fruit. Then said the LORD unto me, The end is come upon my people of Israel; I will not again pass by them any more.

AMOZ • Father of Isaiah.

2Ki 19:2 — And he sent Eliakim, which *was* over the household, and Shebna the scribe, and the elders of the priests, covered with sackcloth, to Isaiah the prophet the son of Amoz.

2Ki 19:20 — Then Isaiah the son of Amoz sent to Hezekiah, saying, Thus saith the LORD God of Israel, *That* which thou hast prayed to me against Sennacherib king of Assyria I have heard.

2Ki 20:1 — In those days was Hezekiah sick unto death. And the prophet Isaiah the son of Amoz came to him, and said unto him, Thus saith the LORD, Set thine house in order; for thou shalt die, and not live.

Isa 1:1 — The vision of Isaiah the son of Amoz, which he saw concerning Judah and Jerusalem in the days of Uzziah, Jotham, Ahaz, *and* Hezekiah, kings of Judah.

Isa 13:1 — The burden of Babylon, which Isaiah the son of Amoz did see.

AMPHIPOLIS • A city of Macedonia.

Ac 17:1 — Now when they had passed through Amphipolis and Apollonia, they came to Thessalonica, where was a synagogue of the Jews:

AMPLIAS • A disciple Paul sends greeting to.

Ro 16:8 — Greet Amplias my beloved in the Lord.

AMRAM

• Father of Moses.

Nu 26:58–59; 1Ch 23:12–13

Ex 6:18 — And the sons of Kohath; Amram, and Izhar, and Hebron, and Uzziel: and the years of the life of Kohath *were* an hundred thirty and three years.

Ex 6:20 — And Amram took him Jochebed his father's sister to wife; and she bare him Aaron and Moses: and the years of the life of Amram *were* an hundred and thirty and seven years.

1Ch 6:3 — And the children of Amram; Aaron, and Moses, and Miriam. The sons also of Aaron; Nadab, and Abihu, Eleazar, and Ithamar.

1Ch 6:18 — And the sons of Kohath *were,* Amram, and Izhar, and Hebron, and Uzziel.

• Head of one of the branches of Levites.

Nu 3:19 — And the sons of Kohath by their families; Amram, and Izehar, Hebron, and Uzziel.

Nu 3:27 — And of Kohath *was* the family of the Amramites, and the family of the Izeharites, and the family of the Hebronites, and the family of the Uzzielites: these *are* the families of the Kohathites.

1Ch 26:23 — Of the Amramites, *and* the Izharites, the Hebronites, *and* the Uzzielites:

• Age of, at death.

Ex 6:20 — And Amram took him Jochebed his father's sister to wife; and she bare him Aaron and Moses: and the years of the life of Amram *were* an hundred and thirty and seven years.

• Son of Bani.

Ezr 10:34 — Of the sons of Bani; Maadai, Amram, and Uel,

• Son of Dishon.

1Ch 1:41 — The sons of Anah; Dishon. And the sons of Dishon; Amram, and Eshban, and Ithran, and Cheran.

AMRAPHEL • King of Shinar.

Ge 14:1 — And it came to pass in the days of Amraphel king of Shinar, Arioch king of Ellasar, Chedorlaomer king of Elam, and Tidal king of nations;

Ge 14:9 — With Chedorlaomer the king of Elam, and with Tidal king of nations, and Amraphel king of Shinar, and Arioch king of Ellasar; four kings with five.

AMUSEMENTS AND WORLDLY PLEASURES

• Belong to the works of the flesh.

Gal 5:19 — Now the works of the flesh are manifest, which are *these;* Adultery, fornication, uncleanness, lasciviousness,

Gal 5:21 — Envyings, murders, drunkenness, revellings, and such like: of the which I tell you before, as I have also told *you* in time past, that they which do such things shall not inherit the kingdom of God.

• Are transitory.

Job 21:12–13

Heb 11:25 — Choosing rather to suffer affliction with the people of God, than to enjoy the pleasures of sin for a season;

• Vain.

Ecc 2:11 — Then I looked on all the works that my hands had wrought, and on the labour that I had laboured to do: and, behold, all *was* vanity and vexation of spirit, and *there was* no profit under the sun.

• Choke the word of God in the heart.

Lk 8:14 — And that which fell among thorns are they, which, when they have heard, go forth, and are choked with cares and riches and pleasures of *this* life, and bring no fruit to perfection.

• Formed a part of idolatrous worship.

Jgs 16:23–25

Ex 32:4 — And he received *them* at their hand, and fashioned it with a graving tool, after he had made it a molten calf: and they said, These *be* thy gods, O Israel, which brought thee up out of the land of Egypt.

Ex 32:6 — And they rose up early on the morrow, and offered burnt offerings, and brought peace offerings; and the people sat down to eat and to drink, and rose up to play.

Ex 32:19 — And it came to pass, as soon as he came nigh unto the camp, that he saw the calf, and the dancing: and Moses' anger waxed hot, and he cast the tables out of his hands, and brake them beneath the mount.

1Co 10:7 — Neither be ye idolaters, as *were* some of them; as it is written, The people sat down to eat and drink, and rose up to play.

• Lead to rejection of God.

Job 21:12–15

• Lead to poverty.

Pr 21:17 — He that loveth pleasure *shall be* a poor man: he that loveth wine and oil shall not be rich.

• Disregard of the judgments and works of God.

Am 6:1–6

Isa 5:12 — And the harp, and the viol, the tabret, and pipe, and wine, are in their feasts: but they regard not the work of the LORD, neither consider the operation of his hands.

• Terminate in sorrow.

Pr 14:13 — Even in laughter the heart is sorrowful; and the end of that mirth *is* heaviness.

• Lead to greater evil.

Mt 14:6–8

Job 1:5 — And it was so, when the days of *their* feasting were gone about, that Job sent and sanctified them, and rose up early in the morning, and offered burnt offerings *according* to the number of them all: for Job said, It may be that my sons have sinned, and cursed God in their hearts. Thus did Job continually.

• The wicked seek for happiness in.

Ecc 2:1 — I said in mine heart, Go to now, I will prove thee with mirth, therefore enjoy pleasure: and, behold, this also *is* vanity.

Ecc 2:8 — I gathered me also silver and gold, and the peculiar treasure of kings and of the provinces: I gat me men singers and women singers, and the delights of the sons of men, *as* musical instruments, and that of all sorts.

• Indulgence in, a proof of folly.

Ecc 7:4 — The heart of the wise *is* in the house of mourning; but the heart of fools *is* in the house of mirth.

• A characteristic of the wicked.

Isa 47:8 — Therefore hear now this, *thou that art* given to pleasures, that dwellest carelessly, that sayest in thine heart, I *am*, and none else beside me; I shall not sit *as* a widow, neither shall I know the loss of children:

Eph 4:17 — This I say therefore, and testify in the Lord, that ye henceforth walk not as other Gentiles walk, in the vanity of their mind,

Eph 4:19 — Who being past feeling have given themselves over unto lasciviousness, to work all uncleanness with greediness.

2Ti 3:4 — Traitors, heady, highminded, lovers of pleasures more than lovers of God;

Tit 3:3 — For we ourselves also were sometimes foolish, disobedient, deceived, serving divers lusts and pleasures, living in malice and envy, hateful, *and* hating one another.

1Pe 4:3 — For the time past of *our* life may suffice us to have wrought the will of the Gentiles, when we walked in lasciviousness, lusts, excess of wine, revellings, banquetings, and abominable idolatries:

• A proof of spiritual death.

1Ti 5:6 — But she that liveth in pleasure is dead while she liveth.

• An abuse of riches.

Jas 5:1 — Go to now, *ye* rich men, weep and howl for your miseries that shall come upon *you.*

Jas 5:5 — Ye have lived in pleasure on the earth, and been wanton; ye have nourished your hearts, as in a day of slaughter.

• Wisdom of abstaining from.

Ecc 7:2–3

• Shunned by the primitive saints.

1Pe 4:3 — For the time past of *our* life may suffice us to have wrought the will of the Gentiles, when we walked in lasciviousness, lusts, excess of wine, revellings, banquetings, and abominable idolatries:

• Abstinence from, seems strange to the wicked.

1Pe 4:4 — Wherein they think it strange that ye run not with *them* to the same excess of riot, speaking evil of *you:*

• Denounced by God.

Isa 5:11–12

• Exclude from the kingdom of God.

Gal 5:21 — Envyings, murders, drunkenness, revellings, and such like: of the which I tell you before, as I have also told *you* in time past, that they which do such things shall not inherit the kingdom of God.

• Punishment of.

Ecc 11:9 — Rejoice, O young man, in thy youth; and let thy heart cheer thee in the days of thy youth, and walk in the ways of thine heart, and in the sight of thine eyes: but know thou, that for all these *things* God will bring thee into judgment.

2Pe 2:13 — And shall receive the reward of unrighteousness, *as* they that count it pleasure to riot in the daytime. Spots *they are* and blemishes, sporting themselves with their own deceivings while they feast with you;

• Renunciation of, exemplified by Moses.

Heb 11:25 — Choosing rather to suffer affliction with the people of God, than to enjoy the pleasures of sin for a season;

See: Dancing

See: Games

See: Pleasure; worldly

See: Worldliness

AMZI

• A Levite.

1Ch 6:46 — The son of Amzi, the son of Bani, the son of Shamer,

• A priest.

Ne 11:12 — And their brethren that did the work of the house *were* eight hundred twenty and two: and Adaiah the son of Jeroham, the son of Pelaliah, the son of Amzi, the son of Zechariah, the son of Pashur, the son of Malchiah,

ANAB • A city of Canaan.

Jos 11:21 — And at that time came Joshua, and cut off the Anakims from the mountains, from Hebron, from Debir, from Anab, and from all the mountains of Judah, and from all the mountains of Israel: Joshua destroyed them utterly with their cities.

Jos 15:50 — And Anab, and Eshtemoh, and Anim,

ANAH

• Son of Seir.

Ge 36:20 — These *are* the sons of Seir the Horite, who inhabited the land; Lotan, and Shobal, and Zibeon, and Anah,

Ge 36:24 — And these *are* the children of Zibeon; both Ajah, and Anah: this *was that* Anah that found the mules in the wilderness, as he fed the asses of Zibeon his father.

Ge 36:29 — These *are* the dukes *that came* of the Horites; duke Lotan, duke Shobal, duke Zibeon, duke Anah,

1Ch 1:38 — And the sons of Seir; Lotan, and Shobal, and Zibeon, and Anah, and Dishon, and Ezar, and Dishan.

• Father-in-law or mother-in-law of Esau.

Ge 36:2 — Esau took his wives of the daughters of Canaan; Adah the daughter of Elon the Hittite, and Aholibamah the daughter of Anah the daughter of Zibeon the Hivite;

Ge 36:14 — And these were the sons of Aholibamah, the daughter of Anah the daughter of Zibeon, Esau's wife: and she bare to Esau Jeush, and Jaalam, and Korah.

Ge 36:24 — And these *are* the children of Zibeon; both Ajah, and Anah: this *was that* Anah that found the mules in the wilderness, as he fed the asses of Zibeon his father.

• Copyist error calls him daughter instead of son of Zibeon the Hivite.

• Called also Beeri.

Ge 26:34 — And Esau was forty years old when he took to wife Judith the daughter of Beeri the Hittite, and Bashemath the daughter of Elon the Hittite:

ANAHARATH • City on the border of Issachar.

Jos 19:19 — And Haphraim, and Shihon, and Anaharath,

ANAIAH • A priest, probably, who stood by Ezra while reading the law.

Ne 8:4 — And Ezra the scribe stood upon a pulpit of wood, which they had made for the purpose; and beside him stood Mattithiah, and Shema, and Anaiah, and Urijah, and Hilkiah, and Maaseiah, on his right hand; and on his left hand, Pedaiah, and Mishael, and Malchiah, and Hashum, and Hashbadana, Zechariah, *and* Meshullam.

Ne 10:22 — Pelatiah, Hanan, Anaiah,

ANAK • Father of three giants.

Jos 15:13–14

Jos 21:11 — And they gave them the city of Arba the father of Anak, which *city is* Hebron, in the hill *country* of Judah, with the suburbs thereof round about it.

ANAKIM

• A race of giants.

Nu 13:28–33

Dt 1:28 — Whither shall we go up? our brethren have discouraged our heart, saying, The people *is* greater and taller than we; the cities *are* great and walled up to heaven; and moreover we have seen the sons of the Anakims there.

Dt 2:10 — The Emims dwelt therein in times past, a people great, and many, and tall, as the Anakims;

Dt 9:2 — A people great and tall, the children of the Anakims, whom thou knowest, and *of whom* thou hast heard *say,* Who can stand before the children of Anak!

• Defeated by Joshua.

Jos 11:21–22

• Defeated by Caleb.

Jos 15:13–14

Jos 14:12 — Now therefore give me this mountain, whereof the LORD spake in that day; for thou heardest in that day how the Anakims *were* there, and *that* the cities *were* great *and* fenced: if so be the LORD *will be* with me, then I shall be able to drive them out, as the LORD said.

Jos 14:15 — And the name of Hebron before *was* Kirjath-arba; *which Arba was* a great man among the Anakims. And the land had rest from war.

Jgs 1:20 — And they gave Hebron unto Caleb, as Moses said: and he expelled thence the three sons of Anak.

See: Hebron

ANAMIM • A tribe descended from Mizraim.

Ge 10:13 — And Mizraim begat Ludim, and Anamim, and Lehabim, and Naphtuhim,

1Ch 1:11 — And Mizraim begat Ludim, and Anamim, and Lehabim, and Napthtuhim,

ANAMMELECH • An Assyrian idol.

2Ki 17:31 — And the Avites made Nibhaz and Tartak, and the Sepharvites burnt their children in fire to Adrammelech and Anammelech, the gods of Sepharvaim.

ANAN • A Jew, returned from Babylonian captivity.

Ne 10:26 — And Ahijah, Hanan, Anan,

ANANI • A descendant of David.

1Ch 3:24 — And the sons of Elioenai *were,* Hodaiah, and Eliashib, and Pelaiah, and Akkub, and Johanan, and Dalaiah, and Anani, seven.

ANANIAH

• Son of Maaseiah.

Ne 3:23 — After him repaired Benjamin and Hashub over against their house. After him repaired Azariah the son of Maaseiah the son of Ananiah by his house.

Ne 8:4 — And Ezra the scribe stood upon a pulpit of wood, which they had made for the purpose; and beside him stood Mattithiah, and Shema, and Anaiah, and Urijah, and Hilkiah, and Maaseiah, on his right hand; and on his left hand, Pedaiah, and Mishael, and Malchiah, and Hashum, and Hashbadana, Zechariah, *and* Meshullam.

• Town of Benjamin.

Ne 11:32 — *And* at Anathoth, Nob, Ananiah,

ANANIAS

• High priest, before whom Paul was tried.

Ac 23:2–5

Ac 24:1 — And after five days Ananias the high priest descended with the elders, and *with* a certain orator *named* Tertullus, who informed the governor against Paul.

Ac 25:2 — Then the high priest and the chief of the Jews informed him against Paul, and besought him,

• A covetous member of church at Jerusalem. Falsehood and death of.

Ac 5:1–11

• A Christian in Damascus.

Ac 9:10–18; 22:12–16

ANARCHY

Isa 3:5–8; Gal 5:13–14; 2Pe 2:10–19; Jude 1:8–13

ANATH • Father of Shamgar.

Jgs 3:31 — And after him was Shamgar the son of Anath, which slew of the Philistines six hundred men with an ox goad: and he also delivered Israel.

ANATHEMA MARAN-ATHA

1Co 16:22 — If any man love not the Lord Jesus Christ, let him be Anathema Maranatha.

***See: Curse**

ANATHOTH

• A Levitical city in Benjamin.

Jos 21:18 — Anathoth with her suburbs, and Almon with her suburbs; four cities.

1Ch 6:60 — And out of the tribe of Benjamin; Geba with her suburbs, and Alemeth with her suburbs, and Anathoth with her suburbs. All their cities throughout their families *were* thirteen cities.

• Abiathar confined in.

1Ki 2:26 — And unto Abiathar the priest said the king, Get thee to Anathoth, unto thine own fields; for thou *art* worthy of death: but I will not at this time put thee to death, because thou barest the ark of the Lord God before David my father, and because thou hast been afflicted in all wherein my father was afflicted.

• Birthplace of Jeremiah.

Jer 32:7–12

Jer 1:1 — The words of Jeremiah the son of Hilkiah, of the priests that *were* in Anathoth in the land of Benjamin:

• Birthplace of Abiezer.

2Sa 23:27 — Abiezer the Anethothite, Mebunnai the Hushathite,

• Birthplace of Jehu.

1Ch 12:3 — The chief *was* Ahiezer, then Joash, the sons of Shemaah the Gibeathite; and Jeziel, and Pelet, the sons of Azmaveth; and Berachah, and Jehu the Antothite,

• Prophecies against.

Jer 11:21–23

• Inhabitants of, after Babylonian captivity.

Ezr 2:23 — The men of Anathoth, an hundred twenty and eight.

Ne 7:27 — The men of Anathoth, an hundred twenty and eight.

• Son of Becher.

1Ch 7:8 — And the sons of Becher; Zemira, and Joash, and Eliezer, and Elioenai, and Omri, and Jerimoth, and Abiah, and Anathoth, and Alameth. All these *are* the sons of Becher.

• A Jew, who returned from Babylon.

Ne 10:19 — Hariph, Anathoth, Nebai,

ANATOMY, Human.

Job 10:11 — Thou hast clothed me with skin and flesh, and hast fenced me with bones and sinews.

ANCHOR

Ac 27:29–30

• Figurative.

Heb 6:19 — Which *hope* we have as an anchor of the soul, both sure and stedfast, and which entereth into that within the veil;

ANCIENT OF DAYS • An appellation of Jehovah.

Da 7:9 — I beheld till the thrones were cast down, and the Ancient of days did sit, whose garment *was* white as snow, and the hair of his head like the pure wool: his throne *was like* the fiery flame, *and* his wheels *as* burning fire.

Da 7:13 — I saw in the night visions, and, behold, *one* like the Son of man came with the clouds of heaven, and came to the Ancient of days, and they brought him near before him.

Da 7:22 — Until the Ancient of days came, and judgment was given to the saints of the most High; and the time came that the saints possessed the kingdom.

ANDREW

• An apostle.

• A fisherman.

Mt 4:18 — And Jesus, walking by the sea of Galilee, saw two brethren, Simon called Peter, and Andrew his brother, casting a net into the sea: for they were fishers.

- **Of Bethsaida.**

Jn 1:44 — Now Philip was of Bethsaida, the city of Andrew and Peter.

- **A disciple of John.**

Jn 1:40 — One of the two which heard John *speak,* and followed him, was Andrew, Simon Peter's brother.

- **Finds Peter, his brother, and brings him to Jesus.**

Jn 1:40–42

- **Call of.**

Mt 4:18 — And Jesus, walking by the sea of Galilee, saw two brethren, Simon called Peter, and Andrew his brother, casting a net into the sea: for they were fishers.

Mk 1:16 — Now as he walked by the sea of Galilee, he saw Simon and Andrew his brother casting a net into the sea: for they were fishers.

- **His name appears in the list of the apostles.**

Mt 10:2 — Now the names of the twelve apostles are these; The first, Simon, who is called Peter, and Andrew his brother; James *the son* of Zebedee, and John his brother;

Mk 3:18 — And Andrew, and Philip, and Bartholomew, and Matthew, and Thomas, and James the *son* of Alphaeus, and Thaddaeus, and Simon the Canaanite,

Lk 6:14 — Simon, (whom he also named Peter,) and Andrew his brother, James and John, Philip and Bartholomew,

- **Asks the Master privately about the destruction of the temple.**

Mk 13:3–4

- **Tells Jesus of the Greeks who sought to see him.**

Jn 12:20–22

- **Reports the number of loaves at the feeding of the five thousand.**

Jn 6:8 — One of his disciples, Andrew, Simon Peter's brother, saith unto him,

- **Meets with the disciples after the Lord's ascension.**

Ac 1:13 — And when they were come in, they went up into an upper room, where abode both Peter, and James, and John, and Andrew, Philip, and Thomas, Bartholomew, and Matthew, James *the son* of Alphaeus, and Simon Zelotes, and Judas *the brother* of James.

ANDRONICUS • Kinsman of Paul.

Ro 16:7 — Salute Andronicus and Junia, my kinsmen, and my fellowprisoners, who are of note among the apostles, who also were in Christ before me.

ANEM • A Levitical city.

1Ch 6:73 — And Ramoth with her suburbs, and Anem with her suburbs:

ANER

- **A Canaanitish chief.**

Ge 14:13 — And there came one that had escaped, and told Abram the Hebrew; for he dwelt in the plain of Mamre the Amorite, brother of Eshcol, and brother of Aner: and these *were* confederate with Abram.

Ge 14:24 — Save only that which the young men have eaten, and the portion of the men which went with me, Aner, Eshcol, and Mamre; let them take their portion.

- **A Levitical city of Manasseh.**

1Ch 6:70 — And out of the half tribe of Manasseh; Aner with her suburbs, and Bileam with her suburbs, for the family of the remnant of the sons of Kohath.

ANGEL

- **One of the Holy Trinity.**
  - **Trinitarian authorities interpret these as referring to Christ, divine presence.**
    - **Called Angel.**

Ac 7:30 — And when forty years were expired, there appeared to him in the wilderness of mount Sina an angel of the Lord in a flame of fire in a bush.

Ac 7:35 — This Moses whom they refused, saying, Who made thee a ruler and a judge? the same did God send *to be* a ruler and a deliverer by the hand of the angel which appeared to him in the bush.

- **Called Mine Angel.**

Ex 32:34 — Therefore now go, lead the people unto *the place* of which I have spoken unto thee: behold, mine Angel shall go before thee: nevertheless in the day when I visit I will visit their sin upon them.

- **Called Angel of God.**

Ex 14:19 — And the angel of God, which went before the camp of Israel, removed and went behind them; and the pillar of the cloud went from before their face, and stood behind them:

Jgs 13:6 — Then the woman came and told her husband, saying, A man of God came unto me, and his countenance *was* like the countenance of an angel of God, very terrible: but I asked him not whence he *was,* neither told he me his name:

2Sa 14:17 — Then thine handmaid said, The word of my lord the king shall now be comfortable: for as an angel of God, so *is* my lord the king to discern good and bad: therefore the LORD thy God will be with thee.

2Sa 14:20 — To fetch about this form of speech hath thy servant Joab done this thing: and my lord *is* wise, according to the wisdom of an angel of God, to know all *things* that *are* in the earth.

- **Called Angel of the Lord.**

Ex 3:2 — And the angel of the LORD appeared unto him in a flame of fire out of the midst of a bush: and he looked, and, behold, the bush burned with fire, and the bush *was* not consumed.

Jgs 2:1 — And an angel of the LORD came up from Gilgal to Bochim, and said, I made you to go up out of Egypt, and have brought you unto the land which I sware unto your fathers; and I said, I will never break my covenant with you.

- **Called Angel of His Presence.**

Isa 63:9 — In all their affliction he was afflicted, and the angel of his presence saved them: in his love and in his pity he redeemed them; and he bare them, and carried them all the days of old.

- **A celestial spirit.**
- **Called Angel of the Lord.**

Mt 1:20 — But while he thought on these things, behold, the angel of the Lord appeared unto him in a dream, saying, Joseph, thou son of David, fear not to take unto thee Mary thy wife: for that which is conceived in her is of the Holy Ghost.

Mt 1:24 — Then Joseph being raised from sleep did as the angel of the Lord had bidden him, and took unto him his wife:

Mt 2:13 — And when they were departed, behold, the angel of the Lord appeareth to Joseph in a dream, saying, Arise, and take the young child and his mother, and flee into Egypt, and be thou there until I bring thee word: for Herod will seek the young child to destroy him.

Mt 2:19 — But when Herod was dead, behold, an angel of the Lord appeareth in a dream to Joseph in Egypt,

Mt 28:2 — And, behold, there was a great earthquake: for the angel of the Lord descended from heaven, and came and rolled back the stone from the door, and sat upon it.

Lk 1:11 — And there appeared unto him an angel of the Lord standing on the right side of the altar of incense.

Ac 5:19 — But the angel of the Lord by night opened the prison doors, and brought them forth, and said,

Ac 8:26 — And the angel of the Lord spake unto Philip, saying, Arise, and go toward the south unto the way that goeth down from Jerusalem unto Gaza, which is desert.

Ac 12:7 — And, behold, the angel of the Lord came upon *him,* and a light shined in the prison: and he smote Peter on the side, and raised him up, saying, Arise up quickly. And his chains fell off from *his* hands.

Ac 12:23 — And immediately the angel of the Lord smote him, because he gave not God the glory: and he was eaten of worms, and gave up the ghost.

- **Called Morning Stars.**

Job 38:7 — When the morning stars sang together, and all the sons of God shouted for joy?

- **Called Hosts.**

Ge 2:1 — Thus the heavens and the earth were finished, and all the host of them.

Ge 32:2 — And when Jacob saw them, he said, This *is* God's host: and he called the name of that place Mahanaim.

Jos 5:14 — And he said, Nay; but *as* captain of the host of the LORD am I now come. And Joshua fell on his face to the earth, and did worship, and said unto him, What saith my lord unto his servant?

1Ch 12:22 — For at *that* time day by day there came to David to help him, until *it was* a great host, like the host of God.

Ps 33:6 — By the word of the LORD were the heavens made; and all the host of them by the breath of his mouth.

Ps 103:21 — Bless ye the LORD, all *ye* his hosts; *ye* ministers of his, that do his pleasure.

Lk 2:13 — And suddenly there was with the angel a multitude of the heavenly host praising God, and saying,

- **Called Principalities, Powers.**

Eph 3:10 — To the intent that now unto the principalities and powers in heavenly *places* might be known by the church the manifold wisdom of God,

Col 1:16 — For by him were all things created, that are in heaven, and that are in earth, visible and invisible, whether *they be* thrones, or dominions, or principalities, or powers: all things were created by him, and for him:

- **Created.**

Ge 2:1 — Thus the heavens and the earth were finished, and all the host of them.

Ne 9:6 — Thou, *even* thou, *art* LORD alone; thou hast made heaven, the heaven of heavens, with all their host, the earth, and all *things* that *are* therein, the seas, and all that *is* therein, and thou preservest them all; and the host of heaven worshippeth thee.

Col 1:16 — For by him were all things created, that are in heaven, and that are in earth, visible and invisible, whether *they be* thrones, or dominions, or principalities, or powers: all things were created by him, and for him:

- **Of different orders.**

Isa 6:2 — Above it stood the seraphims: each one had six wings; with twain he covered his face, and with twain he covered his feet, and with twain he did fly.

1Th 4:16 — For the Lord himself shall descend from heaven with a shout, with the voice of the archangel, and with the trump of God: and the dead in Christ shall rise first:

1Pe 3:22 — Who is gone into heaven, and is on the right hand of God; angels and authorities and powers being made subject unto him.

Jude 1:9 — Yet Michael the archangel, when contending with the devil he disputed about the body of Moses, durst not bring against him a railing accusation, but said, The Lord rebuke thee.

Rev 12:7 — And there was war in heaven: Michael and his angels fought against the dragon; and the dragon fought and his angels,

• **Immortal.**

Lk 20:36 — Neither can they die any more: for they are equal unto the angels; and are the children of God, being the children of the resurrection.

• **Worship God.**

Php 2:9–11

Ne 9:6 — Thou, *even* thou, *art* LORD alone; thou hast made heaven, the heaven of heavens, with all their host, the earth, and all *things* that *are* therein, the seas, and all that *is* therein, and thou preservest them all; and the host of heaven worshippeth thee.

Heb 1:6 — And again, when he bringeth in the firstbegotten into the world, he saith, And let all the angels of God worship him.

• **Not to be worshiped.**

Rev 22:8–9

Col 2:18 — Let no man beguile you of your reward in a voluntary humility and worshipping of angels, intruding into those things which he hath not seen, vainly puffed up by his fleshly mind,

Rev 19:10 — And I fell at his feet to worship him. And he said unto me, See *thou do it* not: I am thy fellowservant, and of thy brethren that have the testimony of Jesus: worship God: for the testimony of Jesus is the spirit of prophecy.

• **Do not marry.**

Mt 22:30 — For in the resurrection they neither marry, nor are given in marriage, but are as the angels of God in heaven.

Mk 12:25 — For when they shall rise from the dead, they neither marry, nor are given in marriage; but are as the angels which are in heaven.

Lk 20:35 — But they which shall be accounted worthy to obtain that world, and the resurrection from the dead, neither marry, nor are given in marriage:

• **Are obedient.**

Ps 103:20 — Bless the LORD, ye his angels, that excel in strength, that do his commandments, hearkening unto the voice of his word.

Mt 6:10 — Thy kingdom come. Thy will be done in earth, as *it is* in heaven.

Lk 11:2 — And he said unto them, When ye pray, say, Our Father which art in heaven, Hallowed be thy name. Thy kingdom come. Thy will be done, as in heaven, so in earth.

1Pe 3:22 — Who is gone into heaven, and is on the right hand of God; angels and authorities and powers being made subject unto him.

2Pe 2:11 — Whereas angels, which are greater in power and might, bring not railing accusation against them before the Lord.

Jude 1:6 — And the angels which kept not their first estate, but left their own habitation, he hath reserved in everlasting chains under darkness unto the judgment of the great day.

• **Have knowledge of, and interest in, earthly affairs.**

Mt 24:36 — But of that day and hour knoweth no *man*, no, not the angels of heaven, but my Father only.

Lk 15:7 — I say unto you, that likewise joy shall be in heaven over one sinner that repenteth, more than over ninety and nine just persons, which need no repentance.

Lk 15:10 — Likewise, I say unto you, there is joy in the presence of the angels of God over one sinner that repenteth.

1Ti 5:21 — I charge *thee* before God, and the Lord Jesus Christ, and the elect angels, that thou observe these things without preferring one before another, doing nothing by partiality.

1Pe 1:12 — Unto whom it was revealed, that not unto themselves, but unto us they did minister the things, which are now reported unto you by them that have preached the gospel unto you with the Holy Ghost sent down from heaven; which things the angels desire to look into.

• **To be judged by men.**

1Co 6:3 — Know ye not that we shall judge angels? how much more things that pertain to this life?

↞**See: Angel; functions of**

• **Men called angels.**

2Sa 19:27 — And he hath slandered thy servant unto my lord the king; but my lord the king *is* as an angel of God: do therefore *what is* good in thine eyes.

• **Are examples of meekness.**

2Pe 2:11 — Whereas angels, which are greater in power and might, bring not railing accusation against them before the Lord.

Jude 1:9 — Yet Michael the archangel, when contending with the devil he disputed about the body of Moses, durst not bring against him a railing accusation, but said, The Lord rebuke thee.

• **Are wise.**

2Sa 14:17 — Then thine handmaid said, The word of my lord the king shall now be comfortable: for as an angel of God, so *is* my lord the king to discern good and bad: therefore the LORD thy God will be with thee.

2Sa 14:20 — To fetch about this form of speech hath thy servant Joab done this thing: and my lord *is* wise, according to the wisdom of an angel of God, to know all *things* that *are* in the earth.

• **Mighty.**

Ps 103:20 — Bless the LORD, ye his angels, that excel in strength, that do his commandments, hearkening unto the voice of his word.

2Pe 2:11 — Whereas angels, which are greater in power and might, bring not railing accusation against them before the Lord.

• **Holy.**

Mt 25:31 — When the Son of man shall come in his glory, and all the holy angels with him, then shall he sit upon the throne of his glory:

Mk 8:38 — Whosoever therefore shall be ashamed of me and of my words in this adulterous and sinful generation; of him also shall the Son of man be ashamed, when he cometh in the glory of his Father with the holy angels.

- **Elect.**

1Ti 5:21 — I charge *thee* before God, and the Lord Jesus Christ, and the elect angels, that thou observe these things without preferring one before another, doing nothing by partiality.

- **Innumerable.**

Dt 33:2 — And he said, The LORD came from Sinai, and rose up from Seir unto them; he shined forth from mount Paran, and he came with ten thousands of saints: from his right hand *went* a fiery law for them.

2Ki 6:17 — And Elisha prayed, and said, LORD, I pray thee, open his eyes, that he may see. And the LORD opened the eyes of the young man; and he saw: and, behold, the mountain *was* full of horses and chariots of fire round about Elisha.

Job 25:3 — Is there any number of his armies? and upon whom doth not his light arise?

Ps 68:17 — The chariots of God *are* twenty thousand, *even* thousands of angels: the Lord *is* among them, *as in* Sinai, in the holy *place.*

Heb 12:22 — But ye are come unto mount Sion, and unto the city of the living God, the heavenly Jerusalem, and to an innumerable company of angels,

Jude 1:14 — And Enoch also, the seventh from Adam, prophesied of these, saying, Behold, the Lord cometh with ten thousands of his saints,

- **Aspects of.**

Jgs 13:6 — Then the woman came and told her husband, saying, A man of God came unto me, and his countenance *was* like the countenance of an angel of God, very terrible: but I asked him not whence he *was,* neither told he me his name:

Isa 6:2 — Above it stood the seraphims: each one had six wings; with twain he covered his face, and with twain he covered his feet, and with twain he did fly.

Da 10:6 — His body also *was* like the beryl, and his face as the appearance of lightning, and his eyes as lamps of fire, and his arms and his feet like in colour to polished brass, and the voice of his words like the voice of a multitude.

Mt 28:3 — His countenance was like lightning, and his raiment white as snow:

See: Angel; unclassified scripture relating to

- **Functions of.**
  - **Guard the way to the tree of life.**

Ge 3:24 — So he drove out the man; and he placed at the east of the garden of Eden Cherubim, and a flaming sword which turned every way, to keep the way of the tree of life.

  - **Law given by.**

Ac 7:53 — Who have received the law by the disposition of angels, and have not kept *it.*

Gal 3:19 — Wherefore then *serveth* the law? It was added because of transgressions, till the seed should come to whom the promise was made; *and it was* ordained by angels in the hand of a mediator.

Heb 2:2 — For if the word spoken by angels was stedfast, and every transgression and disobedience received a just recompence of reward;

- **Medium of revelation to prophets.**

Da 4:13–17; 9:21–27; 10:10–20; Zec 1:9–11; Rev 5:2–14; 7:1–3, 11–17; 8:2–20:15

2Ki 1:15 — And the angel of the LORD said unto Elijah, Go down with him: be not afraid of him. And he arose, and went down with him unto the king.

Da 8:19 — And he said, Behold, I will make thee know what shall be in the last end of the indignation: for at the time appointed the end *shall be.*

Ac 8:26 — And the angel of the Lord spake unto Philip, saying, Arise, and go toward the south unto the way that goeth down from Jerusalem unto Gaza, which is desert.

Gal 3:19 — Wherefore then *serveth* the law? It was added because of transgressions, till the seed should come to whom the promise was made; *and it was* ordained by angels in the hand of a mediator.

Heb 2:2 — For if the word spoken by angels was stedfast, and every transgression and disobedience received a just recompence of reward;

Rev 1:1 — The Revelation of Jesus Christ, which God gave unto him, to shew unto his servants things which must shortly come to pass; and he sent and signified *it* by his angel unto his servant John:

Rev 22:6 — And he said unto me, These sayings *are* faithful and true: and the Lord God of the holy prophets sent his angel to shew unto his servants the things which must shortly be done.

Rev 22:16 — I Jesus have sent mine angel to testify unto you these things in the churches. I am the root and the offspring of David, *and* the bright and morning star.

- **Remonstrates with Balaam.**

Nu 22:22–27

- **Announces the birth of Samson.**

Jgs 13:1–25

- **Announces the birth of John the Baptist.**

Lk 1:11–20

- **Announces the birth of Jesus.**

Mt 1:20–21; Lk 1:28–38; 2:7–15

- **Warns Joseph to escape to Egypt.**

Mt 2:13 — And when they were departed, behold, the angel of the Lord appeareth to Joseph in a dream, saying, Arise, and take the young child and his mother, and flee into Egypt, and be thou there until I bring thee word: for Herod will seek the young child to destroy him.

- **Minister to Jesus after the temptation.**

Mt 4:11 — Then the devil leaveth him, and, behold, angels came and ministered unto him.

Mk 1:13 — And he was there in the wilderness forty days, tempted of Satan; and was with the wild beasts; and the angels ministered unto him.

Jn 1:51 — And he saith unto him, Verily, verily, I say unto you, Hereafter ye shall see heaven open, and the angels of God ascending and descending upon the Son of man.

- **Minister to Jesus during his passion.**

Lk 22:43 — And there appeared an angel unto him from heaven, strengthening him.

- **Present at the tomb of Jesus.**

Mt 28:2–6

- **Present at the ascension.**

Ac 1:11 — Which also said, Ye men of Galilee, why stand ye gazing up into heaven? this same Jesus, which is taken up from you into heaven, shall so come in like manner as ye have seen him go into heaven.

- **Will be with Christ at his second coming.**

Jude 1:14–15

Mt 25:31 — When the Son of man shall come in his glory, and all the holy angels with him, then shall he sit upon the throne of his glory:

Mk 8:38 — Whosoever therefore shall be ashamed of me and of my words in this adulterous and sinful generation; of him also shall the Son of man be ashamed, when he cometh in the glory of his Father with the holy angels.

2Th 1:7 — And to you who are troubled rest with us, when the Lord Jesus shall be revealed from heaven with his mighty angels,

- **At the judgment.**

Mt 13:39 — The enemy that sowed them is the devil; the harvest is the end of the world; and the reapers are the angels.

Mt 13:41 — The Son of man shall send forth his angels, and they shall gather out of his kingdom all things that offend, and them which do iniquity;

Mt 13:49 — So shall it be at the end of the world: the angels shall come forth, and sever the wicked from among the just,

Mt 16:27 — For the Son of man shall come in the glory of his Father with his angels; and then he shall reward every man according to his works.

Mt 24:31 — And he shall send his angels with a great sound of a trumpet, and they shall gather together his elect from the four winds, from one end of heaven to the other.

Mt 25:31 — When the Son of man shall come in his glory, and all the holy angels with him, then shall he sit upon the throne of his glory:

Mk 13:27 — And then shall he send his angels, and shall gather together his elect from the four winds, from the uttermost part of the earth to the uttermost part of heaven.

- **Ministrant to the righteous.**

1Ki 19:5–8; Ps 91:11–12; Lk 4:10–11; Ac 5:19–20; 10:3–6; 12:7–10

Ge 16:7 — And the angel of the LORD found her by a fountain of water in the wilderness, by the fountain in the way to Shur.

Ge 24:7 — The LORD God of heaven, which took me from my father's house, and from the land of my kindred, and which spake unto me, and that sware unto me, saying, Unto thy seed will I give this land; he shall send his angel before thee, and thou shalt take a wife unto my son from thence.

Ge 24:40 — And he said unto me, The LORD, before whom I walk, will send his angel with thee, and prosper thy way; and thou shalt take a wife for my son of my kindred, and of my father's house:

Ex 23:20 — Behold, I send an Angel before thee, to keep thee in the way, and to bring thee into the place which I have prepared.

Ex 23:23 — For mine Angel shall go before thee, and bring thee in unto the Amorites, and the Hittites, and the Perizzites, and the Canaanites, and the Hivites, and the Jebusites: and I will cut them off.

Ex 32:34 — Therefore now go, lead the people unto *the place* of which I have spoken unto thee: behold, mine Angel shall go before thee: nevertheless in the day when I visit I will visit their sin upon them.

Ex 33:2 — And I will send an angel before thee; and I will drive out the Canaanite, the Amorite, and the Hittite, and the Perizzite, the Hivite, and the Jebusite:

Nu 20:16 — And when we cried unto the LORD, he heard our voice, and sent an angel, and hath brought us forth out of Egypt: and, behold, we *are* in Kadesh, a city in the uttermost of thy border:

2Ki 6:17 — And Elisha prayed, and said, LORD, I pray thee, open his eyes, that he may see. And the LORD opened the eyes of the young man; and he saw: and, behold, the mountain *was* full of horses and chariots of fire round about Elisha.

2Ch 18:18 — Again he said, Therefore hear the word of the LORD; I saw the LORD sitting upon his throne, and all the host of heaven standing on his right hand and *on* his left.

Ps 34:7 — The angel of the LORD encampeth round about them that fear him, and delivereth them.

Ps 68:17 — The chariots of God *are* twenty thousand, *even* thousands of angels: the Lord *is* among them, *as in* Sinai, in the holy *place*.

Ps 104:4 — Who maketh his angels spirits; his ministers a flaming fire:

Ecc 5:6 — Suffer not thy mouth to cause thy flesh to sin; neither say thou before the angel, that it *was* an error: wherefore should God be angry at thy voice, and destroy the work of thine hands?

Isa 63:9 — In all their affliction he was afflicted, and the angel of his presence saved them: in his love and in his pity he redeemed them; and he bare them, and carried them all the days of old.

Da 6:22 — My God hath sent his angel, and hath shut the lions' mouths, that they have not hurt me: forasmuch as before him innocency was found in me; and also before thee, O king, have I done no hurt.

Da 7:10 — A fiery stream issued and came forth from before him: thousand thousands ministered unto him, and ten thousand times ten thousand stood before him: the judgment was set, and the books were opened.

Mt 4:6 — And saith unto him, If thou be the Son of God, cast thyself down: for it is written, He shall give his angels charge concerning thee: and in *their* hands they shall bear thee up, lest at any time thou dash thy foot against a stone.

Lk 16:22 — And it came to pass, that the beggar died, and was carried by the angels into Abraham's bosom: the rich man also died, and was buried;

Jn 1:51 — And he saith unto him, Verily, verily, I say unto you, Hereafter ye shall see heaven open, and the angels of God ascending and descending upon the Son of man.

Jn 5:4 — For an angel went down at a certain season into the pool, and troubled the water: whosoever then first after the troubling of the water stepped in was made whole of whatsoever disease he had.

Heb 1:7 — And of the angels he saith, Who maketh his angels spirits, and his ministers a flame of fire.

Heb 1:14 — Are they not all ministering spirits, sent forth to minister for them who shall be heirs of salvation?

Heb 13:2 — Be not forgetful to entertain strangers: for thereby some have entertained angels unawares.

• Execute judgments upon the wicked.

Ge 19:1–25; 2Sa 24:16–17; Ps 35:5–6; 78:1–72; Mt 13:41–42, 49–50; Ac 27:23–24; Jude 1:14–15; Rev 7:1–2

2Sa 19:35 — I *am* this day fourscore years old: *and* can I discern between good and evil? can thy servant taste what I eat or what I drink? can I hear any more the voice of singing men and singing women? wherefore then should thy servant be yet a burden unto my lord the king?

2Ch 32:21 — And the LORD sent an angel, which cut off all the mighty men of valour, and the leaders and captains in the camp of the king of Assyria. So he returned with shame of face to his own land. And when he was come into the house of his god, they that came forth of his own bowels slew him there with the sword.

Isa 37:36 — Then the angel of the LORD went forth, and smote in the camp of the Assyrians a hundred and fourscore and five thousand: and when they arose early in the morning, behold, they *were* all dead corpses.

Ac 12:23 — And immediately the angel of the Lord smote him, because he gave not God the glory: and he was eaten of worms, and gave up the ghost.

Rev 9:15 — And the four angels were loosed, which were prepared for an hour, and a day, and a month, and a year, for to slay the third part of men.

Rev 15:1 — And I saw another sign in heaven, great and marvellous, seven angels having the seven last plagues; for in them is filled up the wrath of God.

• Unclassified scripture relating to.

Job 4:15–19; Ps 103:20–21; Isa 6:2–3, 5–7; Eze 1:4–25; 10:1–22; Da 8:13–14; 9:21–23; Zec 1:12–14; Mt 13:41–42; Lk 9:30–31; 12:8–9; Eph 1:20–21; Heb 1:4–5; Rev 4:8–11; 5:9–11; 7:9–12; 10:1–6; 18:1–3; 22:8–9

Nu 22:35 — And the angel of the LORD said unto Balaam, Go with the men: but only the word that I shall speak unto thee, that thou shalt speak. So Balaam went with the princes of Balak.

Dt 33:2 — And he said, The LORD came from Sinai, and rose up from Seir unto them; he shined forth from mount Paran, and he came with ten thousands of saints: from his right hand *went* a fiery law for them.

2Ki 6:17 — And Elisha prayed, and said, LORD, I pray thee, open his eyes, that he may see. And the LORD opened the eyes of the young man; and he saw: and, behold, the mountain *was* full of horses and chariots of fire round about Elisha.

Ne 9:6 — Thou, *even* thou, *art* LORD alone; thou hast made heaven, the heaven of heavens, with all their host, the earth, and all *things* that *are* therein, the seas, and all that *is* therein, and thou preservest them all; and the host of heaven worshippeth thee.

Job 38:7 — When the morning stars sang together, and all the sons of God shouted for joy?

Ps 8:5 — For thou hast made him a little lower than the angels, and hast crowned him with glory and honour.

Ps 68:17 — The chariots of God *are* twenty thousand, *even* thousands of angels: the Lord *is* among them, *as in* Sinai, in the holy *place*.

Ps 104:4 — Who maketh his angels spirits; his ministers a flaming fire:

Ps 148:2 — Praise ye him, all his angels: praise ye him, all his hosts.

Da 4:13 — I saw in the visions of my head upon my bed, and, behold, a watcher and an holy one came down from heaven;

Da 4:17 — This matter *is* by the decree of the watchers, and the demand by the word of the holy ones: to the intent that the living may know that the most High ruleth in the kingdom of men, and giveth it to whomsoever he will, and setteth up over it the basest of men.

Da 7:10 — A fiery stream issued and came forth from before him: thousand thousands ministered unto him, and ten thousand times ten thousand stood before him: the judgment was set, and the books were opened.

Zec 6:5 — And the angel answered and said unto me, These *are* the four spirits of the heavens, which go forth from standing before the Lord of all the earth.

Mt 4:6 — And saith unto him, If thou be the Son of God, cast thyself down: for it is written, He shall give his angels charge concerning thee: and in *their* hands they shall bear thee up, lest at any time thou dash thy foot against a stone.

Mt 4:11 — Then the devil leaveth him, and, behold, angels came and ministered unto him.

Mt 17:3 — And, behold, there appeared unto them Moses and Elias talking with him.

Mt 18:10 — Take heed that ye despise not one of these little ones; for I say unto you, That in heaven their angels do always behold the face of my Father which is in heaven.

Mt 24:31 — And he shall send his angels with a great sound of a trumpet, and they shall gather together his elect from the four winds, from one end of heaven to the other.

Mt 24:36 — But of that day and hour knoweth no *man*, no, not the angels of heaven, but my Father only.

Mt 25:31 — When the Son of man shall come in his glory, and all the holy angels with him, then shall he sit upon the throne of his glory:

Mt 26:53 — Thinkest thou that I cannot now pray to my Father, and he shall presently give me more than twelve legions of angels?

Mk 1:13 — And he was there in the wilderness forty days, tempted of Satan; and was with the wild beasts; and the angels ministered unto him.

Mk 8:38 — Whosoever therefore shall be ashamed of me and of my words in this adulterous and sinful generation; of him also shall the Son of man be ashamed, when he cometh in the glory of his Father with the holy angels.

Lk 15:7 — I say unto you, that likewise joy shall be in heaven over one sinner that repenteth, more than over ninety and nine just persons, which need no repentance.

Lk 15:10 — Likewise, I say unto you, there is joy in the presence of the angels of God over one sinner that repenteth.

Jn 1:51 — And he saith unto him, Verily, verily, I say unto you, Hereafter ye shall see heaven open, and the angels of God ascending and descending upon the Son of man.

Ac 7:53 — Who have received the law by the disposition of angels, and have not kept *it*.

Ac 8:26 — And the angel of the Lord spake unto Philip, saying, Arise, and go toward the south unto the way that goeth down from Jerusalem unto Gaza, which is desert.

Gal 3:19 — Wherefore then *serveth* the law? It was added because of transgressions, till the seed should come to whom the promise was made; *and it was* ordained by angels in the hand of a mediator.

Eph 3:10 — To the intent that now unto the principalities and powers in heavenly *places* might be known by the church the manifold wisdom of God,

Col 1:16 — For by him were all things created, that are in heaven, and that are in earth, visible and invisible, whether *they be* thrones, or dominions, or principalities, or powers: all things were created by him, and for him:

Col 2:10 — And ye are complete in him, which is the head of all principality and power:

2Th 1:7 — And to you who are troubled rest with us, when the Lord Jesus shall be revealed from heaven with his mighty angels,

1Ti 3:16 — And without controversy great is the mystery of godliness: God was manifest in the flesh, justified in the Spirit, seen of angels, preached unto the Gentiles, believed on in the world, received up into glory.

1Ti 5:21 — I charge *thee* before God, and the Lord Jesus Christ, and the elect angels, that thou observe these things without preferring one before another, doing nothing by partiality.

Heb 1:7 — And of the angels he saith, Who maketh his angels spirits, and his ministers a flame of fire.

Heb 1:13 — But to which of the angels said he at any times, Sit on my right hand, until I make thine enemies thy footstool?

Heb 2:2 — For if the word spoken by angels was stedfast, and every transgression and disobedience received a just recompence of reward;

Heb 2:5 — For unto the angels hath he not put in subjection the world to come, whereof we speak.

Heb 2:7 — Thou madest him a little lower than the angels; thou crownedst him with glory and honour, and didst set him over the works of thy hands:

Heb 2:16 — For verily he took not on *him the nature of* angels; but he took on *him* the seed of Abraham.

Heb 12:22 — But ye are come unto mount Sion, and unto the city of the living God, the heavenly Jerusalem, and to an innumerable company of angels,

Heb 13:2 — Be not forgetful to entertain strangers: for thereby some have entertained angels unawares.

1Pe 1:12 — Unto whom it was revealed, that not unto themselves, but unto us they did minister the things, which are now reported unto you by them that have preached the gospel unto you with the Holy Ghost sent down from heaven; which things the angels desire to look into.

1Pe 3:22 — Who is gone into heaven, and is on the right hand of God; angels and authorities and powers being made subject unto him.

2Pe 2:11 — Whereas angels, which are greater in power and might, bring not railing accusation against them before the Lord.

Rev 14:10 — The same shall drink of the wine of the wrath of God, which is poured out without mixture into the cup of his indignation; and he shall be tormented with fire and brimstone in the presence of the holy angels, and in the presence of the Lamb:

Rev 19:6 — And I heard as it were the voice of a great multitude, and as the voice of many waters, and as the voice of mighty thunderings, saying, Alleluia: for the Lord God omnipotent reigneth.

Rev 19:10 — And I fell at his feet to worship him. And he said unto me, See *thou do it* not: I am thy fellowservant, and of thy brethren that have the testimony of Jesus: worship God: for the testimony of Jesus is the spirit of prophecy.

- **Appearances of.**
  - **To Abraham.**

    Ge 22:11–18

    Ge 18:2 — And he lift up his eyes and looked, and, lo, three men stood by him: and when he saw *them*, he ran to meet them from the tent door, and bowed himself toward the ground,
  - **To Hagar, in the wilderness.**

    Ge 16:7 — And the angel of the LORD found her by a fountain of water in the wilderness, by the fountain in the way to Shur.
  - **To Lot, in Sodom.**

    Ge 19:1–17

• **To Jacob, in his various visions.**

Ge 28:12 — And he dreamed, and behold a ladder set up on the earth, and the top of it reached to heaven: and behold the angels of God ascending and descending on it.

• **To Moses.**

Ex 3:2 — And the angel of the LORD appeared unto him in a flame of fire out of the midst of a bush: and he looked, and, behold, the bush burned with fire, and the bush *was* not consumed.

• **To Israelites.**

Jgs 2:1–4

Ex 14:19 — And the angel of God, which went before the camp of Israel, removed and went behind them; and the pillar of the cloud went from before their face, and stood behind them:

• **To Balaam.**

Nu 22:31 — Then the LORD opened the eyes of Balaam, and he saw the angel of the LORD standing in the way, and his sword drawn in his hand: and he bowed down his head, and fell flat on his face.

• **To Joshua, "the captain of the Lord's host".**

Jos 5:15 — And the captain of the LORD's host said unto Joshua, Loose thy shoe from off thy foot; for the place whereon thou standest *is* holy. And Joshua did so.

• **To Gideon.**

Jgs 6:11–22

• **To Manoah.**

Jgs 13:15–20

Jgs 13:6 — Then the woman came and told her husband, saying, A man of God came unto me, and his countenance *was* like the countenance of an angel of God, very terrible: but I asked him not whence he *was*, neither told he me his name:

• **To David, at the threshing floor of Araunah.**

2Sa 24:16–17; 1Ch 21:15–16

• **To Elijah, while he lay under the juniper tree.**

1Ki 19:5–11

• **To Daniel, in the lions' den.**

Da 10:5–10; 12:5–7

Da 6:22 — My God hath sent his angel, and hath shut the lions' mouths, that they have not hurt me: forasmuch as before him innocency was found in me; and also before thee, O king, have I done no hurt.

Da 8:16 — And I heard a man's voice between *the banks of* Ulai, which called, and said, Gabriel, make this *man* to understand the vision.

Da 9:21 — Yea, whiles I *was* speaking in prayer, even the man Gabriel, whom I had seen in the vision at the beginning, being caused to fly swiftly, touched me about the time of the evening oblation.

Da 10:16 — And, behold, *one* like the similitude of the sons of men touched my lips: then I opened my mouth, and spake, and said unto him that stood before me, O my lord, by the vision my sorrows are turned upon me, and I have retained no strength.

Da 10:18 — Then there came again and touched me *one* like the appearance of a man, and he strengthened me,

• **To Shadrach, Meshach, and Abed-nego, in the fiery furnace.**

Da 3:25 — He answered and said, Lo, I see four men loose, walking in the midst of the fire, and they have no hurt; and the form of the fourth is like the Son of God.

Da 3:28 — *Then* Nebuchadnezzar spake, and said, Blessed *be* the God of Shadrach, Meshach, and Abed-nego, who hath sent his angel, and delivered his servants that trusted in him, and have changed the king's word, and yielded their bodies, that they might not serve nor worship any god, except their own God.

• **To Zechariah, in a vision.**

Zec 3:1–2

Zec 2:3 — And, behold, the angel that talked with me went forth, and another angel went out to meet him,

Zec 4:1 — And the angel that talked with me came again, and waked me, as a man that is wakened out of his sleep,

• **To Joseph, in a dream.**

Mt 1:20 — But while he thought on these things, behold, the angel of the Lord appeared unto him in a dream, saying, Joseph, thou son of David, fear not to take unto thee Mary thy wife: for that which is conceived in her is of the Holy Ghost.

Mt 2:13 — And when they were departed, behold, the angel of the Lord appeareth to Joseph in a dream, saying, Arise, and take the young child and his mother, and flee into Egypt, and be thou there until I bring thee word: for Herod will seek the young child to destroy him.

Mt 2:19 — But when Herod was dead, behold, an angel of the Lord appeareth in a dream to Joseph in Egypt,

• **At the transfiguration of Jesus.**

Lk 9:30–31

Mt 17:3 — And, behold, there appeared unto them Moses and Elias talking with him.

• **To Mary, concerning Jesus.**

Lk 1:26–38

• **To Zacharias.**

Lk 1:11–20, 26–38

• **To the shepherds.**

Lk 2:9–11, 13–14

• **To Jesus, after his temptation.**

Mt 4:11 — Then the devil leaveth him, and, behold, angels came and ministered unto him.

• **To Jesus, in Gethsemane.**

Lk 22:43 — And there appeared an angel unto him from heaven, strengthening him.

• **At the sepulchre.**

Mt 28:2–5; Mk 16:5–7

Lk 24:23 — And when they found not his body, they came, saying, that they had also seen a vision of angels, which said that he was alive.

Jn 20:12 — And seeth two angels in white sitting, the one at the head, and the other at the feet, where the body of Jesus had lain.

• **At the ascension.**

Ac 1:10–11

• **To Peter and John, while in prison.**

Ac 5:19 — But the angel of the Lord by night opened the prison doors, and brought them forth, and said,

• **To Philip.**

Ac 8:26 — And the angel of the Lord spake unto Philip, saying, Arise, and go toward the south unto the way that goeth down from Jerusalem unto Gaza, which is desert.

• **To Cornelius, in a dream.**

Ac 10:30–32

Ac 10:3 — He saw in a vision evidently about the ninth hour of the day an angel of God coming in to him, and saying unto him, Cornelius.

• **To Peter, in prison.**

Ac 12:7–11

• **To Paul, on the way to Damascus.**

Ac 27:23 — For there stood by me this night the angel of God, whose I am, and whom I serve,

• **To John, in Patmos.**

Rev 1:1 — The Revelation of Jesus Christ, which God gave unto him, to shew unto his servants things which must shortly come to pass; and he sent and signified *it* by his angel unto his servant John:

Rev 5:2 — And I saw a strong angel proclaiming with a loud voice, Who is worthy to open the book, and to loose the seals thereof?

Rev 7:11 — And all the angels stood round about the throne, and *about* the elders and the four beasts, and fell before the throne on their faces, and worshipped God,

Rev 10:9 — And I went unto the angel, and said unto him, Give me the little book. And he said unto me, Take *it,* and eat it up; and it shall make thy belly bitter, but it shall be in thy mouth sweet as honey.

Rev 11:1 — And there was given me a reed like unto a rod: and the angel stood, saying, Rise, and measure the temple of God, and the altar, and them that worship therein.

Rev 17:7 — And the angel said unto me, Wherefore didst thou marvel? I will tell thee the mystery of the woman, and of the beast that carrieth her, which hath the seven heads and ten horns.

Rev 19:10 — And I fell at his feet to worship him. And he said unto me, See *thou do it* not: I am thy fellowservant, and of thy brethren that have the testimony of Jesus: worship God: for the testimony of Jesus is the spirit of prophecy.

Rev 22:8 — And I John saw these things, and heard *them.* And when I had heard and seen, I fell down to worship before the feet of the angel which shewed me these things.

• **Fallen.**

Job 4:18 — Behold, he put no trust in his servants; and his angels he charged with folly:

Mt 25:41 — Then shall he say also unto them on the left hand, Depart from me, ye cursed, into everlasting fire, prepared for the devil and his angels:

2Pe 2:4 — For if God spared not the angels that sinned, but cast *them* down to hell, and delivered *them* into chains of darkness, to be reserved unto judgment;

Jude 1:6 — And the angels which kept not their first estate, but left their own habitation, he hath reserved in everlasting chains under darkness unto the judgment of the great day.

Rev 12:9 — And the great dragon was cast out, that old serpent, called the Devil, and Satan, which deceiveth the whole world: he was cast out into the earth, and his angels were cast out with him.

ANGEL OF THE CHURCHES

Rev 1:20–2:1

Rev 2:8 — And unto the angel of the church in Smyrna write; These things saith the first and the last, which was dead, and is alive;

Rev 2:12 — And to the angel of the church in Pergamos write; These things saith he which hath the sharp sword with two edges;

Rev 2:18 — And unto the angel of the church in Thyatira write; These things saith the Son of God, who hath his eyes like unto a flame of fire, and his feet *are* like fine brass;

Rev 3:1 — And unto the angel of the church in Sardis write; These things saith he that hath the seven Spirits of God, and the seven stars; I know thy works, that thou hast a name that thou livest, and art dead.

Rev 3:7 — And to the angel of the church in Philadelphia write; These things saith he that is holy, he that is true, he that hath the key of David, he that openeth, and no man shutteth; and shutteth, and no man openeth;

Rev 3:14 — And unto the angel of the church of the Laodiceans write; These things saith the Amen, the faithful and true witness, the beginning of the creation of God;

ANGER

Pr 19:11–12; 22:24–25; 27:3–4; 29:8–9; Jnh 4:1–11; Gal 5:19–21; Eph 4:22–26, 31–32; Jas 1:19–20

Ge 4:6 — And the LORD said unto Cain, Why art thou wroth? and why is thy countenance fallen?

Ge 49:7 — Cursed *be* their anger, for *it was* fierce; and their wrath, for it was cruel: I will divide them in Jacob, and scatter them in Israel.

2Ch 28:9 — But a prophet of the LORD was there, whose name *was* Oded: and he went out before the host that came to Samaria, and said unto them, Behold, because the LORD God of your fathers was wroth with Judah, he hath delivered them into your hand, and ye have slain them in a rage *that* reacheth up unto heaven.

Job 5:2 — For wrath killeth the foolish man, and envy slayeth the silly one.

Job 19:29 — Be ye afraid of the sword: for wrath *bringeth* the punishments of the sword, that ye may know *there is* a judgment.

Ps 37:8 — Cease from anger, and forsake wrath: fret not thyself in any wise to do evil.

Ps 55:3 — Because of the voice of the enemy, because of the oppression of the wicked: for they cast iniquity upon me, and in wrath they hate me.

Ps 76:10 — Surely the wrath of man shall praise thee: the remainder of wrath shalt thou restrain.

Pr 6:34 — For jealousy *is* the rage of a man: therefore he will not spare in the day of vengeance.

Pr 12:16 — A fool's wrath is presently known: but a prudent *man* covereth shame.

Pr 14:17 — *He that is* soon angry dealeth foolishly: and a man of wicked devices is hated.

Pr 14:29 — *He that is* slow to wrath *is* of great understanding: but *he that is* hasty of spirit exalteth folly.

Pr 15:1 — A soft answer turneth away wrath: but grievous words stir up anger.

Pr 15:18 — A wrathful man stirreth up strife: but *he that is* slow to anger appeaseth strife.

Pr 16:14 — The wrath of a king *is as* messengers of death: but a wise man will pacify it.

Pr 16:29 — A violent man enticeth his neighbour, and leadeth him into the way *that is* not good.

Pr 16:32 — *He that is* slow to anger *is* better than the mighty; and he that ruleth his spirit than he that taketh a city.

Pr 17:14 — The beginning of strife *is as* when one letteth out water: therefore leave off contention, before it be meddled with.

Pr 19:19 — A man of great wrath shall suffer punishment: for if thou deliver *him,* yet thou must do it again.

Pr 21:24 — Proud *and* haughty scorner *is* his name, who dealeth in proud wrath.

Pr 25:28 — He that *hath* no rule over his own spirit *is like* a city *that is* broken down, *and* without walls.

Pr 29:22 — An angry man stirreth up strife, and a furious man aboundeth in transgression.

Pr 30:33 — Surely the churning of milk bringeth forth butter, and the wringing of the nose bringeth forth blood: so the forcing of wrath bringeth forth strife.

Ecc 7:9 — Be not hasty in thy spirit to be angry: for anger resteth in the bosom of fools.

Hos 7:16 — They return, *but* not to the most High: they are like a deceitful bow: their princes shall fall by the sword for the rage of their tongue: this *shall be* their derision in the land of Egypt.

Am 1:11 — Thus saith the LORD; For three transgressions of Edom, and for four, I will not turn away *the punishment* thereof; because he did pursue his brother with the sword, and did cast off all pity, and his anger did tear perpetually, and he kept his wrath for ever:

Mt 5:22 — But I say unto you, That whosoever is angry with his brother without a cause shall be in danger of the judgment: and whosoever shall say to his brother, Raca, shall be in danger of the council: but whosoever shall say, Thou fool, shall be in danger of hell fire.

2Co 12:20 — For I fear, lest, when I come, I shall not find you such as I would, and *that* I shall be found unto you such as ye would not: lest *there be* debates, envyings, wraths, strifes, backbitings, whisperings, swellings, tumults:

Col 3:8 — But now ye also put off all these; anger, wrath, malice, blasphemy, filthy communication out of your mouth.

1Ti 2:8 — I will therefore that men pray every where, lifting up holy hands, without wrath and doubting.

Tit 1:7 — For a bishop must be blameless, as the steward of God; not selfwilled, not soon angry, not given to wine, no striker, not given to filthy lucre;

1Pe 3:7 — Likewise, ye husbands, dwell with *them* according to knowledge, giving honour unto the wife, as unto the weaker vessel, and as being heirs together of the grace of life; that your prayers be not hindered.

- **See: Hatred**
- **See: Jealousy**
- **See: Malice**
- **See: Speaking; evil**
- **See: Strife**
- **See: Kindness**
- **See: Meekness**
- **See: Patience**

- **Instances of.**
  - **Of Cain slaying Abel.**
    Ge 4:5–8
  - **Simeon and Levi, on account of the humbling of their sister, Dinah.**
    Ge 49:5–7
  - **Pharaoh, toward Moses.**
    Ex 10:11; 10:28
  - **Moses, toward Israel.**
    Ex 32:19; Nu 20:10–11
  - **Balaam, toward his ass.**
    Nu 22:27, 29
  - **Balak, toward Balaam.**
    Nu 24:10–11
  - **Ephraimites, toward Gideon, for not soliciting their aid against the Midianites.**
    Jgs 8:1
  - **Jonathan, on account of Saul's persecution of David.**
    1Sa 20:34
  - **Saul, toward Jonathan.**
    1Sa 20:30–34
  - **Ahab, because Naboth would not sell his vineyard.**
    1Ki 21:4
  - **Naaman, because Elisha directed him to wash in the Jordan.**
    2Ki 5:12
  - **Asa, because the prophet reproved him.**
    2Ch 16:10
  - **Ephraimites, toward Judah.**
    2Ch 25:10

• Uzziah, toward Azariah, the priest, because of his reproof of.
2Ch 26:19

• Ahasuerus, toward Vashti.
Est 1:12

• Haman, because Mordecai did not salute him.
Est 3:5

• Ahasuerus, toward Haman.
Est 7:7

• Elihu, because Job had beaten his friends in argument.
Job 32:3

• Moab.
Isa 16:6

• Nebuchadnezzar, on account of the insubordination of the three Hebrews, who refused to worship his idol.
Da 3:13, 19

• Jonah, because the gourd withered.
Jnh 4:1–2, 4, 9

• Herod, toward the wise men who deceived him.
Mt 2:16

• People of Nazareth, toward Jesus.
Lk 4:28

• Paul, toward Ananias.
Ac 23:3

• Jews, against Stephen.
Ac 7:54–58

• Of God.

Nu 16:20–21; 25:3–4; 32:10–11; Dt 6:14–15; 9:13–14, 18–20; 32:21–22; 2Sa 22:8–9; 1Ki 16:2–13; Ps 78:49–50; 103:8–9; Isa 57:16–17; 63:3–6; Jer 21:5–6; 25:15–17, 37–38; Eze 25:14–17; Na 1:2–3; Rev 6:16–17; 14:10–11

Ex 22:24 — And my wrath shall wax hot, and I will kill you with the sword; and your wives shall be widows, and your children fatherless.

Ex 32:10 — Now therefore let me alone, that my wrath may wax hot against them, and that I may consume them: and I will make of thee a great nation.

Ex 33:5 — For the LORD had said unto Moses, Say unto the children of Israel, Ye *are* a stiffnecked people: I will come up into the midst of thee in a moment, and consume thee: therefore now put off thy ornaments from thee, that I may know what to do unto thee.

Nu 11:1 — And *when* the people complained, it displeased the LORD: and the LORD heard *it;* and his anger was kindled; and the fire of the LORD burnt among them, and consumed *them that were* in the uttermost parts of the camp.

Nu 11:10 — Then Moses heard the people weep throughout their families, every man in the door of his tent: and the anger of the LORD was kindled greatly; Moses also was displeased.

Nu 11:33 — And while the flesh *was* yet between their teeth, ere it was chewed, the wrath of the LORD was kindled against the people, and the LORD smote the people with a very great plague.

Nu 12:9 — And the anger of the LORD was kindled against them; and he departed.

Nu 14:11 — And the LORD said unto Moses, How long will this people provoke me? and how long will it be ere they believe me, for all the signs which I have shewed among them?

Nu 16:45 — Get you up from among this congregation, that I may consume them as in a moment. And they fell upon their faces.

Nu 25:11 — Phinehas, the son of Eleazar, the son of Aaron the priest, hath turned my wrath away from the children of Israel, while he was zealous for my sake among them, that I consumed not the children of Israel in my jealousy.

Nu 32:13 — And the LORD'S anger was kindled against Israel, and he made them wander in the wilderness forty years, until all the generation, that had done evil in the sight of the LORD, was consumed.

Jos 7:1 — But the children of Israel committed a trespass in the accursed thing: for Achan, the son of Carmi, the son of Zabdi, the son of Zerah, of the tribe of Judah, took of the accursed thing: and the anger of the LORD was kindled against the children of Israel.

Jos 7:26 — And they raised over him a great heap of stones unto this day. So the LORD turned from the fierceness of his anger. Wherefore the name of that place was called, The valley of Achor, unto this day.

Jos 23:16 — When ye have transgressed the covenant of the LORD your God, which he commanded you, and have gone and served other gods, and bowed yourselves to them; then shall the anger of the LORD be kindled against you, and ye shall perish quickly from off the good land which he hath given unto you.

Jgs 2:12 — And they forsook the LORD God of their fathers, which brought them out of the land of Egypt, and followed other gods, of the gods of the people that *were* round about them, and bowed themselves unto them, and provoked the LORD to anger.

Jgs 3:8 — Therefore the anger of the LORD was hot against Israel, and he sold them into the hand of Chushan-rishathaim king of Mesopotamia: and the children of Israel served Chushan-rishathaim eight years.

Jgs 10:7 — And the anger of the LORD was hot against Israel, and he sold them into the hands of the Philistines, and into the hands of the children of Ammon.

1Sa 28:18 — Because thou obeyedst not the voice of the LORD, nor executedst his fierce wrath upon Amalek, therefore hath the LORD done this thing unto thee this day.

2Sa 6:7 — And the anger of the LORD was kindled against Uzzah; and God smote him there for *his* error; and there he died by the ark of God.

1Ki 11:9 — And the LORD was angry with Solomon, because his heart was turned from the LORD God of Israel, which had appeared unto him twice,

2Ki 13:3 — And the anger of the LORD was kindled against Israel, and he delivered them into the hand of Hazael king of Syria, and into the hand of Benhadad the son of Hazael, all *their* days.

2Ki 17:18 — Therefore the LORD was very angry with Israel, and removed them out of his sight: there was none left but the tribe of Judah only.

2Ki 22:13 — Go ye, enquire of the LORD for me, and for the people, and for all Judah, concerning the words of this book that is found: for great is the wrath of the LORD that is kindled against us, because our fathers have not hearkened unto the words of this book, to do according unto all that which is written concerning us.

2Ki 23:26 — Notwithstanding the LORD turned not from the fierceness of his great wrath, wherewith his anger was kindled against Judah, because of all the provocations that Manasseh had provoked him withal.

Ps 7:11 — God judgeth the righteous, and God is angry *with the wicked* every day.

Ps 69:24 — Pour out thine indignation upon them, and let thy wrathful anger take hold of them.

Ps 74:1 — O God, why hast thou cast us off for ever? *why* doth thine anger smoke against the sheep of thy pasture?

Ps 76:7 — Thou, *even* thou, *art* to be feared: and who may stand in thy sight when once thou art angry?

Ps 78:21 — Therefore the LORD heard *this*, and was wroth: so a fire was kindled against Jacob, and anger also came up against Israel;

Ps 78:38 — But he, *being* full of compassion, forgave *their* iniquity, and destroyed *them* not: yea, many a time turned he his anger away, and did not stir up all his wrath.

Ps 85:3 — Thou hast taken away all thy wrath: thou hast turned *thyself* from the fierceness of thine anger.

Ps 90:11 — Who knoweth the power of thine anger? even according to thy fear, *so is* thy wrath.

Ps 106:23 — Therefore he said that he would destroy them, had not Moses his chosen stood before him in the breach, to turn away his wrath, lest he should destroy *them*.

Ps 106:29 — Thus they provoked *him* to anger with their inventions: and the plague brake in upon them.

Ps 106:32 — They angered *him* also at the waters of strife, so that it went ill with Moses for their sakes:

Ps 110:5 — The Lord at thy right hand shall strike through kings in the day of his wrath.

Isa 5:25 — Therefore is the anger of the LORD kindled against his people, and he hath stretched forth his hand against them, and hath smitten them: and the hills did tremble, and their carcases *were* torn in the midst of the streets. For all this his anger is not turned away, but his hand *is* stretched out still.

Isa 9:17 — Therefore the Lord shall have no joy in their young men, neither shall have mercy on their fatherless and widows: for every one is an hypocrite and an evildoer, and every mouth speaketh folly. For all this his anger is not turned away, but his hand *is* stretched out still.

Isa 9:19 — Through the wrath of the LORD of hosts is the land darkened, and the people shall be as the fuel of the fire: no man shall spare his brother.

Isa 9:21 — Manasseh, Ephraim; and Ephraim, Manasseh: *and* they together *shall be* against Judah. For all this his anger is not turned away, but his hand *is* stretched out still.

Isa 12:1 — And in that day thou shalt say, O LORD, I will praise thee: though thou wast angry with me, thine anger is turned away, and thou comfortedst me.

Isa 13:9 — Behold, the day of the LORD cometh, cruel both with wrath and fierce anger, to lay the land desolate: and he shall destroy the sinners thereof out of it.

Isa 13:13 — Therefore I will shake the heavens, and the earth shall remove out of her place, in the wrath of the LORD of hosts, and in the day of his fierce anger.

Isa 30:27 — Behold, the name of the LORD cometh from far, burning *with* his anger, and the burden *thereof is* heavy: his lips are full of indignation, and his tongue as a devouring fire:

Isa 42:25 — Therefore he hath poured upon him the fury of his anger, and the strength of battle: and it hath set him on fire round about, yet he knew not; and it burned him, yet he laid *it* not to heart.

Isa 48:9 — For my name's sake will I defer mine anger, and for my praise will I refrain for thee, that I cut thee not off.

Isa 66:15 — For, behold, the LORD will come with fire, and with his chariots like a whirlwind, to render his anger with fury, and his rebuke with flames of fire.

Jer 3:12 — Go and proclaim these words toward the north, and say, Return, thou backsliding Israel, saith the LORD; *and* I will not cause mine anger to fall upon you: for I *am* merciful, saith the LORD, *and* I will not keep *anger* for ever.

Jer 4:4 — Circumcise yourselves to the LORD, and take away the foreskins of your heart, ye men of Judah and inhabitants of Jerusalem: lest my fury come forth like fire, and burn that none can quench *it*, because of the evil of your doings.

Jer 4:8 — For this gird you with sackcloth, lament and howl: for the fierce anger of the LORD is not turned back from us.

Jer 4:26 — I beheld, and, lo, the fruitful place *was* a wilderness, and all the cities thereof were broken down at the presence of the LORD, *and* by his fierce anger.

Jer 7:20 — Therefore thus saith the Lord GOD; Behold, mine anger and my fury shall be poured out upon this place, upon man, and upon beast, and upon the trees of the field, and upon the fruit of the ground; and it shall burn, and shall not be quenched.

Jer 10:10 — But the LORD *is* the true God, he *is* the living God, and an everlasting king: at his wrath the earth shall tremble, and the nations shall not be able to abide his indignation.

Jer 17:4 — And thou, even thyself, shalt discontinue from thine heritage that I gave thee; and I will cause thee to serve thine enemies in the land which thou knowest not: for ye have kindled a fire in mine anger, *which* shall burn for ever.

Jer 23:20 — The anger of the LORD shall not return, until he have executed, and till he have performed the thoughts of his heart: in the latter days ye shall consider it perfectly.

Jer 30:24 — The fierce anger of the LORD shall not return, until he have done *it,* and until he have performed the intents of his heart: in the latter days ye shall consider it.

Jer 32:37 — Behold, I will gather them out of all countries, whither I have driven them in mine anger, and in my fury, and in great wrath; and I will bring them again unto this place, and I will cause them to dwell safely:

Jer 33:5 — They come to fight with the Chaldeans, but *it is* fill them with the dead bodies of men, whom I have slain in mine anger and in my fury, and for all whose wickedness I have hid my face from this city.

Jer 36:7 — It may be they will present their supplication before the LORD, and will return every one from his evil way: for great *is* the anger and the fury that the LORD hath pronounced against this people.

Jer 42:18 — For thus saith the LORD of hosts, the God of Israel; As mine anger and my fury hath been poured forth upon the inhabitants of Jerusalem; so shall my fury be poured forth upon you, when ye shall enter into Egypt: and ye shall be an execration, and an astonishment, and a curse, and a reproach; and ye shall see this place no more.

Jer 44:6 — Wherefore my fury and mine anger was poured forth, and was kindled in the cities of Judah and in the streets of Jerusalem; and they are wasted *and* desolate, as at this day.

Jer 51:45 — My people, go ye out of the midst of her, and deliver ye every man his soul from the fierce anger of the LORD.

La 2:1 — How hath the Lord covered the daughter of Zion with a cloud in his anger, *and* cast down from heaven unto the earth the beauty of Israel, and remembered not his footstool in the day of his anger!

La 2:3 — He hath cut off in *his* fierce anger all the horn of Israel: he hath drawn back his right hand from before the enemy, and he burned against Jacob like a flaming fire, *which* devoureth round about.

La 2:6 — And he hath violently taken away his tabernacle, as *if it were of* a garden: he hath destroyed his places of the assembly: the LORD hath caused the solemn feasts and sabbaths to be forgotten in Zion, and hath despised in the indignation of his anger the king and the priest.

La 4:11 — The LORD hath accomplished his fury; he hath poured out his fierce anger, and hath kindled a fire in Zion, and it hath devoured the foundations thereof.

Eze 5:13 — Thus shall mine anger be accomplished, and I will cause my fury to rest upon them, and I will be comforted: and they shall know that I the LORD have spoken *it* in my zeal, when I have accomplished my fury in them.

Eze 5:15 — So it shall be a reproach and a taunt, an instruction and an astonishment unto the nations that *are* round about thee, when I shall execute judgments in thee in anger and in fury and in furious rebukes. I the LORD have spoken *it.*

Da 9:16 — O Lord, according to all thy righteousness, I beseech thee, let thine anger and thy fury be turned away from thy city Jerusalem, thy holy mountain: because for our sins, and for the iniquities of our fathers, Jerusalem and thy people *are become* a reproach to all *that are* about us.

Hos 11:9 — I will not execute the fierceness of mine anger, I will not return to destroy Ephraim: for I *am* God, and not man; the Holy One in the midst of thee: and I will not enter into the city.

Hos 13:11 — I gave thee a king in mine anger, and took *him* away in my wrath.

Hos 14:4 — I will heal their backsliding, I will love them freely: for mine anger is turned away from him.

Na 1:6 — Who can stand before his indignation? and who can abide in the fierceness of his anger? his fury is poured out like fire, and the rocks are thrown down by him.

Mt 22:7 — But when the king heard *thereof,* he was wroth: and he sent forth his armies, and destroyed those murderers, and burned up their city.

Mt 22:13 — Then said the king to the servants, Bind him hand and foot, and take him away, and cast *him* into outer darkness; there shall be weeping and gnashing of teeth.

Ro 1:18 — For the wrath of God is revealed from heaven against all ungodliness and unrighteousness of men, who hold the truth in unrighteousness;

Ro 2:5 — But after thy hardness and impenitent heart treasurest up unto thyself wrath against the day of wrath and revelation of the righteous judgment of God;

Eph 5:6 — Let no man deceive you with vain words: for because of these things cometh the wrath of God upon the children of disobedience.

Col 3:6 — For which things' sake the wrath of God cometh on the children of disobedience:

Heb 3:11 — So I sware in my wrath, They shall not enter into my rest.)

Heb 4:3 — For we which have believed do enter into rest, as he said, As I have sworn in my wrath, if they shall enter into my rest: although the works were finished from the foundation of the world.

Rev 15:1 — And I saw another sign in heaven, great and marvellous, seven angels having the seven last plagues; for in them is filled up the wrath of God.

Rev 15:7 — And one of the four beasts gave unto the seven angels seven golden vials full of the wrath of God, who liveth for ever and ever.

Rev 16:19 — And the great city was divided into three parts, and the cities of the nations fell: and great Babylon came in remembrance before God, to give unto her the cup of the wine of the fierceness of his wrath.

Rev 19:15 — And out of his mouth goeth a sharp sword, that with it he should smite the nations: and he shall rule them with a rod of iron: and he treadeth the winepress of the fierceness and wrath of Almighty God.

ANIAM • Son of Shemidah.

1Ch 7:19 — And the sons of Shemidah were, Ahian, and Shechem, and Likhi, and Aniam.

ANIM • A city of Judah.

Jos 15:50 — And Anab, and Eshtemoh, and Anim,

ANIMALS

• Creation of.

Ge 1:24–25

Ge 2:19 — And out of the ground the LORD God formed every beast of the field, and every fowl of the air; and brought *them* unto Adam to see what he would call them: and whatsoever Adam called every living creature, that *was* the name thereof.

Jer 27:5 — I have made the earth, the man and the beast that *are* upon the ground, by my great power and by my outstretched arm, and have given it unto whom it seemed meet unto me.

• Food of.

Ge 1:30 — And to every beast of the earth, and to every fowl of the air, and to every thing that creepeth upon the earth, wherein *there is* life, *I have given* every green herb for meat: and it was so.

• Named.

Ge 2:20 — And Adam gave names to all cattle, and to the fowl of the air, and to every beast of the field; but for Adam there was not found an help meet for him.

• Ordained as food for man.

Ge 9:2–3; Le 11:21–22; Dt 14:4–6

Le 11:3 — Whatsoever parteth the hoof, and is clovenfooted, *and* cheweth the cud, among the beasts, that shall ye eat.

Le 11:9 — These shall ye eat of all that *are* in the waters: whatsoever hath fins and scales in the waters, in the seas, and in the rivers, them shall ye eat.

Dt 14:9 — These ye shall eat of all that *are* in the waters: all that have fins and scales shall ye eat:

Dt 14:11 — *Of* all clean birds ye shall eat.

Dt 14:20 — *But of* all clean fowls ye may eat.

• God's care of.

Ge 9:9–10

Dt 25:4 — Thou shalt not muzzle the ox when he treadeth out *the corn.*

Job 38:41 — Who provideth for the raven his food? when his young ones cry unto God, they wander for lack of meat.

Ps 36:6 — Thy righteousness *is* like the great mountains; thy judgments *are* a great deep: O LORD, thou preservest man and beast.

Ps 104:11 — They give drink to every beast of the field: the wild asses quench their thirst.

Ps 104:21 — The young lions roar after their prey, and seek their meat from God.

Ps 147:9 — He giveth to the beast his food, *and* to the young ravens which cry.

Jnh 4:11 — And should not I spare Nineveh, that great city, wherein are more than sixscore thousand persons that cannot discern between their right hand and their left hand; and *also* much cattle?

Mt 6:26 — Behold the fowls of the air: for they sow not, neither do they reap, nor gather into barns; yet your heavenly Father feedeth them. Are ye not much better than they?

Mt 10:29 — Are not two sparrows sold for a farthing? and one of them shall not fall on the ground without your Father.

Lk 12:6 — Are not five sparrows sold for two farthings, and not one of them is forgotten before God?

Lk 12:24 — Consider the ravens: for they neither sow nor reap; which neither have storehouse nor barn; and God feedeth them: how much more are ye better than the fowls?

1Co 9:9 — For it is written in the law of Moses, Thou shalt not muzzle the mouth of the ox that treadeth out the corn. Doth God take care for oxen?

• Under the curse.

Ge 3:14 — And the LORD God said unto the serpent, Because thou hast done this, thou *art* cursed above all cattle, and above every beast of the field; upon thy belly shalt thou go, and dust shalt thou eat all the days of thy life:

Ge 6:7 — And the LORD said, I will destroy man whom I have created from the face of the earth; both man, and beast, and the creeping thing, and the fowls of the air; for it repenteth me that I have made them.

Ge 6:17 — And, behold, I, even I, do bring a flood of waters upon the earth, to destroy all flesh, wherein *is* the breath of life, from under heaven; *and* every thing that *is* in the earth shall die.

• Suffer under divine judgments, sent upon man.

Eze 14:19–21; Joel 1:18–20

Jer 7:20 — Therefore thus saith the Lord GOD; Behold, mine anger and my fury shall be poured out upon this place, upon man, and upon beast, and upon the trees of the field, and upon the fruit of the ground; and it shall burn, and shall not be quenched.

Jer 12:4 — How long shall the land mourn, and the herbs of every field wither, for the wickedness of them that dwell therein? the beasts are consumed, and the birds; because they said, He shall not see our last end.

Jer 21:6 — And I will smite the inhabitants of this city, both man and beast: they shall die of a great pestilence.

Eze 14:13 — Son of man, when the land sinneth against me by trespassing grievously, then will I stretch out mine hand upon it, and will break the staff of the bread thereof, and will send famine upon it, and will cut off man and beast from it:

Eze 14:17 — Or *if* I bring a sword upon that land, and say, Sword, go through the land; so that I cut off man and beast from it:

• Two of every sort preserved in the ark.

Ge 6:19–20; 7:2–3

Ge 7:5 — And Noah did according unto all that the LORD commanded him.

Ge 7:9 — There went in two and two unto Noah into the ark, the male and the female, as God had commanded Noah.

Ge 7:14 — They, and every beast after his kind, and all the cattle after their kind, and every creeping thing that creepeth upon the earth after his kind, and every fowl after his kind, every bird of every sort.

Ge 8:19 — Every beast, every creeping thing, and every fowl, *and* whatsoever creepeth upon the earth, after their kinds, went forth out of the ark.

• Suffered the plagues of Egypt.

Ex 9:9–10

Ex 8:17 — And they did so; for Aaron stretched out his hand with his rod, and smote the dust of the earth, and it became lice in man, and in beast; all the dust of the land became lice throughout all the land of Egypt.

Ex 9:19 — Send therefore now, *and* gather thy cattle, and all that thou hast in the field; *for upon* every man and beast which shall be found in the field, and shall not be brought home, the hail shall come down upon them, and they shall die.

Ex 11:5 — And all the firstborn in the land of Egypt shall die, from the firstborn of Pharaoh that sitteth upon his throne, even unto the firstborn of the maidservant that *is* behind the mill; and all the firstborn of beasts.

• Perish at death.

Ecc 3:21 — Who knoweth the spirit of man that goeth upward, and the spirit of the beast that goeth downward to the earth?

Ecc 12:7 — Then shall the dust return to the earth as it was: and the spirit shall return unto God who gave it.

• Possessed of devils.

Mt 8:31–32

Mk 5:13 — And forthwith Jesus gave them leave. And the unclean spirits went out, and entered into the swine: and the herd ran violently down a steep place into the sea, (they were about two thousand;) and were choked in the sea.

Lk 8:33 — Then went the devils out of the man, and entered into the swine: and the herd ran violently down a steep place into the lake, and were choked.

• Clean and unclean.

Le 11:1–47; Dt 14:3–20; Ac 10:11–15; 1Ti 4:3–5

Ge 8:20 — And Noah builded an altar unto the LORD; and took of every clean beast, and of every clean fowl, and offered burnt offerings on the altar.

Le 7:21 — Moreover the soul that shall touch any unclean *thing, as* the uncleanness of man, or *any* unclean beast, or any abominable unclean *thing,* and eat of the flesh of the sacrifice of peace offerings, which *pertain* unto the LORD, even that soul shall be cut off from his people.

Le 20:25 — Ye shall therefore put difference between clean beasts and unclean, and between unclean fowls and clean: and ye shall not make your souls abominable by beast, or by fowl, or by any manner of living thing that creepeth on the ground, which I have separated from you as unclean.

• Offered in sacrifice.

Ge 7:2–8

Ge 4:4 — And Abel, he also brought of the firstlings of his flock and of the fat thereof. And the LORD had respect unto Abel and to his offering:

Ge 8:20 — And Noah builded an altar unto the LORD; and took of every clean beast, and of every clean fowl, and offered burnt offerings on the altar.

See: Offerings

• God's control of.

Ps 91:13 — Thou shalt tread upon the lion and adder: the young lion and the dragon shalt thou trample under feet.

Isa 11:6 — The wolf also shall dwell with the lamb, and the leopard shall lie down with the kid; and the calf and the young lion and the fatling together; and a little child shall lead them.

Isa 11:8 — And the sucking child shall play on the hole of the asp, and the weaned child shall put his hand on the cockatrice' den.

Isa 35:9 — No lion shall be there, nor *any* ravenous beast shall go up thereon, it shall not be found there; but the redeemed shall walk *there:*

Lk 10:19 — Behold, I give unto you power to tread on serpents and scorpions, and over all the power of the enemy: and nothing shall by any means hurt you.

• Instruments of God's will.

Ex 8:1–10:20

Nu 21:6 — And the LORD sent fiery serpents among the people, and they bit the people; and much people of Israel died.

Nu 22:28 — And the LORD opened the mouth of the ass, and she said unto Balaam, What have I done unto thee, that thou hast smitten me these three times?

Jos 24:12 — And I sent the hornet before you, which drave them out from before you, *even* the two kings of the Amorites; *but* not with thy sword, nor with thy bow.

Jer 8:17 — For, behold, I will send serpents, cockatrices, among you, which *will* not *be* charmed, and they shall bite you, saith the LORD.

Joel 1:4 — That which the palmerworm hath left hath the locust eaten; and that which the locust hath left hath the cankerworm eaten; and that which the cankerworm hath left hath the caterpiller eaten.

• Belong to God.

Ps 50:10–12

• Sent in judgment.

Nu 21:6–7

Le 26:22 — I will also send wild beasts among you, which shall rob you of your children, and destroy your cattle, and make you few in number; and your *high* ways shall be desolate.

Dt 8:15 — Who led thee through that great and terrible wilderness, *wherein were* fiery serpents, and scorpions, and drought, where *there was* no water; who brought thee forth water out of the rock of flint;

Dt 28:26 — And thy carcase shall be meat unto all fowls of the air, and unto the beasts of the earth, and no man shall fray *them* away.

Eze 5:17 — So will I send upon you famine and evil beasts, and they shall bereave thee; and pestilence and blood shall pass through thee; and I will bring the sword upon thee. I the LORD have spoken *it.*

Eze 14:15 — If I cause noisome beasts to pass through the land, and they spoil it, so that it be desolate, that no man may pass through because of the beasts:

Eze 32:4 — Then will I leave thee upon the land, I will cast thee forth upon the open field, and will cause all the fowls of the heaven to remain upon thee, and I will fill the beasts of the whole earth with thee.

Rev 6:8 — And I looked, and behold a pale horse: and his name that sat on him was Death, and Hell followed with him. And power was given unto them over the fourth part of the earth, to kill with sword, and with hunger, and with death, and with the beasts of the earth.

• Paul contends with.

1Co 15:32 — If after the manner of men I have fought with beasts at Ephesus, what advantageth it me, if the dead rise not? let us eat and drink; for to morrow we die.

• Nature of.

Job 39:1–30; Ecc 3:18–21

Ps 32:9 — Be ye not as the horse, *or* as the mule, *which* have no understanding: whose mouth must be held in with bit and bridle, lest they come near unto thee.

Ps 49:12 — Nevertheless man *being* in honour abideth not: he is like the beasts *that* perish.

• Habits of.

Job 12:7–8; 39:1–30; Ps 104:20–25; Isa 13:21–22

Job 37:8 — Then the beasts go into dens, and remain in their places.

Job 40:20 — Surely the mountains bring him forth food, where all the beasts of the field play.

Ps 29:9 — The voice of the LORD maketh the hinds to calve, and discovereth the forests: and in his temple doth every one speak of *his* glory.

Isa 34:14 — The wild beasts of the desert shall also meet with the wild beasts of the island, and the satyr shall cry to his fellow; the screech owl also shall rest there, and find for herself a place of rest.

Jas 3:7 — For every kind of beasts, and of birds, and of serpents, and of things in the sea, is tamed, and hath been tamed of mankind:

• Menstruation of.

Jer 2:24 — A wild ass used to the wilderness, *that* snuffeth up the wind at her pleasure; in her occasion who can turn her away? all they that seek her will not weary themselves; in her month they shall find her.

• Facts about breeding.

Ge 30:35–43; 31:8–9

• Instincts of.

Job 39:1–41:34; Ps 104:1–35; Pr 6:6–8; 30:25–28

Dt 32:11 — As an eagle stirreth up her nest, fluttereth over her young, spreadeth abroad her wings, taketh them, beareth them on her wings:

Job 35:11 — Who teacheth us more than the beasts of the earth, and maketh us wiser than the fowls of heaven?

Ps 59:6 — They return at evening: they make a noise like a dog, and go round about the city.

Jer 8:7 — Yea, the stork in the heaven knoweth her appointed times; and the turtle and the crane and the swallow observe the time of their coming; but my people know not the judgment of the LORD.

Mt 24:28 — For wheresoever the carcase is, there will the eagles be gathered together.

• Abodes of.

Job 39:1–30; Ps 104:20–25

Job 24:5 — Behold, *as* wild asses in the desert, go they forth to their work; rising betimes for a prey: the wilderness *yieldeth* food for them *and* for *their* children.

Job 37:8 — Then the beasts go into dens, and remain in their places.

Isa 34:14 — The wild beasts of the desert shall also meet with the wild beasts of the island, and the satyr shall cry to his fellow; the screech owl also shall rest there, and find for herself a place of rest.

Jer 2:24 — A wild ass used to the wilderness, *that* snuffeth up the wind at her pleasure; in her occasion who can turn her away? all they that seek her will not weary themselves; in her month they shall find her.

Jer 50:39 — Therefore the wild beasts of the desert with the wild beasts of the islands shall dwell *there,* and the owls shall dwell therein: and it shall be no more inhabited for ever; neither shall it be dwelt in from generation to generation.

Mk 1:13 — And he was there in the wilderness forty days, tempted of Satan; and was with the wild beasts; and the angels ministered unto him.

See: Birds

See: Cattle, of the bovine species

See: Fish

• Beasts, symbolic.

Rev 4:6–9; 5:6–6:7; 13:1–18; 16:10–13; 17:1–18; 19:19–20

Isa 30:6 — The burden of the beasts of the south: into the land of trouble and anguish, from whence *come* the young and old lion, the viper and fiery flying serpent, they will carry their riches upon the shoulders of young asses, and their treasures upon the bunches of camels, to a people *that* shall not profit *them.*

Da 7:11 — I beheld then because of the voice of the great words which the horn spake: I beheld *even* till the beast was slain, and his body destroyed, and given to the burning flame.

Da 7:17 — These great beasts, which are four, *are* four kings, *which* shall arise out of the earth.

Da 7:19 — Then I would know the truth of the fourth beast, which was diverse from all the others, exceeding dreadful, whose teeth *were of* iron, and his nails *of* brass; *which* devoured, brake in pieces, and stamped the residue with his feet;

Da 8:4 — I saw the ram pushing westward, and northward, and southward; so that no beasts might stand before him, neither *was there any* that could deliver out of his hand; but he did according to his will, and became great.

Ac 10:12 — Wherein were all manner of fourfooted beasts of the earth, and wild beasts, and creeping things, and fowls of the air.

Rev 7:11 — And all the angels stood round about the throne, and *about* the elders and the four beasts, and fell before the throne on their faces, and worshipped God,

Rev 11:7 — And when they shall have finished their testimony, the beast that ascendeth out of the bottomless pit shall make war against them, and shall overcome them, and kill them.

Rev 14:3 — And they sung as it were a new song before the throne, and before the four beasts, and the elders: and no man could learn that song but the hundred *and* forty *and* four thousand, which were redeemed from the earth.

Rev 14:9 — And the third angel followed them, saying with a loud voice, If any man worship the beast and his image, and receive *his* mark in his forehead, or in his hand,

Rev 14:11 — And the smoke of their torment ascendeth up for ever and ever: and they have no rest day nor night, who worship the beast and his image, and whosoever receiveth the mark of his name.

Rev 15:2 — And I saw as it were a sea of glass mingled with fire: and them that had gotten the victory over the beast, and over his image, and over his mark, *and* over the number of his name, stand on the sea of glass, having the harps of God.

Rev 16:2 — And the first went, and poured out his vial upon the earth; and there fell a noisome and grievous sore upon the men which had the mark of the beast, and *upon* them which worshipped his image.

Rev 19:4 — And the four and twenty elders and the four beasts fell down and worshipped God that sat on the throne, saying, Amen; Alleluia.

Rev 20:4 — And I saw thrones, and they sat upon them, and judgment was given unto them: and *I saw* the souls of them that were beheaded for the witness of Jesus, and for the word of God, and which had not worshipped the beast, neither his image, neither had received *his* mark upon their foreheads, or in their hands; and they lived and reigned with Christ a thousand years.

Rev 20:10 — And the devil that deceived them was cast into the lake of fire and brimstone, where the beast and the false prophet *are,* and shall be tormented day and night for ever and ever.

- **Cruelty to.**
  - **Instances of.**
    - **Balaam.**

Nu 22:22–33

- **Houghing horses.**

2Sa 8:4 — And David took from him a thousand *chariots,* and seven hundred horsemen, and twenty thousand footmen: and David houghed all the chariot *horses,* but reserved of them *for* an hundred chariots.

1Ch 18:4 — And David took from him a thousand chariots, and seven thousand horsemen, and twenty thousand footmen: David also houghed all the chariot *horses,* but reserved of them an hundred chariots.

See: Houghing

- **Kindness to.**

Pr 12:10 — A righteous *man* regardeth the life of his beast: but the tender mercies of the wicked *are* cruel.

- **Jacob, in erecting booths for his cattle.**

Ge 33:17 — And Jacob journeyed to Succoth, and built him an house, and made booths for his cattle: therefore the name of the place is called Succoth.

- **People of Gerar, in providing tents for cattle.**

2Ch 14:15 — They smote also the tents of cattle, and carried away sheep and camels in abundance, and returned to Jerusalem.

- **Laws concerning.**

Ex 21:28–22:4; Dt 22:6–7

Ex 20:10 — But the seventh day *is* the sabbath of the LORD thy God: *in it* thou shalt not do any work, thou, nor thy son, nor thy daughter, thy manservant, nor thy maidservant, nor thy cattle, nor thy stranger that *is* within thy gates:

Ex 23:5 — If thou see the ass of him that hateth thee lying under his burden, and wouldest forbear to help him, thou shalt surely help with him.

Ex 23:12 — Six days thou shalt do thy work, and on the seventh day thou shalt rest: that thine ox and thine ass may rest, and the son of thy handmaid, and the stranger, may be refreshed.

Le 19:19 — Ye shall keep my statutes. Thou shalt not let thy cattle gender with a diverse kind: thou shalt not sow thy field with mingled seed: neither shall a garment mingled of linen and woollen come upon thee.

Dt 5:14 — But the seventh day *is* the sabbath of the LORD thy God: *in it* thou shalt not do any work, thou, nor thy son, nor thy daughter, nor thy manservant, nor thy maidservant, nor thine ox, nor thine ass, nor any of thy cattle, nor thy stranger that *is* within thy gates; that thy manservant and thy maidservant may rest as well as thou.

Dt 22:4 — Thou shalt not see thy brother's ass or his ox fall down by the way, and hide thyself from them: thou shalt surely help him to lift *them* up again.

Dt 22:10 — Thou shalt not plow with an ox and an ass together.

Dt 25:4 — Thou shalt not muzzle the ox when he treadeth out *the corn.*

Pr 12:10 — A righteous *man* regardeth the life of his beast: but the tender mercies of the wicked *are* cruel.

1Ti 5:18 — For the scripture saith, Thou shalt not muzzle the ox that treadeth out the corn. And, The labourer *is* worthy of his reward.

- **Firstlings of.**

See: Firstborn

- **Man's dominion over.**

See: Man; dominion of

See: Adder

See: Ant

See: Antelope

- See: Ape
- See: Asp
- See: Ass
- See: Badger
- See: Bat
- See: Bear
- See: Behemoth
- See: Birds
- See: Boar
- See: Camel
- See: Chameleon
- See: Chamois
- See: Chickens
- See: Cockatrice
- See: Coney
- See: Deer
- See: Dog
- See: Dragon
- See: Dromedary
- See: Elephant
- See: Ferret
- See: Fish
- See: Fox
- See: Frogs
- See: Goat
- See: Greyhound
- See: Hare
- See: Hart
- See: Hind
- See: Hippopotamus
- See: Hornet
- See: Horse
- See: Kine
- See: Leopard
- See: Leviathan
- See: Lion
- See: Lizard
- See: Mole
- See: Mouse
- See: Pygarg
- See: Ram
- See: Roe
- See: Satyr
- See: Scorpion
- See: Serpent
- See: Sheep
- See: Swine
- See: Unicorn
- See: Viper
- See: Weasel
- See: Whale
- See: Wolf
- See: Worm
- See: Insects

ANISE • A seed used as a condiment.

Mt 23:23 — Woe unto you, scribes and Pharisees, hypocrites! for ye pay tithe of mint and anise and cummin, and have omitted the weightier *matters* of the law, judgment, mercy, and faith: these ought ye to have done, and not to leave the other undone.

ANNA • A devout widow.

Lk 2:36–37

ANNAS • Associate high priest with Caiaphas.

Lk 3:2 — Annas and Caiaphas being the high priests, the word of God came unto John the son of Zacharias in the wilderness.

Jn 18:13 — And led him away to Annas first; for he was father in law to Caiaphas, which was the high priest that same year.

Jn 18:19 — The high priest then asked Jesus of his disciples, and of his doctrine.

Jn 18:24 — Now Annas had sent him bound unto Caiaphas the high priest.

Ac 4:6 — And Annas the high priest, and Caiaphas, and John, and Alexander, and as many as were of the kindred of the high priest, were gathered together at Jerusalem.

ANOINTING

• Of the body.

Dt 28:40 — Thou shalt have olive trees throughout all thy coasts, but thou shalt not anoint *thyself* with the oil; for thine olive shall cast *his fruit*.

Ru 3:3 — Wash thyself therefore, and anoint thee, and put thy raiment upon thee, and get thee down to the floor: *but* make not thyself known unto the man, until he shall have done eating and drinking.

Est 2:12 — Now when every maid's turn was come to go in to king Ahasuerus, after that she had been twelve months, according to the manner of the women, (for so were the days of their purifications accomplished, *to wit*, six months with oil of myrrh, and six months with sweet odours, and with *other* things for the purifying of the women;)

Ps 92:10 — But my horn shalt thou exalt like *the horn of* an unicorn: I shall be anointed with fresh oil.

Ps 104:15 — And wine *that* maketh glad the heart of man, *and* oil to make *his* face to shine, and bread *which* strengtheneth man's heart.

Ps 141:5 — Let the righteous smite me; *it shall be* a kindness: and let him reprove me; *it shall be* an excellent oil, *which* shall not break my head: for yet my prayer also *shall be* in their calamities.

Pr 27:9 — Ointment and perfume rejoice the heart: so *doth* the sweetness of a man's friend by hearty counsel.

Pr 27:16 — Whosoever hideth her hideth the wind, and the ointment of his right hand, *which* bewrayeth *itself.*

Ecc 9:8 — Let thy garments be always white; and let thy head lack no ointment.

SS 1:3 — Because of the savour of thy good ointments thy name *is as* ointment poured forth, therefore do the virgins love thee.

SS 4:10 — How fair is thy love, my sister, *my* spouse! how much better is thy love than wine! and the smell of thine ointments than all spices!

Isa 57:9 — And thou wentest to the king with ointment, and didst increase thy perfumes, and didst send thy messengers far off, and didst debase *thyself even* unto hell.

Am 6:6 — That drink wine in bowls, and anoint themselves with the chief ointments: but they are not grieved for the affliction of Joseph.

Mic 6:15 — Thou shalt sow, but thou shalt not reap; thou shalt tread the olives, but thou shalt not anoint thee with oil; and sweet wine, but shalt not drink wine.

• Of guests.

2Ch 28:15 — And the men which were expressed by name rose up, and took the captives, and with the spoil clothed all that were naked among them, and arrayed them, and shod them, and gave them to eat and to drink, and anointed them, and carried all the feeble of them upon asses, and brought them to Jericho, the city of palm trees, to their brethren: then they returned to Samaria.

Lk 7:46 — My head with oil thou didst not anoint: but this woman hath anointed my feet with ointment.

• The sick.

Isa 1:6 — From the sole of the foot even unto the head *there is* no soundness in it; *but* wounds, and bruises, and putrifying sores: they have not been closed, neither bound up, neither mollified with ointment.

Mk 6:13 — And they cast out many devils, and anointed with oil many that were sick, and healed *them.*

Lk 10:34 — And went to *him,* and bound up his wounds, pouring in oil and wine, and set him on his own beast, and brought him to an inn, and took care of him.

Jas 5:14 — Is any sick among you? let him call for the elders of the church; and let them pray over him, anointing him with oil in the name of the Lord:

Rev 3:18 — I counsel thee to buy of me gold tried in the fire, that thou mayest be rich; and white raiment, that thou mayest be clothed, and *that* the shame of thy nakedness do not appear; and anoint thine eyes with eyesalve, that thou mayest see.

• The dead.

Mt 26:12 — For in that she hath poured this ointment on my body, she did *it* for my burial.

Mk 14:8 — She hath done what she could: she is come aforehand to anoint my body to the burying.

Mk 16:1 — And when the sabbath was past, Mary Magdalene, and Mary the *mother* of James, and Salome, had bought sweet spices, that they might come and anoint him.

Lk 23:56 — And they returned, and prepared spices and ointments; and rested the sabbath day according to the commandment.

• Of Jesus, as a token of love.

Lk 7:37–38

Lk 7:46 — My head with oil thou didst not anoint: but this woman hath anointed my feet with ointment.

Jn 11:2 — (It was *that* Mary which anointed the Lord with ointment, and wiped his feet with her hair, whose brother Lazarus was sick.)

Jn 12:3 — Then took Mary a pound of ointment of spikenard, very costly, and anointed the feet of Jesus, and wiped his feet with her hair: and the house was filled with the odour of the ointment.

• Omitted in mourning.

2Sa 12:20 — Then David arose from the earth, and washed, and anointed *himself,* and changed his apparel, and came into the house of the LORD, and worshipped: then he came to his own house; and when he required, they set bread before him, and he did eat.

2Sa 14:2 — And Joab sent to Tekoah, and fetched thence a wise woman, and said unto her, I pray thee, feign thyself to be a mourner, and put on now mourning apparel, and anoint not thyself with oil, but be as a woman that had a long time mourned for the dead:

Isa 61:3 — To appoint unto them that mourn in Zion, to give unto them beauty for ashes, the oil of joy for mourning, the garment of praise for the spirit of heaviness; that they might be called trees of righteousness, the planting of the LORD, that he might be glorified.

Da 10:3 — I ate no pleasant bread, neither came flesh nor wine in my mouth, neither did I anoint myself at all, till three whole weeks were fulfilled.

• God preserves those who receive.

Ps 89:20–23

Ps 18:50 — Great deliverance giveth he to his king; and sheweth mercy to his anointed, to David, and to his seed for evermore.

Ps 20:6 — Now know I that the LORD saveth his anointed; he will hear him from his holy heaven with the saving strength of his right hand.

• Saints receive.

Isa 61:3 — To appoint unto them that mourn in Zion, to give unto them beauty for ashes, the oil of joy for mourning, the garment of praise for the spirit of heaviness; that they might be called trees of righteousness, the planting of the LORD, that he might be glorified.

1Jn 2:20 — But ye have an unction from the Holy One, and ye know all things.

• In consecration.

• Of high priests.

Ex 29:7 — Then shalt thou take the anointing oil, and pour *it* upon his head, and anoint him.

Ex 29:29 — And the holy garments of Aaron shall be his sons' after him, to be anointed therein, and to be consecrated in them.

Ex 40:13 — And thou shalt put upon Aaron the holy garments, and anoint him, and sanctify him; that he may minister unto me in the priest's office.

Le 6:20 — This *is* the offering of Aaron and of his sons, which they shall offer unto the LORD in the day when he is anointed; the tenth part of an ephah of fine flour for a meat offering perpetual, half of it in the morning, and half thereof at night.

Le 8:12 — And he poured of the anointing oil upon Aaron's head, and anointed him, to sanctify him.

Le 16:32 — And the priest, whom he shall anoint, and whom he shall consecrate to minister in the priest's office in his father's stead, shall make the atonement, and shall put on the linen clothes, *even* the holy garments:

Nu 35:25 — And the congregation shall deliver the slayer out of the hand of the revenger of blood, and the congregation shall restore him to the city of his refuge, whither he was fled: and he shall abide in it unto the death of the high priest, which was anointed with the holy oil.

Ps 133:2 — *It is* like the precious ointment upon the head, that ran down upon the beard, *even* Aaron's beard: that went down to the skirts of his garments;

• Of priests.

Ex 28:41 — And thou shalt put them upon Aaron thy brother, and his sons with him; and shalt anoint them, and consecrate them, and sanctify them, that they may minister unto me in the priest's office.

Ex 30:30 — And thou shalt anoint Aaron and his sons, and consecrate them, that *they* may minister unto me in the priest's office.

Ex 40:15 — And thou shalt anoint them, as thou didst anoint their father, that they may minister unto me in the priest's office: for their anointing shall surely be an everlasting priesthood throughout their generations.

Le 4:3 — If the priest that is anointed do sin according to the sin of the people; then let him bring for his sin, which he hath sinned, a young bullock without blemish unto the LORD for a sin offering.

Le 8:30 — And Moses took of the anointing oil, and of the blood which *was* upon the altar, and sprinkled *it* upon Aaron, *and* upon his garments, and upon his sons, and upon his sons' garments with him; and sanctified Aaron, *and* his garments, and his sons, and his sons' garments with him.

Nu 3:3 — These *are* the names of the sons of Aaron, the priests which were anointed, whom he consecrated to minister in the priest's office.

• Of kings.

Jgs 9:8 — The trees went forth *on a time* to anoint a king over them; and they said unto the olive tree, Reign thou over us.

Jgs 9:15 — And the bramble said unto the trees, If in truth ye anoint me king over you, *then* come *and* put your trust in my shadow: and if not, let fire come out of the bramble, and devour the cedars of Lebanon.

• Saul.

1Sa 9:16 — To morrow about this time I will send thee a man out of the land of Benjamin, and thou shalt anoint him *to be* captain over my people Israel, that he may save my people out of the hand of the Philistines: for I have looked upon my people, because their cry is come unto me.

1Sa 10:1 — Then Samuel took a vial of oil, and poured *it* upon his head, and kissed him, and said, *Is it* not because the LORD hath anointed thee *to be* captain over his inheritance?

1Sa 15:1 — Samuel also said unto Saul, The LORD sent me to anoint thee *to be* king over his people, over Israel: now therefore hearken thou unto the voice of the words of the LORD.

• David.

1Sa 16:12–13

1Sa 16:3 — And call Jesse to the sacrifice, and I will shew thee what thou shalt do: and thou shalt anoint unto me *him* whom I name unto thee.

2Sa 2:4 — And the men of Judah came, and there they anointed David king over the house of Judah. And they told David, saying, *That* the men of Jabesh-gilead *were they* that buried Saul.

2Sa 5:3 — So all the elders of Israel came to the king to Hebron; and king David made a league with them in Hebron before the LORD: and they anointed David king over Israel.

2Sa 12:7 — And Nathan said to David, Thou *art* the man. Thus saith the LORD God of Israel, I anointed thee king over Israel, and I delivered thee out of the hand of Saul;

2Sa 19:21 — But Abishai the son of Zeruiah answered and said, Shall not Shimei be put to death for this, because he cursed the LORD's anointed?

1Ch 11:3 — Therefore came all the elders of Israel to the king to Hebron; and David made a covenant with them in Hebron before the LORD; and they anointed David king over Israel, according to the word of the LORD by Samuel.

• Solomon.

1Ki 1:39 — And Zadok the priest took an horn of oil out of the tabernacle, and anointed Solomon. And they blew the trumpet; and all the people said, God save king Solomon.

1Ch 29:22 — And did eat and drink before the LORD on that day with great gladness. And they made Solomon the son of David king the second time, and anointed *him* unto the LORD *to be* the chief governor, and Zadok *to be* priest.

• Jehu.

2Ki 9:1–3

1Ki 19:16 — And Jehu the son of Nimshi shalt thou anoint *to be* king over Israel: and Elisha the son of Shaphat of Abel-meholah shalt thou anoint *to be* prophet in thy room.

2Ki 9:6 — And he arose, and went into the house; and he poured the oil on his head, and said unto him, Thus saith the LORD God of Israel, I have anointed thee king over the people of the LORD, *even* over Israel.

2Ki 9:12 — And they said, *It is* false; tell us now. And he said, Thus and thus spake he to me, saying, Thus saith the LORD, I have anointed thee king over Israel.

- **Hazael.**

1Ki 19:15 — And the LORD said unto him, Go, return on thy way to the wilderness of Damascus: and when thou comest, anoint Hazael *to be* king over Syria:

- **Joash.**

2Ki 11:12 — And he brought forth the king's son, and put the crown upon him, and *gave him* the testimony; and they made him king, and anointed him; and they clapped their hands, and said, God save the king.

2Ch 23:11 — Then they brought out the king's son, and put upon him the crown, and *gave him* the testimony, and made him king. And Jehoiada and his sons anointed him, and said, God save the king.

- **Jehoahaz.**

2Ki 23:30 — And his servants carried him in a chariot dead from Megiddo, and brought him to Jerusalem, and buried him in his own sepulchre. And the people of the land took Jehoahaz the son of Josiah, and anointed him, and made him king in his father's stead.

- **Cyrus.**

Isa 45:1 — Thus saith the LORD to his anointed, to Cyrus, whose right hand I have holden, to subdue nations before him; and I will loose the loins of kings, to open before him the two leaved gates; and the gates shall not be shut;

- **Of prophets.**

1Ki 19:16 — And Jehu the son of Nimshi shalt thou anoint *to be* king over Israel: and Elisha the son of Shaphat of Abel-meholah shalt thou anoint *to be* prophet in thy room.

- **Of the tabernacle.**

Ex 30:26 — And thou shalt anoint the tabernacle of the congregation therewith, and the ark of the testimony,

Ex 40:9 — And thou shalt take the anointing oil, and anoint the tabernacle, and all that *is* therein, and shalt hallow it, and all the vessels thereof: and it shall be holy.

Le 8:10 — And Moses took the anointing oil, and anointed the tabernacle and all that *was* therein, and sanctified them.

Nu 7:1 — And it came to pass on the day that Moses had fully set up the tabernacle, and had anointed it, and sanctified it, and all the instruments thereof, both the altar and all the vessels thereof, and had anointed them, and sanctified them;

- **Altars of.**

Ex 30:26–28

Ex 40:10 — And thou shalt anoint the altar of the burnt offering, and all his vessels, and sanctify the altar: and it shall be an altar most holy.

Le 8:11 — And he sprinkled thereof upon the altar seven times, and anointed the altar and all his vessels, both the laver and his foot, to sanctify them.

Nu 7:1 — And it came to pass on the day that Moses had fully set up the tabernacle, and had anointed it, and sanctified it, and all the instruments thereof, both the altar and all the vessels thereof, and had anointed them, and sanctified them;

- **Vessels of.**

Ex 30:27–28; 40:9–10; Le 8:10–11

Nu 7:1 — And it came to pass on the day that Moses had fully set up the tabernacle, and had anointed it, and sanctified it, and all the instruments thereof, both the altar and all the vessels thereof, and had anointed them, and sanctified them;

- **Jacob's Pillar.**
  - **At Bethel.**

Ge 28:18 — And Jacob rose up early in the morning, and took the stone that he had put *for* his pillows, and set it up *for* a pillar, and poured oil upon the top of it.

Ge 31:13 — I *am* the God of Bethel, where thou anointedst the pillar, *and* where thou vowedst a vow unto me: now arise, get thee out from this land, and return unto the land of thy kindred.

Ge 35:14 — And Jacob set up a pillar in the place where he talked with him, *even* a pillar of stone: and he poured a drink offering thereon, and he poured oil thereon.

See: Dedication

- **Figurative.**
  - **Of Christ's kingly and priestly office.**

Ps 45:7 — Thou lovest righteousness, and hatest wickedness: therefore God, thy God, hath anointed thee with the oil of gladness above thy fellows.

Ps 89:20 — I have found David my servant; with my holy oil have I anointed him:

Isa 61:1 — The Spirit of the Lord GOD *is* upon me; because the LORD hath anointed me to preach good tidings unto the meek; he hath sent me to bind up the brokenhearted, to proclaim liberty to the captives, and the opening of the prison to *them that are* bound;

Da 9:24 — Seventy weeks are determined upon thy people and upon thy holy city, to finish the transgression, and to make an end of sins, and to make reconciliation for iniquity, and to bring in everlasting righteousness, and to seal up the vision and prophecy, and to anoint the most Holy.

Lk 4:18 — The Spirit of the Lord is upon me, because he hath anointed me to preach the gospel to the poor; he hath sent me to heal the broken-hearted, to preach deliverance to the captives, and recovering of sight to the blind, to set at liberty them that are bruised,

Ac 4:27 — For of a truth against thy holy child Jesus, whom thou hast anointed, both Herod, and Pontius Pilate, with the Gentiles, and the people of Israel, were gathered together,

Ac 10:38 — How God anointed Jesus of Nazareth with the Holy Ghost and with power: who went about doing good, and healing all that were oppressed of the devil; for God was with him.

Heb 1:9 — Thou hast loved righteousness, and hated iniquity; therefore God, *even* thy God, hath anointed thee with the oil of gladness above thy fellows.

- **Of spiritual gifts.**

2Co 1:21 — Now he which stablisheth us with you in Christ, and hath anointed us, *is* God;

1Jn 2:20 — But ye have an unction from the Holy One, and ye know all things.

1Jn 2:27 — But the anointing which ye have received of him abideth in you, and ye need not that any man teach you: but as the same anointing teacheth you of all things, and is truth, and is no lie, and even as it hath taught you, ye shall abide in him.

- **Typified.**

Ex 40:13–15

Le 8:12 — And he poured of the anointing oil upon Aaron's head, and anointed him, to sanctify him.

1Sa 16:13 — Then Samuel took the horn of oil, and anointed him in the midst of his brethren: and the Spirit of the LORD came upon David from that day forward. So Samuel rose up, and went to Ramah.

1Ki 19:16 — And Jehu the son of Nimshi shalt thou anoint *to be* king over Israel: and Elisha the son of Shaphat of Abel-meholah shalt thou anoint *to be* prophet in thy room.

- **Symbolic of Jesus.**

Mt 26:7–12; Jn 12:3–7

ANOINTING OIL

- **Formula of, given by Moses.**

Ex 30:22–25, 31–33

→See: Oil

→See: Ointment

ANT

Pr 6:6–8

Pr 30:25 — The ants *are* a people not strong, yet they prepare their meat in the summer;

ANTEDILUVIANS

- **Worship God.**

Ge 4:3–4

Ge 4:26 — And to Seth, to him also there was born a son; and he called his name Enos: then began men to call upon the name of the LORD.

- **Occupations of.**

Ge 4:2–3, 20–22

- **Arts of.**

Ge 4:2–3, 20–22; 6:14–22

- **Enoch prophesies to.**

Jude 1:14–15

- **Noah preaches to.**

2Pe 2:5 — And spared not the old world, but saved Noah the eighth *person,* a preacher of righteousness, bringing in the flood upon the world of the ungodly;

- **Wickedness of.**

Ge 6:5–7

- **Destruction of.**

Ge 7:21–23; Job 22:15–17; Mt 24:37–39; Lk 17:26–27

Ge 7:1 — And the LORD said unto Noah, Come thou and all thy house into the ark; for thee have I seen righteous before me in this generation.

2Pe 2:5 — And spared not the old world, but saved Noah the eighth *person,* a preacher of righteousness, bringing in the flood upon the world of the ungodly;

→See: Flood

- **Longevity of.**

→See: Longevity

- **Giants among.**

→See: Giants

ANTELOPE →See: Deer

ANTHROPOMORPHISMS

- **Figures of speech, which attribute human forms, acts, and affections to God.**
- **Miscellaneous figures.**

Ge 2:2–3; 18:17–19; Ps 35:1–3

Ge 2:19 — And out of the ground the LORD God formed every beast of the field, and every fowl of the air; and brought *them* unto Adam to see what he would call them: and whatsoever Adam called every living creature, that *was* the name thereof.

Ge 6:6 — And it repented the LORD that he had made man on the earth, and it grieved him at his heart.

Ge 9:16 — And the bow shall be in the cloud; and I will look upon it, that I may remember the everlasting covenant between God and every living creature of all flesh that *is* upon the earth.

Ge 11:5 — And the LORD came down to see the city and the tower, which the children of men builded.

Ge 11:7 — Go to, let us go down, and there confound their language, that they may not understand one another's speech.

Ge 18:21 — I will go down now, and see whether they have done altogether according to the cry of it, which is come unto me; and if not, I will know.

Ge 18:33 — And the LORD went his way, as soon as he had left communing with Abraham: and Abraham returned unto his place.

Ge 19:29 — And it came to pass, when God destroyed the cities of the plain, that God remembered Abraham, and sent Lot out of the midst of the overthrow, when he overthrew the cities in the which Lot dwelt.

Ge 22:12 — And he said, Lay not thine hand upon the lad, neither do thou any thing unto him: for now I know that thou fearest God, seeing thou hast not withheld thy son, thine only *son* from me.

Ge 28:13 — And, behold, the LORD stood above it, and said, I *am* the LORD God of Abraham thy father, and the God of Isaac: the land whereon thou liest, to thee will I give it, and to thy seed;

Ge 35:13 — And God went up from him in the place where he talked with him.

Ex 2:24 — And God heard their groaning, and God remembered his covenant with Abraham, with Isaac, and with Jacob.

Ex 3:8 — And I am come down to deliver them out of the hand of the Egyptians, and to bring them up out of that land unto a good land and a large, unto a land flowing with milk and honey; unto the place of the Canaanites, and the Hittites, and the Amorites, and the Perizzites, and the Hivites, and the Jebusites.

Ex 14:24 — And it came to pass, that in the morning watch the LORD looked unto the host of the Egyptians through the pillar of fire and of the cloud, and troubled the host of the Egyptians,

Ex 20:5 — Thou shalt not bow down thyself to them, nor serve them: for I the LORD thy God *am* a jealous God, visiting the iniquity of the fathers upon the children unto the third and fourth *generation* of them that hate me;

Ex 31:17 — It *is* a sign between me and the children of Israel for ever: for *in* six days the LORD made heaven and earth, and on the seventh day he rested, and was refreshed.

Ex 32:14 — And the LORD repented of the evil which he thought to do unto his people.

Nu 11:25 — And the LORD came down in a cloud, and spake unto him, and took of the spirit that *was* upon him, and gave *it* unto the seventy elders: and it came to pass, *that,* when the spirit rested upon them, they prophesied, and did not cease.

Jgs 2:18 — And when the LORD raised them up judges, then the LORD was with the judge, and delivered them out of the hand of their enemies all the days of the judge: for it repented the LORD because of their groanings by reason of them that oppressed them and vexed them.

1Sa 15:35 — And Samuel came no more to see Saul until the day of his death: nevertheless Samuel mourned for Saul: and the LORD repented that he had made Saul king over Israel.

2Sa 24:16 — And when the angel stretched out his hand upon Jerusalem to destroy it, the LORD repented him of the evil, and said to the angel that destroyed the people, It is enough: stay now thine hand. And the angel of the LORD was by the threshingplace of Araunah the Jebusite.

1Ch 21:15 — And God sent an angel unto Jerusalem to destroy it: and as he was destroying, the LORD beheld, and he repented him of the evil, and said to the angel that destroyed, It is enough, stay now thine hand. And the angel of the LORD stood by the threshingfloor of Ornan the Jebusite.

Ps 31:2 — Bow down thine ear to me; deliver me speedily: be thou my strong rock, for an house of defence to save me.

Ps 33:6 — By the word of the LORD were the heavens made; and all the host of them by the breath of his mouth.

Ps 36:7 — How excellent *is* thy lovingkindness, O God! therefore the children of men put their trust under the shadow of thy wings.

Ps 57:1 — Be merciful unto me, O God, be merciful unto me: for my soul trusteth in thee: yea, in the shadow of thy wings will I make my refuge, until *these* calamities be overpast.

Ps 68:17 — The chariots of God *are* twenty thousand, *even* thousands of angels: the Lord *is* among them, *as in* Sinai, in the holy *place.*

Ps 94:9 — He that planted the ear, shall he not hear? he that formed the eye, shall he not see?

Ps 106:45 — And he remembered for them his covenant, and repented according to the multitude of his mercies.

Ps 121:4 — Behold, he that keepeth Israel shall neither slumber nor sleep.

Isa 1:15 — And when ye spread forth your hands, I will hide mine eyes from you: yea, when ye make many prayers, I will not hear: your hands are full of blood.

Jer 26:19 — Did Hezekiah king of Judah and all Judah put him at all to death? did he not fear the LORD, and besought the LORD, and the LORD repented him of the evil which he had pronounced against them? Thus might we procure great evil against our souls.

Eze 1:24 — And when they went, I heard the noise of their wings, like the noise of great waters, as the voice of the Almighty, the voice of speech, as the noise of an host: when they stood, they let down their wings.

Eze 1:28 — As the appearance of the bow that is in the cloud in the day of rain, so *was* the appearance of the brightness round about. This *was* the appearance of the likeness of the glory of the LORD. And when I saw *it,* I fell upon my face, and I heard a voice of one that spake.

Am 7:3 — The LORD repented for this: It shall not be, saith the LORD.

Hab 1:13 — *Thou art* of purer eyes than to behold evil, and canst not look on iniquity: wherefore lookest thou upon them that deal treacherously, *and* holdest thy tongue when the wicked devoureth *the man that is* more righteous than he?

1Pe 3:12 — For the eyes of the Lord *are* over the righteous, and his ears *are open* unto their prayers: but the face of the Lord *is* against them that do evil.

• Intellectual faculties attributed to deity.

• Memory.

Isa 43:26 — Put me in remembrance: let us plead together: declare thou, that thou mayest be justified.

Isa 63:11 — Then he remembered the days of old, Moses, *and* his people, *saying,* Where *is* he that brought them up out of the sea with the shepherd of his flock? where *is* he that put his holy Spirit within him?

• **Assisted by tokens.**

Ge 9:16 — And the bow shall be in the cloud; and I will look upon it, that I may remember the everlasting covenant between God and every living creature of all flesh that *is* upon the earth.

• **Reason.**

Isa 1:18 — Come now, and let us reason together, saith the LORD: though your sins be as scarlet, they shall be as white as snow; though they be red like crimson, they shall be as wool.

• **Understanding.**

Ps 147:5 — Great *is* our Lord, and of great power: his understanding *is* infinite.

• **Will.**

Ro 9:19 — Thou wilt say then unto me, Why doth he yet find fault? For who hath resisted his will?

• **Miscellaneous acts and states of mind attributed to.**

• **Walking.**

Ge 3:8 — And they heard the voice of the LORD God walking in the garden in the cool of the day: and Adam and his wife hid themselves from the presence of the LORD God amongst the trees of the garden.

Le 26:12 — And I will walk among you, and will be your God, and ye shall be my people.

Dt 23:14 — For the LORD thy God walketh in the midst of thy camp, to deliver thee, and to give up thine enemies before thee; therefore shall thy camp be holy: that he see no unclean thing in thee, and turn away from thee.

Job 22:14 — Thick clouds *are* a covering to him, that he seeth not; and he walketh in the circuit of heaven.

Hab 3:15 — Thou didst walk through the sea with thine horses, *through* the heap of great waters.

• **Resting.**

Ge 2:2–3

Ex 20:11 — For *in* six days the LORD made heaven and earth, the sea, and all that in them *is,* and rested the seventh day: wherefore the LORD blessed the sabbath day, and hallowed it.

Ex 31:17 — It *is* a sign between me and the children of Israel for ever: for *in* six days the LORD made heaven and earth, and on the seventh day he rested, and was refreshed.

Dt 5:14 — But the seventh day *is* the sabbath of the LORD thy God: *in it* thou shalt not do any work, thou, nor thy son, nor thy daughter, nor thy manservant, nor thy maidservant, nor thine ox, nor thine ass, nor any of thy cattle, nor thy stranger that *is* within thy gates; that thy manservant and thy maidservant may rest as well as thou.

Heb 4:4 — For he spake in a certain place of the seventh *day* on this wise, And God did rest the seventh day from all his works.

Heb 4:10 — For he that is entered into his rest, he also hath ceased from his own works, as God *did* from his.

• **Fainteth not.**

Isa 40:28 — Hast thou not known? hast thou not heard, *that* the everlasting God, the LORD, the Creator of the ends of the earth, fainteth not, neither is weary? *there is* no searching of his understanding.

• **Amazement.**

Isa 59:16 — And he saw that *there was* no man, and wondered that *there was* no intercessor: therefore his arm brought salvation unto him; and his righteousness, it sustained him.

Isa 63:5 — And I looked, and *there was* none to help; and I wondered that *there was* none to uphold: therefore mine own arm brought salvation unto me; and my fury, it upheld me.

Mk 6:6 — And he marvelled because of their unbelief. And he went round about the villages, teaching.

• **Laughing.**

Ps 2:4 — He that sitteth in the heavens shall laugh: the Lord shall have them in derision.

Ps 37:13 — The Lord shall laugh at him: for he seeth that his day is coming.

Ps 59:8 — But thou, O LORD, shalt laugh at them; thou shalt have all the heathen in derision.

Pr 1:26 — I also will laugh at your calamity; I will mock when your fear cometh;

• **Sleeping.**

Ps 44:23 — Awake, why sleepest thou, O Lord? arise, cast *us* not off for ever.

Ps 78:65 — Then the Lord awaked as one out of sleep, *and* like a mighty man that shouteth by reason of wine.

• **Grieved.**

Ge 6:6 — And it repented the LORD that he had made man on the earth, and it grieved him at his heart.

Jgs 10:16 — And they put away the strange gods from among them, and served the LORD: and his soul was grieved for the misery of Israel.

Ps 95:10 — Forty years long was I grieved with *this* generation, and said, It *is* a people that do err in their heart, and they have not known my ways:

Heb 3:10 — Wherefore I was grieved with that generation, and said, They do alway err in *their* heart; and they have not known my ways.

Heb 3:17 — But with whom was he grieved forty years? *was it* not with them that had sinned, whose carcases fell in the wilderness?

• **Oaths.**

Heb 6:16–17

Isa 62:8 — The LORD hath sworn by his right hand, and by the arm of his strength, Surely I will no more give thy corn *to be* meat for thine enemies; and the sons of the stranger shall not drink thy wine, for the which thou hast laboured:

Heb 7:21 — (For those priests were made without an oath; but this with an oath by him that said unto him, The Lord sware and will not repent, Thou *art* a priest for ever after the order of Melchisedec:)

Heb 7:28 — For the law maketh men high priests which have infirmity; but the word of the oath, which was since the law, *maketh* the Son, who is consecrated for evermore.

See: Oath

See: Anger; of God

ANTICHRIST

Mt 24:23–24; Mk 13:21–22; 2Th 2:3–12

Mt 24:5 — For many shall come in my name, saying, I am Christ; and shall deceive many.

Mt 24:26 — Wherefore if they shall say unto you, Behold, *he is* in the desert; go not forth: behold, he is in the secret chambers; believe *it* not.

Mk 13:6 — For many shall come in my name, saying, I am *Christ;* and shall deceive many.

Lk 21:8 — And he said, Take heed that ye be not deceived: for many shall come in my name, saying, I am *Christ;* and the time draweth near: go ye not therefore after them.

1Jn 2:18 — Little children, it is the last time: and as ye have heard that antichrist shall come, even now are there many antichrists; whereby we know that it is the last time.

1Jn 2:22 — Who is a liar but he that denieth that Jesus is the Christ? He is antichrist, that denieth the Father and the Son.

1Jn 4:3 — And every spirit that confesseth not that Jesus Christ is come in the flesh is not of God: and this is that *spirit* of antichrist, whereof ye have heard that it should come; and even now already is it in the world.

2Jn 1:7 — For many deceivers are entered into the world, who confess not that Jesus Christ is come in the flesh. This is a deceiver and an antichrist.

- **To be destroyed.**

Rev 19:20 — And the beast was taken, and with him the false prophet that wrought miracles before him, with which he deceived them that had received the mark of the beast, and them that worshipped his image. These both were cast alive into a lake of fire burning with brimstone.

Rev 20:10 — And the devil that deceived them was cast into the lake of fire and brimstone, where the beast and the false prophet *are,* and shall be tormented day and night for ever and ever.

Rev 20:15 — And whosoever was not found written in the book of life was cast into the lake of fire.

ANTIOCH

- **A city of Syria.**
  - **Disciples first called Christians in.**

    Ac 11:19–30
  - **Church in.**

    Ac 14:26–27

    Ac 13:1 — Now there were in the church that was at Antioch certain prophets and teachers; as Barnabas, and Simeon that was called Niger, and Lucius of Cyrene, and Manaen, which had been brought up with Herod the tetrarch, and Saul.
  - **Barnabas and Paul make second visit to.**

    Ac 14:26–28
  - **Dissension in church of.**

    Ac 15:1–35
  - **Paul and Peter's controversy at.**

    Gal 2:11–15
- **A city of Pisidia.**

  Ac 13:14–52; 14:19–22

  Ac 18:22 — And when he had landed at Caesarea, and gone up, and saluted the church, he went down to Antioch.
  - **Persecutes Paul.**

    2Ti 3:11 — Persecutions, afflictions, which came unto me at Antioch, at Iconium, at Lystra; what persecutions I endured: but out of *them* all the Lord delivered me.

ANTIPAS • A martyr.

Rev 2:13 — I know thy works, and where thou dwellest, *even* where Satan's seat *is:* and thou holdest fast my name, and hast not denied my faith, even in those days wherein Antipas *was* my faithful martyr, who was slain among you, where Satan dwelleth.

ANTIPATRIS • A city in Samaria.

Ac 23:31 — Then the soldiers, as it was commanded them, took Paul, and brought *him* by night to Antipatris.

ANTOTHIJAH • A Benjamite.

1Ch 8:24 — And Hananiah, and Elam, and Antothijah,

ANUB • Son of Coz.

1Ch 4:8 — And Coz begat Anub, and Zobebah, and the families of Aharhel the son of Harum.

ANVIL

Isa 41:7 — So the carpenter encouraged the goldsmith, *and* he that smootheth *with* the hammer him that smote the anvil, saying, It is ready for the sodering: and he fastened it with nails, *that* it should not be moved.

ANXIETY

Php 4:6–7

Pr 29:25 — The fear of man bringeth a snare: but whoso putteth his trust in the LORD shall be safe.

See: Care

APARTHEID

Ac 15:6–11; Eph 3:1–11

Ac 11:15 — And as I began to speak, the Holy Ghost fell on them, as on us at the beginning.

Gal 3:28 — There is neither Jew nor Greek, there is neither bond nor free, there is neither male nor female: for ye are all one in Christ Jesus.

APATHY

Rev 3:14–16

Hos 7:8 — Ephraim, he hath mixed himself among the people; Ephraim is a cake not turned.

APE

• In Solomon's zoological collections.

1Ki 10:22 — For the king had at sea a navy of Tharshish with the navy of Hiram: once in three years came the navy of Tharshish, bringing gold, and silver, ivory, and apes, and peacocks.

2Ch 9:21 — For the king's ships went to Tarshish with the servants of Huram: every three years once came the ships of Tarshish bringing gold, and silver, ivory, and apes, and peacocks.

APELLES • A disciple in Rome.

Ro 16:10 — Salute Apelles approved in Christ. Salute them which are of Aristobulus' *household.*

APHARSACHITES

2Ki 17:1–41

Ezr 5:6 — The copy of the letter that Tatnai, governor on this side the river, and Shethar-boznai, and his companions the Apharsachites, which *were* on this side the river, sent unto Darius the king:

Ezr 6:6 — Now *therefore,* Tatnai, governor beyond the river, Shethar-boznai, and your companions the Apharsachites, which *are* beyond the river, be ye far from thence:

APHARSATHCHITES

2Ki 17:1–41

Ezr 4:9 — Then *wrote* Rehum the chancellor, and Shimshai the scribe, and the rest of their companions; the Dinaites, the Apharsathchites, the Tarpelites, the Apharsites, the Archevites, the Babylonians, the Susanchites, the Dehavites, *and* the Elamites,

APHARSITES

2Ki 17:1–41

Ezr 4:9 — Then *wrote* Rehum the chancellor, and Shimshai the scribe, and the rest of their companions; the Dinaites, the Apharsathchites, the Tarpelites, the Apharsites, the Archevites, the Babylonians, the Susanchites, the Dehavites, *and* the Elamites,

APHEK

• A city of the tribe of Asher.

Jos 19:30 — Ummah also, and Aphek, and Rehob: twenty and two cities with their villages.

• Called Aphik.

Jgs 1:31 — Neither did Asher drive out the inhabitants of Accho, nor the inhabitants of Zidon, nor of Ahlab, nor of Achzib, nor of Helbah, nor of Aphik, nor of Rehob:

• A city of the tribe of Issachar.

• Philistines defeat Israelites at.

1Sa 4:1–11

• Saul slain at.

1Sa 31:1–13

1Sa 29:1 — Now the Philistines gathered together all their armies to Aphek: and the Israelites pitched by a fountain which *is* in Jezreel.

• Probably the same mentioned in Jos 12:18 as a royal city of the Canaanites.

Jos 12:18 — The king of Aphek, one; the king of Lasharon, one;

• A city between Damascus and Palestine. Benhadad defeated at.

1Ki 20:26–30

APHEKAH • A city in the mountains of Judah.

Jos 15:53 — And Janum, and Beth-tappuah, and Aphekah,

APHIAH • A Benjamite.

1Sa 9:1 — Now there was a man of Benjamin, whose name *was* Kish, the son of Abiel, the son of Zeror, the son of Bechorath, the son of Aphiah, a Benjamite, a mighty man of power.

APHIK

• A city of the tribe of Asher.

→See: Aphek

APHRAH

• A city.

Mic 1:10 — Declare ye *it* not at Gath, weep ye not at all: in the house of Aphrah roll thyself in the dust.

• Perhaps identical with Ophrah.

1Ch 4:14 — And Meonothai begat Ophrah: and Seraiah begat Joab, the father of the valley of Charashim; for they were craftsmen.

APHSES • A governor of the temple.

1Ch 24:15 — The seventeenth to Hezir, the eighteenth to Aphses,

APOLLONIA • A city of Macedonia.

Ac 17:1 — Now when they had passed through Amphipolis and Apollonia, they came to Thessalonica, where was a synagogue of the Jews:

APOLLOS

• An eloquent Christian convert at Corinth.

Ac 18:24–19:1; 1Co 3:4–7

1Co 1:12 — Now this I say, that every one of you saith, I am of Paul; and I of Apollos; and I of Cephas; and I of Christ.

• Refuses to return to Rome.

1Co 16:12 — As touching *our* brother Apollos, I greatly desired him to come unto you with the brethren: but his will was not at all to come at this time; but he will come when he shall have convenient time.

• Paul writes Titus about.

Tit 3:13 — Bring Zenas the lawyer and Apollos on their journey diligently, that nothing be wanting unto them.

APOLLYON • Angel of the bottomless pit.

Rev 9:11 — And they had a king over them, *which is* the angel of the bottomless pit, whose name in the

Hebrew tongue *is* Abaddon, but in the Greek tongue hath *his* name Apollyon.

APOLOGETIC

Jn 7:16–17; 2Jn 1:9–10

Ac 2:42 — And they continued stedfastly in the apostles' doctrine and fellowship, and in breaking of bread, and in prayers.

1Ti 4:13 — Till I come, give attendance to reading, to exhortation, to doctrine.

2Ti 1:10 — But is now made manifest by the appearing of our Saviour Jesus Christ, who hath abolished death, and hath brought life and immortality to light through the gospel:

Tit 1:9 — Holding fast the faithful word as he hath been taught, that he may be able by sound doctrine both to exhort and to convince the gainsayers.

Tit 2:1 — But speak thou the things which become sound doctrine:

1Pe 3:15 — But sanctify the Lord God in your hearts: and *be* ready always to *give* an answer to every man that asketh you a reason of the hope that is in you with meekness and fear:

APOSTASY

• Described.

Dt 13:13 — *Certain* men, the children of Belial, are gone out from among you, and have withdrawn the inhabitants of their city, saying, Let us go and serve other gods, which ye have not known;

Heb 3:12 — Take heed, brethren, lest there be in any of you an evil heart of unbelief, in departing from the living God.

• Caused by persecution.

Mt 24:9–10

Lk 8:13 — They on the rock *are they,* which, when they hear, receive the word with joy; and these have no root, which for a while believe, and in time of temptation fall away.

• Caused by worldliness.

2Ti 4:10 — For Demas hath forsaken me, having loved this present world, and is departed unto Thessalonica; Crescens to Galatia, Titus unto Dalmatia.

• Guilt and punishment of.

Zep 1:4–6; Heb 10:25–31; 2Pe 2:20–22

Heb 10:39 — But we are not of them who draw back unto perdition; but of them that believe to the saving of the soul.

2Pe 2:17 — These are wells without water, clouds that are carried with a tempest; to whom the mist of darkness is reserved for ever.

• Cautions against.

Heb 3:12 — Take heed, brethren, lest there be in any of you an evil heart of unbelief, in departing from the living God.

2Pe 3:17 — Ye therefore, beloved, seeing ye know *these things* before, beware lest ye also, being led away with the error of the wicked, fall from your own stedfastness.

• Shall abound in the latter days.

1Ti 4:1–3

Mt 24:12 — And because iniquity shall abound, the love of many shall wax cold.

2Th 2:3 — Let no man deceive you by any means: for *that day shall not come,* except there come a falling away first, and that man of sin be revealed, the son of perdition;

See: Antichrist

• Unclassified scripture relating to.

Isa 1:28–65:11; Jer 17:5–6; Eze 33:12–13; Mt 13:20–21; Mk 4:5–17; Lk 11:24–26; Ac 7:39–43; 2Th 2:11–12; 1Ti 4:1–2; 2Ti 3:1–9; 4:3–4; Heb 6:4–8; 10:26–29; 2Pe 2:20–22; Jude 1:4–6

Dt 32:15 — But Jeshurun waxed fat, and kicked: thou art waxen fat, thou art grown thick, thou art covered *with fatness;* then he forsook God *which* made him, and lightly esteemed the Rock of his salvation.

1Ch 28:9 — And thou, Solomon my son, know thou the God of thy father, and serve him with a perfect heart and with a willing mind: for the LORD searcheth all hearts, and understandeth all the imaginations of the thoughts: if thou seek him, he will be found of thee; but if thou forsake him, he will cast thee off for ever.

Isa 1:16 — Wash you, make you clean; put away the evil of your doings from before mine eyes; cease to do evil;

Eze 3:20 — Again, When a righteous *man* doth turn from his righteousness, and commit iniquity, and I lay a stumblingblock before him, he shall die: because thou hast not given him warning, he shall die in his sin, and his righteousness which he hath done shall not be remembered; but his blood will I require at thine hand.

Eze 18:24 — But when the righteous turneth away from his righteousness, and committeth iniquity, *and* doeth according to all the abominations that the wicked *man* doeth, shall he live? All his righteousness that he hath done shall not be mentioned: in his trespass that he hath trespassed, and in his sin that he hath sinned, in them shall he die.

Eze 18:26 — When a righteous *man* turneth away from his righteousness, and committeth iniquity, and dieth in them; for his iniquity that he hath done shall he die.

Eze 33:18 — When the righteous turneth from his righteousness, and committeth iniquity, he shall even die thereby.

Mt 24:10 — And then shall many be offended, and shall betray one another, and shall hate one another.

Mt 24:12 — And because iniquity shall abound, the love of many shall wax cold.

Lk 8:13 — They on the rock *are they,* which, when they hear, receive the word with joy; and these have no root, which for a while believe, and in time of temptation fall away.

Jn 15:6 — If a man abide not in me, he is cast forth as a branch, and is withered; and men gather them, and cast *them* into the fire, and they are burned.

1Co 9:27 — But I keep under my body, and bring *it* into subjection: lest that by any means, when I have preached to others, I myself should be a castaway.

Gal 5:4 — Christ is become of no effect unto you, whosoever of you are justified by the law; ye are fallen from grace.

2Th 2:3 — Let no man deceive you by any means: for *that day shall not come,* except there come a falling away first, and that man of sin be revealed, the son of perdition;

2Ti 4:10 — For Demas hath forsaken me, having loved this present world, and is departed unto Thessalonica; Crescens to Galatia, Titus unto Dalmatia.

2Pe 2:1 — But there were false prophets also among the people, even as there shall be false teachers among you, who privily shall bring in damnable heresies, even denying the Lord that bought them, and bring upon themselves swift destruction.

2Pe 2:15 — Which have forsaken the right way, and are gone astray, following the way of Balaam *the son* of Bosor, who loved the wages of unrighteousness;

2Pe 2:17 — These are wells without water, clouds that are carried with a tempest; to whom the mist of darkness is reserved for ever.

2Pe 3:17 — Ye therefore, beloved, seeing ye know *these things* before, beware lest ye also, being led away with the error of the wicked, fall from your own stedfastness.

See: Backsliders

See: Reprobacy

• Instances of.

• Israelites.

Ex 32:1–35; Nu 14:1–45

• Saul.

1Sa 15:26–29; 18:12; 28:15, 18

• Amaziah.

2Ch 25:14; 25:27

• Disciples.

Jn 6:66

• Judas.

Mt 26:14–16; 27:3–5; Mk 14:10–11; Lk 22:3–6, 47–48; Ac 1:16–18

• Hymenaeus and Alexander.

1Ti 1:19–20

• Phygellus and Hermogenes.

2Ti 1:15

See: Backsliders; backsliding of Israel

APOSTLE

• An appellation of Jesus.

Heb 3:1 — Wherefore, holy brethren, partakers of the heavenly calling, consider the Apostle and High Priest of our profession, Christ Jesus;

See: Apostles

APOSTLES

• A title distinguishing the twelve disciples, whom Jesus selected to be intimately associated with himself.

Lk 6:13 — And when it was day, he called *unto him* his disciples: and of them he chose twelve, whom also he named apostles;

• Names of.

Mt 10:2–4; Mk 3:16–19; Lk 6:13–16

Ac 1:13 — And when they were come in, they went up into an upper room, where abode both Peter, and James, and John, and Andrew, Philip, and Thomas, Bartholomew, and Matthew, James *the son* of Alphaeus, and Simon Zelotes, and Judas *the brother* of James.

Ac 1:26 — And they gave forth their lots; and the lot fell upon Matthias; and he was numbered with the eleven apostles.

• Selection of.

Mt 4:18–22; 9:9–10; 10:2–4; Mk 3:13–19; Lk 6:13–16

Jn 1:43 — The day following Jesus would go forth into Galilee, and findeth Philip, and saith unto him, Follow me.

• Commission of.

Mt 10:1–42; 28:19–20; Mk 3:14–15; 6:7–11; Lk 9:1–5; 22:28–30; Jn 21:15–19; Ac 1:1–2:47

Mk 16:15 — And he said unto them, Go ye into all the world, and preach the gospel to every creature.

Jn 20:23 — Whose soever sins ye remit, they are remitted unto them; *and* whose soever *sins* ye retain, they are retained.

Ac 10:42 — And he commanded us to preach unto the people, and to testify that it is he which was ordained of God *to be* the Judge of quick and dead.

• Unlearned.

Mt 11:25 — At that time Jesus answered and said, I thank thee, O Father, Lord of heaven and earth, because thou hast hid these things from the wise and prudent, and hast revealed them unto babes.

Ac 4:13 — Now when they saw the boldness of Peter and John, and perceived that they were unlearned and ignorant men, they marvelled; and they took knowledge of them, that they had been with Jesus.

• Miraculous power given to.

Lk 9:1–2; Ac 5:12–16

Mt 10:1 — And when he had called unto *him* his twelve disciples, he gave them power *against* unclean spirits, to cast them out, and to heal all manner of sickness and all manner of disease.

Mk 3:15 — And to have power to heal sicknesses, and to cast out devils:

Mk 6:7 — And he called *unto him* the twelve, and began to send them forth by two and two; and gave them power over unclean spirits;

Mk 16:17 — And these signs shall follow them that believe; In my name shall they cast out devils; they shall speak with new tongues;

Lk 10:9 — And heal the sick that are therein, and say unto them, The kingdom of God is come nigh unto you.

Lk 10:17 — And the seventy returned again with joy, saying, Lord, even the devils are subject unto us through thy name.

Ac 2:4 — And they were all filled with the Holy Ghost, and began to speak with other tongues, as the Spirit gave them utterance.

Ac 2:43 — And fear came upon every soul: and many wonders and signs were done by the apostles.

1Co 14:18 — I thank my God, I speak with tongues more than ye all:

2Co 12:12 — Truly the signs of an apostle were wrought among you in all patience, in signs, and wonders, and mighty deeds.

• Authority of.

Mt 16:19 — And I will give unto thee the keys of the kingdom of heaven: and whatsoever thou shalt bind on earth shall be bound in heaven: and whatsoever thou shalt loose on earth shall be loosed in heaven.

Mt 18:18 — Verily I say unto you, Whatsoever ye shall bind on earth shall be bound in heaven: and whatsoever ye shall loose on earth shall be loosed in heaven.

Mt 19:28 — And Jesus said unto them, Verily I say unto you, That ye which have followed me, in the regeneration when the Son of man shall sit in the throne of his glory, ye also shall sit upon twelve thrones, judging the twelve tribes of Israel.

See: Apostles; commission of

• Inspiration of.

Mt 16:17–19

Mt 10:27 — What I tell you in darkness, *that* speak ye in light: and what ye hear in the ear, *that* preach ye upon the housetops.

Lk 24:45 — Then opened he their understanding, that they might understand the scriptures,

Ac 1:2 — Until the day in which he was taken up, after that he through the Holy Ghost had given commandments unto the apostles whom he had chosen:

Ac 13:9 — Then Saul, (who also *is called* Paul,) filled with the Holy Ghost, set his eyes on him,

• Duties of.

Ac 1:21–22; 10:39–41; 1Jn 1:1–3

Lk 24:48 — And ye are witnesses of these things.

Jn 15:27 — And ye also shall bear witness, because ye have been with me from the beginning.

Ac 1:8 — But ye shall receive power, after that the Holy Ghost is come upon you: and ye shall be witnesses unto me both in Jerusalem, and in all Judaea, and in Samaria, and unto the uttermost part of the earth.

Ac 2:32 — This Jesus hath God raised up, whereof we all are witnesses.

Ac 3:15 — And killed the Prince of life, whom God hath raised from the dead; whereof we are witnesses.

Ac 4:33 — And with great power gave the apostles witness of the resurrection of the Lord Jesus: and great grace was upon them all.

Ac 5:32 — And we are his witnesses of these things; and *so is* also the Holy Ghost, whom God hath given to them that obey him.

Ac 13:31 — And he was seen many days of them which came up with him from Galilee to Jerusalem, who are his witnesses unto the people.

2Pe 1:16 — For we have not followed cunningly devised fables, when we made known unto you the power and coming of our Lord Jesus Christ, but were eyewitnesses of his majesty.

2Pe 1:18 — And this voice which came from heaven we heard, when we were with him in the holy mount.

See: Apostles; commission of

See: Minister, Faithful; instances of; the apostles

• Moral state of, before Pentecost.

Mt 20:20–22; Lk 9:54–55

Mt 17:17 — Then Jesus answered and said, O faithless and perverse generation, how long shall I be with you? how long shall I suffer you? bring him hither to me.

Mt 18:3 — And said, Verily I say unto you, Except ye be converted, and become as little children, ye shall not enter into the kingdom of heaven.

• Slow to receive Jesus, as Messiah.

Mt 14:33 — Then they that were in the ship came and worshipped him, saying, Of a truth thou art the Son of God.

• Forsake Jesus.

Mk 14:50 — And they all forsook him, and fled.

• Fail to comprehend the nature and mission of Jesus, and the nature of the kingdom he came to establish.

Mt 8:25–27; 16:8–12, 21–22; Mk 6:51–52; 8:17–18; 9:9–10, 31–32; 10:13–14; Lk 9:44–45; Jn 4:32–33; 11:12–13; 13:6–8; 14:5–9; 16:17–18

Mt 15:23 — But he answered her not a word. And his disciples came and besought him, saying, Send her away; for she crieth after us.

Mt 19:25 — When his disciples heard *it*, they were exceedingly amazed, saying, Who then can be saved?

Mk 4:13 — And he said unto them, Know ye not this parable? and how then will ye know all parables?

Lk 18:34 — And they understood none of these things: and this saying was hid from them, neither knew they the things which were spoken.

Lk 24:19 — And he said unto them, What things? And they said unto him, Concerning Jesus of Nazareth, which was a prophet mighty in deed and word before God and all the people:

Lk 24:21 — But we trusted that it had been he which should have redeemed Israel: and beside all this, to day is the third day since these things were done.

Jn 10:6 — This parable spake Jesus unto them: but they understood not what things they were which he spake unto them.

Jn 12:16 — These things understood not his disciples at the first: but when Jesus was glorified, then remembered they that these things were written of him, and *that* they had done these things unto him.

Jn 14:22 — Judas saith unto him, not Iscariot, Lord, how is it that thou wilt manifest thyself unto us, and not unto the world?

Jn 16:6 — But because I have said these things unto you, sorrow hath filled your heart.

Jn 16:32 — Behold, the hour cometh, yea, is now come, that ye shall be scattered, every man to his own, and shall leave me alone: and yet I am not alone, because the Father is with me.

Jn 20:9 — For as yet they knew not the scripture, that he must rise again from the dead.

Jn 21:12 — Jesus saith unto them, Come *and* dine. And none of the disciples durst ask him, Who art thou? knowing that it was the Lord.

Ac 1:6 — When they therefore were come together, they asked of him, saying, Lord, wilt thou at this time restore again the kingdom to Israel?

See: Barnabas

See: Matthias

See: Minister, a sacred teacher

See: Minister, Faithful

See: Paul, Ministry, Ac 16–28

See: Paul, Ministry, Ac 9–15

See: Paul, Miscellaneous

See: Paul, through Conversion

• False.

2Co 11:13

Rev 2:2 — I know thy works, and thy labour, and thy patience, and how thou canst not bear them which are evil: and thou hast tried them which say they are apostles, and are not, and hast found them liars:

See: Teachers; false

APOSTROPHE • To death and the grave.

Hos 13:14 — I will ransom them from the power of the grave; I will redeem them from death: O death, I will be thy plagues; O grave, I will be thy destruction: repentance shall be hid from mine eyes.

1Co 15:55 — O death, where *is* thy sting? O grave, where *is* thy victory?

APOTHECARY

• A compounder of drugs.

Ex 30:25 — And thou shalt make it an oil of holy ointment, an ointment compound after the art of the apothecary: it shall be an holy anointing oil.

Ex 30:35 — And thou shalt make it a perfume, a confection after the art of the apothecary, tempered together, pure *and* holy:

Ex 37:29 — And he made the holy anointing oil, and the pure incense of sweet spices, according to the work of the apothecary.

2Ch 16:14 — And they buried him in his own sepulchres, which he had made for himself in the city of David, and laid him in the bed which was filled with sweet odours and divers kinds *of spices* prepared by the apothecaries' art: and they made a very great burning for him.

Ne 3:8 — Next unto him repaired Uzziel the son of Harhaiah, of the goldsmiths. Next unto him also repaired Hananiah the son of *one of* the apothecaries, and they fortified Jerusalem unto the broad wall.

• Ointment of.

Ecc 10:1 — Dead flies cause the ointment of the apothecary to send forth a stinking savour: *so doth* a little folly him that is in reputation for wisdom *and* honour.

APPAIM • Son of Nadab.

1Ch 2:30–31

APPEAL • Paul makes, to Caesar.

Ac 25:10–11, 21–27

Ac 26:32 — Then said Agrippa unto Festus, This man might have been set at liberty, if he had not appealed unto Caesar.

Ac 28:19 — But when the Jews spake against *it,* I was constrained to appeal unto Caesar; not that I had ought to accuse my nation of.

See: Change of Venue

See: Court; superior, and inferior

APPEARANCE

Isa 40:18–31

1Sa 16:7 — But the LORD said unto Samuel, Look not on his countenance, or on the height of his stature; because I have refused him: for *the LORD seeth* not as man seeth; for man looketh on the outward appearance, but the LORD looketh on the heart.

Jn 1:46 — And Nathanael said unto him, Can there any good thing come out of Nazareth? Philip saith unto him, Come and see.

1Ti 4:12 — Let no man despise thy youth; but be thou an example of the believers, in word, in conversation, in charity, in spirit, in faith, in purity.

APPETITE

Pr 23:2 — And put a knife to thy throat, if thou *be* a man given to appetite.

Ro 12:1 — I beseech you therefore, brethren, by the mercies of God, that ye present your bodies a living sacrifice, holy, acceptable unto God, *which is* your reasonable service.

1Co 3:16 — Know ye not that ye are the temple of God, and *that* the Spirit of God dwelleth in you?

• Kept in subjection.

Da 1:8–16

1Co 9:27 — But I keep under my body, and bring *it* into subjection: lest that by any means, when I have preached to others, I myself should be a castaway.

See: Temperance

APPHIA • A Christian at Colosse.

Phm 1:2 — And to *our* beloved Apphia, and Archippus our fellowsoldier, and to the church in thy house:

APPII-FORUM • A market town in Italy.

Ac 28:15 — And from thence, when the brethren heard of us, they came to meet us as far as Appii Forum, and The three taverns: whom when Paul saw, he thanked God, and took courage.

APPLE • A fruit.

Pr 25:11 — A word fitly spoken *is like* apples of gold in pictures of silver.

SS 2:3 — As the apple tree among the trees of the wood, so *is* my beloved among the sons. I sat down under his shadow with great delight, and his fruit *was* sweet to my taste.

SS 2:5 — Stay me with flagons, comfort me with apples: for I *am* sick of love.

SS 7:8 — I said, I will go up to the palm tree, I will take hold of the boughs thereof: now also thy breasts shall be as clusters of the vine, and the smell of thy nose like apples;

SS 8:5 — Who *is* this that cometh up from the wilderness, leaning upon her beloved? I raised thee up under the apple tree: there thy mother brought thee forth: there she brought thee forth *that* bare thee.

Joel 1:12 — The vine is dried up, and the fig tree languisheth; the pomegranate tree, the palm tree also, and the apple tree, *even* all the trees of the field, are withered: because joy is withered away from the sons of men.

AQUILA AND PRISCILLA

• Christians at Corinth.

Ac 18:1–3, 18–19

Ac 18:26 — And he began to speak boldly in the synagogue: whom when Aquila and Priscilla had heard, they took him unto *them,* and expounded unto him the way of God more perfectly.

• Friendship of, for Paul.

Ro 16:3–4

• Paul sends salutations to.

2Ti 4:19 — Salute Prisca and Aquila, and the household of Onesiphorus.

AR

• A city of Moab.

Nu 21:15 — And at the stream of the brooks that goeth down to the dwelling of Ar, and lieth upon the border of Moab.

Dt 2:9 — And the LORD said unto me, Distress not the Moabites, neither contend with them in battle: for I will not give thee of their land *for* a possession; because I have given Ar unto the children of Lot *for* a possession.

Dt 2:18 — Thou art to pass over through Ar, the coast of Moab, this day:

Dt 2:24 — Rise ye up, take your journey, and pass over the river Arnon: behold, I have given into thine hand Sihon the Amorite, king of Heshbon, and his land: begin to possess *it,* and contend with him in battle.

Dt 2:29 — (As the children of Esau which dwell in Seir, and the Moabites which dwell in Ar, did unto me;) until I shall pass over Jordan into the land which the LORD our God giveth us.

• Destruction of.

Nu 21:26–30

Isa 15:1 — The burden of Moab. Because in the night Ar of Moab is laid waste, *and* brought to silence; because in the night Kir of Moab is laid waste, *and* brought to silence;

ARA • Son of Jether.

1Ch 7:38 — And the sons of Jether; Jephunneh, and Pispah, and Ara.

ARAB • A city of Judah.

Jos 15:52 — Arab, and Dumah, and Eshean,

ARABAH • See: Beth-Arabah

ARABIA

• Tributary to Solomon.

2Ch 9:14 — Beside *that which* chapmen and merchants brought. And all the kings of Arabia and governors of the country brought gold and silver to Solomon.

• Tributary to Jehoshaphat.

2Ch 17:11 — Also *some* of the Philistines brought Jehoshaphat presents, and tribute silver; and the Arabians brought him flocks, seven thousand and seven hundred rams, and seven thousand and seven hundred he goats.

• Exports of.

Eze 27:21 — Arabia, and all the princes of Kedar, they occupied with thee in lambs, and rams, and goats: in these *were they* thy merchants.

• Prophecies against.

Isa 21:13 — The burden upon Arabia. In the forest in Arabia shall ye lodge, O ye travelling companies of Dedanim.

Jer 25:24 — And all the kings of Arabia, and all the kings of the mingled people that dwell in the desert,

• Paul visits.

Gal 1:17 — Neither went I up to Jerusalem to them which were apostles before me; but I went into Arabia, and returned again unto Damascus.

ARABIANS

• Pay tribute to Solomon.

2Ch 9:14 — Beside *that which* chapmen and merchants brought. And all the kings of Arabia and governors of the country brought gold and silver to Solomon.

• Pay tribute to Jehoshaphat.

2Ch 17:11 — Also *some* of the Philistines brought Jehoshaphat presents, and tribute silver; and the Arabians brought him flocks, seven thousand and seven hundred rams, and seven thousand and seven hundred he goats.

• Invade and defeat Judah.

2Ch 21:16–17

2Ch 22:1 — And the inhabitants of Jerusalem made Ahaziah his youngest son king in his stead: for the band of men that came with the Arabians to the camp had slain all the eldest. So Ahaziah the son of Jehoram king of Judah reigned.

• Defeated by Uzziah.

2Ch 26:7 — And God helped him against the Philistines, and against the Arabians that dwelt in Gur-baal, and the Mehunims.

• Oppose Nehemiah's rebuilding the walls of Jerusalem.

Ne 2:19 — But when Sanballat the Horonite, and Tobiah the servant, the Ammonite, and Geshem the Arabian, heard *it,* they laughed us to scorn, and despised us, and said, What *is* this thing that ye do? will ye rebel against the king?

Ne 4:7 — But it came to pass, *that* when Sanballat, and Tobiah, and the Arabians, and the Ammonites, and the Ashdodites, heard that the walls of Jerusalem were made up, *and* that the breaches began to be stopped, then they were very wroth,

- **Commerce of.**

  Eze 27:21 — Arabia, and all the princes of Kedar, they occupied with thee in lambs, and rams, and goats: in these *were they* thy merchants.

- **Gospel preached to.**

  Ac 2:11 — Cretes and Arabians, we do hear them speak in our tongues the wonderful works of God.

  Gal 1:17 — Neither went I up to Jerusalem to them which were apostles before me; but I went into Arabia, and returned again unto Damascus.

- **Prophecies concerning.**

  Isa 21:13–17

  Isa 42:11 — Let the wilderness and the cities thereof lift up *their voice,* the villages *that* Kedar doth inhabit: let the inhabitants of the rock sing, let them shout from the top of the mountains.

  Isa 60:7 — All the flocks of Kedar shall be gathered together unto thee, the rams of Nebaioth shall minister unto thee: they shall come up with acceptance on mine altar, and I will glorify the house of my glory.

  Jer 25:24 — And all the kings of Arabia, and all the kings of the mingled people that dwell in the desert,

ARAD

- **A city in the south of Canaan.**

  Nu 21:1 — And *when* king Arad the Canaanite, which dwelt in the south, heard tell that Israel came by the way of the spies; then he fought against Israel, and took *some* of them prisoners.

  Nu 33:40 — And king Arad the Canaanite, which dwelt in the south in the land of Canaan, heard of the coming of the children of Israel.

  - **Subdued by Joshua.**

    Jos 12:14 — The king of Hormah, one; the king of Arad, one;

- **Son of Beriah.**

  1Ch 8:15 — And Zebadiah, and Arad, and Ader,

ARAH

- **Son of Ulla.**

  1Ch 7:39 — And the sons of Ulla; Arah, and Haniel, and Rezia.

- **An Israelite, whose descendants returned from Babylon.**

  Ezr 2:5 — The children of Arah, seven hundred seventy and five.

  Ne 7:10 — The children of Arah, six hundred fifty and two.

  - **Probably identical with Arah in Ne 6:18.**

    Ne 6:18 — For *there were* many in Judah sworn unto him, because he *was* the son in law of Shechaniah the son of Arah; and his son Johanan had taken the daughter of Meshullam the son of Berechiah.

ARAM

- **Name of various regions and of several men; signifies highlands districts of Syria**

- **The region whence Balaam came at Balak's command.**

  Nu 23:7 — And he took up his parable, and said, Balak the king of Moab hath brought me from Aram, out of the mountains of the east, *saying,* Come, curse me Jacob, and come, defy Israel.

- **A region north of Canaan.**

  1Ch 2:23 — And he took Geshur, and Aram, with the towns of Jair, from them, with Kenath, and the towns thereof, *even* threescore cities. All these *belonged to* the sons of Machir the father of Gilead.

- **Son of Shem.**

  Ge 10:22–23

  1Ch 1:17 — The sons of Shem; Elam, and Asshur, and Arphaxad, and Lud, and Aram, and Uz, and Hul, and Gether, and Meshech.

- **Son of Kemuel.**

  Ge 22:21 — Huz his firstborn, and Buz his brother, and Kemuel the father of Aram,

- **Son of Shamer.**

  1Ch 7:34 — And the sons of Shamer; Ahi, and Rohgah, Jehubbah, and Aram.

ARAN • Son of Dishan.

Ge 36:28 — The children of Dishan *are* these: Uz, and Aran.

1Ch 1:42 — The sons of Ezer; Bilhan, and Zavan, *and* Jakan. The sons of Dishan; Uz, and Aran.

ARARAT

- **A district of Armenia.**

  Jer 51:27 — Set ye up a standard in the land, blow the trumpet among the nations, prepare the nations against her, call together against her the kingdoms of Ararat, Minni, and Ashchenaz; appoint a captain against her; cause the horses to come up as the rough caterpillers.

- **Ark rested in mountains of.**

  Ge 8:4 — And the ark rested in the seventh month, on the seventeenth day of the month, upon the mountains of Ararat.

- **Assassins of Sennacherib take refuge in.**

  Isa 37:38 — And it came to pass, as he was worshipping in the house of Nisroch his god, that Adrammelech and Sharezer his sons smote him with the sword; and they escaped into the land of Armenia: and Esar-haddon his son reigned in his stead.

ARAUNAH

- **A Jebusite from whom David bought a site for an altar.**

  2Sa 24:16–24

- **Called also Ornan.**

  1Ch 21:15–25

ARBA

- **Father of Anak.**

  Jos 15:13 — And unto Caleb the son of Jephunneh he gave a part among the children of Judah, according to the commandment of the LORD to Joshua, *even* the city of Arba the father of Anak, which *city is* Hebron.

See: Hebron

ARBITRATION

- **Instances of.**
  - **The two harlots before Solomon.**
    1Ki 3:16–28
  - **Urged by Paul, as a mode of action for Christians.**
    1Co 6:1–8

See: Court

ARCHANGEL

1Th 4:16 — For the Lord himself shall descend from heaven with a shout, with the voice of the archangel, and with the trump of God: and the dead in Christ shall rise first:

Jude 1:9 — Yet Michael the archangel, when contending with the devil he disputed about the body of Moses, durst not bring against him a railing accusation, but said, The Lord rebuke thee.

See: Angel

ARCHELAUS • A ruler of Judaea.

Mt 2:22 — But when he heard that Archelaus did reign in Judaea in the room of his father Herod, he was afraid to go thither: notwithstanding, being warned of God in a dream, he turned aside into the parts of Galilee:

ARCHERY

- **Practiced by Ishmael.**
  Ge 21:20 — And God was with the lad; and he grew, and dwelt in the wilderness, and became an archer.
- **Practiced by Esau.**
  Ge 27:3 — Now therefore take, I pray thee, thy weapons, thy quiver and thy bow, and go out to the field, and take me *some* venison;
- **Practiced by Jonathan.**
  1Sa 20:36–37
  1Sa 20:20 — And I will shoot three arrows on the side *thereof,* as though I shot at a mark.
- **Practiced by sons of Ulam.**
  1Ch 8:40 — And the sons of Ulam were mighty men of valour, archers, and had many sons, and sons' sons, an hundred and fifty. All these *are* of the sons of Benjamin.
- **Practiced by Philistines.**
  1Sa 31:1–3
  1Ch 10:3 — And the battle went sore against Saul, and the archers hit him, and he was wounded of the archers.
- **Practiced by Persians.**
  Isa 13:17–18
- **Practiced by people of Kedar.**
  Isa 21:17 — And the residue of the number of archers, the mighty men of the children of Kedar, shall be diminished: for the LORD God of Israel hath spoken *it.*
- **Practiced by Syrians.**
  1Ki 22:31–34
- **Practiced by Israelites.**
  2Sa 1:18 — (Also he bade them teach the children of Judah *the use of* the bow: behold, it is written in the book of Jasher.)
  1Ch 5:18 — The sons of Reuben, and the Gadites, and half the tribe of Manasseh, of valiant men, men able to bear buckler and sword, and to shoot with bow, and skilful in war, *were* four and forty thousand seven hundred and threescore, that went out to the war.
  1Ch 12:2 — *They were* armed with bows, and could use both the right hand and the left in *hurling* stones and *shooting* arrows out of a bow, *even* of Saul's brethren of Benjamin.
  2Ch 14:8 — And Asa had an army *of men* that bare targets and spears, out of Judah three hundred thousand; and out of Benjamin, that bare shields and drew bows, two hundred and fourscore thousand: all these *were* mighty men of valour.
  2Ch 26:14 — And Uzziah prepared for them throughout all the host shields, and spears, and helmets, and habergeons, and bows, and slings *to cast* stones.
  Ne 4:13 — Therefore set I in the lower places behind the wall, *and* on the higher places, I even set the people after their families with their swords, their spears, and their bows.
  Zec 9:13 — When I have bent Judah for me, filled the bow with Ephraim, and raised up thy sons, O Zion, against thy sons, O Greece, and made thee as the sword of a mighty man.
- **Practiced by Lydians.**
  Jer 46:9 — Come up, ye horses; and rage, ye chariots; and let the mighty men come forth; the Ethiopians and the Libyans, that handle the shield; and the Lydians, that handle *and* bend the bow.
- **In war.**
  Jgs 1:5–11
  Ge 49:23 — The archers have sorely grieved him, and shot *at him,* and hated him:
  1Sa 31:3 — And the battle went sore against Saul, and the archers hit him; and he was sore wounded of the archers.
  Isa 22:3 — All thy rulers are fled together, they are bound by the archers: all that are found in thee are bound together, *which* have fled from far.
  Jer 4:29 — The whole city shall flee for the noise of the horsemen and bowmen; they shall go into thickets, and climb up upon the rocks: every city *shall be* forsaken, and not a man dwell therein.
  Jer 51:3 — Against *him that* bendeth let the archer bend his bow, and against *him that* lifteth himself up in his brigandine: and spare ye not her young men; destroy ye utterly all her host.
  Zec 10:4 — Out of him came forth the corner, out of him the nail, out of him the battle bow, out of him every oppressor together.

See: Arrow

See: Armies

See: Bow

See: War

ARCHEVITES • Inhabitants of Samaria.

Ezr 4:9 — Then *wrote* Rehum the chancellor, and Shimshai the scribe, and the rest of their companions; the Dinaites, the Apharsathchites, the Tarpelites, the Apharsites, the Archevites, the Babylonians, the Susanchites, the Dehavites, *and* the Elamites,

ARCHI • A city of Ephraim.

Jos 16:2 — And goeth out from Bethel to Luz, and passeth along unto the borders of Archi to Ataroth,

ARCHIPPUS • A disciple at Colosse.

Col 4:17 — And say to Archippus, Take heed to the ministry which thou hast received in the Lord, that thou fulfil it.

Phm 1:2 — And to *our* beloved Apphia, and Archippus our fellowsoldier, and to the church in thy house:

ARCHITECTURE

Heb 3:3–4

• Figurative.

Eph 2:21–22

See: Art

See: House

See: Tabernacle

See: Temple

ARCTURUS • Constellation of.

Job 9:9 — Which maketh Arcturus, Orion, and Pleiades, and the chambers of the south.

Job 38:32 — Canst thou bring forth Mazzaroth in his season? or canst thou guide Arcturus with his sons?

ARD

• Son of Benjamin.

Ge 46:21 — And the sons of Benjamin were Belah, and Becher, and Ashbel, Gera, and Naaman, Ehi, and Rosh, Muppim, and Huppim, and Ard.

• Son of Bela.

Nu 26:40 — And the sons of Bela were Ard and Naaman: *of Ard,* the family of the Ardites: *and* of Naaman, the family of the Naamites.

ARDON • Son of Caleb.

1Ch 2:18 — And Caleb the son of Hezron begat *children* of Azubah *his* wife, and of Jerioth: her sons *are* these; Jesher, and Shobab, and Ardon.

ARELI • Son of Gad.

Ge 46:16 — And the sons of Gad; Ziphion, and Haggi, Shuni, and Ezbon, Eri, and Arodi, and Areli.

AREOPAGUS • Mars' hill.

Ac 17:19 — And they took him, and brought him unto Areopagus, saying, May we know what this new doctrine, whereof thou speakest, *is?*

ARETAS • A ruler of Syria.

2Co 11:32 — In Damascus the governor under Aretas the king kept the city of the Damascenes with a garrison, desirous to apprehend me:

ARGOB

• A region east of the Jordan.

Dt 3:13–14

Dt 3:4 — And we took all his cities at that time, there was not a city which we took not from them, threescore cities, all the region of Argob, the kingdom of Og in Bashan.

1Ki 4:13 — The son of Geber, in Ramoth-gilead; to him *pertained* the towns of Jair the son of Manasseh, which *are* in Gilead; to him *also pertained* the region of Argob, which is in Bashan, threescore great cities with walls and brasen bars:

• A courtier of Pekah.

2Ki 15:25 — But Pekah the son of Remaliah, a captain of his, conspired against him, and smote him in Samaria, in the palace of the king's house, with Argob and Arieh, and with him fifty men of the Gileadites: and he killed him, and reigned in his room.

ARIDAI • Son of Haman.

Est 9:9 — And Parmashta, and Arisai, and Aridai, and Vajezatha,

ARIDATHA • Son of Haman.

Est 9:8 — And Poratha, and Adalia, and Aridatha,

ARIEH • A conspirator with Pekah.

2Ki 15:25 — But Pekah the son of Remaliah, a captain of his, conspired against him, and smote him in Samaria, in the palace of the king's house, with Argob and Arieh, and with him fifty men of the Gileadites: and he killed him, and reigned in his room.

ARIEL

• A messenger from Ezra to Iddo.

Ezr 8:16 — Then sent I for Eliezer, for Ariel, for Shemaiah, and for Elnathan, and for Jarib, and for Elnathan, and for Nathan, and for Zechariah, and for Meshullam, chief men; also for Joiarib, and for Elnathan, men of understanding.

• A symbolic name for Jerusalem.

Isa 29:1–2

Isa 29:7 — And the multitude of all the nations that fight against Ariel, even all that fight against her and her munition, and that distress her, shall be as a dream of a night vision.

ARIMATHEA

• Called also Ramah.

• A town five miles north of Jerusalem.

Mt 27:57 — When the even was come, there came a rich man of Arimathaea, named Joseph, who also himself was Jesus' disciple:

Mk 15:43 — Joseph of Arimathaea, an honourable counsellor, which also waited for the kingdom of

God, came, and went in boldly unto Pilate, and craved the body of Jesus.
Lk 23:51 — (The same had not consented to the counsel and deed of them;) *he was* of Arimathaea, a city of the Jews: who also himself waited for the kingdom of God.
Jn 19:38 — And after this Joseph of Arimathaea, being a disciple of Jesus, but secretly for fear of the Jews, besought Pilate that he might take away the body of Jesus: and Pilate gave *him* leave. He came therefore, and took the body of Jesus.

ARIOCH

• King of Ellasar.
Ge 14:1 — And it came to pass in the days of Amraphel king of Shinar, Arioch king of Ellasar, Chedorlaomer king of Elam, and Tidal king of nations;
Ge 14:9 — With Chedorlaomer the king of Elam, and with Tidal king of nations, and Amraphel king of Shinar, and Arioch king of Ellasar; four kings with five.

• Captain of Nebuchadnezzar's guard.
Da 2:14–15; 2:24–25

ARISAI • Son of Haman.

Est 9:9 — And Parmashta, and Arisai, and Aridai, and Vajezatha,

ARISTARCHUS • A companion of Paul.

Ac 19:29 — And the whole city was filled with confusion: and having caught Gaius and Aristarchus, men of Macedonia, Paul's companions in travel, they rushed with one accord into the theatre.
Ac 20:4 — And there accompanied him into Asia Sopater of Berea; and of the Thessalonians, Aristarchus and Secundus; and Gaius of Derbe, and Timotheus; and of Asia, Tychicus and Trophimus.
Ac 27:2 — And entering into a ship of Adramyttium, we launched, meaning to sail by the coasts of Asia; *one* Aristarchus, a Macedonian of Thessalonica, being with us.
Col 4:10 — Aristarchus my fellowprisoner saluteth you, and Marcus, sister's son to Barnabas, (touching whom ye received commandments: if he come unto you, receive him;)
Phm 1:24 — Marcus, Aristarchus, Demas, Lucas, my fellowlabourers.

ARISTOBULUS • A Christian at Rome.

Ro 16:10 — Salute Apelles approved in Christ. Salute them which are of Aristobulus' *household.*

ARK

• Noah's.

• Directions for building of.
Ge 6:14–16

• Noah and family preserved in.
Ge 6:18 — But with thee will I establish my covenant; and thou shalt come into the ark, thou, and thy sons, and thy wife, and thy sons' wives with thee.
Ge 7:8 — Of clean beasts, and of beasts that *are* not clean, and of fowls, and of every thing that creepeth upon the earth,
Mt 24:38 — For as in the days that were before the flood they were eating and drinking, marrying and giving in marriage, until the day that Noe entered into the ark,
Heb 11:7 — By faith Noah, being warned of God of things not seen as yet, moved with fear, prepared an ark to the saving of his house; by the which he condemned the world, and became heir of the righteousness which is by faith.
1Pe 3:20 — Which sometime were disobedient, when once the longsuffering of God waited in the days of Noah, while the ark was a preparing, wherein few, that is, eight souls were saved by water.

• Animals saved in.
Ge 6:19–20; 7:1–16

• Of bulrushes.
Ex 2:3 — And when she could not longer hide him, she took for him an ark of bulrushes, and daubed it with slime and with pitch, and put the child therein; and she laid *it* in the flags by the river's brink.

• In the tabernacle.

• Called Ark of the Covenant.
Jer 3:1–25
Nu 10:33 — And they departed from the mount of the LORD three days' journey: and the ark of the covenant of the LORD went before them in the three days' journey, to search out a resting place for them.
Dt 31:26 — Take this book of the law, and put it in the side of the ark of the covenant of the LORD your God, that it may be there for a witness against thee.
Jos 4:7 — Then ye shall answer them, That the waters of Jordan were cut off before the ark of the covenant of the LORD; when it passed over Jordan, the waters of Jordan were cut off: and these stones shall be for a memorial unto the children of Israel for ever.
1Sa 4:3 — And when the people were come into the camp, the elders of Israel said, Wherefore hath the LORD smitten us to day before the Philistines? Let us fetch the ark of the covenant of the LORD out of Shiloh unto us, that, when it cometh among us, it may save us out of the hand of our enemies.
2Sa 15:24 — And lo Zadok also, and all the Levites *were* with him, bearing the ark of the covenant of God: and they set down the ark of God; and Abiathar went up, until all the people had done passing out of the city.
1Ch 15:25 — So David, and the elders of Israel, and the captains over thousands, went to bring up the ark of the covenant of the LORD out of the house of Obed-edom with joy.
1Ch 17:1 — Now it came to pass, as David sat in his house, that David said to Nathan the prophet, Lo, I dwell in an house of cedars, but the ark of the covenant of the LORD *remaineth* under curtains.

Heb 9:4 — Which had the golden censer, and the ark of the covenant overlaid round about with gold, wherein *was* the golden pot that had manna, and Aaron's rod that budded, and the tables of the covenant;

• Called Ark of the Testimony.

Ex 30:6 — And thou shalt put it before the vail that *is* by the ark of the testimony, before the mercy seat that *is* over the testimony, where I will meet with thee.

• Called Ark of the Lord.

Jos 4:11 — And it came to pass, when all the people were clean passed over, that the ark of the LORD passed over, and the priests, in the presence of the people.

1Sa 4:6 — And when the Philistines heard the noise of the shout, they said, What *meaneth* the noise of this great shout in the camp of the Hebrews? And they understood that the ark of the LORD was come into the camp.

1Sa 6:1 — And the ark of the LORD was in the country of the Philistines seven months.

2Sa 6:9 — And David was afraid of the LORD that day, and said, How shall the ark of the LORD come to me?

1Ki 8:4 — And they brought up the ark of the LORD, and the tabernacle of the congregation, and all the holy vessels that *were* in the tabernacle, even those did the priests and the Levites bring up.

• Called Ark of God.

1Ch 15:1–2

1Sa 3:3 — And ere the lamp of God went out in the temple of the LORD, where the ark of God *was,* and Samuel was laid down *to sleep;*

1Sa 4:11 — And the ark of God was taken; and the two sons of Eli, Hophni and Phinehas, were slain.

1Sa 4:17 — And the messenger answered and said, Israel is fled before the Philistines, and there hath been also a great slaughter among the people, and thy two sons also, Hophni and Phinehas, are dead, and the ark of God is taken.

1Sa 4:22 — And she said, The glory is departed from Israel: for the ark of God is taken.

1Sa 6:3 — And they said, If ye send away the ark of the God of Israel, send it not empty; but in any wise return him a trespass offering: then ye shall be healed, and it shall be known to you why his hand is not removed from you.

1Sa 14:18 — And Saul said unto Ahiah, Bring hither the ark of God. For the ark of God was at that time with the children of Israel.

2Sa 6:7 — And the anger of the LORD was kindled against Uzzah; and God smote him there for *his* error; and there he died by the ark of God.

2Sa 7:2 — That the king said unto Nathan the prophet, See now, I dwell in an house of cedar, but the ark of God dwelleth within curtains.

2Sa 15:25 — And the king said unto Zadok, Carry back the ark of God into the city: if I shall find favour in the eyes of the LORD, he will bring me again, and shew me *both* it, and his habitation:

1Ch 13:12 — And David was afraid of God that day, saying, How shall I bring the ark of God *home* to me?

1Ch 15:15 — And the children of the Levites bare the ark of God upon their shoulders with the staves thereon, as Moses commanded according to the word of the LORD.

1Ch 15:24 — And Shebaniah, and Jehoshaphat, and Nethaneel, and Amasai, and Zechariah, and Benaiah, and Eliezer, the priests, did blow with the trumpets before the ark of God: and Obed-edom and Jehiah *were* doorkeepers for the ark.

1Ch 16:1 — So they brought the ark of God, and set it in the midst of the tent that David had pitched for it: and they offered burnt sacrifices and peace offerings before God.

• Called Ark of God's Strength.

2Ch 6:41 — Now therefore arise, O LORD God, into thy resting place, thou, and the ark of thy strength: let thy priests, O LORD God, be clothed with salvation, and let thy saints rejoice in goodness.

• Sanctification of.

Ex 30:26 — And thou shalt anoint the tabernacle of the congregation therewith, and the ark of the testimony,

• Ceremonies connected with, on the day of atonement.

Le 16:13–15

• Holy.

2Ch 8:11 — And Solomon brought up the daughter of Pharaoh out of the city of David unto the house that he had built for her: for he said, My wife shall not dwell in the house of David king of Israel, because *the places are* holy, whereunto the ark of the LORD hath come.

2Ch 35:3 — And said unto the Levites that taught all Israel, which were holy unto the LORD, Put the holy ark in the house which Solomon the son of David king of Israel did build; *it shall* not *be* a burden upon *your* shoulders: serve now the LORD your God, and his people Israel,

• An oracle of God.

Jos 7:6–15; Jgs 20:27–28; 1Sa 4:3–4

Nu 10:33 — And they departed from the mount of the LORD three days' journey: and the ark of the covenant of the LORD went before them in the three days' journey, to search out a resting place for them.

Nu 14:44 — But they presumed to go up unto the hill top: nevertheless the ark of the covenant of the LORD, and Moses, departed not out of the camp.

1Sa 4:7 — And the Philistines were afraid, for they said, God is come into the camp. And they said, Woe unto us! for there hath not been such a thing heretofore.

1Ch 13:3 — And let us bring again the ark of our God to us: for we enquired not at it in the days of Saul.

1Ch 16:4 — And he appointed *certain* of the Levites to minister before the ark of the LORD, and to record, and to thank and praise the LORD God of Israel:

1Ch 16:37 — So he left there before the ark of the covenant of the LORD Asaph and his brethren, to minister before the ark continually, as every day's work required:

2Ch 6:41 — Now therefore arise, O LORD God, into thy resting place, thou, and the ark of thy strength: let thy priests, O LORD God, be clothed with salvation, and let thy saints rejoice in goodness.

Ps 132:8 — Arise, O LORD, into thy rest; thou, and the ark of thy strength.

See: Mercy Seat

- **Directions for making.**

Ex 25:10–15

Ex 35:12 — The ark, and the staves thereof, *with* the mercy seat, and the vail of the covering,

- **Construction of.**

Ex 37:1–5

Dt 10:3 — And I made an ark *of* shittim wood, and hewed two tables of stone like unto the first, and went up into the mount, having the two tables in mine hand.

- **Contents of.**
  - **The law.**

Ex 25:16 — And thou shalt put into the ark the testimony which I shall give thee.

Ex 25:21 — And thou shalt put the mercy seat above upon the ark; and in the ark thou shalt put the testimony that I shall give thee.

Ex 40:20 — And he took and put the testimony into the ark, and set the staves on the ark, and put the mercy seat above upon the ark:

Dt 10:5 — And I turned myself and came down from the mount, and put the tables in the ark which I had made; and there they be, as the LORD commanded me.

Dt 31:26 — Take this book of the law, and put it in the side of the ark of the covenant of the LORD your God, that it may be there for a witness against thee.

1Ki 8:9 — *There was* nothing in the ark save the two tables of stone, which Moses put there at Horeb, when the LORD made *a covenant* with the children of Israel, when they came out of the land of Egypt.

2Ch 5:10 — *There was* nothing in the ark save the two tables which Moses put *therein* at Horeb, when the LORD made *a covenant* with the children of Israel, when they came out of Egypt.

  - **Aaron's rod.**

Nu 17:10 — And the LORD said unto Moses, Bring Aaron's rod again before the testimony, to be kept for a token against the rebels; and thou shalt quite take away their murmurings from me, that they die not.

Heb 9:4 — Which had the golden censer, and the ark of the covenant overlaid round about with gold, wherein *was* the golden pot that had manna, and Aaron's rod that budded, and the tables of the covenant;

  - **Pot of manna.**

Ex 16:33–34

Heb 9:4 — Which had the golden censer, and the ark of the covenant overlaid round about with gold, wherein *was* the golden pot that had manna, and Aaron's rod that budded, and the tables of the covenant;

- **Place of.**

Heb 9:2–4

Ex 26:33 — And thou shalt hang up the vail under the taches, that thou mayest bring in thither within the vail the ark of the testimony: and the vail shall divide unto you between the holy *place* and the most holy.

Ex 40:21 — And he brought the ark into the tabernacle, and set up the vail of the covering, and covered the ark of the testimony; as the LORD commanded Moses.

1Sa 3:3 — And ere the lamp of God went out in the temple of the LORD, where the ark of God *was,* and Samuel was laid down *to sleep;*

2Sa 7:2 — That the king said unto Nathan the prophet, See now, I dwell in an house of cedar, but the ark of God dwelleth within curtains.

- **How prepared for conveyance.**

Nu 4:5–6

- **Carried by Kohathites.**

Nu 3:30–31

Nu 4:4 — This *shall be* the service of the sons of Kohath in the tabernacle of the congregation, *about* the most holy things:

Nu 4:15 — And when Aaron and his sons have made an end of covering the sanctuary, and all the vessels of the sanctuary, as the camp is to set forward; after that, the sons of Kohath shall come to bear *it:* but they shall not touch *any* holy thing, lest they die. These *things are* the burden of the sons of Kohath in the tabernacle of the congregation.

Dt 10:8 — At that time the LORD separated the tribe of Levi, to bear the ark of the covenant of the LORD, to stand before the LORD to minister unto him, and to bless in his name, unto this day.

1Ch 15:2 — Then David said, None ought to carry the ark of God but the Levites: for them hath the LORD chosen to carry the ark of God, and to minister unto him for ever.

1Ch 15:15 — And the children of the Levites bare the ark of God upon their shoulders with the staves thereon, as Moses commanded according to the word of the LORD.

- **On special occasions carried by priests.**
  - **Crossing Jordan.**

Jos 3:6 — And Joshua spake unto the priests, saying, Take up the ark of the covenant, and pass over before the people. And they took up the ark of the covenant, and went before the people.

Jos 3:14 — And it came to pass, when the people removed from their tents, to pass over Jordan, and the priests bearing the ark of the covenant before the people;

• **Siege of Jericho.**

Jos 6:6 — And Joshua the son of Nun called the priests, and said unto them, Take up the ark of the covenant, and let seven priests bear seven trumpets of rams' horns before the ark of the LORD.

• **Taken to battle.**

Jos 6:6–20; 1Sa 4:3–22

• **Captured by the Philistines.**

1Sa 4:10–11

Ps 78:61 — And delivered his strength into captivity, and his glory into the enemy's hand.

• **Returned by the Philistines.**

1Sa 6:1–21

• **Remains at the house of Abinadab.**

1Sa 7:1–2

2Sa 6:4 — And they brought it out of the house of Abinadab which *was* at Gibeah, accompanying the ark of God: and Ahio went before the ark.

• **In the house of Obed-edom.**

2Sa 6:9–11

• **Set up in Shiloh.**

Jgs 20:27–28; 1Sa 4:3–4

Jos 18:1 — And the whole congregation of the children of Israel assembled together at Shiloh, and set up the tabernacle of the congregation there. And the land was subdued before them.

• **Set up in Jerusalem.**

2Sa 6:12–17; 1Ch 15:1–16:1

1Ch 6:31 — And these *are they* whom David set over the service of song in the house of the LORD, after that the ark had rest.

• **Removed from Jerusalem by Zadok at the time of Absalom's revolt, but returned by command of David.**

2Sa 15:24–29

• **Transferred to Solomon's temple.**

1Ki 8:6–9; 2Ch 5:2–9

2Ch 35:3 — And said unto the Levites that taught all Israel, which were holy unto the LORD, Put the holy ark in the house which Solomon the son of David king of Israel did build; *it shall* not *be* a burden upon *your* shoulders: serve now the LORD your God, and his people Israel,

• **Prophecy concerning.**

Jer 3:16 — And it shall come to pass, when ye be multiplied and increased in the land, in those days, saith the LORD, they shall say no more, The ark of the covenant of the LORD: neither shall it come to mind: neither shall they remember it; neither shall they visit *it;* neither shall *that* be done any more.

• **In John's vision.**

Rev 11:19 — And the temple of God was opened in heaven, and there was seen in his temple the ark of his testament: and there were lightnings, and voices, and thunderings, and an earthquake, and great hail.

ARKITES • Descendants of Canaan.

Ge 10:17 — And the Hivite, and the Arkite, and the Sinite,

1Ch 1:15 — And the Hivite, and the Arkite, and the Sinite,

ARM

• **Figurative use of.**

Isa 40:10–11

Ex 6:6 — Wherefore say unto the children of Israel, I *am* the LORD, and I will bring you out from under the burdens of the Egyptians, and I will rid you out of their bondage, and I will redeem you with a stretched out arm, and with great judgments:

Ex 15:16 — Fear and dread shall fall upon them; by the greatness of thine arm they shall be *as* still as a stone; till thy people pass over, O LORD, till the people pass over, *which* thou hast purchased.

Dt 4:34 — Or hath God assayed to go *and* take him a nation from the midst of another *nation,* by temptations, by signs, and by wonders, and by war, and by a mighty hand, and by a stretched out arm, and by great terrors, according to all that the LORD your God did for you in Egypt before your eyes?

Dt 5:15 — And remember that thou wast a servant in the land of Egypt, and *that* the LORD thy God brought thee out thence through a mighty hand and by a stretched out arm: therefore the LORD thy God commanded thee to keep the sabbath day.

Dt 7:19 — The great temptations which thine eyes saw, and the signs, and the wonders, and the mighty hand, and the stretched out arm, whereby the LORD thy God brought thee out: so shall the LORD thy God do unto all the people of whom thou art afraid.

Dt 9:29 — Yet they *are* thy people and thine inheritance, which thou broughtest out by thy mighty power and by thy stretched out arm.

Dt 11:2 — And know ye this day: for *I speak* not with your children which have not known, and which have not seen the chastisement of the LORD your God, his greatness, his mighty hand, and his stretched out arm,

Dt 26:8 — And the LORD brought us forth out of Egypt with a mighty hand, and with an outstretched arm, and with great terribleness, and with signs, and with wonders:

Dt 33:27 — The eternal God *is thy* refuge, and underneath *are* the everlasting arms: and he shall thrust out the enemy from before thee; and shall say, Destroy *them.*

1Ki 8:42 — (For they shall hear of thy great name, and of thy strong hand, and of thy stretched out arm;) when he shall come and pray toward this house;

2Ki 17:36 — But the LORD, who brought you up out of the land of Egypt with great power and a stretched out arm, him shall ye fear, and him shall ye worship, and to him shall ye do sacrifice.

2Ch 6:32 — Moreover concerning the stranger, which is not of thy people Israel, but is come from a far country for thy great name's sake, and thy mighty hand, and thy stretched out arm; if they come and pray in this house;

Ps 77:15 — Thou hast with *thine* arm redeemed thy people, the sons of Jacob and Joseph. Selah.

Ps 89:10 — Thou hast broken Rahab in pieces, as one that is slain; thou hast scattered thine enemies with thy strong arm.

Ps 89:21 — With whom my hand shall be established: mine arm also shall strengthen him.

Ps 98:1 — O sing unto the LORD a new song; for he hath done marvellous things: his right hand, and his holy arm, hath gotten him the victory.

Ps 136:12 — With a strong hand, and with a stretched out arm: for his mercy *endureth* for ever.

SS 2:6 — His left hand *is* under my head, and his right hand doth embrace me.

Isa 33:2 — O LORD, be gracious unto us; we have waited for thee: be thou their arm every morning, our salvation also in the time of trouble.

Isa 51:5 — My righteousness *is* near; my salvation is gone forth, and mine arms shall judge the people; the isles shall wait upon me, and on mine arm shall they trust.

Isa 51:9 — Awake, awake, put on strength, O arm of the LORD; awake, as in the ancient days, in the generations of old. *Art* thou not it that hath cut Rahab, *and* wounded the dragon?

Isa 52:10 — The LORD hath made bare his holy arm in the eyes of all the nations; and all the ends of the earth shall see the salvation of our God.

Isa 53:1 — Who hath believed our report? and to whom is the arm of the LORD revealed?

Isa 59:16 — And he saw that *there was* no man, and wondered that *there was* no intercessor: therefore his arm brought salvation unto him; and his righteousness, it sustained him.

Isa 62:8 — The LORD hath sworn by his right hand, and by the arm of his strength, Surely I will no more give thy corn *to be* meat for thine enemies; and the sons of the stranger shall not drink thy wine, for the which thou hast laboured:

Isa 63:5 — And I looked, and *there was* none to help; and I wondered that *there was* none to uphold: therefore mine own arm brought salvation unto me; and my fury, it upheld me.

Isa 63:12 — That led *them* by the right hand of Moses with his glorious arm, dividing the water before them, to make himself an everlasting name?

Jer 21:5 — And I myself will fight against you with an outstretched hand and with a strong arm, even in anger, and in fury, and in great wrath.

Jer 27:5 — I have made the earth, the man and the beast that *are* upon the ground, by my great power and by my outstretched arm, and have given it unto whom it seemed meet unto me.

Jer 32:17 — Ah Lord GOD! behold, thou hast made the heaven and the earth by thy great power and stretched out arm, *and* there is nothing too hard for thee:

Eze 20:33 — *As* I live, saith the Lord GOD, surely with a mighty hand, and with a stretched out arm, and with fury poured out, will I rule over you:

Lk 1:51 — He hath shewed strength with his arm; he hath scattered the proud in the imagination of their hearts.

Ac 13:17 — The God of this people of Israel chose our fathers, and exalted the people when they dwelt as strangers in the land of Egypt, and with an high arm brought he them out of it.

See: Anthropomorphisms

ARMAGEDDON • A symbolic name.

Rev 16:16 — And he gathered them together into a place called in the Hebrew tongue Armageddon.

ARMENIA

• A region in western Asia.

2Ki 19:37 — And it came to pass, as he was worshipping in the house of Nisroch his god, that Adrammelech and Sharezer his sons smote him with the sword: and they escaped into the land of Armenia. And Esar-haddon his son reigned in his stead.

Jer 51:27 — Set ye up a standard in the land, blow the trumpet among the nations, prepare the nations against her, call together against her the kingdoms of Ararat, Minni, and Ashchenaz; appoint a captain against her; cause the horses to come up as the rough caterpillers.

• Assassins of Sennacherib take refuge in.

Isa 37:38 — And it came to pass, as he was worshipping in the house of Nisroch his god, that Adrammelech and Sharezer his sons smote him with the sword; and they escaped into the land of Armenia: and Esar-haddon his son reigned in his stead.

ARMIES

• Who of the Israelites were subject to service in.

Nu 1:2–3

Nu 26:2 — Take the sum of all the congregation of the children of Israel, from twenty years old and upward, throughout their fathers' house, all that are able to go to war in Israel.

2Ch 25:5 — Moreover Amaziah gathered Judah together, and made them captains over thousands, and captains over hundreds, according to the houses of *their* fathers, throughout all Judah and Benjamin: and he numbered them from twenty years old and above, and found them three hundred thousand choice *men, able* to go forth to war, that could handle spear and shield.

• Who were exempt from service in.

Nu 1:47–50; Dt 20:5–9

Nu 2:33 — But the Levites were not numbered among the children of Israel; as the LORD commanded Moses.

Jgs 7:3 — Now therefore go to, proclaim in the ears of the people, saying, Whosoever *is* fearful and afraid, let him return and depart early from mount Gilead. And there returned of the people twenty and two thousand; and there remained ten thousand.

• Enumeration of Israel's military forces.

Nu 1:2–3; 2Sa 18:1–2; 24:1–9

Nu 26:2 — Take the sum of all the congregation of the children of Israel, from twenty years old and upward, throughout their fathers' house, all that are able to go to war in Israel.

1Sa 11:8 — And when he numbered them in Bezek, the children of Israel were three hundred thousand, and the men of Judah thirty thousand.

1Ki 20:15 — Then he numbered the young men of the princes of the provinces, and they were two hundred and thirty two: and after them he numbered all the people, *even* all the children of Israel, *being* seven thousand.

2Ch 25:5 — Moreover Amaziah gathered Judah together, and made them captains over thousands, and captains over hundreds, according to the houses of *their* fathers, throughout all Judah and Benjamin: and he numbered them from twenty years old and above, and found them three hundred thousand choice *men, able* to go forth to war, that could handle spear and shield.

• Levies for.

Nu 31:4 — Of every tribe a thousand, throughout all the tribes of Israel, shall ye send to the war.

Jgs 20:10 — And we will take ten men of an hundred throughout all the tribes of Israel, and an hundred of a thousand, and a thousand out of ten thousand, to fetch victual for the people, that they may do, when they come to Gibeah of Benjamin, according to all the folly that they have wrought in Israel.

• Compulsory service in.

1Sa 14:52 — And there was sore war against the Philistines all the days of Saul: and when Saul saw any strong man, or any valiant man, he took him unto him.

↞See: Cowardice

• How officered.

• Commander-in-chief.

1Sa 14:50 — And the name of Saul's wife *was* Ahinoam, the daughter of Ahimaaz: and the name of the captain of his host *was* Abner, the son of Ner, Saul's uncle.

2Sa 2:8 — But Abner the son of Ner, captain of Saul's host, took Ish-bosheth the son of Saul, and brought him over to Mahanaim;

2Sa 8:16 — And Joab the son of Zeruiah *was* over the host; and Jehoshaphat the son of Ahilud *was* recorder;

2Sa 17:25 — And Absalom made Amasa captain of the host instead of Joab: which Amasa was a man's son, whose name *was* Ithra an Israelite, that went in to Abigail the daughter of Nahash, sister to Zeruiah Joab's mother.

2Sa 19:13 — And say ye to Amasa, *Art* thou not of my bone, and of my flesh? God do so to me, and more also, if thou be not captain of the host before me continually in the room of Joab.

2Sa 20:23 — Now Joab *was* over all the host of Israel: and Benaiah the son of Jehoiada *was* over the Cherethites and over the Pelethites:

• Generals of corps and divisions.

Nu 2:3–31; 1Ch 27:1–22; 2Ch 17:12–19

• Captains of thousands.

Nu 31:14 — And Moses was wroth with the officers of the host, *with* the captains over thousands, and captains over hundreds, which came from the battle.

Nu 31:48 — And the officers which *were* over thousands of the host, the captains of thousands, and captains of hundreds, came near unto Moses:

1Sa 17:18 — And carry these ten cheeses unto the captain of *their* thousand, and look how thy brethren fare, and take their pledge.

1Ch 28:1 — And David assembled all the princes of Israel, the princes of the tribes, and the captains of the companies that ministered to the king by course, and the captains over the thousands, and captains over the hundreds, and the stewards over all the substance and possession of the king, and of his sons, with the officers, and with the mighty men, and with all the valiant men, unto Jerusalem.

2Ch 25:5 — Moreover Amaziah gathered Judah together, and made them captains over thousands, and captains over hundreds, according to the houses of *their* fathers, throughout all Judah and Benjamin: and he numbered them from twenty years old and above, and found them three hundred thousand choice *men, able* to go forth to war, that could handle spear and shield.

• Captains of hundreds.

Nu 31:14 — And Moses was wroth with the officers of the host, *with* the captains over thousands, and captains over hundreds, which came from the battle.

Nu 31:48 — And the officers which *were* over thousands of the host, the captains of thousands, and captains of hundreds, came near unto Moses:

2Ki 11:15 — But Jehoiada the priest commanded the captains of the hundreds, the officers of the host, and said unto them, Have her forth without the ranges: and him that followeth her kill with the sword. For the priest had said, Let her not be slain in the house of the LORD.

1Ch 28:1 — And David assembled all the princes of Israel, the princes of the tribes, and the captains of the companies that ministered to the king by course, and the captains over the thousands, and captains over the hundreds, and the stewards over all the substance and possession of the king, and of his sons, with the officers, and with the mighty men, and with all the valiant men, unto Jerusalem.

2Ch 25:5 — Moreover Amaziah gathered Judah together, and made them captains over thousands, and captains over hundreds, according to the houses of *their* fathers, throughout all Judah and Benjamin: and he numbered them from twenty years old and above, and found them three hundred thousand choice *men, able* to go forth to war, that could handle spear and shield.

• Captains of fifties.

2Ki 1:9 — Then the king sent unto him a captain of fifty with his fifty. And he went up to him: and, behold, he sat on the top of an hill. And he spake unto him, Thou man of God, the king hath said, Come down.

Isa 3:3 — The captain of fifty, and the honourable man, and the counsellor, and the cunning artificer, and the eloquent orator.

See: Cavalry

See: Chariot

• Rendezvous of, methods employed in effecting.

• Sounding a trumpet.

1Sa 13:3–4

Nu 10:9 — And if ye go to war in your land against the enemy that oppresseth you, then ye shall blow an alarm with the trumpets; and ye shall be remembered before the LORD your God, and ye shall be saved from your enemies.

Jgs 3:27 — And it came to pass, when he was come, that he blew a trumpet in the mountain of Ephraim, and the children of Israel went down with him from the mount, and he before them.

Jgs 6:34 — But the Spirit of the LORD came upon Gideon, and he blew a trumpet; and Abi-ezer was gathered after him.

• Cutting oxen in pieces, and sending the pieces throughout Israel.

1Sa 11:7 — And he took a yoke of oxen, and hewed them in pieces, and sent *them* throughout all the coasts of Israel by the hands of messengers, saying, Whosoever cometh not forth after Saul and after Samuel, so shall it be done unto his oxen. And the fear of the LORD fell on the people, and they came out with one consent.

• Refusal to obey the summons, instance of.

Jgs 20:1–48; 21:5–11

• Tactics.

• Camp and march.

Nu 2:1–34

• March in ranks.

Ex 13:18 — But God led the people about, *through* the way of the wilderness of the Red sea: and the children of Israel went up harnessed out of the land of Egypt.

1Ch 12:33 — Of Zebulun, such as went forth to battle, expert in war, with all instruments of war, fifty thousand, which could keep rank: *they were* not of double heart.

Joel 2:7 — They shall run like mighty men; they shall climb the wall like men of war; and they shall march every one on his ways, and they shall not break their ranks:

• Move, in attack, in three divisions.

1Sa 13:17–18

Jgs 7:16 — And he divided the three hundred men *into* three companies, and he put a trumpet in every man's hand, with empty pitchers, and lamps within the pitchers.

Jgs 9:43 — And he took the people, and divided them into three companies, and laid wait in the field, and looked, and, behold, the people *were* come forth out of the city; and he rose up against them, and smote them.

1Sa 11:11 — And it was *so* on the morrow, that Saul put the people in three companies; and they came into the midst of the host in the morning watch, and slew the Ammonites until the heat of the day: and it came to pass, that they which remained were scattered, so that two of them were not left together.

2Sa 18:2 — And David sent forth a third part of the people under the hand of Joab, and a third part under the hand of Abishai the son of Zeruiah, Joab's brother, and a third part under the hand of Ittai the Gittite. And the king said unto the people, I will surely go forth with you myself also.

Job 1:17 — While he *was* yet speaking, there came also another, and said, The Chaldeans made out three bands, and fell upon the camels, and have carried them away, yea, and slain the servants with the edge of the sword; and I only am escaped alone to tell thee.

• Flanks called wings.

Isa 8:8 — And he shall pass through Judah; he shall overflow and go over, he shall reach *even* to the neck; and the stretching out of his wings shall fill the breadth of thy land, O Immanuel.

See: Strategy

• Orders delivered with trumpets.

2Sa 2:28 — So Joab blew a trumpet, and all the people stood still, and pursued after Israel no more, neither fought they any more.

2Sa 18:16 — And Joab blew the trumpet, and the people returned from pursuing after Israel: for Joab held back the people.

2Sa 20:1 — And there happened to be there a man of Belial, whose name *was* Sheba, the son of Bichri, a Benjamite: and he blew a trumpet, and said, We have no part in David, neither have we inheritance in the son of Jesse: every man to his tents, O Israel.

2Sa 20:22 — Then the woman went unto all the people in her wisdom. And they cut off the head of Sheba the son of Bichri, and cast *it* out to Joab. And he blew a trumpet, and they retired from the city, every man to his tent. And Joab returned to Jerusalem unto the king.

Ne 4:18 — For the builders, every one had his sword girded by his side, and *so* builded. And he that sounded the trumpet *was* by me.

Ne 4:20 — In what place *therefore* ye hear the sound of the trumpet, resort ye thither unto us: our God shall fight for us.

• Stratagems.

• Ambushes

• Ai.

Jos 8:2–22

• Shechem.

Jgs 9:25 — And the men of Shechem set liers in wait for him in the top of the mountains, and they robbed all that came along that way by them: and it was told Abimelech.

Jgs 9:34 — And Abimelech rose up, and all the people that *were* with him, by night, and they laid wait against Shechem in four companies.

- **Gibeah.**
  Jgs 20:29–43
- **Zemaraim.**
  2Ch 13:13 — But Jeroboam caused an ambushment to come about behind them: so they were before Judah, and the ambushment *was* behind them.
- **By Jehoshaphat.**
  2Ch 20:22 — And when they began to sing and to praise, the LORD set ambushments against the children of Ammon, Moab, and mount Seir, which were come against Judah; and they were smitten.

• Reconnoissances.

- **Of Jericho.**
  Jos 2:1–24
- **Of Ai.**
  Jos 7:2–3
- **Of Bethel.**
  Jgs 1:23–24
- **Of Laish.**
  Jgs 18:2–10
- **Night attacks.**
  Jgs 7:16–22
  Ge 14:15 — And he divided himself against them, he and his servants, by night, and smote them, and pursued them unto Hobah, which *is* on the left hand of Damascus.
- **Decoy.**
  Jos 8:4–22; Jgs 20:29–43; Ne 6:1–19
- **Delay.**
  2Sa 17:7–14

• Celerity of action.

- **Abraham, in pursuit of Chedorlaomer.**
  Ge 14:14–15
- **Joshua, against the Amorites.**
  Jos 10:6 — And the men of Gibeon sent unto Joshua to the camp to Gilgal, saying, Slack not thy hand from thy servants; come up to us quickly, and save us, and help us: for all the kings of the Amorites that dwell in the mountains are gathered together against us.
  Jos 10:9 — Joshua therefore came unto them suddenly, *and* went up from Gilgal all night.
- **The confederated kings.**
  Jos 11:7 — So Joshua came, and all the people of war with him, against them by the waters of Merom suddenly; and they fell upon them.

• David's attack upon the Philistines.
2Sa 5:23–25

• Forced marches.
Isa 5:26–27

• Sieges.
Jer 39:1 — In the ninth year of Zedekiah king of Judah, in the tenth month, came Nebuchadrezzar king of Babylon and all his army against Jerusalem, and they besieged it.

- **Of Jericho.**
  Jos 6:1–27
- **Of Samaria.**
  2Ki 6:24–7:20
- **Of Jerusalem.**
  2Ki 25:1–3

• "Engines" used.
2Ch 26:15 — And he made in Jerusalem engines, invented by cunning men, to be on the towers and upon the bulwarks, to shoot arrows and great stones withal. And his name spread far abroad; for he was marvellously helped, till he was strong.
Jer 6:6 — For thus hath the LORD of hosts said, Hew ye down trees, and cast a mount against Jerusalem: this *is* the city to be visited; she *is* wholly oppression in the midst of her.
Eze 26:9 — And he shall set engines of war against thy walls, and with his axes he shall break down thy towers.

• Fortifications.
Jgs 9:31 — And he sent messengers unto Abimelech privily, saying, Behold, Gaal the son of Ebed and his brethren be come to Shechem; and, behold, they fortify the city against thee.
2Sa 5:9 — So David dwelt in the fort, and called it the city of David. And David built round about from Millo and inward.
2Ki 25:1 — And it came to pass in the ninth year of his reign, in the tenth month, in the tenth *day* of the month, *that* Nebuchadnezzar king of Babylon came, he, and all his host, against Jerusalem, and pitched against it; and they built forts against it round about.
2Ch 11:11 — And he fortified the strong holds, and put captains in them, and store of victual, and of oil and wine.
2Ch 26:9 — Moreover Uzziah built towers in Jerusalem at the corner gate, and at the valley gate, and at the turning *of the wall,* and fortified them.
Ne 3:8 — Next unto him repaired Uzziel the son of Harhaiah, of the goldsmiths. Next unto him also repaired Hananiah the son of *one of* the apothecaries, and they fortified Jerusalem unto the broad wall.
Ne 4:2 — And he spake before his brethren and the army of Samaria, and said, What do these feeble Jews? will they fortify themselves? will they sacrifice? will they make an end in a day? will they revive the stones out of the heaps of the rubbish which are burned?
Isa 22:10 — And ye have numbered the houses of Jerusalem, and the houses have ye broken down to fortify the wall.
Isa 25:12 — And the fortress of the high fort of thy walls shall he bring down, lay low, *and* bring to the ground, *even* to the dust.
Isa 29:3 — And I will camp against thee round about, and will lay siege against thee with a mount, and I will raise forts against thee.
Isa 32:14 — Because the palaces shall be forsaken; the multitude of the city shall be left; the forts and towers shall be for dens for ever, a joy of wild asses, a pasture of flocks;
Jer 6:6 — For thus hath the LORD of hosts said, Hew ye down trees, and cast a mount against Jerusalem: this

is the city to be visited; she *is* wholly oppression in the midst of her.

Jer 32:24 — Behold the mounts, they are come unto the city to take it; and the city is given into the hand of the Chaldeans, that fight against it, because of the sword, and of the famine, and of the pestilence: and what thou hast spoken is come to pass; and, behold, thou seest *it*.

Jer 33:4 — For thus saith the LORD, the God of Israel, concerning the houses of this city, and concerning the houses of the kings of Judah, which are thrown down by the mounts, and by the sword;

Jer 51:53 — Though Babylon should mount up to heaven, and though she should fortify the height of her strength, *yet* from me shall spoilers come unto her, saith the LORD.

Eze 4:2 — And lay siege against it, and build a fort against it, and cast a mount against it; set the camp also against it, and set *battering* rams against it round about.

Eze 17:17 — Neither shall Pharaoh with *his* mighty army and great company make for him in the war, by casting up mounts, and building forts, to cut off many persons:

Eze 21:22 — At his right hand was the divination for Jerusalem, to appoint captains, to open the mouth in the slaughter, to lift up the voice with shouting, to appoint *battering* rams against the gates, to cast a mount, *and* to build a fort.

Eze 26:8 — He shall slay with the sword thy daughters in the field: and he shall make a fort against thee, and cast a mount against thee, and lift up the buckler against thee.

Eze 33:27 — Say thou thus unto them, Thus saith the Lord GOD; *As* I live, surely they that *are* in the wastes shall fall by the sword, and him that *is* in the open field will I give to the beasts to be devoured, and they that be in the forts and in the caves shall die of the pestilence.

Da 11:15 — So the king of the north shall come, and cast up a mount, and take the most fenced cities: and the arms of the south shall not withstand, neither his chosen people, neither *shall there be any* strength to withstand.

Da 11:19 — Then he shall turn his face toward the fort of his own land: but he shall stumble and fall, and not be found.

Na 2:1 — He that dasheth in pieces is come up before thy face: keep the munition, watch the way, make *thy* loins strong, fortify *thy* power mightily.

Na 3:14 — Draw thee waters for the siege, fortify thy strong holds: go into clay, and tread the morter, make strong the brickkiln.

• Standards.

Nu 2:2–3, 17–18

Nu 2:10 — On the south side *shall be* the standard of the camp of Reuben according to their armies: and the captain of the children of Reuben *shall be* Elizur the son of Shedeur.

Nu 2:25 — The standard of the camp of Dan *shall be* on the north side by their armies: and the captain of the children of Dan *shall be* Ahiezer the son of Ammishaddai.

Nu 2:31 — All they that were numbered in the camp of Dan *were* an hundred thousand and fifty and seven thousand and six hundred. They shall go hindmost with their standards.

Nu 2:34 — And the children of Israel did according to all that the LORD commanded Moses: so they pitched by their standards, and so they set forward, every one after their families, according to the house of their fathers.

Nu 10:14 — In the first *place* went the standard of the camp of the children of Judah according to their armies: and over his host *was* Nahshon the son of Amminadab.

Nu 10:18 — And the standard of the camp of Reuben set forward according to their armies: and over his host *was* Elizur the son of Shedeur.

Nu 10:22 — And the standard of the camp of the children of Ephraim set forward according to their armies: and over his host *was* Elishama the son of Ammihud.

Nu 10:25 — And the standard of the camp of the children of Dan set forward, *which was* the rereward of all the camps throughout their hosts: and over his host *was* Ahiezer the son of Ammishaddai.

• Uniforms of.

Eze 23:6 — *Which were* clothed with blue, captains and rulers, all of them desirable young men, horsemen riding upon horses.

Eze 23:12 — She doted upon the Assyrians *her* neighbours, captains and rulers clothed most gorgeously, horsemen riding upon horses, all of them desirable young men.

Na 2:3 — The shield of his mighty men is made red, the valiant men *are* in scarlet: the chariots *shall be* with flaming torches in the day of his preparation, and the fir trees shall be terribly shaken.

• Standing armies.

1Ch 27:1–34; 2Ch 17:12–19; 26:11–15

1Sa 13:2 — Saul chose him three thousand *men* of Israel; *whereof* two thousand were with Saul in Michmash and in mount Bethel, and a thousand were with Jonathan in Gibeah of Benjamin: and the rest of the people he sent every man to his tent.

2Ch 1:14 — And Solomon gathered chariots and horsemen: and he had a thousand and four hundred chariots, and twelve thousand horsemen, which he placed in the chariot cities, and with the king at Jerusalem.

• Religious ceremonies attending.

• Seeking counsel from God before battle.

1Sa 14:37–41; 23:2–12; 1Ki 22:7–28; 2Ki 3:11–19; Jer 37:7–10

Nu 27:21 — And he shall stand before Eleazar the priest, who shall ask *counsel* for him after the judgment of Urim before the LORD: at his word shall they go out, and at his word they shall come in, *both* he, and all the children of Israel with him, even all the congregation.

Jgs 1:1 — Now after the death of Joshua it came to pass, that the children of Israel asked the LORD, saying, Who shall go up for us against the Canaanites first, to fight against them?

1Sa 14:19 — And it came to pass, while Saul talked unto the priest, that the noise that *was* in the host of the Philistines went on and increased: and Saul said unto the priest, Withdraw thine hand.

1Sa 30:8 — And David enquired at the LORD, saying, Shall I pursue after this troop? shall I overtake them? And he answered him, Pursue: for thou shalt surely overtake *them,* and without fail recover *all.*

2Sa 2:1 — And it came to pass after this, that David enquired of the LORD, saying, Shall I go up into any of the cities of Judah? And the LORD said unto him, Go up. And David said, Whither shall I go up? And he said, Unto Hebron.

2Sa 5:19 — And David enquired of the LORD, saying, Shall I go up to the Philistines? wilt thou deliver them into mine hand? And the LORD said unto David, Go up: for I will doubtless deliver the Philistines into thine hand.

2Sa 5:23 — And when David enquired of the LORD, he said, Thou shalt not go up; *but* fetch a compass behind them, and come upon them over against the mulberry trees.

1Ch 14:10 — And David enquired of God, saying, Shall I go up against the Philistines? and wilt thou deliver them into mine hand? And the LORD said unto him, Go up; for I will deliver them into thine hand.

1Ch 14:14 — Therefore David enquired again of God; and God said unto him, Go not up after them; turn away from them, and come upon them over against the mulberry trees.

• Sacrifices.

1Sa 13:11–12

• Purifications.

Nu 31:19–24

• Prophets prophesy before.

2Ch 20:14–17

• Holiness enjoined.

Dt 23:9 — When the host goeth forth against thine enemies, then keep thee from every wicked thing.

• Officers consecrate themselves to God.

2Ch 17:16 — And next him *was* Amasiah the son of Zichri, who willingly offered himself unto the LORD; and with him two hundred thousand mighty men of valour.

• Army choir and songs.

2Ch 20:21–22

• Ark taken to battle.

Jos 6:6–7; 1Sa 4:4–11

Jos 6:13 — And seven priests bearing seven trumpets of rams' horns before the ark of the LORD went on continually, and blew with the trumpets: and the armed men went before them; but the rereward came after the ark of the LORD, *the priests* going on, and blowing with the trumpets.

• Divine assistance to.

• When Aaron and Hur held up Moses' hands.

Ex 17:11–12

• In siege of Jericho.

Jos 6:1–27

• Sun stands still.

Jos 10:11–14

• Gideon's victory.

Jgs 7:1–25

• Samaria's deliverances.

1Ki 20:1–43; 2Ki 7:1–20

• Jehoshaphat's victories.

2Ki 3:1–27; 2Ch 20:1–37

• Angel of the Lord smites the Assyrians.

2Ki 19:35 — And it came to pass that night, that the angel of the LORD went out, and smote in the camp of the Assyrians an hundred fourscore and five thousand: and when they arose early in the morning, behold, they *were* all dead corpses.

• Determine royal succession.

2Sa 2:8–10; 2Ki 11:4–12

1Ki 16:16 — And the people *that were* encamped heard say, Zimri hath conspired, and hath also slain the king: wherefore all Israel made Omri, the captain of the host, king over Israel that day in the camp.

• Composed of insurgents.

1Sa 22:1–2

• Mercenaries.

1Ch 19:6–7; 2Ch 25:5–6

2Sa 10:6 — And when the children of Ammon saw that they stank before David, the children of Ammon sent and hired the Syrians of Beth-rehob, and the Syrians of Zoba, twenty thousand footmen, and of king Maacah a thousand men, and of Ish-tob twelve thousand men.

• Confederated.

Jos 10:1–5; 11:1–5; 2Sa 10:15–16; 1Ki 22:1–4; 2Ki 18:19–21; 1Ch 19:6–7; 2Ch 16:2–9; Ps 83:1–12; Isa 7:1–9; 8:9–12

Jgs 1:3 — And Judah said unto Simeon his brother, Come up with me into my lot, that we may fight against the Canaanites; and I likewise will go with thee into thy lot. So Simeon went with him.

2Sa 10:6 — And when the children of Ammon saw that they stank before David, the children of Ammon sent and hired the Syrians of Beth-rehob, and the Syrians of Zoba, twenty thousand footmen, and of king Maacah a thousand men, and of Ish-tob twelve thousand men.

2Sa 10:19 — And when all the kings *that were* servants to Hadarezer saw that they were smitten before Israel, they made peace with Israel, and served them. So the Syrians feared to help the children of Ammon any more.

1Ki 15:20 — So Ben-hadad hearkened unto king Asa, and sent the captains of the hosts which he had against the cities of Israel, and smote Ijon, and Dan, and Abel-beth-maachah, and all Cinneroth, with all the land of Naphtali.

2Ki 16:9 — And the king of Assyria hearkened unto him: for the king of Assyria went up against Damascus, and took it, and carried *the people of* it captive to Kir, and slew Rezin.

2Ch 18:1 — Now Jehoshaphat had riches and honour in abundance, and joined affinity with Ahab.

2Ch 18:3 — And Ahab king of Israel said unto Jehoshaphat king of Judah, Wilt thou go with me to Ramoth-gilead? And he answered him, I *am* as thou *art,* and my people as thy people; and *we will be* with thee in the war.

2Ch 20:1 — It came to pass after this also, *that* the children of Moab, and the children of Ammon, and with them *other* beside the Ammonites, came against Jehoshaphat to battle.

2Ch 22:5 — He walked also after their counsel, and went with Jehoram the son of Ahab king of Israel to war against Hazael king of Syria at Ramoth-gilead: and the Syrians smote Joram.

2Ch 28:16 — At that time did king Ahaz send unto the kings of Assyria to help him.

2Ch 28:20 — And Tilgath-pilneser king of Assyria came unto him, and distressed him, but strengthened him not.

Isa 54:15 — Behold, they shall surely gather together, *but* not by me: whosoever shall gather together against thee shall fall for thy sake.

- **Exhorted before battle.**

Dt 20:1–9

- **Battle shouts.**

Jgs 7:18 — When I blow with a trumpet, I and all that *are* with me, then blow ye the trumpets also on every side of all the camp, and say, *The sword* of the LORD, and of Gideon.

1Sa 17:20 — And David rose up early in the morning, and left the sheep with a keeper, and took, and went, as Jesse had commanded him; and he came to the trench, as the host was going forth to the fight, and shouted for the battle.

1Sa 17:52 — And the men of Israel and of Judah arose, and shouted, and pursued the Philistines, until thou come to the valley, and to the gates of Ekron. And the wounded of the Philistines fell down by the way to Shaaraim, even unto Gath, and unto Ekron.

- **Triumphs of, celebrated.**
  - **With songs.**

Jgs 5:1–31; 1Sa 18:6–7

  - **With music.**

2Ch 20:28 — And they came to Jerusalem with psalteries and harps and trumpets unto the house of the LORD.

  - **With dancing.**

1Sa 18:6–7

- **Rewards for meritorious conduct.**
  - **The general offers his daughter in marriage.**

Jos 15:16–17

  - **King offers his daughter.**

1Sa 18:17–28

1Sa 17:25 — And the men of Israel said, Have ye seen this man that is come up? surely to defy Israel is he come up: and it shall be, *that* the man who killeth him, the king will enrich him with great riches, and will give him his daughter, and make his father's house free in Israel.

  - **Promotion.**

2Sa 23:8–39; 1Ch 11:10–47

1Ch 11:6 — And David said, Whosoever smiteth the Jebusites first shall be chief and captain. So Joab the son of Zeruiah went first up, and was chief.

  - **Share the spoils.**

Nu 31:25–47

- **Children instructed in military arts.**

2Sa 1:18 — (Also he bade them teach the children of Judah *the use of* the bow: behold, it is written in the book of Jasher.)

- **Insubordination in, punished, Achan.**

Jos 7:1–26

- **Check roll-call.**

Nu 31:48–49

1Sa 14:17 — Then said Saul unto the people that *were* with him, Number now, and see who is gone from us. And when they had numbered, behold, Jonathan and his armourbearer *were* not *there.*

- **Panics.**

Isa 30:17 — One thousand *shall flee* at the rebuke of one; at the rebuke of five shall ye flee: till ye be left as a beacon upon the top of a mountain, and as an ensign on an hill.

  - **Among the Midianites.**

Jgs 7:21 — And they stood every man in his place round about the camp: and all the host ran, and cried, and fled.

  - **Among the Philistines.**

1Sa 14:15–19

  - **Among the Syrians.**

2Ki 7:7–15

- **Soldiers destroy each other to escape captivity.**

1Sa 31:4–6

1Sa 14:20 — And Saul and all the people that *were* with him assembled themselves, and they came to the battle: and, behold, every man's sword was against his fellow, *and there was* a very great discomfiture.

- **Champions fight instead of.**

1Sa 17:8–53; 2Sa 2:14–17; 21:15–22

- **Confidence in, vain.**

Ps 33:16 — There is no king saved by the multitude of an host: a mighty man is not delivered by much strength.

Ps 44:6 — For I will not trust in my bow, neither shall my sword save me.

- **Escort duty performed by.**

Ac 23:23–24, 31–33

2Ki 1:9 — Then the king sent unto him a captain of fifty with his fifty. And he went up to him: and, behold, he sat on the top of an hill. And he spake unto him, Thou man of God, the king hath said, Come down.

- **Roman army.**
  - **Captains of.**

    Ac 22:24–29
  - **Centurions.**

    Mt 8:5 — And when Jesus was entered into Capernaum, there came unto him a centurion, beseeching him,

    Mt 8:8 — The centurion answered and said, Lord, I am not worthy that thou shouldest come under my roof: but speak the word only, and my servant shall be healed.

    Mt 27:54 — Now when the centurion, and they that were with him, watching Jesus, saw the earthquake, and those things that were done, they feared greatly, saying, Truly this was the Son of God.

    Lk 7:2 — And a certain centurion's servant, who was dear unto him, was sick, and ready to die.

    Lk 23:47 — Now when the centurion saw what was done, he glorified God, saying, Certainly this was a righteous man.

    Ac 10:1 — There was a certain man in Caesarea called Cornelius, a centurion of the band called the Italian *band,*

    Ac 10:7 — And when the angel which spake unto Cornelius was departed, he called two of his household servants, and a devout soldier of them that waited on him continually;

    Ac 10:22 — And they said, Cornelius the centurion, a just man, and one that feareth God, and of good report among all the nation of the Jews, was warned from God by an holy angel to send for thee into his house, and to hear words of thee.

    Ac 21:32 — Who immediately took soldiers and centurions, and ran down unto them: and when they saw the chief captain and the soldiers, they left beating of Paul.

    Ac 22:26 — When the centurion heard *that,* he went and told the chief captain, saying, Take heed what thou doest: for this man is a Roman.

    Ac 23:17 — Then Paul called one of the centurions unto *him,* and said, Bring this young man unto the chief captain: for he hath a certain thing to tell him.

    Ac 23:23 — And he called unto *him* two centurions, saying, Make ready two hundred soldiers to go to Caesarea, and horsemen threescore and ten, and spearmen two hundred, at the third hour of the night;

    Ac 24:23 — And he commanded a centurion to keep Paul, and to let *him* have liberty, and that he should forbid none of his acquaintance to minister or come unto him.

    Ac 27:1 — And when it was determined that we should sail into Italy, they delivered Paul and certain other prisoners unto *one* named Julius, a centurion of Augustus' band.

    Ac 27:11 — Nevertheless the centurion believed the master and the owner of the ship, more than those things which were spoken by Paul.

    Ac 27:43 — But the centurion, willing to save Paul, kept them from *their* purpose; and commanded that they which could swim should cast *themselves* first *into the sea,* and get to land:

    Ac 28:16 — And when we came to Rome, the centurion delivered the prisoners to the captain of the guard: but Paul was suffered to dwell by himself with a soldier that kept him.
  - **Divided into "bands".**

    Ac 10:1 — There was a certain man in Caesarea called Cornelius, a centurion of the band called the Italian *band,*

    Ac 27:1 — And when it was determined that we should sail into Italy, they delivered Paul and certain other prisoners unto *one* named Julius, a centurion of Augustus' band.
- **For other than armies of the Israelites and Romans.**
  - ✦See: **Amalekites**
  - ✦See: **Assyria**
  - ✦See: **Babylon**
  - ✦See: **Egyptians**
  - ✦See: **Midianites**
  - ✦See: **Persia**
  - ✦See: **Syria**
- **For commissaries of.**
  - ✦See: **Commissary**
- **For weapons used.**
  - ✦See: **Armor**
  - ✦See: **Ambush**
  - ✦See: **Cavalry**
  - ✦See: **Fort**
  - ✦See: **Garrison**
  - ✦See: **Herald**
  - ✦See: **Hostage**
  - ✦See: **Navy**
  - ✦See: **Reconnoissance**
  - ✦See: **Siege**
  - ✦See: **Soldiers**
  - ✦See: **Spies**
  - ✦See: **Standard**
  - ✦See: **Strategy**
  - ✦See: **Truce**
  - ✦See: **War**
- **Figurative.**

  Dt 33:2 — And he said, The LORD came from Sinai, and rose up from Seir unto them; he shined forth from mount Paran, and he came with ten thousands of saints: from his right hand *went* a fiery law for them.

2Ki 6:17 — And Elisha prayed, and said, LORD, I pray thee, open his eyes, that he may see. And the LORD opened the eyes of the young man; and he saw: and, behold, the mountain *was* full of horses and chariots of fire round about Elisha.

Ps 34:7 — The angel of the LORD encampeth round about them that fear him, and delivereth them.

Ps 68:17 — The chariots of God *are* twenty thousand, *even* thousands of angels: the Lord *is* among them, *as in* Sinai, in the holy *place*.

Rev 9:16 — And the number of the army of the horsemen *were* two hundred thousand thousand: and I heard the number of them.

ARMONI • Son of Saul.

2Sa 21:8 — But the king took the two sons of Rizpah the daughter of Aiah, whom she bare unto Saul, Armoni and Mephibosheth; and the five sons of Michal the daughter of Saul, whom she brought up for Adriel the son of Barzillai the Meholathite:

ARMOR

• The equipment of a soldier.

Jer 46:3–4; Eph 6:14–17

↞See: Breastplate

↞See: Brigandine

↞See: Coat of Mail

↞See: Greaves

↞See: Habergeon

↞See: Helmet

↞See: Shield

• Figurative.

Eph 6:11–18; 1Th 5:5–11

Ro 13:12 — The night is far spent, the day is at hand: let us therefore cast off the works of darkness, and let us put on the armour of light.

2Co 6:7 — By the word of truth, by the power of God, by the armour of righteousness on the right hand and on the left,

2Co 10:4 — (For the weapons of our warfare *are* not carnal, but mighty through God to the pulling down of strong holds;)

ARMOR-BEARER

• An attendant who carried a soldier's equipment.

• Of Abimelech.

Jgs 9:54 — Then he called hastily unto the young man his armourbearer, and said unto him, Draw thy sword, and slay me, that men say not of me, A woman slew him. And his young man thrust him through, and he died.

• Of Jonathan.

1Sa 14:6–7

1Sa 14:12 — And the men of the garrison answered Jonathan and his armourbearer, and said, Come up to us, and we will shew you a thing. And Jonathan said unto his armourbearer, Come up after me: for the LORD hath delivered them into the hand of Israel.

1Sa 14:14 — And that first slaughter, which Jonathan and his armourbearer made, was about twenty men, within as it were an half acre of land, *which* a yoke *of oxen might plow.*

1Sa 14:17 — Then said Saul unto the people that *were* with him, Number now, and see who is gone from us. And when they had numbered, behold, Jonathan and his armourbearer *were* not *there.*

• Of Saul.

1Sa 16:21 — And David came to Saul, and stood before him: and he loved him greatly; and he became his armourbearer.

1Sa 31:6 — So Saul died, and his three sons, and his armourbearer, and all his men, that same day together.

• Of Goliath.

1Sa 17:7 — And the staff of his spear *was* like a weaver's beam; and his spear's head *weighed* six hundred shekels of iron: and one bearing a shield went before him.

• Of Joab.

2Sa 18:15 — And ten young men that bare Joab's armour compassed about and smote Absalom, and slew him.

ARMORY

• A place for the storage of armor.

Ne 3:19 — And next to him repaired Ezer the son of Jeshua, the ruler of Mizpah, another piece over against the going up to the armoury at the turning *of the wall.*

SS 4:4 — Thy neck *is* like the tower of David builded for an armoury, whereon there hang a thousand bucklers, all shields of mighty men.

Isa 22:8 — And he discovered the covering of Judah, and thou didst look in that day to the armour of the house of the forest.

Isa 39:2 — And Hezekiah was glad of them, and shewed them the house of his precious things, the silver, and the gold, and the spices, and the precious ointment, and all the house of his armour, and all that was found in his treasures: there was nothing in his house, nor in all his dominion, that Hezekiah shewed them not.

• In different parts of the kingdom.

1Ki 10:17 — And he made three hundred shields of beaten gold; three pound of gold went to one shield: and the king put them in the house of the forest of Lebanon.

2Ch 11:12 — And in every several city *he put* shields and spears, and made them exceeding strong, having Judah and Benjamin on his side.

↞See: Jerusalem

• Figurative.

Jer 50:25 — The LORD hath opened his armoury, and hath brought forth the weapons of his indignation: for this *is* the work of the Lord GOD of hosts in the land of the Chaldeans.

ARMS

- ✦See: Armor
- ✦See: Arrow
- ✦See: Artillery
- ✦See: Battle-Ax
- ✦See: Battering-Ram
- ✦See: Bow
- ✦See: Chariot
- ✦See: Dagger
- ✦See: Dart
- ✦See: Engine
- ✦See: Javelin
- ✦See: Shield
- ✦See: Sling
- ✦See: Spear
- ✦See: Sword

ARNAN • Patronymic of a family descended from David.

1Ch 3:21 — And the sons of Hananiah; Pelatiah, and Jesaiah: the sons of Rephaiah, the sons of Arnan, the sons of Obadiah, the sons of Shechaniah.

ARNON

• A river emptying into the Dead Sea from the east.

• Boundary between Moabites and Amorites.

Nu 21:13–14

Nu 21:26 — For Heshbon *was* the city of Sihon the king of the Amorites, who had fought against the former king of Moab, and taken all his land out of his hand, even unto Arnon.

Nu 22:36 — And when Balak heard that Balaam was come, he went out to meet him unto a city of Moab, which *is* in the border of Arnon, which *is* in the utmost coast.

Dt 2:24 — Rise ye up, take your journey, and pass over the river Arnon: behold, I have given into thine hand Sihon the Amorite, king of Heshbon, and his land: begin to possess *it,* and contend with him in battle.

Dt 2:36 — From Aroer, which *is* by the brink of the river of Arnon, and *from* the city that *is* by the river, even unto Gilead, there was not one city too strong for us: the LORD our God delivered all unto us:

Dt 3:8 — And we took at that time out of the hand of the two kings of the Amorites the land that *was* on this side Jordan, from the river of Arnon unto mount Hermon;

Dt 3:16 — And unto the Reubenites and unto the Gadites I gave from Gilead even unto the river Arnon half the valley, and the border even unto the river Jabbok, *which is* the border of the children of Ammon;

Jos 12:1 — Now these *are* the kings of the land, which the children of Israel smote, and possessed their land on the other side Jordan toward the rising of the sun, from the river Arnon unto mount Hermon, and all the plain on the east:

• Fords of.

Isa 16:2 — For it shall be, *that,* as a wandering bird cast out of the nest, so the daughters of Moab shall be at the fords of Arnon.

• Miracles at.

Nu 21:14 — Wherefore it is said in the book of the wars of the LORD, What he did in the Red sea, and in the brooks of Arnon,

AROD • A son of Gad.

Nu 26:17 — Of Arod, the family of the Arodites: of Areli, the family of the Arelites.

ARODI • Descendants of Arod.

Ge 46:16 — And the sons of Gad; Ziphion, and Haggi, Shuni, and Ezbon, Eri, and Arodi, and Areli.

AROER

• A city of the Amorites in the valley of the river Arnon.

Dt 4:48 — From Aroer, which *is* by the bank of the river Arnon, even unto mount Sion, which *is* Hermon,

• Conquered by Israelites.

Dt 2:36 — From Aroer, which *is* by the brink of the river of Arnon, and *from* the city that *is* by the river, even unto Gilead, there was not one city too strong for us: the LORD our God delivered all unto us:

Dt 3:12 — And this land, *which* we possessed at that time, from Aroer, which *is* by the river Arnon, and half mount Gilead, and the cities thereof, gave I unto the Reubenites and to the Gadites.

Jgs 11:26 — While Israel dwelt in Heshbon and her towns, and in Aroer and her towns, and in all the cities that *be* along by the coasts of Arnon, three hundred years? why therefore did ye not recover *them* within that time?

• Taken by Hazael.

2Ki 10:33 — From Jordan eastward, all the land of Gilead, the Gadites, and the Reubenites, and the Manassites, from Aroer, which is by the river Arnon, even Gilead and Bashan.

• A city built, or, probaby more correctly, rebuilt, by the Gadites.

Nu 32:34 — And the children of Gad built Dibon, and Ataroth, and Aroer,

Jos 13:25 — And their coast was Jazer, and all the cities of Gilead, and half the land of the children of Ammon, unto Aroer that *is* before Rabbah;

• Jephthah smites the Ammonites at.

Jgs 11:33 — And he smote them from Aroer, even till thou come to Minnith, *even* twenty cities, and unto the plain of the vineyards, with a very great slaughter. Thus the children of Ammon were subdued before the children of Israel.

• **A city in Judah.**

1Sa 30:28 — And to *them* which *were* in Aroer, and to *them* which *were* in Siphmoth, and to *them* which *were* in Eshtemoa,

• **Birthplace of two of David's heroes.**

1Ch 11:44 — Uzzia the Ashterathite, Shama and Jehiel the sons of Hothan the Aroerite,

ARPAD

• **Called also Arphad.**

• **A fortified city of Syria. Perhaps identical with Arvad.**

2Ki 18:34 — Where *are* the gods of Hamath, and of Arpad? where *are* the gods of Sepharvaim, Hena, and Ivah? have they delivered Samaria out of mine hand?

2Ki 19:13 — Where *is* the king of Hamath, and the king of Arpad, and the king of the city of Sepharvaim, of Hena, and Ivah?

• **Idols of.**

Isa 36:19 — Where *are* the gods of Hamath and Arphad? where *are* the gods of Sepharvaim? and have they delivered Samaria out of my hand?

ARPHAD ↞See: Arpad

ARPHAXAD • Son of Shem.

Ge 11:10–13; 1Ch 1:17–18

Ge 10:22 — The children of Shem; Elam, and Asshur, and Arphaxad, and Lud, and Aram.

1Ch 1:24 — Shem, Arphaxad, Shelah,

Lk 3:36 — Which was *the son* of Cainan, which was *the son* of Arphaxad, which was *the son* of Sem, which was *the son* of Noe, which was *the son* of Lamech,

ARREST

• **Of Jesus.**

Mt 26:57 — And they that had laid hold on Jesus led *him* away to Caiaphas the high priest, where the scribes and the elders were assembled.

Mk 14:46 — And they laid their hands on him, and took him.

Lk 22:54 — Then took they him, and led *him,* and brought him into the high priest's house. And Peter followed afar off.

Jn 18:12 — Then the band and the captain and officers of the Jews took Jesus, and bound him,

• **Of apostles.**

Ac 5:17–18

Ac 6:12 — And they stirred up the people, and the elders, and the scribes, and came upon *him,* and caught him, and brought *him* to the council,

• **Of Paul and Silas.**

Ac 16:19 — And when her masters saw that the hope of their gains was gone, they caught Paul and Silas, and drew *them* into the marketplace unto the rulers,

• **Of Paul.**

Ac 21:30 — And all the city was moved, and the people ran together: and they took Paul, and drew him out of the temple: and forthwith the doors were shut.

• **Paul authorized to arrest Christians.**

Ac 9:2 — And desired of him letters to Damascus to the synagogues, that if he found any of this way, whether they were men or women, he might bring them bound unto Jerusalem.

↞See: Extradition

↞See: Prison

↞See: Prisoners

ARROGANCE

1Sa 2:3 — Talk no more so exceeding proudly; let *not* arrogancy come out of your mouth: for the LORD is a God of knowledge, and by him actions are weighed.

Pr 8:13 — The fear of the LORD *is* to hate evil: pride, and arrogancy, and the evil way, and the froward mouth, do I hate.

Isa 13:11 — And I will punish the world for *their* evil, and the wicked for their iniquity; and I will cause the arrogancy of the proud to cease, and will lay low the haughtiness of the terrible.

↞See: Pride

ARROW

• **A weapon.**

• **Used in hunting.**

Ge 21:20 — And God was with the lad; and he grew, and dwelt in the wilderness, and became an archer.

Ge 27:3 — Now therefore take, I pray thee, thy weapons, thy quiver and thy bow, and go out to the field, and take me *some* venison;

• **Used in war.**

1Sa 31:3 — And the battle went sore against Saul, and the archers hit him; and he was sore wounded of the archers.

2Sa 22:15 — And he sent out arrows, and scattered them; lightning, and discomfited them.

1Ki 22:34 — And a *certain* man drew a bow at a venture, and smote the king of Israel between the joints of the harness: wherefore he said unto the driver of his chariot, Turn thine hand, and carry me out of the host; for I am wounded.

2Ki 19:32 — Therefore thus saith the LORD concerning the king of Assyria, He shall not come into this city, nor shoot an arrow there, nor come before it with shield, nor cast a bank against it.

Ps 7:13 — He hath also prepared for him the instruments of death; he ordaineth his arrows against the persecutors.

Isa 22:3 — All thy rulers are fled together, they are bound by the archers: all that are found in thee are bound together, *which* have fled from far.

Jer 51:3 — Against *him that* bendeth let the archer bend his bow, and against *him that* lifteth himself up in his brigandine: and spare ye not her young men; destroy ye utterly all her host.

• **Divination by.**

Eze 21:21 — For the king of Babylon stood at the parting of the way, at the head of the two ways, to use divination: he made *his* arrows bright, he consulted with images, he looked in the liver.

• **Shot by Jonathan as a sign to David.**
1Sa 20:20–42

• **Shot by Joash as a sign against the Syrians.**
2Ki 13:14–19

• **Figurative.**
La 3:12–13
Nu 24:8 — God brought him forth out of Egypt; he hath as it were the strength of an unicorn: he shall eat up the nations his enemies, and shall break their bones, and pierce *them* through with his arrows.
Dt 32:23 — I will heap mischiefs upon them; I will spend mine arrows upon them.
Dt 32:42 — I will make mine arrows drunk with blood, and my sword shall devour flesh; *and that* with the blood of the slain and of the captives, from the beginning of revenges upon the enemy.
Job 6:4 — For the arrows of the Almighty *are* within me, the poison whereof drinketh up my spirit: the terrors of God do set themselves in array against me.
Ps 11:2 — For, lo, the wicked bend *their* bow, they make ready their arrow upon the string, that they may privily shoot at the upright in heart.
Ps 21:12 — Therefore shalt thou make them turn their back, *when* thou shalt make ready *thine arrows* upon thy strings against the face of them.
Ps 38:2 — For thine arrows stick fast in me, and thy hand presseth me sore.
Ps 45:5 — Thine arrows *are* sharp in the heart of the king's enemies; *whereby* the people fall under thee.
Ps 57:4 — My soul *is* among lions: *and* I lie *even among* them that are set on fire, *even* the sons of men, whose teeth *are* spears and arrows, and their tongue a sharp sword.
Ps 58:7 — Let them melt away as waters *which* run continually: *when* he bendeth *his bow to shoot* his arrows, let them be as cut in pieces.
Ps 91:5 — Thou shalt not be afraid for the terror by night; *nor* for the arrow *that* flieth by day;
Ps 120:4 — Sharp arrows of the mighty, with coals of juniper.
Ps 144:6 — Cast forth lightning, and scatter them: shoot out thine arrows, and destroy them.
Pr 25:18 — A man that beareth false witness against his neighbour *is* a maul, and a sword, and a sharp arrow.
Eze 5:16 — When I shall send upon them the evil arrows of famine, which shall be for *their* destruction, *and* which I will send to destroy you: and I will increase the famine upon you, and will break your staff of bread:
Hab 3:11 — The sun *and* moon stood still in their habitation: at the light of thine arrows they went, *and* at the shining of thy glittering spear.

ARSON

Ps 74:7–8

• **Law concerning.**
Ex 22:6 — If fire break out, and catch in thorns, so that the stacks of corn, or the standing corn, or the field, be consumed *therewith;* he that kindled the fire shall surely make restitution.

• **Instances of.**
• **By Samson.**
Jgs 15:4–5
• **By Absalom.**
2Sa 14:30
• **By Zimri.**
1Ki 16:18

ART

• **Primitive.**
• **Invention of musical instruments and instruments of iron and copper.**
Ge 4:21–22
• **Carpentry.**
Ge 6:14–16; Ex 31:2–9
• **Of the apothecary or perfumer.**
Ex 30:25 — And thou shalt make it an oil of holy ointment, an ointment compound after the art of the apothecary: it shall be an holy anointing oil.
Ex 30:35 — And thou shalt make it a perfume, a confection after the art of the apothecary, tempered together, pure *and* holy:
• **Of the armorer.**
1Sa 8:12 — And he will appoint him captains over thousands, and captains over fifties; and *will set them* to ear his ground, and to reap his harvest, and to make his instruments of war, and instruments of his chariots.
• **Of the baker.**
Ge 40:1 — And it came to pass after these things, *that* the butler of the king of Egypt and *his* baker had offended their lord the king of Egypt.
1Sa 8:13 — And he will take your daughters *to be* confectionaries, and *to be* cooks, and *to be* bakers.
• **Of the barber.**
Isa 7:20 — In the same day shall the Lord shave with a razor that is hired, *namely,* by them beyond the river, by the king of Assyria, the head, and the hair of the feet: and it shall also consume the beard.
Eze 5:1 — And thou, son of man, take thee a sharp knife, take thee a barber's razor, and cause *it* to pass upon thine head and upon thy beard: then take thee balances to weigh, and divide the *hair.*
• **Of the brickmaker.**
Ex 5:7–8
Ge 11:3 — And they said one to another, Go to, let us make brick, and burn them throughly. And they had brick for stone, and slime had they for morter.
Ex 5:18 — Go therefore now, *and* work; for there shall no straw be given you, yet shall ye deliver the tale of bricks.
• **Of the calker.**
Eze 27:9 — The ancients of Gebal and the wise *men* thereof were in thee thy calkers: all the ships of the sea with their mariners were in thee to occupy thy merchandise.

Eze 27:27 — Thy riches, and thy fairs, thy merchandise, thy mariners, and thy pilots, thy calkers, and the occupiers of thy merchandise, and all thy men of war, that *are* in thee, and in all thy company which *is* in the midst of thee, shall fall into the midst of the seas in the day of thy ruin.

• Of the compounding confections.

1Sa 8:13 — And he will take your daughters *to be* confectionaries, and *to be* cooks, and *to be* bakers.

• Of the gardener.

Jer 29:5 — Build ye houses, and dwell *in them;* and plant gardens, and eat the fruit of them;

Jn 20:15 — Jesus saith unto her, Woman, why weepest thou? whom seekest thou? She, supposing him to be the gardener, saith unto him, Sir, if thou have borne him hence, tell me where thou hast laid him, and I will take him away.

• Of the goldsmith.

Isa 40:19 — The workman melteth a graven image, and the goldsmith spreadeth it over with gold, and casteth silver chains.

• Of the mariner.

Eze 27:8–9

• Of the mason.

2Sa 5:11 — And Hiram king of Tyre sent messengers to David, and cedar trees, and carpenters, and masons: and they built David an house.

2Ch 24:12 — And the king and Jehoiada gave it to such as did the work of the service of the house of the LORD, and hired masons and carpenters to repair the house of the LORD, and also such as wrought iron and brass to mend the house of the LORD.

• Of the musician.

1Sa 18:6 — And it came to pass as they came, when David was returned from the slaughter of the Philistine, that the women came out of all cities of Israel, singing and dancing, to meet king Saul, with tabrets, with joy, and with instruments of musick.

1Ch 15:16 — And David spake to the chief of the Levites to appoint their brethren *to be* the singers with instruments of musick, psalteries and harps and cymbals, sounding, by lifting up the voice with joy.

• Of the potter.

Isa 64:8 — But now, O LORD, thou *art* our father; we *are* the clay, and thou our potter; and we all *are* the work of thy hand.

Jer 18:3 — Then I went down to the potter's house, and, behold, he wrought a work on the wheels.

La 4:2 — The precious sons of Zion, comparable to fine gold, how are they esteemed as earthen pitchers, the work of the hands of the potter!

Zec 11:13 — And the LORD said unto me, Cast it unto the potter: a goodly price that I was prised at of them. And I took the thirty *pieces* of silver, and cast them to the potter in the house of the LORD.

• Of the refiner of metals.

Mal 3:2–3

1Ch 28:18 — And for the altar of incense refined gold by weight; and gold for the pattern of the chariot of the cherubims, that spread out *their wings,* and covered the ark of the covenant of the LORD.

• Of the ropemaker.

Jgs 16:11 — And he said unto her, If they bind me fast with new ropes that never were occupied, then shall I be weak, and be as another man.

• Of the stonecutter.

Ex 20:25 — And if thou wilt make me an altar of stone, thou shalt not build it of hewn stone: for if thou lift up thy tool upon it, thou hast polluted it.

1Ch 22:15 — Moreover *there are* workmen with thee in abundance, hewers and workers of stone and timber, and all manner of cunning men for every manner of work.

• Of the shipbuilder.

1Ki 9:26 — And king Solomon made a navy of ships in Ezion-geber, which is beside Eloth, on the shore of the Red sea, in the land of Edom.

• Of the smelter of metals.

Job 28:2 — Iron is taken out of the earth, and brass *is* molten *out of* the stone.

• Of the spinner.

Ex 35:25 — And all the women that were wise hearted did spin with their hands, and brought that which they had spun, *both* of blue, and of purple, *and* of scarlet, and of fine linen.

Pr 31:19 — She layeth her hands to the spindle, and her hands hold the distaff.

• Of the tailor.

Ex 28:3 — And thou shalt speak unto all *that are* wise hearted, whom I have filled with the spirit of wisdom, that they may make Aaron's garments to consecrate him, that he may minister unto me in the priest's office.

• Of the tanner.

Ac 9:43 — And it came to pass, that he tarried many days in Joppa with one Simon a tanner.

Ac 10:6 — He lodgeth with one Simon a tanner, whose house is by the sea side: he shall tell thee what thou oughtest to do.

• Of the tentmaker.

Ge 4:20 — And Adah bare Jabal: he was the father of such as dwell in tents, and *of such as have* cattle.

Ac 18:3 — And because he was of the same craft, he abode with them, and wrought: for by their occupation they were tentmakers.

• Of the weaver.

Ex 35:35 — Them hath he filled with wisdom of heart, to work all manner of work, of the engraver, and of the cunning workman, and of the embroiderer, in blue, and in purple, in scarlet, and in fine linen, and of the weaver, *even* of them that do any work, and of those that devise cunning work.

Jn 19:23 — Then the soldiers, when they had crucified Jesus, took his garments, and made four parts, to every soldier a part; and also *his* coat: now the coat was without seam, woven from the top throughout.

• **Of the wine maker.**

Ne 13:15 — In those days saw I in Judah *some* treading winepresses on the sabbath, and bringing in sheaves, and lading asses; as also wine, grapes, and figs, and all *manner of* burdens, which they brought into Jerusalem on the sabbath day: and I testified *against them* in the day wherein they sold victuals.

Isa 63:3 — I have trodden the winepress alone; and of the people *there was* none with me: for I will tread them in mine anger, and trample them in my fury; and their blood shall be sprinkled upon my garments, and I will stain all my raiment.

• **Artisans, skillful.**

• **Jubal.**

Ge 4:21 — And his brother's name *was* Jubal: he was the father of all such as handle the harp and organ.

• **Tubal-cain.**

Ge 4:22 — And Zillah, she also bare Tubal-cain, an instructer of every artificer in brass and iron: and the sister of Tubal-cain *was* Naamah.

• **Bezaleel and Aholiab.**

Ex 31:2–14; 35:30–35

• **Hiram.**

1Ki 7:13–51; 2Ch 2:13–14

• **For the various arts practiced, and products manufactured, in ancient times.**

See: Apothecary
See: Beaten Work
See: Brass, or more probably copper
See: Bread
See: Brick
See: Carpentry
See: Carving
See: Confectioner
See: Copper
See: Drawing
See: Dyeing
See: Embroidery
See: Engraving
See: Fuller
See: Goldsmith
See: Lapidary
See: Leather
See: Lime
See: Mason
See: Master Workman
See: Molding
See: Music
See: Painting
See: Paper
See: Parchment
See: Picture
See: Pottery
See: Rope
See: Ship
See: Silk
See: Silversmith
See: Smith
See: Soap
See: Spinning
See: Sun-Dial
See: Tapestry
See: Tailoring
See: Tent
See: Weaving
See: Wine

ARTAXERXES

• **A Persian king. Probably identical with Ahasuerus.**

• **Prohibits the rebuilding of Jerusalem.**

Ezr 4:7–24

• **King of Persia.**

• **Decrees of, in behalf of the Jews.**

Ezr 7:1–28; Ne 2:1–20

Ne 5:14 — Moreover from the time that I was appointed to be their governor in the land of Judah, from the twentieth year even unto the two and thirtieth year of Artaxerxes the king, *that is,* twelve years, I and my brethren have not eaten the bread of the governor.

ARTEMAS • A companion of Paul.

Tit 3:12 — When I shall send Artemas unto thee, or Tychicus, be diligent to come unto me to Nicopolis: for I have determined there to winter.

ARTILLERY

1Sa 20:40 — And Jonathan gave his artillery unto his lad, and said unto him, Go, carry *them* to the city.

See: Arms

ARTISAN

See: Art
See: Master Workman

ARUBOTH • A district laid under tribute to Solomon's commissariat.

1Ki 4:10 — The son of Hesed, in Aruboth; to him *pertained* Sochoh, and all the land of Hepher:

ARUMAH • A place near Shechem.

Jgs 9:41 — And Abimelech dwelt at Arumah: and Zebul thrust out Gaal and his brethren, that they should not dwell in Shechem.

ARVAD • An island near Zidon.

Eze 27:8 — The inhabitants of Zidon and Arvad were thy mariners: thy wise *men,* O Tyrus, *that* were in thee, were thy pilots.

Eze 27:11 — The men of Arvad with thine army *were* upon thy walls round about, and the Gammadims were in thy towers: they hanged their shields upon thy walls round about; they have made thy beauty perfect.

ARVADITES • Descendants of Canaan.

Ge 10:18 — And the Arvadite, and the Zemarite, and the Hamathite: and afterward were the families of the Canaanites spread abroad.

1Ch 1:16 — And the Arvadite, and the Zemarite, and the Hamathite.

Eze 27:8 — The inhabitants of Zidon and Arvad were thy mariners: thy wise *men,* O Tyrus, *that* were in thee, were thy pilots.

Eze 27:11 — The men of Arvad with thine army *were* upon thy walls round about, and the Gammadims were in thy towers: they hanged their shields upon thy walls round about; they have made thy beauty perfect.

ARZA • A steward of Elah.

1Ki 16:9 — And his servant Zimri, captain of half *his* chariots, conspired against him, as he was in Tirzah, drinking himself drunk in the house of Arza steward of *his* house in Tirzah.

ASA

• King of Judah.

1Ki 15:8–24; 2Ch 14:1–16:14

1Ch 3:10 — And Solomon's son *was* Rehoboam, Abia his son, Asa his son, Jehoshaphat his son,

Mt 1:7 — And Solomon begat Roboam; and Roboam begat Abia; and Abia begat Asa;

• A Levite.

1Ch 9:16 — And Obadiah the son of Shemaiah, the son of Galal, the son of Jeduthun, and Berechiah the son of Asa, the son of Elkanah, that dwelt in the villages of the Netophathites.

ASAHEL

• Nephew of David, and one of his captains.

2Sa 2:18–24

2Sa 2:32 — And they took up Asahel, and buried him in the sepulchre of his father, which *was in* Bethlehem. And Joab and his men went all night, and they came to Hebron at break of day.

2Sa 3:27 — And when Abner was returned to Hebron, Joab took him aside in the gate to speak with him quietly, and smote him there under the fifth *rib,* that he died, for the blood of Asahel his brother.

2Sa 23:24 — Asahel the brother of Joab *was* one of the thirty; Elhanan the son of Dodo of Bethlehem,

1Ch 2:16 — Whose sisters *were* Zeruiah, and Abigail. And the sons of Zeruiah; Abishai, and Joab, and Asahel, three.

1Ch 11:26 — Also the valiant men of the armies *were,* Asahel the brother of Joab, Elhanan the son of Dodo of Bethlehem,

1Ch 27:7 — The fourth *captain* for the fourth month *was* Asahel the brother of Joab, and Zebadiah his son after him: and in his course *were* twenty and four thousand.

• A Levite, commissioned by Jehoshaphat to teach the law to Judah.

2Ch 17:8 — And with them *he sent* Levites, *even* Shemaiah, and Nethaniah, and Zebadiah, and Asahel, and Shemiramoth, and Jehonathan, and Adonijah, and Tobijah, and Tob-adonijah, Levites; and with them Elishama and Jehoram, priests.

• A Levite, who had charge of tithes.

2Ch 31:13 — And Jehiel, and Azaziah, and Nahath, and Asahel, and Jerimoth, and Jozabad, and Eliel, and Ismachiah, and Mahath, and Benaiah, *were* overseers under the hand of Cononiah and Shimei his brother, at the commandment of Hezekiah the king, and Azariah the ruler of the house of God.

• Father of Jonathan.

Ezr 10:15 — Only Jonathan the son of Asahel and Jahaziah the son of Tikvah were employed about this *matter:* and Meshullam and Shabbethai the Levite helped them.

ASAHIAH • An officer of King Josiah.

2Ki 22:12–20; 2Ch 34:20–28

ASAIAH

• A descendant of Simeon.

1Ch 4:36 — And Elioenai, and Jaakobah, and Jeshohaiah, and Asaiah, and Adiel, and Jesimiel, and Benaiah,

• A Levite.

1Ch 6:30 — Shimea his son, Haggiah his son, Asaiah his son.

• Probably identical with a man of same name mentioned in 1Ch 15:6, 11.

• A Shilonite.

1Ch 9:5 — And of the Shilonites; Asaiah the firstborn, and his sons.

ASAPH

• Father of Joah.

2Ki 18:18 — And when they had called to the king, there came out to them Eliakim the son of Hilkiah, which *was* over the household, and Shebna the scribe, and Joah the son of Asaph the recorder.

Isa 36:3 — Then came forth unto him Eliakim, Hilkiah's son, which was over the house, and Shebna the scribe, and Joah, Asaph's son, the recorder.

Isa 36:22 — Then came Eliakim, the son of Hilkiah, that *was* over the household, and Shebna the scribe, and Joah, the son of Asaph, the recorder, to Hezekiah with *their* clothes rent, and told him the words of Rabshakeh.

• Son of Berachiah.

1Ch 15:16–19; 16:5–7; 25:1–9

Ne 12:46 — For in the days of David and Asaph of old *there were* chief of the singers, and songs of praise and thanksgiving unto God.

• One of the three leaders of music in David's organization of the tabernacle service.

2Ch 5:12 — Also the Levites *which were* the singers, all of them of Asaph, of Heman, of Jeduthun, with their sons and their brethren, *being* arrayed in white linen, having cymbals and psalteries and harps, stood at the east end of the altar, and with them an hundred and twenty priests sounding with trumpets:)

2Ch 35:15 — And the singers the sons of Asaph *were* in their place, according to the commandment of David, and Asaph, and Heman, and Jeduthun the king's seer; and the porters *waited* at every gate; they might not depart from their service; for their brethren the Levites prepared for them.

• Appointed to sound the cymbals in the temple choir.

1Ch 15:17 — So the Levites appointed Heman the son of Joel; and of his brethren, Asaph the son of Berechiah; and of the sons of Merari their brethren, Ethan the son of Kushaiah;

1Ch 15:19 — So the singers, Heman, Asaph, and Ethan, *were appointed* to sound with cymbals of brass;

1Ch 16:5 — Asaph the chief, and next to him Zechariah, Jeiel, and Shemiramoth, and Jehiel, and Mattithiah, and Eliab, and Benaiah, and Obed-edom: and Jeiel with psalteries and with harps; but Asaph made a sound with cymbals;

1Ch 16:7 — Then on that day David delivered first *this psalm* to thank the LORD into the hand of Asaph and his brethren.

• A composer of sacred lyrics (Titles of Psalms inclusive).

2Ch 29:13–30

Ps 50:1 — [A Psalm of Asaph.] The mighty God, *even* the LORD, hath spoken, and called the earth from the rising of the sun unto the going down thereof.

Ps 73:1 — [A Psalm of Asaph.] Truly God *is* good to Israel, *even* to such as are of a clean heart.

Ps 74:1 — [Maschil of Asaph.] O God, why hast thou cast us off for ever? *why* doth thine anger smoke against the sheep of thy pasture?

Ps 75:1 — [To the chief Musician, Altaschith, A Psalm *or* song of Asaph.] Unto thee, O God, do we give thanks, *unto thee* do we give thanks: for *that* thy name is near thy wondrous works declare.

Ps 76:1 — [To the chief Musician on Neginoth, A Psalm *or* song of Asaph.] In Judah *is* God known: his name *is* great in Israel.

Ps 77:1 — [To the chief Musician, to Jeduthun, A Psalm of Asaph.] I cried unto God with my voice, *even* unto God with my voice; and he gave ear unto me.

Ps 78:1 — [Maschil of Asaph.] Give ear, O my people, *to* my law: incline your ears to the words of my mouth.

Ps 79:1 — [A Psalm of Asaph.] O God, the heathen are come into thine inheritance; thy holy temple have they defiled; they have laid Jerusalem on heaps.

Ps 80:1 — [To the chief Musician upon Shoshannim-Eduth, A Psalm of Asaph.] Give ear, O Shepherd of Israel, thou that leadest Joseph like a flock; thou that dwellest *between* the cherubims, shine forth.

Ps 81:1 — [To the chief Musician upon Gittith, a Psalm of Asaph.] Sing aloud unto God our strength: make a joyful noise unto the God of Jacob.

Ps 82:1 — [A Psalm of Asaph.] God standeth in the congregation of the mighty; he judgeth among the gods.

Ps 83:1 — [A song *or* Psalm of Asaph.] Keep not thou silence, O God: hold not thy peace, and be not still, O God.

• Descendants of, in the temple choir.

1Ch 25:1–9

2Ch 20:14 — Then upon Jahaziel the son of Zechariah, the son of Benaiah, the son of Jeiel, the son of Mattaniah, a Levite of the sons of Asaph, came the Spirit of the LORD in the midst of the congregation;

2Ch 29:13 — And of the sons of Elizaphan; Shimri, and Jeiel: and of the sons of Asaph; Zechariah, and Mattaniah:

Ezr 2:41 — The singers: the children of Asaph, an hundred twenty and eight.

Ezr 3:10 — And when the builders laid the foundation of the temple of the LORD, they set the priests in their apparel with trumpets, and the Levites the sons of Asaph with cymbals, to praise the LORD, after the ordinance of David king of Israel.

Ne 7:44 — The singers: the children of Asaph, an hundred forty and eight.

Ne 11:22 — The overseer also of the Levites at Jerusalem *was* Uzzi the son of Bani, the son of Hashabiah, the son of Mattaniah, the son of Micha. Of the sons of Asaph, the singers *were* over the business of the house of God.

• A Levite, whose descendants dwelt in Jerusalem after the exile.

1Ch 9:15 — And Bakbakkar, Heresh, and Galal, and Mattaniah the son of Micah, the son of Zichri, the son of Asaph;

• A Kohath Levite.

1Ch 26:1 — Concerning the divisions of the porters: Of the Korhites *was* Meshelemiah the son of Kore, of the sons of Asaph.

• Keeper of forests.

Ne 2:8 — And a letter unto Asaph the keeper of the king's forest, that he may give me timber to make beams for the gates of the palace which *appertained* to the house, and for the wall of the city, and for the house that I shall enter into. And the king granted me, according to the good hand of my God upon me.

ASAREEL • Son of Jehaleleel.

1Ch 4:16 — And the sons of Jehaleleel; Ziph, and Ziphah, Tiria, and Asareel.

ASARELAH

• One of the temple choir.

1Ch 25:2 — Of the sons of Asaph; Zaccur, and Joseph, and Nethaniah, and Asarelah, the sons of Asaph under the hands of Asaph, which prophesied according to the order of the king.

1Ch 25:14 — The seventh to Jesharelah, *he*, his sons, and his brethren, *were* twelve:

• Probably identical with Azareel.

1Ch 25:18 — The eleventh to Azareel, *he*, his sons, and his brethren, *were* twelve:

ASCENSION

• Of Elijah.

2Ki 2:1–18

• Of Jesus.

Mk 16:19–20; Lk 24:50–53; Ac 1:9–12

• Of two witnesses.

Rev 11:12 — And they heard a great voice from heaven saying unto them, Come up hither. And they ascended up to heaven in a cloud; and their enemies beheld them.

ASCETICISM

• A philosophy that teaches self-denial to excess.

• Extreme application of, rebuked by Jesus.

Mt 11:19 — The Son of man came eating and drinking, and they say, Behold a man gluttonous, and a winebibber, a friend of publicans and sinners. But wisdom is justified of her children.

Lk 7:34 — The Son of man is come eating and drinking; and ye say, Behold a gluttonous man, and a winebibber, a friend of publicans and sinners!

• Rebuked by Paul.

Col 2:20–23; 1Ti 4:1–4

1Ti 4:8 — For bodily exercise profiteth little: but godliness is profitable unto all things, having promise of the life that now is, and of that which is to come.

See: Stoicism

• Instances of the practice of.

• John the Baptist.

Mt 11:18; Lk 7:33

• Those who practiced celibacy "for the kingdom of heaven's sake".

Mt 19:12

ASENATH • Wife of Joseph.

Ge 41:45 — And Pharaoh called Joseph's name Zaphnath-paaneah; and he gave him to wife Asenath the daughter of Poti-pherah priest of On. And Joseph went out over *all* the land of Egypt.

Ge 41:50 — And unto Joseph were born two sons before the years of famine came, which Asenath the daughter of Poti-pherah priest of On bare unto him.

Ge 46:20 — And unto Joseph in the land of Egypt were born Manasseh and Ephraim, which Asenath the daughter of Poti-pherah priest of On bare unto him.

ASER See: Asher

ASH • A tree.

Isa 44:14 — He heweth him down cedars, and taketh the cypress and the oak, which he strengtheneth for himself among the trees of the forest: he planteth an ash, and the rain doth nourish *it*.

ASHAN

• A Levitical city of Judah, later of Simeon.

Jos 15:42 — Libnah, and Ether, and Ashan,

Jos 19:7 — Ain, Remmon, and Ether, and Ashan; four cities and their villages:

1Ch 4:32 — And their villages *were*, Etam, and Ain, Rimmon, and Tochen, and Ashan, five cities:

1Ch 6:59 — And Ashan with her suburbs, and Beth-shemesh with her suburbs:

See: Ain

ASHBEA • A descendant of Shelah.

1Ch 4:21 — The sons of Shelah the son of Judah *were*, Er the father of Lecah, and Laadah the father of Mareshah, and the families of the house of them that wrought fine linen, of the house of Ashbea,

ASHBEL • Son of Benjamin.

Ge 46:21 — And the sons of Benjamin were Belah, and Becher, and Ashbel, Gera, and Naaman, Ehi, and Rosh, Muppim, and Huppim, and Ard.

Nu 26:38 — The sons of Benjamin after their families: of Bela, the family of the Belaites: of Ashbel, the family of the Ashbelites: of Ahiram, the family of the Ahiramites:

1Ch 8:1 — Now Benjamin begat Bela his firstborn, Ashbel the second, and Aharah the third,

ASHCHENAZ See: Ashkenaz

ASHDOD

• A city of the Philistines.

Jos 13:3 — From Sihor, which *is* before Egypt, even unto the borders of Ekron northward, *which* is counted to the Canaanite: five lords of the Philistines; the Gazathites, and the Ashdothites, the Eshkalonites, the Gittites, and the Ekronites; also the Avites:

1Sa 6:17 — And these *are* the golden emerods which the Philistines returned *for* a trespass offering unto the LORD; for Ashdod one, for Gaza one, for Askelon one, for Gath one, for Ekron one;

Am 3:9 — Publish in the palaces at Ashdod, and in the palaces in the land of Egypt, and say, Assemble yourselves upon the mountains of Samaria, and behold the great tumults in the midst thereof, and the oppressed in the midst thereof.

• Anakim inhabit.

Jos 11:22 — There was none of the Anakims left in the land of the children of Israel: only in Gaza, in Gath, and in Ashdod, there remained.

• **Assigned to Judah.**

Jos 15:47 — Ashdod with her towns and her villages, Gaza with her towns and her villages, unto the river of Egypt, and the great sea, and the border *thereof*:

• **Dagon's temple in, in which was deposited the ark.**

1Sa 5:1–12

• **Conquest of, by Uzziah.**

2Ch 26:6 — And he went forth and warred against the Philistines, and brake down the wall of Gath, and the wall of Jabneh, and the wall of Ashdod, and built cities about Ashdod, and among the Philistines.

• **Conquest by Tartan.**

Isa 20:1 — In the year that Tartan came unto Ashdod, (when Sargon the king of Assyria sent him,) and fought against Ashdod, and took it;

• **People of, conspire against the Jews.**

Ne 4:7–8

• **Jews intermarry with.**

Ne 13:23–24

• **Prophecies concerning.**

Am 3:1–15

Jer 25:20 — And all the mingled people, and all the kings of the land of Uz, and all the kings of the land of the Philistines, and Ashkelon, and Azzah, and Ekron, and the remnant of Ashdod,

Am 1:8 — And I will cut off the inhabitant from Ashdod, and him that holdeth the sceptre from Ashkelon, and I will turn mine hand against Ekron: and the remnant of the Philistines shall perish, saith the Lord GOD.

Zep 2:4 — For Gaza shall be forsaken, and Ashkelon a desolation: they shall drive out Ashdod at the noonday, and Ekron shall be rooted up.

Zec 9:6 — And a bastard shall dwell in Ashdod, and I will cut off the pride of the Philistines.

• **Called Azotus.**

Ac 8:40 — But Philip was found at Azotus: and passing through he preached in all the cities, till he came to Caesarea.

ASHDOTH-PISGAH • The water courses flowing from Mount Pisgah.

Dt 3:17 — The plain also, and Jordan, and the coast *thereof*, from Chinnereth even unto the sea of the plain, *even* the salt sea, under Ashdoth-pisgah eastward.

Dt 4:49 — And all the plain on this side Jordan eastward, even unto the sea of the plain, under the springs of Pisgah.

Jos 12:3 — And from the plain to the sea of Chinneroth on the east, and unto the sea of the plain, *even* the salt sea on the east, the way to Beth-jeshimoth; and from the south, under Ashdoth-pisgah:

Jos 13:20 — And Beth-peor, and Ashdoth-pisgah, and Beth-jeshimoth,

ASHER

• **Son of Jacob, by Zilpah.**

Ge 30:13 — And Leah said, Happy am I, for the daughters will call me blessed: and she called his name Asher.

Ge 35:26 — And the sons of Zilpah, Leah's handmaid; Gad, and Asher: these *are* the sons of Jacob, which were born to him in Padan-aram.

Ge 49:20 — Out of Asher his bread *shall be* fat, and he shall yield royal dainties.

Ex 1:4 — Dan, and Naphtali, Gad, and Asher.

1Ch 2:2 — Dan, Joseph, and Benjamin, Naphtali, Gad, and Asher.

• **Descendants of.**

Nu 26:44–47

Ge 46:17 — And the sons of Asher; Jimnah, and Ishuah, and Isui, and Beriah, and Serah their sister: and the sons of Beriah; Heber, and Malchiel.

• **Tribe of.**

• **Censes of, by families.**

Nu 1:40–41; 26:44–47

1Ch 7:40 — All these *were* the children of Asher, heads of *their* father's house, choice *and* mighty men of valour, chief of the princes. And the number throughout the genealogy of them that were apt to the war *and* to battle *was* twenty and six thousand men.

1Ch 12:36 — And of Asher, such as went forth to battle, expert in war, forty thousand.

• **Station of, in camp.**

Nu 2:25 — The standard of the camp of Dan *shall be* on the north side by their armies: and the captain of the children of Dan *shall be* Ahiezer the son of Ammishaddai.

Nu 2:27 — And those that encamp by him *shall be* the tribe of Asher: and the captain of the children of Asher *shall be* Pagiel the son of Ocran.

• **Prophecies concerning, by Moses.**

Dt 33:24–25

• **Prophecies concerning, by John.**

Rev 7:6 — Of the tribe of Aser *were* sealed twelve thousand. Of the tribe of Nepthalim *were* sealed twelve thousand. Of the tribe of Manasses *were* sealed twelve thousand.

• **Allotment to, of land in Canaan.**

Jos 19:24–31

Eze 48:2 — And by the border of Dan, from the east side unto the west side, a *portion for* Asher.

• **Upbraided by Deborah.**

Jgs 5:17 — Gilead abode beyond Jordan: and why did Dan remain in ships? Asher continued on the sea shore, and abode in his breaches.

• **Summoned by Gideon.**

Jgs 6:35 — And he sent messengers throughout all Manasseh; who also was gathered after him: and he sent messengers unto Asher, and unto Zebulun, and unto Naphtali; and they came up to meet them.

Jgs 7:23 — And the men of Israel gathered themselves together out of Naphtali, and out of Asher, and out of all Manasseh, and pursued after the Midianites.

- **Join Hezekiah.**

2Ch 30:11 — Nevertheless divers of Asher and Manasseh and of Zebulun humbled themselves, and came to Jerusalem.

- **A city of Shechem.**

Jos 17:7 — And the coast of Manasseh was from Asher to Michmethah, that *lieth* before Shechem; and the border went along on the right hand unto the inhabitants of En-tappuah.

1Ki 4:16 — Baanah the son of Hushai *was* in Asher and in Aloth:

ASHES

- **Uses of, in purification.**

Nu 19:9–10

Nu 19:17 — And for an unclean *person* they shall take of the ashes of the burnt heifer of purification for sin, and running water shall be put thereto in a vessel:

Heb 9:13 — For if the blood of bulls and of goats, and the ashes of an heifer sprinkling the unclean, sanctifieth to the purifying of the flesh:

- **A symbol of mourning.**

2Sa 13:19 — And Tamar put ashes on her head, and rent her garment of divers colours that *was* on her, and laid her hand on her head, and went on crying.

Est 4:1 — When Mordecai perceived all that was done, Mordecai rent his clothes, and put on sackcloth with ashes, and went out into the midst of the city, and cried with a loud and a bitter cry;

Est 4:3 — And in every province, whithersoever the king's commandment and his decree came, *there was* great mourning among the Jews, and fasting, and weeping, and wailing; and many lay in sackcloth and ashes.

- **Sitting in.**

Job 2:8 — And he took him a potsherd to scrape himself withal; and he sat down among the ashes.

Isa 58:5 — Is it such a fast that I have chosen? a day for a man to afflict his soul? *is it* to bow down his head as a bulrush, and to spread sackcloth and ashes *under him?* wilt thou call this a fast, and an acceptable day to the LORD?

Jer 6:26 — O daughter of my people, gird *thee* with sackcloth, and wallow thyself in ashes: make thee mourning, *as for* an only son, most bitter lamentation: for the spoiler shall suddenly come upon us.

Eze 27:30 — And shall cause their voice to be heard against thee, and shall cry bitterly, and shall cast up dust upon their heads, they shall wallow themselves in the ashes:

Jnh 3:6 — For word came unto the king of Nineveh, and he arose from his throne, and he laid his robe from him, and covered *him* with sackcloth, and sat in ashes.

ZZZLk 10:13 — <u>Woe unto thee, Chorazin! woe unto thee, Bethsaida! for if the mighty works had been done in Tyre and Sidon, which have been done in you, they had a great while ago repented, sitting in sackcloth and ashes.</u>

- **Repenting in.**

Job 42:6 — Wherefore I abhor *myself,* and repent in dust and ashes.

Da 9:3 — And I set my face unto the Lord God, to seek by prayer and supplications, with fasting, and sackcloth, and ashes:

Jnh 3:6 — For word came unto the king of Nineveh, and he arose from his throne, and he laid his robe from him, and covered *him* with sackcloth, and sat in ashes.

Mt 11:21 — <u>Woe unto thee, Chorazin! woe unto thee, Bethsaida! for if the mighty works, which were done in you, had been done in Tyre and Sidon, they would have repented long ago in sackcloth and ashes.</u>

Lk 10:13 — <u>Woe unto thee, Chorazin! woe unto thee, Bethsaida! for if the mighty works had been done in Tyre and Sidon, which have been done in you, they had a great while ago repented, sitting in sackcloth and ashes.</u>

- **Disguises in.**

1Ki 20:38 — So the prophet departed, and waited for the king by the way, and disguised himself with ashes upon his face.

1Ki 20:41 — And he hasted, and took the ashes away from his face; and the king of Israel discerned him that he *was* of the prophets.

ASHIMA • An idol.

2Ki 17:30 — And the men of Babylon made Succoth-benoth, and the men of Cuth made Nergal, and the men of Hamath made Ashima,

ASHKELON

- **Called also Askelon.**
- **One of the five chief cities of the Philistines.**

Jos 13:3 — From Sihor, which *is* before Egypt, even unto the borders of Ekron northward, *which* is counted to the Canaanite: five lords of the Philistines; the Gazathites, and the Ashdothites, the Eshkalonites, the Gittites, and the Ekronites; also the Avites:

- **Captured by the people of Judah.**

Jgs 1:18 — Also Judah took Gaza with the coast thereof, and Askelon with the coast thereof, and Ekron with the coast thereof.

- **Samson slays thirty men of.**

Jgs 14:19 — And the Spirit of the LORD came upon him, and he went down to Ashkelon, and slew thirty men of them, and took their spoil, and gave change of garments unto them which expounded the riddle. And his anger was kindled, and he went up to his father's house.

- **Emerods of.**

1Sa 6:17 — And these *are* the golden emerods which the Philistines returned *for* a trespass offering unto the LORD; for Ashdod one, for Gaza one, for Askelon one, for Gath one, for Ekron one;

- **Prophecies concerning.**

Jer 25:20 — And all the mingled people, and all the kings of the land of Uz, and all the kings of the land of the Philistines, and Ashkelon, and Azzah, and Ekron, and the remnant of Ashdod,

Jer 47:5 — Baldness is come upon Gaza; Ashkelon is cut off *with* the remnant of their valley: how long wilt thou cut thyself?

Jer 47:7 — How can it be quiet, seeing the LORD hath given it a charge against Ashkelon, and against the sea shore? there hath he appointed it.

Am 1:8 — And I will cut off the inhabitant from Ashdod, and him that holdeth the sceptre from Ashkelon, and I will turn mine hand against Ekron: and the remnant of the Philistines shall perish, saith the Lord GOD.

Zep 2:4 — For Gaza shall be forsaken, and Ashkelon a desolation: they shall drive out Ashdod at the noonday, and Ekron shall be rooted up.

Zep 2:7 — And the coast shall be for the remnant of the house of Judah; they shall feed thereupon: in the houses of Ashkelon shall they lie down in the evening: for the LORD their God shall visit them, and turn away their captivity.

Zec 9:5 — Ashkelon shall see *it*, and fear; Gaza also *shall see it*, and be very sorrowful, and Ekron; for her expectation shall be ashamed; and the king shall perish from Gaza, and Ashkelon shall not be inhabited.

ASHKENAZ

• Called also Ashchenaz.

• Son of Gomer.

Ge 10:3 — And the sons of Gomer; Ashkenaz, and Riphath, and Togarmah.

1Ch 1:6 — And the sons of Gomer; Ashchenaz, and Riphath, and Togarmah.

• Descendants of.

Jer 51:27 — Set ye up a standard in the land, blow the trumpet among the nations, prepare the nations against her, call together against her the kingdoms of Ararat, Minni, and Ashchenaz; appoint a captain against her; cause the horses to come up as the rough caterpillers.

ASHNAH • Name of two towns in Judah.

Jos 15:33 — *And* in the valley, Eshtaol, and Zoreah, and Ashnah,

Jos 15:43 — And Jiphtah, and Ashnah, and Nezib,

ASHPENAZ • A prince in Nebuchadnezzar's court.

Da 1:3 — And the king spake unto Ashpenaz the master of his eunuchs, that he should bring *certain* of the children of Israel, and of the king's seed, and of the princes;

ASHRIEL • See: Asriel

ASHTAROTH

• Plural form of Ashtoreth, which see.

• The capital city of Bashan.

Dt 1:4 — After he had slain Sihon the king of the Amorites, which dwelt in Heshbon, and Og the king of Bashan, which dwelt at Astaroth in Edrei:

Jos 9:10 — And all that he did to the two kings of the Amorites, that *were* beyond Jordan, to Sihon king of Heshbon, and to Og king of Bashan, which *was* at Ashtaroth.

• Giants dwell at.

Jos 12:4 — And the coast of Og king of Bashan, *which was* of the remnant of the giants, that dwelt at Ashtaroth and at Edrei,

• Allotted to Manasseh.

Jos 13:31 — And half Gilead, and Ashtaroth, and Edrei, cities of the kingdom of Og in Bashan, *were pertaining* unto the children of Machir the son of Manasseh, even to the one half of the children of Machir by their families.

1Ch 6:71 — Unto the sons of Gershom *were given* out of the family of the half tribe of Manasseh, Golan in Bashan with her suburbs, and Ashtaroth with her suburbs:

• Possibly identical with Ashteroth Karnaim, mentioned in Ge 14:5.

Ge 14:5 — And in the fourteenth year came Chedorlaomer, and the kings that *were* with him, and smote the Rephaims in Ashteroth Karnaim, and the Zuzims in Ham, and the Emims in Shaveh Kiriathaim,

ASHTEROTH KARNAIM • An ancient city of Palestine taken by Chedorlaomer.

Ge 14:5 — And in the fourteenth year came Chedorlaomer, and the kings that *were* with him, and smote the Rephaims in Ashteroth Karnaim, and the Zuzims in Ham, and the Emims in Shaveh Kiriathaim,

ASHTORETH

• An idol of the Philistines, Zidonians, and Phenicians. Probably identical with queen of heaven.

Jer 7:18 — The children gather wood, and the fathers kindle the fire, and the women knead *their* dough, to make cakes to the queen of heaven, and to pour out drink offerings unto other gods, that they may provoke me to anger.

• Worshiped by Israelites.

1Sa 7:3-4

Jgs 2:13 — And they forsook the LORD, and served Baal and Ashtaroth.

Jgs 10:6 — And the children of Israel did evil again in the sight of the LORD, and served Baalim, and Ashtaroth, and the gods of Syria, and the gods of Zidon, and the gods of Moab, and the gods of the children of Ammon, and the gods of the Philistines, and forsook the LORD, and served not him.

1Sa 12:10 — And they cried unto the LORD, and said, We have sinned, because we have forsaken the LORD, and have served Baalim and Ashtaroth: but now deliver us out of the hand of our enemies, and we will serve thee.

1Ki 11:5 — For Solomon went after Ashtoreth the goddess of the Zidonians, and after Milcom the abomination of the Ammonites.

1Ki 11:33 — Because that they have forsaken me, and have worshipped Ashtoreth the goddess of the Zidonians, Chemosh the god of the Moabites, and Milcom the god of the children of Ammon, and have not walked in my ways, to do *that which is* right in mine eyes, and *to keep* my statutes and my judgments, as *did* David his father.

2Ki 23:13 — And the high places that *were* before Jerusalem, which *were* on the right hand of the mount of corruption, which Solomon the king of Israel had builded for Ashtoreth the abomination of the Zidonians, and for Chemosh the abomination of the Moabites, and for Milcom the abomination of the children of Ammon, did the king defile.

• Temple of.

1Sa 31:10 — And they put his armour in the house of Ashtaroth: and they fastened his body to the wall of Beth-shan.

• High places of, at Jerusalem, destroyed.

2Ki 23:13 — And the high places that *were* before Jerusalem, which *were* on the right hand of the mount of corruption, which Solomon the king of Israel had builded for Ashtoreth the abomination of the Zidonians, and for Chemosh the abomination of the Moabites, and for Milcom the abomination of the children of Ammon, did the king defile.

ASHUR • Son of Hezron.

1Ch 2:24 — And after that Hezron was dead in Caleb-ephratah, then Abiah Hezron's wife bare him Ashur the father of Tekoa.

1Ch 4:5 — And Ashur the father of Tekoa had two wives, Helah and Naarah.

ASHURITES • Possibly Geshurites.

2Sa 2:9 — And made him king over Gilead, and over the Ashurites, and over Jezreel, and over Ephraim, and over Benjamin, and over all Israel.

Eze 27:6 — *Of* the oaks of Bashan have they made thine oars; the company of the Ashurites have made thy benches *of* ivory, *brought* out of the isles of Chittim.

ASHVATH • Son of Japhlet.

1Ch 7:33 — And the sons of Japhlet; Pasach, and Bimhal, and Ashvath. These *are* the children of Japhlet.

ASIA

• Inhabitants of, in Jerusalem, at Pentecost.

Ac 2:9 — Parthians, and Medes, and Elamites, and the dwellers in Mesopotamia, and in Judaea, and Cappadocia, in Pontus, and Asia,

Ac 21:27 — And when the seven days were almost ended, the Jews which were of Asia, when they saw him in the temple, stirred up all the people, and laid hands on him,

Ac 24:18 — Whereupon certain Jews from Asia found me purified in the temple, neither with multitude, nor with tumult.

• Paul and Silas forbidden by the Holy Ghost to preach in.

Ac 16:6 — Now when they had gone throughout Phrygia and the region of Galatia, and were forbidden of the Holy Ghost to preach the word in Asia,

• Gospel preached in, by Paul.

Ac 19:1–41

Ac 20:4 — And there accompanied him into Asia Sopater of Berea; and of the Thessalonians, Aristarchus and Secundus; and Gaius of Derbe, and Timotheus; and of Asia, Tychicus and Trophimus.

• Paul leaves.

Ac 20:16 — For Paul had determined to sail by Ephesus, because he would not spend the time in Asia: for he hasted, if it were possible for him, to be at Jerusalem the day of Pentecost.

• Churches of.

1Co 16:19 — The churches of Asia salute you. Aquila and Priscilla salute you much in the Lord, with the church that is in their house.

Rev 1:4 — John to the seven churches which are in Asia: Grace *be* unto you, and peace, from him which is, and which was, and which is to come; and from the seven Spirits which are before his throne;

Rev 1:11 — Saying, I am Alpha and Omega, the first and the last: and, What thou seest, write in a book, and send *it* unto the seven churches which are in Asia; unto Ephesus, and unto Smyrna, and unto Pergamos, and unto Thyatira, and unto Sardis, and unto Philadelphia, and unto Laodicea.

ASIEL • Grandfather of Jehu.

1Ch 4:35 — And Joel, and Jehu the son of Josibiah, the son of Seraiah, the son of Asiel,

ASKELON ↞See: Ashkelon

ASNAH • Descendants of, return to Jerusalem.

Ezr 2:50 — The children of Asnah, the children of Mehunim, the children of Nephusim,

ASNAPPER

• A noble Assyrian prince. Colonized Samaria after the captivity to Assyria.

Ezr 4:10 — And the rest of the nations whom the great and noble Asnapper brought over, and set in the cities of Samaria, and the rest *that are* on this side the river, and at such a time.

↞See: Samaria

ASP

• A venomous serpent.

Dt 32:33 — Their wine *is* the poison of dragons, and the cruel venom of asps.

Job 20:14 — *Yet* his meat in his bowels is turned, *it is* the gall of asps within him.

Job 20:16 — He shall suck the poison of asps: the viper's tongue shall slay him.

Isa 11:8 — And the sucking child shall play on the hole of the asp, and the weaned child shall put his hand on the cockatrice' den.

Ro 3:13 — Their throat *is* an open sepulchre; with their tongues they have used deceit; the poison of asps *is* under their lips:

• Venom of, illustrates the speech of the wicked.

Ps 140:3 — They have sharpened their tongues like a serpent; adders' poison *is* under their lips. Selah.

Ro 3:13 — Their throat *is* an open sepulchre; with their tongues they have used deceit; the poison of asps *is* under their lips:

• Injurious effects of wine.

Dt 32:33 — Their wine *is* the poison of dragons, and the cruel venom of asps.

Pr 23:32 — At the last it biteth like a serpent, and stingeth like an adder.

• Deprived of venom, illustrates conversion.

Isa 11:8–9

ASPATHA • Son of Haman.

Est 9:7 — And Parshandatha, and Dalphon, and Aspatha,

ASPHALTUM • See: Slime

ASRIEL

• Called also Ashriel.

• Son of Manasseh.

Jos 17:2 — There was also *a lot* for the rest of the children of Manasseh by their families; for the children of Abiezer, and for the children of Helek, and for the children of Asriel, and for the children of Shechem, and for the children of Hepher, and for the children of Shemida: these *were* the male children of Manasseh the son of Joseph by their families.

1Ch 7:14 — The sons of Manasseh; Ashriel, whom she bare: *(but* his concubine the Aramitess bare Machir the father of Gilead:

ASS

• Domesticated.

• Herds of.

Ge 12:16 — And he entreated Abram well for her sake: and he had sheep, and oxen, and he asses, and menservants, and maidservants, and she asses, and camels.

Ge 24:35 — And the LORD hath blessed my master greatly; and he is become great: and he hath given him flocks, and herds, and silver, and gold, and menservants, and maidservants, and camels, and asses.

Ge 32:5 — And I have oxen, and asses, flocks, and menservants, and womenservants: and I have sent to tell my lord, that I may find grace in thy sight.

Ge 34:28 — They took their sheep, and their oxen, and their asses, and that which *was* in the city, and that which *was* in the field,

Nu 31:34 — And threescore and one thousand asses,

Nu 31:45 — And thirty thousand asses and five hundred,

1Ch 5:21 — And they took away their cattle; of their camels fifty thousand, and of sheep two hundred and fifty thousand, and of asses two thousand, and of men an hundred thousand.

Ezr 2:67 — Their camels, four hundred thirty and five; *their* asses, six thousand seven hundred and twenty.

Ne 7:69 — *Their* camels, four hundred thirty and five: six thousand seven hundred and twenty asses.

• Used for riding.

Nu 22:21–33; Zec 9:1–17

Ge 22:3 — And Abraham rose up early in the morning, and saddled his ass, and took two of his young men with him, and Isaac his son, and clave the wood for the burnt offering, and rose up, and went unto the place of which God had told him.

Jos 15:18 — And it came to pass, as she came *unto him,* that she moved him to ask of her father a field: and she lighted off *her* ass; and Caleb said unto her, What wouldest thou?

Jgs 1:14 — And it came to pass, when she came *to him,* that she moved him to ask of her father a field: and she lighted from off *her* ass; and Caleb said unto her, What wilt thou?

Jgs 5:10 — Speak, ye that ride on white asses, ye that sit in judgment, and walk by the way.

1Sa 25:23 — And when Abigail saw David, she hasted, and lighted off the ass, and fell before David on her face, and bowed herself to the ground,

2Ch 28:15 — And the men which were expressed by name rose up, and took the captives, and with the spoil clothed all that were naked among them, and arrayed them, and shod them, and gave them to eat and to drink, and anointed them, and carried all the feeble of them upon asses, and brought them to Jericho, the city of palm trees, to their brethren: then they returned to Samaria.

• By Jesus.

Jn 12:14–15

Zec 9:9 — Rejoice greatly, O daughter of Zion; shout, O daughter of Jerusalem: behold, thy King cometh unto thee: he *is* just, and having salvation; lowly, and riding upon an ass, and upon a colt the foal of an ass.

Mt 21:2 — Saying unto them, Go into the village over against you, and straightway ye shall find an ass tied, and a colt with her: loose *them,* and bring *them* unto me.

Mt 21:5 — Tell ye the daughter of Sion, Behold, thy King cometh unto thee, meek, and sitting upon an ass, and a colt the foal of an ass.

Lk 13:15 — The Lord then answered him, and said, *Thou* hypocrite, doth not each one of you on the sabbath loose his ox or *his* ass from the stall, and lead *him* away to watering?

• **Carrying burdens.**

Ge 42:26 — And they laded their asses with the corn, and departed thence.

2Sa 16:1 — And when David was a little past the top *of the hill,* behold, Ziba the servant of Mephibosheth met him, with a couple of asses saddled, and upon them two hundred *loaves* of bread, and an hundred bunches of raisins, and an hundred of summer fruits, and a bottle of wine.

Isa 30:6 — The burden of the beasts of the south: into the land of trouble and anguish, from whence *come* the young and old lion, the viper and fiery flying serpent, they will carry their riches upon the shoulders of young asses, and their treasures upon the bunches of camels, to a people *that* shall not profit *them.*

• **Drawing chariots.**

Isa 21:7 — And he saw a chariot *with* a couple of horsemen, a chariot of asses, *and* a chariot of camels; and he hearkened diligently with much heed:

• **For food.**

2Ki 6:25 — And there was a great famine in Samaria: and, behold, they besieged it, until an ass's head was *sold* for fourscore *pieces* of silver, and the fourth part of a cab of dove's dung for five *pieces* of silver.

• **Not to be yoked with an ox.**

Dt 22:10 — Thou shalt not plow with an ox and an ass together.

• **Rest on Sabbath.**

Ex 23:12 — Six days thou shalt do thy work, and on the seventh day thou shalt rest: that thine ox and thine ass may rest, and the son of thy handmaid, and the stranger, may be refreshed.

• **Bridles for.**

Pr 26:3 — A whip for the horse, a bridle for the ass, and a rod for the fool's back.

• **Jawbone of, used by Samson with which to slay Philistines.**

Jgs 15:15–17

• **Firstlings of, redeemed.**

Ex 13:13 — And every firstling of an ass thou shalt redeem with a lamb; and if thou wilt not redeem it, then thou shalt break his neck: and all the firstborn of man among thy children shalt thou redeem.

Ex 34:20 — But the firstling of an ass thou shalt redeem with a lamb: and if thou redeem *him* not, then shalt thou break his neck. All the firstborn of thy sons thou shalt redeem. And none shall appear before me empty.

• **Wild.**

Job 6:5 — Doth the wild ass bray when he hath grass? or loweth the ox over his fodder?

Job 24:5 — Behold, *as* wild asses in the desert, go they forth to their work; rising betimes for a prey: the wilderness *yieldeth* food for them *and* for *their* children.

Job 39:5 — Who hath sent out the wild ass free? or who hath loosed the bands of the wild ass?

Ps 104:11 — They give drink to every beast of the field: the wild asses quench their thirst.

Isa 32:14 — Because the palaces shall be forsaken; the multitude of the city shall be left; the forts and towers shall be for dens for ever, a joy of wild asses, a pasture of flocks;

Jer 2:24 — A wild ass used to the wilderness, *that* snuffeth up the wind at her pleasure; in her occasion who can turn her away? all they that seek her will not weary themselves; in her month they shall find her.

Jer 14:6 — And the wild asses did stand in the high places, they snuffed up the wind like dragons; their eyes did fail, because *there was* no grass.

Hos 8:9 — For they are gone up to Assyria, a wild ass alone by himself: Ephraim hath hired lovers.

ASSASSINATION

• **David's abhorrence of.**

2Sa 4:9–12

• **Laws prohibiting.**

Dt 27:24 — Cursed *be* he that smiteth his neighbour secretly. And all the people shall say, Amen.

• **Instances of.**

• **Of Eglon, by Ehud.**

Jgs 3:15–22

• **Abner, by Joab.**

2Sa 3:27

• **Ish-bosheth, by the sons of Rimmon.**

2Sa 4:5–7

• **Amnon, by Absalom.**

2Sa 13:28–29

• **Amasa, by Joab.**

2Sa 20:9–10

• **Joash, by his servants.**

2Ki 12:20

• **Sennacherib, by his sons.**

2Ki 19:37; Isa 37:38

ASSAULT AND BATTERY

• **Laws concerning.**

Ex 21:18–27; Dt 17:8–12; Mt 5:38–39

Ex 21:15 — And he that smiteth his father, or his mother, shall be surely put to death.

• **The smiting of Jesus.**

• **Prophecies of.**

Isa 50:6 — I gave my back to the smiters, and my cheeks to them that plucked off the hair: I hid not my face from shame and spitting.

La 3:30 — He giveth *his* cheek to him that smiteth him: he is filled full with reproach.

• **The attacks upon.**

Mt 26:67 — Then did they spit in his face, and buffeted him; and others smote *him* with the palms of their hands,

Mt 27:30 — And they spit upon him, and took the reed, and smote him on the head.

Mk 14:65 — And some began to spit on him, and to cover his face, and to buffet him, and to say unto him, Prophesy: and the servants did strike him with the palms of their hands.

Lk 22:63 — And the men that held Jesus mocked him, and smote *him.*

Jn 19:3 — And said, Hail, King of the Jews! and they smote him with their hands.

See: Stripes

See: Stoning

ASSHUR

• Son of Shem, and ancestor of the Assyrians.

Ge 10:11 — Out of that land went forth Asshur, and builded Nineveh, and the city Rehoboth, and Calah,

Ge 10:22 — The children of Shem; Elam, and Asshur, and Arphaxad, and Lud, and Aram.

1Ch 1:17 — The sons of Shem; Elam, and Asshur, and Arphaxad, and Lud, and Aram, and Uz, and Hul, and Gether, and Meshech.

Eze 32:22 — Asshur *is* there and all her company: his graves *are* about him: all of them slain, fallen by the sword:

See: Assyria

ASSHURIM • Descendants of Dedan.

Ge 25:3 — And Jokshan begat Sheba, and Dedan. And the sons of Dedan were Asshurim, and Letushim, and Leummim.

ASSIR

• Son of Korah.

Ex 6:24 — And the sons of Korah; Assir, and Elkanah, and Abiasaph: these *are* the families of the Korhites.

1Ch 6:22 — The sons of Kohath; Amminadab his son, Korah his son, Assir his son,

• Son of Ebiasaph.

1Ch 6:23 — Elkanah his son, and Ebiasaph his son, and Assir his son,

1Ch 6:37 — The son of Tahath, the son of Assir, the son of Ebiasaph, the son of Korah,

• Son of Jeconiah.

1Ch 3:17 — And the sons of Jeconiah; Assir, Salathiel his son,

ASSOS • A seaport in Mysia.

Ac 20:13–14

ASSURANCE

• Produced by faith.

Eph 3:12 — In whom we have boldness and access with confidence by the faith of him.

2Ti 1:12 — For the which cause I also suffer these things: nevertheless I am not ashamed: for I know whom I have believed, and am persuaded that he is able to keep that which I have committed unto him against that day.

Heb 10:22 — Let us draw near with a true heart in full assurance of faith, having our hearts sprinkled from an evil conscience, and our bodies washed with pure water.

• Made full by hope.

Heb 6:11 — And we desire that every one of you do shew the same diligence to the full assurance of hope unto the end:

Heb 6:19 — Which *hope* we have as an anchor of the soul, both sure and stedfast, and which entereth into that within the veil;

• Confirmed by love.

1Jn 3:14 — We know that we have passed from death unto life, because we love the brethren. He that loveth not *his* brother abideth in death.

1Jn 3:19 — And hereby we know that we are of the truth, and shall assure our hearts before him.

1Jn 4:18 — There is no fear in love; but perfect love casteth out fear: because fear hath torment. He that feareth is not made perfect in love.

• Is the effect of righteousness.

Isa 32:17 — And the work of righteousness shall be peace; and the effect of righteousness quietness and assurance for ever.

• Is abundant in the understanding of the gospel.

Col 2:2 — That their hearts might be comforted, being knit together in love, and unto all riches of the full assurance of understanding, to the acknowledgement of the mystery of God, and of the Father, and of Christ;

1Th 1:5 — For our gospel came not unto you in word only, but also in power, and in the Holy Ghost, and in much assurance; as ye know what manner of men we were among you for your sake.

• Saints privileged to have.

• Of their election.

Ps 4:3 — But know that the LORD hath set apart him that is godly for himself: the LORD will hear when I call unto him.

1Th 1:4 — Knowing, brethren beloved, your election of God.

• Their redemption.

Job 19:25 — For I know *that* my redeemer liveth, and *that* he shall stand at the latter *day* upon the earth:

• Their adoption.

Ro 8:16 — The Spirit itself beareth witness with our spirit, that we are the children of God:

1Jn 3:2 — Beloved, now are we the sons of God, and it doth not yet appear what we shall be: but we know that, when he shall appear, we shall be like him; for we shall see him as he is.

• Their salvation.

Isa 12:2 — Behold, God *is* my salvation; I will trust, and not be afraid: for the LORD JEHOVAH *is* my strength and *my* song; he also is become my salvation.

• Eternal life.

1Jn 5:13 — These things have I written unto you that believe on the name of the Son of God; that ye may know that ye have eternal life, and that ye may believe on the name of the Son of God.

- **The unalienable love of God.**

Ro 8:38–39

- **Union with God and Christ.**

1Co 6:15 — Know ye not that your bodies are the members of Christ? shall I then take the members of Christ, and make *them* the members of an harlot? God forbid.

2Co 13:5 — Examine yourselves, whether ye be in the faith; prove your own selves. Know ye not your own selves, how that Jesus Christ is in you, except ye be reprobates?

Eph 5:30 — For we are members of his body, of his flesh, and of his bones.

1Jn 2:5 — But whoso keepeth his word, in him verily is the love of God perfected: hereby know we that we are in him.

1Jn 4:13 — Hereby know we that we dwell in him, and he in us, because he hath given us of his Spirit.

- **Peace with God by Christ.**

Ro 5:1 — Therefore being justified by faith, we have peace with God through our Lord Jesus Christ:

- **Preservation.**

Ps 8:1–9; 27:3–5; 46:1–3

Ps 3:6 — I will not be afraid of ten thousands of people, that have set *themselves* against me round about.

- **Answers to prayer.**

1Jn 5:14–15

1Jn 3:22 — And whatsoever we ask, we receive of him, because we keep his commandments, and do those things that are pleasing in his sight.

- **Comfort in affliction.**

2Co 4:8–10, 16–18

Ps 73:26 — My flesh and my heart faileth: *but* God *is* the strength of my heart, and my portion for ever.

Lk 4:18 — The Spirit of the Lord is upon me, because he hath anointed me to preach the gospel to the poor; he hath sent me to heal the brokenhearted, to preach deliverance to the captives, and recovering of sight to the blind, to set at liberty them that are bruised,

- **Continuance in grace.**

Php 1:6 — Being confident of this very thing, that he which hath begun a good work in you will perform *it* until the day of Jesus Christ:

- **A support in death.**

Ps 23:4 — Yea, though I walk through the valley of the shadow of death, I will fear no evil: for thou *art* with me; thy rod and thy staff they comfort me.

- **A glorious resurrection.**

Job 19:26 — And *though* after my skin *worms* destroy this *body,* yet in my flesh shall I see God:

Ps 17:15 — As for me, I will behold thy face in righteousness: I shall be satisfied, when I awake, with thy likeness.

Php 3:21 — Who shall change our vile body, that it may be fashioned like unto his glorious body, according to the working whereby he is able even to subdue all things unto himself.

1Jn 3:2 — Beloved, now are we the sons of God, and it doth not yet appear what we shall be: but we know that, when he shall appear, we shall be like him; for we shall see him as he is.

- **A kingdom.**

Heb 12:28 — Wherefore we receiving a kingdom which cannot be moved, let us have grace, whereby we may serve God acceptably with reverence and godly fear:

Rev 5:10 — And hast made us unto our God kings and priests: and we shall reign on the earth.

- **A crown.**

2Ti 4:7–8

Jas 1:12 — Blessed *is* the man that endureth temptation: for when he is tried, he shall receive the crown of life, which the Lord hath promised to them that love him.

- **Saints give diligence to attain.**

2Pe 1:10–11

- **Strive to maintain.**

Heb 3:14 — For we are made partakers of Christ, if we hold the beginning of our confidence stedfast unto the end;

Heb 3:18 — And to whom sware he that they should not enter into his rest, but to them that believed not?

- **Confident hope in God restores.**

Ps 42:11 — Why art thou cast down, O my soul? and why art thou disquieted within me? hope thou in God: for I shall yet praise him, *who is* the health of my countenance, and my God.

- **Exemplified.**
- **David.**

Ps 73:24–26

Ps 23:4 — Yea, though I walk through the valley of the shadow of death, I will fear no evil: for thou *art* with me; thy rod and thy staff they comfort me.

- **Paul.**

2Ti 1:12 — For the which cause I also suffer these things: nevertheless I am not ashamed: for I know whom I have believed, and am persuaded that he is able to keep that which I have committed unto him against that day.

2Ti 4:18 — And the Lord shall deliver me from every evil work, and will preserve *me* unto his heavenly kingdom: to whom *be* glory for ever and ever. Amen.

→See: **Faith**

ASSYRIA

- **An empire founded by Nimrod.**

Ge 10:8–12

Mic 5:6 — And they shall waste the land of Assyria with the sword, and the land of Nimrod in the entrances thereof: thus shall he deliver *us* from the Assyrian, when he cometh into our land, and when he treadeth within our borders.

• It extended from east of the Tigris.

Ge 2:14 — And the name of the third river *is* Hiddekel: that *is* it which goeth toward the east of Assyria. And the fourth river *is* Euphrates.

Ge 10:11 — Out of that land went forth Asshur, and builded Nineveh, and the city Rehoboth, and Calah,

• It extended possibly to Egypt.

Ge 25:18 — And they dwelt from Havilah unto Shur, that *is* before Egypt, as thou goest toward Assyria: *and* he died in the presence of all his brethren.

• Its armies invade the land of Israel under Pul.

2Ki 15:19 — *And* Pul the king of Assyria came against the land: and Menahem gave Pul a thousand talents of silver, that his hand might be with him to confirm the kingdom in his hand.

1Ch 5:26 — And the God of Israel stirred up the spirit of Pul king of Assyria, and the spirit of Tilgath-pilneser king of Assyria, and he carried them away, even the Reubenites, and the Gadites, and the half tribe of Manasseh, and brought them unto Halah, and Habor, and Hara, and to the river Gozan, unto this day.

• Its armies invade the land of Israel under Tiglath.

2Ki 15:29 — In the days of Pekah king of Israel came Tiglath-pileser king of Assyria, and took Ijon, and Abel-beth-maachah, and Janoah, and Kedesh, and Hazor, and Gilead, and Galilee, all the land of Naphtali, and carried them captive to Assyria.

1Ch 5:6 — Beerah his son, whom Tilgath-pilneser king of Assyria carried away *captive:* he *was* prince of the Reubenites.

1Ch 5:26 — And the God of Israel stirred up the spirit of Pul king of Assyria, and the spirit of Tilgath-pilneser king of Assyria, and he carried them away, even the Reubenites, and the Gadites, and the half tribe of Manasseh, and brought them unto Halah, and Habor, and Hara, and to the river Gozan, unto this day.

• Its armies invade the land of Israel under Shalmaneser.

2Ki 17:3–6, 24–27; 18:9–12

Jer 50:17 — Israel *is* a scattered sheep; the lions have driven *him* away: first the king of Assyria hath devoured him; and last this Nebuchadrezzar king of Babylon hath broken his bones.

• Its armies invade the land of Israel under Sennacherib.

2Ki 18:13–19:37; 2Ch 32:1–33; Isa 36:1–37:38

• Army of, destroyed by the angel of the Lord.

Isa 37:36 — Then the angel of the LORD went forth, and smote in the camp of the Assyrians a hundred and fourscore and five thousand: and when they arose early in the morning, behold, they *were* all dead corpses.

• Alliances with, sought by Judah and Israel.

Hos 5:13 — When Ephraim saw his sickness, and Judah *saw* his wound, then went Ephraim to the Assyrian, and sent to king Jareb: yet could he not heal you, nor cure you of your wound.

• Israelites subject to.

La 5:6 — We have given the hand *to* the Egyptians, *and to* the Assyrians, to be satisfied with bread.

• Israelites carried captive into.

2Ki 17:3–23

• Jews carried captive to.

2Ki 24:1–25:30; 2Ch 36:5–21

• Invaded by Pharaoh-nechoh.

2Ki 23:29 — In his days Pharaoh-nechoh king of Egypt went up against the king of Assyria to the river Euphrates: and king Josiah went against him; and he slew him at Megiddo, when he had seen him.

• Commerce of.

Eze 27:23 — Haran, and Canneh, and Eden, the merchants of Sheba, Asshur, *and* Chilmad, *were* thy merchants.

• Productiveness of.

Isa 36:17 — Until I come and take you away to a land like your own land, a land of corn and wine, a land of bread and vineyards.

• Prophecies concerning.

Isa 7:17–25; 8:4–10; 10:5–34; 14:24–28; 19:23–20:6; 30:27–33; 31:8–9; 37:21–35; Eze 31:1–18; Jnh 3:1–4; Na 1:1–3:19; Zep 2:13–15

Jer 1:15 — For, lo, I will call all the families of the kingdoms of the north, saith the LORD; and they shall come, and they shall set every one his throne at the entering of the gates of Jerusalem, and against all the walls thereof round about, and against all the cities of Judah.

Zec 10:11 — And he shall pass through the sea with affliction, and shall smite the waves in the sea, and all the deeps of the river shall dry up: and the pride of Assyria shall be brought down, and the sceptre of Egypt shall depart away.

• Prophecies of captivity of Israelites in.

Hos 9:3 — They shall not dwell in the LORD's land; but Ephraim shall return to Egypt, and they shall eat unclean *things* in Assyria.

Hos 11:5 — He shall not return into the land of Egypt, but the Assyrian shall be his king, because they refused to return.

Hos 11:11 — They shall tremble as a bird out of Egypt, and as a dove out of the land of Assyria: and I will place them in their houses, saith the LORD.

• Idols of.

See: Adrammelech

See: Anammelech

See: Nisroch

See: Tartak

ASTROLOGY

Ex 32:1–35; 2Ki 21:1–15; Jer 10:1–2; 44:17–25; Ac 19:18–20; 2Ti 4:3–5

Ge 1:14 — And God said, Let there be lights in the firmament of the heaven to divide the day from the night;

and let them be for signs, and for seasons, and for days, and years:

Dt 4:19 — And lest thou lift up thine eyes unto heaven, and when thou seest the sun, and the moon, and the stars, *even* all the host of heaven, shouldest be driven to worship them, and serve them, which the LORD thy God hath divided unto all nations under the whole heaven.

2Ch 11:15 — And he ordained him priests for the high places, and for the devils, and for the calves which he had made.

Isa 47:13 — Thou art wearied in the multitude of thy counsels. Let now the astrologers, the stargazers, the monthly prognosticators, stand up, and save thee from *these things* that shall come upon thee.

Jer 7:18 — The children gather wood, and the fathers kindle the fire, and the women knead *their* dough, to make cakes to the queen of heaven, and to pour out drink offerings unto other gods, that they may provoke me to anger.

Da 1:20 — And in all matters of wisdom *and* understanding, that the king enquired of them, he found them ten times better than all the magicians *and* astrologers that *were* in all his realm.

Da 2:10 — The Chaldeans answered before the king, and said, There is not a man upon the earth that can shew the king's matter: therefore *there is* no king, lord, nor ruler, *that* asked such things at any magician, or astrologer, or Chaldean.

Da 2:27 — Daniel answered in the presence of the king, and said, The secret which the king hath demanded cannot the wise *men,* the astrologers, the magicians, the soothsayers, shew unto the king;

Da 4:7 — Then came in the magicians, the astrologers, the Chaldeans, and the soothsayers: and I told the dream before them; but they did not make known unto me the interpretation thereof.

Da 5:7 — The king cried aloud to bring in the astrologers, the Chaldeans, and the soothsayers. *And* the king spake, and said to the wise *men* of Babylon, Whosoever shall read this writing, and shew me the interpretation thereof, shall be clothed with scarlet, and *have* a chain of gold about his neck, and shall be the third ruler in the kingdom.

Lk 21:11 — And great earthquakes shall be in divers places, and famines, and pestilences; and fearful sights and great signs shall there be from heaven.

❖See: Astronomy

❖See: Sorcery

ASTRONOMY

Job 38:31–33; Ps 19:1–6; 136:5–9; Jer 31:35–37

Job 26:7 — He stretcheth out the north over the empty place, *and* hangeth the earth upon nothing.

Job 26:13 — By his spirit he hath garnished the heavens; his hand hath formed the crooked serpent.

Job 37:18 — Hast thou with him spread out the sky, *which is* strong, *and* as a molten looking glass?

Ps 8:3 — When I consider thy heavens, the work of thy fingers, the moon and the stars, which thou hast ordained;

Ps 68:33 — To him that rideth upon the heavens of heavens, *which were* of old; lo, he doth send out his voice, *and that* a mighty voice.

Isa 13:10 — For the stars of heaven and the constellations thereof shall not give their light: the sun shall be darkened in his going forth, and the moon shall not cause her light to shine.

Isa 40:22 — *It is* he that sitteth upon the circle of the earth, and the inhabitants thereof *are* as grasshoppers; that stretcheth out the heavens as a curtain, and spreadeth them out as a tent to dwell in:

Isa 40:26 — Lift up your eyes on high, and behold who hath created these *things,* that bringeth out their host by number: he calleth them all by names by the greatness of his might, for that *he is* strong in power; not one faileth.

Isa 47:13 — Thou art wearied in the multitude of thy counsels. Let now the astrologers, the stargazers, the monthly prognosticators, stand up, and save thee from *these things* that shall come upon thee.

Jer 33:22 — As the host of heaven cannot be numbered, neither the sand of the sea measured: so will I multiply the seed of David my servant, and the Levites that minister unto me.

Am 5:8 — *Seek him* that maketh the seven stars and Orion, and turneth the shadow of death into the morning, and maketh the day dark with night: that calleth for the waters of the sea, and poureth them out upon the face of the earth: The LORD *is* his name:

1Co 15:41 — *There is* one glory of the sun, and another glory of the moon, and another glory of the stars: for *one* star differeth from *another* star in glory.

Jude 1:13 — Raging waves of the sea, foaming out their own shame; wandering stars, to whom is reserved the blackness of darkness for ever.

• Sidereal phenomena.

Jos 10:12–14; Job 9:6–9; Eze 32:7–8; Mk 13:24–25; Lk 23:44–45; Ac 2:19–20; Rev 6:12–14; 8:10–12; 9:1–2; 10:1–2; 12:3–4; 16:8–9; 19:11–14

Ecc 1:5 — The sun also ariseth, and the sun goeth down, and hasteth to his place where he arose.

Isa 13:13 — Therefore I will shake the heavens, and the earth shall remove out of her place, in the wrath of the LORD of hosts, and in the day of his fierce anger.

Isa 34:4 — And all the host of heaven shall be dissolved, and the heavens shall be rolled together as a scroll: and all their host shall fall down, as the leaf falleth off from the vine, and as a falling *fig* from the fig tree.

Mt 24:29 — Immediately after the tribulation of those days shall the sun be darkened, and the moon shall not give her light, and the stars shall fall from heaven, and the powers of the heavens shall be shaken:

Mt 24:35 — Heaven and earth shall pass away, but my words shall not pass away.

Mt 27:45 — Now from the sixth hour there was darkness over all the land unto the ninth hour.

Lk 21:25 — And there shall be signs in the sun, and in the moon, and in the stars; and upon the earth distress of nations, with perplexity; the sea and the waves roaring;

2Pe 3:10 — But the day of the Lord will come as a thief in the night; in the which the heavens shall pass away with a great noise, and the elements shall melt with fervent heat, the earth also and the works that are therein shall be burned up.

Rev 13:13 — And he doeth great wonders, so that he maketh fire come down from heaven on the earth in the sight of men,

Rev 21:1 — And I saw a new heaven and a new earth: for the first heaven and the first earth were passed away; and there was no more sea.

See: Constellations
See: Eclipse
See: Heaven
See: Meteorology and Celestial Phenomena
See: Moon
See: Stars
See: Sun

ASUPPIM • A temple gate.

1Ch 26:15 — To Obed-edom southward; and to his sons the house of Asuppim.

1Ch 26:17 — Eastward *were* six Levites, northward four a day, southward four a day, and toward Asuppim two *and* two.

ASYNCRITUS • A disciple at Rome.

Ro 16:14 — Salute Asyncritus, Phlegon, Hermas, Patrobas, Hermes, and the brethren which are with them.

ATAD • The place where the sons of Jacob mourned for their father.

Ge 50:10–11

ATARAH • Wife of Jerahmeel.

1Ch 2:26 — Jerahmeel had also another wife, whose name *was* Atarah; she *was* the mother of Onam.

ATAROTH

• Called also Atroth.

• A city east of Jordan.

Nu 32:3 — Ataroth, and Dibon, and Jazer, and Nimrah, and Heshbon, and Elealeh, and Shebam, and Nebo, and Beon,

Nu 32:34 — And the children of Gad built Dibon, and Ataroth, and Aroer,

• A city, or possibly two different cities, of Ephraim.

Jos 16:2 — And goeth out from Bethel to Luz, and passeth along unto the borders of Archi to Ataroth,

Jos 16:5 — And the border of the children of Ephraim according to their families was *thus:* even the border of their inheritance on the east side was Ataroth-addar, unto Beth-horon the upper;

Jos 16:7 — And it went down from Janohah to Ataroth, and to Naarath, and came to Jericho, and went out at Jordan.

Jos 18:13 — And the border went over from thence toward Luz, to the side of Luz, which is Bethel, southward; and the border descended to Ataroth-adar, near the hill that *lieth* on the south side of the nether Beth-horon.

• A city of Judah. Called Atroth-Beth-Joab.

1Ch 2:54 — The sons of Salma; Bethlehem, and the Netophathites, Ataroth, the house of Joab, and half of the Manahethites, the Zorites.

• A city of Gad.

Nu 32:35 — And Atroth, Shophan, and Jaazer, and Jogbehah,

ATAROTH-ADAR

• Called also Ataroth-Addar.

See: Ataroth; a city, or possibly two different cities, of Ephraim

ATER

• A descendant of Hezekiah, who returned from Babylon.

Ezr 2:16 — The children of Ater of Hezekiah, ninety and eight.

Ne 7:21 — The children of Ater of Hezekiah, ninety and eight.

• A porter.

Ezr 2:42 — The children of the porters: the children of Shallum, the children of Ater, the children of Talmon, the children of Akkub, the children of Hatita, the children of Shobai, *in* all an hundred thirty and nine.

Ne 7:45 — The porters: the children of Shallum, the children of Ater, the children of Talmon, the children of Akkub, the children of Hatita, the children of Shobai, an hundred thirty and eight.

• An Israelite, who subscribed to Nehemiah's covenant.

Ne 10:17 — Ater, Hizkijah, Azzur,

ATHACH • A city of Judah.

1Sa 30:30 — And to *them* which *were* in Hormah, and to *them* which *were* in Chor-ashan, and to *them* which *were* in Athach,

ATHAIAH • Perhaps identical with Asaiah.

Ne 11:4 — And at Jerusalem dwelt *certain* of the children of Judah, and of the children of Benjamin. Of the children of Judah; Athaiah the son of Uzziah, the son of Zechariah, the son of Amariah, the son of Shephatiah, the son of Mahalaleel, of the children of Perez;

ATHALIAH

• Wife of Jehoram, king of Judah.

2Ki 11:1–3, 12–16; 2Ch 22:10–12; 23:12–15

2Ki 8:18 — And he walked in the way of the kings of Israel, as did the house of Ahab: for the daughter of Ahab was his wife: and he did evil in the sight of the LORD.

2Ki 8:26 — Two and twenty years old *was* Ahaziah when he began to reign; and he reigned one year in Jerusalem. And his mother's name *was* Athaliah, the daughter of Omri king of Israel.

2Ki 11:20 — And all the people of the land rejoiced, and the city was in quiet: and they slew Athaliah with the sword *beside* the king's house.

2Ch 23:21 — And all the people of the land rejoiced: and the city was quiet, after that they had slain Athaliah with the sword.

- **Son of Jehoram.**

1Ch 8:26 — And Shamsherai, and Shehariah, and Athaliah,

- **Father of Jeshaiah.**

Ezr 8:7 — And of the sons of Elam; Jeshaiah the son of Athaliah, and with him seventy males.

ATHEISM

Ps 10:4 — The wicked, through the pride of his countenance, will not seek *after God:* God *is* not in all his thoughts.

Ps 14:1 — The fool hath said in his heart, *There is* no God. They are corrupt, they have done abominable works, *there is* none that doeth good.

Ps 53:1 — The fool hath said in his heart, *There is* no God. Corrupt are they, and have done abominable iniquity: *there is* none that doeth good.

Pr 30:9 — Lest I be full, and deny *thee,* and say, Who *is* the LORD? or lest I be poor, and steal, and take the name of my God *in vain.*

Jer 5:12 — They have belied the LORD, and said, *It is* not he; neither shall evil come upon us; neither shall we see sword nor famine:

1Jn 2:22 — Who is a liar but he that denieth that Jesus is the Christ? He is antichrist, that denieth the Father and the Son.

- **Arguments against.**

Job 12:7–25; Ro 1:19–20

See: God

See: Faith

See: Unbelief

ATHENS • A city of Greece.

Ac 17:15–34

1Th 3:1 — Wherefore when we could no longer forbear, we thought it good to be left at Athens alone;

ATHLAI • A son of Bebai.

Ezr 10:28 — Of the sons also of Bebai; Jehohanan, Hananiah, Zabbai, *and* Athlai.

ATOMS OF MATTER

Pr 8:26 — While as yet he had not made the earth, nor the fields, nor the highest part of the dust of the world.

ATONEMENT

- **For tabernacle and furniture.**

Le 16:15–20

Le 16:33 — And he shall make an atonement for the holy sanctuary, and he shall make an atonement for the tabernacle of the congregation, and for the altar, and he shall make an atonement for the priests, and for all the people of the congregation.

- **In consecration of the Levites.**

Nu 8:21 — And the Levites were purified, and they washed their clothes; and Aaron offered them *as* an offering before the LORD; and Aaron made an atonement for them to cleanse them.

- **For those defiled by the dead.**

Nu 6:11 — And the priest shall offer the one for a sin offering, and the other for a burnt offering, and make an atonement for him, for that he sinned by the dead, and shall hallow his head that same day.

- **Made for houses.**

Le 14:53 — But he shall let go the living bird out of the city into the open fields, and make an atonement for the house: and it shall be clean.

- **For sin.**
  - **By meat offerings.**

Le 5:11–13

  - **By jewels.**

Nu 31:50 — We have therefore brought an oblation for the LORD, what every man hath gotten, of jewels of gold, chains, and bracelets, rings, earrings, and tablets, to make an atonement for our souls before the LORD.

  - **By money.**

Ex 30:12–16; Le 5:15–16

2Ki 12:16 — The trespass money and sin money was not brought into the house of the LORD: it was the priests'.

  - **By incense.**

Nu 16:46–50

See: Atonement; made by animal sacrifices

  - **By Jesus.**

See: Atonement; made by Jesus

- **Day of.**
  - **Time of.**

Ex 30:10 — And Aaron shall make an atonement upon the horns of it once in a year with the blood of the sin offering of atonements: once in the year shall he make atonement upon it throughout your generations: it *is* most holy unto the LORD.

Le 23:27 — Also on the tenth *day* of this seventh month *there shall be* a day of atonement: it shall be an holy convocation unto you; and ye shall afflict your souls, and offer an offering made by fire unto the LORD.

Le 25:9 — Then shalt thou cause the trumpet of the jubile to sound on the tenth *day* of the seventh month, in the day of atonement shall ye make the trumpet sound throughout all your land.

Nu 29:7 — And ye shall have on the tenth *day* of this seventh month an holy convocation; and ye shall afflict your souls: ye shall not do any work *therein:*

- **How observed.**

Le 16:2–34; 23:27–32; Nu 29:7–11

Ex 30:10 — And Aaron shall make an atonement upon the horns of it once in a year with the blood of the sin offering of atonements: once in the year shall he make atonement upon it throughout your generations: it *is* most holy unto the LORD.

Heb 5:3 — And by reason hereof he ought, as for the people, so also for himself, to offer for sins.

Heb 9:7 — But into the second *went* the high priest alone once every year, not without blood, which he offered for himself, and *for* the errors of the people:

- **Made by animal sacrifices.**

Le 4:13–15, 17–18; 4:22–35; 5:6–10; 12:6–8; 14:12–32; 16:10–11, 15–19, 24–34; Nu 15:22–28; 29:10–11

Ex 29:36 — And thou shalt offer every day a bullock *for* a sin offering for atonement: and thou shalt cleanse the altar, when thou hast made an atonement for it, and thou shalt anoint it, to sanctify it.

Le 1:4 — And he shall put his hand upon the head of the burnt offering; and it shall be accepted for him to make atonement for him.

Le 4:20 — And he shall do with the bullock as he did with the bullock for a sin offering, so shall he do with this: and the priest shall make an atonement for them, and it shall be forgiven them.

Le 6:7 — And the priest shall make an atonement for him before the LORD: and it shall be forgiven him for any thing of all that he hath done in trespassing therein.

Le 9:7 — And Moses said unto Aaron, Go unto the altar, and offer thy sin offering, and thy burnt offering, and make an atonement for thyself, and for the people: and offer the offering of the people, and make an atonement for them; as the LORD commanded.

Le 10:17 — Wherefore have ye not eaten the sin offering in the holy place, seeing it *is* most holy, and *God* hath given it you to bear the iniquity of the congregation, to make atonement for them before the LORD?

Le 16:6 — And Aaron shall offer his bullock of the sin offering, which *is* for himself, and make an atonement for himself, and for his house.

Le 17:11 — For the life of the flesh *is* in the blood: and I have given it to you upon the altar to make an atonement for your souls: for it *is* the blood *that* maketh an atonement for the soul.

Le 19:22 — And the priest shall make an atonement for him with the ram of the trespass offering before the LORD for his sin which he hath done: and the sin which he hath done shall be forgiven him.

Nu 28:22 — And one goat *for* a sin offering, to make an atonement for you.

Nu 28:30 — *And* one kid of the goats, to make an atonement for you.

Nu 29:5 — And one kid of the goats *for* a sin offering, to make an atonement for you:

Heb 9:22 — And almost all things are by the law purged with blood; and without shedding of blood is no remission.

- **Made by Jesus.**
  - **Divinely ordained.**

Lk 2:30–31; Gal 4:4–5; Eph 1:3–12, 17–22; 2:4–10; Col 1:19–20

1Pe 1:20 — Who verily was foreordained before the foundation of the world, but was manifest in these last times for you,

Rev 13:8 — And all that dwell upon the earth shall worship him, whose names are not written in the book of life of the Lamb slain from the foundation of the world.

- **A mystery.**

1Co 2:7 — But we speak the wisdom of God in a mystery, *even* the hidden *wisdom,* which God ordained before the world unto our glory:

- **With context.**

1Pe 1:8–12

- **Made but once.**

Heb 9:24–28

Heb 7:27 — Who needeth not daily, as those high priests, to offer up sacrifice, first for his own sins, and then for the people's: for this he did once, when he offered up himself.

Heb 10:10 — By the which will we are sanctified through the offering of the body of Jesus Christ once *for all.*

Heb 10:12 — But this man, after he had offered one sacrifice for sins for ever, sat down on the right hand of God;

Heb 10:14 — For by one offering he hath perfected for ever them that are sanctified.

1Pe 3:18 — For Christ also hath once suffered for sins, the just for the unjust, that he might bring us to God, being put to death in the flesh, but quickened by the Spirit:

- **Redemption by.**

Mt 20:28 — Even as the Son of man came not to be ministered unto, but to minister, and to give his life a ransom for many.

Ac 20:28 — Take heed therefore unto yourselves, and to all the flock, over the which the Holy Ghost hath made you overseers, to feed the church of God, which he hath purchased with his own blood.

Gal 3:13 — Christ hath redeemed us from the curse of the law, being made a curse for us: for it is written, Cursed *is* every one that hangeth on a tree:

1Ti 2:6 — Who gave himself a ransom for all, to be testified in due time.

Heb 9:12 — Neither by the blood of goats and calves, but by his own blood he entered in once into the holy place, having obtained eternal redemption *for us.*

Rev 5:9 — And they sung a new song, saying, Thou art worthy to take the book, and to open the seals thereof: for thou wast slain, and hast redeemed us to God by thy blood out of every kindred, and tongue, and people, and nation;

- **Typified.**
  - **1.**

Ge 4:4 — And Abel, he also brought of the firstlings of his flock and of the fat thereof.

And the LORD had respect unto Abel and to his offering:

Heb 11:4 — By faith Abel offered unto God a more excellent sacrifice than Cain, by which he obtained witness that he was righteous, God testifying of his gifts: and by it he being dead yet speaketh.

• **2.**

Ge 22:2 — And he said, Take now thy son, thine only *son* Isaac, whom thou lovest, and get thee into the land of Moriah; and offer him there for a burnt offering upon one of the mountains which I will tell thee of.

Heb 11:17 — By faith Abraham, when he was tried, offered up Isaac: and he that had received the promises offered up his only begotten *son,*

Heb 11:19 — Accounting that God *was* able to raise *him* up, even from the dead; from whence also he received him in a figure.

• **3.**

Ex 12:5 — Your lamb shall be without blemish, a male of the first year: ye shall take *it* out from the sheep, or from the goats:

Ex 12:11 — And thus shall ye eat it; *with* your loins girded, your shoes on your feet, and your staff in your hand; and ye shall eat it in haste: it *is* the LORD's passover.

Ex 12:14 — And this day shall be unto you for a memorial; and ye shall keep it a feast to the LORD throughout your generations; ye shall keep it a feast by an ordinance for ever.

1Co 5:7 — Purge out therefore the old leaven, that ye may be a new lump, as ye are unleavened. For even Christ our passover is sacrificed for us:

• **4.**

Ex 24:8 — And Moses took the blood, and sprinkled *it* on the people, and said, Behold the blood of the covenant, which the LORD hath made with you concerning all these words.

Heb 9:20 — Saying, This *is* the blood of the testament which God hath enjoined unto you.

• **5.**

Le 16:30 — For on that day shall *the priest* make an atonement for you, to cleanse you, *that* ye may be clean from all your sins before the LORD.

Le 16:34 — And this shall be an everlasting statute unto you, to make an atonement for the children of Israel for all their sins once a year. And he did as the LORD commanded Moses.

Heb 9:7 — But into the second *went* the high priest alone once every year, not without blood, which he offered for himself, and *for* the errors of the people:

Heb 9:12 — Neither by the blood of goats and calves, but by his own blood he entered in once into the holy place, having obtained eternal redemption *for us.*

Heb 9:28 — So Christ was once offered to bear the sins of many; and unto them that look for him shall he appear the second time without sin unto salvation.

• **6.**

Le 17:11 — For the life of the flesh *is* in the blood: and I have given it to you upon the altar to make an atonement for your souls: for it *is* the blood *that* maketh an atonement for the soul.

Heb 9:22 — And almost all things are by the law purged with blood; and without shedding of blood is no remission.

See: Salvation; plan of

• Unclassified scripture relating to.

Ps 40:6–8; Isa 53:4–8, 10–12; Da 9:24–27; Lk 24:46–47; Jn 11:49–51; Ac 17:2–3; Ro 3:24–26; 4:25–5:2, 6–11, 15–21; 1Co 1:17–18, 23–24; 2Co 5:18–19; Gal 1:3–4; 4:4–5; Eph 2:13–18; Col 1:19–22; 1Th 5:9–10; 1Ti 2:5–6; Heb 9:12–15, 25–26; 10:1–12, 18–20; 13:20–21; 1Pe 1:18–20

Zec 13:1 — In that day there shall be a fountain opened to the house of David and to the inhabitants of Jerusalem for sin and for uncleanness.

Mt 26:28 — For this is my blood of the new testament, which is shed for many for the remission of sins.

Lk 22:20 — Likewise also the cup after supper, saying, This cup *is* the new testament in my blood, which is shed for you.

Jn 1:29 — The next day John seeth Jesus coming unto him, and saith, Behold the Lamb of God, which taketh away the sin of the world.

Jn 1:36 — And looking upon Jesus as he walked, he saith, Behold the Lamb of God!

Jn 6:51 — I am the living bread which came down from heaven: if any man eat of this bread, he shall live for ever: and the bread that I will give is my flesh, which I will give for the life of the world.

Ac 20:28 — Take heed therefore unto yourselves, and to all the flock, over the which the Holy Ghost hath made you overseers, to feed the church of God, which he hath purchased with his own blood.

1Co 15:3 — For I delivered unto you first of all that which I also received, how that Christ died for our sins according to the scriptures;

Eph 1:7 — In whom we have redemption through his blood, the forgiveness of sins, according to the riches of his grace;

Eph 5:2 — And walk in love, as Christ also hath loved us, and hath given himself for us an offering and a sacrifice to God for a sweetsmelling savour.

Eph 5:25 — Husbands, love your wives, even as Christ also loved the church, and gave himself for it;

Col 1:14 — In whom we have redemption through his blood, *even* the forgiveness of sins:

Tit 2:14 — Who gave himself for us, that he might redeem us from all iniquity, and purify unto himself a peculiar people, zealous of good works.

Heb 1:3 — Who being the brightness of *his* glory, and the express image of his person, and upholding all things by the word of his power, when he had by himself purged our sins, sat down on the right hand of the Majesty on high;

Heb 2:9 — But we see Jesus, who was made a little lower than the angels for the suffering of death, crowned with glory and honour; that he by the grace of God should taste death for every man.

Heb 2:17 — Wherefore in all things it behoved him to be made like unto *his* brethren, that he might be a merciful and faithful high priest in things *pertaining* to God, to make reconciliation for the sins of the people.

Heb 12:24 — And to Jesus the mediator of the new covenant, and to the blood of sprinkling, that speaketh better things than *that of* Abel.

Heb 13:12 — Wherefore Jesus also, that he might sanctify the people with his own blood, suffered without the gate.

1Pe 2:24 — Who his own self bare our sins in his own body on the tree, that we, being dead to sins, should live unto righteousness: by whose stripes ye were healed.

1Pe 3:18 — For Christ also hath once suffered for sins, the just for the unjust, that he might bring us to God, being put to death in the flesh, but quickened by the Spirit:

1Jn 1:7 — But if we walk in the light, as he is in the light, we have fellowship one with another, and the blood of Jesus Christ his Son cleanseth us from all sin.

1Jn 2:2 — And he is the propitiation for our sins: and not for ours only, but also for *the sins of* the whole world.

1Jn 3:5 — And ye know that he was manifested to take away our sins; and in him is no sin.

1Jn 4:10 — Herein is love, not that we loved God, but that he loved us, and sent his Son *to be* the propitiation for our sins.

1Jn 5:6 — This is he that came by water and blood, *even* Jesus Christ; not by water only, but by water and blood. And it is the Spirit that beareth witness, because the Spirit is truth.

Rev 1:5 — And from Jesus Christ, *who is* the faithful witness, *and* the first begotten of the dead, and the prince of the kings of the earth. Unto him that loved us, and washed us from our sins in his own blood,

Rev 5:9 — And they sung a new song, saying, Thou art worthy to take the book, and to open the seals thereof: for thou wast slain, and hast redeemed us to God by thy blood out of every kindred, and tongue, and people, and nation;

Rev 7:14 — And I said unto him, Sir, thou knowest. And he said to me, These are they which came out of great tribulation, and have washed their robes, and made them white in the blood of the Lamb.

Rev 12:11 — And they overcame him by the blood of the Lamb, and by the word of their testimony; and they loved not their lives unto the death.

➜See: Blood

➜See: Jesus, Death of

➜See: Jesus, Mission of

➜See: Jesus, Sufferings of

➜See: Redemption

➜See: Salvation

ATROPHY

• Of the hand.

Mt 12:10–13

ATTAI

• A Gadite warrior.

1Ch 12:11 — Attai the sixth, Eliel the seventh,

• Son of Rehoboam.

2Ch 11:20 — And after her he took Maachah the daughter of Absalom; which bare him Abijah, and Attai, and Ziza, and Shelomith.

• Grandson of Sheshan.

1Ch 2:35–36

ATTALIA • A seaport of Pamphylia.

Ac 14:25 — And when they had preached the word in Perga, they went down into Attalia:

ATTITUDE

Php 4:6–7

Pr 29:25 — The fear of man bringeth a snare: but whoso putteth his trust in the LORD shall be safe.

Php 4:13 — I can do all things through Christ which strengtheneth me.

ATTORNEY

• Employed.

Ac 24:1–2

➜See: Lawyer

ATTRIBUTES OF GOD ➜See: God

AUGUSTUS • A title of Roman emperors.

Lk 2:1 — And it came to pass in those days, that there went out a decree from Caesar Augustus, that all the world should be taxed.

Ac 25:21 — But when Paul had appealed to be reserved unto the hearing of Augustus, I commanded him to be kept till I might send him to Caesar.

Ac 25:25 — But when I found that he had committed nothing worthy of death, and that he himself hath appealed to Augustus, I have determined to send him.

Ac 27:1 — And when it was determined that we should sail into Italy, they delivered Paul and certain other prisoners unto *one* named Julius, a centurion of Augustus' band.

AVA

• Called also Ivah.

• A district near Babylon.

2Ki 17:24 — And the king of Assyria brought *men* from Babylon, and from Cuthah, and from Ava, and from Hamath, and from Sepharvaim, and placed *them* in the cities of Samaria instead of the children of Israel: and they possessed Samaria, and dwelt in the cities thereof.

2Ki 18:34 — Where *are* the gods of Hamath, and of Arpad? where *are* the gods of Sepharvaim, Hena, and Ivah? have they delivered Samaria out of mine hand?

2Ki 19:13 — Where *is* the king of Hamath, and the king of Arpad, and the king of the city of Sepharvaim, of Hena, and Ivah?

Ezr 4:9 — Then *wrote* Rehum the chancellor, and Shimshai the scribe, and the rest of their companions; the Dinaites, the Apharsathchites, the Tarpelites, the Apharsites, the Archevites, the Babylonians, the Susanchites, the Dehavites, *and* the Elamites,

AVARICE

Ecc 4:7–8; 5:10–11; 1Ti 3:2–3

1Ti 6:5 — Perverse disputings of men of corrupt minds, and destitute of the truth, supposing that gain is godliness: from such withdraw thyself.

1Ti 6:10 — For the love of money is the root of all evil: which while some coveted after, they have erred from the faith, and pierced themselves through with many sorrows.

Tit 1:7 — For a bishop must be blameless, as the steward of God; not selfwilled, not soon angry, not given to wine, no striker, not given to filthy lucre;

See: Covetousness

See: Rich

See: Riches

• Instances of.

• The descendants of Joseph.

Jos 17:14–18

AVEN

• "The plain of the Sun".

Am 1:5 — I will break also the bar of Damascus, and cut off the inhabitant from the plain of Aven, and him that holdeth the sceptre from the house of Eden: and the people of Syria shall go into captivity unto Kir, saith the LORD.

• Another name for On.

Eze 30:17 — The young men of Aven and of Pi-beseth shall fall by the sword: and these *cities* shall go into captivity.

• Beth-Aven.

Hos 10:8 — The high places also of Aven, the sin of Israel, shall be destroyed: the thorn and the thistle shall come up on their altars; and they shall say to the mountains, Cover us; and to the hills, Fall on us.

AVENGER OF BLOOD

• Premosaic.

Ge 9:5–6

• Cain fears.

Ge 4:14–15

• Lamech fears.

Ge 4:24 — If Cain shall be avenged sevenfold, truly Lamech seventy and sevenfold.

• Law concerning, set aside by David.

2Sa 14:4–11

See: Homicide

• Figurative.

Ps 8:2 — Out of the mouth of babes and sucklings hast thou ordained strength because of thine enemies, that thou mightest still the enemy and the avenger.

Ps 44:16 — For the voice of him that reproacheth and blasphemeth; by reason of the enemy and avenger.

Ro 13:4 — For he is the minister of God to thee for good. But if thou do that which is evil, be afraid; for he beareth not the sword in vain: for he is the minister of God, a revenger to *execute* wrath upon him that doeth evil.

1Th 4:6 — That no *man* go beyond and defraud his brother in *any* matter: because that the Lord *is* the avenger of all such, as we also have forewarned you and testified.

• Scriptures relating to.

Ge 9:5–6; Nu 35:19–29; Dt 19:4–13; Jos 20:1–9

AVIM

• A city of Benjamin.

Jos 18:23 — And Avim, and Parah, and Ophrah,

• A tribe in southern Palestine.

See: Avites

AVITES

• A nation in southern part of Canaan.

Dt 2:23 — And the Avims which dwelt in Hazerim, *even* unto Azzah, the Caphtorims, which came forth out of Caphtor, destroyed them, and dwelt in their stead.)

Jos 13:3 — From Sihor, which *is* before Egypt, even unto the borders of Ekron northward, *which* is counted to the Canaanite: five lords of the Philistines; the Gazathites, and the Ashdothites, the Eshkalonites, the Gittites, and the Ekronites; also the Avites:

• Colonists of Samaria.

2Ki 17:31 — And the Avites made Nibhaz and Tartak, and the Sepharvites burnt their children in fire to Adrammelech and Anammelech, the gods of Sepharvaim.

AVITH • Capital city of the Edomites.

Ge 36:35 — And Husham died, and Hadad the son of Bedad, who smote Midian in the field of Moab, reigned in his stead: and the name of his city *was* Avith.

1Ch 1:46 — And when Husham was dead, Hadad the son of Bedad, which smote Midian in the field of Moab, reigned in his stead: and the name of his city *was* Avith.

AWL • A tool.

Ex 21:6 — Then his master shall bring him unto the judges; he shall also bring him to the door, or unto the door post; and his master shall bore his ear through with an aul; and he shall serve him for ever.

Dt 15:17 — Then thou shalt take an aul, and thrust *it* through his ear unto the door, and he shall be thy servant for ever. And also unto thy maidservant thou shalt do likewise.

AX

• An implement.

1Sa 13:20–21; Ps 74:5–6

Dt 19:5 — As when a man goeth into the wood with his neighbour to hew wood, and his hand fetcheth a stroke with the axe to cut down the tree, and the head slippeth from the helve, and lighteth upon his neighbour, that he die; he shall flee unto one of those cities, and live:

2Sa 12:31 — And he brought forth the people that *were* therein, and put *them* under saws, and under harrows of iron, and under axes of iron, and made them pass through the brickkiln: and thus did he unto all the cities of the children of Ammon. So David and all the people returned unto Jerusalem.

• Elisha causes to swim.

2Ki 6:5–6

• Battle-ax.

Eze 26:9 — And he shall set engines of war against thy walls, and with his axes he shall break down thy towers.

• Figurative.

Jer 46:22 — The voice thereof shall go like a serpent; for they shall march with an army, and come against her with axes, as hewers of wood.

Jer 51:20 — Thou *art* my battle axe *and* weapons of war: for with thee will I break in pieces the nations, and with thee will I destroy kingdoms;

Mt 3:10 — And now also the axe is laid unto the root of the trees: therefore every tree which bringeth not forth good fruit is hewn down, and cast into the fire.

AXLETREE • Part of a wheeled vehicle.

1Ki 7:32–33

AZAL • A place near Jerusalem.

Zec 14:5 — And ye shall flee *to* the valley of the mountains; for the valley of the mountains shall reach unto Azal: yea, ye shall flee, like as ye fled from before the earthquake in the days of Uzziah king of Judah: and the LORD my God shall come, *and* all the saints with thee.

AZALIAH • Father of Shaphan.

2Ki 22:3 — And it came to pass in the eighteenth year of king Josiah, *that* the king sent Shaphan the son of Azaliah, the son of Meshullam, the scribe, to the house of the LORD, saying,

2Ch 34:8 — Now in the eighteenth year of his reign, when he had purged the land, and the house, he sent Shaphan the son of Azaliah, and Maaseiah the governor of the city, and Joah the son of Joahaz the recorder, to repair the house of the LORD his God.

AZANIAH • Father of Jeshua.

Ne 10:9 — And the Levites: both Jeshua the son of Azaniah, Binnui of the sons of Henadad, Kadmiel;

AZARAEL ✧See: Azareel

AZAREEL

• An Aaronite of the family of Korah.

1Ch 12:6 — Elkanah, and Jesiah, and Azareel, and Joezer, and Jashobeam, the Korhites,

• A musician in the temple.

1Ch 25:18 — The eleventh to Azareel, *he*, his sons, and his brethren, *were* twelve:

• Called Uzziel.

1Ch 25:4 — Of Heman: the sons of Heman; Bukkiah, Mattaniah, Uzziel, Shebuel, and Jerimoth, Hananiah, Hanani, Eliathah, Giddalti, and Romamti-ezer, Joshbekashah, Mallothi, Hothir, *and* Mahazioth:

• A Danite prince.

1Ch 27:22 — Of Dan, Azareel the son of Jeroham. These *were* the princes of the tribes of Israel.

• A son of Bani.

Ezr 10:41 — Azareel, and Shelemiah, Shemariah,

• A priest.

Ne 11:13 — And his brethren, chief of the fathers, two hundred forty and two: and Amashai the son of Azareel, the son of Ahasai, the son of Meshillemoth, the son of Immer,

Ne 12:36 — And his brethren, Shemaiah, and Azarael, Milalai, Gilalai, Maai, Nethaneel, and Judah, Hanani, with the musical instruments of David the man of God, and Ezra the scribe before them.

AZARIAH

• Son of Ethan.

1Ch 2:8 — And the sons of Ethan; Azariah.

• Son of Jehu.

1Ch 2:38–39

• Son of Zadok.

1Ki 4:2 — And these *were* the princes which he had; Azariah the son of Zadok the priest,

• Perhaps identical with a high priest called also Amariah.

• Captain of Solomon's guards.

1Ki 4:5 — And Azariah the son of Nathan *was* over the officers: and Zabud the son of Nathan *was* principal officer, *and* the king's friend:

• A prophet.

2Ch 15:1 — And the Spirit of God came upon Azariah the son of Oded:

• Called Oded.

2Ch 15:8 — And when Asa heard these words, and the prophecy of Oded the prophet, he took courage, and put away the abominable idols out of all the land of Judah and Benjamin, and out of the cities which he had taken from mount Ephraim, and renewed the altar of the LORD, that *was* before the porch of the LORD.

• A high priest.

1Ch 6:9 — And Ahimaaz begat Azariah, and Azariah begat Johanan,

• Called also Amariah.

2Ch 19:11 — And, behold, Amariah the chief priest is over you in all matters of the LORD; and

Zebadiah the son of Ishmael, the ruler of the house of Judah, for all the king's matters: also the Levites *shall be* officers before you. Deal courageously, and the LORD shall be with the good.

• Son of Jehoshaphat.

2Ch 21:2 — And he had brethren the sons of Jehoshaphat, Azariah, and Jehiel, and Zechariah, and Azariah, and Michael, and Shephatiah: all these *were* the sons of Jehoshaphat king of Israel.

• King of Judah.

2Ch 22:6 — And he returned to be healed in Jezreel because of the wounds which were given him at Ramah, when he fought with Hazael king of Syria. And Azariah the son of Jehoram king of Judah went down to see Jehoram the son of Ahab at Jezreel, because he was sick.

See: Ahaziah

• Son of Jeroham.

2Ch 23:1 — And in the seventh year Jehoiada strengthened himself, and took the captains of hundreds, Azariah the son of Jeroham, and Ishmael the son of Jehohanan, and Azariah the son of Obed, and Maaseiah the son of Adaiah, and Elishaphat the son of Zichri, into covenant with him.

• Son of Obed.

2Ch 23:1 — And in the seventh year Jehoiada strengthened himself, and took the captains of hundreds, Azariah the son of Jeroham, and Ishmael the son of Jehohanan, and Azariah the son of Obed, and Maaseiah the son of Adaiah, and Elishaphat the son of Zichri, into covenant with him.

• Son of Johanan. Possibly identical with Zechariah, son of Jehoiada.

1Ch 6:10–11; 2Ch 24:20–22

See: Uzziah; Called Azariah. King of Judah

• Chief of the tribe of Ephraim.

2Ch 28:12 — Then certain of the heads of the children of Ephraim, Azariah the son of Johanan, Berechiah the son of Meshillemoth, and Jehizkiah the son of Shallum, and Amasa the son of Hadlai, stood up against them that came from the war,

• A Levite.

1Ch 6:36 — The son of Elkanah, the son of Joel, the son of Azariah, the son of Zephaniah,

• Called Uzziah.

1Ch 6:24 — Tahath his son, Uriel his son, Uzziah his son, and Shaul his son.

• High priest in Hezekiah's reign.

2Ch 31:10 — And Azariah the chief priest of the house of Zadok answered him, and said, Since *the people* began to bring the offerings into the house of the LORD, we have had enough to eat, and have left plenty: for the LORD hath blessed his people; and that which is left *is* this great store.

2Ch 31:13 — And Jehiel, and Azaziah, and Nahath, and Asahel, and Jerimoth, and Jozabad, and Eliel, and Ismachiah, and Mahath, and Benaiah, *were* overseers under the hand of Cononiah and Shimei his brother, at the commandment of Hezekiah the king, and Azariah the ruler of the house of God.

• Probably identical with Ahitub mentioned in 1Ch 6:11–12.

• Son of Hilkiah.

1Ch 6:13–14

1Ch 9:11 — And Azariah the son of Hilkiah, the son of Meshullam, the son of Zadok, the son of Meraioth, the son of Ahitub, the ruler of the house of God;

Ezr 7:1 — Now after these things, in the reign of Artaxerxes king of Persia, Ezra the son of Seraiah, the son of Azariah, the son of Hilkiah,

Ezr 7:3 — The son of Amariah, the son of Azariah, the son of Meraioth,

• Son of Hoshaiah.

Jer 43:2–7

• Hebrew name of Abed-nego.

Da 1:7 — Unto whom the prince of the eunuchs gave names: for he gave unto Daniel *the name* of Belteshazzar; and to Hananiah, of Shadrach; and to Mishael, of Meshach; and to Azariah, of Abed-nego.

Da 1:19 — And the king communed with them; and among them all was found none like Daniel, Hananiah, Mishael, and Azariah: therefore stood they before the king.

• A captive returned from Babylon.

Ne 7:7 — Who came with Zerubbabel, Jeshua, Nehemiah, Azariah, Raamiah, Nahamani, Mordecai, Bilshan, Mispereth, Bigvai, Nehum, Baanah. The number, *I say,* of the men of the people of Israel *was this;*

Ne 10:2 — Seraiah, Azariah, Jeremiah,

• Called also Seraiah.

Ezr 2:2 — Which came with Zerubbabel: Jeshua, Nehemiah, Seraiah, Reelaiah, Mordecai, Bilshan, Mizpar, Bigvai, Rehum, Baanah. The number of the men of the people of Israel:

AZAZ • Father of Bela.

1Ch 5:8 — And Bela the son of Azaz, the son of Shema, the son of Joel, who dwelt in Aroer, even unto Nebo and Baal-meon:

AZAZEL • The scapegoat.

Le 16:8 — And Aaron shall cast lots upon the two goats; one lot for the LORD, and the other lot for the scapegoat.

Le 16:10 — But the goat, on which the lot fell to be the scapegoat, shall be presented alive before the LORD, to make an atonement with him, *and* to let him go for a scapegoat into the wilderness.

Le 16:26 — And he that let go the goat for the scapegoat shall wash his clothes, and bathe his flesh in water, and afterward come into the camp.

AZAZIAH

• A harper in the temple.

1Ch 15:21 — And Mattithiah, and Elipheleh, and Mikneiah, and Obed-edom, and Jeiel, and Azaziah, with harps on the Sheminith to excel.

• **Father of Hoshea.**

1Ch 27:20 — Of the children of Ephraim, Hoshea the son of Azaziah: of the half tribe of Manasseh, Joel the son of Pedaiah:

• **Overseer in temple.**

2Ch 31:13 — And Jehiel, and Azaziah, and Nahath, and Asahel, and Jerimoth, and Jozabad, and Eliel, and Ismachiah, and Mahath, and Benaiah, *were* overseers under the hand of Cononiah and Shimei his brother, at the commandment of Hezekiah the king, and Azariah the ruler of the house of God.

AZBUK • Father of Nehemiah.

Ne 3:16 — After him repaired Nehemiah the son of Azbuk, the ruler of the half part of Beth-zur, unto *the place* over against the sepulchres of David, and to the pool that was made, and unto the house of the mighty.

AZEKAH • A town of Judah.

Jos 10:10–11

Jos 15:35 — Jarmuth, and Adullam, Socoh, and Azekah,

1Sa 17:1 — Now the Philistines gathered together their armies to battle, and were gathered together at Shochoh, which *belongeth* to Judah, and pitched between Shochoh and Azekah, in Ephes-dammim.

2Ch 11:9 — And Adoraim, and Lachish, and Azekah,

Ne 11:30 — Zanoah, Adullam, and *in* their villages, at Lachish, and the fields thereof, at Azekah, and *in* the villages thereof. And they dwelt from Beer-sheba unto the valley of Hinnom.

Jer 34:7 — When the king of Babylon's army fought against Jerusalem, and against all the cities of Judah that were left, against Lachish, and against Azekah: for these defenced cities remained of the cities of Judah.

AZEL • A Benjamite.

1Ch 8:37–38; 9:43–44

AZEM • A city in the south of Judah. Called also Ezem.

Jos 15:29 — Baalah, and Iim, and Azem,

Jos 19:3 — And Hazar-shual, and Balah, and Azem,

1Ch 4:29 — And at Bilhah, and at Ezem, and at Tolad,

AZGAD

• **Ancestor of certain captives who returned from Babylon.**

Ezr 2:12 — The children of Azgad, a thousand two hundred twenty and two.

Ne 7:17 — The children of Azgad, two thousand three hundred twenty and two.

• **A returned exile.**

Ezr 8:12 — And of the sons of Azgad; Johanan the son of Hakkatan, and with him an hundred and ten males.

• **A chief who signed Nehemiah's covenant.**

Ne 10:15 — Bunni, Azgad, Bebai,

AZIEL • A temple musician.

1Ch 15:20 — And Zechariah, and Aziel, and Shemiramoth, and Jehiel, and Unni, and Eliab, and Maaseiah, and Benaiah, with psalteries on Alamoth;

AZIZA • Son of Zattu.

Ezr 10:27 — And of the sons of Zattu; Elioenai, Eliashib, Mattaniah, and Jeremoth, and Zabad, and Aziza.

AZMAVETH

• **One of David's heroes.**

2Sa 23:31 — Abi-albon the Arbathite, Azmaveth the Barhumite,

1Ch 11:33 — Azmaveth the Baharumite, Eliahba the Shaalbonite,

• **A descendant of Jonathan.**

1Ch 8:36 — And Ahaz begat Jehoadah; and Jehoadah begat Alemeth, and Azmaveth, and Zimri; and Zimri begat Moza,

1Ch 9:42 — And Ahaz begat Jarah; and Jarah begat Alemeth, and Azmaveth, and Zimri; and Zimri begat Moza;

• **Son of Adiel.**

1Ch 27:25 — And over the king's treasures *was* Azmaveth the son of Adiel: and over the storehouses in the fields, in the cities, and in the villages, and in the castles, *was* Jehonathan the son of Uzziah:

• **A village of Judah or Benjamin.**

Ezr 2:24 — The children of Azmaveth, forty and two.

Ne 12:29 — Also from the house of Gilgal, and out of the fields of Geba and Azmaveth: for the singers had builded them villages round about Jerusalem.

• **Called Beth-Azmaveth.**

Ne 7:28 — The men of Beth-azmaveth, forty and two.

AZMON • A place in the south of Canaan.

Nu 34:4–5

Jos 15:4 — *From thence* it passed toward Azmon, and went out unto the river of Egypt; and the goings out of that coast were at the sea: this shall be your south coast.

AZNOTH-TABOR • A town in Naphtali.

Jos 19:34 — And *then* the coast turneth westward to Aznoth-tabor, and goeth out from thence to Hukkok, and reacheth to Zebulun on the south side, and reacheth to Asher on the west side, and to Judah upon Jordan toward the sunrising.

AZOR

• **Ancestor of Jesus.**

Mt 1:13–14

• **Perhaps identical with Azrikam.**

1Ch 3:23 — And the sons of Neariah; Elioenai, and Hezekiah, and Azrikam, three.

AZOTUS See: Ashdod

AZRIEL

• A chief of Manasseh.

1Ch 5:24 — And these *were* the heads of the house of their fathers, even Epher, and Ishi, and Eliel, and Azriel, and Jeremiah, and Hodaviah, and Jahdiel, mighty men of valour, famous men, *and* heads of the house of their fathers.

• Father of Jerimoth.

1Ch 27:19 — Of Zebulun, Ishmaiah the son of Obadiah: of Naphtali, Jerimoth the son of Azriel:

• Father of Seriah.

Jer 36:26 — But the king commanded Jerahmeel the son of Hammelech, and Seraiah the son of Azriel, and Shelemiah the son of Abdeel, to take Baruch the scribe and Jeremiah the prophet: but the LORD hid them.

AZRIKAM

• Son of Neraiah.

1Ch 3:23 — And the sons of Neariah; Elioenai, and Hezekiah, and Azrikam, three.

• Son of Azel.

1Ch 8:38 — And Azel had six sons, whose names *are* these, Azrikam, Bocheru, and Ishmael, and Sheariah, and Obadiah, and Hanan. All these *were* the sons of Azel.

1Ch 9:44 — And Azel had six sons, whose names *are* these, Azrikam, Bocheru, and Ishmael, and Sheariah, and Obadiah, and Hanan: these *were* the sons of Azel.

• A Levite.

1Ch 9:14 — And of the Levites; Shemaiah the son of Hasshub, the son of Azrikam, the son of Hashabiah, of the sons of Merari;

Ne 11:15 — Also of the Levites: Shemaiah the son of Hashub, the son of Azrikam, the son of Hashabiah, the son of Bunni;

• Governor of the house of Ahaz.

2Ch 28:7 — And Zichri, a mighty man of Ephraim, slew Maaseiah the king's son, and Azrikam the governor of the house, and Elkanah *that was* next to the king.

AZUBAH

• Mother of Jehoshaphat.

1Ki 22:42 — Jehoshaphat *was* thirty and five years old when he began to reign; and he reigned twenty and five years in Jerusalem. And his mother's name *was* Azubah the daughter of Shilhi.

2Ch 20:31 — And Jehoshaphat reigned over Judah: *he was* thirty and five years old when he began to reign, and he reigned twenty and five years in Jerusalem. And his mother's name *was* Azubah the daughter of Shilhi.

• Wife of Caleb.

1Ch 2:18–19

AZUR • Father of Jaazaniah.

Eze 11:1 — Moreover the spirit lifted me up, and brought me unto the east gate of the LORD'S house, which looketh eastward: and behold at the door of the gate five and twenty men; among whom I saw Jaazaniah the son of Azur, and Pelatiah the son of Benaiah, the princes of the people.

AZZAH

• A city of the Philistines.

See: Gaza

AZZAN • Father of Paltiel.

Nu 34:26 — And the prince of the tribe of the children of Issachar, Paltiel the son of Azzan.

AZZUR

• An Israelite, who sealed Nehemiah's covenant.

Ne 10:17 — Ater, Hizkijah, Azzur,

• A Gibeonite.

Jer 28:1 — And it came to pass the same year, in the beginning of the reign of Zedekiah king of Judah, in the fourth year, *and* in the fifth month, *that* Hananiah the son of Azur the prophet, which *was* of Gibeon, spake unto me in the house of the LORD, in the presence of the priests and of all the people, saying,

B

BAAL

- **An idol of the Phenicians, god of the sun.**
  - **Wickedly worshiped by the Israelites in the time of the judges.**
    Jgs 2:10–23; 1Sa 7:3–4
  - **Wickedly worshiped by the kingdom of Israel.**
    Hos 1:1–2:23
    2Ki 17:16 — And they left all the commandments of the LORD their God, and made them molten images, *even* two calves, and made a grove, and worshipped all the host of heaven, and served Baal.
    Jer 23:13 — And I have seen folly in the prophets of Samaria; they prophesied in Baal, and caused my people Israel to err.
    Hos 13:1 — When Ephraim spake trembling, he exalted himself in Israel; but when he offended in Baal, he died.
  - **Wickedly worshiped under Ahab.**
    1Ki 16:31–33
    1Ki 18:18 — And he answered, I have not troubled Israel; but thou, and thy father's house, in that ye have forsaken the commandments of the LORD, and thou hast followed Baalim.
    1Ki 19:18 — Yet I have left *me* seven thousand in Israel, all the knees which have not bowed unto Baal, and every mouth which hath not kissed him.
  - **Wickedly worshiped under Jehoram.**
    2Ki 3:2 — And he wrought evil in the sight of the LORD; but not like his father, and like his mother: for he put away the image of Baal that his father had made.
  - **Wickedly worshiped by the Jews.**
    2Ch 22:2–4
    2Ki 21:3 — For he built up again the high places which Hezekiah his father had destroyed; and he reared up altars for Baal, and made a grove, as did Ahab king of Israel; and worshipped all the host of heaven, and served them.
    2Ch 24:7 — For the sons of Athaliah, that wicked woman, had broken up the house of God; and also all the dedicated things of the house of the LORD did they bestow upon Baalim.
    2Ch 28:2 — For he walked in the ways of the kings of Israel, and made also molten images for Baalim.
    2Ch 33:3 — For he built again the high places which Hezekiah his father had broken down, and he reared up altars for Baalim, and made groves, and worshipped all the host of heaven, and served them.
  - **Jeremiah expostulates against the worship of.**
    Jer 2:8 — The priests said not, Where *is* the LORD? and they that handle the law knew me not: the pastors also transgressed against me, and the prophets prophesied by Baal, and walked after *things that* do not profit.
    Jer 2:23 — How canst thou say, I am not polluted, I have not gone after Baalim? see thy way in the valley, know what thou hast done: *thou art* a swift dromedary traversing her ways;
    Jer 7:9 — Will ye steal, murder, and commit adultery, and swear falsely, and burn incense unto Baal, and walk after other gods whom ye know not;
- **Altars of.**
  - **Destroyed by Gideon.**
    Jgs 6:25–32
  - **Destroyed by Jehoiada.**
    2Ki 11:18 — And all the people of the land went into the house of Baal, and brake it down; his altars and his images brake they in pieces thoroughly, and slew Mattan the priest of Baal before the altars. And the priest appointed officers over the house of the LORD.
  - **Destroyed by Josiah.**
    2Ki 23:4–5
- **Prophets of, slain by Elijah.**
  1Ki 18:40 — And Elijah said unto them, Take the prophets of Baal; let not one of them escape. And they took them: and Elijah brought them down to the brook Kishon, and slew them there.
- **All worshipers of, destroyed by Jehu.**
  2Ki 10:18–25
- **A Benjamite.**
  1Ch 8:30 — And his firstborn son Abdon, and Zur, and Kish, and Baal, and Nadab,
  1Ch 9:36 — And his firstborn son Abdon, then Zur, and Kish, and Baal, and Ner, and Nadab,
- **A Reubenite.**
  1Ch 5:5 — Micah his son, Reaia his son, Baal his son,
- **A city in the tribe of Simeon.**
  1Ch 4:33 — And all their villages that *were* round about the same cities, unto Baal. These *were* their habitations, and their genealogy.
  - **Called Baalath-beer.**
    Jos 19:8 — And all the villages that *were* round about these cities to Baalath-beer, Ramath of the south. This is the inheritance of the tribe of the children of Simeon according to their families.

BAAL-BERITH

- **A god of the Shechemites.**
  Jgs 9:4 — And they gave him threescore and ten *pieces* of silver out of the house of Baal-berith, wherewith

Abimelech hired vain and light persons, which followed him.

- **Worshiped by Israelites.**

Jgs 8:33 — And it came to pass, as soon as Gideon was dead, that the children of Israel turned again, and went a whoring after Baalim, and made Baal-berith their god.

- **Called Berith.**

Jgs 9:46 — And when all the men of the tower of Shechem heard *that,* they entered into an hold of the house of the god Berith.

BAAL-GAD

- **A city of the Canaanites.**

Jos 11:17 — *Even* from the mount Halak, that goeth up to Seir, even unto Baal-gad in the valley of Lebanon under mount Hermon: and all their kings he took, and smote them, and slew them.

Jos 12:7 — And these *are* the kings of the country which Joshua and the children of Israel smote on this side Jordan on the west, from Baal-gad in the valley of Lebanon even unto the mount Halak, that goeth up to Seir; which Joshua gave unto the tribes of Israel *for* a possession according to their divisions;

Jos 13:5 — And the land of the Giblites, and all Lebanon, toward the sunrising, from Baal-gad under mount Hermon unto the entering into Hamath.

- **Probably identical with Baal-Hermon.**

Jgs 3:3 — *Namely,* five lords of the Philistines, and all the Canaanites, and the Sidonians, and the Hivites that dwelt in mount Lebanon, from mount Baal-hermon unto the entering in of Hamath.

1Ch 5:23 — And the children of the half tribe of Manasseh dwelt in the land: they increased from Bashan unto Baal-hermon and Senir, and unto mount Hermon.

BAAL-GUR ✦See: Gur-Baal

BAAL-HAMON

- **A place in Mount Ephraim.**

SS 8:11 — Solomon had a vineyard at Baal-hamon; he let out the vineyard unto keepers; every one for the fruit thereof was to bring a thousand *pieces* of silver.

- **Called Hammon.**

Jos 19:28 — And Hebron, and Rehob, and Hammon, and Kanah, *even* unto great Zidon;

BAAL-HANAN

- **A king of Edom.**

Ge 36:38–39; 1Ch 1:49–50

- **One of David's overseers.**

1Ch 27:28 — And over the olive trees and the sycomore trees that *were* in the low plains *was* Baal-hanan the Gederite: and over the cellars of oil *was* Joash:

BAAL-HAZOR • The place where Ammon was slain.

2Sa 13:23 — And it came to pass after two full years, that Absalom had sheepshearers in Baal-hazor, which *is* beside Ephraim: and Absalom invited all the king's sons.

BAAL-HERMON

- **A city near Mount Hermon.**

1Ch 5:23 — And the children of the half tribe of Manasseh dwelt in the land: they increased from Bashan unto Baal-hermon and Senir, and unto mount Hermon.

- **Identical with Baal-Gad.**

✦See: Baal-Gad

- **A mountain of Lebanon.**

Jgs 3:3 — *Namely,* five lords of the Philistines, and all the Canaanites, and the Sidonians, and the Hivites that dwelt in mount Lebanon, from mount Baal-hermon unto the entering in of Hamath.

BAAL-MEON

- **A city of the Reubenites.**

Nu 32:38 — And Nebo, and Baal-meon, (their names being changed,) and Shibmah: and gave other names unto the cities which they builded.

1Ch 5:8 — And Bela the son of Azaz, the son of Shema, the son of Joel, who dwelt in Aroer, even unto Nebo and Baal-meon:

Eze 25:9 — Therefore, behold, I will open the side of Moab from the cities, from his cities *which are* on his frontiers, the glory of the country, Beth-jeshimoth, Baal-meon, and Kiriathaim,

- **Called Beth-Meon.**

Jer 48:23 — And upon Kiriathaim, and upon Beth-gamul, and upon Beth-meon,

- **Called Beth-Baal-Meon.**

Jos 13:17 — Heshbon, and all her cities that *are* in the plain; Dibon, and Bamoth-baal, and Beth-baal-meon,

- **Called Beon.**

Nu 32:3 — Ataroth, and Dibon, and Jazer, and Nimrah, and Heshbon, and Elealeh, and Shebam, and Nebo, and Beon,

BAAL-PEOR • An idol of Moab.

Nu 25:3 — And Israel joined himself unto Baal-peor: and the anger of the LORD was kindled against Israel.

Nu 25:5 — And Moses said unto the judges of Israel, Slay ye every one his men that were joined unto Baal-peor.

Dt 4:3 — Your eyes have seen what the LORD did because of Baal-peor: for all the men that followed Baal-peor, the LORD thy God hath destroyed them from among you.

Ps 106:28 — They joined themselves also unto Baal-peor, and ate the sacrifices of the dead.

Hos 9:10 — I found Israel like grapes in the wilderness; I saw your fathers as the firstripe in the fig tree at her first time: *but* they went to Baal-peor, and separated themselves unto *that* shame; and *their* abominations were according as they loved.

BAAL-PERAZIM

• A place in the valley of Rephaim.

2Sa 5:20 — And David came to Baal-perazim, and David smote them there, and said, The LORD hath broken forth upon mine enemies before me, as the breach of waters. Therefore he called the name of that place Baal-perazim.

1Ch 14:11 — So they came up to Baal-perazim; and David smote them there. Then David said, God hath broken in upon mine enemies by mine hand like the breaking forth of waters: therefore they called the name of that place Baal-perazim.

• Called Perazim.

Isa 28:21 — For the LORD shall rise up as *in* mount Perazim, he shall be wroth as *in* the valley of Gibeon, that he may do his work, his strange work; and bring to pass his act, his strange act.

BAAL-SHALISHA • A place near Gilgal.

1Sa 9:4 — And he passed through mount Ephraim, and passed through the land of Shalisha, but they found *them* not: then they passed through the land of Shalim, and *there they were* not: and he passed through the land of the Benjamites, but they found *them* not.

2Ki 4:42 — And there came a man from Baal-shalisha, and brought the man of God bread of the firstfruits, twenty loaves of barley, and full ears of corn in the husk thereof. And he said, Give unto the people, that they may eat.

BAAL-TAMAR • A place near Gibeah.

Jgs 20:33 — And all the men of Israel rose up out of their place, and put themselves in array at Baal-tamar: and the liers in wait of Israel came forth out of their places, *even* out of the meadows of Gibeah.

BAAL-ZEBUB • A god of the Philistines.

2Ki 1:2–3

2Ki 1:6 — And they said unto him, There came a man up to meet us, and said unto us, Go, turn again unto the king that sent you, and say unto him, Thus saith the LORD, *Is it* not because *there is* not a God in Israel, *that* thou sendest to enquire of Baal-zebub the god of Ekron? therefore thou shalt not come down from that bed on which thou art gone up, but shalt surely die.

2Ki 1:16 — And he said unto him, Thus saith the LORD, Forasmuch as thou hast sent messengers to enquire of Baal-zebub the god of Ekron, *is it* not because *there is* no God in Israel to enquire of his word? therefore thou shalt not come down off that bed on which thou art gone up, but shalt surely die.

BAAL-ZEPHON • An Egyptian city on the Red Sea.

Ex 14:2 — Speak unto the children of Israel, that they turn and encamp before Pi-hahiroth, between Migdol and the sea, over against Baal-zephon: before it shall ye encamp by the sea.

Ex 14:9 — But the Egyptians pursued after them, all the horses *and* chariots of Pharaoh, and his horsemen, and his army, and overtook them encamping by the sea, beside Pi-hahiroth, before Baal-zephon.

Nu 33:7 — And they removed from Etham, and turned again unto Pi-hahiroth, which *is* before Baal-zephon: and they pitched before Migdol.

BAALAH

• A city in the south of Judah.

Jos 15:29 — Baalah, and Iim, and Azem,

• Apparently identical with Balah.

Jos 19:3 — And Hazar-shual, and Balah, and Azem,

• Apparently identical with Bilhah.

1Ch 4:29 — And at Bilhah, and at Ezem, and at Tolad,

• A city in the north of Judah. Called also Kirjath-Jearim, Kirjath-Jerim.

• A mountain in Judah.

Jos 15:11 — And the border went out unto the side of Ekron northward: and the border was drawn to Shicron, and passed along to mount Baalah, and went out unto Jabneel; and the goings out of the border were at the sea.

• Probably identical with Mount Jearim.

Jos 15:10 — And the border compassed from Baalah westward unto mount Seir, and passed along unto the side of mount Jearim, which *is* Chesalon, on the north side, and went down to Beth-shemesh, and passed on to Timnah:

BAALATH • A city of Dan.

Jos 19:44 — And Eltekeh, and Gibbethon, and Baalath,

1Ki 9:18 — and Baalath, and Tadmor in the wilderness, in the land,

2Ch 8:6 — And Baalath, and all the store cities that Solomon had, and all the chariot cities, and the cities of the horsemen, and all that Solomon desired to build in Jerusalem, and in Lebanon, and throughout all the land of his dominion.

BAALATH-BEER

• A city in the tribe of Simeon

See: Baal

BAALE

• A city of Judah.

2Sa 6:2 — And David arose, and went with all the people that *were* with him from Baale of Judah, to bring up from thence the ark of God, whose name is called by the name of the LORD of hosts that dwelleth *between* the cherubims.

See: Kirjath-Jearim

BAALI • An appellation of Jehovah.

Hos 2:16 — And it shall be at that day, saith the LORD, *that* thou shalt call me Ishi; and shall call me no more Baali.

BAALIM

• Plural form of Baal.

Jgs 2:11 — And the children of Israel did evil in the sight of the LORD, and served Baalim:

1Sa 7:4 — Then the children of Israel did put away Baalim and Ashtaroth, and served the LORD only.

Hos 2:13 — And I will visit upon her the days of Baalim, wherein she burned incense to them, and she decked herself with her earrings and her jewels, and she went after her lovers, and forgat me, saith the LORD.

Hos 2:17 — For I will take away the names of Baalim out of her mouth, and they shall no more be remembered by their name.

Hos 11:2 — *As* they called them, so they went from them: they sacrificed unto Baalim, and burned incense to graven images.

See: Baal

BAALIS • King of the Ammonites.

Jer 40:14 — And said unto him, Dost thou certainly know that Baalis the king of the Ammonites hath sent Ishmael the son of Nethaniah to slay thee? But Gedaliah the son of Ahikam believed them not.

BAANA

• Son of Ahilud.

1Ki 4:12 — Baana the son of Ahilud; *to him pertained* Taanach and Megiddo, and all Beth-shean, which is by Zartanah beneath Jezreel, from Beth-shean to Abel-meholah, *even* unto *the place that is* beyond Jokneam:

• Father of Zadok.

Ne 3:4 — And next unto them repaired Meremoth the son of Urijah, the son of Koz. And next unto them repaired Meshullam the son of Berechiah, the son of Meshezabeel. And next unto them repaired Zadok the son of Baana.

BAANAH

• A captain of Ish-bosheth's army.

2Sa 4:5–6

2Sa 4:2 — And Saul's son had two men *that were* captains of bands: the name of the one *was* Baanah, and the name of the other Rechab, the sons of Rimmon a Beerothite, of the children of Benjamin: (for Beeroth also was reckoned to Benjamin:

2Sa 4:9 — And David answered Rechab and Baanah his brother, the sons of Rimmon the Beerothite, and said unto them, As the LORD liveth, who hath redeemed my soul out of all adversity,

• Father of Heleb.

2Sa 23:29 — Heleb the son of Baanah, a Netophathite, Ittai the son of Ribai out of Gibeah of the children of Benjamin,

1Ch 11:30 — Maharai the Netophathite, Heled the son of Baanah the Netophathite,

• A chief Jew of the exile.

Ezr 2:2 — Which came with Zerubbabel: Jeshua, Nehemiah, Seraiah, Reelaiah, Mordecai, Bilshan, Mizpar, Bigvai, Rehum, Baanah. The number of the men of the people of Israel:

Ne 7:7 — Who came with Zerubbabel, Jeshua, Nehemiah, Azariah, Raamiah, Nahamani, Mordecai, Bilshan, Mispereth, Bigvai, Nehum, Baanah. The number, *I say,* of the men of the people of Israel *was this;*

Ne 10:27 — Malluch, Harim, Baanah.

• The name is spelled Baana. Son of Hushai.

1Ki 4:16 — Baanah the son of Hushai *was* in Asher and in Aloth:

BAARA

• Wife of Shaharaim.

1Ch 8:8 — And Shaharaim begat *children* in the country of Moab, after he had sent them away; Hushim and Baara *were* his wives.

• Called Hodesh.

1Ch 8:9 — And he begat of Hodesh his wife, Jobab, and Zibia, and Mesha, and Malcham,

BAASEIAH • A Levite.

1Ch 6:40 — The son of Michael, the son of Baaseiah, the son of Malchiah,

BAASHA • King of Israel.

1Ki 15:16–22; 15:27–16:7; 2Ch 16:1–6

1Ki 21:22 — And will make thine house like the house of Jeroboam the son of Nebat, and like the house of Baasha the son of Ahijah, for the provocation wherewith thou hast provoked *me* to anger, and made Israel to sin.

2Ki 9:9 — And I will make the house of Ahab like the house of Jeroboam the son of Nebat, and like the house of Baasha the son of Ahijah:

Jer 41:9 — Now the pit wherein Ishmael had cast all the dead bodies of the men, whom he had slain because of Gedaliah, *was* it which Asa the king had made for fear of Baasha king of Israel: *and* Ishmael the son of Nethaniah filled it with *them that were* slain.

BABBLER

• A sarcastic epithet applied to St. Paul.

Ac 17:18 — Then certain philosophers of the Epicureans, and of the Stoicks, encountered him. And some said, What will this babbler say? other some, He seemeth to be a setter forth of strange gods: because he preached unto them Jesus, and the resurrection.

BABEL

• A city in the plain of Shinar. Tower built, and tongues confused at.

Ge 11:1–9

See: Babylon

BABES

• In the mouths of, is praise perfected.

Mt 21:16 — And said unto him, Hearest thou what these say? And Jesus saith unto them, Yea; have ye never read, Out of the mouth of babes and sucklings thou hast perfected praise?

- **A symbol of the guileless.**

Ps 8:2 — Out of the mouth of babes and sucklings hast thou ordained strength because of thine enemies, that thou mightest still the enemy and the avenger.

Mt 11:25 — At that time Jesus answered and said, I thank thee, O Father, Lord of heaven and earth, because thou hast hid these things from the wise and prudent, and hast revealed them unto babes.

Lk 10:21 — In that hour Jesus rejoiced in spirit, and said, I thank thee, O Father, Lord of heaven and earth, that thou hast hid these things from the wise and prudent, and hast revealed them unto babes: even so, Father; for so it seemed good in thy sight.

- **A symbol of the children of the kingdom of heaven.**

Mt 18:2–6

Mk 10:15 — Verily I say unto you, Whosoever shall not receive the kingdom of God as a little child, he shall not enter therein.

Lk 18:17 — Verily I say unto you, Whosoever shall not receive the kingdom of God as a little child shall in no wise enter therein.

- **Figurative.**
  - **Of weak Christians.**

Ro 2:20 — An instructor of the foolish, a teacher of babes, which hast the form of knowledge and of the truth in the law.

Heb 5:13 — For every one that useth milk *is* unskilful in the word of righteousness: for he is a babe.

1Pe 2:2 — As newborn babes, desire the sincere milk of the word, that ye may grow thereby:

See: Children

See: Parents

BABYLON

- **City of.**
  - **Built by Nimrod.**

Ge 10:10 — And the beginning of his kingdom was Babel, and Erech, and Accad, and Calneh, in the land of Shinar.

  - **In the land of Shinar.**

Ge 10:10 — And the beginning of his kingdom was Babel, and Erech, and Accad, and Calneh, in the land of Shinar.

Ge 11:2 — And it came to pass, as they journeyed from the east, that they found a plain in the land of Shinar; and they dwelt there.

  - **Tower of.**

Ge 11:1–9

  - **Capital of the kingdom of Babylon.**

2Ch 36:6–7

2Ki 25:13 — And the pillars of brass that *were* in the house of the LORD, and the bases, and the brasen sea that *was* in the house of the LORD, did the Chaldees break in pieces, and carried the brass of them to Babylon.

2Ch 36:10 — And when the year was expired, king Nebuchadnezzar sent, and brought him to Babylon, with the goodly vessels of the house of the LORD, and made Zedekiah his brother king over Judah and Jerusalem.

2Ch 36:18 — And all the vessels of the house of God, great and small, and the treasures of the house of the LORD, and the treasures of the king, and of his princes; all *these* he brought to Babylon.

2Ch 36:20 — And them that had escaped from the sword carried he away to Babylon; where they were servants to him and his sons until the reign of the kingdom of Persia:

Da 4:30 — The king spake, and said, Is not this great Babylon, that I have built for the house of the kingdom by the might of my power, and for the honour of my majesty?

  - **Gates of.**

Isa 45:1–2

Jer 51:58 — Thus saith the LORD of hosts; The broad walls of Babylon shall be utterly broken, and her high gates shall be burned with fire; and the people shall labour in vain, and the folk in the fire, and they shall be weary.

  - **Walled.**

Jer 51:44 — And I will punish Bel in Babylon, and I will bring forth out of his mouth that which he hath swallowed up: and the nations shall not flow together any more unto him: yea, the wall of Babylon shall fall.

Jer 51:58 — Thus saith the LORD of hosts; The broad walls of Babylon shall be utterly broken, and her high gates shall be burned with fire; and the people shall labour in vain, and the folk in the fire, and they shall be weary.

  - **Splendor of.**

Isa 14:4 — That thou shalt take up this proverb against the king of Babylon, and say, How hath the oppressor ceased! the golden city ceased!

- **Peter writes from.**

1Pe 5:13 — The *church that is* at Babylon, elected together with *you,* saluteth you; and *so doth* Marcus my son.

- **Prophecies concerning.**

Ps 137:8–9; Isa 13:1–22; 14:4–26; 21:1–10; 46:1–2; 47:1–15; Jer 21:4–10; 25:12–14; 27:1–11; 34:2–3; 42:11–12; 43:1–13; 46:13–26; 49:28–30; 50:1–51:64; Eze 26:1–21; 29:17–20; Da 2:21–38; 4:10–26; 5:25–29; 7:1–28; Hab 1:5–11; Zec 2:7–9

Ps 87:4 — I will make mention of Rahab and Babylon to them that know me: behold Philistia, and Tyre, with Ethiopia; this *man* was born there.

Isa 48:14 — All ye, assemble yourselves, and hear; which among them hath declared these *things?* The LORD hath loved him: he will do his pleasure on Babylon, and his arm *shall be on* the Chaldeans.

Isa 48:20 — Go ye forth of Babylon, flee ye from the Chaldeans, with a voice of singing declare ye, tell this, utter it *even* to the end of the earth; say ye, The LORD hath redeemed his servant Jacob.

Jer 28:14 — For thus saith the LORD of hosts, the God of Israel; I have put a yoke of iron upon the neck of all these nations, that they may serve Nebuchadnezzar king of Babylon; and they shall serve him: and I have given him the beasts of the field also.

Jer 32:28 — Therefore thus saith the LORD; Behold, I will give this city into the hand of the Chaldeans, and into the hand of Nebuchadrezzar king of Babylon, and he shall take it:

Eze 21:19 — Also, thou son of man, appoint thee two ways, that the sword of the king of Babylon may come: both twain shall come forth out of one land: and choose thou a place, choose *it* at the head of the way to the city.

Eze 30:10 — Thus saith the Lord GOD; I will also make the multitude of Egypt to cease by the hand of Nebuchadrezzar king of Babylon.

Eze 32:11 — For thus saith the Lord GOD; The sword of the king of Babylon shall come upon thee.

• Figurative.

Rev 17:1–18:24

Rev 14:8 — And there followed another angel, saying, Babylon is fallen, is fallen, that great city, because she made all nations drink of the wine of the wrath of her fornication.

Rev 16:19 — And the great city was divided into three parts, and the cities of the nations fell: and great Babylon came in remembrance before God, to give unto her the cup of the wine of the fierceness of his wrath.

• Empire of.

• History of.

See: Assyria

See: Chaldea

See: Persia

• Founded by Nimrod.

Ge 10:10 — And the beginning of his kingdom was Babel, and Erech, and Accad, and Calneh, in the land of Shinar.

• Called Land of Shinar.

Zec 5:1–11

Ge 10:10 — And the beginning of his kingdom was Babel, and Erech, and Accad, and Calneh, in the land of Shinar.

Ge 11:2 — And it came to pass, as they journeyed from the east, that they found a plain in the land of Shinar; and they dwelt there.

Ge 14:1 — And it came to pass in the days of Amraphel king of Shinar, Arioch king of Ellasar, Chedorlaomer king of Elam, and Tidal king of nations;

Ge 14:9 — With Chedorlaomer the king of Elam, and with Tidal king of nations, and Amraphel king of Shinar, and Arioch king of Ellasar; four kings with five.

Isa 11:11 — And it shall come to pass in that day, *that* the Lord shall set his hand again the second time to recover the remnant of his people, which shall be left, from Assyria, and from Egypt, and from Pathros, and from Cush, and from Elam, and from Shinar, and from Hamath, and from the islands of the sea.

Da 1:2 — And the Lord gave Jehoiakim king of Judah into his hand, with part of the vessels of the house of God: which he carried into the land of Shinar to the house of his god; and he brought the vessels into the treasure house of his god.

• Called Sheshach.

Jer 41:1–18; 51:1–64

Jer 25:26 — And all the kings of the north, far and near, one with another, and all the kingdoms of the world, which *are* upon the face of the earth: and the king of Sheshach shall drink after them.

• Called Merathaim.

Jer 50:21 — Go up against the land of Merathaim, *even* against it, and against the inhabitants of Pekod: waste and utterly destroy after them, saith the LORD, and do according to all that I have commanded thee.

• Called also Chaldea.

See: Chaldea

• Divisions of.

Isa 23:12–13

2Ki 17:24 — And the king of Assyria brought *men* from Babylon, and from Cuthah, and from Ava, and from Hamath, and from Sepharvaim, and placed *them* in the cities of Samaria instead of the children of Israel: and they possessed Samaria, and dwelt in the cities thereof.

2Ki 24:7 — And the king of Egypt came not again any more out of his land: for the king of Babylon had taken from the river of Egypt unto the river Euphrates all that pertained to the king of Egypt.

Da 3:1 — Nebuchadnezzar the king made an image of gold, whose height *was* threescore cubits, *and* the breadth thereof six cubits: he set it up in the plain of Dura, in the province of Babylon.

Ac 7:4 — Then came he out of the land of the Chaldaeans, and dwelt in Charran: and from thence, when his father was dead, he removed him into this land, wherein ye now dwell.

• Extent of, at the time of Nebuchadnezzar.

Da 2:37–38

Da 4:1 — Nebuchadnezzar the king, unto all people, nations, and languages, that dwell in all the earth; Peace be multiplied unto you.

Da 6:1 — It pleased Darius to set over the kingdom an hundred and twenty princes, which should be over the whole kingdom;

• Extent of, at the time of Ahasuerus.

Est 1:1 — Now it came to pass in the days of Ahasuerus, (this *is* Ahasuerus which reigned, from India even unto Ethiopia, *over* an hundred and seven and twenty provinces:)

Est 8:9 — Then were the king's scribes called at that time in the third month, that *is,* the month Sivan, on the three and twentieth *day* thereof; and it was written according to all that Mordecai commanded unto the Jews, and to the lieutenants, and the deputies and rulers of the provinces which *are* from India unto

Ethiopia, an hundred twenty and seven provinces, unto every province according to the writing thereof, and unto every people after their language, and to the Jews according to their writing, and according to their language.

Est 9:30 — And he sent the letters unto all the Jews, to the hundred twenty and seven provinces of the kingdom of Ahasuerus, *with* words of peace and truth,

- **Armies of, invade ancient Canaan.**
  Ge 14:1–24
- **Armies of, invade Samaria.**
  2Ki 17:5–24
- **Armies of, invade Judah.**
  2Ki 24:1–16
- **Jews carried to.**
  2Ki 25:1–30; 2Ch 36:17–21; Jer 39:1–18; 52:1–34

  1Ch 9:1 — So all Israel were reckoned by genealogies; and, behold, they *were* written in the book of the kings of Israel and Judah, *who* were carried away to Babylon for their transgression.

  2Ch 33:11 — Wherefore the LORD brought upon them the captains of the host of the king of Assyria, which took Manasseh among the thorns, and bound him with fetters, and carried him to Babylon.

  Jer 32:2 — For then the king of Babylon's army besieged Jerusalem: and Jeremiah the prophet was shut up in the court of the prison, which *was* in the king of Judah's house.
- **Colonists from, sent to Samaria.**
  2Ki 17:29–32; Ezr 4:9–10
- **Conquest of Egypt by.**
  2Ki 24:7 — And the king of Egypt came not again any more out of his land: for the king of Babylon had taken from the river of Egypt unto the river Euphrates all that pertained to the king of Egypt.
- **Prophecies of conquests by.**
  2Ki 20:16–19; Jer 20:4–7; 21:1–22:30; 25:1–11; 27:1–29:32; 32:28–29; 34:1–22; 38:17–18; 43:8–13; 46:13–26; Eze 12:1–28; 17:1–24; 19:1–14; 21:1–32; 24:1–27; 26:1–21; 29:18–20; 30:1–26; 32:1–32

  Jer 36:29 — And thou shalt say to Jehoiakim the king of Judah, Thus saith the LORD; Thou hast burned this roll, saying, Why hast thou written therein, saying, The king of Babylon shall certainly come and destroy this land, and shall cause to cease from thence man and beast?
- **Prophetic denunciations against.**
  Ps 137:8–9; Isa 13:1–22; 43:14–17; 47:1–15; Jer 50:1–51:64

  Isa 14:21 — Prepare slaughter for his children for the iniquity of their fathers; that they do not rise, nor possess the land, nor fill the face of the world with cities.
- **Government of.**
  - **A limited monarchy.**
    Est 1:13–19

    Est 8:8 — Write ye also for the Jews, as it liketh you, in the king's name, and seal *it* with the king's ring: for the writing which is written in the king's name, and sealed with the king's ring, may no man reverse.

    Da 6:8 — Now, O king, establish the decree, and sign the writing, that it be not changed, according to the law of the Medes and Persians, which altereth not.

    Da 6:14 — Then the king, when he heard *these* words, was sore displeased with himself, and set *his* heart on Daniel to deliver him: and he laboured till the going down of the sun to deliver him.

    Da 6:17 — And a stone was brought and laid upon the mouth of the den; and the king sealed it with his own signet, and with the signet of his lords; that the purpose might not be changed concerning Daniel.
  - **Tyrannical.**
    Est 3:7–15; Da 3:1–30
- **Sovereigns of.**
  - **See: Belshazzar**
  - **See: Cyrus; king of Persia**
  - **See: Darius**
  - **See: Evil-Merodach**
  - **See: Nebuchadnezzar**

BACA • Valley of.

Ps 84:6 — *Who* passing through the valley of Baca make it a well; the rain also filleth the pools.

BACKBITING

Ps 15:1–3

Pr 25:23 — The north wind driveth away rain: so *doth* an angry countenance a backbiting tongue.

Ro 1:30 — Backbiters, haters of God, despiteful, proud, boasters, inventors of evil things, disobedient to parents,

2Co 12:20 — For I fear, lest, when I come, I shall not find you such as I would, and *that* I shall be found unto you such as ye would not: lest *there be* debates, envyings, wraths, strifes, backbitings, whisperings, swellings, tumults:

- **See: Accusation, False**
- **See: Slander**
- **See: Speaking; evil**

BACKSLIDERS

Le 26:14–42; Dt 8:11–14; 28:15–68; 29:18–28; 32:15–30; Jos 24:20–27; 1Ki 9:6–9; 2Ch 15:2–4; Job 34:26–27; Ps 44:20–21; Eze 33:12–13; Hos 11:7–8; Mk 4:15–19; Lk 11:21–26; 1Co 10:1–13; 2Co 12:20–21; Gal 1:6–7; 4:9–11; 1Ti 6:20–21; Heb 3:12–13; 5:11–12; 6:4–8; 10:26–29; 10:38–39; 11:14–15; 2Pe 2:20–21; Rev 2:4–5; 2:21–23; 3:2–3

Dt 4:9 — Only take heed to thyself, and keep thy soul diligently, lest thou forget the things which thine eyes have seen, and lest they depart from thy heart all the days of thy life: but teach them thy sons, and thy sons' sons;

Ezr 8:22 — For I was ashamed to require of the king a band of soldiers and horsemen to help us against the enemy in the way: because we had spoken unto the king, saying, The hand of our God *is* upon all them for good that seek him; but his power and his wrath *is* against all them that forsake him.

Ps 73:27 — For, lo, they that are far from thee shall perish: thou hast destroyed all them that go a whoring from thee.

Ps 85:8 — I will hear what God the LORD will speak: for he will speak peace unto his people, and to his saints: but let them not turn again to folly.

Ps 125:5 — As for such as turn aside unto their crooked ways, the LORD shall lead them forth with the workers of iniquity: *but* peace *shall be* upon Israel.

Pr 2:17 — Which forsaketh the guide of her youth, and forgetteth the covenant of her God.

Pr 14:14 — The backslider in heart shall be filled with his own ways: and a good man *shall be satisfied* from himself.

Pr 24:16 — For a just *man* falleth seven times, and riseth up again: but the wicked shall fall into mischief.

Pr 26:11 — As a dog returneth to his vomit, *so* a fool returneth to his folly.

Jer 17:13 — O LORD, the hope of Israel, all that forsake thee shall be ashamed, *and* they that depart from me shall be written in the earth, because they have forsaken the LORD, the fountain of living waters.

Eze 3:20 — Again, When a righteous *man* doth turn from his righteousness, and commit iniquity, and I lay a stumblingblock before him, he shall die: because thou hast not given him warning, he shall die in his sin, and his righteousness which he hath done shall not be remembered; but his blood will I require at thine hand.

Eze 18:24 — But when the righteous turneth away from his righteousness, and committeth iniquity, *and* doeth according to all the abominations that the wicked *man* doeth, shall he live? All his righteousness that he hath done shall not be mentioned: in his trespass that he hath trespassed, and in his sin that he hath sinned, in them shall he die.

Eze 18:26 — When a righteous *man* turneth away from his righteousness, and committeth iniquity, and dieth in them; for his iniquity that he hath done shall he die.

Eze 23:35 — Therefore thus saith the Lord GOD; Because thou hast forgotten me, and cast me behind thy back, therefore bear thou also thy lewdness and thy whoredoms.

Eze 33:18 — When the righteous turneth from his righteousness, and committeth iniquity, he shall even die thereby.

Jnh 2:4 — Then I said, I am cast out of thy sight; yet I will look again toward thy holy temple.

Mt 5:13 — Ye are the salt of the earth: but if the salt have lost his savour, wherewith shall it be salted? it is thenceforth good for nothing, but to be cast out, and to be trodden under foot of men.

Mt 12:45 — Then goeth he, and taketh with himself seven other spirits more wicked than himself, and they enter in and dwell there: and the last *state* of that man is worse than the first. Even so shall it be also unto this wicked generation.

Mt 24:12 — And because iniquity shall abound, the love of many shall wax cold.

Mt 26:31 — Then saith Jesus unto them, All ye shall be offended because of me this night: for it is written, I will smite the shepherd, and the sheep of the flock shall be scattered abroad.

Mk 4:7 — And some fell among thorns, and the thorns grew up, and choked it, and it yielded no fruit.

Mk 8:38 — Whosoever therefore shall be ashamed of me and of my words in this adulterous and sinful generation; of him also shall the Son of man be ashamed, when he cometh in the glory of his Father with the holy angels.

Mk 9:50 — Salt *is* good: but if the salt have lost his saltness, wherewith will ye season it? Have salt in yourselves, and have peace one with another.

Lk 9:62 — And Jesus said unto him, No man, having put his hand to the plough, and looking back, is fit for the kingdom of God.

Lk 17:32 — Remember Lot's wife.

Jn 6:67 — Then said Jesus unto the twelve, Will ye also go away?

Jn 15:6 — If a man abide not in me, he is cast forth as a branch, and is withered; and men gather them, and cast *them* into the fire, and they are burned.

Gal 3:1 — O foolish Galatians, who hath bewitched you, that ye should not obey the truth, before whose eyes Jesus Christ hath been evidently set forth, crucified among you?

Gal 5:7 — Ye did run well; who did hinder you that ye should not obey the truth?

1Ti 1:19 — Holding faith, and a good conscience; which some having put away concerning faith have made shipwreck:

1Ti 5:15 — For some are already turned aside after Satan.

1Ti 6:10 — For the love of money is the root of all evil: which while some coveted after, they have erred from the faith, and pierced themselves through with many sorrows.

2Ti 1:8 — Be not thou therefore ashamed of the testimony of our Lord, nor of me his prisoner: but be thou partaker of the afflictions of the gospel according to the power of God;

2Ti 2:12 — If we suffer, we shall also reign with *him:* if we deny *him,* he also will deny us:

2Ti 4:10 — For Demas hath forsaken me, having loved this present world, and is departed unto Thessalonica; Crescens to Galatia, Titus unto Dalmatia.

Heb 4:1 — Let us therefore fear, lest, a promise being left *us* of entering into his rest, any of you should seem to come short of it.

Heb 4:11 — Let us labour therefore to enter into that rest, lest any man fall after the same example of unbelief.

Heb 12:15 — Looking diligently lest any man fail of the grace of God; lest any root of bitterness springing up trouble *you,* and thereby many be defiled;

2Pe 1:9 — But he that lacketh these things is blind, and cannot see afar off, and hath forgotten that he was purged from his old sins.

2Jn 1:9 — Whosoever transgresseth, and abideth not in the doctrine of Christ, hath not God. He that abideth in the doctrine of Christ, he hath both the Father and the Son.

Rev 21:8 — But the fearful, and unbelieving, and the abominable, and murderers, and whoremongers, and sorcerers, and idolaters, and all liars, shall have their part in the lake which burneth with fire and brimstone: which is the second death.

See: Apostasy

See: Backsliders; backsliding of Israel

See: Church; backslidden

See: Reprobacy

- **Instances of.**
  - **Saul.**
    1Sa 15:11, 26–28
  - **Solomon.**
    1Ki 11:4–40; Ne 13:26
  - **Amon.**
    2Ki 21:22–23
  - **Rehoboam.**
    2Ch 12:1–2
  - **Asa.**
    2Ch 16:7–9
  - **Joash.**
    2Ch 24:24
  - **Amaziah.**
    2Ch 25:27
  - **Syrians.**
    Isa 17:10–11
  - **Jonah.**
    Jnh 1:3
  - **The disciples.**
    Mt 26:56; Jn 6:66
  - **Peter.**
    Mt 26:69–75
  - **Corinthian Christians.**
    1Co 5:1–8; 2Co 12:20–21
  - **Galatians.**
    Gal 1:6; 3:1; 4:9–11; 5:6–7
  - **Hymenaeus and Alexander.**
    1Ti 1:19–20
  - **Phygellus and Hermogenes.**
    2Ti 1:15
  - **Demas.**
    2Ti 4:10
  - **Churches of Asia.**
    1Ti 5:15; Rev 2:4, 14–15, 20; 3:2–3, 15–18
- **Promises to.**

Le 26:40–42; Dt 4:29–31; 30:1–10; 32:28–29; 1Ki 8:33–53; Job 22:23–30; Ps 81:13–14; Isa 57:18–19; Jer 3:4–7, 12–22; 4:1–2; Rev 3:15–21

Dt 32:26 — I said, I would scatter them into corners, I would make the remembrance of them to cease from among men:

2Ch 30:9 — For if ye turn again unto the LORD, your brethren and your children *shall find* compassion before them that lead them captive, so that they shall come again into this land: for the LORD your God *is* gracious and merciful, and will not turn away *his* face from you, if ye return unto him.

Ps 17:5 — Hold up my goings in thy paths, *that* my footsteps slip not.

Ps 56:13 — For thou hast delivered my soul from death: *wilt* not *thou deliver* my feet from falling, that I may walk before God in the light of the living?

Isa 42:3 — A bruised reed shall he not break, and the smoking flax shall he not quench: he shall bring forth judgment unto truth.

Jer 4:14 — O Jerusalem, wash thine heart from wickedness, that thou mayest be saved. How long shall thy vain thoughts lodge within thee?

Jer 6:16 — Thus saith the LORD, Stand ye in the ways, and see, and ask for the old paths, where is the good way, and walk therein, and ye shall find rest for your souls. But they said, We will not walk *therein.*

Hos 14:4 — I will heal their backsliding, I will love them freely: for mine anger is turned away from him.

Zec 10:6 — And I will strengthen the house of Judah, and I will save the house of Joseph, and I will bring them again to place them; for I have mercy upon them: and they shall be as though I had not cast them off: for I *am* the LORD their God, and will hear them.

Mal 3:7 — Even from the days of your fathers ye are gone away from mine ordinances, and have not kept *them.* Return unto me, and I will return unto you, saith the LORD of hosts. But ye said, Wherein shall we return?

Mt 23:37 — O Jerusalem, Jerusalem, *thou* that killest the prophets, and stonest them which are sent unto thee, how often would I have gathered thy children together, even as a hen gathereth her chickens under *her* wings, and ye would not!

Rev 3:8 — I know thy works: behold, I have set before thee an open door, and no man can shut it: for thou hast a little strength, and hast kept my word, and hast not denied my name.

See: Penitence

See: Penitent

See: Seekers

- **Return of.**

Ps 80:3–7, 14–19; Isa 31:6–7; Jer 50:4–6; Hos 6:1–3

Isa 17:7 — At that day shall a man look to his Maker, and his eyes shall have respect to the Holy One of Israel.

Isa 29:24 — They also that erred in spirit shall come to understanding, and they that murmured shall learn doctrine.

Hos 3:5 — Afterward shall the children of Israel return, and seek the LORD their God, and David their king; and shall fear the LORD and his goodness in the latter days.

- **Instances of.**
  - **Jews.**
    Ezr 6:16–21; 10:1–44
  - **David.**
    Ps 51:1–19
  - **Jonah.**
    Jnh 2:1–3:10

- **Peter.**
  Mt 26:75; Mk 14:72; Lk 22:62
- **Thomas.**
  Jn 20:27–29

• Backsliding of Israel.

Dt 4:25–31; 31:16–30; 32:5–6; Jgs 10:12–14; Ezr 9:13–14; Ps 78:10–11, 40–43, 56–64; 106:13–14; Isa 1:4–7, 21–22; 5:12–30; 9:13–21; 17:10–11; 24:5–6; 51:17–20; 65:2–3; Jer 2:11–13, 31–32; 3:1–25; 5:1–31; 7:12–8:22; 10:17–22; 11:9–17; 13:24–25; 15:1–14; 18:13–15; 19:1–15; 32:30–31; Eze 2:3–8; 5:1–17; 11:1–21; 15:1–16:63; 23:1–49; Hos 1:1–9; 2:1–3:5; 5:1–15; 6:4–11; 8:14–9:17; 13:16–14:1; Heb 3:16–18

Ex 17:7 — And he called the name of the place Massah, and Meribah, because of the chiding of the children of Israel, and because they tempted the LORD, saying, Is the LORD among us, or not?

Nu 14:43 — For the Amalekites and the Canaanites *are* there before you, and ye shall fall by the sword: because ye are turned away from the LORD, therefore the LORD will not be with you.

Dt 32:15 — But Jeshurun waxed fat, and kicked: thou art waxen fat, thou art grown thick, thou art covered *with fatness;* then he forsook God *which* made him, and lightly esteemed the Rock of his salvation.

Dt 32:18 — Of the Rock *that* begat thee thou art unmindful, and hast forgotten God that formed thee.

Jgs 2:12 — And they forsook the LORD God of their fathers, which brought them out of the land of Egypt, and followed other gods, of the gods of the people that *were* round about them, and bowed themselves unto them, and provoked the LORD to anger.

2Ki 18:1 — Now it came to pass in the third year of Hoshea son of Elah king of Israel, *that* Hezekiah the son of Ahaz king of Judah began to reign.

2Ki 18:12 — Because they obeyed not the voice of the LORD their God, but transgressed his covenant, *and* all that Moses the servant of the LORD commanded, and would not hear *them,* nor do *them.*

2Ch 13:11 — And they burn unto the LORD every morning and every evening burnt sacrifices and sweet incense: the shewbread also *set they in order* upon the pure table; and the candlestick of gold with the lamps thereof, to burn every evening: for we keep the charge of the LORD our God; but ye have forsaken him.

2Ch 24:20 — And the Spirit of God came upon Zechariah the son of Jehoiada the priest, which stood above the people, and said unto them, Thus saith God, Why transgress ye the commandments of the LORD, that ye cannot prosper? because ye have forsaken the LORD, he hath also forsaken you.

2Ch 27:2 — And he did *that which was* right in the sight of the LORD, according to all that his father Uzziah did: howbeit he entered not into the temple of the LORD. And the people did yet corruptly.

2Ch 29:6 — For our fathers have trespassed, and done *that which was* evil in the eyes of the LORD our God, and have forsaken him, and have turned away their faces from the habitation of the LORD, and turned *their* backs.

2Ch 29:8 — Wherefore the wrath of the LORD was upon Judah and Jerusalem, and he hath delivered them to trouble, to astonishment, and to hissing, as ye see with your eyes.

Ezr 9:10 — And now, O our God, what shall we say after this? for we have forsaken thy commandments,

Ne 9:26 — Nevertheless they were disobedient, and rebelled against thee, and cast thy law behind their backs, and slew thy prophets which testified against them to turn them to thee, and they wrought great provocations.

Isa 2:6 — Therefore thou hast forsaken thy people the house of Jacob, because they be replenished from the east, and *are* soothsayers like the Philistines, and they please themselves in the children of strangers.

Isa 30:9 — That this *is* a rebellious people, lying children, children *that* will not hear the law of the LORD:

Isa 30:15 — For thus saith the Lord GOD, the Holy One of Israel; In returning and rest shall ye be saved; in quietness and in confidence shall be your strength: and ye would not.

Isa 31:6 — Turn ye unto *him from* whom the children of Israel have deeply revolted.

Isa 43:22 — But thou hast not called upon me, O Jacob; but thou hast been weary of me, O Israel.

Isa 43:24 — Thou hast bought me no sweet cane with money, neither hast thou filled me with the fat of thy sacrifices: but thou hast made me to serve with thy sins, thou hast wearied me with thine iniquities.

Isa 50:1 — Thus saith the LORD, Where *is* the bill of your mother's divorcement, whom I have put away? or which of my creditors *is it* to whom I have sold you? Behold, for your iniquities have ye sold yourselves, and for your transgressions is your mother put away.

Isa 63:17 — O LORD, why hast thou made us to err from thy ways, *and* hardened our heart from thy fear? Return for thy servants' sake, the tribes of thine inheritance.

Jer 2:5 — Thus saith the LORD, What iniquity have your fathers found in me, that they are gone far from me, and have walked after vanity, and are become vain?

Jer 2:17 — Hast thou not procured this unto thyself, in that thou hast forsaken the LORD thy God, when he led thee by the way?

Jer 2:19 — Thine own wickedness shall correct thee, and thy backslidings shall reprove thee: know therefore and see that *it is* an evil *thing* and bitter, that thou hast forsaken the LORD thy God, and that my fear *is* not in thee, saith the Lord GOD of hosts.

Jer 2:21 — Yet I had planted thee a noble vine, wholly a right seed: how then art thou turned into the degenerate plant of a strange vine unto me?

Jer 2:27 — Saying to a stock, Thou *art* my father; and to a stone, Thou hast brought me forth: for they have turned *their* back unto me, and not *their* face: but in the time of their trouble they will say, Arise, and save us.

Jer 6:30 — Reprobate silver shall *men* call them, because the LORD hath rejected them.

Jer 12:7 — I have forsaken mine house, I have left mine heritage; I have given the dearly beloved of my soul into the hand of her enemies.

Jer 14:7 — O LORD, though our iniquities testify against us, do thou *it* for thy name's sake: for our backslidings are many; we have sinned against thee.

Jer 14:10 — Thus saith the LORD unto this people, Thus have they loved to wander, they have not refrained their feet, therefore the LORD doth not accept them; he will now remember their iniquity, and visit their sins.

Jer 50:6 — My people hath been lost sheep: their shepherds have caused them to go astray, they have turned them away *on* the mountains: they have gone from mountain to hill, they have forgotten their restingplace.

Eze 22:18 — Son of man, the house of Israel is to me become dross: all they *are* brass, and tin, and iron, and lead, in the midst of the furnace; they are *even* the dross of silver.

Hos 4:6 — My people are destroyed for lack of knowledge: because thou hast rejected knowledge, I will also reject thee, that thou shalt be no priest to me: seeing thou hast forgotten the law of thy God, I will also forget thy children.

Hos 4:10 — For they shall eat, and not have enough: they shall commit whoredom, and shall not increase: because they have left off to take heed to the LORD.

Hos 4:16 — For Israel slideth back as a backsliding heifer: now the LORD will feed them as a lamb in a large place.

Hos 11:2 — *As* they called them, so they went from them: they sacrificed unto Baalim, and burned incense to graven images.

Hos 11:7 — And my people are bent to backsliding from me: though they called them to the most High, none at all would exalt *him*.

Am 2:4 — Thus saith the LORD; For three transgressions of Judah, and for four, I will not turn away *the punishment* thereof; because they have despised the law of the LORD, and have not kept his commandments, and their lies caused them to err, after the which their fathers have walked:

Zep 1:6 — And them that are turned back from the LORD; and *those* that have not sought the LORD, nor enquired for him.

Mal 1:6 — A son honoureth *his* father, and a servant his master: if then I *be* a father, where *is* mine honour? and if I *be* a master, where *is* my fear? saith the LORD of hosts unto you, O priests, that despise my name. And ye say, Wherein have we despised thy name?

Mal 3:7 — Even from the days of your fathers ye are gone away from mine ordinances, and have not kept *them*. Return unto me, and I will return unto you, saith the LORD of hosts. But ye said, Wherein shall we return?

- **Instances of Israel's backsliding.**
  - **At Meribah.**
    Ex 17:1–7
  - **When Aaron made the golden calf.**
    Ex 32:1–35
  - **After Joshua's death.**
    Jgs 2:1–23
  - **During Asa's reign.**
    2Ch 15:1–19
  - **Hezekiah's reign.**
    2Ch 30:2–12

BAD COMPANY

See: Company; evil

BADGER

- **Skins of**
  - **Used for covering of tabernacle.**
    Nu 4:10–12

Ex 25:5 — And rams' skins dyed red, and badgers' skins, and shittim wood,

Ex 26:14 — And thou shalt make a covering for the tent *of* rams' skins dyed red, and a covering above *of* badgers' skins.

Ex 35:7 — And rams' skins dyed red, and badgers' skins, and shittim wood,

Ex 35:23 — And every man, with whom was found blue, and purple, and scarlet, and fine linen, and goats' *hair*, and red skins of rams, and badgers' skins, brought *them*.

Ex 36:19 — And he made a covering for the tent *of* rams' skins dyed red, and a covering *of* badgers' skins above *that*.

Ex 39:34 — And the covering of rams' skins dyed red, and the covering of badgers' skins, and the vail of the covering,

Nu 4:6 — And shall put thereon the covering of badgers' skins, and shall spread over *it* a cloth wholly of blue, and shall put in the staves thereof.

Nu 4:8 — And they shall spread upon them a cloth of scarlet, and cover the same with a covering of badgers' skins, and shall put in the staves thereof.

Nu 4:14 — And they shall put upon it all the vessels thereof, wherewith they minister about it, *even* the censers, the fleshhooks, and the shovels, and the basons, all the vessels of the altar; and they shall spread upon it a covering of badgers' skins, and put to the staves of it.

Nu 4:25 — And they shall bear the curtains of the tabernacle, and the tabernacle of the congregation, his covering, and the covering of the badgers' skins that *is* above upon it, and the hanging for the door of the tabernacle of the congregation,

- **Used for shoes.**

Eze 16:10 — I clothed thee also with broidered work, and shod thee with badgers' skin, and I girded thee about with fine linen, and I covered thee with silk.

BAGPIPE • A musical instrument.

Da 3:5 — *That* at what time ye hear the sound of the cornet, flute, harp, sackbut, psaltery, dulcimer, and all kinds of musick, ye fall down and worship the golden image that Nebuchadnezzar the king hath set up:

BAHURIM • A village between the fords of the Jordan and Jerusalem.

2Sa 3:16 — And her husband went with her along weeping behind her to Bahurim. Then said Abner unto him, Go, return. And he returned.

2Sa 16:5 — And when king David came to Bahurim, behold, thence came out a man of the family of the house of Saul, whose name *was* Shimei, the son of Gera: he came forth, and cursed still as he came.

2Sa 17:18 — Nevertheless a lad saw them, and told Absalom: but they went both of them away quickly, and came to a man's house in Bahurim, which had a well in his court; whither they went down.

2Sa 19:16 — And Shimei the son of Gera, a Benjamite, which *was* of Bahurim, hasted and came down with the men of Judah to meet king David.

1Ki 2:8 — And, behold, *thou hast* with thee Shimei the son of Gera, a Benjamite of Bahurim, which cursed me with a grievous curse in the day when I went to Mahanaim: but he came down to meet me at Jordan, and I sware to him by the LORD, saying, I will not put thee to death with the sword.

BAIL

See: Surety

See: Creditor

See: Debt

See: Debtor

BAJITH • A place of idolatrous worship in Moab.

Isa 15:2 — He is gone up to Bajith, and to Dibon, the high places, to weep: Moab shall howl over Nebo, and over Medeba: on all their heads *shall be* baldness, *and* every beard cut off.

BAKBAKKAR • A Levite.

1Ch 9:15 — And Bakbakkar, Heresh, and Galal, and Mattaniah the son of Micah, the son of Zichri, the son of Asaph;

BAKBUK • An ancestor of the Nethinim.

Ezr 2:51 — The children of Bakbuk, the children of Hakupha, the children of Harhur,

Ne 7:53 — The children of Bakbuk, the children of Hakupha, the children of Harhur,

BAKBUKIAH • A Levite.

Ne 11:17 — And Mattaniah the son of Micha, the son of Zabdi, the son of Asaph, *was* the principal to begin the thanksgiving in prayer: and Bakbukiah the second among his brethren, and Abda the son of Shammua, the son of Galal, the son of Jeduthun.

Ne 12:9 — Also Bakbukiah and Unni, their brethren, *were* over against them in the watches.

Ne 12:25 — Mattaniah, and Bakbukiah, Obadiah, Meshullam, Talmon, Akkub, *were* porters keeping the ward at the thresholds of the gates.

BAKER

1Sa 8:13 — And he will take your daughters *to be* confectionaries, and *to be* cooks, and *to be* bakers.

Jer 37:21 — Then Zedekiah the king commanded that they should commit Jeremiah into the court of the prison, and that they should give him daily a piece of bread out of the bakers' street, until all the bread in the city were spent. Thus Jeremiah remained in the court of the prison.

Hos 7:4 — They *are* all adulterers, as an oven heated by the baker, *who* ceaseth from raising after he hath kneaded the dough, until it be leavened.

Hos 7:6 — For they have made ready their heart like an oven, whiles they lie in wait: their baker sleepeth all the night; in the morning it burneth as a flaming fire.

• Pharaoh's chief baker.

Ge 40:1–23

See: Bread

BALAAM

• Son of Beor.

• From Mesopotamia.

Dt 23:4 — Because they met you not with bread and with water in the way, when ye came forth out of Egypt; and because they hired against thee Balaam the son of Beor of Pethor of Mesopotamia, to curse thee.

• A soothsayer.

Jos 13:22 — Balaam also the son of Beor, the soothsayer, did the children of Israel slay with the sword among them that were slain by them.

• A prophet.

Nu 24:2–9; 2Pe 2:15–16

• Balak sends for, to curse Israel.

Nu 22:5–7

Jos 24:9 — Then Balak the son of Zippor, king of Moab, arose and warred against Israel, and sent and called Balaam the son of Beor to curse you:

Ne 13:2 — Because they met not the children of Israel with bread and with water, but hired Balaam against them, that he should curse them: howbeit our God turned the curse into a blessing.

Mic 6:5 — O my people, remember now what Balak king of Moab consulted, and what Balaam the son of Beor answered him from Shittim unto Gilgal; that ye may know the righteousness of the LORD.

• Anger of, rebuked by his ass.

Nu 22:22–35

2Pe 2:16 — But was rebuked for his iniquity: the dumb ass speaking with man's voice forbad the madness of the prophet.

• Counsel of, an occasion of Israel's corruption with the Midianites.

Rev 2:14–15

Nu 31:16 — Behold, these caused the children of Israel, through the counsel of Balaam, to commit trespass against the LORD in the matter of Peor, and there was a plague among the congregation of the LORD.

• Covetousness of.

2Pe 2:15 — Which have forsaken the right way, and are gone astray, following the way of Balaam *the son* of Bosor, who loved the wages of unrighteousness;

Jude 1:11 — Woe unto them! for they have gone in the way of Cain, and ran greedily after the error of Balaam for reward, and perished in the gainsaying of Core.

• Death of.

Nu 31:8 — And they slew the kings of Midian, beside the rest of them that were slain; *namely,* Evi, and Rekem, and Zur, and Hur, and Reba, five kings of Midian: Balaam also the son of Beor they slew with the sword.

Jos 13:22 — Balaam also the son of Beor, the soothsayer, did the children of Israel slay with the sword among them that were slain by them.

BALAC ⇜See: Balak

BALAH

• A city of Simeon.

Jos 19:3 — And Hazar-shual, and Balah, and Azem,

• Called Bilhah.

1Ch 4:29 — And at Bilhah, and at Ezem, and at Tolad,

BALAK

• King of Moab.

Nu 22:4 — And Moab said unto the elders of Midian, Now shall this company lick up all *that are* round about us, as the ox licketh up the grass of the field. And Balak the son of Zippor *was* king of the Moabites at that time.

Jos 24:9 — Then Balak the son of Zippor, king of Moab, arose and warred against Israel, and sent and called Balaam the son of Beor to curse you:

Jgs 11:25 — And now *art* thou any thing better than Balak the son of Zippor, king of Moab? did he ever strive against Israel, or did he ever fight against them,

Mic 6:5 — O my people, remember now what Balak king of Moab consulted, and what Balaam the son of Beor answered him from Shittim unto Gilgal; that ye may know the righteousness of the LORD.

• Tries to bribe Balaam to curse Israel.

Nu 22:5–7, 15–17

⇜**See: Balaam**

BALANCES

• Used for weighing.

Job 31:6 — Let me be weighed in an even balance, that God may know mine integrity.

Isa 40:12 — Who hath measured the waters in the hollow of his hand, and meted out heaven with the span, and comprehended the dust of the earth in a measure, and weighed the mountains in scales, and the hills in a balance?

Isa 40:15 — Behold, the nations *are* as a drop of a bucket, and are counted as the small dust of the balance: behold, he taketh up the isles as a very little thing.

Eze 5:1 — And thou, son of man, take thee a sharp knife, take thee a barber's razor, and cause *it* to pass upon thine head and upon thy beard: then take thee balances to weigh, and divide the *hair.*

• Money weighed with.

Isa 46:6 — They lavish gold out of the bag, and weigh silver in the balance, *and* hire a goldsmith; and he maketh it a god: they fall down, yea, they worship.

Jer 32:10 — And I subscribed the evidence, and sealed *it,* and took witnesses, and weighed *him* the money in the balances.

• Must be just.

Le 19:36 — Just balances, just weights, a just ephah, and a just hin, shall ye have: I *am* the LORD your God, which brought you out of the land of Egypt.

Pr 16:11 — A just weight and balance *are* the LORD'S: all the weights of the bag *are* his work.

Eze 45:10 — Ye shall have just balances, and a just ephah, and a just bath.

• False balance used.

Hos 12:7 — *He is* a merchant, the balances of deceit *are* in his hand: he loveth to oppress.

Am 8:5 — Saying, When will the new moon be gone, that we may sell corn? and the sabbath, that we may set forth wheat, making the ephah small, and the shekel great, and falsifying the balances by deceit?

Mic 6:11 — Shall I count *them* pure with the wicked balances, and with the bag of deceitful weights?

• An abomination.

Pr 11:1 — A false balance *is* abomination to the LORD: but a just weight *is* his delight.

Pr 20:23 — Divers weights *are* an abomination unto the LORD; and a false balance *is* not good.

• Figurative.

Job 6:2 — O that my grief were throughly weighed, and my calamity laid in the balances together!

Job 31:6 — Let me be weighed in an even balance, that God may know mine integrity.

Ps 62:9 — Surely men of low degree *are* vanity, *and* men of high degree *are* a lie: to be laid in the balance, they *are* altogether *lighter* than vanity.

Isa 40:12 — Who hath measured the waters in the hollow of his hand, and meted out heaven with the span, and comprehended the dust of the earth in a measure, and weighed the mountains in scales, and the hills in a balance?

Da 5:27 — TEKEL; Thou art weighed in the balances, and art found wanting.

Rev 6:5 — And when he had opened the third seal, I heard the third beast say, Come and see. And I beheld, and lo a black horse; and he that sat on him had a pair of balances in his hand.

BALDNESS

Le 13:40–41

• A judgment.

Isa 3:24 — And it shall come to pass, *that* instead of sweet smell there shall be stink; and instead of a girdle a rent; and instead of well set hair baldness; and instead of a stomacher a girding of sackcloth; *and* burning instead of beauty.

Jer 47:5 — Baldness is come upon Gaza; Ashkelon is cut off *with* the remnant of their valley: how long wilt thou cut thyself?

Jer 48:37 — For every head *shall be* bald, and every beard clipped: upon all the hands *shall be* cuttings, and upon the loins sackcloth.

Eze 7:18 — They shall also gird *themselves* with sackcloth, and horror shall cover them; and shame *shall be* upon all faces, and baldness upon all their heads.

• Artificial, a sign of mourning.

Isa 22:12 — And in that day did the Lord God of hosts call to weeping, and to mourning, and to baldness, and to girding with sackcloth:

Jer 16:6 — Both the great and the small shall die in this land: they shall not be buried, neither shall *men* lament for them, nor cut themselves, nor make themselves bald for them:

Eze 27:31 — And they shall make themselves utterly bald for thee, and gird them with sackcloth, and they shall weep for thee with bitterness of heart *and* bitter wailing.

Eze 29:18 — Son of man, Nebuchadrezzar king of Babylon caused his army to serve a great service against Tyrus: every head *was* made bald, and every shoulder *was* peeled: yet had he no wages, nor his army, for Tyrus, for the service that he had served against it:

Am 8:10 — And I will turn your feasts into mourning, and all your songs into lamentation; and I will bring up sackcloth upon all loins, and baldness upon every head; and I will make it as the mourning of an only *son,* and the end thereof as a bitter day.

Mic 1:16 — Make thee bald, and poll thee for thy delicate children; enlarge thy baldness as the eagle; for they are gone into captivity from thee.

• Artificial, as an idolatrous practice, forbidden.

Le 21:5 — They shall not make baldness upon their head, neither shall they shave off the corner of their beard, nor make any cuttings in their flesh.

Dt 14:1 — Ye *are* the children of the Lord your God: ye shall not cut yourselves, nor make any baldness between your eyes for the dead.

• Instances of.

• Elisha.

2Ki 2:23

BALL • Playing at.

Isa 22:18 — He will surely violently turn and toss thee *like* a ball into a large country: there shalt thou die, and there the chariots of thy glory *shall be* the shame of thy lord's house.

BALM • A medicinal balsam.

Ge 37:25 — And they sat down to eat bread: and they lifted up their eyes and looked, and, behold, a company of Ishmeelites came from Gilead with their camels bearing spicery and balm and myrrh, going to carry *it* down to Egypt.

Ge 43:11 — And their father Israel said unto them, If *it must be* so now, do this; take of the best fruits in the land in your vessels, and carry down the man a present, a little balm, and a little honey, spices, and myrrh, nuts, and almonds:

Jer 8:22 — *Is there* no balm in Gilead; *is there* no physician there? why then is not the health of the daughter of my people recovered?

Jer 46:11 — Go up into Gilead, and take balm, O virgin, the daughter of Egypt: in vain shalt thou use many medicines; *for* thou shalt not be cured.

Jer 51:8 — Babylon is suddenly fallen and destroyed: howl for her; take balm for her pain, if so she may be healed.

Eze 27:17 — Judah, and the land of Israel, they *were* thy merchants: they traded in thy market wheat of Minnith, and Pannag, and honey, and oil, and balm.

BAMAH • A high place.

Eze 20:29 — Then I said unto them, What *is* the high place whereunto ye go? And the name thereof is called Bamah unto this day.

BAMOTH

• A camping place of the Israelites.

Nu 21:19–20

• A city of Reuben.

• Called Bamoth-Baal.

Jos 13:17 — Heshbon, and all her cities that *are* in the plain; Dibon, and Bamoth-baal, and Beth-baal-meon,

BANI

• A Gadite.

2Sa 23:36 — Igal the son of Nathan of Zobah, Bani the Gadite,

• A Levite.

1Ch 6:46 — The son of Amzi, the son of Bani, the son of Shamer,

• A descendant of Pharez.

1Ch 9:4 — Uthai the son of Ammihud, the son of Omri, the son of Imri, the son of Bani, of the children of Pharez the son of Judah.

• Father of returned exiles.

Ezr 2:10 — The children of Bani, six hundred forty and two.

Ezr 10:29 — And of the sons of Bani; Meshullam, Malluch, and Adaiah, Jashub, and Sheal, and Ramoth.

• Called Binnui.

Ne 7:15 — The children of Binnui, six hundred forty and eight.

• A Levite of the returned exiles.

Ne 9:4–5

Ne 3:17 — After him repaired the Levites, Rehum the son of Bani. Next unto him repaired Hashabiah, the ruler of the half part of Keilah, in his part.

Ne 8:7 — Also Jeshua, and Bani, and Sherebiah, Jamin, Akkub, Shabbethai, Hodijah, Maaseiah, Kelita, Azariah, Jozabad, Hanan, Pelaiah, and the Levites, caused the people to understand the law: and the people *stood* in their place.

Ne 10:13 — Hodijah, Bani, Beninu.

Ne 11:22 — The overseer also of the Levites at Jerusalem *was* Uzzi the son of Bani, the son of Hashabiah, the son of Mattaniah, the son of Micha. Of the sons of Asaph, the singers *were* over the business of the house of God.

BANISHMENT

Ezr 7:26 — And whosoever will not do the law of thy God, and the law of the king, let judgment be executed speedily upon him, whether *it be* unto death, or to banishment, or to confiscation of goods, or to imprisonment.

• Of Adam and Eve, from Eden.

Ge 3:22–24

• Of Cain, to be "a fugitive and vagabond".

Ge 4:14 — Behold, thou hast driven me out this day from the face of the earth; and from thy face shall I be hid; and I shall be a fugitive and a vagabond in the earth; and it shall come to pass, *that* every one that findeth me shall slay me.

• Of Jews, from Rome.

Ac 18:2 — And found a certain Jew named Aquila, born in Pontus, lately come from Italy, with his wife Priscilla; (because that Claudius had commanded all Jews to depart from Rome:) and came unto them.

• Of John, to Patmos.

Rev 1:9 — I John, who also am your brother, and companion in tribulation, and in the kingdom and patience of Jesus Christ, was in the isle that is called Patmos, for the word of God, and for the testimony of Jesus Christ.

See: Exile

BANNER

• Figurative.

Ps 20:5 — We will rejoice in thy salvation, and in the name of our God we will set up *our* banners: the LORD fulfil all thy petitions.

Ps 60:4 — Thou hast given a banner to them that fear thee, that it may be displayed because of the truth. Selah.

SS 2:4 — He brought me to the banqueting house, and his banner over me *was* love.

SS 6:4 — Thou *art* beautiful, O my love, as Tirzah, comely as Jerusalem, terrible as *an army* with banners.

Isa 13:2 — Lift ye up a banner upon the high mountain, exalt the voice unto them, shake the hand, that they may go into the gates of the nobles.

See: Ensign

See: Standard

BANQUET See: Feasts

BAPTISM

• John's.

Mt 3:5–8, 13–16; Mk 1:4–5, 8–10; Lk 3:7–8; 7:29–30; Jn 1:25–26; Ac 19:3–4

Mt 3:11 — I indeed baptize you with water unto repentance: but he that cometh after me is mightier than I, whose shoes I am not worthy to bear: he shall baptize you with the Holy Ghost, and *with* fire:

Mt 21:25 — The baptism of John, whence was it? from heaven, or of men? And they reasoned with themselves, saying, If we shall say, From heaven; he will say unto us, Why did ye not then believe him?

Mk 11:30 — The baptism of John, was *it* from heaven, or of men? answer me.

Lk 3:12 — Then came also publicans to be baptized, and said unto him, Master, what shall we do?

Lk 3:21 — Now when all the people were baptized, it came to pass, that Jesus also being baptized, and praying, the heaven was opened,

Lk 20:4 — The baptism of John, was it from heaven, or of men?

Jn 1:28 — These things were done in Bethabara beyond Jordan, where John was baptizing.

Jn 1:31 — And I knew him not: but that he should be made manifest to Israel, therefore am I come baptizing with water.

Jn 1:33 — And I knew him not: but he that sent me to baptize with water, the same said unto me, Upon whom thou shalt see the Spirit descending, and remaining on him, the same is he which baptizeth with the Holy Ghost.

Jn 3:23 — And John also was baptizing in Aenon near to Salim, because there was much water there: and they came, and were baptized.

Jn 10:40 — And went away again beyond Jordan into the place where John at first baptized; and there he abode.

Ac 1:5 — For John truly baptized with water; but ye shall be baptized with the Holy Ghost not many days hence.

Ac 1:22 — Beginning from the baptism of John, unto that same day that he was taken up from us, must one be ordained to be a witness with us of his resurrection.

Ac 10:37 — That word, *I say,* ye know, which was published throughout all Judaea, and began from Galilee, after the baptism which John preached;

Ac 11:16 — Then remembered I the word of the Lord, how that he said, John indeed baptized with water; but ye shall be baptized with the Holy Ghost.

Ac 18:25 — This man was instructed in the way of the Lord; and being fervent in the spirit, he spake and taught diligently the things of the Lord, knowing only the baptism of John.

• Christian.

Jn 4:1–2; Ac 8:12–13, 36–38; 10:46–48; 16:14–15; 19:4–5; Ro 6:3–4; 1Co 1:13–17; 10:1–2

Mt 28:19 — Go ye therefore, and teach all nations, baptizing them in the name of the Father, and of the Son, and of the Holy Ghost:

Mk 16:16 — He that believeth and is baptized shall be saved; but he that believeth not shall be damned.

Jn 3:5 — Jesus answered, Verily, verily, I say unto thee, Except a man be born of water and *of* the Spirit, he cannot enter into the kingdom of God.

Jn 3:22 — After these things came Jesus and his disciples into the land of Judaea; and there he tarried with them, and baptized.

Ac 1:5 — For John truly baptized with water; but ye shall be baptized with the Holy Ghost not many days hence.

Ac 1:22 — Beginning from the baptism of John, unto that same day that he was taken up from us, must one be ordained to be a witness with us of his resurrection.

Ac 2:38 — Then Peter said unto them, Repent, and be baptized every one of you in the name of Jesus Christ for the remission of sins, and ye shall receive the gift of the Holy Ghost.

Ac 2:41 — Then they that gladly received his word were baptized: and the same day there were added *unto them* about three thousand souls.

Ac 8:16 — (For as yet he was fallen upon none of them: only they were baptized in the name of the Lord Jesus.)

Ac 9:18 — And immediately there fell from his eyes as it had been scales: and he received sight forthwith, and arose, and was baptized.

Ac 16:33 — And he took them the same hour of the night, and washed *their* stripes; and was baptized, he and all his, straightway.

Ac 18:8 — And Crispus, the chief ruler of the synagogue, believed on the Lord with all his house; and many of the Corinthians hearing believed, and were baptized.

Ac 18:25 — This man was instructed in the way of the Lord; and being fervent in the spirit, he spake and taught diligently the things of the Lord, knowing only the baptism of John.

Ac 22:16 — And now why tarriest thou? arise, and be baptized, and wash away thy sins, calling on the name of the Lord.

1Co 12:13 — For by one Spirit are we all baptized into one body, whether *we be* Jews or Gentiles, whether *we be* bond or free; and have been all made to drink into one Spirit.

1Co 15:29 — Else what shall they do which are baptized for the dead, if the dead rise not at all? why are they then baptized for the dead?

Gal 3:27 — For as many of you as have been baptized into Christ have put on Christ.

Eph 4:5 — One Lord, one faith, one baptism,

Eph 5:26 — That he might sanctify and cleanse it with the washing of water by the word,

Col 2:12 — Buried with him in baptism, wherein also ye are risen with *him* through the faith of the operation of God, who hath raised him from the dead.

Heb 6:2 — Of the doctrine of baptisms, and of laying on of hands, and of resurrection of the dead, and of eternal judgment.

1Pe 3:18 — For Christ also hath once suffered for sins, the just for the unjust, that he might bring us to God, being put to death in the flesh, but quickened by the Spirit:

1Pe 3:21 — The like figure whereunto *even* baptism doth also now save us (not the putting away of the filth of the flesh, but the answer of a good conscience toward God,) by the resurrection of Jesus Christ:

• Of the Holy Ghost.

Joel 2:28–29; Jn 1:32–33; Ac 2:1–4; 8:15–17; 10:44–45; 11:15–16; Tit 3:5–6; 1Pe 3:20–21

Isa 44:3 — For I will pour water upon him that is thirsty, and floods upon the dry ground: I will pour my spirit upon thy seed, and my blessing upon thine offspring:

Zec 12:10 — And I will pour upon the house of David, and upon the inhabitants of Jerusalem, the spirit of grace and of supplications: and they shall look upon me whom they have pierced, and they shall mourn for him, as one mourneth for *his* only *son*, and shall be in bitterness for him, as one that is in bitterness for *his* firstborn.

Mt 3:11 — I indeed baptize you with water unto repentance: but he that cometh after me is mightier than I, whose shoes I am not worthy to bear: he shall baptize you with the Holy Ghost, and *with* fire:

Mt 3:16 — And Jesus, when he was baptized, went up straightway out of the water: and, lo, the heavens were opened unto him, and he saw the Spirit of God descending like a dove, and lighting upon him:

Mk 1:8 — I indeed have baptized you with water: but he shall baptize you with the Holy Ghost.

Lk 3:16 — John answered, saying unto *them* all, I indeed baptize you with water; but one mightier than I cometh, the latchet of whose shoes I am not worthy to unloose: he shall baptize you with the Holy Ghost and with fire:

Lk 3:22 — And the Holy Ghost descended in a bodily shape like a dove upon him, and a voice came from heaven, which said, Thou art my beloved Son; in thee I am well pleased.

Lk 24:49 — And, behold, I send the promise of my Father upon you: but tarry ye in the city of Jerusalem, until ye be endued with power from on high.

Jn 3:5 — Jesus answered, Verily, verily, I say unto thee, Except a man be born of water and *of* the Spirit, he cannot enter into the kingdom of God.

Ac 1:5 — For John truly baptized with water; but ye shall be baptized with the Holy Ghost not many days hence.

Ac 2:38 — Then Peter said unto them, Repent, and be baptized every one of you in the name of Jesus Christ for the remission of sins, and ye shall receive the gift of the Holy Ghost.

Ac 2:41 — Then they that gladly received his word were baptized: and the same day there were added *unto them* about three thousand souls.

Ac 10:38 — How God anointed Jesus of Nazareth with the Holy Ghost and with power: who went about doing good, and healing all that were oppressed of the devil; for God was with him.

Ac 10:47 — Can any man forbid water, that these should not be baptized, which have received the Holy Ghost as well as we?

Ac 19:2 — He said unto them, Have ye received the Holy Ghost since ye believed? And they said unto him, We have not so much as heard whether there be any Holy Ghost.

Ac 19:6 — And when Paul had laid *his* hands upon them, the Holy Ghost came on them; and they spake with tongues, and prophesied.

1Co 12:13 — For by one Spirit are we all baptized into one body, whether *we be* Jews or Gentiles, whether *we be* bond or free; and have been all made to drink into one Spirit.

See: Holy Spirit

BAR-JESUS • A false prophet.

Ac 13:6 — And when they had gone through the isle unto Paphos, they found a certain sorcerer, a false prophet, a Jew, whose name *was* Bar-jesus:

BAR-JONA • Surname of Peter.

Mt 16:17 — And Jesus answered and said unto him, Blessed art thou, Simon Barjona: for flesh and blood hath not revealed *it* unto thee, but my Father which is in heaven.

BARABBAS • A prisoner released by Pilate.

Mt 27:16–26; Mk 15:7–15; Lk 23:18–25

Jn 18:40 — Then cried they all again, saying, Not this man, but Barabbas. Now Barabbas was a robber.

Ac 3:14 — But ye denied the Holy One and the Just, and desired a murderer to be granted unto you;

BARACHEL • Father of Elihu.

Job 32:2 — Then was kindled the wrath of Elihu the son of Barachel the Buzite, of the kindred of Ram: against Job was his wrath kindled, because he justified himself rather than God.

Job 32:6 — And Elihu the son of Barachel the Buzite answered and said, I *am* young, and ye *are* very old; wherefore I was afraid, and durst not shew you mine opinion.

BARACHIAH

• Father of Zechariah.

• Called also Berechiah.

Zec 1:1 — In the eighth month, in the second year of Darius, came the word of the LORD unto Zechariah, the son of Berechiah, the son of Iddo the prophet, saying,

Zec 1:7 — Upon the four and twentieth day of the eleventh month, which *is* the month Sebat, in the second year of Darius, came the word of the LORD unto Zechariah, the son of Berechiah, the son of Iddo the prophet, saying,

• Called Barachias.

Mt 23:35 — That upon you may come all the righteous blood shed upon the earth, from the blood of righteous Abel unto the blood of Zacharias son of Barachias, whom ye slew between the temple and the altar.

BARAK • A judge in Israel.

Jgs 4:1–5:31

Heb 11:32 — And what shall I more say? for the time would fail me to tell of Gedeon, and *of* Barak, and *of* Samson, and *of* Jephthae; *of* David also, and Samuel, and *of* the prophets:

BARBARIAN

• A foreigner.

Ac 28:2–4

Ro 1:14 — I am debtor both to the Greeks, and to the Barbarians; both to the wise, and to the unwise.

1Co 14:11 — Therefore if I know not the meaning of the voice, I shall be unto him that speaketh a barbarian, and he that speaketh *shall be* a barbarian unto me.

Col 3:11 — Where there is neither Greek nor Jew, circumcision nor uncircumcision, Barbarian, Scythian, bond *nor* free: but Christ *is* all, and in all.

See: Strangers

BARBER

Eze 5:1 — And thou, son of man, take thee a sharp knife, take thee a barber's razor, and cause *it* to pass upon thine head and upon thy beard: then take thee balances to weigh, and divide the *hair.*

BARIAH • Son of Shechaniah.

1Ch 3:22 — And the sons of Shechaniah; Shemaiah; and the sons of Shemaiah; Hattush, and Igeal, and Bariah, and Neariah, and Shaphat, six.

BARKOS • A Jew whose descendants returned from exile.

Ezr 2:53 — The children of Barkos, the children of Sisera, the children of Thamah,

Ne 7:55 — The children of Barkos, the children of Sisera, the children of Tamah,

BARLEY

• A product of Egypt.

Ex 9:31 — And the flax and the barley was smitten: for the barley was in the ear, and the flax *was* bolled.

• A product of Palestine.

Dt 8:8 — A land of wheat, and barley, and vines, and fig trees, and pomegranates; a land of oil olive, and honey;

1Ch 11:13 — He was with David at Pas-dammim, and there the Philistines were gathered together to battle, where was a parcel of ground full of barley; and the people fled from before the Philistines.

Jer 41:8 — But ten men were found among them that said unto Ishmael, Slay us not: for we have treasures in the field, of wheat, and of barley, and of oil, and of honey. So he forbare, and slew them not among their brethren.

• Fed to horses.

1Ki 4:28 — Barley also and straw for the horses and dromedaries brought they unto the place where *the officers* were, every man according to his charge.

• Used in offerings.

Nu 5:15 — Then shall the man bring his wife unto the priest, and he shall bring her offering for her, the tenth *part* of an ephah of barley meal; he shall pour no oil upon it, nor put frankincense thereon; for it *is* an offering of jealousy, an offering of memorial, bringing iniquity to remembrance.

Eze 45:15 — And one lamb out of the flock, out of two hundred, out of the fat pastures of Israel; for a meat offering, and for a burnt offering, and for peace offerings, to make reconciliation for them, saith the Lord God.

- **Traffic in.**

2Ch 2:10 — And, behold, I will give to thy servants, the hewers that cut timber, twenty thousand measures of beaten wheat, and twenty thousand measures of barley, and twenty thousand baths of wine, and twenty thousand baths of oil.

Hos 3:2 — So I bought her to me for fifteen *pieces* of silver, and *for* an homer of barley, and an half homer of barley:

- **Tribute in.**

2Ch 27:5 — He fought also with the king of the Ammonites, and prevailed against them. And the children of Ammon gave him the same year an hundred talents of silver, and ten thousand measures of wheat, and ten thousand of barley. So much did the children of Ammon pay unto him, both the second year, and the third.

- **Priests estimated value of.**

Le 27:16 — And if a man shall sanctify unto the Lord *some part* of a field of his possession, then thy estimation shall be according to the seed thereof: an homer of barley seed *shall be valued* at fifty shekels of silver.

2Ki 7:1 — Then Elisha said, Hear ye the word of the Lord; Thus saith the Lord, To morrow about this time *shall* a measure of fine flour *be sold* for a shekel, and two measures of barley for a shekel, in the gate of Samaria.

Rev 6:6 — And I heard a voice in the midst of the four beasts say, A measure of wheat for a penny, and three measures of barley for a penny; and *see* thou hurt not the oil and the wine.

- **Absalom burns Joab's field of.**

2Sa 14:30 — Therefore he said unto his servants, See, Joab's field is near mine, and he hath barley there; go and set it on fire. And Absalom's servants set the field on fire.

- **Loaves of.**

Jn 6:9 — There is a lad here, which hath five barley loaves, and two small fishes: but what are they among so many?

Jn 6:13 — Therefore they gathered *them* together, and filled twelve baskets with the fragments of the five barley loaves, which remained over and above unto them that had eaten.

BARN

2Ki 6:27 — And he said, If the Lord do not help thee, whence shall I help thee? out of the barnfloor, or out of the winepress?

Job 39:12 — Wilt thou believe him, that he will bring home thy seed, and gather *it into* thy barn?

Pr 3:10 — So shall thy barns be filled with plenty, and thy presses shall burst out with new wine.

Joel 1:17 — The seed is rotten under their clods, the garners are laid desolate, the barns are broken down; for the corn is withered.

Hag 2:19 — Is the seed yet in the barn? yea, as yet the vine, and the fig tree, and the pomegranate, and the olive tree, hath not brought forth: from this day will I bless *you*.

Mt 6:26 — Behold the fowls of the air: for they sow not, neither do they reap, nor gather into barns; yet your heavenly Father feedeth them. Are ye not much better than they?

Mt 13:30 — Let both grow together until the harvest: and in the time of harvest I will say to the reapers, Gather ye together first the tares, and bind them in bundles to burn them: but gather the wheat into my barn.

Lk 12:18 — And he said, This will I do: I will pull down my barns, and build greater; and there will I bestow all my fruits and my goods.

Lk 12:24 — Consider the ravens: for they neither sow nor reap; which neither have storehouse nor barn; and God feedeth them: how much more are ye better than the fowls?

See: Garner

BARNABAS

- **Called also Joses.**
- **A prophet.**

Ac 13:1 — Now there were in the church that was at Antioch certain prophets and teachers; as Barnabas, and Simeon that was called Niger, and Lucius of Cyrene, and Manaen, which had been brought up with Herod the tetrarch, and Saul.

- **An apostle.**

Ac 14:14 — *Which* when the apostles, Barnabas and Paul, heard *of*, they rent their clothes, and ran in among the people, crying out,

- **A Levite who gave his possessions to be owned in common with other disciples.**

Ac 4:36–37

- **Goes to Tarsus to find Paul, brings him to Antioch.**

Ac 11:25–26

- **Accompanies Paul to Jerusalem.**

Ac 11:30 — Which also they did, and sent it to the elders by the hands of Barnabas and Saul.

- **Returns with Paul to Antioch.**

Ac 12:25 — And Barnabas and Saul returned from Jerusalem, when they had fulfilled *their* ministry, and took with them John, whose surname was Mark.

- **Goes with Paul to Seleucia.**

Ac 13:1–52

- **Goes with Paul to Iconium.**

Ac 14:1–7

- **Called Jupiter.**

Ac 14:12–18

• **Goes to Derbe.**

Ac 14:20 — Howbeit, as the disciples stood round about him, he rose up, and came into the city: and the next day he departed with Barnabas to Derbe.

• **Is sent as a commissioner to Jerusalem.**

Ac 15:1–41; Gal 2:1–9

• **Disaffected towards Paul.**

Ac 15:36–39

• **Is reconciled to Paul.**

1Co 9:6 — Or I only and Barnabas, have not we power to forbear working?

• **Piety of.**

Ac 11:24 — For he was a good man, and full of the Holy Ghost and of faith: and much people was added unto the Lord.

• **Devotion of, to Jesus.**

Ac 15:26 — Men that have hazarded their lives for the name of our Lord Jesus Christ.

BARREL • An earthen jar.

1Ki 17:12 — And she said, *As* the LORD thy God liveth, I have not a cake, but an handful of meal in a barrel, and a little oil in a cruse: and, behold, I *am* gathering two sticks, that I may go in and dress it for me and my son, that we may eat it, and die.

1Ki 17:14 — For thus saith the LORD God of Israel, The barrel of meal shall not waste, neither shall the cruse of oil fail, until the day *that* the LORD sendeth rain upon the earth.

1Ki 17:16 — *And* the barrel of meal wasted not, neither did the cruse of oil fail, according to the word of the LORD, which he spake by Elijah.

1Ki 18:33 — And he put the wood in order, and cut the bullock in pieces, and laid *him* on the wood, and said, Fill four barrels with water, and pour *it* on the burnt sacrifice, and on the wood.

BARRENNESS, sterility of women

• **A reproach.**

Ge 30:22–23; 1Sa 1:6–7; 2:1–11

Isa 4:1 — And in that day seven women shall take hold of one man, saying, We will eat our own bread, and wear our own apparel: only let us be called by thy name, to take away our reproach.

Lk 1:25 — Thus hath the Lord dealt with me in the days wherein he looked on *me*, to take away my reproach among men.

• **Miraculously removed, instances of.**

• **Sarai.**

Ge 17:15–21

• **Rebekah.**

Ge 25:21 — And Isaac intreated the LORD for his wife, because she *was* barren: and the LORD was intreated of him, and Rebekah his wife conceived.

• **Manoah's wife.**

Jgs 13:1–25

• **Hannah.**

1Sa 1:6–20

• **Elisabeth.**

Lk 1:5–25

• **Sent as a judgment.**

Ge 20:17–18

↞**See: Childlessness**

BARSABAS

• **Surname of Joseph.**

Ac 1:23 — And they appointed two, Joseph called Barsabas, who was surnamed Justus, and Matthias.

• **Judas.**

Ac 15:22 — Then pleased it the apostles and elders, with the whole church, to send chosen men of their own company to Antioch with Paul and Barnabas; *namely,* Judas surnamed Barsabas, and Silas, chief men among the brethren:

BARTER ↞See: Commerce

BARTHOLOMEW • One of the apostles.

Mt 10:3 — Philip, and Bartholomew; Thomas, and Matthew the publican; James *the son* of Alphaeus, and Lebbaeus, whose surname was Thaddaeus;

Mk 3:18 — And Andrew, and Philip, and Bartholomew, and Matthew, and Thomas, and James the *son* of Alphaeus, and Thaddaeus, and Simon the Canaanite,

Lk 6:14 — Simon, (whom he also named Peter,) and Andrew his brother, James and John, Philip and Bartholomew,

Ac 1:13 — And when they were come in, they went up into an upper room, where abode both Peter, and James, and John, and Andrew, Philip, and Thomas, Bartholomew, and Matthew, James *the son* of Alphaeus, and Simon Zelotes, and Judas *the brother* of James.

BARTIMAEUS • A blind man.

Mt 20:29–34; Mk 10:46–52; Lk 18:35–43

Mark 10:46 And they came to Jericho: and as he went out of Jericho with his disciples and a great number of people, blind Bartimaeus, the son of Timaeus, sat by the highway side begging.

BARUCH

• **An amanuensis of Jeremiah.**

Jer 32:12–16; 36:4–32; 43:3–6; 45:1–2

• **Son of Labai.**

Ne 3:20 — After him Baruch the son of Zabbai earnestly repaired the other piece, from the turning *of the wall* unto the door of the house of Eliashib the high priest.

Ne 10:6 — Daniel, Ginnethon, Baruch,

• **A descendant of Pharez.**

Ne 11:5 — And Maaseiah the son of Baruch, the son of Col-hozeh, the son of Hazaiah, the son of Adaiah, the son of Joiarib, the son of Zechariah, the son of Shiloni.

BARZILLAI

• **A friend of David.**

2Sa 17:27–29; 19:31–39

1Ki 2:7 — But shew kindness unto the sons of Barzillai the Gileadite, and let them be of those that eat at thy table: for so they came to me when I fled because of Absalom thy brother.

Ezr 2:61 — And of the children of the priests: the children of Habaiah, the children of Koz, the children of Barzillai; which took a wife of the daughters of Barzillai the Gileadite, and was called after their name:

Ne 7:63 — And of the priests: the children of Habaiah, the children of Koz, the children of Barzillai, which took *one* of the daughters of Barzillai the Gileadite to wife, and was called after their name.

• Father of Adriel.

2Sa 21:8 — But the king took the two sons of Rizpah the daughter of Aiah, whom she bare unto Saul, Armoni and Mephibosheth; and the five sons of Michal the daughter of Saul, whom she brought up for Adriel the son of Barzillai the Meholathite:

• A priest.

Ezr 2:61 — And of the children of the priests: the children of Habaiah, the children of Koz, the children of Barzillai; which took a wife of the daughters of Barzillai the Gileadite, and was called after their name:

Ne 7:63 — And of the priests: the children of Habaiah, the children of Koz, the children of Barzillai, which took *one* of the daughters of Barzillai the Gileadite to wife, and was called after their name.

BASHAN

• A region east of the Jordan and north of Arnon.

Ge 14:5 — And in the fourteenth year came Chedorlaomer, and the kings that *were* with him, and smote the Rephaims in Ashteroth Karnaim, and the Zuzims in Ham, and the Emims in Shaveh Kiriathaim,

• Og, king of.

Jos 13:12 — All the kingdom of Og in Bashan, which reigned in Ashtaroth and in Edrei, who remained of the remnant of the giants: for these did Moses smite, and cast them out.

• Allotted to the two and one-half tribes, which had their possession east of the Jordan.

Dt 3:10–14; Jos 12:4–6; 13:29–31

Nu 32:33 — And Moses gave unto them, *even* to the children of Gad, and to the children of Reuben, and unto half the tribe of Manasseh the son of Joseph, the kingdom of Sihon king of the Amorites, and the kingdom of Og king of Bashan, the land, with the cities thereof in the coasts, *even* the cities of the country round about.

Jos 17:1 — There was also a lot for the tribe of Manasseh; for he *was* the firstborn of Joseph; *to wit,* for Machir the firstborn of Manasseh, the father of Gilead: because he was a man of war, therefore he had Gilead and Bashan.

• Invaded and taken by Hazael, king of Syria.

2Ki 10:32–33

• Retaken by Jehoash.

2Ki 13:25 — And Jehoash the son of Jehoahaz took again out of the hand of Ben-hadad the son of Hazael the cities, which he had taken out of the hand of Jehoahaz his father by war. Three times did Joash beat him, and recovered the cities of Israel.

• Fertility and productiveness of.

Isa 33:9 — The earth mourneth *and* languisheth: Lebanon is ashamed *and* hewn down: Sharon is like a wilderness; and Bashan and Carmel shake off *their fruits.*

Jer 50:19 — And I will bring Israel again to his habitation, and he shall feed on Carmel and Bashan, and his soul shall be satisfied upon mount Ephraim and Gilead.

Na 1:4 — He rebuketh the sea, and maketh it dry, and drieth up all the rivers: Bashan languisheth, and Carmel, and the flower of Lebanon languisheth.

• Forests of, famous.

Isa 2:13 — And upon all the cedars of Lebanon, *that are* high and lifted up, and upon all the oaks of Bashan,

Eze 27:6 — *Of* the oaks of Bashan have they made thine oars; the company of the Ashurites have made thy benches *of* ivory, *brought* out of the isles of Chittim.

Zec 11:2 — Howl, fir tree; for the cedar is fallen; because the mighty are spoiled: howl, O ye oaks of Bashan; for the forest of the vintage is come down.

• Distinguished for its fine cattle.

Dt 32:14 — Butter of kine, and milk of sheep, with fat of lambs, and rams of the breed of Bashan, and goats, with the fat of kidneys of wheat; and thou didst drink the pure blood of the grape.

Ps 22:12 — Many bulls have compassed me: strong *bulls* of Bashan have beset me round.

Eze 39:18 — Ye shall eat the flesh of the mighty, and drink the blood of the princes of the earth, of rams, of lambs, and of goats, of bullocks, all of them fatlings of Bashan.

Am 4:1 — Hear this word, ye kine of Bashan, that *are* in the mountain of Samaria, which oppress the poor, which crush the needy, which say to their masters, Bring, and let us drink.

Mic 7:14 — Feed thy people with thy rod, the flock of thine heritage, which dwell solitarily *in* the wood, in the midst of Carmel: let them feed *in* Bashan and Gilead, as in the days of old.

See: Argob

See: Ashtaroth

See: Edrei

See: Jair

BASHAN-HAVOTH-JAIR • A name given to Argob.

Dt 3:14 — Jair the son of Manasseh took all the country of Argob unto the coasts of Geshuri and Maachathi; and called them after his own name, Bashan-havoth-jair, unto this day.

BASHEMATH • Wife of Esau.

Ge 36:3–4

Ge 26:34 — And Esau was forty years old when he took to wife Judith the daughter of Beeri the Hittite, and Bashemath the daughter of Elon the Hittite:

Ge 36:10 — These *are* the names of Esau's sons; Eliphaz the son of Adah the wife of Esau, Reuel the son of Bashemath the wife of Esau.

Ge 36:13 — And these *are* the sons of Reuel; Nahath, and Zerah, Shammah, and Mizzah: these were the sons of Bashemath Esau's wife.

Ge 36:17 — And these *are* the sons of Reuel Esau's son; duke Nahath, duke Zerah, duke Shammah, duke Mizzah: these *are* the dukes *that came* of Reuel in the land of Edom; these *are* the sons of Bashemath Esau's wife.

BASIN

• Made of gold.

1Ki 7:50 — And the bowls, and the snuffers, and the basons, and the spoons, and the censers *of* pure gold; and the hinges *of* gold, *both* for the doors of the inner house, the most holy *place, and* for the doors of the house, *to wit,* of the temple.

1Ch 28:17 — Also pure gold for the fleshhooks, and the bowls, and the cups: and for the golden basons *he gave gold* by weight for every bason; and *likewise silver* by weight for every bason of silver:

2Ch 4:8 — He made also ten tables, and placed *them* in the temple, five on the right side, and five on the left. And he made an hundred basons of gold.

2Ch 4:22 — And the snuffers, and the basons, and the spoons, and the censers, *of* pure gold: and the entry of the house, the inner doors thereof for the most holy *place,* and the doors of the house of the temple, *were of* gold.

Ezr 1:10 — Thirty basons of gold, silver basons of a second *sort* four hundred and ten, *and* other vessels a thousand.

Ezr 8:27 — Also twenty basons of gold, of a thousand drams; and two vessels of fine copper, precious as gold.

• Made of brass.

Ex 27:3 — And thou shalt make his pans to receive his ashes, and his shovels, and his basons, and his fleshhooks, and his firepans: all the vessels thereof thou shalt make *of* brass.

Ex 38:3 — And he made all the vessels of the altar, the pots, and the shovels, and the basons, *and* the fleshhooks, and the firepans: all the vessels thereof made he *of* brass.

1Ki 7:45 — And the pots, and the shovels, and the basons: and all these vessels, which Hiram made to king Solomon for the house of the LORD, *were of* bright brass.

→See: Tabernacle; furniture of

BASKET

Ge 40:16–17

Ex 29:3 — And thou shalt put them into one basket, and bring them in the basket, with the bullock and the two rams.

Ex 29:23 — And one loaf of bread, and one cake of oiled bread, and one wafer out of the basket of the unleavened bread that *is* before the LORD:

Ex 29:32 — And Aaron and his sons shall eat the flesh of the ram, and the bread that *is* in the basket, *by* the door of the tabernacle of the congregation.

Le 8:2 — Take Aaron and his sons with him, and the garments, and the anointing oil, and a bullock for the sin offering, and two rams, and a basket of unleavened bread;

Nu 6:15 — And a basket of unleavened bread, cakes of fine flour mingled with oil, and wafers of unleavened bread anointed with oil, and their meat offering, and their drink offerings.

Dt 26:2 — That thou shalt take of the first of all the fruit of the earth, which thou shalt bring of thy land that the LORD thy God giveth thee, and shalt put *it* in a basket, and shalt go unto the place which the LORD thy God shall choose to place his name there.

Dt 28:5 — Blessed *shall be* thy basket and thy store.

Dt 28:17 — Cursed *shall be* thy basket and thy store.

2Ki 10:7 — And it came to pass, when the letter came to them, that they took the king's sons, and slew seventy persons, and put their heads in baskets, and sent him *them* to Jezreel.

• Received the fragments after the miracles of the loaves.

Mt 16:9–10

Mt 14:20 — And they did all eat, and were filled: and they took up of the fragments that remained twelve baskets full.

Mt 15:37 — And they did all eat, and were filled: and they took up of the broken *meat* that was left seven baskets full.

• Paul let down from the wall in.

Ac 9:25 — Then the disciples took him by night, and let *him* down by the wall in a basket.

2Co 11:33 — And through a window in a basket was I let down by the wall, and escaped his hands.

BASMATH • Daughter of Solomon.

1Ki 4:15 — Ahimaaz *was* in Naphtali; he also took Basmath the daughter of Solomon to wife:

BASON →See: Basin

BASTARD

• Excluded from the congregation.

Dt 23:2 — A bastard shall not enter into the congregation of the LORD; even to his tenth generation shall he not enter into the congregation of the LORD.

• Instances of.

• Ishmael.

Ge 16:3, 15; Gal 4:22

• Moab and Ammon.

Ge 19:36–37

• Jephthah.

Jgs 11:1

• David's child by Bath-sheba.

2Sa 11:2–5

• **Figurative.**

Zec 9:6 — And a bastard shall dwell in Ashdod, and I will cut off the pride of the Philistines.

Heb 12:8 — But if ye be without chastisement, whereof all are partakers, then are ye bastards, and not sons.

BAT

Le 11:19 — And the stork, the heron after her kind, and the lapwing, and the bat.

Dt 14:18 — And the stork, and the heron after her kind, and the lapwing, and the bat.

Isa 2:20 — In that day a man shall cast his idols of silver, and his idols of gold, which they made *each one* for himself to worship, to the moles and to the bats;

BATH • A Hebrew measure for liquids, containing about eight gallons, three quarts.

Eze 45:10–11

1Ki 7:26 — And it *was* an hand breadth thick, and the brim thereof was wrought like the brim of a cup, with flowers of lilies: it contained two thousand baths.

1Ki 7:38 — Then made he ten lavers of brass: one laver contained forty baths: *and* every laver was four cubits: *and* upon every one of the ten bases one laver.

Ezr 7:22 — Unto an hundred talents of silver, and to an hundred measures of wheat, and to an hundred baths of wine, and to an hundred baths of oil, and salt without prescribing *how much.*

Isa 5:10 — Yea, ten acres of vineyard shall yield one bath, and the seed of an homer shall yield an ephah.

Eze 45:14 — Concerning the ordinance of oil, the bath of oil, *ye shall offer* the tenth part of a bath out of the cor, *which is* an homer of ten baths; for ten baths *are* an homer:

BATH-RABBIM • A gate in the city of Heshbon.

SS 7:4 — Thy neck *is* as a tower of ivory; thine eyes *like* the fishpools in Heshbon, by the gate of Bath-rabbim: thy nose *is* as the tower of Lebanon which looketh toward Damascus.

BATH-SHEBA

• **Wife of Uriah and later wife of David.**

• **Called Bath-Shua.**

1Ch 3:5 — And these were born unto him in Jerusalem; Shimea, and Shobab, and Nathan, and Solomon, four, of Bath-shua the daughter of Ammiel:

• **Adultery of.**

2Sa 11:2–5

• **Solomon's mother.**

1Ki 1:11–31; 2:13–21

1Ch 3:5 — And these were born unto him in Jerusalem; Shimea, and Shobab, and Nathan, and Solomon, four, of Bath-shua the daughter of Ammiel:

BATHING

See: Ablution

See: Purification

BATTERING RAM

2Sa 20:15 — And they came and besieged him in Abel of Beth-maachah, and they cast up a bank against the city, and it stood in the trench: and all the people that *were* with Joab battered the wall, to throw it down.

Eze 4:2 — And lay siege against it, and build a fort against it, and cast a mount against it; set the camp also against it, and set *battering* rams against it round about.

Eze 21:22 — At his right hand was the divination for Jerusalem, to appoint captains, to open the mouth in the slaughter, to lift up the voice with shouting, to appoint *battering* rams against the gates, to cast a mount, *and* to build a fort.

BATTERY See: Assault and Battery

BATTLE

• **Shouting in.**

Jgs 7:20 — And the three companies blew the trumpets, and brake the pitchers, and held the lamps in their left hands, and the trumpets in their right hands to blow *withal:* and they cried, The sword of the LORD, and of Gideon.

1Sa 17:20 — And David rose up early in the morning, and left the sheep with a keeper, and took, and went, as Jesse had commanded him; and he came to the trench, as the host was going forth to the fight, and shouted for the battle.

• **Priests in.**

2Ch 13:12 — And, behold, God himself is with us for *our* captain, and his priests with sounding trumpets to cry alarm against you. O children of Israel, fight ye not against the LORD God of your fathers; for ye shall not prosper.

• **Prayer before.**

• **By Asa.**

2Ch 14:11 — And Asa cried unto the LORD his God, and said, LORD, *it is* nothing with thee to help, whether with many, or with them that have no power: help us, O LORD our God; for we rest on thee, and in thy name we go against this multitude. O LORD, thou *art* our God; let not man prevail against thee.

• **By Jehoshaphat.**

2Ch 20:3–12

See: Armies

See: War

BATTLE-AX

Jer 51:20 — Thou *art* my battle axe *and* weapons of war: for with thee will I break in pieces the nations, and with thee will I destroy kingdoms;

BATTLEMENTS

• **On roofs of houses.**

Dt 22:8 — When thou buildest a new house, then thou shalt make a battlement for thy roof, that thou bring not blood upon thine house, if any man fall from thence.

- **On walls.**

Jer 5:10 — Go ye up upon her walls, and destroy; but make not a full end: take away her battlements; for they *are* not the LORD's.

BAVAI • Builds the wall of Jerusalem.

Ne 3:18 — After him repaired their brethren, Bavai the son of Henadad, the ruler of the half part of Keilah.

BAY TREE

Ps 37:35 — I have seen the wicked in great power, and spreading himself like a green bay tree.

BAZLITH

- **Called also Bazluth.**
- **One of the Nethinim.**

Ezr 2:52 — The children of Bazluth, the children of Mehida, the children of Harsha,

Ne 7:54 — The children of Bazlith, the children of Mehida, the children of Harsha,

BDELLIUM

Ge 2:12 — And the gold of that land *is* good: there *is* bdellium and the onyx stone.

Nu 11:7 — And the manna *was* as coriander seed, and the colour thereof as the colour of bdellium.

BEACON

Isa 30:17 — One thousand *shall flee* at the rebuke of one; at the rebuke of five shall ye flee: till ye be left as a beacon upon the top of a mountain, and as an ensign on an hill.

Jer 6:1 — O ye children of Benjamin, gather yourselves to flee out of the midst of Jerusalem, and blow the trumpet in Tekoa, and set up a sign of fire in Beth-haccerem: for evil appeareth out of the north, and great destruction.

→See: Ensign
→See: Standard

BEALIAH • An Israelite, who joined David at Ziklag.

1Ch 12:5 — Eluzai, and Jerimoth, and Bealiah, and Shemariah, and Shephatiah the Haruphite,

BEAM

- **Weaver's.**

1Sa 17:7 — And the staff of his spear *was* like a weaver's beam; and his spear's head *weighed* six hundred shekels of iron: and one bearing a shield went before him.

2Sa 21:19 — And there was again a battle in Gob with the Philistines, where Elhanan the son of Jaare-oregim, a Bethlehemite, slew *the brother of* Goliath the Gittite, the staff of whose spear *was* like a weaver's beam.

- **Figurative.**

Mt 7:3 — And why beholdest thou the mote that is in thy brother's eye, but considerest not the beam that is in thine own eye?

Lk 6:41 — And why beholdest thou the mote that is in thy brother's eye, but perceivest not the beam that is in thine own eye?

BEAN

2Sa 17:28 — Brought beds, and basons, and earthen vessels, and wheat, and barley, and flour, and parched *corn,* and beans, and lentiles, and parched *pulse,*

Eze 4:9 — Take thou also unto thee wheat, and barley, and beans, and lentiles, and millet, and fitches, and put them in one vessel, and make thee bread thereof, *according* to the number of the days that thou shalt lie upon thy side, three hundred and ninety days shalt thou eat thereof.

BEAR

- **Ferocity of.**

2Sa 17:8 — For, said Hushai, thou knowest thy father and his men, that they *be* mighty men, and they *be* chafed in their minds, as a bear robbed of her whelps in the field: and thy father *is* a man of war, and will not lodge with the people.

Pr 17:12 — Let a bear robbed of her whelps meet a man, rather than a fool in his folly.

Pr 28:15 — *As* a roaring lion, and a ranging bear; *so is* a wicked ruler over the poor people.

Isa 11:7 — And the cow and the bear shall feed; their young ones shall lie down together: and the lion shall eat straw like the ox.

Isa 59:11 — We roar all like bears, and mourn sore like doves: we look for judgment, but *there is* none; for salvation, *but* it is far off from us.

La 3:10 — He *was* unto me *as* a bear lying in wait, *and as* a lion in secret places.

Hos 13:8 — I will meet them as a bear *that is* bereaved *of her whelps,* and will rend the caul of their heart, and there will I devour them like a lion: the wild beast shall tear them.

Am 5:19 — As if a man did flee from a lion, and a bear met him; or went into the house, and leaned his hand on the wall, and a serpent bit him.

- **Killed by David.**

1Sa 17:34–37

- **Two destroy the children of Bethel, who mocked Elisah.**

2Ki 2:24 — And he turned back, and looked on them, and cursed them in the name of the LORD. And there came forth two she bears out of the wood, and tare forty and two children of them.

- **Figurative.**

Da 7:5 — And behold another beast, a second, like to a bear, and it raised up itself on one side, and *it had* three ribs in the mouth of it between the teeth of it: and they said thus unto it, Arise, devour much flesh.

Rev 13:2 — And the beast which I saw was like unto a leopard, and his feet were as *the feet* of a bear, and his mouth as the mouth of a lion: and the dragon gave him his power, and his seat, and great authority.

BEARD

• Worn long by Aaron.

Ps 133:2 — *It is* like the precious ointment upon the head, that ran down upon the beard, *even* Aaron's beard: that went down to the skirts of his garments;

• Worn long by Samson.

Jgs 16:17 — That he told her all his heart, and said unto her. There hath not come a razor upon mine head; for I *have been* a Nazarite unto God from my mother's womb: if I be shaven, then my strength will go from me, and I shall become weak, and be like any *other* man.

• Worn long by David.

1Sa 21:13 — And he changed his behaviour before them, and feigned himself mad in their hands, and scrabbled on the doors of the gate, and let his spittle fall down upon his beard.

• Worn long by Ezekiel.

Eze 5:1 — And thou, son of man, take thee a sharp knife, take thee a barber's razor, and cause *it* to pass upon thine head and upon thy beard: then take thee balances to weigh, and divide the *hair.*

• Shaven by Egyptians.

Ge 41:14 — Then Pharaoh sent and called Joseph, and they brought him hastily out of the dungeon: and he shaved *himself,* and changed his raiment, and came in unto Pharaoh.

• Untrimmed in mourning.

2Sa 19:24 — And Mephibosheth the son of Saul came down to meet the king, and had neither dressed his feet, nor trimmed his beard, nor washed his clothes, from the day the king departed until the day he came *again* in peace.

• Plucked.

Ezr 9:3 — And when I heard this thing, I rent my garment and my mantle, and plucked off the hair of my head and of my beard, and sat down astonied.

• Cut.

Isa 7:20 — In the same day shall the Lord shave with a razor that is hired, *namely,* by them beyond the river, by the king of Assyria, the head, and the hair of the feet: and it shall also consume the beard.

Isa 15:2 — He is gone up to Bajith, and to Dibon, the high places, to weep: Moab shall howl over Nebo, and over Medeba: on all their heads *shall be* baldness, *and* every beard cut off.

Jer 41:5 — That there came certain from Shechem, from Shiloh, and from Samaria, *even* fourscore men, having their beards shaven, and their clothes rent, and having cut themselves, with offerings and incense in their hand, to bring *them* to the house of the LORD.

Jer 48:37 — For every head *shall be* bald, and every beard clipped: upon all the hands *shall be* cuttings, and upon the loins sackcloth.

• Lepers required to shave.

Le 13:29–33

Le 14:9 — But it shall be on the seventh day, that he shall shave all his hair off his head and his beard and his eyebrows, even all his hair he shall shave off: and he shall wash his clothes, also he shall wash his flesh in water, and he shall be clean.

• Idolatrous practice of marring, forbidden.

Le 19:27 — Ye shall not round the corners of your heads, neither shalt thou mar the corners of thy beard.

Le 21:5 — They shall not make baldness upon their head, neither shall they shave off the corner of their beard, nor make any cuttings in their flesh.

• Beards of David's ambassadors half shaven by the king of the Amorites.

2Sa 10:4 — Wherefore Hanun took David's servants, and shaved off the one half of their beards, and cut off their garments in the middle, *even* to their buttocks, and sent them away.

BEASTS ✦See: Animals

BEATEN WORK

• Of metals.

Ex 25:18 — And thou shalt make two cherubims *of* gold, *of* beaten work shalt thou make them, in the two ends of the mercy seat.

Ex 37:17 — And he made the candlestick *of* pure gold: *of* beaten work made he the candlestick; his shaft, and his branch, his bowls, his knops, and his flowers, were of the same:

Ex 37:22 — Their knops and their branches were of the same: all of it *was* one beaten work *of* pure gold.

Nu 8:4 — And this work of the candlestick *was of* beaten gold, unto the shaft thereof, unto the flowers thereof, *was* beaten work: according unto the pattern which the LORD had shewed Moses, so he made the candlestick.

BEATING

• As a punishment.

Ex 5:14 — And the officers of the children of Israel, which Pharaoh's taskmasters had set over them, were beaten, *and* demanded, Wherefore have ye not fulfilled your task in making brick both yesterday and to day, as heretofore?

Dt 25:3 — Forty stripes he may give him, *and* not exceed: lest, *if* he should exceed, and beat him above these with many stripes, then thy brother should seem vile unto thee.

Mk 13:9 — But take heed to yourselves: for they shall deliver you up to councils; and in the synagogues ye shall be beaten: and ye shall be brought before rulers and kings for my sake, for a testimony against them.

Ac 5:40 — And to him they agreed: and when they had called the apostles, and beaten *them,* they commanded that they should not speak in the name of Jesus, and let them go.

Ac 16:22 — And the multitude rose up together against them: and the magistrates rent off their clothes, and commanded to beat *them.*

Ac 16:37 — But Paul said unto them, They have beaten us openly uncondemned, being Romans, and have cast *us* into prison; and now do they thrust us out privily? nay verily; but let them come themselves and fetch us out.

Ac 18:17 — Then all the Greeks took Sosthenes, the chief ruler of the synagogue, and beat *him* before the judgment seat. And Gallio cared for none of those things.

Ac 21:32 — Who immediately took soldiers and centurions, and ran down unto them: and when they saw the chief captain and the soldiers, they left beating of Paul.

Ac 22:19 — And I said, Lord, they know that I imprisoned and beat in every synagogue them that believed on thee:

See: Assault and Battery

See: Punishment

BEAUTY

• Vanity of.

Ps 39:11 — When thou with rebukes dost correct man for iniquity, thou makest his beauty to consume away like a moth: surely every man *is* vanity. Selah.

Pr 6:25 — Lust not after her beauty in thine heart; neither let her take thee with her eyelids.

Pr 31:30 — Favour *is* deceitful, and beauty *is* vain: *but* a woman *that* feareth the LORD, she shall be praised.

Isa 3:24 — And it shall come to pass, *that* instead of sweet smell there shall be stink; and instead of a girdle a rent; and instead of well set hair baldness; and instead of a stomacher a girding of sackcloth; *and* burning instead of beauty.

Eze 16:14 — And thy renown went forth among the heathen for thy beauty: for it *was* perfect through my comeliness, which I had put upon thee, saith the Lord GOD.

Eze 28:17 — Thine heart was lifted up because of thy beauty, thou hast corrupted thy wisdom by reason of thy brightness: I will cast thee to the ground, I will lay thee before kings, that they may behold thee.

• Consumeth away.

Ps 39:11 — When thou with rebukes dost correct man for iniquity, thou makest his beauty to consume away like a moth: surely every man *is* vanity. Selah.

Ps 49:14 — Like sheep they are laid in the grave; death shall feed on them; and the upright shall have dominion over them in the morning; and their beauty shall consume in the grave from their dwelling.

• Instances of.

• Sarah.
Ge 12:11

• Rebekah.
Ge 24:16

• Rachel.
Ge 29:17

• Joseph.
Ge 39:6

• Moses.
Ex 2:2; Heb 11:23

• David.
1Sa 16:12, 18

• Bath-sheba.
2Sa 11:2

• Tamar.
2Sa 13:1

• Absalom.
2Sa 14:25

• Abishag.
1Ki 1:4

• Vashti.
Est 1:11

• Esther.
Est 2:7

• Spiritual.

1Ch 16:29 — Give unto the LORD the glory *due* unto his name: bring an offering, and come before him: worship the LORD in the beauty of holiness.

Ps 27:4 — One *thing* have I desired of the LORD, that will I seek after; that I may dwell in the house of the LORD all the days of my life, to behold the beauty of the LORD, and to enquire in his temple.

Ps 29:2 — Give unto the LORD the glory due unto his name; worship the LORD in the beauty of holiness.

Ps 45:11 — So shall the king greatly desire thy beauty: for he *is* thy Lord; and worship thou him.

Ps 90:17 — And let the beauty of the LORD our God be upon us: and establish thou the work of our hands upon us; yea, the work of our hands establish thou it.

Ps 110:3 — Thy people *shall be* willing in the day of thy power, in the beauties of holiness from the womb of the morning: thou hast the dew of thy youth.

Isa 52:7 — How beautiful upon the mountains are the feet of him that bringeth good tidings, that publisheth peace; that bringeth good tidings of good, that publisheth salvation; that saith unto Zion, Thy God reigneth!

Eze 16:14 — And thy renown went forth among the heathen for thy beauty: for it *was* perfect through my comeliness, which I had put upon thee, saith the Lord GOD.

Zec 9:17 — For how great *is* his goodness, and how great *is* his beauty! corn shall make the young men cheerful, and new wine the maids.

BEAUTY AND BANDS • The staves, broken.

Zec 11:7 — And I will feed the flock of slaughter, *even* you, O poor of the flock. And I took unto me two staves; the one I called Beauty, and the other I called Bands; and I fed the flock.

BEBAI • The name of three Jews whose descendants came from exile.

Ezr 2:11 — The children of Bebai, six hundred twenty and three.

Ezr 8:11 — And of the sons of Bebai; Zechariah the son of Bebai, and with him twenty and eight males.

Ezr 10:28 — Of the sons also of Bebai; Jehohanan, Hananiah, Zabbai, *and* Athlai.

Ne 7:16 — The children of Bebai, six hundred twenty and eight.

Ne 10:15 — Bunni, Azgad, Bebai,

BECHER

• Son of Benjamin.

Ge 46:21 — And the sons of Benjamin were Belah, and Becher, and Ashbel, Gera, and Naaman, Ehi, and Rosh, Muppim, and Huppim, and Ard.

1Ch 7:6 — *The sons* of Benjamin; Bela, and Becher, and Jediael, three.

1Ch 7:8 — And the sons of Becher; Zemira, and Joash, and Eliezer, and Elioenai, and Omri, and Jerimoth, and Abiah, and Anathoth, and Alameth. All these *are* the sons of Becher.

• Son of Ephraim.

Nu 26:35 — These *are* the sons of Ephraim after their families: of Shuthelah, the family of the Shuthalhites: of Becher, the family of the Bachrites: of Tahan, the family of the Tahanites.

• Called Bered.

1Ch 7:20 — And the sons of Ephraim; Shuthelah, and Bered his son, and Tahath his son, and Eladah his son, and Tahath his son,

BECHORATH • Son of Aphiah.

1Sa 9:1 — Now there was a man of Benjamin, whose name *was* Kish, the son of Abiel, the son of Zeror, the son of Bechorath, the son of Aphiah, a Benjamite, a mighty man of power.

BED

• Made of wood.

SS 3:7–9

• Made of iron.

Dt 3:11 — For only Og king of Bashan remained of the remnant of giants; behold, his bedstead *was* a bedstead of iron; is it not in Rabbath of the children of Ammon? nine cubits was the length thereof, and four cubits the breadth of it, after the cubit of a man.

• Made of ivory.

Am 6:4 — That lie upon beds of ivory, and stretch themselves upon their couches, and eat the lambs out of the flock, and the calves out of the midst of the stall;

• Made of gold and silver.

Est 1:6 — *Where were* white, green, and blue, *hangings,* fastened with cords of fine linen and purple to silver rings and pillars of marble: the beds *were of* gold and silver, upon a pavement of red, and blue, and white, and black, marble.

• Used at meals.

Am 6:4 — That lie upon beds of ivory, and stretch themselves upon their couches, and eat the lambs out of the flock, and the calves out of the midst of the stall;

• Exempt from execution for debt.

Pr 22:27 — If thou hast nothing to pay, why should he take away thy bed from under thee?

• Perfumed.

Pr 7:17 — I have perfumed my bed with myrrh, aloes, and cinnamon.

• Figurative.

Ps 139:8 — If I ascend up into heaven, thou *art* there: if I make my bed in hell, behold, thou *art there.*

BEDAN

• One of the deliverers of Israel.

1Sa 12:11 — And the LORD sent Jerubbaal, and Bedan, and Jephthah, and Samuel, and delivered you out of the hand of your enemies on every side, and ye dwelled safe.

• Possibly identical with Abdon.

Judg. 12:13 And after him Abdon the son of Hillel, a Pirathonite, judged Israel.

Judg. 12:15 And Abdon the son of Hillel the Pirathonite died, and was buried in Pirathon in the land of Ephraim, in the mount of the Amalekites.

• Son of Ullam.

1Ch 7:17 — And the sons of Ulam; Bedan. These *were* the sons of Gilead, the son of Machir, the son of Manasseh.

BEE

• In Palestine.

Dt 1:44 — And the Amorites, which dwelt in that mountain, came out against you, and chased you, as bees do, and destroyed you in Seir, *even* unto Hormah.

Jgs 14:8 — And after a time he returned to take her, and he turned aside to see the carcase of the lion: and, behold, *there was* a swarm of bees and honey in the carcase of the lion.

Ps 118:12 — They compassed me about like bees; they are quenched as the fire of thorns: for in the name of the LORD I will destroy them.

Isa 7:18 — And it shall come to pass in that day, *that* the LORD shall hiss for the fly that *is* in the uttermost part of the rivers of Egypt, and for the bee that *is* in the land of Assyria.

• Called by hissing.

Isa 7:18 — And it shall come to pass in that day, *that* the LORD shall hiss for the fly that *is* in the uttermost part of the rivers of Egypt, and for the bee that *is* in the land of Assyria.

See: Honey

BEELIADA

• Son of David.

1Ch 14:7 — And Elishama, and Beeliada, and Eliphalet.

• Called Eliada.

2Sa 5:16 — And Elishama, and Eliada, and Eliphalet.

1Ch 3:8 — And Elishama, and Eliada, and Eliphelet, nine.

BEELZEBUB

• The prince of devils.

Lk 11:18–19

Mt 10:25 — It is enough for the disciple that he be as his master, and the servant as his lord. If they have called the master of the house Beelzebub, how much more *shall they call* them of his household?

Mt 12:24 — But when the Pharisees heard *it,* they said, This *fellow* doth not cast out devils, but by Beelzebub the prince of the devils.

Mt 12:27 — And if I by Beelzebub cast out devils, by whom do your children cast *them* out? therefore they shall be your judges.

Mk 3:22 — And the scribes which came down from Jerusalem said, He hath Beelzebub, and by the prince of the devils casteth he out devils.

Lk 11:15 — But some of them said, He casteth out devils through Beelzebub the chief of the devils.

• Messengers sent to inquire of, by Ahaziah.

2Ki 1:2 — And Ahaziah fell down through a lattice in his upper chamber that *was* in Samaria, and was sick: and he sent messengers, and said unto them, Go, enquire of Baal-zebub the god of Ekron whether I shall recover of this disease.

See: Baal-Zebub

BEER

• A station of the Israelites.

Nu 21:16–18

• A town in the tribe of Judah.

Jgs 9:21 — And Jotham ran away, and fled, and went to Beer, and dwelt there, for fear of Abimelech his brother.

BEER-ELIM • A city of Moab.

Isa 15:8 — For the cry is gone round about the borders of Moab; the howling thereof unto Eglaim, and the howling thereof unto Beer-elim.

BEER-LAHAI-ROI

• Called also Lahai-Roi.

• A well.

Ge 16:14 — Wherefore the well was called Beer-lahai-roi; behold, *it is* between Kadesh and Bered.

Ge 24:62 — And Isaac came from the way of the well Lahai-roi; for he dwelt in the south country.

Ge 25:11 — And it came to pass after the death of Abraham, that God blessed his son Isaac; and Isaac dwelt by the well Lahai-roi.

BEER-SHEBA

• The most southern city of Palestine.

Jgs 20:1 — Then all the children of Israel went out, and the congregation was gathered together as one man, from Dan even to Beer-sheba, with the land of Gilead, unto the LORD in Mizpeh.

• Named by Abraham, who dwelt there.

Ge 21:31–33

Ge 22:19 — So Abraham returned unto his young men, and they rose up and went together to Beer-sheba; and Abraham dwelt at Beer-sheba.

• The dwelling place of Isaac.

Ge 26:23 — And he went up from thence to Beer-sheba.

• Jacob went out from, toward Haran.

Ge 28:10 — And Jacob went out from Beer-sheba, and went toward Haran.

• Sacrifices offered at, by Jacob when journeying to Egypt.

Ge 46:1 — And Israel took his journey with all that he had, and came to Beer-sheba, and offered sacrifices unto the God of his father Isaac.

• In the inheritance of Judah.

Jos 15:20 — This *is* the inheritance of the tribe of the children of Judah according to their families.

Jos 15:28 — And Hazar-shual, and Beer-sheba, and Bizjothjah,

2Sa 24:7 — And came to the strong hold of Tyre, and to all the cities of the Hivites, and of the Canaanites: and they went out to the south of Judah, *even* to Beer-sheba.

• Afterward assigned to Simeon.

Jos 19:2 — And they had in their inheritance Beer-sheba, or Sheba, and Moladah,

Jos 19:9 — Out of the portion of the children of Judah *was* the inheritance of the children of Simeon: for the part of the children of Judah was too much for them: therefore the children of Simeon had their inheritance within the inheritance of them.

1Ch 4:28 — And they dwelt at Beer-sheba, and Moladah, and Hazar-shual,

• Two sons of Samuel were judges at.

1Sa 8:2 — Now the name of his firstborn was Joel; and the name of his second, Abiah: *they were* judges in Beer-sheba.

• Became a seat of idolatrous worship.

Am 5:5 — But seek not Bethel, nor enter into Gilgal, and pass not to Beer-sheba: for Gilgal shall surely go into captivity, and Bethel shall come to nought.

Am 8:14 — They that swear by the sin of Samaria, and say, Thy god, O Dan, liveth; and, The manner of Beer-sheba liveth; even they shall fall, and never rise up again.

• Well of, belonged to Abraham and Isaac.

Ge 21:25–26

• Wilderness of, Hagar miraculously sees a well in.

Ge 21:14–19

• An angel fed Elijah in.

1Ki 19:5 — And as he lay and slept under a juniper tree, behold, then an angel touched him, and said unto him, Arise *and* eat.

1Ki 19:7 — And the angel of the LORD came again the second time, and touched him, and said, Arise *and* eat; because the journey *is* too great for thee.

BEERA • Son of Zophah.

1Ch 7:37 — Bezer, and Hod, and Shamma and Shilshah, and Ithran, and Beera.

BEERAH • A Reubenite.

1Ch 5:6 — Beerah his son, whom Tilgath-pilneser king of Assyria carried away *captive:* he *was* prince of the Reubenites.

BEERI

• A Hittite.

Ge 26:34 — And Esau was forty years old when he took to wife Judith the daughter of Beeri the Hittite, and Bashemath the daughter of Elon the Hittite:

See: Anah

• Father of Hosea.

Hos 1:1 — The word of the LORD that came unto Hosea, the son of Beeri, in the days of Uzziah, Jotham, Ahaz, *and* Hezekiah, kings of Judah, and in the days of Jeroboam the son of Joash, king of Israel.

BEEROTH

• A station of the Israelites.

• Aaron died at.

Dt 10:6 — And the children of Israel took their journey from Beeroth of the children of Jaakan to Mosera: there Aaron died, and there he was buried; and Eleazar his son ministered in the priest's office in his stead.

See: Bene-Jaakan

• A city of the Hivites.

Jos 9:17 — And the children of Israel journeyed, and came unto their cities on the third day. Now their cities *were* Gibeon, and Chephirah, and Beeroth, and Kirjath-jearim.

Jos 18:25 — Gibeon, and Ramah, and Beeroth,

2Sa 4:2 — And Saul's son had two men *that were* captains of bands: the name of the one *was* Baanah, and the name of the other Rechab, the sons of Rimmon a Beerothite, of the children of Benjamin: (for Beeroth also was reckoned to Benjamin:

Ezr 2:25 — The children of Kirjath-arim, Chephirah, and Beeroth, seven hundred and forty and three.

Ne 7:29 — The men of Kirjath-jearim, Chephirah, and Beeroth, seven hundred forty and three.

BEESH-TERAH

• A Levitical city.

Jos 21:27 — And unto the children of Gershon, of the families of the Levites, out of the *other* half tribe of Manasseh *they gave* Golan in Bashan with her suburbs, *to be* a city of refuge for the slayer; and Beesh-terah with her suburbs; two cities.

• Called Ashtaroth.

1Ch 6:71 — Unto the sons of Gershom *were given* out of the family of the half tribe of Manasseh, Golan in Bashan with her suburbs, and Ashtaroth with her suburbs:

BEETLE

• Authorized as food.

Le 11:22 — *Even* these of them ye may eat; the locust after his kind, and the bald locust after his kind, and the beetle after his kind, and the grasshopper after his kind.

BEGGARS

• Set among princes.

1Sa 2:8 — He raiseth up the poor out of the dust, *and* lifteth up the beggar from the dunghill, to set *them* among princes, and to make them inherit the throne of glory: for the pillars of the earth *are* the LORD'S, and he hath set the world upon them.

• Not the seed of the righteous.

Ps 37:25 — I have been young, and *now* am old; yet have I not seen the righteous forsaken, nor his seed begging bread.

• The children of the wicked.

Ps 109:10 — Let his children be continually vagabonds, and beg: let them seek *their bread* also out of their desolate places.

Pr 20:4 — The sluggard will not plow by reason of the cold; *therefore* shall he beg in harvest, and *have* nothing.

Lk 16:3 — Then the steward said within himself, What shall I do? for my lord taketh away from me the stewardship: I cannot dig; to beg I am ashamed.

• Instances of.

• Bartimeus.

Mk 10:46

• Lazarus.

Lk 16:20–22

• The blind man.

Jn 9:8

• The lame man.

Ac 3:2–5

See: Poor

BEHAVIOUR

Rev 5:1–10

Ro 8:17 — And if children, then heirs; heirs of God, and joint-heirs with Christ; if so be that we suffer with *him*, that we may be also glorified together.

1Co 6:2 — Do ye not know that the saints shall judge the world? and if the world shall be judged by you, are ye unworthy to judge the smallest matters?

2Pe 3:11 — *Seeing* then *that* all these things shall be dissolved, what manner *of persons* ought ye to be in *all* holy conversation and godliness,

BEHEADING

• Execution by.

• Of John.

Mt 14:10 — And he sent, and beheaded John in the prison.

Mk 6:27 — And immediately the king sent an executioner, and commanded his head to be brought: and he went and beheaded him in the prison,

• Of James.

Ac 12:2 — And he killed James the brother of John with the sword.

• Of the martyrs.

Rev 20:4 — And I saw thrones, and they sat upon them, and judgment was given unto them: and *I saw* the souls of them that were beheaded for the witness of Jesus, and for the word of God, and which had not worshipped the beast, neither his image, neither had received *his* mark upon their foreheads, or in their hands; and they lived and reigned with Christ a thousand years.

*See: **Punishment**

BEHEMOTH • An amphibious animal.

Job 40:15 — Behold now behemoth, which I made with thee; he eateth grass as an ox.

BEKAH • A half shekel.

Ex 38:26 — A bekah for every man, *that is,* half a shekel, after the shekel of the sanctuary, for every one that went to be numbered, from twenty years old and upward, for six hundred thousand and three thousand and five hundred and fifty *men.*

BEL • A Babylonian god.

Isa 46:1 — Bel boweth down, Nebo stoopeth, their idols were upon the beasts, and upon the cattle: your carriages *were* heavy loaden; *they are* a burden to the weary *beast.*

Jer 50:2 — Declare ye among the nations, and publish, and set up a standard; publish, *and* conceal not: say, Babylon is taken, Bel is confounded, Merodach is broken in pieces; her idols are confounded, her images are broken in pieces.

Jer 51:44 — And I will punish Bel in Babylon, and I will bring forth out of his mouth that which he hath swallowed up: and the nations shall not flow together any more unto him: yea, the wall of Babylon shall fall.

BELA

• A city. Called also Zoar.

Ge 14:2 — *That these* made war with Bera king of Sodom, and with Birsha king of Gomorrah, Shinab king of Admah, and Shemeber king of Zeboiim, and the king of Bela, which is Zoar.

Ge 14:8 — And there went out the king of Sodom, and the king of Gomorrah, and the king of Admah, and the king of Zeboiim, and the king of Bela (the same *is* Zoar;) and they joined battle with them in the vale of Siddim;

• King of Edom.

Ge 36:32–33; 1Ch 1:43–44

• Son of Benjamin.

1Ch 7:6–7

Nu 26:38 — The sons of Benjamin after their families: of Bela, the family of the Belaites: of Ashbel, the family of the Ashbelites: of Ahiram, the family of the Ahiramites:

Nu 26:40 — And the sons of Bela were Ard and Naaman: *of Ard,* the family of the Ardites: *and* of Naaman, the family of the Naamites.

1Ch 8:1 — Now Benjamin begat Bela his firstborn, Ashbel the second, and Aharah the third,

1Ch 8:3 — And the sons of Bela were, Addar, and Gera, and Abihud,

• Called Belah.

Ge 46:21 — And the sons of Benjamin were Belah, and Becher, and Ashbel, Gera, and Naaman, Ehi, and Rosh, Muppim, and Huppim, and Ard.

• Son of Azaz.

1Ch 5:8 — And Bela the son of Azaz, the son of Shema, the son of Joel, who dwelt in Aroer, even unto Nebo and Baal-meon:

BELIAL • Lawlessness.

Dt 13:13 — *Certain* men, the children of Belial, are gone out from among you, and have withdrawn the inhabitants of their city, saying, Let us go and serve other gods, which ye have not known;

2Co 6:15 — And what concord hath Christ with Belial? or what part hath he that believeth with an infidel?

BELIEF

Eph 2:8–9

Jn 3:16 — For God so loved the world, that he gave his only begotten Son, that whosoever believeth in him should not perish, but have everlasting life.

Jn 3:36 — He that believeth on the Son hath everlasting life: and he that believeth not the Son shall not see life; but the wrath of God abideth on him.

Jn 20:31 — But these are written, that ye might believe that Jesus is the Christ, the Son of God; and that believing ye might have life through his name.

Ac 3:16 — And his name through faith in his name hath made this man strong, whom ye see and know: yea, the faith which is by him hath given him this perfect soundness in the presence of you all.

Ac 16:31 — And they said, Believe on the Lord Jesus Christ, and thou shalt be saved, and thy house.

BELIEVER *See: Righteous

BELIEVING *See: Faith

BELL

• Attached to the hem of the priest's robe.

Ex 28:33–34; 39:25–26

• On horses.

Zec 14:20 — In that day shall there be upon the bells of the horses, HOLINESS UNTO THE LORD; and the pots in the LORD's house shall be like the bowls before the altar.

BELLOWS

• Used with the furnace of the founder.

Jer 6:29 — The bellows are burned, the lead is consumed of the fire; the founder melteth in vain: for the wicked are not plucked away.

BELLY

• Used figuratively for the seat of the affections.

Job 15:2 — Should a wise man utter vain knowledge, and fill his belly with the east wind?

Job 15:35 — They conceive mischief, and bring forth vanity, and their belly prepareth deceit.

Job 20:20 — Surely he shall not feel quietness in his belly, he shall not save of that which he desired.

Ps 44:25 — For our soul is bowed down to the dust: our belly cleaveth unto the earth.

Pr 18:20 — A man's belly shall be satisfied with the fruit of his mouth; *and* with the increase of his lips shall he be filled.

Pr 20:27 — The spirit of man *is* the candle of the LORD, searching all the inward parts of the belly.

Pr 20:30 — The blueness of a wound cleanseth away evil: so *do* stripes the inward parts of the belly.

Hab 3:16 — When I heard, my belly trembled; my lips quivered at the voice: rottenness entered into my bones, and I trembled in myself, that I might rest in the day of trouble: when he cometh up unto the people, he will invade them with his troops.

Jn 7:38 — He that believeth on me, as the scripture hath said, out of his belly shall flow rivers of living water.

Tit 1:12 — One of themselves, *even* a prophet of their own, said, The Cretians *are* alway liars, evil beasts, slow bellies.

BELOVED

SS 2:16 — My beloved *is* mine, and I *am* his: he feedeth among the lilies.

SS 6:3 — I *am* my beloved's, and my beloved *is* mine: he feedeth among the lilies.

BELSHAZZAR • King of Babylon.

Da 5:1–30

BELTESHAZZAR

• Name given Daniel.

Da 1:7 — Unto whom the prince of the eunuchs gave names: for he gave unto Daniel *the name* of Belteshazzar; and to Hananiah, of Shadrach; and to Mishael, of Meshach; and to Azariah, of Abed-nego.

→See: Daniel

BEN • A Levite.

1Ch 15:18 — And with them their brethren of the second *degree,* Zechariah, Ben, and Jaaziel, and Shemiramoth, and Jehiel, and Unni, Eliab, and Benaiah, and Maaseiah, and Mattithiah, and Elipheleh, and Mikneiah, and Obed-edom, and Jeiel, the porters.

BEN-ABINADAB →See: Abinadab

BEN-AMMI • Son of Lot.

Ge 19:38 — And the younger, she also bare a son, and called his name Benammi: the same *is* the father of the children of Ammon unto this day.

BEN-DEKAR →See: Dekar

BEN-GEBER →See: Geber

BEN-HADAD

• King of Syria.

1Ki 15:18–20; 2Ch 16:2–4

• A king of Syria, who reigned in the time of Ahab, son of Ben-hadad I.

1Ki 20:1–43; 2Ki 5:1–7:20; 8:7–15

• Son of Hazael and king of Syria.

2Ki 13:24–25

2Ki 13:3 — And the anger of the LORD was kindled against Israel, and he delivered them into the hand of Hazael king of Syria, and into the hand of Ben-hadad the son of Hazael, all *their* days.

Am 1:4 — But I will send a fire into the house of Hazael, which shall devour the palaces of Ben-hadad.

BEN-HAIL • A prince of Judah.

2Ch 17:7 — Also in the third year of his reign he sent to his princes, *even* to Ben-hail, and to Obadiah, and to Zechariah, and to Nethaneel, and to Michaiah, to teach in the cities of Judah.

BEN-HANAN • A son of Shimon.

1Ch 4:20 — And the sons of Shimon *were,* Amnon, and Rinnah, Ben-hanan, and Tilon. And the sons of Ishi *were,* Zoheth, and Ben-zoheth.

BEN-HUR →See: Hur

BEN-ONI • Name given Benjamin by Rachel.

Ge 35:18 — And it came to pass, as her soul was in departing, (for she died) that she called his name Ben-oni: but his father called him Benjamin.

BEN-ZOHETH • Son if Ishi.

1Ch 4:20 — And the sons of Shimon *were,* Amnon, and Rinnah, Ben-hanan, and Tilon. And the sons of Ishi *were,* Zoheth, and Ben-zoheth.

BENAIAH

• Son of Jehoiada, commander of the Cherethites and Pelethites.

2Sa 8:18 — And Benaiah the son of Jehoiada *was over* both the Cherethites and the Pelethites; and David's sons were chief rulers.

1Ki 1:38 — So Zadok the priest, and Nathan the prophet, and Benaiah the son of Jehoiada, and the Cherethites, and the Pelethites, went down, and caused Solomon to ride upon king David's mule, and brought him to Gihon.

• A distinguished warrior.

2Sa 23:20–23; 1Ch 11:22–25; 27:5–6

• Loyal to Solomon.

1Ki 1:2 — Wherefore his servants said unto him, Let there be sought for my lord the king a young virgin: and let her stand before the king, and let her cherish him, and let her lie in thy bosom, that my lord the king may get heat.

1Ki 4:4 — And Benaiah the son of Jehoiada *was* over the host: and Zadok and Abiathar *were* the priests:

- **An Ephraimite, and distinguished warrior.**

2Sa 23:30 — Benaiah the Pirathonite, Hiddai of the brooks of Gaash,

1Ch 11:31 — Ithai the son of Ribai of Gibeah, *that pertained* to the children of Benjamin, Benaiah the Pirathonite,

1Ch 27:14 — The eleventh *captain* for the eleventh month *was* Benaiah the Pirathonite, of the children of Ephraim: and in his course *were* twenty and four thousand.

- **A Levitical musician.**

1Ch 15:18 — And with them their brethren of the second *degree,* Zechariah, Ben, and Jaaziel, and Shemiramoth, and Jehiel, and Unni, Eliab, and Benaiah, and Maaseiah, and Mattithiah, and Elipheleh, and Mikneiah, and Obed-edom, and Jeiel, the porters.

1Ch 15:20 — And Zechariah, and Aziel, and Shemiramoth, and Jehiel, and Unni, and Eliab, and Maaseiah, and Benaiah, with psalteries on Alamoth;

1Ch 16:5 — Asaph the chief, and next to him Zechariah, Jeiel, and Shemiramoth, and Jehiel, and Mattithiah, and Eliab, and Benaiah, and Obed-edom: and Jeiel with psalteries and with harps; but Asaph made a sound with cymbals;

- **A priest.**

1Ch 15:24 — And Shebaniah, and Jehoshaphat, and Nethaneel, and Amasai, and Zechariah, and Benaiah, and Eliezer, the priests, did blow with the trumpets before the ark of God: and Obed-edom and Jehiah *were* doorkeepers for the ark.

1Ch 16:6 — Benaiah also and Jahaziel the priests with trumpets continually before the ark of the covenant of God.

- **Son of Jeiel.**

2Ch 20:14 — Then upon Jahaziel the son of Zechariah, the son of Benaiah, the son of Jeiel, the son of Mattaniah, a Levite of the sons of Asaph, came the Spirit of the LORD in the midst of the congregation;

- **A Levite in time of Hezekiah.**

2Ch 31:13 — And Jehiel, and Azaziah, and Nahath, and Asahel, and Jerimoth, and Jozabad, and Eliel, and Ismachiah, and Mahath, and Benaiah, *were* overseers under the hand of Cononiah and Shimei his brother, at the commandment of Hezekiah the king, and Azariah the ruler of the house of God.

- **A chief of the Simeonites.**

1Ch 4:36 — And Elioenai, and Jaakobah, and Jeshohaiah, and Asaiah, and Adiel, and Jesimiel, and Benaiah,

- **Father of Pelatiah.**

Eze 11:1 — Moreover the spirit lifted me up, and brought me unto the east gate of the LORD'S house, which looketh eastward: and behold at the door of the gate five and twenty men; among whom I saw Jaazaniah the son of Azur, and Pelatiah the son of Benaiah, the princes of the people.

Eze 11:13 — And it came to pass, when I prophesied, that Pelatiah the son of Benaiah died. Then fell I down upon my face, and cried with a loud voice, and said, Ah Lord GOD! wilt thou make a full end of the remnant of Israel?

- **Son of Parosh.**

Ezr 10:25 — Moreover of Israel: of the sons of Parosh; Ramiah, and Jeziah, and Malchiah, and Miamin, and Eleazar, and Malchijah, and Benaiah.

- **Son of Pahath-moab.**

Ezr 10:30 — And of the sons of Pahath-moab; Adna, and Chelal, Benaiah, Maaseiah, Mattaniah, Bezaleel, and Binnui, and Manasseh.

- **Son of Bani.**

Ezr 10:35 — Benaiah, Bedeiah, Chelluh,

- **Son of Nebo.**

Ezr 10:43 — Of the sons of Nebo; Jeiel, Mattithiah, Zabad, Zebina, Jadau, and Joel, Benaiah.

BENCH • Of ivory.

Eze 27:6 — *Of* the oaks of Bashan have they made thine oars; the company of the Ashurites have made thy benches *of* ivory, *brought* out of the isles of Chittim.

BENE-BERAK • A city of Dan.

Jos 19:45 — And Jehud, and Bene-berak, and Gath-rimmon,

BENE-JAAKAN

- **A tribe that gave its name to certain wells in the wilderness.**

Nu 33:31–32

- **Called Beeroth.**

Dt 10:6 — And the children of Israel took their journey from Beeroth of the children of Jaakan to Mosera: there Aaron died, and there he was buried; and Eleazar his son ministered in the priest's office in his stead.

BENEDICTIONS

- **Divinely appointed.**

Nu 6:23–26

Dt 10:8 — At that time the LORD separated the tribe of Levi, to bear the ark of the covenant of the LORD, to stand before the LORD to minister unto him, and to bless in his name, unto this day.

Dt 21:5 — And the priests the sons of Levi shall come near; for them the LORD thy God hath chosen to minister unto him, and to bless in the name of the LORD; and by their word shall every controversy and every stroke be *tried:*

- **Given by God**
  - **Upon creatures he had made.**

Ge 1:22 — And God blessed them, saying, Be fruitful, and multiply, and fill the waters in the seas, and let fowl multiply in the earth.

  - **Upon man.**

Ge 1:28 — And God blessed them, and God said unto them, Be fruitful, and multiply, and replenish the earth, and subdue it: and have dominion over the fish of the sea, and over the fowl of the air, and over every living thing that moveth upon the earth.

• **Upon Noah.**
Ge 9:1–2

• **Instances of.**

• **By Melchizedek, upon Abraham.**
Ge 14:19–20; Heb 7:7

• **By Bethuel's household, upon Rebekah.**
Ge 24:60

• **By Isaac.**

• **Upon Jacob.**
Ge 27:23–29, 37; 28:1–4

• **Upon Esau.**
Ge 27:39–40

• **By Jacob.**

• **Upon Pharaoh.**
Ge 47:7–10

• **Upon Joseph's sons.**
Ge 48:1–22

• **Upon his own sons.**
Ge 49:1–33

• **By Moses, upon the tribes of Israel.**
Dt 33:1–29

• **By Aaron.**
Le 9:22–23

• **By Aaron and by half the tribes, who stood on mount Gerizim.**
Dt 11:29–30; 27:11–13; Jos 8:33

• **By Joshua.**

• **Upon Caleb.**
Jos 14:13

• **Upon the Reubenites and Gadites, and half-tribe of Manasseh.**
Jos 22:6–7

• **By Naomi, upon Ruth and Orpah.**
Ru 1:8–9

• **By the people, upon Ruth.**
Ru 4:11–12

• **By Eli, upon Elkanah.**
1Sa 2:20

• **By David.**

• **Upon the people.**
2Sa 6:18

• **Upon Barzillai.**
2Sa 19:39

• **By Araunah, upon David.**
2Sa 24:23

• **By Solomon, upon the people.**
1Ki 8:14; 8:55–58; 2Ch 6:3

• **By Simeon, upon Jesus.**
Lk 2:34

• **By Jesus.**
Lk 24:50

• **Levitical, forms of.**
Nu 6:23–26

• **Apostolic, forms of.**
Ro 15:5–6; Eph 6:23–24; Heb 13:20–21; 1Pe 5:10–11; 2Pe 1:2–4

Ro 1:7 — To all that be in Rome, beloved of God, called *to be* saints: Grace to you and peace from God our Father, and the Lord Jesus Christ.

Ro 15:13 — Now the God of hope fill you with all joy and peace in believing, that ye may abound in hope, through the power of the Holy Ghost.

Ro 15:33 — Now the God of peace *be* with you all. Amen.

Ro 16:20 — And the God of peace shall bruise Satan under your feet shortly. The grace of our Lord Jesus Christ *be* with you. Amen.

Ro 16:24 — The grace of our Lord Jesus Christ *be* with you all. Amen.

1Co 1:3 — Grace *be* unto you, and peace, from God our Father, and *from* the Lord Jesus Christ.

1Co 16:23 — The grace of our Lord Jesus Christ *be* with you.

2Co 1:2 — Grace be to you and peace from God our Father, and *from* the Lord Jesus Christ.

2Co 13:14 — The grace of the Lord Jesus Christ, and the love of God, and the communion of the Holy Ghost, *be* with you all. Amen.

Gal 1:3 — Grace *be* to you and peace from God the Father, and *from* our Lord Jesus Christ,

Gal 6:16 — And as many as walk according to this rule, peace *be* on them, and mercy, and upon the Israel of God.

Gal 6:18 — Brethren, the grace of our Lord Jesus Christ *be* with your spirit. Amen.

Eph 1:2 — Grace *be* to you, and peace, from God our Father, and *from* the Lord Jesus Christ.

Php 1:2 — Grace *be* unto you, and peace, from God our Father, and *from* the Lord Jesus Christ.

Php 4:23 — The grace of our Lord Jesus Christ *be* with you all. Amen.

Col 1:2 — To the saints and faithful brethren in Christ which are at Colosse: Grace *be* unto you, and peace, from God our Father and the Lord Jesus Christ.

1Th 1:1 — Paul, and Silvanus, and Timotheus, unto the church of the Thessalonians *which is* in God the Father and *in* the Lord Jesus Christ: Grace *be* unto you, and peace, from God our Father, and the Lord Jesus Christ.

1Th 5:28 — The grace of our Lord Jesus Christ *be* with you. Amen.

2Th 1:2 — Grace unto you, and peace, from God our Father and the Lord Jesus Christ.

2Th 3:16 — Now the Lord of peace himself give you peace always by all means. The Lord *be* with you all.

2Th 3:18 — The grace of our Lord Jesus Christ *be* with you all. Amen.

1Ti 1:2 — Unto Timothy, *my* own son in the faith: Grace, mercy, *and* peace, from God our Father and Jesus Christ our Lord.

1Ti 6:21 — Which some professing have erred concerning the faith. Grace *be* with thee. Amen.

2Ti 1:2 — To Timothy, *my* dearly beloved son: Grace, mercy, *and* peace, from God the Father and Christ Jesus our Lord.

2Ti 4:22 — The Lord Jesus Christ *be* with thy spirit. Grace *be* with you. Amen.

Tit 3:15 — All that are with me salute thee. Greet them that love us in the faith. Grace *be* with you all. Amen.

Phm 1:3 — Grace to you, and peace, from God our Father and the Lord Jesus Christ.

Phm 1:25 — The grace of our Lord Jesus Christ *be* with your spirit. Amen.

Heb 13:25 — Grace *be* with you all. Amen.

1Pe 1:2 — Elect according to the foreknowledge of God the Father, through sanctification of the Spirit, unto obedience and sprinkling of the blood of Jesus Christ: Grace unto you, and peace, be multiplied.

1Pe 5:14 — Greet ye one another with a kiss of charity. Peace *be* with you all that are in Christ Jesus. Amen.

2Jn 1:3 — Grace be with you, mercy, *and* peace, from God the Father, and from the Lord Jesus Christ, the Son of the Father, in truth and love.

Jude 1:2 — Mercy unto you, and peace, and love, be multiplied.

Rev 22:21 — The grace of our Lord Jesus Christ *be* with you all. Amen.

BENEFACTOR

Lk 22:25 — And he said unto them, The kings of the Gentiles exercise lordship over them; and they that exercise authority upon them are called benefactors.

BENEFICENCE

Le 25:35–43; Dt 15:7–15; Pr 3:27–28; 25:21–22; Isa 58:6–7, 10–11; Eze 18:7–9; Mt 25:35–45; Ac 6:1–4; 11:29–30; Ro 15:25–27; 1Co 16:1–3; 2Co 8:1–15; 8:24–9:15; Php 4:10–18; Jas 2:15–16

Dt 15:18 — It shall not seem hard unto thee, when thou sendest him away free from thee; for he hath been worth a double hired servant *to thee,* in serving thee six years: and the LORD thy God shall bless thee in all that thou doest.

Ps 41:1 — Blessed *is* he that considereth the poor: the LORD will deliver him in time of trouble.

Ps 112:9 — He hath dispersed, he hath given to the poor; his righteousness endureth for ever; his horn shall be exalted with honour.

Pr 11:25 — The liberal soul shall be made fat: and he that watereth shall be watered also himself.

Pr 22:9 — He that hath a bountiful eye shall be blessed; for he giveth of his bread to the poor.

Pr 28:27 — He that giveth unto the poor shall not lack: but he that hideth his eyes shall have many a curse.

Eze 18:5 — But if a man be just, and do that which is lawful and right,

Mt 5:42 — Give to him that asketh thee, and from him that would borrow of thee turn not thou away.

Mt 19:21 — Jesus said unto him, If thou wilt be perfect, go *and* sell that thou hast, and give to the poor, and thou shalt have treasure in heaven: and come *and* follow me.

Mk 9:41 — For whosoever shall give you a cup of water to drink in my name, because ye belong to Christ, verily I say unto you, he shall not lose his reward.

Mk 10:21 — Then Jesus beholding him loved him, and said unto him, One thing thou lackest: go thy way, sell whatsoever thou hast, and give to the poor, and thou shalt have treasure in heaven: and come, take up the cross, and follow me.

Lk 3:11 — He answereth and saith unto them, He that hath two coats, let him impart to him that hath none; and he that hath meat, let him do likewise.

Lk 11:41 — But rather give alms of such things as ye have; and, behold, all things are clean unto you.

1Co 13:3 — And though I bestow all my goods to feed *the poor,* and though I give my body to be burned, and have not charity, it profiteth me nothing.

Gal 2:10 — Only *they would* that we should remember the poor; the same which I also was forward to do.

1Ti 5:8 — But if any provide not for his own, and specially for those of his own house, he hath denied the faith, and is worse than an infidel.

1Ti 5:16 — If any man or woman that believeth have widows, let them relieve them, and let not the church be charged; that it may relieve them that are widows indeed.

1Ti 6:18 — That they do good, that they be rich in good works, ready to distribute, willing to communicate;

Heb 6:10 — For God *is* not unrighteous to forget your work and labour of love, which ye have shewed toward his name, in that ye have ministered to the saints, and do minister.

Heb 13:16 — But to do good and to communicate forget not: for with such sacrifices God is well pleased.

1Jn 3:17 — But whoso hath this world's good, and seeth his brother have need, and shutteth up his bowels *of compassion* from him, how dwelleth the love of God in him?

See: Alms

See: Liberality

See: Poor; duty to

See: Rich

See: Riches

- **Instances of.**
  - **The old man of Gibeah.**
    Jgs 19:16–21
  - **Boaz.**
    Ru 2:1–23
  - **The returned exile Jews.**
    Ne 5:8–12; 8:10–11
  - **Job.**
    Job 29:11–17; Job 31:16–23
  - **The Temanites.**
    Isa 21:14
  - **The good Samaritan.**
    Lk 10:33–35
  - **Zacchaeus.**
    Lk 19:8
  - **The first Christians.**
    Ac 2:44–46; 4:32–37
  - **Cornelius.**
    Ac 10:2, 4
  - **Onesiphorus.**
    2Ti 1:16–18

See: Alms

See: Poor; duty to

BENEVOLENCE

↞See: Alms

↞See: Beneficence

↞See: Charitableness

↞See: Liberality

↞See: Love

BENINU • A Levite.

Ne 10:13 — Hodijah, Bani, Beninu.

BENJAMIN

• Son of Jacob by Rachel.

Ge 35:18 — And it came to pass, as her soul was in departing, (for she died) that she called his name Ben-oni: but his father called him Benjamin.

Ge 35:24 — The sons of Rachel; Joseph, and Benjamin:

Ge 46:19 — The sons of Rachel Jacob's wife; Joseph, and Benjamin.

• Taken into Egypt.

Ge 42:1–45:28

• Prophecy concerning.

Ge 49:27 — Benjamin shall ravin *as* a wolf: in the morning he shall devour the prey, and at night he shall divide the spoil.

• Descendants of.

Nu 26:38–41

Ge 46:21 — And the sons of Benjamin were Belah, and Becher, and Ashbel, Gera, and Naaman, Ehi, and Rosh, Muppim, and Huppim, and Ard.

• Tribe of.

• Census of, at Sinai.

Nu 1:37 — Those that were numbered of them, *even* of the tribe of Benjamin, *were* thirty and five thousand and four hundred.

• Census of, in the plain of Moab.

Nu 26:41 — These *are* the sons of Benjamin after their families: and they that were numbered of them *were* forty and five thousand and six hundred.

• Clans of.

Nu 26:38–40; 1Ch 7:6–12; 8:1–40

• Position of, in camp and march.

Nu 2:18 — On the west side *shall be* the standard of the camp of Ephraim according to their armies: and the captain of the sons of Ephraim *shall be* Elishama the son of Ammihud.

Nu 2:22 — Then the tribe of Benjamin: and the captain of the sons of Benjamin *shall be* Abidan the son of Gideoni.

• Moses' benediction upon.

Dt 32:12 — *So* the LORD alone did lead him, and *there was* no strange god with him.

• Allotment in the land of Canaan.

Jos 18:11–28

• Reallotment.

Eze 48:23 — As for the rest of the tribes, from the east side unto the west side, Benjamin *shall have* a *portion.*

• Did not exterminate the Jebusites.

Jgs 1:21 — And the children of Benjamin did not drive out the Jebusites that inhabited Jerusalem; but the Jebusites dwell with the children of Benjamin in Jerusalem unto this day.

• Join Deborah in the war against Sisera.

Jgs 5:14 — Out of Ephraim *was there* a root of them against Amalek; after thee, Benjamin, among thy people; out of Machir came down governors, and out of Zebulun they that handle the pen of the writer.

• Territory of, invaded by the Ammonites.

Jgs 10:9 — Moreover the children of Ammon passed over Jordan to fight also against Judah, and against Benjamin, and against the house of Ephraim; so that Israel was sore distressed.

• Did not avenge the crime of the Gibeonites against the Levite's concubine; the war that followed.

Jgs 19:1–20:48

• Saul, the first king of Israel, from.

1Sa 10:20–21

1Sa 9:1 — Now there was a man of Benjamin, whose name *was* Kish, the son of Abiel, the son of Zeror, the son of Bechorath, the son of Aphiah, a Benjamite, a mighty man of power.

1Sa 9:17 — And when Samuel saw Saul, the LORD said unto him, Behold the man whom I spake to thee of! this same shall reign over my people.

• Its rank in the time of Samuel.

1Sa 9:21 — And Saul answered and said, *Am* not I a Benjamite, of the smallest of the tribes of Israel? and my family the least of all the families of the tribe of Benjamin? wherefore then speakest thou so to me?

• Jerusalem within the territory of.

Jer 6:1 — O ye children of Benjamin, gather yourselves to flee out of the midst of Jerusalem, and blow the trumpet in Tekoa, and set up a sign of fire in Beth-haccerem: for evil appeareth out of the north, and great destruction.

• A company of, joins David at Ziklag.

1Ch 12:1–2

1Ch 12:16 — And there came of the children of Benjamin and Judah to the hold unto David.

• Not enrolled by Joab when he took a census of the military forces of Israel.

1Ch 21:6 — But Levi and Benjamin counted he not among them: for the king's word was abominable to Joab.

• Loyal to Ish-bosheth, the son of Saul.

2Sa 2:9 — And made him king over Gilead, and over the Ashurites, and over Jezreel, and over Ephraim, and over Benjamin, and over all Israel.

2Sa 2:15 — Then there arose and went over by number twelve of Benjamin, which *pertained* to

Ish-bosheth the son of Saul, and twelve of the servants of David.

2Sa 2:31 — But the servants of David had smitten of Benjamin, and of Abner's men, *so that* three hundred and threescore men died.

1Ch 12:29 — And of the children of Benjamin, the kindred of Saul, three thousand: for hitherto the greatest part of them had kept the ward of the house of Saul.

• Subsequently joins David.

2Sa 19:16–17

2Sa 3:19 — And Abner also spake in the ears of Benjamin: and Abner went also to speak in the ears of David in Hebron all that seemed good to Israel, and that seemed good to the whole house of Benjamin.

• Loyal to Rehoboam.

1Ki 12:21 — And when Rehoboam was come to Jerusalem, he assembled all the house of Judah, with the tribe of Benjamin, an hundred and fourscore thousand chosen men, which were warriors, to fight against the house of Israel, to bring the kingdom again to Rehoboam the son of Solomon.

2Ch 11:1 — And when Rehoboam was come to Jerusalem, he gathered of the house of Judah and Benjamin an hundred and fourscore thousand chosen *men,* which were warriors, to fight against Israel, that he might bring the kingdom again to Rehoboam.

• Military forces of, in the reign of Asa.

2Ch 14:8 — And Asa had an army *of men* that bare targets and spears, out of Judah three hundred thousand; and out of Benjamin, that bare shields and drew bows, two hundred and fourscore thousand: all these *were* mighty men of valour.

• Military forces of, in the reign of Jehoshaphat.

2Ch 17:17 — And of Benjamin; Eliada a mighty man of valour, and with him armed men with bow and shield two hundred thousand.

• Skill in archery and as slingers of stones.

Jgs 3:15 — But when the children of Israel cried unto the LORD, the LORD raised them up a deliverer, Ehud the son of Gera, a Benjamite, a man lefthanded: and by him the children of Israel sent a present unto Eglon the king of Moab.

Jgs 20:16 — Among all this people *there were* seven hundred chosen men lefthanded; every one could sling stones at an hair *breadth,* and not miss.

1Ch 8:40 — And the sons of Ulam were mighty men of valour, archers, and had many sons, and sons' sons, an hundred and fifty. All these *are* of the sons of Benjamin.

1Ch 12:2 — *They were* armed with bows, and could use both the right hand and the left in *hurling* stones and *shooting* arrows out of a bow, *even* of Saul's brethren of Benjamin.

• Return to Palestine from the exile in Babylon.

Ezr 1:5 — Then rose up the chief of the fathers of Judah and Benjamin, and the priests, and the Levites, with all *them* whose spirit God had raised, to go up to build the house of the LORD which *is* in Jerusalem.

• Saints of, seen in John's vision.

Rev 7:8 — Of the tribe of Zabulon *were* sealed twelve thousand. Of the tribe of Joseph *were* sealed twelve thousand. Of the tribe of Benjamin *were* sealed twelve thousand.

• Paul, of the tribe of.

Ro 11:1 — I say then, Hath God cast away his people? God forbid. For I also am an Israelite, of the seed of Abraham, *of* the tribe of Benjamin.

Php 3:5 — Circumcised the eighth day, of the stock of Israel, *of* the tribe of Benjamin, an Hebrew of the Hebrews; as touching the law, a Pharisee;

➜See: Israel

• Grandson of Benjamin.

1Ch 7:10 — The sons also of Jediael; Bilhan: and the sons of Bilhan; Jeush, and Benjamin, and Ehud, and Chenaanah, and Zethan, and Tharshish, and Ahishahar.

• A son of Harim.

Ezr 10:32 — Benjamin, Malluch, *and* Shemariah.

• Probably identical with the man mentioned in.

Ne 3:23 — After him repaired Benjamin and Hashub over against their house. After him repaired Azariah the son of Maaseiah the son of Ananiah by his house.

• A Jew who assisted in purifying the wall of Jerusalem.

Ne 12:34 — Judah, and Benjamin, and Shemaiah, and Jeremiah,

• A gate of Jerusalem.

Jer 20:2 — Then Pashur smote Jeremiah the prophet, and put him in the stocks that *were* in the high gate of Benjamin, which *was* by the house of the LORD.

Jer 37:13 — And when he was in the gate of Benjamin, a captain of the ward *was* there, whose name *was* Irijah, the son of Shelemiah, the son of Hananiah; and he took Jeremiah the prophet, saying, Thou fallest away to the Chaldeans.

Jer 38:7 — Now when Ebed-melech the Ethiopian, one of the eunuchs which was in the king's house, heard that they had put Jeremiah in the dungeon; the king then sitting in the gate of Benjamin;

Zec 14:10 — All the land shall be turned as a plain from Geba to Rimmon south of Jerusalem: and it shall be lifted up, and inhabited in her place, from Benjamin's gate unto the place of the first gate, unto the corner gate, and *from* the tower of Hananeel unto the king's winepresses.

BENO • A descendant of Merari.

1Ch 24:26–27

BEON

• A place east of Jordan.

Nu 32:3 — Ataroth, and Dibon, and Jazer, and Nimrah, and Heshbon, and Elealeh, and Shebam, and Nebo, and Beon,

• Probably same as Baal-Meon.

Nu 32:38 — And Nebo, and Baal-meon, (their names being changed,) and Shibmah: and gave other names unto the cities which they builded.

BEOR

• Father of Bela.

Ge 36:32 — And Bela the son of Beor reigned in Edom: and the name of his city *was* Dinhabah.

1Ch 1:43 — Now these *are* the kings that reigned in the land of Edom before *any* king reigned over the children of Israel; Bela the son of Beor: and the name of his city *was* Dinhabah.

• Father of Balaam.

Nu 22:5 — He sent messengers therefore unto Balaam the son of Beor to Pethor, which *is* by the river of the land of the children of his people, to call him, saying, Behold, there is a people come out from Egypt: behold, they cover the face of the earth, and they abide over against me:

• Called Bosor.

2Pe 2:15 — Which have forsaken the right way, and are gone astray, following the way of Balaam *the son* of Bosor, who loved the wages of unrighteousness;

BEQUESTS ➜See: Will

BERA • King of Sodom.

Ge 14:2 — *That these* made war with Bera king of Sodom, and with Birsha king of Gomorrah, Shinab king of Admah, and Shemeber king of Zeboiim, and the king of Bela, which is Zoar.

BERACHAH

• An Israelite, who joined David at Ziklag.

1Ch 12:3 — The chief *was* Ahiezer, then Joash, the sons of Shemaah the Gibeathite; and Jeziel, and Pelet, the sons of Azmaveth; and Berachah, and Jehu the Antothite,

• A valley in the south of Judah, where the Israelites blessed the Lord for a victory.

2Ch 20:26 — And on the fourth day they assembled themselves in the valley of Berachah; for there they blessed the LORD: therefore the name of the same place was called, The valley of Berachah, unto this day.

BERACHIAH ➜See: Berechiah

BERAIAH • Son of Shimhi.

1Ch 8:21 — And Adaiah, and Beraiah, and Shimrath, the sons of Shimhi;

BEREA • A city in the south of Macedonia.

Ac 17:10 — And the brethren immediately sent away Paul and Silas by night unto Berea: who coming *thither* went into the synagogue of the Jews.

Ac 17:13 — But when the Jews of Thessalonica had knowledge that the word of God was preached of Paul at Berea, they came thither also, and stirred up the people.

Ac 20:4 — And there accompanied him into Asia Sopater of Berea; and of the Thessalonians, Aristarchus and Secundus; and Gaius of Derbe, and Timotheus; and of Asia, Tychicus and Trophimus.

BEREAVEMENT

• From God.

Ex 12:29 — And it came to pass, that at midnight the LORD smote all the firstborn in the land of Egypt, from the firstborn of Pharaoh that sat on his throne unto the firstborn of the captive that *was* in the dungeon; and all the firstborn of cattle.

Hos 9:12 — Though they bring up their children, yet will I bereave them, *that there shall* not *be* a man *left:* yea, woe also to them when I depart from them!

• Mourning in, forbidden to Aaron, on account of his son's wickedness.

Le 10:6 — And Moses said unto Aaron, and unto Eleazar and unto Ithamar, his sons, Uncover not your heads, neither rend your clothes; lest ye die, and lest wrath come upon all the people: but let your brethren, the whole house of Israel, bewail the burning which the LORD hath kindled.

• Mourning in, forbidden to Ezekiel, for his wife.

Eze 24:16–18

• Instances of.

• Abraham, of Sarah.

Ge 23:2

• Jacob, of Joseph.

Ge 37:34–35

• Joseph, of his father.

Ge 50:1, 4

• The Egyptians, of their firstborn.

Ex 12:29–33

• Naomi, of her husband.

Ru 1:3, 5, 20–21

• David.

• Of his child by Bath-sheba.

2Sa 12:15–23

• Of Absalom.

2Sa 18:33; 19:4

• Resignation in.

2Sa 12:22–23; Job 1:18–21; Ecc 7:2–4; 1Th 4:13–18

➜See: Assurance; saints privileged to have; comfort in affliction

➜See: Afflictions; resignation in

➜See: Resignation

BERECHIAH

• Father of Asaph.

1Ch 15:17 — So the Levites appointed Heman the son of Joel; and of his brethren, Asaph the son of Berechiah; and of the sons of Merari their brethren, Ethan the son of Kushaiah;

1Ch 15:23 — And Berechiah and Elkanah *were* doorkeepers for the ark.

• Called Berachiah.

1Ch 6:39 — And his brother Asaph, who stood on his right hand, *even* Asaph the son of Berachiah, the son of Shimea,

• A warrior of Ephraim.

2Ch 28:12 — Then certain of the heads of the children of Ephraim, Azariah the son of Johanan, Berechiah the son of Meshillemoth, and Jehizkiah the son of Shallum, and Amasa the son of Hadlai, stood up against them that came from the war,

• A brother of Zerubbabel.

1Ch 3:20 — And Hashubah, and Ohel, and Berechiah, and Hasadiah, Jushab-hesed, five.

• Son of Asa.

1Ch 9:16 — And Obadiah the son of Shemaiah, the son of Galal, the son of Jeduthun, and Berechiah the son of Asa, the son of Elkanah, that dwelt in the villages of the Netophathites.

• Son of Iddo.

Zec 1:1 — In the eighth month, in the second year of Darius, came the word of the LORD unto Zechariah, the son of Berechiah, the son of Iddo the prophet, saying,

Zec 1:7 — Upon the four and twentieth day of the eleventh month, which *is* the month Sebat, in the second year of Darius, came the word of the LORD unto Zechariah, the son of Berechiah, the son of Iddo the prophet, saying,

• Son of Meshezabeel.

Ne 3:4 — And next unto them repaired Meremoth the son of Urijah, the son of Koz. And next unto them repaired Meshullam the son of Berechiah, the son of Meshezabeel. And next unto them repaired Zadok the son of Baana.

Ne 3:30 — After him repaired Hananiah the son of Shelemiah, and Hanun the sixth son of Zalaph, another piece. After him repaired Meshullam the son of Berechiah over against his chamber.

Ne 6:18 — For *there were* many in Judah sworn unto him, because he *was* the son in law of Shechaniah the son of Arah; and his son Johanan had taken the daughter of Meshullam the son of Berechiah.

BERED

• A town in the south of Palestine.

Ge 16:14 — Wherefore the well was called Beer-lahai-roi; behold, *it is* between Kadesh and Bered.

• A son of Shuthelah.

1Ch 7:20 — And the sons of Ephraim; Shuthelah, and Bered his son, and Tahath his son, and Eladah his son, and Tahath his son,

• Probably same as Becher.

Nu 26:35 — These *are* the sons of Ephraim after their families: of Shuthelah, the family of the Shuthalhites: of Becher, the family of the Bachrites: of Tahan, the family of the Tahanites.

BERI • Son of Zophah.

1Ch 7:36 — The sons of Zophah; Suah, and Harnepher, and Shual, and Beri, and Imrah,

BERIAH

• Son of Asher.

Nu 26:44–45

Ge 46:17 — And the sons of Asher; Jimnah, and Ishuah, and Isui, and Beriah, and Serah their sister: and the sons of Beriah; Heber, and Malchiel.

1Ch 7:30 — The sons of Asher; Imnah, and Isuah, and Ishuai, and Beriah, and Serah their sister.

• Son of Ephraim.

1Ch 7:20–23

• A Benjamite.

1Ch 8:13 — Beriah also, and Shema, who *were* heads of the fathers of the inhabitants of Aijalon, who drove away the inhabitants of Gath:

• Son of Shimei.

1Ch 23:10–11

BERITH See: Baal-Berith

BERNICE • Daughter of Agrippa.

Ac 25:13 — And after certain days king Agrippa and Bernice came unto Caesarea to salute Festus.

Ac 25:23 — And on the morrow, when Agrippa was come, and Bernice, with great pomp, and was entered into the place of hearing, with the chief captains, and principal men of the city, at Festus' commandment Paul was brought forth.

Ac 26:30 — And when he had thus spoken, the king rose up, and the governor, and Bernice, and they that sat with them:

BERODACH-BALADAN See: Merodach-Baladan

BEROTHAH • Part of the northern boundary of Canaan.

Eze 47:16 — Hamath, Berothah, Sibraim, which *is* between the border of Damascus and the border of Hamath; Hazar-hatticon, which is by the coast of Hauran.

BEROTHAI • A city of Zobah.

2Sa 8:8 — And from Betah, and from Berothai, cities of Hadadezer, king David took exceeding much brass.

BERYL

• A precious stone.

SS 5:14 — His hands *are as* gold rings set with the beryl: his belly *is as* bright ivory overlaid *with* sapphires.

Eze 1:16 — The appearance of the wheels and their work *was* like unto the colour of a beryl: and they four had one likeness: and their appearance and their work was as it were a wheel in the middle of a wheel.

Eze 10:9 — And when I looked, behold the four wheels by the cherubims, one wheel by one cherub, and another wheel by another cherub: and the appearance of the wheels *was* as the colour of a beryl stone.

• Set in the breastplate.

Ex 28:20 — And the fourth row a beryl, and an onyx, and a jasper: they shall be set in gold in their inclosings.

Ex 39:13 — And the fourth row, a beryl, an onyx, and a jasper: *they were* inclosed in ouches of gold in their inclosings.

• John saw, in the foundation of the new Jerusalem.

Rev 21:20 — The fifth, sardonyx; the sixth, sardius; the seventh, chrysolite; the eighth, beryl; the ninth, a topaz; the tenth, a chrysoprasus; the eleventh, a jacinth; the twelfth, an amethyst.

BESAI • One of the Nethinim.

Ezr 2:49 — The children of Uzza, the children of Paseah, the children of Besai,

Ne 7:52 — The children of Besai, the children of Meunim, the children of Nephishesim,

BESODEIAH • Father of Meshullam.

Ne 3:6 — Moreover the old gate repaired Jehoiada the son of Paseah, and Meshullam the son of Besodeiah; they laid the beams thereof, and set up the doors thereof, and the locks thereof, and the bars thereof.

BESOR • A brook near Gaza.

1Sa 30:9–10

1Sa 30:21 — And David came to the two hundred men, which were so faint that they could not follow David, whom they had made also to abide at the brook Besor: and they went forth to meet David, and to meet the people that *were* with him: and when David came near to the people, he saluted them.

BESTIALITY

Ex 22:19 — Whosoever lieth with a beast shall surely be put to death.

Le 18:23 — Neither shalt thou lie with any beast to defile thyself therewith: neither shall any woman stand before a beast to lie down thereto: it *is* confusion.

Le 20:16 — And if a woman approach unto any beast, and lie down thereto, thou shalt kill the woman, and the beast: they shall surely be put to death; their blood *shall be* upon them.

+See: Sodomy

BETAH • A city belonging to Hadadezer.

2Sa 8:8 — And from Betah, and from Berothai, cities of Hadadezer, king David took exceeding much brass.

BETEN • A city of Asher.

Jos 19:25 — And their border was Helkath, and Hali, and Beten, and Achshaph,

BETH-ANATH • A fortified city of Naphtali.

Jos 19:38 — And Iron, and Migdal-el, Horem, and Beth-anath, and Beth-shemesh; nineteen cities with their villages.

Jgs 1:33 — Neither did Naphtali drive out the inhabitants of Beth-shemesh, nor the inhabitants of Beth-anath; but he dwelt among the Canaanites, the inhabitants of the land: nevertheless the inhabitants of Beth-shemesh and of Beth-anath became tributaries unto them.

BETH-ANOTH • A city in Judah.

Jos 15:59 — And Maarath, and Beth-anoth, and Eltekon; six cities with their villages:

BETH-ARABAH

• A city in the valley of the Dead Sea.

Jos 15:6 — And the border went up to Beth-hogla, and passed along by the north of Beth-arabah; and the border went up to the stone of Bohan the son of Reuben:

Jos 15:61 — In the wilderness, Beth-arabah, Middin, and Secacah,

Jos 18:22 — And Beth-arabah, and Zemaraim, and Bethel,

• Called Arabah.

Jos 18:18 — And passed along toward the side over against Arabah northward, and went down unto Arabah:

BETH-ARAM

• A fortified city of Gad.

Jos 13:27 — And in the valley, Beth-aram, and Beth-nimrah, and Succoth, and Zaphon, the rest of the kingdom of Sihon king of Heshbon, Jordan and *his* border, *even* unto the edge of the sea of Chinnereth on the other side Jordan eastward.

• Probably identical with Beth-Haran.

Nu 32:36 — And Beth-nimrah, and Beth-haran, fenced cities: and folds for sheep.

BETH-ARBEL • A city spoiled by Shalman.

Hos 10:14 — Therefore shall a tumult arise among thy people, and all thy fortresses shall be spoiled, as Shalman spoiled Beth-arbel in the day of battle: the mother was dashed in pieces upon *her* children.

BETH-AVEN • A place on the mountains of Benjamin.

Jos 7:2 — And Joshua sent men from Jericho to Ai, which *is* beside Beth-aven, on the east side of Bethel, and spake unto them, saying, Go up and view the country. And the men went up and viewed Ai.

Jos 18:12 — And their border on the north side was from Jordan; and the border went up to the side of

Jericho on the north side, and went up through the mountains westward; and the goings out thereof were at the wilderness of Beth-aven.

1Sa 13:5 — And the Philistines gathered themselves together to fight with Israel, thirty thousand chariots, and six thousand horsemen, and people as the sand which *is* on the sea shore in multitude: and they came up, and pitched in Michmash, eastward from Beth-aven.

1Sa 14:23 — So the LORD saved Israel that day: and the battle passed over unto Beth-aven.

Hos 4:15 — Though thou, Israel, play the harlot, *yet* let not Judah offend; and come not ye unto Gilgal, neither go ye up to Beth-aven, nor swear, The LORD liveth.

Hos 5:8 — Blow ye the cornet in Gibeah, *and* the trumpet in Ramah: cry aloud *at* Beth-aven, after thee, O Benjamin.

Hos 10:5 — The inhabitants of Samaria shall fear because of the calves of Beth-aven: for the people thereof shall mourn over it, and the priests thereof *that* rejoiced on it, for the glory thereof, because it is departed from it.

BETH-AZMAVETH

• A town of Benjamin.

Ne 7:28 — The men of Beth-azmaveth, forty and two.

• Called Azmaveth.

Ezr 2:24 — The children of Azmaveth, forty and two.

Ne 12:29 — Also from the house of Gilgal, and out of the fields of Geba and Azmaveth: for the singers had builded them villages round about Jerusalem.

BETH-BAAL-MEON

• A place in the tribe of Reuben.

Jos 13:17 — Heshbon, and all her cities that *are* in the plain; Dibon, and Bamoth-baal, and Beth-baal-meon,

• Called Baal-Meon.

Nu 32:38 — And Nebo, and Baal-meon, (their names being changed,) and Shibmah: and gave other names unto the cities which they builded.

Eze 25:9 — Therefore, behold, I will open the side of Moab from the cities, from his cities *which are* on his frontiers, the glory of the country, Beth-jeshimoth, Baal-meon, and Kiriathaim,

• Called Beon.

Nu 32:3 — Ataroth, and Dibon, and Jazer, and Nimrah, and Heshbon, and Elealeh, and Shebam, and Nebo, and Beon,

• Called Beth-Meon.

Jer 48:23 — And upon Kiriathaim, and upon Beth-gamul, and upon Beth-meon,

• Subdued by the Israelites.

Nu 32:3–4

• Assigned to the Reubenites.

Jos 13:17 — Heshbon, and all her cities that *are* in the plain; Dibon, and Bamoth-baal, and Beth-baal-meon,

BETH-BARAH • A place east of Jordan.

Jgs 7:24 — And Gideon sent messengers throughout all mount Ephraim, saying, Come down against the Midianites, and take before them the waters unto Beth-barah and Jordan. Then all the men of Ephraim gathered themselves together, and took the waters unto Beth-barah and Jordan.

BETH-BIREI

• A town of Simeon.

1Ch 4:31 — And at Beth-marcaboth, and Hazar-susim, and at Beth-birei, and at Shaaraim. These *were* their cities unto the reign of David.

See: Beth-Lebaoth

BETH-CAR • A place west of Mizpeh.

1Sa 7:11 — And the men of Israel went out of Mizpeh, and pursued the Philistines, and smote them, until *they came* under Beth-car.

BETH-DAGON

• A city of Judah.

Jos 15:41 — And Gederoth, Beth-dagon, and Naamah, and Makkedah; sixteen cities with their villages:

• A city of Asher.

Jos 19:27 — And turneth toward the sunrising to Beth-dagon, and reacheth to Zebulun, and to the valley of Jiphthah-el toward the north side of Beth-emek, and Neiel, and goeth out to Cabul on the left hand,

BETH-DIBLATHAIM

• A city of Moab.

Jer 48:22 — And upon Dibon, and upon Nebo, and upon Beth-diblathaim,

• Called Almon-Diblathaim.

Nu 33:46 — And they removed from Dibon-gad, and encamped in Almon-diblathaim.

BETHEL

• A city north of Jerusalem.

• The ancient city adjacent to, and finally embraced in, was called Luz.

Jgs 1:23–26

Jos 18:13 — And the border went over from thence toward Luz, to the side of Luz, which is Bethel, southward; and the border descended to Ataroth-adar, near the hill that *lieth* on the south side of the nether Beth-horon.

• Abraham establishes an altar at.

Ge 13:3–4

Ge 12:8 — And he removed from thence unto a mountain on the east of Bethel, and pitched his tent, *having* Bethel on the west, and Hai on the east: and there he builded an altar unto the LORD, and called upon the name of the LORD.

• The place where Jacob saw the vision of the ladder.

Ge 28:10–22

Ge 31:13 — I *am* the God of Bethel, where thou anointedst the pillar, *and* where thou vowedst a vow unto me: now arise, get thee out from this land, and return unto the land of thy kindred.

Hos 12:4 — Yea, he had power over the angel, and prevailed: he wept, and made supplication unto him: he found him *in* Bethel, and there he spake with us;

- **The place where Jacob builds an altar.**

Ge 35:1–15

- **Deborah dies at.**

Ge 35:8 — But Deborah Rebekah's nurse died, and she was buried beneath Bethel under an oak: and the name of it was called Allon-bachuth.

- **Conquered by Joshua.**

Jos 8:17 — And there was not a man left in Ai or Bethel, that went not out after Israel: and they left the city open, and pursued after Israel.

Jos 12:16 — The king of Makkedah, one; the king of Bethel, one;

- **Conquered by the house of Joseph.**

Jgs 1:22–26

- **Allotted to Benjamin.**

Jos 18:13 — And the border went over from thence toward Luz, to the side of Luz, which is Bethel, southward; and the border descended to Atarothadar, near the hill that *lieth* on the south side of the nether Beth-horon.

Jos 18:22 — And Beth-arabah, and Zemaraim, and Bethel,

- **Court of justice held at, by Deborah.**

Jgs 4:5 — And she dwelt under the palm tree of Deborah between Ramah and Bethel in mount Ephraim: and the children of Israel came up to her for judgment.

- **Court of justice held at, by Samuel.**

1Sa 7:16 — And he went from year to year in circuit to Bethel, and Gilgal, and Mizpeh, and judged Israel in all those places.

- **Tabernacle at, and called House of God.**

Jgs 20:18 — And the children of Israel arose, and went up to the house of God, and asked counsel of God, and said, Which of us shall go up first to the battle against the children of Benjamin? And the LORD said, Judah *shall go up* first.

Jgs 20:31 — And the children of Benjamin went out against the people, *and* were drawn away from the city; and they began to smite of the people, *and* kill, as at other times, in the highways, of which one goeth up to the house of God, and the other to Gibeah in the field, about thirty men of Israel.

Jgs 21:2 — And the people came to the house of God, and abode there till even before God, and lifted up their voices, and wept sore;

- **Jeroboam institutes idolatrous worship at.**

1Ki 12:25–33

2Ki 10:29 — Howbeit *from* the sins of Jeroboam the son of Nebat, who made Israel to sin, Jehu departed not from after them, *to wit,* the golden calves that *were* in Bethel, and that *were* in Dan.

- **Idolatry at.**

Jer 48:13 — And Moab shall be ashamed of Chemosh, as the house of Israel was ashamed of Bethel their confidence.

Am 4:4 — Come to Bethel, and transgress; at Gilgal multiply transgression; and bring your sacrifices every morning, *and* your tithes after three years:

- **Shalmanezer sends a priest to.**

2Ki 17:27–28

- **Prophecies against the idolatrous altars at.**

1Ki 13:1–6; 2Ki 23:15–20

1Ki 13:32 — For the saying which he cried by the word of the LORD against the altar in Bethel, and against all the houses of the high places which *are* in the cities of Samaria, shall surely come to pass.

2Ki 23:4 — And the king commanded Hilkiah the high priest, and the priests of the second order, and the keepers of the door, to bring forth out of the temple of the LORD all the vessels that were made for Baal, and for the grove, and for all the host of heaven: and he burned them without Jerusalem in the fields of Kidron, and carried the ashes of them unto Bethel.

Am 3:14 — That in the day that I shall visit the transgressions of Israel upon him I will also visit the altars of Bethel: and the horns of the altar shall be cut off, and fall to the ground.

- **The school of prophets at.**

2Ki 2:3 — And the sons of the prophets that *were* at Bethel came forth to Elisha, and said unto him, Knowest thou that the LORD will take away thy master from thy head to day? And he said, Yea, I know *it;* hold ye your peace.

- **Children of, mock Elisha.**

2Ki 2:23–24

- **People of, return from Babylon.**

Ezr 2:28 — The men of Bethel and Ai, two hundred twenty and three.

Ne 7:32 — The men of Bethel and Ai, an hundred twenty and three.

- **Prophecies against.**

Am 5:5 — But seek not Bethel, nor enter into Gilgal, and pass not to Beer-sheba: for Gilgal shall surely go into captivity, and Bethel shall come to nought.

- **A city in the south of Judah.**

1Sa 30:27 — To *them* which *were* in Bethel, and to *them* which *were* in south Ramoth, and to *them* which *were* in Jattir,

- **A mountain.**

1Sa 13:2 — Saul chose him three thousand *men* of Israel; *whereof* two thousand were with Saul in Michmash and in mount Bethel, and a thousand were with Jonathan in Gibeah of Benjamin: and the rest of the people he sent every man to his tent.

BETHEL-APHRAH • A place in Philistia.

Mic 1:10 — Declare ye *it* not at Gath, weep ye not at all: in the house of Aphrah roll thyself in the dust.

BETH-EMEK • A city of Asher.

Jos 19:27 — And turneth toward the sunrising to Beth-dagon, and reacheth to Zebulun, and to the valley of Jiphthah-el toward the north side of Beth-emek, and Neiel, and goeth out to Cabul on the left hand,

BETH-EZEL • A town of Judah.

Mic 1:11 — Pass ye away, thou inhabitant of Saphir, having thy shame naked: the inhabitant of Zaanan came not forth in the mourning of Beth-ezel; he shall receive of you his standing.

BETH-GADER

• A place in Judah.

1Ch 2:51 — Salma the father of Bethlehem, Hareph the father of Beth-gader.

• Probably identical with Geder.

Jos 12:13 — The king of Debir, one; the king of Geder, one;

• Probably identical with Gedor in.

Jos 15:58 — Halhul, Beth-zur, and Gedor,

BETH-GAMUL • A city of Moab.

Jer 48:23 — And upon Kiriathaim, and upon Beth-gamul, and upon Beth-meon,

BETH-HACCEREM • A mountain in Judah.

Ne 3:14 — But the dung gate repaired Malchiah the son of Rechab, the ruler of part of Beth-haccerem; he build it, and set up the doors thereof, the locks thereof, and the bars thereof.

Jer 6:1 — O ye children of Benjamin, gather yourselves to flee out of the midst of Jerusalem, and blow the trumpet in Tekoa, and set up a sign of fire in Beth-haccerem: for evil appeareth out of the north, and great destruction.

BETH-HAGGAN

• A garden house.

2Ki 9:27 — But when Ahaziah the king of Judah saw *this,* he fled by the way of the garden house. And Jehu followed after him, and said, Smite him also in the chariot. *And they did so* at the going up to Gur, which *is* by Ibleam. And he fled to Megiddo, and died there.

• Probably identical with En-Gannim.

Jos 19:21 — And Remeth, and En-gannim, and En-haddah, and Beth-pazzez;

BETH-HANAN **✦See: Elon-Beth-Hanan**

BETH-HARAN

• A fortified city east of Jordan.

Nu 32:36 — And Beth-nimrah, and Beth-haran, fenced cities: and folds for sheep.

• Probably identical with Beth-Aram.

Jos 13:27 — And in the valley, Beth-aram, and Beth-nimrah, and Succoth, and Zaphon, the rest of the kingdom of Sihon king of Heshbon, Jordan and *his* border, *even* unto the edge of the sea of Chinnereth on the other side Jordan eastward.

BETH-HOGLA • A place on the border of Judah.

Jos 15:6 — And the border went up to Beth-hogla, and passed along by the north of Beth-arabah; and the border went up to the stone of Bohan the son of Reuben:

Jos 18:19 — And the border passed along to the side of Beth-hoglah northward: and the outgoings of the border were at the north bay of the salt sea at the south end of Jordan: this *was* the south coast.

Jos 18:21 — Now the cities of the tribe of the children of Benjamin according to their families were Jericho, and Beth-hoglah, and the valley of Keziz,

BETH-HORON

• Two ancient cities of Canaan, near which Joshua defeated the Amorites.

Jos 10:10–11

Jos 16:3 — And goeth down westward to the coast of Japhleti, unto the coast of Beth-horon the nether, and to Gezer: and the goings out thereof are at the sea.

Jos 16:5 — And the border of the children of Ephraim according to their families was *thus:* even the border of their inheritance on the east side was Ataroth-addar, unto Beth-horon the upper;

Jos 18:13 — And the border went over from thence toward Luz, to the side of Luz, which is Bethel, southward; and the border descended to Ataroth-adar, near the hill that *lieth* on the south side of the nether Beth-horon.

1Sa 13:18 — And another company turned the way *to* Beth-horon: and another company turned *to* the way of the border that looketh to the valley of Zeboim toward the wilderness.

1Ch 7:24 — (And his daughter *was* Sherah, who built Beth-horon the nether, and the upper, and Uzzen-sherah.)

• Solomon builds.

1Ki 9:17 — And Solomon built Gezer, and Beth-horon the nether,

2Ch 8:5 — Also he built Beth-horon the upper, and Beth-horon the nether, fenced cities, with walls, gates, and bars;

• Taken from Judah by the ten tribes.

2Ch 25:13 — But the soldiers of the army which Amaziah sent back, that they should not go with him to battle, fell upon the cities of Judah, from Samaria even unto Beth-horon, and smote three thousand of them, and took much spoil.

BETH-JESHIMOTH

• A place in Moab.

Jos 12:3 — And from the plain to the sea of Chinneroth on the east, and unto the sea of the plain, *even* the salt sea on the east, the way to Beth-jeshimoth; and from the south, under Ashdoth-pisgah:

Jos 13:20 — And Beth-peor, and Ashdoth-pisgah, and Beth-jeshimoth,

Eze 25:9 — Therefore, behold, I will open the side of Moab from the cities, from his cities *which are* on his frontiers, the glory of the country, Beth-jeshimoth, Baal-meon, and Kiriathaim,

- **Called Beth-Jesimoth.**

Nu 33:49 — And they pitched by Jordan, from Beth-jesimoth *even* unto Abel-shittim in the plains of Moab.

BETH-JOAB ⇝See: Ataroth

BETH-LEBAOTH

- **A town of Simeon.**

Jos 19:6 — And Beth-lebaoth, and Sharuhen; thirteen cities and their villages:

- **Called Lebaoth.**

Jos 15:32 — And Lebaoth, and Shilhim, and Ain, and Rimmon: all the cities *are* twenty and nine, with their villages:

- **Called Beth-Birel.**

1Ch 4:31 — And at Beth-marcaboth, and Hazar-susim, and at Beth-birei, and at Shaaraim. These *were* their cities unto the reign of David.

BETH-MAACHAH • A city of Manasseh.

2Sa 20:14–15

2Sa 20:18 — Then she spake, saying, They were wont to speak in old time, saying, They shall surely ask *counsel* at Abel: and so they ended *the matter.*

2Ki 15:29 — In the days of Pekah king of Israel came Tiglath-pileser king of Assyria, and took Ijon, and Abel-beth-maachah, and Janoah, and Kedesh, and Hazor, and Gilead, and Galilee, all the land of Naphtali, and carried them captive to Assyria.

BETH-MARCABOTH

- **A town of Simeon.**

Jos 19:5 — And Ziklag, and Beth-marcaboth, and Hazar-susah,

1Ch 4:31 — And at Beth-marcaboth, and Hazar-susim, and at Beth-birei, and at Shaaraim. These *were* their cities unto the reign of David.

- **Probably identical with Madmannah.**

Jos 15:31 — And Ziklag, and Madmannah, and Sansannah,

BETH-MEON ⇝See: Baal-Meon

BETH-NIMRAH

- **A fenced city east of Jordan.**

Jos 13:27 — And in the valley, Beth-aram, and Beth-nimrah, and Succoth, and Zaphon, the rest of the kingdom of Sihon king of Heshbon, Jordan and *his* border, *even* unto the edge of the sea of Chinnereth on the other side Jordan eastward.

  - **Called Nimrah.**

  Nu 32:3 — Ataroth, and Dibon, and Jazer, and Nimrah, and Heshbon, and Elealeh, and Shebam, and Nebo, and Beon,

BETH-PALET

- **A city in Judah.**

Jos 15:27 — And Hazar-gaddah, and Heshmon, and Beth-palet,

- **Called Beth-Phelet.**

Ne 11:26 — And at Jeshua, and at Moladah, and at Beth-phelet,

BETH-PAZZEZ • A town of Issachar.

Jos 19:21 — And Remeth, and En-gannim, and En-haddah, and Beth-pazzez;

BETH-PEOR

- **A place in the tribe of Reuben.**

Dt 3:29 — So we abode in the valley over against Beth-peor.

Dt 4:46 — On this side Jordan, in the valley over against Beth-peor, in the land of Sihon king of the Amorites, who dwelt at Heshbon, whom Moses and the children of Israel smote, after they were come forth out of Egypt:

Dt 34:6 — And he buried him in a valley in the land of Moab, over against Beth-peor: but no man knoweth of his sepulchre unto this day.

- **Near the burial place of Moses.**

Jos 13:20 — And Beth-peor, and Ashdoth-pisgah, and Beth-jeshimoth,

BETH-PHELET ⇝See: Beth-Palet

BETH-RAPHA • Son of Eshton.

1Ch 4:12 — And Eshton begat Beth-rapha, and Paseah, and Tehinnah the father of Ir-nahash. These *are* the men of Rechah.

BETH-REHOB

- **A place in Dan.**

Jgs 18:28 — And *there was* no deliverer, because it *was* far from Zidon, and they had no business with *any* man; and it was in the valley that *lieth* by Beth-rehob. And they built a city, and dwelt therein.

2Sa 10:6 — And when the children of Ammon saw that they stank before David, the children of Ammon sent and hired the Syrians of Beth-rehob, and the Syrians of Zoba, twenty thousand footmen, and of king Maacah a thousand men, and of Ish-tob twelve thousand men.

- **Called Rehob.**

2Sa 10:8 — And the children of Ammon came out, and put the battle in array at the entering in of the gate: and the Syrians of Zoba, and of Rehob, and Ish-tob, and Maacah, *were* by themselves in the field.

BETH-SHAN ⇝See: Beth-Shean

BETH-SHEAN

- **A city of Manasseh.**

Jos 17:11 — And Manasseh had in Issachar and in Asher Beth-shean and her towns, and Ibleam and her towns, and the inhabitants of Dor and her towns, and the inhabitants of Endor and her towns, and the inhabitants of Taanach and her towns, and the inhabitants of Megiddo and her towns, *even* three countries.

1Ch 7:29 — And by the borders of the children of Manasseh, Beth-shean and her towns, Taanach and her towns, Megiddo and her towns, Dor and her towns. In these dwelt the children of Joseph the son of Israel.

• Not subdued.

Jgs 1:27 — Neither did Manasseh drive out *the inhabitants of* Beth-shean and her towns, nor Taanach and her towns, nor the inhabitants of Dor and her towns, nor the inhabitants of Ibleam and her towns, nor the inhabitants of Megiddo and her towns: but the Canaanites would dwell in that land.

• Bodies of Saul and his sons exposed in.

1Sa 31:10 — And they put his armour in the house of Ashtaroth: and they fastened his body to the wall of Beth-shan.

1Sa 31:12 — All the valiant men arose, and went all night, and took the body of Saul and the bodies of his sons from the wall of Beth-shan, and came to Jabesh, and burnt them there.

• Called Beth-Shan.

1Sa 31:10 — And they put his armour in the house of Ashtaroth: and they fastened his body to the wall of Beth-shan.

1Sa 31:12 — All the valiant men arose, and went all night, and took the body of Saul and the bodies of his sons from the wall of Beth-shan, and came to Jabesh, and burnt them there.

2Sa 21:12 — And David went and took the bones of Saul and the bones of Jonathan his son from the men of Jabesh-gilead, which had stolen them from the street of Beth-shan, where the Philistines had hanged them, when the Philistines had slain Saul in Gilboa:

• District of, under tribute to Solomon's commissariat.

1Ki 4:12 — Baana the son of Ahilud; *to him pertained* Taanach and Megiddo, and all Beth-shean, which is by Zartanah beneath Jezreel, from Beth-shean to Abel-meholah, *even* unto *the place that is* beyond Jokneam:

BETH-SHEMESH

• A sacerdotal city of Dan.

Jos 21:16 — And Ain with her suburbs, and Juttah with her suburbs, *and* Beth-shemesh with her suburbs; nine cities out of those two tribes.

1Sa 6:15 — And the Levites took down the ark of the LORD, and the coffer that *was* with it, wherein the jewels of gold *were,* and put *them* on the great stone: and the men of Beth-shemesh offered burnt offerings and sacrificed sacrifices the same day unto the LORD.

1Ch 6:59 — And Ashan with her suburbs, and Beth-shemesh with her suburbs:

• On the northern border of Judah.

Jos 15:10 — And the border compassed from Baalah westward unto mount Seir, and passed along unto the side of mount Jearim, which *is* Chesalon, on the north side, and went down to Beth-shemesh, and passed on to Timnah:

1Sa 6:9 — And see, if it goeth up by the way of his own coast to Beth-shemesh, *then* he hath done us this great evil: but if not, then we shall know that *it is* not his hand *that* smote us; it *was* a chance *that* happened to us.

1Sa 6:12 — And the kine took the straight way to the way of Beth-shemesh, *and* went along the highway, lowing as they went, and turned not aside *to* the right hand or *to* the left; and the lords of the Philistines went after them unto the border of Beth-shemesh.

• In later times transferred to Judah.

2Ki 14:11 — But Amaziah would not hear. Therefore Jehoash king of Israel went up; and he and Amaziah king of Judah looked one another in the face at Beth-shemesh, which *belongeth* to Judah.

• Mentioned in Solomon's commissary districts.

1Ki 4:9 — The son of Dekar, in Makaz, and in Shaalbim, and Beth-shemesh, and Elon-beth-hanan:

• Amaziah taken prisoner at.

2Ki 14:11–13; 2Ch 25:21–23

• Retaken by the Philistines.

2Ch 28:18 — The Philistines also had invaded the cities of the low country, and of the south of Judah, and had taken Beth-shemesh, and Ajalon, and Gederoth, and Shocho with the villages thereof, and Timnah with the villages thereof, Gimzo also and the villages thereof: and they dwelt there.

• Called Ir-Shemesh.

Jos 19:41 — And the coast of their inheritance was Zorah, and Eshtaol, and Ir-shemesh,

• A city near Jerusalem.

Jos 19:22 — And the coast reacheth to Tabor, and Shahazimah, and Beth-shemesh; and the outgoings of their border were at Jordan: sixteen cities with their villages.

• A fortified city of Naphtali.

Jos 19:38 — And Iron, and Migdal-el, Horem, and Beth-anath, and Beth-shemesh; nineteen cities with their villages.

Jgs 1:33 — Neither did Naphtali drive out the inhabitants of Beth-shemesh, nor the inhabitants of Beth-anath; but he dwelt among the Canaanites, the inhabitants of the land: nevertheless the inhabitants of Beth-shemesh and of Beth-anath became tributaries unto them.

• An idolatrous temple.

Jer 43:13 — He shall break also the images of Beth-shemesh, that *is* in the land of Egypt; and the houses of the gods of the Egyptians shall he burn with fire.

BETH-SHITTAH • A place near the Jordan.

Jgs 7:22 — And the three hundred blew the trumpets, and the LORD set every man's sword against his fellow, even throughout all the host: and the host fled to Beth-shittah in Zererath, *and* to the border of Abel-meholah, unto Tabbath.

BETH-TAPPUAH • A town of Judah.

Jos 15:53 — And Janum, and Beth-tappuah, and Aphekah,

BETH-ZUR • A town in Judah.

Jos 15:58 — Halhul, Beth-zur, and Gedor,

1Ch 2:45 — And the son of Shammai *was* Maon: and Maon *was* the father of Beth-zur.

2Ch 11:7 — And Beth-zur, and Shoco, and Adullam,

Ne 3:16 — After him repaired Nehemiah the son of Azbuk, the ruler of the half part of Beth-zur, unto *the place* over against the sepulchres of David, and to the pool that was made, and unto the house of the mighty.

BETHABARA

• A city east of the Jordan.

Jgs 7:24 — And Gideon sent messengers throughout all mount Ephraim, saying, Come down against the Midianites, and take before them the waters unto Beth-barah and Jordan. Then all the men of Ephraim gathered themselves together, and took the waters unto Beth-barah and Jordan.

• John testifies to Christ's messiahship, and baptizes at.

Jn 1:28 — These things were done in Bethabara beyond Jordan, where John was baptizing.

• Jesus at.

Jn 10:39–42

BETHANY

• A village on the eastern slope of the Mount of Olives.

Jn 11:18 — Now Bethany was nigh unto Jerusalem, about fifteen furlongs off:

• Mary, Martha, and Lazarus dwell at.

Lk 10:38–41

• Lazarus dies and is raised to life at.

Jn 11:1–57

• Jesus attends a feast in.

Mt 26:6–13; Jn 12:1–9

• The colt on which Jesus made his triumphal entry into Jerusalem obtained at.

Mk 11:1–11

• Jesus sojourns at.

Mk 11:11–12

Mt 21:17 — And he left them, and went out of the city into Bethany; and he lodged there.

Mk 11:19 — And when even was come, he went out of the city.

BETHER • Mountains of.

SS 2:17 — Until the day break, and the shadows flee away, turn, my beloved, and be thou like a roe or a young hart upon the mountains of Bether.

BETHESDA • Pool of.

Jn 5:2–4

BETHLEHEM

• A city southwest of Jerusalem.

Jgs 17:7 — And there was a young man out of Bethlehemjudah of the family of Judah, who *was* a Levite, and he sojourned there.

Jgs 19:18 — And he said unto him, We *are* passing from Bethlehemjudah toward the side of mount Ephraim; from thence *am* I: and I went to Bethlehemjudah, but I *am now* going to the house of the LORD; and there *is* no man that receiveth me to house.

• Called Ephratah and Ephrath.

Ge 48:7 — And as for me, when I came from Padan, Rachel died by me in the land of Canaan in the way, when yet *there was* but a little way to come unto Ephrath: and I buried her there in the way of Ephrath; the same is Bethlehem.

Ps 132:6 — Lo, we heard of it at Ephratah: we found it in the fields of the wood.

Mic 5:2 — But thou, Bethlehem Ephratah, *though* thou be little among the thousands of Judah, *yet* out of thee shall he come forth unto me *that is* to be ruler in Israel; whose goings forth *have been* from of old, from everlasting.

• Called Bethlehemjudah.

Jgs 17:7–9

Jgs 19:1 — And it came to pass in those days, when *there was* no king in Israel, that there was a certain Levite sojourning on the side of mount Ephraim, who took to him a concubine out of Bethlehemjudah.

Jgs 19:18 — And he said unto him, We *are* passing from Bethlehemjudah toward the side of mount Ephraim; from thence *am* I: and I went to Bethlehemjudah, but I *am now* going to the house of the LORD; and there *is* no man that receiveth me to house.

Ru 1:1 — Now it came to pass in the days when the judges ruled, that there was a famine in the land. And a certain man of Bethlehemjudah went to sojourn in the country of Moab, he, and his wife, and his two sons.

1Sa 17:12 — Now David *was* the son of that Ephrathite of Bethlehemjudah, whose name *was* Jesse; and he had eight sons: and the man went among men *for* an old man in the days of Saul.

• Rachel dies and is buried at.

Ge 35:16 — And they journeyed from Bethel; and there was but a little way to come to Ephrath: and Rachel travailed, and she had hard labour.

Ge 35:19 — And Rachel died, and was buried in the way to Ephrath, which *is* Bethlehem.

Ge 48:7 — And as for me, when I came from Padan, Rachel died by me in the land of Canaan in the way, when yet *there was* but a little way to come unto Ephrath: and I buried her there in the way of Ephrath; the same is Bethlehem.

• The city of Boaz.

Ru 4:1–22

Ru 1:1 — Now it came to pass in the days when the judges ruled, that there was a famine in the land. And a certain man of Bethlehemjudah went to sojourn in the country of Moab, he, and his wife, and his two sons.

Ru 1:19 — So they two went until they came to Bethlehem. And it came to pass, when they were come to Bethlehem, that all the city was moved about them, and they said, *Is* this Naomi?

Ru 2:4 — And behold, Boaz came from Bethlehem, and said unto the reapers, The LORD *be* with you. And they answered him, The LORD bless thee.

• Taken and held by the Philistines.

2Sa 23:14–16

• Jeroboam converts it into a military stronghold.

2Ch 11:6 — He built even Bethlehem, and Etam, and Tekoa,

• The city of Joseph.

Mt 2:5–6

Lk 2:4 — And Joseph also went up from Galilee, out of the city of Nazareth, into Judaea, unto the city of David, which is called Bethlehem; (because he was of the house and lineage of David:)

• Birthplace of Jesus.

Mt 2:1–23

Mic 5:2 — But thou, Bethlehem Ephratah, *though* thou be little among the thousands of Judah, *yet* out of thee shall he come forth unto me *that is* to be ruler in Israel; whose goings forth *have been* from of old, from everlasting.

Lk 2:4 — And Joseph also went up from Galilee, out of the city of Nazareth, into Judaea, unto the city of David, which is called Bethlehem; (because he was of the house and lineage of David:)

Lk 2:15 — And it came to pass, as the angels were gone away from them into heaven, the shepherds said one to another, Let us now go even unto Bethlehem, and see this thing which is come to pass, which the Lord hath made known unto us.

• Herod slays the children of.

Mt 2:16–18

• A town of Zebulun. Six miles west of Nazareth.

Jos 19:15 — And Kattath, and Nahallal, and Shimron, and Idalah, and Bethlehem: twelve cities with their villages.

• Israel judged at.

Jgs 12:10 — Then died Ibzan, and was buried at Bethlehem.

BETHPHAGE • A village on the Mount of Olives.

Mt 21:1 — And when they drew nigh unto Jerusalem, and were come to Bethphage, unto the mount of Olives, then sent Jesus two disciples,

Mk 11:1 — And when they came nigh to Jerusalem, unto Bethphage and Bethany, at the mount of Olives, he sendeth forth two of his disciples,

Lk 19:29 — And it came to pass, when he was come nigh to Bethphage and Bethany, at the mount called *the mount* of Olives, he sent two of his disciples,

BETHSAIDA

• A city of Galilee.

• The city of Philip, Andrew, and Peter.

Jn 1:44 — Now Philip was of Bethsaida, the city of Andrew and Peter.

Jn 12:21 — The same came therefore to Philip, which was of Bethsaida of Galilee, and desired him, saying, Sir, we would see Jesus.

• Jesus visits.

Mk 6:45 — And straightway he constrained his disciples to get into the ship, and to go to the other side before unto Bethsaida, while he sent away the people.

• Jesus cures a blind man in.

Mk 8:22 — And he cometh to Bethsaida; and they bring a blind man unto him, and besought him to touch him.

• Jesus prophecies against.

Mt 11:21 — Woe unto thee, Chorazin! woe unto thee, Bethsaida! for if the mighty works, which were done in you, had been done in Tyre and Sidon, they would have repented long ago in sackcloth and ashes.

Lk 10:13 — Woe unto thee, Chorazin! woe unto thee, Bethsaida! for if the mighty works had been done in Tyre and Sidon, which have been done in you, they had a great while ago repented, sitting in sackcloth and ashes.

• Desert of, east of the sea of Galilee; Jesus feeds five thousand people in.

Mt 14:13 — When Jesus heard *of it,* he departed thence by ship into a desert place apart: and when the people had heard *thereof,* they followed him on foot out of the cities.

Mk 6:32 — And they departed into a desert place by ship privately.

Lk 9:10 — And the apostles, when they were returned, told him all that they had done. And he took them, and went aside privately into a desert place belonging to the city called Bethsaida.

BETHUEL • Son of Nahor and father of Rebekah.

Ge 22:22–23

Ge 24:15 — And it came to pass, before he had done speaking, that, behold, Rebekah came out, who was born to Bethuel, son of Milcah, the wife of Nahor, Abraham's brother, with her pitcher upon her shoulder.

Ge 24:24 — And she said unto him, I *am* the daughter of Bethuel the son of Milcah, which she bare unto Nahor.

Ge 25:20 — And Isaac was forty years old when he took Rebekah to wife, the daughter of Bethuel the Syrian of Padan-aram, the sister to Laban the Syrian.

Ge 28:2 — Arise, go to Padan-aram, to the house of Bethuel thy mother's father; and take thee a wife from thence of the daughters of Laban thy mother's brother.

Ge 28:5 — And Isaac sent away Jacob: and he went to Padan-aram unto Laban, son of Bethuel the Syrian, the brother of Rebekah, Jacob's and Esau's mother.

BETHUL

• A city of Simeon.

Jos 19:4 — And Eltolad, and Bethul, and Hormah,

• Called Chesil.

Jos 15:30 — And Eltolad, and Chesil, and Hormah,

• Called Bethuel.

1Ch 4:30 — And at Bethuel, and at Hormah, and at Ziklag,

BETONIM • A town of Gad.

Jos 13:26 — And from Heshbon unto Ramath-mizpeh, and Betonim; and from Mahanaim unto the border of Debir;

BETRAYAL

• Of Jesus.

Mt 26:14–16, 45–50; Mk 14:10–11; Lk 22:3–6, 47–48

Jn 13:21 — When Jesus had thus said, he was troubled in spirit, and testified, and said, Verily, verily, I say unto you, that one of you shall betray me.

• Of others, foretold.

Mt 20:18 — Behold, we go up to Jerusalem; and the Son of man shall be betrayed unto the chief priests and unto the scribes, and they shall condemn him to death,

Mt 24:10 — And then shall many be offended, and shall betray one another, and shall hate one another.

• Of David, by Doeg.

1Sa 21:1–10; 22:9–10

• Of cities.

Jgs 1:24–25

⁕See: Confidence; betrayed

BETROTHAL

• Of Jacob.

Ge 29:18–30

• Exempts from military duty.

Dt 20:7 — And what man *is there* that hath betrothed a wife, and hath not taken her? let him go and return unto his house, lest he die in the battle, and another man take her.

• A quasi-marriage.

Mt 1:18 — Now the birth of Jesus Christ was on this wise: When as his mother Mary was espoused to Joseph, before they came together, she was found with child of the Holy Ghost.

Lk 1:27 — To a virgin espoused to a man whose name was Joseph, of the house of David; and the virgin's name *was* Mary.

• Figurative.

Hos 2:19–20

Isa 62:4 — Thou shalt no more be termed Forsaken; neither shall thy land any more be termed Desolate: but thou shalt be called Hephzi-bah, and thy land Beulah: for the LORD delighteth in thee, and thy land shall be married.

2Co 11:2 — For I am jealous over you with godly jealousy: for I have espoused you to one husband, that I may present *you as* a chaste virgin to Christ.

⁕See: Marriage

BETTING • By Samson.

Jgs 14:12–19

BEULAH

Isa 62:4 — Thou shalt no more be termed Forsaken; neither shall thy land any more be termed Desolate: but thou shalt be called Hephzi-bah, and thy land Beulah: for the LORD delighteth in thee, and thy land shall be married.

BEZAI

• Head of a Jewish family which returned from Babylon.

Ezr 2:17 — The children of Bezai, three hundred twenty and three.

Ne 7:23 — The children of Bezai, three hundred twenty and four.

• A family that sealed the covenant with Nehemiah.

Ne 10:18 — Hodijah, Hashum, Bezai,

BEZALEEL

• A divinely inspired mechanic and master workman, who built the tabernacle.

Ex 35:30–36:1; 38:1–7

Ex 31:2 — See, I have called by name Bezaleel the son of Uri, the son of Hur, of the tribe of Judah:

Ex 37:1 — And Bezaleel made the ark *of* shittim wood: two cubits and a half *was* the length of it, and a cubit and a half the breadth of it, and a cubit and a half the height of it:

Ex 38:22 — And Bezaleel the son of Uri, the son of Hur, of the tribe of Judah, made all that the LORD commanded Moses.

• Son of Pahath-moab.

Ezr 10:30 — And of the sons of Pahath-moab; Adna, and Chelal, Benaiah, Maaseiah, Mattaniah, Bezaleel, and Binnui, and Manasseh.

BEZEK

• Residence of Adoni-bezek.

Jgs 1:5 — And they found Adoni-bezek in Bezek: and they fought against him, and they slew the Canaanites and the Perizzites.

• A rendezvous of Israel under Saul.

1Sa 11:8 — And when he numbered them in Bezek, the children of Israel were three hundred thousand, and the men of Judah thirty thousand.

BEZER

• A city of refuge. East of the Jordan.

Dt 4:43 — *Namely,* Bezer in the wilderness, in the plain country, of the Reubenites; and Ramoth in Gilead, of the Gadites; and Golan in Bashan, of the Manassites.

Jos 20:8 — And on the other side Jordan by Jericho eastward, they assigned Bezer in the wilderness upon the plain out of the tribe of Reuben, and Ramoth in Gilead out of the tribe of Gad, and Golan in Bashan out of the tribe of Manasseh.

Jos 21:36 — And out of the tribe of Reuben, Bezer with her suburbs, and Jahazah with her suburbs,

1Ch 6:78 — And on the other side Jordan by Jericho, on the east side of Jordan, *were given them* out of the tribe of Reuben, Bezer in the wilderness with her suburbs, and Jahzah with her suburbs,

• Son of Zophah.

1Ch 7:37 — Bezer, and Hod, and Shamma and Shilshah, and Ithran, and Beera.

BIBLE

✧See: Law; of Moses

✧See: Word of God

BICHRI • A Benjamite.

2Sa 20:1–26

BIDKAR • Jehu's captain.

2Ki 9:25 — Then said *Jehu* to Bidkar his captain, Take up, *and* cast him in the portion of the field of Naboth the Jezreelite: for remember how that, when I and thou rode together after Ahab his father, the LORD laid this burden upon him;

BIER

2Sa 3:31 — And David said to Joab, and to all the people that *were* with him, Rend your clothes, and gird you with sackcloth, and mourn before Abner. And king David *himself* followed the bier.

Lk 7:14 — And he came and touched the bier: and they that bare *him* stood still. And he said, Young man, I say unto thee, Arise.

BIGAMY ✧See: Polygamy

BIGOTRY

Lk 9:49–50; 18:9–14; Ac 18:12–13

Isa 65:5 — Which say, Stand by thyself, come not near to me; for I am holier than thou. *These* are a smoke in my nose, a fire that burneth all the day.

Mk 2:16 — And when the scribes and Pharisees saw him eat with publicans and sinners, they said unto his disciples, How is it that he eateth and drinketh with publicans and sinners?

Lk 15:2 — And the Pharisees and scribes murmured, saying, This man receiveth sinners, and eateth with them.

Ac 10:28 — And he said unto them, Ye know how that it is an unlawful thing for a man that is a Jew to keep company, or come unto one of another nation; but God hath shewed me that I should not call any man common or unclean.

Ac 10:45 — And they of the circumcision which believed were astonished, as many as came with Peter, because that on the Gentiles also was poured out the gift of the Holy Ghost.

• Paul's argument against.

Ro 3:1–23; 4:1–16, 23–25

• Instances of.

• Joshua, through envy seeking to suppress Eldad and Medad, who were prophesying.

Nu 11:27–29

• Jews with regard to the Samaritans.

Jn 4:9, 27

• Jews, in rejecting the teachings of Jesus at Nazareth.

Lk 4:28

• Jews, in falsely accusing Jesus of blasphemy.

Jn 5:18

• Jews, in falsely accusing Jesus of being a gluttonous man and winebibber.

Mt 11:18–19

• Jews, in falsely accusing Jesus of keeping company with sinners.

Lk 7:39; 15:2; 19:5–7

• Jews, in falsely accusing Jesus of not conforming to the traditions.

Lk 11:38–39

• Jews, in their treatment of the young man who was born blind, whom Jesus restored to sight.

Jn 9:28–29, 34

• Jews, with regard to Paul's preaching.

Ac 21:28–29; 22:22

• Of the Samaritans in refusing to receive Jesus.

Lk 9:52–53

• Of the disciples in forbidding children to be brought to Jesus.

Mt 19:13; Mk 10:13; Lk 18:15

• Of the early Christians, in opposing the preaching of the gospel to the Gentiles.

Ac 10:45; 11:2–3; 21:20–25

• Of the early Christians, in regard to circumcision.

Ac 15:1–10, 24; Gal 2:3–5

• The Jews.

Ro 10:2–3

• The Jews, in persecutions.

1Th 2:15–16

• Of John in forbidding the casting out of devils by one who followed not Jesus.

Mk 9:38–40; Lk 9:49–50

• James and John in desiring to call down fire upon the Samaritans who would not receive Jesus.

Lk 9:51–56

• Of Saul, in persecuting the Christians.

Ac 9:1–5; 22:3–4; Gal 1:13–14

Ac 26:9 — I verily thought with myself, that I ought to do many things contrary to the name of Jesus of Nazareth.

Php 3:6 — Concerning zeal, persecuting the church; touching the righteousness which is in the law, blameless.

See: Intolerance, Religious

See: Persecution

See: Uncharitableness

BIGTHAN • A conspiring Persian courtier.

Est 2:21–23

Est 6:2 — And it was found written, that Mordecai had told of Bigthana and Teresh, two of the king's chamberlains, the keepers of the door, who sought to lay hand on the king Ahasuerus.

BIGVAI • Head of Jewish family.

Ezr 2:2 — Which came with Zerubbabel: Jeshua, Nehemiah, Seraiah, Reelaiah, Mordecai, Bilshan, Mizpar, Bigvai, Rehum, Baanah. The number of the men of the people of Israel:

Ezr 8:14 — Of the sons also of Bigvai; Uthai, and Zabbud, and with them seventy males.

Ne 7:7 — Who came with Zerubbabel, Jeshua, Nehemiah, Azariah, Raamiah, Nahamani, Mordecai, Bilshan, Mispereth, Bigvai, Nehum, Baanah. The number, *I say,* of the men of the people of Israel *was this;*

Ne 7:19 — The children of Bigvai, two thousand threescore and seven.

Ne 10:16 — Adonijah, Bigvai, Adin,

BILDAD • One of Job's friends.

Job 2:11 — Now when Job's three friends heard of all this evil that was come upon him, they came every one from his own place; Eliphaz the Temanite, and Bildad the Shuhite, and Zophar the Naamathite: for they had made an appointment together to come to mourn with him and to comfort him.

Job 8:1 — Then answered Bildad the Shuhite, and said,

Job 18:1 — Then answered Bildad the Shuhite, and said,

Job 25:1 — Then answered Bildad the Shuhite, and said,

BILEAM

• A town of Manasseh.

1Ch 6:70 — And out of the half tribe of Manasseh; Aner with her suburbs, and Bileam with her suburbs, for the family of the remnant of the sons of Kohath.

• Called Ibleam.

Jos 17:11 — And Manasseh had in Issachar and in Asher Beth-shean and her towns, and Ibleam and her towns, and the inhabitants of Dor and her towns, and the inhabitants of Endor and her towns, and the inhabitants of Taanach and her towns, and the inhabitants of Megiddo and her towns, *even* three countries.

• Called Gath-Rimmon.

Jos 21:25 — And out of the half tribe of Manasseh, Tanach with her suburbs, and Gath-rimmon with her suburbs; two cities.

BILGAH

• One of the chiefs of the sacerdotal courses in the temple.

1Ch 24:14 — The fifteenth to Bilgah, the sixteenth to Immer,

• A priest.

Ne 12:5 — Miamin, Maadiah, Bilgah,

Ne 12:18 — Of Bilgah, Shammua; of Shemaiah, Jehonathan;

• Perhaps identical with Bilgai.

Ne 10:8 — Maaziah, Bilgai, Shemaiah: these *were* the priests.

BILGAI • A priest.

Ne 10:8 — Maaziah, Bilgai, Shemaiah: these *were* the priests.

BILHAH

• Rachael's servant.

Ge 29:29 — And Laban gave to Rachel his daughter Bilhah his handmaid to be her maid.

• Bears children by Jacob.

Ge 30:3–4

Ge 37:2 — These *are* the generations of Jacob. Joseph, *being* seventeen years old, was feeding the flock with his brethren; and the lad *was* with the sons of Bilhah, and with the sons of Zilpah, his father's wives: and Joseph brought unto his father their evil report.

• Mother of Dan and Naphtali.

Ge 30:1–8

Ge 35:25 — And the sons of Bilhah, Rachel's handmaid; Dan, and Naphtali:

Ge 46:23 — And the sons of Dan; Hushim.

Ge 46:25 — These *are* the sons of Bilhah, which Laban gave unto Rachel his daughter, and she bare these unto Jacob: all the souls *were* seven.

• Reuben's incest with.

Ge 35:22 — And it came to pass, when Israel dwelt in that land, that Reuben went and lay with Bilhah his father's concubine: and Israel heard *it.* Now the sons of Jacob were twelve:

Ge 49:4 — Unstable as water, thou shalt not excel; because thou wentest up to thy father's bed; then defiledst thou *it:* he went up to my couch.

• A place in the land of Simeon.

1Ch 4:29 — And at Bilhah, and at Ezem, and at Tolad,

• Called Balah.

Jos 19:3 — And Hazar-shual, and Balah, and Azem,

• Called Baalah.

Jos 15:29 — Baalah, and Iim, and Azem,

BILHAN

• A Horite chief.

Ge 36:27 — The children of Ezer *are* these; Bilhan, and Zaavan, and Akan.

1Ch 1:42 — The sons of Ezer; Bilhan, and Zavan, *and* Jakan. The sons of Dishan; Uz, and Aran.

• A Benjamite.

1Ch 7:10 — The sons also of Jediael; Bilhan: and the sons of Bilhan; Jeush, and Benjamin, and Ehud, and Chenaanah, and Zethan, and Tharshish, and Ahishahar.

BILL OF DIVORCE ✧See: Divorce

BILSHAN • A Jew of the captivity.

Ezr 2:2 — Which came with Zerubbabel: Jeshua, Nehemiah, Seraiah, Reelaiah, Mordecai, Bilshan, Mizpar, Bigvai, Rehum, Baanah. The number of the men of the people of Israel:

Ne 7:7 — Who came with Zerubbabel, Jeshua, Nehemiah, Azariah, Raamiah, Nahamani, Mordecai, Bilshan, Mispereth, Bigvai, Nehum, Baanah. The number, *I say,* of the men of the people of Israel *was this;*

BIMHAL • Son of Japhlet.

1Ch 7:33 — And the sons of Japhlet; Pasach, and Bimhal, and Ashvath. These *are* the children of Japhlet.

BINEA • A descendant of King Saul.

1Ch 8:37 — And Moza begat Binea: Rapha *was* his son, Eleasah his son, Azel his son:

1Ch 9:43 — And Moza begat Binea; and Rephaiah his son, Eleasah his son, Azel his son.

BINNUI

• A Jew of the captivity.

Ne 7:15 — The children of Binnui, six hundred forty and eight.

• Called Bani.

Ezr 2:10 — The children of Bani, six hundred forty and two.

• A Levite of the captivity.

Ne 3:24 — After him repaired Binnui the son of Henadad another piece, from the house of Azariah unto the turning *of the wall,* even unto the corner.

Ne 10:9 — And the Levites: both Jeshua the son of Azaniah, Binnui of the sons of Henadad, Kadmiel;

Ne 12:8 — Moreover the Levites: Jeshua, Binnui, Kadmiel, Sherebiah, Judah, *and* Mattaniah, *which was* over the thanksgiving, he and his brethren.

• Father of Noadiah.

Ezr 8:33 — Now on the fourth day was the silver and the gold and the vessels weighed in the house of our God by the hand of Meremoth the son of Uriah the priest; and with him *was* Eleazar the son of Phinehas; and with them *was* Jozabad the son of Jeshua, and Noadiah the son of Binnui, Levites;

• Son of Pahath-moab.

Ezr 10:30 — And of the sons of Pahath-moab; Adna, and Chelal, Benaiah, Maaseiah, Mattaniah, Bezaleel, and Binnui, and Manasseh.

• Son of Bani.

Ezr 10:38 — And Bani, and Binnui, Shimei,

BIRDS

• Creation of, on the fifth creative day.

Ge 1:20–30

• Man's dominion over.

Ge 9:2–3; Ps 8:5–8

Ge 1:26 — And God said, Let us make man in our image, after our likeness: and let them have dominion over the fish of the sea, and over the fowl of the air, and over the cattle, and over all the earth, and over every creeping thing that creepeth upon the earth.

Ge 1:28 — And God blessed them, and God said unto them, Be fruitful, and multiply, and replenish the earth, and subdue it: and have dominion over the fish of the sea, and over the fowl of the air, and over every living thing that moveth upon the earth.

Jer 27:6 — And now have I given all these lands into the hand of Nebuchadnezzar the king of Babylon, my servant; and the beasts of the field have I given him also to serve him.

Da 2:38 — And wheresoever the children of men dwell, the beasts of the field and the fowls of the heaven hath he given into thine hand, and hath made thee ruler over them all. Thou *art* this head of gold.

Jas 3:7 — For every kind of beasts, and of birds, and of serpents, and of things in the sea, is tamed, and hath been tamed of mankind:

• Appointed for food.

Ge 9:2–3; Dt 14:11–20

• What species were unclean.

Le 11:13–20; Dt 14:12–19

• Used for sacrifice.

✧See: Dove, Turtle

✧See: Pigeon

• Divine care of.

Job 38:41 — Who provideth for the raven his food? when his young ones cry unto God, they wander for lack of meat.

Ps 147:9 — He giveth to the beast his food, *and* to the young ravens which cry.

Mt 10:29 — <u>Are not two sparrows sold for a farthing? and one of them shall not fall on the ground without your Father.</u>

Lk 12:6 — <u>Are not five sparrows sold for two farthings, and not one of them is forgotten before God?</u>

Lk 12:24 — <u>Consider the ravens: for they neither sow nor reap; which neither have storehouse nor barn; and God feedeth them: how much more are ye better than the fowls?</u>

• Songs of, at the break of day.

Ps 104:12 — By them shall the fowls of the heaven have their habitation, *which* sing among the branches.

Ecc 12:4 — And the doors shall be shut in the streets, when the sound of the grinding is low, and he shall rise up at the voice of the bird, and all the daughters of musick shall be brought low;

SS 2:12 — The flowers appear on the earth; the time of the singing *of birds* is come, and the voice of the turtle is heard in our land;

- **Domesticated.**

Job 41:5 — Wilt thou play with him as *with* a bird? or wilt thou bind him for thy maidens?

Jas 3:7 — For every kind of beasts, and of birds, and of serpents, and of things in the sea, is tamed, and hath been tamed of mankind:

- **Solomon's proverbs of.**

1Ki 4:33 — And he spake of trees, from the cedar tree that *is* in Lebanon even unto the hyssop that springeth out of the wall: he spake also of beasts, and of fowl, and of creeping things, and of fishes.

- **Nests of.**

Ps 104:17 — Where the birds make their nests: *as for* the stork, the fir trees *are* her house.

Mt 8:20 — And Jesus saith unto him, The foxes have holes, and the birds of the air *have* nests; but the Son of man hath not where to lay *his* head.

Mt 13:32 — Which indeed is the least of all seeds: but when it is grown, it is the greatest among herbs, and becometh a tree, so that the birds of the air come and lodge in the branches thereof.

- **Instincts of.**

Pr 1:17 — Surely in vain the net is spread in the sight of any bird.

- **Habits of.**

Job 39:13–18; Job 39:26–30

- **Migrate.**

Jer 8:7 — Yea, the stork in the heaven knoweth her appointed times; and the turtle and the crane and the swallow observe the time of their coming; but my people know not the judgment of the LORD.

- **Mosaic law protected the mother from being taken with the young.**

Dt 22:6–7

- **Cages of.**

Jer 5:27 — As a cage is full of birds, so *are* their houses full of deceit: therefore they are become great, and waxen rich.

Rev 18:2 — And he cried mightily with a strong voice, saying, Babylon the great is fallen, is fallen, and is become the habitation of devils, and the hold of every foul spirit, and a cage of every unclean and hateful bird.

See: Snare

- **Figurative.**

Isa 16:2 — For it shall be, *that,* as a wandering bird cast out of the nest, so the daughters of Moab shall be at the fords of Arnon.

Isa 46:11 — Calling a ravenous bird from the east, the man that executeth my counsel from a far country: yea, I have spoken *it,* I will also bring it to pass; I have purposed *it,* I will also do it.

Jer 12:9 — Mine heritage *is* unto me *as* a speckled bird, the birds round about *are* against her; come ye, assemble all the beasts of the field, come to devour.

Eze 39:4 — Thou shalt fall upon the mountains of Israel, thou, and all thy bands, and the people that *is* with thee: I will give thee unto the ravenous birds of every sort, and *to* the beasts of the field to be devoured.

- **Symbolic.**

Da 7:6 — After this I beheld, and lo another, like a leopard, which had upon the back of it four wings of a fowl; the beast had also four heads; and dominion was given to it.

See: Bittern
See: Chickens
See: Cormorant
See: Crane
See: Cuckoo
See: Dove, Turtle
See: Eagle
See: Falcon
See: Glede
See: Hawk
See: Hen
See: Heron
See: Kite
See: Lapwing
See: Night Hawk
See: Osprey
See: Ossifrage
See: Ostriches
See: Owl
See: Partridge
See: Peacock
See: Pelican
See: Pigeon
See: Quail
See: Raven
See: Sparrow
See: Stork
See: Swallow
See: Swan
See: Vulture

BIRSHA • A king of Gomorrah.

Ge 14:2–10

BIRTH

- **Pangs in giving.**

Ps 48:6 — Fear took hold upon them there, *and* pain, as of a woman in travail.

Isa 13:8 — And they shall be afraid: pangs and sorrows shall take hold of them; they shall be in pain as a woman that travaileth: they shall be amazed one at another; their faces *shall be as* flames.

Isa 21:3 — Therefore are my loins filled with pain: pangs have taken hold upon me, as the pangs of a woman that travaileth: I was bowed down at the hearing *of it;* I was dismayed at the seeing *of it.*

Jer 4:31 — For I have heard a voice as of a woman in travail, *and* the anguish as of her that bringeth forth her first child, the voice of the daughter of Zion, *that* bewaileth herself, *that* spreadeth her hands, *saying,* Woe *is* me now! for my soul is wearied because of murderers.

Jer 6:24 — We have heard the fame thereof: our hands wax feeble: anguish hath taken hold of us, *and* pain, as of a woman in travail.

Jer 30:6 — Ask ye now, and see whether a man doth travail with child? wherefore do I see every man with his hands on his loins, as a woman in travail, and all faces are turned into paleness?

Jer 31:8 — Behold, I will bring them from the north country, and gather them from the coasts of the earth, *and* with them the blind and the lame, the woman with child and her that travaileth with child together: a great company shall return thither.

• Giving, ordained to be in sorrow.

Ge 3:16 — Unto the woman he said, I will greatly multiply thy sorrow and thy conception; in sorrow thou shalt bring forth children; and thy desire *shall be* to thy husband, and he shall rule over thee.

➜See: Abortion

➜See: Children

BIRTHDAY

• Celebrated by feasts.

Ge 40:20 — And it came to pass the third day, *which was* Pharaoh's birthday, that he made a feast unto all his servants: and he lifted up the head of the chief butler and of the chief baker among his servants.

Mt 14:6 — But when Herod's birthday was kept, the daughter of Herodias danced before them, and pleased Herod.

• Cursed.

Job 3:1–26

Jer 20:14 — Cursed *be* the day wherein I was born: let not the day wherein my mother bare me be blessed.

Jer 20:18 — Wherefore came I forth out of the womb to see labour and sorrow, that my days should be consumed with shame?

BIRTHRIGHT

• Belonged to the firstborn.

Dt 21:15–16

• Entitled the firstborn to a double portion of inheritance.

Dt 21:15–17

• Entitled the firstborn to royal succession.

2Ch 21:3 — And their father gave them great gifts of silver, and of gold, and of precious things, with fenced cities in Judah: but the kingdom gave he to Jehoram; because he *was* the firstborn.

• An honorable title.

Ex 4:22 — And thou shalt say unto Pharaoh, Thus saith the LORD, Israel *is* my son, *even* my firstborn:

Ps 89:27 — Also I will make him *my* firstborn, higher than the kings of the earth.

Jer 31:9 — They shall come with weeping, and with supplications will I lead them: I will cause them to walk by the rivers of waters in a straight way, wherein they shall not stumble: for I am a father to Israel, and Ephraim *is* my firstborn.

Ro 8:29 — For whom he did foreknow, he also did predestinate *to be* conformed to the image of his Son, that he might be the firstborn among many brethren.

Col 1:15 — Who is the image of the invisible God, the firstborn of every creature:

Heb 1:6 — And again, when he bringeth in the firstbegotten into the world, he saith, And let all the angels of God worship him.

Heb 12:23 — To the general assembly and church of the firstborn, which are written in heaven, and to God the Judge of all, and to the spirits of just men made perfect,

Rev 1:5 — And from Jesus Christ, *who is* the faithful witness, *and* the first begotten of the dead, and the prince of the kings of the earth. Unto him that loved us, and washed us from our sins in his own blood,

• Sold by Esau.

Ge 25:29–34; Ro 9:12–13

Ge 27:36 — And he said, Is not he rightly named Jacob? for he hath supplanted me these two times: he took away my birthright; and, behold, now he hath taken away my blessing. And he said, Hast thou not reserved a blessing for me?

Heb 12:16 — Lest there *be* any fornicator, or profane person, as Esau, who for one morsel of meat sold his birthright.

• Forfeited by Reuben.

1Ch 5:1–2

• Set aside, that of Manasseh.

Ge 48:15–20

• Set aside, that of Adonijah.

1Ki 2:15 — And he said, Thou knowest that the kingdom was mine, and *that* all Israel set their faces on me, that I should reign: howbeit the kingdom is turned about, and is become my brother's: for it was his from the LORD.

• Hosah's son.

1Ch 26:10 — Also Hosah, of the children of Merari, had sons; Simri the chief, (for *though* he was not the firstborn, yet his father made him the chief;)

➜See: Firstborn

BIRZAVITH • A descendant of Ahser.

1Ch 7:31 — And the sons of Beriah; Heber, and Malchiel, who *is* the father of Birzavith.

BISHLAM • A Samaritan who obstructed the rebuilding of the temple at Jerusalem.

Ezr 4:7–24

BISHOP

1Ti 3:2–7; Tit 1:5–11

Ac 20:28 — Take heed therefore unto yourselves, and to all the flock, over the which the Holy Ghost hath made you overseers, to feed the church of God, which he hath purchased with his own blood.

Php 1:1 — Paul and Timotheus, the servants of Jesus Christ, to all the saints in Christ Jesus which are at Philippi, with the bishops and deacons:

• A title of Jesus.

1Pe 2:25 — For ye were as sheep going astray; but are now returned unto the Shepherd and Bishop of your souls.

See: Elder

BIT • Part of a bridle.

Ps 32:9 — Be ye not as the horse, *or* as the mule, *which* have no understanding: whose mouth must be held in with bit and bridle, lest they come near unto thee.

Jas 3:3 — Behold, we put bits in the horses' mouths, that they may obey us; and we turn about their whole body.

BITHIAH • Daughter of Pharaoh.

1Ch 4:18 — And his wife Jehudijah bare Jered the father of Gedor, and Heber the father of Socho, and Jekuthiel the father of Zanoah. And these *are* the sons of Bithiah the daughter of Pharaoh, which Mered took.

BITHRON • A district bordering on the Jordan.

2Sa 2:29 — And Abner and his men walked all that night through the plain, and passed over Jordan, and went through all Bithron, and they came to Mahanaim.

BITHYNIA • A Roman province in Asia Minor.

Ac 16:7 — After they were come to Mysia, they assayed to go into Bithynia: but the Spirit suffered them not.

1Pe 1:1 — Peter, an apostle of Jesus Christ, to the strangers scattered throughout Pontus, Galatia, Cappadocia, Asia, and Bithynia,

BITTER HERBS

• Eaten symbolicly with the passover.

Ex 12:8 — And they shall eat the flesh in that night, roast with fire, and unleavened bread; *and* with bitter *herbs* they shall eat it.

Nu 9:11 — The fourteenth day of the second month at even they shall keep it, *and* eat it with unleavened bread and bitter *herbs*.

BITTER WATER

• At Marah.

Ex 15:23 — And when they came to Marah, they could not drink of the waters of Marah, for they *were* bitter: therefore the name of it was called Marah.

• A ceremonial water used by the priest.

Nu 5:18–27

BITTERN

Isa 14:23 — I will also make it a possession for the bittern, and pools of water: and I will sweep it with the besom of destruction, saith the LORD of hosts.

Isa 34:11 — But the cormorant and the bittern shall possess it; the owl also and the raven shall dwell in it: and he shall stretch out upon it the line of confusion, and the stones of emptiness.

Zep 2:14 — And flocks shall lie down in the midst of her, all the beasts of the nations: both the cormorant and the bittern shall lodge in the upper lintels of it; *their* voice shall sing in the windows; desolation *shall be* in the thresholds: for he shall uncover the cedar work.

BITUMEN

• An inflammable mineral.

Ge 11:3 — And they said one to another, Go to, let us make brick, and burn them throughly. And they had brick for stone, and slime had they for morter.

Ge 14:10 — And the vale of Siddim *was full of* slimepits; and the kings of Sodom and Gomorrah fled, and fell there; and they that remained fled to the mountain.

Ex 2:3 — And when she could not longer hide him, she took for him an ark of bulrushes, and daubed it with slime and with pitch, and put the child therein; and she laid *it* in the flags by the river's brink.

See: Petroleum

BIZJOTHJAH

• A town in Judah.

Jos 15:28 — And Hazar-shual, and Beer-sheba, and Bizjothjah,

• Called Bizjothjah-Baalah.

Jos 15:32 — And Lebaoth, and Shilhim, and Ain, and Rimmon: all the cities *are* twenty and nine, with their villages:

• Called Baalath-Beer.

Jos 19:8 — And all the villages that *were* round about these cities to Baalath-beer, Ramath of the south. This is the inheritance of the tribe of the children of Simeon according to their families.

• Called Balah.

Jos 19:3 — And Hazar-shual, and Balah, and Azem,

BIZTHA • A Persian chamberlain.

Est 1:10 — On the seventh day, when the heart of the king was merry with wine, he commanded Mehuman, Biztha, Harbona, Bigtha, and Abagtha, Zethar, and Carcas, the seven chamberlains that served in the presence of Ahasuerus the king,

BLACKNESS

• Figurative.

Job 30:30 — My skin is black upon me, and my bones are burned with heat.

Joel 2:6 — Before their face the people shall be much pained: all faces shall gather blackness.

• **Blackness of darkness.**

Jude 1:13 — Raging waves of the sea, foaming out their own shame; wandering stars, to whom is reserved the blackness of darkness for ever.

See: Colors; symbolic uses of

BLACKSMITH See: Smith

BLAIN • An inflammatory abscess.

Ex 9:9–10

BLASPHEMY

Le 24:10–16; Job 9:16–18, 34–35; 10:2–7; 13:7–9, 25–27; 15:25–26; 16:11–14; 19:6–7, 21–22; 21:13–14; 22:12–14; 33:10–11; 34:5–6, 16–19; Ps 78:19–20; Pr 30:7–9; Isa 8:21–22; 29:15–16; 36:20–21; Eze 33:17–20; 35:12–13; Da 11:36–37; Zec 5:3–4; Mal 3:13–14; Mt 12:31–32; Mk 3:29–30; 7:21–23

Ex 20:7 — Thou shalt not take the name of the LORD thy God in vain; for the LORD will not hold him guiltless that taketh his name in vain.

Le 19:12 — And ye shall not swear by my name falsely, neither shalt thou profane the name of thy God: I *am* the LORD.

Le 22:32 — Neither shall ye profane my holy name; but I will be hallowed among the children of Israel: I *am* the LORD which hallow you,

Dt 5:11 — Thou shalt not take the name of the LORD thy God in vain: for the LORD will not hold *him* guiltless that taketh his name in vain.

2Sa 12:14 — Howbeit, because by this deed thou hast given great occasion to the enemies of the LORD to blaspheme, the child also *that is* born unto thee shall surely die.

2Ki 19:22 — Whom hast thou reproached and blasphemed? and against whom hast thou exalted *thy* voice, and lifted up thine eyes on high? *even* against the Holy *One* of Israel.

2Ch 32:19 — And they spake against the God of Jerusalem, as against the gods of the people of the earth, *which were* the work of the hands of man.

Job 15:13 — That thou turnest thy spirit against God, and lettest *such* words go out of thy mouth?

Job 16:9 — He teareth *me* in his wrath, who hateth me: he gnasheth upon me with his teeth; mine enemy sharpeneth his eyes upon me.

Job 22:17 — Which said unto God, Depart from us: and what can the Almighty do for them?

Job 30:21 — Thou art become cruel to me: with thy strong hand thou opposest thyself against me.

Job 34:9 — For he hath said, It profiteth a man nothing that he should delight himself with God.

Job 34:37 — For he addeth rebellion unto his sin, he clappeth *his hands* among us, and multiplieth his words against God.

Job 37:20 — Shall it be told him that I speak? if a man speak, surely he shall be swallowed up.

Job 40:2 — Shall he that contendeth with the Almighty instruct *him?* he that reproveth God, let him answer it.

Ps 10:11 — He hath said in his heart, God hath forgotten: he hideth his face; he will never see *it.*

Ps 10:13 — Wherefore doth the wicked contemn God? he hath said in his heart, Thou wilt not require *it.*

Ps 50:21 — These *things* hast thou done, and I kept silence; thou thoughtest that I was altogether *such an one* as thyself: *but* I will reprove thee, and set *them* in order before thine eyes.

Ps 73:9 — They set their mouth against the heavens, and their tongue walketh through the earth.

Ps 73:11 — And they say, How doth God know? and is there knowledge in the most High?

Ps 74:18 — Remember this, *that* the enemy hath reproached, O LORD, and *that* the foolish people have blasphemed thy name.

Ps 94:7 — Yet they say, The LORD shall not see, neither shall the God of Jacob regard *it.*

Ps 139:20 — For they speak against thee wickedly, *and* thine enemies take *thy name* in vain.

Isa 36:15 — Neither let Hezekiah make you trust in the LORD, saying, The LORD will surely deliver us: this city shall not be delivered into the hand of the king of Assyria.

Isa 36:18 — *Beware* lest Hezekiah persuade you, saying, The LORD will deliver us. Hath any of the gods of the nations delivered his land out of the hand of the king of Assyria?

Isa 37:10 — Thus shall ye speak to Hezekiah king of Judah, saying, Let not thy God, in whom thou trustest, deceive thee, saying, Jerusalem shall not be given into the hand of the king of Assyria.

Isa 37:23 — Whom hast thou reproached and blasphemed? and against whom hast thou exalted *thy* voice, and lifted up thine eyes on high? *even* against the Holy One of Israel.

Isa 40:27 — Why sayest thou, O Jacob, and speakest, O Israel, My way is hid from the LORD, and my judgment is passed over from my God?

Isa 45:9 — Woe unto him that striveth with his Maker! *Let* the potsherd *strive* with the potsherds of the earth. Shall the clay say to him that fashioneth it, What makest thou? or thy work, He hath no hands?

Isa 52:5 — Now therefore, what have I here, saith the LORD, that my people is taken away for nought? they that rule over them make them to howl, saith the LORD; and my name continually every day is blasphemed.

Isa 65:7 — Your iniquities, and the iniquities of your fathers together, saith the LORD, which have burned incense upon the mountains, and blasphemed me upon the hills: therefore will I measure their former work into their bosom.

Jer 4:10 — Then said I, Ah, Lord GOD! surely thou hast greatly deceived this people and Jerusalem, saying, Ye shall have peace; whereas the sword reacheth unto the soul.

Jer 17:15 — Behold, they say unto me, Where *is* the word of the LORD? let it come now.

Jer 20:7 — O LORD, thou hast deceived me, and I was deceived: thou art stronger than I, and hast prevailed: I am in derision daily, every one mocketh me.

Jer 23:10 — For the land is full of adulterers; for because of swearing the land mourneth; the pleasant places of the wilderness are dried up, and their course is evil, and their force *is* not right.

Eze 8:12 — Then said he unto me, Son of man, hast thou seen what the ancients of the house of Israel do in the dark, every man in the chambers of his imagery? for they say, The LORD seeth us not; the LORD hath forsaken the earth.

Eze 9:9 — Then said he unto me, The iniquity of the house of Israel and Judah *is* exceeding great, and the land is full of blood, and the city full of perverseness: for they say, The LORD hath forsaken the earth, and the LORD seeth not.

Eze 18:25 — Yet ye say, The way of the Lord is not equal. Hear now, O house of Israel; Is not my way equal? are not your ways unequal?

Eze 20:27 — Therefore, son of man, speak unto the house of Israel, and say unto them, Thus saith the Lord GOD; Yet in this your fathers have blasphemed me, in that they have committed a trespass against me.

Da 7:25 — And he shall speak *great* words against the most High, and shall wear out the saints of the most High, and think to change times and laws: and they shall be given into his hand until a time and times and the dividing of time.

Hos 7:13 — Woe unto them! for they have fled from me: destruction unto them! because they have transgressed against me: though I have redeemed them, yet they have spoken lies against me.

Zep 1:12 — And it shall come to pass at that time, *that* I will search Jerusalem with candles, and punish the men that are settled on their lees: that say in their heart, The LORD will not do good, neither will he do evil.

Mt 10:25 — It is enough for the disciple that he be as his master, and the servant as his lord. If they have called the master of the house Beelzebub, how much more *shall they call* them of his household?

Mt 15:19 — For out of the heart proceed evil thoughts, murders, adulteries, fornications, thefts, false witness, blasphemies:

Lk 12:10 — And whosoever shall speak a word against the Son of man, it shall be forgiven him: but unto him that blasphemeth against the Holy Ghost it shall not be forgiven.

Jn 19:7 — The Jews answered him, We have a law, and by our law he ought to die, because he made himself the Son of God.

Ro 2:24 — For the name of God is blasphemed among the Gentiles through you, as it is written.

1Co 12:3 — Wherefore I give you to understand, that no man speaking by the Spirit of God calleth Jesus accursed: and *that* no man can say that Jesus is the Lord, but by the Holy Ghost.

Col 3:8 — But now ye also put off all these; anger, wrath, malice, blasphemy, filthy communication out of your mouth.

2Th 2:4 — Who opposeth and exalteth himself above all that is called God, or that is worshipped; so that he as God sitteth in the temple of God, shewing himself that he is God.

2Ti 3:2 — For men shall be lovers of their own selves, covetous, boasters, proud, blasphemers, disobedient to parents, unthankful, unholy,

Heb 10:29 — Of how much sorer punishment, suppose ye, shall he be thought worthy, who hath trodden under foot the Son of God, and hath counted the blood of the covenant, wherewith he was sanctified, an unholy thing, and hath done despite unto the Spirit of grace?

Jas 2:7 — Do not they blaspheme that worthy name by the which ye are called?

Jas 3:10 — Out of the same mouth proceedeth blessing and cursing. My brethren, these things ought not so to be.

Jas 5:12 — But above all things, my brethren, swear not, neither by heaven, neither by the earth, neither by any other oath: but let your yea be yea; and *your* nay, nay; lest ye fall into condemnation.

2Pe 3:3 — Knowing this first, that there shall come in the last days scoffers, walking after their own lusts,

Rev 13:1 — And I stood upon the sand of the sea, and saw a beast rise up out of the sea, having seven heads and ten horns, and upon his horns ten crowns, and upon his heads the name of blasphemy.

Rev 13:6 — And he opened his mouth in blasphemy against God, to blaspheme his name, and his tabernacle, and them that dwell in heaven.

Rev 16:9 — And men were scorched with great heat, and blasphemed the name of God, which hath power over these plagues: and they repented not to give him glory.

Rev 16:11 — And blasphemed the God of heaven because of their pains and their sores, and repented not of their deeds.

Rev 16:21 — And there fell upon men a great hail out of heaven, *every stone* about the weight of a talent: and men blasphemed God because of the plague of the hail; for the plague thereof was exceeding great.

Rev 17:3 — So he carried me away in the spirit into the wilderness: and I saw a woman sit upon a scarlet coloured beast, full of names of blasphemy, having seven heads and ten horns.

• Prophecy of.

Rev 13:5–6

Rev 13:1 — And I stood upon the sand of the sea, and saw a beast rise up out of the sea, having seven heads and ten horns, and upon his horns ten crowns, and upon his heads the name of blasphemy.

Rev 16:9 — And men were scorched with great heat, and blasphemed the name of God, which hath power over these plagues: and they repented not to give him glory.

Rev 16:11 — And blasphemed the God of heaven because of their pains and their sores, and repented not of their deeds.

Rev 16:21 — And there fell upon men a great hail out of heaven, *every stone* about the weight of a talent: and men blasphemed God because of the plague of the hail; for the plague thereof was exceeding great.

Rev 17:3 — So he carried me away in the spirit into the wilderness: and I saw a woman sit upon a scarlet coloured beast, full of names of blasphemy, having seven heads and ten horns.

• Instances of.

• The depraved son of Shelomith, who, in an altercation with an Israelite, cursed God.

Le 24:10–16

• **Of the Israelites, in murmuring against God.**
Nu 21:5–6

• **Infidels, who used the adultery of David as an occasion to blaspheme.**
2Sa 12:14

• **Shimei, in his malice toward David.**
2Sa 16:5

• **Rabshaken, in the siege of Jerusalem.**
2Ki 18:22; 19:1–37; Isa 36:15–20; 37:10–33

• **Job's wife, when she exhorted Job to curse God and die.**
Job 2:9

• **Peter, when accused of being a disciple of Jesus.**
Mt 26:74; Mk 14:71

• **The revilers of Jesus, when he was crucified.**
Mt 27:40–44; 27:63

• **The early Christians, persecuted by Saul of Tarsus, compelled to blaspheme the name of Jesus.**
Ac 26:11; 1Ti 1:13

• **Two disciples were delivered unto Satan to learn not to blaspheme.**
1Ti 1:20

• **Man of sin.**
2Th 2:3–4

• **Backslidden Ephesians.**
Rev 2:9

• **False indictments for.**

• **Of Naboth.**
1Ki 21:13 — And there came in two men, children of Belial, and sat before him: and the men of Belial witnessed against him, *even* against Naboth, in the presence of the people, saying, Naboth did blaspheme God and the king. Then they carried him forth out of the city, and stoned him with stones, that he died.

• **Of Jesus.**
Lk 22:70–71
Mt 26:65 — Then the high priest rent his clothes, saying, He hath spoken blasphemy; what further need have we of witnesses? behold, now ye have heard his blasphemy.
Mk 14:58 — We heard him say, I will destroy this temple that is made with hands, and within three days I will build another made without hands.
Jn 19:7 — The Jews answered him, We have a law, and by our law he ought to die, because he made himself the Son of God.

• **Of Stephen.**
Ac 6:11 — Then they suborned men, which said, We have heard him speak blasphemous words against Moses, and *against* God.
Ac 6:13 — And set up false witnesses, which said, This man ceaseth not to speak blasphemous words against this holy place, and the law:

• **Jesus falsely accused of, previous to his trial.**
Mk 2:7 — Why doth this *man* thus speak blasphemies? who can forgive sins but God only?
Lk 5:21 — And the scribes and the Pharisees began to reason, saying, Who is this which speaketh blasphemies? Who can forgive sins, but God alone?

BLASTING

• **Blight.**
1Ki 8:37 — If there be in the land famine, if there be pestilence, blasting, mildew, locust, *or* if there be caterpiller; if their enemy besiege them in the land of their cities; whatsoever plague, whatsoever sickness *there be;*

• **Sent as a judgment.**
Dt 28:22 — The LORD shall smite thee with a consumption, and with a fever, and with an inflammation, and with an extreme burning, and with the sword, and with blasting, and with mildew; and they shall pursue thee until thou perish.
2Ki 19:7 — Behold, I will send a blast upon him, and he shall hear a rumour, and shall return to his own land; and I will cause him to fall by the sword in his own land.
Isa 37:7 — Behold, I will send a blast upon him, and he shall hear a rumour, and return to his own land; and I will cause him to fall by the sword in his own land.
Am 4:9 — I have smitten you with blasting and mildew: when your gardens and your vineyards and your fig trees and your olive trees increased, the palmerworm devoured *them:* yet have ye not returned unto me, saith the LORD.
Hag 2:17 — I smote you with blasting and with mildew and with hail in all the labours of your hands; yet ye *turned* not to me, saith the LORD.

• **Figurative.**
Ex 15:8 — And with the blast of thy nostrils the waters were gathered together, the floods stood upright as an heap, *and* the depths were congealed in the heart of the sea.
2Sa 22:16 — And the channels of the sea appeared, the foundations of the world were discovered, at the rebuking of the LORD, at the blast of the breath of his nostrils.
Job 4:9 — By the blast of God they perish, and by the breath of his nostrils are they consumed.
Ps 18:15 — Then the channels of waters were seen, and the foundations of the world were discovered at thy rebuke, O LORD, at the blast of the breath of thy nostrils.

BLASTUS • One of Herod's officers.

Ac 12:20 — And Herod was highly displeased with them of Tyre and Sidon: but they came with one accord to him, and, having made Blastus the king's chamberlain their friend, desired peace; because their country was nourished by the king's *country.*

BLEMISH

• A physical deformity.

• Debarred sons of Aaron from exercise of priestly offices.

Le 21:17–23

• Animals with, forbidden to be used for sacrifice.

Le 22:19–25

• Figurative.

Eph 5:27 — That he might present it to himself a glorious church, not having spot, or wrinkle, or any such thing; but that it should be holy and without blemish.

1Pe 1:19 — But with the precious blood of Christ, as of a lamb without blemish and without spot:

BLESSING

• For blessing before eating.

→See: Prayer

→See: Prayer; thanksgiving and, before taking food

→See: Benedictions

• Responsive blessings of the law.

Dt 28:1–14

• For the responsive curses of the law.

→See: Curse

• Divine, contingent upon obedience.

Le 26:3–43; Dt 7:12–15; 11:26–28; 15:4–5; 28:1–14; 30:1–10, 15–20; 1Ki 2:3–4; 9:3–9; 1Ch 28:7–8; 2Ch 7:17–22; Pr 3:1–2; Jer 7:3–7; 11:1–5; 15:19–21; 17:24–27; 22:4–5, 15–16; Mal 3:10–12; Col 1:22–23; Heb 6:11–12

Ex 15:26 — And said, If thou wilt diligently hearken to the voice of the LORD thy God, and wilt do that which is right in his sight, and wilt give ear to his commandments, and keep all his statutes, I will put none of these diseases upon thee, which I have brought upon the Egyptians: for I *am* the LORD that healeth thee.

Ex 19:5 — Now therefore, if ye will obey my voice indeed, and keep my covenant, then ye shall be a peculiar treasure unto me above all people: for all the earth *is* mine:

Ex 20:6 — And shewing mercy unto thousands of them that love me, and keep my commandments.

Ex 23:22 — But if thou shalt indeed obey his voice, and do all that I speak; then I will be an enemy unto thine enemies, and an adversary unto thine adversaries.

Dt 4:1 — Now therefore hearken, O Israel, unto the statutes and unto the judgments, which I teach you, for to do *them,* that ye may live, and go in and possess the land which the LORD God of your fathers giveth you.

Dt 4:40 — Thou shalt keep therefore his statutes, and his commandments, which I command thee this day, that it may go well with thee, and with thy children after thee, and that thou mayest prolong *thy* days upon the earth, which the LORD thy God giveth thee, for ever.

Dt 5:10 — And shewing mercy unto thousands of them that love me and keep my commandments.

Dt 5:29 — O that there were such an heart in them, that they would fear me, and keep all my commandments always, that it might be well with them, and with their children for ever!

Dt 7:9 — Know therefore that the LORD thy God, he *is* God, the faithful God, which keepeth covenant and mercy with them that love him and keep his commandments to a thousand generations;

Dt 12:28 — Observe and hear all these words which I command thee, that it may go well with thee, and with thy children after thee for ever, when thou doest *that which is* good and right in the sight of the LORD thy God.

Dt 29:9 — Keep therefore the words of this covenant, and do them, that ye may prosper in all that ye do.

Jos 1:8 — This book of the law shall not depart out of thy mouth; but thou shalt meditate therein day and night, that thou mayest observe to do according to all that is written therein: for then thou shalt make thy way prosperous, and then thou shalt have good success.

1Ki 3:14 — And if thou wilt walk in my ways, to keep my statutes and my commandments, as thy father David did walk, then I will lengthen thy days.

1Ki 8:23 — And he said, LORD God of Israel, *there is* no God like thee, in heaven above, or on earth beneath, who keepest covenant and mercy with thy servants that walk before thee with all their heart:

1Ch 22:13 — Then shalt thou prosper, if thou takest heed to fulfil the statutes and judgments which the LORD charged Moses with concerning Israel: be strong, and of good courage; dread not, nor be dismayed.

2Ch 26:5 — And he sought God in the days of Zechariah, who had understanding in the visions of God: and as long as he sought the LORD, God made him to prosper.

2Ch 27:6 — So Jotham became mighty, because he prepared his ways before the LORD his God.

2Ch 30:9 — For if ye turn again unto the LORD, your brethren and your children *shall find* compassion before them that lead them captive, so that they shall come again into this land: for the LORD your God *is* gracious and merciful, and will not turn away *his* face from you, if ye return unto him.

2Ch 31:10 — And Azariah the chief priest of the house of Zadok answered him, and said, Since *the people* began to bring the offerings into the house of the LORD, we have had enough to eat, and have left plenty: for the LORD hath blessed his people; and that which is left *is* this great store.

Job 36:11 — If they obey and serve *him,* they shall spend their days in prosperity, and their years in pleasures.

Pr 16:7 — When a man's ways please the LORD, he maketh even his enemies to be at peace with him.

Isa 1:19 — If ye be willing and obedient, ye shall eat the good of the land:

Jer 7:23 — But this thing commanded I them, saying, Obey my voice, and I will be your God, and ye shall be my people: and walk ye in all the ways that I have commanded you, that it may be well unto you.

Jer 12:16 — And it shall come to pass, if they will diligently learn the ways of my people, to swear by my name, The LORD liveth; as they taught my people to swear by Baal; then shall they be built in the midst of my people.

Zec 3:7 — Thus saith the LORD of hosts; If thou wilt walk in my ways, and if thou wilt keep my charge, then thou shalt also judge my house, and shalt also keep my courts, and I will give thee places to walk among these that stand by.

Mt 10:22 — And ye shall be hated of all *men* for my name's sake: but he that endureth to the end shall be saved.

Mt 24:13 — But he that shall endure unto the end, the same shall be saved.

Mk 13:13 — And ye shall be hated of all *men* for my name's sake: but he that shall endure unto the end, the same shall be saved.

Heb 3:6 — But Christ as a son over his own house; whose house are we, if we hold fast the confidence and the rejoicing of the hope firm unto the end.

Heb 3:14 — For we are made partakers of Christ, if we hold the beginning of our confidence stedfast unto the end;

Heb 10:36 — For ye have need of patience, that, after ye have done the will of God, ye might receive the promise.

Rev 2:10 — Fear none of those things which thou shalt suffer: behold, the devil shall cast *some* of you into prison, that ye may be tried; and ye shall have tribulation ten days: be thou faithful unto death, and I will give thee a crown of life.

See: Faithfulness

See: Contingencies

• Spiritual, from God.

Ps 18:1–2, 35–36; 23:2–3; 92:12–14; 94:17–18; 132:15–16; 144:1–2; Isa 4:3–4; 6:6–7; 33:5–6; 41:13–14, 17–18; 58:10–11; Hos 14:5–8; Mal 3:2–3; 2Co 1:21–22; Col 1:11–12; Heb 12:10–11; Jas 1:17–18; 2Pe 1:2–4

Ge 49:24 — But his bow abode in strength, and the arms of his hands were made strong by the hands of the mighty *God* of Jacob; (from thence *is* the shepherd, the stone of Israel:)

Ex 15:2 — The LORD *is* my strength and song, and he is become my salvation: he *is* my God, and I will prepare him an habitation; my father's God, and I will exalt him.

Ex 31:13 — Speak thou also unto the children of Israel, saying, Verily my sabbaths ye shall keep: for it is a sign between me and you throughout your generations; that ye may know that I *am* the LORD that doth sanctify you.

Ex 33:16 — For wherein shall it be known here that I and thy people have found grace in thy sight? *is it* not in that thou goest with us? so shall we be separated, I and thy people, from all the people that *are* upon the face of the earth.

Le 21:8 — Thou shalt sanctify him therefore; for he offereth the bread of thy God: he shall be holy unto thee: for I the LORD, which sanctify you, *am* holy.

Dt 33:25 — Thy shoes *shall be* iron and brass; and as thy days, *so shall* thy strength *be.*

Dt 33:27 — The eternal God *is thy* refuge, and underneath *are* the everlasting arms: and he shall thrust out the enemy from before thee; and shall say, Destroy *them.*

1Sa 2:4 — The bows of the mighty men *are* broken, and they that stumbled are girded with strength.

Ne 8:10 — Then he said unto them, Go your way, eat the fat, and drink the sweet, and send portions unto them for whom nothing is prepared: for *this* day *is* holy unto our Lord: neither be ye sorry; for the joy of the LORD is your strength.

Job 23:6 — Will he plead against me with *his* great power? No; but he would put *strength* in me.

Ps 1:3 — And he shall be like a tree planted by the rivers of water, that bringeth forth his fruit in his season; his leaf also shall not wither; and whatsoever he doeth shall prosper.

Ps 18:28 — For thou wilt light my candle: the LORD my God will enlighten my darkness.

Ps 18:32 — *It is* God that girdeth me with strength, and maketh my way perfect.

Ps 27:14 — Wait on the LORD: be of good courage, and he shall strengthen thine heart: wait, I say, on the LORD.

Ps 28:8 — The LORD *is* their strength, and he *is* the saving strength of his anointed.

Ps 29:11 — The LORD will give strength unto his people; the LORD will bless his people with peace.

Ps 30:7 — LORD, by thy favour thou hast made my mountain to stand strong: thou didst hide thy face, *and* I was troubled.

Ps 31:24 — Be of good courage, and he shall strengthen your heart, all ye that hope in the LORD.

Ps 37:6 — And he shall bring forth thy righteousness as the light, and thy judgment as the noonday.

Ps 37:17 — For the arms of the wicked shall be broken: but the LORD upholdeth the righteous.

Ps 37:24 — Though he fall, he shall not be utterly cast down: for the LORD upholdeth *him with* his hand.

Ps 37:39 — But the salvation of the righteous *is* of the LORD: *he is* their strength in the time of trouble.

Ps 52:8 — But I *am* like a green olive tree in the house of God: I trust in the mercy of God for ever and ever.

Ps 55:22 — Cast thy burden upon the LORD, and he shall sustain thee: he shall never suffer the righteous to be moved.

Ps 61:5 — For thou, O God, hast heard my vows: thou hast given *me* the heritage of those that fear thy name.

Ps 63:8 — My soul followeth hard after thee: thy right hand upholdeth me.

Ps 66:9 — Which holdeth our soul in life, and suffereth not our feet to be moved.

Ps 68:18 — Thou hast ascended on high, thou hast led captivity captive: thou hast received gifts for men;

yea, *for* the rebellious also, that the LORD God might dwell *among them.*

Ps 68:28 — Thy God hath commanded thy strength: strengthen, O God, that which thou hast wrought for us.

Ps 68:35 — O God, *thou art* terrible out of thy holy places: the God of Israel *is* he that giveth strength and power unto *his* people. Blessed *be* God.

Ps 71:16 — I will go in the strength of the Lord GOD: I will make mention of thy righteousness, *even* of thine only.

Ps 72:6 — He shall come down like rain upon the mown grass: as showers *that* water the earth.

Ps 72:17 — His name shall endure for ever: his name shall be continued as long as the sun: and *men* shall be blessed in him: all nations shall call him blessed.

Ps 73:23 — Nevertheless I *am* continually with thee: thou hast holden *me* by my right hand.

Ps 73:26 — My flesh and my heart faileth: *but* God *is* the strength of my heart, and my portion for ever.

Ps 81:10 — I *am* the LORD thy God, which brought thee out of the land of Egypt: open thy mouth wide, and I will fill it.

Ps 84:5 — Blessed *is* the man whose strength *is* in thee; in whose heart *are* the ways *of them.*

Ps 84:11 — For the LORD God *is* a sun and shield: the LORD will give grace and glory: no good *thing* will he withhold from them that walk uprightly.

Ps 89:17 — For thou *art* the glory of their strength: and in thy favour our horn shall be exalted.

Ps 105:4 — Seek the LORD, and his strength: seek his face evermore.

Ps 119:32 — I will run the way of thy commandments, when thou shalt enlarge my heart.

Ps 119:102 — I have not departed from thy judgments: for thou hast taught me.

Ps 138:3 — In the day when I cried thou answeredst me, *and* strengthenedst me *with* strength in my soul.

Ps 138:8 — The LORD will perfect *that which* concerneth me: thy mercy, O LORD, *endureth* for ever: forsake not the works of thine own hands.

Ps 146:5 — Happy *is he* that *hath* the God of Jacob for his help, whose hope *is* in the LORD his God:

Pr 10:29 — The way of the LORD *is* strength to the upright: but destruction *shall be* to the workers of iniquity.

Pr 16:6 — By mercy and truth iniquity is purged: and by the fear of the LORD *men* depart from evil.

Isa 1:25 — And I will turn my hand upon thee, and purely purge away thy dross, and take away all thy tin:

Isa 26:12 — LORD, thou wilt ordain peace for us: for thou also hast wrought all our works in us.

Isa 28:6 — And for a spirit of judgment to him that sitteth in judgment, and for strength to them that turn the battle to the gate.

Isa 40:11 — He shall feed his flock like a shepherd: he shall gather the lambs with his arm, and carry *them* in his bosom, *and* shall gently lead those that are with young.

Isa 40:29 — He giveth power to the faint; and to *them that have* no might he increaseth strength.

Isa 40:31 — But they that wait upon the LORD shall renew *their* strength; they shall mount up with wings as eagles; they shall run, and not be weary; *and* they shall walk, and not faint.

Isa 41:10 — Fear thou not; for I *am* with thee: be not dismayed; for I *am* thy God: I will strengthen thee; yea, I will help thee; yea, I will uphold thee with the right hand of my righteousness.

Isa 44:3 — For I will pour water upon him that is thirsty, and floods upon the dry ground: I will pour my spirit upon thy seed, and my blessing upon thine offspring:

Isa 45:8 — Drop down, ye heavens, from above, and let the skies pour down righteousness: let the earth open, and let them bring forth salvation, and let righteousness spring up together; I the LORD have created it.

Isa 45:24 — Surely, shall *one* say, in the LORD have I righteousness and strength: *even* to him shall *men* come; and all that are incensed against him shall be ashamed.

Isa 54:17 — No weapon that is formed against thee shall prosper; and every tongue *that* shall rise against thee in judgment thou shalt condemn. This *is* the heritage of the servants of the LORD, and their righteousness *is* of me, saith the LORD.

Isa 57:19 — I create the fruit of the lips; Peace, peace to *him that is* far off, and to *him that is* near, saith the LORD; and I will heal him.

Isa 58:8 — Then shall thy light break forth as the morning, and thine health shall spring forth speedily: and thy righteousness shall go before thee; the glory of the LORD shall be thy rereward.

Jer 31:12 — Therefore they shall come and sing in the height of Zion, and shall flow together to the goodness of the LORD, for wheat, and for wine, and for oil, and for the young of the flock and of the herd: and their soul shall be as a watered garden; and they shall not sorrow any more at all.

Jer 31:14 — And I will satiate the soul of the priests with fatness, and my people shall be satisfied with my goodness, saith the LORD.

Jer 31:33 — But this *shall be* the covenant that I will make with the house of Israel; After those days, saith the LORD, I will put my law in their inward parts, and write it in their hearts; and will be their God, and they shall be my people.

Eze 16:14 — And thy renown went forth among the heathen for thy beauty: for it *was* perfect through my comeliness, which I had put upon thee, saith the Lord GOD.

Da 11:32 — And such as do wickedly against the covenant shall he corrupt by flatteries: but the people that do know their God shall be strong, and do *exploits.*

Hos 6:3 — Then shall we know, *if* we follow on to know the LORD: his going forth is prepared as the morning; and he shall come unto us as the rain, as the latter *and* former rain unto the earth.

Hab 3:19 — The LORD God *is* my strength, and he will make my feet like hinds' *feet,* and he will make me to walk upon mine high places. To the chief singer on my stringed instruments.

Zec 10:12 — And I will strengthen them in the LORD; and they shall walk up and down in his name, saith the LORD.

Zec 12:8 — In that day shall the LORD defend the inhabitants of Jerusalem; and he that is feeble among them at that day shall be as David; and the house of David *shall be* as God, as the angel of the LORD before them.

Mal 4:2 — But unto you that fear my name shall the Sun of righteousness arise with healing in his wings; and ye shall go forth, and grow up as calves of the stall.

Jn 1:16 — And of his fulness have all we received, and grace for grace.

Jn 17:11 — And now I am no more in the world, but these are in the world, and I come to thee. Holy Father, keep through thine own name those whom thou hast given me, that they may be one, as we *are.*

Ac 20:32 — And now, brethren, I commend you to God, and to the word of his grace, which is able to build you up, and to give you an inheritance among all them which are sanctified.

Ro 9:23 — And that he might make known the riches of his glory on the vessels of mercy, which he had afore prepared unto glory,

Ro 14:4 — Who art thou that judgest another man's servant? to his own master he standeth or falleth. Yea, he shall be holden up: for God is able to make him stand.

1Co 12:6 — And there are diversities of operations, but it is the same God which worketh all in all.

1Co 13:10 — But when that which is perfect is come, then that which is in part shall be done away.

1Co 13:12 — For now we see through a glass, darkly; but then face to face: now I know in part; but then shall I know even as also I am known.

1Co 15:10 — But by the grace of God I am what I am: and his grace *which was bestowed* upon me was not in vain; but I laboured more abundantly than they all: yet not I, but the grace of God which was with me.

2Co 3:5 — Not that we are sufficient of ourselves to think any thing as of ourselves; but our sufficiency *is* of God;

2Co 5:5 — Now he that hath wrought us for the selfsame thing *is* God, who also hath given unto us the earnest of the Spirit.

2Co 9:8 — And God *is* able to make all grace abound toward you; that ye, always having all sufficiency in all *things,* may abound to every good work:

2Co 10:4 — (For the weapons of our warfare *are* not carnal, but mighty through God to the pulling down of strong holds;)

Eph 3:20 — Now unto him that is able to do exceeding abundantly above all that we ask or think, according to the power that worketh in us,

Php 1:6 — Being confident of this very thing, that he which hath begun a good work in you will perform *it* until the day of Jesus Christ:

Php 2:13 — For it is God which worketh in you both to will and to do of *his* good pleasure.

Php 4:7 — And the peace of God, which passeth all understanding, shall keep your hearts and minds through Christ Jesus.

Php 4:19 — But my God shall supply all your need according to his riches in glory by Christ Jesus.

1Th 5:24 — Faithful *is* he that calleth you, who also will do *it.*

1Pe 1:5 — Who are kept by the power of God through faith unto salvation ready to be revealed in the last time.

1Jn 1:9 — If we confess our sins, he is faithful and just to forgive us *our* sins, and to cleanse us from all unrighteousness.

1Jn 4:4 — Ye are of God, little children, and have overcome them: because greater is he that is in you, than he that is in the world.

Jude 1:1 — Jude, the servant of Jesus Christ, and brother of James, to them that are sanctified by God the Father, and preserved in Jesus Christ, *and* called:

Jude 1:24 — Now unto him that is able to keep you from falling, and to present *you* faultless before the presence of his glory with exceeding joy,

See: Regeneration

See: Sanctification

- **Temporal, from God.**

Ge 8:22–9:3; 26:4–5; 28:20–21; 49:11–12, 24–25; Ex 23:25–26; Le 25:20–22; 26:4–10; Dt 6:2–25; 7:13–24; 8:1–10, 15–18; 11:12–15; 26:18–19; 28:7–8; 32:13–14; 1Sa 2:7–8; 2Sa 7:8–9; 1Ch 17:7–8; Job 37:16–17; Job 38:1–41; Ps 21:3–5; 65:8–13; 68:9–10; 69:35–36; 81:13–16; 91:1–15; 103:2–5; 104:1–35; 107:35–38; 127:1–5; 136:1–26; 144:12–15; 145:15–16; 146:5–9; 147:8–9, 13–14; Isa 30:23–26; 31:1–2; 33:15–16; Jer 27:4–6; Eze 36:28–38; Mal 3:10–12; Mt 6:30–33; Lk 12:22–31; 2Co 9:8–10; 2Pe 2:7–9

Ge 1:30 — And to every beast of the earth, and to every fowl of the air, and to every thing that creepeth upon the earth, wherein *there is* life, *I have given* every green herb for meat: and it was so.

Ge 22:17 — That in blessing I will bless thee, and in multiplying I will multiply thy seed as the stars of the heaven, and as the sand which *is* upon the sea shore; and thy seed shall possess the gate of his enemies;

Ge 49:20 — Out of Asher his bread *shall be* fat, and he shall yield royal dainties.

Ex 15:26 — And said, If thou wilt diligently hearken to the voice of the LORD thy God, and wilt do that which is right in his sight, and wilt give ear to his commandments, and keep all his statutes, I will put none of these diseases upon thee, which I have brought upon the Egyptians: for I *am* the LORD that healeth thee.

Ex 23:22 — But if thou shalt indeed obey his voice, and do all that I speak; then I will be an enemy unto thine enemies, and an adversary unto thine adversaries.

Ex 34:24 — For I will cast out the nations before thee, and enlarge thy borders: neither shall any man desire thy land, when thou shalt go up to appear before the LORD thy God thrice in the year.

Nu 10:29 — And Moses said unto Hobab, the son of Raguel the Midianite, Moses' father in law, We are journeying unto the place of which the LORD said, I will give it you: come thou with us, and we will do thee good: for the LORD hath spoken good concerning Israel.

Dt 1:10 — The LORD your God hath multiplied you, and, behold, ye *are* this day as the stars of heaven for multitude.

Dt 2:7 — For the LORD thy God hath blessed thee in all the works of thy hand: he knoweth thy walking through this great wilderness: these forty years the LORD thy God *hath been* with thee; thou hast lacked nothing.

Dt 4:4 — But ye that did cleave unto the LORD your God *are* alive every one of you this day.

Dt 4:40 — Thou shalt keep therefore his statutes, and his commandments, which I command thee this day, that it may go well with thee, and with thy children after thee, and that thou mayest prolong *thy* days upon the earth, which the LORD thy God giveth thee, for ever.

Dt 5:33 — Ye shall walk in all the ways which the LORD your God hath commanded you, that ye may live, and *that it may be* well with you, and *that* ye may prolong *your* days in the land which ye shall possess.

Dt 10:18 — He doth execute the judgment of the fatherless and widow, and loveth the stranger, in giving him food and raiment.

Dt 12:7 — And there ye shall eat before the LORD your God, and ye shall rejoice in all that ye put your hand unto, ye and your households, wherein the LORD thy God hath blessed thee.

Dt 12:28 — Observe and hear all these words which I command thee, that it may go well with thee, and with thy children after thee for ever, when thou doest *that which is* good and right in the sight of the LORD thy God.

Dt 15:4 — Save when there shall be no poor among you; for the LORD shall greatly bless thee in the land which the LORD thy God giveth thee *for* an inheritance to possess it:

Dt 15:6 — For the LORD thy God blesseth thee, as he promised thee: and thou shalt lend unto many nations, but thou shalt not borrow; and thou shalt reign over many nations, but they shall not reign over thee.

Dt 29:5 — And I have led you forty years in the wilderness: your clothes are not waxen old upon you, and thy shoe is not waxen old upon thy foot.

Jos 1:8 — This book of the law shall not depart out of thy mouth; but thou shalt meditate therein day and night, that thou mayest observe to do according to all that is written therein: for then thou shalt make thy way prosperous, and then thou shalt have good success.

Ru 1:6 — Then she arose with her daughters in law, that she might return from the country of Moab: for she had heard in the country of Moab how that the LORD had visited his people in giving them bread.

1Ch 29:12 — Both riches and honour *come* of thee, and thou reignest over all; and in thine hand *is* power and might; and in thine hand *it is* to make great, and to give strength unto all.

1Ch 29:14 — But who *am* I, and what *is* my people, that we should be able to offer so willingly after this sort? for all things *come* of thee, and of thine own have we given thee.

1Ch 29:16 — O LORD our God, all this store that we have prepared to build thee an house for thine holy name *cometh* of thine hand, and *is* all thine own.

2Ch 1:12 — Wisdom and knowledge *is* granted unto thee; and I will give thee riches, and wealth, and honour, such as none of the kings have had that *have been* before thee, neither shall there any after thee have the like.

2Ch 31:10 — And Azariah the chief priest of the house of Zadok answered him, and said, Since *the people* began to bring the offerings into the house of the LORD, we have had enough to eat, and have left plenty: for the LORD hath blessed his people; and that which is left *is* this great store.

Ezr 8:22 — For I was ashamed to require of the king a band of soldiers and horsemen to help us against the enemy in the way: because we had spoken unto the king, saying, The hand of our God *is* upon all them for good that seek him; but his power and his wrath *is* against all them that forsake him.

Ne 8:10 — Then he said unto them, Go your way, eat the fat, and drink the sweet, and send portions unto them for whom nothing is prepared: for *this* day *is* holy unto our Lord: neither be ye sorry; for the joy of the LORD is your strength.

Job 5:10 — Who giveth rain upon the earth, and sendeth waters upon the fields:

Job 12:23 — He increaseth the nations, and destroyeth them: he enlargeth the nations, and straiteneth them *again.*

Job 22:18 — Yet he filled their houses with good *things:* but the counsel of the wicked is far from me.

Job 37:6 — For he saith to the snow, Be thou *on* the earth; likewise to the small rain, and to the great rain of his strength.

Job 37:10 — By the breath of God frost is given: and the breadth of the waters is straitened.

Job 37:13 — He causeth it to come, whether for correction, or for his land, or for mercy.

Ps 23:1 — The LORD *is* my shepherd; I shall not want.

Ps 23:5 — Thou preparest a table before me in the presence of mine enemies: thou anointest my head with oil; my cup runneth over.

Ps 34:10 — The young lions do lack, and suffer hunger: but they that seek the LORD shall not want any good *thing.*

Ps 36:6 — Thy righteousness *is* like the great mountains; thy judgments *are* a great deep: O LORD, thou preservest man and beast.

Ps 44:3 — For they got not the land in possession by their own sword, neither did their own arm save them: but thy right hand, and thine arm, and the light of thy countenance, because thou hadst a favour unto them.

Ps 68:6 — God setteth the solitary in families: he bringeth out those which are bound with chains: but the rebellious dwell in a dry *land.*

Ps 68:19 — Blessed *be* the Lord, *who* daily loadeth us *with benefits, even* the God of our salvation. Selah.

Ps 85:12 — Yea, the LORD shall give *that which is* good; and our land shall yield her increase.

Ps 105:24 — And he increased his people greatly; and made them stronger than their enemies.

Ps 111:5 — He hath given meat unto them that fear him: he will ever be mindful of his covenant.

Ps 113:9 — He maketh the barren woman to keep house, *and to be* a joyful mother of children. Praise ye the LORD.

Ps 115:16 — The heaven, *even* the heavens, *are* the LORD'S: but the earth hath he given to the children of men.

Ps 135:7 — He causeth the vapours to ascend from the ends of the earth; he maketh lightnings for the rain; he bringeth the wind out of his treasuries.

Ecc 2:24 — *There is* nothing better for a man, *than* that he should eat and drink, and *that* he should make his soul enjoy good in his labour. This also I saw, that it *was* from the hand of God.

Ecc 3:13 — And also that every man should eat and drink, and enjoy the good of all his labour, it *is* the gift of God.

Ecc 5:19 — Every man also to whom God hath given riches and wealth, and hath given him power to eat thereof, and to take his portion, and to rejoice in his labour; this *is* the gift of God.

Isa 25:4 — For thou hast been a strength to the poor, a strength to the needy in his distress, a refuge from the storm, a shadow from the heat, when the blast of the terrible ones *is* as a storm *against* the wall.

Isa 43:20 — The beast of the field shall honour me, the dragons and the owls: because I give waters in the wilderness, *and* rivers in the desert, to give drink to my people, my chosen.

Isa 48:21 — And they thirsted not *when* he led them through the deserts: he caused the waters to flow out of the rock for them: he clave the rock also, and the waters gushed out.

Isa 51:2 — Look unto Abraham your father, and unto Sarah *that* bare you: for I called him alone, and blessed him, and increased him.

Isa 55:10 — For as the rain cometh down, and the snow from heaven, and returneth not thither, but watereth the earth, and maketh it bring forth and bud, that it may give seed to the sower, and bread to the eater:

Jer 5:24 — Neither say they in their heart, Let us now fear the LORD our God, that giveth rain, both the former and the latter, in his season: he reserveth unto us the appointed weeks of the harvest.

Jer 10:13 — When he uttereth his voice, *there is* a multitude of waters in the heavens, and he causeth the vapors to ascend from the ends of the earth; he maketh lightnings with rain, and bringeth forth the wind out of his treasures.

Jer 14:22 — Are there *any* among the vanities of the Gentiles that can cause rain? or can the heavens give showers? *art* not thou he, O LORD our God? therefore we will wait upon thee: for thou hast made all these *things.*

Jer 30:19 — And out of them shall proceed thanksgiving and the voice of them that make merry: and I will multiply them, and they shall not be few; I will also glorify them, and they shall not be small.

Jer 31:35 — Thus saith the LORD, which giveth the sun for a light by day, *and* the ordinances of the moon and of the stars for a light by night, which divideth the sea when the waves thereof roar; The LORD of hosts *is* his name:

Jer 51:16 — When he uttereth *his* voice, *there is* a multitude of waters in the heavens; and he causeth the vapors to ascend from the ends of the earth: he maketh lightnings with rain, and bringeth forth the wind out of his treasures.

Da 5:18 — O thou king, the most high God gave Nebuchadnezzar thy father a kingdom, and majesty, and glory, and honour:

Da 6:20 — And when he came to the den, he cried with a lamentable voice unto Daniel: *and* the king spake and said to Daniel, O Daniel, servant of the living God, is thy God, whom thou servest continually, able to deliver thee from the lions?

Da 6:22 — My God hath sent his angel, and hath shut the lions' mouths, that they have not hurt me: forasmuch as before him innocency was found in me; and also before thee, O king, have I done no hurt.

Hos 2:8 — For she did not know that I gave her corn, and wine, and oil, and multiplied her silver and gold, *which* they prepared for Baal.

Hos 11:3 — I taught Ephraim also to go, taking them by their arms; but they knew not that I healed them.

Joel 2:21 — Fear not, O land; be glad and rejoice: for the LORD will do great things.

Joel 2:23 — Be glad then, ye children of Zion, and rejoice in the LORD your God: for he hath given you the former rain moderately, and he will cause to come down for you the rain, the former rain, and the latter rain in the first *month.*

Joel 2:26 — And ye shall eat in plenty, and be satisfied, and praise the name of the LORD your God, that hath dealt wondrously with you: and my people shall never be ashamed.

Am 4:7 — And also I have withholden the rain from you, when *there were* yet three months to the harvest: and I caused it to rain upon one city, and caused it not to rain upon another city: one piece was rained upon, and the piece whereupon it rained not withered.

Jnh 4:6 — And the LORD God prepared a gourd, and made *it* to come up over Jonah, that it might be a shadow over his head, to deliver him from his grief. So Jonah was exceeding glad of the gourd.

Zec 10:1 — Ask ye of the LORD rain in the time of the latter rain; *so* the LORD shall make bright clouds, and give them showers of rain, to every one grass in the field.

Mt 5:45 — That ye may be the children of your Father which is in heaven: for he maketh his sun to rise on the evil and on the good, and sendeth rain on the just and on the unjust.

Mt 6:26 — Behold the fowls of the air: for they sow not, neither do they reap, nor gather into barns; yet your heavenly Father feedeth them. Are ye not much better than they?

Mt 10:29 — Are not two sparrows sold for a farthing? and one of them shall not fall on the ground without your Father.

Jn 6:31 — Our fathers did eat manna in the desert; as it is written, He gave them bread from heaven to eat.

Ac 14:17 — Nevertheless he left not himself without witness, in that he did good, and gave us rain from heaven, and fruitful seasons, filling our hearts with food and gladness.

1Co 2:9 — But as it is written, Eye hath not seen, nor ear heard, neither have entered into the heart of man, the things which God hath prepared for them that love him.

1Co 16:2 — Upon the first *day* of the week let every one of you lay by him in store, as *God* hath prospered him, that there be no gatherings when I come.

2Co 7:6 — Nevertheless God, that comforteth those that are cast down, comforted us by the coming of Titus;

Php 4:19 — But my God shall supply all your need according to his riches in glory by Christ Jesus.

See: God, Goodness of

See: God, Providence of

• Temporal, from God, exemplified.

• To Noah, at the time of the flood.

Ge 7:1 — And the LORD said unto Noah, Come thou and all thy house into the ark; for thee have I seen righteous before me in this generation.

• To Abraham.

Ge 24:1 — And Abraham was old, *and* well stricken in age: and the LORD had blessed Abraham in all things.

• To Isaac.

Ge 26:12–24

Ge 26:28 — And they said, We saw certainly that the LORD was with thee: and we said, Let there be now an oath betwixt us, *even* betwixt us and thee, and let us make a covenant with thee;

• To Jacob.

Ge 35:9–15

• To Israelites, in Egypt.

Ex 11:3 — And the LORD gave the people favour in the sight of the Egyptians. Moreover the man Moses *was* very great in the land of Egypt, in the sight of Pharaoh's servants, and in the sight of the people.

• To Israelites, in the wilderness, supplying water.

Ex 17:1–7; Nu 20:10–11; Ps 78:15–20

Ps 105:41 — He opened the rock, and the waters gushed out; they ran in the dry places *like* a river.

• To Israelites, in the wilderness, supplying manna.

Nu 11:7–9; Ps 78:23–24

Ex 16:14 — And when the dew that lay was gone up, behold, upon the face of the wilderness *there lay* a small round thing, *as* small as the hoar frost on the ground.

Ex 16:31 — And the house of Israel called the name thereof Manna: and it *was* like coriander seed, white; and the taste of it *was* like wafers *made* with honey.

Ne 9:15 — And gavest them bread from heaven for their hunger, and broughtest forth water for them out of the rock for their thirst, and promisedst them that they should go in to possess the land which thou hadst sworn to give them.

• To Israelites, in the wilderness, supplying quails.

Nu 11:31–33; Ps 78:23–30

Ps 105:40 — *The people* asked, and he brought quails, and satisfied them with the bread of heaven.

• To David.

2Sa 5:10 — And David went on, and grew great, and the LORD God of hosts *was* with him.

1Ch 14:17 — And the fame of David went out into all lands; and the LORD brought the fear of him upon all nations.

• To Obed-edom.

2Sa 6:11 — And the ark of the LORD continued in the house of Obed-edom the Gittite three months: and the LORD blessed Obed-edom, and all his household.

• To Solomon.

1Ki 3:13 — And I have also given thee that which thou hast not asked, both riches, and honour: so that there shall not be any among the kings like unto thee all thy days.

1Ch 29:25 — And the LORD magnified Solomon exceedingly in the sight of all Israel, and bestowed upon him *such* royal majesty as had not been on any king before him in Israel.

2Ch 1:1 — And Solomon the son of David was strengthened in his kingdom, and the LORD his God *was* with him, and magnified him exceedingly.

• To Elijah, fed by ravens.

1Ki 17:2–7

• To Elijah, by an angel.

1Ki 19:5–8

• To the widow of Zerephath.

1Ki 17:12–16

• Hezekiah prospered.

2Ki 18:6–7

2Ch 32:29 — Moreover he provided him cities, and possessions of flocks and herds in abundance: for God had given him substance very much.

• Hezekiah restored to health.

2Ki 20:1–7

• To Asa.

2Ch 14:6–7

• To Jehoshaphat.

2Ch 17:3–5

2Ch 20:30 — So the realm of Jehoshaphat was quiet: for his God gave him rest round about.

• **To Uzziah.**

2Ch 26:5–15

• **To Jotham.**

2Ch 27:6 — So Jotham became mighty, because he prepared his ways before the LORD his God.

• **To Job.**

Job 1:10 — Hast not thou made an hedge about him, and about his house, and about all that he hath on every side? thou hast blessed the work of his hands, and his substance is increased in the land.

Job 42:10 — And the LORD turned the captivity of Job, when he prayed for his friends: also the LORD gave Job twice as much as he had before.

Job 42:12 — So the LORD blessed the latter end of Job more than his beginning: for he had fourteen thousand sheep, and six thousand camels, and a thousand yoke of oxen, and a thousand she asses.

• **To Daniel.**

Da 1:9 — Now God had brought Daniel into favour and tender love with the prince of the eunuchs.

• **Temporal, prayer for.**

Ge 27:28–29; 28:3–4, 20–21; Dt 33:13–16; 1Ki 8:35–50

Ge 48:16 — The Angel which redeemed me from all evil, bless the lads; and let my name be named on them, and the name of my fathers Abraham and Isaac; and let them grow into a multitude in the midst of the earth.

Dt 1:11 — (The LORD God of your fathers make you a thousand times so many more as ye *are*, and bless you, as he hath promised you!)

Dt 26:15 — Look down from thy holy habitation, from heaven, and bless thy people Israel, and the land which thou hast given us, as thou swarest unto our fathers, a land that floweth with milk and honey.

Dt 33:11 — Bless, LORD, his substance, and accept the work of his hands: smite through the loins of them that rise against him, and of them that hate him, that they rise not again.

Dt 33:24 — And of Asher he said, *Let* Asher *be* blessed with children; let him be acceptable to his brethren, and let him dip his foot in oil.

1Ch 4:10 — And Jabez called on the God of Israel, saying, Oh that thou wouldest bless me indeed, and enlarge my coast, and that thine hand might be with me, and that thou wouldest keep *me* from evil, that it may not grieve me! And God granted him that which he requested.

1Ch 17:27 — Now therefore let it please thee to bless the house of thy servant, that it may be before thee for ever: for thou blessest, O LORD, and *it shall be* blessed for ever.

Ps 28:9 — Save thy people, and bless thine inheritance: feed them also, and lift them up for ever.

Ps 36:11 — Let not the foot of pride come against me, and let not the hand of the wicked remove me.

Pr 30:8 — Remove far from me vanity and lies: give me neither poverty nor riches; feed me with food convenient for me:

Mt 6:11 — Give us this day our daily bread.

Ro 1:10 — Making request, if by any means now at length I might have a prosperous journey by the will of God to come unto you.

1Th 3:11 — Now God himself and our Father, and our Lord Jesus Christ, direct our way unto you.

3Jn 1:2 — Beloved, I wish above all things that thou mayest prosper and be in health, even as thy soul prospereth.

See: Afflictions; prayer in

See: Prayer

See: Prosperity

• **Temporal blessings, prayer for.**

• **Instances of.**

• **Abraham.**

Ge 15:2–4

• **Abraham's servant.**

Ge 24:12 — And he said, O LORD God of my master Abraham, I pray thee, send me good speed this day, and shew kindness unto my master Abraham.

• **Laban.**

Ge 24:60 — And they blessed Rebekah, and said unto her, Thou *art* our sister, be thou *the mother* of thousands of millions, and let thy seed possess the gate of those which hate them.

• **Isaac.**

Ge 25:21 — And Isaac intreated the LORD for his wife, because she *was* barren: and the LORD was intreated of him, and Rebekah his wife conceived.

• **Hannah.**

1Sa 1:11 — And she vowed a vow, and said, O LORD of hosts, if thou wilt indeed look on the affliction of thine handmaid, and remember me, and not forget thine handmaid, but wilt give unto thine handmaid a man child, then I will give him unto the LORD all the days of his life, and there shall no razor come upon his head.

• **Elijah.**

1Ki 17:20–21; Jas 5:17–18

1Ki 18:42 — So Ahab went up to eat and to drink. And Elijah went up to the top of Carmel; and he cast himself down upon the earth, and put his face between his knees,

1Ki 18:44 — And it came to pass at the seventh time, that he said, Behold, there ariseth a little cloud out of the sea, like a man's hand. And he said, Go up, say unto Ahab, Prepare *thy chariot,* and get thee down, that the rain stop thee not.

• **Ezra.**

Ezr 8:21–23

• **Nehemiah.**

Ne 1:11 — O Lord, I beseech thee, let now thine ear be attentive to the prayer of thy servant, and to the prayer of thy servants, who desire to fear thy name: and prosper, I pray thee, thy servant this day, and grant him mercy in the sight of this man. For I was the king's cupbearer.

Ne 2:4 — Then the king said unto me, For what dost thou make request? So I prayed to the God of heaven.

Ne 6:9 — For they all made us afraid, saying, Their hands shall be weakened from the work, that it be not done. Now therefore, *O God,* strengthen my hands.

BLIND

Lk 7:22 — Then Jesus answering said unto them, Go your way, and tell John what things ye have seen and heard; how that the blind see, the lame walk, the lepers are cleansed, the deaf hear, the dead are raised, to the poor the gospel is preached.

Jn 9:25 — He answered and said, Whether he be a sinner *or no,* I know not: one thing I know, that, whereas I was blind, now I see.

Ro 2:19 — And art confident that thou thyself art a guide of the blind, a light of them which are in darkness,

2Pe 1:9 — But he that lacketh these things is blind, and cannot see afar off, and hath forgotten that he was purged from his old sins.

Rev 3:17 — Because thou sayest, I am rich, and increased with goods, and have need of nothing; and knowest not that thou art wretched, and miserable, and poor, and blind, and naked:

- **Cruelty to, forbidden.**

Le 19:14 — Thou shalt not curse the deaf, nor put a stumblingblock before the blind, but shalt fear thy God: I *am* the LORD.

Dt 27:18 — Cursed *be* he that maketh the blind to wander out of the way. And all the people shall say, Amen.

- **Hated by David.**

2Sa 5:8 — And David said on that day, Whosoever getteth up to the gutter, and smiteth the Jebusites, and the lame and the blind, *that are* hated of David's soul, *he shall be chief and captain.* Wherefore they said, The blind and the lame shall not come into the house.

See: Blindness

BLINDNESS

- **Disqualified for priestly office.**

Le 21:18 — For whatsoever man *he be* that hath a blemish, he shall not approach: a blind man, or a lame, or he that hath a flat nose, or any thing superfluous,

- **Of animals, disqualified for a sacrifice.**

Le 22:22 — Blind, or broken, or maimed, or having a wen, or scurvy, or scabbed, ye shall not offer these unto the LORD, nor make an offering by fire of them upon the altar unto the LORD.

Dt 15:21 — And if there be *any* blemish therein, *as if it be* lame, or blind, *or have* any ill blemish, thou shalt not sacrifice it unto the LORD thy God.

Mal 1:8 — And if ye offer the blind for sacrifice, *is it* not evil? and if ye offer the lame and sick, *is it* not evil? offer it now unto thy governor; will he be pleased with thee, or accept thy person? saith the LORD of hosts.

- **Miraculously inflicted upon the Sodomites.**

Ge 19:11 — And they smote the men that *were* at the door of the house with blindness, both small and great: so that they wearied themselves to find the door.

- **Miraculously inflicted upon the Syrians.**

2Ki 6:18–23

- **Miraculously inflicted upon Saul of Tarsus.**

Ac 9:8–9

- **Miraculously inflicted upon Elymas.**

Ac 13:11 — And now, behold, the hand of the Lord *is* upon thee, and thou shalt be blind, not seeing the sun for a season. And immediately there fell on him a mist and a darkness; and he went about seeking some to lead him by the hand.

- **Sent as a judgment.**

Dt 28:28 — The LORD shall smite thee with madness, and blindness, and astonishment of heart:

- **Miraculous healing of.**

Mt 9:27–30

Mt 11:5 — The blind receive their sight, and the lame walk, the lepers are cleansed, and the deaf hear, the dead are raised up, and the poor have the gospel preached to them.

Mt 12:22 — Then was brought unto him one possessed with a devil, blind, and dumb: and he healed him, insomuch that the blind and dumb both spake and saw.

Mt 21:14 — And the blind and the lame came to him in the temple; and he healed them.

  - **Bartimaeus.**

    Mt 20:30–34; Mk 10:46–52

  - **Man of Bethsaida.**

    Mk 8:22–25

  - **A man born blind.**

    Jn 9:1–7

- **Instances of.**
  - **Isaac.**

    Ge 27:1

  - **Jacob.**

    Ge 48:10

  - **Eli.**

    1Sa 4:15

  - **Ahijah.**

    1Ki 14:4

- **Spiritual.**

Dt 32:28–29; Job 22:13–14; Ps 10:5–6; 73:2–28; 94:7–8; Pr 1:29–30; 7:7–23; 19:2–3; Isa 6:9–10; 26:10–11; 29:10–12; 40:27–28; 42:6–7, 18–20; 44:18–20; Jer 5:4–5; 8:7–9; Mt 5:15–16; 13:13–16; 23:16–24; Mk 4:11–12; Jn 3:9–12, 19–20; 4:10–11; 8:42–43, 54–55; 9:29–39; 12:38–41; 16:2–3; Ro 1:19–22; 1:28–32; 1Co 1:20–21; 2:14–15; 2Co 3:14–15; 4:3–4; 1Th 4:4–5; 5:4–7; 2Th 2:11–12; Heb 5:11–12

Ex 5:2 — And Pharaoh said, Who *is* the LORD, that I should obey his voice to let Israel go? I know not the LORD, neither will I let Israel go.

Dt 29:4 — Yet the LORD hath not given you an heart to perceive, and eyes to see, and ears to hear, unto this day.

Jgs 16:20 — And she said, The Philistines *be* upon thee, Samson. And he awoke out of his sleep, and said, I will go out as at other times before, and shake myself. And he wist not that the LORD was departed from him.

Job 21:14 — Therefore they say unto God, Depart from us; for we desire not the knowledge of thy ways.

Ps 14:1 — The fool hath said in his heart, *There is* no God. They are corrupt, they have done abominable works, *there is* none that doeth good.

Ps 14:4 — Have all the workers of iniquity no knowledge? who eat up my people *as* they eat bread, and call not upon the LORD.

Ps 79:6 — Pour out thy wrath upon the heathen that have not known thee, and upon the kingdoms that have not called upon thy name.

Ps 82:5 — They know not, neither will they understand; they walk on in darkness: all the foundations of the earth are out of course.

Ps 92:6 — A brutish man knoweth not; neither doth a fool understand this.

Ps 95:10 — Forty years long was I grieved with *this* generation, and said, It *is* a people that do err in their heart, and they have not known my ways:

Ps 119:18 — Open thou mine eyes, that I may behold wondrous things out of thy law.

Pr 1:7 — The fear of the LORD *is* the beginning of knowledge: *but* fools despise wisdom and instruction.

Pr 1:22 — How long, ye simple ones, will ye love simplicity? and the scorners delight in their scorning, and fools hate knowledge?

Pr 4:19 — The way of the wicked *is* as darkness: they know not at what they stumble.

Pr 10:21 — The lips of the righteous feed many: but fools die for want of wisdom.

Pr 13:18 — Poverty and shame *shall be to* him that refuseth instruction: but he that regardeth reproof shall be honoured.

Pr 14:12 — There is a way which seemeth right unto a man, but the end thereof *are* the ways of death.

Pr 17:16 — Wherefore *is there* a price in the hand of a fool to get wisdom, seeing *he hath* no heart *to it?*

Pr 28:5 — Evil men understand not judgment: but they that seek the LORD understand all *things.*

Ecc 7:25 — I applied mine heart to know, and to search, and to seek out wisdom, and the reason *of things,* and to know the wickedness of folly, even of foolishness *and* madness:

Isa 1:3 — The ox knoweth his owner, and the ass his master's crib: *but* Israel doth not know, my people doth not consider.

Isa 5:13 — Therefore my people are gone into captivity, because *they have* no knowledge: and their honourable men *are* famished, and their multitude dried up with thirst.

Isa 5:20 — Woe unto them that call evil good, and good evil; that put darkness for light, and light for darkness; that put bitter for sweet, and sweet for bitter!

Isa 9:2 — The people that walked in darkness have seen a great light: they that dwell in the land of the shadow of death, upon them hath the light shined.

Isa 27:11 — When the boughs thereof are withered, they shall be broken off: the women come, *and* set them on fire: for it *is* a people of no understanding: therefore he that made them will not have mercy on them, and he that formed them will shew them no favour.

Isa 28:13 — But the word of the LORD was unto them precept upon precept, precept upon precept; line upon line, line upon line; here a little, *and* there a little; that they might go, and fall backward, and be broken, and snared, and taken.

Isa 28:15 — Because ye have said, We have made a covenant with death, and with hell are we at agreement; when the overflowing scourge shall pass through, it shall not come unto us: for we have made lies our refuge, and under falsehood have we hid ourselves:

Isa 40:21 — Have ye not known? have ye not heard? hath it not been told you from the beginning? have ye not understood from the foundations of the earth?

Isa 48:8 — Yea, thou heardest not; yea, thou knewest not; yea, from that time *that* thine ear was not opened: for I knew that thou wouldest deal very treacherously, and wast called a transgressor from the womb.

Isa 53:1 — Who hath believed our report? and to whom is the arm of the LORD revealed?

Isa 56:10 — His watchmen *are* blind: they are all ignorant, they *are* all dumb dogs, they cannot bark; sleeping, lying down, loving to slumber.

Isa 60:2 — For, behold, the darkness shall cover the earth, and gross darkness the people: but the LORD shall arise upon thee, and his glory shall be seen upon thee.

Jer 2:8 — The priests said not, Where *is* the LORD? and they that handle the law knew me not: the pastors also transgressed against me, and the prophets prophesied by Baal, and walked after *things that* do not profit.

Jer 4:22 — For my people *is* foolish, they have not known me; they *are* sottish children, and they have none understanding: they *are* wise to do evil, but to do good they have no knowledge.

Jer 5:21 — Hear now this, O foolish people, and without understanding; which have eyes, and see not; which have ears, and hear not:

Jer 9:3 — And they bend their tongues *like* their bow *for* lies: but they are not valiant for the truth upon the earth; for they proceed from evil to evil, and they know not me, saith the LORD.

Jer 9:6 — Thine habitation *is* in the midst of deceit; through deceit they refuse to know me, saith the LORD.

Jer 16:10 — And it shall come to pass, when thou shalt shew this people all these words, and they shall say unto thee, Wherefore hath the LORD pronounced all this great evil against us? or what *is* our iniquity? or what *is* our sin that we have committed against the LORD our God?

Jer 17:9 — The heart *is* deceitful above all *things,* and desperately wicked: who can know it?

Eze 12:2 — Son of man, thou dwellest in the midst of a rebellious house, which have eyes to see, and see not; they have ears to hear, and hear not: for they *are* a rebellious house.

Da 12:10 — Many shall be purified, and made white, and tried; but the wicked shall do wickedly: and none of the wicked shall understand; but the wise shall understand.

Hos 4:1 — Hear the word of the LORD, ye children of Israel: for the LORD hath a controversy with the inhabitants of the land, because *there is* no truth, nor mercy, nor knowledge of God in the land.

Hos 4:6 — My people are destroyed for lack of knowledge: because thou hast rejected knowledge, I will also reject thee, that thou shalt be no priest to me: seeing thou hast forgotten the law of thy God, I will also forget thy children.

Hos 4:14 — I will not punish your daughters when they commit whoredom, nor your spouses when they commit adultery: for themselves are separated with whores, and they sacrifice with harlots: therefore the people *that* doth not understand shall fall.

Hos 5:4 — They will not frame their doings to turn unto their God: for the spirit of whoredoms *is* in the midst of them, and they have not known the LORD.

Hos 7:11 — Ephraim also is like a silly dove without heart: they call to Egypt, they go to Assyria.

Am 9:10 — All the sinners of my people shall die by the sword, which say, The evil shall not overtake nor prevent us.

Mic 4:12 — But they know not the thoughts of the LORD, neither understand they his counsel: for he shall gather them as the sheaves into the floor.

Mt 6:23 — But if thine eye be evil, thy whole body shall be full of darkness. If therefore the light that is in thee be darkness, how great *is* that darkness!

Mt 13:19 — When any one heareth the word of the kingdom, and understandeth *it* not, then cometh the wicked *one,* and catcheth away that which was sown in his heart. This is he which received seed by the way side.

Mt 15:14 — Let them alone: they be blind leaders of the blind. And if the blind lead the blind, both shall fall into the ditch.

Mt 16:3 — And in the morning, *It will be* foul weather to day: for the sky is red and lowring. O *ye* hypocrites, ye can discern the face of the sky; but can ye not *discern* the signs of the times?

Mt 22:29 — Jesus answered and said unto them, Ye do err, not knowing the scriptures, nor the power of God.

Mk 4:15 — And these are they by the way side, where the word is sown; but when they have heard, Satan cometh immediately, and taketh away the word that was sown in their hearts.

Mk 6:52 — For they considered not *the miracle* of the loaves: for their heart was hardened.

Mk 7:18 — And he saith unto them, Are ye so without understanding also? Do ye not perceive, that whatsoever thing from without entereth into the man, *it* cannot defile him;

Mk 12:24 — And Jesus answering said unto them, Do ye not therefore err, because ye know not the scriptures, neither the power of God?

Lk 4:18 — The Spirit of the Lord is upon me, because he hath anointed me to preach the gospel to the poor; he hath sent me to heal the brokenhearted, to preach deliverance to the captives, and recovering of sight to the blind, to set at liberty them that are bruised,

Lk 8:10 — And he said, Unto you it is given to know the mysteries of the kingdom of God: but to others in parables; that seeing they might not see, and hearing they might not understand.

Lk 8:12 — Those by the way side are they that hear; then cometh the devil, and taketh away the word out of their hearts, lest they should believe and be saved.

Lk 11:52 — Woe unto you, lawyers! for ye have taken away the key of knowledge: ye entered not in yourselves, and them that were entering in ye hindered.

Lk 12:48 — But he that knew not, and did commit things worthy of stripes, shall be beaten with few *stripes.* For unto whomsoever much is given, of him shall be much required: and to whom men have committed much, of him they will ask the more.

Lk 12:57 — Yea, and why even of yourselves judge ye not what is right?

Lk 19:42 — Saying, If thou hadst known, even thou, at least in this thy day, the things *which belong* unto thy peace! but now they are hid from thine eyes.

Lk 23:34 — Then said Jesus, Father, forgive them; for they know not what they do. And they parted his raiment, and cast lots.

Jn 1:5 — And the light shineth in darkness; and the darkness comprehended it not.

Jn 1:10 — He was in the world, and the world was made by him, and the world knew him not.

Jn 3:4 — Nicodemus saith unto him, How can a man be born when he is old? can he enter the second time into his mother's womb, and be born?

Jn 3:31 — He that cometh from above is above all: he that is of the earth is earthly, and speaketh of the earth: he that cometh from heaven is above all.

Jn 4:15 — The woman saith unto him, Sir, give me this water, that I thirst not, neither come hither to draw.

Jn 4:22 — Ye worship ye know not what: we know what we worship: for salvation is of the Jews.

Jn 6:52 — The Jews therefore strove among themselves, saying, How can this man give us *his* flesh to eat?

Jn 6:60 — Many therefore of his disciples, when they had heard *this,* said, This is an hard saying; who can hear it?

Jn 7:28 — Then cried Jesus in the temple as he taught, saying, Ye both know me, and ye know whence I am: and I am not come of myself, but he that sent me is true, whom ye know not.

Jn 8:12 — Then spake Jesus again unto them, saying, I am the light of the world: he that followeth me shall not walk in darkness, but shall have the light of life.

Jn 8:15 — Ye judge after the flesh; I judge no man.

Jn 8:19 — Then said they unto him, Where is thy Father? Jesus answered, Ye neither know me, nor my

Father: if ye had known me, ye should have known my Father also.

Jn 8:27 — They understood not that he spake to them of the Father.

Jn 8:33 — They answered him, We be Abraham's seed, and were never in bondage to any man: how sayest thou, Ye shall be made free?

Jn 8:52 — Then said the Jews unto him, Now we know that thou hast a devil. Abraham is dead, and the prophets; and thou sayest, If a man keep my saying, he shall never taste of death.

Jn 8:57 — Then said the Jews unto him, Thou art not yet fifty years old, and hast thou seen Abraham?

Jn 14:17 — *Even* the Spirit of truth; whom the world cannot receive, because it seeth him not, neither knoweth him: but ye know him; for he dwelleth with you, and shall be in you.

Jn 15:21 — But all these things will they do unto you for my name's sake, because they know not him that sent me.

Jn 17:25 — O righteous Father, the world hath not known thee: but I have known thee, and these have known that thou hast sent me.

Ac 3:17 — And now, brethren, I wot that through ignorance ye did *it,* as *did* also your rulers.

Ac 13:27 — For they that dwell at Jerusalem, and their rulers, because they knew him not, nor yet the voices of the prophets which are read every sabbath day, they have fulfilled *them* in condemning *him.*

Ac 17:23 — For as I passed by, and beheld your devotions, I found an altar with this inscription, TO THE UNKNOWN GOD. Whom therefore ye ignorantly worship, him declare I unto you.

Ac 19:2 — He said unto them, Have ye received the Holy Ghost since ye believed? And they said unto him, We have not so much as heard whether there be any Holy Ghost.

Ac 26:18 — To open their eyes, *and* to turn *them* from darkness to light, and *from* the power of Satan unto God, that they may receive forgiveness of sins, and inheritance among them which are sanctified by faith that is in me.

Ro 2:4 — Or despisest thou the riches of his goodness and forbearance and longsuffering; not knowing that the goodness of God leadeth thee to repentance?

Ro 11:25 — For I would not, brethren, that ye should be ignorant of this mystery, lest ye should be wise in your own conceits; that blindness in part is happened to Israel, until the fulness of the Gentiles be come in.

1Co 1:18 — For the preaching of the cross is to them that perish foolishness; but unto us which are saved it is the power of God.

1Co 2:8 — Which none of the princes of this world knew: for had they known *it,* they would not have crucified the Lord of glory.

1Co 15:34 — Awake to righteousness, and sin not; for some have not the knowledge of God: I speak *this* to your shame.

2Co 4:6 — For God, who commanded the light to shine out of darkness, hath shined in our hearts, to *give* the light of the knowledge of the glory of God in the face of Jesus Christ.

Gal 4:8 — Howbeit then, when ye knew not God, ye did service unto them which by nature are no gods.

Eph 4:18 — Having the understanding darkened, being alienated from the life of God through the ignorance that is in them, because of the blindness of their heart:

Eph 5:8 — For ye were sometimes darkness, but now *are ye* light in the Lord: walk as children of light:

Col 1:13 — Who hath delivered us from the power of darkness, and hath translated *us* into the kingdom of his dear Son:

2Th 1:8 — In flaming fire taking vengeance on them that know not God, and that obey not the gospel of our Lord Jesus Christ:

2Ti 3:7 — Ever learning, and never able to come to the knowledge of the truth.

2Ti 3:13 — But evil men and seducers shall wax worse and worse, deceiving, and being deceived.

Tit 1:16 — They profess that they know God; but in works they deny *him,* being abominable, and disobedient, and unto every good work reprobate.

1Pe 1:14 — As obedient children, not fashioning yourselves according to the former lusts in your ignorance:

1Pe 2:9 — But ye *are* a chosen generation, a royal priesthood, an holy nation, a peculiar people; that ye should shew forth the praises of him who hath called you out of darkness into his marvellous light:

2Pe 1:9 — But he that lacketh these things is blind, and cannot see afar off, and hath forgotten that he was purged from his old sins.

2Pe 3:16 — As also in all *his* epistles, speaking in them of these things; in which are some things hard to be understood, which they that are unlearned and unstable wrest, as *they do* also the other scriptures, unto their own destruction.

1Jn 1:6 — If we say that we have fellowship with him, and walk in darkness, we lie, and do not the truth:

1Jn 1:8 — If we say that we have no sin, we deceive ourselves, and the truth is not in us.

1Jn 2:4 — He that saith, I know him, and keepeth not his commandments, is a liar, and the truth is not in him.

1Jn 2:9 — He that saith he is in the light, and hateth his brother, is in darkness even until now.

1Jn 2:11 — But he that hateth his brother is in darkness, and walketh in darkness, and knoweth not whither he goeth, because that darkness hath blinded his eyes.

1Jn 3:1 — Behold, what manner of love the Father hath bestowed upon us, that we should be called the sons of God: therefore the world knoweth us not, because it knew him not.

1Jn 3:6 — Whosoever abideth in him sinneth not: whosoever sinneth hath not seen him, neither known him.

1Jn 4:8 — He that loveth not knoweth not God; for God is love.

3Jn 1:11 — Beloved, follow not that which is evil, but that which is good. He that doeth good is of God: but he that doeth evil hath not seen God.

Jude 1:10 — But these speak evil of those things which they know not: but what they know naturally, as brute beasts, in those things they corrupt themselves.

Rev 3:17 — Because thou sayest, I am rich, and increased with goods, and have need of nothing; and knowest not that thou art wretched, and miserable, and poor, and blind, and naked:

See: Afflictions; obduracy in

See: Man; ignorance of

See: God, Providence of, Mysterious and Misinterpreted

• Instances of.

• Israelites.

Nu 16:1–17:13

• Moab.

2Ki 3:27

• Scribes.

Mt 9:3

BLOOD

• Is the life.

Ge 9:4 — But flesh with the life thereof, *which is* the blood thereof, shall ye not eat.

Le 17:11 — For the life of the flesh *is* in the blood: and I have given it to you upon the altar to make an atonement for your souls: for it *is* the blood *that* maketh an atonement for the soul.

Le 17:14 — For *it is* the life of all flesh; the blood of it *is* for the life thereof: therefore I said unto the children of Israel, Ye shall eat the blood of no manner of flesh: for the life of all flesh *is* the blood thereof: whosoever eateth it shall be cut off.

Le 19:16 — Thou shalt not go up and down *as* a talebearer among thy people: neither shalt thou stand against the blood of thy neighbour: I *am* the LORD.

Dt 12:23 — Only be sure that thou eat not the blood: for the blood *is* the life; and thou mayest not eat the life with the flesh.

Mt 27:4 — Saying, I have sinned in that I have betrayed the innocent blood. And they said, What *is that* to us? see thou *to that.*

Mt 27:24 — When Pilate saw that he could prevail nothing, but *that* rather a tumult was made, he took water, and washed *his* hands before the multitude, saying, I am innocent of the blood of this just person: see ye *to it.*

• Forbidden to be used as food.

Le 7:26–27; 17:10–14

Ge 9:4 — But flesh with the life thereof, *which is* the blood thereof, shall ye not eat.

Le 3:17 — *It shall be* a perpetual statute for your generations throughout all your dwellings, that ye eat neither fat nor blood.

Le 19:26 — Ye shall not eat *any thing* with the blood: neither shall ye use enchantment, nor observe times.

Dt 12:16 — Only ye shall not eat the blood; ye shall pour it upon the earth as water.

Dt 12:23 — Only be sure that thou eat not the blood: for the blood *is* the life; and thou mayest not eat the life with the flesh.

Dt 15:23 — Only thou shalt not eat the blood thereof; thou shalt pour it upon the ground as water.

Eze 33:25 — Wherefore say unto them, Thus saith the Lord GOD; Ye eat with the blood, and lift up your eyes toward your idols, and shed blood: and shall ye possess the land?

Ac 15:20 — But that we write unto them, that they abstain from pollutions of idols, and *from* fornication, and *from* things strangled, and *from* blood.

Ac 15:29 — That ye abstain from meats offered to idols, and from blood, and from things strangled, and from fornication: from which if ye keep yourselves, ye shall do well. Fare ye well.

Ac 21:25 — As touching the Gentiles which believe, we have written *and* concluded that they observe no such thing, save only that they keep themselves from *things* offered to idols, and from blood, and from strangled, and from fornication.

• Plague of.

Ex 7:17–25

Ps 78:44 — And had turned their rivers into blood; and their floods, that they could not drink.

Ps 105:29 — He turned their waters into blood, and slew their fish.

• Sacrificial.

• Without shedding of, no remission.

Heb 9:22 — And almost all things are by the law purged with blood; and without shedding of blood is no remission.

• Sprinkled on altar and people.

Ex 24:6–8

Eze 43:18 — And he said unto me, Son of man, thus saith the Lord GOD; These *are* the ordinances of the altar in the day when they shall make it, to offer burnt offerings thereon, and to sprinkle blood thereon.

Eze 43:20 — And thou shalt take of the blood thereof, and put *it* on the four horns of it, and on the four corners of the settle, and upon the border round about: thus shalt thou cleanse and purge it.

• Sprinkled on doorposts.

Ex 12:7–23

Heb 11:28 — Through faith he kept the passover, and the sprinkling of blood, lest he that destroyed the firstborn should touch them.

• Of sin offering.

• Sprinkled seven times before the vail.

Le 4:5–6

Le 4:17 — And the priest shall dip his finger *in some* of the blood, and sprinkle *it* seven times before the LORD, *even* before the vail.

• **Sprinkled on horns of the altar of sweet incense, and at the bottom of the altar of burnt offering.**

Ex 30:10 — And Aaron shall make an atonement upon the horns of it once in a year with the blood of the sin offering of atonements: once in the year shall he make atonement upon it throughout your generations: it *is* most holy unto the LORD.

Le 4:7 — And the priest shall put *some* of the blood upon the horns of the altar of sweet incense before the LORD, which *is* in the tabernacle of the congregation: and shall pour all the blood of the bullock at the bottom of the altar of the burnt offering, which *is at* the door of the tabernacle of the congregation.

Le 4:18 — And he shall put *some* of the blood upon the horns of the altar which *is* before the LORD, that *is* in the tabernacle of the congregation, and shall pour out all the blood at the bottom of the altar of the burnt offering, which *is at* the door of the tabernacle of the congregation.

Le 4:25 — And the priest shall take of the blood of the sin offering with his finger, and put *it* upon the horns of the altar of burnt offering, and shall pour out his blood at the bottom of the altar of burnt offering.

Le 4:30 — And the priest shall take of the blood thereof with his finger, and put *it* upon the horns of the altar of burnt offering, and shall pour out all the blood thereof at the bottom of the altar.

Le 5:9 — And he shall sprinkle of the blood of the sin offering upon the side of the altar; and the rest of the blood shall be wrung out at the bottom of the altar: it *is* a sin offering.

Le 9:9 — And the sons of Aaron brought the blood unto him: and he dipped his finger in the blood, and put *it* upon the horns of the altar, and poured out the blood at the bottom of the altar:

Le 9:12 — And he slew the burnt offering; and Aaron's sons presented unto him the blood, which he sprinkled round about upon the altar.

• **Of bullock of sin offering, put on the horns of the altar.**

Ex 29:12 — And thou shalt take of the blood of the bullock, and put *it* upon the horns of the altar with thy finger, and pour all the blood beside the bottom of the altar.

Le 8:15 — And he slew *it;* and Moses took the blood, and put *it* upon the horns of the altar round about with his finger, and purified the altar, and poured the blood at the bottom of the altar, and sanctified it, to make reconciliation upon it.

• **Of bullock of sin offering, poured at the bottom of the altar.**

Ex 29:12 — And thou shalt take of the blood of the bullock, and put *it* upon the horns of the altar with thy finger, and pour all the blood beside the bottom of the altar.

Le 8:15 — And he slew *it;* and Moses took the blood, and put *it* upon the horns of the altar round about with his finger, and purified the altar, and poured the blood at the bottom of the altar, and sanctified it, to make reconciliation upon it.

See: Offerings

• **Of trespass offering.**

• **Sprinkled on the altar.**

Le 7:2 — In the place where they kill the burnt offering shall they kill the trespass offering: and the blood thereof shall he sprinkle round about upon the altar.

See: Offerings

• **Of burnt offering.**

• **Sprinkled round about, and upon the altar.**

Le 1:1–17

Ex 29:16 — And thou shalt slay the ram, and thou shalt take his blood, and sprinkle *it* round about upon the altar.

Le 5:11 — But if he be not able to bring two turtledoves, or two young pigeons, then he that sinned shall bring for his offering the tenth part of an ephah of fine flour for a sin offering; he shall put no oil upon it, neither shall he put *any* frankincense thereon: for it *is* a sin offering.

Le 5:15 — If a soul commit a trespass, and sin through ignorance, in the holy things of the LORD; then he shall bring for his trespass unto the LORD a ram without blemish out of the flocks, with thy estimation by shekels of silver, after the shekel of the sanctuary, for a trespass offering:

Le 8:19 — And he killed *it;* and Moses sprinkled the blood upon the altar round about.

Dt 12:27 — And thou shalt offer thy burnt offerings, the flesh and the blood, upon the altar of the LORD thy God: and the blood of thy sacrifices shall be poured out upon the altar of the LORD thy God, and thou shalt eat the flesh.

See: Offerings

• **Used for cleansing of leprosy.**

Le 14:6–7, 51–52

Le 14:17 — And of the rest of the oil that *is* in his hand shall the priest put upon the tip of the right ear of him that is to be cleansed, and upon the thumb of his right hand, and upon the great toe of his right foot, upon the blood of the trespass offering:

Le 14:28 — And the priest shall put of the oil that *is* in his hand upon the tip of the right ear of him that is to be cleansed, and upon the thumb of his right hand, and upon the great toe of his right foot, upon the place of the blood of the trespass offering:

See: Offerings

• **Of peace offering.**

• **Sprinkled about the altar.**

Le 3:2 — And he shall lay his hand upon the head of his offering, and kill it *at* the door of the tabernacle of the congregation: and Aaron's sons the priests shall sprinkle the blood upon the altar round about.

Le 3:8 — And he shall lay his hand upon the head of his offering, and kill it before the tabernacle of the congregation: and Aaron's sons shall sprinkle the blood thereof round about upon the altar.

Le 3:13 — And he shall lay his hand upon the head of it, and kill it before the tabernacle of the congregation: and the sons of Aaron shall sprinkle the blood thereof upon the altar round about.

Le 9:19 — And the fat of the bullock and of the ram, the rump, and that which covereth *the inwards,* and the kidneys, and the caul *above* the liver:

- **Blood of the ram put on Aaron and his sons.**

Ex 29:20–21; Le 8:23–24

Le 8:30 — And Moses took of the anointing oil, and of the blood which *was* upon the altar, and sprinkled *it* upon Aaron, *and* upon his garments, and upon his sons, and upon his sons' garments with him; and sanctified Aaron, *and* his garments, and his sons, and his sons' garments with him.

See: **Offerings**

- **Of atonement.**
  - **Sprinkled on mercy seat.**

Le 16:14–15, 18–19

Le 16:27 — And the bullock *for* the sin offering, and the goat *for* the sin offering, whose blood was brought in to make atonement in the holy *place,* shall *one* carry forth without the camp; and they shall burn in the fire their skins, and their flesh, and their dung.

Le 17:11 — For the life of the flesh *is* in the blood: and I have given it to you upon the altar to make an atonement for your souls: for it *is* the blood *that* maketh an atonement for the soul.

See: **Offerings**

- **Blood of the covenant.**

Ex 24:5–8; Heb 9:18–19

Zec 9:11 — As for thee also, by the blood of thy covenant I have sent forth thy prisoners out of the pit wherein *is* no water.

Mt 26:28 — <u>For this is my blood of the new testament, which is shed for many for the remission of sins.</u>

Heb 9:22 — And almost all things are by the law purged with blood; and without shedding of blood is no remission.

Heb 10:29 — Of how much sorer punishment, suppose ye, shall he be thought worthy, who hath trodden under foot the Son of God, and hath counted the blood of the covenant, wherewith he was sanctified, an unholy thing, and hath done despite unto the Spirit of grace?

Heb 13:20 — Now the God of peace, that brought again from the dead our Lord Jesus, that great shepherd of the sheep, through the blood of the everlasting covenant,

See: **Offerings**

- **Figurative.**
  - **Of victories.**

Ps 58:10 — The righteous shall rejoice when he seeth the vengeance: he shall wash his feet in the blood of the wicked.

- **Of oppression and cruelty.**

Hab 2:12 — Woe to him that buildeth a town with blood, and stablisheth a city by iniquity!

- **Of destruction.**

Eze 35:6 — Therefore, *as* I live, saith the Lord GOD, I will prepare thee unto blood, and blood shall pursue thee: sith thou hast not hated blood, even blood shall pursue thee.

- **Of guilt.**

Le 20:9 — For every one that curseth his father or his mother shall be surely put to death: he hath cursed his father or his mother; his blood *shall be* upon him.

2Sa 1:16 — And David said unto him, Thy blood *be* upon thy head; for thy mouth hath testified against thee, saying, I have slain the LORD'S anointed.

Eze 18:13 — Hath given forth upon usury, and hath taken increase: shall he then live? he shall not live: he hath done all these abominations; he shall surely die; his blood shall be upon him.

- **Of judgments.**

Eze 16:38 — And I will judge thee, as women that break wedlock and shed blood are judged; and I will give thee blood in fury and jealousy.

Rev 16:6 — For they have shed the blood of saints and prophets, and thou hast given them blood to drink; for they are worthy.

- **Of sacrifices, typical of the atoning blood of Christ.**

Heb 9:6–28

- **Of Christ.**

Jn 6:53–56; Ro 3:24–25; Heb 9:12–14; 10:19–20; 1Pe 1:18–19; Rev 1:5–6

Mt 26:28 — <u>For this is my blood of the new testament, which is shed for many for the remission of sins.</u>

Mk 14:24 — And he said unto them, <u>This is my blood of the new testament, which is shed for many.</u>

Lk 22:20 — Likewise also the cup after supper, saying, <u>This cup *is* the new testament in my blood, which is shed for you.</u>

Jn 19:34 — But one of the soldiers with a spear pierced his side, and forthwith came there out blood and water.

Ac 20:28 — Take heed therefore unto yourselves, and to all the flock, over the which the Holy Ghost hath made you overseers, to feed the church of God, which he hath purchased with his own blood.

Ro 5:9 — Much more then, being now justified by his blood, we shall be saved from wrath through him.

1Co 10:16 — The cup of blessing which we bless, is it not the communion of the blood of Christ? The bread which we break, is it not the communion of the body of Christ?

1Co 11:25 — After the same manner also *he took* the cup, when he had supped, saying, This cup is the new testament in my blood: this do ye, as oft as ye drink *it*, in remembrance of me.

Eph 1:7 — In whom we have redemption through his blood, the forgiveness of sins, according to the riches of his grace;

Eph 2:13 — But now in Christ Jesus ye who sometimes were far off are made nigh by the blood of Christ.

Eph 2:16 — And that he might reconcile both unto God in one body by the cross, having slain the enmity thereby:

Col 1:14 — In whom we have redemption through his blood, *even* the forgiveness of sins:

Col 1:20 — And, having made peace through the blood of his cross, by him to reconcile all things unto himself; by him, *I say*, whether *they be* things in earth, or things in heaven.

Heb 10:29 — Of how much sorer punishment, suppose ye, shall he be thought worthy, who hath trodden under foot the Son of God, and hath counted the blood of the covenant, wherewith he was sanctified, an unholy thing, and hath done despite unto the Spirit of grace?

Heb 12:24 — And to Jesus the mediator of the new covenant, and to the blood of sprinkling, that speaketh better things than *that of* Abel.

Heb 13:12 — Wherefore Jesus also, that he might sanctify the people with his own blood, suffered without the gate.

Heb 13:20 — Now the God of peace, that brought again from the dead our Lord Jesus, that great shepherd of the sheep, through the blood of the everlasting covenant,

1Pe 1:2 — Elect according to the foreknowledge of God the Father, through sanctification of the Spirit, unto obedience and sprinkling of the blood of Jesus Christ: Grace unto you, and peace, be multiplied.

1Jn 1:7 — But if we walk in the light, as he is in the light, we have fellowship one with another, and the blood of Jesus Christ his Son cleanseth us from all sin.

1Jn 5:6 — This is he that came by water and blood, *even* Jesus Christ; not by water only, but by water and blood. And it is the Spirit that beareth witness, because the Spirit is truth.

1Jn 5:8 — And there are three that bear witness in earth, the spirit, and the water, and the blood: and these three agree in one.

Rev 5:9 — And they sung a new song, saying, Thou art worthy to take the book, and to open the seals thereof: for thou wast slain, and hast redeemed us to God by thy blood out of every kindred, and tongue, and people, and nation;

Rev 7:14 — And I said unto him, Sir, thou knowest. And he said to me, These are they which came out of great tribulation, and have washed their robes, and made them white in the blood of the Lamb.

Rev 12:11 — And they overcame him by the blood of the Lamb, and by the word of their testimony; and they loved not their lives unto the death.

⌖See: Atonement
⌖See: Jesus, Mission of
⌖See: Jesus, Sufferings of

BLUE ⌖See: Colors

BLUSHING

• With shame.

Ezr 9:6 — And said, O my God, I am ashamed and blush to lift up my face to thee, my God: for our iniquities are increased over *our* head, and our trespass is grown up unto the heavens.

Jer 6:15 — Were they ashamed when they had committed abomination? nay, they were not at all ashamed, neither could they blush: therefore they shall fall among them that fall: at the time *that* I visit them they shall be cast down, saith the LORD.

Jer 8:12 — Were they ashamed when they had committed abomination? nay, they were not at all ashamed, neither could they blush: therefore shall they fall among them that fall: in the time of their visitation they shall be cast down, saith the LORD.

BOANERGES • Surname of the sons of Zebedee.

Mk 3:17 — And James the *son* of Zebedee, and John the brother of James; and he surnamed them Boanerges, which is, The sons of thunder:

BOAR

• Wild.

Ps 80:13 — The boar out of the wood doth waste it, and the wild beast of the field doth devour it.

⌖See: Swine

BOASTING

Pr 20:14 — *It is* naught, *it is* naught, saith the buyer: but when he is gone his way, then he boasteth.

Pr 25:14 — Whoso boasteth himself of a false gift *is like* clouds and wind without rain.

Pr 27:1 — Boast not thyself of to morrow; for thou knowest not what a day may bring forth.

Isa 10:15 — Shall the axe boast itself against him that heweth therewith? *or* shall the saw magnify itself against him that shaketh it? as if the rod should shake *itself* against them that lift it up, *or* as if the staff should lift up *itself, as if it were* no wood.

Jer 9:23 — Thus saith the LORD, Let not the wise *man* glory in his wisdom, neither let the mighty *man* glory in his might, let not the rich *man* glory in his riches:

Ro 1:30 — Backbiters, haters of God, despiteful, proud, boasters, inventors of evil things, disobedient to parents,

Jas 3:5 — Even so the tongue is a little member, and boasteth great things. Behold, how great a matter a little fire kindleth!

Jas 4:16 — But now ye rejoice in your boastings: all such rejoicing is evil.

• **Of evil.**

Ps 52:1 — Why boastest thou thyself in mischief, O mighty man? the goodness of God *endureth* continually.

• **Instances of.**

• **Goliath.**

1Sa 17:1–58

• **Benhadad.**

1Ki 20:10

• **Sennacherib.**

2Ki 18:19; Isa 10:8–15

• **The disciples.**

Lk 10:17, 20

• **Spiritual.**

Ps 49:6–9; Ro 3:1–31; 11:17–21; 1Co 1:17–31; 4:6–7; 2Co 10:12–18; Eph 2:8–10

Ps 52:1 — Why boastest thou thyself in mischief, O mighty man? the goodness of God *endureth* continually.

Ps 94:4 — *How long* shall they utter *and* speak hard things? *and* all the workers of iniquity boast themselves?

BOAT ⇾See: Ship

BOAZ

• **An ancestor of Jesus.**

Mt 1:5 — And Salmon begat Booz of Rachab; and Booz begat Obed of Ruth; and Obed begat Jesse;

Lk 3:32 — Which was *the son* of Jesse, which was *the son* of Obed, which was *the son* of Booz, which was *the son* of Salmon, which was *the son* of Naasson,

• **History of, Ruth.**

Ru 2:1–4:22

• **One of the brazen pillars of the temple.**

1Ki 7:21 — And he set up the pillars in the porch of the temple: and he set up the right pillar, and called the name thereof Jachin: and he set up the left pillar, and he called the name thereof Boaz.

2Ch 3:17 — And he reared up the pillars before the temple, one on the right hand, and the other on the left; and called the name of that on the right hand Jachin, and the name of that on the left Boaz.

BOCHERU • Son of Azel.

1Ch 8:38 — And Azel had six sons, whose names *are* these, Azrikam, Bocheru, and Ishmael, and Sheariah, and Obadiah, and Hanan. All these *were* the sons of Azel.

1Ch 9:44 — And Azel had six sons, whose names *are* these, Azrikam, Bocheru, and Ishmael, and Sheariah, and Obadiah, and Hanan: these *were* the sons of Azel.

BOCHIM • A place west of Jordan. Near Gilgal.

Jgs 2:1 — And an angel of the LORD came up from Gilgal to Bochim, and said, I made you to go up out of Egypt, and have brought you unto the land which I sware unto your fathers; and I said, I will never break my covenant with you.

Jgs 2:5 — And they called the name of that place Bochim: and they sacrificed there unto the LORD.

BODY

• **Made a slave.**

1Co 9:27 — But I keep under my body, and bring *it* into subjection: lest that by any means, when I have preached to others, I myself should be a castaway.

• **Called House.**

2Co 5:1 — For we know that if our earthly house of *this* tabernacle were dissolved, we have a building of God, an house not made with hands, eternal in the heavens.

• **Called House of Clay.**

Job 4:19 — How much less *in* them that dwell in houses of clay, whose foundation *is* in the dust, *which* are crushed before the moth?

• **Called the Temple of God.**

Eph 2:20–21

1Co 3:16 — Know ye not that ye are the temple of God, and *that* the Spirit of God dwelleth in you?

1Co 6:15 — Know ye not that your bodies are the members of Christ? shall I then take the members of Christ, and make *them* the members of an harlot? God forbid.

1Co 6:19 — What? know ye not that your body is the temple of the Holy Ghost *which is* in you, which ye have of God, and ye are not your own?

1Pe 2:5 — Ye also, as lively stones, are built up a spiritual house, an holy priesthood, to offer up spiritual sacrifices, acceptable to God by Jesus Christ.

• **Corruptible.**

1Co 15:53–54

Job 17:14 — I have said to corruption, Thou *art* my father: to the worm, *Thou art* my mother, and my sister.

• **Resurrection of.**

1Co 15:19–54

⇾**See: Resurrection**

BOHAN • A Reubenite.

Jos 15:6 — And the border went up to Beth-hogla, and passed along by the north of Beth-arabah; and the border went up to the stone of Bohan the son of Reuben:

Jos 18:17 — And was drawn from the north, and went forth to En-shemesh, and went forth toward Geliloth, which *is* over against the going up of Adummim, and descended to the stone of Bohan the son of Reuben,

BOIL

• **A tumor.**

• **Plague of.**

• **On the Egyptians.**

Ex 9:9–10

Dt 28:27 — The LORD will smite thee with the botch of Egypt, and with the emerods, and with the scab, and with the itch, whereof thou canst not be healed.

Dt 28:35 — The LORD shall smite thee in the knees, and in the legs, with a sore botch that cannot be healed, from the sole of thy foot unto the top of thy head.

- **On the Philistines.**

1Sa 5:6 — But the hand of the LORD was heavy upon them of Ashdod, and he destroyed them, and smote them with emerods, *even* Ashdod and the coasts thereof.

1Sa 5:9 — And it was *so*, that, after they had carried it about, the hand of the LORD was against the city with a very great destruction: and he smote the men of the city, both small and great, and they had emerods in their secret parts.

1Sa 6:5 — Wherefore ye shall make images of your emerods, and images of your mice that mar the land; and ye shall give glory unto the God of Israel: peradventure he will lighten his hand from off you, and from off your gods, and from off your land.

- **Of Hezekiah, healed.**

2Ki 20:7 — And Isaiah said, Take a lump of figs. And they took and laid *it* on the boil, and he recovered.

Isa 38:21 — For Isaiah had said, Let them take a lump of figs, and lay *it* for a plaister upon the boil, and he shall recover.

- **Of Job.**

Job 2:7–8

- **Levitical ceremonies prescribed for.**

Le 13:18–23

BOILING POT

- **Parable of.**

Eze 24:3–5

BOLDNESS

Ac 4:23–32

Ac 1:8 — But ye shall receive power, after that the Holy Ghost is come upon you: and ye shall be witnesses unto me both in Jerusalem, and in all Judaea, and in Samaria, and unto the uttermost part of the earth.

- **Of the righteous.**

Pr 14:26 — In the fear of the LORD *is* strong confidence: and his children shall have a place of refuge.

Pr 28:1 — The wicked flee when no man pursueth: but the righteous are bold as a lion.

Eph 3:12 — In whom we have boldness and access with confidence by the faith of him.

Heb 4:16 — Let us therefore come boldly unto the throne of grace, that we may obtain mercy, and find grace to help in time of need.

Heb 10:19 — Having therefore, brethren, boldness to enter into the holiest by the blood of Jesus,

Heb 13:6 — So that we may boldly say, The Lord *is* my helper, and I will not fear what man shall do unto me.

1Jn 2:28 — And now, little children, abide in him; that, when he shall appear, we may have confidence, and not be ashamed before him at his coming.

1Jn 4:17 — Herein is our love made perfect, that we may have boldness in the day of judgment: because as he is, so are we in this world.

- **Instances of, in prayer.**
  - **Abraham.**

Ge 18:23–32

  - **Moses.**

Ex 33:12–18

See: Courage

BOLT

- **Fiery.**

Hab 3:5 — Before him went the pestilence, and burning coals went forth at his feet.

BOND

- **To keep the peace.**

Ac 17:9 — And when they had taken security of Jason, and of the other, they let them go.

BONDAGE

- **Of Israelites in Egypt.**

Ex 1:14 — And they made their lives bitter with hard bondage, in morter, and in brick, and in all manner of service in the field: all their service, wherein they made them serve, *was* with rigour.

Ex 2:23 — And it came to pass in process of time, that the king of Egypt died: and the children of Israel sighed by reason of the bondage, and they cried, and their cry came up unto God by reason of the bondage.

Ex 6:6 — Wherefore say unto the children of Israel, I *am* the LORD, and I will bring you out from under the burdens of the Egyptians, and I will rid you out of their bondage, and I will redeem you with a stretched out arm, and with great judgments:

- **Of Israelites in Persia.**

Ezr 9:9 — For we *were* bondmen; yet our God hath not forsaken us in our bondage, but hath extended mercy unto us in the sight of the kings of Persia, to give us a reviving, to set up the house of our God, and to repair the desolations thereof, and to give us a wall in Judah and in Jerusalem.

See: Emancipation

See: Servant

BONDMAN **See: Servant**

BONES

- **Vision of the dry.**

Eze 37:1–14

- **None of Christ's broken.**

Ps 34:20 — He keepeth all his bones: not one of them is broken.

Jn 19:36 — For these things were done, that the scripture should be fulfilled, A bone of him shall not be broken.

BONNET

- **A turban.**
- **Worn by priests.**

Ex 28:40 — And for Aaron's sons thou shalt make coats, and thou shalt make for them girdles, and bonnets shalt thou make for them, for glory and for beauty.

Ex 29:9 — And thou shalt gird them with girdles, Aaron and his sons, and put the bonnets on them: and the priest's office shall be theirs for a perpetual statute: and thou shalt consecrate Aaron and his sons.

Ex 39:28 — And a mitre *of* fine linen, and goodly bonnets *of* fine linen, and linen breeches *of* fine twined linen,

Le 8:13 — And Moses brought Aaron's sons, and put coats upon them, and girded them with girdles, and put bonnets upon them; as the LORD commanded Moses.

Eze 44:18 — They shall have linen bonnets upon their heads, and shall have linen breeches upon their loins; they shall not gird *themselves* with any thing that causeth sweat.

• Worn by women.

Isa 3:20 — The bonnets, and the ornaments of the legs, and the headbands, and the tablets, and the earrings,

See: Dress

BOOK

• Genealogies kept in.

Ge 5:1 — This *is* the book of the generations of Adam. In the day that God created man, in the likeness of God made he him;

• Law of Moses written in.

Nu 5:23 — And the priest shall write these curses in a book, and he shall blot *them* out with the bitter water:

Dt 17:18 — And it shall be, when he sitteth upon the throne of his kingdom, that he shall write him a copy of this law in a book out of *that which is* before the priests the Levites:

Dt 31:9 — And Moses wrote this law, and delivered it unto the priests the sons of Levi, which bare the ark of the covenant of the LORD, and unto all the elders of Israel.

Dt 31:24 — And it came to pass, when Moses had made an end of writing the words of this law in a book, until they were finished,

Dt 31:26 — Take this book of the law, and put it in the side of the ark of the covenant of the LORD your God, that it may be there for a witness against thee.

2Ki 22:8 — And Hilkiah the high priest said unto Shaphan the scribe, I have found the book of the law in the house of the LORD. And Hilkiah gave the book to Shaphan, and he read it.

• Topography of Palestine, recorded in.

Jos 18:9 — And the men went and passed through the land, and described it by cities into seven parts in a book, and came *again* to Joshua to the host at Shiloh.

• Chronicles of the times kept in.

• By Jasher.

Jos 10:13 — And the sun stood still, and the moon stayed, until the people had avenged themselves upon their enemies. *Is* not this written in the book of Jasher? So the sun stood still in the midst of heaven, and hasted not to go down about a whole day.

2Sa 1:18 — (Also he bade them teach the children of Judah *the use of* the bow: behold, it is written in the book of Jasher.)

• By Samuel, Nathan, and Gad.

1Sa 10:25 — Then Samuel told the people the manner of the kingdom, and wrote *it* in a book, and laid *it* up before the LORD. And Samuel sent all the people away, every man to his house.

1Ch 29:29 — Now the acts of David the king, first and last, behold, they *are* written in the book of Samuel the seer, and in the book of Nathan the prophet, and in the book of Gad the seer,

• By Iddo.

2Ch 12:15 — Now the acts of Rehoboam, first and last, *are* they not written in the book of Shemaiah the prophet, and of Iddo the seer concerning genealogies? And *there were* wars between Rehoboam and Jeroboam continually.

2Ch 13:22 — And the rest of the acts of Abijah, and his ways, and his sayings, *are* written in the story of the prophet Iddo.

• By Isaiah.

2Ch 26:22 — Now the rest of the acts of Uzziah, first and last, did Isaiah the prophet, the son of Amoz, write.

2Ch 32:32 — Now the rest of the acts of Hezekiah, and his goodness, behold, they *are* written in the vision of Isaiah the prophet, the son of Amoz, *and* in the book of the kings of Judah and Israel.

Isa 8:1 — Moreover the LORD said unto me, Take thee a great roll, and write in it with a man's pen concerning Maher-shalal-hash-baz.

• Of the kings of Judah and Israel.

• Of David.

1Ch 27:24 — Joab the son of Zeruiah began to number, but he finished not, because there fell wrath for it against Israel; neither was the number put in the account of the chronicles of king David.

• Of Solomon.

1Ki 11:41 — And the rest of the acts of Solomon, and all that he did, and his wisdom, *are* they not written in the book of the acts of Solomon?

• Of Jehu.

2Ch 20:34 — Now the rest of the acts of Jehoshaphat, first and last, behold, they *are* written in the book of Jehu the son of Hanani, who is mentioned in the book of the kings of Israel.

• Of other kings.

2Ch 16:11 — And, behold, the acts of Asa, first and last, lo, they *are* written in the book of the kings of Judah and Israel.

2Ch 24:27 — Now *concerning* his sons, and the greatness of the burdens *laid* upon him, and the repairing of the house of God, behold, they *are* written in the story of the book of the kings. And Amaziah his son reigned in his stead.

2Ch 25:26 — Now the rest of the acts of Amaziah, first and last, behold, *are* they not written in the book of the kings of Judah and Israel?

2Ch 27:7 — Now the rest of the acts of Jotham, and all his wars, and his ways, lo, they *are* written in the book of the kings of Israel and Judah.

2Ch 28:26 — Now the rest of his acts and of all his ways, first and last, behold, they *are* written in the book of the kings of Judah and Israel.

2Ch 35:27 — And his deeds, first and last, behold, they *are* written in the book of the kings of Israel and Judah.

2Ch 36:8 — Now the rest of the acts of Jehoiakim, and his abominations which he did, and that which was found in him, behold, they *are* written in the book of the kings of Israel and Judah: and Jehoiachin his son reigned in his stead.

• Of the kings of Israel.

1Ki 14:19 — And the rest of the acts of Jeroboam, how he warred, and how he reigned, behold, they *are* written in the book of the chronicles of the kings of Israel.

2Ch 20:34 — Now the rest of the acts of Jehoshaphat, first and last, behold, they *are* written in the book of Jehu the son of Hanani, who is mentioned in the book of the kings of Israel.

2Ch 33:18 — Now the rest of the acts of Manasseh, and his prayer unto his God, and the words of the seers that spake to him in the name of the LORD God of Israel, behold, they *are written* in the book of the kings of Israel.

• Other records kept in.

Ezr 6:1–2

Ezr 4:15 — That search may be made in the book of the records of thy fathers: so shalt thou find in the book of the records, and know that this city *is* a rebellious city, and hurtful unto kings and provinces, and that they have moved sedition within the same of old time: for which cause was this city destroyed.

Est 6:1 — On that night could not the king sleep, and he commanded to bring the book of records of the chronicles; and they were read before the king.

Est 9:32 — And the decree of Esther confirmed these matters of Purim; and it was written in the book.

Jer 32:12 — And I gave the evidence of the purchase unto Baruch the son of Neriah, the son of Maaseiah, in the sight of Hanameel mine uncle's *son,* and in the presence of the witnesses that subscribed the book of the purchase, before all the Jews that sat in the court of the prison.

Ac 19:19 — Many of them also which used curious arts brought their books together, and burned them before all *men:* and they counted the price of them, and found it fifty thousand *pieces* of silver.

• Prophecies written in, by Jeremiah.

Jer 25:13 — And I will bring upon that land all my words which I have pronounced against it, *even* all that is written in this book, which Jeremiah hath prophesied against all the nations.

Jer 30:2 — Thus speaketh the LORD God of Israel, saying, Write thee all the words that I have spoken unto thee in a book.

Jer 45:1 — The word that Jeremiah the prophet spake unto Baruch the son of Neriah, when he had written these words in a book at the mouth of Jeremiah, in the fourth year of Jehoiakim the son of Josiah king of Judah, saying,

Jer 51:60 — So Jeremiah wrote in a book all the evil that should come upon Babylon, *even* all these words that are written against Babylon.

Jer 51:63 — And it shall be, when thou hast made an end of reading this book, *that* thou shalt bind a stone to it, and cast it into the midst of Euphrates:

Da 9:2 — In the first year of his reign I Daniel understood by books the number of the years, whereof the word of the LORD came to Jeremiah the prophet, that he would accomplish seventy years in the desolations of Jerusalem.

• Other prophecies written in.

2Ch 33:18–19

• Lamentations written in.

2Ch 35:25 — And Jeremiah lamented for Josiah: and all the singing men and the singing women spake of Josiah in their lamentations to this day, and made them an ordinance in Israel: and, behold, they *are* written in the lamentations.

• Numerous.

Ecc 12:12 — And further, by these, my son, be admonished: of making many books *there is* no end; and much study *is* a weariness of the flesh.

• Eating of.

Eze 2:8–3:3; Rev 10:2–10

Jer 15:16 — Thy words were found, and I did eat them; and thy word was unto me the joy and rejoicing of mine heart: for I am called by thy name, O LORD God of hosts.

• Of magic.

Ac 19:19 — Many of them also which used curious arts brought their books together, and burned them before all *men:* and they counted the price of them, and found it fifty thousand *pieces* of silver.

• Paul's left at Troas.

2Ti 4:13 — The cloke that I left at Troas with Carpus, when thou comest, bring *with thee,* and the books, *but* especially the parchments.

• Made in a roll.

Jer 36:4 — Then Jeremiah called Baruch the son of Neriah: and Baruch wrote from the mouth of Jeremiah all the words of the LORD, which he had spoken unto him, upon a roll of a book.

Zec 5:1 — Then I turned, and lifted up mine eyes, and looked, and behold a flying roll.

• Sealed.

Rev 5:1–5

Isa 29:11 — And the vision of all is become unto you as the words of a book that is sealed, which *men* deliver to one that is learned, saying, Read this, I pray thee: and he saith, I cannot; for it *is* sealed:

Da 12:4 — But thou, O Daniel, shut up the words, and seal the book, *even* to the time of the end: many shall run to and fro, and knowledge shall be increased.

- **Kirjath-jearim was called Kirjath-sepher, which signifies a city of books.**

Jos 15:15–16; Jgs 1:11–12

- **Of life.**

Ex 32:32–33

Ps 69:28 — Let them be blotted out of the book of the living, and not be written with the righteous.

Ps 87:6 — The LORD shall count, when he writeth up the people, that this man was born there. Selah.

Da 12:1 — And at that time shall Michael stand up, the great prince which standeth for the children of thy people: and there shall be a time of trouble, such as never was since there was a nation *even* to that same time: and at that time thy people shall be delivered, every one that shall be found written in the book.

Lk 10:20 — Notwithstanding in this rejoice not, that the spirits are subject unto you; but rather rejoice, because your names are written in heaven.

Php 4:3 — And I intreat thee also, true yokefellow, help those women which laboured with me in the gospel, with Clement also, and *with* other my fellowlabourers, whose names *are* in the book of life.

Rev 3:5 — He that overcometh, the same shall be clothed in white raiment; and I will not blot out his name out of the book of life, but I will confess his name before my Father, and before his angels.

Rev 13:8 — And all that dwell upon the earth shall worship him, whose names are not written in the book of life of the Lamb slain from the foundation of the world.

Rev 17:8 — The beast that thou sawest was, and is not; and shall ascend out of the bottomless pit, and go into perdition: and they that dwell on the earth shall wonder, whose names were not written in the book of life from the foundation of the world, when they behold the beast that was, and is not, and yet is.

Rev 20:12 — And I saw the dead, small and great, stand before God; and the books were opened: and another book was opened, which is *the book* of life: and the dead were judged out of those things which were written in the books, according to their works.

Rev 20:15 — And whosoever was not found written in the book of life was cast into the lake of fire.

Rev 21:27 — And there shall in no wise enter into it any thing that defileth, neither *whatsoever* worketh abomination, or *maketh* a lie: but they which are written in the Lamb's book of life.

Rev 22:19 — And if any man shall take away from the words of the book of this prophecy, God shall take away his part out of the book of life, and out of the holy city, and *from* the things which are written in this book.

- **Of remembrance.**

Ps 56:8 — Thou tellest my wanderings: put thou my tears into thy bottle: *are they* not in thy book?

Ps 139:16 — Thine eyes did see my substance, yet being unperfect; and in thy book all *my members* were written, *which* in continuance were fashioned, when *as yet there was* none of them.

Mal 3:16 — Then they that feared the LORD spake often one to another: and the LORD hearkened, and heard *it*, and a book of remembrance was written before him for them that feared the LORD, and that thought upon his name.

BOOTH

- **Made of boughs.**

Jnh 4:5 — So Jonah went out of the city, and sat on the east side of the city, and there made him a booth, and sat under it in the shadow, till he might see what would become of the city.

- **Made for cattle.**

Ge 33:17 — And Jacob journeyed to Succoth, and built him an house, and made booths for his cattle: therefore the name of the place is called Succoth.

- **Made for watchmen.**

Job 27:18 — He buildeth his house as a moth, and as a booth *that* the keeper maketh.

Isa 1:8 — And the daughter of Zion is left as a cottage in a vineyard, as a lodge in a garden of cucumbers, as a besieged city.

Isa 24:20 — The earth shall reel to and fro like a drunkard, and shall be removed like a cottage; and the transgression thereof shall be heavy upon it; and it shall fall, and not rise again.

- **Dwelling for the Israelites during the Feast of Tabernacles.**

Le 23:40–43; Ne 8:15–16

BOOZ ⇜See: Boaz

BORING THE EAR

- **A token of servitude for life.**

Ex 21:6 — Then his master shall bring him unto the judges; he shall also bring him to the door, or unto the door post; and his master shall bore his ear through with an aul; and he shall serve him for ever.

BORROWING

Ex 22:14–15; Ne 5:1–13

Ps 37:21 — The wicked borroweth, and payeth not again: but the righteous sheweth mercy, and giveth.

Pr 22:7 — The rich ruleth over the poor, and the borrower *is* servant to the lender.

Mt 5:42 — Give to him that asketh thee, and from him that would borrow of thee turn not thou away.

⇜**See: Lending**

⇜**See: Interest**

- **Instances of.**
  - **Israelites from the Egyptians.**

    Ex 3:22; 11:2; 12:35

- **Borrowing trouble.**

⇜**See: Trouble; borrowing**

BOSCATH ⇜See: Bozkath

BOSOR

✦See: Beor
✦See: Bozrah

BOSS

• Of a shield.

Job 15:26 — He runneth upon him, *even* on *his* neck, upon the thick bosses of his bucklers:

BOTANICAL GARDENS

Ecc 2:5–6

1Ki 4:33 — And he spake of trees, from the cedar tree that *is* in Lebanon even unto the hyssop that springeth out of the wall: he spake also of beasts, and of fowl, and of creeping things, and of fishes.

1Ki 10:22 — For the king had at sea a navy of Tharshish with the navy of Hiram: once in three years came the navy of Tharshish, bringing gold, and silver, ivory, and apes, and peacocks.

BOTANY

• Laws of nature in the vegetable kingdom uniform in action.

Mt 7:16–18; Lk 6:43–44; 1Co 15:36–38

Mt 7:20 — Wherefore by their fruits ye shall know them.

Gal 6:7 — Be not deceived; God is not mocked: for whatsoever a man soweth, that shall he also reap.

• Lily, beauty of.

Mt 6:28–29

2Co 9:6 — But this *I say,* He which soweth sparingly shall reap also sparingly; and he which soweth bountifully shall reap also bountifully.

✦See: Algum
✦See: Almond
✦See: Aloes
✦See: Anise
✦See: Apple
✦See: Ash
✦See: Balm
✦See: Barley
✦See: Bay Tree
✦See: Bean
✦See: Box
✦See: Bramble
✦See: Bulrush
✦See: Camphire
✦See: Cane
✦See: Cassia
✦See: Cedar
✦See: Chestnut Tree
✦See: Cinnamon
✦See: Cockle
✦See: Coriander
✦See: Corn
✦See: Cucumber
✦See: Cummin
✦See: Cypress
✦See: Date
✦See: Ebony
✦See: Elm
✦See: Fig Tree
✦See: Fir Tree
✦See: Fitch
✦See: Flag
✦See: Flax
✦See: Frankincense
✦See: Galbanum
✦See: Gall
✦See: Garlic
✦See: Gopher Wood
✦See: Gourd
✦See: Grass
✦See: Hazel
✦See: Heath
✦See: Hemlock
✦See: Husk
✦See: Hyssop
✦See: Juniper
✦See: Leek
✦See: Lentiles
✦See: Lily
✦See: Mallows
✦See: Mandrake
✦See: Melon
✦See: Millet
✦See: Mint
✦See: Mulberry Tree
✦See: Mustard
✦See: Myrrh
✦See: Myrtle
✦See: Nettles
✦See: Nut
✦See: Oak
✦See: Olive
✦See: Onion
✦See: Palm Tree
✦See: Pine
✦See: Pomegranate
✦See: Poplar
✦See: Reed
✦See: Rose

↞See: Rue
↞See: Rye
↞See: Shittim
↞See: Spikenard
↞See: Stacte
↞See: Sycamine
↞See: Sycamore
↞See: Tares
↞See: Teil Tree
↞See: Thistle
↞See: Thorn
↞See: Thyine
↞See: Vine
↞See: Wheat
↞See: Willow
↞See: Wormwood

BOTCH ↞See: Boil

BOTTLE

Ge 21:14 — And Abraham rose up early in the morning, and took bread, and a bottle of water, and gave *it* unto Hagar, putting *it* on her shoulder, and the child, and sent her away: and she departed, and wandered in the wilderness of Beer-sheba.

- **Made of skins.**

Lk 5:37–38

Jos 9:4 — They did work wilily, and went and made as if they had been ambassadors, and took old sacks upon their asses, and wine bottles, old, and rent, and bound up;

Jos 9:13 — And these bottles of wine, which we filled, *were* new; and, behold, they be rent: and these our garments and our shoes are become old by reason of the very long journey.

Job 32:19 — Behold, my belly *is* as wine *which* hath no vent; it is ready to burst like new bottles.

Ps 119:83 — For I am become like a bottle in the smoke; *yet* do I not forget thy statutes.

Mt 9:17 — Neither do men put new wine into old bottles: else the bottles break, and the wine runneth out, and the bottles perish: but they put new wine into new bottles, and both are preserved.

Mk 2:22 — And no man putteth new wine into old bottles: else the new wine doth burst the bottles, and the wine is spilled, and the bottles will be marred: but new wine must be put into new bottles.

- **Made of clay.**

Isa 30:14 — And he shall break it as the breaking of the potters' vessel that is broken in pieces; he shall not spare: so that there shall not be found in the bursting of it a sherd to take fire from the hearth, or to take water *withal* out of the pit.

Jer 19:1 — Thus saith the LORD, Go and get a potter's earthen bottle, and *take* of the ancients of the people, and of the ancients of the priests;

Jer 19:10 — Then shalt thou break the bottle in the sight of the men that go with thee,

Jer 48:12 — Therefore, behold, the days come, saith the LORD, that I will send unto him wanderers, that shall cause him to wander, and shall empty his vessels, and break their bottles.

- **Used as a lachrymatory.**

Ps 56:8 — Thou tellest my wanderings: put thou my tears into thy bottle: *are they* not in thy book?

↞See: Pitcher

BOW

- **A weapon.**

Ge 21:16 — And she went, and sat her down over against *him* a good way off, as it were a bowshot: for she said, Let me not see the death of the child. And she sat over against *him*, and lift up her voice, and wept.

Ge 21:20 — And God was with the lad; and he grew, and dwelt in the wilderness, and became an archer.

- **Made of brass.**

2Sa 22:35 — He teacheth my hands to war; so that a bow of steel is broken by mine arms.

Job 20:24 — He shall flee from the iron weapon, *and* the bow of steel shall strike him through.

Ps 18:34 — He teacheth my hands to war, so that a bow of steel is broken by mine arms.

- **Made of wood.**

Eze 39:9 — And they that dwell in the cities of Israel shall go forth, and shall set on fire and burn the weapons, both the shields and the bucklers, the bows and the arrows, and the handstaves, and the spears, and they shall burn them with fire seven years:

- **Used in war.**

Isa 13:18 — *Their* bows also shall dash the young men to pieces; and they shall have no pity on the fruit of the womb; their eye shall not spare children.

La 2:4 — He hath bent his bow like an enemy: he stood with his right hand as an adversary, and slew all *that were* pleasant to the eye in the tabernacle of the daughter of Zion: he poured out his fury like fire.

Eze 39:3 — And I will smite thy bow out of thy left hand, and will cause thine arrows to fall out of thy right hand.

- **Used by the Elamites.**

Jer 49:35 — Thus saith the LORD of hosts; Behold, I will break the bow of Elam, the chief of their might.

- **David instructed the Israelites in the use of, by writing war song to.**

2Sa 1:18 — (Also he bade them teach the children of Judah *the use of* the bow: behold, it is written in the book of Jasher.)

- **Used in hunting.**

↞See: Archery
↞See: Arrow

- **Figurative.**

Ge 49:24 — But his bow abode in strength, and the arms of his hands were made strong by the hands of the mighty *God* of Jacob; (from thence *is* the shepherd, the stone of Israel:)

Job 16:13 — His archers compass me round about, he cleaveth my reins asunder, and doth not spare; he poureth out my gall upon the ground.

Job 29:20 — My glory *was* fresh in me, and my bow was renewed in my hand.

Ps 78:57 — But turned back, and dealt unfaithfully like their fathers: they were turned aside like a deceitful bow.

La 3:12 — He hath bent his bow, and set me as a mark for the arrow.

Hos 1:5 — And it shall come to pass at that day, that I will break the bow of Israel in the valley of Jezreel.

Hab 3:9 — Thy bow was made quite naked, *according* to the oaths of the tribes, *even thy* word. Selah. Thou didst cleave the earth with rivers.

Rev 6:2 — And I saw, and behold a white horse: and he that sat on him had a bow; and a crown was given unto him: and he went forth conquering, and to conquer.

- **A token in the clouds.**

Ge 9:8–17

Eze 1:28 — As the appearance of the bow that is in the cloud in the day of rain, so *was* the appearance of the brightness round about. This *was* the appearance of the likeness of the glory of the LORD. And when I saw *it*, I fell upon my face, and I heard a voice of one that spake.

Rev 4:3 — And he that sat was to look upon like a jasper and a sardine stone: and *there was* a rainbow round about the throne, in sight like unto an emerald.

Rev 10:1 — And I saw another mighty angel come down from heaven, clothed with a cloud: and a rainbow *was* upon his head, and his face *was* as it were the sun, and his feet as pillars of fire:

BOW, as in worship

Ge 24:26 — And the man bowed down his head, and worshipped the LORD.

Ex 4:31 — And the people believed: and when they heard that the LORD had visited the children of Israel, and that he had looked upon their affliction, then they bowed their heads and worshipped.

Ex 34:8 — And Moses made haste, and bowed his head toward the earth, and worshipped.

2Ch 7:3 — And when all the children of Israel saw how the fire came down, and the glory of the LORD upon the house, they bowed themselves with their faces to the ground upon the pavement, and worshipped, and praised the LORD, *saying*, For *he is* good; for his mercy *endureth* for ever.

BOWELS

- **Diseased.**

2Ch 21:15–20

- **Judas', gushed out.**

Ac 1:18 — Now this man purchased a field with the reward of iniquity; and falling headlong, he burst asunder in the midst, and all his bowels gushed out.

- **Figurative.**
  - **Of the sensibilities.**

Ge 43:30 — And Joseph made haste; for his bowels did yearn upon his brother: and he sought *where* to weep; and he entered into *his* chamber, and wept there.

1Ki 3:26 — Then spake the woman whose the living child *was* unto the king, for her bowels yearned upon her son, and she said, O my lord, give her the living child, and in no wise slay it. But the other said, Let it be neither mine nor thine, *but* divide *it*.

Job 30:27 — My bowels boiled, and rested not: the days of affliction prevented me.

Ps 22:14 — I am poured out like water, and all my bones are out of joint: my heart is like wax; it is melted in the midst of my bowels.

SS 5:4 — My beloved put in his hand by the hole *of the door*, and my bowels were moved for him.

Jer 4:19 — My bowels, my bowels! I am pained at my very heart; my heart maketh a noise in me; I cannot hold my peace, because thou hast heard, O my soul, the sound of the trump, the alarm of war.

Jer 31:20 — *Is* Ephraim my dear son? *is he* a pleasant child? for since I spake against him, I do earnestly remember him still: therefore my bowels are troubled for him; I will surely have mercy upon him, saith the LORD.

La 1:20 — Behold, O LORD; for I *am* in distress: my bowels are troubled; mine heart is turned within me; for I have grievously rebelled: abroad the sword bereaveth, at home *there is* as death.

Php 1:8 — For God is my record, how greatly I long after you all in the bowels of Jesus Christ.

Php 2:1 — If *there be* therefore any consolation in Christ, if any comfort of love, if any fellowship of the Spirit, if any bowels and mercies,

Col 3:12 — Put on therefore, as the elect of God, holy and beloved, bowels of mercies, kindness, humbleness of mind, meekness, longsuffering;

1Jn 3:17 — But whoso hath this world's good, and seeth his brother have need, and shutteth up his bowels *of compassion* from him, how dwelleth the love of God in him?

See: Heart

See: Worship; attitudes in

BOWL

- **Made of gold.**
  - **For the tabernacle.**

Ex 25:29 — And thou shalt make the dishes thereof, and spoons thereof, and covers thereof, and bowls thereof, to cover withal: *of* pure gold shalt thou make them.

Ex 37:16 — And he made the vessels which *were* upon the table, his dishes, and his spoons, and his bowls, and his covers to cover withal, *of* pure gold.

- **For the temple.**

1Ki 7:50 — And the bowls, and the snuffers, and the basons, and the spoons, and the censers *of* pure gold; and the hinges *of* gold, *both* for the doors of the inner house, the most holy *place, and* for the doors of the house, *to wit,* of the temple.

1Ch 28:17 — Also pure gold for the fleshhooks, and the bowls, and the cups: and for the golden basons *he gave gold* by weight for every bason; and *likewise silver* by weight for every bason of silver:

2Ch 4:8 — He made also ten tables, and placed *them* in the temple, five on the right side, and five on the left. And he made an hundred basons of gold.

- **Made of silver.**

Nu 4:7 — And upon the table of shewbread they shall spread a cloth of blue, and put thereon the dishes, and the spoons, and the bowls, and covers to cover withal: and the continual bread shall be thereon:

Nu 7:13 — And his offering *was* one silver charger, the weight thereof *was* an hundred and thirty *shekels,* one silver bowl of seventy shekels, after the shekel of the sanctuary; both of them *were* full of fine flour mingled with oil for a meat offering:

Nu 7:19 — He offered *for* his offering one silver charger, the weight whereof *was* an hundred and thirty *shekels,* one silver bowl of seventy shekels, after the shekel of the sanctuary; both of them full of fine flour mingled with oil for a meat offering:

Nu 7:25 — His offering *was* one silver charger, the weight whereof *was* an hundred and thirty *shekels,* one silver bowl of seventy shekels, after the shekel of the sanctuary; both of them full of fine flour mingled with oil for a meat offering:

Nu 7:31 — His offering *was* one silver charger of the weight of an hundred and thirty *shekels,* one silver bowl of seventy shekels, after the shekel of the sanctuary; both of them full of fine flour mingled with oil for a meat offering:

Nu 7:37 — His offering *was* one silver charger, the weight whereof *was* an hundred and thirty *shekels,* one silver bowl of seventy shekels, after the shekel of the sanctuary; both of them full of fine flour mingled with oil for a meat offering:

Nu 7:43 — His offering *was* one silver charger of the weight of an hundred and thirty *shekels,* a silver bowl of seventy shekels, after the shekel of the sanctuary; both of them full of fine flour mingled with oil for a meat offering:

Nu 7:49 — His offering *was* one silver charger, the weight whereof *was* an hundred and thirty *shekels,* one silver bowl of seventy shekels, after the shekel of the sanctuary; both of them full of fine flour mingled with oil for a meat offering:

Nu 7:55 — His offering *was* one silver charger of the weight of an hundred and thirty *shekels,* one silver bowl of seventy shekels, after the shekel of the sanctuary; both of them full of fine flour mingled with oil for a meat offering:

Nu 7:61 — His offering *was* one silver charger, the weight whereof *was* an hundred and thirty *shekels,* one silver bowl of seventy shekels, after the shekel of the sanctuary; both of them full of fine flour mingled with oil for a meat offering:

Nu 7:67 — His offering *was* one silver charger, the weight whereof *was* an hundred and thirty *shekels,* one silver bowl of seventy shekels, after the shekel of the sanctuary; both of them full of fine flour mingled with oil for a meat offering:

Nu 7:73 — His offering *was* one silver charger, the weight whereof *was* an hundred and thirty *shekels,* one silver bowl of seventy shekels, after the shekel of the sanctuary; both of them full of fine flour mingled with oil for a meat offering:

Nu 7:79 — His offering *was* one silver charger, the weight whereof *was* an hundred and thirty *shekels,* one silver bowl of seventy shekels, after the shekel of the sanctuary; both of them full of fine flour mingled with oil for a meat offering:

Nu 7:84 — This *was* the dedication of the altar, in the day when it was anointed, by the princes of Israel: twelve chargers of silver, twelve silver bowls, twelve spoons of gold:

- **Stamped "Holiness to the Lord".**

Zec 14:20–21

See: Basin

- **Figurative.**

Ecc 12:6 — Or ever the silver cord be loosed, or the golden bowl be broken, or the pitcher be broken at the fountain, or the wheel broken at the cistern.

BOX

- **For oil.**

2Ki 9:1–3

- **Made of alabaster.**

Mt 26:7 — There came unto him a woman having an alabaster box of very precious ointment, and poured it on his head, as he sat *at meat.*

Mk 14:3 — And being in Bethany in the house of Simon the leper, as he sat at meat, there came a woman having an alabaster box of ointment of spikenard very precious; and she brake the box, and poured *it* on his head.

Lk 7:37 — And, behold, a woman in the city, which was a sinner, when she knew that *Jesus* sat at meat in the Pharisee's house, brought an alabaster box of ointment,

BOX TREE

Isa 41:19 — I will plant in the wilderness the cedar, the shittah tree, and the myrtle, and the oil tree; I will set in the desert the fir tree, *and* the pine, and the box tree together:

Isa 60:13 — The glory of Lebanon shall come unto thee, the fir tree, the pine tree, and the box together, to beautify the place of my sanctuary; and I will make the place of my feet glorious.

BOXING

• Figurative.

1Co 9:26 — I therefore so run, not as uncertainly; so fight I, not as one that beateth the air:

BOZEZ • A rock near Gibeah.

1Sa 14:4 — And between the passages, by which Jonathan sought to go over unto the Philistines' garrison, *there was* a sharp rock on the one side and a sharp rock on the other side: and the name of the one *was* Bozez, and the name of the other Seneh.

BOZKATH • A city of Judah.

Jos 15:39 — Lachish, and Bozkath, and Eglon,

2Ki 22:1 — Josiah *was* eight years old when he began to reign, and he reigned thirty and one years in Jerusalem. And his mother's name *was* Jedidah, the daughter of Adaiah of Boscath.

BOZRAH

• A city of Edom.

Ge 36:33 — And Bela died, and Jobab the son of Zerah of Bozrah reigned in his stead.

• Sheep of.

Mic 2:12 — I will surely assemble, O Jacob, all of thee; I will surely gather the remnant of Israel; I will put them together as the sheep of Bozrah, as the flock in the midst of their fold: they shall make great noise by reason of *the multitude of* men.

• Prophecies concerning.

Isa 34:6 — The sword of the LORD is filled with blood, it is made fat with fatness, *and* with the blood of lambs and goats, with the fat of the kidneys of rams: for the LORD hath a sacrifice in Bozrah, and a great slaughter in the land of Idumea.

Isa 63:1 — Who *is* this that cometh from Edom, with dyed garments from Bozrah? this *that is* glorious in his apparel, travelling in the greatness of his strength? I that speak in righteousness, mighty to save.

Jer 49:13 — For I have sworn by myself, saith the LORD, that Bozrah shall become a desolation, a reproach, a waste, and a curse; and all the cities thereof shall be perpetual wastes.

Jer 49:22 — Behold, he shall come up and fly as the eagle, and spread his wings over Bozrah: and at that day shall the heart of the mighty men of Edom be as the heart of a woman in her pangs.

Am 1:12 — But I will send a fire upon Teman, which shall devour the palaces of Bozrah.

• A town of Moab.

Jer 48:24 — And upon Kerioth, and upon Bozrah, and upon all the cities of the land of Moab, far or near.

BRACELET

• Present of.

Ge 24:22 — And it came to pass, as the camels had done drinking, that the man took a golden earring of half a shekel weight, and two bracelets for her hands of ten *shekels* weight of gold;

• Worn by women.

Ge 24:30 — And it came to pass, when he saw the earring and bracelets upon his sister's hands, and when he heard the words of Rebekah his sister, saying, Thus spake the man unto me; that he came unto the man; and, behold, he stood by the camels at the well.

Isa 3:19 — The chains, and the bracelets, and the mufflers,

• Worn by men.

Ge 38:18 — And he said, What pledge shall I give thee? And she said, Thy signet, and thy bracelets, and thy staff that *is* in thine hand. And he gave *it* her, and came in unto her, and she conceived by him.

Ge 38:25 — When she *was* brought forth, she sent to her father in law, saying, By the man, whose these *are*, *am* I with child: and she said, Discern, I pray thee, whose *are* these, the signet, and bracelets, and staff.

• Dedicated to the tabernacle.

Ex 35:22 — And they came, both men and women, as many as were willing hearted, *and* brought bracelets, and earrings, and rings, and tablets, all jewels of gold: and every man that offered *offered* an offering of gold unto the LORD.

Nu 31:50 — We have therefore brought an oblation for the LORD, what every man hath gotten, of jewels of gold, chains, and bracelets, rings, earrings, and tablets, to make an atonement for our souls before the LORD.

• Taken as spoils.

Nu 31:50 — We have therefore brought an oblation for the LORD, what every man hath gotten, of jewels of gold, chains, and bracelets, rings, earrings, and tablets, to make an atonement for our souls before the LORD.

2Sa 1:10 — So I stood upon him, and slew him, because I was sure that he could not live after that he was fallen: and I took the crown that *was* upon his head, and the bracelet that *was* on his arm, and have brought them hither unto my lord.

• Figurative.

Eze 16:11 — I decked thee also with ornaments, and I put bracelets upon thy hands, and a chain on thy neck.

BRAMBLE

Isa 34:13 — And thorns shall come up in her palaces, nettles and brambles in the fortresses thereof: and it shall be an habitation of dragons, *and* a court for owls.

Lk 6:44 — For every tree is known by his own fruit. For of thorns men do not gather figs, nor of a bramble bush gather they grapes.

• Allegory of.

Jgs 9:14–15

BRANCH

• Figurative.

Jn 15:2–5

Pr 11:28 — He that trusteth in his riches shall fall: but the righteous shall flourish as a branch.

Isa 60:21 — Thy people also *shall be* all righteous: they shall inherit the land for ever, the branch of my planting, the work of my hands, that I may be glorified.

Hos 14:6 — His branches shall spread, and his beauty shall be as the olive tree, and his smell as Lebanon.

- **Pruning of.**

Isa 18:5 — For afore the harvest, when the bud is perfect, and the sour grape is ripening in the flower, he shall both cut off the sprigs with pruninghooks, and take away *and* cut down the branches.

Da 4:14 — He cried aloud, and said thus, Hew down the tree, and cut off his branches, shake off his leaves, and scatter his fruit: let the beasts get away from under it, and the fowls from his branches:

Jn 15:6 — If a man abide not in me, he is cast forth as a branch, and is withered; and men gather them, and cast *them* into the fire, and they are burned.

Ro 11:17 — And if some of the branches be broken off, and thou, being a wild olive tree, wert graffed in among them, and with them partakest of the root and fatness of the olive tree;

Ro 11:21 — For if God spared not the natural branches, *take heed* lest he also spare not thee.

- **Fruitless, cut off.**

Jn 15:2 — Every branch in me that beareth not fruit he taketh away: and every *branch* that beareth fruit, he purgeth it, that it may bring forth more fruit.

Jn 15:6 — If a man abide not in me, he is cast forth as a branch, and is withered; and men gather them, and cast *them* into the fire, and they are burned.

- **A title of Christ.**

Ps 80:15— And the vineyard which thy right hand hath planted, and the branch *that* thou madest strong for thyself.

Isa 4:2 — In that day shall the branch of the LORD be beautiful and glorious, and the fruit of the earth *shall be* excellent and comely for them that are escaped of Israel.

Isa 11:1 — And there shall come forth a rod out of the stem of Jesse, and a Branch shall grow out of his roots:

Jer 23:5 — Behold, the days come, saith the LORD, that I will raise unto David a righteous Branch, and a King shall reign and prosper, and shall execute judgment and justice in the earth.

Jer 33:15 — In those days, and at that time, will I cause the Branch of righteousness to grow up unto David; and he shall execute judgment and righteousness in the land.

Zec 3:8 — Hear now, O Joshua the high priest, thou, and thy fellows that sit before thee: for they *are* men wondered at: for, behold, I will bring forth my servant the BRANCH.

Zec 6:12 — And speak unto him, saying, Thus speaketh the LORD of hosts, saying, Behold the man whose name *is* The BRANCH; and he shall grow up out of his place, and he shall build the temple of the LORD:

- **Symbolic name of Joshua.**

Zec 6:12 — And speak unto him, saying, Thus speaketh the LORD of hosts, saying, Behold the man whose name *is* The BRANCH; and he shall grow up out of his place, and he shall build the temple of the LORD:

See: Grafting

BRASS, or more probably copper

- **Smelted.**

Job 28:2 — Iron is taken out of the earth, and brass *is* molten *out of* the stone.

Eze 22:20 — *As* they gather silver, and brass, and iron, and lead, and tin, into the midst of the furnace, to blow the fire upon it, to melt *it;* so will I gather *you* in mine anger and in my fury, and I will leave *you there,* and melt you.

- **A mineral of Canaan.**

Dt 8:9 — A land wherein thou shalt eat bread without scarceness, thou shalt not lack any *thing* in it; a land whose stones are iron, and out of whose hills thou mayest dig brass.

Jos 22:8 — And he spake unto them, saying, Return with much riches unto your tents, and with very much cattle, with silver, and with gold, and with brass, and with iron, and with very much raiment: divide the spoil of your enemies with your brethren.

- **A mineral of Syria.**

2Sa 8:8 — And from Betah, and from Berothai, cities of Hadadezer, king David took exceeding much brass.

- **Tyrians traded in.**

Eze 27:13 — Javan, Tubal, and Meshech, they *were* thy merchants: they traded the persons of men and vessels of brass in thy market.

- **Abundance of, for the temple.**

1Ki 7:47 — And Solomon left all the vessels *unweighed,* because they were exceeding many: neither was the weight of the brass found out.

1Ch 22:14 — Now, behold, in my trouble I have prepared for the house of the LORD an hundred thousand talents of gold, and a thousand thousand talents of silver; and of brass and iron without weight; for it is in abundance: timber also and stone have I prepared; and thou mayest add thereto.

- **Articles made of.**
  - **Altar, vessels, and other articles of the tabernacle and temple.**

Ex 38:28–31; 1Ki 7:14–47

Ezr 8:27 — Also twenty basons of gold, of a thousand drams; and two vessels of fine copper, precious as gold.

  - **Cymbals.**

1Ch 15:19 — So the singers, Heman, Asaph, and Ethan, *were appointed* to sound with cymbals of brass;

- **Trumpets.**
  1Co 13:1 — Though I speak with the tongues of men and of angels, and have not charity, I am become *as* sounding brass, or a tinkling cymbal.
- **Armor.**
  1Sa 17:5–6
  2Ch 12:10 — Instead of which king Rehoboam made shields of brass, and committed *them* to the hands of the chief of the guard, that kept the entrance of the king's house.
- **Bows.**

See: Bow

- **Fetters.**
  Jgs 16:21 — But the Philistines took him, and put out his eyes, and brought him down to Gaza, and bound him with fetters of brass; and he did grind in the prison house.
  2Ki 25:7 — And they slew the sons of Zedekiah before his eyes, and put out the eyes of Zedekiah, and bound him with fetters of brass, and carried him to Babylon.
- **Gates.**
  Ps 107:16 — For he hath broken the gates of brass, and cut the bars of iron in sunder.
  Isa 45:2 — I will go before thee, and make the crooked places straight: I will break in pieces the gates of brass, and cut in sunder the bars of iron:
- **Bars.**
  1Ki 4:13 — The son of Geber, in Ramoth-gilead; to him *pertained* the towns of Jair the son of Manasseh, which *are* in Gilead; to him *also pertained* the region of Argob, which is in Bashan, threescore great cities with walls and brasen bars:
- **Idols.**
  Da 5:4 — They drank wine, and praised the gods of gold, and of silver, of brass, of iron, of wood, and of stone.
  Rev 9:20 — And the rest of the men which were not killed by these plagues yet repented not of the works of their hands, that they should not worship devils, and idols of gold, and silver, and brass, and stone, and of wood: which neither can see, nor hear, nor walk:
- **Mirrors.**
  Ex 38:8 — And he made the laver *of* brass, and the foot of it *of* brass, of the lookingglasses of *the women* assembling, which assembled *at* the door of the tabernacle of the congregation.
- **Household vessels.**
  Mk 7:4 — And *when they come* from the market, except they wash, they eat not. And many other things there be, which they have received to hold, *as* the washing of cups, and pots, brasen vessels, and of tables.
- **Money.**
  Mt 10:9 — Provide neither gold, nor silver, nor brass in your purses,
  Mk 12:41 — And Jesus sat over against the treasury, and beheld how the people cast money into the treasury: and many that were rich cast in much.

- **Workers in.**
  - **Tubal-cain.**
    Ge 4:22 — And Zillah, she also bare Tubal-cain, an instructer of every artificer in brass and iron: and the sister of Tubal-cain *was* Naamah.
  - **Hiram.**
    1Ki 7:14 — He *was* a widow's son of the tribe of Naphtali, and his father *was* a man of Tyre, a worker in brass: and he was filled with wisdom, and understanding, and cunning to work all works in brass. And he came to king Solomon, and wrought all his work.
  - **Alexander.**
    2Ti 4:14 — Alexander the coppersmith did me much evil: the Lord reward him according to his works:

See: Brazier

See: Copper

See: Molding

- **Figurative.**
  Da 10:1–21
  Le 26:19 — And I will break the pride of your power; and I will make your heaven as iron, and your earth as brass:
  Dt 33:25 — Thy shoes *shall be* iron and brass; and as thy days, *so shall* thy strength *be.*
  Isa 48:4 — Because I knew that thou *art* obstinate, and thy neck *is* an iron sinew, and thy brow brass;
  Jer 1:18 — For, behold, I have made thee this day a defenced city, and an iron pillar, and brasen walls against the whole land, against the kings of Judah, against the princes thereof, against the priests thereof, and against the people of the land.
  Eze 1:7 — And their feet *were* straight feet; and the sole of their feet *was* like the sole of a calf's foot: and they sparkled like the colour of burnished brass.
  Da 2:32 — This image's head *was* of fine gold, his breast and his arms of silver, his belly and his thighs of brass,
  Da 2:39 — And after thee shall arise another kingdom inferior to thee, and another third kingdom of brass, which shall bear rule over all the earth.
  Da 7:19 — Then I would know the truth of the fourth beast, which was diverse from all the others, exceeding dreadful, whose teeth *were of* iron, and his nails *of* brass; *which* devoured, brake in pieces, and stamped the residue with his feet;
  Zec 6:1 — And I turned, and lifted up mine eyes, and looked, and, behold, there came four chariots out from between two mountains; and the mountains *were* mountains of brass.
  Rev 1:15 — And his feet like unto fine brass, as if they burned in a furnace; and his voice as the sound of many waters.

BRAVERY

See: Boldness

See: Courage

BRAY • To pound.

Pr 27:22 — Though thou shouldest bray a fool in a mortar among wheat with a pestle, *yet* will not his foolishness depart from him.

BRAZEN SEA ➜See: Laver

BRAZEN SERPENT

• Made by Moses for the healing of the Israelites.

Nu 21:9 — And Moses made a serpent of brass, and put it upon a pole, and it came to pass, that if a serpent had bitten any man, when he beheld the serpent of brass, he lived.

• Worshiped by Israelites.

2Ki 18:4 — He removed the high places, and brake the images, and cut down the groves, and brake in pieces the brasen serpent that Moses had made: for unto those days the children of Israel did burn incense to it: and he called it Nehushtan.

• A symbol of Christ.

Jn 3:14–15

BRAZIER

• An artificer in brass and copper.

Ge 4:22 — And Zillah, she also bare Tubal-cain, an instructer of every artificer in brass and iron: and the sister of Tubal-cain *was* Naamah.

2Ti 4:14 — Alexander the coppersmith did me much evil: the Lord reward him according to his works:

• A utensil used for warming houses.

Jer 36:22–24

BREAD

• Called the Staff of Life.

Eze 4:16 — Moreover he said unto me, Son of man, behold, I will break the staff of bread in Jerusalem: and they shall eat bread by weight, and with care; and they shall drink water by measure, and with astonishment:

Eze 5:16 — When I shall send upon them the evil arrows of famine, which shall be for *their* destruction, *and* which I will send to destroy you: and I will increase the famine upon you, and will break your staff of bread:

Eze 14:13 — Son of man, when the land sinneth against me by trespassing grievously, then will I stretch out mine hand upon it, and will break the staff of the bread thereof, and will send famine upon it, and will cut off man and beast from it:

• Kinds of.

• Bread of affliction.

1Ki 22:27 — And say, Thus saith the king, Put this *fellow* in the prison, and feed him with bread of affliction and with water of affliction, until I come in peace.

Ps 127:2 — *It is* vain for you to rise up early, to sit up late, to eat the bread of sorrows: *for* so he giveth his beloved sleep.

Isa 30:20 — And *though* the Lord give you the bread of adversity, and the water of affliction, yet shall not thy teachers be removed into a corner any more, but thine eyes shall see thy teachers:

Hos 9:4 — They shall not offer wine *offerings* to the LORD, neither shall they be pleasing unto him: their sacrifices *shall be* unto them as the bread of mourners; all that eat thereof shall be polluted: for their bread for their soul shall not come into the house of the LORD.

• Leavened.

Le 7:13 — Besides the cakes, he shall offer *for* his offering leavened bread with the sacrifice of thanksgiving of his peace offerings.

Le 23:17 — Ye shall bring out of your habitations two wave loaves of two tenth deals: they shall be of fine flour; they shall be baken with leaven; *they are* the firstfruits unto the LORD.

Hos 7:4 — They *are* all adulterers, as an oven heated by the baker, *who* ceaseth from raising after he hath kneaded the dough, until it be leavened.

Am 4:5 — And offer a sacrifice of thanksgiving with leaven, and proclaim *and* publish the free offerings: for this liketh you, O ye children of Israel, saith the Lord GOD.

Mt 13:33 — Another parable spake he unto them; The kingdom of heaven is like unto leaven, which a woman took, and hid in three measures of meal, till the whole was leavened.

• Unleavened.

Ge 19:3 — And he pressed upon them greatly; and they turned in unto him, and entered into his house; and he made them a feast, and did bake unleavened bread, and they did eat.

Ex 29:2 — And unleavened bread, and cakes unleavened tempered with oil, and wafers unleavened anointed with oil: *of* wheaten flour shalt thou make them.

Jgs 6:19 — And Gideon went in, and made ready a kid, and unleavened cakes of an ephah of flour: the flesh he put in a basket, and he put the broth in a pot, and brought *it* out unto him under the oak, and presented *it*.

1Sa 28:24 — And the woman had a fat calf in the house; and she hasted, and killed it, and took flour, and kneaded *it*, and did bake unleavened bread thereof:

• Made of wheat flour.

Ex 29:2 — And unleavened bread, and cakes unleavened tempered with oil, and wafers unleavened anointed with oil: *of* wheaten flour shalt thou make them.

1Ki 4:22 — And Solomon's provision for one day was thirty measures of fine flour, and threescore measures of meal,

1Ki 5:11 — And Solomon gave Hiram twenty thousand measures of wheat *for* food to his household, and twenty measures of pure oil: thus gave Solomon to Hiram year by year.

Ps 81:16 — He should have fed them also with the finest of the wheat: and with honey out of the rock should I have satisfied thee.

• Made of manna.

Nu 11:8 — *And* the people went about, and gathered *it,* and ground *it* in mills, or beat *it* in a mortar, and baked *it* in pans, and made cakes of it: and the taste of it was as the taste of fresh oil.

• Made of meal.

1Ki 17:12 — And she said, *As* the LORD thy God liveth, I have not a cake, but an handful of meal in a barrel, and a little oil in a cruse: and, behold, I *am* gathering two sticks, that I may go in and dress it for me and my son, that we may eat it, and die.

• Made of barley.

Jgs 7:13 — And when Gideon was come, behold, *there was* a man that told a dream unto his fellow, and said, Behold, I dreamed a dream, and, lo, a cake of barley bread tumbled into the host of Midian, and came unto a tent, and smote it that it fell, and overturned it, that the tent lay along.

• How prepared.

• Mixed with oil.

Ex 29:2 — And unleavened bread, and cakes unleavened tempered with oil, and wafers unleavened anointed with oil: *of* wheaten flour shalt thou make them.

Ex 29:23 — And one loaf of bread, and one cake of oiled bread, and one wafer out of the basket of the unleavened bread that *is* before the LORD:

• Mixed with honey.

Ex 16:31 — And the house of Israel called the name thereof Manna: and it *was* like coriander seed, white; and the taste of it *was* like wafers *made* with honey.

• Mixed with leaven, or ferment.

Ge 18:6 — And Abraham hastened into the tent unto Sarah, and said, Make ready quickly three measures of fine meal, knead *it,* and make cakes upon the hearth.

Ex 8:3 — And the river shall bring forth frogs abundantly, which shall go up and come into thine house, and into thy bedchamber, and upon thy bed, and into the house of thy servants, and upon thy people, and into thine ovens, and into thy kneadingtroughs:

Ex 12:34 — And the people took their dough before it was leavened, their kneadingtroughs being bound up in their clothes upon their shoulders.

1Sa 28:24 — And the woman had a fat calf in the house; and she hasted, and killed it, and took flour, and kneaded *it,* and did bake unleavened bread thereof:

2Sa 13:8 — So Tamar went to her brother Amnon's house; and he was laid down. And she took flour, and kneaded *it,* and made cakes in his sight, and did bake the cakes.

Jer 7:18 — The children gather wood, and the fathers kindle the fire, and the women knead *their* dough, to make cakes to the queen of heaven, and to pour out drink offerings unto other gods, that they may provoke me to anger.

Hos 7:4 — They *are* all adulterers, as an oven heated by the baker, *who* ceaseth from raising after he hath kneaded the dough, until it be leavened.

↞See: Bread; kinds of; leavened

↞See: Leaven

• Made into loaves.

1Sa 10:3 — Then shalt thou go on forward from thence, and thou shalt come to the plain of Tabor, and there shall meet thee three men going up to God to Bethel, one carrying three kids, and another carrying three loaves of bread, and another carrying a bottle of wine:

1Sa 17:17 — And Jesse said unto David his son, Take now for thy brethren an ephah of this parched *corn,* and these ten loaves, and run to the camp to thy brethren;

1Sa 25:18 — Then Abigail made haste, and took two hundred loaves, and two bottles of wine, and five sheep ready dressed, and five measures of parched *corn,* and an hundred clusters of raisins, and two hundred cakes of figs, and laid *them* on asses.

1Ki 14:3 — And take with thee ten loaves, and cracknels, and a cruse of honey, and go to him: he shall tell thee what shall become of the child.

Mk 8:14 — Now *the disciples* had forgotten to take bread, neither had they in the ship with them more than one loaf.

• Made into cakes.

2Sa 6:19 — And he dealt among all the people, *even* among the whole multitude of Israel, as well to the women as men, to every one a cake of bread, and a good piece *of flesh,* and a flagon *of wine.* So all the people departed every one to his house.

1Ki 17:12 — And she said, *As* the LORD thy God liveth, I have not a cake, but an handful of meal in a barrel, and a little oil in a cruse: and, behold, I *am* gathering two sticks, that I may go in and dress it for me and my son, that we may eat it, and die.

• Made into wafers.

Ex 16:21 — And they gathered it every morning, every man according to his eating: and when the sun waxed hot, it melted.

Ex 29:23 — And one loaf of bread, and one cake of oiled bread, and one wafer out of the basket of the unleavened bread that *is* before the LORD:

• Made into cracknels.

1Ki 14:3 — And take with thee ten loaves, and cracknels, and a cruse of honey, and go to him: he shall tell thee what shall become of the child.

• Baked in ovens.

Ex 8:3 — And the river shall bring forth frogs abundantly, which shall go up and come into thine house, and into thy bedchamber, and upon thy bed, and into the house of thy servants, and upon thy people, and into thine ovens, and into thy kneadingtroughs:

Le 2:4 — And if thou bring an oblation of a meat offering baken in the oven, *it shall be* unleavened cakes of fine flour mingled with oil, or unleavened wafers anointed with oil.

Le 7:9 — And all the meat offering that is baken in the oven, and all that is dressed in the fryingpan, and in the pan, shall be the priest's that offereth it.

Le 11:35 — And every *thing* whereupon *any part* of their carcase falleth shall be unclean; *whether it be* oven, or ranges for pots, they shall be broken down: *for* they *are* unclean, and shall be unclean unto you.

Le 26:26 — *And* when I have broken the staff of your bread, ten women shall bake your bread in one oven, and they shall deliver *you* your bread again by weight: and ye shall eat, and not be satisfied.

Hos 7:4 — They *are* all adulterers, as an oven heated by the baker, *who* ceaseth from raising after he hath kneaded the dough, until it be leavened.

- **Baked in pans.**

2Sa 13:6–9

Le 2:5 — And if thy oblation *be* a meat offering *baken* in a pan, it shall be *of* fine flour unleavened, mingled with oil.

Le 2:7 — And if thy oblation *be* a meat offering *baken* in the frying pan, it shall be made *of* fine flour with oil.

- **Baked on hearths.**

Ge 18:6 — And Abraham hastened into the tent unto Sarah, and said, Make ready quickly three measures of fine meal, knead *it,* and make cakes upon the hearth.

- **Baked on coals.**

1Ki 19:6 — And he looked, and, behold, *there was* a cake baken on the coals, and a cruse of water at his head. And he did eat and drink, and laid him down again.

Isa 44:19 — And none considereth in his heart, neither *is there* knowledge nor understanding to say, I have burned part of it in the fire; yea, also I have baked bread upon the coals thereof; I have roasted flesh, and eaten *it:* and shall I make the residue thereof an abomination? shall I fall down to the stock of a tree?

Jn 21:9 — As soon then as they were come to land, they saw a fire of coals there, and fish laid thereon, and bread.

- **Made by men.**

Ge 40:2 — And Pharaoh was wroth against two *of* his officers, against the chief of the butlers, and against the chief of the bakers.

- **Made by women.**

Le 26:26 — *And* when I have broken the staff of your bread, ten women shall bake your bread in one oven, and they shall deliver *you* your bread again by weight: and ye shall eat, and not be satisfied.

1Sa 8:13 — And he will take your daughters *to be* confectionaries, and *to be* cooks, and *to be* bakers.

Jer 7:18 — The children gather wood, and the fathers kindle the fire, and the women knead *their* dough, to make cakes to the queen of heaven, and to pour out drink offerings unto other gods, that they may provoke me to anger.

- **Traffic in.**

Jer 37:21 — Then Zedekiah the king commanded that they should commit Jeremiah into the court of the prison, and that they should give him daily a piece of bread out of the bakers' street, until all the bread in the city were spent. Thus Jeremiah remained in the court of the prison.

Mk 6:37 — He answered and said unto them, Give ye them to eat. And they say unto him, Shall we go and buy two hundred pennyworth of bread, and give them to eat?

- **Sacrificed.**

Le 21:21–22

Le 21:6 — They shall be holy unto their God, and not profane the name of their God: for the offerings of the LORD made by fire, *and* the bread of their God, they do offer: therefore they shall be holy.

Le 21:8 — Thou shalt sanctify him therefore; for he offereth the bread of thy God: he shall be holy unto thee: for I the LORD, which sanctify you, *am* holy.

Le 21:17 — Speak unto Aaron, saying, Whosoever *he be* of thy seed in their generations that hath *any* blemish, let him not approach to offer the bread of his God.

Le 22:25 — Neither from a stranger's hand shall ye offer the bread of your God of any of these; because their corruption *is* in them, *and* blemishes *be* in them: they shall not be accepted for you.

1Sa 2:36 — And it shall come to pass, *that* every one that is left in thine house shall come *and* crouch to him for a piece of silver and a morsel of bread, and shall say, Put me, I pray thee, into one of the priests' offices, that I may eat a piece of bread.

2Ki 23:9 — Nevertheless the priests of the high places came not up to the altar of the LORD in Jerusalem, but they did eat of the unleavened bread among their brethren.

- **By idolaters.**

Jer 7:18 — The children gather wood, and the fathers kindle the fire, and the women knead *their* dough, to make cakes to the queen of heaven, and to pour out drink offerings unto other gods, that they may provoke me to anger.

Jer 44:19 — And when we burned incense to the queen of heaven, and poured out drink offerings unto her, did we make her cakes to worship her, and pour out drink offerings unto her, without our men?

See: Shewbread

See: Offerings

- **Figurative.**

Isa 55:2 — Wherefore do ye spend money for *that which is* not bread? and your labour for *that which* satisfieth not? hearken diligently unto me, and eat ye *that which is* good, and let your soul delight itself in fatness.

1Co 10:17 — For we *being* many are one bread, *and* one body: for we are all partakers of that one bread.

2Co 9:10 — Now he that ministereth seed to the sower both minister bread for *your* food, and multiply your seed sown, and increase the fruits of your righteousness;)

• **Christ.**

Jn 6:32–35

• **Symbolic.**

• **Of the body of Christ.**

1Co 11:23–24

Mt 26:26 — And as they were eating, Jesus took bread, and blessed *it,* and brake *it,* and gave *it* to the disciples, and said, Take, eat; this is my body.

Ac 20:7 — And upon the first *day* of the week, when the disciples came together to break bread, Paul preached unto them, ready to depart on the morrow; and continued his speech until midnight.

BREASTPLATE

• **For high priest.**

Ex 25:7 — Onyx stones, and stones to be set in the ephod, and in the breastplate.

• **Directions for the making of.**

Ex 28:15–30

• **Made by Bezaleel.**

Ex 39:8 — And he made the breastplate *of* cunning work, like the work of the ephod; *of* gold, blue, and purple, and scarlet, and fine twined linen.

Ex 39:21 — And they did bind the breastplate by his rings unto the rings of the ephod with a lace of blue, that it might be above the curious girdle of the ephod, and that the breastplate might not be loosed from the ephod; as the LORD commanded Moses.

• **Freewill offering of materials for.**

Ex 35:9 — And onyx stones, and stones to be set for the ephod, and for the breastplate.

Ex 35:27 — And the rulers brought onyx stones, and stones to be set, for the ephod, and for the breastplate;

• **Worn by Aaron.**

Ex 29:5 — And thou shalt take the garments, and put upon Aaron the coat, and the robe of the ephod, and the ephod, and the breastplate, and gird him with the curious girdle of the ephod:

Le 8:8 — And he put the breastplate upon him: also he put in the breastplate the Urim and the Thummim.

• **Armor for soldiers.**

Rev 9:9 — And they had breastplates, as it were breastplates of iron; and the sound of their wings *was* as the sound of chariots of many horses running to battle.

Rev 9:17 — And thus I saw the horses in the vision, and them that sat on them, having breastplates of fire, and of jacinth, and brimstone: and the heads of the horses *were* as the heads of lions; and out of their mouths issued fire and smoke and brimstone.

• **Figurative.**

Isa 59:17 — For he put on righteousness as a breastplate, and an helmet of salvation upon his head; and he put on the garments of vengeance *for* clothing, and was clad with zeal as a cloke.

Eph 6:14 — Stand therefore, having your loins girt about with truth, and having on the breastplate of righteousness;

1Th 5:8 — But let us, who are of the day, be sober, putting on the breastplate of faith and love; and for an helmet, the hope of salvation.

BREATH

• **Of life.**

Ge 2:7 — And the LORD God formed man *of* the dust of the ground, and breathed into his nostrils the breath of life; and man became a living soul.

Ge 7:22 — All in whose nostrils *was* the breath of life, of all that *was* in the dry *land,* died.

Ac 17:25 — Neither is worshipped with men's hands, as though he needed any thing, seeing he giveth to all life, and breath, and all things;

• **Of God.**

2Sa 22:16 — And the channels of the sea appeared, the foundations of the world were discovered, at the rebuking of the LORD, at the blast of the breath of his nostrils.

Job 4:9 — By the blast of God they perish, and by the breath of his nostrils are they consumed.

Job 15:30 — He shall not depart out of darkness; the flame shall dry up his branches, and by the breath of his mouth shall he go away.

Job 33:4 — The Spirit of God hath made me, and the breath of the Almighty hath given me life.

Job 37:10 — By the breath of God frost is given: and the breadth of the waters is straitened.

Ps 18:15 — Then the channels of waters were seen, and the foundations of the world were discovered at thy rebuke, O LORD, at the blast of the breath of thy nostrils.

Ps 33:6 — By the word of the LORD were the heavens made; and all the host of them by the breath of his mouth.

Isa 30:33 — For Tophet *is* ordained of old; yea, for the king it is prepared; he hath made *it* deep *and* large: the pile thereof *is* fire and much wood; the breath of the LORD, like a stream of brimstone, doth kindle it.

• **Figurative.**

Eze 37:9 — Then said he unto me, Prophesy unto the wind, prophesy, son of man, and say to the wind, Thus saith the Lord GOD; Come from the four winds, O breath, and breathe upon these slain, that they may live.

BREECHES

• **For the priests.**

Ex 28:42 — And thou shalt make them linen breeches to cover their nakedness; from the loins even unto the thighs they shall reach:

Ex 39:28 — And a mitre *of* fine linen, and goodly bonnets *of* fine linen, and linen breeches *of* fine twined linen,

Le 6:10 — And the priest shall put on his linen garment, and his linen breeches shall he put upon his flesh, and take up the ashes which the fire hath consumed with the burnt offering on the altar, and he shall put them beside the altar.

Le 16:4 — He shall put on the holy linen coat, and he shall have the linen breeches upon his flesh, and shall be girded with a linen girdle, and with the linen mitre shall he be attired: these *are* holy garments; therefore shall he wash his flesh in water, and *so* put them on.

Eze 44:18 — They shall have linen bonnets upon their heads, and shall have linen breeches upon their loins; they shall not gird *themselves* with any thing that causeth sweat.

BRIBERY

Dt 16:18–19; Ps 26:9–10; Isa 5:22–23; 33:15–16; Eze 22:12–13

Ex 23:8 — And thou shalt take no gift: for the gift blindeth the wise, and perverteth the words of the righteous.

Dt 27:25 — Cursed *be* he that taketh reward to slay an innocent person. And all the people shall say, Amen.

1Sa 8:1 — And it came to pass, when Samuel was old, that he made his sons judges over Israel.

1Sa 8:3 — And his sons walked not in his ways, but turned aside after lucre, and took bribes, and perverted judgment.

Job 15:34 — For the congregation of hypocrites *shall be* desolate, and fire shall consume the tabernacles of bribery.

Pr 15:27 — He that is greedy of gain troubleth his own house; but he that hateth gifts shall live.

Pr 17:8 — A gift *is as* a precious stone in the eyes of him that hath it: whithersoever it turneth, it prospereth.

Pr 17:23 — A wicked *man* taketh a gift out of the bosom to pervert the ways of judgment.

Pr 18:16 — A man's gift maketh room for him, and bringeth him before great men.

Pr 21:14 — A gift in secret pacifieth anger: and a reward in the bosom strong wrath.

Pr 25:14 — Whoso boasteth himself of a false gift *is like* clouds and wind without rain.

Pr 28:21 — To have respect of persons *is* not good: for for a piece of bread *that* man will transgress.

Pr 29:4 — The king by judgment establisheth the land: but he that receiveth gifts overthroweth it.

Ecc 7:7 — Surely oppression maketh a wise man mad; and a gift destroyeth the heart.

Isa 1:23 — Thy princes *are* rebellious, and companions of thieves: every one loveth gifts, and followeth after rewards: they judge not the fatherless, neither doth the cause of the widow come unto them.

Eze 13:19 — And will ye pollute me among my people for handfuls of barley and for pieces of bread, to slay the souls that should not die, and to save the souls alive that should not live, by your lying to my people that hear *your* lies?

Am 2:6 — Thus saith the LORD; For three transgressions of Israel, and for four, I will not turn away *the punishment* thereof; because they sold the righteous for silver, and the poor for a pair of shoes;

Am 5:12 — For I know your manifold transgressions and your mighty sins: they afflict the just, they take a bribe, and they turn aside the poor in the gate *from their right.*

Mic 7:3 — That they may do evil with both hands earnestly, the prince asketh, and the judge *asketh* for a reward; and the great *man,* he uttereth his mischievous desire: so they wrap it up.

• Instances of.

• Delilah.

Jgs 16:5

• Samuel's sons.

1Sa 8:1, 3

• The false prophet, Shemaiah.

Ne 6:10–13

• Ben-hadad.

1Ki 15:19

• Haman bribes Ahasuerus to destroy the Jews.

Est 3:9

• Chief priests bribe Judas.

Mt 26:15; 27:3–9; Mk 14:11; Lk 22:5

• Soldiers bribed to declare that the disciples stole the body of Jesus.

Mt 28:12–15

• Felix seeks a bribe from Paul.

Ac 24:26

BRICK

• Used in building.

• Babel.

Ge 11:3 — And they said one to another, Go to, let us make brick, and burn them throughly. And they had brick for stone, and slime had they for morter.

• Cities in Egypt.

Ex 1:11 — Therefore they did set over them taskmasters to afflict them with their burdens. And they built for Pharaoh treasure cities, Pithom and Raamses.

Ex 1:14 — And they made their lives bitter with hard bondage, in morter, and in brick, and in all manner of service in the field: all their service, wherein they made them serve, *was* with rigour.

• Houses.

Isa 9:10 — The bricks are fallen down, but we will build with hewn stones: the sycomores are cut down, but we will change *them into* cedars.

• Altars.

Isa 65:3 — A people that provoketh me to anger continually to my face; that sacrificeth in gardens, and burneth incense upon altars of brick;

• Made by Israelites.

Ex 5:7–19

2Sa 12:31 — And he brought forth the people that *were* therein, and put *them* under saws, and under harrows of iron, and under axes of iron, and made them pass through the brickkiln: and thus did he unto all the cities of the children of Ammon. So David and all the people returned unto Jerusalem.

Jer 43:9 — Take great stones in thine hand, and hide them in the clay in the brickkiln, which *is* at the entry of Pharaoh's house in Tahpanhes, in the sight of the men of Judah;

Na 3:14 — Draw thee waters for the siege, fortify thy strong holds: go into clay, and tread the morter, make strong the brickkiln.

BRICK-KILN

Jer 43:9 — Take great stones in thine hand, and hide them in the clay in the brickkiln, which *is* at the entry of Pharaoh's house in Tahpanhes, in the sight of the men of Judah;

Na 3:14 — Draw thee waters for the siege, fortify thy strong holds: go into clay, and tread the morter, make strong the brickkiln.

• Captives tortured in.

2Sa 12:31 — And he brought forth the people that *were* therein, and put *them* under saws, and under harrows of iron, and under axes of iron, and made them pass through the brickkiln: and thus did he unto all the cities of the children of Ammon. So David and all the people returned unto Jerusalem.

BRIDE

• Ornaments of.

Isa 49:18 — Lift up thine eyes round about, and behold: all these gather themselves together, *and* come to thee. *As* I live, saith the LORD, thou shalt surely clothe thee with them all, as with an ornament, and bind them *on thee,* as a bride *doeth.*

Isa 61:10 — I will greatly rejoice in the LORD, my soul shall be joyful in my God; for he hath clothed me with the garments of salvation, he hath covered me with the robe of righteousness, as a bridegroom decketh *himself* with ornaments, and as a bride adorneth *herself* with her jewels.

Jer 2:32 — Can a maid forget her ornaments, *or* a bride her attire? yet my people have forgotten me days without number.

Rev 21:2 — And I John saw the holy city, new Jerusalem, coming down from God out of heaven, prepared as a bride adorned for her husband.

• Presents to.

Ge 24:53 — And the servant brought forth jewels of silver, and jewels of gold, and raiment, and gave *them* to Rebekah: he gave also to her brother and to her mother precious things.

• Maids of.

Ge 24:59 — And they sent away Rebekah their sister, and her nurse, and Abraham's servant, and his men.

Ge 24:61 — And Rebekah arose, and her damsels, and they rode upon the camels, and followed the man: and the servant took Rebekah, and went his way.

Ge 29:24 — And Laban gave unto his daughter Leah Zilpah his maid *for* an handmaid.

Ge 29:29 — And Laban gave to Rachel his daughter Bilhah his handmaid to be her maid.

• Figurative.

Ps 45:10–17; Eze 16:8–14; Rev 19:7–8

2Co 11:2 — For I am jealous over you with godly jealousy: for I have espoused you to one husband, that I may present *you as* a chaste virgin to Christ.

Rev 21:2 — And I John saw the holy city, new Jerusalem, coming down from God out of heaven, prepared as a bride adorned for her husband.

Rev 21:9 — And there came unto me one of the seven angels which had the seven vials full of the seven last plagues, and talked with me, saying, Come hither, I will shew thee the bride, the Lamb's wife.

Rev 22:17 — And the Spirit and the bride say, Come. And let him that heareth say, Come. And let him that is athirst come. And whosoever will, let him take the water of life freely.

BRIDEGROOM

• Ornaments of.

Isa 61:10 — I will greatly rejoice in the LORD, my soul shall be joyful in my God; for he hath clothed me with the garments of salvation, he hath covered me with the robe of righteousness, as a bridegroom decketh *himself* with ornaments, and as a bride adorneth *herself* with her jewels.

• Exempt from military duty.

Dt 24:5 — When a man hath taken a new wife, he shall not go out to war, neither shall he be charged with any business: *but* he shall be free at home one year, and shall cheer up his wife which he hath taken.

• Companions of.

Jgs 14:11 — And it came to pass, when they saw him, that they brought thirty companions to be with him.

• Joy with.

Mk 2:19–20; Lk 5:34–35

Mt 9:15 — And Jesus said unto them, Can the children of the bridechamber mourn, as long as the bridegroom is with them? but the days will come, when the bridegroom shall be taken from them, and then shall they fast.

• Parable of.

Mt 25:1–3

• Song of.

SS 4:7–16

• Figurative.

Eze 16:8–14

BRIDLE

Ps 32:9 — Be ye not as the horse, *or* as the mule, *which* have no understanding: whose mouth must be held in with bit and bridle, lest they come near unto thee.

Pr 26:3 — A whip for the horse, a bridle for the ass, and a rod for the fool's back.

Rev 14:20 — And the winepress was trodden without the city, and blood came out of the winepress, even unto the horse bridles, by the space of a thousand *and* six hundred furlongs.

• Figurative.

2Ki 19:28 — Because thy rage against me and thy tumult is come up into mine ears, therefore I will put my hook in thy nose, and my bridle in thy lips, and I will turn thee back by the way by which thou camest.

Ps 39:1 — I said, I will take heed to my ways, that I sin not with my tongue: I will keep my mouth with a bridle, while the wicked is before me.

See: Bit

BRIER

• Figurative.

Isa 5:6 — And I will lay it waste: it shall not be pruned, nor digged; but there shall come up briers and thorns: I will also command the clouds that they rain no rain upon it.

Isa 55:13 — Instead of the thorn shall come up the fir tree, and instead of the brier shall come up the myrtle tree: and it shall be to the LORD for a name, for an everlasting sign *that* shall not be cut off.

Eze 2:6 — And thou, son of man, be not afraid of them, neither be afraid of their words, though briers and thorns *be* with thee, and thou dost dwell among scorpions: be not afraid of their words, nor be dismayed at their looks, though they *be* a rebellious house.

Eze 28:24 — And there shall be no more a pricking brier unto the house of Israel, nor *any* grieving thorn of all *that are* round about them, that despised them; and they shall know that I *am* the Lord GOD.

BRIGANDINE • A coat of mail.

Jer 46:4 — Harness the horses; and get up, ye horsemen, and stand forth with *your* helmets; furbish the spears, *and* put on the brigandines.

Jer 51:3 — Against *him that* bendeth let the archer bend his bow, and against *him that* lifteth himself up in his brigandine: and spare ye not her young men; destroy ye utterly all her host.

BRIMSTONE

• Fire and, rained upon Sodom.

Ge 19:24 — Then the LORD rained upon Sodom and upon Gomorrah brimstone and fire from the LORD out of heaven;

Lk 17:29 — But the same day that Lot went out of Sodom it rained fire and brimstone from heaven, and destroyed *them* all.

• In Palestine.

Dt 29:23 — *And that* the whole land thereof *is* brimstone, and salt, *and* burning, *that* it is not sown, nor beareth, nor any grass groweth therein, like the overthrow of Sodom, and Gomorrah, Admah, and Zeboim, which the LORD overthrew in his anger, and in his wrath:

• Figurative.

Rev 9:17–18

Job 18:15 — It shall dwell in his tabernacle, because *it is* none of his: brimstone shall be scattered upon his habitation.

Ps 11:6 — Upon the wicked he shall rain snares, fire and brimstone, and an horrible tempest: *this shall be* the portion of their cup.

Isa 30:33 — For Tophet *is* ordained of old; yea, for the king it is prepared; he hath made *it* deep *and* large: the pile thereof *is* fire and much wood; the breath of the LORD, like a stream of brimstone, doth kindle it.

Eze 38:22 — And I will plead against him with pestilence and with blood; and I will rain upon him, and upon his bands, and upon the many people that *are* with him, an overflowing rain, and great hailstones, fire, and brimstone.

Rev 14:10 — The same shall drink of the wine of the wrath of God, which is poured out without mixture into the cup of his indignation; and he shall be tormented with fire and brimstone in the presence of the holy angels, and in the presence of the Lamb:

Rev 19:20 — And the beast was taken, and with him the false prophet that wrought miracles before him, with which he deceived them that had received the mark of the beast, and them that worshipped his image. These both were cast alive into a lake of fire burning with brimstone.

Rev 21:8 — But the fearful, and unbelieving, and the abominable, and murderers, and whoremongers, and sorcerers, and idolaters, and all liars, shall have their part in the lake which burneth with fire and brimstone: which is the second death.

BROOK See: River

BROTH

Jgs 6:19–20

2Ki 4:38 — And Elisha came again to Gilgal: and *there was* a dearth in the land; and the sons of the prophets *were* sitting before him: and he said unto his servant, Set on the great pot, and seethe pottage for the sons of the prophets.

Isa 65:4 — Which remain among the graves, and lodge in the monuments, which eat swine's flesh, and broth of abominable *things is in* their vessels;

• Symbolic.

Eze 24:5 — Take the choice of the flock, and burn also the bones under it, *and* make it boil well, and let them seethe the bones of it therein.

BROTHEL See: High Places

BROTHER

• Signifies a relative.

Ge 14:16 — And he brought back all the goods, and also brought again his brother Lot, and his goods, and the women also, and the people.

Ge 29:12 — And Jacob told Rachel that he *was* her father's brother, and that he *was* Rebekah's son: and she ran and told her father.

• Signifies a neighbor.

Dt 23:7 — Thou shalt not abhor an Edomite; for he *is* thy brother: thou shalt not abhor an Egyptian; because thou wast a stranger in his land.

Jgs 21:6 — And the children of Israel repented them for Benjamin their brother, and said, There is one tribe cut off from Israel this day.

Ne 5:7 — Then I consulted with myself, and I rebuked the nobles, and the rulers, and said unto them, Ye exact usury, every one of his brother. And I set a great assembly against them.

- **Signifies any Israelite.**

Jer 34:9 — That every man should let his manservant, and every man his maidservant, *being* an Hebrew or an Hebrewess, go free; that none should serve himself of them, *to wit,* of a Jew his brother.

Ob 1:10 — For *thy* violence against thy brother Jacob shame shall cover thee, and thou shalt be cut off for ever.

- **Signifies mankind.**

Ge 9:5 — And surely your blood of your lives will I require; at the hand of every beast will I require it, and at the hand of man; at the hand of every man's brother will I require the life of man.

Mt 18:35 — So likewise shall my heavenly Father do also unto you, if ye from your hearts forgive not every one his brother their trespasses.

1Jn 3:15 — Whosoever hateth his brother is a murderer: and ye know that no murderer hath eternal life abiding in him.

- **Signifies companion.**

2Sa 1:26 — I am distressed for thee, my brother Jonathan: very pleasant hast thou been unto me: thy love to me was wonderful, passing the love of women.

1Ki 13:30 — And he laid his carcase in his own grave; and they mourned over him, *saying,* Alas, my brother!

1Ki 20:33 — Now the men did diligently observe whether *any thing would come* from him, and did hastily catch *it:* and they said, Thy brother Benhadad. Then he said, Go ye, bring him. Then Benhadad came forth to him; and he caused him to come up into the chariot.

- **Love of.**

Pr 17:17 — A friend loveth at all times, and a brother is born for adversity.

Pr 18:24 — A man *that hath* friends must shew himself friendly: and there is a friend *that* sticketh closer than a brother.

SS 8:1 — O that thou *wert* as my brother, that sucked the breasts of my mother! *when* I should find thee without, I would kiss thee; yea, I should not be despised.

- **Unfaithful.**

Pr 27:10 — Thine own friend, and thy father's friend, forsake not; neither go into thy brother's house in the day of thy calamity: *for* better *is* a neighbour *that is* near than a brother far off.

- **Reuben's love for Joseph.**

Ge 37:21–22

- **Joseph's love for his brethren.**

Ge 43:30–34; 45:1–5; 50:19–25

- **A fraternal epithet, especially among Christians.**

Heb 2:11–12

- **Instituted by Christ.**

Mt 12:50 — For whosoever shall do the will of my Father which is in heaven, the same is my brother, and sister, and mother.

Mt 25:40 — And the King shall answer and say unto them, Verily I say unto you, Inasmuch as ye have done *it* unto one of the least of these my brethren, ye have done *it* unto me.

- **Used by disciples.**

Ac 9:17 — And Ananias went his way, and entered into the house; and putting his hands on him said, Brother Saul, the Lord, *even* Jesus, that appeared unto thee in the way as thou camest, hath sent me, that thou mightest receive thy sight, and be filled with the Holy Ghost.

Ac 21:20 — And when they heard *it,* they glorified the Lord, and said unto him, Thou seest, brother, how many thousands of Jews there are which believe; and they are all zealous of the law:

Ro 16:23 — Gaius mine host, and of the whole church, saluteth you. Erastus the chamberlain of the city saluteth you, and Quartus a brother.

1Co 7:12 — But to the rest speak I, not the Lord: If any brother hath a wife that believeth not, and she be pleased to dwell with him, let him not put her away.

2Co 2:13 — I had no rest in my spirit, because I found not Titus my brother: but taking my leave of them, I went from thence into Macedonia.

- **Used by Peter.**

1Pe 1:22 — Seeing ye have purified your souls in obeying the truth through the Spirit unto unfeigned love of the brethren, *see that ye* love one another with a pure heart fervently:

- **Used among the Israelites.**

Dt 22:1–4

Le 19:17 — Thou shalt not hate thy brother in thine heart: thou shalt in any wise rebuke thy neighbour, and not suffer sin upon him.

- **Brother's widow, law concerning Levite marriage of.**

Dt 25:5–10

Mt 22:24 — Saying, Master, Moses said, If a man die, having no children, his brother shall marry his wife, and raise up seed unto his brother.

Mk 12:19 — Master, Moses wrote unto us, If a man's brother die, and leave *his* wife *behind him,* and leave no children, that his brother should take his wife, and raise up seed unto his brother.

Lk 20:28 — Saying, Master, Moses wrote unto us, If any man's brother die, having a wife, and he die without children, that his brother should take his wife, and raise up seed unto his brother.

BROTHERLY KINDNESS

✦**See: Brother**

✦**See: Charitableness**

✦**See: Fellowship**

✦**See: Fraternity**

✦**See: Friendship**

✦**See: Love**

BUCKET

Nu 24:7 — He shall pour the water out of his buckets, and his seed *shall be* in many waters, and his king shall be higher than Agag, and his kingdom shall be exalted.

Isa 40:15 — Behold, the nations *are* as a drop of a bucket, and are counted as the small dust of the balance: behold, he taketh up the isles as a very little thing.

BUCKLER ✦See: Shield

BUILDER

• Of the tabernacle.

✦See: Bezaleel

✦See: Master Workman

• Figurative.

Ps 118:22 — The stone *which* the builders refused is become the head *stone* of the corner.

Mt 21:42 — Jesus saith unto them, Did ye never read in the scriptures, The stone which the builders rejected, the same is become the head of the corner: this is the Lord's doing, and it is marvellous in our eyes?

Ac 4:11 — This is the stone which was set at nought of you builders, which is become the head of the corner.

Heb 11:10 — For he looked for a city which hath foundations, whose builder and maker *is* God.

1Pe 2:7 — Unto you therefore which believe *he is* precious: but unto them which be disobedient, the stone which the builders disallowed, the same is made the head of the corner,

✦See: Carpentry

BUILDING

• Figurative.

2Co 5:1 — For we know that if our earthly house of *this* tabernacle were dissolved, we have a building of God, an house not made with hands, eternal in the heavens.

BUKKI

• Son of Abishua.

1Ch 6:5 — And Abishua begat Bukki, and Bukki begat Uzzi,

1Ch 6:41 — The son of Ethni, the son of Zerah, the son of Adaiah,

Ezr 7:4 — The son of Zerahiah, the son of Uzzi, the son of Bukki,

• A prince of Dan.

Nu 34:22 — And the prince of the tribe of the children of Dan, Bukki the son of Jogli.

BUKKIAH • A Levite.

1Ch 25:4 — Of Heman: the sons of Heman; Bukkiah, Mattaniah, Uzziel, Shebuel, and Jerimoth, Hananiah, Hanani, Eliathah, Giddalti, and Romamti-ezer, Joshbekashah, Mallothi, Hothir, *and* Mahazioth:

1Ch 25:13 — The sixth to Bukkiah, *he,* his sons, and his brethren, *were* twelve:

BUL

• The eighth month, November.

• The temple completed in.

1Ki 6:38 — And in the eleventh year, in the month Bul, which *is* the eighth month, was the house finished throughout all the parts thereof, and according to all the fashion of it. So was he seven years in building it.

• Jeroboam institutes an idolatrous feast in, to correspond with the Feast of Tabernacles.

1Ki 12:32–33

1Ch 27:11 — The eighth *captain* for the eighth month *was* Sibbecai the Hushathite, of the Zarhites: and in his course *were* twenty and four thousand.

BULL

• Wild, caught in nets.

Isa 51:20 — Thy sons have fainted, they lie at the head of all the streets, as a wild bull in a net: they are full of the fury of the LORD, the rebuke of thy God.

• Blood of, in sacrifice.

Heb 9:13 — For if the blood of bulls and of goats, and the ashes of an heifer sprinkling the unclean, sanctifieth to the purifying of the flesh:

Heb 10:4 — For *it is* not possible that the blood of bulls and of goats should take away sins.

✦See: Bullock, or ox

✦See: Offerings

BULLOCK, or ox

• Uses of.

• For sacrifice.

Ex 29:10–14; Nu 7:87–88; 28:11–29:40

Ex 29:3 — And thou shalt put them into one basket, and bring them in the basket, with the bullock and the two rams.

Ex 29:36 — And thou shalt offer every day a bullock *for* a sin offering for atonement: and thou shalt cleanse the altar, when thou hast made an atonement for it, and thou shalt anoint it, to sanctify it.

Le 4:8 — And he shall take off from it all the fat of the bullock for the sin offering; the fat that covereth the inwards, and all the fat that *is* upon the inwards,

Le 4:16 — And the priest that is anointed shall bring of the bullock's blood to the tabernacle of the congregation:

• For plowing.

1Sa 14:14 — And that first slaughter, which Jonathan and his armourbearer made, was about twenty men, within as it were an half acre of land, *which* a yoke *of oxen might plow.*

1Ki 19:19 — So he departed thence, and found Elisha the son of Shaphat, who *was* plowing *with* twelve yoke *of oxen* before him, and he with the twelfth: and Elijah passed by him, and cast his mantle upon him.

Pr 14:4 — Where no oxen *are,* the crib *is* clean: but much increase *is* by the strength of the ox.

Isa 32:20 — Blessed *are* ye that sow beside all waters, that send forth *thither* the feet of the ox and the ass.

Jer 31:18 — I have surely heard Ephraim bemoaning himself *thus;* Thou hast chastised me, and I was chastised, as a bullock unaccustomed *to the yoke:* turn thou me, and I shall be turned; for thou *art* the LORD my God.

- **For treading out corn.**

Dt 25:4 — Thou shalt not muzzle the ox when he treadeth out *the corn.*

- **With wagons.**

Nu 7:3–8; 2Sa 6:3–6

- **Laws concerning.**
- **Trespass by.**

Ex 21:28–36

- **Theft of.**

Ex 22:1–10

- **Rest for.**

Ex 23:12 — Six days thou shalt do thy work, and on the seventh day thou shalt rest: that thine ox and thine ass may rest, and the son of thy handmaid, and the stranger, may be refreshed.

- **Not to be muzzled, when treading grain.**

Dt 25:4 — Thou shalt not muzzle the ox when he treadeth out *the corn.*

1Co 9:9 — For it is written in the law of Moses, Thou shalt not muzzle the mouth of the ox that treadeth out the corn. Doth God take care for oxen?

1Ti 5:18 — For the scripture saith, Thou shalt not muzzle the ox that treadeth out the corn. And, The labourer *is* worthy of his reward.

- **Not to be yoked with an ass.**

Dt 22:10 — Thou shalt not plow with an ox and an ass together.

- **Twelve brazen, under the molten sea in Solomon's temple.**

1Ki 7:25 — It stood upon twelve oxen, three looking toward the north, and three looking toward the west, and three looking toward the south, and three looking toward the east: and the sea *was set* above upon them, and all their hinder parts *were* inward.

2Ch 4:4 — It stood upon twelve oxen, three looking toward the north, and three looking toward the west, and three looking toward the south, and three looking toward the east: and the sea *was set* above upon them, and all their hinder parts *were* inward.

Jer 52:20 — The two pillars, one sea, and twelve brasen bulls that *were* under the bases, which king Solomon had made in the house of the LORD: the brass of all these vessels was without weight.

See: Bull

See: Cattle, of the bovine species

- **Symbolic.**

Eze 1:10 — As for the likeness of their faces, they four had the face of a man, and the face of a lion, on the right side: and they four had the face of an ox on the left side; they four also had the face of an eagle.

Rev 4:7 — And the first beast *was* like a lion, and the second beast like a calf, and the third beast had a face as a man, and the fourth beast *was* like a flying eagle.

BULRUSH

- **Moses' ark of.**

Ex 2:3 — And when she could not longer hide him, she took for him an ark of bulrushes, and daubed it with slime and with pitch, and put the child therein; and she laid *it* in the flags by the river's brink.

- **Boats made of.**

Isa 18:2 — That sendeth ambassadors by the sea, even in vessels of bulrushes upon the waters, *saying,* Go, ye swift messengers, to a nation scattered and peeled, to a people terrible from their beginning hitherto; a nation meted out and trodden down, whose land the rivers have spoiled!

- **Figurative.**

Isa 58:5 — Is it such a fast that I have chosen? a day for a man to afflict his soul? *is it* to bow down his head as a bulrush, and to spread sackcloth and ashes *under him?* wilt thou call this a fast, and an acceptable day to the LORD?

BULWARK

Dt 20:20 — Only the trees which thou knowest that they *be* not trees for meat, thou shalt destroy and cut them down; and thou shalt build bulwarks against the city that maketh war with thee, until it be subdued.

2Ch 26:15 — And he made in Jerusalem engines, invented by cunning men, to be on the towers and upon the bulwarks, to shoot arrows and great stones withal. And his name spread far abroad; for he was marvellously helped, till he was strong.

Ecc 9:14 — *There was* a little city, and few men within it; and there came a great king against it, and besieged it, and built great bulwarks against it:

- **Figurative.**

Ps 48:13 — Mark ye well her bulwarks, consider her palaces; that ye may tell *it* to the generation following.

Isa 26:1 — In that day shall this song be sung in the land of Judah; We have a strong city; salvation will *God* appoint *for* walls and bulwarks.

BUNAH • Son of Jerahmeel.

1Ch 2:25 — And the sons of Jerahmeel the firstborn of Hezron were, Ram the firstborn, and Bunah, and Oren, and Ozem, *and* Ahijah.

BUNNI

- **A Levite and teacher with Ezra.**

Ne 9:4 — Then stood up upon the stairs, of the Levites, Jeshua, and Bani, Kadmiel, Shebaniah, Bunni, Sherebiah, Bani, *and* Chenani, and cried with a loud voice unto the LORD their God.

- **Ancestor of Shemaiah.**

Ne 11:15 — Also of the Levites: Shemaiah the son of Hashub, the son of Azrikam, the son of Hashabiah, the son of Bunni;

- **A family of Jews.**

Ne 10:15 — Bunni, Azgad, Bebai,

BURDEN

• Figurative.

• Of oppressions.

Isa 58:6 — *Is* not this the fast that I have chosen? to loose the bands of wickedness, to undo the heavy burdens, and to let the oppressed go free, and that ye break every yoke?

Mt 23:4 — For they bind heavy burdens and grievous to be borne, and lay *them* on men's shoulders; but they *themselves* will not move them with one of their fingers.

Lk 11:46 — And he said, Woe unto you also, *ye* lawyers! for ye lade men with burdens grievous to be borne, and ye yourselves touch not the burdens with one of your fingers.

Gal 6:2 — Bear ye one another's burdens, and so fulfil the law of Christ.

• Of the prophetic message.

Isa 13:1 — The burden of Babylon, which Isaiah the son of Amoz did see.

Isa 15:1 — The burden of Moab. Because in the night Ar of Moab is laid waste, *and* brought to silence; because in the night Kir of Moab is laid waste, *and* brought to silence;

Isa 17:1 — The burden of Damascus. Behold, Damascus is taken away from *being* a city, and it shall be a ruinous heap.

Isa 19:1 — The burden of Egypt. Behold, the LORD rideth upon a swift cloud, and shall come into Egypt: and the idols of Egypt shall be moved at his presence, and the heart of Egypt shall melt in the midst of it.

BURGLARY ↞See: Theft and Thieves

BURIAL

• Rites of.

Jer 34:5 — *But* thou shalt die in peace: and with the burnings of thy fathers, the former kings which were before thee, so shall they burn *odours* for thee; and they will lament thee, *saying,* Ah lord! for I have pronounced the word, saith the LORD.

• Soon after death.

Jn 19:38–42; Ac 5:9–10

Dt 21:23 — His body shall not remain all night upon the tree, but thou shalt in any wise bury him that day; (for he that is hanged *is* accursed of God;) that thy land be not defiled, which the LORD thy God giveth thee *for* an inheritance.

Jos 8:29 — And the king of Ai he hanged on a tree until eventide: and as soon as the sun was down, Joshua commanded that they should take his carcase down from the tree, and cast it at the entering of the gate of the city, and raise thereon a great heap of stones, *that remaineth* unto this day.

• With spices.

2Ch 16:14 — And they buried him in his own sepulchres, which he had made for himself in the city of David, and laid him in the bed which was filled with sweet odours and divers kinds *of spices* prepared by the apothecaries' art: and they made a very great burning for him.

Mk 16:1 — And when the sabbath was past, Mary Magdalene, and Mary the *mother* of James, and Salome, had bought sweet spices, that they might come and anoint him.

Lk 23:56 — And they returned, and prepared spices and ointments; and rested the sabbath day according to the commandment.

• Bier used at.

2Sa 3:31 — And David said to Joab, and to all the people that *were* with him, Rend your clothes, and gird you with sackcloth, and mourn before Abner. And king David *himself* followed the bier.

Lk 7:14 — And he came and touched the bier: and they that bare *him* stood still. And he said, Young man, I say unto thee, Arise.

• Attended by relatives and friends.

• Of Jacob.

Ge 50:5–9

• Of Abner.

2Sa 3:31 — And David said to Joab, and to all the people that *were* with him, Rend your clothes, and gird you with sackcloth, and mourn before Abner. And king David *himself* followed the bier.

• Child of Jeroboam.

1Ki 14:13 — And all Israel shall mourn for him, and bury him: for he only of Jeroboam shall come to the grave, because in him there is found *some* good thing toward the LORD God of Israel in the house of Jeroboam.

• The son of the widow of Nain.

Lk 7:12–13

• Of Stephen.

Ac 8:2 — And devout men carried Stephen *to his burial,* and made great lamentation over him.

• Lack of, a disgrace.

2Ki 9:10 — And the dogs shall eat Jezebel in the portion of Jezreel, and *there shall be* none to bury *her.* And he opened the door, and fled.

Pr 30:17 — The eye *that* mocketh at *his* father, and despiseth to obey *his* mother, the ravens of the valley shall pick it out, and the young eagles shall eat it.

Jer 16:4 — They shall die of grievous deaths; they shall not be lamented; neither shall they be buried; *but* they shall be as dung upon the face of the earth: and they shall be consumed by the sword, and by famine; and their carcases shall be meat for the fowls of heaven, and for the beasts of the earth.

Jer 22:19 — He shall be buried with the burial of an ass, drawn and cast forth beyond the gates of Jerusalem.

Eze 39:15 — And the passengers *that* pass through the land, when *any* seeth a man's bone, then shall he set up a sign by it, till the buriers have buried it in the valley of Hamon-gog.

• Directions given about, before death

• By Jacob.

Ge 49:29–30

• **By Joseph.**

Ge 50:25 — And Joseph took an oath of the children of Israel, saying, God will surely visit you, and ye shall carry up my bones from hence.

• **Burial of Gog, (multitude) requiring 7 months.**

Eze 39:12–13

• **Burying places.**

• **Bought by Abraham.**

Ge 23:1–20

Ge 25:9 — And his sons Isaac and Ishmael buried him in the cave of Machpelah, in the field of Ephron the son of Zohar the Hittite, which *is* before Mamre;

• **Prepared by.**

• **Jacob.**

Ge 50:5 — My father made me swear, saying, Lo, I die: in my grave which I have digged for me in the land of Canaan, there shalt thou bury me. Now therefore let me go up, I pray thee, and bury my father, and I will come again.

• **By Asa.**

2Ch 16:14 — And they buried him in his own sepulchres, which he had made for himself in the city of David, and laid him in the bed which was filled with sweet odours and divers kinds *of spices* prepared by the apothecaries' art: and they made a very great burning for him.

• **By Joseph.**

Mt 27:60 — And laid it in his own new tomb, which he had hewn out in the rock: and he rolled a great stone to the door of the sepulchre, and departed.

• **On hills.**

Jos 24:33 — And Eleazar the son of Aaron died; and they buried him in a hill *that pertained to* Phinehas his son, which was given him in mount Ephraim.

2Ki 23:16 — And as Josiah turned himself, he spied the sepulchres that *were* there in the mount, and sent, and took the bones out of the sepulchres, and burned *them* upon the altar, and polluted it, according to the word of the LORD which the man of God proclaimed, who proclaimed these words.

• **In valleys.**

Jer 7:32 — Therefore, behold, the days come, saith the LORD, that it shall no more be called Tophet, nor the valley of the son of Hinnom, but the valley of slaughter: for they shall bury in Tophet, till there be no place.

• **Family.**

Ge 47:30 — But I will lie with my fathers, and thou shalt carry me out of Egypt, and bury me in their buryingplace. And he said, I will do as thou hast said.

Ge 49:29 — And he charged them, and said unto them, I am to be gathered unto my people: bury me with my fathers in the cave that *is* in the field of Ephron the Hittite,

Ac 7:16 — And were carried over into Sychem, and laid in the sepulchre that Abraham bought for a sum of money of the sons of Emmor *the father* of Sychem.

• **Of kings.**

1Ki 2:10 — So David slept with his fathers, and was buried in the city of David.

2Ch 32:33 — And Hezekiah slept with his fathers, and they buried him in the chiefest of the sepulchres of the sons of David: and all Judah and the inhabitants of Jerusalem did him honour at his death. And Manasseh his son reigned in his stead.

• **A place of honor.**

2Ch 21:20 — Thirty and two years old was he when he began to reign, and he reigned in Jerusalem eight years, and departed without being desired. Howbeit they buried him in the city of David, but not in the sepulchres of the kings.

2Ch 24:16 — And they buried him in the city of David among the kings, because he had done good in Israel, both toward God, and toward his house.

2Ch 24:25 — And when they were departed from him, (for they left him in great diseases,) his own servants conspired against him for the blood of the sons of Jehoiada the priest, and slew him on his bed, and he died: and they buried him in the city of David, but they buried him not in the sepulchres of the kings.

• **For poor and strangers.**

Jer 26:23 — And they fetched forth Urijah out of Egypt, and brought him unto Jehoiakim the king; who slew him with the sword, and cast his dead body into the graves of the common people.

Mt 27:7 — And they took counsel, and bought with them the potter's field, to bury strangers in.

• **Tombs.**

• **In houses.**

1Sa 25:1 — And Samuel died; and all the Israelites were gathered together, and lamented him, and buried him in his house at Ramah. And David arose, and went down to the wilderness of Paran.

1Ki 2:34 — So Benaiah the son of Jehoiada went up, and fell upon him, and slew him: and he was buried in his own house in the wilderness.

• **In gardens.**

2Ki 21:18 — And Manasseh slept with his fathers, and was buried in the garden of his own house, in the garden of Uzza: and Amon his son reigned in his stead.

2Ki 21:26 — And he was buried in his sepulchre in the garden of Uzza: and Josiah his son reigned in his stead.

Jn 19:41 — Now in the place where he was crucified there was a garden; and in the garden a new sepulchre, wherein was never man yet laid.

• **In caves.**

Ge 23:9 — That he may give me the cave of Machpelah, which he hath, which *is* in the end of his field; for as much money as it is worth he shall give it me for a possession of a buryingplace amongst you.

• **Under trees, Deborah's.**

Ge 35:8 — But Deborah Rebekah's nurse died, and she was buried beneath Bethel under an oak: and the name of it was called Allon-bachuth.

• **King Saul's.**

1Sa 31:13 — And they took their bones, and buried *them* under a tree at Jabesh, and fasted seven days.

• **Closed with stones.**

Mt 27:60 — And laid it in his own new tomb, which he had hewn out in the rock: and he rolled a great stone to the door of the sepulchre, and departed.

Mt 27:66 — So they went, and made the sepulchre sure, sealing the stone, and setting a watch.

Jn 11:38 — Jesus therefore again groaning in himself cometh to the grave. It was a cave, and a stone lay upon it.

Jn 20:1 — The first *day* of the week cometh Mary Magdalene early, when it was yet dark, unto the sepulchre, and seeth the stone taken away from the sepulchre.

• **Sealed.**

Mt 27:66 — So they went, and made the sepulchre sure, sealing the stone, and setting a watch.

• **Marked with pillars, Rachel's.**

Ge 35:20 — And Jacob set a pillar upon her grave: that *is* the pillar of Rachel's grave unto this day.

• **Marked with pillars and inscriptions.**

2Ki 23:17 — Then he said, What title *is* that that I see? And the men of the city told him, *It is* the sepulchre of the man of God, which came from Judah, and proclaimed these things that thou hast done against the altar of Bethel.

• **Painted and garnished.**

Mt 23:27 — Woe unto you, scribes and Pharisees, hypocrites! for ye are like unto whited sepulchres, which indeed appear beautiful outward, but are within full of dead *men's* bones, and of all uncleanness.

Mt 23:29 — Woe unto you, scribes and Pharisees, hypocrites! because ye build the tombs of the prophets, and garnish the sepulchres of the righteous,

• **With shelves.**

Isa 14:15 — Yet thou shalt be brought down to hell, to the sides of the pit.

• **Demoniacs dwelt in.**

Mt 8:28 — And when he was come to the other side into the country of the Gergesenes, there met him two possessed with devils, coming out of the tombs, exceeding fierce, so that no man might pass by that way.

• **Any who touched were unclean.**

Nu 19:16 — And whosoever toucheth one that is slain with a sword in the open fields, or a dead body, or a bone of a man, or a grave, shall be unclean seven days.

Nu 19:18 — And a clean person shall take hyssop, and dip *it* in the water, and sprinkle *it* upon the tent, and upon all the vessels, and upon the persons that were there, and upon him that touched a bone, or one slain, or one dead, or a grave:

Isa 65:4 — Which remain among the graves, and lodge in the monuments, which eat swine's flesh, and broth of abominable *things is in* their vessels;

• **Refused to the dead.**

Rev 11:9 — And they of the people and kindreds and tongues and nations shall see their dead bodies three days and an half, and shall not suffer their dead bodies to be put in graves.

• **Robbed.**

Jer 8:1 — At that time, saith the LORD, they shall bring out the bones of the kings of Judah, and the bones of his princes, and the bones of the priests, and the bones of the prophets, and the bones of the inhabitants of Jerusalem, out of their graves:

See: Cremation

See: Dead

See: Death

See: Elegy

See: Grave

See: Mourning

• **Figurative.**

Isa 22:16 — What hast thou here? and whom hast thou here, that thou hast hewed thee out a sepulchre here, *as* he that heweth him out a sepulchre on high, *and* that graveth an habitation for himself in a rock?

Ro 6:4 — Therefore we are buried with him by baptism into death: that like as Christ was raised up from the dead by the glory of the Father, even so we also should walk in newness of life.

Col 2:12 — Buried with him in baptism, wherein also ye are risen with *him* through the faith of the operation of God, who hath raised him from the dead.

BURNING

• **As a punishment.**

See: Punishment

BURNING BUSH

Ex 3:2–5

Ac 7:30 — And when forty years were expired, there appeared to him in the wilderness of mount Sina an angel of the Lord in a flame of fire in a bush.

BURNT OFFERING **See: Offerings; burnt**

BUSH, BURNING **See: Burning Bush**

BUSHEL • About one peck.

Mt 5:15 — Neither do men light a candle, and put it under a bushel, but on a candlestick; and it giveth light unto all that are in the house.

Mk 4:21 — And he said unto them, Is a candle brought to be put under a bushel, or under a bed? and not to be set on a candlestick?

Lk 11:33 — No man, when he hath lighted a candle, putteth *it* in a secret place, neither under a bushel, but on a candlestick, that they which come in may see the light.

BUSYBODY

2Th 3:11–12

Le 19:16 — Thou shalt not go up and down *as* a talebearer among thy people: neither shalt thou stand against the blood of thy neighbour: I *am* the LORD.

Pr 20:3 — *It is* an honour for a man to cease from strife: but every fool will be meddling.

1Ti 5:13 — And withal they learn *to be* idle, wandering about from house to house; and not only idle, but tattlers also and busybodies, speaking things which they ought not.

1Pe 4:15 — But let none of you suffer as a murderer, or *as* a thief, or *as* an evildoer, or as a busybody in other men's matters.

See: Talebearer

See: Speaking; evil

BUTLER

• Pharaoh's, imprisoned and released.

Ge 40:1–23; Ne 1:11–2:1

1Ki 10:5 — And the meat of his table, and the sitting of his servants, and the attendance of his ministers, and their apparel, and his cupbearers, and his ascent by which he went up unto the house of the LORD; there was no more spirit in her.

2Ch 9:4 — And the meat of his table, and the sitting of his servants, and the attendance of his ministers, and their apparel; his cupbearers also, and their apparel; and his ascent by which he went up into the house of the LORD; there was no more spirit in her.

BUTTER

Ge 18:8 — And he took butter, and milk, and the calf which he had dressed, and set *it* before them; and he stood by them under the tree, and they did eat.

Dt 32:14 — Butter of kine, and milk of sheep, with fat of lambs, and rams of the breed of Bashan, and goats, with the fat of kidneys of wheat; and thou didst drink the pure blood of the grape.

Jgs 5:25 — He asked water, *and* she gave *him* milk; she brought forth butter in a lordly dish.

2Sa 17:29 — And honey, and butter, and sheep, and cheese of kine, for David, and for the people that *were* with him, to eat: for they said, The people *is* hungry, and weary, and thirsty, in the wilderness.

Job 20:17 — He shall not see the rivers, the floods, the brooks of honey and butter.

Isa 7:15 — Butter and honey shall he eat, that he may know to refuse the evil, and choose the good.

Isa 7:22 — And it shall come to pass, for the abundance of milk *that* they shall give he shall eat butter: for butter and honey shall every one eat that is left in the land.

• Made by churning.

Pr 30:33 — Surely the churning of milk bringeth forth butter, and the wringing of the nose bringeth forth blood: so the forcing of wrath bringeth forth strife.

BUZ

• Son of Nahor.

Ge 22:21 — Huz his firstborn, and Buz his brother, and Kemuel the father of Aram,

• Father of Jahdo.

1Ch 5:14 — These *are* the children of Abihail the son of Huri, the son of Jaroah, the son of Gilead, the son of Michael, the son of Jeshishai, the son of Jahdo, the son of Buz;

BUZZI • Father of Ezekiel.

Eze 1:3 — The word of the LORD came expressly unto Ezekiel the priest, the son of Buzi, in the land of the Chaldeans by the river Chebar; and the hand of the LORD was there upon him.

C

CAB

• A dry measure containing about two quarts.

2Ki 6:25 — And there was a great famine in Samaria: and, behold, they besieged it, until an ass's head was *sold* for fourscore *pieces* of silver, and the fourth part of a cab of dove's dung for five *pieces* of silver.

See: Measure

CABBON • A place in Judah.

Jos 15:40 — And Cabbon, and Lahmam, and Kithlish,

CABINET

• Heads of departments in government.

• David's.

2Sa 8:15–18; 20:23–26; 1Ch 27:32–34

2Sa 15:12 — And Absalom sent for Ahithophel the Gilonite, David's counsellor, from his city, *even* from Giloh, while he offered sacrifices. And the conspiracy was strong; for the people increased continually with Absalom.

• Solomon's.

1Ki 4:1–7

• Hezekiah's.

Isa 36:3 — Then came forth unto him Eliakim, Hilkiah's son, which was over the house, and Shebna the scribe, and Joah, Asaph's son, the recorder.

• Artaxerxes'.

Ezr 7:14 — Forasmuch as thou art sent of the king, and of his seven counsellors, to enquire concerning Judah and Jerusalem, according to the law of thy God which *is* in thine hand;

See: Counsellor

CABUL

• A city in the north of Palestine.

Jos 19:27 — And turneth toward the sunrising to Beth-dagon, and reacheth to Zebulun, and to the valley of Jiphthah-el toward the north side of Bethemek, and Neiel, and goeth out to Cabul on the left hand,

• Name given by Hiram to certain cities in Galilee.

1Ki 9:13 — And he said, What cities *are* these which thou hast given me, my brother? And he called them the land of Cabul unto this day.

CAESAR

• Augustus.

Lk 2:1 — And it came to pass in those days, that there went out a decree from Caesar Augustus, that all the world should be taxed.

• Tiberius.

Lk 3:1 — Now in the fifteenth year of the reign of Tiberius Caesar, Pontius Pilate being governor of Judaea, and Herod being tetrarch of Galilee, and his brother Philip tetrarch of Ituraea and of the region of Trachonitis, and Lysanias the tetrarch of Abilene,

Lk 20:22 — Is it lawful for us to give tribute unto Caesar, or no?

• Claudius.

Ac 11:28 — And there stood up one of them named Agabus, and signified by the spirit that there should be great dearth throughout all the world: which came to pass in the days of Claudius Caesar.

• Nero.

Php 4:22 — All the saints salute you, chiefly they that are of Caesar's household.

CAESAREA

• A seaport in Palestine.

• Home of Philip.

Ac 8:40 — But Philip was found at Azotus: and passing through he preached in all the cities, till he came to Caesarea.

Ac 21:8 — And the next *day* we that were of Paul's company departed, and came unto Caesarea: and we entered into the house of Philip the evangelist, which was *one* of the seven; and abode with him.

• Home of Cornelius, the centurion.

Ac 10:1 — There was a certain man in Caesarea called Cornelius, a centurion of the band called the Italian *band*,

Ac 10:24 — And the morrow after they entered into Caesarea. And Cornelius waited for them, and had called together his kinsmen and near friends.

• Home of Herod.

Ac 12:19–23

• Home of Felix.

Ac 23:23–24

• Paul conveyed to, by the disciples to save him from his enemies.

Ac 9:30 — *Which* when the brethren knew, they brought him down to Caesarea, and sent him forth to Tarsus.

• Paul conveyed to, by Roman soldiers to be tried by Felix.

Ac 23:23–25

CAESAREA PHILIPPI

• A city in the north of Palestine.

• Visited by Jesus.

Mt 16:13 — When Jesus came into the coasts of Caesarea Philippi, he asked his disciples, saying, Whom do men say that I the Son of man am?

Mk 8:27 — And Jesus went out, and his disciples, into the towns of Caesarea Philippi: and by the way he asked his disciples, saying unto them, Whom do men say that I am?

Lk 9:18 — And it came to pass, as he was alone praying, his disciples were with him: and he asked them, saying, Whom say the people that I am?

CAGE

• For birds, unclean.

Jer 5:27 — As a cage is full of birds, so *are* their houses full of deceit: therefore they are become great, and waxen rich.

Rev 18:2 — And he cried mightily with a strong voice, saying, Babylon the great is fallen, is fallen, and is become the habitation of devils, and the hold of every foul spirit, and a cage of every unclean and hateful bird.

CAIAPHAS

• High priest.

Lk 3:2 — Annas and Caiaphas being the high priests, the word of God came unto John the son of Zacharias in the wilderness.

• Son-in-law of Annas.

Jn 18:13 — And led him away to Annas first; for he was father in law to Caiaphas, which was the high priest that same year.

• Prophesies concerning Jesus.

Jn 11:49–51

Jn 18:14 — Now Caiaphas was he, which gave counsel to the Jews, that it was expedient that one man should die for the people.

• Jesus tried before.

Mt 26:2–3; 26:63–65

Mt 26:57 — And they that had laid hold on Jesus led *him* away to Caiaphas the high priest, where the scribes and the elders were assembled.

Jn 18:24 — Now Annas had sent him bound unto Caiaphas the high priest.

Jn 18:28 — Then led they Jesus from Caiaphas unto the hall of judgment: and it was early; and they themselves went not into the judgment hall, lest they should be defiled; but that they might eat the passover.

• Peter and other disciples accused before.

Ac 4:1–22

CAIN

• Son of Adam.

Ge 4:1 — And Adam knew Eve his wife; and she conceived, and bare Cain, and said, I have gotten a man from the LORD.

• Jealousy and crime of.

Ge 4:3–15

Heb 11:4 — By faith Abel offered unto God a more excellent sacrifice than Cain, by which he obtained witness that he was righteous, God testifying of his gifts: and by it he being dead yet speaketh.

1Jn 3:12 — Not as Cain, *who* was of that wicked one, and slew his brother. And wherefore slew he him? Because his own works were evil, and his brother's righteous.

Jude 1:11 — Woe unto them! for they have gone in the way of Cain, and ran greedily after the error of Balaam for reward, and perished in the gainsaying of Core.

• Sojourns in the land of Nod.

Ge 4:16 — And Cain went out from the presence of the LORD, and dwelt in the land of Nod, on the east of Eden.

• Children and descendants of.

Ge 4:17–18

• A city of Judah.

Jos 15:57 — Cain, Gibeah, and Timnah; ten cities with their villages:

CAINAN

• Called also Kenan.

• Son of Enos.

Ge 5:9–15

1Ch 1:2 — Kenan, Mahalaleel, Jered,

Lk 3:37 — Which was *the son* of Mathusala, which was *the son* of Enoch, which was *the son* of Jared, which was *the son* of Maleleel, which was *the son* of Cainan,

• Son of Arphaxad.

Lk 3:36 — Which was *the son* of Cainan, which was *the son* of Arphaxad, which was *the son* of Sem, which was *the son* of Noe, which was *the son* of Lamech,

CALAH • An ancient city of Assyria.

Ge 10:11–12

CALAMUS

• A sweet cane of Palestine.

SS 4:14 — Spikenard and saffron; calamus and cinnamon, with all trees of frankincense; myrrh and aloes, with all the chief spices:

Eze 27:19 — Dan also and Javan going to and fro occupied in thy fairs: bright iron, cassia, and calamus, were in thy market.

• An ingredient of the holy ointment.

Ex 30:23 — Take thou also unto thee principal spices, of pure myrrh five hundred *shekels,* and of sweet cinnamon half so much, *even* two hundred and fifty *shekels,* and of sweet calamus two hundred and fifty *shekels,*

Isa 43:24 — Thou hast bought me no sweet cane with money, neither hast thou filled me with the fat of thy sacrifices: but thou hast made me to serve with thy sins, thou hast wearied me with thine iniquities.

• Commerce in.

Jer 6:20 — To what purpose cometh there to me incense from Sheba, and the sweet cane from a far country? your burnt offerings *are* not acceptable, nor your sacrifices sweet unto me.

Eze 27:19 — Dan also and Javan going to and fro occupied in thy fairs: bright iron, cassia, and calamus, were in thy market.

CALCOL • Son of Zerah.

1Ch 2:6 — And the sons of Zerah; Zimri, and Ethan, and Heman, and Calcol, and Dara: five of them in all.

CALDRON

• In the tabernacle.

1Sa 2:14 — And he struck *it* into the pan, or kettle, or caldron, or pot; all that the fleshhook brought up the priest took for himself. So they did in Shiloh unto all the Israelites that came thither.

• In the temple.

Jer 52:18–19

2Ch 35:13 — And they roasted the passover with fire according to the ordinance: but the *other* holy *offerings* sod they in pots, and in caldrons, and in pans, and divided *them* speedily among all the people.

• Figurative.

Eze 11:3–11

CALEB

• One of the two survivors of the Israelites permitted to enter the land of promise.

Nu 26:63–65; 32:11–13; Dt 1:34–36; Jos 14:6–15

Nu 14:30 — Doubtless ye shall not come into the land, *concerning* which I sware to make you dwell therein, save Caleb the son of Jephunneh, and Joshua the son of Nun.

Nu 14:38 — But Joshua the son of Nun, and Caleb the son of Jephunneh, *which were* of the men that went to search the land, lived *still.*

• Sent to Canaan as a spy.

Nu 13:6 — Of the tribe of Judah, Caleb the son of Jephunneh

• Brings favorable report.

Nu 13:26–30; 14:6–9

• Assists in dividing Canaan.

Nu 34:19 — And the names of the men *are* these: Of the tribe of Judah, Caleb the son of Jephunneh

• Life of, miraculously saved.

Nu 14:10–12

• Leader of the Israelites after Joshua's death.

Jgs 1:11–12

• Age of.

Jos 14:7–10

• Inheritance of.

Jos 14:6–15; 15:13–16

• Descendants of.

1Ch 4:15 — And the sons of Caleb the son of Jephunneh; Iru, Elah, and Naam: and the sons of Elah, even Kenaz.

CALEB-EPHRATAH • A place near Bethlehem.

1Ch 2:24 — And after that Hezron was dead in Caleb-ephratah, then Abiah Hezron's wife bare him Ashur the father of Tekoa.

CALF

• Offered in sacrifice.

Mic 6:6 — Wherewith shall I come before the LORD, *and* bow myself before the high God? shall I come before him with burnt offerings, with calves of a year old?

• Golden, made by Aaron.

Ex 32:1–35

Dt 9:16 — And I looked, and, behold, ye had sinned against the LORD your God, *and* had made you a molten calf: ye had turned aside quickly out of the way which the LORD had commanded you.

Ne 9:18 — Yea, when they had made them a molten calf, and said, This *is* thy God that brought thee up out of Egypt, and had wrought great provocations;

Ps 106:19 — They made a calf in Horeb, and worshipped the molten image.

Ac 7:41 — And they made a calf in those days, and offered sacrifice unto the idol, and rejoiced in the works of their own hands.

• Images of, set up in Bethel and Dan by Jeroboam.

1Ki 12:28–33

2Ki 10:29 — Howbeit *from* the sins of Jeroboam the son of Nebat, who made Israel to sin, Jehu departed not from after them, *to wit,* the golden calves that *were* in Bethel, and that *were* in Dan.

• Worshiped by Jehu.

2Ki 10:29 — Howbeit *from* the sins of Jeroboam the son of Nebat, who made Israel to sin, Jehu departed not from after them, *to wit,* the golden calves that *were* in Bethel, and that *were* in Dan.

• Prophecies against the golden calves at Bethel.

1Ki 13:1–5; Hos 8:5–6; 10:5–6

1Ki 13:32 — For the saying which he cried by the word of the LORD against the altar in Bethel, and against all the houses of the high places which *are* in the cities of Samaria, shall surely come to pass.

Jer 48:13 — And Moab shall be ashamed of Chemosh, as the house of Israel was ashamed of Bethel their confidence.

Hos 10:15 — So shall Bethel do unto you because of your great wickedness: in a morning shall the king of Israel utterly be cut off.

Hos 13:2 — And now they sin more and more, and have made them molten images of their silver, *and* idols according to their own understanding, all of it the work of the craftsmen: they say of them, Let the men that sacrifice kiss the calves.

Am 3:14 — That in the day that I shall visit the transgressions of Israel upon him I will also visit the altars of Bethel: and the horns of the altar shall be cut off, and fall to the ground.

Am 4:4 — Come to Bethel, and transgress; at Gilgal multiply transgression; and bring your sacrifices every morning, *and* your tithes after three years:

Am 8:14 — They that swear by the sin of Samaria, and say, Thy god, O Dan, liveth; and, The manner of

Beer-sheba liveth; even they shall fall, and never rise up again.

- **Altars of, destroyed.**

2Ki 23:15–20

2Ki 23:4 — And the king commanded Hilkiah the high priest, and the priests of the second order, and the keepers of the door, to bring forth out of the temple of the LORD all the vessels that were made for Baal, and for the grove, and for all the host of heaven: and he burned them without Jerusalem in the fields of Kidron, and carried the ashes of them unto Bethel.

- **"Calves of the lips," a metaphor signifying worship.**

Hos 14:2 — Take with you words, and turn to the LORD: say unto him, Take away all iniquity, and receive *us* graciously: so will we render the calves of our lips.

CALKERS

Eze 27:9 — The ancients of Gebal and the wise *men* thereof were in thee thy calkers: all the ships of the sea with their mariners were in thee to occupy thy merchandise.

Eze 27:27 — Thy riches, and thy fairs, thy merchandise, thy mariners, and thy pilots, thy calkers, and the occupiers of thy merchandise, and all thy men of war, that *are* in thee, and in all thy company which *is* in the midst of thee, shall fall into the midst of the seas in the day of thy ruin.

CALL, Personal

- **By Christ.**

Isa 55:5 — Behold, thou shalt call a nation *that* thou knowest not, and nations *that* knew not thee shall run unto thee because of the LORD thy God, and for the Holy One of Israel; for he hath glorified thee.

Ro 1:6 — Among whom are ye also the called of Jesus Christ:

- **By his Spirit.**

Rev 22:17 — And the Spirit and the bride say, Come. And let him that heareth say, Come. And let him that is athirst come. And whosoever will, let him take the water of life freely.

- **By his works.**

Ps 19:2–3

Ro 1:20 — For the invisible things of him from the creation of the world are clearly seen, being understood by the things that are made, *even* his eternal power and Godhead; so that they are without excuse:

- **By his ministers.**

Jer 35:15 — I have sent also unto you all my servants the prophets, rising up early and sending *them,* saying, Return ye now every man from his evil way, and amend your doings, and go not after other gods to serve them, and ye shall dwell in the land which I have given to you and to your fathers: but ye have not inclined your ear, nor hearkened unto me.

2Co 5:20 — Now then we are ambassadors for Christ, as though God did beseech *you* by us: we pray *you* in Christ's stead, be ye reconciled to God.

- **By his gospel.**

2Th 2:14 — Whereunto he called you by our gospel, to the obtaining of the glory of our Lord Jesus Christ.

- **Is from darkness to light.**

1Pe 2:9 — But ye *are* a chosen generation, a royal priesthood, an holy nation, a peculiar people; that ye should shew forth the praises of him who hath called you out of darkness into his marvellous light:

- **Addressed to all.**

Isa 45:22 — Look unto me, and be ye saved, all the ends of the earth: for I *am* God, and *there is* none else.

Mt 20:16 — <u>So the last shall be first, and the first last: for many be called, but few chosen.</u>

- **Most reject.**

Pr 1:24 — Because I have called, and ye refused; I have stretched out my hand, and no man regarded;

Mt 20:16 — <u>So the last shall be first, and the first last: for many be called, but few chosen.</u>

- **Effectual to saints.**

Ps 110:3 — Thy people *shall be* willing in the day of thy power, in the beauties of holiness from the womb of the morning: thou hast the dew of thy youth.

Ac 13:48 — And when the Gentiles heard this, they were glad, and glorified the word of the Lord: and as many as were ordained to eternal life believed.

1Co 1:24 — But unto them which are called, both Jews and Greeks, Christ the power of God, and the wisdom of God.

- **Not to many wise.**

1Co 1:26 — For ye see your calling, brethren, how that not many wise men after the flesh, not many mighty, not many noble, *are called:*

- **To saints, is of grace.**

Gal 1:6 — I marvel that ye are so soon removed from him that called you into the grace of Christ unto another gospel:

2Ti 1:9 — Who hath saved us, and called *us* with an holy calling, not according to our works, but according to his own purpose and grace, which was given us in Christ Jesus before the world began,

- **To saints, according to the purpose of God.**

Ro 9:23–24

Ro 8:28 — And we know that all things work together for good to them that love God, to them who are the called according to *his* purpose.

Ro 9:11 — (For *the children* being not yet born, neither having done any good or evil, that the purpose of God according to election might stand, not of works, but of him that calleth;)

- **To saints, without repentance.**

Ro 11:29 — For the gifts and calling of God *are* without repentance.

- **To saints, high.**

Php 3:14 — I press toward the mark for the prize of the high calling of God in Christ Jesus.

- **To saints, holy.**

2Ti 1:9 — Who hath saved us, and called *us* with an holy calling, not according to our works, but according to his own purpose and grace, which was given us in Christ Jesus before the world began,

- **To saints, heavenly.**

Heb 3:1 — Wherefore, holy brethren, partakers of the heavenly calling, consider the Apostle and High Priest of our profession, Christ Jesus;

- **To saints, to fellowship with Christ.**

1Co 1:9 — God *is* faithful, by whom ye were called unto the fellowship of his Son Jesus Christ our Lord.

- **To saints, holiness.**

1Th 4:7 — For God hath not called us unto uncleanness, but unto holiness.

- **To saints, to a price.**

Php 3:14 — I press toward the mark for the prize of the high calling of God in Christ Jesus.

- **To saints, to liberty.**

Gal 5:13 — For, brethren, ye have been called unto liberty; only *use* not liberty for an occasion to the flesh, but by love serve one another.

- **To saints, to peace.**

1Co 7:15 — But if the unbelieving depart, let him depart. A brother or a sister is not under bondage in such *cases:* but God hath called us to peace.

Col 3:15 — And let the peace of God rule in your hearts, to the which also ye are called in one body; and be ye thankful.

- **To saints, to glory and virtue.**

2Pe 1:3 — According as his divine power hath given unto us all things that *pertain* unto life and godliness, through the knowledge of him that hath called us to glory and virtue:

- **To saints, to the eternal glory of Christ.**

2Th 2:14 — Whereunto he called you by our gospel, to the obtaining of the glory of our Lord Jesus Christ.

1Pe 5:10 — But the God of all grace, who hath called us unto his eternal glory by Christ Jesus, after that ye have suffered a while, make you perfect, stablish, strengthen, settle *you.*

- **To saints, to eternal life.**

1Ti 6:12 — Fight the good fight of faith, lay hold on eternal life, whereunto thou art also called, and hast professed a good profession before many witnesses.

- **Partakers of, justified.**

Ro 8:30 — Moreover whom he did predestinate, them he also called: and whom he called, them he also justified: and whom he justified, them he also glorified.

- **Walk worthy of.**

Eph 4:1 — I therefore, the prisoner of the Lord, beseech you that ye walk worthy of the vocation wherewith ye are called,

2Th 1:11 — Wherefore also we pray always for you, that our God would count you worthy of *this* calling, and fulfil all the good pleasure of *his* goodness, and the work of faith with power:

- **Blessedness of receiving.**

Rev 19:9 — And he saith unto me, Write, Blessed *are* they which are called unto the marriage supper of the Lamb. And he saith unto me, These are the true sayings of God.

- **To be made sure.**

2Pe 1:10 — Wherefore the rather, brethren, give diligence to make your calling and election sure: for if ye do these things, ye shall never fall:

- **Praise God for.**

1Pe 2:9 — But ye *are* a chosen generation, a royal priesthood, an holy nation, a peculiar people; that ye should shew forth the praises of him who hath called you out of darkness into his marvellous light:

- **Illustrated.**

Pr 8:3–4; Mt 23:3–9

- **Rejection of, leads to judicial blindness.**

Ac 28:24–27; Ro 11:8–10

Isa 6:9 — And he said, Go, and tell this people, Hear ye indeed, but understand not; and see ye indeed, but perceive not.

- **Delusion.**

2Th 2:10–11

Isa 66:4 — I also will choose their delusions, and will bring their fears upon them; because when I called, none did answer; when I spake, they did not hear: but they did evil before mine eyes, and chose *that* in which I delighted not.

- **Withdrawal of the means of grace.**

Jer 26:4–6

Ac 13:46 — Then Paul and Barnabas waxed bold, and said, It was necessary that the word of God should first have been spoken to you: but seeing ye put it from you, and judge yourselves unworthy of everlasting life, lo, we turn to the Gentiles.

Ac 18:6 — And when they opposed themselves, and blasphemed, he shook *his* raiment, and said unto them, Your blood *be* upon your own heads; I *am* clean: from henceforth I will go unto the Gentiles.

Rev 2:5 — Remember therefore from whence thou art fallen, and repent, and do the first works; or else I will come unto thee quickly, and will remove thy candlestick out of his place, except thou repent.

- **Temporal judgments.**

Zec 7:12–14

Isa 28:12 — To whom he said, This *is* the rest *wherewith* ye may cause the weary to rest; and this *is* the refreshing: yet they would not hear.

Jer 6:16 — Thus saith the LORD, Stand ye in the ways, and see, and ask for the old paths, where is the good way, and walk therein, and ye shall find rest for your souls. But they said, We will not walk *therein.*

Jer 6:19 — Hear, O earth: behold, I will bring evil upon this people, *even* the fruit of their thoughts, because they have not hearkened unto my words, nor to my law, but rejected it.

Jer 35:17 — Therefore thus saith the LORD God of hosts, the God of Israel; Behold, I will bring upon Judah and upon all the inhabitants of Jerusalem all the evil that I have pronounced against them: because I have spoken unto them, but they have not heard; and I have called unto them, but they have not answered.

- **Rejection by God.**

Pr 1:24–32

Jer 6:19 — Hear, O earth: behold, I will bring evil upon this people, *even* the fruit of their thoughts, because they have not hearkened unto my words, nor to my law, but rejected it.

Jer 6:30 — Reprobate silver shall *men* call them, because the LORD hath rejected them.

• Condemnation.

Heb 2:1–3

Jn 12:48 — He that rejecteth me, and receiveth not my words, hath one that judgeth him: the word that I have spoken, the same shall judge him in the last day.

Heb 12:25 — See that ye refuse not him that speaketh. For if they escaped not who refused him that spake on earth, much more *shall not* we *escape*, if we turn away from him that *speaketh* from heaven:

• Destruction.

Mt 22:3–7

Pr 29:1 — He, that being often reproved hardeneth *his* neck, shall suddenly be destroyed, and that without remedy.

CALL, Special Religious Duty

• Of Abraham.

Ge 12:1 — Now the LORD had said unto Abram, Get thee out of thy country, and from thy kindred, and from thy father's house, unto a land that I will shew thee:

Isa 51:2 — Look unto Abraham your father, and unto Sarah *that* bare you: for I called him alone, and blessed him, and increased him.

Heb 11:8 — By faith Abraham, when he was called to go out into a place which he should after receive for an inheritance, obeyed; and he went out, not knowing whither he went.

• Moses.

Ex 4:1–16; Ac 7:34–35

Ex 3:2 — And the angel of the LORD appeared unto him in a flame of fire out of the midst of a bush: and he looked, and, behold, the bush burned with fire, and the bush *was* not consumed.

Ex 3:4 — And when the LORD saw that he turned aside to see, God called unto him out of the midst of the bush, and said, Moses, Moses. And he said, Here *am* I.

Ex 3:10 — Come now therefore, and I will send thee unto Pharaoh, that thou mayest bring forth my people the children of Israel out of Egypt.

Ps 105:26 — He sent Moses his servant; *and* Aaron whom he had chosen.

• Aaron and his sons.

Ex 4:14–16

Ex 28:1 — And take thou unto thee Aaron thy brother, and his sons with him, from among the children of Israel, that he may minister unto me in the priest's office, *even* Aaron, Nadab and Abihu, Eleazar and Ithamar, Aaron's sons.

Ps 105:26 — He sent Moses his servant; *and* Aaron whom he had chosen.

Heb 5:4 — And no man taketh this honour unto himself, but he that is called of God, as *was* Aaron.

✳See: Moses

• Joshua.

Nu 27:18–19, 22–23; Jos 1:1–9

Dt 31:14 — And the LORD said unto Moses, Behold, thy days approach that thou must die: call Joshua, and present yourselves in the tabernacle of the congregation, that I may give him a charge. And Moses and Joshua went, and presented themselves in the tabernacle of the congregation.

Dt 31:23 — And he gave Joshua the son of Nun a charge, and said, Be strong and of a good courage: for thou shalt bring the children of Israel into the land which I sware unto them: and I will be with thee.

• Gideon.

Jgs 6:11–16

• Samuel.

1Sa 3:4–10

• Solomon.

1Ch 28:6 — And he said unto me, Solomon thy son, he shall build my house and my courts: for I have chosen him *to be* my son, and I will be his father.

1Ch 28:10 — Take heed now; for the LORD hath chosen thee to build an house for the sanctuary: be strong, and do *it*.

• Jehu.

2Ki 9:6–7

2Ch 22:7 — And the destruction of Ahaziah was of God by coming to Joram: for when he was come, he went out with Jehoram against Jehu the son of Nimshi, whom the LORD had anointed to cut off the house of Ahab.

• Cyrus.

Isa 45:1–4

• Amos.

Am 7:14–15

• Apostles.

Mt 4:18–22; Mk 1:16–17; 3:13–19; Lk 6:13–15

Mt 9:9 — And as Jesus passed forth from thence, he saw a man, named Matthew, sitting at the receipt of custom: and he saith unto him, Follow me. And he arose, and followed him.

Mk 2:14 — And as he passed by, he saw Levi the *son* of Alphaeus sitting at the receipt of custom, and said unto him, Follow me. And he arose and followed him.

Lk 5:27 — And after these things he went forth, and saw a publican, named Levi, sitting at the receipt of custom: and he said unto him, Follow me.

Jn 15:16 — Ye have not chosen me, but I have chosen you, and ordained you, that ye should go and bring forth fruit, and *that* your fruit should remain: that whatsoever ye shall ask of the Father in my name, he may give it you.

• The rich young man.

Mk 10:21–22

• Paul.

Ac 9:4–6, 15–16; 13:2–3

Ro 1:1 — Paul, a servant of Jesus Christ, called *to be* an apostle, separated unto the gospel of God,

1Co 1:1 — Paul, called *to be* an apostle of Jesus Christ through the will of God, and Sosthenes *our* brother,

2Co 1:1 — Paul, an apostle of Jesus Christ by the will of God, and Timothy *our* brother, unto the church of God which is at Corinth, with all the saints which are in all Achaia:

Gal 1:1 — Paul, an apostle, (not of men, neither by man, but by Jesus Christ, and God the Father, who raised him from the dead;)

Eph 1:1 — Paul, an apostle of Jesus Christ by the will of God, to the saints which are at Ephesus, and to the faithful in Christ Jesus:

Col 1:1 — Paul, an apostle of Jesus Christ by the will of God, and Timotheus *our* brother,

1Ti 1:1 — Paul, an apostle of Jesus Christ by the commandment of God our Saviour, and Lord Jesus Christ, *which is* our hope;

2Ti 1:1 — Paul, an apostle of Jesus Christ by the will of God, according to the promise of life which is in Christ Jesus,

• All who are called of God.

1Th 2:11–12; 2Th 2:13–14; Heb 3:1–2, 7–8

Ro 8:30 — Moreover whom he did predestinate, them he also called: and whom he called, them he also justified: and whom he justified, them he also glorified.

1Co 1:2 — Unto the church of God which is at Corinth, to them that are sanctified in Christ Jesus, called *to be* saints, with all that in every place call upon the name of Jesus Christ our Lord, both theirs and ours:

1Co 1:9 — God *is* faithful, by whom ye were called unto the fellowship of his Son Jesus Christ our Lord.

1Co 1:24 — But unto them which are called, both Jews and Greeks, Christ the power of God, and the wisdom of God.

2Ti 1:9 — Who hath saved us, and called *us* with an holy calling, not according to our works, but according to his own purpose and grace, which was given us in Christ Jesus before the world began,

1Pe 5:10 — But the God of all grace, who hath called us unto his eternal glory by Christ Jesus, after that ye have suffered a while, make you perfect, stablish, strengthen, settle *you.*

2Pe 1:3 — According as his divine power hath given unto us all things that *pertain* unto life and godliness, through the knowledge of him that hath called us to glory and virtue:

2Pe 1:10 — Wherefore the rather, brethren, give diligence to make your calling and election sure: for if ye do these things, ye shall never fall:

Jude 1:1 — Jude, the servant of Jesus Christ, and brother of James, to them that are sanctified by God the Father, and preserved in Jesus Christ, *and* called:

Rev 17:14 — These shall make war with the Lamb, and the Lamb shall overcome them: for he is Lord of lords, and King of kings: and they that are with him *are* called, and chosen, and faithful.

See: Minister, a sacred teacher; call of

See: Backsliders

See: Seekers

CALNEH

• Called also Canneh and Calno.

• A city of Assyria.

Ge 10:10 — And the beginning of his kingdom was Babel, and Erech, and Accad, and Calneh, in the land of Shinar.

Isa 10:9 — *Is* not Calno as Carchemish? *is* not Hamath as Arpad? *is* not Samaria as Damascus?

Eze 27:23 — Haran, and Canneh, and Eden, the merchants of Sheba, Asshur, *and* Chilmad, *were* thy merchants.

Am 6:2 — Pass ye unto Calneh, and see; and from thence go ye to Hamath the great: then go down to Gath of the Philistines: *be they* better than these kingdoms? or their border greater than your border?

CALVARY

• Called also Golgotha.

• Place where Jesus was crucified.

Mt 27:33 — And when they were come unto a place called Golgotha, that is to say, a place of a skull,

Mk 15:22 — And they bring him unto the place Golgotha, which is, being interpreted, The place of a skull.

Lk 23:33 — And when they were come to the place, which is called Calvary, there they crucified him, and the malefactors, one on the right hand, and the other on the left.

Jn 19:17 — And he bearing his cross went forth into a place called *the place* of a skull, which is called in the Hebrew Golgotha:

CAMEL

• Herds of.

Ge 12:16 — And he entreated Abram well for her sake: and he had sheep, and oxen, and he asses, and menservants, and maidservants, and she asses, and camels.

Ge 24:35 — And the LORD hath blessed my master greatly; and he is become great: and he hath given him flocks, and herds, and silver, and gold, and menservants, and maidservants, and camels, and asses.

Ge 30:43 — And the man increased exceedingly, and had much cattle, and maidservants, and menservants, and camels, and asses.

1Sa 30:17 — And David smote them from the twilight even unto the evening of the next day: and there escaped not a man of them, save four hundred young men, which rode upon camels, and fled.

1Ch 27:30 — Over the camels also was Obil the Ishmaelite: and over the asses *was* Jehdeiah the Meronothite:

Job 1:3 — His substance also was seven thousand sheep, and three thousand camels, and five hundred yoke of oxen, and five hundred she asses, and a very great household; so that this man was the greatest of all the men of the east.

Job 1:17 — While he *was* yet speaking, there came also another, and said, The Chaldeans made out three bands, and fell upon the camels, and have carried them away, yea, and slain the servants with the edge of the sword; and I only am escaped alone to tell thee.

Isa 60:6 — The multitude of camels shall cover thee, the dromedaries of Midian and Ephah; all they from Sheba shall come: they shall bring gold and incense; and they shall shew forth the praises of the LORD.

• Docility of.

Ge 24:11 — And he made his camels to kneel down without the city by a well of water at the time of the evening, *even* the time that women go out to draw *water.*

• Uses of.

• For riding.

Ge 24:10 — And the servant took ten camels of the camels of his master, and departed; for all the goods of his master *were* in his hand: and he arose, and went to Mesopotamia, unto the city of Nahor.

Ge 24:61 — And Rebekah arose, and her damsels, and they rode upon the camels, and followed the man: and the servant took Rebekah, and went his way.

Ge 24:64 — And Rebekah lifted up her eyes, and when she saw Isaac, she lighted off the camel.

Ge 31:17 — Then Jacob rose up, and set his sons and his wives upon camels;

• For posts.

Est 8:10 — And he wrote in the king Ahasuerus' name, and sealed it with the king's ring, and sent letters by posts on horseback, *and* riders on mules, camels, *and* young dromedaries:

Est 8:14 — *So* the posts that rode upon mules *and* camels went out, being hastened and pressed on by the king's commandment. And the decree was given at Shushan the palace.

Jer 2:23 — How canst thou say, I am not polluted, I have not gone after Baalim? see thy way in the valley, know what thou hast done: *thou art* a swift dromedary traversing her ways;

• For drawing chariots.

Isa 21:7 — And he saw a chariot *with* a couple of horsemen, a chariot of asses, *and* a chariot of camels; and he hearkened diligently with much heed:

• For carrying burdens.

Ge 24:10 — And the servant took ten camels of the camels of his master, and departed; for all the goods of his master *were* in his hand: and he arose, and went to Mesopotamia, unto the city of Nahor.

Ge 37:25 — And they sat down to eat bread: and they lifted up their eyes and looked, and, behold, a company of Ishmeelites came from Gilead with their camels bearing spicery and balm and myrrh, going to carry *it* down to Egypt.

1Ki 10:2 — And she came to Jerusalem with a very great train, with camels that bare spices, and very much gold, and precious stones: and when she was come to Solomon, she communed with him of all that was in her heart.

2Ki 8:9 — So Hazael went to meet him, and took a present with him, even of every good thing of Damascus, forty camels' burden, and came and stood before him, and said, Thy son Ben-hadad king of Syria hath sent me to thee, saying, Shall I recover of this disease?

1Ch 12:40 — Moreover they that were nigh them, *even* unto Issachar and Zebulun and Naphtali, brought bread on asses, and on camels, and on mules, and on oxen, *and* meat, meal, cakes of figs, and bunches of raisins, and wine, and oil, and oxen, and sheep abundantly: for *there was* joy in Israel.

Isa 30:6 — The burden of the beasts of the south: into the land of trouble and anguish, from whence *come* the young and old lion, the viper and fiery flying serpent, they will carry their riches upon the shoulders of young asses, and their treasures upon the bunches of camels, to a people *that* shall not profit *them.*

• For cavalry.

1Sa 30:17 — And David smote them from the twilight even unto the evening of the next day: and there escaped not a man of them, save four hundred young men, which rode upon camels, and fled.

• For milk.

Ge 32:15 — Thirty milch camels with their colts, forty kine, and ten bulls, twenty she asses, and ten foals.

• Forbidden as food.

Le 11:4 — Nevertheless these shall ye not eat of them that chew the cud, or of them that divide the hoof: *as* the camel, because he cheweth the cud, but divideth not the hoof; he is unclean unto you.

• Hair of, made into cloth.

Mt 3:4 — And the same John had his raiment of camel's hair, and a leathern girdle about his loins; and his meat was locusts and wild honey.

Mk 1:6 — And John was clothed with camel's hair, and with a girdle of a skin about his loins; and he did eat locusts and wild honey;

• Ornaments of.

Jgs 8:21 — Then Zebah and Zalmunna said, Rise thou, and fall upon us: for as the man *is, so is* his strength. And Gideon arose, and slew Zebah and Zalmunna, and took away the ornaments that *were* on their camels' necks.

Jgs 8:26 — And the weight of the golden earrings that he requested was a thousand and seven hundred *shekels* of gold; beside ornaments, and collars, and purple raiment that *was* on the kings of Midian, and beside the chains that *were* about their camels' necks.

• Stables for.

Eze 25:5 — And I will make Rabbah a stable for camels, and the Ammonites a couchingplace for flocks: and ye shall know that I *am* the LORD.

CAMON • Place where Jair was buried.

Jgs 10:5 — And Jair died, and was buried in Camon.

CAMP

• Of the Israelites about the tabernacle.

Nu 2:1–3:51

See: Itinerary

CAMPHIRE • A shrub bearing fragrant flowers, not related to camphor.

SS 1:14 — My beloved *is* unto me *as* a cluster of camphire in the vineyards of En-gedi.

SS 4:13 — Thy plants *are* an orchard of pomegranates, with pleasant fruits; camphire, with spikenard,

CANA

• Marriage at.

Jn 2:1–11

• Nobleman's son healed at.

Jn 4:46–47

• Nathanael's home at.

Jn 21:2 — There were together Simon Peter, and Thomas called Didymus, and Nathanael of Cana in Galilee, and the *sons* of Zebedee, and two other of his disciples.

CANAAN

• Son of Ham.

Ge 9:25–27

Ge 9:18 — And the sons of Noah, that went forth of the ark, were Shem, and Ham, and Japheth: and Ham is the father of Canaan.

Ge 9:22 — And Ham, the father of Canaan, saw the nakedness of his father, and told his two brethren without.

• Descendants of.

Ge 10:6 — And the sons of Ham; Cush, and Mizraim, and Phut, and Canaan.

Ge 10:15 — And Canaan begat Sidon his firstborn, and Heth,

1Ch 1:8 — The sons of Ham; Cush, and Mizraim, Put, and Canaan.

1Ch 1:13 — And Canaan begat Zidon his firstborn, and Heth,

• Land of.

Ge 11:31 — And Terah took Abram his son, and Lot the son of Haran his son's son, and Sarai his daughter in law, his son Abram's wife; and they went forth with them from Ur of the Chaldees, to go into the land of Canaan; and they came unto Haran, and dwelt there.

Ge 17:8 — And I will give unto thee, and to thy seed after thee, the land wherein thou art a stranger, all the land of Canaan, for an everlasting possession; and I will be their God.

Ge 23:2 — And Sarah died in Kirjath-arba; the same *is* Hebron in the land of Canaan: and Abraham came to mourn for Sarah, and to weep for her.

See: Israel, The Revolt of the Ten Tribes; history of

See: Canaanites

• Called the Sanctuary.

Ex 15:17 — Thou shalt bring them in, and plant them in the mountain of thine inheritance, *in* the place, O LORD, *which* thou hast made for thee to dwell in, in the Sanctuary, O Lord, *which* thy hands have established.

• Called Palestine.

Ex 15:14 — The people shall hear, *and* be afraid: sorrow shall take hold on the inhabitants of Palestina.

• Called Land of Israel.

1Sa 13:19 — Now there was no smith found throughout all the land of Israel: for the Philistines said, Lest the Hebrews make *them* swords or spears:

• Called of the Hebrews.

Ge 40:15 — For indeed I was stolen away out of the land of the Hebrews: and here also have I done nothing that they should put me into the dungeon.

• Called of the Jews.

Ac 10:39 — And we are witnesses of all things which he did both in the land of the Jews, and in Jerusalem; whom they slew and hanged on a tree:

• Called of Promise.

Heb 11:9 — By faith he sojourned in the land of promise, as *in* a strange country, dwelling in tabernacles with Isaac and Jacob, the heirs with him of the same promise:

• Called Holy Land.

Zec 2:12 — And the LORD shall inherit Judah his portion in the holy land, and shall choose Jerusalem again.

• Called Lord's Land.

Hos 9:3 — They shall not dwell in the LORD's land; but Ephraim shall return to Egypt, and they shall eat unclean *things* in Assyria.

• Called Immanuel's Land.

Isa 8:8 — And he shall pass through Judah; he shall overflow and go over, he shall reach *even* to the neck; and the stretching out of his wings shall fill the breadth of thy land, O Immanuel.

• Called Beulah.

Isa 62:4 — Thou shalt no more be termed Forsaken; neither shall thy land any more be termed Desolate: but thou shalt be called Hephzi-bah, and thy land Beulah: for the LORD delighteth in thee, and thy land shall be married.

• Promised to Abraham and his seed.

Ge 12:1–7; 13:14–17; 15:18–21; Dt 12:9–10

Ge 17:8 — And I will give unto thee, and to thy seed after thee, the land wherein thou art a stranger, all the land of Canaan, for an everlasting possession; and I will be their God.

Ps 105:11 — Saying, Unto thee will I give the land of Canaan, the lot of your inheritance:

• Renewed to Isaac.

Ge 26:3 — Sojourn in this land, and I will be with thee, and will bless thee; for unto thee, and unto thy seed, I will give all these countries, and I will perform the oath which I sware unto Abraham thy father;

• **Extent of.**

• **According to the promise.**

Ge 15:18 — In the same day the LORD made a covenant with Abram, saying, Unto thy seed have I given this land, from the river of Egypt unto the great river, the river Euphrates:

Ex 23:31 — And I will set thy bounds from the Red sea even unto the sea of the Philistines, and from the desert unto the river: for I will deliver the inhabitants of the land into your hand; and thou shalt drive them out before thee.

Dt 11:24 — Every place whereon the soles of your feet shall tread shall be yours: from the wilderness and Lebanon, from the river, the river Euphrates, even unto the uttermost sea shall your coast be.

Jos 1:4 — From the wilderness and this Lebanon even unto the great river, the river Euphrates, all the land of the Hittites, and unto the great sea toward the going down of the sun, shall be your coast.

Jos 15:1 — *This* then was the lot of the tribe of the children of Judah by their families; *even* to the border of Edom the wilderness of Zin southward *was* the uttermost part of the south coast.

• **After the conquest by Joshua.**

Jos 12:1–8

• **In Solomon's time.**

1Ki 4:21 — And Solomon reigned over all kingdoms from the river unto the land of the Philistines, and unto the border of Egypt: they brought presents, and served Solomon all the days of his life.

1Ki 4:24 — For he had dominion over all *the region* on this side the river, from Tiphsah even to Azzah, over all the kings on this side the river: and he had peace on all sides round about him.

2Ch 7:8 — Also at the same time Solomon kept the feast seven days, and all Israel with him, a very great congregation, from the entering in of Hamath unto the river of Egypt.

2Ch 9:26 — And he reigned over all the kings from the river even unto the land of the Philistines, and to the border of Egypt.

• **Prophecy concerning, after the restoration of Israel.**

Eze 47:13–20

• **Fertility of.**

Dt 8:7–9; 11:10–13

• **Fruitfulness of.**

Nu 14:7–8

Nu 13:27 — And they told him, and said, We came unto the land whither thou sentest us, and surely it floweth with milk and honey; and this *is* the fruit of it.

Jer 2:7 — And I brought you into a plentiful country, to eat the fruit thereof and the goodness thereof; but when ye entered, ye defiled my land, and made mine heritage an abomination.

Jer 32:22 — And hast given them this land, which thou didst swear to their fathers to give them, a land flowing with milk and honey;

• **Products of.**

• **Fruits.**

Dt 8:8 — A land of wheat, and barley, and vines, and fig trees, and pomegranates; a land of oil olive, and honey;

Jer 40:10 — As for me, behold, I will dwell at Mizpah to serve the Chaldeans, which will come unto us: but ye, gather ye wine, and summer fruits, and oil, and put *them* in your vessels, and dwell in your cities that ye have taken.

Jer 40:12 — Even all the Jews returned out of all places whither they were driven, and came to the land of Judah, to Gedaliah, unto Mizpah, and gathered wine and summer fruits very much.

• **Mineral.**

Dt 8:9 — A land wherein thou shalt eat bread without scarceness, thou shalt not lack any *thing* in it; a land whose stones are iron, and out of whose hills thou mayest dig brass.

• **Exports of.**

Eze 27:17 — Judah, and the land of Israel, they *were* thy merchants: they traded in thy market wheat of Minnith, and Pannag, and honey, and oil, and balm.

• **Famines in.**

1Ki 17:1–24

Ge 12:10 — And there was a famine in the land: and Abram went down into Egypt to sojourn there; for the famine *was* grievous in the land.

Ge 26:1 — And there was a famine in the land, beside the first famine that was in the days of Abraham. And Isaac went unto Abimelech king of the Philistines unto Gerar.

Ge 47:13 — And *there was* no bread in all the land; for the famine *was* very sore, so that the land of Egypt and *all* the land of Canaan fainted by reason of the famine.

Ru 1:1 — Now it came to pass in the days when the judges ruled, that there was a famine in the land. And a certain man of Bethlehemjudah went to sojourn in the country of Moab, he, and his wife, and his two sons.

2Sa 21:1 — Then there was a famine in the days of David three years, year after year; and David enquired of the LORD. And the LORD answered, *It is* for Saul, and for *his* bloody house, because he slew the Gibeonites.

See: Famine

• **Spies sent into, by Moses.**

Nu 13:17–29

• **Conquest of, by the Israelites.**

Nu 21:21–35; Dt 3:3–6; Jos 6:1–12:24; Ps 44:1–3

• **Divided by lot among the twelve tribes and families.**

Nu 26:55–56

Nu 33:54 — And ye shall divide the land by lot for an inheritance among your families: *and* to the more ye shall give the more inheritance, and to the fewer ye shall give the less inheritance: every man's *inheritance* shall be in the place where his lot falleth; according to the tribes of your fathers ye shall inherit.

Nu 34:13 — And Moses commanded the children of Israel, saying, This *is* the land which ye shall inherit by lot, which the LORD commanded to give unto the nine tribes, and to the half tribe:

• **Divided by Joshua, Eleazar and a prince from each tribe.**

Nu 34:16–35:8; Jos 14:1–19:51

• **Divided into twelve provinces by Solomon.**

1Ki 4:7–19

• **Divided into two kingdoms, Judah and Israel.**

1Ki 11:29–36; 12:16–21

• **Roman provinces of.**

Jn 4:3–4

Lk 3:1 — Now in the fifteenth year of the reign of Tiberius Caesar, Pontius Pilate being governor of Judaea, and Herod being tetrarch of Galilee, and his brother Philip tetrarch of Ituraea and of the region of Trachonitis, and Lysanias the tetrarch of Abilene,

CANAANITES

• **Eleven nations, descended from Canaan.**

Ge 10:15–19; 1Ch 1:13–16

Dt 7:1 — When the LORD thy God shall bring thee into the land whither thou goest to possess it, and hath cast out many nations before thee, the Hittites, and the Girgashites, and the Amorites, and the Canaanites, and the Perizzites, and the Hivites, and the Jebusites, seven nations greater and mightier than thou;

• **Territory of.**

Nu 34:1–12; Dt 7:1–3; Jos 5:1–15; Ps 135:11–12

Ge 10:19 — And the border of the Canaanites was from Sidon, as thou comest to Gerar, unto Gaza; as thou goest, unto Sodom, and Gomorrah, and Admah, and Zeboim, even unto Lasha.

Ge 12:6 — And Abram passed through the land unto the place of Sichem, unto the plain of Moreh. And the Canaanite *was* then in the land.

Ge 15:18 — In the same day the LORD made a covenant with Abram, saying, Unto thy seed have I given this land, from the river of Egypt unto the great river, the river Euphrates:

Ex 23:31 — And I will set thy bounds from the Red sea even unto the sea of the Philistines, and from the desert unto the river: for I will deliver the inhabitants of the land into your hand; and thou shalt drive them out before thee.

Nu 13:29 — The Amalekites dwell in the land of the south: and the Hittites, and the Jebusites, and the Amorites, dwell in the mountains: and the Canaanites dwell by the sea, and by the coast of Jordan.

Dt 32:49 — Get thee up into this mountain Abarim, *unto* mount Nebo, which *is* in the land of Moab, that *is* over against Jericho; and behold the land of Canaan, which I give unto the children of Israel for a possession:

Jos 1:4 — From the wilderness and this Lebanon even unto the great river, the river Euphrates, all the land of the Hittites, and unto the great sea toward the going down of the sun, shall be your coast.

• **Given to Israelites.**

Ge 12:6–7

Ge 15:18 — In the same day the LORD made a covenant with Abram, saying, Unto thy seed have I given this land, from the river of Egypt unto the great river, the river Euphrates:

Ge 17:8 — And I will give unto thee, and to thy seed after thee, the land wherein thou art a stranger, all the land of Canaan, for an everlasting possession; and I will be their God.

Ex 23:23 — For mine Angel shall go before thee, and bring thee in unto the Amorites, and the Hittites, and the Perizzites, and the Canaanites, and the Hivites, and the Jebusites: and I will cut them off.

• **Wickedness of.**

Le 18:27–28

Ge 13:13 — But the men of Sodom *were* wicked and sinners before the LORD exceedingly.

Le 18:25 — And the land is defiled: therefore I do visit the iniquity thereof upon it, and the land itself vomiteth out her inhabitants.

Le 20:23 — And ye shall not walk in the manners of the nation, which I cast out before you: for they committed all these things, and therefore I abhorred them.

• **To be expelled from the land.**

Ex 33:2 — And I will send an angel before thee; and I will drive out the Canaanite, the Amorite, and the Hittite, and the Perizzite, the Hivite, and the Jebusite:

Ex 34:11 — Observe thou that which I command thee this day: behold, I drive out before thee the Amorite, and the Canaanite, and the Hittite, and the Perizzite, and the Hivite, and the Jebusite.

• **To be destroyed.**

Ex 23:23–24; Dt 31:3–5

Dt 19:1 — When the LORD thy God hath cut off the nations, whose land the LORD thy God giveth thee, and thou succeedest them, and dwellest in their cities, and in their houses;

• **Not expelled.**

Jos 17:12–18; Jgs 1:1–33; 3:1–3

• **Defeat the Israelites.**

Jgs 4:1–3

Nu 14:45 — Then the Amalekites came down, and the Canaanites which dwelt in that hill, and smote them, and discomfited them, *even* unto Hormah.

• **Defeated by the Israelites.**

Nu 21:1–3; Jos 11:1–6; Jgs 4:4–24

• **Defeated by the Egyptians.**

1Ki 9:16 — *For* Pharaoh king of Egypt had gone up, and taken Gezer, and burnt it with fire, and slain the Canaanites that dwelt in the city, and given it *for* a present unto his daughter, Solomon's wife.

• **Chariots of.**

Jos 17:18 — But the mountain shall be thine; for it *is* a wood, and thou shalt cut it down: and the outgoings of it shall be thine: for thou shalt drive out the Canaanites, though they have iron chariots, *and* though they *be* strong.

• Isaac forbidden by Abraham to take a wife from.

Ge 28:1 — And Isaac called Jacob, and blessed him, and charged him, and said unto him, Thou shalt not take a wife of the daughters of Canaan.

• Judah marries a woman of.

Ge 38:2 — And Judah saw there a daughter of a certain Canaanite, whose name *was* Shuah; and he took her, and went in unto her.

1Ch 2:3 — The sons of Judah; Er, and Onan, and Shelah: *which* three were born unto him of the daughter of Shua the Canaanitess. And Er, the firstborn of Judah, was evil in the sight of the LORD; and he slew him.

• The exile Jews take wives from.

Ezr 9:2 — For they have taken of their daughters for themselves, and for their sons: so that the holy seed have mingled themselves with the people of *those* lands: yea, the hand of the princes and rulers hath been chief in this trespass.

• Prophecy conerning.

Ge 9:25–27

CANDACE • Queen of Ethiopia.

Ac 8:27 — And he arose and went: and, behold, a man of Ethiopia, an eunuch of great authority under Candace queen of the Ethiopians, who had the charge of all her treasure, and had come to Jerusalem for to worship,

CANDIDATE

• Refuses to make promises.

2Ch 10:3–16

• Electioneering by, instance of, Absalom.

2Sa 15:1–6

CANDLE

• Lamp is used for candle throughout the Scriptures.

See: Lamp

CANDLESTICK

• Of the tabernacle.

• Made after divine pattern.

Ex 25:31–40; 37:17–24

Nu 8:4 — And this work of the candlestick *was of* beaten gold, unto the shaft thereof, unto the flowers thereof, *was* beaten work: according unto the pattern which the LORD had shewed Moses, so he made the candlestick.

• Place of.

Ex 40:24–25

Ex 26:35 — And thou shalt set the table without the vail, and the candlestick over against the table on the side of the tabernacle toward the south: and thou shalt put the table on the north side.

Heb 9:2 — For there was a tabernacle made; the first, wherein *was* the candlestick, and the table, and the shewbread; which is called the sanctuary.

• Furniture of.

Nu 4:9–10

Ex 25:38 — And the tongs thereof, and the snuffdishes thereof, *shall be of* pure gold.

Ex 37:23 — And he made his seven lamps, and his snuffers, and his snuffdishes, *of* pure gold.

• Burned every night.

Ex 27:20–21

• Trimmed every morning.

Ex 30:7 — And Aaron shall burn thereon sweet incense every morning: when he dresseth the lamps, he shall burn incense upon it.

• Carried by Kohathites.

Nu 4:4 — This *shall be* the service of the sons of Kohath in the tabernacle of the congregation, *about* the most holy things:

Nu 4:15 — And when Aaron and his sons have made an end of covering the sanctuary, and all the vessels of the sanctuary, as the camp is to set forward; after that, the sons of Kohath shall come to bear *it:* but they shall not touch *any* holy thing, lest they die. These *things are* the burden of the sons of Kohath in the tabernacle of the congregation.

• Called the Lamp of God.

1Sa 3:3 — And ere the lamp of God went out in the temple of the LORD, where the ark of God *was*, and Samuel was laid down *to sleep;*

• Of the temple.

• Ten branches of.

1Ki 7:49–50

• Of gold.

1Ch 28:15 — Even the weight for the candlesticks of gold, and for their lamps of gold, by weight for every candlestick, and for the lamps thereof: and for the candlesticks of silver by weight, *both* for the candlestick, and *also* for the lamps thereof, according to the use of every candlestick.

2Ch 4:20 — Moreover the candlesticks with their lamps, that they should burn after the manner before the oracle, of pure gold;

• Taken with other spoils to Babylon.

Jer 52:19 — And the basons, and the firepans, and the bowls, and the caldrons, and the candlesticks, and the spoons, and the cups; *that* which *was* of gold *in* gold, and *that* which *was* of silver *in* silver, took the captain of the guard away.

• Symbolic.

Rev 1:12–13

Zec 4:2 — And said unto me, What seest thou? And I said, I have looked, and behold a candlestick all *of* gold, with a bowl upon the top of it, and his seven lamps thereon, and seven pipes to the seven lamps, which *are* upon the top thereof:

Zec 4:11 — Then answered I, and said unto him, What *are* these two olive trees upon the right *side* of the candlestick and upon the left *side* thereof?

Rev 1:20 — The mystery of the seven stars which thou sawest in my right hand, and the seven golden candlesticks. The seven stars are the angels of the seven churches: and the seven candlesticks which thou sawest are the seven churches.

Rev 2:5 — Remember therefore from whence thou art fallen, and repent, and do the first works; or else I will come unto thee quickly, and will remove thy candlestick out of his place, except thou repent.

Rev 11:4 — These are the two olive trees, and the two candlesticks standing before the God of the earth.

CANE ✦See: Calamus

CANKER

• Figurative.

2Ti 2:17 — And their word will eat as doth a canker: of whom is Hymenaeus and Philetus;

CANKERWORM

• Sent as a judgment.

Na 3:15–16

Joel 1:4 — That which the palmerworm hath left hath the locust eaten; and that which the locust hath left hath the cankerworm eaten; and that which the cankerworm hath left hath the caterpiller eaten.

Joel 2:25 — And I will restore to you the years that the locust hath eaten, the cankerworm, and the caterpiller, and the palmerworm, my great army which I sent among you.

CANNEH ✦See: Calneh

CANNIBALISM

Dt 28:53–57; 2Ki 6:28–29

Le 26:29 — And ye shall eat the flesh of your sons, and the flesh of your daughters shall ye eat.

Jer 19:9 — And I will cause them to eat the flesh of their sons and the flesh of their daughters, and they shall eat every one the flesh of his friend in the siege and straitness, wherewith their enemies, and they that seek their lives, shall straiten them.

La 2:20 — Behold, O LORD, and consider to whom thou hast done this. Shall the women eat their fruit, *and* children of a span long? shall the priest and the prophet be slain in the sanctuary of the Lord?

La 4:10 — The hands of the pitiful women have sodden their own children: they were their meat in the destruction of the daughter of my people.

Eze 5:10 — Therefore the fathers shall eat the sons in the midst of thee, and the sons shall eat their fathers; and I will execute judgments in thee, and the whole remnant of thee will I scatter into all the winds.

CAPERNAUM

• A city on the shore of the Sea of Galilee.

Lk 4:31 — And came down to Capernaum, a city of Galilee, and taught them on the sabbath days.

• Jesus chose as the place of his abode.

Mt 4:13 — And leaving Nazareth, he came and dwelt in Capernaum, which is upon the sea coast, in the borders of Zabulon and Nephthalim:

• Miracles of Jesus performed at.

Mt 17:24–27; Mk 1:21–3:6; Lk 7:1–10; Jn 4:46–53; 6:17–25

Mt 9:1 — And he entered into a ship, and passed over, and came into his own city.

Mt 9:26 — And the fame hereof went abroad into all that land.

Jn 6:59 — These things said he in the synagogue, as he taught in Capernaum.

• His prophecy against.

Mt 11:23 — And thou, Capernaum, which art exalted unto heaven, shalt be brought down to hell: for if the mighty works, which have been done in thee, had been done in Sodom, it would have remained until this day.

Lk 10:15 — And thou, Capernaum, which art exalted to heaven, shalt be thrust down to hell.

CAPHTOR • A country now unknown.

Dt 2:23 — And the Avims which dwelt in Hazerim, *even* unto Azzah, the Caphtorims, which came forth out of Caphtor, destroyed them, and dwelt in their stead.)

CAPHTORIM • People of Caphtor.

Ge 10:14 — And Pathrusim, and Casluhim, (out of whom came Philistim,) and Caphtorim.

Dt 2:23 — And the Avims which dwelt in Hazerim, *even* unto Azzah, the Caphtorims, which came forth out of Caphtor, destroyed them, and dwelt in their stead.)

1Ch 1:12 — And Pathrusim, and Casluhim, (of whom came the Philistines,) and Caphthorim.

Jer 47:4 — Because of the day that cometh to spoil all the Philistines, *and* to cut off from Tyrus and Zidon every helper that remaineth: for the LORD will spoil the Philistines, the remnant of the country of Caphtor.

Am 9:7 — *Are* ye not as children of the Ethiopians unto me, O children of Israel? saith the LORD. Have not I brought up Israel out of the land of Egypt? and the Philistines from Caphtor, and the Syrians from Kir?

CAPITAL AND LABOR

• Strife between.

Mt 21:33–41; Mk 12:1–9; Lk 20:9–16

✦See: Employee

✦See: Employer

✦See: Master

✦See: Rich; the

✦See: Servant

CAPITAL PUNISHMENT

Ge 9:6 — Whoso sheddeth man's blood, by man shall his blood be shed: for in the image of God made he man.

✦See: Punishment

CAPPADOCIA • Easternmost province of Asia Minor.

Ac 2:9 — Parthians, and Medes, and Elamites, and the dwellers in Mesopotamia, and in Judaea, and Cappadocia, in Pontus, and Asia,

1Pe 1:1 — Peter, an apostle of Jesus Christ, to the strangers scattered throughout Pontus, Galatia, Cappadocia, Asia, and Bithynia,

CAPTAIN

• Commander-in-chief of an army.

Dt 20:9 — And it shall be, when the officers have made an end of speaking unto the people, that they shall make captains of the armies to lead the people.

Jgs 4:2 — And the LORD sold them into the hand of Jabin king of Canaan, that reigned in Hazor; the captain of whose host *was* Sisera, which dwelt in Harosheth of the Gentiles.

1Sa 14:50 — And the name of Saul's wife *was* Ahinoam, the daughter of Ahimaaz: and the name of the captain of his host *was* Abner, the son of Ner, Saul's uncle.

1Ki 2:35 — And the king put Benaiah the son of Jehoiada in his room over the host: and Zadok the priest did the king put in the room of Abiathar.

1Ki 16:16 — And the people *that were* encamped heard say, Zimri hath conspired, and hath also slain the king: wherefore all Israel made Omri, the captain of the host, king over Israel that day in the camp.

1Ch 27:34 — And after Ahithophel *was* Jehoiada the son of Benaiah, and Abiathar: and the general of the king's army *was* Joab.

• Of the tribes.

Nu 2:1–34

• Of thousands.

Nu 31:48 — And the officers which *were* over thousands of the host, the captains of thousands, and captains of hundreds, came near unto Moses:

1Sa 17:18 — And carry these ten cheeses unto the captain of *their* thousand, and look how thy brethren fare, and take their pledge.

1Ch 28:1 — And David assembled all the princes of Israel, the princes of the tribes, and the captains of the companies that ministered to the king by course, and the captains over the thousands, and captains over the hundreds, and the stewards over all the substance and possession of the king, and of his sons, with the officers, and with the mighty men, and with all the valiant men, unto Jerusalem.

• Of hundreds.

2Ki 11:15 — But Jehoiada the priest commanded the captains of the hundreds, the officers of the host, and said unto them, Have her forth without the ranges: and him that followeth her kill with the sword. For the priest had said, Let her not be slain in the house of the LORD.

***See: Centurion**

• Of fifties.

2Ki 1:9 — Then the king sent unto him a captain of fifty with his fifty. And he went up to him: and, behold, he sat on the top of an hill. And he spake unto him, Thou man of God, the king hath said, Come down.

Isa 3:3 — The captain of fifty, and the honourable man, and the counsellor, and the cunning artificer, and the eloquent orator.

• Of the guard.

Ge 37:36 — And the Midianites sold him into Egypt unto Potiphar, an officer of Pharaoh's, *and* captain of the guard.

2Ki 25:8 — And in the fifth month, on the seventh *day* of the month, which *is* the nineteenth year of king Nebuchadnezzar king of Babylon, came Nebuzaradan, captain of the guard, a servant of the king of Babylon, unto Jerusalem:

• Of the ward.

Jer 37:13 — And when he was in the gate of Benjamin, a captain of the ward *was* there, whose name *was* Irijah, the son of Shelemiah, the son of Hananiah; and he took Jeremiah the prophet, saying, Thou fallest away to the Chaldeans.

• Signifying any commander.

1Sa 9:16 — To morrow about this time I will send thee a man out of the land of Benjamin, and thou shalt anoint him *to be* captain over my people Israel, that he may save my people out of the hand of the Philistines: for I have looked upon my people, because their cry is come unto me.

1Sa 22:2 — And every one *that was* in distress, and every one that *was* in debt, and every one *that was* discontented, gathered themselves unto him; and he became a captain over them: and there were with him about four hundred men.

2Ki 20:5 — Turn again, and tell Hezekiah the captain of my people, Thus saith the LORD, the God of David thy father, I have heard thy prayer, I have seen thy tears: behold, I will heal thee: on the third day thou shalt go up unto the house of the LORD.

• Signifying any commander, as leader.

2Ch 17:14–19

1Ch 11:21 — Of the three, he was more honourable than the two; for he was their captain: howbeit he attained not to the *first* three.

1Ch 12:34 — And of Naphtali a thousand captains, and with them with shield and spear thirty and seven thousand.

Jn 18:12 — Then the band and the captain and officers of the Jews took Jesus, and bound him,

• David's captains, or chief heroes.

2Sa 23:1–39; 1Ch 11:1–47

• King appoints.

1Sa 18:13 — Therefore Saul removed him from him, and made him his captain over a thousand; and he went out and came in before the people.

2Sa 17:25 — And Absalom made Amasa captain of the host instead of Joab: which Amasa was a man's son, whose name *was* Ithra an Israelite, that went in to Abigail the daughter of Nahash, sister to Zeruiah Joab's mother.

2Sa 18:1 — And David numbered the people that *were* with him, and set captains of thousands and captains of hundreds over them.

• Angel of the Lord, called.

Jos 5:14 — And he said, Nay; but *as* captain of the host of the LORD am I now come. And Joshua fell on his face to the earth, and did worship, and said unto him, What saith my lord unto his servant?

2Ch 13:12 — And, behold, God himself is with us for *our* captain, and his priests with sounding trumpets to cry alarm against you. O children of Israel, fight ye not against the LORD God of your fathers; for ye shall not prosper.

• Christ called.

Heb 2:10 — For it became him, for whom *are* all things, and by whom *are* all things, in bringing many sons unto glory, to make the captain of their salvation perfect through sufferings.

See: Armies

CAPTIVE

• Prisoner of war.

1Sa 30:1–2

Ge 14:12 — And they took Lot, Abram's brother's son, who dwelt in Sodom, and his goods, and departed.

• Cruelty to.

• Putting to death.

Nu 31:9–20; Jos 10:15–40; 1Sa 15:32–33

Dt 20:13 — And when the LORD thy God hath delivered it into thine hands, thou shalt smite every male thereof with the edge of the sword:

Dt 21:10 — When thou goest forth to war against thine enemies, and the LORD thy God hath delivered them into thine hands, and thou hast taken them captive,

Jos 8:29 — And the king of Ai he hanged on a tree until eventide: and as soon as the sun was down, Joshua commanded that they should take his carcase down from the tree, and cast it at the entering of the gate of the city, and raise thereon a great heap of stones, *that remaineth* unto this day.

Jos 11:11 — And they smote all the souls that *were* therein with the edge of the sword, utterly destroying *them:* there was not any left to breathe: and he burnt Hazor with fire.

Jgs 7:25 — And they took two princes of the Midianites, Oreb and Zeeb; and they slew Oreb upon the rock Oreb, and Zeeb they slew at the winepress of Zeeb, and pursued Midian, and brought the heads of Oreb and Zeeb to Gideon on the other side Jordan.

Jgs 8:21 — Then Zebah and Zalmunna said, Rise thou, and fall upon us: for as the man *is, so is* his strength. And Gideon arose, and slew Zebah and Zalmunna, and took away the ornaments that *were* on their camels' necks.

Jgs 21:11 — And this *is* the thing that ye shall do, Ye shall utterly destroy every male, and every woman that hath lain by man.

2Sa 8:2 — And he smote Moab, and measured them with a line, casting them down to the ground; even with two lines measured he to put to death, and with one full line to keep alive. And so the Moabites became David's servants, *and* brought gifts.

2Ki 8:12 — And Hazael said, Why weepeth my lord? And he answered, Because I know the evil that thou wilt do unto the children of Israel: their strong holds wilt thou set on fire, and their young men wilt thou slay with the sword, and wilt dash their children, and rip up their women with child.

Jer 39:6 — Then the king of Babylon slew the sons of Zedekiah in Riblah before his eyes: also the king of Babylon slew all the nobles of Judah.

• Putting to death twenty thousand, by Amaziah.

2Ch 25:11–12

• Ripping women with child.

2Ki 8:12 — And Hazael said, Why weepeth my lord? And he answered, Because I know the evil that thou wilt do unto the children of Israel: their strong holds wilt thou set on fire, and their young men wilt thou slay with the sword, and wilt dash their children, and rip up their women with child.

2Ki 15:16 — Then Menahem smote Tiphsah, and all that *were* therein, and the coasts thereof from Tirzah: because they opened not *to him,* therefore he smote *it; and* all the women therein that were with child he ripped up.

Am 1:13 — Thus saith the LORD; For three transgressions of the children of Ammon, and for four, I will not turn away *the punishment* thereof; because they have ripped up the women with child of Gilead, that they might enlarge their border:

• Tortured under saws and harrows.

2Sa 12:31 — And he brought forth the people that *were* therein, and put *them* under saws, and under harrows of iron, and under axes of iron, and made them pass through the brickkiln: and thus did he unto all the cities of the children of Ammon. So David and all the people returned unto Jerusalem.

1Ch 20:3 — And he brought out the people that *were* in it, and cut *them* with saws, and with harrows of iron, and with axes. Even so dealt David with all the cities of the children of Ammon. And David and all the people returned to Jerusalem.

• Blinded.

Jgs 16:21 — But the Philistines took him, and put out his eyes, and brought him down to Gaza, and bound him with fetters of brass; and he did grind in the prison house.

Jer 39:7 — Moreover he put out Zedekiah's eyes, and bound him with chains, to carry him to Babylon.

• Maimed.

Jgs 1:6–7

• Ravished.

La 5:11–13

Zec 14:2 — For I will gather all nations against Jerusalem to battle; and the city shall be taken, and the houses rifled, and the women ravished; and half of the city shall go forth into captivity, and the residue of the people shall not be cut off from the city.

• **Enslaved.**

Dt 20:14 — But the women, and the little ones, and the cattle, and all that is in the city, *even* all the spoil thereof, shalt thou take unto thyself; and thou shalt eat the spoil of thine enemies, which the LORD thy God hath given thee.

2Ki 5:2 — And the Syrians had gone out by companies, and had brought away captive out of the land of Israel a little maid; and she waited on Naaman's wife.

Ps 44:12 — Thou sellest thy people for nought, and dost not increase *thy wealth* by their price.

Joel 3:6 — The children also of Judah and the children of Jerusalem have ye sold unto the Grecians, that ye might remove them far from their border.

• **Robbed.**

Eze 23:25–26

• **Confined in pits.**

Isa 51:14 — The captive exile hasteneth that he may be loosed, and that he should not die in the pit, nor that his bread should fail.

• **Other indignities to.**

Isa 20:4 — So shall the king of Assyria lead away the Egyptians prisoners, and the Ethiopians captives, young and old, naked and barefoot, even with *their* buttocks uncovered, to the shame of Egypt.

• **Kindness to.**

2Ki 25:27–30

Ps 106:46 — He made them also to be pitied of all those that carried them captives.

• **Advanced to positions in state.**

Ge 41:39–45; Da 1:1–21

Est 2:8 — So it came to pass, when the king's commandment and his decree was heard, and when many maidens were gathered together unto Shushan the palace, to the custody of Hegai, that Esther was brought also unto the king's house, to the custody of Hegai, keeper of the women.

CAPTIVITY

• **Of the Israelites foretold.**

Le 26:33 — And I will scatter you among the heathen, and will draw out a sword after you: and your land shall be desolate, and your cities waste.

Dt 28:36 — The LORD shall bring thee, and thy king which thou shalt set over thee, unto a nation which neither thou nor thy fathers have known; and there shalt thou serve other gods, wood and stone.

• **Of the ten tribes.**

2Ki 17:23–24; 18:9–12

2Ki 17:6 — In the ninth year of Hoshea the king of Assyria took Samaria, and carried Israel away into Assyria, and placed them in Halah and in Habor *by* the river of Gozan, and in the cities of the Medes.

• **Of Judah in Babylon, prophecy of.**

Jer 25:2–11

Isa 39:6 — Behold, the days come, that all that *is* in thine house, and *that* which thy fathers have laid up in store until this day, shall be carried to Babylon: nothing shall be left, saith the LORD.

Jer 13:19 — The cities of the south shall be shut up, and none shall open *them:* Judah shall be carried away captive all of it, it shall be wholly carried away captive.

Jer 20:4 — For thus saith the LORD, Behold, I will make thee a terror to thyself, and to all thy friends: and they shall fall by the sword of their enemies, and thine eyes shall behold *it:* and I will give all Judah into the hand of the king of Babylon, and he shall carry them captive into Babylon, and shall slay them with the sword.

Jer 32:28 — Therefore thus saith the LORD; Behold, I will give this city into the hand of the Chaldeans, and into the hand of Nebuchadrezzar king of Babylon, and he shall take it:

• **Of Judah in Babylon, prophecy of fulfilled.**

2Ki 24:11–16; 25:1–30; 2Ch 36:1–23; Jer 52:28–30

• **Jews return from.**

Ezr 2:1–3:13; 8:1–36

• **Israelites in, promises to.**

Ne 1:9 — But *if* ye turn unto me, and keep my commandments, and do them; though there were of you cast out unto the uttermost part of the heaven, *yet* will I gather them from thence, and will bring them unto the place that I have chosen to set my name there.

• **As a judgment.**

Jer 29:17–19; La 1:3–5; Eze 39:23–24

Ezr 5:12 — But after that our fathers had provoked the God of heaven unto wrath, he gave them into the hand of Nebuchadnezzar the king of Babylon, the Chaldean, who destroyed this house, and carried the people away into Babylon.

Ezr 9:7 — Since the days of our fathers *have* we *been* in a great trespass unto this day; and for our iniquities have we, our kings, and *our* priests, been delivered into the hand of the kings of the lands, to the sword, to captivity, and to a spoil, and to confusion of face, as *it is* this day.

Isa 5:13 — Therefore my people are gone into captivity, because *they have* no knowledge: and their honourable men *are* famished, and their multitude dried up with thirst.

• **Figurative.**

Isa 61:1 — The Spirit of the Lord GOD *is* upon me; because the LORD hath anointed me to preach good tidings unto the meek; he hath sent me to bind up the brokenhearted, to proclaim liberty to the captives, and the opening of the prison to *them that are* bound;

Ro 7:23 — But I see another law in my members, warring against the law of my mind, and bringing me into captivity to the law of sin which is in my members.

1Co 9:27 — But I keep under my body, and bring *it* into subjection: lest that by any means, when I have preached to others, I myself should be a castaway.

2Co 10:5 — Casting down imaginations, and every high thing that exalteth itself against the knowledge of God, and bringing into captivity every thought to the obedience of Christ;

2Ti 2:26 — And *that* they may recover themselves out of the snare of the devil, who are taken captive by him at his will.

2Ti 3:6 — For of this sort are they which creep into houses, and lead captive silly women laden with sins, led away with divers lusts,

- **"Captivity led captive".**

Jgs 5:12 — Awake, awake, Deborah: awake, awake, utter a song: arise, Barak, and lead thy captivity captive, thou son of Abinoam.

Ps 68:18 — Thou hast ascended on high, thou hast led captivity captive: thou hast received gifts for men; yea, *for* the rebellious also, that the LORD God might dwell *among them.*

Eph 4:8 — Wherefore he saith, When he ascended up on high, he led captivity captive, and gave gifts unto men.

CARBUNCLE

- **A precious stone.**

Isa 54:12 — And I will make thy windows of agates, and thy gates of carbuncles, and all thy borders of pleasant stones.

Eze 28:13 — Thou hast been in Eden the garden of God; every precious stone *was* thy covering, the sardius, topaz, and the diamond, the beryl, the onyx, and the jasper, the sapphire, the emerald, and the carbuncle, and gold: the workmanship of thy tabrets and of thy pipes was prepared in thee in the day that thou wast created.

- **One of the precious stones set in the breastplate.**

Ex 28:17 — And thou shalt set in it settings of stones, *even* four rows of stones: *the first* row *shall be* a sardius, a topaz, and a carbuncle: *this shall be* the first row.

Ex 39:10 — And they set in it four rows of stones: *the first* row *was* a sardius, a topaz, and a carbuncle: this *was* the first row.

CARCAS • A Persian chamberlain.

Est 1:10 — On the seventh day, when the heart of the king was merry with wine, he commanded Mehuman, Biztha, Harbona, Bigtha, and Abagtha, Zethar, and Carcas, the seven chamberlains that served in the presence of Ahasuerus the king,

CARCHEMISH • A Babylonian city on the Euphrates, against which the king of Egypt made war.

2Ch 35:20 — After all this, when Josiah had prepared the temple, Necho king of Egypt came up to fight against Charchemish by Euphrates: and Josiah went out against him.

Isa 10:9 — *Is* not Calno as Carchemish? *is* not Hamath as Arpad? *is* not Samaria as Damascus?

Jer 46:2 — Against Egypt, against the army of Pharaoh-necho king of Egypt, which was by the river Euphrates in Carchemish, which Nebuchadrezzar king of Babylon smote in the fourth year of Jehoiakim the son of Josiah king of Judah.

CARE

1Co 12:25 — That there should be no schism in the body; but *that* the members should have the same care one for another.

2Co 8:16 — But thanks *be* to God, which put the same earnest care into the heart of Titus for you.

Php 2:20 — For I have no man likeminded, who will naturally care for your state.

1Ti 3:5 — (For if a man know not how to rule his own house, how shall he take care of the church of God?)

1Pe 2:25 — For ye were as sheep going astray; but are now returned unto the Shepherd and Bishop of your souls.

1Pe 5:4 — And when the chief Shepherd shall appear, ye shall receive a crown of glory that fadeth not away.

- **Worldly.**

Mt 6:25–34; Lk 14:18–20; 1Co 7:32–33

Ps 39:6 — Surely every man walketh in a vain shew: surely they are disquieted in vain: he heapeth up *riches,* and knoweth not who shall gather them.

Ps 127:2 — *It is* vain for you to rise up early, to sit up late, to eat the bread of sorrows: *for* so he giveth his beloved sleep.

Ecc 4:8 — There is one *alone,* and *there is* not a second; yea, he hath neither child nor brother: yet *is there* no end of all his labour; neither is his eye satisfied with riches; neither *saith he,* For whom do I labour, and bereave my soul of good? This *is* also vanity, yea, it *is* a sore travail.

Mt 13:22 — He also that received seed among the thorns is he that heareth the word; and the care of this world, and the deceitfulness of riches, choke the word, and he becometh unfruitful.

Mk 4:19 — And the cares of this world, and the deceitfulness of riches, and the lusts of other things entering in, choke the word, and it becometh unfruitful.

Lk 8:14 — And that which fell among thorns are they, which, when they have heard, go forth, and are choked with cares and riches and pleasures of *this* life, and bring no fruit to perfection.

Lk 12:27 — Consider the lilies how they grow: they toil not, they spin not; and yet I say unto you, that Solomon in all his glory was not arrayed like one of these.

Lk 21:34 — And take heed to yourselves, lest at any time your hearts be overcharged with surfeiting, and drunkenness, and cares of this life, and so that day come upon you unawares.

Php 4:6 — Be careful for nothing; but in every thing by prayer and supplication with thanksgiving let your requests be made known unto God.

2Ti 2:4 — No man that warreth entangleth himself with the affairs of *this* life; that he may please him who hath chosen him to be a soldier.

See: Carnal Mindedness
See: Riches
See: Worldliness

• Remedy for.

Jer 17:7–8; Mt 6:26–34; Lk 12:22–32; Php 4:6–7; 1Pe 5:6–7

Ps 37:5 — Commit thy way unto the LORD; trust also in him; and he shall bring *it* to pass.

Ps 55:22 — Cast thy burden upon the LORD, and he shall sustain thee: he shall never suffer the righteous to be moved.

Pr 16:3 — Commit thy works unto the LORD, and thy thoughts shall be established.

Heb 13:5 — *Let your* conversation *be* without covetousness; *and be* content with such things as ye have: for he hath said, I will never leave thee, nor forsake thee.

• Instances of.

• Martha.

Lk 10:40–41

• Certain persons who desired to follow Jesus.

Mt 8:19–22; Lk 9:57–62

⇒See: Rich; the

CAREAH ⇒See: Kareah

CARMEL

• A fertile and picturesque mountain in Palestine.

SS 7:5 — Thine head upon thee *is* like Carmel, and the hair of thine head like purple; the king *is* held in the galleries.

Isa 33:9 — The earth mourneth *and* languisheth: Lebanon is ashamed *and* hewn down: Sharon is like a wilderness; and Bashan and Carmel shake off *their fruits.*

Isa 35:2 — It shall blossom abundantly, and rejoice even with joy and singing: the glory of Lebanon shall be given unto it, the excellency of Carmel and Sharon, they shall see the glory of the LORD, *and* the excellency of our God.

Jer 46:18 — *As* I live, saith the King, whose name *is* the LORD of hosts, Surely as Tabor *is* among the mountains, and as Carmel by the sea, *so* shall he come.

Jer 50:19 — And I will bring Israel again to his habitation, and he shall feed on Carmel and Bashan, and his soul shall be satisfied upon mount Ephraim and Gilead.

Am 1:2 — And he said, The LORD will roar from Zion, and utter his voice from Jerusalem; and the habitations of the shepherds shall mourn, and the top of Carmel shall wither.

• Forests of.

2Ki 19:23 — By the messengers thou hast reproached the Lord, and hast said, With the multitude of my chariots I am come up to the height of the mountains, to the sides of Lebanon, and will cut down the tall cedar trees thereof, *and* the choice fir trees thereof: and I will enter into the lodgings of his borders, *and into* the forest of his Carmel.

• Caves of.

Am 9:3 — And though they hide themselves in the top of Carmel, I will search and take them out thence; and though they be hid from my sight in the bottom of the sea, thence will I command the serpent, and he shall bite them:

Mic 7:14 — Feed thy people with thy rod, the flock of thine heritage, which dwell solitarily *in* the wood, in the midst of Carmel: let them feed *in* Bashan and Gilead, as in the days of old.

• An idolatrous high place where Elijah challenged the prophets of Baal.

1Ki 18:17–46

• Elisha's abode in.

2Ki 2:25 — And he went from thence to mount Carmel, and from thence he returned to Samaria.

2Ki 4:25 — So she went and came unto the man of God to mount Carmel. And it came to pass, when the man of God saw her afar off, that he said to Gehazi his servant, Behold, *yonder is* that Shunammite:

• A city of Judah.

Jos 15:55 — Maon, Carmel, and Ziph, and Juttah,

• Saul erects a memorial at.

1Sa 15:12 — And when Samuel rose early to meet Saul in the morning, it was told Samuel, saying, Saul came to Carmel, and, behold, he set him up a place, and is gone about, and passed on, and gone down to Gilgal.

• Nabal's possessions at.

1Sa 25:2 — And *there was* a man in Maon, whose possessions *were* in Carmel; and the man *was* very great, and he had three thousand sheep, and a thousand goats: and he was shearing his sheep in Carmel.

• King Uzziah, who delighted in agriculture, had vineyards at.

2Ch 26:10 — Also he built towers in the desert, and digged many wells: for he had much cattle, both in the low country, and in the plains: husbandmen *also,* and vine dressers in the mountains, and in Carmel: for he loved husbandry.

CARMI

• Son of Reuben.

Ge 46:9 — And the sons of Reuben; Hanoch, and Phallu, and Hezron, and Carmi.

Ex 6:14 — These *be* the heads of their fathers' houses: The sons of Reuben the firstborn of Israel; Hanoch, and Pallu, Hezron, and Carmi: these *be* the families of Reuben.

• Son of Hezron.

1Ch 4:1 — The sons of Judah; Pharez, Hezron, and Carmi, and Hur, and Shobal.

• Called Chelubai.

1Ch 2:9 — The sons also of Hezron, that were born unto him; Jerahmeel, and Ram, and Chelubai.

• **Called Caleb.**

1Ch 2:18 — And Caleb the son of Hezron begat *children* of Azubah *his* wife, and of Jerioth: her sons *are* these; Jesher, and Shobab, and Ardon.

• **Father of Achan.**

Jos 7:1 — But the children of Israel committed a trespass in the accursed thing: for Achan, the son of Carmi, the son of Zabdi, the son of Zerah, of the tribe of Judah, took of the accursed thing: and the anger of the LORD was kindled against the children of Israel.

Jos 7:18 — And he brought his household man by man; and Achan, the son of Carmi, the son of Zabdi, the son of Zerah, of the tribe of Judah, was taken.

1Ch 2:7 — And the sons of Carmi; Achar, the troubler of Israel, who transgressed in the thing accursed.

CARNAL MINDEDNESS

Ro 8:6–8

Gal 6:8 — For he that soweth to his flesh shall of the flesh reap corruption; but he that soweth to the Spirit shall of the Spirit reap life everlasting.

Jas 4:4 — Ye adulterers and adulteresses, know ye not that the friendship of the world is enmity with God? whosoever therefore will be a friend of the world is the enemy of God.

See: Care; worldly

See: Riches

See: Sin; fruits of

See: Worldliness

CARPENTRY

• **Building the ark.**

Ge 6:14–16

• **Tabernacle, and furniture of.**

Ex 31:2–9

See: Tabernacle

• **David's palace.**

2Sa 5:11 — And Hiram king of Tyre sent messengers to David, and cedar trees, and carpenters, and masons: and they built David an house.

• **Temple.**

2Ki 12:11 — And they gave the money, being told, into the hands of them that did the work, that had the oversight of the house of the LORD: and they laid it out to the carpenters and builders, that wrought upon the house of the LORD,

2Ki 22:6 — Unto carpenters, and builders, and masons, and to buy timber and hewn stone to repair the house.

See: Temple

• **Making idols.**

Isa 41:7 — So the carpenter encouraged the goldsmith, *and* he that smootheth *with* the hammer him that smote the anvil, saying, It is ready for the sodering: and he fastened it with nails, *that* it should not be moved.

Isa 44:13 — The carpenter stretcheth out *his* rule; he marketh it out with a line; he fitteth it with planes, and he marketh it out with the compass, and maketh it after the figure of a man, according to the beauty of a man; that it may remain in the house.

• **Carpenters.**

Jer 24:1 — The LORD shewed me, and, behold, two baskets of figs *were* set before the temple of the LORD, after that Nebuchadrezzar king of Babylon had carried away captive Jeconiah the son of Jehoiakim king of Judah, and the princes of Judah, with the carpenters and smiths, from Jerusalem, and had brought them to Babylon.

Zec 1:20 — And the LORD shewed me four carpenters.

• **Joseph.**

Mt 13:55 — Is not this the carpenter's son? is not his mother called Mary? and his brethren, James, and Joses, and Simon, and Judas?

• **Jesus.**

Mk 6:3 — Is not this the carpenter, the son of Mary, the brother of James, and Joses, and of Juda, and Simon? and are not his sisters here with us? And they were offended at him.

See: Carving

See: Master Workman

CARPET

Pr 31:22 — She maketh herself coverings of tapestry; her clothing *is* silk and purple.

CARPUS • A Christian at Troas.

2Ti 4:13 — The cloke that I left at Troas with Carpus, when thou comest, bring *with thee,* and the books, *but* especially the parchments.

CARSHENA • A Persian prince.

Est 1:14 — And the next unto him *was* Carshena, Shethar, Admatha, Tarshish, Meres, Marsena, *and* Memucan, the seven princes of Persia and Media, which saw the king's face, *and* which sat the first in the kingdom;)

CART

1Sa 6:7–14; Isa 28:27–28

2Sa 6:3 — And they set the ark of God upon a new cart, and brought it out of the house of Abinadab that *was* in Gibeah: and Uzzah and Ahio, the sons of Abinadab, drave the new cart.

See: Wagon

CARVING

• **Woodwork of the temple was decorated with carvings of flowers, cherubim, and palm trees.**

1Ki 6:18 — And the cedar of the house within *was* carved with knops and open flowers: all *was* cedar; there was no stone seen.

1Ki 6:29 — And he carved all the walls of the house round about with carved figures of cherubims and palm trees and open flowers, within and without.

1Ki 6:32 — The two doors also *were of* olive tree; and he carved upon them carvings of cherubims and palm trees and open flowers, and overlaid *them* with gold, and spread gold upon the cherubims, and upon the palm trees.

1Ki 6:35 — And he carved *thereon* cherubims and palm trees and open flowers: and covered *them* with gold fitted upon the carved work.

Ps 74:6 — But now they break down the carved work thereof at once with axes and hammers.

• Beds decorated with.

Pr 7:16 — I have decked my bed with coverings of tapestry, with carved *works,* with fine linen of Egypt.

• Idols manufactured by.

Isa 44:9–17; Hab 2:18–19

Dt 7:5 — But thus shall ye deal with them; ye shall destroy their altars, and break down their images, and cut down their groves, and burn their graven images with fire.

Isa 45:20 — Assemble yourselves and come; draw near together, ye *that are* escaped of the nations: they have no knowledge that set up the wood of their graven image, and pray unto a god *that* cannot save.

• Persons skilled in.

• Bezaleel.

Ex 31:5 — And in cutting of stones, to set *them,* and in carving of timber, to work in all manner of workmanship.

• Hiram.

1Ki 7:13–51; 2Ch 2:13–14

CASIPHIA • A place in the Persian empire.

Ezr 8:17 — And I sent them with commandment unto Iddo the chief at the place Casiphia, and I told them what they should say unto Iddo, *and* to his brethren the Nethinims, at the place Casiphia, that they should bring unto us ministers for the house of our God.

CASLUHIM • A people whose progenitor was a son of Mizraim.

Ge 10:14 — And Pathrusim, and Casluhim, (out of whom came Philistim,) and Caphtorim.

1Ch 1:12 — And Pathrusim, and Casluhim, (of whom came the Philistines,) and Caphthorim.

CASSIA

• An aromatic plant. Probably cinnamon.

Ps 45:8 — All thy garments *smell* of myrrh, and aloes, *and* cassia, out of the ivory palaces, whereby they have made thee glad.

Eze 27:19 — Dan also and Javan going to and fro occupied in thy fairs: bright iron, cassia, and calamus, were in thy market.

• An ingredient of the sacred oil.

Ex 30:24 — And of cassia five hundred *shekels,* after the shekel of the sanctuary, and of oil olive an hin:

CASTING ➔See: Molding

CASTLE

• A tower.

Ge 25:16 — These *are* the sons of Ishmael, and these *are* their names, by their towns, and by their castles; twelve princes according to their nations.

Nu 31:10 — And they burnt all their cities wherein they dwelt, and all their goodly castles, with fire.

1Ch 11:5 — And the inhabitants of Jebus said to David, Thou shalt not come hither. Nevertheless David took the castle of Zion, which *is* the city of David.

1Ch 11:7 — And David dwelt in the castle; therefore they called it the city of David.

2Ch 17:12 — And Jehoshaphat waxed great exceedingly; and he built in Judah castles, and cities of store.

2Ch 27:4 — Moreover he built cities in the mountains of Judah, and in the forests he built castles and towers.

Ac 21:34 — And some cried one thing, some another, among the multitude: and when he could not know the certainty for the tumult, he commanded him to be carried into the castle.

Ac 21:37 — And as Paul was to be led into the castle, he said unto the chief captain, May I speak unto thee? Who said, Canst thou speak Greek?

Ac 23:10 — And when there arose a great dissension, the chief captain, fearing lest Paul should have been pulled in pieces of them, commanded the soldiers to go down, and to take him by force from among them, and to bring *him* into the castle.

Ac 23:16 — And when Paul's sister's son heard of their lying in wait, he went and entered into the castle, and told Paul.

Ac 23:32 — On the morrow they left the horsemen to go with him, and returned to the castle:

• Bars of.

Pr 18:19 — A brother offended *is harder to be won* than a strong city: and *their* contentions *are* like the bars of a castle.

• For the doctrine, "The house is my castle".

Dt 24:10–11

➔**See: Fort**

➔**See: Tower**

CASTOR AND POLLUX • Name of a ship.

Ac 28:11 — And after three months we departed in a ship of Alexandria, which had wintered in the isle, whose sign was Castor and Pollux.

CATERPILLER

• Sent as a judgment.

1Ki 8:37 — If there be in the land famine, if there be pestilence, blasting, mildew, locust, *or* if there be caterpiller; if their enemy besiege them in the land of their cities; whatsoever plague, whatsoever sickness *there be;*

Ps 78:46 — He gave also their increase unto the caterpiller, and their labour unto the locust.

Ps 105:34 — He spake, and the locusts came, and caterpillers, and that without number,

Jer 51:27 — Set ye up a standard in the land, blow the trumpet among the nations, prepare the nations against her, call together against her the kingdoms of

Ararat, Minni, and Ashchenaz; appoint a captain against her; cause the horses to come up as the rough caterpillers.

Joel 1:4 — That which the palmerworm hath left hath the locust eaten; and that which the locust hath left hath the cankerworm eaten; and that which the cankerworm hath left hath the caterpiller eaten.

Joel 2:25 — And I will restore to you the years that the locust hath eaten, the cankerworm, and the caterpiller, and the palmerworm, my great army which I sent among you.

CATHOLICITY

- **A liberality of religious sentiment.**
- **Inculcated.**

Mk 9:38–41; Lk 9:49–50; Ac 10:1–48; 11:17–18; 15:1–31; Ro 1:1–7, 14–16; 3:20–5:2; Gal 3:27–28; Eph 2:14–17; Col 3:11–15

See: Heathen

See: Strangers

- **Instances of.**
  - **Solomon, in his prayer.**

    1Ki 8:41–43
  - **Paul, in recognizing devout heathen.**

    Ac 13:16, 26, 42–43
  - **Peter.**

    Ac 10:34–35
  - **Rulers of the synagogue at Salamis, permitting the apostles to preach.**

    Ac 13:5

CATTLE, of the bovine species

- **Used for sacrifice.**

1Ki 8:63 — And Solomon offered a sacrifice of peace offerings, which he offered unto the LORD, two and twenty thousand oxen, and an hundred and twenty thousand sheep. So the king and all the children of Israel dedicated the house of the LORD.

See: Heifer

See: Offerings

- **Sheltered.**

Ge 33:17 — And Jacob journeyed to Succoth, and built him an house, and made booths for his cattle: therefore the name of the place is called Succoth.

- **Stall-fed.**

Pr 15:17 — Better *is* a dinner of herbs where love is, than a stalled ox and hatred therewith.

- **Gilead adapted to the raising of.**

Nu 32:1–4

- **Gilead adapted to the raising of Bashan.**

Ps 22:12 — Many bulls have compassed me: strong *bulls* of Bashan have beset me round.

Eze 39:18 — Ye shall eat the flesh of the mighty, and drink the blood of the princes of the earth, of rams, of lambs, and of goats, of bullocks, all of them fatlings of Bashan.

Am 4:1 — Hear this word, ye kine of Bashan, that *are* in the mountain of Samaria, which oppress the poor, which crush the needy, which say to their masters, Bring, and let us drink.

See: Animals

See: Bull

See: Bullock, or ox

See: Cow

See: Heifer

See: Kine

See: Offerings

CAUL

- **Probably the upper lobe of the liver.**
  - **Burnt with sacrifice.**

Ex 29:13 — And thou shalt take all the fat that covereth the inwards, and the caul *that is* above the liver, and the two kidneys, and the fat that is upon them, and burn *them* upon the altar.

Ex 29:22 — Also thou shalt take of the ram the fat and the rump, and the fat that covereth the inwards, and the *caul* above the liver, and the two kidneys, and the fat that *is* upon them, and the right shoulder; for it *is* a ram of consecration:

Le 3:4 — And the two kidneys, and the fat that *is* on them, which *is* by the flanks, and the caul above the liver, with the kidneys, it shall he take away.

Le 3:10 — And the two kidneys, and the fat that *is* upon them, which *is* by the flanks, and the caul above the liver, with the kidneys, it shall he take away.

Le 3:15 — And the two kidneys, and the fat that *is* upon them, which *is* by the flanks, and the caul above the liver, with the kidneys, it shall he take away.

Le 4:9 — And the two kidneys, and the fat that *is* upon them, which *is* by the flanks, and the caul above the liver, with the kidneys, it shall he take away,

Le 7:4 — And the two kidneys, and the fat that *is* on them, which *is* by the flanks, and the caul *that is* above the liver, with the kidneys, it shall he take away:

Le 8:16 — And he took all the fat that *was* upon the inwards, and caul *above* the liver, and the two kidneys, and their fat, and Moses burned *it* upon the altar.

Le 8:25 — And he took the fat, and the rump, and all the fat that *was* upon the inwards, and the caul *above* the liver, and the two kidneys, and their fat, and the right shoulder:

Le 9:10 — But the fat, and the kidneys, and the caul above the liver of the sin offering, he burnt upon the altar; as the LORD commanded Moses.

Le 9:19 — And the fat of the bullock and of the ram, the rump, and that which covereth *the inwards,* and the kidneys, and the caul *above* the liver:

• **Netted caps.**

Isa 3:18 — In that day the Lord will take away the bravery of *their* tinkling ornaments *about their feet,* and *their* cauls, and *their* round tires like the moon,

CAUSE ✦See: Actions at Law

CAUTION

✦See: Expediency

✦See: Prudence

CAVALRY

• **Mounted on horses.**

Rev 9:16–18

Ex 14:23 — And the Egyptians pursued, and went in after them to the midst of the sea, *even* all Pharaoh's horses, his chariots, and his horsemen.

1Sa 13:5 — And the Philistines gathered themselves together to fight with Israel, thirty thousand chariots, and six thousand horsemen, and people as the sand which *is* on the sea shore in multitude: and they came up, and pitched in Michmash, eastward from Beth-aven.

2Sa 8:4 — And David took from him a thousand *chariots,* and seven hundred horsemen, and twenty thousand footmen: and David houghed all the chariot *horses,* but reserved of them *for* an hundred chariots.

1Ki 4:26 — And Solomon had forty thousand stalls of horses for his chariots, and twelve thousand horsemen.

2Ch 8:6 — And Baalath, and all the store cities that Solomon had, and all the chariot cities, and the cities of the horsemen, and all that Solomon desired to build in Jerusalem, and in Lebanon, and throughout all the land of his dominion.

2Ch 9:25 — And Solomon had four thousand stalls for horses and chariots, and twelve thousand horsemen; whom he bestowed in the chariot cities, and with the king at Jerusalem.

2Ch 12:3 — With twelve hundred chariots, and threescore thousand horsemen: and the people *were* without number that came with him out of Egypt; the Lubim, the Sukkiims, and the Ethiopians.

Isa 30:16 — But ye said, No; for we will flee upon horses; therefore shall ye flee: and, We will ride upon the swift; therefore shall they that pursue you be swift.

Isa 31:1 — Woe to them that go down to Egypt for help; and stay on horses, and trust in chariots, because *they are* many; and in horsemen, because they are very strong; but they look not unto the Holy One of Israel, neither seek the LORD!

Jer 4:29 — The whole city shall flee for the noise of the horsemen and bowmen; they shall go into thickets, and climb up upon the rocks: every city *shall be* forsaken, and not a man dwell therein.

Zec 10:5 — And they shall be as mighty *men,* which tread down *their enemies* in the mire of the streets in the battle: and they shall fight, because the LORD *is* with them, and the riders on horses shall be confounded.

• **Mounted on camels.**

1Sa 30:17 — And David smote them from the twilight even unto the evening of the next day: and there escaped not a man of them, save four hundred young men, which rode upon camels, and fled.

✦See: Armies

CAVE

• **Used as a dwelling.**

• **By Lot.**

Ge 19:30 — And Lot went up out of Zoar, and dwelt in the mountain, and his two daughters with him; for he feared to dwell in Zoar: and he dwelt in a cave, he and his two daughters.

• **By Elijah.**

1Ki 19:9 — And he came thither unto a cave, and lodged there; and, behold, the word of the LORD *came* to him, and he said unto him, What doest thou here, Elijah?

• **By Israelites.**

Eze 33:27 — Say thou thus unto them, Thus saith the Lord GOD; *As* I live, surely they that *are* in the wastes shall fall by the sword, and him that *is* in the open field will I give to the beasts to be devoured, and they that be in the forts and in the caves shall die of the pestilence.

• **By saints.**

Heb 11:38 — (Of whom the world was not worthy:) they wandered in deserts, and *in* mountains, and *in* dens and caves of the earth.

• **Place of refuge.**

Jos 10:16–27

Jgs 6:2 — And the hand of Midian prevailed against Israel: *and* because of the Midianites the children of Israel made them the dens which *are* in the mountains, and caves, and strong holds.

1Sa 13:6 — When the men of Israel saw that they were in a strait, (for the people were distressed,) then the people did hide themselves in caves, and in thickets, and in rocks, and in high places, and in pits.

1Ki 18:4 — For it was *so,* when Jezebel cut off the prophets of the LORD, that Obadiah took an hundred prophets, and hid them by fifty in a cave, and fed them with bread and water.)

1Ki 18:13 — Was it not told my lord what I did when Jezebel slew the prophets of the LORD, how I hid an hundred men of the LORD's prophets by fifty in a cave, and fed them with bread and water?

1Ki 19:9 — And he came thither unto a cave, and lodged there; and, behold, the word of the LORD *came* to him, and he said unto him, What doest thou here, Elijah?

1Ki 19:13 — And it was *so,* when Elijah heard *it,* that he wrapped his face in his mantle, and went out, and stood in the entering in of the cave. And, behold, *there came* a voice unto him, and said, What doest thou here, Elijah?

• **Burial place.**

Ge 23:9–20; 49:29–32

Ge 25:9 — And his sons Isaac and Ishmael buried him in the cave of Machpelah, in the field of Ephron the son of Zohar the Hittite, which *is* before Mamre;

Ge 50:13 — For his sons carried him into the land of Canaan, and buried him in the cave of the field of Machpelah, which Abraham bought with the field for a possession of a buryingplace of Ephron the Hittite, before Mamre.

Jn 11:38 — Jesus therefore again groaning in himself cometh to the grave. It was a cave, and a stone lay upon it.

• Of Adullam.

1Sa 22:1 — David therefore departed thence, and escaped to the cave Adullam: and when his brethren and all his father's house heard it, they went down thither to him.

2Sa 23:13 — And three of the thirty chief went down, and came to David in the harvest time unto the cave of Adullam: and the troop of the Philistines pitched in the valley of Rephaim.

1Ch 11:15 — Now three of the thirty captains went down to the rock to David, into the cave of Adullam; and the host of the Philistines encamped in the valley of Rephaim.

• Of En-gedi.

1Sa 24:3–8

CEDAR

• Valuable for building purposes.

Isa 9:10 — The bricks are fallen down, but we will build with hewn stones: the sycomores are cut down, but we will change *them into* cedars.

• David's ample provision of, in Jerusalem, for the temple.

2Ch 1:15 — And the king made silver and gold at Jerusalem *as plenteous* as stones, and cedar trees made he as the sycomore trees that *are* in the vale for abundance.

2Ch 22:4 — Wherefore he did evil in the sight of the LORD like the house of Ahab: for they were his counsellors after the death of his father to his destruction.

• Furnished by Hiram, king of Tyre, for Solomon's temple.

1Ki 5:6–10

1Ki 9:11 — (*Now* Hiram the king of Tyre had furnished Solomon with cedar trees and fir trees, and with gold, according to all his desire,) that then king Solomon gave Hiram twenty cities in the land of Galilee.

2Ch 2:16 — And we will cut wood out of Lebanon, as much as thou shalt need: and we will bring it to thee in flotes by sea to Joppa; and thou shall carry it up to Jerusalem.

• Used in rebuilding the temple.

Ezr 3:7 — They gave money also unto the masons, and to the carpenters; and meat, and drink, and oil, unto them of Zidon, and to them of Tyre, to bring cedar trees from Lebanon to the sea of Joppa, according to the grant that they had of Cyrus king of Persia.

• Used in David's palace.

2Sa 5:11 — And Hiram king of Tyre sent messengers to David, and cedar trees, and carpenters, and masons: and they built David an house.

1Ch 17:1 — Now it came to pass, as David sat in his house, that David said to Nathan the prophet, Lo, I dwell in an house of cedars, but the ark of the covenant of the LORD *remaineth* under curtains.

• Used in Solomon's palace.

1Ki 7:2 — He built also the house of the forest of Lebanon; the length thereof *was* an hundred cubits, and the breadth thereof fifty cubits, and the height thereof thirty cubits, upon four rows of cedar pillars, with cedar beams upon the pillars.

• Used for masts of ships.

Eze 27:5 — They have made all thy *ship* boards of fir trees of Senir: they have taken cedars from Lebanon to make masts for thee.

• Used in purifications.

Le 14:49–52

Le 14:4 — Then shall the priest command to take for him that is to be cleansed two birds alive *and* clean, and cedar wood, and scarlet, and hyssop:

Le 14:6 — As for the living bird, he shall take it, and the cedar wood, and the scarlet, and the hyssop, and shall dip them and the living bird in the blood of the bird *that was* killed over the running water:

Nu 19:6 — And the priest shall take cedar wood, and hyssop, and scarlet, and cast *it* into the midst of the burning of the heifer.

• Figurative.

Ps 72:16 — There shall be an handful of corn in the earth upon the top of the mountains; the fruit thereof shall shake like Lebanon: and *they* of the city shall flourish like grass of the earth.

Ps 92:12 — The righteous shall flourish like the palm tree: he shall grow like a cedar in Lebanon.

Isa 2:13 — And upon all the cedars of Lebanon, *that are* high and lifted up, and upon all the oaks of Bashan,

Isa 14:8 — Yea, the fir trees rejoice at thee, *and* the cedars of Lebanon, *saying,* Since thou art laid down, no feller is come up against us.

Jer 22:7 — And I will prepare destroyers against thee, every one with his weapons: and they shall cut down thy choice cedars, and cast *them* into the fire.

Eze 31:3 — Behold, the Assyrian *was* a cedar in Lebanon with fair branches, and with a shadowing shroud, and of an high stature; and his top was among the thick boughs.

Zec 11:2 — Howl, fir tree; for the cedar is fallen; because the mighty are spoiled: howl, O ye oaks of Bashan; for the forest of the vintage is come down.

CEDRON

• Called also Kidron.

• Brook of, running south under the eastern wall of Jerusalem.

1Ki 2:37 — For it shall be, *that* on the day thou goest out, and passest over the brook Kidron, thou shalt know for certain that thou shalt surely die: thy blood shall be upon thine own head.

Ne 2:15 — Then went I up in the night by the brook, and viewed the wall, and turned back, and entered by the gate of the valley, and *so* returned.

Jer 31:40 — And the whole valley of the dead bodies, and of the ashes, and all the fields unto the brook of Kidron, unto the corner of the horse gate toward the east, *shall be* holy unto the LORD; it shall not be plucked up, nor thrown down any more for ever.

• Idols destroyed on the banks of.

• By Asa.

1Ki 15:13 — And also Maachah his mother, even her he removed from *being* queen, because she had made an idol in a grove; and Asa destroyed her idol, and burnt *it* by the brook Kidron.

• By Josiah.

2Ki 23:6 — And he brought out the grove from the house of the LORD, without Jerusalem, unto the brook Kidron, and burned it at the brook Kidron, and stamped *it* small to powder, and cast the powder thereof upon the graves of the children of the people.

2Ki 23:12 — And the altars that *were* on the top of the upper chamber of Ahaz, which the kings of Judah had made, and the altars which Manasseh had made in the two courts of the house of the LORD, did the king beat down, and brake *them* down from thence, and cast the dust of them into the brook Kidron.

• By Hezekiah.

2Ch 29:16 — And the priests went into the inner part of the house of the LORD, to cleanse *it,* and brought out all the uncleanness that they found in the temple of the LORD into the court of the house of the LORD. And the Levites took *it,* to carry *it* out abroad into the brook Kidron.

• Its channel changed by Hezekiah.

2Ch 32:4 — So there was gathered much people together, who stopped all the fountains, and the brook that ran through the midst of the land, saying, Why should the kings of Assyria come, and find much water?

CELIBACY

Mt 19:10–12; 1Co 7:1–2, 7–9, 25–26, 32–40; 1Ti 4:1–3; Rev 14:1–5

1Co 9:5 — Have we not power to lead about a sister, a wife, as well as other apostles, and *as* the brethren of the Lord, and Cephas?

CELLAR

• For wine.

1Ch 27:27 — And over the vineyards was Shimei the Ramathite: over the increase of the vineyards for the wine cellars *was* Zabdi the Shiphmite:

• For oil.

1Ch 27:28 — And over the olive trees and the sycomore trees that *were* in the low plains *was* Baalhanan the Gederite: and over the cellars of oil *was* Joash:

CENCHREA • A city of Corinth.

Ac 18:18 — And Paul *after this* tarried *there* yet a good while, and then took his leave of the brethren, and sailed thence into Syria, and with him Priscilla and Aquila; having shorn *his* head in Cenchrea: for he had a vow.

Ro 16:1 — I commend unto you Phebe our sister, which is a servant of the church which is at Cenchrea:

CENSER

• Used for offering incense.

Nu 16:6–7, 16–18

Le 16:12 — And he shall take a censer full of burning coals of fire from off the altar before the LORD, and his hands full of sweet incense beaten small, and bring *it* within the vail:

Nu 4:14 — And they shall put upon it all the vessels thereof, wherewith they minister about it, *even* the censers, the fleshhooks, and the shovels, and the basons, all the vessels of the altar; and they shall spread upon it a covering of badgers' skins, and put to the staves of it.

Nu 16:46 — And Moses said unto Aaron, Take a censer, and put fire therein from off the altar, and put on incense, and go quickly unto the congregation, and make an atonement for them: for there is wrath gone out from the LORD; the plague is begun.

Rev 8:3 — And another angel came and stood at the altar, having a golden censer; and there was given unto him much incense, that he should offer *it* with the prayers of all saints upon the golden altar which was before the throne.

• For the temple, made of gold.

1Ki 7:50 — And the bowls, and the snuffers, and the basons, and the spoons, and the censers *of* pure gold; and the hinges *of* gold, *both* for the doors of the inner house, the most holy *place, and* for the doors of the house, *to wit,* of the temple.

2Ch 4:22 — And the snuffers, and the basons, and the spoons, and the censers, *of* pure gold: and the entry of the house, the inner doors thereof for the most holy *place,* and the doors of the house of the temple, *were of* gold.

Heb 9:4 — Which had the golden censer, and the ark of the covenant overlaid round about with gold, wherein *was* the golden pot that had manna, and Aaron's rod that budded, and the tables of the covenant;

• Those which Korah used were converted into plates.

Nu 16:37–39

• Used in idolatrous rites.

Eze 8:11 — And there stood before them seventy men of the ancients of the house of Israel, and in the midst of them stood Jaazaniah the son of Shaphan, with every man his censer in his hand; and a thick cloud of incense went up.

• Symbolic.

Rev 8:3 — And another angel came and stood at the altar, having a golden censer; and there was given unto him much incense, that he should offer *it* with the prayers of all saints upon the golden altar which was before the throne.

Rev 8:5 — And the angel took the censer, and filled it with fire of the altar, and cast *it* into the earth: and there were voices, and thunderings, and lightnings, and an earthquake.

CENSORIOUSNESS

See: Uncharitableness

See: Speaking; evil

See: Charitableness

CENSUS

• Numbering of Israel

• By Moses.

Nu 1:1–54; 3:14–43; 26:1–65

Ex 38:26 — A bekah for every man, *that is,* half a shekel, after the shekel of the sanctuary, for every one that went to be numbered, from twenty years old and upward, for six hundred thousand and three thousand and five hundred and fifty *men.*

• By David.

2Sa 24:1–9; 1Ch 21:1–8

1Ch 27:24 — Joab the son of Zeruiah began to number, but he finished not, because there fell wrath for it against Israel; neither was the number put in the account of the chronicles of king David.

• A poll tax to be levied at each.

Ex 30:12–16

Ex 38:26 — A bekah for every man, *that is,* half a shekel, after the shekel of the sanctuary, for every one that went to be numbered, from twenty years old and upward, for six hundred thousand and three thousand and five hundred and fifty *men.*

• Of the Roman Empire, by Caesar.

Lk 2:1–3

CENTURION

• A commander of one hundred soldiers in the Roman army.

Mk 15:44–45; Ac 22:25–26

Ac 21:32 — Who immediately took soldiers and centurions, and ran down unto them: and when they saw the chief captain and the soldiers, they left beating of Paul.

Ac 23:17 — Then Paul called one of the centurions unto *him,* and said, Bring this young man unto the chief captain: for he hath a certain thing to tell him.

Ac 23:23 — And he called unto *him* two centurions, saying, Make ready two hundred soldiers to go to Caesarea, and horsemen threescore and ten, and spearmen two hundred, at the third hour of the night;

Ac 24:23 — And he commanded a centurion to keep Paul, and to let *him* have liberty, and that he should forbid none of his acquaintance to minister or come unto him.

• Of Capernaum, comes to Jesus in behalf of his servant.

Mt 8:5–13; Lk 7:1–10

• In charge of the soldiers who crucified Jesus, testifies, "Truly this was the Son of God".

Mt 27:54 — Now when the centurion, and they that were with him, watching Jesus, saw the earthquake, and those things that were done, they feared greatly, saying, Truly this was the Son of God.

Mk 15:39 — And when the centurion, which stood over against him, saw that he so cried out, and gave up the ghost, he said, Truly this man was the Son of God.

Lk 23:47 — Now when the centurion saw what was done, he glorified God, saying, Certainly this was a righteous man.

See: Cornelius

CEPHAS See: Peter

CESAR See: Caesar

CESAREA See: Caesarea

CESAREA PHILIPPI See: Caesarea Philippi

CHAFF

• Figurative.

Job 21:18 — They are as stubble before the wind, and as chaff that the storm carrieth away.

Ps 1:4 — The ungodly *are* not so: but *are* like the chaff which the wind driveth away.

Ps 35:5 — Let them be as chaff before the wind: and let the angel of the LORD chase *them.*

Isa 17:13 — The nations shall rush like the rushing of many waters: but *God* shall rebuke them, and they shall flee far off, and shall be chased as the chaff of the mountains before the wind, and like a rolling thing before the whirlwind.

Da 2:35 — Then was the iron, the clay, the brass, the silver, and the gold, broken to pieces together, and became like the chaff of the summer threshingfloors; and the wind carried them away, that no place was found for them: and the stone that smote the image became a great mountain, and filled the whole earth.

Hos 13:3 — Therefore they shall be as the morning cloud, and as the early dew that passeth away, as the chaff *that* is driven with the whirlwind out of the floor, and as the smoke out of the chimney.

Mt 3:12 — Whose fan *is* in his hand, and he will throughly purge his floor, and gather his wheat into the garner; but he will burn up the chaff with unquenchable fire.

Lk 3:17 — Whose fan *is* in his hand, and he will throughly purge his floor, and will gather the wheat into his garner; but the chaff he will burn with fire unquenchable.

CHAINS

• Used as ornaments.

• Worn by princes.

Ge 41:42 — And Pharaoh took off his ring from his hand, and put it upon Joseph's hand, and arrayed him in vestures of fine linen, and put a gold chain about his neck;

Da 5:7 — The king cried aloud to bring in the astrologers, the Chaldeans, and the soothsayers. *And* the king spake, and said to the wise *men* of Babylon, Whosoever shall read this writing, and shew me the interpretation thereof, shall be clothed with scarlet, and *have* a chain of gold about his neck, and shall be the third ruler in the kingdom.

Da 5:29 — Then commanded Belshazzar, and they clothed Daniel with scarlet, and *put* a chain of gold about his neck, and made a proclamation concerning him, that he should be the third ruler in the kingdom.

• Worn on ankles.

Nu 31:50 — We have therefore brought an oblation for the LORD, what every man hath gotten, of jewels of gold, chains, and bracelets, rings, earrings, and tablets, to make an atonement for our souls before the LORD.

Isa 3:19 — The chains, and the bracelets, and the mufflers,

• Worn on the breastplate of high priest.

Ex 28:14 — And two chains *of* pure gold at the ends; *of* wreathen work shalt thou make them, and fasten the wreathen chains to the ouches.

Ex 39:15 — And they made upon the breastplate chains at the ends, *of* wreathen work *of* pure gold.

• Used on camels.

Jgs 8:26 — And the weight of the golden earrings that he requested was a thousand and seven hundred *shekels* of gold; beside ornaments, and collars, and purple raiment that *was* on the kings of Midian, and beside the chains that *were* about their camels' necks.

• A partition of, in the temple.

1Ki 6:21 — So Solomon overlaid the house within with pure gold: and he made a partition by the chains of gold before the oracle; and he overlaid it with gold.

1Ki 7:17 — *And* nets of checker work, and wreaths of chain work, for the chapiters which *were* upon the top of the pillars; seven for the one chapiter, and seven for the other chapiter.

• Used to confine prisoners.

Ac 12:6–7

Ps 68:6 — God setteth the solitary in families: he bringeth out those which are bound with chains: but the rebellious dwell in a dry *land.*

Ps 149:8 — To bind their kings with chains, and their nobles with fetters of iron;

Jer 40:4 — And now, behold, I loose thee this day from the chains which *were* upon thine hand. If it seem good unto thee to come with me into Babylon, come; and I will look well unto thee: but if it seem ill unto thee to come with me into Babylon, forbear: behold, all the land *is* before thee: whither it seemeth good and convenient for thee to go, thither go.

Ac 21:33 — Then the chief captain came near, and took him, and commanded *him* to be bound with two chains; and demanded who he was, and what he had done.

Ac 28:20 — For this cause therefore have I called for you, to see *you,* and to speak with *you:* because that for the hope of Israel I am bound with this chain.

2Ti 1:16 — The Lord give mercy unto the house of Onesiphorus; for he oft refreshed me, and was not ashamed of my chain:

→See: Fetters

• Figurative.

Eze 7:23–27

Ps 73:6 — Therefore pride compasseth them about as a chain; violence covereth them *as* a garment.

Pr 1:9 — For they *shall be* an ornament of grace unto thy head, and chains about thy neck.

La 3:7 — He hath hedged me about, that I cannot get out: he hath made my chain heavy.

2Pe 2:4 — For if God spared not the angels that sinned, but cast *them* down to hell, and delivered *them* into chains of darkness, to be reserved unto judgment;

Jude 1:6 — And the angels which kept not their first estate, but left their own habitation, he hath reserved in everlasting chains under darkness unto the judgment of the great day.

Rev 20:1 — And I saw an angel come down from heaven, having the key of the bottomless pit and a great chain in his hand.

CHALCEDONY • A precious stone.

Rev 21:19 — And the foundations of the wall of the city *were* garnished with all manner of precious stones. The first foundation *was* jasper; the second, sapphire; the third, a chalcedony; the fourth, an emerald;

CHALCOL

• Called also Calcol.

• Son of Nahor.

1Ki 4:31 — For he was wiser than all men; than Ethan the Ezrahite, and Heman, and Chalcol, and Darda, the sons of Mahol: and his fame was in all nations round about.

1Ch 2:6 — And the sons of Zerah; Zimri, and Ethan, and Heman, and Calcol, and Dara: five of them in all.

CHALDEA

• The southern portion of Babylonia.

• Often used interchangeably with Babylon, as the name of the empire founded in the valley of the Euphrates.

• Abraham a native of.

Ge 11:28 — And Haran died before his father Terah in the land of his nativity, in Ur of the Chaldees.

Ge 11:31 — And Terah took Abram his son, and Lot the son of Haran his son's son, and Sarai his daughter in law, his son Abram's wife; and they went forth with them from Ur of the Chaldees, to go into the land of Canaan; and they came unto Haran, and dwelt there.

Ge 15:7 — And he said unto him, I *am* the LORD that brought thee out of Ur of the Chaldees, to give thee this land to inherit it.

• Founded by the Assyrians.

Isa 23:13 — Behold the land of the Chaldeans; this people was not, *til* the Assyrian founded it for them that dwell in the wilderness: they set up the towers thereof, they raised up the palaces thereof; *and* he brought it to ruin.

• Character of its people.

Hab 1:6 — For, lo, I raise up the Chaldeans, *that* bitter and hasty nation, which shall march through the breadth of the land, to possess the dwellingplaces *that are* not theirs.

See: Babylon

See: Chaldeans

CHALDEANS

• Learned and wise men of the East.

Jer 50:35 — A sword *is* upon the Chaldeans, saith the LORD, and upon the inhabitants of Babylon, and upon her princes, and upon her wise *men*.

Da 1:4 — Children in whom *was* no blemish, but well favoured, and skilful in all wisdom, and cunning in knowledge, and understanding science, and such as *had* ability in them to stand in the king's palace, and whom they might teach the learning and the tongue of the Chaldeans.

Da 2:2 — Then the king commanded to call the magicians, and the astrologers, and the sorcerers, and the Chaldeans, for to shew the king his dreams. So they came and stood before the king.

Da 4:7 — Then came in the magicians, the astrologers, the Chaldeans, and the soothsayers: and I told the dream before them; but they did not make known unto me the interpretation thereof.

Da 5:7 — The king cried aloud to bring in the astrologers, the Chaldeans, and the soothsayers. *And* the king spake, and said to the wise *men* of Babylon, Whosoever shall read this writing, and shew me the interpretation thereof, shall be clothed with scarlet, and *have* a chain of gold about his neck, and shall be the third ruler in the kingdom.

CHALK

Isa 27:9 — By this therefore shall the iniquity of Jacob be purged; and this is all the fruit to take away his sin; when he maketh all the stones of the altar as chalkstones that are beaten in sunder, the groves and images shall not stand up.

CHAMBERLAIN • An officer of a king.

Est 1:10–15; 2:3–21; 4:4–5

2Ki 23:11 — And he took away the horses that the kings of Judah had given to the sun, at the entering in of the house of the LORD, by the chamber of Nathanmelech the chamberlain, which *was* in the suburbs, and burned the chariots of the sun with fire.

Ac 12:20 — And Herod was highly displeased with them of Tyre and Sidon: but they came with one accord to him, and, having made Blastus the king's chamberlain their friend, desired peace; because their country was nourished by the king's *country*.

Ro 16:23 — Gaius mine host, and of the whole church, saluteth you. Erastus the chamberlain of the city saluteth you, and Quartus a brother.

CHAMELEON

• Forbidden as food.

Le 11:30 — And the ferret, and the chameleon, and the lizard, and the snail, and the mole.

CHAMOIS • A species of antelope.

Dt 14:5 — The hart, and the roebuck, and the fallow deer, and the wild goat, and the pygarg, and the wild ox, and the chamois.

CHAMPAIGN • A flat, open country.

Dt 11:30 — *Are* they not on the other side Jordan, by the way where the sun goeth down, in the land of the Canaanites, which dwell in the champaign over against Gilgal, beside the plains of Moreh?

CHAMPIONSHIP

• Battles were decided by.

• Instances of.

• Goliath and David.

1Sa 17:8–53

• Young men of David's and Abner's armies.

2Sa 2:14–17

• Representatives of the Philistines' and David's armies.

2Sa 21:15–22

CHANAAN See: Canaan

CHANCELLOR

• A state officer.

Ezr 4:8–9

Ezr 4:17 — *Then* sent the king an answer unto Rehum the chancellor, and *to* Shimshai the scribe, and *to* the rest of their companions that dwell in Samaria, and *unto* the rest beyond the river, Peace, and at such a time.

See: Cabinet

CHANGE OF VENUE

• Granted Paul.

Ac 23:17–35

• Declined by Paul.

Ac 25:9 — But Festus, willing to do the Jews a pleasure, answered Paul, and said, Wilt thou go up to Jerusalem, and there be judged of these things before me?

Ac 25:11 — For if I be an offender, or have committed any thing worthy of death, I refuse not to die: but if there be none of these things whereof these accuse me, no man may deliver me unto them. I appeal unto Caesar.

CHAPITER • Head of a pillar.

1Ki 7:16–42; 2Ch 4:12–13

Ex 36:38 — And the five pillars of it with their hooks: and he overlaid their chapiters and their fillets with gold: but their five sockets *were of* brass.

2Ki 25:17 — The height of the one pillar *was* eighteen cubits, and the chapiter upon it *was* brass: and the height of the chapiter three cubits; and the wreathen work, and pomegranates upon the chapiter round about, all of brass: and like unto these had the second pillar with wreathen work.

Jer 52:22 — And a chapiter of brass *was* upon it; and the height of one chapiter *was* five cubits, with network and pomegranates upon the chapiters round about, all of brass. The second pillar also and the pomegranates *were* like unto these.

CHARACTER, of Saints

• Attentive to Christ's voice.

Jn 10:3–4

• Blameless and harmless.

Php 2:15 — That ye may be blameless and harmless, the sons of God, without rebuke, in the midst of a crooked and perverse nation, among whom ye shine as lights in the world;

• Bold.

Pr 28:1 — The wicked flee when no man pursueth: but the righteous are bold as a lion.

• Contrite.

Isa 57:15 — For thus saith the high and lofty One that inhabiteth eternity, whose name *is* Holy; I dwell in the high and holy *place,* with him also *that is* of a contrite and humble spirit, to revive the spirit of the humble, and to revive the heart of the contrite ones.

Isa 66:2 — For all those *things* hath mine hand made, and all those *things* have been, saith the LORD: but to this *man* will I look, *even* to *him that is* poor and of a contrite spirit, and trembleth at my word.

• Devout.

Ac 8:2 — And devout men carried Stephen *to his burial,* and made great lamentation over him.

Ac 22:12 — And one Ananias, a devout man according to the law, having a good report of all the Jews which dwelt *there,*

• Faithful.

Rev 17:14 — These shall make war with the Lamb, and the Lamb shall overcome them: for he is Lord of lords, and King of kings: and they that are with him *are* called, and chosen, and faithful.

• Fearing God.

Mal 3:16 — Then they that feared the LORD spake often one to another: and the LORD hearkened, and heard *it,* and a book of remembrance was written before him for them that feared the LORD, and that thought upon his name.

Ac 10:2 — A devout *man,* and one that feared God with all his house, which gave much alms to the people, and prayed to God alway.

• Following Christ.

Jn 10:4 — And when he putteth forth his own sheep, he goeth before them, and the sheep follow him: for they know his voice.

Jn 10:27 — My sheep hear my voice, and I know them, and they follow me:

• Godly.

Ps 4:3 — But know that the LORD hath set apart him that is godly for himself: the LORD will hear when I call unto him.

2Pe 2:9 — The Lord knoweth how to deliver the godly out of temptations, and to reserve the unjust unto the day of judgment to be punished:

• Guileless.

Jn 1:47 — Jesus saw Nathanael coming to him, and saith of him, Behold an Israelite indeed, in whom is no guile!

• Holy.

Dt 7:6 — For thou *art* an holy people unto the LORD thy God: the LORD thy God hath chosen thee to be a special people unto himself, above all people that *are* upon the face of the earth.

Dt 14:2 — For thou *art* an holy people unto the LORD thy God, and the LORD hath chosen thee to be a peculiar people unto himself, above all the nations that *are* upon the earth.

Col 3:12 — Put on therefore, as the elect of God, holy and beloved, bowels of mercies, kindness, humbleness of mind, meekness, longsuffering;

• Humble.

Ps 34:2 — My soul shall make her boast in the LORD: the humble shall hear *thereof,* and be glad.

1Pe 5:5 — Likewise, ye younger, submit yourselves unto the elder. Yea, all *of you* be subject one to another, and be clothed with humility: for God resisteth the proud, and giveth grace to the humble.

• Hungering for righteousness.

Mt 5:6 — Blessed *are* they which do hunger and thirst after righteousness: for they shall be filled.

• Just.

Ge 6:9 — These *are* the generations of Noah: Noah was a just man *and* perfect in his generations, *and* Noah walked with God.

Hab 2:4 — Behold, his soul *which* is lifted up is not upright in him: but the just shall live by his faith.

Lk 2:25 — And, behold, there was a man in Jerusalem, whose name *was* Simeon; and the same man *was* just and devout, waiting for the consolation of Israel: and the Holy Ghost was upon him.

• Led by the Spirit.

Ro 8:14 — For as many as are led by the Spirit of God, they are the sons of God.

• Liberal.

Isa 32:8 — But the liberal deviseth liberal things; and by liberal things shall he stand.

2Co 9:13 — Whiles by the experiment of this ministration they glorify God for your professed subjection into the gospel of Christ, and for *your* liberal distribution unto them, and unto all *men;*

- **Loathing themselves.**

Eze 20:43 — And there shall ye remember your ways, and all your doings, wherein ye have been defiled; and ye shall lothe yourselves in your own sight for all your evils that ye have committed.

- **Loving.**

Col 1:4 — Since we heard of your faith in Christ Jesus, and of the love *which ye have* to all the saints,

1Th 4:9 — But as touching brotherly love ye need not that I write unto you: for ye yourselves are taught of God to love one another.

- **Lowly.**

Pr 16:19 — Better *it is to be* of an humble spirit with the lowly, than to divide the spoil with the proud.

- **Meek.**

Isa 29:19 — The meek also shall increase *their* joy in the LORD, and the poor among men shall rejoice in the Holy One of Israel.

Mt 5:5 — Blessed *are* the meek: for they shall inherit the earth.

- **Merciful.**

Ps 37:26 — *He is* ever merciful, and lendeth; and his seed *is* blessed.

Mt 5:7 — Blessed *are* the merciful: for they shall obtain mercy.

- **New creatures.**

2Co 5:17 — Therefore if any man *be* in Christ, *he is* a new creature: old things are passed away; behold, all things are become new.

Eph 2:10 — For we are his workmanship, created in Christ Jesus unto good works, which God hath before ordained that we should walk in them.

- **Obedient.**

Ro 16:19 — For your obedience is come abroad unto all *men.* I am glad therefore on your behalf: but yet I would have you wise unto that which is good, and simple concerning evil.

1Pe 1:14 — As obedient children, not fashioning yourselves according to the former lusts in your ignorance:

- **Poor in spirit.**

Mt 5:3 — Blessed *are* the poor in spirit: for theirs is the kingdom of heaven.

- **Prudent.**

Pr 16:21 — The wise in heart shall be called prudent: and the sweetness of the lips increaseth learning.

- **Pure in heart.**

Mt 5:8 — Blessed *are* the pure in heart: for they shall see God.

1Jn 3:3 — And every man that hath this hope in him purifieth himself, even as he is pure.

- **Righteous.**

Isa 60:21 — Thy people also *shall be* all righteous: they shall inherit the land for ever, the branch of my planting, the work of my hands, that I may be glorified.

Lk 1:6 — And they were both righteous before God, walking in all the commandments and ordinances of the Lord blameless.

- **Sincere.**

2Co 1:12 — For our rejoicing is this, the testimony of our conscience, that in simplicity and godly sincerity, not with fleshly wisdom, but by the grace of God, we have had our conversation in the world, and more abundantly to you-ward.

2Co 2:17 — For we are not as many, which corrupt the word of God: but as of sincerity, but as of God, in the sight of God speak we in Christ.

- **Steadfast.**

Ac 2:42 — And they continued stedfastly in the apostles' doctrine and fellowship, and in breaking of bread, and in prayers.

Col 2:5 — For though I be absent in the flesh, yet am I with you in the spirit, joying and beholding your order, and the stedfastness of your faith in Christ.

- **Taught of God.**

Isa 54:13 — And all thy children *shall be* taught of the LORD; and great *shall be* the peace of thy children.

1Jn 2:27 — But the anointing which ye have received of him abideth in you, and ye need not that any man teach you: but as the same anointing teacheth you of all things, and is truth, and is no lie, and even as it hath taught you, ye shall abide in him.

- **True.**

2Co 6:8 — By honour and dishonour, by evil report and good report: as deceivers, and *yet* true;

- **Undefiled.**

Ps 119:1 — Blessed *are* the undefiled in the way, who walk in the law of the LORD.

- **Upright.**

1Ki 3:6 — And Solomon said, Thou hast shewed unto thy servant David my father great mercy, according as he walked before thee in truth, and in righteousness, and in uprightness of heart with thee; and thou hast kept for him this great kindness, that thou hast given him a son to sit on his throne, as *it is* this day.

Ps 15:2 — He that walketh uprightly, and worketh righteousness, and speaketh the truth in his heart.

- **Watchful.**

Lk 12:37 — Blessed *are* those servants, whom the lord when he cometh shall find watching: verily I say unto you, that he shall gird himself, and make them to sit down to meat, and will come forth and serve them.

- **Zealous of good works.**

Tit 2:14 — Who gave himself for us, that he might redeem us from all iniquity, and purify unto himself a peculiar people, zealous of good works.

See: Righteous; described

CHARACTER, of the Wicked

- **Abominable.**

Rev 21:8 — But the fearful, and unbelieving, and the abominable, and murderers, and whoremongers, and sorcerers, and idolaters, and all liars, shall have their part in the lake which burneth with fire and brimstone: which is the second death.

- **Alienated from God.**

Col 1:1–29

Eph 4:18 — Having the understanding darkened, being alienated from the life of God through the ignorance that is in them, because of the blindness of their heart:

• Blasphemous.

Lk 22:65 — And many other things blasphemously spake they against him.

Rev 16:9 — And men were scorched with great heat, and blasphemed the name of God, which hath power over these plagues: and they repented not to give him glory.

• Blinded.

2Co 4:4 — In whom the god of this world hath blinded the minds of them which believe not, lest the light of the glorious gospel of Christ, who is the image of God, should shine unto them.

Eph 4:18 — Having the understanding darkened, being alienated from the life of God through the ignorance that is in them, because of the blindness of their heart:

• Boastful.

Ps 10:3 — For the wicked boasteth of his heart's desire, and blesseth the covetous, *whom* the LORD abhorreth.

Ps 49:6 — They that trust in their wealth, and boast themselves in the multitude of their riches;

• Conspiring against saints.

Ne 4:8 — And conspired all of them together to come *and* to fight against Jerusalem, and to hinder it.

Ne 6:2 — That Sanballat and Geshem sent unto me, saying, Come, let us meet together in *some one of* the villages in the plain of Ono. But they thought to do me mischief.

Ps 38:12 — They also that seek after my life lay snares *for me:* and they that seek my hurt speak mischievous things, and imagine deceits all the day long.

• Corrupt.

Mt 7:17 — Even so every good tree bringeth forth good fruit; but a corrupt tree bringeth forth evil fruit.

Eph 4:22 — That ye put off concerning the former conversation the old man, which is corrupt according to the deceitful lusts;

• Covetous.

Mic 2:2 — And they covet fields, and take *them* by violence; and houses, and take *them* away: so they oppress a man and his house, even a man and his heritage.

Ro 1:29 — Being filled with all unrighteousness, fornication, wickedness, covetousness, maliciousness; full of envy, murder, debate, deceit, malignity; whisperers,

• Deceitful.

Ps 5:6 — Thou shalt destroy them that speak leasing: the LORD will abhor the bloody and deceitful man.

Ro 3:13 — Their throat *is* an open sepulchre; with their tongues they have used deceit; the poison of asps *is* under their lips:

• Delighting in the iniquity of others.

Pr 2:14 — Who rejoice to do evil, *and* delight in the frowardness of the wicked;

Ro 1:32 — Who knowing the judgment of God, that they which commit such things are worthy of death, not only do the same, but have pleasure in them that do them.

• Despising saints.

2Ti 3:3–4

Ne 2:19 — But when Sanballat the Horonite, and Tobiah the servant, the Ammonite, and Geshem the Arabian, heard *it,* they laughed us to scorn, and despised us, and said, What *is* this thing that ye do? will ye rebel against the king?

Ne 4:2 — And he spake before his brethren and the army of Samaria, and said, What do these feeble Jews? will they fortify themselves? will they sacrifice? will they make an end in a day? will they revive the stones out of the heaps of the rubbish which are burned?

• Destructive.

Isa 59:7 — Their feet run to evil, and they make haste to shed innocent blood: their thoughts *are* thoughts of iniquity; wasting and destruction *are* in their paths.

• Disobedient.

Ne 9:26 — Nevertheless they were disobedient, and rebelled against thee, and cast thy law behind their backs, and slew thy prophets which testified against them to turn them to thee, and they wrought great provocations.

Tit 3:3 — For we ourselves also were sometimes foolish, disobedient, deceived, serving divers lusts and pleasures, living in malice and envy, hateful, *and* hating one another.

1Pe 2:7 — Unto you therefore which believe *he is* precious: but unto them which be disobedient, the stone which the builders disallowed, the same is made the head of the corner,

• Enticing to evil.

Pr 1:10–14

2Ti 3:6 — For of this sort are they which creep into houses, and lead captive silly women laden with sins, led away with divers lusts,

• Envious.

Ne 2:10 — When Sanballat the Horonite, and Tobiah the servant, the Ammonite, heard *of it,* it grieved them exceedingly that there was come a man to seek the welfare of the children of Israel.

Tit 3:3 — For we ourselves also were sometimes foolish, disobedient, deceived, serving divers lusts and pleasures, living in malice and envy, hateful, *and* hating one another.

• Evildoers.

Jer 13:23 — Can the Ethiopian change his skin, or the leopard his spots? *then* may ye also do good, that are accustomed to do evil.

Mic 7:3 — That they may do evil with both hands earnestly, the prince asketh, and the judge *asketh* for a reward; and the great *man,* he uttereth his mischievous desire: so they wrap it up.

- **Fearful.**

Pr 28:1 — The wicked flee when no man pursueth: but the righteous are bold as a lion.

Rev 21:8 — But the fearful, and unbelieving, and the abominable, and murderers, and whoremongers, and sorcerers, and idolaters, and all liars, shall have their part in the lake which burneth with fire and brimstone: which is the second death.

- **Fierce.**

Pr 16:29 — A violent man enticeth his neighbour, and leadeth him into the way *that is* not good.

2Ti 3:3 — Without natural affection, trucebreakers, false accusers, incontinent, fierce, despisers of those that are good,

- **Foolish.**

Dt 32:6 — Do ye thus requite the LORD, O foolish people and unwise? *is* not he thy father *that* hath bought thee? hath he not made thee, and established thee?

Ps 5:5 — The foolish shall not stand in thy sight: thou hatest all workers of iniquity.

- **Forgetting God.**

Job 8:13 — So *are* the paths of all that forget God; and the hypocrite's hope shall perish:

- **Fraudulent.**

Ps 37:21 — The wicked borroweth, and payeth not again: but the righteous sheweth mercy, and giveth.

Mic 6:11 — Shall I count *them* pure with the wicked balances, and with the bag of deceitful weights?

- **Froward.**

Pr 21:8 — The way of man *is* froward and strange: but *as for* the pure, his work *is* right.

Isa 57:17 — For the iniquity of his covetousness was I wroth, and smote him: I hid me, and was wroth, and he went on frowardly in the way of his heart.

- **Glorying in their shame.**

Php 3:19 — Whose end *is* destruction, whose God *is their* belly, and *whose* glory *is* in their shame, who mind earthly things.)

- **Hard-hearted.**

Eze 3:7 — But the house of Israel will not hearken unto thee; for they will not hearken unto me: for all the house of Israel *are* impudent and hardhearted.

- **Hating the light.**

Job 24:13 — They are of those that rebel against the light; they know not the ways thereof, nor abide in the paths thereof.

Jn 3:20 — For every one that doeth evil hateth the light, neither cometh to the light, lest his deeds should be reproved.

- **Heady and highminded.**

2Ti 3:4 — Traitors, heady, highminded, lovers of pleasures more than lovers of God;

- **Hostile to God.**

Ro 8:7 — Because the carnal mind *is* enmity against God: for it is not subject to the law of God, neither indeed can be.

Col 1:21 — And you, that were sometime alienated and enemies in *your* mind by wicked works, yet now hath he reconciled:

- **Hypocritical.**

Isa 29:13 — Wherefore the Lord said, Forasmuch as this people draw near *me* with their mouth, and with their lips do honour me, but have removed their heart far from me, and their fear toward me is taught by the precept of men:

2Ti 3:5 — Having a form of godliness, but denying the power thereof: from such turn away.

- **Ignorant of God.**

Hos 4:1 — Hear the word of the LORD, ye children of Israel: for the LORD hath a controversy with the inhabitants of the land, because *there is* no truth, nor mercy, nor knowledge of God in the land.

2Th 1:8 — In flaming fire taking vengeance on them that know not God, and that obey not the gospel of our Lord Jesus Christ:

- **Impudent.**

Eze 2:4 — For *they are* impudent children and stiffhearted. I do send thee unto them; and thou shalt say unto them, Thus saith the Lord GOD.

- **Incontinent.**

2Ti 3:3 — Without natural affection, trucebreakers, false accusers, incontinent, fierce, despisers of those that are good,

- **Infidel.**

Ps 10:4 — The wicked, through the pride of his countenance, will not seek *after God:* God *is* not in all his thoughts.

Ps 14:1 — The fool hath said in his heart, *There is* no God. They are corrupt, they have done abominable works, *there is* none that doeth good.

- **Loathsome.**

Pr 13:5 — A righteous *man* hateth lying: but a wicked *man* is loathsome, and cometh to shame.

- **Lovers of pleasure, not of God.**

2Ti 3:4 — Traitors, heady, highminded, lovers of pleasures more than lovers of God;

- **Lying.**

Ps 58:3 — The wicked are estranged from the womb: they go astray as soon as they be born, speaking lies.

Ps 62:4 — They only consult to cast *him* down from his excellency: they delight in lies: they bless with their mouth, but they curse inwardly. Selah.

Isa 59:4 — None calleth for justice, nor *any* pleadeth for truth: they trust in vanity, and speak lies; they conceive mischief, and bring forth iniquity.

- **Mischievous.**

Pr 24:8 — He that deviseth to do evil shall be called a mischievous person.

Mic 7:3 — That they may do evil with both hands earnestly, the prince asketh, and the judge *asketh* for a reward; and the great *man,* he uttereth his mischievous desire: so they wrap it up.

- **Murderous.**

Ps 10:8 — He sitteth in the lurking places of the villages: in the secret places doth he murder the innocent: his eyes are privily set against the poor.

Ps 94:6 — They slay the widow and the stranger, and murder the fatherless.

Ro 1:29 — Being filled with all unrighteousness, fornication, wickedness, covetousness, maliciousness; full of envy, murder, debate, deceit, malignity; whisperers,

• Prayerless.

Job 21:15 — What *is* the Almighty, that we should serve him? and what profit should we have, if we pray unto him?

Ps 53:4 — Have the workers of iniquity no knowledge? who eat up my people *as* they eat bread: they have not called upon God.

• Persecuting.

Ps 69:26 — For they persecute *him* whom thou hast smitten; and they talk to the grief of those whom thou hast wounded.

Ps 109:16 — Because that he remembered not to shew mercy, but persecuted the poor and needy man, that he might even slay the broken in heart.

• Perverse.

Dt 32:5 — They have corrupted themselves, their spot *is* not *the spot* of his children: *they are* a perverse and crooked generation.

• Proud.

Ps 59:12 — *For* the sin of their mouth *and* the words of their lips let them even be taken in their pride: and for cursing and lying *which* they speak.

Ob 1:3 — The pride of thine heart hath deceived thee, thou that dwellest in the clefts of the rock, whose habitation *is* high; that saith in his heart, Who shall bring me down to the ground?

2Ti 3:2 — For men shall be lovers of their own selves, covetous, boasters, proud, blasphemers, disobedient to parents, unthankful, unholy,

• Rebellious.

Isa 1:2 — Hear, O heavens, and give ear, O earth: for the LORD hath spoken, I have nourished and brought up children, and they have rebelled against me.

Isa 30:9 — That this *is* a rebellious people, lying children, children *that* will not hear the law of the LORD:

• Rejoicing in the affliction of saints.

Ps 35:15 — But in mine adversity they rejoiced, and gathered themselves together: *yea,* the abjects gathered themselves together against me, and I knew *it* not; they did tear *me,* and ceased not:

• Reprobate.

2Co 13:5 — Examine yourselves, whether ye be in the faith; prove your own selves. Know ye not your own selves, how that Jesus Christ is in you, except ye be reprobates?

2Ti 3:8 — Now as Jannes and Jambres withstood Moses, so do these also resist the truth: men of corrupt minds, reprobate concerning the faith.

Tit 1:16 — They profess that they know God; but in works they deny *him,* being abominable, and disobedient, and unto every good work reprobate.

• Selfish.

2Ti 3:2 — For men shall be lovers of their own selves, covetous, boasters, proud, blasphemers, disobedient to parents, unthankful, unholy,

• Sensual.

Php 3:19 — Whose end *is* destruction, whose God *is* *their* belly, and *whose* glory *is* in their shame, who mind earthly things.)

Jude 1:19 — These be they who separate themselves, sensual, having not the Spirit.

• Sold under sin.

1Ki 21:20 — And Ahab said to Elijah, Hast thou found me, O mine enemy? And he answered, I have found *thee:* because thou hast sold thyself to work evil in the sight of the LORD.

2Ki 17:17 — And they caused their sons and their daughters to pass through the fire, and used divination and enchantments, and sold themselves to do evil in the sight of the LORD, to provoke him to anger.

• Stiff-hearted.

Eze 2:4 — For *they are* impudent children and stiffhearted. I do send thee unto them; and thou shalt say unto them, Thus saith the Lord GOD.

• Stiffnecked.

Ex 33:5 — For the LORD had said unto Moses, Say unto the children of Israel, Ye *are* a stiffnecked people: I will come up into the midst of thee in a moment, and consume thee: therefore now put off thy ornaments from thee, that I may know what to do unto thee.

Ac 7:51 — Ye stiffnecked and uncircumcised in heart and ears, ye do always resist the Holy Ghost: as your fathers *did,* so *do* ye.

• Uncircumcised in heart.

Jer 9:26 — Egypt, and Judah, and Edom, and the children of Ammon, and Moab, and all *that are* in the utmost corners, that dwell in the wilderness: for all *these* nations *are* uncircumcised, and all the house of Israel *are* uncircumcised in the heart.

• Unclean.

Isa 64:6 — But we are all as an unclean *thing,* and all our righteousnesses *are* as filthy rags; and we all do fade as a leaf; and our iniquities, like the wind, have taken us away.

Eph 4:19 — Who being past feeling have given themselves over unto lasciviousness, to work all uncleanness with greediness.

• Unjust.

Pr 11:7 — When a wicked man dieth, *his* expectation shall perish: and the hope of unjust *men* perisheth.

Isa 26:18 — We have been with child, we have been in pain, we have as it were brought forth wind; we have not wrought any deliverance in the earth; neither have the inhabitants of the world fallen.

• Unmerciful.

Ro 1:31 — Without understanding, covenantbreakers, without natural affection, implacable, unmerciful:

• Ungodly.

Pr 16:27 — An ungodly man diggeth up evil: and in his lips *there is* as a burning fire.

- **Unholy.**
  2Ti 3:2 — For men shall be lovers of their own selves, covetous, boasters, proud, blasphemers, disobedient to parents, unthankful, unholy,
- **Unprofitable.**
  Mt 25:30 — And cast ye the unprofitable servant into outer darkness: there shall be weeping and gnashing of teeth.
  Ro 3:12 — They are all gone out of the way, they are together become unprofitable; there is none that doeth good, no, not one.
- **Unruly.**
  Tit 1:10 — For there are many unruly and vain talkers and deceivers, specially they of the circumcision:
- **Unthankful.**
  Lk 6:35 — But love ye your enemies, and do good, and lend, hoping for nothing again; and your reward shall be great, and ye shall be the children of the Highest: for he is kind unto the unthankful and *to* the evil.
  2Ti 3:2 — For men shall be lovers of their own selves, covetous, boasters, proud, blasphemers, disobedient to parents, unthankful, unholy,
- **Untoward.**
  Ac 2:40 — And with many other words did he testify and exhort, saying, Save yourselves from this untoward generation.
- **Unwise.**
  Dt 32:6 — Do ye thus requite the LORD, O foolish people and unwise? *is* not he thy father *that* hath bought thee? hath he not made thee, and established thee?

See: Wicked; described

CHARACTER, Miscellaneous

- **Good.**
  Pr 22:1 — A *good* name *is* rather to be chosen than great riches, *and* loving favour rather than silver and gold.
  Ecc 7:1 — A good name *is* better than precious ointment; and the day of death than the day of one's birth.
- **Defamation of, punished.**
  Dt 22:13–19
- **Revealed in countenance.**
  Isa 3:9 — The shew of their countenance doth witness against them; and they declare their sin as Sodom, they hide *it* not. Woe unto their soul! for they have rewarded evil unto themselves.

  See: Countenance

  See: Face
- **Firmness of.**
  Ps 57:7 — My heart is fixed, O God, my heart is fixed: I will sing and give praise.
  Ps 108:1 — O God, my heart is fixed; I will sing and give praise, even with my glory.
  Ps 112:7 — He shall not be afraid of evil tidings: his heart is fixed, trusting in the LORD.
  Mt 10:22 — And ye shall be hated of all *men* for my name's sake: but he that endureth to the end shall be saved.
  Mk 4:20 — And these are they which are sown on good ground; such as hear the word, and receive *it*, and bring forth fruit, some thirtyfold, some sixty, and some an hundred.
  1Co 7:20 — Let every man abide in the same calling wherein he was called.
  2Th 2:15 — Therefore, brethren, stand fast, and hold the traditions which ye have been taught, whether by word, or our epistle.
  2Th 3:3 — But the Lord is faithful, who shall stablish you, and keep *you* from evil.
  Heb 10:23 — Let us hold fast the profession of *our* faith without wavering; (for he is faithful that promised;)
  Heb 13:9 — Be not carried about with divers and strange doctrines. For *it is* a good thing that the heart be established with grace; not with meats, which have not profited them that have been occupied therein.
  Jas 1:25 — But whoso looketh into the perfect law of liberty, and continueth *therein*, he being not a forgetful hearer, but a doer of the work, this man shall be blessed in his deed.
- **Instances of firmness.**
  - **Joseph in resisting Potiphar's wife.**
    Ge 39:7–12
  - **Pilate.**
    Jn 19:22
  - **Paul.**
    Ac 20:22–24; 21:13–14

  See: Decision

  See: Stability
- **Instability of.**
  Pr 24:21–22; Mt 8:19–22; 13:19–22; Mk 4:15–19; Lk 8:5–15; 9:59–62; Jas 1:6–8
  Pr 27:8 — As a bird that wandereth from her nest, so *is* a man that wandereth from his place.
  Jer 2:36 — Why gaddest thou about so much to change thy way? thou also shalt be ashamed of Egypt, as thou wast ashamed of Assyria.
  Hos 6:4 — O Ephraim, what shall I do unto thee? O Judah, what shall I do unto thee? for your goodness *is* as a morning cloud, and as the early dew it goeth away.
  Hos 7:8 — Ephraim, he hath mixed himself among the people; Ephraim is a cake not turned.
  Hos 10:2 — Their heart is divided; now shall they be found faulty: he shall break down their altars, he shall spoil their images.
  Eph 4:14 — That we *henceforth* be no more children, tossed to and fro, and carried about with every wind of doctrine, by the sleight of men, *and* cunning craftiness, whereby they lie in wait to deceive;
  Jas 4:8 — Draw nigh to God, and he will draw nigh to you. Cleanse *your* hands, *ye* sinners; and purify *your* hearts, *ye* double minded.

2Pe 2:14 — Having eyes full of adultery, and that cannot cease from sin; beguiling unstable souls: an heart they have exercised with covetous practices; cursed children:

See: Indecision

See: Instability

See: Perseverance

See: Stability

- **Instances of instability.**
  - **Reuben.**
    Ge 49:3–4
  - **Pharaoh.**
    Ex 8:15, 32; 9:34; 14:5
  - **Solomon.**
    1Ki 11:4–8
  - **Israelites.**
    Ex 32:8; Jgs 2:17, 19; 2Ch 11:17; 12:1
  - **King Saul in his treatment of David.**
    1Sa 18:1–19:24

CHARASHIM • Valley of.

1Ch 4:14 — And Meonothai begat Ophrah: and Seraiah begat Joab, the father of the valley of Charashim; for they were craftsmen.

Ne 11:35 — Lod, and Ono, the valley of craftsmen.

CHARGE

- **Delivered to ministers.**

See: Minister, a sacred teacher

CHARGER

- **A dish.**
- **Dedicated to the tabernacle.**

Nu 7:84–85

Nu 7:13 — And his offering *was* one silver charger, the weight thereof *was* an hundred and thirty *shekels,* one silver bowl of seventy shekels, after the shekel of the sanctuary; both of them *were* full of fine flour mingled with oil for a meat offering:

Nu 7:19 — He offered *for* his offering one silver charger, the weight whereof *was* an hundred and thirty *shekels,* one silver bowl of seventy shekels, after the shekel of the sanctuary; both of them full of fine flour mingled with oil for a meat offering:

Nu 7:25 — His offering *was* one silver charger, the weight whereof *was* an hundred and thirty *shekels,* one silver bowl of seventy shekels, after the shekel of the sanctuary; both of them full of fine flour mingled with oil for a meat offering:

Nu 7:31 — His offering *was* one silver charger of the weight of an hundred and thirty *shekels,* one silver bowl of seventy shekels, after the shekel of the sanctuary; both of them full of fine flour mingled with oil for a meat offering:

Nu 7:37 — His offering *was* one silver charger, the weight whereof *was* an hundred and thirty *shekels,* one silver bowl of seventy shekels, after the shekel of the sanctuary; both of them full of fine flour mingled with oil for a meat offering:

Nu 7:43 — His offering *was* one silver charger of the weight of an hundred and thirty *shekels,* a silver bowl of seventy shekels, after the shekel of the sanctuary; both of them full of fine flour mingled with oil for a meat offering:

Nu 7:49 — His offering *was* one silver charger, the weight whereof *was* an hundred and thirty *shekels,* one silver bowl of seventy shekels, after the shekel of the sanctuary; both of them full of fine flour mingled with oil for a meat offering:

Nu 7:55 — His offering *was* one silver charger of the weight of an hundred and thirty *shekels,* one silver bowl of seventy shekels, after the shekel of the sanctuary; both of them full of fine flour mingled with oil for a meat offering:

Nu 7:61 — His offering *was* one silver charger, the weight whereof *was* an hundred and thirty *shekels,* one silver bowl of seventy shekels, after the shekel of the sanctuary; both of them full of fine flour mingled with oil for a meat offering:

Nu 7:67 — His offering *was* one silver charger, the weight whereof *was* an hundred and thirty *shekels,* one silver bowl of seventy shekels, after the shekel of the sanctuary; both of them full of fine flour mingled with oil for a meat offering:

Nu 7:73 — His offering *was* one silver charger, the weight whereof *was* an hundred and thirty *shekels,* one silver bowl of seventy shekels, after the shekel of the sanctuary; both of them full of fine flour mingled with oil for a meat offering:

Nu 7:79 — His offering *was* one silver charger, the weight whereof *was* an hundred and thirty *shekels,* one silver bowl of seventy shekels, after the shekel of the sanctuary; both of them full of fine flour mingled with oil for a meat offering:

- **John the Baptist's head carried on.**

Mt 14:8 — And she, being before instructed of her mother, said, Give me here John Baptist's head in a charger.

Mt 14:11 — And his head was brought in a charger, and given to the damsel: and she brought *it* to her mother.

CHARIOT

- **For war.**

2Ch 12:2–3; Na 2:3–4

Ex 14:7 — And he took six hundred chosen chariots, and all the chariots of Egypt, and captains over every one of them.

Ex 14:9 — But the Egyptians pursued after them, all the horses *and* chariots of Pharaoh, and his horsemen, and his army, and overtook them encamping by the sea, beside Pi-hahiroth, before Baal-zephon.

Ex 14:25 — And took off their chariot wheels, that they drave them heavily: so that the Egyptians said, Let us flee from the face of Israel; for the LORD fighteth for them against the Egyptians.

Jos 11:4 — And they went out, they and all their hosts with them, much people, even as the sand that *is* upon the sea shore in multitude, with horses and chariots very many.

1Sa 13:5 — And the Philistines gathered themselves together to fight with Israel, thirty thousand chariots, and six thousand horsemen, and people as the sand which *is* on the sea shore in multitude: and they came up, and pitched in Michmash, eastward from Beth-aven.

1Ki 20:1 — And Ben-hadad the king of Syria gathered all his host together: and *there were* thirty and two kings with him, and horses, and chariots: and he went up and besieged Samaria, and warred against it.

1Ki 20:25 — And number thee an army, like the army that thou hast lost, horse for horse, and chariot for chariot: and we will fight against them in the plain, *and* surely we shall be stronger than they. And he hearkened unto their voice, and did so.

2Ki 6:14 — Therefore sent he thither horses, and chariots, and a great host: and they came by night, and compassed the city about.

Ps 20:7 — Some *trust* in chariots, and some in horses: but we will remember the name of the LORD our God.

Ps 46:9 — He maketh wars to cease unto the end of the earth; he breaketh the bow, and cutteth the spear in sunder; he burneth the chariot in the fire.

Jer 46:9 — Come up, ye horses; and rage, ye chariots; and let the mighty men come forth; the Ethiopians and the Libyans, that handle the shield; and the Lydians, that handle *and* bend the bow.

Jer 47:3 — At the noise of the stamping of the hoofs of his strong *horses,* at the rushing of his chariots, *and at* the rumbling of his wheels, the fathers shall not look back to *their* children for feebleness of hands;

Jer 51:21 — And with thee will I break in pieces the horse and his rider; and with thee will I break in pieces the chariot and his rider;

Joel 2:5 — Like the noise of chariots on the tops of mountains shall they leap, like the noise of a flame of fire that devoureth the stubble, as a strong people set in battle array.

Na 3:2 — The noise of a whip, and the noise of the rattling of the wheels, and of the pransing horses, and of the jumping chariots.

• Wheels of Pharaoh's, providentially taken off.

Ex 14:25 — And took off their chariot wheels, that they drave them heavily: so that the Egyptians said, Let us flee from the face of Israel; for the LORD fighteth for them against the Egyptians.

• Commanded by captains.

1Ki 22:31–33

Ex 14:7 — And he took six hundred chosen chariots, and all the chariots of Egypt, and captains over every one of them.

1Ki 9:22 — But of the children of Israel did Solomon make no bondmen: but they *were* men of war, and his servants, and his princes, and his captains, and rulers of his chariots, and his horsemen.

2Ki 8:21 — So Joram went over to Zair, and all the chariots with him: and he rose by night, and smote the Edomites which compassed him about, and the captains of the chariots: and the people fled into their tents.

• Made of iron.

Jos 17:18 — But the mountain shall be thine; for it *is* a wood, and thou shalt cut it down: and the outgoings of it shall be thine: for thou shalt drive out the Canaanites, though they have iron chariots, *and* though they *be* strong.

Jgs 1:19 — And the LORD was with Judah; and he drave out the inhabitants of the mountain; but could not drive out *the inhabitants of* the valley, because they had chariots of iron.

• Introduced among Israelites by David.

2Sa 8:4 — And David took from him a thousand *chariots,* and seven hundred horsemen, and twenty thousand footmen: and David houghed all the chariot *horses,* but reserved of them *for* an hundred chariots.

• Imported from Egypt by Solomon.

1Ki 10:26–29

• Cities for.

1Ki 9:19 — And all the cities of store that Solomon had, and cities for his chariots, and cities for his horsemen, and that which Solomon desired to build in Jerusalem, and in Lebanon, and in all the land of his dominion.

2Ch 1:14 — And Solomon gathered chariots and horsemen: and he had a thousand and four hundred chariots, and twelve thousand horsemen, which he placed in the chariot cities, and with the king at Jerusalem.

2Ch 8:6 — And Baalath, and all the store cities that Solomon had, and all the chariot cities, and the cities of the horsemen, and all that Solomon desired to build in Jerusalem, and in Lebanon, and throughout all the land of his dominion.

2Ch 9:25 — And Solomon had four thousand stalls for horses and chariots, and twelve thousand horsemen; whom he bestowed in the chariot cities, and with the king at Jerusalem.

• Royal.

Ge 41:43 — And he made him to ride in the second chariot which he had; and they cried before him, Bow the knee: and he made him *ruler* over all the land of Egypt.

Ge 46:29 — And Joseph made ready his chariot, and went up to meet Israel his father, to Goshen, and presented himself unto him; and he fell on his neck, and wept on his neck a good while.

2Ki 5:9 — So Naaman came with his horses and with his chariot, and stood at the door of the house of Elisha.

2Ch 35:24 — His servants therefore took him out of that chariot, and put him in the second chariot that he had; and they brought him to Jerusalem, and he died, and was buried in *one of* the sepulchres of his fathers. And all Judah and Jerusalem mourned for Josiah.

Jer 17:25 — Then shall there enter into the gates of this city kings and princes sitting upon the throne of David, riding in chariots and on horses, they, and their princes, the men of Judah, and the inhabitants of Jerusalem: and this city shall remain for ever.

Ac 8:29 — Then the Spirit said unto Philip, Go near, and join thyself to this chariot.

- **Drawn by camels.**

Isa 21:7 — And he saw a chariot *with* a couple of horsemen, a chariot of asses, *and* a chariot of camels; and he hearkened diligently with much heed:

Mic 1:13 — O thou inhabitant of Lachish, bind the chariot to the swift beast: she *is* the beginning of the sin to the daughter of Zion: for the transgressions of Israel were found in thee.

- **Traffic in.**

Rev 18:13 — And cinnamon, and odours, and ointments, and frankincense, and wine, and oil, and fine flour, and wheat, and beasts, and sheep, and horses, and chariots, and slaves, and souls of men.

- **Kings ride in.**

2Ch 35:24 — His servants therefore took him out of that chariot, and put him in the second chariot that he had; and they brought him to Jerusalem, and he died, and was buried in *one of* the sepulchres of his fathers. And all Judah and Jerusalem mourned for Josiah.

Jer 17:25 — Then shall there enter into the gates of this city kings and princes sitting upon the throne of David, riding in chariots and on horses, they, and their princes, the men of Judah, and the inhabitants of Jerusalem: and this city shall remain for ever.

Jer 22:4 — For if ye do this thing indeed, then shall there enter in by the gates of this house kings sitting upon the throne of David, riding in chariots and on horses, he, and his servants, and his people.

- **Cherubim in Solomon's temple mounted on.**

1Ch 28:18 — And for the altar of incense refined gold by weight; and gold for the pattern of the chariot of the cherubims, that spread out *their wings,* and covered the ark of the covenant of the LORD.

- **Figurative.**
  - **Chariots of God.**

2Ki 6:17 — And Elisha prayed, and said, LORD, I pray thee, open his eyes, that he may see. And the LORD opened the eyes of the young man; and he saw: and, behold, the mountain *was* full of horses and chariots of fire round about Elisha.

Ps 68:17 — The chariots of God *are* twenty thousand, *even* thousands of angels: the Lord *is* among them, *as in* Sinai, in the holy *place.*

Ps 104:3 — Who layeth the beams of his chambers in the waters: who maketh the clouds his chariot: who walketh upon the wings of the wind:

Isa 66:15 — For, behold, the LORD will come with fire, and with his chariots like a whirlwind, to render his anger with fury, and his rebuke with flames of fire.

Hab 3:8 — Was the LORD displeased against the rivers? *was* thine anger against the rivers? *was* thy wrath against the sea, that thou didst ride upon thine horses *and* thy chariots of salvation?

Rev 9:9 — And they had breastplates, as it were breastplates of iron; and the sound of their wings *was* as the sound of chariots of many horses running to battle.

- **Symbolic.**

2Ki 2:11–12; Zec 6:1–8

CHARISMATA

- **Inspired gifts bestowed on the apostles and early Christians.**

Mk 16:17–18; Ac 10:44–46; 1Co 12:1–31

Mt 10:1 — And when he had called unto *him* his twelve disciples, he gave them power *against* unclean spirits, to cast them out, and to heal all manner of sickness and all manner of disease.

Mt 10:8 — Heal the sick, cleanse the lepers, raise the dead, cast out devils: freely ye have received, freely give.

Lk 10:1 — After these things the Lord appointed other seventy also, and sent them two and two before his face into every city and place, whither he himself would come.

Lk 10:9 — And heal the sick that are therein, and say unto them, The kingdom of God is come nigh unto you.

Lk 10:17 — And the seventy returned again with joy, saying, Lord, even the devils are subject unto us through thy name.

Lk 10:19 — Behold, I give unto you power to tread on serpents and scorpions, and over all the power of the enemy: and nothing shall by any means hurt you.

Ac 2:4 — And they were all filled with the Holy Ghost, and began to speak with other tongues, as the Spirit gave them utterance.

Ac 19:6 — And when Paul had laid *his* hands upon them, the Holy Ghost came on them; and they spake with tongues, and prophesied.

See: Miracles of the disciples

See: Tongues

CHARITABLENESS

Mt 5:23–24; 6:14–15; 7:1–5; 18:21–35; Lk 6:36–42; 17:3–4; Ro 14:1–23; 1Co 10:28–33; 13:1–13; Col 3:13–14; Jas 4:11–12

Pr 10:12 — Hatred stirreth up strifes: but love covereth all sins.

Pr 17:9 — He that covereth a transgression seeketh love; but he that repeateth a matter separateth *very* friends.

Jn 7:24 — Judge not according to the appearance, but judge righteous judgment.

1Co 4:5 — Therefore judge nothing before the time, until the Lord come, who both will bring to light the hidden things of darkness, and will make manifest the counsels of the hearts: and then shall every man have praise of God.

1Co 16:14 — Let all your things be done with charity.

Gal 6:1 — Brethren, if a man be overtaken in a fault, ye which are spiritual, restore such an one in the spirit of meekness; considering thyself, lest thou also be tempted.

Eph 4:32 — And be ye kind one to another, tenderhearted, forgiving one another, even as God for Christ's sake hath forgiven you.

1Ti 1:5 — Now the end of the commandment is charity out of a pure heart, and *of* a good conscience, and *of* faith unfeigned:

1Ti 4:12 — Let no man despise thy youth; but be thou an example of the believers, in word, in conversation, in charity, in spirit, in faith, in purity.

2Ti 2:22 — Flee also youthful lusts: but follow righteousness, faith, charity, peace, with them that call on the Lord out of a pure heart.

Jas 2:13 — For he shall have judgment without mercy, that hath shewed no mercy; and mercy rejoiceth against judgment.

1Pe 3:9 — Not rendering evil for evil, or railing for railing: but contrariwise blessing; knowing that ye are thereunto called, that ye should inherit a blessing.

1Pe 4:8 — And above all things have fervent charity among yourselves: for charity shall cover the multitude of sins.

See: Love

See: Uncharitableness

CHARITY

See: Alms

See: Beneficence

See: Liberality

See: Love

CHARMERS AND CHARMING

Isa 19:3 — And the spirit of Egypt shall fail in the midst thereof; and I will destroy the counsel thereof: and they shall seek to the idols, and to the charmers, and to them that have familiar spirits, and to the wizards.

Jer 8:17 — For, behold, I will send serpents, cockatrices, among you, which *will* not *be* charmed, and they shall bite you, saith the LORD.

• Prohibited.

Dt 18:11 — Or a charmer, or a consulter with familiar spirits, or a wizard, or a necromancer.

• Of serpents.

Ps 58:4–5

Jer 8:17 — For, behold, I will send serpents, cockatrices, among you, which *will* not *be* charmed, and they shall bite you, saith the LORD.

See: Sorcery

CHARRAN **See: Haran**

CHASTEN

1Pe 4:12–19

Job 23:10 — But he knoweth the way that I take: *when* he hath tried me, I shall come forth as gold.

Pr 3:11 — My son, despise not the chastening of the LORD; neither be weary of his correction:

Isa 26:16 — LORD, in trouble have they visited thee, they poured out a prayer *when* thy chastening *was* upon them.

Heb 12:5 — And ye have forgotten the exhortation which speaketh unto you as unto children, My son, despise not thou the chastening of the Lord, nor faint when thou art rebuked of him:

CHASTISEMENT

• From God.

Dt 11:2–9; 2Sa 7:14–15; 2Ch 6:24–31; 7:13–14; Ps 94:12–13; 106:41–44; 107:17–21, 23–31; Pr 3:11–12; Isa 53:4–5; 57:16–18; Jer 31:18–20; Heb 12:5–11

Le 26:28 — Then I will walk contrary unto you also in fury; and I, even I, will chastise you seven times for your sins.

Job 5:17 — Behold, happy *is* the man whom God correcteth: therefore despise not thou the chastening of the Almighty:

Job 33:19 — He is chastened also with pain upon his bed, and the multitude of his bones with strong *pain:*

Ps 6:1 — O LORD, rebuke me not in thine anger, neither chasten me in thy hot displeasure.

Ps 38:1 — O LORD, rebuke me not in thy wrath: neither chasten me in thy hot displeasure.

Ps 73:14 — For all the day long have I been plagued, and chastened every morning.

Ps 89:32 — Then will I visit their transgression with the rod, and their iniquity with stripes.

Ps 118:18 — The LORD hath chastened me sore: but he hath not given me over unto death.

Ps 119:67 — Before I was afflicted I went astray: but now have I kept thy word.

Ps 119:75 — I know, O LORD, that thy judgments *are* right, and that *thou* in faithfulness hast afflicted me.

Isa 26:16 — LORD, in trouble have they visited thee, they poured out a prayer *when* thy chastening *was* upon them.

Isa 42:25 — Therefore he hath poured upon him the fury of his anger, and the strength of battle: and it hath set him on fire round about, yet he knew not; and it burned him, yet he laid *it* not to heart.

Jer 2:30 — In vain have I smitten your children; they received no correction: your own sword hath devoured your prophets, like a destroying lion.

Jer 30:14 — All thy lovers have forgotten thee; they seek thee not; for I have wounded thee with the wound of an enemy, with the chastisement of a cruel one, for the multitude of thine iniquity; *because* thy sins were increased.

Jer 46:28 — Fear thou not, O Jacob my servant, saith the LORD: for I *am* with thee; for I will make a full end of all the nations whither I have driven thee: but I will not make a full end of thee, but correct thee in measure; yet will I not leave thee wholly unpunished.

La 1:5 — Her adversaries are the chief, her enemies prosper; for the LORD hath afflicted her for the multitude of her transgressions: her children are gone into captivity before the enemy.

Hos 7:12 — When they shall go, I will spread my net upon them; I will bring them down as the fowls of the heaven; I will chastise them, as their congregation hath heard.

Hos 10:10 — *It is* in my desire that I should chastise them; and the people shall be gathered against them, when they shall bind themselves in their two furrows.

Hag 2:17 — I smote you with blasting and with mildew and with hail in all the labours of your hands; yet ye *turned* not to me, saith the LORD.

Rev 3:19 — As many as I love, I rebuke and chasten: be zealous therefore, and repent.

✦See: Afflictions; design of

✦See: Judgments

✦See: Punishment

✦See: Wicked; punishment of

CHASTITY

Pr 2:10–11,16–22; 5:15–21; 6:24–25; 7:1–5; 1Co 6:13–19; 7:1–2, 7–9, 25–26, 36–37; Rev 14:1–5

Ex 20:14 — Thou shalt not commit adultery.

Job 31:1 — I made a covenant with mine eyes; why then should I think upon a maid?

Pr 31:3 — Give not thy strength unto women, nor thy ways to that which destroyeth kings.

Mt 5:28 — But I say unto you, That whosoever looketh on a woman to lust after her hath committed adultery with her already in his heart.

Ac 15:20 — But that we write unto them, that they abstain from pollutions of idols, and *from* fornication, and *from* things strangled, and *from* blood.

Ro 13:13 — Let us walk honestly, as in the day; not in rioting and drunkenness, not in chambering and wantonness, not in strife and envying.

Eph 5:3 — But fornication, and all uncleanness, or covetousness, let it not be once named among you, as becometh saints;

Col 3:5 — Mortify therefore your members which are upon the earth; fornication, uncleanness, inordinate affection, evil concupiscence, and covetousness, which is idolatry:

1Th 4:3 — For this is the will of God, *even* your sanctification, that ye should abstain from fornication:

1Th 4:7 — For God hath not called us unto uncleanness, but unto holiness.

✦See: Continence

• Instances of.

• Joseph.

Ge 39:7–20

• Boaz.

Ru 3:6–13

• Paul.

1Co 7:1–40

CHEATING ✦See: Dishonesty

CHEBAR • A river of Mesopotamia.

Eze 1:1 — Now it came to pass in the thirtieth year, in the fourth *month,* in the fifth *day* of the month, as I *was* among the captives by the river of Chebar, *that* the heavens were opened, and I saw visions of God.

Eze 1:3 — The word of the LORD came expressly unto Ezekiel the priest, the son of Buzi, in the land of the Chaldeans by the river Chebar; and the hand of the LORD was there upon him.

Eze 3:15 — Then I came to them of the captivity at Tel-abib, that dwelt by the river of Chebar, and I sat where they sat, and remained there astonished among them seven days.

Eze 3:23 — Then I arose, and went forth into the plain: and, behold, the glory of the LORD stood there, as the glory which I saw by the river of Chebar: and I fell on my face.

Eze 10:15 — And the cherubims were lifted up. This *is* the living creature that I saw by the river of Chebar.

Eze 10:22 — And the likeness of their faces *was* the same faces which I saw by the river of Chebar, their appearances and themselves: they went every one straight forward.

Eze 43:3 — And *it was* according to the appearance of the vision which I saw, *even* according to the vision that I saw when I came to destroy the city: and the visions *were* like the vision that I saw by the river Chebar; and I fell upon my face.

CHEDORLAOMER • King of Elam.

Ge 14:1–16

CHEERFULNESS ✦See: Contentment

CHEESE

1Sa 17:18 — And carry these ten cheeses unto the captain of *their* thousand, and look how thy brethren fare, and take their pledge.

2Sa 17:29 — And honey, and butter, and sheep, and cheese of kine, for David, and for the people that *were* with him, to eat: for they said, The people *is* hungry, and weary, and thirsty, in the wilderness.

Job 10:10 — Hast thou not poured me out as milk, and curdled me like cheese?

CHELAL • Son of Pahath-moab.

Ezr 10:30 — And of the sons of Pahath-moab; Adna, and Chelal, Benaiah, Maaseiah, Mattaniah, Bezaleel, and Binnui, and Manasseh.

CHELLUH • Son of Bani.

Ezr 10:35 — Benaiah, Bedeiah, Chelluh,

CHELUB

• A descendant of Caleb.

1Ch 4:11 — And Chelub the brother of Shuah begat Mehir, which *was* the father of Eshton.

• Father of Ezri.

1Ch 27:26 — And over them that did the work of the field for tillage of the ground *was* Ezri the son of Chelub:

CHELUBI

• Son of Hezron.

1Ch 2:9 — The sons also of Hezron, that were born unto him; Jerahmeel, and Ram, and Chelubai.

• Called Caleb.

1Ch 2:18 — And Caleb the son of Hezron begat *children* of Azubah *his* wife, and of Jerioth: her sons *are* these; Jesher, and Shobab, and Ardon.

1Ch 2:42 — Now the sons of Caleb the brother of Jerahmeel *were,* Mesha his firstborn, which was the father of Ziph; and the sons of Mareshah the father of Hebron.

CHEMARIM • A term descriptive of idolatrous priests.

2Ki 23:15 — Moreover the altar that *was* at Bethel, *and* the high place which Jeroboam the son of Nebat, who made Israel to sin, had made, both that altar and the high place he brake down, and burned the high place, *and* stamped *it* small to powder, and burned the grove.

Hos 10:5 — The inhabitants of Samaria shall fear because of the calves of Beth-aven: for the people thereof shall mourn over it, and the priests thereof *that* rejoiced on it, for the glory thereof, because it is departed from it.

Zep 1:4 — I will also stretch out mine hand upon Judah, and upon all the inhabitants of Jerusalem; and I will cut off the remnant of Baal from this place, *and* the name of the Chemarims with the priests;

CHEMOSH

• An idol of the Moabites and Ammonites.

1Ki 11:7 — Then did Solomon build an high place for Chemosh, the abomination of Moab, in the hill that *is* before Jerusalem, and for Molech, the abomination of the children of Ammon.

1Ki 11:33 — Because that they have forsaken me, and have worshipped Ashtoreth the goddess of the Zidonians, Chemosh the god of the Moabites, and Milcom the god of the children of Ammon, and have not walked in my ways, to do *that which is* right in mine eyes, and *to keep* my statutes and my judgments, as *did* David his father.

2Ki 23:13 — And the high places that *were* before Jerusalem, which *were* on the right hand of the mount of corruption, which Solomon the king of Israel had builded for Ashtoreth the abomination of the Zidonians, and for Chemosh the abomination of the Moabites, and for Milcom the abomination of the children of Ammon, did the king defile.

Jer 48:7 — For because thou hast trusted in thy works and in thy treasures, thou shalt also be taken: and Chemosh shall go forth into captivity *with* his priests and his princes together.

Jer 48:13 — And Moab shall be ashamed of Chemosh, as the house of Israel was ashamed of Bethel their confidence.

Jer 48:46 — Woe be unto thee, O Moab! the people of Chemosh perisheth: for thy sons are taken captives, and thy daughters captives.

• An idol of the Amorites.

Jgs 11:24 — Wilt not thou possess that which Chemosh thy god giveth thee to possess? So whomsoever the LORD our God shall drive out from before us, them will we possess.

CHENAANAH

• Father of the false prophet Zedekiah.

1Ki 22:11 — And Zedekiah the son of Chenaanah made him horns of iron: and he said, Thus saith the LORD, With these shalt thou push the Syrians, until thou have consumed them.

1Ki 22:24 — But Zedekiah the son of Chenaanah went near, and smote Micaiah on the cheek, and said, Which way went the Spirit of the LORD from me to speak unto thee?

2Ch 18:10 — And Zedekiah the son of Chenaanah had made him horns of iron, and said, Thus saith the LORD, With these thou shalt push Syria until they be consumed.

2Ch 18:23 — Then Zedekiah the son of Chenaanah came near, and smote Micaiah upon the cheek, and said, Which way went the Spirit of the LORD from me to speak unto thee?

• Brother of Ehud.

1Ch 7:10 — The sons also of Jediael; Bilhan: and the sons of Bilhan; Jeush, and Benjamin, and Ehud, and Chenaanah, and Zethan, and Tharshish, and Ahishahar.

CHENANI • A Levite.

Ne 9:4 — Then stood up upon the stairs, of the Levites, Jeshua, and Bani, Kadmiel, Shebaniah, Bunni, Sherebiah, Bani, *and* Chenani, and cried with a loud voice unto the LORD their God.

CHENANIAH • A Levite.

1Ch 15:22 — And Chenaniah, chief of the Levites, *was* for song: he instructed about the song, because he *was* skilful.

1Ch 15:27 — And David *was* clothed with a robe of fine linen, and all the Levites that bare the ark, and the singers, and Chenaniah the master of the song with the singers: David also *had* upon him an ephod of linen.

• An Izharite.

1Ch 26:29 — Of the Izharites, Chenaniah and his sons *were* for the outward business over Israel, for officers and judges.

CHEPHAR-HAAMMONAI • A town of Benjamin.

Jos 18:24 — And Chephar-haammonai, and Ophni, and Gaba; twelve cities with their villages:

CHEPHIRAH • A city of the Hivites.

Jos 9:17 — And the children of Israel journeyed, and came unto their cities on the third day. Now their cities *were* Gibeon, and Chephirah, and Beeroth, and Kirjath-jearim.

Jos 18:26 — And Mizpeh, and Chephirah, and Mozah,

Ezr 2:25 — The children of Kirjath-arim, Chephirah, and Beeroth, seven hundred and forty and three.

Ne 7:29 — The men of Kirjath-jearim, Chephirah, and Beeroth, seven hundred forty and three.

CHERAN • A Horite.

Ge 36:26 — And these *are* the children of Dishon; Hemdan, and Eshban, and Ithran, and Cheran.

1Ch 1:41 — The sons of Anah; Dishon. And the sons of Dishon; Amram, and Eshban, and Ithran, and Cheran.

CHERETHITES

• A Philistine tribe, which adhered to David, and with the Pelethites formed his bodyguard.

1Sa 30:14 — We made an invasion *upon* the south of the Cherethites, and upon *the coast* which *belongeth* to Judah, and upon the south of Caleb; and we burned Ziklag with fire.

1Sa 30:16 — And when he had brought him down, behold, *they were* spread abroad upon all the earth, eating and drinking, and dancing, because of all the great spoil that they had taken out of the land of the Philistines, and out of the land of Judah.

2Sa 8:18 — And Benaiah the son of Jehoiada *was over* both the Cherethites and the Pelethites; and David's sons were chief rulers.

2Sa 15:18 — And all his servants passed on beside him; and all the Cherethites, and all the Pelethites, and all the Gittites, six hundred men which came after him from Gath, passed on before the king.

2Sa 20:7 — And there went out after him Joab's men, and the Cherethites, and the Pelethites, and all the mighty men: and they went out of Jerusalem, to pursue after Sheba the son of Bichri.

2Sa 20:23 — Now Joab *was* over all the host of Israel: and Benaiah the son of Jehoiada *was* over the Cherethites and over the Pelethites:

1Ki 1:38 — So Zadok the priest, and Nathan the prophet, and Benaiah the son of Jehoiada, and the Cherethites, and the Pelethites, went down, and caused Solomon to ride upon king David's mule, and brought him to Gihon.

1Ki 1:44 — And the king hath sent with him Zadok the priest, and Nathan the prophet, and Benaiah the son of Jehoiada, and the Cherethites, and the Pelethites, and they have caused him to ride upon the king's mule:

1Ch 18:17 — And Benaiah the son of Jehoiada *was* over the Cherethites and the Pelethites; and the sons of David *were* chief about the king.

Eze 25:16 — Therefore thus saith the Lord GOD; Behold, I will stretch out mine hand upon the Philistines, and I will cut off the Cherethims, and destroy the remnant of the sea coast.

Zep 2:5 — Woe unto the inhabitants of the sea coast, the nation of the Cherethites! the word of the LORD *is* against you; O Canaan, the land of the Philistines, I will even destroy thee, that there shall be no inhabitant.

• Solomon's escort at his coronation.

1Ki 1:38 — So Zadok the priest, and Nathan the prophet, and Benaiah the son of Jehoiada, and the Cherethites, and the Pelethites, went down, and caused Solomon to ride upon king David's mule, and brought him to Gihon.

CHERITH • A brook near Jericho.

1Ki 17:3–7

CHERUB • Name of a place or person.

Ezr 2:59 — And these *were* they which went up from Tel-melah, Tel-harsa, Cherub, Addan, *and* Immer: but they could not shew their father's house, and their seed, whether they *were* of Israel:

Ne 7:61 — And these *were* they which went up *also* from Telmelah, Telharesha, Cherub, Addon, and Immer: but they could not shew their father's house, nor their seed, whether they *were* of Israel.

CHERUBIM

• Eastward of the garden of Eden.

Ge 3:24 — So he drove out the man; and he placed at the east of the garden of Eden Cherubim, and a flaming sword which turned every way, to keep the way of the tree of life.

• In the tabernacle.

Ex 25:18–20; 37:7–9

• Ark rested beneath the wings of.

1Ki 8:6–7; 2Ch 5:7–8

Heb 9:5 — And over it the cherubims of glory shadowing the mercyseat; of which we cannot now speak particularly.

• Figures of.

• Embroidered on walls of tabernacle.

Ex 26:1 — Moreover thou shalt make the tabernacle *with* ten curtains *of* fine twined linen, and blue, and purple, and scarlet: *with* cherubims of cunning work shalt thou make them.

Ex 36:8 — And every wise hearted man among them that wrought the work of the tabernacle made ten curtains *of* fine twined linen, and blue, and purple, and scarlet: *with* cherubims of cunning work made he them.

• Embroidered on the vail.

Ex 26:31 — And thou shalt make a vail *of* blue, and purple, and scarlet, and fine twined linen of cunning work: with cherubims shall it be made:

Ex 36:35 — And he made a vail *of* blue, and purple, and scarlet, and fine twined linen: *with* cherubims made he it of cunning work.

• In the temple.

1Ki 6:23–29; 2Ch 3:10–13

• On the vail.

2Ch 3:14 — And he made the vail *of* blue, and purple, and crimson, and fine linen, and wrought cherubims thereon.

• On the walls.

1Ki 6:29–35

2Ch 3:7 — He overlaid also the house, the beams, the posts, and the walls thereof, and the doors thereof, with gold; and graved cherubims on the walls.

• On the lavers.

1Ki 7:29 — And on the borders that *were* between the ledges *were* lions, oxen, and cherubims: and upon the ledges *there was* a base above: and beneath the lions and oxen *were* certain additions made of thin work.

1Ki 7:36 — For on the plates of the ledges thereof, and on the borders thereof, he graved cherubims, lions, and palm trees, according to the proportion of every one, and additions round about.

• In Ezekiel's vision of the temple.

Eze 41:18–20

Eze 41:25 — And *there were* made on them, on the doors of the temple, cherubims and palm trees, like as *were* made upon the walls; and *there were* thick planks upon the face of the porch without.

• Figurative.

Eze 28:14 — Thou *art* the anointed cherub that covereth; and I have set thee *so:* thou wast upon the holy mountain of God; thou hast walked up and down in the midst of the stones of fire.

Eze 28:16 — By the multitude of thy merchandise they have filled the midst of thee with violence, and thou hast sinned: therefore I will cast thee as profane out of the mountain of God: and I will destroy thee, O covering cherub, from the midst of the stones of fire.

• Symbolic.

Eze 1:1–28; 10:1–22

CHESALON • A landmark in the north boundary of Jeda.

Jos 15:10 — And the border compassed from Baalah westward unto mount Seir, and passed along unto the side of mount Jearim, which *is* Chesalon, on the north side, and went down to Beth-shemesh, and passed on to Timnah:

CHESED • Son of Nahor.

Ge 22:22 — And Chesed, and Hazo, and Pildash, and Jidlaph, and Bethuel.

CHESIL

• A town in the south of Palestine.

Jos 15:30 — And Eltolad, and Chesil, and Hormah,

• Probably identical with Bethul.

Jos 19:4 — And Eltolad, and Bethul, and Hormah,

• Probably identical with Bethuel.

1Ch 4:30 — And at Bethuel, and at Hormah, and at Ziklag,

CHEST

• For money.

2Ch 24:8–11

2Ki 12:9 — But Jehoiada the priest took a chest, and bored a hole in the lid of it, and set it beside the altar, on the right side as one cometh into the house of the LORD: and the priests that kept the door put therein all the money *that was* brought into the house of the LORD.

CHESTNUT TREE

Ge 30:37 — And Jacob took him rods of green poplar, and of the hazel and chesnut tree; and pilled white strakes in them, and made the white appear which *was* in the rods.

Eze 31:8 — The cedars in the garden of God could not hide him: the fir trees were not like his boughs, and the chesnut trees were not like his branches; nor any tree in the garden of God was like unto him in his beauty.

CHESULLOTH

• A city of Issachar.

Jos 19:18 — And their border was toward Jezreel, and Chesulloth, and Shunem,

• Probably identical with Chisloth-Tabor.

Jos 19:12 — And turned from Sarid eastward toward the sunrising unto the border of Chisloth-tabor, and then goeth out to Daberath, and goeth up to Japhia,

• Probably identical with Tabor.

1Ch 6:77 — Unto the rest of the children of Merari *were given* out of the tribe of Zebulun, Rimmon with her suburbs, Tabor with her suburbs:

CHEZIB

• Birthplace of Shelah.

Ge 38:5 — And she yet again conceived, and bare a son; and called his name Shelah: and he was at Chezib, when she bare him.

• Probably identical with Chozeba.

1Ch 4:22 — And Jokim, and the men of Chozeba, and Joash, and Saraph, who had the dominion in Moab, and Jashubi-lehem. And *these are* ancient things.

• Probably identical with Achzib.

Jos 15:44 — And Keilah, and Achzib, and Mareshah; nine cities with their villages:

CHICKENS

• Broods her young.

Mt 23:37 — O Jerusalem, Jerusalem, *thou* that killest the prophets, and stonest them which are sent unto thee, how often would I have gathered thy children together, even as a hen gathereth her chickens under *her* wings, and ye would not!

Lk 13:34 — O Jerusalem, Jerusalem, which killest the prophets, and stonest them that are sent unto thee; how often would I have gathered thy children together, as a hen *doth gather* her brood under *her* wings, and ye would not!

CHIDING

• Cain chides God.

Ge 4:13–14

• Pharaoh chides Abraham, for calling his wife his sister.

Ge 12:18–19

• Abimelech chides Abraham for a like offense.

Ge 20:9–10

• Abimelech chides Isaac for similar conduct.

Ge 26:9–10

• Isaac and Laban chide each other.

Ge 31:26–42

• Jacob chides Simeon and Levi for slaying Hamor and Shechem.

Ge 34:30 — And Jacob said to Simeon and Levi, Ye have troubled me to make me to stink among the inhabitants of the land, among the Canaanites and the Perizzites: and I *being* few in number, they shall gather themselves together against me, and slay me; and I shall be destroyed, I and my house.

- **Reuben chides his brethren for their treatment of Joseph.**

Ge 42:22 — And Reuben answered them, saying, Spake I not unto you, saying, Do not sin against the child; and ye would not hear? therefore, behold, also his blood is required.

- **Israelites chide Moses and tempt God.**

Ex 17:7 — And he called the name of the place Massah, and Meribah, because of the chiding of the children of Israel, and because they tempted the LORD, saying, Is the LORD among us, or not?

- **Deborah chides Israel in her epic.**

Jgs 5:16–23

- **David chides Joab for slaying Abner.**

2Sa 3:28–31

- **Joab chides David for lamenting the death of Absalom.**

2Sa 19:5–7

- **Jesus chides his disciples**
  - **On account of their unbelief.**

Mt 16:8–11

Mt 8:26 — And he saith unto them, Why are ye fearful, O ye of little faith? Then he arose, and rebuked the winds and the sea; and there was a great calm.

Mt 14:31 — And immediately Jesus stretched forth *his* hand, and caught him, and said unto him, O thou of little faith, wherefore didst thou doubt?

Mt 17:17 — Then Jesus answered and said, O faithless and perverse generation, how long shall I be with you? how long shall I suffer you? bring him hither to me.

Mk 4:40 — And he said unto them, Why are ye so fearful? how is it that ye have no faith?

Lk 8:25 — And he said unto them, Where is your faith? And they being afraid wondered, saying one to another, What manner of man is this! for he commandeth even the winds and water, and they obey him.

  - **For slowness of heart.**

Mt 16:8–9

Mt 15:16 — And Jesus said, Are ye also yet without understanding?

Mt 16:11 — How is it that ye do not understand that I spake *it* not to you concerning bread, that ye should beware of the leaven of the Pharisees and of the Sadducees?

Mk 7:18 — And he saith unto them, Are ye so without understanding also? Do ye not perceive, that whatsoever thing from without entereth into the man, *it* cannot defile him;

Lk 24:25 — Then he said unto them, O fools, and slow of heart to believe all that the prophets have spoken:

Jn 14:9 — Jesus saith unto him, Have I been so long time with you, and yet hast thou not known me, Philip? he that hath seen me hath seen the Father; and how sayest thou *then,* Shew us the Father?

  - **For sleeping in Gethsemane.**

Mt 26:40 — And he cometh unto the disciples, and findeth them asleep, and saith unto Peter, What, could ye not watch with me one hour?

Mk 14:27 — And Jesus saith unto them, All ye shall be offended because of me this night: for it is written, I will smite the shepherd, and the sheep shall be scattered.

- **For forbidding children to be brought to him.**

Mt 19:14 — But Jesus said, Suffer little children, and forbid them not, to come unto me: for of such is the kingdom of heaven.

Mk 10:14 — But when Jesus saw *it,* he was much displeased, and said unto them, Suffer the little children to come unto me, and forbid them not: for of such is the kingdom of God.

Lk 18:16 — But Jesus called them *unto him,* and said, Suffer little children to come unto me, and forbid them not: for of such is the kingdom of God.

CHIDON

- **Place where Uzza was stricken to death.**

1Ch 13:9 — And when they came unto the threshingfloor of Chidon, Uzza put forth his hand to hold the ark; for the oxen stumbled.

- **Called Nachon's threshing floor.**

2Sa 6:6 — And when they came to Nachon's threshingfloor, Uzzah put forth *his hand* to the ark of God, and took hold of it; for the oxen shook *it.*

CHILDLESSNESS

- **A reproach.**

Ge 30:1–3

Ge 16:2 — And Sarai said unto Abram, Behold now, the LORD hath restrained me from bearing: I pray thee, go in unto my maid; it may be that I may obtain children by her. And Abram hearkened to the voice of Sarai.

Ge 29:32 — And Leah conceived, and bare a son, and she called his name Reuben: for she said, Surely the LORD hath looked upon my affliction; now therefore my husband will love me.

Ge 30:13 — And Leah said, Happy am I, for the daughters will call me blessed: and she called his name Asher.

1Sa 1:6 — And her adversary also provoked her sore, for to make her fret, because the LORD had shut up her womb.

Isa 4:1 — And in that day seven women shall take hold of one man, saying, We will eat our own bread, and wear our own apparel: only let us be called by thy name, to take away our reproach.

Lk 1:25 — Thus hath the Lord dealt with me in the days wherein he looked on *me,* to take away my reproach among men.

See: Barrenness, sterility of women

CHILDREN

• Unclassified scriptures relating to.

Mt 21:15–16

Ne 12:43 — Also that day they offered great sacrifices, and rejoiced: for God had made them rejoice with great joy: the wives also and the children rejoiced: so that the joy of Jerusalem was heard even afar off.

Ps 8:2 — Out of the mouth of babes and sucklings hast thou ordained strength because of thine enemies, that thou mightest still the enemy and the avenger.

Pr 10:1 — The proverbs of Solomon. A wise son maketh a glad father: but a foolish son *is* the heaviness of his mother.

Pr 13:1 — A wise son *heareth* his father's instruction: but a scorner heareth not rebuke.

Pr 15:5 — A fool despiseth his father's instruction: but he that regardeth reproof is prudent.

Pr 15:20 — A wise son maketh a glad father: but a foolish man despiseth his mother.

Pr 28:7 — Whoso keepeth the law *is* a wise son: but he that is a companion of riotous *men* shameth his father.

Ecc 4:13 — Better *is* a poor and a wise child than an old and foolish king, who will no more be admonished.

Mal 1:6 — A son honoureth *his* father, and a servant his master: if then I *be* a father, where *is* mine honour? and if I *be* a master, where *is* my fear? saith the LORD of hosts unto you, O priests, that despise my name. And ye say, Wherein have we despised thy name?

• Instances of.

• Shem and Japheth.
Ge 9:23

• Isaac.
Ge 22:6–12

• Esau.
Ge 28:6–9

• Judah.
Ge 44:18–34

• Joseph.
Ge 45:9–13; 46:29; 47:11; 48:12; 50:1–13

• Moses.
Ex 15:2; 18:7

• Jephthah's daughter.
Jgs 11:36

• Samson.
Jgs 13:24

• Ruth.
Ru 1:15–17

• Samuel.
1Sa 2:26; 3:10

• Saul.
1Sa 9:5

• David.
1Sa 22:3–4; Ps 71:5, 17

• Solomon.
1Ki 2:19–20; 3:3–13

• Abijah.
1Ki 14:13

• Obadiah.
1Ki 18:12

• Jehoshaphat.
1Ki 22:43; 2Ch 17:3

• The Israelitish maid, captive in Syria.
2Ki 5:2–4

• Jewish children.
2Ch 20:13; Ne 8:3

• Josiah.
2Ch 34:1–3

• Job.
Job 29:4

• Elihu.
Job 32:4–7

• Jeremiah.
Jer 1:5–7

• Children in the temple.
Mt 21:15

• John.
Lk 1:80

• Jesus.
Lk 2:52

• Timothy.
2Ti 1:5; 3:15

• Worship, attend divine.

Ne 8:2–3

Jos 8:35 — There was not a word of all that Moses commanded, which Joshua read not before all the congregation of Israel, with the women, and the little ones, and the strangers that were conversant among them.

2Ch 20:13 — And all Judah stood before the LORD, with their little ones, their wives, and their children.

2Ch 31:16 — Beside their genealogy of males, from three years old and upward, *even* unto every one that entereth into the house of the LORD, his daily portion for their service in their charges according to their courses;

Ezr 8:21 — Then I proclaimed a fast there, at the river of Ahava, that we might afflict ourselves before our God, to seek of him a right way for us, and for our little ones, and for all our substance.

Ne 12:43 — Also that day they offered great sacrifices, and rejoiced: for God had made them rejoice with great joy: the wives also and the children rejoiced: so that the joy of Jerusalem was heard even afar off.

Mt 21:15 — And when the chief priests and scribes saw the wonderful things that he did, and the children crying in the temple, and saying, Hosanna to the Son of David; they were sore displeased,

Lk 2:46 — And it came to pass, that after three days they found him in the temple, sitting in the midst of the doctors, both hearing them, and asking them questions.

• Symbolic of the regenerated.

Mt 18:2–6; Mk 9:36–37; Lk 9:46–48

Mk 10:15 — Verily I say unto you, Whosoever shall not receive the kingdom of God as a little child, he shall not enter therein.

- **Figurative.**

1Co 13:11 — When I was a child, I spake as a child, I understood as a child, I thought as a child: but when I became a man, I put away childish things.

1Co 14:20 — Brethren, be not children in understanding: howbeit in malice be ye children, but in understanding be men.

1Pe 2:2 — As newborn babes, desire the sincere milk of the word, that ye may grow thereby:

See: Babes

See: Young Men

CHILDREN OF GOD **See: Righteous**

CHILDREN, Commandments to

Ps 148:12–13; Pr 1:8–9; 3:1–3; 4:1–4, 10–11, 20–22; 5:1–2; 6:20–25; 8:32–33; Eph 6:1–3; Col 3:1–25

Ex 20:12 — Honour thy father and thy mother: that thy days may be long upon the land which the LORD thy God giveth thee.

Le 19:3 — Ye shall fear every man his mother, and his father, and keep my sabbaths: I *am* the LORD your God.

Le 19:32 — Thou shalt rise up before the hoary head, and honour the face of the old man, and fear thy God: I *am* the LORD.

Dt 5:16 — Honour thy father and thy mother, as the LORD thy God hath commanded thee; that thy days may be prolonged, and that it may go well with thee, in the land which the LORD thy God giveth thee.

Ps 119:9 — Wherewithal shall a young man cleanse his way? by taking heed *thereto* according to thy word.

Pr 23:22 — Hearken unto thy father that begat thee, and despise not thy mother when she is old.

Pr 23:26 — My son, give me thine heart, and let thine eyes observe my ways.

Pr 27:11 — My son, be wise, and make my heart glad, that I may answer him that reproacheth me.

Ecc 12:1 — Remember now thy Creator in the days of thy youth, while the evil days come not, nor the years draw nigh, when thou shalt say, I have no pleasure in them;

La 3:27 — *It is* good for a man that he bear the yoke in his youth.

Mt 15:4 — For God commanded, saying, Honour thy father and mother: and, He that curseth father or mother, let him die the death.

Mt 19:19 — Honour thy father and *thy* mother: and, Thou shalt love thy neighbour as thyself.

Mk 10:19 — Thou knowest the commandments, Do not commit adultery, Do not kill, Do not steal, Do not bear false witness, Defraud not, Honour thy father and mother.

Lk 18:20 — Thou knowest the commandments, Do not commit adultery, Do not kill, Do not steal, Do not bear false witness, Honour thy father and thy mother.

1Ti 4:12 — Let no man despise thy youth; but be thou an example of the believers, in word, in conversation, in charity, in spirit, in faith, in purity.

2Ti 2:22 — Flee also youthful lusts: but follow righteousness, faith, charity, peace, with them that call on the Lord out of a pure heart.

Tit 2:6 — Young men likewise exhort to be sober minded.

See: Young Men

- **Counsel of parents to.**

1Ki 2:1–4; 1Ch 22:6–13; 28:9–10

1Ch 28:20 — And David said to Solomon his son, Be strong and of good courage, and do *it:* fear not, nor be dismayed: for the LORD God, *even* my God, *will be* with thee; he will not fail thee, nor forsake thee, until thou hast finished all the work for the service of the house of the LORD.

See: Parents

- **Instruction of.**

Ex 13:8–10, 14–16; Dt 4:9–10; 6:6–9; 11:19–20; 31:12–13; Ps 78:1–8; Isa 28:9–10

Jos 8:35 — There was not a word of all that Moses commanded, which Joshua read not before all the congregation of Israel, with the women, and the little ones, and the strangers that were conversant among them.

Ps 34:11 — Come, ye children, hearken unto me: I will teach you the fear of the LORD.

Pr 1:1 — The proverbs of Solomon the son of David, king of Israel;

Pr 1:4 — To give subtilty to the simple, to the young man knowledge and discretion.

Pr 22:6 — Train up a child in the way he should go: and when he is old, he will not depart from it.

Joel 1:3 — Tell ye your children of it, and *let* your children *tell* their children, and their children another generation.

Jn 21:15 — So when they had dined, Jesus saith to Simon Peter, Simon, *son* of Jonas, lovest thou me more than these? He saith unto him, Yea, Lord; thou knowest that I love thee. He saith unto him, Feed my lambs.

Ac 22:3 — I am verily a man *which am* a Jew, born in Tarsus, a city in Cilicia, yet brought up in this city at the feet of Gamaliel, *and* taught according to the perfect manner of the law of the fathers, and was zealous toward God, as ye all are this day.

See: Instruction

See: Young Men

See: Tutor

- **False instruction of.**

Mk 7:9–13

- **Prayer in behalf of.**

Ge 17:18 — And Abraham said unto God, O that Ishmael might live before thee!

2Sa 12:16 — David therefore besought God for the child; and David fasted, and went in, and lay all night upon the earth.

1Ch 22:12 — Only the LORD give thee wisdom and understanding, and give thee charge concerning Israel, that thou mayest keep the law of the LORD thy God.

1Ch 29:19 — And give unto Solomon my son a perfect heart, to keep thy commandments, thy testimonies, and thy statutes, and to do all *these things,* and to build the palace, for the which I have made provision.

Job 1:5 — And it was so, when the days of *their* feasting were gone about, that Job sent and sanctified them, and rose up early in the morning, and offered burnt offerings *according* to the number of them all: for Job said, It may be that my sons have sinned, and cursed God in their hearts. Thus did Job continually.

• Promises and assurances to.

Pr 3:1–10; 23:15–16, 24–25; Mt 18:4–5; 19:14–15; Mk 10:13–16; Lk 18:15–16; 1Jn 2:12–13

Pr 8:17 — I love them that love me; and those that seek me early shall find me.

Pr 8:32 — Now therefore hearken unto me, O ye children: for blessed *are they that* keep my ways.

Pr 29:3 — Whoso loveth wisdom rejoiceth his father: but he that keepeth company with harlots spendeth *his* substance.

Isa 40:11 — He shall feed his flock like a shepherd: he shall gather the lambs with his arm, and carry *them* in his bosom, *and* shall gently lead those that are with young.

Isa 54:13 — And all thy children *shall be* taught of the LORD; and great *shall be* the peace of thy children.

Mt 18:10 — Take heed that ye despise not one of these little ones; for I say unto you, That in heaven their angels do always behold the face of my Father which is in heaven.

Mk 9:37 — Whosoever shall receive one of such children in my name, receiveth me: and whosoever shall receive me, receiveth not me, but him that sent me.

Lk 9:48 — And said unto them, Whosoever shall receive this child in my name receiveth me: and whosoever shall receive me receiveth him that sent me: for he that is least among you all, the same shall be great.

Ac 2:39 — For the promise is unto you, and to your children, and to all that are afar off, *even* as many as the Lord our God shall call.

See: Young Men

• Of the righteous, blessed of God.

Ge 17:7–8; 19:15–16; 26:3–4; Le 26:44–45; Ps 103:17–18; 112:2–3; Isa 44:3–5

Ge 6:18 — But with thee will I establish my covenant; and thou shalt come into the ark, thou, and thy sons, and thy wife, and thy sons' wives with thee.

Ge 7:1 — And the LORD said unto Noah, Come thou and all thy house into the ark; for thee have I seen righteous before me in this generation.

Ge 12:7 — And the LORD appeared unto Abram, and said, Unto thy seed will I give this land: and there builded he an altar unto the LORD, who appeared unto him.

Ge 13:15 — For all the land which thou seest, to thee will I give it, and to thy seed for ever.

Ge 19:12 — And the men said unto Lot, Hast thou here any besides? son in law, and thy sons, and thy daughters, and whatsoever thou hast in the city, bring *them* out of this place:

Ge 21:13 — And also of the son of the bondwoman will I make a nation, because he *is* thy seed.

Ge 26:24 — And the LORD appeared unto him the same night, and said, I *am* the God of Abraham thy father: fear not, for I *am* with thee, and will bless thee, and multiply thy seed for my servant Abraham's sake.

Dt 4:37 — And because he loved thy fathers, therefore he chose their seed after them, and brought thee out in his sight with his mighty power out of Egypt;

Dt 10:15 — Only the LORD had a delight in thy fathers to love them, and he chose their seed after them, *even* you above all people, as *it is* this day.

Dt 12:28 — Observe and hear all these words which I command thee, that it may go well with thee, and with thy children after thee for ever, when thou doest *that which is* good and right in the sight of the LORD thy God.

1Ki 11:13 — Howbeit I will not rend away all the kingdom; *but* will give one tribe to thy son for David my servant's sake, and for Jerusalem's sake which I have chosen.

1Ki 15:4 — Nevertheless for David's sake did the LORD his God give him a lamp in Jerusalem, to set up his son after him, and to establish Jerusalem:

2Ki 8:19 — Yet the LORD would not destroy Judah for David his servant's sake, as he promised him to give him alway a light, *and* to his children.

Ps 37:26 — *He is* ever merciful, and lendeth; and his seed *is* blessed.

Ps 102:28 — The children of thy servants shall continue, and their seed shall be established before thee.

Pr 3:33 — The curse of the LORD *is* in the house of the wicked: but he blesseth the habitation of the just.

Pr 11:21 — *Though* hand *join* in hand, the wicked shall not be unpunished: but the seed of the righteous shall be delivered.

Pr 12:7 — The wicked are overthrown, and *are* not: but the house of the righteous shall stand.

Pr 13:22 — A good *man* leaveth an inheritance to his children's children: and the wealth of the sinner is laid up for the just.

Pr 20:7 — The just *man* walketh in his integrity: his children *are* blessed after him.

Isa 65:23 — They shall not labour in vain, nor bring forth for trouble; for they *are* the seed of the blessed of the LORD, and their offspring with them.

Jer 32:39 — And I will give them one heart, and one way, that they may fear me for ever, for the good of them, and of their children after them:

Ac 2:39 — For the promise is unto you, and to your children, and to all that are afar off, *even* as many as the Lord our God shall call.

1Co 7:14 — For the unbelieving husband is sanctified by the wife, and the unbelieving wife is sanctified by the husband: else were your children unclean; but now are they holy.

• Correction of.

Pr 23:13–14

Pr 13:24 — He that spareth his rod hateth his son: but he that loveth him chasteneth him betimes.

Pr 19:18 — Chasten thy son while there is hope, and let not thy soul spare for his crying.

Pr 22:15 — Foolishness *is* bound in the heart of a child; *but* the rod of correction shall drive it far from him.

Pr 29:15 — The rod and reproof give wisdom: but a child left *to himself* bringeth his mother to shame.

Pr 29:17 — Correct thy son, and he shall give thee rest; yea, he shall give delight unto thy soul.

Eph 6:4 — And, ye fathers, provoke not your children to wrath: but bring them up in the nurture and admonition of the Lord.

Col 3:21 — Fathers, provoke not your children *to anger,* lest they be discouraged.

- **Punishment of.**

Dt 21:18–21

Ex 21:15 — And he that smiteth his father, or his mother, shall be surely put to death.

Ex 21:17 — And he that curseth his father, or his mother, shall surely be put to death.

Le 20:9 — For every one that curseth his father or his mother shall be surely put to death: he hath cursed his father or his mother; his blood *shall be* upon him.

Dt 27:16 — Cursed *be* he that setteth light by his father or his mother. And all the people shall say, Amen.

Mt 15:4 — For God commanded, saying, Honour thy father and mother: and, He that curseth father or mother, let him die the death.

Mk 7:10 — For Moses said, Honour thy father and thy mother; and, Whoso curseth father or mother, let him die the death:

CHILDREN, Good

- **The Lord is with.**

1Sa 3:19 — And Samuel grew, and the LORD was with him, and did let none of his words fall to the ground.

- **Know the Scriptures.**

2Ti 3:15 — And that from a child thou hast known the holy scriptures, which are able to make thee wise unto salvation through faith which is in Christ Jesus.

- **Their obedience to parents is well pleasing to God.**

Col 3:20 — Children, obey *your* parents in all things: for this is well pleasing unto the Lord.

- **Partake of the promises of God.**

Ac 2:39 — For the promise is unto you, and to your children, and to all that are afar off, *even* as many as the Lord our God shall call.

- **Shall be blessed.**

Pr 3:1–4; Eph 6:2–3

- **Show love to parents.**

Ge 46:29 — And Joseph made ready his chariot, and went up to meet Israel his father, to Goshen, and presented himself unto him; and he fell on his neck, and wept on his neck a good while.

- **Obey parents.**

Ge 28:7 — And that Jacob obeyed his father and his mother, and was gone to Padan-aram;

Ge 47:30 — But I will lie with my fathers, and thou shalt carry me out of Egypt, and bury me in their buryingplace. And he said, I will do as thou hast said.

- **Attend to parental teaching.**

Pr 13:1 — A wise son *heareth* his father's instruction: but a scorner heareth not rebuke.

- **Take care of parents.**

Ge 45:9–11

Ge 47:12 — And Joseph nourished his father, and his brethren, and all his father's household, with bread, according to *their* families.

Mt 15:5 — But ye say, Whosoever shall say to *his* father or *his* mother, *It is* a gift, by whatsoever thou mightest be profited by me;

- **Make their parents' hearts glad.**

Pr 10:1 — The proverbs of Solomon. A wise son maketh a glad father: but a foolish son *is* the heaviness of his mother.

Pr 23:24 — The father of the righteous shall greatly rejoice: and he that begetteth a wise *child* shall have joy of him.

Pr 29:17 — Correct thy son, and he shall give thee rest; yea, he shall give delight unto thy soul.

- **Honor the aged.**

Job 32:6–7

- **Character of, illustrates conversion.**

Mt 18:3 — And said, Verily I say unto you, Except ye be converted, and become as little children, ye shall not enter into the kingdom of heaven.

- **Illustrative of a teachable spirit.**

Mt 18:4 — Whosoever therefore shall humble himself as this little child, the same is greatest in the kingdom of heaven.

CHILDREN, Miscellaneous

- **In answer to prayer.**
  - **To Abraham.**

    Ge 15:2–5; 21:1–2
  - **To Isaac.**

    Ge 25:21 — And Isaac intreated the LORD for his wife, because she *was* barren: and the LORD was intreated of him, and Rebekah his wife conceived.
  - **To Leah.**

    Ge 30:17–22
  - **To Rachel.**

    Ge 30:22–24
  - **To Hannah.**

    1Sa 1:9–20
  - **To Zacharias.**

    Lk 1:13 — But the angel said unto him, Fear not, Zacharias: for thy prayer is heard; and thy wife Elisabeth shall bear thee a son, and thou shalt call his name John.

- **Treatment of, at birth.**

Eze 16:4–6

Lk 2:7 — And she brought forth her firstborn son, and wrapped him in swaddling clothes, and laid him in a manger; because there was no room for them in the inn.

Lk 2:12 — And this *shall be* a sign unto you; Ye shall find the babe wrapped in swaddling clothes, lying in a manger.

- **Circumcision of.**

  ➜See: Circumcision

- **Dedicated to God in infancy.**
  - **Samson.**

    Jgs 13:5 — For, lo, thou shalt conceive, and bear a son; and no razor shall come on his head: for the child shall be a Nazarite unto God from the womb: and he shall begin to deliver Israel out of the hand of the Philistines.

    Jgs 13:7 — But he said unto me, Behold, thou shalt conceive, and bear a son; and now drink no wine nor strong drink, neither eat any unclean *thing:* for the child shall be a Nazarite to God from the womb to the day of his death.

  - **Samuel.**

    1Sa 1:24–28

- **Promised to the righteous.**

  Ps 128:2–4

  Dt 7:12 — Wherefore it shall come to pass, if ye hearken to these judgments, and keep, and do them, that the LORD thy God shall keep unto thee the covenant and the mercy which he sware unto thy fathers:

  Dt 7:14 — Thou shalt be blessed above all people: there shall not be male or female barren among you, or among your cattle.

  Job 5:25 — Thou shalt know also that thy seed *shall be* great, and thine offspring as the grass of the earth.

  Ps 128:6 — Yea, thou shalt see thy children's children, *and* peace upon Israel.

- **Weaning of.**

  Ge 21:8 — And the child grew, and was weaned: and Abraham made a great feast the *same* day that Isaac was weaned.

  1Sa 1:22 — But Hannah went not up; for she said unto her husband, *I will not go up* until the child be weaned, and *then* I will bring him, that he may appear before the LORD, and there abide for ever.

  1Ki 11:20 — And the sister of Tahpenes bare him Genubath his son, whom Tahpenes weaned in Pharaoh's house: and Genubath was in Pharaoh's household among the sons of Pharaoh.

  Ps 131:2 — Surely I have behaved and quieted myself, as a child that is weaned of his mother: my soul *is* even as a weaned child.

  Isa 28:9 — Whom shall he teach knowledge? and whom shall he make to understand doctrine? *them that are* weaned from the milk, *and* drawn from the breasts.

- **Nurses for.**

  Ex 2:7–9

  Ru 4:16 — And Naomi took the child, and laid it in her bosom, and became nurse unto it.

  2Sa 4:4 — And Jonathan, Saul's son, had a son *that was* lame of *his* feet. He was five years old when the tidings came of Saul and Jonathan out of Jezreel, and his nurse took him up, and fled: and it came to pass, as she made haste to flee, that he fell, and became lame. And his name *was* Mephibosheth.

  2Ki 11:2 — But Jehosheba, the daughter of king Joram, sister of Ahaziah, took Joash the son of Ahaziah and stole him from among the king's sons *which were* slain; and they hid him, *even* him and his nurse, in the bedchamber from Athaliah, so that he was not slain.

  Ac 7:20 — In which time Moses was born, and was exceeding fair, and nourished up in his father's house three months:

- **Taught to walk.**

  Hos 11:3 — I taught Ephraim also to go, taking them by their arms; but they knew not that I healed them.

- **Tutors and governors for.**

  Gal 4:1–2

  2Ki 10:1 — And Ahab had seventy sons in Samaria. And Jehu wrote letters, and sent to Samaria, unto the rulers of Jezreel, to the elders, and to them that brought up Ahab's *children,* saying,

  Ac 22:3 — I am verily a man *which am* a Jew, born in Tarsus, a city in Cilicia, yet brought up in this city at the feet of Gamaliel, *and* taught according to the perfect manner of the law of the fathers, and was zealous toward God, as ye all are this day.

  Gal 3:24 — Wherefore the law was our schoolmaster *to bring us* unto Christ, that we might be justified by faith.

- **Bastard, excluded from the privileges of the congregation.**

  Dt 23:2 — A bastard shall not enter into the congregation of the LORD; even to his tenth generation shall he not enter into the congregation of the LORD.

  Heb 12:8 — But if ye be without chastisement, whereof all are partakers, then are ye bastards, and not sons.

- **Early piety of.**
  - **Samuel.**

    1Sa 3:1–21

    1Sa 2:18 — But Samuel ministered before the LORD, *being* a child, girded with a linen ephod.

  - **Jeremiah.**

    Jer 1:5–7

  - **John the Baptist.**

    Lk 1:15 — For he shall be great in the sight of the Lord, and shall drink neither wine nor strong drink; and he shall be filled with the Holy Ghost, even from his mother's womb.

    Lk 1:80 — And the child grew, and waxed strong in spirit, and was in the deserts till the day of his shewing unto Israel.

  - **Jesus.**

    Lk 2:46–47

Lk 2:40 — And the child grew, and waxed strong in spirit, filled with wisdom: and the grace of God was upon him.

Lk 2:52 — And Jesus increased in wisdom and stature, and in favour with God and man.

• Difference made between male and female, in Mosaic law.

Le 12:1–8

• Partiality of parents among.

• Rebekah for Jacob.

Ge 27:6–17

• Jacob for Joseph.

Ge 37:3–4

• Partiality among, forbidden.

Dt 21:15–17

• Love of, for parents.

• Of Ruth.

Ru 1:16–18

• Jesus.

Jn 19:26–27

• Sacrificed.

Eze 16:20–21

2Ki 17:31 — And the Avites made Nibhaz and Tartak, and the Sepharvites burnt their children in fire to Adrammelech and Anammelech, the gods of Sepharvaim.

• Caused to pass through fire.

2Ki 16:3 — But he walked in the way of the kings of Israel, yea, and made his son to pass through the fire, according to the abominations of the heathen, whom the LORD cast out from before the children of Israel.

Jer 32:35 — And they built the high places of Baal, which *are* in the valley of the son of Hinnom, to cause their sons and their daughters to pass through *the fire* unto Molech; which I commanded them not, neither came it into my mind, that they should do this abomination, to cause Judah to sin.

Eze 16:21 — That thou hast slain my children, and delivered them to cause them to pass through *the fire* for them?

• Sold for debt.

2Ki 4:1 — Now there cried a certain woman of the wives of the sons of the prophets unto Elisha, saying, Thy servant my husband is dead; and thou knowest that thy servant did fear the LORD: and the creditor is come to take unto him my two sons to be bondmen.

Ne 5:5 — Yet now our flesh *is* as the flesh of our brethren, our children as their children: and, lo, we bring into bondage our sons and our daughters to be servants, and *some* of our daughters are brought unto bondage *already:* neither *is it* in our power *to redeem them;* for other men have our lands and vineyards.

Job 24:9 — They pluck the fatherless from the breast, and take a pledge of the poor.

Mt 18:25 — But forasmuch as he had not to pay, his lord commanded him to be sold, and his wife, and children, and all that he had, and payment to be made.

• Sold in marriage, law concerning.

Ex 21:7–11

• Sold in marriage, instance of, Leah and Rachel.

Ge 29:15–30

• Edict to murder.

• Of Pharaoh.

Ex 1:22 — And Pharaoh charged all his people, saying, Every son that is born ye shall cast into the river, and every daughter ye shall save alive.

• Of Jehu.

2Ki 10:1–8

• Of Herod.

Mt 2:16–18

• Eaten.

See: Cannibalism

• Share benefits of covenant privileges guaranteed to parents.

Ge 17:7–8; 26:3–5; Le 26:44–45

Ge 6:18 — But with thee will I establish my covenant; and thou shalt come into the ark, thou, and thy sons, and thy wife, and thy sons' wives with thee.

Ge 12:7 — And the LORD appeared unto Abram, and said, Unto thy seed will I give this land: and there builded he an altar unto the LORD, who appeared unto him.

Ge 13:15 — For all the land which thou seest, to thee will I give it, and to thy seed for ever.

Ge 19:12 — And the men said unto Lot, Hast thou here any besides? son in law, and thy sons, and thy daughters, and whatsoever thou hast in the city, bring *them* out of this place:

Ge 21:13 — And also of the son of the bondwoman will I make a nation, because he *is* thy seed.

Ge 26:24 — And the LORD appeared unto him the same night, and said, I *am* the God of Abraham thy father: fear not, for I *am* with thee, and will bless thee, and multiply thy seed for my servant Abraham's sake.

Isa 65:23 — They shall not labour in vain, nor bring forth for trouble; for they *are* the seed of the blessed of the LORD, and their offspring with them.

1Co 7:14 — For the unbelieving husband is sanctified by the wife, and the unbelieving wife is sanctified by the husband: else were your children unclean; but now are they holy.

• Bound by covenants of parents.

Ge 17:9–14

• Involved in guilt of parents.

Le 26:39–42; Isa 14:20–21; 65:6–7

Ex 20:5 — Thou shalt not bow down thyself to them, nor serve them: for I the LORD thy God *am* a jealous God, visiting the iniquity of the fathers upon the children unto the third and fourth *generation* of them that hate me;

Ex 34:7 — Keeping mercy for thousands, forgiving iniquity and transgression and sin, and that will by no means clear *the guilty;* visiting the iniquity of the fathers upon the children, and upon the children's children, unto the third and to the fourth *generation.*

Le 20:5 — Then I will set my face against that man, and against his family, and will cut him off, and all that go a whoring after him, to commit whoredom with Molech, from among their people.

Nu 14:18 — The LORD *is* longsuffering, and of great mercy, forgiving iniquity and transgression, and by no means clearing *the guilty,* visiting the iniquity of the fathers upon the children unto the third and fourth *generation.*

Nu 14:33 — And your children shall wander in the wilderness forty years, and bear your whoredoms, until your carcases be wasted in the wilderness.

1Ki 21:29 — Seest thou how Ahab humbleth himself before me? because he humbleth himself before me, I will not bring the evil in his days: *but* in his son's days will I bring the evil upon his house.

Job 21:19 — God layeth up his iniquity for his children: he rewardeth him, and he shall know *it.*

Ps 37:28 — For the LORD loveth judgment, and forsaketh not his saints; they are preserved for ever: but the seed of the wicked shall be cut off.

Jer 32:18 — Thou shewest lovingkindness unto thousands, and recompensest the iniquity of the fathers into the bosom of their children after them: the Great, the Mighty God, the LORD of hosts, *is* his name,

Da 6:24 — And the king commanded, and they brought those men which had accused Daniel, and they cast *them* into the den of lions, them, their children, and their wives; and the lions had the mastery of them, and brake all their bones in pieces or ever they came at the bottom of the den.

- **Not punished for parents' sake.**

Jer 31:29–30; Eze 18:1–30

- **Death of, as a judgment upon parents.**
  - **Firstborn of Egypt.**

Ex 12:29 — And it came to pass, that at midnight the LORD smote all the firstborn in the land of Egypt, from the firstborn of Pharaoh that sat on his throne unto the firstborn of the captive that *was* in the dungeon; and all the firstborn of cattle.

  - **Sons of Eli.**

1Sa 3:13–14

  - **Sons of Saul.**

1Sa 28:18–19

  - **David's child by Uriah's wife.**

2Sa 12:14–19

- **Miracles in behalf of.**
  - **Raised from the dead by Elijah.**

1Ki 17:17–23

  - **By Elisha.**

2Ki 4:17–36

  - **By Jesus.**

Mt 9:24–26; Mk 5:35–42; Lk 7:13–15; 8:49–56

Mt 9:18 — While he spake these things unto them, behold, there came a certain ruler, and worshipped him, saying, My daughter is even now dead: but come and lay thy hand upon her, and she shall live.

  - **Healing of.**

Mk 7:29–30; 9:23–27; Lk 8:42–56; 9:38–42; Jn 4:46–54

Mt 15:28 — Then Jesus answered and said unto her, O woman, great *is* thy faith: be it unto thee even as thou wilt. And her daughter was made whole from that very hour.

Mt 17:18 — And Jesus rebuked the devil; and he departed out of him: and the child was cured from that very hour.

- **Character of, known by conduct.**

Pr 20:11 — Even a child is known by his doings, whether his work *be* pure, and whether *it be* right.

- **Blessed by Jesus.**

Mt 19:13–15; Mk 10:13–16; Lk 18:15–16

- **Future state of.**

Mt 18:10 — Take heed that ye despise not one of these little ones; for I say unto you, That in heaven their angels do always behold the face of my Father which is in heaven.

Mt 19:14 — But Jesus said, Suffer little children, and forbid them not, to come unto me: for of such is the kingdom of heaven.

- **Minors.**

Gal 4:1–2

- **Of ministers.**

1Ti 3:4 — One that ruleth well his own house, having his children in subjection with all gravity;

Tit 1:6 — If any be blameless, the husband of one wife, having faithful children not accused of riot or unruly.

- **Alienated, Ishmael, to gratify Sarah.**

Ge 21:9–15

- **Amusements of.**

Mt 11:16–17; Lk 7:31–32

Job 21:11 — They send forth their little ones like a flock, and their children dance.

Zec 8:5 — And the streets of the city shall be full of boys and girls playing in the streets thereof.

- **Adopted.**

*See: Adoption

CHILDREN, the Gift of God

Ge 29:32–35; 30:17–20, 22–24

Ge 4:1 — And Adam knew Eve his wife; and she conceived, and bare Cain, and said, I have gotten a man from the LORD.

Ge 4:25 — And Adam knew his wife again; and she bare a son, and called his name Seth: For God, *said she,* hath appointed me another seed instead of Abel, whom Cain slew.

Ge 17:16 — And I will bless her, and give thee a son also of her: yea, I will bless her, and she shall be *a mother* of nations; kings of people shall be of her.

Ge 17:20 — And as for Ishmael, I have heard thee: Behold, I have blessed him, and will make him fruitful, and will multiply him exceedingly; twelve princes shall he beget, and I will make him a great nation.

Ge 28:3 — And God Almighty bless thee, and make thee fruitful, and multiply thee, that thou mayest be a multitude of people;

Ge 30:2 — And Jacob's anger was kindled against Rachel: and he said, *Am* I in God's stead, who hath withheld from thee the fruit of the womb?

Ge 30:6 — And Rachel said, God hath judged me, and hath also heard my voice, and hath given me a son: therefore called she his name Dan.

Ge 33:5 — And he lifted up his eyes, and saw the women and the children; and said, Who *are* those with thee? And he said, The children which God hath graciously given thy servant.

Ru 4:13 — So Boaz took Ruth, and she was his wife: and when he went in unto her, the LORD gave her conception, and she bare a son.

Job 1:21 — And said, Naked came I out of my mother's womb, and naked shall I return thither: the LORD gave, and the LORD hath taken away; blessed be the name of the LORD.

Ps 107:38 — He blesseth them also, so that they are multiplied greatly; and suffereth not their cattle to decrease.

Ps 107:41 — Yet setteth he the poor on high from affliction, and maketh *him* families like a flock.

Ps 113:9 — He maketh the barren woman to keep house, *and to be* a joyful mother of children. Praise ye the LORD.

Ps 127:3 — Lo, children *are* an heritage of the LORD: *and* the fruit of the womb *is his* reward.

• God's care of.

Ex 22:22–24; Ps 10:17–18

Dt 10:18 — He doth execute the judgment of the fatherless and widow, and loveth the stranger, in giving him food and raiment.

Dt 14:29 — And the Levite, (because he hath no part nor inheritance with thee,) and the stranger, and the fatherless, and the widow, which *are* within thy gates, shall come, and shall eat and be satisfied; that the LORD thy God may bless thee in all the work of thine hand which thou doest.

Job 29:12 — Because I delivered the poor that cried, and the fatherless, and *him that had* none to help him.

Ps 10:14 — Thou hast seen *it;* for thou beholdest mischief and spite, to requite *it* with thy hand: the poor committeth himself unto thee; thou art the helper of the fatherless.

Ps 27:10 — When my father and my mother forsake me, then the LORD will take me up.

Ps 68:5 — A father of the fatherless, and a judge of the widows, *is* God in his holy habitation.

Ps 146:9 — The LORD preserveth the strangers; he relieveth the fatherless and widow: but the way of the wicked he turneth upside down.

Jer 49:11 — Leave thy fatherless children, I will preserve *them* alive; and let thy widows trust in me.

Hos 14:3 — Asshur shall not save us; we will not ride upon horses: neither will we say any more to the work of our hands, *Ye are* our gods: for in thee the fatherless findeth mercy.

Mal 3:5 — And I will come near to you to judgment; and I will be a swift witness against the sorcerers, and against the adulterers, and against false swearers, and against those that oppress the hireling in *his* wages, the widow, and the fatherless, and that turn aside the stranger *from his right,* and fear not me, saith the LORD of hosts.

• A blessing.

Ps 127:3–5

Ge 5:29 — And he called his name Noah, saying, This *same* shall comfort us concerning our work and toil of our hands, because of the ground which the LORD hath cursed.

Ge 30:1 — And when Rachel saw that she bare Jacob no children, Rachel envied her sister; and said unto Jacob, Give me children, or else I die.

Pr 17:6 — Children's children *are* the crown of old men; and the glory of children *are* their fathers.

Isa 54:1 — Sing, O barren, thou *that* didst not bear; break forth into singing, and cry aloud, thou *that* didst not travail with child: for more *are* the children of the desolate than the children of the married wife, saith the LORD.

Jer 20:15 — Cursed *be* the man who brought tidings to my father, saying, A man child is born unto thee; making him very glad.

CHILDREN, Wicked

Dt 21:18–21; Ps 144:7–8; Ecc 11:9–10; Jer 7:17–18

Ge 8:21 — And the LORD smelled a sweet savour; and the LORD said in his heart, I will not again curse the ground any more for man's sake; for the imagination of man's heart *is* evil from his youth; neither will I again smite any more every thing living, as I have done.

Ex 21:15 — And he that smiteth his father, or his mother, shall be surely put to death.

Ex 21:17 — And he that curseth his father, or his mother, shall surely be put to death.

Nu 32:14 — And, behold, ye are risen up in your fathers' stead, an increase of sinful men, to augment yet the fierce anger of the LORD toward Israel.

Dt 27:16 — Cursed *be* he that setteth light by his father or his mother. And all the people shall say, Amen.

Job 13:26 — For thou writest bitter things against me, and makest me to possess the iniquities of my youth.

Job 19:18 — Yea, young children despised me; I arose, and they spake against me.

Job 20:11 — His bones are full *of the sin* of his youth, which shall lie down with him in the dust.

Job 30:1 — But now *they that are* younger than I have me in derision, whose fathers I would have disdained to have set with the dogs of my flock.

Job 30:12 — Upon *my* right *hand* rise the youth; they push away my feet, and they raise up against me the ways of their destruction.

Ps 144:11 — Rid me, and deliver me from the hand of strange children, whose mouth speaketh vanity, and their right hand *is* a right hand of falsehood:

Pr 7:7 — And beheld among the simple ones, I discerned among the youths, a young man void of understanding,

Pr 10:1 — The proverbs of Solomon. A wise son maketh a glad father: but a foolish son *is* the heaviness of his mother.

Pr 13:1 — A wise son *heareth* his father's instruction: but a scorner heareth not rebuke.

Pr 15:5 — A fool despiseth his father's instruction: but he that regardeth reproof is prudent.

Pr 15:20 — A wise son maketh a glad father: but a foolish man despiseth his mother.

Pr 17:2 — A wise servant shall have rule over a son that causeth shame, and shall have part of the inheritance among the brethren.

Pr 17:21 — He that begetteth a fool *doeth it* to his sorrow: and the father of a fool hath no joy.

Pr 17:25 — A foolish son *is* a grief to his father, and bitterness to her that bare him.

Pr 19:13 — A foolish son *is* the calamity of his father: and the contentions of a wife *are* a continual dropping.

Pr 19:26 — He that wasteth *his* father, *and* chaseth away *his* mother, *is* a son that causeth shame, and bringeth reproach.

Pr 20:20 — Whoso curseth his father or his mother, his lamp shall be put out in obscure darkness.

Pr 22:15 — Foolishness *is* bound in the heart of a child; *but* the rod of correction shall drive it far from him.

Pr 23:22 — Hearken unto thy father that begat thee, and despise not thy mother when she is old.

Pr 28:7 — Whoso keepeth the law *is* a wise son: but he that is a companion of riotous *men* shameth his father.

Pr 28:24 — Whoso robbeth his father or his mother, and saith, *It is* no transgression; the same *is* the companion of a destroyer.

Pr 30:11 — *There is* a generation *that* curseth their father, and doth not bless their mother.

Pr 30:17 — The eye *that* mocketh at *his* father, and despiseth to obey *his* mother, the ravens of the valley shall pick it out, and the young eagles shall eat it.

Isa 3:5 — And the people shall be oppressed, every one by another, and every one by his neighbour: the child shall behave himself proudly against the ancient, and the base against the honourable.

Jer 3:25 — We lie down in our shame, and our confusion covereth us: for we have sinned against the LORD our God, we and our fathers, from our youth even unto this day, and have not obeyed the voice of the LORD our God.

Jer 32:30 — For the children of Israel and the children of Judah have only done evil before me from their youth: for the children of Israel have only provoked me to anger with the work of their hands, saith the LORD.

Eze 22:7 — In thee have they set light by father and mother: in the midst of thee have they dealt by oppression with the stranger: in thee have they vexed the fatherless and the widow.

Mic 7:6 — For the son dishonoureth the father, the daughter riseth up against her mother, the daughter in law against her mother in law; a man's enemies *are* the men of his own house.

Mk 7:10 — For Moses said, Honour thy father and thy mother; and, Whoso curseth father or mother, let him die the death:

Mk 13:12 — Now the brother shall betray the brother to death, and the father the son; and children shall rise up against *their* parents, and shall cause them to be put to death.

Ro 1:30 — Backbiters, haters of God, despiteful, proud, boasters, inventors of evil things, disobedient to parents,

2Ti 3:2 — For men shall be lovers of their own selves, covetous, boasters, proud, blasphemers, disobedient to parents, unthankful, unholy,

- **Instances of.**
  - **Canaan.**

    Ge 9:25 — And he said, Cursed *be* Canaan; a servant of servants shall he be unto his brethren.
  - **Lot's daughters.**

    Ge 19:30–38

    Ge 19:14 — And Lot went out, and spake unto his sons in law, which married his daughters, and said, Up, get you out of this place; for the LORD will destroy this city. But he seemed as one that mocked unto his sons in law.
  - **Ishmael.**

    Ge 21:9 — And Sarah saw the son of Hagar the Egyptian, which she had born unto Abraham, mocking.
  - **Eli's sons.**

    1Sa 2:22–25

    1Sa 2:12 — Now the sons of Eli *were* sons of Belial; they knew not the LORD.
  - **Samuel's sons.**

    1Sa 8:3 — And his sons walked not in his ways, but turned aside after lucre, and took bribes, and perverted judgment.
  - **Absalom.**

    2Sa 15:1–37
  - **Adonijah.**

    1Ki 1:5 — Then Adonijah the son of Haggith exalted himself, saying, I will be king: and he prepared him chariots and horsemen, and fifty men to run before him.
  - **Abijam.**

    1Ki 15:3 — And he walked in all the sins of his father, which he had done before him: and his heart was not perfect with the LORD his God, as the heart of David his father.
  - **Ahaziah.**

    1Ki 22:52 — And he did evil in the sight of the LORD, and walked in the way of his father, and in the way of his mother, and in the way of Jeroboam the son of Nebat, who made Israel to sin:
  - **Children at Bethel.**

    2Ki 2:23–24
  - **Samaritans' descendants.**

    2Ki 17:41 — So these nations feared the LORD, and served their graven images, both their children, and their children's children: as did their fathers, so do they unto this day.
  - **Adrammelech and Sharezer.**

    2Ki 19:37 — And it came to pass, as he was worshipping in the house of Nisroch his god, that Adrammelech and Sharezer his sons smote him with the sword: and they escaped into the land of Armenia. And Esar-haddon his son reigned in his stead.

2Ch 32:21 — And the LORD sent an angel, which cut off all the mighty men of valour, and the leaders and captains in the camp of the king of Assyria. So he returned with shame of face to his own land. And when he was come into the house of his god, they that came forth of his own bowels slew him there with the sword.

• **Amon.**

2Ki 21:21 — And he walked in all the way that his father walked in, and served the idols that his father served, and worshipped them:

CHILEAB

• **A son of David.**

2Sa 3:3 — And his second, Chileab, of Abigail the wife of Nabal the Carmelite; and the third, Absalom the son of Maacah the daughter of Talmai king of Geshur;

• **Called Daniel.**

1Ch 3:1 — Now these were the sons of David, which were born unto him in Hebron; the firstborn Amnon, of Ahinoam the Jezreelitess; the second Daniel, of Abigail the Carmelitess:

CHILION • A son of Naomi.

Ru 1:4–5

Ru 1:2 — And the name of the man *was* Elimelech, and the name of his wife Naomi, and the name of his two sons Mahlon and Chilion, Ephrathites of Bethlehemjudah. And they came into the country of Moab, and continued there.

Ru 4:9 — And Boaz said unto the elders, and *unto* all the people, Ye *are* witnesses this day, that I have bought all that *was* Elimelech's, and all that *was* Chilion's and Mahlon's, of the hand of Naomi.

CHILMAD

• **Merchants of.**

Eze 27:23 — Haran, and Canneh, and Eden, the merchants of Sheba, Asshur, *and* Chilmad, *were* thy merchants.

CHIMHAM • A Gileadite.

2Sa 19:37–38

2Sa 19:40 — Then the king went on to Gilgal, and Chimham went on with him: and all the people of Judah conducted the king, and also half the people of Israel.

Jer 41:17 — And they departed, and dwelt in the habitation of Chimham, which is by Bethlehem, to go to enter into Egypt,

CHIMNEY

Hos 13:3 — Therefore they shall be as the morning cloud, and as the early dew that passeth away, as the chaff *that* is driven with the whirlwind out of the floor, and as the smoke out of the chimney.

CHINESE

• **Sinim in Isa 49:12 is believed by many authorities to be a reference to the Chinese.**

Isa 49:12 — Behold, these shall come from far: and, lo, these from the north and from the west; and these from the land of Sinim.

CHINNERETH

• **Called also Chinneroth, Cinnereth and Cinneroth.**

• **A district in the north of Palestine.**

Jos 11:2 — And to the kings that *were* on the north of the mountains, and of the plains south of Chinneroth, and in the valley, and in the borders of Dor on the west,

1Ki 15:20 — So Ben-hadad hearkened unto king Asa, and sent the captains of the hosts which he had against the cities of Israel, and smote Ijon, and Dan, and Abel-beth-maachah, and all Cinneroth, with all the land of Naphtali.

• **A city in Naphtali.**

Jos 19:35 — And the fenced cities *are* Ziddim, Zer, and Hammath, Rakkath, and Chinnereth,

• **The sea of.**

Nu 34:11 — And the coast shall go down from Shepham to Riblah, on the east side of Ain; and the border shall descend, and shall reach unto the side of the sea of Chinnereth eastward:

Jos 12:3 — And from the plain to the sea of Chinneroth on the east, and unto the sea of the plain, *even* the salt sea on the east, the way to Beth-jeshimoth; and from the south, under Ashdoth-pisgah:

Jos 13:27 — And in the valley, Beth-aram, and Beth-nimrah, and Succoth, and Zaphon, the rest of the kingdom of Sihon king of Heshbon, Jordan and *his* border, *even* unto the edge of the sea of Chinnereth on the other side Jordan eastward.

See: Galilee; Sea of

CHINNEROTH **See: Chinnereth**

CHIOS • An island west of Smyrna.

Ac 20:15 — And we sailed thence, and came the next *day* over against Chios; and the next *day* we arrived at Samos, and tarried at Trogyllium; and the next *day* we came to Miletus.

CHISLEU • Ninth month in the Israelitish calendar.

Ezr 10:9 — Then all the men of Judah and Benjamin gathered themselves together unto Jerusalem within three days. It *was* the ninth month, on the twentieth *day* of the month; and all the people sat in the street of the house of God, trembling because of *this* matter, and for the great rain.

Ne 1:1 — The words of Nehemiah the son of Hachaliah. And it came to pass in the month Chisleu, in the twentieth year, as I was in Shushan the palace,

Jer 36:22 — Now the king sat in the winterhouse in the ninth month: and *there was a fire* on the hearth burning before him.

CHISLON • Father of Eldad.

Nu 34:21 — Of the tribe of Benjamin, Elidad the son of Chislon.

CHISLOTH-TABOR

• A place on the border of Zebulun.

Jos 19:12 — And turned from Sarid eastward toward the sunrising unto the border of Chisloth-tabor, and then goeth out to Daberath, and goeth up to Japhia,

• Called Tabor.

1Ch 6:77 — Unto the rest of the children of Merari *were given* out of the tribe of Zebulun, Rimmon with her suburbs, Tabor with her suburbs:

• Probably same as Chesulloth.

Jos 19:18 — And their border was toward Jezreel, and Chesulloth, and Shunem,

CHITTIM

• Descendants of Javan.

Ge 10:4 — And the sons of Javan; Elishah, and Tarshish, Kittim, and Dodanim.

• Probably inhabited islands of the Mediterranean.

Isa 23:1 — The burden of Tyre. Howl, ye ships of Tarshish; for it is laid waste, so that there is no house, no entering in: from the land of Chittim it is revealed to them.

Isa 23:12 — And he said, Thou shalt no more rejoice, O thou oppressed virgin, daughter of Zidon: arise, pass over to Chittim; there also shalt thou have no rest.

Jer 2:10 — For pass over the isles of Chittim, and see; and send unto Kedar, and consider diligently, and see if there be such a thing.

• Their commerce.

Eze 27:6 — *Of* the oaks of Bashan have they made thine oars; the company of the Ashurites have made thy benches *of* ivory, *brought* out of the isles of Chittim.

• Prophecies concerning.

Nu 24:24 — And ships *shall come* from the coast of Chittim, and shall afflict Asshur, and shall afflict Eber, and he also shall perish for ever.

Da 11:30 — For the ships of Chittim shall come against him: therefore he shall be grieved, and return, and have indignation against the holy covenant: so shall he do; he shall even return, and have intelligence with them that forsake the holy covenant.

CHIUN

• Called also Remphan.

• A god of the Phenicians.

Am 5:26 — But ye have borne the tabernacle of your Moloch and Chiun your images, the star of your god, which ye made to yourselves.

Ac 7:43 — Yea, ye took up the tabernacle of Moloch, and the star of your god Remphan, figures which ye made to worship them: and I will carry you away beyond Babylon.

CHLOE • A Christian of Corinth.

1Co 1:11 — For it hath been declared unto me of you, my brethren, by them *which are of the house* of Chloe, that there are contentions among you.

CHOICE

• Between judgments, by David.

1Ch 21:11–13

2Sa 24:12 — Go and say unto David, Thus saith the LORD, I offer thee three *things;* choose thee one of them, that I may *do it* unto thee.

• The sinner's.

Dt 30:19–20; Jos 24:15–18

1Ki 18:21 — And Elijah came unto all the people, and said, How long halt ye between two opinions? if the LORD *be* God, follow him: but if Baal, *then* follow him. And the people answered him not a word.

See: Contingencies

See: Blessing; divine, contingent upon obedience

CHOOSING See: Choice

CHOR-ASHAN

• A town in Judah.

1Sa 30:30 — And to *them* which *were* in Hormah, and to *them* which *were* in Chor-ashan, and to *them* which *were* in Athach,

• Perhaps identical with Ashan.

Jos 15:42 — Libnah, and Ether, and Ashan,

CHORAZIN

• Denunciation against.

Mt 11:21 — Woe unto thee, Chorazin! woe unto thee, Bethsaida! for if the mighty works, which were done in you, had been done in Tyre and Sidon, they would have repented long ago in sackcloth and ashes.

Lk 10:13 — Woe unto thee, Chorazin! woe unto thee, Bethsaida! for if the mighty works had been done in Tyre and Sidon, which have been done in you, they had a great while ago repented, sitting in sackcloth and ashes.

CHORUSES See: Music

CHOSEN, or Elected

Mt 20:16 — So the last shall be first, and the first last: for many be called, but few chosen.

Mt 22:14 — For many are called, but few *are* chosen.

1Pe 2:9 — But ye *are* a chosen generation, a royal priesthood, an holy nation, a peculiar people; that ye should shew forth the praises of him who hath called you out of darkness into his marvellous light:

Rev 17:14 — These shall make war with the Lamb, and the Lamb shall overcome them: for he is Lord of lords, and King of kings: and they that are with him *are* called, and chosen, and faithful.

See: Foreknowledge of God

See: Predestination

CHOZEBA

• A city of Judah.

1Ch 4:22 — And Jokim, and the men of Chozeba, and Joash, and Saraph, who had the dominion in Moab, and Jashubi-lehem. And *these are* ancient things.

See: Chezib

See: Achzib

CHRIST See: Jesus, Names, Appellations, and Titles of; The Christ

CHRISTIAN

• Believers called.

Ac 11:26 — And when he had found him, he brought him unto Antioch. And it came to pass, that a whole year they assembled themselves with the church, and taught much people. And the disciples were called Christians first in Antioch.

Ac 26:28 — Then Agrippa said unto Paul, Almost thou persuadest me to be a Christian.

1Pe 4:16 — Yet if *any man suffer* as a Christian, let him not be ashamed; but let him glorify God on this behalf.

See: Righteous

CHRONOLOGY

• Jewish year instituted.

Ex 12:2 — This month *shall be* unto you the beginning of months: it *shall be* the first month of the year to you.

See: Time

CHRYSOLYTE • A precious stone.

Rev 21:20 — The fifth, sardonyx; the sixth, sardius; the seventh, chrysolite; the eighth, beryl; the ninth, a topaz; the tenth, a chrysoprasus; the eleventh, a jacinth; the twelfth, an amethyst.

CHRYSOPRASUS • A precious stone.

Rev 21:20 — The fifth, sardonyx; the sixth, sardius; the seventh, chrysolite; the eighth, beryl; the ninth, a topaz; the tenth, a chrysoprasus; the eleventh, a jacinth; the twelfth, an amethyst.

CHUB • A people who were an ally tribe to Egypt, and probably inhabited Africa.

Eze 30:5 — Ethiopia, and Libya, and Lydia, and all the mingled people, and Chub, and the men of the land that is in league, shall fall with them by the sword.

CHUN

• A Syrian city.

1Ch 18:8 — Likewise from Tibhath, and from Chun, cities of Hadarezer, brought David very much brass, wherewith Solomon made the brasen sea, and the pillars, and the vessels of brass.

See: Betah

See: Berothai

CHURCH

• Backslidden.

Ps 80:1–19; Isa 1:2–27; 17:9–11; 43:22–28; Jer 2:5–34; 3:1–25; 8:5–9:3; 10:19–22; 18:11–17; 50:4–7; Eze 2:3–5; 5:5–17; Hos 2:1–23; 4:1–19; 6:1–11; Joel 2:1–32; Am 6:1–14; Mt 21:33–46; Mk 12:1–12; Lk 13:6–9; Rev 2:1–5, 12–16, 18–25; 3:1–4, 14–20

Ps 12:1 — Help, LORD; for the godly man ceaseth; for the faithful fail from among the children of men.

Eze 16:23 — And it came to pass after all thy wickedness, (woe, woe unto thee! saith the Lord GOD;)

• Backslidings of Israel.

See: Church; corruption in

See: Backsliders

See: Backsliders; backsliding of Israel

• Beneficence of.

See: Beneficence

See: Giving

See: Liberality

• Christ, Head of.

Ps 118:22–23; Mt 21:42–43; Lk 20:17–18; Jn 15:1–8; Eph 1:22–23; 2:20–22; 5:23–32; Rev 2:12–13, 18–19; 21:22–23

Isa 33:22 — For the LORD *is* our judge, the LORD *is* our lawgiver, the LORD *is* our king; he will save us.

Isa 55:4 — Behold, I have given him *for* a witness to the people, a leader and commander to the people.

Mt 12:6 — But I say unto you, That in this place is *one* greater than the temple.

Mt 12:8 — For the Son of man is Lord even of the sabbath day.

Mt 23:8 — But be not ye called Rabbi: for one is your Master, *even* Christ; and all ye are brethren.

Mt 23:10 — Neither be ye called masters: for one is your Master, *even* Christ.

Mk 2:28 — Therefore the Son of man is Lord also of the sabbath.

Mk 12:10 — And have ye not read this scripture; The stone which the builders rejected is become the head of the corner:

Lk 6:5 — And he said unto them, That the Son of man is Lord also of the sabbath.

Jn 13:13 — Ye call me Master and Lord: and ye say well; for so I am.

Ac 2:36 — Therefore let all the house of Israel know assuredly, that God hath made that same Jesus, whom ye have crucified, both Lord and Christ.

Ro 8:29 — For whom he did foreknow, he also did predestinate *to be* conformed to the image of his Son, that he might be the firstborn among many brethren.

Ro 9:5 — Whose *are* the fathers, and of whom as concerning the flesh Christ *came,* who is over all, God blessed for ever. Amen.

1Co 3:11 — For other foundation can no man lay than that is laid, which is Jesus Christ.

1Co 11:3 — But I would have you know, that the head of every man is Christ; and the head of the woman *is* the man; and the head of Christ *is* God.

1Co 12:5 — And there are differences of administrations, but the same Lord.

Eph 1:10 — That in the dispensation of the fulness of times he might gather together in one all things in Christ, both which are in heaven, and which are on earth; *even* in him:

Eph 4:15 — But speaking the truth in love, may grow up into him in all things, which is the head, *even* Christ:

Col 1:13 — Who hath delivered us from the power of darkness, and hath translated *us* into the kingdom of his dear Son:

Col 1:18 — And he is the head of the body, the church: who is the beginning, the firstborn from the dead; that in all *things* he might have the preeminence.

Col 2:10 — And ye are complete in him, which is the head of all principality and power:

Col 2:19 — And not holding the Head, from which all the body by joints and bands having nourishment ministered, and knit together, increaseth with the increase of God.

Col 3:11 — Where there is neither Greek nor Jew, circumcision nor uncircumcision, Barbarian, Scythian, bond *nor* free: but Christ *is* all, and in all.

Heb 3:3 — For this *man* was counted worthy of more glory than Moses, inasmuch as he who hath builded the house hath more honour than the house.

Heb 3:6 — But Christ as a son over his own house; whose house are we, if we hold fast the confidence and the rejoicing of the hope firm unto the end.

1Pe 2:7 — Unto you therefore which believe *he is* precious: but unto them which be disobedient, the stone which the builders disallowed, the same is made the head of the corner,

Rev 1:13 — And in the midst of the seven candlesticks *one* like unto the Son of man, clothed with a garment down to the foot, and girt about the paps with a golden girdle.

Rev 2:1 — Unto the angel of the church of Ephesus write; These things saith he that holdeth the seven stars in his right hand, who walketh in the midst of the seven golden candlesticks;

Rev 2:9 — I know thy works, and tribulation, and poverty, (but thou art rich) and *I know* the blasphemy of them which say they are Jews, and are not, but *are* the synagogue of Satan.

Rev 3:1 — And unto the angel of the church in Sardis write; These things saith he that hath the seven Spirits of God, and the seven stars; I know thy works, that thou hast a name that thou livest, and art dead.

Rev 3:7 — And to the angel of the church in Philadelphia write; These things saith he that is holy, he that is true, he that hath the key of David, he that openeth, and no man shutteth; and shutteth, and no man openeth;

Rev 5:6 — And I beheld, and, lo, in the midst of the throne and of the four beasts, and in the midst of the elders, stood a Lamb as it had been slain, having seven horns and seven eyes, which are the seven Spirits of God sent forth into all the earth.

Rev 22:16 — I Jesus have sent mine angel to testify unto you these things in the churches. I am the root and the offspring of David, *and* the bright and morning star.

See: Jesus, Kingdom of

• Christian, divinely established.

Mt 16:15–18; Eph 2:20–22

1Th 1:1 — Paul, and Silvanus, and Timotheus, unto the church of the Thessalonians *which is* in God the Father and *in* the Lord Jesus Christ: Grace *be* unto you, and peace, from God our Father, and the Lord Jesus Christ.

2Th 1:1 — Paul, and Silvanus, and Timotheus, unto the church of the Thessalonians in God our Father and the Lord Jesus Christ:

1Ti 3:15 — But if I tarry long, that thou mayest know how thou oughtest to behave thyself in the house of God, which is the church of the living God, the pillar and ground of the truth.

• Corruption in.

Mic 3:1–4; Mt 21:33–41; 23:2–7, 13–33; 26:14–16, 59–68; Mk 12:1–12; 14:10–11; Lk 22:3–6

Hos 4:9 — And there shall be, like people, like priest: and I will punish them for their ways, and reward them their doings.

Mic 3:9 — Hear this, I pray you, ye heads of the house of Jacob, and princes of the house of Israel, that abhor judgment, and pervert all equity.

Mic 3:11 — The heads thereof judge for reward, and the priests thereof teach for hire, and the prophets thereof divine for money: yet will they lean upon the LORD, and say, *Is* not the LORD among us? none evil can come upon us.

Mt 21:45 — And when the chief priests and Pharisees had heard his parables, they perceived that he spake of them.

See: Backsliders; backsliding of Israel

• Decrees of.

Ac 15:28–29

Ac 16:4 — And as they went through the cities, they delivered them the decrees for to keep, that were ordained of the apostles and elders which were at Jerusalem.

• Design of.

Eph 2:20–22

Ro 3:2 — Much every way: chiefly, because that unto them were committed the oracles of God.

Ro 9:4 — Who are Israelites; to whom *pertaineth* the adoption, and the glory, and the covenants, and the giving of the law, and the service *of God*, and the promises;

1Ti 3:15 — But if I tarry long, that thou mayest know how thou oughtest to behave thyself in the house of God, which is the church of the living God, the pillar and ground of the truth.

• Dissensions in.

1Co 1:11–13; 3:3–4; 11:18–19; 2Co 12:20–21

• Duty of, to ministers.

1Co 16:10–11; Php 4:10–12, 14–18; 1Th 5:12–13

Dt 12:19 — Take heed to thyself that thou forsake not the Levite as long as thou livest upon the earth.

Php 2:29 — Receive him therefore in the Lord with all gladness; and hold such in reputation:

1Ti 5:17 — Let the elders that rule well be counted worthy of double honour, especially they who labour in the word and doctrine.

Heb 13:7 — Remember them which have the rule over you, who have spoken unto you the word of God: whose faith follow, considering the end of *their* conversation.

Heb 13:17 — Obey them that have the rule over you, and submit yourselves: for they watch for your souls, as they that must give account, that they may do it with joy, and not with grief: for that *is* unprofitable for you.

See: Minister, a sacred teacher; duties of the church to

• Government of, Mosaic and Christian.

Dt 17:8–13; Lk 9:46–48; 22:24–30; Ac 1:23–26; 6:2–3, 5–6; 11:29–30; 15:1–31; 16:4–5; 1Co 11:33–34; 2Co 2:2–11; Gal 2:9–10; Eph 4:11–12; 1Ti 3:1–13; Jas 5:14–15; 1Pe 5:1–3; 3Jn 1:9–10; Jude 1:22–23

Mt 16:19 — And I will give unto thee the keys of the kingdom of heaven: and whatsoever thou shalt bind on earth shall be bound in heaven: and whatsoever thou shalt loose on earth shall be loosed in heaven.

Jn 20:23 — Whose soever sins ye remit, they are remitted unto them; *and* whose soever *sins* ye retain, they are retained.

Ac 1:15 — And in those days Peter stood up in the midst of the disciples, and said, (the number of names together were about an hundred and twenty,)

Ac 11:22 — Then tidings of these things came unto the ears of the church which was in Jerusalem: and they sent forth Barnabas, that he should go as far as Antioch.

Ac 13:1 — Now there were in the church that was at Antioch certain prophets and teachers; as Barnabas, and Simeon that was called Niger, and Lucius of Cyrene, and Manaen, which had been brought up with Herod the tetrarch, and Saul.

Ac 13:3 — And when they had fasted and prayed, and laid *their* hands on them, they sent *them* away.

Ac 13:5 — And when they were at Salamis, they preached the word of God in the synagogues of the Jews: and they had also John to *their* minister.

Ac 14:23 — And when they had ordained them elders in every church, and had prayed with fasting, they commended them to the Lord, on whom they believed.

Ac 20:17 — And from Miletus he sent to Ephesus, and called the elders of the church.

Ac 20:28 — Take heed therefore unto yourselves, and to all the flock, over the which the Holy Ghost hath made you overseers, to feed the church of God, which he hath purchased with his own blood.

1Co 7:17 — But as God hath distributed to every man, as the Lord hath called every one, so let him walk. And so ordain I in all churches.

1Co 11:2 — Now I praise you, brethren, that ye remember me in all things, and keep the ordinances, as I delivered *them* to you.

1Co 12:5 — And there are differences of administrations, but the same Lord.

1Co 12:28 — And God hath set some in the church, first apostles, secondarily prophets, thirdly teachers, after that miracles, then gifts of healings, helps, governments, diversities of tongues.

1Co 14:26 — How is it then, brethren? when ye come together, every one of you hath a psalm, hath a doctrine, hath a tongue, hath a revelation, hath an interpretation. Let all things be done unto edifying.

1Co 14:33 — For God is not *the author* of confusion, but of peace, as in all churches of the saints.

1Co 14:40 — Let all things be done decently and in order.

1Co 16:3 — And when I come, whomsoever ye shall approve by *your* letters, them will I send to bring your liberality unto Jerusalem.

1Co 16:16 — That ye submit yourselves unto such, and to every one that helpeth with *us,* and laboureth.

Php 1:1 — Paul and Timotheus, the servants of Jesus Christ, to all the saints in Christ Jesus which are at Philippi, with the bishops and deacons:

1Ti 4:14 — Neglect not the gift that is in thee, which was given thee by prophecy, with the laying on of the hands of the presbytery.

1Ti 5:1 — Rebuke not an elder, but intreat *him* as a father; *and* the younger men as brethren;

1Ti 5:17 — Let the elders that rule well be counted worthy of double honour, especially they who labour in the word and doctrine.

1Ti 5:22 — Lay hands suddenly on no man, neither be partaker of other men's sins: keep thyself pure.

2Ti 1:6 — Wherefore I put thee in remembrance that thou stir up the gift of God, which is in thee by the putting on of my hands.

Tit 1:5 — For this cause left I thee in Crete, that thou shouldest set in order the things that are wanting, and ordain elders in every city, as I had appointed thee:

Heb 13:17 — Obey them that have the rule over you, and submit yourselves: for they watch for your souls, as they that must give account, that they may do it with joy, and not with grief: for that *is* unprofitable for you.

Heb 13:24 — Salute all them that have the rule over you, and all the saints. They of Italy salute you.

See: Minister, a sacred teacher; duties of

• Rules of discipline in, Mosaic and Christian.

Ex 30:37–38; Le 17:8–9; 19:5–8; Dt 13:12–18; 17:2–13; 19:16–21; 21:1–9, 18–21; 22:13–29; Ezr 10:1–44; Mt 18:15–18; Jn 9:1–41; Ro 15:1–3; 1Co 4:21–5:2; 5:4–7, 11–13; 2Co 2:6–8, 10–11; 6:14–15; 10:1–11; 13:1–2; 2Th 3:14–15; 1Ti 1:19–20; 5:1–2, 19–20; 6:3–5; Tit 3:10–11; 2Jn 1:10–11; Jude 1:22–23; Rev 22:1–21

Ge 17:14 — And the uncircumcised man child whose flesh of his foreskin is not circumcised, that soul shall be cut off from his people; he hath broken my covenant.

Ex 12:15 — Seven days shall ye eat unleavened bread; even the first day ye shall put away leaven out of your houses: for whosoever eateth leavened bread from the first day until the seventh day, that soul shall be cut off from Israel.

Ex 30:33 — Whosoever compoundeth *any* like it, or whosoever putteth *any* of it upon a stranger, shall even be cut off from his people.

Le 7:27 — Whatsoever soul *it be* that eateth any manner of blood, even that soul shall be cut off from his people.

Le 20:18 — And if a man shall lie with a woman having her sickness, and shall uncover her nakedness; he hath discovered her fountain, and she hath uncovered the fountain of her blood: and both of them shall be cut off from among their people.

Le 22:3 — Say unto them, Whosoever *he be* of all your seed among your generations, that goeth unto the holy things, which the children of Israel hallow unto the LORD, having his uncleanness upon him, that soul shall be cut off from my presence: I *am* the LORD.

Nu 9:13 — But the man that *is* clean, and is not in a journey, and forbeareth to keep the passover, even the same soul shall be cut off from among his people: because he brought not the offering of the LORD in his appointed season, that man shall bear his sin.

Nu 15:31 — Because he hath despised the word of the LORD, and hath broken his commandment, that soul shall utterly be cut off; his iniquity *shall be* upon him.

Nu 19:13 — Whosoever toucheth the dead body of any man that is dead, and purifieth not himself, defileth the tabernacle of the LORD; and that soul shall be cut off from Israel: because the water of separation was not sprinkled upon him, he shall be unclean; his uncleanness *is* yet upon him.

Nu 19:20 — But the man that shall be unclean, and shall not purify himself, that soul shall be cut off from among the congregation, because he hath defiled the sanctuary of the LORD: the water of separation hath not been sprinkled upon him; he *is* unclean.

Mt 16:19 — And I will give unto thee the keys of the kingdom of heaven: and whatsoever thou shalt bind on earth shall be bound in heaven: and whatsoever thou shalt loose on earth shall be loosed in heaven.

Jn 16:2 — They shall put you out of the synagogues: yea, the time cometh, that whosoever killeth you will think that he doeth God service.

Jn 20:23 — Whose soever sins ye remit, they are remitted unto them; *and* whose soever *sins* ye retain, they are retained.

Ro 14:1 — Him that is weak in the faith receive ye, *but* not to doubtful disputations.

Ro 16:17 — Now I beseech you, brethren, mark them which cause divisions and offences contrary to the doctrine which ye have learned; and avoid them.

1Co 4:19 — But I will come to you shortly, if the Lord will, and will know, not the speech of them which are puffed up, but the power.

1Co 16:22 — If any man love not the Lord Jesus Christ, let him be Anathema Maranatha.

2Co 7:8 — For though I made you sorry with a letter, I do not repent, though I did repent: for I perceive that the same epistle hath made you sorry, though *it were* but for a season.

2Co 13:10 — Therefore I write these things being absent, lest being present I should use sharpness, according to the power which the Lord hath given me to edification, and not to destruction.

Gal 5:10 — I have confidence in you through the Lord, that ye will be none otherwise minded: but he that troubleth you shall bear his judgment, whosoever he be.

Gal 5:12 — I would they were even cut off which trouble you.

Gal 6:1 — Brethren, if a man be overtaken in a fault, ye which are spiritual, restore such an one in the spirit of meekness; considering thyself, lest thou also be tempted.

1Th 5:14 — Now we exhort you, brethren, warn them that are unruly, comfort the feebleminded, support the weak, be patient toward all *men*.

2Th 3:6 — Now we command you, brethren, in the name of our Lord Jesus Christ, that ye withdraw yourselves from every brother that walketh disorderly, and not after the tradition which he received of us.

2Ti 4:2 — Preach the word; be instant in season, out of season; reprove, rebuke, exhort with all longsuffering and doctrine.

Tit 1:13 — This witness is true. Wherefore rebuke them sharply, that they may be sound in the faith;

Tit 2:15 — These things speak, and exhort, and rebuke with all authority. Let no man despise thee.

See: Excommunication

See: Minister, a sacred teacher; duties of

- **Love for.**

Ps 137:1–6; Isa 62:6–7; 66:13–14; Jer 51:50–51; La 1:1–5:22

Ps 102:14 — For thy servants take pleasure in her stones, and favour the dust thereof.

Ps 122:6 — Pray for the peace of Jerusalem: they shall prosper that love thee.

Ps 128:5 — The LORD shall bless thee out of Zion: and thou shalt see the good of Jerusalem all the days of thy life.

Isa 22:4 — Therefore said I, Look away from me; I will weep bitterly, labour not to comfort me, because of the spoiling of the daughter of my people.

Isa 58:12 — And *they that shall be* of thee shall build the old waste places: thou shalt raise up the foundations of many generations; and thou shalt be called, The repairer of the breach, The restorer of paths to dwell in.

Isa 62:1 — For Zion's sake will I not hold my peace, and for Jerusalem's sake I will not rest, until the righteousness thereof go forth as brightness, and the salvation thereof as a lamp *that* burneth.

Isa 66:10 — Rejoice ye with Jerusalem, and be glad with her, all ye that love her: rejoice for joy with her, all ye that mourn for her:

Jer 9:1 — Oh that my head were waters, and mine eyes a fountain of tears, that I might weep day and night for the slain of the daughter of my people!

- **Membership in.**

Eze 44:6–7; Jn 15:1–27; Ro 12:4–5; 1Co 3:11–15; 12:12–28

Isa 44:5 — One shall say, I *am* the LORD'S; and another shall call *himself* by the name of Jacob; and another shall subscribe *with* his hand unto the LORD, and surname *himself* by the name of Israel.

Eze 44:9 — Thus saith the Lord GOD; No stranger, uncircumcised in heart, nor uncircumcised in flesh, shall enter into my sanctuary, of any stranger that *is* among the children of Israel.

Mt 12:50 — For whosoever shall do the will of my Father which is in heaven, the same is my brother, and sister, and mother.

Mt 19:14 — But Jesus said, Suffer little children, and forbid them not, to come unto me: for of such is the kingdom of heaven.

Mk 10:14 — But when Jesus saw *it*, he was much displeased, and said unto them, Suffer the little children to come unto me, and forbid them not: for of such is the kingdom of God.

Lk 18:16 — But Jesus called them *unto him*, and said, Suffer little children to come unto me, and forbid them not: for of such is the kingdom of God.

Ac 2:41 — Then they that gladly received his word were baptized: and the same day there were added *unto them* about three thousand souls.

Ac 2:47 — Praising God, and having favour with all the people. And the Lord added to the church daily such as should be saved.

Ac 4:4 — Howbeit many of them which heard the word believed; and the number of the men was about five thousand.

Ac 5:14 — And believers were the more added to the Lord, multitudes both of men and women.)

Ac 9:35 — And all that dwelt at Lydda and Saron saw him, and turned to the Lord.

Ac 9:42 — And it was known throughout all Joppa; and many believed in the Lord.

Ac 11:21 — And the hand of the Lord was with them: and a great number believed, and turned unto the Lord.

Eph 4:25 — Wherefore putting away lying, speak every man truth with his neighbour: for we are members one of another.

Eph 5:30 — For we are members of his body, of his flesh, and of his bones.

Php 4:3 — And I intreat thee also, true yokefellow, help those women which laboured with me in the gospel, with Clement also, and *with* other my fellowlabourers, whose names *are* in the book of life.

Rev 21:27 — And there shall in no wise enter into it any thing that defileth, neither *whatsoever* worketh abomination, or *maketh* a lie: but they which are written in the Lamb's book of life.

✣See: Righteous; described

- **Prophecies concerning prosperity of.**

Ps 22:27–31; 68:31–32; 69:35–36; 72:1–20; 85:10–12; 89:1–37; 96:1–13; 102:13–16, 18–22; 110:1–7; 126:5–6; 132:15–18; 138:4–5; 145:10–11; Isa 2:2–5; 4:2–3, 5–6; 9:1–7; 11:1–10; 19:24–25; 23:17–18; 25:6–8; 29:18–24; 32:1–20; 33:13–24; 35:1–10; 40:4–11; 41:17–20; 42:1–12; 44:3–5; 45:23–24; 46:12–13; 49:6–12, 18–23; 51:3–16; 52:1–15; 53:10–55:13; 56:3–8; 59:19–62:12; 65:1–25; 66:7–23; Jer 16:19–21; 31:7–9; Eze 17:22–24; 34:23–31; 47:1–12; Da 2:44–45; 7:13–14; 12:1–13; Joel 2:26–32; Am 9:11–12; Mic 4:1–7; 5:2–15; Zep 3:9–20; Hag 2:7–9; Zec 2:10–11; 8:20–9:1; 9:9–17; 14:8–21; Mt 13:16–17; 13:31–33; Mk 4:26–32; Ac 2:1–47; Ro 1:5–7; 1Co 15:24–28; Heb 12:23–24, 27–28; Rev 5:13–14; 20:4–6; 21:9–22:5

Ge 12:3 — And I will bless them that bless thee, and curse him that curseth thee: and in thee shall all families of the earth be blessed.

Ge 49:10 — The sceptre shall not depart from Judah, nor a lawgiver from between his feet, until Shiloh come; and unto him *shall* the gathering of the people *be*.

Dt 32:21 — They have moved me to jealousy with *that which is* not God; they have provoked me to anger with their vanities: and I will move them to jealousy with *those which are* not a people; I will provoke them to anger with a foolish nation.

Ps 2:8 — Ask of me, and I shall give *thee* the heathen *for* thine inheritance, and the uttermost parts of the earth *for* thy possession.

Ps 46:4 — *There is* a river, the streams whereof shall make glad the city of God, the holy *place* of the tabernacles of the most High.

Ps 46:10 — Be still, and know that I *am* God: I will be exalted among the heathen, I will be exalted in the earth.

Ps 65:2 — O thou that hearest prayer, unto thee shall all flesh come.

Ps 66:4 — All the earth shall worship thee, and shall sing unto thee; they shall sing *to* thy name. Selah.

Ps 86:9 — All nations whom thou hast made shall come and worship before thee, O Lord; and shall glorify thy name.

Ps 87:4 — I will make mention of Rahab and Babylon to them that know me: behold Philistia, and Tyre, with Ethiopia; this *man* was born there.

Ps 113:3 — From the rising of the sun unto the going down of the same the LORD'S name *is* to be praised.

Ps 118:24 — This *is* the day *which* the LORD hath made; we will rejoice and be glad in it.

Isa 18:7 — In that time shall the present be brought unto the LORD of hosts of a people scattered and peeled, and from a people terrible from their beginning hitherto; a nation meted out and trodden under foot, whose land the rivers have spoiled, to the place of the name of the LORD of hosts, the mount Zion.

Isa 24:16 — From the uttermost part of the earth have we heard songs, *even* glory to the righteous. But I said, My leanness, my leanness, woe unto me! the treacherous dealers have dealt treacherously; yea, the treacherous dealers have dealt very treacherously.

Isa 30:20 — And *though* the Lord give you the bread of adversity, and the water of affliction, yet shall not thy teachers be removed into a corner any more, but thine eyes shall see thy teachers:

Isa 33:5 — The LORD is exalted; for he dwelleth on high: he hath filled Zion with judgment and righteousness.

Isa 45:6 — That they may know from the rising of the sun, and from the west, that *there is* none beside me. I *am* the LORD, and *there is* none else.

Isa 45:8 — Drop down, ye heavens, from above, and let the skies pour down righteousness: let the earth open, and let them bring forth salvation, and let righteousness spring up together; I the LORD have created it.

Isa 45:14 — Thus saith the LORD, The labour of Egypt, and merchandise of Ethiopia and of the Sabeans, men of stature, shall come over unto thee, and they shall be thine: they shall come after thee; in chains they shall come over, and they shall fall down unto thee, they shall make supplication unto thee, *saying,* Surely God *is* in thee; and *there is* none else, *there is* no God.

Jer 3:17 — At that time they shall call Jerusalem the throne of the LORD; and all the nations shall be gathered unto it, to the name of the LORD, to Jerusalem: neither shall they walk any more after the imagination of their evil heart.

Jer 4:2 — And thou shalt swear, The LORD liveth, in truth, in judgment, and in righteousness; and the nations shall bless themselves in him, and in him shall they glory.

Jer 31:34 — And they shall teach no more every man his neighbour, and every man his brother, saying, Know the LORD: for they shall all know me, from the least of them unto the greatest of them, saith the LORD; for I will forgive their iniquity, and I will remember their sin no more.

Jer 33:22 — As the host of heaven cannot be numbered, neither the sand of the sea measured: so will I multiply the seed of David my servant, and the Levites that minister unto me.

Da 2:35 — Then was the iron, the clay, the brass, the silver, and the gold, broken to pieces together, and became like the chaff of the summer threshingfloors; and the wind carried them away, that no place was found for them: and the stone that smote the image became a great mountain, and filled the whole earth.

Da 7:18 — But the saints of the most High shall take the kingdom, and possess the kingdom for ever, even for ever and ever.

Da 7:22 — Until the Ancient of days came, and judgment was given to the saints of the most High; and the time came that the saints possessed the kingdom.

Da 7:27 — And the kingdom and dominion, and the greatness of the kingdom under the whole heaven, shall be given to the people of the saints of the most High, whose kingdom *is* an everlasting kingdom, and all dominions shall serve and obey him.

Joel 3:18 — And it shall come to pass in that day, *that* the mountains shall drop down new wine, and the hills shall flow with milk, and all the rivers of Judah shall flow with waters, and a fountain shall come forth of the house of the LORD, and shall water the valley of Shittim.

Hab 2:14 — For the earth shall be filled with the knowledge of the glory of the LORD, as the waters cover the sea.

Zep 2:11 — The LORD *will be* terrible unto them: for he will famish all the gods of the earth; and *men* shall worship him, every one from his place, *even* all the isles of the heathen.

Zec 6:15 — And they *that are* far off shall come and build in the temple of the LORD, and ye shall know that the LORD of hosts hath sent me unto you. And *this* shall come to pass, if ye will diligently obey the voice of the LORD your God.

Mal 1:11 — For from the rising of the sun even unto the going down of the same my name *shall be* great among the Gentiles; and in every place incense *shall be* offered unto my name, and a pure offering: for my name *shall be* great among the heathen, saith the LORD of hosts.

Mt 8:11 — And I say unto you, That many shall come from the east and west, and shall sit down with Abraham, and Isaac, and Jacob, in the kingdom of heaven.

Mt 11:5 — The blind receive their sight, and the lame walk, the lepers are cleansed, and the deaf hear, the dead are raised up, and the poor have the gospel preached to them.

Mt 11:11 — Verily I say unto you, Among them that are born of women there hath not risen a greater than John the Baptist: notwithstanding he that is least in the kingdom of heaven is greater than he.

Mt 16:18 — And I say also unto thee, That thou art Peter, and upon this rock I will build my church; and the gates of hell shall not prevail against it.

Lk 7:22 — Then Jesus answering said unto them, Go your way, and tell John what things ye have seen and heard; how that the blind see, the lame walk, the lepers are cleansed, the deaf hear, the dead are raised, to the poor the gospel is preached.

Jn 8:35 — And the servant abideth not in the house for ever: *but* the Son abideth ever.

Jn 10:16 — And other sheep I have, which are not of this fold: them also I must bring, and they shall hear my voice; and there shall be one fold, *and* one shepherd.

Eph 1:10 — That in the dispensation of the fulness of times he might gather together in one all things in Christ, both which are in heaven, and which are on earth; *even* in him:

Rev 5:10 — And hast made us unto our God kings and priests: and we shall reign on the earth.

Rev 11:15 — And the seventh angel sounded; and there were great voices in heaven, saying, The kingdoms of this world are become *the kingdoms* of our Lord, and of his Christ; and he shall reign for ever and ever.

Rev 12:10 — And I heard a loud voice saying in heaven, Now is come salvation, and strength, and the kingdom of our God, and the power of his Christ: for the accuser of our brethren is cast down, which accused them before our God day and night.

Rev 15:4 — Who shall not fear thee, O Lord, and glorify thy name? for *thou* only *art* holy: for all nations shall come and worship before thee; for thy judgments are made manifest.

See: Jesus, Kingdom of

CHURCH AND STATE

• Ecclesiastical power superior to civil.

• Appoints kings.

1Sa 10:1 — Then Samuel took a vial of oil, and poured *it* upon his head, and kissed him, and said, *Is it* not because the LORD hath anointed thee *to be* captain over his inheritance?

• Directs administration.

1Sa 15:1–4

• Reproves ruler.

1Sa 15:14–35

• Withdraws support and anoints a successor.

1Sa 16:1–13; 2Ki 9:1–26; 11:4–12

• Attempted usurpation of ecclesiastical functions by civil authorities, reproved.

1Sa 13:8–14; 2Ch 26:16–21

• State superior to the church.

• David, in organizing the priests, Levites, musicians, and details of services.

1Ch 23:1–25:31

2Ch 35:4 — And prepare *yourselves* by the houses of your fathers, after your courses, according to the writing of David king of Israel, and according to the writing of Solomon his son.

• Solomon, in thrusting Abiathar out of the high priest's office.

1Ki 2:26–27

• Solomon, in officiating the dedication of the Temple.

1Ki 5:1–8:66

• Hezekiah, in reorganizing temple service.

2Ch 31:2–19

• Jeroboam, in subverting the Jewish religion.

1Ki 12:26–33

• Manasseh in subverting and afterward restoring the true religion.

2Ch 33:2–9, 15–17

• Jehoash, in supervising the repairs of the temple.

2Ki 12:4–18

• Ahaz, in transforming the altars.

2Ki 16:10–16

• Josiah, in exercising the function of the priests in the temple.

2Ch 34:29–33

• State favorable to the church.

• Cyrus, in his proclamation to restore the temple at Jerusalem.

2Ch 36:22–23; Ezr 1:1–11

• Darius, in his edict furthering the restoration of the temple.

Ezr 6:1–14

• Artaxerxes, in exempting priests, Levites, and other temple functionaries from taxes.

Ezr 7:24 — Also we certify you, that touching any of the priests and Levites, singers, porters, Nethinims, or ministers of this house of God, it shall not be lawful to impose toll, tribute, or custom, upon them.

See: Government

See: Tax

CHURCH, Christian Churches

• List of Christian Churches.

• Antioch.

Ac 13:1 — Now there were in the church that was at Antioch certain prophets and teachers; as Barnabas, and Simeon that was called Niger, and Lucius of Cyrene, and Manaen, which had been brought up with Herod the tetrarch, and Saul.

• Asia.

1Co 16:19 — The churches of Asia salute you. Aquila and Priscilla salute you much in the Lord, with the church that is in their house.

Rev 1:4 — John to the seven churches which are in Asia: Grace *be* unto you, and peace, from him which is, and which was, and which is to come; and from the seven Spirits which are before his throne;

• Babylon.

1Pe 5:13 — The *church that is* at Babylon, elected together with *you,* saluteth you; and *so doth* Marcus my son.

• Caesarea.

Ac 18:22 — And when he had landed at Caesarea, and gone up, and saluted the church, he went down to Antioch.

• Cenchrea.

Ro 16:1 — I commend unto you Phebe our sister, which is a servant of the church which is at Cenchrea:

• Cilicia.

Ac 15:41 — And he went through Syria and Cilicia, confirming the churches.

• Corinth.

1Co 1:2 — Unto the church of God which is at Corinth, to them that are sanctified in Christ Jesus, called *to be* saints, with all that in every place call upon the name of Jesus Christ our Lord, both theirs and ours:

• Ephesus.

Eph 1:22 — And hath put all *things* under his feet, and gave him *to be* the head over all *things* to the church,

Rev 2:1 — Unto the angel of the church of Ephesus write; These things saith he that holdeth the seven stars in his right hand, who walketh in the midst of the seven golden candlesticks;

• Galatia.

Gal 1:2 — And all the brethren which are with me, unto the churches of Galatia:

• Galilee.

Ac 9:31 — Then had the churches rest throughout all Judaea and Galilee and Samaria, and were edified; and walking in the fear of the Lord, and in the comfort of the Holy Ghost, were multiplied.

• **Jerusalem.**

Ac 15:4 — And when they were come to Jerusalem, they were received of the church, and *of* the apostles and elders, and they declared all things that God had done with them.

• **Joppa.**

Ac 9:42 — And it was known throughout all Joppa; and many believed in the Lord.

• **Judaea.**

Ac 9:31 — Then had the churches rest throughout all Judaea and Galilee and Samaria, and were edified; and walking in the fear of the Lord, and in the comfort of the Holy Ghost, were multiplied.

• **Laodicea.**

Rev 3:14 — And unto the angel of the church of the Laodiceans write; These things saith the Amen, the faithful and true witness, the beginning of the creation of God;

• **Pergamos.**

Rev 2:12 — And to the angel of the church in Pergamos write; These things saith he which hath the sharp sword with two edges;

• **Philadelphia.**

Rev 3:7 — And to the angel of the church in Philadelphia write; These things saith he that is holy, he that is true, he that hath the key of David, he that openeth, and no man shutteth; and shutteth, and no man openeth;

• **Samaria.**

Ac 9:31 — Then had the churches rest throughout all Judaea and Galilee and Samaria, and were edified; and walking in the fear of the Lord, and in the comfort of the Holy Ghost, were multiplied.

• **Sardis.**

Rev 3:1 — And unto the angel of the church in Sardis write; These things saith he that hath the seven Spirits of God, and the seven stars; I know thy works, that thou hast a name that thou livest, and art dead.

• **Smyrna.**

Rev 2:8 — And unto the angel of the church in Smyrna write; These things saith the first and the last, which was dead, and is alive;

• **Syria.**

Ac 15:41 — And he went through Syria and Cilicia, confirming the churches.

• **Thessalonica.**

1Th 1:1 — Paul, and Silvanus, and Timotheus, unto the church of the Thessalonians *which is* in God the Father and *in* the Lord Jesus Christ: Grace *be* unto you, and peace, from God our Father, and the Lord Jesus Christ.

• **Thyatira.**

Rev 2:18 — And unto the angel of the church in Thyatira write; These things saith the Son of God, who hath his eyes like unto a flame of fire, and his feet *are* like fine brass;

• **Unity of.**

Jn 17:21–23; Ro 12:4–5; 1Co 12:12–27; Gal 3:26–28; Eph 2:14–19; 4:4–5, 12–13

Ps 133:1 — Behold, how good and how pleasant *it is* for brethren to dwell together in unity!

Jn 10:16 — And other sheep I have, which are not of this fold: them also I must bring, and they shall hear my voice; and there shall be one fold, *and* one shepherd.

Jn 17:11 — And now I am no more in the world, but these are in the world, and I come to thee. Holy Father, keep through thine own name those whom thou hast given me, that they may be one, as we *are.*

1Co 10:17 — For we *being* many are one bread, *and* one body: for we are all partakers of that one bread.

1Co 12:5 — And there are differences of administrations, but the same Lord.

Eph 1:10 — That in the dispensation of the fulness of times he might gather together in one all things in Christ, both which are in heaven, and which are on earth; *even* in him:

Eph 2:21 — In whom all the building fitly framed together groweth unto an holy temple in the Lord:

Eph 3:6 — That the Gentiles should be fellowheirs, and of the same body, and partakers of his promise in Christ by the gospel:

Eph 3:15 — Of whom the whole family in heaven and earth is named,

Eph 4:16 — From whom the whole body fitly joined together and compacted by that which every joint supplieth, according to the effectual working in the measure of every part, maketh increase of the body unto the edifying of itself in love.

Eph 4:25 — Wherefore putting away lying, speak every man truth with his neighbour: for we are members one of another.

Col 3:11 — Where there is neither Greek nor Jew, circumcision nor uncircumcision, Barbarian, Scythian, bond *nor* free: but Christ *is* all, and in all.

Col 3:15 — And let the peace of God rule in your hearts, to the which also ye are called in one body; and be ye thankful.

See: Ecclesiasticism

• **Triumphant.**

Heb 12:22–23

Gal 4:26 — But Jerusalem which is above is free, which is the mother of us all.

Rev 3:12 — Him that overcometh will I make a pillar in the temple of my God, and he shall go no more out: and I will write upon him the name of my God, and the name of the city of my God, *which is* new Jerusalem, which cometh down out of heaven from my God: and *I will write upon him* my new name.

Rev 21:3 — And I heard a great voice out of heaven saying, Behold, the tabernacle of God *is* with men, and he will dwell with them, and they shall be his people, and God himself shall be with them, *and be* their God.

Rev 21:10 — And he carried me away in the spirit to a great and high mountain, and shewed me that great city, the holy Jerusalem, descending out of heaven from God,

CHURCH, Miscellany of Minor Sub-Topics

• Miscellany of Minor Sub-Topics

• Called in the Old Testament, the Congregation.

Ex 16:1–2; 16:9–10

Ex 12:3 — Speak ye unto all the congregation of Israel, saying, In the tenth *day* of this month they shall take to them every man a lamb, according to the house of *their* fathers, a lamb for an house:

Ex 12:6 — And ye shall keep it up until the fourteenth day of the same month: and the whole assembly of the congregation of Israel shall kill it in the evening.

Ex 12:19 — Seven days shall there be no leaven found in your houses: for whosoever eateth that which is leavened, even that soul shall be cut off from the congregation of Israel, whether he be a stranger, or born in the land.

Ex 12:47 — All the congregation of Israel shall keep it.

Ex 16:22 — And it came to pass, *that* on the sixth day they gathered twice as much bread, two omers for one *man:* and all the rulers of the congregation came and told Moses.

Le 4:13 — And if the whole congregation of Israel sin through ignorance, and the thing be hid from the eyes of the assembly, and they have done *somewhat against* any of the commandments of the LORD *concerning things* which should not be done, and are guilty;

Le 4:15 — And the elders of the congregation shall lay their hands upon the head of the bullock before the LORD: and the bullock shall be killed before the LORD.

Le 10:17 — Wherefore have ye not eaten the sin offering in the holy place, seeing it *is* most holy, and *God* hath given it you to bear the iniquity of the congregation, to make atonement for them before the LORD?

Le 24:14 — Bring forth him that hath cursed without the camp; and let all that heard *him* lay their hands upon his head, and let all the congregation stone him.

• Called in the New Testament, Church.

1Co 14:33–34

Mt 16:18 — And I say also unto thee, That thou art Peter, and upon this rock I will build my church; and the gates of hell shall not prevail against it.

Mt 18:17 — And if he shall neglect to hear them, tell *it* unto the church: but if he neglect to hear the church, let him be unto thee as an heathen man and a publican.

Ac 2:47 — Praising God, and having favour with all the people. And the Lord added to the church daily such as should be saved.

1Co 11:18 — For first of all, when ye come together in the church, I hear that there be divisions among you; and I partly believe it.

1Co 14:19 — Yet in the church I had rather speak five words with my understanding, that *by my voice* I might teach others also, than ten thousand words in an *unknown* tongue.

1Co 14:23 — If therefore the whole church be come together into one place, and all speak with tongues, and there come in *those that are* unlearned, or unbelievers, will they not say that ye are mad?

1Co 14:28 — But if there be no interpreter, let him keep silence in the church; and let him speak to himself, and to God.

1Co 15:9 — For I am the least of the apostles, that am not meet to be called an apostle, because I persecuted the church of God.

Gal 1:13 — For ye have heard of my conversation in time past in the Jews' religion, how that beyond measure I persecuted the church of God, and wasted it:

• Assembly of the Saints.

Ps 89:7 — God is greatly to be feared in the assembly of the saints, and to be had in reverence of all *them that are* about him.

• Assembly of the Upright.

Ps 111:1 — Praise ye the LORD. I will praise the LORD with *my* whole heart, in the assembly of the upright, and *in* the congregation.

• Body of Christ.

Eph 1:22–23

Col 1:24 — Who now rejoice in my sufferings for you, and fill up that which is behind of the afflictions of Christ in my flesh for his body's sake, which is the church:

• Branch of God's Planting.

Isa 60:21 — Thy people also *shall be* all righteous: they shall inherit the land for ever, the branch of my planting, the work of my hands, that I may be glorified.

• Bride of Christ.

Rev 21:9 — And there came unto me one of the seven angels which had the seven vials full of the seven last plagues, and talked with me, saying, Come hither, I will shew thee the bride, the Lamb's wife.

• Church of God.

Ac 20:28 — Take heed therefore unto yourselves, and to all the flock, over the which the Holy Ghost hath made you overseers, to feed the church of God, which he hath purchased with his own blood.

• Church of the Living God.

1Ti 3:15 — But if I tarry long, that thou mayest know how thou oughtest to behave thyself in the house of God, which is the church of the living God, the pillar and ground of the truth.

• Church of the Firstborn.

Heb 12:23 — To the general assembly and church of the firstborn, which are written in heaven, and to God the Judge of all, and to the spirits of just men made perfect,

• **City of the Living God.**

Heb 12:22 — But ye are come unto mount Sion, and unto the city of the living God, the heavenly Jerusalem, and to an innumerable company of angels,

• **Congregation of Saints.**

Ps 149:1 — Praise ye the LORD. Sing unto the LORD a new song, *and* his praise in the congregation of saints.

• **Congregation of the Lord's Poor.**

Ps 74:19 — O deliver not the soul of thy turtledove unto the multitude *of the wicked:* forget not the congregation of thy poor for ever.

• **Dove.**

SS 2:14 — O my dove, *that art* in the clefts of the rock, in the secret *places* of the stairs, let me see thy countenance, let me hear thy voice; for sweet *is* thy voice, and thy countenance *is* comely.

SS 5:2 — I sleep, but my heart waketh: *it is* the voice of my beloved that knocketh, *saying,* Open to me, my sister, my love, my dove, my undefiled: for my head is filled with dew, *and* my locks with the drops of the night.

• **Family in Heaven and Earth.**

Eph 3:15 — Of whom the whole family in heaven and earth is named,

• **Flock of God.**

Eze 34:15 — I will feed my flock, and I will cause them to lie down, saith the Lord GOD.

1Pe 5:2 — Feed the flock of God which is among you, taking the oversight *thereof,* not by constraint, but willingly; not for filthy lucre, but of a ready mind;

• **Fold of Christ.**

Jn 10:16 — And other sheep I have, which are not of this fold: them also I must bring, and they shall hear my voice; and there shall be one fold, *and* one shepherd.

• **General Assembly of the Firstborn.**

Heb 12:23 — To the general assembly and church of the firstborn, which are written in heaven, and to God the Judge of all, and to the spirits of just men made perfect,

• **God's Building.**

1Co 3:9 — For we are labourers together with God: ye are God's husbandry, *ye are* God's building.

• **God's Husbandry.**

1Co 3:9 — For we are labourers together with God: ye are God's husbandry, *ye are* God's building.

• **God's Heritage.**

Joel 3:2 — I will also gather all nations, and will bring them down into the valley of Jehoshaphat, and will plead with them there for my people and *for* my heritage Israel, whom they have scattered among the nations, and parted my land.

1Pe 5:3 — Neither as being lords over *God's* heritage, but being ensamples to the flock.

• **Golden Candlestick.**

Rev 1:20 — The mystery of the seven stars which thou sawest in my right hand, and the seven golden candlesticks. The seven stars are the angels of the seven churches: and the seven candlesticks which thou sawest are the seven churches.

• **Habitation of God.**

Eph 2:22 — In whom ye also are builded together for an habitation of God through the Spirit.

• **Heavenly Jerusalem.**

Gal 4:26 — But Jerusalem which is above is free, which is the mother of us all.

Heb 12:22 — But ye are come unto mount Sion, and unto the city of the living God, the heavenly Jerusalem, and to an innumerable company of angels,

• **Holy City.**

Rev 21:2 — And I John saw the holy city, new Jerusalem, coming down from God out of heaven, prepared as a bride adorned for her husband.

• **Holy Hill.**

Ps 2:6 — Yet have I set my king upon my holy hill of Zion.

Ps 15:1 — LORD, who shall abide in thy tabernacle? who shall dwell in thy holy hill?

• **Holy Mountain.**

Zec 8:3 — Thus saith the LORD; I am returned unto Zion, and will dwell in the midst of Jerusalem: and Jerusalem shall be called a city of truth; and the mountain of the LORD of hosts the holy mountain.

• **House of God.**

1Ti 3:15 — But if I tarry long, that thou mayest know how thou oughtest to behave thyself in the house of God, which is the church of the living God, the pillar and ground of the truth.

Heb 10:21 — And *having* an high priest over the house of God;

• **House of the God of Jacob.**

Isa 2:3 — And many people shall go and say, Come ye, and let us go up to the mountain of the LORD, to the house of the God of Jacob; and he will teach us of his ways, and we will walk in his paths: for out of Zion shall go forth the law, and the word of the LORD from Jerusalem.

• **House of Christ.**

Heb 3:6 — But Christ as a son over his own house; whose house are we, if we hold fast the confidence and the rejoicing of the hope firm unto the end.

• **Household of God.**

Eph 2:19 — Now therefore ye are no more strangers and foreigners, but fellowcitizens with the saints, and of the household of God;

• **Inheritance.**

Ps 28:9 — Save thy people, and bless thine inheritance: feed them also, and lift them up for ever.

Isa 19:25 — Whom the LORD of hosts shall bless, saying, Blessed *be* Egypt my people, and Assyria the work of my hands, and Israel mine inheritance.

- **Israel of God.**

Gal 6:16 — And as many as walk according to this rule, peace *be* on them, and mercy, and upon the Israel of God.

- **King's Daughter.**

Ps 45:13 — The king's daughter *is* all glorious within: her clothing *is* of wrought gold.

- **Kingdom of God.**

Mt 6:33 — But seek ye first the kingdom of God, and his righteousness; and all these things shall be added unto you.

Mt 12:28 — But if I cast out devils by the Spirit of God, then the kingdom of God is come unto you.

Mt 19:24 — And again I say unto you, It is easier for a camel to go through the eye of a needle, than for a rich man to enter into the kingdom of God.

Mt 21:31 — Whether of them twain did the will of *his* father? They say unto him, The first. Jesus saith unto them, Verily I say unto you, That the publicans and the harlots go into the kingdom of God before you.

- **Kingdom of Heaven.**

Mt 5:19–20

Mt 3:2 — And saying, Repent ye: for the kingdom of heaven is at hand.

Mt 4:17 — From that time Jesus began to preach, and to say, Repent: for the kingdom of heaven is at hand.

Mt 5:3 — Blessed *are* the poor in spirit: for theirs is the kingdom of heaven.

Mt 5:10 — Blessed *are* they which are persecuted for righteousness' sake: for theirs is the kingdom of heaven.

Mt 10:7 — And as ye go, preach, saying, The kingdom of heaven is at hand.

- **His Kingdom.**

Ps 103:19 — The LORD hath prepared his throne in the heavens; and his kingdom ruleth over all.

Ps 145:12 — To make known to the sons of men his mighty acts, and the glorious majesty of his kingdom.

Mt 16:28 — Verily I say unto you, There be some standing here, which shall not taste of death, till they see the Son of man coming in his kingdom.

Lk 1:33 — And he shall reign over the house of Jacob for ever; and of his kingdom there shall be no end.

- **My Kingdom.**

Jn 18:36 — Jesus answered, My kingdom is not of this world: if my kingdom were of this world, then would my servants fight, that I should not be delivered to the Jews: but now is my kingdom not from hence.

- **Thy Kingdom.**

Ps 45:6 — Thy throne, O God, *is* for ever and ever: the sceptre of thy kingdom *is* a right sceptre.

Ps 145:11 — They shall speak of the glory of thy kingdom, and talk of thy power;

Ps 145:13 — Thy kingdom *is* an everlasting kingdom, and thy dominion *endureth* throughout all generations.

Mt 6:10 — Thy kingdom come. Thy will be done in earth, as *it is* in heaven.

Lk 23:42 — And he said unto Jesus, Lord, remember me when thou comest into thy kingdom.

- **Lamb's Bride.**

Eph 5:22–32

Rev 22:17 — And the Spirit and the bride say, Come. And let him that heareth say, Come. And let him that is athirst come. And whosoever will, let him take the water of life freely.

- **Lamb's Wife.**

Rev 19:7–9

Rev 21:9 — And there came unto me one of the seven angels which had the seven vials full of the seven last plagues, and talked with me, saying, Come hither, I will shew thee the bride, the Lamb's wife.

- **Lot of God's Inheritance.**

Dt 32:9 — For the LORD'S portion *is* his people; Jacob *is* the lot of his inheritance.

- **Mount Zion.**

Heb 12:22 — But ye are come unto mount Sion, and unto the city of the living God, the heavenly Jerusalem, and to an innumerable company of angels,

- **Mountain of the Lord's House.**

Isa 2:2 — And it shall come to pass in the last days, *that* the mountain of the LORD'S house shall be established in the top of the mountains, and shall be exalted above the hills; and all nations shall flow unto it.

- **New Jerusalem.**

Rev 21:2 — And I John saw the holy city, new Jerusalem, coming down from God out of heaven, prepared as a bride adorned for her husband.

- **Pillar and Ground of the Truth.**

1Ti 3:15 — But if I tarry long, that thou mayest know how thou oughtest to behave thyself in the house of God, which is the church of the living God, the pillar and ground of the truth.

- **Place of God's Throne.**

Eze 43:7 — And he said unto me, Son of man, the place of my throne, and the place of the soles of my feet, where I will dwell in the midst of the children of Israel for ever, and my holy name, shall the house of Israel no more defile, *neither* they, nor their kings, by their whoredom, nor by the carcases of their kings in their high places.

- **Pleasant Portion.**
  Jer 12:10 — Many pastors have destroyed my vineyard, they have trodden my portion under foot, they have made my pleasant portion a desolate wilderness.
- **Sanctuary of God.**
  Ps 114:2 — Judah was his sanctuary, *and* Israel his dominion.
- **Sister of Christ.**
  SS 4:12 — A garden inclosed *is* my sister, *my* spouse; a spring shut up, a fountain sealed.
  SS 5:2 — I sleep, but my heart waketh: *it is* the voice of my beloved that knocketh, *saying,* Open to me, my sister, my love, my dove, my undefiled: for my head is filled with dew, *and* my locks with the drops of the night.
- **Spiritual House.**
  1Pe 2:5 — Ye also, as lively stones, are built up a spiritual house, an holy priesthood, to offer up spiritual sacrifices, acceptable to God by Jesus Christ.
- **Spouse of Christ.**
  SS 4:12 — A garden inclosed *is* my sister, *my* spouse; a spring shut up, a fountain sealed.
  SS 5:1 — I am come into my garden, my sister, *my* spouse: I have gathered my myrrh with my spice; I have eaten my honeycomb with my honey; I have drunk my wine with my milk: eat, O friends; drink, yea, drink abundantly, O beloved.
- **Strength and Glory of God.**
  Ps 78:61 — And delivered his strength into captivity, and his glory into the enemy's hand.
- **Sought Out, a City Not Forsaken.**
  Isa 62:12 — And they shall call them, The holy people, The redeemed of the LORD: and thou shalt be called, Sought out, A city not forsaken.
- **the Lord's Portion.**
  Dt 32:9 — For the LORD's portion *is* his people; Jacob *is* the lot of his inheritance.
- **Temple of God.**
  1Co 3:16–17
- **Temple of the Living God.**
  2Co 6:16 — And what agreement hath the temple of God with idols? for ye are the temple of the living God; as God hath said, I will dwell in them, and walk in *them;* and I will be their God, and they shall be my people.
- **Vineyard.**
  Jer 12:10 — Many pastors have destroyed my vineyard, they have trodden my portion under foot, they have made my pleasant portion a desolate wilderness.
  Mt 21:41 — They say unto him, He will miserably destroy those wicked men, and will let out *his* vineyard unto other husbandmen, which shall render him the fruits in their seasons.

• Christ's love for.

Jn 10:11–12; Eph 5:25–32

Jn 10:8 — All that ever came before me are thieves and robbers: but the sheep did not hear them.

Rev 3:9 — Behold, I will make them of the synagogue of Satan, which say they are Jews, and are not, but do lie; behold, I will make them to come and worship before thy feet, and to know that I have loved thee.

• Loved by believers.

Ps 87:7 — As well the singers as the players on instruments *shall be there:* all my springs *are* in thee.

Ps 137:5 — If I forget thee, O Jerusalem, let my right hand forget *her cunning.*

1Co 12:25 — That there should be no schism in the body; but *that* the members should have the same care one for another.

1Th 4:9 — But as touching brotherly love ye need not that I write unto you: for ye yourselves are taught of God to love one another.

• Is prayed for.

Ps 122:6 — Pray for the peace of Jerusalem: they shall prosper that love thee.

Isa 62:6 — I have set watchmen upon thy walls, O Jerusalem, *which* shall never hold their peace day nor night: ye that make mention of the LORD, keep not silence,

• Dear to God.

Isa 43:4 — Since thou wast precious in my sight, thou hast been honourable, and I have loved thee: therefore will I give men for thee, and people for thy life.

• Safe under his care.

Ps 46:1–2

Ps 46:5 — God *is* in the midst of her; she shall not be moved: God shall help her, *and that* right early.

• Salt and light of the world.

Mt 5:13 — Ye are the salt of the earth: but if the salt have lost his savour, wherewith shall it be salted? it is thenceforth good for nothing, but to be cast out, and to be trodden under foot of men.

• Militant.

SS 6:10 — Who *is* she *that* looketh forth as the morning, fair as the moon, clear as the sun, *and* terrible as *an army* with banners?

Php 2:25 — Yet I supposed it necessary to send to you Epaphroditus, my brother, and companion in labour, and fellow soldier, but your messenger, and he that ministered to my wants.

2Ti 2:3 — Thou therefore endure hardness, as a good soldier of Jesus Christ.

2Ti 4:7 — I have fought a good fight, I have finished *my* course, I have kept the faith:

Phm 1:2 — And to *our* beloved Apphia, and Archippus our fellowsoldier, and to the church in thy house:

• God defends.

Ps 89:18 — For the LORD *is* our defence; and the Holy One of Israel *is* our king.

Isa 4:5 — And the LORD will create upon every dwelling place of mount Zion, and upon her assemblies, a cloud and smoke by day, and the shining of a flaming fire by night: for upon all the glory *shall be* a defence.

Isa 49:25 — But thus saith the LORD, Even the captives of the mighty shall be taken away, and the prey of the terrible shall be delivered: for I will contend with him that contendeth with thee, and I will save thy children.

Mt 16:18 — And I say also unto thee, That thou art Peter, and upon this rock I will build my church; and the gates of hell shall not prevail against it.

• God provides ministers for.

Eph 4:11–12

Jer 3:15 — And I will give you pastors according to mine heart, which shall feed you with knowledge and understanding.

• Is glorious.

Ps 45:13 — The king's daughter *is* all glorious within: her clothing *is* of wrought gold.

Eph 5:27 — That he might present it to himself a glorious church, not having spot, or wrinkle, or any such thing; but that it should be holy and without blemish.

• Is clothed in righteousness.

Rev 19:8 — And to her was granted that she should be arrayed in fine linen, clean and white: for the fine linen is the righteousness of saints.

• Believers continually added to, by the Lord.

Ac 2:47 — Praising God, and having favour with all the people. And the Lord added to the church daily such as should be saved.

Ac 5:14 — And believers were the more added to the Lord, multitudes both of men and women.)

Ac 11:24 — For he was a good man, and full of the Holy Ghost and of faith: and much people was added unto the Lord.

• Unity of.

Ro 12:5 — So we, *being* many, are one body in Christ, and every one members one of another.

1Co 10:17 — For we *being* many are one bread, *and* one body: for we are all partakers of that one bread.

1Co 12:12 — For as the body is one, and hath many members, and all the members of that one body, being many, are one body: so also *is* Christ.

Gal 3:28 — There is neither Jew nor Greek, there is neither bond nor free, there is neither male nor female: for ye are all one in Christ Jesus.

Eph 4:4 — *There is* one body, and one Spirit, even as ye are called in one hope of your calling;

• Privileges of.

Ps 36:8 — They shall be abundantly satisfied with the fatness of thy house; and thou shalt make them drink of the river of thy pleasures.

Ps 87:5 — And of Zion it shall be said, This and *that man* was born in her: and the highest himself shall establish her.

• Worship of, to be attended.

Heb 10:25 — Not forsaking the assembling of ourselves together, as the manner of some *is;* but exhorting *one another:* and so much the more, as ye see the day approaching.

• Harmonious fellowship of.

Ps 133:1–3; 1Jn 3:1–4:21

Jn 13:34 — A new commandment I give unto you, That ye love one another; as I have loved you, that ye also love one another.

Ac 4:32 — And the multitude of them that believed were of one heart and of one soul: neither said any *of them* that ought of the things which he possessed was his own; but they had all things common.

Php 1:4 — Always in every prayer of mine for you all making request with joy,

Php 2:1 — If *there be* therefore any consolation in Christ, if any comfort of love, if any fellowship of the Spirit, if any bowels and mercies,

• Divisions in, to be shunned.

Ro 16:17 — Now I beseech you, brethren, mark them which cause divisions and offences contrary to the doctrine which ye have learned; and avoid them.

1Co 1:10 — Now I beseech you, brethren, by the name of our Lord Jesus Christ, that ye all speak the same thing, and *that* there be no divisions among you; but *that* ye be perfectly joined together in the same mind and in the same judgment.

1Co 3:3 — For ye are yet carnal: for whereas *there is* among you envying, and strife, and divisions, are ye not carnal, and walk as men?

• Baptized into by one Spirit.

1Co 12:13 — For by one Spirit are we all baptized into one body, whether *we be* Jews or Gentiles, whether *we be* bond or free; and have been all made to drink into one Spirit.

• Ministers commanded to feed.

Ac 20:28 — Take heed therefore unto yourselves, and to all the flock, over the which the Holy Ghost hath made you overseers, to feed the church of God, which he hath purchased with his own blood.

• Is edified by the word.

Eph 4:15–16

Ro 12:6 — Having then gifts differing according to the grace that is given to us, whether prophecy, *let us prophesy* according to the proportion of faith;

1Co 14:4 — He that speaketh in an *unknown* tongue edifieth himself; but he that prophesieth edifieth the church.

1Co 14:13 — Wherefore let him that speaketh in an *unknown* tongue pray that he may interpret.

Col 3:16 — Let the word of Christ dwell in you richly in all wisdom; teaching and admonishing one another in psalms and hymns and spiritual songs, singing with grace in your hearts to the Lord.

• The wicked persecute.

Ac 8:1–3; 1Th 2:14–15

• Not to be despised.

1Co 11:22 — What? have ye not houses to eat and to drink in? or despise ye the church of God, and shame them that have not? What shall I say to you? shall I praise you in this? I praise *you* not.

• Defiling of will be punished.

1Co 3:17 — If any man defile the temple of God, him shall God destroy; for the temple of God is holy, which *temple* ye are.

• Extent of, predicted.

Eze 17:22–24; Da 2:34–35

Isa 2:2 — And it shall come to pass in the last days, *that* the mountain of the LORD's house shall be established in the top of the mountains, and shall be exalted above the hills; and all nations shall flow unto it.

✦See: Ecclesiasticism

✦See: Jesus, Kingdom of

✦See: Minister, a Sacred Teacher

✦See: Minister, Miscellany of Minor Sub-Topics

✦See: Usurpation; in ecclesiastical affairs

- **Unclassified scripture relating to.**

Ps 46:4–5; 48:1–2, 11–13; 69:35–36; 84:1–10; 87:1–6; 102:13–14, 19–21; 126:1–2; 132:13–16; 133:1–134:3; 137:1–6; Isa 4:2–6; 27:2–3; 31:4–5; 33:20–24; 35:1–10; 40:9–11; 43:1–7; 49:14–17; 52:1–2, 7–12; 60:1–6, 19–21; 61:1–3; 62:11–12; Jer 3:14–15; 31:6–7; Joel 2:15–17; Eph 1:22–23; 2:21–22; 5:23–27; 1Ti 3:14–15; Heb 12:22–23; Rev 21:10–11

Dt 32:9 — For the LORD'S portion *is* his people; Jacob *is* the lot of his inheritance.

Ps 2:6 — Yet have I set my king upon my holy hill of Zion.

Ps 9:11 — Sing praises to the LORD, which dwelleth in Zion: declare among the people his doings.

Ps 9:14 — That I may shew forth all thy praise in the gates of the daughter of Zion: I will rejoice in thy salvation.

Ps 14:7 — Oh that the salvation of Israel *were come* out of Zion! when the LORD bringeth back the captivity of his people, Jacob shall rejoice, *and* Israel shall be glad.

Ps 20:2 — Send thee help from the sanctuary, and strengthen thee out of Zion;

Ps 50:2 — Out of Zion, the perfection of beauty, God hath shined.

Ps 51:18 — Do good in thy good pleasure unto Zion: build thou the walls of Jerusalem.

Ps 53:6 — Oh that the salvation of Israel *were come* out of Zion! When God bringeth back the captivity of his people, Jacob shall rejoice, *and* Israel shall be glad.

Ps 65:1 — Praise waiteth for thee, O God, in Sion: and unto thee shall the vow be performed.

Ps 74:2 — Remember thy congregation, *which* thou hast purchased of old; the rod of thine inheritance, *which* thou hast redeemed; this mount Zion, wherein thou hast dwelt.

Ps 99:2 — The LORD *is* great in Zion; and he *is* high above all the people.

Ps 102:16 — When the LORD shall build up Zion, he shall appear in his glory.

Ps 110:2 — The LORD shall send the rod of thy strength out of Zion: rule thou in the midst of thine enemies.

Ps 111:1 — Praise ye the LORD. I will praise the LORD with *my* whole heart, in the assembly of the upright, and *in* the congregation.

Ps 114:2 — Judah was his sanctuary, *and* Israel his dominion.

Ps 125:1 — They that trust in the LORD *shall be* as mount Zion, *which* cannot be removed, *but* abideth for ever.

Ps 129:5 — Let them all be confounded and turned back that hate Zion.

Ps 149:2 — Let Israel rejoice in him that made him: let the children of Zion be joyful in their King.

Isa 1:8 — And the daughter of Zion is left as a cottage in a vineyard, as a lodge in a garden of cucumbers, as a besieged city.

Isa 1:27 — Zion shall be redeemed with judgment, and her converts with righteousness.

Isa 2:3 — And many people shall go and say, Come ye, and let us go up to the mountain of the LORD, to the house of the God of Jacob; and he will teach us of his ways, and we will walk in his paths: for out of Zion shall go forth the law, and the word of the LORD from Jerusalem.

Isa 12:6 — Cry out and shout, thou inhabitant of Zion: for great *is* the Holy One of Israel in the midst of thee.

Isa 14:32 — What shall *one* then answer the messengers of the nation? That the LORD hath founded Zion, and the poor of his people shall trust in it.

Isa 24:23 — Then the moon shall be confounded, and the sun ashamed, when the LORD of hosts shall reign in mount Zion, and in Jerusalem, and before his ancients gloriously.

Isa 28:5 — In that day shall the LORD of hosts be for a crown of glory, and for a diadem of beauty, unto the residue of his people,

Isa 28:16 — Therefore thus saith the Lord GOD, Behold, I lay in Zion for a foundation a stone, a tried stone, a precious corner *stone,* a sure foundation: he that believeth shall not make haste.

Isa 33:5 — The LORD is exalted; for he dwelleth on high: he hath filled Zion with judgment and righteousness.

Isa 33:14 — The sinners in Zion are afraid; fearfulness hath surprised the hypocrites. Who among us shall dwell with the devouring fire? who among us shall dwell with everlasting burnings?

Isa 43:21 — This people have I formed for myself; they shall shew forth my praise.

Isa 43:25 — I, *even* I, *am* he that blotteth out thy transgressions for mine own sake, and will not remember thy sins.

Isa 44:23 — Sing, O ye heavens; for the LORD hath done *it:* shout, ye lower parts of the earth: break forth into singing, ye mountains, O forest, and every tree therein: for the LORD hath redeemed Jacob, and glorified himself in Israel.

Isa 59:20 — And the Redeemer shall come to Zion, and unto them that turn from transgression in Jacob, saith the LORD.

Isa 62:1 — For Zion's sake will I not hold my peace, and for Jerusalem's sake I will not rest, until the righteousness thereof go forth as brightness, and the salvation thereof as a lamp *that* burneth.

Isa 62:3 — Thou shalt also be a crown of glory in the hand of the LORD, and a royal diadem in the hand of thy God.

Isa 66:8 — Who hath heard such a thing? who hath seen such things? Shall the earth be made to bring forth in one day? *or* shall a nation be born at once? for as soon as Zion travailed, she brought forth her children.

Isa 66:18 — For I *know* their works and their thoughts: it shall come, that I will gather all nations and tongues; and they shall come, and see my glory.

Jer 12:10 — Many pastors have destroyed my vineyard, they have trodden my portion under foot, they have made my pleasant portion a desolate wilderness.

Jer 13:11 — For as the girdle cleaveth to the loins of a man, so have I caused to cleave unto me the whole house of Israel and the whole house of Judah, saith the LORD; that they might be unto me for a people, and for a name, and for a praise, and for a glory: but they would not hear.

Jer 31:12 — Therefore they shall come and sing in the height of Zion, and shall flow together to the goodness of the LORD, for wheat, and for wine, and for oil, and for the young of the flock and of the herd: and their soul shall be as a watered garden; and they shall not sorrow any more at all.

Jer 31:23 — Thus saith the LORD of hosts, the God of Israel; As yet they shall use this speech in the land of Judah and in the cities thereof, when I shall bring again their captivity; The LORD bless thee, O habitation of justice, *and* mountain of holiness.

Jer 33:9 — And it shall be to me a name of joy, a praise and an honour before all the nations of the earth, which shall hear all the good that I do unto them: and they shall fear and tremble for all the goodness and for all the prosperity that I procure unto it.

Eze 43:7 — And he said unto me, Son of man, the place of my throne, and the place of the soles of my feet, where I will dwell in the midst of the children of Israel for ever, and my holy name, shall the house of Israel no more defile, *neither* they, nor their kings, by their whoredom, nor by the carcases of their kings in their high places.

Joel 2:1 — Blow ye the trumpet in Zion, and sound an alarm in my holy mountain: let all the inhabitants of the land tremble: for the day of the LORD cometh, for *it is* nigh at hand;

Zec 8:3 — Thus saith the LORD; I am returned unto Zion, and will dwell in the midst of Jerusalem: and Jerusalem shall be called a city of truth; and the mountain of the LORD of hosts the holy mountain.

Mt 13:24 — Another parable put he forth unto them, saying, The kingdom of heaven is likened unto a man which sowed good seed in his field:

Mt 16:18 — And I say also unto thee, That thou art Peter, and upon this rock I will build my church; and the gates of hell shall not prevail against it.

Ac 7:38 — This is he, that was in the church in the wilderness with the angel which spake to him in the mount Sina, and *with* our fathers: who received the lively oracles to give unto us:

Ac 20:28 — Take heed therefore unto yourselves, and to all the flock, over the which the Holy Ghost hath made you overseers, to feed the church of God, which he hath purchased with his own blood.

1Co 3:9 — For we are labourers together with God: ye are God's husbandry, *ye are* God's building.

1Co 12:28 — And God hath set some in the church, first apostles, secondarily prophets, thirdly teachers, after that miracles, then gifts of healings, helps, governments, diversities of tongues.

1Co 15:9 — For I am the least of the apostles, that am not meet to be called an apostle, because I persecuted the church of God.

2Co 8:1 — Moreover, brethren, we do you to wit of the grace of God bestowed on the churches of Macedonia;

Eph 3:15 — Of whom the whole family in heaven and earth is named,

Eph 3:21— Unto him *be* glory in the church by Christ Jesus throughout all ages, world without end. Amen.

Eph 5:29 — For no man ever yet hated his own flesh; but nourisheth and cherisheth it, even as the Lord the church:

Col 1:24 — Who now rejoice in my sufferings for you, and fill up that which is behind of the afflictions of Christ in my flesh for his body's sake, which is the church:

Heb 3:6 — But Christ as a son over his own house; whose house are we, if we hold fast the confidence and the rejoicing of the hope firm unto the end.

1Pe 2:5 — Ye also, as lively stones, are built up a spiritual house, an holy priesthood, to offer up spiritual sacrifices, acceptable to God by Jesus Christ.

Rev 1:20 — The mystery of the seven stars which thou sawest in my right hand, and the seven golden candlesticks. The seven stars are the angels of the seven churches: and the seven candlesticks which thou sawest are the seven churches.

Rev 21:2 — And I John saw the holy city, new Jerusalem, coming down from God out of heaven, prepared as a bride adorned for her husband.

Rev 21:23 — And the city had no need of the sun, neither of the moon, to shine in it: for the glory of God did lighten it, and the Lamb *is* the light thereof.

CHURCH, Place of Worship

• Called Courts.

Ps 65:4 — Blessed *is the man whom* thou choosest, and causest to approach *unto thee, that* he may dwell in thy courts: we shall be satisfied with the goodness of thy house, *even* of thy holy temple.

Ps 84:2 — My soul longeth, yea, even fainteth for the courts of the LORD: my heart and my flesh crieth out for the living God.

Ps 84:10 — For a day in thy courts *is* better than a thousand. I had rather be a doorkeeper in the house of my God, than to dwell in the tents of wickedness.

Ps 92:13 — Those that be planted in the house of the LORD shall flourish in the courts of our God.

Ps 96:8 — Give unto the LORD the glory *due unto* his name: bring an offering, and come into his courts.

Ps 100:4 — Enter into his gates with thanksgiving, *and* into his courts with praise: be thankful unto him, *and* bless his name.

Ps 116:19 — In the courts of the LORD'S house, in the midst of thee, O Jerusalem. Praise ye the LORD.

Isa 1:12 — When ye come to appear before me, who hath required this at your hand, to tread my courts?

Isa 62:9 — But they that have gathered it shall eat it, and praise the LORD; and they that have brought it together shall drink it in the courts of my holiness.

Zec 3:7 — Thus saith the LORD of hosts; If thou wilt walk in my ways, and if thou wilt keep my charge, then thou shalt also judge my house, and shalt also keep my courts, and I will give thee places to walk among these that stand by.

• Called House of God.

Ge 28:17 — And he was afraid, and said, How dreadful *is* this place! this is none other but the house of God, and this *is* the gate of heaven.

Ge 28:22 — And this stone, which I have set *for* a pillar, shall be God's house: and of all that thou shalt give me I will surely give the tenth unto thee.

Jos 9:23 — Now therefore ye *are* cursed, and there shall none of you be freed from being bondmen, and hewers of wood and drawers of water for the house of my God.

Jgs 18:31 — And they set them up Micah's graven image, which he made, all the time that the house of God was in Shiloh.

Jgs 20:18 — And the children of Israel arose, and went up to the house of God, and asked counsel of God, and said, Which of us shall go up first to the battle against the children of Benjamin? And the LORD said, Judah *shall go up* first.

Jgs 20:26 — Then all the children of Israel, and all the people, went up, and came unto the house of God, and wept, and sat there before the LORD, and fasted that day until even, and offered burnt offerings and peace offerings before the LORD.

Jgs 21:2 — And the people came to the house of God, and abode there till even before God, and lifted up their voices, and wept sore;

1Ch 9:11 — And Azariah the son of Hilkiah, the son of Meshullam, the son of Zadok, the son of Meraioth, the son of Ahitub, the ruler of the house of God;

1Ch 24:5 — Thus were they divided by lot, one sort with another; for the governors of the sanctuary, and governors *of the house* of God, were of the sons of Eleazar, and of the sons of Ithamar.

2Ch 5:14 — So that the priests could not stand to minister by reason of the cloud: for the glory of the LORD had filled the house of God.

2Ch 22:12 — And he was with them hid in the house of God six years: and Athaliah reigned over the land.

2Ch 24:13 — So the workmen wrought, and the work was perfected by them, and they set the house of God in his state, and strengthened it.

2Ch 33:7 — And he set a carved image, the idol which he had made, in the house of God, of which God had said to David and to Solomon his son, In this house, and in Jerusalem, which I have chosen before all the tribes of Israel, will I put my name for ever:

2Ch 36:19 — And they burnt the house of God, and brake down the wall of Jerusalem, and burnt all the palaces thereof with fire, and destroyed all the goodly vessels thereof.

Ezr 5:8 — Be it known unto the king, that we went into the province of Judea, to the house of the great God, which is builded with great stones, and timber is laid in the walls, and this work goeth fast on, and prospereth in their hands.

Ezr 5:15 — And said unto him, Take these vessels, go, carry them into the temple that *is* in Jerusalem, and let the house of God be builded in his place.

Ezr 7:20 — And whatsoever more shall be needful for the house of thy God, which thou shalt have occasion to bestow, bestow *it* out of the king's treasure house.

Ezr 7:23 — Whatsoever is commanded by the God of heaven, let it be diligently done for the house of the God of heaven: for why should there be wrath against the realm of the king and his sons?

Ne 6:10 — Afterward I came unto the house of Shemaiah the son of Delaiah the son of Mehetabeel, who *was* shut up; and he said, Let us meet together in the house of God, within the temple, and let us shut the doors of the temple: for they will come to slay thee; yea, in the night will they come to slay thee.

Ne 11:11 — Seraiah the son of Hilkiah, the son of Meshullam, the son of Zadok, the son of Meraioth, the son of Ahitub, *was* the ruler of the house of God.

Ne 13:11 — Then contended I with the rulers, and said, Why is the house of God forsaken? And I gathered them together, and set them in their place.

Ps 42:4 — When I remember these *things,* I pour out my soul in me: for I had gone with the multitude, I went with them to the house of God, with the voice of joy and praise, with a multitude that kept holyday.

Ps 52:8 — But I *am* like a green olive tree in the house of God: I trust in the mercy of God for ever and ever.

Ps 55:14 — We took sweet counsel together, *and* walked unto the house of God in company.

Ps 84:10 — For a day in thy courts *is* better than a thousand. I had rather be a doorkeeper in the house of my God, than to dwell in the tents of wickedness.

Ecc 5:1 — Keep thy foot when thou goest to the house of God, and be more ready to hear, than to give the sacrifice of fools: for they consider not that they do evil.

Isa 2:3 — And many people shall go and say, Come ye, and let us go up to the mountain of the LORD, to the house of the God of Jacob; and he will teach us of his ways, and we will walk in his paths: for out of Zion shall go forth the law, and the word of the LORD from Jerusalem.

Hos 9:8 — The watchman of Ephraim *was* with my God: *but* the prophet *is* a snare of a fowler in all his ways, *and* hatred in the house of his God.

Joel 1:16 — Is not the meat cut off before our eyes, *yea,* joy and gladness from the house of our God?

Mic 4:2 — And many nations shall come, and say, Come, and let us go up to the mountain of the LORD, and to the house of the God of Jacob; and he will teach us of his ways, and we will walk in his paths: for the law shall go forth of Zion, and the word of the LORD from Jerusalem.

Zec 7:2 — When they had sent unto the house of God Sherezer and Regem-melech, and their men, to pray before the LORD,

Mt 12:4 — How he entered into the house of God, and did eat the shewbread, which was not lawful for him to eat, neither for them which were with him, but only for the priests?

1Ti 3:15 — But if I tarry long, that thou mayest know how thou oughtest to behave thyself in the house of God, which is the church of the living God, the pillar and ground of the truth.

Heb 10:21 — And *having* an high priest over the house of God;

1Pe 4:17 — For the time *is come* that judgment must begin at the house of God: and if *it* first *begin* at us, what shall the end *be* of them that obey not the gospel of God?

• Called House of the Lord.

2Ki 11:3–4, 18–19; 12:9–10; Jer 20:1–2; 36:5–6

Ex 23:19 — The first of the firstfruits of thy land thou shalt bring into the house of the LORD thy God. Thou shalt not seethe a kid in his mother's milk.

Ex 34:26 — The first of the firstfruits of thy land thou shalt bring unto the house of the LORD thy God. Thou shalt not seethe a kid in his mother's milk.

Dt 23:18 — Thou shalt not bring the hire of a whore, or the price of a dog, into the house of the LORD thy God for any vow: for even both these *are* abomination unto the LORD thy God.

Jos 6:24 — And they burnt the city with fire, and all that *was* therein: only the silver, and the gold, and the vessels of brass and of iron, they put into the treasury of the house of the LORD.

Jgs 19:18 — And he said unto him, We *are* passing from Bethlehemjudah toward the side of mount Ephraim; from thence *am* I: and I went to Bethlehemjudah, but I *am now* going to the house of the LORD; and there *is* no man that receiveth me to house.

1Sa 1:7 — And *as* he did so year by year, when she went up to the house of the LORD, so she provoked her; therefore she wept, and did not eat.

1Sa 1:24 — And when she had weaned him, she took him up with her, with three bullocks, and one ephah of flour, and a bottle of wine, and brought him unto the house of the LORD in Shiloh: and the child *was* young.

2Sa 12:20 — Then David arose from the earth, and washed, and anointed *himself*, and changed his apparel, and came into the house of the LORD, and worshipped: then he came to his own house; and when he required, they set bread before him, and he did eat.

1Ki 3:1 — And Solomon made affinity with Pharaoh king of Egypt, and took Pharaoh's daughter, and brought her into the city of David, until he had made an end of building his own house, and the house of the LORD, and the wall of Jerusalem round about.

1Ki 6:37 — In the fourth year was the foundation of the house of the LORD laid, in the month Zif:

1Ki 7:40 — And Hiram made the lavers, and the shovels, and the basons. So Hiram made an end of doing all the work that he made king Solomon for the house of the LORD:

1Ki 8:10 — And it came to pass, when the priests were come out of the holy *place*, that the cloud filled the house of the LORD,

1Ki 8:63 — And Solomon offered a sacrifice of peace offerings, which he offered unto the LORD, two and twenty thousand oxen, and an hundred and twenty thousand sheep. So the king and all the children of Israel dedicated the house of the LORD.

1Ki 10:5 — And the meat of his table, and the sitting of his servants, and the attendance of his ministers, and their apparel, and his cupbearers, and his ascent by which he went up unto the house of the LORD; there was no more spirit in her.

2Ki 11:15 — But Jehoiada the priest commanded the captains of the hundreds, the officers of the host, and said unto them, Have her forth without the ranges: and him that followeth her kill with the sword. For the priest had said, Let her not be slain in the house of the LORD.

2Ki 12:4 — And Jehoash said to the priests, All the money of the dedicated things that is brought into the house of the LORD, *even* the money of every one that passeth *the account*, the money that every man is set at, *and* all the money that cometh into any man's heart to bring into the house of the LORD,

2Ki 12:13 — Howbeit there were not made for the house of the LORD bowls of silver, snuffers, basons, trumpets, any vessels of gold, or vessels of silver, of the money *that was* brought into the house of the LORD:

2Ki 12:16 — The trespass money and sin money was not brought into the house of the LORD: it was the priests'.

2Ki 16:18 — And the covert for the sabbath that they had built in the house, and the king's entry without, turned he from the house of the LORD for the king of Assyria.

2Ki 20:8 — And Hezekiah said unto Isaiah, What *shall be* the sign that the LORD will heal me, and that I shall go up into the house of the LORD the third day?

2Ki 23:2 — And the king went up into the house of the LORD, and all the men of Judah and all the inhabitants of Jerusalem with him, and the priests, and the prophets, and all the people, both small and great: and he read in their ears all the words of the book of the covenant which was found in the house of the LORD.

2Ki 23:7 — And he brake down the houses of the sodomites, that *were* by the house of the LORD, where the women wove hangings for the grove.

2Ki 23:11 — And he took away the horses that the kings of Judah had given to the sun, at the entering in of the house of the LORD, by the chamber of Nathanmelech the chamberlain, which *was* in the suburbs, and burned the chariots of the sun with fire.

2Ki 25:9 — And he burnt the house of the LORD, and the king's house, and all the houses of Jerusalem, and every great *man's* house burnt he with fire.

1Ch 6:31 — And these *are they* whom David set over the service of song in the house of the LORD, after that the ark had rest.

1Ch 22:1 — Then David said, This *is* the house of the LORD God, and this *is* the altar of the burnt offering for Israel.

1Ch 22:11 — Now, my son, the LORD be with thee; and prosper thou, and build the house of the LORD thy God, as he hath said of thee.

1Ch 22:14 — Now, behold, in my trouble I have prepared for the house of the LORD an hundred thousand talents of gold, and a thousand thousand talents of silver; and of brass and iron without weight; for it is in abundance: timber also and stone have I prepared; and thou mayest add thereto.

1Ch 23:4 — Of which, twenty and four thousand *were* to set forward the work of the house of the LORD; and six thousand *were* officers and judges:

1Ch 26:12 — Among these *were* the divisions of the porters, *even* among the chief men, *having* wards one against another, to minister in the house of the LORD.

2Ch 8:16 — Now all the work of Solomon was prepared unto the day of the foundation of the house of the LORD, and until it was finished. So the house of the LORD was perfected.

2Ch 26:21 — And Uzziah the king was a leper unto the day of his death, and dwelt in a several house, *being* a leper; for he was cut off from the house of the LORD: and Jotham his son *was* over the king's house, judging the people of the land.

2Ch 29:5 — And said unto them, Hear me, ye Levites, sanctify now yourselves, and sanctify the house of the LORD God of your fathers, and carry forth the filthiness out of the holy *place*.

2Ch 29:15 — And they gathered their brethren, and sanctified themselves, and came, according to the commandment of the king, by the words of the LORD, to cleanse the house of the LORD.

2Ch 33:15 — And he took away the strange gods, and the idol out of the house of the LORD, and all the altars that he had built in the mount of the house of the LORD, and in Jerusalem, and cast *them* out of the city.

2Ch 34:15 — And Hilkiah answered and said to Shaphan the scribe, I have found the book of the law in the house of the LORD. And Hilkiah delivered the book to Shaphan.

2Ch 36:14 — Moreover all the chief of the priests, and the people, transgressed very much after all the abominations of the heathen; and polluted the house of the LORD which he had hallowed in Jerusalem.

Ezr 7:27 — Blessed *be* the LORD God of our fathers, which hath put *such a thing* as this in the king's heart, to beautify the house of the LORD which *is* in Jerusalem:

Ps 23:6 — Surely goodness and mercy shall follow me all the days of my life: and I will dwell in the house of the LORD for ever.

Ps 27:4 — One *thing* have I desired of the LORD, that will I seek after; that I may dwell in the house of the LORD all the days of my life, to behold the beauty of the LORD, and to enquire in his temple.

Ps 92:13 — Those that be planted in the house of the LORD shall flourish in the courts of our God.

Ps 116:19 — In the courts of the LORD'S house, in the midst of thee, O Jerusalem. Praise ye the LORD.

Ps 118:26 — Blessed *be* he that cometh in the name of the LORD: we have blessed you out of the house of the LORD.

Ps 122:1 — I was glad when they said unto me, Let us go into the house of the LORD.

Ps 122:9 — Because of the house of the LORD our God I will seek thy good.

Ps 134:1 — Behold, bless ye the LORD, all *ye* servants of the LORD, which by night stand in the house of the LORD.

Isa 2:2 — And it shall come to pass in the last days, *that* the mountain of the LORD'S house shall be established in the top of the mountains, and shall be exalted above the hills; and all nations shall flow unto it.

Isa 37:14 — And Hezekiah received the letter from the hand of the messengers, and read it: and Hezekiah went up unto the house of the LORD, and spread it before the LORD.

Jer 17:26 — And they shall come from the cities of Judah, and from the places about Jerusalem, and from the land of Benjamin, and from the plain, and from the mountains, and from the south, bringing burnt offerings, and sacrifices, and meat offerings, and incense, and bringing sacrifices of praise, unto the house of the LORD.

Jer 26:2 — Thus saith the LORD; Stand in the court of the LORD'S house, and speak unto all the cities of Judah, which come to worship in the LORD'S house, all the words that I command thee to speak unto them; diminish not a word:

Jer 26:7 — So the priests and the prophets and all the people heard Jeremiah speaking these words in the house of the LORD.

Jer 28:1 — And it came to pass the same year, in the beginning of the reign of Zedekiah king of Judah, in the fourth year, *and* in the fifth month, *that* Hananiah the son of Azur the prophet, which *was* of Gibeon, spake unto me in the house of the LORD, in the presence of the priests and of all the people, saying,

Jer 28:5 — Then the prophet Jeremiah said unto the prophet Hananiah in the presence of the priests, and in the presence of all the people that stood in the house of the LORD,

Jer 29:26 — The LORD hath made thee priest in the stead of Jehoiada the priest, that ye should be officers in the house of the LORD, for every man *that is* mad, and maketh himself a prophet, that thou shouldest put him in prison, and in the stocks.

Jer 35:2 — Go unto the house of the Rechabites, and speak unto them, and bring them into the house of the LORD, into one of the chambers, and give them wine to drink.

Jer 38:14 — Then Zedekiah the king sent, and took Jeremiah the prophet unto him into the third entry that *is* in the house of the LORD: and the king said unto Jeremiah, I will ask thee a thing; hide nothing from me.

Jer 41:5 — That there came certain from Shechem, from Shiloh, and from Samaria, *even* fourscore men, having their beards shaven, and their clothes rent, and having cut themselves, with offerings and incense in their hand, to bring *them* to the house of the LORD.

Jer 51:51 — We are confounded, because we have heard reproach: shame hath covered our faces: for strangers are come into the sanctuaries of the LORD'S house.

La 2:7 — The Lord hath cast off his altar, he hath abhorred his sanctuary, he hath given up into the hand of the enemy the walls of her palaces; they have made a noise in the house of the LORD, as in the day of a solemn feast.

Eze 44:4 — Then brought he me the way of the north gate before the house: and I looked, and, behold, the glory of the LORD filled the house of the LORD: and I fell upon my face.

Hag 1:2 — Thus speaketh the LORD of hosts, saying, This people say, The time is not come, the time that the LORD'S house should be built.

Zec 8:9 — Thus saith the LORD of hosts; Let your hands be strong, ye that hear in these days these words by the mouth of the prophets, which *were* in the day *that* the foundation of the house of the LORD of hosts was laid, that the temple might be built.

- **Called Sanctuary.**

Da 8:13–14; Heb 9:1–2

Ex 25:8 — And let them make me a sanctuary; that I may dwell among them.

Le 19:30 — Ye shall keep my sabbaths, and reverence my sanctuary: I *am* the LORD.

Le 21:12 — Neither shall he go out of the sanctuary, nor profane the sanctuary of his God; for the crown of the anointing oil of his God *is* upon him: I *am* the LORD.

Nu 3:28 — In the number of all the males, from a month old and upward, *were* eight thousand and six hundred, keeping the charge of the sanctuary.

Nu 4:12 — And they shall take all the instruments of ministry, wherewith they minister in the sanctuary, and put *them* in a cloth of blue, and cover them with a covering of badgers' skins, and shall put *them* on a bar:

Nu 7:9 — But unto the sons of Kohath he gave none: because the service of the sanctuary belonging unto them *was that* they should bear upon their shoulders.

Nu 8:19 — And I have given the Levites *as* a gift to Aaron and to his sons from among the children of Israel, to do the service of the children of Israel in the tabernacle of the congregation, and to make an atonement for the children of Israel: that there be no plague among the children of Israel, when the children of Israel come nigh unto the sanctuary.

Nu 10:21 — And the Kohathites set forward, bearing the sanctuary: and *the other* did set up the tabernacle against they came.

Nu 18:1 — And the LORD said unto Aaron, Thou and thy sons and thy father's house with thee shall bear the iniquity of the sanctuary: and thou and thy sons with thee shall bear the iniquity of your priesthood.

Nu 18:5 — And ye shall keep the charge of the sanctuary, and the charge of the altar: that there be no wrath any more upon the children of Israel.

Nu 19:20 — But the man that shall be unclean, and shall not purify himself, that soul shall be cut off from among the congregation, because he hath defiled the sanctuary of the LORD: the water of separation hath not been sprinkled upon him; he *is* unclean.

1Ch 9:29 — *Some* of them also *were* appointed to oversee the vessels, and all the instruments of the sanctuary, and the fine flour, and the wine, and the oil, and the frankincense, and the spices.

1Ch 22:19 — Now set your heart and your soul to seek the LORD your God; arise therefore, and build ye the sanctuary of the LORD God, to bring the ark of the covenant of the LORD, and the holy vessels of God, into the house that is to be built to the name of the LORD.

1Ch 24:5 — Thus were they divided by lot, one sort with another; for the governors of the sanctuary, and governors *of the house* of God, were of the sons of Eleazar, and of the sons of Ithamar.

1Ch 28:10 — Take heed now; for the LORD hath chosen thee to build an house for the sanctuary: be strong, and do *it*.

2Ch 20:8 — And they dwelt therein, and have built thee a sanctuary therein for thy name, saying,

2Ch 26:18 — And they withstood Uzziah the king, and said unto him, *It appertaineth* not unto thee, Uzziah, to burn incense unto the LORD, but to the priests the sons of Aaron, that are consecrated to burn incense: go out of the sanctuary; for thou hast trespassed; neither *shall it be* for thine honour from the LORD God.

2Ch 29:21 — And they brought seven bullocks, and seven rams, and seven lambs, and seven he goats, for a sin offering for the kingdom, and for the sanctuary, and for Judah. And he commanded the priests the sons of Aaron to offer *them* on the altar of the LORD.

2Ch 30:8 — Now be ye not stiffnecked, as your fathers *were, but* yield yourselves unto the LORD, and enter into his sanctuary, which he hath sanctified for ever: and serve the LORD your God, that the fierceness of his wrath may turn away from you.

2Ch 30:19 — *That* prepareth his heart to seek God, the LORD God of his fathers, though *he be* not *cleansed* according to the purification of the sanctuary.

Ne 10:39 — For the children of Israel and the children of Levi shall bring the offering of the corn, of the new wine, and the oil, unto the chambers, where *are* the vessels of the sanctuary, and the priests that minister, and the porters, and the singers: and we will not forsake the house of our God.

Ps 20:2 — Send thee help from the sanctuary, and strengthen thee out of Zion;

Ps 28:2 — Hear the voice of my supplications, when I cry unto thee, when I lift up my hands toward thy holy oracle.

Ps 63:2 — To see thy power and thy glory, so *as* I have seen thee in the sanctuary.

Ps 68:24 — They have seen thy goings, O God; *even* the goings of my God, my King, in the sanctuary.

Ps 73:17 — Until I went into the sanctuary of God; *then* understood I their end.

Ps 74:3 — Lift up thy feet unto the perpetual desolations; *even* all *that* the enemy hath done wickedly in the sanctuary.

Ps 74:7 — They have cast fire into thy sanctuary, they have defiled *by casting down* the dwelling place of thy name to the ground.

Ps 77:13 — Thy way, O God, *is* in the sanctuary: who *is so* great a God as *our* God?

Ps 78:69 — And he built his sanctuary like high *palaces,* like the earth which he hath established for ever.

Ps 150:1 — Praise ye the LORD. Praise God in his sanctuary: praise him in the firmament of his power.

Isa 16:12 — And it shall come to pass, when it is seen that Moab is weary on the high place, that he shall come to his sanctuary to pray; but he shall not prevail.

Isa 63:18 — The people of thy holiness have possessed *it* but a little while: our adversaries have trodden down thy sanctuary.

La 2:7 — The Lord hath cast off his altar, he hath abhorred his sanctuary, he hath given up into the hand of the enemy the walls of her palaces; they have made a noise in the house of the LORD, as in the day of a solemn feast.

La 2:20 — Behold, O LORD, and consider to whom thou hast done this. Shall the women eat their fruit, *and* children of a span long? shall the priest and the prophet be slain in the sanctuary of the Lord?

La 4:1 — How is the gold become dim! *how* is the most fine gold changed! the stones of the sanctuary are poured out in the top of every street.

Eze 5:11 — Wherefore, *as* I live, saith the Lord GOD; Surely, because thou hast defiled my sanctuary with all thy detestable things, and with all thine abominations, therefore will I also diminish *thee;* neither shall mine eye spare, neither will I have any pity.

Eze 42:20 — He measured it by the four sides: it had a wall round about, five hundred *reeds* long, and five hundred broad, to make a separation between the sanctuary and the profane place.

Eze 44:5 — And the LORD said unto me, Son of man, mark well, and behold with thine eyes, and hear with thine ears all that I say unto thee concerning all the ordinances of the house of the LORD, and all the laws thereof; and mark well the entering in of the house, with every going forth of the sanctuary.

Eze 44:27 — And in the day that he goeth into the sanctuary, unto the inner court, to minister in the sanctuary, he shall offer his sin offering, saith the Lord GOD.

Eze 45:3 — And of this measure shalt thou measure the length of five and twenty thousand, and the breadth of ten thousand: and in it shall be the sanctuary *and* the most holy *place.*

Eze 48:8 — And by the border of Judah, from the east side unto the west side, shall be the offering which ye shall offer of five and twenty thousand *reeds in* breadth, and *in* length as one of the *other* parts, from the east side unto the west side: and the sanctuary shall be in the midst of it.

Eze 48:21 — And the residue *shall be* for the prince, on the one side and on the other of the holy oblation, and of the possession of the city, over against the five and twenty thousand of the oblation toward the east border, and westward over against the five and twenty thousand toward the west border, over against the portions for the prince: and it shall be the holy oblation; and the sanctuary of the house *shall be* in the midst thereof.

Da 8:11 — Yea, he magnified *himself* even to the prince of the host, and by him the daily *sacrifice* was taken away, and the place of his sanctuary was cast down.

Da 9:17 — Now therefore, O our God, hear the prayer of thy servant, and his supplications, and cause thy face to shine upon thy sanctuary that is desolate, for the Lord's sake.

Da 9:26 — And after threescore and two weeks shall Messiah be cut off, but not for himself: and the people of the prince that shall come shall destroy the city and the sanctuary; and the end thereof *shall be* with a flood, and unto the end of the war desolations are determined.

Da 11:31 — And arms shall stand on his part, and they shall pollute the sanctuary of strength, and shall take away the daily *sacrifice,* and they shall place the abomination that maketh desolate.

Heb 8:2 — A minister of the sanctuary, and of the true tabernacle, which the Lord pitched, and not man.

• Called House of Prayer.

Isa 56:7 — Even them will I bring to my holy mountain, and make them joyful in my house of prayer: their burnt offerings and their sacrifices *shall be* accepted upon mine altar; for mine house shall be called an house of prayer for all people.

Mt 21:13 — And said unto them, It is written, My house shall be called the house of prayer; but ye have made it a den of thieves.

• Called Tabernacle.

Ex 26:1 — Moreover thou shalt make the tabernacle *with* ten curtains *of* fine twined linen, and blue, and purple, and scarlet: *with* cherubims of cunning work shalt thou make them.

Le 26:11 — And I will set my tabernacle among you: and my soul shall not abhor you.

Jos 22:19 — Notwithstanding, if the land of your possession *be* unclean, *then* pass ye over unto the land of the possession of the LORD, wherein the LORD'S tabernacle dwelleth, and take possession among us: but rebel not against the LORD, nor rebel against us, in building you an altar beside the altar of the LORD our God.

Ps 15:1 — LORD, who shall abide in thy tabernacle? who shall dwell in thy holy hill?

Ps 61:4 — I will abide in thy tabernacle for ever: I will trust in the covert of thy wings. Selah.

Ps 76:2 — In Salem also is his tabernacle, and his dwelling place in Zion.

Heb 8:2 — A minister of the sanctuary, and of the true tabernacle, which the Lord pitched, and not man.

Heb 8:5 — Who serve unto the example and shadow of heavenly things, as Moses was admonished of God when he was about to make the tabernacle: for, See, saith he, *that* thou make all things according to the pattern shewed to thee in the mount.

Heb 9:2 — For there was a tabernacle made; the first, wherein *was* the candlestick, and the table, and the shewbread; which is called the sanctuary.

Heb 9:11 — But Christ being come an high priest of good things to come, by a greater and more perfect tabernacle, not made with hands, that is to say, not of this building;

Rev 13:6 — And he opened his mouth in blasphemy against God, to blaspheme his name, and his tabernacle, and them that dwell in heaven.

Rev 21:3 — And I heard a great voice out of heaven saying, Behold, the tabernacle of God *is* with men, and he will dwell with them, and they shall be his people, and God himself shall be with them, *and be* their God.

• Called Temple.

1Sa 1:9 — So Hannah rose up after they had eaten in Shiloh, and after they had drunk. Now Eli the priest sat upon a seat by a post of the temple of the LORD.

1Sa 3:3 — And ere the lamp of God went out in the temple of the LORD, where the ark of God *was,* and Samuel was laid down *to sleep;*

2Ki 11:10 — And to the captains over hundreds did the priest give king David's spears and shields, that *were* in the temple of the LORD.

2Ki 11:13 — And when Athaliah heard the noise of the guard *and* of the people, she came to the people into the temple of the LORD.

Ezr 4:1 — Now when the adversaries of Judah and Benjamin heard that the children of the captivity builded the temple unto the LORD God of Israel;

Ps 5:7 — But as for me, I will come *into* thy house in the multitude of thy mercy: *and* in thy fear will I worship toward thy holy temple.

Ps 11:4 — The LORD *is* in his holy temple, the LORD'S throne *is* in heaven: his eyes behold, his eyelids try, the children of men.

Ps 27:4 — One *thing* have I desired of the LORD, that will I seek after; that I may dwell in the house of the LORD all the days of my life, to behold the beauty of the LORD, and to enquire in his temple.

Ps 29:9 — The voice of the LORD maketh the hinds to calve, and discovereth the forests: and in his temple doth every one speak of *his* glory.

Ps 48:9 — We have thought of thy lovingkindness, O God, in the midst of thy temple.

Ps 68:29 — Because of thy temple at Jerusalem shall kings bring presents unto thee.

Isa 6:1 — In the year that king Uzziah died I saw also the Lord sitting upon a throne, high and lifted up, and his train filled the temple.

Mal 3:1 — Behold, I will send my messenger, and he shall prepare the way before me: and the Lord, whom ye seek, shall suddenly come to his temple, even the messenger of the covenant, whom ye delight in: behold, he shall come, saith the LORD of hosts.

Mt 4:5 — Then the devil taketh him up into the holy city, and setteth him on a pinnacle of the temple,

Mt 23:16 — Woe unto you, *ye* blind guides, which say, Whosoever shall swear by the temple, it is nothing; but whosoever shall swear by the gold of the temple, he is a debtor!

Lk 18:10 — Two men went up into the temple to pray; the one a Pharisee, and the other a publican.

Lk 24:53 — And were continually in the temple, praising and blessing God. Amen.

• Called Zion.

Ps 9:11 — Sing praises to the LORD, which dwelleth in Zion: declare among the people his doings.

Ps 48:11 — Let mount Zion rejoice, let the daughters of Judah be glad, because of thy judgments.

Ps 74:2 — Remember thy congregation, *which* thou hast purchased of old; the rod of thine inheritance, *which* thou hast redeemed; this mount Zion, wherein thou hast dwelt.

Ps 132:13 — For the LORD hath chosen Zion; he hath desired *it* for his habitation.

Ps 137:1 — By the rivers of Babylon, there we sat down, yea, we wept, when we remembered Zion.

Isa 35:10 — And the ransomed of the LORD shall return, and come to Zion with songs and everlasting joy upon their heads: they shall obtain joy and gladness, and sorrow and sighing shall flee away.

Jer 31:6 — For there shall be a day, *that* the watchmen upon the mount Ephraim shall cry, Arise ye, and let us go up to Zion unto the LORD our God.

Jer 50:5 — They shall ask the way to Zion with their faces thitherward, *saying,* Come, and let us join ourselves to the LORD in a perpetual covenant *that* shall not be forgotten.

Joel 2:1 — Blow ye the trumpet in Zion, and sound an alarm in my holy mountain: let all the inhabitants of the land tremble: for the day of the LORD cometh, for *it is* nigh at hand;

Joel 2:15 — Blow the trumpet in Zion, sanctify a fast, call a solemn assembly:

• Called Holy Place.

Le 16:2–24

Ex 28:29 — And Aaron shall bear the names of the children of Israel in the breastplate of judgment upon his heart, when he goeth in unto the holy *place,* for a memorial before the LORD continually.

Ex 38:24 — All the gold that was occupied for the work in all the work of the holy *place,* even the gold of the offering, was twenty and nine talents, and seven hundred and thirty shekels, after the shekel of the sanctuary.

Le 6:16 — And the remainder thereof shall Aaron and his sons eat: with unleavened bread shall it be eaten in the holy place; in the court of the tabernacle of the congregation they shall eat it.

Le 10:17 — Wherefore have ye not eaten the sin offering in the holy place, seeing it *is* most holy, and *God* hath given it you to bear the iniquity of the congregation, to make atonement for them before the LORD?

Le 14:13 — And he shall slay the lamb in the place where he shall kill the sin offering and the burnt offering, in the holy place: for as the sin offering *is* the priest's, *so is* the trespass offering: it *is* most holy:

Jos 5:15 — And the captain of the LORD's host said unto Joshua, Loose thy shoe from off thy foot; for the place whereon thou standest *is* holy. And Joshua did so.

1Ki 8:8 — And they drew out the staves, that the ends of the staves were seen out in the holy *place* before the oracle, and they were not seen without: and there they are unto this day.

1Ch 23:32 — And that they should keep the charge of the tabernacle of the congregation, and the charge of the holy *place,* and the charge of the sons of Aaron their brethren, in the service of the house of the LORD.

2Ch 29:5 — And said unto them, Hear me, ye Levites, sanctify now yourselves, and sanctify the house of the LORD God of your fathers, and carry forth the filthiness out of the holy *place.*

2Ch 30:27 — Then the priests the Levites arose and blessed the people: and their voice was heard, and their prayer came *up* to his holy dwelling place, *even* unto heaven.

2Ch 35:5 — And stand in the holy *place* according to the divisions of the families of the fathers of your brethren the people, and *after* the division of the families of the Levites.

Ezr 9:8 — And now for a little space grace hath been *shewed* from the LORD our God, to leave us a remnant to escape, and to give us a nail in his holy place, that our God may lighten our eyes, and give us a little reviving in our bondage.

Ps 24:3 — Who shall ascend into the hill of the LORD? or who shall stand in his holy place?

Ps 46:4 — *There is* a river, the streams whereof shall make glad the city of God, the holy *place* of the tabernacles of the most High.

Ps 68:17 — The chariots of God *are* twenty thousand, *even* thousands of angels: the Lord *is* among them, *as in* Sinai, in the holy *place.*

Ecc 8:10 — And so I saw the wicked buried, who had come and gone from the place of the holy, and they were forgotten in the city where they had so done: this *is* also vanity.

Isa 57:15 — For thus saith the high and lofty One that inhabiteth eternity, whose name *is* Holy; I dwell in the high and holy *place,* with him also *that is* of a contrite and humble spirit, to revive the spirit of the humble, and to revive the heart of the contrite ones.

Eze 41:4 — So he measured the length thereof, twenty cubits; and the breadth, twenty cubits, before the temple: and he said unto me, This *is* the most holy *place.*

Eze 42:13 — Then said he unto me, The north chambers *and* the south chambers, which *are* before the separate place, they *be* holy chambers, where the priests that approach unto the LORD shall eat the most holy things: there shall they lay the most holy things, and the meat offering, and the sin offering, and the trespass offering; for the place *is* holy.

Eze 45:4 — The holy *portion* of the land shall be for the priests the ministers of the sanctuary, which shall come near to minister unto the LORD: and it shall be a place for their houses, and an holy place for the sanctuary.

Mt 24:15 — When ye therefore shall see the abomination of desolation, spoken of by Daniel the prophet, stand in the holy place, (whoso readeth, let him understand:)

Ac 6:13 — And set up false witnesses, which said, This man ceaseth not to speak blasphemous words against this holy place, and the law:

Ac 21:28 — Crying out, Men of Israel, help: This is the man, that teacheth all *men* every where against the people, and the law, and this place: and further brought Greeks also into the temple, and hath polluted this holy place.

Heb 9:12 — Neither by the blood of goats and calves, but by his own blood he entered in once into the holy place, having obtained eternal redemption *for us.*

Heb 9:25 — Nor yet that he should offer himself often, as the high priest entereth into the holy place every year with blood of others;

• Called Holy Temple.

Ps 5:7 — But as for me, I will come *into* thy house in the multitude of thy mercy: *and* in thy fear will I worship toward thy holy temple.

Ps 11:4 — The LORD *is* in his holy temple, the LORD'S throne *is* in heaven: his eyes behold, his eyelids try, the children of men.

Ps 65:4 — Blessed *is the man whom* thou choosest, and causest to approach *unto thee, that* he may dwell in thy courts: we shall be satisfied with the goodness of thy house, *even* of thy holy temple.

Ps 79:1 — O God, the heathen are come into thine inheritance; thy holy temple have they defiled; they have laid Jerusalem on heaps.

Ps 138:2 — I will worship toward thy holy temple, and praise thy name for thy lovingkindness and for thy truth: for thou hast magnified thy word above all thy name.

Jnh 2:4 — Then I said, I am cast out of thy sight; yet I will look again toward thy holy temple.

Jnh 2:7 — When my soul fainted within me I remembered the LORD: and my prayer came in unto thee, into thine holy temple.

Mic 1:2 — Hear, all ye people; hearken, O earth, and all that therein is: and let the Lord GOD be witness against you, the Lord from his holy temple.

Hab 2:20 — But the LORD *is* in his holy temple: let all the earth keep silence before him.

Eph 2:21 — In whom all the building fitly framed together groweth unto an holy temple in the Lord:

Eph 3:17 — That Christ may dwell in your hearts by faith; that ye, being rooted and grounded in love,

• Called My Father's House.

Jn 2:16 — And said unto them that sold doves, Take these things hence; make not my Father's house an house of merchandise.

Jn 14:2 — In my Father's house are many mansions: if *it were* not so, I would have told you. I go to prepare a place for you.

• Holy.

Ex 30:26–29; Le 8:10–11

Ex 40:9 — And thou shalt take the anointing oil, and anoint the tabernacle, and all that *is* therein, and shalt hallow it, and all the vessels thereof: and it shall be holy.

Le 16:33 — And he shall make an atonement for the holy sanctuary, and he shall make an atonement for the tabernacle of the congregation, and for the altar, and he shall make an atonement for the priests, and for all the people of the congregation.

Le 19:30 — Ye shall keep my sabbaths, and reverence my sanctuary: I *am* the LORD.

Le 21:12 — Neither shall he go out of the sanctuary, nor profane the sanctuary of his God; for the crown of the anointing oil of his God *is* upon him: I *am* the LORD.

Nu 7:1 — And it came to pass on the day that Moses had fully set up the tabernacle, and had anointed it, and sanctified it, and all the instruments thereof, both the altar and all the vessels thereof, and had anointed them, and sanctified them;

1Ki 9:3 — And the LORD said unto him, I have heard thy prayer and thy supplication, that thou hast made before me: I have hallowed this house, which thou hast built, to put my name there for ever; and mine eyes and mine heart shall be there perpetually.

1Ch 29:3 — Moreover, because I have set my affection to the house of my God, I have of mine own proper good, of gold and silver, *which* I have given to the house of my God, over and above all that I have prepared for the holy house,

2Ch 3:8 — And he made the most holy house, the length whereof *was* according to the breadth of the house, twenty cubits, and the breadth thereof twenty cubits: and he overlaid it with fine gold, *amounting* to six hundred talents.

Isa 64:11 — Our holy and our beautiful house, where our fathers praised thee, is burned up with fire: and all our pleasant things are laid waste.

Eze 23:39 — For when they had slain their children to their idols, then they came the same day into my sanctuary to profane it; and, lo, thus have they done in the midst of mine house.

1Co 3:17 — If any man defile the temple of God, him shall God destroy; for the temple of God is holy, which *temple* ye are.

• Edifices.

See: Synagogue

See: Tabernacle

See: Temple

CHURNING

Pr 30:33 — Surely the churning of milk bringeth forth butter, and the wringing of the nose bringeth forth blood: so the forcing of wrath bringeth forth strife.

See: Butter

CHUSHAN-RISHATHAIM • King of Mesopotamia.

Jgs 3:8–10

CHUZA • Herod's steward.

Lk 8:3 — And Joanna the wife of Chuza Herod's steward, and Susanna, and many others, which ministered unto him of their substance.

CILICIA

• Maritime province of Asia Minor.

• Jews dwell in.

Ac 6:9 — Then there arose certain of *the synagogue,* which is called the synagogue of the Libertines, and Cyrenians, and Alexandrians, and of them of Cilicia and of Asia, disputing with Stephen.

• Churches of.

Ac 15:23 — And they wrote *letters* by them after this manner; The apostles and elders and brethren *send* greeting unto the brethren which are of the Gentiles in Antioch and Syria and Cilicia:

Ac 15:41 — And he went through Syria and Cilicia, confirming the churches.

Gal 1:21 — Afterwards I came into the regions of Syria and Cilicia;

• Sea of.

Ac 27:5 — And when we had sailed over the sea of Cilicia and Pamphylia, we came to Myra, *a city* of Lycia.

CINNAMON

• A spice.

Pr 7:17 — I have perfumed my bed with myrrh, aloes, and cinnamon.

SS 4:14 — Spikenard and saffron; calamus and cinnamon, with all trees of frankincense; myrrh and aloes, with all the chief spices:

Rev 18:13 — And cinnamon, and odours, and ointments, and frankincense, and wine, and oil, and fine flour, and wheat, and beasts, and sheep, and horses, and chariots, and slaves, and souls of men.

• An ingredient of the sacred oil.

Ex 30:23 — Take thou also unto thee principal spices, of pure myrrh five hundred *shekels,* and of sweet cinnamon half so much, *even* two hundred and fifty *shekels,* and of sweet calamus two hundred and fifty *shekels,*

CINNERETH

See: Chinnereth

See: Galilee; Sea of

CIRCUMCISION

• Institution of.

Ge 17:10–24

Le 12:3 — And in the eighth day the flesh of his foreskin shall be circumcised.

Jn 7:22 — Moses therefore gave unto you circumcision; (not because it is of Moses, but of the fathers;) and ye on the sabbath day circumcise a man.

Ac 7:8 — And he gave him the covenant of circumcision: and so *Abraham* begat Isaac, and circumcised him the eighth day; and Isaac *begat* Jacob; and Jacob *begat* the twelve patriarchs.

Ro 4:11 — And he received the sign of circumcision, a seal of the righteousness of the faith which *he had yet* being uncircumcised: that he might be the father of all them that believe, though they be not circumcised; that righteousness might be imputed unto them also:

• A seal of righteousness.

Ro 2:25–29

Ro 4:11 — And he received the sign of circumcision, a seal of the righteousness of the faith which *he had yet* being uncircumcised: that he might be the father of all them that believe, though they be not circumcised; that righteousness might be imputed unto them also:

• Performed on all males on the eighth day.

Ge 17:12–13

Le 12:3 — And in the eighth day the flesh of his foreskin shall be circumcised.

Php 3:5 — Circumcised the eighth day, of the stock of Israel, *of* the tribe of Benjamin, an Hebrew of the Hebrews; as touching the law, a Pharisee;

• Rite of, observed on the Sabbath.

Jn 7:23 — If a man on the sabbath day receive circumcision, that the law of Moses should not be broken; are ye angry at me, because I have made a man every whit whole on the sabbath day?

• A prerequisite of the privileges of the passover.

Ex 12:48 — And when a stranger shall sojourn with thee, and will keep the passover to the LORD, let all his males be circumcised, and then let him come near and keep it; and he shall be as one that is born in the land: for no uncircumcised person shall eat thereof.

• Child named at the time of.

Ge 21:3–4

Lk 1:59 — And it came to pass, that on the eighth day they came to circumcise the child; and they called him Zacharias, after the name of his father.

Lk 2:21 — And when eight days were accomplished for the circumcising of the child, his name was called JESUS, which was so named of the angel before he was conceived in the womb.

• Neglect of, punished.

Ge 17:14 — And the uncircumcised man child whose flesh of his foreskin is not circumcised, that soul shall be cut off from his people; he hath broken my covenant.

Ex 4:24 — And it came to pass by the way in the inn, that the LORD met him, and sought to kill him.

• Neglected.

Jos 5:7 — And their children, *whom* he raised up in their stead, them Joshua circumcised: for they were uncircumcised, because they had not circumcised them by the way.

• Covenant promises of.

Ge 17:4–14; Ro 9:7–13

Ac 7:8 — And he gave him the covenant of circumcision: and so *Abraham* begat Isaac, and circumcised him the eighth day; and Isaac *begat* Jacob; and Jacob *begat* the twelve patriarchs.

Ro 3:1 — What advantage then hath the Jew? or what profit *is there* of circumcision?

Ro 4:11 — And he received the sign of circumcision, a seal of the righteousness of the faith which *he had yet* being uncircumcised: that he might be the father of all them that believe, though they be not circumcised; that righteousness might be imputed unto them also:

Gal 5:3 — For I testify again to every man that is circumcised, that he is a debtor to do the whole law.

• Necessity of, falsely taught by Judaizing Christians.

Ac 15:1 — And certain men which came down from Judaea taught the brethren, *and said,* Except ye be circumcised after the manner of Moses, ye cannot be saved.

• Paul's argument against the continuance of.

Ro 2:25 — For circumcision verily profiteth, if thou keep the law: but if thou be a breaker of the law, thy circumcision is made uncircumcision.

Ro 2:28 — For he is not a Jew, which is one outwardly; neither *is that* circumcision, which is outward in the flesh:

Gal 6:13 — For neither they themselves who are circumcised keep the law; but desire to have you circumcised, that they may glory in your flesh.

• Characterized by Paul as a yoke.

Ac 15:10 — Now therefore why tempt ye God, to put a yoke upon the neck of the disciples, which neither our fathers nor we were able to bear?

• Abrogated.

Ac 15:5–29; Ro 4:9–11; 1Co 7:18–19; Gal 2:3–4; 5:2–11

Ro 3:30 — Seeing *it is* one God, which shall justify the circumcision by faith, and uncircumcision through faith.

Gal 6:12 — As many as desire to make a fair shew in the flesh, they constrain you to be circumcised; only lest they should suffer persecution for the cross of Christ.

Eph 2:11 — Wherefore remember, that ye *being* in time past Gentiles in the flesh, who are called Uncircumcision by that which is called the Circumcision in the flesh made by hands;

Eph 2:15 — Having abolished in his flesh the enmity, *even* the law of commandments *contained* in ordinances; for to make in himself of twain one new man, *so* making peace;

Col 2:11 — In whom also ye are circumcised with the circumcision made without hands, in putting off the body of the sins of the flesh by the circumcision of Christ:

Col 3:11 — Where there is neither Greek nor Jew, circumcision nor uncircumcision, Barbarian, Scythian, bond *nor* free: but Christ *is* all, and in all.

- **Instances of.**
  - **Abraham.**
    Ge 17:23–27; 21:3–4
  - **Shechemites.**
    Ge 34:24
  - **Moses.**
    Ex 4:25
  - **Israelites at Gilgal.**
    Jos 5:2–9
  - **John the Baptist.**
    Lk 1:59
  - **Jesus.**
    Lk 2:21
  - **Paul.**
    Php 3:5
  - **Timothy.**
    Ac 16:3
- **Figurative.**

Ro 2:28–29

Ex 6:12 — And Moses spake before the LORD, saying, Behold, the children of Israel have not hearkened unto me; how then shall Pharaoh hear me, who *am* of uncircumcised lips?

Dt 10:16 — Circumcise therefore the foreskin of your heart, and be no more stiffnecked.

Dt 30:6 — And the LORD thy God will circumcise thine heart, and the heart of thy seed, to love the LORD thy God with all thine heart, and with all thy soul, that thou mayest live.

Jer 4:4 — Circumcise yourselves to the LORD, and take away the foreskins of your heart, ye men of Judah and inhabitants of Jerusalem: lest my fury come forth like fire, and burn that none can quench *it,* because of the evil of your doings.

Jer 6:10 — To whom shall I speak, and give warning, that they may hear? behold, their ear *is* uncircumcised, and they cannot hearken: behold, the word of the LORD is unto them a reproach; they have no delight in it.

Jer 9:26 — Egypt, and Judah, and Edom, and the children of Ammon, and Moab, and all *that are* in the utmost corners, that dwell in the wilderness: for all *these* nations *are* uncircumcised, and all the house of Israel *are* uncircumcised in the heart.

Ro 15:8 — Now I say that Jesus Christ was a minister of the circumcision for the truth of God, to confirm the promises *made* unto the fathers:

Php 3:3 — For we are the circumcision, which worship God in the spirit, and rejoice in Christ Jesus, and have no confidence in the flesh.

Col 2:11 — In whom also ye are circumcised with the circumcision made without hands, in putting off the body of the sins of the flesh by the circumcision of Christ:

Col 3:11 — Where there is neither Greek nor Jew, circumcision nor uncircumcision, Barbarian, Scythian, bond *nor* free: but Christ *is* all, and in all.

- **A designation of the Jews.**

Ac 10:45 — And they of the circumcision which believed were astonished, as many as came with Peter, because that on the Gentiles also was poured out the gift of the Holy Ghost.

Ac 11:2 — And when Peter was come up to Jerusalem, they that were of the circumcision contended with him,

Gal 2:9 — And when James, Cephas, and John, who seemed to be pillars, perceived the grace that was given unto me, they gave to me and Barnabas the right hands of fellowship; that we *should go* unto the heathen, and they unto the circumcision.

Eph 2:11 — Wherefore remember, that ye *being* in time past Gentiles in the flesh, who are called Uncircumcision by that which is called the Circumcision in the flesh made by hands;

Col 4:11 — And Jesus, which is called Justus, who are of the circumcision. These only *are my* fellow workers unto the kingdom of God, which have been a comfort unto me.

Tit 1:10 — For there are many unruly and vain talkers and deceivers, specially they of the circumcision:

- **A designation of Christians.**

Php 3:3 — For we are the circumcision, which worship God in the spirit, and rejoice in Christ Jesus, and have no confidence in the flesh.

CIRCUMSTANCE

Ro 8:35–39

Php 4:11 — Not that I speak in respect of want: for I have learned, in whatsoever state I am, *therewith* to be content.

1Ti 6:6 — But godliness with contentment is great gain.

CIS ✦See: Kish

CISTERN

- **Broken.**

Jer 2:13 — For my people have committed two evils; they have forsaken me the fountain of living waters, *and* hewed them out cisterns, broken cisterns, that can hold no water.

- **Figurative.**

2Ki 18:31 — Hearken not to Hezekiah: for thus saith the king of Assyria, Make *an agreement* with me by a present, and come out to me, and *then* eat ye every man of his own vine, and every one of his fig tree, and drink ye every one the waters of his cistern:

Pr 5:15 — Drink waters out of thine own cistern, and running waters out of thine own well.

Ecc 12:6 — Or ever the silver cord be loosed, or the golden bowl be broken, or the pitcher be broken at the fountain, or the wheel broken at the cistern.

Isa 36:16 — Hearken not to Hezekiah: for thus saith the king of Assyria, Make *an agreement* with me *by* a present, and come out to me: and eat ye every one of his vine, and every one of his fig tree, and drink ye every one the waters of his own cistern;

✦See: Wells

CITIES

- **Ancient.**
  Ge 10:10–12

Ge 4:17 — And Cain knew his wife; and she conceived, and bare Enoch: and he builded a city, and called the name of the city, after the name of his son, Enoch.

• Fortified.

2Ch 11:10–12

Nu 32:36 — And Beth-nimrah, and Beth-haran, fenced cities: and folds for sheep.

Dt 9:1 — Hear, O Israel: Thou *art* to pass over Jordan this day, to go in to possess nations greater and mightier than thyself, cities great and fenced up to heaven,

Jos 10:20 — And it came to pass, when Joshua and the children of Israel had made an end of slaying them with a very great slaughter, till they were consumed, that the rest *which* remained of them entered into fenced cities.

Jos 14:12 — Now therefore give me this mountain, whereof the LORD spake in that day; for thou heardest in that day how the Anakims *were* there, and *that* the cities *were* great *and* fenced: if so be the LORD *will be* with me, then I shall be able to drive them out, as the LORD said.

2Ch 8:5 — Also he built Beth-horon the upper, and Beth-horon the nether, fenced cities, with walls, gates, and bars;

2Ch 17:2 — And he placed forces in all the fenced cities of Judah, and set garrisons in the land of Judah, and in the cities of Ephraim, which Asa his father had taken.

2Ch 17:19 — These waited on the king, beside *those* whom the king put in the fenced cities throughout all Judah.

2Ch 21:3 — And their father gave them great gifts of silver, and of gold, and of precious things, with fenced cities in Judah: but the kingdom gave he to Jehoram; because he *was* the firstborn.

Isa 23:11 — He stretched out his hand over the sea, he shook the kingdoms: the LORD hath given a commandment against the merchant *city,* to destroy the strong holds thereof.

• Gates of.

See: Gates

• Designated as.

• Royal.

Jos 10:2 — That they feared greatly, because Gibeon *was* a great city, as one of the royal cities, and because it *was* greater than Ai, and all the men thereof *were* mighty.

1Sa 27:5 — And David said unto Achish, If I have now found grace in thine eyes, let them give me a place in some town in the country, that I may dwell there: for why should thy servant dwell in the royal city with thee?

2Sa 12:26 — And Joab fought against Rabbah of the children of Ammon, and took the royal city.

1Ch 11:7 — And David dwelt in the castle; therefore they called it the city of David.

• Treasure.

Ge 41:48 — And he gathered up all the food of the seven years, which were in the land of Egypt, and laid up the food in the cities: the food of the field, which *was* round about every city, laid he up in the same.

Ex 1:11 — Therefore they did set over them taskmasters to afflict them with their burdens. And they built for Pharaoh treasure cities, Pithom and Raamses.

1Ki 9:19 — And all the cities of store that Solomon had, and cities for his chariots, and cities for his horsemen, and that which Solomon desired to build in Jerusalem, and in Lebanon, and in all the land of his dominion.

2Ch 8:4 — And he built Tadmor in the wilderness, and all the store cities, which he built in Hamath.

2Ch 16:4 — And Ben-hadad hearkened unto king Asa, and sent the captains of his armies against the cities of Israel; and they smote Ijon, and Dan, and Abel-maim, and all the store cities of Naphtali.

2Ch 17:12 — And Jehoshaphat waxed great exceedingly; and he built in Judah castles, and cities of store.

• Chariot.

2Ch 1:14 — And Solomon gathered chariots and horsemen: and he had a thousand and four hundred chariots, and twelve thousand horsemen, which he placed in the chariot cities, and with the king at Jerusalem.

2Ch 8:6 — And Baalath, and all the store cities that Solomon had, and all the chariot cities, and the cities of the horsemen, and all that Solomon desired to build in Jerusalem, and in Lebanon, and throughout all the land of his dominion.

2Ch 9:25 — And Solomon had four thousand stalls for horses and chariots, and twelve thousand horsemen; whom he bestowed in the chariot cities, and with the king at Jerusalem.

• Merchant.

Isa 23:11 — He stretched out his hand over the sea, he shook the kingdoms: the LORD hath given a commandment against the merchant *city,* to destroy the strong holds thereof.

Eze 17:4 — He cropped off the top of his young twigs, and carried it into a land of traffick; he set it in a city of merchants.

Eze 27:3 — And say unto Tyrus, O thou that art situate at the entry of the sea, *which art* a merchant of the people for many isles, Thus saith the Lord GOD; O Tyrus, thou hast said, I *am* of perfect beauty.

• Town clerk of.

Ac 19:35 — And when the townclerk had appeased the people, he said, *Ye* men of Ephesus, what man is there that knoweth not how that the city of the Ephesians is a worshipper of the great goddess Diana, and of the *image* which fell down from Jupiter?

• Government of, by rulers.

Ne 3:17–18

Ne 3:9 — And next unto them repaired Rephaiah the son of Hur, the ruler of the half part of Jerusalem.

Ne 3:12 — And next unto him repaired Shallum the son of Halohesh, the ruler of the half part of Jerusalem, he and his daughters.

Ne 7:2 — That I gave my brother Hanani, and Hananiah the ruler of the palace, charge over Jerusalem: for he *was* a faithful man, and feared God above many.

See: Government

- **Suburbs of.**

Nu 35:3–5

Jos 14:4 — For the children of Joseph were two tribes, Manasseh and Ephraim: therefore they gave no part unto the Levites in the land, save cities to dwell *in*, with their suburbs for their cattle and for their substance.

- **Watchmen of.**

See: Watchman

- **Figurative.**

Heb 11:10 — For he looked for a city which hath foundations, whose builder and maker *is* God.

Heb 11:16 — But now they desire a better *country*, that is, an heavenly: wherefore God is not ashamed to be called their God: for he hath prepared for them a city.

Heb 12:22 — But ye are come unto mount Sion, and unto the city of the living God, the heavenly Jerusalem, and to an innumerable company of angels,

Heb 13:14 — For here have we no continuing city, but we seek one to come.

CITIES OF REFUGE **See: Refuge; Cities of**

CITIZENS

- **Duties of.**

Pr 16:14–15; 25:6–7; Ecc 8:2–4; Mt 17:24–27; 22:17–21; Mk 12:14–17; Lk 20:22–25; Ac 19:35–41; Ro 13:1–3, 5–7; 1Ti 2:1–2; 1Pe 2:13–17

Ex 22:28 — Thou shalt not revile the gods, nor curse the ruler of thy people.

Nu 27:20 — And thou shalt put some of thine honour upon him, that all the congregation of the children of Israel may be obedient.

Ezr 6:10 — That they may offer sacrifices of sweet savours unto the God of heaven, and pray for the life of the king, and of his sons.

Ezr 7:26 — And whosoever will not do the law of thy God, and the law of the king, let judgment be executed speedily upon him, whether *it be* unto death, or to banishment, or to confiscation of goods, or to imprisonment.

Ezr 10:8 — And that whosoever would not come within three days, according to the counsel of the princes and the elders, all his substance should be forfeited, and himself separated from the congregation of those that had been carried away.

Pr 24:21 — My son, fear thou the LORD and the king: *and* meddle not with them that are given to change:

Pr 25:15 — By long forbearing is a prince persuaded, and a soft tongue breaketh the bone.

Ecc 10:4 — If the spirit of the ruler rise up against thee, leave not thy place; for yielding pacifieth great offences.

Ecc 10:20 — Curse not the king, no not in thy thought; and curse not the rich in thy bedchamber: for a bird of the air shall carry the voice, and that which hath wings shall tell the matter.

Jer 29:7 — And seek the peace of the city whither I have caused you to be carried away captives, and pray unto the LORD for it: for in the peace thereof shall ye have peace.

Ac 23:5 — Then said Paul, I wist not, brethren, that he was the high priest: for it is written, Thou shalt not speak evil of the ruler of thy people.

Tit 3:1 — Put them in mind to be subject to principalities and powers, to obey magistrates, to be ready to every good work,

- **Rights of.**

Pr 23:1–3; Ac 19:36–39; 22:25–29; 24:18–19

Job 34:18 — *Is it fit* to say to a king, *Thou art* wicked? *and* to princes, *Ye are* ungodly?

Pr 14:28 — In the multitude of people *is* the king's honour: but in the want of people *is* the destruction of the prince.

Pr 14:35 — The king's favour *is* toward a wise servant: but his wrath is *against* him that causeth shame.

Pr 22:11 — He that loveth pureness of heart, *for* the grace of his lips the king *shall be* his friend.

Ac 16:37 — But Paul said unto them, They have beaten us openly uncondemned, being Romans, and have cast *us* into prison; and now do they thrust us out privily? nay verily; but let them come themselves and fetch us out.

Ac 25:5 — Let them therefore, said he, which among you are able, go down with *me*, and accuse this man, if there be any wickedness in him.

Ac 25:10 — Then said Paul, I stand at Caesar's judgment seat, where I ought to be judged: to the Jews have I done no wrong, as thou very well knowest.

Ac 25:16 — To whom I answered, It is not the manner of the Romans to deliver any man to die, before that he which is accused have the accusers face to face, and have licence to answer for himself concerning the crime laid against him.

See: Change of Venue

See: Court

See: Government

See: Justice

- **Loyal.**
  - **Instances of.**
    - **Israelites.**

Jos 1:16–18; 2Sa 3:36–37

2Sa 15:23 — And all the country wept with a loud voice, and all the people passed over: the king also himself passed over the brook Kidron, and all the people passed over, toward the way of the wilderness.

2Sa 15:30 — And David went up by the ascent of *mount* Olivet, and wept as he went up, and had his head covered, and he went barefoot: and all the people that *was* with him covered every man his head, and they went up, weeping as they went up.

2Sa 18:3 — But the people answered, Thou shalt not go forth: for if we flee away, they will not care for us; neither if half of us die, will they care for us: but now *thou art* worth ten thousand of us: therefore now *it is* better that thou succour us out of the city.

2Sa 21:17 — But Abishai the son of Zeruiah succoured him, and smote the Philistine, and killed him. Then the men of David sware unto him, saying, Thou shalt go no more out with us to battle, that thou quench not the light of Israel.

1Ch 12:38 — All these men of war, that could keep rank, came with a perfect heart to Hebron, to make David king over all Israel: and all the rest also of Israel *were* of one heart to make David king.

- **David.**
  1Sa 24:6–10; 26:6–16
  2Sa 1:14 — And David said unto him, How wast thou not afraid to stretch forth thine hand to destroy the LORD's anointed?
- **Hushai.**
  2Sa 17:15–16
- **David's soldiers.**
  2Sa 18:12–13; 23:15–16
- **Joab.**
  2Sa 19:5–6
- **Barzillai.**
  2Sa 19:32 — Now Barzillai was a very aged man, *even* fourscore years old: and he had provided the king of sustenance while he lay at Mahanaim; for he *was* a very great man.
- **Jehoiada.**
  2Ki 11:4–12
- **Mordecai.**
  Est 2:21–23

• Wicked and treasonable.

2Ti 3:1–4

Pr 17:11 — An evil *man* seeketh only rebellion: therefore a cruel messenger shall be sent against him.

Pr 19:10 — Delight is not seemly for a fool; much less for a servant to have rule over princes.

Pr 19:12 — The king's wrath *is* as the roaring of a lion; but his favour *is* as dew upon the grass.

Pr 20:2 — The fear of a king *is* as the roaring of a lion: *whoso* provoketh him to anger sinneth *against* his own soul.

2Pe 2:10 — But chiefly them that walk after the flesh in the lust of uncleanness, and despise government. Presumptuous *are they,* selfwilled, they are not afraid to speak evil of dignities.

Jude 1:8 — Likewise also these *filthy* dreamers defile the flesh, despise dominion, and speak evil of dignities.

See: Anarchy

• Instances of wicked.

- **Miriam and Aaron.**
  Nu 12:1–11
- **Korah, Dathan and Abiram.**
  Nu 16:1–50; 26:9
- **Shechemites.**
  Jgs 9:22
- **Ephraimites.**
  Jgs 12:1–4
- **Israelites.**
  1Sa 10:27; 1Ki 12:16–19
- **Absalom.**
  2Sa 15:10–13
- **Ahithophel.**
  2Sa 17:1–4
- **Sheba.**
  2Sa 20:1–2
- **Adonijah.**
  1Ki 1:5–7
- **Hadad and Jeroboam.**
  1Ki 11:14–26
- **Baasha.**
  1Ki 15:27
- **Zimri.**
  1Ki 16:9
- **Jozachar and Jozabad.**
  2Ki 12:19–21; 14:5
- **Amaziah.**
  2Ki 14:19
- **Amon.**
  2Ki 21:23
- **Shallum.**
  2Ki 15:10
- **Menahem.**
  2Ki 15:14
- **Pekah.**
  2Ki 15:25
- **Hoshea.**
  2Ki 15:30
- **Sons, Sennacherib.**
  2Ki 19:37
- **Ishmael.**
  Jer 40:14–41:18
- **Bigthan and Teresh.**
  Est 2:21
- **Jews.**
  Eze 17:12–20
- **Barabbas.**
  Mk 15:7
- **Theudas and four hundred seditious persons.**
  Acts 5:36–37
- **An Egyptian.**
  Acts 21:38

See: Country; love of

See: Government

See: Patriotism

See: Rulers

• **Figurative.**

Eph 2:19 — Now therefore ye are no more strangers and foreigners, but fellowcitizens with the saints, and of the household of God;

Php 3:20 — For our conversation is in heaven; from whence also we look for the Saviour, the Lord Jesus Christ:

CIVIL DAMAGES ↞See: Damages and Compensation

CIVIL ENGINEERING

Job 28:9–11

Jos 18:9 — And the men went and passed through the land, and described it by cities into seven parts in a book, and came *again* to Joshua to the host at Shiloh.

CIVIL SERVICE

• **School for.**

Da 1:3–5; 1:17–21

• **Appointment in, on account of merit.**

Ge 39:1–6; 41:38–44; Est 6:1–11; Da 1:17–21; Mt 25:14–15, 23–30; Lk 19:12–27

1Ki 11:28 — And the man Jeroboam *was* a mighty man of valour: and Solomon seeing the young man that he was industrious, he made him ruler over all the charge of the house of Joseph.

• **Corruption in.**

Da 6:4–17

Ne 5:15 — But the former governors that *had been* before me were chargeable unto the people, and had taken of them bread and wine, beside forty shekels of silver; yea, even their servants bare rule over the people: but so did not I, because of the fear of God.

Mk 15:15 — And *so* Pilate, willing to content the people, released Barabbas unto them, and delivered Jesus, when he had scourged *him,* to be crucified.

Ac 24:26 — He hoped also that money should have been given him of Paul, that he might loose him: wherefore he sent for him the oftener, and communed with him.

↞**See: Bribery**

• **Reform in.**

Ne 5:14–15

• **Influence in.**

1Ki 1:5–40; Mt 20:20–23

2Ki 4:13 — And he said unto him, Say now unto her, Behold, thou hast been careful for us with all this care; what *is* to be done for thee? wouldest thou be spoken for to the king, or to the captain of the host? And she answered, I dwell among mine own people.

Mk 10:35 — And James and John, the sons of Zebedee, come unto him, saying, Master, we would that thou shouldest do for us whatsoever we shall desire.

CLAIRVOYANCE

1Sa 28:13–14; 2Ki 6:15–17

↞**See: Sorcery**

CLAP

Ps 47:1 — O clap your hands, all ye people; shout unto God with the voice of triumph.

CLAUDA • An island near Crete.

Ac 27:16 — And running under a certain island which is called Clauda, we had much work to come by the boat:

CLAUDIA • A female disciple.

2Ti 4:21 — Do thy diligence to come before winter. Eubulus greeteth thee, and Pudens, and Linus, and Claudia, and all the brethren.

CLAUDIUS • Emperor of Rome.

Ac 11:28 — And there stood up one of them named Agabus, and signified by the spirit that there should be great dearth throughout all the world: which came to pass in the days of Claudius Caesar.

Ac 18:2 — And found a certain Jew named Aquila, born in Pontus, lately come from Italy, with his wife Priscilla; (because that Claudius had commanded all Jews to depart from Rome:) and came unto them.

CLAUDIUS LYSIUS

• **A Roman military officer.**

Ac 21:31–40; 22:23–30

• **Sends Paul to Felix.**

Ac 23:10–35

CLAY

• **Man formed from.**

Job 33:6 — Behold, I *am* according to thy wish in God's stead: I also am formed out of the clay.

• **Seals made of.**

Job 38:14 — It is turned as clay *to* the seal; and they stand as a garment.

• **Used by potter.**

Isa 29:16 — Surely your turning of things upside down shall be esteemed as the potter's clay: for shall the work say of him that made it, He made me not? or shall the thing framed say of him that framed it, He had no understanding?

Isa 41:25 — I have raised up *one* from the north, and he shall come: from the rising of the sun shall he call upon my name: and he shall come upon princes as *upon* morter, and as the potter treadeth clay.

Isa 45:9 — Woe unto him that striveth with his Maker! *Let* the potsherd *strive* with the potsherds of the earth. Shall the clay say to him that fashioneth it, What makest thou? or thy work, He hath no hands?

• **Blind man's eyes anointed with.**

Jn 9:6 — When he had thus spoken, he spat on the ground, and made clay of the spittle, and he anointed the eyes of the blind man with the clay,

• **Figurative.**

Job 4:19 — How much less *in* them that dwell in houses of clay, whose foundation *is* in the dust, *which* are crushed before the moth?

Ps 40:2 — He brought me up also out of an horrible pit, out of the miry clay, and set my feet upon a rock, *and* established my goings.

Isa 45:9 — Woe unto him that striveth with his Maker! *Let* the potsherd *strive* with the potsherds of the earth. Shall the clay say to him that fashioneth it, What makest thou? or thy work, He hath no hands?

Isa 64:8 — But now, O LORD, thou *art* our father; we *are* the clay, and thou our potter; and we all *are* the work of thy hand.

Jer 18:6 — O house of Israel, cannot I do with you as this potter? saith the LORD. Behold, as the clay *is* in the potter's hand, so *are* ye in mine hand, O house of Israel.

Ro 9:21 — Hath not the potter power over the clay, of the same lump to make one vessel unto honour, and another unto dishonour?

• Symbolic.

Da 2:33–41

CLEAN AND UNCLEAN ANIMALS

⇜See: Animals

⇜See: Birds; what species were unclean

⇜See: Fish; clean and unclean

⇜See: Insects

CLEANLINESS

• Taught by frequent ablutions.

⇜See: Ablution

⇜See: Purification

• Regulation relating to, in camp.

Dt 23:12–14

• Figurative.

Ps 51:7 — Purge me with hyssop, and I shall be clean: wash me, and I shall be whiter than snow.

Ps 51:10 — Create in me a clean heart, O God; and renew a right spirit within me.

Ps 73:1 — Truly God *is* good to Israel, *even* to such as are of a clean heart.

Pr 20:9 — Who can say, I have made my heart clean, I am pure from my sin?

Isa 1:16 — Wash you, make you clean; put away the evil of your doings from before mine eyes; cease to do evil;

Eze 36:25 — Then will I sprinkle clean water upon you, and ye shall be clean: from all your filthiness, and from all your idols, will I cleanse you.

1Jn 1:7 — But if we walk in the light, as he is in the light, we have fellowship one with another, and the blood of Jesus Christ his Son cleanseth us from all sin.

1Jn 1:9 — If we confess our sins, he is faithful and just to forgive us *our* sins, and to cleanse us from all unrighteousness.

Rev 1:5 — And from Jesus Christ, *who is* the faithful witness, *and* the first begotten of the dead, and the prince of the kings of the earth. Unto him that loved us, and washed us from our sins in his own blood,

CLEANSING ⇜See: Ablution

CLEMENCY

• Of David toward disloyal subjects.

• Shimei.

2Sa 16:5–13; 19:16–23

• Amasa.

2Sa 17:25 — And Absalom made Amasa captain of the host instead of Joab: which Amasa was a man's son, whose name *was* Ithra an Israelite, that went in to Abigail the daughter of Nahash, sister to Zeruiah Joab's mother.

2Sa 19:13 — And say ye to Amasa, *Art* thou not of my bone, and of my flesh? God do so to me, and more also, if thou be not captain of the host before me continually in the room of Joab.

• Divine.

⇜See: God, Long-Suffering of

⇜See: God, Mercy of

CLEMENT • A disciple at Philippi.

Php 4:3 — And I intreat thee also, true yokefellow, help those women which laboured with me in the gospel, with Clement also, and *with* other my fellowlabourers, whose names *are* in the book of life.

CLEOPAS • A disciple to whom Jesus appeared after his resurrection.

Lk 24:18 — And the one of them, whose name was Cleopas, answering said unto him, Art thou only a stranger in Jerusalem, and hast not known the things which are come to pass there in these days?

CLEOPHAS • Husband of one of the Marys.

Jn 19:25 — Now there stood by the cross of Jesus his mother, and his mother's sister, Mary the *wife* of Cleophas, and Mary Magdalene.

CLERGYMAN

⇜See: Minister, a Sacred Teacher

⇜See: Minister, Miscellany of Minor Sub-Topics

CLERK

• Town.

Ac 19:35 — And when the townclerk had appeased the people, he said, *Ye* men of Ephesus, what man is there that knoweth not how that the city of the Ephesians is a worshipper of the great goddess Diana, and of the *image* which fell down from Jupiter?

CLOKE (CLOAK)

• Paul's, left at Troas.

2Ti 4:13 — The cloke that I left at Troas with Carpus, when thou comest, bring *with thee,* and the books, *but* especially the parchments.

• **Figurative.**

Jn 15:22 — If I had not come and spoken unto them, they had not had sin: but now they have no cloke for their sin.

1Pe 2:16 — As free, and not using *your* liberty for a cloke of maliciousness, but as the servants of God.

CLOSET

• **Used as a place for prayer.**

Mt 6:6 — But thou, when thou prayest, enter into thy closet, and when thou hast shut thy door, pray to thy Father which is in secret; and thy Father which seeth in secret shall reward thee openly.

CLOTHING

• **Of the Israelites, waxed not old.**

Dt 8:4 — Thy raiment waxed not old upon thee, neither did thy foot swell, these forty years.

Dt 29:5 — And I have led you forty years in the wilderness: your clothes are not waxen old upon you, and thy shoe is not waxen old upon thy foot.

Ne 9:21 — Yea, forty years didst thou sustain them in the wilderness, *so that* they lacked nothing; their clothes waxed not old, and their feet swelled not.

See: Dress

CLOUD

• **Figurative.**

Jer 4:13 — Behold, he shall come up as clouds, and his chariots *shall be* as a whirlwind: his horses are swifter than eagles. Woe unto us! for we are spoiled.

Hos 6:4 — O Ephraim, what shall I do unto thee? O Judah, what shall I do unto thee? for your goodness *is* as a morning cloud, and as the early dew it goeth away.

Hos 13:3 — Therefore they shall be as the morning cloud, and as the early dew that passeth away, as the chaff *that* is driven with the whirlwind out of the floor, and as the smoke out of the chimney.

• **Symbolic.**

Rev 14:14 — And I looked, and behold a white cloud, and upon the cloud *one* sat like unto the Son of man, having on his head a golden crown, and in his hand a sharp sickle.

• **Pillar of.**

Ex 13:21–22; 24:16–18; 33:9–10; 40:36–38; Nu 9:15–23; 10:11–12, 33–36; 1Ki 8:10–11; 2Ch 7:1–3; Eze 10:18–19; 11:22–23; Lk 2:8–9; 9:34–35

Ex 14:19 — And the angel of God, which went before the camp of Israel, removed and went behind them; and the pillar of the cloud went from before their face, and stood behind them:

Ex 14:24 — And it came to pass, that in the morning watch the LORD looked unto the host of the Egyptians through the pillar of fire and of the cloud, and troubled the host of the Egyptians,

Ex 16:10 — And it came to pass, as Aaron spake unto the whole congregation of the children of Israel, that they looked toward the wilderness, and, behold, the glory of the LORD appeared in the cloud.

Ex 19:9 — And the LORD said unto Moses, Lo, I come unto thee in a thick cloud, that the people may hear when I speak with thee, and believe thee for ever. And Moses told the words of the people unto the LORD.

Ex 19:16 — And it came to pass on the third day in the morning, that there were thunders and lightnings, and a thick cloud upon the mount, and the voice of the trumpet exceeding loud; so that all the people that *was* in the camp trembled.

Ex 34:5 — And the LORD descended in the cloud, and stood with him there, and proclaimed the name of the LORD.

Le 16:2 — And the LORD said unto Moses, Speak unto Aaron thy brother, that he come not at all times into the holy *place* within the vail before the mercy seat, which *is* upon the ark; that he die not: for I will appear in the cloud upon the mercy seat.

Nu 11:25 — And the LORD came down in a cloud, and spake unto him, and took of the spirit that *was* upon him, and gave *it* unto the seventy elders: and it came to pass, *that,* when the spirit rested upon them, they prophesied, and did not cease.

Nu 12:5 — And the LORD came down in the pillar of the cloud, and stood in the door of the tabernacle, and called Aaron and Miriam: and they both came forth.

Nu 12:10 — And the cloud departed from off the tabernacle; and, behold, Miriam *became* leprous, *white* as snow: and Aaron looked upon Miriam, and, behold, *she was* leprous.

Nu 14:10 — But all the congregation bade stone them with stones. And the glory of the LORD appeared in the tabernacle of the congregation before all the children of Israel.

Nu 16:19 — And Korah gathered all the congregation against them unto the door of the tabernacle of the congregation: and the glory of the LORD appeared unto all the congregation.

Nu 16:42 — And it came to pass, when the congregation was gathered against Moses and against Aaron, that they looked toward the tabernacle of the congregation: and, behold, the cloud covered it, and the glory of the LORD appeared.

Dt 1:33 — Who went in the way before you, to search you out a place to pitch your tents *in,* in fire by night, to shew you by what way ye should go, and in a cloud by day.

Dt 31:15 — And the LORD appeared in the tabernacle in a pillar of a cloud: and the pillar of the cloud stood over the door of the tabernacle.

Ne 9:12 — Moreover thou leddest them in the day by a cloudy pillar; and in the night by a pillar of fire, to give them light in the way wherein they should go.

Ne 9:19 — Yet thou in thy manifold mercies forsookest them not in the wilderness: the pillar of the cloud departed not from them by day, to lead them in the way; neither the pillar of fire by night, to shew them light, and the way wherein they should go.

Ps 78:14 — In the daytime also he led them with a cloud, and all the night with a light of fire.

Ps 105:39 — He spread a cloud for a covering; and fire to give light in the night.

Isa 4:5 — And the LORD will create upon every dwelling place of mount Zion, and upon her assemblies, a cloud and smoke by day, and the shining of a flaming fire by night: for upon all the glory *shall be* a defence.

Isa 6:1 — In the year that king Uzziah died I saw also the Lord sitting upon a throne, high and lifted up, and his train filled the temple.

Isa 6:4 — And the posts of the door moved at the voice of him that cried, and the house was filled with smoke.

Mt 17:5 — While he yet spake, behold, a bright cloud overshadowed them: and behold a voice out of the cloud, which said, This is my beloved Son, in whom I am well pleased; hear ye him.

- **Appearances of.**
  - **In Ezekiel's vision.**

Eze 10:3–4; 11:22–23

Eze 10:18 — Then the glory of the LORD departed from off the threshold of the house, and stood over the cherubims.

CNIDUS

- **A city in Asia Minor.**

Ac 27:7 — And when we had sailed slowly many days, and scarce were come over against Cnidus, the wind not suffering us, we sailed under Crete, over against Salmone;

COAL

- **Figurative.**

Pr 25:22 — For thou shalt heap coals of fire upon his head, and the LORD shall reward thee.

- **Symbolic.**

Isa 6:6–7

2Sa 14:7 — And, behold, the whole family is risen against thine handmaid, and they said, Deliver him that smote his brother, that we may kill him, for the life of his brother whom he slew; and we will destroy the heir also: and so they shall quench my coal which is left, and shall not leave to my husband *neither* name nor remainder upon the earth.

COAL OIL ⇜See: Oil

COAT OF MAIL

1Sa 17:5 — And *he had* an helmet of brass upon his head, and he *was* armed with a coat of mail; and the weight of the coat *was* five thousand shekels of brass.

1Sa 17:38 — And Saul armed David with his armour, and he put an helmet of brass upon his head; also he armed him with a coat of mail.

1Ki 22:34 — And a *certain* man drew a bow at a venture, and smote the king of Israel between the joints of the harness: wherefore he said unto the driver of his chariot, Turn thine hand, and carry me out of the host; for I am wounded.

2Ch 18:33 — And a *certain* man drew a bow at a venture, and smote the king of Israel between the joints of the harness: therefore he said to his chariot man, Turn thine hand, that thou mayest carry me out of the host; for I am wounded.

COCK CROWING

Mt 26:74–75

Mt 26:34 — Jesus said unto him, Verily I say unto thee, That this night, before the cock crow, thou shalt deny me thrice.

Mk 13:35 — Watch ye therefore: for ye know not when the master of the house cometh, at even, or at midnight, or at the cockcrowing, or in the morning:

Mk 14:30 — And Jesus saith unto him, Verily I say unto thee, That this day, *even* in this night, before the cock crow twice, thou shalt deny me thrice.

Mk 14:68 — But he denied, saying, I know not, neither understand I what thou sayest. And he went out into the porch; and the cock crew.

Mk 14:72 — And the second time the cock crew. And Peter called to mind the word that Jesus said unto him, Before the cock crow twice, thou shalt deny me thrice. And when he thought thereon, he wept.

COCKATRICE

- **A fabulous serpent.**
- **Figurative.**

Isa 11:8 — And the sucking child shall play on the hole of the asp, and the weaned child shall put his hand on the cockatrice's den.

Isa 14:29 — Rejoice not thou, whole Palestina, because the rod of him that smote thee is broken: for out of the serpent's root shall come forth a cockatrice, and his fruit *shall be* a fiery flying serpent.

Isa 59:5 — They hatch cockatrice' eggs, and weave the spider's web: he that eateth of their eggs dieth, and that which is crushed breaketh out into a viper.

Jer 8:17 — For, behold, I will send serpents, cockatrices, among you, which *will* not *be* charmed, and they shall bite you, saith the LORD.

COCKLE • A general term for obnoxious plants.

Job 31:40 — Let thistles grow instead of wheat, and cockle instead of barley. The words of Job are ended.

COERCION

- **Religious.**

2Ch 15:12–15; Da 3:1–30; 6:26–27

Ex 22:20 — He that sacrificeth unto *any* god, save unto the LORD only, he shall be utterly destroyed.

⇜See: Intolerance, Religious

COFFER

- **A chest.**

1Sa 6:8 — And take the ark of the LORD, and lay it upon the cart; and put the jewels of gold, which ye return him *for* a trespass offering, in a coffer by the side thereof; and send it away, that it may go.

1Sa 6:11 — And they laid the ark of the LORD upon the cart, and the coffer with the mice of gold and the images of their emerods.

1Sa 6:15 — And the Levites took down the ark of the LORD, and the coffer that *was* with it, wherein the jewels of gold *were,* and put *them* on the great stone: and the men of Beth-shemesh offered burnt offerings and sacrificed sacrifices the same day unto the LORD.

Eze 27:24 — These *were* thy merchants in all sorts *of things,* in blue clothes, and broidered work, and in chests of rich apparel, bound with cords, and made of cedar, among thy merchandise.

COFFIN

Ge 50:26 — So Joseph died, *being* an hundred and ten years old: and they embalmed him, and he was put in a coffin in Egypt.

See: Burial

COIN **See: Money**

COL-HOZEH • Father of Baruch.

Ne 11:5 — And Maaseiah the son of Baruch, the son of Col-hozeh, the son of Hazaiah, the son of Adaiah, the son of Joiarib, the son of Zechariah, the son of Shiloni.

COLLECTION

• Of money, for the poor.

See: Alms

See: Beneficence

See: Giving

See: Liberality

COLLEGE

• Second quarter of the city of Jerusalem.

2Ki 22:14 — So Hilkiah the priest, and Ahikam, and Achbor, and Shaphan, and Asahiah, went unto Huldah the prophetess, the wife of Shallum the son of Tikvah, the son of Harhas, keeper of the wardrobe; (now she dwelt in Jerusalem in the college;) and they communed with her.

2Ch 34:22 — And Hilkiah, and *they* that the king *had appointed,* went to Huldah the prophetess, the wife of Shallum the son of Tikvath, the son of Hasrah, keeper of the wardrobe; (now she dwelt in Jerusalem in the college:) and they spake to her to that *effect.*

See: School

COLLUSION

• In sin.

Le 20:4–5

See: Complicity

See: Connivance

COLONIZATION

• Of conquered countries and people.

Ezr 4:9–10

2Ki 17:6 — In the ninth year of Hoshea the king of Assyria took Samaria, and carried Israel away into Assyria, and placed them in Halah and in Habor *by* the river of Gozan, and in the cities of the Medes.

2Ki 17:24 — And the king of Assyria brought *men* from Babylon, and from Cuthah, and from Ava, and from Hamath, and from Sepharvaim, and placed *them* in the cities of Samaria instead of the children of Israel: and they possessed Samaria, and dwelt in the cities thereof.

COLORS

• Symbolic uses of.

• Black: a symbol of affliction and calamity.

Job 10:20–22; Ps 107:10–11; Joel 3:14–15; Zep 1:14–15

Job 3:5 — Let darkness and the shadow of death stain it; let a cloud dwell upon it; let the blackness of the day terrify it.

Job 30:26 — When I looked for good, then evil came *unto me:* and when I waited for light, there came darkness.

Ps 143:3 — For the enemy hath persecuted my soul; he hath smitten my life down to the ground; he hath made me to dwell in darkness, as those that have been long dead.

Isa 5:30 — And in that day they shall roar against them like the roaring of the sea: and if *one* look unto the land, behold darkness *and* sorrow, and the light is darkened in the heavens thereof.

Isa 8:22 — And they shall look unto the earth; and behold trouble and darkness, dimness of anguish; and *they shall be* driven to darkness.

Isa 9:19 — Through the wrath of the LORD of hosts is the land darkened, and the people shall be as the fuel of the fire: no man shall spare his brother.

Isa 24:11 — *There is* a crying for wine in the streets; all joy is darkened, the mirth of the land is gone.

Isa 50:3 — I clothe the heavens with blackness, and I make sackcloth their covering.

Joel 2:6 — Before their face the people shall be much pained: all faces shall gather blackness.

Joel 2:10 — The earth shall quake before them; the heavens shall tremble: the sun and the moon shall be dark, and the stars shall withdraw their shining:

Am 5:8 — *Seek him* that maketh the seven stars and Orion, and turneth the shadow of death into the morning, and maketh the day dark with night: that calleth for the waters of the sea, and poureth them out upon the face of the earth: The LORD *is* his name:

Na 2:10 — She is empty, and void, and waste: and the heart melteth, and the knees smite together, and much pain *is* in all loins, and the faces of them all gather blackness.

Mt 8:12 — But the children of the kingdom shall be cast out into outer darkness: there shall be weeping and gnashing of teeth.

Mt 22:13 — Then said the king to the servants, Bind him hand and foot, and take him away, and cast *him* into outer darkness; there shall be weeping and gnashing of teeth.

Mt 25:30 — And cast ye the unprofitable servant into outer darkness: there shall be weeping and gnashing of teeth.

2Pe 2:4 — For if God spared not the angels that sinned, but cast *them* down to hell, and delivered *them* into chains of darkness, to be reserved unto judgment;

Jude 1:13 — Raging waves of the sea, foaming out their own shame; wandering stars, to whom is reserved the blackness of darkness for ever.

Rev 16:10 — And the fifth angel poured out his vial upon the seat of the beast; and his kingdom was full of darkness; and they gnawed their tongues for pain,

• Blue: symbol of deity.

Ex 25:3–4; 39:1–5; Nu 4:5–12; 15:38–40

Ex 24:10 — And they saw the God of Israel: and *there was* under his feet as it were a paved work of a sapphire stone, and as it were the body of heaven in *his* clearness.

Ex 26:1 — Moreover thou shalt make the tabernacle *with* ten curtains *of* fine twined linen, and blue, and purple, and scarlet: *with* cherubims of cunning work shalt thou make them.

Ex 28:28 — And they shall bind the breastplate by the rings thereof unto the rings of the ephod with a lace of blue, that *it* may be above the curious girdle of the ephod, and that the breastplate be not loosed from the ephod.

Ex 28:37 — And thou shalt put it on a blue lace, that it may be upon the mitre; upon the forefront of the mitre it shall be.

Ex 38:18 — And the hanging for the gate of the court *was* needlework, *of* blue, and purple, and scarlet, and fine twined linen: and twenty cubits *was* the length, and the height in the breadth *was* five cubits, answerable to the hangings of the court.

Ex 39:21 — And they did bind the breastplate by his rings unto the rings of the ephod with a lace of blue, that it might be above the curious girdle of the ephod, and that the breastplate might not be loosed from the ephod; as the LORD commanded Moses.

Ex 39:24 — And they made upon the hems of the robe pomegranates *of* blue, and purple, and scarlet, *and* twined *linen.*

Ex 39:29 — And a girdle *of* fine twined linen, and blue, and purple, and scarlet, *of* needlework; as the LORD commanded Moses.

Ex 39:31 — And they tied unto it a lace of blue, to fasten *it* on high upon the mitre; as the LORD commanded Moses.

2Ch 2:7 — Send me now therefore a man cunning to work in gold, and in silver, and in brass, and in iron, and in purple, and crimson, and blue, and that can skill to grave with the cunning men that *are* with me in Judah and in Jerusalem, whom David my father did provide.

2Ch 2:14 — The son of a woman of the daughters of Dan, and his father *was* a man of Tyre, skilful to work in gold, and in silver, in brass, in iron, in stone, and in timber, in purple, in blue, and in fine linen, and in crimson; also to grave any manner of graving, and to find out every device which shall be put to him, with thy cunning men, and with the cunning men of my lord David thy father.

2Ch 3:14 — And he made the vail *of* blue, and purple, and crimson, and fine linen, and wrought cherubims thereon.

Jer 10:9 — Silver spread into plates is brought from Tarshish, and gold from Uphaz, the work of the workman, and of the hands of the founder: blue and purple is their clothing: they *are* all the work of cunning *men.*

Eze 1:26 — And above the firmament that *was* over their heads *was* the likeness of a throne, as the appearance of a sapphire stone: and upon the likeness of the throne *was* the likeness as the appearance of a man above upon it.

Eze 10:1 — Then I looked, and, behold, in the firmament that was above the head of the cherubims there appeared over them as it were a sapphire stone, as the appearance of the likeness of a throne.

• Symbol of royalty.

Est 8:15 — And Mordecai went out from the presence of the king in royal apparel of blue and white, and with a great crown of gold, and with a garment of fine linen and purple: and the city of Shushan rejoiced and was glad.

Eze 23:6 — *Which were* clothed with blue, captains and rulers, all of them desirable young men, horsemen riding upon horses.

• Crimson, red, purple, and scarlet: symbols of various ideas.

• Of iniquity.

Rev 17:3–4

Isa 1:18 — Come now, and let us reason together, saith the LORD: though your sins be as scarlet, they shall be as white as snow; though they be red like crimson, they shall be as wool.

Rev 18:12 — The merchandise of gold, and silver, and precious stones, and of pearls, and fine linen, and purple, and silk, and scarlet, and all thyine wood, and all manner vessels of ivory, and all manner vessels of most precious wood, and of brass, and iron, and marble,

Rev 18:16 — And saying, Alas, alas, that great city, that was clothed in fine linen, and purple, and scarlet, and decked with gold, and precious stones, and pearls!

• Of royalty.

Jgs 8:26 — And the weight of the golden earrings that he requested was a thousand and seven hundred *shekels* of gold; beside ornaments, and collars, and purple raiment that *was* on the kings of Midian, and beside the chains that *were* about their camels' necks.

Da 5:7 — The king cried aloud to bring in the astrologers, the Chaldeans, and the soothsayers. *And* the king spake, and said to the wise *men* of Babylon, Whosoever shall read this writing, and shew me the interpretation thereof, shall be clothed with scarlet, and *have* a chain of gold about his neck, and shall be the third ruler in the kingdom.

Da 5:16 — And I have heard of thee, that thou canst make interpretations, and dissolve doubts: now if thou canst read the writing, and make known to me the interpretation thereof, thou shalt be clothed with scarlet, and *have* a chain of gold about thy neck, and shalt be the third ruler in the kingdom.

Da 5:29 — Then commanded Belshazzar, and they clothed Daniel with scarlet, and *put* a chain of gold about his neck, and made a proclamation concerning him, that he should be the third ruler in the kingdom.

Mt 27:28 — And they stripped him, and put on him a scarlet robe.

• Prosperity.

2Sa 1:24 — Ye daughters of Israel, weep over Saul, who clothed you in scarlet, with *other* delights, who put on ornaments of gold upon your apparel.

Pr 31:21 — She is not afraid of the snow for her household: for all her household *are* clothed with scarlet.

La 4:5 — They that did feed delicately are desolate in the streets: they that were brought up in scarlet embrace dunghills.

• Conquest.

Na 2:3 — The shield of his mighty men is made red, the valiant men *are* in scarlet: the chariots *shall be* with flaming torches in the day of his preparation, and the fir trees shall be terribly shaken.

Rev 12:3 — And there appeared another wonder in heaven; and behold a great red dragon, having seven heads and ten horns, and seven crowns upon his heads.

• These colors symbolize types and shadows of the atonement.

Ex 25:3–5; 28:4–6; 35:5–7; 39:1–43; Le 14:51–52; Nu 4:7–8; 19:5–6; Isa 63:1–3; Heb 9:19–23

Ex 26:1 — Moreover thou shalt make the tabernacle *with* ten curtains *of* fine twined linen, and blue, and purple, and scarlet: *with* cherubims of cunning work shalt thou make them.

Ex 26:14 — And thou shalt make a covering for the tent *of* rams' skins dyed red, and a covering above *of* badgers' skins.

Ex 26:31 — And thou shalt make a vail *of* blue, and purple, and scarlet, and fine twined linen of cunning work: with cherubims shall it be made:

Ex 26:36 — And thou shalt make an hanging for the door of the tent, *of* blue, and purple, and scarlet, and fine twined linen, wrought with needlework.

Ex 27:16 — And for the gate of the court *shall be* an hanging of twenty cubits, *of* blue, and purple, and scarlet, and fine twined linen, wrought with needlework: *and* their pillars *shall be* four, and their sockets four.

Ex 28:8 — And the curious girdle of the ephod, which *is* upon it, shall be of the same, according to the work thereof; *even of* gold, *of* blue, and purple, and scarlet, and fine twined linen.

Ex 28:15 — And thou shalt make the breastplate of judgment with cunning work; after the work of the ephod thou shalt make it; *of* gold, *of* blue, and *of* purple, and *of* scarlet, and *of* fine twined linen, shalt thou make it.

Ex 28:31 — And thou shalt make the robe of the ephod all *of* blue.

Ex 28:33 — And *beneath* upon the hem of it thou shalt make pomegranates *of* blue, and *of* purple, and *of* scarlet, round about the hem thereof; and bells of gold between them round about:

Ex 35:23 — And every man, with whom was found blue, and purple, and scarlet, and fine linen, and goats' *hair,* and red skins of rams, and badgers' skins, brought *them.*

Ex 35:25 — And all the women that were wise hearted did spin with their hands, and brought that which they had spun, *both* of blue, and of purple, *and* of scarlet, and of fine linen.

Ex 35:35 — Them hath he filled with wisdom of heart, to work all manner of work, of the engraver, and of the cunning workman, and of the embroiderer, in blue, and in purple, in scarlet, and in fine linen, and of the weaver, *even* of them that do any work, and of those that devise cunning work.

Ex 36:8 — And every wise hearted man among them that wrought the work of the tabernacle made ten curtains *of* fine twined linen, and blue, and purple, and scarlet: *with* cherubims of cunning work made he them.

Ex 36:19 — And he made a covering for the tent *of* rams' skins dyed red, and a covering *of* badgers' skins above *that.*

Ex 36:35 — And he made a vail *of* blue, and purple, and scarlet, and fine twined linen: *with* cherubims made he it of cunning work.

Ex 36:37 — And he made an hanging for the tabernacle door *of* blue, and purple, and scarlet, and fine twined linen, of needlework;

Ex 38:18 — And the hanging for the gate of the court *was* needlework, *of* blue, and purple, and scarlet, and fine twined linen: and twenty cubits *was* the length, and the height in the breadth *was* five cubits, answerable to the hangings of the court.

Ex 38:23 — And with him *was* Aholiab, son of Ahisamach, of the tribe of Dan, an engraver, and a cunning workman, and an embroiderer in blue, and in purple, and in scarlet, and fine linen.

Le 14:4 — Then shall the priest command to take for him that is to be cleansed two birds alive *and* clean, and cedar wood, and scarlet, and hyssop:

Le 14:6 — As for the living bird, he shall take it, and the cedar wood, and the scarlet, and the hyssop, and shall dip them and the living bird in the blood of the bird *that was* killed over the running water:

Le 14:49 — And he shall take to cleanse the house two birds, and cedar wood, and scarlet, and hyssop:

Nu 4:13 — And they shall take away the ashes from the altar, and spread a purple cloth thereon:

Nu 19:2 — This *is* the ordinance of the law which the LORD hath commanded, saying, Speak unto the children of Israel, that they bring thee a red heifer without spot, wherein *is* no blemish, *and* upon which never came yoke:

- **White: symbol of holiness.**
  - **The high priest's holy garments were of white linen.**

Le 16:4 — He shall put on the holy linen coat, and he shall have the linen breeches upon his flesh, and shall be girded with a linen girdle, and with the linen mitre shall he be attired: these *are* holy garments; therefore shall he wash his flesh in water, and *so* put them on.

Le 16:32 — And the priest, whom he shall anoint, and whom he shall consecrate to minister in the priest's office in his father's stead, shall make the atonement, and shall put on the linen clothes, *even* the holy garments:

- **Choir singers arrayed in white.**

2Ch 5:12 — Also the Levites *which were* the singers, all of them of Asaph, of Heman, of Jeduthun, with their sons and their brethren, *being* arrayed in white linen, having cymbals and psalteries and harps, stood at the east end of the altar, and with them an hundred and twenty priests sounding with trumpets:)

- **Scriptures employing the symbol.**

Mt 17:1–2; 28:2–3; Rev 1:13–14; 3:4–5; 7:13–14

Ps 51:7 — Purge me with hyssop, and I shall be clean: wash me, and I shall be whiter than snow.

Ecc 9:8 — Let thy garments be always white; and let thy head lack no ointment.

Isa 1:18 — Come now, and let us reason together, saith the LORD: though your sins be as scarlet, they shall be as white as snow; though they be red like crimson, they shall be as wool.

Da 7:9 — I beheld till the thrones were cast down, and the Ancient of days did sit, whose garment *was* white as snow, and the hair of his head like the pure wool: his throne *was like* the fiery flame, *and* his wheels *as* burning fire.

Da 11:35 — And *some* of them of understanding shall fall, to try them, and to purge, and to make *them* white, *even* to the time of the end: because *it is* yet for a time appointed.

Da 12:10 — Many shall be purified, and made white, and tried; but the wicked shall do wickedly: and none of the wicked shall understand; but the wise shall understand.

Mk 9:3 — And his raiment became shining, exceeding white as snow; so as no fuller on earth can white them.

Rev 2:17 — He that hath an ear, let him hear what the Spirit saith unto the churches; To him that overcometh will I give to eat of the hidden manna, and will give him a white stone, and in the stone a new name written, which no man knoweth saving he that receiveth *it*.

Rev 3:18 — I counsel thee to buy of me gold tried in the fire, that thou mayest be rich; and white raiment, that thou mayest be clothed, and *that* the shame of thy nakedness do not appear; and anoint thine eyes with eyesalve, that thou mayest see.

Rev 4:4 — And round about the throne *were* four and twenty seats: and upon the seats I saw four and twenty elders sitting, clothed in white raiment; and they had on their heads crowns of gold.

Rev 6:2 — And I saw, and behold a white horse: and he that sat on him had a bow; and a crown was given unto him: and he went forth conquering, and to conquer.

Rev 6:11 — And white robes were given unto every one of them; and it was said unto them, that they should rest yet for a little season, until their fellowservants also and their brethren, that should be killed as they *were*, should be fulfilled.

Rev 7:9 — After this I beheld, and, lo, a great multitude, which no man could number, of all nations, and kindreds, and people, and tongues, stood before the throne, and before the Lamb, clothed with white robes, and palms in their hands;

Rev 15:6 — And the seven angels came out of the temple, having the seven plagues, clothed in pure and white linen, and having their breasts girded with golden girdles.

Rev 19:8 — And to her was granted that she should be arrayed in fine linen, clean and white: for the fine linen is the righteousness of saints.

Rev 19:11 — And I saw heaven opened, and behold a white horse; and he that sat upon him *was* called Faithful and True, and in righteousness he doth judge and make war.

Rev 19:14 — And the armies *which were* in heaven followed him upon white horses, clothed in fine linen, white and clean.

Rev 20:11 — And I saw a great white throne, and him that sat on it, from whose face the earth and the heaven fled away; and there was found no place for them.

COLOSSE • A city of Phrygia.

Col 1:7–8

Col 1:2 — To the saints and faithful brethren in Christ which are at Colosse: Grace *be* unto you, and peace, from God our Father and the Lord Jesus Christ.

COLT

- **Ridden by Jesus.**

Mt 21:2 — Saying unto them, Go into the village over against you, and straightway ye shall find an ass tied, and a colt with her: loose *them*, and bring *them* unto me.

Mt 21:5 — Tell ye the daughter of Sion, Behold, thy King cometh unto thee, meek, and sitting upon an ass, and a colt the foal of an ass.

Mt 21:7 — And brought the ass, and the colt, and put on them their clothes, and they set *him* thereon.

Mk 11:2 — And saith unto them, Go your way into the village over against you: and as soon as ye be entered into it, ye shall find a colt tied, whereon never man sat; loose him, and bring *him*.

Jn 12:15 — Fear not, daughter of Sion: behold, thy King cometh, sitting on an ass's colt.

COMFORT

➜See: **Afflictions; consolation in**

➜See: **Righteous; promises to, expressed or implied**

COMFORTER

➜See: **God, Grace of**

➜See: **Holy Spirit**

COMMANDMENTS

Ex 13:8–10; 20:3–17; Dt 4:9–10; 5:6–21; 6:4–9; 11:18–21; 32:46–47; Jos 8:30–35; 2Ch 17:7–9; Ne 8:2–8; Ps 78:1–7; Pr 3:3–4; 6:20–21; 7:1–4; Zec 7:9–10; 8:16–17

Dt 4:5 — Behold, I have taught you statutes and judgments, even as the LORD my God commanded me, that ye should do so in the land whither ye go to possess it.

Isa 57:8 — Behind the doors also and the posts hast thou set up thy remembrance: for thou hast discovered *thyself to another* than me, and art gone up; thou hast enlarged thy bed, and made thee *a covenant* with them; thou lovedst their bed where thou sawest *it*.

Jer 11:4 — Which I commanded your fathers in the day *that* I brought them forth out of the land of Egypt, from the iron furnace, saying, Obey my voice, and do them, according to all which I command you: so shall ye be my people, and I will be your God:

- **Precepts of Jesus.**
  - **Explicitly stated, or implied in didactic discourse.**

Mt 5:22–24; 5:27–6:4; 6:6–8, 16–25; 6:31–7:29; 10:5–42; 18:8–10, 15–17, 21–22; 19:16–19; 20:25–28; 22:34–40; 24:42–51; 25:34–46; Mk 6:7–11; 9:38–39, 42–50; 10:11–12, 17–22; 13:33–37; Lk 6:27–42; 10:28–37; 12:12–31; Jn 13:34–35; 14:23–24; 15:4–5, 7–12, 20–22

Mt 5:16 — Let your light so shine before men, that they may see your good works, and glorify your Father which is in heaven.

Mt 16:24 — Then said Jesus unto his disciples, If any *man* will come after me, let him deny himself, and take up his cross, and follow me.

Mt 22:21 — They say unto him, Caesar's. Then saith he unto them, Render therefore unto Caesar the things which are Caesar's; and unto God the things that are God's.

Mk 8:34 — And when he had called the people *unto him* with his disciples also, he said unto them, Whosoever will come after me, let him deny himself, and take up his cross, and follow me.

Mk 9:35 — And he sat down, and called the twelve, and saith unto them, If any man desire to be first, *the same* shall be last of all, and servant of all.

Mk 10:9 — What therefore God hath joined together, let not man put asunder.

Mk 11:22 — And Jesus answering saith unto them, Have faith in God.

Mk 12:17 — And Jesus answering said unto them, Render to Caesar the things that are Caesar's, and to God the things that are God's. And they marvelled at him.

Lk 13:24 — Strive to enter in at the strait gate: for many, I say unto you, will seek to enter in, and shall not be able.

Jn 7:24 — Judge not according to the appearance, but judge righteous judgment.

Jn 14:11 — Believe me that I *am* in the Father, and the Father in me: or else believe me for the very works' sake.

Jn 14:15 — If ye love me, keep my commandments.

Jn 15:2 — Every branch in me that beareth not fruit he taketh away: and every *branch* that beareth fruit, he purgeth it, that it may bring forth more fruit.

Jn 15:14 — Ye are my friends, if ye do whatsoever I command you.

Jn 15:17 — These things I command you, that ye love one another.

➜See: **Decalogue**

➜See: **Table**

- **Precepts of St. Paul.**
  - **Explicitly stated or implied in didactic epistles.**

Ro 12:1–3, 6–21; 13:8–14; 14:19–21; 15:1–2; 1Co 8:7–13; 10:7–10, 28–29, 31–32; 16:13–14; Gal 6:1–2; Eph 4:1–3; 4:26–5:6; 5:15–21; 6:10–11, 13–18; Php 1:27–28; 2:2–8, 12–15; 4:4–6, 8–9; Col 2:20–3:2; 3:8–9, 12–17; 1Th 4:5–6, 9–12; 5:12–22; 2Th 3:6–15; 1Ti 2:1–2, 8–12; 3:2–13; 4:1–7; 4:12–5:14; 5:16–21; 6:11–14, 17–20; 2Ti 1:13–14; 2:22–25; 3:2–5; Tit 1:5–14; 2:2–5, 9–12; 3:1–2; Heb 6:11–12; 10:22–25; 12:1–5, 12–16; 13:1–3, 15–17

1Co 8:1 — Now as touching things offered unto idols, we know that we all have knowledge. Knowledge puffeth up, but charity edifieth.

1Co 10:24 — Let no man seek his own, but every man another's *wealth*.

1Co 14:20 — Brethren, be not children in understanding: howbeit in malice be ye children, but in understanding be men.

2Co 13:7 — Now I pray to God that ye do no evil; not that we should appear approved, but that ye should do that which is honest, though we be as reprobates.

Gal 5:1 — Stand fast therefore in the liberty wherewith Christ hath made us free, and be not entangled again with the yoke of bondage.

Gal 5:16 — *This* I say then, Walk in the Spirit, and ye shall not fulfil the lust of the flesh.

Eph 5:11 — And have no fellowship with the unfruitful works of darkness, but rather reprove *them*.

Col 2:6 — As ye have therefore received Christ Jesus the Lord, *so* walk ye in him:

Col 2:16 — Let no man therefore judge you in meat, or in drink, or in respect of an holyday, or of the new moon, or of the sabbath *days*:

Col 3:5 — Mortify therefore your members which are upon the earth; fornication, uncleanness, inordinate affection, evil concupiscence, and covetousness, which is idolatry:

Col 3:23 — And whatsoever ye do, do *it* heartily, as to the Lord, and not unto men;

1Th 3:12 — And the Lord make you to increase and abound in love one toward another, and toward all *men,* even as we *do* toward you:

1Th 4:1 — Furthermore then we beseech you, brethren, and exhort *you* by the Lord Jesus, that as ye have received of us how ye ought to walk and to please God, *so* ye would abound more and more.

1Th 4:3 — For this is the will of God, *even* your sanctification, that ye should abstain from fornication:

1Th 5:6 — Therefore let us not sleep, as *do* others; but let us watch and be sober.

1Th 5:8 — But let us, who are of the day, be sober, putting on the breastplate of faith and love; and for an helmet, the hope of salvation.

2Th 2:15 — Therefore, brethren, stand fast, and hold the traditions which ye have been taught, whether by word, or our epistle.

1Ti 1:4 — Neither give heed to fables and endless genealogies, which minister questions, rather than godly edifying which is in faith: *so do.*

2Ti 2:19 — Nevertheless the foundation of God standeth sure, having this seal, The Lord knoweth them that are his. And, Let every one that nameth the name of Christ depart from iniquity.

Tit 3:8 — *This is* a faithful saying, and these things I will that thou affirm constantly, that they which have believed in God might be careful to maintain good works. These things are good and profitable unto men.

Heb 6:1 — Therefore leaving the principles of the doctrine of Christ, let us go on unto perfection; not laying again the foundation of repentance from dead works, and of faith toward God,

Heb 13:5 — *Let your* conversation *be* without covetousness; *and be* content with such things as ye have: for he hath said, I will never leave thee, nor forsake thee.

Heb 13:7 — Remember them which have the rule over you, who have spoken unto you the word of God: whose faith follow, considering the end of *their* conversation.

Heb 13:9 — Be not carried about with divers and strange doctrines. For *it is* a good thing that the heart be established with grace; not with meats, which have not profited them that have been occupied therein.

• Precepts of other apostles.

• Explicitly stated or implied in didactic epistles.

Jas 1:21–22; 2:1–4, 8–12; 4:7–11, 13–15; 5:7–12; 1Pe 1:13–17; 2:11–25; 3:8–12, 15–17; 4:1–16; 5:1–3, 5–9; 2Pe 1:5–7; 1Jn 3:10–23; 4:7–8, 11–12, 15–16; 2Jn 1:5–6; Jude 1:3–4, 20–23; Rev 3:18–19

Jas 1:16 — Do not err, my beloved brethren.

Jas 1:19 — Wherefore, my beloved brethren, let every man be swift to hear, slow to speak, slow to wrath:

Jas 3:1 — My brethren, be not many masters, knowing that we shall receive the greater condemnation.

Jas 5:16 — Confess *your* faults one to another, and pray one for another, that ye may be healed. The effectual fervent prayer of a righteous man availeth much.

2Pe 1:10 — Wherefore the rather, brethren, give diligence to make your calling and election sure: for if ye do these things, ye shall never fall:

2Pe 3:14 — Wherefore, beloved, seeing that ye look for such things, be diligent that ye may be found of him in peace, without spot, and blameless.

2Pe 3:18 — But grow in grace, and *in* the knowledge of our Lord and Saviour Jesus Christ. To him *be* glory both now and for ever. Amen.

1Jn 2:15 — Love not the world, neither the things *that are* in the world. If any man love the world, the love of the Father is not in him.

1Jn 2:28 — And now, little children, abide in him; that, when he shall appear, we may have confidence, and not be ashamed before him at his coming.

1Jn 4:1 — Beloved, believe not every spirit, but try the spirits whether they are of God: because many false prophets are gone out into the world.

1Jn 4:21 — And this commandment have we from him, That he who loveth God love his brother also.

1Jn 5:21 — Little children, keep yourselves from idols. Amen.

3Jn 1:11 — Beloved, follow not that which is evil, but that which is good. He that doeth good is of God: but he that doeth evil hath not seen God.

Rev 3:11 — Behold, I come quickly: hold that fast which thou hast, that no man take thy crown.

Rev 22:17 — And the Spirit and the bride say, Come. And let him that heareth say, Come. And let him that is athirst come. And whosoever will, let him take the water of life freely.

See: Adultery

See: Children

See: Citizens

See: Homicide

See: Instruction

See: Minister, a sacred teacher

See: Obedience; enjoined

See: Servant

See: Theft and Thieves

See: Wife

See: Women

• Precepts of men.

Mt 15:2–20; Mk 7:2–23; Ro 14:1–6, 10–23; 1Ti 4:1–3

Isa 29:13 — Wherefore the Lord said, Forasmuch as this people draw near *me* with their mouth, and with their lips do honour me, but have removed their heart far from me, and their fear toward me is taught by the precept of men:

COMMERCE

• Laws concerning.

Le 19:36–37

Le 25:14 — And if thou sell *ought* unto thy neighbour, or buyest ought of thy neighbour's hand, ye shall not oppress one another:

Le 25:17 — Ye shall not therefore oppress one another; but thou shalt fear thy God: for I *am* the LORD your God.

• Carried on by means of caravans.

Ge 37:25 — And they sat down to eat bread: and they lifted up their eyes and looked, and, behold, a company of Ishmeelites came from Gilead with their camels bearing spicery and balm and myrrh, going to carry *it* down to Egypt.

Ge 37:27 — Come, and let us sell him to the Ishmeelites, and let not our hand be upon him; for he *is* our brother *and* our flesh. And his brethren were content.

Isa 60:6 — The multitude of camels shall cover thee, the dromedaries of Midian and Ephah; all they from Sheba shall come: they shall bring gold and incense; and they shall shew forth the praises of the LORD.

• Carried on by means of ships.

1Ki 9:27–28; Ps 107:23–30

1Ki 10:11 — And the navy also of Hiram, that brought gold from Ophir, brought in from Ophir great plenty of almug trees, and precious stones.

1Ki 22:48 — Jehoshaphat made ships of Tharshish to go to Ophir for gold: but they went not; for the ships were broken at Ezion-geber.

Pr 31:14 — She is like the merchants' ships; she bringeth her food from afar.

Rev 18:19 — And they cast dust on their heads, and cried, weeping and wailing, saying, Alas, alas, that great city, wherein were made rich all that had ships in the sea by reason of her costliness! for in one hour is she made desolate.

• Conducted in fairs.

Eze 27:12 — Tarshish *was* thy merchant by reason of the multitude of all *kind of* riches; with silver, iron, tin, and lead, they traded in thy fairs.

Eze 27:19 — Dan also and Javan going to and fro occupied in thy fairs: bright iron, cassia, and calamus, were in thy market.

Mt 11:16 — But whereunto shall I liken this generation? It is like unto children sitting in the markets, and calling unto their fellows,

• Of the Arabians.

Eze 27:21–24

Isa 60:6 — The multitude of camels shall cover thee, the dromedaries of Midian and Ephah; all they from Sheba shall come: they shall bring gold and incense; and they shall shew forth the praises of the LORD.

Jer 6:20 — To what purpose cometh there to me incense from Sheba, and the sweet cane from a far country? your burnt offerings *are* not acceptable, nor your sacrifices sweet unto me.

• Of the Egyptians.

Ge 42:2–34

• Of the Ethiopians.

Isa 45:14 — Thus saith the LORD, The labour of Egypt, and merchandise of Ethiopia and of the Sabeans, men of stature, shall come over unto thee, and they shall be thine: they shall come after thee; in chains they shall come over, and they shall fall down unto thee, they shall make supplication unto thee, *saying,* Surely God *is* in thee; and *there is* none else, *there is* no God.

• Of the Ishmaelites.

Ge 37:27–28

• Of the Israelites.

1Ki 9:26–28; Ne 3:31–32

Eze 27:17 — Judah, and the land of Israel, they *were* thy merchants: they traded in thy market wheat of Minnith, and Pannag, and honey, and oil, and balm.

• Of the Ninevites.

Na 3:16 — Thou hast multiplied thy merchants above the stars of heaven: the cankerworm spoileth, and fleeth away.

• Of the Syrians.

Eze 27:16 — Syria *was* thy merchant by reason of the multitude of the wares of thy making: they occupied in thy fairs with emeralds, purple, and broidered work, and fine linen, and coral, and agate.

Eze 27:18 — Damascus *was* thy merchant in the multitude of the wares of thy making, for the multitude of all riches; in the wine of Helbon, and white wool.

• Of the Tyrians.

Eze 27:1–36

2Sa 5:11 — And Hiram king of Tyre sent messengers to David, and cedar trees, and carpenters, and masons: and they built David an house.

1Ki 5:6 — Now therefore command thou that they hew me cedar trees out of Lebanon; and my servants shall be with thy servants: and unto thee will I give hire for thy servants according to all that thou shalt appoint: for thou knowest that *there is* not among us any that can skill to hew timber like unto the Sidonians.

Isa 23:8 — Who hath taken this counsel against Tyre, the crowning *city,* whose merchants *are* princes, whose traffickers *are* the honourable of the earth?

Eze 28:5 — By thy great wisdom *and* by thy traffick hast thou increased thy riches, and thine heart is lifted up because of thy riches:

• Of the Zidonians.

Isa 23:2 — Be still, ye inhabitants of the isle; thou whom the merchants of Zidon, that pass over the sea, have replenished.

Eze 27:8 — The inhabitants of Zidon and Arvad were thy mariners: thy wise *men,* O Tyrus, *that* were in thee, were thy pilots.

• Of the Babylonians.

Rev 18:11–13

Rev 18:3 — For all nations have drunk of the wine of the wrath of her fornication, and the kings of the earth have committed fornication with her, and the merchants of the earth are waxed rich through the abundance of her delicacies.

- **Of the Jews.**

Eze 27:17 — Judah, and the land of Israel, they *were* thy merchants: they traded in thy market wheat of Minnith, and Pannag, and honey, and oil, and balm.

- **From Tarshish.**

Jer 10:9 — Silver spread into plates is brought from Tarshish, and gold from Uphaz, the work of the workman, and of the hands of the founder: blue and purple is their clothing: they *are* all the work of cunning *men.*

Eze 27:25 — The ships of Tarshish did sing of thee in thy market: and thou wast replenished, and made very glorious in the midst of the seas.

- **Evil practices connected with.**

Pr 29:14 — The king that faithfully judgeth the poor, his throne shall be established for ever.

Eze 22:13 — Behold, therefore I have smitten mine hand at thy dishonest gain which thou hast made, and at thy blood which hath been in the midst of thee.

Hos 12:7 — *He is* a merchant, the balances of deceit *are* in his hand: he loveth to oppress.

- **Articles of.**

- **Apes.**

1Ki 10:22 — For the king had at sea a navy of Tharshish with the navy of Hiram: once in three years came the navy of Tharshish, bringing gold, and silver, ivory, and apes, and peacocks.

- **Balm.**

Ge 37:25 — And they sat down to eat bread: and they lifted up their eyes and looked, and, behold, a company of Ishmeelites came from Gilead with their camels bearing spicery and balm and myrrh, going to carry *it* down to Egypt.

- **Blue cloth.**

Eze 27:24 — These *were* thy merchants in all sorts *of things,* in blue clothes, and broidered work, and in chests of rich apparel, bound with cords, and made of cedar, among thy merchandise.

- **Brass.**

Eze 27:13 — Javan, Tubal, and Meshech, they *were* thy merchants: they traded the persons of men and vessels of brass in thy market.

Rev 18:12 — The merchandise of gold, and silver, and precious stones, and of pearls, and fine linen, and purple, and silk, and scarlet, and all thyine wood, and all manner vessels of ivory, and all manner vessels of most precious wood, and of brass, and iron, and marble,

- **Cinnamon.**

Rev 18:13 — And cinnamon, and odours, and ointments, and frankincense, and wine, and oil, and fine flour, and wheat, and beasts, and sheep, and horses, and chariots, and slaves, and souls of men.

- **Corn.**

1Ki 5:11 — And Solomon gave Hiram twenty thousand measures of wheat *for* food to his household, and twenty measures of pure oil: thus gave Solomon to Hiram year by year.

Eze 27:17 — Judah, and the land of Israel, they *were* thy merchants: they traded in thy market wheat of Minnith, and Pannag, and honey, and oil, and balm.

- **Cattle.**

Eze 27:21 — Arabia, and all the princes of Kedar, they occupied with thee in lambs, and rams, and goats: in these *were they* thy merchants.

- **Chest of rich apparel.**

Eze 27:24 — These *were* thy merchants in all sorts *of things,* in blue clothes, and broidered work, and in chests of rich apparel, bound with cords, and made of cedar, among thy merchandise.

- **Chariots.**

1Ki 10:29 — And a chariot came up and went out of Egypt for six hundred *shekels* of silver, and an horse for an hundred and fifty: and so for all the kings of the Hittites, and for the kings of Syria, did they bring *them* out by their means.

Rev 18:13 — And cinnamon, and odours, and ointments, and frankincense, and wine, and oil, and fine flour, and wheat, and beasts, and sheep, and horses, and chariots, and slaves, and souls of men.

- **Clothes for chariots.**

Eze 27:20 — Dedan *was* thy merchant in precious clothes for chariots.

- **Embroidery.**

Eze 27:16 — Syria *was* thy merchant by reason of the multitude of the wares of thy making: they occupied in thy fairs with emeralds, purple, and broidered work, and fine linen, and coral, and agate.

Eze 27:24 — These *were* thy merchants in all sorts *of things,* in blue clothes, and broidered work, and in chests of rich apparel, bound with cords, and made of cedar, among thy merchandise.

- **Frankincense.**

Jer 6:20 — To what purpose cometh there to me incense from Sheba, and the sweet cane from a far country? your burnt offerings *are* not acceptable, nor your sacrifices sweet unto me.

Rev 18:13 — And cinnamon, and odours, and ointments, and frankincense, and wine, and oil, and fine flour, and wheat, and beasts, and sheep, and horses, and chariots, and slaves, and souls of men.

- **Gold.**

1Ki 9:28 — And they came to Ophir, and fetched from thence gold, four hundred and twenty talents, and brought *it* to king Solomon.

1Ki 10:22 — For the king had at sea a navy of Tharshish with the navy of Hiram: once in three years came the navy of Tharshish, bringing gold, and silver, ivory, and apes, and peacocks.

2Ch 8:18 — And Huram sent him by the hands of his servants ships, and servants that had knowledge of the sea; and they went with the servants of Solomon to Ophir, and took thence four hundred and fifty talents of gold, and brought *them* to king Solomon.

Isa 60:6 — The multitude of camels shall cover thee, the dromedaries of Midian and Ephah; all they from Sheba shall come: they shall bring gold and incense; and they shall shew forth the praises of the LORD.

Rev 18:12 — The merchandise of gold, and silver, and precious stones, and of pearls, and fine linen, and purple, and silk, and scarlet, and all thyine wood, and all manner vessels of ivory, and all manner vessels of most precious wood, and of brass, and iron, and marble,

• Honey.

Eze 27:17 — Judah, and the land of Israel, they *were* thy merchants: they traded in thy market wheat of Minnith, and Pannag, and honey, and oil, and balm.

• Horses.

1Ki 10:29 — And a chariot came up and went out of Egypt for six hundred *shekels* of silver, and an horse for an hundred and fifty: and so for all the kings of the Hittites, and for the kings of Syria, did they bring *them* out by their means.

Eze 27:14 — They of the house of Togarmah traded in thy fairs with horses and horsemen and mules.

Rev 18:13 — And cinnamon, and odours, and ointments, and frankincense, and wine, and oil, and fine flour, and wheat, and beasts, and sheep, and horses, and chariots, and slaves, and souls of men.

• Ivory.

1Ki 10:22 — For the king had at sea a navy of Tharshish with the navy of Hiram: once in three years came the navy of Tharshish, bringing gold, and silver, ivory, and apes, and peacocks.

2Ch 9:21 — For the king's ships went to Tarshish with the servants of Huram: every three years once came the ships of Tarshish bringing gold, and silver, ivory, and apes, and peacocks.

Eze 27:15 — The men of Dedan *were* thy merchants; many isles *were* the merchandise of thine hand: they brought thee *for* a present horns of ivory and ebony.

Rev 18:12 — The merchandise of gold, and silver, and precious stones, and of pearls, and fine linen, and purple, and silk, and scarlet, and all thyine wood, and all manner vessels of ivory, and all manner vessels of most precious wood, and of brass, and iron, and marble,

• Iron and steel.

Eze 27:12 — Tarshish *was* thy merchant by reason of the multitude of all *kind of* riches; with silver, iron, tin, and lead, they traded in thy fairs.

Eze 27:19 — Dan also and Javan going to and fro occupied in thy fairs: bright iron, cassia, and calamus, were in thy market.

• Land.

Ge 23:13–16

Ru 4:3 — And he said unto the kinsman, Naomi, that is come again out of the country of Moab, selleth a parcel of land, which *was* our brother Elimelech's:

• Lead.

Eze 27:12 — Tarshish *was* thy merchant by reason of the multitude of all *kind of* riches; with silver, iron, tin, and lead, they traded in thy fairs.

• Linen.

1Ki 10:28 — And Solomon had horses brought out of Egypt, and linen yarn: the king's merchants received the linen yarn at a price.

Rev 18:12 — The merchandise of gold, and silver, and precious stones, and of pearls, and fine linen, and purple, and silk, and scarlet, and all thyine wood, and all manner vessels of ivory, and all manner vessels of most precious wood, and of brass, and iron, and marble,

• Oil.

Ex 27:1–21

1Ki 5:11 — And Solomon gave Hiram twenty thousand measures of wheat *for* food to his household, and twenty measures of pure oil: thus gave Solomon to Hiram year by year.

• Pearls.

Rev 18:12 — The merchandise of gold, and silver, and precious stones, and of pearls, and fine linen, and purple, and silk, and scarlet, and all thyine wood, and all manner vessels of ivory, and all manner vessels of most precious wood, and of brass, and iron, and marble,

• Peacocks.

1Ki 10:22 — For the king had at sea a navy of Tharshish with the navy of Hiram: once in three years came the navy of Tharshish, bringing gold, and silver, ivory, and apes, and peacocks.

• Perfumes.

SS 2:6 — His left hand *is* under my head, and his right hand doth embrace me.

• Precious stones.

Eze 27:16 — Syria *was* thy merchant by reason of the multitude of the wares of thy making: they occupied in thy fairs with emeralds, purple, and broidered work, and fine linen, and coral, and agate.

Eze 27:22 — The merchants of Sheba and Raamah, they *were* thy merchants: they occupied in thy fairs with chief of all spices, and with all precious stones, and gold.

Eze 28:13 — Thou hast been in Eden the garden of God; every precious stone *was* thy covering, the sardius, topaz, and the diamond, the beryl, the onyx, and the jasper, the sapphire, the emerald, and the carbuncle, and gold: the workmanship of thy tabrets and of thy pipes was prepared in thee in the day that thou wast created.

Eze 28:16 — By the multitude of thy merchandise they have filled the midst of thee with violence, and thou hast sinned: therefore I will cast thee as profane out of the mountain of God: and I will destroy thee, O covering cherub, from the midst of the stones of fire.

Rev 18:12 — The merchandise of gold, and silver, and precious stones, and of pearls, and fine linen, and purple, and silk, and scarlet, and all thyine wood, and all manner vessels of ivory, and all manner vessels of most precious wood, and of brass, and iron, and marble,

• **Purple.**

Eze 27:16 — Syria *was* thy merchant by reason of the multitude of the wares of thy making: they occupied in thy fairs with emeralds, purple, and broidered work, and fine linen, and coral, and agate.

Rev 18:12 — The merchandise of gold, and silver, and precious stones, and of pearls, and fine linen, and purple, and silk, and scarlet, and all thyine wood, and all manner vessels of ivory, and all manner vessels of most precious wood, and of brass, and iron, and marble,

• **Sheep.**

Rev 18:13 — And cinnamon, and odours, and ointments, and frankincense, and wine, and oil, and fine flour, and wheat, and beasts, and sheep, and horses, and chariots, and slaves, and souls of men.

• **Slaves.**

Ge 37:28 — Then there passed by Midianites merchantmen; and they drew and lifted up Joseph out of the pit, and sold Joseph to the Ishmeelites for twenty *pieces* of silver: and they brought Joseph into Egypt.

Ge 37:36 — And the Midianites sold him into Egypt unto Potiphar, an officer of Pharaoh's, *and* captain of the guard.

Dt 24:7 — If a man be found stealing any of his brethren of the children of Israel, and maketh merchandise of him, or selleth him; then that thief shall die; and thou shalt put evil away from among you.

• **Silk.**

Rev 18:12 — The merchandise of gold, and silver, and precious stones, and of pearls, and fine linen, and purple, and silk, and scarlet, and all thyine wood, and all manner vessels of ivory, and all manner vessels of most precious wood, and of brass, and iron, and marble,

• **Silver.**

1Ki 10:22 — For the king had at sea a navy of Tharshish with the navy of Hiram: once in three years came the navy of Tharshish, bringing gold, and silver, ivory, and apes, and peacocks.

2Ch 9:21 — For the king's ships went to Tarshish with the servants of Huram: every three years once came the ships of Tarshish bringing gold, and silver, ivory, and apes, and peacocks.

Rev 18:12 — The merchandise of gold, and silver, and precious stones, and of pearls, and fine linen, and purple, and silk, and scarlet, and all thyine wood, and all manner vessels of ivory, and all manner vessels of most precious wood, and of brass, and iron, and marble,

• **Sweet cane.**

Jer 6:20 — To what purpose cometh there to me incense from Sheba, and the sweet cane from a far country? your burnt offerings *are* not acceptable, nor your sacrifices sweet unto me.

• **Thyine wood.**

Rev 18:12 — The merchandise of gold, and silver, and precious stones, and of pearls, and fine linen, and purple, and silk, and scarlet, and all thyine wood, and all manner vessels of ivory, and all manner vessels of most precious wood, and of brass, and iron, and marble,

• **Timber.**

1Ki 5:6 — Now therefore command thou that they hew me cedar trees out of Lebanon; and my servants shall be with thy servants: and unto thee will I give hire for thy servants according to all that thou shalt appoint: for thou knowest that *there is* not among us any that can skill to hew timber like unto the Sidonians.

1Ki 5:8 — And Hiram sent to Solomon, saying, I have considered the things which thou sentest to me for: *and* I will do all thy desire concerning timber of cedar, and concerning timber of fir.

• **Tin.**

Eze 27:12 — Tarshish *was* thy merchant by reason of the multitude of all *kind of* riches; with silver, iron, tin, and lead, they traded in thy fairs.

• **Wheat.**

Rev 18:13 — And cinnamon, and odours, and ointments, and frankincense, and wine, and oil, and fine flour, and wheat, and beasts, and sheep, and horses, and chariots, and slaves, and souls of men.

• **White wool.**

Eze 27:18 — Damascus *was* thy merchant in the multitude of the wares of thy making, for the multitude of all riches; in the wine of Helbon, and white wool.

• **Wine.**

2Ch 2:15 — Now therefore the wheat, and the barley, the oil, and the wine, which my lord hath spoken of, let him send unto his servants:

Eze 27:18 — Damascus *was* thy merchant in the multitude of the wares of thy making, for the multitude of all riches; in the wine of Helbon, and white wool.

Rev 18:13 — And cinnamon, and odours, and ointments, and frankincense, and wine, and oil, and fine flour, and wheat, and beasts, and sheep, and horses, and chariots, and slaves, and souls of men.

• **Bodies and souls of men.**

Rev 18:13 — And cinnamon, and odours, and ointments, and frankincense, and wine, and oil, and fine flour, and wheat, and beasts, and sheep, and horses, and chariots, and slaves, and souls of men.

• **Transportation of passengers.**

Jnh 1:3 — But Jonah rose up to flee unto Tarshish from the presence of the LORD, and went down to Joppa; and he found a ship going to Tarshish: so he paid the fare thereof, and went down into it, to go with them unto Tarshish from the presence of the LORD.

Ac 21:2 — And finding a ship sailing over unto Phenicia, we went aboard, and set forth.

Ac 27:2 — And entering into a ship of Adramyttium, we launched, meaning to sail by the coasts of Asia; *one* Aristarchus, a Macedonian of Thessalonica, being with us.

Ac 27:6 — And there the centurion found a ship of Alexandria sailing into Italy; and he put us therein.

Ac 27:37 — And we were in all in the ship two hundred threescore and sixteen souls.

See: Merchant

See: Tarshish

See: Trade

See: Traffic

COMMISSARY

• **For armies, cattle drive with.**

2Ki 3:9 — So the king of Israel went, and the king of Judah, and the king of Edom: and they fetched a compass of seven days' journey: and there was no water for the host, and for the cattle that followed them.

See: Armies

• **For royal households.**

1Ki 4:7–19, 27–28

COMMISSION

Mt 28:19–20; Ac 1:7–8

Jn 14:12 — Verily, verily, I say unto you, He that believeth on me, the works that I do shall he do also; and greater *works* than these shall he do; because I go unto my Father.

Jn 20:21 — Then said Jesus to them again, Peace *be* unto you: as *my* Father hath sent me, even so send I you.

COMMITMENT

Ex 32:29 — For Moses had said, Consecrate yourselves to day to the LORD, even every man upon his son, and upon his brother; that he may bestow upon you a blessing this day.

1Ch 29:5 — The gold for *things* of gold, and the silver for *things* of silver, and for all manner of work *to be made* by the hands of artificers. And who *then* is willing to consecrate his service this day unto the LORD?

Pr 23:26 — My son, give me thine heart, and let thine eyes observe my ways.

Ro 12:1 — I beseech you therefore, brethren, by the mercies of God, that ye present your bodies a living sacrifice, holy, acceptable unto God, *which is* your reasonable service.

COMMONWEALTH

• **Figurative.**

Php 3:20 — For our conversation is in heaven; from whence also we look for the Saviour, the Lord Jesus Christ:

COMMUNICATE

Pr 18:13 — He that answereth a matter before he heareth *it*, it *is* folly and shame unto him.

Jas 1:19 — Wherefore, my beloved brethren, let every man be swift to hear, slow to speak, slow to wrath:

COMMUNION

See: Passover; Lord's Supper ordained at

• **With God.**

Jn 14:16–18; Php 2:1–2

Ps 16:7 — I will bless the LORD, who hath given me counsel: my reins also instruct me in the night seasons.

Jn 14:23 — Jesus answered and said unto him, If a man love me, he will keep my words: and my Father will love him, and we will come unto him, and make our abode with him.

1Co 10:16 — The cup of blessing which we bless, is it not the communion of the blood of Christ? The bread which we break, is it not the communion of the body of Christ?

2Co 6:16 — And what agreement hath the temple of God with idols? for ye are the temple of the living God; as God hath said, I will dwell in them, and walk in *them;* and I will be their God, and they shall be my people.

2Co 13:14 — The grace of the Lord Jesus Christ, and the love of God, and the communion of the Holy Ghost, *be* with you all. Amen.

Gal 4:6 — And because ye are sons, God hath sent forth the Spirit of his Son into your hearts, crying, Abba, Father.

1Jn 1:3 — That which we have seen and heard declare we unto you, that ye also may have fellowship with us: and truly our fellowship *is* with the Father, and with his Son Jesus Christ.

Rev 3:20 — Behold, I stand at the door, and knock: if any man hear my voice, and open the door, I will come in to him, and will sup with him, and he with me.

See: Fellowship

• **Instances of.**

• **Enoch.**

Ge 5:22, 24

• **Noah.**

Ge 6:9, 13–22; 8:15–17

• **Abraham.**

Ge 12:1–3, 7; 17:1–2; 18:1–33; 22:1–2, 11–12, 16–18

• **Hagar.**

Ge 16:8–12

• **Isaac.**

Ge 26:2, 24

• **Isaac, in dreams.**

Ge 28:13, 15; 31:3; 35:1, 7; 46:2–4

- **Moses.**
  Ex 3:1–4:17; 33:9, 11; 34:28; Nu 12:8
- **Joshua.**
  Jos 1:1–9; 6:2–5; 7:10–15; 8:1–2; 20:1–6
- **Gideon.**
  Jgs 6:11–24
- **Solomon.**
  1Ki 3:5–14; 2Ch 1:7–12

• **Of saints.**

Ps 133:1–3; Jn 17:20–21; 1Co 10:16–17; 12:12–13; 2Co 6:14–18; Eph 4:1–3; Heb 10:24–25; Jas 5:1–20

1Sa 23:16 — And Jonathan Saul's son arose, and went to David into the wood, and strengthened his hand in God.

Ps 55:14 — We took sweet counsel together, *and* walked unto the house of God in company.

Ps 119:63 — I *am* a companion of all *them* that fear thee, and of them that keep thy precepts.

Am 3:3 — Can two walk together, except they be agreed?

Mal 3:16 — Then they that feared the LORD spake often one to another: and the LORD hearkened, and heard *it,* and a book of remembrance was written before him for them that feared the LORD, and that thought upon his name.

Lk 22:32 — But I have prayed for thee, that thy faith fail not: and when thou art converted, strengthen thy brethren.

Lk 24:17 — And he said unto them, What manner of communications *are* these that ye have one to another, as ye walk, and are sad?

Lk 24:32 — And they said one to another, Did not our heart burn within us, while he talked with us by the way, and while he opened to us the scriptures?

Ac 2:42 — And they continued stedfastly in the apostles' doctrine and fellowship, and in breaking of bread, and in prayers.

Ro 12:15 — Rejoice with them that do rejoice, and weep with them that weep.

Eph 5:11 — And have no fellowship with the unfruitful works of darkness, but rather reprove *them.*

Col 3:16 — Let the word of Christ dwell in you richly in all wisdom; teaching and admonishing one another in psalms and hymns and spiritual songs, singing with grace in your hearts to the Lord.

1Th 4:18 — Wherefore comfort one another with these words.

1Th 5:11 — Wherefore comfort yourselves together, and edify one another, even as also ye do.

1Th 5:14 — Now we exhort you, brethren, warn them that are unruly, comfort the feebleminded, support the weak, be patient toward all *men.*

Heb 3:13 — But exhort one another daily, while it is called To day; lest any of you be hardened through the deceitfulness of sin.

1Jn 1:3 — That which we have seen and heard declare we unto you, that ye also may have fellowship with us: and truly our fellowship *is* with the Father, and with his Son Jesus Christ.

1Jn 1:7 — But if we walk in the light, as he is in the light, we have fellowship one with another, and the blood of Jesus Christ his Son cleanseth us from all sin.

See: Fellowship

COMMUNISM

Ac 2:44–45; 4:34–5:10

Ac 4:32 — And the multitude of them that believed were of one heart and of one soul: neither said any *of them* that ought of the things which he possessed was his own; but they had all things common.

Heb 13:3 — Remember them that are in bonds, as bound with them; *and* them which suffer adversity, as being yourselves also in the body.

COMPANY

• **Evil.**

Ex 23:32–33; 34:12–15; Nu 16:21–26; Dt 7:2–4; Jos 23:6–13; Jgs 2:1–3; 2Sa 23:6–7; Ps 26:4–5; 106:34–35; 120:5–7; 139:21–22; Pr 1:10–11, 14–15; 2:11–12; 4:14–15; 22:24–25; Isa 8:11–12; Hos 7:8–9; Ro 16:17–18; 1Co 5:9–11; 2Co 6:14–15; Eph 5:6–7; 2Ti 3:4–5; 2Pe 2:7–8; 2Jn 1:10–11

Ge 19:15 — And when the morning arose, then the angels hastened Lot, saying, Arise, take thy wife, and thy two daughters, which are here; lest thou be consumed in the iniquity of the city.

Ge 49:6 — O my soul, come not thou into their secret; unto their assembly, mine honour, be not thou united: for in their anger they slew a man, and in their selfwill they digged down a wall.

Ex 23:2 — Thou shalt not follow a multitude to *do* evil; neither shalt thou speak in a cause to decline after many to wrest *judgment:*

Le 18:3 — After the doings of the land of Egypt, wherein ye dwelt, shall ye not do: and after the doings of the land of Canaan, whither I bring you, shall ye not do: neither shall ye walk in their ordinances.

Le 20:23 — And ye shall not walk in the manners of the nation, which I cast out before you: for they committed all these things, and therefore I abhorred them.

Nu 33:55 — But if ye will not drive out the inhabitants of the land from before you; then it shall come to pass, that those which ye let remain of them *shall be* pricks in your eyes, and thorns in your sides, and shall vex you in the land wherein ye dwell.

Dt 12:30 — Take heed to thyself that thou be not snared by following them, after that they be destroyed from before thee; and that thou enquire not after their gods, saying, How did these nations serve their gods? even so will I do likewise.

2Ch 19:2 — And Jehu the son of Hanani the seer went out to meet him, and said to king Jehoshaphat, Shouldest thou help the ungodly, and love them that hate the LORD? therefore is wrath upon thee from before the LORD.

Ezr 9:14 — Should we again break thy commandments, and join in affinity with the people of these abominations? wouldest not thou be angry with us till thou hadst consumed *us*, so that *there should be* no remnant nor escaping?

Ps 1:1 — Blessed *is* the man that walketh not in the counsel of the ungodly, nor standeth in the way of sinners, nor sitteth in the seat of the scornful.

Ps 6:8 — Depart from me, all ye workers of iniquity; for the LORD hath heard the voice of my weeping.

Ps 15:4 — In whose eyes a vile person is contemned; but he honoureth them that fear the LORD. *He that* sweareth to *his own* hurt, and changeth not.

Ps 26:9 — Gather not my soul with sinners, nor my life with bloody men:

Ps 28:3 — Draw me not away with the wicked, and with the workers of iniquity, which speak peace to their neighbours, but mischief *is* in their hearts.

Ps 31:6 — I have hated them that regard lying vanities: but I trust in the LORD.

Ps 50:18 — When thou sawest a thief, then thou consentedst with him, and hast been partaker with adulterers.

Ps 84:10 — For a day in thy courts *is* better than a thousand. I had rather be a doorkeeper in the house of my God, than to dwell in the tents of wickedness.

Ps 101:4 — A froward heart shall depart from me: I will not know a wicked *person*.

Ps 101:7 — He that worketh deceit shall not dwell within my house: he that telleth lies shall not tarry in my sight.

Ps 119:115 — Depart from me, ye evildoers: for I will keep the commandments of my God.

Ps 139:19 — Surely thou wilt slay the wicked, O God: depart from me therefore, ye bloody men.

Ps 141:4 — Incline not my heart to *any* evil thing, to practise wicked works with men that work iniquity: and let me not eat of their dainties.

Pr 2:16 — To deliver thee from the strange woman, *even* from the stranger *which* flattereth with her words;

Pr 2:19 — None that go unto her return again, neither take they hold of the paths of life.

Pr 5:8 — Remove thy way far from her, and come not nigh the door of her house:

Pr 9:6 — Forsake the foolish, and live; and go in the way of understanding.

Pr 12:11 — He that tilleth his land shall be satisfied with bread: but he that followeth vain *persons is* void of understanding.

Pr 12:26 — The righteous *is* more excellent than his neighbour: but the way of the wicked seduceth them.

Pr 13:20 — He that walketh with wise *men* shall be wise: but a companion of fools shall be destroyed.

Pr 14:7 — Go from the presence of a foolish man, when thou perceivest not *in him* the lips of knowledge.

Pr 16:29 — A violent man enticeth his neighbour, and leadeth him into the way *that is* not good.

Pr 17:12 — Let a bear robbed of her whelps meet a man, rather than a fool in his folly.

Pr 20:19 — He that goeth about *as* a talebearer revealeth secrets: therefore meddle not with him that flattereth with his lips.

Pr 22:5 — Thorns *and* snares *are* in the way of the froward: he that doth keep his soul shall be far from them.

Pr 22:10 — Cast out the scorner, and contention shall go out; yea, strife and reproach shall cease.

Pr 23:6 — Eat thou not the bread of *him that hath* an evil eye, neither desire thou his dainty meats:

Pr 23:20 — Be not among winebibbers; among riotous eaters of flesh:

Pr 24:1 — Be not thou envious against evil men, neither desire to be with them.

Pr 28:7 — Whoso keepeth the law *is* a wise son: but he that is a companion of riotous *men* shameth his father.

Pr 28:19 — He that tilleth his land shall have plenty of bread: but he that followeth after vain *persons* shall have poverty enough.

Pr 29:16 — When the wicked are multiplied, transgression increaseth: but the righteous shall see their fall.

Pr 29:24 — Whoso is partner with a thief hateth his own soul: he heareth cursing, and bewrayeth *it* not.

Ecc 9:18 — Wisdom *is* better than weapons of war: but one sinner destroyeth much good.

Isa 1:23 — Thy princes *are* rebellious, and companions of thieves: every one loveth gifts, and followeth after rewards: they judge not the fatherless, neither doth the cause of the widow come unto them.

Isa 6:5 — Then said I, Woe *is* me! for I am undone; because I *am* a man of unclean lips, and I dwell in the midst of a people of unclean lips: for mine eyes have seen the King, the LORD of hosts.

Jer 2:25 — Withhold thy foot from being unshod, and thy throat from thirst: but thou saidst, There is no hope: no; for I have loved strangers, and after them will I go.

Jer 9:2 — Oh that I had in the wilderness a lodging place of wayfaring men; that I might leave my people, and go from them! for they *be* all adulterers, an assembly of treacherous men.

Jer 15:17 — I sat not in the assembly of the mockers, nor rejoiced; I sat alone because of thy hand: for thou hast filled me with indignation.

Jer 51:6 — Flee out of the midst of Babylon, and deliver every man his soul: be not cut off in her iniquity; for this *is* the time of the LORD'S vengeance; he will render unto her a recompence.

Jer 51:45 — My people, go ye out of the midst of her, and deliver ye every man his soul from the fierce anger of the LORD.

Hos 4:17 — Ephraim *is* joined to idols: let him alone.

Hos 7:5 — In the day of our king the princes have made *him* sick with bottles of wine; he stretched out his hand with scorners.

Mic 6:16 — For the statutes of Omri are kept, and all the works of the house of Ahab, and ye walk in their counsels; that I should make thee a desolation, and the inhabitants thereof an hissing: therefore ye shall bear the reproach of my people.

Mt 24:12 — <u>And because iniquity shall abound, the love of many shall wax cold.</u>

1Co 5:6 — Your glorying *is* not good. Know ye not that a little leaven leaveneth the whole lump?

1Co 15:33 — Be not deceived: evil communications corrupt good manners.

2Co 6:17 — Wherefore come out from among them, and be ye separate, saith the Lord, and touch not the unclean *thing;* and I will receive you,

Gal 5:9 — A little leaven leaveneth the whole lump.

Eph 5:11 — And have no fellowship with the unfruitful works of darkness, but rather reprove *them.*

2Th 3:6 — Now we command you, brethren, in the name of our Lord Jesus Christ, that ye withdraw yourselves from every brother that walketh disorderly, and not after the tradition which he received of us.

1Ti 5:22 — Lay hands suddenly on no man, neither be partaker of other men's sins: keep thyself pure.

1Ti 6:5 — Perverse disputings of men of corrupt minds, and destitute of the truth, supposing that gain is godliness: from such withdraw thyself.

2Pe 2:18 — For when they speak great swelling *words* of vanity, they allure through the lusts of the flesh, *through much* wantonness, those that were clean escaped from them who live in error.

Rev 2:2 — I know thy works, and thy labour, and thy patience, and how thou canst not bear them which are evil: and thou hast tried them which say they are apostles, and are not, and hast found them liars:

Rev 18:4 — And I heard another voice from heaven, saying, Come out of her, my people, that ye be not partakers of her sins, and that ye receive not of her plagues.

- **Good.**

Pr 13:20 — He that walketh with wise *men* shall be wise: but a companion of fools shall be destroyed.

See: Communion; of saints

See: Example

See: Fellowship

See: Influence

COMPASSES

- **Carpenter's.**

Isa 44:13 — The carpenter stretcheth out *his* rule; he marketh it out with a line; he fitteth it with planes, and he marketh it out with the compass, and maketh it after the figure of a man, according to the beauty of a man; that it may remain in the house.

COMPASSION

Lk 10:34 — And went to *him,* and bound up his wounds, pouring in oil and wine, and set him on his own beast, and brought him to an inn, and took care of him.

Ac 16:33 — And he took them the same hour of the night, and washed *their* stripes; and was baptized, he and all his, straightway.

Ac 28:2 — And the barbarous people shewed us no little kindness: for they kindled a fire, and received us every one, because of the present rain, and because of the cold.

- **Of God.**

See: God, Mercy of

- **Of Christ.**

See: Jesus, Compassion of

COMPLACENT

Pr 1:32 — For the turning away of the simple shall slay them, and the prosperity of fools shall destroy them.

Eze 30:9 — In that day shall messengers go forth from me in ships to make the careless Ethiopians afraid, and great pain shall come upon them, as in the day of Egypt: for, lo, it cometh.

Am 6:1 — Woe to them *that are* at ease in Zion, and trust in the mountain of Samaria, *which are* named chief of the nations, to whom the house of Israel came!

Zep 1:12 — And it shall come to pass at that time, *that* I will search Jerusalem with candles, and punish the men that are settled on their lees: that say in their heart, The LORD will not do good, neither will he do evil.

COMPLAINT **See: Murmuring**

COMPLICITY

2Jn 1:10–11

Ps 50:18 — When thou sawest a thief, then thou consentedst with him, and hast been partaker with adulterers.

Pr 29:24 — Whoso is partner with a thief hateth his own soul: he heareth cursing, and bewrayeth *it* not.

Ro 1:32 — Who knowing the judgment of God, that they which commit such things are worthy of death, not only do the same, but have pleasure in them that do them.

- **Instances of.**
  - **The daughter of Herodias, in asking for the head of John the Baptist.**
    Mt 14:8; Mk 6:25
  - **Pilate, in the death of Jesus.**
    Mt 27:17–26; Mk 15:9–15; Lk 23:13–25; Jn 19:13–16
  - **Paul, in the stoning of Stephen.**
    Ac 7:58

See: Collusion

See: Connivance

See: Conspiracy

COMPROMISE

- **Before litigation, enjoined.**

Pr 25:8–10; Mt 5:25–26; Lk 12:58–59

See: Adjudication at Law

See: Arbitration

See: Court

See: Justice

CONCEIT

Lk 18:11–12

Pr 3:5 — Trust in the LORD with all thine heart; and lean not unto thine own understanding.

Pr 3:7 — Be not wise in thine own eyes: fear the LORD, and depart from evil.

Pr 12:15 — The way of a fool *is* right in his own eyes: but he that hearkeneth unto counsel *is* wise.

Pr 23:4 — Labour not to be rich: cease from thine own wisdom.

Pr 26:5 — Answer a fool according to his folly, lest he be wise in his own conceit.

Pr 26:12 — Seest thou a man wise in his own conceit? *there is* more hope of a fool than of him.

Pr 26:16 — The sluggard *is* wiser in his own conceit than seven men that can render a reason.

Pr 28:11 — The rich man *is* wise in his own conceit; but the poor that hath understanding searcheth him out.

Pr 28:26 — He that trusteth in his own heart is a fool: but whoso walketh wisely, he shall be delivered.

Isa 5:21 — Woe unto *them that are* wise in their own eyes, and prudent in their own sight!

Jer 9:23 — Thus saith the LORD, Let not the wise *man* glory in his wisdom, neither let the mighty *man* glory in his might, let not the rich *man* glory in his riches:

Ro 1:22 — Professing themselves to be wise, they became fools,

Ro 11:25 — For I would not, brethren, that ye should be ignorant of this mystery, lest ye should be wise in your own conceits; that blindness in part is happened to Israel, until the fulness of the Gentiles be come in.

Ro 12:16 — *Be* of the same mind one toward another. Mind not high things, but condescend to men of low estate. Be not wise in your own conceits.

✧See: Hypocrisy

✧See: Pride

CONCEPTION

• Miraculous.

• Sarah.

Ge 21:1–2

• Rebekah.

Ge 25:21 — And Isaac intreated the LORD for his wife, because she *was* barren: and the LORD was intreated of him, and Rebekah his wife conceived.

• Rachel.

Ge 30:22 — And God remembered Rachel, and God hearkened to her, and opened her womb.

• Manoah's wife.

Jgs 13:3–24

• Hannah.

1Sa 1:19–20

• Elisabeth.

Lk 1:24–25, 36–37

Lk 1:58 — And her neighbours and her cousins heard how the Lord had shewed great mercy upon her; and they rejoiced with her.

• Mary.

Lk 1:31–35

Mt 1:18 — Now the birth of Jesus Christ was on this wise: When as his mother Mary was espoused to Joseph, before they came together, she was found with child of the Holy Ghost.

Mt 1:20 — But while he thought on these things, behold, the angel of the Lord appeared unto him in a dream, saying, Joseph, thou son of David, fear not to take unto thee Mary thy wife: for that which is conceived in her is of the Holy Ghost.

CONCISION • A term for circumcision.

Php 3:2 — Beware of dogs, beware of evil workers, beware of the concision.

CONCUBINAGE

• Laws concerning.

Ex 21:7–11; Le 19:20–22; Dt 21:10–14

• Concubines might be dismissed.

Ge 21:9–14

• Called wives.

Jgs 19:3–5

Ge 37:2 — These *are* the generations of Jacob. Joseph, *being* seventeen years old, was feeding the flock with his brethren; and the lad *was* with the sons of Bilhah, and with the sons of Zilpah, his father's wives: and Joseph brought unto his father their evil report.

• Children of, not heirs.

Ge 15:4 — And, behold, the word of the LORD *came* unto him, saying, This shall not be thine heir; but he that shall come forth out of thine own bowels shall be thine heir.

Ge 21:10 — Wherefore she said unto Abraham, Cast out this bondwoman and her son: for the son of this bondwoman shall not be heir with my son, *even* with Isaac.

• Practiced by Abraham.

Ge 16:3 — And Sarai Abram's wife took Hagar her maid the Egyptian, after Abram had dwelt ten years in the land of Canaan, and gave her to her husband Abram to be his wife.

Ge 25:6 — But unto the sons of the concubines, which Abraham had, Abraham gave gifts, and sent them away from Isaac his son, while he yet lived, eastward, unto the east country.

1Ch 1:32 — Now the sons of Keturah, Abraham's concubine: she bare Zimran, and Jokshan, and Medan, and Midian, and Ishbak, and Shuah. And the sons of Jokshan; Sheba, and Dedan.

• Practiced by Nahor.

Ge 22:23–24

• Practiced by Jacob.

Ge 30:4 — And she gave him Bilhah her handmaid to wife: and Jacob went in unto her.

• Practiced by Eliphaz.

Ge 36:12 — And Timna was concubine to Eliphaz Esau's son; and she bare to Eliphaz Amalek: these *were* the sons of Adah Esau's wife.

• Practiced by Gideon.

Jgs 8:31 — And his concubine that *was* in Shechem, she also bare him a son, whose name he called Abimelech.

• Practiced by a Levite.

Jgs 19:1 — And it came to pass in those days, when *there was* no king in Israel, that there was a certain Levite sojourning on the side of mount Ephraim, who took to him a concubine out of Bethlehemjudah.

• Practiced by Caleb.

1Ch 2:46–48

- **Practiced by Manasseh.**
  1Ch 7:14 — The sons of Manasseh; Ashriel, whom she bare: (*but* his concubine the Aramitess bare Machir the father of Gilead:
- **Practiced by Saul.**
  2Sa 3:7 — And Saul had a concubine, whose name *was* Rizpah, the daughter of Aiah: and *Ish-bosheth* said to Abner, Wherefore hast thou gone in unto my father's concubine?
- **Practiced by David.**
  2Sa 5:13 — And David took *him* more concubines and wives out of Jerusalem, after he was come from Hebron: and there were yet sons and daughters born to David.
  2Sa 15:16 — And the king went forth, and all his household after him. And the king left ten women, *which were* concubines, to keep the house.
- **Practiced by Solomon.**
  1Ki 11:3 — And he had seven hundred wives, princesses, and three hundred concubines: and his wives turned away his heart.
- **Practiced by Rehoboam.**
  2Ch 11:21 — And Rehoboam loved Maachah the daughter of Absalom above all his wives and his concubines: (for he took eighteen wives, and threescore concubines; and begat twenty and eight sons, and threescore daughters.)
- **Practiced by Abijah.**
  2Ch 13:21 — But Abijah waxed mighty, and married fourteen wives, and begat twenty and two sons, and sixteen daughters.
- **Practiced by Belshazzar.**
  Da 5:2 — Belshazzar, whiles he tasted the wine, commanded to bring the golden and silver vessels which his father Nebuchadnezzar had taken out of the temple which *was* in Jerusalem; that the king, and his princes, his wives, and his concubines, might drink therein.

See: Marriage
See: Polygamy

CONCUPISCENCE See: Lasciviousness

CONDEMNATION, SELF See: Self-Condemnation

CONDESCENSION OF GOD

- **In reasoning with his creatures.**
  - **Sets forth his reasons for sending the flood.**
    Ge 6:11–13
  - **Enters into covenant with Abraham.**
    Ge 15:1–21; 18:1–22
  - **Indulges Abraham's intercession for Sodom.**
    Ge 18:23–33
  - **Warns Abimelech in a dream.**
    Ge 20:3–7
  - **Reasons with Moses.**
    Ex 4:2–17
  - **Sends flesh to the Israelites in consequence of their murmuring.**
    Ex 16:12 — I have heard the murmurings of the children of Israel: speak unto them, saying, At even ye shall eat flesh, and in the morning ye shall be filled with bread; and ye shall know that I *am* the LORD your God.
  - **Indulges Moses' prayer to behold his glory.**
    Ex 33:18–23
  - **Indulges Gideon's tests.**
    Jgs 6:36–40
  - **Reasons with Job.**
    Job 38:1–41:34
  - **Invites sinners, saying, "Come now, and let us reason together".**
    Isa 1:18–20
  - **Expostulates with backsliding Israel.**
    Isa 41:21–24; 43:1–19; 65:1–16; Jer 3:1–15; 4:1–31; 7:1–34; Eze 18:25–32; 33:10–20; Hos 2:1–23; Mic 6:1–9; Mal 3:7–15
- **Scriptures relating to.**
  Ps 8:4–6; 113:5–6; Heb 6:17–18
  Ps 144:3 — LORD, what *is* man, that thou takest knowledge of him! *or* the son of man, that thou makest account of him!
  Isa 45:11 — Thus saith the LORD, the Holy One of Israel, and his Maker, Ask me of things to come concerning my sons, and concerning the work of my hands command ye me.
  Jn 3:16 — For God so loved the world, that he gave his only begotten Son, that whosoever believeth in him should not perish, but have everlasting life.
  Jn 3:19 — And this is the condemnation, that light is come into the world, and men loved darkness rather than light, because their deeds were evil.
  Jn 3:36 — He that believeth on the Son hath everlasting life: and he that believeth not the Son shall not see life; but the wrath of God abideth on him.
  Ro 5:8 — But God commendeth his love toward us, in that, while we were yet sinners, Christ died for us.
  Ro 5:18 — Therefore as by the offence of one *judgment came* upon all men to condemnation; even so by the righteousness of one *the free gift came* upon all men unto justification of life.
  1Co 11:34 — And if any man hunger, let him eat at home; that ye come not together unto condemnation. And the rest will I set in order when I come.
  1Ti 3:6 — Not a novice, lest being lifted up with pride he fall into the condemnation of the devil.
  Heb 2:11 — For both he that sanctifieth and they who are sanctified *are* all of one: for which cause he is not ashamed to call them brethren,
  Jas 5:12 — But above all things, my brethren, swear not, neither by heaven, neither by the earth, neither by any other oath: but let your yea be yea; and *your* nay, nay; lest ye fall into condemnation.

1Jn 4:10 — Herein is love, not that we loved God, but that he loved us, and sent his Son *to be* the propitiation for our sins.

1Jn 4:19 — We love him, because he first loved us.

CONDOLENCE

• Instances of.

• David, to Hanun.
2Sa 10:2

• King of Babylon, to Hezekiah.
2Ki 20:12–13

• The three friends of, to Job.
Job 2:11

• Jesus, to Mary and Martha.
Jn 11:23–35

See: Assurance; saints privileged to have; comfort in affliction

See: Sympathy

CONEY

Le 11:5 — And the coney, because he cheweth the cud, but divideth not the hoof; he *is* unclean unto you.

Dt 14:7 — Nevertheless these ye shall not eat of them that chew the cud, or of them that divide the cloven hoof; *as* the camel, and the hare, and the coney: for they chew the cud, but divide not the hoof; *therefore* they *are* unclean unto you.

Ps 104:18 — The high hills *are* a refuge for the wild goats; *and* the rocks for the conies.

Pr 30:26 — The conies *are but* a feeble folk, yet make they their houses in the rocks;

CONFECTIONER

1Sa 8:13 — And he will take your daughters *to be* confectionaries, and *to be* cooks, and *to be* bakers.

CONFEDERACIES

• Instances of.

• Of kings.
Ge 14:1–2; Jos 10:1–5; 11:1–5; 1Ki 20:1

See: Alliances

CONFESSION

• Of Christ.

Mt 7:21–23; 10:32–33; Jn 1:15–18; 9:22–38; 12:42–43; Ac 8:35–37; 19:4–5; Ro 10:9–11; 1Jn 4:2–3

Mt 3:11 — I indeed baptize you with water unto repentance: but he that cometh after me is mightier than I, whose shoes I am not worthy to bear: he shall baptize you with the Holy Ghost, and *with* fire:

Lk 12:8 — Also I say unto you, Whosoever shall confess me before men, him shall the Son of man also confess before the angels of God:

Ac 18:5 — And when Silas and Timotheus were come from Macedonia, Paul was pressed in the spirit, and testified to the Jews *that* Jesus *was* Christ.

1Co 12:3 — Wherefore I give you to understand, that no man speaking by the Spirit of God calleth Jesus accursed: and *that* no man can say that Jesus is the Lord, but by the Holy Ghost.

1Jn 1:6 — If we say that we have fellowship with him, and walk in darkness, we lie, and do not the truth:

1Jn 2:4 — He that saith, I know him, and keepeth not his commandments, is a liar, and the truth is not in him.

1Jn 4:15 — Whosoever shall confess that Jesus is the Son of God, God dwelleth in him, and he in God.

See: Testimony; religious

• Of sin.

See: Sin; confession of

CONFIDENCE

• Betrayed.

• Instances of.

• Joshua, by the Gibeonites.
Jos 9:3–15

• Eglon, by Ehud.
Jgs 3:15–23

• Ahimelech, by David.
1Sa 21:1–9

• Abner, by Joab.
2Sa 3:27 — And when Abner was returned to Hebron, Joab took him aside in the gate to speak with him quietly, and smote him there under the fifth *rib,* that he died, for the blood of Asahel his brother.

• Amasa, by Joab.
2Sa 20:9–10

• The worshipers of Baal, by Jehu.
2Ki 10:18–28

See: Betrayal

• False.

Dt 29:18–19; Ps 20:7–8; 33:16–17; 49:6–7; Isa 9:9–10; 30:1–2, 15–16; 47:7–8; Jer 2:22–23; 49:4–5; Eze 13:10–11; 29:6–7; Hos 7:11–16; Am 6:1–7; Mt 26:33–35; Mk 14:29–31; Lk 12:19–20; 17:26–30; 18:9–14; 22:33–34; Jn 13:37–38; Gal 6:7–8; Jas 4:13–15; Rev 18:7–8

1Ki 20:11 — And the king of Israel answered and said, Tell *him,* Let not him that girdeth on *his harness* boast himself as he that putteth it off.

2Ki 18:21 — Now, behold, thou trustest upon the staff of this bruised reed, *even* upon Egypt, on which if a man lean, it will go into his hand, and pierce it: so is Pharaoh king of Egypt unto all that trust on him.

Job 11:20 — But the eyes of the wicked shall fail, and they shall not escape, and their hope *shall be as* the giving up of the ghost.

Job 15:31 — Let not him that is deceived trust in vanity: for vanity shall be his recompence.

Job 29:18 — Then I said, I shall die in my nest, and I shall multiply *my* days as the sand.

Ps 10:6 — He hath said in his heart, I shall not be moved: for *I shall* never *be* in adversity.

Ps 30:6 — And in my prosperity I said, I shall never be moved.

Ps 36:2 — For he flattereth himself in his own eyes, until his iniquity be found to be hateful.

Ps 44:6 — For I will not trust in my bow, neither shall my sword save me.

Ps 52:7 — Lo, *this is* the man *that* made not God his strength; but trusted in the abundance of his riches, *and* strengthened himself in his wickedness.

Ps 60:11 — Give us help from trouble: for vain *is* the help of man.

Ps 108:12 — Give us help from trouble: for vain *is* the help of man.

Pr 14:16 — A wise *man* feareth, and departeth from evil: but the fool rageth, and is confident.

Pr 16:25 — There is a way that seemeth right unto a man, but the end thereof *are* the ways of death.

Pr 18:11 — The rich man's wealth *is* his strong city, and as an high wall in his own conceit.

Pr 23:4 — Labour not to be rich: cease from thine own wisdom.

Pr 26:12 — Seest thou a man wise in his own conceit? *there is* more hope of a fool than of him.

Pr 28:26 — He that trusteth in his own heart is a fool: but whoso walketh wisely, he shall be delivered.

Pr 29:26 — Many seek the ruler's favour; but *every* man's judgment *cometh* from the LORD.

Isa 2:22 — Cease ye from man, whose breath *is* in his nostrils: for wherein is he to be accounted of?

Isa 5:21 — Woe unto *them that are* wise in their own eyes, and prudent in their own sight!

Isa 8:12 — Say ye not, A confederacy, to all *them to* whom this people shall say, A confederacy; neither fear ye their fear, nor be afraid.

Isa 20:5 — And they shall be afraid and ashamed of Ethiopia their expectation, and of Egypt their glory.

Isa 22:11 — Ye made also a ditch between the two walls for the water of the old pool: but ye have not looked unto the maker thereof, neither had respect unto him that fashioned it long ago.

Isa 28:15 — Because ye have said, We have made a covenant with death, and with hell are we at agreement; when the overflowing scourge shall pass through, it shall not come unto us: for we have made lies our refuge, and under falsehood have we hid ourselves:

Isa 28:18 — And your covenant with death shall be disannulled, and your agreement with hell shall not stand; when the overflowing scourge shall pass through, then ye shall be trodden down by it.

Isa 30:5 — They were all ashamed of a people *that* could not profit them, nor be an help nor profit, but a shame, and also a reproach.

Isa 30:7 — For the Egyptians shall help in vain, and to no purpose: therefore have I cried concerning this, Their strength *is* to sit still.

Isa 30:10 — Which say to the seers, See not; and to the prophets, Prophesy not unto us right things, speak unto us smooth things, prophesy deceits:

Isa 31:1 — Woe to them that go down to Egypt for help; and stay on horses, and trust in chariots, because *they are* many; and in horsemen, because they are very strong; but they look not unto the Holy One of Israel, neither seek the LORD!

Isa 31:3 — Now the Egyptians *are* men, and not God; and their horses flesh, and not spirit. When the LORD shall stretch out his hand, both he that helpeth shall fall, and he that is holpen shall fall down, and they all shall fail together.

Isa 36:6 — Lo, thou trustest in the staff of this broken reed, on Egypt; whereon if a man lean, it will go into his hand, and pierce it: so *is* Pharaoh king of Egypt to all that trust in him.

Isa 47:10 — For thou hast trusted in thy wickedness: thou hast said, None seeth me. Thy wisdom and thy knowledge, it hath perverted thee; and thou hast said in thine heart, I *am,* and none else beside me.

Isa 56:12 — Come ye, *say they,* I will fetch wine, and we will fill ourselves with strong drink; and to morrow shall be as this day, *and* much more abundant.

Isa 57:13 — When thou criest, let thy companies deliver thee; but the wind shall carry them all away; vanity shall take *them:* but he that putteth his trust in me shall possess the land, and shall inherit my holy mountain;

Jer 2:13 — For my people have committed two evils; they have forsaken me the fountain of living waters, *and* hewed them out cisterns, broken cisterns, that can hold no water.

Jer 2:18 — And now what hast thou to do in the way of Egypt, to drink the waters of Sihor? or what hast thou to do in the way of Assyria, to drink the waters of the river?

Jer 2:37 — Yea, thou shalt go forth from him, and thine hands upon thine head: for the LORD hath rejected thy confidences, and thou shalt not prosper in them.

Jer 3:23 — Truly in vain *is salvation hoped for* from the hills, *and from* the multitude of mountains: truly in the LORD our God *is* the salvation of Israel.

Jer 5:17 — And they shall eat up thine harvest, and thy bread, *which* thy sons and thy daughters should eat: they shall eat up thy flocks and thine herds: they shall eat up thy vines and thy fig trees: they shall impoverish thy fenced cities, wherein thou trustedst, with the sword.

Jer 6:14 — They have healed also the hurt *of the daughter* of my people slightly, saying, Peace, peace; when *there is* no peace.

Jer 7:8 — Behold, ye trust in lying words, that cannot profit.

Jer 8:11 — For they have healed the hurt of the daughter of my people slightly, saying, Peace, peace; when *there is* no peace.

Jer 12:5 — If thou hast run with the footmen, and they have wearied thee, then how canst thou contend with horses? and *if* in the land of peace, *wherein* thou trustedst, *they wearied thee,* then how wilt thou do in the swelling of Jordan?

Jer 14:13 — Then said I, Ah, Lord GOD! behold, the prophets say unto them, Ye shall not see the sword, neither shall ye have famine; but I will give you assured peace in this place.

Jer 17:5 — Thus saith the LORD; Cursed be the man that trusteth in man, and maketh flesh his arm, and whose heart departeth from the LORD.

Jer 21:13 — Behold, I *am* against thee, O inhabitant of the valley, *and* rock of the plain, saith the LORD;

which say, Who shall come down against us? or who shall enter into our habitations?

Jer 23:17 — They say still unto them that despise me, The LORD hath said, Ye shall have peace; and they say unto every one that walketh after the imagination of his own heart, No evil shall come upon you.

Jer 48:7 — For because thou hast trusted in thy works and in thy treasures, thou shalt also be taken: and Chemosh shall go forth into captivity *with* his priests and his princes together.

Jer 48:11 — Moab hath been at ease from his youth, and he hath settled on his lees, and hath not been emptied from vessel to vessel, neither hath he gone into captivity: therefore his taste remained in him, and his scent is not changed.

La 4:17 — As for us, our eyes as yet failed for our vain help: in our watching we have watched for a nation *that* could not save *us*.

Eze 8:12 — Then said he unto me, Son of man, hast thou seen what the ancients of the house of Israel do in the dark, every man in the chambers of his imagery? for they say, The LORD seeth us not; the LORD hath forsaken the earth.

Eze 30:8 — And they shall know that I *am* the LORD, when I have set a fire in Egypt, and *when* all her helpers shall be destroyed.

Hos 5:13 — When Ephraim saw his sickness, and Judah *saw* his wound, then went Ephraim to the Assyrian, and sent to king Jareb: yet could he not heal you, nor cure you of your wound.

Hos 7:9 — Strangers have devoured his strength, and he knoweth *it* not: yea, gray hairs are here and there upon him, yet he knoweth not.

Hos 10:13 — Ye have plowed wickedness, ye have reaped iniquity; ye have eaten the fruit of lies: because thou didst trust in thy way, in the multitude of thy mighty men.

Hos 12:1 — Ephraim feedeth on wind, and followeth after the east wind: he daily increaseth lies and desolation; and they do make a covenant with the Assyrians, and oil is carried into Egypt.

Hos 14:3 — Asshur shall not save us; we will not ride upon horses: neither will we say any more to the work of our hands, *Ye are* our gods: for in thee the fatherless findeth mercy.

Am 6:13 — Ye which rejoice in a thing of nought, which say, Have we not taken to us horns by our own strength?

Am 9:10 — All the sinners of my people shall die by the sword, which say, The evil shall not overtake nor prevent us.

Ob 1:3 — The pride of thine heart hath deceived thee, thou that dwellest in the clefts of the rock, whose habitation *is* high; that saith in his heart, Who shall bring me down to the ground?

Mic 3:11 — The heads thereof judge for reward, and the priests thereof teach for hire, and the prophets thereof divine for money: yet will they lean upon the LORD, and say, *Is* not the LORD among us? none evil can come upon us.

Zep 1:12 — And it shall come to pass at that time, *that* I will search Jerusalem with candles, and punish the men that are settled on their lees: that say in their heart, The LORD will not do good, neither will he do evil.

Zep 2:15 — This *is* the rejoicing city that dwelt carelessly, that said in her heart, I *am*, and *there is* none beside me: how is she become a desolation, a place for beasts to lie down in! every one that passeth by her shall hiss, *and* wag his hand.

Zec 4:6 — Then he answered and spake unto me, saying, This *is* the word of the LORD unto Zerubbabel, saying, Not by might, nor by power, but by my spirit, saith the LORD of hosts.

Mt 25:5 — While the bridegroom tarried, they all slumbered and slept.

Mk 10:24 — And the disciples were astonished at his words. But Jesus answereth again, and saith unto them, Children, how hard is it for them that trust in riches to enter into the kingdom of God!

Lk 11:35 — Take heed therefore that the light which is in thee be not darkness.

Jn 5:45 — Do not think that I will accuse you to the Father: there is *one* that accuseth you, *even* Moses, in whom ye trust.

Ro 2:3 — And thinkest thou this, O man, that judgest them which do such things, and doest the same, that thou shalt escape the judgment of God?

Ro 12:16 — *Be* of the same mind one toward another. Mind not high things, but condescend to men of low estate. Be not wise in your own conceits.

1Co 3:21 — Therefore let no man glory in men. For all things are yours;

2Co 1:9 — But we had the sentence of death in ourselves, that we should not trust in ourselves, but in God which raiseth the dead:

1Th 5:3 — For when they shall say, Peace and safety; then sudden destruction cometh upon them, as travail upon a woman with child; and they shall not escape.

1Ti 6:17 — Charge them that are rich in this world, that they be not highminded, nor trust in uncertain riches, but in the living God, who giveth us richly all things to enjoy;

See: Blindness; spiritual

See: Conceit

- **Instances of.**
  - **Builders of Babel.**
    Ge 11:4
  - **Saul.**
    1Sa 13:8–14
  - **Sennacherib.**
    2Ki 19:23
  - **Asa.**
    2Ch 16:7–9
  - **Hezekiah.**
    Isa 22:11
  - **Jonah.**
    Jnh 1:3–5
  - **Peter.**
    Mt 26:33–35; Lk 22:33–34

• **Paul.**
Php 1:25; 2:23–24

CONFISCATION

• Of property.

• By David, that of Mephibosheth.
2Sa 16:4 — Then said the king to Ziba, Behold, thine *are* all that *pertained* unto Mephibosheth. And Ziba said, I humbly beseech thee *that* I may find grace in thy sight, my lord, O king.

• By Ahab, of Naboth's vineyard.
1Ki 21:7–16

• By Ahasuerus, of Haman's house.
Est 8:1 — On that day did the king Ahasuerus give the house of Haman the Jews' enemy unto Esther the queen. And Mordecai came before the king; for Esther had told what he *was* unto her.

• As a penalty.
Ezr 10:8 — And that whosoever would not come within three days, according to the counsel of the princes and the elders, all his substance should be forfeited, and himself separated from the congregation of those that had been carried away.

CONFLICT

1Ki 3:16–28; Mt 5:23–26; Ac 15:1–29, 36–41; Php 4:1–3

CONFUSION

• Of tongues.
Ge 11:1–9

CONGESTION

Le 13:28 — And if the bright spot stay in his place, *and* spread not in the skin, but it *be* somewhat dark; it *is* a rising of the burning, and the priest shall pronounce him clean: for it *is* an inflammation of the burning.

Dt 28:22 — The LORD shall smite thee with a consumption, and with a fever, and with an inflammation, and with an extreme burning, and with the sword, and with blasting, and with mildew; and they shall pursue thee until thou perish.

CONGREGATION

• Those who were exluded from.
Dt 23:1–3

See: Church

See: Excommunication

CONIAH **See: Jehoiachin**

CONNIVANCE

1Sa 3:11–13

Pr 10:10 — He that winketh with the eye causeth sorrow: but a prating fool shall fall.

See: Collusion

See: Complicity

See: Conspiracy

CONONIAH • Name of two Israelites.

2Ch 31:12–13

2Ch 35:9 — Conaniah also, and Shemaiah and Nethaneel, his brethren, and Hashabiah and Jeiel and Jozabad, chief of the Levites, gave unto the Levites for passover offerings five thousand *small cattle,* and five hundred oxen.

CONSCIENCE

Mt 5:15–16; 6:22–23; Lk 11:33–36; Ro 2:14–15; 7:15–23; 14:1–23; 1Co 8:9–13; 10:27–32; 1Jn 3:20–21

Job 15:21 — A dreadful sound *is* in his ears: in prosperity the destroyer shall come upon him.

Job 15:24 — Trouble and anguish shall make him afraid; they shall prevail against him, as a king ready to the battle.

Job 27:6 — My righteousness I hold fast, and will not let it go: my heart shall not reproach *me* so long as I live.

Pr 20:12 — The hearing ear, and the seeing eye, the LORD hath made even both of them.

Ac 23:1 — And Paul, earnestly beholding the council, said, Men *and* brethren, I have lived in all good conscience before God until this day.

Ac 24:16 — And herein do I exercise myself, to have always a conscience void of offence toward God, and *toward* men.

Ro 9:1 — I say the truth in Christ, I lie not, my conscience also bearing me witness in the Holy Ghost,

1Co 8:7 — Howbeit *there is* not in every man that knowledge: for some with conscience of the idol unto this hour eat *it* as a thing offered unto an idol; and their conscience being weak is defiled.

2Co 1:12 — For our rejoicing is this, the testimony of our conscience, that in simplicity and godly sincerity, not with fleshly wisdom, but by the grace of God, we have had our conversation in the world, and more abundantly to you-ward.

2Co 4:2 — But have renounced the hidden things of dishonesty, not walking in craftiness, nor handling the word of God deceitfully; but by manifestation of the truth commending ourselves to every man's conscience in the sight of God.

2Co 5:11 — Knowing therefore the terror of the Lord, we persuade men; but we are made manifest unto God; and I trust also are made manifest in your consciences.

1Ti 1:5 — Now the end of the commandment is charity out of a pure heart, and *of* a good conscience, and *of* faith unfeigned:

1Ti 1:19 — Holding faith, and a good conscience; which some having put away concerning faith have made shipwreck:

1Ti 3:9 — Holding the mystery of the faith in a pure conscience.

Heb 9:14 — How much more shall the blood of Christ, who through the eternal Spirit offered himself without spot to God, purge your conscience from dead works to serve the living God?

Heb 10:22 — Let us draw near with a true heart in full assurance of faith, having our hearts sprinkled from an evil conscience, and our bodies washed with pure water.

Heb 13:18 — Pray for us: for we trust we have a good conscience, in all things willing to live honestly.

1Pe 2:19 — For this *is* thankworthy, if a man for conscience toward God endure grief, suffering wrongfully.

1Pe 3:16 — Having a good conscience; that, whereas they speak evil of you, as of evildoers, they may be ashamed that falsely accuse your good conversation in Christ.

1Pe 3:21 — The like figure whereunto *even* baptism doth also now save us (not the putting away of the filth of the flesh, but the answer of a good conscience toward God,) by the resurrection of Jesus Christ:

- **Faithful.**
  - **Instances of.**
    - **Of Pharaoh, when he took Abraham's wife for a concubine.**

      Ge 12:18–19
    - **Of Abimelech, when he took Isaac's wife for a concubine.**

      Ge 26:9–11
    - **Of Jacob, in his care of Laban's property.**

      Ge 31:39 — That which was torn *of beasts* I brought not unto thee; I bare the loss of it; of my hand didst thou require it, *whether* stolen by day, or stolen by night.
    - **Of Joseph, when Potiphar's wife tried to seduce him.**

      Ge 39:7–12
    - **Of Nehemiah, in the matter of taxes.**

      Ne 5:15 — But the former governors that *had been* before me were chargeable unto the people, and had taken of them bread and wine, beside forty shekels of silver; yea, even their servants bare rule over the people: but so did not I, because of the fear of God.
    - **Of Daniel, in refusing to eat of the king's meat and wine.**

      Da 1:8 — But Daniel purposed in his heart that he would not defile himself with the portion of the king's meat, nor with the wine which he drank: therefore he requested of the prince of the eunuchs that he might not defile himself.
    - **Of Peter, in declaring the whole counsel of God.**

      Ac 4:19–20

      Ac 5:29 — Then Peter and the *other* apostles answered and said, We ought to obey God rather than men.

  See: Honesty

  See: Integrity
- **Guilty.**

  Ps 51:1–4, 7–14; Isa 59:9–14; Mt 14:1–2; 27:3–5; Heb 10:26–27

  Job 15:21 — A dreadful sound *is* in his ears: in prosperity the destroyer shall come upon him.

  Job 15:24 — Trouble and anguish shall make him afraid; they shall prevail against him, as a king ready to the battle.

  Ps 73:21 — Thus my heart was grieved, and I was pricked in my reins.

  Pr 28:1 — The wicked flee when no man pursueth: but the righteous are bold as a lion.

  Mk 6:14 — And king Herod heard *of him;* (for his name was spread abroad:) and he said, That John the Baptist was risen from the dead, and therefore mighty works do shew forth themselves in him.

  Mk 6:16 — But when Herod heard *thereof,* he said, It is John, whom I beheaded: he is risen from the dead.

  Jn 8:9 — And they which heard *it,* being convicted by *their own* conscience, went out one by one, beginning at the eldest, *even* unto the last: and Jesus was left alone, and the woman standing in the midst.

  Ac 2:37 — Now when they heard *this,* they were pricked in their heart, and said unto Peter and to the rest of the apostles, Men *and* brethren, what shall we do?

  1Ti 4:2 — Speaking lies in hypocrisy; having their conscience seared with a hot iron;

  Tit 1:15 — Unto the pure all things *are* pure: but unto them that are defiled and unbelieving *is* nothing pure; but even their mind and conscience is defiled.

  Heb 9:14 — How much more shall the blood of Christ, who through the eternal Spirit offered himself without spot to God, purge your conscience from dead works to serve the living God?
  - **Instances of.**
    - **Of Adam and Eve, after they sinned.**

      Ge 3:7–8
    - **Of Jacob, after he defrauded Esau.**

      Ge 33:1–12
    - **Of Joseph's brethren.**

      Ge 42:21 — And they said one to another, We *are* verily guilty concerning our brother, in that we saw the anguish of his soul, when he besought us, and we would not hear; therefore is this distress come upon us.

      Ge 44:16 — And Judah said, What shall we say unto my lord? what shall we speak? or how shall we clear ourselves? God hath found out the iniquity of thy servants: behold, we *are* my lord's servants, both we, and *he* also with whom the cup is found.
    - **Of Pharaoh, after the plagues.**

      Ex 9:27 — And Pharaoh sent, and called for Moses and Aaron, and said unto them, I have sinned this time: the LORD *is* righteous, and I and my people *are* wicked.
    - **Of Micah, after stealing.**

      Jgs 17:2 — And he said unto his mother, The eleven hundred *shekels* of silver that were taken from thee, about which thou cursedst, and spakest of also in mine ears, behold, the silver is with me; I took it. And his mother said, Blessed *be thou* of the LORD, my son.
    - **Of David, for having cut off Saul's skirt.**

      1Sa 24:5 — And it came to pass afterward, that David's heart smote him, because he had cut off Saul's skirt.
    - **Of David, for having numbered the children of Israel.**

      2Sa 24:10 — And David's heart smote him after that he had numbered the people. And David said unto the LORD, I have sinned greatly in that I have done: and now, I beseech thee, O

LORD, take away the iniquity of thy servant; for I have done very foolishly.

• **Of David, for his adultery, and murder of Uriah.**

Ps 32:1–11; 38:1–22; 40:11–12; 51:1–19

• **Of Joab, for numbering Israel.**

1Ch 21:1–7

• **Of the lepers of Samaria.**

2Ki 7:8–10

• **Of the old prophet of Bethel.**

1Ki 13:29–32

• **Of Herod, for beheading John the Baptist.**

Mt 14:2 — And said unto his servants, This is John the Baptist; he is risen from the dead; and therefore mighty works do shew forth themselves in him.

Lk 9:7 — Now Herod the tetrarch heard of all that was done by him: and he was perplexed, because that it was said of some, that John was risen from the dead;

• **Of Peter, after denying the Lord.**

Mt 26:75 — And Peter remembered the word of Jesus, which said unto him, Before the cock crow, thou shalt deny me thrice. And he went out, and wept bitterly.

Mk 14:72 — And the second time the cock crew. And Peter called to mind the word that Jesus said unto him, Before the cock crow twice, thou shalt deny me thrice. And when he thought thereon, he wept.

Lk 22:62 — And Peter went out, and wept bitterly.

• **Of Judas, after betraying the Lord.**

Mt 27:3–5

• **The accusers of the woman taken in adultery.**

Jn 8:9 — And they which heard *it,* being convicted by *their own* conscience, went out one by one, beginning at the eldest, *even* unto the last: and Jesus was left alone, and the woman standing in the midst.

• **Dead.**

Am 6:3–6; Jn 16:2–3; Ro 1:21–25; Eph 4:17–19

Pr 16:25 — There is a way that seemeth right unto a man, but the end thereof *are* the ways of death.

Pr 30:20 — Such *is* the way of an adulterous woman; she eateth, and wipeth her mouth, and saith, I have done no wickedness.

Jer 6:15 — Were they ashamed when they had committed abomination? nay, they were not at all ashamed, neither could they blush: therefore they shall fall among them that fall: at the time *that* I visit them they shall be cast down, saith the LORD.

Am 6:1 — Woe to them *that are* at ease in Zion, and trust in the mountain of Samaria, *which are* named chief of the nations, to whom the house of Israel came!

1Ti 4:2 — Speaking lies in hypocrisy; having their conscience seared with a hot iron;

Tit 1:15 — Unto the pure all things *are* pure: but unto them that are defiled and unbelieving *is* nothing pure; but even their mind and conscience is defiled.

See: Blindness; spiritual

CONSCIENCE MONEY

Mt 27:3–5

Jgs 17:2 — And he said unto his mother, The eleven hundred *shekels* of silver that were taken from thee, about which thou cursedst, and spakest of also in mine ears, behold, the silver is with me; I took it. And his mother said, Blessed *be thou* of the LORD, my son.

2Ki 12:16 — The trespass money and sin money was not brought into the house of the LORD: it was the priests'.

See: Money; sin

CONSCIENTIOUSNESS See: Integrity

CONSCRIPTION

• **Of soldiers.**

1Sa 14:52 — And there was sore war against the Philistines all the days of Saul: and when Saul saw any strong man, or any valiant man, he took him unto him.

See: Armies

CONSECRATED THINGS

• **Laws regarding.**

Le 27:1–34; Nu 18:8–32

See: Firstborn

See: First Fruits

CONSECRATION

• **Of Aaron.**

See: Aaron

• **Of priests.**

See: Priest, Mosaic

• **Of the altar.**

See: Altar

• **Of the temple.**

See: Temple, Solomon's; facts about; dedication of

See: Offerings

• **Personal.**

Mt 13:44–46

1Ch 29:5 — The gold for *things* of gold, and the silver for *things* of silver, and for all manner of work *to be made* by the hands of artificers. And who *then* is willing to consecrate his service this day unto the LORD?

Ps 51:17 — The sacrifices of God *are* a broken spirit: a broken and a contrite heart, O God, thou wilt not despise.

Pr 23:26 — My son, give me thine heart, and let thine eyes observe my ways.

Ro 6:13 — Neither yield ye your members *as* instruments of unrighteousness unto sin: but yield yourselves unto God, as those that are alive from the dead, and your members *as* instruments of righteousness unto God.

Ro 6:16 — Know ye not, that to whom ye yield yourselves servants to obey, his servants ye are to whom ye obey; whether of sin unto death, or of obedience unto righteousness?

Ro 6:19 — I speak after the manner of men because of the infirmity of your flesh: for as ye have yielded your members servants to uncleanness and to iniquity unto iniquity; even so now yield your members servants to righteousness unto holiness.

Ro 12:1 — I beseech you therefore, brethren, by the mercies of God, that ye present your bodies a living sacrifice, holy, acceptable unto God, *which is* your reasonable service.

2Co 8:5 — And *this they did,* not as we hoped, but first gave their own selves to the Lord, and unto us by the will of God.

- **Conditional.**
  Ge 28:20–22; 2Sa 15:7–8
  ✦See: Dedication
  ✦See: Offerings
- **Instances of.**
  - **Cain and Abel.**
    Ge 4:4–7
  - **Abraham, of Isaac.**
    Ge 22:9–12
  - **The people of Israel.**
    Ex 32:29
  - **Jephthah, of his daughter.**
    Jgs 11:30–31, 34–40
  - **Hannah, of Samuel.**
    1Sa 1:11, 24–28
  - **David consecrates the water obtained by his valiant warriors.**
    2Sa 23:16
  - **Zichri, of himself.**
    2Ch 17:16

CONSISTENCY

Ne 5:9 — Also I said, It *is* not good that ye do: ought ye not to walk in the fear of our God because of the reproach of the heathen our enemies?

Mt 6:24 — No man can serve two masters: for either he will hate the one, and love the other; or else he will hold to the one, and despise the other. Ye cannot serve God and mammon.

Lk 16:13 — No servant can serve two masters: for either he will hate the one, and love the other; or else he will hold to the one, and despise the other. Ye cannot serve God and mammon.

Ro 14:22 — Hast thou faith? have *it* to thyself before God. Happy *is* he that condemneth not himself in that thing which he alloweth.

1Co 10:21 — Ye cannot drink the cup of the Lord, and the cup of devils: ye cannot be partakers of the Lord's table, and of the table of devils.

✦See: Deceit
✦See: Expediency
✦See: Hypocrisy
✦See: Inconsistency
✦See: Obduracy
✦See: Prudence

CONSOLATION

✦See: Afflictions; consolation in
✦See: Holy Spirit

CONSPIRACY

- **Law against.**
  Ex 23:1–33
- **Instances of.**
  - **Joseph's brethren, against Joseph.**
    Ge 37:18–20
  - **Miriam and Aaron, against Moses.**
    Nu 12:1–16; 14:4; 16:1–35
  - **Abimelech, against Gideon's sons.**
    Jgs 9:1–6
  - **Gaal, against Abimelech.**
    Jgs 9:23–41
  - **Delilah, against Samson.**
    Jgs 16:4–21
  - **Abner, against Ish-bosheth.**
    2Sa 3:7–21
  - **Of Absalom.**
    2Sa 15:10–13
  - **Of Jeroboam.**
    1Ki 14:2
  - **Of Baasha.**
    1Ki 15:27
  - **Of Zimri.**
    1Ki 16:9
  - **Of Jezebel, against Naboth.**
    1Ki 21:8–13
  - **Of Jehu.**
    2Ki 9:14–26
  - **Of Jehoiada.**
    2Ki 11:4–16
  - **Of servants, against Joash.**
    2Ki 12:20
  - **People in Jerusalem, against Amaziah.**
    2Ki 14:19
  - **Shallum, against Zachariah.**
    2Ki 15:10
  - **Pekahiah.**
    2Ki 15:23–25
  - **Pekah.**
    2Ki 15:30
  - **Amon.**
    2Ki 21:23
  - **Sennacherib.**
    2Ki 19:37
  - **Amaziah.**
    2Ch 25:27
  - **Ahasuerus.**
    Est 2:21–23
  - **Jeremiah.**
    Jer 18:18

- **Daniel.**
  Da 6:4–17
- **Shadrach, Meshach, and Abed-nego.**
  Da 3:8–18
- **Against Jesus.**
  Jer 11:9, 19; Mt 12:14; 21:38–41; 26:3–4; 27:1–2; Mk 3:6
- **Paul.**
  Ac 18:12; 23:12–15

• Falsely accused of.

- **Jonathan.**
  1Sa 22:8 — That all of you have conspired against me, and *there is* none that sheweth me that my son hath made a league with the son of Jesse, and *there is* none of you that is sorry for me, or sheweth unto me that my son hath stirred up my servant against me, to lie in wait, as at this day?

CONSTANCY

• In obedience.

Ps 119:31 — I have stuck unto thy testimonies: O LORD, put me not to shame.

Ps 119:33 — Teach me, O LORD, the way of thy statutes; and I shall keep it *unto* the end.

• In friendship.

Pr 27:10 — Thine own friend, and thy father's friend, forsake not; neither go into thy brother's house in the day of thy calamity: *for* better *is* a neighbour *that is* near than a brother far off.

• Under suffering.

1Pe 4:12–16

Mt 5:12 — Rejoice, and be exceeding glad: for great *is* your reward in heaven: for so persecuted they the prophets which were before you.

Heb 12:5 — And ye have forgotten the exhortation which speaketh unto you as unto children, My son, despise not thou the chastening of the Lord, nor faint when thou art rebuked of him:

• In prayer.

Lk 18:1 — And he spake a parable unto them *to this end,* that men ought always to pray, and not to faint;

Ro 12:12 — Rejoicing in hope; patient in tribulation; continuing instant in prayer;

Eph 6:18 — Praying always with all prayer and supplication in the Spirit, and watching thereunto with all perseverance and supplication for all saints;

Col 4:2 — Continue in prayer, and watch in the same with thanksgiving;

1Th 5:17 — Pray without ceasing.

• In beneficence.

Gal 6:9 — And let us not be weary in well doing: for in due season we shall reap, if we faint not.

• In profession.

Heb 10:23 — Let us hold fast the profession of *our* faith without wavering; (for he is faithful that promised;)

• Instances of.

Ru 1:14

- **Jonathan.**
  1Sa 18:1; 20:16
- **Priscilla and Aquila.**
  Ro 16:3–4

✦See: Character of Saints

✦See: Stability

CONSTELLATIONS

Isa 13:10 — For the stars of heaven and the constellations thereof shall not give their light: the sun shall be darkened in his going forth, and the moon shall not cause her light to shine.

• The serpent.

Job 26:13 — By his spirit he hath garnished the heavens; his hand hath formed the crooked serpent.

• Orion.

Job 9:9 — Which maketh Arcturus, Orion, and Pleiades, and the chambers of the south.

Am 5:8 — *Seek him* that maketh the seven stars and Orion, and turneth the shadow of death into the morning, and maketh the day dark with night: that calleth for the waters of the sea, and poureth them out upon the face of the earth: The LORD *is* his name:

✦See: Astronomy

CONSTITUTION • Agreement between the ruler and people.

Dt 17:18–20; 2Ch 23:2–3; Jer 34:8–11; Da 6:12–15

2Sa 5:3 — So all the elders of Israel came to the king to Hebron; and king David made a league with them in Hebron before the LORD: and they anointed David king over Israel.

CONSUMPTION

Le 26:16 — I also will do this unto you; I will even appoint over you terror, consumption, and the burning ague, that shall consume the eyes, and cause sorrow of heart: and ye shall sow your seed in vain, for your enemies shall eat it.

Dt 28:22 — The LORD shall smite thee with a consumption, and with a fever, and with an inflammation, and with an extreme burning, and with the sword, and with blasting, and with mildew; and they shall pursue thee until thou perish.

CONTEMPT OF COURT ✦See: Court

CONTENTION ✦See: Strife

CONTENTMENT

Ecc 3:12–13; 6:7–9; 9:7–9; 1Co 7:20–21; Php 4:11–12; 1Ti 6:6–8

Ps 16:6 — The lines are fallen unto me in pleasant *places;* yea, I have a goodly heritage.

Ps 37:7 — Rest in the LORD, and wait patiently for him: fret not thyself because of him who prospereth in his way, because of the man who bringeth wicked devices to pass.

Ps 37:16 — A little that a righteous man hath *is* better than the riches of many wicked.

Pr 14:10 — The heart knoweth his own bitterness; and a stranger doth not intermeddle with his joy.

Pr 14:14 — The backslider in heart shall be filled with his own ways: and a good man *shall be satisfied* from himself.
Pr 15:13 — A merry heart maketh a cheerful countenance: but by sorrow of the heart the spirit is broken.
Pr 15:15 — All the days of the afflicted *are* evil: but he that is of a merry heart *hath* a continual feast.
Pr 15:30 — The light of the eyes rejoiceth the heart: *and* a good report maketh the bones fat.
Pr 16:8 — Better *is* a little with righteousness than great revenues without right.
Pr 17:1 — Better *is* a dry morsel, and quietness therewith, than an house full of sacrifices *with* strife.
Pr 17:22 — A merry heart doeth good *like* a medicine: but a broken spirit drieth the bones.
Pr 30:8 — Remove far from me vanity and lies: give me neither poverty nor riches; feed me with food convenient for me:
Ecc 2:24 — *There is* nothing better for a man, *than* that he should eat and drink, and *that* he should make his soul enjoy good in his labour. This also I saw, that it *was* from the hand of God.
Ecc 4:6 — Better *is* an handful *with* quietness, than both the hands full *with* travail and vexation of spirit.
Ecc 5:12 — The sleep of a labouring man *is* sweet, whether he eat little or much: but the abundance of the rich will not suffer him to sleep.
Ecc 8:15 — Then I commended mirth, because a man hath no better thing under the sun, than to eat, and to drink, and to be merry: for that shall abide with him of his labour the days of his life, which God giveth him under the sun.
Lk 3:14 — And the soldiers likewise demanded of him, saying, And what shall we do? And he said unto them, Do violence to no man, neither accuse *any* falsely; and be content with your wages.
1Co 7:17 — But as God hath distributed to every man, as the Lord hath called every one, so let him walk. And so ordain I in all churches.
1Co 7:24 — Brethren, let every man, wherein he is called, therein abide with God.
Gal 5:26 — Let us not be desirous of vain glory, provoking one another, envying one another.
Heb 13:5 — *Let your* conversation *be* without covetousness; *and be* content with such things as ye have: for he hath said, I will never leave thee, nor forsake thee.

See: Afflictions; resignation in

See: Resignation

- **Instances of.**
  - **Esau, in refusing Jacob's present.**
    Ge 33:9
  - **Barzillai, in refusing to go with David to Jerusalem.**
    2Sa 19:33–37
  - **The Shunammite, in refusing to make a request of Elisah.**
    2Ki 4:13

CONTINENCE

Mt 5:27–28; 1Co 7:1–9; 7:25–29, 36–38; 1Ti 5:1–2; Rev 14:4–5
Job 31:1 — I made a covenant with mine eyes; why then should I think upon a maid?
Mt 19:12 — For there are some eunuchs, which were so born from *their* mother's womb: and there are some eunuchs, which were made eunuchs of men: and there be eunuchs, which have made themselves eunuchs for the kingdom of heaven's sake. He that is able to receive *it*, let him receive *it*.
Ro 13:13 — Let us walk honestly, as in the day; not in rioting and drunkenness, not in chambering and wantonness, not in strife and envying.
1Co 9:27 — But I keep under my body, and bring *it* into subjection: lest that by any means, when I have preached to others, I myself should be a castaway.
Col 3:5 — Mortify therefore your members which are upon the earth; fornication, uncleanness, inordinate affection, evil concupiscence, and covetousness, which is idolatry:
1Ti 4:12 — Let no man despise thy youth; but be thou an example of the believers, in word, in conversation, in charity, in spirit, in faith, in purity.
Rev 14:1 — And I looked, and, lo, a Lamb stood on the mount Sion, and with him an hundred forty *and* four thousand, having his Father's name written in their foreheads.

See: Chastity

- **Instances of.**
  - **Joseph.**
    Ge 39:7–12
  - **Uriah.**
    2Sa 11:8–13
  - **Boaz.**
    Ru 3:6–13
  - **Joseph, husband of Mary.**
    Mt 1:24–25
  - **Paul.**
    1Co 7:8

CONTINENTS

Ge 1:9–10; Job 28:8–11; Job 38:4–18; Ps 104:5–9
Job 26:7 — He stretcheth out the north over the empty place, *and* hangeth the earth upon nothing.
Job 26:10 — He hath compassed the waters with bounds, until the day and night come to an end.
Ps 95:5 — The sea *is* his, and he made it: and his hands formed the dry *land*.
Ps 136:6 — To him that stretched out the earth above the waters: for his mercy *endureth* for ever.
Pr 8:29 — When he gave to the sea his decree, that the waters should not pass his commandment: when he appointed the foundations of the earth:
Pr 30:4 — Who hath ascended up into heaven, or descended? who hath gathered the wind in his fists? who hath bound the waters in a garment? who hath established all the ends of the earth? what *is* his name, and what *is* his son's name, if thou canst tell?

See: Geology

CONTINGENCIES

• In divine government of man.

Ge 2:16–17; Le 26:3–28; Dt 7:12–26; 11:26–28; 30:15–16; 2Sa 24:12–14; Job 36:11–12; Jer 18:8–10; 22:4–5; Eze 33:14–16; Jn 15:6–7; Col 1:22–23; 2Th 2:8–10

Ge 3:3 — But of the fruit of the tree which *is* in the midst of the garden, God hath said, Ye shall not eat of it, neither shall ye touch it, lest ye die.

Ge 4:7 — If thou doest well, shalt thou not be accepted? and if thou doest not well, sin lieth at the door. And unto thee *shall be* his desire, and thou shalt rule over him.

Ge 18:19 — For I know him, that he will command his children and his household after him, and they shall keep the way of the LORD, to do justice and judgment; that the LORD may bring upon Abraham that which he hath spoken of him.

Ex 19:5 — Now therefore, if ye will obey my voice indeed, and keep my covenant, then ye shall be a peculiar treasure unto me above all people: for all the earth *is* mine:

Dt 30:19 — I call heaven and earth to record this day against you, *that* I have set before you life and death, blessing and cursing: therefore choose life, that both thou and thy seed may live:

Jos 24:15 — And if it seem evil unto you to serve the LORD, choose you this day whom ye will serve; whether the gods which your fathers served that *were* on the other side of the flood, or the gods of the Amorites, in whose land ye dwell: but as for me and my house, we will serve the LORD.

1Ki 3:14 — And if thou wilt walk in my ways, to keep my statutes and my commandments, as thy father David did walk, then I will lengthen thy days.

1Ki 20:42 — And he said unto him, Thus saith the LORD, Because thou hast let go out of *thy* hand a man whom I appointed to utter destruction, therefore thy life shall go for his life, and thy people for his people.

1Ch 28:7 — Moreover I will establish his kingdom for ever, if he be constant to do my commandments and my judgments, as at this day.

2Ch 26:5 — And he sought God in the days of Zechariah, who had understanding in the visions of God: and as long as he sought the LORD, God made him to prosper.

Jer 11:4 — Which I commanded your fathers in the day *that* I brought them forth out of the land of Egypt, from the iron furnace, saying, Obey my voice, and do them, according to all which I command you: so shall ye be my people, and I will be your God:

Jer 12:17 — But if they will not obey, I will utterly pluck up and destroy that nation, saith the LORD.

Jnh 3:10 — And God saw their works, that they turned from their evil way; and God repented of the evil, that he had said that he would do unto them; and he did *it* not.

Mt 19:17 — And he said unto him, Why callest thou me good? *there is* none good but one, *that is,* God: but if thou wilt enter into life, keep the commandments.

Mt 23:37 — O Jerusalem, Jerusalem, *thou* that killest the prophets, and stonest them which are sent unto thee, how often would I have gathered thy children together, even as a hen gathereth her chickens under *her* wings, and ye would not!

Mt 26:39 — And he went a little farther, and fell on his face, and prayed, saying, O my Father, if it be possible, let this cup pass from me: nevertheless not as I will, but as thou *wilt.*

Mt 26:42 — He went away again the second time, and prayed, saying, O my Father, if this cup may not pass away from me, except I drink it, thy will be done.

Mk 11:26 — But if ye do not forgive, neither will your Father which is in heaven forgive your trespasses.

Jn 9:41 — Jesus said unto them, If ye were blind, ye should have no sin: but now ye say, We see; therefore your sin remaineth.

Jn 14:23 — Jesus answered and said unto him, If a man love me, he will keep my words: and my Father will love him, and we will come unto him, and make our abode with him.

Heb 3:14 — For we are made partakers of Christ, if we hold the beginning of our confidence stedfast unto the end;

Rev 2:22 — Behold, I will cast her into a bed, and them that commit adultery with her into great tribulation, except they repent of their deeds.

Rev 3:3 — Remember therefore how thou hast received and heard, and hold fast, and repent. If therefore thou shalt not watch, I will come on thee as a thief, and thou shalt not know what hour I will come upon thee.

Rev 22:17 — And the Spirit and the bride say, Come. And let him that heareth say, Come. And let him that is athirst come. And whosoever will, let him take the water of life freely.

See: Blessing; divine, contingent upon obedience

See: Predestination

See: Will

CONTRACTS

• Between Abraham and Abimelech, concerning wells of water.

Ge 21:25–32

• Contract violated.

Ge 26:15 — For all the wells which his father's servants had digged in the days of Abraham his father, the Philistines had stopped them, and filled them with earth.

• First contract between Laban and Jacob for Laban's daughter.

Ge 29:15–20, 27–30

• Contract violated.

Ge 29:23–27

• Second contract between Laban and Jacob for Laban's daughter.

Ge 30:28–34

• **Contract violated.**

Ge 30:37–43

Ge 31:7 — And your father hath deceived me, and changed my wages ten times; but God suffered him not to hurt me.

• **Contract between Laban and Jacob for cattle.**

Ge 30:27–29, 31–34

See: Fraud

• **Between Solomon and Hiram.**

1Ki 5:9–11

1Ki 9:11 — (*Now* Hiram the king of Tyre had furnished Solomon with cedar trees and fir trees, and with gold, according to all his desire,) that then king Solomon gave Hiram twenty cities in the land of Galilee.

• **Dissolved.**

• **By mutual consent.**

Ex 4:18 — And Moses went and returned to Jethro his father in law, and said unto him, Let me go, I pray thee, and return unto my brethren which *are* in Egypt, and see whether they be yet alive. And Jethro said to Moses, Go in peace.

• **By blotting out.**

Col 2:14 — Blotting out the handwriting of ordinances that was against us, which was contrary to us, and took it out of the way, nailing it to his cross;

• **Modes of ratifying.**

• **By giving presents.**

Ge 21:25–30

1Sa 18:4 — And Jonathan stripped himself of the robe that *was* upon him, and gave it to David, and his garments, even to his sword, and to his bow, and to his girdle.

• **By consummating in the presence of the public at the gate of the city.**

Ru 4:1–2

Ge 23:18 — Unto Abraham for a possession in the presence of the children of Heth, before all that went in at the gate of his city.

• **By erecting a heap of stones.**

Ge 31:44–54

• **By oaths.**

Heb 6:16–17

Ge 26:3 — Sojourn in this land, and I will be with thee, and will bless thee; for unto thee, and unto thy seed, I will give all these countries, and I will perform the oath which I sware unto Abraham thy father;

Ge 26:31 — And they rose up betimes in the morning, and sware one to another: and Isaac sent them away, and they departed from him in peace.

Jos 9:15 — And Joshua made peace with them, and made a league with them, to let them live: and the princes of the congregation sware unto them.

Jos 9:20 — This we will do to them; we will even let them live, lest wrath be upon us, because of the oath which we sware unto them.

1Ch 16:16 — *Even of the covenant* which he made with Abraham, and of his oath unto Isaac;

• **By joining hands.**

Pr 6:1 — My son, if thou be surety for thy friend, *if* thou hast stricken thy hand with a stranger,

Pr 11:21 — *Though* hand *join* in hand, the wicked shall not be unpunished: but the seed of the righteous shall be delivered.

Pr 17:18 — A man void of understanding striketh hands, *and* becometh surety in the presence of his friend.

Pr 22:26 — Be not thou *one* of them that strike hands, *or* of them that are sureties for debts.

Eze 17:18 — Seeing he despised the oath by breaking the covenant, when, lo, he had given his hand, and hath done all these *things,* he shall not escape.

• **With salt.**

Nu 18:19 — All the heave offerings of the holy things, which the children of Israel offer unto the LORD, have I given thee, and thy sons and thy daughters with thee, by a statute for ever: it is a covenant of salt for ever before the LORD unto thee and to thy seed with thee.

• **By taking off the shoe.**

Ru 4:6–8

• **By written instrument.**

Jer 32:10–15

See: Covenant

See: Vows

• **Scriptures illustrative of the binding force of.**

Ex 21:2–6; Le 6:1–2, 4–7; Jos 9:3–9, 15–16, 18–27; Mt 20:1–16

Gal 3:15 — Brethren, I speak after the manner of men; Though *it be* but a man's covenant, yet *if it be* confirmed, no man disannulleth, or addeth thereto.

See: Covenant

See: Land

CONTRITION

See: Repentance

See: Sin; confession of

CONVENTION

• **For counsel.**

Pr 15:22 — Without counsel purposes are disappointed: but in the multitude of counsellors they are established.

CONVERSATION

Mt 12:35–37

Mt 5:37 — But let your communication be, Yea, yea; Nay, nay: for whatsoever is more than these cometh of evil.

Eph 4:29 — Let no corrupt communication proceed out of your mouth, but that which is good to the use of edifying, that it may minister grace unto the hearers.

Col 3:8 — But now ye also put off all these; anger, wrath, malice, blasphemy, filthy communication out of your mouth.

Col 4:6 — Let your speech *be* alway with grace, seasoned with salt, that ye may know how ye ought to answer every man.

Jas 5:12 — But above all things, my brethren, swear not, neither by heaven, neither by the earth, neither by any other oath: but let your yea be yea; and *your* nay, nay; lest ye fall into condemnation.

See: Tongue

CONVERSION

See: Regeneration

- **Instances of.**

See: Converts

CONVERTS

- **"Wayside".**

Mt 13:4 — And when he sowed, some *seeds* fell by the way side, and the fowls came and devoured them up:

Mt 13:19 — When any one heareth the word of the kingdom, and understandeth *it* not, then cometh the wicked *one*, and catcheth away that which was sown in his heart. This is he which received seed by the way side.

- **"Stony ground".**

Mt 13:20–21

Mt 13:5 — Some fell upon stony places, where they had not much earth: and forthwith they sprung up, because they had no deepness of earth:

- **"Choked".**

Mt 13:7 — And some fell among thorns; and the thorns sprung up, and choked them:

Mt 13:22 — He also that received seed among the thorns is he that heareth the word; and the care of this world, and the deceitfulness of riches, choke the word, and he becometh unfruitful.

- **"Good ground".**

Lk 8:4–15

Mt 13:8 — But other fell into good ground, and brought forth fruit, some an hundredfold, some sixtyfold, some thirtyfold.

Mt 13:23 — But he that received seed into the good ground is he that heareth the word, and understandeth *it;* which also beareth fruit, and bringeth forth, some an hundredfold, some sixty, some thirty.

See: Backsliders

See: Proselyte

See: Revivals

- **Instances of.**
  - **Ruth.**

Ru 1:16

  - **Nebuchadnezzar.**

Da 4:1–37

  - **The mariners with Jonah.**

Jnh 1:5–6, 9, 14, 16

  - **Ninevites.**

Jnh 3:1–10

  - **Gadarenes.**

Lk 8:35–39

  - **The Samaritans.**

Jn 4:28–42

  - **The thief on the cross.**

Lk 23:39–43

  - **At Pentecost, three thousand.**

Ac 2:41

  - **Post-pentecostal.**

Ac 4:4

  - **The eunuch.**

Ac 8:35–38

  - **Saul of Tarsus.**

Ac 9:3–18

  - **Sergius Paulus.**

Ac 13:7, 12; 26:12–23

  - **Cornelius.**

Ac 10:1–48

  - **Jews and Greeks at Antioch.**

Ac 13:43

  - **Lydia.**

Ac 16:14–15

  - **Jailer.**

Ac 16:27–34

  - **Greeks.**

Ac 17:4, 12

- **Zealous.**
  - **Instances of.**
    - **Nebuchadnezzar.**

Da 4:1–37

Da 3:29 — Therefore I make a decree, That every people, nation, and language, which speak any thing amiss against the God of Shadrach, Meshach, and Abed-nego, shall be cut in pieces, and their houses shall be made a dunghill: because there is no other God that can deliver after this sort.

    - **Andrew.**

Jn 1:40–41

    - **Philip.**

Jn 1:43–45

    - **The woman of Samaria.**

Jn 4:28–29

    - **The man possessed of demons.**

Lk 8:39 — Return to thine own house, and shew how great things God hath done unto thee. And he went his way, and published throughout the whole city how great things Jesus had done unto him.

    - **The blind men.**

Jn 9:8–38

Mt 9:31 — But they, when they were departed, spread abroad his fame in all that country.

• **The dumb man.**

Mk 7:36 — And he charged them that they should tell no man: but the more he charged them, so much the more a great deal they published *it;*

CONVEYANCE

• **Of land.**

See: Land

CONVICTION

• **Of sin.**

Dt 28:65–67; Job 40:4–5; Ps 38:1–22; 51:1–4, 7–17; Eze 7:16–18, 25–26; Ac 16:29–30; 1Co 14:24–25

Ge 4:13 — And Cain said unto the LORD, My punishment *is* greater than I can bear.

Ps 31:10 — For my life is spent with grief, and my years with sighing: my strength faileth because of mine iniquity, and my bones are consumed.

Isa 6:5 — Then said I, Woe *is* me! for I am undone; because I *am* a man of unclean lips, and I dwell in the midst of a people of unclean lips: for mine eyes have seen the King, the LORD of hosts.

La 1:20 — Behold, O LORD; for I *am* in distress: my bowels are troubled; mine heart is turned within me; for I have grievously rebelled: abroad the sword bereaveth, at home *there is* as death.

Eze 33:10 — Therefore, O thou son of man, speak unto the house of Israel; Thus ye speak, saying, If our transgressions and our sins *be* upon us, and we pine away in them, how should we then live?

Mic 7:17 — They shall lick the dust like a serpent, they shall move out of their holes like worms of the earth: they shall be afraid of the LORD our God, and shall fear because of thee.

Lk 5:8 — When Simon Peter saw *it,* he fell down at Jesus' knees, saying, Depart from me; for I am a sinful man, O Lord.

Ac 2:37 — Now when they heard *this,* they were pricked in their heart, and said unto Peter and to the rest of the apostles, Men *and* brethren, what shall we do?

Ac 9:6 — And he trembling and astonished said, Lord, what wilt thou have me to do? And the Lord *said* unto him, Arise, and go into the city, and it shall be told thee what thou must do.

Ro 2:15 — Which shew the work of the law written in their hearts, their conscience also bearing witness, and *their* thoughts the mean while accusing or else excusing one another;)

See: Sin; confession of

• **Instances of.**

• **Adam and Eve, after their disobedience.**

Ge 3:8–10

• **Joseph's brethren, on account of their cruelty to Joseph.**

Ge 42:21–22; 44:16; 45:3; 50:15–21

• **Pharaoh.**

• **After the plague of hail.**

Ex 9:27–28

• **After the plague of locusts.**

Ex 10:16–17

• **After the death of the firstborn.**

Ex 12:31 — And he called for Moses and Aaron by night, and said, Rise up, *and* get you forth from among my people, both ye and the children of Israel; and go, serve the LORD, as ye have said.

• **The Israelites.**

• **After being rebuked and punished for worshiping the golden calf.**

Ex 33:4 — And when the people heard these evil tidings, they mourned: and no man did put on him his ornaments.

• **After the death of the ten spies, and their being sentenced to wander forty years.**

Nu 14:39–40

• **After their murmuring against God and being bitten by fiery serpents.**

Nu 21:7 — Therefore the people came to Moses, and said, We have sinned, for we have spoken against the LORD, and against thee; pray unto the LORD, that he take away the serpents from us. And Moses prayed for the people.

• **Saul, after sparing Agag and the best of the spoils.**

1Sa 15:24 — And Saul said unto Samuel, I have sinned: for I have transgressed the commandment of the LORD, and thy words: because I feared the people, and obeyed their voice.

• **David, after the pestilence sent on account of his numbering the people.**

1Ch 21:30 — But David could not go before it to enquire of God: for he was afraid because of the sword of the angel of the LORD.

See: Psalms; penitential

• **Widow of Zrephath, when her son died.**

1Ki 17:18 — And she said unto Elijah, What have I to do with thee, O thou man of God? art thou come unto me to call my sin to remembrance, and to slay my son?

• **Belshazzar, when he "saw the part of the hand that wrote".**

Da 5:6 — Then the king's countenance was changed, and his thoughts troubled him, so that the joints of his loins were loosed, and his knees smote one against another.

• Darius, when Daniel was in the lions' den.

Da 6:18 — Then the king went to his palace, and passed the night fasting: neither were instruments of musick brought before him: and his sleep went from him.

• **Mariners.**

• **After casting Jonah into the sea.**

Jnh 1:16 — Then the men feared the LORD exceedingly, and offered a sacrifice unto the LORD, and made vows.

• **At the preaching of Jonah.**

Jnh 3:1–10

Mt 12:41 — The men of Nineveh shall rise in judgment with this generation, and shall condemn it: because they repented at the preaching of Jonas; and, behold, a greater than Jonas *is* here.

Lk 11:32 — The men of Nineve shall rise up in the judgment with this generation, and shall condemn it: for they repented at the preaching of Jonas; and, behold, a greater than Jonas *is* here.

• Jonah, in the whale's belly.

Jnh 2:1–10

• Herod, when he heard of the fame of Jesus.

Mt 14:2 — And said unto his servants, This is John the Baptist; he is risen from the dead; and therefore mighty works do shew forth themselves in him.

Mk 6:14 — And king Herod heard *of him;* (for his name was spread abroad:) and he said, That John the Baptist was risen from the dead, and therefore mighty works do shew forth themselves in him.

Lk 9:7 — Now Herod the tetrarch heard of all that was done by him: and he was perplexed, because that it was said of some, that John was risen from the dead;

• Jews, when Jesus commanded the guiltless man to cast the first stone at the woman taken in adultery.

Jn 8:9 — And they which heard *it,* being convicted by *their own* conscience, went out one by one, beginning at the eldest, *even* unto the last: and Jesus was left alone, and the woman standing in the midst.

• Judas, after his betrayal of Jesus.

Mt 27:3–5

• Saul of Tarsus, when he saw Jesus on the way to Damascus.

Ac 9:6 — And he trembling and astonished said, Lord, what wilt thou have me to do? And the Lord *said* unto him, Arise, and go into the city, and it shall be told thee what thou must do.

• Felix, under the preaching of Paul.

Ac 24:25 — And as he reasoned of righteousness, temperance, and judgment to come Felix trembled, and answered, Go thy way for this time; when I have a convenient season, I will call for thee.

• Philippian jailer, after the earthquake.

Ac 16:30 — And brought them out, and said, Sirs, what must I do to be saved?

✦See: Wicked

• From God.

Job 33:14–30; Jn 6:44–45; 16:7–11

Ac 16:14 — And a certain woman named Lydia, a seller of purple, of the city of Thyatira, which worshipped God, heard *us:* whose heart the Lord opened, that she attended unto the things which were spoken of Paul.

✦See: Penitent

✦See: Remorse

✦See: Repentance

✦See: Sin; confession of

• Unjust, of innocent persons.

✦See: Accusation, False

✦See: Indictments

• Unclassified scripture relating to.

Ex 22:30 — Likewise shalt thou do with thine oxen, *and* with thy sheep: seven days it shall be with his dam; on the eighth day thou shalt give it me.

Ps 94:16 — Who will rise up for me against the evildoers? *or* who will stand up for me against the workers of iniquity?

1Ti 6:12 — Fight the good fight of faith, lay hold on eternal life, whereunto thou art also called, and hast professed a good profession before many witnesses.

2Ti 2:2 — And the things that thou hast heard of me among many witnesses, the same commit thou to faithful men, who shall be able to teach others also.

2Ti 4:7 — I have fought a good fight, I have finished *my* course, I have kept the faith:

CONVOCATION

• Holy.

• Three held annually by the Israelites.

Le 23:1–44

✦See: Feasts

COOKING

• A kid might not be seethed in the mother's milk.

Dt 14:21 — Ye shall not eat *of* any thing that dieth of itself: thou shalt give it unto the stranger that *is* in thy gates, that he may eat it; or thou mayest sell it unto an alien: for thou *art* an holy people unto the LORD thy God. Thou shalt not seethe a kid in his mother's milk.

• Spice used in.

Eze 24:10 — Heap on wood, kindle the fire, consume the flesh, and spice it well, and let the bones be burned.

• Ephraim, a cake unturned.

Hos 7:8 — Ephraim, he hath mixed himself among the people; Ephraim is a cake not turned.

• In the temple.

Eze 46:19–24

✦See: Bread

✦See: Oven

COOS • An island, Paul visits, in the Mediterranean.

Ac 21:1 — And it came to pass, that after we were gotten from them, and had launched, we came with a straight course unto Coos, and the *day* following unto Rhodes, and from thence unto Patara:

COPPER

• Incorrectly translated brass.

Dt 8:9 — A land wherein thou shalt eat bread without scarceness, thou shalt not lack any *thing* in it; a land whose stones are iron, and out of whose hills thou mayest dig brass.

See: Brass, or more probably copper

COPULATION

• Forbidden between persons near of kin.

Le 18:6–16

• During menses.

Le 15:19 — And if a woman have an issue, *and* her issue in her flesh be blood, she shall be put apart seven days: and whosoever toucheth her shall be unclean until the even.

Le 18:19 — Also thou shalt not approach unto a woman to uncover her nakedness, as long as she is put apart for her uncleanness.

• With animals.

See: Adultery

See: Lasciviousness

See: Sodomy

COR

• A measure for liquids and solids, containing ten ephahs, or baths, and equal to the homer.

Eze 45:14 — Concerning the ordinance of oil, the bath of oil, *ye shall offer* the tenth part of a bath out of the cor, *which is* an homer of ten baths; for ten baths *are* an homer:

• Rendered measure in.

1Ki 4:22 — And Solomon's provision for one day was thirty measures of fine flour, and threescore measures of meal,

1Ki 5:11 — And Solomon gave Hiram twenty thousand measures of wheat *for* food to his household, and twenty measures of pure oil: thus gave Solomon to Hiram year by year.

2Ch 2:10 — And, behold, I will give to thy servants, the hewers that cut timber, twenty thousand measures of beaten wheat, and twenty thousand measures of barley, and twenty thousand baths of wine, and twenty thousand baths of oil.

2Ch 27:5 — He fought also with the king of the Ammonites, and prevailed against them. And the children of Ammon gave him the same year an hundred talents of silver, and ten thousand measures of wheat, and ten thousand of barley. So much did the children of Ammon pay unto him, both the second year, and the third.

Ezr 7:22 — Unto an hundred talents of silver, and to an hundred measures of wheat, and to an hundred baths of wine, and to an hundred baths of oil, and salt without prescribing *how much.*

Lk 16:7 — Then said he to another, And how much owest thou? And he said, An hundred measures of wheat. And he said unto him, Take thy bill, and write fourscore.

See: Measure

CORAL

Job 28:18 — No mention shall be made of coral, or of pearls: for the price of wisdom *is* above rubies.

Eze 27:16 — Syria *was* thy merchant by reason of the multitude of the wares of thy making: they occupied in thy fairs with emeralds, purple, and broidered work, and fine linen, and coral, and agate.

CORBAN • An oblation.

Mk 7:11 — But ye say, If a man shall say to his father or mother, *It is* Corban, that is to say, a gift, by whatsoever thou mightest be profited by me; *he shall be free.*

CORD

• Ancient uses of.

• In casting lots.

Mic 2:5 — Therefore thou shalt have none that shall cast a cord by lot in the congregation of the LORD.

• In fastening tents.

Ex 35:18 — The pins of the tabernacle, and the pins of the court, and their cords,

Ex 39:40 — The hangings of the court, his pillars, and his sockets, and the hanging for the court gate, his cords, and his pins, and all the vessels of the service of the tabernacle, for the tent of the congregation,

Isa 54:2 — Enlarge the place of thy tent, and let them stretch forth the curtains of thine habitations: spare not, lengthen thy cords, and strengthen thy stakes;

• In leading or binding animals.

Ps 118:27 — God *is* the LORD, which hath shewed us light: bind the sacrifice with cords, *even* unto the horns of the altar.

Hos 11:4 — I drew them with cords of a man, with bands of love: and I was to them as they that take off the yoke on their jaws, and I laid meat unto them.

• In hitching to cart or plough.

Job 39:10 — Canst thou bind the unicorn with his band in the furrow? or will he harrow the valleys after thee?

• In binding prisoners.

Jgs 15:13 — And they spake unto him, saying, No; but we will bind thee fast, and deliver thee into their hand: but surely we will not kill thee. And they bound him with two new cords, and brought him up from the rock.

• In measuring ground.

Jos 17:14 — And the children of Joseph spake unto Joshua, saying, Why hast thou given me *but* one lot and one portion to inherit, seeing I *am* a great people, forasmuch as the LORD hath blessed me hitherto?

2Sa 8:2 — And he smote Moab, and measured them with a line, casting them down to the ground; even with two lines measured he to put to death, and with one full line to keep alive. And so the Moabites became David's servants, *and* brought gifts.

Ps 78:55 — He cast out the heathen also before them, and divided them an inheritance by line, and made the tribes of Israel to dwell in their tents.

Am 7:17 — Therefore thus saith the LORD; Thy wife shall be an harlot in the city, and thy sons and thy daughters shall fall by the sword, and thy land shall be divided by line; and thou shalt die in a polluted land: and Israel shall surely go into captivity forth of his land.

Zec 2:1 — I lifted up mine eyes again, and looked, and behold a man with a measuring line in his hand.

• Worn on the head as a sign of submission.

1Ki 20:31 — And his servants said unto him, Behold now, we have heard that the kings of the house of Israel *are* merciful kings: let us, I pray thee, put sackcloth on our loins, and ropes upon our heads, and go out to the king of Israel: peradventure he will save thy life.

• Figurative.

• Of spiritual blessings.

Ps 16:6 — The lines are fallen unto me in pleasant *places;* yea, I have a goodly heritage.

• Of sin.

Pr 5:22 — His own iniquities shall take the wicked himself, and he shall be holden with the cords of his sins.

• Of life.

Ecc 12:6 — Or ever the silver cord be loosed, or the golden bowl be broken, or the pitcher be broken at the fountain, or the wheel broken at the cistern.

• Of friendship.

Ecc 4:12 — And if one prevail against him, two shall withstand him; and a threefold cord is not quickly broken.

Hos 11:4 — I drew them with cords of a man, with bands of love: and I was to them as they that take off the yoke on their jaws, and I laid meat unto them.

• Symbolic uses of.

• Token in mourning.

1Ki 20:31–33

Job 36:8 — And if *they be* bound in fetters, *and* be holden in cords of affliction;

• Signifying an inheritance.

Jos 17:14 — And the children of Joseph spake unto Joshua, saying, Why hast thou given me *but* one lot and one portion to inherit, seeing I *am* a great people, forasmuch as the LORD hath blessed me hitherto?

CORIANDER • A spice.

Ex 16:31 — And the house of Israel called the name thereof Manna: and it *was* like coriander seed, white; and the taste of it *was* like wafers *made* with honey.

Nu 11:7 — And the manna *was* as coriander seed, and the colour thereof as the colour of bdellium.

CORINTH

• A city of Achaia.

• Visited.

• By Paul.

Ac 18:1–28; 1Co 16:5–7

2Co 1:16 — And to pass by you into Macedonia, and to come again out of Macedonia unto you, and of you to be brought on my way toward Judaea.

2Co 12:14 — Behold, the third time I am ready to come to you; and I will not be burdensome to you: for I seek not yours, but you: for the children ought not to lay up for the parents, but the parents for the children.

2Co 13:1 — This *is* the third *time* I am coming to you. In the mouth of two or three witnesses shall every word be established.

• By Apollos.

Tit 1:1–3:15

Ac 19:1 — And it came to pass, that, while Apollos was at Corinth, Paul having passed through the upper coasts came to Ephesus: and finding certain disciples,

• By Titus.

2Co 8:16–17

2Co 12:18 — I desired Titus, and with *him* I sent a brother. Did Titus make a gain of you? walked we not in the same spirit? *walked we* not in the same steps?

• By Erastus, a Christian of.

Ro 16:23 — Gaius mine host, and of the whole church, saluteth you. Erastus the chamberlain of the city saluteth you, and Quartus a brother.

2Ti 4:20 — Erastus abode at Corinth: but Trophimus have I left at Miletum sick.

• Church of.

• Schism in.

1Co 1:12 — Now this I say, that every one of you saith, I am of Paul; and I of Apollos; and I of Cephas; and I of Christ.

1Co 3:4 — For while one saith, I am of Paul; and another, I *am* of Apollos; are ye not carnal?

• Immoralities in.

1Co 5:1–13; 11:1–34

• Writes to Paul.

1Co 7:1 — Now concerning the things whereof ye wrote unto me: *It is* good for a man not to touch a woman.

• Alienation of, from Paul.

2Co 10:1–18

• Abuse of ordinances in.

1Co 14:1–40

1Co 11:22 — What? have ye not houses to eat and to drink in? or despise ye the church of God, and shame them that have not? What shall I say to you? shall I praise you in this? I praise *you* not.

• **Heresies in.**

2Co 11:1–33

1Co 15:12 — Now if Christ be preached that he rose from the dead, how say some among you that there is no resurrection of the dead?

• **Lawsuits in.**

1Co 6:1–20

• **Liberality of.**

2Co 9:1–15

• **Paul's letters to.**

1Co 16:21–24

1Co 1:2 — Unto the church of God which is at Corinth, to them that are sanctified in Christ Jesus, called *to be* saints, with all that in every place call upon the name of Jesus Christ our Lord, both theirs and ours:

2Co 1:1 — Paul, an apostle of Jesus Christ by the will of God, and Timothy *our* brother, unto the church of God which is at Corinth, with all the saints which are in all Achaia:

2Co 1:13 — For we write none other things unto you, than what ye read or acknowledge; and I trust ye shall acknowledge even to the end;

CORMORANT

• **A bird.**

• **Forbidden as food.**

Le 11:17 — And the little owl, and the cormorant, and the great owl,

Dt 14:17 — And the pelican, and the gier eagle, and the cormorant,

Isa 34:11 — But the cormorant and the bittern shall possess it; the owl also and the raven shall dwell in it: and he shall stretch out upon it the line of confusion, and the stones of emptiness.

Zep 2:14 — And flocks shall lie down in the midst of her, all the beasts of the nations: both the cormorant and the bittern shall lodge in the upper lintels of it; *their* voice shall sing in the windows; desolation *shall be* in the thresholds: for he shall uncover the cedar work.

CORN

• **A general term applied to all grains.**

• **In valleys.**

Ps 65:13 — The pastures are clothed with flocks; the valleys also are covered over with corn; they shout for joy, they also sing.

Mk 4:28 — For the earth bringeth forth fruit of herself; first the blade, then the ear, after that the full corn in the ear.

• **A product of Egypt.**

Ge 41:47–49

• **A product of Palestine.**

Dt 33:28 — Israel then shall dwell in safety alone: the fountain of Jacob *shall be* upon a land of corn and wine; also his heavens shall drop down dew.

Eze 27:17 — Judah, and the land of Israel, they *were* thy merchants: they traded in thy market wheat of Minnith, and Pannag, and honey, and oil, and balm.

• **Parched.**

Ru 2:14 — And Boaz said unto her, At mealtime come thou hither, and eat of the bread, and dip thy morsel in the vinegar. And she sat beside the reapers: and he reached her parched *corn,* and she did eat, and was sufficed, and left.

1Sa 17:17 — And Jesse said unto David his son, Take now for thy brethren an ephah of this parched *corn,* and these ten loaves, and run to the camp to thy brethren;

1Sa 25:18 — Then Abigail made haste, and took two hundred loaves, and two bottles of wine, and five sheep ready dressed, and five measures of parched *corn,* and an hundred clusters of raisins, and two hundred cakes of figs, and laid *them* on asses.

2Sa 17:28 — Brought beds, and basons, and earthen vessels, and wheat, and barley, and flour, and parched *corn,* and beans, and lentiles, and parched *pulse,*

• **Ground.**

2Sa 17:19 — And the woman took and spread a covering over the well's mouth, and spread ground corn thereon; and the thing was not known.

• **Eaten by the Israelites.**

Jos 5:11–12

• **Shocks of, burnt.**

Jgs 15:5 — And when he had set the brands on fire, he *let* them go into the standing corn of the Philistines, and burnt up both the shocks, and also the standing corn, with the vineyards *and* olives.

• **Heads of, plucked by Christ's disciples.**

Mt 12:1 — At that time Jesus went on the sabbath day through the corn; and his disciples were an hungred, and began to pluck the ears of corn, and to eat.

• **Mosaic laws concerning.**

Ex 22:6 — If fire break out, and catch in thorns, so that the stacks of corn, or the standing corn, or the field, be consumed *therewith;* he that kindled the fire shall surely make restitution.

Dt 23:25 — When thou comest into the standing corn of thy neighbour, then thou mayest pluck the ears with thine hand; but thou shalt not move a sickle unto thy neighbour's standing corn.

• **Figurative.**

Ps 72:16 — There shall be an handful of corn in the earth upon the top of the mountains; the fruit thereof shall shake like Lebanon: and *they* of the city shall flourish like grass of the earth.

Hos 14:7 — They that dwell under his shadow shall return; they shall revive *as* the corn, and grow as the vine: the scent thereof *shall be* as the wine of Lebanon.

Jn 12:24 — Verily, verily, I say unto you, Except a corn of wheat fall into the ground and die, it abideth alone: but if it die, it bringeth forth much fruit.

• **Symbolic.**

Ge 41:5 — And he slept and dreamed the second time: and, behold, seven ears of corn came up upon one stalk, rank and good.

See: Barley

See: Barn

See: Bread

See: First Fruits

See: Gleaning

See: Harvest

See: Reaping

See: Rye

See: Threshing

See: Tithes

See: Wheat

CORNELIUS • A Roman centurion.

Ac 10:1–48

CORNER STONE

• **Figurative.**

Job 38:6 — Whereupon are the foundations thereof fastened? or who laid the corner stone thereof;

Ps 144:12 — That our sons *may be* as plants grown up in their youth; *that* our daughters *may be* as corner stones, polished *after* the similitude of a palace:

See: Stones

• **Of Christ.**

Ps 118:22 — The stone *which* the builders refused is become the head *stone* of the corner.

Isa 28:16 — Therefore thus saith the Lord GOD, Behold, I lay in Zion for a foundation a stone, a tried stone, a precious corner *stone,* a sure foundation: he that believeth shall not make haste.

Mt 21:42 — Jesus saith unto them, Did ye never read in the scriptures, The stone which the builders rejected, the same is become the head of the corner: this is the Lord's doing, and it is marvellous in our eyes?

Mk 12:10 — And have ye not read this scripture; The stone which the builders rejected is become the head of the corner:

Lk 20:17 — And he beheld them, and said, What is this then that is written, The stone which the builders rejected, the same is become the head of the corner?

Ac 4:11 — This is the stone which was set at nought of you builders, which is become the head of the corner.

1Co 3:11 — For other foundation can no man lay than that is laid, which is Jesus Christ.

Eph 2:20 — And are built upon the foundation of the apostles and prophets, Jesus Christ himself being the chief corner *stone;*

1Pe 2:6 — Wherefore also it is contained in the scripture, Behold, I lay in Sion a chief corner stone, elect, precious: and he that believeth on him shall not be confounded.

CORNET **See: Trumpet**

CORPORAL PUNISHMENT **See: Punishment**

CORPULENCY

• **Instances of.**

• **Eglon.**

Jgs 3:17

• **Eli.**

1Sa 4:18

CORRECTION

See: Afflictions; design of

See: Chastisement

See: Children, Commandments to; correction of

See: Parents

See: Punishment

See: Scourging

CORRUPTION

• **Physical decomposition.**

Le 22:25 — Neither from a stranger's hand shall ye offer the bread of your God of any of these; because their corruption *is* in them, *and* blemishes *be* in them: they shall not be accepted for you.

• **After death.**

Ecc 12:1–14; Ac 13:34–37

Ge 3:19 — In the sweat of thy face shalt thou eat bread, till thou return unto the ground; for out of it wast thou taken: for dust thou *art,* and unto dust shalt thou return.

Job 17:14 — I have said to corruption, Thou *art* my father: to the worm, *Thou art* my mother, and my sister.

Job 21:26 — They shall lie down alike in the dust, and the worms shall cover them.

Job 34:15 — All flesh shall perish together, and man shall turn again unto dust.

Ps 16:10 — For thou wilt not leave my soul in hell; neither wilt thou suffer thine Holy One to see corruption.

Ps 49:9 — That he should still live for ever, *and* not see corruption.

Ps 104:29 — Thou hidest thy face, they are troubled: thou takest away their breath, they die, and return to their dust.

Ecc 3:20 — All go unto one place; all are of the dust, and all turn to dust again.

Jnh 2:6 — I went down to the bottoms of the mountains; the earth with her bars *was* about me for ever: yet hast thou brought up my life from corruption, O LORD my God.

Ac 2:27 — Because thou wilt not leave my soul in hell, neither wilt thou suffer thine Holy One to see corruption.

Ac 2:31 — He seeing this before spake of the resurrection of Christ, that his soul was not left in hell, neither his flesh did see corruption.

1Co 15:42 — So also *is* the resurrection of the dead. It is sown in corruption; it is raised in incorruption:

1Co 15:50 — Now this I say, brethren, that flesh and blood cannot inherit the kingdom of God; neither doth corruption inherit incorruption.

• **Figurative.**

• **Of sin.**

Isa 38:17 — Behold, for peace I had great bitterness: but thou hast in love to my soul *delivered it* from the pit of corruption: for thou hast cast all my sins behind thy back.

Ro 8:21 — Because the creature itself also shall be delivered from the bondage of corruption into the glorious liberty of the children of God.

Gal 6:8 — For he that soweth to his flesh shall of the flesh reap corruption; but he that soweth to the Spirit shall of the Spirit reap life everlasting.

2Pe 1:4 — Whereby are given unto us exceeding great and precious promises: that by these ye might be partakers of the divine nature, having escaped the corruption that is in the world through lust.

2Pe 2:12 — But these, as natural brute beasts, made to be taken and destroyed, speak evil of the things that they understand not; and shall utterly perish in their own corruption;

2Pe 2:19 — While they promise them liberty, they themselves are the servants of corruption: for of whom a man is overcome, of the same is he brought in bondage.

• **Mount of.**

2Ki 23:13 — And the high places that *were* before Jerusalem, which *were* on the right hand of the mount of corruption, which Solomon the king of Israel had builded for Ashtoreth the abomination of the Zidonians, and for Chemosh the abomination of the Moabites, and for Milcom the abomination of the children of Ammon, did the king defile.

• **Judicial.**

See: Court

See: Government

See: Judge

• **Ecclesiastical.**

See: Church; corruption in

See: Minister, False and Corrupt

• **Political.**

See: Bribery

See: Civil Service

See: Government

See: Politics, Statecraft

COSMETICS

2Ki 9:30 — And when Jehu was come to Jezreel, Jezebel heard *of it;* and she painted her face, and tired her head, and looked out at a window.

Jer 4:30 — And *when* thou *art* spoiled, what wilt thou do? Though thou clothest thyself with crimson, though thou deckest thee with ornaments of gold, though thou rentest thy face with painting, in vain shalt thou make thyself fair; *thy* lovers will despise thee, they will seek thy life.

Eze 23:40 — And furthermore, that ye have sent for men to come from far, unto whom a messenger *was* sent; and, lo, they came: for whom thou didst wash thyself, paintedst thy eyes, and deckedst thyself with ornaments,

COTTON

Ex 25:4 — And blue, and purple, and scarlet, and fine linen, and goats' *hair,*

COUNCIL

• **Apostolic.**

Ac 15:1–29

• **Of war.**

2Sa 17:1–15

2Sa 16:20 — Then said Absalom to Ahithophel, Give counsel among you what we shall do.

COUNSEL

1Ki 22:5 — And Jehoshaphat said unto the king of Israel, Enquire, I pray thee, at the word of the LORD to day.

Ps 1:1 — Blessed *is* the man that walketh not in the counsel of the ungodly, nor standeth in the way of sinners, nor sitteth in the seat of the scornful.

Ps 73:24 — Thou shalt guide me with thy counsel, and afterward receive me *to* glory.

Pr 1:5 — A wise *man* will hear, and will increase learning; and a man of understanding shall attain unto wise counsels:

Pr 9:9 — Give *instruction* to a wise *man,* and he will be yet wiser: teach a just *man,* and he will increase in learning.

Pr 11:14 — Where no counsel *is,* the people fall: but in the multitude of counsellors *there is* safety.

Pr 12:15 — The way of a fool *is* right in his own eyes: but he that hearkeneth unto counsel *is* wise.

Pr 15:22 — Without counsel purposes are disappointed: but in the multitude of counsellors they are established.

Pr 19:20 — Hear counsel, and receive instruction, that thou mayest be wise in thy latter end.

Pr 20:18 — *Every* purpose is established by counsel: and with good advice make war.

Pr 24:6 — For by wise counsel thou shalt make thy war: and in multitude of counsellors *there is* safety.

Pr 27:9 — Ointment and perfume rejoice the heart: so *doth* the sweetness of a man's friend by hearty counsel.

1Th 5:11 — Wherefore comfort yourselves together, and edify one another, even as also ye do.

1Th 5:14 — Now we exhort you, brethren, warn them that are unruly, comfort the feebleminded, support the weak, be patient toward all *men.*

See: Prudence

• **Rejected.**
Pr 1:24–33

• **Instances of.**

• **By Rehoboam.**
1Ki 12:8–16

• **By the rich young ruler.**
Mt 19:22

COUNSELLOR

• **A wise man, versed in law and diplomacy.**
1Ch 27:32–33

• **Ahithophel was, to David.**
2Sa 16:23 — And the counsel of Ahithophel, which he counselled in those days, *was* as if a man had enquired at the oracle of God: so *was* all the counsel of Ahithophel both with David and with Absalom.

1Ch 27:33 — And Ahithophel *was* the king's counsellor: and Hushai the Archite *was* the king's companion:

• **Ahithophel was, to Absalom.**
2Sa 16:23 — And the counsel of Ahithophel, which he counselled in those days, *was* as if a man had enquired at the oracle of God: so *was* all the counsel of Ahithophel both with David and with Absalom.

• **Was member of the Sanhedrin at Jerusalem.**
Lk 23:50–51

Mk 15:43 — Joseph of Arimathaea, an honourable counsellor, which also waited for the kingdom of God, came, and went in boldly unto Pilate, and craved the body of Jesus.

• **A title of Christ.**
Isa 9:6 — For unto us a child is born, unto us a son is given: and the government shall be upon his shoulder: and his name shall be called Wonderful, Counsellor, The mighty God, The everlasting Father, The Prince of Peace.

COUNTENANCE

• **Angry.**
Pr 25:23 — The north wind driveth away rain: so *doth* an angry countenance a backbiting tongue.

• **Cheerful.**
Job 29:24 — *If* I laughed on them, they believed *it* not; and the light of my countenance they cast not down.

Ps 4:6 — *There be* many that say, Who will shew us *any* good? LORD, lift thou up the light of thy countenance upon us.

Ps 21:6 — For thou hast made him most blessed for ever: thou hast made him exceeding glad with thy countenance.

Ps 44:3 — For they got not the land in possession by their own sword, neither did their own arm save them: but thy right hand, and thine arm, and the light of thy countenance, because thou hadst a favour unto them.

Pr 15:13 — A merry heart maketh a cheerful countenance: but by sorrow of the heart the spirit is broken.

Pr 27:17 — Iron sharpeneth iron; so a man sharpeneth the countenance of his friend.

• **Fierce.**
Dt 28:50 — A nation of fierce countenance, which shall not regard the person of the old, nor shew favour to the young:

Da 8:23 — And in the latter time of their kingdom, when the transgressors are come to the full, a king of fierce countenance, and understanding dark sentences, shall stand up.

• **Guilty.**
Ge 4:5 — But unto Cain and to his offering he had not respect. And Cain was very wroth, and his countenance fell.

Isa 3:9 — The shew of their countenance doth witness against them; and they declare their sin as Sodom, they hide *it* not. Woe unto their soul! for they have rewarded evil unto themselves.

• **Health indicated in.**
Ps 42:11 — Why art thou cast down, O my soul? and why art thou disquieted within me? hope thou in God: for I shall yet praise him, *who is* the health of my countenance, and my God.

Ps 43:5 — Why art thou cast down, O my soul? and why art thou disquieted within me? hope in God: for I shall yet praise him, *who is* the health of my countenance, and my God.

• **Pride in.**
2Ki 5:1 — Now Naaman, captain of the host of the king of Syria, was a great man with his master, and honourable, because by him the LORD had given deliverance unto Syria: he was also a mighty man in valour, *but he was* a leper.

Ps 10:4 — The wicked, through the pride of his countenance, will not seek *after God:* God *is* not in all his thoughts.

• **Reading of.**
Ge 31:2 — And Jacob beheld the countenance of Laban, and, behold, it *was* not toward him as before.

Ge 31:5 — And said unto them, I see your father's countenance, that it *is* not toward me as before; but the God of my father hath been with me.

• **Sad.**
Ne 2:2–3

1Sa 1:18 — And she said, Let thine handmaid find grace in thy sight. So the woman went her way, and did eat, and her countenance was no more *sad.*

Ecc 7:3 — Sorrow *is* better than laughter: for by the sadness of the countenance the heart is made better.

Eze 27:35 — All the inhabitants of the isles shall be astonished at thee, and their kings shall be sore afraid, they shall be troubled in *their* countenance.

Da 1:15 — And at the end of ten days their countenances appeared fairer and fatter in flesh than all the children which did eat the portion of the king's meat.

Da 5:6 — Then the king's countenance was changed, and his thoughts troubled him, so that the joints of his loins were loosed, and his knees smote one against another.

• **Transfigured.**
Ex 34:29–35

Lk 9:29 — And as he prayed, the fashion of his countenance was altered, and his raiment *was* white *and* glistering.

2Co 3:7 — But if the ministration of death, written *and* engraven in stones, was glorious, so that the children of Israel could not stedfastly behold the face of Moses for the glory of his countenance; which *glory* was to be done away:

2Co 3:13 — And not as Moses, *which* put a vail over his face, that the children of Israel could not stedfastly look to the end of that which is abolished:

See: Face

COUNTRY

- **Love of.**

Jgs 5:1–31; Ne 1:1–6:19; Ps 137:1–6

2Sa 10:12 — Be of good courage, and let us play the men for our people, and for the cities of our God: and the LORD do that which seemeth him good.

- **The Jews held church and country as one.**

See: Church; love for

See: Patriotism

COURAGE

- **Enjoined upon Joshua.**

Dt 31:7–8, 22–23; Jos 1:1–9

- **Enjoined upon the Israelites.**

Le 26:6–8; 2Ch 32:7–8

- **Enjoined upon Solomon.**

1Ch 22:13 — Then shalt thou prosper, if thou takest heed to fulfil the statutes and judgments which the LORD charged Moses with concerning Israel: be strong, and of good courage; dread not, nor be dismayed.

1Ch 28:20 — And David said to Solomon his son, Be strong and of good courage, and do *it:* fear not, nor be dismayed: for the LORD God, *even* my God, *will be* with thee; he will not fail thee, nor forsake thee, until thou hast finished all the work for the service of the house of the LORD.

- **Enjoined upon Asa.**

2Ch 15:1–7

- **Enjoined by Jehoshaphat upon the judicial and executive officers he appointed.**

2Ch 19:11 — And, behold, Amariah the chief priest is over you in all matters of the LORD; and Zebadiah the son of Ishmael, the ruler of the house of Judah, for all the king's matters: also the Levites *shall be* officers before you. Deal courageously, and the LORD shall be with the good.

- **Scriptures relating to.**

Php 1:27–28

Pr 28:1 — The wicked flee when no man pursueth: but the righteous are bold as a lion.

Eze 2:6 — And thou, son of man, be not afraid of them, neither be afraid of their words, though briers and thorns *be* with thee, and thou dost dwell among scorpions: be not afraid of their words, nor be dismayed at their looks, though they *be* a rebellious house.

Eze 3:9 — As an adamant harder than flint have I made thy forehead: fear them not, neither be dismayed at their looks, though they *be* a rebellious house.

1Co 16:13 — Watch ye, stand fast in the faith, quit you like men, be strong.

2Ti 1:7 — For God hath not given us the spirit of fear; but of power, and of love, and of a sound mind.

- **Instances of the courage of conviction.**
  - **Abraham, in leaving his fatherland.**

    Ge 12:1–9
  - **Abraham, in offering Isaac.**

    Ge 22:1–14
  - **Gideon, in destroying the altar of Baal.**

    Jgs 6:25–31
  - **Ezra, in undertaking the perilous journey from Babylon to Palestine without a guard.**

    Ezr 8:22–23
  - **The Jews, in returning answer to Tatnai.**

    Ezr 5:11
  - **The three Hebrews, who refused to bow down to the image of Nebuchadnezzar.**

    Da 3:16–18
  - **Daniel, in persisting in prayer, regardless of the edict against praying.**

    Da 6:10
  - **Peter and John, in refusing to obey men, rather than God.**

    Ac 4:19; 5:29

  See: Minister, a sacred teacher; courage of

  See: Reproof

- **Instances of personal bravery.**
  - **Joshua and Caleb, in advising that Israel go at once and possess the land.**

    Nu 13:30; 14:6–12
  - **Othniel, in smiting Kirjathsepher.**

    Jos 15:16–17
  - **Gideon, in attacking the confederate armies of the Midianites and Amalekites with three hundred men.**

    Jgs 7:7–23
  - **Deborah, in leading Israel's armies.**

    Jgs 4:1–24
  - **Jael, in slaying Sisera.**

    Jgs 4:18–22
  - **Agag, in the indifference with which he faced death.**

    1Sa 15:32–33
  - **David, in slaying Goliath.**

    1Sa 17:32–50
  - **David, in entering into the tent of Saul, and carrying away Saul's spear.**

    1Sa 26:7–12

- **David's captains.**
  2Sa 23:1–39
- **Joab, in reproving King David.**
  2Sa 19:5–7
- **Nehemiah, in refusing to take refuge in the temple.**
  Ne 6:10–13
- **Esther, in going to the king to save her people.**
  Est 4:8, 16; 5:1–7:10
- **Joseph of Arimathaea, in caring for the body of Jesus.**
  Mk 15:43
- **Thomas, in being willing to die with Jesus.**
  Jn 11:16
- **Peter and other disciples.**
  Ac 3:12–26; 4:9–13, 19–20, 31
- **The apostles, under persecution.**
  Ac 5:21, 29–32
- **Paul, in going to Jerusalem, despite his impressions that bonds and imprisonments awaited him.**
  Ac 20:22–24; 24:14, 25

See: Boldness; of the righteous

See: Minister, a sacred teacher; courage of

See: Reproof; faithfulness in

See: Cowardice

COURT

- **Ecclesiastical.**
  1Ch 26:29–32; 2Ch 19:8–11; Mt 18:15–18
  Jn 20:23 — Whose soever sins ye remit, they are remitted unto them; *and* whose soever *sins* ye retain, they are retained.

  See: Church; rules of discipline in, Mosaic and Christian
- **Civil.**
  - **Held at the tabernacle.**
    Nu 27:2 — And they stood before Moses, and before Eleazar the priest, and before the princes and all the congregation, *by* the door of the tabernacle of the congregation, saying,
  - **Held at the gates of cities.**
    Dt 21:19 — Then shall his father and his mother lay hold on him, and bring him out unto the elders of his city, and unto the gate of his place;
    Dt 22:15 — Then shall the father of the damsel, and her mother, take and bring forth *the tokens of* the damsel's virginity unto the elders of the city in the gate:
    Dt 25:7 — And if the man like not to take his brother's wife, then let his brother's wife go up to the gate unto the elders, and say, My husband's brother refuseth to raise up unto his brother a name in Israel, he will not perform the duty of my husband's brother.
    Jos 20:4 — And when he that doth flee unto one of those cities shall stand at the entering of the gate of the city, and shall declare his cause in the ears of the elders of that city, they shall take him into the city unto them, and give him a place, that he may dwell among them.
    Ru 4:1 — Then went Boaz up to the gate, and sat him down there: and, behold, the kinsman of whom Boaz spake came by; unto whom he said, Ho, such a one! turn aside, sit down here. And he turned aside, and sat down.
    Zec 8:16 — These *are* the things that ye shall do; Speak ye every man the truth to his neighbour; execute the judgment of truth and peace in your gates:
  - **Held under a palm tree.**
    Jgs 4:5 — And she dwelt under the palm tree of Deborah between Ramah and Bethel in mount Ephraim: and the children of Israel came up to her for judgment.
- **Composition of, and mode of procedure.**
  Ex 18:25–26; Dt 1:15–17; Ru 4:2–5; 1Ch 26:29–32; 2Ch 19:8–11; Mt 26:54–71; Mk 14:55–65; Lk 22:50–71; Jn 18:13–28; Ac 5:17–21, 25–28, 38–41
  Dt 17:9 — And thou shalt come unto the priests the Levites, and unto the judge that shall be in those days, and enquire; and they shall shew thee the sentence of judgment:
  Mk 14:53 — And they led Jesus away to the high priest: and with him were assembled all the chief priests and the elders and the scribes.
  Mk 15:1 — And straightway in the morning the chief priests held a consultation with the elders and scribes and the whole council, and bound Jesus, and carried *him* away, and delivered *him* to Pilate.
  Ac 5:34 — Then stood there up one in the council, a Pharisee, named Gamaliel, a doctor of the law, had in reputation among all the people, and commanded to put the apostles forth a little space;

  See: Judge

  See: Justice

  See: Priest, High; duties of; judicial
- **Circuit.**
  1Sa 7:15–17
- **Superior, and inferior.**
  Ex 18:21–26; Dt 1:15–17; 17:8–13; 2Ch 19:5–10
- **Justice required of.**
  Ex 23:2–3, 6–8; Dt 1:16–17; 2Ch 19:5–10
  Dt 25:1 — If there be a controversy between men, and they come unto judgment, that *the judges* may judge them; then they shall justify the righteous, and condemn the wicked.

  See: Judge

  See: Justice
- **Sentence of, final and obligatory.**
  Dt 17:8–12

• **Contempt of.**

Dt 17:8–12; Ac 23:1–5

Mic 5:1 — Now gather thyself in troops, O daughter of troops: he hath laid siege against us: they shall smite the judge of Israel with a rod upon the cheek.

• **Corrupt.**

Isa 10:1–2; Mt 26:59–62; 27:18–26; Mk 14:55–65; Ac 4:15–18; 6:11–14; 24:26–27

Pr 17:15 — He that justifieth the wicked, and he that condemneth the just, even they both *are* abomination to the LORD.

Pr 29:26 — Many seek the ruler's favour; but *every* man's judgment *cometh* from the LORD.

Isa 1:23 — Thy princes *are* rebellious, and companions of thieves: every one loveth gifts, and followeth after rewards: they judge not the fatherless, neither doth the cause of the widow come unto them.

Isa 5:23 — Which justify the wicked for reward, and take away the righteousness of the righteous from him!

Mic 3:11 — The heads thereof judge for reward, and the priests thereof teach for hire, and the prophets thereof divine for money: yet will they lean upon the LORD, and say, *Is* not the LORD among us? none evil can come upon us.

Mic 7:3 — That they may do evil with both hands earnestly, the prince asketh, and the judge *asketh* for a reward; and the great *man,* he uttereth his mischievous desire: so they wrap it up.

Zep 3:3 — Her princes within her *are* roaring lions; her judges *are* evening wolves; they gnaw not the bones till the morrow.

Mk 14:53 — And they led Jesus away to the high priest: and with him were assembled all the chief priests and the elders and the scribes.

Mk 15:10 — For he knew that the chief priests had delivered him for envy.

See: Bribery

See: Judge

See: Justice

• **Accused spoke in his own defense.**

Jer 26:11–16; Mk 15:3–5; Ac 4:8–12, 18–20; 5:29–32; 7:1–56; 23:1–7; 26:1–32

See: Appeal

See: Punishment

See: Witness

COURTESY

See: Manners

COURTSHIP

• **Ancient customs of.**

• **Suitor visited the maid.**

Jgs 14:7 — And he went down, and talked with the woman; and she pleased Samson well.

• **Women proposed marriage.**

Ru 3:9–13

See: Marriage

COVENANT

• **Sacred.**

Jos 9:18–21

Gal 3:15 — Brethren, I speak after the manner of men; Though *it be* but a man's covenant, yet *if it be* confirmed, no man disannulleth, or addeth thereto.

• **Binding.**

Jos 9:18–20; Jer 34:8–21; Eze 17:14–18

Gal 3:15 — Brethren, I speak after the manner of men; Though *it be* but a man's covenant, yet *if it be* confirmed, no man disannulleth, or addeth thereto.

• **Binding, not only on those who make them, but on those who are represented.**

Dt 29:14–15

• **Blood of.**

Ex 24:8 — And Moses took the blood, and sprinkled *it* on the people, and said, Behold the blood of the covenant, which the LORD hath made with you concerning all these words.

• **Book of.**

Ex 24:7 — And he took the book of the covenant, and read in the audience of the people: and they said, All that the LORD hath said will we do, and be obedient.

• **The Mosaic law called a covenant.**

Ex 34:28 — And he was there with the LORD forty days and forty nights; he did neither eat bread, nor drink water. And he wrote upon the tables the words of the covenant, the ten commandments.

See: Contracts

See: Vows

• **Of men with men.**

• **Breach of, punished.**

2Sa 21:1–6; Jer 34:8–22; Eze 17:13–19

• **National.**

See: Alliances

• **Ratified.**

• **By giving the hand.**

Ezr 10:19 — And they gave their hands that they would put away their wives; and *being* guilty, *they offered* a ram of the flock for their trespass.

La 5:6 — We have given the hand *to* the Egyptians, *and to* the Assyrians, to be satisfied with bread.

Eze 17:18 — Seeing he despised the oath by breaking the covenant, when, lo, he had given his hand, and hath done all these *things,* he shall not escape.

• **By loosing the shoe.**

Ru 4:7–11

• **Written and sealed.**

Jer 32:10–12

Ne 9:38 — And because of all this we make a sure *covenant,* and write *it;* and our princes, Levites, *and* priests, seal *unto it.*

• **By giving presents.**

Ge 21:27–30; 1Sa 18:3–4

- **By making a feast.**
  Ge 26:30 — And he made them a feast, and they did eat and drink.
- **By a monument.**
  Ge 31:45–46, 49–53
- **By salting.**
  Le 2:13 — And every oblation of thy meat offering shalt thou season with salt; neither shalt thou suffer the salt of the covenant of thy God to be lacking from thy meat offering: with all thine offerings thou shalt offer salt.
  Nu 18:19 — All the heave offerings of the holy things, which the children of Israel offer unto the LORD, have I given thee, and thy sons and thy daughters with thee, by a statute for ever: it is a covenant of salt for ever before the LORD unto thee and to thy seed with thee.
  2Ch 13:5 — Ought ye not to know that the LORD God of Israel gave the kingdom over Israel to David for ever, *even* to him and to his sons by a covenant of salt?
- **By offering a sacrifice.**
  Ge 15:9–17; Jer 34:18–19
- **By oath.**

➛See: Contracts
➛See: Oath

- **Instances of.**
  - **Abraham and Abimelech.**
    Ge 21:22–32
  - **Abimelech and Isaac.**
    Ge 26:26–31
  - **Jacob and Laban.**
    Ge 31:44–54
  - **Jonathan and David.**
    1Sa 18:3–4; 20:16, 42; 2Sa 21:7
  - **Jews with each other, to serve God.**
    2Ch 15:12–15; Ne 10:28–32
  - **King Zedekiah and his subjects.**
    Jer 34:8
  - **Ahab with Benhadad.**
    1Ki 20:34
  - **Subjects with sovereign.**
    2Ch 23:1–3, 16
- **Of God with men.**
  - **Confirmed with an oath.**
    Heb 6:17–18
    Ge 22:16 — And said, By myself have I sworn, saith the LORD, for because thou hast done this thing, and hast not withheld thy son, thine only *son:*
    Ge 26:3 — Sojourn in this land, and I will be with thee, and will bless thee; for unto thee, and unto thy seed, I will give all these countries, and I will perform the oath which I sware unto Abraham thy father;
    Ge 50:24 — And Joseph said unto his brethren, I die: and God will surely visit you, and bring you out of this land unto the land which he sware to Abraham, to Isaac, and to Jacob.
    Ps 89:35 — Once have I sworn by my holiness that I will not lie unto David.
    Ps 105:9 — Which *covenant* he made with Abraham, and his oath unto Isaac;
    Lk 1:73 — The oath which he sware to our father Abraham,
    Heb 6:13 — For when God made promise to Abraham, because he could swear by no greater, he sware by himself,
  - **Binding.**
    Le 26:1–46; Jer 11:2–3
    Gal 3:15 — Brethren, I speak after the manner of men; Though *it be* but a man's covenant, yet *if it be* confirmed, no man disannulleth, or addeth thereto.
  - **Everlasting.**
    Ge 8:20–9:17
    Ps 105:8 — He hath remembered his covenant for ever, the word *which* he commanded to a thousand generations.
    Ps 105:10 — And confirmed the same unto Jacob for a law, *and* to Israel *for* an everlasting covenant:
    Isa 54:10 — For the mountains shall depart, and the hills be removed; but my kindness shall not depart from thee, neither shall the covenant of my peace be removed, saith the LORD that hath mercy on thee.
    Isa 61:8 — For I the LORD love judgment, I hate robbery for burnt offering; and I will direct their work in truth, and I will make an everlasting covenant with them.
  - **God faithful to.**
    Le 26:44–45; Dt 7:8–9; Ps 105:8–11
    Dt 4:31 — (For the LORD thy God *is* a merciful God;) he will not forsake thee, neither destroy thee, nor forget the covenant of thy fathers which he sware unto them.
    Jgs 2:1 — And an angel of the LORD came up from Gilgal to Bochim, and said, I made you to go up out of Egypt, and have brought you unto the land which I sware unto your fathers; and I said, I will never break my covenant with you.
    1Ki 8:23 — And he said, LORD God of Israel, *there is* no God like thee, in heaven above, or on earth beneath, who keepest covenant and mercy with thy servants that walk before thee with all their heart:
    Ps 106:45 — And he remembered for them his covenant, and repented according to the multitude of his mercies.
    Ps 111:5 — He hath given meat unto them that fear him: he will ever be mindful of his covenant.
    Mic 7:20 — Thou wilt perform the truth to Jacob, *and* the mercy to Abraham, which thou hast sworn unto our fathers from the days of old.
  - **Repudiated by God on account of Jews' idolatry.**
    Jer 44:26–27
    Heb 8:9 — Not according to the covenant that I made with their fathers in the day when I took them by the hand to lead them out of the land

of Egypt; because they continued not in my covenant, and I regarded them not, saith the Lord.

• **Broken by the Jews.**

Jer 22:9 — Then they shall answer, Because they have forsaken the covenant of the LORD their God, and worshipped other gods, and served them.

Eze 16:59 — For thus saith the Lord GOD; I will even deal with thee as thou hast done, which hast despised the oath in breaking the covenant.

Heb 8:9 — Not according to the covenant that I made with their fathers in the day when I took them by the hand to lead them out of the land of Egypt; because they continued not in my covenant, and I regarded them not, saith the Lord.

• **Punishments for breaking of.**

Le 26:25–46

• **Instances of.**

• **Of the Sabbath.**

Ex 31:16

• **Of the Ten Commandments.**

Ex 34:28; Dt 5:2–3; 9:9

• **With Adam.**

Ge 2:16–17

• **With Noah.**

Ge 8:16; 9:8–17

• **With Abraham.**

Ge 12:1–3; 15:1–21; 17:1–22; Ex 6:4–8; Ps 105:8–11; Ro 9:7–13; Gal 3:1–29

See: Circumcision

• **With Isaac.**

Ge 17:19

• **With Jacob.**

Ge 28:13–15

• **With the Israelites to deliver them from Egypt.**

Ex 6:4–8

• **With Phinehas.**

Nu 25:12–13

• **With Israel, at Horeb.**

Dt 5:2–3

• **With Israel, in Moab.**

Dt 29:1–15

• **Of the Levites.**

Ne 13:29; Mal 2:4–5

• **With David.**

2Sa 7:12–16; 1Ch 17:11–14; 2Ch 6:16

• **With David and his house.**

2Sa 23:5; Ps 89:20–37; Jer 33:21

• **With his people.**

Isa 55:3; 59:21

• **To be confirmed.**

Da 9:27

• **The second covenant.**

Jer 31:31–34; Heb 8:4–13; 12:18–24

Heb 13:20 — Now the God of peace, that brought again from the dead our Lord Jesus, that great shepherd of the sheep, through the blood of the everlasting covenant,

• **Of man with God.**

• **Jacob.**

Ge 28:20–22

• **Joshua.**

Jos 24:19–28

• **Absalom.**

2Sa 15:7–8

• **Jehoiada and Joash.**

2Ki 11:17 — And Jehoiada made a covenant between the LORD and the king and the people that they should be the LORD'S people; between the king also and the people.

• **Josiah.**

2Ki 23:3 — And the king stood by a pillar, and made a covenant before the LORD, to walk after the LORD, and to keep his commandments and his testimonies and his statutes with all *their* heart and all *their* soul, to perform the words of this covenant that were written in this book. And all the people stood to the covenant.

• **Asa.**

2Ch 15:12–15

• **Nehemiah.**

Ne 9:38–10:39

• **Israelites.**

Jer 50:5 — They shall ask the way to Zion with their faces thitherward, *saying,* Come, and let us join ourselves to the LORD in a perpetual covenant *that* shall not be forgotten.

See: Vows

COVERING

Pr 10:12 — Hatred stirreth up strifes: but love covereth all sins.

Pr 17:9 — He that covereth a transgression seeketh love; but he that repeateth a matter separateth *very* friends.

Pr 28:13 — He that covereth his sins shall not prosper: but whoso confesseth and forsaketh *them* shall have mercy.

Ro 3:25 — Whom God hath set forth *to be* a propitiation through faith in his blood, to declare his righteousness for the remission of sins that are past, through the forbearance of God;

1Co 13:7 — Beareth all things, believeth all things, hopeth all things, endureth all things.

1Pe 4:8 — And above all things have fervent charity among yourselves: for charity shall cover the multitude of sins.

1Jn 2:2 — And he is the propitiation for our sins: and not for ours only, but also for *the sins of* the whole world.

1Jn 4:10 — Herein is love, not that we loved God, but that he loved us, and sent his Son *to be* the propitiation for our sins.

COVETOUSNESS

Job 31:24–25; Pr 21:25–26; 23:4–5; 30:8–9; Ecc 1:2–8; 5:10–11; Eze 22:12–13; Hab 1:15–16; 2:5–9; Mt 6:19–21, 24–25, 31–33; 19:23–24; 22:1–14; Mk 7:21–23; Lk 12:15–21, 33–34; 14:16–24; 18:24–25; Jn 6:26–27; Ro 13:1–14; Php 3:18–19; Col 3:5–6; 1Ti 6:5–11; Jas 4:13–17; 2Pe 2:14–16; 1Jn 2:15–17

Ex 18:21 — Moreover thou shalt provide out of all the people able men, such as fear God, men of truth, hating covetousness; and place *such* over them, *to be* rulers of thousands, *and* rulers of hundreds, rulers of fifties, and rulers of tens:

Ex 20:17 — Thou shalt not covet thy neighbour's house, thou shalt not covet thy neighbour's wife, nor his manservant, nor his maidservant, nor his ox, nor his ass, nor any thing that *is* thy neighbour's.

Dt 5:21 — Neither shalt thou desire thy neighbour's wife, neither shalt thou covet thy neighbour's house, his field, or his manservant, or his maidservant, his ox, or his ass, or any *thing* that *is* thy neighbour's.

Ne 5:7 — Then I consulted with myself, and I rebuked the nobles, and the rulers, and said unto them, Ye exact usury, every one of his brother. And I set a great assembly against them.

Job 20:15 — He hath swallowed down riches, and he shall vomit them up again: God shall cast them out of his belly.

Job 31:28 — This also *were* an iniquity *to be punished by* the judge: for I should have denied the God *that is* above.

Ps 10:3 — For the wicked boasteth of his heart's desire, and blesseth the covetous, *whom* the LORD abhorreth.

Ps 119:36 — Incline my heart unto thy testimonies, and not to covetousness.

Pr 1:19 — So *are* the ways of every one that is greedy of gain; *which* taketh away the life of the owners thereof.

Pr 11:24 — There is that scattereth, and yet increaseth; and *there is* that withholdeth more than is meet, but *it tendeth* to poverty.

Pr 11:26 — He that withholdeth corn, the people shall curse him: but blessing *shall be* upon the head of him that selleth *it*.

Pr 15:27 — He that is greedy of gain troubleth his own house; but he that hateth gifts shall live.

Pr 22:16 — He that oppresseth the poor to increase his *riches, and* he that giveth to the rich, *shall* surely *come* to want.

Ecc 4:8 — There is one *alone,* and *there is* not a second; yea, he hath neither child nor brother: yet *is there* no end of all his labour; neither is his eye satisfied with riches; neither *saith he,* For whom do I labour, and bereave my soul of good? This *is* also vanity, yea, it *is* a sore travail.

Isa 1:23 — Thy princes *are* rebellious, and companions of thieves: every one loveth gifts, and followeth after rewards: they judge not the fatherless, neither doth the cause of the widow come unto them.

Isa 5:8 — Woe unto them that join house to house, *that* lay field to field, till *there be* no place, that they may be placed alone in the midst of the earth!

Isa 56:11 — Yea, *they are* greedy dogs *which* can never have enough, and they *are* shepherds *that* cannot understand: they all look to their own way, every one for his gain, from his quarter.

Isa 57:17 — For the iniquity of his covetousness was I wroth, and smote him: I hid me, and was wroth, and he went on frowardly in the way of his heart.

Jer 6:13 — For from the least of them even unto the greatest of them every one *is* given to covetousness; and from the prophet even unto the priest every one dealeth falsely.

Jer 8:10 — Therefore will I give their wives unto others, *and* their fields to them that shall inherit *them:* for every one from the least even unto the greatest is given to covetousness, from the prophet even unto the priest every one dealeth falsely.

Jer 17:11 — As the partridge sitteth *on eggs,* and hatcheth *them* not; *so* he that getteth riches, and not by right, shall leave them in the midst of his days, and at his end shall be a fool.

Jer 22:17 — But thine eyes and thine heart *are* not but for thy covetousness, and for to shed innocent blood, and for oppression, and for violence, to do *it.*

Jer 51:13 — O thou that dwellest upon many waters, abundant in treasures, thine end is come, *and* the measure of thy covetousness.

Eze 33:31 — And they come unto thee as the people cometh, and they sit before thee as my people, and they hear thy words, but they will not do them: for with their mouth they shew much love, *but* their heart goeth after their covetousness.

Hos 4:18 — Their drink is sour: they have committed whoredom continually: her rulers *with* shame do love, Give ye.

Hos 10:1 — Israel *is* an empty vine, he bringeth forth fruit unto himself: according to the multitude of his fruit he hath increased the altars; according to the goodness of his land they have made goodly images.

Mic 2:2 — And they covet fields, and take *them* by violence; and houses, and take *them* away: so they oppress a man and his house, even a man and his heritage.

Mic 3:11 — The heads thereof judge for reward, and the priests thereof teach for hire, and the prophets thereof divine for money: yet will they lean upon the LORD, and say, *Is* not the LORD among us? none evil can come upon us.

Mic 7:3 — That they may do evil with both hands earnestly, the prince asketh, and the judge *asketh* for a reward; and the great *man,* he uttereth his mischievous desire: so they wrap it up.

Hag 1:6 — Ye have sown much, and bring in little; ye eat, but ye have not enough; ye drink, but ye are not filled with drink; ye clothe you, but there is none warm; and he that earneth wages earneth wages *to put it* into a bag with holes.

Mal 1:10 — Who *is there* even among you that would shut the doors *for nought?* neither do ye kindle *fire* on mine altar for nought. I have no pleasure in you, saith the LORD of hosts, neither will I accept an offering at your hand.

Mt 13:22 — He also that received seed among the thorns is he that heareth the word; and the care of this world, and the deceitfulness of riches, choke the word, and he becometh unfruitful.

Mt 16:26 — For what is a man profited, if he shall gain the whole world, and lose his own soul? or what shall a man give in exchange for his soul?

Mk 4:19 — And the cares of this world, and the deceitfulness of riches, and the lusts of other things entering in, choke the word, and it becometh unfruitful.

Lk 7:14 — And he came and touched the bier: and they that bare *him* stood still. And he said, Young man, I say unto thee, Arise.

Ro 1:29 — Being filled with all unrighteousness, fornication, wickedness, covetousness, maliciousness; full of envy, murder, debate, deceit, malignity; whisperers,

1Co 5:11 — But now I have written unto you not to keep company, if any man that is called a brother be a fornicator, or covetous, or an idolater, or a railer, or a drunkard, or an extortioner; with such an one no not to eat.

1Co 6:10 — Nor thieves, nor covetous, nor drunkards, nor revilers, nor extortioners, shall inherit the kingdom of God.

Eph 5:3 — But fornication, and all uncleanness, or covetousness, let it not be once named among you, as becometh saints;

Eph 5:5 — For this ye know, that no whoremonger, nor unclean person, nor covetous man, who is an idolater, hath any inheritance in the kingdom of Christ and of God.

Col 3:2 — Set your affection on things above, not on things on the earth.

1Th 2:5 — For neither at any time used we flattering words, as ye know, nor a cloke of covetousness; God *is* witness:

1Ti 3:3 — Not given to wine, no striker, not greedy of filthy lucre; but patient, not a brawler, not covetous;

1Ti 6:17 — Charge them that are rich in this world, that they be not highminded, nor trust in uncertain riches, but in the living God, who giveth us richly all things to enjoy;

2Ti 3:2 — For men shall be lovers of their own selves, covetous, boasters, proud, blasphemers, disobedient to parents, unthankful, unholy,

Tit 1:7 — For a bishop must be blameless, as the steward of God; not selfwilled, not soon angry, not given to wine, no striker, not given to filthy lucre;

Tit 1:11 — Whose mouths must be stopped, who subvert whole houses, teaching things which they ought not, for filthy lucre's sake.

Heb 13:5 — *Let your* conversation *be* without covetousness; *and be* content with such things as ye have: for he hath said, I will never leave thee, nor forsake thee.

Jas 4:2 — Ye lust, and have not: ye kill, and desire to have, and cannot obtain: ye fight and war, yet ye have not, because ye ask not.

1Pe 5:2 — Feed the flock of God which is among you, taking the oversight *thereof,* not by constraint, but willingly; not for filthy lucre, but of a ready mind;

2Pe 2:3 — And through covetousness shall they with feigned words make merchandise of you: whose judgment now of a long time lingereth not, and their damnation slumbereth not.

Jude 1:11 — Woe unto them! for they have gone in the way of Cain, and ran greedily after the error of Balaam for reward, and perished in the gainsaying of Core.

See: Avarice

See: Rich

See: Riches

See: Worldliness

• Instances of.

• Eve, in desiring the forbidden fruit.
Ge 3:6

• Lot, in choosing the plain of the Jordan.
Ge 13:10–13

• Laban, in giving Rebekah to be Isaac's wife.
Ge 24:29–51

• Laban, in deceiving Jacob when he served him seven years for Rachel.
Ge 29:15–30

• Laban, in deceiving Jacob in wages.
Ge 31:7; 31:15; 31:41–42

• Jacob, in defrauding Esau of his father's blessing.
Ge 27:6–29

• Jacob, in defrauding Laban of his flocks and herds.
Ge 30:35–43

• Jacob, in buying Esau's birthright.
Ge 25:31

• Balaam, in loving the wages of unrighteousness.
Nu 22:1–41; 2Pe 2:15

• Achan, in hiding the treasure.
Jos 7:21

• Eli's sons, in taking the flesh of the sacrifice.
1Sa 2:13–17

• Samuel's sons, in taking bribes.
1Sa 8:3

• Saul, in sparing Agag and the booty.
1Sa 15:8–9

• David, of Bath-sheba.
2Sa 11:2–5

• Ahab, in desiring Naboth's vineyard.
1Ki 21:2–16

• Gehazi, in taking a gift from Naaman.
2Ki 5:20–27

• Jews, in exacting usury of their brethren.
Ne 5:1–11

• Jews, in keeping back the portion of the Levites.
Ne 13:10

• Jews, in building fine houses while the house of the Lord lay waste.
Hag 1:4–9

• Jews, in following Jesus for the loaves and fishes.
Jn 6:26

• Money changers in the temple.
Mt 21:12–13; Lk 19:45–46; Jn 2:14–16

• The rich young ruler.
Mt 19:16–22

• The rich fool.
Lk 12:15–21

- **Judas, in betraying Jesus for twenty pieces of silver.**
  Mt 26:15–16; Mk 14:10–11; Lk 22:3–6; Jn 12:6
- **The unjust steward.**
  Lk 16:1–8
- **The Pharisees.**
  Lk 16:14
- **Simon Magus, in trying to buy the gift of the Holy Ghost.**
  Ac 8:18–23
- **The sorcerers, in filing complaint against Paul and Silas.**
  Ac 16:19
- **Demetrius, in raising a riot against Paul and Silas.**
  Ac 19:24, 27
- **Felix, in hoping for a bribe from Paul.**
  Ac 24:26
- **Demas, in forsaking Paul for love of the world.**
  2Ti 4:10

See: Avarice
See: Bribery
See: Rich
See: Riches

COW

- **Used for draught.**
  1Sa 6:7–12
  Hos 10:11 — And Ephraim *is as* an heifer *that is* taught, *and* loveth to tread out *the corn;* but I passed over upon her fair neck: I will make Ephraim to ride; Judah shall plow, *and* Jacob shall break his clods.
- **Milk of, used for food.**
  See: Milk
  See: Cattle, of the bovine species
  See: Kine
- **Figurative.**
  Am 4:1 — Hear this word, ye kine of Bashan, that *are* in the mountain of Samaria, which oppress the poor, which crush the needy, which say to their masters, Bring, and let us drink.

COWARDICE

Le 26:36–37; Isa 51:12–13

Dt 20:8 — And the officers shall speak further unto the people, and they shall say, What man *is there that is* fearful and fainthearted? let him go and return unto his house, lest his brethren's heart faint as well as his heart.

Dt 32:30 — How should one chase a thousand, and two put ten thousand to flight, except their Rock had sold them, and the LORD had shut them up?

Jos 7:5 — And the men of Ai smote of them about thirty and six men: for they chased them *from* before the gate *even* unto Shebarim, and smote them in the going down: wherefore the hearts of the people melted, and became as water.

Jos 23:10 — One man of you shall chase a thousand: for the LORD your God, he *it is* that fighteth for you, as he hath promised you.

Jgs 7:3 — Now therefore go to, proclaim in the ears of the people, saying, Whosoever *is* fearful and afraid, let him return and depart early from mount Gilead. And there returned of the people twenty and two thousand; and there remained ten thousand.

Job 15:24 — Trouble and anguish shall make him afraid; they shall prevail against him, as a king ready to the battle.

Job 18:11 — Terrors shall make him afraid on every side, and shall drive him to his feet.

Pr 28:1 — The wicked flee when no man pursueth: but the righteous are bold as a lion.

Pr 29:25 — The fear of man bringeth a snare: but whoso putteth his trust in the LORD shall be safe.

Gal 6:12 — As many as desire to make a fair shew in the flesh, they constrain you to be circumcised; only lest they should suffer persecution for the cross of Christ.

2Ti 4:16 — At my first answer no man stood with me, but all *men* forsook me: *I pray God* that it may not be laid to their charge.

See: Courage

- **Instances of.**
  - **Adam, in attempting to shift responsibility for his sin upon Eve.**
    Ge 3:12
  - **Abraham, in calling his wife his sister.**
    Ge 12:11–19; 20:2–12
  - **Isaac, in calling his wife his sister.**
    Ge 26:7–9
  - **Jacob, in flying from Laban.**
    Ge 31:31
  - **Aaron, in yielding to the Israelites, when they demanded an idol.**
    Ex 32:22–24
  - **The ten spies.**
    Nu 13:28, 31–33
  - **Israelites, in fearing to attempt the conquest of Canaan.**
    Nu 14:1–5; Dt 1:26–28
  - **Israelites, in the battle with the people of Ai.**
    Jos 7:5
  - **Israelites, to meet Goliath.**
    1Sa 17:24
  - **Israelites, to fight with the Philistines.**
    1Sa 13:6–7
  - **Twenty thousand of Gideon's army.**
    Jgs 7:3
  - **Ephraimites.**
    Ps 78:9
  - **Ephraimites and Manassehites.**
    Jos 17:14–18
  - **Amoritish kings.**
    Jos 10:16
  - **Canaanites.**
    Jos 2:11; 5:1

• **Samuel, fearing to obey God's command to anoint a king in Saul's stead.**
1Sa 16:2

• **David, in fleeing from Absalom.**
2Sa 15:13–17

• **Nicodemus, in coming to Jesus by night.**
Jn 3:1–2

• **Joseph of Arimathaea, secretly a disciple.**
Jn 19:38

• **Parents of the blind man, who was restored to sight.**
Jn 9:22

• **Early converts among the rulers.**
Jn 12:42–43

• **Disciples, in the storm at sea.**
Mt 8:26; Mk 4:38; Lk 8:25

• **Disciples, when they saw Jesus walking on the sea.**
Mt 14:25; Mk 6:50; Jn 6:19

• **Disciples, when Jesus was apprehended.**
Mt 26:56

• **Peter, in denying the Lord.**
Mt 26:69–74; Mk 14:66–72; Lk 22:54–60; Jn 18:16–17, 25, 27

• **Pilate, in condemning Jesus, through fear of the people.**
Jn 19:12–16

• **Guards of the sepulchre of Jesus.**
Mt 28:4

• **The Philippian jailer.**
Ac 16:27

• **Peter and other Christians, at Antioch.**
Gal 2:11–14

COZ • Father of Anub.

1Ch 4:8 — And Coz begat Anub, and Zobebah, and the families of Aharhel the son of Harum.

COZBI • Daughter of Zur.

Nu 25:15 — And the name of the Midianitish woman that was slain *was* Cozbi, the daughter of Zur; he *was* head over a people, *and* of a chief house in Midian.

Nu 25:18 — For they vex you with their wiles, wherewith they have beguiled you in the matter of Peor, and in the matter of Cozbi, the daughter of a prince of Midian, their sister, which was slain in the day of the plague for Peor's sake.

CRACKNEL • A biscuit or cake, hard baked.

1Ki 14:3 — And take with thee ten loaves, and cracknels, and a cruse of honey, and go to him: he shall tell thee what shall become of the child.

CRAFTINESS

• Instances of.

• **Satan, in the temptation of Eve.**
Ge 3:1–5

• **Jacob, in purchase of Esau's birthright.**
Ge 25:31–33

• **Jacob, obtaining Isaac's blessing.**
Ge 27:6–29

• **Jacob, in management of Laban's flocks and herds.**
Ge 30:31–43

• **Gibeonites, in deceiving Joshua and the Israelites into a treaty.**
Jos 9:3–15

• **Sanballat, in trying to deceive Nehemiah into a conference.**
Ne 6:1–19

• **Jews, in seeking to entangle the Master.**
Mt 22:15–17, 24–28; Mk 12:13–14, 18–23; Lk 20:19–26

• **Jews, in seeking to slay Jesus.**
Mt 26:4; Mk 14:1

CRAFTSMAN

➜See: Art

➜See: Master Workman

CRANE • An amphibious bird.

Isa 38:14 — Like a crane *or* a swallow, so did I chatter: I did mourn as a dove: mine eyes fail *with looking* upward: O LORD, I am oppressed; undertake for me.

Jer 8:7 — Yea, the stork in the heaven knoweth her appointed times; and the turtle and the crane and the swallow observe the time of their coming; but my people know not the judgment of the LORD.

CREATION

Col 1:16 — For by him were all things created, that are in heaven, and that are in earth, visible and invisible, whether *they be* thrones, or dominions, or principalities, or powers: all things were created by him, and for him:

Heb 11:3 — Through faith we understand that the worlds were framed by the word of God, so that things which are seen were not made of things which do appear.

• Beginning of.

Ge 1:1 — In the beginning God created the heaven and the earth.

• History of.

Ge 1:1–2:25

➜See: Animals

➜See: Birds

➜See: Earth

➜See: Fish

➜See: Grass

➜See: Heaven

➜See: Man

➜See: Moon

➜See: Sea

➜See: Stars

➜See: Sun

➜See: Water

*See: **Women**
*See: **God, Creator**
*See: **Jesus, Creator**

CREATURE

*See: **Creation**
*See: **God, Creator**
*See: **Man; created**

• New Creature.

2Co 5:17 — Therefore if any man *be* in Christ, *he is* a new creature: old things are passed away; behold, all things are become new.

Gal 6:15 — For in Christ Jesus neither circumcision availeth any thing, nor uncircumcision, but a new creature.

*See: **Regeneration**

CREDITOR

• Laws concerning.

Ex 21:2–6; 22:25–27; Le 25:14–17, 35–37; Dt 15:2–3; 23:19–20; 24:10–13

Dt 24:6 — No man shall take the nether or the upper millstone to pledge: for he taketh *a man's* life to pledge.

Dt 24:17 — Thou shalt not pervert the judgment of the stranger, *nor* of the fatherless; nor take a widow's raiment to pledge:

Mt 5:42 — Give to him that asketh thee, and from him that would borrow of thee turn not thou away.

Lk 6:34 — And if ye lend *to them* of whom ye hope to receive, what thank have ye? for sinners also lend to sinners, to receive as much again.

• Oppressions of.

Ne 5:1–13; Job 20:18–20; 24:9–10; Pr 22:26–27; Mt 5:25–26; 18:28–35; Lk 12:58–59

2Ki 4:1 — Now there cried a certain woman of the wives of the sons of the prophets unto Elisha, saying, Thy servant my husband is dead; and thou knowest that thy servant did fear the LORD: and the creditor is come to take unto him my two sons to be bondmen.

Job 22:6 — For thou hast taken a pledge from thy brother for nought, and stripped the naked of their clothing.

Job 24:3 — They drive away the ass of the fatherless, they take the widow's ox for a pledge.

• Merciful.

Mt 18:23–27; Lk 7:41–43

Ps 112:5 — A good man sheweth favour, and lendeth: he will guide his affairs with discretion.

*See: **Debt**
*See: **Debtor**
*See: **Jubilee**
*See: **Surety**

CREED

*See: **Decrees**
*See: **Law; of Moses**
*See: **Ecclesiasticism**
*See: **Tradition**

CREEPING THINGS

• A general term for animals.

Le 11:20–23, 29–31

Ge 1:26 — And God said, Let us make man in our image, after our likeness: and let them have dominion over the fish of the sea, and over the fowl of the air, and over the cattle, and over all the earth, and over every creeping thing that creepeth upon the earth.

Le 11:42 — Whatsoever goeth upon the belly, and whatsoever goeth upon *all* four, or whatsoever hath more feet among all creeping things that creep upon the earth, them ye shall not eat; for they *are* an abomination.

Ps 104:20 — Thou makest darkness, and it is night: wherein all the beasts of the forest do creep *forth*.

Ps 104:25 — *So is* this great and wide sea, wherein *are* things creeping innumerable, both small and great beasts.

Ro 1:23 — And changed the glory of the uncorruptible God into an image made like to corruptible man, and to birds, and fourfooted beasts, and creeping things.

• Unclean.

Le 11:29–44

Le 5:2 — Or if a soul touch any unclean thing, whether *it be* a carcase of an unclean beast, or a carcase of unclean cattle, or the carcase of unclean creeping things, and *if* it be hidden from him; he also shall be unclean, and guilty.

Le 11:20 — All fowls that creep, going upon *all* four, *shall be* an abomination unto you.

Dt 14:19 — And every creeping thing that flieth *is* unclean unto you: they shall not be eaten.

• Clean.

Le 11:21–22

• Uses of, in idolatrous worship.

Eze 8:10 — So I went in and saw; and behold every form of creeping things, and abominable beasts, and all the idols of the house of Israel, pourtrayed upon the wall round about.

CREMATION

Jos 7:25 — And Joshua said, Why hast thou troubled us? the LORD shall trouble thee this day. And all Israel stoned him with stones, and burned them with fire, after they had stoned them with stones.

1Sa 31:12 — All the valiant men arose, and went all night, and took the body of Saul and the bodies of his sons from the wall of Beth-shan, and came to Jabesh, and burnt them there.

2Ki 23:20 — And he slew all the priests of the high places that *were* there upon the altars, and burned men's bones upon them, and returned to Jerusalem.

Am 2:1 — Thus saith the LORD; For three transgressions of Moab, and for four, I will not turn away *the punishment* thereof; because he burned the bones of the king of Edom into lime:

Am 6:10 — And a man's uncle shall take him up, and he that burneth him, to bring out the bones out of the house, and shall say unto him that *is* by the sides of the house, *Is there* yet *any* with thee? and he shall say, No. Then shall he say, Hold thy tongue: for we may not make mention of the name of the LORD.

See: Burial

CRESCENS • A disciple with Paul at Rome.

2Ti 4:10 — For Demas hath forsaken me, having loved this present world, and is departed unto Thessalonica; Crescens to Galatia, Titus unto Dalmatia.

CRETE

• An island in the Mediterranean Sea.

• Visited by Paul.

Ac 27:12–13

Ac 27:7 — And when we had sailed slowly many days, and scarce were come over against Cnidus, the wind not suffering us, we sailed under Crete, over against Salmone;

Ac 27:21 — But after long abstinence Paul stood forth in the midst of them, and said, Sirs, ye should have hearkened unto me, and not have loosed from Crete, and to have gained this harm and loss.

• Visited by Titus.

Tit 1:5 — For this cause left I thee in Crete, that thou shouldest set in order the things that are wanting, and ordain elders in every city, as I had appointed thee:

• Character of the inhabitants of.

Ac 2:11 — Cretes and Arabians, we do hear them speak in our tongues the wonderful works of God.

Tit 1:12 — One of themselves, *even* a prophet of their own, said, The Cretians *are* alway liars, evil beasts, slow bellies.

CRIB

• Used for grain.

Job 39:9 — Will the unicorn be willing to serve thee, or abide by thy crib?

Pr 14:4 — Where no oxen *are,* the crib *is* clean: but much increase *is* by the strength of the ox.

Isa 1:3 — The ox knoweth his owner, and the ass his master's crib: *but* Israel doth not know, my people doth not consider.

CRIME

• Partial lists of (also see specific crimes).

Eze 22:8–12, 27–30; Hos 4:1–2; Mk 7:21–22; Ro 1:29–32; 3:14–18; Gal 5:19–21

Mt 15:19 — For out of the heart proceed evil thoughts, murders, adulteries, fornications, thefts, false witness, blasphemies:

Ro 1:24 — Wherefore God also gave them up to uncleanness through the lusts of their own hearts, to dishonour their own bodies between themselves:

Ro 13:9 — For this, Thou shalt not commit adultery, Thou shalt not kill, Thou shalt not steal, Thou shalt not bear false witness, Thou shalt not covet; and if *there be* any other commandment, it is briefly comprehended in this saying, namely, Thou shalt love thy neighbour as thyself.

1Co 5:11 — But now I have written unto you not to keep company, if any man that is called a brother be a fornicator, or covetous, or an idolater, or a railer, or a drunkard, or an extortioner; with such an one no not to eat.

See: Adultery

See: Arson

See: Homicide

See: Theft and Thieves

See: Punishment

CRIMINALS

• Released at feasts.

Mt 27:15 — Now at *that* feast the governor was wont to release unto the people a prisoner, whom they would.

Mt 27:21 — The governor answered and said unto them, Whether of the twain will ye that I release unto you? They said, Barabbas.

Mk 15:6 — Now at *that* feast he released unto them one prisoner, whomsoever they desired.

Lk 23:17 — (For of necessity he must release one unto them at the feast.)

• Confined in prisons.

Ge 39:20–23; Ac 12:4–5; 16:19–40

Ezr 7:26 — And whosoever will not do the law of thy God, and the law of the king, let judgment be executed speedily upon him, whether *it be* unto death, or to banishment, or to confiscation of goods, or to imprisonment.

Ac 4:3 — And they laid hands on them, and put *them* in hold unto the next day: for it was now eventide.

• Confined in dungeons.

Ge 40:15 — For indeed I was stolen away out of the land of the Hebrews: and here also have I done nothing that they should put me into the dungeon.

Ge 41:14 — Then Pharaoh sent and called Joseph, and they brought him hastily out of the dungeon: and he shaved *himself,* and changed his raiment, and came in unto Pharaoh.

Ex 12:29 — And it came to pass, that at midnight the LORD smote all the firstborn in the land of Egypt, from the firstborn of Pharaoh that sat on his throne unto the firstborn of the captive that *was* in the dungeon; and all the firstborn of cattle.

Isa 24:22 — And they shall be gathered together, *as* prisoners are gathered in the pit, and shall be shut up in the prison, and after many days shall they be visited.

Jer 37:16 — When Jeremiah was entered into the dungeon, and into the cabins, and Jeremiah had remained there many days;

Jer 38:10 — Then the king commanded Ebed-melech the Ethiopian, saying, Take from hence thirty men with thee, and take up Jeremiah the prophet out of the dungeon, before he die.

La 3:53 — They have cut off my life in the dungeon, and cast a stone upon me.

La 3:55 — I called upon thy name, O LORD, out of the low dungeon.

• Cruelty to.

✦See: Mocking

✦See: Scourging

✦See: Stoning

• Punishment of.

✦See: Adultery

✦See: Arson

✦See: Homicide

✦See: Punishment

CRIMINATION ✦See: Self-Crimination

CRIMSON ✦See: Colors

CRISIS

Heb 11:32–39; 12:7–11; Jas 5:10–11

Jn 15:2 — Every branch in me that beareth not fruit he taketh away: and every *branch* that beareth fruit, he purgeth it, that it may bring forth more fruit.

CRISPING PINS

Isa 3:22 — The changeable suits of apparel, and the mantles, and the wimples, and the crisping pins,

CRISPUS • A ruler at Corinth.

Ac 18:8 — And Crispus, the chief ruler of the synagogue, believed on the Lord with all his house; and many of the Corinthians hearing believed, and were baptized.

1Co 1:14 — I thank God that I baptized none of you, but Crispus and Gaius;

CRITICISM, Unjust ✦See: Uncharitableness

CROCODILE ✦See: Dragon

CROSS

• Jesus crucified on.

Mt 27:32 — And as they came out, they found a man of Cyrene, Simon by name: him they compelled to bear his cross.

Mk 15:21 — And they compel one Simon a Cyrenian, who passed by, coming out of the country, the father of Alexander and Rufus, to bear his cross.

Lk 23:26 — And as they led him away, they laid hold upon one Simon, a Cyrenian, coming out of the country, and on him they laid the cross, that he might bear *it* after Jesus.

Ac 2:23 — Him, being delivered by the determinate counsel and foreknowledge of God, ye have taken, and by wicked hands have crucified and slain:

Ac 2:36 — Therefore let all the house of Israel know assuredly, that God hath made that same Jesus, whom ye have crucified, both Lord and Christ.

Ac 4:10 — Be it known unto you all, and to all the people of Israel, that by the name of Jesus Christ of Nazareth, whom ye crucified, whom God raised from the dead, *even* by him doth this man stand here before you whole.

1Co 1:23 — But we preach Christ crucified, unto the Jews a stumblingblock, and unto the Greeks foolishness;

1Co 2:2 — For I determined not to know any thing among you, save Jesus Christ, and him crucified.

1Co 2:8 — Which none of the princes of this world knew: for had they known *it,* they would not have crucified the Lord of glory.

Eph 2:16 — And that he might reconcile both unto God in one body by the cross, having slain the enmity thereby:

Php 2:8 — And being found in fashion as a man, he humbled himself, and became obedient unto death, even the death of the cross.

Col 1:20 — And, having made peace through the blood of his cross, by him to reconcile all things unto himself; by him, *I say,* whether *they be* things in earth, or things in heaven.

Col 2:14 — Blotting out the handwriting of ordinances that was against us, which was contrary to us, and took it out of the way, nailing it to his cross;

Heb 12:2 — Looking unto Jesus the author and finisher of *our* faith; who for the joy that was set before him endured the cross, despising the shame, and is set down at the right hand of the throne of God.

• Borne by Simon.

Mt 27:32 — And as they came out, they found a man of Cyrene, Simon by name: him they compelled to bear his cross.

Mk 15:21 — And they compel one Simon a Cyrenian, who passed by, coming out of the country, the father of Alexander and Rufus, to bear his cross.

Lk 23:26 — And as they led him away, they laid hold upon one Simon, a Cyrenian, coming out of the country, and on him they laid the cross, that he might bear *it* after Jesus.

• Borne by Jesus.

Jn 19:17 — And he bearing his cross went forth into a place called *the place* of a skull, which is called in the Hebrew Golgotha:

• Figurative.

1Co 1:17–18; Gal 5:11–12

Mt 10:38 — And he that taketh not his cross, and followeth after me, is not worthy of me.

Mt 16:24 — Then said Jesus unto his disciples, If any *man* will come after me, let him deny himself, and take up his cross, and follow me.

Mk 8:34 — And when he had called the people *unto him* with his disciples also, he said unto them, Whosoever will come after me, let him deny himself, and take up his cross, and follow me.

Mk 10:21 — Then Jesus beholding him loved him, and said unto him, One thing thou lackest: go thy way, sell whatsoever thou hast, and give to the poor, and thou shalt have treasure in heaven: and come, take up the cross, and follow me.

Lk 9:23 — And he said to *them* all, If any *man* will come after me, let him deny himself, and take up his cross daily, and follow me.

Lk 14:27 — And whosoever doth not bear his cross, and come after me, cannot be my disciple.

Gal 6:12 — As many as desire to make a fair shew in the flesh, they constrain you to be circumcised; only lest they should suffer persecution for the cross of Christ.

Gal 6:14 — But God forbid that I should glory, save in the cross of our Lord Jesus Christ, by whom the world is crucified unto me, and I unto the world.

Php 2:8 — And being found in fashion as a man, he humbled himself, and became obedient unto death, even the death of the cross.

Php 3:18 — (For many walk, of whom I have told you often, and now tell you even weeping, *that they are* the enemies of the cross of Christ:

Col 1:20 — And, having made peace through the blood of his cross, by him to reconcile all things unto himself; by him, *I say,* whether *they be* things in earth, or things in heaven.

See: Crucifixion

See: Self-Denial

CROSS-QUESTIONING

Pr 20:5 — Counsel in the heart of man *is like* deep water; but a man of understanding will draw it out.

See: Witness

CROWN

• Prescribed for priests.

Ex 29:6 — And thou shalt put the mitre upon his head, and put the holy crown upon the mitre.

Ex 39:30 — And they made the plate of the holy crown *of* pure gold, and wrote upon it a writing, *like to* the engravings of a signet, HOLINESS TO THE LORD.

Le 8:9 — And he put the mitre upon his head; also upon the mitre, *even* upon his forefront, did he put the golden plate, the holy crown; as the LORD commanded Moses.

• Worn by kings.

2Sa 1:10 — So I stood upon him, and slew him, because I was sure that he could not live after that he was fallen: and I took the crown that *was* upon his head, and the bracelet that *was* on his arm, and have brought them hither unto my lord.

2Sa 12:30 — And he took their king's crown from off his head, the weight whereof *was* a talent of gold with the precious stones: and it was *set* on David's head. And he brought forth the spoil of the city in great abundance.

2Ki 11:12 — And he brought forth the king's son, and put the crown upon him, and *gave him* the testimony; and they made him king, and anointed him; and they clapped their hands, and said, God save the king.

Est 6:8 — Let the royal apparel be brought which the king *useth* to wear, and the horse that the king rideth upon, and the crown royal which is set upon his head:

SS 3:11 — Go forth, O ye daughters of Zion, and behold king Solomon with the crown wherewith his mother crowned him in the day of his espousals, and in the day of the gladness of his heart.

Rev 6:2 — And I saw, and behold a white horse: and he that sat on him had a bow; and a crown was given unto him: and he went forth conquering, and to conquer.

• Worn by queens.

Est 1:11 — To bring Vashti the queen before the king with the crown royal, to shew the people and the princes her beauty: for she *was* fair to look on.

Est 2:17 — And the king loved Esther above all the women, and she obtained grace and favour in his sight more than all the virgins; so that he set the royal crown upon her head, and made her queen instead of Vashti.

Est 8:15 — And Mordecai went out from the presence of the king in royal apparel of blue and white, and with a great crown of gold, and with a garment of fine linen and purple: and the city of Shushan rejoiced and was glad.

• Made of gold.

Ps 21:3 — For thou preventest him with the blessings of goodness: thou settest a crown of pure gold on his head.

Zec 6:11 — Then take silver and gold, and make crowns, and set *them* upon the head of Joshua the son of Josedech, the high priest;

• Of victory.

2Ti 2:5 — And if a man also strive for masteries, *yet* is he not crowned, except he strive lawfully.

• An ornament.

Eze 16:12 — And I put a jewel on thy forehead, and earrings in thine ears, and a beautiful crown upon thine head.

Eze 23:42 — And a voice of a multitude being at ease *was* with her: and with the men of the common sort *were* brought Sabeans from the wilderness, which put bracelets upon their hands, and beautiful crowns upon their heads.

• Set with gems.

2Sa 12:30 — And he took their king's crown from off his head, the weight whereof *was* a talent of gold with the precious stones: and it was *set* on David's head. And he brought forth the spoil of the city in great abundance.

1Ch 20:2 — And David took the crown of their king from off his head, and found it to weigh a talent of gold, and *there were* precious stones in it; and it was set upon David's head: and he brought also exceeding much spoil out of the city.

Isa 62:3 — Thou shalt also be a crown of glory in the hand of the LORD, and a royal diadem in the hand of thy God.

Zec 9:16 — And the LORD their God shall save them in that day as the flock of his people: for they *shall be as* the stones of a crown, lifted up as an ensign upon his land.

• Of thorns.

Mt 27:29 — And when they had platted a crown of thorns, they put *it* upon his head, and a reed in his right hand: and they bowed the knee before him, and mocked him, saying, Hail, King of the Jews!

Mk 15:17 — And they clothed him with purple, and platted a crown of thorns, and put it about his *head,*

Jn 19:5 — Then came Jesus forth, wearing the crown of thorns, and the purple robe. And *Pilate* saith unto them, Behold the man!

• Figurative.

Isa 28:5 — In that day shall the LORD of hosts be for a crown of glory, and for a diadem of beauty, unto the residue of his people,

1Co 9:25 — And every man that striveth for the mastery is temperate in all things. Now they *do it* to obtain a corruptible crown; but we an incorruptible.

2Ti 4:8 — Henceforth there is laid up for me a crown of righteousness, which the Lord, the righteous judge, shall give me at that day: and not to me only, but unto all them also that love his appearing.

Jas 1:12 — Blessed *is* the man that endureth temptation: for when he is tried, he shall receive the crown of life, which the Lord hath promised to them that love him.

1Pe 5:4 — And when the chief Shepherd shall appear, ye shall receive a crown of glory that fadeth not away.

Rev 2:10 — Fear none of those things which thou shalt suffer: behold, the devil shall cast *some* of you into prison, that ye may be tried; and ye shall have tribulation ten days: be thou faithful unto death, and I will give thee a crown of life.

Rev 3:11 — Behold, I come quickly: hold that fast which thou hast, that no man take thy crown.

• Symbolic.

Rev 4:4 — And round about the throne *were* four and twenty seats: and upon the seats I saw four and twenty elders sitting, clothed in white raiment; and they had on their heads crowns of gold.

Rev 4:10 — The four and twenty elders fall down before him that sat on the throne, and worship him that liveth for ever and ever, and cast their crowns before the throne, saying,

Rev 6:2 — And I saw, and behold a white horse: and he that sat on him had a bow; and a crown was given unto him: and he went forth conquering, and to conquer.

Rev 9:7 — And the shapes of the locusts *were* like unto horses prepared unto battle; and on their heads *were* as it were crowns like gold, and their faces *were* as the faces of men.

Rev 12:1 — And there appeared a great wonder in heaven; a woman clothed with the sun, and the moon under her feet, and upon her head a crown of twelve stars:

Rev 12:3 — And there appeared another wonder in heaven; and behold a great red dragon, having seven heads and ten horns, and seven crowns upon his heads.

Rev 13:1 — And I stood upon the sand of the sea, and saw a beast rise up out of the sea, having seven heads and ten horns, and upon his horns ten crowns, and upon his heads the name of blasphemy.

Rev 14:14 — And I looked, and behold a white cloud, and upon the cloud *one* sat like unto the Son of man, having on his head a golden crown, and in his hand a sharp sickle.

Rev 19:12 — His eyes *were* as a flame of fire, and on his head *were* many crowns; and he had a name written, that no man knew, but he himself.

CRUCIFIXION

• The reproach of.

Gal 3:13 — Christ hath redeemed us from the curse of the law, being made a curse for us: for it is written, Cursed *is* every one that hangeth on a tree:

Gal 5:11 — And I, brethren, if I yet preach circumcision, why do I yet suffer persecution? then is the offence of the cross ceased.

• Of Jesus.

See: Jesus, History of

• Of two malefactors.

Mt 27:38 — Then were there two thieves crucified with him, one on the right hand, and another on the left.

• Of disciples, foretold.

Mt 23:34 — Wherefore, behold, I send unto you prophets, and wise men, and scribes: and *some* of them ye shall kill and crucify; and *some* of them shall ye scourge in your synagogues, and persecute *them* from city to city:

See: Cross

• Figurative.

Ro 6:6 — Knowing this, that our old man is crucified with *him,* that the body of sin might be destroyed, that henceforth we should not serve sin.

Gal 2:20 — I am crucified with Christ: nevertheless I live; yet not I, but Christ liveth in me: and the life which I now live in the flesh I live by the faith of the Son of God, who loved me, and gave himself for me.

Gal 5:24 — And they that are Christ's have crucified the flesh with the affections and lusts.

Gal 6:14 — But God forbid that I should glory, save in the cross of our Lord Jesus Christ, by whom the world is crucified unto me, and I unto the world.

See: Cross; figurative

CRUELTY

• Instances of.

• Of Sarah to Hagar.

Ge 16:6; 21:9–14

• Egyptians to the Israelites.

Ex 5:6–18

• Peninnah to Hannah.

1Sa 1:4–7; 2:3

• Of Jews to Jesus.

Mt 26:67; 27:28–31

• Of soldiers to Jesus.

Lk 22:64; Jn 19:3

• In war.

Isa 13:16, 18

See: Animals; cruelty to

➜**See: Kindness**

➜**See: Love**

➜**See: Malice**

➜**See: Prisoners; of war**

CRUSE • A vessel for liquids.

1Sa 26:11 — The LORD forbid that I should stretch forth mine hand against the LORD'S anointed: but, I pray thee, take thou now the spear that *is* at his bolster, and the cruse of water, and let us go.

1Ki 14:3 — And take with thee ten loaves, and cracknels, and a cruse of honey, and go to him: he shall tell thee what shall become of the child.

2Ki 2:20 — And he said, Bring me a new cruse, and put salt therein. And they bring *it* to him.

CRY

Lk 18:3–8

Ex 3:7 — And the LORD said, I have surely seen the affliction of my people which *are* in Egypt, and have heard their cry by reason of their taskmasters; for I know their sorrows;

Ex 22:23 — If thou afflict them in any wise, and they cry at all unto me, I will surely hear their cry;

2Sa 22:7 — In my distress I called upon the LORD, and cried to my God: and he did hear my voice out of his temple, and my cry *did enter* into his ears.

CRYSTAL • A precious stone.

Job 28:17 — The gold and the crystal cannot equal it: and the exchange of it *shall not be for* jewels of fine gold.

Eze 1:22 — And the likeness of the firmament upon the heads of the living creature *was* as the colour of the terrible crystal, stretched forth over their heads above.

Rev 4:6 — And before the throne *there was* a sea of glass like unto crystal: and in the midst of the throne, and round about the throne, *were* four beasts full of eyes before and behind.

Rev 21:11 — Having the glory of God: and her light *was* like unto a stone most precious, even like a jasper stone, clear as crystal;

Rev 22:1 — And he shewed me a pure river of water of life, clear as crystal, proceeding out of the throne of God and of the Lamb.

CUBIT • A measure of distance, probably 20.24 in.–21.888 in.

Ge 6:16 — A window shalt thou make to the ark, and in a cubit shalt thou finish it above; and the door of the ark shalt thou set in the side thereof; *with* lower, second, and third *stories* shalt thou make it.

Dt 3:11 — For only Og king of Bashan remained of the remnant of giants; behold, his bedstead *was* a bedstead of iron; is it not in Rabbath of the children of Ammon? nine cubits was the length thereof, and four cubits the breadth of it, after the cubit of a man.

Eze 40:5 — And behold a wall on the outside of the house round about, and in the man's hand a measuring reed of six cubits *long* by the cubit and an hand breadth: so he measured the breadth of the building, one reed; and the height, one reed.

Eze 43:13 — And these *are* the measures of the altar after the cubits: The cubit *is* a cubit and an hand breadth; even the bottom *shall be* a cubit, and the breadth a cubit, and the border thereof by the edge thereof round about *shall be* a span: and this *shall be* the higher place of the altar.

Rev 21:17 — And he measured the wall thereof, an hundred *and* forty *and* four cubits, *according to* the measure of a man, that is, of the angel.

• Who can add to his height.

Mt 6:27 — Which of you by taking thought can add one cubit unto his stature?

Lk 12:25 — And which of you with taking thought can add to his stature one cubit?

CUCKOO (CUCKOW)

• A bird.

• Forbidden as food.

Le 11:16 — And the owl, and the night hawk, and the cuckow, and the hawk after his kind,

Dt 14:15 — And the owl, and the night hawk, and the cuckow, and the hawk after his kind,

CUCUMBER

Nu 11:5 — We remember the fish, which we did eat in Egypt freely; the cucumbers, and the melons, and the leeks, and the onions, and the garlick:

Isa 1:8 — And the daughter of Zion is left as a cottage in a vineyard, as a lodge in a garden of cucumbers, as a besieged city.

CUD

• Chewing of, was one of the facts by which clean and unclean animals were distinguished.

Le 11:3–8; Dt 14:3–8

CULTS

2Jn 1:10–11

2Ti 4:3 — For the time will come when they will not endure sound doctrine; but after their own lusts shall they heap to themselves teachers, having itching ears;

Tit 1:9 — Holding fast the faithful word as he hath been taught, that he may be able by sound doctrine both to exhort and to convince the gainsayers.

CUMMIN • A plant bearing a small aromatic seed.

Isa 28:25 — When he hath made plain the face thereof, doth he not cast abroad the fitches, and scatter the cummin, and cast in the principal wheat and the appointed barley and rie in their place?

Isa 28:27 — For the fitches are not threshed with a threshing instrument, neither is a cart wheel turned about upon the cummin; but the fitches are beaten out with a staff, and the cummin with a rod.

Mt 23:23 — Woe unto you, scribes and Pharisees, hypocrites! for ye pay tithe of mint and anise and cummin, and have omitted the weightier *matters* of the law, judgment, mercy, and faith: these ought ye to have done, and not to leave the other undone.

CUP

Ge 40:11 — And Pharaoh's cup *was* in my hand: and I took the grapes, and pressed them into Pharaoh's cup, and I gave the cup into Pharaoh's hand.

2Sa 12:3 — But the poor *man* had nothing, save one little ewe lamb, which he had bought and nourished up: and it grew up together with him, and with his children; it did eat of his own meat, and drank of his own cup, and lay in his bosom, and was unto him as a daughter.

1Ki 7:26 — And it *was* an hand breadth thick, and the brim thereof was wrought like the brim of a cup, with flowers of lilies: it contained two thousand baths.

Mt 23:25 — Woe unto you, scribes and Pharisees, hypocrites! for ye make clean the outside of the cup and of the platter, but within they are full of extortion and excess.

• Made of silver.

Ge 44:2 — And put my cup, the silver cup, in the sack's mouth of the youngest, and his corn money. And he did according to the word that Joseph had spoken.

• Made of gold.

1Ch 28:17 — Also pure gold for the fleshhooks, and the bowls, and the cups: and for the golden basons *he gave gold* by weight for every bason; and *likewise silver* by weight for every bason of silver:

Jer 52:19 — And the basons, and the firepans, and the bowls, and the caldrons, and the candlesticks, and the spoons, and the cups; *that* which *was* of gold *in* gold, and *that* which *was* of silver *in* silver, took the captain of the guard away.

• Used in the institution of the Lord's Supper.

Mt 26:27 — And he took the cup, and gave thanks, and gave *it* to them, saying, Drink ye all of it;

Mk 14:23 — And he took the cup, and when he had given thanks, he gave *it* to them: and they all drank of it.

Lk 22:20 — Likewise also the cup after supper, saying, This cup *is* the new testament in my blood, which is shed for you.

1Co 10:21 — Ye cannot drink the cup of the Lord, and the cup of devils: ye cannot be partakers of the Lord's table, and of the table of devils.

• Of the table of devils.

1Co 10:21 — Ye cannot drink the cup of the Lord, and the cup of devils: ye cannot be partakers of the Lord's table, and of the table of devils.

• Figurative.

• Of sorrow.

Jer 25:15–28; Eze 23:31–34; Mt 20:22–23

Ps 11:6 — Upon the wicked he shall rain snares, fire and brimstone, and an horrible tempest: *this shall be* the portion of their cup.

Ps 73:10 — Therefore his people return hither: and waters of a full *cup* are wrung out to them.

Ps 75:8 — For in the hand of the LORD *there is* a cup, and the wine is red; it is full of mixture; and he poureth out of the same: but the dregs thereof, all the wicked of the earth shall wring *them* out, *and* drink *them.*

Isa 51:17 — Awake, awake, stand up, O Jerusalem, which hast drunk at the hand of the LORD the cup of his fury; thou hast drunken the dregs of the cup of trembling, *and* wrung *them* out.

Isa 51:22 — Thus saith thy Lord the LORD, and thy God *that* pleadeth the cause of his people, Behold, I have taken out of thine hand the cup of trembling, *even* the dregs of the cup of my fury; thou shalt no more drink it again:

Mt 26:39 — And he went a little farther, and fell on his face, and prayed, saying, O my Father, if it be possible, let this cup pass from me: nevertheless not as I will, but as thou *wilt.*

Mk 14:36 — And he said, Abba, Father, all things *are* possible unto thee; take away this cup from me: nevertheless not what I will, but what thou wilt.

Lk 22:42 — Saying, Father, if thou be willing, remove this cup from me: nevertheless not my will, but thine, be done.

Jn 18:11 — Then said Jesus unto Peter, Put up thy sword into the sheath: the cup which my Father hath given me, shall I not drink it?

Rev 14:10 — The same shall drink of the wine of the wrath of God, which is poured out without mixture into the cup of his indignation; and he shall be tormented with fire and brimstone in the presence of the holy angels, and in the presence of the Lamb:

• Of consolation.

Jer 16:7 — Neither shall *men* tear *themselves* for them in mourning, to comfort them for the dead; neither shall *men* give them the cup of consolation to drink for their father or for their mother.

• Of joy.

Ps 23:5 — Thou preparest a table before me in the presence of mine enemies: thou anointest my head with oil; my cup runneth over.

• Of salvation.

Ps 116:13 — I will take the cup of salvation, and call upon the name of the LORD.

CUPBEARER

Ge 40:1 — And it came to pass after these things, *that* the butler of the king of Egypt and *his* baker had offended their lord the king of Egypt.

Ge 40:11 — And Pharaoh's cup *was* in my hand: and I took the grapes, and pressed them into Pharaoh's cup, and I gave the cup into Pharaoh's hand.

1Ki 10:5 — And the meat of his table, and the sitting of his servants, and the attendance of his ministers, and their apparel, and his cupbearers, and his ascent by which he went up unto the house of the LORD; there was no more spirit in her.

2Ch 9:4 — And the meat of his table, and the sitting of his servants, and the attendance of his ministers, and their apparel; his cupbearers also, and their apparel; and his ascent by which he went up into the house of the LORD; there was no more spirit in her.

Ne 1:11 — O Lord, I beseech thee, let now thine ear be attentive to the prayer of thy servant, and to the prayer of thy servants, who desire to fear thy name: and prosper, I pray thee, thy servant this day, and grant him mercy in the sight of this man. For I was the king's cupbearer.

CUPIDITY

✧See: Avarice
✧See: Covetousness
✧See: Lust

CURES

- **Miraculous.**

✧See: Miracles of the Disciples
✧See: Miracles, Joshua-Jonah
✧See: Miracles, of Jesus, in chronological order
✧See: Disease
✧See: Physician

CURIOSITY

Pr 27:20 — Hell and destruction are never full; so the eyes of man are never satisfied.

Ecc 7:21 — Also take no heed unto all words that are spoken; lest thou hear thy servant curse thee:

- **Instances of.**
  - **Of Eve.**
    Ge 3:6
  - **Of Abraham, to know whether God would destroy the righteous in Sodom.**
    Ge 18:23–32
  - **Of Jacob, to know the name of the angel.**
    Ge 32:29
  - **Of the Israelites, to see God.**
    Ex 19:21, 24
  - **Of the Israelites, to witness the offering in the Holy of Holies.**
    Nu 4:19–20
  - **Of Manoah, to know the name of an angel.**
    Jgs 13:17–18
  - **Of the people of Beth-shemish, to see inside the ark.**
    1Sa 6:19
  - **Of the Babylonians, to see Hezekiah's treasures.**
    2Ki 20:13
  - **Of Daniel, to know a vision.**
    Da 12:8–9
  - **Of Peter, to know what was being done with Jesus.**
    Mt 26:58
  - **Of Peter, to know what John would be appointed to do.**
    Jn 21:21–22
  - **A disciple, to know if there be few that be saved.**
    Lk 13:23
  - **Of Herod, to see Jesus.**
    Lk 9:9; 23:8
  - **Of the Jews, to see Lazarus, after he was raised from the dead.**
    Jn 12:9
  - **Of the Jews, to see Lazarus, after he was raised from the dead and to see Jesus.**
    Jn 12:20–21
  - **Of the disciples, to know whether Jesus would restore the kingdom of the Jews.**
    Ac 1:6–7
  - **Of the Athenians, to hear some new thing.**
    Ac 17:19–21
  - **Of angels, to look into the mysteries of salvation.**
    1Pe 1:12

CURSE

- **Denounced against.**
  - **The serpent.**
    Ge 3:14–15
  - **Adam and Eve.**
    Ge 3:15–19
  - **The ground.**
    Ge 3:17–18
  - **Cain.**
    Ge 4:11–16
  - **Canaan, Noah's son.**
    Ge 9:24–27
  - **Meroz.**
    Jgs 5:23 — Curse ye Meroz, said the angel of the LORD, curse ye bitterly the inhabitants thereof; because they came not to the help of the LORD, to the help of the LORD against the mighty.
  - **Gehazi.**
    2Ki 5:27 — The leprosy therefore of Naaman shall cleave unto thee, and unto thy seed for ever. And he went out from his presence a leper *as white* as snow.
- **Barak commands Balaam to curse Israel.**

Nu 22:6 — Come now therefore, I pray thee, curse me this people; for they *are* too mighty for me: peradventure I shall prevail, *that* we may smite them, and *that* I may drive them out of the land: for I wot that he whom thou blessest *is* blessed, and he whom thou cursest is cursed.

Nu 23:11 — And Balak said unto Balaam, What hast thou done unto me? I took thee to curse mine enemies, and, behold, thou hast blessed *them* altogether.

✧See: Benedictions

- **Curses of the Mosaic law.**

Dt 27:1–26; Jos 8:30–34

✧See: Blessing

CURSING

• Of parents.

Ex 21:17 — And he that curseth his father, or his mother, shall surely be put to death.

Mt 15:4 — For God commanded, saying, Honour thy father and mother: and, He that curseth father or mother, let him die the death.

Mk 7:10 — For Moses said, Honour thy father and thy mother; and, Whoso curseth father or mother, let him die the death:

• Shimei curses David.

2Sa 16:5–8

• The precepts of Jesus concerning.

Mt 5:44 — But I say unto you, Love your enemies, bless them that curse you, do good to them that hate you, and pray for them which despitefully use you, and persecute you;

Lk 6:28 — Bless them that curse you, and pray for them which despitefully use you.

• Apostolic.

Ro 12:4 — For as we have many members in one body, and all members have not the same office:

✦See: Anathema Maran-Atha

✦See: Blasphemy

✦See: God; name of; not to be profaned

✦See: Oath

CURTAINS

• For tabernacle.

Ex 26:1–37; 27:9–18; 36:8–18

• In the palace of Ahasuerus.

Est 1:6 — *Where were* white, green, and blue, *hangings,* fastened with cords of fine linen and purple to silver rings and pillars of marble: the beds *were of* gold and silver, upon a pavement of red, and blue, and white, and black, marble.

✦See: Tabernacle

✦See: Tapestry

• Figurative.

Isa 40:22 — *It is* he that sitteth upon the circle of the earth, and the inhabitants thereof *are* as grasshoppers; that stretcheth out the heavens as a curtain, and spreadeth them out as a tent to dwell in:

Isa 54:2 — Enlarge the place of thy tent, and let them stretch forth the curtains of thine habitations: spare not, lengthen thy cords, and strengthen thy stakes;

Jer 4:20 — Destruction upon destruction is cried; for the whole land is spoiled: suddenly are my tents spoiled, *and* my curtains in a moment.

Jer 10:20 — My tabernacle is spoiled, and all my cords are broken: my children are gone forth of me, and they *are* not: *there is* none to stretch forth my tent any more, and to set up my curtains.

Jer 49:29 — Their tents and their flocks shall they take away: they shall take to themselves their curtains, and all their vessels, and their camels; and they shall cry unto them, Fear *is* on every side.

CUSH

• Son of Ham.

Ge 10:6–8; 1Ch 1:8–10

• A Benjamite, title of.

Ps 7:1–17

• Land of.

Ge 2:13 — And the name of the second river *is* Gihon: the same *is* it that compasseth the whole land of Ethiopia.

Ps 68:31 — Princes shall come out of Egypt; Ethiopia shall soon stretch out her hands unto God.

Isa 18:1 — Woe to the land shadowing with wings, which *is* beyond the rivers of Ethiopia:

✦See: Ethiopia

CUSHAN

• Poetic form of Cush.

Hab 3:7 — I saw the tents of Cushan in affliction: *and* the curtains of the land of Midian did tremble.

✦See: Ethiopia

CUSHI

• A messenger who brought tidings to David.

2Sa 18:21–32

• Father of Shelemiah.

Jer 36:14 — Therefore all the princes sent Jehudi the son of Nethaniah, the son of Shelemiah, the son of Cushi, unto Baruch, saying, Take in thine hand the roll wherein thou hast read in the ears of the people, and come. So Baruch the son of Neriah took the roll in his hand, and came unto them.

• Father of Zephaniah.

Zep 1:1 — The word of the LORD which came unto Zephaniah the son of Cushi, the son of Gedaliah, the son of Amariah, the son of Hizkiah, in the days of Josiah the son of Amon, king of Judah.

CUTH

• Called also Cuthah.

• A district of Asia, from which colonists were transported to Samaria.

2Ki 17:24–30

Ezr 4:10 — And the rest of the nations whom the great and noble Asnapper brought over, and set in the cities of Samaria, and the rest *that are* on this side the river, and at such a time.

CUTTING, the Flesh for the Dead

• Forbidden.

Le 19:28 — Ye shall not make any cuttings in your flesh for the dead, nor print any marks upon you: I *am* the LORD.

Le 21:5 — They shall not make baldness upon their head, neither shall they shave off the corner of their beard, nor make any cuttings in their flesh.

Dt 14:1 — Ye *are* the children of the LORD your God: ye shall not cut yourselves, nor make any baldness between your eyes for the dead.

Jer 16:6 — Both the great and the small shall die in this land: they shall not be buried, neither shall *men* lament for them, nor cut themselves, nor make themselves bald for them:

CYMBAL

• A musical instrument made of brass.

1Ch 15:19 — So the singers, Heman, Asaph, and Ethan, *were appointed* to sound with cymbals of brass;

1Ch 15:28 — Thus all Israel brought up the ark of the covenant of the LORD with shouting, and with sound of the cornet, and with trumpets, and with cymbals, making a noise with psalteries and harps.

1Co 13:1 — Though I speak with the tongues of men and of angels, and have not charity, I am become *as* sounding brass, or a tinkling cymbal.

• Used in the tabernacle service.

2Sa 6:5 — And David and all the house of Israel played before the LORD on all manner of *instruments made of* fir wood, even on harps, and on psalteries, and on timbrels, and on cornets, and on cymbals.

1Ch 13:8 — And David and all Israel played before God with all *their* might, and with singing, and with harps, and with psalteries, and with timbrels, and with cymbals, and with trumpets.

1Ch 15:16 — And David spake to the chief of the Levites to appoint their brethren *to be* the singers with instruments of musick, psalteries and harps and cymbals, sounding, by lifting up the voice with joy.

1Ch 15:19 — So the singers, Heman, Asaph, and Ethan, *were appointed* to sound with cymbals of brass;

1Ch 15:28 — Thus all Israel brought up the ark of the covenant of the LORD with shouting, and with sound of the cornet, and with trumpets, and with cymbals, making a noise with psalteries and harps.

• Used in the temple service.

2Ch 5:12–13

1Ch 16:5 — Asaph the chief, and next to him Zechariah, Jeiel, and Shemiramoth, and Jehiel, and Mattithiah, and Eliab, and Benaiah, and Obed-edom: and Jeiel with psalteries and with harps; but Asaph made a sound with cymbals;

1Ch 16:42 — And with them Heman and Jeduthun with trumpets and cymbals for those that should make a sound, and with musical instruments of God. And the sons of Jeduthun *were* porters.

1Ch 25:1 — Moreover David and the captains of the host separated to the service of the sons of Asaph, and of Heman, and of Jeduthun, who should prophesy with harps, with psalteries, and with cymbals: and the number of the workmen according to their service was:

1Ch 25:6 — All these *were* under the hands of their father for song *in* the house of the LORD, with cymbals, psalteries, and harps, for the service of the house of God, according to the king's order to Asaph, Jeduthun, and Heman.

Ps 150:5 — Praise him upon the loud cymbals: praise him upon the high sounding cymbals.

• Used on special occasions.

• Day of atonement.

2Ch 29:25 — And he set the Levites in the house of the LORD with cymbals, with psalteries, and with harps, according to the commandment of David, and of Gad the king's seer, and Nathan the prophet: for *so was* the commandment of the LORD by his prophets.

• Laying of the foundation of the second temple.

Ezr 3:10–11

• Dedication of the wall.

Ne 12:27 — And at the dedication of the wall of Jerusalem they sought the Levites out of all their places, to bring them to Jerusalem, to keep the dedication with gladness, both with thanksgivings, and with singing, *with* cymbals, psalteries, and with harps.

Ne 12:36 — And his brethren, Shemaiah, and Azarael, Milalai, Gilalai, Maai, Nethaneel, and Judah, Hanani, with the musical instruments of David the man of God, and Ezra the scribe before them.

CYPRESS

SS 1:14 — My beloved *is* unto me *as* a cluster of camphire in the vineyards of En-gedi.

SS 4:13 — Thy plants *are* an orchard of pomegranates, with pleasant fruits; camphire, with spikenard,

Isa 44:14 — He heweth him down cedars, and taketh the cypress and the oak, which he strengtheneth for himself among the trees of the forest: he planteth an ash, and the rain doth nourish *it*.

CYPRUS

• An island.

Ac 21:3 — Now when we had discovered Cyprus, we left it on the left hand, and sailed into Syria, and landed at Tyre: for there the ship was to unlade her burden.

Ac 27:4 — And when we had launched from thence, we sailed under Cyprus, because the winds were contrary.

• Barnabas born in.

Ac 4:36 — And Joses, who by the apostles was surnamed Barnabas, (which is, being interpreted, The son of consolation,) a Levite, *and* of the country of Cyprus,

• Persecuted Jews preached the gospel at.

Ac 11:19–20

• Visited by.

• Barnabas and Saul.

Ac 13:4–12

• Barnabas and Mark.

Ac 15:39 — And the contention was so sharp between them, that they departed asunder one from the other: and so Barnabas took Mark, and sailed unto Cyprus;

• Mnason, a disciple of.

Ac 21:16 — There went with us also *certain* of the disciples of Caesarea, and brought with them one Mnason of Cyprus, an old disciple, with whom we should lodge.

CYRENE

• A city in Libya.

Ac 2:10 — Phrygia, and Pamphylia, in Egypt, and in the parts of Libya about Cyrene, and strangers of Rome, Jews and proselytes,

• Contained a synagogue.

Ac 6:9 — Then there arose certain of *the synagogue,* which is called the synagogue of the Libertines, and Cyrenians, and Alexandrians, and of them of Cilicia and of Asia, disputing with Stephen.

• Simon and Lucius belonged to.

Mk 15:21 — And they compel one Simon a Cyrenian, who passed by, coming out of the country, the father of Alexander and Rufus, to bear his cross.

Ac 11:20 — And some of them were men of Cyprus and Cyrene, which, when they were come to Antioch, spake unto the Grecians, preaching the Lord Jesus.

Ac 13:1 — Now there were in the church that was at Antioch certain prophets and teachers; as Barnabas, and Simeon that was called Niger, and Lucius of Cyrene, and Manaen, which had been brought up with Herod the tetrarch, and Saul.

CYRENIUS • Governor of Syria.

Lk 2:2 — (*And* this taxing was first made when Cyrenius was governor of Syria.)

CYRUS

• King of Persia.

• Issues a decree for the emancipation of the Jews and rebuilding the temple.

2Ch 36:22–23; Ezr 1:1–11; 5:13–14

Ezr 3:7 — They gave money also unto the masons, and to the carpenters; and meat, and drink, and oil, unto them of Zidon, and to them of Tyre, to bring cedar trees from Lebanon to the sea of Joppa, according to the grant that they had of Cyrus king of Persia.

Ezr 4:3 — But Zerubbabel, and Jeshua, and the rest of the chief of the fathers of Israel, said unto them, Ye have nothing to do with us to build an house unto our God; but we ourselves together will build unto the LORD God of Israel, as king Cyrus the king of Persia hath commanded us.

Ezr 6:3 — In the first year of Cyrus the king *the same* Cyrus the king made a decree *concerning* the house of God at Jerusalem, Let the house be builded, the place where they offered sacrifices, and let the foundations thereof be strongly laid; the height thereof threescore cubits, *and* the breadth thereof threescore cubits;

• Prophecies concerning.

Isa 13:17–22; 44:28–45:4; 48:14–15

Isa 21:2 — A grievous vision is declared unto me; the treacherous dealer dealeth treacherously, and the spoiler spoileth. Go up, O Elam: besiege, O Media; all the sighing thereof have I made to cease.

Isa 41:2 — Who raised up the righteous *man* from the east, called him to his foot, gave the nations before him, and made *him* rule over kings? he gave *them* as the dust to his sword, *and* as driven stubble to his bow.

Isa 45:13 — I have raised him up in righteousness, and I will direct all his ways: he shall build my city, and he shall let go my captives, not for price nor reward, saith the LORD of hosts.

Isa 46:11 — Calling a ravenous bird from the east, the man that executeth my counsel from a far country: yea, I have spoken *it,* I will also bring it to pass; I have purposed *it,* I will also do it.

D

DABAREH ✦See: Daberath

DABBASHETH • A place on the boundary line of Zebulun.

Jos 19:11 — And their border went up toward the sea, and Maralah, and reached to Dabbasheth, and reached to the river that *is* before Jokneam;

DABERATH

• Called also Dabareh.

• A town of Issachar.

Jos 19:12 — And turned from Sarid eastward toward the sunrising unto the border of Chisloth-tabor, and then goeth out to Daberath, and goeth up to Japhia,

Jos 21:28 — And out of the tribe of Issachar, Kishon with her suburbs, Dabareh with her suburbs,

• Assigned to the Levites.

1Ch 6:72 — And out of the tribe of Issachar; Kedesh with her suburbs, Daberath with her suburbs,

DAGGER • A short sword.

Jgs 3:16–22

DAGON

• An idol of the Philistines.

1Sa 5:1–12

Jgs 16:23 — Then the lords of the Philistines gathered them together for to offer a great sacrifice unto Dagon their god, and to rejoice: for they said, Our god hath delivered Samson our enemy into our hand.

• Temple of.

1Ch 10:10 — And they put his armour in the house of their gods, and fastened his head in the temple of Dagon.

DAILY OFFERING

• Sacrificial.

Ex 29:38–42; 30:7–9; Nu 28:3–8; Ezr 3:4–6; Eze 46:13–15; Da 9:26–27

Da 9:21 — Yea, whiles I *was* speaking in prayer, even the man Gabriel, whom I had seen in the vision at the beginning, being caused to fly swiftly, touched me about the time of the evening oblation.

Da 11:31 — And arms shall stand on his part, and they shall pollute the sanctuary of strength, and shall take away the daily *sacrifice,* and they shall place the abomination that maketh desolate.

Ac 3:1 — Now Peter and John went up together into the temple at the hour of prayer, *being* the ninth *hour.*

✦See: Offerings

• Figurative.

Jn 1:29 — The next day John seeth Jesus coming unto him, and saith, Behold the Lamb of God, which taketh away the sin of the world.

Jn 1:36 — And looking upon Jesus as he walked, he saith, Behold the Lamb of God!

1Pe 1:19 — But with the precious blood of Christ, as of a lamb without blemish and without spot:

DALAIAH ✦See: Delaiah

DALMANUTHA • A town on the west coast of the Sea of Galilee.

Mk 8:10 — And straightway he entered into a ship with his disciples, and came into the parts of Dalmanutha.

DALMATIA • A country on the eastern shore of the Adriatic.

2Ti 4:10 — For Demas hath forsaken me, having loved this present world, and is departed unto Thessalonica; Crescens to Galatia, Titus unto Dalmatia.

DALPHON • Son of Haman.

Est 9:7 — And Parshandatha, and Dalphon, and Aspatha,

DAMAGES AND COMPENSATION

Ex 21:18–19, 28–34; Le 6:1–5; Dt 22:13–19, 28–29

Ex 21:22 — If men strive, and hurt a woman with child, so that her fruit depart *from her,* and yet no mischief follow: he shall be surely punished, according as the woman's husband will lay upon him; and he shall pay as the judges *determine.*

DAMARIS • A female convert of Athens.

Ac 17:34 — Howbeit certain men clave unto him, and believed: among the which *was* Dionysius the Areopagite, and a woman named Damaris, and others with them.

DAMASCUS

• An ancient city.

Ge 14:15 — And he divided himself against them, he and his servants, by night, and smote them, and pursued them unto Hobah, which *is* on the left hand of Damascus.

Ge 15:2 — And Abram said, Lord GOD, what wilt thou give me, seeing I go childless, and the steward of my house is this Eliezer of Damascus?

• Capital of Syria.

Jer 49:23–29; Eze 47:16–17

1Ki 20:34 — And *Ben-hadad* said unto him, The cities, which my father took from thy father, I will restore; and thou shalt make streets for thee in Damascus, as my father made in Samaria. Then *said*

Ahab, I will send thee away with this covenant. So he made a covenant with him, and sent him away.

Isa 7:8 — For the head of Syria *is* Damascus, and the head of Damascus *is* Rezin; and within threescore and five years shall Ephraim be broken, that it be not a people.

- **Laid under tribute to David.**

2Sa 8:5–6

- **Besieged by Rezon.**

1Ki 11:23–24

- **Recovered by Jeroboam.**

2Ki 14:28 — Now the rest of the acts of Jeroboam, and all that he did, and his might, how he warred, and how he recovered Damascus, and Hamath, *which belonged* to Judah, for Israel, are they not written in the book of the chronicles of the kings of Israel?

- **Taken by king of Assyria.**

2Ki 16:9 — And the king of Assyria hearkened unto him: for the king of Assyria went up against Damascus, and took it, and carried *the people of* it captive to Kir, and slew Rezin.

- **Walled.**

Jer 49:27 — And I will kindle a fire in the wall of Damascus, and it shall consume the palaces of Ben-hadad.

2Co 11:33 — And through a window in a basket was I let down by the wall, and escaped his hands.

- **Garrisoned.**

2Co 11:32 — In Damascus the governor under Aretas the king kept the city of the Damascenes with a garrison, desirous to apprehend me:

- **Luxury in.**

Am 3:12 — Thus saith the LORD; As the shepherd taketh out of the mouth of the lion two legs, or a piece of an ear; so shall the children of Israel be taken out that dwell in Samaria in the corner of a bed, and in Damascus *in* a couch.

- **Paul's experiences in.**

Ac 9:1–43; 22:5–16; 26:12–20

2Co 11:32 — In Damascus the governor under Aretas the king kept the city of the Damascenes with a garrison, desirous to apprehend me:

Gal 1:17 — Neither went I up to Jerusalem to them which were apostles before me; but I went into Arabia, and returned again unto Damascus.

- **Prophecies concerning.**

Isa 17:1–2; Jer 49:23–29

Isa 8:4 — For before the child shall have knowledge to cry, My father, and my mother, the riches of Damascus and the spoil of Samaria shall be taken away before the king of Assyria.

Am 1:3 — Thus saith the LORD; For three transgressions of Damascus, and for four, I will not turn away *the punishment* thereof; because they have threshed Gilead with threshing instruments of iron:

Am 1:5 — I will break also the bar of Damascus, and cut off the inhabitant from the plain of Aven, and him that holdeth the sceptre from the house of Eden: and the people of Syria shall go into captivity unto Kir, saith the LORD.

Zec 9:1 — The burden of the word of the LORD in the land of Hadrach, and Damascus *shall be* the rest thereof: when the eyes of man, as of all the tribes of Israel, *shall be* toward the LORD.

- **Wilderness of.**

1Ki 19:15 — And the LORD said unto him, Go, return on thy way to the wilderness of Damascus: and when thou comest, anoint Hazael *to be* king over Syria:

See: Syria

DAMNED **See: Wicked; punishment of**

DAN

- **Fifth son of Jacob and Bilhah.**

Ge 30:6 — And Rachel said, God hath judged me, and hath also heard my voice, and hath given me a son: therefore called she his name Dan.

Ge 35:25 — And the sons of Bilhah, Rachel's handmaid; Dan, and Naphtali:

  - **Descendants of.**

  Nu 26:42–43

  Ge 46:23 — And the sons of Dan; Hushim.

  See: Dan; tribe of

  - **Blessed of Jacob.**

  Ge 49:16–17

- **Tribe of.**

  - **Census of.**

  Nu 26:42–43

  Nu 1:39 — Those that were numbered of them, *even* of the tribe of Dan, *were* threescore and two thousand and seven hundred.

  - **Inheritance of, according to the allotment of Joshua.**

  Jos 19:40–47

  - **Inheritance of, according to the allotment of Ezekiel.**

  Eze 48:1 — Now these *are* the names of the tribes. From the north end to the coast of the way of Hethlon, as one goeth to Hamath, Hazar-enan, the border of Damascus northward, to the coast of Hamath; for these are his sides east *and* west; a *portion for* Dan.

  - **Position of, in journey and camp, during the Exodus.**

  Nu 2:25 — The standard of the camp of Dan *shall be* on the north side by their armies: and the captain of the children of Dan *shall be* Ahiezer the son of Ammishaddai.

  Nu 2:31 — All they that were numbered in the camp of Dan *were* an hundred thousand and fifty and seven thousand and six hundred. They shall go hindmost with their standards.

  Nu 10:25 — And the standard of the camp of the children of Dan set forward, *which was* the rereward of all the camps throughout their hosts: and over his host *was* Ahiezer the son of Ammishaddai.

  - **Blessed by Moses.**

  Dt 33:22 — And of Dan he said, Dan *is* a lion's whelp: he shall leap from Bashan.

• Fail to conquer the Amorites.

Jgs 1:34–35

• Conquests by.

Jgs 18:27–29

Jos 19:47 — And the coast of the children of Dan went out *too little* for them: therefore the children of Dan went up to fight against Leshem, and took it, and smote it with the edge of the sword, and possessed it, and dwelt therein, and called Leshem, Dan, after the name of Dan their father.

• Deborah upbraids, for cowardice.

Jgs 5:17 — Gilead abode beyond Jordan: and why did Dan remain in ships? Asher continued on the sea shore, and abode in his breaches.

• Idolatry of.

Jgs 18:1–31

• Commerce of.

Jgs 5:17 — Gilead abode beyond Jordan: and why did Dan remain in ships? Asher continued on the sea shore, and abode in his breaches.

Eze 27:19 — Dan also and Javan going to and fro occupied in thy fairs: bright iron, cassia, and calamus, were in thy market.

See: Israel, Name Given to Descendants of Jacob; tribes of Israel were named after the sons of Jacob

• A city of the tribe of Dan, called also Laish and Leshem.

Ge 14:14 — And when Abram heard that his brother was taken captive, he armed his trained *servants,* born in his own house, three hundred and eighteen, and pursued *them* unto Dan.

Dt 34:1 — And Moses went up from the plains of Moab unto the mountain of Nebo, to the top of Pisgah, that *is* over against Jericho. And the LORD shewed him all the land of Gilead, unto Dan,

Jgs 20:1 — Then all the children of Israel went out, and the congregation was gathered together as one man, from Dan even to Beer-sheba, with the land of Gilead, unto the LORD in Mizpeh.

Jer 8:16 — The snorting of his horses was heard from Dan: the whole land trembled at the sound of the neighing of his strong ones; for they are come, and have devoured the land, and all that is in it; the city, and those that dwell therein.

• Captured by the people of Dan.

Jos 19:47 — And the coast of the children of Dan went out *too little* for them: therefore the children of Dan went up to fight against Leshem, and took it, and smote it with the edge of the sword, and possessed it, and dwelt therein, and called Leshem, Dan, after the name of Dan their father.

• Idolatry established at.

Jgs 18:1–31; 1Ki 12:28–29

Am 8:14 — They that swear by the sin of Samaria, and say, Thy god, O Dan, liveth; and, The manner of Beer-sheba liveth; even they shall fall, and never rise up again.

• Captured by Ben-hadad.

1Ki 15:20 — So Ben-hadad hearkened unto king Asa, and sent the captains of the hosts which he had against the cities of Israel, and smote Ijon, and Dan, and Abel-beth-maachah, and all Cinneroth, with all the land of Naphtali.

2Ch 16:4 — And Ben-hadad hearkened unto king Asa, and sent the captains of his armies against the cities of Israel; and they smote Ijon, and Dan, and Abel-maim, and all the store cities of Naphtali.

DAN-JAAN • A place near the source of the Jordan.

2Sa 24:6 — Then they came to Gilead, and to the land of Tahtim-hodshi; and they came to Dan-jaan, and about to Zidon,

DANCE

2Sa 6:14 — And David danced before the LORD with all *his* might; and David *was* girded with a linen ephod.

Mt 14:6 — But when Herod's birthday was kept, the daughter of Herodias danced before them, and pleased Herod.

DANCING

Jgs 21:19–21; 2Sa 6:14–16; Lk 15:23–25

Ex 15:20 — And Miriam the prophetess, the sister of Aaron, took a timbrel in her hand; and all the women went out after her with timbrels and with dances.

Ex 32:19 — And it came to pass, as soon as he came nigh unto the camp, that he saw the calf, and the dancing: and Moses' anger waxed hot, and he cast the tables out of his hands, and brake them beneath the mount.

Jgs 11:34 — And Jephthah came to Mizpeh unto his house, and, behold, his daughter came out to meet him with timbrels and with dances: and she *was his* only child; beside her he had neither son nor daughter.

1Sa 18:6 — And it came to pass as they came, when David was returned from the slaughter of the Philistine, that the women came out of all cities of Israel, singing and dancing, to meet king Saul, with tabrets, with joy, and with instruments of musick.

1Sa 21:11 — And the servants of Achish said unto him, *Is* not this David the king of the land? did they not sing one to another of him in dances, saying, Saul hath slain his thousands, and David his ten thousands?

1Sa 30:16 — And when he had brought him down, behold, *they were* spread abroad upon all the earth, eating and drinking, and dancing, because of all the great spoil that they had taken out of the land of the Philistines, and out of the land of Judah.

Job 21:11 — They send forth their little ones like a flock, and their children dance.

Ps 30:11 — Thou hast turned for me my mourning into dancing: thou hast put off my sackcloth, and girded me with gladness;

Ps 149:3 — Let them praise his name in the dance: let them sing praises unto him with the timbrel and harp.

Ps 150:4 — Praise him with the timbrel and dance: praise him with stringed instruments and organs.

Ecc 3:4 — A time to weep, and a time to laugh; a time to mourn, and a time to dance;

Jer 31:4 — Again I will build thee, and thou shalt be built, O virgin of Israel: thou shalt again be adorned with thy tabrets, and shalt go forth in the dances of them that make merry.

Jer 31:13 — Then shall the virgin rejoice in the dance, both young men and old together: for I will turn their mourning into joy, and will comfort them, and make them rejoice from their sorrow.

La 5:15 — The joy of our heart is ceased; our dance is turned into mourning.

Mt 11:17 — And saying, We have piped unto you, and ye have not danced; we have mourned unto you, and ye have not lamented.

• Herodias, daughter of Herod, dances before him.

Mt 14:6 — But when Herod's birthday was kept, the daughter of Herodias danced before them, and pleased Herod.

Mk 6:22 — And when the daughter of the said Herodias came in, and danced, and pleased Herod and them that sat with him, the king said unto the damsel, Ask of me whatsoever thou wilt, and I will give *it* thee.

• Idolatrous.

Ex 32:19 — And it came to pass, as soon as he came nigh unto the camp, that he saw the calf, and the dancing: and Moses' anger waxed hot, and he cast the tables out of his hands, and brake them beneath the mount.

Ex 32:25 — And when Moses saw that the people *were* naked; (for Aaron had made them naked unto *their* shame among their enemies:)

DANIEL

• A Jewish captive, called also Beltheshazzar.

• Educated at king's court.

Da 1:1–21

• Interprets visions.

Da 2:1–49; 4:1–5:31

• Promotion and executive authority of.

Da 2:48–49

Da 5:11 — There is a man in thy kingdom, in whom *is* the spirit of the holy gods; and in the days of thy father light and understanding and wisdom, like the wisdom of the gods, was found in him; whom the king Nebuchadnezzar thy father, the king, *I say*, thy father, made master of the magicians, astrologers, Chaldeans, *and* soothsayers;

Da 5:29 — Then commanded Belshazzar, and they clothed Daniel with scarlet, and *put* a chain of gold about his neck, and made a proclamation concerning him, that he should be the third ruler in the kingdom.

Da 6:2 — And over these three presidents; of whom Daniel *was* first: that the princes might give accounts unto them, and the king should have no damage.

• Conspiracy against, cast into the lions' den.

Da 6:1–28

• Prophecies of.

Da 4:8–9; 7:1–12:13

Mt 24:15 — When ye therefore shall see the abomination of desolation, spoken of by Daniel the prophet, stand in the holy place, (whoso readeth, let him understand:)

• Abstinence of.

Da 1:8–16

• Wisdom of.

Eze 28:3 — Behold, thou *art* wiser than Daniel; there is no secret that they can hide from thee:

Da 1:17 — As for these four children, God gave them knowledge and skill in all learning and wisdom: and Daniel had understanding in all visions and dreams.

• Devoutness of.

Da 6:1–28; 9:1–10:21; 12:1–13

Eze 14:14 — Though these three men, Noah, Daniel, and Job, were in it, they should deliver *but* their own souls by their righteousness, saith the Lord GOD.

Da 2:18 — That they would desire mercies of the God of heaven concerning this secret; that Daniel and his fellows should not perish with the rest of the wise *men* of Babylon.

• Courage and fidelity of.

Da 5:17–23; 6:10–23

Da 4:27 — Wherefore, O king, let my counsel be acceptable unto thee, and break off thy sins by righteousness, and thine iniquities by shewing mercy to the poor; if it may be a lengthening of thy tranquility.

• Worshiped by Nebuchadnezzar.

Da 2:6 — But if ye shew the dream, and the interpretation thereof, ye shall receive of me gifts and rewards and great honour: therefore shew me the dream, and the interpretation thereof.

• David's son, called also Chileab.

2Sa 3:3 — And his second, Chileab, of Abigail the wife of Nabal the Carmelite; and the third, Absalom the son of Maacah the daughter of Talmai king of Geshur;

1Ch 3:1 — Now these were the sons of David, which were born unto him in Hebron; the firstborn Amnon, of Ahinoam the Jezreelitess; the second Daniel, of Abigail the Carmelitess:

• A descendant of Ithamar, and a companion of Ezra.

Ezr 8:2 — Of the sons of Phinehas; Gershom: of the sons of Ithamar; Daniel: of the sons of David; Hattush.

Ne 10:6 — Daniel, Ginnethon, Baruch,

DANNAH • A city in the mountains of Judah.

Jos 15:49 — And Dannah, and Kirjath-sannah, which *is* Debir,

DARA ✦See: Darda

DARDA

• Called also Dara.

• A famous wise man.

1Ki 4:31 — For he was wiser than all men; than Ethan the Ezrahite, and Heman, and Chalcol, and Darda, the sons of Mahol: and his fame was in all nations round about.

1Ch 2:6 — And the sons of Zerah; Zimri, and Ethan, and Heman, and Calcol, and Dara: five of them in all.

DARIUS

• The Mede, king of Persia.

Da 5:31–6:28

Da 9:1 — In the first year of Darius the son of Ahasuerus, of the seed of the Medes, which was made king over the realm of the Chaldeans;

• King of Persia.

• Emancipates the Jews.

Ezr 5:1–6:22

Hag 1:1 — In the second year of Darius the king, in the sixth month, in the first day of the month, came the word of the LORD by Haggai the prophet unto Zerubbabel the son of Shealtiel, governor of Judah, and to Joshua the son of Josedech, the high priest, saying,

Hag 1:15 — In the four and twentieth day of the sixth month, in the second year of Darius the king.

Zec 1:1 — In the eighth month, in the second year of Darius, came the word of the LORD unto Zechariah, the son of Berechiah, the son of Iddo the prophet, saying,

• The Persian.

Ne 12:22 — The Levites in the days of Eliashib, Joiada, and Johanan, and Jaddua, *were* recorded chief of the fathers: also the priests, to the reign of Darius the Persian.

DARKNESS

• Over the face of the earth.

Ge 1:2 — And the earth was without form, and void; and darkness *was* upon the face of the deep. And the Spirit of God moved upon the face of the waters.

Job 38:9 — When I made the cloud the garment thereof, and thick darkness a swaddlingband for it,

Jer 4:23 — I beheld the earth, and, lo, *it was* without form, and void; and the heavens, and they *had* no light.

• Called night.

Ge 1:5 — And God called the light Day, and the darkness he called Night. And the evening and the morning were the first day.

• God creates.

Isa 45:7 — I form the light, and create darkness: I make peace, and create evil: I the LORD do all these *things.*

• Miraculous.

• In Egypt.

Ex 10:21–22

Ps 105:28 — He sent darkness, and made it dark; and they rebelled not against his word.

• At Sinai.

Ex 20:21 — And the people stood afar off, and Moses drew near unto the thick darkness where God *was.*

Heb 12:18 — For ye are not come unto the mount that might be touched, and that burned with fire, nor unto blackness, and darkness, and tempest,

• At the crucifixion.

Mt 27:45 — Now from the sixth hour there was darkness over all the land unto the ninth hour.

Mk 15:33 — And when the sixth hour was come, there was darkness over the whole land until the ninth hour.

• Figurative.

• Of judgments.

Eze 32:7–8

Pr 20:20 — Whoso curseth his father or his mother, his lamp shall be put out in obscure darkness.

Isa 8:22 — And they shall look unto the earth; and behold trouble and darkness, dimness of anguish; and *they shall be* driven to darkness.

Isa 13:10 — For the stars of heaven and the constellations thereof shall not give their light: the sun shall be darkened in his going forth, and the moon shall not cause her light to shine.

Jer 4:28 — For this shall the earth mourn, and the heavens above be black: because I have spoken *it,* I have purposed *it,* and will not repent, neither will I turn back from it.

Jer 13:16 — Give glory to the LORD your God, before he cause darkness, and before your feet stumble upon the dark mountains, and, while ye look for light, he turn it into the shadow of death, *and* make *it* gross darkness.

La 3:2 — He hath led me, and brought *me into* darkness, but not *into* light.

Joel 2:2 — A day of darkness and of gloominess, a day of clouds and of thick darkness, as the morning spread upon the mountains: a great people and a strong; there hath not been ever the like, neither shall be any more after it, *even* to the years of many generations.

Joel 2:10 — The earth shall quake before them; the heavens shall tremble: the sun and the moon shall be dark, and the stars shall withdraw their shining:

Am 4:13 — For, lo, he that formeth the mountains, and createth the wind, and declareth unto man what *is* his thought, that maketh the morning darkness, and treadeth upon the high places of the earth, The LORD, The God of hosts, *is* his name.

Am 5:18 — Woe unto you that desire the day of the LORD! to what end *is* it for you? the day of the LORD *is* darkness, and not light.

Am 5:20 — *Shall* not the day of the LORD *be* darkness, and not light? even very dark, and no brightness in it?

Am 8:9 — And it shall come to pass in that day, saith the Lord GOD, that I will cause the sun to go down at noon, and I will darken the earth in the clear day:

Mic 7:8 — Rejoice not against me, O mine enemy: when I fall, I shall arise; when I sit in darkness, the LORD *shall be* a light unto me.

Mt 24:29 — Immediately after the tribulation of those days shall the sun be darkened, and the moon shall not give her light, and the stars shall fall from heaven, and the powers of the heavens shall be shaken:

Mk 13:24 — But in those days, after that tribulation, the sun shall be darkened, and the moon shall not give her light,

Lk 23:45 — And the sun was darkened, and the veil of the temple was rent in the midst.

Rev 8:12 — And the fourth angel sounded, and the third part of the sun was smitten, and the third part of the moon, and the third part of the stars; so as the third part of them was darkened, and the day shone not for a third part of it, and the night likewise.

Rev 9:2 — And he opened the bottomless pit; and there arose a smoke out of the pit, as the smoke of a great furnace; and the sun and the air were darkened by reason of the smoke of the pit.

• Called outer darkness.

Mt 8:12 — But the children of the kingdom shall be cast out into outer darkness: there shall be weeping and gnashing of teeth.

Mt 22:13 — Then said the king to the servants, Bind him hand and foot, and take him away, and cast *him* into outer darkness; there shall be weeping and gnashing of teeth.

Mt 25:30 — And cast ye the unprofitable servant into outer darkness: there shall be weeping and gnashing of teeth.

• Of powers of darkness.

Lk 22:53 — When I was daily with you in the temple, ye stretched forth no hands against me: but this is your hour, and the power of darkness.

Eph 6:12 — For we wrestle not against flesh and blood, but against principalities, against powers, against the rulers of the darkness of this world, against spiritual wickedness in high *places.*

Col 1:13 — Who hath delivered us from the power of darkness, and hath translated *us* into the kingdom of his dear Son:

1Th 5:5 — Ye are all the children of light, and the children of the day: we are not of the night, nor of darkness.

Rev 16:10 — And the fifth angel poured out his vial upon the seat of the beast; and his kingdom was full of darkness; and they gnawed their tongues for pain,

• Of spiritual blindness.

Mt 6:22–23; Jn 3:19–21; 11:9–10; Ro 13:12–13; 1Th 5:4–5; 1Jn 1:5–7; 2:8–11

Isa 9:2 — The people that walked in darkness have seen a great light: they that dwell in the land of the shadow of death, upon them hath the light shined.

Isa 42:16 — And I will bring the blind by a way *that* they knew not; I will lead them in paths *that* they have not known: I will make darkness light before them, and crooked things straight. These things will I do unto them, and not forsake them.

Isa 50:10 — Who *is* among you that feareth the LORD, that obeyeth the voice of his servant, that walketh *in* darkness, and hath no light? let him trust in the name of the LORD, and stay upon his God.

Mt 4:16 — The people which sat in darkness saw great light; and to them which sat in the region and shadow of death light is sprung up.

Mt 8:12 — But the children of the kingdom shall be cast out into outer darkness: there shall be weeping and gnashing of teeth.

Lk 1:79 — To give light to them that sit in darkness and *in* the shadow of death, to guide our feet into the way of peace.

Lk 11:34 — The light of the body is the eye: therefore when thine eye is single, thy whole body also is full of light; but when *thine eye* is evil, thy body also *is* full of darkness.

Jn 1:5 — And the light shineth in darkness; and the darkness comprehended it not.

Jn 8:12 — Then spake Jesus again unto them, saying, I am the light of the world: he that followeth me shall not walk in darkness, but shall have the light of life.

Ac 26:18 — To open their eyes, *and* to turn *them* from darkness to light, and *from* the power of Satan unto God, that they may receive forgiveness of sins, and inheritance among them which are sanctified by faith that is in me.

Ro 1:21 — Because that, when they knew God, they glorified *him* not as God, neither were thankful; but became vain in their imaginations, and their foolish heart was darkened.

1Co 4:5 — Therefore judge nothing before the time, until the Lord come, who both will bring to light the hidden things of darkness, and will make manifest the counsels of the hearts: and then shall every man have praise of God.

2Co 4:6 — For God, who commanded the light to shine out of darkness, hath shined in our hearts, to *give* the light of the knowledge of the glory of God in the face of Jesus Christ.

2Co 6:14 — Be ye not unequally yoked together with unbelievers: for what fellowship hath righteousness with unrighteousness? and what communion hath light with darkness?

Eph 5:8 — For ye were sometimes darkness, but now *are ye* light in the Lord: walk as children of light:

Eph 5:11 — And have no fellowship with the unfruitful works of darkness, but rather reprove *them.*

1Pe 2:9 — But ye *are* a chosen generation, a royal priesthood, an holy nation, a peculiar people; that ye should shew forth the praises of him who hath called you out of darkness into his marvellous light:

See: Blindness; spiritual

• The darkness of the Holy of Holies was symbolic of the dwelling place of Jehovah.

2Sa 22:10–12

Ex 19:16 — And it came to pass on the third day in the morning, that there were thunders and lightnings, and a thick cloud upon the mount, and the voice of the trumpet exceeding loud; so that all the people that *was* in the camp trembled.

2Ch 6:1 — Then said Solomon, The LORD hath said that he would dwell in the thick darkness.

1Ki 8:12 — Then spake Solomon, The LORD said that he would dwell in thick darkness.

Ps 18:11 — He made darkness his secret place; his pavilion round about him *were* dark waters *and* thick clouds of the skies.

Ps 97:2 — Clouds and darkness *are* round about him: righteousness and judgment *are* the habitation of his throne.

Heb 12:18 — For ye are not come unto the mount that might be touched, and that burned with fire, nor unto blackness, and darkness, and tempest,

See: Tabernacle; description of; the Most Holy Place

DARKON • A servant of Solomon.

Ezr 2:56 — The children of Jaalah, the children of Darkon, the children of Giddel,

Ne 7:58 — The children of Jaala, the children of Darkon, the children of Giddel,

DART • A light javelin.

Nu 25:7 — And when Phinehas, the son of Eleazar, the son of Aaron the priest, saw *it,* he rose up from among the congregation, and took a javelin in his hand;

1Sa 18:10 — And it came to pass on the morrow, that the evil spirit from God came upon Saul, and he prophesied in the midst of the house: and David played with his hand, as at other times: and *there was* a javelin in Saul's hand.

2Sa 18:14 — Then said Joab, I may not tarry thus with thee. And he took three darts in his hand, and thrust them through the heart of Absalom, while he *was* yet alive in the midst of the oak.

Job 41:29 — Darts are counted as stubble: he laugheth at the shaking of a spear.

• Figurative.

Eph 6:16 — Above all, taking the shield of faith, wherewith ye shall be able to quench all the fiery darts of the wicked.

DATE • A fruit.

2Ch 31:5 — And as soon as the commandment came abroad, the children of Israel brought in abundance the firstfruits of corn, wine, and oil, and honey, and of all the increase of the field; and the tithe of all *things* brought they in abundantly.

DATHAN • A conspirator against Moses.

Nu 16:1–35

Nu 26:9 — And the sons of Eliab; Nemuel, and Dathan, and Abiram. This *is that* Dathan and Abiram, *which were* famous in the congregation, who strove against Moses and against Aaron in the company of Korah, when they strove against the LORD:

Dt 11:6 — And what he did unto Dathan and Abiram, the sons of Eliab, the son of Reuben: how the earth opened her mouth, and swallowed them up, and their households, and their tents, and all the substance that *was* in their possession, in the midst of all Israel:

Ps 106:17 — The earth opened and swallowed up Dathan, and covered the company of Abiram.

DATING

1Co 7:1–9, 25–40

DAUGHTER

• Forbidden to be wife of her mother's husband.

Le 20:14 — And if a man take a wife and her mother, it *is* wickedness: they shall be burnt with fire, both he and they; that there be no wickedness among you.

• Sold in concubinage.

Ex 21:7–10

• Given in marriage by parents.

Jgs 1:12–13; 1Sa 18:20–21

1Sa 17:25 — And the men of Israel said, Have ye seen this man that is come up? surely to defy Israel is he come up: and it shall be, *that* the man who killeth him, the king will enrich him with great riches, and will give him his daughter, and make his father's house free in Israel.

• Property rights of.

Nu 27:1–11; 36:1–13; Jos 17:3–6

Ru 4:3 — And he said unto the kinsman, Naomi, that is come again out of the country of Moab, selleth a parcel of land, which *was* our brother Elimelech's:

• Used also for granddaughter.

Ge 36:2 — Esau took his wives of the daughters of Canaan; Adah the daughter of Elon the Hittite, and Aholibamah the daughter of Anah the daughter of Zibeon the Hivite;

DAUGHTER-IN-LAW

• Filial.

• Instances of.

• Ruth.

Ru 1:11–18

Ru 4:15 — And he shall be unto thee a restorer of *thy* life, and a nourisher of thine old age: for thy daughter in law, which loveth thee, which is better to thee than seven sons, hath born him.

• **Unfilial.**

• **Prophecy of.**

Mic 7:6 — For the son dishonoureth the father, the daughter riseth up against her mother, the daughter in law against her mother in law; a man's enemies *are* the men of his own house.

Mt 10:35 — For I am come to set a man at variance against his father, and the daughter against her mother, and the daughter in law against her mother in law.

DAVID

• **King of Israel.**

• **Genealogy of.**

Ru 4:18–22; 1Ch 2:3–15; Mt 1:1–6; Lk 3:31–38

1Sa 16:11 — And Samuel said unto Jesse, Are here all *thy* children? And he said, There remaineth yet the youngest, and, behold, he keepeth the sheep. And Samuel said unto Jesse, Send and fetch him: for we will not sit down till he come hither.

1Sa 17:12 — Now David *was* the son of that Ephrathite of Bethlehemjudah, whose name *was* Jesse; and he had eight sons: and the man went among men *for* an old man in the days of Saul.

• **A shepherd.**

1Sa 16:11 — And Samuel said unto Jesse, Are here all *thy* children? And he said, There remaineth yet the youngest, and, behold, he keepeth the sheep. And Samuel said unto Jesse, Send and fetch him: for we will not sit down till he come hither.

• **Kills a lion and a bear.**

1Sa 17:34–36

• **Anointed king, while a youth, by the prophet Samuel, and inspired.**

Ps 89:19–37

1Sa 16:1 — And the LORD said unto Samuel, How long wilt thou mourn for Saul, seeing I have rejected him from reigning over Israel? fill thine horn with oil, and go, I will send thee to Jesse the Bethlehemite: for I have provided me a king among his sons.

1Sa 16:13 — Then Samuel took the horn of oil, and anointed him in the midst of his brethren: and the Spirit of the LORD came upon David from that day forward. So Samuel rose up, and went to Ramah.

• **Chosen of God.**

Ps 78:70 — He chose David also his servant, and took him from the sheepfolds:

• **Described to Saul.**

1Sa 16:18 — Then answered one of the servants, and said, Behold, I have seen a son of Jesse the Bethlehemite, *that is* cunning in playing, and a mighty valiant man, and a man of war, and prudent in matters, and a comely person, and the LORD *is* with him.

• **Detailed as armorbearer and musician at Saul's court.**

1Sa 16:21–23

• **Slays Goliath.**

1Sa 17:1–58

• **Love of Jonathan for.**

1Sa 18:1–4

• **Popularity and discreetness of.**

1Sa 18:1–30

• **Saul's jealousy of.**

1Sa 18:8–30

• **Is defrauded of Merab, and given Michal to wife.**

1Sa 18:17–27

• **Jonathan intercedes for.**

1Sa 19:1–7

• **At this time probably writes Ps 11.**

Ps 11:1–7

• **Conducts a campaign against and defeats the Philistines.**

1Sa 19:8 — And there was war again: and David went out, and fought with the Philistines, and slew them with a great slaughter; and they fled from him.

• **Saul attempts to slay him; escapes to Ramah.**

1Sa 19:9–24

• **About this time writes Ps 59.**

Ps 59:1–17

• **Returns, and Jonathan makes a covenant with.**

1Sa 20:1–42

• **Escapes by way of Nob, where he obtains shewbread and Goliath's sword from Abimelech.**

1Sa 21:1–6; Mt 12:3–4

• **Escapes to Gath.**

1Sa 21:10–15

• **At this time probably writes Pss 34, 35, 52, 56, 120.**

Ps 34:1–35:28; 52:1–9; 56:1–13; 120:1–7

• **Recruits an army of insurgents.**

1Sa 22:1–23

• **About this time probably writes Pss 17, 35, 52, 58, 64, 109, 142.**

Ps 17:1–15; 35:1–28; 52:1–9; 58:1–11; 64:1–10; 109:1–31; 142:1–7

• **Saves Keilah.**

1Sa 23:1–13

• **Makes second covenant with Jonathan.**

1Sa 23:16–18

• **Goes to wilderness of Ziph; betrayed to Saul (writes on betrayal, Ps 54), probably others.**

1Sa 23:13–26; Ps 22:1–31; 31:1–24; 34:1–22; 140:1–13

• **Saul is diverted from pursuit of.**

1Sa 23:27–28

• **At this time probably writes Ps 12.**

Ps 12:1–8; 22:1–31

• **Goes to En-gedi.**

1Sa 23:29 — And David went up from thence, and dwelt in strong holds at En-gedi.

• Refrains from slaying Saul (writes Ps 57).
1Sa 24:1–22; Ps 57:1–11

• Covenants with Saul.
1Sa 26:1–25

• Marries Nabal's widow, Abigail, and Ahinoam.
1Sa 25:1–44

• Dwells in wilderness of Ziph; opportunity to slay Saul, but takes spear only; Saul is contrite.
1Sa 26:1–25

• Flees to Achish and dwells in Ziklag.
1Sa 27:1–12

• List of men who join him.
1Ch 12:1–22

• Conducts an expedition against Amalekites; misstates the facts to Achish.
1Sa 27:8–12

• At this time probably writes Ps 141.
Ps 141:1–10

• Is refused permission to accompany the Philistines to battle against the Israelites.
1Sa 28:1–2; 29:1–11

• Rescues the people of Ziklag, who had been captured by the Amalekites.
1Sa 30:1–31

• At this time probably writes Ps 13.
Ps 13:1–6

• Death and burial of Saul and his sons.
1Sa 31:1–13; 2Sa 21:1–14

• Slays the murderer of Saul.
2Sa 1:1–16

• Lamentation over Saul.
2Sa 1:17–27

• After dwelling one year and four months at Ziklag, goes to Hebron, and is anointed king by Judah.
2Sa 2:1–4; 1Ch 11:1–3

1Sa 27:7 — And the time that David dwelt in the country of the Philistines was a full year and four months.

2Sa 2:11 — And the time that David was king in Hebron over the house of Judah was seven years and six months.

2Sa 5:5 — In Hebron he reigned over Judah seven years and six months: and in Jerusalem he reigned thirty and three years over all Israel and Judah.

1Ki 2:11 — And the days that David reigned over Israel *were* forty years: seven years reigned he in Hebron, and thirty and three years reigned he in Jerusalem.

1Ch 3:4 — *These* six were born unto him in Hebron; and there he reigned seven years and six months: and in Jerusalem he reigned thirty and three years.

• List of those who join him at Hebron.
1Ch 12:23–40

• Ish-bosheth, son of Saul, crowned.
2Sa 2:1–4:12

• Wages war against, and defeats, Ish-bosheth.
2Sa 2:13–32

2Sa 3:4 — And the fourth, Adonijah the son of Haggith; and the fifth, Shephatiah the son of Abital;

• Demands the restoration of Michal, his wife.
2Sa 3:14–16

• Abner revolts from Ish-bosheth, and joins him, but is slain by Joab.
2Sa 3:1–39

• Punishes Ish-bosheth's murderers.
2Sa 4:1–12

• Anointed king over all Israel.
1Ch 11:1–3; 12:23–40

2Sa 2:11 — And the time that David was king in Hebron over the house of Judah was seven years and six months.

2Sa 5:5 — In Hebron he reigned over Judah seven years and six months: and in Jerusalem he reigned thirty and three years over all Israel and Judah.

1Ch 3:4 — *These* six were born unto him in Hebron; and there he reigned seven years and six months: and in Jerusalem he reigned thirty and three years.

1Ch 29:27 — And the time that he reigned over Israel *was* forty years; seven years reigned he in Hebron, and thirty and three *years* reigned he in Jerusalem.

• Makes conquest of Jerusalem.
1Ch 11:4–8

2Sa 5:6 — And the king and his men went to Jerusalem unto the Jebusites, the inhabitants of the land: which spake unto David, saying, Except thou take away the blind and the lame, thou shalt not come in hither: thinking, David cannot come in hither.

Isa 29:1 — Woe to Ariel, to Ariel, the city *where* David dwelt! add ye year to year; let them kill sacrifices.

• Builds a palace.

2Sa 5:11 — And Hiram king of Tyre sent messengers to David, and cedar trees, and carpenters, and masons: and they built David an house.

2Ch 2:3 — And Solomon sent to Huram the king of Tyre, saying, As thou didst deal with David my father, and didst send him cedars to build him an house to dwell therein, *even so deal with me.*

• Friendship of Hiram, king of Tyre.

2Sa 5:11 — And Hiram king of Tyre sent messengers to David, and cedar trees, and carpenters, and masons: and they built David an house.

1Ki 5:1 — And Hiram king of Tyre sent his servants unto Solomon; for he had heard that they had anointed him king in the room of his father: for Hiram was ever a lover of David.

• Prospered of God.

2Sa 5:10 — And David went on, and grew great, and the LORD God of hosts *was* with him.

1Ch 11:9 — So David waxed greater and greater: for the LORD of hosts *was* with him.

• **Fame of.**

1Ch 14:17 — And the fame of David went out into all lands; and the LORD brought the fear of him upon all nations.

• **Philistines make war against, and are defeated.**

2Sa 5:17 — But when the Philistines heard that they had anointed David king over Israel, all the Philistines came up to seek David; and David heard *of it,* and went down to the hold.

2Sa 5:25 — And David did so, as the LORD had commanded him; and smote the Philistines from Geba until thou come to Gazer.

• **Assembles thirty thousand men to escort the ark to Jerusalem with music and thanksgiving.**

2Sa 6:1–5

• **Uzzah is stricken when he attempts to steady the ark.**

2Sa 6:6–11

• **Is terrified, and leaves the ark at the house of Obed-edom.**

2Sa 6:9–11

• **After three months brings the ark to Jerusalem with dancing and great joy.**

2Sa 6:12–16; 1Ch 13:1–14

• **Organizes the tabernacle service.**

1Ch 15:16–24; 16:4–6, 37–43

1Ch 9:22 — All these *which were* chosen to be porters in the gates were two hundred and twelve. These were reckoned by their genealogy in their villages, whom David and Samuel the seer did ordain in their set office.

• **Offers sacrifice, distributes gifts, and blesses the people.**

2Sa 6:17–19

• **Michal upbraids him for his religious enthusiasm.**

2Sa 6:20–23

• **Desires to build a temple; is forbidden, but receives promise that his seed should reign forever.**

2Sa 7:12–16; 1Ch 17:11–14; Ps 89:3–4; 132:11–12

2Sa 23:5 — Although my house *be* not so with God; yet he hath made with me an everlasting covenant, ordered in all *things,* and sure: for *this is* all my salvation, and all *my* desire, although he make *it* not to grow.

2Ch 6:16 — Now therefore, O LORD God of Israel, keep with thy servant David my father that which thou hast promised him, saying, There shall not fail thee a man in my sight to sit upon the throne of Israel; yet so that thy children take heed to their way to walk in my law, as thou hast walked before me.

Ac 15:16 — After this I will return, and will build again the tabernacle of David, which is fallen down; and I will build again the ruins thereof, and I will set it up:

Ro 15:12 — And again, Esaias saith, There shall be a root of Jesse, and he that shall rise to reign over the Gentiles; in him shall the Gentiles trust.

• **Interpretation and fulfillment of this prophecy.**

Ac 13:22–23

• **At this time probably writes Pss 15, 16, 24, 101, 138.**

Ps 15:1–16:11; 24:1–10; 101:1–8; 138:1–8

• **Conquers the Philistines, Moabites, and Syria.**

2Sa 8:1–18

• **Treats Mephibosheth, the lame son of Saul, with great kindness.**

2Sa 19:24–30

2Sa 9:6 — Now when Mephibosheth, the son of Jonathan, the son of Saul, was come unto David, he fell on his face, and did reverence. And David said, Mephibosheth. And he answered, Behold thy servant!

• **Sends message of sympathy to Hanun.**

2Sa 10:1–19; 1Ch 19:1–19

• **Probably writes Pss 18, 20, 21.**

Ps 18:1–50; 20:1–21:13

• **Commits adultery with Bath-sheba.**

2Sa 11:2–5

• **Wickedly causes the death of Uriah.**

2Sa 11:6–25

• **Takes Bath-sheba to be his wife.**

2Sa 11:26–27

• **Is rebuked by the prophet Nathan.**

2Sa 12:1–14

• **Repents of his crime and confesses his guilt.**

Ps 6:1–10; 32:1–11; 38:1–40:17; 51:1–19

• **Is chastised with grievous affliction on account of his crime.**

Ps 38:1–22; 41:1–13; 69:1–36

• **Death of his infant son by Bath-sheba.**

2Sa 12:15–23

• **Solomon is born to.**

2Sa 12:24–25

• **Ammonites defeated and tortured.**

2Sa 12:26–31

• **Amnon's crime, his murder by Absalom, and Absalom's flight.**

2Sa 13:1–39

• **Absalom's return.**

2Sa 14:1–24

• **Absalom's usurpation.**

2Sa 14:1–15:37

• **Flees from Jerusalem.**

2Sa 15:13–37; Ps 5:1–12; 7:1–17; 26:1–12; 61:1–8; 63:1–11; 69:1–70:5; 86:1–17; 143:1–12

• **At this time he probably writes Pss 5, 7, 26, 61, 63, 69, 70, 86, 143.**

• **Shimei curses him.**

2Sa 16:1–23

• **Crosses the Jordan.**
2Sa 17:21–29

• **Absalom's defeat and death.**
2Sa 18:1–33

• **Laments the death of Absalom.**
2Sa 18:33–19:4

• **Upbraided by Joab.**
2Sa 19:5–7

• **Upbraids the priests for not showing loyalty amid the murmurings of the people.**
2Sa 19:9–15

• **Shimei sues for clemency.**
2Sa 19:16–23

• **Mephibosheth sues for the king's favor.**
2Sa 19:24–30

• **Barzillai rewarded.**
2Sa 19:31–40

• **Judah accused by the ten tribes of stealing him away.**
2Sa 19:41–43

• **Returns to Jerusalem.**
2Sa 20:1–3

• **At this time probably writes Pss 27, 66, 122, 144.**

• **Sheba's conspiracy against him, and his death.**
2Sa 20:1–26

• **Makes Amasa general.**
2Sa 19:13 — And say ye to Amasa, *Art* thou not of my bone, and of my flesh? God do so to me, and more also, if thou be not captain of the host before me continually in the room of Joab.

• **Amasa is slain.**
2Sa 20:4–10

• **Consigns seven sons of Saul to the Gibeonites to be slain to atone for Saul's persecution of the Gibeonites.**
2Sa 21:1–14

• **Buries Saul's bones, and his sons'.**
2Sa 21:12–14

• **Defeats the Philistines.**
2Sa 21:15–22; 1Ch 20:4–8

• **Takes the military strength of Israel without divine authority, and is reproved.**
2Sa 24:1–25; 1Ch 21:1–30

1Ch 27:24 — Joab the son of Zeruiah began to number, but he finished not, because there fell wrath for it against Israel; neither was the number put in the account of the chronicles of king David.

• **Probably composes Pss 30, 131.**
Ps 30:1–12; 131:1–3

• **Marries Abishag.**
1Ki 1:1–4

• **Probably composes Pss 19, 111.**
Ps 19:1–14; 111:1–10

• **Reorganizes the tabernacle service.**
1Ch 22:1–26:32; 2Ch 29:27–30

2Ch 7:6 — And the priests waited on their offices: the Levites also with instruments of musick of the LORD, which David the king had made to praise the LORD, because his mercy *endureth* for ever, when David praised by their ministry; and the priests sounded trumpets before them, and all Israel stood.

2Ch 8:14 — And he appointed, according to the order of David his father, the courses of the priests to their service, and the Levites to their charges, to praise and minister before the priests, as the duty of every day required: the porters also by their courses at every gate: for so had David the man of God commanded.

2Ch 23:18 — Also Jehoiada appointed the offices of the house of the LORD by the hand of the priests the Levites, whom David had distributed in the house of the LORD, to offer the burnt offerings of the LORD, as *it is* written in the law of Moses, with rejoicing and with singing, *as it was ordained* by David.

2Ch 35:15 — And the singers the sons of Asaph *were* in their place, according to the commandment of David, and Asaph, and Heman, and Jeduthun the king's seer; and the porters *waited* at every gate; they might not depart from their service; for their brethren the Levites prepared for them.

Ezr 3:10 — And when the builders laid the foundation of the temple of the LORD, they set the priests in their apparel with trumpets, and the Levites the sons of Asaph with cymbals, to praise the LORD, after the ordinance of David king of Israel.

Ezr 8:20 — Also of the Nethinims, whom David and the princes had appointed for the service of the Levites, two hundred and twenty Nethinims: all of them were expressed by name.

• **Adonijah usurps the sceptre; Solomon appointed to the throne.**
1Ki 1:1–53

1Ch 23:1 — So when David was old and full of days, he made Solomon his son king over Israel.

• **Delivers his charge to Solomon.**
1Ki 2:1–11; 1Ch 22:6–19; 28:1–29:30

• **Probably composes Pss 23, 145.**
Ps 23:1–6; 145:1–21

• **Last words of.**
2Sa 23:1–7

• **Death of.**
Ac 2:29–30

1Ki 2:10 — So David slept with his fathers, and was buried in the city of David.

1Ch 29:28 — And he died in a good old age, full of days, riches, and honour: and Solomon his son reigned in his stead.

• **Sepulchre of.**
Ac 2:29 — Men *and* brethren, let me freely speak unto you of the patriarch David, that he is both dead and buried, and his sepulchre is with us unto this day.

• **Age of, at death.**
2Sa 5:4–5

1Ch 29:28 — And he died in a good old age, full of days, riches, and honour: and Solomon his son reigned in his stead.

• Length of reign, forty years.

1Ch 29:27–28

1Ki 2:11 — And the days that David reigned over Israel *were* forty years: seven years reigned he in Hebron, and thirty and three years reigned he in Jerusalem.

• Wives of.

2Sa 3:1–39

• Children born at Hebron.

2Sa 3:2–5

1Ch 3:4 — *These* six were born unto him in Hebron; and there he reigned seven years and six months: and in Jerusalem he reigned thirty and three years.

• Children born at Jerusalem.

2Sa 5:14–16; 1Ch 3:5–8; 14:4–7

• Descendants of.

1Ch 3:1–24

• Civil and military officers of.

2Sa 8:16–18

→See: Cabinet

• Lists of his heroes, and of their exploits.

2Sa 23:1–39; 1Ch 11:1–47; 12:23–40

• Devoutness of.

2Sa 6:14–18; 7:18–29; 1Ch 17:16–27; Ps 6:1–7:17; 11:1–7; 13:1–6; 17:1–15; 22:1–31; 26:1–12; 27:7–28:9; 31:1–24; 35:1–28; 37:1–39:13; 40:11–17; 42:1–43:5; 51:1–19; 54:1–57:11; 59:1–62:12; 64:1–6; 66:1–20; 69:1–71:24; 86:1–17; 101:1–8; 108:1–13; 120:1–2; 140:1–144:15

1Sa 13:14 — But now thy kingdom shall not continue: the LORD hath sought him a man after his own heart, and the LORD hath commanded him *to be* captain over his people, because thou hast not kept *that* which the LORD commanded thee.

2Sa 6:5 — And David and all the house of Israel played before the LORD on all manner of *instruments made of* fir wood, even on harps, and on psalteries, and on timbrels, and on cornets, and on cymbals.

2Sa 8:11 — Which also king David did dedicate unto the LORD, with the silver and gold that he had dedicated of all nations which he subdued;

2Sa 24:25 — And David built there an altar unto the LORD, and offered burnt offerings and peace offerings. So the LORD was intreated for the land, and the plague was stayed from Israel.

1Ki 3:14 — And if thou wilt walk in my ways, to keep my statutes and my commandments, as thy father David did walk, then I will lengthen thy days.

1Ch 29:10 — Wherefore David blessed the LORD before all the congregation: and David said, Blessed *be* thou, LORD God of Israel our father, for ever and ever.

2Ch 7:17 — And as for thee, if thou wilt walk before me, as David thy father walked, and do according to all that I have commanded thee, and shalt observe my statutes and my judgments;

Zec 12:8 — In that day shall the LORD defend the inhabitants of Jerusalem; and he that is feeble among them at that day shall be as David; and the house of David *shall be* as God, as the angel of the LORD before them.

Ac 13:22 — And when he had removed him, he raised up unto them David to be their king; to whom also he gave testimony, and said, I have found David the *son* of Jesse, a man after mine own heart, which shall fulfil all my will.

• Justice in the administration of.

2Sa 8:15 — And David reigned over all Israel; and David executed judgment and justice unto all his people.

1Ch 18:14 — So David reigned over all Israel, and executed judgment and justice among all his people.

• Discreetness of.

1Sa 18:14 — And David behaved himself wisely in all his ways; and the LORD *was* with him.

1Sa 18:30 — Then the princes of the Philistines went forth: and it came to pass, after they went forth, *that* David behaved himself more wisely than all the servants of Saul; so that his name was much set by.

• Meekness of.

2Sa 19:22–23

1Sa 24:7 — So David stayed his servants with these words, and suffered them not to rise against Saul. But Saul rose up out of the cave, and went on *his* way.

1Sa 26:11 — The LORD forbid that I should stretch forth mine hand against the LORD's anointed: but, I pray thee, take thou now the spear that *is* at his bolster, and the cruse of water, and let us go.

2Sa 16:11 — And David said to Abishai, and to all his servants, Behold, my son, which came forth of my bowels, seeketh my life: how much more now *may this* Benjamite *do it?* let him alone, and let him curse; for the LORD hath bidden him.

• Merciful.

2Sa 19:23 — Therefore the king said unto Shimei, Thou shalt not die. And the king sware unto him.

• David as musician.

1Sa 16:21–23

1Ch 15:16 — And David spake to the chief of the Levites to appoint their brethren *to be* the singers with instruments of musick, psalteries and harps and cymbals, sounding, by lifting up the voice with joy.

1Ch 23:5 — Moreover four thousand *were* porters; and four thousand praised the LORD with the instruments which I made, *said David,* to praise *therewith.*

2Ch 7:6 — And the priests waited on their offices: the Levites also with instruments of musick of the LORD, which David the king had made to praise the LORD, because his mercy *endureth* for ever, when David praised by their ministry; and the priests sounded trumpets before them, and all Israel stood.

2Ch 29:26 — And the Levites stood with the instruments of David, and the priests with the trumpets.

Ne 12:36 — And his brethren, Shemaiah, and Azarael, Milalai, Gilalai, Maai, Nethaneel, and Judah, Hanani, with the musical instruments of David the man of God, and Ezra the scribe before them.

Am 6:5 — That chant to the sound of the viol, *and* invent to themselves instruments of musick, like David;

• **David as poet.**

2Sa 22:1–51

See: Psalms; of David

• **David as prophet.**

2Sa 23:2–7; Mt 22:41–46; Ac 2:25–38

1Ch 28:19 — All *this, said David,* the LORD made me understand in writing by *his* hand upon me, *even* all the works of this pattern.

Ac 4:25 — Who by the mouth of thy servant David hast said, Why did the heathen rage, and the people imagine vain things?

• **Type of Christ.**

Ps 2:1–12; 16:1–11; 69:7–9, 20–21; 89:19–37

Ps 18:43 — Thou hast delivered me from the strivings of the people; *and* thou hast made me the head of the heathen: a people *whom* I have not known shall serve me.

Ps 69:26 — For they persecute *him* whom thou hast smitten; and they talk to the grief of those whom thou hast wounded.

Ps 69:29 — But I *am* poor and sorrowful: let thy salvation, O God, set me up on high.

• **Jesus called son of.**

Mt 20:30–31; Mk 10:47–48

Mt 9:27 — And when Jesus departed thence, two blind men followed him, crying, and saying, *Thou* Son of David, have mercy on us.

Mt 12:23 — And all the people were amazed, and said, Is not this the son of David?

Mt 15:22 — And, behold, a woman of Canaan came out of the same coasts, and cried unto him, saying, Have mercy on me, O Lord, *thou* Son of David; my daughter is grievously vexed with a devil.

Mt 21:9 — And the multitudes that went before, and that followed, cried, saying, Hosanna to the Son of David: Blessed *is* he that cometh in the name of the Lord; Hosanna in the highest.

Mt 22:42 — Saying, What think ye of Christ? whose son is he? They say unto him, *The Son* of David.

Lk 18:37 — And they told him, that Jesus of Nazareth passeth by.

Lk 18:39 — And they which went before rebuked him, that he should hold his peace: but he cried so much the more, *Thou* Son of David, have mercy on me.

• **Prophecies concerning him and his kingdom.**

2Sa 7:11–16; 1Ch 17:9–14; 22:1–19; 2Ch 6:5–17; Ps 89:19–37; Isa 22:20–25; Jer 33:15–26; Lk 1:32–33

Nu 24:17 — I shall see him, but not now: I shall behold him, but not nigh: there shall come a Star out of Jacob, and a Sceptre shall rise out of Israel, and shall smite the corners of Moab, and destroy all the children of Sheth.

Nu 24:19 — Out of Jacob shall come he that shall have dominion, and shall destroy him that remaineth of the city.

2Ch 13:5 — Ought ye not to know that the LORD God of Israel gave the kingdom over Israel to David for ever, *even* to him and to his sons by a covenant of salt?

2Ch 21:7 — Howbeit the LORD would not destroy the house of David, because of the covenant that he had made with David, and as he promised to give a light to him and to his sons for ever.

Isa 9:7 — Of the increase of *his* government and peace *there shall be* no end, upon the throne of David, and upon his kingdom, to order it, and to establish it with judgment and with justice from henceforth even for ever. The zeal of the LORD of hosts will perform this.

Isa 16:5 — And in mercy shall the throne be established: and he shall sit upon it in truth in the tabernacle of David, judging, and seeking judgment, and hasting righteousness.

Jer 23:5 — Behold, the days come, saith the LORD, that I will raise unto David a righteous Branch, and a King shall reign and prosper, and shall execute judgment and justice in the earth.

• **Chronicles of, written by Samuel, Nathan, and Gad.**

1Ch 29:29–30

• **A prophetic name for Christ.**

Eze 34:23–24; 37:24–25

Jer 30:9 — But they shall serve the LORD their God, and David their king, whom I will raise up unto them.

Hos 3:5 — Afterward shall the children of Israel return, and seek the LORD their God, and David their king; and shall fear the LORD and his goodness in the latter days.

DAY

• **A creative period.**

Ge 1:5 — And God called the light Day, and the darkness he called Night. And the evening and the morning were the first day.

Ge 1:8 — And God called the firmament Heaven. And the evening and the morning were the second day.

Ge 1:13 — And the evening and the morning were the third day.

Ge 1:19 — And the evening and the morning were the fourth day.

Ge 1:23 — And the evening and the morning were the fifth day.

Ge 1:31 — And God saw every thing that he had made, and, behold, *it was* very good. And the evening and the morning were the sixth day.

Ge 2:2 — And on the seventh day God ended his work which he had made; and he rested on the seventh day from all his work which he had made.

• **Divided into twelve hours.**

Jn 11:9 — Jesus answered, Are there not twelve hours in the day? If any man walk in the day, he stumbleth not, because he seeth the light of this world.

• **Prophetic.**

Da 9:24–27; 12:11–12

Da 8:14 — And he said unto me, Unto two thousand and three hundred days; then shall the sanctuary be cleansed.

2Pe 3:8 — But, beloved, be not ignorant of this one thing, that one day *is* with the Lord as a thousand years, and a thousand years as one day.

Rev 9:15 — And the four angels were loosed, which were prepared for an hour, and a day, and a month, and a year, for to slay the third part of men.

Rev 11:3 — And I will give *power* unto my two witnesses, and they shall prophesy a thousand two hundred *and* threescore days, clothed in sackcloth.

Rev 12:6 — And the woman fled into the wilderness, where she hath a place prepared of God, that they should feed her there a thousand two hundred *and* threescore days.

• Six working days ordained.

Ex 20:9 — Six days shalt thou labour, and do all thy work:

Eze 46:1 — Thus saith the Lord GOD; The gate of the inner court that looketh toward the east shall be shut the six working days; but on the sabbath it shall be opened, and in the day of the new moon it shall be opened.

• Sixth day of the week called preparation day.

Mk 15:42 — And now when the even was come, because it was the preparation, that is, the day before the sabbath,

Jn 19:14 — And it was the preparation of the passover, and about the sixth hour: and he saith unto the Jews, Behold your King!

Jn 19:31 — The Jews therefore, because it was the preparation, that the bodies should not remain upon the cross on the sabbath day, (for that sabbath day was an high day,) besought Pilate that their legs might be broken, and *that* they might be taken away.

Jn 19:42 — There laid they Jesus therefore because of the Jews' preparation *day;* for the sepulchre was nigh at hand.

• First day of the week called the Lord's day.

Rev 1:10 — I was in the Spirit on the Lord's day, and heard behind me a great voice, as of a trumpet,

• With the Lord as a thousand years.

2Pe 3:8 — But, beloved, be not ignorant of this one thing, that one day *is* with the Lord as a thousand years, and a thousand years as one day.

• Day's journey, eighteen or twenty miles.

Ex 3:18 — And they shall hearken to thy voice: and thou shalt come, thou and the elders of Israel, unto the king of Egypt, and ye shall say unto him, The LORD God of the Hebrews hath met with us: and now let us go, we beseech thee, three days' journey into the wilderness, that we may sacrifice to the LORD our God.

1Ki 19:4 — But he himself went a day's journey into the wilderness, and came and sat down under a juniper tree: and he requested for himself that he might die; and said, It is enough; now, O LORD, take away my life; for I *am* not better than my fathers.

Jnh 3:4 — And Jonah began to enter into the city a day's journey, and he cried, and said, Yet forty days, and Nineveh shall be overthrown.

• Sabbath day's journey, about two thousand paces.

Ac 1:12 — Then returned they unto Jerusalem from the mount called Olivet, which is from Jerusalem a sabbath day's journey.

• The seventh of the week ordained as a day of rest.

See: Sabbath

• Times of adversity called Day of the Lord.

Zep 2:2–3

Isa 2:12 — For the day of the LORD of hosts *shall be* upon every *one that is* proud and lofty, and upon every *one that is* lifted up; and he shall be brought low:

Isa 13:6 — Howl ye; for the day of the LORD *is* at hand; it shall come as a destruction from the Almighty.

Isa 13:9 — Behold, the day of the LORD cometh, cruel both with wrath and fierce anger, to lay the land desolate: and he shall destroy the sinners thereof out of it.

Isa 34:8 — For *it is* the day of the LORD's vengeance, *and* the year of recompences for the controversy of Zion.

Jer 46:10 — For this *is* the day of the Lord GOD of hosts, a day of vengeance, that he may avenge him of his adversaries: and the sword shall devour, and it shall be satiate and made drunk with their blood: for the Lord GOD of hosts hath a sacrifice in the north country by the river Euphrates.

La 2:22 — Thou hast called as in a solemn day my terrors round about, so that in the day of the LORD's anger none escaped nor remained: those that I have swaddled and brought up hath mine enemy consumed.

Eze 30:3 — For the day *is* near, even the day of the LORD *is* near, a cloudy day; it shall be the time of the heathen.

Joel 2:1 — Blow ye the trumpet in Zion, and sound an alarm in my holy mountain: let all the inhabitants of the land tremble: for the day of the LORD cometh, for *it is* nigh at hand;

Am 5:18 — Woe unto you that desire the day of the LORD! to what end *is* it for you? the day of the LORD *is* darkness, and not light.

Ob 1:15 — For the day of the LORD *is* near upon all the heathen: as thou hast done, it shall be done unto thee: thy reward shall return upon thine own head.

Zep 1:8 — And it shall come to pass in the day of the LORD's sacrifice, that I will punish the princes, and the king's children, and all such as are clothed with strange apparel.

Zep 1:18 — Neither their silver nor their gold shall be able to deliver them in the day of the LORD's wrath; but the whole land shall be devoured by the fire of his jealousy: for he shall make even a speedy riddance of all them that dwell in the land.

Zec 14:1 — Behold, the day of the LORD cometh, and thy spoil shall be divided in the midst of thee.

• **Judgment.**

• **Called Day of the Lord.**

Mal 4:5 — Behold, I will send you Elijah the prophet before the coming of the great and dreadful day of the LORD:

1Co 5:5 — To deliver such an one unto Satan for the destruction of the flesh, that the spirit may be saved in the day of the Lord Jesus.

2Co 1:14 — As also ye have acknowledged us in part, that we are your rejoicing, even as ye also *are* ours in the day of the Lord Jesus.

1Th 5:2 — For yourselves know perfectly that the day of the Lord so cometh as a thief in the night.

2Pe 3:10 — But the day of the Lord will come as a thief in the night; in the which the heavens shall pass away with a great noise, and the elements shall melt with fervent heat, the earth also and the works that are therein shall be burned up.

See: Judgment

• **A figure of spiritual illumination.**

Pr 4:18 — But the path of the just *is* as the shining light, that shineth more and more unto the perfect day.

1Th 5:8 — But let us, who are of the day, be sober, putting on the breastplate of faith and love; and for an helmet, the hope of salvation.

DAYSMAN • A mediator.

Job 9:33 — Neither is there any daysman betwixt us, *that* might lay his hand upon us both.

DAYSTAR

• **Figurative of spiritual life.**

2Pe 1:19 — We have also a more sure word of prophecy; whereunto ye do well that ye take heed, as unto a light that shineth in a dark place, until the day dawn, and the day star arise in your hearts:

DEACON

• **An ecclesiastic charged with the temporal affairs of the church; ordained by the apostles.**

Ac 6:1–6

• **Qualifications of.**

1Ti 3:8–13

• **The Greek word translated deacon signifies servant, and is so translated.**

Mt 23:11 — But he that is greatest among you shall be your servant.

Jn 12:26 — If any man serve me, let him follow me; and where I am, there shall also my servant be: if any man serve me, him will *my* Father honour.

• **Also translated minister.**

Mk 10:43 — But so shall it not be among you: but whosoever will be great among you, shall be your minister:

1Co 3:5 — Who then is Paul, and who *is* Apollos, but ministers by whom ye believed, even as the Lord gave to every man?

1Th 3:2 — And sent Timotheus, our brother, and minister of God, and our fellowlabourer in the gospel of Christ, to establish you, and to comfort you concerning your faith:

DEACONESS

Ro 16:1 — I commend unto you Phebe our sister, which is a servant of the church which is at Cenchrea:

DEAD

• **Raised to life, instances of.**

• **Son of the widow of Zarephath.**

1Ki 17:17–23

• **Shunammite's son.**

2Ki 4:32–37

• **Young man laid in Elisha's sepulchre.**

2Ki 13:21 — And it came to pass, as they were burying a man, that, behold, they spied a band *of men;* and they cast the man into the sepulchre of Elisha: and when the man was let down, and touched the bones of Elisha, he revived, and stood up on his feet.

• **Widow's son.**

Lk 7:12–15

• **Jairus' daughter.**

Lk 8:49–55

• **Lazarus.**

Jn 11:43–44

• **Dorcas.**

Ac 9:37–40

• **Eutychus.**

Ac 20:9–12

Heb 11:35 — Women received their dead raised to life again: and others were tortured, not accepting deliverance; that they might obtain a better resurrection:

• **Prepared for burial by washing.**

Ac 9:37 — And it came to pass in those days, that she was sick, and died: whom when they had washed, they laid *her* in an upper chamber.

• **Prepared for burial by anointing.**

Mt 26:12 — For in that she hath poured this ointment on my body, she did *it* for my burial.

• **Prepared for burial by wrapping in linen.**

Mt 27:59 — And when Joseph had taken the body, he wrapped it in a clean linen cloth,

• **Burned.**

See: Cremation

• **Burnings of incense made for.**

2Ch 16:14 — And they buried him in his own sepulchres, which he had made for himself in the city of David, and laid him in the bed which was filled with sweet odours and divers kinds *of spices* prepared by the apothecaries' art: and they made a very great burning for him.

2Ch 21:19 — And it came to pass, that in process of time, after the end of two years, his bowels fell out by reason of his sickness: so he died of sore diseases. And his people made no burning for him, like the burning of his fathers.

Jer 34:5 — *But* thou shalt die in peace: and with the burnings of thy fathers, the former kings which were before thee, so shall they burn *odours* for thee; and they will lament thee, *saying,* Ah lord! for I have pronounced the word, saith the LORD.

✣See: Burial

✣See: Cremation

✣See: Embalming

• Unclassified scripture relating to.

Job 3:13–19; 14:11–15; 17:13–16; Ps 88:10–12; Ecc 9:5–6; Lk 9:30–31; 16:19–31; 20:35–36

Job 14:21 — His sons come to honour, and he knoweth *it* not; and they are brought low, but he perceiveth *it* not of them.

Ps 6:5 — For in death *there is* no remembrance of thee: in the grave who shall give thee thanks?

Ps 30:9 — What profit *is there* in my blood, when I go down to the pit? Shall the dust praise thee? shall it declare thy truth?

Ps 49:15 — But God will redeem my soul from the power of the grave: for he shall receive me. Selah.

Ps 115:17 — The dead praise not the LORD, neither any that go down into silence.

Pr 21:16 — The man that wandereth out of the way of understanding shall remain in the congregation of the dead.

Eze 32:31 — Pharaoh shall see them, and shall be comforted over all his multitude, *even* Pharaoh and all his army slain by the sword, saith the Lord GOD.

Da 12:2 — And many of them that sleep in the dust of the earth shall awake, some to everlasting life, and some to shame *and* everlasting contempt.

Lk 23:43 — And Jesus said unto him, Verily I say unto thee, To day shalt thou be with me in paradise.

Jn 11:25 — Jesus said unto her, I am the resurrection, and the life: he that believeth in me, though he were dead, yet shall he live:

✣See: Burial

✣See: Death

✣See: Mourning

✣See: Resurrection

✣See: Righteous; promises to, expressed or implied

✣See: Wicked; punishment of

DEAD SEA

• Lies southeast of Jerusalem.

• Also called.

• Salt Sea.

Ge 14:3 — All these were joined together in the vale of Siddim, which is the salt sea.

Nu 34:12 — And the border shall go down to Jordan, and the goings out of it shall be at the salt sea: this shall be your land with the coasts thereof round about.

• Sea of the Plain.

Dt 3:17 — The plain also, and Jordan, and the coast *thereof,* from Chinnereth even unto the sea of the plain, *even* the salt sea, under Ashdoth-pisgah eastward.

Dt 4:49 — And all the plain on this side Jordan eastward, even unto the sea of the plain, under the springs of Pisgah.

Jos 3:16 — That the waters which came down from above stood *and* rose up upon an heap very far from the city Adam, that *is* beside Zaretan: and those that came down toward the sea of the plain, *even* the salt sea, failed, *and* were cut off: and the people passed over right against Jericho.

• East Sea.

Joel 2:20 — But I will remove far off from you the northern *army,* and will drive him into a land barren and desolate, with his face toward the east sea, and his hinder part toward the utmost sea, and his stink shall come up, and his ill savour shall come up, because he hath done great things.

• Former Sea.

Zec 14:8 — And it shall be in that day, *that* living waters shall go out from Jerusalem; half of them toward the former sea, and half of them toward the hinder sea: in summer and in winter shall it be.

• Prophecy concerning.

Eze 47:7–10

Eze 47:18 — And the east side ye shall measure from Hauran, and from Damascus, and from Gilead, and from the land of Israel by Jordan, from the border unto the east sea. And *this is* the east side.

DEAFNESS

• Law concerning.

Le 19:14 — Thou shalt not curse the deaf, nor put a stumblingblock before the blind, but shalt fear thy God: I *am* the LORD.

• Inflicted by God.

Ex 4:11 — And the LORD said unto him, Who hath made man's mouth? or who maketh the dumb, or deaf, or the seeing, or the blind? have not I the LORD?

• Miraculous cure of.

Mt 11:5 — The blind receive their sight, and the lame walk, the lepers are cleansed, and the deaf hear, the dead are raised up, and the poor have the gospel preached to them.

Mk 7:32 — And they bring unto him one that was deaf, and had an impediment in his speech; and they beseech him to put his hand upon him.

Mk 9:25 — When Jesus saw that the people came running together, he rebuked the foul spirit, saying unto him, *Thou* dumb and deaf spirit, I charge thee, come out of him, and enter no more into him.

• Figurative.

• Of moral insensibility.

Ac 28:26–27

Isa 6:10 — Make the heart of this people fat, and make their ears heavy, and shut their eyes; lest they see with their eyes, and hear with their ears, and understand with their heart, and convert, and be healed.

Isa 29:18 — And in that day shall the deaf hear the words of the book, and the eyes of the blind shall see out of obscurity, and out of darkness.

Isa 35:5 — Then the eyes of the blind shall be opened, and the ears of the deaf shall be unstopped.

Eze 12:2 — Son of man, thou dwellest in the midst of a rebellious house, which have eyes to see, and see not; they have ears to hear, and hear not: for they *are* a rebellious house.

Mt 13:15 — For this people's heart is waxed gross, and *their* ears are dull of hearing, and *their* eyes they have closed; lest at any time they should see with their eyes, and hear with *their* ears, and should understand with *their* heart, and should be converted, and I should heal them.

Jn 12:40 — He hath blinded their eyes, and hardened their heart; that they should not see with *their* eyes, nor understand with *their* heart, and be converted, and I should heal them.

See: Blindness; spiritual

See: Conscience; dead

See: Impenitence

See: Obduracy

DEATH

• Referred to as.

• Giving up the Ghost.

Ge 25:8 — Then Abraham gave up the ghost, and died in a good old age, an old man, and full *of years;* and was gathered to his people.

Ge 35:29 — And Isaac gave up the ghost, and died, and was gathered unto his people, *being* old and full of days: and his sons Esau and Jacob buried him.

La 1:19 — I called for my lovers, *but* they deceived me: my priests and mine elders gave up the ghost in the city, while they sought their meat to relieve their souls.

Ac 5:10 — Then fell she down straightway at his feet, and yielded up the ghost: and the young men came in, and found her dead, and, carrying *her* forth, buried *her* by her husband.

• King of Terrors.

Job 18:14 — His confidence shall be rooted out of his tabernacle, and it shall bring him to the king of terrors.

• A Change.

Job 14:14 — If a man die, shall he live *again?* all the days of my appointed time will I wait, till my change come.

• Going to thy Fathers.

Ge 15:15 — And thou shalt go to thy fathers in peace; thou shalt be buried in a good old age.

Ge 25:8 — Then Abraham gave up the ghost, and died in a good old age, an old man, and full *of years;* and was gathered to his people.

Ge 35:29 — And Isaac gave up the ghost, and died, and was gathered unto his people, *being* old and full of days: and his sons Esau and Jacob buried him.

• Putting Off this Tabernacle.

2Pe 1:14 — Knowing that shortly I must put off *this* my tabernacle, even as our Lord Jesus Christ hath shewed me.

• Requiring the Soul.

Lk 12:20 — But God said unto him, *Thou* fool, this night thy soul shall be required of thee: then whose shall those things be, which thou hast provided?

• Going the Way Whence there is No Return.

Job 16:22 — When a few years are come, then I shall go the way *whence* I shall not return.

• Being Gathered to our People.

Ge 49:33 — And when Jacob had made an end of commanding his sons, he gathered up his feet into the bed, and yielded up the ghost, and was gathered unto his people.

• Going Down into Silence.

Ps 115:17 — The dead praise not the LORD, neither any that go down into silence.

• Returning to Dust.

Ge 3:19 — In the sweat of thy face shalt thou eat bread, till thou return unto the ground; for out of it wast thou taken: for dust thou *art,* and unto dust shalt thou return.

Ps 104:29 — Thou hidest thy face, they are troubled: thou takest away their breath, they die, and return to their dust.

• Being Cut Down.

Job 14:2 — He cometh forth like a flower, and is cut down: he fleeth also as a shadow, and continueth not.

• Fleeing as a Shadow.

Job 14:2 — He cometh forth like a flower, and is cut down: he fleeth also as a shadow, and continueth not.

• Departing.

Php 1:23 — For I am in a strait betwixt two, having a desire to depart, and to be with Christ; which is far better:

• Sleep.

1Th 4:14–15

Dt 31:16 — And the LORD said unto Moses, Behold, thou shalt sleep with thy fathers; and this people will rise up, and go a whoring after the gods of the strangers of the land, whither they go *to be* among them, and will forsake me, and break my covenant which I have made with them.

Job 7:21 — And why dost thou not pardon my transgression, and take away mine iniquity? for now shall I sleep in the dust; and thou shalt seek me in the morning, but I *shall* not *be.*

Job 14:12 — So man lieth down, and riseth not: till the heavens *be* no more, they shall not awake, nor be raised out of their sleep.

Jer 51:39 — In their heat I will make their feasts, and I will make them drunken, that they may rejoice, and sleep a perpetual sleep, and not wake, saith the LORD.

Da 12:2 — And many of them that sleep in the dust of the earth shall awake, some to everlasting life, and some to shame *and* everlasting contempt.

Jn 11:11 — These things said he: and after that he saith unto them, Our friend Lazarus sleepeth; but I go, that I may awake him out of sleep.

Ac 7:60 — And he kneeled down, and cried with a loud voice, Lord, lay not this sin to their charge. And when he had said this, he fell asleep.

Ac 13:36 — For David, after he had served his own generation by the will of God, fell on sleep, and was laid unto his fathers, and saw corruption:

1Co 15:6 — After that, he was seen of above five hundred brethren at once; of whom the greater part remain unto this present, but some are fallen asleep.

1Co 15:18 — Then they also which are fallen asleep in Christ are perished.

1Co 15:51 — Behold, I shew you a mystery; We shall not all sleep, but we shall all be changed,

• Exemption from.

• Enoch.

Ge 5:24 — And Enoch walked with God: and he *was* not; for God took him.

Heb 11:5 — By faith Enoch was translated that he should not see death; and was not found, because God had translated him: for before his translation he had this testimony, that he pleased God.

• Elijah.

2Ki 2:1–25

• Promised to saints at the second coming of Christ.

1Co 15:51 — Behold, I shew you a mystery; We shall not all sleep, but we shall all be changed,

1Th 4:15 — For this we say unto you by the word of the Lord, that we which are alive *and* remain unto the coming of the Lord shall not prevent them which are asleep.

1Th 4:17 — Then we which are alive *and* remain shall be caught up together with them in the clouds, to meet the Lord in the air: and so shall we ever be with the Lord.

• In heaven.

Lk 20:36 — Neither can they die any more: for they are equal unto the angels; and are the children of God, being the children of the resurrection.

Rev 21:4 — And God shall wipe away all tears from their eyes; and there shall be no more death, neither sorrow, nor crying, neither shall there be any more pain: for the former things are passed away.

• Desired.

Jer 8:3 — And death shall be chosen rather than life by all the residue of them that remain of this evil family, which remain in all the places whither I have driven them, saith the LORD of hosts.

Rev 9:6 — And in those days shall men seek death, and shall not find it; and shall desire to die, and death shall flee from them.

• By Moses.

Nu 11:15 — And if thou deal thus with me, kill me, I pray thee, out of hand, if I have found favour in thy sight; and let me not see my wretchedness.

• By Elijah.

1Ki 19:4 — But he himself went a day's journey into the wilderness, and came and sat down under a juniper tree: and he requested for himself that he might die; and said, It is enough; now, O LORD, take away my life; for I *am* not better than my fathers.

• By Job.

Job 3:1–26; 6:8–11; 7:1–3, 15–16

Job 10:1 — My soul is weary of my life; I will leave my complaint upon myself; I will speak in the bitterness of my soul.

Job 14:13 — Oh that thou wouldest hide me in the grave, that thou wouldest keep me secret, until thy wrath be past, that thou wouldest appoint me a set time, and remember me!

• By Jonah.

Jnh 4:8 — And it came to pass, when the sun did arise, that God prepared a vehement east wind; and the sun beat upon the head of Jonah, that he fainted, and wished in himself to die, and said, *It is* better for me to die than to live.

• By Simeon.

Lk 2:29 — Lord, now lettest thou thy servant depart in peace, according to thy word:

• By Paul.

Php 1:20–23

2Co 5:2 — For in this we groan, earnestly desiring to be clothed upon with our house which is from heaven:

2Co 5:8 — We are confident, *I say,* and willing rather to be absent from the body, and to be present with the Lord.

• As a judgment.

• Upon the Antediluvians.

Ge 6:11–13

Ge 6:7 — And the LORD said, I will destroy man whom I have created from the face of the earth; both man, and beast, and the creeping thing, and the fowls of the air; for it repenteth me that I have made them.

• Upon the Sodomites.

Ge 19:12–13, 24–25

• Upon Saul.

1Ch 10:13–14

• Symbolized.

• By the pale horse.

Rev 6:8 — And I looked, and behold a pale horse: and his name that sat on him was Death, and Hell followed with him. And power was given unto them over the fourth part of the earth, to kill with sword, and with hunger, and with death, and with the beasts of the earth.

- **By King of Terrors.**

Job 18:14 — His confidence shall be rooted out of his tabernacle, and it shall bring him to the king of terrors.

- **Apostrophe to.**

Hos 13:14 — I will ransom them from the power of the grave; I will redeem them from death: O death, I will be thy plagues; O grave, I will be thy destruction: repentance shall be hid from mine eyes.

1Co 15:55 — O death, where *is* thy sting? O grave, where *is* thy victory?

- **Unclassified scripture relating to.**

1Sa 20:2–3; Job 3:17–19; 7:8–10; 10:21–22; 14:5–12, 19–21; 17:13–14; 21:25–26, 32–33; 34:14–15; 36:18–19; Ps 88:9–14; 103:14–16; Ecc 2:14–18; 3:19–21; 7:1–2; 9:5–6; Isa 38:10–13; Lk 20:34–38; 23:39–43; 1Co 15:21–22, 55–57; Heb 2:14–15; Jas 1:10–11; Rev 20:12–14

Ge 2:17 — But of the tree of the knowledge of good and evil, thou shalt not eat of it: for in the day that thou eatest thereof thou shalt surely die.

Ge 3:19 — In the sweat of thy face shalt thou eat bread, till thou return unto the ground; for out of it wast thou taken: for dust thou *art,* and unto dust shalt thou return.

Ge 27:2 — And he said, Behold now, I am old, I know not the day of my death:

Dt 32:39 — See now that I, *even* I, *am* he, and *there is* no god with me: I kill, and I make alive; I wound, and I heal: neither *is there any* that can deliver out of my hand.

Jos 23:14 — And, behold, this day I *am* going the way of all the earth: and ye know in all your hearts and in all your souls, that not one thing hath failed of all the good things which the LORD your God spake concerning you; all are come to pass unto you, *and* not one thing hath failed thereof.

1Sa 2:6 — The LORD killeth, and maketh alive: he bringeth down to the grave, and bringeth up.

2Sa 1:23 — Saul and Jonathan *were* lovely and pleasant in their lives, and in their death they were not divided: they were swifter than eagles, they were stronger than lions.

2Sa 14:14 — For we must needs die, and *are* as water spilt on the ground, which cannot be gathered up again; neither doth God respect *any* person: yet doth he devise means, that his banished be not expelled from him.

Job 1:21 — And said, Naked came I out of my mother's womb, and naked shall I return thither: the LORD gave, and the LORD hath taken away; blessed be the name of the LORD.

Job 3:13 — For now should I have lain still and been quiet, I should have slept: then had I been at rest,

Job 7:1 — *Is there* not an appointed time to man upon earth? *are not* his days also like the days of an hireling?

Job 7:21 — And why dost thou not pardon my transgression, and take away mine iniquity? for now shall I sleep in the dust; and thou shalt seek me in the morning, but I *shall* not *be.*

Job 14:2 — He cometh forth like a flower, and is cut down: he fleeth also as a shadow, and continueth not.

Job 14:14 — If a man die, shall he live *again?* all the days of my appointed time will I wait, till my change come.

Job 16:22 — When a few years are come, then I shall go the way *whence* I shall not return.

Job 17:16 — They shall go down to the bars of the pit, when *our* rest together *is* in the dust.

Job 21:23 — One dieth in his full strength, being wholly at ease and quiet.

Job 30:23 — For I know *that* thou wilt bring me *to* death, and *to* the house appointed for all living.

Job 38:17 — Have the gates of death been opened unto thee? or hast thou seen the doors of the shadow of death?

Ps 6:5 — For in death *there is* no remembrance of thee: in the grave who shall give thee thanks?

Ps 23:4 — Yea, though I walk through the valley of the shadow of death, I will fear no evil: for thou *art* with me; thy rod and thy staff they comfort me.

Ps 30:9 — What profit *is there* in my blood, when I go down to the pit? Shall the dust praise thee? shall it declare thy truth?

Ps 39:4 — LORD, make me to know mine end, and the measure of my days, what it *is; that* I may know how frail I *am.*

Ps 39:13 — O spare me, that I may recover strength, before I go hence, and be no more.

Ps 49:7 — None *of them* can by any means redeem his brother, nor give to God a ransom for him:

Ps 49:9 — That he should still live for ever, *and* not see corruption.

Ps 68:20 — *He that is* our God *is* the God of salvation; and unto God the Lord *belong* the issues from death.

Ps 82:7 — But ye shall die like men, and fall like one of the princes.

Ps 89:48 — What man *is he that* liveth, and shall not see death? shall he deliver his soul from the hand of the grave? Selah.

Ps 90:3 — Thou turnest man to destruction; and sayest, Return, ye children of men.

Ps 104:29 — Thou hidest thy face, they are troubled: thou takest away their breath, they die, and return to their dust.

Ps 115:17 — The dead praise not the LORD, neither any that go down into silence.

Ps 143:3 — For the enemy hath persecuted my soul; he hath smitten my life down to the ground; he hath made me to dwell in darkness, as those that have been long dead.

Ps 144:4 — Man is like to vanity: his days *are* as a shadow that passeth away.

Ps 146:4 — His breath goeth forth, he returneth to his earth; in that very day his thoughts perish.

Ecc 3:2 — A time to be born, and a time to die; a time to plant, and a time to pluck up *that which is* planted;

Ecc 4:2 — Wherefore I praised the dead which are already dead more than the living which are yet alive.

Ecc 5:15 — As he came forth of his mother's womb, naked shall he return to go as he came, and shall take nothing of his labour, which he may carry away in his hand.

Ecc 6:6 — Yea, though he live a thousand years twice *told,* yet hath he seen no good: do not all go to one place?

Ecc 6:10 — That which hath been is named already, and it is known that it *is* man: neither may he contend with him that is mightier than he.

Ecc 7:15 — All *things* have I seen in the days of my vanity: there is a just *man* that perisheth in his righteousness, and there is a wicked *man* that prolongeth *his life* in his wickedness.

Ecc 8:8 — *There is* no man that hath power over the spirit to retain the spirit; neither *hath he* power in the day of death: and *there is* no discharge in *that* war; neither shall wickedness deliver those that are given to it.

Ecc 9:3 — This *is* an evil among all *things* that are done under the sun, that *there is* one event unto all: yea, also the heart of the sons of men is full of evil, and madness is in their heart while they live, and after that *they go* to the dead.

Ecc 9:10 — Whatsoever thy hand findeth to do, do *it* with thy might; for *there is* no work, nor device, nor knowledge, nor wisdom, in the grave, whither thou goest.

Ecc 12:5 — Also *when* they shall be afraid of *that which is* high, and fears *shall be* in the way, and the almond tree shall flourish, and the grasshopper shall be a burden, and desire shall fail: because man goeth to his long home, and the mourners go about the streets:

Ecc 12:7 — Then shall the dust return to the earth as it was: and the spirit shall return unto God who gave it.

Isa 25:8 — He will swallow up death in victory; and the Lord GOD will wipe away tears from off all faces; and the rebuke of his people shall he take away from off all the earth: for the LORD hath spoken *it.*

Isa 38:1 — In those days was Hezekiah sick unto death. And Isaiah the prophet the son of Amoz came unto him, and said unto him, Thus saith the LORD, Set thine house in order: for thou shalt die, and not live.

Isa 38:18 — For the grave cannot praise thee, death can *not* celebrate thee: they that go down into the pit cannot hope for thy truth.

Isa 40:7 — The grass withereth, the flower fadeth: because the spirit of the LORD bloweth upon it: surely the people *is* grass.

Isa 51:12 — I, *even* I, *am* he that comforteth you: who *art* thou, that thou shouldest be afraid of a man *that* shall die, and of the son of man *which* shall be made as grass;

Jer 9:21 — For death is come up into our windows, *and* is entered into our palaces, to cut off the children from without, *and* the young men from the streets.

La 3:6 — He hath set me in dark places, as *they that be* dead of old.

Hos 13:14 — I will ransom them from the power of the grave; I will redeem them from death: O death, I will be thy plagues; O grave, I will be thy destruction: repentance shall be hid from mine eyes.

Zec 1:5 — Your fathers, where *are* they? and the prophets, do they live for ever?

Mt 10:28 — <u>And fear not them which kill the body, but are not able to kill the soul: but rather fear him which is able to destroy both soul and body in hell.</u>

Jn 9:4 — <u>I must work the works of him that sent me, while it is day: the night cometh, when no man can work.</u>

Ro 5:12 — Wherefore, as by one man sin entered into the world, and death by sin; and so death passed upon all men, for that all have sinned:

Ro 5:14 — Nevertheless death reigned from Adam to Moses, even over them that had not sinned after the similitude of Adam's transgression, who is the figure of him that was to come.

1Co 15:26 — The last enemy *that* shall be destroyed *is* death.

1Ti 6:7 — For we brought nothing into *this* world, *and it is* certain we can carry nothing out.

2Ti 1:10 — But is now made manifest by the appearing of our Saviour Jesus Christ, who hath abolished death, and hath brought life and immortality to light through the gospel:

Heb 9:27 — And as it is appointed unto men once to die, but after this the judgment:

Heb 13:14 — For here have we no continuing city, but we seek one to come.

1Pe 1:24 — For all flesh *is* as grass, and all the glory of man as the flower of grass. The grass withereth, and the flower thereof falleth away:

Rev 1:18 — <u>I *am* he that liveth, and was dead; and, behold, I am alive for evermore, Amen; and have the keys of hell and of death.</u>

Rev 21:4 — And God shall wipe away all tears from their eyes; and there shall be no more death, neither sorrow, nor crying, neither shall there be any more pain: for the former things are passed away.

• Preparation for.

Ecc 11:7–8; Isa 38:18–19; Lk 12:35–37

Dt 32:29 — O that they were wise, *that* they understood this, *that* they would consider their latter end!

2Ki 20:1 — In those days was Hezekiah sick unto death. And the prophet Isaiah the son of Amoz came to him, and said unto him, Thus saith the LORD, Set thine house in order; for thou shalt die, and not live.

Ps 39:4 — LORD, make me to know mine end, and the measure of my days, what it *is; that* I may know how frail I *am.*

Ps 39:13 — O spare me, that I may recover strength, before I go hence, and be no more.

Ps 90:12 — So teach *us* to number our days, that we may apply *our* hearts unto wisdom.

Ecc 9:4 — For to him that is joined to all the living there is hope: for a living dog is better than a dead lion.

Ecc 9:10 — Whatsoever thy hand findeth to do, do *it* with thy might; for *there is* no work, nor device, nor knowledge, nor wisdom, in the grave, whither thou goest.

Jn 9:4 — I must work the works of him that sent me, while it is day: the night cometh, when no man can work.

Ro 14:8 — For whether we live, we live unto the Lord; and whether we die, we die unto the Lord: whether we live therefore, or die, we are the Lord's.

Php 1:21 — For to me to live *is* Christ, and to die *is* gain.

Heb 13:14 — For here have we no continuing city, but we seek one to come.

Jas 4:15 — For that ye *ought* to say, If the Lord will, we shall live, and do this, or that.

1Pe 1:17 — And if ye call on the Father, who without respect of persons judgeth according to every man's work, pass the time of your sojourning *here* in fear:

- **Of the righteous.**

2Ki 22:19–20; Isa 57:1–2; Ro 14:7–8; 1Co 3:21–23; 15:51–57; 2Co 1:9–10; Php 1:20–21, 23–24; 1Th 4:13–14; 5:9–10; 2Ti 4:6–8; Heb 2:14–15

Nu 23:10 — Who can count the dust of Jacob, and the number of the fourth *part* of Israel? Let me die the death of the righteous, and let my last end be like his!

2Sa 12:23 — But now he is dead, wherefore should I fast? can I bring him back again? I shall go to him, but he shall not return to me.

Ps 23:4 — Yea, though I walk through the valley of the shadow of death, I will fear no evil: for thou *art* with me; thy rod and thy staff they comfort me.

Ps 31:5 — Into thine hand I commit my spirit: thou hast redeemed me, O LORD God of truth.

Ps 37:37 — Mark the perfect *man,* and behold the upright: for the end of *that* man *is* peace.

Ps 49:15 — But God will redeem my soul from the power of the grave: for he shall receive me. Selah.

Ps 73:24 — Thou shalt guide me with thy counsel, and afterward receive me *to* glory.

Ps 116:15 — Precious in the sight of the LORD *is* the death of his saints.

Pr 14:32 — The wicked is driven away in his wickedness: but the righteous hath hope in his death.

Ecc 7:1 — A good name *is* better than precious ointment; and the day of death than the day of one's birth.

Da 12:13 — But go thou thy way till the end *be:* for thou shalt rest, and stand in thy lot at the end of the days.

Lk 2:29 — Lord, now lettest thou thy servant depart in peace, according to thy word:

Lk 16:22 — And it came to pass, that the beggar died, and was carried by the angels into Abraham's bosom: the rich man also died, and was buried;

Lk 23:43 — And Jesus said unto him, Verily I say unto thee, To day shalt thou be with me in paradise.

Jn 11:11 — These things said he: and after that he saith unto them, Our friend Lazarus sleepeth; but I go, that I may awake him out of sleep.

Ac 7:59 — And they stoned Stephen, calling upon *God,* and saying, Lord Jesus, receive my spirit.

2Co 5:1 — For we know that if our earthly house of *this* tabernacle were dissolved, we have a building of God, an house not made with hands, eternal in the heavens.

2Co 5:4 — For we that are in *this* tabernacle do groan, being burdened: not for that we would be unclothed, but clothed upon, that mortality might be swallowed up of life.

2Co 5:8 — We are confident, *I say,* and willing rather to be absent from the body, and to be present with the Lord.

Heb 11:13 — These all died in faith, not having received the promises, but having seen them afar off, and were persuaded of *them,* and embraced *them,* and confessed that they were strangers and pilgrims on the earth.

2Pe 1:11 — For so an entrance shall be ministered unto you abundantly into the everlasting kingdom of our Lord and Saviour Jesus Christ.

2Pe 1:14 — Knowing that shortly I must put off *this* my tabernacle, even as our Lord Jesus Christ hath shewed me.

Rev 14:13 — And I heard a voice from heaven saying unto me, Write, Blessed *are* the dead which die in the Lord from henceforth: Yea, saith the Spirit, that they may rest from their labours; and their works do follow them.

- **Anticipated.**
  - **By Isaac.**

Ge 27:1–4, 22–40

- **Scenes of.**
  - **Of Jacob.**

Ge 49:1–33

Heb 11:21 — By faith Jacob, when he was a dying, blessed both the sons of Joseph; and worshipped, *leaning* upon the top of his staff.

  - **Of Aaron.**

Nu 20:23–28

  - **Of Moses.**

Dt 31:14–16; 31:21–34:7

Dt 31:19 — Now therefore write ye this song for you, and teach it the children of Israel: put it in their mouths, that this song may be a witness for me against the children of Israel.

  - **Of Joshua.**

Jos 24:1–29

  - **Of Samson.**

Jgs 16:25–30

  - **Of Eli.**

1Sa 4:12–18

  - **Of the wife of Phinehas.**

1Sa 4:19–21

  - **Of David.**

1Ki 2:1–10

  - **Of Zechariah.**

2Ch 24:22 — Thus Joash the king remembered not the kindness which Jehoiada his father had done to him, but slew his son. And when he died, he said, The LORD look upon *it,* and require *it.*

- **Of Jesus.**
  Mt 27:34–53; Mk 15:23–38; Lk 23:27–49; Jn 19:16–30
- **Of Stephen.**
  Ac 7:59–60
- **Of Paul.**
  2Ti 4:6–8

• Of the wicked.

Job 20:4–5; 21:17–18, 23–26; 27:19–23; Ps 37:1–2, 9–10, 35–36; 49:9–10, 19–20; 73:3–4, 17–20; Pr 5:22–23; Jer 16:3–4; Lk 16:22–28; Ac 5:3–10

Nu 16:30 — But if the LORD make a new thing, and the earth open her mouth, and swallow them up, with all that *appertain* unto them, and they go down quick into the pit; then ye shall understand that these men have provoked the LORD.

1Sa 25:38 — And it came to pass about ten days *after,* that the LORD smote Nabal, that he died.

2Ch 21:6 — And he walked in the way of the kings of Israel, like as did the house of Ahab: for he had the daughter of Ahab to wife: and he wrought *that which was* evil in the eyes of the LORD.

2Ch 21:20 — Thirty and two years old was he when he began to reign, and he reigned in Jerusalem eight years, and departed without being desired. Howbeit they buried him in the city of David, but not in the sepulchres of the kings.

Job 4:21 — Doth not their excellency *which is* in them go away? they die, even without wisdom.

Job 18:14 — His confidence shall be rooted out of his tabernacle, and it shall bring him to the king of terrors.

Job 18:18 — He shall be driven from light into darkness, and chased out of the world.

Job 20:8 — He shall fly away as a dream, and shall not be found: yea, he shall be chased away as a vision of the night.

Job 20:11 — His bones are full *of the sin* of his youth, which shall lie down with him in the dust.

Job 21:13 — They spend their days in wealth, and in a moment go down to the grave.

Job 24:20 — The womb shall forget him; the worm shall feed sweetly on him; he shall be no more remembered; and wickedness shall be broken as a tree.

Job 24:24 — They are exalted for a little while, but are gone and brought low; they are taken out of the way as all *other,* and cut off as the tops of the ears of corn.

Job 27:8 — For what *is* the hope of the hypocrite, though he hath gained, when God taketh away his soul?

Job 34:20 — In a moment shall they die, and the people shall be troubled at midnight, and pass away: and the mighty shall be taken away without hand.

Job 36:12 — But if they obey not, they shall perish by the sword, and they shall die without knowledge.

Job 36:14 — They die in youth, and their life *is* among the unclean.

Job 36:18 — Because *there is* wrath, *beware* lest he take thee away with *his* stroke: then a great ransom cannot deliver thee.

Job 36:20 — Desire not the night, when people are cut off in their place.

Ps 49:7 — None *of them* can by any means redeem his brother, nor give to God a ransom for him:

Ps 49:14 — Like sheep they are laid in the grave; death shall feed on them; and the upright shall have dominion over them in the morning; and their beauty shall consume in the grave from their dwelling.

Ps 49:17 — For when he dieth he shall carry nothing away: his glory shall not descend after him.

Ps 55:15 — Let death seize upon them, *and* let them go down quick into hell: for wickedness is in their dwellings, *and* among them.

Ps 55:23 — But thou, O God, shalt bring them down into the pit of destruction: bloody and deceitful men shall not live out half their days; but I will trust in thee.

Ps 58:9 — Before your pots can feel the thorns, he shall take them away as with a whirlwind, both living, and in *his* wrath.

Ps 78:50 — He made a way to his anger; he spared not their soul from death, but gave their life over to the pestilence;

Ps 92:7 — When the wicked spring as the grass, and when all the workers of iniquity do flourish; *it is* that they shall be destroyed for ever:

Pr 2:22 — But the wicked shall be cut off from the earth, and the transgressors shall be rooted out of it.

Pr 10:25 — As the whirlwind passeth, so *is* the wicked no *more:* but the righteous *is* an everlasting foundation.

Pr 10:27 — The fear of the LORD prolongeth days: but the years of the wicked shall be shortened.

Pr 11:7 — When a wicked man dieth, *his* expectation shall perish: and the hope of unjust *men* perisheth.

Pr 11:10 — When it goeth well with the righteous, the city rejoiceth: and when the wicked perish, *there is* shouting.

Pr 13:9 — The light of the righteous rejoiceth: but the lamp of the wicked shall be put out.

Pr 14:32 — The wicked is driven away in his wickedness: but the righteous hath hope in his death.

Pr 21:16 — The man that wandereth out of the way of understanding shall remain in the congregation of the dead.

Pr 24:20 — For there shall be no reward to the evil *man;* the candle of the wicked shall be put out.

Pr 29:1 — He, that being often reproved hardeneth *his* neck, shall suddenly be destroyed, and that without remedy.

Pr 29:16 — When the wicked are multiplied, transgression increaseth: but the righteous shall see their fall.

Ecc 8:10 — And so I saw the wicked buried, who had come and gone from the place of the holy, and they were forgotten in the city where they had so done: this *is* also vanity.

Isa 14:11 — Thy pomp is brought down to the grave, *and* the noise of thy viols: the worm is spread under thee, and the worms cover thee.

Isa 14:15 — Yet thou shalt be brought down to hell, to the sides of the pit.

Isa 17:14 — And behold at eveningtide trouble; *and* before the morning he *is* not. This *is* the portion of them that spoil us, and the lot of them that rob us.

Isa 26:14 — *They are* dead, they shall not live; *they are* deceased, they shall not rise: therefore hast thou visited and destroyed them, and made all their memory to perish.

Eze 28:8 — They shall bring thee down to the pit, and thou shalt die the deaths of *them that are* slain in the midst of the seas.

Eze 28:10 — Thou shalt die the deaths of the uncircumcised by the hand of strangers: for I have spoken *it,* saith the Lord GOD.

Am 9:10 — All the sinners of my people shall die by the sword, which say, The evil shall not overtake nor prevent us.

Lk 12:20 — But God said unto him, *Thou* fool, this night thy soul shall be required of thee: then whose shall those things be, which thou hast provided?

1Th 5:3 — For when they shall say, Peace and safety; then sudden destruction cometh upon them, as travail upon a woman with child; and they shall not escape.

- **Spiritual.**

Jn 5:24–26; 6:50–51; Ro 8:5–6, 12–13; Eph 2:5–6

Lk 1:79 — To give light to them that sit in darkness and *in* the shadow of death, to guide our feet into the way of peace.

Jn 6:53 — Then Jesus said unto them, Verily, verily, I say unto you, Except ye eat the flesh of the Son of man, and drink his blood, ye have no life in you.

Jn 11:26 — And whosoever liveth and believeth in me shall never die. Believest thou this?

Ro 5:12 — Wherefore, as by one man sin entered into the world, and death by sin; and so death passed upon all men, for that all have sinned:

Ro 5:15 — But not as the offence, so also *is* the free gift. For if through the offence of one many be dead, much more the grace of God, and the gift by grace, *which is* by one man, Jesus Christ, hath abounded unto many.

Ro 7:11 — For sin, taking occasion by the commandment, deceived me, and by it slew *me.*

2Co 5:14 — For the love of Christ constraineth us; because we thus judge, that if one died for all, then were all dead:

Eph 2:1 — And you *hath he quickened,* who were dead in trespasses and sins;

Eph 4:18 — Having the understanding darkened, being alienated from the life of God through the ignorance that is in them, because of the blindness of their heart:

Eph 5:14 — Wherefore he saith, Awake thou that sleepest, and arise from the dead, and Christ shall give thee light.

Col 2:13 — And you, being dead in your sins and the uncircumcision of your flesh, hath he quickened together with him, having forgiven you all trespasses;

1Ti 5:6 — But she that liveth in pleasure is dead while she liveth.

1Pe 2:24 — Who his own self bare our sins in his own body on the tree, that we, being dead to sins, should live unto righteousness: by whose stripes ye were healed.

1Jn 5:12 — He that hath the Son hath life; *and* he that hath not the Son of God hath not life.

✦See: Depravity of Man

✦See: Man; state of, after the fall

✦See: Reprobacy

- **Second.**

Eze 18:23–24; 33:8–9, 14–16; Mk 9:43–44

Pr 14:12 — There is a way which seemeth right unto a man, but the end thereof *are* the ways of death.

Eze 18:4 — Behold, all souls are mine; as the soul of the father, so also the soul of the son is mine: the soul that sinneth, it shall die.

Eze 18:10 — If he beget a son *that is* a robber, a shedder of blood, and *that* doeth the like to *any* one of these *things,*

Eze 18:13 — Hath given forth upon usury, and hath taken increase: shall he then live? he shall not live: he hath done all these abominations; he shall surely die; his blood shall be upon him.

Eze 18:21 — But if the wicked will turn from all his sins that he hath committed, and keep all my statutes, and do that which is lawful and right, he shall surely live, he shall not die.

Eze 33:11 — Say unto them, *As* I live, saith the Lord GOD, I have no pleasure in the death of the wicked; but that the wicked turn from his way and live: turn ye, turn ye from your evil ways; for why will ye die, O house of Israel?

Mt 7:13 — Enter ye in at the strait gate: for wide *is* the gate, and broad *is* the way, that leadeth to destruction, and many there be which go in thereat:

Mt 10:28 — And fear not them which kill the body, but are not able to kill the soul: but rather fear him which is able to destroy both soul and body in hell.

Mt 25:30 — And cast ye the unprofitable servant into outer darkness: there shall be weeping and gnashing of teeth.

Mt 25:41 — Then shall he say also unto them on the left hand, Depart from me, ye cursed, into everlasting fire, prepared for the devil and his angels:

Mt 25:46 — And these shall go away into everlasting punishment: but the righteous into life eternal.

Ro 1:32 — Who knowing the judgment of God, that they which commit such things are worthy of death, not only do the same, but have pleasure in them that do them.

Ro 6:16 — Know ye not, that to whom ye yield yourselves servants to obey, his servants ye are to whom ye obey; whether of sin unto death, or of obedience unto righteousness?

Ro 6:21 — What fruit had ye then in those things whereof ye are now ashamed? for the end of those things *is* death.

Ro 6:23 — For the wages of sin *is* death; but the gift of God *is* eternal life through Jesus Christ our Lord.

Ro 8:13 — For if ye live after the flesh, ye shall die: but if ye through the Spirit do mortify the deeds of the body, ye shall live.

Ro 9:22 — *What* if God, willing to shew *his* wrath, and to make his power known, endured with much longsuffering the vessels of wrath fitted to destruction:

2Th 1:9 — Who shall be punished with everlasting destruction from the presence of the Lord, and from the glory of his power;

Jas 1:15 — Then when lust hath conceived, it bringeth forth sin: and sin, when it is finished, bringeth forth death.

Jas 4:12 — There is one lawgiver, who is able to save and to destroy: who art thou that judgest another?

2Pe 2:12 — But these, as natural brute beasts, made to be taken and destroyed, speak evil of the things that they understand not; and shall utterly perish in their own corruption;

Rev 2:11 — He that hath an ear, let him hear what the Spirit saith unto the churches; He that overcometh shall not be hurt of the second death.

Rev 19:20 — And the beast was taken, and with him the false prophet that wrought miracles before him, with which he deceived them that had received the mark of the beast, and them that worshipped his image. These both were cast alive into a lake of fire burning with brimstone.

Rev 20:14 — And death and hell were cast into the lake of fire. This is the second death.

Rev 21:8 — But the fearful, and unbelieving, and the abominable, and murderers, and whoremongers, and sorcerers, and idolaters, and all liars, shall have their part in the lake which burneth with fire and brimstone: which is the second death.

+See: Hell

+See: Wicked; punishment of

- **Figurative of regeneration.**

Ro 6:2–11; 7:1–11; 8:10–11

Col 2:20 — Wherefore if ye be dead with Christ from the rudiments of the world, why, as though living in the world, are ye subject to ordinances,

+See: Dead

+See: Regeneration

DEBIR

- **King of Eglon.**

Jos 10:3–27

- **A town in the mountains of Judah.**
  - **Called also Kirjath-Sannah and Kirjath-Sepher, which signifies a city of books.**

Jos 15:15–16

  - **Anakim expelled from, by Joshua.**

Jos 11:21 — And at that time came Joshua, and cut off the Anakims from the mountains, from Hebron, from Debir, from Anab, and from all the mountains of Judah, and from all the mountains of Israel: Joshua destroyed them utterly with their cities.

  - **Taken by Othniel.**

Jos 15:15–17; Jgs 1:12–13

Jos 15:49 — And Dannah, and Kirjath-sannah, which *is* Debir,

  - **Allotted to the Aaronites.**

Jos 21:15 — And Holon with her suburbs, and Debir with her suburbs,

- **A place near the valley of Achor.**

Jos 15:7 — And the border went up toward Debir from the valley of Achor, and so northward, looking toward Gilgal, *that is* before the going up to Adummim, which *is* on the south side of the river: and the border passed toward the waters of En-shemesh, and the goings out thereof were at En-rogel:

DEBORAH

- **Nurse to Rebekah.**

Ge 24:59 — And they sent away Rebekah their sister, and her nurse, and Abraham's servant, and his men.

  - **Buried beneath an oak under Bethel.**

Ge 35:8 — But Deborah Rebekah's nurse died, and she was buried beneath Bethel under an oak: and the name of it was called Allon-bachuth.

- **The prophetess, a judge of Israel.**

Jgs 4:4–5

Jgs 5:7 — *The inhabitants of* the villages ceased, they ceased in Israel, until that I Deborah arose, that I arose a mother in Israel.

  - **Inspires Barak to defeat Sisera.**

Jgs 4:6–16

  - **Triumphant song of.**

Jgs 5:1–31

DEBT

Ro 13:1–8; 1Ti 2:1–3

Da 4:32 — And they shall drive thee from men, and thy dwelling *shall be* with the beasts of the field: they shall make thee to eat grass as oxen, and seven times shall pass over thee, until thou know that the most High ruleth in the kingdom of men, and giveth it to whomsoever he will.

- **Security for.**

Ex 22:25–27; Dt 24:10–13; Ne 5:3–4

Dt 24:6 — No man shall take the nether or the upper millstone to pledge: for he taketh *a man's* life to pledge.

Job 22:6 — For thou hast taken a pledge from thy brother for nought, and stripped the naked of their clothing.

Job 24:9 — They pluck the fatherless from the breast, and take a pledge of the poor.

Pr 11:15 — He that is surety for a stranger shall smart *for it:* and he that hateth suretiship is sure.

Pr 22:26 — Be not thou *one* of them that strike hands, *or* of them that are sureties for debts.

Am 2:8 — And they lay *themselves* down upon clothes laid to pledge by every altar, and they drink the wine of the condemned in the house of their god.

+See: Creditor

+See: Debtor

+See: Surety

DEBTOR

• Laws concerning.

Ex 21:2–6; 22:10–15; Le 25:14–17, 25–41, 47–55; Mt 5:25–26

Ne 10:31 — And *if* the people of the land bring ware or any victuals on the sabbath day to sell, *that* we would not buy it of them on the sabbath, or on the holy day: and *that* we would leave the seventh year, and the exaction of every debt.

Mt 5:40 — And if any man will sue thee at the law, and take away thy coat, let him have *thy* cloke also.

Mt 18:25 — But forasmuch as he had not to pay, his lord commanded him to be sold, and his wife, and children, and all that he had, and payment to be made.

• Unclassified scripture relating to.

2Ki 4:1–7; Ne 5:3–5; Job 20:18–19; Mt 18:23–33; Lk 20:9–16

See: Creditor
See: Debt
See: Surety

DECALOGUE

• Written by God.

Ex 24:12 — And the LORD said unto Moses, Come up to me into the mount, and be there: and I will give thee tables of stone, and a law, and commandments which I have written; that thou mayest teach them.

Ex 31:18 — And he gave unto Moses, when he had made an end of communing with him upon mount Sinai, two tables of testimony, tables of stone, written with the finger of God.

Ex 32:16 — And the tables *were* the work of God, and the writing *was* the writing of God, graven upon the tables.

Dt 5:22 — These words the LORD spake unto all your assembly in the mount out of the midst of the fire, of the cloud, and of the thick darkness, with a great voice: and he added no more. And he wrote them in two tables of stone, and delivered them unto me.

Dt 9:10 — And the LORD delivered unto me two tables of stone written with the finger of God; and on them *was written* according to all the words, which the LORD spake with you in the mount out of the midst of the fire in the day of the assembly.

Hos 8:12 — I have written to him the great things of my law, *but* they were counted as a strange thing.

• Divine authority of.

Ex 34:27–28; Dt 5:4–22

Ex 20:1 — And God spake all these words, saying,

• Called Words of the Covenant.

Ex 34:28 — And he was there with the LORD forty days and forty nights; he did neither eat bread, nor drink water. And he wrote upon the tables the words of the covenant, the ten commandments.

Dt 4:13 — And he declared unto you his covenant, which he commanded you to perform, *even* ten commandments; and he wrote them upon two tables of stone.

• Tables of Testimony.

Ex 20:1–17; Dt 5:7–21; Mt 19:18–19; 22:34–40; Lk 10:25–28; Ro 13:8–10

Ex 31:18 — And he gave unto Moses, when he had made an end of communing with him upon mount Sinai, two tables of testimony, tables of stone, written with the finger of God.

Ex 34:29 — And it came to pass, when Moses came down from mount Sinai with the two tables of testimony in Moses' hand, when he came down from the mount, that Moses wist not that the skin of his face shone while he talked with him.

Ex 40:20 — And he took and put the testimony into the ark, and set the staves on the ark, and put the mercy seat above upon the ark:

See: Commandments

DECAPOLIS

• Ten cities situated in one district on the east of the Sea of Galilee.

Mt 4:25 — And there followed him great multitudes of people from Galilee, and *from* Decapolis, and *from* Jerusalem, and *from* Judaea, and *from* beyond Jordan.

Mk 5:20 — And he departed, and began to publish in Decapolis how great things Jesus had done for him: and all *men* did marvel.

Mk 7:31 — And again, departing from the coasts of Tyre and Sidon, he came unto the sea of Galilee, through the midst of the coasts of Decapolis.

DECEIT

• Is falsehood.

Ps 119:118 — Thou hast trodden down all them that err from thy statutes: for their deceit *is* falsehood.

• The tongue an instrument of.

Ro 3:13 — Their throat *is* an open sepulchre; with their tongues they have used deceit; the poison of asps *is* under their lips:

• Comes from the heart.

Mk 7:22 — Thefts, covetousness, wickedness, deceit, lasciviousness, an evil eye, blasphemy, pride, foolishness:

• Characteristic of the heart.

Jer 17:9 — The heart *is* deceitful above all *things*, and desperately wicked: who can know it?

• God abhors.

Ps 5:6 — Thou shalt destroy them that speak leasing: the LORD will abhor the bloody and deceitful man.

• Forbidden.

Pr 24:28 — Be not a witness against thy neighbour without cause; and deceive *not* with thy lips.

1Pe 3:10 — For he that will love life, and see good days, let him refrain his tongue from evil, and his lips that they speak no guile:

• Christ was perfectly free from.

Isa 53:9 — And he made his grave with the wicked, and with the rich in his death; because he had done no violence, neither *was any* deceit in his mouth.

1Pe 2:22 — Who did no sin, neither was guile found in his mouth:

• Saints free from.

Ps 24:4 — He that hath clean hands, and a pure heart; who hath not lifted up his soul unto vanity, nor sworn deceitfully.

Zep 3:13 — The remnant of Israel shall not do iniquity, nor speak lies; neither shall a deceitful tongue be found in their mouth: for they shall feed and lie down, and none shall make *them* afraid.

Rev 14:5 — And in their mouth was found no guile: for they are without fault before the throne of God.

• Saints purpose against.

Job 27:4 — My lips shall not speak wickedness, nor my tongue utter deceit.

• Saints avoid.

Job 31:5 — If I have walked with vanity, or if my foot hath hasted to deceit;

• Saints shun those addicted to.

Ps 101:7 — He that worketh deceit shall not dwell within my house: he that telleth lies shall not tarry in my sight.

• Saints pray for deliverance from those who use.

Ps 43:1 — Judge me, O God, and plead my cause against an ungodly nation: O deliver me from the deceitful and unjust man.

Ps 120:2 — Deliver my soul, O LORD, from lying lips, *and* from a deceitful tongue.

• Saints delivered from those who use.

Ps 72:14 — He shall redeem their soul from deceit and violence: and precious shall their blood be in his sight.

• Saints should beware of those who teach.

Eph 5:6 — Let no man deceive you with vain words: for because of these things cometh the wrath of God upon the children of disobedience.

Col 2:8 — Beware lest any man spoil you through philosophy and vain deceit, after the tradition of men, after the rudiments of the world, and not after Christ.

• Saints should lay aside, in seeking truth.

1Pe 2:1 — Wherefore laying aside all malice, and all guile, and hypocrisies, and envies, and all evil speakings,

• Ministers should lay aside.

2Co 4:2 — But have renounced the hidden things of dishonesty, not walking in craftiness, nor handling the word of God deceitfully; but by manifestation of the truth commending ourselves to every man's conscience in the sight of God.

1Th 2:3 — For our exhortation *was* not of deceit, nor of uncleanness, nor in guile:

• The wicked are full of.

Ro 1:29 — Being filled with all unrighteousness, fornication, wickedness, covetousness, maliciousness; full of envy, murder, debate, deceit, malignity; whisperers,

• The wicked devise.

Ps 35:20 — For they speak not peace: but they devise deceitful matters against *them that are* quiet in the land.

Ps 38:12 — They also that seek after my life lay snares *for me:* and they that seek my hurt speak mischievous things, and imagine deceits all the day long.

Pr 12:5 — The thoughts of the righteous *are* right: *but* the counsels of the wicked *are* deceit.

• The wicked utter.

Ps 10:7 — His mouth is full of cursing and deceit and fraud: under his tongue *is* mischief and vanity.

Ps 36:3 — The words of his mouth *are* iniquity and deceit: he hath left off to be wise, *and* to do good.

• The wicked work.

Pr 11:18 — The wicked worketh a deceitful work: but to him that soweth righteousness *shall be* a sure reward.

• The wicked increase in.

2Ti 3:13 — But evil men and seducers shall wax worse and worse, deceiving, and being deceived.

• The wicked use, to each other.

Jer 9:5 — And they will deceive every one his neighbour, and will not speak the truth: they have taught their tongue to speak lies, *and* weary themselves to commit iniquity.

• The wicked use, to themselves.

Jer 37:9 — Thus saith the LORD; Deceive not yourselves, saying, The Chaldeans shall surely depart from us: for they shall not depart.

Ob 1:3 — The pride of thine heart hath deceived thee, thou that dwellest in the clefts of the rock, whose habitation *is* high; that saith in his heart, Who shall bring me down to the ground?

Ob 1:7 — All the men of thy confederacy have brought thee *even* to the border: the men that were at peace with thee have deceived thee, *and* prevailed against thee; *they that eat* thy bread have laid a wound under thee: *there is* none understanding in him.

• The wicked delight in.

Pr 20:17 — Bread of deceit *is* sweet to a man; but afterwards his mouth shall be filled with gravel.

• False teachers are workers of.

2Co 11:13 — For such *are* false apostles, deceitful workers, transforming themselves into the apostles of Christ.

• False teachers preach.

Jer 14:14 — Then the LORD said unto me, The prophets prophesy lies in my name: I sent them not, neither have I commanded them, neither spake unto them: they prophesy unto you a false vision and divination, and a thing of nought, and the deceit of their heart.

Jer 23:26 — How long shall *this* be in the heart of the prophets that prophesy lies? yea, *they are* prophets of the deceit of their own heart;

• False teachers impose on others by.

Ro 16:18 — For they that are such serve not our Lord Jesus Christ, but their own belly; and by good words and fair speeches deceive the hearts of the simple.

Eph 4:14 — That we *henceforth* be no more children, tossed to and fro, and carried about with every wind of doctrine, by the sleight of men, *and* cunning craftiness, whereby they lie in wait to deceive;

- **False teachers sport themselves with.**
  2Pe 2:13 — And shall receive the reward of unrighteousness, *as* they that count it pleasure to riot in the daytime. Spots *they are* and blemishes, sporting themselves with their own deceivings while they feast with you;
- **Hypocrites devise.**
  Job 15:35 — They conceive mischief, and bring forth vanity, and their belly prepareth deceit.
- **Hypocrites practice.**
  Hos 11:12 — Ephraim compasseth me about with lies, and the house of Israel with deceit: but Judah yet ruleth with God, and is faithful with the saints.
- **False witnesses use.**
  Pr 12:17 — *He that* speaketh truth sheweth forth righteousness: but a false witness deceit.
- **A characteristic of antichrist.**
  2Jn 1:7 — For many deceivers are entered into the world, who confess not that Jesus Christ is come in the flesh. This is a deceiver and an antichrist.
- **Characteristic of the apostasy.**
  2Th 2:10 — And with all deceivableness of unrighteousness in them that perish; because they received not the love of the truth, that they might be saved.
- **Evil of.**
  - **Hinders knowledge of God.**
    Jer 9:6 — Thine habitation *is* in the midst of deceit; through deceit they refuse to know me, saith the LORD.
  - **Keeps from turning to God.**
    Jer 8:5 — Why *then* is this people of Jerusalem slidden back by a perpetual backsliding? they hold fast deceit, they refuse to return.
  - **Leads to pride and oppression.**
    Jer 5:27–28
  - **Leads to lying.**
    Pr 14:25 — A true witness delivereth souls: but a deceitful *witness* speaketh lies.
  - **Often accompanied by fraud and injustice.**
    Ps 10:7 — His mouth is full of cursing and deceit and fraud: under his tongue *is* mischief and vanity.
    Ps 43:1 — Judge me, O God, and plead my cause against an ungodly nation: O deliver me from the deceitful and unjust man.
  - **Hatred often concealed by.**
    Pr 26:24–26
  - **The folly of fools is.**
    Pr 14:8 — The wisdom of the prudent *is* to understand his way: but the folly of fools *is* deceit.
  - **Blessedness of being free from.**
    Ps 24:4–5
    Ps 32:2 — Blessed *is* the man unto whom the LORD imputeth not iniquity, and in whose spirit *there is* no guile.
  - **Punishment of.**
    Jer 9:7–9
    Ps 55:23 — But thou, O God, shalt bring them down into the pit of destruction: bloody and deceitful men shall not live out half their days; but I will trust in thee.

See: Confidence; false
See: Deception
See: Falsehood
See: Flattery
See: Hypocrisy

DECEPTION

Mt 24:4 — And Jesus answered and said unto them, Take heed that no man deceive you.

1Co 6:9 — Know ye not that the unrighteous shall not inherit the kingdom of God? Be not deceived: neither fornicators, nor idolaters, nor adulterers, nor effeminate, nor abusers of themselves with mankind,

Gal 6:7 — Be not deceived; God is not mocked: for whatsoever a man soweth, that shall he also reap.

2Th 2:3 — Let no man deceive you by any means: for *that day shall not come,* except there come a falling away first, and that man of sin be revealed, the son of perdition;

- **Instances of.**
  - **By Satan.**
    Ge 3:4
  - **Abraham, in stating that Sarah was his sister.**
    Ge 12:13; 20:2
  - **Isaac, in stating that his wife was his sister.**
    Ge 26:7
  - **Jacob and Rebekah, in imposing Jacob on his father, and Jacob's impersonating Esau.**
    Ge 27:6–23
  - **Jacob's sons, in entrapping the Shechemites.**
    Ge 34:13–31
  - **Jacob's sons, in representing to their father that Joseph had been destroyed by wild beasts.**
    Ge 37:29–35
  - **Joseph, in his ruse with his brethren.**
    Ge 42:1–44:34
  - **The Gibeonites, in misrepresenting their habitat.**
    Jos 9:3–15
  - **Ehud deceives Eglon, and slays him.**
    Jgs 3:15–30
  - **Delilah deceives Samson.**
    Jgs 16:4–20
  - **David feigns madness.**
    1Sa 21:10–15
  - **Amnon deceives Tamar by feigning sickness.**
    2Sa 13:6–14
  - **Hushai deceives Absalom.**
    2Sa 16:15–19

- **Sanballat tries to deceive Nehemiah.**
  Ne 6:1–19
- **Absalom, when he avenged his sister.**
  2Sa 13:24–28
- **Absalom, when he began his conspiracy.**
  2Sa 15:7
- **The old prophet.**
  1Ki 13:18
- **Gehazi.**
  2Ki 5:20
- **Job's friends.**
  Job 6:15
- **Doeg.**
  Ps 52:2
- **Herod.**
  Mt 2:8
- **Pharisees.**
  Mt 22:16
- **Chief priests.**
  Mk 14:1
- **Lawyer.**
  Lk 10:25
- **Ananias and Sapphira.**
  Ac 5:1

See: Deceit
See: Falsehood
See: Falsehood, False Witness
See: Hypocrisy

- **Self.**

See: Confidence; false
See: Flattery

DECISION

Pr 4:25–27; Jn 15:4–5; Ro 8:38–39; 2Th 3:13–14; 2Ti 1:13–14; Tit 1:7–9; Heb 3:6–8; 1Pe 5:8–9; 2Pe 1:10–11; 3:17–18; Jude 1:20–21; Rev 2:10–11, 25–26; 3:11–12

Dt 30:19 — I call heaven and earth to record this day against you, *that* I have set before you life and death, blessing and cursing: therefore choose life, that both thou and thy seed may live:

Jos 23:8 — But cleave unto the LORD your God, as ye have done unto this day.

Jos 24:15 — And if it seem evil unto you to serve the LORD, choose you this day whom ye will serve; whether the gods which your fathers served that *were* on the other side of the flood, or the gods of the Amorites, in whose land ye dwell: but as for me and my house, we will serve the LORD.

1Sa 12:20 — And Samuel said unto the people, Fear not: ye have done all this wickedness: yet turn not aside from following the LORD, but serve the LORD with all your heart;

1Ki 18:21 — And Elijah came unto all the people, and said, How long halt ye between two opinions? if the LORD *be* God, follow him: but if Baal, *then* follow him. And the people answered him not a word.

Ps 37:34 — Wait on the LORD, and keep his way, and he shall exalt thee to inherit the land: when the wicked are cut off, thou shalt see *it*.

Ps 69:13 — But as for me, my prayer *is* unto thee, O LORD, *in* an acceptable time: O God, in the multitude of thy mercy hear me, in the truth of thy salvation.

Isa 50:7 — For the Lord GOD will help me; therefore shall I not be confounded: therefore have I set my face like a flint, and I know that I shall not be ashamed.

Mt 10:22 — And ye shall be hated of *all* men for my name's sake: but he that endureth to the end shall be saved.

Mt 11:6 — And blessed is *he*, whosoever shall not be offended in me.

Mt 24:13 — But he that shall endure unto the end, the same shall be saved.

Mt 25:23 — His lord said unto him, Well done, good and faithful servant; thou hast been faithful over a few things, I will make thee ruler over many things: enter thou into the joy of thy lord.

Mk 13:13 — And ye shall be hated of all *men* for my name's sake: but he that shall endure unto the end, the same shall be saved.

Lk 7:23 — And blessed is *he*, whosoever shall not be offended in me.

Jn 8:31 — Then said Jesus to those Jews which believed on him, If ye continue in my word, *then* are ye my disciples indeed;

Jn 15:7 — If ye abide in me, and my words abide in you, ye shall ask what ye will, and it shall be done unto you.

Jn 15:9 — As the Father hath loved me, so have I loved you: continue ye in my love.

Ac 11:23 — Who, when he came, and had seen the grace of God, was glad, and exhorted them all, that with purpose of heart they would cleave unto the Lord.

Ac 13:43 — Now when the congregation was broken up, many of the Jews and religious proselytes followed Paul and Barnabas: who, speaking to them, persuaded them to continue in the grace of God.

Ac 14:22 — Confirming the souls of the disciples, *and* exhorting them to continue in the faith, and that we must through much tribulation enter into the kingdom of God.

Ro 2:7 — To them who by patient continuance in well doing seek for glory and honour and immortality, eternal life:

Ro 11:22 — Behold therefore the goodness and severity of God: on them which fell, severity; but toward thee, goodness, if thou continue in *his* goodness: otherwise thou also shalt be cut off.

1Co 15:58 — Therefore, my beloved brethren, be ye stedfast, unmovable, always abounding in the work of the Lord, forasmuch as ye know that your labour is not in vain in the Lord.

1Co 16:13 — Watch ye, stand fast in the faith, quit you like men, be strong.

Gal 5:1 — Stand fast therefore in the liberty wherewith Christ hath made us free, and be not entangled again with the yoke of bondage.

Gal 5:10 — I have confidence in you through the Lord, that ye will be none otherwise minded: but he that troubleth you shall bear his judgment, whosoever he be.

Gal 6:9 — And let us not be weary in well doing: for in due season we shall reap, if we faint not.

Eph 4:14 — That we *henceforth* be no more children, tossed to and fro, and carried about with every wind of doctrine, by the sleight of men, *and* cunning craftiness, whereby they lie in wait to deceive;

Eph 6:13 — Wherefore take unto you the whole armour of God, that ye may be able to withstand in the evil day, and having done all, to stand.

Php 1:27 — Only let your conversation be as it becometh the gospel of Christ: that whether I come and see you, or else be absent, I may hear of your affairs, that ye stand fast in one spirit, with one mind striving together for the faith of the gospel;

Php 4:1 — Therefore, my brethren dearly beloved and longed for, my joy and crown, so stand fast in the Lord, *my* dearly beloved.

Col 1:23 — If ye continue in the faith grounded and settled, and *be* not moved away from the hope of the gospel, which ye have heard, *and* which was preached to every creature which is under heaven; whereof I Paul am made a minister;

1Th 3:8 — For now we live, if ye stand fast in the Lord.

1Th 3:13 — To the end he may stablish your hearts unblameable in holiness before God, even our Father, at the coming of our Lord Jesus Christ with all his saints.

2Th 2:15 — Therefore, brethren, stand fast, and hold the traditions which ye have been taught, whether by word, or our epistle.

2Th 2:17 — Comfort your hearts, and stablish you in every good word and work.

2Ti 2:1 — Thou therefore, my son, be strong in the grace that is in Christ Jesus.

2Ti 2:3 — Thou therefore endure hardness, as a good soldier of Jesus Christ.

2Ti 3:14 — But continue thou in the things which thou hast learned and hast been assured of, knowing of whom thou hast learned *them;*

Heb 2:1 — Therefore we ought to give the more earnest heed to the things which we have heard, lest at any time we should let *them* slip.

Heb 3:14 — For we are made partakers of Christ, if we hold the beginning of our confidence stedfast unto the end;

Heb 4:14 — Seeing then that we have a great high priest, that is passed into the heavens, Jesus the Son of God, let us hold fast *our* profession.

Heb 10:23 — Let us hold fast the profession of *our* faith without wavering; (for he is faithful that promised;)

Heb 10:35 — Cast not away therefore your confidence, which hath great recompence of reward.

Heb 12:1 — Wherefore seeing we also are compassed about with so great a cloud of witnesses, let us lay aside every weight, and the sin which doth so easily beset us, and let us run with patience the race that is set before us,

Heb 13:9 — Be not carried about with divers and strange doctrines. For *it is* a good thing that the heart be established with grace; not with meats, which have not profited them that have been occupied therein.

Heb 13:13 — Let us go forth therefore unto him without the camp, bearing his reproach.

Jas 1:4 — But let patience have *her* perfect work, that ye may be perfect and entire, wanting nothing.

Jas 1:12 — Blessed *is* the man that endureth temptation: for when he is tried, he shall receive the crown of life, which the Lord hath promised to them that love him.

Jas 1:25 — But whoso looketh into the perfect law of liberty, and continueth *therein,* he being not a forgetful hearer, but a doer of the work, this man shall be blessed in his deed.

1Pe 1:13 — Wherefore gird up the loins of your mind, be sober, and hope to the end for the grace that is to be brought unto you at the revelation of Jesus Christ;

1Jn 2:24 — Let that therefore abide in you, which ye have heard from the beginning. If that which ye have heard from the beginning shall remain in you, ye also shall continue in the Son, and in the Father.

1Jn 2:28 — And now, little children, abide in him; that, when he shall appear, we may have confidence, and not be ashamed before him at his coming.

2Jn 1:8 — Look to yourselves, that we lose not those things which we have wrought, but that we receive a full reward.

Rev 2:7 — <u>He that hath an ear, let him hear what the Spirit saith unto the churches; To him that overcometh will I give to eat of the tree of life, which is in the midst of the paradise of God.</u>

Rev 2:17 — <u>He that hath an ear, let him hear what the Spirit saith unto the churches; To him that overcometh will I give to eat of the hidden manna, and will give him a white stone, and in the stone a new name written, which no man knoweth saving he that receiveth *it.*</u>

Rev 3:5 — <u>He that overcometh, the same shall be clothed in white raiment; and I will not blot out his name out of the book of life, but I will confess his name before my Father, and before his angels.</u>

Rev 3:21 — <u>To him that overcometh will I grant to sit with me in my throne, even as I also overcame, and am set down with my Father in his throne.</u>

Rev 15:2 — And I saw as it were a sea of glass mingled with fire: and them that had gotten the victory over the beast, and over his image, and over his mark, *and* over the number of his name, stand on the sea of glass, having the harps of God.

Rev 21:7 — He that overcometh shall inherit all things; and I will be his God, and he shall be my son.

Rev 22:11 — He that is unjust, let him be unjust still: and he which is filthy, let him be filthy still: and he that is righteous, let him be righteous still: and he that is holy, let him be holy still.

↞See: Character of Saints

↞See: Perseverance

↞See: Stability

↞See: Indecision

↞See: Instability

• Exhortation to.

Mt 8:21–22; Lk 9:59–62; Col 2:6–7; 1Ti 6:11–14

Jos 1:7 — Only be thou strong and very courageous, that thou mayest observe to do according to all the law, which Moses my servant commanded thee: turn not from it *to* the right hand or *to* the left, that thou mayest prosper whithersoever thou goest.

1Ch 16:15 — Be ye mindful always of his covenant; the word *which* he commanded to a thousand generations;

2Ch 19:11 — And, behold, Amariah the chief priest is over you in all matters of the LORD; and Zebadiah the son of Ishmael, the ruler of the house of Judah, for all the king's matters: also the Levites *shall be* officers before you. Deal courageously, and the LORD shall be with the good.

Mt 4:17 — From that time Jesus began to preach, and to say, Repent: for the kingdom of heaven is at hand.

Mt 6:24 — No man can serve two masters: for either he will hate the one, and love the other; or else he will hold to the one, and despise the other. Ye cannot serve God and mammon.

Mt 10:32 — Whosoever therefore shall confess me before men, him will I confess also before my Father which is in heaven.

Mt 12:30 — He that is not with me is against me; and he that gathereth not with me scattereth abroad.

Lk 11:23 — He that is not with me is against me: and he that gathereth not with me scattereth.

Lk 12:8 — Also I say unto you, Whosoever shall confess me before men, him shall the Son of man also confess before the angels of God:

Lk 16:13 — No servant can serve two masters: for either he will hate the one, and love the other; or else he will hold to the one, and despise the other. Ye cannot serve God and mammon.

Lk 17:32 — Remember Lot's wife.

- **Instances of.**
  - **Abel.**
    Heb 11:4
  - **Enoch.**
    Heb 11:5–6
  - **Noah.**
    Heb 11:7
  - **Abraham.**
    Heb 11:8, 17–19
  - **Jacob.**
    Ge 28:20–21
  - **Joseph.**
    Ge 39:7–20
  - **Moses.**
    Nu 12:7; Heb 3:5; 11:24–26
  - **Israelites.**
    Ex 19:7–8; 24:3, 7; Dt 4:4; 5:27; 26:17; 29:12; Jos 22:34; 24:21–25; 1Ki 19:18; 2Ki 11:17; 2Ch 11:16; 13:10–11; 15:12, 15; 23:16; 29:10; Ezr 10:3–44; Ne 9:38–10:39; Ps 50:5; Jer 34:15; 42:5–6; 50:5; Hos 11:12
  - **Caleb.**
    Nu 14:6–10, 24, 37–38; Dt 1:36; Jos 14:14
  - **Balaam.**
    Nu 22:15–18
  - **Phinehas.**
    Nu 25:7–13
  - **Joshua.**
    Jos 24:15, 18–24
  - **Gideon.**
    Jgs 6:25–7:25
  - **Ruth.**
    Ru 1:16
  - **Saul.**
    1Sa 11:4–7
  - **Abigail.**
    1Sa 25:4–37
  - **David.**
    1Sa 17:20–54; 2Sa 22:22–24
  - **Psalmist.**
    Ps 17:3; 26:6, 11; 40:9–10; 56:12; 57:7–8; 66:16; 71:17; 86:11; 101:2–3; 108:1; 116:9, 13–14, 16; 119:8, 30–31, 38, 44–46, 57, 94, 106, 115, 125, 145–146; 143:12
  - **A prophet.**
    1Ki 13:8–10
  - **Elijah.**
    1Ki 18:22
  - **Jehoshaphat.**
    1Ki 22:7; 2Ch 18:6
  - **Naaman.**
    2Ki 5:15, 17
  - **Jehu.**
    2Ki 9:11–10:36
  - **Hezekiah.**
    2Ki 18:6; 2Ch 15:17
  - **Josiah.**
    2Ki 22:2; 23:3, 25; 2Ch 34:31
  - **Nehemiah.**
    Ne 2:1–20
  - **Mordecai.**
    Est 3:2–3
  - **Esther.**
    Est 4:16
  - **Job.**
    Job 2:3; 23:11–12
  - **Matthew.**
    Mt 9:9
  - **Joseph.**
    Mk 15:43
  - **Nathanael.**
    Jn 1:49
  - **Martha.**
    Jn 11:27
  - **The disciples.**
    Lk 18:28; Jn 6:68–69; Ac 2:42
  - **Paul.**
    Ac 9:29; 26:6; Ro 1:16; Php 1:20–21; Col 2:5; 2Ti 4:7–8
  - **Ephesians.**
    Rev 2:2–3
  - **Church of Sardis.**
    Rev 3:4, 8, 10
  - **Saints.**
    Rev 14:4

✦See: **Perseverance**

✦See: **Stability**

✦See: **Zeal, Religious**

• Valley of.

Joel 3:14 — Multitudes, multitudes in the valley of decision: for the day of the LORD *is* near in the valley of decision.

DECREES

• Of the Medes, irrevocable.

Da 6:14–15

• Ecclesiastical, of the church at Jerusalem.

Ac 15:28–29

Ac 16:14 — And a certain woman named Lydia, a seller of purple, of the city of Thyatira, which worshipped God, heard *us:* whose heart the Lord opened, that she attended unto the things which were spoken of Paul.

• Divine.

✦See: **Predestination**

DEDAN

• Son of Raamah.

Ge 10:7 — And the sons of Cush; Seba, and Havilah, and Sabtah, and Raamah, and Sabtechah: and the sons of Raamah; Sheba, and Dedan.

1Ch 1:9 — And the sons of Cush; Seba, and Havilah, and Sabta, and Raamah, and Sabtecha. And the sons of Raamah; Sheba, and Dedan.

• Son of Jokshan.

Ge 25:3 — And Jokshan begat Sheba, and Dedan. And the sons of Dedan were Asshurim, and Letushim, and Leummim.

1Ch 1:32 — Now the sons of Keturah, Abraham's concubine: she bare Zimran, and Jokshan, and Medan, and Midian, and Ishbak, and Shuah. And the sons of Jokshan; Sheba, and Dedan.

• A country, probably bordering on Edom.

Eze 20:1–49

Jer 49:8 — Flee ye, turn back, dwell deep, O inhabitants of Dedan; for I will bring the calamity of Esau upon him, the time *that* I will visit him.

Eze 25:13 — Therefore thus saith the Lord GOD; I will also stretch out mine hand upon Edom, and will cut off man and beast from it; and I will make it desolate from Teman; and they of Dedan shall fall by the sword.

Eze 27:15 — The men of Dedan *were* thy merchants; many isles *were* the merchandise of thine hand: they brought thee *for* a present horns of ivory and ebony.

Eze 38:13 — Sheba, and Dedan, and the merchants of Tarshish, with all the young lions thereof, shall say unto thee, Art thou come to take a spoil? hast thou gathered thy company to take a prey? to carry away silver and gold, to take away cattle and goods, to take a great spoil?

DEDANIM • Descendants of Dedan.

Isa 21:13 — The burden upon Arabia. In the forest in Arabia shall ye lodge, O ye travelling companies of Dedanim.

DEDICATION

• Law concerning dedicated things.

Le 27:1–34; 1Ch 26:26–27

Nu 18:14 — Every thing devoted in Israel shall be thine.

• Must be without blemish.

Le 22:18–23

Mal 1:14 — But cursed *be* the deceiver, which hath in his flock a male, and voweth, and sacrificeth unto the LORD a corrupt thing: for I *am* a great King, saith the LORD of hosts, and my name *is* dreadful among the heathen.

• Not redeemable.

Le 27:28–29

• Must be voluntary.

Le 1:3 — If his offering *be* a burnt sacrifice of the herd, let him offer a male without blemish: he shall offer it of his own voluntary will at the door of the tabernacle of the congregation before the LORD.

Le 22:19 — *Ye shall offer* at your own will a male without blemish, of the beeves, of the sheep, or of the goats.

✦See: **Offerings**

✦See: **Vows**

• Of the tabernacle.

Nu 7:1–89

• Of Solomon's temple.

1Ki 8:1–66

2Ch 7:5 — And king Solomon offered a sacrifice of twenty and two thousand oxen, and an hundred and twenty thousand sheep: so the king and all the people dedicated the house of God.

• Of the second temple.

Ezr 6:16–17

• Of the wall of Jerusalem.

Ne 12:27–43

• Of houses.

Dt 20:5 — And the officers shall speak unto the people, saying, What man *is there* that hath built a new house, and hath not dedicated it? let him go and return to his house, lest he die in the battle, and another man dedicate it.

• Of Samuel by his mother.

1Sa 1:11 — And she vowed a vow, and said, O LORD of hosts, if thou wilt indeed look on the affliction of thine handmaid, and remember me, and not forget thine handmaid, but wilt give unto thine handmaid a man child, then I will give him unto the LORD all the days of his life, and there shall no razor come upon his head.

1Sa 1:22 — But Hannah went not up; for she said unto her husband, *I will not go up* until the child be weaned, and *then* I will bring him, that he may appear before the LORD, and there abide for ever.

• **Of self.**

↠**See: Consecration**

• **For instances of liberality in dedicated things.**

↠**See: Liberality**

• **Feast of.**

2Ch 7:8–10

1Ki 8:65 — And at that time Solomon held a feast, and all Israel with him, a great congregation, from the entering in of Hamath unto the river of Egypt, before the LORD our God, seven days and seven days, *even* fourteen days.

Jn 10:22 — And it was at Jerusalem the feast of the dedication, and it was winter.

DEED

• **To land.**

Jer 44:1–30

Jer 32:12 — And I gave the evidence of the purchase unto Baruch the son of Neriah, the son of Maaseiah, in the sight of Hanameel mine uncle's *son,* and in the presence of the witnesses that subscribed the book of the purchase, before all the Jews that sat in the court of the prison.

Jer 32:14 — Thus saith the LORD of hosts, the God of Israel; Take these evidences, this evidence of the purchase, both which is sealed, and this evidence which is open; and put them in an earthen vessel, that they may continue many days.

↠**See: Land**

DEER

• **Called also Fallow Deer, Hart, Hind, Roebuck.**

• **Designated among the clean animals, to be eaten.**

Dt 12:15 — Notwithstanding thou mayest kill and eat flesh in all thy gates, whatsoever thy soul lusteth after, according to the blessing of the LORD thy God which he hath given thee: the unclean and the clean may eat thereof, as of the roebuck, and as of the hart.

Dt 14:5 — The hart, and the roebuck, and the fallow deer, and the wild goat, and the pygarg, and the wild ox, and the chamois.

• **Provided for Solomon's household.**

1Ki 4:23 — Ten fat oxen, and twenty oxen out of the pastures, and an hundred sheep, beside harts, and roebucks, and fallowdeer, and fatted fowl.

• **Fleetness of.**

2Sa 2:18 — And there were three sons of Zeruiah there, Joab, and Abishai, and Asahel: and Asahel *was as* light of foot as a wild roe.

1Ch 12:8 — And of the Gadites there separated themselves unto David into the hold to the wilderness men of might, *and* men of war *fit* for the battle, that could handle shield and buckler, whose faces *were like* the faces of lions, and *were* as swift as the roes upon the mountains;

Pr 6:5 — Deliver thyself as a roe from the hand *of the hunter,* and as a bird from the hand of the fowler.

SS 8:14 — Make haste, my beloved, and be thou like to a roe or to a young hart upon the mountains of spices.

Isa 35:6 — Then shall the lame *man* leap as an hart, and the tongue of the dumb sing: for in the wilderness shall waters break out, and streams in the desert.

• **Surefootedness of.**

2Sa 22:34 — He maketh my feet like hinds' *feet:* and setteth me upon my high places.

• **Gentleness of.**

Pr 5:19 — *Let her be as* the loving hind and pleasant roe; let her breasts satisfy thee at all times; and be thou ravished always with her love.

DEFENSE

• **An argument made before a court.**

• **Of Jeremiah.**

Jer 26:12–16

• **Of Peter.**

Ac 4:8–13; 5:23–29

• **Of Stephen.**

Ac 7:1–60

• **Of Paul.**

Ac 22:1–23:6; 24:10–21; 26:1–23

• **Military defenses.**

↠**See: Fort**

↠**See: Armies**

DEFILEMENT

• **Laws relating to.**

Le 7:18–21; 22:2–7

Le 11:43 — Ye shall not make yourselves abominable with any creeping thing that creepeth, neither shall ye make yourselves unclean with them, that ye should be defiled thereby.

• **Caused by**

• **Leprosy.**

Le 13:44–46; 14:1–57; 22:4–7

Le 13:3 — And the priest shall look on the plague in the skin of the flesh: and *when* the hair in the plague is turned white, and the plague in sight *be* deeper than the skin of his flesh, it *is* a plague of leprosy: and the priest shall look on him, and pronounce him unclean.

• **Gonorrhea.**

Le 15:1–15

Le 22:4 — What man soever of the seed of Aaron *is* a leper, or hath a running issue; he shall not eat of the holy things, until he be clean. And whoso toucheth any thing *that is* unclean *by* the dead, or a man whose seed goeth from him;

• **Copulation.**

Le 15:17 — And every garment, and every skin, whereon is the seed of copulation, shall be washed with water, and be unclean until the even.

- **Spermatorrhea.**
  Le 15:16–17
- **Childbirth.**
  Le 12:2–8
  Lk 2:22 — And when the days of her purification according to the law of Moses were accomplished, they brought him to Jerusalem, to present *him* to the Lord;
- **Menses.**
  Le 15:19–33
  2Sa 11:4 — And David sent messengers, and took her; and she came in unto him, and he lay with her; for she was purified from her uncleanness: and she returned unto her house.
- **Touching the dead.**
  Nu 19:11–22; 31:19–20
- **Touching carcass of any unclean animal.**
  Le 11:39–40; 17:15–16
  Le 22:8 — That which dieth of itself, or is torn *with beasts,* he shall not eat to defile himself therewith: I *am* the LORD.
- **Touching carcass of an unclean thing.**
  Le 5:2–13; 11:24–2831–38; 14:46–57; 15:5–11; Dt 23:10–11
  Le 11:8 — Of their flesh shall ye not eat, and their carcase shall ye not touch; they *are* unclean to you.
- **Slaying in battle.**
  Nu 31:19–20

• Contact with sinners falsely supposed to cause.

Jn 18:28 — Then led they Jesus from Caiaphas unto the hall of judgment: and it was early; and they themselves went not into the judgment hall, lest they should be defiled; but that they might eat the passover.

• Of priests.

Nu 19:7–10; Eze 44:25–26

Le 16:26 — And he that let go the goat for the scapegoat shall wash his clothes, and bathe his flesh in water, and afterward come into the camp.

Le 16:28 — And he that burneth them shall wash his clothes, and bathe his flesh in water, and afterward he shall come into the camp.

• Egyptian usage, concerning.

Ge 43:32 — And they set on for him by himself, and for them by themselves, and for the Egyptians, which did eat with him, by themselves: because the Egyptians might not eat bread with the Hebrews; for that *is* an abomination unto the Egyptians.

See: Ablution

See: Purification

See: Uncleanness

DEFORMITY See: Blemish

DEGREES

• Or steps in the dial of Ahaz.

2Ki 20:9–11

DEHAVITES

Ezr 4:9 — Then *wrote* Rehum the chancellor, and Shimshai the scribe, and the rest of their companions; the Dinaites, the Apharsathchites, the Tarpelites, the Apharsites, the Archevites, the Babylonians, the Susanchites, the Dehavites, *and* the Elamites,

DEKAR • Father of one of Solomon's purveyors.

1Ki 4:9 — The son of Dekar, in Makaz, and in Shaalbim, and Beth-shemesh, and Elon-beth-hanan:

DELAIAH

• Head of the twenty-third division of the priestly order.

1Ch 24:18 — The three and twentieth to Delaiah, the four and twentieth to Maaziah.

• A prince of Judah.

Jer 36:12 — Then he went down into the king's house, into the scribe's chamber: and, lo, all the princes sat there, *even* Elishama the scribe, and Delaiah the son of Shemaiah, and Elnathan the son of Achbor, and Gemariah the son of Shaphan, and Zedekiah the son of Hananiah, and all the princes.

Jer 36:25 — Nevertheless Elnathan and Delaiah and Gemariah had made intercession to the king that he would not burn the roll: but he would not hear them.

• A progenitor of certain Babylonish captives.

Ezr 2:60 — The children of Delaiah, the children of Tobiah, the children of Nekoda, six hundred fifty and two.

Ne 7:62 — The children of Delaiah, the children of Tobiah, the children of Nekoda, six hundred forty and two.

• Father of a false prophet.

Ne 6:10 — Afterward I came unto the house of Shemaiah the son of Delaiah the son of Mehetabeel, who *was* shut up; and he said, Let us meet together in the house of God, within the temple, and let us shut the doors of the temple: for they will come to slay thee; yea, in the night will they come to slay thee.

• A descendant of the royal line of Judah, called also Dalaiah.

1Ch 3:24 — And the sons of Elioenai *were,* Hodaiah, and Eliashib, and Pelaiah, and Akkub, and Johanan, and Dalaiah, and Anani, seven.

DELEGATE

Ex 18:13–26; Ac 6:1–6; Eph 4:11–16

DELILAH • Samson's paramour.

Jgs 16:4–18

DELIVERANCE

See: Afflictions

See: God, Providence of

See: Prayer; answered

DELIVERER

• Appellation of Jesus.

Ro 11:26 — And so all Israel shall be saved: as it is written, There shall come out of Sion the Deliverer, and shall turn away ungodliness from Jacob:

DELUGE ↞See: Flood

DELUSION

• Self.

↞See: Self-Delusion

DEMAGOGISM

• Instances of.

• Absalom.

2Sa 15:2–6

• Felix.

Ac 24:27

• Herod.

Ac 12:3

• Pilate.

Mt 27:17–26; Mk 15:15; Lk 23:13–24; Jn 18:38–40; 19:6–13

DEMAS

• A companion of Paul.

Col 4:14 — Luke, the beloved physician, and Demas, greet you.

Phm 1:24 — Marcus, Aristarchus, Demas, Lucas, my fellowlabourers.

• Deserts Paul.

2Ti 4:10 — For Demas hath forsaken me, having loved this present world, and is departed unto Thessalonica; Crescens to Galatia, Titus unto Dalmatia.

DEMETRIUS • A silversmith, noted for raising a riot.

Ac 19:24–38

3Jn 1:12 — Demetrius hath good report of all *men,* and of the truth itself: yea, and we *also* bear record; and ye know that our record is true.

DEMONS

• Worship of.

1Co 10:20–21

Le 17:7 — And they shall no more offer their sacrifices unto devils, after whom they have gone a whoring. This shall be a statute for ever unto them throughout their generations.

Dt 32:17 — They sacrificed unto devils, not to God; to gods whom they knew not, to new *gods that* came newly up, whom your fathers feared not.

2Ch 11:15 — And he ordained him priests for the high places, and for the devils, and for the calves which he had made.

Ps 106:37 — Yea, they sacrificed their sons and their daughters unto devils,

Mt 4:9 — And saith unto him, All these things will I give thee, if thou wilt fall down and worship me.

Lk 4:7 — If thou therefore wilt worship me, all shall be thine.

1Ti 4:1 — Now the Spirit speaketh expressly, that in the latter times some shall depart from the faith, giving heed to seducing spirits, and doctrines of devils;

Rev 13:4 — And they worshipped the dragon which gave power unto the beast: and they worshipped the beast, saying, Who *is* like unto the beast? who is able to make war with him?

• Worship of, forbidden.

Le 17:7 — And they shall no more offer their sacrifices unto devils, after whom they have gone a whoring. This shall be a statute for ever unto them throughout their generations.

Zec 13:2 — And it shall come to pass in that day, saith the LORD of hosts, *that* I will cut off the names of the idols out of the land, and they shall no more be remembered: and also I will cause the prophets and the unclean spirit to pass out of the land.

Rev 9:20 — And the rest of the men which were not killed by these plagues yet repented not of the works of their hands, that they should not worship devils, and idols of gold, and silver, and brass, and stone, and of wood: which neither can see, nor hear, nor walk:

• Possession by, instances of.

• Saul.

1Sa 16:14–23; 18:10–11; 19:9–10

• Two men of the Gergesens.

Mt 8:28–34; Mk 5:2–20

• The dumb man.

Mt 9:32–33

• The blind and dumb man.

Mt 12:22 — Then was brought unto him one possessed with a devil, blind, and dumb: and he healed him, insomuch that the blind and dumb both spake and saw.

Lk 11:14 — And he was casting out a devil, and it was dumb. And it came to pass, when the devil was gone out, the dumb spake; and the people wondered.

• The daughter of the Syrophenician.

Mt 15:22–29; Mk 7:25–30

• The lunatic child.

Mt 17:14–18; Mk 9:17–27; Lk 9:37–42

• The man in the synagogue.

Mk 1:23–26; Lk 4:33–35

• Mary Magdalene.

Lk 8:2–3

Mk 16:9 — Now when *Jesus* was risen early the first *day* of the week, he appeared first to Mary Magdalene, out of whom he had cast seven devils.

• The herd of swine.

Mt 8:30–32

• Cast out by Jesus.

Mt 4:24 — And his fame went throughout all Syria: and they brought unto him all sick people that were taken with divers diseases and torments, and those which were possessed with devils, and those which were lunatick, and those that had the palsy; and he healed them.

Mt 8:16 — When the even was come, they brought unto him many that were possessed with devils: and he cast out the spirits with *his* word, and healed all that were sick:

Mk 3:22 — And the scribes which came down from Jerusalem said, He hath Beelzebub, and by the prince of the devils casteth he out devils.

Lk 4:41 — And devils also came out of many, crying out, and saying, Thou art Christ the Son of God. And he rebuking *them* suffered them not to speak: for they knew that he was Christ.

• Power over, given the disciples.

Mt 10:1 — And when he had called unto *him* his twelve disciples, he gave them power *against* unclean spirits, to cast them out, and to heal all manner of sickness and all manner of disease.

Mk 6:7 — And he called *unto him* the twelve, and began to send them forth by two and two; and gave them power over unclean spirits;

Mk 16:17 — And these signs shall follow them that believe; In my name shall they cast out devils; they shall speak with new tongues;

• Cast out by the disciples.

Mk 9:38 — And John answered him, saying, Master, we saw one casting out devils in thy name, and he followeth not us: and we forbad him, because he followeth not us.

Lk 10:17 — And the seventy returned again with joy, saying, Lord, even the devils are subject unto us through thy name.

• Cast out by Peter.

Ac 5:16 — There came also a multitude *out* of the cities round about unto Jerusalem, bringing sick folks, and them which were vexed with unclean spirits: and they were healed every one.

• Cast out by Paul.

Ac 16:16–18

Ac 19:12 — So that from his body were brought unto the sick handkerchiefs or aprons, and the diseases departed from them, and the evil spirits went out of them.

• Cast out by Philip.

Ac 8:7 — For unclean spirits, crying with loud voice, came out of many that were possessed *with them:* and many taken with palsies, and that were lame, were healed.

• Disciples could not expel.

Mk 9:28–29

Mk 9:18 — And wheresoever he taketh him, he teareth him: and he foameth, and gnasheth with his teeth, and pineth away: and I spake to thy disciples that they should cast him out; and they could not.

• Sceva's sons exorcise.

Ac 19:13–16

• Parable of the man repossessed.

Mt 12:43–45

• Jesus falsely accused of being possessed of.

Mk 3:22–30

Jn 7:20 — The people answered and said, Thou hast a devil: who goeth about to kill thee?

Jn 8:48 — Then answered the Jews, and said unto him, Say we not well that thou art a Samaritan, and hast a devil?

Jn 10:20 — And many of them said, He hath a devil, and is mad; why hear ye him?

• Testify to the divinity of Jesus.

Mk 1:23–24

Mt 8:29 — And, behold, they cried out, saying, What have we to do with thee, Jesus, thou Son of God? art thou come hither to torment us before the time?

Mk 3:11 — And unclean spirits, when they saw him, fell down before him, and cried, saying, Thou art the Son of God.

Mk 5:7 — And cried with a loud voice, and said, What have I to do with thee, Jesus, *thou* Son of the most high God? I adjure thee by God, that thou torment me not.

Lk 8:28 — When he saw Jesus, he cried out, and fell down before him, and with a loud voice said, What have I to do with thee, Jesus, *thou* Son of God most high? I beseech thee, torment me not.

Ac 19:15 — And the evil spirit answered and said, Jesus I know, and Paul I know; but who are ye?

• Adversaries of men.

Mt 12:45 — Then goeth he, and taketh with himself seven other spirits more wicked than himself, and they enter in and dwell there: and the last *state* of that man is worse than the first. Even so shall it be also unto this wicked generation.

• Sent to foment trouble between Abimelech and the Shechemites.

Jgs 9:23 — Then God sent an evil spirit between Abimelech and the men of Shechem; and the men of Shechem dealt treacherously with Abimelech:

• Messages given false prophets by.

1Ki 22:21–23

• Believe and tremble.

Jas 2:19 — Thou believest that there is one God; thou doest well: the devils also believe, and tremble.

• To be judged at the general judgment.

Mt 8:29 — And, behold, they cried out, saying, What have we to do with thee, Jesus, thou Son of God? art thou come hither to torment us before the time?

2Pe 2:4 — For if God spared not the angels that sinned, but cast *them* down to hell, and delivered *them* into chains of darkness, to be reserved unto judgment;

Jude 1:6 — And the angels which kept not their first estate, but left their own habitation, he hath reserved in everlasting chains under darkness unto the judgment of the great day.

• Punishment of.

Rev 12:7–9

Mt 8:29 — And, behold, they cried out, saying, What have we to do with thee, Jesus, thou Son of God? art thou come hither to torment us before the time?

Mt 25:41 — Then shall he say also unto them on the left hand, Depart from me, ye cursed, into everlasting fire, prepared for the devil and his angels:

Lk 8:28 — When he saw Jesus, he cried out, and fell down before him, and with a loud voice said, What have I to do with thee, Jesus, *thou* Son of God most high? I beseech thee, torment me not.

2Pe 2:4 — For if God spared not the angels that sinned, but cast *them* down to hell, and delivered *them* into chains of darkness, to be reserved unto judgment;

Jude 1:6 — And the angels which kept not their first estate, but left their own habitation, he hath reserved in everlasting chains under darkness unto the judgment of the great day.

See: Satan

DENOMINATION

1Co 1:12 — Now this I say, that every one of you saith, I am of Paul; and I of Apollos; and I of Cephas; and I of Christ.

1Co 3:4 — For while one saith, I am of Paul; and another, I *am* of Apollos; are ye not carnal?

1Co 3:12 — Now if any man build upon this foundation gold, silver, precious stones, wood, hay, stubble;

DENS

• Used as places of refuge.

Jgs 6:2 — And the hand of Midian prevailed against Israel: *and* because of the Midianites the children of Israel made them the dens which *are* in the mountains, and caves, and strong holds.

Heb 11:38 — (Of whom the world was not worthy:) they wandered in deserts, and *in* mountains, and *in* dens and caves of the earth.

Rev 6:15 — And the kings of the earth, and the great men, and the rich men, and the chief captains, and the mighty men, and every bondman, and every free man, hid themselves in the dens and in the rocks of the mountains;

DENYING JESUS **See: Jesus, Rejected**

DEPRAVITY OF MAN

Ge 6:5–7, 11–13; Job 4:17–19; 9:2–3, 29–31; 15:14–16; 25:4–6; Ps 14:1–3; 53:1–3; 58:1–5; Isa 1:5–6; 42:6–7; Eze 36:25–26; 37:1–3; Mic 7:2–4; Mt 12:34–35; Mk 7:21–23; Jn 1:10–11; Ro 3:9–19; 5:12–14; 6:19–20; 7:13–15, 18–21; 8:5–8; 1Co 5:9–10; 2Co 3:4–5; Gal 3:10–11; 5:19–21; Eph 2:1–3, 11–12; 4:17–19

Ge 8:21 — And the LORD smelled a sweet savour; and the LORD said in his heart, I will not again curse the ground any more for man's sake; for the imagination of man's heart *is* evil from his youth; neither will I again smite any more every thing living, as I have done.

Dt 32:10 — He found him in a desert land, and in the waste howling wilderness; he led him about, he instructed him, he kept him as the apple of his eye.

2Ch 6:36 — If they sin against thee, (for *there is* no man which sinneth not,) and thou be angry with them, and deliver them over before *their* enemies, and they carry them away captives unto a land far off or near;

Job 9:20 — If I justify myself, mine own mouth shall condemn me: *if I say, I am* perfect, it shall also prove me perverse.

Job 11:12 — For vain man would be wise, though man be born *like* a wild ass's colt.

Job 14:4 — Who can bring a clean *thing* out of an unclean? not one.

Ps 5:9 — For *there is* no faithfulness in their mouth; their inward part *is* very wickedness; their throat *is* an open sepulchre; they flatter with their tongue.

Ps 51:5 — Behold, I was shapen in iniquity; and in sin did my mother conceive me.

Ps 94:11 — The LORD knoweth the thoughts of man, that they *are* vanity.

Ps 130:3 — If thou, LORD, shouldest mark iniquities, O Lord, who shall stand?

Ps 143:2 — And enter not into judgment with thy servant: for in thy sight shall no man living be justified.

Pr 10:20 — The tongue of the just *is as* choice silver: the heart of the wicked *is* little worth.

Pr 20:6 — Most men will proclaim every one his own goodness: but a faithful man who can find?

Pr 20:9 — Who can say, I have made my heart clean, I am pure from my sin?

Pr 21:8 — The way of man *is* froward and strange: but *as for* the pure, his work *is* right.

Ecc 7:20 — For *there is* not a just man upon earth, that doeth good, and sinneth not.

Ecc 7:29 — Lo, this only have I found, that God hath made man upright; but they have sought out many inventions.

Ecc 8:11 — Because sentence against an evil work is not executed speedily, therefore the heart of the sons of men is fully set in them to do evil.

Ecc 9:3 — This *is* an evil among all *things* that are done under the sun, that *there is* one event unto all: yea, also the heart of the sons of men is full of evil, and madness is in their heart while they live, and after that *they go* to the dead.

Isa 43:8 — Bring forth the blind people that have eyes, and the deaf that have ears.

Isa 48:8 — Yea, thou heardest not; yea, thou knewest not; yea, from that time *that* thine ear was not opened: for I knew that thou wouldest deal very treacherously, and wast called a transgressor from the womb.

Isa 51:1 — Hearken to me, ye that follow after righteousness, ye that seek the LORD: look unto the rock *whence* ye are hewn, and to the hole of the pit *whence* ye are digged.

Isa 53:6 — All we like sheep have gone astray; we have turned every one to his own way; and the LORD hath laid on him the iniquity of us all.

Isa 64:6 — But we are all as an unclean *thing,* and all our righteousnesses *are* as filthy rags; and we all do fade as a leaf; and our iniquities, like the wind, have taken us away.

Jer 2:22 — For though thou wash thee with nitre, and take thee much sope, *yet* thine iniquity is marked before me, saith the Lord GOD.

Jer 2:29 — Wherefore will ye plead with me? ye all have transgressed against me, saith the LORD.

Jer 6:7 — As a fountain casteth out her waters, so she casteth out her wickedness: violence and spoil is heard in her; before me continually is grief and wounds.

Jer 13:23 — Can the Ethiopian change his skin, or the leopard his spots? *then* may ye also do good, that are accustomed to do evil.

Jer 16:12 — And ye have done worse than your fathers; for, behold, ye walk every one after the imagination of his evil heart, that they may not hearken unto me:

Jer 17:9 — The heart *is* deceitful above all *things,* and desperately wicked: who can know it?

Eze 16:6 — And when I passed by thee, and saw thee polluted in thine own blood, I said unto thee *when thou wast* in thy blood, Live; yea, I said unto thee *when thou wast* in thy blood, Live.

Hos 6:7 — But they like men have transgressed the covenant: there have they dealt treacherously against me.

Hos 14:9 — Who *is* wise, and he shall understand these *things?* prudent, and he shall know them? for the ways of the LORD *are* right, and the just shall walk in them: but the transgressors shall fall therein.

Mt 7:17 — Even so every good tree bringeth forth good fruit; but a corrupt tree bringeth forth evil fruit.

Mt 15:19 — For out of the heart proceed evil thoughts, murders, adulteries, fornications, thefts, false witness, blasphemies:

Lk 1:79 — To give light to them that sit in darkness and *in* the shadow of death, to guide our feet into the way of peace.

Jn 3:19 — And this is the condemnation, that light is come into the world, and men loved darkness rather than light, because their deeds were evil.

Jn 8:23 — And he said unto them, Ye are from beneath; I am from above: ye are of this world; I am not of this world.

Jn 14:17 — *Even* the Spirit of truth; whom the world cannot receive, because it seeth him not, neither knoweth him: but ye know him; for he dwelleth with you, and shall be in you.

Ac 8:23 — For I perceive that thou art in the gall of bitterness, and *in* the bond of iniquity.

Ro 2:1 — Therefore thou art inexcusable, O man, whosoever thou art that judgest: for wherein thou judgest another, thou condemnest thyself; for thou that judgest doest the same things.

Ro 3:23 — For all have sinned, and come short of the glory of God;

Ro 5:6 — For when we were yet without strength, in due time Christ died for the ungodly.

Ro 6:6 — Knowing this, that our old man is crucified with *him,* that the body of sin might be destroyed, that henceforth we should not serve sin.

Ro 6:17 — But God be thanked, that ye were the servants of sin, but ye have obeyed from the heart that form of doctrine which was delivered you.

Ro 7:5 — For when we were in the flesh, the motions of sins, which were by the law, did work in our members to bring forth fruit unto death.

Ro 7:11 — For sin, taking occasion by the commandment, deceived me, and by it slew *me.*

Ro 7:23 — But I see another law in my members, warring against the law of my mind, and bringing me into captivity to the law of sin which is in my members.

Ro 7:25 — I thank God through Jesus Christ our Lord. So then with the mind I myself serve the law of God; but with the flesh the law of sin.

Ro 8:13 — For if ye live after the flesh, ye shall die: but if ye through the Spirit do mortify the deeds of the body, ye shall live.

Ro 11:32 — For God hath concluded them all in unbelief, that he might have mercy upon all.

1Co 2:14 — But the natural man receiveth not the things of the Spirit of God: for they are foolishness unto him: neither can he know *them,* because they are spiritually discerned.

1Co 3:3 — For ye are yet carnal: for whereas *there is* among you envying, and strife, and divisions, are ye not carnal, and walk as men?

2Co 5:14 — For the love of Christ constraineth us; because we thus judge, that if one died for all, then were all dead:

Gal 3:22 — But the scripture hath concluded all under sin, that the promise by faith of Jesus Christ might be given to them that believe.

Gal 5:17 — For the flesh lusteth against the Spirit, and the Spirit against the flesh: and these are contrary the one to the other: so that ye cannot do the things that ye would.

Eph 4:22 — That ye put off concerning the former conversation the old man, which is corrupt according to the deceitful lusts;

Eph 5:8 — For ye were sometimes darkness, but now *are ye* light in the Lord: walk as children of light:

Eph 5:14 — Wherefore he saith, Awake thou that sleepest, and arise from the dead, and Christ shall give thee light.

Col 1:13 — Who hath delivered us from the power of darkness, and hath translated *us* into the kingdom of his dear Son:

Col 1:21 — And you, that were sometime alienated and enemies in *your* mind by wicked works, yet now hath he reconciled:

Col 2:13 — And you, being dead in your sins and the uncircumcision of your flesh, hath he quickened together with him, having forgiven you all trespasses;

Col 3:5 — Mortify therefore your members which are upon the earth; fornication, uncleanness, inordinate affection, evil concupiscence, and covetousness, which is idolatry:

Col 3:7 — In the which ye also walked some time, when ye lived in them.

2Ti 2:26 — And *that* they may recover themselves out of the snare of the devil, who are taken captive by him at his will.

Tit 3:3 — For we ourselves also were sometimes foolish, disobedient, deceived, serving divers lusts and pleasures, living in malice and envy, hateful, *and* hating one another.

Jas 3:2 — For in many things we offend all. If any man offend not in word, the same *is* a perfect man, *and* able also to bridle the whole body.

Jas 4:5 — Do ye think that the scripture saith in vain, The spirit that dwelleth in us lusteth to envy?

1Pe 1:18 — Forasmuch as ye know that ye were not redeemed with corruptible things, *as* silver and gold, from your vain conversation *received* by tradition from your fathers;

1Pe 2:9 — But ye *are* a chosen generation, a royal priesthood, an holy nation, a peculiar people; that ye should shew forth the praises of him who hath called you out of darkness into his marvellous light:

1Pe 2:25 — For ye were as sheep going astray; but are now returned unto the Shepherd and Bishop of your souls.

1Jn 1:8 — If we say that we have no sin, we deceive ourselves, and the truth is not in us.

1Jn 1:10 — If we say that we have not sinned, we make him a liar, and his word is not in us.

1Jn 2:16 — For all that *is* in the world, the lust of the flesh, and the lust of the eyes, and the pride of life, is not of the Father, but is of the world.

1Jn 3:10 — In this the children of God are manifest, and the children of the devil: whosoever doeth not righteousness is not of God, neither he that loveth not his brother.

1Jn 5:19 — And we know that we are of God, and the whole world lieth in wickedness.

Rev 3:17 — Because thou sayest, I am rich, and increased with goods, and have need of nothing; and knowest not that thou art wretched, and miserable, and poor, and blind, and naked:

See: Fall of Man

See: Sin

DEPRESSION

1Ki 18:46–19:18

Php 4:6 — Be careful for nothing; but in every thing by prayer and supplication with thanksgiving let your requests be made known unto God.

1Th 5:14 — Now we exhort you, brethren, warn them that are unruly, comfort the feebleminded, support the weak, be patient toward all *men.*

DEPUTY • An officer who administers the functions of a superior in his absence.

Ac 13:7–8

1Ki 22:47 — *There was* then no king in Edom: a deputy *was* king.

Ac 18:12 — And when Gallio was the deputy of Achaia, the Jews made insurrection with one accord against Paul, and brought him to the judgment seat,

Ac 19:38 — Wherefore if Demetrius, and the craftsmen which are with him, have a matter against any man, the law is open, and there are deputies: let them implead one another.

DERBE

• A city of Lycaonia.

• Paul flees to.

Ac 14:6 — They were ware of *it,* and fled unto Lystra and Derbe, cities of Lycaonia, and unto the region that lieth round about:

Ac 14:20 — Howbeit, as the disciples stood round about him, he rose up, and came into the city: and the next day he departed with Barnabas to Derbe.

• Visited by Paul and Silas.

Ac 16:1 — Then came he to Derbe and Lystra: and, behold, a certain disciple was there, named Timotheus, the son of a certain woman, which was a Jewess, and believed; but his father *was* a Greek:

• Gaius born in.

Ac 20:4 — And there accompanied him into Asia Sopater of Berea; and of the Thessalonians, Aristarchus and Secundus; and Gaius of Derbe, and Timotheus; and of Asia, Tychicus and Trophimus.

DERISION

• The wicked held in, by God.

Ps 2:4 — He that sitteth in the heavens shall laugh: the Lord shall have them in derision.

Pr 1:26 — I also will laugh at your calamity; I will mock when your fear cometh;

• Instances of.

• Sarah, when the angels gave her the promise of a child.

Ge 18:12

• The evil children of Bethel deride Elisha.

2Ki 2:23

• The people of Israel scoff at Hezekiah.

2Ch 30:1–10

See: Irony

See: Sarcasm

See: Scoffing

DESERT

• An arid region bearing only a sparse vegetation.

Le 16:22 — And the goat shall bear upon him all their iniquities unto a land not inhabited: and he shall let go the goat in the wilderness.

Dt 8:15 — Who led thee through that great and terrible wilderness, *wherein were* fiery serpents, and scorpions, and drought, where *there was* no water; who brought thee forth water out of the rock of flint;

Jer 2:2 — Go and cry in the ears of Jerusalem, saying, Thus saith the LORD; I remember thee, the kindness of thy youth, the love of thine espousals, when thou wentest after me in the wilderness, in a land *that was* not sown.

Jer 2:6 — Neither said they, Where *is* the LORD that brought us up out of the land of Egypt, that led us through the wilderness, through a land of deserts and of pits, through a land of drought, and of the shadow of death, through a land that no man passed through, and where no man dwelt?

Jer 17:6 — For he shall be like the heath in the desert, and shall not see when good cometh; but shall inhabit the parched places in the wilderness, *in* a salt land and not inhabited.

• **Figurative.**

Isa 35:1 — The wilderness and the solitary place shall be glad for them; and the desert shall rejoice, and blossom as the rose.

DESERTING

Isa 6:1–8; Mk 4:3–25; Lk 9:51–62; 2Ti 4:10–18

Ac 15:38 — But Paul thought not good to take him with them, who departed from them from Pamphylia, and went not with them to the work.

DESIGN

• **In nature, evidence of.**

Job 12:7–11

Pr 16:4 — The LORD hath made all *things* for himself: yea, even the wicked for the day of evil.

DESIRE

• **Spiritual.**

Ps 42:1–11; 51:1–17; 86:11–12; 119:19–20; 116–117; 123:1–2; 130:5–6; 143:5–6; Pr 2:3–5; Isa 26:8–9; 55:1–2; La 3:25–26; Jn 12:20–21; Php 3:12–14

Dt 4:29 — But if from thence thou shalt seek the LORD thy God, thou shalt find *him,* if thou seek him with all thy heart and with all thy soul.

2Ch 15:15 — And all Judah rejoiced at the oath: for they had sworn with all their heart, and sought him with their whole desire; and he was found of them: and the LORD gave them rest round about.

Ps 9:1 — I will praise *thee,* O LORD, with my whole heart; I will shew forth all thy marvellous works.

Ps 17:1 — Hear the right, O LORD, attend unto my cry, give ear unto my prayer, *that goeth* not out of feigned lips.

Ps 22:26 — The meek shall eat and be satisfied: they shall praise the LORD that seek him: your heart shall live for ever.

Ps 24:6 — This *is* the generation of them that seek him, that seek thy face, O Jacob. Selah.

Ps 25:5 — Lead me in thy truth, and teach me: for thou *art* the God of my salvation; on thee do I wait all the day.

Ps 25:15 — Mine eyes *are* ever toward the LORD; for he shall pluck my feet out of the net.

Ps 27:8 — *When thou saidst,* Seek ye my face; my heart said unto thee, Thy face, LORD, will I seek.

Ps 27:14 — Wait on the LORD: be of good courage, and he shall strengthen thine heart: wait, I say, on the LORD.

Ps 33:20 — Our soul waiteth for the LORD: he *is* our help and our shield.

Ps 34:10 — The young lions do lack, and suffer hunger: but they that seek the LORD shall not want any good *thing.*

Ps 37:4 — Delight thyself also in the LORD; and he shall give thee the desires of thine heart.

Ps 37:7 — Rest in the LORD, and wait patiently for him: fret not thyself because of him who prospereth in his way, because of the man who bringeth wicked devices to pass.

Ps 37:9 — For evildoers shall be cut off: but those that wait upon the LORD, they shall inherit the earth.

Ps 37:34 — Wait on the LORD, and keep his way, and he shall exalt thee to inherit the land: when the wicked are cut off, thou shalt see *it.*

Ps 38:9 — Lord, all my desire *is* before thee; and my groaning is not hid from thee.

Ps 39:12 — Hear my prayer, O LORD, and give ear unto my cry; hold not thy peace at my tears: for I *am* a stranger with thee, *and* a sojourner, as all my fathers *were.*

Ps 40:1 — I waited patiently for the LORD; and he inclined unto me, and heard my cry.

Ps 62:1 — Truly my soul waiteth upon God: from him *cometh* my salvation.

Ps 63:1 — O God, thou *art* my God; early will I seek thee: my soul thirsteth for thee, my flesh longeth for thee in a dry and thirsty land, where no water is;

Ps 63:8 — My soul followeth hard after thee: thy right hand upholdeth me.

Ps 68:28 — Thy God hath commanded thy strength: strengthen, O God, that which thou hast wrought for us.

Ps 69:3 — I am weary of my crying: my throat is dried: mine eyes fail while I wait for my God.

Ps 69:32 — The humble shall see *this, and* be glad: and your heart shall live that seek God.

Ps 70:4 — Let all those that seek thee rejoice and be glad in thee: and let such as love thy salvation say continually, Let God be magnified.

Ps 73:25 — Whom have I in heaven *but thee?* and *there is* none upon earth *that* I desire beside thee.

Ps 81:10 — I *am* the LORD thy God, which brought thee out of the land of Egypt: open thy mouth wide, and I will fill it.

Ps 84:2 — My soul longeth, yea, even fainteth for the courts of the LORD: my heart and my flesh crieth out for the living God.

Ps 86:16 — O turn unto me, and have mercy upon me; give thy strength unto thy servant, and save the son of thine handmaid.

Ps 94:19 — In the multitude of my thoughts within me thy comforts delight my soul.

Ps 105:4 — Seek the LORD, and his strength: seek his face evermore.

Ps 118:17 — I shall not die, but live, and declare the works of the LORD.

Ps 119:2 — Blessed *are* they that keep his testimonies, *and that* seek him with the whole heart.

Ps 119:10 — With my whole heart have I sought thee: O let me not wander from thy commandments.

Ps 119:40 — Behold, I have longed after thy precepts: quicken me in thy righteousness.

Ps 119:77 — Let thy tender mercies come unto me, that I may live: for thy law *is* my delight.

Ps 119:88 — Quicken me after thy lovingkindness; so shall I keep the testimony of thy mouth.

Ps 119:107 — I am afflicted very much: quicken me, O LORD, according unto thy word.

Ps 119:122 — Be surety for thy servant for good: let not the proud oppress me.

Ps 119:133 — Order my steps in thy word: and let not any iniquity have dominion over me.

Ps 119:149 — Hear my voice according unto thy lovingkindness: O LORD, quicken me according to thy judgment.

Ps 119:154 — Plead my cause, and deliver me: quicken me according to thy word.

Ps 119:156 — Great *are* thy tender mercies, O LORD: quicken me according to thy judgments.

Ps 119:159 — Consider how I love thy precepts: quicken me, O LORD, according to thy lovingkindness.

Pr 8:17 — I love them that love me; and those that seek me early shall find me.

Pr 8:34 — Blessed *is* the man that heareth me, watching daily at my gates, waiting at the posts of my doors.

Isa 8:17 — And I will wait upon the LORD, that hideth his face from the house of Jacob, and I will look for him.

Isa 8:19 — And when they shall say unto you, Seek unto them that have familiar spirits, and unto wizards that peep, and that mutter: should not a people seek unto their God? for the living to the dead?

Isa 40:31 — But they that wait upon the LORD shall renew *their* strength; they shall mount up with wings as eagles; they shall run, and not be weary; *and* they shall walk, and not faint.

Isa 55:6 — Seek ye the LORD while he may be found, call ye upon him while he is near:

Jer 29:13 — And ye shall seek me, and find *me*, when ye shall search for me with all your heart.

La 3:41 — Let us lift up our heart with *our* hands unto God in the heavens.

Hos 10:12 — Sow to yourselves in righteousness, reap in mercy; break up your fallow ground: for *it is* time to seek the LORD, till he come and rain righteousness upon you.

Hab 3:2 — O LORD, I have heard thy speech, *and* was afraid: O LORD, revive thy work in the midst of the years, in the midst of the years make known; in wrath remember mercy.

• Mt 5:6 — Blessed *are* they which do hunger and thirst after righteousness: for they shall be filled.

Lk 6:21 — Blessed *are* ye that hunger now: for ye shall be filled. Blessed *are* ye that weep now: for ye shall laugh.

Lk 10:42 — But one thing is needful: and Mary hath chosen that good part, which shall not be taken away from her.

Heb 11:6 — But without faith *it is* impossible to please *him:* for he that cometh to God must believe that he is, and *that* he is a rewarder of them that diligently seek him.

See: Hunger; spiritual

See: Thirst; figurative, the ardent desire of the devout mind

• Evil.

See: Imagination

See: Lust

DESPAIR See: Despondency

DESPONDENCY

Nu 17:12–13; Dt 28:65–67; Job 3:1–26; 17:13–16; Ps 77:7–9; La 3:1–21; Jnh 2:2–4; Mic 7:1–7; Lk 13:27–28; 23:29–30; Rev 6:14–17; 9:5–6

Ps 31:22 — For I said in my haste, I am cut off from before thine eyes: nevertheless thou heardest the voice of my supplications when I cried unto thee.

Pr 13:12 — Hope deferred maketh the heart sick: but *when* the desire cometh, *it is* a tree of life.

Isa 2:19 — And they shall go into the holes of the rocks, and into the caves of the earth, for fear of the LORD, and for the glory of his majesty, when he ariseth to shake terribly the earth.

Jer 2:25 — Withhold thy foot from being unshod, and thy throat from thirst: but thou saidst, There is no hope: no; for I have loved strangers, and after them will I go.

Jer 8:20 — The harvest is past, the summer is ended, and we are not saved.

Jer 18:12 — And they said, There is no hope: but we will walk after our own devices, and we will every one do the imagination of his evil heart.

La 5:22 — But thou hast utterly rejected us; thou art very wroth against us.

Hos 10:8 — The high places also of Aven, the sin of Israel, shall be destroyed: the thorn and the thistle shall come up on their altars; and they shall say to the mountains, Cover us; and to the hills, Fall on us.

Mt 24:30 — And then shall appear the sign of the Son of man in heaven: and then shall all the tribes of the earth mourn, and they shall see the Son of man coming in the clouds of heaven with power and great glory.

See: Afflictions

See: Resignation

See: Sorrow

See: Suffering

• Instances of.

• Cain, when God pronounced judgment upon him for the murder of Abel.

Ge 4:13–14

• Hagar, when cast out of the household of Abraham on account of the jealousy of Sarah.

Ge 21:15–16

• Moses.

• When sent on his mission to the Israelites.

Ex 4:1, 10, 13; 6:12

• At the Red Sea.

Ex 14:15

• When the people lusted for flesh.

Nu 11:15

• The Israelites, on account of the cruel oppressions of the Egyptians.

Ex 6:9

• Elijah, when he fled from Jezebel to the wilderness and sat under the juniper tree, and wished to die.

1Ki 19:4

• Jonah, after he had preached to the Ninevites.

Jnh 4:3, 8

• The mariners with Paul.

Ac 27:20

• Job.

Job 3:1–26

• Jeremiah.

La 3:1–31

La 5:22 — But thou hast utterly rejected us; thou art very wroth against us.

• Comfort in.

Isa 35:3–4; Lk 18:1–8; Heb 12:12–13

See: Afflictions; consolation in

See: Righteous; promises to, expressed or implied

DESPOTISM

See: Government; monarchical

See: Government; monarchical; tyranny in

DETECTIVES

Lk 20:20 — And they watched *him,* and sent forth spies, which should feign themselves just men, that they might take hold of his words, that so they might deliver him unto the power and authority of the governor.

See: Spies

DEUEL

• Called also Reuel.

• Captain of the tribe of Dan.

Nu 1:14 — Of Gad; Eliasaph the son of Deuel.

Nu 2:14 — Then the tribe of Gad: and the captain of the sons of Gad *shall be* Eliasaph the son of Reuel.

Nu 7:42 — On the sixth day Eliasaph the son of Deuel, prince of the children of Gad, *offered:*

Nu 10:20 — And over the host of the tribe of the children of Gad was Eliasaph the son of Deuel.

DEVIL

See: Demons

See: Satan

DEVOTION

• To God.

See: Religion

• For conspicuous instances of.

See: Enoch

See: Noah

See: Abraham

See: Moses

See: David (later history)

See: Solomon (earlier life)

See: Josiah

See: Asa

See: Isaiah

See: Elijah

See: Jeremiah

See: Daniel

See: Shadrach

See: Meshach

See: Abednego

• To Jesus.

See: Peter

See: John, the Apostle

See: Paul, Ministry, Ac 16–28

See: Paul, Ministry, Ac 9–15

See: Paul, Miscellaneous

See: Mary Magdalene

• For elaborated topics covering the subject.

See: Love; of man for God

See: Consecration

See: Zeal, Religious

DEW

• A merciful providence.

Dt 33:13

• Forms imperceptibly.

2Sa 17:12 — So shall we come upon him in some place where he shall be found, and we will light upon him as the dew falleth on the ground: and of him and of all the men that *are* with him there shall not be left so much as one.

• Forms in the night.

Job 29:19 — My root *was* spread out by the waters, and the dew lay all night upon my branch.

• From the clouds.

Pr 3:20 — By his knowledge the depths are broken up, and the clouds drop down the dew.

• Called the dew of heaven.

Da 4:15 — Nevertheless leave the stump of his roots in the earth, even with a band of iron and brass, in the tender grass of the field; and let it be wet with the dew of heaven, and *let* his portion *be* with the beasts in the grass of the earth:

• Absence of.

1Ki 17:1 — And Elijah the Tishbite, *who was* of the inhabitants of Gilead, said unto Ahab, *As* the LORD God of Israel liveth, before whom I stand, there shall not be dew nor rain these years, but according to my word.

• Miraculous profusion and absence of.

Jgs 6:36–40

See: Meteorology and Celestial Phenomena

• **Figurative.**

Ps 110:3 — Thy people *shall be* willing in the day of thy power, in the beauties of holiness from the womb of the morning: thou hast the dew of thy youth.

Isa 26:19 — Thy dead *men* shall live, *together with* my dead body shall they arise. Awake and sing, ye that dwell in dust: for thy dew *is as* the dew of herbs, and the earth shall cast out the dead.

Hos 6:4 — O Ephraim, what shall I do unto thee? O Judah, what shall I do unto thee? for your goodness *is* as a morning cloud, and as the early dew it goeth away.

Hos 13:3 — Therefore they shall be as the morning cloud, and as the early dew that passeth away, as the chaff *that* is driven with the whirlwind out of the floor, and as the smoke out of the chimney.

Hos 14:5 — I will be as the dew unto Israel: he shall grow as the lily, and cast forth his roots as Lebanon.

DIADEM

Eze 21:26 — Thus saith the Lord GOD; Remove the diadem, and take off the crown: this *shall* not *be* the same: exalt *him that is* low, and abase *him that is* high.

DIAL • A contrivance for indicating time by the sun's rays.

2Ki 20:11 — And Isaiah the prophet cried unto the LORD: and he brought the shadow ten degrees backward, by which it had gone down in the dial of Ahaz.

Isa 38:8 — Behold, I will bring again the shadow of the degrees, which is gone down in the sun dial of Ahaz, ten degrees backward. So the sun returned ten degrees, by which degrees it was gone down.

DIAMOND

• **One of the jewels in the breastplate.**

Ex 28:18 — And the second row *shall be* an emerald, a sapphire, and a diamond.

Ex 39:11 — And the second row, an emerald, a sapphire, and a diamond.

Jer 17:1 — The sin of Judah *is* written with a pen of iron, *and* with the point of a diamond: *it is* graven upon the table of their heart, and upon the horns of your altars;

Eze 28:13 — Thou hast been in Eden the garden of God; every precious stone *was* thy covering, the sardius, topaz, and the diamond, the beryl, the onyx, and the jasper, the sapphire, the emerald, and the carbuncle, and gold: the workmanship of thy tabrets and of thy pipes was prepared in thee in the day that thou wast created.

DIANA • Goddess of the Ephesians.

Ac 19:27–28

Ac 19:24 — For a certain *man* named Demetrius, a silversmith, which made silver shrines for Diana, brought no small gain unto the craftsmen;

Ac 19:35 — And when the townclerk had appeased the people, he said, *Ye* men of Ephesus, what man is there that knoweth not how that the city of the Ephesians is a worshipper of the great goddess Diana, and of the *image* which fell down from Jupiter?

DIBLAIM • Father of Hosea's wife.

Hos 1:3 — So he went and took Gomer the daughter of Diblaim; which conceived, and bare him a son.

DIBLATH • An unknown place.

Eze 6:14 — So will I stretch out my hand upon them, and make the land desolate, yea, more desolate than the wilderness toward Diblath, in all their habitations: and they shall know that I *am* the LORD.

DIBON

• **Called also Dibon-Gad and Dimon.**

• **A city on the northern banks of the Arnon.**

Nu 21:30 — We have shot at them; Heshbon is perished even unto Dibon, and we have laid them waste even unto Nophah, which *reacheth* unto Medeba.

• **Israelites encamp at.**

Nu 33:45 — And they departed from Iim, and pitched in Dibon-gad.

• **Allotted to Gad and Reuben.**

Nu 32:3 — Ataroth, and Dibon, and Jazer, and Nimrah, and Heshbon, and Elealeh, and Shebam, and Nebo, and Beon,

Nu 32:34 — And the children of Gad built Dibon, and Ataroth, and Aroer,

Jos 13:9 — From Aroer, that *is* upon the bank of the river Arnon, and the city that *is* in the midst of the river, and all the plain of Medeba unto Dibon;

Jos 13:17 — Heshbon, and all her cities that *are* in the plain; Dibon, and Bamoth-baal, and Beth-baal-meon,

• **Taken by Moab.**

Isa 15:2 — He is gone up to Bajith, and to Dibon, the high places, to weep: Moab shall howl over Nebo, and over Medeba: on all their heads *shall be* baldness, *and* every beard cut off.

Isa 15:9 — For the waters of Dimon shall be full of blood: for I will bring more upon Dimon, lions upon him that escapeth of Moab, and upon the remnant of the land.

Jer 48:18 — Thou daughter that dost inhabit Dibon, come down from *thy* glory, and sit in thirst; for the spoiler of Moab shall come upon thee, *and* he shall destroy thy strong holds.

Jer 48:22 — And upon Dibon, and upon Nebo, and upon Beth-diblathaim,

• **A city in the tribe of Judah.**

Ne 11:25 — And for the villages, with their fields, *some* of the children of Judah dwelt at Kirjath-arba, and *in* the villages thereof, and at Dibon, and in the villages thereof, and at Jekabzeel, and *in* the villages thereof,

• **Probably identical with Dimonah.**

Jos 15:22 — And Kinah, and Dimonah, and Adadah,

DIBRI • Father of Shelomith.

Le 24:11 — And the Israelitish woman's son blasphemed the name *of the LORD*, and cursed. And they brought him unto Moses: (and his mother's name *was* Shelomith, the daughter of Dibri, of the tribe of Dan:)

DIDYMUS • Surname of Thomas.

Jn 11:16 — Then said Thomas, which is called Didymus, unto his fellowdisciples, Let us also go, that we may die with him.

DIKLAH • Son of Joktan, and name of a district inhabited by his descendants.

Ge 10:27 — And Hadoram, and Uzal, and Diklah,

DILEAN • A city of Judah.

Jos 15:38 — And Dilean, and Mizpeh, and Joktheel,

DILIGENCE

• Jesus an example of.

Mk 1:35 — And in the morning, rising up a great while before day, he went out, and departed into a solitary place, and there prayed.

Lk 2:49 — And he said unto them, How is it that ye sought me? wist ye not that I must be about my Father's business?

• Required by God.

• In seeking him.

1Ch 22:19 — Now set your heart and your soul to seek the LORD your God; arise therefore, and build ye the sanctuary of the LORD God, to bring the ark of the covenant of the LORD, and the holy vessels of God, into the house that is to be built to the name of the LORD.

Heb 11:6 — But without faith *it is* impossible to please *him:* for he that cometh to God must believe that he is, and *that* he is a rewarder of them that diligently seek him.

• In obeying him.

Dt 6:17 — Ye shall diligently keep the commandments of the LORD your God, and his testimonies, and his statutes, which he hath commanded thee.

Dt 11:13 — And it shall come to pass, if ye shall hearken diligently unto my commandments which I command you this day, to love the LORD your God, and to serve him with all your heart and with all your soul,

• In hearkening to him.

Isa 55:2 — Wherefore do ye spend money for *that which is* not bread? and your labour for *that which* satisfieth not? hearken diligently unto me, and eat ye *that which is* good, and let your soul delight itself in fatness.

• In striving after perfection.

Php 3:13–14

• In cultivating Christian graces.

2Pe 1:5 — And beside this, giving all diligence, add to your faith virtue; and to virtue knowledge;

• In keeping the soul.

Dt 4:9 — Only take heed to thyself, and keep thy soul diligently, lest thou forget the things which thine eyes have seen, and lest they depart from thy heart all the days of thy life: but teach them thy sons, and thy sons' sons;

• In keeping the heart.

Pr 4:23 — Keep thy heart with all diligence; for out of it *are* the issues of life.

• In labors of love.

Heb 6:10–12

• In following every good work.

1Ti 3:10 — And let these also first be proved; then let them use the office of a deacon, being *found* blameless.

• In guarding against defilement.

Heb 12:15 — Looking diligently lest any man fail of the grace of God; lest any root of bitterness springing up trouble *you,* and thereby many be defiled;

• In seeking to be found spotless.

2Pe 3:14 — Wherefore, beloved, seeing that ye look for such things, be diligent that ye may be found of him in peace, without spot, and blameless.

• In making our calling sure.

2Pe 1:10 — Wherefore the rather, brethren, give diligence to make your calling and election sure: for if ye do these things, ye shall never fall:

• In self-examination.

Ps 77:6 — I call to remembrance my song in the night: I commune with mine own heart: and my spirit made diligent search.

• In lawful business.

Pr 27:23 — Be thou diligent to know the state of thy flocks, *and* look well to thy herds.

Ecc 9:10 — Whatsoever thy hand findeth to do, do *it* with thy might; for *there is* no work, nor device, nor knowledge, nor wisdom, in the grave, whither thou goest.

• In teaching religion.

2Ti 4:2 — Preach the word; be instant in season, out of season; reprove, rebuke, exhort with all longsuffering and doctrine.

Jude 1:3 — Beloved, when I gave all diligence to write unto you of the common salvation, it was needful for me to write unto you, and exhort *you* that ye should earnestly contend for the faith which was once delivered unto the saints.

• In instructing children.

Dt 6:7 — And thou shalt teach them diligently unto thy children, and shalt talk of them when thou sittest in thine house, and when thou walkest by the way, and when thou liest down, and when thou risest up.

Dt 11:19 — And ye shall teach them your children, speaking of them when thou sittest in thine house, and when thou walkest by the way, when thou liest down, and when thou risest up.

• In discharging official duties.

Dt 19:18 — And the judges shall make diligent inquisition: and, behold, *if* the witness *be* a false witness, *and* hath testified falsely against his brother;

- **That saints should abound in.**
  2Co 8:7 — Therefore, as ye abound in every *thing, in* faith, and utterance, and knowledge, and *in* all diligence, and *in* your love to us, *see* that ye abound in this grace also.
- **In the service of God.**
  Jn 9:4 — I must work the works of him that sent me, while it is day: the night cometh, when no man can work.
  Gal 6:9 — And let us not be weary in well doing: for in due season we shall reap, if we faint not.

- **Is not in vain.**
  1Co 15:58 — Therefore, my beloved brethren, be ye stedfast, unmovable, always abounding in the work of the Lord, forasmuch as ye know that your labour is not in vain in the Lord.
- **Preserves from evil.**
  Ex 15:26 — And said, If thou wilt diligently hearken to the voice of the LORD thy God, and wilt do that which is right in his sight, and wilt give ear to his commandments, and keep all his statutes, I will put none of these diseases upon thee, which I have brought upon the Egyptians: for I *am* the LORD that healeth thee.
- **Leads to assured hope.**
  Heb 6:11 — And we desire that every one of you do shew the same diligence to the full assurance of hope unto the end:
- **God rewards.**
  Dt 11:14 — That I will give *you* the rain of your land in his due season, the first rain and the latter rain, that thou mayest gather in thy corn, and thy wine, and thine oil.
  Heb 11:6 — But without faith *it is* impossible to please *him:* for he that cometh to God must believe that he is, and *that* he is a rewarder of them that diligently seek him.
- **In temporal matters leads to favor.**
  Pr 11:27 — He that diligently seeketh good procureth favour: but he that seeketh mischief, it shall come unto him.
- **In temporal matters leads to prosperity.**
  Pr 10:4 — He becometh poor that dealeth *with* a slack hand: but the hand of the diligent maketh rich.
  Pr 13:4 — The soul of the sluggard desireth, and *hath* nothing: but the soul of the diligent shall be made fat.
- **In temporal matters leads to honor.**
  Pr 12:24 — The hand of the diligent shall bear rule: but the slothful shall be under tribute.
  Pr 22:29 — Seest thou a man diligent in his business? he shall stand before kings; he shall not stand before mean *men.*
- **Figurative.**
  Pr 6:6–8
- **Exempified.**
  - **Ruth.**
    Ru 2:17 — So she gleaned in the field until even, and beat out that she had gleaned: and it was about an ephah of barley.
  - **Hezekiah.**
    2Ch 31:21 — And in every work that he began in the service of the house of God, and in the law, and in the commandments, to seek his God, he did *it* with all his heart, and prospered.
  - **Nehemiah and his helpers.**
    Ne 4:6 — So built we the wall; and all the wall was joined together unto the half thereof: for the people had a mind to work.
  - **Psalmist.**
    Ps 119:60 — I made haste, and delayed not to keep thy commandments.
  - **Apostles.**
    Ac 5:42 — And daily in the temple, and in every house, they ceased not to teach and preach Jesus Christ.
  - **Apollos.**
    Ac 18:25 — This man was instructed in the way of the Lord; and being fervent in the spirit, he spake and taught diligently the things of the Lord, knowing only the baptism of John.
  - **Titus.**
    2Co 8:22 — And we have sent with them our brother, whom we have oftentimes proved diligent in many things, but now much more diligent, upon the great confidence which *I have* in you.
  - **Paul.**
    1Th 2:9 — For ye remember, brethren, our labour and travail: for labouring night and day, because we would not be chargeable unto any of you, we preached unto you the gospel of God.
  - **Onesiphorus.**
    2Ti 1:17 — But, when he was in Rome, he sought me out very diligently, and found *me.*

See: Industry
See: Zeal, Religious
See: Idleness
See: Slothfulness

DILIGENT

Lk 16:9–12
Pr 22:29 — Seest thou a man diligent in his business? he shall stand before kings; he shall not stand before mean *men.*
1Co 4:2 — Moreover it is required in stewards, that a man be found faithful.
1Ti 3:7 — Moreover he must have a good report of them which are without; lest he fall into reproach and the snare of the devil.

DIMNAH • A Levitical city of Zebulun.

Jos 21:35 — Dimnah with her suburbs, Nahalal with her suburbs; four cities.

DIMON See: Dibon

DIMONAH See: Dibon; a city in the tribe of Judah

DINAH

• Daughter of Jacob and Leah.

Ge 30:21 — And afterwards she bare a daughter, and called her name Dinah.

• Ravishment of.

Ge 34:1–31

DINHABAH • A city of Edom.

Ge 36:32 — And Bela the son of Beor reigned in Edom: and the name of his city *was* Dinhabah.

1Ch 1:43 — Now these *are* the kings that reigned in the land of Edom before *any* king reigned over the children of Israel; Bela the son of Beor: and the name of his city *was* Dinhabah.

DINNER

• Eaten at noon.

Ge 43:16 — And when Joseph saw Benjamin with them, he said to the ruler of his house, Bring *these* men home, and slay, and make ready; for *these* men shall dine with me at noon.

✦See: Feasts

DIONYSIUS • A convert of Paul.

Ac 17:34 — Howbeit certain men clave unto him, and believed: among the which *was* Dionysius the Areopagite, and a woman named Damaris, and others with them.

DIOTREPHES • A false teacher.

3Jn 1:9 — I wrote unto the church: but Diotrephes, who loveth to have the preeminence among them, receiveth us not.

DIPLOMACY

1Co 9:20–23

✦See: Tact

• Instances of.

• Abimelech.

Ge 21:22–23; 26:26–31

• The Gibeonites, in securing a league with the Israelites through deception.

Jos 9:3–16

• Jephthah, with the king of Moab, unsuccessful.

Jgs 11:12–28

• Abigail.

1Sa 25:23–31

• Hiram, to secure the good will of David.

2Sa 5:11

• Toi, to promote the friendship of David.

2Sa 8:10

• David, in sending Hushai to Absalom's court.

2Sa 15:32–37; 16:15–19; 17:1–14

• The wise woman of Abel.

2Sa 20:16–22

• Absalom winning the people.

2Sa 15:2–6

• Solomon, in his alliance with Hiram.

1Ki 5:1–12; 9:10–14, 26–27; 10:11

• Solomon, by intermarriage with other nations.

1Ki 1:1–5

• Ambassadors from Ben-hadad to Ahab.

1Ki 20:31–34

• Jehoash purchases peace from Hazael.

2Ki 12:18

• Ahaz purchases aid from the king of Assyria.

2Ki 16:7–9

• Rab-shakeh, in trying to induce Jerusalem to capitulate by bombastic harangue.

2Ki 18:17–19:13; Isa 36:11–22

• Sanballat, in an attempt to prevent the rebuilding of Jerusalem by Nehemiah.

Ne 6:1–19

• The people of Tyre and Sidon, in securing the favor of Herod.

Ac 12:20–22

• Paul, in arraying the Pharisees and Sadducees against each other at his trial.

Ac 23:6–10

• Ecclesiastical.

• Paul, in circumcising Timothy.

Ac 16:3 — Him would Paul have to go forth with him; and took and circumcised him because of the Jews which were in those quarters: for they knew all that his father was a Greek.

• Paul, in performing certain temple services to placate the Jews.

Ac 21:20–25

Gal 6:12 — As many as desire to make a fair shew in the flesh, they constrain you to be circumcised; only lest they should suffer persecution for the cross of Christ.

• Corrupt practices in.

• The officers of Nebuchadnezzar's court to secure the destruction of Daniel.

Da 6:4–15

DISBELIEF ✦See: Unbelief

DISCIPLE

• A name given to the followers of any teacher.

Mt 28:19–20; Ac 16:1–3

2Ti 2:2 — And the things that thou hast heard of me among many witnesses, the same commit thou to faithful men, who shall be able to teach others also.

• Of John the Baptist.

Mt 9:14 — Then came to him the disciples of John, saying, Why do we and the Pharisees fast oft, but thy disciples fast not?

• **Of Jesus.**

Mt 10:1 — And when he had called unto *him* his twelve disciples, he gave them power *against* unclean spirits, to cast them out, and to heal all manner of sickness and all manner of disease.

Mt 20:17 — And Jesus going up to Jerusalem took the twelve disciples apart in the way, and said unto them,

Ac 9:26 — And when Saul was come to Jerusalem, he assayed to join himself to the disciples: but they were all afraid of him, and believed not that he was a disciple.

Ac 14:2 — But the unbelieving Jews stirred up the Gentiles, and made their minds evil affected against the brethren.

Ac 21:4 — And finding disciples, we tarried there seven days: who said to Paul through the Spirit, that he should not go up to Jerusalem.

• **The seventy sent forth.**

Lk 10:1 — After these things the Lord appointed other seventy also, and sent them two and two before his face into every city and place, whither he himself would come.

• **First called Christians at Antioch.**

Ac 11:26 — And when he had found him, he brought him unto Antioch. And it came to pass, that a whole year they assembled themselves with the church, and taught much people. And the disciples were called Christians first in Antioch.

See: Apostles

See: Righteous

DISCIPLESHIP

• **Tests of.**

Mt 10:32–39; Lk 14:26–27; Jn 21:15–19

Lk 14:33 — So likewise, whosoever he be of you that forsaketh not all that he hath, he cannot be my disciple.

See: Commandments

DISCIPLINE

Pr 3:11 — My son, despise not the chastening of the LORD; neither be weary of his correction:

Heb 12:7 — If ye endure chastening, God dealeth with you as with sons; for what son is he whom the father chasteneth not?

Heb 12:11 — Now no chastening for the present seemeth to be joyous, but grievous: nevertheless afterward it yieldeth the peaceable fruit of righteousness unto them which are exercised thereby.

• **Of armies, for disobedience of order.**

Jos 7:10–26; Jgs 21:5–12

See: Armies

• **Church discipline.**

See: Church; rules of discipline in, Mosaic and Christian

DISCONTENTMENT

See: Murmuring

See: Contentment

DISCOURAGE

2Ti 2:1–7; Heb 12:1–3, 12–13

Mk 7:34 — And looking up to heaven, he sighed, and saith unto him, Ephphatha, that is, Be opened.

DISCOURAGEMENT See: Despondency

DISEASE

• **Sent from God.**

Le 14:34 — When ye be come into the land of Canaan, which I give to you for a possession, and I put the plague of leprosy in a house of the land of your possession;

• **As judgment.**

Ps 107:17 — Fools because of their transgression, and because of their iniquities, are afflicted.

Isa 3:17 — Therefore the LORD will smite with a scab the crown of the head of the daughters of Zion, and the LORD will discover their secret parts.

• **Instances of.**

- **Egyptians.**

  See: Plague

- **Nabal.**

  1Sa 25:38

- **David's child.**

  2Sa 12:15

- **Gehazi.**

  2Ki 5:27

- **Jeroboam.**

  2Ch 13:20

- **Jehoram.**

  2Ch 21:12–19

- **Uzziah.**

  2Ch 26:17–20

• **Threatened as judgment.**

Dt 28:27–28

Le 26:16 — I also will do this unto you; I will even appoint over you terror, consumption, and the burning ague, that shall consume the eyes, and cause sorrow of heart: and ye shall sow your seed in vain, for your enemies shall eat it.

Dt 7:15 — And the LORD will take away from thee all sickness, and will put none of the evil diseases of Egypt, which thou knowest, upon thee; but will lay them upon all *them* that hate thee.

Dt 28:22 — The LORD shall smite thee with a consumption, and with a fever, and with an inflammation, and with an extreme burning, and with the sword, and with blasting, and with mildew; and they shall pursue thee until thou perish.

Dt 28:35 — The LORD shall smite thee in the knees, and in the legs, with a sore botch that cannot be healed, from the sole of thy foot unto the top of thy head.

Dt 29:22 — So that the generation to come of your children that shall rise up after you, and the stranger that shall come from a far land, shall say, when they see the plagues of that land, and the sicknesses which the LORD hath laid upon it;

- **Healing of, from God.**

Ex 15:26 — And said, If thou wilt diligently hearken to the voice of the LORD thy God, and wilt do that which is right in his sight, and wilt give ear to his commandments, and keep all his statutes, I will put none of these diseases upon thee, which I have brought upon the Egyptians: for I *am* the LORD that healeth thee.

Ex 23:25 — And ye shall serve the LORD your God, and he shall bless thy bread, and thy water; and I will take sickness away from the midst of thee.

Dt 7:15 — And the LORD will take away from thee all sickness, and will put none of the evil diseases of Egypt, which thou knowest, upon thee; but will lay them upon all *them* that hate thee.

2Ch 16:12 — And Asa in the thirty and ninth year of his reign was diseased in his feet, until his disease *was* exceeding *great:* yet in his disease he sought not to the LORD, but to the physicians.

Ps 103:3 — Who forgiveth all thine iniquities; who healeth all thy diseases;

Ps 107:20 — He sent his word, and healed them, and delivered *them* from their destructions.

- **In answer to prayer.**
  - **Of Hezekiah.**

2Ki 20:1–11; Isa 38:1–8

  - **Of David.**

Ps 116:3–8

Ps 21:4 — He asked life of thee, *and* thou gavest *it* him, *even* length of days for ever and ever.

- **Miraculous healing of, a sign to accompany the preaching of the word.**

Mk 16:18 — They shall take up serpents; and if they drink any deadly thing, it shall not hurt them; they shall lay hands on the sick, and they shall recover.

See: Miracles of the Disciples

See: Miracles, Joshua-Jonah

See: Miracles, of Jesus, in chronological order

- **Physicians employed for.**

2Ch 16:12 — And Asa in the thirty and ninth year of his reign was diseased in his feet, until his disease *was* exceeding *great:* yet in his disease he sought not to the LORD, but to the physicians.

Jer 8:22 — *Is there* no balm in Gilead; *is there* no physician there? why then is not the health of the daughter of my people recovered?

Mt 9:12 — But when Jesus heard *that,* he said unto them, They that be whole need not a physician, but they that are sick.

Mk 5:26 — And had suffered many things of many physicians, and had spent all that she had, and was nothing bettered, but rather grew worse,

Lk 4:23 — And he said unto them, Ye will surely say unto me this proverb, Physician, heal thyself: whatsoever we have heard done in Capernaum, do also here in thy country.

- **Remedies used.**

Pr 17:22 — A merry heart doeth good *like* a medicine: but a broken spirit drieth the bones.

Pr 20:30 — The blueness of a wound cleanseth away evil: so *do* stripes the inward parts of the belly.

Isa 38:21 — For Isaiah had said, Let them take a lump of figs, and lay *it* for a plaister upon the boil, and he shall recover.

Jer 30:13 — *There is* none to plead thy cause, that thou mayest be bound up: thou hast no healing medicines.

Jer 46:11 — Go up into Gilead, and take balm, O virgin, the daughter of Egypt: in vain shalt thou use many medicines; *for* thou shalt not be cured.

  - **Poultices.**

2Ki 20:7 — And Isaiah said, Take a lump of figs. And they took and laid *it* on the boil, and he recovered.

  - **Ointments.**

Isa 1:6 — From the sole of the foot even unto the head *there is* no soundness in it; *but* wounds, and bruises, and putrifying sores: they have not been closed, neither bound up, neither mollified with ointment.

Jer 8:22 — *Is there* no balm in Gilead; *is there* no physician there? why then is not the health of the daughter of my people recovered?

  - **Emulsions.**

Lk 10:34 — And went to *him,* and bound up his wounds, pouring in oil and wine, and set him on his own beast, and brought him to an inn, and took care of him.

- **Of the sexual organs.**

Le 15:1–33

Le 22:4 — What man soever of the seed of Aaron *is* a leper, or hath a running issue; he shall not eat of the holy things, until he be clean. And whoso toucheth any thing *that is* unclean *by* the dead, or a man whose seed goeth from him;

Nu 5:2 — Command the children of Israel, that they put out of the camp every leper, and every one that hath an issue, and whosoever is defiled by the dead:

Dt 23:10 — If there be among you any man, that is not clean by reason of uncleanness that chanceth him by night, then shall he go abroad out of the camp, he shall not come within the camp:

See: Circumcision

See: Menstruation

See: Gonorrhea

- **Treatment of fractures.**

Eze 30:21 — Son of man, I have broken the arm of Pharaoh king of Egypt; and, lo, it shall not be bound up to be healed, to put a roller to bind it, to make it strong to hold the sword.

See: Afflictions

- **Figurative.**

Ps 38:7 — For my loins are filled with a loathsome *disease:* and *there is* no soundness in my flesh.

Isa 1:6 — From the sole of the foot even unto the head *there is* no soundness in it; *but* wounds, and bruises, and putrifying sores: they have not been closed, neither bound up, neither mollified with ointment.

Jer 30:12 — For thus saith the LORD, Thy bruise *is* incurable, *and* thy wound *is* grievous.

- **Various kinds of.**
  - **See: Abortion**
  - **See: Ague**
  - **See: Atrophy**
  - **See: Blain**
  - **See: Blemish**
  - **See: Blindness**
  - **See: Boil**
  - **See: Congestion**
  - **See: Consumption**
  - **See: Deafness**
  - **See: Demons**
  - **See: Dropsy**
  - **See: Dysentery**
  - **See: Dyspepsia**
  - **See: Epilepsy**
  - **See: Fever**
  - **See: Gonorrhea**
  - **See: Gout**
  - **See: Hemorrhage**
  - **See: Hemorrhoids**
  - **See: Insanity**
  - **See: Itch**
  - **See: Lameness**
  - **See: Leprosy**
  - **See: Murrain**
  - **See: Paralysis**
  - **See: Pestilence**
  - **See: Scab**
  - **See: Scall**
  - **See: Scurvy**
  - **See: Spermatorrhea**
  - **See: Stammering**
  - **See: Sunstroke**
  - **See: Tumor**
  - **See: Worm**
- **Of the bowels.**
  - **See: Bowels**

DISHAN • Son of Seir.

Ge 36:21 — And Dishon, and Ezer, and Dishan: these *are* the dukes of the Horites, the children of Seir in the land of Edom.

Ge 36:30 — Duke Dishon, duke Ezer, duke Dishan: these *are* the dukes *that came* of Hori, among their dukes in the land of Seir.

1Ch 1:38 — And the sons of Seir; Lotan, and Shobal, and Zibeon, and Anah, and Dishon, and Ezar, and Dishan.

DISHON

- **Son of Seir.**

Ge 36:21 — And Dishon, and Ezer, and Dishan: these *are* the dukes of the Horites, the children of Seir in the land of Edom.

Ge 36:30 — Duke Dishon, duke Ezer, duke Dishan: these *are* the dukes *that came* of Hori, among their dukes in the land of Seir.

1Ch 1:38 — And the sons of Seir; Lotan, and Shobal, and Zibeon, and Anah, and Dishon, and Ezar, and Dishan.

- **Grandson of Seir.**

Ge 36:25 — And the children of Anah *were* these; Dishon, and Aholibamah the daughter of Anah.

1Ch 1:41 — The sons of Anah; Dishon. And the sons of Dishon; Amram, and Eshban, and Ithran, and Cheran.

DISHONESTY

Le 6:2–7; 19:35–36; Dt 25:13–16; Job 24:2–11; Pr 3:27–28; Jer 7:8–10; 9:4–6; Hos 4:1–2; Mic 6:10–11; Zec 5:3–4; Lk 16:1–8

Le 19:13 — Thou shalt not defraud thy neighbour, neither rob *him:* the wages of him that is hired shall not abide with thee all night until the morning.

Ps 37:21 — The wicked borroweth, and payeth not again: but the righteous sheweth mercy, and giveth.

Ps 50:18 — When thou sawest a thief, then thou consentedst with him, and hast been partaker with adulterers.

Ps 62:10 — Trust not in oppression, and become not vain in robbery: if riches increase, set not your heart *upon them.*

Pr 11:1 — A false balance *is* abomination to the LORD: but a just weight *is* his delight.

Pr 20:10 — Divers weights, *and* divers measures, both of them *are* alike abomination to the LORD.

Pr 20:14 — *It is* naught, *it is* naught, saith the buyer: but when he is gone his way, then he boasteth.

Pr 20:17 — Bread of deceit *is* sweet to a man; but afterwards his mouth shall be filled with gravel.

Pr 20:23 — Divers weights *are* an abomination unto the LORD; and a false balance *is* not good.

Isa 32:7 — The instruments also of the churl *are* evil: he deviseth wicked devices to destroy the poor with lying words, even when the needy speaketh right.

Jer 9:8 — Their tongue *is as* an arrow shot out; it speaketh deceit: *one* speaketh peaceably to his neighbour with his mouth, but in heart he layeth his wait.

Jer 22:13 — Woe unto him that buildeth his house by unrighteousness, and his chambers by wrong; *that* useth his neighbour's service without wages, and giveth him not for his work;

Eze 22:29 — The people of the land have used oppression, and exercised robbery, and have vexed the poor and needy: yea, they have oppressed the stranger wrongfully.

Hos 12:7 — *He is* a merchant, the balances of deceit *are* in his hand: he loveth to oppress.

Am 3:10 — For they know not to do right, saith the LORD, who store up violence and robbery in their palaces.

Am 8:5 — Saying, When will the new moon be gone, that we may sell corn? and the sabbath, that we may set forth wheat, making the ephah small, and the shekel great, and falsifying the balances by deceit?

Na 3:1 — Woe to the bloody city! it is all full of lies *and* robbery; the prey departeth not;

Zep 1:9 — In the same day also will I punish all those that leap on the threshold, which fill their masters' houses with violence and deceit.

1Th 4:6 — That no *man* go beyond and defraud his brother in *any* matter: because that the Lord *is* the avenger of all such, as we also have forewarned you and testified.

Jas 5:4 — Behold, the hire of the labourers who have reaped down your fields, which is of you kept back by fraud, crieth: and the cries of them which have reaped are entered into the ears of the Lord of sabaoth.

- **Instances of.**
  - **Abimelech's servants usurp a well of water.**
    Ge 21:25; 26:15–22
  - **Jacob obtains his brother's birthright by unjust advantage.**
    Ge 25:29–33
  - **Jacob steals his father's blessing.**
    Ge 27:6–29
  - **Jacob steals Laban's flocks by skillful manipulation.**
    Ge 30:31–43
  - **Rebekah's guile in Jacob's behalf.**
    Ge 27:6–17
  - **Laban's treatment of Jacob.**
    Ge 29:21–30; 31:36–42
  - **Rachel steals the household gods.**
    Ge 31:19
  - **Simeon and Levi deceive the Shechemites.**
    Ge 34:15–31
  - **Achan hides the wedge of gold and the Babylonish garment.**
    Jos 7:11–26
  - **Micah steals eleven hundred pieces of silver.**
    Jgs 17:2
  - **Micah's priest steals his images.**
    Jgs 18:14–21
  - **Joab's guile in securing Absalom's return.**
    2Sa 14:2–20
  - **Ahab usurps Naboth's vineyard.**
    1Ki 21:2–16
  - **Judas' hypocritical sympathy for the poor.**
    Jn 12:6

  See: Diplomacy

  See: Hypocrisy

  See: Injustice

  See: Treason

DISOBEDIENCE TO GOD

- **Denunciations against.**
  Le 26:14–46; Nu 14:11–12, 22–24; 32:8–13; Dt 28:15–68

  Dt 18:19 — And it shall come to pass, *that* whosoever will not hearken unto my words which he shall speak in my name, I will require *it* of him.
- **Punishment of.**
  - **Of the Egyptians by plagues.**

  See: Plague

  See: Sin; punishment of
- **Instances of.**
  - **Adam and Eve, eating the forbidden fruit.**
    Ge 3:6–11
  - **Lot, in refusing to go to the mountain, as commanded by the angels.**
    Ge 19:19–20
  - **Lot's wife, in looking back upon Sodom.**
    Ge 19:26
  - **Moses, in making excuses when commissioned to deliver Israel.**
    Ex 4:13–14
  - **Moses, when he smote the rock.**
    Nu 20:11; 20:23–24
  - **Aaron, at the smiting of the rock by Moses.**
    Nu 20:23–24
  - **Pharaoh, in refusing to let the children of Israel go.**
    Ex 5:2; 7:13, 22–23; 8:15, 19, 32; 9:12, 34; 10:20, 27; 11:10; 14:8
  - **The children of Israel, in gathering excessive quantities of manna.**
    Ex 16:19–20
  - **The children of Israel, in refusing to enter the promised land.**
    Nu 14:1–10; Dt 1:26; Jos 5:6; Ps 106:24–25
  - **Nadab and Abihu, in offering strange fire.**
    Le 10:1–2
  - **Balaam, in accompanying the messengers from Balak.**
    Nu 22:22
  - **Achan, in secreting the wedge of gold and the Babylonian garment.**
    Jos 7:15–26
  - **Saul, in offering a sacrifice.**
    1Sa 13:13
  - **Saul, in sparing Agag and the spoils of the Amalekites.**
    1Sa 15:1–35; 28:18
  - **David, in his adultery, and in the slaying of Uriah.**
    2Sa 12:9
  - **Solomon, in building places for idolatrous worship.**
    1Ki 11:7–10

• **The prophet of Judah, in not keeping the commandment to deliver his message to Jeroboam without delay.**
1Ki 13:1–34

• **A man of Israel, who refused to smite the prophet.**
1Ki 20:35–36

• **Ahab, in suffering the king of Assyria to escape out of his hands.**
1Ki 20:42

• **Priests, in not performing their functions after the due order.**
1Ch 15:13

• **The people of Judah.**
Jer 43:7

• **The people of Judah, in going to dwell in Egypt contrary to divine command.**
Jer 44:12–14

• **Jonah, in refusing to deliver the message to the Ninevites.**
Jnh 1:1–17

• **The blind men Jesus healed and commanded not to publish their healing.**
Mt 9:30–31

• **The leper whom Jesus healed and commanded not to publish the fact.**
Mk 1:45

• **Paul, in going to Jerusalem contrary to repeated admonitions.**
Ac 21:4; 21:10–14

• **Children.**

✣See: Children, commandments to

• **The righteous.**

✣See: Commandments

• **Unclassified scriptures relating to.**

Dt 11:28 — And a curse, if ye will not obey the commandments of the LORD your God, but turn aside out of the way which I command you this day, to go after other gods, which ye have not known.

1Sa 12:15 — But if ye will not obey the voice of the LORD, but rebel against the commandment of the LORD, then shall the hand of the LORD be against you, as *it was* against your fathers.

Eph 5:6 — Let no man deceive you with vain words: for because of these things cometh the wrath of God upon the children of disobedience.

1Th 1:8 — For from you sounded out the word of the Lord not only in Macedonia and Achaia, but also in every place your faith to God-ward is spread abroad; so that we need not to speak any thing.

DISPERSION

• **Of the descendants of Noah.**
Ge 10:1–32

• **After building the tower of Babel.**
Ge 11:1–9

Dt 32:8 — When the most High divided to the nations their inheritance, when he separated the sons of Adam, he set the bounds of the people according to the number of the children of Israel.

• **Of the Jews, foretold.**

Jer 16:15 — But, The LORD liveth, that brought up the children of Israel from the land of the north, and from all the lands whither he had driven them: and I will bring them again into their land that I gave unto their fathers.

Jer 24:9 — And I will deliver them to be removed into all the kingdoms of the earth for *their* hurt, *to be* a reproach and a proverb, a taunt and a curse, in all places whither I shall drive them.

Jn 7:35 — Then said the Jews among themselves, Whither will he go, that we shall not find him? will he go unto the dispersed among the Gentiles, and teach the Gentiles?

DISPUTE

• **About property.**

✣See: Property

DISSEMBLING

• **Instances of.**

• **Joseph.**
Ge 42:7–20; 43:26–34

• **David.**
1Sa 21:13–15

✣See: Deception

✣See: Hypocrisy

DISSENSION

• **In churches.**
1Co 1:10–13; 3:3–4; 11:18–19

DISSIPATION

• **Dangers of.**

Job 1:5 — And it was so, when the days of *their* feasting were gone about, that Job sent and sanctified them, and rose up early in the morning, and offered burnt offerings *according* to the number of them all: for Job said, It may be that my sons have sinned, and cursed God in their hearts. Thus did Job continually.

✣See: Drunkenness

DISTAFF

Pr 31:19 — She layeth her hands to the spindle, and her hands hold the distaff.

DITCH

• **Figurative.**

Pr 23:27 — For a whore *is* a deep ditch; and a strange woman *is* a narrow pit.

DIVINATION ✣See: Sorcery

DIVINITY

• **Of Christ.**

✣See: Jesus, Divinity of

DIVORCE

Ex 21:7–11; Dt 21:10–14; 24:1–4; Ezr 10:1–16; Ne 13:23–30; Mal 2:14–16; Mt 5:31–32; 19:3–12; 1Co 7:10–17

Jer 3:1 — They say, If a man put away his wife, and she go from him, and become another man's, shall he return unto her again? shall not that land be greatly polluted? but thou hast played the harlot with many lovers; yet return again to me, saith the LORD.

Mic 2:9 — The women of my people have ye cast out from their pleasant houses; from their children have ye taken away my glory for ever.

Mk 10:2 — And the Pharisees came to him, and asked him, Is it lawful for a man to put away *his* wife? tempting him.

Lk 16:18 — Whosoever putteth away his wife, and marrieth another, committeth adultery: and whosoever marrieth her that is put away from *her* husband committeth adultery.

• Disobedience of the wife to the husband, a sufficient cause for, in the Persian empire.

Est 1:10–22

See: Marriage

• Figurative.

Isa 50:1 — Thus saith the LORD, Where *is* the bill of your mother's divorcement, whom I have put away? or which of my creditors *is it* to whom I have sold you? Behold, for your iniquities have ye sold yourselves, and for your transgressions is your mother put away.

Isa 54:4 — Fear not; for thou shalt not be ashamed: neither be thou confounded; for thou shalt not be put to shame: for thou shalt forget the shame of thy youth, and shalt not remember the reproach of thy widowhood any more.

Jer 3:8 — And I saw, when for all the causes whereby backsliding Israel committed adultery I had put her away, and given her a bill of divorce; yet her treacherous sister Judah feared not, but went and played the harlot also.

DOCTOR

• A teacher, or master.

Mt 8:19 — And a certain scribe came, and said unto him, Master, I will follow thee whithersoever thou goest.

Lk 2:46 — And it came to pass, that after three days they found him in the temple, sitting in the midst of the doctors, both hearing them, and asking them questions.

Lk 5:17 — And it came to pass on a certain day, as he was teaching, that there were Pharisees and doctors of the law sitting by, which were come out of every town of Galilee, and Judaea, and Jerusalem: and the power of the Lord was *present* to heal them.

Ac 5:34 — Then stood there up one in the council, a Pharisee, named Gamaliel, a doctor of the law, had in reputation among all the people, and commanded to put the apostles forth a little space;

1Ti 1:7 — Desiring to be teachers of the law; understanding neither what they say, nor whereof they affirm.

See: Physician

See: Disease

DOCTRINES

Jn 7:16–17

Ac 2:42 — And they continued stedfastly in the apostles' doctrine and fellowship, and in breaking of bread, and in prayers.

1Ti 4:13 — Till I come, give attendance to reading, to exhortation, to doctrine.

2Ti 1:10 — But is now made manifest by the appearing of our Saviour Jesus Christ, who hath abolished death, and hath brought life and immortality to light through the gospel:

Tit 1:9 — Holding fast the faithful word as he hath been taught, that he may be able by sound doctrine both to exhort and to convince the gainsayers.

Tit 2:1 — But speak thou the things which become sound doctrine:

1Pe 3:15 — But sanctify the Lord God in your hearts: and *be* ready always to *give* an answer to every man that asketh you a reason of the hope that is in you with meekness and fear:

• Set forth by church councils.

Ac 15:6–29

• False.

Ro 16:17–18; 1Co 3:1–4; 11:18–19; 2Co 11:3–4; Gal 1:6–8; Col 2:18–23; 1Ti 1:3–4, 6–7; 4:1–3; 6:3–5, 20–21; 2Ti 2:16–18; 3:6–9; Tit 1:10–11; 3:10–11; 2Pe 2:1–22; 2Jn 1:9–11

Mt 5:19 — Whosoever therefore shall break one of these least commandments, and shall teach men so, he shall be called the least in the kingdom of heaven: but whosoever shall do and teach *them,* the same shall be called great in the kingdom of heaven.

Mt 15:9 — But in vain they do worship me, teaching *for* doctrines the commandments of men.

Mt 15:13 — But he answered and said, Every plant, which my heavenly Father hath not planted, shall be rooted up.

1Co 3:11 — For other foundation can no man lay than that is laid, which is Jesus Christ.

1Co 3:21 — Therefore let no man glory in men. For all things are yours;

2Co 2:17 — For we are not as many, which corrupt the word of God: but as of sincerity, but as of God, in the sight of God speak we in Christ.

Eph 4:14 — That we *henceforth* be no more children, tossed to and fro, and carried about with every wind of doctrine, by the sleight of men, *and* cunning craftiness, whereby they lie in wait to deceive;

Col 2:4 — And this I say, lest any man should beguile you with enticing words.

Col 2:8 — Beware lest any man spoil you through philosophy and vain deceit, after the tradition of men, after the rudiments of the world, and not after Christ.

1Ti 1:19 — Holding faith, and a good conscience; which some having put away concerning faith have made shipwreck:

1Ti 4:7 — But refuse profane and old wives' fables, and exercise thyself *rather* unto godliness.

2Ti 2:14 — Of these things put *them* in remembrance, charging *them* before the Lord that they strive not about words to no profit, *but* to the subverting of the hearers.

2Ti 3:13 — But evil men and seducers shall wax worse and worse, deceiving, and being deceived.

2Ti 4:3 — For the time will come when they will not endure sound doctrine; but after their own lusts shall they heap to themselves teachers, having itching ears;

Tit 1:14 — Not giving heed to Jewish fables, and commandments of men, that turn from the truth.

Heb 13:9 — Be not carried about with divers and strange doctrines. For *it is* a good thing that the heart be established with grace; not with meats, which have not profited them that have been occupied therein.

1Jn 4:3 — And every spirit that confesseth not that Jesus Christ is come in the flesh is not of God: and this is that *spirit* of antichrist, whereof ye have heard that it should come; and even now already is it in the world.

2Jn 1:7 — For many deceivers are entered into the world, who confess not that Jesus Christ is come in the flesh. This is a deceiver and an antichrist.

Jude 1:4 — For there are certain men crept in unawares, who were before of old ordained to this condemnation, ungodly men, turning the grace of our God into lasciviousness, and denying the only Lord God, and our Lord Jesus Christ.

Jude 1:11 — Woe unto them! for they have gone in the way of Cain, and ran greedily after the error of Balaam for reward, and perished in the gainsaying of Core.

See: Minister, False and Corrupt
See: Corinth; church of; schism in
See: Teachers; false

DODAI See: Dodo

DODANIM

• Descendants of Noah.

Ge 10:4 — And the sons of Javan; Elishah, and Tarshish, Kittim, and Dodanim.

• Called Rodanim.

1Ch 1:7 — And the sons of Javan; Elishah, and Tarshish, Kittim, and Dodanim.

DODAVAH • A prophet.

2Ch 20:37 — Then Eliezer the son of Dodavah of Mareshah prophesied against Jehoshaphat, saying, Because thou hast joined thyself with Ahaziah, the LORD hath broken thy works. And the ships were broken, that they were not able to go to Tarshish.

DODO

• A descendant of Issachar.

Jgs 10:1 — And after Abimelech there arose to defend Israel Tola the son of Puah, the son of Dodo, a man of Issachar; and he dwelt in Shamir in mount Ephraim.

• One of David's heroes.

2Sa 23:9 — And after him *was* Eleazar the son of Dodo the Ahohite, *one* of the three mighty men with David, when they defied the Philistines *that* were there gathered together to battle, and the men of Israel were gone away:

1Ch 11:12 — And after him *was* Eleazar the son of Dodo, the Ahohite, who *was one* of the three mighties.

• Called Dodai.

1Ch 27:4 — And over the course of the second month *was* Dodai an Ahohite, and of his course *was* Mikloth also the ruler: in his course likewise *were* twenty and four thousand.

• A Bethlehemite.

2Sa 23:24 — Asahel the brother of Joab *was* one of the thirty; Elhanan the son of Dodo of Bethlehem,

1Ch 11:26 — Also the valiant men of the armies *were,* Asahel the brother of Joab, Elhanan the son of Dodo of Bethlehem,

DOEG

• An Edomite, present when Ahimelech helped David.

Ps 52:1–9

1Sa 21:7 — Now a certain man of the servants of Saul *was* there that day, detained before the LORD; and his name *was* Doeg, an Edomite, the chiefest of the herdmen that *belonged* to Saul.

1Sa 22:9 — Then answered Doeg the Edomite, which was set over the servants of Saul, and said, I saw the son of Jesse coming to Nob, to Ahimelech the son of Ahitub.

1Sa 22:22 — And David said unto Abiathar, I knew *it* that day, when Doeg the Edomite *was* there, that he would surely tell Saul: I have occasioned *the death* of all the persons of thy father's house.

• Slew eighty-five priests.

1Sa 22:18–19

DOER

• Of the word.

Ro 2:13–15; Jas 1:22–27

Mt 7:21 — Not every one that saith unto me, Lord, Lord, shall enter into the kingdom of heaven; but he that doeth the will of my Father which is in heaven.

Mt 12:50 — For whosoever shall do the will of my Father which is in heaven, the same is my brother, and sister, and mother.

Lk 11:28 — But he said, Yea rather, blessed *are* they that hear the word of God, and keep it.

2Co 8:11 — Now therefore perform the doing *of it;* that as *there was* a readiness to will, so *there may be* a performance also out of that which ye have.

Jas 4:11 — Speak not evil one of another, brethren. He that speaketh evil of *his* brother, and judgeth his brother, speaketh evil of the law, and judgeth the law: but if thou judge the law, thou art not a doer of the law, but a judge.

See: Hearers

DOERS

Jas 1:22 — But be ye doers of the word, and not hearers only, deceiving your own selves.

Jas 4:17 — Therefore to him that knoweth to do good, and doeth *it* not, to him it is sin.

DOG

• Price of, not to be brought into the sanctuary.

Dt 23:18 — Thou shalt not bring the hire of a whore, or the price of a dog, into the house of the LORD thy God for any vow: for even both these *are* abomination unto the LORD thy God.

• Shepherd dogs.

Job 30:1 — But now *they that are* younger than I have me in derision, whose fathers I would have disdained to have set with the dogs of my flock.

• Habits of.

• Licking blood.

1Ki 21:19 — And thou shalt speak unto him, saying, Thus saith the LORD, Hast thou killed, and also taken possession? And thou shalt speak unto him, saying, Thus saith the LORD, In the place where dogs licked the blood of Naboth shall dogs lick thy blood, even thine.

1Ki 22:38 — And *one* washed the chariot in the pool of Samaria; and the dogs licked up his blood; and they washed his armour; according unto the word of the LORD which he spake.

• Licking sores.

Lk 16:21 — And desiring to be fed with the crumbs which fell from the rich man's table: moreover the dogs came and licked his sores.

• Returns to his vomit.

Pr 26:11 — As a dog returneth to his vomit, *so* a fool returneth to his folly.

2Pe 2:22 — But it is happened unto them according to the true proverb, The dog *is* turned to his own vomit again; and the sow that was washed to her wallowing in the mire.

• Lapping of.

Jgs 7:5 — So he brought down the people unto the water: and the LORD said unto Gideon, Every one that lappeth of the water with his tongue, as a dog lappeth, him shalt thou set by himself; likewise every one that boweth down upon his knees to drink.

• Dumb and sleeping.

Isa 56:10–11

• Greyhound.

Pr 30:31 — A greyhound; an he goat also; and a king, against whom *there is* no rising up.

• Epithet of contempt.

Isa 56:10–11

1Sa 17:43 — And the Philistine said unto David, *Am* I a dog, that thou comest to me with staves? And the Philistine cursed David by his gods.

1Sa 24:14 — After whom is the king of Israel come out? after whom dost thou pursue? after a dead dog, after a flea.

2Sa 3:8 — Then was Abner very wroth for the words of Ish-bosheth, and said, *Am* I a dog's head, which against Judah do shew kindness this day unto the house of Saul thy father, to his brethren, and to his friends, and have not delivered thee into the hand of David, that thou chargest me to day with a fault concerning this woman?

2Sa 9:8 — And he bowed himself, and said, What is thy servant, that thou shouldest look upon such a dead dog as I *am?*

2Sa 16:9 — Then said Abishai the son of Zeruiah unto the king, Why should this dead dog curse my lord the king? let me go over, I pray thee, and take off his head.

2Ki 8:13 — And Hazael said, But what, *is* thy servant a dog, that he should do this great thing? And Elisha answered, The LORD hath shewed me that thou *shalt be* king over Syria.

Mt 15:26 — But he answered and said, It is not meet to take the children's bread, and to cast *it* to dogs.

• Figurative.

Php 3:2 — Beware of dogs, beware of evil workers, beware of the concision.

Rev 22:15 — For without *are* dogs, and sorcerers, and whoremongers, and murderers, and idolaters, and whosoever loveth and maketh a lie.

DOGMATISM **See: Commandments; precepts of men**

DOMICILE

• Right of.

Dt 24:10–11

DOMINION

• Of man.

See: Man; dominion of

DONATIONS **See: Liberality**

DOOR

• Posts of, sprinkled with the blood of the paschal lamb.

Ex 12:22 — And ye shall take a bunch of hyssop, and dip *it* in the blood that *is* in the bason, and strike the lintel and the two side posts with the blood that *is* in the bason; and none of you shall go out at the door of his house until the morning.

• Posts of, the law to be written on.

Dt 11:20 — And thou shalt write them upon the door posts of thine house, and upon thy gates:

• Hinges for.

Pr 26:14 — *As* the door turneth upon his hinges, so *doth* the slothful upon his bed.

• Made of gold.

1Ki 7:50 — And the bowls, and the snuffers, and the basons, and the spoons, and the censers *of* pure gold; and the hinges *of* gold, *both* for the doors of the inner house, the most holy *place, and* for the doors of the house, *to wit,* of the temple.

• Doors of the temple made of two leaves, cherubim and flowers carved upon, covered with gold.

1Ki 6:31–35

• Figurative.

• Door of hope.

Hos 2:15 — And I will give her her vineyards from thence, and the valley of Achor for a door of hope: and she shall sing there, as in the days of her youth, and as in the day when she came up out of the land of Egypt.

• Door of opportunity.

1Co 16:9 — For a great door and effectual is opened unto me, and *there are* many adversaries.

Rev 3:8 — I know thy works: behold, I have set before thee an open door, and no man can shut it: for thou hast a little strength, and hast kept my word, and hast not denied my name.

• Door closed.

Mt 25:10 — And while they went to buy, the bridegroom came; and they that were ready went in with him to the marriage: and the door was shut.

Lk 13:25 — When once the master of the house is risen up, and hath shut to the door, and ye begin to stand without, and to knock at the door, saying, Lord, Lord, open unto us; and he shall answer and say unto you, I know you not whence ye are:

Rev 3:7 — And to the angel of the church in Philadelphia write; These things saith he that is holy, he that is true, he that hath the key of David, he that openeth, and no man shutteth; and shutteth, and no man openeth;

DOORKEEPERS

• Of the temple.

2Ki 25:18 — And the captain of the guard took Seraiah the chief priest, and Zephaniah the second priest, and the three keepers of the door:

• Of palaces.

Jn 18:17 — Then saith the damsel that kept the door unto Peter, Art not thou also *one* of this man's disciples? He saith, I am not.

DOPHKAH • Camping place of the Israelites.

Nu 33:12 — And they took their journey out of the wilderness of Sin, and encamped in Dophkah.

DOR

• A town and district of Palestine.

Jos 11:2 — And to the kings that *were* on the north of the mountains, and of the plains south of Chinneroth, and in the valley, and in the borders of Dor on the west,

• Conquered by Joshua.

Jos 12:23 — The king of Dor in the coast of Dor, one; the king of the nations of Gilgal, one;

1Ki 4:11 — The son of Abinadab, in all the region of Dor; which had Taphath the daughter of Solomon to wife:

• Allotted to Manasseh, although situated in the territory of Asher.

Jos 17:11 — And Manasseh had in Issachar and in Asher Beth-shean and her towns, and Ibleam and her towns, and the inhabitants of Dor and her towns, and the inhabitants of Endor and her towns, and the inhabitants of Taanach and her towns, and the inhabitants of Megiddo and her towns, *even* three countries.

Jgs 1:27 — Neither did Manasseh drive out *the inhabitants of* Beth-shean and her towns, nor Taanach and her towns, nor the inhabitants of Dor and her towns, nor the inhabitants of Ibleam and her towns, nor the inhabitants of Megiddo and her towns: but the Canaanites would dwell in that land.

DORCAS

• Called also Tabitha.

• A pious woman of Joppa.

Ac 9:36–42

DOTHAN

• A district and town in Palestine.

Ge 37:17 — And the man said, They are departed hence; for I heard them say, Let us go to Dothan. And Joseph went after his brethren, and found them in Dothan.

• Syrian army made blind at.

2Ki 6:13–19

DOUBTING

Job 3:1–26; 4:3–6; 9:16–23; 16:1–17:16; 23:15–17; 30:20–21; Ps 42:5–6; 73:13–17; Isa 40:27–28; 49:14–15; La 1:1–5:22

Ps 22:2 — O my God, I cry in the daytime, but thou hearest not; and in the night season, and am not silent.

Ps 31:22 — For I said in my haste, I am cut off from before thine eyes: nevertheless thou heardest the voice of my supplications when I cried unto thee.

Ps 49:5 — Wherefore should I fear in the days of evil, *when* the iniquity of my heels shall compass me about?

Ps 77:3 — I remembered God, and was troubled: I complained, and my spirit was overwhelmed. Selah.

Ps 77:7 — Will the Lord cast off for ever? and will he be favourable no more?

Ps 77:9 — Hath God forgotten to be gracious? hath he in anger shut up his tender mercies? Selah.

Pr 24:10 — *If* thou faint in the day of adversity, thy strength *is* small.

Isa 50:2 — Wherefore, when I came, *was there* no man? when I called, *was there* none to answer? Is my hand shortened at all, that it cannot redeem? or have I no power to deliver? behold, at my rebuke I dry up the sea, I make the rivers a wilderness: their fish stinketh, because *there is* no water, and dieth for thirst.

Jer 8:18 — *When* I would comfort myself against sorrow, my heart *is* faint in me.

Jer 15:18 — Why is my pain perpetual, and my wound incurable, *which* refuseth to be healed? wilt thou be altogether unto me as a liar, *and as* waters *that* fail?

Jer 45:3 — Thou didst say, Woe is me now! for the LORD hath added grief to my sorrow; I fainted in my sighing, and I find no rest.

Hos 10:3 — For now they shall say, We have no king, because we feared not the LORD; what then should a king do to us?

Mt 8:26 — And he saith unto them, Why are ye fearful, O ye of little faith? Then he arose, and rebuked the winds and the sea; and there was a great calm.

Mt 14:31 — And immediately Jesus stretched forth *his* hand, and caught him, and said unto him, O thou of little faith, wherefore didst thou doubt?

Mt 17:17 — Then Jesus answered and said, O faithless and perverse generation, how long shall I be with you? how long shall I suffer you? bring him hither to me.

Mk 4:38 — And he was in the hinder part of the ship, asleep on a pillow: and they awake him, and say unto him, Master, carest thou not that we perish?

Mk 4:40 — And he said unto them, Why are ye so fearful? how is it that ye have no faith?

Mk 9:19 — He answereth him, and saith, O faithless generation, how long shall I be with you? how long shall I suffer you? bring him unto me.

Lk 8:25 — And he said unto them, Where is your faith? And they being afraid wondered, saying one to another, What manner of man is this! for he commandeth even the winds and water, and they obey him.

Lk 9:40 — And I besought thy disciples to cast him out; and they could not.

Lk 24:25 — Then he said unto them, O fools, and slow of heart to believe all that the prophets have spoken:

1Pe 1:6 — Wherein ye greatly rejoice, though now for a season, if need be, ye are in heaviness through manifold temptations:

• Exemplified.

Ge 12:12–13; 18:12–14; Ex 5:22–23; 14:10–12; Nu 11:21–22; 1Sa 16:1–2; 22:3–4; 1Ki 18:7–14; 19:13–18; 2Ki 13:18–19; Jer 32:24–25; La 1:1–5:22; Mt 8:23–27; 11:2–3; 14:29–31; 17:14–21; Mk 9:14–29; 16:10–11; Jn 14:8–11; Ac 9:13–14

Ge 15:8 — And he said, Lord GOD, whereby shall I know that I shall inherit it?

Ge 19:30 — And Lot went up out of Zoar, and dwelt in the mountain, and his two daughters with him; for he feared to dwell in Zoar: and he dwelt in a cave, he and his two daughters.

Ge 20:2 — And Abraham said of Sarah his wife, She *is* my sister: and Abimelech king of Gerar sent, and took Sarah.

Ge 20:11 — And Abraham said, Because I thought, Surely the fear of God *is* not in this place; and they will slay me for my wife's sake.

Ge 26:7 — And the men of the place asked *him* of his wife; and he said, She *is* my sister: for he feared to say, *She is* my wife; lest, *said he,* the men of the place should kill me for Rebekah; because she *was* fair to look upon.

Ex 3:11 — And Moses said unto God, Who *am* I, that I should go unto Pharaoh, and that I should bring forth the children of Israel out of Egypt?

Ex 4:1 — And Moses answered and said, But, behold, they will not believe me, nor hearken unto my voice: for they will say, The LORD hath not appeared unto thee.

Ex 4:10 — And Moses said unto the LORD, O my Lord, I *am* not eloquent, neither heretofore, nor since thou hast spoken unto thy servant: but I *am* slow of speech, and of a slow tongue.

Ex 4:13 — And he said, O my Lord, send, I pray thee, by the hand *of him whom* thou wilt send.

Ex 6:12 — And Moses spake before the LORD, saying, Behold, the children of Israel have not hearkened unto me; how then shall Pharaoh hear me, who *am* of uncircumcised lips?

Ex 14:15 — And the LORD said unto Moses, Wherefore criest thou unto me? speak unto the children of Israel, that they go forward:

Jgs 6:13 — And Gideon said unto him, Oh my Lord, if the LORD be with us, why then is all this befallen us? and where *be* all his miracles which our fathers told us of, saying, Did not the LORD bring us up from Egypt? but now the LORD hath forsaken us, and delivered us into the hands of the Midianites.

Jgs 6:15 — And he said unto him, Oh my Lord, wherewith shall I save Israel? behold, my family is poor in Manasseh, and I *am* the least in my father's house.

1Sa 17:11 — When Saul and all Israel heard those words of the Philistine, they were dismayed, and greatly afraid.

1Sa 17:24 — And all the men of Israel, when they saw the man, fled from him, and were sore afraid.

Jer 1:6 — Then said I, Ah, Lord GOD! behold, I cannot speak: for I *am* a child.

Mt 28:17 — And when they saw him, they worshipped him: but some doubted.

➜See: Cowardice

➜See: Murmuring

DOUGH

• First of, offered to God.

Nu 15:19–21

Ne 10:37 — And *that* we should bring the firstfruits of our dough, and our offerings, and the fruit of all manner of trees, of wine and of oil, unto the priests, to the chambers of the house of our God; and the tithes of our ground unto the Levites, that the same Levites might have the tithes in all the cities of our tillage.

- **Kneaded.**

Jer 7:18 — The children gather wood, and the fathers kindle the fire, and the women knead *their* dough, to make cakes to the queen of heaven, and to pour out drink offerings unto other gods, that they may provoke me to anger.

Hos 7:4 — They *are* all adulterers, as an oven heated by the baker, *who* ceaseth from raising after he hath kneaded the dough, until it be leavened.

- **Part of, for priest.**

Eze 44:30 — And the first of all the firstfruits of all *things,* and every oblation of all, of every *sort* of your oblations, shall be the priest's: ye shall also give unto the priest the first of your dough, that he may cause the blessing to rest in thine house.

See: Bread

See: Oven

DOVE, TURTLE

- **Sent out from the ark by Noah.**

Ge 8:8–11

- **Mourning of.**

Isa 38:14 — Like a crane *or* a swallow, so did I chatter: I did mourn as a dove: mine eyes fail *with looking* upward: O LORD, I am oppressed; undertake for me.

Isa 59:11 — We roar all like bears, and mourn sore like doves: we look for judgment, but *there is* none; for salvation, *but* it is far off from us.

Na 2:7 — And Huzzab shall be led away captive, she shall be brought up, and her maids shall lead *her* as with the voice of doves, tabering upon their breasts.

- **Domesticated.**

Isa 60:8 — Who *are* these *that* fly as a cloud, and as the doves to their windows?

- **Nests of.**

Jer 48:28 — O ye that dwell in Moab, leave the cities, and dwell in the rock, and be like the dove *that* maketh her nest in the sides of the hole's mouth.

- **Harmlessness of, typical of Christ's gentleness.**

Mt 10:16 — Behold, I send you forth as sheep in the midst of wolves: be ye therefore wise as serpents, and harmless as doves.

- **Sacrificial uses of.**

Ge 15:9 — And he said unto him, Take me an heifer of three years old, and a she goat of three years old, and a ram of three years old, and a turtledove, and a young pigeon.

- **Prescribed for purification.**
  - **Of women.**

Le 12:6 — And when the days of her purifying are fulfilled, for a son, or for a daughter, she shall bring a lamb of the first year for a burnt offering, and a young pigeon, or a turtledove, for a sin offering, unto the door of the tabernacle of the congregation, unto the priest:

Le 12:8 — And if she be not able to bring a lamb, then she shall bring two turtles, or two young pigeons; the one for the burnt offering, and the other for a sin offering: and the priest shall make an atonement for her, and she shall be clean.

Lk 2:24 — And to offer a sacrifice according to that which is said in the law of the Lord, A pair of turtledoves, or two young pigeons.

  - **Of Nazarites.**

Nu 6:10 — And on the eighth day he shall bring two turtles, or two young pigeons, to the priest, to the door of the tabernacle of the congregation:

  - **Of lepers.**

Le 14:22 — And two turtledoves, or two young pigeons, such as he is able to get; and the one shall be a sin offering, and the other a burnt offering.

- **Burnt offering of.**

Le 1:14–17

- **Trespass offering of, for the impecunious.**

Le 5:7–10

Le 12:8 — And if she be not able to bring a lamb, then she shall bring two turtles, or two young pigeons; the one for the burnt offering, and the other for a sin offering: and the priest shall make an atonement for her, and she shall be clean.

- **Sin offering, for those who touched any dead body.**

Nu 6:10 — And on the eighth day he shall bring two turtles, or two young pigeons, to the priest, to the door of the tabernacle of the congregation:

- **Market for, in the temple.**

Mt 21:12 — And Jesus went into the temple of God, and cast out all them that sold and bought in the temple, and overthrew the tables of the moneychangers, and the seats of them that sold doves,

Jn 2:14 — And found in the temple those that sold oxen and sheep and doves, and the changers of money sitting:

- **Symbolic.**
  - **Of the Holy Spirit.**

Mt 3:16 — And Jesus, when he was baptized, went up straightway out of the water: and, lo, the heavens were opened unto him, and he saw the Spirit of God descending like a dove, and lighting upon him:

Lk 3:22 — And the Holy Ghost descended in a bodily shape like a dove upon him, and a voice came from heaven, which said, Thou art my beloved Son; in thee I am well pleased.

Jn 1:32 — And John bare record, saying, I saw the Spirit descending from heaven like a dove, and it abode upon him.

See: Pigeon

DOWRY

Ex 22:16–17; Ru 4:3–9

See: Women

DOXOLOGY See: Praise

DRAGON

• Any terrible creature, as a venomous serpent.

Dt 32:33 — Their wine *is* the poison of dragons, and the cruel venom of asps.

• A serpent of the desert.

Ps 91:13 — Thou shalt tread upon the lion and adder: the young lion and the dragon shalt thou trample under feet.

Isa 34:13 — And thorns shall come up in her palaces, nettles and brambles in the fortresses thereof: and it shall be an habitation of dragons, *and* a court for owls.

Jer 9:11 — And I will make Jerusalem heaps, *and* a den of dragons; and I will make the cities of Judah desolate, without an inhabitant.

Jer 51:37 — And Babylon shall become heaps, a dwelling place for dragons, an astonishment, and an hissing, without an inhabitant.

• A sea serpent.

Ps 74:13 — Thou didst divide the sea by thy strength: thou brakest the heads of the dragons in the waters.

Ps 148:7 — Praise the LORD from the earth, ye dragons, and all deeps:

Isa 27:1 — In that day the LORD with his sore and great and strong sword shall punish leviathan the piercing serpent, even leviathan that crooked serpent; and he shall slay the dragon that *is* in the sea.

• A jackal.

Isa 13:22 — And the wild beasts of the islands shall cry in their desolate houses, and dragons in *their* pleasant palaces: and her time *is* near to come, and her days shall not be prolonged.

Isa 34:13 — And thorns shall come up in her palaces, nettles and brambles in the fortresses thereof: and it shall be an habitation of dragons, *and* a court for owls.

Isa 35:7 — And the parched ground shall become a pool, and the thirsty land springs of water: in the habitation of dragons, where each lay, *shall be* grass with reeds and rushes.

Isa 43:20 — The beast of the field shall honour me, the dragons and the owls: because I give waters in the wilderness, *and* rivers in the desert, to give drink to my people, my chosen.

Jer 9:11 — And I will make Jerusalem heaps, *and* a den of dragons; and I will make the cities of Judah desolate, without an inhabitant.

Jer 10:22 — Behold, the noise of the bruit is come, and a great commotion out of the north country, to make the cities of Judah desolate, *and* a den of dragons.

Jer 14:6 — And the wild asses did stand in the high places, they snuffed up the wind like dragons; their eyes did fail, because *there was* no grass.

Jer 49:33 — And Hazor shall be a dwelling for dragons, *and* a desolation for ever: there shall no man abide there, nor *any* son of man dwell in it.

Jer 51:37 — And Babylon shall become heaps, a dwelling place for dragons, an astonishment, and an hissing, without an inhabitant.

Mic 1:8 — Therefore I will wail and howl, I will go stripped and naked: I will make a wailing like the dragons, and mourning as the owls.

Mal 1:3 — And I hated Esau, and laid his mountains and his heritage waste for the dragons of the wilderness.

• Interperted as a whale.

Ge 1:21 — And God created great whales, and every living creature that moveth, which the waters brought forth abundantly, after their kind, and every winged fowl after his kind: and God saw that *it was* good.

Job 7:12 — *Am* I a sea, or a whale, that thou settest a watch over me?

• Serpent.

Ex 7:9 — When Pharaoh shall speak unto you, saying, Shew a miracle for you: then thou shalt say unto Aaron, Take thy rod, and cast *it* before Pharaoh, *and* it shall become a serpent.

• A term applied to Pharaoh.

Isa 51:9 — Awake, awake, put on strength, O arm of the LORD; awake, as in the ancient days, in the generations of old. *Art* thou not it that hath cut Rahab, *and* wounded the dragon?

• A term applied to Satan.

Rev 20:2 — And he laid hold on the dragon, that old serpent, which is the Devil, and Satan, and bound him a thousand years,

• Symbolic.

Rev 12:1–13:18

Eze 29:3 — Speak, and say, Thus saith the Lord GOD; Behold, I *am* against thee, Pharaoh king of Egypt, the great dragon that lieth in the midst of his rivers, which hath said, My river *is* mine own, and I have made *it* for myself.

Eze 32:2 — Son of man, take up a lamentation for Pharaoh king of Egypt, and say unto him, Thou art like a young lion of the nations, and thou *art* as a whale in the seas: and thou camest forth with thy rivers, and troubledst the waters with thy feet, and fouledst their rivers.

Rev 16:13 — And I saw three unclean spirits like frogs *come* out of the mouth of the dragon, and out of the mouth of the beast, and out of the mouth of the false prophet.

DRAM

• Called also Drachm.

• A Persian coin of differently estimated value.

Ne 7:70–72

1Ch 29:7 — And gave for the service of the house of God of gold five thousand talents and ten thousand drams, and of silver ten thousand talents, and of brass eighteen thousand talents, and one hundred thousand talents of iron.

Ezr 2:69 — They gave after their ability unto the treasure of the work threescore and one thousand drams of gold, and five thousand pound of silver, and one hundred priests' garments.

Ezr 8:27 — Also twenty basons of gold, of a thousand drams; and two vessels of fine copper, precious as gold.

DRAMA ⇛See: Pantomime

DRAWING

- **Of pictures on tile.**

Eze 4:1 — Thou also, son of man, take thee a tile, and lay it before thee, and pourtray upon it the city, *even* Jerusalem:

DREAM

- **Evanescent.**

Job 20:8 — He shall fly away as a dream, and shall not be found: yea, he shall be chased away as a vision of the night.

- **Vanity of.**

Ecc 5:3 — For a dream cometh through the multitude of business; and a fool's voice *is known* by multitude of words.

Ecc 5:7 — For in the multitude of dreams and many words *there are* also *divers* vanities: but fear thou God.

- **Revelations by.**

Job 33:15–17

Nu 12:6 — And he said, Hear now my words: If there be a prophet among you, *I* the LORD will make myself known unto him in a vision, *and* will speak unto him in a dream.

Jer 23:28 — The prophet that hath a dream, let him tell a dream; and he that hath my word, let him speak my word faithfully. What *is* the chaff to the wheat? saith the LORD.

Joel 2:28 — And it shall come to pass afterward, *that* I will pour out my spirit upon all flesh; and your sons and your daughters shall prophesy, your old men shall dream dreams, your young men shall see visions:

Ac 2:17 — And it shall come to pass in the last days, saith God, I will pour out of my Spirit upon all flesh: and your sons and your daughters shall prophesy, and your young men shall see visions, and your old men shall dream dreams:

- **The dreams of the butler and baker.**

Ge 40:8–23

- **The dream of Pharaoh.**

Ge 41:1–36

- **Interpreted by Joseph.**

Ge 40:12–13, 18–19; 41:25–32

- **Interpreted by Daniel.**

Da 2:16–23, 28–30; 4:1–37

- **Delusive.**

Isa 29:7–8

- **False prophets pretended to receive revelations through.**

Dt 13:1–5; Jer 23:25–32

Jer 27:9 — Therefore hearken not ye to your prophets, nor to your diviners, nor to your dreamers, nor to your enchanters, nor to your sorcerers, which speak unto you, saying, Ye shall not serve the king of Babylon:

Jer 29:8 — For thus saith the LORD of hosts, the God of Israel; Let not your prophets and your diviners, that *be* in the midst of you, deceive you, neither hearken to your dreams which ye cause to be dreamed.

Zec 10:2 — For the idols have spoken vanity, and the diviners have seen a lie, and have told false dreams; they comfort in vain: therefore they went their way as a flock, they were troubled, because *there was* no shepherd.

⇛See: Vision, New Testament

- **Instances of.**
  - **Abimelech, concerning Sarah.**
    Ge 20:3
  - **Jacob.**
    - **Concerning the ladder.**
      Ge 28:12
    - **Concerning the ring-straked cattle.**
      Ge 31:10–13
    - **Concerning his going down into Egypt.**
      Ge 46:2
  - **Joseph, concerning the sheaves.**
    Ge 37:5–10
  - **Laban, concerning Jacob.**
    Ge 31:24
  - **The Midianite, concerning the cake of barley.**
    Jgs 7:13
  - **Solomon, concerning his choice of wisdom.**
    1Ki 3:3–15
  - **Eliphaz, of a spirit speaking to him.**
    Job 4:12–21
  - **Daniel, concerning the four beasts.**
    Da 7:1–28
  - **Joseph.**
    - **Concerning Mary's innocence.**
      Mt 1:20–21
    - **Concerning the flight into Egypt.**
      Mt 2:13
    - **Concerning the return into Palestine.**
      Mt 2:19–22
  - **Pilate's wife, concerning Jesus.**
    Mt 27:19
  - **Cornelius' vision, concerning Peter.**
    Ac 10:3–6
  - **Peter's vision of the unclean beasts.**
    Ac 10:10–16
  - **Paul's visions.**
    - **The man in Macedonia, crying, "Come over into Macedonia".**
      Ac 16:9
    - **Relating to his going to Rome.**
      Ac 23:11
    - **Concerning the shipwreck, and the safety of all on board.**
      Ac 27:23–24

DRESS

• **Of fig leaves.**

Ge 3:7 — And the eyes of them both were opened, and they knew that they *were* naked; and they sewed fig leaves together, and made themselves aprons.

• **Of skins.**

Ge 3:21 — Unto Adam also and to his wife did the LORD God make coats of skins, and clothed them.

• **Of other materials.**

See: Goat; hair of

See: Hair

See: Leather

See: Linen

See: Sackcloth

See: Silk

See: Wool

• **Mixed materials in, forbidden.**

Dt 22:11 — Thou shalt not wear a garment of divers sorts, *as* of woollen and linen together.

• **Men forbidden to wear women's, and women forbidden to wear men's.**

Dt 22:5 — The woman shall not wear that which pertaineth unto a man, neither shall a man put on a woman's garment: for all that do so *are* abomination unto the LORD thy God.

• **Rules with respect to women's.**

1Ti 2:9–10; 1Pe 3:1–6

Mt 5:28 — But I say unto you, That whosoever looketh on a woman to lust after her hath committed adultery with her already in his heart.

• **Not to be held over night as a pledge for debt.**

Ex 22:26 — If thou at all take thy neighbour's raiment to pledge, thou shalt deliver it unto him by that the sun goeth down:

• **Ceremonial purification of.**

Le 13:47–59

Le 11:32 — And upon whatsoever *any* of them, when they are dead, doth fall, it shall be unclean; whether *it be* any vessel of wood, or raiment, or skin, or sack, whatsoever vessel *it be,* wherein *any* work is done, it must be put into water, and it shall be unclean until the even; so it shall be cleansed.

Nu 31:20 — And purify all *your* raiment, and all that is made of skins, and all work of goats' *hair,* and all things made of wood.

• **Rending of.**

See: Mourning

• **Of the head.**

• **Bonnets, prescribed by Moses, for the priests.**

Ex 28:40 — And for Aaron's sons thou shalt make coats, and thou shalt make for them girdles, and bonnets shalt thou make for them, for glory and for beauty.

Ex 29:9 — And thou shalt gird them with girdles, Aaron and his sons, and put the bonnets on them: and the priest's office shall be theirs for a perpetual statute: and thou shalt consecrate Aaron and his sons.

Ex 39:28 — And a mitre *of* fine linen, and goodly bonnets *of* fine linen, and linen breeches *of* fine twined linen,

• **Bonnets, prescribed by Ezekiel.**

Eze 44:18 — They shall have linen bonnets upon their heads, and shall have linen breeches upon their loins; they shall not gird *themselves* with any thing that causeth sweat.

• **Hats worn by men.**

Da 3:21 — Then these men were bound in their coats, their hosen, and their hats, and their *other* garments, and were cast into the midst of the burning fiery furnace.

• **Bonnets worn by women.**

Isa 3:20 — The bonnets, and the ornaments of the legs, and the headbands, and the tablets, and the earrings,

Eze 24:17 — Forbear to cry, make no mourning for the dead, bind the tire of thine head upon thee, and put on thy shoes upon thy feet, and cover not *thy* lips, and eat not the bread of men.

Eze 24:23 — And your tires *shall be* upon your heads, and your shoes upon your feet: ye shall not mourn nor weep; but ye shall pine away for your iniquities, and mourn one toward another.

• **Hoods.**

Isa 3:23 — The glasses, and the fine linen, and the hoods, and the vails.

• **Kerchiefs.**

Eze 13:18 — And say, Thus saith the Lord GOD; Woe to the *women* that sew pillows to all armholes, and make kerchiefs upon the head of every stature to hunt souls! Will ye hunt the souls of my people, and will ye save the souls alive *that come* unto you?

Eze 13:21 — Your kerchiefs also will I tear, and deliver my people out of your hand, and they shall be no more in your hand to be hunted; and ye shall know that I *am* the LORD.

• **Various articles of.**

• **Mantle.**

1Ki 19:13 — And it was *so,* when Elijah heard *it,* that he wrapped his face in his mantle, and went out, and stood in the entering in of the cave. And, behold, *there came* a voice unto him, and said, What doest thou here, Elijah?

1Ch 15:27 — And David *was* clothed with a robe of fine linen, and all the Levites that bare the ark, and the singers, and Chenaniah the master of the song with the singers: David also *had* upon him an ephod of linen.

Ezr 9:3 — And when I heard this thing, I rent my garment and my mantle, and plucked off the hair of my head and of my beard, and sat down astonied.

Job 1:20 — Then Job arose, and rent his mantle, and shaved his head, and fell down upon the ground, and worshipped,

• **Many colored.**

2Sa 13:18 — And *she had* a garment of divers colours upon her: for with such robes were the king's daughters *that were* virgins apparelled. Then his servant brought her out, and bolted the door after her.

• **Purple.**

Jn 19:2 — And the soldiers platted a crown of thorns, and put *it* on his head, and they put on him a purple robe,

Jn 19:5 — Then came Jesus forth, wearing the crown of thorns, and the purple robe. And *Pilate* saith unto them, Behold the man!

• **Robe.**

Ex 28:4 — And these *are* the garments which they shall make; a breastplate, and an ephod, and a robe, and a broidered coat, a mitre, and a girdle: and they shall make holy garments for Aaron thy brother, and his sons, that he may minister unto me in the priest's office.

1Sa 18:4 — And Jonathan stripped himself of the robe that *was* upon him, and gave it to David, and his garments, even to his sword, and to his bow, and to his girdle.

• **Shawls.**

Isa 3:22 — The changeable suits of apparel, and the mantles, and the wimples, and the crisping pins,

• **Embroidered coat.**

Ex 28:4 — And these *are* the garments which they shall make; a breastplate, and an ephod, and a robe, and a broidered coat, a mitre, and a girdle: and they shall make holy garments for Aaron thy brother, and his sons, that he may minister unto me in the priest's office.

Ex 28:40 — And for Aaron's sons thou shalt make coats, and thou shalt make for them girdles, and bonnets shalt thou make for them, for glory and for beauty.

1Sa 2:19 — Moreover his mother made him a little coat, and brought *it* to him from year to year, when she came up with her husband to offer the yearly sacrifice.

Da 3:21 — Then these men were bound in their coats, their hosen, and their hats, and their *other* garments, and were cast into the midst of the burning fiery furnace.

• **Sleeveless shirt, called coat.**

Mt 5:40 — And if any man will sue thee at the law, and take away thy coat, let him have *thy* cloke also.

Lk 6:29 — And unto him that smiteth thee on the *one* cheek offer also the other; and him that taketh away thy cloke forbid not *to take thy* coat also.

Jn 19:23 — Then the soldiers, when they had crucified Jesus, took his garments, and made four parts, to every soldier a part; and also *his* coat: now the coat was without seam, woven from the top throughout.

Ac 9:39 — Then Peter arose and went with them. When he was come, they brought him into the upper chamber: and all the widows stood by him weeping, and shewing the coats and garments which Dorcas made, while she was with them.

• **Cloak.**

Jn 19:2 — And the soldiers platted a crown of thorns, and put *it* on his head, and they put on him a purple robe,

Jn 19:5 — Then came Jesus forth, wearing the crown of thorns, and the purple robe. And *Pilate* saith unto them, Behold the man!

2Ti 4:13 — The cloke that I left at Troas with Carpus, when thou comest, bring *with thee*, and the books, *but* especially the parchments.

• **Hosen.**

Da 3:21 — Then these men were bound in their coats, their hosen, and their hats, and their *other* garments, and were cast into the midst of the burning fiery furnace.

• **Skirts.**

Eze 5:3 — Thou shalt also take thereof a few in number, and bind them in thy skirts.

• **Mufflers.**

Isa 3:19 — The chains, and the bracelets, and the mufflers,

• **Wimples.**

Isa 3:22 — The changeable suits of apparel, and the mantles, and the wimples, and the crisping pins,

• **Sashes.**

Isa 3:20 — The bonnets, and the ornaments of the legs, and the headbands, and the tablets, and the earrings,

✦**See: Vail**

• **Changes of raiment, the folly of excessive.**

Job 27:16 — Though he heap up silver as the dust, and prepare raiment as the clay;

• **Uniform vestments kept in store for worshipers of Baal.**

2Ki 10:22–23

Zep 1:8 — And it shall come to pass in the day of the LORD'S sacrifice, that I will punish the princes, and the king's children, and all such as are clothed with strange apparel.

• **Uniform vestments kept in store for wedding feasts.**

Mt 22:11 — And when the king came in to see the guests, he saw there a man which had not on a wedding garment:

• **Presents made of changes of raiment.**

Ge 45:22 — To all of them he gave each man changes of raiment; but to Benjamin he gave three hundred *pieces* of silver, and five changes of raiment.

1Sa 18:4 — And Jonathan stripped himself of the robe that *was* upon him, and gave it to David, and his garments, even to his sword, and to his bow, and to his girdle.

2Ki 5:5 — And the king of Syria said, Go to, go, and I will send a letter unto the king of Israel. And he departed, and took with him ten talents of silver, and six thousand *pieces* of gold, and ten changes of raiment.

Est 6:8 — Let the royal apparel be brought which the king *useth* to wear, and the horse that the king rideth upon, and the crown royal which is set upon his head:

Da 5:7 — The king cried aloud to bring in the astrologers, the Chaldeans, and the soothsayers. *And* the king spake, and said to the wise *men* of Babylon, Whosoever shall read this writing, and shew me the interpretation thereof, shall be clothed with scarlet, and *have* a chain of gold about his neck, and shall be the third ruler in the kingdom.

- **Vestments of priests.**
  - **See: Priest, High**
  - **See: Priest, Mosaic**
- **Vestments of mourning.**
  - **See: Mourning**
- **Figurative.**
  - **Filthy, of unrighteousness.**

    Isa 64:6 — But we are all as an unclean *thing,* and all our righteousnesses *are* as filthy rags; and we all do fade as a leaf; and our iniquities, like the wind, have taken us away.
  - **Of righteousness and of iniquity.**
  - **See: Colors; symbolic uses of**
- **Symbolic.**
  - **Filthy, of iniquity.**

    Zec 3:3–4

DRINK

- **Intoxicating.**
  - **See: Abstinence, Total**
  - **See: Drunkard**
  - **See: Drunkenness**
  - **See: Wine**

DRINK OFFERING

See: Offerings

DRIVING

- **Rapid by Jehu.**

  2Ki 9:20 — And the watchman told, saying, He came even unto them, and cometh not again: and the driving is like the driving of Jehu the son of Nimshi; for he driveth furiously.

DROMEDARY

1Ki 4:28 — Barley also and straw for the horses and dromedaries brought they unto the place where *the officers* were, every man according to his charge.

Est 8:10 — And he wrote in the king Ahasuerus' name, and sealed it with the king's ring, and sent letters by posts on horseback, *and* riders on mules, camels, *and* young dromedaries:

Isa 60:6 — The multitude of camels shall cover thee, the dromedaries of Midian and Ephah; all they from Sheba shall come: they shall bring gold and incense; and they shall shew forth the praises of the LORD.

DROPSY

Lk 14:2 — And, behold, there was a certain man before him which had the dropsy.

DROSS

- **Figurative.**

  Eze 22:18–19

  Ps 119:119 — Thou puttest away all the wicked of the earth *like* dross: therefore I love thy testimonies.

  Pr 25:4 — Take away the dross from the silver, and there shall come forth a vessel for the finer.

  Pr 26:23 — Burning lips and a wicked heart *are like* a potsherd covered with silver dross.

  Isa 1:22 — Thy silver is become dross, thy wine mixed with water:

DROUGHT

1Ki 17:1–24; Jer 14:1–6

Ge 31:40 — *Thus* I was; in the day the drought consumed me, and the frost by night; and my sleep departed from mine eyes.

- **Sent by God as a judgment.**

  Dt 28:23–24

  1Ki 8:35 — When heaven is shut up, and there is no rain, because they have sinned against thee; if they pray toward this place, and confess thy name, and turn from their sin, when thou afflictest them:

  2Ch 6:26 — When the heaven is shut up, and there is no rain, because they have sinned against thee; *yet* if they pray toward this place, and confess thy name, and turn from their sin, when thou dost afflict them;

  2Ch 7:13 — If I shut up heaven that there be no rain, or if I command the locusts to devour the land, or if I send pestilence among my people;

  Hos 13:15 — Though he be fruitful among *his* brethren, an east wind shall come, the wind of the LORD shall come up from the wilderness, and his spring shall become dry, and his fountain shall be dried up: he shall spoil the treasure of all pleasant vessels.

  - **See: Famine**
  - **See: Meteorology and Celestial Phenomena**
  - **See: Rain**
- **Figurative.**

  Ps 32:4 — For day and night thy hand was heavy upon me: my moisture is turned into the drought of summer. Selah.

  Isa 44:3 — For I will pour water upon him that is thirsty, and floods upon the dry ground: I will pour my spirit upon thy seed, and my blessing upon thine offspring:

DRUGS

1Co 3:16 — Know ye not that ye are the temple of God, and *that* the Spirit of God dwelleth in you?

1Co 6:20 — For ye are bought with a price: therefore glorify God in your body, and in your spirit, which are God's.

DRUNKARD

Dt 21:20–21; 1Co 6:9–10

Ps 69:12 — They that sit in the gate speak against me; and I *was* the song of the drunkards.

Pr 23:21 — For the drunkard and the glutton shall come to poverty: and drowsiness shall clothe *a man* with rags.

Isa 28:1 — Woe to the crown of pride, to the drunkards of Ephraim, whose glorious beauty is a fading flower, which *are* on the head of the fat valleys of them that are overcome with wine!

Isa 28:3 — The crown of pride, the drunkards of Ephraim, shall be trodden under feet:

Joel 1:5 — Awake, ye drunkards, and weep; and howl, all ye drinkers of wine, because of the new wine; for it is cut off from your mouth.

Na 1:10 — For while *they be* folden together *as* thorns, and while they are drunken *as* drunkards, they shall be devoured as stubble fully dry.

1Co 5:11 — But now I have written unto you not to keep company, if any man that is called a brother be a fornicator, or covetous, or an idolater, or a railer, or a drunkard, or an extortioner; with such an one no not to eat.

+See: Drunkenness

DRUNKENNESS

Dt 21:20–21; 29:19–21; Pr 23:20–21, 29–35; 31:4–7; Isa 5:11–12; 28:7–8; Hab 2:15–17; Gal 5:19–21; 1Th 5:7–8

1Sa 1:14 — And Eli said unto her, How long wilt thou be drunken? put away thy wine from thee.

Ps 69:12 — They that sit in the gate speak against me; and I *was* the song of the drunkards.

Pr 20:1 — Wine *is* a mocker, strong drink *is* raging: and whosoever is deceived thereby is not wise.

Pr 21:17 — He that loveth pleasure *shall be* a poor man: he that loveth wine and oil shall not be rich.

Isa 5:22 — Woe unto *them that are* mighty to drink wine, and men of strength to mingle strong drink:

Isa 19:14 — The LORD hath mingled a perverse spirit in the midst thereof: and they have caused Egypt to err in every work thereof, as a drunken *man* staggereth in his vomit.

Isa 24:9 — They shall not drink wine with a song; strong drink shall be bitter to them that drink it.

Isa 24:11 — *There is* a crying for wine in the streets; all joy is darkened, the mirth of the land is gone.

Isa 28:1 — Woe to the crown of pride, to the drunkards of Ephraim, whose glorious beauty is a fading flower, which *are* on the head of the fat valleys of them that are overcome with wine!

Isa 28:3 — The crown of pride, the drunkards of Ephraim, shall be trodden under feet:

Isa 56:12 — Come ye, *say they,* I will fetch wine, and we will fill ourselves with strong drink; and to morrow shall be as this day, *and* much more abundant.

Jer 25:27 — Therefore thou shalt say unto them, Thus saith the LORD of hosts, the God of Israel; Drink ye, and be drunken, and spue, and fall, and rise no more, because of the sword which I will send among you.

Hos 4:11 — Whoredom and wine and new wine take away the heart.

Hos 7:5 — In the day of our king the princes have made *him* sick with bottles of wine; he stretched out his hand with scorners.

Hos 7:14 — And they have not cried unto me with their heart, when they howled upon their beds: they assemble themselves for corn and wine, *and* they rebel against me.

Joel 1:5 — Awake, ye drunkards, and weep; and howl, all ye drinkers of wine, because of the new wine; for it is cut off from your mouth.

Joel 3:3 — And they have cast lots for my people; and have given a boy for an harlot, and sold a girl for wine, that they might drink.

Am 2:8 — And they lay *themselves* down upon clothes laid to pledge by every altar, and they drink the wine of the condemned in the house of their god.

Am 2:12 — But ye gave the Nazarites wine to drink; and commanded the prophets, saying, Prophesy not.

Am 6:1 — Woe to them *that are* at ease in Zion, and trust in the mountain of Samaria, *which are* named chief of the nations, to whom the house of Israel came!

Am 6:6 — That drink wine in bowls, and anoint themselves with the chief ointments: but they are not grieved for the affliction of Joseph.

Mic 2:11 — If a man walking in the spirit and falsehood do lie, *saying,* I will prophesy unto thee of wine and of strong drink; he shall even be the prophet of this people.

Na 1:10 — For while *they be* folden together *as* thorns, and while they are drunken *as* drunkards, they shall be devoured as stubble fully dry.

Mt 24:49 — And shall begin to smite *his* fellowservants, and to eat and drink with the drunken;

Lk 12:45 — But and if that servant say in his heart, My lord delayeth his coming; and shall begin to beat the menservants and maidens, and to eat and drink, and to be drunken;

Lk 21:34 — And take heed to yourselves, lest at any time your hearts be overcharged with surfeiting, and drunkenness, and cares of this life, and so that day come upon you unawares.

Ro 13:13 — Let us walk honestly, as in the day; not in rioting and drunkenness, not in chambering and wantonness, not in strife and envying.

Eph 5:18 — And be not drunk with wine, wherein is excess; but be filled with the Spirit;

• Figurative.

Isa 51:21–23; Jer 25:15–16, 27–28; 51:7–9; Eze 23:31–34; Hab 2:15–16

Ps 73:10 — Therefore his people return hither: and waters of a full *cup* are wrung out to them.

Ps 75:8 — For in the hand of the LORD *there is* a cup, and the wine is red; it is full of mixture; and he poureth out of the same: but the dregs thereof, all the wicked of the earth shall wring *them* out, *and* drink *them.*

Pr 26:9 — *As* a thorn goeth up into the hand of a drunkard, so *is* a parable in the mouth of fools.

Isa 28:8 — For all tables are full of vomit *and* filthiness, *so that there is* no place *clean.*

Isa 51:17 — Awake, awake, stand up, O Jerusalem, which hast drunk at the hand of the LORD the cup of his fury; thou hast drunken the dregs of the cup of trembling, *and* wrung *them* out.

Isa 63:6 — And I will tread down the people in mine anger, and make them drunk in my fury, and I will bring down their strength to the earth.

La 3:15 — He hath filled me with bitterness, he hath made me drunken with wormwood.

See: Abstinence, Total

See: Drunkard

See: Sobriety

See: Wine

- **Instances of.**
  - **Noah.**
    Ge 9:21
  - **Lot.**
    Ge 19:33
  - **Nabal.**
    1Sa 25:36
  - **Uriah.**
    2Sa 11:13
  - **Amnon.**
    2Sa 13:28
  - **Elah.**
    1Ki 16:9
  - **Ben-hadad and his thirty-two confederate kings.**
    1Ki 20:16
  - **Ahasuerus.**
    Est 1:10–11
  - **Belshazzar.**
    Da 5:1–6
- **Falsely accused of.**
  - **Hannah.**
    1Sa 1:12–16
  - **Jesus.**
    Mt 11:19 — The Son of man came eating and drinking, and they say, Behold a man gluttonous, and a winebibber, a friend of publicans and sinners. But wisdom is justified of her children.
  - **The apostles.**
    Ac 2:13–15

DRUSILLA • Wife of Felix.

Ac 24:24 — And after certain days, when Felix came with his wife Drusilla, which was a Jewess, he sent for Paul, and heard him concerning the faith in Christ.

DUKE

- **Title of the princes of Edom.**

Ge 36:15–43; 1Ch 1:51–54

Ex 15:15 — Then the dukes of Edom shall be amazed; the mighty men of Moab, trembling shall take hold upon them; all the inhabitants of Canaan shall melt away.

- **Of the Midianites.**

Jos 13:21 — And all the cities of the plain, and all the kingdom of Sihon king of the Amorites, which reigned in Heshbon, whom Moses smote with the princes of Midian, Evi, and Rekem, and Zur, and Hur, and Reba, *which were* dukes of Sihon, dwelling in the country.

DULCIMER

- **Bagpipe.**

Da 3:5 — *That* at what time ye hear the sound of the cornet, flute, harp, sackbut, psaltery, dulcimer, and all kinds of musick, ye fall down and worship the golden image that Nebuchadnezzar the king hath set up:

Da 3:10 — Thou, O king, hast made a decree, that every man that shall hear the sound of the cornet, flute, harp, sackbut, psaltery, and dulcimer, and all kinds of musick, shall fall down and worship the golden image:

Da 3:15 — Now if ye be ready that at what time ye hear the sound of the cornet, flute, harp, sackbut, psaltery, and dulcimer, and all kinds of musick, ye fall down and worship the image which I have made; *well:* but if ye worship not, ye shall be cast the same hour into the midst of a burning fiery furnace; and who *is* that God that shall deliver you out of my hands?

See: Music; instruments of

DUMAH

- **Son of Ishmael.**

Isa 21:11–12

Ge 25:14 — And Mishma, and Dumah, and Massa,

1Ch 1:30 — Mishma and Dumah, Massa, Hadad, and Tema,

- **A city of Canaan assigned to Judah.**

Jos 15:52 — Arab, and Dumah, and Eshean,

DUMB

- **Stricken of God.**

Ex 4:11 — And the LORD said unto him, Who hath made man's mouth? or who maketh the dumb, or deaf, or the seeing, or the blind? have not I the LORD?

Lk 1:20 — And, behold, thou shalt be dumb, and not able to speak, until the day that these things shall be performed, because thou believest not my words, which shall be fulfilled in their season.

Lk 1:64 — And his mouth was opened immediately, and his tongue *loosed,* and he spake, and praised God.

- **Miraculous healing of, by Jesus.**

Mt 9:32–33; 15:30–31; Mk 9:25–26

Mt 12:22 — Then was brought unto him one possessed with a devil, blind, and dumb: and he healed him, insomuch that the blind and dumb both spake and saw.

Mk 7:37 — And were beyond measure astonished, saying, He hath done all things well: he maketh both the deaf to hear, and the dumb to speak.

Mk 9:17 — And one of the multitude answered and said, Master, I have brought unto thee my son, which hath a dumb spirit;

See: Deafness

DUNGEON

• In prisons.

Jer 38:6 — Then took they Jeremiah, and cast him into the dungeon of Malchiah the son of Hammelech, that *was* in the court of the prison: and they let down Jeremiah with cords. And in the dungeon *there was* no water, but mire: so Jeremiah sunk in the mire.

La 3:53 — They have cut off my life in the dungeon, and cast a stone upon me.

See: Prison

DURA • Plain of.

Da 3:1 — Nebuchadnezzar the king made an image of gold, whose height *was* threescore cubits, *and* the breadth thereof six cubits: he set it up in the plain of Dura, in the province of Babylon.

DUST

• Man made from.

Ge 2:7 — And the LORD God formed man *of* the dust of the ground, and breathed into his nostrils the breath of life; and man became a living soul.

Ge 3:19 — In the sweat of thy face shalt thou eat bread, till thou return unto the ground; for out of it wast thou taken: for dust thou *art,* and unto dust shalt thou return.

Ge 3:23 — Therefore the LORD God sent him forth from the garden of Eden, to till the ground from whence he was taken.

Ecc 3:20 — All go unto one place; all are of the dust, and all turn to dust again.

• Casting of, in anger.

2Sa 16:13 — And as David and his men went by the way, Shimei went along on the hill's side over against him, and cursed as he went, and threw stones at him, and cast dust.

• Shaking from feet.

Mt 10:14 — And whosoever shall not receive you, nor hear your words, when ye depart out of that house or city, shake off the dust of your feet.

Ac 13:51 — But they shook off the dust of their feet against them, and came unto Iconium.

• Put on the head in mourning.

Jos 7:6 — And Joshua rent his clothes, and fell to the earth upon his face before the ark of the LORD until the eventide, he and the elders of Israel, and put dust upon their heads.

1Sa 4:12 — And there ran a man of Benjamin out of the army, and came to Shiloh the same day with his clothes rent, and with earth upon his head.

2Sa 1:2 — It came even to pass on the third day, that, behold, a man came out of the camp from Saul with his clothes rent, and earth upon his head: and *so* it was, when he came to David, that he fell to the earth, and did obeisance.

2Sa 15:30 — And David went up by the ascent of *mount* Olivet, and wept as he went up, and had his head covered, and he went barefoot: and all the people that *was* with him covered every man his head, and they went up, weeping as they went up.

Job 2:12 — And when they lifted up their eyes afar off, and knew him not, they lifted up their voice, and wept; and they rent every one his mantle, and sprinkled dust upon their heads toward heaven.

Job 42:6 — Wherefore I abhor *myself,* and repent in dust and ashes.

DUTY

• Tribute levied on foreign commerce by Solomon.

1Ki 10:15 — Beside *that he had* of the merchantmen, and of the traffick of the spice merchants, and of all the kings of Arabia, and of the governors of the country.

• Of man to God.

Dt 10:12–13; 30:15–20; Mt 22:36–40; Lk 21:3–4; Ac 4:19–20

Dt 6:5 — And thou shalt love the LORD thy God with all thine heart, and with all thy soul, and with all thy might.

Dt 11:1 — Therefore thou shalt love the LORD thy God, and keep his charge, and his statutes, and his judgments, and his commandments, alway.

Jos 22:5 — But take diligent heed to do the commandment and the law, which Moses the servant of the LORD charged you, to love the LORD your God, and to walk in all his ways, and to keep his commandments, and to cleave unto him, and to serve him with all your heart and with all your soul.

Jos 23:11 — Take good heed therefore unto yourselves, that ye love the LORD your God.

Ps 31:23 — O love the LORD, all ye his saints: *for* the LORD preserveth the faithful, and plentifully rewardeth the proud doer.

Pr 23:26 — My son, give me thine heart, and let thine eyes observe my ways.

Mt 4:10 — Then saith Jesus unto him, Get thee hence, Satan: for it is written, Thou shalt worship the Lord thy God, and him only shalt thou serve.

Mt 12:50 — For whosoever shall do the will of my Father which is in heaven, the same is my brother, and sister, and mother.

Mt 22:21 — They say unto him, Caesar's. Then saith he unto them, Render therefore unto Caesar the things which are Caesar's; and unto God the things that are God's.

Lk 17:10 — So likewise ye, when ye shall have done all those things which are commanded you, say, We are unprofitable servants: we have done that which was our duty to do.

Jn 4:34 — Jesus saith unto them, My meat is to do the will of him that sent me, and to finish his work.

Jn 6:38 — For I came down from heaven, not to do mine own will, but the will of him that sent me.

Jn 14:15 — If ye love me, keep my commandments.

Jn 14:21 — He that hath my commandments, and keepeth them, he it is that loveth me: and he that loveth me shall be loved of my Father, and I will love him, and will manifest myself to him.

Jn 15:14 — Ye are my friends, if ye do whatsoever I command you.

Ac 5:29 — Then Peter and the *other* apostles answered and said, We ought to obey God rather than men.

Jude 1:21 — Keep yourselves in the love of God, looking for the mercy of our Lord Jesus Christ unto eternal life.

✦See: Commandments

✦See: Faithfulness

✦See: Obedience

• Of man to man.

Isa 58:6–7; Mt 25:34–46; Lk 10:25–37

Le 19:18 — Thou shalt not avenge, nor bear any grudge against the children of thy people, but thou shalt love thy neighbour as thyself: I *am* the LORD.

Mt 7:12 — Therefore all things whatsoever ye would that men should do to you, do ye even so to them: for this is the law and the prophets.

✦See: Children

✦See: Commandments

✦See: Husband

✦See: Minister, a Sacred Teacher; duties of

✦See: Parents

✦See: Wife

DWARFS

• Forbidden to be priests.

Le 21:20 — Or crookbackt, or a dwarf, or that hath a blemish in his eye, or be scurvy, or scabbed, or hath his stones broken;

DYEING

Ex 25:5 — And rams' skins dyed red, and badgers' skins, and shittim wood,

Ex 26:14 — And thou shalt make a covering for the tent *of* rams' skins dyed red, and a covering above *of* badgers' skins.

Isa 63:1 — Who *is* this that cometh from Edom, with dyed garments from Bozrah? this *that is* glorious in his apparel, travelling in the greatness of his strength? I that speak in righteousness, mighty to save.

Eze 23:15 — Girded with girdles upon their loins, exceeding in dyed attire upon their heads, all of them princes to look to, after the manner of the Babylonians of Chaldea, the land of their nativity:

DYING ✦See: Death

DYSENTERY

Ac 28:8 — And it came to pass, that the father of Publius lay sick of a fever and of a bloody flux: to whom Paul entered in, and prayed, and laid his hands on him, and healed him.

DYSPEPSIA

• Of Timothy.

1Ti 5:23 — Drink no longer water, but use a little wine for thy stomach's sake and thine often infirmities.

E

EAGLE

• Forbidden as food.

Le 11:13 — And these *are they which ye* shall have in abomination among the fowls; they shall not be eaten, they *are* an abomination: the eagle, and the ossifrage, and the ospray,

Dt 14:12 — But these *are they* of which ye shall not eat: the eagle, and ossifrage, and the ospray,

• Swift flight of.

Dt 28:49 — The LORD shall bring a nation against thee from far, from the end of the earth, *as swift* as the eagle flieth; a nation whose tongue thou shalt not understand;

Job 9:26 — They are passed away as the swift ships: as the eagle *that* hasteth to the prey.

Pr 30:19 — The way of an eagle in the air; the way of a serpent upon a rock; the way of a ship in the midst of the sea; and the way of a man with a maid.

Jer 4:13 — Behold, he shall come up as clouds, and his chariots *shall be* as a whirlwind: his horses are swifter than eagles. Woe unto us! for we are spoiled.

Jer 49:22 — Behold, he shall come up and fly as the eagle, and spread his wings over Bozrah: and at that day shall the heart of the mighty men of Edom be as the heart of a woman in her pangs.

La 4:19 — Our persecutors are swifter than the eagles of the heaven: they pursued us upon the mountains, they laid wait for us in the wilderness.

• Nest of.

Job 39:27–30

Dt 32:11 — As an eagle stirreth up her nest, fluttereth over her young, spreadeth abroad her wings, taketh them, beareth them on her wings:

Jer 49:16 — Thy terribleness hath deceived thee, *and* the pride of thine heart, O thou that dwellest in the clefts of the rock, that holdest the height of the hill: though thou shouldest make thy nest as high as the eagle, I will bring thee down from thence, saith the LORD.

• Bears her young on her wings.

Ex 19:4 — Ye have seen what I did unto the Egyptians, and *how* I bare you on eagles' wings, and brought you unto myself.

Dt 32:11 — As an eagle stirreth up her nest, fluttereth over her young, spreadeth abroad her wings, taketh them, beareth them on her wings:

• Long life of.

Ps 103:5 — Who satisfieth thy mouth with good *things; so that* thy youth is renewed like the eagle's.

• Bald.

Mic 1:16 — Make thee bald, and poll thee for thy delicate children; enlarge thy baldness as the eagle; for they are gone into captivity from thee.

• Gier-eagle.

Le 11:18 — And the swan, and the pelican, and the gier eagle,

• Figurative.

Ex 19:4 — Ye have seen what I did unto the Egyptians, and *how* I bare you on eagles' wings, and brought you unto myself.

Dt 32:11 — As an eagle stirreth up her nest, fluttereth over her young, spreadeth abroad her wings, taketh them, beareth them on her wings:

Jer 48:40 — For thus saith the LORD; Behold, he shall fly as an eagle, and shall spread his wings over Moab.

Hos 8:1 — *Set* the trumpet to thy mouth. *He shall come* as an eagle against the house of the LORD, because they have transgressed my covenant, and trespassed against my law.

• Symbolic.

Eze 1:10 — As for the likeness of their faces, they four had the face of a man, and the face of a lion, on the right side: and they four had the face of an ox on the left side; they four also had the face of an eagle.

Eze 10:14 — And every one had four faces: the first face *was* the face of a cherub, and the second face *was* the face of a man, and the third the face of a lion, and the fourth the face of an eagle.

Eze 17:3 — And say, Thus saith the Lord GOD; A great eagle with great wings, longwinged, full of feathers, which had divers colours, came unto Lebanon, and took the highest branch of the cedar:

Da 7:4 — The first *was* like a lion, and had eagle's wings: I beheld till the wings thereof were plucked, and it was lifted up from the earth, and made stand upon the feet as a man, and a man's heart was given to it.

Rev 4:7 — And the first beast *was* like a lion, and the second beast like a calf, and the third beast had a face as a man, and the fourth beast *was* like a flying eagle.

Rev 12:14 — And to the woman were given two wings of a great eagle, that she might fly into the wilderness, into her place, where she is nourished for a time, and times, and half a time, from the face of the serpent.

EAR

• Blood put upon, in consecration of priests.

Ex 29:20 — Then shalt thou kill the ram, and take of his blood, and put *it* upon the tip of the right ear of Aaron, and upon the tip of the right ear of his sons, and upon the thumb of their right hand, and upon the great toe of their right foot, and sprinkle the blood upon the altar round about.

Le 8:23 — And he slew *it;* and Moses took of the blood of it, and put *it* upon the tip of Aaron's right ear, and upon the thumb of his right hand, and upon the great toe of his right foot.

• **Blood put upon, in cleansing lepers.**

Le 14:14 — And the priest shall take *some* of the blood of the trespass offering, and the priest shall put *it* upon the tip of the right ear of him that is to be cleansed, and upon the thumb of his right hand, and upon the great toe of his right foot:

Le 14:25 — And he shall kill the lamb of the trespass offering, and the priest shall take *some* of the blood of the trespass offering, and put *it* upon the tip of the right ear of him that is to be cleansed, and upon the thumb of his right hand, and upon the great toe of his right foot:

• **Anointed with oil in purifications.**

Le 14:17 — And of the rest of the oil that *is* in his hand shall the priest put upon the tip of the right ear of him that is to be cleansed, and upon the thumb of his right hand, and upon the great toe of his right foot, upon the blood of the trespass offering:

Le 14:28 — And the priest shall put of the oil that *is* in his hand upon the tip of the right ear of him that is to be cleansed, and upon the thumb of his right hand, and upon the great toe of his right foot, upon the place of the blood of the trespass offering:

• **Bored as a sign of servitude.**

Ex 21:5–6; Ps 46:1–11

➾See: Deafness

• **Figurative.**

• **Anthropomorphic uses of.**

Ps 17:6 — I have called upon thee, for thou wilt hear me, O God: incline thine ear unto me, *and hear* my speech.

Ps 39:12 — Hear my prayer, O LORD, and give ear unto my cry; hold not thy peace at my tears: for I *am* a stranger with thee, *and* a sojourner, as all my fathers *were*.

Ps 77:1 — I cried unto God with my voice, *even* unto God with my voice; and he gave ear unto me.

Ps 80:1 — Give ear, O Shepherd of Israel, thou that leadest Joseph like a flock; thou that dwellest *between* the cherubims, shine forth.

Ps 84:8 — O LORD God of hosts, hear my prayer: give ear, O God of Jacob. Selah.

• **For more extended anthropomorphic uses, consult concordances.**

EARRING

• **Of gold.**

Pr 25:12 — *As* an earring of gold, and an ornament of fine gold, *so is* a wise reprover upon an obedient ear.

• **Offering of, for the golden calf.**

Ex 32:2–3

• **Offering of, for the tabernacle.**

Ex 35:22 — And they came, both men and women, as many as were willing hearted, *and* brought bracelets, and earrings, and rings, and tablets, all jewels of gold: and every man that offered *offered* an offering of gold unto the LORD.

• **Worn for idolatrous purposes.**

Ge 35:4 — And they gave unto Jacob all the strange gods which *were* in their hand, and *all their* earrings which *were* in their ears; and Jacob hid them under the oak which *was* by Shechem.

Isa 3:20 — The bonnets, and the ornaments of the legs, and the headbands, and the tablets, and the ear-rings,

EARNEST

• **A pledge or token.**

Ps 86:17 — Shew me a token for good; that they which hate me may see *it*, and be ashamed: because thou, LORD, hast holpen me, and comforted me.

2Co 1:22 — Who hath also sealed us, and given the earnest of the Spirit in our hearts.

2Co 5:5 — Now he that hath wrought us for the selfsame thing *is* God, who also hath given unto us the earnest of the Spirit.

Eph 1:14 — Which is the earnest of our inheritance until the redemption of the purchased possession, unto the praise of his glory.

➾See: Token

EARNESTNESS ➾See: Zeal, Religious

EARTH

• **Primitive condition of.**

Ge 1:6–7; Ps 104:5–9

Ge 1:2 — And the earth was without form, and void; and darkness *was* upon the face of the deep. And the Spirit of God moved upon the face of the waters.

Job 26:7 — He stretcheth out the north over the empty place, *and* hangeth the earth upon nothing.

Jer 4:23 — I beheld the earth, and, lo, *it was* without form, and void; and the heavens, and they *had* no light.

• **Design of.**

Isa 45:18 — For thus saith the LORD that created the heavens; God himself that formed the earth and made it; he hath established it, he created it not in vain, he formed it to be inhabited: I *am* the LORD; and *there is* none else.

• **Ancient notions concerning.**

1Sa 2:8 — He raiseth up the poor out of the dust, *and* lifteth up the beggar from the dunghill, to set *them* among princes, and to make them inherit the throne of glory: for the pillars of the earth *are* the LORD'S, and he hath set the world upon them.

Job 9:6 — Which shaketh the earth out of her place, and the pillars thereof tremble.

Rev 7:1 — And after these things I saw four angels standing on the four corners of the earth, holding the four winds of the earth, that the wind should not blow on the earth, nor on the sea, nor on any tree.

• **Cursed of God.**

Ge 3:17–18; Ro 8:19–22

• **Circle of.**

Isa 40:22 — *It is* he that sitteth upon the circle of the earth, and the inhabitants thereof *are* as grasshoppers; that stretcheth out the heavens as a curtain, and spreadeth them out as a tent to dwell in:

• God's footstool.

Isa 66:1 — Thus saith the LORD, The heaven *is* my throne, and the earth *is* my footstool: where *is* the house that ye build unto me? and where *is* the place of my rest?

La 2:1 — How hath the Lord covered the daughter of Zion with a cloud in his anger, *and* cast down from heaven unto the earth the beauty of Israel, and remembered not his footstool in the day of his anger!

• Given to man.

Ps 115:16 — The heaven, *even* the heavens, *are* the LORD'S: but the earth hath he given to the children of men.

• Early divisions of.

Ge 10:1–11:32

Dt 32:8 — When the most High divided to the nations their inheritance, when he separated the sons of Adam, he set the bounds of the people according to the number of the children of Israel.

• Perpetuity of.

Ge 49:26 — The blessings of thy father have prevailed above the blessings of my progenitors unto the utmost bound of the everlasting hills: they shall be on the head of Joseph, and on the crown of the head of him that was separate from his brethren.

Dt 33:15 — And for the chief things of the ancient mountains, and for the precious things of the lasting hills,

Ps 78:69 — And he built his sanctuary like high *palaces,* like the earth which he hath established for ever.

Ps 104:5 — *Who* laid the foundations of the earth, *that* it should not be removed for ever.

Ecc 1:4 — *One* generation passeth away, and *another* generation cometh: but the earth abideth for ever.

Hab 3:6 — He stood, and measured the earth: he beheld, and drove asunder the nations; and the everlasting mountains were scattered, the perpetual hills did bow: his ways *are* everlasting.

• A new earth.

Isa 65:17 — For, behold, I create new heavens and a new earth: and the former shall not be remembered, nor come into mind.

Isa 66:22 — For as the new heavens and the new earth, which I will make, shall remain before me, saith the LORD, so shall your seed and your name remain.

Rev 21:1 — And I saw a new heaven and a new earth: for the first heaven and the first earth were passed away; and there was no more sea.

• Created by God.

Pr 8:22–26

Ge 1:1 — In the beginning God created the heaven and the earth.

2Ki 19:15 — And Hezekiah prayed before the LORD, and said, O LORD God of Israel, which dwellest *between* the cherubims, thou art the God, *even* thou alone, of all the kingdoms of the earth: thou hast made heaven and earth.

2Ch 2:12 — Huram said moreover, Blessed *be* the LORD God of Israel, that made heaven and earth, who hath given to David the king a wise son, endued with prudence and understanding, that might build an house for the LORD, and an house for his kingdom.

Ne 9:6 — Thou, *even* thou, *art* LORD alone; thou hast made heaven, the heaven of heavens, with all their host, the earth, and all *things* that *are* therein, the seas, and all that *is* therein, and thou preservest them all; and the host of heaven worshippeth thee.

Ps 90:2 — Before the mountains were brought forth, or ever thou hadst formed the earth and the world, even from everlasting to everlasting, thou *art* God.

Ps 102:25 — Of old hast thou laid the foundation of the earth: and the heavens *are* the work of thy hands.

Ps 115:15 — Ye *are* blessed of the LORD which made heaven and earth.

Ps 146:6 — Which made heaven, and earth, the sea, and all that therein *is:* which keepeth truth for ever:

Isa 37:16 — O LORD of hosts, God of Israel, that dwellest *between* the cherubims, thou *art* the God, *even* thou alone, of all the kingdoms of the earth: thou hast made heaven and earth.

Isa 45:18 — For thus saith the LORD that created the heavens; God himself that formed the earth and made it; he hath established it, he created it not in vain, he formed it to be inhabited: I *am* the LORD; and *there is* none else.

Jer 10:12 — He hath made the earth by his power, he hath established the world by his wisdom, and hath stretched out the heavens by his discretion.

Jer 27:5 — I have made the earth, the man and the beast that *are* upon the ground, by my great power and by my outstretched arm, and have given it unto whom it seemed meet unto me.

Jer 32:17 — Ah Lord GOD! behold, thou hast made the heaven and the earth by thy great power and stretched out arm, *and* there is nothing too hard for thee:

Jer 51:15 — He hath made the earth by his power, he hath established the world by his wisdom, and hath stretched out the heaven by his understanding.

Jn 17:24 — Father, I will that they also, whom thou hast given me, be with me where I am; that they may behold my glory, which thou hast given me: for thou lovedst me before the foundation of the world.

2Pe 3:5 — For this they willingly are ignorant of, that by the word of God the heavens were of old, and the earth standing out of the water and in the water:

Rev 10:6 — And sware by him that liveth for ever and ever, who created heaven, and the things that therein are, and the earth, and the things that therein are, and the sea, and the things which are therein, that there should be time no longer:

Rev 14:7 — Saying with a loud voice, Fear God, and give glory to him; for the hour of his judgment is come: and worship him that made heaven, and earth, and the sea, and the fountains of waters.

- **Created by Christ.**

Jn 1:3 — All things were made by him; and without him was not any thing made that was made.

Jn 1:10 — He was in the world, and the world was made by him, and the world knew him not.

Heb 1:10 — And, Thou, Lord, in the beginning hast laid the foundation of the earth; and the heavens are the works of thine hands:

↞See: Creation

↞See: God, Creator

- **Destruction of.**

Ps 102:25–27; Isa 24:19–20; Mt 24:29–31, 35–39; Mk 13:24–37; Lk 21:26–36; Heb 1:10–12; 2Pe 3:10–13

Isa 51:6 — Lift up your eyes to the heavens, and look upon the earth beneath: for the heavens shall vanish away like smoke, and the earth shall wax old like a garment, and they that dwell therein shall die in like manner: but my salvation shall be for ever, and my righteousness shall not be abolished.

Mt 5:18 — For verily I say unto you, Till heaven and earth pass, one jot or one tittle shall in no wise pass from the law, till all be fulfilled.

Mt 24:3 — And as he sat upon the mount of Olives, the disciples came unto him privately, saying, Tell us, when shall these things be? and what *shall be* the sign of thy coming, and of the end of the world?

Mt 24:14 — And this gospel of the kingdom shall be preached in all the world for a witness unto all nations; and then shall the end come.

Rev 20:11 — And I saw a great white throne, and him that sat on it, from whose face the earth and the heaven fled away; and there was found no place for them.

Rev 21:1 — And I saw a new heaven and a new earth: for the first heaven and the first earth were passed away; and there was no more sea.

EARTHENWARE ↞See: Pottery

EARTHQUAKES

Ps 46:2–3

Job 9:6 — Which shaketh the earth out of her place, and the pillars thereof tremble.

Ps 18:7 — Then the earth shook and trembled; the foundations also of the hills moved and were shaken, because he was wroth.

Ps 104:32 — He looketh on the earth, and it trembleth: he toucheth the hills, and they smoke.

Jer 4:24 — I beheld the mountains, and, lo, they trembled, and all the hills moved lightly.

- **As judgments.**

Isa 13:13–14; 24:19–20

Ps 18:15 — Then the channels of waters were seen, and the foundations of the world were discovered at thy rebuke, O LORD, at the blast of the breath of thy nostrils.

Ps 60:2 — Thou hast made the earth to tremble; thou hast broken it: heal the breaches thereof; for it shaketh.

Isa 29:6 — Thou shalt be visited of the LORD of hosts with thunder, and with earthquake, and great noise, with storm and tempest, and the flame of devouring fire.

Na 1:5 — The mountains quake at him, and the hills melt, and the earth is burned at his presence, yea, the world, and all that dwell therein.

- **Prophecies of.**

Eze 38:19 — For in my jealousy *and* in the fire of my wrath have I spoken, Surely in that day there shall be a great shaking in the land of Israel;

Zec 14:4 — And his feet shall stand in that day upon the mount of Olives, which *is* before Jerusalem on the east, and the mount of Olives shall cleave in the midst thereof toward the east and toward the west, *and there shall be* a very great valley; and half of the mountain shall remove toward the north, and half of it toward the south.

Mt 24:7 — For nation shall rise against nation, and kingdom against kingdom: and there shall be famines, and pestilences, and earthquakes, in divers places.

Mk 13:8 — For nation shall rise against nation, and kingdom against kingdom: and there shall be earthquakes in divers places, and there shall be famines and troubles: these *are* the beginnings of sorrows.

Lk 21:11 — And great earthquakes shall be in divers places, and famines, and pestilences; and fearful sights and great signs shall there be from heaven.

Rev 11:19 — And the temple of God was opened in heaven, and there was seen in his temple the ark of his testament: and there were lightnings, and voices, and thunderings, and an earthquake, and great hail.

- **Instances of.**
  - **At Sinai.**

Ex 19:18; Ps 68:8; 77:18; 114:4–7; Heb 12:26

  - **When Korah, Dathan, and Abiram were swallowed up.**

Nu 16:31–32

  - **When Jonathan and his armorbearer attacked the garrison at Gibeah.**

1Sa 14:15

  - **When the Lord revealed himself to Elijah in the still small voice.**

1Ki 19:11

  - **In Canaan, in the days of Uzziah, king of Judah.**

Am 1:1; Zec 14:5

  - **At the crucifixion of Jesus.**

Mt 27:51

  - **At the resurrection of Jesus.**

Mt 28:2

  - **When Paul and Silas were in prison at Philippi.**

Ac 16:26

- **Figurative.**

Ps 60:2 — Thou hast made the earth to tremble; thou hast broken it: heal the breaches thereof; for it shaketh.

- **Symbolic.**

Rev 6:12–14

Rev 11:13 — And the same hour was there a great earthquake, and the tenth part of the city fell, and in the earthquake were slain of men seven thousand: and the remnant were affrighted, and gave glory to the God of heaven.

Rev 16:18 — And there were voices, and thunders, and lightnings; and there was a great earthquake, such as was not since men were upon the earth, so mighty an earthquake, *and* so great.

Rev 16:20 — And every island fled away, and the mountains were not found.

EAST SEA ⇜See: Dead Sea

EAST WIND ⇜See: Wind

EASTER

Ac 12:4 — And when he had apprehended him, he put *him* in prison, and delivered *him* to four quaternions of soldiers to keep him; intending after Easter to bring him forth to the people.

EATING

• The host acting as a waiter.

Ge 18:8 — And he took butter, and milk, and the calf which he had dressed, and set *it* before them; and he stood by them under the tree, and they did eat.

• Favored guests served an extra portion.

Ge 43:34 — And he took *and sent* messes unto them from before him: but Benjamin's mess was five times so much as any of theirs. And they drank, and were merry with him.

• Table used in.

Jgs 1:7 — And Adoni-bezek said, Threescore and ten kings, having their thumbs and their great toes cut off, gathered *their meat* under my table: as I have done, so God hath requited me. And they brought him to Jerusalem, and there he died.

• Sitting at table.

Ex 32:6 — And they rose up early on the morrow, and offered burnt offerings, and brought peace offerings; and the people sat down to eat and to drink, and rose up to play.

• Reclining on couches.

Lk 7:37–38

Am 6:4 — That lie upon beds of ivory, and stretch themselves upon their couches, and eat the lambs out of the flock, and the calves out of the midst of the stall;

Am 6:7 — Therefore now shall they go captive with the first that go captive, and the banquet of them that stretched themselves shall be removed.

Jn 13:25 — He then lying on Jesus' breast saith unto him, Lord, who is it?

• Ablutions before.

Mt 15:2 — Why do thy disciples transgress the tradition of the elders? for they wash not their hands when they eat bread.

⇜See: Feasts

⇜See: Food

⇜See: Gluttony

EBAL

• Son of Joktan.

1Ch 1:22 — And Ebal, and Abimael, and Sheba,

• A Horite.

Ge 36:23 — And the children of Shobal *were* these; Alvan, and Manahath, and Ebal, Shepho, and Onam.

1Ch 1:40 — The sons of Shobal; Alian, and Manahath, and Ebal, Shephi, and Onam. And the sons of Zibeon; Aiah, and Anah.

• A mountain of Ephraim.

• Half of the tribes of Israel stand on, to respond "Amen" to the curses of the law.

Dt 27:12–13

Dt 11:29 — And it shall come to pass, when the LORD thy God hath brought thee in unto the land whither thou goest to possess it, that thou shalt put the blessing upon mount Gerizim, and the curse upon mount Ebal.

Jos 8:33 — And all Israel, and their elders, and officers, and their judges, stood on this side the ark and on that side before the priests the Levites, which bare the ark of the covenant of the LORD, as well the stranger, as he that was born among them; half of them over against mount Gerizim, and half of them over against mount Ebal; as Moses the servant of the LORD had commanded before, that they should bless the people of Israel.

• Altar built on.

Jos 8:30 — Then Joshua built an altar unto the LORD God of Israel in mount Ebal,

⇜See: Gerizim

EBED

• Father of Gaal.

Jgs 9:26–35

• A captive returned from Babylon.

Ezr 8:6 — Of the sons also of Adin; Ebed the son of Jonathan, and with him fifty males.

EBED-MELECH

• An Ethiopian.

• Jeremiah rescued by.

Jer 38:7–13

• Prophecy concerning.

Jer 39:16–18

EBENEZER

• Name of a memorial stone.

1Sa 7:12 — Then Samuel took a stone, and set *it* between Mizpeh and Shen, and called the name of it Eben-ezer, saying, Hitherto hath the LORD helped us.

• Philistines defeat the Israelites at.

1Sa 4:1–22

• Philistines remove the ark from.

1Sa 5:1 — And the Philistines took the ark of God, and brought it from Eben-ezer unto Ashdod.

EBER

- **Called also Heber.**
- **The probable founder of the Hebrew race.**

Ge 10:21–25

Ge 11:14 — And Salah lived thirty years, and begat Eber:

1Ch 1:19 — And unto Eber were born two sons: the name of the one *was* Peleg; because in his days the earth was divided: and his brother's name *was* Joktan.

1Ch 1:25 — Eber, Peleg, Reu,

Lk 3:35 — Which was *the son* of Saruch, which was *the son* of Ragau, which was *the son* of Phalec, which was *the son* of Heber, which was *the son* of Sala,

- **Prophecy concerning.**

Nu 24:24 — And ships *shall come* from the coast of Chittim, and shall afflict Asshur, and shall afflict Eber, and he also shall perish for ever.

- **A Gadite, called Heber.**

1Ch 5:13 — And their brethren of the house of their fathers *were,* Michael, and Meshullam, and Sheba, and Jorai, and Jachan, and Zia, and Heber, seven.

- **A Benjamite.**

1Ch 8:12 — The sons of Elpaal; Eber, and Misham, and Shamed, who built Ono, and Lod, with the towns thereof:

- **A Benjamite of Jerusalem.**

1Ch 8:22 — And Ishpan, and Heber, and Eliel,

- **A priest.**

Ne 12:20 — Of Sallai, Kallai; of Amok, Eber;

EBIASAPH

- **Called also Asaph.**
- **A son of Korah.**

1Ch 6:23 — Elkanah his son, and Ebiasaph his son, and Assir his son,

1Ch 9:19 — And Shallum the son of Kore, the son of Ebiasaph, the son of Korah, and his brethren, of the house of his father, the Korahites, *were* over the work of the service, keepers of the gates of the tabernacle: and their fathers, *being* over the host of the LORD, *were* keepers of the entry.

1Ch 26:1 — Concerning the divisions of the porters: Of the Korhites *was* Meshelemiah the son of Kore, of the sons of Asaph.

EBONY

- **A fossil.**
- **Merchandise in.**

Eze 27:15 — The men of Dedan *were* thy merchants; many isles *were* the merchandise of thine hand: they brought thee *for* a present horns of ivory and ebony.

EBRONAH • The thirtieth camping place of the Israelites.

Nu 33:34–35

ECCLESIASTICISM

- **The Jewish, rebuked by Jesus.**

Mt 9:10–13; 23:2–4, 8–10, 13–35; Mk 9:49–50

- **The Jewish, to be overthrown.**

Mt 21:19–20, 28–44

- **Traditional rules of the Jewish.**

Mt 15:1–20; Mk 7:2–23

See: Commandments; precepts of men

- **Arrogance of.**

Mt 12:2–7

Mt 23:4 — For they bind heavy burdens and grievous to be borne, and lay *them* on men's shoulders; but they *themselves* will not move them with one of their fingers.

See: Church

See: Minister, False and Corrupt

See: Usurpation; in ecclesiastical affairs

ECLIPSE

- **Of the sun and moon.**

Eze 32:7–8; Rev 6:12–13

Isa 13:10 — For the stars of heaven and the constellations thereof shall not give their light: the sun shall be darkened in his going forth, and the moon shall not cause her light to shine.

Joel 2:10 — The earth shall quake before them; the heavens shall tremble: the sun and the moon shall be dark, and the stars shall withdraw their shining:

Joel 2:31 — The sun shall be turned into darkness, and the moon into blood, before the great and the terrible day of the LORD come.

Joel 3:15 — The sun and the moon shall be darkened, and the stars shall withdraw their shining.

Am 8:9 — And it shall come to pass in that day, saith the Lord GOD, that I will cause the sun to go down at noon, and I will darken the earth in the clear day:

Mic 3:6 — Therefore night *shall be* unto you, that ye shall not have a vision; and it shall be dark unto you, that ye shall not divine; and the sun shall go down over the prophets, and the day shall be dark over them.

Mt 24:29 — Immediately after the tribulation of those days shall the sun be darkened, and the moon shall not give her light, and the stars shall fall from heaven, and the powers of the heavens shall be shaken:

Mk 13:24 — But in those days, after that tribulation, the sun shall be darkened, and the moon shall not give her light,

Ac 2:20 — The sun shall be turned into darkness, and the moon into blood, before that great and notable day of the Lord come:

Rev 8:12 — And the fourth angel sounded, and the third part of the sun was smitten, and the third part of the moon, and the third part of the stars; so as the third part of them was darkened, and the day shone not for a third part of it, and the night likewise.

See: Moon

See: Sun

- **Figurative.**

Isa 60:19 — The sun shall be no more thy light by day; neither for brightness shall the moon give light unto thee: but the LORD shall be unto thee an everlasting light, and thy God thy glory.

ECONOMICS

• Political.

Ge 41:33 — Now therefore let Pharaoh look out a man discreet and wise, and set him over the land of Egypt.

Ge 41:57 — And all countries came into Egypt to Joseph for to buy *corn;* because that the famine was so sore in all lands.

• Household.

Pr 31:10–31; Ecc 11:4–6; Jn 6:12–13

Pr 24:27 — Prepare thy work without, and make it fit for thyself in the field; and afterwards build thine house.

See: Family

See: Frugality

See: Industry

ECONOMY

• Political.

See: Economics

See: Government

ED • Name of the altar erected by the tribes Reuben, Gad, and Manasseh at the fords of the Jordan.

Jos 22:34 — And the children of Reuben and the children of Gad called the altar *Ed:* for it *shall be* a witness between us that the LORD *is* God.

EDAR • A tower.

Ge 35:21 — And Israel journeyed, and spread his tent beyond the tower of Edar.

Mic 4:8 — And thou, O tower of the flock, the strong hold of the daughter of Zion, unto thee shall it come, even the first dominion; the kingdom shall come to the daughter of Jerusalem.

EDEN

• The garden of Eden.

Ge 2:8–17; 3:23–24

Ge 4:16 — And Cain went out from the presence of the LORD, and dwelt in the land of Nod, on the east of Eden.

Isa 51:3 — For the LORD shall comfort Zion: he will comfort all her waste places; and he will make her wilderness like Eden, and her desert like the garden of the LORD; joy and gladness shall be found therein, thanksgiving, and the voice of melody.

Eze 28:13 — Thou hast been in Eden the garden of God; every precious stone *was* thy covering, the sardius, topaz, and the diamond, the beryl, the onyx, and the jasper, the sapphire, the emerald, and the carbuncle, and gold: the workmanship of thy tabrets and of thy pipes was prepared in thee in the day that thou wast created.

Eze 31:9 — I have made him fair by the multitude of his branches: so that all the trees of Eden, that *were* in the garden of God, envied him.

Eze 31:16 — I made the nations to shake at the sound of his fall, when I cast him down to hell with them that descend into the pit: and all the trees of Eden, the choice and best of Lebanon, all that drink water, shall be comforted in the nether parts of the earth.

Eze 31:18 — To whom art thou thus like in glory and in greatness among the trees of Eden? yet shalt thou be brought down with the trees of Eden unto the nether parts of the earth: thou shalt lie in the midst of the uncircumcised with *them that be* slain by the sword. This *is* Pharaoh and all his multitude, saith the Lord GOD.

Eze 36:35 — And they shall say, This land that was desolate is become like the garden of Eden; and the waste and desolate and ruined cities *are become* fenced, *and* are inhabited.

Joel 2:3 — A fire devoureth before them; and behind them a flame burneth: the land *is* as the garden of Eden before them, and behind them a desolate wilderness; yea, and nothing shall escape them.

• A mart of costly merchandise.

2Ki 19:12 — Have the gods of the nations delivered them which my fathers have destroyed; *as* Gozan, and Haran, and Rezeph, and the children of Eden which *were* in Thelasar?

Isa 37:12 — Have the gods of the nations delivered them which my fathers have destroyed, *as* Gozan, and Haran, and Rezeph, and the children of Eden which *were* in Telassar?

Eze 27:23 — Haran, and Canneh, and Eden, the merchants of Sheba, Asshur, *and* Chilmad, *were* thy merchants.

Am 1:5 — I will break also the bar of Damascus, and cut off the inhabitant from the plain of Aven, and him that holdeth the sceptre from the house of Eden: and the people of Syria shall go into captivity unto Kir, saith the LORD.

• A Gershonite.

2Ch 29:12 — Then the Levites arose, Mahath the son of Amasai, and Joel the son of Azariah, of the sons of the Kohathites: and of the sons of Merari, Kish the son of Abdi, and Azariah the son of Jehalelel: and of the Gershonites; Joah the son of Zimmah, and Eden the son of Joah:

• A Levite.

2Ch 31:15 — And next him *were* Eden, and Miniamin, and Jeshua, and Shemaiah, Amariah, and Shecaniah, in the cities of the priests, in *their* set office, to give to their brethren by courses, as well to the great as to the small:

EDER

• Called also Edar.

• A place near Ephrath.

Ge 35:21 — And Israel journeyed, and spread his tent beyond the tower of Edar.

• **A city of Judah.**

Jos 15:21 — And the uttermost cities of the tribe of the children of Judah toward the coast of Edom southward were Kabzeel, and Eder, and Jagur,

• **A grandson of Merari.**

1Ch 23:23 — The sons of Mushi; Mahli, and Eder, and Jeremoth, three.

1Ch 24:30 — The sons also of Mushi; Mahli, and Eder, and Jerimoth. These *were* the sons of the Levites after the house of their fathers.

EDOM

• **Signifies red.**

• **A name of Esau, possibly on account of his being covered with red hair.**

Ge 25:25 — And the first came out red, all over like an hairy garment; and they called his name Esau.

Ge 25:30 — And Esau said to Jacob, Feed me, I pray thee, with that same red *pottage;* for I *am* faint: therefore was his name called Edom.

Ge 36:1 — Now these *are* the generations of Esau, who *is* Edom.

Ge 36:8 — Thus dwelt Esau in mount Seir: Esau *is* Edom.

Ge 36:19 — These *are* the sons of Esau, who *is* Edom, and these *are* their dukes.

• **Land occupied by descendants of Esau; extended from the Elanitic Gulf to the Red Sea.**

Ge 36:16–17

Ge 32:3 — And Jacob sent messengers before him to Esau his brother unto the land of Seir, the country of Edom.

Ge 36:21 — And Dishon, and Ezer, and Dishan: these *are* the dukes of the Horites, the children of Seir in the land of Edom.

Jer 40:11 — Likewise when all the Jews that *were* in Moab, and among the Ammonites, and in Edom, and that *were* in all the countries, heard that the king of Babylon had left a remnant of Judah, and that he had set over them Gedaliah the son of Ahikam the son of Shaphan;

See: Idumea

• **Noted for its wise men.**

Ob 1:8 — Shall I not in that day, saith the LORD, even destroy the wise *men* out of Edom, and understanding out of the mount of Esau?

• **Sins of.**

Ob 1:10–14

• **Prophecies concerning.**

Jer 25:21–23; 27:1–11

Da 11:41 — He shall enter also into the glorious land, and many *countries* shall be overthrown: but these shall escape out of his hand, *even* Edom, and Moab, and the chief of the children of Ammon.

See: Edomites

• **Figurative.**

• **Of the foes of Zion.**

Isa 63:1 — Who *is* this that cometh from Edom, with dyed garments from Bozrah? this *that is* glorious in his apparel, travelling in the greatness of his strength? I that speak in righteousness, mighty to save.

• **Wilderness of.**

2Ki 3:8 — And he said, Which way shall we go up? And he answered, The way through the wilderness of Edom.

EDOMITES

• **Called also Edom.**

• **Descendants of Esau.**

Ge 36:1–43

• **Kings of.**

Ge 36:31–39; 1Ch 1:43–50

Nu 20:14 — And Moses sent messengers from Kadesh unto the king of Edom, Thus saith thy brother Israel, Thou knowest all the travail that hath befallen us:

Eze 32:29 — There *is* Edom, her kings, and all her princes, which with their might are laid by *them that were* slain by the sword: they shall lie with the uncircumcised, and with them that go down to the pit.

Am 2:1 — Thus saith the LORD; For three transgressions of Moab, and for four, I will not turn away *the punishment* thereof; because he burned the bones of the king of Edom into lime:

• **Dukes of.**

Ge 36:9–43; 1Ch 1:51–54

Ex 15:15 — Then the dukes of Edom shall be amazed; the mighty men of Moab, trembling shall take hold upon them; all the inhabitants of Canaan shall melt away.

• **Land of.**

Dt 2:4–5

Ge 32:3 — And Jacob sent messengers before him to Esau his brother unto the land of Seir, the country of Edom.

Dt 2:12 — The Horims also dwelt in Seir beforetime; but the children of Esau succeeded them, when they had destroyed them from before them, and dwelt in their stead; as Israel did unto the land of his possession, which the LORD gave unto them.

• **Protected by divine command from desolation by the Israelites.**

Dt 2:4–6

• **Protected from being held in abhorrence by the Israelites.**

Dt 23:7 — Thou shalt not abhor an Edomite; for he *is* thy brother: thou shalt not abhor an Egyptian; because thou wast a stranger in his land.

• **Refuse the Israelites passage through their country.**

Nu 20:18–21

• **Saul makes war against.**

1Sa 14:47 — So Saul took the kingdom over Israel, and fought against all his enemies on every side, against Moab, and against the children of Ammon, and against Edom, and against the kings of Zobah, and against the Philistines: and whithersoever he turned himself, he vexed *them.*

• David makes conquest of.

1Ki 11:14–16; 1Ch 18:11–13

• David makes conquest of garrisons.

2Sa 8:14 — And he put garrisons in Edom; throughout all Edom put he garrisons, and all they of Edom became David's servants. And the LORD preserved David whithersoever he went.

• David writes battle songs concerning his conquest of.

Ps 60:8–9; 108:9–10

• Become confederates of Jehoshaphat.

2Ki 3:9 — So the king of Israel went, and the king of Judah, and the king of Edom: and they fetched a compass of seven days' journey: and there was no water for the host, and for the cattle that followed them.

2Ki 3:26 — And when the king of Moab saw that the battle was too sore for him, he took with him seven hundred men that drew swords, to break through *even* unto the king of Edom: but they could not.

• Ruled by a deputy king.

1Ki 22:47 — *There was* then no king in Edom: a deputy *was* king.

• The Lord delivers the army of into the hands of Jehoshaphat.

2Ch 20:20 — And they rose early in the morning, and went forth into the wilderness of Tekoa: and as they went forth, Jehoshaphat stood and said, Hear me, O Judah, and ye inhabitants of Jerusalem; Believe in the LORD your God, so shall ye be established; believe his prophets, so shall ye prosper.

2Ch 20:23 — For the children of Ammon and Moab stood up against the inhabitants of mount Seir, utterly to slay and destroy *them:* and when they had made an end of the inhabitants of Seir, every one helped to destroy another.

• Revolt in the days of Joram.

2Ki 8:20–22; 2Ch 21:8–10

• Amaziah, king of Judah, invades the territory of.

2Ki 14:5–7; 2Ch 25:11–12

2Ki 14:10 — Thou hast indeed smitten Edom, and thine heart hath lifted thee up: glory *of this,* and tarry at home: for why shouldest thou meddle to *thy* hurt, that thou shouldest fall, *even* thou, and Judah with thee?

2Ch 28:17 — For again the Edomites had come and smitten Judah, and carried away captives.

• Join Babylon in war against the Israelites.

Am 1:9–11; Ob 1:11–16

Eze 35:5 — Because thou hast had a perpetual hatred, and hast shed *the blood of* the children of Israel by the force of the sword in the time of their calamity, in the time *that their* iniquity *had* an end:

• A Jewish prophet in Babylon denounces.

Eze 25:12–14; 35:3–10

Ps 137:7 — Remember, O LORD, the children of Edom in the day of Jerusalem; who said, Rase *it,* rase *it, even* to the foundation thereof.

• Children of the third generation might be received into the congregation of Israel.

Dt 23:8 — The children that are begotten of them shall enter into the congregation of the LORD in their third generation.

• Prophecies concerning.

Ge 27:37–40; Isa 21:11–12; 34:1–17; 63:1–4; Jer 9:25–26; 27:1–11; 49:7–22; La 4:21–22; Eze 25:12–14; 32:29–30; 35:1–15; Am 1:11–12; Ob 1:1–21; Mal 1:2–5

Ge 25:23 — And the LORD said unto her, Two nations *are* in thy womb, and two manner of people shall be separated from thy bowels; and *the one* people shall be stronger than *the other* people; and the elder shall serve the younger.

Ge 27:29 — Let people serve thee, and nations bow down to thee: be lord over thy brethren, and let thy mother's sons bow down to thee: cursed *be* every one that curseth thee, and blessed *be* he that blesseth thee.

Nu 24:18 — And Edom shall be a possession, Seir also shall be a possession for his enemies; and Israel shall do valiantly.

Isa 11:14 — But they shall fly upon the shoulders of the Philistines toward the west; they shall spoil them of the east together: they shall lay their hand upon Edom and Moab; and the children of Ammon shall obey them.

Eze 36:5 — Therefore thus saith the Lord GOD; Surely in the fire of my jealousy have I spoken against the residue of the heathen, and against all Idumea, which have appointed my land into their possession with the joy of all *their* heart, with despiteful minds, to cast it out for a prey.

Joel 3:19 — Egypt shall be a desolation, and Edom shall be a desolate wilderness, for the violence *against* the children of Judah, because they have shed innocent blood in their land.

Am 9:12 — That they may possess the remnant of Edom, and of all the heathen, which are called by my name, saith the LORD that doeth this.

EDREI

• A town of Bashan.

• Allotted to Manasseh.

Jos 13:31 — And half Gilead, and Ashtaroth, and Edrei, cities of the kingdom of Og in Bashan, *were pertaining* unto the children of Machir the son of Manasseh, even to the one half of the children of Machir by their families.

• Joshua defeats Og at.

Nu 21:33–35; Dt 3:1–3

Dt 1:4 — After he had slain Sihon the king of the Amorites, which dwelt in Heshbon, and Og the king of Bashan, which dwelt at Astaroth in Edrei:

EDUCATION

- See: Instruction
- See: Teachers
- See: School

EGLAH • Wife of David.

2Sa 3:5 — And the sixth, Ithream, by Eglah David's wife. These were born to David in Hebron.

1Ch 3:3 — The fifth, Shephatiah of Abital: the sixth, Ithream by Eglah his wife.

EGLAIM • City of Moab.

Isa 15:8 — For the cry is gone round about the borders of Moab; the howling thereof unto Eglaim, and the howling thereof unto Beer-elim.

EGLON

• King of Moab.

• Assassinated by Ehud.

Jgs 3:12–30

• An ancient city of Canaan.

• Taken by Joshua.

Jos 10:23 — And they did so, and brought forth those five kings unto him out of the cave, the king of Jerusalem, the king of Hebron, the king of Jarmuth, the king of Lachish, *and* the king of Eglon.

Jos 10:35 — And they took it on that day, and smote it with the edge of the sword, and all the souls that *were* therein he utterly destroyed that day, according to all that he had done to Lachish.

• Allotted to Judah.

Jos 15:39 — Lachish, and Bozkath, and Eglon,

EGO

Ro 12:1–3

1Th 5:11 — Wherefore comfort yourselves together, and edify one another, even as also ye do.

1Th 5:14 — Now we exhort you, brethren, warn them that are unruly, comfort the feebleminded, support the weak, be patient toward all *men*.

EGOTISM

- See: Conceit

EGYPT

• The country of.

• Called Rahab.

Ps 87:4 — I will make mention of Rahab and Babylon to them that know me: behold Philistia, and Tyre, with Ethiopia; this *man* was born there.

Ps 89:10 — Thou hast broken Rahab in pieces, as one that is slain; thou hast scattered thine enemies with thy strong arm.

• Called Land of Ham.

Ps 105:23 — Israel also came into Egypt; and Jacob sojourned in the land of Ham.

Ps 106:22 — Wondrous works in the land of Ham, *and* terrible things by the Red sea.

• Limits of.

Eze 29:10 — Behold, therefore I *am* against thee, and against thy rivers, and I will make the land of Egypt utterly waste *and* desolate, from the tower of Syene even unto the border of Ethiopia.

• Fertility of.

Ge 13:10 — And Lot lifted up his eyes, and beheld all the plain of Jordan, that it *was* well watered every where, before the LORD destroyed Sodom and Gomorrah, *even* as the garden of the LORD, like the land of Egypt, as thou comest unto Zoar.

• Productions of.

Isa 19:5–9

Nu 11:5 — We remember the fish, which we did eat in Egypt freely; the cucumbers, and the melons, and the leeks, and the onions, and the garlick:

Ps 78:47 — He destroyed their vines with hail, and their sycomore trees with frost.

Pr 7:16 — I have decked my bed with coverings of tapestry, with carved *works*, with fine linen of Egypt.

• Irrigation employed in.

Dt 11:10 — For the land, whither thou goest in to possess it, *is* not as the land of Egypt, from whence ye came out, where thou sowedst thy seed, and wateredst *it* with thy foot, as a garden of herbs:

• Imports of.

Ge 37:25 — And they sat down to eat bread: and they lifted up their eyes and looked, and, behold, a company of Ishmeelites came from Gilead with their camels bearing spicery and balm and myrrh, going to carry *it* down to Egypt.

Ge 37:36 — And the Midianites sold him into Egypt unto Potiphar, an officer of Pharaoh's, *and* captain of the guard.

• Exports of.

Ge 37:25 — And they sat down to eat bread: and they lifted up their eyes and looked, and, behold, a company of Ishmeelites came from Gilead with their camels bearing spicery and balm and myrrh, going to carry *it* down to Egypt.

Ge 37:36 — And the Midianites sold him into Egypt unto Potiphar, an officer of Pharaoh's, *and* captain of the guard.

Ex 27:7 — And the staves shall be put into the rings, and the staves shall be upon the two sides of the altar, to bear it.

Pr 7:16 — I have decked my bed with coverings of tapestry, with carved *works*, with fine linen of Egypt.

Eze 27:7 — Fine linen with broidered work from Egypt was that which thou spreadest forth to be thy sail; blue and purple from the isles of Elishah was that which covered thee.

• Exports of horses.

1Ki 10:28–29

• Famine in.

Ge 41:1–57

Ac 7:11 — Now there came a dearth over all the land of Egypt and Chanaan, and great affliction: and our fathers found no sustenance.

• Armies of.

Ex 14:7 — And he took six hundred chosen chariots, and all the chariots of Egypt, and captains over every one of them.

Isa 31:1 — Woe to them that go down to Egypt for help; and stay on horses, and trust in chariots, because *they are* many; and in horsemen, because they are very strong; but they look not unto the Holy One of Israel, neither seek the LORD!

• Army of, destroyed in the Red Sea.

Ex 14:5–31

Isa 43:17 — Which bringeth forth the chariot and horse, the army and the power; they shall lie down together, they shall not rise: they are extinct, they are quenched as tow.

• Magi of.

Ge 41:8 — And it came to pass in the morning that his spirit was troubled; and he sent and called for all the magicians of Egypt, and all the wise men thereof: and Pharaoh told them his dream; but *there was* none that could interpret them unto Pharaoh.

Ex 7:11 — Then Pharaoh also called the wise men and the sorcerers: now the magicians of Egypt, they also did in like manner with their enchantments.

1Ki 4:30 — And Solomon's wisdom excelled the wisdom of all the children of the east country, and all the wisdom of Egypt.

Ac 7:22 — And Moses was learned in all the wisdom of the Egyptians, and was mighty in words and in deeds.

• Priests of.

Ge 41:45 — And Pharaoh called Joseph's name Zaphnath-paaneah; and he gave him to wife Asenath the daughter of Poti-pherah priest of On. And Joseph went out over *all* the land of Egypt.

Ge 47:22 — Only the land of the priests bought he not; for the priests had a portion *assigned them* of Pharaoh, and did eat their portion which Pharaoh gave them: wherefore they sold not their lands.

• Idols of.

Eze 20:7–8

• Overflowed by the Nile.

Am 8:8 — Shall not the land tremble for this, and every one mourn that dwelleth therein? and it shall rise up wholly as a flood; and it shall be cast out and drowned, as *by* the flood of Egypt.

Am 9:5 — And the Lord GOD of hosts *is* he that toucheth the land, and it shall melt, and all that dwell therein shall mourn: and it shall rise up wholly like a flood; and shall be drowned, as *by* the flood of Egypt.

• Plagues in.

See: Plague

• Joseph's captivity in, and subsequent rule over.

See: Joseph, Son of Jacob

• Civil war in.

Isa 19:2 — And I will set the Egyptians against the Egyptians: and they shall fight every one against his brother, and every one against his neighbour; city against city, *and* kingdom against kingdom.

• The king acquires title to land of.

Ge 47:18–26

• Abraham dwells in.

Ge 12:10–13:1

• Israelites in bondage in.

See: Israelites

• Joseph takes Jesus to.

Mt 2:13–20

• Prophecies against.

Ge 15:13–14; Isa 19:1–25; 20:2–6; Jer 9:25–26; 43:8–13; 46:1–28; Eze 29:1–32:32

Isa 45:14 — Thus saith the LORD, The labour of Egypt, and merchandise of Ethiopia and of the Sabeans, men of stature, shall come over unto thee, and they shall be thine: they shall come after thee; in chains they shall come over, and they shall fall down unto thee, they shall make supplication unto thee, *saying,* Surely God *is* in thee; and *there is* none else, *there is* no God.

Jer 44:30 — Thus saith the LORD; Behold, I will give Pharaoh-hophra king of Egypt into the hand of his enemies, and into the hand of them that seek his life; as I gave Zedekiah king of Judah into the hand of Nebuchadrezzar king of Babylon, his enemy, and that sought his life.

Hos 8:13 — They sacrifice flesh *for* the sacrifices of mine offerings, and *eat it;* but the LORD accepteth them not; now will he remember their iniquity, and visit their sins: they shall return to Egypt.

Joel 3:11 — Assemble yourselves, and come, all ye heathen, and gather yourselves together round about: thither cause thy mighty ones to come down, O LORD.

Zec 10:11 — And he shall pass through the sea with affliction, and shall smite the waves in the sea, and all the deeps of the river shall dry up: and the pride of Assyria shall be brought down, and the sceptre of Egypt shall depart away.

See: Egyptians

• Symbolic.

Rev 11:8 — And their dead bodies *shall lie* in the street of the great city, which spiritually is called Sodom and Egypt, where also our Lord was crucified.

• River, or brook of.

• Perhaps identical with Sihor.

See: Sihor

• A small stream flowing into the Mediterranean Sea. The western boundary of the land promised to the children of Israel.

Ge 15:18 — In the same day the LORD made a covenant with Abram, saying, Unto thy seed have I given this land, from the river of Egypt unto the great river, the river Euphrates:

Nu 34:5 — And the border shall fetch a compass from Azmon unto the river of Egypt, and the goings out of it shall be at the sea.

Jos 13:3 — From Sihor, which *is* before Egypt, even unto the borders of Ekron northward, *which* is counted to the Canaanite: five lords of the Philistines; the Gazathites, and the Ashdothites, the Eshkalonites, the Gittites, and the Ekronites; also the Avites:

Jos 15:4 — *From thence* it passed toward Azmon, and went out unto the river of Egypt; and the goings out of that coast were at the sea: this shall be your south coast.

Jos 15:47 — Ashdod with her towns and her villages, Gaza with her towns and her villages, unto the river of Egypt, and the great sea, and the border *thereof*:

1Ki 8:65 — And at that time Solomon held a feast, and all Israel with him, a great congregation, from the entering in of Hamath unto the river of Egypt, before the LORD our God, seven days and seven days, *even* fourteen days.

2Ki 24:7 — And the king of Egypt came not again any more out of his land: for the king of Babylon had taken from the river of Egypt unto the river Euphrates all that pertained to the king of Egypt.

Isa 27:12 — And it shall come to pass in that day, *that* the LORD shall beat off from the channel of the river unto the stream of Egypt, and ye shall be gathered one by one, O ye children of Israel.

Eze 47:19 — And the south side southward, from Tamar *even* to the waters of strife *in* Kadesh, the river to the great sea. And *this is* the south side southward.

Eze 48:28 — And by the border of Gad, at the south side southward, the border shall be even from Tamar *unto* the waters of strife *in* Kadesh, *and* to the river toward the great sea.

EGYPTIANS

• Descendants of the Mizraim.

Ge 10:13–14

Ge 10:6 — And the sons of Ham; Cush, and Mizraim, and Phut, and Canaan.

• Wisdom of.

1Ki 4:30 — And Solomon's wisdom excelled the wisdom of all the children of the east country, and all the wisdom of Egypt.

• The art of embalming the dead practiced by.

Ge 50:2–3

Ge 50:26 — So Joseph died, *being* an hundred and ten years old: and they embalmed him, and he was put in a coffin in Egypt.

• Hospitality of, to Abraham.

Ge 12:10–20

• Slaves bought by.

Ge 37:36 — And the Midianites sold him into Egypt unto Potiphar, an officer of Pharaoh's, *and* captain of the guard.

• Oppress the Israelites.

Ex 1:1–22

• Refuse to release the Israelites.

Ex 5:1–10:29

• Visited by plagues.

Ex 7:1–12:51; Ps 78:43–51

• Visited by plagues, firstborn of, destroyed.

Ex 12:29 — And it came to pass, that at midnight the LORD smote all the firstborn in the land of Egypt, from the firstborn of Pharaoh that sat on his throne unto the firstborn of the captive that *was* in the dungeon; and all the firstborn of cattle.

Ps 78:51 — And smote all the firstborn in Egypt; the chief of *their* strength in the tabernacles of Ham:

Ps 105:36 — He smote also all the firstborn in their land, the chief of all their strength.

Ps 136:10 — To him that smote Egypt in their firstborn: for his mercy *endureth* for ever:

• Send the Israelites away.

Ex 12:29–36

• Pursue Israelites, and the army of, destroyed.

Ex 14:5–30

Ps 106:11 — And the waters covered their enemies: there was not one of them left.

Heb 11:29 — By faith they passed through the Red sea as by dry *land:* which the Egyptians assaying to do were drowned.

• Abhorred shepherds.

Ge 46:34 — That ye shall say, Thy servants' trade hath been about cattle from our youth even until now, both we, *and* also our fathers: that ye may dwell in the land of Goshen; for every shepherd *is* an abomination unto the Egyptians.

• Refused to eat with Hebrews.

Ge 43:32 — And they set on for him by himself, and for them by themselves, and for the Egyptians, which did eat with him, by themselves: because the Egyptians might not eat bread with the Hebrews; for that *is* an abomination unto the Egyptians.

• Alliances with, forbidden to the Israelites.

Isa 30:2 — That walk to go down into Egypt, and have not asked at my mouth; to strengthen themselves in the strength of Pharaoh, and to trust in the shadow of Egypt!

Isa 31:1 — Woe to them that go down to Egypt for help; and stay on horses, and trust in chariots, because *they are* many; and in horsemen, because they are very strong; but they look not unto the Holy One of Israel, neither seek the LORD!

Isa 36:6 — Lo, thou trustest in the staff of this broken reed, on Egypt; whereon if a man lean, it will go into his hand, and pierce it: so *is* Pharaoh king of Egypt to all that trust in him.

Eze 17:15 — But he rebelled against him in sending his ambassadors into Egypt, that they might give him horses and much people. Shall he prosper? shall he escape that doeth such *things?* or shall he break the covenant, and be delivered?

Eze 29:6 — And all the inhabitants of Egypt shall know that I *am* the LORD, because they have been a staff of reed to the house of Israel.

• **Eligible to membership in Israelitish congregation in the third generation.**
Dt 23:7–8

• **Invade the land of Israel.**

• **Under Shishak.**
1Ki 14:25–26; 2Ch 12:2–9

• **Pharaoh-nechoh.**
2Ki 23:29–35; 2Ch 35:20–24; 36:3–4

• **Aid the Israelites against the Chaldeans.**
Jer 37:5–11

• **Intermarry with the Jews.**
1Ki 3:1 — And Solomon made affinity with Pharaoh king of Egypt, and took Pharaoh's daughter, and brought her into the city of David, until he had made an end of building his own house, and the house of the LORD, and the wall of Jerusalem round about.

• **An enthusiastic Egyptian instigated rebellion against Roman government.**
Ac 21:38 — Art not thou that Egyptian, which before these days madest an uproar, and leddest out into the wilderness four thousand men that were murderers?

• **Prophecies of dispersion and restoration of.**
Eze 29:12–15
Eze 30:23 — And I will scatter the Egyptians among the nations, and will disperse them through the countries.
Eze 30:26 — And I will scatter the Egyptians among the nations, and disperse them among the countries; and they shall know that I *am* the LORD.

• **Conversion of, foretold.**
Isa 19:18 — In that day shall five cities in the land of Egypt speak the language of Canaan, and swear to the LORD of hosts; one shall be called, The city of destruction.

See: Egypt

EHI See: Ehud

EHUD

• **A descendant of Benjamin.**
1Ch 8:6 — And these *are* the sons of Ehud: these are the heads of the fathers of the inhabitants of Geba, and they removed them to Manahath:

• **Called Ehi.**
Ge 46:21 — And the sons of Benjamin were Belah, and Becher, and Ashbel, Gera, and Naaman, Ehi, and Rosh, Muppim, and Huppim, and Ard.

• **Probably identical with.**

• **Ahiram, mentioned in Nu 26:38.**
Nu 26:38 — The sons of Benjamin after their families: of Bela, the family of the Belaites: of Ashbel, the family of the Ashbelites: of Ahiram, the family of the Ahiramites:

• **Aharah.**
1Ch 8:1 — Now Benjamin begat Bela his firstborn, Ashbel the second, and Aharah the third,

• **Ahoah.**
1Ch 8:4 — And Abishua, and Naaman, and Ahoah,

• **Ahiah.**
1Ch 8:7 — And Naaman, and Ahiah, and Gera, he removed them, and begat Uzza, and Ahihud.

• **Aher.**
1Ch 7:12 — Shuppim also, and Huppim, the children of Ir, *and* Hushim, the sons of Aher.

• **Son of Bilhan.**
1Ch 7:10 — The sons also of Jediael; Bilhan: and the sons of Bilhan; Jeush, and Benjamin, and Ehud, and Chenaanah, and Zethan, and Tharshish, and Ahishahar.

• **A Benjamite, the assassin of Eglon.**
Jgs 3:16 — But Ehud made him a dagger which had two edges, of a cubit length; and he did gird it under his raiment upon his right thigh.

EKER • Son of Ram.
1Ch 2:27 — And the sons of Ram the firstborn of Jerahmeel were, Maaz, and Jamin, and Eker.

EKRON

• **One of the five chief cities of the Philistines.**
Jos 13:3 — From Sihor, which *is* before Egypt, even unto the borders of Ekron northward, *which* is counted to the Canaanite: five lords of the Philistines; the Gazathites, and the Ashdothites, the Eshkalonites, the Gittites, and the Ekronites; also the Avites:

• **Conquered and allotted to Judah.**
Jos 15:11 — And the border went out unto the side of Ekron northward: and the border was drawn to Shicron, and passed along to mount Baalah, and went out unto Jabneel; and the goings out of the border were at the sea.
Jos 15:45 — Ekron, with her towns and her villages:
Jgs 1:18 — Also Judah took Gaza with the coast thereof, and Askelon with the coast thereof, and Ekron with the coast thereof.

• **Allotted to Dan.**
Jos 19:43 — And Elon, and Thimnathah, and Ekron,

• **The ark of God taken to.**
1Sa 5:10 — Therefore they sent the ark of God to Ekron. And it came to pass, as the ark of God came to Ekron, that the Ekronites cried out, saying, They have brought about the ark of the God of Israel to us, to slay us and our people.

• **Temple of Baal-zebub at.**
2Ki 1:2 — And Ahaziah fell down through a lattice in his upper chamber that *was* in Samaria, and was sick: and he sent messengers, and said unto them, Go, enquire of Baal-zebub the god of Ekron whether I shall recover of this disease.

• **Prophecies against.**
Jer 25:20 — And all the mingled people, and all the kings of the land of Uz, and all the kings of the land of the Philistines, and Ashkelon, and Azzah, and Ekron, and the remnant of Ashdod,

Am 1:8 — And I will cut off the inhabitant from Ashdod, and him that holdeth the sceptre from Ashkelon, and I will turn mine hand against Ekron: and the remnant of the Philistines shall perish, saith the Lord God.

Zep 2:4 — For Gaza shall be forsaken, and Ashkelon a desolation: they shall drive out Ashdod at the noon-day, and Ekron shall be rooted up.

Zec 9:5 — Ashkelon shall see *it,* and fear; Gaza also *shall see it,* and be very sorrowful, and Ekron; for her expectation shall be ashamed; and the king shall perish from Gaza, and Ashkelon shall not be inhabited.

EL-BETH-EL • Name of the altar erected by Jacob where he had the vision of angels.

Ge 35:7 — And he built there an altar, and called the place El-beth-el: because there God appeared unto him, when he fled from the face of his brother.

EL-ELOHE-ISRAEL • Name of Jacob's altar at Salem.

Ge 33:20 — And he erected there an altar, and called it El-elohe-Israel.

ELADAH• Son of Ephraim.

1Ch 7:20 — And the sons of Ephraim; Shuthelah, and Bered his son, and Tahath his son, and Eladah his son, and Tahath his son,

ELAH

• A valley where David slew Goliath.

1Sa 17:2 — And Saul and the men of Israel were gathered together, and pitched by the valley of Elah, and set the battle in array against the Philistines.

1Sa 17:19 — Now Saul, and they, and all the men of Israel, *were* in the valley of Elah, fighting with the Philistines.

1Sa 21:9 — And the priest said, The sword of Goliath the Philistine, whom thou slewest in the valley of Elah, behold, it *is here* wrapped in a cloth behind the ephod: if thou wilt take that, take *it:* for *there is* no other save that here. And David said, *There is* none like that; give it me.

• An Edomitish duke.

Ge 36:41 — Duke Aholibamah, duke Elah, duke Pinon,

1Ch 1:52 — Duke Aholibamah, duke Elah, duke Pinon,

• Son of Caleb.

1Ch 4:15 — And the sons of Caleb the son of Jephunneh; Iru, Elah, and Naam: and the sons of Elah, even Kenaz.

• Father of Shimei.

1Ki 4:18 — Shimei the son of Elah, in Benjamin:

• Son and successor of Baasha, king of Israel.

1Ki 16:6–14

• Father of Hoshea.

2Ki 15:30 — And Hoshea the son of Elah made a conspiracy against Pekah the son of Remaliah, and smote him, and slew him, and reigned in his stead, in the twentieth year of Jotham the son of Uzziah.

2Ki 17:1 — In the twelfth year of Ahaz king of Judah began Hoshea the son of Elah to reign in Samaria over Israel nine years.

• A Benjamite chief.

1Ch 9:8 — And Ibneiah the son of Jeroham, and Elah the son of Uzzi, the son of Michri, and Meshullam the son of Shephatiah, the son of Reuel, the son of Ibnijah;

ELAM

• A district southeast of Babylon, on Persian Gulf.

Ge 14:1 — And it came to pass in the days of Amraphel king of Shinar, Arioch king of Ellasar, Chedorlaomer king of Elam, and Tidal king of nations;

Ge 14:9 — With Chedorlaomer the king of Elam, and with Tidal king of nations, and Amraphel king of Shinar, and Arioch king of Ellasar; four kings with five.

Da 8:2 — And I saw in a vision; and it came to pass, when I saw, that I *was* at Shushan *in* the palace, which *is* in the province of Elam; and I saw in a vision, and I was by the river of Ulai.

• Prophecies concerning.

Jer 49:34–39

Isa 11:11 — And it shall come to pass in that day, *that* the Lord shall set his hand again the second time to recover the remnant of his people, which shall be left, from Assyria, and from Egypt, and from Pathros, and from Cush, and from Elam, and from Shinar, and from Hamath, and from the islands of the sea.

Isa 21:2 — A grievous vision is declared unto me; the treacherous dealer dealeth treacherously, and the spoiler spoileth. Go up, O Elam: besiege, O Media; all the sighing thereof have I made to cease.

Isa 22:6 — And Elam bare the quiver with chariots of men *and* horsemen, and Kir uncovered the shield.

Jer 25:25 — And all the kings of Zimri, and all the kings of Elam, and all the kings of the Medes,

Eze 32:24 — There *is* Elam and all her multitude round about her grave, all of them slain, fallen by the sword, which are gone down uncircumcised into the nether parts of the earth, which caused their terror in the land of the living; yet have they borne their shame with them that go down to the pit.

• Jews from.

Ac 2:9 — Parthians, and Medes, and Elamites, and the dwellers in Mesopotamia, and in Judaea, and Cappadocia, in Pontus, and Asia,

See: Elamites

• A Korhite Levite.

1Ch 26:3 — Elam the fifth, Jehohanan the sixth, Elioenai the seventh.

• A Benjamite chief.

1Ch 8:24 — And Hananiah, and Elam, and Antothijah,

• Designated as "the other Elam".

Ezr 2:31 — The children of the other Elam, a thousand two hundred fifty and four.

Ne 7:34 — The children of the other Elam, a thousand two hundred fifty and four.

• A Jewish captive, whose descendants, to the number of twelve hundred and fifty-four, returned from Babylon.

Ezr 2:7 — The children of Elam, a thousand two hundred fifty and four.

Ezr 8:7 — And of the sons of Elam; Jeshaiah the son of Athaliah, and with him seventy males.

Ne 7:12 — The children of Elam, a thousand two hundred fifty and four.

• A Levite musician.

Ne 12:42 — And Maaseiah, and Shemaiah, and Eleazar, and Uzzi, and Jehohanan, and Malchijah, and Elam, and Ezer. And the singers sang loud, with Jezrahiah *their* overseer.

• One of the Israelitish chiefs with Nehemiah.

Ne 10:14 — The chief of the people; Parosh, Pahathmoab, Elam, Zatthu, Bani,

ELAMITES

• Descendants of Elam, whose name was given to the district of Elam.

Ge 10:22 — The children of Shem; Elam, and Asshur, and Arphaxad, and Lud, and Aram.

• Present at Pentecost.

Ac 2:9 — Parthians, and Medes, and Elamites, and the dwellers in Mesopotamia, and in Judaea, and Cappadocia, in Pontus, and Asia,

ELASAH

• Son of Helez, called Eleasah.

1Ch 2:39 — And Azariah begat Helez, and Helez begat Eleasah,

• Son of Shaphan.

Jer 29:3 — By the hand of Elasah the son of Shaphan, and Gemariah the son of Hilkiah, (whom Zedekiah king of Judah sent unto Babylon to Nebuchadnezzar king of Babylon) saying,

• Son of Pashur.

Ezr 10:22 — And of the sons of Pashur; Elioenai, Maaseiah, Ishmael, Nethaneel, Jozabad, and Elasah.

ELATH

• Called also Eloth.

• A city of Idumea.

Dt 2:8 — And when we passed by from our brethren the children of Esau, which dwelt in Seir, through the way of the plain from Elath, and from Ezion-gaber, we turned and passed by the way of the wilderness of Moab.

1Ki 9:26 — And king Solomon made a navy of ships in Ezion-geber, which is beside Eloth, on the shore of the Red sea, in the land of Edom.

2Ch 8:17 — Then went Solomon to Ezion-geber, and to Eloth, at the sea side in the land of Edom.

• Conquest of, by Uzziah.

2Ch 26:2 — He built Eloth, and restored it to Judah, after that the king slept with his fathers.

• Conquest of, by the Syrians.

2Ki 16:6 — At that time Rezin king of Syria recovered Elath to Syria, and drave the Jews from Elath: and the Syrians came to Elath, and dwelt there unto this day.

ELDAAH • A descendant of Abraham.

Ge 25:4 — And the sons of Midian; Ephah, and Epher, and Hanoch, and Abidah, and Eldaah. All these *were* the children of Keturah.

1Ch 1:33 — And the sons of Midian; Ephah, and Epher, and Henoch, and Abida, and Eldaah. All these *are* the sons of Keturah.

ELDAD • Prophesies in the camp of the Israelites.

Nu 11:26–29

ELDER

• In the Mosaic system.

• Equivalent to the title and role of senator.

Dt 1:13 — Take you wise men, and understanding, and known among your tribes, and I will make them rulers over you.

Dt 1:15 — So I took the chief of your tribes, wise men, and known, and made them heads over you, captains over thousands, and captains over hundreds, and captains over fifties, and captains over tens, and officers among your tribes.

See: Government; Mosaic

• In the Christian church.

Ac 11:29–30; 15:1–35; 16:4–5; 20:28–32; 1Ti 5:17–19; Tit 1:5–9; Jas 5:14–15; 1Pe 5:1–5

Ac 14:23 — And when they had ordained them elders in every church, and had prayed with fasting, they commended them to the Lord, on whom they believed.

Ac 20:17 — And from Miletus he sent to Ephesus, and called the elders of the church.

Ac 21:18 — And the *day* following Paul went in with us unto James; and all the elders were present.

1Ti 4:14 — Neglect not the gift that is in thee, which was given thee by prophecy, with the laying on of the hands of the presbytery.

Heb 11:2 — For by it the elders obtained a good report.

2Jn 1:1 — The elder unto the elect lady and her children, whom I love in the truth; and not I only, but also all they that have known the truth;

3Jn 1:1 — The elder unto the wellbeloved Gaius, whom I love in the truth.

• Apocalyptic vision of.

Rev 5:5–6

Rev 4:4 — And round about the throne *were* four and twenty seats: and upon the seats I saw four and twenty elders sitting, clothed in white raiment; and they had on their heads crowns of gold.

Rev 4:10 — The four and twenty elders fall down before him that sat on the throne, and worship him that liveth for ever and ever, and cast their crowns before the throne, saying,

Rev 5:8 — And when he had taken the book, the four beasts and four *and* twenty elders fell down before the Lamb, having every one of them harps, and golden vials full of odours, which are the prayers of saints.

Rev 5:11 — And I beheld, and I heard the voice of many angels round about the throne and the beasts and the elders: and the number of them was ten thousand times ten thousand, and thousands of thousands;

Rev 5:14 — And the four beasts said, Amen. And the four *and* twenty elders fell down and worshipped him that liveth for ever and ever.

Rev 7:11 — And all the angels stood round about the throne, and *about* the elders and the four beasts, and fell before the throne on their faces, and worshipped God,

Rev 7:13 — And one of the elders answered, saying unto me, What are these which are arrayed in white robes? and whence came they?

Rev 11:16 — And the four and twenty elders, which sat before God on their seats, fell upon their faces, and worshipped God,

Rev 14:3 — And they sung as it were a new song before the throne, and before the four beasts, and the elders: and no man could learn that song but the hundred *and* forty *and* four thousand, which were redeemed from the earth.

Rev 19:4 — And the four and twenty elders and the four beasts fell down and worshipped God that sat on the throne, saying, Amen; Alleluia.

↞See: Church; government of, Mosaic and Christian

↞See: Deacon

ELDERLY

1Ti 5:1–16

Pr 16:31 — The hoary head *is* a crown of glory, *if* it be found in the way of righteousness.

Phm 1:9 — Yet for love's sake I rather beseech *thee*, being such an one as Paul the aged, and now also a prisoner of Jesus Christ.

Jas 1:27 — Pure religion and undefiled before God and the Father is this, To visit the fatherless and widows in their affliction, *and* to keep himself unspotted from the world.

ELEAD • A descendant of Ephraim.

1Ch 7:21 — And Zabad his son, and Shuthelah his son, and Ezer, and Elead, whom the men of Gath *that were* born in *that* land slew, because they came down to take away their cattle.

ELEALEH

• A city of Moab.

• Taken by the Israelites.

Nu 32:3 — Ataroth, and Dibon, and Jazer, and Nimrah, and Heshbon, and Elealeh, and Shebam, and Nebo, and Beon,

Nu 32:37 — And the children of Reuben built Heshbon, and Elealeh, and Kirjathaim,

• Repossessed by the Moabites.

Isa 15:4 — And Heshbon shall cry, and Elealeh: their voice shall be heard *even* unto Jahaz: therefore the armed soldiers of Moab shall cry out; his life shall be grievous unto him.

Isa 16:9 — Therefore I will bewail with the weeping of Jazer the vine of Sibmah: I will water thee with my tears, O Heshbon, and Elealeh: for the shouting for thy summer fruits and for thy harvest is fallen.

ELEASAH

• Name of two men, or of one man, uncertain which.

• Called also Elasah.

• Compare.

1Ch 2:39 — And Azariah begat Helez, and Helez begat Eleasah,

1Ch 8:37 — And Moza begat Binea: Rapha *was* his son, Eleasah his son, Azel his son:

1Ch 9:43 — And Moza begat Binea; and Rephaiah his son, Eleasah his son, Azel his son.

Ezr 10:22 — And of the sons of Pashur; Elioenai, Maaseiah, Ishmael, Nethaneel, Jozabad, and Elasah.

Jer 29:3 — By the hand of Elasah the son of Shaphan, and Gemariah the son of Hilkiah, (whom Zedekiah king of Judah sent unto Babylon to Nebuchadnezzar king of Babylon) saying,

ELEAZER

• Son of Aaron.

Ex 6:23 — And Aaron took him Elisheba, daughter of Amminadab, sister of Naashon, to wife; and she bare him Nadab, and Abihu, Eleazar, and Ithamar.

Ex 28:1 — And take thou unto thee Aaron thy brother, and his sons with him, from among the children of Israel, that he may minister unto me in the priest's office, *even* Aaron, Nadab and Abihu, Eleazar and Ithamar, Aaron's sons.

• Marries a daughter of Putiel, who bore him Phinehas.

Ex 6:25 — And Eleazar Aaron's son took him *one* of the daughters of Putiel to wife; and she bare him Phinehas: these *are* the heads of the fathers of the Levites according to their families.

• After the death of Nadab and Abihu is made chief of the tribe of Levi.

Nu 3:32 — And Eleazar the son of Aaron the priest *shall be* chief over the chief of the Levites, *and have* the oversight of them that keep the charge of the sanctuary.

• **Duties of.**

Nu 4:16 — And to the office of Eleazar the son of Aaron the priest *pertaineth* the oil for the light, and the sweet incense, and the daily meat offering, and the anointing oil, *and* the oversight of all the tabernacle, and of all that therein *is*, in the sanctuary, and in the vessels thereof.

• **Succeeds Aaron as high priest.**

Nu 20:26 — And strip Aaron of his garments, and put them upon Eleazar his son: and Aaron shall be gathered *unto his people*, and shall die there.

Nu 20:28 — And Moses stripped Aaron of his garments, and put them upon Eleazar his son; and Aaron died there in the top of the mount: and Moses and Eleazar came down from the mount.

Dt 10:6 — And the children of Israel took their journey from Beeroth of the children of Jaakan to Mosera: there Aaron died, and there he was buried; and Eleazar his son ministered in the priest's office in his stead.

• **Assists Moses in the census.**

Nu 26:63 — These *are* they that were numbered by Moses and Eleazar the priest, who numbered the children of Israel in the plains of Moab by Jordan *near* Jericho.

• **With Joshua, divides Palestine.**

Nu 34:17 — These *are* the names of the men which shall divide the land unto you: Eleazar the priest, and Joshua the son of Nun.

• **Death and burial of.**

Jos 24:33 — And Eleazar the son of Aaron died; and they buried him in a hill *that pertained to* Phinehas his son, which was given him in mount Ephraim.

• **Descendants of.**

1Ch 24:1–19

• **An inhabitant of Kirjath-jearim who attended the ark.**

1Sa 7:1–2

• **A Merarite Levite.**

1Ch 23:21–22

1Ch 24:28 — Of Mahli *came* Eleazar, who had no sons.

• **Son of Dodo, and one of David's distinguished heroes.**

2Sa 23:9–10

2Sa 23:13 — And three of the thirty chief went down, and came to David in the harvest time unto the cave of Adullam: and the troop of the Philistines pitched in the valley of Rephaim.

1Ch 11:12 — And after him *was* Eleazar the son of Dodo, the Ahohite, who *was one* of the three mighties.

• **Son of Phinehas.**

Ezr 8:33 — Now on the fourth day was the silver and the gold and the vessels weighed in the house of our God by the hand of Meremoth the son of Uriah the priest; and with him *was* Eleazar the son of Phinehas; and with them *was* Jozabad the son of Jeshua, and Noadiah the son of Binnui, Levites;

Ne 12:42 — And Maaseiah, and Shemaiah, and Eleazar, and Uzzi, and Jehohanan, and Malchijah, and Elam, and Ezer. And the singers sang loud, with Jezrahiah *their* overseer.

• **A returned Israelitish exile.**

Ezr 10:25 — Moreover of Israel: of the sons of Parosh; Ramiah, and Jeziah, and Malchiah, and Miamin, and Eleazar, and Malchijah, and Benaiah.

ELECTION

• **Of rulers.**

• **By lot.**

Ne 11:1 — And the rulers of the people dwelt at Jerusalem: the rest of the people also cast lots, to bring one of ten to dwell in Jerusalem the holy city, and nine parts *to dwell* in *other* cities.

• **Of grace.**

Jn 15:16 — Ye have not chosen me, but I have chosen you, and ordained you, that ye should go and bring forth fruit, and *that* your fruit should remain: that whatsoever ye shall ask of the Father in my name, he may give it you.

Jn 17:6 — I have manifested thy name unto the men which thou gavest me out of the world: thine they were, and thou gavest them me; and they have kept thy word.

Eph 1:4 — According as he hath chosen us in him before the foundation of the world, that we should be holy and without blame before him in love:

Eph 2:10 — For we are his workmanship, created in Christ Jesus unto good works, which God hath before ordained that we should walk in them.

2Th 2:13 — But we are bound to give thanks alway to God for you, brethren beloved of the Lord, because God hath from the beginning chosen you to salvation through sanctification of the Spirit and belief of the truth:

• **Of Christ as Messiah.**

Isa 42:1 — Behold my servant, whom I uphold; mine elect, *in whom* my soul delighteth; I have put my spirit upon him: he shall bring forth judgment to the Gentiles.

1Pe 2:6 — Wherefore also it is contained in the scripture, Behold, I lay in Sion a chief corner stone, elect, precious: and he that believeth on him shall not be confounded.

• **Of good angels.**

1Ti 5:21 — I charge *thee* before God, and the Lord Jesus Christ, and the elect angels, that thou observe these things without preferring one before another, doing nothing by partiality.

• **Of Israel.**

Dt 7:6 — For thou *art* an holy people unto the LORD thy God: the LORD thy God hath chosen thee to be a special people unto himself, above all people that *are* upon the face of the earth.

Isa 45:4 — For Jacob my servant's sake, and Israel mine elect, I have even called thee by thy name: I have surnamed thee, though thou hast not known me.

• Of ministers.

Lk 6:13 — And when it was day, he called *unto him* his disciples: and of them he chose twelve, whom also he named apostles;

Ac 9:15 — But the Lord said unto him, Go thy way: for he is a chosen vessel unto me, to bear my name before the Gentiles, and kings, and the children of Israel:

• Of churches.

1Pe 5:13 — The *church that is* at Babylon, elected together with *you*, saluteth you; and *so doth* Marcus my son.

See: Predestination

ELECTIONEERING

• By Absalom.

2Sa 15:1–6

• By Adonijah.

1Ki 1:7 — And he conferred with Joab the son of Zeruiah, and with Abiathar the priest: and they following Adonijah helped *him*.

ELEGY

• David's, on Saul and Jonathan.

2Sa 1:19–27

2Sa 1:17 — And David lamented with this lamentation over Saul and over Jonathan his son:

• On Abner.

2Sa 3:33–34; La 3:1–66

See: Poetry

ELEPH • A town allotted to Benjamin.

Jos 18:28 — And Zelah, Eleph, and Jebusi, which *is* Jerusalem, Gibeath, *and* Kirjath; fourteen cities with their villages. This *is* the inheritance of the children of Benjamin according to their families.

ELEPHANT

Job 40:15 — Behold now behemoth, which I made with thee; he eateth grass as an ox.

See: Ivory

ELHANAN

• A distinguished warrior in the time of David, who slew Lahmi, the brother of Goliath, the Gittite.

2Sa 21:19 — And there was again a battle in Gob with the Philistines, where Elhanan the son of Jaare-oregim, a Bethlehemite, slew *the brother of* Goliath the Gittite, the staff of whose spear *was* like a weaver's beam.

• Compare.

1Ch 20:5 — And there was war again with the Philistines; and Elhanan the son of Jair slew Lahmi the brother of Goliath the Gittite, whose spear staff *was* like a weaver's beam.

• Son of Dodo, and one of David's heroes.

2Sa 23:24 — Asahel the brother of Joab *was* one of the thirty; Elhanan the son of Dodo of Bethlehem,

1Ch 11:26 — Also the valiant men of the armies *were*, Asahel the brother of Joab, Elhanan the son of Dodo of Bethlehem,

ELI

• High priest.

1Sa 1:25 — And they slew a bullock, and brought the child to Eli.

1Sa 2:11 — And Elkanah went to Ramah to his house. And the child did minister unto the LORD before Eli the priest.

1Ki 2:27 — So Solomon thrust out Abiathar from being priest unto the LORD; that he might fulfil the word of the LORD, which he spake concerning the house of Eli in Shiloh.

• Judge of Israel.

1Sa 4:18 — And it came to pass, when he made mention of the ark of God, that he fell from off the seat backward by the side of the gate, and his neck brake, and he died: for he was an old man, and heavy. And he had judged Israel forty years.

• Misjudges and rebukes Hannah.

1Sa 1:17–18

1Sa 1:14 — And Eli said unto her, How long wilt thou be drunken? put away thy wine from thee.

1Sa 2:20 — And Eli blessed Elkanah and his wife, and said, The LORD give thee seed of this woman for the loan which is lent to the LORD. And they went unto their own home.

• His benediction upon Hannah.

1Sa 1:17–18

1Sa 2:20 — And Eli blessed Elkanah and his wife, and said, The LORD give thee seed of this woman for the loan which is lent to the LORD. And they went unto their own home.

• Officiates when Samuel is presented at the tabernacle.

1Sa 1:24–28

• Indulgent to his corrupt sons.

1Sa 2:22–25; 3:11–14

1Sa 2:29 — Wherefore kick ye at my sacrifice and at mine offering, which I have commanded *in my* habitation; and honourest thy sons above me, to make yourselves fat with the chiefest of all the offerings of Israel my people?

• His solicitude for the ark.

1Sa 4:11–18

• Death of.

1Sa 4:18 — And it came to pass, when he made mention of the ark of God, that he fell from off the seat backward by the side of the gate, and his neck brake, and he died: for he was an old man, and heavy. And he had judged Israel forty years.

• Prophecies of judgments upon his house.

1Sa 2:27–3:21

1Ki 2:27 — So Solomon thrust out Abiathar from being priest unto the LORD; that he might fulfil the word of the LORD, which he spake concerning the house of Eli in Shiloh.

ELIAB

• A Reubenite, progenitor of Dathan and Abiram.

Nu 26:8–9

Nu 16:1 — Now Korah, the son of Izhar, the son of Kohath, the son of Levi, and Dathan and Abiram, the sons of Eliab, and On, the son of Peleth, sons of Reuben, took *men:*

Nu 16:12 — And Moses sent to call Dathan and Abiram, the sons of Eliab: which said, We will not come up:

Dt 11:6 — And what he did unto Dathan and Abiram, the sons of Eliab, the son of Reuben: how the earth opened her mouth, and swallowed them up, and their households, and their tents, and all the substance that *was* in their possession, in the midst of all Israel:

• Son of Helon.

Nu 1:9 — Of Zebulun; Eliab the son of Helon.

Nu 2:7 — *Then* the tribe of Zebulun: and Eliab the son of Helon *shall be* captain of the children of Zebulun.

Nu 7:24 — On the third day Eliab the son of Helon, prince of the children of Zebulun, *did offer:*

Nu 7:29 — And for a sacrifice of peace offerings, two oxen, five rams, five he goats, five lambs of the first year: this *was* the offering of Eliab the son of Helon.

Nu 10:16 — And over the host of the tribe of the children of Zebulun *was* Eliab the son of Helon.

• Ancestor of Samuel.

1Ch 6:27 — Eliab his son, Jeroham his son, Elkanah his son.

• Called also Elihu.

1Sa 1:1 — Now there was a certain man of Ramathaim-zophim, of mount Ephraim, and his name was Elkanah, the son of Jeroham, the son of Elihu, the son of Tohu, the son of Zuph, an Ephrathite:

• Called also Eliel.

1Ch 6:34 — The son of Elkanah, the son of Jeroham, the son of Eliel, the son of Toah,

• Son of Jesse, and eldest brother of David.

1Sa 16:6 — And it came to pass, when they were come, that he looked on Eliab, and said, Surely the LORD's anointed *is* before him.

1Sa 17:13 — And the three eldest sons of Jesse went *and* followed Saul to the battle: and the names of his three sons that went to the battle *were* Eliab the first born, and next unto him Abinadab, and the third Shammah.

1Sa 17:28 — And Eliab his eldest brother heard when he spake unto the men; and Eliab's anger was kindled against David, and he said, Why camest thou down hither? and with whom hast thou left those few sheep in the wilderness? I know thy pride, and the naughtiness of thine heart; for thou art come down that thou mightest see the battle.

1Ch 2:13 — And Jesse begat his firstborn Eliab, and Abinadab the second, and Shimma the third,

• A prince in the tribe of Judah.

1Ch 27:18 — Of Judah, Elihu, *one* of the brethren of David: of Issachar, Omri the son of Michael:

• A hero of the tribe of Gad.

1Ch 12:9 — Ezer the first, Obadiah the second, Eliab the third,

• A Levite, a porter and musician.

1Ch 15:18 — And with them their brethren of the second *degree,* Zechariah, Ben, and Jaaziel, and Shemiramoth, and Jehiel, and Unni, Eliab, and Benaiah, and Maaseiah, and Mattithiah, and Elipheleh, and Mikneiah, and Obed-edom, and Jeiel, the porters.

1Ch 15:20 — And Zechariah, and Aziel, and Shemiramoth, and Jehiel, and Unni, and Eliab, and Maaseiah, and Benaiah, with psalteries on Alamoth;

1Ch 16:5 — Asaph the chief, and next to him Zechariah, Jeiel, and Shemiramoth, and Jehiel, and Mattithiah, and Eliab, and Benaiah, and Obed-edom: and Jeiel with psalteries and with harps; but Asaph made a sound with cymbals;

ELIADA

• Son of David.

2Sa 5:16 — And Elishama, and Eliada, and Eliphalet.

1Ch 3:8 — And Elishama, and Eliada, and Eliphelet, nine.

• Called Beeliada.

1Ch 14:7 — And Elishama, and Beeliada, and Eliphalet.

• A Benjamite.

2Ch 17:17 — And of Benjamin; Eliada a mighty man of valour, and with him armed men with bow and shield two hundred thousand.

ELIADAH • An Aramite.

1Ki 11:23 — And God stirred him up *another* adversary, Rezon the son of Eliadah, which fled from his lord Hadadezer king of Zobah:

ELIAH ⇨See: Elijah; called also Eliah

ELIAHBA • One of David's heroes.

2Sa 23:32 — Eliahba the Shaalbonite, of the sons of Jashen, Jonathan,

1Ch 11:33 — Azmaveth the Baharumite, Eliahba the Shaalbonite,

ELIAKIM

• Son of Melea.

Lk 3:30 — Which was *the son* of Simeon, which was *the son* of Juda, which was *the son* of Joseph, which was *the son* of Jonan, which was *the son* of Eliakim,

• Son of Hilkiah, deputy of Hezekiah.

2Ki 18:18 — And when they had called to the king, there came out to them Eliakim the son of Hilkiah, which *was* over the household, and Shebna the scribe, and Joah the son of Asaph the recorder.

2Ki 19:2 — And he sent Eliakim, which *was* over the household, and Shebna the scribe, and the elders of the priests, covered with sackcloth, to Isaiah the prophet the son of Amoz.

Isa 36:3 — Then came forth unto him Eliakim, Hilkiah's son, which was over the house, and Shebna the scribe, and Joah, Asaph's son, the recorder.

Isa 36:11 — Then said Eliakim and Shebna and Joah unto Rabshakeh, Speak, I pray thee, unto thy servants in the Syrian language; for we understand *it:* and speak not to us in the Jews' language, in the ears of the people that *are* on the wall.

Isa 36:22 — Then came Eliakim, the son of Hilkiah, that *was* over the household, and Shebna the scribe, and Joah, the son of Asaph, the recorder, to Hezekiah with *their* clothes rent, and told him the words of Rabshakeh.

Isa 37:2 — And he sent Eliakim, who *was* over the household, and Shebna the scribe, and the elders of the priests covered with sackcloth, unto Isaiah the prophet the son of Amoz.

• Original name of Jehoiakim, king of Judah.

2Ki 23:34 — And Pharaoh-nechoh made Eliakim the son of Josiah king in the room of Josiah his father, and turned his name to Jehoiakim, and took Jehoahaz away: and he came to Egypt, and died there.

2Ch 36:4 — And the king of Egypt made Eliakim his brother king over Judah and Jerusalem, and turned his name to Jehoiakim. And Necho took Jehoahaz his brother, and carried him to Egypt.

• Son of Abiud.

Mt 1:13 — And Zorobabel begat Abiud; and Abiud begat Eliakim; and Eliakim begat Azor;

• Probably same as Shechaniah.

1Ch 3:21 — And the sons of Hananiah; Pelatiah, and Jesaiah: the sons of Rephaiah, the sons of Arnan, the sons of Obadiah, the sons of Shechaniah.

• A priest.

Ne 12:41 — And the priests; Eliakim, Maaseiah, Miniamin, Michaiah, Elioenai, Zechariah, *and* Hananiah, with trumpets;

ELIAM

• Father of Bath-sheba.

2Sa 11:3 — And David sent and enquired after the woman. And *one* said, *Is* not this Bath-sheba, the daughter of Eliam, the wife of Uriah the Hittite?

• Called Ammiel.

1Ch 3:5 — And these were born unto him in Jerusalem; Shimea, and Shobab, and Nathan, and Solomon, four, of Bath-shua the daughter of Ammiel:

• One of David's valiant men.

2Sa 23:34 — Eliphelet the son of Ahasbai, the son of the Maachathite, Eliam the son of Ahithophel the Gilonite,

• Called Ahijah.

1Ch 11:36 — Hepher the Mecherathite, Ahijah the Pelonite,

ELIAS • See: Elijah

ELIASAPH

• A chief of the tribe of Dan.

Nu 1:14 — Of Gad; Eliasaph the son of Deuel.

Nu 2:14 — Then the tribe of Gad: and the captain of the sons of Gad *shall be* Eliasaph the son of Reuel.

Nu 7:42 — On the sixth day Eliasaph the son of Deuel, prince of the children of Gad, *offered:*

Nu 7:47 — And for a sacrifice of peace offerings, two oxen, five rams, five he goats, five lambs of the first year: this *was* the offering of Eliasaph the son of Deuel.

Nu 10:20 — And over the host of the tribe of the children of Gad was Eliasaph the son of Deuel.

• Son of Lael.

Nu 3:24 — And the chief of the house of the father of the Gershonites *shall be* Eliasaph the son of Lael.

ELIASHIB

• A priest.

1Ch 24:12 — The eleventh to Eliashib, the twelfth to Jakim,

• Name of three Israelites, mentioned in.

Ezr 10:24 — Of the singers also; Eliashib: and of the porters; Shallum, and Telem, and Uri.

Ezr 10:27 — And of the sons of Zattu; Elioenai, Eliashib, Mattaniah, and Jeremoth, and Zabad, and Aziza.

Ezr 10:36 — Vaniah, Meremoth, Eliashib,

• High priest.

Ne 13:4–9

Ne 3:1 — Then Eliashib the high priest rose up with his brethren the priests, and they builded the sheep gate; they sanctified it, and set up the doors of it; even unto the tower of Meah they sanctified it, unto the tower of Hananeel.

Ne 12:10 — And Jeshua begat Joiakim, Joiakim also begat Eliashib, and Eliashib begat Joiada,

Ne 13:28 — And *one* of the sons of Joiada, the son of Eliashib the high priest, *was* son in law to Sanballat the Horonite: therefore I chased him from me.

• Son of Elioenai.

1Ch 3:24 — And the sons of Elioenai *were*, Hodaiah, and Eliashib, and Pelaiah, and Akkub, and Johanan, and Dalaiah, and Anani, seven.

ELIATHAH • A musician.

1Ch 25:4 — Of Heman: the sons of Heman; Bukkiah, Mattaniah, Uzziel, Shebuel, and Jerimoth, Hananiah, Hanani, Eliathah, Giddalti, and Romamti-ezer, Joshbekashah, Mallothi, Hothir, *and* Mahazioth:

1Ch 25:27 — The twentieth to Eliathah, *he*, his sons, and his brethren, *were* twelve:

ELIDAD • A prince of Benjamin.

Nu 34:21 — Of the tribe of Benjamin, Elidad the son of Chislon.

ELIEL

• A chief of Manasseh.

1Ch 5:24 — And these *were* the heads of the house of their fathers, even Epher, and Ishi, and Eliel, and

Azriel, and Jeremiah, and Hodaviah, and Jahdiel, mighty men of valour, famous men, *and* heads of the house of their fathers.

- **Son of Toah.**
  1Ch 6:34 — The son of Elkanah, the son of Jeroham, the son of Eliel, the son of Toah,
- **Two Benjamite chiefs.**
  1Ch 8:20 — And Elienai, and Zilthai, and Eliel,
  1Ch 8:22 — And Ishpan, and Heber, and Eliel,
- **Three of David's heroes, bearing the same name.**
  1Ch 11:46–47
  1Ch 12:11 — Attai the sixth, Eliel the seventh,
- **Chief of Levites.**
  1Ch 15:9 — Of the sons of Hebron; Eliel the chief, and his brethren fourscore:
  1Ch 15:11 — And David called for Zadok and Abiathar the priests, and for the Levites, for Uriel, Asaiah, and Joel, Shemaiah, and Eliel, and Amminadab,
- **A Levite, who had charge of the temple.**
  2Ch 31:13 — And Jehiel, and Azaziah, and Nahath, and Asahel, and Jerimoth, and Jozabad, and Eliel, and Ismachiah, and Mahath, and Benaiah, *were* overseers under the hand of Cononiah and Shimei his brother, at the commandment of Hezekiah the king, and Azariah the ruler of the house of God.

ELIENAI • A Benjamite citizen of Jerusalem.

1Ch 8:20 — And Elienai, and Zilthai, and Eliel,

ELIEZER

- **Abraham's servant.**
  Ge 24:1–67
  Ge 15:2 — And Abram said, Lord GOD, what wilt thou give me, seeing I go childless, and the steward of my house is this Eliezer of Damascus?
- **Son of Becher.**
  1Ch 7:8 — And the sons of Becher; Zemira, and Joash, and Eliezer, and Elioenai, and Omri, and Jerimoth, and Abiah, and Anathoth, and Alameth. All these *are* the sons of Becher.
- **Son of Moses.**
  Ex 18:4 — And the name of the other *was* Eliezer; for the God of my father, *said he, was* mine help, and delivered me from the sword of Pharaoh:
  1Ch 23:15 — The sons of Moses *were,* Gershom, and Eliezer.
  1Ch 23:17 — And the sons of Eliezer *were,* Rehabiah the chief. And Eliezer had none other sons; but the sons of Rehabiah were very many.
- **A priest.**
  1Ch 15:24 — And Shebaniah, and Jehoshaphat, and Nethaneel, and Amasai, and Zechariah, and Benaiah, and Eliezer, the priests, did blow with the trumpets before the ark of God: and Obed-edom and Jehiah *were* doorkeepers for the ark.
- **Son of Zichri.**
  1Ch 27:16 — Furthermore over the tribes of Israel: the ruler of the Reubenites *was* Eliezer the son of Zichri: of the Simeonites, Shephatiah the son of Maachah:
- **A prophet.**
  2Ch 20:37 — Then Eliezer the son of Dodavah of Mareshah prophesied against Jehoshaphat, saying, Because thou hast joined thyself with Ahaziah, the LORD hath broken thy works. And the ships were broken, that they were not able to go to Tarshish.
- **Son of Jorim.**
  Lk 3:29 — Which was *the son* of Jose, which was *the son* of Eliezer, which was *the son* of Jorim, which was *the son* of Matthat, which was *the son* of Levi,
- **A Jewish exile.**
  Ezr 8:16 — Then sent I for Eliezer, for Ariel, for Shemaiah, and for Elnathan, and for Jarib, and for Elnathan, and for Nathan, and for Zechariah, and for Meshullam, chief men; also for Joiarib, and for Elnathan, men of understanding.
- **A priest after the exile.**
  Ezr 10:18 — And among the sons of the priests there were found that had taken strange wives: *namely,* of the sons of Jeshua the son of Jozadak, and his brethren; Maaseiah, and Eliezer, and Jarib, and Gedaliah.
- **A Levite.**
  Ezr 10:23 — Also of the Levites; Jozabad, and Shimei, and Kelaiah, (the same *is* Kelita,) Pethahiah, Judah, and Eliezer.
- **An Israelite after the exile.**
  Ezr 10:31 — And *of* the sons of Harim; Eliezer, Ishijah, Malchiah, Shemaiah, Shimeon,

ELIHOENAI

- **A Levite.**
  1Ch 26:3 — Elam the fifth, Jehohanan the sixth, Elioenai the seventh.
- **Son of Zerahiah.**
  Ezr 8:4 — Of the sons of Pahath-moab; Elihoenai the son of Zerahiah, and with him two hundred males.

ELIHOREPH • Son of Shisha.

1Ki 4:3 — Elihoreph and Ahiah, the sons of Shisha, scribes; Jehoshaphat the son of Ahilud, the recorder.

ELIHU

- **A Buzite and one of Job's three friends.**
  Job 32:1–37:24
- **Son of Tohu.**
  1Sa 1:1 — Now there was a certain man of Ramathaim-zophim, of mount Ephraim, and his name was Elkanah, the son of Jeroham, the son of Elihu, the son of Tohu, the son of Zuph, an Ephrathite:
  - **Probably identical with.**
    - **Eliel.**
      1Ch 6:34 — The son of Elkanah, the son of Jeroham, the son of Eliel, the son of Toah,
    - **Eliab.**
      1Ch 6:27 — Eliab his son, Jeroham his son, Elkanah his son.

• A Manassite warrior, who joined David at Ziklag.

1Ch 12:20 — As he went to Ziklag, there fell to him of Manasseh, Adnah, and Jozabad, and Jediael, and Michael, and Jozabad, and Elihu, and Zilthai, captains of the thousands that *were* of Manasseh.

• A porter of the temple.

1Ch 26:7 — The sons of Shemaiah; Othni, and Rephael, and Obed, Elzabad, whose brethren *were* strong men, Elihu, and Semachiah.

• A chief of the tribe of Judah.

1Ch 27:18 — Of Judah, Elihu, *one* of the brethren of David: of Issachar, Omri the son of Michael:

• Possibly Eliab, the oldest brother of David.

1Sa 16:6 — And it came to pass, when they were come, that he looked on Eliab, and said, Surely the LORD's anointed *is* before him.

ELIJAH

• The Tishbite, a Gileadite and prophet. Called Elias in the King James Version of the New Testament.

• Persecuted by Ahab.

1Ki 17:2–7; 18:7–10

• Escapes to the wilderness, where he is miraculously fed by ravens.

1Ki 17:1–7

• By divine direction, goes to Zarephath where he is sustained by a widow.

1Ki 17:8–16

• Returns, and sends a message to Ahab.

1Ki 18:1–16

• Meets Ahab and directs him to assemble the prophets of Baal.

1Ki 18:17–20

• Derisively challenges the priests of Baal to offer sacrifices.

1Ki 18:25–29

• Slays the prophets of Baal.

1Ki 18:40 — And Elijah said unto them, Take the prophets of Baal; let not one of them escape. And they took them: and Elijah brought them down to the brook Kishon, and slew them there.

• Escapes to the wilderness from the fierceness of Jezebel.

1Ki 19:1–18

• Fasts forty days.

1Ki 19:8 — And he arose, and did eat and drink, and went in the strength of that meat forty days and forty nights unto Horeb the mount of God.

• Despondency and murmuring of.

1Ki 19:10 — And he said, I have been very jealous for the LORD God of hosts: for the children of Israel have forsaken thy covenant, thrown down thine altars, and slain thy prophets with the sword; and I, *even* I only, am left; and they seek my life, to take it away.

1Ki 19:14 — And he said, I have been very jealous for the LORD God of hosts: because the children of Israel have forsaken thy covenant, thrown down thine altars, and slain thy prophets with the sword; and I, *even* I only, am left; and they seek my life, to take it away.

• Consolation given to.

1Ki 9:11–18

• Flees to wilderness of Damascus; directed to anoint kings.

1Ki 19:9–21

• Personal aspect of.

2Ki 1:8 — And they answered him, *He was* an hairy man, and girt with a girdle of leather about his loins. And he said, It *is* Elijah the Tishbite.

• Piety of.

1Ki 19:10 — And he said, I have been very jealous for the LORD God of hosts: for the children of Israel have forsaken thy covenant, thrown down thine altars, and slain thy prophets with the sword; and I, *even* I only, am left; and they seek my life, to take it away.

1Ki 19:14 — And he said, I have been very jealous for the LORD God of hosts: because the children of Israel have forsaken thy covenant, thrown down thine altars, and slain thy prophets with the sword; and I, *even* I only, am left; and they seek my life, to take it away.

Lk 1:17 — And he shall go before him in the spirit and power of Elias, to turn the hearts of the fathers to the children, and the disobedient to the wisdom of the just; to make ready a people prepared for the Lord.

Ro 11:2 — God hath not cast away his people which he foreknew. Wot ye not what the scripture saith of Elias? how he maketh intercession to God against Israel, saying,

Jas 5:17 — Elias was a man subject to like passions as we are, and he prayed earnestly that it might not rain: and it rained not on the earth by the space of three years and six months.

• His translation.

2Ki 2:11 — And it came to pass, as they still went on, and talked, that, behold, *there appeared* a chariot of fire, and horses of fire, and parted them both asunder; and Elijah went up by a whirlwind into heaven.

• Appears to Jesus at his transfiguration.

Mt 17:3–4

Mk 9:4 — And there appeared unto them Elias with Moses: and they were talking with Jesus.

Lk 9:30 — And, behold, there talked with him two men, which were Moses and Elias:

• Antitype of John the Baptist.

Mt 17:10–12; Mk 9:12–13; Jn 1:21–25

Mt 11:14 — And if ye will receive *it*, this is Elias, which was for to come.

Mt 16:14 — And they said, Some *say that thou art* John the Baptist: some, Elias; and others, Jeremias, or one of the prophets.

Lk 1:17 — And he shall go before him in the spirit and power of Elias, to turn the hearts of the fathers to the children, and the disobedient to the wisdom of the just; to make ready a people prepared for the Lord.

• Miracles of.

• Increases the oil of the widow of Zarephath.

1Ki 17:14–16

• Raises from the dead the son of the woman of Zarephath.

1Ki 17:17–24

• Causes rain after a drought of three and a half years.

1Ki 18:41–45; Jas 5:17–18

• Causes fire to consume the sacrifice.

1Ki 18:36–38

1Ki 18:24 — And call ye on the name of your gods, and I will call on the name of the LORD: and the God that answereth by fire, let him be God. And all the people answered and said, It is well spoken.

• Calls fire down upon the soldiers of Ahaziah.

2Ki 1:10–12

Lk 9:54 — And when his disciples James and John saw *this,* they said, Lord, wilt thou that we command fire to come down from heaven, and consume them, even as Elias did?

• Prophecies of.

• Foretells a drought.

1Ki 17:3 — Get thee hence, and turn thee eastward, and hide thyself by the brook Cherith, that *is* before Jordan.

• Foretells the destruction of Ahab and his house.

1Ki 21:17–29; 2Ki 9:25–37

• Foretells the death of Ahaziah.

2Ki 1:2–17

• Foretells the plague sent as a judgment upon the people in the time of Jehoram, king of Israel.

2Ch 21:12–15

• Called also Eliah.

• A Benjamite chief.

1Ch 8:27 — And Jaresiah, and Eliah, and Zichri, the sons of Jeroham.

• A post-exile Jew.

Ezr 10:21 — And of the sons of Harim; Maaseiah, and Elijah, and Shemaiah, and Jehiel, and Uzziah.

ELIKA • One of David's chiefs.

2Sa 23:25 — Shammah the Harodite, Elika the Harodite,

ELIM • Second camp of the Israelites after crossing the Red Sea.

Ex 15:27 — And they came to Elim, where *were* twelve wells of water, and threescore and ten palm trees: and they encamped there by the waters.

Nu 33:9 — And they removed from Marah, and came unto Elim: and in Elim *were* twelve fountains of water, and threescore and ten palm trees; and they pitched there.

ELIMELECH

• With Naomi, his wife, and two sons, emigrate to Moab.

Ru 1:2–3; 2:1–2

Ru 4:3 — And he said unto the kinsman, Naomi, that is come again out of the country of Moab, selleth a parcel of land, which *was* our brother Elimelech's:

Ru 4:9 — And Boaz said unto the elders, and *unto* all the people, Ye *are* witnesses this day, that I have bought all that *was* Elimelech's, and all that *was* Chilion's and Mahlon's, of the hand of Naomi.

ELIOENAI

See: Elihoenai

• Son of Becher.

1Ch 7:8 — And the sons of Becher; Zemira, and Joash, and Eliezer, and Elioenai, and Omri, and Jerimoth, and Abiah, and Anathoth, and Alameth. All these *are* the sons of Becher.

• A chief of Simeon.

1Ch 4:36 — And Elioenai, and Jaakobah, and Jeshohaiah, and Asaiah, and Adiel, and Jesimiel, and Benaiah,

• A priest.

Ezr 10:22 — And of the sons of Pashur; Elioenai, Maaseiah, Ishmael, Nethaneel, Jozabad, and Elasah.

• Possibly identical with one mentioned in Ne 12:41.

Ne 12:41 — And the priests; Eliakim, Maaseiah, Miniamin, Michaiah, Elioenai, Zechariah, *and* Hananiah, with trumpets;

• An Israelite.

Ezr 10:27 — And of the sons of Zattu; Elioenai, Eliashib, Mattaniah, and Jeremoth, and Zabad, and Aziza.

• Son of Neariah.

1Ch 3:23–24

ELIPHAL • A captain in David's army.

1Ch 11:35 — Ahiam the son of Sacar the Hararite, Eliphal the son of Ur,

ELIPHALET See: Eliphelet

ELIPHAZ

• Son of Esau.

Ge 36:10–16

Ge 36:4 — And Adah bare to Esau Eliphaz; and Bashemath bare Reuel;

1Ch 1:35 — The sons of Esau; Eliphaz, Reuel, and Jeush, and Jaalam, and Korah.

• Friend of Job.

Job 4:1–5:27; 22:1–30; 42:7–9

Job 2:11 — Now when Job's three friends heard of all this evil that was come upon him, they came every one from his own place; Eliphaz the Temanite, and Bildad the Shuhite, and Zophar the Naamathite: for they had made an appointment together to come to mourn with him and to comfort him.

ELIPHELEH • A Levite of the second degree.

1Ch 15:18 — And with them their brethren of the second *degree,* Zechariah, Ben, and Jaaziel, and Shemiramoth, and Jehiel, and Unni, Eliab, and Benaiah, and Maaseiah, and Mattithiah, and Elipheleh, and Mikneiah, and Obed-edom, and Jeiel, the porters.

1Ch 15:21 — And Mattithiah, and Elipheleh, and Mikneiah, and Obed-edom, and Jeiel, and Azaziah, with harps on the Sheminith to excel.

ELIPHELET

• A distinguished warrior.

2Sa 23:34 — Eliphelet the son of Ahasbai, the son of the Maachathite, Eliam the son of Ahithophel the Gilonite,

• A son of David.

1Ch 3:6 — Ibhar also, and Elishama, and Eliphelet,

• Called Elpalet.

1Ch 14:5 — And Ibhar, and Elishua, and Elpalet,

• Probably identical with a son of David.

2Sa 5:16 — And Elishama, and Eliada, and Eliphalet.

1Ch 3:8 — And Elishama, and Eliada, and Eliphelet, nine.

1Ch 14:7 — And Elishama, and Beeliada, and Eliphalet.

• A descendant of Saul.

1Ch 8:39 — And the sons of Eshek his brother *were,* Ulam his firstborn, Jehush the second, and Eliphelet the third.

• A companion of Ezra.

Ezr 8:13 — And of the last sons of Adonikam, whose names *are* these, Eliphelet, Jeiel, and Shemaiah, and with them threescore males.

• An Israelite. Probably identical with a companion of Ezra.

Ezr 10:33 — Of the sons of Hashum; Mattenai, Mattathah, Zabad, Eliphelet, Jeremai, Manasseh, *and* Shimei.

ELISABETH • Wife of Zacharias and mother of John the Baptist.

Lk 1:5–60

ELISEUS

Lk 4:27 — And many lepers were in Israel in the time of Eliseus the prophet; and none of them was cleansed, saving Naaman the Syrian.

See: Elisha

ELISHA

• Successor to the prophet Elijah.

• Elijah instructed to anoint.

1Ki 19:16 — And Jehu the son of Nimshi shalt thou anoint *to be* king over Israel: and Elisha the son of Shaphat of Abel-meholah shalt thou anoint *to be* prophet in thy room.

• Called by Elijah.

1Ki 19:19 — So he departed thence, and found Elisha the son of Shaphat, who *was* plowing *with* twelve yoke *of oxen* before him, and he with the twelfth: and Elijah passed by him, and cast his mantle upon him.

• Ministers unto Elijah.

1Ki 19:21 — And he returned back from him, and took a yoke of oxen, and slew them, and boiled their flesh with the instruments of the oxen, and gave unto the people, and they did eat. Then he arose, and went after Elijah, and ministered unto him.

• Witnesses Elijah's translation; receives a double portion of his spirit.

2Ki 2:1–15

2Ki 3:11 — But Jehoshaphat said, *Is there* not here a prophet of the LORD, that we may enquire of the LORD by him? And one of the king of Israel's servants answered and said, Here *is* Elisha the son of Shaphat, which poured water on the hands of Elijah.

• Mocked by the children of Bethel.

2Ki 2:23–24

• Causes the king to restore the property of the hospitable Shunammite.

2Ki 8:1–6

• Instructs that Jehu be anointed king of Israel.

2Ki 9:1–3

• Life of, sought by Jehoram.

2Ki 6:31–33

• Death of.

2Ki 13:14–20

• Bones of, restore a dead man to life.

2Ki 13:21 — And it came to pass, as they were burying a man, that, behold, they spied a band *of men;* and they cast the man into the sepulchre of Elisha: and when the man was let down, and touched the bones of Elisha, he revived, and stood up on his feet.

• Miracles of.

• Divides the Jordan.

2Ki 2:14 — And he took the mantle of Elijah that fell from him, and smote the waters, and said, Where *is* the LORD God of Elijah? and when he also had smitten the waters, they parted hither and thither: and Elisha went over.

• Purifies the waters of Jericho by casting salt into the fountain.

2Ki 2:19–22

• Increases the oil of the woman whose sons were to be sold for debt.

2Ki 4:1–7

• Raises from the dead the son of the Shunammite.

2Ki 4:18–37

• Neutralizes the poison of the pottage.

2Ki 4:38–41

• Increases the bread to feed one hundred men.

2Ki 4:42–44

- **Heals Naaman the leper.**
  2Ki 5:1–19
  Lk 4:27 — And many lepers were in Israel in the time of Eliseus the prophet; and none of them was cleansed, saving Naaman the Syrian.
- **Sends leprosy as a judgment upon Gehazi.**
  2Ki 5:26–27
- **Recovers the ax that had fallen into a stream by causing it to float.**
  2Ki 6:6 — And the man of God said, Where fell it? And he shewed him the place. And he cut down a stick, and cast *it* in thither; and the iron did swim.
- **Reveals the counsel of the king of Syria.**
  2Ki 6:12 — And one of his servants said, None, my lord, O king: but Elisha, the prophet that *is* in Israel, telleth the king of Israel the words that thou speakest in thy bedchamber.
- **Opens the eyes of his servant to see the hosts of the Lord.**
  2Ki 6:17 — And Elisha prayed, and said, LORD, I pray thee, open his eyes, that he may see. And the LORD opened the eyes of the young man; and he saw: and, behold, the mountain *was* full of horses and chariots of fire round about Elisha.
- **Brings blindness upon the army of Syria.**
  2Ki 6:18 — And when they came down to him, Elisha prayed unto the LORD, and said, Smite this people, I pray thee, with blindness. And he smote them with blindness according to the word of Elisha.

• Prophecies of.

- **Foretells a son to the Shunammite woman.**
  2Ki 4:16 — And he said, About this season, according to the time of life, thou shalt embrace a son. And she said, Nay, my lord, *thou* man of God, do not lie unto thine handmaid.
- **Foretells plenty to the starving in Samaria.**
  2Ki 7:1 — Then Elisha said, Hear ye the word of the LORD; Thus saith the LORD, To morrow about this time *shall* a measure of fine flour *be sold* for a shekel, and two measures of barley for a shekel, in the gate of Samaria.
- **Foretells death of the unbelieving prince.**
  2Ki 7:2 — Then a lord on whose hand the king leaned answered the man of God, and said, Behold, *if* the LORD would make windows in heaven, might this thing be? And he said, Behold, thou shalt see *it* with thine eyes, but shalt not eat thereof.
- **Foretells seven years' famine in the land of Canaan.**
  2Ki 8:1–3
- **Foretells death of Ben-hadad, king of Syria.**
  2Ki 8:7–10
- **Foretells elevation of Hazael to the throne.**
  2Ki 8:11–15
- **Foretells the victory of Jehoash over Syria.**
  2Ki 13:14–19

ELISHAH

• A descendant of Noah.

Ge 10:4 — And the sons of Javan; Elishah, and Tarshish, Kittim, and Dodanim.

1Ch 1:7 — And the sons of Javan; Elishah, and Tarshish, Kittim, and Dodanim.

• Islands of the Mediterranean bear the name of.

Eze 27:7 — Fine linen with broidered work from Egypt was that which thou spreadest forth to be thy sail; blue and purple from the isles of Elishah was that which covered thee.

ELISHAMA

• Grandfather of Joshua.

Nu 1:10 — Of the children of Joseph: of Ephraim; Elishama the son of Ammihud: of Manasseh; Gamaliel the son of Pedahzur.

Nu 2:18 — On the west side *shall be* the standard of the camp of Ephraim according to their armies: and the captain of the sons of Ephraim *shall be* Elishama the son of Ammihud.

Nu 7:48 — On the seventh day Elishama the son of Ammihud, prince of the children of Ephraim, *offered:*

Nu 7:53 — And for a sacrifice of peace offerings, two oxen, five rams, five he goats, five lambs of the first year: this *was* the offering of Elishama the son of Ammihud.

Nu 10:22 — And the standard of the camp of the children of Ephraim set forward according to their armies: and over his host *was* Elishama the son of Ammihud.

1Ch 7:26 — Laadan his son, Ammihud his son, Elishama his son,

• A son of David.

2Sa 5:16 — And Elishama, and Eliada, and Eliphalet.

1Ch 3:8 — And Elishama, and Eliada, and Eliphelet, nine.

1Ch 14:7 — And Elishama, and Beeliada, and Eliphalet.

• Another son of David.

1Ch 3:6 — Ibhar also, and Elishama, and Eliphelet,

- **Elsewhere called Elishua.**
  2Sa 5:15 — Ibhar also, and Elishua, and Nepheg, and Japhia,
  1Ch 14:5 — And Ibhar, and Elishua, and Elpalet,

See: Elishua

• A descendant of Judah.

1Ch 2:41 — And Shallum begat Jekamiah, and Jekamiah begat Elishama.

• Probably identical with a descendant of Judah.

2Ki 25:25 — But it came to pass in the seventh month, that Ishmael the son of Nethaniah, the son of Elishama, of the seed royal, came, and ten men with him, and smote Gedaliah, that he died, and the Jews and the Chaldees that were with him at Mizpah.

Jer 41:1 — Now it came to pass in the seventh month, *that* Ishmael the son of Nethaniah the son of Elishama, of the seed royal, and the princes of the king, even ten men with him, came unto Gedaliah the son of Ahikam to Mizpah; and there they did eat bread together in Mizpah.

• A secretary to Jehoiakim.

Jer 36:20–21

Jer 36:12 — Then he went down into the king's house, into the scribe's chamber: and, lo, all the princes sat there, *even* Elishama the scribe, and Delaiah the son of Shemaiah, and Elnathan the son of Achbor, and Gemariah the son of Shaphan, and Zedekiah the son of Hananiah, and all the princes.

• A priest sent by Jehoshaphat to teach the law.

2Ch 17:8 — And with them *he sent* Levites, *even* Shemaiah, and Nethaniah, and Zebadiah, and Asahel, and Shemiramoth, and Jehonathan, and Adonijah, and Tobijah, and Tob-adonijah, Levites; and with them Elishama and Jehoram, priests.

ELISHAPHAT • A Jewish captain.

2Ch 23:1 — And in the seventh year Jehoiada strengthened himself, and took the captains of hundreds, Azariah the son of Jeroham, and Ishmael the son of Jehohanan, and Azariah the son of Obed, and Maaseiah the son of Adaiah, and Elishaphat the son of Zichri, into covenant with him.

ELISHEBA • Wife of Aaron.

Ex 6:23 — And Aaron took him Elisheba, daughter of Amminadab, sister of Naashon, to wife; and she bare him Nadab, and Abihu, Eleazar, and Ithamar.

ELISHUA

• A son of David.

2Sa 5:15 — Ibhar also, and Elishua, and Nepheg, and Japhia,

1Ch 14:5 — And Ibhar, and Elishua, and Elpalet,

• Called Elishama.

1Ch 3:6 — Ibhar also, and Elishama, and Eliphelet,

ELIUD • An ancestor of Jesus.

Mt 1:14–15

ELIZAPHAN

• A Levite.

Ex 6:22 — And the sons of Uzziel; Mishael, and Elzaphan, and Zithri.

Le 10:4 — And Moses called Mishael and Elzaphan, the sons of Uzziel the uncle of Aaron, and said unto them, Come near, carry your brethren from before the sanctuary out of the camp.

Nu 3:30 — And the chief of the house of the father of the families of the Kohathites *shall be* Elizaphan the son of Uzziel.

1Ch 15:8 — Of the sons of Elizaphan; Shemaiah the chief, and his brethren two hundred:

• A prince of Zebulun.

Nu 34:25 — And the prince of the tribe of the children of Zebulun, Elizaphan the son of Parnach.

• Probably identical with a Levite.

2Ch 29:13 — And of the sons of Elizaphan; Shimri, and Jeiel: and of the sons of Asaph; Zechariah, and Mattaniah:

ELIZUR • A chief of Reuben.

Nu 1:5 — And these *are* the names of the men that shall stand with you: of *the tribe of* Reuben; Elizur the son of Shedeur.

Nu 2:10 — On the south side *shall be* the standard of the camp of Reuben according to their armies: and the captain of the children of Reuben *shall be* Elizur the son of Shedeur.

Nu 7:30 — On the fourth day Elizur the son of Shedeur, prince of the children of Reuben, *did offer:*

Nu 7:35 — And for a sacrifice of peace offerings, two oxen, five rams, five he goats, five lambs of the first year: this *was* the offering of Elizur the son of Shedeur.

Nu 10:18 — And the standard of the camp of Reuben set forward according to their armies: and over his host *was* Elizur the son of Shedeur.

ELKANAH

• Grandson of Korah.

Ex 6:24 — And the sons of Korah; Assir, and Elkanah, and Abiasaph: these *are* the families of the Korhites.

1Ch 6:23 — Elkanah his son, and Ebiasaph his son, and Assir his son,

• Father of Samuel. A descendant of preceding.

1Sa 1:1 — Now there was a certain man of Ramathaim-zophim, of mount Ephraim, and his name was Elkanah, the son of Jeroham, the son of Elihu, the son of Tohu, the son of Zuph, an Ephrathite:

1Sa 1:4 — And when the time was that Elkanah offered, he gave to Peninnah his wife, and to all her sons and her daughters, portions:

1Sa 1:8 — Then said Elkanah her husband to her, Hannah, why weepest thou? and why eatest thou not? and why is thy heart grieved? *am* not I better to thee than ten sons?

1Sa 1:19 — And they rose up in the morning early, and worshipped before the LORD, and returned, and came to their house to Ramah: and Elkanah knew Hannah his wife; and the LORD remembered her.

1Sa 1:21 — And the man Elkanah, and all his house, went up to offer unto the LORD the yearly sacrifice, and his vow.

1Sa 1:23 — And Elkanah her husband said unto her, Do what seemeth thee good; tarry until thou have weaned him; only the LORD establish his word. So the woman abode, and gave her son suck until she weaned him.

1Sa 2:11 — And Elkanah went to Ramah to his house. And the child did minister unto the LORD before Eli the priest.

1Sa 2:20 — And Eli blessed Elkanah and his wife, and said, The LORD give thee seed of this woman for the loan which is lent to the LORD. And they went unto their own home.

1Ch 6:27 — Eliab his son, Jeroham his son, Elkanah his son.

1Ch 6:34 — The son of Elkanah, the son of Jeroham, the son of Eliel, the son of Toah,

• A Levite.

1Ch 6:25 — And the sons of Elkanah; Amasai, and Ahimoth.

1Ch 6:36 — The son of Elkanah, the son of Joel, the son of Azariah, the son of Zephaniah,

• Possibly identical with a Levite.

1Ch 6:25 — And the sons of Elkanah; Amasai, and Ahimoth.

1Ch 6:36 — The son of Elkanah, the son of Joel, the son of Azariah, the son of Zephaniah,

• A Levite.

1Ch 9:16 — And Obadiah the son of Shemaiah, the son of Galal, the son of Jeduthun, and Berechiah the son of Asa, the son of Elkanah, that dwelt in the villages of the Netophathites.

• A Levite who joined David at Ziklag.

1Ch 12:6 — Elkanah, and Jesiah, and Azareel, and Joezer, and Jashobeam, the Korhites,

• A doorkeeper for the ark. Perhaps identical with a Levite who joined David at Ziklag.

1Ch 15:23 — And Berechiah and Elkanah *were* doorkeepers for the ark.

• A prince of Ahaz.

2Ch 28:7 — And Zichri, a mighty man of Ephraim, slew Maaseiah the king's son, and Azrikam the governor of the house, and Elkanah *that was* next to the king.

ELLASAR

• A city of Chaldea.

• Its king invades Canaan.

Ge 14:1 — And it came to pass in the days of Amraphel king of Shinar, Arioch king of Ellasar, Chedorlaomer king of Elam, and Tidal king of nations;

Ge 14:9 — With Chedorlaomer the king of Elam, and with Tidal king of nations, and Amraphel king of Shinar, and Arioch king of Ellasar; four kings with five.

ELM

Hos 4:13 — They sacrifice upon the tops of the mountains, and burn incense upon the hills, under oaks and poplars and elms, because the shadow thereof *is* good: therefore your daughters shall commit whoredom, and your spouses shall commit adultery.

ELMODAM • An ancestor of Jesus.

Lk 3:28 — Which was *the son* of Melchi, which was *the son* of Addi, which was *the son* of Cosam, which was *the son* of Elmodam, which was *the son* of Er,

ELNAAM • Father of two distinguished warriors.

1Ch 11:46 — Eliel the Mahavite, and Jeribai, and Joshaviah, the sons of Elnaam, and Ithmah the Moabite,

ELNATHAN

• Father of Nehushta, the mother of king Jehoiachin.

2Ki 24:8 — Jehoiachin *was* eighteen years old when he began to reign, and he reigned in Jerusalem three months. And his mother's name *was* Nehushta, the daughter of Elnathan of Jerusalem.

Jer 26:22 — And Jehoiakim the king sent men into Egypt, *namely,* Elnathan the son of Achbor, and *certain* men with him into Egypt.

Jer 36:12 — Then he went down into the king's house, into the scribe's chamber: and, lo, all the princes sat there, *even* Elishama the scribe, and Delaiah the son of Shemaiah, and Elnathan the son of Achbor, and Gemariah the son of Shaphan, and Zedekiah the son of Hananiah, and all the princes.

Jer 36:25 — Nevertheless Elnathan and Delaiah and Gemariah had made intercession to the king that he would not burn the roll: but he would not hear them.

• Name of three Levites in the time of Ezra.

Ezr 8:16 — Then sent I for Eliezer, for Ariel, for Shemaiah, and for Elnathan, and for Jarib, and for Elnathan, and for Nathan, and for Zechariah, and for Meshullam, chief men; also for Joiarib, and for Elnathan, men of understanding.

ELOI

Mk 15:34 — And at the ninth hour Jesus cried with a loud voice, saying, Eloi, Eloi, lama sabachthani? which is, being interpreted, My God, my God, why hast thou forsaken me?

ELON

• Father-in-law of Esau.

Ge 26:34 — And Esau was forty years old when he took to wife Judith the daughter of Beeri the Hittite, and Bashemath the daughter of Elon the Hittite:

Ge 36:2 — Esau took his wives of the daughters of Canaan; Adah the daughter of Elon the Hittite, and Aholibamah the daughter of Anah the daughter of Zibeon the Hivite;

• A son of Zebulun.

Ge 46:14 — And the sons of Zebulun; Sered, and Elon, and Jahleel.

Nu 26:26 — *Of* the sons of Zebulun after their families: of Sered, the family of the Sardites: of Elon, the family of the Elonites: of Jahleel, the family of the Jahleelites.

• A town of Dan.

Jos 19:43 — And Elon, and Thimnathah, and Ekron,

• **A Hebrew judge.**
Jgs 12:11–12

ELON-BETH-HANAN

• **A town of Dan.**
1Ki 4:9 — The son of Dekar, in Makaz, and in Shaalbim, and Beth-shemesh, and Elon-beth-hanan:

• **Perhaps identical with Elon in Jos 19:43.**
Jos 19:43 — And Elon, and Thimnathah, and Ekron,

ELONITES

• **Descendants of Elon, son of Zebulun.**
Nu 26:26 — *Of* the sons of Zebulun after their families: of Sered, the family of the Sardites: of Elon, the family of the Elonites: of Jahleel, the family of the Jahleelites.

ELOTH *See:* Elath

ELPAAL • A Benjamite.

1Ch 8:11–12
1Ch 8:18 — Ishmerai also, and Jezliah, and Jobab, the sons of Elpaal;

ELPALET

• **A son of David.**
1Ch 14:5 — And Ibhar, and Elishua, and Elpalet,

• **Called Eliphalet in.**
1Ch 3:6 — Ibhar also, and Elishama, and Eliphelet,

ELPARAN • A place in the wilderness of Paran.

Ge 14:6 — And the Horites in their mount Seir, unto El-paran, which *is* by the wilderness.

ELTEKEH • A city of Dan.

Jos 19:44 — And Eltekeh, and Gibbethon, and Baalath,
Jos 21:23 — And out of the tribe of Dan, Eltekeh with her suburbs, Gibbethon with her suburbs,

ELTEKON • A city of Judah.

Jos 15:59 — And Maarath, and Beth-anoth, and Eltekon; six cities with their villages:

ELTOLAD

• **A city of Judah.**
Jos 15:30 — And Eltolad, and Chesil, and Hormah,
Jos 19:4 — And Eltolad, and Bethul, and Hormah,

• **Called Tolad in 1Ch 4:29.**
1Ch 4:29 — And at Bilhah, and at Ezem, and at Tolad,

ELUL

• **Sixth month (September).**

• **The Jews finish the wall of Jerusalem in.**
Ne 6:15 — So the wall was finished in the twenty and fifth *day* of *the month* Elul, in fifty and two days.

• **Zerubbabel builds the temple in Hag 1:14–15.**
Hag 1:14–15

ELUZAI • A Benjamite.

1Ch 12:5 — Eluzai, and Jerimoth, and Bealiah, and Shemariah, and Shephatiah the Haruphite,

ELYMAS

• **A false prophet, punished with blindness.**
Ac 13:8 — But Elymas the sorcerer (for so is his name by interpretation) withstood them, seeking to turn away the deputy from the faith.
Ac 13:10 — And said, O full of all subtilty and all mischief, *thou* child of the devil, *thou* enemy of all righteousness, wilt thou not cease to pervert the right ways of the Lord?

ELZABAD

• **A Gadite.**
1Ch 12:12 — Johanan the eighth, Elzabad the ninth,

• **A Korhite.**
1Ch 26:7 — The sons of Shemaiah; Othni, and Rephael, and Obed, Elzabad, whose brethren *were* strong men, Elihu, and Semachiah.

ELZAPHAN *See:* Elizaphan

EMANCIPATION

• **Of all Jewish servants, at the jubilee.**
Le 25:8–17, 39–41
Ex 21:2 — If thou buy an Hebrew servant, six years he shall serve: and in the seventh he shall go out free for nothing.
Dt 15:12 — *And* if thy brother, an Hebrew man, or an Hebrew woman, be sold unto thee, and serve thee six years; then in the seventh year thou shalt let him go free from thee.

• **Proclamation of.**
  • **By Zedekiah.**
  Jer 34:8–11
  • **By Cyrus.**
  Ezr 1:1–4
  2Ch 36:23 — Thus saith Cyrus king of Persia, All the kingdoms of the earth hath the LORD God of heaven given me; and he hath charged me to build him an house in Jerusalem, which *is* in Judah. Who *is there* among you of all his people? The LORD his God *be* with him, and let him go up.

See: Exodus
See: Jubilee

EMBALMING

• **Of Jacob.**
Ge 50:2–3

• **Of Joseph.**
Ge 50:26 — So Joseph died, *being* an hundred and ten years old: and they embalmed him, and he was put in a coffin in Egypt.

• **Of Asa.**
2Ch 16:14 — And they buried him in his own sepulchres, which he had made for himself in the city of David, and laid him in the bed which was filled with sweet odours and divers kinds *of spices* prepared by

the apothecaries' art: and they made a very great burning for him.

- **Of Jesus.**

Jn 19:39–40

Mk 15:46 — And he bought fine linen, and took him down, and wrapped him in the linen, and laid him in a sepulchre which was hewn out of a rock, and rolled a stone unto the door of the sepulchre.

Mk 16:1 — And when the sabbath was past, Mary Magdalene, and Mary the *mother* of James, and Salome, had bought sweet spices, that they might come and anoint him.

EMBEZZLEMENT

Lk 16:1–7

See: Dishonesty

See: Fraud

EMBROIDERY

- **In blue and purple and scarlet on the curtains of the tabernacle.**

Ex 26:1 — Moreover thou shalt make the tabernacle *with* ten curtains *of* fine twined linen, and blue, and purple, and scarlet: *with* cherubims of cunning work shalt thou make them.

Ex 26:36 — And thou shalt make an hanging for the door of the tent, *of* blue, and purple, and scarlet, and fine twined linen, wrought with needlework.

Ex 27:16 — And for the gate of the court *shall be* an hanging of twenty cubits, *of* blue, and purple, and scarlet, and fine twined linen, wrought with needlework: *and* their pillars *shall be* four, and their sockets four.

- **On the girdle and coat of the high priest, mingled with gold.**

Ex 28:4 — And these *are* the garments which they shall make; a breastplate, and an ephod, and a robe, and a broidered coat, a mitre, and a girdle: and they shall make holy garments for Aaron thy brother, and his sons, that he may minister unto me in the priest's office.

Ex 28:39 — And thou shalt embroider the coat of fine linen, and thou shalt make the mitre *of* fine linen, and thou shalt make the girdle *of* needlework.

- **On the garments of.**
  - **Sisera.**

Jgs 5:30 — Have they not sped? have they *not* divided the prey; to every man a damsel *or* two; to Sisera a prey of divers colours, a prey of divers colours of needlework, of divers colours of needlework on both sides, *meet* for the necks of *them that take* the spoil?

  - **Princes.**

Eze 26:16 — Then all the princes of the sea shall come down from their thrones, and lay away their robes, and put off their broidered garments: they shall clothe themselves with trembling; they shall sit upon the ground, and shall tremble at *every* moment, and be astonished at thee.

  - **Women.**

Ps 45:14 — She shall be brought unto the king in raiment of needlework: the virgins her companions that follow her shall be brought unto thee.

Eze 16:10 — I clothed thee also with broidered work, and shod thee with badgers' skin, and I girded thee about with fine linen, and I covered thee with silk.

Eze 16:13 — Thus wast thou decked with gold and silver; and thy raiment *was of* fine linen, and silk, and broidered work; thou didst eat fine flour, and honey, and oil: and thou wast exceeding beautiful, and thou didst prosper into a kingdom.

Eze 16:18 — And tookest thy broidered garments, and coveredst them: and thou hast set mine oil and mine incense before them.

- **Bezaleel and Aholiab divinely inspired for, in the work of the tabernacle.**

Ex 35:30–35; 38:22–23

See: Tapestry

EMERALD

- **A precious stone.**
- **Color of the rainbow.**

Rev 4:3 — And he that sat was to look upon like a jasper and a sardine stone: and *there* was a rainbow round about the throne, in sight like unto an emerald.

- **Merchandise of, in Tyre.**

Eze 27:16 — Syria *was* thy merchant by reason of the multitude of the wares of thy making: they occupied in thy fairs with emeralds, purple, and broidered work, and fine linen, and coral, and agate.

Eze 28:13 — Thou hast been in Eden the garden of God; every precious stone *was* thy covering, the sardius, topaz, and the diamond, the beryl, the onyx, and the jasper, the sapphire, the emerald, and the carbuncle, and gold: the workmanship of thy tabrets and of thy pipes was prepared in thee in the day that thou wast created.

- **Set in the breastplate.**

Ex 28:18 — And the second row *shall be* an emerald, a sapphire, and a diamond.

- **Symbolic.**
  - **In the foundation of the holy city.**

Rev 21:19 — And the foundations of the wall of the city *were* garnished with all manner of precious stones. The first foundation *was* jasper; the second, sapphire; the third, a chalcedony; the fourth, an emerald;

EMERGENCY

Jos 7:10–13

Ex 14:15 — And the LORD said unto Moses, Wherefore criest thou unto me? speak unto the children of Israel, that they go forward:

See: Decision

EMERODS **See: Hemorrhoids**

EMIMS • A race of giants.

Dt 2:10–11

Ge 14:5 — And in the fourteenth year came Chedorlaomer, and the kings that *were* with him, and smote the Rephaims in Ashteroth Karnaim, and the Zuzims in Ham, and the Emims in Shaveh Kiriathaim,

EMMANUEL

Mt 1:23 — Behold, a virgin shall be with child, and shall bring forth a son, and they shall call his name Emmanuel, which being interpreted is, God with us.

See: Immanuel

See: Jesus, Names, Appellations, and Titles of; Emmanuel

EMMAUS

• A village about threescore furlongs from Jerusalem.

• Appearance of Jesus in, after his resurrection.

Lk 24:13 — And, behold, two of them went that same day to a village called Emmaus, which was from Jerusalem *about* threescore furlongs.

EMMOR

Ac 7:16 — And were carried over into Sychem, and laid in the sepulchre that Abraham bought for a sum of money of the sons of Emmor *the father* of Sychem.

See: Hamor

EMPLOYEE

Dt 24:14–15

Le 19:13 — Thou shalt not defraud thy neighbour, neither rob *him:* the wages of him that is hired shall not abide with thee all night until the morning.

Le 25:6 — And the sabbath of the land shall be meat for you; for thee, and for thy servant, and for thy maid, and for thy hired servant, and for thy stranger that sojourneth with thee,

Dt 15:18 — It shall not seem hard unto thee, when thou sendest him away free from thee; for he hath been worth a double hired servant *to thee,* in serving thee six years: and the LORD thy God shall bless thee in all that thou doest.

Mt 10:10 — Nor scrip for *your* journey, neither two coats, neither shoes, nor yet staves: for the workman is worthy of his meat.

Lk 10:7 — And in the same house remain, eating and drinking such things as they give: for the labourer is worthy of his hire. Go not from house to house.

Ro 4:4 — Now to him that worketh is the reward not reckoned of grace, but of debt.

1Ti 5:18 — For the scripture saith, Thou shalt not muzzle the ox that treadeth out the corn. And, The labourer *is* worthy of his reward.

• Character of unrighteous.

Job 7:1–3; Mt 20:1–15; 21:33–41; Jn 10:12–13

Job 14:1 — Man *that is* born of a woman *is* of few days, and full of trouble.

Job 14:6 — Turn from him, that he may rest, till he shall accomplish, as an hireling, his day.

• Kindness to.

Ru 2:4 — And behold, Boaz came from Bethlehem, and said unto the reapers, The LORD *be* with you. And they answered him, The LORD bless thee.

Lk 15:17 — And when he came to himself, he said, How many hired servants of my father's have bread enough and to spare, and I perish with hunger!

Lk 15:19 — And am no more worthy to be called thy son: make me as one of thy hired servants.

• Oppressions of.

Lk 15:15–16

Pr 22:16 — He that oppresseth the poor to increase his *riches, and* he that giveth to the rich, *shall* surely *come* to want.

Mal 3:5 — And I will come near to you to judgment; and I will be a swift witness against the sorcerers, and against the adulterers, and against false swearers, and against those that oppress the hireling in *his* wages, the widow, and the fatherless, and that turn aside the stranger *from his right,* and fear not me, saith the LORD of hosts.

Jas 5:4 — Behold, the hire of the labourers who have reaped down your fields, which is of you kept back by fraud, crieth: and the cries of them which have reaped are entered into the ears of the Lord of sabaoth.

See: Servant

See: Employer

See: Master

EMPLOYER

Dt 24:14–15; Job 31:13–15; Mt 20:1–15; Phm 1:15–16; Jas 5:4–5

Le 19:13 — Thou shalt not defraud thy neighbour, neither rob *him:* the wages of him that is hired shall not abide with thee all night until the morning.

Le 25:43 — Thou shalt not rule over him with rigour; but shalt fear thy God.

Dt 5:14 — But the seventh day *is* the sabbath of the LORD thy God: *in it* thou shalt not do any work, thou, nor thy son, nor thy daughter, nor thy manservant, nor thy maidservant, nor thine ox, nor thine ass, nor any of thy cattle, nor thy stranger that *is* within thy gates; that thy manservant and thy maidservant may rest as well as thou.

Pr 22:16 — He that oppresseth the poor to increase his *riches, and* he that giveth to the rich, *shall* surely *come* to want.

Pr 29:21 — He that delicately bringeth up his servant from a child shall have him become *his* son at the length.

Jer 22:13 — Woe unto him that buildeth his house by unrighteousness, and his chambers by wrong; *that* useth his neighbour's service without wages, and giveth him not for his work;

Mal 3:5 — And I will come near to you to judgment; and I will be a swift witness against the sorcerers, and against the adulterers, and against false swearers, and against those that oppress the hireling in *his* wages, the widow, and the fatherless, and that turn aside the stranger *from his right,* and fear not me, saith the LORD of hosts.

Mt 10:10 — Nor scrip for *your* journey, neither two coats, neither shoes, nor yet staves: for the workman is worthy of his meat.

Lk 10:7 — And in the same house remain, eating and drinking such things as they give: for the labourer is worthy of his hire. Go not from house to house.

Ro 4:4 — Now to him that worketh is the reward not reckoned of grace, but of debt.

Eph 6:9 — And, ye masters, do the same things unto them, forbearing threatening: knowing that your Master also is in heaven; neither is there respect of persons with him.

Col 4:1 — Masters, give unto *your* servants that which is just and equal; knowing that ye also have a Master in heaven.

1Ti 5:18 — For the scripture saith, Thou shalt not muzzle the ox that treadeth out the corn. And, The labourer *is* worthy of his reward.

See: Master

See: Labor

See: Servant

EMULATION

2Co 8:1–8; 9:1–5

Ro 11:11 — I say then, Have they stumbled that they should fall? God forbid: but *rather* through their fall salvation *is come* unto the Gentiles, for to provoke them to jealousy.

Ro 11:14 — If by any means I may provoke to emulation *them which are* my flesh, and might save some of them.

Heb 10:24 — And let us consider one another to provoke unto love and to good works:

• **Illustrated.**

• **In Esau's marriages.**
Ge 28:6–9

• **In Jacob's household.**
Ge 30:1–24

EN-DOR

• **A city of Manasseh.**

Jos 17:11 — And Manasseh had in Issachar and in Asher Beth-shean and her towns, and Ibleam and her towns, and the inhabitants of Dor and her towns, and the inhabitants of Endor and her towns, and the inhabitants of Taanach and her towns, and the inhabitants of Megiddo and her towns, *even* three countries.

• **The witch of, consulted by Saul.**
1Sa 28:7–25

• **Deborah triumphs at, over Sisera.**
Jgs 4:1–24

Ps 83:10 — *Which* perished at Endor: they became *as* dung for the earth.

EN-GANNIM

• **A city of Judah.**

Jos 15:34 — And Zanoah, and En-gannim, Tappuah, and Enam,

• **A city of Issachar.**

Jos 19:21 — And Remeth, and En-gannim, and En-haddah, and Beth-pazzez;

Jos 21:29 — Jarmuth with her suburbs, En-gannim with her suburbs; four cities.

EN-GEDI

• **Called also Hazezon-Tamar.**

• **A city allotted to Judah.**

Jos 15:62 — And Nibshan, and the city of Salt, and En-gedi; six cities with their villages.

• **Built by the Amorites.**

Ge 14:7 — And they returned, and came to En-mishpat, which *is* Kadesh, and smote all the country of the Amalekites, and also the Amorites that dwelt in Hazezon-tamar.

2Ch 20:2 — Then there came some that told Jehoshaphat, saying, There cometh a great multitude against thee from beyond the sea on this side Syria; and, behold, they *be* Hazazon-tamar, which *is* En-gedi.

• **Famous for its vineyards.**

SS 1:14 — My beloved *is* unto me *as* a cluster of camphire in the vineyards of En-gedi.

• **Wilderness of, in the vicinity of the Dead Sea; David uses as a stronghold.**
1Sa 23:29–24:22

• **Cave of.**

1Sa 24:3 — And he came to the sheepcotes by the way, where *was* a cave; and Saul went in to cover his feet: and David and his men remained in the sides of the cave.

EN-HADDAH • A city of Issachar.

Jos 19:21 — And Remeth, and En-gannim, and En-haddah, and Beth-pazzez;

EN-HAKKORE

• **A spring.**

• **Miraculously supplied to Samson.**

Jgs 15:19 — But God clave an hollow place that *was* in the jaw, and there came water thereout; and when he had drunk, his spirit came again, and he revived: wherefore he called the name thereof En-hakkore, which *is* in Lehi unto this day.

EN-HAZOR • A city of Naphtali.

Jos 19:37 — And Kedesh, and Edrei, and En-hazor,

EN-MISHPAT

• **Ancient name of Kadesh.**

Ge 14:7 — And they returned, and came to En-mishpat, which *is* Kadesh, and smote all the country of the Amalekites, and also the Amorites that dwelt in Hazezon-tamar.

See: Kadesh

EN-RIMMON

• A city of Judah.

Ne 11:29 — And at En-rimmon, and at Zareah, and at Jarmuth,

• Probably identical with Ain and Rimmon.

Jo 15:32 — And Lebaoth, and Shilhim, and Ain, and Rimmon: all the cities are twenty and nine, with their villages:

EN-ROGEL

• A spring near Jerusalem.

Jos 15:7 — And the border went up toward Debir from the valley of Achor, and so northward, looking toward Gilgal, *that is* before the going up to Adummim, which *is* on the south side of the river: and the border passed toward the waters of En-shemesh, and the goings out thereof were at En-rogel:

Jos 18:16 — And the border came down to the end of the mountain that *lieth* before the valley of the son of Hinnom, *and* which *is* in the valley of the giants on the north, and descended to the valley of Hinnom, to the side of Jebusi on the south, and descended to En-rogel,

2Sa 17:17 — Now Jonathan and Ahimaaz stayed by En-rogel; for they might not be seen to come into the city: and a wench went and told them; and they went and told king David.

• A rebellious feast at.

1Ki 1:9 — And Adonijah slew sheep and oxen and fat cattle by the stone of Zoheleth, which *is* by En-rogel, and called all his brethren the king's sons, and all the men of Judah the king's servants:

EN-SHEMESH • A spring between Judah and Benjamin.

Jos 15:7 — And the border went up toward Debir from the valley of Achor, and so northward, looking toward Gilgal, *that is* before the going up to Adummim, which *is* on the south side of the river: and the border passed toward the waters of En-shemesh, and the goings out thereof were at En-rogel:

Jos 18:17 — And was drawn from the north, and went forth to En-shemesh, and went forth toward Geliloth, which *is* over against the going up of Adummim, and descended to the stone of Bohan the son of Reuben,

EN-TAPPUAH • A spring near Tappuah.

Jos 17:7 — And the coast of Manasseh was from Asher to Michmethah, that *lieth* before Shechem; and the border went along on the right hand unto the inhabitants of En-tappuah.

ENAM • A city of Judah.

Jos 15:34 — And Zanoah, and En-gannim, Tappuah, and Enam,

ENAN • A man of Naphtali.

Nu 1:15 — Of Naphtali; Ahira the son of Enan.

Nu 2:29 — Then the tribe of Naphtali: and the captain of the children of Naphtali *shall be* Ahira the son of Enan.

Nu 7:78 — On the twelfth day Ahira the son of Enan, prince of the children of Naphtali, *offered:*

Nu 7:83 — And for a sacrifice of peace offerings, two oxen, five rams, five he goats, five lambs of the first year: this *was* the offering of Ahira the son of Enan.

Nu 10:27 — And over the host of the tribe of the children of Naphtali *was* Ahira the son of Enan.

ENCHANTMENT

✦See: Magician
✦See: Sorcery

ENCOURAGE

2Co 1:3–4; 2:1–14; Php 2:25–30; 1Ti 6:12–21; Heb 12:1–3

Pr 12:25 — Heaviness in the heart of man maketh it stoop: but a good word maketh it glad.

Pr 15:23 — A man hath joy by the answer of his mouth: and a word *spoken* in due season, how good *is it!*

Pr 25:11 — A word fitly spoken *is like* apples of gold in pictures of silver.

Mt 25:21 — His lord said unto him, Well done, *thou* good and faithful servant: thou hast been faithful over a few things, I will make thee ruler over many things: enter thou into the joy of thy lord.

Mt 25:23 — His lord said unto him, Well done, good and faithful servant; thou hast been faithful over a few things, I will make thee ruler over many things: enter thou into the joy of thy lord.

Php 4:13 — I can do all things through Christ which strengtheneth me.

2Ti 4:7 — I have fought a good fight, I have finished *my* course, I have kept the faith:

Heb 3:13 — But exhort one another daily, while it is called To day; lest any of you be hardened through the deceitfulness of sin.

ENDURANCE ✦See: Perseverance

ENEAS ✦See: Aeneas

ENEGLAIM • A place near the Dead Sea.

Eze 47:10 — And it shall come to pass, *that* the fishers shall stand upon it from En-gedi even unto Eneglaim; they shall be a *place* to spread forth nets; their fish shall be according to their kinds, as the fish of the great sea, exceeding many.

ENEMY

Job 31:29–30; Ps 35:1–28; Pr 24:17–18; 25:21–22; Mt 5:43–48; Lk 6:27–36

Ex 23:5 — If thou see the ass of him that hateth thee lying under his burden, and wouldest forbear to help him, thou shalt surely help with him.

Ro 12:14 — Bless them which persecute you: bless, and curse not.

Ro 12:20 — Therefore if thine enemy hunger, feed him; if he thirst, give him drink: for in so doing thou shalt heap coals of fire on his head.

• The wickedness of David's.

Ps 109:2–5; 129:1–3

Ps 56:5 — Every day they wrest my words: all their thoughts *are* against me for evil.

Ps 57:4 — My soul *is* among lions: *and* I lie *even among* them that are set on fire, *even* the sons of men, whose teeth *are* spears and arrows, and their tongue a sharp sword.

Ps 57:6 — They have prepared a net for my steps; my soul is bowed down: they have digged a pit before me, into the midst whereof they are fallen *themselves.* Selah.

Ps 62:4 — They only consult to cast *him* down from his excellency: they delight in lies: they bless with their mouth, but they curse inwardly. Selah.

Ps 69:4 — They that hate me without a cause are more than the hairs of mine head: they that would destroy me, *being* mine enemies wrongfully, are mighty: then I restored *that* which I took not away.

Ps 69:9 — For the zeal of thine house hath eaten me up; and the reproaches of them that reproached thee are fallen upon me.

Ps 71:10 — For mine enemies speak against me; and they that lay wait for my soul take counsel together,

Ps 102:8 — Mine enemies reproach me all the day; *and* they that are mad against me are sworn against me.

- **His imprecations against.**
  - **See: Prayer, Miscellany of Minor Subtopics; imprecatory**
- **Instances of forgiveness of.**
  - **David, of Absalom, and co-conspirators.**
    2Sa 19:6, 12–13
  - **Jesus, of his persecutors.**
    Lk 23:34
  - **Stephen, of his murderers.**
    Ac 7:60

ENGINE

- **Of war.**

2Ch 26:15 — And he made in Jerusalem engines, invented by cunning men, to be on the towers and upon the bulwarks, to shoot arrows and great stones withal. And his name spread far abroad; for he was marvellously helped, till he was strong.

Eze 26:9 — And he shall set engines of war against thy walls, and with his axes he shall break down thy towers.

See: Armies

See: Fort

ENGRAFTING See: Grafting

ENGRAVING

- **In making idols.**

Ex 32:4 — And he received *them* at their hand, and fashioned it with a graving tool, after he had made it a molten calf: and they said, These *be* thy gods, O Israel, which brought thee up out of the land of Egypt.

- **On the stones set in the priest's breastplate.**

Ex 28:9–11; 39:8–14

Ex 28:21 — And the stones shall be with the names of the children of Israel, twelve, according to their names, *like* the engravings of a signet; every one with his name shall they be according to the twelve tribes.

Ex 28:36 — And thou shalt make a plate *of* pure gold, and grave upon it, *like* the engravings of a signet, HOLINESS TO THE LORD.

- **On the stones set in the priest's girdle.**

Ex 39:6 — And they wrought onyx stones inclosed in ouches of gold, graven, as signets are graven, with the names of the children of Israel.

- **On the stones set in the priest's crown.**

Ex 39:30 — And they made the plate of the holy crown *of* pure gold, and wrote upon it a writing, *like to* the engravings of a signet, HOLINESS TO THE LORD.

ENOCH

- **Eldest son of Cain.**

Ge 4:17–18

- **A city built by Cain.**

Ge 4:17 — And Cain knew his wife; and she conceived, and bare Enoch: and he builded a city, and called the name of the city, after the name of his son, Enoch.

- **Father of Methuselah.**
  - **Translation of.**

Ge 5:18–24

Lk 3:37 — Which was *the son* of Mathusala, which was *the son* of Enoch, which was *the son* of Jared, which was *the son* of Maleleel, which was *the son* of Cainan,

Heb 11:5 — By faith Enoch was translated that he should not see death; and was not found, because God had translated him: for before his translation he had this testimony, that he pleased God.

Jude 1:14 — And Enoch also, the seventh from Adam, prophesied of these, saying, Behold, the Lord cometh with ten thousands of his saints,

- **Called Henoch.**

1Ch 1:3 — Henoch, Methuselah, Lamech,

ENON

- **A place east of the Jordan.**
- **John baptized near.**

Jn 3:23 — And John also was baptizing in Aenon near to Salim, because there was much water there: and they came, and were baptized.

ENOS

- **Son of Seth.**

Ge 5:6–11

Ge 4:26 — And to Seth, to him also there was born a son; and he called his name Enos: then began men to call upon the name of the LORD.

Lk 3:38 — Which was *the son* of Enos, which was *the son* of Seth, which was *the son* of Adam, which was *the son* of God.

- **Called Enosh.**

1Ch 1:1 — Adam, Sheth, Enosh,

ENQUIRING OF GOD

⇾See: Afflictions; prayer in

⇾See: Prayer

ENSIGN

Ps 74:4 — Thine enemies roar in the midst of thy congregations; they set up their ensigns *for* signs.

Isa 5:26 — And he will lift up an ensign to the nations from far, and will hiss unto them from the end of the earth: and, behold, they shall come with speed swiftly:

Isa 11:10 — And in that day there shall be a root of Jesse, which shall stand for an ensign of the people; to it shall the Gentiles seek: and his rest shall be glorious.

Isa 11:12 — And he shall set up an ensign for the nations, and shall assemble the outcasts of Israel, and gather together the dispersed of Judah from the four corners of the earth.

Isa 18:3 — All ye inhabitants of the world, and dwellers on the earth, see ye, when he lifteth up an ensign on the mountains; and when he bloweth a trumpet, hear ye.

Isa 30:17 — One thousand *shall flee* at the rebuke of one; at the rebuke of five shall ye flee: till ye be left as a beacon upon the top of a mountain, and as an ensign on an hill.

Isa 31:9 — And he shall pass over to his strong hold for fear, and his princes shall be afraid of the ensign, saith the LORD, whose fire *is* in Zion, and his furnace in Jerusalem.

Zec 9:16 — And the LORD their God shall save them in that day as the flock of his people: for they *shall be as* the stones of a crown, lifted up as an ensign upon his land.

⇾See: Banner

⇾See: Standard

ENTHUSIASM

- **Instances of.**
  - **Gideon.**
    Jgs 6:1–40
  - **Jehu.**
    2Ki 9:1–14; 10:1–28

⇾See: Zeal, Religious

ENUMERATION ⇾See: Census

ENVY

Job 5:2–3; Ps 73:17–20; Gal 5:19–21; 1Ti 6:4–5

Ps 37:1 — Fret not thyself because of evildoers, neither be thou envious against the workers of iniquity.

Ps 37:7 — Rest in the LORD, and wait patiently for him: fret not thyself because of him who prospereth in his way, because of the man who bringeth wicked devices to pass.

Ps 49:16 — Be not thou afraid when one is made rich, when the glory of his house is increased;

Ps 73:3 — For I was envious at the foolish, *when* I saw the prosperity of the wicked.

Ps 112:10 — The wicked shall see *it,* and be grieved; he shall gnash with his teeth, and melt away: the desire of the wicked shall perish.

Pr 3:31 — Envy thou not the oppressor, and choose none of his ways.

Pr 14:30 — A sound heart *is* the life of the flesh: but envy the rottenness of the bones.

Pr 23:17 — Let not thine heart envy sinners: but *be thou* in the fear of the LORD all the day long.

Pr 24:1 — Be not thou envious against evil men, neither desire to be with them.

Pr 24:19 — Fret not thyself because of evil *men,* neither be thou envious at the wicked;

Pr 27:4 — Wrath *is* cruel, and anger *is* outrageous; but who *is* able to stand before envy?

Ecc 4:4 — Again, I considered all travail, and every right work, that for this a man is envied of his neighbour. This *is* also vanity and vexation of spirit.

SS 8:6 — Set me as a seal upon thine heart, as a seal upon thine arm: for love *is* strong as death; jealousy *is* cruel as the grave: the coals thereof *are* coals of fire, *which hath a* most vehement flame.

Isa 26:11 — LORD, *when* thy hand is lifted up, they will not see: *but* they shall see, and be ashamed for *their* envy at the people; yea, the fire of thine enemies shall devour them.

Eze 35:11 — Therefore, as I live, saith the Lord GOD, I will even do according to thine anger, and according to thine envy which thou hast used out of thy hatred against them; and I will make myself known among them, when I have judged thee.

Mt 27:18 — For he knew that for envy they had delivered him.

Ro 1:29 — Being filled with all unrighteousness, fornication, wickedness, covetousness, maliciousness; full of envy, murder, debate, deceit, malignity; whisperers,

Ro 13:13 — Let us walk honestly, as in the day; not in rioting and drunkenness, not in chambering and wantonness, not in strife and envying.

1Co 3:3 — For ye are yet carnal: for whereas *there is* among you envying, and strife, and divisions, are ye not carnal, and walk as men?

1Co 13:4 — Charity suffereth long, *and* is kind; charity envieth not; charity vaunteth not itself, is not puffed up,

2Co 12:20 — For I fear, lest, when I come, I shall not find you such as I would, and *that* I shall be found unto you such as ye would not: lest *there be* debates, envyings, wraths, strifes, backbitings, whisperings, swellings, tumults:

Gal 5:26 — Let us not be desirous of vain glory, provoking one another, envying one another.

Tit 3:3 — For we ourselves also were sometimes foolish, disobedient, deceived, serving divers lusts and pleasures, living in malice and envy, hateful, *and* hating one another.

Jas 3:14 — But if ye have bitter envying and strife in your hearts, glory not, and lie not against the truth.

Jas 3:16 — For where envying and strife *is,* there *is* confusion and every evil work.

Jas 4:5 — Do ye think that the scripture saith in vain, The spirit that dwelleth in us lusteth to envy?

Jas 5:9 — Grudge not one against another, brethren, lest ye be condemned: behold, the judge standeth before the door.

1Pe 2:1 — Wherefore laying aside all malice, and all guile, and hypocrisies, and envies, and all evil speakings,

- **Instances of.**
  - **Cain, of Abel.**
    Ge 4:4–8
  - **Sarah, of Hagar.**
    Ge 16:5–6; 21:9–10
  - **Philistines, of Isaac.**
    Ge 26:14
  - **Rachel, of Leah.**
    Ge 30:1
  - **Leah, of Rachel.**
    Ge 30:15
  - **Laban's sons, of Jacob.**
    Ge 31:1
  - **Joseph's brethren, of Joseph.**
    Ge 37:4–11, 19–20; Ac 7:9
  - **Joshua, of Eldad and Medad.**
    Nu 11:28–30
  - **Miriam and Aaron, of Moses.**
    Nu 12:1–10
  - **Korah, Dathan, and Abiram, of Moses.**
    Nu 16:3; Ps 106:16–18
  - **Saul, of David.**
    1Sa 18:8–9, 29; 20:31
  - **Haman, of Mordecai.**
    Est 5:13
  - **The princes of Babylon, of Daniel.**
    Da 6:4
  - **Priests, of Jesus.**
    Mt 27:18; Mk 15:10; Jn 11:47
  - **Jews, of Paul and Barnabas.**
    Ac 13:45; 17:5

EPAPHRAS • A co-laborer with Paul.

Col 1:7 — As ye also learned of Epaphras our dear fellowservant, who is for you a faithful minister of Christ;

Col 4:12 — Epaphras, who is *one* of you, a servant of Christ, saluteth you, always labouring fervently for you in prayers, that ye may stand perfect and complete in all the will of God.

Phm 1:23 — There salute thee Epaphras, my fellowprisoner in Christ Jesus;

EPAPHRODITUS

- **A messenger of Paul.**

Php 2:25 — Yet I supposed it necessary to send to you Epaphroditus, my brother, and companion in labour, and fellow soldier, but your messenger, and he that ministered to my wants.

Php 4:18 — But I have all, and abound: I am full, having received of Epaphroditus the things *which were sent* from you, an odour of a sweet smell, a sacrifice acceptable, wellpleasing to God.

- **Sick at Rome.**

Php 2:26–27

Php 2:30 — Because for the work of Christ he was nigh unto death, not regarding his life, to supply your lack of service toward me.

EPENETUS • A friend of Paul.

Ro 16:5 — Likewise *greet* the church that is in their house. Salute my wellbeloved Epaenetus, who is the firstfruits of Achaia unto Christ.

EPHAH • A son of Midian.

Ge 25:4 — And the sons of Midian; Ephah, and Epher, and Hanoch, and Abidah, and Eldaah. All these *were* the children of Keturah.

1Ch 1:33 — And the sons of Midian; Ephah, and Epher, and Henoch, and Abida, and Eldaah. All these *are* the sons of Keturah.

Isa 60:6 — The multitude of camels shall cover thee, the dromedaries of Midian and Ephah; all they from Sheba shall come: they shall bring gold and incense; and they shall shew forth the praises of the LORD.

- **Caleb's concubine.**

1Ch 2:46 — And Ephah, Caleb's concubine, bare Haran, and Moza, and Gazez: and Haran begat Gazez.

- **Son of Jahdai.**

1Ch 2:47 — And the sons of Jahdai; Regem, and Jotham, and Gesham, and Pelet, and Ephah, and Shaaph.

- **A measure of about three pecks.**

✧See: **Measure; dry**

EPHAI • An Israelite.

Jer 40:8 — Then they came to Gedaliah to Mizpah, even Ishmael the son of Nethaniah, and Johanan and Jonathan the sons of Kareah, and Seraiah the son of Tanhumeth, and the sons of Ephai the Netophathite, and Jezaniah the son of a Maachathite, they and their men.

EPHER

- **A son of Midian.**

Ge 25:4 — And the sons of Midian; Ephah, and Epher, and Hanoch, and Abidah, and Eldaah. All these *were* the children of Keturah.

1Ch 1:33 — And the sons of Midian; Ephah, and Epher, and Henoch, and Abida, and Eldaah. All these *are* the sons of Keturah.

- **Son of Ezra.**

1Ch 4:17 — And the sons of Ezra *were*, Jether, and Mered, and Epher, and Jalon: and she bare Miriam, and Shammai, and Ishbah the father of Eshtemoa.

- **A chief of Manasseh.**

1Ch 5:24 — And these *were* the heads of the house of their fathers, even Epher, and Ishi, and Eliel, and Azriel, and Jeremiah, and Hodaviah, and Jahdiel, mighty men of valour, famous men, *and* heads of the house of their fathers.

EPHES-DAMMIM • A place in Judah.

1Sa 17:1 — Now the Philistines gathered together their armies to battle, and were gathered together at

Shochoh, which *belongeth* to Judah, and pitched between Shochoh and Azekah, in Ephes-dammim.

EPHESIANS

• Paul's letter to.

Eph 1:1–6:24

→See: Ephesus

EPHESUS

• Paul visits and preaches in.

Ac 18:19–21; 19:1–41; 20:16–38

• Apollos visits and preaches in.

Ac 18:18–28

• Sceva's sons attempt to expel a demon in.

Ac 19:13–16

• Timothy directed by Paul to remain at.

1Ti 1:3 — As I besought thee to abide still at Ephesus, when I went into Macedonia, that thou mightest charge some that they teach no other doctrine,

• Paul sends Tychicus to.

2Ti 4:12 — And Tychicus have I sent to Ephesus.

• Onesiphorus lives at.

2Ti 1:18 — The Lord grant unto him that he may find mercy of the Lord in that day: and in how many things he ministered unto me at Ephesus, thou knowest very well.

• Church at.

Eph 1:1–23

Rev 1:11 — Saying, I am Alpha and Omega, the first and the last: and, What thou seest, write in a book, and send *it* unto the seven churches which are in Asia; unto Ephesus, and unto Smyrna, and unto Pergamos, and unto Thyatira, and unto Sardis, and unto Philadelphia, and unto Laodicea.

• Apocalyptic message to.

Eph 2:1–22; Rev 2:1–7

EPHLAL • A descendant of Pharez.

1Ch 2:37 — And Zabad begat Ephlal, and Ephlal begat Obed,

EPHOD

• A sacred vestment worn by the high priest.

• Described.

Ex 28:6–14, 31–35

Ex 25:7 — Onyx stones, and stones to be set in the ephod, and in the breastplate.

• Making of.

Ex 39:2–26

• Breastplate attached to.

Ex 28:22–29

• Worn by Aaron.

Ex 39:5 — And the curious girdle of his ephod, that *was* upon it, *was* of the same, according to the work thereof; *of* gold, blue, and purple, and scarlet, and fine twined linen; as the LORD commanded Moses.

• Used as an oracle.

1Sa 30:7–8

1Sa 23:9 — And David knew that Saul secretly practised mischief against him; and he said to Abiathar the priest, Bring hither the ephod.

1Sa 23:12 — Then said David, Will the men of Keilah deliver me and my men into the hand of Saul? And the LORD said, They will deliver *thee* up.

• An inferior, was worn by the common priests.

1Sa 22:18 — And the king said to Doeg, Turn thou, and fall upon the priests. And Doeg the Edomite turned, and he fell upon the priests, and slew on that day fourscore and five persons that did wear a linen ephod.

• An inferior, was worn by Samuel.

1Sa 2:18 — But Samuel ministered before the LORD, *being* a child, girded with a linen ephod.

• An inferior, was worn by David.

2Sa 6:14 — And David danced before the LORD with all *his* might; and David *was* girded with a linen ephod.

• Was called coat.

Ex 28:40 — And for Aaron's sons thou shalt make coats, and thou shalt make for them girdles, and bonnets shalt thou make for them, for glory and for beauty.

Ex 29:8 — And thou shalt bring his sons, and put coats upon them.

Ex 39:27 — And they made coats *of* fine linen *of* woven work for Aaron, and for his sons,

Ex 40:14 — And thou shalt bring his sons, and clothe them with coats:

Le 8:13 — And Moses brought Aaron's sons, and put coats upon them, and girded them with girdles, and put bonnets upon them; as the LORD commanded Moses.

Le 10:5 — So they went near, and carried them in their coats out of the camp; as Moses had said.

• Made by Gideon, became an idolatrous snare to Israel.

Jgs 8:27 — And Gideon made an ephod thereof, and put it in his city, *even* in Ophrah: and all Israel went thither a whoring after it: which thing became a snare unto Gideon, and to his house.

Jgs 17:5 — And the man Micah had an house of gods, and made an ephod, and teraphim, and consecrated one of his sons, who became his priest.

Jgs 18:14 — Then answered the five men that went to spy out the country of Laish, and said unto their brethren, Do ye know that there is in these houses an ephod, and teraphim, and a graven image, and a molten image? now therefore consider what ye have to do.

• Prophecy concerning the absence of the ephod from Israel.

Hos 3:4 — For the children of Israel shall abide many days without a king, and without a prince, and without a sacrifice, and without an image, and without an ephod, and *without* teraphim:

• A man of Manasseh.

Nu 34:23 — The prince of the children of Joseph, for the tribe of the children of Manasseh, Hanniel the son of Ephod.

EPHRAIM

• Second son of Joseph.

Ge 41:52 — And the name of the second called he Ephraim: For God hath caused me to be fruitful in the land of my affliction.

• Adopted by Jacob.

Ge 48:5 — And now thy two sons, Ephraim and Manasseh, which were born unto thee in the land of Egypt before I came unto thee into Egypt, *are* mine; as Reuben and Simeon, they shall be mine.

• Blessed before Manasseh; prophecies concerning.

Ge 48:14–20

• Descendants of.

Nu 26:35–37; 1Ch 7:20–27

• Mourns for his sons.

1Ch 7:21–22

• A tribe of Israel.

• Prophecy concerning.

Ge 49:25–26; Isa 7:1–25; 9:18–21; Jer 31:1–40

Isa 11:13 — The envy also of Ephraim shall depart, and the adversaries of Judah shall be cut off: Ephraim shall not envy Judah, and Judah shall not vex Ephraim.

Isa 28:1 — Woe to the crown of pride, to the drunkards of Ephraim, whose glorious beauty is a fading flower, which *are* on the head of the fat valleys of them that are overcome with wine!

Hos 5:14 — For I will *be* unto Ephraim as a lion, and as a young lion to the house of Judah: I, *even* I, will tear and go away; I will take away, and none shall rescue *him.*

Zec 9:10 — And I will cut off the chariot from Ephraim, and the horse from Jerusalem, and the battle bow shall be cut off: and he shall speak peace unto the heathen: and his dominion *shall be* from sea *even* to sea, and from river *even* to the ends of the earth.

Zec 10:7 — And *they of* Ephraim shall be like a mighty *man,* and their heart shall rejoice as through wine: yea, their children shall see *it,* and be glad; their heart shall rejoice in the LORD.

• Numbered at Sinai and in plains of Moab.

Nu 1:33 — Those that were numbered of them, *even* of the tribe of Ephraim, *were* forty thousand and five hundred.

Nu 26:37 — These *are* the families of the sons of Ephraim according to those that were numbered of them, thirty and two thousand and five hundred. These *are* the sons of Joseph after their families.

• Place in camp and march.

Nu 2:18 — On the west side *shall be* the standard of the camp of Ephraim according to their armies: and the captain of the sons of Ephraim *shall be* Elishama the son of Ammihud.

Nu 2:24 — All that were numbered of the camp of Ephraim *were* an hundred thousand and eight thousand and an hundred, throughout their armies. And they shall go forward in the third rank.

Nu 10:22 — And the standard of the camp of the children of Ephraim set forward according to their armies: and over his host *was* Elishama the son of Ammihud.

• Blessed by Moses.

Dt 33:13–17

• Territory allotted to, after the conquest of Canaan.

Jos 16:5–9; 17:9–10, 15–18; 1Ch 7:28–29

• Fail to expel the Canaanites.

Jos 16:10 — And they drave not out the Canaanites that dwelt in Gezer: but the Canaanites dwell among the Ephraimites unto this day, and serve under tribute.

• Take Bethel in battle.

Jgs 1:22–25

• Upbraid Gideon for not summoning them to join the war against the Midianites.

Jgs 8:1 — And the men of Ephraim said unto him, Why hast thou served us thus, that thou calledst us not, when thou wentest to fight with the Midianites? And they did chide with him sharply.

• Join Gideon against the Midianites.

Jgs 7:24–25

• Their jealousy of Jephthah.

Jgs 12:1 — And the men of Ephraim gathered themselves together, and went northward, and said unto Jephthah, Wherefore passedst thou over to fight against the children of Ammon, and didst not call us to go with thee? we will burn thine house upon thee with fire.

• Defeated by him.

Jgs 12:4–6

• Receive Ish-bosheth as king.

2Sa 2:9 — And made him king over Gilead, and over the Ashurites, and over Jezreel, and over Ephraim, and over Benjamin, and over all Israel.

• Jeroboam set up a golden calf in Bethel.

1Ki 12:29 — And he set the one in Bethel, and the other put he in Dan.

• Revolt from house of David.

1Ki 12:25 — Then Jeroboam built Shechem in mount Ephraim, and dwelt therein; and went out from thence, and built Penuel.

2Ch 10:16 — And when all Israel *saw* that the king would not hearken unto them, the people answered the king, saying, What portion have we in David? and *we have* none inheritance in the son of Jesse: every man to your tents, O Israel: *and* now, David, see to thine own house. So all Israel went to their tents.

• **Some of tribe join Judah under Asa.**

2Ch 15:9 — And he gathered all Judah and Benjamin, and the strangers with them out of Ephraim and Manasseh, and out of Simeon: for they fell to him out of Israel in abundance, when they saw that the LORD his God *was* with him.

• **Chastise Ahaz and Judah.**

2Ch 28:7 — And Zichri, a mighty man of Ephraim, slew Maaseiah the king's son, and Azrikam the governor of the house, and Elkanah *that was* next to the king.

• **Join Hezekiah in reinstituting the passover.**

2Ch 30:18 — For a multitude of the people, *even* many of Ephraim, and Manasseh, Issachar, and Zebulun, had not cleansed themselves, yet did they eat the passover otherwise than it was written. But Hezekiah prayed for them, saying, The good LORD pardon every one

• **Join in the destruction of idolatrous forms in Jerusalem.**

2Ch 31:1 — Now when all this was finished, all Israel that were present went out to the cities of Judah, and brake the images in pieces, and cut down the groves, and threw down the high places and the altars out of all Judah and Benjamin, in Ephraim also and Manasseh, until they had utterly destroyed them all. Then all the children of Israel returned, every man to his possession, into their own cities.

• **Submit to the scepter of Josiah.**

2Ch 34:1–6

• **Envied by other tribes.**

Isa 11:13 — The envy also of Ephraim shall depart, and the adversaries of Judah shall be cut off: Ephraim shall not envy Judah, and Judah shall not vex Ephraim.

Jer 7:15 — And I will cast you out of my sight, as I have cast out all your brethren, *even* the whole seed of Ephraim.

Eze 37:16 — Moreover, thou son of man, take thee one stick, and write upon it, For Judah, and for the children of Israel his companions: then take another stick, and write upon it, For Joseph, the stick of Ephraim, and *for* all the house of Israel his companions:

Eze 37:19 — Say unto them, Thus saith the Lord GOD; Behold, I will take the stick of Joseph, which *is* in the hand of Ephraim, and the tribes of Israel his fellows, and will put them with him, *even* with the stick of Judah, and make them one stick, and they shall be one in mine hand.

Hos 13:1 — When Ephraim spake trembling, he exalted himself in Israel; but when he offended in Baal, he died.

• **Worshiped Baal.**

Hos 13:1 — When Ephraim spake trembling, he exalted himself in Israel; but when he offended in Baal, he died.

• **Sin of, remembered by God.**

Hos 13:12 — The iniquity of Ephraim *is* bound up; his sin *is* hid.

• **Reallotment of territory to, by Ezekiel.**

Eze 48:5 — And by the border of Manasseh, from the east side unto the west side, a *portion for* Ephraim.

• **Name of, applied to the ten tribes.**

2Ch 25:6–7; Isa 7:8–9; 11:12–13

2Ch 17:2 — And he placed forces in all the fenced cities of Judah, and set garrisons in the land of Judah, and in the cities of Ephraim, which Asa his father had taken.

Isa 17:3 — The fortress also shall cease from Ephraim, and the kingdom from Damascus, and the remnant of Syria: they shall be as the glory of the children of Israel, saith the LORD of hosts.

Jer 31:18 — I have surely heard Ephraim bemoaning himself *thus;* Thou hast chastised me, and I was chastised, as a bullock unaccustomed *to the yoke:* turn thou me, and I shall be turned; for thou *art* the LORD my God.

Jer 31:20 — *Is* Ephraim my dear son? *is he* a pleasant child? for since I spake against him, I do earnestly remember him still: therefore my bowels are troubled for him; I will surely have mercy upon him, saith the LORD.

Hos 4:17 — Ephraim *is* joined to idols: let him alone.

Hos 5:3 — I know Ephraim, and Israel is not hid from me: for now, O Ephraim, thou committest whoredom, *and* Israel is defiled.

Hos 5:5 — And the pride of Israel doth testify to his face: therefore shall Israel and Ephraim fall in their iniquity; Judah also shall fall with them.

Hos 6:4 — O Ephraim, what shall I do unto thee? O Judah, what shall I do unto thee? for your goodness *is* as a morning cloud, and as the early dew it goeth away.

Hos 6:10 — I have seen an horrible thing in the house of Israel: there *is* the whoredom of Ephraim, Israel is defiled.

Hos 8:11 — Because Ephraim hath made many altars to sin, altars shall be unto him to sin.

Hos 12:14 — Ephraim provoked *him* to anger most bitterly: therefore shall he leave his blood upon him, and his reproach shall his Lord return unto him.

• **Tribe of, called Joseph.**

Rev 7:8 — Of the tribe of Zabulon *were* sealed twelve thousand. Of the tribe of Joseph *were* sealed twelve thousand. Of the tribe of Benjamin *were* sealed twelve thousand.

• Mount of.

• **A range of low mountains.**

Jos 17:15–18

• **Joshua has his inheritance in.**

Jgs 2:9 — And they buried him in the border of his inheritance in Timnath-heres, in the mount of Ephraim, on the north side of the hill Gaash.

• **Residence of Micah.**

Jgs 17:8 — And the man departed out of the city from Bethlehemjudah to sojourn where he could find *a place:* and he came to mount Ephraim to the house of Micah, as he journeyed.

- **A place of hiding for Israelites.**

1Sa 14:22 — Likewise all the men of Israel which had hid themselves in mount Ephraim, *when* they heard that the Philistines fled, even they also followed hard after them in the battle.

- **Sheba resides in.**

2Sa 20:21 — The matter *is* not so: but a man of mount Ephraim, Sheba the son of Bichri by name, hath lifted up his hand against the king, *even* against David: deliver him only, and I will depart from the city. And the woman said unto Joab, Behold, his head shall be thrown to thee over the wall.

- **Noted for rich pastures.**

Jer 50:19 — And I will bring Israel again to his habitation, and he shall feed on Carmel and Bashan, and his soul shall be satisfied upon mount Ephraim and Gilead.

- **Prophecy concerning its conversion.**

Jer 31:6 — For there shall be a day, *that* the watchmen upon the mount Ephraim shall cry, Arise ye, and let us go up to Zion unto the LORD our God.

- **A wood east of the Jordan.**

- **Absalom slain in.**

2Sa 18:6–17

- **A gate of Jerusalem.**

2Ki 14:13 — And Jehoash king of Israel took Amaziah king of Judah, the son of Jehoash the son of Ahaziah, at Beth-shemesh, and came to Jerusalem, and brake down the wall of Jerusalem from the gate of Ephraim unto the corner gate, four hundred cubits.

2Ch 25:23 — And Joash the king of Israel took Amaziah king of Judah, the son of Joash, the son of Jehoahaz, at Beth-shemesh, and brought him to Jerusalem, and brake down the wall of Jerusalem from the gate of Ephraim to the corner gate, four hundred cubits.

Ne 8:16 — So the people went forth, and brought *them,* and made themselves booths, every one upon the roof of his house, and in their courts, and in the courts of the house of God, and in the street of the water gate, and in the street of the gate of Ephraim.

Ne 12:39 — And from above the gate of Ephraim, and above the old gate, and above the fish gate, and the tower of Hananeel, and the tower of Meah, even unto the sheep gate: and they stood still in the prison gate.

- **A city in the territory of Ephraim.**

2Ch 13:19 — And Abijah pursued after Jeroboam, and took cities from him, Bethel with the towns thereof, and Jeshanah with the towns thereof, and Ephrain with the towns thereof.

- **Jesus escapes to, from the persecution of Caiaphas.**

Jn 11:54 — Jesus therefore walked no more openly among the Jews; but went thence unto a country near to the wilderness, into a city called Ephraim, and there continued with his disciples.

EPHRAIMITES ⇜See: Ephraim; a tribe of Israel

EPHRAIN • A city in Benjamin.

2Ch 13:19 — And Abijah pursued after Jeroboam, and took cities from him, Bethel with the towns thereof, and Jeshanah with the towns thereof, and Ephrain with the towns thereof.

⇜See: Ephraim; a city in the territory of Ehriam

EPHRATAH

- **The ancient name of Bethlehem.**

Ru 4:11 — And all the people that *were* in the gate, and the elders, said, *We are* witnesses. The LORD make the woman that is come into thine house like Rachel and like Leah, which two did build the house of Israel: and do thou worthily in Ephratah, and be famous in Bethlehem:

Ps 132:6 — Lo, we heard of it at Ephratah: we found it in the fields of the wood.

Mic 5:2 — But thou, Bethlehem Ephratah, *though* thou be little among the thousands of Judah, *yet* out of thee shall he come forth unto me *that is* to be ruler in Israel; whose goings forth *have been* from of old, from everlasting.

- **Called also Ephrath.**

Ge 35:16 — And they journeyed from Bethel; and there was but a little way to come to Ephrath: and Rachel travailed, and she had hard labour.

Ge 35:19 — And Rachel died, and was buried in the way to Ephrath, which *is* Bethlehem.

Ge 48:7 — And as for me, when I came from Padan, Rachel died by me in the land of Canaan in the way, when yet *there was* but a little way to come unto Ephrath: and I buried her there in the way of Ephrath; the same is Bethlehem.

- **Second wife of Caleb, mother of Hur.**

1Ch 2:19 — And when Azubah was dead, Caleb took unto him Ephrath, which bare him Hur.

1Ch 2:50 — These were the sons of Caleb the son of Hur, the firstborn of Ephratah; Shobal the father of Kirjath-jearim,

1Ch 4:4 — And Penuel the father of Gedor and Ezer the father of Hushah. These *are* the sons of Hur, the firstborn of Ephratah, the father of Bethlehem.

EPHRATH ⇜See: Ephratah

EPHRON

- **Son of Zohar, the Hittite.**

- **Sells to Abraham the field containing the cave Machpelah.**

Ge 23:8–17; 49:29–30

Ge 25:9 — And his sons Isaac and Ishmael buried him in the cave of Machpelah, in the field of Ephron the son of Zohar the Hittite, which *is* before Mamre;

Ge 50:13 — For his sons carried him into the land of Canaan, and buried him in the cave of the field of Machpelah, which Abraham bought with the field for a possession of a buryingplace of Ephron the Hittite, before Mamre.

• A mountain on the boundary line between Judah and Benjamin.

Jos 15:9 — And the border was drawn from the top of the hill unto the fountain of the water of Nephtoah, and went out to the cities of mount Ephron; and the border was drawn to Baalah, which *is* Kirjath-jearim:

EPIC

• Heroic poetry.

• Miriam's song.

Ex 15:1–19

Ex 15:21 — And Miriam answered them, Sing ye to the LORD, for he hath triumphed gloriously; the horse and his rider hath he thrown into the sea.

• Deborah's song.

Jgs 5:1–31

• David's war song.

2Sa 22:1–51

→See: Poetry

EPICUREANS

• Reject John the Baptist.

Mt 11:18 — For John came neither eating nor drinking, and they say, He hath a devil.

Lk 7:33 — For John the Baptist came neither eating bread nor drinking wine; and ye say, He hath a devil.

• Doctrines propagated by, familiar to Solomon.

Ecc 2:1–10

• Doctrines propagated by, familiar to Paul.

1Co 15:32 — If after the manner of men I have fought with beasts at Ephesus, what advantageth it me, if the dead rise not? let us eat and drink; for to morrow we die.

• Dispute with Paul.

Ac 17:18 — Then certain philosophers of the Epicureans, and of the Stoicks, encountered him. And some said, What will this babbler say? other some, He seemeth to be a setter forth of strange gods: because he preached unto them Jesus, and the resurrection.

EPILEPSY

Mk 9:17–22

→See: Disease

EPISTLES

• From the church at Jerusalem to the Gentiles.

Ac 15:23–29

• Of Luke to Theophilus.

Lk 1:1–4

Ac 1:1 — The former treatise have I made, O Theophilus, of all that Jesus began both to do and teach,

• Of Paul.

Ro 1:1; Tit 3:15

• Of James, Peter and John.

Jas 1:1–3; Jn 1:14

→See: Letters

EQUALITY

• Of men.

→See: Man; equality of

EQUITY →See: Justice

ER

• Son of Judah.

Ge 38:3, 6–7

Ge 46:12 — And the sons of Judah; Er, and Onan, and Shelah, and Pharez, and Zarah: but Er and Onan died in the land of Canaan. And the sons of Pharez were Hezron and Hamul.

Nu 26:19 — The sons of Judah *were* Er and Onan: and Er and Onan died in the land of Canaan.

1Ch 2:3 — The sons of Judah; Er, and Onan, and Shelah: *which* three were born unto him of the daughter of Shua the Canaanitess. And Er, the firstborn of Judah, was evil in the sight of the LORD; and he slew him.

• A son of Shelah.

1Ch 4:21 — The sons of Shelah the son of Judah *were*, Er the father of Lecah, and Laadah the father of Mareshah, and the families of the house of them that wrought fine linen, of the house of Ashbea,

• An ancestor of Jesus.

Lk 3:28 — Which was *the son* of Melchi, which was *the son* of Addi, which was *the son* of Cosam, which was *the son* of Elmodam, which was *the son* of Er,

ERAN • A grandson of Ephraim.

Nu 26:36 — And these *are* the sons of Shuthelah: of Eran, the family of the Eranites.

ERASTUS

• A friend of Paul.

Ac 19:22 — So he sent into Macedonia two of them that ministered unto him, Timotheus and Erastus; but he himself stayed in Asia for a season.

2Ti 4:20 — Erastus abode at Corinth: but Trophimus have I left at Miletum sick.

• Convert of Paul's. Probably same as preceding.

Ro 16:23 — Gaius mine host, and of the whole church, saluteth you. Erastus the chamberlain of the city saluteth you, and Quartus a brother.

ERECH • A city of Shinar.

Ge 10:10 — And the beginning of his kingdom was Babel, and Erech, and Accad, and Calneh, in the land of Shinar.

ERI • A son of Gad.

Ge 46:16 — And the sons of Gad; Ziphion, and Haggi, Shuni, and Ezbon, Eri, and Arodi, and Areli.

Nu 26:16 — Of Ozni, the family of the Oznites: of Eri, the family of the Erites:

ERRORS

• In teachers and doctrines.

↞See: Teachers; false

ESAIAS ↞See: Isaiah

ESAR-HADDON

• King of Assyria.

• Succeeds Sennacherib.

2Ki 19:37 — And it came to pass, as he was worshipping in the house of Nisroch his god, that Adrammelech and Sharezer his sons smote him with the sword: and they escaped into the land of Armenia. And Esar-haddon his son reigned in his stead.

Isa 37:38 — And it came to pass, as he was worshipping in the house of Nisroch his god, that Adrammelech and Sharezer his sons smote him with the sword; and they escaped into the land of Armenia: and Esar-haddon his son reigned in his stead.

• Called Asnapper.

Ezr 4:2 — Then they came to Zerubbabel, and to the chief of the fathers, and said unto them, Let us build with you: for we seek your God, as ye *do;* and we do sacrifice unto him since the days of Esar-haddon king of Assur, which brought us up hither.

Ezr 4:10 — And the rest of the nations whom the great and noble Asnapper brought over, and set in the cities of Samaria, and the rest *that are* on this side the river, and at such a time.

ESAU

• Eldest of twin sons born to Isaac and Rebekah.

• Birth of.

Ge 25:19–26

1Ch 1:34 — And Abraham begat Isaac. The sons of Isaac; Esau and Israel.

• Called Edom.

Ge 36:1 — Now these *are* the generations of Esau, who *is* Edom.

Ge 36:8 — Thus dwelt Esau in mount Seir: Esau *is* Edom.

• A hunter.

Ge 25:27–28

• Beloved by Isaac.

Ge 25:27–28

• Sells his birthright for a mess of pottage.

Ge 25:29–34

Mal 1:2 — I have loved you, saith the LORD. Yet ye say, Wherein hast thou loved us? *Was* not Esau Jacob's brother? saith the LORD: yet I loved Jacob,

Ro 9:13 — As it is written, Jacob have I loved, but Esau have I hated.

Heb 12:16 — Lest there *be* any fornicator, or profane person, as Esau, who for one morsel of meat sold his birthright.

• Marries a Hittite.

Ge 26:34 — And Esau was forty years old when he took to wife Judith the daughter of Beeri the Hittite, and Bashemath the daughter of Elon the Hittite:

• His marriage to, a grief to Isaac and Rebekah.

Ge 26:35 — Which were a grief of mind unto Isaac and to Rebekah.

• Polygamy of.

Ge 36:2–3

Ge 26:34 — And Esau was forty years old when he took to wife Judith the daughter of Beeri the Hittite, and Bashemath the daughter of Elon the Hittite:

Ge 28:9 — Then went Esau unto Ishmael, and took unto the wives which he had Mahalath the daughter of Ishmael Abraham's son, the sister of Nebajoth, to be his wife.

• Is defrauded of his father's blessing by Jacob.

Ge 27:1–46

Heb 11:20 — By faith Isaac blessed Jacob and Esau concerning things to come.

• Meets Jacob on the return of the latter from Haran.

Ge 33:1 — And Jacob lifted up his eyes, and looked, and, behold, Esau came, and with him four hundred men. And he divided the children unto Leah, and unto Rachel, and unto the two handmaids.

• With Jacob, buries his father.

Ge 35:29 — And Isaac gave up the ghost, and died, and was gathered unto his people, *being* old and full of days: and his sons Esau and Jacob buried him.

• Descendants of.

Ge 36:1–43; 1Ch 1:35–37

• Enmity of descendants of, toward descendants of Jacob.

Ob 1:10–14

• Ancestor of Edomites.

Jer 49:8 — Flee ye, turn back, dwell deep, O inhabitants of Dedan; for I will bring the calamity of Esau upon him, the time *that* I will visit him.

• Mount of Edom, called Mount of Esau.

Ob 1:8–9, 18–19

Ob 1:21 — And saviours shall come up on mount Zion to judge the mount of Esau; and the kingdom shall be the LORD'S.

• His name used to denote his descendants and their country.

Dt 2:5 — Meddle not with them; for I will not give you of their land, no, not so much as a footbreadth; because I have given mount Seir unto Esau *for* a possession.

Jer 49:8 — Flee ye, turn back, dwell deep, O inhabitants of Dedan; for I will bring the calamity of Esau upon him, the time *that* I will visit him.

Jer 49:10 — But I have made Esau bare, I have uncovered his secret places, and he shall not be able to hide himself: his seed is spoiled, and his brethren, and his neighbours, and he is not.

Ob 1:6 — How are *the things* of Esau searched out! *how* are his hidden things sought up!

• Prophecies concerning.

Ob 1:18 — And the house of Jacob shall be a fire, and the house of Joseph a flame, and the house of Esau for stubble, and they shall kindle in them, and devour them; and there shall not be *any* remaining of the house of Esau; for the LORD hath spoken *it.*

ESCAPE

• None, from the judgments of God.

Ge 3:7–11; 4:9–11; Job 34:21–22; 1Th 5:2–3; Heb 2:2–3; 12:25–26; Rev 6:15–17

Isa 10:3 — And what will ye do in the day of visitation, and in the desolation *which* shall come from far? to whom will ye flee for help? and where will ye leave your glory?

Mt 23:33 — *Ye* serpents, *ye* generation of vipers, how can ye escape the damnation of hell?

Ro 2:3 — And thinkest thou this, O man, that judgest them which do such things, and doest the same, that thou shalt escape the judgment of God?

See: Judgments; no escape from

See: Sin; fruits of

See: Sin; punishment of

ESCHEAT See: Confiscation

ESEK • A well dug by the servants of Isaac.

Ge 26:20 — And the herdmen of Gerar did strive with Isaac's herdmen, saying, The water *is* ours: and he called the name of the well Esek; because they strove with him.

ESH-BAAL See: Ish-Bosheth

ESHBAN • A son of Dishon.

Ge 36:26 — And these *are* the children of Dishon; Hemdan, and Eshban, and Ithran, and Cheran.

1Ch 1:41 — The sons of Anah; Dishon. And the sons of Dishon; Amram, and Eshban, and Ithran, and Cheran.

ESHCOL

• An Amorite, and ally of Abraham.

Ge 14:13 — And there came one that had escaped, and told Abram the Hebrew; for he dwelt in the plain of Mamre the Amorite, brother of Eshcol, and brother of Aner: and these *were* confederate with Abram.

Ge 14:24 — Save only that which the young men have eaten, and the portion of the men which went with me, Aner, Eshcol, and Mamre; let them take their portion.

• A valley or brook near Hebron.

Nu 13:23–24

Nu 32:9 — For when they went up unto the valley of Eshcol, and saw the land, they discouraged the heart of the children of Israel, that they should not go into the land which the LORD had given them.

Dt 1:24 — And they turned and went up into the mountain, and came unto the valley of Eshcol, and searched it out.

ESHEAN • A city in Judah.

Jos 15:52 — Arab, and Dumah, and Eshean,

ESHEK • A Benjamite.

1Ch 8:39 — And the sons of Eshek his brother *were,* Ulam his firstborn, Jehush the second, and Eliphelet the third.

ESHTAOL

• A town of Judah.

Jos 15:33 — *And* in the valley, Eshtaol, and Zoreah, and Ashnah,

• Allotted to Dan.

Jos 19:41 — And the coast of their inheritance was Zorah, and Eshtaol, and Ir-shemesh,

Jgs 18:2 — And the children of Dan sent of their family five men from their coasts, men of valour, from Zorah, and from Eshtaol, to spy out the land, and to search it; and they said unto them, Go, search the land: who when they came to mount Ephraim, to the house of Micah, they lodged there.

Jgs 18:8 — And they came unto their brethren to Zorah and Eshtaol: and their brethren said unto them, What *say* ye?

Jgs 18:11 — And there went from thence of the family of the Danites, out of Zorah and out of Eshtaol, six hundred men appointed with weapons of war.

• Samson moved by the spirit of the Lord near.

Jgs 13:25 — And the Spirit of the LORD began to move him at times in the camp of Dan between Zorah and Eshtaol.

• Samson buried near.

Jgs 16:31 — Then his brethren and all the house of his father came down, and took him, and brought *him* up, and buried him between Zorah and Eshtaol in the buryingplace of Manoah his father. And he judged Israel twenty years.

ESHTEMOA

• A town of Canaan assigned to Judah.

• Called also Eshtemoh.

Jos 15:50 — And Anab, and Eshtemoh, and Anim,

• Allotted to the Aaronites.

Jos 21:14 — And Jattir with her suburbs, and Eshtemoa with her suburbs,

1Ch 6:57 — And to the sons of Aaron they gave the cities of Judah, *namely,* Hebron, *the city* of refuge, and Libnah with her suburbs, and Jattir, and Eshtemoa, with their suburbs,

• David shared spoil with.

1Sa 30:28 — And to *them* which *were* in Aroer, and to *them* which *were* in Siphmoth, and to *them* which *were* in Eshtemoa,

- **A descendant of Ezra.**

1Ch 4:17 — And the sons of Ezra *were,* Jether, and Mered, and Epher, and Jalon: and she bare Miriam, and Shammai, and Ishbah the father of Eshtemoa.

1Ch 4:19 — And the sons of *his* wife Hodiah the sister of Naham, the father of Keilah the Garmite, and Eshtemoa the Maachathite.

ESHTON • Son of Mehir.

1Ch 4:11–12

ESLI • An ancestor of Jesus.

Lk 3:25 — Which was *the son* of Mattathias, which was *the son* of Amos, which was *the son* of Naum, which was *the son* of Esli, which was *the son* of Nagge,

ESROM • An ancestor of Jesus.

Mt 1:3 — And Judas begat Phares and Zara of Thamar; and Phares begat Esrom; and Esrom begat Aram;

Lk 3:33 — Which was *the son* of Aminadab, which was *the son* of Aram, which was *the son* of Esrom, which was *the son* of Phares, which was *the son* of Juda,

ESTATE

- **Vast land.**

Isa 5:8 — Woe unto them that join house to house, *that* lay field to field, till *there be* no place, that they may be placed alone in the midst of the earth!

✦See: Land

ESTHER

- **Called also Hadassah.**
- **Niece of Mordecai.**

Est 2:7 — And he brought up Hadassah, that *is,* Esther, his uncle's daughter: for she had neither father nor mother, and the maid *was* fair and beautiful; whom Mordecai, when her father and mother were dead, took for his own daughter.

Est 2:15 — Now when the turn of Esther, the daughter of Abihail the uncle of Mordecai, who had taken her for his daughter, was come to go in unto the king, she required nothing but what Hegai the king's chamberlain, the keeper of the women, appointed. And Esther obtained favour in the sight of all them that looked upon her.

- **Chosen queen.**

Est 2:17 — And the king loved Esther above all the women, and she obtained grace and favour in his sight more than all the virgins; so that he set the royal crown upon her head, and made her queen instead of Vashti.

- **Tells the king of the plot against his life.**

Est 2:22 — And the thing was known to Mordecai, who told it unto Esther the queen; and Esther certified the king *thereof* in Mordecai's name.

- **Fasts on account of the decree to destroy the Israelites; accuses Haman to the king; intercedes for her people.**

Est 4:1–9:32

ETAM

- **A village of Simeon.**

1Ch 4:32 — And their villages *were,* Etam, and Ain, Rimmon, and Tochen, and Ashan, five cities:

- **A city in Judah.**

2Ch 11:6 — He built even Bethlehem, and Etam, and Tekoa,

- **A name in list of Judah's descendants, but probably referring to a city in Judah.**

1Ch 4:3 — And these *were of* the father of Etam; Jezreel, and Ishma, and Idbash: and the name of their sister *was* Hazelelponi:

- **A rock where Samson was bound and delivered to the Philistines.**

Jgs 15:11–13

Jgs 15:8 — And he smote them hip and thigh with a great slaughter: and he went down and dwelt in the top of the rock Etam.

ETERNAL LIFE ✦See: Life; everlasting

ETERNAL PUNISHMENT ✦See: Punishment; eternal

ETERNITY

- **God inhabiteth.**

Isa 57:15 — For thus saith the high and lofty One that inhabiteth eternity, whose name *is* Holy; I dwell in the high and holy *place,* with him also *that is* of a contrite and humble spirit, to revive the spirit of the humble, and to revive the heart of the contrite ones.

Mic 5:2 — But thou, Bethlehem Ephratah, *though* thou be little among the thousands of Judah, *yet* out of thee shall he come forth unto me *that is* to be ruler in Israel; whose goings forth *have been* from of old, from everlasting.

- **God rules.**

Jer 10:10 — But the LORD *is* the true God, he *is* the living God, and an everlasting king: at his wrath the earth shall tremble, and the nations shall not be able to abide his indignation.

✦See: God, Eternity of

- **Unclassified scripture relating to.**

Ps 30:12 — To the end that *my* glory may sing praise to thee, and not be silent. O LORD my God, I will give thanks unto thee for ever.

Ps 41:13 — Blessed *be* the LORD God of Israel from everlasting, and to everlasting. Amen, and Amen.

Ps 72:17 — His name shall endure for ever: his name shall be continued as long as the sun: and *men* shall be blessed in him: all nations shall call him blessed.

Ps 90:2 — Before the mountains were brought forth, or ever thou hadst formed the earth and the world, even from everlasting to everlasting, thou *art* God.

Ps 110:4 — The LORD hath sworn, and will not repent, Thou *art* a priest for ever after the order of Melchizedek.

Ps 119:142 — Thy righteousness *is* an everlasting righteousness, and thy law *is* the truth.

Mt 6:13 — And lead us not into temptation, but deliver us from evil: For thine is the kingdom, and the power, and the glory, for ever. Amen.

Mt 18:8 — Wherefore if thy hand or thy foot offend thee, cut them off, and cast *them* from thee: it is better for thee to enter into life halt or maimed, rather than having two hands or two feet to be cast into everlasting fire.

2Co 9:9 — (As it is written, He hath dispersed abroad; he hath given to the poor: his righteousness remaineth for ever.

Jude 1:6 — And the angels which kept not their first estate, but left their own habitation, he hath reserved in everlasting chains under darkness unto the judgment of the great day.

See: Life; everlasting

See: Punishment; eternal

ETHAM • Second camping place of Israel.

Nu 33:6–7

Ex 13:20 — And they took their journey from Succoth, and encamped in Etham, in the edge of the wilderness.

ETHAN

• A renowned sage.

1Ki 4:31 — For he was wiser than all men; than Ethan the Ezrahite, and Heman, and Chalcol, and Darda, the sons of Mahol: and his fame was in all nations round about.

Ps 89:1 — [Maschil of Ethan the Ezrahite.] I will sing of the mercies of the LORD for ever: with my mouth will I make known thy faithfulness to all generations.

• Son of Zerah.

1Ch 2:6 — And the sons of Zerah; Zimri, and Ethan, and Heman, and Calcol, and Dara: five of them in all.

1Ch 2:8 — And the sons of Ethan; Azariah.

• Two Levites.

1Ch 6:42 — The son of Ethan, the son of Zimmah, the son of Shimei,

1Ch 6:44 — And their brethren the sons of Merari *stood* on the left hand: Ethan the son of Kishi, the son of Abdi, the son of Malluch,

1Ch 15:17 — So the Levites appointed Heman the son of Joel; and of his brethren, Asaph the son of Berechiah; and of the sons of Merari their brethren, Ethan the son of Kushaiah;

1Ch 15:19 — So the singers, Heman, Asaph, and Ethan, *were appointed* to sound with cymbals of brass;

ETHANIM

• Seventh month (October).

• Feast of Trumpets in.

Le 23:23–25

• Day of atonement, on the tenth day of.

Le 23:26–32

• Feast of Tabernacles in.

Le 23:33–43

• Jubilee proclaimed on the tenth day of.

Le 25:9 — Then shalt thou cause the trumpet of the jubile to sound on the tenth *day* of the seventh month, in the day of atonement shall ye make the trumpet sound throughout all your land.

• Temple dedicated in.

1Ki 8:2 — And all the men of Israel assembled themselves unto king Solomon at the feast in the month Ethanim, which *is* the seventh month.

• Altar restored in, after the captivity.

Ezr 3:1 — And when the seventh month was come, and the children of Israel *were* in the cities, the people gathered themselves together as one man to Jerusalem.

Ezr 3:6 — From the first day of the seventh month began they to offer burnt offerings unto the LORD. But the foundation of the temple of the LORD was not *yet* laid.

ETHBAAL • King of Sidon.

1Ki 16:31 — And it came to pass, as if it had been a light thing for him to walk in the sins of Jeroboam the son of Nebat, that he took to wife Jezebel the daughter of Ethbaal king of the Zidonians, and went and served Baal, and worshipped him.

ETHER

• A city of Canaan.

• Assigned to Judah.

Jos 15:42 — Libnah, and Ether, and Ashan,

• Subsequently allotted to Simeon.

Jos 19:7 — Ain, Remmon, and Ether, and Ashan; four cities and their villages:

• Called Tochen.

1Ch 4:32 — And their villages *were*, Etam, and Ain, Rimmon, and Tochen, and Ashan, five cities:

ETHICS

Pr 22:29 — Seest thou a man diligent in his business? he shall stand before kings; he shall not stand before mean *men*.

Ecc 5:3 — For a dream cometh through the multitude of business; and a fool's voice *is known* by multitude of words.

Ecc 8:16 — When I applied mine heart to know wisdom, and to see the business that is done upon the earth: (for also *there is that* neither day nor night seeth sleep with his eyes:)

Ro 12:11 — Not slothful in business; fervent in spirit; serving the Lord;

ETHIOPIA

• A region in Africa, inhabited by the descendants of Ham.

• The inhabitants of, dark-skinned.

Jer 13:23 — Can the Ethiopian change his skin, or the leopard his spots? *then* may ye also do good, that are accustomed to do evil.

• Within the Babylonian empire.

Est 1:1 — Now it came to pass in the days of Ahasuerus, (this *is* Ahasuerus which reigned, from India even unto Ethiopia, *over* an hundred and seven and twenty provinces:)

• Rivers of.

Ge 10:6 — And the sons of Ham; Cush, and Mizraim, and Phut, and Canaan.

Isa 18:1 — Woe to the land shadowing with wings, which *is* beyond the rivers of Ethiopia:

• Bordered Egypt on the south.

Eze 29:10 — Behold, therefore I *am* against thee, and against thy rivers, and I will make the land of Egypt utterly waste *and* desolate, from the tower of Syene even unto the border of Ethiopia.

• Was called the land of Cush.

Ge 10:6 — And the sons of Ham; Cush, and Mizraim, and Phut, and Canaan.

1Ch 1:9 — And the sons of Cush; Seba, and Havilah, and Sabta, and Raamah, and Sabtecha. And the sons of Raamah; Sheba, and Dedan.

Isa 11:11 — And it shall come to pass in that day, *that* the Lord shall set his hand again the second time to recover the remnant of his people, which shall be left, from Assyria, and from Egypt, and from Pathros, and from Cush, and from Elam, and from Shinar, and from Hamath, and from the islands of the sea.

• Warriors of.

2Ch 12:3 — With twelve hundred chariots, and threescore thousand horsemen: and the people *were* without number that came with him out of Egypt; the Lubim, the Sukkiims, and the Ethiopians.

Jer 46:9 — Come up, ye horses; and rage, ye chariots; and let the mighty men come forth; the Ethiopians and the Libyans, that handle the shield; and the Lydians, that handle *and* bend the bow.

Eze 38:5 — Persia, Ethiopia, and Libya with them; all of them with shield and helmet:

• Defeated by Asa.

2Ch 14:9–15

2Ch 16:8 — Were not the Ethiopians and the Lubims a huge host, with very many chariots and horsemen? yet, because thou didst rely on the LORD, he delivered them into thine hand.

• Invaded Syria.

2Ki 19:9 — And when he heard say of Tirhakah king of Ethiopia, Behold, he is come out to fight against thee: he sent messengers again unto Hezekiah, saying,

• Merchandise of.

Isa 45:14 — Thus saith the LORD, The labour of Egypt, and merchandise of Ethiopia and of the Sabeans, men of stature, shall come over unto thee, and they shall be thine: they shall come after thee; in chains they shall come over, and they shall fall down unto thee, they shall make supplication unto thee, *saying*, Surely God *is* in thee; and *there is* none else, *there is* no God.

• Moses marries a woman of.

Nu 12:1 — And Miriam and Aaron spake against Moses because of the Ethiopian woman whom he had married: for he had married an Ethiopian woman.

• Ebel-melech, at the court of Babylon, native of, kindly treats Jeremiah.

Jer 38:7–13; 39:15–18

• Candace, queen of.

Ac 8:27 — And he arose and went: and, behold, a man of Ethiopia, an eunuch of great authority under Candace queen of the Ethiopians, who had the charge of all her treasure, and had come to Jerusalem for to worship,

• A eunuch from, becomes a disciple under the preaching of Philip.

Ac 8:27–39

• Prophecies concerning the conversion of.

Ps 68:31 — Princes shall come out of Egypt; Ethiopia shall soon stretch out her hands unto God.

Ps 87:4 — I will make mention of Rahab and Babylon to them that know me: behold Philistia, and Tyre, with Ethiopia; this *man* was born there.

Isa 45:14 — Thus saith the LORD, The labour of Egypt, and merchandise of Ethiopia and of the Sabeans, men of stature, shall come over unto thee, and they shall be thine: they shall come after thee; in chains they shall come over, and they shall fall down unto thee, they shall make supplication unto thee, *saying*, Surely God *is* in thee; and *there is* none else, *there is* no God.

Da 11:43 — But he shall have power over the treasures of gold and of silver, and over all the precious things of Egypt: and the Libyans and the Ethiopians *shall be* at his steps.

• Desolation of.

Isa 18:1–6; 20:2–6; Eze 30:4–9

Isa 43:3 — For I *am* the LORD thy God, the Holy One of Israel, thy Saviour: I gave Egypt *for* thy ransom, Ethiopia and Seba for thee.

Hab 3:7 — I saw the tents of Cushan in affliction: *and* the curtains of the land of Midian did tremble.

Zep 2:12 — Ye Ethiopians also, ye *shall be* slain by my sword.

ETHNAN • Grandson of Ashur.

1Ch 4:7 — And the sons of Helah *were*, Zereth, and Jezoar, and Ethnan.

ETHNI • An ancestor of Asaph.

1Ch 6:41 — The son of Ethni, the son of Zerah, the son of Adaiah,

ETIQUETTE ✦See: Manners

EUBULUS • A friend of Paul.

2Ti 4:21 — Do thy diligence to come before winter. Eubulus greeteth thee, and Pudens, and Linus, and Claudia, and all the brethren.

EUCHARIST

Mt 26:17–30; Mk 14:22–24; Lk 22:19–20; Jn 13:1–4; Ac 2:46–47; 1Co 10:16–17, 21–22; 11:20–34

Lk 13:26 — Then shall ye begin to say, We have eaten and drunk in thy presence, and thou hast taught in our streets.

Ac 2:42 — And they continued stedfastly in the apostles' doctrine and fellowship, and in breaking of bread, and in prayers.

Ac 20:7 — And upon the first *day* of the week, when the disciples came together to break bread, Paul preached unto them, ready to depart on the morrow; and continued his speech until midnight.

EUNICE • Timothy's mother.

Ac 16:1 — Then came he to Derbe and Lystra: and, behold, a certain disciple was there, named Timotheus, the son of a certain woman, which was a Jewess, and believed; but his father *was* a Greek:

2Ti 1:5 — When I call to remembrance the unfeigned faith that is in thee, which dwelt first in thy grandmother Lois, and thy mother Eunice; and I am persuaded that in thee also.

EUNUCH

Mt 19:12 — For there are some eunuchs, which were so born from *their* mother's womb: and there are some eunuchs, which were made eunuchs of men: and there be eunuchs, which have made themselves eunuchs for the kingdom of heaven's sake. He that is able to receive *it*, let him receive *it*.

• Prohibited from certain privileges of the congregation.

Isa 56:3–5

Dt 23:1 — He that is wounded in the stones, or hath his privy member cut off, shall not enter into the congregation of the LORD.

• Influential court officials.

Jer 38:7–13

Jer 52:25 — He took also out of the city an eunuch, which had the charge of the men of war; and seven men of them that were near the king's person, which were found in the city; and the principal scribe of the host, who mustered the people of the land; and threescore men of the people of the land, that were found in the midst of the city.

Da 1:3 — And the king spake unto Ashpenaz the master of his eunuchs, that he should bring *certain* of the children of Israel, and of the king's seed, and of the princes;

• Those who voluntarily became (continent, probably) for the kingdom of heaven's sake.

Mt 19:12 — For there are some eunuchs, which were so born from *their* mother's womb: and there are some eunuchs, which were made eunuchs of men: and there be eunuchs, which have made themselves eunuchs for the kingdom of heaven's sake. He that is able to receive *it*, let him receive *it*.

• Baptism of the Ethiopian.

Ac 8:26–29

EUODIAS • A Christian woman of Philippi.

Php 4:2 — I beseech Euodias, and beseech Syntyche, that they be of the same mind in the Lord.

EUPHRATES

• A river in the garden of Eden.

Ge 2:14 — And the name of the third river *is* Hiddekel: that *is* it which goeth toward the east of Assyria. And the fourth river *is* Euphrates.

• The eastern limit of the kingdom of Israel.

Ge 15:18 — In the same day the LORD made a covenant with Abram, saying, Unto thy seed have I given this land, from the river of Egypt unto the great river, the river Euphrates:

Ex 23:31 — And I will set thy bounds from the Red sea even unto the sea of the Philistines, and from the desert unto the river: for I will deliver the inhabitants of the land into your hand; and thou shalt drive them out before thee.

Dt 1:7 — Turn you, and take your journey, and go to the mount of the Amorites, and unto all *the places* nigh thereunto, in the plain, in the hills, and in the vale, and in the south, and by the sea side, to the land of the Canaanites, and unto Lebanon, unto the great river, the river Euphrates.

Dt 11:24 — Every place whereon the soles of your feet shall tread shall be yours: from the wilderness and Lebanon, from the river, the river Euphrates, even unto the uttermost sea shall your coast be.

Jos 1:4 — From the wilderness and this Lebanon even unto the great river, the river Euphrates, all the land of the Hittites, and unto the great sea toward the going down of the sun, shall be your coast.

2Sa 8:3 — David smote also Hadadezer, the son of Rehob, king of Zobah, as he went to recover his border at the river Euphrates.

1Ki 4:21 — And Solomon reigned over all kingdoms from the river unto the land of the Philistines, and unto the border of Egypt: they brought presents, and served Solomon all the days of his life.

1Ch 5:9 — And eastward he inhabited unto the entering in of the wilderness from the river Euphrates: because their cattle were multiplied in the *land* of Gilead.

1Ch 18:3 — And David smote Hadarezer king of Zobah unto Hamath, as he went to stablish his dominion by the river Euphrates.

• Pharaoh-nechoh, king of Egypt, made conquest to.

Jer 46:2–10

2Ki 24:7 — And the king of Egypt came not again any more out of his land: for the king of Babylon had taken from the river of Egypt unto the river Euphrates all that pertained to the king of Egypt.

• On the banks of, Jeremiah symbolically buries his girdle.

Jer 13:1–7

• Jeremiah casts the roll containing the prophecies against Babylon into.

Jer 51:59–64

• Symbolic.

• The inundations of, of the extension of the empire of Assyria.

Isa 8:6–8

• In the symbolisms of the apocalypse.

Rev 9:14 — Saying to the sixth angel which had the trumpet, Loose the four angels which are bound in the great river Euphrates.

Rev 16:12 — And the sixth angel poured out his vial upon the great river Euphrates; and the water thereof was dried up, that the way of the kings of the east might be prepared.

EUROCLYDON • A tempestuous wind.

Ac 27:14 — But not long after there arose against it a tempestuous wind, called Euroclydon.

EUTYCHUS • A young man of Troas, restored to life by Paul.

Ac 20:9–11

EVANGELISM

Mt 28:19–20; Ac 16:1–3

Ro 11:14 — If by any means I may provoke to emulation *them which are* my flesh, and might save some of them.

1Co 9:22 — To the weak became I as weak, that I might gain the weak: I am made all things to all *men,* that I might by all means save some.

2Ti 2:2 — And the things that thou hast heard of me among many witnesses, the same commit thou to faithful men, who shall be able to teach others also.

Jas 5:20 — Let him know, that he which converteth the sinner from the error of his way shall save a soul from death, and shall hide a multitude of sins.

1Pe 3:15 — But sanctify the Lord God in your hearts: and *be* ready always to *give* an answer to every man that asketh you a reason of the hope that is in you with meekness and fear:

Jude 1:23 — And others save with fear, pulling *them* out of the fire; hating even the garment spotted by the flesh.

→See: Minister, a sacred teacher; duties of

→See: Zeal, Religious

EVAPORATION

Ps 135:7 — He causeth the vapours to ascend from the ends of the earth; he maketh lightnings for the rain; he bringeth the wind out of his treasuries.

Jer 10:13 — When he uttereth his voice, *there is* a multitude of waters in the heavens, and he causeth the vapors to ascend from the ends of the earth; he maketh lightnings with rain, and bringeth forth the wind out of his treasures.

Jer 51:16 — When he uttereth *his* voice, *there is* a multitude of waters in the heavens; and he causeth the vapors to ascend from the ends of the earth: he maketh lightnings with rain, and bringeth forth the wind out of his treasures.

Am 5:8 — *Seek him* that maketh the seven stars and Orion, and turneth the shadow of death into the morning, and maketh the day dark with night: that calleth for the waters of the sea, and poureth them out upon the face of the earth: The LORD *is* his name:

Am 9:6 — *It is* he that buildeth his stories in the heaven, and hath founded his troop in the earth; he that calleth for the waters of the sea, and poureth them out upon the face of the earth: The LORD *is* his name.

EVE

• Creation of.

Ge 1:26–28; 2:21–24

1Ti 2:13 — For Adam was first formed, then Eve.

• Named by Adam.

Ge 2:23 — And Adam said, This *is* now bone of my bones, and flesh of my flesh: she shall be called Woman, because she was taken out of Man.

Ge 3:20 — And Adam called his wife's name Eve; because she was the mother of all living.

• Beguiled by Satan.

Ge 3:1–24

2Co 11:3 — But I fear, lest by any means, as the serpent beguiled Eve through his subtilty, so your minds should be corrupted from the simplicity that is in Christ.

1Ti 2:14 — And Adam was not deceived, but the woman being deceived was in the transgression.

• Clothed with fig leaves.

Ge 3:7 — And the eyes of them both were opened, and they knew that they *were* naked; and they sewed fig leaves together, and made themselves aprons.

• Clothed with skins.

Ge 3:21 — Unto Adam also and to his wife did the LORD God make coats of skins, and clothed them.

• Curse denounced against.

Ge 3:16 — Unto the woman he said, I will greatly multiply thy sorrow and thy conception; in sorrow thou shalt bring forth children; and thy desire *shall be* to thy husband, and he shall rule over thee.

• Messiah promised to.

Ge 3:15 — And I will put enmity between thee and the woman, and between thy seed and her seed; it shall bruise thy head, and thou shalt bruise his heel.

• Children of.

Ge 4:1–2; 5:3–4

Ge 4:25 — And Adam knew his wife again; and she bare a son, and called his name Seth: For God, *said she,* hath appointed me another seed instead of Abel, whom Cain slew.

EVERLASTING FIRE →See: Fire; figurative; everlasting fire

EVERLASTING LIFE →See: Life; everlasting

EVERLASTING PUNISHMENT ✢See: Punishment; eternal

EVI • Prince of Midian, slain.

Nu 31:8 — And they slew the kings of Midian, beside the rest of them that were slain; *namely,* Evi, and Rekem, and Zur, and Hur, and Reba, five kings of Midian: Balaam also the son of Beor they slew with the sword.

Jos 13:21 — And all the cities of the plain, and all the kingdom of Sihon king of the Amorites, which reigned in Heshbon, whom Moses smote with the princes of Midian, Evi, and Rekem, and Zur, and Hur, and Reba, *which were* dukes of Sihon, dwelling in the country.

EVICTION

• Of tenants.

Mt 21:41 — They say unto him, He will miserably destroy those wicked men, and will let out *his* vineyard unto other husbandmen, which shall render him the fruits in their seasons.

Mk 12:9 — What shall therefore the lord of the vineyard do? he will come and destroy the husbandmen, and will give the vineyard unto others.

EVIDENCE

• Laws concerning.

Dt 17:6–7; 19:15–21

Ex 20:16 — Thou shalt not bear false witness against thy neighbour.

Ex 23:1 — Thou shalt not raise a false report: put not thine hand with the wicked to be an unrighteous witness.

Ex 23:7 — Keep thee far from a false matter; and the innocent and righteous slay thou not: for I will not justify the wicked.

Le 5:1 — And if a soul sin, and hear the voice of swearing, and *is* a witness, whether he hath seen or known *of it;* if he do not utter *it,* then he shall bear his iniquity.

Le 24:14 — Bring forth him that hath cursed without the camp; and let all that heard *him* lay their hands upon his head, and let all the congregation stone him.

Nu 35:30 — Whoso killeth any person, the murderer shall be put to death by the mouth of witnesses: but one witness shall not testify against any person *to cause him* to die.

Pr 24:28 — Be not a witness against thy neighbour without cause; and deceive *not* with thy lips.

Mt 18:16 — But if he will not hear *thee, then* take with thee one or two more, that in the mouth of two or three witnesses every word may be established.

Mt 19:18 — He saith unto him, Which? Jesus said, Thou shalt do no murder, Thou shalt not commit adultery, Thou shalt not steal, Thou shalt not bear false witness,

Heb 10:28 — He that despised Moses' law died without mercy under two or three witnesses:

• Self-Criminating.

Jos 7:19–21

✢See: Accusation, False

✢See: Falsehood, False Witness

✢See: Self-Crimination

✢See: Witness

EVIL

Jn 8:44 — Ye are of your father the devil, and the lusts of *your* father ye will do. He was a murderer from the beginning, and abode not in the truth, because there is no truth in him. When he speaketh a lie, he speaketh of his own: for he is a liar, and the father of it.

Jn 8:49 — Jesus answered, I have not a devil; but I honour my Father, and ye do dishonour me.

Jas 1:13 — Let no man say when he is tempted, I am tempted of God: for God cannot be tempted with evil, neither tempteth he any man:

• Appearance of, to be avoided.

Ro 14:1–23; 1Co 8:7–13; 10:28–33; 1Th 4:11–12

1Th 5:22 — Abstain from all appearance of evil.

• Instances of.

• Paul, in refusing to eat that which had been offered to idols.

1Co 8:13

• Paul, in supporting himself.

1Co 9:7–23

EVIL FOR EVIL ✢See: Retaliation

EVIL FOR GOOD

Ps 7:4–5

Ps 35:12 — They rewarded me evil for good *to* the spoiling of my soul.

Ps 109:5 — And they have rewarded me evil for good, and hatred for my love.

Pr 17:13 — Whoso rewardeth evil for good, evil shall not depart from his house.

• Instances of.

• Joseph accuses his brethren of rendering.

Ge 44:4

• Israelites, to Moses.

Ex 5:21; 14:11; 15:24; 16:2–3; 17:3–4

• Nabal returns, to David.

1Sa 25:21

• Saul returns, to David.

1Sa 19:1, 4–5, 10

• David, to Uriah.

2Sa 11:1–27

• David, to Joab.

1Ki 2:4–6

✢See: Enemy

✢See: Good for Evil

EVIL SPEAKING ✢See: Speaking; evil

EVIL-MERODACH

- **Son and successor of Nebuchadnezzar.**
- **Released Jehoiachin from prison.**

2Ki 25:27–30; Jer 52:31–34

EVOLUTION

Ge 1:1 — In the beginning God created the heaven and the earth.

Col 1:16 — For by him were all things created, that are in heaven, and that are in earth, visible and invisible, whether *they be* thrones, or dominions, or principalities, or powers: all things were created by him, and for him:

Heb 11:3 — Through faith we understand that the worlds were framed by the word of God, so that things which are seen were not made of things which do appear.

EXALTATION

- **Of Christ.**

See: Jesus, Exaltation of

- **Of self.**

See: Self-Exaltation

EXAMPLE

- **Bad, admonitions against.**

Le 18:2–3; Pr 22:24–25; Jer 17:1–2; Mt 23:1–3; 1Co 8:9–13

Le 20:23 — And ye shall not walk in the manners of the nation, which I cast out before you: for they committed all these things, and therefore I abhorred them.

Dt 18:9 — When thou art come into the land which the LORD thy God giveth thee, thou shalt not learn to do after the abominations of those nations.

2Ch 30:7 — And be not ye like your fathers, and like your brethren, which trespassed against the LORD God of their fathers, *who* therefore gave them up to desolation, as ye see.

Isa 8:11 — For the LORD spake thus to me with a strong hand, and instructed me that I should not walk in the way of this people, saying,

Jer 16:12 — And ye have done worse than your fathers; for, behold, ye walk every one after the imagination of his evil heart, that they may not hearken unto me:

Eze 20:18 — But I said unto their children in the wilderness, Walk ye not in the statutes of your fathers, neither observe their judgments, nor defile yourselves with their idols:

Hos 4:9 — And there shall be, like people, like priest: and I will punish them for their ways, and reward them their doings.

Hos 4:15 — Though thou, Israel, play the harlot, *yet* let not Judah offend; and come not ye unto Gilgal, neither go ye up to Beth-aven, nor swear, The LORD liveth.

Hos 5:5 — And the pride of Israel doth testify to his face: therefore shall Israel and Ephraim fall in their iniquity; Judah also shall fall with them.

Zec 1:4 — Be ye not as your fathers, unto whom the former prophets have cried, saying, Thus saith the LORD of hosts; Turn ye now from your evil ways, and *from* your evil doings: but they did not hear, nor hearken unto me, saith the LORD.

1Co 10:6 — Now these things were our examples, to the intent we should not lust after evil things, as they also lusted.

Eph 4:17 — This I say therefore, and testify in the Lord, that ye henceforth walk not as other Gentiles walk, in the vanity of their mind,

3Jn 1:11 — Beloved, follow not that which is evil, but that which is good. He that doeth good is of God: but he that doeth evil hath not seen God.

See: Influence

- **Good.**

Ne 5:8–19; 1Th 1:6–8; Tit 2:7–8; Jas 5:10–11; 1Pe 2:11–25; 3:5–6

Ps 101:2 — I will behave myself wisely in a perfect way. O when wilt thou come unto me? I will walk within my house with a perfect heart.

1Ti 4:12 — Let no man despise thy youth; but be thou an example of the believers, in word, in conversation, in charity, in spirit, in faith, in purity.

Heb 13:7 — Remember them which have the rule over you, who have spoken unto you the word of God: whose faith follow, considering the end of *their* conversation.

1Pe 4:15 — But let none of you suffer as a murderer, or *as* a thief, or *as* an evildoer, or as a busybody in other men's matters.

1Pe 5:3 — Neither as being lords over *God's* heritage, but being ensamples to the flock.

See: Influence

- **God, our.**

Le 11:44 — For I *am* the LORD your God: ye shall therefore sanctify yourselves, and ye shall be holy; for I *am* holy: neither shall ye defile yourselves with any manner of creeping thing that creepeth upon the earth.

Le 19:2 — Speak unto all the congregation of the children of Israel, and say unto them, Ye shall be holy: for I the LORD your God *am* holy.

Mt 5:48 — Be ye therefore perfect, even as your Father which is in heaven is perfect.

Lk 6:36 — Be ye therefore merciful, as your Father also is merciful.

Eph 6:9 — And, ye masters, do the same things unto them, forbearing threatening: knowing that your Master also is in heaven; neither is there respect of persons with him.

- **Christ, our.**

Mk 10:43–45; Jn 13:13–17; Ro 15:2–7; Eph 5:1–2; Php 2:5–8; Heb 12:2–3; 1Pe 3:17–18

Mt 20:28 — Even as the Son of man came not to be ministered unto, but to minister, and to give his life a ransom for many.

Lk 22:27 — For whether *is* greater, he that sitteth at meat, or he that serveth? *is* not he that sitteth at meat? but I am among you as he that serveth.

Jn 13:34 — A new commandment I give unto you, That ye love one another; as I have loved you, that ye also love one another.

2Co 8:9 — For ye know the grace of our Lord Jesus Christ, that, though he was rich, yet for your sakes he became poor, that ye through his poverty might be rich.

2Co 10:1 — Now I Paul myself beseech you by the meekness and gentleness of Christ, who in presence *am* base among you, but being absent am bold toward you:

Col 3:13 — Forbearing one another, and forgiving one another, if any man have a quarrel against any: even as Christ forgave you, so also *do* ye.

1Pe 2:21 — For even hereunto were ye called: because Christ also suffered for us, leaving us an example, that ye should follow his steps:

1Pe 4:1 — Forasmuch then as Christ hath suffered for us in the flesh, arm yourselves likewise with the same mind: for he that hath suffered in the flesh hath ceased from sin;

1Jn 2:6 — He that saith he abideth in him ought himself also so to walk, even as he walked.

1Jn 3:16 — Hereby perceive we the love *of God,* because he laid down his life for us: and we ought to lay down *our* lives for the brethren.

Rev 3:21 — To him that overcometh will I grant to sit with me in my throne, even as I also overcame, and am set down with my Father in his throne.

- **Paul, our.**

1Co 7:7–8; 2Th 3:7–10

Ac 20:35 — I have shewed you all things, how that so labouring ye ought to support the weak, and to remember the words of the Lord Jesus, how he said, It is more blessed to give than to receive.

1Co 4:16 — Wherefore I beseech you, be ye followers of me.

1Co 11:1 — Be ye followers of me, even as I also *am* of Christ.

Php 3:17 — Brethren, be followers together of me, and mark them which walk so as ye have us for an ensample.

Php 4:9 — Those things, which ye have both learned, and received, and heard, and seen in me, do: and the God of peace shall be with you.

1Ti 1:16 — Howbeit for this cause I obtained mercy, that in me first Jesus Christ might shew forth all longsuffering, for a pattern to them which should hereafter believe on him to life everlasting.

2Ti 1:13 — Hold fast the form of sound words, which thou hast heard of me, in faith and love which is in Christ Jesus.

⇜See: Influence

EXCHANGERS ⇜See: Money Changers

EXCOMMUNICATION

⇜See: Church; government of, Mosaic and Christian

⇜See: Church; rules of discipline in, Mosaic and Christian

EXCUSES

Ge 3:12–13; Ex 4:10–14; 32:22–24; Dt 30:11–14; Jgs 6:12–17; 1Ki 19:19–21; 2Ki 5:10–14; Jer 1:4–10; Lk 9:59–62; 14:18–20

Ex 4:1 — And Moses answered and said, But, behold, they will not believe me, nor hearken unto my voice: for they will say, The LORD hath not appeared unto thee.

Jer 1:1 — The words of Jeremiah the son of Hilkiah, of the priests that *were* in Anathoth in the land of Benjamin:

Mt 8:21 — And another of his disciples said unto him, Lord, suffer me first to go and bury my father.

Ac 24:25 — And as he reasoned of righteousness, temperance, and judgment to come Felix trembled, and answered, Go thy way for this time; when I have a convenient season, I will call for thee.

Ro 1:20 — For the invisible things of him from the creation of the world are clearly seen, being understood by the things that are made, *even* his eternal power and Godhead; so that they are without excuse:

Ro 2:1 — Therefore thou art inexcusable, O man, whosoever thou art that judgest: for wherein thou judgest another, thou condemnest thyself; for thou that judgest doest the same things.

EXECUTIONER

Ge 37:36 — And the Midianites sold him into Egypt unto Potiphar, an officer of Pharaoh's, *and* captain of the guard.

Pr 16:14 — The wrath of a king *is as* messengers of death: but a wise man will pacify it.

Jer 39:9 — Then Nebuzar-adan the captain of the guard carried away captive into Babylon the remnant of the people that remained in the city, and those that fell away, that fell to him, with the rest of the people that remained.

Da 2:14 — Then Daniel answered with counsel and wisdom to Arioch the captain of the king's guard, which was gone forth to slay the wise *men* of Babylon:

Mt 14:10 — And he sent, and beheaded John in the prison.

⇜See: Punishment

EXILE

- **Absalom.**

2Sa 14:13–14

2Sa 14:24 — And the king said, Let him turn to his own house, and let him not see my face. So Absalom returned to his own house, and saw not the king's face.

- **Ittai.**

2Sa 15:19 — Then said the king to Ittai the Gittite, Wherefore goest thou also with us? return to thy place, and abide with the king: for thou *art* a stranger, and also an exile.

EXODUS

• Of early tribes.

Ge 11:2 — And it came to pass, as they journeyed from the east, that they found a plain in the land of Shinar; and they dwelt there.

• Of Israel from Egypt.

→See: Israel

EXORCISM

• Casting out evil spirits by sorcery.

→See: Sorcery

EXPEDIENCY

Ro 14:14–22; 1Co 8:8–13; 9:19–23; 10:23–33

1Co 6:12 — All things are lawful unto me, but all things are not expedient: all things are lawful for me, but I will not be brought under the power of any.

→See: Evil; appearance of, to be avoided

→See: Prudence

EXPERIENCE

• Solomon's.

Ecc 1:2 — Vanity of vanities, saith the Preacher, vanity of vanities; all *is* vanity.

• Religious, relating of.

→See: Testimony; religious

EXPERIMENT • In worldly pleasure, Solomon's.

Ecc 1:1–2:26

EXPIATION →See: Atonement

EXPORTS

• From Egypt.

• Of horses and chariots, and linen yarn.

1Ki 10:28–29; 2Ch 1:16–17

• Of corn.

Ge 42:1–43:34

• From Gilead.

• Of spices.

Ge 37:25 — And they sat down to eat bread: and they lifted up their eyes and looked, and, behold, a company of Ishmeelites came from Gilead with their camels bearing spicery and balm and myrrh, going to carry *it* down to Egypt.

• From Ophir.

• Of gold.

1Ki 10:11 — And the navy also of Hiram, that brought gold from Ophir, brought in from Ophir great plenty of almug trees, and precious stones.

1Ki 22:48 — Jehoshaphat made ships of Tharshish to go to Ophir for gold: but they went not; for the ships were broken at Ezion-geber.

1Ch 29:4 — *Even* three thousand talents of gold, of the gold of Ophir, and seven thousand talents of refined silver, to overlay the walls of the houses *withal:*

• From Tarshish.

• Of gold.

1Ki 10:22 — For the king had at sea a navy of Tharshish with the navy of Hiram: once in three years came the navy of Tharshish, bringing gold, and silver, ivory, and apes, and peacocks.

• Of ivory, apes, and peacocks.

1Ki 10:22 — For the king had at sea a navy of Tharshish with the navy of Hiram: once in three years came the navy of Tharshish, bringing gold, and silver, ivory, and apes, and peacocks.

• Of silver, iron, tin, lead, brass, slaves.

Eze 27:12–13

• From Arabia.

• Of sheep and goats.

Eze 27:21 — Arabia, and all the princes of Kedar, they occupied with thee in lambs, and rams, and goats: in these *were they* thy merchants.

• From Palestine.

• Honey.

Eze 27:17 — Judah, and the land of Israel, they *were* thy merchants: they traded in thy market wheat of Minnith, and Pannag, and honey, and oil, and balm.

→See: Commerce

→See: Imports

EXPOSTULATION →See: Reproof

EXTERMINATION →See: War; of extermination

EXTORTION

Mic 3:2–3; 1Co 5:10–11

Ps 109:11 — Let the extortioner catch all that he hath; and let the strangers spoil his labour.

Isa 16:4 — Let mine outcasts dwell with thee, Moab; be thou a covert to them from the face of the spoiler: for the extortioner is at an end, the spoiler ceaseth, the oppressors are consumed out of the land.

Eze 22:12 — In thee have they taken gifts to shed blood; thou hast taken usury and increase, and thou hast greedily gained of thy neighbours by extortion, and hast forgotten me, saith the Lord GOD.

Mt 23:35 — That upon you may come all the righteous blood shed upon the earth, from the blood of righteous Abel unto the blood of Zacharias son of Barachias, whom ye slew between the temple and the altar.

Lk 18:11 — The Pharisee stood and prayed thus with himself, God, I thank thee, that I am not as other men *are,* extortioners, unjust, adulterers, or even as this publican.

1Co 6:10 — Nor thieves, nor covetous, nor drunkards, nor revilers, nor extortioners, shall inherit the kingdom of God.

→See: Usury

- **Instances of.**
  - **Jacob in demanding Esau's birthright for a mess of pottage.**

    Ge 25:31
  - **Pharaoh in exacting of the Egyptians lands and persons, for corn.**

    Ge 47:13–26

EXTRADITION

Jer 26:21–23

1Ki 18:7 — And as Obadiah was in the way, behold, Elijah met him: and he knew him, and fell on his face, and said, *Art* thou that my lord Elijah?

1Ki 18:10 — *As* the LORD thy God liveth, there is no nation or kingdom, whither my lord hath not sent to seek thee: and when they said, *He is* not *there;* he took an oath of the kingdom and nation, that they found thee not.

Ac 9:2 — And desired of him letters to Damascus to the synagogues, that if he found any of this way, whether they were men or women, he might bring them bound unto Jerusalem.

Ac 9:14 — And here he hath authority from the chief priests to bind all that call on thy name.

Ac 22:5 — As also the high priest doth bear me witness, and all the estate of the elders: from whom also I received letters unto the brethren, and went to Damascus, to bring them which were there bound unto Jerusalem, for to be punished.

EXTRAVAGANCE

Pr 21:17 — He that loveth pleasure *shall be* a poor man: he that loveth wine and oil shall not be rich.

Pr 21:20 — *There is* treasure to be desired and oil in the dwelling of the wise; but a foolish man spendeth it up.

Lk 16:19 — There was a certain rich man, which was clothed in purple and fine linen, and fared sumptuously every day:

See: Gluttony

EYE

- **Anthropomorphic uses of.**

  Ps 33:18–19; 121:3–5

  Ps 34:15 — The eyes of the LORD *are* upon the righteous, and his ears *are open* unto their cry.

  Isa 1:15 — And when ye spread forth your hands, I will hide mine eyes from you: yea, when ye make many prayers, I will not hear: your hands are full of blood.

  Isa 3:8 — For Jerusalem is ruined, and Judah is fallen: because their tongue and their doings *are* against the LORD, to provoke the eyes of his glory.

  Am 9:8 — Behold, the eyes of the Lord GOD *are* upon the sinful kingdom, and I will destroy it from off the face of the earth; saving that I will not utterly destroy the house of Jacob, saith the LORD.

  Hab 1:13 — *Thou art* of purer eyes than to behold evil, and canst not look on iniquity: wherefore lookest thou upon them that deal treacherously, *and* holdest thy tongue when the wicked devoureth *the man that is* more righteous than he?

  1Pe 3:12 — For the eyes of the Lord *are* over the righteous, and his ears *are open* unto their prayers: but the face of the Lord *is* against them that do evil.
- **For additional anthropomorphic uses of.**

  See: Anthropomorphisms
- **Figurative.**
  - **Of evil desire, never satisfied.**

    Pr 27:20 — Hell and destruction are never full; so the eyes of man are never satisfied.

    Ecc 1:8 — All things *are* full of labour; man cannot utter *it:* the eye is not satisfied with seeing, nor the ear filled with hearing.

    1Jn 2:16 — For all that *is* in the world, the lust of the flesh, and the lust of the eyes, and the pride of life, is not of the Father, but is of the world.
  - **The offending.**

    Mt 5:29 — And if thy right eye offend thee, pluck it out, and cast *it* from thee: for it is profitable for thee that one of thy members should perish, and not *that* thy whole body should be cast into hell.

EYE FOR EYE **See: Retaliation**

EYELIDS • Painted.

Eze 23:40 — And furthermore, that ye have sent for men to come from far, unto whom a messenger *was* sent; and, lo, they came: for whom thou didst wash thyself, paintedst thy eyes, and deckedst thyself with ornaments,

EYES

Ps 119:37 — Turn away mine eyes from beholding vanity; *and* quicken thou me in thy way.

Pr 4:25 — Let thine eyes look right on, and let thine eyelids look straight before thee.

Isa 33:15 — He that walketh righteously, and speaketh uprightly; he that despiseth the gain of oppressions, that shaketh his hands from holding of bribes, that stoppeth his ears from hearing of blood, and shutteth his eyes from seeing evil;

Mt 5:29 — And if thy right eye offend thee, pluck it out, and cast *it* from thee: for it is profitable for thee that one of thy members should perish, and not *that* thy whole body should be cast into hell.

EZBAI

- **Father of Naarai.**

  1Ch 11:37 — Hezro the Carmelite, Naarai the son of Ezbai,
- **Possibly identical with Paarai.**

  2Sa 23:35 — Hezrai the Carmelite, Paarai the Arbite,

EZBON

- **A son of Gad.**

  Ge 46:16 — And the sons of Gad; Ziphion, and Haggi, Shuni, and Ezbon, Eri, and Arodi, and Areli.
  - **Called Ozni.**

    Nu 26:16 — Of Ozni, the family of the Oznites: of Eri, the family of the Erites:

• Son of Bela.
1Ch 7:7 — And the sons of Bela; Ezbon, and Uzzi, and Uzziel, and Jerimoth, and Iri, five; heads of the house of *their* fathers, mighty men of valour; and were reckoned by their genealogies twenty and two thousand and thirty and four.

EZEKIAS ✦See: Hezekiah

EZEKIEL

• A priest.

• Time of his prophecy.
Eze 1:1–3

• Persecution of.
Eze 3:25 — But thou, O son of man, behold, they shall put bands upon thee, and shall bind thee with them, and thou shalt not go out among them:

• Visions of.

• Of God's glory.
Eze 1:1–28; 8:1–18; 10:1–22
Eze 11:22 — Then did the cherubims lift up their wings, and the wheels beside them; and the glory of the God of Israel *was* over them above.

• Of Jews' abominations.
Eze 8:5–6

• Of their punishment.
Eze 9:10 — And as for me also, mine eye shall not spare, neither will I have pity, *but* I will recompense their way upon their head.

• Of the valley of dry bones.
Eze 37:1–14

• Of a man with measuring line.
Eze 40:1–48:35

• Of the river.
Eze 47:1–5

• Teaches by pantomime.

• Feigns dumbness.
Eze 3:26 — And I will make thy tongue cleave to the roof of thy mouth, that thou shalt be dumb, and shalt not be to them a reprover: for they *are* a rebellious house.
Eze 24:27 — In that day shall thy mouth be opened to him which is escaped, and thou shalt speak, and be no more dumb: and thou shalt be a sign unto them; and they shall know that I *am* the LORD.
Eze 33:22 — Now the hand of the LORD was upon me in the evening, afore he that was escaped came; and had opened my mouth, until he came to me in the morning; and my mouth was opened, and I was no more dumb.

• Symbolizes the siege of Jerusalem by drawings on a tile.
Eze 4:1–17

• Shaves himself.
Eze 5:1–4

• Removes his belongings to illustrate the approaching Jewish captivity.
Eze 12:3–7

• Sighs.
Eze 21:6–7

• Employs a boiling pot to symbolize the destruction of Jerusalem.
Eze 24:1–14

• Omits mourning at the death of his wife.
Eze 24:16–27

• Prophesies by parable of an eagle.
Eze 17:2–10

• Other parables.
Eze 15:1–16:63; 19:1–14; 23:1–49

• Prophecies of, concerning various nations.
Eze 25:1–29:21

• His popularity.
Eze 33:31–32

EZEL

• A stone near Saul's residence.

• David and Jonathan meet at.
1Sa 20:19 — And *when* thou hast stayed three days, *then* thou shalt go down quickly, and come to the place where thou didst hide thyself when the business was *in hand,* and shalt remain by the stone Ezel.

EZEM

• Called also Azem.

• A city of Simeon.
Jos 15:29 — Baalah, and Iim, and Azem,
Jos 19:3 — And Hazar-shual, and Balah, and Azem,
1Ch 4:29 — And at Bilhah, and at Ezem, and at Tolad,

EZER

• Called also Ezar, a Horite duke.
Ge 36:21 — And Dishon, and Ezer, and Dishan: these *are* the dukes of the Horites, the children of Seir in the land of Edom.
Ge 36:27 — The children of Ezer *are* these; Bilhan, and Zaavan, and Akan.
Ge 36:30 — Duke Dishon, duke Ezer, duke Dishan: these *are* the dukes *that came* of Hori, among their dukes in the land of Seir.
1Ch 1:38 — And the sons of Seir; Lotan, and Shobal, and Zibeon, and Anah, and Dishon, and Ezar, and Dishan.
1Ch 1:42 — The sons of Ezer; Bilhan, and Zavan, *and* Jakan. The sons of Dishan; Uz, and Aran.

• A son of Ephraim.
1Ch 7:21 — And Zabad his son, and Shuthelah his son, and Ezer, and Elead, whom the men of Gath *that were* born in *that* land slew, because they came down to take away their cattle.

• A priest.
Ne 12:42 — And Maaseiah, and Shemaiah, and Eleazar, and Uzzi, and Jehohanan, and Malchijah, and Elam, and Ezer. And the singers sang loud, with Jezrahiah *their* overseer.

• A man of Judah.
1Ch 4:4 — And Penuel the father of Gedor and Ezer the father of Hushah. These *are* the sons of Hur, the firstborn of Ephratah, the father of Bethlehem.

- **Perhaps identical with the Ezra of 1Ch 4:17.**
  1Ch 4:17 — And the sons of Ezra *were,* Jether, and Mered, and Epher, and Jalon: and she bare Miriam, and Shammai, and Ishbah the father of Eshtemoa.

- **A Gadite warrior.**
  1Ch 12:9 — Ezer the first, Obadiah the second, Eliab the third,

- **A Levite.**
  Ne 3:19 — And next to him repaired Ezer the son of Jeshua, the ruler of Mizpah, another piece over against the going up to the armoury at the turning *of the wall.*

EZION-GABER

- **Last encampment of Israel before coming to the "wilderness of Zin".**
  Nu 33:35–36
  Dt 2:8 — And when we passed by from our brethren the children of Esau, which dwelt in Seir, through the way of the plain from Elath, and from Ezion-gaber, we turned and passed by the way of the wilderness of Moab.

- **Solomon built a navy at.**
  1Ki 9:26 — And king Solomon made a navy of ships in Ezion-geber, which is beside Eloth, on the shore of the Red sea, in the land of Edom.

- **Solomon visits.**
  2Ch 8:17 — Then went Solomon to Ezion-geber, and to Eloth, at the sea side in the land of Edom.

- **Jehoshaphat built a navy at.**
  2Ch 20:36 — And he joined himself with him to make ships to go to Tarshish: and they made the ships in Ezion-gaber.

- **Ships of Jehoshaphat wrecked at.**
  1Ki 22:48 — Jehoshaphat made ships of Tharshish to go to Ophir for gold: but they went not; for the ships were broken at Ezion-geber.

EZRA

- **A famous scribe and priest.**
  Ezr 7:1–6
  Ezr 7:10 — For Ezra had prepared his heart to seek the law of the LORD, and to do *it,* and to teach in Israel statutes and judgments.
  Ezr 7:21 — And I, *even* I Artaxerxes the king, do make a decree to all the treasurers which *are* beyond the river, that whatsoever Ezra the priest, the scribe of the law of the God of heaven, shall require of you, it be done speedily,
  Ne 12:36 — And his brethren, Shemaiah, and Azarael, Milalai, Gilalai, Maai, Nethaneel, and Judah, Hanani, with the musical instruments of David the man of God, and Ezra the scribe before them.

  - **Appoints a fast.**
    Ezr 8:21 — Then I proclaimed a fast there, at the river of Ahava, that we might afflict ourselves before our God, to seek of him a right way for us, and for our little ones, and for all our substance.

  - **Commissioned by Artaxerxes; returns to Jerusalem with a large company of Jews.**
    Ezr 7:8 — And he came to Jerusalem in the fifth month, which *was* in the seventh year of the king.

  - **His charge to the priests.**
    Ezr 8:29 — Watch ye, and keep *them,* until ye weigh *them* before the chief of the priests and the Levites, and chief of the fathers of Israel, at Jerusalem, in the chambers of the house of the Lord.

  - **Exhorts people to put away their heathen wives.**
    Ezr 9:1–10:17

  - **Reads the law.**
    Ne 8:1–18

  - **Reforms corruptions.**
    Ezr 10:1–44; Ne 13:1–31

  - **Dedicates the wall of Jerusalem.**
    Ne 12:27–43

- **A leading priest among the colonists under Zerubbabel.**
  Ne 12:1 — Now these *are* the priests and the Levites that went up with Zerubbabel the son of Shealtiel, and Jeshua: Seraiah, Jeremiah, Ezra,

  - **Probably identical with Azariah in.**
    Ezr 7:1 — Now after these things, in the reign of Artaxerxes king of Persia, Ezra the son of Seraiah, the son of Azariah, the son of Hilkiah,
    Ne 10:2 — Seraiah, Azariah, Jeremiah,

- **A descendant of Judah.**
  1Ch 4:17 — And the sons of Ezra *were,* Jether, and Mered, and Epher, and Jalon: and she bare Miriam, and Shammai, and Ishbah the father of Eshtemoa.

EZRI • An overseer of King David.

1Ch 27:26 — And over them that did the work of the field for tillage of the ground *was* Ezri the son of Chelub:

F

FABLE

1Ti 1:4 — Neither give heed to fables and endless genealogies, which minister questions, rather than godly edifying which is in faith: *so do.*

1Ti 4:7 — But refuse profane and old wives' fables, and exercise thyself *rather* unto godliness.

2Ti 4:4 — And they shall turn away *their* ears from the truth, and shall be turned unto fables.

Tit 1:14 — Not giving heed to Jewish fables, and commandments of men, that turn from the truth.

2Pe 1:16 — For we have not followed cunningly devised fables, when we made known unto you the power and coming of our Lord Jesus Christ, but were eyewitnesses of his majesty.

FACE

- **Character revealed in.**

  Isa 3:9 — The shew of their countenance doth witness against them; and they declare their sin as Sodom, they hide *it* not. Woe unto their soul! for they have rewarded evil unto themselves.

- **Transfigured.**
  - **Of Moses.**

    Ex 34:29–35
  - **Of Jesus.**

    Mt 17:2 — And was transfigured before them: and his face did shine as the sun, and his raiment was white as the light.

    Lk 9:29 — And as he prayed, the fashion of his countenance was altered, and his raiment *was* white *and* glistering.

- **Covering of.**

  Isa 6:2 — Above it stood the seraphims: each one had six wings; with twain he covered his face, and with twain he covered his feet, and with twain he did fly.

- **Disfiguring of, in fasting.**

  Mt 6:16 — Moreover when ye fast, be not, as the hypocrites, of a sad countenance: for they disfigure their faces, that they may appear unto men to fast. Verily I say unto you, They have their reward.

FADS

1Co 7:31 — And they that use this world, as not abusing *it:* for the fashion of this world passeth away.

1Jn 2:17 — And the world passeth away, and the lust thereof: but he that doeth the will of God abideth for ever.

FAILURE

Hag 1:5–6

1Sa 16:7 — But the LORD said unto Samuel, Look not on his countenance, or on the height of his stature; because I have refused him: for *the LORD seeth* not as man seeth; for man looketh on the outward appearance, but the LORD looketh on the heart.

Ps 42:5 — Why art thou cast down, O my soul? and why *art* thou disquieted in me? hope thou in God: for I shall yet praise him *for* the help of his countenance.

Ps 52:7 — Lo, *this is* the man *that* made not God his strength; but trusted in the abundance of his riches, *and* strengthened himself in his wickedness.

Ps 146:3 — Put not your trust in princes, *nor* in the son of man, in whom *there is* no help.

Pr 28:26 — He that trusteth in his own heart is a fool: but whoso walketh wisely, he shall be delivered.

Isa 31:1 — Woe to them that go down to Egypt for help; and stay on horses, and trust in chariots, because *they are* many; and in horsemen, because they are very strong; but they look not unto the Holy One of Israel, neither seek the LORD!

FAINTING

La 2:12 — They say to their mothers, Where *is* corn and wine? when they swooned as the wounded in the streets of the city, when their soul was poured out into their mothers' bosom.

Da 8:27 — And I Daniel fainted, and was sick *certain* days; afterward I rose up, and did the king's business; and I was astonished at the vision, but none understood *it.*

FAIR HAVENS

- **A harbor in Crete.**
- **Paul tarries at, on his way to Rome.**

  Ac 27:8 — And, hardly passing it, came unto a place which is called The fair havens; nigh whereunto was the city *of* Lasea.

FAITH

Ps 9:9–10; 33:18–19; 34:1–8; 78:5–7; 112:7–8; 118:8–9; Isa 57:1–21; Jer 17:7–8; Mt 21:21–22; Mk 9:23–24; 11:23–24; Lk 8:48–50; Jn 11:25–27; Ro 1:16–17; 4:1–5:1; 9:31–33; 10:6–10; 1Co 12:8–9; Gal 3:1–29; 1Ti 6:11–12; 2Ti 4:7–8; Heb 4:1–11; 10:38–11:3; 13:5–6; Jas 2:1–26

2Sa 22:31 — *As for* God, his way *is* perfect; the word of the LORD *is* tried: he *is* a buckler to all them that trust in him.

Ps 2:12 — Kiss the Son, lest he be angry, and ye perish *from* the way, when his wrath is kindled but a little. Blessed *are* all they that put their trust in him.

Ps 5:11 — But let all those that put their trust in thee rejoice: let them ever shout for joy, because thou defendest them: let them also that love thy name be joyful in thee.

Ps 7:1 — O Lord my God, in thee do I put my trust: save me from all them that persecute me, and deliver me:

Ps 18:30 — *As for* God, his way *is* perfect: the word of the LORD is tried: he *is* a buckler to all those that trust in him.

Ps 32:10 — Many sorrows *shall be* to the wicked: but he that trusteth in the LORD, mercy shall compass him about.

Ps 34:22 — The LORD redeemeth the soul of his servants: and none of them that trust in him shall be desolate.

Ps 36:7 — How excellent *is* thy lovingkindness, O God! therefore the children of men put their trust under the shadow of thy wings.

Ps 40:4 — Blessed *is* that man that maketh the LORD his trust, and respecteth not the proud, nor such as turn aside to lies.

Ps 64:10 — The righteous shall be glad in the LORD, and shall trust in him; and all the upright in heart shall glory.

Ps 84:5 — Blessed *is* the man whose strength *is* in thee; in whose heart *are* the ways *of them.*

Ps 84:12 — O LORD of hosts, blessed *is* the man that trusteth in thee.

Ps 112:5 — A good man sheweth favour, and lendeth: he will guide his affairs with discretion.

Ps 125:1 — They that trust in the LORD *shall be* as mount Zion, *which* cannot be removed, *but* abideth for ever.

Ps 147:11 — The LORD taketh pleasure in them that fear him, in those that hope in his mercy.

Pr 3:5 — Trust in the LORD with all thine heart; and lean not unto thine own understanding.

Pr 14:26 — In the fear of the LORD *is* strong confidence: and his children shall have a place of refuge.

Pr 22:19 — That thy trust may be in the LORD, I have made known to thee this day, even to thee.

Pr 28:25 — He that is of a proud heart stirreth up strife: but he that putteth his trust in the LORD shall be made fat.

Pr 29:25 — The fear of man bringeth a snare: but whoso putteth his trust in the LORD shall be safe.

Pr 30:5 — Every word of God *is* pure: he *is* a shield unto them that put their trust in him.

Isa 10:20 — And it shall come to pass in that day, *that* the remnant of Israel, and such as are escaped of the house of Jacob, shall no more again stay upon him that smote them; but shall stay upon the LORD, the Holy One of Israel, in truth.

Isa 14:32 — What shall *one* then answer the messengers of the nation? That the LORD hath founded Zion, and the poor of his people shall trust in it.

Isa 26:3 — Thou wilt keep *him* in perfect peace, *whose* mind *is* stayed *on thee:* because he trusteth in thee.

Isa 30:15 — For thus saith the Lord GOD, the Holy One of Israel; In returning and rest shall ye be saved; in quietness and in confidence shall be your strength: and ye would not.

Jer 39:18 — For I will surely deliver thee, and thou shalt not fall by the sword, but thy life shall be for a prey unto thee: because thou hast put thy trust in me, saith the LORD.

Na 1:7 — The LORD *is* good, a strong hold in the day of trouble; and he knoweth them that trust in him.

Mt 9:22 — But Jesus turned him about, and when he saw her, he said, Daughter, be of good comfort; thy faith hath made thee whole. And the woman was made whole from that hour.

Lk 7:50 — And he said to the woman, Thy faith hath saved thee; go in peace.

Lk 17:5 — And the apostles said unto the Lord, Increase our faith.

Lk 18:8 — I tell you that he will avenge them speedily. Nevertheless when the Son of man cometh, shall he find faith on the earth?

Ac 3:16 — And his name through faith in his name hath made this man strong, whom ye see and know: yea, the faith which is by him hath given him this perfect soundness in the presence of you all.

Ac 13:48 — And when the Gentiles heard this, they were glad, and glorified the word of the Lord: and as many as were ordained to eternal life believed.

Ac 26:18 — To open their eyes, *and* to turn *them* from darkness to light, and *from* the power of Satan unto God, that they may receive forgiveness of sins, and inheritance among them which are sanctified by faith that is in me.

Ro 11:20 — Well; because of unbelief they were broken off, and thou standest by faith. Be not highminded, but fear:

Ro 11:23 — And they also, if they abide not still in unbelief, shall be graffed in: for God is able to graff them in again.

Ro 14:23 — And he that doubteth is damned if he eat, because *he eateth* not of faith: for whatsoever *is* not of faith is sin.

Ro 15:13 — Now the God of hope fill you with all joy and peace in believing, that ye may abound in hope, through the power of the Holy Ghost.

1Co 1:21 — For after that in the wisdom of God the world by wisdom knew not God, it pleased God by the foolishness of preaching to save them that believe.

1Co 2:5 — That your faith should not stand in the wisdom of men, but in the power of God.

2Co 1:24 — Not for that we have dominion over your faith, but are helpers of your joy: for by faith ye stand.

Gal 5:6 — For in Jesus Christ neither circumcision availeth any thing, nor uncircumcision; but faith which worketh by love.

Gal 5:22 — But the fruit of the Spirit is love, joy, peace, longsuffering, gentleness, goodness, faith,

Eph 2:8 — For by grace are ye saved through faith; and that not of yourselves: *it is* the gift of God:

Eph 6:16 — Above all, taking the shield of faith, wherewith ye shall be able to quench all the fiery darts of the wicked.

Col 1:23 — If ye continue in the faith grounded and settled, and *be* not moved away from the hope of the gospel, which ye have heard, *and* which was preached to every creature which is under heaven; whereof I Paul am made a minister;

Col 2:12 — Buried with him in baptism, wherein also ye are risen with *him* through the faith of the operation of God, who hath raised him from the dead.

1Th 2:13 — For this cause also thank we God without ceasing, because, when ye received the word of God which ye heard of us, ye received *it* not *as* the word of men, but as it is in truth, the word of God, which effectually worketh also in you that believe.

1Th 5:8 — But let us, who are of the day, be sober, putting on the breastplate of faith and love; and for an helmet, the hope of salvation.

2Th 2:13 — But we are bound to give thanks alway to God for you, brethren beloved of the Lord, because God hath from the beginning chosen you to salvation through sanctification of the Spirit and belief of the truth:

1Ti 1:5 — Now the end of the commandment is charity out of a pure heart, and *of* a good conscience, and *of* faith unfeigned:

1Ti 1:19 — Holding faith, and a good conscience; which some having put away concerning faith have made shipwreck:

1Ti 2:15 — Notwithstanding she shall be saved in childbearing, if they continue in faith and charity and holiness with sobriety.

1Ti 4:10 — For therefore we both labour and suffer reproach, because we trust in the living God, who is the Saviour of all men, specially of those that believe.

1Ti 6:17 — Charge them that are rich in this world, that they be not highminded, nor trust in uncertain riches, but in the living God, who giveth us richly all things to enjoy;

Heb 6:1 — Therefore leaving the principles of the doctrine of Christ, let us go on unto perfection; not laying again the foundation of repentance from dead works, and of faith toward God,

Heb 6:7 — For the earth which drinketh in the rain that cometh oft upon it, and bringeth forth herbs meet for them by whom it is dressed, receiveth blessing from God:

Heb 6:12 — That ye be not slothful, but followers of them who through faith and patience inherit the promises.

Heb 6:18 — That by two immutable things, in which *it was* impossible for God to lie, we might have a strong consolation, who have fled for refuge to lay hold upon the hope set before us:

Heb 10:35 — Cast not away therefore your confidence, which hath great recompence of reward.

Heb 11:6 — But without faith *it is* impossible to please *him:* for he that cometh to God must believe that he is, and *that* he is a rewarder of them that diligently seek him.

Jas 1:6 — But let him ask in faith, nothing wavering. For he that wavereth is like a wave of the sea driven with the wind and tossed.

1Pe 1:5 — Who are kept by the power of God through faith unto salvation ready to be revealed in the last time.

1Pe 1:7 — That the trial of your faith, being much more precious than of gold that perisheth, though it be tried with fire, might be found unto praise and honour and glory at the appearing of Jesus Christ:

1Pe 1:9 — Receiving the end of your faith, *even* the salvation of *your* souls.

1Pe 1:21 — Who by him do believe in God, that raised him up from the dead, and gave him glory; that your faith and hope might be in God.

1Pe 3:5 — For after this manner in the old time the holy women also, who trusted in God, adorned themselves, being in subjection unto their own husbands:

1Jn 3:21 — Beloved, if our heart condemn us not, *then* have we confidence toward God.

1Jn 5:4 — For whatsoever is born of God overcometh the world: and this is the victory that overcometh the world, *even* our faith.

Rev 22:7 — Behold, I come quickly: blessed is he that keepeth the sayings of the prophecy of this book.

➜See: Faith in Christ

• Enjoined.

Dt 1:21–31; 7:17–21; 31:6–8; Jos 1:5–9; Jgs 6:14–16; 2Ki 19:6–7; 2Ch 32:7–8; Ps 37:39–40; Pr 3:5–6, 24–26; Isa 35:3–4; 41:13–14; 43:1–2; Hab 2:3–4; Zep 3:16–17; Mt 6:25–34; 17:18–20; Mk 11:22–24; Lk 12:22–32

Ex 14:13 — And Moses said unto the people, Fear ye not, stand still, and see the salvation of the LORD, which he will shew to you to day: for the Egyptians whom ye have seen to day, ye shall see them again no more for ever.

Nu 21:34 — And the LORD said unto Moses, Fear him not: for I have delivered him into thy hand, and all his people, and his land; and thou shalt do to him as thou didst unto Sihon king of the Amorites, which dwelt at Heshbon.

Dt 3:2 — And the LORD said unto me, Fear him not: for I will deliver him, and all his people, and his land, into thy hand; and thou shalt do unto him as thou didst unto Sihon king of the Amorites, which dwelt at Heshbon.

Dt 3:22 — Ye shall not fear them: for the LORD your God he shall fight for you.

Dt 20:1 — When thou goest out to battle against thine enemies, and seest horses, and chariots, *and* a people more than thou, be not afraid of them: for the LORD thy God *is* with thee, which brought thee up out of the land of Egypt.

Dt 31:23 — And he gave Joshua the son of Nun a charge, and said, Be strong and of a good courage: for thou shalt bring the children of Israel into the land which I sware unto them: and I will be with thee.

Jos 10:25 — And Joshua said unto them, Fear not, nor be dismayed, be strong and of good courage: for thus shall the LORD do to all your enemies against whom ye fight.

2Ch 15:7 — Be ye strong therefore, and let not your hands be weak: for your work shall be rewarded.

2Ch 16:9 — For the eyes of the LORD run to and fro throughout the whole earth, to shew himself strong in the behalf of *them* whose heart *is* perfect toward him. Herein thou hast done foolishly: therefore from henceforth thou shalt have wars.

2Ch 20:15 — And he said, Hearken ye, all Judah, and ye inhabitants of Jerusalem, and thou king Jehoshaphat, Thus saith the LORD unto you, Be not afraid nor dismayed by reason of this great multitude; for the battle *is* not yours, but God's.

2Ch 20:17 — Ye shall not *need* to fight in this *battle:* set yourselves, stand ye *still,* and see the salvation of the LORD with you, O Judah and Jerusalem: fear not, nor be dismayed; to morrow go out against them: for the LORD *will be* with you.

2Ch 20:20 — And they rose early in the morning, and went forth into the wilderness of Tekoa: and as they went forth, Jehoshaphat stood and said, Hear me, O Judah, and ye inhabitants of Jerusalem; Believe in the LORD your God, so shall ye be established; believe his prophets, so shall ye prosper.

Ne 4:14 — And I looked, and rose up, and said unto the nobles, and to the rulers, and to the rest of the people, Be not ye afraid of them: remember the Lord, *which is* great and terrible, and fight for your brethren, your sons, and your daughters, your wives, and your houses.

Job 35:14 — Although thou sayest thou shalt not see him, *yet* judgment *is* before him; therefore trust thou in him.

Ps 4:5 — Offer the sacrifices of righteousness, and put your trust in the LORD.

Ps 27:14 — Wait on the LORD: be of good courage, and he shall strengthen thine heart: wait, I say, on the LORD.

Ps 31:19 — *Oh* how great *is* thy goodness, which thou hast laid up for them that fear thee; *which* thou hast wrought for them that trust in thee before the sons of men!

Ps 31:24 — Be of good courage, and he shall strengthen your heart, all ye that hope in the LORD.

Ps 37:3 — Trust in the LORD, and do good; *so* shalt thou dwell in the land, and verily thou shalt be fed.

Ps 37:5 — Commit thy way unto the LORD; trust also in him; and he shall bring *it* to pass.

Ps 37:7 — Rest in the LORD, and wait patiently for him: fret not thyself because of him who prospereth in his way, because of the man who bringeth wicked devices to pass.

Ps 55:22 — Cast thy burden upon the LORD, and he shall sustain thee: he shall never suffer the righteous to be moved.

Ps 62:8 — Trust in him at all times; *ye* people, pour out your heart before him: God *is* a refuge for us. Selah.

Ps 115:9 — O Israel, trust thou in the LORD: he *is* their help and their shield.

Ps 115:11 — Ye that fear the LORD, trust in the LORD: he *is* their help and their shield.

Ps 130:7 — Let Israel hope in the LORD: for with the LORD *there is* mercy, and with him *is* plenteous redemption.

Pr 16:3 — Commit thy works unto the LORD, and thy thoughts shall be established.

Isa 26:4 — Trust ye in the LORD for ever: for in the LORD JEHOVAH *is* everlasting strength:

Isa 26:20 — Come, my people, enter thou into thy chambers, and shut thy doors about thee: hide thyself as it were for a little moment, until the indignation be overpast.

Isa 37:6 — And Isaiah said unto them, Thus shall ye say unto your master, Thus saith the LORD, Be not afraid of the words that thou hast heard, wherewith the servants of the king of Assyria have blasphemed me.

Isa 41:10 — Fear thou not; for I *am* with thee: be not dismayed; for I *am* thy God: I will strengthen thee; yea, I will help thee; yea, I will uphold thee with the right hand of my righteousness.

Isa 43:5 — Fear not: for I *am* with thee: I will bring thy seed from the east, and gather thee from the west;

Isa 43:10 — Ye *are* my witnesses, saith the LORD, and my servant whom I have chosen: that ye may know and believe me, and understand that I *am* he: before me there was no God formed, neither shall there be after me.

Isa 44:2 — Thus saith the LORD that made thee, and formed thee from the womb, *which* will help thee; Fear not, O Jacob, my servant; and thou, Jesurun, whom I have chosen.

Isa 44:8 — Fear ye not, neither be afraid: have not I told thee from that time, and have declared *it?* ye *are* even my witnesses. Is there a God beside me? yea, *there is* no God; I know not *any.*

Isa 50:10 — Who *is* among you that feareth the LORD, that obeyeth the voice of his servant, that walketh *in* darkness, and hath no light? let him trust in the name of the LORD, and stay upon his God.

Jer 42:11 — Be not afraid of the king of Babylon, of whom ye are afraid; be not afraid of him, saith the LORD: for I *am* with you to save you, and to deliver you from his hand.

Jer 49:11 — Leave thy fatherless children, I will preserve *them* alive; and let thy widows trust in me.

Joel 2:21 — Fear not, O land; be glad and rejoice: for the LORD will do great things.

Joel 3:16 — The LORD also shall roar out of Zion, and utter his voice from Jerusalem; and the heavens and the earth shall shake: but the LORD *will be* the hope of his people, and the strength of the children of Israel.

Zec 8:9 — Thus saith the LORD of hosts; Let your hands be strong, ye that hear in these days these words by the mouth of the prophets, which *were* in the day *that* the foundation of the house of the LORD of hosts was laid, that the temple might be built.

Zec 9:12 — Turn you to the strong hold, ye prisoners of hope: even to day do I declare *that* I will render double unto thee;

Mk 1:15 — And saying, <u>The time is fulfilled, and the kingdom of God is at hand: repent ye, and believe the gospel.</u>

Lk 17:6 — And the Lord said, <u>If ye had faith as a grain of mustard seed, ye might say unto this sycamine tree, Be thou plucked up by the root, and be thou planted in the sea; and it should obey you.</u>

- **Exemplified.**

Ex 15:1–19; Nu 14:8–9; 1Sa 17:36–37, 45–47; 2Sa 22:2–5; 2Ch 13:10–11; 32:7–8; Ne 1:8–10; Job 4:7–21; 5:8–9; 13:15–16; 19:25–27; Ps 3:5–6; 6:8–9; 9:3–4; 16:1–2; 18:1–3, 28–29; 20:5–7; 22:4–5; 23:1–6; 25:1–2; 26:12–27:1; 27:5–6; 31:3–6, 14–15; 33:20–22; 40:3–4; 42:5–6; 46:1–3; 47:3–4; 55:16–17; 56:3–4, 8–9; 57:1–3; 59:9–10; 60:9–10; 61:6–7; 62:5–7; 63:6–7; 69:35–36; 70:5–71:1, 71:5–7, 20–21; 73:23–24; 77:10–12; 91:1–2, 9–10; 94:14–15, 17–18; 108:10–13; 115:12–14; 118:6–7; 119:42–43; 130:5–6; 138:7–8; 140:6–7; 143:8–9; Isa 50:7–9; La 3:24–32; Da 3:16–17; Jnh 2:2–9; Mic 7:7–9; Hab 3:17–19; Ac 24:14–15; Ro

8:38–39; 2Co 4:8–9, 16–18; Php 1:19–21; 2Ti 2:11–13; Heb 11:4–5, 7–11, 13–14, 16–39

Ge 6:22 — Thus did Noah; according to all that God commanded him, so did he.

Ge 16:13 — And she called the name of the LORD that spake unto her, Thou God seest me: for she said, Have I also here looked after him that seeth me?

Ge 24:7 — The LORD God of heaven, which took me from my father's house, and from the land of my kindred, and which spake unto me, and that sware unto me, saying, Unto thy seed will I give this land; he shall send his angel before thee, and thou shalt take a wife unto my son from thence.

Ge 24:40 — And he said unto me, The LORD, before whom I walk, will send his angel with thee, and prosper thy way; and thou shalt take a wife for my son of my kindred, and of my father's house:

Ge 48:21 — And Israel said unto Joseph, Behold, I die: but God shall be with you, and bring you again unto the land of your fathers.

Ge 50:20 — But as for you, ye thought evil against me; *but* God meant it unto good, to bring to pass, as *it is* this day, to save much people alive.

Ge 50:24 — And Joseph said unto his brethren, I die: and God will surely visit you, and bring you out of this land unto the land which he sware to Abraham, to Isaac, and to Jacob.

Ex 18:11 — Now I know that the LORD *is* greater than all gods: for in the thing wherein they dealt proudly *he was* above them.

Nu 10:29 — And Moses said unto Hobab, the son of Raguel the Midianite, Moses' father in law, We are journeying unto the place of which the LORD said, I will give it you: come thou with us, and we will do thee good: for the LORD hath spoken good concerning Israel.

Jos 14:12 — Now therefore give me this mountain, whereof the LORD spake in that day; for thou heardest in that day how the Anakims *were* there, and *that* the cities *were* great *and* fenced: if so be the LORD *will be* with me, then I shall be able to drive them out, as the LORD said.

1Sa 14:6 — And Jonathan said to the young man that bare his armour, Come, and let us go over unto the garrison of these uncircumcised: it may be that the LORD will work for us: for *there is* no restraint to the LORD to save by many or by few.

2Sa 7:28 — And now, O Lord GOD, thou *art* that God, and thy words be true, and thou hast promised this goodness unto thy servant:

2Sa 23:5 — Although my house *be* not so with God; yet he hath made with me an everlasting covenant, ordered in all *things,* and sure: for *this is* all my salvation, and all *my* desire, although he make *it* not to grow.

2Ki 18:5 — He trusted in the LORD God of Israel; so that after him was none like him among all the kings of Judah, nor *any* that were before him.

1Ch 28:20 — And David said to Solomon his son, Be strong and of good courage, and do *it:* fear not, nor be dismayed: for the LORD God, *even* my God, *will be* with thee; he will not fail thee, nor forsake thee, until thou hast finished all the work for the service of the house of the LORD.

2Ch 14:11 — And Asa cried unto the LORD his God, and said, LORD, *it is* nothing with thee to help, whether with many, or with them that have no power: help us, O LORD our God; for we rest on thee, and in thy name we go against this multitude. O LORD, thou *art* our God; let not man prevail against thee.

2Ch 20:12 — O our God, wilt thou not judge them? for we have no might against this great company that cometh against us; neither know we what to do: but our eyes *are* upon thee.

Ezr 8:22 — For I was ashamed to require of the king a band of soldiers and horsemen to help us against the enemy in the way: because we had spoken unto the king, saying, The hand of our God *is* upon all them for good that seek him; but his power and his wrath *is* against all them that forsake him.

Ne 2:20 — Then answered I them, and said unto them, The God of heaven, he will prosper us; therefore we his servants will arise and build: but ye have no portion, nor right, nor memorial, in Jerusalem.

Job 10:12 — Thou hast granted me life and favour, and thy visitation hath preserved my spirit.

Job 14:15 — Thou shalt call, and I will answer thee: thou wilt have a desire to the work of thine hands.

Job 16:19 — Also now, behold, my witness *is* in heaven, and my record *is* on high.

Job 23:6 — Will he plead against me with *his* great power? No; but he would put *strength* in me.

Job 42:2 — I know that thou canst do every *thing,* and *that* no thought can be withholden from thee.

Ps 3:3 — But thou, O LORD, *art* a shield for me; my glory, and the lifter up of mine head.

Ps 4:3 — But know that the LORD hath set apart him that is godly for himself: the LORD will hear when I call unto him.

Ps 4:8 — I will both lay me down in peace, and sleep: for thou, LORD, only makest me dwell in safety.

Ps 7:1 — O Lord my God, in thee do I put my trust: save me from all them that persecute me, and deliver me:

Ps 7:10 — My defence *is* of God, which saveth the upright in heart.

Ps 11:1 — In the LORD put I my trust: How say ye to my soul, Flee *as* a bird to your mountain?

Ps 13:5 — But I have trusted in thy mercy; my heart shall rejoice in thy salvation.

Ps 16:5 — The LORD *is* the portion of mine inheritance and of my cup: thou maintainest my lot.

Ps 16:8 — I have set the LORD always before me: because *he is* at my right hand, I shall not be moved.

Ps 16:11 — Thou wilt shew me the path of life: in thy presence *is* fulness of joy; at thy right hand *there are* pleasures for evermore.

Ps 17:6 — I have called upon thee, for thou wilt hear me, O God: incline thine ear unto me, *and hear* my speech.

Ps 18:18 — They prevented me in the day of my calamity: but the LORD was my stay.

Ps 21:7 — For the king trusteth in the LORD, and through the mercy of the most High he shall not be moved.
Ps 25:5 — Lead me in thy truth, and teach me: for thou *art* the God of my salvation; on thee do I wait all the day.
Ps 25:15 — Mine eyes *are* ever toward the LORD; for he shall pluck my feet out of the net.
Ps 25:20 — O keep my soul, and deliver me: let me not be ashamed; for I put my trust in thee.
Ps 26:1 — Judge me, O LORD; for I have walked in mine integrity: I have trusted also in the LORD; *therefore* I shall not slide.
Ps 27:10 — When my father and my mother forsake me, then the LORD will take me up.
Ps 28:7 — The LORD *is* my strength and my shield; my heart trusted in him, and I am helped: therefore my heart greatly rejoiceth; and with my song will I praise him.
Ps 31:1 — In thee, O LORD, do I put my trust; let me never be ashamed: deliver me in thy righteousness.
Ps 32:7 — Thou *art* my hiding place; thou shalt preserve me from trouble; thou shalt compass me about with songs of deliverance. Selah.
Ps 35:10 — All my bones shall say, LORD, who *is* like unto thee, which deliverest the poor from him that is too strong for him, yea, the poor and the needy from him that spoileth him?
Ps 38:9 — Lord, all my desire *is* before thee; and my groaning is not hid from thee.
Ps 38:15 — For in thee, O LORD, do I hope: thou wilt hear, O Lord my God.
Ps 39:7 — And now, Lord, what wait I for? my hope *is* in thee.
Ps 40:17 — But I *am* poor and needy; *yet* the Lord thinketh upon me: thou *art* my help and my deliverer; make no tarrying, O my God.
Ps 41:12 — And as for me, thou upholdest me in mine integrity, and settest me before thy face for ever.
Ps 42:8 — *Yet* the LORD will command his lovingkindness in the daytime, and in the night his song *shall be* with me, *and* my prayer unto the God of my life.
Ps 43:5 — Why art thou cast down, O my soul? and why art thou disquieted within me? hope in God: for I shall yet praise him, *who is* the health of my countenance, and my God.
Ps 44:5 — Through thee will we push down our enemies: through thy name will we tread them under that rise up against us.
Ps 44:8 — In God we boast all the day long, and praise thy name for ever. Selah.
Ps 46:5 — God *is* in the midst of her; she shall not be moved: God shall help her, *and that* right early.
Ps 46:7 — The LORD of hosts *is* with us; the God of Jacob *is* our refuge. Selah.
Ps 48:8 — As we have heard, so have we seen in the city of the LORD of hosts, in the city of our God: God will establish it for ever. Selah.
Ps 48:14 — For this God *is* our God for ever and ever: he will be our guide *even* unto death.
Ps 52:8 — But I *am* like a green olive tree in the house of God: I trust in the mercy of God for ever and ever.
Ps 54:4 — Behold, God *is* mine helper: the Lord *is* with them that uphold my soul.
Ps 55:23 — But thou, O God, shalt bring them down into the pit of destruction: bloody and deceitful men shall not live out half their days; but I will trust in thee.
Ps 56:11 — In God have I put my trust: I will not be afraid what man can do unto me.
Ps 59:17 — Unto thee, O my strength, will I sing: for God *is* my defence, *and* the God of my mercy.
Ps 60:12 — Through God we shall do valiantly: for he *it is that* shall tread down our enemies.
Ps 61:2 — From the end of the earth will I cry unto thee, when my heart is overwhelmed: lead me to the rock *that* is higher than I.
Ps 61:4 — I will abide in thy tabernacle for ever: I will trust in the covert of thy wings. Selah.
Ps 62:1 — Truly my soul waiteth upon God: from him *cometh* my salvation.
Ps 66:9 — Which holdeth our soul in life, and suffereth not our feet to be moved.
Ps 67:6 — *Then* shall the earth yield her increase; *and* God, *even* our own God, shall bless us.
Ps 69:19 — Thou hast known my reproach, and my shame, and my dishonour: mine adversaries *are* all before thee.
Ps 71:3 — Be thou my strong habitation, whereunto I may continually resort: thou hast given commandment to save me; for thou *art* my rock and my fortress.
Ps 71:14 — But I will hope continually, and will yet praise thee more and more.
Ps 71:16 — I will go in the strength of the Lord GOD: I will make mention of thy righteousness, *even* of thine only.
Ps 73:26 — My flesh and my heart faileth: *but* God *is* the strength of my heart, and my portion for ever.
Ps 73:28 — But *it is* good for me to draw near to God: I have put my trust in the Lord GOD, that I may declare all thy works.
Ps 74:12 — For God *is* my King of old, working salvation in the midst of the earth.
Ps 86:2 — Preserve my soul; for I *am* holy: O thou my God, save thy servant that trusteth in thee.
Ps 86:7 — In the day of my trouble I will call upon thee: for thou wilt answer me.
Ps 89:18 — For the LORD *is* our defence; and the Holy One of Israel *is* our king.
Ps 89:26 — He shall cry unto me, Thou *art* my father, my God, and the rock of my salvation.
Ps 90:1 — LORD, thou hast been our dwelling place in all generations.
Ps 92:10 — But my horn shalt thou exalt like *the horn of* an unicorn: I shall be anointed with fresh oil.
Ps 92:15 — To shew that the LORD *is* upright: *he is* my rock, and *there is* no unrighteousness in him.
Ps 94:22 — But the LORD is my defence; and my God *is* the rock of my refuge.
Ps 102:13 — Thou shalt arise, *and* have mercy upon Zion: for the time to favour her, yea, the set time, is come.

Ps 116:7 — Return unto thy rest, O my soul; for the LORD hath dealt bountifully with thee.

Ps 118:10 — All nations compassed me about: but in the name of the LORD will I destroy them.

Ps 118:14 — The LORD *is* my strength and song, and is become my salvation.

Ps 118:17 — I shall not die, but live, and declare the works of the LORD.

Ps 119:57 — *Thou art* my portion, O LORD: I have said that I would keep thy words.

Ps 119:74 — They that fear thee will be glad when they see me; because I have hoped in thy word.

Ps 119:81 — My soul fainteth for thy salvation: *but* I hope in thy word.

Ps 119:114 — Thou *art* my hiding place and my shield: I hope in thy word.

Ps 119:151 — Thou *art* near, O LORD; and all thy commandments *are* truth.

Ps 119:166 — LORD, I have hoped for thy salvation, and done thy commandments.

Ps 121:2 — My help *cometh* from the LORD, which made heaven and earth.

Ps 124:8 — Our help *is* in the name of the LORD, who made heaven and earth.

Ps 140:12 — I know that the LORD will maintain the cause of the afflicted, *and* the right of the poor.

Ps 141:8 — But mine eyes *are* unto thee, O GOD the Lord: in thee is my trust; leave not my soul destitute.

Ps 142:3 — When my spirit was overwhelmed within me, then thou knewest my path. In the way wherein I walked have they privily laid a snare for me.

Ps 142:5 — I cried unto thee, O LORD: I said, Thou *art* my refuge *and* my portion in the land of the living.

Ps 144:2 — My goodness, and my fortress; my high tower, and my deliverer; my shield, and *he* in whom I trust; who subdueth my people under me.

Ps 144:10 — *It is he* that giveth salvation unto kings: who delivereth David his servant from the hurtful sword.

Ecc 11:1 — Cast thy bread upon the waters: for thou shalt find it after many days.

Isa 8:10 — Take counsel together, and it shall come to nought; speak the word, and it shall not stand: for God *is* with us.

Isa 8:17 — And I will wait upon the LORD, that hideth his face from the house of Jacob, and I will look for him.

Isa 12:2 — Behold, God *is* my salvation; I will trust, and not be afraid: for the LORD JEHOVAH *is* my strength and *my* song; he also is become my salvation.

Isa 25:9 — And it shall be said in that day, Lo, this *is* our God; we have waited for him, and he will save us: this *is* the LORD; we have waited for him, we will be glad and rejoice in his salvation.

Isa 26:1 — In that day shall this song be sung in the land of Judah; We have a strong city; salvation will *God* appoint *for* walls and bulwarks.

Isa 26:8 — Yea, in the way of thy judgments, O LORD, have we waited for thee; the desire of *our* soul *is* to thy name, and to the remembrance of thee.

Isa 33:2 — O LORD, be gracious unto us; we have waited for thee: be thou their arm every morning, our salvation also in the time of trouble.

Isa 33:22 — For the LORD *is* our judge, the LORD *is* our lawgiver, the LORD *is* our king; he will save us.

Isa 38:16 — O Lord, by these *things men* live, and in all these *things is* the life of my spirit: so wilt thou recover me, and make me to live.

Isa 63:16 — Doubtless thou *art* our father, though Abraham be ignorant of us, and Israel acknowledge us not: thou, O LORD, *art* our father, our redeemer; thy name *is* from everlasting.

Isa 64:8 — But now, O LORD, thou *art* our father; we *are* the clay, and thou our potter; and we all *are* the work of thy hand.

Jer 10:23 — O LORD, I know that the way of man *is* not in himself: *it is* not in man that walketh to direct his steps.

Jer 14:9 — Why shouldest thou be as a man astonied, as a mighty man *that* cannot save? yet thou, O LORD, *art* in the midst of us, and we are called by thy name; leave us not.

Jer 14:22 — Are there *any* among the vanities of the Gentiles that can cause rain? or can the heavens give showers? *art* not thou he, O LORD our God? therefore we will wait upon thee: for thou hast made all these *things.*

Jer 16:19 — O LORD, my strength, and my fortress, and my refuge in the day of affliction, the Gentiles shall come unto thee from the ends of the earth, and shall say, Surely our fathers have inherited lies, vanity, and *things* wherein *there is* no profit.

Jer 17:12 — A glorious high throne from the beginning *is* the place of our sanctuary.

Jer 17:17 — Be not a terror unto me: thou *art* my hope in the day of evil.

Jer 20:11 — But the LORD *is* with me as a mighty terrible one: therefore my persecutors shall stumble, and they shall not prevail: they shall be greatly ashamed; for they shall not prosper: *their* everlasting confusion shall never be forgotten.

Da 6:16 — Then the king commanded, and they brought Daniel, and cast *him* into the den of lions. *Now* the king spake and said unto Daniel, Thy God whom thou servest continually, he will deliver thee.

Mic 7:20 — Thou wilt perform the truth to Jacob, *and* the mercy to Abraham, which thou hast sworn unto our fathers from the days of old.

Hab 1:12 — *Art* thou not from everlasting, O LORD my God, mine Holy One? We shall not die. O LORD, thou hast ordained them for judgment; and, O mighty God, thou hast established them for correction.

Zep 3:12 — I will also leave in the midst of thee an afflicted and poor people, and they shall trust in the name of the LORD.

Lk 1:38 — And Mary said, Behold the handmaid of the Lord; be it unto me according to thy word. And the angel departed from her.

Lk 7:50 — And he said to the woman, <u>Thy faith hath saved thee; go in peace.</u>

Jn 3:33 — He that hath received his testimony hath set to his seal that God is true.

Ac 16:34 — And when he had brought them into his house, he set meat before them, and rejoiced, believing in God with all his house.

Ac 27:25 — Wherefore, sirs, be of good cheer: for I believe God, that it shall be even as it was told me.

Ro 8:18 — For I reckon that the sufferings of this present time *are* not worthy *to be compared* with the glory which shall be revealed in us.

Ro 8:28 — And we know that all things work together for good to them that love God, to them who are the called according to *his* purpose.

Ro 15:29 — And I am sure that, when I come unto you, I shall come in the fulness of the blessing of the gospel of Christ.

1Co 9:26 — I therefore so run, not as uncertainly; so fight I, not as one that beateth the air:

2Co 1:10 — Who delivered us from so great a death, and doth deliver: in whom we trust that he will yet deliver *us;*

2Co 4:13 — We having the same spirit of faith, according as it is written, I believed, and therefore have I spoken; we also believe, and therefore speak;

2Co 5:7 — (For we walk by faith, not by sight:)

Gal 5:5 — For we through the Spirit wait for the hope of righteousness by faith.

1Ti 4:10 — For therefore we both labour and suffer reproach, because we trust in the living God, who is the Saviour of all men, specially of those that believe.

2Ti 1:12 — For the which cause I also suffer these things: nevertheless I am not ashamed: for I know whom I have believed, and am persuaded that he is able to keep that which I have committed unto him against that day.

Heb 10:34 — For ye had compassion of me in my bonds, and took joyfully the spoiling of your goods, knowing in yourselves that ye have in heaven a better and an enduring substance.

Heb 13:14 — For here have we no continuing city, but we seek one to come.

2Pe 3:13 — Nevertheless we, according to his promise, look for new heavens and a new earth, wherein dwelleth righteousness.

1Jn 4:16 — And we have known and believed the love that God hath to us. God is love; and he that dwelleth in love dwelleth in God, and God in him.

- **Instances of.**
  - **Noah, in building the ark.**
    Ge 6:14–22; Heb 11:7
  - **Abraham.**
    - **In forsaking the land of his nativity at the command of God.**
      Ge 12:1–4
    - **Believing the promise of many descendants.**
      Ge 12:7; 15:4–8
    - **In the offering up of Isaac.**
      Ge 22:1–10; Ro 4:18–21; Heb 11:8–19
  - **Jacob, in blessing Joseph's sons.**
    Heb 11:21
  - **Joseph, concerning God's providence in his being sold into Egypt, and the final deliverance of Israel.**
    Ge 50:20; Heb 11:22
  - **Jochebed, in caring for Moses.**
    Ex 2:2; Heb 11:23
  - **Pharaoh's servants, who obeyed the Lord.**
    Ex 9:20
  - **Moses.**
    - **In espousing the cause of his people.**
      Heb 11:24–28
    - **At the death of Korah.**
      Nu 16:28–29
  - **The Israelites.**
    - **When Aaron declared the mission of himself and Moses.**
      Ex 4:31
    - **In the battle with the Canaanites.**
      1Ch 5:20
    - **In other conquests.**
      2Ch 13:8–18
    - **See: Moses; miracles of**
  - **Caleb, in advising to take the land of promise.**
    Nu 13:30; 14:6–9
  - **Rahab, in hospitality to the spies.**
    Jos 2:9, 11; Heb 11:31
  - **The spies, sent to reconnoiter Jericho.**
    Jos 2:24
  - **Conquest of Jericho.**
    Jos 6:1–27
  - **Manoah's wife.**
    Jgs 13:23
  - **Hannah.**
    1Sa 1:1–28
  - **Jonathan, in smiting the Philistines.**
    1Sa 14:6
  - **David.**
    - **In smiting Goliath.**
      1Sa 17:37, 46–47
    - **In choosing to fall into the hands of the Almighty in his punishment for numbering Israel.**
      2Sa 24:14
    - **In believing God's promise, that his kingdom would be a perpetual kingdom.**
      Ac 2:30
  - **Elijah, in his controversy with the priests of Baal.**
    1Ki 18:32–38
  - **Widow of Zarephath in feeding Elijah.**
    1Ki 17:13–15
  - **Amaziah in obeying God and going to battle alone.**
    2Ch 25:7–10
  - **Hezekiah.**
    2Ki 18:5; 19:1–20:11

- **Daniel, in the lions' den.**
  Da 6:1–28
- **The three Hebrews, who refused to worship Nebuchadnezzar's idol.**
  Da 3:13–27
- **Ninevites, in obeying Jonah.**
  Jnh 3:5
- **Ezra, in making the journey from Babylon to Jerusalem without a military escort.**
  Ezr 8:22
- **Joseph, in obeying the vision about Mary and to flee into Egypt.**
  Mt 1:18–24; 2:13–14
- **Abel.**
  Heb 11:4
- **Eliphaz, in the overruling providence of God, that afflictions are for the good of the righteous.**
  Job 5:6–27
- **Mordecai, in the deliverance of the Jews.**
  Est 4:14
- **Simeon, when he saw Jesus in the temple.**
  Lk 2:25–35
- **Conquests by.**
  Heb 11:32–34

See: Faith, Trial of
See: Faith in Christ; instances of

FAITH in Christ

Mt 7:24–25; 11:28–30; Lk 6:46–49; Jn 3:14–16; 11:25–26; 14:11–12; Ro 3:22–28; Gal 3:1–29; Eph 1:12–14; 1Pe 2:6–7; 1Jn 5:4–5, 13–14

Isa 28:16 — Therefore thus saith the Lord GOD, Behold, I lay in Zion for a foundation a stone, a tried stone, a precious corner *stone,* a sure foundation: he that believeth shall not make haste.

Mt 8:2 — And, behold, there came a leper and worshipped him, saying, Lord, if thou wilt, thou canst make me clean.

Mt 8:13 — And Jesus said unto the centurion, Go thy way; and as thou hast believed, so be it done unto thee. And his servant was healed in the selfsame hour.

Mt 9:22 — But Jesus turned him about, and when he saw her, he said, Daughter, be of good comfort; thy faith hath made thee whole. And the woman was made whole from that hour.

Mt 9:29 — Then touched he their eyes, saying, According to your faith be it unto you.

Mt 11:6 — And blessed is *he,* whosoever shall not be offended in me.

Mt 14:27 — But straightway Jesus spake unto them, saying, Be of good cheer; it is I; be not afraid.

Mt 15:28 — Then Jesus answered and said unto her, O woman, great *is* thy faith: be it unto thee even as thou wilt. And her daughter was made whole from that very hour.

Mt 17:7 — And Jesus came and touched them, and said, Arise, and be not afraid.

Mk 5:36 — As soon as Jesus heard the word that was spoken, he saith unto the ruler of the synagogue, Be not afraid, only believe.

Mk 9:23 — Jesus said unto him, If thou canst believe, all things *are* possible to him that believeth.

Mk 16:16 — He that believeth and is baptized shall be saved; but he that believeth not shall be damned.

Lk 7:9 — When Jesus heard these things, he marvelled at him, and turned him about, and said unto the people that followed him, I say unto you, I have not found so great faith, no, not in Israel.

Lk 7:50 — And he said to the woman, Thy faith hath saved thee; go in peace.

Lk 8:50 — But when Jesus heard *it,* he answered him, saying, Fear not: believe only, and she shall be made whole.

Lk 17:6 — And the Lord said, If ye had faith as a grain of mustard seed, ye might say unto this sycamine tree, Be thou plucked up by the root, and be thou planted in the sea; and it should obey you.

Lk 18:42 — And Jesus said unto him, Receive thy sight: thy faith hath saved thee.

Jn 1:12 — But as many as received him, to them gave he power to become the sons of God, *even* to them that believe on his name:

Jn 3:18 — He that believeth on him is not condemned: but he that believeth not is condemned already, because he hath not believed in the name of the only begotten Son of God.

Jn 3:36 — He that believeth on the Son hath everlasting life: and he that believeth not the Son shall not see life; but the wrath of God abideth on him.

Jn 5:24 — Verily, verily, I say unto you, He that heareth my word, and believeth on him that sent me, hath everlasting life, and shall not come into condemnation; but is passed from death unto life.

Jn 6:20 — But he saith unto them, It is I; be not afraid.

Jn 6:29 — Jesus answered and said unto them, This is the work of God, that ye believe on him whom he hath sent.

Jn 6:35 — And Jesus said unto them, I am the bread of life: he that cometh to me shall never hunger; and he that believeth on me shall never thirst.

Jn 6:45 — It is written in the prophets, And they shall be all taught of God. Every man therefore that hath heard, and hath learned of the Father, cometh unto me.

Jn 6:47 — Verily, verily, I say unto you, He that believeth on me hath everlasting life.

Jn 7:38 — He that believeth on me, as the scripture hath said, out of his belly shall flow rivers of living water.

Jn 9:35 — Jesus heard that they had cast him out; and when he had found him, he said unto him, Dost thou believe on the Son of God?

Jn 11:40 — Jesus saith unto her, Said I not unto thee, that, if thou wouldest believe, thou shouldest see the glory of God?

Jn 12:36 — While ye have light, believe in the light, that ye may be the children of light. These things spake Jesus, and departed, and did hide himself from them.

Jn 12:44 — Jesus cried and said, He that believeth on me, believeth not on me, but on him that sent me.

Jn 12:46 — I am come a light into the world, that whosoever believeth on me should not abide in darkness.

Jn 13:7 — Jesus answered and said unto him, What I do thou knowest not now; but thou shalt know hereafter.

Jn 13:20 — Verily, verily, I say unto you, He that receiveth whomsoever I send receiveth me; and he that receiveth me receiveth him that sent me.

Jn 14:1 — Let not your heart be troubled: ye believe in God, believe also in me.

Jn 16:27 — For the Father himself loveth you, because ye have loved me, and have believed that I came out from God.

Jn 16:33 — These things I have spoken unto you, that in me ye might have peace. In the world ye shall have tribulation: but be of good cheer; I have overcome the world.

Jn 18:37 — Pilate therefore said unto him, Art thou a king then? Jesus answered, Thou sayest that I am a king. To this end was I born, and for this cause came I into the world, that I should bear witness unto the truth. Every one that is of the truth heareth my voice.

Jn 20:27 — Then saith he to Thomas, reach hither thy finger, and behold my hands; and reach hither thy hand, and thrust *it* into my side: and be not faithless, but believing.

Jn 20:29 — Jesus saith unto him, Thomas, because thou hast seen me, thou hast believed: blessed *are* they that have not seen, and *yet* have believed.

Jn 20:31 — But these are written, that ye might believe that Jesus is the Christ, the Son of God; and that believing ye might have life through his name.

Ac 3:16 — And his name through faith in his name hath made this man strong, whom ye see and know: yea, the faith which is by him hath given him this perfect soundness in the presence of you all.

Ac 10:43 — To him give all the prophets witness, that through his name whosoever believeth in him shall receive remission of sins.

Ac 15:9 — And put no difference between us and them, purifying their hearts by faith.

Ac 15:11 — But we believe that through the grace of the Lord Jesus Christ we shall be saved, even as they.

Ac 16:31 — And they said, Believe on the Lord Jesus Christ, and thou shalt be saved, and thy house.

Ac 20:21 — Testifying both to the Jews, and also to the Greeks, repentance toward God, and faith toward our Lord Jesus Christ.

Ac 26:18 — To open their eyes, *and* to turn *them* from darkness to light, and *from* the power of Satan unto God, that they may receive forgiveness of sins, and inheritance among them which are sanctified by faith that is in me.

Ro 9:33 — As it is written, Behold, I lay in Sion a stumblingstone and rock of offence: and whosoever believeth on him shall not be ashamed.

Ro 10:4 — For Christ *is* the end of the law for righteousness to every one that believeth.

Ro 10:9 — That if thou shalt confess with thy mouth the Lord Jesus, and shalt believe in thine heart that God hath raised him from the dead, thou shalt be saved.

Gal 2:16 — Knowing that a man is not justified by the works of the law, but by the faith of Jesus Christ, even we have believed in Jesus Christ, that we might be justified by the faith of Christ, and not by the works of the law: for by the works of the law shall no flesh be justified.

Gal 5:6 — For in Jesus Christ neither circumcision availeth any thing, nor uncircumcision; but faith which worketh by love.

Eph 3:12 — In whom we have boldness and access with confidence by the faith of him.

Eph 3:17 — That Christ may dwell in your hearts by faith; that ye, being rooted and grounded in love,

Eph 4:13 — Till we all come in the unity of the faith, and of the knowledge of the Son of God, unto a perfect man, unto the measure of the stature of the fulness of Christ:

Php 3:9 — And be found in him, not having mine own righteousness, which is of the law, but that which is through the faith of Christ, the righteousness which is of God by faith:

Col 2:7 — Rooted and built up in him, and stablished in the faith, as ye have been taught, abounding therein with thanksgiving.

1Ti 1:16 — Howbeit for this cause I obtained mercy, that in me first Jesus Christ might shew forth all longsuffering, for a pattern to them which should hereafter believe on him to life everlasting.

2Ti 1:13 — Hold fast the form of sound words, which thou hast heard of me, in faith and love which is in Christ Jesus.

2Ti 2:1 — Thou therefore, my son, be strong in the grace that is in Christ Jesus.

2Ti 3:15 — And that from a child thou hast known the holy scriptures, which are able to make thee wise unto salvation through faith which is in Christ Jesus.

Heb 4:16 — Let us therefore come boldly unto the throne of grace, that we may obtain mercy, and find grace to help in time of need.

Heb 6:19 — Which *hope* we have as an anchor of the soul, both sure and stedfast, and which entereth into that within the veil;

Heb 10:22 — Let us draw near with a true heart in full assurance of faith, having our hearts sprinkled from an evil conscience, and our bodies washed with pure water.

Heb 12:2 — Looking unto Jesus the author and finisher of *our* faith; who for the joy that was set before him endured the cross, despising the shame, and is set down at the right hand of the throne of God.

Heb 13:7 — Remember them which have the rule over you, who have spoken unto you the word of God: whose faith follow, considering the end of *their* conversation.

1Pe 1:8 — Whom having not seen, ye love; in whom, though now ye see *him* not, yet believing, ye rejoice with joy unspeakable and full of glory:

2Pe 1:1 — Simon Peter, a servant and an apostle of Jesus Christ, to them that have obtained like precious faith with us through the righteousness of God and our Saviour Jesus Christ:

1Jn 3:23 — And this is his commandment, That we should believe on the name of his Son Jesus Christ, and love one another, as he gave us commandment.

1Jn 5:10 — He that believeth on the Son of God hath the witness in himself: he that believeth not God hath made him a liar; because he believeth not the record that God gave of his Son.

Jude 1:21 — Keep yourselves in the love of God, looking for the mercy of our Lord Jesus Christ unto eternal life.

Rev 1:17 — And when I saw him, I fell at his feet as dead. And he laid his right hand upon me, saying unto me, Fear not; I am the first and the last:

Rev 3:18 — I counsel thee to buy of me gold tried in the fire, that thou mayest be rich; and white raiment, that thou mayest be clothed, and *that* the shame of thy nakedness do not appear; and anoint thine eyes with eyesalve, that thou mayest see.

Rev 3:20 — Behold, I stand at the door, and knock: if any man hear my voice, and open the door, I will come in to him, and will sup with him, and he with me.

- **Exemplified.**

Mt 8:5–10; 15:26–28; Mk 7:27–30; Lk 7:3–9; Jn 6:68–69; 10:41–42; 11:21–22; Ro 7:24–25; 2Co 12:9–10

Mt 8:2 — And, behold, there came a leper and worshipped him, saying, Lord, if thou wilt, thou canst make me clean.

Mt 9:18 — While he spake these things unto them, behold, there came a certain ruler, and worshipped him, saying, My daughter is even now dead: but come and lay thy hand upon her, and she shall live.

Mt 9:21 — For she said within herself, If I may but touch his garment, I shall be whole.

Mt 9:28 — And when he was come into the house, the blind men came to him: and Jesus saith unto them, Believe ye that I am able to do this? They said unto him, Yea, Lord.

Mt 14:33 — Then they that were in the ship came and worshipped him, saying, Of a truth thou art the Son of God.

Mt 16:16 — And Simon Peter answered and said, Thou art the Christ, the Son of the living God.

Mk 5:28 — For she said, If I may touch but his clothes, I shall be whole.

Mk 9:24 — And straightway the father of the child cried out, and said with tears, Lord, I believe; help thou mine unbelief.

Lk 5:5 — And Simon answering said unto him, Master, we have toiled all the night, and have taken nothing: nevertheless at thy word I will let down the net.

Lk 8:48 — And he said unto her, Daughter, be of good comfort: thy faith hath made thee whole; go in peace.

Lk 23:42 — And he said unto Jesus, Lord, remember me when thou comest into thy kingdom.

Jn 4:29 — Come, see a man, which told me all things that ever I did: is not this the Christ?

Jn 4:42 — And said unto the woman, Now we believe, not because of thy saying: for we have heard *him* ourselves, and know that this is indeed the Christ, the Saviour of the world.

Jn 6:14 — Then those men, when they had seen the miracle that Jesus did, said, This is of a truth that prophet that should come into the world.

Jn 7:31 — And many of the people believed on him, and said, When Christ cometh, will he do more miracles than these which this *man* hath done?

Jn 9:38 — And he said, Lord, I believe. And he worshipped him.

Jn 11:27 — She saith unto him, Yea, Lord: I believe that thou art the Christ, the Son of God, which should come into the world.

Jn 11:32 — Then when Mary was come where Jesus was, and saw him, she fell down at his feet, saying unto him, Lord, if thou hadst been here, my brother had not died.

Jn 16:30 — Now are we sure that thou knowest all things, and needest not that any man should ask thee: by this we believe that thou camest forth from God.

Jn 20:28 — And Thomas answered and said unto him, My Lord and my God.

Ac 8:37 — And Philip said, If thou believest with all thine heart, thou mayest. And he answered and said, I believe that Jesus Christ is the Son of God.

Ac 11:17 — Forasmuch then as God gave them the like gift as *he did* unto us, who believed on the Lord Jesus Christ; what was I, that I could withstand God?

Ro 8:35 — Who shall separate us from the love of Christ? *shall* tribulation, or distress, or persecution, or famine, or nakedness, or peril, or sword?

Ro 8:37 — Nay, in all these things we are more than conquerors through him that loved us.

Gal 2:20 — I am crucified with Christ: nevertheless I live; yet not I, but Christ liveth in me: and the life which I now live in the flesh I live by the faith of the Son of God, who loved me, and gave himself for me.

Php 4:13 — I can do all things through Christ which strengtheneth me.

1Ti 1:14 — And the grace of our Lord was exceeding abundant with faith and love which is in Christ Jesus.

2Ti 1:12 — For the which cause I also suffer these things: nevertheless I am not ashamed: for I know whom I have believed, and am persuaded that he is able to keep that which I have committed unto him against that day.

2Ti 4:18 — And the Lord shall deliver me from every evil work, and will preserve *me* unto his heavenly kingdom: to whom *be* glory for ever and ever. Amen.

- **Instances of.**
  - **The wise men of the east.**

    Mt 2:1–2, 11
  - **Peter.**

    Mt 4:18–22; Mk 1:16–20; Lk 5:4–5; Jn 6:68–69
  - **Andrew.**

    Mt 4:18–22; Mk 1:16–20; Jn 1:41
  - **James and John.**

    Mt 4:21–22; Mk 1:19–20
  - **The woman with the issue of blood.**

    Mt 9:21–22
  - **Jairus, for the healing of his daughter.**

    Mt 9:18, 23–25
  - **Two blind men.**

    Mt 9:29–30
  - **Blind Bartimaeus and a fellow blind man.**

    Mt 20:30–34; Mk 10:46–52; Lk 18:35–42

- **The Samaritan leper.**
  Lk 17:11–19
- **The sick of Gennesaret.**
  Mt 14:36; Mk 3:10; 6:54–56
- **Those who brought the paralytic to Jesus.**
  Lk 5:18–20
- **The Syrophenician woman.**
  Mt 15:22–28; Mk 7:25–30
- **The woman who anointed Jesus' feet.**
  Lk 7:36–50
- **Those who brought sick of palsy.**
  Mt 9:2
- **Philip.**
  Jn 1:45–46
- **Nathanael.**
  Jn 1:49
- **The Samaritans, who believed through the preaching of Jesus.**
  Jn 4:39–42
- **The Samaritans, through the preaching of Philip.**
  Ac 8:9–12
- **The nobleman whose child was sick.**
  Jn 4:46–53
- **Abraham.**
  Jn 8:56
- **The blind man whom Jesus healed on the Sabbath.**
  Jn 9:13–38
- **Mary, the sister of Martha.**
  Lk 10:38–42; Jn 11:32
- **John the disciple.**
  Jn 20:8
- **The disciples, through the miracle at Cana of Galilee.**
  Jn 2:11
- **Jews at Jerusalem.**
  Jn 2:23; 8:30; 11:45; 12:11
- **Three thousand at Pentecost.**
  Ac 2:41
- **Five thousand.**
  Ac 4:4
- **Multitudes.**
  Ac 5:14
- **The cripple at Lystra.**
  Ac 14:9
- **Stephen.**
  Ac 6:8
- **Ethiopian eunuch.**
  Ac 8:37
- **People of Lydda and Saron.**
  Ac 9:35
- **People of Joppa.**
  Ac 9:42
- **People of Antioch.**
  Ac 11:21–24
- **Barnabas.**
  Ac 11:24
- **Eunice, Lois, and Timothy.**
  Ac 16:1; 2Ti 1:5
- **Lydia.**
  Ac 16:14
- **Philippian jailer.**
  Ac 16:31–34
- **Crispus.**
  Ac 18:8
- **The Corinthians.**
  Ac 18:8; 1Co 15:11
- **Jews at Rome.**
  Ac 28:24
- **Ephesians.**
  Eph 1:13, 15
- **Colossians.**
  Col 1:2, 4
- **Thessalonians.**
  1Th 1:3–4, 6; 3:6–8
- **Philemon.**
  Phm 1:5
- **Church at Thyatira.**
  Rev 2:19

FAITH, Trial of

Mt 13:19–22; 24:21–25; Lk 8:13–14; 2Th 1:3–5; Heb 6:13–15

1Ch 29:17 — I know also, my God, that thou triest the heart, and hast pleasure in uprightness. As for me, in the uprightness of mine heart I have willingly offered all these things: and now have I seen with joy thy people, which are present here, to offer willingly unto thee.

Ps 26:2 — Examine me, O LORD, and prove me; try my reins and my heart.

Ps 81:7 — Thou calledst in trouble, and I delivered thee; I answered thee in the secret place of thunder: I proved thee at the waters of Meribah. Selah.

Jas 1:3 — Knowing *this,* that the trying of your faith worketh patience.

Jas 1:12 — Blessed *is* the man that endureth temptation: for when he is tried, he shall receive the crown of life, which the Lord hath promised to them that love him.

1Pe 1:7 — That the trial of your faith, being much more precious than of gold that perisheth, though it be tried with fire, might be found unto praise and honour and glory at the appearing of Jesus Christ:

See: Temptation

- **Instances of trial of.**
  - **Noah.**
    Ge 6:14–22; Heb 11:7
  - **Abraham.**
    - **When commanded to leave his native land and go he knew not whither.**
      Ge 12:1–4; Heb 11:8
    - **When commanded to offer Isaac.**
      Ge 22:1–19; Heb 11:17–19
  - **Moses.**
    - **When sent to Pharaoh.**
      Ex 3:11–12; 4:10–17; Heb 11:25–29

• **At the Red Sea, by the murmurings of the people.**
Ex 14:1–15:27

• **Joshua and the children of Israel, in the method of taking Jericho.**
Jos 6:1–27; Heb 11:30

• **Gideon, when commanded to deliver Israel.**
Jgs 6:36–7:25; Heb 11:32

• **Job, by affliction and adversity.**
Job 1:1–2:13

• **Ezra, in leaving Babylon without a military escort.**
Ezr 8:22

• **Daniel, when forbidden to pray to Jehovah.**
Da 6:4–23; Heb 11:32–33

• **The three Hebrews, when commanded to worship the image.**
Da 3:8–30; Heb 11:32–34

• **The Syrophenician woman.**
Mt 15:21–28; Mk 7:24–30

• **The two blind men who appealed to Jesus for sight.**
Mt 9:28

• **The disicples, when Jesus came walking on the Sea of Galilee.**
Mt 14:25–33

• **The disciples.**

• **By the question of Jesus, as to who he was.**
Mt 16:15–20; Lk 9:20–21

• **By their inability to cast out the evil spirit from the lunatic.**
Mt 17:14–21; Mk 9:14–29; Lk 9:37–42

• **In the tempest at sea.**
Mt 8:23–27; Mk 4:36–41; Lk 8:22–26

• **Of Philip, when questioned by Jesus as to how the multitude would be fed.**
Jn 6:5–6

• **Of Peter, when asked whether he loved Jesus.**
Jn 21:16–17

See: Afflictions; design of

• **Strengthened by miracles.**

See: Miracles, Other; design of

• **Sum total of religious belief and life.**

Ro 1:8 — First, I thank my God through Jesus Christ for you all, that your faith is spoken of throughout the whole world.

Jude 1:3 — Beloved, when I gave all diligence to write unto you of the common salvation, it was needful for me to write unto you, and exhort *you* that ye should earnestly contend for the faith which was once delivered unto the saints.

• **Weak.**

See: Doubting

FAITHFULNESS

Mt 24:45–47; 25:14–23; Lk 12:42–44; 16:10–12; 19:12–27; Eph 6:5–9

Ps 12:1 — Help, LORD; for the godly man ceaseth; for the faithful fail from among the children of men.

Ps 31:23 — O love the LORD, all ye his saints: *for* the LORD preserveth the faithful, and plentifully rewardeth the proud doer.

Pr 20:6 — Most men will proclaim every one his own goodness: but a faithful man who can find?

Pr 28:20 — A faithful man shall abound with blessings: but he that maketh haste to be rich shall not be innocent.

Mt 10:22 — And ye shall be hated of all *men* for my name's sake: but he that endureth to the end shall be saved.

1Co 4:2 — Moreover it is required in stewards, that a man be found faithful.

Col 3:22 — Servants, obey in all things *your* masters according to the flesh; not with eyeservice, as menpleasers; but in singleness of heart, fearing God:

Rev 2:10 — Fear none of those things which thou shalt suffer: behold, the devil shall cast *some* of you into prison, that ye may be tried; and ye shall have tribulation ten days: be thou faithful unto death, and I will give thee a crown of life.

See: Minister, Faithful

See: Obedience

See: Perseverance

See: Reproof; faithfulness in

• **Instances of.**

• **Abraham.**
Gal 3:9

• **Moses.**
Heb 3:5

• **David.**
2Sa 22:22–25

• **Elijah.**
1Ki 19:10, 14

• **Abijah.**
2Ch 13:4–20

• **Jehoshaphat.**
2Ch 20:1–30

• **Job.**
Job 1:21–22; 2:9–10

See: Hezekiah

See: Josiah

See: Joash

See: Daniel

• **Of God.**

See: God, Faithfulness of

FALCON • A carnivorous bird.

Le 11:14 — And the vulture, and the kite after his kind;

Dt 14:13 — And the glede, and the kite, and the vulture after his kind,

FALL OF MAN

Ge 2:16–17; 3:1–19; Ro 5:18–21; 1Co 15:21–22

Job 31:33 — If I covered my transgressions as Adam, by hiding mine iniquity in my bosom:

Ecc 7:29 — Lo, this only have I found, that God hath made man upright; but they have sought out many inventions.

Isa 43:27 — Thy first father hath sinned, and thy teachers have transgressed against me.

Hos 6:7 — But they like men have transgressed the covenant: there have they dealt treacherously against me.

Ro 5:12 — Wherefore, as by one man sin entered into the world, and death by sin; and so death passed upon all men, for that all have sinned:

Ro 5:14 — Nevertheless death reigned from Adam to Moses, even over them that had not sinned after the similitude of Adam's transgression, who is the figure of him that was to come.

2Co 11:3 — But I fear, lest by any means, as the serpent beguiled Eve through his subtilty, so your minds should be corrupted from the simplicity that is in Christ.

1Ti 2:14 — And Adam was not deceived, but the woman being deceived was in the transgression.

✢See: Depravity of Man

FALSE ACCUSATION ✢See:

Accusation, False

FALSE CONFIDENCE

• In self.

Dt 29:19 — And it come to pass, when he heareth the words of this curse, that he bless himself in his heart, saying, I shall have peace, though I walk in the imagination of mine heart, to add drunkenness to thirst:

1Ki 20:11 — And the king of Israel answered and said, Tell *him,* Let not him that girdeth on *his harness* boast himself as he that putteth it off.

Pr 3:5 — Trust in the LORD with all thine heart; and lean not unto thine own understanding.

Pr 23:4 — Labour not to be rich: cease from thine own wisdom.

Pr 26:12 — Seest thou a man wise in his own conceit? *there is* more hope of a fool than of him.

Pr 28:26 — He that trusteth in his own heart is a fool: but whoso walketh wisely, he shall be delivered.

Isa 5:21 — Woe unto *them that are* wise in their own eyes, and prudent in their own sight!

Ro 12:16 — *Be* of the same mind one toward another. Mind not high things, but condescend to men of low estate. Be not wise in your own conceits.

2Co 1:9 — But we had the sentence of death in ourselves, that we should not trust in ourselves, but in God which raiseth the dead:

• In outward resources.

Isa 31:1–3

Ps 20:7 — Some *trust* in chariots, and some in horses: but we will remember the name of the LORD our God.

Ps 33:17 — An horse *is* a vain thing for safety: neither shall he deliver *any* by his great strength.

Ps 44:6 — For I will not trust in my bow, neither shall my sword save me.

Ps 49:6 — They that trust in their wealth, and boast themselves in the multitude of their riches;

Pr 11:28 — He that trusteth in his riches shall fall: but the righteous shall flourish as a branch.

Isa 22:11 — Ye made also a ditch between the two walls for the water of the old pool: but ye have not looked unto the maker thereof, neither had respect unto him that fashioned it long ago.

Jer 48:7 — For because thou hast trusted in thy works and in thy treasures, thou shalt also be taken: and Chemosh shall go forth into captivity *with* his priests and his princes together.

Zec 4:6 — Then he answered and spake unto me, saying, This *is* the word of the LORD unto Zerubbabel, saying, Not by might, nor by power, but by my spirit, saith the LORD of hosts.

Mk 10:24 — And the disciples were astonished at his words. But Jesus answereth again, and saith unto them, Children, how hard is it for them that trust in riches to enter into the kingdom of God!

• In man.

Ps 146:3–4

Ps 33:16 — There is no king saved by the multitude of an host: a mighty man is not delivered by much strength.

Ps 62:9 — Surely men of low degree *are* vanity, *and* men of high degree *are* a lie: to be laid in the balance, they *are* altogether *lighter* than vanity.

Ps 118:8 — *It is* better to trust in the LORD than to put confidence in man.

Isa 2:22 — Cease ye from man, whose breath *is* in his nostrils: for wherein is he to be accounted of?

Jer 17:5 — Thus saith the LORD; Cursed be the man that trusteth in man, and maketh flesh his arm, and whose heart departeth from the LORD.

Hos 5:13 — When Ephraim saw his sickness, and Judah *saw* his wound, then went Ephraim to the Assyrian, and sent to king Jareb: yet could he not heal you, nor cure you of your wound.

Hos 7:11 — Ephraim also is like a silly dove without heart: they call to Egypt, they go to Assyria.

• Instances of.

• At Babel.

Ge 11:4

• Sennacherib, in the siege of Jerusalem.

2Ki 19:23

• Asa, in relying on Syria rather than on God.

2Ch 16:7–9

• Hezekiah, in the defenses of Jerusalem.

Isa 22:11

• Peter, in asserting his devotion to Jesus.

Mt 26:35; Lk 22:33–34; Jn 13:37–38

✢See: Confidence; false

FALSEHOOD

Le 6:2–7; 19:11–12; Job 31:5–6; Ps 12:2–3; 50:19–20; 52:2–5; 120:2–4; Pr 2:12–15; 6:12–13, 16–19; 10:9–10;

12:19–20; 26:18–19, 24–26; Isa 59:3–4, 12–13; Jer 9:5–6; Hos 4:1–2; Mt 25:44–46; Jn 8:44–45; 1Ti 1:9–10

Ex 20:16 — Thou shalt not bear false witness against thy neighbour.

Ex 23:1 — Thou shalt not raise a false report: put not thine hand with the wicked to be an unrighteous witness.

Le 19:16 — Thou shalt not go up and down *as* a talebearer among thy people: neither shalt thou stand against the blood of thy neighbour: I *am* the LORD.

Job 13:4 — But ye *are* forgers of lies, ye *are* all physicians of no value.

Job 21:34 — How then comfort ye me in vain, seeing in your answers there remaineth falsehood?

Job 27:4 — My lips shall not speak wickedness, nor my tongue utter deceit.

Job 31:33 — If I covered my transgressions as Adam, by hiding mine iniquity in my bosom:

Job 36:4 — For truly my words *shall* not *be* false: he that is perfect in knowledge *is* with thee.

Ps 5:6 — Thou shalt destroy them that speak leasing: the LORD will abhor the bloody and deceitful man.

Ps 5:9 — For *there is* no faithfulness in their mouth; their inward part *is* very wickedness; their throat *is* an open sepulchre; they flatter with their tongue.

Ps 10:7 — His mouth is full of cursing and deceit and fraud: under his tongue *is* mischief and vanity.

Ps 28:3 — Draw me not away with the wicked, and with the workers of iniquity, which speak peace to their neighbours, but mischief *is* in their hearts.

Ps 31:18 — Let the lying lips be put to silence; which speak grievous things proudly and contemptuously against the righteous.

Ps 34:13 — Keep thy tongue from evil, and thy lips from speaking guile.

Ps 36:3 — The words of his mouth *are* iniquity and deceit: he hath left off to be wise, *and* to do good.

Ps 55:21 — *The words* of his mouth were smoother than butter, but war *was* in his heart: his words were softer than oil, yet *were* they drawn swords.

Ps 55:23 — But thou, O God, shalt bring them down into the pit of destruction: bloody and deceitful men shall not live out half their days; but I will trust in thee.

Ps 58:3 — The wicked are estranged from the womb: they go astray as soon as they be born, speaking lies.

Ps 59:12 — *For* the sin of their mouth *and* the words of their lips let them even be taken in their pride: and for cursing and lying *which* they speak.

Ps 62:4 — They only consult to cast *him* down from his excellency: they delight in lies: they bless with their mouth, but they curse inwardly. Selah.

Ps 63:11 — But the king shall rejoice in God; every one that sweareth by him shall glory: but the mouth of them that speak lies shall be stopped.

Ps 101:5 — Whoso privily slandereth his neighbour, him will I cut off: him that hath an high look and a proud heart will not I suffer.

Ps 101:7 — He that worketh deceit shall not dwell within my house: he that telleth lies shall not tarry in my sight.

Ps 109:2 — For the mouth of the wicked and the mouth of the deceitful are opened against me: they have spoken against me with a lying tongue.

Ps 116:11 — I said in my haste, All men *are* liars.

Ps 119:29 — Remove from me the way of lying: and grant me thy law graciously.

Ps 119:69 — The proud have forged a lie against me: *but* I will keep thy precepts with *my* whole heart.

Ps 119:163 — I hate and abhor lying: *but* thy law do I love.

Ps 144:8 — Whose mouth speaketh vanity, and their right hand *is* a right hand of falsehood.

Ps 144:11 — Rid me, and deliver me from the hand of strange children, whose mouth speaketh vanity, and their right hand *is* a right hand of falsehood:

Pr 3:3 — Let not mercy and truth forsake thee: bind them about thy neck; write them upon the table of thine heart:

Pr 10:18 — He that hideth hatred *with* lying lips, and he that uttereth a slander, *is* a fool.

Pr 10:31 — The mouth of the just bringeth forth wisdom: but the froward tongue shall be cut out.

Pr 11:9 — An hypocrite with *his* mouth destroyeth his neighbour: but through knowledge shall the just be delivered.

Pr 12:17 — *He that* speaketh truth sheweth forth righteousness: but a false witness deceit.

Pr 12:22 — Lying lips *are* abomination to the LORD: but they that deal truly *are* his delight.

Pr 13:5 — A righteous *man* hateth lying: but a wicked *man* is loathsome, and cometh to shame.

Pr 14:5 — A faithful witness will not lie: but a false witness will utter lies.

Pr 14:8 — The wisdom of the prudent *is* to understand his way: but the folly of fools *is* deceit.

Pr 14:25 — A true witness delivereth souls: but a deceitful *witness* speaketh lies.

Pr 17:4 — A wicked doer giveth heed to false lips; *and* a liar giveth ear to a naughty tongue.

Pr 17:7 — Excellent speech becometh not a fool: much less do lying lips a prince.

Pr 19:5 — A false witness shall not be unpunished, and *he that* speaketh lies shall not escape.

Pr 19:9 — A false witness shall not be unpunished, and he that speaketh lies shall perish.

Pr 19:22 — The desire of a man *is* his kindness: and a poor man *is* better than a liar.

Pr 19:28 — An ungodly witness scorneth judgment: and the mouth of the wicked devoureth iniquity.

Pr 20:17 — Bread of deceit *is* sweet to a man; but afterwards his mouth shall be filled with gravel.

Pr 21:6 — The getting of treasures by a lying tongue *is* a vanity tossed to and fro of them that seek death.

Pr 26:28 — A lying tongue hateth *those that are* afflicted by it; and a flattering mouth worketh ruin.

Pr 27:14 — He that blesseth his friend with a loud voice, rising early in the morning, it shall be counted a curse to him.

Ecc 5:6 — Suffer not thy mouth to cause thy flesh to sin; neither say thou before the angel, that it *was* an error: wherefore should God be angry at thy voice, and destroy the work of thine hands?

Isa 28:15 — Because ye have said, We have made a covenant with death, and with hell are we at agreement; when the overflowing scourge shall pass through, it shall not come unto us: for we have made lies our refuge, and under falsehood have we hid ourselves:

Isa 32:7 — The instruments also of the churl *are* evil: he deviseth wicked devices to destroy the poor with lying words, even when the needy speaketh right.

Isa 57:11 — And of whom hast thou been afraid or feared, that thou hast lied, and hast not remembered me, nor laid *it* to thy heart? have not I held my peace even of old, and thou fearest me not?

Isa 63:8 — For he said, Surely they *are* my people, children *that* will not lie: so he was their Saviour.

Jer 7:8 — Behold, ye trust in lying words, that cannot profit.

Jer 7:28 — But thou shalt say unto them, This *is* a nation that obeyeth not the voice of the LORD their God, nor receiveth correction: truth is perished, and is cut off from their mouth.

Jer 9:3 — And they bend their tongues *like* their bow *for* lies: but they are not valiant for the truth upon the earth; for they proceed from evil to evil, and they know not me, saith the LORD.

Jer 9:8 — Their tongue *is as* an arrow shot out; it speaketh deceit: *one* speaketh peaceably to his neighbour with his mouth, but in heart he layeth his wait.

Jer 12:6 — For even thy brethren, and the house of thy father, even they have dealt treacherously with thee; yea, they have called a multitude after thee: believe them not, though they speak fair words unto thee.

Jer 50:36 — A sword *is* upon the liars; and they shall dote: a sword *is* upon her mighty men; and they shall be dismayed.

Eze 22:9 — In thee are men that carry tales to shed blood: and in thee they eat upon the mountains: in the midst of thee they commit lewdness.

Ob 1:7 — All the men of thy confederacy have brought thee *even* to the border: the men that were at peace with thee have deceived thee, *and* prevailed against thee; *they that eat* thy bread have laid a wound under thee: *there is* none understanding in him.

Mic 6:12 — For the rich men thereof are full of violence, and the inhabitants thereof have spoken lies, and their tongue *is* deceitful in their mouth.

Na 3:1 — Woe to the bloody city! it is all full of lies *and* robbery; the prey departeth not;

Zep 3:13 — The remnant of Israel shall not do iniquity, nor speak lies; neither shall a deceitful tongue be found in their mouth: for they shall feed and lie down, and none shall make *them* afraid.

Eph 4:25 — Wherefore putting away lying, speak every man truth with his neighbour: for we are members one of another.

Eph 4:29 — Let no corrupt communication proceed out of your mouth, but that which is good to the use of edifying, that it may minister grace unto the hearers.

Col 3:9 — Lie not one to another, seeing that ye have put off the old man with his deeds;

1Ti 4:2 — Speaking lies in hypocrisy; having their conscience seared with a hot iron;

1Pe 3:10 — For he that will love life, and see good days, let him refrain his tongue from evil, and his lips that they speak no guile:

1Pe 3:16 — Having a good conscience; that, whereas they speak evil of you, as of evildoers, they may be ashamed that falsely accuse your good conversation in Christ.

Rev 21:8 — But the fearful, and unbelieving, and the abominable, and murderers, and whoremongers, and sorcerers, and idolaters, and all liars, shall have their part in the lake which burneth with fire and brimstone: which is the second death.

Rev 21:27 — And there shall in no wise enter into it any thing that defileth, neither *whatsoever* worketh abomination, or *maketh* a lie: but they which are written in the Lamb's book of life.

Rev 22:15 — For without *are* dogs, and sorcerers, and whoremongers, and murderers, and idolaters, and whosoever loveth and maketh a lie.

See: Accusation, False

See: Conspiracy

See: Deceit

See: Deception

See: Falsehood, False Witness

See: Flattery

See: Hypocrisy

See: Perjury

See: Teachers; false

- **Instances of, Old Testament.**
  - **Satan.**
    - **In deceiving Eve.**
      Ge 3:4–5
    - **In inpugning Job's motives for being righteous.**
      Job 1:9–10; 2:4–5
  - **Adam and Eve, in attempting to evade responsibility.**
    Ge 3:12–13
  - **Cain, in denying knowledge of his brother.**
    Ge 4:9
  - **Abraham, in denying that Sarah was his wife.**
    Ge 12:11–19; 20:2
  - **Sarah.**
    - **To the angels, denying her derisive laugh of unbelief.**
      Ge 18:15
    - **In denying to the king of Gerar, that she was Abraham's wife.**
      Ge 20:5, 16
  - **Isaac, denying that Rebekah was his wife.**
    Ge 26:7–10
  - **Rebekah and Isaac, in the conspiracy against Esau.**
    Ge 27:6–24, 46

• Jacob's sons, in the scheme to destroy the Shechemites by first having them circumcised.

Ge 34:1–31

• Joseph's brethren, in deceiving their father into a belief that Joseph was killed by wild beasts.

Ge 37:29–35

• Potiphar's wife, in falsely accusing Joseph.

Ge 39:14–17

• Joseph, in the deception he carried on with his brethren.

Ge 42:1–44:34

• Pharaoh, in dealing deceitfully with the Israelites.

Ex 7:1–12:51

• Aaron, in attempting to shift responsibility for the making of the golden calf.

Ex 32:1–24

• Rahab, in denying that the spies were in her house.

Jos 2:4–6

• The Gibeonites, deception of.

Jos 9:1–27

• Ehud in plot to assassinate king of Moab.

Jgs 3:16–23

• Sisera, who instructed Jael to mislead his pursuers.

Jgs 4:20

• Saul.

• In lying to Samuel.

1Sa 15:1–26

• In acusing Ahimelech of conspiring with David against himself.

1Sa 22:11–16

• David.

• In lying to Ahimelech.

1Sa 21:1–15

• In feigning madness.

1Sa 21:13–15

• In other deceits with the Philistines.

1Sa 27:8–12

• In the falsehood he put in the mouth of Hushai, of friendship to Absalom.

2Sa 15:34–37

• Michal, in the false statement that David was sick, in order to save him from Saul's violence.

1Sa 19:12–17

• The Amalekite who claimed to have slain Saul.

2Sa 1:10–12

• Hushai.

• In false professions to Absalom.

2Sa 16:16–19

• In his deceitful counsel to Absalom.

2Sa 17:7–14

• The wife of the Bahurimite who saved the lives of Hushai's messengers.

2Sa 17:15–22

• The murder, under false pretense.

• Of Adonijah.

1Ki 2:23 — Then king Solomon sware by the LORD, saying, God do so to me, and more also, if Adonijah have not spoken this word against his own life.

• Of Shimei.

1Ki 2:42–43

• Of Jeroboam's wife.

1Ki 14:2 — And Jeroboam said to his wife, Arise, I pray thee, and disguise thyself, that thou be not known to be the wife of Jeroboam; and get thee to Shiloh: behold, there *is* Ahijah the prophet, which told me that *I should be* king over this people.

• The old prophet of Bethel who misguided the prophet of Judah.

1Ki 13:11–22

• Jeroboam's wife, feigning herself another woman.

1Ki 14:5–7

• The conspirators against Naboth.

1Ki 21:7–13

• Gehazi's greed.

2Ki 5:20–24

• Hazael lies to the king in regard to his recovery.

2Ki 8:7–15

• Jehu lied to the worshipers of Baal in order to gain advantage over them, and destroy them.

2Ki 10:18–28

• Zedekiah, in violating his oath of allegiance to Nebuchadnezzar.

Eze 17:15–20

2Ch 36:13 — And he also rebelled against king Nebuchadnezzar, who had made him swear by God: but he stiffened his neck, and hardened his heart from turning unto the LORD God of Israel.

Eze 16:59 — For thus saith the Lord GOD; I will even deal with thee as thou hast done, which hast despised the oath in breaking the covenant.

• Samaritans, in their efforts to hinder the rebuilding of the temple at Jerusalem.

Ezr 4:1–24

• Sanballat, in trying to obstruct the rebuilding of Jerusalem.

Ne 6:1–19

• Haman, in his conspiracy against the Jews.

Est 3:8 — And Haman said unto king Ahasuerus, There is a certain people scattered abroad and dispersed among the people in all the provinces of thy kingdom; and their laws *are* diverse from all people; neither keep they the king's laws: therefore it *is* not for the king's profit to suffer them.

- **Jeremiah's adversaries, in accusing him of joining the Chaldeans.**
  Jer 37:13–15
- **Princes of Israel, when they went to Jeremiah for a vision from the Lord.**
  Jer 42:20 — For ye dissembled in your hearts, when ye sent me unto the LORD your God, saying, Pray for us unto the LORD our God; and according unto all that the LORD our God shall say, so declare unto us, and we will do *it.*

- **Instances of, New Testament.**
  - **Satan, in his false pretentions to Jesus.**
    Mt 4:8–9; Lk 4:6–7
  - **Herod, to the wise men, in professing to desire to worship Jesus.**
    Mt 2:8
  - **The Jews.**
    - **In falsely accusing Jesus of being gluttonous and a winebibber.**
      Mt 11:19
    - **In refusing to bear truthful testimony concerning John the Baptist.**
      Mt 21:24–27
    - **In falsely accusing Jesus of blasphemy, when he remitted sin.**
      Mt 9:2–6; Mk 2:7; Lk 5:21
    - **In falsely accusing Jesus when he announced that he was the Son of God.**
      Mt 26:65; Mk 14:64; Jn 10:33–38
  - **Peter, in denying Jesus.**
    Mt 26:69–75; Mk 14:68–71; Lk 22:56–62; Jn 18:25–27
  - **The Roman soldiers, who said the disciples stole the body of Jesus.**
    Mt 28:13, 15
  - **The disobedient son, who promised to work in the vineyard, but did not.**
    Mt 21:30
  - **Ananias and Sapphira falsely state that they had sold their land for a given sum.**
    Ac 5:1–10
  - **Stephen's accusers, who falsely accused him of blaspheming Moses and God.**
    Ac 6:11–14
  - **Paul's traducers, falsely accusing him of treason to Caesar.**
    Ac 16:20–21; 17:5–7; 24:5; 25:7–8
  - **The Cretians are always liars, evil beasts, slow bellies.**
    Tit 1:12

✦See: Accusation, False
✦See: Conspiracy
✦See: Falsehood, False Witness
✦See: Hypocrisy
✦See: Perjury
✦See: Teachers; false

- **False teachers.**
  ✦See: Teachers; false

FALSEHOOD, False Witness

Le 19:11–12; Dt 19:16–20; Pr 6:16–18; Zec 5:3–4; 1Ti 1:9–10

Ex 20:16 — Thou shalt not bear false witness against thy neighbour.

Ex 23:1 — Thou shalt not raise a false report: put not thine hand with the wicked to be an unrighteous witness.

Le 6:3 — Or have found that which was lost, and lieth concerning it, and sweareth falsely; in any of all these that a man doeth, sinning therein:

Le 19:16 — Thou shalt not go up and down *as* a talebearer among thy people: neither shalt thou stand against the blood of thy neighbour: I *am* the LORD.

Dt 5:20 — Neither shalt thou bear false witness against thy neighbour.

Ps 27:12 — Deliver me not over unto the will of mine enemies: for false witnesses are risen up against me, and such as breathe out cruelty.

Ps 35:11 — False witnesses did rise up; they laid to my charge *things* that I knew not.

Pr 12:17 — *He that* speaketh truth sheweth forth righteousness: but a false witness deceit.

Pr 14:5 — A faithful witness will not lie: but a false witness will utter lies.

Pr 14:8 — The wisdom of the prudent *is* to understand his way: but the folly of fools *is* deceit.

Pr 14:25 — A true witness delivereth souls: but a deceitful *witness* speaketh lies.

Pr 18:5 — *It is* not good to accept the person of the wicked, to overthrow the righteous in judgment.

Pr 19:9 — A false witness shall not be unpunished, and he that speaketh lies shall perish.

Pr 19:22 — The desire of a man *is* his kindness: and a poor man *is* better than a liar.

Pr 19:28 — An ungodly witness scorneth judgment: and the mouth of the wicked devoureth iniquity.

Pr 21:28 — A false witness shall perish: but the man that heareth speaketh constantly.

Pr 24:28 — Be not a witness against thy neighbour without cause; and deceive *not* with thy lips.

Pr 25:18 — A man that beareth false witness against his neighbour *is* a maul, and a sword, and a sharp arrow.

Mt 15:19 — For out of the heart proceed evil thoughts, murders, adulteries, fornications, thefts, false witness, blasphemies:

Mt 19:18 — He saith unto him, Which? Jesus said, Thou shalt do no murder, Thou shalt not commit adultery, Thou shalt not steal, Thou shalt not bear false witness,

Lk 3:14 — And the soldiers likewise demanded of him, saying, And what shall we do? And he said unto them, Do violence to no man, neither accuse *any* falsely; and be content with your wages.

Lk 18:20 — Thou knowest the commandments, Do not commit adultery, Do not kill, Do not steal, Do not bear false witness, Honour thy father and thy mother.

Ro 13:9 — For this, Thou shalt not commit adultery, Thou shalt not kill, Thou shalt not steal, Thou shalt not bear false witness, Thou shalt not covet; and if *there be* any other commandment, it is briefly comprehended in this saying, namely, Thou shalt love thy neighbour as thyself.

- **See: Evidence; laws concerning**
- **See: Falsehood**
- **See: Perjury**
- **See: Witness**

• Instances of.

• Witnesses against Naboth.
1Ki 21:13

• Witnesses against Jesus.
Mt 26:59–61; Mk 14:54–59

• Witnesses against Stephen.
Ac 6:11, 13

• Witnesses against Paul.
Ac 16:20–21; 17:5–7; 24:5; 25:7–8

FAMILIAR SPIRITS

• Consulting of, forbidden.
Dt 18:10–11

Le 19:31 — Regard not them that have familiar spirits, neither seek after wizards, to be defiled by them: I *am* the LORD your God.

Le 20:6 — And the soul that turneth after such as have familiar spirits, and after wizards, to go a whoring after them, I will even set my face against that soul, and will cut him off from among his people.

Le 20:27 — A man also or woman that hath a familiar spirit, or that is a wizard, shall surely be put to death: they shall stone them with stones: their blood *shall be* upon them.

• Vain.

Isa 8:19 — And when they shall say unto you, Seek unto them that have familiar spirits, and unto wizards that peep, and that mutter: should not a people seek unto their God? for the living to the dead?

Isa 19:3 — And the spirit of Egypt shall fail in the midst thereof; and I will destroy the counsel thereof: and they shall seek to the idols, and to the charmers, and to them that have familiar spirits, and to the wizards.

• Those who consulted, to be cut off.

Le 20:6 — And the soul that turneth after such as have familiar spirits, and after wizards, to go a whoring after them, I will even set my face against that soul, and will cut him off from among his people.

Le 20:27 — A man also or woman that hath a familiar spirit, or that is a wizard, shall surely be put to death: they shall stone them with stones: their blood *shall be* upon them.

• Instances of those who consulted.

• Saul.
1Sa 28:3–25; 1Ch 10:13

- **See: Demons**
- **See: Necromancy**
- **See: Witchcraft**

FAMILY

• Of saints.

• Blessed.

Ps 128:3 — Thy wife *shall be* as a fruitful vine by the sides of thine house: thy children like olive plants round about thy table.

Ps 128:6 — Yea, thou shalt see thy children's children, *and* peace upon Israel.

• Should be taught God's word.
Dt 4:9–10

• Worship God together.

1Co 16:19 — The churches of Asia salute you. Aquila and Priscilla salute you much in the Lord, with the church that is in their house.

• Be duly regulated.
1Ti 3:4–5

Pr 31:27 — She looketh well to the ways of her household, and eateth not the bread of idleness.

1Ti 3:12 — Let the deacons be the husbands of one wife, ruling their children and their own houses well.

• Live in unity.

Ge 45:24 — So he sent his brethren away, and they departed: and he said unto them, See that ye fall not out by the way.

Ps 133:1 — Behold, how good and how pleasant *it is* for brethren to dwell together in unity!

• Live in mutual forbearance.
Ge 50:17–21; Mt 18:21–22

• Rejoice together before God.

Dt 14:26 — And thou shalt bestow that money for whatsoever thy soul lusteth after, for oxen, or for sheep, or for wine, or for strong drink, or for whatsoever thy soul desireth: and thou shalt eat there before the LORD thy God, and thou shalt rejoice, thou, and thine household,

• Deceivers and liars should be removed from.

Ps 101:7 — He that worketh deceit shall not dwell within my house: he that telleth lies shall not tarry in my sight.

• Warned against departing from God.

Dt 29:18 — Lest there should be among you man, or woman, or family, or tribe, whose heart turneth away this day from the LORD our God, to go *and* serve the gods of these nations; lest there should be among you a root that beareth gall and wormwood;

• Punishment of irreligious.

Jer 10:25 — Pour out thy fury upon the heathen that know thee not, and upon the families that call not on thy name: for they have eaten up Jacob, and devoured him, and consumed him, and have made his habitation desolate.

• Good, exemplified.

• Abraham.

Ge 18:19 — For I know him, that he will command his children and his household after him, and they shall keep the way of the LORD, to do justice and judgment; that the LORD may bring upon Abraham that which he hath spoken of him.

• **Jacob.**

Ge 35:2 — Then Jacob said unto his household, and to all that *were* with him, Put away the strange gods that *are* among you, and be clean, and change your garments:

• **Joshua.**

Jos 24:15 — And if it seem evil unto you to serve the LORD, choose you this day whom ye will serve; whether the gods which your fathers served that *were* on the other side of the flood, or the gods of the Amorites, in whose land ye dwell: but as for me and my house, we will serve the LORD.

• **David.**

2Sa 6:20 — Then David returned to bless his household. And Michal the daughter of Saul came out to meet David, and said, How glorious was the king of Israel to day, who uncovered himself to day in the eyes of the handmaids of his servants, as one of the vain fellows shamelessly uncovereth himself!

• **Job.**

Job 1:5 — And it was so, when the days of *their* feasting were gone about, that Job sent and sanctified them, and rose up early in the morning, and offered burnt offerings *according* to the number of them all: for Job said, It may be that my sons have sinned, and cursed God in their hearts. Thus did Job continually.

• **Lazarus of Bethany.**

Jn 11:1–5

• **Cornelius.**

Ac 10:2 — A devout *man,* and one that feared God with all his house, which gave much alms to the people, and prayed to God alway.

Ac 10:33 — Immediately therefore I sent to thee; and thou hast well done that thou art come. Now therefore are we all here present before God, to hear all things that are commanded thee of God.

• **Lydia.**

Ac 16:15 — And when she was baptized, and her household, she besought *us,* saying, If ye have judged me to be faithful to the Lord, come into my house, and abide *there.* And she constrained us.

• **Jailer of Philippi.**

Ac 16:31–34

• **Crispus.**

Ac 18:8 — And Crispus, the chief ruler of the synagogue, believed on the Lord with all his house; and many of the Corinthians hearing believed, and were baptized.

• **Lois.**

2Ti 1:5 — When I call to remembrance the unfeigned faith that is in thee, which dwelt first in thy grandmother Lois, and thy mother Eunice; and I am persuaded that in thee also.

See: Children

See: Husband

See: Orphan

See: Widow

See: Wife

• **Instituted.**

Ge 2:23–24

• **Government of.**

1Co 11:7–9; Eph 5:22–24; 1Ti 3:4–5

Ge 3:16 — Unto the woman he said, I will greatly multiply thy sorrow and thy conception; in sorrow thou shalt bring forth children; and thy desire *shall be* to thy husband, and he shall rule over thee.

Ge 18:19 — For I know him, that he will command his children and his household after him, and they shall keep the way of the LORD, to do justice and judgment; that the LORD may bring upon Abraham that which he hath spoken of him.

Est 1:20 — And when the king's decree which he shall make shall be published throughout all his empire, (for it is great,) all the wives shall give to their husbands honour, both to great and small.

Est 1:22 — For he sent letters into all the king's provinces, into every province according to the writing thereof, and to every people after their language, that every man should bear rule in his own house, and that *it* should be published according to the language of every people.

1Co 7:10 — And unto the married I command, *yet* not I, but the Lord, Let not the wife depart from *her* husband:

1Co 11:3 — But I would have you know, that the head of every man is Christ; and the head of the woman *is* the man; and the head of Christ *is* God.

Col 3:18 — Wives, submit yourselves unto your own husbands, as it is fit in the Lord.

1Ti 3:2 — A bishop then must be blameless, the husband of one wife, vigilant, sober, of good behaviour, given to hospitality, apt to teach;

1Pe 3:1 — Likewise, ye wives, *be* in subjection to your own husbands; that, if any obey not the word, they also may without the word be won by the conversation of the wives;

1Pe 3:6 — Even as Sarah obeyed Abraham, calling him lord: whose daughters ye are, as long as ye do well, and are not afraid with any amazement.

• **Infelicity in.**

Pr 27:15–16

Pr 11:22 — *As* a jewel of gold in a swine's snout, *so is* a fair woman which is without discretion.

Pr 12:4 — A virtuous woman *is* a crown to her husband: but she that maketh ashamed *is* as rottenness in his bones.

Pr 14:1 — Every wise woman buildeth her house: but the foolish plucketh it down with her hands.

Pr 15:27 — He that is greedy of gain troubleth his own house; but he that hateth gifts shall live.

Pr 18:19 — A brother offended *is harder to be won* than a strong city: and *their* contentions *are* like the bars of a castle.

Pr 19:13 — A foolish son *is* the calamity of his father: and the contentions of a wife *are* a continual dropping.

Pr 21:9 — *It is* better to dwell in a corner of the housetop, than with a brawling woman in a wide house.

Pr 21:19 — *It is* better to dwell in the wilderness, than with a contentious and an angry woman.

Pr 25:24 — *It is* better to dwell in the corner of the housetop, than with a brawling woman and in a wide house.

Pr 30:21 — For three *things* the earth is disquieted, and for four *which* it cannot bear:

Pr 30:23 — For an odious *woman* when she is married; and an handmaid that is heir to her mistress.

- **Instances of infelicity in.**
  - **Abraham, on account of Hagar.**
    Ge 16:5; 21:10–11
  - **Isaac, on account of disagreement between Jacob and Esau.**
    Ge 27:4–46
  - **Jacob, bigamic jealousy between Leah and Rachel.**
    Ge 29:30–34; 30:1–25
  - **Moses and Zipporah.**
    Ex 4:25–26
  - **Elkanah, on account of bigamic feuds.**
    1Sa 1:4–7
  - **David and Michal.**
    2Sa 6:16, 20–23
  - **Ahasuerus, on account of Vashti's refusing to appear before his drunken courtiers.**
    Est 1:10–22
- **Persian, domestic customs.**
  Est 1:10–22

  See: Harem
- **Religion of the.**
  Ge 12:7–8; 13:3–4; 17:12–14; Dt 4:9–10; 11:19–20; 12:5–7, 11–12; Ac 10:1–6, 47–48; 16:25–34

Ge 18:19 — For I know him, that he will command his children and his household after him, and they shall keep the way of the LORD, to do justice and judgment; that the LORD may bring upon Abraham that which he hath spoken of him.

Jos 24:15 — And if it seem evil unto you to serve the LORD, choose you this day whom ye will serve; whether the gods which your fathers served that *were* on the other side of the flood, or the gods of the Amorites, in whose land ye dwell: but as for me and my house, we will serve the LORD.

Ps 101:2 — I will behave myself wisely in a perfect way. O when wilt thou come unto me? I will walk within my house with a perfect heart.

Jer 7:18 — The children gather wood, and the fathers kindle the fire, and the women knead *their* dough, to make cakes to the queen of heaven, and to pour out drink offerings unto other gods, that they may provoke me to anger.

Ac 10:33 — Immediately therefore I sent to thee; and thou hast well done that thou art come. Now therefore are we all here present before God, to hear all things that are commanded thee of God.

Ac 10:44 — While Peter yet spake these words, the Holy Ghost fell on all them which heard the word.

Ac 18:8 — And Crispus, the chief ruler of the synagogue, believed on the Lord with all his house; and many of the Corinthians hearing believed, and were baptized.

1Co 1:16 — And I baptized also the household of Stephanas: besides, I know not whether I baptized any other.

FAMINE

- **Pharaoh forewarned of, in dreams.**
  Ge 41:1–57
- **Described.**
  Dt 28:53–57; Isa 9:18–21; Jer 14:1–6; La 2:11–22; 4:4–10; Joel 1:17–20

Isa 5:13 — Therefore my people are gone into captivity, because *they have* no knowledge: and their honourable men *are* famished, and their multitude dried up with thirst.

Isa 17:11 — In the day shalt thou make thy plant to grow, and in the morning shalt thou make thy seed to flourish: *but* the harvest *shall be* a heap in the day of grief and of desperate sorrow.

Jer 5:17 — And they shall eat up thine harvest, and thy bread, *which* thy sons and thy daughters should eat: they shall eat up thy flocks and thine herds: they shall eat up thy vines and thy fig trees: they shall impoverish thy fenced cities, wherein thou trustedst, with the sword.

Jer 48:33 — And joy and gladness is taken from the plentiful field, and from the land of Moab; and I have caused wine to fail from the winepresses: none shall tread with shouting; *their* shouting *shall be* no shouting.

La 1:11 — All her people sigh, they seek bread; they have given their pleasant things for meat to relieve the soul: see, O LORD, and consider; for I am become vile.

La 1:19 — I called for my lovers, *but* they deceived me: my priests and mine elders gave up the ghost in the city, while they sought their meat to relieve their souls.

- **Sent as a judgment.**
  Le 26:19–29; Dt 28:23–24, 38–42; Ps 107:33–34; Isa 3:1–8; Jer 14:15–22; La 5:4–5; Eze 4:16–17; 5:16–17; Joel 1:15–16; Am 4:6–9; 5:16–17; Hag 1:10–11; Rev 6:5–8

1Ki 17:1 — And Elijah the Tishbite, *who was* of the inhabitants of Gilead, said unto Ahab, *As* the LORD God of Israel liveth, before whom I stand, there shall not be dew nor rain these years, but according to my word.

2Ki 8:1 — Then spake Elisha unto the woman, whose son he had restored to life, saying, Arise, and go thou and thine household, and sojourn wheresoever thou canst sojourn: for the LORD hath called for a famine; and it shall also come upon the land seven years.

1Ch 21:12 — Either three years' famine; or three months to be destroyed before thy foes, while that the sword of thine enemies overtaketh *thee;* or else three days the sword of the LORD, even the pestilence, in the land, and the angel of the LORD destroying throughout all the coasts of Israel. Now therefore advise thyself what word I shall bring again to him that sent me.

Ps 105:16 — Moreover he called for a famine upon the land: he brake the whole staff of bread.

Isa 14:30 — And the firstborn of the poor shall feed, and the needy shall lie down in safety: and I will kill thy root with famine, and he shall slay thy remnant.

Jer 19:9 — And I will cause them to eat the flesh of their sons and the flesh of their daughters, and they shall eat every one the flesh of his friend in the siege and straitness, wherewith their enemies, and they that seek their lives, shall straiten them.

Jer 29:17 — Thus saith the LORD of hosts; Behold, I will send upon them the sword, the famine, and the pestilence, and will make them like vile figs, that cannot be eaten, they are so evil.

Jer 29:19 — Because they have not hearkened to my words, saith the LORD, which I sent unto them by my servants the prophets, rising up early and sending *them;* but ye would not hear, saith the LORD.

La 5:10 — Our skin was black like an oven because of the terrible famine.

Eze 14:13 — Son of man, when the land sinneth against me by trespassing grievously, then will I stretch out mine hand upon it, and will break the staff of the bread thereof, and will send famine upon it, and will cut off man and beast from it:

Mt 24:7 — For nation shall rise against nation, and kingdom against kingdom: and there shall be famines, and pestilences, and earthquakes, in divers places.

Lk 21:11 — And great earthquakes shall be in divers places, and famines, and pestilences; and fearful sights and great signs shall there be from heaven.

- **Cannibalism in.**

Dt 28:53 — And thou shalt eat the fruit of thine own body, the flesh of thy sons and of thy daughters, which the LORD thy God hath given thee, in the siege, and in the straitness, wherewith thine enemies shall distress thee:

2Ki 6:28 — And the king said unto her, What aileth thee? And she answered, This woman said unto me, Give thy son, that we may eat him to day, and we will eat my son to morrow.

- **Righteous delivered from.**

Job 5:20 — In famine he shall redeem thee from death: and in war from the power of the sword.

Ps 33:19 — To deliver their soul from death, and to keep them alive in famine.

Ps 37:19 — They shall not be ashamed in the evil time: and in the days of famine they shall be satisfied.

- **Figurative.**

Am 8:11 — Behold, the days come, saith the Lord GOD, that I will send a famine in the land, not a famine of bread, nor a thirst for water, but of hearing the words of the LORD:

- **Instances of.**
  - **In Canaan.**

Ge 12:10; 26:1; 2Sa 21:1; 1Ki 17:1–18:1; 2Ki 6:25–29; 7:4

  - **In Jerusalem, from siege.**

2Ki 25:3; Jer 52:6

  - **In Egypt.**

Ge 41:53–57

  - **Universal.**

Ac 11:28

FAN

- **Used for winnowing grain.**

Isa 30:24 — The oxen likewise and the young asses that ear the ground shall eat clean provender, which hath been winnowed with the shovel and with the fan.

Jer 15:7 — And I will fan them with a fan in the gates of the land; I will bereave *them* of children, I will destroy my people, *since* they return not from their ways.

Jer 51:2 — And will send unto Babylon fanners, that shall fan her, and shall empty her land: for in the day of trouble they shall be against her round about.

Mt 3:12 — Whose fan *is* in his hand, and he will throughly purge his floor, and gather his wheat into the garner; but he will burn up the chaff with unquenchable fire.

FARMING

See: Agriculture

See: Vineyard

FARTHING

- **This word is used to translate two different words in the Greek text.**
  - **Assarion.**
    - **A Roman coin.**

Mt 10:29 — Are not two sparrows sold for a farthing? and one of them shall not fall on the ground without your Father.

Lk 12:6 — Are not five sparrows sold for two farthings, and not one of them is forgotten before God?

  - **Kodrantes.**
    - **American money, about two-fifths of a cent; English money, less than a farthing.**

Mt 5:26 — Verily I say unto thee, Thou shalt by no means come out thence, till thou hast paid the uttermost farthing.

Mk 12:42 — And there came a certain poor widow, and she threw in two mites, which make a farthing.

FASTING

• **Observed on occasions of.**

• **Public calamities.**

2Sa 1:12 — And they mourned, and wept, and fasted until even, for Saul, and for Jonathan his son, and for the people of the LORD, and for the house of Israel; because they were fallen by the sword.

• **Afflictions.**

Ps 35:13 — But as for me, when they were sick, my clothing *was* sackcloth: I humbled my soul with fasting; and my prayer returned into mine own bosom.

Da 6:18 — Then the king went to his palace, and passed the night fasting: neither were instruments of musick brought before him: and his sleep went from him.

• **Private afflictions.**

2Sa 12:16 — David therefore besought God for the child; and David fasted, and went in, and lay all night upon the earth.

• **Approaching danger.**

Est 4:16 — Go, gather together all the Jews that are present in Shushan, and fast ye for me, and neither eat nor drink three days, night or day: I also and my maidens will fast likewise; and so will I go in unto the king, which *is* not according to the law: and if I perish, I perish.

• **Ordination of ministers.**

Ac 13:3 — And when they had fasted and prayed, and laid *their* hands on them, they sent *them* away.

Ac 14:23 — And when they had ordained them elders in every church, and had prayed with fasting, they commended them to the Lord, on whom they believed.

• **Accompanied by.**

• **Prayer.**

Da 9:3 — And I set my face unto the Lord God, to seek by prayer and supplications, with fasting, and sackcloth, and ashes:

• **Confession of sin.**

Ne 9:1–2

1Sa 7:6 — And they gathered together to Mizpeh, and drew water, and poured *it* out before the LORD, and fasted on that day, and said there, We have sinned against the LORD. And Samuel judged the children of Israel in Mizpeh.

• **Humiliation.**

Dt 9:18 — And I fell down before the LORD, as at the first, forty days and forty nights: I did neither eat bread, nor drink water, because of all your sins which ye sinned, in doing wickedly in the sight of the LORD, to provoke him to anger.

Ne 9:1 — Now in the twenty and fourth day of this month the children of Israel were assembled with fasting, and with sackclothes, and earth upon them.

• **Reading of the Scriptures.**

Jer 36:6 — Therefore go thou, and read in the roll, which thou hast written from my mouth, the words of the LORD in the ears of the people in the LORD'S house upon the fasting day: and also thou shalt read them in the ears of all Judah that come out of their cities.

• **During 40 days, Moses.**

Dt 9:9 — When I was gone up into the mount to receive the tables of stone, *even* the tables of the covenant which the LORD made with you, then I abode in the mount forty days and forty nights, I neither did eat bread nor drink water:

Dt 9:18 — And I fell down before the LORD, as at the first, forty days and forty nights: I did neither eat bread, nor drink water, because of all your sins which ye sinned, in doing wickedly in the sight of the LORD, to provoke him to anger.

• **Habitual.**

• **By John's disciples.**

Mt 9:14 — Then came to him the disciples of John, saying, Why do we and the Pharisees fast oft, but thy disciples fast not?

• **By Anna.**

Lk 2:37 — And she *was* a widow of about fourscore and four years, which departed not from the temple, but served *God* with fastings and prayers night and day.

• **By Pharisees.**

Mt 9:14 — Then came to him the disciples of John, saying, Why do we and the Pharisees fast oft, but thy disciples fast not?

Mk 2:18 — And the disciples of John and of the Pharisees used to fast: and they come and say unto him, Why do the disciples of John and of the Pharisees fast, but thy disciples fast not?

Lk 18:12 — <u>I fast twice in the week, I give tithes of all that I possess.</u>

• **By Cornelius.**

Ac 10:30 — And Cornelius said, Four days ago I was fasting until this hour; and at the ninth hour I prayed in my house, and, behold, a man stood before me in bright clothing,

• **By Paul.**

2Co 6:5 — In stripes, in imprisonments, in tumults, in labours, in watchings, in fastings;

2Co 11:27 — In weariness and painfulness, in watchings often, in hunger and thirst, in fastings often, in cold and nakedness.

• **In times of bereavement.**

• **Of the people of Jabesh-gilead, for Saul and his sons.**

1Sa 31:13 — And they took their bones, and buried *them* under a tree at Jabesh, and fasted seven days.

1Ch 10:12 — They arose, all the valiant men, and took away the body of Saul, and the bodies of his sons, and brought them to Jabesh, and buried their bones under the oak in Jabesh, and fasted seven days.

• **Of David, at the time of Saul's death.**

2Sa 1:12 — And they mourned, and wept, and fasted until even, for Saul, and for Jonathan his son, and for the people of the LORD, and for the house of Israel; because they were fallen by the sword.

- **Of his child's sickness.**
  2Sa 12:21–23
  2Sa 12:16 — David therefore besought God for the child; and David fasted, and went in, and lay all night upon the earth.
- **Of Abner's death.**
  2Sa 3:35 — And when all the people came to cause David to eat meat while it was yet day, David sware, saying, So do God to me, and more also, if I taste bread, or ought else, till the sun be down.

- **Prolonged.**
  - **For three weeks, by Daniel.**
    Da 10:2–3
  - **For forty days, by Moses.**
    Ex 24:18 — And Moses went into the midst of the cloud, and gat him up into the mount: and Moses was in the mount forty days and forty nights.
    Ex 34:28 — And he was there with the LORD forty days and forty nights; he did neither eat bread, nor drink water. And he wrote upon the tables the words of the covenant, the ten commandments.
    Dt 9:9 — When I was gone up into the mount to receive the tables of stone, *even* the tables of the covenant which the LORD made with you, then I abode in the mount forty days and forty nights, I neither did eat bread nor drink water:
    Dt 9:18 — And I fell down before the LORD, as at the first, forty days and forty nights: I did neither eat bread, nor drink water, because of all your sins which ye sinned, in doing wickedly in the sight of the LORD, to provoke him to anger.
  - **Elijah.**
    1Ki 19:8 — And he arose, and did eat and drink, and went in the strength of that meat forty days and forty nights unto Horeb the mount of God.
  - **Jesus.**
    Mt 4:1–2; Mk 1:12–13; Lk 4:1–2
  - **Humiliation.**

See: Humility

- **Unclassified scripture relating to.**
  Ezr 8:21–23; Isa 58:3–7; Da 10:2–3; Joel 2:12–13; Mt 6:16–18; 9:14–15; Ac 27:33–34
  Ps 35:13 — But as for me, when they were sick, my clothing *was* sackcloth: I humbled my soul with fasting; and my prayer returned into mine own bosom.
  Ps 69:10 — When I wept, *and chastened* my soul with fasting, that was to my reproach.
  Jer 14:12 — When they fast, I will not hear their cry; and when they offer burnt offering and an oblation, I will not accept them: but I will consume them by the sword, and by the famine, and by the pestilence.
  Joel 1:14 — Sanctify ye a fast, call a solemn assembly, gather the elders *and* all the inhabitants of the land *into* the house of the LORD your God, and cry unto the LORD,
  Zec 7:5 — Speak unto all the people of the land, and to the priests, saying, When ye fasted and mourned in the fifth and seventh *month,* even those seventy years, did ye at all fast unto me, *even* to me?
  Zec 8:19 — Thus saith the LORD of hosts; The fast of the fourth *month,* and the fast of the fifth, and the fast of the seventh, and the fast of the tenth, shall be to the house of Judah joy and gladness, and cheerful feasts; therefore love the truth and peace.
  Mt 17:21 — Howbeit this kind goeth not out but by prayer and fasting.
  Ac 27:9 — Now when much time was spent, and when sailing was now dangerous, because the fast was now already past, Paul admonished *them,*
  1Co 7:5 — Defraud ye not one the other, except *it be* with consent for a time, that ye may give yourselves to fasting and prayer; and come together again, that Satan tempt you not for your incontinency.

- **Instances of.**
  - **The Israelites on account of the wrong suffered by a Levite's concubine.**
    Jgs 20:26
  - **The Israelites, when they went to Mizpeh for the ark.**
    1Sa 7:6
  - **David.**
    - **At the death of Saul.**
      2Sa 1:12
    - **During the sickness of the child born to him by Bath-sheba.**
      2Sa 12:16–22
    - **While interceding in prayer for his friends.**
      Ps 35:13
    - **In his zeal for Zion.**
      Ps 69:10
    - **In prayer for himself and his adversaries.**
      Ps 109:4, 24
  - **Ahab, when Elijah prophesied the destruction of himself and his house.**
    1Ki 21:20–29
  - **Jehoshaphat, at the time of the invasion of the confederated armies of the Canaanites and Syrians.**
    2Ch 20:3
  - **Ezra, on account of the idolatrous marriages of the Jews.**
    Ezr 10:6
  - **Nehemiah, on account of the desolation of Jerusalem and the temple.**
    Ne 1:4
  - **The Jews.**
    - **When Jeremiah prophesied against Judea and Jerusalem.**
      Jer 36:9
    - **In Babylon, with prayer for divine deliverance and guidance.**
      Ezr 8:21; 8:23
  - **Darius, when he put Daniel in the lions' den.**
    Da 6:18

• **Daniel.**

• **On account of the captivity of the people, with prayer for their deliverance.**

Da 9:3

• **At the time of his vision.**

Da 10:1–3

• **Ninevites, when Jonah preached to them.**

Jnh 3:5–10

• **Paul, at the time of his conversion.**

Ac 9:9

• **The disciples, at the time of the consecration of Barnabas and Saul.**

Ac 13:2–3

• **The consecration of the elders.**

Ac 14:23

FAT

• **Offered in sacrifice.**

Le 3:3–5, 9–11, 14–16; 4:8–10; 7:3–5; 8:25–26; 1Sa 2:15–16

Ex 23:18 — Thou shalt not offer the blood of my sacrifice with leavened bread; neither shall the fat of my sacrifice remain until the morning.

Ex 29:13 — And thou shalt take all the fat that covereth the inwards, and the caul *that is* above the liver, and the two kidneys, and the fat that is upon them, and burn *them* upon the altar.

Ex 29:22 — Also thou shalt take of the ram the fat and the rump, and the fat that covereth the inwards, and the *caul* above the liver, and the two kidneys, and the fat that *is* upon them, and the right shoulder; for it *is* a ram of consecration:

Le 1:8 — And the priests, Aaron's sons, shall lay the parts, the head, and the fat, in order upon the wood that *is* on the fire which *is* upon the altar:

Le 8:16 — And he took all the fat that *was* upon the inwards, and caul *above* the liver, and the two kidneys, and their fat, and Moses burned *it* upon the altar.

Le 10:15 — The heave shoulder and the wave breast shall they bring with the offerings made by fire of the fat, to wave *it for* a wave offering before the LORD; and it shall be thine, and thy sons' with thee, by a statute for ever; as the LORD hath commanded.

Le 17:6 — And the priest shall sprinkle the blood upon the altar of the LORD *at* the door of the tabernacle of the congregation, and burn the fat for a sweet savour unto the LORD.

Isa 43:24 — Thou hast bought me no sweet cane with money, neither hast thou filled me with the fat of thy sacrifices: but thou hast made me to serve with thy sins, thou hast wearied me with thine iniquities.

• **Belonged to the Lord.**

Le 3:16 — And the priest shall burn them upon the altar: *it is* the food of the offering made by fire for a sweet savour: all the fat *is* the LORD'S.

• **Forbidden as food.**

Le 3:16–17

Le 7:23 — Speak unto the children of Israel, saying, Ye shall eat no manner of fat, of ox, or of sheep, or of goat.

• **Idolatrous sacrifices of.**

Dt 32:38 — Which did eat the fat of their sacrifices, *and* drank the wine of their drink offerings? let them rise up and help you, *and* be your protection.

• **Figurative.**

Ge 45:18 — And take your father and your households, and come unto me: and I will give you the good of the land of Egypt, and ye shall eat the fat of the land.

Ge 49:20 — Out of Asher his bread *shall be* fat, and he shall yield royal dainties.

Ps 37:20 — But the wicked shall perish, and the enemies of the LORD *shall be* as the fat of lambs: they shall consume; into smoke shall they consume away.

Ps 81:16 — He should have fed them also with the finest of the wheat: and with honey out of the rock should I have satisfied thee.

Isa 25:6 — And in this mountain shall the LORD of hosts make unto all people a feast of fat things, a feast of wines on the lees, of fat things full of marrow, of wines on the lees well refined.

FATHER

• **An idolatrous title of priests.**

Jgs 17:10 — And Micah said unto him, Dwell with me, and be unto me a father and a priest, and I will give thee ten *shekels* of silver by the year, and a suit of apparel, and thy victuals. So the Levite went in.

• **Forbidden to be used as a title among the disciples.**

Mt 23:9 — And call no *man* your father upon the earth: for one is your Father, which is in heaven.

See: God, Fatherhood of

See: Parents

FATHER-IN-LAW

• **Hospitable to son-in-law, a man of Bethlehem-judah.**

Jgs 19:3–9

• **Unjust, Laban to Jacob.**

Ge 29:21–23; 31:39–42

Ge 31:7 — And your father hath deceived me, and changed my wages ten times; but God suffered him not to hurt me.

FATHERHOOD

• **Of God.**

See: God, Fatherhood of

FATHERLESS **See: Orphan**

FATHOM

Ac 27:28 — And sounded, and found *it* twenty fathoms: and when they had gone a little further, they sounded again, and found *it* fifteen fathoms.

FATTED CALF

Lk 15:23 — And bring hither the fatted calf, and kill *it*; and let us eat, and be merry:

FAULT FINDING

✧See: **Murmuring**
✧See: **Uncharitableness**

FAVOR ✧See: God, Grace of

FAVORITISM

• **Instances of.**

• **Jacob, for Rachel.**
Ge 29:30, 34

• **Elkanah, for Hannah.**
1Sa 1:4–5

• **Rebekah, for Jacob.**
Ge 27:6–17

• **Jacob, for Joseph.**
Ge 37:3–4

• **Joseph, for Benjamin.**
Ge 43:34

• **Forbidden in parents.**
Dt 21:15–17

✧See: **Partiality**

FEAR

✧See: **Cowardice**
✧See: **Fear of God**

FEAR OF GOD

• **Reverence.**

Ex 20:18–20; Dt 10:20–21; Ps 25:12–14; 111:10–112:1; Pr 14:26–27; Isa 2:19–21; Jer 32:39–40; Mic 7:16–17; Heb 12:28–29; 1Pe 2:17–18; 1Jn 4:16–18

Ge 35:5 — And they journeyed: and the terror of God was upon the cities that *were* round about them, and they did not pursue after the sons of Jacob.

Ex 18:21 — Moreover thou shalt provide out of all the people able men, such as fear God, men of truth, hating covetousness; and place *such* over them, *to be* rulers of thousands, *and* rulers of hundreds, rulers of fifties, and rulers of tens:

Le 22:32 — Neither shall ye profane my holy name; but I will be hallowed among the children of Israel: I *am* the LORD which hallow you,

Dt 4:10 — *Specially* the day that thou stoodest before the LORD thy God in Horeb, when the LORD said unto me, Gather me the people together, and I will make them hear my words, that they may learn to fear me all the days that they shall live upon the earth, and *that* they may teach their children.

Dt 5:29 — O that there were such an heart in them, that they would fear me, and keep all my commandments always, that it might be well with them, and with their children for ever!

Dt 6:2 — That thou mightest fear the LORD thy God, to keep all his statutes and his commandments, which I command thee, thou, and thy son, and thy son's son, all the days of thy life; and that thy days may be prolonged.

Dt 6:13 — Thou shalt fear the LORD thy God, and serve him, and shalt swear by his name.

Dt 10:12 — And now, Israel, what doth the LORD thy God require of thee, but to fear the LORD thy God, to walk in all his ways, and to love him, and to serve the LORD thy God with all thy heart and with all thy soul,

Dt 13:4 — Ye shall walk after the LORD your God, and fear him, and keep his commandments, and obey his voice, and ye shall serve him, and cleave unto him.

Dt 14:23 — And thou shalt eat before the LORD thy God, in the place which he shall choose to place his name there, the tithe of thy corn, of thy wine, and of thine oil, and the firstlings of thy herds and of thy flocks; that thou mayest learn to fear the LORD thy God always.

Dt 28:49 — The LORD shall bring a nation against thee from far, from the end of the earth, *as swift* as the eagle flieth; a nation whose tongue thou shalt not understand;

Dt 28:58 — If thou wilt not observe to do all the words of this law that are written in this book, that thou mayest fear this glorious and fearful name, THE LORD THY GOD;

Jos 4:24 — That all the people of the earth might know the hand of the LORD, that it *is* mighty: that ye might fear the LORD your God for ever.

Jos 24:14 — Now therefore fear the LORD, and serve him in sincerity and in truth: and put away the gods which your fathers served on the other side of the flood, and in Egypt; and serve ye the LORD.

1Sa 2:30 — Wherefore the LORD God of Israel saith, I said indeed *that* thy house, and the house of thy father, should walk before me for ever: but now the LORD saith, Be it far from me; for them that honour me I will honour, and they that despise me shall be lightly esteemed.

1Sa 12:14 — If ye will fear the LORD, and serve him, and obey his voice, and not rebel against the commandment of the LORD, then shall both ye and also the king that reigneth over you continue following the LORD your God:

1Sa 12:24 — Only fear the LORD, and serve him in truth with all your heart: for consider how great *things* he hath done for you.

2Sa 23:3 — The God of Israel said, the Rock of Israel spake to me, He that ruleth over men *must be* just, ruling in the fear of God.

1Ki 8:40 — That they may fear thee all the days that they live in the land which thou gavest unto our fathers.

2Ki 17:28 — Then one of the priests whom they had carried away from Samaria came and dwelt in Bethel, and taught them how they should fear the LORD.

2Ki 17:36 — But the LORD, who brought you up out of the land of Egypt with great power and a stretched out arm, him shall ye fear, and him shall ye worship, and to him shall ye do sacrifice.

2Ki 17:39 — But the LORD your God ye shall fear; and he shall deliver you out of the hand of all your enemies.

1Ch 16:30 — Fear before him, all the earth: the world also shall be stable, that it be not moved.

2Ch 19:7 — Wherefore now let the fear of the LORD be upon you; take heed and do *it:* for *there is* no iniquity with the LORD our God, nor respect of persons, nor taking of gifts.

2Ch 19:9 — And he charged them, saying, Thus shall ye do in the fear of the LORD, faithfully, and with a perfect heart.

Ezr 10:3 — Now therefore let us make a covenant with our God to put away all the wives, and such as are born of them, according to the counsel of my lord, and of those that tremble at the commandment of our God; and let it be done according to the law.

Ne 5:9 — Also I said, It *is* not good that ye do: ought ye not to walk in the fear of our God because of the reproach of the heathen our enemies?

Job 28:28 — And unto man he said, Behold, the fear of the Lord, that *is* wisdom; and to depart from evil *is* understanding.

Job 37:24 — Men do therefore fear him: he respecteth not any *that are* wise of heart.

Ps 2:11 — Serve the LORD with fear, and rejoice with trembling.

Ps 4:4 — Stand in awe, and sin not: commune with your own heart upon your bed, and be still. Selah.

Ps 15:4 — In whose eyes a vile person is contemned; but he honoureth them that fear the LORD. *He that* sweareth to *his own* hurt, and changeth not.

Ps 19:9 — The fear of the LORD *is* clean, enduring for ever: the judgments of the LORD *are* true *and* righteous altogether.

Ps 22:23 — Ye that fear the LORD, praise him; all ye the seed of Jacob, glorify him; and fear him, all ye the seed of Israel.

Ps 22:25 — My praise *shall be* of thee in the great congregation: I will pay my vows before them that fear him.

Ps 31:19 — *Oh* how great *is* thy goodness, which thou hast laid up for them that fear thee; *which* thou hast wrought for them that trust in thee before the sons of men!

Ps 33:8 — Let all the earth fear the LORD: let all the inhabitants of the world stand in awe of him.

Ps 33:18 — Behold, the eye of the LORD *is* upon them that fear him, upon them that hope in his mercy;

Ps 34:7 — The angel of the LORD encampeth round about them that fear him, and delivereth them.

Ps 34:9 — O fear the LORD, ye his saints: for *there is* no want to them that fear him.

Ps 34:11 — Come, ye children, hearken unto me: I will teach you the fear of the LORD.

Ps 46:10 — Be still, and know that I *am* God: I will be exalted among the heathen, I will be exalted in the earth.

Ps 52:6 — The righteous also shall see, and fear, and shall laugh at him:

Ps 60:4 — Thou hast given a banner to them that fear thee, that it may be displayed because of the truth. Selah.

Ps 64:9 — And all men shall fear, and shall declare the work of God; for they shall wisely consider of his doing.

Ps 66:16 — Come *and* hear, all ye that fear God, and I will declare what he hath done for my soul.

Ps 67:7 — God shall bless us; and all the ends of the earth shall fear him.

Ps 72:5 — They shall fear thee as long as the sun and moon endure, throughout all generations.

Ps 76:7 — Thou, *even* thou, *art* to be feared: and who may stand in thy sight when once thou art angry?

Ps 76:11 — Vow, and pay unto the LORD your God: let all that be round about him bring presents unto him that ought to be feared.

Ps 85:9 — Surely his salvation *is* nigh them that fear him; that glory may dwell in our land.

Ps 86:11 — Teach me thy way, O LORD; I will walk in thy truth: unite my heart to fear thy name.

Ps 89:7 — God is greatly to be feared in the assembly of the saints, and to be had in reverence of all *them that are* about him.

Ps 90:11 — Who knoweth the power of thine anger? even according to thy fear, *so is* thy wrath.

Ps 96:4 — For the LORD *is* great, and greatly to be praised: he *is* to be feared above all gods.

Ps 96:9 — O worship the LORD in the beauty of holiness: fear before him, all the earth.

Ps 99:1 — The LORD reigneth; let the people tremble: he sitteth *between* the cherubims; let the earth be moved.

Ps 102:15 — So the heathen shall fear the name of the LORD, and all the kings of the earth thy glory.

Ps 103:11 — For as the heaven is high above the earth, *so* great is his mercy toward them that fear him.

Ps 103:13 — Like as a father pitieth *his* children, *so* the LORD pitieth them that fear him.

Ps 103:17 — But the mercy of the LORD *is* from everlasting to everlasting upon them that fear him, and his righteousness unto children's children;

Ps 111:5 — He hath given meat unto them that fear him: he will ever be mindful of his covenant.

Ps 115:11 — Ye that fear the LORD, trust in the LORD: he *is* their help and their shield.

Ps 115:13 — He will bless them that fear the LORD, *both* small and great.

Ps 118:4 — Let them now that fear the LORD say, that his mercy *endureth* for ever.

Ps 119:63 — I *am* a companion of all *them* that fear thee, and of them that keep thy precepts.

Ps 119:74 — They that fear thee will be glad when they see me; because I have hoped in thy word.

Ps 119:79 — Let those that fear thee turn unto me, and those that have known thy testimonies.

Ps 128:1 — Blessed *is* every one that feareth the LORD; that walketh in his ways.

Ps 128:4 — Behold, that thus shall the man be blessed that feareth the LORD.

Ps 130:4 — But *there is* forgiveness with thee, that thou mayest be feared.

Ps 135:20 — Bless the LORD, O house of Levi: ye that fear the LORD, bless the LORD.

Ps 145:19 — He will fulfil the desire of them that fear him: he also will hear their cry, and will save them.

Ps 147:11 — The LORD taketh pleasure in them that fear him, in those that hope in his mercy.

Pr 1:7 — The fear of the LORD *is* the beginning of knowledge: *but* fools despise wisdom and instruction.

Pr 2:5 — Then shalt thou understand the fear of the LORD, and find the knowledge of God.

Pr 3:7 — Be not wise in thine own eyes: fear the LORD, and depart from evil.

Pr 8:13 — The fear of the LORD *is* to hate evil: pride, and arrogancy, and the evil way, and the froward mouth, do I hate.

Pr 9:10 — The fear of the LORD *is* the beginning of wisdom: and the knowledge of the holy *is* understanding.

Pr 10:27 — The fear of the LORD prolongeth days: but the years of the wicked shall be shortened.

Pr 13:13 — Whoso despiseth the word shall be destroyed: but he that feareth the commandment shall be rewarded.

Pr 14:2 — He that walketh in his uprightness feareth the LORD: but *he that is* perverse in his ways despiseth him.

Pr 14:16 — A wise *man* feareth, and departeth from evil: but the fool rageth, and is confident.

Pr 15:16 — Better *is* little with the fear of the LORD than great treasure and trouble therewith.

Pr 15:33 — The fear of the LORD *is* the instruction of wisdom; and before honour *is* humility.

Pr 16:6 — By mercy and truth iniquity is purged: and by the fear of the LORD *men* depart from evil.

Pr 19:23 — The fear of the LORD *tendeth* to life: and *he that hath it* shall abide satisfied; he shall not be visited with evil.

Pr 22:4 — By humility *and* the fear of the LORD *are* riches, and honour, and life.

Pr 23:17 — Let not thine heart envy sinners: but *be thou* in the fear of the LORD all the day long.

Pr 24:21 — My son, fear thou the LORD and the king: *and* meddle not with them that are given to change:

Pr 28:14 — Happy *is* the man that feareth alway: but he that hardeneth his heart shall fall into mischief.

Pr 31:30 — Favour *is* deceitful, and beauty *is* vain: *but* a woman *that* feareth the LORD, she shall be praised.

Ecc 3:14 — I know that, whatsoever God doeth, it shall be for ever: nothing can be put to it, nor any thing taken from it: and God doeth *it*, that *men* should fear before him.

Ecc 5:7 — For in the multitude of dreams and many words *there are* also *divers* vanities: but fear thou God.

Ecc 7:18 — *It is* good that thou shouldest take hold of this; yea, also from this withdraw not thine hand: for he that feareth God shall come forth of them all.

Ecc 8:12 — Though a sinner do evil an hundred times, and his *days* be prolonged, yet surely I know that it shall be well with them that fear God, which fear before him:

Ecc 12:13 — Let us hear the conclusion of the whole matter: Fear God, and keep his commandments: for this *is* the whole *duty* of man.

Isa 2:10 — Enter into the rock, and hide thee in the dust, for fear of the LORD, and for the glory of his majesty.

Isa 8:13 — Sanctify the LORD of hosts himself; and *let* him *be* your fear, and *let* him *be* your dread.

Isa 25:3 — Therefore shall the strong people glorify thee, the city of the terrible nations shall fear thee.

Isa 29:13 — Wherefore the Lord said, Forasmuch as this people draw near *me* with their mouth, and with their lips do honour me, but have removed their heart far from me, and their fear toward me is taught by the precept of men:

Isa 29:23 — But when he seeth his children, the work of mine hands, in the midst of him, they shall sanctify my name, and sanctify the Holy One of Jacob, and shall fear the God of Israel.

Isa 33:6 — And wisdom and knowledge shall be the stability of thy times, *and* strength of salvation: the fear of the LORD *is* his treasure.

Isa 33:13 — Hear, ye *that are* far off, what I have done; and, ye *that are* near, acknowledge my might.

Isa 50:10 — Who *is* among you that feareth the LORD, that obeyeth the voice of his servant, that walketh *in* darkness, and hath no light? let him trust in the name of the LORD, and stay upon his God.

Isa 59:19 — So shall they fear the name of the LORD from the west, and his glory from the rising of the sun. When the enemy shall come in like a flood, the Spirit of the LORD shall lift up a standard against him.

Isa 60:5 — Then thou shalt see, and flow together, and thine heart shall fear, and be enlarged; because the abundance of the sea shall be converted unto thee, the forces of the Gentiles shall come unto thee.

Jer 5:22 — Fear ye not me? saith the LORD: will ye not tremble at my presence, which have placed the sand *for* the bound of the sea by a perpetual decree, that it cannot pass it: and though the waves thereof toss themselves, yet can they not prevail; though they roar, yet can they not pass over it?

Jer 10:7 — Who would not fear thee, O King of nations? for to thee doth it appertain: forasmuch as among all the wise *men* of the nations, and in all their kingdoms, *there is* none like unto thee.

Jer 33:9 — And it shall be to me a name of joy, a praise and an honour before all the nations of the earth, which shall hear all the good that I do unto them: and they shall fear and tremble for all the goodness and for all the prosperity that I procure unto it.

Hos 3:5 — Afterward shall the children of Israel return, and seek the LORD their God, and David their king; and shall fear the LORD and his goodness in the latter days.

Zep 1:7 — Hold thy peace at the presence of the Lord GOD: for the day of the LORD *is* at hand: for the LORD hath prepared a sacrifice, he hath bid his guests.

Zep 3:7 — I said, Surely thou wilt fear me, thou wilt receive instruction; so their dwelling should not be cut off, howsoever I punished them: but they rose early, *and* corrupted all their doings.

Zec 2:13 — Be silent, O all flesh, before the LORD: for he is raised up out of his holy habitation.

Mal 1:6 — A son honoureth *his* father, and a servant his master: if then I *be* a father, where *is* mine honour? and if I *be* a master, where *is* my fear? saith the LORD of hosts unto you, O priests, that despise my name. And ye say, Wherein have we despised thy name?

Mal 3:16 — Then they that feared the LORD spake often one to another: and the LORD hearkened, and heard *it*, and a book of remembrance was written before him for them that feared the LORD, and that thought upon his name.

Mal 4:2 — But unto you that fear my name shall the Sun of righteousness arise with healing in his wings; and ye shall go forth, and grow up as calves of the stall.

Mt 10:28 — And fear not them which kill the body, but are not able to kill the soul: but rather fear him which is able to destroy both soul and body in hell.

Lk 1:50 — And his mercy *is* on them that fear him from generation to generation.

Lk 12:5 — But I will forewarn you whom ye shall fear: Fear him, which after he hath killed hath power to cast into hell; yea, I say unto you, Fear him.

Lk 23:40 — But the other answering rebuked him, saying, Dost not thou fear God, seeing thou art in the same condemnation?

Ac 10:35 — But in every nation he that feareth him, and worketh righteousness, is accepted with him.

Ac 13:16 — Then Paul stood up, and beckoning with *his* hand said, Men of Israel, and ye that fear God, give audience.

Ac 13:26 — Men *and* brethren, children of the stock of Abraham, and whosoever among you feareth God, to you is the word of this salvation sent.

Ro 11:20 — Well; because of unbelief they were broken off, and thou standest by faith. Be not highminded, but fear:

2Co 7:1 — Having therefore these promises, dearly beloved, let us cleanse ourselves from all filthiness of the flesh and spirit, perfecting holiness in the fear of God.

Eph 5:21 — Submitting yourselves one to another in the fear of God.

Eph 6:5 — Servants, be obedient to them that are *your* masters according to the flesh, with fear and trembling, in singleness of your heart, as unto Christ;

Col 3:22 — Servants, obey in all things *your* masters according to the flesh; not with eyeservice, as menpleasers; but in singleness of heart, fearing God:

Heb 5:5 — So also Christ glorified not himself to be made an high priest; but he that said unto him, Thou art my Son, to day have I begotten thee.

Heb 5:7 — Who in the days of his flesh, when he had offered up prayers and supplications with strong crying and tears unto him that was able to save him from death, and was heard in that he feared;

Jas 2:19 — Thou believest that there is one God; thou doest well: the devils also believe, and tremble.

1Pe 1:17 — And if ye call on the Father, who without respect of persons judgeth according to every man's work, pass the time of your sojourning *here* in fear:

1Pe 2:12 — Having your conversation honest among the Gentiles: that, whereas they speak against you as evildoers, they may by *your* good works, which they shall behold, glorify God in the day of visitation.

1Pe 3:2 — While they behold your chaste conversation *coupled* with fear.

1Pe 3:15 — But sanctify the Lord God in your hearts: and *be* ready always to *give* an answer to every man that asketh you a reason of the hope that is in you with meekness and fear:

Rev 11:18 — And the nations were angry, and thy wrath is come, and the time of the dead, that they should be judged, and that thou shouldest give reward unto thy servants the prophets, and to the saints, and them that fear thy name, small and great; and shouldest destroy them which destroy the earth.

Rev 14:7 — Saying with a loud voice, Fear God, and give glory to him; for the hour of his judgment is come: and worship him that made heaven, and earth, and the sea, and the fountains of waters.

Rev 19:5 — And a voice came out of the throne, saying, Praise our God, all ye his servants, and ye that fear him, both small and great.

• Conspicuous instances of those who feared.

• Noah, in preparing the ark.

Heb 11:7 — By faith Noah, being warned of God of things not seen as yet, moved with fear, prepared an ark to the saving of his house; by the which he condemned the world, and became heir of the righteousness which is by faith.

• Abraham, tested in the offering of his son Isaac.

Ge 22:12 — And he said, Lay not thine hand upon the lad, neither do thou any thing unto him: for now I know that thou fearest God, seeing thou hast not withheld thy son, thine only *son* from me.

• Jacob, in the vision of the ladder, and the covenant of God.

Ge 28:16–17

Ge 42:18 — And Joseph said unto them the third day, This do, and live; *for* I fear God:

• The midwives of Egypt, in refusing to take the lives of the Hebrew children.

Ex 1:17 — But the midwives feared God, and did not as the king of Egypt commanded them, but saved the men children alive.

Ex 1:21 — And it came to pass, because the midwives feared God, that he made them houses.

• The Egyptians, at the time of the plague of thunder and hail and fire.

Ex 9:20 — He that feared the word of the LORD among the servants of Pharaoh made his servants and his cattle flee into the houses:

• The nine and one-half tribes of Israel west of Jordan.

Jos 22:15–20

• Phinehas, in turning away the anger of God at the time of the plague.

Nu 25:6–15

• Obadiah, in sheltering one hundred prophets against the wrath of Jezebel.

1Ki 18:3–4

• Jehoshaphat, in proclaiming a feast, when land was about to be invaded.

2Ch 20:3 — And Jehoshaphat feared, and set himself to seek the LORD, and proclaimed a fast throughout all Judah.

• Nehemiah, in his reform of the public administration.

Ne 5:15 — But the former governors that *had been* before me were chargeable unto the people, and had taken of them bread and wine, beside forty shekels of silver; yea, even their servants bare rule over the people: but so did not I, because of the fear of God.

• Hanani, which qualified him to be ruler over Jerusalem.

Ne 7:2 — That I gave my brother Hanani, and Hananiah the ruler of the palace, charge over Jerusalem: for he *was* a faithful man, and feared God above many.

• Job, according to the testimony of Satan.

Job 1:8 — And the LORD said unto Satan, Hast thou considered my servant Job, that *there is* none like him in the earth, a perfect and an upright man, one that feareth God, and escheweth evil?

• David.

Ps 5:7 — But as for me, I will come *into* thy house in the multitude of thy mercy: *and* in thy fear will I worship toward thy holy temple.

Ps 119:38 — Stablish thy word unto thy servant, who *is devoted* to thy fear.

• Hezekiah, in his treatment of the prophet Micah, who prophesied evil against Jerusalem.

Jer 26:19 — Did Hezekiah king of Judah and all Judah put him at all to death? did he not fear the LORD, and besought the LORD, and the LORD repented him of the evil which he had pronounced against them? Thus might we procure great evil against our souls.

• Jonah, in the tempest.

Jnh 1:9 — And he said unto them, I *am* an Hebrew; and I fear the LORD, the God of heaven, which hath made the sea and the dry *land.*

• The Jews, in obeying the voice of the Lord.

Hag 1:12 — Then Zerubbabel the son of Shealtiel, and Joshua the son of Josedech, the high priest, with all the remnant of the people, obeyed the voice of the LORD their God, and the words of Haggai the prophet, as the LORD their God had sent him, and the people did fear before the LORD.

• Levi, in receiving the covenant of life and peace.

Hag 1:5 — Now therefore thus saith the LORD of hosts; Consider your ways.

• The women at the sepulchre.

Mt 28:8 — And they departed quickly from the sepulchre with fear and great joy; and did run to bring his disciples word.

• Cornelius, who feared God with all his house.

Ac 10:2 — A devout *man,* and one that feared God with all his house, which gave much alms to the people, and prayed to God alway.

✦See: Conviction; of sin

✦See: Faith

• Cultivated.

Ex 19:12–13; Heb 12:18–24

Ex 3:5 — And he said, Draw not nigh hither: put off thy shoes from off thy feet, for the place whereon thou standest is holy ground.

• Guilty.

Job 15:20–25; Pr 1:24–27

Job 18:11 — Terrors shall make him afraid on every side, and shall drive him to his feet.

Pr 10:24 — The fear of the wicked, it shall come upon him: but the desire of the righteous shall be granted.

Da 5:6 — Then the king's countenance was changed, and his thoughts troubled him, so that the joints of his loins were loosed, and his knees smote one against another.

Jas 2:19 — Thou believest that there is one God; thou doest well: the devils also believe, and tremble.

• Instances of guilty fear.

• Adam and Eve.

Ge 3:8–13

• The guards at Jesus' tomb.

Mt 28:4

• Judas.

Mt 27:3–5

• Devils.

Jas 2:19

✦See: Conviction; of sin

• A motive of obedience.

Dt 6:13–15; 8:5–6; 10:12–13; 13:6–11; 17:11–13; 19:16–20; 21:18–21; 28:14–68; 31:11–13; Jos 23:11–16; 1Sa 12:14–15, 24–25; Job 31:1–4, 13–15; Lk 12:4–5; 2Co 5:10–11; 2Ti 4:1–2; 2Pe 3:10–12; Rev 14:9–10

Le 19:14 — Thou shalt not curse the deaf, nor put a stumblingblock before the blind, but shalt fear thy God: I *am* the LORD.

Le 19:32 — Thou shalt rise up before the hoary head, and honour the face of the old man, and fear thy God: I *am* the LORD.

Le 25:17 — Ye shall not therefore oppress one another; but thou shalt fear thy God: for I *am* the LORD your God.

Le 25:36 — Take thou no usury of him, or increase: but fear thy God; that thy brother may live with thee.

Le 25:43 — Thou shalt not rule over him with rigour; but shalt fear thy God.

Nu 32:15 — For if ye turn away from after him, he will yet again leave them in the wilderness; and ye shall destroy all this people.

Dt 7:4 — For they will turn away thy son from following me, that they may serve other gods: so will the anger of the LORD be kindled against you, and destroy thee suddenly.

Dt 10:20 — Thou shalt fear the LORD thy God; him shalt thou serve, and to him shalt thou cleave, and swear by his name.

Dt 13:4 — Ye shall walk after the LORD your God, and fear him, and keep his commandments, and obey his voice, and ye shall serve him, and cleave unto him.

Dt 14:23 — And thou shalt eat before the LORD thy God, in the place which he shall choose to place his name there, the tithe of thy corn, of thy wine, and of thine oil, and the firstlings of thy herds and of thy flocks; that thou mayest learn to fear the LORD thy God always.

Dt 15:9 — Beware that there be not a thought in thy wicked heart, saying, The seventh year, the year of release, is at hand; and thine eye be evil against thy poor brother, and thou givest him nought; and he cry unto the LORD against thee, and it be sin unto thee.

Job 13:21 — Withdraw thine hand far from me: and let not thy dread make me afraid.

Job 31:23 — For destruction *from* God *was* a terror to me, and by reason of his highness I could not endure.

Pr 16:6 — By mercy and truth iniquity is purged: and by the fear of the LORD *men* depart from evil.

Isa 1:20 — But if ye refuse and rebel, ye shall be devoured with the sword: for the mouth of the LORD hath spoken *it.*

Jer 4:4 — Circumcise yourselves to the LORD, and take away the foreskins of your heart, ye men of Judah and inhabitants of Jerusalem: lest my fury come forth like fire, and burn that none can quench *it,* because of the evil of your doings.

Jer 22:5 — But if ye will not hear these words, I swear by myself, saith the LORD, that this house shall become a desolation.

Mt 10:28 — And fear not them which kill the body, but are not able to kill the soul: but rather fear him which is able to destroy both soul and body in hell.

See: Punishment; design of; to secure obedience

See: Reward; a motive to faithfulness

FEAR of Jews

Jn 7:45–53

Ps 107:2 — Let the redeemed of the LORD say so, whom he hath redeemed from the hand of the enemy;

Pr 29:25 — The fear of man bringeth a snare: but whoso putteth his trust in the LORD shall be safe.

Jn 9:22 — These *words* spake his parents, because they feared the Jews: for the Jews had agreed already, that if any man did confess that he was Christ, he should be put out of the synagogue.

Jn 19:38 — And after this Joseph of Arimathaea, being a disciple of Jesus, but secretly for fear of the Jews, besought Pilate that he might take away the body of Jesus: and Pilate gave *him* leave. He came therefore, and took the body of Jesus.

FEASTS

• Ancient customs at.

• Men alone present at.

Ge 40:20 — And it came to pass the third day, *which was* Pharaoh's birthday, that he made a feast unto all his servants: and he lifted up the head of the chief butler and of the chief baker among his servants.

Ge 43:32 — And they set on for him by himself, and for them by themselves, and for the Egyptians, which did eat with him, by themselves: because the Egyptians might not eat bread with the Hebrews; for that *is* an abomination unto the Egyptians.

Ge 43:34 — And he took *and sent* messes unto them from before him: but Benjamin's mess was five times so much as any of theirs. And they drank, and were merry with him.

1Sa 9:22 — And Samuel took Saul and his servant, and brought them into the parlour, and made them sit in the chiefest place among them that were bidden, which *were* about thirty persons.

Est 1:8 — And the drinking *was* according to the law; none did compel: for so the king had appointed to all the officers of his house, that they should do according to every man's pleasure.

Mk 6:21 — And when a convenient day was come, that Herod on his birthday made a supper to his lords, high captains, and chief *estates* of Galilee;

Lk 14:24 — For I say unto you, That none of those men which were bidden shall taste of my supper.

• Women alone.

Est 1:9 — Also Vashti the queen made a feast for the women *in* the royal house which *belonged* to king Ahasuerus.

• Men and women attend.

Ex 32:2–3; Da 5:1–3

Ex 32:6 — And they rose up early on the morrow, and offered burnt offerings, and brought peace offerings; and the people sat down to eat and to drink, and rose up to play.

• Riddles propounded at.

Jgs 14:12 — And Samson said unto them, I will now put forth a riddle unto you: if ye can certainly declare it me within the seven days of the feast, and find *it* out, then I will give you thirty sheets and thirty change of garments:

• Marriage feasts provided by the bridegroom.

Jgs 14:10 — So his father went down unto the woman: and Samson made there a feast; for so used the young men to do.

Jgs 14:17 — And she wept before him the seven days, while their feast lasted: and it came to pass on the seventh day, that he told her, because she lay sore upon him: and she told the riddle to the children of her people.

- **Guests arranged according to age.**

Ge 43:33 — And they sat before him, the firstborn according to his birthright, and the youngest according to his youth: and the men marvelled one at another.

- **Guests arranged according to rank.**

Lk 14:8–10

1Sa 9:22 — And Samuel took Saul and his servant, and brought them into the parlour, and made them sit in the chiefest place among them that were bidden, which *were* about thirty persons.

- **Reclined on couches.**

Am 6:4 — That lie upon beds of ivory, and stretch themselves upon their couches, and eat the lambs out of the flock, and the calves out of the midst of the stall;

Am 6:7 — Therefore now shall they go captive with the first that go captive, and the banquet of them that stretched themselves shall be removed.

Lk 7:38 — And stood at his feet behind *him* weeping, and began to wash his feet with tears, and did wipe *them* with the hairs of her head, and kissed his feet, and anointed *them* with the ointment.

Jn 13:25 — He then lying on Jesus' breast saith unto him, Lord, who is it?

- **Served in one dish.**

Mt 26:23 — And he answered and said, He that dippeth *his* hand with me in the dish, the same shall betray me.

- **Were presided over by a governor.**

Jn 2:8–9

- **Host served.**

Ge 18:8 — And he took butter, and milk, and the calf which he had dressed, and set *it* before them; and he stood by them under the tree, and they did eat.

- **Wine served at.**

Est 5:6 — And the king said unto Esther at the banquet of wine, What *is* thy petition? and it shall be granted thee: and what *is* thy request? even to the half of the kingdom it shall be performed.

Est 7:7 — And the king arising from the banquet of wine in his wrath *went* into the palace garden: and Haman stood up to make request for his life to Esther the queen; for he saw that there was evil determined against him by the king.

- **Music at.**

Am 6:4–5

Isa 5:12 — And the harp, and the viol, the tabret, and pipe, and wine, are in their feasts: but they regard not the work of the LORD, neither consider the operation of his hands.

Lk 15:25 — Now his elder son was in the field: and as he came and drew nigh to the house, he heard musick and dancing.

- **Dancing at.**

Mt 14:6 — But when Herod's birthday was kept, the daughter of Herodias danced before them, and pleased Herod.

Lk 15:25 — Now his elder son was in the field: and as he came and drew nigh to the house, he heard musick and dancing.

- **Given by kings.**

Est 1:3–8; Da 5:1–4

1Sa 20:5 — And David said unto Jonathan, Behold, to morrow *is* the new moon, and I should not fail to sit with the king at meat: but let me go, that I may hide myself in the field unto the third *day* at even.

1Sa 25:36 — And Abigail came to Nabal; and, behold, he held a feast in his house, like the feast of a king; and Nabal's heart *was* merry within him, for he *was* very drunken: wherefore she told him nothing, less or more, until the morning light.

2Sa 9:10 — Thou therefore, and thy sons, and thy servants, shall till the land for him, and thou shalt bring in *the fruits*, that thy master's son may have food to eat: but Mephibosheth thy master's son shall eat bread alway at my table. Now Ziba had fifteen sons and twenty servants.

1Ki 2:7 — But shew kindness unto the sons of Barzillai the Gileadite, and let them be of those that eat at thy table: for so they came to me when I fled because of Absalom thy brother.

1Ki 4:22 — And Solomon's provision for one day was thirty measures of fine flour, and threescore measures of meal,

1Ki 18:19 — Now therefore send, *and* gather to me all Israel unto mount Carmel, and the prophets of Baal four hundred and fifty, and the prophets of the groves four hundred, which eat at Jezebel's table.

- **Drunkenness at.**

Da 5:1–4

1Sa 25:36 — And Abigail came to Nabal; and, behold, he held a feast in his house, like the feast of a king; and Nabal's heart *was* merry within him, for he *was* very drunken: wherefore she told him nothing, less or more, until the morning light.

Est 1:10 — On the seventh day, when the heart of the king was merry with wine, he commanded Mehuman, Biztha, Harbona, Bigtha, and Abagtha, Zethar, and Carcas, the seven chamberlains that served in the presence of Ahasuerus the king,

- **Covenants ratified by.**

Ge 26:28–30

- **Celebrations by.**
  - **Birthdays.**

Ge 40:20 — And it came to pass the third day, *which was* Pharaoh's birthday, that he made a feast unto all his servants: and he lifted up the head of the chief butler and of the chief baker among his servants.

Mk 6:21 — And when a convenient day was come, that Herod on his birthday made a supper to his lords, high captains, and chief *estates* of Galilee;

- **Coronations.**

1Ch 12:38–40

1Ki 1:25 — For he is gone down this day, and hath slain oxen and fat cattle and sheep in abundance, and hath called all the king's sons, and the captains of the host, and Abiathar the priest; and, behold, they eat and drink before him, and say, God save king Adonijah.

- **National deliverances.**

Est 9:17–19

Est 8:17 — And in every province, and in every city, whithersoever the king's commandment and his decree came, the Jews had joy and gladness, a feast and a good day. And many of the people of the land became Jews; for the fear of the Jews fell upon them.

- **Figurative.**

Mt 22:1–14; Lk 14:16–24

Rev 19:9 — And he saith unto me, Write, Blessed *are* they which are called unto the marriage supper of the Lamb. And he saith unto me, These are the true sayings of God.

Rev 19:17 — And I saw an angel standing in the sun; and he cried with a loud voice, saying to all the fowls that fly in the midst of heaven, Come and gather yourselves together unto the supper of the great God;

- **Annual festivals.**
  - **Instituted by Moses.**
  - **Designated as Solemn Feasts.**

Nu 15:3 — And will make an offering by fire unto the LORD, a burnt offering, or a sacrifice in performing a vow, or in a freewill offering, or in your solemn feasts, to make a sweet savour unto the LORD, of the herd, or of the flock:

2Ch 8:13 — Even after a certain rate every day, offering according to the commandment of Moses, on the sabbaths, and on the new moons, and on the solemn feasts, three times in the year, *even* in the feast of unleavened bread, and in the feast of weeks, and in the feast of tabernacles.

La 2:6 — And he hath violently taken away his tabernacle, as *if it were of* a garden: he hath destroyed his places of the assembly: the LORD hath caused the solemn feasts and sabbaths to be forgotten in Zion, and hath despised in the indignation of his anger the king and the priest.

Eze 46:9 — But when the people of the land shall come before the LORD in the solemn feasts, he that entereth in by the way of the north gate to worship shall go out by the way of the south gate; and he that entereth by the way of the south gate shall go forth by the way of the north gate: he shall not return by the way of the gate whereby he came in, but shall go forth over against it.

  - **Set feasts.**

Nu 29:39 — These *things* ye shall do unto the LORD in your set feasts, beside your vows, and your freewill offerings, for your burnt offerings, and for your meat offerings, and for your drink offerings, and for your peace offerings.

Ezr 3:5 — And afterward *offered* the continual burnt offering, both of the new moons, and of all the set feasts of the LORD that were consecrated, and of every one that willingly offered a freewill offering unto the LORD.

  - **Appointed feasts.**

Isa 1:14 — Your new moons and your appointed feasts my soul hateth: they are a trouble unto me; I am weary to bear *them.*

  - **Holy convocations.**

Le 23:4 — These *are* the feasts of the LORD, *even* holy convocations, which ye shall proclaim in their seasons.

  - **First and last days were Sabbatic.**

Le 23:39–40; Nu 28:18–25; Ne 8:1–18

Nu 29:12 — And on the fifteenth day of the seventh month ye shall have an holy convocation; ye shall do no servile work, and ye shall keep a feast unto the LORD seven days:

Nu 29:35 — On the eighth day ye shall have a solemn assembly: ye shall do no servile work *therein:*

  - **Kept with rejoicing.**

Dt 16:11–14; 2Ch 30:21–26; Ne 8:9–12

Le 23:40 — And ye shall take you on the first day the boughs of goodly trees, branches of palm trees, and the boughs of thick trees, and willows of the brook; and ye shall rejoice before the LORD your God seven days.

Ezr 6:22 — And kept the feast of unleavened bread seven days with joy: for the LORD had made them joyful, and turned the heart of the king of Assyria unto them, to strengthen their hands in the work of the house of God, the God of Israel.

Ne 8:17 — And all the congregation of them that were come again out of the captivity made booths, and sat under the booths: for since the days of Jeshua the son of Nun unto that day had not the children of Israel done so. And there was very great gladness.

Ps 42:4 — When I remember these *things,* I pour out my soul in me: for I had gone with the multitude, I went with them to the house of God, with the voice of joy and praise, with a multitude that kept holyday.

Ps 122:4 — Whither the tribes go up, the tribes of the LORD, unto the testimony of Israel, to give thanks unto the name of the LORD.

Isa 30:29 — Ye shall have a song, as in the night *when* a holy solemnity is kept; and gladness of heart, as when one goeth with a pipe to come into the mountain of the LORD, to the mighty One of Israel.

Zec 8:19 — Thus saith the LORD of hosts; The fast of the fourth *month,* and the fast of the fifth, and the fast of the seventh, and the fast of the tenth, shall be to the house of Judah joy and gladness, and cheerful feasts; therefore love the truth and peace.

• **Divine protection given during.**

Ex 34:24 — For I will cast out the nations before thee, and enlarge thy borders: neither shall any man desire thy land, when thou shalt go up to appear before the LORD thy God thrice in the year.

• **Three principal, were Passover, Pentecost, Tabernacles; males required to attend.**

Jn 7:1–53

Ex 23:17 — Three times in the year all thy males shall appear before the Lord GOD.

Ex 34:23 — Thrice in the year shall all your men children appear before the Lord GOD, the God of Israel.

Dt 16:16 — Three times in a year shall all thy males appear before the LORD thy God in the place which he shall choose; in the feast of unleavened bread, and in the feast of weeks, and in the feast of tabernacles: and they shall not appear before the LORD empty:

Ps 42:4 — When I remember these *things,* I pour out my soul in me: for I had gone with the multitude, I went with them to the house of God, with the voice of joy and praise, with a multitude that kept holyday.

Ps 122:4 — Whither the tribes go up, the tribes of the LORD, unto the testimony of Israel, to give thanks unto the name of the LORD.

Eze 36:38 — As the holy flock, as the flock of Jerusalem in her solemn feasts; so shall the waste cities be filled with flocks of men: and they shall know that I *am* the LORD.

Lk 2:44 — But they, supposing him to have been in the company, went a day's journey; and they sought him among *their* kinsfolk and acquaintance.

Jn 4:45 — Then when he was come into Galilee, the Galilaeans received him, having seen all the things that he did at Jerusalem at the feast: for they also went unto the feast.

• **Aliens permitted to attend.**

Ac 2:1–11

Jn 12:20 — And there were certain Greeks among them that came up to worship at the feast:

• **Attended by women.**

1Sa 1:3 — And this man went up out of his city yearly to worship and to sacrifice unto the LORD of hosts in Shiloh. And the two sons of Eli, Hophni and Phinehas, the priests of the LORD, *were* there.

1Sa 1:9 — So Hannah rose up after they had eaten in Shiloh, and after they had drunk. Now Eli the priest sat upon a seat by a post of the temple of the LORD.

Lk 2:41 — Now his parents went to Jerusalem every year at the feast of the passover.

• **Observed.**

• **By Jesus.**

Mt 26:17–20; Lk 2:41–42

Lk 22:15 — And he said unto them, With desire I have desired to eat this passover with you before I suffer:

Jn 2:13 — And the Jews' passover was at hand, and Jesus went up to Jerusalem,

Jn 2:23 — Now when he was in Jerusalem at the passover, in the feast *day,* many believed in his name, when they saw the miracles which he did.

Jn 5:1 — After this there was a feast of the Jews; and Jesus went up to Jerusalem.

Jn 7:10 — But when his brethren were gone up, then went he also up unto the feast, not openly, but as it were in secret.

Jn 10:22 — And it was at Jerusalem the feast of the dedication, and it was winter.

• **By Paul.**

Ac 18:21 — But bade them farewell, saying, I must by all means keep this feast that cometh in Jerusalem: but I will return again unto you, if God will. And he sailed from Ephesus.

Ac 19:21 — After these things were ended, Paul purposed in the spirit, when he had passed through Macedonia and Achaia, to go to Jerusalem, saying, After I have been there, I must also see Rome.

Ac 20:6 — And we sailed away from Philippi after the days of unleavened bread, and came unto them to Troas in five days; where we abode seven days.

Ac 20:16 — For Paul had determined to sail by Ephesus, because he would not spend the time in Asia: for he hasted, if it were possible for him, to be at Jerusalem the day of Pentecost.

Ac 24:11 — Because that thou mayest understand, that there are yet but twelve days since I went up to Jerusalem for to worship.

Ac 24:17 — Now after many years I came to bring alms to my nation, and offerings.

• **For full treatment of annual feasts.**

See: Passover

See: Pentecost

See: Purim

See: Tabernacle

See: Trumpets

FEET

• **Bells worn on.**

Isa 3:16 — Moreover the LORD saith, Because the daughters of Zion are haughty, and walk with stretched forth necks and wanton eyes, walking and mincing *as* they go, and making a tinkling with their feet:

Isa 3:18 — In that day the Lord will take away the bravery of *their* tinkling ornaments *about their feet,* and *their* cauls, and *their* round tires like the moon,

• **Washing of, as an example, by Jesus.**

Jn 13:4–14

• **Sitting at.**

Dt 33:3 — Yea, he loved the people; all his saints *are* in thy hand: and they sat down at thy feet; *every one* shall receive of thy words.

Lk 10:39 — And she had a sister called Mary, which also sat at Jesus' feet, and heard his word.

Ac 22:3 — I am verily a man *which am* a Jew, born in Tarsus, a city in Cilicia, yet brought up in this city at the feet of Gamaliel, *and* taught according to the perfect manner of the law of the fathers, and was zealous toward God, as ye all are this day.

See: Ablution

FELIX

• Governor of Judaea.

• Paul tried before.

Ac 23:24–24:27

• Trembles under Paul's preaching.

Ac 24:25 — And as he reasoned of righteousness, temperance, and judgment to come Felix trembled, and answered, Go thy way for this time; when I have a convenient season, I will call for thee.

• Leaves Paul in bonds.

Ac 24:26–27

Ac 25:14 — And when they had been there many days, Festus declared Paul's cause unto the king, saying, There is a certain man left in bonds by Felix:

FELLOWSHIP

Ecc 4:9–12

Am 3:3 — Can two walk together, except they be agreed?

See: Fellowship

See: Fraternity

• With God.

Ex 33:14–17; 1Jn 1:5–7; Rev 21:3–4

Ge 5:22 — And Enoch walked with God after he begat Methuselah three hundred years, and begat sons and daughters:

Ge 5:24 — And Enoch walked with God: and he *was* not; for God took him.

Ge 6:9 — These *are* the generations of Noah: Noah was a just man *and* perfect in his generations, *and* Noah walked with God.

Ex 29:45 — And I will dwell among the children of Israel, and will be their God.

Le 26:12 — And I will walk among you, and will be your God, and ye shall be my people.

Isa 57:15 — For thus saith the high and lofty One that inhabiteth eternity, whose name *is* Holy; I dwell in the high and holy *place,* with him also *that is* of a contrite and humble spirit, to revive the spirit of the humble, and to revive the heart of the contrite ones.

Zec 2:10 — Sing and rejoice, O daughter of Zion: for, lo, I come, and I will dwell in the midst of thee, saith the LORD.

Mk 9:37 — Whosoever shall receive one of such children in my name, receiveth me: and whosoever shall receive me, receiveth not me, but him that sent me.

Jn 14:23 — Jesus answered and said unto him, If a man love me, he will keep my words: and my Father will love him, and we will come unto him, and make our abode with him.

Jn 17:21 — That they all may be one; as thou, Father, *art* in me, and I in thee, that they also may be one in us: that the world may believe that thou hast sent me.

Jn 17:23 — I in them, and thou in me, that they may be made perfect in one; and that the world may know that thou hast sent me, and hast loved them, as thou hast loved me.

2Co 6:16 — And what agreement hath the temple of God with idols? for ye are the temple of the living God; as God hath said, I will dwell in them, and walk in *them;* and I will be their God, and they shall be my people.

2Co 13:11 — Finally, brethren, farewell. Be perfect, be of good comfort, be of one mind, live in peace; and the God of love and peace shall be with you.

1Jn 1:3 — That which we have seen and heard declare we unto you, that ye also may have fellowship with us: and truly our fellowship *is* with the Father, and with his Son Jesus Christ.

1Jn 3:24 — And he that keepeth his commandments dwelleth in him, and he in him. And hereby we know that he abideth in us, by the Spirit which he hath given us.

See: Communion; with God

• With Christ.

Ps 45:9–16; SS 1:1–8:14; Mt 12:48–50; Jn 6:51–57; 14:20–23; 15:1–8; 17:21–23; 1Co 6:13–15; 1Th 5:9–10

Mt 18:20 — For where two or three are gathered together in my name, there am I in the midst of them.

Mk 9:37 — Whosoever shall receive one of such children in my name, receiveth me: and whosoever shall receive me, receiveth not me, but him that sent me.

Lk 8:21 — And he answered and said unto them, My mother and my brethren are these which hear the word of God, and do it.

Lk 24:32 — And they said one to another, Did not our heart burn within us, while he talked with us by the way, and while he opened to us the scriptures?

Jn 17:26 — And I have declared unto them thy name, and will declare *it:* that the love wherewith thou hast loved me may be in them, and I in them.

Ro 7:4 — Wherefore, my brethren, ye also are become dead to the law by the body of Christ; that ye should be married to another, *even* to him who is raised from the dead, that we should bring forth fruit unto God.

Ro 8:1 — *There is* therefore now no condemnation to them which are in Christ Jesus, who walk not after the flesh, but after the Spirit.

Ro 8:10 — And if Christ *be* in you, the body *is* dead because of sin; but the Spirit *is* life because of righteousness.

Ro 8:17 — And if children, then heirs; heirs of God, and joint-heirs with Christ; if so be that we suffer with *him,* that we may be also glorified together.

Ro 11:17 — And if some of the branches be broken off, and thou, being a wild olive tree, wert graffed in among them, and with them partakest of the root and fatness of the olive tree;

Ro 12:5 — So we, *being* many, are one body in Christ, and every one members one of another.

1Co 1:9 — God *is* faithful, by whom ye were called unto the fellowship of his Son Jesus Christ our Lord.

1Co 6:17 — But he that is joined unto the Lord is one spirit.

1Co 10:16 — The cup of blessing which we bless, is it not the communion of the blood of Christ? The bread which we break, is it not the communion of the body of Christ?

1Co 12:12 — For as the body is one, and hath many members, and all the members of that one body, being many, are one body: so also *is* Christ.

1Co 12:27 — Now ye are the body of Christ, and members in particular.

2Co 11:2 — For I am jealous over you with godly jealousy: for I have espoused you to one husband, that I may present *you as* a chaste virgin to Christ.

2Co 13:5 — Examine yourselves, whether ye be in the faith; prove your own selves. Know ye not your own selves, how that Jesus Christ is in you, except ye be reprobates?

Eph 5:30 — For we are members of his body, of his flesh, and of his bones.

Eph 5:32 — This is a great mystery: but I speak concerning Christ and the church.

Col 1:27 — To whom God would make known what *is* the riches of the glory of this mystery among the Gentiles; which is Christ in you, the hope of glory:

Col 3:3 — For ye are dead, and your life is hid with Christ in God.

Heb 2:11 — For both he that sanctifieth and they who are sanctified *are* all of one: for which cause he is not ashamed to call them brethren,

1Jn 2:6 — He that saith he abideth in him ought himself also so to walk, even as he walked.

1Jn 2:24 — Let that therefore abide in you, which ye have heard from the beginning. If that which ye have heard from the beginning shall remain in you, ye also shall continue in the Son, and in the Father.

1Jn 2:28 — And now, little children, abide in him; that, when he shall appear, we may have confidence, and not be ashamed before him at his coming.

1Jn 3:6 — Whosoever abideth in him sinneth not: whosoever sinneth hath not seen him, neither known him.

1Jn 3:24 — And he that keepeth his commandments dwelleth in him, and he in him. And hereby we know that he abideth in us, by the Spirit which he hath given us.

1Jn 4:13 — Hereby know we that we dwell in him, and he in us, because he hath given us of his Spirit.

1Jn 5:12 — He that hath the Son hath life; *and* he that hath not the Son of God hath not life.

1Jn 5:20 — *And* we know that the Son of God is come, and hath given us an understanding, that we may know him that is true, and we are in him that is true, *even* in his Son Jesus Christ. This is the true God, and eternal life.

2Jn 1:9 — Whosoever transgresseth, and abideth not in the doctrine of Christ, hath not God. He that abideth in the doctrine of Christ, he hath both the Father and the Son.

Rev 3:20 — Behold, I stand at the door, and knock: if any man hear my voice, and open the door, I will come in to him, and will sup with him, and he with me.

See: Communion

• Of the Holy Spirit.

Ro 8:9 — But ye are not in the flesh, but in the Spirit, if so be that the Spirit of God dwell in you. Now if any man have not the Spirit of Christ, he is none of his.

1Co 3:16 — Know ye not that ye are the temple of God, and *that* the Spirit of God dwelleth in you?

2Co 13:14 — The grace of the Lord Jesus Christ, and the love of God, and the communion of the Holy Ghost, *be* with you all. Amen.

See: Communion

See: Holy Spirit

• Of the righteous.

Mt 20:25–28; Mk 10:42–45; Lk 24:13–15; Jn 17:21–23; Ac 2:44–47; Ro 14:1–4, 13–16, 18–21; 15:1–7; 1Co 10:16–17; 16:19–20; Eph 2:14–22; Php 2:1–2; Heb 10:24–25; 1Pe 3:8–9; 1Jn 4:7–8, 11–13

Ps 55:14 — We took sweet counsel together, *and* walked unto the house of God in company.

Ps 119:63 — I *am* a companion of all *them* that fear thee, and of them that keep thy precepts.

Am 3:3 — Can two walk together, except they be agreed?

Mal 3:16 — Then they that feared the LORD spake often one to another: and the LORD hearkened, and heard *it*, and a book of remembrance was written before him for them that feared the LORD, and that thought upon his name.

Mt 17:4 — Then answered Peter, and said unto Jesus, Lord, it is good for us to be here: if thou wilt, let us make here three tabernacles; one for thee, and one for Moses, and one for Elias.

Mt 23:8 — But be not ye called Rabbi: for one is your Master, *even* Christ; and all ye are brethren.

Lk 22:32 — But I have prayed for thee, that thy faith fail not: and when thou art converted, strengthen thy brethren.

Jn 13:34 — A new commandment I give unto you, That ye love one another; as I have loved you, that ye also love one another.

Jn 15:12 — This is my commandment, That ye love one another, as I have loved you.

Jn 17:11 — And now I am no more in the world, but these are in the world, and I come to thee. Holy Father, keep through thine own name those whom thou hast given me, that they may be one, as we *are*.

Ac 1:14 — These all continued with one accord in prayer and supplication, with the women, and Mary the mother of Jesus, and with his brethren.

Ac 2:1 — And when the day of Pentecost was fully come, they were all with one accord in one place.

Ac 2:42 — And they continued stedfastly in the apostles' doctrine and fellowship, and in breaking of bread, and in prayers.

Ac 17:4 — And some of them believed, and consorted with Paul and Silas; and of the devout Greeks a great multitude, and of the chief women not a few.

Ac 20:35 — I have shewed you all things, how that so labouring ye ought to support the weak, and to remember the words of the Lord Jesus, how he said, It is more blessed to give than to receive.

Ro 1:12 — That is, that I may be comforted together with you by the mutual faith both of you and me.

Ro 14:10 — But why dost thou judge thy brother? or why dost thou set at nought thy brother? for we shall all stand before the judgment seat of Christ.

1Co 1:10 — Now I beseech you, brethren, by the name of our Lord Jesus Christ, that ye all speak the same thing, and *that* there be no divisions among you; but *that* ye be perfectly joined together in the same mind and in the same judgment.

1Co 12:13 — For by one Spirit are we all baptized into one body, whether *we be* Jews or Gentiles, whether *we be* bond or free; and have been all made to drink into one Spirit.

Gal 2:9 — And when James, Cephas, and John, who seemed to be pillars, perceived the grace that was given unto me, they gave to me and Barnabas the right hands of fellowship; that we *should go* unto the heathen, and they unto the circumcision.

Gal 6:2 — Bear ye one another's burdens, and so fulfil the law of Christ.

Gal 6:10 — As we have therefore opportunity, let us do good unto all *men,* especially unto them who are of the household of faith.

Eph 5:2 — And walk in love, as Christ also hath loved us, and hath given himself for us an offering and a sacrifice to God for a sweetsmelling savour.

Eph 5:19 — Speaking to yourselves in psalms and hymns and spiritual songs, singing and making melody in your heart to the Lord;

Eph 5:30 — For we are members of his body, of his flesh, and of his bones.

Php 1:3 — I thank my God upon every remembrance of you,

Php 1:5 — For your fellowship in the gospel from the first day until now;

Php 1:27 — Only let your conversation be as it becometh the gospel of Christ: that whether I come and see you, or else be absent, I may hear of your affairs, that ye stand fast in one spirit, with one mind striving together for the faith of the gospel;

Col 2:2 — That their hearts might be comforted, being knit together in love, and unto all riches of the full assurance of understanding, to the acknowledgement of the mystery of God, and of the Father, and of Christ;

Col 3:16 — Let the word of Christ dwell in you richly in all wisdom; teaching and admonishing one another in psalms and hymns and spiritual songs, singing with grace in your hearts to the Lord.

1Th 4:18 — Wherefore comfort one another with these words.

1Th 5:11 — Wherefore comfort yourselves together, and edify one another, even as also ye do.

1Th 5:14 — Now we exhort you, brethren, warn them that are unruly, comfort the feebleminded, support the weak, be patient toward all *men.*

Heb 3:13 — But exhort one another daily, while it is called To day; lest any of you be hardened through the deceitfulness of sin.

Heb 13:1 — Let brotherly love continue.

Jas 5:16 — Confess *your* faults one to another, and pray one for another, that ye may be healed. The effectual fervent prayer of a righteous man availeth much.

1Pe 2:17 — Honour all *men.* Love the brotherhood. Fear God. Honour the king.

1Jn 1:3 — That which we have seen and heard declare we unto you, that ye also may have fellowship with us: and truly our fellowship *is* with the Father, and with his Son Jesus Christ.

1Jn 1:7 — But if we walk in the light, as he is in the light, we have fellowship one with another, and the blood of Jesus Christ his Son cleanseth us from all sin.

1Jn 3:14 — We know that we have passed from death unto life, because we love the brethren. He that loveth not *his* brother abideth in death.

See: Communion; of saints

• With the wicked.

Ex 33:15–16; 34:13–16; Nu 25:1–8; Dt 31:16–17; Jos 23:12–13; Ezr 6:21–22; Ps 26:4–5; 102:6–8; 2Pe 2:18–19

Ge 49:6 — O my soul, come not thou into their secret; unto their assembly, mine honour, be not thou united: for in their anger they slew a man, and in their selfwill they digged down a wall.

Ezr 9:14 — Should we again break thy commandments, and join in affinity with the people of these abominations? wouldest not thou be angry with us till thou hadst consumed *us,* so that *there should be* no remnant nor escaping?

Ps 6:8 — Depart from me, all ye workers of iniquity; for the LORD hath heard the voice of my weeping.

Ps 50:18 — When thou sawest a thief, then thou consentedst with him, and hast been partaker with adulterers.

Pr 12:11 — He that tilleth his land shall be satisfied with bread: but he that followeth vain *persons is* void of understanding.

Pr 28:19 — He that tilleth his land shall have plenty of bread: but he that followeth after vain *persons* shall have poverty enough.

Pr 29:24 — Whoso is partner with a thief hateth his own soul: he heareth cursing, and bewrayeth *it* not.

1Co 5:11 — But now I have written unto you not to keep company, if any man that is called a brother be a fornicator, or covetous, or an idolater, or a railer, or a drunkard, or an extortioner; with such an one no not to eat.

1Co 15:33 — Be not deceived: evil communications corrupt good manners.

2Pe 3:17 — Ye therefore, beloved, seeing ye know *these things* before, beware lest ye also, being led away with the error of the wicked, fall from your own stedfastness.

- **Punishment of.**

Jgs 3:5–8; Ps 106:41–42; Rev 2:22–23

Nu 33:56 — Moreover it shall come to pass, *that* I shall do unto you, as I thought to do unto them.

Jos 23:13 — Know for a certainty that the LORD your God will no more drive out *any of* these nations from before you; but they shall be snares and traps unto you, and scourges in your sides, and thorns in your eyes, until ye perish from off this good land which the LORD your God hath given you.

Jgs 2:3 — Wherefore I also said, I will not drive them out from before you; but they shall be *as thorns* in your sides, and their gods shall be a snare unto you.

Ezr 9:7 — Since the days of our fathers *have we been* in a great trespass unto this day; and for our iniquities have we, our kings, and *our* priests, been delivered into the hand of the kings of the lands, to the sword, to captivity, and to a spoil, and to confusion of face, as *it is* this day.

Ezr 9:14 — Should we again break thy commandments, and join in affinity with the people of these abominations? wouldest not thou be angry with us till thou hadst consumed *us,* so that *there should be* no remnant nor escaping?

Rev 2:16 — Repent; or else I will come unto thee quickly, and will fight against them with the sword of my mouth.

✦See: Company; evil

✦See: Influence

- **With the wicked forbidden.**

Ex 23:32–33; Dt 7:2–4; 13:6–11; Jos 23:6–7; Ezr 9:1–2; Pr 1:10–15; 4:14–15; 1Co 5:9–11; 2Co 6:14–17; 2Th 3:14–15; 1Ti 6:3–5; 2Ti 3:2–7; 2Jn 1:9–11; Rev 18:1–4

Ex 34:12 — Take heed to thyself, lest thou make a covenant with the inhabitants of the land whither thou goest, lest it be for a snare in the midst of thee:

Nu 16:26 — And he spake unto the congregation, saying, Depart, I pray you, from the tents of these wicked men, and touch nothing of theirs, lest ye be consumed in all their sins.

Dt 12:30 — Take heed to thyself that thou be not snared by following them, after that they be destroyed from before thee; and that thou enquire not after their gods, saying, How did these nations serve their gods? even so will I do likewise.

Jos 23:13 — Know for a certainty that the LORD your God will no more drive out *any of* these nations from before you; but they shall be snares and traps unto you, and scourges in your sides, and thorns in your eyes, until ye perish from off this good land which the LORD your God hath given you.

Jgs 2:2 — And ye shall make no league with the inhabitants of this land; ye shall throw down their altars: but ye have not obeyed my voice: why have ye done this?

Ezr 9:12 — Now therefore give not your daughters unto their sons, neither take their daughters unto your sons, nor seek their peace or their wealth for ever: that ye may be strong, and eat the good of the land, and leave *it* for an inheritance to your children for ever.

Ezr 10:11 — Now therefore make confession unto the LORD God of your fathers, and do his pleasure: and separate yourselves from the people of the land, and from the strange wives.

Ps 1:1 — Blessed *is* the man that walketh not in the counsel of the ungodly, nor standeth in the way of sinners, nor sitteth in the seat of the scornful.

Pr 9:6 — Forsake the foolish, and live; and go in the way of understanding.

Pr 14:7 — Go from the presence of a foolish man, when thou perceivest not *in him* the lips of knowledge.

Mt 18:17 — And if he shall neglect to hear them, tell *it* unto the church: but if he neglect to hear the church, let him be unto thee as an heathen man and a publican.

Ro 16:17 — Now I beseech you, brethren, mark them which cause divisions and offences contrary to the doctrine which ye have learned; and avoid them.

Eph 5:11 — And have no fellowship with the unfruitful works of darkness, but rather reprove *them.*

2Th 3:6 — Now we command you, brethren, in the name of our Lord Jesus Christ, that ye withdraw yourselves from every brother that walketh disorderly, and not after the tradition which he received of us.

2Pe 3:17 — Ye therefore, beloved, seeing ye know *these things* before, beware lest ye also, being led away with the error of the wicked, fall from your own stedfastness.

- **The evil of fellowship with the wicked exemplified.**

  - **By Solomon.**

1Ki 11:1–8

  - **By Rehoboam.**

1Ki 12:8–9

  - **By Jehoshaphat.**

2Ch 20:35–37

2Ch 18:3 — And Ahab king of Israel said unto Jehoshaphat king of Judah, Wilt thou go with me to Ramoth-gilead? And he answered him, I *am* as thou *art,* and my people as thy people; and *we will be* with thee in the war.

2Ch 19:2 — And Jehu the son of Hanani the seer went out to meet him, and said to king Jehoshaphat, Shouldest thou help the ungodly, and love them that hate the LORD? therefore is wrath upon thee from before the LORD.

  - **By Jehoram.**

2Ch 21:6 — And he walked in the way of the kings of Israel, like as did the house of Ahab: for he had the daughter of Ahab to wife: and he wrought *that which was* evil in the eyes of the LORD.

  - **By Ahaziah.**

2Ch 22:3–5

  - **By Israelites.**

Ezr 9:1–2

- **By Israel.**
  Eze 44:7 — In that ye have brought *into my sanctuary* strangers, uncircumcised in heart, and uncircumcised in flesh, to be in my sanctuary, to pollute it, *even* my house, when ye offer my bread, the fat and the blood, and they have broken my covenant because of all your abominations.
- **By Judas Iscariot.**
  Mt 26:14–16

- **Instances of those who avoided fellowship with the wicked.**
  - **Man of God.**
    1Ki 13:7–10
  - **Nehemiah.**
    Ne 6:2–4; 10:29–31
  - **David.**
    Ps 101:4–7; 119:115
  - **Jeremiah.**
    Jer 15:17
  - **Joseph of Arimathaea.**
    Lk 23:51
  - **Church of Ephesus.**
    Rev 2:6

  See: Company; evil
  See: Influence; evil

FENCE

SS 4:12 — A garden inclosed *is* my sister, *my* spouse; a spring shut up, a fountain sealed.

- **Made of stone walls.**
  Pr 24:30–31
  Nu 22:24 — But the angel of the LORD stood in a path of the vineyards, a wall *being* on this side, and a wall on that side.
  Ps 62:3 — How long will ye imagine mischief against a man? ye shall be slain all of you: as a bowing wall *shall ye be, and as* a tottering fence.
  Isa 5:2 — And he fenced it, and gathered out the stones thereof, and planted it with the choicest vine, and built a tower in the midst of it, and also made a winepress therein: and he looked that it should bring forth grapes, and it brought forth wild grapes.
  Mic 7:11 — *In* the day that thy walls are to be built, *in* that day shall the decree be far removed.
- **Hedge.**
  Pr 15:19 — The way of the slothful *man is* as an hedge of thorns: but the way of the righteous *is* made plain.
  Ecc 10:8 — He that diggeth a pit shall fall into it; and whoso breaketh an hedge, a serpent shall bite him.
  Isa 5:5 — And now go to; I will tell you what I will do to my vineyard: I will take away the hedge thereof, and it shall be eaten up; *and* break down the wall thereof, and it shall be trodden down:
  Hos 2:6 — Therefore, behold, I will hedge up thy way with thorns, and make a wall, that she shall not find her paths.
  Na 3:17 — Thy crowned *are* as the locusts, and thy captains as the great grasshoppers, which camp in the hedges in the cold day, *but* when the sun ariseth they flee away, and their place is not known where they *are.*
  Mt 21:33 — Hear another parable: There was a certain householder, which planted a vineyard, and hedged it round about, and digged a winepress in it, and built a tower, and let it out to husbandmen, and went into a far country:
- **Figurative.**
  Eze 22:30 — And I sought for a man among them, that should make up the hedge, and stand in the gap before me for the land, that I should not destroy it: but I found none.

FERRET

Le 11:30 — And the ferret, and the chameleon, and the lizard, and the snail, and the mole.

FERRYBOAT

2Sa 19:18 — And there went over a ferry boat to carry over the king's household, and to do what he thought good. And Shimei the son of Gera fell down before the king, as he was come over Jordan;

FESTIVALS **See: Feasts**

FESTUS

- **Governor of Judaea, and successor to Felix.**
- **Called also Porcius Festus.**
  Ac 24:27 — But after two years Porcius Festus came into Felix' room: and Felix, willing to shew the Jews a pleasure, left Paul bound.
- **Tries Paul.**
  Ac 25:1–27

FETTERS

- **Used for securing prisoners.**
  2Ch 33:11 — Wherefore the LORD brought upon them the captains of the host of the king of Assyria, which took Manasseh among the thorns, and bound him with fetters, and carried him to Babylon.
  2Ch 36:6 — Against him came up Nebuchadnezzar king of Babylon, and bound him in fetters, to carry him to Babylon.
  Mk 5:4 — Because that he had been often bound with fetters and chains, and the chains had been plucked asunder by him, and the fetters broken in pieces: neither could any *man* tame him.
- **Made of brass.**
  Jgs 16:21 — But the Philistines took him, and put out his eyes, and brought him down to Gaza, and bound him with fetters of brass; and he did grind in the prison house.
  2Ki 25:7 — And they slew the sons of Zedekiah before his eyes, and put out the eyes of Zedekiah, and bound him with fetters of brass, and carried him to Babylon.
- **Made of iron.**

  See: Chains

FEVER

Le 26:16 — I also will do this unto you; I will even appoint over you terror, consumption, and the burning ague, that shall consume the eyes, and cause sorrow of heart: and ye shall sow your seed in vain, for your enemies shall eat it.

Dt 28:22 — The LORD shall smite thee with a consumption, and with a fever, and with an inflammation, and with an extreme burning, and with the sword, and with blasting, and with mildew; and they shall pursue thee until thou perish.

Job 30:30 — My skin is black upon me, and my bones are burned with heat.

Ps 22:15 — My strength is dried up like a potsherd; and my tongue cleaveth to my jaws; and thou hast brought me into the dust of death.

Mt 8:14 — And when Jesus was come into Peter's house, he saw his wife's mother laid, and sick of a fever.

Ac 28:8 — And it came to pass, that the father of Publius lay sick of a fever and of a bloody flux: to whom Paul entered in, and prayed, and laid his hands on him, and healed him.

FICKLENESS ⇽See: Instability

FIG

• Common to Palestine.

Nu 13:23 — And they came unto the brook of Eshcol, and cut down from thence a branch with one cluster of grapes, and they bare it between two upon a staff; and *they brought* of the pomegranates, and of the figs.

Dt 8:8 — A land of wheat, and barley, and vines, and fig trees, and pomegranates; a land of oil olive, and honey;

• Common to Egypt.

Ps 105:33 — He smote their vines also and their fig trees; and brake the trees of their coasts.

• Employed as a remedy.

2Ki 20:7 — And Isaiah said, Take a lump of figs. And they took and laid *it* on the boil, and he recovered.

Isa 38:21 — For Isaiah had said, Let them take a lump of figs, and lay *it* for a plaister upon the boil, and he shall recover.

• Traffic in.

Ne 13:15 — In those days saw I in Judah *some* treading winepresses on the sabbath, and bringing in sheaves, and lading asses; as also wine, grapes, and figs, and all *manner of* burdens, which they brought into Jerusalem on the sabbath day: and I testified *against them* in the day wherein they sold victuals.

• Dried and preserved.

1Sa 30:12 — And they gave him a piece of a cake of figs, and two clusters of raisins: and when he had eaten, his spirit came again to him: for he had eaten no bread, nor drunk *any* water, three days and three nights.

• Cakes of, sent by Abigail to David.

1Sa 25:18–35

• Aprons made of fig leaves, by Adam and Eve.

Ge 3:7 — And the eyes of them both were opened, and they knew that they *were* naked; and they sewed fig leaves together, and made themselves aprons.

FIG TREE

• In an allegory.

Jgs 9:11 — But the fig tree said unto them, Should I forsake my sweetness, and my good fruit, and go to be promoted over the trees?

• Jeremiah's parable of.

Jer 24:2–3

• Barren, parable of.

Lk 13:6–9; 21:29–31

• Figurative.

Mt 24:32 — Now learn a parable of the fig tree; When his branch is yet tender, and putteth forth leaves, ye know that summer is nigh:

Rev 6:13 — And the stars of heaven fell unto the earth, even as a fig tree casteth her untimely figs, when she is shaken of a mighty wind.

FIGHT OF FAITH

2Ch 20:17 — Ye shall not *need* to fight in this *battle:* set yourselves, stand ye *still,* and see the salvation of the LORD with you, O Judah and Jerusalem: fear not, nor be dismayed; to morrow go out against them: for the LORD *will be* with you.

1Ti 6:12 — Fight the good fight of faith, lay hold on eternal life, whereunto thou art also called, and hast professed a good profession before many witnesses.

2Ti 4:7 — I have fought a good fight, I have finished *my* course, I have kept the faith:

Heb 10:32 — But call to remembrance the former days, in which, after ye were illuminated, ye endured a great fight of afflictions;

Heb 11:34 — Quenched the violence of fire, escaped the edge of the sword, out of weakness were made strong, waxed valiant in fight, turned to flight the armies of the aliens.

FIGURE

• Figurative under principal topics throughout the work.

⇽See: Allegory

⇽See: Pantomime

⇽See: Parables

⇽See: Symbols and Similitudes

⇽See: Types

FILE

• Used for sharpening edged tools.

1Sa 13:21 — Yet they had a file for the mattocks, and for the coulters, and for the forks, and for the axes, and to sharpen the goads.

FINANCES

• Methods of raising money.

⇽See: Money

⇽See: Temple

⇽See: Tribute

FINE

• A penalty.

Ex 22:7–9; Le 5:15–16; 6:5–6; Nu 5:5–8; Pr 6:30–31

Ex 22:1 — If a man shall steal an ox, or a sheep, and kill it, or sell it; he shall restore five oxen for an ox, and four sheep for a sheep.

Ex 22:4 — If the theft be certainly found in his hand alive, whether it be ox, or ass, or sheep; he shall restore double.

See: Damages and Compensation

FINGER

• Six on one hand.

2Sa 21:20 — And there was yet a battle in Gath, where was a man of *great* stature, that had on every hand six fingers, and on every foot six toes, four and twenty in number; and he also was born to the giant.

FINGERBREADTH • A unit of measurement.

Jer 52:21 — And *concerning* the pillars, the height of one pillar *was* eighteen cubits; and a fillet of twelve cubits did compass it; and the thickness thereof *was* four fingers: *it was* hollow.

FIR TREE

• Wood of, used for building.

1Ki 6:15 — And he built the walls of the house within with boards of cedar, both the floor of the house, and the walls of the cieling: *and* he covered *them* on the inside with wood, and covered the floor of the house with planks of fir.

1Ki 6:34 — And the two doors *were of* fir tree: the two leaves of the one door *were* folding, and the two leaves of the other door *were* folding.

SS 1:17 — The beams of our house *are* cedar, *and* our rafters of fir.

• Ships made of.

Eze 27:5 — They have made all thy *ship* boards of fir trees of Senir: they have taken cedars from Lebanon to make masts for thee.

• Instruments of music made of.

2Sa 6:5 — And David and all the house of Israel played before the LORD on all manner of *instruments made of* fir wood, even on harps, and on psalteries, and on timbrels, and on cornets, and on cymbals.

FIRE

• Used as a signal in war.

Jer 6:1 — O ye children of Benjamin, gather yourselves to flee out of the midst of Jerusalem, and blow the trumpet in Tekoa, and set up a sign of fire in Beth-haccerem: for evil appeareth out of the north, and great destruction.

• Furnaces of.

Da 3:6 — And whoso falleth not down and worshippeth shall the same hour be cast into the midst of a burning fiery furnace.

• Children caused to pass through.

2Ki 16:3 — But he walked in the way of the kings of Israel, yea, and made his son to pass through the fire, according to the abominations of the heathen, whom the LORD cast out from before the children of Israel.

2Ki 17:17 — And they caused their sons and their daughters to pass through the fire, and used divination and enchantments, and sold themselves to do evil in the sight of the LORD, to provoke him to anger.

• Miracles connected with.

• Miraculously descends upon, and consumes, Abraham's sacrifice.

Ge 15:17 — And it came to pass, that, when the sun went down, and it was dark, behold a smoking furnace, and a burning lamp that passed between those pieces.

• David's.

1Ch 21:26 — And David built there an altar unto the LORD, and offered burnt offerings and peace offerings, and called upon the LORD; and he answered him from heaven by fire upon the altar of burnt offering.

• Elijah's.

1Ki 18:38 — Then the fire of the LORD fell, and consumed the burnt sacrifice, and the wood, and the stones, and the dust, and licked up the water that *was* in the trench.

• Solomon's, at dedication of the temple.

2Ch 7:1 — Now when Solomon had made an end of praying, the fire came down from heaven, and consumed the burnt offering and the sacrifices; and the glory of the LORD filled the house.

• Display of, in the plagues of Egypt.

Ex 9:24 — So there was hail, and fire mingled with the hail, very grievous, such as there was none like it in all the land of Egypt since it became a nation.

• Display of, at Elijah's translation.

2Ki 2:11 — And it came to pass, as they still went on, and talked, that, behold, *there appeared* a chariot of fire, and horses of fire, and parted them both asunder; and Elijah went up by a whirlwind into heaven.

• Consumes the conspirators with Korah, Dathan, and Abiram.

Nu 16:35 — And there came out a fire from the LORD, and consumed the two hundred and fifty men that offered incense.

• Consumes the captains and their fifties.

2Ki 1:9–12

• Torture by.

Da 3:1–30

Le 21:9 — And the daughter of any priest, if she profane herself by playing the whore, she profaneth her father: she shall be burnt with fire.

Jer 29:22 — And of them shall be taken up a curse by all the captivity of Judah which *are* in Babylon, saying, The LORD make thee like Zedekiah and like Ahab, whom the king of Babylon roasted in the fire;

Eze 23:25 — And I will set my jealousy against thee, and they shall deal furiously with thee: they shall take away thy nose and thine ears; and thy remnant shall fall by the sword: they shall take thy sons and thy daughters; and thy residue shall be devoured by the fire.

Eze 23:47 — And the company shall stone them with stones, and dispatch them with their swords; they shall slay their sons and their daughters, and burn up their houses with fire.

• Pillar of fire.

Ex 13:21–22; Nu 9:15–23

Ex 14:19 — And the angel of God, which went before the camp of Israel, removed and went behind them; and the pillar of the cloud went from before their face, and stood behind them:

Ex 14:24 — And it came to pass, that in the morning watch the LORD looked unto the host of the Egyptians through the pillar of fire and of the cloud, and troubled the host of the Egyptians,

Ex 40:38 — For the cloud of the LORD *was* upon the tabernacle by day, and fire was on it by night, in the sight of all the house of Israel, throughout all their journeys.

See: Cloud; pillar of

• Figurative.

• Of cleansing.

Isa 6:6–7

• Of spiritual power.

Ps 104:4 — Who maketh his angels spirits; his ministers a flaming fire:

Jer 20:9 — Then I said, I will not make mention of him, nor speak any more in his name. But *his word* was in mine heart as a burning fire shut up in my bones, and I was weary with forbearing, and I could not *stay.*

Mt 3:11 — I indeed baptize you with water unto repentance: but he that cometh after me is mightier than I, whose shoes I am not worthy to bear: he shall baptize you with the Holy Ghost, and *with* fire:

Lk 3:16 — John answered, saying unto *them* all, I indeed baptize you with water; but one mightier than I cometh, the latchet of whose shoes I am not worthy to unloose: he shall baptize you with the Holy Ghost and with fire:

• Of judgments.

Dt 4:24 — For the LORD thy God *is* a consuming fire, *even* a jealous God.

Dt 32:22 — For a fire is kindled in mine anger, and shall burn unto the lowest hell, and shall consume the earth with her increase, and set on fire the foundations of the mountains.

Isa 33:14 — The sinners in Zion are afraid; fearfulness hath surprised the hypocrites. Who among us shall dwell with the devouring fire? who among us shall dwell with everlasting burnings?

Jer 23:29 — *Is* not my word like as a fire? saith the LORD; and like a hammer *that* breaketh the rock in pieces?

Am 1:4 — But I will send a fire into the house of Hazael, which shall devour the palaces of Benhadad.

Am 1:7 — But I will send a fire on the wall of Gaza, which shall devour the palaces thereof:

Am 1:10 — But I will send a fire on the wall of Tyrus, which shall devour the palaces thereof.

Am 1:12 — But I will send a fire upon Teman, which shall devour the palaces of Bozrah.

Am 1:14 — But I will kindle a fire in the wall of Rabbah, and it shall devour the palaces thereof, with shouting in the day of battle, with a tempest in the day of the whirlwind:

Am 2:2 — But I will send a fire upon Moab, and it shall devour the palaces of Kirioth: and Moab shall die with tumult, with shouting, *and* with the sound of the trumpet:

Mal 3:2 — But who may abide the day of his coming? and who shall stand when he appeareth? for he *is* like a refiner's fire, and like fullers' sope:

Lk 12:49 — I am come to send fire on the earth; and what will I if it be already kindled?

Rev 20:9 — And they went up on the breadth of the earth, and compassed the camp of the saints about, and the beloved city: and fire came down from God out of heaven, and devoured them.

• Of the destruction of the wicked.

Mt 13:42 — And shall cast them into a furnace of fire: there shall be wailing and gnashing of teeth.

Mt 13:50 — And shall cast them into the furnace of fire: there shall be wailing and gnashing of teeth.

Mt 25:41 — Then shall he say also unto them on the left hand, Depart from me, ye cursed, into everlasting fire, prepared for the devil and his angels:

Mk 9:44 — Where their worm dieth not, and the fire is not quenched.

Rev 9:2 — And he opened the bottomless pit; and there arose a smoke out of the pit, as the smoke of a great furnace; and the sun and the air were darkened by reason of the smoke of the pit.

Rev 21:8 — But the fearful, and unbelieving, and the abominable, and murderers, and whoremongers, and sorcerers, and idolaters, and all liars, shall have their part in the lake which burneth with fire and brimstone: which is the second death.

• Everlasting fire.

Isa 33:14 — The sinners in Zion are afraid; fearfulness hath surprised the hypocrites. Who among us shall dwell with the devouring fire? who among us shall dwell with everlasting burnings?

Mt 18:8 — Wherefore if thy hand or thy foot offend thee, cut them off, and cast *them* from thee: it is better for thee to enter into life halt or maimed, rather than having two hands or two feet to be cast into everlasting fire.

Mt 25:41 — Then shall he say also unto them on the left hand, Depart from me, ye cursed, into everlasting fire, prepared for the devil and his angels:

Mk 9:44 — Where their worm dieth not, and the fire is not quenched.

• **A symbol of God's presence.**

Ge 15:17 — And it came to pass, that, when the sun went down, and it was dark, behold a smoking furnace, and a burning lamp that passed between those pieces.

• **In the burning bush.**

Ex 3:2 — And the angel of the LORD appeared unto him in a flame of fire out of the midst of a bush: and he looked, and, behold, the bush burned with fire, and the bush *was* not consumed.

• **On Sinai.**

Ex 19:18 — And mount Sinai was altogether on a smoke, because the LORD descended upon it in fire: and the smoke thereof ascended as the smoke of a furnace, and the whole mount quaked greatly.

• **Tongues of, on the apostles.**

Ac 2:3 — And there appeared unto them cloven tongues like as of fire, and it sat upon each of them.

➔**See: Arson**

FIREBRAND

• **Used by Samson.**

Jgs 15:4 — And Samson went and caught three hundred foxes, and took firebrands, and turned tail to tail, and put a firebrand in the midst between two tails.

• **Figurative.**

Pr 26:18 — As a mad *man* who casteth firebrands, arrows, and death,

Am 4:11 — I have overthrown *some* of you, as God overthrew Sodom and Gomorrah, and ye were as a firebrand plucked out of the burning: yet have ye not returned unto me, saith the LORD.

Zec 3:2 — And the LORD said unto Satan, The LORD rebuke thee, O Satan; even the LORD that hath chosen Jerusalem rebuke thee: *is* not this a brand plucked out of the fire?

FIREPAN

Ex 38:3 — And he made all the vessels of the altar, the pots, and the shovels, and the basons, *and* the fleshhooks, and the firepans: all the vessels thereof made he *of* brass.

2Ki 25:15 — And the firepans, and the bowls, *and* such things as *were* of gold, *in* gold, and of silver, *in* silver, the captain of the guard took away.

FIRKIN • About nine gallons.

Jn 2:6 — And there were set there six waterpots of stone, after the manner of the purifying of the Jews, containing two or three firkins apiece.

FIRMAMENT • The expanse above the earth.

Ge 1:6–8, 14–17

Ge 1:20 — And God said, Let the waters bring forth abundantly the moving creature that hath life, and fowl *that* may fly above the earth in the open firmament of heaven.

Ps 19:1 — The heavens declare the glory of God; and the firmament sheweth his handywork.

Da 12:3 — And they that be wise shall shine as the brightness of the firmament; and they that turn many to righteousness as the stars for ever and ever.

FIRSTFRUITS

• **First ripe of fruits, grain, oil, wine, and first of fleece, required as an offering.**

Le 2:12–16

Ex 22:29 — Thou shalt not delay *to offer* the first of thy ripe fruits, and of thy liquors: the firstborn of thy sons shalt thou give unto me.

Nu 18:12 — All the best of the oil, and all the best of the wine, and of the wheat, the firstfruits of them which they shall offer unto the LORD, them have I given thee.

Dt 18:4 — The firstfruit *also* of thy corn, of thy wine, and of thine oil, and the first of the fleece of thy sheep, shalt thou give him.

2Ch 31:5 — And as soon as the commandment came abroad, the children of Israel brought in abundance the firstfruits of corn, wine, and oil, and honey, and of all the increase of the field; and the tithe of all *things* brought they in abundantly.

Ne 10:35 — And to bring the firstfruits of our ground, and the firstfruits of all fruit of all trees, year by year, unto the house of the LORD:

Ne 10:37 — And *that* we should bring the firstfruits of our dough, and our offerings, and the fruit of all manner of trees, of wine and of oil, unto the priests, to the chambers of the house of our God; and the tithes of our ground unto the Levites, that the same Levites might have the tithes in all the cities of our tillage.

Ne 10:39 — For the children of Israel and the children of Levi shall bring the offering of the corn, of the new wine, and the oil, unto the chambers, where *are* the vessels of the sanctuary, and the priests that minister, and the porters, and the singers: and we will not forsake the house of our God.

Pr 3:9 — Honour the LORD with thy substance, and with the firstfruits of all thine increase:

Jer 2:3 — Israel *was* holiness unto the LORD, *and* the firstfruits of his increase: all that devour him shall offend; evil shall come upon them, saith the LORD.

Ro 11:16 — For if the firstfruit *be* holy, the lump *is* also *holy:* and if the root *be* holy, so *are* the branches.

• **Offerings of, must be free from blemish.**

Nu 18:12 — All the best of the oil, and all the best of the wine, and of the wheat, the firstfruits of them which they shall offer unto the LORD, them have I given thee.

• **Offerings of, presented at the tabernacle.**

Dt 26:3–10

Ex 22:29 — Thou shalt not delay *to offer* the first of thy ripe fruits, and of thy liquors: the firstborn of thy sons shalt thou give unto me.

Ex 23:19 — The first of the firstfruits of thy land thou shalt bring into the house of the LORD thy God. Thou shalt not seethe a kid in his mother's milk.

Ex 34:26 — The first of the firstfruits of thy land thou shalt bring unto the house of the LORD thy God. Thou shalt not seethe a kid in his mother's milk.

• Offerings of, belonged to the priests.

Nu 18:12–13; Dt 18:3–5

Le 23:20 — And the priest shall wave them with the bread of the first fruits *for* a wave offering before the LORD, with the two lambs: they shall be holy to the LORD for the priest.

• Freewill offerings of, given to the prophets.

2Ki 4:42 — And there came a man from Baal-shalisha, and brought the man of God bread of the firstfruits, twenty loaves of barley, and full ears of corn in the husk thereof. And he said, Give unto the people, that they may eat.

• Wave offering of.

Le 23:10–14

Le 23:17 — Ye shall bring out of your habitations two wave loaves of two tenth deals: they shall be of fine flour; they shall be baken with leaven; *they are* the firstfruits unto the LORD.

• As a heave offering.

Nu 15:20 — Ye shall offer up a cake of the first of your dough *for* an heave offering: as *ye do* the heave offering of the threshingfloor, so shall ye heave it.

Ne 10:37 — And *that* we should bring the firstfruits of our dough, and our offerings, and the fruit of all manner of trees, of wine and of oil, unto the priests, to the chambers of the house of our God; and the tithes of our ground unto the Levites, that the same Levites might have the tithes in all the cities of our tillage.

Eze 44:30 — And the first of all the firstfruits of all *things,* and every oblation of all, of every *sort* of your oblations, shall be the priest's: ye shall also give unto the priest the first of your dough, that he may cause the blessing to rest in thine house.

• To be offered as a thank offering upon entrance into the land of promise.

Dt 26:3–10

• Figurative.

Ro 8:23 — And not only *they,* but ourselves also, which have the firstfruits of the Spirit, even we ourselves groan within ourselves, waiting for the adoption, *to wit,* the redemption of our body.

Ro 11:16 — For if the firstfruit *be* holy, the lump *is* also *holy:* and if the root *be* holy, so *are* the branches.

1Co 15:20 — But now is Christ risen from the dead, *and* become the firstfruits of them that slept.

1Co 15:23 — But every man in his own order: Christ the firstfruits; afterward they that are Christ's at his coming.

Jas 1:18 — Of his own will begat he us with the word of truth, that we should be a kind of firstfruits of his creatures.

FIRSTBORN

• Of man and beast, reserved to himself by God.

Ex 13:12–16; 22:29–30; 34:19–20; Nu 8:17–18; Dt 15:19–23

Ex 13:2 — Sanctify unto me all the firstborn, whatsoever openeth the womb among the children of Israel, *both* of man and of beast: it *is* mine.

Le 27:26 — Only the firstling of the beasts, which should be the LORD'S firstling, no man shall sanctify it; whether *it be* ox, or sheep: it *is* the LORD'S.

Nu 3:13 — Because all the firstborn *are* mine; *for* on the day that I smote all the firstborn in the land of Egypt I hallowed unto me all the firstborn in Israel, both man and beast: mine shall they be: I *am* the LORD.

Ne 10:36 — Also the firstborn of our sons, and of our cattle, as *it is* written in the law, and the firstlings of our herds and of our flocks, to bring to the house of our God, unto the priests that minister in the house of our God:

• Redemption of.

Nu 3:40–51; 18:15–17

Ex 13:13 — And every firstling of an ass thou shalt redeem with a lamb; and if thou wilt not redeem it, then thou shalt break his neck: and all the firstborn of man among thy children shalt thou redeem.

Ex 34:20 — But the firstling of an ass thou shalt redeem with a lamb: and if thou redeem *him* not, then shalt thou break his neck. All the firstborn of thy sons thou shalt redeem. And none shall appear before me empty.

Le 27:27 — And if *it be* of an unclean beast, then he shall redeem it according to thine estimation, and shall add a fifth *part* of it thereto: or if it be not redeemed, then it shall be sold according to thy estimation.

• Levites taken instead of firstborn of the families of Israel.

Nu 3:40–45; 8:16–18

Nu 3:12 — And I, behold, I have taken the Levites from among the children of Israel instead of all the firstborn that openeth the matrix among the children of Israel: therefore the Levites shall be mine;

• Of Egyptians slain.

Ex 11:5 — And all the firstborn in the land of Egypt shall die, from the firstborn of Pharaoh that sitteth upon his throne, even unto the firstborn of the maidservant that *is* behind the mill; and all the firstborn of beasts.

Ex 12:12 — For I will pass through the land of Egypt this night, and will smite all the firstborn in the land of Egypt, both man and beast; and against all the gods of Egypt I will execute judgment: I *am* the LORD.

Ex 12:29 — And it came to pass, that at midnight the LORD smote all the firstborn in the land of Egypt, from the firstborn of Pharaoh that sat on his throne unto the firstborn of the captive that *was* in the dungeon; and all the firstborn of cattle.

Ex 13:15 — And it came to pass, when Pharaoh would hardly let us go, that the LORD slew all the firstborn in the land of Egypt, both the firstborn of man, and the firstborn of beast: therefore I sacrifice to the LORD all that openeth the matrix, being males; but all the firstborn of my children I redeem.

Nu 33:4 — For the Egyptians buried all *their* firstborn, which the LORD had smitten among them: upon their gods also the LORD executed judgments.

Ps 105:36 — He smote also all the firstborn in their land, the chief of all their strength.

Ps 136:10 — To him that smote Egypt in their firstborn: for his mercy *endureth* for ever:

• Of idolators, sacrificed.

Eze 20:26 — And I polluted them in their own gifts, in that they caused to pass through *the fire* all that openeth the womb, that I might make them desolate, to the end that they might know that I *am* the LORD.

• Birthright of the.

• Head precedence over other sons of the family.

Ge 4:7 — If thou doest well, shalt thou not be accepted? and if thou doest not well, sin lieth at the door. And unto thee *shall be* his desire, and thou shalt rule over him.

• Had a double portion of inheritance.

Dt 21:15–17

• Had royal succession.

2Ch 21:3 — And their father gave them great gifts of silver, and of gold, and of precious things, with fenced cities in Judah: but the kingdom gave he to Jehoram; because he *was* the firstborn.

• Honorable distinction of.

Ex 4:22 — And thou shalt say unto Pharaoh, Thus saith the LORD, Israel *is* my son, *even* my firstborn:

Ps 89:27 — Also I will make him *my* firstborn, higher than the kings of the earth.

Jer 31:9 — They shall come with weeping, and with supplications will I lead them: I will cause them to walk by the rivers of waters in a straight way, wherein they shall not stumble: for I am a father to Israel, and Ephraim *is* my firstborn.

Ro 8:29 — For whom he did foreknow, he also did predestinate *to be* conformed to the image of his Son, that he might be the firstborn among many brethren.

Col 1:15 — Who is the image of the invisible God, the firstborn of every creature:

Heb 1:6 — And again, when he bringeth in the firstbegotten into the world, he saith, And let all the angels of God worship him.

Heb 12:23 — To the general assembly and church of the firstborn, which are written in heaven, and to God the Judge of all, and to the spirits of just men made perfect,

Rev 1:5 — And from Jesus Christ, *who is* the faithful witness, *and* the first begotten of the dead, and the prince of the kings of the earth. Unto him that loved us, and washed us from our sins in his own blood,

• Sold by Esau.

Ge 25:29–34; Ro 9:12–13

Ge 27:36 — And he said, Is not he rightly named Jacob? for he hath supplanted me these two times: he took away my birthright; and, behold, now he hath taken away my blessing. And he said, Hast thou not reserved a blessing for me?

Heb 12:16 — Lest there *be* any fornicator, or profane person, as Esau, who for one morsel of meat sold his birthright.

• Forfeited by Reuben.

Ge 49:3–4; 1Ch 5:1–2

• Set aside.

• That of Manasseh.

Ge 48:15–20

1Ch 5:1 — Now the sons of Reuben the firstborn of Israel, (for he *was* the firstborn; but, forasmuch as he defiled his father's bed, his birthright was given unto the sons of Joseph the son of Israel: and the genealogy is not to be reckoned after the birthright.

• Adonijah.

1Ki 2:15 — And he said, Thou knowest that the kingdom was mine, and *that* all Israel set their faces on me, that I should reign: howbeit the kingdom is turned about, and is become my brother's: for it was his from the LORD.

• Hosah's son.

1Ch 26:10 — Also Hosah, of the children of Merari, had sons; Simri the chief, (for *though* he was not the firstborn, yet his father made him the chief;)

See: Birthright

FIRSTLING See: Firstborn

FISH

• Creation of.

Ge 1:20–22

• Appointed for food.

Ge 9:2–3

• Clean and unclean.

Le 11:9–12; Dt 14:9–10

• Taken with nets.

Hab 1:14–17; Lk 5:2–6; Jn 21:6–8

Ecc 9:12 — For man also knoweth not his time: as the fishes that are taken in an evil net, and as the birds that are caught in the snare; so *are* the sons of men snared in an evil time, when it falleth suddenly upon them.

Mt 4:21 — And going on from thence, he saw other two brethren, James *the son* of Zebedee, and John his brother, in a ship with Zebedee their father, mending their nets; and he called them.

• Taken with hooks.

Isa 19:8 — The fishers also shall mourn, and all they that cast angle into the brooks shall lament, and they that spread nets upon the waters shall languish.

Am 4:2 — The Lord GOD hath sworn by his holiness, that, lo, the days shall come upon you, that he will take you away with hooks, and your posterity with fishhooks.

Mt 17:27 — Notwithstanding, lest we should offend them, go thou to the sea, and cast an hook, and take up the fish that first cometh up; and when thou hast opened his mouth, thou shalt find a piece of money: that take, and give unto them for me and thee.

• Taken with spears.

Job 41:7 — Canst thou fill his skin with barbed irons? or his head with fish spears?

• Ponds for.

• In Heshbon.

SS 7:4 — Thy neck *is* as a tower of ivory; thine eyes *like* the fishpools in Heshbon, by the gate of Bath-rabbim: thy nose *is* as the tower of Lebanon which looketh toward Damascus.

• In Egypt.

Isa 19:10 — And they shall be broken in the purposes thereof, all that make sluices *and* ponds for fish.

• Traffic in.

Ne 13:16 — There dwelt men of Tyre also therein, which brought fish, and all manner of ware, and sold on the sabbath unto the children of Judah, and in Jerusalem.

Jn 21:13 — Jesus then cometh, and taketh bread, and giveth them, and fish likewise.

• Broiled.

Jn 21:9–13

Lk 24:42 — And they gave him a piece of a broiled fish, and of an honeycomb.

• Miracles connected with.

• Jonah swallowed by.

Jnh 1:17–2:10

Mt 12:40 — For as Jonas was three days and three nights in the whale's belly; so shall the Son of man be three days and three nights in the heart of the earth.

• Of the loaves and fishes.

Lk 9:3–17

Mt 14:19 — And he commanded the multitude to sit down on the grass, and took the five loaves, and the two fishes, and looking up to heaven, he blessed, and brake, and gave the loaves to *his* disciples, and the disciples to the multitude.

Mt 15:36 — And he took the seven loaves and the fishes, and gave thanks, and brake *them,* and gave to his disciples, and the disciples to the multitude.

Lk 5:6 — And when they had this done, they inclosed a great multitude of fishes: and their net brake.

• Coin obtained from mouth of.

Mt 17:27 — Notwithstanding, lest we should offend them, go thou to the sea, and cast an hook, and take up the fish that first cometh up; and when thou hast opened his mouth, thou shalt find a piece of money: that take, and give unto them for me and thee.

• Great draught of.

Lk 5:4–7

Jn 21:6 — And he said unto them, Cast the net on the right side of the ship, and ye shall find. They cast therefore, and now they were not able to draw it for the multitude of fishes.

• Furnished to the disciples by Jesus after his resurrection.

Jn 21:9–13

Lk 24:42 — And they gave him a piece of a broiled fish, and of an honeycomb.

• Figurative.

Eze 47:9–10

FISH GATE

2Ch 33:14 — Now after this he built a wall without the city of David, on the west side of Gihon, in the valley, even to the entering in at the fish gate, and compassed about Ophel, and raised it up a very great height, and put captains of war in all the fenced cities of Judah.

Ne 3:3 — But the fish gate did the sons of Hassenaah build, who *also* laid the beams thereof, and set up the doors thereof, the locks thereof, and the bars thereof.

Zep 1:10 — And it shall come to pass in that day, saith the LORD, *that there shall be* the noise of a cry from the fish gate, and an howling from the second, and a great crashing from the hills.

FISH SPEAR

Job 41:7 — Canst thou fill his skin with barbed irons? or his head with fish spears?

FISHERMEN

• Certain apostles.

Mt 4:18–21; Jn 21:2–3

Mk 1:16 — Now as he walked by the sea of Galilee, he saw Simon and Andrew his brother casting a net into the sea: for they were fishers.

Mk 1:19 — And when he had gone a little farther thence, he saw James the *son* of Zebedee, and John his brother, who also were in the ship mending their nets.

• Figurative.

Jer 16:16 — Behold, I will send for many fishers, saith the LORD, and they shall fish them; and after will I send for many hunters, and they shall hunt them from every mountain, and from every hill, and out of the holes of the rocks.

Mt 4:19 — And he saith unto them, Follow me, and I will make you fishers of men.

FISHHOOK

Am 4:2 — The Lord GOD hath sworn by his holiness, that, lo, the days shall come upon you, that he will take you away with hooks, and your posterity with fishhooks.

FISHPOOL

SS 7:4 — Thy neck *is* as a tower of ivory; thine eyes *like* the fishpools in Heshbon, by the gate of Bath-rabbim: thy nose *is* as the tower of Lebanon which looketh toward Damascus.

FITCH

Isa 28:25–27

Eze 4:9 — Take thou also unto thee wheat, and barley, and beans, and lentiles, and millet, and fitches, and put them in one vessel, and make thee bread thereof, *according* to the number of the days that thou shalt lie upon thy side, three hundred and ninety days shalt thou eat thereof.

FLAG

Ex 2:3 — And when she could not longer hide him, she took for him an ark of bulrushes, and daubed it with slime and with pitch, and put the child therein; and she laid *it* in the flags by the river's brink.

Ex 2:5 — And the daughter of Pharaoh came down to wash *herself* at the river; and her maidens walked along by the river's side; and when she saw the ark among the flags, she sent her maid to fetch it.

Job 8:11 — Can the rush grow up without mire? can the flag grow without water?

Isa 19:6 — And they shall turn the rivers far away; *and* the brooks of defence shall be emptied and dried up: the reeds and flags shall wither.

Jnh 2:5 — The waters compassed me about, *even* to the soul: the depth closed me round about, the weeds were wrapped about my head.

• An ensign.

See: Ensign

FLAGON

• Erroneously translated flagon of wine, but more accurately cake of raisin.

2Sa 6:19 — And he dealt among all the people, *even* among the whole multitude of Israel, as well to the women as men, to every one a cake of bread, and a good piece *of flesh,* and a flagon *of wine.* So all the people departed every one to his house.

SS 2:15 — Take us the foxes, the little foxes, that spoil the vines: for our vines *have* tender grapes.

Hos 3:1 — Then said the LORD unto me, Go yet, love a woman beloved of *her* friend, yet an adulteress, according to the love of the LORD toward the children of Israel, who look to other gods, and love flagons of wine.

FLATTERY

Job 32:21–22; Ps 5:8–9; 12:2–3; 1Th 2:4–6

Job 17:5 — He that speaketh flattery to *his* friends, even the eyes of his children shall fail.

Ps 36:2 — For he flattereth himself in his own eyes, until his iniquity be found to be hateful.

Ps 49:13 — This their way *is* their folly: yet their posterity approve their sayings. Selah.

Ps 49:18 — Though while he lived he blessed his soul: and *men* will praise thee, when thou doest well to thyself.

Ps 78:36 — Nevertheless they did flatter him with their mouth, and they lied unto him with their tongues.

Pr 5:3 — For the lips of a strange woman drop *as* an honeycomb, and her mouth *is* smoother than oil:

Pr 6:24 — To keep thee from the evil woman, from the flattery of the tongue of a strange woman.

Pr 7:5 — That they may keep thee from the strange woman, from the stranger *which* flattereth with her words.

Pr 7:21 — With her much fair speech she caused him to yield, with the flattering of her lips she forced him.

Pr 14:20 — The poor is hated even of his own neighbour: but the rich *hath* many friends.

Pr 19:4 — Wealth maketh many friends; but the poor is separated from his neighbour.

Pr 19:6 — Many will intreat the favour of the prince: and every man *is* a friend to him that giveth gifts.

Pr 20:19 — He that goeth about *as* a talebearer revealeth secrets: therefore meddle not with him that flattereth with his lips.

Pr 22:16 — He that oppresseth the poor to increase his *riches, and* he that giveth to the rich, *shall* surely *come* to want.

Pr 24:24 — He that saith unto the wicked, Thou *art* righteous; him shall the people curse, nations shall abhor him:

Pr 25:26 — A righteous man falling down before the wicked *is as* a troubled fountain, and a corrupt spring.

Pr 26:28 — A lying tongue hateth *those that are* afflicted by it; and a flattering mouth worketh ruin.

Pr 27:21 — *As* the fining pot for silver, and the furnace for gold; so *is* a man to his praise.

Pr 28:23 — He that rebuketh a man afterwards shall find more favour than he that flattereth with the tongue.

Pr 29:5 — A man that flattereth his neighbour spreadeth a net for his feet.

Da 11:21 — And in his estate shall stand up a vile person, to whom they shall not give the honour of the kingdom: but he shall come in peaceably, and obtain the kingdom by flatteries.

Da 11:34 — Now when they shall fall, they shall be holpen with a little help: but many shall cleave to them with flatteries.

Lk 6:26 — Woe unto you, when all men shall speak well of you! for so did their fathers to the false prophets.

Ro 16:18 — For they that are such serve not our Lord Jesus Christ, but their own belly; and by good words and fair speeches deceive the hearts of the simple.

Gal 1:10 — For do I now persuade men, or God? or do I seek to please men? for if I yet pleased men, I should not be the servant of Christ.

Jude 1:16 — These are murmurers, complainers, walking after their own lusts; and their mouth speaketh great swelling *words,* having men's persons in admiration because of advantage.

• Instances of.

• By Jacob.

Ge 33:10

• By Gideon.

Jgs 8:1–3

• By Mephibosheth.

2Sa 9:8

• By woman of Tekoah.

2Sa 14:17–20

• By Absalom.

2Sa 15:2–6

• **By Israel and Judah.**
2Sa 19:41–43

• **By Adonijah.**
1Ki 1:42

• **By Ahab.**
1Ki 20:4

• **By false prophets.**
1Ki 22:13

• **By Darius's courtiers.**
Da 6:7

• **By Herodians.**
Lk 20:21

• **By Tyrians.**
Ac 12:22

• **Tertullus flatters Felix.**
Ac 24:2–4

• **Paul flatters Felix.**
Ac 24:10 — Then Paul, after that the governor had beckoned unto him to speak, answered, Forasmuch as I know that thou hast been of many years a judge unto this nation, I do the more cheerfully answer for myself:

• **By Agrippa.**
Ac 26:2–3

FLAX

• **In Egypt.**
Ex 9:31 — And the flax and the barley was smitten: for the barley was in the ear, and the flax *was* bolled.

• **In Palestine.**
Jos 2:6 — But she had brought them up to the roof of the house, and hid them with the stalks of flax, which she had laid in order upon the roof.

• **Linen made from.**
Pr 31:13 — She seeketh wool, and flax, and worketh willingly with her hands.

Isa 19:6 — And they shall turn the rivers far away; *and* the brooks of defence shall be emptied and dried up: the reeds and flags shall wither.

Hos 2:5— For their mother hath played the harlot: she that conceived them hath done shamefully: for she said, I will go after my lovers, that give *me* my bread and my water, my wool and my flax, mine oil and my drink.

Hos 2:9 — Therefore will I return, and take away my corn in the time thereof, and my wine in the season thereof, and will recover my wool and my flax *given* to cover her nakedness.

• **Robes made of.**
Est 1:16 — And Memucan answered before the king and the princes, Vashti the queen hath not done wrong to the king only, but also to all the princes, and to all the people that *are* in all the provinces of the king Ahasuerus.

Eze 40:3 — And he brought me thither, and, behold, *there was* a man, whose appearance was like the appearance of brass, with a line of flax in his hand, and a measuring reed; and he stood in the gate.

→**See: Linen**

• **Figurative.**

• **Smoking flax not quenched.**
Isa 42:3 — A bruised reed shall he not break, and the smoking flax shall he not quench: he shall bring forth judgment unto truth.

Mt 12:20 — A bruised reed shall he not break, and smoking flax shall he not quench, till he send forth judgment unto victory.

FLEA

1Sa 24:14 — After whom is the king of Israel come out? after whom dost thou pursue? after a dead dog, after a flea.

1Sa 26:20 — Now therefore, let not my blood fall to the earth before the face of the LORD: for the king of Israel is come out to seek a flea, as when one doth hunt a partridge in the mountains.

FLESH

• **Figurative.**

• **Fruits of.**
Gal 5:19–21

• **Symbolic.**

• **Body of Christ symbolized by the bread of the holy eucharist.**
Jn 6:51–63

FLESHHOOK

• **Used in the tabernacle.**
1Sa 2:13–14

Ex 27:3 — And thou shalt make his pans to receive his ashes, and his shovels, and his basons, and his fleshhooks, and his firepans: all the vessels thereof thou shalt make *of* brass.

Ex 38:3 — And he made all the vessels of the altar, the pots, and the shovels, and the basons, *and* the fleshhooks, and the firepans: all the vessels thereof made he *of* brass.

Nu 4:14 — And they shall put upon it all the vessels thereof, wherewith they minister about it, *even* the censers, the fleshhooks, and the shovels, and the basons, all the vessels of the altar; and they shall spread upon it a covering of badgers' skins, and put to the staves of it.

• **Made of gold.**
1Ch 28:17 — Also pure gold for the fleshhooks, and the bowls, and the cups: and for the golden basons *he gave gold* by weight for every bason; and *likewise silver* by weight for every bason of silver:

• **Made of brass.**
2Ch 4:16 — The pots also, and the shovels, and the fleshhooks, and all their instruments, did Huram his father make to king Solomon for the house of the LORD of bright brass.

FLIES

Ecc 10:1 — Dead flies cause the ointment of the apothecary to send forth a stinking savour: *so doth* a little folly him that is in reputation for wisdom *and* honour.

• **Plague of.**
Ex 8:21–31

Ps 78:45 — He sent divers sorts of flies among them, which devoured them; and frogs, which destroyed them.

Ps 105:31 — He spake, and there came divers sorts of flies, *and* lice in all their coasts.

- **Figurative.**

Isa 7:18 — And it shall come to pass in that day, *that* the LORD shall hiss for the fly that *is* in the uttermost part of the rivers of Egypt, and for the bee that *is* in the land of Assyria.

FLINT

Dt 8:15 — Who led thee through that great and terrible wilderness, *wherein were* fiery serpents, and scorpions, and drought, where *there was* no water; who brought thee forth water out of the rock of flint;

Dt 32:13 — He made him ride on the high places of the earth, that he might eat the increase of the fields; and he made him to suck honey out of the rock, and oil out of the flinty rock;

Ps 114:8 — Which turned the rock *into* a standing water, the flint into a fountain of waters.

Isa 50:7 — For the Lord GOD will help me; therefore shall I not be confounded: therefore have I set my face like a flint, and I know that I shall not be ashamed.

Eze 3:9 — As an adamant harder than flint have I made thy forehead: fear them not, neither be dismayed at their looks, though they *be* a rebellious house.

FLOOD

- **The deluge.**
- **Foretold.**

Ge 6:13 — And God said unto Noah, The end of all flesh is come before me; for the earth is filled with violence through them; and, behold, I will destroy them with the earth.

Ge 6:17 — And, behold, I, even I, do bring a flood of waters upon the earth, to destroy all flesh, wherein *is* the breath of life, from under heaven; *and* every thing that *is* in the earth shall die.

- **History of.**

Ge 6:1–8:22

- **References to.**

Lk 17:26–27

Job 22:16 — Which were cut down out of time, whose foundation was overflown with a flood:

Ps 90:5 — Thou carriest them away as with a flood; they are *as* a sleep: in the morning *they are* like grass *which* groweth up.

Mt 24:38 — <u>For as in the days that were before the flood they were eating and drinking, marrying and giving in marriage, until the day that Noe entered into the ark,</u>

Heb 11:7 — By faith Noah, being warned of God of things not seen as yet, moved with fear, prepared an ark to the saving of his house; by the which he condemned the world, and became heir of the righteousness which is by faith.

1Pe 3:20 — Which sometime were disobedient, when once the longsuffering of God waited in the days of Noah, while the ark was a preparing, wherein few, that is, eight souls were saved by water.

2Pe 2:5 — And spared not the old world, but saved Noah the eighth *person,* a preacher of righteousness, bringing in the flood upon the world of the ungodly;

- **The promise that it should not recur.**

Ge 8:20–21

Isa 54:9 — For this *is as* the waters of Noah unto me: for *as* I have sworn that the waters of Noah should no more go over the earth; so have I sworn that I would not be wroth with thee, nor rebuke thee.

See: Meteorology and Celestial Phenomena

FLOUR

See: Barley

See: Bread

See: Offerings

See: Wheat

FLOWERS See: Botany

FLUTE

Da 3:5 — *That* at what time ye hear the sound of the cornet, flute, harp, sackbut, psaltery, dulcimer, and all kinds of musick, ye fall down and worship the golden image that Nebuchadnezzar the king hath set up:

Da 3:7 — Therefore at that time, when all the people heard the sound of the cornet, flute, harp, sackbut, psaltery, and all kinds of musick, all the people, the nations, and the languages, fell down *and* worshipped the golden image that Nebuchadnezzar the king had set up.

Da 3:10 — Thou, O king, hast made a decree, that every man that shall hear the sound of the cornet, flute, harp, sackbut, psaltery, and dulcimer, and all kinds of musick, shall fall down and worship the golden image:

Da 3:15 — Now if ye be ready that at what time ye hear the sound of the cornet, flute, harp, sackbut, psaltery, and dulcimer, and all kinds of musick, ye fall down and worship the image which I have made; *well:* but if ye worship not, ye shall be cast the same hour into the midst of a burning fiery furnace; and who *is* that God that shall deliver you out of my hands?

See: Music; instruments of

FLY See: Flies

FOOD

- **Articles of.**
  - **Milk.**

Ge 49:12 — His eyes *shall be* red with wine, and his teeth white with milk.

Pr 27:27 — And *thou shalt have* goats' milk enough for thy food, for the food of thy household, and *for* the maintenance for thy maidens.

  - **Butter.**

Dt 32:14 — Butter of kine, and milk of sheep, with fat of lambs, and rams of the breed of Bashan, and goats, with the fat of kidneys of wheat; and thou didst drink the pure blood of the grape.

2Sa 17:29 — And honey, and butter, and sheep, and cheese of kine, for David, and for the people that *were* with him, to eat: for they said, The people *is* hungry, and weary, and thirsty, in the wilderness.

- **Cheese.**

1Sa 17:18 — And carry these ten cheeses unto the captain of *their* thousand, and look how thy brethren fare, and take their pledge.

Job 10:10 — Hast thou not poured me out as milk, and curdled me like cheese?

- **Bread.**

Ge 18:5 — And I will fetch a morsel of bread, and comfort ye your hearts; after that ye shall pass on: for therefore are ye come to your servant. And they said, So do, as thou hast said.

1Sa 17:17 — And Jesse said unto David his son, Take now for thy brethren an ephah of this parched *corn,* and these ten loaves, and run to the camp to thy brethren;

- **Parched corn.**

Ru 2:14 — And Boaz said unto her, At mealtime come thou hither, and eat of the bread, and dip thy morsel in the vinegar. And she sat beside the reapers: and he reached her parched *corn,* and she did eat, and was sufficed, and left.

1Sa 17:17 — And Jesse said unto David his son, Take now for thy brethren an ephah of this parched *corn,* and these ten loaves, and run to the camp to thy brethren;

- **Flesh.**

2Sa 6:19 — And he dealt among all the people, *even* among the whole multitude of Israel, as well to the women as men, to every one a cake of bread, and a good piece *of flesh,* and a flagon *of wine.* So all the people departed every one to his house.

Pr 9:2 — She hath killed her beasts; she hath mingled her wine; she hath also furnished her table.

- **Fish.**

Mt 7:10 — Or if he ask a fish, will he give him a serpent?

Lk 24:42 — And they gave him a piece of a broiled fish, and of an honeycomb.

- **Herbs.**

Pr 15:17 — Better *is* a dinner of herbs where love is, than a stalled ox and hatred therewith.

Ro 14:2 — For one believeth that he may eat all things: another, who is weak, eateth herbs.

Heb 6:7 — For the earth which drinketh in the rain that cometh oft upon it, and bringeth forth herbs meet for them by whom it is dressed, receiveth blessing from God:

- **Fruit.**

2Sa 16:2 — And the king said unto Ziba, What meanest thou by these? And Ziba said, The asses *be* for the king's household to ride on; and the bread and summer fruit for the young men to eat; and the wine, that such as be faint in the wilderness may drink.

- **Dried fruit.**

1Sa 25:18 — Then Abigail made haste, and took two hundred loaves, and two bottles of wine, and five sheep ready dressed, and five measures of parched *corn,* and an hundred clusters of raisins, and two hundred cakes of figs, and laid *them* on asses.

1Sa 30:12 — And they gave him a piece of a cake of figs, and two clusters of raisins: and when he had eaten, his spirit came again to him: for he had eaten no bread, nor drunk *any* water, three days and three nights.

- **Honey.**

SS 5:1 — I am come into my garden, my sister, *my* spouse: I have gathered my myrrh with my spice; I have eaten my honeycomb with my honey; I have drunk my wine with my milk: eat, O friends; drink, yea, drink abundantly, O beloved.

Isa 7:15 — Butter and honey shall he eat, that he may know to refuse the evil, and choose the good.

- **Oil.**

Dt 12:17 — Thou mayest not eat within thy gates the tithe of thy corn, or of thy wine, or of thy oil, or the firstlings of thy herds or of thy flock, nor any of thy vows which thou vowest, nor thy freewill offerings, or heave offering of thine hand:

Pr 21:17 — He that loveth pleasure *shall be* a poor man: he that loveth wine and oil shall not be rich.

Eze 16:13 — Thus wast thou decked with gold and silver; and thy raiment *was of* fine linen, and silk, and broidered work; thou didst eat fine flour, and honey, and oil: and thou wast exceeding beautiful, and thou didst prosper into a kingdom.

- **Vinegar.**

Nu 6:3 — He shall separate *himself* from wine and strong drink, and shall drink no vinegar of wine, or vinegar of strong drink, neither shall he drink any liquor of grapes, nor eat moist grapes, or dried.

Ru 2:14 — And Boaz said unto her, At mealtime come thou hither, and eat of the bread, and dip thy morsel in the vinegar. And she sat beside the reapers: and he reached her parched *corn,* and she did eat, and was sufficed, and left.

- **Wine.**

2Sa 6:19 — And he dealt among all the people, *even* among the whole multitude of Israel, as well to the women as men, to every one a cake of bread, and a good piece *of flesh,* and a flagon *of wine.* So all the people departed every one to his house.

Jn 2:3 — And when they wanted wine, the mother of Jesus saith unto him, They have no wine.

Jn 2:10 — And saith unto him, Every man at the beginning doth set forth good wine; and when men have well drunk, then that which is worse: *but* thou hast kept the good wine until now.

- **Prepared by females.**

Ge 27:9 — Go now to the flock, and fetch me from thence two good kids of the goats; and I will make them savoury meat for thy father, such as he loveth:

1Sa 8:13 — And he will take your daughters *to be* confectionaries, and *to be* cooks, and *to be* bakers.

Pr 31:15 — She riseth also while it is yet night, and giveth meat to her household, and a portion to her maidens.

• **Thanks given before.**

Mk 8:6 — And he commanded the people to sit down on the ground: and he took the seven loaves, and gave thanks, and brake, and gave to his disciples to set before *them;* and they did set *them* before the people.

Ac 27:35 — And when he had thus spoken, he took bread, and gave thanks to God in presence of them all: and when he had broken *it,* he began to eat.

• **A hymn sung after.**

Mt 26:30 — And when they had sung an hymn, they went out into the mount of Olives.

• **Men and women did not partake together.**

Ge 18:8–9

Est 1:3 — In the third year of his reign, he made a feast unto all his princes and his servants; the power of Persia and Media, the nobles and princes of the provinces, *being* before him:

Est 1:9 — Also Vashti the queen made a feast for the women *in* the royal house which *belonged* to king Ahasuerus.

See: Bread

See: Eating

See: Oven

• **From God.**

Ge 1:29–30; Ps 104:14–15; 1Ti 4:3–5

Ge 9:3 — Every moving thing that liveth shall be meat for you; even as the green herb have I given you all things.

Ge 48:15 — And he blessed Joseph, and said, God, before whom my fathers Abraham and Isaac did walk, the God which fed me all my life long unto this day,

Ps 23:5 — Thou preparest a table before me in the presence of mine enemies: thou anointest my head with oil; my cup runneth over.

Ps 103:5 — Who satisfieth thy mouth with good *things; so that* thy youth is renewed like the eagle's.

Ps 111:5 — He hath given meat unto them that fear him: he will ever be mindful of his covenant.

Ps 136:25 — Who giveth food to all flesh: for his mercy *endureth* for ever.

Ps 145:15 — The eyes of all wait upon thee; and thou givest them their meat in due season.

Ps 147:9 — He giveth to the beast his food, *and* to the young ravens which cry.

Pr 30:8 — Remove far from me vanity and lies: give me neither poverty nor riches; feed me with food convenient for me:

Isa 3:1 — For, behold, the Lord, the LORD of hosts, doth take away from Jerusalem and from Judah the stay and the staff, the whole stay of bread, and the whole stay of water,

Mt 6:11 — Give us this day our daily bread.

Ro 14:14 — I know, and am persuaded by the Lord Jesus, that *there is* nothing unclean of itself: but to him that esteemeth any thing to be unclean, to him *it is* unclean.

Ro 14:21 — *It is* good neither to eat flesh, nor to drink wine, nor *any thing* whereby thy brother stumbleth, or is offended, or is made weak.

• **Things prohibited as food.**

Le 11:1–47; 17:13–15; Dt 14:1–29

Ex 22:31 — And ye shall be holy men unto me: neither shall ye eat *any* flesh *that is* torn of beasts in the field; ye shall cast it to the dogs.

FOOL

Pr 9:6–8, 13–17; 10:13–14; 14:7–9; 15:20–21; 17:24–25; 18:6–7; 26:3–12; Ecc 10:11–15; Mt 7:26–27

Ps 5:5 — The foolish shall not stand in thy sight: thou hatest all workers of iniquity.

Ps 14:1 — The fool hath said in his heart, *There is* no God. They are corrupt, they have done abominable works, *there is* none that doeth good.

Ps 74:18 — Remember this, *that* the enemy hath reproached, O LORD, and *that* the foolish people have blasphemed thy name.

Ps 74:22 — Arise, O God, plead thine own cause: remember how the foolish man reproacheth thee daily.

Ps 107:17 — Fools because of their transgression, and because of their iniquities, are afflicted.

Pr 1:7 — The fear of the LORD *is* the beginning of knowledge: *but* fools despise wisdom and instruction.

Pr 1:22 — How long, ye simple ones, will ye love simplicity? and the scorners delight in their scorning, and fools hate knowledge?

Pr 3:35 — The wise shall inherit glory: but shame shall be the promotion of fools.

Pr 10:1 — The proverbs of Solomon. A wise son maketh a glad father: but a foolish son *is* the heaviness of his mother.

Pr 10:8 — The wise in heart will receive commandments: but a prating fool shall fall.

Pr 10:10 — He that winketh with the eye causeth sorrow: but a prating fool shall fall.

Pr 10:18 — He that hideth hatred *with* lying lips, and he that uttereth a slander, *is* a fool.

Pr 10:23 — *It is* as sport to a fool to do mischief: but a man of understanding hath wisdom.

Pr 14:1 — Every wise woman buildeth her house: but the foolish plucketh it down with her hands.

Pr 14:15 — The simple believeth every word: but the prudent *man* looketh well to his going.

Pr 15:7 — The lips of the wise disperse knowledge: but the heart of the foolish *doeth* not so.

Pr 18:2 — A fool hath no delight in understanding, but that his heart may discover itself.

Pr 19:13 — A foolish son *is* the calamity of his father: and the contentions of a wife *are* a continual dropping.

Pr 20:3 — *It is* an honour for a man to cease from strife: but every fool will be meddling.

Pr 21:20 — *There is* treasure to be desired and oil in the dwelling of the wise; but a foolish man spendeth it up.

Pr 29:9 — *If* a wise man contendeth with a foolish man, whether he rage or laugh, *there is* no rest.

Pr 29:11 — A fool uttereth all his mind: but a wise *man* keepeth it in till afterwards.

Ecc 4:5 — The fool foldeth his hands together, and eateth his own flesh.

Ecc 7:9 — Be not hasty in thy spirit to be angry: for anger resteth in the bosom of fools.

Tit 3:3 — For we ourselves also were sometimes foolish, disobedient, deceived, serving divers lusts and pleasures, living in malice and envy, hateful, *and* hating one another.

- **Parables of.**
  - **The foolish virgins.**
    Mt 25:1–13
  - **The rich fool.**
    Lk 12:16–20

FOOT

- **Washing the feet of the disciples by Jesus.**
  Jn 13:4–16
- **Washing the feet by disciples.**
  1Ti 5:10 — Well reported of for good works; if she have brought up children, if she have lodged strangers, if she have washed the saints' feet, if she have relieved the afflicted, if she have diligently followed every good work.

  See: Ablution

  See: Purification

  See: Shoe
- **Figurative.**
  Mt 18:8 — Wherefore if thy hand or thy foot offend thee, cut them off, and cast *them* from thee: it is better for thee to enter into life halt or maimed, rather than having two hands or two feet to be cast into everlasting fire.

FOOTMAN • A runner before kings and princes.

1Sa 8:11 — And he said, This will be the manner of the king that shall reign over you: He will take your sons, and appoint *them* for himself, for his chariots, and to be his horsemen; and *some* shall run before his chariots.

2Sa 15:1 — And it came to pass after this, that Absalom prepared him chariots and horses, and fifty men to run before him.

1Ki 1:5 — Then Adonijah the son of Haggith exalted himself, saying, I will be king: and he prepared him chariots and horsemen, and fifty men to run before him.

FOOTSTOOL

- **Figurative.**
  - **The earth is God's.**
    Isa 60:13 — The glory of Lebanon shall come unto thee, the fir tree, the pine tree, and the box together, to beautify the place of my sanctuary; and I will make the place of my feet glorious.

    Isa 66:1 — Thus saith the LORD, The heaven *is* my throne, and the earth *is* my footstool: where *is* the house that ye build unto me? and where *is* the place of my rest?

    La 2:1 — How hath the Lord covered the daughter of Zion with a cloud in his anger, *and* cast down from heaven unto the earth the beauty of Israel, and remembered not his footstool in the day of his anger!

    Ac 7:49 — Heaven *is* my throne, and earth *is* my footstool: what house will ye build me? saith the Lord: or what *is* the place of my rest?

FOREIGN

Le 19:10 — And thou shalt not glean thy vineyard, neither shalt thou gather *every* grape of thy vineyard; thou shalt leave them for the poor and stranger: I *am* the LORD your God.

Dt 24:21 — When thou gatherest the grapes of thy vineyard, thou shalt not glean *it* afterward: it shall be for the stranger, for the fatherless, and for the widow.

Gal 6:10 — As we have therefore opportunity, let us do good unto all *men,* especially unto them who are of the household of faith.

Heb 13:2 — Be not forgetful to entertain strangers: for thereby some have entertained angels unawares.

FOREIGNER

Le 19:10 — And thou shalt not glean thy vineyard, neither shalt thou gather *every* grape of thy vineyard; thou shalt leave them for the poor and stranger: I *am* the LORD your God.

Dt 24:21 — When thou gatherest the grapes of thy vineyard, thou shalt not glean *it* afterward: it shall be for the stranger, for the fatherless, and for the widow.

Gal 6:10 — As we have therefore opportunity, let us do good unto all *men,* especially unto them who are of the household of faith.

Heb 13:2 — Be not forgetful to entertain strangers: for thereby some have entertained angels unawares.

- **Figurative.**
  Eph 2:19 — Now therefore ye are no more strangers and foreigners, but fellowcitizens with the saints, and of the household of God;

  See: Aliens

  See: Gentiles

  See: Strangers

FOREKNOWLEDGE OF GOD

See: God, Foreknowledge of

See: God, Wisdom of

FOREMAN **See: Master Workman**

FOREORDINATION **See: Predestination**

FORERUNNER

- **Figurative of Christ.**
  Heb 6:20 — Whither the forerunner is for us entered, *even* Jesus, made an high priest for ever after the order of Melchisedec.

FORGERY

• By Jezebel.

1Ki 21:8 — So she wrote letters in Ahab's name, and sealed *them* with his seal, and sent the letters unto the elders and to the nobles that *were* in his city, dwelling with Naboth.

FORGETTING GOD

• A characteristic of the wicked.

Pr 2:17 — Which forsaketh the guide of her youth, and forgetteth the covenant of her God.

Isa 65:11 — But ye *are* they that forsake the LORD, that forget my holy mountain, that prepare a table for that troop, and that furnish the drink offering unto that number.

• Backsliders guilty of.

Jer 2:32 — Can a maid forget her ornaments, *or* a bride her attire? yet my people have forgotten me days without number.

Jer 3:21 — A voice was heard upon the high places, weeping *and* supplications of the children of Israel: for they have perverted their way, *and* they have forgotten the LORD their God.

• Is forgetting his covenant.

Dt 4:23 — Take heed unto yourselves, lest ye forget the covenant of the LORD your God, which he made with you, and make you a graven image, *or* the likeness of any *thing*, which the LORD thy God hath forbidden thee.

2Ki 17:38 — And the covenant that I have made with you ye shall not forget; neither shall ye fear other gods.

• Is forgetting his works.

Ps 78:7 — That they might set their hope in God, and not forget the works of God, but keep his commandments:

Ps 78:11 — And forgat his works, and his wonders that he had shewed them.

Ps 106:13 — They soon forgat his works; they waited not for his counsel:

• Is forgetting his benefits.

Ps 103:2 — Bless the LORD, O my soul, and forget not all his benefits:

Ps 106:7 — Our fathers understood not thy wonders in Egypt; they remembered not the multitude of thy mercies; but provoked *him* at the sea, *even* at the Red sea.

• Is forgetting his word.

Heb 12:5 — And ye have forgotten the exhortation which speaketh unto you as unto children, My son, despise not thou the chastening of the Lord, nor faint when thou art rebuked of him:

Jas 1:25 — But whoso looketh into the perfect law of liberty, and continueth *therein*, he being not a forgetful hearer, but a doer of the work, this man shall be blessed in his deed.

• Is forgetting his law.

Ps 119:153 — Consider mine affliction, and deliver me: for I do not forget thy law.

Ps 119:176 — I have gone astray like a lost sheep; seek thy servant; for I do not forget thy commandments.

Hos 4:6 — My people are destroyed for lack of knowledge: because thou hast rejected knowledge, I will also reject thee, that thou shalt be no priest to me: seeing thou hast forgotten the law of thy God, I will also forget thy children.

• Is forgetting his church.

Ps 137:5 — If I forget thee, O Jerusalem, let my right hand forget *her cunning*.

• Is forgetting his past deliverances.

Jgs 8:34 — And the children of Israel remembered not the LORD their God, who had delivered them out of the hands of all their enemies on every side:

Ps 78:42 — They remembered not his hand, *nor* the day when he delivered them from the enemy.

• Is forgetting his power to deliver.

Isa 51:13–15

• Encouraged by false teachers.

Jer 23:27 — Which think to cause my people to forget my name by their dreams which they tell every man to his neighbour, as their fathers have forgotten my name for Baal.

• Prosperity leads to.

Dt 8:12–14

Hos 13:6 — According to their pasture, so were they filled; they were filled, and their heart was exalted; therefore have they forgotten me.

• Trials should not lead to.

Ps 44:17–20

• Resolve against.

Ps 119:16 — I will delight myself in thy statutes: I will not forget thy word.

Ps 119:93 — I will never forget thy precepts: for with them thou hast quickened me.

• Cautions against.

Dt 6:12 — *Then* beware lest thou forget the LORD, which brought thee forth out of the land of Egypt, from the house of bondage.

Dt 8:11 — Beware that thou forget not the LORD thy God, in not keeping his commandments, and his judgments, and his statutes, which I command thee this day:

• Exhortation to those guilty of.

Ps 50:22 — Now consider this, ye that forget God, lest I tear *you* in pieces, and *there be* none to deliver.

• Punishment of.

Job 8:12–13; Isa 17:10–11

Ps 9:17 — The wicked shall be turned into hell, *and* all the nations that forget God.

Eze 23:35 — Therefore thus saith the Lord GOD; Because thou hast forgotten me, and cast me behind thy back, therefore bear thou also thy lewdness and thy whoredoms.

Hos 8:14 — For Israel hath forgotten his Maker, and buildeth temples; and Judah hath multiplied fenced cities: but I will send a fire upon his cities, and it shall devour the palaces thereof.

• **Punishment threatened.**

Job 8:13 — So *are* the paths of all that forget God; and the hypocrite's hope shall perish:

Ps 9:17 — The wicked shall be turned into hell, *and* all the nations that forget God.

Ps 50:22 — Now consider this, ye that forget God, lest I tear *you* in pieces, and *there be* none to deliver.

Isa 17:10 — Because thou hast forgotten the God of thy salvation, and hast not been mindful of the rock of thy strength, therefore shalt thou plant pleasant plants, and shalt set it with strange slips:

Jer 2:32 — Can a maid forget her ornaments, *or* a bride her attire? yet my people have forgotten me days without number.

Hos 8:14 — For Israel hath forgotten his Maker, and buildeth temples; and Judah hath multiplied fenced cities: but I will send a fire upon his cities, and it shall devour the palaces thereof.

See: Backsliders

FORGIVENESS

• **Of enemies.**

Ex 23:4–5; Pr 25:21–22; Mt 5:39–41, 43–48; 6:14–15; 18:21–35; Mk 11:25–26; Lk 6:27–37; 17:3–4; Ro 12:19–21; 1Co 4:12–13

Pr 19:11 — The discretion of a man deferreth his anger; and *it is* his glory to pass over a transgression.

Pr 24:17 — Rejoice not when thine enemy falleth, and let not thine heart be glad when he stumbleth:

Pr 24:29 — Say not, I will do so to him as he hath done to me: I will render to the man according to his work.

Ecc 7:21 — Also take no heed unto all words that are spoken; lest thou hear thy servant curse thee:

Mt 5:7 — Blessed *are* the merciful: for they shall obtain mercy.

Mt 6:12 — And forgive us our debts, as we forgive our debtors.

Lk 11:4 — And forgive us our sins; for we also forgive every one that is indebted to us. And lead us not into temptation; but deliver us from evil.

Ro 12:14 — Bless them which persecute you: bless, and curse not.

Ro 12:17 — Recompense to no man evil for evil. Provide things honest in the sight of all men.

Eph 4:32 — And be ye kind one to another, tenderhearted, forgiving one another, even as God for Christ's sake hath forgiven you.

Col 3:13 — Forbearing one another, and forgiving one another, if any man have a quarrel against any: even as Christ forgave you, so also *do* ye.

Phm 1:10 — I beseech thee for my son Onesimus, whom I have begotten in my bonds:

Phm 1:18 — If he hath wronged thee, or oweth *thee* ought, put that on mine account;

1Pe 3:9 — Not rendering evil for evil, or railing for railing: but contrariwise blessing; knowing that ye are thereunto called, that ye should inherit a blessing.

See: Enemy

• **Instances of.**

• **Esau forgives Jacob.**

Ge 33:4 — And Esau ran to meet him, and embraced him, and fell on his neck, and kissed him: and they wept.

Ge 33:11 — Take, I pray thee, my blessing that is brought to thee; because God hath dealt graciously with me, and because I have enough. And he urged him, and he took *it.*

• **Joseph, his brethren.**

Ge 45:5–15; 50:19–21

• **Moses, the Israelites.**

Nu 12:1–13

• **David forgives Saul.**

1Sa 24:10–12; 2Sa 1:14–17

1Sa 26:9 — And David said to Abishai, Destroy him not: for who can stretch forth his hand against the LORD's anointed, and be guiltless?

1Sa 26:23 — The LORD render to every man his righteousness and his faithfulness: for the LORD delivered thee into *my* hand to day, but I would not stretch forth mine hand against the LORD's anointed.

• **David forgives Shimei.**

2Sa 16:9–13; 1Ki 2:8–9

2Sa 19:23 — Therefore the king said unto Shimei, Thou shalt not die. And the king sware unto him.

• **Solomon forgives Adonijah.**

1Ki 1:53 — So king Solomon sent, and they brought him down from the altar. And he came and bowed himself to king Solomon: and Solomon said unto him, Go to thine house.

• **The prophet of Judah forgives Jeroboam.**

1Ki 13:3–6

• **Jesus forgives his enemies.**

Lk 23:34 — Then said Jesus, Father, forgive them; for they know not what they do. And they parted his raiment, and cast lots.

• **Of sins.**

See: Sin; forgiveness of

FORK

• **An agricultural implement.**

1Sa 13:21 — Yet they had a file for the mattocks, and for the coulters, and for the forks, and for the axes, and to sharpen the goads.

See: Fleshhook

FORM

• **In religious service.**

1Ch 15:13–14

2Ch 29:34 — But the priests were too few, so that they could not flay all the burnt offerings: wherefore their brethren the Levites did help them, till the work was ended, and until the *other* priests had sanctified themselves: for the Levites *were* more upright in heart to sanctify themselves than the priests.

- **Irregularity in.**

2Ch 30:2–5, 17–20; Mt 12:3–4

See: Church and State

- **Formalism.**

Ps 50:8–15; 51:16–17; 69:30–31; Isa 1:11–15; 29:13–16; Am 5:21–23; Mic 6:6–7; Mal 1:13–14; Mt 15:8–9; Lk 13:24–27; Ro 2:17–29; Php 3:4–7; 2Ti 3:1–5

1Sa 15:22 — And Samuel said, Hath the LORD *as great* delight in burnt offerings and sacrifices, as in obeying the voice of the LORD? Behold, to obey *is* better than sacrifice, *and* to hearken than the fat of rams.

Ecc 5:1 — Keep thy foot when thou goest to the house of God, and be more ready to hear, than to give the sacrifice of fools: for they consider not that they do evil.

Jer 6:20 — To what purpose cometh there to me incense from Sheba, and the sweet cane from a far country? your burnt offerings *are* not acceptable, nor your sacrifices sweet unto me.

Jer 14:12 — When they fast, I will not hear their cry; and when they offer burnt offering and an oblation, I will not accept them: but I will consume them by the sword, and by the famine, and by the pestilence.

Hos 6:6 — For I desired mercy, and not sacrifice; and the knowledge of God more than burnt offerings.

Mal 1:6 — A son honoureth *his* father, and a servant his master: if then I *be* a father, where *is* mine honour? and if I *be* a master, where *is* my fear? saith the LORD of hosts unto you, O priests, that despise my name. And ye say, Wherein have we despised thy name?

Mal 1:8 — And if ye offer the blind for sacrifice, *is it* not evil? and if ye offer the lame and sick, *is it* not evil? offer it now unto thy governor; will he be pleased with thee, or accept thy person? saith the LORD of hosts.

Mal 1:10 — Who *is there* even among you that would shut the doors *for nought?* neither do ye kindle *fire* on mine altar for nought. I have no pleasure in you, saith the LORD of hosts, neither will I accept an offering at your hand.

Mt 9:13 — But go ye and learn what *that* meaneth, I will have mercy, and not sacrifice: for I am not come to call the righteous, but sinners to repentance.

Mt 12:7 — But if ye had known what *this* meaneth, I will have mercy, and not sacrifice, ye would not have condemned the guiltless.

1Co 7:19 — Circumcision is nothing, and uncircumcision is nothing, but the keeping of the commandments of God.

See: Ordinance

See: Works

FORNICATION

See: Adultery

See: Lasciviousness

FORT

- **A military defense.**
- **Field fortifications.**

Dt 20:19–20

2Ki 25:1 — And it came to pass in the ninth year of his reign, in the tenth month, in the tenth *day* of the month, *that* Nebuchadnezzar king of Babylon came, he, and all his host, against Jerusalem, and pitched against it; and they built forts against it round about.

Eze 4:2 — And lay siege against it, and build a fort against it, and cast a mount against it; set the camp also against it, and set *battering* rams against it round about.

Eze 17:17 — Neither shall Pharaoh with *his* mighty army and great company make for him in the war, by casting up mounts, and building forts, to cut off many persons:

Eze 26:8 — He shall slay with the sword thy daughters in the field: and he shall make a fort against thee, and cast a mount against thee, and lift up the buckler against thee.

- **Defenses of cities.**

2Ch 26:15 — And he made in Jerusalem engines, invented by cunning men, to be on the towers and upon the bulwarks, to shoot arrows and great stones withal. And his name spread far abroad; for he was marvellously helped, till he was strong.

Isa 25:12 — And the fortress of the high fort of thy walls shall he bring down, lay low, *and* bring to the ground, *even* to the dust.

See: Castle

See: Tower

See: Walls, of the cities

- **Erected in vineyards and herding grounds.**

2Ch 26:10 — Also he built towers in the desert, and digged many wells: for he had much cattle, both in the low country, and in the plains: husbandmen *also,* and vine dressers in the mountains, and in Carmel: for he loved husbandry.

Isa 5:2 — And he fenced it, and gathered out the stones thereof, and planted it with the choicest vine, and built a tower in the midst of it, and also made a winepress therein: and he looked that it should bring forth grapes, and it brought forth wild grapes.

Mt 21:33 — Hear another parable: There was a certain householder, which planted a vineyard, and hedged it round about, and digged a winepress in it, and built a tower, and let it out to husbandmen, and went into a far country:

Mk 12:1 — And he began to speak unto them by parables. A *certain* man planted a vineyard, and set an hedge about *it,* and digged *a place for* the winefat, and built a tower, and let it out to husbandmen, and went into a far country.

Lk 20:9 — Then began he to speak to the people this parable; A certain man planted a vineyard, and let it forth to husbandmen, and went into a far country for a long time.

• **Caves used for.**

Jgs 6:2 — And the hand of Midian prevailed against Israel: *and* because of the Midianites the children of Israel made them the dens which *are* in the mountains, and caves, and strong holds.

1Sa 23:29 — And David went up from thence, and dwelt in strong holds at En-gedi.

Isa 33:16 — He shall dwell on high: his place of defence *shall be* the munitions of rocks: bread shall be given him; his waters *shall be* sure.

• **Figurative.**

• **Of God's care.**

2Sa 22:2–3

2Sa 22:47 — The LORD liveth; and blessed *be* my rock; and exalted be the God of the rock of my salvation.

Ps 18:2 — The LORD *is* my rock, and my fortress, and my deliverer; my God, my strength, in whom I will trust; my buckler, and the horn of my salvation, *and* my high tower.

Ps 31:3 — For thou *art* my rock and my fortress; therefore for thy name's sake lead me, and guide me.

Ps 71:3 — Be thou my strong habitation, whereunto I may continually resort: thou hast given commandment to save me; for thou *art* my rock and my fortress.

Ps 91:2 — I will say of the LORD, *He is* my refuge and my fortress: my God; in him will I trust.

Ps 144:2 — My goodness, and my fortress; my high tower, and my deliverer; my shield, and *he* in whom I trust; who subdueth my people under me.

Pr 18:10 — The name of the LORD *is* a strong tower: the righteous runneth into it, and is safe.

Na 1:7 — The LORD *is* good, a strong hold in the day of trouble; and he knoweth them that trust in him.

FORTITUDE ✦See: Courage

FORTUNATUS • A Christian of Corinth.

1Co 16:17 — I am glad of the coming of Stephanas and Fortunatus and Achaicus: for that which was lacking on your part they have supplied.

FORTUNE

• **Changes of.**

Ge 40:1–23

✦**See: Daniel**

✦**See: David**

✦**See: Esther**

✦**See: Haman**

✦**See: Jeroboam**

✦**See: Joseph, Son of Jacob**

✦**See: Job**

✦**See: Mordecai**

FORTUNE TELLING ✦See: Sorcery

FORTY

• **Remarkable coincidences in the number.**

• **Days.**

• **Of rain, at the time of the flood.**

Ge 7:17 — And the flood was forty days upon the earth; and the waters increased, and bare up the ark, and it was lift up above the earth.

• **Of flood, before sending forth the raven.**

Ge 8:6 — And it came to pass at the end of forty days, that Noah opened the window of the ark which he had made:

• **For embalming.**

Ge 50:3 — And forty days were fulfilled for him; for so are fulfilled the days of those which are embalmed: and the Egyptians mourned for him threescore and ten days.

• **Of fasting.**

• **By Moses.**

Ex 24:18 — And Moses went into the midst of the cloud, and gat him up into the mount: and Moses was in the mount forty days and forty nights.

Ex 34:28 — And he was there with the LORD forty days and forty nights; he did neither eat bread, nor drink water. And he wrote upon the tables the words of the covenant, the ten commandments.

Dt 9:9 — When I was gone up into the mount to receive the tables of stone, *even* the tables of the covenant which the LORD made with you, then I abode in the mount forty days and forty nights, I neither did eat bread nor drink water:

Dt 9:25 — Thus I fell down before the LORD forty days and forty nights, as I fell down *at the first;* because the LORD had said he would destroy you.

• **By Elijah.**

1Ki 19:8 — And he arose, and did eat and drink, and went in the strength of that meat forty days and forty nights unto Horeb the mount of God.

• **By Jesus.**

Mt 4:2 — And when he had fasted forty days and forty nights, he was afterward an hungred.

• **Spies in the land of promise.**

Nu 13:25 — And they returned from searching of the land after forty days.

• **Of probation, given to the Ninevites.**

Jnh 3:4 — And Jonah began to enter into the city a day's journey, and he cried, and said, Yet forty days, and Nineveh shall be overthrown.

• **Christ's stay after the resurrection.**

Ac 1:3 — To whom also he shewed himself alive after his passion by many infallible proofs, being seen of them forty days, and speaking of the things pertaining to the kingdom of God:

• **Symbolic.**

Eze 4:6 — And when thou hast accomplished them, lie again on thy right side, and thou shalt bear the iniquity of the house of Judah forty days: I have appointed thee each day for a year.

• **Years.**

• **Wanderings of the Israelites in the wilderness.**

Ex 16:35 — And the children of Israel did eat manna forty years, until they came to a land inhabited; they did eat manna, until they came unto the borders of the land of Canaan.

Nu 14:34 — After the number of the days in which ye searched the land, *even* forty days, each day for a year, shall ye bear your iniquities, *even* forty years, and ye shall know my breach of promise.

• **Peace in Israel.**

Jgs 3:11 — And the land had rest forty years. And Othniel the son of Kenaz died.

Jgs 5:31 — So let all thine enemies perish, O LORD: but *let* them that love him *be* as the sun when he goeth forth in his might. And the land had rest forty years.

Jgs 8:28 — Thus was Midian subdued before the children of Israel, so that they lifted up their heads no more. And the country was in quietness forty years in the days of Gideon.

• **Egypt to be desolated.**

Eze 29:11 — No foot of man shall pass through it, nor foot of beast shall pass through it, neither shall it be inhabited forty years.

• **Egypt to be restored after.**

Eze 29:13 — Yet thus saith the Lord GOD; At the end of forty years will I gather the Egyptians from the people whither they were scattered:

• **Stripes.**

• **Administered in punishing criminals.**

Dt 25:3 — Forty stripes he may give him, *and* not exceed: lest, *if* he should exceed, and beat him above these with many stripes, then thy brother should seem vile unto thee.

2Co 11:24 — Of the Jews five times received I forty *stripes* save one.

FOUNDING ⇢See: Molding

FOUNTAIN

• **Figurative.**

• **Of divine grace.**

Ps 36:9 — For with thee *is* the fountain of life: in thy light shall we see light.

Jer 2:13 — For my people have committed two evils; they have forsaken me the fountain of living waters, *and* hewed them out cisterns, broken cisterns, that can hold no water.

• **Of the salvation of the gospel.**

Joel 3:18 — And it shall come to pass in that day, *that* the mountains shall drop down new wine, and the hills shall flow with milk, and all the rivers of Judah shall flow with waters, and a fountain shall come forth of the house of the LORD, and shall water the valley of Shittim.

Zec 13:1 — In that day there shall be a fountain opened to the house of David and to the inhabitants of Jerusalem for sin and for uncleanness.

Jn 4:14 — But whosoever drinketh of the water that I shall give him shall never thirst; but the water that I shall give him shall be in him a well of water springing up into everlasting life.

Rev 7:17 — For the Lamb which is in the midst of the throne shall feed them, and shall lead them unto living fountains of waters: and God shall wipe away all tears from their eyes.

Rev 21:6 — And he said unto me, It is done. I am Alpha and Omega, the beginning and the end. I will give unto him that is athirst of the fountain of the water of life freely.

• **The turgid, of the debasement of character.**

Pr 25:26 — A righteous man falling down before the wicked *is as* a troubled fountain, and a corrupt spring.

FOX

• **Dens of.**

Mt 8:20 — And Jesus saith unto him, The foxes have holes, and the birds of the air *have* nests; but the Son of man hath not where to lay *his* head.

Lk 9:58 — And Jesus said unto him, Foxes have holes, and birds of the air *have* nests; but the Son of man hath not where to lay *his* head.

• **Samson uses, to burn the field of the Philistines.**

Jgs 15:4 — And Samson went and caught three hundred foxes, and took firebrands, and turned tail to tail, and put a firebrand in the midst between two tails.

• **Depredations of.**

Ps 63:10 — They shall fall by the sword: they shall be a portion for foxes.

SS 2:15 — Take us the foxes, the little foxes, that spoil the vines: for our vines *have* tender grapes.

• **Held in contempt.**

Ne 4:3 — Now Tobiah the Ammonite *was* by him, and he said, Even that which they build, if a fox go up, he shall even break down their stone wall.

• **Figurative.**

• **Of unfaithful prophets.**

Eze 13:4 — O Israel, thy prophets are like the foxes in the deserts.

• **Of craftiness.**

Lk 13:32 — And he said unto them, Go ye, and tell that fox, Behold, I cast out devils, and I do cures to day and to morrow, and the third *day* I shall be perfected.

• **Of heretics.**

SS 2:15 — Take us the foxes, the little foxes, that spoil the vines: for our vines *have* tender grapes.

FRACTURES

• **Treatment of.**

Eze 30:21 — Son of man, I have broken the arm of Pharaoh king of Egypt; and, lo, it shall not be bound up to be healed, to put a roller to bind it, to make it strong to hold the sword.

FRANKINCENSE

• An ingredient of the sacred oil.

Ex 30:34 — And the LORD said unto Moses, Take unto thee sweet spices, stacte, and onycha, and galbanum; *these* sweet spices with pure frankincense: of each shall there be a like *weight:*

• Used with showbread.

Le 24:7 — And thou shalt put pure frankincense upon *each* row, that it may be on the bread for a memorial, *even* an offering made by fire unto the LORD.

• Used with meat offerings.

Le 2:1–2, 15–16

Le 6:15 — And he shall take of it his handful, of the flour of the meat offering, and of the oil thereof, and all the frankincense which *is* upon the meat offering, and shall burn *it* upon the altar *for* a sweet savour, *even* the memorial of it, unto the LORD.

• Prohibited, in sin offerings when they consist of turtledoves or pigeons.

Le 5:11 — But if he be not able to bring two turtledoves, or two young pigeons, then he that sinned shall bring for his offering the tenth part of an ephah of fine flour for a sin offering; he shall put no oil upon it, neither shall he put *any* frankincense thereon: for it *is* a sin offering.

• Prohibited, in making an offering of memorial.

Nu 5:15 — Then shall the man bring his wife unto the priest, and he shall bring her offering for her, the tenth *part* of an ephah of barley meal; he shall pour no oil upon it, nor put frankincense thereon; for it *is* an offering of jealousy, an offering of memorial, bringing iniquity to remembrance.

• A perfume.

SS 3:6 — Who *is* this that cometh out of the wilderness like pillars of smoke, perfumed with myrrh and frankincense, with all powders of the merchant?

• Commerce in.

Rev 18:11–13

• Used as an incense.

Isa 43:23 — Thou hast not brought me the small cattle of thy burnt offerings; neither hast thou honoured me with thy sacrifices. I have not caused thee to serve with an offering, nor wearied thee with incense.

Isa 60:6 — The multitude of camels shall cover thee, the dromedaries of Midian and Ephah; all they from Sheba shall come: they shall bring gold and incense; and they shall shew forth the praises of the LORD.

Isa 66:3 — He that killeth an ox *is as if* he slew a man; he that sacrificeth a lamb, *as if* he cut off a dog's neck; he that offereth an oblation, *as if he offered* swine's blood; he that burneth incense, *as if* he blessed an idol. Yea, they have chosen their own ways, and their soul delighteth in their abominations.

Jer 6:20 — To what purpose cometh there to me incense from Sheba, and the sweet cane from a far country? your burnt offerings *are* not acceptable, nor your sacrifices sweet unto me.

• Gift of.

Mt 2:11 — And when they were come into the house, they saw the young child with Mary his mother, and fell down, and worshipped him: and when they had opened their treasures, they presented unto him gifts; gold, and frankincense, and myrrh.

FRATERNITY

Dt 15:7–15; Ps 133:1–3; Mt 5:22–24; 18:15–18, 21–22; 1Co 6:1–8; 8:1–13; Gal 6:1–2; 2Th 3:14–15; 1Jn 2:9–11

Ge 13:8 — And Abram said unto Lot, Let there be no strife, I pray thee, between me and thee, and between my herdmen and thy herdmen; for we *be* brethren.

Ps 22:22 — I will declare thy name unto my brethren: in the midst of the congregation will I praise thee.

Zec 11:14 — Then I cut asunder mine other staff, *even* Bands, that I might break the brotherhood between Judah and Israel.

Mal 2:10 — Have we not all one father? hath not one God created us? why do we deal treacherously every man against his brother, by profaning the covenant of our fathers?

Mt 18:35 — So likewise shall my heavenly Father do also unto you, if ye from your hearts forgive not every one his brother their trespasses.

Mt 23:8 — But be not ye called Rabbi: for one is your Master, *even* Christ; and all ye are brethren.

Mt 25:40 — And the King shall answer and say unto them, Verily I say unto you, Inasmuch as ye have done *it* unto one of the least of these my brethren, ye have done *it* unto me.

Jn 13:34 — A new commandment I give unto you, That ye love one another; as I have loved you, that ye also love one another.

Jn 15:12 — This is my commandment, That ye love one another, as I have loved you.

Jn 20:17 — Jesus saith unto her, Touch me not; for I am not yet ascended to my Father: but go to my brethren, and say unto them, I ascend unto my Father, and your Father; and *to* my God, and your God.

Ro 12:10 — *Be* kindly affectioned one to another with brotherly love; in honour preferring one another;

1Th 4:9 — But as touching brotherly love ye need not that I write unto you: for ye yourselves are taught of God to love one another.

Heb 13:1 — Let brotherly love continue.

1Pe 1:22 — Seeing ye have purified your souls in obeying the truth through the Spirit unto unfeigned love of the brethren, *see that ye* love one another with a pure heart fervently:

1Pe 2:17 — Honour all *men.* Love the brotherhood. Fear God. Honour the king.

1Pe 3:8 — Finally, *be ye* all of one mind, having compassion one of another, love as brethren, *be* pitiful, *be* courteous:

2Pe 1:5 — And beside this, giving all diligence, add to your faith virtue; and to virtue knowledge;

2Pe 1:7 — And to godliness brotherly kindness; and to brotherly kindness charity.

1Jn 3:17 — But whoso hath this world's good, and seeth his brother have need, and shutteth up his bowels *of compassion* from him, how dwelleth the love of God in him?

See: Brother

See: Church

See: Fellowship

See: Friendship

- **Instances of.**
  - **The Nazarites, vows of.**
    Nu 6:1–21; La 4:7; Am 2:11–12; Ac 21:24–31

See: Nazarite

FRATRICIDE

- **Instances of.**
  - **Cain.**
    Ge 4:8
  - **Abimelech.**
    Jgs 9:5
  - **Absalom.**
    2Sa 13:28–29
  - **Solomon.**
    1Ki 2:23–25
  - **Jehoram.**
    2Ch 21:4

See: Homicide

FRAUD **See: Dishonesty**

FREE WILL **See: Blessing; divine, contingent upon obedience**

FREEDMEN

- **Synagogue of.**
  Ac 6:9 — Then there arose certain of *the synagogue,* which is called the synagogue of the Libertines, and Cyrenians, and Alexandrians, and of them of Cilicia and of Asia, disputing with Stephen.

See: Emancipation

FREEDOM

- **From servitude.**

See: Emancipation

See: Jubilee

FREEWILL OFFERINGS

Le 22:21 — And whosoever offereth a sacrifice of peace offerings unto the LORD to accomplish *his* vow, or a freewill offering in beeves or sheep, it shall be perfect to be accepted; there shall be no blemish therein.

Le 22:23 — Either a bullock or a lamb that hath any thing superfluous or lacking in his parts, that mayest thou offer *for* a freewill offering; but for a vow it shall not be accepted.

Le 23:38 — Beside the sabbaths of the LORD, and beside your gifts, and beside all your vows, and beside all your freewill offerings, which ye give unto the LORD.

Nu 29:39 — These *things* ye shall do unto the LORD in your set feasts, beside your vows, and your freewill offerings, for your burnt offerings, and for your meat offerings, and for your drink offerings, and for your peace offerings.

Dt 12:6 — And thither ye shall bring your burnt offerings, and your sacrifices, and your tithes, and heave offerings of your hand, and your vows, and your freewill offerings, and the firstlings of your herds and of your flocks:

Dt 12:17 — Thou mayest not eat within thy gates the tithe of thy corn, or of thy wine, or of thy oil, or the firstlings of thy herds or of thy flock, nor any of thy vows which thou vowest, nor thy freewill offerings, or heave offering of thine hand:

2Ch 31:14 — And Kore the son of Imnah the Levite, the porter toward the east, *was* over the freewill offerings of God, to distribute the oblations of the LORD, and the most holy things.

Ezr 3:5 — And afterward *offered* the continual burnt offering, both of the new moons, and of all the set feasts of the LORD that were consecrated, and of every one that willingly offered a freewill offering unto the LORD.

Ezr 7:16 — And all the silver and gold that thou canst find in all the province of Babylon, with the freewill offering of the people, and of the priests, offering willingly for the house of their God which *is* in Jerusalem:

Ezr 8:28 — And I said unto them, Ye *are* holy unto the LORD; the vessels *are* holy also; and the silver and the gold *are* a freewill offering unto the LORD God of your fathers.

Ps 119:108 — Accept, I beseech thee, the freewill offerings of my mouth, O LORD, and teach me thy judgments.

See: Beneficence

See: Gifts from God

See: Giving

See: Liberality

See: Offerings

FRIENDS

- **Jesus calls his disciples.**
  Jn 15:14–15
- **False friends.**
  - **Instances of.**
    - **Pharaoh's butler false to Joseph.**
      Ge 40:23 — Yet did not the chief butler remember Joseph, but forgat him.
    - **Delilah to Samson.**
      Jgs 16:1–20
    - **The Ephraimite's wife.**
      Jgs 19:1–2
    - **David to Joab.**
      1Ki 2:5–6
    - **David to Uriah.**
      2Sa 11:1–27
    - **Ahithophel to David.**
      2Sa 15:12 — And Absalom sent for Ahithophel the Gilonite, David's counsellor, from his city, *even* from Giloh, while he offered sacrifices. And the conspiracy was strong; for the people increased continually with Absalom.

• **David's friends to David.**

Ps 35:11–16; 55:12–14, 20–21

Ps 41:9 — Yea, mine own familiar friend, in whom I trusted, which did eat of my bread, hath lifted up *his* heel against me.

Ps 88:8 — Thou hast put away mine acquaintance far from me; thou hast made me an abomination unto them: *I am* shut up, and I cannot come forth.

Ps 88:18 — Lover and friend hast thou put far from me, *and* mine acquaintance into darkness.

• **Judas.**

Mt 26:48–49

• **Disciples.**

Mt 26:56 — But all this was done, that the scriptures of the prophets might be fulfilled. Then all the disciples forsook him, and fled.

Mt 26:58 — But Peter followed him afar off unto the high priest's palace, and went in, and sat with the servants, to see the end.

✣See: Hypocrisy

FRIENDSHIP

Dt 13:6–9; Job 6:14–15; 19:13–22; Ps 35:13–14; 55:12–14; Pr 22:24–27; 27:9–10; Ecc 4:9–12; Php 4:14–19

Job 16:2 — I have heard many such things: miserable comforters *are* ye all.

Job 16:20 — My friends scorn me: *but* mine eye poureth out *tears* unto God.

Ps 41:9 — Yea, mine own familiar friend, in whom I trusted, which did eat of my bread, hath lifted up *his* heel against me.

Ps 88:8 — Thou hast put away mine acquaintance far from me; thou hast made me an abomination unto them: *I am* shut up, and I cannot come forth.

Ps 88:18 — Lover and friend hast thou put far from me, *and* mine acquaintance into darkness.

Pr 11:13 — A talebearer revealeth secrets: but he that is of a faithful spirit concealeth the matter.

Pr 17:9 — He that covereth a transgression seeketh love; but he that repeateth a matter separateth *very* friends.

Pr 17:17 — A friend loveth at all times, and a brother is born for adversity.

Pr 18:24 — A man *that hath* friends must shew himself friendly: and there is a friend *that* sticketh closer than a brother.

Pr 22:11 — He that loveth pureness of heart, *for* the grace of his lips the king *shall be* his friend.

Pr 25:17 — Withdraw thy foot from thy neighbour's house; lest he be weary of thee, and *so* hate thee.

Pr 25:19 — Confidence in an unfaithful man in time of trouble *is like* a broken tooth, and a foot out of joint.

Pr 27:6 — Faithful *are* the wounds of a friend; but the kisses of an enemy *are* deceitful.

Pr 27:14 — He that blesseth his friend with a loud voice, rising early in the morning, it shall be counted a curse to him.

Pr 27:17 — Iron sharpeneth iron; so a man sharpeneth the countenance of his friend.

Pr 27:19 — As in water face *answereth* to face, so the heart of man to man.

Am 3:3 — Can two walk together, except they be agreed?

Php 2:27 — For indeed he was sick nigh unto death: but God had mercy on him; and not on him only, but on me also, lest I should have sorrow upon sorrow.

Php 2:30 — Because for the work of Christ he was nigh unto death, not regarding his life, to supply your lack of service toward me.

2Ti 4:16 — At my first answer no man stood with me, but all *men* forsook me: *I pray God* that it may not be laid to their charge.

• **Instances of.**

• **Abraham and Lot.**

Ge 14:14–16

• **Ruth and Naomi.**

Ru 1:16–17

• **Samuel and Saul.**

1Sa 15:35–16:1

• **David and Jonathan.**

1Sa 18:1–4; 20:1–42; 23:16–18; 2Sa 1:17–27; 9:1–13

• **David and Abiathar.**

1Sa 22:23

• **David and Nahash.**

2Sa 10:2

• **David and Hiram.**

1Ki 5:1

• **David and Mephibosheth.**

2Sa 9:1–13

• **David and Hushai.**

2Sa 15:32–17:22

• **David and Ittai.**

2Sa 15:19–21

• **Joram and Ahaziah.**

2Ki 8:28–29; 9:16

• **Jehu and Jehonadab.**

2Ki 10:15–27

• **Job and his three friends.**

Job 2:11–13

• **Daniel and his three companions.**

Da 2:49

• **Mary, Martha, and Lazarus, and Jesus.**

Lk 10:38–42; Jn 11:1–46

• **The Marys, and Joseph of Arimathaea, for Jesus.**

Mt 27:55–61; 28:1–8; Lk 24:10; Jn 20:11–18

• **Luke and Theophilus.**

Ac 1:1

• **Paul and his nephew.**

Ac 23:16

• **Paul, Priscilla, and Aquila.**

Ro 16:3–4

• **Paul, Timothy, and Epaphroditus.**

Php 2:19–20, 22, 25

FRINGES

• **Prescribed for vesture worn by the Israelites.**

Nu 15:37–41

Dt 22:12 — Thou shalt make thee fringes upon the four quarters of thy vesture, wherewith thou coverest *thyself.*

- **Made broad by the Pharisees.**

Mt 23:5 — But all their works they do for to be seen of men: they make broad their phylacteries, and enlarge the borders of their garments,

FROGS

- **Plague.**

Ex 8:2–14

Ps 78:45 — He sent divers sorts of flies among them, which devoured them; and frogs, which destroyed them.

Ps 105:30 — Their land brought forth frogs in abundance, in the chambers of their kings.

- **Symbolic.**

Rev 16:13 — And I saw three unclean spirits like frogs *come* out of the mouth of the dragon, and out of the mouth of the beast, and out of the mouth of the false prophet.

FRONTLETS

- **A leather band worn on the forehead containing certain commandments.**

Ex 13:6–16; Dt 6:1–8

Dt 11:18 — Therefore shall ye lay up these my words in your heart and in your soul, and bind them for a sign upon your hand, that they may be as frontlets between your eyes.

See: Phylactery

FRUGALITY

1Ki 17:5–6, 10–13; Pr 23:20–21; Mk 14:4–5

Pr 11:16 — A gracious woman retaineth honour: and strong *men* retain riches.

Pr 12:27 — The slothful *man* roasteth not that which he took in hunting: but the substance of a diligent man *is* precious.

Pr 13:22 — A good *man* leaveth an inheritance to his children's children: and the wealth of the sinner is laid up for the just.

Pr 21:17 — He that loveth pleasure *shall be* a poor man: he that loveth wine and oil shall not be rich.

Pr 21:20 — *There is* treasure to be desired and oil in the dwelling of the wise; but a foolish man spendeth it up.

Pr 22:3 — A prudent *man* foreseeth the evil, and hideth himself: but the simple pass on, and are punished.

Pr 31:27 — She looketh well to the ways of her household, and eateth not the bread of idleness.

Mt 14:20 — And they did all eat, and were filled: and they took up of the fragments that remained twelve baskets full.

Mt 15:37 — And they did all eat, and were filled: and they took up of the broken *meat* that was left seven baskets full.

Mk 7:28 — And she answered and said unto him, Yes, Lord: yet the dogs under the table eat of the children's crumbs.

Eph 4:28 — Let him that stole steal no more: but rather let him labour, working with *his* hands the thing which is good, that he may have to give to him that needeth.

See: Extravagance

See: Industry

- **Instances of.**
  - **The provisions made by the Egyptians against famine.**

    Ge 41:48–49, 53–54
  - **The gathering of manna.**

    Ex 16:17–18, 22–24

FRUIT TREES

- **Care for.**

Dt 20:19–20

FRUITS

- **Natural (look under the respective headings).**

Ge 1:11–12, 27–29

- **Spiritual.**

See: Righteousness; fruits of

See: Sin; fruits of

FRYING PAN

Le 2:7 — And if thy oblation *be* a meat offering *baken* in the frying pan, it shall be made *of* fine flour with oil.

Le 7:9 — And all the meat offering that is baken in the oven, and all that is dressed in the fryingpan, and in the pan, shall be the priest's that offereth it.

FUEL

- **For temple, how provided.**

Ne 13:30–31

Ne 10:34 — And we cast the lots among the priests, the Levites, and the people, for the wood offering, to bring *it* into the house of our God, after the houses of our fathers, at times appointed year by year, to burn upon the altar of the LORD our God, as *it is* written in the law:

FUGITIVES

- **From servitude, not to be returned.**

Dt 23:15–16

- **Instances of.**
  - **From slavery, Shimei's servants.**

    1Ki 2:39
  - **From slavery, Onesimus.**

    Phm 1:1
  - **From justice.**
    - **Moses.**

      Ex 2:15 — Now when Pharaoh heard this thing, he sought to slay Moses. But Moses fled from the face of Pharaoh, and dwelt in the land of Midian: and he sat down by a well.
    - **Absalom.**

      2Sa 13:34–38

- **From the wrath of the king.**
  - **David.**
    1Sa 21:10 — And David arose, and fled that day for fear of Saul, and went to Achish the king of Gath.
  - **Jeroboam.**
    1Ki 11:40 — Solomon sought therefore to kill Jeroboam. And Jeroboam arose, and fled into Egypt, unto Shishak king of Egypt, and was in Egypt until the death of Solomon.
  - **Joseph, to Egypt.**
    Mt 2:13–15

FULLER

Mal 3:2 — But who may abide the day of his coming? and who shall stand when he appeareth? for he *is* like a refiner's fire, and like fullers' sope:

Mk 9:3 — And his raiment became shining, exceeding white as snow; so as no fuller on earth can white them.

FULLER'S FIELD • A post near Jerusalem.

2Ki 18:17 — And the king of Assyria sent Tartan and Rabsaris and Rab-shakeh from Lachish to king Hezekiah with a great host against Jerusalem. And they went up and came to Jerusalem. And when they were come up, they came and stood by the conduit of the upper pool, which is in the highway of the fuller's field.

Isa 7:3 — Then said the LORD unto Isaiah, Go forth now to meet Ahaz, thou, and Shear-jashub thy son, at the end of the conduit of the upper pool in the highway of the fuller's field;

Isa 36:2 — And the king of Assyria sent Rabshakeh from Lachish to Jerusalem unto king Hezekiah with a great army. And he stood by the conduit of the upper pool in the highway of the fuller's field.

FUNERALS

↞See: Burial

↞See: Elegy

FURLONG • One eighth of a mile.

Lk 24:13 — And, behold, two of them went that same day to a village called Emmaus, which was from Jerusalem *about* threescore furlongs.

Jn 11:18 — Now Bethany was nigh unto Jerusalem, about fifteen furlongs off:

Rev 21:16 — And the city lieth foursquare, and the length is as large as the breadth: and he measured the city with the reed, twelve thousand furlongs. The length and the breadth and the height of it are equal.

FURNACE

- **Uses of.**
  - **For refining silver.**
    Eze 22:22 — As silver is melted in the midst of the furnace, so shall ye be melted in the midst thereof; and ye shall know that I the LORD have poured out my fury upon you.
    Mal 3:3 — And he shall sit *as* a refiner and purifier of silver: and he shall purify the sons of Levi, and purge them as gold and silver, that they may offer unto the LORD an offering in righteousness.
  - **For refining gold.**
    Pr 17:3 — The fining pot *is* for silver, and the furnace for gold: but the LORD trieth the hearts.
  - **For melting lead and tin.**
    Eze 22:20 — *As* they gather silver, and brass, and iron, and lead, and tin, into the midst of the furnace, to blow the fire upon it, to melt *it;* so will I gather *you* in mine anger and in my fury, and I will leave *you there,* and melt you.
  - **For capital punishment, Shadrach, Meshach, and Abed-nego cast into, by Nebuchadnezzar.**
    Da 3:6–26
- **Figurative.**
  - **Of affliction.**
    Dt 4:20 — But the LORD hath taken you, and brought you forth out of the iron furnace, *even* out of Egypt, to be unto him a people of inheritance, as *ye are* this day.
    1Ki 8:51 — For they *be* thy people, and thine inheritance, which thou broughtest forth out of Egypt, from the midst of the furnace of iron:
    Ps 12:6 — The words of the LORD *are* pure words: *as* silver tried in a furnace of earth, purified seven times.
    Isa 48:10 — Behold, I have refined thee, but not with silver; I have chosen thee in the furnace of affliction.
    Jer 11:4 — Which I commanded your fathers in the day *that* I brought them forth out of the land of Egypt, from the iron furnace, saying, Obey my voice, and do them, according to all which I command you: so shall ye be my people, and I will be your God:
  - **Of lust.**
    Hos 7:4 — They *are* all adulterers, as an oven heated by the baker, *who* ceaseth from raising after he hath kneaded the dough, until it be leavened.
  - **Of hell.**
    Mal 4:1 — For, behold, the day cometh, that shall burn as an oven; and all the proud, yea, and all that do wickedly, shall be stubble: and the day that cometh shall burn them up, saith the LORD of hosts, that it shall leave them neither root nor branch.
    Mt 13:42 — <u>And shall cast them into a furnace of fire: there shall be wailing and gnashing of teeth.</u>
    Mt 13:50 — <u>And shall cast them into the furnace of fire: there shall be wailing and gnashing of teeth.</u>
    Rev 9:2 — And he opened the bottomless pit; and there arose a smoke out of the pit, as the smoke of a great furnace; and the sun and the air were darkened by reason of the smoke of the pit.

FUTURE PUNISHMENT ↞See: Punishment; eternal

G

GAAL • Conspires against and is defeated by Abimelech.

Jgs 9:26–41

GAASH

• A foothill of Mount Ephraim.

• Joshua's inheritance embraced.

Jos 24:30 — And they buried him in the border of his inheritance in Timnath-serah, which *is* in mount Ephraim, on the north side of the hill of Gaash.

• Joshua buried on the north side of.

Jos 24:30 — And they buried him in the border of his inheritance in Timnath-serah, which *is* in mount Ephraim, on the north side of the hill of Gaash.

Jgs 2:9 — And they buried him in the border of his inheritance in Timnath-heres, in the mount of Ephraim, on the north side of the hill Gaash.

• Brooks of.

2Sa 23:30 — Benaiah the Pirathonite, Hiddai of the brooks of Gaash,

GABA

• Called also Geba.

• A city of Canaan allotted to Benjamin.

Jos 18:24 — And Chephar-haammonai, and Ophni, and Gaba; twelve cities with their villages:

Ezr 2:26 — The children of Ramah and Gaba, six hundred twenty and one.

Ne 7:30 — The men of Ramah and Gaba, six hundred twenty and one.

GABBAI • A Benjamite chief.

Ne 11:8 — And after him Gabbai, Sallai, nine hundred twenty and eight.

GABBATHA • A place of judgment in Jerusalem, where Pilate passed sentence on Jesus.

Jn 19:13 — When Pilate therefore heard that saying, he brought Jesus forth, and sat down in the judgment seat in a place that is called the Pavement, but in the Hebrew, Gabbatha.

GABRIEL

• A messenger of God.

• Appeared to.

• Daniel.

Da 8:16 — And I heard a man's voice between *the banks of* Ulai, which called, and said, Gabriel, make this *man* to understand the vision.

Da 9:21 — Yea, whiles I *was* speaking in prayer, even the man Gabriel, whom I had seen in the vision at the beginning, being caused to fly swiftly, touched me about the time of the evening oblation.

• Zacharias.

Lk 1:11–19

• Mary.

Lk 1:26–29

GAD

• Jacob's seventh son.

Ge 30:11 — And Leah said, A troop cometh: and she called his name Gad.

Ge 35:26 — And the sons of Zilpah, Leah's handmaid; Gad, and Asher: these *are* the sons of Jacob, which were born to him in Padan-aram.

Ex 1:4 — Dan, and Naphtali, Gad, and Asher.

• Children of.

Nu 26:15–18

Ge 46:16 — And the sons of Gad; Ziphion, and Haggi, Shuni, and Ezbon, Eri, and Arodi, and Areli.

1Ch 5:11 — And the children of Gad dwelt over against them, in the land of Bashan unto Salchah:

• Prophecy concerning.

Ge 49:19 — Gad, a troop shall overcome him: but he shall overcome at the last.

• A tribe of Israel.

• Blessed by Moses.

Dt 33:20 — And of Gad he said, Blessed *be* he that enlargeth Gad: he dwelleth as a lion, and teareth the arm with the crown of the head.

• Enumeration of.

• At Sinai.

Nu 1:24–25

Nu 1:14 — Of Gad; Eliasaph the son of Deuel.

• In the plains of Moab.

Nu 26:15–18

• In the reign of Jotham.

1Ch 5:11–17

• Place of, in camp and march.

Nu 2:10 — On the south side *shall be* the standard of the camp of Reuben according to their armies: and the captain of the children of Reuben *shall be* Elizur the son of Shedeur.

Nu 2:14 — Then the tribe of Gad: and the captain of the sons of Gad *shall be* Eliasaph the son of Reuel.

Nu 2:16 — All that were numbered in the camp of Reuben *were* an hundred thousand and fifty and one thousand and four hundred and fifty, throughout their armies. And they shall set forth in the second rank.

• Wealth of, in cattle, and spoils.

Nu 32:1 — Now the children of Reuben and the children of Gad had a very great multitude of cattle: and when they saw the land of Jazer, and the land of Gilead, that, behold, the place *was* a place for cattle;

Jos 22:8 — And he spake unto them, saying, Return with much riches unto your tents, and with very much cattle, with silver, and with gold, and with brass, and with iron, and with very much raiment: divide the spoil of your enemies with your brethren.

• Petition for their portion of land east of the Jordan.

Nu 32:1–5; Dt 3:16–17

Dt 3:12 — And this land, *which* we possessed at that time, from Aroer, which *is* by the river Arnon, and half mount Gilead, and the cities thereof, gave I unto the Reubenites and to the Gadites.

Dt 29:8 — And we took their land, and gave it for an inheritance unto the Reubenites, and to the Gadites, and to the half tribe of Manasseh.

• Boundaries of territory.

Jos 13:24–28

1Ch 5:11 — And the children of Gad dwelt over against them, in the land of Bashan unto Salchah:

• Aid in the conquest of the region west of the Jordan.

Nu 32:16–32; Jos 4:12–13; 22:1–8

• Erect a monument to signify the unity of the tribes east of the Jordan with the tribes west of the river.

Jos 22:10–14

• Disaffected toward Saul as king, and joined the faction under David in the wilderness of Hebron.

1Ch 12:8–15, 37–38

• Join the Reubenites in the war against the Hagarites.

1Ch 5:18–22

1Ch 5:10 — And in the days of Saul they made war with the Hagarites, who fell by their hand: and they dwelt in their tents throughout all the east land of Gilead.

• Smitten by the king of Syria.

2Ki 10:32–33

• Carried into captivity to Assyria.

1Ch 5:26 — And the God of Israel stirred up the spirit of Pul king of Assyria, and the spirit of Tilgath-pilneser king of Assyria, and he carried them away, even the Reubenites, and the Gadites, and the half tribe of Manasseh, and brought them unto Halah, and Habor, and Hara, and to the river Gozan, unto this day.

• Land of, occupied by the Ammonites, after the tribe is carried into captivity.

Jer 49:1 — Concerning the Ammonites, thus saith the LORD; Hath Israel no sons? hath he no heir? why *then* doth their king inherit Gad, and his people dwell in his cities?

• Reallotment of territory to, by Ezekiel.

Eze 48:27 — And by the border of Zebulun, from the east side unto the west side, Gad a *portion*.

Eze 48:29 — This *is* the land which ye shall divide by lot unto the tribes of Israel for inheritance, and these *are* their portions, saith the Lord GOD.

• A prophet of David.

2Sa 24:11 — For when David was up in the morning, the word of the LORD came unto the prophet Gad, David's seer, saying,

• Bids David leave Adullam.

1Sa 22:5 — And the prophet Gad said unto David, Abide not in the hold; depart, and get thee into the land of Judah. Then David departed, and came into the forest of Hareth.

• Offers David choice between three evils, for his presumption in numbering Israel.

2Sa 24:11–14; 1Ch 21:9–13

• Bids David build an altar on threshing floor of Ornan.

2Sa 24:18–19; 1Ch 21:18–19

• Assists David in arranging temple service.

2Ch 29:25 — And he set the Levites in the house of the LORD with cymbals, with psalteries, and with harps, according to the commandment of David, and of Gad the king's seer, and Nathan the prophet: for *so was* the commandment of the LORD by his prophets.

• Writings of.

1Ch 29:29 — Now the acts of David the king, first and last, behold, they *are* written in the book of Samuel the seer, and in the book of Nathan the prophet, and in the book of Gad the seer,

GADARENES

• Called also Gergesenes.

• Jesus visits and works miracles among, but is rejected.

Mt 8:28–34; Mk 5:1–19

GADDI

• A chief of Manasseh.

• One of the twelve spies who explored Canaan.

Nu 13:11 — Of the tribe of Joseph, namely, of the tribe of Manasseh, Gaddi the son of Susi.

GADDIEL

• A chief of Zebulun.

• One of the twelve spies.

Nu 13:10 — Of the tribe of Zebulun, Gaddiel the son of Sodi.

GADI • Father of Menahem.

2Ki 15:14 — For Menahem the son of Gadi went up from Tirzah, and came to Samaria, and smote Shallum the son of Jabesh in Samaria, and slew him, and reigned in his stead.

2Ki 15:17 — In the nine and thirtieth year of Azariah king of Judah began Menahem the son of Gadi to reign over Israel, *and reigned* ten years in Samaria.

GAHAM • Son of Nahor.

Ge 22:24 — And his concubine, whose name *was* Reumah, she bare also Tebah, and Gaham, and Thahash, and Maachah.

GAHAR • One of the Nethinim.

Ezr 2:47 — The children of Giddel, the children of Gahar, the children of Reaiah,

Ne 7:49 — The children of Hanan, the children of Giddel, the children of Gahar,

GAIUS

• A Macedonian, and a companion of Paul.

• Seized at Ephesus.

Ac 19:29 — And the whole city was filled with confusion: and having caught Gaius and Aristarchus, men of Macedonia, Paul's companions in travel, they rushed with one accord into the theatre.

• A man of Derbe, accompanied Paul from Macedonia.

Ac 20:4 — And there accompanied him into Asia Sopater of Berea; and of the Thessalonians, Aristarchus and Secundus; and Gaius of Derbe, and Timotheus; and of Asia, Tychicus and Trophimus.

• A Corinthian, whom Paul baptized.

Ro 16:23 — Gaius mine host, and of the whole church, saluteth you. Erastus the chamberlain of the city saluteth you, and Quartus a brother.

1Co 1:14 — I thank God that I baptized none of you, but Crispus and Gaius;

• Man to whom John's third epistle was addressed.

3Jn 1:1–14

GALAL

• A Levite.

1Ch 9:15 — And Bakbakkar, Heresh, and Galal, and Mattaniah the son of Micah, the son of Zichri, the son of Asaph;

• Son of Jeduthun.

1Ch 9:16 — And Obadiah the son of Shemaiah, the son of Galal, the son of Jeduthun, and Berechiah the son of Asa, the son of Elkanah, that dwelt in the villages of the Netophathites.

Ne 11:17 — And Mattaniah the son of Micha, the son of Zabdi, the son of Asaph, *was* the principal to begin the thanksgiving in prayer: and Bakbukiah the second among his brethren, and Abda the son of Shammua, the son of Galal, the son of Jeduthun.

GALATIA

• A province of Asia Minor.

• Its churches visited by Paul.

Ac 16:6 — Now when they had gone throughout Phrygia and the region of Galatia, and were forbidden of the Holy Ghost to preach the word in Asia,

Ac 18:23 — And after he had spent some time *there,* he departed, and went over *all* the country of Galatia and Phrygia in order, strengthening all the disciples.

• Collection taken in, for Christians at Jerusalem.

1Co 16:1 — Now concerning the collection for the saints, as I have given order to the churches of Galatia, even so do ye.

• Peter's address to.

1Pe 1:1 — Peter, an apostle of Jesus Christ, to the strangers scattered throughout Pontus, Galatia, Cappadocia, Asia, and Bithynia,

• Churches in.

Gal 1:1–24

GALBANUM • A fragrant gum used in the sacred oil.

Ex 30:34 — And the LORD said unto Moses, Take unto thee sweet spices, stacte, and onycha, and galbanum; *these* sweet spices with pure frankincense: of each shall there be a like *weight:*

GALEED

• Called also Jegar-Sahadutha.

• The memorial of Jacob's and Laban's covenant.

Ge 31:47–48

GALILEE

• The northern district of Palestine.

• A city of refuge in.

Jos 20:7 — And they appointed Kedesh in Galilee in mount Naphtali, and Shechem in mount Ephraim, and Kirjath-arba, which *is* Hebron, in the mountain of Judah.

Jos 21:32 — And out of the tribe of Naphtali, Kedesh in Galilee with her suburbs, *to be* a city of refuge for the slayer; and Hammoth-dor with her suburbs, and Kartan with her suburbs; three cities.

1Ch 6:76 — And out of the tribe of Naphtali; Kedesh in Galilee with her suburbs, and Hammon with her suburbs, and Kirjathaim with her suburbs.

• Cities in, given to Hiram.

1Ki 9:11–12

• Taken by king of Assyria.

2Ki 15:29 — In the days of Pekah king of Israel came Tiglath-pileser king of Assyria, and took Ijon, and Abel-beth-maachah, and Janoah, and Kedesh, and Hazor, and Gilead, and Galilee, all the land of Naphtali, and carried them captive to Assyria.

• Prophecy concerning.

Isa 9:1 — Nevertheless the dimness *shall* not *be* such as *was* in her vexation, when at the first he lightly afflicted the land of Zebulun and the land of Naphtali, and afterward did more grievously afflict *her by* the way of the sea, beyond Jordan, in Galilee of the nations.

Mt 4:15 — The land of Zabulon, and the land of Nephthalim, *by* the way of the sea, beyond Jordan, Galilee of the Gentiles;

• Called Galilee of the Nations.

Isa 9:1 — Nevertheless the dimness *shall* not *be* such as *was* in her vexation, when at the first he lightly afflicted the land of Zebulun and the land of Naphtali, and afterward did more grievously afflict *her by* the way of the sea, beyond Jordan, in Galilee of the nations.

• Herod, tetrarch of.

Lk 23:6–7

Mk 6:21 — And when a convenient day was come, that Herod on his birthday made a supper to his lords, high captains, and chief *estates* of Galilee;

Lk 3:1 — Now in the fifteenth year of the reign of Tiberius Caesar, Pontius Pilate being governor of Judaea, and Herod being tetrarch of Galilee, and his brother Philip tetrarch of Ituraea and of the region of Trachonitis, and Lysanias the tetrarch of Abilene,

• Jesus resides in.

Mt 17:22 — And while they abode in Galilee, Jesus said unto them, The Son of man shall be betrayed into the hands of men:

Mt 19:1 — And it came to pass, *that* when Jesus had finished these sayings, he departed from Galilee, and came into the coasts of Judaea beyond Jordan;

Jn 7:1 — After these things Jesus walked in Galilee: for he would not walk in Jewry, because the Jews sought to kill him.

Jn 7:9 — When he had said these words unto them, he abode *still* in Galilee.

• Teaching and miracles of Jesus in.

Mt 15:29–31; Jn 4:43–45

Mt 4:23 — And Jesus went about all Galilee, teaching in their synagogues, and preaching the gospel of the kingdom, and healing all manner of sickness and all manner of disease among the people.

Mt 4:25 — And there followed him great multitudes of people from Galilee, and *from* Decapolis, and *from* Jerusalem, and *from* Judaea, and *from* beyond Jordan.

Mk 1:14 — Now after that John was put in prison, Jesus came into Galilee, preaching the gospel of the kingdom of God,

Mk 1:28 — And immediately his fame spread abroad throughout all the region round about Galilee.

Mk 1:39 — And he preached in their synagogues throughout all Galilee, and cast out devils.

Mk 3:7 — But Jesus withdrew himself with his disciples to the sea: and a great multitude from Galilee followed him, and from Judaea,

Lk 4:14 — And Jesus returned in the power of the Spirit into Galilee: and there went out a fame of him through all the region round about.

Lk 4:44 — And he preached in the synagogues of Galilee.

Lk 5:17 — And it came to pass on a certain day, as he was teaching, that there were Pharisees and doctors of the law sitting by, which were come out of every town of Galilee, and Judaea, and Jerusalem: and the power of the Lord was *present* to heal them.

Lk 23:5 — And they were the more fierce, saying, He stirreth up the people, teaching throughout all Jewry, beginning from Galilee to this place.

Jn 1:43 — The day following Jesus would go forth into Galilee, and findeth Philip, and saith unto him, Follow me.

Jn 4:3 — He left Judaea, and departed again into Galilee.

Ac 10:37 — That word, *I say,* ye know, which was published throughout all Judaea, and began from Galilee, after the baptism which John preached;

• People of, receive Jesus.

Jn 4:45 — Then when he was come into Galilee, the Galilaeans received him, having seen all the things that he did at Jerusalem at the feast: for they also went unto the feast.

Jn 4:53 — So the father knew that *it was* at the same hour, in the which Jesus said unto him, Thy son liveth: and himself believed, and his whole house.

• Disciples were chiefly from.

Ac 1:11 — Which also said, Ye men of Galilee, why stand ye gazing up into heaven? this same Jesus, which is taken up from you into heaven, shall so come in like manner as ye have seen him go into heaven.

Ac 2:7 — And they were all amazed and marvelled, saying one to another, Behold, are not all these which speak Galilaeans?

• Women from, ministered to Jesus.

Mt 27:55–56

Mk 15:41 — (Who also, when he was in Galilee, followed him, and ministered unto him;) and many other women which came up with him unto Jerusalem.

Lk 23:49 — And all his acquaintance, and the women that followed him from Galilee, stood afar off, beholding these things.

Lk 23:55 — And the women also, which came with him from Galilee, followed after, and beheld the sepulchre, and how his body was laid.

• Jesus appeared to his disciples in, after his resurrection.

Mt 28:16–17; Jn 21:1–25

Mt 26:32 — But after I am risen again, I will go before you into Galilee.

Mt 28:7 — And go quickly, and tell his disciples that he is risen from the dead; and, behold, he goeth before you into Galilee; there shall ye see him: lo, I have told you.

Mt 28:10 — Then said Jesus unto them, Be not afraid: go tell my brethren that they go into Galilee, and there shall they see me.

Mk 14:28 — But after that I am risen, I will go before you into Galilee.

Mk 16:7 — But go your way, tell his disciples and Peter that he goeth before you into Galilee: there shall ye see him, as he said unto you.

- **Routes from, to Judaea.**
  Jn 4:3–5
  Jgs 21:19 — Then they said, Behold, *there is* a feast of the LORD in Shiloh yearly *in a place* which *is* on the north side of Bethel, on the east side of the highway that goeth up from Bethel to Shechem, and on the south of Lebonah.
- **Dialect of.**
  Mk 14:70 — And he denied it again. And a little after, they that stood by said again to Peter, Surely thou art *one* of them: for thou art a Galilaean, and thy speech agreeth *thereto.*
- **Called Gennesaret.**
  Mt 14:34 — And when they were gone over, they came into the land of Gennesaret.
  Mk 6:53 — And when they had passed over, they came into the land of Gennesaret, and drew to the shore.
- **Churches in.**
  Ac 9:31 — Then had the churches rest throughout all Judaea and Galilee and Samaria, and were edified; and walking in the fear of the Lord, and in the comfort of the Holy Ghost, were multiplied.

- **Sea of.**
  - **Called Sea of Tiberias.**
    Jn 21:1 — After these things Jesus shewed himself again to the disciples at the sea of Tiberias; and on this wise shewed he *himself.*
  - **Called Lake of Gennesaret.**
    Lk 5:1 — And it came to pass, that, as the people pressed upon him to hear the word of God, he stood by the lake of Gennesaret,
  - **Called Sea of Chinnereth.**
    Nu 34:11 — And the coast shall go down from Shepham to Riblah, on the east side of Ain; and the border shall descend, and shall reach unto the side of the sea of Chinnereth eastward:
    Dt 3:17 — The plain also, and Jordan, and the coast *thereof,* from Chinnereth even unto the sea of the plain, *even* the salt sea, under Ashdoth-pisgah eastward.
    Jos 13:27 — And in the valley, Beth-aram, and Beth-nimrah, and Succoth, and Zaphon, the rest of the kingdom of Sihon king of Heshbon, Jordan and *his* border, *even* unto the edge of the sea of Chinnereth on the other side Jordan eastward.
  - **Called Sea of Cinneroth.**
    Jos 12:3 — And from the plain to the sea of Chinneroth on the east, and unto the sea of the plain, *even* the salt sea on the east, the way to Beth-jeshimoth; and from the south, under Ashdoth-pisgah:
  - **Jesus calls disciples on the shore of.**
    Mt 4:18–22; Lk 5:1–11
  - **Jesus teaches from a ship on.**
    Mt 13:1–3
  - **Miracles of Jesus on.**
    Mt 8:24–32; 14:22–33; Mk 4:37–39; Lk 5:1–9; 8:22–24; Jn 21:1–11
    Mt 17:27 — Notwithstanding, lest we should offend them, go thou to the sea, and cast an hook, and take up the fish that first cometh up; and when thou hast opened his mouth, thou shalt find a piece of money: that take, and give unto them for me and thee.

GALL

- **Any bitter or poisonous substance, as the bile.**
  Job 16:13 — His archers compass me round about, he cleaveth my reins asunder, and doth not spare; he poureth out my gall upon the ground.
- **Any venom of serpents.**
  Job 20:14 — *Yet* his meat in his bowels is turned, *it is* the gall of asps within him.
- **A bitter herb.**
  Dt 29:18 — Lest there should be among you man, or woman, or family, or tribe, whose heart turneth away this day from the LORD our God, to go *and* serve the gods of these nations; lest there should be among you a root that beareth gall and wormwood;
- **Given Jesus.**
  Ps 69:21 — They gave me also gall for my meat; and in my thirst they gave me vinegar to drink.
  Mt 27:34 — They gave him vinegar to drink mingled with gall: and when he had tasted *thereof,* he would not drink.
- **Figurative.**
  - **Gall of bitterness.**
    Ac 8:23 — For I perceive that thou art in the gall of bitterness, and *in* the bond of iniquity.

GALLERIES

- **In temple of Ezekiel's vision.**
  Eze 42:3 — Over against the twenty *cubits* which *were* for the inner court, and over against the pavement which *was* for the utter court, *was* gallery against gallery in three *stories.*

GALLIM

- **A town.**
- **Probably in tribe of Benjamin.**
  1Sa 25:44 — But Saul had given Michal his daughter, David's wife, to Phalti the son of Laish, which *was* of Gallim.
  Isa 10:30 — Lift up thy voice, O daughter of Gallim: cause it to be heard unto Laish, O poor Anathoth.

GALLIO

- **Proconsul of Achaia.**
- **Dismisses complaint of Jews against Paul.**
  Ac 18:12–17

GALLOWS

- **Used for execution of criminals.**
  Est 7:9–10
  Est 2:23 — And when inquisition was made of the matter, it was found out; therefore they were both

hanged on a tree: and it was written in the book of the chronicles before the king.

Est 5:14 — Then said Zeresh his wife and all his friends unto him, Let a gallows be made of fifty cubits high, and to morrow speak thou unto the king that Mordecai may be hanged thereon: then go thou in merrily with the king unto the banquet. And the thing pleased Haman; and he caused the gallows to be made.

Est 6:4 — And the king said, Who *is* in the court? Now Haman was come into the outward court of the king's house, to speak unto the king to hang Mordecai on the gallows that he had prepared for him.

Est 9:13 — Then said Esther, If it please the king, let it be granted to the Jews which *are* in Shushan to do to morrow also according unto this day's decree, and let Haman's ten sons be hanged upon the gallows.

Est 9:25 — But when *Esther* came before the king, he commanded by letters that his wicked device, which he devised against the Jews, should return upon his own head, and that he and his sons should be hanged on the gallows.

- **Reproach of being hanged upon.**

Gal 3:13 — Christ hath redeemed us from the curse of the law, being made a curse for us: for it is written, Cursed *is* every one that hangeth on a tree:

See: Punishment

GAMALIEL

- **A celebrated teacher.**
  - **Speech of, before the Sanhedrin.**

Ac 5:33–40

  - **Paul's teacher.**

Ac 22:3 — I am verily a man *which am* a Jew, born in Tarsus, a city in Cilicia, yet brought up in this city at the feet of Gamaliel, *and* taught according to the perfect manner of the law of the fathers, and was zealous toward God, as ye all are this day.

- **A captain of Manasseh.**

Nu 1:10 — Of the children of Joseph: of Ephraim; Elishama the son of Ammihud: of Manasseh; Gamaliel the son of Pedahzur.

Nu 2:20 — And by him *shall be* the tribe of Manasseh: and the captain of the children of Manasseh *shall be* Gamaliel the son of Pedahzur.

Nu 10:23 — And over the host of the tribe of the children of Manasseh *was* Gamaliel the son of Pedahzur.

  - **Offering of, at dedication of tabernacle.**

Nu 7:54–59

GAMBLING

Pr 28:19–20; Mt 25:14–30

Ps 62:10 — Trust not in oppression, and become not vain in robbery: if riches increase, set not your heart *upon them.*

Pr 13:11 — Wealth *gotten* by vanity shall be diminished: but he that gathereth by labour shall increase.

Lk 12:15 — And he said unto them, Take heed, and beware of covetousness: for a man's life consisteth not in the abundance of the things which he possesseth.

1Ti 6:9 — But they that will be rich fall into temptation and a snare, and *into* many foolish and hurtful lusts, which drown men in destruction and perdition.

Heb 13:5 — *Let your* conversation *be* without covetousness; *and be* content with such things as ye have: for he hath said, I will never leave thee, nor forsake thee.

GAMES

- **Foot races.**

1Co 9:24 — Know ye not that they which run in a race run all, but one receiveth the prize? So run, that ye may obtain.

1Co 9:26 — I therefore so run, not as uncertainly; so fight I, not as one that beateth the air:

Gal 2:2 — And I went up by revelation, and communicated unto them that gospel which I preach among the Gentiles, but privately to them which were of reputation, lest by any means I should run, or had run, in vain.

Php 2:16 — Holding forth the word of life; that I may rejoice in the day of Christ, that I have not run in vain, neither laboured in vain.

Heb 12:1 — Wherefore seeing we also are compassed about with so great a cloud of witnesses, let us lay aside every weight, and the sin which doth so easily beset us, and let us run with patience the race that is set before us,

- **Gladiatorial.**

1Co 4:9 — For I think that God hath set forth us the apostles last, as it were appointed to death: for we are made a spectacle unto the world, and to angels, and to men.

1Co 9:26 — I therefore so run, not as uncertainly; so fight I, not as one that beateth the air:

1Co 15:32 — If after the manner of men I have fought with beasts at Ephesus, what advantageth it me, if the dead rise not? let us eat and drink; for to morrow we die.

2Ti 4:7 — I have fought a good fight, I have finished *my* course, I have kept the faith:

- **Figurative.**
  - **Of the Christian life.**

1Co 9:24 — Know ye not that they which run in a race run all, but one receiveth the prize? So run, that ye may obtain.

1Co 9:26 — I therefore so run, not as uncertainly; so fight I, not as one that beateth the air:

Gal 5:7 — Ye did run well; who did hinder you that ye should not obey the truth?

Php 2:16 — Holding forth the word of life; that I may rejoice in the day of Christ, that I have not run in vain, neither laboured in vain.

Php 3:14 — I press toward the mark for the prize of the high calling of God in Christ Jesus.

Heb 12:1 — Wherefore seeing we also are compassed about with so great a cloud of witnesses, let us lay aside every weight, and the sin which doth so easily beset us, and let us run with patience the race that is set before us,

- **Of a successful ministry.**

Gal 2:2 — And I went up by revelation, and communicated unto them that gospel which I preach among the Gentiles, but privately to them which were of reputation, lest by any means I should run, or had run, in vain.

Php 2:16 — Holding forth the word of life; that I may rejoice in the day of Christ, that I have not run in vain, neither laboured in vain.

- **Fighting wild beasts, of spiritual conflict.**

1Co 4:9 — For I think that God hath set forth us the apostles last, as it were appointed to death: for we are made a spectacle unto the world, and to angels, and to men.

1Co 9:26 — I therefore so run, not as uncertainly; so fight I, not as one that beateth the air:

1Co 15:32 — If after the manner of men I have fought with beasts at Ephesus, what advantageth it me, if the dead rise not? let us eat and drink; for to morrow we die.

2Ti 4:7 — I have fought a good fight, I have finished *my* course, I have kept the faith:

GAMMADIM • Warriors or watchmen.

Eze 27:11 — The men of Arvad with thine army *were* upon thy walls round about, and the Gammadims were in thy towers: they hanged their shields upon thy walls round about; they have made thy beauty perfect.

GAMUL • A priest in the time of David.

1Ch 24:17 — The one and twentieth to Jachin, the two and twentieth to Gamul,

GARDEN

- **Of Eden.**

  ✦**See: Eden**

- **Of Gethsemane.**

  ✦**See: Gethsemane**

GAREB

- **One of David's mighty men.**

2Sa 23:38 — Ira an Ithrite, Gareb an Ithrite,

1Ch 11:40 — Ira the Ithrite, Gareb the Ithrite,

- **A hill.**

Jer 31:39 — And the measuring line shall yet go forth over against it upon the hill Gareb, and shall compass about to Goath.

GARLANDS

Ac 14:13 — Then the priest of Jupiter, which was before their city, brought oxen and garlands unto the gates, and would have done sacrifice with the people.

GARLIC

Nu 11:5 — We remember the fish, which we did eat in Egypt freely; the cucumbers, and the melons, and the leeks, and the onions, and the garlick:

GARMENT

- **Of righteousness.**

Isa 61:10 — I will greatly rejoice in the LORD, my soul shall be joyful in my God; for he hath clothed me with the garments of salvation, he hath covered me with the robe of righteousness, as a bridegroom decketh *himself* with ornaments, and as a bride adorneth *herself* with her jewels.

Mt 22:11 — And when the king came in to see the guests, he saw there a man which had not on a wedding garment:

2Co 5:3 — If so be that being clothed we shall not be found naked.

Rev 3:18 — I counsel thee to buy of me gold tried in the fire, that thou mayest be rich; and white raiment, that thou mayest be clothed, and *that* the shame of thy nakedness do not appear; and anoint thine eyes with eyesalve, that thou mayest see.

Rev 7:14 — And I said unto him, Sir, thou knowest. And he said to me, These are they which came out of great tribulation, and have washed their robes, and made them white in the blood of the Lamb.

Rev 16:15 — Behold, I come as a thief. Blessed *is* he that watcheth, and keepeth his garments, lest he walk naked, and they see his shame.

Rev 19:8 — And to her was granted that she should be arrayed in fine linen, clean and white: for the fine linen is the righteousness of saints.

✦**See: Dress**

✦**See: Robe**

GARNER

Mt 3:12 — Whose fan *is* in his hand, and he will throughly purge his floor, and gather his wheat into the garner; but he will burn up the chaff with unquenchable fire.

GARRISON • A military camp.

1Sa 13:3 — And Jonathan smote the garrison of the Philistines that *was* in Geba, and the Philistines heard *of it*. And Saul blew the trumpet throughout all the land, saying, Let the Hebrews hear.

1Sa 14:1 — Now it came to pass upon a day, that Jonathan the son of Saul said unto the young man that bare his armour, Come, and let us go over to the Philistines' garrison, that *is* on the other side. But he told not his father.

2Sa 8:6 — Then David put garrisons in Syria of Damascus: and the Syrians became servants to David, *and* brought gifts. And the LORD preserved David whithersoever he went.

2Sa 8:14 — And he put garrisons in Edom; throughout all Edom put he garrisons, and all they of Edom became David's servants. And the LORD preserved David whithersoever he went.

2Sa 23:14 — And David *was* then in an hold, and the garrison of the Philistines *was* then *in* Bethlehem.

GASHMU

• Called also Geshem.

• A Samaritan.

Ne 6:1 — Now it came to pass, when Sanballat, and Tobiah, and Geshem the Arabian, and the rest of our enemies, heard that I had builded the wall, and *that* there was no breach left therein; (though at that time I had not set up the doors upon the gates;)

Ne 6:6 — Wherein *was* written, It is reported among the heathen, and Gashmu saith *it, that* thou and the Jews think to rebel: for which cause thou buildest the wall, that thou mayest be their king, according to these words.

GATAM • Grandson of Esau.

Ge 36:11 — And the sons of Eliphaz were Teman, Omar, Zepho, and Gatam, and Kenaz.

Ge 36:16 — Duke Korah, duke Gatam, *and* duke Amalek: these *are* the dukes *that came* of Eliphaz in the land of Edom; these *were* the sons of Adah.

1Ch 1:36 — The sons of Eliphaz; Teman, and Omar, Zephi, and Gatam, Kenaz, and Timna, and Amalek.

GATES

• Of cities.

Dt 3:5 — All these cities *were* fenced with high walls, gates, and bars; beside unwalled towns a great many.

Jos 6:26 — And Joshua adjured *them* at that time, saying, Cursed *be* the man before the LORD, that riseth up and buildeth this city Jericho: he shall lay the foundation thereof in his firstborn, and in his youngest *son* shall he set up the gates of it.

1Sa 23:7 — And it was told Saul that David was come to Keilah. And Saul said, God hath delivered him into mine hand; for he is shut in, by entering into a town that hath gates and bars.

2Sa 18:24 — And David sat between the two gates: and the watchman went up to the roof over the gate unto the wall, and lifted up his eyes, and looked, and behold a man running alone.

2Ch 8:5 — Also he built Beth-horon the upper, and Beth-horon the nether, fenced cities, with walls, gates, and bars;

• Made of iron.

Ac 12:10 — When they were past the first and the second ward, they came unto the iron gate that leadeth unto the city; which opened to them of his own accord: and they went out, and passed on through one street; and forthwith the angel departed from him.

• Made of wood.

Ne 1:3 — And they said unto me, The remnant that are left of the captivity there in the province *are* in great affliction and reproach: the wall of Jerusalem also *is* broken down, and the gates thereof are burned with fire.

• Made of brass.

Ps 107:16 — For he hath broken the gates of brass, and cut the bars of iron in sunder.

Isa 45:2 — I will go before thee, and make the crooked places straight: I will break in pieces the gates of brass, and cut in sunder the bars of iron:

• Double doors.

Isa 45:1 — Thus saith the LORD to his anointed, to Cyrus, whose right hand I have holden, to subdue nations before him; and I will loose the loins of kings, to open before him the two leaved gates; and the gates shall not be shut;

Eze 41:24 — And the doors had two leaves *apiece*, two turning leaves; two *leaves* for the one door, and two leaves for the other *door.*

• The open square of, a place for idlers.

Jer 17:19–20

Ge 19:1 — And there came two angels to Sodom at even; and Lot sat in the gate of Sodom: and Lot seeing *them* rose up to meet them; and he bowed himself with his face toward the ground;

1Sa 4:18 — And it came to pass, when he made mention of the ark of God, that he fell from off the seat backward by the side of the gate, and his neck brake, and he died: for he was an old man, and heavy. And he had judged Israel forty years.

Ps 69:12 — They that sit in the gate speak against me; and I *was* the song of the drunkards.

Pr 1:21 — She crieth in the chief place of concourse, in the openings of the gates: in the city she uttereth her words, *saying,*

• Religious services held at.

Ac 14:13 — Then the priest of Jupiter, which was before their city, brought oxen and garlands unto the gates, and would have done sacrifice with the people.

• The law read at.

Ne 8:1–18

• Place for the transaction of public business, announcement of legal transactions.

Ge 23:10 — And Ephron dwelt among the children of Heth: and Ephron the Hittite answered Abraham in the audience of the children of Heth, *even* of all that went in at the gate of his city, saying,

Ge 23:16 — And Abraham hearkened unto Ephron; and Abraham weighed to Ephron the silver, which he had named in the audience of the sons of Heth, four hundred shekels of silver, current *money* with the merchant.

• Place for conferences on public affairs.

Ge 34:20 — And Hamor and Shechem his son came unto the gate of their city, and communed with the men of their city, saying,

• Place for holding courts of justice.

Dt 16:18 — Judges and officers shalt thou make thee in all thy gates, which the LORD thy God giveth thee, throughout thy tribes: and they shall judge the people with just judgment.

Dt 21:19 — Then shall his father and his mother lay hold on him, and bring him out unto the elders of his city, and unto the gate of his place;

Dt 22:15 — Then shall the father of the damsel, and her mother, take and bring forth *the tokens of* the damsel's virginity unto the elders of the city in the gate:

Jos 20:4 — And when he that doth flee unto one of those cities shall stand at the entering of the gate of the city, and shall declare his cause in the ears of the elders of that city, they shall take him into the city unto them, and give him a place, that he may dwell among them.

Ru 4:1 — Then went Boaz up to the gate, and sat him down there: and, behold, the kinsman of whom Boaz spake came by; unto whom he said, Ho, such a one! turn aside, sit down here. And he turned aside, and sat down.

2Sa 15:2 — And Absalom rose up early, and stood beside the way of the gate: and it was so, that when any man that had a controversy came to the king for judgment, then Absalom called unto him, and said, Of what city *art* thou? And he said, Thy servant is of one of the tribes of Israel.

Pr 22:22 — Rob not the poor, because he *is* poor: neither oppress the afflicted in the gate:

Zec 8:16 — These *are* the things that ye shall do; Speak ye every man the truth to his neighbour; execute the judgment of truth and peace in your gates:

• Place for public concourse.

Ge 23:10 — And Ephron dwelt among the children of Heth: and Ephron the Hittite answered Abraham in the audience of the children of Heth, *even* of all that went in at the gate of his city, saying,

Pr 1:21 — She crieth in the chief place of concourse, in the openings of the gates: in the city she uttereth her words, *saying,*

Pr 8:3 — She crieth at the gates, at the entry of the city, at the coming in at the doors.

Jer 14:2 — Judah mourneth, and the gates thereof languish; they are black unto the ground; and the cry of Jerusalem is gone up.

Jer 22:2 — And say, Hear the word of the LORD, O king of Judah, that sittest upon the throne of David, thou, and thy servants, and thy people that enter in by these gates:

• Thrones of kings at.

1Ki 22:10 — And the king of Israel and Jehoshaphat the king of Judah sat each on his throne, having put on their robes, in a void place in the entrance of the gate of Samaria; and all the prophets prophesied before them.

2Ch 18:9 — And the king of Israel and Jehoshaphat king of Judah sat either of them on his throne, clothed in *their* robes, and they sat in a void place at the entering in of the gate of Samaria; and all the prophets prophesied before them.

Jer 38:7 — Now when Ebed-melech the Ethiopian, one of the eunuchs which was in the king's house, heard that they had put Jeremiah in the dungeon; the king then sitting in the gate of Benjamin;

Jer 39:3 — And all the princes of the king of Babylon came in, and sat in the middle gate, *even* Nergal-sharezer, Samgar-nebo, Sarsechim, Rab-saris, Nergal-sharezer, Rabmag, with all the residue of the princes of the king of Babylon.

• Punishment of criminals outside of.

Dt 17:5 — Then shalt thou bring forth that man or that woman, which have committed that wicked thing, unto thy gates, *even* that man or that woman, and shalt stone them with stones, till they die.

Jer 20:2 — Then Pashur smote Jeremiah the prophet, and put him in the stocks that *were* in the high gate of Benjamin, which *was* by the house of the LORD.

Ac 7:58 — And cast *him* out of the city, and stoned *him:* and the witnesses laid down their clothes at a young man's feet, whose name was Saul.

Heb 13:12 — Wherefore Jesus also, that he might sanctify the people with his own blood, suffered without the gate.

• Closed at night.

Jos 2:5 — And it came to pass *about the time* of shutting of the gate, when it was dark, that the men went out: whither the men went I wot not: pursue after them quickly; for ye shall overtake them.

Jos 2:7 — And the men pursued after them the way to Jordan unto the fords: and as soon as they which pursued after them were gone out, they shut the gate.

• Closed on the Sabbath.

Ne 13:19 — And it came to pass, that when the gates of Jerusalem began to be dark before the sabbath, I commanded that the gates should be shut, and charged that they should not be opened till after the sabbath: and *some* of my servants set I at the gates, *that* there should no burden be brought in on the sabbath day.

• Guards at.

2Ki 7:17 — And the king appointed the lord on whose hand he leaned to have the charge of the gate: and the people trode upon him in the gate, and he died, as the man of God had said, who spake when the king came down to him.

Ne 13:19 — And it came to pass, that when the gates of Jerusalem began to be dark before the sabbath, I commanded that the gates should be shut, and charged that they should not be opened till after the sabbath: and *some* of my servants set I at the gates, *that* there should no burden be brought in on the sabbath day.

Ne 13:22 — And I commanded the Levites that they should cleanse themselves, and *that* they should come *and* keep the gates, to sanctify the sabbath day. Remember me, O my God, *concerning* this also, and spare me according to the greatness of thy mercy.

• Jails made in the towers of.

Jer 20:2 — Then Pashur smote Jeremiah the prophet, and put him in the stocks that *were* in the high gate of Benjamin, which *was* by the house of the LORD.

• Bodies of criminals exposed to view at.

2Ki 10:8 — And there came a messenger, and told him, saying, They have brought the heads of the king's sons. And he said, Lay ye them in two heaps at the entering in of the gate until the morning.

• **Figurative.**

• **Of the people of a city.**

Isa 3:26 — And her gates shall lament and mourn; and she *being* desolate shall sit upon the ground.

• **Of the gospel.**

Isa 60:11 — Therefore thy gates shall be open continually; they shall not be shut day nor night; that *men* may bring unto thee the forces of the Gentiles, and *that* their kings *may be* brought.

• **Of the powers of hell.**

Mt 16:18 — And I say also unto thee, That thou art Peter, and upon this rock I will build my church; and the gates of hell shall not prevail against it.

• **Of death.**

Job 38:17 — Have the gates of death been opened unto thee? or hast thou seen the doors of the shadow of death?

Ps 9:13 — Have mercy upon me, O LORD; consider my trouble *which I suffer* of them that hate me, thou that liftest me up from the gates of death:

Isa 38:10 — I said in the cutting off of my days, I shall go to the gates of the grave: I am deprived of the residue of my years.

• **Of the grave.**

Isa 38:10 — I said in the cutting off of my days, I shall go to the gates of the grave: I am deprived of the residue of my years.

• **Of righteousness.**

Ps 118:19 — Open to me the gates of righteousness: I will go into them, *and* I will praise the LORD:

• **Of salvation.**

Ps 118:19–20

Ge 28:17 — And he was afraid, and said, How dreadful *is* this place! this is none other but the house of God, and this *is* the gate of heaven.

Ps 24:7 — Lift up your heads, O ye gates; and be ye lift up, ye everlasting doors; and the King of glory shall come in.

Isa 26:2 — Open ye the gates, that the righteous nation which keepeth the truth may enter in.

Mt 7:13 — Enter ye in at the strait gate: for wide *is* the gate, and broad *is* the way, that leadeth to destruction, and many there be which go in thereat:

• **Symbolic.**

Rev 21:12–13

Rev 21:21 — And the twelve gates *were* twelve pearls; every several gate was of one pearl: and the street of the city *was* pure gold, as it were transparent glass.

Rev 21:25 — And the gates of it shall not be shut at all by day: for there shall be no night there.

GATH

• **One of the five chief cities of the Philistines.**

Jos 13:3 — From Sihor, which *is* before Egypt, even unto the borders of Ekron northward, *which* is counted to the Canaanite: five lords of the Philistines; the Gazathites, and the Ashdothites, the Eshkalonites, the Gittites, and the Ekronites; also the Avites:

1Sa 6:17 — And these *are* the golden emerods which the Philistines returned *for* a trespass offering unto the LORD; for Ashdod one, for Gaza one, for Askelon one, for Gath one, for Ekron one;

Am 6:2 — Pass ye unto Calneh, and see; and from thence go ye to Hamath the great: then go down to Gath of the Philistines: *be they* better than these kingdoms? or their border greater than your border?

Mic 1:10 — Declare ye *it* not at Gath, weep ye not at all: in the house of Aphrah roll thyself in the dust.

• **Anakim, a race of giants, inhabitants of.**

Jos 11:22 — There was none of the Anakims left in the land of the children of Israel: only in Gaza, in Gath, and in Ashdod, there remained.

• **Goliath dwelt in.**

1Ch 20:5–8

1Sa 17:4 — And there went out a champion out of the camp of the Philistines, named Goliath, of Gath, whose height *was* six cubits and a span.

• **Obed-edom belonged to.**

2Sa 6:10 — So David would not remove the ark of the LORD unto him into the city of David: but David carried it aside into the house of Obed-edom the Gittite.

• **The ark taken to.**

1Sa 5:8 — They sent therefore and gathered all the lords of the Philistines unto them, and said, What shall we do with the ark of the God of Israel? And they answered, Let the ark of the God of Israel be carried about unto Gath. And they carried the ark of the God of Israel about *thither.*

• **Inhabitants of, called Gittites.**

Jos 13:3 — From Sihor, which *is* before Egypt, even unto the borders of Ekron northward, *which* is counted to the Canaanite: five lords of the Philistines; the Gazathites, and the Ashdothites, the Eshkalonites, the Gittites, and the Ekronites; also the Avites:

• **David takes refuge at.**

1Sa 21:10–15; 27:2–7

• **Band of Gittites, attached to David.**

2Sa 15:18–22

• **Taken by David.**

1Ch 18:1 — Now after this it came to pass, that David smote the Philistines, and subdued them, and took Gath and her towns out of the hand of the Philistines.

• **Shimei's servants escape to.**

1Ki 2:39–41

• **Fortified by Rehoboam.**

2Ch 11:8 — And Gath, and Mareshah, and Ziph,

• **Taken, by Hazael.**

2Ki 12:17 — Then Hazael king of Syria went up, and fought against Gath, and took it: and Hazael set his face to go up to Jerusalem.

• **Recovered, by Jehoash.**

2Ki 13:25 — And Jehoash the son of Jehoahaz took again out of the hand of Ben-hadad the son of Hazael the cities, which he had taken out of the hand of Jehoahaz his father by war. Three times did Joash beat him, and recovered the cities of Israel.

- **Besieged, by Uzziah.**
  2Ch 26:6 — And he went forth and warred against the Philistines, and brake down the wall of Gath, and the wall of Jabneh, and the wall of Ashdod, and built cities about Ashdod, and among the Philistines.
- **Called Methegammah.**
  2Sa 8:1 — And after this it came to pass, that David smote the Philistines, and subdued them: and David took Metheg-ammah out of the hand of the Philistines.

GATH-HEPHER • A city of Zebulun.

2Ki 14:25 — He restored the coast of Israel from the entering of Hamath unto the sea of the plain, according to the word of the LORD God of Israel, which he spake by the hand of his servant Jonah, the son of Amittai, the prophet, which *was* of Gath-hepher.

GATH-RIMMON

- **A Levitical city of Dan.**
  Jos 19:45 — And Jehud, and Bene-berak, and Gath-rimmon,
- **A city of Manasseh.**
  Jos 21:24–25
  1Ch 6:69 — And Aijalon with her suburbs, and Gath-rimmon with her suburbs:
  - **Called also Bileam.**
    1Ch 6:70 — And out of the half tribe of Manasseh; Aner with her suburbs, and Bileam with her suburbs, for the family of the remnant of the sons of Kohath.

GAZA

- **Called also Azzah.**
  - **A city of the Philistines.**
    Jos 13:3 — From Sihor, which *is* before Egypt, even unto the borders of Ekron northward, *which* is counted to the Canaanite: five lords of the Philistines; the Gazathites, and the Ashdothites, the Eshkalonites, the Gittites, and the Ekronites; also the Avites:
    Jer 25:20 — And all the mingled people, and all the kings of the land of Uz, and all the kings of the land of the Philistines, and Ashkelon, and Azzah, and Ekron, and the remnant of Ashdod,
  - **One of the border cities of the Canaanites.**
    Ge 10:19 — And the border of the Canaanites was from Sidon, as thou comest to Gerar, unto Gaza; as thou goest, unto Sodom, and Gomorrah, and Admah, and Zeboim, even unto Lasha.
  - **A city of the Avim and Anakim.**
    Dt 2:23 — And the Avims which dwelt in Hazerim, *even* unto Azzah, the Caphtorims, which came forth out of Caphtor, destroyed them, and dwelt in their stead.)
    Jos 11:22 — There was none of the Anakims left in the land of the children of Israel: only in Gaza, in Gath, and in Ashdod, there remained.
  - **Allotted to Judah.**
    Jos 15:47 — Ashdod with her towns and her villages, Gaza with her towns and her villages, unto the river of Egypt, and the great sea, and the border *thereof:*
    Jgs 1:18 — Also Judah took Gaza with the coast thereof, and Askelon with the coast thereof, and Ekron with the coast thereof.
  - **A temple of Dagon, situated at.**
    Jgs 16:23 — Then the lords of the Philistines gathered them together for to offer a great sacrifice unto Dagon their god, and to rejoice: for they said, Our god hath delivered Samson our enemy into our hand.
  - **Samson dies at.**
    Jgs 16:21–31
  - **On the western boundary of the kingdom of Israel in the time of Solomon.**
    1Ki 4:24 — For he had dominion over all *the region* on this side the river, from Tiphsah even to Azzah, over all the kings on this side the river: and he had peace on all sides round about him.
  - **Smitten by Pharaoh.**
    Jer 47:1 — The word of the LORD that came to Jeremiah the prophet against the Philistines, before that Pharaoh smote Gaza.
  - **Prophecies relating to.**
    Am 1:6–7
    Zep 2:4 — For Gaza shall be forsaken, and Ashkelon a desolation: they shall drive out Ashdod at the noonday, and Ekron shall be rooted up.
    Zec 9:5 — Ashkelon shall see *it,* and fear; Gaza also *shall see it,* and be very sorrowful, and Ekron; for her expectation shall be ashamed; and the king shall perish from Gaza, and Ashkelon shall not be inhabited.
  - **Desert of.**
    Ac 8:26–39
- **A city of Ephraim.**
  Jgs 6:4 — And they encamped against them, and destroyed the increase of the earth, till thou come unto Gaza, and left no sustenance for Israel, neither sheep, nor ox, nor ass.
  1Ch 7:28 — And their possessions and habitations *were,* Bethel and the towns thereof, and eastward Naaran, and westward Gezer, with the towns thereof; Shechem also and the towns thereof, unto Gaza and the towns thereof:

GAZATHITES

- **Inhabitants of Gaza.**
  Jos 13:3 — From Sihor, which *is* before Egypt, even unto the borders of Ekron northward, *which* is counted to the Canaanite: five lords of the Philistines; the Gazathites, and the Ashdothites, the Eshkalonites, the Gittites, and the Ekronites; also the Avites:
- **Called Gazites.**
  Jgs 16:2 — *And it was told* the Gazites, saying, Samson is come hither. And they compassed *him* in, and laid wait for him all night in the gate of the city,

and were quiet all the night, saying, In the morning, when it is day, we shall kill him.

GAZER • Called also Gezer.

2Sa 5:25 — And David did so, as the LORD had commanded him; and smote the Philistines from Geba until thou come to Gazer.

1Ch 14:16 — David therefore did as God commanded him: and they smote the host of the Philistines from Gibeon even to Gazer.

GAZEZ

• A son of Caleb.

1Ch 2:46 — And Ephah, Caleb's concubine, bare Haran, and Moza, and Gazez: and Haran begat Gazez.

• A grandson of Caleb.

1Ch 2:46 — And Ephah, Caleb's concubine, bare Haran, and Moza, and Gazez: and Haran begat Gazez.

GAZZAM • One of the Nethinim.

Ezr 2:48 — The children of Rezin, the children of Nekoda, the children of Gazzam,

Ne 7:51 — The children of Gazzam, the children of Uzza, the children of Phaseah,

GEBA

• Called also Gaba.

• A city of Benjamin. Assigned to the sons of Aaron.

Jos 21:17 — And out of the tribe of Benjamin, Gibeon with her suburbs, Geba with her suburbs,

1Sa 13:3 — And Jonathan smote the garrison of the Philistines that *was* in Geba, and the Philistines heard *of it.* And Saul blew the trumpet throughout all the land, saying, Let the Hebrews hear.

2Sa 5:25 — And David did so, as the LORD had commanded him; and smote the Philistines from Geba until thou come to Gazer.

1Ki 15:22 — Then king Asa made a proclamation throughout all Judah; none *was* exempted: and they took away the stones of Ramah, and the timber thereof, wherewith Baasha had builded; and king Asa built with them Geba of Benjamin, and Mizpah.

2Ki 23:8 — And he brought all the priests out of the cities of Judah, and defiled the high places where the priests had burned incense, from Geba to Beer-sheba, and brake down the high places of the gates that *were* in the entering in of the gate of Joshua the governor of the city, which *were* on a man's left hand at the gate of the city.

1Ch 6:60 — And out of the tribe of Benjamin; Geba with her suburbs, and Alemeth with her suburbs, and Anathoth with her suburbs. All their cities throughout their families *were* thirteen cities.

1Ch 8:6 — And these *are* the sons of Ehud: these are the heads of the fathers of the inhabitants of Geba, and they removed them to Manahath:

2Ch 16:6 — Then Asa the king took all Judah; and they carried away the stones of Ramah, and the timber thereof, wherewith Baasha was building; and he built therewith Geba and Mizpah.

Ne 11:31 — The children also of Benjamin from Geba *dwelt* at Michmash, and Aija, and Bethel, and *in* their villages,

Ne 12:29 — Also from the house of Gilgal, and out of the fields of Geba and Azmaveth: for the singers had builded them villages round about Jerusalem.

Isa 10:29 — They are gone over the passage: they have taken up their lodging at Geba; Ramah is afraid; Gibeah of Saul is fled.

Zec 14:10 — All the land shall be turned as a plain from Geba to Rimmon south of Jerusalem: and it shall be lifted up, and inhabited in her place, from Benjamin's gate unto the place of the first gate, unto the corner gate, and *from* the tower of Hananeel unto the king's winepresses.

GEBAL

• A city south of Sidon.

• Given to Reuben.

Jos 13:5 — And the land of the Giblites, and all Lebanon, toward the sunrising, from Baal-gad under mount Hermon unto the entering into Hamath.

• People of, work for Solomon.

1Ki 5:18 — And Solomon's builders and Hiram's builders did hew *them,* and the stonesquarers: so they prepared timber and stones to build the house.

• Shipbuilders in.

Eze 27:9 — The ancients of Gebal and the wise *men* thereof were in thee thy calkers: all the ships of the sea with their mariners were in thee to occupy thy merchandise.

• A district near the Dead Sea.

Ps 83:7 — Gebal, and Ammon, and Amalek; the Philistines with the inhabitants of Tyre;

GEBER • Name of two men, officers of Solomon.

1Ki 4:13 — The son of Geber, in Ramoth-gilead; to him *pertained* the towns of Jair the son of Manasseh, which *are* in Gilead; to him *also pertained* the region of Argob, which is in Bashan, threescore great cities with walls and brasen bars:

1Ki 4:19 — Geber the son of Uri *was* in the country of Gilead, *in* the country of Sihon king of the Amorites, and of Og king of Bashan; and *he was* the only officer which *was* in the land.

GEBIM • A city of Benjamin.

Isa 10:31 — Madmenah is removed; the inhabitants of Gebim gather themselves to flee.

GEDALIAH

• Governor appointed by Nebuchadnezzar after carrying the Jews into captivity.

2Ki 25:22–24

• Jeremiah committed to the care of.

Jer 40:5–6

Jer 39:14 — Even they sent, and took Jeremiah out of the court of the prison, and committed him unto Gedaliah the son of Ahikam the son of Shaphan, that he should carry him home: so he dwelt among the people.

• Warned of the conspiracy of Ishmael by Johanan, and the captains of his army.

Jer 40:13–16

• Slain by Ishmael.

2Ki 25:25–26; Jer 41:1–10

• A musician.

1Ch 25:3 — Of Jeduthun: the sons of Jeduthun; Gedaliah, and Zeri, and Jeshaiah, Hashabiah, and Mattithiah, six, under the hands of their father Jeduthun, who prophesied with a harp, to give thanks and to praise the LORD.

1Ch 25:9 — Now the first lot came forth for Asaph to Joseph: the second to Gedaliah, who with his brethren and sons *were* twelve:

• A priest, who divorced his Gentile wife after the exile.

Ezr 10:18 — And among the sons of the priests there were found that had taken strange wives: *namely,* of the sons of Jeshua the son of Jozadak, and his brethren; Maaseiah, and Eliezer, and Jarib, and Gedaliah.

• Ancestor of Zephaniah.

Zep 1:1 — The word of the LORD which came unto Zephaniah the son of Cushi, the son of Gedaliah, the son of Amariah, the son of Hizkiah, in the days of Josiah the son of Amon, king of Judah.

• A prince who caused imprisonment of Jeremiah.

Jer 38:1 — Then Shephatiah the son of Mattan, and Gedaliah the son of Pashur, and Jucal the son of Shelemiah, and Pashur the son of Malchiah, heard the words that Jeremiah had spoken unto all the people, saying,

GEDEON ↞See: Gideon

GEDER

• An ancient city of Canaan.

Jos 12:13 — The king of Debir, one; the king of Geder, one;

• Possibly identical with Gedor, the town of Heroham, or the valley of taken by Simeonites.

GEDERAH • A city in plain of Judah.

Jos 15:36 — And Sharaim, and Adithaim, and Gederah, and Gederothaim; fourteen cities with their villages:

GEDEROTH • A city in plain of Judah.

Jos 15:41 — And Gederoth, Beth-dagon, and Naamah, and Makkedah; sixteen cities with their villages:

2Ch 28:18 — The Philistines also had invaded the cities of the low country, and of the south of Judah, and had taken Beth-shemesh, and Ajalon, and Gederoth, and Shocho with the villages thereof, and Timnah with the villages thereof, Gimzo also and the villages thereof: and they dwelt there.

GEDEROTHAIM • A city in plain of Judah.

Jos 15:36 — And Sharaim, and Adithaim, and Gederah, and Gederothaim; fourteen cities with their villages:

GEDOR

• A city in mountains of Judah.

Jos 15:58 — Halhul, Beth-zur, and Gedor,

• The town of Jeroham.

1Ch 12:7 — And Joelah, and Zebadiah, the sons of Jeroham of Gedor.

• Possibly identical with Geder.

↞See: Geder

• Valley of, taken by Simeonites.

1Ch 4:39 — And they went to the entrance of Gedor, *even* unto the east side of the valley, to seek pasture for their flocks.

↞See: Geder

• An ancestor of Saul.

1Ch 8:31 — And Gedor, and Ahio, and Zacher.

1Ch 9:37 — And Gedor, and Ahio, and Zechariah, and Mikloth.

• Either a place or a person. Authorities disagree.

1Ch 4:4 — And Penuel the father of Gedor and Ezer the father of Hushah. These *are* the sons of Hur, the firstborn of Ephratah, the father of Bethlehem.

1Ch 4:18 — And his wife Jehudijah bare Jered the father of Gedor, and Heber the father of Socho, and Jekuthiel the father of Zanoah. And these *are* the sons of Bithiah the daughter of Pharaoh, which Mered took.

GEHAZI

• Servant of Elisha.

2Ki 4:12 — And he said to Gehazi his servant, Call this Shunammite. And when he had called her, she stood before him.

2Ki 4:29 — Then he said to Gehazi, Gird up thy loins, and take my staff in thine hand, and go thy way: if thou meet any man, salute him not; and if any salute thee, answer him not again: and lay my staff upon the face of the child.

2Ki 4:31 — And Gehazi passed on before them, and laid the staff upon the face of the child; but *there was* neither voice, nor hearing. Wherefore he went again to meet him, and told him, saying, The child is not awaked.

• Covetousness of, and the judgment of leprosy upon.

2Ki 5:20–27

• Mentions to King Jehoram the miracles of Elisha, his master.

2Ki 8:4–5

GEHENNA ↞See: Hell

GELILOTH

• A place mentioned in Jos 18:17.

Jos 18:17 — And was drawn from the north, and went forth to En-shemesh, and went forth toward Geliloth, which *is* over against the going up of Adummim, and descended to the stone of Bohan the son of Reuben,

• A place as marking the boundary of Benjamin (Gilgal is substituted).

Jos 15:7 — And the border went up toward Debir from the valley of Achor, and so northward, looking toward Gilgal, *that is* before the going up to Adummim, which *is* on the south side of the river: and the border passed toward the waters of En-shemesh, and the goings out thereof were at En-rogel:

GEMALLI • Father of Ammiel.

Nu 13:12 — Of the tribe of Dan, Ammiel the son of Gemalli.

GEMARIAH

• Son of Shaphan.

Jer 36:10–12

Jer 36:25 — Nevertheless Elnathan and Delaiah and Gemariah had made intercession to the king that he would not burn the roll: but he would not hear them.

• An ambassador of Zedekiah to Nebuchadnezzar.

Jer 29:3 — By the hand of Elasah the son of Shaphan, and Gemariah the son of Hilkiah, (whom Zedekiah king of Judah sent unto Babylon to Nebuchadnezzar king of Babylon) saying,

GENEALOGY

Nu 1:18 — And they assembled all the congregation together on the first *day* of the second month, and they declared their pedigrees after their families, by the house of their fathers, according to the number of the names, from twenty years old and upward, by their polls.

2Ch 12:15 — Now the acts of Rehoboam, first and last, *are* they not written in the book of Shemaiah the prophet, and of Iddo the seer concerning genealogies? And *there were* wars between Rehoboam and Jeroboam continually.

Ezr 2:59 — And these *were* they which went up from Tel-melah, Tel-harsa, Cherub, Addan, *and* Immer: but they could not shew their father's house, and their seed, whether they *were* of Israel:

Ne 7:5 — And my God put into mine heart to gather together the nobles, and the rulers, and the people, that they might be reckoned by genealogy. And I found a register of the genealogy of them which came up at the first, and found written therein,

Heb 7:3 — Without father, without mother, without descent, having neither beginning of days, nor end of life; but made like unto the Son of God; abideth a priest continually.

• Of no spiritual significance.

Mt 3:9 — And think not to say within yourselves, We have Abraham to *our* father: for I say unto you, that God is able of these stones to raise up children unto Abraham.

1Ti 1:4 — Neither give heed to fables and endless genealogies, which minister questions, rather than godly edifying which is in faith: *so do.*

Tit 3:9 — But avoid foolish questions, and genealogies, and contentions, and strivings about the law; for they are unprofitable and vain.

• From Adam to Noah.

Ge 4:16–22; 5:1–32; 1Ch 1:1–4; Lk 3:36–38

• From Adam to Abraham.

Ge 11:10–32; 1Ch 1:4–27; Lk 3:34–38

• From Adam to Jesus.

Mt 1:1–16; Lk 3:23–38

• Of the descendants of.

• Noah.

Ge 10:1–32

• Nahor.

Ge 22:20–24

• Abraham, by his wife Keturah.

Ge 25:1–4; 1Ch 1:32–33

• Ishmael.

Ge 25:12–16; 1Ch 1:28–31

• Esau.

Ge 36:1–43; 1Ch 1:35–54

• Jacob.

Ge 35:23–26; Ex 6:14–27; Nu 26:1–65; 1Ch 2:1–9:44

Ex 1:5 — And all the souls that came out of the loins of Jacob were seventy souls: for Joseph was in Egypt *already.*

• Pharez to David.

Ru 4:18–22

• Of the Jews who returned from the captivity.

Ezr 7:1–5; 8:1–15; Ne 7:1–73

Ne 11:12 — And their brethren that did the work of the house *were* eight hundred twenty and two: and Adaiah the son of Jeroham, the son of Pelaliah, the son of Amzi, the son of Zechariah, the son of Pashur, the son of Malchiah,

• Of Joseph.

Mt 1:1–25; Lk 3:23–38

GENERALS

• Distinguished.

See: Abraham

See: Amasa

See: Benaiah

See: Ben-Hadad

See: Captain

See: David

See: Gideon

See: Jephthah

See: Joab

See: Joshua

See: Naaman

See: Saul

See: Sennacherib

GENEROSITY See: Liberality

GENETIC

Isa 14:12–14

Ro 1:25 — Who changed the truth of God into a lie, and worshipped and served the creature more than the Creator, who is blessed for ever. Amen.

GENIUS

• Mechanical, a divine inspiration.

Ex 31:2–11; 35:30–36:1

Ex 28:3 — And thou shalt speak unto all *that are* wise hearted, whom I have filled with the spirit of wisdom, that they may make Aaron's garments to consecrate him, that he may minister unto me in the priest's office.

GENNESARET See: Galilee

GENTILES

• Unclassified scriptures relating to.

Jer 10:2–3; Mt 6:7–8, 31–32; Ac 17:16–17, 22–27; Ro 1:18–2:15; Eph 4:17–19; 1Pe 4:3–4

Ac 14:16 — Who in times past suffered all nations to walk in their own ways.

Ac 17:4 — And some of them believed, and consorted with Paul and Silas; and of the devout Greeks a great multitude, and of the chief women not a few.

1Co 10:20 — But *I say,* that the things which the Gentiles sacrifice, they sacrifice to devils, and not to God: and I would not that ye should have fellowship with devils.

1Co 12:2 — Ye know that ye were Gentiles, carried away unto these dumb idols, even as ye were led.

Gal 2:15 — We *who are* Jews by nature, and not sinners of the Gentiles,

Eph 2:12 — That at that time ye were without Christ, being aliens from the commonwealth of Israel, and strangers from the covenants of promise, having no hope, and without God in the world:

Eph 5:12 — For it is a shame even to speak of those things which are done of them in secret.

1Th 4:5 — Not in the lust of concupiscence, even as the Gentiles which know not God:

See: Idolatry

See: Missions

• Prophecies of the conversion of.

Ps 22:27–31; 68:31–32; 72:1–20; 102:18–22; 145:10–11; Isa 2:2–5; 9:1–7; 11:1–10; 35:1–10; 40:4–11; 42:1–12; 45:22–24; 49:5–6, 18–23; 54:1–3; 56:6–8; 60:3–5, 8–14; 66:7–23; Jer 16:19–21; Eze 47:3–5; Da 2:44–45; 7:13–14; Joel 2:28–32; Am 9:11–12; Mic 4:3–4; Zec 2:10–11; 8:1–9:1; 9:9–17; 14:8–21; Mt 12:17–21; Lk 13:29–30

Ge 12:3 — And I will bless them that bless thee, and curse him that curseth thee: and in thee shall all families of the earth be blessed.

Ge 12:5 — And Abram took Sarai his wife, and Lot his brother's son, and all their substance that they had gathered, and the souls that they had gotten in Haran; and they went forth to go into the land of Canaan; and into the land of Canaan they came.

Ge 22:18 — And in thy seed shall all the nations of the earth be blessed; because thou hast obeyed my voice.

Ge 49:10 — The sceptre shall not depart from Judah, nor a lawgiver from between his feet, until Shiloh come; and unto him *shall* the gathering of the people *be.*

Dt 32:21 — They have moved me to jealousy with *that which is* not God; they have provoked me to anger with their vanities: and I will move them to jealousy with *those which are* not a people; I will provoke them to anger with a foolish nation.

Ps 2:8 — Ask of me, and I shall give *thee* the heathen *for* thine inheritance, and the uttermost parts of the earth *for* thy possession.

Ps 46:4 — *There is* a river, the streams whereof shall make glad the city of God, the holy *place* of the tabernacles of the most High.

Ps 46:10 — Be still, and know that I *am* God: I will be exalted among the heathen, I will be exalted in the earth.

Ps 65:2 — O thou that hearest prayer, unto thee shall all flesh come.

Ps 65:5 — By terrible things in righteousness wilt thou answer us, O God of our salvation; *who art* the confidence of all the ends of the earth, and of them that are afar off *upon* the sea:

Ps 66:4 — All the earth shall worship thee, and shall sing unto thee; they shall sing *to* thy name. Selah.

Ps 86:9 — All nations whom thou hast made shall come and worship before thee, O Lord; and shall glorify thy name.

Ps 102:15 — So the heathen shall fear the name of the LORD, and all the kings of the earth thy glory.

Isa 18:7 — In that time shall the present be brought unto the LORD of hosts of a people scattered and peeled, and from a people terrible from their beginning hitherto; a nation meted out and trodden under foot, whose land the rivers have spoiled, to the place of the name of the LORD of hosts, the mount Zion.

Isa 24:16 — From the uttermost part of the earth have we heard songs, *even* glory to the righteous. But I said, My leanness, my leanness, woe unto me! the treacherous dealers have dealt treacherously; yea, the treacherous dealers have dealt very treacherously.

Isa 45:6 — That they may know from the rising of the sun, and from the west, that *there is* none beside me. I *am* the LORD, and *there is* none else.

Isa 45:8 — Drop down, ye heavens, from above, and let the skies pour down righteousness: let the earth open, and let them bring forth salvation, and let righteousness spring up together; I the LORD have created it.

Isa 49:1 — Listen, O isles, unto me; and hearken, ye people, from far; The LORD hath called me from the womb; from the bowels of my mother hath he made mention of my name.

Isa 55:5 — Behold, thou shalt call a nation *that* thou knowest not, and nations *that* knew not thee shall run unto thee because of the LORD thy God, and for the Holy One of Israel; for he hath glorified thee.

Isa 56:3 — Neither let the son of the stranger, that hath joined himself to the LORD, speak, saying, The LORD hath utterly separated me from his people: neither let the eunuch say, Behold, I *am* a dry tree.

Isa 60:1 — Arise, shine; for thy light is come, and the glory of the LORD is risen upon thee.

Isa 65:1 — I am sought of *them that* asked not *for me;* I am found of *them that* sought me not: I said, Behold me, behold me, unto a nation *that* was not called by my name.

Jer 3:17 — At that time they shall call Jerusalem the throne of the LORD; and all the nations shall be gathered unto it, to the name of the LORD, to Jerusalem: neither shall they walk any more after the imagination of their evil heart.

Jer 4:2 — And thou shalt swear, The LORD liveth, in truth, in judgment, and in righteousness; and the nations shall bless themselves in him, and in him shall they glory.

Da 2:35 — Then was the iron, the clay, the brass, the silver, and the gold, broken to pieces together, and became like the chaff of the summer threshingfloors; and the wind carried them away, that no place was found for them: and the stone that smote the image became a great mountain, and filled the whole earth.

Hos 2:23 — And I will sow her unto me in the earth; and I will have mercy upon her that had not obtained mercy; and I will say to *them which were* not my people, Thou *art* my people; and they shall say, *Thou art* my God.

Hag 2:7 — And I will shake all nations, and the desire of all nations shall come: and I will fill this house with glory, saith the LORD of hosts.

Zec 6:15 — And they *that are* far off shall come and build in the temple of the LORD, and ye shall know that the LORD of hosts hath sent me unto you. And *this* shall come to pass, if ye will diligently obey the voice of the LORD your God.

Mal 1:11 — For from the rising of the sun even unto the going down of the same my name *shall be* great among the Gentiles; and in every place incense *shall be* offered unto my name, and a pure offering: for my name *shall be* great among the heathen, saith the LORD of hosts.

Mt 3:9 — And think not to say within yourselves, We have Abraham to *our* father: for I say unto you, that God is able of these stones to raise up children unto Abraham.

Mt 8:11 — And I say unto you, That many shall come from the east and west, and shall sit down with Abraham, and Isaac, and Jacob, in the kingdom of heaven.

Mt 19:30 — But many *that are* first shall be last; and the last *shall be* first.

Mk 10:31 — But many *that are* first shall be last; and the last first.

Lk 21:24 — And they shall fall by the edge of the sword, and shall be led away captive into all nations: and Jerusalem shall be trodden down of the Gentiles, until the times of the Gentiles be fulfilled.

Jn 10:16 — And other sheep I have, which are not of this fold: them also I must bring, and they shall hear my voice; and there shall be one fold, *and* one shepherd.

Ac 9:15 — But the Lord said unto him, Go thy way: for he is a chosen vessel unto me, to bear my name before the Gentiles, and kings, and the children of Israel:

See: Church; prophecies concerning prosperity of

• Conversion of.

Ac 11:1–18; 13:46–48; 15:7–9, 12–31; 18:4–6; 26:16–18; Ro 1:5–7; 9:22–30; 10:19–20; 11:11–13, 17–21; 15:9–12; Gal 1:15–16; Eph 3:1–8

Ac 10:45 — And they of the circumcision which believed were astonished, as many as came with Peter, because that on the Gentiles also was poured out the gift of the Holy Ghost.

Ac 13:2 — As they ministered to the Lord, and fasted, the Holy Ghost said, Separate me Barnabas and Saul for the work whereunto I have called them.

Ac 14:27 — And when they were come, and had gathered the church together, they rehearsed all that God had done with them, and how he had opened the door of faith unto the Gentiles.

Ac 28:28 — Be it known therefore unto you, that the salvation of God is sent unto the Gentiles, and *that* they will hear it.

Gal 2:2 — And I went up by revelation, and communicated unto them that gospel which I preach among the Gentiles, but privately to them which were of reputation, lest by any means I should run, or had run, in vain.

Gal 3:14 — That the blessing of Abraham might come on the Gentiles through Jesus Christ; that we might receive the promise of the Spirit through faith.

Col 3:11 — Where there is neither Greek nor Jew, circumcision nor uncircumcision, Barbarian, Scythian, bond *nor* free: but Christ *is* all, and in all.

1Th 2:16 — Forbidding us to speak to the Gentiles that they might be saved, to fill up their sins alway: for the wrath is come upon them to the uttermost.

1Ti 3:16 — And without controversy great is the mystery of godliness: God was manifest in the flesh, justified in the Spirit, seen of angels, preached unto the Gentiles, believed on in the world, received up into glory.

2Ti 1:11 — Whereunto I am appointed a preacher, and an apostle, and a teacher of the Gentiles.

Rev 11:15 — And the seventh angel sounded; and there were great voices in heaven, saying, The kingdoms of this world are become *the kingdoms* of our Lord, and of his Christ; and he shall reign for ever and ever.

Rev 15:4 — Who shall not fear thee, O Lord, and glorify thy name? for *thou* only *art* holy: for all nations shall come and worship before thee; for thy judgments are made manifest.

↞See: **Church; prophecies concerning prosperity of**

↞See: **Jesus, Kingdom of; prophecies concerning**

↞See: **Missions**

GENTLENESS

• Of Christ.

2Ch 10:1 — And Rehoboam went to Shechem: for to Shechem were all Israel come to make him king.

Isa 40:11 — He shall feed his flock like a shepherd: he shall gather the lambs with his arm, and carry *them* in his bosom, *and* shall gently lead those that are with young.

Mt 11:29 — Take my yoke upon you, and learn of me; for I am meek and lowly in heart: and ye shall find rest unto your souls.

↞See: **Jesus, Compassion of**

↞See: **Jesus, Humility of**

↞See: **Jesus, Meekness of**

• Of God.

2Sa 22:36 — Thou hast also given me the shield of thy salvation: and thy gentleness hath made me great.

Ps 18:35 — Thou hast also given me the shield of thy salvation: and thy right hand hath holden me up, and thy gentleness hath made me great.

Isa 40:11 — He shall feed his flock like a shepherd: he shall gather the lambs with his arm, and carry *them* in his bosom, *and* shall gently lead those that are with young.

↞See: **God, Compassion of**

↞See: **God, Long-Suffering of**

• Of Paul.

1Th 2:7 — But we were gentle among you, even as a nurse cherisheth her children:

• Exhortations to.

2Ti 2:24–26; Tit 3:1–2

Gal 5:22 — But the fruit of the Spirit is love, joy, peace, longsuffering, gentleness, goodness, faith,

Jas 3:17 — But the wisdom that is from above is first pure, then peaceable, gentle, *and* easy to be intreated, full of mercy and good fruits, without partiality, and without hypocrisy.

↞See: **Humility**

↞See: **Kindness**

↞See: **Meekness**

↞See: **Patience**

GENUBATH • Son of Hadad.

1Ki 11:20 — And the sister of Tahpenes bare him Genubath his son, whom Tahpenes weaned in Pharaoh's house: and Genubath was in Pharaoh's household among the sons of Pharaoh.

GEOLOGY

Ge 1:9–10; Job 12:8–9; 28:9–11; Ps 24:1–2; 104:5–13; 2Pe 3:5–7

1Sa 2:8 — He raiseth up the poor out of the dust, *and* lifteth up the beggar from the dunghill, to set *them* among princes, and to make them inherit the throne of glory: for the pillars of the earth *are* the LORD'S, and he hath set the world upon them.

2Sa 22:16 — And the channels of the sea appeared, the foundations of the world were discovered, at the rebuking of the LORD, at the blast of the breath of his nostrils.

Ps 18:15 — Then the channels of waters were seen, and the foundations of the world were discovered at thy rebuke, O LORD, at the blast of the breath of thy nostrils.

Ps 136:6 — To him that stretched out the earth above the waters: for his mercy *endureth* for ever.

Pr 30:4 — Who hath ascended up into heaven, or descended? who hath gathered the wind in his fists? who hath bound the waters in a garment? who hath established all the ends of the earth? what *is* his name, and what *is* his son's name, if thou canst tell?

Jer 31:37 — Thus saith the LORD; If heaven above can be measured, and the foundations of the earth searched out beneath, I will also cast off all the seed of Israel for all that they have done, saith the LORD.

Hab 3:9 — Thy bow was made quite naked, *according* to the oaths of the tribes, *even thy* word. Selah. Thou didst cleave the earth with rivers.

↞See: **Astronomy**

↞See: **Creation**

↞See: **Earth**

↞See: **Hot Springs**

↞See: **Meteorology and Celestial Phenomena**

GERA

• Possibly the name of three men.

• More probably of one, the son of Bela.

Ge 46:21 — And the sons of Benjamin were Belah, and Becher, and Ashbel, Gera, and Naaman, Ehi, and Rosh, Muppim, and Huppim, and Ard.

Jgs 3:15 — But when the children of Israel cried unto the LORD, the LORD raised them up a deliverer, Ehud the son of Gera, a Benjamite, a man lefthanded: and by him the children of Israel sent a present unto Eglon the king of Moab.

2Sa 16:5 — And when king David came to Bahurim, behold, thence came out a man of the family of the house of Saul, whose name *was* Shimei, the son of Gera: he came forth, and cursed still as he came.

2Sa 19:16 — And Shimei the son of Gera, a Benjamite, which *was* of Bahurim, hasted and came down with the men of Judah to meet king David.

2Sa 19:18 — And there went over a ferry boat to carry over the king's household, and to do what he thought good. And Shimei the son of Gera fell down before the king, as he was come over Jordan;

1Ki 2:8 — And, behold, *thou hast* with thee Shimei the son of Gera, a Benjamite of Bahurim, which cursed me with a grievous curse in the day when I went to Mahanaim: but he came down to meet me at Jordan, and I sware to him by the LORD, saying, I will not put thee to death with the sword.

1Ch 8:3 — And the sons of Bela were, Addar, and Gera, and Abihud,

1Ch 8:5 — And Gera, and Shephuphan, and Huram.

1Ch 8:7 — And Naaman, and Ahiah, and Gera, he removed them, and begat Uzza, and Ahihud.

GERAH

Le 25:1–55; 27:1–34

Ex 30:13 — This they shall give, every one that passeth among them that are numbered, half a shekel after the shekel of the sanctuary: (a shekel *is* twenty gerahs:) an half shekel *shall be* the offering of the LORD.

Nu 3:47 — Thou shalt even take five shekels apiece by the poll, after the shekel of the sanctuary shalt thou take *them:* (the shekel *is* twenty gerahs:)

• Paris, a weight equal to thirteen and seven tenths grains.

GERAR

• A city of the Philistines.

Ge 10:19 — And the border of the Canaanites was from Sidon, as thou comest to Gerar, unto Gaza; as thou goest, unto Sodom, and Gomorrah, and Admah, and Zeboim, even unto Lasha.

• Abimelech, king of.

Ge 20:1 — And Abraham journeyed from thence toward the south country, and dwelled between Kadesh and Shur, and sojourned in Gerar.

Ge 26:6 — And Isaac dwelt in Gerar:

• Visited by Abraham.

Ge 20:1 — And Abraham journeyed from thence toward the south country, and dwelled between Kadesh and Shur, and sojourned in Gerar.

• Visited by Isaac.

2Ch 14:13–14

Ge 26:1 — And there was a famine in the land, beside the first famine that was in the days of Abraham. And Isaac went unto Abimelech king of the Philistines unto Gerar.

• A valley.

Ge 26:17–22

GERGESENES ✣See: Gadarenes

GERIZIM

• Mount of blessing.

Dt 11:29 — And it shall come to pass, when the LORD thy God hath brought thee in unto the land whither thou goest to possess it, that thou shalt put the blessing upon mount Gerizim, and the curse upon mount Ebal.

Dt 27:12 — These shall stand upon mount Gerizim to bless the people, when ye are come over Jordan; Simeon, and Levi, and Judah, and Issachar, and Joseph, and Benjamin:

Jos 8:33 — And all Israel, and their elders, and officers, and their judges, stood on this side the ark and on that side before the priests the Levites, which bare the ark of the covenant of the LORD, as well the stranger, as he that was born among them; half of them over against mount Gerizim, and half of them over against mount Ebal; as Moses the servant of the LORD had commanded before, that they should bless the people of Israel.

• Jotham addresses the Shechemites from, against the conspiracy of Abimelech.

Jgs 9:7 — And when they told *it* to Jotham, he went and stood in the top of mount Gerizim, and lifted up his voice, and cried, and said unto them, Hearken unto me, ye men of Shechem, that God may hearken unto you.

• Samaritans worship at.

Jn 4:20 — Our fathers worshipped in this mountain; and ye say, that in Jerusalem is the place where men ought to worship.

GERSHOM

• Son of Moses.

1Ch 23:15–16

Ex 2:22 — And she bare *him* a son, and he called his name Gershom: for he said, I have been a stranger in a strange land.

Ex 18:3 — And her two sons; of which the name of the one *was* Gershom; for he said, I have been an alien in a strange land:

1Ch 26:24 — And Shebuel the son of Gershom, the son of Moses, *was* ruler of the treasures.

✣**See: Gershon**

• A descendant of Phinehas.

Ezr 8:2 — Of the sons of Phinehas; Gershom: of the sons of Ithamar; Daniel: of the sons of David; Hattush.

• A Levite.

Jgs 18:30 — And the children of Dan set up the graven image: and Jonathan, the son of Gershom, the son of Manasseh, he and his sons were priests to the tribe of Dan until the day of the captivity of the land.

GERSHON

• Called also Gershom.

• Son of Levi.

Ex 6:16–17; Nu 3:17–26; 4:22–28; 1Ch 6:16–17

Ge 46:11 — And the sons of Levi; Gershon, Kohath, and Merari.

Nu 4:38 — And those that were numbered of the sons of Gershon, throughout their families, and by the house of their fathers,

Nu 7:7 — Two wagons and four oxen he gave unto the sons of Gershon, according to their service:

Nu 10:17 — And the tabernacle was taken down; and the sons of Gershon and the sons of Merari set forward, bearing the tabernacle.

Nu 26:57 — And these *are* they that were numbered of the Levites after their families: of Gershon, the family of the Gershonites: of Kohath, the family of the Kohathites: of Merari, the family of the Merarites.

Jos 21:6 — And the children of Gershon *had* by lot out of the families of the tribe of Issachar, and out of the tribe of Asher, and out of the tribe of Naphtali, and out of the half tribe of Manasseh in Bashan, thirteen cities.

1Ch 6:1 — The sons of Levi; Gershon, Kohath, and Merari.

1Ch 6:20 — Of Gershom; Libni his son, Jahath his son, Zimmah his son,

1Ch 6:43 — The son of Jahath, the son of Gershom, the son of Levi.

1Ch 6:62 — And to the sons of Gershom throughout their families out of the tribe of Issachar, and out of the tribe of Asher, and out of the tribe of Naphtali, and out of the tribe of Manasseh in Bashan, thirteen cities.

1Ch 6:71 — Unto the sons of Gershom *were given* out of the family of the half tribe of Manasseh, Golan in Bashan with her suburbs, and Ashtaroth with her suburbs:

1Ch 15:7 — Of the sons of Gershom; Joel the chief, and his brethren an hundred and thirty:

1Ch 23:6 — And David divided them into courses among the sons of Levi, *namely,* Gershon, Kohath, and Merari.

GESHAM • A descendant of Caleb.

1Ch 2:47 — And the sons of Jahdai; Regem, and Jotham, and Gesham, and Pelet, and Ephah, and Shaaph.

GESHEM

• Called also Gashmu, an Arabian.

• Opposed Nehemiah in building Jerusalem.

Ne 6:1–6

Ne 2:19 — But when Sanballat the Horonite, and Tobiah the servant, the Ammonite, and Geshem the Arabian, heard *it,* they laughed us to scorn, and despised us, and said, What *is* this thing that ye do? will ye rebel against the king?

GESHUR

• District east of the sources of the Jordan.

• The inhabitants of, not subdued by the Israelites.

Jos 13:2–13

Dt 3:14 — Jair the son of Manasseh took all the country of Argob unto the coasts of Geshuri and Maachathi; and called them after his own name, Bashan-havoth-jair, unto this day.

1Ch 2:23 — And he took Geshur, and Aram, with the towns of Jair, from them, with Kenath, and the towns thereof, *even* threescore cities. All these *belonged to* the sons of Machir the father of Gilead.

• Inhabitants of one of the villages of, exterminated, and the spoils taken by David.

1Sa 27:8 — And David and his men went up, and invaded the Geshurites, and the Gezrites, and the Amalekites: for those *nations were* of old the inhabitants of the land, as thou goest to Shur, even unto the land of Egypt.

• David marries a princess of.

2Sa 3:3 — And his second, Chileab, of Abigail the wife of Nabal the Carmelite; and the third, Absalom the son of Maacah the daughter of Talmai king of Geshur;

1Ch 3:2 — The third, Absalom the son of Maachah the daughter of Talmai king of Geshur: the fourth, Adonijah the son of Haggith:

• Absalom takes refuge in, after the murder of Amnon.

2Sa 13:37–38

2Sa 15:8 — For thy servant vowed a vow while I abode at Geshur in Syria, saying, If the LORD shall bring me again indeed to Jerusalem, then I will serve the LORD.

GETHSEMANE

• A garden near Jerusalem.

• Jesus betrayed in.

Mt 26:36–50; Mk 14:32–46; Lk 22:39–49; Jn 18:1–2

GEZER

• Called also Gazer, Gazara, Gazera, and Gob.

• A Canaanitish royal city; king of, defeated by Joshua.

Jos 10:33 — Then Horam king of Gezer came up to help Lachish; and Joshua smote him and his people, until he had left him none remaining.

Jos 12:12 — The king of Eglon, one; the king of Gezer, one;

• Canaanites not all expelled from, but made to pay tribute.

Jos 16:10 — And they drave not out the Canaanites that dwelt in Gezer: but the Canaanites dwell among the Ephraimites unto this day, and serve under tribute.

Jgs 1:29 — Neither did Ephraim drive out the Canaanites that dwelt in Gezer; but the Canaanites dwelt in Gezer among them.

• Allotted to Ephraim.

Jos 16:3 — And goeth down westward to the coast of Japhleti, unto the coast of Beth-horon the nether, and to Gezer: and the goings out thereof are at the sea.

Jos 16:10 — And they drave not out the Canaanites that dwelt in Gezer: but the Canaanites dwell among the Ephraimites unto this day, and serve under tribute.

1Ch 7:28 — And their possessions and habitations *were,* Bethel and the towns thereof, and eastward Naaran, and westward Gezer, with the towns thereof; Shechem also and the towns thereof, unto Gaza and the towns thereof:

• Assigned to Levites.

Jos 2:21 — And she said, According unto your words, so *be* it. And she sent them away, and they departed: and she bound the scarlet line in the window.

• Battle with Philistines at.

2Sa 21:18 — And it came to pass after this, that there was again a battle with the Philistines at Gob: then Sibbechai the Hushathite slew Saph, which *was* of the sons of the giant.

1Ch 20:4 — And it came to pass after this, that there arose war at Gezer with the Philistines; at which time Sibbechai the Hushathite slew Sippai, *that was* of the children of the giant: and they were subdued.

• Smitten by David.

1Sa 27:8 — And David and his men went up, and invaded the Geshurites, and the Gezrites, and the Amalekites: for those *nations were* of old the inhabitants of the land, as thou goest to Shur, even unto the land of Egypt.

• Fortified by Solomon.

1Ki 9:15–17

GHOST

• Soul.

Ac 5:5 — And Ananias hearing these words fell down, and gave up the ghost: and great fear came on all them that heard these things.

Ac 5:10 — Then fell she down straightway at his feet, and yielded up the ghost: and the young men came in, and found her dead, and, carrying *her* forth, buried *her* by her husband.

Ac 12:23 — And immediately the angel of the Lord smote him, because he gave not God the glory: and he was eaten of worms, and gave up the ghost.

See: Man; spirit

See: Spirit

GIAH • A place on the way to the wilderness of Gibeon.

2Sa 2:24 — Joab also and Abishai pursued after Abner: and the sun went down when they were come to the hill of Ammah, that *lieth* before Giah by the way of the wilderness of Gibeon.

GIANTS

Ge 6:4 — There were giants in the earth in those days; and also after that, when the sons of God came in unto the daughters of men, and they bare *children* to them, the same *became* mighty men which *were* of old, men of renown.

See: Anakim

See: Emims

See: Goliath

See: Ishbi-Benob

See: Og, king of Bashan

See: Rephaim

See: Zamzummims

GIBBAR

Ezr 2:20 — The children of Gibbar, ninety and five.

See: Gibeon

GIBBETHON

• A city of Dan.

Jos 19:44 — And Eltekeh, and Gibbethon, and Baalath,

• Allotted to the Levites.

Jos 21:23 — And out of the tribe of Dan, Eltekeh with her suburbs, Gibbethon with her suburbs,

• Besieged by Israel, while in possession of Philistines.

1Ki 15:27 — And Baasha the son of Ahijah, of the house of Issachar, conspired against him; and Baasha smote him at Gibbethon, which *belonged* to the Philistines; for Nadab and all Israel laid siege to Gibbethon.

1Ki 16:15 — In the twenty and seventh year of Asa king of Judah did Zimri reign seven days in Tirzah. And the people *were* encamped against Gibbethon, which *belonged* to the Philistines.

1Ki 16:17 — And Omri went up from Gibbethon, and all Israel with him, and they besieged Tirzah.

GIBEA • A descendant of Judah.

1Ch 2:49 — She bare also Shaaph the father of Madmannah, Sheva the father of Machbenah, and the father of Gibea: and the daughter of Caleb *was* Achsa.

GIBEAH

• Of Judah.

Jos 15:57 — Cain, Gibeah, and Timnah; ten cities with their villages:

• Of Saul.

• Called also Gibeah of Benjamin. The people's wickedness.

Jgs 19:12–30

Hos 9:9 — They have deeply corrupted *themselves,* as in the days of Gibeah: *therefore* he will remember their iniquity, he will visit their sins.

Hos 10:9 — O Israel, thou hast sinned from the days of Gibeah: there they stood: the battle in Gibeah against the children of iniquity did not overtake them.

• Destroyed by the Israelites.

Jgs 20:1–48

• The city of Saul.

1Sa 10:26 — And Saul also went home to Gibeah; and there went with him a band of men, whose hearts God had touched.

1Sa 15:34 — Then Samuel went to Ramah; and Saul went up to his house to Gibeah of Saul.

1Sa 22:6 — When Saul heard that David was discovered, and the men that *were* with him, (now Saul abode in Gibeah under a tree in Ramah, having his spear in his hand, and all his servants *were* standing about him;)

• The ark of the covenant conveyed to, by the Philistines.

1Sa 7:1 — And the men of Kirjath-jearim came, and brought up the ark of the LORD, and brought it into the house of Abinadab in the hill, and sanctified Eleazar his son to keep the ark of the LORD.

2Sa 6:3 — And they set the ark of God upon a new cart, and brought it out of the house of Abinadab that *was* in Gibeah: and Uzzah and Ahio, the sons of Abinadab, drave the new cart.

• Deserted.

Isa 10:29 — They are gone over the passage: they have taken up their lodging at Geba; Ramah is afraid; Gibeah of Saul is fled.

• Another town in Benjamin. Called also Gibeath.

Jos 18:28 — And Zelah, Eleph, and Jebusi, which *is* Jerusalem, Gibeath, *and* Kirjath; fourteen cities with their villages. This *is* the inheritance of the children of Benjamin according to their families.

• Gibeah in the Field.

Jgs 20:31 — And the children of Benjamin went out against the people, *and* were drawn away from the city; and they began to smite of the people, *and* kill, as at other times, in the highways, of which one goeth up to the house of God, and the other to Gibeah in the field, about thirty men of Israel.

• Probably identical with Geba.

See: Geba

GIBEON

• A city of the Hivites.

Jos 9:3 — And when the inhabitants of Gibeon heard what Joshua had done unto Jericho and to Ai,

Jos 9:17 — And the children of Israel journeyed, and came unto their cities on the third day. Now their cities *were* Gibeon, and Chephirah, and Beeroth, and Kirjath-jearim.

2Sa 21:2 — And the king called the Gibeonites, and said unto them; (now the Gibeonites *were* not of the children of Israel, but of the remnant of the Amorites; and the children of Israel had sworn unto them: and Saul sought to slay them in his zeal to the children of Israel and Judah.)

• The people of, adroitly draw Joshua into a treaty.

Jos 9:1–27

• Made servants by the Israelites, when their sharp practice was discovered.

Jos 9:27 — And Joshua made them that day hewers of wood and drawers of water for the congregation, and for the altar of the LORD, even unto this day, in the place which he should choose.

• The sun stands still over, during Joshua's battle with the five confederated kings.

Jos 10:12–14

• Allotted to Benjamin.

Jos 18:25 — Gibeon, and Ramah, and Beeroth,

• Assigned to the Aaronites.

Jos 21:17 — And out of the tribe of Benjamin, Gibeon with her suburbs, Geba with her suburbs,

• The tabernacle located at.

2Ch 1:2–3

1Ki 3:4 — And the king went to Gibeon to sacrifice there; for that *was* the great high place: a thousand burnt offerings did Solomon offer upon that altar.

1Ch 16:39 — And Zadok the priest, and his brethren the priests, before the tabernacle of the LORD in the high place that *was* at Gibeon,

1Ch 21:29 — For the tabernacle of the LORD, which Moses made in the wilderness, and the altar of the burnt offering, *were* at that season in the high place at Gibeon.

2Ch 1:13 — Then Solomon came *from his journey* to the high place that *was* at Gibeon to Jerusalem, from before the tabernacle of the congregation, and reigned over Israel.

• Smitten by David.

1Ch 14:16 — David therefore did as God commanded him: and they smote the host of the Philistines from Gibeon even to Gazer.

• Seven sons of Saul slain at, to avenge the inhabitants of.

2Sa 21:1–9

• Solomon worships at, and offers sacrifices.

1Ki 3:4 — And the king went to Gibeon to sacrifice there; for that *was* the great high place: a thousand burnt offerings did Solomon offer upon that altar.

• God appears to him in dreams.

1Ki 3:5 — In Gibeon the LORD appeared to Solomon in a dream by night: and God said, Ask what I shall give thee.

1Ki 9:2 — That the LORD appeared to Solomon the second time, as he had appeared unto him at Gibeon.

• Abner slays Asahel at.

2Sa 3:30 — So Joab and Abishai his brother slew Abner, because he had slain their brother Asahel at Gibeon in the battle.

• Ishmael, the son of Nethaniah, defeated at, by Jonathan.

Jer 41:11–16

• Pool of.

2Sa 2:13 — And Joab the son of Zeruiah, and the servants of David, went out, and met together by the pool of Gibeon: and they sat down, the one on the one side of the pool, and the other on the other side of the pool.

Jer 41:12 — Then they took all the men, and went to fight with Ishmael the son of Nethaniah, and found him by the great waters that *are* in Gibeon.

GIDDALTI • A son of Heman.

1Ch 25:4 — Of Heman: the sons of Heman; Bukkiah, Mattaniah, Uzziel, Shebuel, and Jerimoth, Hananiah, Hanani, Eliathah, Giddalti, and Romamti-ezer, Joshbekashah, Mallothi, Hothir, *and* Mahazioth:

1Ch 25:29 — The two and twentieth to Giddalti, *he*, his sons, and his brethren, *were* twelve:

GIDDEL

• One of the Nethinim.

Ezr 2:47 — The children of Giddel, the children of Gahar, the children of Reaiah,

Ne 7:49 — The children of Hanan, the children of Giddel, the children of Gahar,

• One of Solomon's servants.

Ezr 2:56 — The children of Jaalah, the children of Darkon, the children of Giddel,

Ne 7:58 — The children of Jaala, the children of Darkon, the children of Giddel,

GIDEON

• Call of, by an angel.

Jgs 6:11 — And there came an angel of the LORD, and sat under an oak which *was* in Ophrah, that *pertained* unto Joash the Abi-ezrite: and his son Gideon threshed wheat by the winepress, to hide *it* from the Midianites.

Jgs 6:14 — And the LORD looked upon him, and said, Go in this thy might, and thou shalt save Israel from the hand of the Midianites: have not I sent thee?

• His excuses.

Jgs 6:15 — And he said unto him, Oh my Lord, wherewith shall I save Israel? behold, my family is poor in Manasseh, and I *am* the least in my father's house.

• Promises of the Lord to.

Jgs 6:16 — And the LORD said unto him, Surely I will be with thee, and thou shalt smite the Midianites as one man.

• Angel attests the call to, by miracle.

Jgs 6:21–24

• He destroys the altar of Baal, and builds one to the Lord.

Jgs 6:25–27

• His prayer tests.

Jgs 6:36–40

• Leads an army against, and defeats the Midianites.

Jgs 6:33–35; 7:1–25; 8:4–12

• Ephraimites chide, for not inviting them to join in the campaign against the Midianites.

Jgs 8:1–3

• Avenges himself upon the people of Succoth.

Jgs 8:14–17

• Israel desires to make him king, he refuses.

Jgs 8:22–23

• Makes an ephod which becomes a snare to the Israelites.

Jgs 8:24–27

• Had seventy sons.

Jgs 8:30 — And Gideon had threescore and ten sons of his body begotten: for he had many wives.

• Death of.

Jgs 8:32 — And Gideon the son of Joash died in a good old age, and was buried in the sepulchre of Joash his father, in Ophrah of the Abi-ezrites.

• Faith of.

Heb 11:32 — And what shall I more say? for the time would fail me to tell of Gedeon, and *of* Barak, and *of* Samson, and *of* Jephthae; *of* David also, and Samuel, and *of* the prophets:

GIDEONI • Father of Abidan.

Nu 1:11 — Of Benjamin; Abidan the son of Gideoni.

Nu 2:22 — Then the tribe of Benjamin: and the captain of the sons of Benjamin *shall be* Abidan the son of Gideoni.

Nu 7:60 — On the ninth day Abidan the son of Gideoni, prince of the children of Benjamin, *offered:*

Nu 7:65 — And for a sacrifice of peace offerings, two oxen, five rams, five he goats, five lambs of the first year: this *was* the offering of Abidan the son of Gideoni.

Nu 10:24 — And over the host of the tribe of the children of Benjamin *was* Abidan the son of Gideoni.

GIDOM • Limit of pursuit after battle of Gibeah.

Jgs 20:45 — And they turned and fled toward the wilderness unto the rock of Rimmon: and they gleaned of them in the highways five thousand men; and pursued hard after them unto Gidom, and slew two thousand men of them.

GIFTS FROM GOD

• Spiritual.

• Christ, the Saviour.

Jn 6:32–33

Isa 42:6 — I the LORD have called thee in righteousness, and will hold thine hand, and will keep thee, and give thee for a covenant of the people, for a light of the Gentiles;

Isa 55:4 — Behold, I have given him *for* a witness to the people, a leader and commander to the people.

Jn 3:16 — For God so loved the world, that he gave his only begotten Son, that whosoever believeth in him should not perish, but have everlasting life.

Jn 4:10 — Jesus answered and said unto her, If thou knewest the gift of God, and who it is that saith to thee, Give me to drink; thou wouldest have asked of him, and he would have given thee living water.

• The Holy Spirit, the Comforter.

See: Holy Spirit

• Grace.

Jas 4:6 — But he giveth more grace. Wherefore he saith, God resisteth the proud, but giveth grace unto the humble.

• Wisdom.

Pr 2:6 — For the LORD giveth wisdom: out of his mouth *cometh* knowledge and understanding.

Jas 1:5 — If any of you lack wisdom, let him ask of God, that giveth to all *men* liberally, and upbraideth not; and it shall be given him.

• Repentance.

Ac 11:18 — When they heard these things, they held their peace, and glorified God, saying, Then hath God also to the Gentiles granted repentance unto life.

• Faith.

Eph 2:8 — For by grace are ye saved through faith; and that not of yourselves: *it is* the gift of God:

Php 1:29 — For unto you it is given in the behalf of Christ, not only to believe on him, but also to suffer for his sake;

• Temporal.

• Food and raiment.

Mt 6:25 — Therefore I say unto you, Take no thought for your life, what ye shall eat, or what ye shall drink; nor yet for your body, what ye shall put on. Is not the life more than meat, and the body than raiment?

Mt 6:33 — But seek ye first the kingdom of God, and his righteousness; and all these things shall be added unto you.

• Rain and fruitful seasons.

Le 26:4–5

Ge 8:22 — While the earth remaineth, seedtime and harvest, and cold and heat, and summer and winter, and day and night shall not cease.

Ge 27:28 — Therefore God give thee of the dew of heaven, and the fatness of the earth, and plenty of corn and wine:

Isa 30:23 — Then shall he give the rain of thy seed, that thou shalt sow the ground withal; and bread of the increase of the earth, and it shall be fat and plenteous: in that day shall thy cattle feed in large pastures.

• Wisdom.

2Ch 1:12 — Wisdom and knowledge *is* granted unto thee; and I will give thee riches, and wealth, and honour, such as none of the kings have had that *have been* before thee, neither shall there any after thee have the like.

• Peace.

Le 26:6 — And I will give peace in the land, and ye shall lie down, and none shall make *you* afraid: and I will rid evil beasts out of the land, neither shall the sword go through your land.

1Ch 22:9 — Behold, a son shall be born to thee, who shall be a man of rest; and I will give him rest from all his enemies round about: for his name shall be Solomon, and I will give peace and quietness unto Israel in his days.

• To be used and enjoyed.

Ecc 5:19–20; 1Ti 4:4–5

Ecc 3:13 — And also that every man should eat and drink, and enjoy the good of all his labour, it *is* the gift of God.

• Should cause us to remember God.

Dt 8:18 — But thou shalt remember the LORD thy God: for *it is* he that giveth thee power to get wealth, that he may establish his covenant which he sware unto thy fathers, as *it is* this day.

• All creatures partake of.

Ps 145:15–16

Ps 136:25 — Who giveth food to all flesh: for his mercy *endureth* for ever.

• Prayer for.

Zec 10:1 — Ask ye of the LORD rain in the time of the latter rain; *so* the LORD shall make bright clouds, and give them showers of rain, to every one grass in the field.

Mt 6:11 — Give us this day our daily bread.

• Unclassified scriptures relating to, both temporal and spiritual.

Da 2:21–23; Mt 25:14–30; Jn 16:23–24; Ro 5:16–18; 12:6–8; 1Co 1:5–7; 12:4–11; Eph 4:7–8; Jas 1:1–27

Ps 4:7 — Thou hast put gladness in my heart, more than in the time *that* their corn and their wine increased.

Ps 21:2 — Thou hast given him his heart's desire, and hast not withholden the request of his lips. Selah.

Ps 29:11 — The LORD will give strength unto his people; the LORD will bless his people with peace.

Ps 34:10 — The young lions do lack, and suffer hunger: but they that seek the LORD shall not want any good *thing.*

Ps 68:18 — Thou hast ascended on high, thou hast led captivity captive: thou hast received gifts for men; yea, *for* the rebellious also, that the LORD God might dwell *among them.*

Ps 68:35 — O God, *thou art* terrible out of thy holy places: the God of Israel *is* he that giveth strength and power unto *his* people. Blessed *be* God.

Ps 84:11 — For the LORD God *is* a sun and shield: the LORD will give grace and glory: no good *thing* will he withhold from them that walk uprightly.

Ecc 2:26 — For *God* giveth to a man that *is* good in his sight wisdom, and knowledge, and joy: but to the sinner he giveth travail, to gather and to heap up, that he may give to *him that is* good before God. This also *is* vanity and vexation of spirit.

Isa 42:5 — Thus saith God the LORD, he that created the heavens, and stretched them out; he that spread forth the earth, and that which cometh out of it; he that giveth breath unto the people upon it, and spirit to them that walk therein:

Eze 11:19 — And I will give them one heart, and I will put a new spirit within you; and I will take the stony heart out of their flesh, and will give them an heart of flesh:

Mt 11:28 — Come unto me, all *ye* that labour and are heavy laden, and I will give you rest.

Jn 6:27 — Labour not for the meat which perisheth, but for that meat which endureth unto everlasting life, which the Son of man shall give unto you: for him hath God the Father sealed.

Jn 17:22 — And the glory which thou gavest me I have given them; that they may be one, even as we are one:

Ro 6:23 — For the wages of sin *is* death; but the gift of God *is* eternal life through Jesus Christ our Lord.

Ro 8:32 — He that spared not his own Son, but delivered him up for us all, how shall he not with him also freely give us all things?

Ro 11:29 — For the gifts and calling of God *are* without repentance.

1Co 7:7 — For I would that all men were even as I myself. But every man hath his proper gift of God, one after this manner, and another after that.

1Co 13:2 — And though I have *the gift of* prophecy, and understand all mysteries, and all knowledge; and though I have all faith, so that I could remove mountains, and have not charity, I am nothing.

1Ti 6:17 — Charge them that are rich in this world, that they be not highminded, nor trust in uncertain riches, but in the living God, who giveth us richly all things to enjoy;

1Pe 4:10 — As every man hath received the gift, *even so* minister the same one to another, as good stewards of the manifold grace of God.

2Pe 1:3 — According as his divine power hath given unto us all things that *pertain* unto life and godliness, through the knowledge of him that hath called us to glory and virtue:

See: Beneficence

See: Blessing; temporal, from God

See: Giving

See: Liberality

GIHON

• A river in Egypt.

Ge 2:13 — And the name of the second river *is* Gihon: the same *is* it that compasseth the whole land of Ethiopia.

• Pools near Jerusalem.

1Ki 1:33 — The king also said unto them, Take with you the servants of your lord, and cause Solomon my son to ride upon mine own mule, and bring him down to Gihon:

1Ki 1:38 — So Zadok the priest, and Nathan the prophet, and Benaiah the son of Jehoiada, and the Cherethites, and the Pelethites, went down, and caused Solomon to ride upon king David's mule, and brought him to Gihon.

1Ki 1:45 — And Zadok the priest and Nathan the prophet have anointed him king in Gihon: and they are come up from thence rejoicing, so that the city rang again. This *is* the noise that ye have heard.

• Hezekiah brings the waters of the upper pool by an aqueduct into the city of Jerusalem.

Ne 2:13–15; 3:13–16; Isa 22:9–11

2Ch 32:4 — So there was gathered much people together, who stopped all the fountains, and the brook that ran through the midst of the land, saying, Why should the kings of Assyria come, and find much water?

2Ch 32:30 — This same Hezekiah also stopped the upper watercourse of Gihon, and brought it straight down to the west side of the city of David. And Hezekiah prospered in all his works.

2Ch 33:14 — Now after this he built a wall without the city of David, on the west side of Gihon, in the valley, even to the entering in at the fish gate, and compassed about Ophel, and raised it up a very great height, and put captains of war in all the fenced cities of Judah.

Isa 7:3 — Then said the LORD unto Isaiah, Go forth now to meet Ahaz, thou, and Shear-jashub thy son, at the end of the conduit of the upper pool in the highway of the fuller's field;

Isa 36:2 — And the king of Assyria sent Rabshakeh from Lachish to Jerusalem unto king Hezekiah with a great army. And he stood by the conduit of the upper pool in the highway of the fuller's field.

GILALAI • A priest and musician.

Ne 12:36 — And his brethren, Shemaiah, and Azarael, Milalai, Gilalai, Maai, Nethaneel, and Judah, Hanani, with the musical instruments of David the man of God, and Ezra the scribe before them.

GILBOA • A hill south of Jezreel, where Saul was defeated by the Philistines, and died.

1Sa 31:1–8; 1Ch 10:1–8

1Sa 28:4 — And the Philistines gathered themselves together, and came and pitched in Shunem: and Saul gathered all Israel together, and they pitched in Gilboa.

GILEAD

• A region east of the Jordan allotted to the tribes of Reuben and Gad and half tribe of Manasseh.

Nu 32:1–30

Dt 3:13 — And the rest of Gilead, and all Bashan, *being* the kingdom of Og, gave I unto the half tribe of Manasseh; all the region of Argob, with all Bashan, which was called the land of giants.

Dt 34:1 — And Moses went up from the plains of Moab unto the mountain of Nebo, to the top of Pisgah, that *is* over against Jericho. And the LORD shewed him all the land of Gilead, unto Dan,

2Ki 10:33 — From Jordan eastward, all the land of Gilead, the Gadites, and the Reubenites, and the Manassites, from Aroer, which is by the river Arnon, even Gilead and Bashan.

• Reubenites expel the Hagarites from.

1Ch 5:9–10, 18–22

• Ammonites make war against; defeated by Jephthah.

Jgs 11:1–40

Am 1:13 — Thus saith the LORD; For three transgressions of the children of Ammon, and for four, I will not turn away *the punishment* thereof; because they have ripped up the women with child of Gilead, that they might enlarge their border:

• The prophet Elijah a native of.

1Ki 17:1 — And Elijah the Tishbite, *who was* of the inhabitants of Gilead, said unto Ahab, *As* the LORD God of Israel liveth, before whom I stand, there shall not be dew nor rain these years, but according to my word.

• David retreats to, at the time of Absalom's rebellion.

2Sa 17:16 — Now therefore send quickly, and tell David, saying, Lodge not this night in the plains of the wilderness, but speedily pass over; lest the king be swallowed up, and all the people that *are* with him.

2Sa 17:22 — Then David arose, and all the people that *were* with him, and they passed over Jordan: by the morning light there lacked not one of them that was not gone over Jordan.

2Sa 17:24 — Then David came to Mahanaim. And Absalom passed over Jordan, he and all the men of Israel with him.

• Pursued into, by Absalom.

2Sa 17:26 — So Israel and Absalom pitched in the land of Gilead.

• Absalom defeated and slain in the forests of.

2Sa 18:9 — And Absalom met the servants of David. And Absalom rode upon a mule, and the mule went under the thick boughs of a great oak, and his head caught hold of the oak, and he was taken up between the heaven and the earth; and the mule that *was* under him went away.

• Hazael, king of Syria, smites the land of.

2Ki 10:32–33

Am 1:3 — Thus saith the LORD; For three transgressions of Damascus, and for four, I will not turn away *the punishment* thereof; because they have threshed Gilead with threshing instruments of iron:

• Invaded by Tiglath-pileser, king of Syria.

2Ki 15:29 — In the days of Pekah king of Israel came Tiglath-pileser king of Assyria, and took Ijon, and Abel-beth-maachah, and Janoah, and Kedesh, and Hazor, and Gilead, and Galilee, all the land of Naphtali, and carried them captive to Assyria.

• A grazing country.

Nu 32:1 — Now the children of Reuben and the children of Gad had a very great multitude of cattle: and when they saw the land of Jazer, and the land of Gilead, that, behold, the place *was* a place for cattle;

1Ch 5:9 — And eastward he inhabited unto the entering in of the wilderness from the river Euphrates: because their cattle were multiplied in the *land* of Gilead.

• Exported spices, balm, and myrrh.

Ge 37:25 — And they sat down to eat bread: and they lifted up their eyes and looked, and, behold, a company of Ishmeelites came from Gilead with their camels bearing spicery and balm and myrrh, going to carry *it* down to Egypt.

Jer 8:22 — *Is there* no balm in Gilead; *is there* no physician there? why then is not the health of the daughter of my people recovered?

Jer 46:11 — Go up into Gilead, and take balm, O virgin, the daughter of Egypt: in vain shalt thou use many medicines; *for* thou shalt not be cured.

• Figurative.

• Of prosperity.

Jer 22:6 — For thus saith the LORD unto the king's house of Judah; Thou *art* Gilead unto me, *and* the head of Lebanon: *yet* surely I will make thee a wilderness, *and* cities *which* are not inhabited.

Jer 50:19 — And I will bring Israel again to his habitation, and he shall feed on Carmel and Bashan, and his soul shall be satisfied upon mount Ephraim and Gilead.

• A mountain.

Jgs 7:3 — Now therefore go to, proclaim in the ears of the people, saying, Whosoever *is* fearful and afraid, let him return and depart early from mount Gilead. And there returned of the people twenty and two thousand; and there remained ten thousand.

SS 4:1 — Behold, thou *art* fair, my love; behold, thou *art* fair; thou *hast* doves' eyes within thy locks: thy hair *is* as a flock of goats, that appear from mount Gilead.

SS 6:5 — Turn away thine eyes from me, for they have overcome me: thy hair *is* as a flock of goats that appear from Gilead.

• Laban overtakes Jacob at.

Ge 31:21–25

• A city.

Hos 6:8 — Gilead *is* a city of them that work iniquity, *and is* polluted with blood.

Hos 12:11 — *Is there* iniquity *in* Gilead? surely they are vanity: they sacrifice bullocks in Gilgal; yea, their altars *are* as heaps in the furrows of the fields.

• Grandson of Manasseh.

Nu 26:29–30

Nu 27:1 — Then came the daughters of Zelophehad, the son of Hepher, the son of Gilead, the son of Machir, the son of Manasseh, of the families of Manasseh the son of Joseph: and these are the names of his daughters; Mahlah, Noah, and Hoglah, and Milcah, and Tirzah.

Nu 36:1 — And the chief fathers of the families of the children of Gilead, the son of Machir, the son of Manasseh, of the families of the sons of Joseph, came near, and spake before Moses, and before the princes, the chief fathers of the children of Israel:

Jos 17:1 — There was also a lot for the tribe of Manasseh; for he *was* the firstborn of Joseph; *to wit,* for Machir the firstborn of Manasseh, the father of Gilead: because he was a man of war, therefore he had Gilead and Bashan.

Jos 17:3 — But Zelophehad, the son of Hepher, the son of Gilead, the son of Machir, the son of Manasseh, had no sons, but daughters: and these *are* the names of his daughters, Mahlah, and Noah, Hoglah, Milcah, and Tirzah.

1Ch 2:21 — And afterward Hezron went in to the daughter of Machir the father of Gilead, whom he married when he *was* threescore years old; and she bare him Segub.

1Ch 2:23 — And he took Geshur, and Aram, with the towns of Jair, from them, with Kenath, and the towns thereof, *even* threescore cities. All these *belonged to* the sons of Machir the father of Gilead.

1Ch 7:14 — The sons of Manasseh; Ashriel, whom she bare: *(but* his concubine the Aramitess bare Machir the father of Gilead:

1Ch 7:17 — And the sons of Ulam; Bedan. These *were* the sons of Gilead, the son of Machir, the son of Manasseh.

• Father of Jephthah.

Jgs 11:1–2

• A chief of Gad.

1Ch 5:14 — These *are* the children of Abihail the son of Huri, the son of Jaroah, the son of Gilead, the son of Michael, the son of Jeshishai, the son of Jahdo, the son of Buz;

GILGAL

• Place of the first encampment of the Israelites west of the Jordan.

Jos 4:19 — And the people came up out of Jordan on the tenth *day* of the first month, and encamped in Gilgal, in the east border of Jericho.

Jos 9:6 — And they went to Joshua unto the camp at Gilgal, and said unto him, and to the men of Israel, We be come from a far country: now therefore make ye a league with us.

Jos 10:6 — And the men of Gibeon sent unto Joshua to the camp to Gilgal, saying, Slack not thy hand from thy servants; come up to us quickly, and save us, and help us: for all the kings of the Amorites that dwell in the mountains are gathered together against us.

Jos 10:43 — And Joshua returned, and all Israel with him, unto the camp to Gilgal.

Jos 14:6 — Then the children of Judah came unto Joshua in Gilgal: and Caleb the son of Jephunneh the Kenezite said unto him, Thou knowest the thing that the LORD said unto Moses the man of God concerning me and thee in Kadesh-barnea.

• Monument erected in, to commemorate the passage of the Jordan by the children of Israel.

Jos 4:19–24

• Circumcision renewed at.

Jos 5:2–9

• Passover kept at.

Jos 5:10–11

• Manna ceased at, after the passover.

Jos 5:12 — And the manna ceased on the morrow after they had eaten of the old corn of the land; neither had the children of Israel manna any more; but they did eat of the fruit of the land of Canaan that year.

• Quarries at.

Jgs 3:19 — But he himself turned again from the quarries that *were* by Gilgal, and said, I have a secret errand unto thee, O king: who said, Keep silence. And all that stood by him went out from him.

• Eglon, king of Moab, resides and is slain at.

Jgs 3:14–26

• A judgment seat, where Israel, in that district, came to be judged by Samuel.

1Sa 7:16 — And he went from year to year in circuit to Bethel, and Gilgal, and Mizpeh, and judged Israel in all those places.

• Saul proclaimed king over all Israel at.

1Sa 11:15 — And all the people went to Gilgal; and there they made Saul king before the LORD in Gilgal; and there they sacrificed sacrifices of peace offerings before the LORD; and there Saul and all the men of Israel rejoiced greatly.

• An altar built at, and sacrifice offered.

1Sa 13:4–15; 15:6–23

1Sa 11:15 — And all the people went to Gilgal; and there they made Saul king before the LORD in Gilgal; and there they sacrificed sacrifices of peace offerings before the LORD; and there Saul and all the men of Israel rejoiced greatly.

• Agag, king of the Amalekites, slain at, by Samuel.

1Sa 15:33 — And Samuel said, As thy sword hath made women childless, so shall thy mother be childless among women. And Samuel hewed Agag in pieces before the LORD in Gilgal.

• Tribe of Judah assembles at.

2Sa 19:14–15, 40–43

• A school of the prophets at.

2Ki 4:38–40

• Prophecies concerning.

Hos 4:15 — Though thou, Israel, play the harlot, *yet* let not Judah offend; and come not ye unto Gilgal, neither go ye up to Beth-aven, nor swear, The LORD liveth.

Hos 9:15 — All their wickedness *is* in Gilgal: for there I hated them: for the wickedness of their doings I will drive them out of mine house, I will love them no more: all their princes *are* revolters.

Hos 12:11 — *Is there* iniquity *in* Gilead? surely they are vanity: they sacrifice bullocks in Gilgal; yea, their altars *are* as heaps in the furrows of the fields.

Am 4:4 — Come to Bethel, and transgress; at Gilgal multiply transgression; and bring your sacrifices every morning, *and* your tithes after three years:

Am 5:5 — But seek not Bethel, nor enter into Gilgal, and pass not to Beer-sheba: for Gilgal shall surely go into captivity, and Bethel shall come to nought.

• A royal city in Canaan, conquered by Joshua.

Jos 12:23 — The king of Dor in the coast of Dor, one; the king of the nations of Gilgal, one;

GILOH • A town in Judah.

Jos 15:51 — And Goshen, and Holon, and Giloh; eleven cities with their villages:

2Sa 15:12 — And Absalom sent for Ahithophel the Gilonite, David's counsellor, from his city, *even* from Giloh, while he offered sacrifices. And the conspiracy was strong; for the people increased continually with Absalom.

GIMZO • A city of Judah.

2Ch 28:18 — The Philistines also had invaded the cities of the low country, and of the south of Judah, and had taken Beth-shemesh, and Ajalon, and

Gederoth, and Shocho with the villages thereof, and Timnah with the villages thereof, Gimzo also and the villages thereof: and they dwelt there.

GIN

• A snare.

Am 3:5 — Can a bird fall in a snare upon the earth, where no gin *is* for him? shall *one* take up a snare from the earth, and have taken nothing at all?

✧See: Snare

GINATH • Father of Tibni.

1Ki 16:21–22

GINNETHON

• Called also Ginnetho.

• A companion of Nehemiah.

Ne 10:6 — Daniel, Ginnethon, Baruch,

Ne 12:4 — Iddo, Ginnetho, Abijah,

Ne 12:16 — Of Iddo, Zechariah; of Ginnethon, Meshullam;

GIRDLE

• Worn by the high priest.

Ex 28:4 — And these *are* the garments which they shall make; a breastplate, and an ephod, and a robe, and a broidered coat, a mitre, and a girdle: and they shall make holy garments for Aaron thy brother, and his sons, that he may minister unto me in the priest's office.

Ex 28:39 — And thou shalt embroider the coat of fine linen, and thou shalt make the mitre *of* fine linen, and thou shalt make the girdle *of* needlework.

Ex 39:29 — And a girdle *of* fine twined linen, and blue, and purple, and scarlet, *of* needlework; as the LORD commanded Moses.

Le 8:7 — And he put upon him the coat, and girded him with the girdle, and clothed him with the robe, and put the ephod upon him, and he girded him with the curious girdle of the ephod, and bound *it* unto him therewith.

Le 16:4 — He shall put on the holy linen coat, and he shall have the linen breeches upon his flesh, and shall be girded with a linen girdle, and with the linen mitre shall he be attired: these *are* holy garments; therefore shall he wash his flesh in water, and *so* put them on.

• Worn by other priests.

Ex 28:40 — And for Aaron's sons thou shalt make coats, and thou shalt make for them girdles, and bonnets shalt thou make for them, for glory and for beauty.

Ex 29:9 — And thou shalt gird them with girdles, Aaron and his sons, and put the bonnets on them: and the priest's office shall be theirs for a perpetual statute: and thou shalt consecrate Aaron and his sons.

Le 8:13 — And Moses brought Aaron's sons, and put coats upon them, and girded them with girdles, and put bonnets upon them; as the LORD commanded Moses.

• Worn by women.

Isa 3:24 — And it shall come to pass, *that* instead of sweet smell there shall be stink; and instead of a girdle a rent; and instead of well set hair baldness; and instead of a stomacher a girding of sackcloth; *and* burning instead of beauty.

• Embroidered.

Ex 28:27–28

Ex 28:8 — And the curious girdle of the ephod, which *is* upon it, shall be of the same, according to the work thereof; *even of* gold, *of* blue, and purple, and scarlet, and fine twined linen.

Ex 29:5 — And thou shalt take the garments, and put upon Aaron the coat, and the robe of the ephod, and the ephod, and the breastplate, and gird him with the curious girdle of the ephod:

Le 8:7 — And he put upon him the coat, and girded him with the girdle, and clothed him with the robe, and put the ephod upon him, and he girded him with the curious girdle of the ephod, and bound *it* unto him therewith.

• Made of linen.

Pr 31:24 — She maketh fine linen, and selleth *it;* and delivereth girdles unto the merchant.

• Made of leather.

2Ki 1:8 — And they answered him, *He was* an hairy man, and girt with a girdle of leather about his loins. And he said, It *is* Elijah the Tishbite.

Mt 3:4 — And the same John had his raiment of camel's hair, and a leathern girdle about his loins; and his meat was locusts and wild honey.

• Traffic in.

Pr 31:24 — She maketh fine linen, and selleth *it;* and delivereth girdles unto the merchant.

• Used to bear arms.

1Sa 18:4 — And Jonathan stripped himself of the robe that *was* upon him, and gave it to David, and his garments, even to his sword, and to his bow, and to his girdle.

2Sa 20:8 — When they *were* at the great stone which *is* in Gibeon, Amasa went before them. And Joab's garment that he had put on was girded unto him, and upon it a girdle *with* a sword fastened upon his loins in the sheath thereof; and as he went forth it fell out.

2Ki 3:21 — And when all the Moabites heard that the kings were come up to fight against them, they gathered all that were able to put on armour, and upward, and stood in the border.

• Figurative.

Isa 11:5 — And righteousness shall be the girdle of his loins, and faithfulness the girdle of his reins.

Isa 22:21 — And I will clothe him with thy robe, and strengthen him with thy girdle, and I will commit thy government into his hand: and he shall be a father to the inhabitants of Jerusalem, and to the house of Judah.

Eph 6:14 — Stand therefore, having your loins girt about with truth, and having on the breastplate of righteousness;

• Symbolic.

Jer 13:1–11

Ac 21:11 — And when he was come unto us, he took Paul's girdle, and bound his own hands and feet, and said, Thus saith the Holy Ghost, So shall the Jews at Jerusalem bind the man that owneth this girdle, and shall deliver *him* into the hands of the Gentiles.

Rev 15:6 — And the seven angels came out of the temple, having the seven plagues, clothed in pure and white linen, and having their breasts girded with golden girdles.

GIRGASHITES

• Land of, given to Abraham and his descendants.

Ge 15:21 — And the Amorites, and the Canaanites, and the Girgashites, and the Jebusites.

Dt 7:1 — When the LORD thy God shall bring thee into the land whither thou goest to possess it, and hath cast out many nations before thee, the Hittites, and the Girgashites, and the Amorites, and the Canaanites, and the Perizzites, and the Hivites, and the Jebusites, seven nations greater and mightier than thou;

Jos 3:10 — And Joshua said, Hereby ye shall know that the living God *is* among you, and *that* he will without fail drive out from before you the Canaanites, and the Hittites, and the Hivites, and the Perizzites, and the Girgashites, and the Amorites, and the Jebusites.

Ne 9:8 — And foundest his heart faithful before thee, and madest a covenant with him to give the land of the Canaanites, the Hittites, the Amorites, and the Perizzites, and the Jebusites, and the Girgashites, to give *it, I say,* to his seed, and hast performed thy words; for thou *art* righteous:

• Delivered to the children of Israel.

Jos 24:11 — And ye went over Jordan, and came unto Jericho: and the men of Jericho fought against you, the Amorites, and the Perizzites, and the Canaanites, and the Hittites, and the Girgashites, the Hivites, and the Jebusites; and I delivered them into your hand.

GISPA

• Called also Gispha.

• An overseer of the Nethinim.

Ne 11:21 — But the Nethinims dwelt in Ophel: and Ziha and Gispa *were* over the Nethinims.

GITTAH-HEPHER

• A prolonged form of Gath-Hepher.

Jos 19:13 — And from thence passeth on along on the east to Gittah-hepher, to Ittah-kazin, and goeth out to Remmon-methoar to Neah;

See: Gath-Hepher

GITTAIM • A place of which little is known.

2Sa 4:3 — And the Beerothites fled to Gittaim, and were sojourners there until this day.)

Ne 11:33 — Hazor, Ramah, Gittaim,

GITTITE See: Gath

GITTITH See: Music

GIVING

• Rules for.

Mt 6:1–4; 2Co 8:11–12; 9:6–7

1Co 16:2 — Upon the first *day* of the week let every one of you lay by him in store, as *God* hath prospered him, that there be no gatherings when I come.

2Co 8:14 — But by an equality, *that* now at this time your abundance *may be a supply* for their want, that their abundance also may be *a supply* for your want: that there may be equality:

See: Alms

See: Beneficence

See: Liberality

GIZONITE • A man or town of Judah.

1Ch 11:34 — The sons of Hashem the Gizonite, Jonathan the son of Shage the Hararite,

GLADIATOR

• Contend with wild beasts.

1Co 15:32 — If after the manner of men I have fought with beasts at Ephesus, what advantageth it me, if the dead rise not? let us eat and drink; for to morrow we die.

GLADNESS See: Joy

GLASS

Job 28:17 — The gold and the crystal cannot equal it: and the exchange of it *shall not be for* jewels of fine gold.

• Symbolic.

Rev 21:18 — And the building of the wall of it was *of* jasper: and the city *was* pure gold, like unto clear glass.

Rev 21:21 — And the twelve gates *were* twelve pearls; every several gate was of one pearl: and the street of the city *was* pure gold, as it were transparent glass.

• Sea of.

Rev 15:2 — And I saw as it were a sea of glass mingled with fire: and them that had gotten the victory over the beast, and over his image, and over his mark, *and* over the number of his name, stand on the sea of glass, having the harps of God.

See: Mirror

GLEANING

• Laws concerning.

Le 19:9–10; Dt 24:19–20

Le 23:22 — And when ye reap the harvest of your land, thou shalt not make clean riddance of the corners of thy field when thou reapest, neither shalt thou gather any gleaning of thy harvest: thou shalt leave them unto the poor, and to the stranger: I *am* the LORD your God.

See: Orphan

See: Strangers

See: Widow

• **Figurative.**

Jgs 8:2 — And he said unto them, What have I done now in comparison of you? *Is* not the gleaning of the grapes of Ephraim better than the vintage of Abi-ezer?

Isa 17:6 — Yet gleaning grapes shall be left in it, as the shaking of an olive tree, two *or* three berries in the top of the uppermost bough, four *or* five in the outmost fruitful branches thereof, saith the LORD God of Israel.

Jer 49:9 — If grapegatherers come to thee, would they not leave *some* gleaning grapes? if thieves by night, they will destroy till they have enough.

Mic 7:1 — Woe is me! for I am as when they have gathered the summer fruits, as the grapegleanings of the vintage: *there is* no cluster to eat: my soul desired the firstripe fruit.

• **Instances of.**

• **Ruth in the field of Boaz.**

Ru 2:2–3

GLEDE • A carnivorous bird.

Dt 14:13 — And the glede, and the kite, and the vulture after his kind,

GLORIFYING GOD

• **Commanded.**

1Ch 16:28 — Give unto the LORD, ye kindreds of the people, give unto the LORD glory and strength.

Ps 22:23 — Ye that fear the LORD, praise him; all ye the seed of Jacob, glorify him; and fear him, all ye the seed of Israel.

Isa 42:12 — Let them give glory unto the LORD, and declare his praise in the islands.

• **Due to him.**

1Ch 16:29 — Give unto the LORD the glory *due* unto his name: bring an offering, and come before him: worship the LORD in the beauty of holiness.

• **For his holiness.**

Ps 99:9 — Exalt the LORD our God, and worship at his holy hill; for the LORD our God *is* holy.

Rev 15:4 — Who shall not fear thee, O Lord, and glorify thy name? for *thou* only *art* holy: for all nations shall come and worship before thee; for thy judgments are made manifest.

• **For mercy and truth.**

Ps 115:1 — Not unto us, O LORD, not unto us, but unto thy name give glory, for thy mercy, *and* for thy truth's sake.

Ro 15:9 — And that the Gentiles might glorify God for *his* mercy; as it is written, For this cause I will confess to thee among the Gentiles, and sing unto thy name.

• **For faithfulness and truth.**

Isa 25:1 — O LORD, thou *art* my God; I will exalt thee, I will praise thy name; for thou hast done wonderful *things; thy* counsels of old *are* faithfulness *and* truth.

• **For wondrous works.**

Mt 15:31 — Insomuch that the multitude wondered, when they saw the dumb to speak, the maimed to be whole, the lame to walk, and the blind to see: and they glorified the God of Israel.

Ac 4:21 — So when they had further threatened them, they let them go, finding nothing how they might punish them, because of the people: for all *men* glorified God for that which was done.

• **For judgments.**

Isa 25:3 — Therefore shall the strong people glorify thee, the city of the terrible nations shall fear thee.

Eze 28:22 — And say, Thus saith the Lord GOD; Behold, I *am* against thee, O Zidon; and I will be glorified in the midst of thee: and they shall know that I *am* the LORD, when I shall have executed judgments in her, and shall be sanctified in her.

Rev 14:7 — Saying with a loud voice, Fear God, and give glory to him; for the hour of his judgment is come: and worship him that made heaven, and earth, and the sea, and the fountains of waters.

• **For deliverances.**

Ps 50:15 — And call upon me in the day of trouble: I will deliver thee, and thou shalt glorify me.

• **For grace to others.**

Ac 11:18 — When they heard these things, they held their peace, and glorified God, saying, Then hath God also to the Gentiles granted repentance unto life.

2Co 9:13 — Whiles by the experiment of this ministration they glorify God for your professed subjection into the gospel of Christ, and for *your* liberal distribution unto them, and unto all *men;*

Gal 1:24 — And they glorified God in me.

• **Accomplished by.**

• **Relying on his promises.**

Ro 4:20 — He staggered not at the promise of God through unbelief; but was strong in faith, giving glory to God;

• **Praising him.**

Ps 50:23 — Whoso offereth praise glorifieth me: and to him that ordereth *his* conversation *aright* will I shew the salvation of God.

• **Doing all to glorify him.**

1Co 10:31 — Whether therefore ye eat, or drink, or whatsoever ye do, do all to the glory of God.

• **Dying for him.**

Jn 21:19 — This spake he, signifying by what death he should glorify God. And when he had spoken this, he saith unto him, Follow me.

• **Suffering for Christ.**

1Pe 4:14 — If ye be reproached for the name of Christ, happy *are ye;* for the spirit of glory and of God resteth upon you: on their part he is evil spoken of, but on your part he is glorified.

1Pe 4:16 — Yet if *any man suffer* as a Christian, let him not be ashamed; but let him glorify God on this behalf.

• **Glorifying Christ.**

Ac 19:17 — And this was known to all the Jews and Greeks also dwelling at Ephesus; and fear fell on them all, and the name of the Lord Jesus was magnified.

2Th 1:12 — That the name of our Lord Jesus Christ may be glorified in you, and ye in him, according to the grace of our God and the Lord Jesus Christ.

- **Bringing forth fruits of righteousness.**

Jn 15:8 — Herein is my Father glorified, that ye bear much fruit; so shall ye be my disciples.

Php 1:11 — Being filled with the fruits of righteousness, which are by Jesus Christ, unto the glory and praise of God.

- **Having patience in affliction.**

Isa 24:15 — Wherefore glorify ye the LORD in the fires, *even* the name of the LORD God of Israel in the isles of the sea.

- **Faithfulness.**

1Pe 4:11 — If any man speak, *let him speak* as the oracles of God; if any man minister, *let him do it* as of the ability which God giveth: that God in all things may be glorified through Jesus Christ, to whom be praise and dominion for ever and ever. Amen.

- **Required in body and spirit.**

1Co 6:20 — For ye are bought with a price: therefore glorify God in your body, and in your spirit, which are God's.

- **Shall be universal.**

Ps 86:9 — All nations whom thou hast made shall come and worship before thee, O Lord; and shall glorify thy name.

Rev 5:13 — And every creature which is in heaven, and on the earth, and under the earth, and such as are in the sea, and all that are in them, heard I saying, Blessing, and honour, and glory, and power, *be* unto him that sitteth upon the throne, and unto the Lamb for ever and ever.

- **Saints.**
  - **Should resolve on.**

Ps 69:30 — I will praise the name of God with a song, and will magnify him with thanksgiving.

Ps 118:28 — Thou *art* my God, and I will praise thee: *thou art* my God, I will exalt thee.

  - **Unite in.**

Ps 34:3 — O magnify the LORD with me, and let us exalt his name together.

Ro 15:6 — That ye may with one mind *and* one mouth glorify God, even the Father of our Lord Jesus Christ.

  - **Persevere in.**

Ps 86:12 — I will praise thee, O Lord my God, with all my heart: and I will glorify thy name for evermore.

- **All the blessings of God are designed to lead to.**

Isa 60:21 — Thy people also *shall be* all righteous: they shall inherit the land for ever, the branch of my planting, the work of my hands, that I may be glorified.

Isa 61:3 — To appoint unto them that mourn in Zion, to give unto them beauty for ashes, the oil of joy for mourning, the garment of praise for the spirit of heaviness; that they might be called trees of righteousness, the planting of the LORD, that he might be glorified.

- **The holy example of the saints may lead others to.**

Mt 5:16 — Let your light so shine before men, that they may see your good works, and glorify your Father which is in heaven.

1Pe 2:12 — Having your conversation honest among the Gentiles: that, whereas they speak against you as evildoers, they may by *your* good works, which they shall behold, glorify God in the day of visitation.

- **All, by nature, fail in.**

Ro 3:23 — For all have sinned, and come short of the glory of God;

- **The wicked averse to.**

Da 5:23 — But hast lifted up thyself against the Lord of heaven; and they have brought the vessels of his house before thee, and thou, and thy lords, thy wives, and thy concubines, have drunk wine in them; and thou hast praised the gods of silver, and gold, of brass, iron, wood, and stone, which see not, nor hear, nor know: and the God in whose hand thy breath *is,* and whose *are* all thy ways, hast thou not glorified:

Ro 1:21 — Because that, when they knew God, they glorified *him* not as God, neither were thankful; but became vain in their imaginations, and their foolish heart was darkened.

- **Punishment for not.**

Da 5:23 — But hast lifted up thyself against the Lord of heaven; and they have brought the vessels of his house before thee, and thou, and thy lords, thy wives, and thy concubines, have drunk wine in them; and thou hast praised the gods of silver, and gold, of brass, iron, wood, and stone, which see not, nor hear, nor know: and the God in whose hand thy breath *is,* and whose *are* all thy ways, hast thou not glorified:

Da 5:30 — In that night was Belshazzar the king of the Chaldeans slain.

Mal 2:2 — If ye will not hear, and if ye will not lay *it* to heart, to give glory unto my name, saith the LORD of hosts, I will even send a curse upon you, and I will curse your blessings: yea, I have cursed them already, because ye do not lay *it* to heart.

Ac 12:23 — And immediately the angel of the Lord smote him, because he gave not God the glory: and he was eaten of worms, and gave up the ghost.

Ro 1:21 — Because that, when they knew God, they glorified *him* not as God, neither were thankful; but became vain in their imaginations, and their foolish heart was darkened.

- **Heavenly hosts engaged in.**

Rev 4:11 — Thou art worthy, O Lord, to receive glory and honour and power: for thou hast created all things, and for thy pleasure they are and were created.

- **Exemplified by.**
  - **David.**

    Ps 57:5 — Be thou exalted, O God, above the heavens; *let* thy glory *be* above all the earth.
  - **The multitude.**

    Mt 9:8 — But when the multitudes saw *it,* they marvelled, and glorified God, which had given such power unto men.

    Mt 15:31 — Insomuch that the multitude wondered, when they saw the dumb to speak, the maimed to be whole, the lame to walk, and the blind to see: and they glorified the God of Israel.
  - **The virgin Mary.**

    Lk 1:46 — And Mary said, My soul doth magnify the Lord,
  - **The angels.**

    Lk 2:14 — Glory to God in the highest, and on earth peace, good will toward men.
  - **The shepherds.**

    Lk 2:20 — And the shepherds returned, glorifying and praising God for all the things that they had heard and seen, as it was told unto them.
  - **Jesus.**

    Jn 17:4 — I have glorified thee on the earth: I have finished the work which thou gavest me to do.
  - **The man sick of the palsy.**

    Lk 5:25 — And immediately he rose up before them, and took up that whereon he lay, and departed to his own house, glorifying God.
  - **The woman with infirmity.**

    Lk 13:13 — And he laid *his* hands on her: and immediately she was made straight, and glorified God.
  - **The leper whom Jesus healed.**

    Lk 17:15 — And one of them, when he saw that he was healed, turned back, and with a loud voice glorified God,
  - **The blind man.**

    Lk 18:43 — And immediately he received his sight, and followed him, glorifying God: and all the people, when they saw *it,* gave praise unto God.
  - **The centurion.**

    Lk 23:47 — Now when the centurion saw what was done, he glorified God, saying, Certainly this was a righteous man.
  - **The church at Jerusalem.**

    Ac 11:18 — When they heard these things, they held their peace, and glorified God, saying, Then hath God also to the Gentiles granted repentance unto life.
  - **The Gentiles at Antioch.**

    Ac 13:48 — And when the Gentiles heard this, they were glad, and glorified the word of the Lord: and as many as were ordained to eternal life believed.
  - **Abraham.**

    Ro 4:20 — He staggered not at the promise of God through unbelief; but was strong in faith, giving glory to God;
  - **Paul.**

    Ro 11:36 — For of him, and through him, and to him, *are* all things: to whom *be* glory for ever. Amen.

GLORY

- **God is, to his people.**

  Ps 3:3 — But thou, O LORD, *art* a shield for me; my glory, and the lifter up of mine head.

  Zec 2:5 — For I, saith the LORD, will be unto her a wall of fire round about, and will be the glory in the midst of her.
- **Christ is, to his people.**

  Isa 60:1 — Arise, shine; for thy light is come, and the glory of the LORD is risen upon thee.

  Lk 2:32 — A light to lighten the Gentiles, and the glory of thy people Israel.
- **The gospel ordained to be, to saints.**

  1Co 2:7 — But we speak the wisdom of God in a mystery, *even* the hidden *wisdom,* which God ordained before the world unto our glory:
- **Of the gospel exceeds that of the law.**

  2Co 3:9–10
- **The joy of saints is full of.**

  1Pe 1:8 — Whom having not seen, ye love; in whom, though now ye see *him* not, yet believing, ye rejoice with joy unspeakable and full of glory:
- **Spiritual.**
  - **Is given by God.**

    Ps 84:11 — For the LORD God *is* a sun and shield: the LORD will give grace and glory: no good *thing* will he withhold from them that walk uprightly.
  - **Is given by Christ.**

    Jn 17:22 — And the glory which thou gavest me I have given them; that they may be one, even as we are one:
  - **Is the work of the Holy Ghost.**

    2Co 3:18 — But we all, with open face beholding as in a glass the glory of the Lord, are changed into the same image from glory to glory, *even* as by the Spirit of the Lord.
- **Eternal.**
  - **Procured by the death of Christ.**

    Heb 2:10 — For it became him, for whom *are* all things, and by whom *are* all things, in bringing many sons unto glory, to make the captain of their salvation perfect through sufferings.
  - **Accompanies salvation by Christ.**

    2Ti 2:10 — Therefore I endure all things for the elect's sakes, that they may also obtain the salvation which is in Christ Jesus with eternal glory.
  - **Inherited by saints.**

    1Sa 2:8 — He raiseth up the poor out of the dust, *and* lifteth up the beggar from the dunghill, to set *them* among princes, and to make them inherit the throne of glory: for the pillars of the earth *are* the LORD'S, and he hath set the world upon them.

    Ps 73:24 — Thou shalt guide me with thy counsel, and afterward receive me *to* glory.

Pr 3:35 — The wise shall inherit glory: but shame shall be the promotion of fools.

Col 3:4 — When Christ, *who is* our life, shall appear, then shall ye also appear with him in glory.

1Pe 5:10 — But the God of all grace, who hath called us unto his eternal glory by Christ Jesus, after that ye have suffered a while, make you perfect, stablish, strengthen, settle *you.*

- **Saints called to.**

2Th 2:14 — Whereunto he called you by our gospel, to the obtaining of the glory of our Lord Jesus Christ.

1Pe 5:10 — But the God of all grace, who hath called us unto his eternal glory by Christ Jesus, after that ye have suffered a while, make you perfect, stablish, strengthen, settle *you.*

- **Saints prepared unto.**

Ro 9:23 — And that he might make known the riches of his glory on the vessels of mercy, which he had afore prepared unto glory,

- **Enhanced by afflictions.**

2Co 4:17 — For our light affliction, which is but for a moment, worketh for us a far more exceeding *and* eternal weight of glory;

- **Present afflictions not worthy to be compared with.**

Ro 8:18 — For I reckon that the sufferings of this present time *are* not worthy *to be compared* with the glory which shall be revealed in us.

- **Of the church shall be rich and abundant.**

Isa 60:11–13

- **The bodies of saints shall be raised in.**

1Co 15:43 — It is sown in dishonour; it is raised in glory: it is sown in weakness; it is raised in power:

Php 3:21 — Who shall change our vile body, that it may be fashioned like unto his glorious body, according to the working whereby he is able even to subdue all things unto himself.

- **Saints shall be, of their ministers.**

1Th 2:19–20

- **Afflictions of ministers are, to saints.**

Eph 3:13 — Wherefore I desire that ye faint not at my tribulations for you, which is your glory.

- **Temporal.**

- **Is given by God.**

Da 2:37 — Thou, O king, *art* a king of kings: for the God of heaven hath given thee a kingdom, power, and strength, and glory.

- **Passeth away.**

1Pe 1:24 — For all flesh *is* as grass, and all the glory of man as the flower of grass. The grass withereth, and the flower thereof falleth away:

- **The devil tries to seduce by.**

Mt 4:8 — Again, the devil taketh him up into an exceeding high mountain, and sheweth him all the kingdoms of the world, and the glory of them;

- **Of hypocrites turned to shame.**

Hos 4:7 — As they were increased, so they sinned against me: *therefore* will I change their glory into shame.

- **Seek not, from man.**

Mt 6:2 — Therefore when thou doest *thine* alms, do not sound a trumpet before thee, as the hypocrites do in the synagogues and in the streets, that they may have glory of men. Verily I say unto you, They have their reward.

1Th 2:6 — Nor of men sought we glory, neither of you, nor *yet* of others, when we might have been burdensome, as the apostles of Christ.

- **Of the wicked is in their shame.**

Php 3:19 — Whose end *is* destruction, whose God *is their* belly, and *whose* glory *is* in their shame, who mind earthly things.)

- **Ends in destruction.**

Isa 5:14 — Therefore hell hath enlarged herself, and opened her mouth without measure: and their glory, and their multitude, and their pomp, and he that rejoiceth, shall descend into it.

- **Of God.**

- **Exhibited in Christ.**

Jn 1:14 — And the Word was made flesh, and dwelt among us, (and we beheld his glory, the glory as of the only begotten of the Father,) full of grace and truth.

2Co 4:6 — For God, who commanded the light to shine out of darkness, hath shined in our hearts, to *give* the light of the knowledge of the glory of God in the face of Jesus Christ.

Heb 1:3 — Who being the brightness of *his* glory, and the express image of his person, and upholding all things by the word of his power, when he had by himself purged our sins, sat down on the right hand of the Majesty on high;

- **Ascribed to God.**

Gal 1:5 — To whom *be* glory for ever and ever. Amen.

- **Exhibited in his name.**

Dt 28:58 — If thou wilt not observe to do all the words of this law that are written in this book, that thou mayest fear this glorious and fearful name, THE LORD THY GOD;

Ne 9:5 — Then the Levites, Jeshua, and Kadmiel, Bani, Hashabniah, Sherebiah, Hodijah, Shebaniah, *and* Pethahiah, said, Stand up *and* bless the LORD your God for ever and ever: and blessed be thy glorious name, which is exalted above all blessing and praise.

- **Exhibited in his majesty.**

Job 37:22 — Fair weather cometh out of the north: with God is terrible majesty.

Ps 93:1 — The LORD reigneth, he is clothed with majesty; the LORD is clothed with strength, *wherewith* he hath girded himself: the world also is stablished, that it cannot be moved.

Ps 104:1 — Bless the LORD, O my soul. O LORD my God, thou art very great; thou art clothed with honour and majesty.

Ps 145:5 — I will speak of the glorious honour of thy majesty, and of thy wondrous works.

Ps 145:12 — To make known to the sons of men his mighty acts, and the glorious majesty of his kingdom.

Isa 2:10 — Enter into the rock, and hide thee in the dust, for fear of the LORD, and for the glory of his majesty.

• Exhibited in his power.

Ex 15:1 — Then sang Moses and the children of Israel this song unto the LORD, and spake, saying, I will sing unto the LORD, for he hath triumphed gloriously: the horse and his rider hath he thrown into the sea.

Ex 15:6 — Thy right hand, O LORD, is become glorious in power: thy right hand, O LORD, hath dashed in pieces the enemy.

Ro 6:4 — Therefore we are buried with him by baptism into death: that like as Christ was raised up from the dead by the glory of the Father, even so we also should walk in newness of life.

• Exhibited in his works.

Ps 19:1 — The heavens declare the glory of God; and the firmament sheweth his handywork.

Ps 111:3 — His work *is* honourable and glorious: and his righteousness endureth for ever.

• Exhibited in his holiness.

Ex 15:11 — Who *is* like unto thee, O LORD, among the gods? who *is* like thee, glorious in holiness, fearful *in* praises, doing wonders?

• Described as great.

Ps 138:5 — Yea, they shall sing in the ways of the LORD: for great *is* the glory of the LORD.

• Described as eternal.

Ps 104:31 — The glory of the LORD shall endure for ever: the LORD shall rejoice in his works.

• Described as rich.

Eph 3:16 — That he would grant you, according to the riches of his glory, to be strengthened with might by his Spirit in the inner man;

• Described as highly exalted.

Ps 8:1 — O LORD our Lord, how excellent *is* thy name in all the earth! who hast set thy glory above the heavens.

Ps 113:4 — The LORD *is* high above all nations, *and* his glory above the heavens.

• Exhibited to Moses.

Ex 33:18–23; 34:5–7

• Exhibited to Stephen.

Ac 7:55 — But he, being full of the Holy Ghost, looked up stedfastly into heaven, and saw the glory of God, and Jesus standing on the right hand of God,

• Exhibited by his church.

Dt 5:24 — And ye said, Behold, the LORD our God hath shewed us his glory and his greatness, and we have heard his voice out of the midst of the fire: we have seen this day that God doth talk with man, and he liveth.

Ps 102:16 — When the LORD shall build up Zion, he shall appear in his glory.

• Enlightens the church.

Isa 60:1–2

Rev 21:11 — Having the glory of God: and her light *was* like unto a stone most precious, even like a jasper stone, clear as crystal;

Rev 21:23 — And the city had no need of the sun, neither of the moon, to shine in it: for the glory of God did lighten it, and the Lamb *is* the light thereof.

• Saints desire to behold.

Ps 63:2 — To see thy power and thy glory, so *as* I have seen thee in the sanctuary.

Ps 90:16 — Let thy work appear unto thy servants, and thy glory unto their children.

• God is jealous of.

Isa 42:8 — I *am* the LORD: that *is* my name: and my glory will I not give to another, neither my praise to graven images.

• The earth is full of.

Isa 6:3 — And one cried unto another, and said, Holy, holy, holy, *is* the LORD of hosts: the whole earth *is* full of his glory.

• The knowledge of, shall fill the earth.

Hab 2:14 — For the earth shall be filled with the knowledge of the glory of the LORD, as the waters cover the sea.

GLUTTONY

Ex 16:20–21; Nu 11:32–33; Dt 21:20–21; Pr 30:21–22; Am 6:4–7; Lk 12:19–20, 45–46; Ro 13:13–14

Ex 16:27 — And it came to pass, *that* there went out *some* of the people on the seventh day for to gather, and they found none.

Pr 23:21 — For the drunkard and the glutton shall come to poverty: and drowsiness shall clothe *a man* with rags.

Ecc 10:17 — Blessed *art* thou, O land, when thy king *is* the son of nobles, and thy princes eat in due season, for strength, and not for drunkenness!

Isa 22:13 — And behold joy and gladness, slaying oxen, and killing sheep, eating flesh, and drinking wine: let us eat and drink; for to morrow we shall die.

Lk 21:34 — And take heed to yourselves, lest at any time your hearts be overcharged with surfeiting, and drunkenness, and cares of this life, and so that day come upon you unawares.

1Co 15:32 — If after the manner of men I have fought with beasts at Ephesus, what advantageth it me, if the dead rise not? let us eat and drink; for to morrow we die.

Php 3:19 — Whose end *is* destruction, whose God *is their* belly, and *whose* glory *is* in their shame, who mind earthly things.)

1Pe 4:3 — For the time past of *our* life may suffice us to have wrought the will of the Gentiles, when we walked in lasciviousness, lusts, excess of wine, revellings, banquetings, and abominable idolatries:

Jude 1:12 — These are spots in your feasts of charity, when they feast with you, feeding themselves without fear: clouds *they are* without water, carried about of winds; trees whose fruit withereth, without fruit, twice dead, plucked up by the roots;

- **Instances of.**
  - **Esau.**
    Ge 25:30–34; Heb 12:16–17
  - **Israel.**
    Nu 11:4; Ps 78:18
  - **Sons of Eli.**
    1Sa 2:12–17
  - **Belshazzar.**
    Da 5:1

GNASHING OF TEETH

Job 16:9 — He teareth *me* in his wrath, who hateth me: he gnasheth upon me with his teeth; mine enemy sharpeneth his eyes upon me.

Ps 35:16 — With hypocritical mockers in feasts, they gnashed upon me with their teeth.

Ps 37:12 — The wicked plotteth against the just, and gnasheth upon him with his teeth.

Ps 112:10 — The wicked shall see *it*, and be grieved; he shall gnash with his teeth, and melt away: the desire of the wicked shall perish.

La 2:16 — All thine enemies have opened their mouth against thee: they hiss and gnash the teeth: they say, We have swallowed *her* up: certainly this *is* the day that we looked for; we have found, we have seen *it*.

Mt 8:12 — But the children of the kingdom shall be cast out into outer darkness: there shall be weeping and gnashing of teeth.

Mt 13:42 — And shall cast them into a furnace of fire: there shall be wailing and gnashing of teeth.

Mt 22:13 — Then said the king to the servants, Bind him hand and foot, and take him away, and cast *him* into outer darkness; there shall be weeping and gnashing of teeth.

Mt 24:51 — And shall cut him asunder, and appoint *him* his portion with the hypocrites: there shall be weeping and gnashing of teeth.

Mt 25:30 — And cast ye the unprofitable servant into outer darkness: there shall be weeping and gnashing of teeth.

Lk 13:28 — There shall be weeping and gnashing of teeth, when ye shall see Abraham, and Isaac, and Jacob, and all the prophets, in the kingdom of God, and you *yourselves* thrust out.

See: Teeth

GOAD

- **An instrument of torture.**
  1Sa 13:21 — Yet they had a file for the mattocks, and for the coulters, and for the forks, and for the axes, and to sharpen the goads.
- **Six hundred men slain with, by Shamgar, a judge of Israel.**
  Jgs 3:31 — And after him was Shamgar the son of Anath, which slew of the Philistines six hundred men with an ox goad: and he also delivered Israel.
- **Figurative.**
  - **Of mental incentive.**
    Ecc 12:11 — The words of the wise *are* as goads, and as nails fastened by the masters of assemblies, *which* are given from one shepherd.

GOALS

Mt 22:36–38; Jas 4:13–17

Pr 16:9 — A man's heart deviseth his way: but the LORD directeth his steps.

1Co 10:31 — Whether therefore ye eat, or drink, or whatsoever ye do, do all to the glory of God.

GOAT

- **Designated as one of the clean animals to be eaten.**
  Le 11:1–8
  Dt 14:4 — These *are* the beasts which ye shall eat: the ox, the sheep, and the goat,
- **Used for food.**
  Ge 27:9 — Go now to the flock, and fetch me from thence two good kids of the goats; and I will make them savoury meat for thy father, such as he loveth:
  1Sa 16:20 — And Jesse took an ass *laden* with bread, and a bottle of wine, and a kid, and sent *them* by David his son unto Saul.
- **Used for the paschal feast.**
  Ex 12:5 — Your lamb shall be without blemish, a male of the first year: ye shall take *it* out from the sheep, or from the goats:
  2Ch 35:7 — And Josiah gave to the people, of the flock, lambs and kids, all for the passover offerings, for all that were present, to the number of thirty thousand, and three thousand bullocks: these *were* of the king's substance.
- **Used as a sacrifice by Abraham.**
  Ge 15:9 — And he said unto him, Take me an heifer of three years old, and a she goat of three years old, and a ram of three years old, and a turtledove, and a young pigeon.
- **Used by Gideon.**
  Jgs 6:19 — And Gideon went in, and made ready a kid, and unleavened cakes of an ephah of flour: the flesh he put in a basket, and he put the broth in a pot, and brought *it* out unto him under the oak, and presented *it*.
- **Used by Manoah.**
  Jgs 13:19 — So Manoah took a kid with a meat offering, and offered *it* upon a rock unto the LORD: and *the angel* did wonderously; and Manoah and his wife looked on.
- **Milk of, used for food.**
  Pr 27:27 — And *thou shalt have* goats' milk enough for thy food, for the food of thy household, and *for* the maintenance for thy maidens.
- **Hair of.**
  - **Used for clothing.**
    Nu 31:20 — And purify all *your* raiment, and all that is made of skins, and all work of goats' *hair*, and all things made of wood.

• **Used for pillows.**

1Sa 19:13 — And Michal took an image, and laid *it* in the bed, and put a pillow of goats' *hair* for his bolster, and covered *it* with a cloth.

• **Used for curtains of the tabernacle.**

Ex 26:7 — And thou shalt make curtains *of* goats' *hair* to be a covering upon the tabernacle: eleven curtains shalt thou make.

Ex 35:23 — And every man, with whom was found blue, and purple, and scarlet, and fine linen, and goats' *hair,* and red skins of rams, and badgers' skins, brought *them.*

Ex 36:14 — And he made curtains *of* goats' *hair* for the tent over the tabernacle: eleven curtains he made them.

• **Used for tents.**

See: Tabernacle

• **Mosaic law concerning.**

• **Kid should not be killed for food before it was eight days old.**

Le 22:27 — When a bullock, or a sheep, or a goat, is brought forth, then it shall be seven days under the dam; and from the eighth day and thenceforth it shall be accepted for an offering made by fire unto the LORD.

• **Kid should not be killed nor seethed in its mother's milk.**

Ex 23:19 — The first of the firstfruits of thy land thou shalt bring into the house of the LORD thy God. Thou shalt not seethe a kid in his mother's milk.

• **Numerous.**

Dt 32:14 — Butter of kine, and milk of sheep, with fat of lambs, and rams of the breed of Bashan, and goats, with the fat of kidneys of wheat; and thou didst drink the pure blood of the grape.

1Sa 25:2 — And *there was* a man in Maon, whose possessions *were* in Carmel; and the man *was* very great, and he had three thousand sheep, and a thousand goats: and he was shearing his sheep in Carmel.

2Ch 17:11 — Also *some* of the Philistines brought Jehoshaphat presents, and tribute silver; and the Arabians brought him flocks, seven thousand and seven hundred rams, and seven thousand and seven hundred he goats.

SS 4:1 — Behold, thou *art* fair, my love; behold, thou *art* fair; thou *hast* doves' eyes within thy locks: thy hair *is* as a flock of goats, that appear from mount Gilead.

SS 6:5 — Turn away thine eyes from me, for they have overcome me: thy hair *is* as a flock of goats that appear from Gilead.

• **Wild, in Palestine.**

1Sa 24:2 — Then Saul took three thousand chosen men out of all Israel, and went to seek David and his men upon the rocks of the wild goats.

Ps 104:18 — The high hills *are* a refuge for the wild goats; *and* the rocks for the conies.

GOATH • A place near Jerusalem.

Jer 31:39 — And the measuring line shall yet go forth over against it upon the hill Gareb, and shall compass about to Goath.

GOB

• **Called also Gezer.**

See: Gezer

GOBLET

See: Cup

GOD

• **Appearances of, to.**

• **Adam.**

Ge 3:8–21

• **Abraham.**

Ge 18:2–33

• **Jacob, at Bethel.**

Ge 35:7 — And he built there an altar, and called the place El-beth-el: because there God appeared unto him, when he fled from the face of his brother.

Ge 35:9 — And God appeared unto Jacob again, when he came out of Padan-aram, and blessed him.

• **Moses, in the flaming bush.**

Ex 3:2 — And the angel of the LORD appeared unto him in a flame of fire out of the midst of a bush: and he looked, and, behold, the bush burned with fire, and the bush *was* not consumed.

• **Moses, at Sinai.**

Ex 19:16–24

Ex 24:10 — And they saw the God of Israel: and *there was* under his feet as it were a paved work of a sapphire stone, and as it were the body of heaven in *his* clearness.

• **Moses and Joshua.**

Dt 31:14–15

• **Israel.**

Jgs 2:1–5

• **Gideon.**

Jgs 6:11–24

• **Solomon.**

2Ch 1:7–12; 7:12–22

1Ki 3:5 — In Gibeon the LORD appeared to Solomon in a dream by night: and God said, Ask what I shall give thee.

1Ki 9:2 — That the LORD appeared to Solomon the second time, as he had appeared unto him at Gibeon.

1Ki 11:9 — And the LORD was angry with Solomon, because his heart was turned from the LORD God of Israel, which had appeared unto him twice,

• **Isaiah.**

Isa 6:1–5

• **Ezekiel.**

Eze 1:26–28

• **Name of.**

• **Proclaimed.**

Ex 6:3 — And I appeared unto Abraham, unto Isaac, and unto Jacob, by *the name of* God Almighty, but by my name JEHOVAH was I not known to them.

Ex 15:3 — The LORD *is* a man of war: the LORD *is* his name.

Ex 34:5 — And the LORD descended in the cloud, and stood with him there, and proclaimed the name of the LORD.

Ex 34:14 — For thou shalt worship no other god: for the LORD, whose name *is* Jealous, *is* a jealous God:

Ps 83:18 — That *men* may know that thou, whose name alone *is* JEHOVAH, *art* the most high over all the earth.

• **To be reverenced.**

Ex 20:7 — Thou shalt not take the name of the LORD thy God in vain; for the LORD will not hold him guiltless that taketh his name in vain.

Dt 5:11 — Thou shalt not take the name of the LORD thy God in vain: for the LORD will not hold *him* guiltless that taketh his name in vain.

Dt 28:58 — If thou wilt not observe to do all the words of this law that are written in this book, that thou mayest fear this glorious and fearful name, THE LORD THY GOD;

Ps 111:9 — He sent redemption unto his people: he hath commanded his covenant for ever: holy and reverend *is* his name.

Mic 4:5 — For all people will walk every one in the name of his god, and we will walk in the name of the LORD our God for ever and ever.

1Ti 6:1 — Let as many servants as are under the yoke count their own masters worthy of all honour, that the name of God and *his* doctrine be not blasphemed.

• **Praised.**

Ps 34:3 — O magnify the LORD with me, and let us exalt his name together.

Ps 72:17 — His name shall endure for ever: his name shall be continued as long as the sun: and *men* shall be blessed in him: all nations shall call him blessed.

• **Not to be profaned.**

Ex 20:7 — Thou shalt not take the name of the LORD thy God in vain; for the LORD will not hold him guiltless that taketh his name in vain.

Le 18:21 — And thou shalt not let any of thy seed pass through *the fire* to Molech, neither shalt thou profane the name of thy God: I *am* the LORD.

Le 19:12 — And ye shall not swear by my name falsely, neither shalt thou profane the name of thy God: I *am* the LORD.

Le 20:3 — And I will set my face against that man, and will cut him off from among his people; because he hath given of his seed unto Molech, to defile my sanctuary, and to profane my holy name.

Le 21:6 — They shall be holy unto their God, and not profane the name of their God: for the offerings of the LORD made by fire, *and* the bread of their God, they do offer: therefore they shall be holy.

Le 22:2 — Speak unto Aaron and to his sons, that they separate themselves from the holy things of the children of Israel, and that they profane not my holy name *in those things* which they hallow unto me: I *am* the LORD.

Le 22:32 — Neither shall ye profane my holy name; but I will be hallowed among the children of Israel: I *am* the LORD which hallow you,

Dt 5:11 — Thou shalt not take the name of the LORD thy God in vain: for the LORD will not hold *him* guiltless that taketh his name in vain.

Ps 139:20 — For they speak against thee wickedly, *and* thine enemies take *thy name* in vain.

Pr 30:9 — Lest I be full, and deny *thee,* and say, Who *is* the LORD? or lest I be poor, and steal, and take the name of my God *in vain.*

Isa 52:5 — Now therefore, what have I here, saith the LORD, that my people is taken away for nought? they that rule over them make them to howl, saith the LORD; and my name continually every day is blasphemed.

Ro 2:24 — For the name of God is blasphemed among the Gentiles through you, as it is written.

Rev 16:9 — And men were scorched with great heat, and blasphemed the name of God, which hath power over these plagues: and they repented not to give him glory.

• **Profaned.**

Ps 139:20 — For they speak against thee wickedly, *and* thine enemies take *thy name* in vain.

Mt 26:74 — Then began he to curse and to swear, *saying,* I know not the man. And immediately the cock crew.

See: Blasphemy

See: Perjury

• **Repentance attributed to.**

Ge 6:6–7

Ex 32:14 — And the LORD repented of the evil which he thought to do unto his people.

Jgs 2:18 — And when the LORD raised them up judges, then the LORD was with the judge, and delivered them out of the hand of their enemies all the days of the judge: for it repented the LORD because of their groanings by reason of them that oppressed them and vexed them.

1Sa 15:35 — And Samuel came no more to see Saul until the day of his death: nevertheless Samuel mourned for Saul: and the LORD repented that he had made Saul king over Israel.

2Sa 24:16 — And when the angel stretched out his hand upon Jerusalem to destroy it, the LORD repented him of the evil, and said to the angel that destroyed the people, It is enough: stay now thine hand. And the angel of the LORD was by the threshingplace of Araunah the Jebusite.

1Ch 21:15 — And God sent an angel unto Jerusalem to destroy it: and as he was destroying, the LORD beheld, and he repented him of the evil, and said to the angel that destroyed, It is enough, stay now thine hand. And the angel of the LORD stood by the threshingfloor of Ornan the Jebusite.

Ps 106:45 — And he remembered for them his covenant, and repented according to the multitude of his mercies.

Jer 26:19 — Did Hezekiah king of Judah and all Judah put him at all to death? did he not fear the LORD, and besought the LORD, and the LORD repented him of the evil which he had pronounced against them? Thus might we procure great evil against our souls.

Am 7:3 — The LORD repented for this: It shall not be, saith the LORD.

Jnh 3:10 — And God saw their works, that they turned from their evil way; and God repented of the evil, that he had said that he would do unto them; and he did *it* not.

• For other anthropomorphic scriptures.

See: Anthropomorphisms

• Rejected by.

• Israel.

1Sa 8:7–8

Isa 65:12 — Therefore will I number you to the sword, and ye shall all bow down to the slaughter: because when I called, ye did not answer; when I spake, ye did not hear; but did evil before mine eyes, and did choose *that* wherein I delighted not.

Isa 66:4 — I also will choose their delusions, and will bring their fears upon them; because when I called, none did answer; when I spake, they did not hear: but they did evil before mine eyes, and chose *that* in which I delighted not.

• Saul.

1Sa 15:26 — And Samuel said unto Saul, I will not return with thee: for thou hast rejected the word of the LORD, and the LORD hath rejected thee from being king over Israel.

See: Jesus, Rejected

• Comforter.

Job 35:10 — But none saith, Where *is* God my maker, who giveth songs in the night;

See: Afflictions; consolation in

See: Holy Spirit

• Covenant keeping.

See: Covenant

• Anger of.

See: Anger; of God

• Attributes of, look at specific attribute for references.

• Condescension of.

See: Condescension of God

• Unclassified scripture relating to.

Job 5:8–20; 9:2–35; 10:2–18; 12:7–20; 26:7–14; 33:12–30; 34:10–30; 37:1–39:29; 40:1–42:6; Ps 8:3–6; 104:1–32; 107:23–26; 119:90–91; 147:15–18; 148:3–6; Ecc 3:14–15; Isa 50:2–3; Jer 31:35–37; 33:20–21, 25–26; Na 1:3–6; Ro 1:19–20

Ps 97:6 — The heavens declare his righteousness, and all the people see his glory.

Ps 135:6 — Whatsoever the LORD pleased, *that* did he in heaven, and in earth, in the seas, and all deep places.

Isa 2:19 — And they shall go into the holes of the rocks, and into the caves of the earth, for fear of the LORD, and for the glory of his majesty, when he ariseth to shake terribly the earth.

Isa 13:13 — Therefore I will shake the heavens, and the earth shall remove out of her place, in the wrath of the LORD of hosts, and in the day of his fierce anger.

Isa 29:6 — Thou shalt be visited of the LORD of hosts with thunder, and with earthquake, and great noise, with storm and tempest, and the flame of devouring fire.

Isa 48:13 — Mine hand also hath laid the foundation of the earth, and my right hand hath spanned the heavens: *when* I call unto them, they stand up together.

Isa 64:3 — When thou didst terrible things *which* we looked not for, thou camest down, the mountains flowed down at thy presence.

Jer 5:24 — Neither say they in their heart, Let us now fear the LORD our God, that giveth rain, both the former and the latter, in his season: he reserveth unto us the appointed weeks of the harvest.

Jer 10:2 — Thus saith the LORD, Learn not the way of the heathen, and be not dismayed at the signs of heaven; for the heathen are dismayed at them.

Jer 10:13 — When he uttereth his voice, *there is* a multitude of waters in the heavens, and he causeth the vapors to ascend from the ends of the earth; he maketh lightnings with rain, and bringeth forth the wind out of his treasures.

Jer 51:16 — When he uttereth *his* voice, *there is* a multitude of waters in the heavens; and he causeth the vapors to ascend from the ends of the earth: he maketh lightnings with rain, and bringeth forth the wind out of his treasures.

Da 2:21 — And he changeth the times and the seasons: he removeth kings, and setteth up kings: he giveth wisdom unto the wise, and knowledge to them that know understanding:

Am 5:8 — *Seek him* that maketh the seven stars and Orion, and turneth the shadow of death into the morning, and maketh the day dark with night: that calleth for the waters of the sea, and poureth them out upon the face of the earth: The LORD *is* his name:

GOD, a Spirit

Nu 16:22 — And they fell upon their faces, and said, O God, the God of the spirits of all flesh, shall one man sin, and wilt thou be wroth with all the congregation?

Nu 27:16 — Let the LORD, the God of the spirits of all flesh, set a man over the congregation,

Jn 4:24 — God *is* a Spirit: and they that worship him must worship *him* in spirit and in truth.

Ac 17:29 — Forasmuch then as we are the offspring of God, we ought not to think that the Godhead is like unto gold, or silver, or stone, graven by art and man's device.

See: Holy Spirit

See: Life; spiritual

GOD, Access to

Ps 24:3–4; 145:18–19; Col 1:21–22

Dt 4:7 — For what nation *is there so* great, who *hath* God *so* nigh unto them, as the LORD our God *is* in all *things that* we call upon him *for?*

Ps 27:4 — One *thing* have I desired of the LORD, that will I seek after; that I may dwell in the house of the LORD all the days of my life, to behold the beauty of the LORD, and to enquire in his temple.

Ps 43:2 — For thou *art* the God of my strength: why dost thou cast me off? why go I mourning because of the oppression of the enemy?

Ps 65:4 — Blessed *is the man whom* thou choosest, and causest to approach *unto thee, that* he may dwell in thy courts: we shall be satisfied with the goodness of thy house, *even* of thy holy temple.

Isa 55:3 — Incline your ear, and come unto me: hear, and your soul shall live; and I will make an everlasting covenant with you, *even* the sure mercies of David.

Mt 6:6 — But thou, when thou prayest, enter into thy closet, and when thou hast shut thy door, pray to thy Father which is in secret; and thy Father which seeth in secret shall reward thee openly.

Jn 10:7 — Then said Jesus unto them again, Verily, verily, I say unto you, I am the door of the sheep.

Jn 10:9 — I am the door: by me if any man enter in, he shall be saved, and shall go in and out, and find pasture.

Jn 14:6 — Jesus saith unto him, I am the way, the truth, and the life: no man cometh unto the Father, but by me.

Ac 14:27 — And when they were come, and had gathered the church together, they rehearsed all that God had done with them, and how he had opened the door of faith unto the Gentiles.

Ro 5:2 — By whom also we have access by faith into this grace wherein we stand, and rejoice in hope of the glory of God.

Eph 2:13 — But now in Christ Jesus ye who sometimes were far off are made nigh by the blood of Christ.

Eph 2:18 — For through him we both have access by one Spirit unto the Father.

Eph 3:12 — In whom we have boldness and access with confidence by the faith of him.

Heb 4:16 — Let us therefore come boldly unto the throne of grace, that we may obtain mercy, and find grace to help in time of need.

Heb 7:19 — For the law made nothing perfect, but the bringing in of a better hope *did;* by the which we draw nigh unto God.

Heb 7:25 — Wherefore he is able also to save them to the uttermost that come unto God by him, seeing he ever liveth to make intercession for them.

Heb 10:19 — Having therefore, brethren, boldness to enter into the holiest by the blood of Jesus,

Heb 10:22 — Let us draw near with a true heart in full assurance of faith, having our hearts sprinkled from an evil conscience, and our bodies washed with pure water.

Heb 11:6 — But without faith *it is* impossible to please *him:* for he that cometh to God must believe that he is, and *that* he is a rewarder of them that diligently seek him.

Jas 4:8 — Draw nigh to God, and he will draw nigh to you. Cleanse *your* hands, *ye* sinners; and purify *your* hearts, *ye* double minded.

1Pe 1:17 — And if ye call on the Father, who without respect of persons judgeth according to every man's work, pass the time of your sojourning *here* in fear:

1Pe 3:18 — For Christ also hath once suffered for sins, the just for the unjust, that he might bring us to God, being put to death in the flesh, but quickened by the Spirit:

1Jn 4:16 — And we have known and believed the love that God hath to us. God is love; and he that dwelleth in love dwelleth in God, and God in him.

See: Penitent

See: Repentance

See: Seekers

GOD, Compassion of

See: God, Long-Suffering of

See: God, Mercy of

GOD, Creator

Ge 1:1–28, 1:31–2:25; 5:1–2; Job 9:8–9; 12:7–9; 26:7–13; 28:23–26; 38:4–38; Ps 24:1–2; 33:6–7; 74:16–17; 89:11–12; 95:4–5; 104:2–3, 5–6, 30–31; 119:90–91; 136:5–9; 146:5–6; 148:5–6; Pr 8:26–29; Jer 10:12–13; 51:15–16; Ac 17:24–26; Heb 1:1–2

Ge 9:6 — Whoso sheddeth man's blood, by man shall his blood be shed: for in the image of God made he man.

Ex 20:11 — For *in* six days the LORD made heaven and earth, the sea, and all that in them *is,* and rested the seventh day: wherefore the LORD blessed the sabbath day, and hallowed it.

1Sa 2:8 — He raiseth up the poor out of the dust, *and* lifteth up the beggar from the dunghill, to set *them* among princes, and to make them inherit the throne of glory: for the pillars of the earth *are* the LORD'S, and he hath set the world upon them.

2Ki 19:15 — And Hezekiah prayed before the LORD, and said, O LORD God of Israel, which dwellest *between* the cherubims, thou art the God, *even* thou alone, of all the kingdoms of the earth: thou hast made heaven and earth.

1Ch 16:26 — For all the gods of the people *are* idols: but the LORD made the heavens.

Ne 9:6 — Thou, *even* thou, *art* LORD alone; thou hast made heaven, the heaven of heavens, with all their host, the earth, and all *things* that *are* therein, the seas, and all that *is* therein, and thou preservest them all; and the host of heaven worshippeth thee.

Job 10:3 — *Is it* good unto thee that thou shouldest oppress, that thou shouldest despise the work of thine hands, and shine upon the counsel of the wicked?

Job 10:8 — Thine hands have made me and fashioned me together round about; yet thou dost destroy me.

Job 37:16 — Dost thou know the balancings of the clouds, the wondrous works of him which is perfect in knowledge?

Job 37:18 — Hast thou with him spread out the sky, *which is* strong, *and* as a molten looking glass?

Ps 8:3 — When I consider thy heavens, the work of thy fingers, the moon and the stars, which thou hast ordained;

Ps 19:1 — The heavens declare the glory of God; and the firmament sheweth his handywork.

Ps 19:4 — Their line is gone out through all the earth, and their words to the end of the world. In them hath he set a tabernacle for the sun,

Ps 33:9 — For he spake, and it was *done;* he commanded, and it stood fast.

Ps 65:6 — Which by his strength setteth fast the mountains; *being* girded with power:

Ps 78:69 — And he built his sanctuary like high *palaces,* like the earth which he hath established for ever.

Ps 89:47 — Remember how short my time is: wherefore hast thou made all men in vain?

Ps 90:2 — Before the mountains were brought forth, or ever thou hadst formed the earth and the world, even from everlasting to everlasting, thou *art* God.

Ps 96:5 — For all the gods of the nations *are* idols: but the LORD made the heavens.

Ps 102:25 — Of old hast thou laid the foundation of the earth: and the heavens *are* the work of thy hands.

Ps 103:22 — Bless the LORD, all his works in all places of his dominion: bless the LORD, O my soul.

Ps 104:24 — O LORD, how manifold are thy works! in wisdom hast thou made them all: the earth is full of thy riches.

Ps 121:2 — My help *cometh* from the LORD, which made heaven and earth.

Ps 124:8 — Our help *is* in the name of the LORD, who made heaven and earth.

Pr 3:19 — The LORD by wisdom hath founded the earth; by understanding hath he established the heavens.

Pr 16:4 — The LORD hath made all *things* for himself: yea, even the wicked for the day of evil.

Pr 22:2 — The rich and poor meet together: the LORD *is* the maker of them all.

Pr 26:10 — The great *God* that formed all *things* both rewardeth the fool, and rewardeth transgressors.

Pr 30:4 — Who hath ascended up into heaven, or descended? who hath gathered the wind in his fists? who hath bound the waters in a garment? who hath established all the ends of the earth? what *is* his name, and what *is* his son's name, if thou canst tell?

Ecc 3:11 — He hath made every *thing* beautiful in his time: also he hath set the world in their heart, so that no man can find out the work that God maketh from the beginning to the end.

Ecc 7:29 — Lo, this only have I found, that God hath made man upright; but they have sought out many inventions.

Ecc 11:5 — As thou knowest not what *is* the way of the spirit, *nor* how the bones *do grow* in the womb of her that is with child: even so thou knowest not the works of God who maketh all.

Isa 17:7 — At that day shall a man look to his Maker, and his eyes shall have respect to the Holy One of Israel.

Isa 37:16 — O LORD of hosts, God of Israel, that dwellest *between* the cherubims, thou *art* the God, *even* thou alone, of all the kingdoms of the earth: thou hast made heaven and earth.

Isa 40:12 — Who hath measured the waters in the hollow of his hand, and meted out heaven with the span, and comprehended the dust of the earth in a measure, and weighed the mountains in scales, and the hills in a balance?

Isa 40:26 — Lift up your eyes on high, and behold who hath created these *things,* that bringeth out their host by number: he calleth them all by names by the greatness of his might, for that *he is* strong in power; not one faileth.

Isa 40:28 — Hast thou not known? hast thou not heard, *that* the everlasting God, the LORD, the Creator of the ends of the earth, fainteth not, neither is weary? *there is* no searching of his understanding.

Isa 42:5 — Thus saith God the LORD, he that created the heavens, and stretched them out; he that spread forth the earth, and that which cometh out of it; he that giveth breath unto the people upon it, and spirit to them that walk therein:

Isa 44:24 — Thus saith the LORD, thy redeemer, and he that formed thee from the womb, I *am* the LORD that maketh all *things;* that stretcheth forth the heavens alone; that spreadeth abroad the earth by myself;

Isa 45:7 — I form the light, and create darkness: I make peace, and create evil: I the LORD do all these *things.*

Isa 45:12 — I have made the earth, and created man upon it: I, *even* my hands, have stretched out the heavens, and all their host have I commanded.

Isa 45:18 — For thus saith the LORD that created the heavens; God himself that formed the earth and made it; he hath established it, he created it not in vain, he formed it to be inhabited: I *am* the LORD; and *there is* none else.

Isa 48:13 — Mine hand also hath laid the foundation of the earth, and my right hand hath spanned the heavens: *when* I call unto them, they stand up together.

Isa 51:13 — And forgettest the LORD thy maker, that hath stretched forth the heavens, and laid the foundations of the earth; and hast feared continually every day because of the fury of the oppressor, as if he were ready to destroy? and where *is* the fury of the oppressor?

Isa 51:16 — And I have put my words in thy mouth, and I have covered thee in the shadow of mine hand, that I may plant the heavens, and lay the foundations of the earth, and say unto Zion, Thou *art* my people.

Isa 66:2 — For all those *things* hath mine hand made, and all those *things* have been, saith the LORD: but to this *man* will I look, *even* to *him that is* poor and of a contrite spirit, and trembleth at my word.

Jer 5:22 — Fear ye not me? saith the LORD: will ye not tremble at my presence, which have placed the sand *for* the bound of the sea by a perpetual decree, that it cannot pass it: and though the waves thereof toss themselves, yet can they not prevail; though they roar, yet can they not pass over it?

Jer 10:16 — The portion of Jacob *is* not like them: for he *is* the former of all *things;* and Israel *is* the rod of his inheritance: The LORD of hosts *is* his name.

Jer 27:5 — I have made the earth, the man and the beast that *are* upon the ground, by my great power and by my outstretched arm, and have given it unto whom it seemed meet unto me.

Jer 31:35 — Thus saith the LORD, which giveth the sun for a light by day, *and* the ordinances of the moon and of the stars for a light by night, which divideth the sea when the waves thereof roar; The LORD of hosts *is* his name:

Jer 32:17 — Ah Lord GOD! behold, thou hast made the heaven and the earth by thy great power and stretched out arm, *and* there is nothing too hard for thee:

Jer 33:2 — Thus saith the LORD the maker thereof, the LORD that formed it, to establish it; the LORD *is* his name;

Jer 51:19 — The portion of Jacob *is* not like them; for he *is* the former of all things: and *Israel is* the rod of his inheritance: the LORD of hosts is his name.

Am 4:13 — For, lo, he that formeth the mountains, and createth the wind, and declareth unto man what *is* his thought, that maketh the morning darkness, and treadeth upon the high places of the earth, The LORD, The God of hosts, *is* his name.

Am 5:8 — *Seek him* that maketh the seven stars and Orion, and turneth the shadow of death into the morning, and maketh the day dark with night: that calleth for the waters of the sea, and poureth them out upon the face of the earth: The LORD *is* his name:

Am 9:6 — *It is* he that buildeth his stories in the heaven, and hath founded his troop in the earth; he that calleth for the waters of the sea, and poureth them out upon the face of the earth: The LORD *is* his name.

Jnh 1:9 — And he said unto them, I *am* an Hebrew; and I fear the LORD, the God of heaven, which hath made the sea and the dry *land*.

Zec 12:1 — The burden of the word of the LORD for Israel, saith the LORD, which stretcheth forth the heavens, and layeth the foundation of the earth, and formeth the spirit of man within him.

Mk 10:6 — But from the beginning of the creation God made them male and female.

Mk 13:19 — For *in* those days shall be affliction, such as was not from the beginning of the creation which God created unto this time, neither shall be.

Ac 4:24 — And when they heard that, they lifted up their voice to God with one accord, and said, Lord, thou *art* God, which hast made heaven, and earth, and the sea, and all that in them is:

Ac 7:50 — Hath not my hand made all these things?

Ac 14:15 — And saying, Sirs, why do ye these things? We also are men of like passions with you, and preach unto you that ye should turn from these vanities unto the living God, which made heaven, and earth, and the sea, and all things that are therein:

Ro 1:20— For the invisible things of him from the creation of the world are clearly seen, being understood by the things that are made, *even* his eternal power and Godhead; so that they are without excuse:

Ro 11:36 — For of him, and through him, and to him, *are* all things: to whom *be* glory for ever. Amen.

1Co 8:6 — But to us *there is but* one God, the Father, of whom *are* all things, and we in him; and one Lord Jesus Christ, by whom *are* all things, and we by him.

1Co 11:12 — For as the woman *is* of the man, even so *is* the man also by the woman; but all things of God.

2Co 4:6 — For God, who commanded the light to shine out of darkness, hath shined in our hearts, to *give* the light of the knowledge of the glory of God in the face of Jesus Christ.

2Co 5:5 — Now he that hath wrought us for the selfsame thing *is* God, who also hath given unto us the earnest of the Spirit.

2Co 5:18 — And all things *are* of God, who hath reconciled us to himself by Jesus Christ, and hath given to us the ministry of reconciliation;

Eph 3:9 — And to make all *men* see what *is* the fellowship of the mystery, which from the beginning of the world hath been hid in God, who created all things by Jesus Christ:

1Ti 6:13 — I give thee charge in the sight of God, who quickeneth all things, and *before* Christ Jesus, who before Pontius Pilate witnessed a good confession;

Heb 2:10 — For it became him, for whom *are* all things, and by whom *are* all things, in bringing many sons unto glory, to make the captain of their salvation perfect through sufferings.

Heb 3:4 — For every house is builded by some *man;* but he that built all things *is* God.

Heb 11:3 — Through faith we understand that the worlds were framed by the word of God, so that things which are seen were not made of things which do appear.

Heb 11:10 — For he looked for a city which hath foundations, whose builder and maker *is* God.

Rev 4:11 — Thou art worthy, O Lord, to receive glory and honour and power: for thou hast created all things, and for thy pleasure they are and were created.

Rev 10:6 — And sware by him that liveth for ever and ever, who created heaven, and the things that therein are, and the earth, and the things that therein are, and the sea, and the things which are therein, that there should be time no longer:

Rev 14:7 — Saying with a loud voice, Fear God, and give glory to him; for the hour of his judgment is come: and worship him that made heaven, and earth, and the sea, and the fountains of waters.

GOD, Creator of Man

Ge 1:26–27; 5:1–2; Job 10:8–9, 11–12; Ac 17:24–26, 28–29; 1Co 12:24–25

Ge 2:7 — And the LORD God formed man *of* the dust of the ground, and breathed into his nostrils the breath of life; and man became a living soul.

Ge 9:6 — Whoso sheddeth man's blood, by man shall his blood be shed: for in the image of God made he man.

Ex 4:11 — And the LORD said unto him, Who hath made man's mouth? or who maketh the dumb, or deaf, or the seeing, or the blind? have not I the LORD?

Nu 16:22 — And they fell upon their faces, and said, O God, the God of the spirits of all flesh, shall one man sin, and wilt thou be wroth with all the congregation?

Nu 27:16 — Let the LORD, the God of the spirits of all flesh, set a man over the congregation,

Dt 4:32 — For ask now of the days that are past, which were before thee, since the day that God created man upon the earth, and *ask* from the one side of heaven unto the other, whether there hath been *any such thing* as this great thing *is,* or hath been heard like it?

Dt 32:6 — Do ye thus requite the LORD, O foolish people and unwise? *is* not he thy father *that* hath bought thee? hath he not made thee, and established thee?

Dt 32:15 — But Jeshurun waxed fat, and kicked: thou art waxen fat, thou art grown thick, thou art covered *with fatness;* then he forsook God *which* made him, and lightly esteemed the Rock of his salvation.

Dt 32:18 — Of the Rock *that* begat thee thou art unmindful, and hast forgotten God that formed thee.

Job 12:10 — In whose hand *is* the soul of every living thing, and the breath of all mankind.

Job 27:3 — All the while my breath *is* in me, and the spirit of God *is* in my nostrils;

Job 31:15 — Did not he that made me in the womb make him? and did not one fashion us in the womb?

Job 33:4 — The Spirit of God hath made me, and the breath of the Almighty hath given me life.

Job 34:19 — *How much less to him* that accepteth not the persons of princes, nor regardeth the rich more than the poor? for they all *are* the work of his hands.

Job 38:36 — Who hath put wisdom in the inward parts? or who hath given understanding to the heart?

Ps 33:15 — He fashioneth their hearts alike; he considereth all their works.

Ps 86:9 — All nations whom thou hast made shall come and worship before thee, O Lord; and shall glorify thy name.

Ps 94:9 — He that planted the ear, shall he not hear? he that formed the eye, shall he not see?

Ps 95:6 — O come, let us worship and bow down: let us kneel before the LORD our maker.

Ps 100:3 — Know ye that the LORD he *is* God: *it is* he *that* hath made us, and not we ourselves; *we are* his people, and the sheep of his pasture.

Ps 119:73 — Thy hands have made me and fashioned me: give me understanding, that I may learn thy commandments.

Ps 139:13 — For thou hast possessed my reins: thou hast covered me in my mother's womb.

Ps 149:2 — Let Israel rejoice in him that made him: let the children of Zion be joyful in their King.

Pr 16:4 — The LORD hath made all *things* for himself: yea, even the wicked for the day of evil.

Pr 20:12 — The hearing ear, and the seeing eye, the LORD hath made even both of them.

Pr 22:2 — The rich and poor meet together: the LORD *is* the maker of them all.

Ecc 11:5 — As thou knowest not what *is* the way of the spirit, *nor* how the bones *do grow* in the womb of her that is with child: even so thou knowest not the works of God who maketh all.

Ecc 12:1 — Remember now thy Creator in the days of thy youth, while the evil days come not, nor the years draw nigh, when thou shalt say, I have no pleasure in them;

Isa 42:5 — Thus saith God the LORD, he that created the heavens, and stretched them out; he that spread forth the earth, and that which cometh out of it; he that giveth breath unto the people upon it, and spirit to them that walk therein:

Isa 43:1 — But now thus saith the LORD that created thee, O Jacob, and he that formed thee, O Israel, Fear not: for I have redeemed thee, I have called *thee* by thy name; thou *art* mine.

Isa 43:7 — *Even* every one that is called by my name: for I have created him for my glory, I have formed him; yea, I have made him.

Isa 44:2 — Thus saith the LORD that made thee, and formed thee from the womb, *which* will help thee; Fear not, O Jacob, my servant; and thou, Jesurun, whom I have chosen.

Isa 44:24 — Thus saith the LORD, thy redeemer, and he that formed thee from the womb, I *am* the LORD that maketh all *things;* that stretcheth forth the heavens alone; that spreadeth abroad the earth by myself;

Isa 45:12 — I have made the earth, and created man upon it: I, *even* my hands, have stretched out the heavens, and all their host have I commanded.

Isa 45:18 — For thus saith the LORD that created the heavens; God himself that formed the earth and made it; he hath established it, he created it not in vain, he formed it to be inhabited: I *am* the LORD; and *there is* none else.

Isa 51:13 — And forgettest the LORD thy maker, that hath stretched forth the heavens, and laid the foundations of the earth; and hast feared continually every day because of the fury of the oppressor, as if he were ready to destroy? and where *is* the fury of the oppressor?

Isa 64:8 — But now, O LORD, thou *art* our father; we *are* the clay, and thou our potter; and we all *are* the work of thy hand.

Jer 27:5 — I have made the earth, the man and the beast that *are* upon the ground, by my great power and by my outstretched arm, and have given it unto whom it seemed meet unto me.

Da 5:23 — But hast lifted up thyself against the Lord of heaven; and they have brought the vessels of his house before thee, and thou, and thy lords, thy wives, and thy concubines, have drunk wine in them; and thou hast praised the gods of silver, and gold, of brass, iron, wood, and stone, which see not, nor hear, nor know: and the God in whose hand thy breath *is,* and whose *are* all thy ways, hast thou not glorified:

Zec 12:1 — The burden of the word of the LORD for Israel, saith the LORD, which stretcheth forth the heavens, and layeth the foundation of the earth, and formeth the spirit of man within him.

Mal 2:10 — Have we not all one father? hath not one God created us? why do we deal treacherously every man against his brother, by profaning the covenant of our fathers?

1Co 12:18 — But now hath God set the members every one of them in the body, as it hath pleased him.

1Co 15:38 — But God giveth it a body as it hath pleased him, and to every seed his own body.

Heb 12:9 — Furthermore we have had fathers of our flesh which corrected *us,* and we gave *them* reverence: shall we not much rather be in subjection unto the Father of spirits, and live?

1Pe 4:19 — Wherefore let them that suffer according to the will of God commit the keeping of their souls *to him* in well doing, as unto a faithful Creator.

See: Life; from God

See: Man

GOD, Eternity of

Ps 90:1–2; 102:24–27; Pr 8:23–25; 1Ti 6:15–16; Rev 4:8–10

Ge 21:33 — And *Abraham* planted a grove in Beer-sheba, and called there on the name of the LORD, the everlasting God.

Ex 3:15 — And God said moreover unto Moses, Thus shalt thou say unto the children of Israel, The LORD God of your fathers, the God of Abraham, the God of Isaac, and the God of Jacob, hath sent me unto you: this *is* my name for ever, and this *is* my memorial unto all generations.

Ex 15:18 — The LORD shall reign for ever and ever.

Dt 32:40 — For I lift up my hand to heaven, and say, I live for ever.

Dt 33:27 — The eternal God *is thy* refuge, and underneath *are* the everlasting arms: and he shall thrust out the enemy from before thee; and shall say, Destroy *them*.

1Ch 16:36 — Blessed *be* the LORD God of Israel for ever and ever. And all the people said, Amen, and praised the LORD.

1Ch 29:10 — Wherefore David blessed the LORD before all the congregation: and David said, Blessed *be* thou, LORD God of Israel our father, for ever and ever.

Ne 9:5 — Then the Levites, Jeshua, and Kadmiel, Bani, Hashabniah, Sherebiah, Hodijah, Shebaniah, *and* Pethahiah, said, Stand up *and* bless the LORD your God for ever and ever: and blessed be thy glorious name, which is exalted above all blessing and praise.

Job 36:26 — Behold, God *is* great, and we know *him* not, neither can the number of his years be searched out.

Ps 9:7 — But the LORD shall endure for ever: he hath prepared his throne for judgment.

Ps 33:11 — The counsel of the LORD standeth for ever, the thoughts of his heart to all generations.

Ps 41:13 — Blessed *be* the LORD God of Israel from everlasting, and to everlasting. Amen, and Amen.

Ps 55:19 — God shall hear, and afflict them, even he that abideth of old. Selah. Because they have no changes, therefore they fear not God.

Ps 68:33 — To him that rideth upon the heavens of heavens, *which were* of old; lo, he doth send out his voice, *and that* a mighty voice.

Ps 90:4 — For a thousand years in thy sight *are but* as yesterday when it is past, and *as* a watch in the night.

Ps 92:8 — But thou, LORD, *art most* high for evermore.

Ps 93:2 — Thy throne *is* established of old: thou *art* from everlasting.

Ps 102:12 — But thou, O LORD, shalt endure for ever; and thy remembrance unto all generations.

Ps 104:31 — The glory of the LORD shall endure for ever: the LORD shall rejoice in his works.

Ps 111:3 — His work *is* honourable and glorious: and his righteousness endureth for ever.

Ps 135:13 — Thy name, O LORD, *endureth* for ever; *and* thy memorial, O LORD, throughout all generations.

Ps 145:13 — Thy kingdom *is* an everlasting kingdom, and thy dominion *endureth* throughout all generations.

Ps 146:10 — The LORD shall reign for ever, *even* thy God, O Zion, unto all generations. Praise ye the LORD.

Isa 26:4 — Trust ye in the LORD for ever: for in the LORD JEHOVAH *is* everlasting strength:

Isa 40:28 — Hast thou not known? hast thou not heard, *that* the everlasting God, the LORD, the Creator of the ends of the earth, fainteth not, neither is weary? *there is* no searching of his understanding.

Isa 41:4 — Who hath wrought and done *it*, calling the generations from the beginning? I the LORD, the first, and with the last; I *am* he.

Isa 43:13 — Yea, before the day *was* I *am* he; and *there is* none that can deliver out of my hand: I will work, and who shall let it?

Isa 44:6 — Thus saith the LORD the King of Israel, and his redeemer the LORD of hosts; I *am* the first, and I *am* the last; and beside me *there is* no God.

Isa 46:4 — And *even* to *your* old age I *am* he; and *even* to hoar hairs will I carry *you*: I have made, and I will bear; even I will carry, and will deliver *you*.

Isa 48:12 — Hearken unto me, O Jacob and Israel, my called; I *am* he; I *am* the first, I also *am* the last.

Isa 57:15 — For thus saith the high and lofty One that inhabiteth eternity, whose name *is* Holy; I dwell in the high and holy *place*, with him also *that is* of a contrite and humble spirit, to revive the spirit of the humble, and to revive the heart of the contrite ones.

Isa 63:16 — Doubtless thou *art* our father, though Abraham be ignorant of us, and Israel acknowledge us not: thou, O LORD, *art* our father, our redeemer; thy name *is* from everlasting.

Jer 10:10 — But the LORD *is* the true God, he *is* the living God, and an everlasting king: at his wrath the earth shall tremble, and the nations shall not be able to abide his indignation.

Jer 17:12 — A glorious high throne from the beginning *is* the place of our sanctuary.

La 5:19 — Thou, O LORD, remainest for ever; thy throne from generation to generation.

Da 4:3 — How great *are* his signs! and how mighty *are* his wonders! his kingdom *is* an everlasting kingdom, and his dominion *is* from generation to generation.

Da 4:34 — And at the end of the days I Nebuchadnezzar lifted up mine eyes unto heaven, and mine understanding returned unto me, and I blessed the most High, and I praised and honoured him that liveth for ever, whose dominion *is* an everlasting dominion, and his kingdom *is* from generation to generation:

Mic 5:2 — But thou, Bethlehem Ephratah, *though* thou be little among the thousands of Judah, *yet* out of thee shall he come forth unto me *that is* to be ruler in Israel; whose goings forth *have been* from of old, from everlasting.

Hab 1:12 — *Art* thou not from everlasting, O LORD my God, mine Holy One? We shall not die. O LORD, thou hast ordained them for judgment; and, O mighty God, thou hast established them for correction.

Hab 3:6 — He stood, and measured the earth: he beheld, and drove asunder the nations; and the everlasting mountains were scattered, the perpetual hills did bow: his ways *are* everlasting.

Ro 1:20 — For the invisible things of him from the creation of the world are clearly seen, being understood by the things that are made, *even* his eternal power and Godhead; so that they are without excuse:

Ro 16:26 — But now is made manifest, and by the scriptures of the prophets, according to the commandment of the everlasting God, made known to all nations for the obedience of faith:

Eph 3:21 — Unto him *be* glory in the church by Christ Jesus throughout all ages, world without end. Amen.

1Ti 1:17 — Now unto the King eternal, immortal, invisible, the only wise God, *be* honour and glory for ever and ever. Amen.

Heb 1:8 — But unto the Son *he saith,* Thy throne, O God, *is* for ever and ever: a sceptre of righteousness *is* the sceptre of thy kingdom.

Heb 9:14 — How much more shall the blood of Christ, who through the eternal Spirit offered himself without spot to God, purge your conscience from dead works to serve the living God?

2Pe 3:8 — But, beloved, be not ignorant of this one thing, that one day *is* with the Lord as a thousand years, and a thousand years as one day.

1Jn 2:13 — I write unto you, fathers, because ye have known him *that is* from the beginning. I write unto you, young men, because ye have overcome the wicked one. I write unto you, little children, because ye have known the Father.

Rev 1:4 — John to the seven churches which are in Asia: Grace *be* unto you, and peace, from him which is, and which was, and which is to come; and from the seven Spirits which are before his throne;

Rev 1:6 — And hath made us kings and priests unto God and his Father; to him *be* glory and dominion for ever and ever. Amen.

Rev 5:14 — And the four beasts said, Amen. And the four *and* twenty elders fell down and worshipped him that liveth for ever and ever.

Rev 10:6 — And sware by him that liveth for ever and ever, who created heaven, and the things that therein are, and the earth, and the things that therein are, and the sea, and the things which are therein, that there should be time no longer:

Rev 11:17 — Saying, We give thee thanks, O Lord God Almighty, which art, and wast, and art to come; because thou hast taken to thee thy great power, and hast reigned.

Rev 15:7 — And one of the four beasts gave unto the seven angels seven golden vials full of the wrath of God, who liveth for ever and ever.

Rev 16:5 — And I heard the angel of the waters say, Thou art righteous, O Lord, which art, and wast, and shalt be, because thou hast judged thus.

➜See: God, Self-Existent

GOD, Faithfulness of

Ge 9:15–16; Ex 6:4–5; Le 26:44–45; Dt 7:8–9; 2Sa 7:14–15; 1Ki 8:23–24; 2Ch 6:4–15; Ne 9:7–8; Ps 89:1–2, 33–34; 92:1–2, 14–15; 111:7–9; 119:89–90; 121:3–4; Isa 54:9–10; Jer 31:36–37; 33:20–21, 25–26; Hos 2:19–20; Mt 24:34–35; Lk 1:54–55, 68–70, 72–73; Ac 13:32–33; Ro 3:3–4; 11:1–2; Heb 6:13–19; 10:22–23

Ge 6:18 — But with thee will I establish my covenant; and thou shalt come into the ark, thou, and thy sons, and thy wife, and thy sons' wives with thee.

Ge 21:1 — And the LORD visited Sarah as he had said, and the LORD did unto Sarah as he had spoken.

Ge 24:27 — And he said, Blessed *be* the LORD God of my master Abraham, who hath not left destitute my master of his mercy and his truth: I *being* in the way, the LORD led me to the house of my master's brethren.

Ge 28:15 — And, behold, I *am* with thee, and will keep thee in all *places* whither thou goest, and will bring thee again into this land; for I will not leave thee, until I have done *that* which I have spoken to thee of.

Ge 32:10 — I am not worthy of the least of all the mercies, and of all the truth, which thou hast shewed unto thy servant; for with my staff I passed over this Jordan; and now I am become two bands.

Ex 2:24 — And God heard their groaning, and God remembered his covenant with Abraham, with Isaac, and with Jacob.

Ex 12:41 — And it came to pass at the end of the four hundred and thirty years, even the selfsame day it came to pass, that all the hosts of the LORD went out from the land of Egypt.

Ex 34:6 — And the LORD passed by before him, and proclaimed, The LORD, The LORD God, merciful and gracious, longsuffering, and abundant in goodness and truth,

Dt 4:31 — (For the LORD thy God *is* a merciful God;) he will not forsake thee, neither destroy thee, nor forget the covenant of thy fathers which he sware unto them.

Dt 9:5 — Not for thy righteousness, or for the uprightness of thine heart, dost thou go to possess their land: but for the wickedness of these nations the LORD thy God doth drive them out from before thee, and that he may perform the word which the LORD sware unto thy fathers, Abraham, Isaac, and Jacob.

Dt 31:6 — Be strong and of a good courage, fear not, nor be afraid of them: for the LORD thy God, he *it is* that doth go with thee; he will not fail thee, nor forsake thee.

Dt 32:4 — *He is* the Rock, his work *is* perfect: for all his ways *are* judgment: a God of truth and without iniquity, just and right *is* he.

Jos 21:45 — There failed not ought of any good thing which the LORD had spoken unto the house of Israel; all came to pass.

Jos 23:14 — And, behold, this day I *am* going the way of all the earth: and ye know in all your hearts and in all your souls, that not one thing hath failed of all the good things which the LORD your God spake concerning you; all are come to pass unto you, *and* not one thing hath failed thereof.

Jgs 2:1 — And an angel of the LORD came up from Gilgal to Bochim, and said, I made you to go up out of Egypt, and have brought you unto the land which I sware unto your fathers; and I said, I will never break my covenant with you.

1Sa 12:22 — For the LORD will not forsake his people for his great name's sake: because it hath pleased the LORD to make you his people.

2Sa 7:28 — And now, O Lord GOD, thou *art* that God, and thy words be true, and thou hast promised this goodness unto thy servant:

2Sa 22:31 — *As for* God, his way *is* perfect; the word of the LORD *is* tried: he *is* a buckler to all them that trust in him.

2Sa 23:5 — Although my house *be* not so with God; yet he hath made with me an everlasting covenant, ordered in all *things,* and sure: for *this is* all my salvation, and all *my* desire, although he make *it* not to grow.

1Ki 8:15 — And he said, Blessed *be* the LORD God of Israel, which spake with his mouth unto David my father, and hath with his hand fulfilled *it,* saying,

1Ki 8:20 — And the LORD hath performed his word that he spake, and I am risen up in the room of David my father, and sit on the throne of Israel, as the LORD promised, and have built an house for the name of the LORD God of Israel.

1Ki 8:56 — Blessed *be* the LORD, that hath given rest unto his people Israel, according to all that he promised: there hath not failed one word of all his good promise, which he promised by the hand of Moses his servant.

2Ki 8:19 — Yet the LORD would not destroy Judah for David his servant's sake, as he promised him to give him alway a light, *and* to his children.

2Ki 13:23 — And the LORD was gracious unto them, and had compassion on them, and had respect unto them, because of his covenant with Abraham, Isaac, and Jacob, and would not destroy them, neither cast he them from his presence as yet.

1Ch 17:27 — Now therefore let it please thee to bless the house of thy servant, that it may be before thee for ever: for thou blessest, O LORD, and *it shall be* blessed for ever.

1Ch 28:20 — And David said to Solomon his son, Be strong and of good courage, and do *it:* fear not, nor be dismayed: for the LORD God, *even* my God, *will be* with thee; he will not fail thee, nor forsake thee, until thou hast finished all the work for the service of the house of the LORD.

2Ch 21:7 — Howbeit the LORD would not destroy the house of David, because of the covenant that he had made with David, and as he promised to give a light to him and to his sons for ever.

Ezr 9:9 — For we *were* bondmen; yet our God hath not forsaken us in our bondage, but hath extended mercy unto us in the sight of the kings of Persia, to give us a reviving, to set up the house of our God, and to repair the desolations thereof, and to give us a wall in Judah and in Jerusalem.

Ne 1:5 — And said, I beseech thee, O LORD God of heaven, the great and terrible God, that keepeth covenant and mercy for them that love him and observe his commandments:

Ne 9:32 — Now therefore, our God, the great, the mighty, and the terrible God, who keepest covenant and mercy, let not all the trouble seem little before thee, that hath come upon us, on our kings, on our princes, and on our priests, and on our prophets, and on our fathers, and on all thy people, since the time of the kings of Assyria unto this day.

Ps 9:10 — And they that know thy name will put their trust in thee: for thou, LORD, hast not forsaken them that seek thee.

Ps 18:30 — *As for* God, his way *is* perfect: the word of the LORD is tried: he *is* a buckler to all those that trust in him.

Ps 19:9 — The fear of the LORD *is* clean, enduring for ever: the judgments of the LORD *are* true *and* righteous altogether.

Ps 25:10 — All the paths of the LORD *are* mercy and truth unto such as keep his covenant and his testimonies.

Ps 31:5 — Into thine hand I commit my spirit: thou hast redeemed me, O LORD God of truth.

Ps 33:4 — For the word of the LORD *is* right; and all his works *are done* in truth.

Ps 36:5 — Thy mercy, O LORD, *is* in the heavens; *and* thy faithfulness *reacheth* unto the clouds.

Ps 37:28 — For the LORD loveth judgment, and forsaketh not his saints; they are preserved for ever: but the seed of the wicked shall be cut off.

Ps 40:10 — I have not hid thy righteousness within my heart; I have declared thy faithfulness and thy salvation: I have not concealed thy lovingkindness and thy truth from the great congregation.

Ps 89:5 — And the heavens shall praise thy wonders, O LORD: thy faithfulness also in the congregation of the saints.

Ps 89:8 — O LORD God of hosts, who *is* a strong LORD like unto thee? or to thy faithfulness round about thee?

Ps 89:14 — Justice and judgment *are* the habitation of thy throne: mercy and truth shall go before thy face.

Ps 89:24 — But my faithfulness and my mercy *shall be* with him: and in my name shall his horn be exalted.

Ps 89:28 — My mercy will I keep for him for evermore, and my covenant shall stand fast with him.

Ps 94:14 — For the LORD will not cast off his people, neither will he forsake his inheritance.

Ps 98:3 — He hath remembered his mercy and his truth toward the house of Israel: all the ends of the earth have seen the salvation of our God.

Ps 100:5 — For the LORD *is* good; his mercy *is* everlasting; and his truth *endureth* to all generations.

Ps 103:17 — But the mercy of the LORD *is* from everlasting to everlasting upon them that fear him, and his righteousness unto children's children;

Ps 105:8 — He hath remembered his covenant for ever, the word *which* he commanded to a thousand generations.

Ps 105:42 — For he remembered his holy promise, *and* Abraham his servant.

Ps 111:5 — He hath given meat unto them that fear him: he will ever be mindful of his covenant.

Ps 117:2 — For his merciful kindness is great toward us: and the truth of the LORD *endureth* for ever. Praise ye the LORD.

Ps 119:65 — Thou hast dealt well with thy servant, O LORD, according unto thy word.

Ps 132:11 — The LORD hath sworn *in* truth unto David; he will not turn from it; Of the fruit of thy body will I set upon thy throne.

Ps 138:2 — I will worship toward thy holy temple, and praise thy name for thy lovingkindness and for thy truth: for thou hast magnified thy word above all thy name.

Ps 146:6 — Which made heaven, and earth, the sea, and all that therein *is:* which keepeth truth for ever:

Isa 11:5 — And righteousness shall be the girdle of his loins, and faithfulness the girdle of his reins.

Isa 25:1 — O LORD, thou *art* my God; I will exalt thee, I will praise thy name; for thou hast done wonderful *things; thy* counsels of old *are* faithfulness *and* truth.

Isa 42:16 — And I will bring the blind by a way *that* they knew not; I will lead them in paths *that* they have not known: I will make darkness light before them, and crooked things straight. These things will I do unto them, and not forsake them.

Isa 44:21 — Remember these, O Jacob and Israel; for thou *art* my servant: I have formed thee; thou *art* my servant: O Israel, thou shalt not be forgotten of me.

Isa 49:7 — Thus saith the LORD, the Redeemer of Israel, *and* his Holy One, to him whom man despiseth, to him whom the nation abhorreth, to a servant of rulers, Kings shall see and arise, princes also shall worship, because of the LORD that is faithful, *and* the Holy One of Israel, and he shall choose thee.

Isa 49:16 — Behold, I have graven thee upon the palms of *my* hands; thy walls *are* continually before me.

Isa 51:6 — Lift up your eyes to the heavens, and look upon the earth beneath: for the heavens shall vanish away like smoke, and the earth shall wax old like a garment, and they that dwell therein shall die in like manner: but my salvation shall be for ever, and my righteousness shall not be abolished.

Isa 51:8 — For the moth shall eat them up like a garment, and the worm shall eat them like wool: but my righteousness shall be for ever, and my salvation from generation to generation.

Isa 65:16 — That he who blesseth himself in the earth shall bless himself in the God of truth; and he that sweareth in the earth shall swear by the God of truth; because the former troubles are forgotten, and because they are hid from mine eyes.

Jer 29:10 — For thus saith the LORD, That after seventy years be accomplished at Babylon I will visit you, and perform my good word toward you, in causing you to return to this place.

Jer 32:40 — And I will make an everlasting covenant with them, that I will not turn away from them, to do them good; but I will put my fear in their hearts, that they shall not depart from me.

Jer 33:14 — Behold, the days come, saith the LORD, that I will perform that good thing which I have promised unto the house of Israel and to the house of Judah.

Jer 51:5 — For Israel *hath* not *been* forsaken, nor Judah of his God, of the LORD of hosts; though their land was filled with sin against the Holy One of Israel.

La 3:23 — *They are* new every morning: great *is* thy faithfulness.

Eze 16:60 — Nevertheless I will remember my covenant with thee in the days of thy youth, and I will establish unto thee an everlasting covenant.

Eze 16:62 — And I will establish my covenant with thee; and thou shalt know that I *am* the LORD:

Da 9:4 — And I prayed unto the LORD my God, and made my confession, and said, O Lord, the great and dreadful God, keeping the covenant and mercy to them that love him, and to them that keep his commandments;

Mic 7:20 — Thou wilt perform the truth to Jacob, *and* the mercy to Abraham, which thou hast sworn unto our fathers from the days of old.

Hag 2:5 — *According to* the word that I covenanted with you when ye came out of Egypt, so my spirit remaineth among you: fear ye not.

Zec 9:11 — As for thee also, by the blood of thy covenant I have sent forth thy prisoners out of the pit wherein *is* no water.

Jn 8:26 — I have many things to say and to judge of you: but he that sent me is true; and I speak to the world those things which I have heard of him.

Ro 11:29 — For the gifts and calling of God *are* without repentance.

Ro 15:8 — Now I say that Jesus Christ was a minister of the circumcision for the truth of God, to confirm the promises *made* unto the fathers:

1Co 1:9 — God *is* faithful, by whom ye were called unto the fellowship of his Son Jesus Christ our Lord.

1Co 10:13 — There hath no temptation taken you but such as is common to man: but God *is* faithful, who will not suffer you to be tempted above that ye are able; but will with the temptation also make a way to escape, that ye may be able to bear *it.*

2Co 1:20 — For all the promises of God in him *are* yea, and in him Amen, unto the glory of God by us.

1Th 5:24 — Faithful *is* he that calleth you, who also will do *it.*

2Ti 2:13 — If we believe not, *yet* he abideth faithful: he cannot deny himself.

2Ti 2:19 — Nevertheless the foundation of God standeth sure, having this seal, The Lord knoweth them that are his. And, Let every one that nameth the name of Christ depart from iniquity.

Tit 1:2 — In hope of eternal life, which God, that cannot lie, promised before the world began;

Heb 6:10 — For God *is* not unrighteous to forget your work and labour of love, which ye have shewed toward his name, in that ye have ministered to the saints, and do minister.

Heb 10:37 — For yet a little while, and he that shall come will come, and will not tarry.

1Pe 4:19 — Wherefore let them that suffer according to the will of God commit the keeping of their souls *to him* in well doing, as unto a faithful Creator.

2Pe 3:9 — The Lord is not slack concerning his promise, as some men count slackness; but is longsuffering to us-ward, not willing that any should perish, but that all should come to repentance.

1Jn 1:9 — If we confess our sins, he is faithful and just to forgive us *our* sins, and to cleanse us from all unrighteousness.

Rev 6:10 — And they cried with a loud voice, saying, How long, O Lord, holy and true, dost thou not judge and avenge our blood on them that dwell on the earth?

Rev 15:3 — And they sing the song of Moses the servant of God, and the song of the Lamb, saying, Great and marvellous *are* thy works, Lord God Almighty; just and true *are* thy ways, thou King of saints.

GOD, Fatherhood of

Dt 32:5–6; Mt 6:8–9; 10:32–33; 11:25–27; Mk 11:25–26; Lk 10:21–22; Jn 5:17–23, 36–37; 6:44–46; 8:41–42; 10:29–30, 32–33, 36–38; 12:26–28; 14:6–13, 20–21, 23–24; 15:8–10, 23–24; 16:25–28; Ro 1:3–4; Gal 1:3–4; 4:4–7; Eph 1:2–3; Col 1:2–3; 2Th 1:1–2; Heb 1:5–6; 1Pe 1:2–3; 1Jn 2:22–24; 2Jn 1:3–4; Rev 1:5–6

Ex 4:22 — And thou shalt say unto Pharaoh, Thus saith the LORD, Israel *is* my son, *even* my firstborn:

Dt 14:1 — Ye *are* the children of the LORD your God: ye shall not cut yourselves, nor make any baldness between your eyes for the dead.

2Sa 7:14 — I will be his father, and he shall be my son. If he commit iniquity, I will chasten him with the rod of men, and with the stripes of the children of men:

1Ch 28:6 — And he said unto me, Solomon thy son, he shall build my house and my courts: for I have chosen him *to be* my son, and I will be his father.

1Ch 29:10 — Wherefore David blessed the LORD before all the congregation: and David said, Blessed *be* thou, LORD God of Israel our father, for ever and ever.

Ps 68:5 — A father of the fatherless, and a judge of the widows, *is* God in his holy habitation.

Ps 89:26 — He shall cry unto me, Thou *art* my father, my God, and the rock of my salvation.

Isa 1:2 — Hear, O heavens, and give ear, O earth: for the LORD hath spoken, I have nourished and brought up children, and they have rebelled against me.

Isa 8:18 — Behold, I and the children whom the LORD hath given me *are* for signs and for wonders in Israel from the LORD of hosts, which dwelleth in mount Zion.

Isa 9:6 — For unto us a child is born, unto us a son is given: and the government shall be upon his shoulder: and his name shall be called Wonderful, Counsellor, The mighty God, The everlasting Father, The Prince of Peace.

Isa 63:16 — Doubtless thou *art* our father, though Abraham be ignorant of us, and Israel acknowledge us not: thou, O LORD, *art* our father, our redeemer; thy name *is* from everlasting.

Isa 64:8 — But now, O LORD, thou *art* our father; we *are* the clay, and thou our potter; and we all *are* the work of thy hand.

Jer 3:19 — But I said, How shall I put thee among the children, and give thee a pleasant land, a goodly heritage of the hosts of nations? and I said, Thou shalt call me, My father; and shalt not turn away from me.

Hos 1:10 — Yet the number of the children of Israel shall be as the sand of the sea, which cannot be measured nor numbered; and it shall come to pass, *that* in the place where it was said unto them, Ye *are* not my people, *there* it shall be said unto them, *Ye are* the sons of the living God.

Hos 11:1 — When Israel *was* a child, then I loved him, and called my son out of Egypt.

Mt 3:17 — And lo a voice from heaven, saying, This is my beloved Son, in whom I am well pleased.

Mt 5:45 — That ye may be the children of your Father which is in heaven: for he maketh his sun to rise on the evil and on the good, and sendeth rain on the just and on the unjust.

Mt 6:4 — That thine alms may be in secret: and thy Father which seeth in secret himself shall reward thee openly.

Mt 6:6 — But thou, when thou prayest, enter into thy closet, and when thou hast shut thy door, pray to thy Father which is in secret; and thy Father which seeth in secret shall reward thee openly.

Mt 7:11 — If ye then, being evil, know how to give good gifts unto your children, how much more shall your Father which is in heaven give good things to them that ask him?

Mt 10:20 — For it is not ye that speak, but the Spirit of your Father which speaketh in you.

Mt 10:29 — Are not two sparrows sold for a farthing? and one of them shall not fall on the ground without your Father.

Mt 11:2 — Now when John had heard in the prison the works of Christ, he sent two of his disciples,

Mt 12:50 — For whosoever shall do the will of my Father which is in heaven, the same is my brother, and sister, and mother.

Mt 13:43 — Then shall the righteous shine forth as the sun in the kingdom of their Father. Who hath ears to hear, let him hear.

Mt 15:13 — But he answered and said, Every plant, which my heavenly Father hath not planted, shall be rooted up.

Mt 16:17 — And Jesus answered and said unto him, Blessed art thou, Simon Barjona: for flesh and blood hath not revealed *it* unto thee, but my Father which is in heaven.

Mt 16:27 — For the Son of man shall come in the glory of his Father with his angels; and then he shall reward every man according to his works.

Mt 18:10 — Take heed that ye despise not one of these little ones; for I say unto you, That in heaven their angels do always behold the face of my Father which is in heaven.

Mt 18:14 — Even so it is not the will of your Father which is in heaven, that one of these little ones should perish.

Mt 18:19 — Again I say unto you, That if two of you shall agree on earth as touching any thing that they shall ask, it shall be done for them of my Father which is in heaven.

Mt 20:23 — And he saith unto them, Ye shall drink indeed of my cup, and be baptized with the baptism that I am baptized with: but to sit on my right hand, and on my left, is not mine to give, but *it shall be given to them* for whom it is prepared of my Father.

Mt 26:29 — But I say unto you, I will not drink henceforth of this fruit of the vine, until that day when I drink it new with you in my Father's kingdom.

Mt 26:39— And he went a little farther, and fell on his face, and prayed, saying, O my Father, if it be possible, let this cup pass from me: nevertheless not as I will, but as thou *wilt.*

Mt 26:42 — He went away again the second time, and prayed, saying, O my Father, if this cup may not pass away from me, except I drink it, thy will be done.

Mk 8:38 — Whosoever therefore shall be ashamed of me and of my words in this adulterous and sinful generation; of him also shall the Son of man be ashamed, when he cometh in the glory of his Father with the holy angels.

Mk 13:32 — But of that day and *that* hour knoweth no man, no, not the angels which are in heaven, neither the Son, but the Father.

Lk 2:49 — And he said unto them, How is it that ye sought me? wist ye not that I must be about my Father's business?

Lk 11:13 — If ye then, being evil, know how to give good gifts unto your children: how much more shall *your* heavenly Father give the Holy Spirit to them that ask him?

Lk 22:29 — And I appoint unto you a kingdom, as my Father hath appointed unto me;

Lk 23:46 — And when Jesus had cried with a loud voice, he said, Father, into thy hands I commend my spirit: and having said thus, he gave up the ghost.

Lk 24:49 — And, behold, I send the promise of my Father upon you: but tarry ye in the city of Jerusalem, until ye be endued with power from on high.

Jn 1:14 — And the Word was made flesh, and dwelt among us, (and we beheld his glory, the glory as of the only begotten of the Father,) full of grace and truth.

Jn 1:18 — No man hath seen God at any time; the only begotten Son, which is in the bosom of the Father, he hath declared *him.*

Jn 2:16 — And said unto them that sold doves, Take these things hence; make not my Father's house an house of merchandise.

Jn 4:21 — Jesus saith unto her, Woman, believe me, the hour cometh, when ye shall neither in this mountain, nor yet at Jerusalem, worship the Father.

Jn 4:23 — But the hour cometh, and now is, when the true worshippers shall worship the Father in spirit and in truth: for the Father seeketh such to worship him.

Jn 5:43 — I am come in my Father's name, and ye receive me not: if another shall come in his own name, him ye will receive.

Jn 6:27 — Labour not for the meat which perisheth, but for that meat which endureth unto everlasting life, which the Son of man shall give unto you: for him hath God the Father sealed.

Jn 6:32 — Then Jesus said unto them, Verily, verily, I say unto you, Moses gave you not that bread from heaven; but my Father giveth you the true bread from heaven.

Jn 8:19 — Then said they unto him, Where is thy Father? Jesus answered, Ye neither know me, nor my Father: if ye had known me, ye should have known my Father also.

Jn 8:27 — They understood not that he spake to them of the Father.

Jn 8:38 — I speak that which I have seen with my Father: and ye do that which ye have seen with your father.

Jn 8:49 — Jesus answered, I have not a devil; but I honour my Father, and ye do dishonour me.

Jn 10:15 — As the Father knoweth me, even so know I the Father: and I lay down my life for the sheep.

Jn 12:50 — And I know that his commandment is life everlasting: whatsoever I speak therefore, even as the Father said unto me, so I speak.

Jn 13:3 — Jesus knowing that the Father had given all things into his hands, and that he was come from God, and went to God;

Jn 14:2 — In my Father's house are many mansions: if *it were* not so, I would have told you. I go to prepare a place for you.

Jn 14:16 — And I will pray the Father, and he shall give you another Comforter, that he may abide with you for ever;

Jn 14:26 — But the Comforter, *which is* the Holy Ghost, whom the Father will send in my name, he shall teach you all things, and bring all things to your remembrance, whatsoever I have said unto you.

Jn 14:31 — But that the world may know that I love the Father; and as the Father gave me commandment, even so I do. Arise, let us go hence.

Jn 15:16 — Ye have not chosen me, but I have chosen you, and ordained you, that ye should go and bring forth fruit, and *that* your fruit should remain: that whatsoever ye shall ask of the Father in my name, he may give it you.

Jn 15:26 — But when the Comforter is come, whom I will send unto you from the Father, *even* the Spirit of truth, which proceedeth from the Father, he shall testify of me:

Jn 16:3 — And these things will they do unto you, because they have not known the Father, nor me.

Jn 16:10 — Of righteousness, because I go to my Father, and ye see me no more;

Jn 16:15 — All things that the Father hath are mine: therefore said I, that he shall take of mine, and shall shew *it* unto you.

Jn 16:23 — And in that day ye shall ask me nothing. Verily, verily, I say unto you, Whatsoever ye shall ask the Father in my name, he will give *it* you.

Jn 17:1 — These words spake Jesus, and lifted up his eyes to heaven, and said, Father, the hour is come; glorify thy Son, that thy Son also may glorify thee:

Jn 17:5 — And now, O Father, glorify thou me with thine own self with the glory which I had with thee before the world was.

Jn 17:11 — And now I am no more in the world, but these are in the world, and I come to thee. Holy Father, keep through thine own name those whom thou hast given me, that they may be one, as we *are.*

Jn 17:21 — That they all may be one; as thou, Father, *art* in me, and I in thee, that they also may be one in us: that the world may believe that thou hast sent me.

Jn 17:24 — Father, I will that they also, whom thou hast given me, be with me where I am; that they may behold my glory, which thou hast given me: for thou lovedst me before the foundation of the world.

Jn 20:17 — Jesus saith unto her, Touch me not; for I am not yet ascended to my Father: but go to my brethren, and say unto them, I ascend unto my Father, and your Father; and *to* my God, and your God.

Jn 20:21 — Then said Jesus to them again, Peace *be* unto you: as *my* Father hath sent me, even so send I you.

Ac 1:4 — And, being assembled together with *them,* commanded them that they should not depart from Jerusalem, but wait for the promise of the Father, which, *saith he,* ye have heard of me.

Ac 2:33 — Therefore being by the right hand of God exalted, and having received of the Father the promise of the Holy Ghost, he hath shed forth this, which ye now see and hear.

Ro 1:7 — To all that be in Rome, beloved of God, called *to be* saints: Grace to you and peace from God our Father, and the Lord Jesus Christ.

Ro 8:15 — For ye have not received the spirit of bondage again to fear; but ye have received the Spirit of adoption, whereby we cry, Abba, Father.

1Co 1:3 — Grace *be* unto you, and peace, from God our Father, and *from* the Lord Jesus Christ.

1Co 8:6 — But to us *there is but* one God, the Father, of whom *are* all things, and we in him; and one Lord Jesus Christ, by whom *are* all things, and we by him.

1Co 15:24 — Then *cometh* the end, when he shall have delivered up the kingdom to God, even the Father; when he shall have put down all rule and all authority and power.

2Co 1:3 — Blessed *be* God, even the Father of our Lord Jesus Christ, the Father of mercies, and the God of all comfort;

2Co 6:18 — And will be a Father unto you, and ye shall be my sons and daughters, saith the Lord Almighty.

Gal 1:1 — Paul, an apostle, (not of men, neither by man, but by Jesus Christ, and God the Father, who raised him from the dead;)

Eph 1:17 — That the God of our Lord Jesus Christ, the Father of glory, may give unto you the spirit of wisdom and revelation in the knowledge of him:

Eph 2:18 — For through him we both have access by one Spirit unto the Father.

Eph 3:14 — For this cause I bow my knees unto the Father of our Lord Jesus Christ,

Eph 4:6 — One God and Father of all, who *is* above all, and through all, and in you all.

Eph 5:20 — Giving thanks always for all things unto God and the Father in the name of our Lord Jesus Christ;

Eph 6:23 — Peace *be* to the brethren, and love with faith, from God the Father and the Lord Jesus Christ.

Php 1:2 — Grace *be* unto you, and peace, from God our Father, and *from* the Lord Jesus Christ.

Col 1:12 — Giving thanks unto the Father, which hath made us meet to be partakers of the inheritance of the saints in light:

Col 2:2 — That their hearts might be comforted, being knit together in love, and unto all riches of the full assurance of understanding, to the acknowledgement of the mystery of God, and of the Father, and of Christ;

Col 3:17 — And whatsoever ye do in word or deed, *do* all in the name of the Lord Jesus, giving thanks to God and the Father by him.

1Th 1:1 — Paul, and Silvanus, and Timotheus, unto the church of the Thessalonians *which is* in God the Father and *in* the Lord Jesus Christ: Grace *be* unto you, and peace, from God our Father, and the Lord Jesus Christ.

1Th 1:3 — Remembering without ceasing your work of faith, and labour of love, and patience of hope in our Lord Jesus Christ, in the sight of God and our Father;

1Th 3:11 — Now God himself and our Father, and our Lord Jesus Christ, direct our way unto you.

1Th 3:13 — To the end he may stablish your hearts unblameable in holiness before God, even our Father, at the coming of our Lord Jesus Christ with all his saints.

2Th 2:16 — Now our Lord Jesus Christ himself, and God, even our Father, which hath loved us, and hath given *us* everlasting consolation and good hope through grace,

Tit 1:4 — To Titus, *mine* own son after the common faith: Grace, mercy, *and* peace, from God the Father and the Lord Jesus Christ our Saviour.

Heb 12:9 — Furthermore we have had fathers of our flesh which corrected *us,* and we gave *them* reverence: shall we not much rather be in subjection unto the Father of spirits, and live?

Jas 1:17 — Every good gift and every perfect gift is from above, and cometh down from the Father of lights, with whom is no variableness, neither shadow of turning.

Jas 1:27 — Pure religion and undefiled before God and the Father is this, To visit the fatherless and widows in their affliction, *and* to keep himself unspotted from the world.

Jas 3:9 — Therewith bless we God, even the Father; and therewith curse we men, which are made after the similitude of God.

1Pe 1:17 — And if ye call on the Father, who without respect of persons judgeth according to every man's work, pass the time of your sojourning *here* in fear:

1Jn 1:2 — (For the life was manifested, and we have seen *it,* and bear witness, and shew unto you that eternal life, which was with the Father, and was manifested unto us;)

1Jn 2:1 — My little children, these things write I unto you, that ye sin not. And if any man sin, we have an advocate with the Father, Jesus Christ the righteous:

1Jn 2:13 — I write unto you, fathers, because ye have known him *that is* from the beginning. I write unto you, young men, because ye have overcome the wicked one. I write unto you, little children, because ye have known the Father.

1Jn 2:15 — Love not the world, neither the things *that are* in the world. If any man love the world, the love of the Father is not in him.

1Jn 3:1 — Behold, what manner of love the Father hath bestowed upon us, that we should be called the sons of God: therefore the world knoweth us not, because it knew him not.

1Jn 4:14 — And we have seen and do testify that the Father sent the Son *to be* the Saviour of the world.

2Jn 1:9 — Whosoever transgresseth, and abideth not in the doctrine of Christ, hath not God. He that abideth in the doctrine of Christ, he hath both the Father and the Son.

Jude 1:1 — Jude, the servant of Jesus Christ, and brother of James, to them that are sanctified by God the Father, and preserved in Jesus Christ, *and* called:

Rev 3:5 — He that overcometh, the same shall be clothed in white raiment; and I will not blot out his name out of the book of life, but I will confess his name before my Father, and before his angels.

Rev 14:1 — And I looked, and, lo, a Lamb stood on the mount Sion, and with him an hundred forty *and* four thousand, having his Father's name written in their foreheads.

→See: Adoption

GOD, Favor of ✦See: God, Grace of

GOD, Foreknowledge of

1Sa 23:10–12; Isa 46:9–10; 48:5–6; Da 2:28–29

Isa 42:9 — Behold, the former things are come to pass, and new things do I declare: before they spring forth I tell you of them.

Isa 44:7 — And who, as I, shall call, and shall declare it, and set it in order for me, since I appointed the ancient people? and the things that are coming, and shall come, let them shew unto them.

Isa 45:11 — Thus saith the LORD, the Holy One of Israel, and his Maker, Ask me of things to come concerning my sons, and concerning the work of my hands command ye me.

Isa 48:3 — I have declared the former things from the beginning; and they went forth out of my mouth, and I shewed them; I did *them* suddenly, and they came to pass.

Jer 1:5 — Before I formed thee in the belly I knew thee; and before thou camest forth out of the womb I sanctified thee, *and* I ordained thee a prophet unto the nations.

Mt 6:8 — Be not ye therefore like unto them: for your Father knoweth what things ye have need of, before ye ask him.

Mt 24:36 — But of that day and hour knoweth no *man*, no, not the angels of heaven, but my Father only.

Ac 15:18 — Known unto God are all his works from the beginning of the world.

Ro 8:29 — For whom he did foreknow, he also did predestinate *to be* conformed to the image of his Son, that he might be the firstborn among many brethren.

Ro 11:2 — God hath not cast away his people which he foreknew. Wot ye not what the scripture saith of Elias? how he maketh intercession to God against Israel, saying,

1Pe 1:2 — Elect according to the foreknowledge of God the Father, through sanctification of the Spirit, unto obedience and sprinkling of the blood of Jesus Christ: Grace unto you, and peace, be multiplied.

✦See: God, Knowledge of

✦See: God, Wisdom of

✦See: Predestination

GOD, Glory of

Ex 19:18–19; 20:18–19; 33:18–20, 22–23; 34:29–35; 40:34–35; Dt 4:11–12; 5:24–25; 2Sa 22:1–51; 1Ch 16:24–25; Job 9:32–33; 35:5–7; 37:4–5; Ps 18:7–15; 19:1–4; 24:8–10; 29:2–4; 72:18–19; 96:3–4, 6–7; 97:2–6; 102:21–22; 145:11–12; Isa 6:1–5; 60:1–2, 19–21; 66:1–2; Eze 1:26–28; 36:22–23; 43:4–5; Hab 3:3–6; Jn 13:31–32; 1Ti 6:15–16; Heb 12:18–21; Rev 21:10–11

Ex 3:2 — And the angel of the LORD appeared unto him in a flame of fire out of the midst of a bush: and he looked, and, behold, the bush burned with fire, and the bush *was* not consumed.

Ex 19:16 — And it came to pass on the third day in the morning, that there were thunders and lightnings, and a thick cloud upon the mount, and the voice of the trumpet exceeding loud; so that all the people that *was* in the camp trembled.

Ex 24:10 — And they saw the God of Israel: and *there was* under his feet as it were a paved work of a sapphire stone, and as it were the body of heaven in *his* clearness.

Ex 24:17 — And the sight of the glory of the LORD *was* like devouring fire on the top of the mount in the eyes of the children of Israel.

Ex 34:5 — And the LORD descended in the cloud, and stood with him there, and proclaimed the name of the LORD.

Dt 4:33 — Did *ever* people hear the voice of God speaking out of the midst of the fire, as thou hast heard, and live?

Dt 4:36 — Out of heaven he made thee to hear his voice, that he might instruct thee: and upon earth he shewed thee his great fire; and thou heardest his words out of the midst of the fire.

Dt 5:5 — (I stood between the LORD and you at that time, to shew you the word of the LORD: for ye were afraid by reason of the fire, and went not up into the mount;) saying,

Dt 7:21 — Thou shalt not be affrighted at them: for the LORD thy God *is* among you, a mighty God and terrible.

Dt 10:17 — For the LORD your God *is* God of gods, and Lord of lords, a great God, a mighty, and a terrible, which regardeth not persons, nor taketh reward:

Dt 28:58 — If thou wilt not observe to do all the words of this law that are written in this book, that thou mayest fear this glorious and fearful name, THE LORD THY GOD;

Dt 33:2 — And he said, The LORD came from Sinai, and rose up from Seir unto them; he shined forth from mount Paran, and he came with ten thousands of saints: from his right hand *went* a fiery law for them.

Dt 33:26 — *There is* none like unto the God of Jeshurun, *who* rideth upon the heaven in thy help, and in his excellency on the sky.

1Ki 19:12 — And after the earthquake a fire; *but* the LORD *was* not in the fire: and after the fire a still small voice.

Job 13:11 — Shall not his excellency make you afraid? and his dread fall upon you?

Job 22:12 — *Is* not God in the height of heaven? and behold the height of the stars, how high they are!

Job 25:3 — Is there any number of his armies? and upon whom doth not his light arise?

Job 37:22 — Fair weather cometh out of the north: with God is terrible majesty.

Ps 8:9 — O LORD our Lord, how excellent is thy name in all the earth!

Ps 46:10 — Be still, and know that I *am* God: I will be exalted among the heathen, I will be exalted in the earth.

Ps 57:5 — Be thou exalted, O God, above the heavens; *let* thy glory *be* above all the earth.

Ps 57:11 — Be thou exalted, O God, above the heavens: *let* thy glory *be* above all the earth.

Ps 68:24 — They have seen thy goings, O God; *even* the goings of my God, my King, in the sanctuary.

Ps 76:4 — Thou *art* more glorious *and* excellent than the mountains of prey.

Ps 97:9 — For thou, LORD, *art* high above all the earth: thou art exalted far above all gods.

Ps 102:16 — When the LORD shall build up Zion, he shall appear in his glory.

Ps 104:31 — The glory of the LORD shall endure for ever: the LORD shall rejoice in his works.

Ps 106:8 — Nevertheless he saved them for his name's sake, that he might make his mighty power to be known.

Ps 113:4 — The LORD *is* high above all nations, *and* his glory above the heavens.

Ps 145:5 — I will speak of the glorious honour of thy majesty, and of thy wondrous works.

Isa 1:24 — Therefore saith the Lord, the LORD of hosts, the mighty One of Israel, Ah, I will ease me of mine adversaries, and avenge me of mine enemies:

Isa 2:10 — Enter into the rock, and hide thee in the dust, for fear of the LORD, and for the glory of his majesty.

Isa 12:6 — Cry out and shout, thou inhabitant of Zion: for great *is* the Holy One of Israel in the midst of thee.

Isa 24:23 — Then the moon shall be confounded, and the sun ashamed, when the LORD of hosts shall reign in mount Zion, and in Jerusalem, and before his ancients gloriously.

Isa 26:15 — Thou hast increased the nation, O LORD, thou hast increased the nation: thou art glorified: thou hadst removed *it* far *unto* all the ends of the earth.

Isa 28:5 — In that day shall the LORD of hosts be for a crown of glory, and for a diadem of beauty, unto the residue of his people,

Isa 29:23 — But when he seeth his children, the work of mine hands, in the midst of him, they shall sanctify my name, and sanctify the Holy One of Jacob, and shall fear the God of Israel.

Isa 30:30 — And the LORD shall cause his glorious voice to be heard, and shall shew the lighting down of his arm, with the indignation of *his* anger, and *with* the flame of a devouring fire, *with* scattering, and tempest, and hailstones.

Isa 33:5 — The LORD is exalted; for he dwelleth on high: he hath filled Zion with judgment and righteousness.

Isa 33:10 — Now will I rise, saith the LORD; now will I be exalted; now will I lift up myself.

Isa 35:2 — It shall blossom abundantly, and rejoice even with joy and singing: the glory of Lebanon shall be given unto it, the excellency of Carmel and Sharon, they shall see the glory of the LORD, *and* the excellency of our God.

Isa 40:5 — And the glory of the LORD shall be revealed, and all flesh shall see *it* together: for the mouth of the LORD hath spoken *it.*

Isa 43:7 — *Even* every one that is called by my name: for I have created him for my glory, I have formed him; yea, I have made him.

Isa 43:21 — This people have I formed for myself; they shall shew forth my praise.

Isa 44:23 — Sing, O ye heavens; for the LORD hath done *it:* shout, ye lower parts of the earth: break forth into singing, ye mountains, O forest, and every tree therein: for the LORD hath redeemed Jacob, and glorified himself in Israel.

Isa 48:9 — For my name's sake will I defer mine anger, and for my praise will I refrain for thee, that I cut thee not off.

Isa 48:11 — For mine own sake, *even* for mine own sake, will I do *it:* for how should *my name* be polluted? and I will not give my glory unto another.

Isa 49:3 — And said unto me, Thou *art* my servant, O Israel, in whom I will be glorified.

Isa 49:26 — And I will feed them that oppress thee with their own flesh; and they shall be drunken with their own blood, as with sweet wine: and all flesh shall know that I the LORD *am* thy Saviour and thy Redeemer, the mighty One of Jacob.

Isa 52:10 — The LORD hath made bare his holy arm in the eyes of all the nations; and all the ends of the earth shall see the salvation of our God.

Isa 55:9 — For *as* the heavens are higher than the earth, so are my ways higher than your ways, and my thoughts than your thoughts.

Isa 57:15 — For thus saith the high and lofty One that inhabiteth eternity, whose name *is* Holy; I dwell in the high and holy *place,* with him also *that is* of a contrite and humble spirit, to revive the spirit of the humble, and to revive the heart of the contrite ones.

Isa 60:6 — The multitude of camels shall cover thee, the dromedaries of Midian and Ephah; all they from Sheba shall come: they shall bring gold and incense; and they shall shew forth the praises of the LORD.

Isa 61:3 — To appoint unto them that mourn in Zion, to give unto them beauty for ashes, the oil of joy for mourning, the garment of praise for the spirit of heaviness; that they might be called trees of righteousness, the planting of the LORD, that he might be glorified.

Isa 62:3 — Thou shalt also be a crown of glory in the hand of the LORD, and a royal diadem in the hand of thy God.

Isa 63:12 — That led *them* by the right hand of Moses with his glorious arm, dividing the water before them, to make himself an everlasting name?

Isa 63:14 — As a beast goeth down into the valley, the Spirit of the LORD caused him to rest: so didst thou lead thy people, to make thyself a glorious name.

Isa 66:18 — For I *know* their works and their thoughts: it shall come, that I will gather all nations and tongues; and they shall come, and see my glory.

Jer 13:11 — For as the girdle cleaveth to the loins of a man, so have I caused to cleave unto me the whole house of Israel and the whole house of Judah, saith the LORD; that they might be unto me for a people, and for a name, and for a praise, and for a glory: but they would not hear.

Jer 17:12 — A glorious high throne from the beginning *is* the place of our sanctuary.

Jer 33:9 — And it shall be to me a name of joy, a praise and an honour before all the nations of the earth, which shall hear all the good that I do unto them: and they shall fear and tremble for all the goodness and for all the prosperity that I procure unto it.

Eze 3:12 — Then the spirit took me up, and I heard behind me a voice of a great rushing, *saying,* Blessed *be* the glory of the LORD from his place.

Eze 3:23 — Then I arose, and went forth into the plain: and, behold, the glory of the LORD stood there, as the glory which I saw by the river of Chebar: and I fell on my face.

Eze 8:4 — And, behold, the glory of the God of Israel *was* there, according to the vision that I saw in the plain.

Eze 20:14 — But I wrought for my name's sake, that it should not be polluted before the heathen, in whose sight I brought them out.

Eze 20:44 — And ye shall know that I *am* the LORD, when I have wrought with you for my name's sake, not according to your wicked ways, nor according to your corrupt doings, O ye house of Israel, saith the Lord GOD.

Mt 6:9 — After this manner therefore pray ye: Our Father which art in heaven, Hallowed be thy name.

Mt 6:13 — And lead us not into temptation, but deliver us from evil: For thine is the kingdom, and the power, and the glory, for ever. Amen.

Lk 2:14 — Glory to God in the highest, and on earth peace, good will toward men.

Jn 8:50 — And I seek not mine own glory: there is one that seeketh and judgeth.

Jn 12:28 — Father, glorify thy name. Then came there a voice from heaven, *saying,* I have both glorified *it,* and will glorify *it* again.

Jn 14:13 — And whatsoever ye shall ask in my name, that will I do, that the Father may be glorified in the Son.

Jn 17:1 — These words spake Jesus, and lifted up his eyes to heaven, and said, Father, the hour is come; glorify thy Son, that thy Son also may glorify thee:

Jn 17:10 — And all mine are thine, and thine are mine; and I am glorified in them.

Ac 7:55 — But he, being full of the Holy Ghost, looked up stedfastly into heaven, and saw the glory of God, and Jesus standing on the right hand of God,

Ro 1:23 — And changed the glory of the uncorruptible God into an image made like to corruptible man, and to birds, and fourfooted beasts, and creeping things.

Ro 11:36 — For of him, and through him, and to him, *are* all things: to whom *be* glory for ever. Amen.

2Co 1:20 — For all the promises of God in him *are* yea, and in him Amen, unto the glory of God by us.

2Co 4:15 — For all things *are* for your sakes, that the abundant grace might through the thanksgiving of many redound to the glory of God.

Eph 1:6 — To the praise of the glory of his grace, wherein he hath made us accepted in the beloved.

Eph 1:12 — That we should be to the praise of his glory, who first trusted in Christ.

Eph 1:14 — Which is the earnest of our inheritance until the redemption of the purchased possession, unto the praise of his glory.

Eph 2:7 — That in the ages to come he might shew the exceeding riches of his grace in *his* kindness toward us through Christ Jesus.

Eph 3:21 — Unto him *be* glory in the church by Christ Jesus throughout all ages, world without end. Amen.

Php 1:11 — Being filled with the fruits of righteousness, which are by Jesus Christ, unto the glory and praise of God.

Php 2:11 — And *that* every tongue should confess that Jesus Christ *is* Lord, to the glory of God the Father.

Php 4:19 — But my God shall supply all your need according to his riches in glory by Christ Jesus.

Jude 1:25 — To the only wise God our Saviour, *be* glory and majesty, dominion and power, both now and ever. Amen.

Rev 4:11 — Thou art worthy, O Lord, to receive glory and honour and power: for thou hast created all things, and for thy pleasure they are and were created.

Rev 15:8 — And the temple was filled with smoke from the glory of God, and from his power; and no man was able to enter into the temple, till the seven plagues of the seven angels were fulfilled.

Rev 21:23 — And the city had no need of the sun, neither of the moon, to shine in it: for the glory of God did lighten it, and the Lamb *is* the light thereof.

See: Glory

See: Praise

GOD, Goodness of

Ps 8:1–9; 25:8–10; 107:8–9; 139:17–18

Ex 33:19 — And he said, I will make all my goodness pass before thee, and I will proclaim the name of the LORD before thee; and will be gracious to whom I will be gracious, and will shew mercy on whom I will shew mercy.

Ex 34:6 — And the LORD passed by before him, and proclaimed, The LORD, The LORD God, merciful and gracious, longsuffering, and abundant in goodness and truth,

Dt 30:9 — And the LORD thy God will make thee plenteous in every work of thine hand, in the fruit of thy body, and in the fruit of thy cattle, and in the fruit of thy land, for good: for the LORD will again rejoice over thee for good, as he rejoiced over thy fathers:

1Ch 16:34 — O give thanks unto the LORD; for *he is* good; for his mercy *endureth* for ever.

2Ch 5:13 — It came even to pass, as the trumpeters and singers *were* as one, to make one sound to be heard in praising and thanking the LORD; and when they lifted up *their* voice with the trumpets and cymbals and instruments of musick, and praised the LORD, *saying,* For *he is* good; for his mercy *endureth* for ever: that *then* the house was filled with a cloud, *even* the house of the LORD;

2Ch 7:3 — And when all the children of Israel saw how the fire came down, and the glory of the LORD upon the house, they bowed themselves with their faces to the ground upon the pavement, and worshipped, and praised the LORD, *saying,* For *he is* good; for his mercy *endureth* for ever.

Ps 17:7 — Shew thy marvellous lovingkindness, O thou that savest by thy right hand them which put their trust *in thee* from those that rise up *against them.*

Ps 33:5 — He loveth righteousness and judgment: the earth is full of the goodness of the LORD.

Ps 34:8 — O taste and see that the LORD *is* good: blessed *is* the man *that* trusteth in him.

Ps 36:7 — How excellent *is* thy lovingkindness, O God! therefore the children of men put their trust under the shadow of thy wings.

Ps 52:1 — Why boastest thou thyself in mischief, O mighty man? the goodness of God *endureth* continually.

Ps 52:9 — I will praise thee for ever, because thou hast done *it:* and I will wait on thy name; for *it is* good before thy saints.

Ps 68:19 — Blessed *be* the Lord, *who* daily loadeth us *with benefits, even* the God of our salvation. Selah.

Ps 69:16 — Hear me, O LORD; for thy lovingkindness *is* good: turn unto me according to the multitude of thy tender mercies.

Ps 73:1 — Truly God *is* good to Israel, *even* to such as are of a clean heart.

Ps 86:5 — For thou, Lord, *art* good, and ready to forgive; and plenteous in mercy unto all them that call upon thee.

Ps 100:5 — For the LORD *is* good; his mercy *is* everlasting; and his truth *endureth* to all generations.

Ps 106:1 — Praise ye the LORD. O give thanks unto the LORD; for *he is* good: for his mercy *endureth* for ever.

Ps 107:43 — Whoso *is* wise, and will observe these *things,* even they shall understand the lovingkindness of the LORD.

Ps 118:29 — O give thanks unto the LORD; for *he is* good: for his mercy *endureth* for ever.

Ps 119:64 — The earth, O LORD, is full of thy mercy: teach me thy statutes.

Ps 119:68 — Thou *art* good, and doest good; teach me thy statutes.

Ps 135:3 — Praise the LORD; for the LORD *is* good: sing praises unto his name; for *it is* pleasant.

Ps 136:1 — O give thanks unto the LORD; for *he is* good: for his mercy *endureth* for ever.

Ps 143:10 — Teach me to do thy will; for thou *art* my God: thy spirit *is* good; lead me into the land of uprightness.

Ps 144:3 — LORD, what *is* man, that thou takest knowledge of him! *or* the son of man, that thou makest account of him!

Ps 145:7 — They shall abundantly utter the memory of thy great goodness, and shall sing of thy righteousness.

Ps 145:9 — The LORD *is* good to all: and his tender mercies *are* over all his works.

Isa 63:7 — I will mention the lovingkindnesses of the LORD, *and* the praises of the LORD, according to all that the LORD hath bestowed on us, and the great goodness toward the house of Israel, which he hath bestowed on them according to his mercies, and according to the multitude of his lovingkindnesses.

Jer 9:24 — But let him that glorieth glory in this, that he understandeth and knoweth me, that I *am* the LORD which exercise lovingkindness, judgment, and righteousness, in the earth: for in these *things* I delight, saith the LORD.

La 3:25 — The LORD *is* good unto them that wait for him, to the soul *that* seeketh him.

Hos 3:5 — Afterward shall the children of Israel return, and seek the LORD their God, and David their king; and shall fear the LORD and his goodness in the latter days.

Na 1:7 — The LORD *is* good, a strong hold in the day of trouble; and he knoweth them that trust in him.

Mt 7:11 — If ye then, being evil, know how to give good gifts unto your children, how much more shall your Father which is in heaven give good things to them that ask him?

Mt 19:17 — And he said unto him, Why callest thou me good? *there is* none good but one, *that is,* God: but if thou wilt enter into life, keep the commandments.

Mk 10:18 — And Jesus said unto him, Why callest thou me good? *there is* none good but one, *that is,* God.

Lk 1:53 — He hath filled the hungry with good things; and the rich he hath sent empty away.

Lk 6:35 — But love ye your enemies, and do good, and lend, hoping for nothing again; and your reward shall be great, and ye shall be the children of the Highest: for he is kind unto the unthankful and *to* the evil.

Lk 18:19 — And Jesus said unto him, Why callest thou me good? none *is* good, save one, *that is,* God.

Ro 2:4 — Or despisest thou the riches of his goodness and forbearance and longsuffering; not knowing that the goodness of God leadeth thee to repentance?

Ro 11:22 — Behold therefore the goodness and severity of God: on them which fell, severity; but toward thee, goodness, if thou continue in *his* goodness: otherwise thou also shalt be cut off.

2Th 1:11 — Wherefore also we pray always for you, that our God would count you worthy of *this* calling, and fulfil all the good pleasure of *his* goodness, and the work of faith with power:

Tit 3:4 — But after that the kindness and love of God our Saviour toward man appeared,

Jas 1:5 — If any of you lack wisdom, let him ask of God, that giveth to all *men* liberally, and upbraideth not; and it shall be given him.

Jas 1:17 — Every good gift and every perfect gift is from above, and cometh down from the Father of lights, with whom is no variableness, neither shadow of turning.

1Jn 4:8 — He that loveth not knoweth not God; for God is love.

➔See: God, Grace of

➔See: God, Long-Suffering of

➔See: God, Love of

➔See: God, Mercy of

GOD, Grace of

Ge 6:8–9; Ex 33:11–12, 22–23; Le 26:11–12; Nu 23:20–21; Job 29:3–5; Ps 18:25–26; 24:4–5; 41:11–12; 115:12–13; 132:13–14; Isa 33:21–22; Joel 2:26–27; 3:16–17, 20–21; Jn 14:16–21; 1Co 3:21–23; Eph 2:13–14, 18–19; 1Jn 4:17–18; Rev 1:5–6

Ge 18:26 — And the LORD said, If I find in Sodom fifty righteous within the city, then I will spare all the place for their sakes.

Ge 18:28 — Peradventure there shall lack five of the fifty righteous: wilt thou destroy all the city for *lack of* five? And he said, If I find there forty and five, I will not destroy *it.*

Ge 18:30 — And he said *unto him,* Oh let not the Lord be angry, and I will speak: Peradventure there shall thirty be found there. And he said, I will not do *it,* if I find thirty there.

Ge 18:32 — And he said, Oh let not the Lord be angry, and I will speak yet but this once: Peradventure ten shall be found there. And he said, I will not destroy *it* for ten's sake.

Ge 32:28 — And he said, Thy name shall be called no more Jacob, but Israel: for as a prince hast thou power with God and with men, and hast prevailed.

Ge 46:4 — I will go down with thee into Egypt; and I will also surely bring thee up *again:* and Joseph shall put his hand upon thine eyes.

Ex 3:12 — And he said, Certainly I will be with thee; and this *shall be* a token unto thee, that I have sent thee: When thou hast brought forth the people out of Egypt, ye shall serve God upon this mountain.

Ex 20:21 — And the people stood afar off, and Moses drew near unto the thick darkness where God *was.*

Ex 20:24 — An altar of earth thou shalt make unto me, and shalt sacrifice thereon thy burnt offerings, and thy peace offerings, thy sheep, and thine oxen: in all places where I record my name I will come unto thee, and I will bless thee.

Ex 24:2 — And Moses alone shall come near the LORD: but they shall not come nigh; neither shall the people go up with him.

Ex 33:17 — And the LORD said unto Moses, I will do this thing also that thou hast spoken: for thou hast found grace in my sight, and I know thee by name.

Nu 5:3 — Both male and female shall ye put out, without the camp shall ye put them; that they defile not their camps, in the midst whereof I dwell.

Nu 6:27 — And they shall put my name upon the children of Israel; and I will bless them.

Nu 14:14 — And they will tell *it* to the inhabitants of this land: *for* they have heard that thou LORD *art* among this people, that thou LORD art seen face to face, and *that* thy cloud standeth over them, and *that* thou goest before them, by daytime in a pillar of a cloud, and in a pillar of fire by night.

Nu 22:12 — And God said unto Balaam, Thou shalt not go with them; thou shalt not curse the people: for they *are* blessed.

Nu 24:1 — And when Balaam saw that it pleased the LORD to bless Israel, he went not, as at other times, to seek for enchantments, but he set his face toward the wilderness.

Dt 4:7 — For what nation *is there so* great, who *hath* God *so* nigh unto them, as the LORD our God *is* in all *things that* we call upon him *for?*

Dt 31:6 — Be strong and of a good courage, fear not, nor be afraid of them: for the LORD thy God, he *it is* that doth go with thee; he will not fail thee, nor forsake thee.

Dt 31:8 — And the LORD, he *it is* that doth go before thee; he will be with thee, he will not fail thee, neither forsake thee: fear not, neither be dismayed.

Dt 33:23 — And of Naphtali he said, O Naphtali, satisfied with favour, and full with the blessing of the LORD: possess thou the west and the south.

Jos 1:5 — There shall not any man be able to stand before thee all the days of thy life: as I was with Moses, *so* I will be with thee: I will not fail thee, nor forsake thee.

Jos 1:9 — Have not I commanded thee? Be strong and of a good courage; be not afraid, neither be thou dismayed: for the LORD thy God *is* with thee whithersoever thou goest.

1Sa 2:26 — And the child Samuel grew on, and was in favour both with the LORD, and also with men.

2Sa 22:20 — He brought me forth also into a large place: he delivered me, because he delighted in me.

1Ki 6:13 — And I will dwell among the children of Israel, and will not forsake my people Israel.

2Ch 15:2 — And he went out to meet Asa, and said unto him, Hear ye me, Asa, and all Judah and Benjamin; The LORD *is* with you, while ye be with him; and if ye seek him, he will be found of you; but if ye forsake him, he will forsake you.

Job 10:12 — Thou hast granted me life and favour, and thy visitation hath preserved my spirit.

Job 22:27 — Thou shalt make thy prayer unto him, and he shall hear thee, and thou shalt pay thy vows.

Ps 3:8 — Salvation *belongeth* unto the LORD: thy blessing *is* upon thy people. Selah.

Ps 5:12 — For thou, LORD, wilt bless the righteous; with favour wilt thou compass him as *with* a shield.

Ps 11:7 — For the righteous LORD loveth righteousness; his countenance doth behold the upright.

Ps 18:19 — He brought me forth also into a large place; he delivered me, because he delighted in me.

Ps 25:14 — The secret of the LORD *is* with them that fear him; and he will shew them his covenant.

Ps 30:7 — LORD, by thy favour thou hast made my mountain to stand strong: thou didst hide thy face, *and* I was troubled.

Ps 36:9 — For with thee *is* the fountain of life: in thy light shall we see light.

Ps 37:18 — The LORD knoweth the days of the upright: and their inheritance shall be for ever.

Ps 37:23 — The steps of a *good* man are ordered by the LORD: and he delighteth in his way.

Ps 44:3 — For they got not the land in possession by their own sword, neither did their own arm save them: but thy right hand, and thine arm, and the light of thy countenance, because thou hadst a favour unto them.

Ps 46:7 — The LORD of hosts *is* with us; the God of Jacob *is* our refuge. Selah.

Ps 58:11 — So that a man shall say, Verily *there is* a reward for the righteous: verily he is a God that judgeth in the earth.

Ps 68:16 — Why leap ye, ye high hills? *this is* the hill *which* God desireth to dwell in; yea, the LORD will dwell *in it* for ever.

Ps 68:18 — Thou hast ascended on high, thou hast led captivity captive: thou hast received gifts for men; yea, *for* the rebellious also, that the LORD God might dwell *among them.*

Ps 75:10 — All the horns of the wicked also will I cut off; *but* the horns of the righteous shall be exalted.

Ps 84:11 — For the LORD God *is* a sun and shield: the LORD will give grace and glory: no good *thing* will he withhold from them that walk uprightly.

Ps 89:17 — For thou *art* the glory of their strength: and in thy favour our horn shall be exalted.
Ps 92:10 — But my horn shalt thou exalt like *the horn of* an unicorn: I shall be anointed with fresh oil.
Ps 94:19 — In the multitude of my thoughts within me thy comforts delight my soul.
Ps 102:13 — Thou shalt arise, *and* have mercy upon Zion: for the time to favour her, yea, the set time, is come.
Ps 112:9 — He hath dispersed, he hath given to the poor; his righteousness endureth for ever; his horn shall be exalted with honour.
Ps 115:15 — Ye *are* blessed of the LORD which made heaven and earth.
Ps 147:11 — The LORD taketh pleasure in them that fear him, in those that hope in his mercy.
Ps 149:4 — For the LORD taketh pleasure in his people: he will beautify the meek with salvation.
Pr 3:4 — So shalt thou find favour and good understanding in the sight of God and man.
Pr 3:23 — Then shalt thou walk in thy way safely, and thy foot shall not stumble.
Pr 3:32 — For the froward *is* abomination to the LORD: but his secret *is* with the righteous.
Pr 3:35 — The wise shall inherit glory: but shame shall be the promotion of fools.
Pr 8:35 — For whoso findeth me findeth life, and shall obtain favour of the LORD.
Pr 10:6 — Blessings *are* upon the head of the just: but violence covereth the mouth of the wicked.
Pr 10:22 — The blessing of the LORD, it maketh rich, and he addeth no sorrow with it.
Pr 10:24 — The fear of the wicked, it shall come upon him: but the desire of the righteous shall be granted.
Pr 11:20 — They that are of a froward heart *are* abomination to the LORD: but *such as are* upright in *their* way *are* his delight.
Pr 11:27 — He that diligently seeketh good procureth favour: but he that seeketh mischief, it shall come unto him.
Pr 12:2 — A good *man* obtaineth favour of the LORD: but a man of wicked devices will he condemn.
Pr 14:9 — Fools make a mock at sin: but among the righteous *there is* favour.
Pr 16:7 — When a man's ways please the LORD, he maketh even his enemies to be at peace with him.
Isa 28:5 — In that day shall the LORD of hosts be for a crown of glory, and for a diadem of beauty, unto the residue of his people,
Isa 30:26 — Moreover the light of the moon shall be as the light of the sun, and the light of the sun shall be sevenfold, as the light of seven days, in the day that the LORD bindeth up the breach of his people, and healeth the stroke of their wound.
Isa 33:17 — Thine eyes shall see the king in his beauty: they shall behold the land that is very far off.
Isa 41:10 — Fear thou not; for I *am* with thee: be not dismayed; for I *am* thy God: I will strengthen thee; yea, I will help thee; yea, I will uphold thee with the right hand of my righteousness.
Isa 43:5 — Fear not: for I *am* with thee: I will bring thy seed from the east, and gather thee from the west;
Isa 43:21 — This people have I formed for myself; they shall shew forth my praise.
Isa 54:8 — In a little wrath I hid my face from thee for a moment; but with everlasting kindness will I have mercy on thee, saith the LORD thy Redeemer.
Isa 60:10 — And the sons of strangers shall build up thy walls, and their kings shall minister unto thee: for in my wrath I smote thee, but in my favour have I had mercy on thee.
Jer 15:20 — And I will make thee unto this people a fenced brasen wall: and they shall fight against thee, but they shall not prevail against thee: for I *am* with thee to save thee and to deliver thee, saith the LORD.
La 3:24 — The LORD *is* my portion, saith my soul; therefore will I hope in him.
Eze 37:27 — My tabernacle also shall be with them: yea, I will be their God, and they shall be my people.
Eze 39:29 — Neither will I hide my face any more from them: for I have poured out my spirit upon the house of Israel, saith the Lord GOD.
Eze 48:35 — *It was* round about eighteen thousand *measures:* and the name of the city from *that* day *shall be,* The LORD *is* there.
Hos 14:4 — I will heal their backsliding, I will love them freely: for mine anger is turned away from him.
Am 3:2 — You only have I known of all the families of the earth: therefore I will punish you for all your iniquities.
Zep 3:15 — The LORD hath taken away thy judgments, he hath cast out thine enemy: the king of Israel, *even* the LORD, *is* in the midst of thee: thou shalt not see evil any more.
Zep 3:17 — The LORD thy God in the midst of thee *is* mighty; he will save, he will rejoice over thee with joy; he will rest in his love, he will joy over thee with singing.
Hag 1:13 — Then spake Haggai the LORD'S messenger in the LORD'S message unto the people, saying, I *am* with you, saith the LORD.
Zec 2:5 — For I, saith the LORD, will be unto her a wall of fire round about, and will be the glory in the midst of her.
Zec 8:3 — Thus saith the LORD; I am returned unto Zion, and will dwell in the midst of Jerusalem: and Jerusalem shall be called a city of truth; and the mountain of the LORD of hosts the holy mountain.
Zec 9:16 — And the LORD their God shall save them in that day as the flock of his people: for they *shall be as* the stones of a crown, lifted up as an ensign upon his land.
Lk 1:28 — And the angel came in unto her, and said, Hail, *thou that art* highly favoured, the Lord *is* with thee: blessed *art* thou among women.
Lk 1:30 — And the angel said unto her, Fear not, Mary: for thou hast found favour with God.
Lk 1:66 — And all they that heard *them* laid *them* up in their hearts, saying, What manner of child shall this be! And the hand of the Lord was with him.
Lk 2:52 — And Jesus increased in wisdom and stature, and in favour with God and man.
Jn 14:23 — Jesus answered and said unto him, If a man love me, he will keep my words: and my Father will love him, and we will come unto him, and make our abode with him.

Jn 15:15 — Henceforth I call you not servants; for the servant knoweth not what his lord doeth: but I have called you friends; for all things that I have heard of my Father I have made known unto you.

Ac 4:33 — And with great power gave the apostles witness of the resurrection of the Lord Jesus: and great grace was upon them all.

Ac 10:35 — But in every nation he that feareth him, and worketh righteousness, is accepted with him.

Ro 2:29 — But he *is* a Jew, which is one inwardly; and circumcision *is that* of the heart, in the spirit, *and* not in the letter; whose praise *is* not of men, but of God.

Ro 5:2 — By whom also we have access by faith into this grace wherein we stand, and rejoice in hope of the glory of God.

1Co 1:9 — God *is* faithful, by whom ye were called unto the fellowship of his Son Jesus Christ our Lord.

2Co 4:15 — For all things *are* for your sakes, that the abundant grace might through the thanksgiving of many redound to the glory of God.

2Co 10:18 — For not he that commendeth himself is approved, but whom the Lord commendeth.

Gal 4:6 — And because ye are sons, God hath sent forth the Spirit of his Son into your hearts, crying, Abba, Father.

Eph 1:6 — To the praise of the glory of his grace, wherein he hath made us accepted in the beloved.

Eph 2:16 — And that he might reconcile both unto God in one body by the cross, having slain the enmity thereby:

Eph 2:22 — In whom ye also are builded together for an habitation of God through the Spirit.

Eph 3:12 — In whom we have boldness and access with confidence by the faith of him.

Heb 4:16 — Let us therefore come boldly unto the throne of grace, that we may obtain mercy, and find grace to help in time of need.

Heb 10:19 — Having therefore, brethren, boldness to enter into the holiest by the blood of Jesus,

Heb 10:22 — Let us draw near with a true heart in full assurance of faith, having our hearts sprinkled from an evil conscience, and our bodies washed with pure water.

Heb 11:5 — By faith Enoch was translated that he should not see death; and was not found, because God had translated him: for before his translation he had this testimony, that he pleased God.

1Pe 2:9 — But ye *are* a chosen generation, a royal priesthood, an holy nation, a peculiar people; that ye should shew forth the praises of him who hath called you out of darkness into his marvellous light:

1Jn 1:3 — That which we have seen and heard declare we unto you, that ye also may have fellowship with us: and truly our fellowship *is* with the Father, and with his Son Jesus Christ.

1Jn 3:19 — And hereby we know that we are of the truth, and shall assure our hearts before him.

Rev 3:20 — Behold, I stand at the door, and knock: if any man hear my voice, and open the door, I will come in to him, and will sup with him, and he with me.

Rev 19:9 — And he saith unto me, Write, Blessed *are* they which are called unto the marriage supper of the Lamb. And he saith unto me, These are the true sayings of God.

Rev 21:3 — And I heard a great voice out of heaven saying, Behold, the tabernacle of God *is* with men, and he will dwell with them, and they shall be his people, and God himself shall be with them, *and be* their God.

✧See: Grace of God

• Instances of special grace.

• To Enoch.
Ge 5:24

• To Noah.
Ge 6:8

• To Abraham.
Ge 12:2

• To Jacob.
Ge 32:28; 46:4

• To Moses.
Ex 3:12; 33:12, 14

• To Solomon.
1Ch 22:18

GOD, Guide

Ex 33:13–15; Ne 9:19–20; Ps 23:2–3; 139:9–10; Jn 10:3–4

Ge 12:1 — Now the LORD had said unto Abram, Get thee out of thy country, and from thy kindred, and from thy father's house, unto a land that I will shew thee:

Ex 13:21 — And the LORD went before them by day in a pillar of a cloud, to lead them the way; and by night in a pillar of fire, to give them light; to go by day and night:

Ex 15:13 — Thou in thy mercy hast led forth the people *which* thou hast redeemed: thou hast guided *them* in thy strength unto thy holy habitation.

Nu 10:33 — And they departed from the mount of the LORD three days' journey: and the ark of the covenant of the LORD went before them in the three days' journey, to search out a resting place for them.

Dt 32:10 — He found him in a desert land, and in the waste howling wilderness; he led him about, he instructed him, he kept him as the apple of his eye.

Dt 32:12 — *So* the LORD alone did lead him, and *there was* no strange god with him.

2Sa 22:29 — For thou *art* my lamp, O LORD: and the LORD will lighten my darkness.

2Ch 32:22 — Thus the LORD saved Hezekiah and the inhabitants of Jerusalem from the hand of Sennacherib the king of Assyria, and from the hand of all *other,* and guided them on every side.

Ps 5:8 — Lead me, O LORD, in thy righteousness because of mine enemies; make thy way straight before my face.

Ps 25:5 — Lead me in thy truth, and teach me: for thou *art* the God of my salvation; on thee do I wait all the day.

Ps 25:9 — The meek will he guide in judgment: and the meek will he teach his way.

Ps 27:11 — Teach me thy way, O LORD, and lead me in a plain path, because of mine enemies.

Ps 31:3 — For thou *art* my rock and my fortress; therefore for thy name's sake lead me, and guide me.

Ps 32:8 — I will instruct thee and teach thee in the way which thou shalt go: I will guide thee with mine eye.

Ps 48:14 — For this God *is* our God for ever and ever: he will be our guide *even* unto death.

Ps 61:2 — From the end of the earth will I cry unto thee, when my heart is overwhelmed: lead me to the rock *that* is higher than I.

Ps 73:24 — Thou shalt guide me with thy counsel, and afterward receive me *to* glory.

Ps 78:52 — But made his own people to go forth like sheep, and guided them in the wilderness like a flock.

Ps 80:1 — Give ear, O Shepherd of Israel, thou that leadest Joseph like a flock; thou that dwellest *between* the cherubims, shine forth.

Ps 107:7 — And he led them forth by the right way, that they might go to a city of habitation.

Ps 139:24 — And see if *there be any* wicked way in me, and lead me in the way everlasting.

Pr 8:20 — I lead in the way of righteousness, in the midst of the paths of judgment:

Isa 40:11 — He shall feed his flock like a shepherd: he shall gather the lambs with his arm, and carry *them* in his bosom, *and* shall gently lead those that are with young.

Isa 42:16 — And I will bring the blind by a way *that* they knew not; I will lead them in paths *that* they have not known: I will make darkness light before them, and crooked things straight. These things will I do unto them, and not forsake them.

Isa 48:17 — Thus saith the LORD, thy Redeemer, the Holy One of Israel; I *am* the LORD thy God which teacheth thee to profit, which leadeth thee by the way *that* thou shouldest go.

Isa 55:4 — Behold, I have given him *for* a witness to the people, a leader and commander to the people.

Isa 57:18 — I have seen his ways, and will heal him: I will lead him also, and restore comforts unto him and to his mourners.

Isa 58:11 — And the LORD shall guide thee continually, and satisfy thy soul in drought, and make fat thy bones: and thou shalt be like a watered garden, and like a spring of water, whose waters fail not.

Jer 3:4 — Wilt thou not from this time cry unto me, My father, thou art the guide of my youth?

Lk 1:79 — To give light to them that sit in darkness and *in* the shadow of death, to guide our feet into the way of peace.

Jn 16:13 — Howbeit when he, the Spirit of truth, is come, he will guide you into all truth: for he shall not speak of himself; but whatsoever he shall hear, *that* shall he speak: and he will shew you things to come.

See: God, Providence of

GOD, His Preserving Care Exemplified

• To Noah and his family, at the time of the flood.

Ge 6:13–21; 7:1–8:1, 15–16

Ge 6:8 — But Noah found grace in the eyes of the LORD.

• To Abraham and Sarah, in Egypt.

Ge 12:17 — And the LORD plagued Pharaoh and his house with great plagues because of Sarai Abram's wife.

• To Abraham and Sarah, in Gerar.

Ge 20:3 — But God came to Abimelech in a dream by night, and said to him, Behold, thou *art but* a dead man, for the woman which thou hast taken; for she *is* a man's wife.

• To Lot, when Sodom was destroyed.

Ge 19:1–38

• To Hagar, when Abraham cast her out.

Ge 21:17 — And God heard the voice of the lad; and the angel of God called Hagar out of heaven, and said unto her, What aileth thee, Hagar? fear not; for God hath heard the voice of the lad where he *is*.

Ge 21:19 — And God opened her eyes, and she saw a well of water; and she went, and filled the bottle with water, and gave the lad drink.

• To Jacob, when he fled from Laban, his father-in-law.

Ge 31:24 — And God came to Laban the Syrian in a dream by night, and said unto him, Take heed that thou speak not to Jacob either good or bad.

Ge 31:29 — It is in the power of my hand to do you hurt: but the God of your father spake unto me yesternight, saying, Take thou heed that thou speak not to Jacob either good or bad.

• To Jacob, when he met Esau.

Ge 33:1–20

• To Jacob, as he journeyed in the land of Canaan.

Ge 35:5 — And they journeyed: and the terror of God was upon the cities that *were* round about them, and they did not pursue after the sons of Jacob.

• To Joseph, in Egypt.

Ge 39:2 — And the LORD was with Joseph, and he was a prosperous man; and he was in the house of his master the Egyptian.

Ge 39:21 — But the LORD was with Joseph, and shewed him mercy, and gave him favour in the sight of the keeper of the prison.

• To Moses, in his infancy.

Ex 2:1–10

• To the Israelites.

• In bringing about their deliverance from bondage.

Ex 1:9–12; 2:23–25; 3:7–9

• In exempting the land of Goshen from the plague of flies.

Ex 8:22 — And I will sever in that day the land of Goshen, in which my people dwell, that no swarms *of flies* shall be there; to the end thou mayest know that I *am* the LORD in the midst of the earth.

• In preserving their cattle from the plague of murrain.

Ex 9:4–7

• In exempting the land of Goshen from the plague of darkness.

Ex 10:21–23

• **In saving the firstborn, when the plague of death destroyed the firstborn of Egypt.**

Ex 12:13 — And the blood shall be to you for a token upon the houses where ye *are:* and when I see the blood, I will pass over you, and the plague shall not be upon you to destroy *you,* when I smite the land of Egypt.

Ex 12:23 — For the LORD will pass through to smite the Egyptians; and when he seeth the blood upon the lintel, and on the two side posts, the LORD will pass over the door, and will not suffer the destroyer to come in unto your houses to smite *you.*

• **In deliverance from Egypt.**

Ex 13:17–14:31

Ex 13:3 — And Moses said unto the people, Remember this day, in which ye came out from Egypt, out of the house of bondage; for by strength of hand the LORD brought you out from this *place:* there shall no leavened bread be eaten.

Ex 19:4 — Ye have seen what I did unto the Egyptians, and *how* I bare you on eagles' wings, and brought you unto myself.

Le 26:13 — I *am* the LORD your God, which brought you forth out of the land of Egypt, that ye should not be their bondmen; and I have broken the bands of your yoke, and made you go upright.

• **In the wilderness.**

Ex 40:36–38; Nu 9:17–23

Nu 10:33 — And they departed from the mount of the LORD three days' journey: and the ark of the covenant of the LORD went before them in the three days' journey, to search out a resting place for them.

Nu 22:12 — And God said unto Balaam, Thou shalt not go with them; thou shalt not curse the people: for they *are* blessed.

Nu 23:8 — How shall I curse, whom God hath not cursed? or how shall I defy, *whom* the LORD hath not defied?

Dt 1:31 — And in the wilderness, where thou hast seen how that the LORD thy God bare thee, as a man doth bear his son, in all the way that ye went, until ye came into this place.

Dt 23:5 — Nevertheless the LORD thy God would not hearken unto Balaam; but the LORD thy God turned the curse into a blessing unto thee, because the LORD thy God loved thee.

• **Victories under**

• **Joshua.**

Jos 6:1–11:23; 24:11–13

• **Othniel.**

Jgs 3:9–11

• **Ehud.**

Jgs 3:15–30

• **Shamgar.**

Jgs 3:31 — And after him was Shamgar the son of Anath, which slew of the Philistines six hundred men with an ox goad: and he also delivered Israel.

• **Deborah.**

Jgs 4:5 — And she dwelt under the palm tree of Deborah between Ramah and Bethel in mount Ephraim: and the children of Israel came up to her for judgment.

• **Gideon.**

Jgs 7:1–8:23

• **Jephthah.**

Jgs 11:29–40

• **David.**

1Sa 17:45–49

• **Ahab.**

1Ki 20:1–43

• **Victories on account of Samuel's intercession.**

1Sa 7:7–10

• **Delivering the kingdom of Israel from Syria.**

2Sa 7:1–29

• **Delivering Israel by Jeroboam II.**

2Ki 14:26–27

• **Delivering Israel by Abijah.**

2Ch 13:4–18

• **Delivering Israel from the oppressions of the king of Syria.**

2Ki 13:2–5

• **To the kingdom of Judah.**

• **In delivering from Egypt.**

2Ch 12:2–12

• **In delivering the Ethiopian host.**

2Ch 14:11–14

• **In giving peace with other nations.**

2Ch 17:1–19

• **In delivering them from the army of the Assyrians.**

2Ki 19:1–37

• **To David.**

2Sa 7:1–29; 1Ch 11:13–14

• **To Hezekiah.**

2Ki 19:1–37; Job 1:9–12

Job 2:6 — And the LORD said unto Satan, Behold, he *is* in thine hand; but save his life.

• **To Jeremiah and Baruch.**

Jer 36:26 — But the king commanded Jerahmeel the son of Hammelech, and Seraiah the son of Azriel, and Shelemiah the son of Abdeel, to take Baruch the scribe and Jeremiah the prophet: but the LORD hid them.

• **To Daniel and the three Hebrew captives.**

Da 2:18–23; 6:1–28

Da 3:27 — And the princes, governors, and captains, and the king's counsellors, being gathered together, saw these men, upon whose bodies the fire had no power, nor was an hair of their head singed, neither were their coats changed, nor the smell of fire had passed on them.

- **Jonah.**

Jnh 1:17 — Now the LORD had prepared a great fish to swallow up Jonah. And Jonah was in the belly of the fish three days and three nights.

- **The wise men of the east.**

Mt 2:12 — And being warned of God in a dream that they should not return to Herod, they departed into their own country another way.

- **Jesus and his parents.**

Mt 2:19–22

Mt 2:13 — And when they were departed, behold, the angel of the Lord appeareth to Joseph in a dream, saying, Arise, and take the young child and his mother, and flee into Egypt, and be thou there until I bring thee word: for Herod will seek the young child to destroy him.

- **Peter.**

Ac 12:3–17

- **Paul and Silas.**

Ac 16:26–39

- **Paul.**

Ac 28:5–6

Mk 16:18 — They shall take up serpents; and if they drink any deadly thing, it shall not hurt them; they shall lay hands on the sick, and they shall recover.

Ac 27:24 — Saying, Fear not, Paul; thou must be brought before Caesar: and, lo, God hath given thee all them that sail with thee.

See: Assurance; saints privileged to have; comfort in affliction

See: Faith

See: God

See: God, Grace of

See: God, Providence of; instances of

See: Poor; God's care of

See: Saviour

GOD, Holiness of

Job 4:17–19; Ps 33:4–5; Isa 43:14–15; Eze 36:21–22; Hab 1:12–13; 1Pe 1:15–16

Ex 3:5 — And he said, Draw not nigh hither: put off thy shoes from off thy feet, for the place whereon thou standest is holy ground.

Ex 15:11 — Who *is* like unto thee, O LORD, among the gods? who *is* like thee, glorious in holiness, fearful *in* praises, doing wonders?

Le 11:44 — For I *am* the LORD your God: ye shall therefore sanctify yourselves, and ye shall be holy; for I *am* holy: neither shall ye defile yourselves with any manner of creeping thing that creepeth upon the earth.

Le 19:2 — Speak unto all the congregation of the children of Israel, and say unto them, Ye shall be holy: for I the LORD your God *am* holy.

Le 20:26 — And ye shall be holy unto me: for I the LORD *am* holy, and have severed you from *other* people, that ye should be mine.

Le 21:8 — Thou shalt sanctify him therefore; for he offereth the bread of thy God: he shall be holy unto thee: for I the LORD, which sanctify you, *am* holy.

Dt 32:4 — *He is* the Rock, his work *is* perfect: for all his ways *are* judgment: a God of truth and without iniquity, just and right *is* he.

Jos 5:15 — And the captain of the LORD'S host said unto Joshua, Loose thy shoe from off thy foot; for the place whereon thou standest *is* holy. And Joshua did so.

Jos 24:19 — And Joshua said unto the people, Ye cannot serve the LORD: for he *is* an holy God; he *is* a jealous God; he will not forgive your transgressions nor your sins.

1Sa 2:2 — *There is* none holy as the LORD: for *there is* none beside thee: neither *is there* any rock like our God.

1Sa 6:20 — And the men of Beth-shemesh said, Who is able to stand before this holy LORD God? and to whom shall he go up from us?

1Ch 16:10 — Glory ye in his holy name: let the heart of them rejoice that seek the LORD.

Job 6:10 — Then should I yet have comfort; yea, I would harden myself in sorrow: let him not spare; for I have not concealed the words of the Holy One.

Job 15:15 — Behold, he putteth no trust in his saints; yea, the heavens are not clean in his sight.

Job 25:5 — Behold even to the moon, and it shineth not; yea, the stars are not pure in his sight.

Job 34:10 — Therefore hearken unto me, ye men of understanding: far be it from God, *that he should do* wickedness; and *from* the Almighty, *that he should commit* iniquity.

Job 36:23 — Who hath enjoined him his way? or who can say, Thou hast wrought iniquity?

Ps 11:7 — For the righteous LORD loveth righteousness; his countenance doth behold the upright.

Ps 18:30 — *As for* God, his way *is* perfect: the word of the LORD is tried: he *is* a buckler to all those that trust in him.

Ps 22:3 — But thou *art* holy, *O thou* that inhabitest the praises of Israel.

Ps 30:4 — Sing unto the LORD, O ye saints of his, and give thanks at the remembrance of his holiness.

Ps 36:6 — Thy righteousness *is* like the great mountains; thy judgments *are* a great deep: O LORD, thou preservest man and beast.

Ps 47:8 — God reigneth over the heathen: God sitteth upon the throne of his holiness.

Ps 48:1 — Great *is* the LORD, and greatly to be praised in the city of our God, *in* the mountain of his holiness.

Ps 48:10 — According to thy name, O God, so *is* thy praise unto the ends of the earth: thy right hand is full of righteousness.

Ps 60:6 — God hath spoken in his holiness; I will rejoice, I will divide Shechem, and mete out the valley of Succoth.

Ps 89:35 — Once have I sworn by my holiness that I will not lie unto David.

Ps 92:15 — To shew that the LORD *is* upright: *he is* my rock, and *there is* no unrighteousness in him.

Ps 98:1 — O sing unto the LORD a new song; for he hath done marvellous things: his right hand, and his holy arm, hath gotten him the victory.

Ps 99:3 — Let them praise thy great and terrible name; *for* it *is* holy.

Ps 99:5 — Exalt ye the LORD our God, and worship at his footstool; *for* he *is* holy.

Ps 99:9 — Exalt the LORD our God, and worship at his holy hill; for the LORD our God *is* holy.

Ps 105:3 — Glory ye in his holy name: let the heart of them rejoice that seek the LORD.

Ps 108:7 — God hath spoken in his holiness; I will rejoice, I will divide Shechem, and mete out the valley of Succoth.

Ps 111:9 — He sent redemption unto his people: he hath commanded his covenant for ever: holy and reverend *is* his name.

Ps 119:142 — Thy righteousness *is* an everlasting righteousness, and thy law *is* the truth.

Ps 145:17 — The LORD *is* righteous in all his ways, and holy in all his works.

Pr 9:10 — The fear of the LORD *is* the beginning of wisdom: and the knowledge of the holy *is* understanding.

Isa 5:16 — But the LORD of hosts shall be exalted in judgment, and God that is holy shall be sanctified in righteousness.

Isa 6:3 — And one cried unto another, and said, Holy, holy, holy, *is* the LORD of hosts: the whole earth *is* full of his glory.

Isa 12:6 — Cry out and shout, thou inhabitant of Zion: for great *is* the Holy One of Israel in the midst of thee.

Isa 29:19 — The meek also shall increase *their* joy in the LORD, and the poor among men shall rejoice in the Holy One of Israel.

Isa 29:23 — But when he seeth his children, the work of mine hands, in the midst of him, they shall sanctify my name, and sanctify the Holy One of Jacob, and shall fear the God of Israel.

Isa 41:14 — Fear not, thou worm Jacob, *and* ye men of Israel; I will help thee, saith the LORD, and thy redeemer, the Holy One of Israel.

Isa 45:19 — I have not spoken in secret, in a dark place of the earth: I said not unto the seed of Jacob, Seek ye me in vain: I the LORD speak righteousness, I declare things that are right.

Isa 47:4 — *As for* our redeemer, the LORD of hosts *is* his name, the Holy One of Israel.

Isa 49:7 — Thus saith the LORD, the Redeemer of Israel, *and* his Holy One, to him whom man despiseth, to him whom the nation abhorreth, to a servant of rulers, Kings shall see and arise, princes also shall worship, because of the LORD that is faithful, *and* the Holy One of Israel, and he shall choose thee.

Isa 52:10 — The LORD hath made bare his holy arm in the eyes of all the nations; and all the ends of the earth shall see the salvation of our God.

Isa 57:15 — For thus saith the high and lofty One that inhabiteth eternity, whose name *is* Holy; I dwell in the high and holy *place,* with him also *that is* of a contrite and humble spirit, to revive the spirit of the humble, and to revive the heart of the contrite ones.

Jer 2:5 — Thus saith the LORD, What iniquity have your fathers found in me, that they are gone far from me, and have walked after vanity, and are become vain?

La 3:38 — Out of the mouth of the most High proceedeth not evil and good?

Eze 39:7 — So will I make my holy name known in the midst of my people Israel; and I will not *let them* pollute my holy name any more: and the heathen shall know that I *am* the LORD, the Holy One in Israel.

Eze 39:25 — Therefore thus saith the Lord GOD; Now will I bring again the captivity of Jacob, and have mercy upon the whole house of Israel, and will be jealous for my holy name;

Da 4:8 — But at the last Daniel came in before me, whose name *was* Belteshazzar, according to the name of my god, and in whom is the spirit of the holy gods: and before him I told the dream, *saying,*

Hos 11:9 — I will not execute the fierceness of mine anger, I will not return to destroy Ephraim: for I *am* God, and not man; the Holy One in the midst of thee: and I will not enter into the city.

Mt 5:48 — Be ye therefore perfect, even as your Father which is in heaven is perfect.

Mt 19:17 — And he said unto him, Why callest thou me good? *there is* none good but one, *that is,* God: but if thou wilt enter into life, keep the commandments.

Mk 10:18 — And Jesus said unto him, Why callest thou me good? *there is* none good but one, *that is,* God.

Lk 1:49 — For he that is mighty hath done to me great things; and holy *is* his name.

Lk 18:19 — And Jesus said unto him, Why callest thou me good? none *is* good, save one, *that is,* God.

Jn 7:28 — Then cried Jesus in the temple as he taught, saying, Ye both know me, and ye know whence I am: and I am not come of myself, but he that sent me is true, whom ye know not.

Jn 17:11 — And now I am no more in the world, but these are in the world, and I come to thee. Holy Father, keep through thine own name those whom thou hast given me, that they may be one, as we *are.*

Ro 1:23 — And changed the glory of the uncorruptible God into an image made like to corruptible man, and to birds, and fourfooted beasts, and creeping things.

Heb 1:8 — But unto the Son *he saith,* Thy throne, O God, *is* for ever and ever: a sceptre of righteousness *is* the sceptre of thy kingdom.

Jas 1:13 — Let no man say when he is tempted, I am tempted of God: for God cannot be tempted with evil, neither tempteth he any man:

1Jn 1:5 — This then is the message which we have heard of him, and declare unto you, that God is light, and in him is no darkness at all.

1Jn 2:20 — But ye have an unction from the Holy One, and ye know all things.

Rev 4:8 — And the four beasts had each of them six wings about *him;* and *they were* full of eyes within: and they rest not day and night, saying, Holy, holy, holy, Lord God Almighty, which was, and is, and is to come.

Rev 6:10 — And they cried with a loud voice, saying, How long, O Lord, holy and true, dost thou not judge and avenge our blood on them that dwell on the earth?

Rev 15:4 — Who shall not fear thee, O Lord, and glorify thy name? for *thou* only *art* holy: for all nations shall come and worship before thee; for thy judgments are made manifest.

See: God, Perfection of

See: God, Righteousness of

See: Sin; separates from God

GOD, Human Forms and Appearance of ➛See: Anthropomorphisms

GOD, Immutable

Nu 23:19–20; Ps 119:89–91; Heb 6:17–18

1Sa 15:29 — And also the Strength of Israel will not lie nor repent: for he *is* not a man, that he should repent.

Job 23:13 — But he *is* in one *mind,* and who can turn him? and *what* his soul desireth, even *that* he doeth.

Ps 33:11 — The counsel of the LORD standeth for ever, the thoughts of his heart to all generations.

Pr 19:21 — *There are* many devices in a man's heart; nevertheless the counsel of the LORD, that shall stand.

Ecc 3:14 — I know that, whatsoever God doeth, it shall be for ever: nothing can be put to it, nor any thing taken from it: and God doeth *it,* that *men* should fear before him.

Ecc 7:13 — Consider the work of God: for who can make *that* straight, which he hath made crooked?

Isa 31:2 — Yet he also *is* wise, and will bring evil, and will not call back his words: but will arise against the house of the evildoers, and against the help of them that work iniquity.

Isa 40:28 — Hast thou not known? hast thou not heard, *that* the everlasting God, the LORD, the Creator of the ends of the earth, fainteth not, neither is weary? *there is* no searching of his understanding.

Isa 59:1 — Behold, the LORD'S hand is not shortened, that it cannot save; neither his ear heavy, that it cannot hear:

Hos 13:14 — I will ransom them from the power of the grave; I will redeem them from death: O death, I will be thy plagues; O grave, I will be thy destruction: repentance shall be hid from mine eyes.

Mal 3:6 — For I *am* the LORD, I change not; therefore ye sons of Jacob are not consumed.

Ro 11:29 — For the gifts and calling of God *are* without repentance.

Jas 1:17 — Every good gift and every perfect gift is from above, and cometh down from the Father of lights, with whom is no variableness, neither shadow of turning.

GOD, Impartial

Ac 10:34–35

Dt 10:17 — For the LORD your God *is* God of gods, and Lord of lords, a great God, a mighty, and a terrible, which regardeth not persons, nor taketh reward:

Job 36:5 — Behold, God *is* mighty, and despiseth not *any: he is* mighty in strength *and* wisdom.

Job 37:24 — Men do therefore fear him: he respecteth not any *that are* wise of heart.

Ro 2:6 — Who will render to every man according to his deeds:

Ro 2:11 — For there is no respect of persons with God.

Gal 2:6 — But of these who seemed to be somewhat, (whatsoever they were, it maketh no matter to me: God accepteth no man's person:) for they who seemed *to be somewhat* in conference added nothing to me:

Eph 6:8 — Knowing that whatsoever good thing any man doeth, the same shall he receive of the Lord, whether *he be* bond or free.

Col 3:25 — But he that doeth wrong shall receive for the wrong which he hath done: and there is no respect of persons.

1Pe 1:17 — And if ye call on the Father, who without respect of persons judgeth according to every man's work, pass the time of your sojourning *here* in fear:

GOD, Incomprehensible

Job 11:7–9; 37:1–24; Isa 40:12–31; 55:8–9

Ex 20:21 — And the people stood afar off, and Moses drew near unto the thick darkness where God *was.*

Dt 4:11 — And ye came near and stood under the mountain; and the mountain burned with fire unto the midst of heaven, with darkness, clouds, and thick darkness.

Dt 5:22 — These words the LORD spake unto all your assembly in the mount out of the midst of the fire, of the cloud, and of the thick darkness, with a great voice: and he added no more. And he wrote them in two tables of stone, and delivered them unto me.

1Ki 8:12 — Then spake Solomon, The LORD said that he would dwell in thick darkness.

Job 15:8 — Hast thou heard the secret of God? and dost thou restrain wisdom to thyself?

Ps 18:11 — He made darkness his secret place; his pavilion round about him *were* dark waters *and* thick clouds of the skies.

Ps 97:2 — Clouds and darkness *are* round about him: righteousness and judgment *are* the habitation of his throne.

Ecc 3:11 — He hath made every *thing* beautiful in his time: also he hath set the world in their heart, so that no man can find out the work that God maketh from the beginning to the end.

1Co 2:16 — For who hath known the mind of the Lord, that he may instruct him? But we have the mind of Christ.

- **Symbolized by.**
  - **The pillar of fire.**
    Ex 14:19–20
  - **The darkness of the Holy of Holies in the tabernacle.**
    1Ki 8:12 — Then spake Solomon, The LORD said that he would dwell in thick darkness.
  - **The general structure of the Most Holy Place.**
    Le 16:2 — And the LORD said unto Moses, Speak unto Aaron thy brother, that he come not at all times into the holy *place* within the vail before the mercy seat, which *is* upon the ark; that he die not: for I will appear in the cloud upon the mercy seat.

➛See: God, Unsearchable

GOD, Infinite

1Ki 8:27 — But will God indeed dwell on the earth? behold, the heaven and heaven of heavens cannot contain thee; how much less this house that I have builded?

2Ch 2:6 — But who is able to build him an house, seeing the heaven and heaven of heavens cannot contain him? who *am* I then, that I should build him an house, save only to burn sacrifice before him?

2Ch 6:1 — Then said Solomon, The LORD hath said that he would dwell in the thick darkness.

2Ch 6:18 — But will God in very deed dwell with men on the earth? behold, heaven and the heaven of heavens cannot contain thee; how much less this house which I have built!

Ps 147:5 — Great *is* our Lord, and of great power: his understanding *is* infinite.

Jer 23:24 — Can any hide himself in secret places that I shall not see him? saith the LORD. Do not I fill heaven and earth? saith the LORD.

✦See: God, Incomprehensible
✦See: God, Ubiquitous
✦See: God, Unsearchable

GOD, Invisible

Job 23:8–9; Col 1:13–15

Ex 20:21 — And the people stood afar off, and Moses drew near unto the thick darkness where God *was.*

Ex 33:20 — And he said, Thou canst not see my face: for there shall no man see me, and live.

Dt 4:11 — And ye came near and stood under the mountain; and the mountain burned with fire unto the midst of heaven, with darkness, clouds, and thick darkness.

Dt 4:15 — Take ye therefore good heed unto yourselves; for ye saw no manner of similitude on the day *that* the LORD spake unto you in Horeb out of the midst of the fire:

Dt 5:22 — These words the LORD spake unto all your assembly in the mount out of the midst of the fire, of the cloud, and of the thick darkness, with a great voice: and he added no more. And he wrote them in two tables of stone, and delivered them unto me.

1Ki 8:12 — Then spake Solomon, The LORD said that he would dwell in thick darkness.

Job 9:11 — Lo, he goeth by me, and I see *him* not: he passeth on also, but I perceive him not.

Ps 18:11 — He made darkness his secret place; his pavilion round about him *were* dark waters *and* thick clouds of the skies.

Ps 97:2 — Clouds and darkness *are* round about him: righteousness and judgment *are* the habitation of his throne.

Jn 1:18 — No man hath seen God at any time; the only begotten Son, which is in the bosom of the Father, he hath declared *him.*

Jn 5:37 — And the Father himself, which hath sent me, hath borne witness of me. Ye have neither heard his voice at any time, nor seen his shape.

Jn 6:46 — Not that any man hath seen the Father, save he which is of God, he hath seen the Father.

Ro 1:20 — For the invisible things of him from the creation of the world are clearly seen, being understood by the things that are made, *even* his eternal power and Godhead; so that they are without excuse:

1Ti 1:17 — Now unto the King eternal, immortal, invisible, the only wise God, *be* honour and glory for ever and ever. Amen.

1Ti 6:16 — Who only hath immortality, dwelling in the light which no man can approach unto; whom no man hath seen, nor can see: to whom *be* honour and power everlasting. Amen.

Heb 11:27 — By faith he forsook Egypt, not fearing the wrath of the king: for he endured, as seeing him who is invisible.

1Jn 4:12 — No man hath seen God at any time. If we love one another, God dwelleth in us, and his love is perfected in us.

✦See: God, Incomprehensible
✦See: God, Infinite
✦See: God, Unsearchable

GOD, Jealous

2Ch 16:7–10; Isa 30:1–2

Ex 20:5 — Thou shalt not bow down thyself to them, nor serve them: for I the LORD thy God *am* a jealous God, visiting the iniquity of the fathers upon the children unto the third and fourth *generation* of them that hate me;

Ex 20:7 — Thou shalt not take the name of the LORD thy God in vain; for the LORD will not hold him guiltless that taketh his name in vain.

Ex 34:14 — For thou shalt worship no other god: for the LORD, whose name *is* Jealous, *is* a jealous God:

Dt 4:24 — For the LORD thy God *is* a consuming fire, *even* a jealous God.

Dt 5:9 — Thou shalt not bow down thyself unto them, nor serve them: for I the LORD thy God *am* a jealous God, visiting the iniquity of the fathers upon the children unto the third and fourth *generation* of them that hate me,

Dt 5:11 — Thou shalt not take the name of the LORD thy God in vain: for the LORD will not hold *him* guiltless that taketh his name in vain.

Dt 6:15 — (For the LORD thy God *is* a jealous God among you) lest the anger of the LORD thy God be kindled against thee, and destroy thee from off the face of the earth.

Dt 29:20 — The LORD will not spare him, but then the anger of the LORD and his jealousy shall smoke against that man, and all the curses that are written in this book shall lie upon him, and the LORD shall blot out his name from under heaven.

Dt 32:16 — They provoked him to jealousy with strange *gods,* with abominations provoked they him to anger.

Dt 32:21 — They have moved me to jealousy with *that which is* not God; they have provoked me to anger with their vanities: and I will move them to jealousy with *those which are* not a people; I will provoke them to anger with a foolish nation.

Jos 24:19 — And Joshua said unto the people, Ye cannot serve the LORD: for he *is* an holy God; he *is* a jealous God; he will not forgive your transgressions nor your sins.

Isa 31:1 — Woe to them that go down to Egypt for help; and stay on horses, and trust in chariots, because *they are* many; and in horsemen, because they are very strong; but they look not unto the Holy One of Israel, neither seek the LORD!

Isa 31:3 — Now the Egyptians *are* men, and not God; and their horses flesh, and not spirit. When the LORD shall stretch out his hand, both he that helpeth shall fall, and he that is holpen shall fall down, and they all shall fail together.

Eze 23:25 — And I will set my jealousy against thee, and they shall deal furiously with thee: they shall take away thy nose and thine ears; and thy remnant shall fall by the sword: they shall take thy sons and thy daughters; and thy residue shall be devoured by the fire.

Eze 36:5 — Therefore thus saith the Lord GOD; Surely in the fire of my jealousy have I spoken against the residue of the heathen, and against all Idumea, which have appointed my land into their possession with the joy of all *their* heart, with despiteful minds, to cast it out for a prey.

Eze 39:25 — Therefore thus saith the Lord GOD; Now will I bring again the captivity of Jacob, and have mercy upon the whole house of Israel, and will be jealous for my holy name;

Joel 2:18 — Then will the LORD be jealous for his land, and pity his people.

Na 1:2 — God *is* jealous, and the LORD revengeth; the LORD revengeth, and *is* furious; the LORD will take vengeance on his adversaries, and he reserveth *wrath* for his enemies.

Zec 1:14 — So the angel that communed with me said unto me, Cry thou, saying, Thus saith the LORD of hosts; I am jealous for Jerusalem and for Zion with a great jealousy.

1Co 10:22 — Do we provoke the Lord to jealousy? are we stronger than he?

GOD, Judge, and His Justice

Ge 18:20–21; Jgs 9:56–57; 2Sa 22:25–27; 2Ch 6:22–23; Job 31:13–15; 34:10–12; Ps 7:8–9; 9:7–8; 11:4–5; 18:25–26; 26:1–2; 76:8–9; 94:1–2; 98:2–3; Pr 21:2–3; Isa 3:13–14; 10:17–18; Eze 18:29–30; 33:7–19; Da 7:9–10; Ro 2:5–16; 3:4–6; Eph 6:8–9; 2Th 1:4–6; Heb 10:30–31; 12:22–23; Rev 6:16–17; 16:5–7

Ge 16:5 — And Sarai said unto Abram, My wrong *be* upon thee: I have given my maid into thy bosom; and when she saw that she had conceived, I was despised in her eyes: the LORD judge between me and thee.

Ge 18:25 — That be far from thee to do after this manner, to slay the righteous with the wicked: and that the righteous should be as the wicked, that be far from thee: Shall not the Judge of all the earth do right?

Ex 20:5 — Thou shalt not bow down thyself to them, nor serve them: for I the LORD thy God *am* a jealous God, visiting the iniquity of the fathers upon the children unto the third and fourth *generation* of them that hate me;

Ex 34:7 — Keeping mercy for thousands, forgiving iniquity and transgression and sin, and that will by no means clear *the guilty;* visiting the iniquity of the fathers upon the children, and upon the children's children, unto the third and to the fourth *generation.*

Nu 16:22 — And they fell upon their faces, and said, O God, the God of the spirits of all flesh, shall one man sin, and wilt thou be wroth with all the congregation?

Dt 4:24 — For the LORD thy God *is* a consuming fire, *even* a jealous God.

Dt 10:17 — For the LORD your God *is* God of gods, and Lord of lords, a great God, a mighty, and a terrible, which regardeth not persons, nor taketh reward:

Dt 32:4 — *He is* the Rock, his work *is* perfect: for all his ways *are* judgment: a God of truth and without iniquity, just and right *is* he.

Dt 32:35 — To me *belongeth* vengeance, and recompence; their foot shall slide in *due* time: for the day of their calamity *is* at hand, and the things that shall come upon them make haste.

Jos 24:19 — And Joshua said unto the people, Ye cannot serve the LORD: for he *is* an holy God; he *is* a jealous God; he will not forgive your transgressions nor your sins.

Jgs 11:27 — Wherefore I have not sinned against thee, but thou doest me wrong to war against me: the LORD the Judge be judge this day between the children of Israel and the children of Ammon.

1Sa 2:3 — Talk no more so exceeding proudly; let *not* arrogancy come out of your mouth: for the LORD is a God of knowledge, and by him actions are weighed.

1Sa 2:10 — The adversaries of the LORD shall be broken to pieces; out of heaven shall he thunder upon them: the LORD shall judge the ends of the earth; and he shall give strength unto his king, and exalt the horn of his anointed.

1Sa 24:12 — The LORD judge between me and thee, and the LORD avenge me of thee: but mine hand shall not be upon thee.

1Sa 24:15 — The LORD therefore be judge, and judge between me and thee, and see, and plead my cause, and deliver me out of thine hand.

2Sa 14:14 — For we must needs die, and *are* as water spilt on the ground, which cannot be gathered up again; neither doth God respect *any* person: yet doth he devise means, that his banished be not expelled from him.

1Ki 8:32 — Then hear thou in heaven, and do, and judge thy servants, condemning the wicked, to bring his way upon his head; and justifying the righteous, to give him according to his righteousness.

1Ch 16:33 — Then shall the trees of the wood sing out at the presence of the LORD, because he cometh to judge the earth.

2Ch 19:7 — Wherefore now let the fear of the LORD be upon you; take heed and do *it:* for *there is* no iniquity with the LORD our God, nor respect of persons, nor taking of gifts.

Ne 9:33 — Howbeit thou *art* just in all that is brought upon us; for thou hast done right, but we have done wickedly:

Job 4:17 — Shall mortal man be more just than God? shall a man be more pure than his maker?

Job 8:3 — Doth God pervert judgment? or doth the Almighty pervert justice?

Job 9:15 — Whom, though I were righteous, *yet* would I not answer, *but* I would make supplication to my judge.

Job 9:28 — I am afraid of all my sorrows, I know that thou wilt not hold me innocent.

Job 21:22 — Shall *any* teach God knowledge? seeing he judgeth those that are high.

Job 23:7 — There the righteous might dispute with him; so should I be delivered for ever from my judge.

Job 34:17 — Shall even he that hateth right govern? and wilt thou condemn him that is most just?

Job 34:19 — *How much less to him* that accepteth not the persons of princes, nor regardeth the rich more than the poor? for they all *are* the work of his hands.

Job 34:23 — For he will not lay upon man more *than right;* that he should enter into judgment with God.

Job 35:14 — Although thou sayest thou shalt not see him, *yet* judgment *is* before him; therefore trust thou in him.

Job 36:3 — I will fetch my knowledge from afar, and will ascribe righteousness to my Maker.

Job 36:19 — Will he esteem thy riches? *no,* not gold, nor all the forces of strength.

Job 37:23 — *Touching* the Almighty, we cannot find him out: *he is* excellent in power, and in judgment, and in plenty of justice: he will not afflict.

Ps 7:11 — God judgeth the righteous, and God is angry *with the wicked* every day.

Ps 9:4 — For thou hast maintained my right and my cause; thou satest in the throne judging right.

Ps 11:7 — For the righteous LORD loveth righteousness; his countenance doth behold the upright.

Ps 19:9 — The fear of the LORD *is* clean, enduring for ever: the judgments of the LORD *are* true *and* righteous altogether.

Ps 33:5 — He loveth righteousness and judgment: the earth is full of the goodness of the LORD.

Ps 35:24 — Judge me, O LORD my God, according to thy righteousness; and let them not rejoice over me.

Ps 43:1 — Judge me, O God, and plead my cause against an ungodly nation: O deliver me from the deceitful and unjust man.

Ps 50:4 — He shall call to the heavens from above, and to the earth, that he may judge his people.

Ps 50:6 — And the heavens shall declare his righteousness: for God *is* judge himself. Selah.

Ps 51:4 — Against thee, thee only, have I sinned, and done *this* evil in thy sight: that thou mightest be justified when thou speakest, *and* be clear when thou judgest.

Ps 58:11 — So that a man shall say, Verily *there is* a reward for the righteous: verily he is a God that judgeth in the earth.

Ps 62:12 — Also unto thee, O Lord, *belongeth* mercy: for thou renderest to every man according to his work.

Ps 67:4 — O let the nations be glad and sing for joy: for thou shalt judge the people righteously, and govern the nations upon earth. Selah.

Ps 71:19 — Thy righteousness also, O God, *is* very high, who hast done great things: O God, who *is* like unto thee!

Ps 75:7 — But God *is* the judge: he putteth down one, and setteth up another.

Ps 82:8 — Arise, O God, judge the earth: for thou shalt inherit all nations.

Ps 85:10 — Mercy and truth are met together; righteousness and peace have kissed *each other.*

Ps 89:14 — Justice and judgment *are* the habitation of thy throne: mercy and truth shall go before thy face.

Ps 90:8 — Thou hast set our iniquities before thee, our secret *sins* in the light of thy countenance.

Ps 90:11 — Who knoweth the power of thine anger? even according to thy fear, *so is* thy wrath.

Ps 92:15 — To shew that the LORD *is* upright: *he is* my rock, and *there is* no unrighteousness in him.

Ps 94:10 — He that chastiseth the heathen, shall not he correct? he that teacheth man knowledge, *shall not he know?*

Ps 96:10 — Say among the heathen *that* the LORD reigneth: the world also shall be established that it shall not be moved: he shall judge the people righteously.

Ps 96:13 — Before the LORD: for he cometh, for he cometh to judge the earth: he shall judge the world with righteousness, and the people with his truth.

Ps 97:2 — Clouds and darkness *are* round about him: righteousness and judgment *are* the habitation of his throne.

Ps 98:9 — Before the LORD; for he cometh to judge the earth: with righteousness shall he judge the world, and the people with equity.

Ps 99:4 — The king's strength also loveth judgment; thou dost establish equity, thou executest judgment and righteousness in Jacob.

Ps 99:8 — Thou answeredst them, O LORD our God: thou wast a God that forgavest them, though thou tookest vengeance of their inventions.

Ps 103:6 — The LORD executeth righteousness and judgment for all that are oppressed.

Ps 111:7 — The works of his hands *are* verity and judgment; all his commandments *are* sure.

Ps 119:137 — Righteous *art* thou, O LORD, and upright *are* thy judgments.

Ps 129:4 — The LORD *is* righteous: he hath cut asunder the cords of the wicked.

Ps 135:14 — For the LORD will judge his people, and he will repent himself concerning his servants.

Ps 143:2 — And enter not into judgment with thy servant: for in thy sight shall no man living be justified.

Ps 145:17 — The LORD *is* righteous in all his ways, and holy in all his works.

Pr 11:31 — Behold, the righteous shall be recompensed in the earth: much more the wicked and the sinner.

Pr 16:2 — All the ways of a man *are* clean in his own eyes; but the LORD weigheth the spirits.

Pr 17:3 — The fining pot *is* for silver, and the furnace for gold: but the LORD trieth the hearts.

Pr 24:12 — If thou sayest, Behold, we knew it not; doth not he that pondereth the heart consider *it?* and he that keepeth thy soul, doth *not* he know *it?* and shall *not* he render to *every* man according to his works?

Pr 29:13 — The poor and the deceitful man meet together: the LORD lighteneth both their eyes.

Pr 29:26 — Many seek the ruler's favour; but *every* man's judgment *cometh* from the LORD.

Ecc 3:15 — That which hath been is now; and that which is to be hath already been; and God requireth that which is past.

Ecc 3:17 — I said in mine heart, God shall judge the righteous and the wicked: for *there is* a time there for every purpose and for every work.

Ecc 11:9 — Rejoice, O young man, in thy youth; and let thy heart cheer thee in the days of thy youth, and walk in the ways of thine heart, and in the sight of thine eyes: but know thou, that for all these *things* God will bring thee into judgment.

Ecc 12:14 — For God shall bring every work into judgment, with every secret thing, whether *it be* good, or whether *it be* evil.

Isa 1:27 — Zion shall be redeemed with judgment, and her converts with righteousness.

Isa 26:7 — The way of the just *is* uprightness: thou, most upright, dost weigh the path of the just.

Isa 28:17 — Judgment also will I lay to the line, and righteousness to the plummet: and the hail shall sweep away the refuge of lies, and the waters shall overflow the hiding place.

Isa 28:21 — For the LORD shall rise up as *in* mount Perazim, he shall be wroth as *in* the valley of Gibeon, that he may do his work, his strange work; and bring to pass his act, his strange act.

Isa 30:18 — And therefore will the LORD wait, that he may be gracious unto you, and therefore will he be exalted, that he may have mercy upon you: for the LORD *is* a God of judgment: blessed *are* all they that wait for him.

Isa 30:27 — Behold, the name of the LORD cometh from far, burning *with* his anger, and the burden *thereof is* heavy: his lips are full of indignation, and his tongue as a devouring fire:

Isa 30:30 — And the LORD shall cause his glorious voice to be heard, and shall shew the lighting down of his arm, with the indignation of *his* anger, and *with* the flame of a devouring fire, *with* scattering, and tempest, and hailstones.

Isa 31:2 — Yet he also *is* wise, and will bring evil, and will not call back his words: but will arise against the house of the evildoers, and against the help of them that work iniquity.

Isa 33:22 — For the LORD *is* our judge, the LORD *is* our lawgiver, the LORD *is* our king; he will save us.

Isa 45:21 — Tell ye, and bring *them* near; yea, let them take counsel together: who hath declared this from ancient time? *who* hath told it from that time? *have* not I the LORD? and *there is* no God else beside me; a just God and a Saviour; *there is* none beside me.

Isa 61:8 — For I the LORD love judgment, I hate robbery for burnt offering; and I will direct their work in truth, and I will make an everlasting covenant with them.

Jer 9:24 — But let him that glorieth glory in this, that he understandeth and knoweth me, that I *am* the LORD which exercise lovingkindness, judgment, and righteousness, in the earth: for in these *things* I delight, saith the LORD.

Jer 10:10 — But the LORD *is* the true God, he *is* the living God, and an everlasting king: at his wrath the earth shall tremble, and the nations shall not be able to abide his indignation.

Jer 11:20 — But, O LORD of hosts, that judgest righteously, that triest the reins and the heart, let me see thy vengeance on them: for unto thee have I revealed my cause.

Jer 12:1 — Righteous *art* thou, O LORD, when I plead with thee: yet let me talk with thee of *thy* judgments: Wherefore doth the way of the wicked prosper? *wherefore* are all they happy that deal very treacherously?

Jer 20:12 — But, O LORD of hosts, that triest the righteous, *and* seest the reins and the heart, let me see thy vengeance on them: for unto thee have I opened my cause.

Jer 32:19 — Great in counsel, and mighty in work: for thine eyes *are* open upon all the ways of the sons of men: to give every one according to his ways, and according to the fruit of his doings:

Jer 50:7 — All that found them have devoured them: and their adversaries said, We offend not, because they have sinned against the LORD, the habitation of justice, even the LORD, the hope of their fathers.

Jer 51:10 — The LORD hath brought forth our righteousness: come, and let us declare in Zion the work of the LORD our God.

La 1:18 — The LORD is righteous; for I have rebelled against his commandment: hear, I pray you, all people, and behold my sorrow: my virgins and my young men are gone into captivity.

Eze 14:23 — And they shall comfort you, when ye see their ways and their doings: and ye shall know that I have not done without cause all that I have done in it, saith the Lord GOD.

Eze 18:25 — Yet ye say, The way of the Lord is not equal. Hear now, O house of Israel; Is not my way equal? are not your ways unequal?

Da 4:37 — Now I Nebuchadnezzar praise and extol and honour the King of heaven, all whose works *are* truth, and his ways judgment: and those that walk in pride he is able to abase.

Da 9:7 — O Lord, righteousness *belongeth* unto thee, but unto us confusion of faces, as at this day; to the men of Judah, and to the inhabitants of Jerusalem, and unto all Israel, *that are* near, and *that are* far off, through all the countries whither thou hast driven them, because of their trespass that they have trespassed against thee.

Da 9:14 — Therefore hath the LORD watched upon the evil, and brought it upon us: for the LORD our God *is* righteous in all his works which he doeth: for we obeyed not his voice.

Hos 10:10 — *It is* in my desire that I should chastise them; and the people shall be gathered against them, when they shall bind themselves in their two furrows.

Am 8:7 — The LORD hath sworn by the excellency of Jacob, Surely I will never forget any of their works.

Na 1:3 — The LORD *is* slow to anger, and great in power, and will not at all acquit *the wicked:* the LORD hath his way in the whirlwind and in the storm, and the clouds *are* the dust of his feet.

Na 1:6 — Who can stand before his indignation? and who can abide in the fierceness of his anger? his fury is poured out like fire, and the rocks are thrown down by him.

Zep 3:5 — The just LORD *is* in the midst thereof; he will not do iniquity: every morning doth he bring his judgment to light, he faileth not; but the unjust knoweth no shame.

Mal 3:5 — And I will come near to you to judgment; and I will be a swift witness against the sorcerers, and against the adulterers, and against false swearers, and against those that oppress the hireling in *his* wages, the widow, and the fatherless, and that turn aside the stranger *from his right,* and fear not me, saith the LORD of hosts.

Mal 3:18 — Then shall ye return, and discern between the righteous and the wicked, between him that serveth God and him that serveth him not.

Ac 10:34 — Then Peter opened *his* mouth, and said, Of a truth I perceive that God is no respecter of persons:

Ac 17:31 — Because he hath appointed a day, in the which he will judge the world in righteousness by *that* man whom he hath ordained; *whereof* he hath given assurance unto all *men*, in that he hath raised him from the dead.

Ro 1:32 — Who knowing the judgment of God, that they which commit such things are worthy of death, not only do the same, but have pleasure in them that do them.

Ro 2:2 — But we are sure that the judgment of God is according to truth against them which commit such things.

Ro 3:26 — To declare, *I say*, at this time his righteousness: that he might be just, and the justifier of him which believeth in Jesus.

Ro 9:14 — What shall we say then? *Is there* unrighteousness with God? God forbid.

Ro 11:22 — Behold therefore the goodness and severity of God: on them which fell, severity; but toward thee, goodness, if thou continue in *his* goodness: otherwise thou also shalt be cut off.

Col 3:25 — But he that doeth wrong shall receive for the wrong which he hath done: and there is no respect of persons.

Heb 6:10 — For God *is* not unrighteous to forget your work and labour of love, which ye have shewed toward his name, in that ye have ministered to the saints, and do minister.

Heb 12:29 — For our God *is* a consuming fire.

1Pe 1:17 — And if ye call on the Father, who without respect of persons judgeth according to every man's work, pass the time of your sojourning *here* in fear:

2Pe 2:9 — The Lord knoweth how to deliver the godly out of temptations, and to reserve the unjust unto the day of judgment to be punished:

1Jn 1:9 — If we confess our sins, he is faithful and just to forgive us *our* sins, and to cleanse us from all unrighteousness.

Jude 1:6 — And the angels which kept not their first estate, but left their own habitation, he hath reserved in everlasting chains under darkness unto the judgment of the great day.

Rev 11:18 — And the nations were angry, and thy wrath is come, and the time of the dead, that they should be judged, and that thou shouldest give reward unto thy servants the prophets, and to the saints, and them that fear thy name, small and great; and shouldest destroy them which destroy the earth.

Rev 15:3 — And they sing the song of Moses the servant of God, and the song of the Lamb, saying, Great and marvellous *are* thy works, Lord God Almighty; just and true *are* thy ways, thou King of saints.

Rev 18:8 — Therefore shall her plagues come in one day, death, and mourning, and famine; and she shall be utterly burned with fire: for strong *is* the Lord God who judgeth her.

Rev 19:2 — For true and righteous *are* his judgments: for he hath judged the great whore, which did corrupt the earth with her fornication, and hath avenged the blood of his servants at her hand.

→See: God, Holiness of

→See: God, Righteousness of

→See: Government; God in

→See: Jesus, Judge

→See: Judgment; the general

→See: Judgments

→See: Sin; punishment of

GOD, King →See: God, Sovereign

GOD, Knowledge of

Ex 3:19–20; 14:3–4; Job 22:13–14; 34:21–22; 36:4–5; Ps 33:13–15; 94:9–11; 121:3–4; 139:1–24; 147:4–5; Pr 3:19–20; Isa 29:15–16; 40:13–14, 26–28; 48:5–6; Am 9:2–4; Mt 10:29–30; Ro 11:33–34

Ge 16:13 — And she called the name of the LORD that spake unto her, Thou God seest me: for she said, Have I also here looked after him that seeth me?

Ex 3:3 — And Moses said, I will now turn aside, and see this great sight, why the bush is not burnt.

Ex 3:7 — And the LORD said, I have surely seen the affliction of my people which *are* in Egypt, and have heard their cry by reason of their taskmasters; for I know their sorrows;

Ex 3:9 — Now therefore, behold, the cry of the children of Israel is come unto me: and I have also seen the oppression wherewith the Egyptians oppress them.

Ex 6:1 — Then the LORD said unto Moses, Now shalt thou see what I will do to Pharaoh: for with a strong hand shall he let them go, and with a strong hand shall he drive them out of his land.

Ex 11:1 — And the LORD said unto Moses, Yet will I bring one plague *more* upon Pharaoh, and upon Egypt; afterwards he will let you go hence: when he shall let *you* go, he shall surely thrust you out hence altogether.

Nu 14:27 — How long *shall I bear with* this evil congregation, which murmur against me? I have heard the murmurings of the children of Israel, which they murmur against me.

Dt 2:7 — For the LORD thy God hath blessed thee in all the works of thy hand: he knoweth thy walking through this great wilderness: these forty years the LORD thy God *hath been* with thee; thou hast lacked nothing.

Dt 31:21 — And it shall come to pass, when many evils and troubles are befallen them, that this song shall testify against them as a witness; for it shall not be forgotten out of the mouths of their seed: for I know their imagination which they go about, even now, before I have brought them into the land which I sware.

1Sa 2:3 — Talk no more so exceeding proudly; let *not* arrogancy come out of your mouth: for the LORD is a God of knowledge, and by him actions are weighed.

1Sa 16:7 — But the LORD said unto Samuel, Look not on his countenance, or on the height of his stature; because I have refused him: for *the LORD seeth* not as man seeth; for man looketh on the outward appearance, but the LORD looketh on the heart.

2Sa 7:20 — And what can David say more unto thee? for thou, Lord God, knowest thy servant.

1Ki 8:39 — Then hear thou in heaven thy dwelling place, and forgive, and do, and give to every man according to his ways, whose heart thou knowest; (for thou, *even* thou only, knowest the hearts of all the children of men;)

2Ki 19:27 — But I know thy abode, and thy going out, and thy coming in, and thy rage against me.

1Ch 28:9 — And thou, Solomon my son, know thou the God of thy father, and serve him with a perfect heart and with a willing mind: for the LORD searcheth all hearts, and understandeth all the imaginations of the thoughts: if thou seek him, he will be found of thee; but if thou forsake him, he will cast thee off for ever.

1Ch 29:17 — I know also, my God, that thou triest the heart, and hast pleasure in uprightness. As for me, in the uprightness of mine heart I have willingly offered all these things: and now have I seen with joy thy people, which are present here, to offer willingly unto thee.

2Ch 6:30 — Then hear thou from heaven thy dwelling place, and forgive, and render unto every man according unto all his ways, whose heart thou knowest; (for thou only knowest the hearts of the children of men:)

2Ch 16:9 — For the eyes of the LORD run to and fro throughout the whole earth, to shew himself strong in the behalf of *them* whose heart *is* perfect toward him. Herein thou hast done foolishly: therefore from henceforth thou shalt have wars.

Ne 9:10 — And shewedst signs and wonders upon Pharaoh, and on all his servants, and on all the people of his land: for thou knewest that they dealt proudly against them. So didst thou get thee a name, as *it is* this day.

Job 11:11 — For he knoweth vain men: he seeth wickedness also; will he not then consider *it?*

Job 12:13 — With him *is* wisdom and strength, he hath counsel and understanding.

Job 12:16 — With him *is* strength and wisdom: the deceived and the deceiver *are* his.

Job 12:22 — He discovereth deep things out of darkness, and bringeth out to light the shadow of death.

Job 21:22 — Shall *any* teach God knowledge? seeing he judgeth those that are high.

Job 23:10 — But he knoweth the way that I take: *when* he hath tried me, I shall come forth as gold.

Job 24:1 — Why, seeing times are not hidden from the Almighty, do they that know him not see his days?

Job 24:23 — *Though* it be given him *to be* in safety, whereon he resteth; yet his eyes *are* upon their ways.

Job 26:6 — Hell *is* naked before him, and destruction hath no covering.

Job 28:10 — He cutteth out rivers among the rocks; and his eye seeth every precious thing.

Job 28:24 — For he looketh to the ends of the earth, *and* seeth under the whole heaven;

Job 31:4 — Doth not he see my ways, and count all my steps?

Job 34:25 — Therefore he knoweth their works, and he overturneth *them* in the night, so that they are destroyed.

Job 37:16 — Dost thou know the balancings of the clouds, the wondrous works of him which is perfect in knowledge?

Job 42:2 — I know that thou canst do every *thing,* and *that* no thought can be withholden from thee.

Ps 1:6 — For the LORD knoweth the way of the righteous: but the way of the ungodly shall perish.

Ps 7:9 — Oh let the wickedness of the wicked come to an end; but establish the just: for the righteous God trieth the hearts and reins.

Ps 10:11 — He hath said in his heart, God hath forgotten: he hideth his face; he will never see *it.*

Ps 11:4 — The LORD *is* in his holy temple, the LORD'S throne *is* in heaven: his eyes behold, his eyelids try, the children of men.

Ps 37:18 — The LORD knoweth the days of the upright: and their inheritance shall be for ever.

Ps 38:9 — Lord, all my desire *is* before thee; and my groaning is not hid from thee.

Ps 44:21 — Shall not God search this out? for he knoweth the secrets of the heart.

Ps 66:7 — He ruleth by his power for ever; his eyes behold the nations: let not the rebellious exalt themselves. Selah.

Ps 69:19 — Thou hast known my reproach, and my shame, and my dishonour: mine adversaries *are* all before thee.

Ps 73:11 — And they say, How doth God know? and is there knowledge in the most High?

Ps 92:5 — O LORD, how great are thy works! *and* thy thoughts are very deep.

Ps 94:7 — Yet they say, The LORD shall not see, neither shall the God of Jacob regard *it.*

Ps 103:14 — For he knoweth our frame; he remembereth that we *are* dust.

Ps 104:24 — O LORD, how manifold are thy works! in wisdom hast thou made them all: the earth is full of thy riches.

Ps 119:168 — I have kept thy precepts and thy testimonies: for all my ways *are* before thee.

Ps 136:5 — To him that by wisdom made the heavens: for his mercy *endureth* for ever.

Ps 142:3 — When my spirit was overwhelmed within me, then thou knewest my path. In the way wherein I walked have they privily laid a snare for me.

Pr 5:21 — For the ways of man *are* before the eyes of the LORD, and he pondereth all his goings.

Pr 15:3 — The eyes of the LORD *are* in every place, beholding the evil and the good.

Pr 15:11 — Hell and destruction *are* before the LORD: how much more then the hearts of the children of men?

Pr 16:2 — All the ways of a man *are* clean in his own eyes; but the LORD weigheth the spirits.

Pr 17:3 — The fining pot *is* for silver, and the furnace for gold: but the LORD trieth the hearts.

Pr 21:2 — Every way of a man *is* right in his own eyes: but the LORD pondereth the hearts.

Pr 24:12 — If thou sayest, Behold, we knew it not; doth not he that pondereth the heart consider *it?* and he that keepeth thy soul, doth *not* he know *it?* and shall *not* he render to *every* man according to his works?

Isa 28:29 — This also cometh forth from the LORD of hosts, *which* is wonderful in counsel, *and* excellent in working.

Isa 37:28 — But I know thy abode, and thy going out, and thy coming in, and thy rage against me.

Isa 41:4 — Who hath wrought and done *it,* calling the generations from the beginning? I the LORD, the first, and with the last; I *am* he.

Isa 42:9 — Behold, the former things are come to pass, and new things do I declare: before they spring forth I tell you of them.

Isa 44:7 — And who, as I, shall call, and shall declare it, and set it in order for me, since I appointed the ancient people? and the things that are coming, and shall come, let them shew unto them.

Isa 45:4 — For Jacob my servant's sake, and Israel mine elect, I have even called thee by thy name: I have surnamed thee, though thou hast not known me.

Isa 45:21 — Tell ye, and bring *them* near; yea, let them take counsel together: who hath declared this from ancient time? *who* hath told it from that time? *have* not I the LORD? and *there is* no God else beside me; a just God and a Saviour; *there is* none beside me.

Isa 46:10 — Declaring the end from the beginning, and from ancient times *the things* that are not *yet* done, saying, My counsel shall stand, and I will do all my pleasure:

Isa 48:3 — I have declared the former things from the beginning; and they went forth out of my mouth, and I shewed them; I did *them* suddenly, and they came to pass.

Isa 66:18 — For I *know* their works and their thoughts: it shall come, that I will gather all nations and tongues; and they shall come, and see my glory.

Jer 5:3 — O LORD, *are* not thine eyes upon the truth? thou hast stricken them, but they have not grieved; thou hast consumed them, *but* they have refused to receive correction: they have made their faces harder than a rock; they have refused to return.

Jer 10:7 — Who would not fear thee, O King of nations? for to thee doth it appertain: forasmuch as among all the wise *men* of the nations, and in all their kingdoms, *there is* none like unto thee.

Jer 10:12 — He hath made the earth by his power, he hath established the world by his wisdom, and hath stretched out the heavens by his discretion.

Jer 11:20 — But, O LORD of hosts, that judgest righteously, that triest the reins and the heart, let me see thy vengeance on them: for unto thee have I revealed my cause.

Jer 17:10 — I the LORD search the heart, *I* try the reins, even to give every man according to his ways, *and* according to the fruit of his doings.

Jer 20:12 — But, O LORD of hosts, that triest the righteous, *and* seest the reins and the heart, let me see thy vengeance on them: for unto thee have I opened my cause.

Jer 23:24 — Can any hide himself in secret places that I shall not see him? saith the LORD. Do not I fill heaven and earth? saith the LORD.

Jer 32:19 — Great in counsel, and mighty in work: for thine eyes *are* open upon all the ways of the sons of men: to give every one according to his ways, and according to the fruit of his doings:

Jer 51:15 — He hath made the earth by his power, he hath established the world by his wisdom, and hath stretched out the heaven by his understanding.

Eze 9:9 — Then said he unto me, The iniquity of the house of Israel and Judah *is* exceeding great, and the land is full of blood, and the city full of perverseness: for they say, The LORD hath forsaken the earth, and the LORD seeth not.

Eze 11:5 — And the Spirit of the LORD fell upon me, and said unto me, Speak; Thus saith the LORD; Thus have ye said, O house of Israel: for I know the things that come into your mind, *every one of* them.

Da 2:20 — Daniel answered and said, Blessed be the name of God for ever and ever: for wisdom and might are his:

Da 2:22 — He revealeth the deep and secret things: he knoweth what *is* in the darkness, and the light dwelleth with him.

Da 2:28 — But there is a God in heaven that revealeth secrets, and maketh known to the king Nebuchadnezzar what shall be in the latter days. Thy dream, and the visions of thy head upon thy bed, are these;

Am 4:13 — For, lo, he that formeth the mountains, and createth the wind, and declareth unto man what *is* his thought, that maketh the morning darkness, and treadeth upon the high places of the earth, The LORD, The God of hosts, *is* his name.

Zec 4:10 — For who hath despised the day of small things? for they shall rejoice, and shall see the plummet in the hand of Zerubbabel *with* those seven; they *are* the eyes of the LORD, which run to and fro through the whole earth.

Mt 6:4 — That thine alms may be in secret: and thy Father which seeth in secret himself shall reward thee openly.

Mt 6:8 — Be not ye therefore like unto them: for your Father knoweth what things ye have need of, before ye ask him.

Mt 6:18 — That thou appear not unto men to fast, but unto thy Father which is in secret: and thy Father, which seeth in secret, shall reward thee openly.

Mt 6:32 — (For after all these things do the Gentiles seek:) for your heavenly Father knoweth that ye have need of all these things.

Mt 24:36 — But of that day and hour knoweth no *man,* no, not the angels of heaven, but my Father only.

Mk 13:32 — But of that day and *that* hour knoweth no man, no, not the angels which are in heaven, neither the Son, but the Father.

Lk 16:15 — And he said unto them, Ye are they which justify yourselves before men; but God knoweth your hearts: for that which is highly esteemed among men is abomination in the sight of God.

Ac 1:24 — And they prayed, and said, Thou, Lord, which knowest the hearts of all *men,* shew whether of these two thou hast chosen,

Ac 2:23 — Him, being delivered by the determinate counsel and foreknowledge of God, ye have taken, and by wicked hands have crucified and slain:

Ac 15:8 — And God, which knoweth the hearts, bare them witness, giving them the Holy Ghost, even as *he did* unto us;

Ac 15:18 — Known unto God are all his works from the beginning of the world.

Ro 8:27 — And he that searcheth the hearts knoweth what *is* the mind of the Spirit, because he maketh intercession for the saints according to *the will of* God.

Ro 8:29 — For whom he did foreknow, he also did predestinate *to be* conformed to the image of his Son, that he might be the firstborn among many brethren.

Ro 16:27 — To God only wise, *be* glory through Jesus Christ for ever. Amen.

1Co 1:25 — Because the foolishness of God is wiser than men; and the weakness of God is stronger than men.

1Co 2:7 — But we speak the wisdom of God in a mystery, *even* the hidden *wisdom,* which God ordained before the world unto our glory:

1Co 3:20 — And again, The Lord knoweth the thoughts of the wise, that they are vain.

1Co 8:3 — But if any man love God, the same is known of him.

Gal 4:9 — But now, after that ye have known God, or rather are known of God, how turn ye again to the weak and beggarly elements, whereunto ye desire again to be in bondage?

Eph 1:8 — Wherein he hath abounded toward us in all wisdom and prudence;

Eph 3:10 — To the intent that now unto the principalities and powers in heavenly *places* might be known by the church the manifold wisdom of God,

1Th 2:4 — But as we were allowed of God to be put in trust with the gospel, even so we speak; not as pleasing men, but God, which trieth our hearts.

1Ti 1:17 — Now unto the King eternal, immortal, invisible, the only wise God, *be* honour and glory for ever and ever. Amen.

2Ti 2:19 — Nevertheless the foundation of God standeth sure, having this seal, The Lord knoweth them that are his. And, Let every one that nameth the name of Christ depart from iniquity.

Heb 4:13 — Neither is there any creature that is not manifest in his sight: but all things *are* naked and opened unto the eyes of him with whom we have to do.

1Pe 1:2 — Elect according to the foreknowledge of God the Father, through sanctification of the Spirit, unto obedience and sprinkling of the blood of Jesus Christ: Grace unto you, and peace, be multiplied.

1Jn 1:5 — This then is the message which we have heard of him, and declare unto you, that God is light, and in him is no darkness at all.

1Jn 3:20 — For if our heart condemn us, God is greater than our heart, and knoweth all things.

Jude 1:25 — To the only wise God our Saviour, *be* glory and majesty, dominion and power, both now and ever. Amen.

See: God, Foreknowledge of

See: God, Wisdom of

GOD, Longsuffering of

Ps 103:8–10; Isa 5:1–4; Jer 7:23–25; Hab 1:2–4; Mt 21:33–41; Mk 12:1–9; Lk 13:6–9; 20:9–16; Ro 9:22–23; Rev 2:21–22

Ge 6:3 — And the LORD said, My spirit shall not always strive with man, for that he also *is* flesh: yet his days shall be an hundred and twenty years.

Ge 15:16 — But in the fourth generation they shall come hither again: for the iniquity of the Amorites *is* not yet full.

Ex 34:6 — And the LORD passed by before him, and proclaimed, The LORD, The LORD God, merciful and gracious, longsuffering, and abundant in goodness and truth,

Nu 14:18 — The LORD *is* longsuffering, and of great mercy, forgiving iniquity and transgression, and by no means clearing *the guilty,* visiting the iniquity of the fathers upon the children unto the third and fourth *generation.*

Ps 86:15 — But thou, O Lord, *art* a God full of compassion, and gracious, longsuffering, and plenteous in mercy and truth.

Isa 30:18 — And therefore will the LORD wait, that he may be gracious unto you, and therefore will he be exalted, that he may have mercy upon you: for the LORD *is* a God of judgment: blessed *are* all they that wait for him.

Isa 42:14 — I have long time holden my peace; I have been still, *and* refrained myself: *now* will I cry like a travailing woman; I will destroy and devour at once.

Isa 48:9 — For my name's sake will I defer mine anger, and for my praise will I refrain for thee, that I cut thee not off.

Isa 48:11 — For mine own sake, *even* for mine own sake, will I do *it:* for how should *my name* be polluted? and I will not give my glory unto another.

Jer 7:13 — And now, because ye have done all these works, saith the LORD, and I spake unto you, rising up early and speaking, but ye heard not; and I called you, but ye answered not;

Jer 11:7 — For I earnestly protested unto your fathers in the day *that* I brought them up out of the land of Egypt, *even* unto this day, rising early and protesting, saying, Obey my voice.

Jer 15:15 — O LORD, thou knowest: remember me, and visit me, and revenge me of my persecutors; take me not away in thy longsuffering: know that for thy sake I have suffered rebuke.

Eze 20:17 — Nevertheless mine eye spared them from destroying them, neither did I make an end of them in the wilderness.

Joel 2:13 — And rend your heart, and not your garments, and turn unto the LORD your God: for he *is* gracious and merciful, slow to anger, and of great kindness, and repenteth him of the evil.

Mt 19:8 — He saith unto them, Moses because of the hardness of your hearts suffered you to put away your wives: but from the beginning it was not so.

Mt 23:37 — O Jerusalem, Jerusalem, *thou* that killest the prophets, and stonest them which are sent unto thee, how often would I have gathered thy children together, even as a hen gathereth her chickens under *her* wings, and ye would not!

Lk 13:34 — O Jerusalem, Jerusalem, which killest the prophets, and stonest them that are sent unto thee; how often would I have gathered thy children together, as a hen *doth gather* her brood under *her* wings, and ye would not!

Ac 14:16 — Who in times past suffered all nations to walk in their own ways.

Ac 17:30 — And the times of this ignorance God winked at; but now commandeth all men every where to repent:

Ro 2:4 — Or despisest thou the riches of his goodness and forbearance and longsuffering; not knowing that the goodness of God leadeth thee to repentance?

Ro 3:25 — Whom God hath set forth *to be* a propitiation through faith in his blood, to declare his righteousness for the remission of sins that are past, through the forbearance of God;

Ro 15:5 — Now the God of patience and consolation grant you to be likeminded one toward another according to Christ Jesus:

1Pe 3:20 — Which sometime were disobedient, when once the longsuffering of God waited in the days of Noah, while the ark was a preparing, wherein few, that is, eight souls were saved by water.

2Pe 3:9 — The Lord is not slack concerning his promise, as some men count slackness; but is longsuffering to us-ward, not willing that any should perish, but that all should come to repentance.

2Pe 3:15 — And account *that* the longsuffering of our Lord *is* salvation; even as our beloved brother Paul also according to the wisdom given unto him hath written unto you;

See: God, Love of

See: God, Mercy of

GOD, Long-Suffering of, Abused

Ne 9:28–31; Pr 1:24–27; Mt 24:48–51; Lk 13:6–9

Pr 29:1 — He, that being often reproved hardeneth *his* neck, shall suddenly be destroyed, and that without remedy.

Ecc 8:11 — Because sentence against an evil work is not executed speedily, therefore the heart of the sons of men is fully set in them to do evil.

GOD, Love of

Dt 7:7–8; 1Ki 8:51–53; Ps 78:61–62; Eph 2:4–5; Tit 3:4–5; 1Jn 4:8–10, 12–13, 15–16

Dt 4:37 — And because he loved thy fathers, therefore he chose their seed after them, and brought thee out in his sight with his mighty power out of Egypt;

Dt 7:13 — And he will love thee, and bless thee, and multiply thee: he will also bless the fruit of thy womb, and the fruit of thy land, thy corn, and thy wine, and thine oil, the increase of thy kine, and the flocks of thy sheep, in the land which he sware unto thy fathers to give thee.

Dt 9:29 — Yet they *are* thy people and thine inheritance, which thou broughtest out by thy mighty power and by thy stretched out arm.

Dt 10:15 — Only the LORD had a delight in thy fathers to love them, and he chose their seed after them, *even* you above all people, as *it is* this day.

Dt 10:18 — He doth execute the judgment of the fatherless and widow, and loveth the stranger, in giving him food and raiment.

Dt 23:5 — Nevertheless the LORD thy God would not hearken unto Balaam; but the LORD thy God turned the curse into a blessing unto thee, because the LORD thy God loved thee.

Dt 33:3 — Yea, he loved the people; all his saints *are* in thy hand: and they sat down at thy feet; *every one* shall receive of thy words.

Dt 33:12 — *And* of Benjamin he said, The beloved of the LORD shall dwell in safety by him; *and the LORD* shall cover him all the day long, and he shall dwell between his shoulders.

2Sa 12:24 — And David comforted Bath-sheba his wife, and went in unto her, and lay with her: and she bare a son, and he called his name Solomon: and the LORD loved him.

Ne 13:26 — Did not Solomon king of Israel sin by these things? yet among many nations was there no king like him, who was beloved of his God, and God made him king over all Israel: nevertheless even him did outlandish women cause to sin.

Job 7:17 — What *is* man, that thou shouldest magnify him? and that thou shouldest set thine heart upon him?

Ps 42:8 — *Yet* the LORD will command his lovingkindness in the daytime, and in the night his song *shall be* with me, *and* my prayer unto the God of my life.

Ps 47:4 — He shall choose our inheritance for us, the excellency of Jacob whom he loved. Selah.

Ps 63:3 — Because thy lovingkindness *is* better than life, my lips shall praise thee.

Ps 78:65 — Then the Lord awaked as one out of sleep, *and* like a mighty man that shouteth by reason of wine.

Ps 78:68 — But chose the tribe of Judah, the mount Zion which he loved.

Ps 89:33 — Nevertheless my lovingkindness will I not utterly take from him, nor suffer my faithfulness to fail.

Ps 103:13 — Like as a father pitieth *his* children, *so* the LORD pitieth them that fear him.

Ps 146:8 — The LORD openeth *the eyes of* the blind: the LORD raiseth them that are bowed down: the LORD loveth the righteous:

Pr 15:9 — The way of the wicked *is* an abomination unto the LORD: but he loveth him that followeth after righteousness.

Isa 38:17 — Behold, for peace I had great bitterness: but thou hast in love to my soul *delivered it* from the pit of corruption: for thou hast cast all my sins behind thy back.

Isa 43:4 — Since thou wast precious in my sight, thou hast been honourable, and I have loved thee: therefore will I give men for thee, and people for thy life.

Jer 31:3 — The LORD hath appeared of old unto me, *saying,* Yea, I have loved thee with an everlasting love: therefore with lovingkindness have I drawn thee.

Hos 11:1 — When Israel *was* a child, then I loved him, and called my son out of Egypt.

Mal 1:2 — I have loved you, saith the LORD. Yet ye say, Wherein hast thou loved us? *Was* not Esau Jacob's brother? saith the LORD: yet I loved Jacob,

Jn 3:16 — For God so loved the world, that he gave his only begotten Son, that whosoever believeth in him should not perish, but have everlasting life.

Jn 5:20 — For the Father loveth the Son, and sheweth him all things that himself doeth: and he will shew him greater works than these, that ye may marvel.

Jn 14:21 — He that hath my commandments, and keepeth them, he it is that loveth me: and he that loveth me shall be loved of my Father, and I will love him, and will manifest myself to him.

Jn 14:23 — Jesus answered and said unto him, If a man love me, he will keep my words: and my Father will love him, and we will come unto him, and make our abode with him.

Jn 16:27 — For the Father himself loveth you, because ye have loved me, and have believed that I came out from God.

Jn 17:10 — And all mine are thine, and thine are mine; and I am glorified in them.

Jn 17:23 — I in them, and thou in me, that they may be made perfect in one; and that the world may know that thou hast sent me, and hast loved them, as thou hast loved me.

Jn 17:26 — And I have declared unto them thy name, and will declare *it:* that the love wherewith thou hast loved me may be in them, and I in them.

Jn 20:17 — Jesus saith unto her, Touch me not; for I am not yet ascended to my Father: but go to my brethren, and say unto them, I ascend unto my Father, and your Father; and *to* my God, and your God.

Ro 1:7 — To all that be in Rome, beloved of God, called *to be* saints: Grace to you and peace from God our Father, and the Lord Jesus Christ.

Ro 5:8 — But God commendeth his love toward us, in that, while we were yet sinners, Christ died for us.

Ro 9:13 — As it is written, Jacob have I loved, but Esau have I hated.

Ro 11:28 — As concerning the gospel, *they are* enemies for your sakes: but as touching the election, *they are* beloved for the fathers' sakes.

2Co 9:7 — Every man according as he purposeth in his heart, *so let him give;* not grudgingly, or of necessity: for God loveth a cheerful giver.

2Co 13:11 — Finally, brethren, farewell. Be perfect, be of good comfort, be of one mind, live in peace; and the God of love and peace shall be with you.

2Th 2:16 — Now our Lord Jesus Christ himself, and God, even our Father, which hath loved us, and hath given *us* everlasting consolation and good hope through grace,

Heb 12:6 — For whom the Lord loveth he chasteneth, and scourgeth every son whom he receiveth.

1Jn 3:1 — Behold, what manner of love the Father hath bestowed upon us, that we should be called the sons of God: therefore the world knoweth us not, because it knew him not.

1Jn 4:19 — We love him, because he first loved us.

Jude 1:21 — Keep yourselves in the love of God, looking for the mercy of our Lord Jesus Christ unto eternal life.

Rev 3:12 — Him that overcometh will I make a pillar in the temple of my God, and he shall go no more out: and I will write upon him the name of my God, and the name of the city of my God, *which is* new Jerusalem, which cometh down out of heaven from my God: and *I will write upon him* my new name.

Rev 14:1 — And I looked, and, lo, a Lamb stood on the mount Sion, and with him an hundred forty *and* four thousand, having his Father's name written in their foreheads.

GOD, Love of, Exemplified

Ex 19:4–6; 29:45–46; Le 11:44–45; 22:32–33; Dt 7:6–8; 26:18–19; 28:9–10; 32:9–12; 2Sa 7:23–24; 1Ki 8:51–53; Ps 78:61–62; Isa 41:8–10; 43:1–4; 44:1–2, 21–22; 49:13–17; 54:5–6; 62:4–5; 63:7–9; Jer 3:14–15; Eze 16:1–14; Hos 2:19–20; 11:3–4; Mal 1:2–3; 3:16–17; Mt 18:11–14; Lk 15:4–7, 11–27; Ro 8:31–32; 1Co 6:19–20; 2Co 5:18–21; Eph 1:3–6

Ge 17:7 — And I will establish my covenant between me and thee and thy seed after thee in their generations for an everlasting covenant, to be a God unto thee, and to thy seed after thee.

Ge 46:3 — And he said, I *am* God, the God of thy father: fear not to go down into Egypt; for I will there make of thee a great nation:

Ex 3:6 — Moreover he said, I *am* the God of thy father, the God of Abraham, the God of Isaac, and the God of Jacob. And Moses hid his face; for he was afraid to look upon God.

Ex 6:7 — And I will take you to me for a people, and I will be to you a God: and ye shall know that I *am* the LORD your God, which bringeth you out from under the burdens of the Egyptians.

Le 20:24 — But I have said unto you, Ye shall inherit their land, and I will give it unto you to possess it, a land that floweth with milk and honey: I *am* the LORD your God, which have separated you from *other* people.

Le 20:26 — And ye shall be holy unto me: for I the LORD *am* holy, and have severed you from *other* people, that ye should be mine.

Le 25:23 — The land shall not be sold for ever: for the land *is* mine; for ye *are* strangers and sojourners with me.

Le 25:38 — I *am* the LORD your God, which brought you forth out of the land of Egypt, to give you the land of Canaan, *and* to be your God.

Le 25:42 — For they *are* my servants, which I brought forth out of the land of Egypt: they shall not be sold as bondmen.

Le 25:55 — For unto me the children of Israel *are* servants; they *are* my servants whom I brought forth out of the land of Egypt: I *am* the LORD your God.

Le 26:12 — And I will walk among you, and will be your God, and ye shall be my people.

Nu 15:41 — I *am* the LORD your God, which brought you out of the land of Egypt, to be your God: I *am* the LORD your God.

Dt 4:20 — But the LORD hath taken you, and brought you forth out of the iron furnace, *even* out of Egypt, to be unto him a people of inheritance, as *ye are* this day.

Dt 4:34 — Or hath God assayed to go *and* take him a nation from the midst of another *nation,* by temptations, by signs, and by wonders, and by war, and by a mighty hand, and by a stretched out arm, and by great terrors, according to all that the LORD your God did for you in Egypt before your eyes?

Dt 4:37 — And because he loved thy fathers, therefore he chose their seed after them, and brought thee out in his sight with his mighty power out of Egypt;

Dt 7:13 — And he will love thee, and bless thee, and multiply thee: he will also bless the fruit of thy womb, and the fruit of thy land, thy corn, and thy wine, and thine oil, the increase of thy kine, and the flocks of thy sheep, in the land which he sware unto thy fathers to give thee.

Dt 9:29 — Yet they *are* thy people and thine inheritance, which thou broughtest out by thy mighty power and by thy stretched out arm.

Dt 10:15 — Only the LORD had a delight in thy fathers to love them, and he chose their seed after them, *even* you above all people, as *it is* this day.

Dt 14:2 — for thou *art* an holy people unto the LORD thy God, and the LORD hath chosen thee to be a peculiar people unto himself, above all the nations that *are* upon the earth.

Dt 23:5 — Nevertheless the LORD thy God would not hearken unto Balaam; but the LORD thy God turned the curse into a blessing unto thee, because the LORD thy God loved thee.

Dt 27:9 — And Moses and the priests the Levites spake unto all Israel, saying, Take heed, and hearken, O Israel; this day thou art become the people of the LORD thy God.

Dt 29:13 — That he may establish thee to day for a people unto himself, and *that* he may be unto thee a God, as he hath said unto thee, and as he hath sworn unto thy fathers, to Abraham, to Isaac, and to Jacob.

Dt 33:3 — Yea, he loved the people; all his saints *are* in thy hand: and they sat down at thy feet; *every one* shall receive of thy words.

Dt 33:12 — *And* of Benjamin he said, The beloved of the LORD shall dwell in safety by him; *and the LORD* shall cover him all the day long, and he shall dwell between his shoulders.

2Sa 12:24 — And David comforted Bath-sheba his wife, and went in unto her, and lay with her: and she bare a son, and he called his name Solomon: and the LORD loved him.

Ne 13:26 — Did not Solomon king of Israel sin by these things? yet among many nations was there no king like him, who was beloved of his God, and God made him king over all Israel: nevertheless even him did outlandish women cause to sin.

Ps 4:3 — But know that the LORD hath set apart him that is godly for himself: the LORD will hear when I call unto him.

Ps 31:19 — *Oh* how great *is* thy goodness, which thou hast laid up for them that fear thee; *which* thou hast wrought for them that trust in thee before the sons of men!

Ps 31:21 — Blessed *be* the LORD: for he hath shewed me his marvellous kindness in a strong city.

Ps 42:8 — *Yet* the LORD will command his lovingkindness in the daytime, and in the night his song *shall be* with me, *and* my prayer unto the God of my life.

Ps 47:4 — He shall choose our inheritance for us, the excellency of Jacob whom he loved. Selah.

Ps 48:9 — We have thought of thy lovingkindness, O God, in the midst of thy temple.

Ps 48:14 — For this God *is* our God for ever and ever: he will be our guide *even* unto death.

Ps 50:5 — Gather my saints together unto me; those that have made a covenant with me by sacrifice.

Ps 50:7 — Hear, O my people, and I will speak; O Israel, and I will testify against thee: I *am* God, *even* thy God.

Ps 63:3 — Because thy lovingkindness *is* better than life, my lips shall praise thee.

Ps 73:1 — Truly God *is* good to Israel, *even* to such as are of a clean heart.

Ps 74:2 — Remember thy congregation, *which* thou hast purchased of old; the rod of thine inheritance, *which* thou hast redeemed; this mount Zion, wherein thou hast dwelt.

Ps 78:65 — Then the Lord awaked as one out of sleep, *and* like a mighty man that shouteth by reason of wine.

Ps 78:68 — But chose the tribe of Judah, the mount Zion which he loved.

Ps 79:13 — So we thy people and sheep of thy pasture will give thee thanks for ever: we will shew forth thy praise to all generations.

Ps 81:13 — Oh that my people had hearkened unto me, *and* Israel had walked in my ways!

Ps 89:33 — Nevertheless my lovingkindness will I not utterly take from him, nor suffer my faithfulness to fail.

Ps 90:1 — LORD, thou hast been our dwelling place in all generations.

Ps 95:7 — For he *is* our God; and we *are* the people of his pasture, and the sheep of his hand. To day if ye will hear his voice,

Ps 100:3 — Know ye that the LORD he *is* God: *it is* he *that* hath made us, and not we ourselves; *we are* his people, and the sheep of his pasture.

Ps 103:4 — Who redeemeth thy life from destruction; who crowneth thee with lovingkindness and tender mercies;

Ps 105:6 — O ye seed of Abraham his servant, ye children of Jacob his chosen.

Ps 114:2 — Judah was his sanctuary, *and* Israel his dominion.

Ps 135:4 — For the LORD hath chosen Jacob unto himself, *and* Israel for his peculiar treasure.

Ps 148:14 — He also exalteth the horn of his people, the praise of all his saints; *even* of the children of Israel, a people near unto him. Praise ye the LORD.

Pr 11:20 — They that are of a froward heart *are* abomination to the LORD: but *such as are* upright in *their* way *are* his delight.

Pr 15:9 — The way of the wicked *is* an abomination unto the LORD: but he loveth him that followeth after righteousness.

Isa 5:7 — For the vineyard of the LORD of hosts *is* the house of Israel, and the men of Judah his pleasant plant: and he looked for judgment, but behold oppression; for righteousness, but behold a cry.

Isa 43:7 — *Even* every one that is called by my name: for I have created him for my glory, I have formed him; yea, I have made him.

Isa 48:12 — Hearken unto me, O Jacob and Israel, my called; I *am* he; I *am* the first, I also *am* the last.

Isa 51:16 — And I have put my words in thy mouth, and I have covered thee in the shadow of mine hand, that I may plant the heavens, and lay the foundations of the earth, and say unto Zion, Thou *art* my people.

Isa 54:10 — For the mountains shall depart, and the hills be removed; but my kindness shall not depart from thee, neither shall the covenant of my peace be removed, saith the LORD that hath mercy on thee.

Isa 64:4 — For since the beginning of the world *men* have not heard, nor perceived by the ear, neither hath the eye seen, O God, beside thee, *what* he hath prepared for him that waiteth for him.

Isa 65:19 — And I will rejoice in Jerusalem, and joy in my people: and the voice of weeping shall be no more heard in her, nor the voice of crying.

Isa 66:13 — As one whom his mother comforteth, so will I comfort you; and ye shall be comforted in Jerusalem.

Jer 10:16 — The portion of Jacob *is* not like them: for he *is* the former of all *things;* and Israel *is* the rod of his inheritance: The LORD of hosts *is* his name.

Jer 12:7 — I have forsaken mine house, I have left mine heritage; I have given the dearly beloved of my soul into the hand of her enemies.

Jer 13:11 — For as the girdle cleaveth to the loins of a man, so have I caused to cleave unto me the whole house of Israel and the whole house of Judah, saith the LORD; that they might be unto me for a people, and for a name, and for a praise, and for a glory: but they would not hear.

Jer 15:16 — Thy words were found, and I did eat them; and thy word was unto me the joy and rejoicing of mine heart: for I am called by thy name, O LORD God of hosts.

Jer 30:22 — And ye shall be my people, and I will be your God.

Jer 31:3 — The LORD hath appeared of old unto me, *saying,* Yea, I have loved thee with an everlasting love: therefore with lovingkindness have I drawn thee.

Jer 31:14 — And I will satiate the soul of the priests with fatness, and my people shall be satisfied with my goodness, saith the LORD.

Jer 31:32 — Not according to the covenant that I made with their fathers in the day *that* I took them by the hand to bring them out of the land of Egypt; which my covenant they brake, although I was an husband unto them, saith the LORD:

Jer 32:41 — Yea, I will rejoice over them to do them good, and I will plant them in this land assuredly with my whole heart and with my whole soul.

Jer 51:19 — The portion of Jacob *is* not like them; for he *is* the former of all things: and *Israel is* the rod of his inheritance: the LORD of hosts is his name.

Eze 34:31 — And ye my flock, the flock of my pasture, *are* men, *and* I *am* your God, saith the Lord GOD.

Eze 37:27 — My tabernacle also shall be with them: yea, I will be their God, and they shall be my people.

Hos 2:23 — And I will sow her unto me in the earth; and I will have mercy upon her that had not obtained mercy; and I will say to *them which were* not my people, Thou *art* my people; and they shall say, *Thou art* my God.

Hos 9:10 — I found Israel like grapes in the wilderness; I saw your fathers as the firstripe in the fig tree at her first time: *but* they went to Baal-peor, and separated themselves unto *that* shame; and *their* abominations were according as they loved.

Hos 11:1 — When Israel *was* a child, then I loved him, and called my son out of Egypt.

Zep 3:17 — The LORD thy God in the midst of thee *is* mighty; he will save, he will rejoice over thee with joy; he will rest in his love, he will joy over thee with singing.

Hag 2:23 — In that day, saith the LORD of hosts, will I take thee, O Zerubbabel, my servant, the son of Shealtiel, saith the LORD, and will make thee as a signet: for I have chosen thee, saith the LORD of hosts.

Zec 1:14 — So the angel that communed with me said unto me, Cry thou, saying, Thus saith the LORD of hosts; I am jealous for Jerusalem and for Zion with a great jealousy.

Zec 2:8 — For thus saith the LORD of hosts; After the glory hath he sent me unto the nations which spoiled you: for he that toucheth you toucheth the apple of his eye.

Zec 8:8 — And I will bring them, and they shall dwell in the midst of Jerusalem: and they shall be my people, and I will be their God, in truth and in righteousness.

Zec 13:9 — And I will bring the third part through the fire, and will refine them as silver is refined, and will try them as gold is tried: they shall call on my name, and I will hear them: I will say, It *is* my people: and they shall say, The LORD *is* my God.

Jn 14:21 — He that hath my commandments, and keepeth them, he it is that loveth me: and he that loveth me shall be loved of my Father, and I will love him, and will manifest myself to him.

Jn 14:23 — Jesus answered and said unto him, If a man love me, he will keep my words: and my Father will love him, and we will come unto him, and make our abode with him.

Jn 16:27 — For the Father himself loveth you, because ye have loved me, and have believed that I came out from God.

Jn 17:10 — And all mine are thine, and thine are mine; and I am glorified in them.

Jn 17:23 — I in them, and thou in me, that they may be made perfect in one; and that the world may know that thou hast sent me, and hast loved them, as thou hast loved me.

Jn 17:26 — And I have declared unto them thy name, and will declare *it:* that the love wherewith thou hast loved me may be in them, and I in them.

Ro 1:7 — To all that be in Rome, beloved of God, called *to be* saints: Grace to you and peace from God our Father, and the Lord Jesus Christ.

Ro 5:8 — But God commendeth his love toward us, in that, while we were yet sinners, Christ died for us.

Ro 8:39 — Nor height, nor depth, nor any other creature, shall be able to separate us from the love of God, which is in Christ Jesus our Lord.

Ro 11:28 — As concerning the gospel, *they are* enemies for your sakes: but as touching the election, *they are* beloved for the fathers' sakes.

1Co 2:9 — But as it is written, Eye hath not seen, nor ear heard, neither have entered into the heart of man, the things which God hath prepared for them that love him.

1Co 3:9 — For we are labourers together with God: ye are God's husbandry, *ye are* God's building.

1Co 7:23 — Ye are bought with a price; be not ye the servants of men.

2Co 6:16 — And what agreement hath the temple of God with idols? for ye are the temple of the living God; as God hath said, I will dwell in them, and walk in *them;* and I will be their God, and they shall be my people.

2Co 13:14 — The grace of the Lord Jesus Christ, and the love of God, and the communion of the Holy Ghost, *be* with you all. Amen.

Col 3:12 — Put on therefore, as the elect of God, holy and beloved, bowels of mercies, kindness, humbleness of mind, meekness, longsuffering;

Heb 11:16 — But now they desire a better *country,* that is, an heavenly: wherefore God is not ashamed to be called their God: for he hath prepared for them a city.

Jas 1:18 — Of his own will begat he us with the word of truth, that we should be a kind of firstfruits of his creatures.

1Pe 2:10 — Which in time past *were* not a people, but *are* now the people of God: which had not obtained mercy, but now have obtained mercy.

GOD, Mercy of

Ge 18:26–32; Ex 2:24–25; 34:6–7; Le 26:40–45; Nu 14:18–20; 2Ki 14:26–27; Ezr 9:7–14; Ne 9:17–20, 27–31; Job 23:2–6; 33:1–33; Ps 32:1–2; 78:4–72; 85:2–3; 103:8–14; 106:43–46; 117:2–118:4; 130:3–4, 7–8; 136:3–26; 145:8–9; 146:7–8; Isa 55:7–9; 57:15–16, 18–19; Jer 3:1–22; La 3:22–23, 31–33; Eze 18:31–32; 20:11–44; Da 4:22–27; Hos 2:14–23; 11:8–9; 14:1–8; Jnh 4:10–11; Mic 7:18–19; Zec 1:16–17; Mt 18:11–14, 23–27; Lk 1:77–78; 15:4–7; Ro 10:12–13; Eph 1:6–8; 2:4–7

Ge 8:21 — And the LORD smelled a sweet savour; and the LORD said in his heart, I will not again curse the ground any more for man's sake; for the imagination of man's heart *is* evil from his youth; neither will I again smite any more every thing living, as I have done.

Ge 19:16 — And while he lingered, the men laid hold upon his hand, and upon the hand of his wife, and upon the hand of his two daughters; the LORD being merciful unto him: and they brought him forth, and set him without the city.

Ex 15:13 — Thou in thy mercy hast led forth the people *which* thou hast redeemed: thou hast guided *them* in thy strength unto thy holy habitation.

Ex 20:2 — I *am* the LORD thy God, which have brought thee out of the land of Egypt, out of the house of bondage.

Ex 20:6 — And shewing mercy unto thousands of them that love me, and keep my commandments.

Ex 20:22 — And the LORD said unto Moses, Thus thou shalt say unto the children of Israel, Ye have seen that I have talked with you from heaven.

Ex 22:27 — For that *is* his covering only, it *is* his raiment for his skin: wherein shall he sleep? and it shall come to pass, when he crieth unto me, that I will hear; for I *am* gracious.

Ex 25:17 — And thou shalt make a mercy seat *of* pure gold: two cubits and a half *shall be* the length thereof, and a cubit and a half the breadth thereof.

Ex 32:14 — And the LORD repented of the evil which he thought to do unto his people.

Ex 32:34 — Therefore now go, lead the people unto *the place* of which I have spoken unto thee: behold, mine Angel shall go before thee: nevertheless in the day when I visit I will visit their sin upon them.

Ex 33:19 — And he said, I will make all my goodness pass before thee, and I will proclaim the name of the LORD before thee; and will be gracious to whom I will be gracious, and will shew mercy on whom I will shew mercy.

Nu 16:48 — And he stood between the dead and the living; and the plague was stayed.

Nu 21:8 — And the LORD said unto Moses, Make thee a fiery serpent, and set it upon a pole: and it shall come to pass, that every one that is bitten, when he looketh upon it, shall live.

Dt 4:31 — (For the LORD thy God *is* a merciful God;) he will not forsake thee, neither destroy thee, nor forget the covenant of thy fathers which he sware unto them.

Dt 5:10 — And shewing mercy unto thousands of them that love me and keep my commandments.

Dt 5:29 — O that there were such an heart in them, that they would fear me, and keep all my commandments always, that it might be well with them, and with their children for ever!

Dt 7:9 — Know therefore that the LORD thy God, he *is* God, the faithful God, which keepeth covenant and mercy with them that love him and keep his commandments to a thousand generations;

Dt 32:29 — O that they were wise, *that* they understood this, *that* they would consider their latter end!

Dt 32:36 — For the LORD shall judge his people, and repent himself for his servants, when he seeth that *their* power is gone, and *there is* none shut up, or left.

Dt 32:43 — Rejoice, O ye nations, *with* his people: for he will avenge the blood of his servants, and will render vengeance to his adversaries, and will be merciful unto his land, *and* to his people.

Jgs 2:18 — And when the LORD raised them up judges, then the LORD was with the judge, and delivered them out of the hand of their enemies all the days of the judge: for it repented the LORD because of their groanings by reason of them that oppressed them and vexed them.

Jgs 3:9 — And when the children of Israel cried unto the LORD, the LORD raised up a deliverer to the children of Israel, who delivered them, *even* Othniel the son of Kenaz, Caleb's younger brother.

Jgs 3:15 — But when the children of Israel cried unto the LORD, the LORD raised them up a deliverer, Ehud the son of Gera, a Benjamite, a man lefthanded: and by him the children of Israel sent a present unto Eglon the king of Moab.

Jgs 10:16 — And they put away the strange gods from among them, and served the LORD: and his soul was grieved for the misery of Israel.

2Sa 12:13 — And David said unto Nathan, I have sinned against the LORD. And Nathan said unto David, The LORD also hath put away thy sin; thou shalt not die.

2Sa 14:14 — For we must needs die, and *are* as water spilt on the ground, which cannot be gathered up again; neither doth God respect *any* person: yet doth he devise means, that his banished be not expelled from him.

2Sa 24:14 — And David said unto Gad, I am in a great strait: let us fall now into the hand of the LORD; for his mercies *are* great: and let me not fall into the hand of man.

2Sa 24:16 — And when the angel stretched out his hand upon Jerusalem to destroy it, the LORD repented him of the evil, and said to the angel that destroyed the people, It is enough: stay now thine hand. And the angel of the LORD was by the threshingplace of Araunah the Jebusite.

1Ki 8:23 — And he said, LORD God of Israel, *there is* no God like thee, in heaven above, or on earth beneath, who keepest covenant and mercy with thy servants that walk before thee with all their heart:

1Ki 11:39 — And I will for this afflict the seed of David, but not for ever.

2Ki 13:23 — And the LORD was gracious unto them, and had compassion on them, and had respect unto them, because of his covenant with Abraham, Isaac, and Jacob, and would not destroy them, neither cast he them from his presence as yet.

1Ch 16:34 — O give thanks unto the LORD; for *he is* good; for his mercy *endureth* for ever.

2Ch 5:13 — It came even to pass, as the trumpeters and singers *were* as one, to make one sound to be heard in praising and thanking the LORD; and when they lifted up *their* voice with the trumpets and cymbals and instruments of musick, and praised the LORD, *saying,* For *he is* good; for his mercy *endureth* for ever: that *then* the house was filled with a cloud, *even* the house of the LORD;

2Ch 7:3 — And when all the children of Israel saw how the fire came down, and the glory of the LORD upon the house, they bowed themselves with their faces to the ground upon the pavement, and worshipped, and praised the LORD, *saying,* For *he is* good; for his mercy *endureth* for ever.

2Ch 7:6 — And the priests waited on their offices: the Levites also with instruments of musick of the LORD, which David the king had made to praise the LORD, because his mercy *endureth* for ever, when David praised by their ministry; and the priests sounded trumpets before them, and all Israel stood.

2Ch 7:14 — If my people, which are called by my name, shall humble themselves, and pray, and seek my face, and turn from their wicked ways; then will I hear from heaven, and will forgive their sin, and will heal their land.

2Ch 24:19 — Yet he sent prophets to them, to bring them again unto the LORD; and they testified against them: but they would not give ear.

2Ch 30:9 — For if ye turn again unto the LORD, your brethren and your children *shall find* compassion before them that lead them captive, so that they shall come again into this land: for the LORD your God *is* gracious and merciful, and will not turn away *his* face from you, if ye return unto him.

2Ch 36:15 — And the LORD God of their fathers sent to them by his messengers, rising up betimes, and sending; because he had compassion on his people, and on his dwelling place:

Ne 1:10 — Now these *are* thy servants and thy people, whom thou hast redeemed by thy great power, and by thy strong hand.

Job 11:6 — And that he would shew thee the secrets of wisdom, that *they are* double to that which is! Know therefore that God exacteth of thee *less* than thine iniquity *deserveth.*

Job 24:12 — Men groan from out of the city, and the soul of the wounded crieth out: yet God layeth not folly *to them.*

Ps 18:50 — Great deliverance giveth he to his king; and sheweth mercy to his anointed, to David, and to his seed for evermore.

Ps 25:6 — Remember, O LORD, thy tender mercies and thy lovingkindnesses; for they *have been* ever of old.

Ps 25:8 — Good and upright *is* the LORD: therefore will he teach sinners in the way.

Ps 30:5 — For his anger *endureth but* a moment; in his favour is life: weeping may endure for a night, but joy *cometh* in the morning.

Ps 31:7 — I will be glad and rejoice in thy mercy: for thou hast considered my trouble; thou hast known my soul in adversities;

Ps 32:5 — I acknowledged my sin unto thee, and mine iniquity have I not hid. I said, I will confess my transgressions unto the LORD; and thou forgavest the iniquity of my sin. Selah.

Ps 36:5 — Thy mercy, O LORD, *is* in the heavens; *and* thy faithfulness *reacheth* unto the clouds.

Ps 50:21 — These *things* hast thou done, and I kept silence; thou thoughtest that I was altogether *such an one* as thyself: *but* I will reprove thee, and set *them* in order before thine eyes.

Ps 57:10 — For thy mercy is great unto the heavens, and thy truth unto the clouds.

Ps 62:12 — Also unto thee, O Lord, *belongeth* mercy: for thou renderest to every man according to his work.

Ps 65:3 — Iniquities prevail against me: *as for* our transgressions, thou shalt purge them away.

Ps 69:16 — Hear me, O LORD; for thy lovingkindness *is* good: turn unto me according to the multitude of thy tender mercies.

Ps 80:1 — Give ear, O Shepherd of Israel, thou that leadest Joseph like a flock; thou that dwellest *between* the cherubims, shine forth.

Ps 85:10 — Mercy and truth are met together; righteousness and peace have kissed *each other.*

Ps 86:5 — For thou, Lord, *art* good, and ready to forgive; and plenteous in mercy unto all them that call upon thee.

Ps 86:13 — For great *is* thy mercy toward me: and thou hast delivered my soul from the lowest hell.

Ps 86:15 — But thou, O Lord, *art* a God full of compassion, and gracious, longsuffering, and plenteous in mercy and truth.

Ps 89:2 — For I have said, Mercy shall be built up for ever: thy faithfulness shalt thou establish in the very heavens.

Ps 89:14 — Justice and judgment *are* the habitation of thy throne: mercy and truth shall go before thy face.

Ps 89:28 — My mercy will I keep for him for evermore, and my covenant shall stand fast with him.

Ps 99:8 — Thou answeredst them, O LORD our God: thou wast a God that forgavest them, though thou tookest vengeance of their inventions.

Ps 100:5 — For the LORD *is* good; his mercy *is* everlasting; and his truth *endureth* to all generations.

Ps 103:3 — Who forgiveth all thine iniquities; who healeth all thy diseases;

Ps 103:17 — But the mercy of the LORD *is* from everlasting to everlasting upon them that fear him, and his righteousness unto children's children;

Ps 106:1 — Praise ye the LORD. O give thanks unto the LORD; for *he is* good: for his mercy *endureth* for ever.

Ps 107:1 — O give thanks unto the LORD, for *he is* good: for his mercy *endureth* for ever.

Ps 108:4 — For thy mercy *is* great above the heavens: and thy truth *reacheth* unto the clouds.

Ps 111:4 — He hath made his wonderful works to be remembered: the LORD *is* gracious and full of compassion.

Ps 116:5 — Gracious *is* the LORD, and righteous; yea, our God *is* merciful.

Ps 118:29 — O give thanks unto the LORD; for *he is* good: for his mercy *endureth* for ever.

Ps 119:64 — The earth, O LORD, is full of thy mercy: teach me thy statutes.

Ps 119:156 — Great *are* thy tender mercies, O LORD: quicken me according to thy judgments.

Ps 135:14 — For the LORD will judge his people, and he will repent himself concerning his servants.

Ps 138:2 — I will worship toward thy holy temple, and praise thy name for thy lovingkindness and for thy truth: for thou hast magnified thy word above all thy name.

Pr 16:6 — By mercy and truth iniquity is purged: and by the fear of the LORD *men* depart from evil.

Pr 28:13 — He that covereth his sins shall not prosper: but whoso confesseth and forsaketh *them* shall have mercy.

Isa 1:5 — Why should ye be stricken any more? ye will revolt more and more: the whole head is sick, and the whole heart faint.

Isa 1:18 — Come now, and let us reason together, saith the LORD: though your sins be as scarlet, they shall be as white as snow; though they be red like crimson, they shall be as wool.

Isa 6:7 — And he laid *it* upon my mouth, and said, Lo, this hath touched thy lips; and thine iniquity is taken away, and thy sin purged.

Isa 12:1 — And in that day thou shalt say, O LORD, I will praise thee: though thou wast angry with me, thine anger is turned away, and thou comfortedst me.

Isa 17:6 — Yet gleaning grapes shall be left in it, as the shaking of an olive tree, two *or* three berries in the top of the uppermost bough, four *or* five in the outmost fruitful branches thereof, saith the LORD God of Israel.

Isa 24:13 — When thus it shall be in the midst of the land among the people, *there shall be* as the shaking of an olive tree, *and* as the gleaning grapes when the vintage is done.

Isa 54:9 — For this *is as* the waters of Noah unto me: for *as* I have sworn that the waters of Noah should no more go over the earth; so have I sworn that I would not be wroth with thee, nor rebuke thee.

Isa 57:11 — And of whom hast thou been afraid or feared, that thou hast lied, and hast not remembered me, nor laid *it* to thy heart? have not I held my peace even of old, and thou fearest me not?

Isa 60:10 — And the sons of strangers shall build up thy walls, and their kings shall minister unto thee: for in my wrath I smote thee, but in my favour have I had mercy on thee.

Isa 65:2 — I have spread out my hands all the day unto a rebellious people, which walketh in a way *that was* not good, after their own thoughts;

Isa 65:8 — Thus saith the LORD, As the new wine is found in the cluster, and *one* saith, Destroy it not; for a blessing *is* in it: so will I do for my servants' sakes, that I may not destroy them all.

Jer 2:9 — Wherefore I will yet plead with you, saith the LORD, and with your children's children will I plead.

Jer 4:27 — For thus hath the LORD said, The whole land shall be desolate; yet will I not make a full end.

Jer 5:10 — Go ye up upon her walls, and destroy; but make not a full end: take away her battlements; for they *are* not the LORD'S.

Jer 7:25 — Since the day that your fathers came forth out of the land of Egypt unto this day I have even sent unto you all my servants the prophets, daily rising up early and sending *them:*

Jer 9:24 — But let him that glorieth glory in this, that he understandeth and knoweth me, that I *am* the LORD which exercise lovingkindness, judgment, and righteousness, in the earth: for in these *things* I delight, saith the LORD.

Jer 29:11 — For I know the thoughts that I think toward you, saith the LORD, thoughts of peace, and not of evil, to give you an expected end.

Jer 30:11 — For I *am* with thee, saith the LORD, to save thee: though I make a full end of all nations whither I have scattered thee, yet will I not make a full end of thee: but I will correct thee in measure, and will not leave thee altogether unpunished.

Jer 31:20 — *Is* Ephraim my dear son? *is he* a pleasant child? for since I spake against him, I do earnestly remember him still: therefore my bowels are troubled for him; I will surely have mercy upon him, saith the LORD.

Jer 31:34 — And they shall teach no more every man his neighbour, and every man his brother, saying, Know the LORD: for they shall all know me, from the least of them unto the greatest of them, saith the LORD; for I will forgive their iniquity, and I will remember their sin no more.

Jer 31:37 — Thus saith the LORD; If heaven above can be measured, and the foundations of the earth searched out beneath, I will also cast off all the seed of Israel for all that they have done, saith the LORD.

Jer 32:18 — Thou shewest lovingkindness unto thousands, and recompensest the iniquity of the fathers into the bosom of their children after them: the Great, the Mighty God, the LORD of hosts, *is* his name,

Jer 33:8 — And I will cleanse them from all their iniquity, whereby they have sinned against me; and I will pardon all their iniquities, whereby they have sinned, and whereby they have transgressed against me.

Jer 33:11 — The voice of joy, and the voice of gladness, the voice of the bridegroom, and the voice of the bride, the voice of them that shall say, Praise the LORD of hosts: for the LORD *is* good; for his mercy *endureth* for ever: *and* of them that shall bring the sacrifice of praise into the house of the LORD. For I will cause to return the captivity of the land, as at the first, saith the LORD.

Jer 36:3 — It may be that the house of Judah will hear all the evil which I purpose to do unto them; that they may return every man from his evil way; that I may forgive their iniquity and their sin.

Jer 46:28 — Fear thou not, O Jacob my servant, saith the LORD: for I *am* with thee; for I will make a full end of all the nations whither I have driven thee: but I will not make a full end of thee, but correct thee in measure; yet will I not leave thee wholly unpunished.

Jer 50:20 — In those days, and in that time, saith the LORD, the iniquity of Israel shall be sought for, and *there shall be* none; and the sins of Judah, and they shall not be found: for I will pardon them whom I reserve.

Jer 51:5 — For Israel *hath* not *been* forsaken, nor Judah of his God, of the LORD of hosts; though their land was filled with sin against the Holy One of Israel.

Eze 14:22 — Yet, behold, therein shall be left a remnant that shall be brought forth, *both* sons and daughters: behold, they shall come forth unto you, and ye shall see their way and their doings: and ye shall be comforted concerning the evil that I have brought upon Jerusalem, *even* concerning all that I have brought upon it.

Eze 16:6 — And when I passed by thee, and saw thee polluted in thine own blood, I said unto thee *when thou wast* in thy blood, Live; yea, I said unto thee *when thou wast* in thy blood, Live.

Eze 16:42 — So will I make my fury toward thee to rest, and my jealousy shall depart from thee, and I will be quiet, and will be no more angry.

Eze 16:63 — That thou mayest remember, and be confounded, and never open thy mouth any more because of thy shame, when I am pacified toward thee for all that thou hast done, saith the Lord GOD.

Eze 18:23 — Have I any pleasure at all that the wicked should die? saith the Lord GOD: *and* not that he should return from his ways, and live?

Eze 33:11 — Say unto them, *As* I live, saith the Lord GOD, I have no pleasure in the death of the wicked; but that the wicked turn from his way and live: turn ye, turn ye from your evil ways; for why will ye die, O house of Israel?

Eze 36:25 — Then will I sprinkle clean water upon you, and ye shall be clean: from all your filthiness, and from all your idols, will I cleanse you.

Da 9:4 — And I prayed unto the LORD my God, and made my confession, and said, O Lord, the great and dreadful God, keeping the covenant and mercy to them that love him, and to them that keep his commandments;

Da 9:9 — To the Lord our God *belong* mercies and forgivenesses, though we have rebelled against him;

Joel 2:13 — And rend your heart, and not your garments, and turn unto the LORD your God: for he *is* gracious and merciful, slow to anger, and of great kindness, and repenteth him of the evil.

Joel 2:18 — Then will the LORD be jealous for his land, and pity his people.

Joel 3:21 — For I will cleanse their blood *that* I have not cleansed: for the LORD dwelleth in Zion.

Am 7:3 — The LORD repented for this: It shall not be, saith the LORD.

Jnh 4:2 — And he prayed unto the LORD, and said, I pray thee, O LORD, *was* not this my saying, when I was yet in my country? Therefore I fled before unto Tarshish: for I knew that thou *art* a gracious God, and merciful, slow to anger, and of great kindness, and repentest thee of the evil.

Na 1:3 — The LORD *is* slow to anger, and great in power, and will not at all acquit *the wicked:* the LORD hath his way in the whirlwind and in the storm, and the clouds *are* the dust of his feet.

Zep 2:7 — And the coast shall be for the remnant of the house of Judah; they shall feed thereupon: in the houses of Ashkelon shall they lie down in the evening: for the LORD their God shall visit them, and turn away their captivity.

Zec 3:9 — For behold the stone that I have laid before Joshua; upon one stone *shall be* seven eyes: behold, I will engrave the graving thereof, saith the LORD of hosts, and I will remove the iniquity of that land in one day.

Zec 10:6 — And I will strengthen the house of Judah, and I will save the house of Joseph, and I will bring them again to place them; for I have mercy upon them: and they shall be as though I had not cast them off: for I *am* the LORD their God, and will hear them.

Mal 3:6 — For I *am* the LORD, I change not; therefore ye sons of Jacob are not consumed.

Mt 6:14 — For if ye forgive men their trespasses, your heavenly Father will also forgive you:

Lk 1:50 — And his mercy *is* on them that fear him from generation to generation.

Lk 6:36 — Be ye therefore merciful, as your Father also is merciful.

Ac 3:19 — Repent ye therefore, and be converted, that your sins may be blotted out, when the times of refreshing shall come from the presence of the Lord;

Ac 17:30 — And the times of this ignorance God winked at; but now commandeth all men every where to repent:

Ac 26:18 — To open their eyes, *and* to turn *them* from darkness to light, and *from* the power of Satan unto God, that they may receive forgiveness of sins, and inheritance among them which are sanctified by faith that is in me.

Ro 9:15 — For he saith to Moses, I will have mercy on whom I will have mercy, and I will have compassion on whom I will have compassion.

Ro 9:18 — Therefore hath he mercy on whom he will *have mercy,* and whom he will he hardeneth.

Ro 11:32 — For God hath concluded them all in unbelief, that he might have mercy upon all.

Ro 15:9 — And that the Gentiles might glorify God for *his* mercy; as it is written, For this cause I will confess to thee among the Gentiles, and sing unto thy name.

1Co 15:10 — But by the grace of God I am what I am: and his grace *which was bestowed* upon me was not in vain; but I laboured more abundantly than they all: yet not I, but the grace of God which was with me.

2Co 1:3 — Blessed *be* God, even the Father of our Lord Jesus Christ, the Father of mercies, and the God of all comfort;

2Co 4:15 — For all things *are* for your sakes, that the abundant grace might through the thanksgiving of many redound to the glory of God.

2Co 12:9 — And he said unto me, My grace is sufficient for thee: for my strength is made perfect in weakness. Most gladly therefore will I rather glory in my infirmities, that the power of Christ may rest upon me.

1Ti 1:13 — Who was before a blasphemer, and a persecutor, and injurious: but I obtained mercy, because I did *it* ignorantly in unbelief.

Tit 3:5 — Not by works of righteousness which we have done, but according to his mercy he saved us, by the washing of regeneration, and renewing of the Holy Ghost;

Heb 4:16 — Let us therefore come boldly unto the throne of grace, that we may obtain mercy, and find grace to help in time of need.

Heb 8:12 — For I will be merciful to their unrighteousness, and their sins and their iniquities will I remember no more.

Jas 2:13 — For he shall have judgment without mercy, that hath shewed no mercy; and mercy rejoiceth against judgment.

Jas 4:8 — Draw nigh to God, and he will draw nigh to you. Cleanse *your* hands, *ye* sinners; and purify *your* hearts, *ye* double minded.

Jas 5:11 — Behold, we count them happy which endure. Ye have heard of the patience of Job, and have seen the end of the Lord; that the Lord is very pitiful, and of tender mercy.

Jas 5:15 — And the prayer of faith shall save the sick, and the Lord shall raise him up; and if he have committed sins, they shall be forgiven him.

1Pe 1:3 — Blessed *be* the God and Father of our Lord Jesus Christ, which according to his abundant mercy hath begotten us again unto a lively hope by the resurrection of Jesus Christ from the dead,

1Pe 2:10 — Which in time past *were* not a people, but *are* now the people of God: which had not obtained mercy, but now have obtained mercy.

1Pe 5:10 — But the God of all grace, who hath called us unto his eternal glory by Christ Jesus, after that ye have suffered a while, make you perfect, stablish, strengthen, settle *you.*

2Pe 3:9 — The Lord is not slack concerning his promise, as some men count slackness; but is longsuffering to us-ward, not willing that any should perish, but that all should come to repentance.

2Pe 3:15 — And account *that* the longsuffering of our Lord *is* salvation; even as our beloved brother Paul also according to the wisdom given unto him hath written unto you;

1Jn 1:9 — If we confess our sins, he is faithful and just to forgive us *our* sins, and to cleanse us from all unrighteousness.

Rev 2:21 — And I gave her space to repent of her fornication; and she repented not.

See: God, Long-Suffering of

See: God, Love of

GOD, Omnipotent

Ge 17:1 — And when Abram was ninety years old and nine, the LORD appeared to Abram, and said unto him, I *am* the Almighty God; walk before me, and be thou perfect.

Ge 18:14 — Is any thing too hard for the LORD? At the time appointed I will return unto thee, according to the time of life, and Sarah shall have a son.

Job 42:2 — I know that thou canst do every *thing,* and *that* no thought can be withholden from thee.

Isa 26:4 — Trust ye in the LORD for ever: for in the LORD JEHOVAH *is* everlasting strength:

Mt 19:26 — But Jesus beheld *them,* and said unto them, With men this is impossible; but with God all things are possible.

Lk 1:37 — For with God nothing shall be impossible.

Ac 26:8 — Why should it be thought a thing incredible with you, that God should raise the dead?

Rev 19:6 — And I heard as it were the voice of a great multitude, and as the voice of many waters, and as the voice of mighty thunderings, saying, Alleluia: for the Lord God omnipotent reigneth.

Rev 21:22 — And I saw no temple therein: for the Lord God Almighty and the Lamb are the temple of it.

- **For uses of the term Almighty, consult concordances.**

See: God, Creator

See: God, Power of

See: God, Preserver

GOD, Omnipresent

Ps 139:7–10; Jer 23:23–24; Ac 7:48–49; 17:27–28

Ge 28:16 — And Jacob awaked out of his sleep, and he said, Surely the LORD is in this place; and I knew *it* not.

1Ki 8:27 — But will God indeed dwell on the earth? behold, the heaven and heaven of heavens cannot contain thee; how much less this house that I have builded?

2Ch 2:6 — But who is able to build him an house, seeing the heaven and heaven of heavens cannot contain him? who *am* I then, that I should build him an house, save only to burn sacrifice before him?

Ps 139:3 — Thou compassest my path and my lying down, and art acquainted *with* all my ways.

Ps 139:5 — Thou hast beset me behind and before, and laid thine hand upon me.

Ac 17:24 — God that made the world and all things therein, seeing that he is Lord of heaven and earth, dwelleth not in temples made with hands;

See: God, Presence of

See: God, Ubiquitous

GOD, Omniscient

↞See: God, Knowledge of
↞See: God, Wisdom of

GOD, Perfection of

Dt 32:4 — *He is* the Rock, his work *is* perfect: for all his ways *are* judgment: a God of truth and without iniquity, just and right *is* he.

2Sa 22:31 — *As for* God, his way *is* perfect; the word of the LORD *is* tried: he *is* a buckler to all them that trust in him.

Ps 18:30 — *As for* God, his way *is* perfect: the word of the LORD is tried: he *is* a buckler to all those that trust in him.

Mt 5:48 — Be ye therefore perfect, even as your Father which is in heaven is perfect.

Ro 12:2 — And be not conformed to this world: but be ye transformed by the renewing of your mind, that ye may prove what is that good, and acceptable, and perfect, will of God.

Jas 1:17 — Every good gift and every perfect gift is from above, and cometh down from the Father of lights, with whom is no variableness, neither shadow of turning.

↞See: God, Holiness of
↞See: God, Judge, and His Justice
↞See: Knowledge
↞See: Wisdom

GOD, Personality of

Isa 43:10–11; 45:5–6, 21–22; Jer 10:6–7; 1Co 8:4–6; Col 1:1–29

Ex 3:14 — And God said unto Moses, I AM THAT I AM: and he said, Thus shalt thou say unto the children of Israel, I AM hath sent me unto you.

Ex 8:10 — And he said, To morrow. And he said, *Be it* according to thy word: that thou mayest know that *there is* none like unto the LORD our God.

Ex 15:11 — Who *is* like unto thee, O LORD, among the gods? who *is* like thee, glorious in holiness, fearful *in* praises, doing wonders?

Ex 20:3 — Thou shalt have no other gods before me.

Ex 34:14 — For thou shalt worship no other god: for the LORD, whose name *is* Jealous, *is* a jealous God:

Dt 4:35 — Unto thee it was shewed, that thou mightest know that the LORD he *is* God; *there is* none else beside him.

Dt 4:39 — Know therefore this day, and consider *it* in thine heart, that the LORD he *is* God in heaven above, and upon the earth beneath: *there is* none else.

Dt 5:7 — Thou shalt have none other gods before me.

Dt 6:4 — Hear, O Israel: The LORD our God *is* one LORD:

Dt 10:17 — For the LORD your God *is* God of gods, and Lord of lords, a great God, a mighty, and a terrible, which regardeth not persons, nor taketh reward:

Dt 32:12 — *So* the LORD alone did lead him, and *there was* no strange god with him.

Dt 32:39 — See now that I, *even* I, *am* he, and *there is* no god with me: I kill, and I make alive; I wound, and I heal: neither *is there any* that can deliver out of my hand.

Jos 22:22 — The LORD God of gods, the LORD God of gods, he knoweth, and Israel he shall know; if *it be* in rebellion, or if in transgression against the LORD, (save us not this day,)

Jgs 13:16 — And the angel of the LORD said unto Manoah, Though thou detain me, I will not eat of thy bread: and if thou wilt offer a burnt offering, thou must offer it unto the LORD. For Manoah knew not that he *was* an angel of the LORD.

1Sa 2:2 — *There is* none holy as the LORD: for *there is* none beside thee: neither *is there* any rock like our God.

1Sa 7:3 — And Samuel spake unto all the house of Israel, saying, If ye do return unto the LORD with all your hearts, *then* put away the strange gods and Ashtaroth from among you, and prepare your hearts unto the LORD, and serve him only: and he will deliver you out of the hand of the Philistines.

2Sa 7:22 — Wherefore thou art great, O LORD God: for *there is* none like thee, neither *is there any* God beside thee, according to all that we have heard with our ears.

2Sa 22:32 — For who *is* God, save the LORD? and who *is* a rock, save our God?

1Ki 8:23 — And he said, LORD God of Israel, *there is* no God like thee, in heaven above, or on earth beneath, who keepest covenant and mercy with thy servants that walk before thee with all their heart:

1Ki 8:60 — That all the people of the earth may know that the LORD *is* God, *and that there is* none else.

2Ki 17:36 — But the LORD, who brought you up out of the land of Egypt with great power and a stretched out arm, him shall ye fear, and him shall ye worship, and to him shall ye do sacrifice.

2Ki 19:15 — And Hezekiah prayed before the LORD, and said, O LORD God of Israel, which dwellest *between* the cherubims, thou art the God, *even* thou alone, of all the kingdoms of the earth: thou hast made heaven and earth.

2Ch 6:14 — And said, O LORD God of Israel, *there is* no God like thee in the heaven, nor in the earth; which keepest covenant, and *shewest* mercy unto thy servants, that walk before thee with all their hearts:

Ezr 1:3 — Who *is there* among you of all his people? his God be with him, and let him go up to Jerusalem, which is in Judah, and build the house of the LORD God of Israel, (he *is* the God,) which *is* in Jerusalem.

Ne 9:6 — Thou, *even* thou, *art* LORD alone; thou hast made heaven, the heaven of heavens, with all their host, the earth, and all *things* that *are* therein, the seas, and all that *is* therein, and thou preservest them all; and the host of heaven worshippeth thee.

Ps 18:31 — For who *is* God save the LORD? or who *is* a rock save our God?

Ps 86:10 — For thou *art* great, and doest wondrous things: thou *art* God alone.

Ps 96:5 — For all the gods of the nations *are* idols: but the LORD made the heavens.

Isa 37:16 — O LORD of hosts, God of Israel, that dwellest *between* the cherubims, thou *art* the God, *even* thou alone, of all the kingdoms of the earth: thou hast made heaven and earth.

Isa 40:25 — To whom then will ye liken me, or shall I be equal? saith the Holy One.

Isa 42:8 — I *am* the LORD: that *is* my name: and my glory will I not give to another, neither my praise to graven images.

Isa 44:6 — Thus saith the LORD the King of Israel, and his redeemer the LORD of hosts; I *am* the first, and I *am* the last; and beside me *there is* no God.

Isa 44:8 — Fear ye not, neither be afraid: have not I told thee from that time, and have declared *it?* ye *are* even my witnesses. Is there a God beside me? yea, *there is* no God; I know not *any.*

Isa 45:18 — For thus saith the LORD that created the heavens; God himself that formed the earth and made it; he hath established it, he created it not in vain, he formed it to be inhabited: I *am* the LORD; and *there is* none else.

Isa 46:5 — To whom will ye liken me, and make *me* equal, and compare me, that we may be like?

Isa 46:9 — Remember the former things of old: for I *am* God, and *there is* none else; *I am* God, and *there is* none like me,

Jer 10:10 — But the LORD *is* the true God, he *is* the living God, and an everlasting king: at his wrath the earth shall tremble, and the nations shall not be able to abide his indignation.

Jer 14:22 — Are there *any* among the vanities of the Gentiles that can cause rain? or can the heavens give showers? *art* not thou he, O LORD our God? therefore we will wait upon thee: for thou hast made all these *things.*

Jer 32:27 — Behold, I *am* the LORD, the God of all flesh: is there any thing too hard for me?

Hos 13:4 — Yet I *am* the LORD thy God from the land of Egypt, and thou shalt know no god but me: for *there is* no saviour beside me.

Mal 2:10 — Have we not all one father? hath not one God created us? why do we deal treacherously every man against his brother, by profaning the covenant of our fathers?

Mt 4:10 — Then saith Jesus unto him, Get thee hence, Satan: for it is written, Thou shalt worship the Lord thy God, and him only shalt thou serve.

Mt 23:9 — And call no *man* your father upon the earth: for one is your Father, which is in heaven.

Mk 12:32 — And the scribe said unto him, Well, Master, thou hast said the truth: for there is one God; and there is none other but he:

Jn 14:9 — Jesus saith unto him, Have I been so long time with you, and yet hast thou not known me, Philip? he that hath seen me hath seen the Father; and how sayest thou *then,* Shew us the Father?

Jn 17:3 — And this is life eternal, that they might know thee the only true God, and Jesus Christ, whom thou hast sent.

Ro 1:25 — Who changed the truth of God into a lie, and worshipped and served the creature more than the Creator, who is blessed for ever. Amen.

Ro 3:29 — *Is he* the God of the Jews only? *is he* not also of the Gentiles? Yes, of the Gentiles also:

2Co 4:4 — In whom the god of this world hath blinded the minds of them which believe not, lest the light of the glorious gospel of Christ, who is the image of God, should shine unto them.

Gal 3:20 — Now a mediator is not *a mediator* of one, but God is one.

Eph 4:6 — One God and Father of all, who *is* above all, and through all, and in you all.

1Th 1:9 — For they themselves shew of us what manner of entering in we had unto you, and how ye turned to God from idols to serve the living and true God;

1Ti 2:5 — For *there is* one God, and one mediator between God and men, the man Christ Jesus;

Heb 1:3 — Who being the brightness of *his* glory, and the express image of his person, and upholding all things by the word of his power, when he had by himself purged our sins, sat down on the right hand of the Majesty on high;

See: God, Unity of

GOD, Power of

Ex 15:6–8, 10–12; Dt 33:26–27; 1Sa 2:6–8; 1Ch 29:11–12; 2Ch 25:8–9; Job 9:4–7, 12–13; 12:14–16; 23:13–14; 26:11–12; 34:14–15; 36:27–37:23; 41:10–11; Ps 2:4–5; 18:1–50; 29:3–9; 65:6–7; 68:33–35; 76:6–7; 78:12–16, 43–51; 89:8–9; 97:3–5; 104:29–30; 105:1–45; 114:3–8; 135:8–12; 136:10–22; Isa 43:16–17; 46:10–11; 50:2–3; Jer 10:12–13; Am 9:5–6; Mic 1:3–4; Na 1:3–6; Hab 3:9–11; 2Co 13:1–14; Eph 1:19–20; 3:20–21

Ex 15:3 — The LORD *is* a man of war: the LORD *is* his name.

Nu 11:23 — And the LORD said unto Moses, Is the LORD'S hand waxed short? thou shalt see now whether my word shall come to pass unto thee or not.

Nu 23:20 — Behold, I have received *commandment* to bless: and he hath blessed; and I cannot reverse it.

Dt 3:24 — O Lord GOD, thou hast begun to shew thy servant thy greatness, and thy mighty hand: for what God *is there* in heaven or in earth, that can do according to thy works, and according to thy might?

Dt 7:21 — Thou shalt not be affrighted at them: for the LORD thy God *is* among you, a mighty God and terrible.

Dt 11:2 — And know ye this day: for *I speak* not with your children which have not known, and which have not seen the chastisement of the LORD your God, his greatness, his mighty hand, and his stretched out arm,

Dt 32:39 — See now that I, *even* I, *am* he, and *there is* no god with me: I kill, and I make alive; I wound, and I heal: neither *is there any* that can deliver out of my hand.

Jos 4:24 — That all the people of the earth might know the hand of the LORD, that it *is* mighty: that ye might fear the LORD your God for ever.

1Sa 2:10 — The adversaries of the LORD shall be broken to pieces; out of heaven shall he thunder upon them: the LORD shall judge the ends of the earth; and he shall give strength unto his king, and exalt the horn of his anointed.

1Sa 14:6 — And Jonathan said to the young man that bare his armour, Come, and let us go over unto the garrison of these uncircumcised: it may be that the LORD will work for us: for *there is* no restraint to the LORD to save by many or by few.

2Sa 22:13 — Through the brightness before him were coals of fire kindled.

2Sa 22:16 — And the channels of the sea appeared, the foundations of the world were discovered, at the rebuking of the LORD, at the blast of the breath of his nostrils.

2Ch 14:11 — And Asa cried unto the LORD his God, and said, LORD, *it is* nothing with thee to help, whether with many, or with them that have no power: help us, O LORD our God; for we rest on thee, and in thy name we go against this multitude. O LORD, thou *art* our God; let not man prevail against thee.

2Ch 16:9 — For the eyes of the LORD run to and fro throughout the whole earth, to shew himself strong in the behalf of *them* whose heart *is* perfect toward him. Herein thou hast done foolishly: therefore from henceforth thou shalt have wars.

2Ch 20:6 — And said, O LORD God of our fathers, *art* not thou God in heaven? and rulest *not* thou over all the kingdoms of the heathen? and in thine hand *is there not* power and might, so that none is able to withstand thee?

Ezr 8:22 — For I was ashamed to require of the king a band of soldiers and horsemen to help us against the enemy in the way: because we had spoken unto the king, saying, The hand of our God *is* upon all them for good that seek him; but his power and his wrath *is* against all them that forsake him.

Ne 1:10 — Now these *are* thy servants and thy people, whom thou hast redeemed by thy great power, and by thy strong hand.

Job 5:9 — Which doeth great things and unsearchable; marvellous things without number:

Job 9:10 — Which doeth great things past finding out; yea, and wonders without number.

Job 9:19 — If *I speak* of strength, lo, *he is* strong: and if of judgment, who shall set me a time *to plead?*

Job 10:7 — Thou knowest that I am not wicked; and *there is* none that can deliver out of thine hand.

Job 11:10 — If he cut off, and shut up, or gather together, then who can hinder him?

Job 14:20 — Thou prevailest for ever against him, and he passeth: thou changest his countenance, and sendest him away.

Job 26:14 — Lo, these *are* parts of his ways: but how little a portion is heard of him? but the thunder of his power who can understand?

Job 36:5 — Behold, God *is* mighty, and despiseth not *any: he is* mighty in strength *and* wisdom.

Job 38:8 — Or *who* shut up the sea with doors, when it brake forth, *as if* it had issued out of the womb?

Job 38:11 — And said, Hitherto shalt thou come, but no further: and here shall thy proud waves be stayed?

Job 38:37 — Who can number the clouds in wisdom? or who can stay the bottles of heaven,

Job 40:9 — Hast thou an arm like God? or canst thou thunder with a voice like him?

Job 42:2 — I know that thou canst do every *thing,* and *that* no thought can be withholden from thee.

Ps 21:13 — Be thou exalted, LORD, in thine own strength: *so* will we sing and praise thy power.

Ps 33:9 — For he spake, and it was *done;* he commanded, and it stood fast.

Ps 46:6 — The heathen raged, the kingdoms were moved: he uttered his voice, the earth melted.

Ps 62:11 — God hath spoken once; twice have I heard this; that power *belongeth* unto God.

Ps 66:3 — Say unto God, How terrible *art thou in* thy works! through the greatness of thy power shall thine enemies submit themselves unto thee.

Ps 66:7 — He ruleth by his power for ever; his eyes behold the nations: let not the rebellious exalt themselves. Selah.

Ps 74:13 — Thou didst divide the sea by thy strength: thou brakest the heads of the dragons in the waters.

Ps 74:15 — Thou didst cleave the fountain and the flood: thou driedst up mighty rivers.

Ps 77:14 — Thou *art* the God that doest wonders: thou hast declared thy strength among the people.

Ps 77:16 — The waters saw thee, O God, the waters saw thee; they were afraid: the depths also were troubled.

Ps 77:18 — The voice of thy thunder *was* in the heaven: the lightnings lightened the world: the earth trembled and shook.

Ps 78:26 — He caused an east wind to blow in the heaven: and by his power he brought in the south wind.

Ps 79:11 — Let the sighing of the prisoner come before thee; according to the greatness of thy power preserve thou those that are appointed to die;

Ps 89:13 — Thou hast a mighty arm: strong is thy hand, *and* high is thy right hand.

Ps 90:3 — Thou turnest man to destruction; and sayest, Return, ye children of men.

Ps 93:1 — The LORD reigneth, he is clothed with majesty; the LORD is clothed with strength, *wherewith* he hath girded himself: the world also is stablished, that it cannot be moved.

Ps 93:4 — The LORD on high *is* mightier than the noise of many waters, *yea, than* the mighty waves of the sea.

Ps 104:7 — At thy rebuke they fled; at the voice of thy thunder they hasted away.

Ps 104:9 — Thou hast set a bound that they may not pass over; that they turn not again to cover the earth.

Ps 104:32 — He looketh on the earth, and it trembleth: he toucheth the hills, and they smoke.

Ps 106:8 — Nevertheless he saved them for his name's sake, that he might make his mighty power to be known.

Ps 107:25 — For he commandeth, and raiseth the stormy wind, which lifteth up the waves thereof.

Ps 107:29 — He maketh the storm a calm, so that the waves thereof are still.

Ps 111:6 — He hath shewed his people the power of his works, that he may give them the heritage of the heathen.

Ps 115:3 — But our God *is* in the heavens: he hath done whatsoever he hath pleased.

Ps 118:16 — The right hand of the LORD is exalted: the right hand of the LORD doeth valiantly.

Ps 135:6 — Whatsoever the LORD pleased, *that* did he in heaven, and in earth, in the seas, and all deep places.

Ps 144:5 — Bow thy heavens, O LORD, and come down: touch the mountains, and they shall smoke.

Ps 145:6 — And *men* shall speak of the might of thy terrible acts: and I will declare thy greatness.

Ps 145:16 — Thou openest thine hand, and satisfiest the desire of every living thing.

Ps 147:5 — Great *is* our Lord, and of great power: his understanding *is* infinite.

Ps 147:16 — He giveth snow like wool: he scattereth the hoar frost like ashes.

Ps 147:18 — He sendeth out his word, and melteth them: he causeth his wind to blow, *and* the waters flow.

Ps 148:5 — Let them praise the name of the LORD: for he commanded, and they were created.

Pr 21:30 — *There is* no wisdom nor understanding nor counsel against the LORD.

Pr 30:4 — Who hath ascended up into heaven, or descended? who hath gathered the wind in his fists? who hath bound the waters in a garment? who hath established all the ends of the earth? what *is* his name, and what *is* his son's name, if thou canst tell?

Isa 14:24 — The LORD of hosts hath sworn, saying, Surely as I have thought, so shall it come to pass; and as I have purposed, *so* shall it stand:

Isa 14:27 — For the LORD of hosts hath purposed, and who shall disannul *it?* and his hand *is* stretched out, and who shall turn it back?

Isa 17:13 — The nations shall rush like the rushing of many waters: but *God* shall rebuke them, and they shall flee far off, and shall be chased as the chaff of the mountains before the wind, and like a rolling thing before the whirlwind.

Isa 19:1 — The burden of Egypt. Behold, the LORD rideth upon a swift cloud, and shall come into Egypt: and the idols of Egypt shall be moved at his presence, and the heart of Egypt shall melt in the midst of it.

Isa 23:11 — He stretched out his hand over the sea, he shook the kingdoms: the LORD hath given a commandment against the merchant *city*, to destroy the strong holds thereof.

Isa 26:4 — Trust ye in the LORD for ever: for in the LORD JEHOVAH *is* everlasting strength:

Isa 27:4 — Fury *is* not in me: who would set the briers *and* thorns against me in battle? I would go through them, I would burn them together.

Isa 31:3 — Now the Egyptians *are* men, and not God; and their horses flesh, and not spirit. When the LORD shall stretch out his hand, both he that helpeth shall fall, and he that is holpen shall fall down, and they all shall fail together.

Isa 33:3 — At the noise of the tumult the people fled; at the lifting up of thyself the nations were scattered.

Isa 33:13 — Hear, ye *that are* far off, what I have done; and, ye *that are* near, acknowledge my might.

Isa 40:12 — Who hath measured the waters in the hollow of his hand, and meted out heaven with the span, and comprehended the dust of the earth in a measure, and weighed the mountains in scales, and the hills in a balance?

Isa 40:22 — *It is* he that sitteth upon the circle of the earth, and the inhabitants thereof *are* as grasshoppers; that stretcheth out the heavens as a curtain, and spreadeth them out as a tent to dwell in:

Isa 40:24 — Yea, they shall not be planted; yea, they shall not be sown: yea, their stock shall not take root in the earth: and he shall also blow upon them, and they shall wither, and the whirlwind shall take them away as stubble.

Isa 40:26 — Lift up your eyes on high, and behold who hath created these *things*, that bringeth out their host by number: he calleth them all by names by the greatness of his might, for that *he is* strong in power; not one faileth.

Isa 40:28 — Hast thou not known? hast thou not heard, *that* the everlasting God, the LORD, the Creator of the ends of the earth, fainteth not, neither is weary? *there is* no searching of his understanding.

Isa 43:13 — Yea, before the day *was* I *am* he; and *there is* none that can deliver out of my hand: I will work, and who shall let it?

Isa 44:27 — That saith to the deep, Be dry, and I will dry up thy rivers:

Isa 48:13 — Mine hand also hath laid the foundation of the earth, and my right hand hath spanned the heavens: *when* I call unto them, they stand up together.

Isa 51:10 — *Art* thou not it which hath dried the sea, the waters of the great deep; that hath made the depths of the sea a way for the ransomed to pass over?

Isa 51:15 — But I *am* the LORD thy God, that divided the sea, whose waves roared: The LORD of hosts *is* his name.

Isa 52:10 — The LORD hath made bare his holy arm in the eyes of all the nations; and all the ends of the earth shall see the salvation of our God.

Isa 59:1 — Behold, the LORD'S hand is not shortened, that it cannot save; neither his ear heavy, that it cannot hear:

Isa 60:16 — Thou shalt also suck the milk of the Gentiles, and shalt suck the breast of kings: and thou shalt know that I the LORD *am* thy Saviour and thy Redeemer, the mighty One of Jacob.

Isa 63:12 — That led *them* by the right hand of Moses with his glorious arm, dividing the water before them, to make himself an everlasting name?

Jer 5:22 — Fear ye not me? saith the LORD: will ye not tremble at my presence, which have placed the sand *for* the bound of the sea by a perpetual decree, that it cannot pass it: and though the waves thereof toss themselves, yet can they not prevail; though they roar, yet can they not pass over it?

Jer 10:6 — Forasmuch as *there is* none like unto thee, O LORD; thou *art* great, and thy name is great in might.

Jer 20:11 — But the LORD *is* with me as a mighty terrible one: therefore my persecutors shall stumble, and they shall not prevail: they shall be greatly ashamed; for they shall not prosper: *their* everlasting confusion shall never be forgotten.

Jer 27:5 — I have made the earth, the man and the beast that *are* upon the ground, by my great power and by my outstretched arm, and have given it unto whom it seemed meet unto me.

Jer 32:17 — Ah Lord GOD! behold, thou hast made the heaven and the earth by thy great power and stretched out arm, *and* there is nothing too hard for thee:

Jer 32:27 — Behold, I *am* the LORD, the God of all flesh: is there any thing too hard for me?

Jer 50:44 — Behold, he shall come up like a lion from the swelling of Jordan unto the habitation of the strong: but I will make them suddenly run away from her: and who *is* a chosen *man, that* I may appoint over her? for who *is* like me? and who will appoint me the time? and who *is* that shepherd that will stand before me?

Jer 51:15 — He hath made the earth by his power, he hath established the world by his wisdom, and hath stretched out the heaven by his understanding.

Da 2:20 — Daniel answered and said, Blessed be the name of God for ever and ever: for wisdom and might are his:

Da 3:17 — If it be *so,* our God whom we serve is able to deliver us from the burning fiery furnace, and he will deliver *us* out of thine hand, O king.

Da 4:35 — And all the inhabitants of the earth *are* reputed as nothing: and he doeth according to his will in the army of heaven, and *among* the inhabitants of the earth: and none can stay his hand, or say unto him, What doest thou?

Da 6:27 — He delivereth and rescueth, and he worketh signs and wonders in heaven and in earth, who hath delivered Daniel from the power of the lions.

Joel 2:11 — And the LORD shall utter his voice before his army: for his camp *is* very great: for *he is* strong that executeth his word: for the day of the LORD *is* great and very terrible; and who can abide it?

Joel 3:16 — The LORD also shall roar out of Zion, and utter his voice from Jerusalem; and the heavens and the earth shall shake: but the LORD *will be* the hope of his people, and the strength of the children of Israel.

Am 1:2 — And he said, The LORD will roar from Zion, and utter his voice from Jerusalem; and the habitations of the shepherds shall mourn, and the top of Carmel shall wither.

Am 4:13 — For, lo, he that formeth the mountains, and createth the wind, and declareth unto man what *is* his thought, that maketh the morning darkness, and treadeth upon the high places of the earth, The LORD, The God of hosts, *is* his name.

Hab 3:6 — He stood, and measured the earth: he beheld, and drove asunder the nations; and the everlasting mountains were scattered, the perpetual hills did bow: his ways *are* everlasting.

Hab 3:15 — Thou didst walk through the sea with thine horses, *through* the heap of great waters.

Zec 9:14 — And the LORD shall be seen over them, and his arrow shall go forth as the lightning: and the LORD GOD shall blow the trumpet, and shall go with whirlwinds of the south.

Mt 3:9 — And think not to say within yourselves, We have Abraham to *our* father: for I say unto you, that God is able of these stones to raise up children unto Abraham.

Mt 6:13 — And lead us not into temptation, but deliver us from evil: For thine is the kingdom, and the power, and the glory, for ever. Amen.

Mt 10:28 — And fear not them which kill the body, but are not able to kill the soul: but rather fear him which is able to destroy both soul and body in hell.

Mt 19:26 — But Jesus beheld *them,* and said unto them, With men this is impossible; but with God all things are possible.

Mt 22:29 — Jesus answered and said unto them, Ye do err, not knowing the scriptures, nor the power of God.

Mk 10:27 — And Jesus looking upon them saith, With men *it is* impossible, but not with God: for with God all things are possible.

Mk 14:36 — And he said, Abba, Father, all things *are* possible unto thee; take away this cup from me: nevertheless not what I will, but what thou wilt.

Lk 1:37 — For with God nothing shall be impossible.

Lk 1:49 — For he that is mighty hath done to me great things; and holy *is* his name.

Lk 1:51 — He hath shewed strength with his arm; he hath scattered the proud in the imagination of their hearts.

Lk 11:20 — But if I with the finger of God cast out devils, no doubt the kingdom of God is come upon you.

Lk 18:27 — And he said, The things which are impossible with men are possible with God.

Ro 1:20 — For the invisible things of him from the creation of the world are clearly seen, being understood by the things that are made, *even* his eternal power and Godhead; so that they are without excuse:

Ro 4:21 — And being fully persuaded that, what he had promised, he was able also to perform.

1Co 6:14 — And God hath both raised up the Lord, and will also raise up us by his own power.

Heb 1:3 — Who being the brightness of *his* glory, and the express image of his person, and upholding all things by the word of his power, when he had by himself purged our sins, sat down on the right hand of the Majesty on high;

Heb 12:26 — Whose voice then shook the earth: but now he hath promised, saying, Yet once more I shake not the earth only, but also heaven.

Heb 12:29 — For our God *is* a consuming fire.

Jas 4:12 — There is one lawgiver, who is able to save and to destroy: who art thou that judgest another?

1Pe 1:5 — Who are kept by the power of God through faith unto salvation ready to be revealed in the last time.

Rev 4:11 — Thou art worthy, O Lord, to receive glory and honour and power: for thou hast created all things, and for thy pleasure they are and were created.

Rev 5:13 — And every creature which is in heaven, and on the earth, and under the earth, and such as are in the sea, and all that are in them, heard I saying, Blessing, and honour, and glory, and power, *be* unto him that sitteth upon the throne, and unto the Lamb for ever and ever.

Rev 11:17 — Saying, We give thee thanks, O Lord God Almighty, which art, and wast, and art to come; because thou hast taken to thee thy great power, and hast reigned.

Rev 19:1 — And after these things I heard a great voice of much people in heaven, saying, Alleluia; Salvation, and glory, and honour, and power, unto the Lord our God:

Rev 19:6 — And I heard as it were the voice of a great multitude, and as the voice of many waters, and as the voice of mighty thunderings, saying, Alleluia: for the Lord God omnipotent reigneth.

↞See: God, Omnipotent

GOD, Presence of

Dt 4:34–36; Ps 139:7–10; Jer 23:23–24; 32:18–19; Jnh 1:3–4; Ac 7:48–49; 17:27–28

Ge 16:13 — And she called the name of the LORD that spake unto her, Thou God seest me: for she said, Have I also here looked after him that seeth me?

Ge 28:16 — And Jacob awaked out of his sleep, and he said, Surely the LORD is in this place; and I knew *it* not.

Ex 20:24 — An altar of earth thou shalt make unto me, and shalt sacrifice thereon thy burnt offerings, and thy peace offerings, thy sheep, and thine oxen: in all places where I record my name I will come unto thee, and I will bless thee.

Dt 4:39 — Know therefore this day, and consider *it* in thine heart, that the LORD he *is* God in heaven above, and upon the earth beneath: *there is* none else.

1Ki 8:27 — But will God indeed dwell on the earth? behold, the heaven and heaven of heavens cannot contain thee; how much less this house that I have builded?

2Ch 2:6 — But who is able to build him an house, seeing the heaven and heaven of heavens cannot contain him? who *am* I then, that I should build him an house, save only to burn sacrifice before him?

Ps 139:3 — Thou compassest my path and my lying down, and art acquainted *with* all my ways.

Ps 139:5 — Thou hast beset me behind and before, and laid thine hand upon me.

Isa 57:15 — For thus saith the high and lofty One that inhabiteth eternity, whose name *is* Holy; I dwell in the high and holy *place,* with him also *that is* of a contrite and humble spirit, to revive the spirit of the humble, and to revive the heart of the contrite ones.

Isa 66:1 — Thus saith the LORD, The heaven *is* my throne, and the earth *is* my footstool: where *is* the house that ye build unto me? and where *is* the place of my rest?

Ac 17:24 — God that made the world and all things therein, seeing that he is Lord of heaven and earth, dwelleth not in temples made with hands;

1Co 12:6 — And there are diversities of operations, but it is the same God which worketh all in all.

Eph 1:23 — Which is his body, the fulness of him that filleth all in all.

See: God, Omnipresent

See: God, Preserver

GOD, Preserver

Ge 48:15–16; 49:24–25; Ex 6:6–7; 8:22–23; 13:21–22; 14:29–30; 15:16–17; 23:20–31; Dt 1:30–31; 7:21–22; 33:25–29; Ezr 8:22–23; Job 5:18–24; 11:18–19; 27:3–4; Ps 10:17–18; 14:5–6; 25:8–9; 34:19–22; 37:23–24, 32–33; 41:1–3; 91:1–16; 102:19–20; 103:2–5; 121:3–8; 124:1–125:3; 145:19–20; 146:7–8; 147:2–3; Pr 2:7–8; 3:23–24; Isa 4:5–6; 31:4–5; 46:3–4; 51:9–10; 54:14–15; Jer 30:7–8; 31:9–10; Eze 34:11–16; Da 3:27–28; Am 5:8–9; Zep 3:19–20; Zec 4:6–7; 9:14–16; Mt 10:29–31; Lk 12:6–7; 18:7–8; 1Pe 3:12–13

Ge 14:20 — And blessed be the most high God, which hath delivered thine enemies into thy hand. And he gave him tithes of all.

Ge 28:15 — And, behold, I *am* with thee, and will keep thee in all *places* whither thou goest, and will bring thee again into this land; for I will not leave thee, until I have done *that* which I have spoken to thee of.

Ge 31:3 — And the LORD said unto Jacob, Return unto the land of thy fathers, and to thy kindred; and I will be with thee.

Ge 31:13 — I *am* the God of Bethel, where thou anointedst the pillar, *and* where thou vowedst a vow unto me: now arise, get thee out from this land, and return unto the land of thy kindred.

Ex 3:17 — And I have said, I will bring you up out of the affliction of Egypt unto the land of the Canaanites, and the Hittites, and the Amorites, and the Perizzites, and the Hivites, and the Jebusites, unto a land flowing with milk and honey.

Ex 9:26 — Only in the land of Goshen, where the children of Israel *were,* was there no hail.

Ex 11:7 — But against any of the children of Israel shall not a dog move his tongue, against man or beast: that ye may know how that the LORD doth put a difference between the Egyptians and Israel.

Ex 12:13 — And the blood shall be to you for a token upon the houses where ye *are:* and when I see the blood, I will pass over you, and the plague shall not be upon you to destroy *you,* when I smite the land of Egypt.

Ex 12:17 — And ye shall observe *the feast of* unleavened bread; for in this selfsame day have I brought your armies out of the land of Egypt: therefore shall ye observe this day in your generations by an ordinance for ever.

Ex 12:23 — For the LORD will pass through to smite the Egyptians; and when he seeth the blood upon the lintel, and on the two side posts, the LORD will pass over the door, and will not suffer the destroyer to come in unto your houses to smite *you.*

Ex 15:2 — The LORD *is* my strength and song, and he is become my salvation: he *is* my God, and I will prepare him an habitation; my father's God, and I will exalt him.

Ex 15:13 — Thou in thy mercy hast led forth the people *which* thou hast redeemed: thou hast guided *them* in thy strength unto thy holy habitation.

Ex 16:15 — And when the children of Israel saw *it,* they said one to another, It *is* manna: for they wist not what it *was.* And Moses said unto them, This *is* the bread which the LORD hath given you to eat.

Ex 19:4 — Ye have seen what I did unto the Egyptians, and *how* I bare you on eagles' wings, and brought you unto myself.

Ex 34:24 — For I will cast out the nations before thee, and enlarge thy borders: neither shall any man desire thy land, when thou shalt go up to appear before the LORD thy God thrice in the year.

Nu 10:33 — And they departed from the mount of the LORD three days' journey: and the ark of the covenant of the LORD went before them in the three days' journey, to search out a resting place for them.

Nu 23:23 — Surely *there is* no enchantment against Jacob, neither *is there* any divination against Israel: according to this time it shall be said of Jacob and of Israel, What hath God wrought!

Dt 9:3 — Understand therefore this day, that the LORD thy God *is* he which goeth over before thee; *as* a consuming fire he shall destroy them, and he shall bring them down before thy face: so shalt thou drive them out, and destroy them quickly, as the LORD hath said unto thee.

Dt 11:25 — There shall no man be able to stand before you: *for* the LORD your God shall lay the fear of you and the dread of you upon all the land that ye shall tread upon, as he hath said unto you.

Dt 23:14 — For the LORD thy God walketh in the midst of thy camp, to deliver thee, and to give up thine enemies before thee; therefore shall thy camp be holy: that he see no unclean thing in thee, and turn away from thee.

Dt 30:4 — If *any* of thine be driven out unto the outmost *parts* of heaven, from thence will the LORD thy God gather thee, and from thence will he fetch thee:

Dt 30:20 — That thou mayest love the LORD thy God, *and* that thou mayest obey his voice, and that thou mayest cleave unto him: for he *is* thy life, and the length of thy days: that thou mayest dwell in the land which the LORD sware unto thy fathers, to Abraham, to Isaac, and to Jacob, to give them.

Dt 31:3 — The LORD thy God, he will go over before thee, *and* he will destroy these nations from before thee, and thou shalt possess them: *and* Joshua, he shall go over before thee, as the LORD hath said.

Dt 32:10 — He found him in a desert land, and in the waste howling wilderness; he led him about, he instructed him, he kept him as the apple of his eye.

Dt 33:12 — *And* of Benjamin he said, The beloved of the LORD shall dwell in safety by him; *and the LORD* shall cover him all the day long, and he shall dwell between his shoulders.

Jos 23:10 — One man of you shall chase a thousand: for the LORD your God, he *it is* that fighteth for you, as he hath promised you.

1Sa 2:6 — The LORD killeth, and maketh alive: he bringeth down to the grave, and bringeth up.

1Sa 2:9 — He will keep the feet of his saints, and the wicked shall be silent in darkness; for by strength shall no man prevail.

1Sa 9:16 — To morrow about this time I will send thee a man out of the land of Benjamin, and thou shalt anoint him *to be* captain over my people Israel, that he may save my people out of the hand of the Philistines: for I have looked upon my people, because their cry is come unto me.

2Sa 22:28 — And the afflicted people thou wilt save: but thine eyes *are* upon the haughty, *that* thou mayest bring *them* down.

2Ki 20:6 — And I will add unto thy days fifteen years; and I will deliver thee and this city out of the hand of the king of Assyria; and I will defend this city for mine own sake, and for my servant David's sake.

2Ch 16:9 — For the eyes of the LORD run to and fro throughout the whole earth, to shew himself strong in the behalf of *them* whose heart *is* perfect toward him. Herein thou hast done foolishly: therefore from henceforth thou shalt have wars.

2Ch 20:15 — And he said, Hearken ye, all Judah, and ye inhabitants of Jerusalem, and thou king Jehoshaphat, Thus saith the LORD unto you, Be not afraid nor dismayed by reason of this great multitude; for the battle *is* not yours, but God's.

2Ch 20:17 — Ye shall not *need* to fight in this *battle:* set yourselves, stand ye *still,* and see the salvation of the LORD with you, O Judah and Jerusalem: fear not, nor be dismayed; to morrow go out against them: for the LORD *will be* with you.

Ne 9:6 — Thou, *even* thou, *art* LORD alone; thou hast made heaven, the heaven of heavens, with all their host, the earth, and all *things* that *are* therein, the seas, and all that *is* therein, and thou preservest them all; and the host of heaven worshippeth thee.

Job 1:10 — Hast not thou made an hedge about him, and about his house, and about all that he hath on every side? thou hast blessed the work of his hands, and his substance is increased in the land.

Job 4:7 — Remember, I pray thee, who *ever* perished, being innocent? or where were the righteous cut off?

Job 5:11 — To set up on high those that be low; that those which mourn may be exalted to safety.

Job 10:12 — Thou hast granted me life and favour, and thy visitation hath preserved my spirit.

Job 22:25 — Yea, the Almighty shall be thy defence, and thou shalt have plenty of silver.

Job 33:18 — He keepeth back his soul from the pit, and his life from perishing by the sword.

Job 36:7 — He withdraweth not his eyes from the righteous: but with kings *are they* on the throne; yea, he doth establish them for ever, and they are exalted.

Job 36:16 — Even so would he have removed thee out of the strait *into* a broad place, where *there is* no straitness; and that which *should be* set on thy table should be full of fatness.

Ps 1:6 — For the LORD knoweth the way of the righteous: but the way of the ungodly shall perish.

Ps 3:3 — But thou, O LORD, *art* a shield for me; my glory, and the lifter up of mine head.

Ps 9:9 — The LORD also will be a refuge for the oppressed, a refuge in times of trouble.

Ps 12:7 — Thou shalt keep them, O LORD, thou shalt preserve them from this generation for ever.

Ps 17:7 — Shew thy marvellous lovingkindness, O thou that savest by thy right hand them which put their trust *in thee* from those that rise up *against them.*

Ps 18:17 — He delivered me from my strong enemy, and from them which hated me: for they were too strong for me.

Ps 18:27 — For thou wilt save the afflicted people; but wilt bring down high looks.

Ps 19:14 — Let the words of my mouth, and the meditation of my heart, be acceptable in thy sight, O LORD, my strength, and my redeemer.

Ps 25:12 — What man *is* he that feareth the LORD? him shall he teach in the way *that* he shall choose.

Ps 31:20 — Thou shalt hide them in the secret of thy presence from the pride of man: thou shalt keep them secretly in a pavilion from the strife of tongues.

Ps 31:23 — O love the LORD, all ye his saints: *for* the LORD preserveth the faithful, and plentifully rewardeth the proud doer.

Ps 32:6 — For this shall every one that is godly pray unto thee in a time when thou mayest be found: surely in the floods of great waters they shall not come nigh unto him.

Ps 34:15 — The eyes of the LORD *are* upon the righteous, and his ears *are open* unto their cry.
Ps 34:17 — *The righteous* cry, and the LORD heareth, and delivereth them out of all their troubles.
Ps 37:17 — For the arms of the wicked shall be broken: but the LORD upholdeth the righteous.
Ps 37:28 — For the LORD loveth judgment, and forsaketh not his saints; they are preserved for ever: but the seed of the wicked shall be cut off.
Ps 46:1 — God *is* our refuge and strength, a very present help in trouble.
Ps 46:5 — God *is* in the midst of her; she shall not be moved: God shall help her, *and that* right early.
Ps 46:7 — The LORD of hosts *is* with us; the God of Jacob *is* our refuge. Selah.
Ps 48:3 — God is known in her palaces for a refuge.
Ps 50:15 — And call upon me in the day of trouble: I will deliver thee, and thou shalt glorify me.
Ps 61:3 — For thou hast been a shelter for me, *and* a strong tower from the enemy.
Ps 61:6 — Thou wilt prolong the king's life: *and* his years as many generations.
Ps 68:6 — God setteth the solitary in families: he bringeth out those which are bound with chains: but the rebellious dwell in a dry *land*.
Ps 68:22 — The Lord said, I will bring again from Bashan, I will bring *my people* again from the depths of the sea:
Ps 72:14 — He shall redeem their soul from deceit and violence: and precious shall their blood be in his sight.
Ps 73:23 — Nevertheless I *am* continually with thee: thou hast holden *me* by my right hand.
Ps 80:1 — Give ear, O Shepherd of Israel, thou that leadest Joseph like a flock; thou that dwellest *between* the cherubims, shine forth.
Ps 84:11 — For the LORD God *is* a sun and shield: the LORD will give grace and glory: no good *thing* will he withhold from them that walk uprightly.
Ps 87:5 — And of Zion it shall be said, This and *that man* was born in her: and the highest himself shall establish her.
Ps 94:13 — That thou mayest give him rest from the days of adversity, until the pit be digged for the wicked.
Ps 97:10 — Ye that love the LORD, hate evil: he preserveth the souls of his saints; he delivereth them out of the hand of the wicked.
Ps 107:9 — For he satisfieth the longing soul, and filleth the hungry soul with goodness.
Ps 112:4 — Unto the upright there ariseth light in the darkness: *he is* gracious, and full of compassion, and righteous.
Ps 115:10 — O house of Aaron, trust in the LORD: he *is* their help and their shield.
Ps 116:6 — The LORD preserveth the simple: I was brought low, and he helped me.
Ps 118:13 — Thou hast thrust sore at me that I might fall: but the LORD helped me.
Ps 127:1 — Except the LORD build the house, they labour in vain that build it: except the LORD keep the city, the watchman waketh *but* in vain.
Ps 145:14 — The LORD upholdeth all that fall, and raiseth up all *those that be* bowed down.
Pr 3:6 — In all thy ways acknowledge him, and he shall direct thy paths.
Pr 10:3 — The LORD will not suffer the soul of the righteous to famish: but he casteth away the substance of the wicked.
Pr 10:30 — The righteous shall never be removed: but the wicked shall not inhabit the earth.
Pr 11:8 — The righteous is delivered out of trouble, and the wicked cometh in his stead.
Pr 12:3 — A man shall not be established by wickedness: but the root of the righteous shall not be moved.
Pr 12:13 — The wicked is snared by the transgression of *his* lips: but the just shall come out of trouble.
Pr 12:21 — There shall no evil happen to the just: but the wicked shall be filled with mischief.
Pr 14:26 — In the fear of the LORD *is* strong confidence: and his children shall have a place of refuge.
Pr 15:19 — The way of the slothful *man is* as an hedge of thorns: but the way of the righteous *is* made plain.
Pr 16:9 — A man's heart deviseth his way: but the LORD directeth his steps.
Pr 16:33 — The lot is cast into the lap; but the whole disposing thereof *is* of the LORD.
Pr 19:23 — The fear of the LORD *tendeth* to life: and *he that hath it* shall abide satisfied; he shall not be visited with evil.
Pr 20:22 — Say not thou, I will recompense evil; *but* wait on the LORD, and he shall save thee.
Pr 20:24 — Man's goings *are* of the LORD; how can a man then understand his own way?
Pr 21:31 — The horse *is* prepared against the day of battle: but safety *is* of the LORD.
Pr 22:12 — The eyes of the LORD preserve knowledge, and he overthroweth the words of the transgressor.
Pr 24:16 — For a just *man* falleth seven times, and riseth up again: but the wicked shall fall into mischief.
Isa 10:27 — And it shall come to pass in that day, *that* his burden shall be taken away from off thy shoulder, and his yoke from off thy neck, and the yoke shall be destroyed because of the anointing.
Isa 14:3 — And it shall come to pass in the day that the LORD shall give thee rest from thy sorrow, and from thy fear, and from the hard bondage wherein thou wast made to serve,
Isa 26:7 — The way of the just *is* uprightness: thou, most upright, dost weigh the path of the just.
Isa 27:3 — I the LORD do keep it; I will water it every moment: lest *any* hurt it, I will keep it night and day.
Isa 30:21 — And thine ears shall hear a word behind thee, saying, This *is* the way, walk ye in it, when ye turn to the right hand, and when ye turn to the left.
Isa 30:26 — Moreover the light of the moon shall be as the light of the sun, and the light of the sun shall be sevenfold, as the light of seven days, in the day that the LORD bindeth up the breach of his people, and healeth the stroke of their wound.
Isa 31:9 — And he shall pass over to his strong hold for fear, and his princes shall be afraid of the ensign, saith the LORD, whose fire *is* in Zion, and his furnace in Jerusalem.
Isa 32:2 — And a man shall be as an hiding place from the wind, and a covert from the tempest; as rivers of

water in a dry place, as the shadow of a great rock in a weary land.

Isa 32:18 — And my people shall dwell in a peaceable habitation, and in sure dwellings, and in quiet resting places;

Isa 33:16 — He shall dwell on high: his place of defence *shall be* the munitions of rocks: bread shall be given him; his waters *shall be* sure.

Isa 33:20 — Look upon Zion, the city of our solemnities: thine eyes shall see Jerusalem a quiet habitation, a tabernacle *that* shall not be taken down; not one of the stakes thereof shall ever be removed, neither shall any of the cords thereof be broken.

Isa 35:9 — No lion shall be there, nor *any* ravenous beast shall go up thereon, it shall not be found there; but the redeemed shall walk *there:*

Isa 37:32 — For out of Jerusalem shall go forth a remnant, and they that escape out of mount Zion: the zeal of the LORD of hosts shall do this.

Isa 37:35 — For I will defend this city to save it for mine own sake, and for my servant David's sake.

Isa 40:11 — He shall feed his flock like a shepherd: he shall gather the lambs with his arm, and carry *them* in his bosom, *and* shall gently lead those that are with young.

Isa 40:29 — He giveth power to the faint; and to *them that have* no might he increaseth strength.

Isa 40:31 — But they that wait upon the LORD shall renew *their* strength; they shall mount up with wings as eagles; they shall run, and not be weary; *and* they shall walk, and not faint.

Isa 42:13 — The LORD shall go forth as a mighty man, he shall stir up jealousy like a man of war: he shall cry, yea, roar; he shall prevail against his enemies.

Isa 42:16 — And I will bring the blind by a way *that* they knew not; I will lead them in paths *that* they have not known: I will make darkness light before them, and crooked things straight. These things will I do unto them, and not forsake them.

Isa 43:2 — When thou passest through the waters, I *will be* with thee; and through the rivers, they shall not overflow thee: when thou walkest through the fire, thou shalt not be burned; neither shall the flame kindle upon thee.

Isa 45:2 — I will go before thee, and make the crooked places straight: I will break in pieces the gates of brass, and cut in sunder the bars of iron:

Isa 45:4 — For Jacob my servant's sake, and Israel mine elect, I have even called thee by thy name: I have surnamed thee, though thou hast not known me.

Isa 48:17 — Thus saith the LORD, thy Redeemer, the Holy One of Israel; I *am* the LORD thy God which teacheth thee to profit, which leadeth thee by the way *that* thou shouldest go.

Isa 49:9 — That thou mayest say to the prisoners, Go forth; to them that *are* in darkness, Shew yourselves. They shall feed in the ways, and their pastures *shall be* in all high places.

Isa 49:17 — Thy children shall make haste; thy destroyers and they that made thee waste shall go forth of thee.

Isa 49:25 — But thus saith the LORD, Even the captives of the mighty shall be taken away, and the prey of the terrible shall be delivered: for I will contend with him that contendeth with thee, and I will save thy children.

Isa 51:22 — Thus saith thy Lord the LORD, and thy God *that* pleadeth the cause of his people, Behold, I have taken out of thine hand the cup of trembling, *even* the dregs of the cup of my fury; thou shalt no more drink it again:

Isa 52:12 — For ye shall not go out with haste, nor go by flight: for the LORD will go before you; and the God of Israel *will be* your rereward.

Isa 54:17 — No weapon that is formed against thee shall prosper; and every tongue *that* shall rise against thee in judgment thou shalt condemn. This *is* the heritage of the servants of the LORD, and their righteousness *is* of me, saith the LORD.

Isa 57:14 — And shall say, Cast ye up, cast ye up, prepare the way, take up the stumblingblock out of the way of my people.

Isa 58:11 — And the LORD shall guide thee continually, and satisfy thy soul in drought, and make fat thy bones: and thou shalt be like a watered garden, and like a spring of water, whose waters fail not.

Isa 59:19 — So shall they fear the name of the LORD from the west, and his glory from the rising of the sun. When the enemy shall come in like a flood, the Spirit of the LORD shall lift up a standard against him.

Isa 63:9 — In all their affliction he was afflicted, and the angel of his presence saved them: in his love and in his pity he redeemed them; and he bare them, and carried them all the days of old.

Jer 2:3 — Israel *was* holiness unto the LORD, *and* the firstfruits of his increase: all that devour him shall offend; evil shall come upon them, saith the LORD.

Jer 2:6 — Neither said they, Where *is* the LORD that brought us up out of the land of Egypt, that led us through the wilderness, through a land of deserts and of pits, through a land of drought, and of the shadow of death, through a land that no man passed through, and where no man dwelt?

Jer 2:20 — For of old time I have broken thy yoke, *and* burst thy bands; and thou saidst, I will not transgress; when upon every high hill and under every green tree thou wanderest, playing the harlot.

Jer 3:4 — Wilt thou not from this time cry unto me, My father, thou art the guide of my youth?

Jer 11:4 — Which I commanded your fathers in the day *that* I brought them forth out of the land of Egypt, from the iron furnace, saying, Obey my voice, and do them, according to all which I command you: so shall ye be my people, and I will be your God:

Jer 30:11 — For I *am* with thee, saith the LORD, to save thee: though I make a full end of all nations whither I have scattered thee, yet will I not make a full end of thee: but I will correct thee in measure, and will not leave thee altogether unpunished.

Jer 30:17 — For I will restore health unto thee, and I will heal thee of thy wounds, saith the LORD; because they called thee an Outcast, *saying,* This *is* Zion, whom no man seeketh after.

Jer 31:28 — And it shall come to pass, *that* like as I have watched over them, to pluck up, and to break down, and to throw down, and to destroy, and to afflict; so will I watch over them, to build, and to plant, saith the LORD.

Eze 9:4 — And the LORD said unto him, Go through the midst of the city, through the midst of Jerusalem, and set a mark upon the foreheads of the men that sigh and that cry for all the abominations that be done in the midst thereof.

Eze 9:6 — Slay utterly old *and* young, both maids, and little children, and women: but come not near any man upon whom *is* the mark; and begin at my sanctuary. Then they began at the ancient men which *were* before the house.

Eze 11:16 — Therefore say, Thus saith the Lord GOD; Although I have cast them far off among the heathen, and although I have scattered them among the countries, yet will I be to them as a little sanctuary in the countries where they shall come.

Eze 34:22 — Therefore will I save my flock, and they shall no more be a prey; and I will judge between cattle and cattle.

Eze 34:31 — And ye my flock, the flock of my pasture, *are* men, *and* I *am* your God, saith the Lord GOD.

Da 12:1 — And at that time shall Michael stand up, the great prince which standeth for the children of thy people: and there shall be a time of trouble, such as never was since there was a nation *even* to that same time: and at that time thy people shall be delivered, every one that shall be found written in the book.

Hos 2:18 — And in that day will I make a covenant for them with the beasts of the field, and with the fowls of heaven, and *with* the creeping things of the ground: and I will break the bow and the sword and the battle out of the earth, and will make them to lie down safely.

Hos 13:10 — I will be thy king: where *is any other* that may save thee in all thy cities? and thy judges of whom thou saidst, Give me a king and princes?

Joel 2:18 — Then will the LORD be jealous for his land, and pity his people.

Am 9:9 — For, lo, I will command, and I will sift the house of Israel among all nations, like as *corn* is sifted in a sieve, yet shall not the least grain fall upon the earth.

Mic 2:13 — The breaker is come up before them: they have broken up, and have passed through the gate, and are gone out by it: and their king shall pass before them, and the LORD on the head of them.

Na 1:12 — Thus saith the LORD: Though *they be* quiet, and likewise many, yet thus shall they be cut down, when he shall pass through. Though I have afflicted thee, I will afflict thee no more.

Zep 3:13 — The remnant of Israel shall not do iniquity, nor speak lies; neither shall a deceitful tongue be found in their mouth: for they shall feed and lie down, and none shall make *them* afraid.

Zep 3:15 — The LORD hath taken away thy judgments, he hath cast out thine enemy: the king of Israel, *even* the LORD, *is* in the midst of thee: thou shalt not see evil any more.

Zep 3:17 — The LORD thy God in the midst of thee *is* mighty; he will save, he will rejoice over thee with joy; he will rest in his love, he will joy over thee with singing.

Zec 2:5 — For I, saith the LORD, will be unto her a wall of fire round about, and will be the glory in the midst of her.

Zec 2:8 — For thus saith the LORD of hosts; After the glory hath he sent me unto the nations which spoiled you: for he that toucheth you toucheth the apple of his eye.

Zec 4:10 — For who hath despised the day of small things? for they shall rejoice, and shall see the plummet in the hand of Zerubbabel *with* those seven; they *are* the eyes of the LORD, which run to and fro through the whole earth.

Zec 9:8 — And I will encamp about mine house because of the army, because of him that passeth by, and because of him that returneth: and no oppressor shall pass through them any more: for now have I seen with mine eyes.

Zec 12:8 — In that day shall the LORD defend the inhabitants of Jerusalem; and he that is feeble among them at that day shall be as David; and the house of David *shall be* as God, as the angel of the LORD before them.

Mt 4:6 — And saith unto him, If thou be the Son of God, cast thyself down: for it is written, He shall give his angels charge concerning thee: and in *their* hands they shall bear thee up, lest at any time thou dash thy foot against a stone.

Mt 24:22 — And except those days should be shortened, there should no flesh be saved: but for the elect's sake those days shall be shortened.

Mt 24:31 — And he shall send his angels with a great sound of a trumpet, and they shall gather together his elect from the four winds, from one end of heaven to the other.

Mk 13:20 — And except that the Lord had shortened those days, no flesh should be saved: but for the elect's sake, whom he hath chosen, he hath shortened the days.

Lk 21:18 — But there shall not an hair of your head perish.

Ac 17:28 — For in him we live, and move, and have our being; as certain also of your own poets have said, For we are also his offspring.

Ro 8:28 — And we know that all things work together for good to them that love God, to them who are the called according to *his* purpose.

1Co 10:13 — There hath no temptation taken you but such as is common to man: but God *is* faithful, who will not suffer you to be tempted above that ye are able; but will with the temptation also make a way to escape, that ye may be able to bear *it*.

2Th 3:3 — But the Lord is faithful, who shall stablish you, and keep *you* from evil.

Heb 1:14 — Are they not all ministering spirits, sent forth to minister for them who shall be heirs of salvation?

Jas 4:15 — For that ye *ought* to say, If the Lord will, we shall live, and do this, or that.

2Pe 2:9 — The Lord knoweth how to deliver the godly out of temptations, and to reserve the unjust unto the day of judgment to be punished:

Rev 3:10 — Because thou hast kept the word of my patience, I also will keep thee from the hour of temptation, which shall come upon all the world, to try them that dwell upon the earth.

Rev 7:3 — Saying, Hurt not the earth, neither the sea, nor the trees, till we have sealed the servants of our God in their foreheads.

Rev 12:6 — And the woman fled into the wilderness, where she hath a place prepared of God, that they should feed her there a thousand two hundred *and* threescore days.

GOD, Providence of

Ge 1:29–30; 8:22–9:3; 26:4–5; 28:20–21; 49:11–12, 24–25; Ex 23:25–26; Le 25:18–22; 26:4–6; Dt 6:2–25; 7:13–24; 8:3–4; 11:7–8, 12–15; 13:17–18; 15:4–6; 28:2–13; 30:15–20; 32:11–14; 1Sa 2:7–8; 2Sa 7:8–9; 1Ki 2:3–4; 9:4–5; 1Ch 17:7–8; 2Ch 7:17–18; 20:3–30; Job 5:6–11, 24–26; 8:6–7, 20–21; 11:17–19; 22:24–25; 29:19–20; 33:14–30; 37:6–24; 38:25–27; 39:5–6; Ps 21:3–5; 23:1–6; 34:9–10; 36:6–7; 44:1–3; 65:9–13; 68:9–10; 69:35–36; 71:6–7; 78:52–55; 81:13–16; 103:3–5; 104:10–19, 24–30; 105:14–45; 107:1–43; 113:6–9; 116:1–15; 118:5–6, 13–14; 127:1–5; 128:2–6; 135:6–12; 136:5–25; 144:12–15; 145:15–16; 146:7–9; 147:8–9, 13–14; Pr 3:1–2; 11:10–11; Isa 30:23–26; 46:3–4; Jer 22:15–16; Eze 36:9–11, 28–38; Da 6:20–22; Hos 2:21–22; Joel 2:18–26; Am 4:7–12; Zec 9:17–10:1; Mal 3:10–12; Mt 6:30–33; 10:29–31; Lk 12:6–7, 24–28; Ac 7:34–36; 2Co 9:8–10

Ge 2:16 — And the LORD God commanded the man, saying, Of every tree of the garden thou mayest freely eat:

Ge 22:14 — And Abraham called the name of that place Jehovah-jireh: as it is said *to* this day, In the mount of the LORD it shall be seen.

Ge 22:17 — That in blessing I will bless thee, and in multiplying I will multiply thy seed as the stars of the heaven, and as the sand which *is* upon the sea shore; and thy seed shall possess the gate of his enemies;

Ge 49:20 — Out of Asher his bread *shall be* fat, and he shall yield royal dainties.

Ex 15:26 — And said, If thou wilt diligently hearken to the voice of the LORD thy God, and wilt do that which is right in his sight, and wilt give ear to his commandments, and keep all his statutes, I will put none of these diseases upon thee, which I have brought upon the Egyptians: for I *am* the LORD that healeth thee.

Ex 23:22 — But if thou shalt indeed obey his voice, and do all that I speak; then I will be an enemy unto thine enemies, and an adversary unto thine adversaries.

Ex 34:24 — For I will cast out the nations before thee, and enlarge thy borders: neither shall any man desire thy land, when thou shalt go up to appear before the LORD thy God thrice in the year.

Le 26:10 — And ye shall eat old store, and bring forth the old because of the new.

Nu 10:29 — And Moses said unto Hobab, the son of Raguel the Midianite, Moses' father in law, We are journeying unto the place of which the LORD said, I will give it you: come thou with us, and we will do thee good: for the LORD hath spoken good concerning Israel.

Dt 1:10 — The LORD your God hath multiplied you, and, behold, ye *are* this day as the stars of heaven for multitude.

Dt 2:7 — For the LORD thy God hath blessed thee in all the works of thy hand: he knoweth thy walking through this great wilderness: these forty years the LORD thy God *hath been* with thee; thou hast lacked nothing.

Dt 4:4 — But ye that did cleave unto the LORD your God *are* alive every one of you this day.

Dt 4:40 — Thou shalt keep therefore his statutes, and his commandments, which I command thee this day, that it may go well with thee, and with thy children after thee, and that thou mayest prolong *thy* days upon the earth, which the LORD thy God giveth thee, for ever.

Dt 5:29 — O that there were such an heart in them, that they would fear me, and keep all my commandments always, that it might be well with them, and with their children for ever!

Dt 5:33 — Ye shall walk in all the ways which the LORD your God hath commanded you, that ye may live, and *that it may be* well with you, and *that* ye may prolong *your* days in the land which ye shall possess.

Dt 8:18 — But thou shalt remember the LORD thy God: for *it is* he that giveth thee power to get wealth, that he may establish his covenant which he sware unto thy fathers, as *it is* this day.

Dt 10:18 — He doth execute the judgment of the fatherless and widow, and loveth the stranger, in giving him food and raiment.

Dt 12:7 — And there ye shall eat before the LORD your God, and ye shall rejoice in all that ye put your hand unto, ye and your households, wherein the LORD thy God hath blessed thee.

Dt 12:28 — Observe and hear all these words which I command thee, that it may go well with thee, and with thy children after thee for ever, when thou doest *that which is* good and right in the sight of the LORD thy God.

Dt 26:19 — And to make thee high above all nations which he hath made, in praise, and in name, and in honour; and that thou mayest be an holy people unto the LORD thy God, as he hath spoken.

Dt 29:5 — And I have led you forty years in the wilderness: your clothes are not waxen old upon you, and thy shoe is not waxen old upon thy foot.

Dt 29:9 — Keep therefore the words of this covenant, and do them, that ye may prosper in all that ye do.

Dt 32:47 — For it *is* not a vain thing for you; because it *is* your life: and through this thing ye shall prolong *your* days in the land, whither ye go over Jordan to possess it.

Jos 1:8 — This book of the law shall not depart out of thy mouth; but thou shalt meditate therein day and night, that thou mayest observe to do according to all that is written therein: for then thou shalt make thy way prosperous, and then thou shalt have good success.

Ru 1:6 — Then she arose with her daughters in law, that she might return from the country of Moab: for she had heard in the country of Moab how that the LORD had visited his people in giving them bread.

1Sa 14:6 — And Jonathan said to the young man that bare his armour, Come, and let us go over unto the garrison of these uncircumcised: it may be that the LORD will work for us: for *there is* no restraint to the LORD to save by many or by few.

1Ch 22:9 — Behold, a son shall be born to thee, who shall be a man of rest; and I will give him rest from all his enemies round about: for his name shall be Solomon, and I will give peace and quietness unto Israel in his days.

1Ch 22:13 — Then shalt thou prosper, if thou takest heed to fulfil the statutes and judgments which the LORD charged Moses with concerning Israel: be strong, and of good courage; dread not, nor be dismayed.

1Ch 28:8 — Now therefore in the sight of all Israel the congregation of the LORD, and in the audience of our God, keep and seek for all the commandments of the LORD your God: that ye may possess this good land, and leave *it* for an inheritance for your children after you for ever.

1Ch 29:12 — Both riches and honour *come* of thee, and thou reignest over all; and in thine hand *is* power and might; and in thine hand *it is* to make great, and to give strength unto all.

1Ch 29:14 — But who *am* I, and what *is* my people, that we should be able to offer so willingly after this sort? for all things *come* of thee, and of thine own have we given thee.

1Ch 29:16 — O LORD our God, all this store that we have prepared to build thee an house for thine holy name *cometh* of thine hand, and *is* all thine own.

2Ch 1:12 — Wisdom and knowledge *is* granted unto thee; and I will give thee riches, and wealth, and honour, such as none of the kings have had that *have been* before thee, neither shall there any after thee have the like.

2Ch 30:9 — For if ye turn again unto the LORD, your brethren and your children *shall find* compassion before them that lead them captive, so that they shall come again into this land: for the LORD your God *is* gracious and merciful, and will not turn away *his* face from you, if ye return unto him.

2Ch 31:10 — And Azariah the chief priest of the house of Zadok answered him, and said, Since *the people* began to bring the offerings into the house of the LORD, we have had enough to eat, and have left plenty: for the LORD hath blessed his people; and that which is left *is* this great store.

Ezr 8:22 — For I was ashamed to require of the king a band of soldiers and horsemen to help us against the enemy in the way: because we had spoken unto the king, saying, The hand of our God *is* upon all them for good that seek him; but his power and his wrath *is* against all them that forsake him.

Ne 9:25 — And they took strong cities, and a fat land, and possessed houses full of all goods, wells digged, vineyards, and oliveyards, and fruit trees in abundance: so they did eat, and were filled, and became fat, and delighted themselves in thy great goodness.

Job 12:23 — He increaseth the nations, and destroyeth them: he enlargeth the nations, and straiteneth them *again.*

Job 22:18 — Yet he filled their houses with good *things:* but the counsel of the wicked is far from me.

Job 22:28 — Thou shalt also decree a thing, and it shall be established unto thee: and the light shall shine upon thy ways.

Job 29:5 — When the Almighty *was* yet with me, *when* my children *were* about me;

Job 36:11 — If they obey and serve *him,* they shall spend their days in prosperity, and their years in pleasures.

Job 38:41 — Who provideth for the raven his food? when his young ones cry unto God, they wander for lack of meat.

Ps 33:12 — Blessed *is* the nation whose God *is* the LORD: *and* the people *whom* he hath chosen for his own inheritance.

Ps 33:15 — He fashioneth their hearts alike; he considereth all their works.

Ps 34:7 — The angel of the LORD encampeth round about them that fear him, and delivereth them.

Ps 37:3 — Trust in the LORD, and do good; *so* shalt thou dwell in the land, and verily thou shalt be fed.

Ps 37:19 — They shall not be ashamed in the evil time: and in the days of famine they shall be satisfied.

Ps 37:22 — For *such as be* blessed of him shall inherit the earth; and *they that be* cursed of him shall be cut off.

Ps 37:25 — I have been young, and *now* am old; yet have I not seen the righteous forsaken, nor his seed begging bread.

Ps 37:34 — Wait on the LORD, and keep his way, and he shall exalt thee to inherit the land: when the wicked are cut off, thou shalt see *it.*

Ps 40:5 — Many, O LORD my God, *are* thy wonderful works *which* thou hast done, and thy thoughts *which are* to us-ward: they cannot be reckoned up in order unto thee: *if* I would declare and speak *of them,* they are more than can be numbered.

Ps 67:6 — *Then* shall the earth yield her increase; *and* God, *even* our own God, shall bless us.

Ps 68:6 — God setteth the solitary in families: he bringeth out those which are bound with chains: but the rebellious dwell in a dry *land.*

Ps 71:15 — My mouth shall shew forth thy righteousness *and* thy salvation all the day; for I know not the numbers *thereof.*

Ps 72:16 — There shall be an handful of corn in the earth upon the top of the mountains; the fruit thereof shall shake like Lebanon: and *they* of the city shall flourish like grass of the earth.

Ps 85:12 — Yea, the LORD shall give *that which is* good; and our land shall yield her increase.

Ps 87:5 — And of Zion it shall be said, This and *that man* was born in her: and the highest himself shall establish her.

Ps 100:3 — Know ye that the LORD he *is* God: *it is* he *that* hath made us, and not we ourselves; *we are* his people, and the sheep of his pasture.

Ps 111:5 — He hath given meat unto them that fear him: he will ever be mindful of his covenant.

Ps 115:16 — The heaven, *even* the heavens, *are* the LORD'S: but the earth hath he given to the children of men.

Ps 122:9 — Because of the house of the LORD our God I will seek thy good.

Pr 2:21 — For the upright shall dwell in the land, and the perfect shall remain in it.

Pr 10:22 — The blessing of the LORD, it maketh rich, and he addeth no sorrow with it.

Pr 10:27 — The fear of the LORD prolongeth days: but the years of the wicked shall be shortened.

Pr 11:31 — Behold, the righteous shall be recompensed in the earth: much more the wicked and the sinner.

Pr 13:25 — The righteous eateth to the satisfying of his soul: but the belly of the wicked shall want.

Pr 14:11 — The house of the wicked shall be overthrown: but the tabernacle of the upright shall flourish.

Pr 14:19 — The evil bow before the good; and the wicked at the gates of the righteous.

Pr 14:34 — Righteousness exalteth a nation: but sin *is* a reproach to any people.

Pr 15:6 — In the house of the righteous *is* much treasure: but in the revenues of the wicked is trouble.

Pr 16:7 — When a man's ways please the LORD, he maketh even his enemies to be at peace with him.

Pr 16:9 — A man's heart deviseth his way: but the LORD directeth his steps.

Pr 28:10 — Whoso causeth the righteous to go astray in an evil way, he shall fall himself into his own pit: but the upright shall have good *things* in possession.

Ecc 2:24 — *There is* nothing better for a man, *than* that he should eat and drink, and *that* he should make his soul enjoy good in his labour. This also I saw, that it *was* from the hand of God.

Ecc 2:26 — For *God* giveth to a man that *is* good in his sight wisdom, and knowledge, and joy: but to the sinner he giveth travail, to gather and to heap up, that he may give to *him that is* good before God. This also *is* vanity and vexation of spirit.

Ecc 3:13 — And also that every man should eat and drink, and enjoy the good of all his labour, it *is* the gift of God.

Ecc 5:19 — Every man also to whom God hath given riches and wealth, and hath given him power to eat thereof, and to take his portion, and to rejoice in his labour; this *is* the gift of God.

Isa 1:19 — If ye be willing and obedient, ye shall eat the good of the land:

Isa 25:4 — For thou hast been a strength to the poor, a strength to the needy in his distress, a refuge from the storm, a shadow from the heat, when the blast of the terrible ones *is* as a storm *against* the wall.

Isa 33:16 — He shall dwell on high: his place of defence *shall be* the munitions of rocks: bread shall be given him; his waters *shall be* sure.

Isa 43:20 — The beast of the field shall honour me, the dragons and the owls: because I give waters in the wilderness, *and* rivers in the desert, to give drink to my people, my chosen.

Isa 48:17 — Thus saith the LORD, thy Redeemer, the Holy One of Israel; I *am* the LORD thy God which teacheth thee to profit, which leadeth thee by the way *that* thou shouldest go.

Isa 48:21 — And they thirsted not *when* he led them through the deserts: he caused the waters to flow out of the rock for them: he clave the rock also, and the waters gushed out.

Isa 51:2 — Look unto Abraham your father, and unto Sarah *that* bare you: for I called him alone, and blessed him, and increased him.

Isa 55:10 — For as the rain cometh down, and the snow from heaven, and returneth not thither, but watereth the earth, and maketh it bring forth and bud, that it may give seed to the sower, and bread to the eater:

Isa 61:9 — And their seed shall be known among the Gentiles, and their offspring among the people: all that see them shall acknowledge them, that they *are* the seed *which* the LORD hath blessed.

Isa 62:9 — But they that have gathered it shall eat it, and praise the LORD; and they that have brought it together shall drink it in the courts of my holiness.

Isa 65:13 — Therefore thus saith the Lord GOD, Behold, my servants shall eat, but ye shall be hungry: behold, my servants shall drink, but ye shall be thirsty: behold, my servants shall rejoice, but ye shall be ashamed:

Isa 65:23 — They shall not labour in vain, nor bring forth for trouble; for they *are* the seed of the blessed of the LORD, and their offspring with them.

Jer 5:24 — Neither say they in their heart, Let us now fear the LORD our God, that giveth rain, both the former and the latter, in his season: he reserveth unto us the appointed weeks of the harvest.

Jer 10:13 — When he uttereth his voice, *there is* a multitude of waters in the heavens, and he causeth the vapors to ascend from the ends of the earth; he maketh lightnings with rain, and bringeth forth the wind out of his treasures.

Jer 14:22 — Are there *any* among the vanities of the Gentiles that can cause rain? or can the heavens give showers? *art* not thou he, O LORD our God? therefore we will wait upon thee: for thou hast made all these *things.*

Jer 27:6 — And now have I given all these lands into the hand of Nebuchadnezzar the king of Babylon, my servant; and the beasts of the field have I given him also to serve him.

Jer 30:19 — And out of them shall proceed thanksgiving and the voice of them that make merry: and I will multiply them, and they shall not be few; I will also glorify them, and they shall not be small.

Jer 31:35 — Thus saith the LORD, which giveth the sun for a light by day, *and* the ordinances of the moon and of the stars for a light by night, which divideth the sea when the waves thereof roar; The LORD of hosts *is* his name:

Jer 33:11 — The voice of joy, and the voice of gladness, the voice of the bridegroom, and the voice of the bride, the voice of them that shall say, Praise the LORD of hosts: for the LORD *is* good; for his mercy *endureth* for ever: *and* of them that shall bring the sacrifice of praise into the house of the LORD. For I will cause to return the captivity of the land, as at the first, saith the LORD.

Jer 51:16 — When he uttereth *his* voice, *there is* a multitude of waters in the heavens; and he causeth the vapors to ascend from the ends of the earth: he maketh lightnings with rain, and bringeth forth the wind out of his treasures.

Da 5:18 — O thou king, the most high God gave Nebuchadnezzar thy father a kingdom, and majesty, and glory, and honour:

Hos 2:8 — For she did not know that I gave her corn, and wine, and oil, and multiplied her silver and gold, *which* they prepared for Baal.

Hos 11:3 — I taught Ephraim also to go, taking them by their arms; but they knew not that I healed them.

Am 9:13 — Behold, the days come, saith the LORD, that the plowman shall overtake the reaper, and the treader of grapes him that soweth seed; and the mountains shall drop sweet wine, and all the hills shall melt.

Jnh 4:6 — And the LORD God prepared a gourd, and made *it* to come up over Jonah, that it might be a shadow over his head, to deliver him from his grief. So Jonah was exceeding glad of the gourd.

Hag 2:19 — Is the seed yet in the barn? yea, as yet the vine, and the fig tree, and the pomegranate, and the olive tree, hath not brought forth: from this day will I bless *you.*

Zec 3:7 — Thus saith the LORD of hosts; If thou wilt walk in my ways, and if thou wilt keep my charge, then thou shalt also judge my house, and shalt also keep my courts, and I will give thee places to walk among these that stand by.

Zec 8:12 — For the seed *shall be* prosperous; the vine shall give her fruit, and the ground shall give her increase, and the heavens shall give their dew; and I will cause the remnant of this people to possess all these *things.*

Mt 5:5 — Blessed *are* the meek: for they shall inherit the earth.

Mt 5:45 — That ye may be the children of your Father which is in heaven: for he maketh his sun to rise on the evil and on the good, and sendeth rain on the just and on the unjust.

Mt 6:26 — Behold the fowls of the air: for they sow not, neither do they reap, nor gather into barns; yet your heavenly Father feedeth them. Are ye not much better than they?

Lk 22:35 — And he said unto them, When I sent you without purse, and scrip, and shoes, lacked ye any thing? And they said, Nothing.

Jn 6:31 — Our fathers did eat manna in the desert; as it is written, He gave them bread from heaven to eat.

Ac 14:17 — Nevertheless he left not himself without witness, in that he did good, and gave us rain from heaven, and fruitful seasons, filling our hearts with food and gladness.

1Co 2:9 — But as it is written, Eye hath not seen, nor ear heard, neither have entered into the heart of man, the things which God hath prepared for them that love him.

1Co 16:2 — Upon the first *day* of the week let every one of you lay by him in store, as *God* hath prospered him, that there be no gatherings when I come.

- **Instances of.**
  - **Saving Noah.**
    Ge 7:1
  - **The call of Abraham.**
    Ge 12:1
  - **Protecting Abraham, Sarah, and Abimelech.**
    Ge 20:3–6
  - **Deliverance of Lot.**
    Ge 19:1–38
  - **Care of Isaac.**
    Ge 26:2–3
  - **The mission of Joseph.**
    Ge 39:2–3, 23; 45:7–8; 50:20; Ps 105:17–22
  - **Warning Pharaoh of famine.**
    Ge 41:1–57
  - **Delivering the Israelites.**
    Ex 3:8; 11:3; 13:18; Ac 7:34–36
  - **The pillar of cloud.**
    Ex 13:21; 14:19–20
  - **Dividing the Red Sea.**
    Ex 14:21
  - **Delaying and destroying Pharaoh.**
    Ex 14:25–30
  - **Purifying the waters of Marah.**
    Ex 15:25
  - **Supplying manna and quail.**
    Ex 16:13–15; Nu 11:31–32
  - **Supplying water at Meribah.**
    Nu 20:7–11; Ne 9:10–25
  - **Protection of homes while at feasts.**
    Ex 34:24
  - **In the conquest of Canaan.**
    Ps 44:2–3
  - **Saving David's army.**
    2Sa 5:23–25
  - **The revolt of the ten tribes.**
    1Ki 12:15, 24; 2Ch 10:15
  - **Fighting the battles of Israel.**
    2Ch 13:12, 18; 14:9–14; 16:7–9; 20:15, 17, 22–23; 32:21–22
  - **Restoring Manasseh after his conversion.**
    2Ch 33:12–13
  - **Feeding Elijah and the widow.**
    1Ki 17:1–24; 19:1–8
  - **In prospering Hezekiah.**
    2Ki 18:6–7; 2Ch 32:29
  - **In prospering Asa.**
    2Ch 14:6–7
  - **In prospering Jehoshaphat.**
    2Ch 17:3, 5; 20:30
  - **In prospering Uzziah.**
    2Ch 26:5–15
  - **In prospering Jotham.**
    2Ch 27:6
  - **In prospering Job.**
    Job 1:10; 42:10, 12
  - **In prospering Daniel.**
    Da 1:9
  - **In turning the heart of the king of Assyria to favor the Jews.**
    Ezr 6:22
  - **In rescuing Jeremiah.**
    Jer 38:6–13; La 3:52–58
  - **Restoration of the Jews.**
    2Ch 36:22–23; Ezr 1:1
  - **Rescuing the Jews from Haman's plot.**
    Est 1:1–10:3
  - **Rebuilding the walls of Jerusalem.**
    Ne 6:16

- **Warning Joseph in dreams.**
  Mt 1:20; 2:13, 19–20
- **Warning the wise men of the east.**
  Mt 2:12–13
- **Restoring Epaphroditus.**
  Php 2:27
- **In the banishment of John to Patmos.**
  Rev 1:9

See: God, Goodness of

See: God, Preserver

See: God, Providence of, Overruling Interpositions of the

GOD, Providence of, Mysterious and Misinterpreted

Job 24:1–12; Ps 73:2–5, 12–17; Ecc 8:12–17; Jer 12:1–2; Hab 1:2–3, 13–14; Mal 3:14–15

Job 10:15 — If I be wicked, woe unto me; and *if* I be righteous, *yet* will I not lift up my head. *I am* full of confusion; therefore see thou mine affliction;

Job 12:6 — The tabernacles of robbers prosper, and they that provoke God are secure; into whose hand God bringeth *abundantly.*

Job 21:7 — Wherefore do the wicked live, become old, yea, are mighty in power?

Job 33:13 — Why dost thou strive against him? for he giveth not account of any of his matters.

Ps 10:5 — His ways are always grievous; thy judgments *are* far above out of his sight: *as for* all his enemies, he puffeth at them.

Ps 89:47 — Remember how short my time is: wherefore hast thou made all men in vain?

Pr 28:5 — Evil men understand not judgment: but they that seek the LORD understand all *things.*

Ecc 7:15 — All *things* have I seen in the days of my vanity: there is a just *man* that perisheth in his righteousness, and there is a wicked *man* that prolongeth *his life* in his wickedness.

Ecc 9:2 — All *things come* alike to all: *there is* one event to the righteous, and to the wicked; to the good and to the clean, and to the unclean; to him that sacrificeth, and to him that sacrificeth not: as *is* the good, so *is* the sinner; *and* he that sweareth, as *he* that feareth an oath.

Ecc 9:11 — I returned, and saw under the sun, that the race *is* not to the swift, nor the battle to the strong, neither yet bread to the wise, nor yet riches to men of understanding, nor yet favour to men of skill; but time and chance happeneth to them all.

Jer 50:7 — All that found them have devoured them: and their adversaries said, We offend not, because they have sinned against the LORD, the habitation of justice, even the LORD, the hope of their fathers.

Da 12:10 — Many shall be purified, and made white, and tried; but the wicked shall do wickedly: and none of the wicked shall understand; but the wise shall understand.

Mic 4:12 — But they know not the thoughts of the LORD, neither understand they his counsel: for he shall gather them as the sheaves into the floor.

Hab 1:11 — Then shall *his* mind change, and he shall pass over, and offend, *imputing* this his power unto his god.

See: Blindness; spiritual

- **Instances of.**
  - **Elijah's trials.**
    1Ki 19:1–21
  - **Job's.**
    Job 1:1–2:13; 3:19–23
  - **Israelites.**
    Ex 5:20–23

GOD, Providence of, Overruling Interpositions of the

Ge 45:5–7; Nu 22:12–18; 23:1–30; 24:10–13; Dt 23:4–5; Jgs 9:23–24; 1Sa 2:6–9; 1Ki 11:14–40; 2Ch 36:22–23; Est 6:1–12; Job 5:12–13; Ps 17:13–14; 127:1–2; Ecc 2:26–3:1; Isa 8:9–10; 10:5–7; 13:3–5; 44:28–45:6; 48:14–15; 54:16–17; Jer 51:20–21; Eze 21:26–27; 29:19–20; Ac 3:17–18; 5:38–39; 7:9–10

Ge 50:20 — But as for you, ye thought evil against me; *but* God meant it unto good, to bring to pass, as *it is* this day, to save much people alive.

Ex 14:4 — And I will harden Pharaoh's heart, that he shall follow after them; and I will be honoured upon Pharaoh, and upon all his host; that the Egyptians may know that I *am* the LORD. And they did so.

Dt 2:30 — But Sihon king of Heshbon would not let us pass by him: for the LORD thy God hardened his spirit, and made his heart obstinate, that he might deliver him into thy hand, as *appeareth* this day.

Jos 11:20 — For it was of the LORD to harden their hearts, that they should come against Israel in battle, that he might destroy them utterly, *and* that they might have no favour, but that he might destroy them, as the LORD commanded Moses.

2Sa 17:14 — And Absalom and all the men of Israel said, The counsel of Hushai the Archite *is* better than the counsel of Ahithophel. For the LORD had appointed to defeat the good counsel of Ahithophel, to the intent that the LORD might bring evil upon Absalom.

1Ki 12:15 — Wherefore the king hearkened not unto the people; for the cause was from the LORD, that he might perform his saying, which the LORD spake by Ahijah the Shilonite unto Jeroboam the son of Nebat.

1Ch 5:26 — And the God of Israel stirred up the spirit of Pul king of Assyria, and the spirit of Tilgath-pilneser king of Assyria, and he carried them away, even the Reubenites, and the Gadites, and the half tribe of Manasseh, and brought them unto Halah, and Habor, and Hara, and to the river Gozan, unto this day.

2Ch 10:15 — So the king hearkened not unto the people: for the cause was of God, that the LORD might perform his word, which he spake by the hand of Ahijah the Shilonite to Jeroboam the son of Nebat.

Ezr 1:1 — Now in the first year of Cyrus king of Persia, that the word of the LORD by the mouth of Jeremiah might be fulfilled, the LORD stirred up the spirit of Cyrus king of Persia, that he made a proclamation throughout all his kingdom, and *put it* also in writing, saying,

Ezr 5:5 — But the eye of their God was upon the elders of the Jews, that they could not cause them to cease, till the matter came to Darius: and then they returned answer by letter concerning this *matter.*

Ezr 6:22 — And kept the feast of unleavened bread seven days with joy: for the LORD had made them joyful, and turned the heart of the king of Assyria unto them, to strengthen their hands in the work of the house of God, the God of Israel.

Ne 6:16 — And it came to pass, that when all our enemies heard *thereof,* and all the heathen that *were* about us saw *these things,* they were much cast down in their own eyes: for they perceived that this work was wrought of our God.

Est 7:10 — So they hanged Haman on the gallows that he had prepared for Mordecai. Then was the king's wrath pacified.

Est 9:1 — Now in the twelfth month, that *is,* the month Adar, on the thirteenth day of the same, when the king's commandment and his decree drew near to be put in execution, in the day that the enemies of the Jews hoped to have power over them, (though it was turned to the contrary, that the Jews had rule over them that hated them;)

Est 9:25 — But when *Esther* came before the king, he commanded by letters that his wicked device, which he devised against the Jews, should return upon his own head, and that he and his sons should be hanged on the gallows.

Ps 33:10 — The LORD bringeth the counsel of the heathen to nought: he maketh the devices of the people of none effect.

Ps 75:7 — But God *is* the judge: he putteth down one, and setteth up another.

Ps 76:10 — Surely the wrath of man shall praise thee: the remainder of wrath shalt thou restrain.

Ps 105:17 — He sent a man before them, *even* Joseph, *who* was sold for a servant:

Pr 13:22 — A good *man* leaveth an inheritance to his children's children: and the wealth of the sinner is laid up for the just.

Pr 14:19 — The evil bow before the good; and the wicked at the gates of the righteous.

Pr 16:7 — When a man's ways please the LORD, he maketh even his enemies to be at peace with him.

Pr 16:33 — The lot is cast into the lap; but the whole disposing thereof *is* of the LORD.

Pr 19:21 — *There are* many devices in a man's heart; nevertheless the counsel of the LORD, that shall stand.

Pr 21:1 — The king's heart *is* in the hand of the LORD, *as* the rivers of water: he turneth it whithersoever he will.

Pr 21:18 — The wicked *shall be* a ransom for the righteous, and the transgressor for the upright.

Pr 28:8 — He that by usury and unjust gain increaseth his substance, he shall gather it for him that will pity the poor.

Ecc 3:10 — I have seen the travail, which God hath given to the sons of men to be exercised in it.

Isa 41:2 — Who raised up the righteous *man* from the east, called him to his foot, gave the nations before him, and made *him* rule over kings? he gave *them* as the dust to his sword, *and* as driven stubble to his bow.

Isa 41:4 — Who hath wrought and done *it,* calling the generations from the beginning? I the LORD, the first, and with the last; I *am* he.

Isa 43:14 — Thus saith the LORD, your redeemer, the Holy One of Israel; For your sake I have sent to Babylon, and have brought down all their nobles, and the Chaldeans, whose cry *is* in the ships.

Isa 45:13 — I have raised him up in righteousness, and I will direct all his ways: he shall build my city, and he shall let go my captives, not for price nor reward, saith the LORD of hosts.

Jer 52:3 — For through the anger of the LORD it came to pass in Jerusalem and Judah, till he had cast them out from his presence, that Zedekiah rebelled against the king of Babylon.

Da 11:27 — And both these kings' hearts *shall be* to do mischief, and they shall speak lies at one table; but it shall not prosper: for yet the end *shall be* at the time appointed.

Ro 1:10 — Making request, if by any means now at length I might have a prosperous journey by the will of God to come unto you.

Ro 8:28 — And we know that all things work together for good to them that love God, to them who are the called according to *his* purpose.

1Co 4:19 — But I will come to you shortly, if the Lord will, and will know, not the speech of them which are puffed up, but the power.

1Co 16:7 — For I will not see you now by the way; but I trust to tarry a while with you, if the Lord permit.

Php 1:12 — But I would ye should understand, brethren, that the things *which happened* unto me have fallen out rather unto the furtherance of the gospel;

Php 1:19 — For I know that this shall turn to my salvation through your prayer, and the supply of the Spirit of Jesus Christ,

Phm 1:15 — For perhaps he therefore departed for a season, that thou shouldest receive him for ever;

Jas 4:15 — For that ye *ought* to say, If the Lord will, we shall live, and do this, or that.

Rev 17:17 — For God hath put in their hearts to fulfil his will, and to agree, and give their kingdom unto the beast, until the words of God shall be fulfilled.

⇜See: God, Goodness of

⇜See: God, Preserver

GOD, Righteousness of

La 3:34–36; Ro 3:4–6, 21–22; 10:3–4

Jgs 5:11 — *They that are delivered* from the noise of archers in the places of drawing water, there shall they rehearse the righteous acts of the LORD, *even* the righteous acts *toward the inhabitants* of his villages in Israel: then shall the people of the LORD go down to the gates.

Ezr 9:15 — O LORD God of Israel, thou *art* righteous: for we remain yet escaped, as *it is* this day: behold, we *are* before thee in our trespasses: for we cannot stand before thee because of this.

Job 36:3 — I will fetch my knowledge from afar, and will ascribe righteousness to my Maker.

Ps 5:8 — Lead me, O LORD, in thy righteousness because of mine enemies; make thy way straight before my face.

Ps 7:9 — Oh let the wickedness of the wicked come to an end; but establish the just: for the righteous God trieth the hearts and reins.

Ps 48:10 — According to thy name, O God, so *is* thy praise unto the ends of the earth: thy right hand is full of righteousness.

Ps 50:6 — And the heavens shall declare his righteousness: for God *is* judge himself. Selah.

Ps 71:15 — My mouth shall shew forth thy righteousness *and* thy salvation all the day; for I know not the numbers *thereof.*

Ps 71:19 — Thy righteousness also, O God, *is* very high, who hast done great things: O God, who *is* like unto thee!

Ps 72:1 — Give the king thy judgments, O God, and thy righteousness unto the king's son.

Ps 88:12 — Shall thy wonders be known in the dark? and thy righteousness in the land of forgetfulness?

Ps 89:16 — In thy name shall they rejoice all the day: and in thy righteousness shall they be exalted.

Ps 97:2 — Clouds and darkness *are* round about him: righteousness and judgment *are* the habitation of his throne.

Ps 111:3 — His work *is* honourable and glorious: and his righteousness endureth for ever.

Ps 112:4 — Unto the upright there ariseth light in the darkness: *he is* gracious, and full of compassion, and righteous.

Ps 116:5 — Gracious *is* the LORD, and righteous; yea, our God *is* merciful.

Ps 119:40 — Behold, I have longed after thy precepts: quicken me in thy righteousness.

Ps 119:137 — Righteous *art* thou, O LORD, and upright *are* thy judgments.

Ps 119:142 — Thy righteousness *is* an everlasting righteousness, and thy law *is* the truth.

Ps 119:144 — The righteousness of thy testimonies *is* everlasting: give me understanding, and I shall live.

Ps 119:172 — My tongue shall speak of thy word: for all thy commandments *are* righteousness.

Ps 143:1 — Hear my prayer, O LORD, give ear to my supplications: in thy faithfulness answer me, *and* in thy righteousness.

Ps 145:7 — They shall abundantly utter the memory of thy great goodness, and shall sing of thy righteousness.

Ps 145:17 — The LORD *is* righteous in all his ways, and holy in all his works.

Isa 41:10 — Fear thou not; for I *am* with thee: be not dismayed; for I *am* thy God: I will strengthen thee; yea, I will help thee; yea, I will uphold thee with the right hand of my righteousness.

Isa 51:8 — For the moth shall eat them up like a garment, and the worm shall eat them like wool: but my righteousness shall be for ever, and my salvation from generation to generation.

Isa 56:1 — Thus saith the LORD, Keep ye judgment, and do justice: for my salvation *is* near to come, and my righteousness to be revealed.

Jer 4:2 — And thou shalt swear, The LORD liveth, in truth, in judgment, and in righteousness; and the nations shall bless themselves in him, and in him shall they glory.

Jer 9:24 — But let him that glorieth glory in this, that he understandeth and knoweth me, that I *am* the LORD which exercise lovingkindness, judgment, and righteousness, in the earth: for in these *things* I delight, saith the LORD.

Jer 12:1 — Righteous *art* thou, O LORD, when I plead with thee: yet let me talk with thee of *thy* judgments: Wherefore doth the way of the wicked prosper? *wherefore* are all they happy that deal very treacherously?

Da 9:7 — O Lord, righteousness *belongeth* unto thee, but unto us confusion of faces, as at this day; to the men of Judah, and to the inhabitants of Jerusalem, and unto all Israel, *that are* near, and *that are* far off, through all the countries whither thou hast driven them, because of their trespass that they have trespassed against thee.

Da 9:14 — Therefore hath the LORD watched upon the evil, and brought it upon us: for the LORD our God *is* righteous in all his works which he doeth: for we obeyed not his voice.

Hos 14:9 — Who *is* wise, and he shall understand these *things?* prudent, and he shall know them? for the ways of the LORD *are* right, and the just shall walk in them: but the transgressors shall fall therein.

Mic 7:9 — I will bear the indignation of the LORD, because I have sinned against him, until he plead my cause, and execute judgment for me: he will bring me forth to the light, *and* I shall behold his righteousness.

Mt 6:33 — But seek ye first the kingdom of God, and his righteousness; and all these things shall be added unto you.

Jn 17:25 — O righteous Father, the world hath not known thee: but I have known thee, and these have known that thou hast sent me.

Ac 17:31 — Because he hath appointed a day, in the which he will judge the world in righteousness by *that* man whom he hath ordained; *whereof* he hath given assurance unto all *men,* in that he hath raised him from the dead.

Ro 1:17 — For therein is the righteousness of God revealed from faith to faith: as it is written, The just shall live by faith.

Ro 9:14 — What shall we say then? *Is there* unrighteousness with God? God forbid.

2Ti 4:8 — Henceforth there is laid up for me a crown of righteousness, which the Lord, the righteous judge, shall give me at that day: and not to me only, but unto all them also that love his appearing.

1Pe 2:23 — Who, when he was reviled, reviled not again; when he suffered, he threatened not; but committed *himself* to him that judgeth righteously:

2Pe 1:1 — Simon Peter, a servant and an apostle of Jesus Christ, to them that have obtained like precious faith with us through the righteousness of God and our Saviour Jesus Christ:

1Jn 2:1 — My little children, these things write I unto you, that ye sin not. And if any man sin, we have an advocate with the Father, Jesus Christ the righteous:

Rev 16:5 — And I heard the angel of the waters say, Thou art righteous, O Lord, which art, and wast, and shalt be, because thou hast judged thus.

See: God, Holiness of

See: God, Judge, and His Justice

GOD, Saviour

Dt 33:25–29; Job 33:27–30; Ps 18:30–31; 33:18–19; 37:39–40; 62:1–2, 6–7; 68:19–20; 76:8–9; 98:2–3; Isa 43:11–12; 44:22–24; 45:21–22; 46:12–13; 52:9–10; Zec 9:11–12; Jn 3:16–17; Ro 8:30–32; 2Th 2:16–17; 1Ti 2:3–4; Tit 1:2–3; 2:10–11; 3:4–5; 1Jn 4:9–10

Ge 48:16 — The Angel which redeemed me from all evil, bless the lads; and let my name be named on them, and the name of my fathers Abraham and Isaac; and let them grow into a multitude in the midst of the earth.

Ex 15:2 — The LORD *is* my strength and song, and he is become my salvation: he *is* my God, and I will prepare him an habitation; my father's God, and I will exalt him.

Dt 32:15 — But Jeshurun waxed fat, and kicked: thou art waxen fat, thou art grown thick, thou art covered *with fatness;* then he forsook God *which* made him, and lightly esteemed the Rock of his salvation.

Dt 32:31 — For their rock *is* not as our Rock, even our enemies themselves *being* judges.

Dt 32:39 — See now that I, *even* I, *am* he, and *there is* no god with me: I kill, and I make alive; I wound, and I heal: neither *is there any* that can deliver out of my hand.

1Sa 2:2 — *There is* none holy as the LORD: for *there is* none beside thee: neither *is there* any rock like our God.

Job 33:24 — Then he is gracious unto him, and saith, Deliver him from going down to the pit: I have found a ransom.

Ps 3:8 — Salvation *belongeth* unto the LORD: thy blessing *is* upon thy people. Selah.

Ps 19:14 — Let the words of my mouth, and the meditation of my heart, be acceptable in thy sight, O LORD, my strength, and my redeemer.

Ps 25:5 — Lead me in thy truth, and teach me: for thou *art* the God of my salvation; on thee do I wait all the day.

Ps 27:1 — The LORD *is* my light and my salvation; whom shall I fear? the LORD *is* the strength of my life; of whom shall I be afraid?

Ps 28:8 — The LORD *is* their strength, and he *is* the saving strength of his anointed.

Ps 31:5 — Into thine hand I commit my spirit: thou hast redeemed me, O LORD God of truth.

Ps 34:22 — The LORD redeemeth the soul of his servants: and none of them that trust in him shall be desolate.

Ps 36:9 — For with thee *is* the fountain of life: in thy light shall we see light.

Ps 50:23 — Whoso offereth praise glorifieth me: and to him that ordereth *his* conversation *aright* will I shew the salvation of God.

Ps 65:5 — By terrible things in righteousness wilt thou answer us, O God of our salvation; *who art* the confidence of all the ends of the earth, and of them that are afar off *upon* the sea:

Ps 71:16 — I will go in the strength of the Lord GOD: I will make mention of thy righteousness, *even* of thine only.

Ps 74:12 — For God *is* my King of old, working salvation in the midst of the earth.

Ps 85:9 — Surely his salvation *is* nigh them that fear him; that glory may dwell in our land.

Ps 88:1 — O LORD God of my salvation, I have cried day *and* night before thee:

Ps 96:2 — Sing unto the LORD, bless his name; shew forth his salvation from day to day.

Ps 111:9 — He sent redemption unto his people: he hath commanded his covenant for ever: holy and reverend *is* his name.

Ps 118:14 — The LORD *is* my strength and song, and is become my salvation.

Ps 118:21 — I will praise thee: for thou hast heard me, and art become my salvation.

Ps 118:27 — God *is* the LORD, which hath shewed us light: bind the sacrifice with cords, *even* unto the horns of the altar.

Ps 121:7 — The LORD shall preserve thee from all evil: he shall preserve thy soul.

Ps 133:3 — As the dew of Hermon, *and as the dew* that descended upon the mountains of Zion: for there the LORD commanded the blessing, *even* life for evermore.

Ps 145:9 — The LORD *is* good to all: and his tender mercies *are* over all his works.

Ps 149:4 — For the LORD taketh pleasure in his people: he will beautify the meek with salvation.

Isa 12:2 — Behold, God *is* my salvation; I will trust, and not be afraid: for the LORD JEHOVAH *is* my strength and *my* song; he also is become my salvation.

Isa 25:4 — For thou hast been a strength to the poor, a strength to the needy in his distress, a refuge from the storm, a shadow from the heat, when the blast of the terrible ones *is* as a storm *against* the wall.

Isa 25:9 — And it shall be said in that day, Lo, this *is* our God; we have waited for him, and he will save us: this *is* the LORD; we have waited for him, we will be glad and rejoice in his salvation.

Isa 26:1 — In that day shall this song be sung in the land of Judah; We have a strong city; salvation will *God* appoint *for* walls and bulwarks.

Isa 33:22 — For the LORD *is* our judge, the LORD *is* our lawgiver, the LORD *is* our king; he will save us.

Isa 35:4 — Say to them *that are* of a fearful heart, Be strong, fear not: behold, your God will come *with* vengeance, *even* God *with* a recompence; he will come and save you.

Isa 41:14 — Fear not, thou worm Jacob, *and* ye men of Israel; I will help thee, saith the LORD, and thy redeemer, the Holy One of Israel.

Isa 43:3 — For I *am* the LORD thy God, the Holy One of Israel, thy Saviour: I gave Egypt *for* thy ransom, Ethiopia and Seba for thee.

Isa 43:14 — Thus saith the LORD, your redeemer, the Holy One of Israel; For your sake I have sent to Babylon, and have brought down all their nobles, and the Chaldeans, whose cry *is* in the ships.

Isa 44:6 — Thus saith the LORD the King of Israel, and his redeemer the LORD of hosts; I *am* the first, and I *am* the last; and beside me *there is* no God.

Isa 45:15 — Verily thou *art* a God that hidest thyself, O God of Israel, the Saviour.

Isa 45:17 — *But* Israel shall be saved in the LORD with an everlasting salvation: ye shall not be ashamed nor confounded world without end.

Isa 47:4 — *As for* our redeemer, the LORD of hosts *is* his name, the Holy One of Israel.

Isa 48:17 — Thus saith the LORD, thy Redeemer, the Holy One of Israel; I *am* the LORD thy God which teacheth thee to profit, which leadeth thee by the way *that* thou shouldest go.

Isa 49:25 — But thus saith the LORD, Even the captives of the mighty shall be taken away, and the prey of the terrible shall be delivered: for I will contend with him that contendeth with thee, and I will save thy children.

Isa 50:2 — Wherefore, when I came, *was there* no man? when I called, *was there* none to answer? Is my hand shortened at all, that it cannot redeem? or have I no power to deliver? behold, at my rebuke I dry up the sea, I make the rivers a wilderness: their fish stinketh, because *there is* no water, and dieth for thirst.

Isa 52:3 — For thus saith the LORD, Ye have sold yourselves for nought; and ye shall be redeemed without money.

Isa 59:1 — Behold, the LORD's hand is not shortened, that it cannot save; neither his ear heavy, that it cannot hear:

Isa 60:16 — Thou shalt also suck the milk of the Gentiles, and shalt suck the breast of kings: and thou shalt know that I the LORD *am* thy Saviour and thy Redeemer, the mighty One of Jacob.

Isa 63:8 — For he said, Surely they *are* my people, children *that* will not lie: so he was their Saviour.

Isa 63:16 — Doubtless thou *art* our father, though Abraham be ignorant of us, and Israel acknowledge us not: thou, O LORD, *art* our father, our redeemer; thy name *is* from everlasting.

Jer 3:23 — Truly in vain *is salvation hoped for* from the hills, *and from* the multitude of mountains: truly in the LORD our God *is* the salvation of Israel.

Jer 8:22 — *Is there* no balm in Gilead; *is there* no physician there? why then is not the health of the daughter of my people recovered?

Jer 14:8 — O the hope of Israel, the saviour thereof in time of trouble, why shouldest thou be as a stranger in the land, and as a wayfaring man *that* turneth aside to tarry for a night?

Jer 30:17 — For I will restore health unto thee, and I will heal thee of thy wounds, saith the LORD; because they called thee an Outcast, *saying,* This *is* Zion, whom no man seeketh after.

Jer 33:6 — Behold, I will bring it health and cure, and I will cure them, and will reveal unto them the abundance of peace and truth.

Jer 50:34 — Their Redeemer *is* strong; the LORD of hosts *is* his name: he shall throughly plead their cause, that he may give rest to the land, and disquiet the inhabitants of Babylon.

Eze 37:23 — Neither shall they defile themselves any more with their idols, nor with their detestable things, nor with any of their transgressions: but I will save them out of all their dwellingplaces, wherein they have sinned, and will cleanse them: so shall they be my people, and I will be their God.

Hos 1:7 — But I will have mercy upon the house of Judah, and will save them by the LORD their God, and will not save them by bow, nor by sword, nor by battle, by horses, nor by horsemen.

Hos 13:4 — Yet I *am* the LORD thy God from the land of Egypt, and thou shalt know no god but me: for *there is* no saviour beside me.

Hos 13:9 — O Israel, thou hast destroyed thyself; but in me *is* thine help.

Joel 3:16 — The LORD also shall roar out of Zion, and utter his voice from Jerusalem; and the heavens and the earth shall shake: but the LORD *will be* the hope of his people, and the strength of the children of Israel.

Jnh 2:9 — But I will sacrifice unto thee with the voice of thanksgiving; I will pay *that* that I have vowed. Salvation *is* of the LORD.

Zec 9:16 — And the LORD their God shall save them in that day as the flock of his people: for they *shall be as* the stones of a crown, lifted up as an ensign upon his land.

Lk 1:68 — Blessed *be* the Lord God of Israel; for he hath visited and redeemed his people,

Jn 6:39 — And this is the Father's will which hath sent me, that of all which he hath given me I should lose nothing, but should raise it up again at the last day.

Ro 1:16 — For I am not ashamed of the gospel of Christ: for it is the power of God unto salvation to every one that believeth; to the Jew first, and also to the Greek.

Ro 6:23 — For the wages of sin *is* death; but the gift of God *is* eternal life through Jesus Christ our Lord.

1Co 1:18 — For the preaching of the cross is to them that perish foolishness; but unto us which are saved it is the power of God.

2Co 5:18 — And all things *are* of God, who hath reconciled us to himself by Jesus Christ, and hath given to us the ministry of reconciliation;

Eph 1:3 — Blessed *be* the God and Father of our Lord Jesus Christ, who hath blessed us with all spiritual blessings in heavenly *places* in Christ:

Eph 1:5 — Having predestinated us unto the adoption of children by Jesus Christ to himself, according to the good pleasure of his will,

1Th 5:9 — For God hath not appointed us to wrath, but to obtain salvation by our Lord Jesus Christ,

1Ti 4:10 — For therefore we both labour and suffer reproach, because we trust in the living God, who is the Saviour of all men, specially of those that believe.

2Ti 1:9 — Who hath saved us, and called *us* with an holy calling, not according to our works, but according to his own purpose and grace, which was given us in Christ Jesus before the world began,

1Pe 1:5 — Who are kept by the power of God through faith unto salvation ready to be revealed in the last time.

1Jn 5:11 — And this is the record, that God hath given to us eternal life, and this life is in his Son.

Rev 7:10 — And cried with a loud voice, saying, Salvation to our God which sitteth upon the throne, and unto the Lamb.

Rev 19:1 — And after these things I heard a great voice of much people in heaven, saying, Alleluia; Salvation, and glory, and honour, and power, unto the Lord our God:

➜See: God, Preserver

GOD, Self-Existent

Job 35:6–8; Ac 17:24–25

Ex 3:14 — And God said unto Moses, I AM THAT I AM: and he said, Thus shalt thou say unto the children of Israel, I AM hath sent me unto you.

Dt 32:40 — For I lift up my hand to heaven, and say, I live for ever.

Isa 44:6 — Thus saith the LORD the King of Israel, and his redeemer the LORD of hosts; I *am* the first, and I *am* the last; and beside me *there is* no God.

Jer 10:10 — But the LORD *is* the true God, he *is* the living God, and an everlasting king: at his wrath the earth shall tremble, and the nations shall not be able to abide his indignation.

Jn 5:26 — For as the Father hath life in himself; so hath he given to the Son to have life in himself;

See: God, Eternity of

GOD, Sovereign

Ge 14:18–20; Dt 32:41–43; 1Sa 2:6–8; 1Ch 29:11–12; Job 12:9–10, 16–17; 36:1–33; Ps 22:28–29; 47:2–3, 7–8; 50:10–12; 75:6–7; 76:11–12; 93:1–2; 95:3–5; 97:1–2; 135:5–6; 136:2–3; 145:11–13; Isa 40:22–23; Jer 18:1–23; 27:5–7; 32:27–28; La 3:37–38; Da 2:20–21; 4:34–35; 5:26–28; Ac 17:24–26; 1Ti 6:15–16

Ge 14:22 — And Abram said to the king of Sodom, I have lift up mine hand unto the LORD, the most high God, the possessor of heaven and earth,

Ge 24:3 — And I will make thee swear by the LORD, the God of heaven, and the God of the earth, that thou shalt not take a wife unto my son of the daughters of the Canaanites, among whom I dwell:

Ex 8:22 — And I will sever in that day the land of Goshen, in which my people dwell, that no swarms *of flies* shall be there; to the end thou mayest know that I *am* the LORD in the midst of the earth.

Ex 9:29 — And Moses said unto him, As soon as I am gone out of the city, I will spread abroad my hands unto the LORD; *and* the thunder shall cease, neither shall there be any more hail; that thou mayest know how that the earth *is* the LORD'S.

Ex 15:18 — The LORD shall reign for ever and ever.

Ex 18:11 — Now I know that the LORD *is* greater than all gods: for in the thing wherein they dealt proudly *he was* above them.

Ex 19:5 — Now therefore, if ye will obey my voice indeed, and keep my covenant, then ye shall be a peculiar treasure unto me above all people: for all the earth *is* mine:

Nu 27:16 — Let the LORD, the God of the spirits of all flesh, set a man over the congregation,

Dt 2:19 — And *when* thou comest nigh over against the children of Ammon, distress them not, nor meddle with them: for I will not give thee of the land of the children of Ammon *any* possession; because I have given it unto the children of Lot *for* a possession.

Dt 4:39 — Know therefore this day, and consider *it* in thine heart, that the LORD he *is* God in heaven above, and upon the earth beneath: *there is* none else.

Dt 10:14 — Behold, the heaven and the heaven of heavens *is* the LORD'S thy God, the earth *also*, with all that therein *is*.

Dt 10:17 — For the LORD your God *is* God of gods, and Lord of lords, a great God, a mighty, and a terrible, which regardeth not persons, nor taketh reward:

Dt 32:8 — When the most High divided to the nations their inheritance, when he separated the sons of Adam, he set the bounds of the people according to the number of the children of Israel.

Dt 32:39 — See now that I, *even* I, *am* he, and *there is* no god with me: I kill, and I make alive; I wound, and I heal: neither *is there any* that can deliver out of my hand.

Jos 2:11 — And as soon as we had heard *these things*, our hearts did melt, neither did there remain any more courage in any man, because of you: for the LORD your God, he *is* God in heaven above, and in earth beneath.

Jos 3:11 — Behold, the ark of the covenant of the Lord of all the earth passeth over before you into Jordan.

2Ki 19:15 — And Hezekiah prayed before the LORD, and said, O LORD God of Israel, which dwellest *between* the cherubims, thou art the God, *even* thou alone, of all the kingdoms of the earth: thou hast made heaven and earth.

2Ch 20:6 — And said, O LORD God of our fathers, *art* not thou God in heaven? and rulest *not* thou over all the kingdoms of the heathen? and in thine hand *is there not* power and might, so that none is able to withstand thee?

Ne 9:6 — Thou, *even* thou, *art* LORD alone; thou hast made heaven, the heaven of heavens, with all their host, the earth, and all *things* that *are* therein, the seas, and all that *is* therein, and thou preservest them all; and the host of heaven worshippeth thee.

Job 9:12 — Behold, he taketh away, who can hinder him? who will say unto him, What doest thou?

Job 25:2 — Dominion and fear *are* with him, he maketh peace in his high places.

Job 33:13 — Why dost thou strive against him? for he giveth not account of any of his matters.

Job 34:13 — Who hath given him a charge over the earth? or who hath disposed the whole world?

Job 34:24 — He shall break in pieces mighty men without number, and set others in their stead.

Job 34:33 — *Should it be* according to thy mind? he will recompense it, whether thou refuse, or whether thou choose; and not I: therefore speak what thou knowest.

Job 41:11 — Who hath prevented me, that I should repay *him? whatsoever is* under the whole heaven is mine.

Ps 10:16 — The LORD *is* King for ever and ever: the heathen are perished out of his land.

Ps 24:1 — The earth *is* the LORD'S, and the fulness thereof; the world, and they that dwell therein.

Ps 24:10 — Who is this King of glory? The LORD of hosts, he *is* the King of glory. Selah.

Ps 29:10 — The LORD sitteth upon the flood; yea, the LORD sitteth King for ever.

Ps 44:4 — Thou art my King, O God: command deliverances for Jacob.

Ps 59:13 — Consume *them* in wrath, consume *them*, that they *may* not *be:* and let them know that God ruleth in Jacob unto the ends of the earth. Selah.

Ps 65:5 — By terrible things in righteousness wilt thou answer us, O God of our salvation; *who art* the confidence of all the ends of the earth, and of them that are afar off *upon* the sea:

Ps 66:7 — He ruleth by his power for ever; his eyes behold the nations: let not the rebellious exalt themselves. Selah.

Ps 67:4 — O let the nations be glad and sing for joy: for thou shalt judge the people righteously, and govern the nations upon earth. Selah.

Ps 74:12 — For God *is* my King of old, working salvation in the midst of the earth.

Ps 82:1 — God standeth in the congregation of the mighty; he judgeth among the gods.

Ps 82:8 — Arise, O God, judge the earth: for thou shalt inherit all nations.

Ps 83:18 — That *men* may know that thou, whose name alone *is* JEHOVAH, *art* the most high over all the earth.

Ps 89:11 — The heavens *are* thine, the earth also *is* thine: *as for* the world and the fulness thereof, thou hast founded them.

Ps 89:18 — For the LORD *is* our defence; and the Holy One of Israel *is* our king.

Ps 96:10 — Say among the heathen *that* the LORD reigneth: the world also shall be established that it shall not be moved: he shall judge the people righteously.

Ps 97:5 — The hills melted like wax at the presence of the LORD, at the presence of the Lord of the whole earth.

Ps 97:9 — For thou, LORD, *art* high above all the earth: thou art exalted far above all gods.

Ps 98:6 — With trumpets and sound of cornet make a joyful noise before the LORD, the King.

Ps 99:1 — The LORD reigneth; let the people tremble: he sitteth *between* the cherubims; let the earth be moved.

Ps 103:19 — The LORD hath prepared his throne in the heavens; and his kingdom ruleth over all.

Ps 105:7 — He *is* the LORD our God: his judgments *are* in all the earth.

Ps 113:4 — The LORD *is* high above all nations, *and* his glory above the heavens.

Ps 115:3 — But our God *is* in the heavens: he hath done whatsoever he hath pleased.

Ps 115:16 — The heaven, *even* the heavens, *are* the LORD'S: but the earth hath he given to the children of men.

Ps 146:10 — The LORD shall reign for ever, *even* thy God, O Zion, unto all generations. Praise ye the LORD.

Ecc 9:1 — For all this I considered in my heart even to declare all this, that the righteous, and the wise, and their works, are in the hand of God: no man knoweth either love or hatred *by* all *that is* before them.

Isa 24:23 — Then the moon shall be confounded, and the sun ashamed, when the LORD of hosts shall reign in mount Zion, and in Jerusalem, and before his ancients gloriously.

Isa 33:22 — For the LORD *is* our judge, the LORD *is* our lawgiver, the LORD *is* our king; he will save us.

Isa 37:16 — O LORD of hosts, God of Israel, that dwellest *between* the cherubims, thou *art* the God, *even* thou alone, of all the kingdoms of the earth: thou hast made heaven and earth.

Isa 43:15 — I *am* the LORD, your Holy One, the creator of Israel, your King.

Isa 44:6 — Thus saith the LORD the King of Israel, and his redeemer the LORD of hosts; I *am* the first, and I *am* the last; and beside me *there is* no God.

Isa 45:7 — I form the light, and create darkness: I make peace, and create evil: I the LORD do all these *things*.

Isa 45:23 — I have sworn by myself, the word is gone out of my mouth *in* righteousness, and shall not return, That unto me every knee shall bow, every tongue shall swear.

Isa 52:7 — How beautiful upon the mountains are the feet of him that bringeth good tidings, that publisheth peace; that bringeth good tidings of good, that publisheth salvation; that saith unto Zion, Thy God reigneth!

Isa 54:5 — For thy Maker *is* thine husband; the LORD of hosts *is* his name; and thy Redeemer the Holy One of Israel; The God of the whole earth shall he be called.

Jer 10:10 — But the LORD *is* the true God, he *is* the living God, and an everlasting king: at his wrath the earth shall tremble, and the nations shall not be able to abide his indignation.

La 5:19 — Thou, O LORD, remainest for ever; thy throne from generation to generation.

Eze 16:50 — And they were haughty, and committed abomination before me: therefore I took them away as I saw *good*.

Eze 17:24 — And all the trees of the field shall know that I the LORD have brought down the high tree, have exalted the low tree, have dried up the green tree, and have made the dry tree to flourish: I the LORD have brought down the high tree, have exalted the low tree, have dried up the green tree, and have made the dry tree to flourish: I the LORD have spoken and have done *it*.

Eze 18:4 — Behold, all souls are mine; as the soul of the father, so also the soul of the son is mine: the soul that sinneth, it shall die.

Da 2:47 — The king answered unto Daniel, and said, Of a truth *it is*, that your God is a God of gods, and a Lord of kings, and a revealer of secrets, seeing thou couldst reveal this secret.

Da 4:3 — How great *are* his signs! and how mighty *are* his wonders! his kingdom *is* an everlasting kingdom, and his dominion *is* from generation to generation.

Da 4:17 — This matter *is* by the decree of the watchers, and the demand by the word of the holy ones: to the intent that the living may know that the most High ruleth in the kingdom of men, and giveth it to whomsoever he will, and setteth up over it the basest of men.

Da 4:25 — That they shall drive thee from men, and thy dwelling shall be with the beasts of the field, and they shall make thee to eat grass as oxen, and they shall wet thee with the dew of heaven, and seven times shall pass over thee, till thou know that the most High ruleth in the kingdom of men, and giveth it to whomsoever he will.

Da 4:37 — Now I Nebuchadnezzar praise and extol and honour the King of heaven, all whose works *are* truth, and his ways judgment: and those that walk in pride he is able to abase.

Da 5:18 — O thou king, the most high God gave Nebuchadnezzar thy father a kingdom, and majesty, and glory, and honour:

Da 6:26 — I make a decree, That in every dominion of my kingdom men tremble and fear before the God of Daniel: for he is the living God, and stedfast for ever, and his kingdom *that* which shall not be destroyed, and his dominion *shall be even* unto the end.

Mic 4:7 — And I will make her that halted a remnant, and her that was cast far off a strong nation: and the LORD shall reign over them in mount Zion from henceforth, even for ever.

Mic 4:13 — Arise and thresh, O daughter of Zion: for I will make thine horn iron, and I will make thy hoofs brass: and thou shalt beat in pieces many people: and I will consecrate their gain unto the LORD, and their substance unto the Lord of the whole earth.

Hag 2:8 — The silver *is* mine, and the gold *is* mine, saith the LORD of hosts.

Mal 1:14 — But cursed *be* the deceiver, which hath in his flock a male, and voweth, and sacrificeth unto the LORD a corrupt thing: for I *am* a great King, saith the LORD of hosts, and my name *is* dreadful among the heathen.

Mt 6:10 — Thy kingdom come. Thy will be done in earth, as *it is* in heaven.

Mt 6:13 — And lead us not into temptation, but deliver us from evil: For thine is the kingdom, and the power, and the glory, for ever. Amen.

Mt 11:25 — At that time Jesus answered and said, I thank thee, O Father, Lord of heaven and earth, because thou hast hid these things from the wise and prudent, and hast revealed them unto babes.

Mt 20:15 — Is it not lawful for me to do what I will with mine own? Is thine eye evil, because I am good?

Lk 1:53 — He hath filled the hungry with good things; and the rich he hath sent empty away.

Lk 10:21 — In that hour Jesus rejoiced in spirit, and said, I thank thee, O Father, Lord of heaven and earth, that thou hast hid these things from the wise and prudent, and hast revealed them unto babes: even so, Father; for so it seemed good in thy sight.

Jn 10:29 — My Father, which gave *them* me, is greater than all; and no *man* is able to pluck *them* out of my Father's hand.

Jn 19:11 — Jesus answered, Thou couldest have no power *at all* against me, except it were given thee from above: therefore he that delivered me unto thee hath the greater sin.

Ro 9:19 — Thou wilt say then unto me, Why doth he yet find fault? For who hath resisted his will?

Ro 14:11 — For it is written, *As* I live, saith the Lord, every knee shall bow to me, and every tongue shall confess to God.

1Co 10:26 — For the earth *is* the Lord's, and the fulness thereof.

Eph 4:6 — One God and Father of all, who *is* above all, and through all, and in you all.

Heb 1:3 — Who being the brightness of *his* glory, and the express image of his person, and upholding all things by the word of his power, when he had by himself purged our sins, sat down on the right hand of the Majesty on high;

Jas 4:12 — There is one lawgiver, who is able to save and to destroy: who art thou that judgest another?

Rev 1:6 — And hath made us kings and priests unto God and his Father; to him *be* glory and dominion for ever and ever. Amen.

Rev 4:11 — Thou art worthy, O Lord, to receive glory and honour and power: for thou hast created all things, and for thy pleasure they are and were created.

Rev 11:4 — These are the two olive trees, and the two candlesticks standing before the God of the earth.

Rev 11:13 — And the same hour was there a great earthquake, and the tenth part of the city fell, and in the earthquake were slain of men seven thousand: and the remnant were affrighted, and gave glory to the God of heaven.

Rev 11:17 — Saying, We give thee thanks, O Lord God Almighty, which art, and wast, and art to come; because thou hast taken to thee thy great power, and hast reigned.

Rev 19:6 — And I heard as it were the voice of a great multitude, and as the voice of many waters, and as the voice of mighty thunderings, saying, Alleluia: for the Lord God omnipotent reigneth.

See: God, Power of

GOD, Truth

Nu 23:19 — God *is* not a man, that he should lie; neither the son of man, that he should repent: hath he said, and shall he not do *it?* or hath he spoken, and shall he not make it good?

Dt 32:4 — *He is* the Rock, his work *is* perfect: for all his ways *are* judgment: a God of truth and without iniquity, just and right *is* he.

1Sa 15:29 — And also the Strength of Israel will not lie nor repent: for he *is* not a man, that he should repent.

Ps 25:10 — All the paths of the LORD *are* mercy and truth unto such as keep his covenant and his testimonies.

Ps 31:5 — Into thine hand I commit my spirit: thou hast redeemed me, O LORD God of truth.

Ps 33:4 — For the word of the LORD *is* right; and all his works *are done* in truth.

Ps 40:10 — I have not hid thy righteousness within my heart; I have declared thy faithfulness and thy salvation: I have not concealed thy lovingkindness and thy truth from the great congregation.

Ps 43:3 — O send out thy light and thy truth: let them lead me; let them bring me unto thy holy hill, and to thy tabernacles.

Ps 57:3 — He shall send from heaven, and save *from* the reproach of him that would swallow me up. Selah. God shall send forth his mercy and his truth.

Ps 57:10 — For thy mercy is great unto the heavens, and thy truth unto the clouds.

Ps 71:22 — I will also praise thee with the psaltery, *even* thy truth, O my God: unto thee will I sing with the harp, O thou Holy One of Israel.

Ps 86:11 — Teach me thy way, O LORD; I will walk in thy truth: unite my heart to fear thy name.

Ps 86:15 — But thou, O Lord, *art* a God full of compassion, and gracious, longsuffering, and plenteous in mercy and truth.

Ps 89:14 — Justice and judgment *are* the habitation of thy throne: mercy and truth shall go before thy face.

Ps 91:4 — He shall cover thee with his feathers, and under his wings shalt thou trust: his truth *shall be thy* shield and buckler.

Ps 100:5 — For the LORD *is* good; his mercy *is* everlasting; and his truth *endureth* to all generations.

Ps 108:4 — For thy mercy *is* great above the heavens: and thy truth *reacheth* unto the clouds.

Ps 117:2 — For his merciful kindness is great toward us: and the truth of the LORD *endureth* for ever. Praise ye the LORD.

Ps 132:11 — The LORD hath sworn *in* truth unto David; he will not turn from it; Of the fruit of thy body will I set upon thy throne.

Ps 138:2 — I will worship toward thy holy temple, and praise thy name for thy lovingkindness and for thy truth: for thou hast magnified thy word above all thy name.

Ps 146:6 — Which made heaven, and earth, the sea, and all that therein *is:* which keepeth truth for ever:

Isa 25:1 — O LORD, thou *art* my God; I will exalt thee, I will praise thy name; for thou hast done wonderful *things; thy* counsels of old *are* faithfulness *and* truth.

Isa 65:16 — That he who blesseth himself in the earth shall bless himself in the God of truth; and he that sweareth in the earth shall swear by the God of truth; because the former troubles are forgotten, and because they are hid from mine eyes.

Jer 10:10 — But the LORD *is* the true God, he *is* the living God, and an everlasting king: at his wrath the earth shall tremble, and the nations shall not be able to abide his indignation.

Da 4:37 — Now I Nebuchadnezzar praise and extol and honour the King of heaven, all whose works *are* truth, and his ways judgment: and those that walk in pride he is able to abase.

Da 9:13 — As *it is* written in the law of Moses, all this evil is come upon us: yet made we not our prayer before the LORD our God, that we might turn from our iniquities, and understand thy truth.

Jn 8:26 — I have many things to say and to judge of you: but he that sent me is true; and I speak to the world those things which I have heard of him.

Jn 17:17 — Sanctify them through thy truth: thy word is truth.

Jn 17:19 — And for their sakes I sanctify myself, that they also might be sanctified through the truth.

Ro 3:4 — God forbid: yea, let God be true, but every man a liar; as it is written, That thou mightest be justified in thy sayings, and mightest overcome when thou art judged.

Ro 3:7 — For if the truth of God hath more abounded through my lie unto his glory; why yet am I also judged as a sinner?

Tit 1:2 — In hope of eternal life, which God, that cannot lie, promised before the world began;

Rev 6:10 — And they cried with a loud voice, saying, How long, O Lord, holy and true, dost thou not judge and avenge our blood on them that dwell on the earth?

Rev 15:3 — And they sing the song of Moses the servant of God, and the song of the Lamb, saying, Great and marvellous *are* thy works, Lord God Almighty; just and true *are* thy ways, thou King of saints.

See: God, Faithfulness of
See: God, Judge, and His Justice
See: God, Righteousness of
See: Truth

GOD, Ubiquitous

Ps 139:7–10; Jer 23:23–24; Ac 7:48–49

1Ki 8:27 — But will God indeed dwell on the earth? behold, the heaven and heaven of heavens cannot contain thee; how much less this house that I have builded?

2Ch 2:6 — But who is able to build him an house, seeing the heaven and heaven of heavens cannot contain him? who *am* I then, that I should build him an house, save only to burn sacrifice before him?

Ps 139:3 — Thou compassest my path and my lying down, and art acquainted *with* all my ways.

Ps 139:5 — Thou hast beset me behind and before, and laid thine hand upon me.

See: God, Eternity of
See: God, Infinite
See: God, Omnipresent
See: God, Power of
See: God, Presence of
See: God, Providence of

GOD, Unchangeable See: God, Immutable

GOD, Unity of

Dt 6:4 — Hear, O Israel: The LORD our God *is* one LORD:

1Ki 8:60 — That all the people of the earth may know that the LORD *is* God, *and that there is* none else.

1Ki 20:28 — And there came a man of God, and spake unto the king of Israel, and said, Thus saith the LORD, Because the Syrians have said, The LORD *is* God of the hills, but he *is* not God of the valleys, therefore will I deliver all this great multitude into thine hand, and ye shall know that I *am* the LORD.

Isa 42:8 — I *am* the LORD: that *is* my name: and my glory will I not give to another, neither my praise to graven images.

Mk 12:29 — And Jesus answered him, The first of all the commandments *is,* Hear, O Israel; The Lord our God is one Lord:

Mk 12:32 — And the scribe said unto him, Well, Master, thou hast said the truth: for there is one God; and there is none other but he:

Jn 17:3 — And this is life eternal, that they might know thee the only true God, and Jesus Christ, whom thou hast sent.

1Co 8:4 — As concerning therefore the eating of those things that are offered in sacrifice unto idols, we know that an idol *is* nothing in the world, and that *there is* none other God but one.

1Co 8:6 — But to us *there is but* one God, the Father, of whom *are* all things, and we in him; and one Lord Jesus Christ, by whom *are* all things, and we by him.

Gal 3:20 — Now a mediator is not *a mediator* of one, but God is one.

1Ti 2:5 — For *there is* one God, and one mediator between God and men, the man Christ Jesus;

Jas 2:19 — Thou believest that there is one God; thou doest well: the devils also believe, and tremble.

GOD, Unsearchable

Job 5:8–9; 11:7–9; Isa 55:8–9; Ro 11:33–34; 1Co 2:10–11

Ge 32:29 — And Jacob asked *him,* and said, Tell *me,* I pray thee, thy name. And he said, Wherefore *is it that* thou dost ask after my name? And he blessed him there.

Dt 29:29 — The secret *things belong* unto the LORD our God: but *those things which* are revealed *belong* unto us and to our children for ever, that *we* may do all the words of this law.

Jgs 13:18 — And the angel of the LORD said unto him, Why askest thou thus after my name, seeing it is secret?

1Ki 8:12 — Then spake Solomon, The LORD said that he would dwell in thick darkness.

1Ki 8:27 — But will God indeed dwell on the earth? behold, the heaven and heaven of heavens cannot contain thee; how much less this house that I have builded?

2Ch 2:6 — But who is able to build him an house, seeing the heaven and heaven of heavens cannot contain him? who *am* I then, that I should build him an house, save only to burn sacrifice before him?

2Ch 6:1 — Then said Solomon, The LORD hath said that he would dwell in the thick darkness.

2Ch 6:18 — But will God in very deed dwell with men on the earth? behold, heaven and the heaven of heavens cannot contain thee; how much less this house which I have built!

Job 9:10 — Which doeth great things past finding out; yea, and wonders without number.

Job 26:9 — He holdeth back the face of his throne, *and* spreadeth his cloud upon it.

Job 26:14 — Lo, these *are* parts of his ways: but how little a portion is heard of him? but the thunder of his power who can understand?

Job 36:26 — Behold, God *is* great, and we know *him* not, neither can the number of his years be searched out.

Job 37:5 — God thundereth marvellously with his voice; great things doeth he, which we cannot comprehend.

Job 37:23 — *Touching* the Almighty, we cannot find him out: *he is* excellent in power, and in judgment, and in plenty of justice: he will not afflict.

Ps 77:19 — Thy way *is* in the sea, and thy path in the great waters, and thy footsteps are not known.

Ps 92:5 — O LORD, how great are thy works! *and* thy thoughts are very deep.

Ps 97:2 — Clouds and darkness *are* round about him: righteousness and judgment *are* the habitation of his throne.

Ps 139:6 — *Such* knowledge *is* too wonderful for me; it is high, I cannot *attain* unto it.

Ps 145:3 — Great *is* the LORD, and greatly to be praised; and his greatness *is* unsearchable.

Pr 25:2 — *It is* the glory of God to conceal a thing: but the honour of kings *is* to search out a matter.

Pr 30:4 — Who hath ascended up into heaven, or descended? who hath gathered the wind in his fists? who hath bound the waters in a garment? who hath established all the ends of the earth? what *is* his name, and what *is* his son's name, if thou canst tell?

Ecc 3:11 — He hath made every *thing* beautiful in his time: also he hath set the world in their heart, so that no man can find out the work that God maketh from the beginning to the end.

Ecc 7:24 — That which is far off, and exceeding deep, who can find it out?

Ecc 11:5 — As thou knowest not what *is* the way of the spirit, *nor* how the bones *do grow* in the womb of her that is with child: even so thou knowest not the works of God who maketh all.

Isa 40:28 — Hast thou not known? hast thou not heard, *that* the everlasting God, the LORD, the Creator of the ends of the earth, fainteth not, neither is weary? *there is* no searching of his understanding.

Isa 45:15 — Verily thou *art* a God that hidest thyself, O God of Israel, the Saviour.

Jer 23:24 — Can any hide himself in secret places that I shall not see him? saith the LORD. Do not I fill heaven and earth? saith the LORD.

Na 1:3 — The LORD *is* slow to anger, and great in power, and will not at all acquit *the wicked:* the LORD hath his way in the whirlwind and in the storm, and the clouds *are* the dust of his feet.

Mt 11:27 — All things are delivered unto me of my Father: and no man knoweth the Son, but the Father; neither knoweth any man the Father, save the Son, and *he* to whomsoever the Son will reveal *him.*

1Co 2:16 — For who hath known the mind of the Lord, that he may instruct him? But we have the mind of Christ.

Eph 3:8 — Unto me, who am less than the least of all saints, is this grace given, that I should preach among the Gentiles the unsearchable riches of Christ;

⇜See: Mysteries

GOD, Voice of ⇜See: Anthropomorphisms

GOD, Wisdom of

Pr 3:19–20; 8:27–31; Da 2:20–22; 1Co 1:24–25

Ezr 7:25 — And thou, Ezra, after the wisdom of thy God, that *is* in thine hand, set magistrates and judges, which may judge all the people that *are* beyond the river, all such as know the laws of thy God; and teach ye them that know *them* not.

Job 9:4 — *He is* wise in heart, and mighty in strength: who hath hardened *himself* against him, and hath prospered?

Job 12:13 — With him *is* wisdom and strength, he hath counsel and understanding.

Job 12:16 — With him *is* strength and wisdom: the deceived and the deceiver *are* his.

Ps 104:24 — O LORD, how manifold are thy works! in wisdom hast thou made them all: the earth is full of thy riches.

Ps 136:5 — To him that by wisdom made the heavens: for his mercy *endureth* for ever.

Ps 147:5 — Great *is* our Lord, and of great power: his understanding *is* infinite.

Pr 8:12 — I wisdom dwell with prudence, and find out knowledge of witty inventions.

Pr 8:22 — The LORD possessed me in the beginning of his way, before his works of old.

Isa 31:2 — Yet he also *is* wise, and will bring evil, and will not call back his words: but will arise against the house of the evildoers, and against the help of them that work iniquity.

Jer 10:7 — Who would not fear thee, O King of nations? for to thee doth it appertain: forasmuch as among all the wise *men* of the nations, and in all their kingdoms, *there is* none like unto thee.

Jer 10:12 — He hath made the earth by his power, he hath established the world by his wisdom, and hath stretched out the heavens by his discretion.

Jer 51:15 — He hath made the earth by his power, he hath established the world by his wisdom, and hath stretched out the heaven by his understanding.

Da 2:28 — But there is a God in heaven that revealeth secrets, and maketh known to the king Nebuchadnezzar what shall be in the latter days. Thy dream, and the visions of thy head upon thy bed, are these;

Ro 16:27 — To God only wise, *be* glory through Jesus Christ for ever. Amen.

Eph 1:8 — Wherein he hath abounded toward us in all wisdom and prudence;

Eph 3:10 — To the intent that now unto the principalities and powers in heavenly *places* might be known by the church the manifold wisdom of God,

1Ti 1:17 — Now unto the King eternal, immortal, invisible, the only wise God, *be* honour and glory for ever and ever. Amen.

Jude 1:25 — To the only wise God our Saviour, *be* glory and majesty, dominion and power, both now and ever. Amen.

Rev 7:12 — Saying, Amen: Blessing, and glory, and wisdom, and thanksgiving, and honour, and power, and might, *be* unto our God for ever and ever. Amen.

See: God, Knowledge of

See: God, Omniscient

GOD, Works of

Job 9:1–35; 37:1–41:34; Ps 8:1–9; 19:1–14; 89:1–52; 92:4–5; 104:1–35; 111:1–10; 136:1–26; 145:1–21; 147:1–148:14

Ge 1:10 — And God called the dry *land* Earth; and the gathering together of the waters called he Seas: and God saw that *it was* good.

Ge 1:18 — And to rule over the day and over the night, and to divide the light from the darkness: and God saw that *it was* good.

Ge 1:21 — And God created great whales, and every living creature that moveth, which the waters brought forth abundantly, after their kind, and every winged fowl after his kind: and God saw that *it was* good.

Ge 1:25 — And God made the beast of the earth after his kind, and cattle after their kind, and every thing that creepeth upon the earth after his kind: and God saw that *it was* good.

Dt 32:4 — *He is* the Rock, his work *is* perfect: for all his ways *are* judgment: a God of truth and without iniquity, just and right *is* he.

Ps 26:7 — That I may publish with the voice of thanksgiving, and tell of all thy wondrous works.

Ps 33:4 — For the word of the LORD *is* right; and all his works *are done* in truth.

Ps 40:5 — Many, O LORD my God, *are* thy wonderful works *which* thou hast done, and thy thoughts *which are* to us-ward: they cannot be reckoned up in order unto thee: *if* I would declare and speak *of them,* they are more than can be numbered.

Ps 66:3 — Say unto God, How terrible *art thou in* thy works! through the greatness of thy power shall thine enemies submit themselves unto thee.

Ps 75:1 — Unto thee, O God, do we give thanks, *unto thee* do we give thanks: for *that* thy name is near thy wondrous works declare.

Ps 86:8 — Among the gods *there is* none like unto thee, O Lord; neither *are there any works* like unto thy works.

Ps 118:17 — I shall not die, but live, and declare the works of the LORD.

Ps 139:14 — I will praise thee; for I am fearfully *and* wonderfully made: marvellous *are* thy works; and *that* my soul knoweth right well.

Ecc 3:11 — He hath made every *thing* beautiful in his time: also he hath set the world in their heart, so that no man can find out the work that God maketh from the beginning to the end.

Ecc 3:14 — I know that, whatsoever God doeth, it shall be for ever: nothing can be put to it, nor any thing taken from it: and God doeth *it,* that *men* should fear before him.

Jer 10:12 — He hath made the earth by his power, he hath established the world by his wisdom, and hath stretched out the heavens by his discretion.

See: Creation

See: God, Creator

See: Works

GODLESSNESS

Job 8:11–13; Ps 14:2–3; 53:2–4; Isa 30:1–2, 9–13; Hos 7:2–4; Jn 15:23–25; Ro 1:21–22; 8:6–8; Heb 10:26–27

Dt 7:10 — And repayeth them that hate him to their face, to destroy them: he will not be slack to him that hateth him, he will repay him to his face.

Dt 32:15 — But Jeshurun waxed fat, and kicked: thou art waxen fat, thou art grown thick, thou art covered *with fatness;* then he forsook God *which* made him, and lightly esteemed the Rock of his salvation.

1Sa 2:30 — Wherefore the LORD God of Israel saith, I said indeed *that* thy house, and the house of thy father, should walk before me for ever: but now the LORD saith, Be it far from me; for them that honour me I will honour, and they that despise me shall be lightly esteemed.

Job 35:10 — But none saith, Where *is* God my maker, who giveth songs in the night;

Ps 2:2 — The kings of the earth set themselves, and the rulers take counsel together, against the LORD, and against his anointed, *saying,*

Ps 2:4 — He that sitteth in the heavens shall laugh: the Lord shall have them in derision.

Ps 9:17 — The wicked shall be turned into hell, *and* all the nations that forget God.

Ps 10:4 — The wicked, through the pride of his countenance, will not seek *after God:* God *is* not in all his thoughts.

Ps 28:5 — Because they regard not the works of the LORD, nor the operation of his hands, he shall destroy them, and not build them up.

Ps 36:1 — The transgression of the wicked saith within my heart, *that there is* no fear of God before his eyes.

Ps 50:22 — Now consider this, ye that forget God, lest I tear *you* in pieces, and *there be* none to deliver.

Ps 52:7 — Lo, *this is* the man *that* made not God his strength; but trusted in the abundance of his riches, *and* strengthened himself in his wickedness.

Ps 54:3 — For strangers are risen up against me, and oppressors seek after my soul: they have not set God before them. Selah.

Ps 55:19 — God shall hear, and afflict them, even he that abideth of old. Selah. Because they have no changes, therefore they fear not God.

Ps 86:14 — O God, the proud are risen against me, and the assemblies of violent *men* have sought after my soul; and have not set thee before them.

Pr 14:2 — He that walketh in his uprightness feareth the LORD: but *he that is* perverse in his ways despiseth him.

Isa 1:3 — The ox knoweth his owner, and the ass his master's crib: *but* Israel doth not know, my people doth not consider.

Isa 5:12 — And the harp, and the viol, the tabret, and pipe, and wine, are in their feasts: but they regard not the work of the LORD, neither consider the operation of his hands.

Isa 17:10 — Because thou hast forgotten the God of thy salvation, and hast not been mindful of the rock of thy strength, therefore shalt thou plant pleasant plants, and shalt set it with strange slips:

Isa 22:11 — Ye made also a ditch between the two walls for the water of the old pool: but ye have not looked unto the maker thereof, neither had respect unto him that fashioned it long ago.

Isa 31:1 — Woe to them that go down to Egypt for help; and stay on horses, and trust in chariots, because *they are* many; and in horsemen, because they are very strong; but they look not unto the Holy One of Israel, neither seek the LORD!

Jer 2:32 — Can a maid forget her ornaments, *or* a bride her attire? yet my people have forgotten me days without number.

Da 5:23 — But hast lifted up thyself against the Lord of heaven; and they have brought the vessels of his house before thee, and thou, and thy lords, thy wives, and thy concubines, have drunk wine in them; and thou hast praised the gods of silver, and gold, of brass, iron, wood, and stone, which see not, nor hear, nor know: and the God in whose hand thy breath *is,* and whose *are* all thy ways, hast thou not glorified:

Mal 2:17 — Ye have wearied the LORD with your words. Yet ye say, Wherein have we wearied *him?* When ye say, Every one that doeth evil *is* good in the sight of the LORD, and he delighteth in them; or, Where *is* the God of judgment?

Mal 3:8 — Will a man rob God? Yet ye have robbed me. But ye say, Wherein have we robbed thee? In tithes and offerings.

Jn 5:42 — But I know you, that ye have not the love of God in you.

Jn 5:44 — How can ye believe, which receive honour one of another, and seek not the honour that *cometh* from God only?

Ro 1:28 — And even as they did not like to retain God in *their* knowledge, God gave them over to a reprobate mind, to do those things which are not convenient;

Ro 3:11 — There is none that understandeth, there is none that seeketh after God.

Ro 3:18 — There is no fear of God before their eyes.

Eph 4:18 — Having the understanding darkened, being alienated from the life of God through the ignorance that is in them, because of the blindness of their heart:

Col 1:21 — And you, that were sometime alienated and enemies in *your* mind by wicked works, yet now hath he reconciled:

Jas 4:4 — Ye adulterers and adulteresses, know ye not that the friendship of the world is enmity with God? whosoever therefore will be a friend of the world is the enemy of God.

See: Impenitence
See: Obduracy
See: Prayerlessness
See: Reprobacy
See: Unbelief
See: Wicked

GODLINESS

See: Holiness
See: Righteousness

GODLY **See: Righteous**

GODS

See: Idol
See: Idolatry
See: Image

GOG

- **A Reubenite.**

1Ch 5:4 — The sons of Joel; Shemaiah his son, Gog his son, Shimei his son,

- **A Scythian prince.**
  - **Prophecy against.**

Eze 38:1–39:29

Rev 20:8 — And shall go out to deceive the nations which are in the four quarters of the earth, Gog and Magog, to gather them together to battle: the number of whom *is* as the sand of the sea.

GOLAN

- **A town in Bashan.**
- **Given to Manasseh as a city of refuge.**

Dt 4:43 — *Namely,* Bezer in the wilderness, in the plain country, of the Reubenites; and Ramoth in Gilead, of the Gadites; and Golan in Bashan, of the Manassites.

Jos 20:8 — And on the other side Jordan by Jericho eastward, they assigned Bezer in the wilderness upon the plain out of the tribe of Reuben, and Ramoth in Gilead out of the tribe of Gad, and Golan in Bashan out of the tribe of Manasseh.

- **A Levitical city.**

Jos 21:27 — And unto the children of Gershon, of the families of the Levites, out of the *other* half tribe of Manasseh *they gave* Golan in Bashan with her suburbs, *to be* a city of refuge for the slayer; and Beeshterah with her suburbs; two cities.

1Ch 6:71 — Unto the sons of Gershom *were given* out of the family of the half tribe of Manasseh, Golan in Bashan with her suburbs, and Ashtaroth with her suburbs:

GOLD

- **Exported from Havilah.**

Ge 2:11–12

- **From Ophir.**

1Ki 9:28 — And they came to Ophir, and fetched from thence gold, four hundred and twenty talents, and brought *it* to king Solomon.

1Ki 10:11 — And the navy also of Hiram, that brought gold from Ophir, brought in from Ophir great plenty of almug trees, and precious stones.

1Ch 29:4 — *Even* three thousand talents of gold, of the gold of Ophir, and seven thousand talents of refined silver, to overlay the walls of the houses *withal:*

2Ch 8:18 — And Huram sent him by the hands of his servants ships, and servants that had knowledge of the sea; and they went with the servants of Solomon to Ophir, and took thence four hundred and fifty talents of gold, and brought *them* to king Solomon.

Job 22:24 — Then shalt thou lay up gold as dust, and the *gold* of Ophir as the stones of the brooks.

- **From Tarshish.**

1Ki 22:48 — Jehoshaphat made ships of Tharshish to go to Ophir for gold: but they went not; for the ships were broken at Ezion-geber.

- **From Parvaim.**

2Ch 3:6 — And he garnished the house with precious stones for beauty: and the gold *was* gold of Parvaim.

- **From Sheba.**

1Ki 10:10 — And she gave the king an hundred and twenty talents of gold, and of spices very great store, and precious stones: there came no more such abundance of spices as these which the queen of Sheba gave to king Solomon.

2Ch 9:9 — And she gave the king an hundred and twenty talents of gold, and of spices great abundance, and precious stones: neither was there any such spice as the queen of Sheba gave king Solomon.

Ps 72:15 — And he shall live, and to him shall be given of the gold of Sheba: prayer also shall be made for him continually; *and* daily shall he be praised.

- **From Uphaz.**

Jer 10:9 — Silver spread into plates is brought from Tarshish, and gold from Uphaz, the work of the workman, and of the hands of the founder: blue and purple is their clothing: they *are* all the work of cunning *men.*

- **Refine.**

Job 28:19 — The topaz of Ethiopia shall not equal it, neither shall it be valued with pure gold.

Job 31:24 — If I have made gold my hope, or have said to the fine gold, *Thou art* my confidence;

Pr 8:19 — My fruit *is* better than gold, yea, than fine gold; and my revenue than choice silver.

Pr 17:3 — The fining pot *is* for silver, and the furnace for gold: but the LORD trieth the hearts.

Pr 27:21 — *As* the fining pot for silver, and the furnace for gold; so *is* a man to his praise.

Zec 13:9 — And I will bring the third part through the fire, and will refine them as silver is refined, and will try them as gold is tried: they shall call on my name, and I will hear them: I will say, It *is* my people: and they shall say, The LORD *is* my God.

Mal 3:3 — And he shall sit *as* a refiner and purifier of silver: and he shall purify the sons of Levi, and purge them as gold and silver, that they may offer unto the LORD an offering in righteousness.

- **Used in the arts.**
  - **Beaten work.**

2Ch 9:15 — And king Solomon made two hundred targets of beaten gold: six hundred *shekels* of beaten gold went to one target.

  - **Made into wire threads and wrought into embroidered tapestry.**

Ex 39:3 — And they did beat the gold into thin plates, and cut *it into* wires, to work *it* in the blue, and in the purple, and in the scarlet, and in the fine linen, *with* cunning work.

  - **Made into apparel.**

Ps 45:9 — Kings' daughters *were* among thy honourable women: upon thy right hand did stand the queen in gold of Ophir.

Ps 45:13 — The king's daughter *is* all glorious within: her clothing *is* of wrought gold.

  - **In ornamenting the priests' garments.**

Ex 39:1–43

  - **Modeled into forms of fruits.**

Pr 25:11 — A word fitly spoken *is like* apples of gold in pictures of silver.

  - **Modeled into ornaments.**

Nu 31:50–51

Ge 24:22 — And it came to pass, as the camels had done drinking, that the man took a golden earring of half a shekel weight, and two bracelets for her hands of ten *shekels* weight of gold;

Ex 3:22 — But every woman shall borrow of her neighbour, and of her that sojourneth in her house, jewels of silver, and jewels of gold, and raiment: and ye shall put *them* upon your sons, and upon your daughters; and ye shall spoil the Egyptians.

Ex 11:2 — Speak now in the ears of the people, and let every man borrow of his neighbour, and every woman of her neighbour, jewels of silver, and jewels of gold.

Ex 28:11 — With the work of an engraver in stone, *like* the engravings of a signet, shalt thou engrave the two stones with the names of the children of Israel: thou shalt make them to be set in ouches of gold.

SS 1:10 — Thy cheeks are comely with rows *of jewels,* thy neck with chains *of gold.*

SS 5:14 — His hands *are as* gold rings set with the beryl: his belly *is as* bright ivory overlaid *with* sapphires.

Eze 16:17 — Thou hast also taken thy fair jewels of my gold and of my silver, which I had given thee, and madest to thyself images of men, and didst commit whoredom with them,

- **Crowns made of.**

Ex 37:2–11

Ex 25:25 — And thou shalt make unto it a border of an hand breadth round about, and thou shalt make a golden crown to the border thereof round about.

Ex 39:30 — And they made the plate of the holy crown *of* pure gold, and wrote upon it a writing, *like to* the engravings of a signet, HOLINESS TO THE LORD.

Est 8:15 — And Mordecai went out from the presence of the king in royal apparel of blue and white, and with a great crown of gold, and with a garment of fine linen and purple: and the city of Shushan rejoiced and was glad.

Ps 21:3 — For thou preventest him with the blessings of goodness: thou settest a crown of pure gold on his head.

Zec 6:11 — Then take silver and gold, and make crowns, and set *them* upon the head of Joshua the son of Josedech, the high priest;

- **Candlesticks made of, for the tabernacle.**

Ex 25:31–38; 37:17–24

- **Shields of.**

1Ki 10:16–17

- **Overlaying with.**

Ex 25:1–40; 1Ki 6:20–22

Ex 26:27 — And five bars for the boards of the other side of the tabernacle, and five bars for the boards of the side of the tabernacle, for the two sides westward.

Ex 26:29 — And thou shalt overlay the boards with gold, and make their rings *of* gold *for* places for the bars: and thou shalt overlay the bars with gold.

Ex 30:5 — And thou shalt make the staves *of* shittim wood, and overlay them with gold.

Ex 36:34 — And he overlaid the boards with gold, and made their rings *of* gold *to be* places for the bars, and overlaid the bars with gold.

Ex 36:36 — And he made thereunto four pillars *of* shittim *wood,* and overlaid them with gold: their hooks *were of* gold; and he cast for them four sockets of silver.

Ex 36:38 — And the five pillars of it with their hooks: and he overlaid their chapiters and their fillets with gold: but their five sockets *were of* brass.

Ex 37:2 — And he overlaid it with pure gold within and without, and made a crown of gold to it round about.

Ex 37:4 — And he made staves *of* shittim wood, and overlaid them with gold.

Ex 37:11 — And he overlaid it with pure gold, and made thereunto a crown of gold round about.

Ex 37:15 — And he made the staves *of* shittim wood, and overlaid them with gold, to bear the table.

1Ki 6:28 — And he overlaid the cherubims with gold.

1Ki 6:30 — And the floor of the house he overlaid with gold, within and without.

1Ki 6:32 — The two doors also *were of* olive tree; and he carved upon them carvings of cherubims and palm trees and open flowers, and overlaid *them* with gold, and spread gold upon the cherubims, and upon the palm trees.

1Ki 6:35 — And he carved *thereon* cherubims and palm trees and open flowers: and covered *them* with gold fitted upon the carved work.

- **Bedsteads made of.**

Est 1:6 — *Where were* white, green, and blue, *hangings,* fastened with cords of fine linen and purple to silver rings and pillars of marble: the beds *were of* gold and silver, upon a pavement of red, and blue, and white, and black, marble.

- **Wedge of.**

Jos 7:21 — When I saw among the spoils a goodly Babylonish garment, and two hundred shekels of silver, and a wedge of gold of fifty shekels weight, then I coveted them, and took them; and, behold, they *are* hid in the earth in the midst of my tent, and the silver under it.

Isa 13:12 — I will make a man more precious than fine gold; even a man than the golden wedge of Ophir.

- **Used as money.**

Ezr 8:25–28

Ge 44:1 — And he commanded the steward of his house, saying, Fill the men's sacks *with* food, as much as they can carry, and put every man's money in his sack's mouth.

Ge 44:8 — Behold, the money, which we found in our sacks' mouths, we brought again unto thee out of the land of Canaan: how then should we steal out of thy lord's house silver or gold?

1Ch 21:25 — So David gave to Ornan for the place six hundred shekels of gold by weight.

Isa 13:17 — Behold, I will stir up the Medes against them, which shall not regard silver; and *as for* gold, they shall not delight in it.

Isa 60:9 — Surely the isles shall wait for me, and the ships of Tarshish first, to bring thy sons from far, their silver and their gold with them, unto the name of the LORD thy God, and to the Holy One of Israel, because he hath glorified thee.

Eze 7:19 — They shall cast their silver in the streets, and their gold shall be removed: their silver and their gold shall not be able to deliver them in the day of the wrath of the LORD: they shall not satisfy their souls, neither fill their bowels: because it is the stumblingblock of their iniquity.

Eze 28:4 — With thy wisdom and with thine understanding thou hast gotten thee riches, and hast gotten gold and silver into thy treasures:

Mt 2:11 — And when they were come into the house, they saw the young child with Mary his mother, and fell down, and worshipped him: and when they had opened their treasures, they presented unto him gifts; gold, and frankincense, and myrrh.

Mt 10:9 — Provide neither gold, nor silver, nor brass in your purses,

Ac 3:6 — Then Peter said, Silver and gold have I none; but such as I have give I thee: In the name of Jesus Christ of Nazareth rise up and walk.

Ac 20:33 — I have coveted no man's silver, or gold, or apparel.

1Pe 1:18 — Forasmuch as ye know that ye were not redeemed with corruptible things, *as* silver and gold, from your vain conversation *received* by tradition from your fathers;

• Solomon rich in.

1Ki 10:2 — And she came to Jerusalem with a very great train, with camels that bare spices, and very much gold, and precious stones: and when she was come to Solomon, she communed with him of all that was in her heart.

1Ki 10:14 — Now the weight of gold that came to Solomon in one year was six hundred threescore and six talents of gold.

1Ki 10:21 — And all king Solomon's drinking vessels *were of* gold, and all the vessels of the house of the forest of Lebanon *were of* pure gold; none *were of* silver: it was nothing accounted of in the days of Solomon.

• Vessels and utensils made of, for the tabernacle.

Ex 25:38–39

Ex 25:26 — And thou shalt make for it four rings of gold, and put the rings in the four corners that *are* on the four feet thereof.

Ex 25:29 — And thou shalt make the dishes thereof, and spoons thereof, and covers thereof, and bowls thereof, to cover withal: *of* pure gold shalt thou make them.

Ex 37:16 — And he made the vessels which *were* upon the table, his dishes, and his spoons, and his bowls, and his covers to cover withal, *of* pure gold.

• Vessels and utensils made of, for the temple.

1Ch 29:2–7

1Ch 18:11 — Them also king David dedicated unto the LORD, with the silver and the gold that he brought from all *these* nations; from Edom, and from Moab, and from the children of Ammon, and from the Philistines, and from Amalek.

1Ch 22:14 — Now, behold, in my trouble I have prepared for the house of the LORD an hundred thousand talents of gold, and a thousand thousand talents of silver; and of brass and iron without weight; for it is in abundance: timber also and stone have I prepared; and thou mayest add thereto.

1Ch 22:16 — Of the gold, the silver, and the brass, and the iron, *there is* no number. Arise *therefore*, and be doing, and the LORD be with thee.

• Altar, lamps, and other articles made of.

1Ki 7:48–51

2Ki 25:15 — And the firepans, and the bowls, *and* such things as *were* of gold, *in* gold, and of silver, *in* silver, the captain of the guard took away.

Ezr 8:27 — Also twenty basons of gold, of a thousand drams; and two vessels of fine copper, precious as gold.

Jer 52:19 — And the basons, and the firepans, and the bowls, and the caldrons, and the candlesticks, and the spoons, and the cups; *that* which *was* of gold *in* gold, and *that* which *was* of silver *in* silver, took the captain of the guard away.

Da 5:3 — Then they brought the golden vessels that were taken out of the temple of the house of God which *was* at Jerusalem; and the king, and his princes, his wives, and his concubines, drank in them.

See: Gold; used in the arts; overlaying with

• Belongs to God.

Eze 16:17 — Thou hast also taken thy fair jewels of my gold and of my silver, which I had given thee, and madest to thyself images of men, and didst commit whoredom with them,

• Figurative.

Ecc 12:6 — Or ever the silver cord be loosed, or the golden bowl be broken, or the pitcher be broken at the fountain, or the wheel broken at the cistern.

Jer 51:7 — Babylon *hath been* a golden cup in the LORD'S hand, that made all the earth drunken: the nations have drunken of her wine; therefore the nations are mad.

La 4:1 — How is the gold become dim! *how* is the most fine gold changed! the stones of the sanctuary are poured out in the top of every street.

1Co 3:12 — Now if any man build upon this foundation gold, silver, precious stones, wood, hay, stubble;

• Symbolic.

Da 2:32–45

Rev 21:18 — And the building of the wall of it was *of* jasper: and the city *was* pure gold, like unto clear glass.

Rev 21:21 — And the twelve gates *were* twelve pearls; every several gate was of one pearl: and the street of the city *was* pure gold, as it were transparent glass.

See: Goldsmith

GOLDEN ALTAR ⇜See: Altar

GOLDEN CANDLESTICK ⇜See: Candlestick

GOLDEN RULE

Dt 5:14–15

Le 19:18 — Thou shalt not avenge, nor bear any grudge against the children of thy people, but thou shalt love thy neighbour as thyself: I *am* the LORD.

Mt 7:12 — Therefore all things whatsoever ye would that men should do to you, do ye even so to them: for this is the law and the prophets.

Lk 6:31 — And as ye would that men should do to you, do ye also to them likewise.

Ro 13:9 — For this, Thou shalt not commit adultery, Thou shalt not kill, Thou shalt not steal, Thou shalt not bear false witness, Thou shalt not covet; and if *there be* any other commandment, it is briefly comprehended in this saying, namely, Thou shalt love thy neighbour as thyself.

Gal 5:14 — For all the law is fulfilled in one word, *even* in this; Thou shalt love thy neighbour as thyself.

GOLDSMITH

Ne 3:31–32

2Ch 2:7 — Send me now therefore a man cunning to work in gold, and in silver, and in brass, and in iron, and in purple, and crimson, and blue, and that can skill to grave with the cunning men that *are* with me in Judah and in Jerusalem, whom David my father did provide.

2Ch 2:14 — The son of a woman of the daughters of Dan, and his father *was* a man of Tyre, skilful to work in gold, and in silver, in brass, in iron, in stone, and in timber, in purple, in blue, and in fine linen, and in crimson; also to grave any manner of graving, and to find out every device which shall be put to him, with thy cunning men, and with the cunning men of my lord David thy father.

Ne 3:8 — Next unto him repaired Uzziel the son of Harhaiah, of the goldsmiths. Next unto him also repaired Hananiah the son of *one of* the apothecaries, and they fortified Jerusalem unto the broad wall.

Isa 40:19 — The workman melteth a graven image, and the goldsmith spreadeth it over with gold, and casteth silver chains.

Isa 41:7 — So the carpenter encouraged the goldsmith, *and* he that smootheth *with* the hammer him that smote the anvil, saying, It is ready for the sodering: and he fastened it with nails, *that* it should not be moved.

Isa 46:6 — They lavish gold out of the bag, and weigh silver in the balance, *and* hire a goldsmith; and he maketh it a god: they fall down, yea, they worship.

⇜See: Gold

GOLGOTHA

• Hebrew name of the place where Jesus was crucified.

Mt 27:33 — And when they were come unto a place called Golgotha, that is to say, a place of a skull,

Mk 15:22 — And they bring him unto the place Golgotha, which is, being interpreted, The place of a skull.

Jn 19:17 — And he bearing his cross went forth into a place called *the place* of a skull, which is called in the Hebrew Golgotha:

⇜See: Calvary

GOLIATH

• A giant champion of Gath.

• Defied armies of Israel and is slain by David.

1Sa 17:1–58

1Sa 21:9 — And the priest said, The sword of Goliath the Philistine, whom thou slewest in the valley of Elah, behold, it *is here* wrapped in a cloth behind the ephod: if thou wilt take that, take *it:* for *there is* no other save that here. And David said, *There is* none like that; give it me.

1Sa 22:10 — And he enquired of the LORD for him, and gave him victuals, and gave him the sword of Goliath the Philistine.

• His sons.

2Sa 21:15–22; 1Ch 20:4–8

GOMER

• Son of Japheth.

Ge 10:2–3; 1Ch 1:5–6

• A people descended from Gomer.

Eze 38:6 — Gomer, and all his bands; the house of Togarmah of the north quarters, and all his bands: *and* many people with thee.

• Wife, or concubine, of Hosea.

Hos 1:3 — So he went and took Gomer the daughter of Diblaim; which conceived, and bare him a son.

GOMORRAH

• One of the "cities of the plain".

Ge 10:19 — And the border of the Canaanites was from Sidon, as thou comest to Gerar, unto Gaza; as thou goest, unto Sodom, and Gomorrah, and Admah, and Zeboim, even unto Lasha.

Ge 13:10 — And Lot lifted up his eyes, and beheld all the plain of Jordan, that it *was* well watered every where, before the LORD destroyed Sodom and Gomorrah, *even* as the garden of the LORD, like the land of Egypt, as thou comest unto Zoar.

• Its king defeated by Chedorlaomer.

Ge 14:8–11

Ge 14:2 — *That these* made war with Bera king of Sodom, and with Birsha king of Gomorrah, Shinab king of Admah, and Shemeber king of Zeboiim, and the king of Bela, which is Zoar.

• Wickedness of.

Ge 18:20 — And the LORD said, Because the cry of Sodom and Gomorrah is great, and because their sin is very grievous;

• Destroyed.

Ge 19:24–28; Isa 1:9–10

Dt 29:23 — *And that* the whole land thereof *is* brimstone, and salt, *and* burning, *that* it is not sown, nor beareth, nor any grass groweth therein, like the overthrow of Sodom, and Gomorrah, Admah, and Zeboim, which the LORD overthrew in his anger, and in his wrath:

Dt 32:32 — For their vine *is* of the vine of Sodom, and of the fields of Gomorrah: their grapes *are* grapes of gall, their clusters *are* bitter:

Isa 13:19 — And Babylon, the glory of kingdoms, the beauty of the Chaldees' excellency, shall be as when God overthrew Sodom and Gomorrah.

Jer 23:14 — I have seen also in the prophets of Jerusalem an horrible thing: they commit adultery, and walk in lies: they strengthen also the hands of evildoers, that none doth return from his wickedness: they are all of them unto me as Sodom, and the inhabitants thereof as Gomorrah.

Jer 49:18 — As in the overthrow of Sodom and Gomorrah and the neighbour *cities* thereof, saith the LORD, no man shall abide there, neither shall a son of man dwell in it.

Jer 50:40 — As God overthrew Sodom and Gomorrah and the neighbour *cities* thereof, saith the LORD; *so* shall no man abide there, neither shall any son of man dwell therein.

Am 4:11 — I have overthrown *some* of you, as God overthrew Sodom and Gomorrah, and ye were as a firebrand plucked out of the burning: yet have ye not returned unto me, saith the LORD.

Zep 2:9 — Therefore *as* I live, saith the LORD of hosts, the God of Israel, Surely Moab shall be as Sodom, and the children of Ammon as Gomorrah, *even* the breeding of nettles, and saltpits, and a perpetual desolation: the residue of my people shall spoil them, and the remnant of my people shall possess them.

Mt 10:15 — Verily I say unto you, It shall be more tolerable for the land of Sodom and Gomorrha in the day of judgment, than for that city.

Mk 6:11 — And whosoever shall not receive you, nor hear you, when ye depart thence, shake off the dust under your feet for a testimony against them. Verily I say unto you, It shall be more tolerable for Sodom and Gomorrha in the day of judgment, than for that city.

Ro 9:29 — And as Esaias said before, Except the Lord of Sabaoth had left us a seed, we had been as Sodoma, and been made like unto Gomorrha.

2Pe 2:6 — And turning the cities of Sodom and Gomorrah into ashes condemned *them* with an overthrow, making *them* an ensample unto those that after should live ungodly;

Jude 1:7 — Even as Sodom and Gomorrha, and the cities about them in like manner, giving themselves over to fornication, and going after strange flesh, are set forth for an example, suffering the vengeance of eternal fire.

GONORRHEA

Le 15:1–33

See: Disease

GOOD AND EVIL

- **Choice between, by Adam and Eve.**

  Ge 3:1–24

- **Exhortation to choose between.**

  Jos 24:15 — And if it seem evil unto you to serve the LORD, choose you this day whom ye will serve; whether the gods which your fathers served that *were* on the other side of the flood, or the gods of the Amorites, in whose land ye dwell: but as for me and my house, we will serve the LORD.

- **Conflict between.**

  Rev 16:13–21

- **Subjective conflict between.**

  Ro 7:9–25

GOOD FOR EVIL

Mt 5:44–48; Lk 6:27–36

- **Returning.**
  - **Instances of.**
    - **Abraham to Abimelech.**

      Ge 20:14–18
    - **David, to Saul.**

      1Sa 26:1–25

      1Sa 24:17 — And he said to David, Thou *art* more righteous than I: for thou hast rewarded me good, whereas I have rewarded thee evil.
    - **Elisha, to the Syrians.**

      2Ki 6:22–23
    - **David, to his enemies.**

      Ps 35:12–14
    - **Jesus, to his crucifiers.**

      Lk 23:34 — Then said Jesus, Father, forgive them; for they know not what they do. And they parted his raiment, and cast lots.
    - **Stephen.**

      Ac 7:60 — And he kneeled down, and cried with a loud voice, Lord, lay not this sin to their charge. And when he had said this, he fell asleep.

  See: Golden Rule

  See: Evil for Good

GOOD NEWS

Pr 15:30 — The light of the eyes rejoiceth the heart: *and* a good report maketh the bones fat.

Pr 25:25 — *As* cold waters to a thirsty soul, so *is* good news from a far country.

GOOD WORKS

Mt 5:16 — Let your light so shine before men, that they may see your good works, and glorify your Father which is in heaven.

Jn 15:8 — Herein is my Father glorified, that ye bear much fruit; so shall ye be my disciples.

Ac 9:36 — Now there was at Joppa a certain disciple named Tabitha, which by interpretation is called Dorcas: this woman was full of good works and almsdeeds which she did.

Eph 2:10 — For we are his workmanship, created in Christ Jesus unto good works, which God hath before ordained that we should walk in them.
1Ti 2:10 — But (which becometh women professing godliness) with good works.
1Ti 5:10 — Well reported of for good works; if she have brought up children, if she have lodged strangers, if she have washed the saints' feet, if she have relieved the afflicted, if she have diligently followed every good work.
1Ti 5:25 — Likewise also the good works *of some* are manifest beforehand; and they that are otherwise cannot be hid.
1Ti 6:18 — That they do good, that they be rich in good works, ready to distribute, willing to communicate;
Tit 2:14 — Who gave himself for us, that he might redeem us from all iniquity, and purify unto himself a peculiar people, zealous of good works.
Tit 3:10 — A man that is an heretick after the first and second admonition reject;
Heb 10:2 — For then would they not have ceased to be offered? because that the worshippers once purged should have had no more conscience of sins.
Heb 10:24 — And let us consider one another to provoke unto love and to good works:
Jas 2:17 — Even so faith, if it hath not works, is dead, being alone.
1Pe 2:12 — Having your conversation honest among the Gentiles: that, whereas they speak against you as evildoers, they may by *your* good works, which they shall behold, glorify God in the day of visitation.

GOPHER WOOD

• Noah's ark made of.

Ge 6:14 — Make thee an ark of gopher wood; rooms shalt thou make in the ark, and shalt pitch it within and without with pitch.

GOSHEN

• A district in Egypt especially adapted to herds and flocks.

• Israelites dwelt in.

Ge 47:1–31
Ge 45:10 — And thou shalt dwell in the land of Goshen, and thou shalt be near unto me, thou, and thy children, and thy children's children, and thy flocks, and thy herds, and all that thou hast:
Ge 46:28 — And he sent Judah before him unto Joseph, to direct his face unto Goshen; and they came into the land of Goshen.

• Exempted from plagues.

Ex 8:22 — And I will sever in that day the land of Goshen, in which my people dwell, that no swarms *of flies* shall be there; to the end thou mayest know that I *am* the LORD in the midst of the earth.
Ex 9:26 — Only in the land of Goshen, where the children of Israel *were*, was there no hail.

• A town and district of Judah.

Jos 10:41 — And Joshua smote them from Kadesh-barnea even unto Gaza, and all the country of Goshen, even unto Gibeon.
Jos 11:16 — So Joshua took all that land, the hills, and all the south country, and all the land of Goshen, and the valley, and the plain, and the mountain of Israel, and the valley of the same;
Jos 15:51 — And Goshen, and Holon, and Giloh; eleven cities with their villages:

GOSPEL

• Called.

• Gospel of the Kingdom.

Mt 4:23 — And Jesus went about all Galilee, teaching in their synagogues, and preaching the gospel of the kingdom, and healing all manner of sickness and all manner of disease among the people.
Mt 24:14 — And this gospel of the kingdom shall be preached in all the world for a witness unto all nations; and then shall the end come.

• Gospel of God.

Ro 1:1 — Paul, a servant of Jesus Christ, called *to be* an apostle, separated unto the gospel of God,
Ro 15:16 — That I should be the minister of Jesus Christ to the Gentiles, ministering the gospel of God, that the offering up of the Gentiles might be acceptable, being sanctified by the Holy Ghost.
1Th 2:8 — So being affectionately desirous of you, we were willing to have imparted unto you, not the gospel of God only, but also our own souls, because ye were dear unto us.
1Ti 1:11 — According to the glorious gospel of the blessed God, which was committed to my trust.
1Pe 4:17 — For the time *is come* that judgment must begin at the house of God: and if *it* first *begin* at us, what shall the end *be* of them that obey not the gospel of God?

• Gospel of Jesus Christ.

Mk 1:1 — The beginning of the gospel of Jesus Christ, the Son of God;

• Gospel of Christ.

Ro 1:16 — For I am not ashamed of the gospel of Christ: for it is the power of God unto salvation to every one that believeth; to the Jew first, and also to the Greek.
1Co 9:12 — If others be partakers of *this* power over you, *are* not we rather? Nevertheless we have not used this power; but suffer all things, lest we should hinder the gospel of Christ.
1Co 9:18 — What is my reward then? *Verily* that, when I preach the gospel, I may make the gospel of Christ without charge, that I abuse not my power in the gospel.
Gal 1:7 — Which is not another; but there be some that trouble you, and would pervert the gospel of Christ.
Php 1:27 — Only let your conversation be as it becometh the gospel of Christ: that whether I come and see you, or else be absent, I may hear of your affairs, that ye stand fast in one spirit, with one mind striving together for the faith of the gospel;
1Th 3:2 — And sent Timotheus, our brother, and minister of God, and our fellowlabourer in the

gospel of Christ, to establish you, and to comfort you concerning your faith:

- **The Dispensation of the Grace of God.**
  Eph 3:2 — If ye have heard of the dispensation of the grace of God which is given me to youward:
- **The Grace of God.**
  Ac 20:24 — But none of these things move me, neither count I my life dear unto myself, so that I might finish my course with joy, and the ministry, which I have received of the Lord Jesus, to testify the gospel of the grace of God.
- **Gospel of Salvation.**
  Eph 1:13 — In whom ye also *trusted,* after that ye heard the word of truth, the gospel of your salvation: in whom also after that ye believed, ye were sealed with that holy Spirit of promise,
- **Gospel of Peace.**
  Eph 6:15 — And your feet shod with the preparation of the gospel of peace;
- **The Kingdom of God.**
  Lk 16:16 — The law and the prophets *were* until John: since that time the kingdom of God is preached, and every man presseth into it.
- **Glorious Gospel of Christ.**
  2Co 4:4 — In whom the god of this world hath blinded the minds of them which believe not, lest the light of the glorious gospel of Christ, who is the image of God, should shine unto them.
- **Preaching of Jesus Christ.**
  Ro 16:25 — Now to him that is of power to stablish you according to my gospel, and the preaching of Jesus Christ, according to the revelation of the mystery, which was kept secret since the world began,
- **Mystery of Christ.**
  Eph 3:4 — Whereby, when ye read, ye may understand my knowledge in the mystery of Christ)
- **Mystery of the Gospel.**
  Eph 6:19 — And for me, that utterance may be given unto me, that I may open my mouth boldly, to make known the mystery of the gospel,
- **Word of God.**
  1Th 2:13 — For this cause also thank we God without ceasing, because, when ye received the word of God which ye heard of us, ye received *it* not *as* the word of men, but as it is in truth, the word of God, which effectually worketh also in you that believe.
- **Word of Christ.**
  Col 3:16 — Let the word of Christ dwell in you richly in all wisdom; teaching and admonishing one another in psalms and hymns and spiritual songs, singing with grace in your hearts to the Lord.
- **Word of Salvation.**
  Ac 13:26 — Men *and* brethren, children of the stock of Abraham, and whosoever among you feareth God, to you is the word of this salvation sent.
- **Word of Reconciliation.**
  2Co 5:19 — To wit, that God was in Christ, reconciling the world unto himself, not imputing their trespasses unto them; and hath committed unto us the word of reconciliation.
- **Word of Truth.**
  2Co 6:7 — By the word of truth, by the power of God, by the armour of righteousness on the right hand and on the left,
  Eph 1:13 — In whom ye also *trusted,* after that ye heard the word of truth, the gospel of your salvation: in whom also after that ye believed, ye were sealed with that holy Spirit of promise,
- **Word of Faith.**
  Ro 10:8 — But what saith it? The word is nigh thee, *even* in thy mouth, and in thy heart: that is, the word of faith, which we preach;
- **Word of Life.**
  Php 2:16 — Holding forth the word of life; that I may rejoice in the day of Christ, that I have not run in vain, neither laboured in vain.
- **Ministration of the Spirit.**
  2Co 3:8 — How shall not the ministration of the spirit be rather glorious?
- **Doctrine According to Godliness.**
  1Ti 6:3 — If any man teach otherwise, and consent not to wholesome words, *even* the words of our Lord Jesus Christ, and to the doctrine which is according to godliness;
- **Form of Sound Words.**
  2Ti 1:13 — Hold fast the form of sound words, which thou hast heard of me, in faith and love which is in Christ Jesus.

• Likened to.

- **A mustard seed.**
  Mt 13:31–32; Mk 4:30–33
  Lk 13:18 — Then said he, Unto what is the kingdom of God like? and whereunto shall I resemble it?
- **Good seed.**
  Mt 13:24–30, 36–43
- **Leaven.**
  Mt 13:33 — Another parable spake he unto them; The kingdom of heaven is like unto leaven, which a woman took, and hid in three measures of meal, till the whole was leavened.
- **A pearl of great price.**
  Mt 13:45–46; Lk 13:20–21
- **Treasure hidden in a field.**
  Mt 13:44 — Again, the kingdom of heaven is like unto treasure hid in a field; the which when a man hath found, he hideth, and for joy thereof goeth and selleth all that he hath, and buyeth that field.
- **A householder.**
  Mt 20:1–16
- **A feast.**
  Lk 14:16–24

• Unclassified scripture relating to.

Ps 46:4–5; Mt 11:4–6; 28:18–20; Mk 1:14–15; Lk 1:67–79; 2:10–14; 4:18–19; 10:23–24; 17:20–21; Jn

1:16–17; 17:7–8; Ac 13:32–33; Ro 1:16–17; 10:15–18; 16:25–26; 1Co 1:24–25; 2:4–7; 9:16–18; 15:1–2; 2Co 3:6–11; 4:3–4; 10:4–5; Eph 1:13–14; 3:8–11; 6:19–20; Col 1:5–6, 26–29; 1Ti 1:10–11; Rev 14:6–7

Ps 89:15 — Blessed *is* the people that know the joyful sound: they shall walk, O LORD, in the light of thy countenance.

Isa 40:8 — The grass withereth, the flower fadeth: but the word of our God shall stand for ever.

Mt 4:23 — And Jesus went about all Galilee, teaching in their synagogues, and preaching the gospel of the kingdom, and healing all manner of sickness and all manner of disease among the people.

Mt 13:17 — For verily I say unto you, That many prophets and righteous *men* have desired to see *those things* which ye see, and have not seen *them;* and to hear *those things* which ye hear, and have not heard *them.*

Mt 24:14 — And this gospel of the kingdom shall be preached in all the world for a witness unto all nations; and then shall the end come.

Mk 13:10 — And the gospel must first be published among all nations.

Mk 16:15 — And he said unto them, Go ye into all the world, and preach the gospel to every creature.

Lk 2:34 — And Simeon blessed them, and said unto Mary his mother, Behold, this *child* is set for the fall and rising again of many in Israel; and for a sign which shall be spoken against;

Lk 7:22 — Then Jesus answering said unto them, Go your way, and tell John what things ye have seen and heard; how that the blind see, the lame walk, the lepers are cleansed, the deaf hear, the dead are raised, to the poor the gospel is preached.

Lk 16:16 — The law and the prophets *were* until John: since that time the kingdom of God is preached, and every man presseth into it.

Jn 4:14 — But whosoever drinketh of the water that I shall give him shall never thirst; but the water that I shall give him shall be in him a well of water springing up into everlasting life.

Jn 8:32 — And ye shall know the truth, and the truth shall make you free.

Jn 12:35 — Then Jesus said unto them, Yet a little while is the light with you. Walk while ye have the light, lest darkness come upon you: for he that walketh in darkness knoweth not whither he goeth.

Jn 12:50 — And I know that his commandment is life everlasting: whatsoever I speak therefore, even as the Father said unto me, so I speak.

Jn 13:20 — Verily, verily, I say unto you, He that receiveth whomsoever I send receiveth me; and he that receiveth me receiveth him that sent me.

Jn 18:36 — Jesus answered, My kingdom is not of this world: if my kingdom were of this world, then would my servants fight, that I should not be delivered to the Jews: but now is my kingdom not from hence.

Ac 2:11 — Cretes and Arabians, we do hear them speak in our tongues the wonderful works of God.

Ac 5:20 — Go, stand and speak in the temple to the people all the words of this life.

Ac 10:36 — The word which *God* sent unto the children of Israel, preaching peace by Jesus Christ: (he is Lord of all:)

Ac 12:24 — But the word of God grew and multiplied.

Ac 14:3 — Long time therefore abode they speaking boldly in the Lord, which gave testimony unto the word of his grace, and granted signs and wonders to be done by their hands.

Ac 16:17 — The same followed Paul and us, and cried, saying, These men are the servants of the most high God, which shew unto us the way of salvation.

Ac 19:20 — So mightily grew the word of God and prevailed.

Ac 20:24 — But none of these things move me, neither count I my life dear unto myself, so that I might finish my course with joy, and the ministry, which I have received of the Lord Jesus, to testify the gospel of the grace of God.

Ac 20:32 — And now, brethren, I commend you to God, and to the word of his grace, which is able to build you up, and to give you an inheritance among all them which are sanctified.

Ro 15:29 — And I am sure that, when I come unto you, I shall come in the fulness of the blessing of the gospel of Christ.

1Co 1:18 — For the preaching of the cross is to them that perish foolishness; but unto us which are saved it is the power of God.

1Co 1:21 — For after that in the wisdom of God the world by wisdom knew not God, it pleased God by the foolishness of preaching to save them that believe.

1Co 2:9 — But as it is written, Eye hath not seen, nor ear heard, neither have entered into the heart of man, the things which God hath prepared for them that love him.

1Co 4:20 — For the kingdom of God *is* not in word, but in power.

2Co 3:18 — But we all, with open face beholding as in a glass the glory of the Lord, are changed into the same image from glory to glory, *even* as by the Spirit of the Lord.

2Co 4:6 — For God, who commanded the light to shine out of darkness, hath shined in our hearts, to *give* the light of the knowledge of the glory of God in the face of Jesus Christ.

2Co 9:15 — Thanks *be* unto God for his unspeakable gift.

Gal 2:2 — And I went up by revelation, and communicated unto them that gospel which I preach among the Gentiles, but privately to them which were of reputation, lest by any means I should run, or had run, in vain.

Gal 3:8 — And the scripture, foreseeing that God would justify the heathen through faith, preached before the gospel unto Abraham, *saying,* In thee shall all nations be blessed.

Eph 6:15 — And your feet shod with the preparation of the gospel of peace;

Eph 6:17 — And take the helmet of salvation, and the sword of the Spirit, which is the word of God:

Col 1:23 — If ye continue in the faith grounded and settled, and *be* not moved away from the hope of the gospel, which ye have heard, *and* which was preached to every creature which is under heaven; whereof I Paul am made a minister;

1Th 1:5 — For our gospel came not unto you in word only, but also in power, and in the Holy Ghost, and in much assurance; as ye know what manner of men we were among you for your sake.

1Th 2:13 — For this cause also thank we God without ceasing, because, when ye received the word of God which ye heard of us, ye received *it* not *as* the word of men, but as it is in truth, the word of God, which effectually worketh also in you that believe.

2Th 1:10 — When he shall come to be glorified in his saints, and to be admired in all them that believe (because our testimony among you was believed) in that day.

2Th 2:10 — And with all deceivableness of unrighteousness in them that perish; because they received not the love of the truth, that they might be saved.

2Th 2:14 — Whereunto he called you by our gospel, to the obtaining of the glory of our Lord Jesus Christ.

1Ti 2:4 — Who will have all men to be saved, and to come unto the knowledge of the truth.

1Ti 3:16 — And without controversy great is the mystery of godliness: God was manifest in the flesh, justified in the Spirit, seen of angels, preached unto the Gentiles, believed on in the world, received up into glory.

1Ti 4:6 — If thou put the brethren in remembrance of these things, thou shalt be a good minister of Jesus Christ, nourished up in the words of faith and of good doctrine, whereunto thou hast attained.

2Ti 1:10 — But is now made manifest by the appearing of our Saviour Jesus Christ, who hath abolished death, and hath brought life and immortality to light through the gospel:

2Ti 2:3 — Thou therefore endure hardness, as a good soldier of Jesus Christ.

Heb 4:2 — For unto us was the gospel preached, as well as unto them: but the word preached did not profit them, not being mixed with faith in them that heard *it*.

Heb 5:13 — For every one that useth milk *is* unskilful in the word of righteousness: for he is a babe.

Heb 6:1 — Therefore leaving the principles of the doctrine of Christ, let us go on unto perfection; not laying again the foundation of repentance from dead works, and of faith toward God,

Heb 7:19 — For the law made nothing perfect, but the bringing in of a better hope *did;* by the which we draw nigh unto God.

Jas 1:18 — Of his own will begat he us with the word of truth, that we should be a kind of firstfruits of his creatures.

Jas 1:21 — Wherefore lay apart all filthiness and superfluity of naughtiness, and receive with meekness the engrafted word, which is able to save your souls.

Jas 1:25 — But whoso looketh into the perfect law of liberty, and continueth *therein,* he being not a forgetful hearer, but a doer of the work, this man shall be blessed in his deed.

1Pe 1:23 — Being born again, not of corruptible seed, but of incorruptible, by the word of God, which liveth and abideth for ever.

1Pe 1:25 — But the word of the Lord endureth for ever. And this is the word which by the gospel is preached unto you.

1Pe 4:6 — For for this cause was the gospel preached also to them that are dead, that they might be judged according to men in the flesh, but live according to God in the spirit.

1Pe 5:12 — By Silvanus, a faithful brother unto you, as I suppose, I have written briefly, exhorting, and testifying that this is the true grace of God wherein ye stand.

2Pe 1:16 — For we have not followed cunningly devised fables, when we made known unto you the power and coming of our Lord Jesus Christ, but were eyewitnesses of his majesty.

2Pe 1:19 — We have also a more sure word of prophecy; whereunto ye do well that ye take heed, as unto a light that shineth in a dark place, until the day dawn, and the day star arise in your hearts:

2Pe 2:2 — And many shall follow their pernicious ways; by reason of whom the way of truth shall be evil spoken of.

2Pe 2:21 — For it had been better for them not to have known the way of righteousness, than, after they have known *it,* to turn from the holy commandment delivered unto them.

1Jn 2:8 — Again, a new commandment I write unto you, which thing is true in him and in you: because the darkness is past, and the true light now shineth.

Jude 1:3 — Beloved, when I gave all diligence to write unto you of the common salvation, it was needful for me to write unto you, and exhort *you* that ye should earnestly contend for the faith which was once delivered unto the saints.

• Called the New Covenant.

Jer 31:31–34; Heb 8:6–13; 9:8–15; 12:22–24

Heb 7:22 — By so much was Jesus made a surety of a better testament.

Heb 10:9 — Then said he, Lo, I come to do thy will, O God. He taketh away the first, that he may establish the second.

• Prophecies relating to.

Isa 2:3–5; 4:2–6; 9:6–7; 42:6–7; 43:18–21; 51:4–6; 55:1–5; 60:1–61:3; Eze 34:23–31; 47:1–12; Joel 2:28–32; Mic 4:1–7

Ps 46:4 — *There is* a river, the streams whereof shall make glad the city of God, the holy *place* of the tabernacles of the most High.

Isa 9:2 — The people that walked in darkness have seen a great light: they that dwell in the land of the shadow of death, upon them hath the light shined.

Isa 25:7 — And he will destroy in this mountain the face of the covering cast over all people, and the vail that is spread over all nations.

Isa 29:18 — And in that day shall the deaf hear the words of the book, and the eyes of the blind shall see out of obscurity, and out of darkness.

Isa 29:24 — They also that erred in spirit shall come to understanding, and they that murmured shall learn doctrine.

Isa 32:3 — And the eyes of them that see shall not be dim, and the ears of them that hear shall hearken.

Isa 35:5 — Then the eyes of the blind shall be opened, and the ears of the deaf shall be unstopped.

Isa 40:9 — O Zion, that bringest good tidings, get thee up into the high mountain; O Jerusalem, that bringest good tidings, lift up thy voice with strength; lift *it* up, be not afraid; say unto the cities of Judah, Behold your God!

Isa 41:27 — The first *shall say* to Zion, Behold, behold them: and I will give to Jerusalem one that bringeth good tidings.

Isa 46:13 — I bring near my righteousness; it shall not be far off, and my salvation shall not tarry: and I will place salvation in Zion for Israel my glory.

Isa 49:13 — Sing, O heavens; and be joyful, O earth; and break forth into singing, O mountains: for the LORD hath comforted his people, and will have mercy upon his afflicted.

Isa 52:7 — How beautiful upon the mountains are the feet of him that bringeth good tidings, that publisheth peace; that bringeth good tidings of good, that publisheth salvation; that saith unto Zion, Thy God reigneth!

Mt 24:14 — And this gospel of the kingdom shall be preached in all the world for a witness unto all nations; and then shall the end come.

See: Church; prophecies concerning prosperity of

See: Jesus, Kingdom of

See: Jesus, Mission of

See: Kingdom of Heaven

GOSSIP

• Forbidden.

Le 19:16 — Thou shalt not go up and down *as* a talebearer among thy people: neither shalt thou stand against the blood of thy neighbour: I *am* the LORD.

Ps 50:20 — Thou sittest *and* speakest against thy brother; thou slanderest thine own mother's son.

Pr 11:13 — A talebearer revealeth secrets: but he that is of a faithful spirit concealeth the matter.

Pr 20:19 — He that goeth about *as* a talebearer revealeth secrets: therefore meddle not with him that flattereth with his lips.

Eze 22:9 — In thee are men that carry tales to shed blood: and in thee they eat upon the mountains: in the midst of thee they commit lewdness.

See: Slander

See: Speaking; evil

GOURD

• Jonah's, resembled the squash; used in Assyria to cover booths.

Jnh 4:6–10

• The wild gourd is supposed to be a plant in appearance like the cucumber.

2Ki 4:39 — And one went out into the field to gather herbs, and found a wild vine, and gathered thereof wild gourds his lap full, and came and shred *them* into the pot of pottage: for they knew *them* not.

GOUT

2Ch 16:12 — And Asa in the thirty and ninth year of his reign was diseased in his feet, until his disease *was* exceeding *great:* yet in his disease he sought not to the LORD, but to the physicians.

GOVERNMENT

• Paternal functions of.

Ge 41:25–57

• Civil service school provided by.

Da 1:3–20

• Maintains a system of public instruction.

2Ch 17:7–9

• Executive departments in.

See: Cabinet

See: King

See: Rulers

• Judicial department in.

See: Court

See: Judge

See: Justice

See: Levites

See: Priest, High

• Mosaic.

• Administrative and judicial system.

Ex 18:13–26; Nu 11:16–17, 24–25; Dt 1:9–17

• Popular, by a National Assembly, or its representatives.

• Accepted, and agreed to, the law given by Moses.

Ex 19:7–8; Dt 29:10–15

Ex 24:3 — And Moses came and told the people all the words of the LORD, and all the judgments: and all the people answered with one voice, and said, All the words which the LORD hath said will we do.

Ex 24:7 — And he took the book of the covenant, and read in the audience of the people: and they said, All that the LORD hath said will we do, and be obedient.

• Refused to make conquest of Canaan.

Nu 14:1–10

• Chose, or ratified, the chief ruler.

Nu 27:18–23; 1Sa 8:4–22; 11:14–15; 2Sa 3:17–21; 5:1–3

1Sa 10:24 — And Samuel said to all the people, See ye him whom the LORD hath chosen, that *there is* none like him among all the people? And all the people shouted, and said, God save the king.

1Ch 29:22 — And did eat and drink before the LORD on that day with great gladness. And they made Solomon the son of David king the second time, and anointed *him* unto the LORD *to be* the chief governor, and Zadok *to be* priest.

2Ch 23:3 — And all the congregation made a covenant with the king in the house of God. And he said unto them, Behold, the king's son shall reign, as the LORD hath said of the sons of David.

• **Possessed veto power over the king's purposes.**

1Sa 14:44–45

• **The court in certain capital cases.**

Nu 35:24–25

Nu 35:12 — And they shall be unto you cities for refuge from the avenger; that the manslayer die not, until he stand before the congregation in judgment.

• **The delegated, senatorial council.**

• **Closely associated with Moses and subsequent leaders.**

Ex 4:29–31; 17:5–6; 19:7–8; Nu 11:16–18; Dt 1:13–15; 29:10–15; Jos 8:32–33; 23:2–3; 24:24–25; Jgs 21:16–25; Ac 5:21–41

Ex 3:16 — Go, and gather the elders of Israel together, and say unto them, The LORD God of your fathers, the God of Abraham, of Isaac, and of Jacob, appeared unto me, saying, I have surely visited you, and *seen* that which is done to you in Egypt:

Ex 12:21 — Then Moses called for all the elders of Israel, and said unto them, Draw out and take you a lamb according to your families, and kill the passover.

Ex 18:12 — And Jethro, Moses' father in law, took a burnt offering and sacrifices for God: and Aaron came, and all the elders of Israel, to eat bread with Moses' father in law before God.

Ex 24:1 — And he said unto Moses, Come up unto the LORD, thou, and Aaron, Nadab, and Abihu, and seventy of the elders of Israel; and worship ye afar off.

Ex 24:14 — And he said unto the elders, Tarry ye here for us, until we come again unto you: and, behold, Aaron and Hur *are* with you: if any man have any matters to do, let him come unto them.

Le 4:15 — And the elders of the congregation shall lay their hands upon the head of the bullock before the LORD: and the bullock shall be killed before the LORD.

Le 9:1 — And it came to pass on the eighth day, *that* Moses called Aaron and his sons, and the elders of Israel;

Nu 11:30 — And Moses gat him into the camp, he and the elders of Israel.

Nu 16:25 — And Moses rose up and went unto Dathan and Abiram; and the elders of Israel followed him.

Dt 5:23 — And it came to pass, when ye heard the voice out of the midst of the darkness, (for the mountain did burn with fire,) that ye came near unto me, *even* all the heads of your tribes, and your elders;

Dt 27:1 — And Moses with the elders of Israel commanded the people, saying, Keep all the commandments which I command you this day.

Dt 31:9 — And Moses wrote this law, and delivered it unto the priests the sons of Levi, which bare the ark of the covenant of the LORD, and unto all the elders of Israel.

Dt 31:28 — Gather unto me all the elders of your tribes, and your officers, that I may speak these words in their ears, and call heaven and earth to record against them.

Jos 7:6 — And Joshua rent his clothes, and fell to the earth upon his face before the ark of the LORD until the eventide, he and the elders of Israel, and put dust upon their heads.

Jos 8:10 — And Joshua rose up early in the morning, and numbered the people, and went up, he and the elders of Israel, before the people to Ai.

Jos 23:6 — Be ye therefore very courageous to keep and to do all that is written in the book of the law of Moses, that ye turn not aside therefrom *to* the right hand or *to* the left;

Jos 24:1 — And Joshua gathered all the tribes of Israel to Shechem, and called for the elders of Israel, and for their heads, and for their judges, and for their officers; and they presented themselves before God.

Ac 5:17 — Then the high priest rose up, and all they that were with him, (which is the sect of the Sadducees,) and were filled with indignation,

• **Miscellany of facts relating to the Senate.**

• **Demands a king.**

1Sa 8:4–10, 19–22

• **Saul pleads to be honored before.**

1Sa 15:30 — Then he said, I have sinned: *yet* honour me now, I pray thee, before the elders of my people, and before Israel, and turn again with me, that I may worship the LORD thy God.

• **Chooses David as king.**

2Sa 3:17–21

2Sa 5:3 — So all the elders of Israel came to the king to Hebron; and king David made a league with them in Hebron before the LORD: and they anointed David king over Israel.

1Ch 11:3 — Therefore came all the elders of Israel to the king to Hebron; and David made a covenant with them in Hebron before the LORD; and they anointed David king over

Israel, according to the word of the LORD by Samuel.

• Closely associated with David.

2Sa 12:17 — And the elders of his house arose, *and went* to him, to raise him up from the earth: but he would not, neither did he eat bread with them.

1Ch 15:25 — So David, and the elders of Israel, and the captains over thousands, went to bring up the ark of the covenant of the LORD out of the house of Obed-edom with joy.

1Ch 21:16 — And David lifted up his eyes, and saw the angel of the LORD stand between the earth and the heaven, having a drawn sword in his hand stretched out over Jerusalem. Then David and the elders *of Israel, who were* clothed in sackcloth, fell upon their faces.

• Joins Absalom in his usurpation.

2Sa 17:4 — And the saying pleased Absalom well, and all the elders of Israel.

• David upbraids.

2Sa 19:11 — And king David sent to Zadok and to Abiathar the priests, saying, Speak unto the elders of Judah, saying, Why are ye the last to bring the king back to his house? seeing the speech of all Israel is come to the king, *even* to his house.

• Assists Solomon at the dedication of the temple.

1Ki 8:1–3; 2Ch 5:2–4

• Counsels king Rehoboam.

1Ki 12:6–8

1Ki 12:13 — And the king answered the people roughly, and forsook the old men's counsel that they gave him;

• Counsels king Ahab.

1Ki 20:7–8

• Josiah assembles to hear the law of the Lord.

2Ki 23:1 — And the king sent, and they gathered unto him all the elders of Judah and of Jerusalem.

2Ch 34:29 — Then the king sent and gathered together all the elders of Judah and Jerusalem.

2Ch 34:31 — And the king stood in his place, and made a covenant before the LORD, to walk after the LORD, and to keep his commandments, and his testimonies, and his statutes, with all his heart, and with all his soul, to perform the words of the covenant which are written in this book.

• Legislates with Ezra in reforming certain marriages with the heathen.

Ezr 10:8–14

Ezr 9:1 — Now when these things were done, the princes came to me, saying, The people of Israel, and the priests, and the Levites, have not separated themselves from the people of the lands, *doing* according to their abominations, *even* of the Canaanites, the Hittites, the Perizzites, the Jebusites, the Ammonites, the Moabites, the Egyptians, and the Amorites.

• Legislates in later times.

Mt 15:7–9; Mk 7:1–13

Mt 15:2 — Why do thy disciples transgress the tradition of the elders? for they wash not their hands when they eat bread.

• Sits as a court.

Jer 26:10–24

• Constitutes, with priests and scribes, a court for the trial of both civil and ecclesiastical causes.

Mt 26:3–5, 57–68; 27:1–2; Mk 14:43–65; Lk 22:52–71; Ac 4:1–21; 6:9–7:59

Mt 21:23 — And when he was come into the temple, the chief priests and the elders of the people came unto him as he was teaching, and said, By what authority doest thou these things? and who gave thee this authority?

Mk 8:31 — And he began to teach them, that the Son of man must suffer many things, and be rejected of the elders, and *of* the chief priests, and scribes, and be killed, and after three days rise again.

Mk 15:1 — And straightway in the morning the chief priests held a consultation with the elders and scribes and the whole council, and bound Jesus, and carried *him* away, and delivered *him* to Pilate.

• Unfaithful to the city.

La 1:19 — I called for my lovers, *but* they deceived me: my priests and mine elders gave up the ghost in the city, while they sought their meat to relieve their souls.

• Seeks counsel from prophets.

Eze 8:1 — And it came to pass in the sixth year, in the sixth *month,* in the fifth *day* of the month, *as* I sat in mine house, and the elders of Judah sat before me, that the hand of the Lord GOD fell there upon me.

Eze 14:1 — Then came certain of the elders of Israel unto me, and sat before me.

Eze 20:1 — And it came to pass in the seventh year, in the fifth *month,* the tenth *day* of the month, *that* certain of the elders of Israel came to enquire of the LORD, and sat before me.

Eze 20:3 — Son of man, speak unto the elders of Israel, and say unto them, Thus saith the Lord GOD; Are ye come to enquire of me? *As* I live, saith the Lord GOD, I will not be enquired of by you.

Joel 1:14 — Sanctify ye a fast, call a solemn assembly, gather the elders *and* all the inhabitants of the land *into* the house of the LORD your God, and cry unto the LORD,

Joel 2:16 — Gather the people, sanctify the congregation, assemble the elders, gather the children, and those that suck the breasts: let the bridegroom go forth of his chamber, and the bride out of her closet.

• Corrupt.

1Ki 21:8–14; Eze 8:11–12; Mt 26:14–15; 27:3–4

- **A similar senate existed among.**
  - **The Egyptians.**

Ge 41:37–38

Ge 50:7 — And Joseph went up to bury his father: and with him went up all the servants of Pharaoh, the elders of his house, and all the elders of the land of Egypt,

Ex 10:1 — And the LORD said unto Moses, Go in unto Pharaoh: for I have hardened his heart, and the heart of his servants, that I might shew these my signs before him:

Ex 10:7 — And Pharaoh's servants said unto him, How long shall this man be a snare unto us? let the men go, that they may serve the LORD their God: knowest thou not yet that Egypt is destroyed?

Ex 12:30 — And Pharaoh rose up in the night, he, and all his servants, and all the Egyptians; and there was a great cry in Egypt; for *there was* not a house where *there was* not one dead.

Ex 14:5 — And it was told the king of Egypt that the people fled: and the heart of Pharaoh and of his servants was turned against the people, and they said, Why have we done this, that we have let Israel go from serving us?

  - **The Midianites and Moabites.**

Nu 22:4 — And Moab said unto the elders of Midian, Now shall this company lick up all *that are* round about us, as the ox licketh up the grass of the field. And Balak the son of Zippor *was* king of the Moabites at that time.

Nu 22:7 — And the elders of Moab and the elders of Midian departed with the rewards of divination in their hand; and they came unto Balaam, and spake unto him the words of Balak.

  - **The Gibeonites.**

Jos 9:11 — Wherefore our elders and all the inhabitants of our country spake to us, saying, Take victuals with you for the journey, and go to meet them, and say unto them, We *are* your servants: therefore now make ye a league with us.

- **Executive officers of tribes and cities, called princes or nobles, members of the National Assembly.**

Nu 1:4–16; 7:2–3, 10–11; 31:13–14; 34:18–29; Jos 9:15–21; 22:13–32; 1Ki 21:11–13; Ne 3:18–19

Nu 1:44 — These *are* those that were numbered, which Moses and Aaron numbered, and the princes of Israel, *being* twelve men: each one was for the house of his fathers.

Nu 7:18 — On the second day Nethaneel the son of Zuar, prince of Issachar, did offer:

Nu 7:24 — On the third day Eliab the son of Helon, prince of the children of Zebulun, *did offer:*

Nu 7:54 — On the eighth day *offered* Gamaliel the son of Pedahzur, prince of the children of Manasseh:

Nu 7:84 — This *was* the dedication of the altar, in the day when it was anointed, by the princes of Israel: twelve chargers of silver, twelve silver bowls, twelve spoons of gold:

Nu 10:4 — And if they blow *but* with one *trumpet,* then the princes, *which are* heads of the thousands of Israel, shall gather themselves unto thee.

Nu 16:2 — And they rose up before Moses, with certain of the children of Israel, two hundred and fifty princes of the assembly, famous in the congregation, men of renown:

Nu 17:2 — Speak unto the children of Israel, and take of every one of them a rod according to the house of *their* fathers, of all their princes according to the house of their fathers twelve rods: write thou every man's name upon his rod.

Nu 17:6 — And Moses spake unto the children of Israel, and every one of their princes gave him a rod apiece, for each prince one, according to their fathers' houses, *even* twelve rods: and the rod of Aaron *was* among their rods.

Nu 27:2 — And they stood before Moses, and before Eleazar the priest, and before the princes and all the congregation, *by* the door of the tabernacle of the congregation, saying,

Nu 32:2 — The children of Gad and the children of Reuben came and spake unto Moses, and to Eleazar the priest, and unto the princes of the congregation, saying,

Nu 36:1 — And the chief fathers of the families of the children of Gilead, the son of Machir, the son of Manasseh, of the families of the sons of Joseph, came near, and spake before Moses, and before the princes, the chief fathers of the children of Israel:

Jos 17:4 — And they came near before Eleazar the priest, and before Joshua the son of Nun, and before the princes, saying, The LORD commanded Moses to give us an inheritance among our brethren. Therefore according to the commandment of the LORD he gave them an inheritance among the brethren of their father.

Ne 3:9 — And next unto them repaired Rephaiah the son of Hur, the ruler of the half part of Jerusalem.

Ne 3:12 — And next unto him repaired Shallum the son of Halohesh, the ruler of the half part of Jerusalem, he and his daughters.

Ne 3:16 — After him repaired Nehemiah the son of Azbuk, the ruler of the half part of Beth-zur, unto *the place* over against the sepulchres of David, and to the pool that was made, and unto the house of the mighty.

- **The Mosaic judicial system.**

See: Court

See: Judge

See: Levites

See: Priest, Mosaic

See: Rulers

See: Sanhedrin

See: Synagogue

- **Forms and facts of government after the death of Moses and the princes who survived Moses.**
  - **See: Israel, Under Judges**
  - **See: Israel, Under Kings**
- **Constitutional.**
  - **See: Constitution**
- **Ecclesiastical.**
  - **See: Church; government of, Mosaic and Christian**
  - **See: Priest, High**
- **Imperial.**

Da 6:1–3

Ge 14:1 — And it came to pass in the days of Amraphel king of Shinar, Arioch king of Ellasar, Chedorlaomer king of Elam, and Tidal king of nations;

Jos 11:10 — And Joshua at that time turned back, and took Hazor, and smote the king thereof with the sword: for Hazor beforetime was the head of all those kingdoms.

Est 1:1 — Now it came to pass in the days of Ahasuerus, (this *is* Ahasuerus which reigned, from India even unto Ethiopia, *over* an hundred and seven and twenty provinces:)

Da 4:1 — Nebuchadnezzar the king, unto all people, nations, and languages, that dwell in all the earth; Peace be multiplied unto you.

Lk 2:1 — And it came to pass in those days, that there went out a decree from Caesar Augustus, that all the world should be taxed.

- **Monarchical.**
  - **Tyranny in.**
    - **Instances of.**
      - **By Saul.**

1Sa 22:12–19

1Sa 22:6 — When Saul heard that David was discovered, and the men that *were* with him, (now Saul abode in Gibeah under a tree in Ramah, having his spear in his hand, and all his servants *were* standing about him;)

- **By David.**

2Sa 1:13–16; 4:9–12; 11:14–17

- **By Solomon.**

1Ki 2:23–25, 28–34, 36–46; 12:1–16; 21:7–16; 2Ki 10:1–36

- **By Ahasuerus.**

Est 2:1–3:15

- **By Nebuchadnezzar.**

Da 2:5–13

Da 1:10 — And the prince of the eunuchs said unto Daniel, I fear my lord the king, who hath appointed your meat and your drink: for why should he see your faces worse liking than the children which *are* of your sort? then shall ye make *me* endanger my head to the king.

Da 5:19 — And for the majesty that he gave him, all people, nations, and languages, trembled and feared before him: whom he would he slew; and whom he would he kept alive; and whom he would he set up; and whom he would he put down.

- **By Herod.**

Mk 6:27–28

- **See: Assyria**
- **See: Babylon**
- **See: Chaldea**
- **See: Israel, Under Kings**
- **See: Syria**
- **Limited.**
  - **See: Constitution**
- **Municipal.**
  - **Devolving on a local senate and executive officers.**

Dt 21:2–8, 18–21; 22:13–21; 25:7–9; Jgs 8:14–16; 11:5–11; Ru 4:2–11; 1Ki 21:8–14; 2Ki 10:1–7; Ne 3:18–19

Dt 19:12 — Then the elders of his city shall send and fetch him thence, and deliver him into the hand of the avenger of blood, that he may die.

Jos 20:4 — And when he that doth flee unto one of those cities shall stand at the entering of the gate of the city, and shall declare his cause in the ears of the elders of that city, they shall take him into the city unto them, and give him a place, that he may dwell among them.

1Sa 11:3 — And the elders of Jabesh said unto him, Give us seven days' respite, that we may send messengers unto all the coasts of Israel: and then, if *there be* no man to save us, we will come out to thee.

1Sa 16:4 — And Samuel did that which the LORD spake, and came to Bethlehem. And the elders of the town trembled at his coming, and said, Comest thou peaceably?

1Sa 30:26 — And when David came to Ziklag, he sent of the spoil unto the elders of Judah, *even* to his friends, saying, Behold a present for you of the spoil of the enemies of the LORD;

Ezr 10:8 — And that whosoever would not come within three days, according to the counsel of the princes and the elders, all his substance should be forfeited, and himself separated from the congregation of those that had been carried away.

Ezr 10:14 — Let now our rulers of all the congregation stand, and let all them which have taken strange wives in our cities come at appointed times, and with them the elders of every city, and the judges thereof, until the fierce wrath of our God for this matter be turned from us.

Ne 3:9 — And next unto them repaired Rephaiah the son of Hur, the ruler of the half part of Jerusalem.

Ne 3:12 — And next unto him repaired Shallum the son of Halohesh, the ruler of the half part of Jerusalem, he and his daughters.

Ne 3:16 — After him repaired Nehemiah the son of Azbuk, the ruler of the half part of Beth-zur, unto *the place* over against the sepulchres of David, and to the pool that was made, and unto the house of the mighty.

La 5:14 — The elders have ceased from the gate, the young men from their musick.

• **Patriarchal.**

Ge 27:29 — Let people serve thee, and nations bow down to thee: be lord over thy brethren, and let thy mother's sons bow down to thee: cursed *be* every one that curseth thee, and blessed *be* he that blesseth thee.

Ge 27:37 — And Isaac answered and said unto Esau, Behold, I have made him thy lord, and all his brethren have I given to him for servants; and with corn and wine have I sustained him: and what shall I do now unto thee, my son?

• **Provincial.**

Ezr 4:8–9; Da 6:1–3

Ezr 5:3 — At the same time came to them Tatnai, governor on this side the river, and Shethar-boznai, and their companions, and said thus unto them, Who hath commanded you to build this house, and to make up this wall?

Ezr 5:6 — The copy of the letter that Tatnai, governor on this side the river, and Shethar-boznai, and his companions the Apharsachites, which *were* on this side the river, sent unto Darius the king:

Ezr 6:6 — Now *therefore,* Tatnai, governor beyond the river, Shethar-boznai, and your companions the Apharsachites, which *are* beyond the river, be ye far from thence:

Ezr 8:36 — And they delivered the king's commissions unto the king's lieutenants, and to the governors on this side the river: and they furthered the people, and the house of God.

Ne 2:7 — Moreover I said unto the king, If it please the king, let letters be given me to the governors beyond the river, that they may convey me over till I come into Judah;

Ne 2:9 — Then I came to the governors beyond the river, and gave them the king's letters. Now the king had sent captains of the army and horsemen with me.

Ne 5:14 — Moreover from the time that I was appointed to be their governor in the land of Judah, from the twentieth year even unto the two and thirtieth year of Artaxerxes the king, *that is,* twelve years, I and my brethren have not eaten the bread of the governor.

Mt 27:2 — And when they had bound him, they led *him* away, and delivered him to Pontius Pilate the governor.

Mt 28:14 — And if this come to the governor's ears, we will persuade him, and secure you.

Lk 3:1 — Now in the fifteenth year of the reign of Tiberius Caesar, Pontius Pilate being governor of Judaea, and Herod being tetrarch of Galilee, and his brother Philip tetrarch of Ituraea and of the region of Trachonitis, and Lysanias the tetrarch of Abilene,

Ac 24:1 — And after five days Ananias the high priest descended with the elders, and *with* a certain orator *named* Tertullus, who informed the governor against Paul.

➜See: Herod

➜See: Pilate, Pontius

• **Representative.**

Dt 1:13–15

Jos 9:11 — Wherefore our elders and all the inhabitants of our country spake to us, saying, Take victuals with you for the journey, and go to meet them, and say unto them, We *are* your servants: therefore now make ye a league with us.

➜See: Elder

➜See: Government; Mosaic; the delegated, senatorial council

• **Theocratic.**

Ex 19:3–8; Dt 26:16–19; 29:1–13; 1Sa 8:6–7

➜See: Church and State

➜See: Elder

➜See: Government; God in

➜See: Judge

➜See: Rulers

• **Corruption in.**

1Ki 21:5–13; Mic 3:1–4, 9–11

Pr 25:5 — Take away the wicked *from* before the king, and his throne shall be established in righteousness.

➜See: Church; corruption in

➜See: Court; corrupt

• **Instances of.**

• **Pilate, in delivering Jesus to death to please the clamoring multitude.**

Jn 19:12–16

Mt 27:24 — When Pilate saw that he could prevail nothing, but *that* rather a tumult was made, he took water, and washed *his* hands before the multitude, saying, I am innocent of the blood of this just person: see ye *to it.*

• **Felix, who expected money from Paul.**

Ac 24:26 — He hoped also that money should have been given him of Paul, that he might loose him: wherefore he sent for him the oftener, and communed with him.

➜See: Rulers, Wicked; instances of

• **Duty of citizens to.**

Mt 22:17–21; Ro 13:1–7; 1Pe 2:13–17

Lk 20:25 — And he said unto them, Render therefore unto Caesar the things which be Caesar's, and unto God the things which be God's.

Tit 3:1 — Put them in mind to be subject to principalities and powers, to obey magistrates, to be ready to every good work,

➜See: Citizens

• **God in.**

• **In appointment of Saul as king.**

1Sa 9:15–17

1Sa 10:1 — Then Samuel took a vial of oil, and poured *it* upon his head, and kissed him, and said, *Is it* not because the LORD hath anointed thee *to be* captain over his inheritance?

- **In Saul's rejection.**

1Sa 15:26–28

Ac 13:22 — And when he had removed him, he raised up unto them David to be their king; to whom also he gave testimony, and said, I have found David the *son* of Jesse, a man after mine own heart, which shall fulfil all my will.

- **In appointment of David.**

2Sa 7:13–16; Ps 89:19–37

1Sa 16:1 — And the LORD said unto Samuel, How long wilt thou mourn for Saul, seeing I have rejected him from reigning over Israel? fill thine horn with oil, and go, I will send thee to Jesse the Bethlehemite: for I have provided me a king among his sons.

1Sa 16:7 — But the LORD said unto Samuel, Look not on his countenance, or on the height of his stature; because I have refused him: for *the LORD seeth* not as man seeth; for man looketh on the outward appearance, but the LORD looketh on the heart.

1Sa 16:13 — Then Samuel took the horn of oil, and anointed him in the midst of his brethren: and the Spirit of the LORD came upon David from that day forward. So Samuel rose up, and went to Ramah.

Ac 13:22 — And when he had removed him, he raised up unto them David to be their king; to whom also he gave testimony, and said, I have found David the *son* of Jesse, a man after mine own heart, which shall fulfil all my will.

- **In counseling Solomon.**

1Ki 9:2–9

- **In magnifying him.**

1Ch 29:25 — And the LORD magnified Solomon exceedingly in the sight of all Israel, and bestowed upon him *such* royal majesty as had not been on any king before him in Israel.

- **In denouncing Solomon's wickedness.**

1Ki 11:9–13

- **In raising adversaries against Solomon.**

1Ki 11:14 — And the LORD stirred up an adversary unto Solomon, Hadad the Edomite: he *was* of the king's seed in Edom.

1Ki 11:23 — And God stirred him up *another* adversary, Rezon the son of Eliadah, which fled from his lord Hadadezer king of Zobah:

- **In rending the Jewish nation in twain.**

1Ki 12:1–24

1Ki 11:13 — Howbeit I will not rend away all the kingdom; *but* will give one tribe to thy son for David my servant's sake, and for Jerusalem's sake which I have chosen.

2Ch 10:15 — So the king hearkened not unto the people: for the cause was of God, that the LORD might perform his word, which he spake by the hand of Ahijah the Shilonite to Jeroboam the son of Nebat.

2Ch 11:4 — Thus saith the LORD, Ye shall not go up, nor fight against your brethren: return every man to his house: for this thing is done of me. And they obeyed the words of the LORD, and returned from going against Jeroboam.

2Ch 22:7 — And the destruction of Ahaziah was of God by coming to Joram: for when he was come, he went out with Jehoram against Jehu the son of Nimshi, whom the LORD had anointed to cut off the house of Ahab.

- **In blotting out the house of Jeroboam.**

1Ki 14:7–16; 15:27–30

- **In appointment of kings.**

1Ki 16:1–4; 1Ch 28:4–5; Pr 8:15–16; Da 2:20–21; 5:20–24

1Ki 14:14 — Moreover the LORD shall raise him up a king over Israel, who shall cut off the house of Jeroboam that day: but what? even now.

1Ch 29:25 — And the LORD magnified Solomon exceedingly in the sight of all Israel, and bestowed upon him *such* royal majesty as had not been on any king before him in Israel.

Ps 22:28 — For the kingdom *is* the LORD'S: and he *is* the governor among the nations.

Da 2:37 — Thou, O king, *art* a king of kings: for the God of heaven hath given thee a kingdom, power, and strength, and glory.

- **In destruction of nations.**

Am 9:8 — Behold, the eyes of the Lord GOD *are* upon the sinful kingdom, and I will destroy it from off the face of the earth; saving that I will not utterly destroy the house of Jacob, saith the LORD.

See: Government; theocratic

See: God, Sovereign

- **Unclassified scripture relating to.**

Pr 8:15–16; Isa 9:6–7; Jer 1:9–10; 18:6–10; 25:12–33; Eze 21:25–27; 29:19–20; Da 2:20–21; 5:18–28; Hag 2:21–22; Jn 19:10–11

Ps 22:28 — For the kingdom *is* the LORD'S: and he *is* the governor among the nations.

Da 2:37 — Thou, O king, *art* a king of kings: for the God of heaven hath given thee a kingdom, power, and strength, and glory.

Da 4:17 — This matter *is* by the decree of the watchers, and the demand by the word of the holy ones: to the intent that the living may know that the most High ruleth in the kingdom of men, and giveth it to whomsoever he will, and setteth up over it the basest of men.

Da 10:13 — But the prince of the kingdom of Persia withstood me one and twenty days: but, lo, Michael, one of the chief princes, came to help me; and I remained there with the kings of Persia.

Hos 8:4 — They have set up kings, but not by me: they have made princes, and I knew *it* not: of their silver and their gold have they made them idols, that they may be cut off.

Am 9:8 — Behold, the eyes of the Lord GOD *are* upon the sinful kingdom, and I will destroy it from off the face of the earth; saving that I will not utterly destroy the house of Jacob, saith the LORD.

See: God, Sovereign

See: Jesus, Kingdom of

GOZAN

• A district of Mesopotamia.

• Israelites taken in captivity to, by the king of Assyria, after the conquest of Samaria.

2Ki 17:6 — In the ninth year of Hoshea the king of Assyria took Samaria, and carried Israel away into Assyria, and placed them in Halah and in Habor *by* the river of Gozan, and in the cities of the Medes.

2Ki 18:11 — And the king of Assyria did carry away Israel unto Assyria, and put them in Halah and in Habor *by* the river of Gozan, and in the cities of the Medes:

2Ki 19:12 — Have the gods of the nations delivered them which my fathers have destroyed; *as* Gozan, and Haran, and Rezeph, and the children of Eden which *were* in Thelasar?

1Ch 5:26 — And the God of Israel stirred up the spirit of Pul king of Assyria, and the spirit of Tilgath-pilneser king of Assyria, and he carried them away, even the Reubenites, and the Gadites, and the half tribe of Manasseh, and brought them unto Halah, and Habor, and Hara, and to the river Gozan, unto this day.

GRACE OF GOD

Dt 7:6–9; 9:4–6; Job 22:2–3; Ps 94:17–19; Da 10:18–19; Jn 6:44–45; 17:11–12; Ac 4:29–30; Ro 3:22–24; 4:4–5; 5:6–8, 15–21; 9:10–16; 11:5–6; 1Co 1:4–8; Gal 1:15–16; Eph 1:5–9, 11–12; 2:8–9; Jude 1:24–25

Ge 15:6 — And he believed in the LORD; and he counted it to him for righteousness.

Ge 20:6 — And God said unto him in a dream, Yea, I know that thou didst this in the integrity of thy heart; for I also withheld thee from sinning against me: therefore suffered I thee not to touch her.

Job 10:12 — Thou hast granted me life and favour, and thy visitation hath preserved my spirit.

Ps 138:3 — In the day when I cried thou answeredst me, *and* strengthenedst me *with* strength in my soul.

Ps 143:11 — Quicken me, O LORD, for thy name's sake: for thy righteousness' sake bring my soul out of trouble.

Da 9:18 — O my God, incline thine ear, and hear; open thine eyes, and behold our desolations, and the city which is called by thy name: for we do not present our supplications before thee for our righteousnesses, but for thy great mercies.

Jn 17:15 — I pray not that thou shouldest take them out of the world, but that thou shouldest keep them from the evil.

Ac 26:22 — Having therefore obtained help of God, I continue unto this day, witnessing both to small and great, saying none other things than those which the prophets and Moses did say should come:

Ro 4:16 — Therefore *it is* of faith, that *it might be* by grace; to the end the promise might be sure to all the seed; not to that only which is of the law, but to that also which is of the faith of Abraham; who is the father of us all,

Ro 5:2 — By whom also we have access by faith into this grace wherein we stand, and rejoice in hope of the glory of God.

1Co 10:13 — There hath no temptation taken you but such as is common to man: but God *is* faithful, who will not suffer you to be tempted above that ye are able; but will with the temptation also make a way to escape, that ye may be able to bear *it*.

1Co 15:10 — But by the grace of God I am what I am: and his grace *which was bestowed* upon me was not in vain; but I laboured more abundantly than they all: yet not I, but the grace of God which was with me.

2Co 1:12 — For our rejoicing is this, the testimony of our conscience, that in simplicity and godly sincerity, not with fleshly wisdom, but by the grace of God, we have had our conversation in the world, and more abundantly to you-ward.

Eph 3:16 — That he would grant you, according to the riches of his glory, to be strengthened with might by his Spirit in the inner man;

Eph 4:7 — But unto every one of us is given grace according to the measure of the gift of Christ.

Eph 6:10 — Finally, my brethren, be strong in the Lord, and in the power of his might.

Php 1:19 — For I know that this shall turn to my salvation through your prayer, and the supply of the Spirit of Jesus Christ,

Php 2:13 — For it is God which worketh in you both to will and to do of *his* good pleasure.

1Th 1:1 — Paul, and Silvanus, and Timotheus, unto the church of the Thessalonians *which is* in God the Father and *in* the Lord Jesus Christ: Grace *be* unto you, and peace, from God our Father, and the Lord Jesus Christ.

1Th 5:28 — The grace of our Lord Jesus Christ *be* with you. Amen.

1Ti 1:14 — And the grace of our Lord was exceeding abundant with faith and love which is in Christ Jesus.

2Ti 1:1 — Paul, an apostle of Jesus Christ by the will of God, according to the promise of life which is in Christ Jesus,

2Ti 1:9 — Who hath saved us, and called *us* with an holy calling, not according to our works, but according to his own purpose and grace, which was given us in Christ Jesus before the world began,

Tit 3:7 — That being justified by his grace, we should be made heirs according to the hope of eternal life.

1Pe 1:5 — Who are kept by the power of God through faith unto salvation ready to be revealed in the last time.

1Pe 4:10 — As every man hath received the gift, *even so* minister the same one to another, as good stewards of the manifold grace of God.

1Pe 5:10 — But the God of all grace, who hath called us unto his eternal glory by Christ Jesus, after that ye have suffered a while, make you perfect, stablish, strengthen, settle *you*.

2Pe 1:2 — Grace and peace be multiplied unto you through the knowledge of God, and of Jesus our Lord,

Jude 1:1 — Jude, the servant of Jesus Christ, and brother of James, to them that are sanctified by God the Father, and preserved in Jesus Christ, *and* called:

Jude 1:21 — Keep yourselves in the love of God, looking for the mercy of our Lord Jesus Christ unto eternal life.

Rev 3:10 — Because thou hast kept the word of my patience, I also will keep thee from the hour of temptation, which shall come upon all the world, to try them that dwell upon the earth.

See: God, Grace of

• **Growth in.**

Php 1:9–11; 3:12–15; Col 1:10–11; 1Th 3:12–13; Heb 6:1–3; 1Pe 2:1–3

Ps 84:7 — They go from strength to strength, *every one of them* in Zion appeareth before God.

Pr 4:18 — But the path of the just *is* as the shining light, that shineth more and more unto the perfect day.

Php 1:6 — Being confident of this very thing, that he which hath begun a good work in you will perform *it* until the day of Jesus Christ:

Col 2:19 — And not holding the Head, from which all the body by joints and bands having nourishment ministered, and knit together, increaseth with the increase of God.

1Th 3:10 — Night and day praying exceedingly that we might see your face, and might perfect that which is lacking in your faith?

2Th 1:3 — We are bound to thank God always for you, brethren, as it is meet, because that your faith groweth exceedingly, and the charity of every one of you all toward each other aboundeth;

2Pe 3:18 — But grow in grace, and *in* the knowledge of our Lord and Saviour Jesus Christ. To him *be* glory both now and for ever. Amen.

GRACES

• **Christian.**

Mt 5:3–11; Ro 5:3–5; 1Co 13:1–8; Gal 5:22–23; 2Pe 1:5–9

1Co 13:13 — And now abideth faith, hope, charity, these three; but the greatest of these *is* charity.

See: Character of Saints

See: Charitableness

See: Courage

See: Gentleness

See: Hope

See: Kindness

See: Knowledge

See: Long-Suffering

See: Love

See: Meekness

See: Mercy

See: Patience

See: Peace

See: Perseverance

See: Purity

See: Righteousness; fruits of

See: Stability

See: Temperance

See: Wisdom

GRAFTING

Ro 11:17–24

GRANDFATHER

• **Called father.**

Ge 10:21 — Unto Shem also, the father of all the children of Eber, the brother of Japheth the elder, even to him were *children* born.

GRAPE

• **Cultivated in vineyards by.**

• **Noah.**

Ge 9:20 — And Noah began *to be* an husbandman, and he planted a vineyard:

• **The Canaanites.**

Nu 13:24 — The place was called the brook Eshcol, because of the cluster of grapes which the children of Israel cut down from thence.

Dt 6:11 — And houses full of all good *things,* which thou filledst not, and wells digged, which thou diggedst not, vineyards and olive trees, which thou plantedst not; when thou shalt have eaten and be full;

Jos 24:13 — And I have given you a land for which ye did not labour, and cities which ye built not, and ye dwell in them; of the vineyards and oliveyards which ye planted not do ye eat.

• **The Edomites.**

Nu 20:17 — Let us pass, I pray thee, through thy country: we will not pass through the fields, or through the vineyards, neither will we drink *of* the water of the wells: we will go by the king's *high* way, we will not turn to the right hand nor to the left, until we have passed thy borders.

• **The Amorites.**

Isa 16:8–9

Nu 21:22 — Let me pass through thy land: we will not turn into the fields, or into the vineyards; we will not drink *of* the waters of the well: *but* we will go along by the king's *high* way, until we be past thy borders.

• **The Philistines.**

Jgs 15:5 — And when he had set the brands on fire, he *let* them go into the standing corn of the Philistines, and burnt up both the shocks, and also the standing corn, with the vineyards *and* olives.

• **Grown at.**

• **Abel.**

Jgs 11:33 — And he smote them from Aroer, even till thou come to Minnith, *even* twenty cities, and unto the plain of the vineyards, with a very great slaughter. Thus the children of Ammon were subdued before the children of Israel.

• **Baal-hamon.**

SS 8:11 — Solomon had a vineyard at Baal-hamon; he let out the vineyard unto keepers; every one for the fruit thereof was to bring a thousand *pieces* of silver.

• **Carmel.**

2Ch 26:10 — Also he built towers in the desert, and digged many wells: for he had much cattle, both in the low country, and in the plains: husbandmen *also,* and vine dressers in the mountains, and in Carmel: for he loved husbandry.

- **En-gedi.**
  SS 1:14 — My beloved *is* unto me *as* a cluster of camphire in the vineyards of En-gedi.
- **Jezreel.**
  1Ki 21:1 — And it came to pass after these things, *that* Naboth the Jezreelite had a vineyard, which *was* in Jezreel, hard by the palace of Ahab king of Samaria.
- **Lebanon.**
  Hos 14:7 — They that dwell under his shadow shall return; they shall revive *as* the corn, and grow as the vine: the scent thereof *shall be* as the wine of Lebanon.
- **Samaria.**
  Jer 31:5 — Thou shalt yet plant vines upon the mountains of Samaria: the planters shall plant, and shall eat *them* as common things.
- **Shechem.**
  Jgs 9:27 — And they went out into the fields, and gathered their vineyards, and trode *the grapes,* and made merry, and went into the house of their god, and did eat and drink, and cursed Abimelech.
- **Shiloah.**
  Jgs 21:20–21
- **Timnath.**
  Jgs 14:5 — Then went Samson down, and his father and his mother, to Timnath, and came to the vineyards of Timnath: and, behold, a young lion roared against him.

• Culture of.

Le 25:3 — Six years thou shalt sow thy field, and six years thou shalt prune thy vineyard, and gather in the fruit thereof;

Le 25:11 — A jubile shall that fiftieth year be unto you: ye shall not sow, neither reap that which groweth of itself in it, nor gather *the grapes* in it of thy vine undressed.

Dt 28:39 — Thou shalt plant vineyards, and dress *them,* but shalt neither drink *of* the wine, nor gather *the grapes;* for the worms shall eat them.

2Ch 26:10 — Also he built towers in the desert, and digged many wells: for he had much cattle, both in the low country, and in the plains: husbandmen *also,* and vine dressers in the mountains, and in Carmel: for he loved husbandry.

SS 6:11 — I went down into the garden of nuts to see the fruits of the valley, *and* to see whether the vine flourished, *and* the pomegranates budded.

Isa 5:1 — Now will I sing to my wellbeloved a song of my beloved touching his vineyard. My wellbeloved hath a vineyard in a very fruitful hill:

Jer 31:5 — Thou shalt yet plant vines upon the mountains of Samaria: the planters shall plant, and shall eat *them* as common things.

• Wine made of.

Jer 25:30 — Therefore prophesy thou against them all these words, and say unto them, The LORD shall roar from on high, and utter his voice from his holy habitation; he shall mightily roar upon his habitation; he shall give a shout, as they that tread *the grapes,* against all the inhabitants of the earth.

• Wine of, forbidden to Nazarites.

Nu 6:4 — All the days of his separation shall he eat nothing that is made of the vine tree, from the kernels even to the husk.

See: Nazarite
See: Vine
See: Vineyard
See: Wine

• Figurative.

Eze 15:1–8; Rev 14:18–20

Dt 32:32 — For their vine *is* of the vine of Sodom, and of the fields of Gomorrah: their grapes *are* grapes of gall, their clusters *are* bitter:

Ps 128:3 — Thy wife *shall be* as a fruitful vine by the sides of thine house: thy children like olive plants round about thy table.

Jer 2:21 — Yet I had planted thee a noble vine, wholly a right seed: how then art thou turned into the degenerate plant of a strange vine unto me?

Hos 10:1 — Israel *is* an empty vine, he bringeth forth fruit unto himself: according to the multitude of his fruit he hath increased the altars; according to the goodness of his land they have made goodly images.

- **Fable of.**
  Jgs 9:12–13
- **Parables of the vine.**
  Ps 80:8–14; Eze 17:6–10; 19:10–14; Jn 15:1–5
- **Proverb of.**
  Eze 18:2 — What mean ye, that ye use this proverb concerning the land of Israel, saying, The fathers have eaten sour grapes, and the children's teeth are set on edge?

See: Vine
See: Vineyard
See: Wine

GRASS

• Created on the third creative day.

Ge 1:11 — And God said, Let the earth bring forth grass, the herb yielding seed, *and* the fruit tree yielding fruit after his kind, whose seed *is* in itself, upon the earth: and it was so.

• Mown.

Ps 72:6 — He shall come down like rain upon the mown grass: as showers *that* water the earth.

• God's care of.

Mt 6:30 — Wherefore, if God so clothe the grass of the field, which to day is, and to morrow is cast into the oven, *shall he* not much more *clothe* you, O ye of little faith?

Lk 12:28 — If then God so clothe the grass, which is to day in the field, and to morrow is cast into the oven; how much more *will he clothe* you, O ye of little faith?

• On roofs of houses.

Ps 129:6 — Let them be as the grass *upon* the housetops, which withereth afore it groweth up:

• Figurative.

Ps 90:5–6; Jas 1:10–11

Isa 40:6 — The voice said, Cry. And he said, What shall I cry? All flesh *is* grass, and all the goodliness thereof *is* as the flower of the field:

1Pe 1:24 — For all flesh *is* as grass, and all the glory of man as the flower of grass. The grass withereth, and the flower thereof falleth away:

GRASSHOPPER

Nu 13:33 — And there we saw the giants, the sons of Anak, *which come* of the giants: and we were in our own sight as grasshoppers, and so we were in their sight.

Ecc 12:5 — Also *when* they shall be afraid of *that which is* high, and fears *shall be* in the way, and the almond tree shall flourish, and the grasshopper shall be a burden, and desire shall fail: because man goeth to his long home, and the mourners go about the streets:

Isa 40:22 — *It is* he that sitteth upon the circle of the earth, and the inhabitants thereof *are* as grasshoppers; that stretcheth out the heavens as a curtain, and spreadeth them out as a tent to dwell in:

Na 3:17 — Thy crowned *are* as the locusts, and thy captains as the great grasshoppers, which camp in the hedges in the cold day, *but* when the sun ariseth they flee away, and their place is not known where they *are.*

✦See: Locust

GRATE

Ex 27:4–5; 38:4–5

GRATITUDE ✦See: Thankfulness

GRAVE

Hos 13:14 — I will ransom them from the power of the grave; I will redeem them from death: O death, I will be thy plagues; O grave, I will be thy destruction: repentance shall be hid from mine eyes.

1Co 15:55 — O death, where *is* thy sting? O grave, where *is* thy victory?

• Prepared by Jacob.

Ge 50:5 — My father made me swear, saying, Lo, I die: in my grave which I have digged for me in the land of Canaan, there shalt thou bury me. Now therefore let me go up, I pray thee, and bury my father, and I will come again.

• Defilement from touching.

Nu 19:16 — And whosoever toucheth one that is slain with a sword in the open fields, or a dead body, or a bone of a man, or a grave, shall be unclean seven days.

Nu 19:18 — And a clean person shall take hyssop, and dip *it* in the water, and sprinkle *it* upon the tent, and upon all the vessels, and upon the persons that were there, and upon him that touched a bone, or one slain, or one dead, or a grave:

• Weeping at.

2Sa 3:32 — And they buried Abner in Hebron: and the king lifted up his voice, and wept at the grave of Abner; and all the people wept.

Jn 11:31 — The Jews then which were with her in the house, and comforted her, when they saw Mary, that she rose up hastily and went out, followed her, saying, She goeth unto the grave to weep there.

Jn 20:11 — But Mary stood without at the sepulchre weeping: and as she wept, she stooped down, *and looked* into the sepulchre,

• Of parents, honored.

2Sa 19:37 — Let thy servant, I pray thee, turn back again, that I may die in mine own city, *and be buried* by the grave of my father and of my mother. But behold thy servant Chimham; let him go over with my lord the king; and do to him what shall seem good unto thee.

• Welcomed.

Job 3:20–22

• Resurrection from.

• Of Lazarus.

Jn 11:43–44

Jn 12:17 — The people therefore that was with him when he called Lazarus out of his grave, and raised him from the dead, bare record.

• Of Jesus.

Mt 28:5–6; 1Co 15:12–20

• Of saints after Jesus' resurrection.

Mt 27:52–53

• Of all the dead, foretold.

1Co 15:22–54

Jn 5:28 — Marvel not at this: for the hour is coming, in the which all that are in the graves shall hear his voice,

✦See: Burial

GRAVEL

• Figurative.

Pr 20:17 — Bread of deceit *is* sweet to a man; but afterwards his mouth shall be filled with gravel.

GRAVING ✦See: Engraving

GREAT SEA ✦See: Mediterranean Sea

GREAVES

1Sa 17:6 — And *he had* greaves of brass upon his legs, and a target of brass between his shoulders.

GREECE

• Inhabitants of, called Gentiles.

Mk 7:26 — The woman was a Greek, a Syrophenician by nation; and she besought him that he would cast forth the devil out of her daughter.

Jn 7:35 — Then said the Jews among themselves, Whither will he go, that we shall not find him? will he go unto the dispersed among the Gentiles, and teach the Gentiles?

Ro 2:10 — But glory, honour, and peace, to every man that worketh good, to the Jew first, and also to the Gentile:

Ro 3:9 — What then? are we better *than they?* No, in no wise: for we have before proved both Jews and Gentiles, that they are all under sin;

1Co 10:32 — Give none offence, neither to the Jews, nor to the Gentiles, nor to the church of God:

1Co 12:13 — For by one Spirit are we all baptized into one body, whether *we be* Jews or Gentiles, whether *we be* bond or free; and have been all made to drink into one Spirit.

- **Desire to see Jesus.**

Jn 12:20–23

- **Marry among the Jews.**

Ac 16:1 — Then came he to Derbe and Lystra: and, behold, a certain disciple was there, named Timotheus, the son of a certain woman, which was a Jewess, and believed; but his father *was* a Greek:

- **Accept the Messiah.**

Ac 17:2–4

Ac 17:12 — Therefore many of them believed; also of honourable women which were Greeks, and of men, not a few.

Ac 17:24 — God that made the world and all things therein, seeing that he is Lord of heaven and earth, dwelleth not in temples made with hands;

- **Persecute the early Christians.**

Ac 6:9–14

Ac 9:29 — And he spake boldly in the name of the Lord Jesus, and disputed against the Grecians: but they went about to slay him.

Ac 18:17 — Then all the Greeks took Sosthenes, the chief ruler of the synagogue, and beat *him* before the judgment seat. And Gallio cared for none of those things.

- **Gentiles called Greeks.**

Ro 10:12 — For there is no difference between the Jew and the Greek: for the same Lord over all is rich unto all that call upon him.

Gal 3:28 — There is neither Jew nor Greek, there is neither bond nor free, there is neither male nor female: for ye are all one in Christ Jesus.

Col 3:11 — Where there is neither Greek nor Jew, circumcision nor uncircumcision, Barbarian, Scythian, bond *nor* free: but Christ *is* all, and in all.

- **Schools of philosophy in Athens.**

Ac 19:9 — But when divers were hardened, and believed not, but spake evil of that way before the multitude, he departed from them, and separated the disciples, disputing daily in the school of one Tyrannus.

- **Philosophy of.**

1Co 1:22–23

- **Poets of.**

Ac 17:28 — For in him we live, and move, and have our being; as certain also of your own poets have said, For we are also his offspring.

- **Prophecies concerning.**

Da 10:20 — Then said he, Knowest thou wherefore I come unto thee? and now will I return to fight with the prince of Persia: and when I am gone forth, lo, the prince of Grecia shall come.

Zec 9:13 — When I have bent Judah for me, filled the bow with Ephraim, and raised up thy sons, O Zion, against thy sons, O Greece, and made thee as the sword of a mighty man.

See: Athens

See: Epicureans

See: Stoicism

GREED **See: Covetousness**

GREEK

- **Philosophy of.**

1Co 1:22–23

See: Greece

GREYHOUND

Pr 30:31 — A greyhound; an he goat also; and a king, against whom *there is* no rising up.

GRIEF

- **Attributed to the Holy Spirit.**

Eph 4:30 — And grieve not the holy Spirit of God, whereby ye are sealed unto the day of redemption.

Heb 3:10 — Wherefore I was grieved with that generation, and said, They do alway err in *their* heart; and they have not known my ways.

Heb 3:17 — But with whom was he grieved forty years? *was it* not with them that had sinned, whose carcases fell in the wilderness?

See: Afflictions

See: Sorrow

GRINDING **See: Mill**

GROUND

- **Man made from.**

Ge 2:7 — And the LORD God formed man *of* the dust of the ground, and breathed into his nostrils the breath of life; and man became a living soul.

Ge 3:19 — In the sweat of thy face shalt thou eat bread, till thou return unto the ground; for out of it wast thou taken: for dust thou *art,* and unto dust shalt thou return.

Ge 3:23 — Therefore the LORD God sent him forth from the garden of Eden, to till the ground from whence he was taken.

Job 4:19 — How much less *in* them that dwell in houses of clay, whose foundation *is* in the dust, *which* are crushed before the moth?

Job 33:6 — Behold, I *am* according to thy wish in God's stead: I also am formed out of the clay.

- **Animals from.**

Ge 2:19 — And out of the ground the LORD God formed every beast of the field, and every fowl of the air; and brought *them* unto Adam to see what he would call them: and whatsoever Adam called every living creature, that *was* the name thereof.

• **Vegetables from.**

Ge 2:9 — And out of the ground made the LORD God to grow every tree that is pleasant to the sight, and good for food; the tree of life also in the midst of the garden, and the tree of knowledge of good and evil.

• **Cursed.**

Ge 3:17 — And unto Adam he said, Because thou hast hearkened unto the voice of thy wife, and hast eaten of the tree, of which I commanded thee, saying, Thou shalt not eat of it: cursed *is* the ground for thy sake; in sorrow shalt thou eat *of* it all the days of thy life;

Ge 5:29 — And he called his name Noah, saying, This *same* shall comfort us concerning our work and toil of our hands, because of the ground which the LORD hath cursed.

GROVES

• **Probably an image or images of the Canaanitish goddess Asherah.**

See: Ashtoreth

• **Forbidden to be established.**

Dt 16:21 — Thou shalt not plant thee a grove of any trees near unto the altar of the LORD thy God, which thou shalt make thee.

Isa 1:29 — For they shall be ashamed of the oaks which ye have desired, and ye shall be confounded for the gardens that ye have chosen.

Isa 17:8 — And he shall not look to the altars, the work of his hands, neither shall respect *that* which his fingers have made, either the groves, or the images.

Isa 27:9 — By this therefore shall the iniquity of Jacob be purged; and this is all the fruit to take away his sin; when he maketh all the stones of the altar as chalkstones that are beaten in sunder, the groves and images shall not stand up.

Mic 5:14 — And I will pluck up thy groves out of the midst of thee: so will I destroy thy cities.

• **Worshiped by Israelites.**

2Ki 21:3–7

Jgs 3:7 — And the children of Israel did evil in the sight of the LORD, and forgat the LORD their God, and served Baalim and the groves.

1Ki 14:15 — For the LORD shall smite Israel, as a reed is shaken in the water, and he shall root up Israel out of this good land, which he gave to their fathers, and shall scatter them beyond the river, because they have made their groves, provoking the LORD to anger.

1Ki 14:23 — For they also built them high places, and images, and groves, on every high hill, and under every green tree.

1Ki 15:13 — And also Maachah his mother, even her he removed from *being* queen, because she had made an idol in a grove; and Asa destroyed her idol, and burnt *it* by the brook Kidron.

1Ki 18:19 — Now therefore send, *and* gather to me all Israel unto mount Carmel, and the prophets of Baal four hundred and fifty, and the prophets of the groves four hundred, which eat at Jezebel's table.

2Ki 13:6 — Nevertheless they departed not from the sins of the house of Jeroboam, who made Israel sin, *but* walked therein: and there remained the grove also in Samaria.)

2Ki 17:10 — And they set them up images and groves in every high hill, and under every green tree:

2Ki 17:16 — And they left all the commandments of the LORD their God, and made them molten images, *even* two calves, and made a grove, and worshipped all the host of heaven, and served Baal.

2Ch 24:18 — And they left the house of the LORD God of their fathers, and served groves and idols: and wrath came upon Judah and Jerusalem for this their trespass.

Jer 17:2 — Whilst their children remember their altars and their groves by the green trees upon the high hills.

• **Destroyed by.**

• **Gideon.**

Jgs 6:28 — And when the men of the city arose early in the morning, behold, the altar of Baal was cast down, and the grove was cut down that *was* by it, and the second bullock was offered upon the altar *that was* built.

• **Hezekiah.**

2Ki 18:4 — He removed the high places, and brake the images, and cut down the groves, and brake in pieces the brasen serpent that Moses had made: for unto those days the children of Israel did burn incense to it: and he called it Nehushtan.

• **Josiah.**

2Ch 34:3–4

2Ki 23:14 — And he brake in pieces the images, and cut down the groves, and filled their places with the bones of men.

• **Asa.**

2Ch 14:3 — For he took away the altars of the strange *gods*, and the high places, and brake down the images, and cut down the groves:

• **Jehoshaphat.**

2Ch 17:6 — And his heart was lifted up in the ways of the LORD: moreover he took away the high places and groves out of Judah.

2Ch 19:3 — Nevertheless there are good things found in thee, in that thou hast taken away the groves out of the land, and hast prepared thine heart to seek God.

See: Idolatry

GROWTH

Mt 13:1–30; 28:19–20; Heb 5:12–13

2Co 5:17 — Therefore if any man *be* in Christ, *he is* a new creature: old things are passed away; behold, all things are become new.

Eph 4:14 — That we *henceforth* be no more children, tossed to and fro, and carried about with every wind of doctrine, by the sleight of men, *and* cunning craftiness, whereby they lie in wait to deceive;

1Pe 2:2 — As newborn babes, desire the sincere milk of the word, that ye may grow thereby:

GUARD ✧See: Watchman

GUDGODAH

• A station of the Israelites in the wilderness.

Dt 10:7 — From thence they journeyed unto Gudgodah; and from Gudgodah to Jotbath, a land of rivers of waters.

• Probably identical with Hor-Hagidgad.

Nu 33:32–33

GUEST

• Salutations to.

Ge 18:2 — And he lift up his eyes and looked, and, lo, three men stood by him: and when he saw *them,* he ran to meet them from the tent door, and bowed himself toward the ground,

• Abraham's hospitality to.

✧See: Hospitality

• Rules for the conduct of.

Pr 23:1–3, 6–8; 25:6–7; Lk 10:5–7; 14:7–11

Pr 25:17 — Withdraw thy foot from thy neighbour's house; lest he be weary of thee, and *so* hate thee.

1Co 10:27 — If any of them that believe not bid you *to a feast,* and ye be disposed to go; whatsoever is set before you, eat, asking no question for conscience sake.

✧See: Hospitality

GUIDANCE ✧See: God, Guide

GUILE

✧See: Conspiracy

✧See: Deceit

✧See: Fraud

✧See: Hypocrisy

GUILT

✧See: Conscience

✧See: Conviction

✧See: Sin

GUNI

• Son of Naphtali.

Ge 46:24 — And the sons of Naphtali; Jahzeel, and Guni, and Jezer, and Shillem.

Nu 26:48 — *Of* the sons of Naphtali after their families: of Jahzeel, the family of the Jahzeelites: of Guni, the family of the Gunites:

1Ch 7:13 — The sons of Naphtali; Jahziel, and Guni, and Jezer, and Shallum, the sons of Bilhah.

• Father of Abdiel.

1Ch 5:15 — Ahi the son of Abdiel, the son of Guni, chief of the house of their fathers.

GUR • Place where Jehu slew Ahaziah.

2Ki 9:27 — But when Ahaziah the king of Judah saw *this,* he fled by the way of the garden house. And Jehu followed after him, and said, Smite him also in the chariot. *And they did so* at the going up to Gur, which *is* by Ibleam. And he fled to Megiddo, and died there.

GUR-BAAL • A town between Canaan and Arabia.

2Ch 26:7 — And God helped him against the Philistines, and against the Arabians that dwelt in Gur-baal, and the Mehunims.

H

HAAHASHTARI • Son of Naarah.

1Ch 4:6 — And Naarah bare him Ahuzam, and Hepher, and Temeni, and Haahashtari. These *were* the sons of Naarah.

HABAIAH • A priest, whose descendants returned from captivity.

Ezr 2:61 — And of the children of the priests: the children of Habaiah, the children of Koz, the children of Barzillai; which took a wife of the daughters of Barzillai the Gileadite, and was called after their name:

Ne 7:63 — And of the priests: the children of Habaiah, the children of Koz, the children of Barzillai, which took *one* of the daughters of Barzillai the Gileadite to wife, and was called after their name.

HABAKKUK

• A prophet and poet, who prophesied after the destruction of Nineveh, probably.

Hab 1:1 — The burden which Habakkuk the prophet did see.

Hab 3:1 — A prayer of Habakkuk the prophet upon Shigionoth.

• His hymn of praise of the majesty of God.

Hab 3:1–19

HABAZINIAH • Head of the family of Rechabites.

Jer 35:3 — Then I took Jaazaniah the son of Jeremiah, the son of Habaziniah, and his brethren, and all his sons, and the whole house of the Rechabites;

HABERGEON

• A part of the defensive armor of a soldier.

Ex 28:32 — And there shall be an hole in the top of it, in the midst thereof: it shall have a binding of woven work round about the hole of it, as it were the hole of an habergeon, that it be not rent.

Ex 39:23 — And *there was* an hole in the midst of the robe, as the hole of an habergeon, *with* a band round about the hole, that it should not rend.

See: Breastplate

HABOR • A river of Mesopotamia.

2Ki 17:6 — In the ninth year of Hoshea the king of Assyria took Samaria, and carried Israel away into Assyria, and placed them in Halah and in Habor *by* the river of Gozan, and in the cities of the Medes.

2Ki 18:11 — And the king of Assyria did carry away Israel unto Assyria, and put them in Halah and in Habor *by* the river of Gozan, and in the cities of the Medes:

1Ch 5:26 — And the God of Israel stirred up the spirit of Pul king of Assyria, and the spirit of Tilgath-pilneser king of Assyria, and he carried them away, even the Reubenites, and the Gadites, and the half tribe of Manasseh, and brought them unto Halah, and Habor, and Hara, and to the river Gozan, unto this day.

HACHALIAH • Father of Nehemiah.

Ne 1:1 — The words of Nehemiah the son of Hachaliah. And it came to pass in the month Chisleu, in the twentieth year, as I was in Shushan the palace,

Ne 10:1 — Now those that sealed *were,* Nehemiah, the Tirshatha, the son of Hachaliah, and Zidkijah,

HACHILAH • A hill in Judah where David and his followers hid from Saul.

1Sa 23:19 — Then came up the Ziphites to Saul to Gibeah, saying, Doth not David hide himself with us in strong holds in the wood, in the hill of Hachilah, which *is* on the south of Jeshimon?

1Sa 26:3 — And Saul pitched in the hill of Hachilah, which *is* before Jeshimon, by the way. But David abode in the wilderness, and he saw that Saul came after him into the wilderness.

HACHMONI • Father of Jehiel.

1Ch 11:11 — And this *is* the number of the mighty men whom David had; Jashobeam, and Hachmonite, the chief of the captains: he lifted up his spear against three hundred slain *by him* at one time.

1Ch 27:32 — Also Jonathan David's uncle was a counsellor, a wise man, and a scribe: and Jehiel the son of Hachmoni *was* with the king's sons:

HADAD

• A successor of Husham as king of Edom. Vanquished the Midianites on the field of Moab.

Ge 36:35 — And Husham died, and Hadad the son of Bedad, who smote Midian in the field of Moab, reigned in his stead: and the name of his city *was* Avith.

1Ch 1:46 — And when Husham was dead, Hadad the son of Bedad, which smote Midian in the field of Moab, reigned in his stead: and the name of his city *was* Avith.

• A son of Ishmael.

1Ch 1:30 — Mishma and Dumah, Massa, Hadad, and Tema,

• Called Hadar.

Ge 25:15 — Hadar, and Tema, Jetur, Naphish, and Kedemah:

• Successor of Baal-hanan, king of Edom.

1Ch 1:50 — And when Baal-hanan was dead, Hadad reigned in his stead: and the name of his city *was* Pai; and his wife's name *was* Mehetabel, the daughter of Matred, the daughter of Mezahab.

• **Called Hadar.**

Ge 36:39 — And Baal-hanan the son of Achbor died, and Hadar reigned in his stead: and the name of his city *was* Pau; and his wife's name *was* Mehetabel, the daughter of Matred, the daughter of Mezahab.

• **A prince of Edom.**

• **Adversary of Solomon.**

1Ki 11:14–22

1Ki 11:25 — And he was an adversary to Israel all the days of Solomon, beside the mischief that Hadad *did:* and he abhorred Israel, and reigned over Syria.

HADADEZER

• **Called also Hadarezer.**

• **King of Zobah. Vanquished by David.**

2Sa 8:3–13; 10:15–19; 1Ch 18:3–10; 19:6–19

1Ki 11:23 — And God stirred him up *another* adversary, Rezon the son of Eliadah, which fled from his lord Hadadezer king of Zobah:

HADADRIMMON • A place in the valley of Megiddon.

Zec 12:11 — In that day shall there be a great mourning in Jerusalem, as the mourning of Hadadrimmon in the valley of Megiddon.

HADAR ⇜See: Hadad

HADAREZER ⇜See: Hadadezer

HADASHAH • A town in Judah.

Jos 15:37 — Zenan, and Hadashah, and Migdal-gad,

HADASSAH

• **Jewish name of Esther.**

Est 2:7 — And he brought up Hadassah, that *is,* Esther, his uncle's daughter: for she had neither father nor mother, and the maid *was* fair and beautiful; whom Mordecai, when her father and mother were dead, took for his own daughter.

⇜**See: Esther**

HADATTAH • Probably an adjective qualifying Hazor, making it equivalent to New Hazor.

Jos 15:25 — And Hazor, Hadattah, and Kerioth, *and* Hezron, which *is* Hazor,

HADES

• **The unseen world, translated hell in KJV.**

Rev 20:13–14

Mt 10:28 — And fear not them which kill the body, but are not able to kill the soul: but rather fear him which is able to destroy both soul and body in hell.

Mt 11:23 — And thou, Capernaum, which art exalted unto heaven, shalt be brought down to hell: for if the mighty works, which have been done in thee, had been done in Sodom, it would have remained until this day.

Mt 16:18 — And I say also unto thee, That thou art Peter, and upon this rock I will build my church; and the gates of hell shall not prevail against it.

Lk 10:15 — And thou, Capernaum, which art exalted to heaven, shalt be thrust down to hell.

Lk 16:23 — And in hell he lift up his eyes, being in torments, and seeth Abraham afar off, and Lazarus in his bosom.

Ac 2:27 — Because thou wilt not leave my soul in hell, neither wilt thou suffer thine Holy One to see corruption.

Ac 2:31 — He seeing this before spake of the resurrection of Christ, that his soul was not left in hell, neither his flesh did see corruption.

Rev 1:18 — I *am* he that liveth, and was dead; and, behold, I am alive for evermore, Amen; and have the keys of hell and of death.

Rev 6:8 — And I looked, and behold a pale horse: and his name that sat on him was Death, and Hell followed with him. And power was given unto them over the fourth part of the earth, to kill with sword, and with hunger, and with death, and with the beasts of the earth.

⇜**See: Hell**

• **Realm, or state, of the dead.**

• **Usually expressed in Hebrew by Sheol and in Greek by Hades.**

Ps 88:10–12; Ecc 9:4–6; Lk 23:42–43

2Sa 22:6 — The sorrows of hell compassed me about; the snares of death prevented me;

Job 26:5 — Dead *things* are formed from under the waters, and the inhabitants thereof.

Ps 6:5 — For in death *there is* no remembrance of thee: in the grave who shall give thee thanks?

Ps 17:15 — As for me, I will behold thy face in righteousness: I shall be satisfied, when I awake, with thy likeness.

Ps 30:9 — What profit *is there* in my blood, when I go down to the pit? Shall the dust praise thee? shall it declare thy truth?

Ps 49:15 — But God will redeem my soul from the power of the grave: for he shall receive me. Selah.

Ps 86:13 — For great *is* thy mercy toward me: and thou hast delivered my soul from the lowest hell.

Ps 115:17 — The dead praise not the LORD, neither any that go down into silence.

Ps 116:3 — The sorrows of death compassed me, and the pains of hell gat hold upon me: I found trouble and sorrow.

Pr 15:24 — The way of life *is* above to the wise, that he may depart from hell beneath.

Pr 21:16 — The man that wandereth out of the way of understanding shall remain in the congregation of the dead.

Pr 27:20 — Hell and destruction are never full; so the eyes of man are never satisfied.

Isa 5:14 — Therefore hell hath enlarged herself, and opened her mouth without measure: and their glory, and their multitude, and their pomp, and he that rejoiceth, shall descend into it.

Jnh 2:2 — And said, I cried by reason of mine affliction unto the LORD, and he heard me; out of the belly of hell cried I, *and* thou heardest my voice.

Jn 8:22 — Then said the Jews, Will he kill himself? because he saith, Whither I go, ye cannot come.

2Co 12:4— How that he was caught up into paradise, and heard unspeakable words, which it is not lawful for a man to utter.

See: Hell

See: Immortality

See: Paradise

See: Righteous

See: Spirit

See: Wicked; punishment of

HADID

• A city of Benjamin.

• Captives of, returned from Babylon.

Ezr 2:33 — The children of Lod, Hadid, and Ono, seven hundred twenty and five.

Ne 7:37 — The children of Lod, Hadid, and Ono, seven hundred twenty and one.

Ne 11:34 — Hadid, Zeboim, Neballat,

HADLAI • An Ephraimite.

2Ch 28:12 — Then certain of the heads of the children of Ephraim, Azariah the son of Johanan, Berechiah the son of Meshillemoth, and Jehizkiah the son of Shallum, and Amasa the son of Hadlai, stood up against them that came from the war,

HADORAM

• Descendant of Shem.

Ge 10:27 — And Hadoram, and Uzal, and Diklah,

1Ch 1:21 — Hadoram also, and Uzal, and Diklah,

• Son of Ton, or Toi.

1Ch 18:10 — He sent Hadoram his son to king David, to enquire of his welfare, and to congratulate him, because he had fought against Hadarezer, and smitten him; (for Hadarezer had war with Tou;) and *with him* all manner of vessels of gold and silver and brass.

• Called Joram.

2Sa 8:10 — Then Toi sent Joram his son unto king David, to salute him, and to bless him, because he had fought against Hadadezer, and smitten him: for Hadadezer had wars with Toi. And *Joram* brought with him vessels of silver, and vessels of gold, and vessels of brass:

• Chief officer of the tribute under Rehoboam.

2Ch 10:18 — Then king Rehoboam sent Hadoram that *was* over the tribute; and the children of Israel stoned him with stones, that he died. But king Rehoboam made speed to get him up to *his* chariot, to flee to Jerusalem.

• Probably identical with Adoniram.

1Ki 4:6 — And Ahishar *was* over the household: and Adoniram the son of Abda *was* over the tribute.

1Ki 5:14 — And he sent them to Lebanon ten thousand a month by courses: a month they were in Lebanon, *and* two months at home: and Adoniram *was* over the levy.

• Probably identical with Adoram.

2Sa 20:24 — And Adoram *was* over the tribute: and Jehoshaphat the son of Ahilud *was* recorder:

HADRACH • A district of Syria.

Zec 9:1 — The burden of the word of the LORD in the land of Hadrach, and Damascus *shall be* the rest thereof: when the eyes of man, as of all the tribes of Israel, *shall be* toward the LORD.

HAGAB • One of the Nethinim.

Ezr 2:46 — The children of Hagab, the children of Shalmai, the children of Hanan,

HAGABA

• Called also Hagabah.

• One of the Nethinim.

Ezr 2:45 — The children of Lebanah, the children of Hagabah, the children of Akkub,

Ne 7:48 — The children of Lebana, the children of Hagaba, the children of Shalmai,

HAGAR

• A servant of Abraham and handmaid of Sarah.

• Given by Sarah to Abraham to be his wife.

Ge 16:1–16

• Descendants of.

Ge 25:12–15; 1Ch 5:19–22

1Ch 5:10 — And in the days of Saul they made war with the Hagarites, who fell by their hand: and they dwelt in their tents throughout all the east land of Gilead.

Ps 83:6 — The tabernacles of Edom, and the Ishmaelites; of Moab, and the Hagarenes;

• Called Agar.

Gal 4:24–25

HAGGAI

• One of the minor prophets.

• Urges the Jews to rebuild the temple.

Hag 1:1–2:23

Ezr 5:1 — Then the prophets, Hag the prophet, and Zechariah the son of Iddo, prophesied unto the Jews that *were* in Judah and Jerusalem in the name of the God of Israel, *even* unto them.

Ezr 6:14 — And the elders of the Jews builded, and they prospered through the prophesying of Hag the prophet and Zechariah the son of Iddo. And they builded, and finished *it,* according to the commandment of the God of Israel, and according to the commandment of Cyrus, and Darius, and Artaxerxes king of Persia.

HAGGERI • Father of Mibhar.

1Ch 11:38 — Joel the brother of Nathan, Mibhar the son of Haggeri,

HAGGI • Son of Gad.

Ge 46:16 — And the sons of Gad; Ziphion, and Haggi, Shuni, and Ezbon, Eri, and Arodi, and Areli.

Nu 26:15 — The children of Gad after their families: of Zephon, the family of the Zephonites: of Haggi, the family of the Haggites: of Shuni, the family of the Shunites:

HAGGIAH • A Levite.

1Ch 6:30 — Shimea his son, Haggiah his son, Asaiah his son.

HAGGITH

• Wife of David.

• Mother of Adonijah.

2Sa 3:4 — And the fourth, Adonijah the son of Haggith; and the fifth, Shephatiah the son of Abital;

1Ki 1:5 — Then Adonijah the son of Haggith exalted himself, saying, I will be king: and he prepared him chariots and horsemen, and fifty men to run before him.

1Ki 1:11 — Wherefore Nathan spake unto Bath-sheba the mother of Solomon, saying, Hast thou not heard that Adonijah the son of Haggith doth reign, and David our lord knoweth *it* not?

1Ki 2:13 — And Adonijah the son of Haggith came to Bath-sheba the mother of Solomon. And she said, Comest thou peaceably? And he said, Peaceably.

1Ch 3:2 — The third, Absalom the son of Maachah the daughter of Talmai king of Geshur: the fourth, Adonijah the son of Haggith:

HAI

Ge 12:8 — And he removed from thence unto a mountain on the east of Bethel, and pitched his tent, *having* Bethel on the west, and Hai on the east: and there he builded an altar unto the LORD, and called upon the name of the LORD.

Ge 13:3 — And he went on his journeys from the south even to Bethel, unto the place where his tent had been at the beginning, between Bethel and Hai;

See: Ai

HAIL

Job 38:22 — Hast thou entered into the treasures of the snow? or hast thou seen the treasures of the hail,

Hag 2:17 — I smote you with blasting and with mildew and with hail in all the labours of your hands; yet ye *turned* not to me, saith the LORD.

• Plague of, in Egypt.

Ex 9:18–29

Ps 78:48 — He gave up their cattle also to the hail, and their flocks to hot thunderbolts.

Ps 105:32 — He gave them hail for rain, *and* flaming fire in their land.

• Destroys army of the Amorites.

Jos 10:11 — And it came to pass, as they fled from before Israel, *and* were in the going down to Beth-horon, that the LORD cast down great stones from heaven upon them unto Azekah, and they died: *they were* more which died with hailstones than they whom the children of Israel slew with the sword.

• Figurative.

Isa 28:2 — Behold, the Lord hath a mighty and strong one, *which* as a tempest of hail *and* a destroying storm, as a flood of mighty waters overflowing, shall cast down to the earth with the hand.

Rev 8:7 — The first angel sounded, and there followed hail and fire mingled with blood, and they were cast upon the earth: and the third part of trees was burnt up, and all green grass was burnt up.

Rev 11:19 — And the temple of God was opened in heaven, and there was seen in his temple the ark of his testament: and there were lightnings, and voices, and thunderings, and an earthquake, and great hail.

Rev 16:21 — And there fell upon men a great hail out of heaven, *every stone* about the weight of a talent: and men blasphemed God because of the plague of the hail; for the plague thereof was exceeding great.

HAIR

• Numbered.

Mt 10:30 — <u>But the very hairs of your head are all numbered.</u>

Lk 12:7 — <u>But even the very hairs of your head are all numbered. Fear not therefore: ye are of more value than many sparrows.</u>

• Worn long by women.

1Co 11:5–6

Isa 3:24 — And it shall come to pass, *that* instead of sweet smell there shall be stink; and instead of a girdle a rent; and instead of well set hair baldness; and instead of a stomacher a girding of sackcloth; *and* burning instead of beauty.

Lk 7:38 — And stood at his feet behind *him* weeping, and began to wash his feet with tears, and did wipe *them* with the hairs of her head, and kissed his feet, and anointed *them* with the ointment.

1Co 11:15 — But if a woman have long hair, it is a glory to her: for *her* hair is given her for a covering.

1Ti 2:9 — In like manner also, that women adorn themselves in modest apparel, with shamefacedness and sobriety; not with broided hair, or gold, or pearls, or costly array;

1Pe 3:3 — Whose adorning let it not be that outward *adorning* of plaiting the hair, and of wearing of gold, or of putting on of apparel;

Rev 9:8 — And they had hair as the hair of women, and their teeth were as *the teeth* of lions.

• Worn long by Absalom.

2Sa 14:26 — And when he polled his head, (for it was at every year's end that he polled *it:* because *the hair* was heavy on him, therefore he polled it:) he weighed the hair of his head at two hundred shekels after the king's weight.

• Worn short by men.

1Co 11:14 — Doth not even nature itself teach you, that, if a man have long hair, it is a shame unto him?

• Symbolic dividing of.

Eze 5:1–2

➜See: Baldness

➜See: Caul

➜See: Leprosy

➜See: Mourning

➜See: Nazarite

HAKKATAN • Father of Johanan.

Ezr 8:12 — And of the sons of Azgad; Johanan the son of Hakkatan, and with him an hundred and ten males.

HAKKOZ

• A priest.

1Ch 24:10 — The seventh to Hakkoz, the eighth to Abijah,

• Called Koz.

Ezr 2:61 — And of the children of the priests: the children of Habaiah, the children of Koz, the children of Barzillai; which took a wife of the daughters of Barzillai the Gileadite, and was called after their name:

Ne 3:4 — And next unto them repaired Meremoth the son of Urijah, the son of Koz. And next unto them repaired Meshullam the son of Berechiah, the son of Meshezabeel. And next unto them repaired Zadok the son of Baana.

Ne 3:21 — After him repaired Meremoth the son of Urijah the son of Koz another piece, from the door of the house of Eliashib even to the end of the house of Eliashib.

HAKUPHA • One of the Nethinim.

Ezr 2:51 — The children of Bakbuk, the children of Hakupha, the children of Harhur,

Ne 7:53 — The children of Bakbuk, the children of Hakupha, the children of Harhur,

HALAH • A place to which Israelite captives were transported.

2Ki 17:6 — In the ninth year of Hoshea the king of Assyria took Samaria, and carried Israel away into Assyria, and placed them in Halah and in Habor *by* the river of Gozan, and in the cities of the Medes.

2Ki 18:11 — And the king of Assyria did carry away Israel unto Assyria, and put them in Halah and in Habor *by* the river of Gozan, and in the cities of the Medes:

1Ch 5:26 — And the God of Israel stirred up the spirit of Pul king of Assyria, and the spirit of Tilgath-pilneser king of Assyria, and he carried them away, even the Reubenites, and the Gadites, and the half tribe of Manasseh, and brought them unto Halah, and Habor, and Hara, and to the river Gozan, unto this day.

HALAK • A mountain, the southern limit of Joshua's conquests.

Jos 11:17 — *Even* from the mount Halak, that goeth up to Seir, even unto Baal-gad in the valley of Lebanon under mount Hermon: and all their kings he took, and smote them, and slew them.

Jos 12:7 — And these *are* the kings of the country which Joshua and the children of Israel smote on this side Jordan on the west, from Baal-gad in the valley of Lebanon even unto the mount Halak, that goeth up to Seir; which Joshua gave unto the tribes of Israel *for* a possession according to their divisions;

HALF-HOMER

• A measure of about seven or eight gallons.

➜See: Measure; dry

HALHUL • A city in Judah.

Jos 15:58 — Halhul, Beth-zur, and Gedor,

HALI • A border town of Asher.

Jos 19:25 — And their border was Helkath, and Hali, and Beten, and Achshaph,

HALLELUJAH

• An exclamatory expression of praise or adoration: "Praise ye the LORD"

Ps 146:10–147:1

Ps 106:1 — Praise ye the LORD. O give thanks unto the LORD; for *he is* good: for his mercy *endureth* for ever.

Ps 111:1 — Praise ye the LORD. I will praise the LORD with *my* whole heart, in the assembly of the upright, and *in* the congregation.

Ps 112:1 — Praise ye the LORD. Blessed *is* the man *that* feareth the LORD, *that* delighteth greatly in his commandments.

Ps 113:1 — Praise ye the LORD. Praise, O ye servants of the LORD, praise the name of the LORD.

Ps 117:1 — O praise the LORD, all ye nations: praise him, all ye people.

Ps 135:1 — Praise ye the LORD. Praise ye the name of the LORD; praise *him,* O ye servants of the LORD.

Ps 146:1 — Praise ye the LORD. Praise the LORD, O my soul.

Ps 148:1 — Praise ye the LORD. Praise ye the LORD from the heavens: praise him in the heights.

Rev 19:1 — And after these things I heard a great voice of much people in heaven, saying, Alleluia; Salvation, and glory, and honour, and power, unto the Lord our God:

➜See: Praise

HALOHESH

• Called also Hallohesh.

• Father of Shallum.

Ne 3:12 — And next unto him repaired Shallum the son of Halohesh, the ruler of the half part of Jerusalem, he and his daughters.

• **Sealed the covenant with Nehemiah.**
Ne 10:24 — Hallohesh, Pileha, Shobek,

HAM

• **Son of Noah.**
Ge 5:32 — And Noah was five hundred years old: and Noah begat Shem, Ham, and Japheth.
Ge 9:18 — And the sons of Noah, that went forth of the ark, were Shem, and Ham, and Japheth: and Ham is the father of Canaan.
Ge 9:24 — And Noah awoke from his wine, and knew what his younger son had done unto him.
1Ch 1:4 — Noah, Shem, Ham, and Japheth.

• **Provokes his father's wrath and is cursed by him.**
Ge 9:18–27

• **His children.**
Ge 10:6–20; 1Ch 1:8–16

• **Patronymic of the descendants of Ham.**
1Ch 4:40 — And they found fat pasture and good, and the land *was* wide, and quiet, and peaceable; for *they* of Ham had dwelt there of old.
Ps 78:51 — And smote all the firstborn in Egypt; the chief of *their* strength in the tabernacles of Ham:
Ps 105:23 — Israel also came into Egypt; and Jacob sojourned in the land of Ham.
Ps 105:27 — They shewed his signs among them, and wonders in the land of Ham.
Ps 106:22 — Wondrous works in the land of Ham, *and* terrible things by the Red sea.

• **Place where Chedorlaomer smote the Zuzims.**
Ge 14:5 — And in the fourteenth year came Chedorlaomer, and the kings that *were* with him, and smote the Rephaims in Ashteroth Karnaim, and the Zuzims in Ham, and the Emims in Shaveh Kiriathaim,

HAMAN

• **Prime minister of Ahasuerus.**
Est 3:1 — After these things did king Ahasuerus promote Haman the son of Hammedatha the Agagite, and advanced him, and set his seat above all the princes that *were* with him.

• **Plotted against Esther and the Jews, thwarted by Esther and Mordecai, hanged.**
Est 3:1–9:32

HAMATH

• **Called also Hemath.**

• **A city of upper Syria.**
Nu 13:21 — So they went up, and searched the land from the wilderness of Zin unto Rehob, as men come to Hamath.
Nu 34:8 — From mount Hor ye shall point out *your border* unto the entrance of Hamath; and the goings forth of the border shall be to Zedad:
Jos 13:5 — And the land of the Giblites, and all Lebanon, toward the sunrising, from Baal-gad under mount Hermon unto the entering into Hamath.
1Ki 8:65 — And at that time Solomon held a feast, and all Israel with him, a great congregation, from the entering in of Hamath unto the river of Egypt, before the LORD our God, seven days and seven days, *even* fourteen days.
Eze 47:16 — Hamath, Berothah, Sibraim, which *is* between the border of Damascus and the border of Hamath; Hazar-hatticon, which is by the coast of Hauran.

• **Inhabited by Canaanites.**
Ge 10:18 — And the Arvadite, and the Zemarite, and the Hamathite: and afterward were the families of the Canaanites spread abroad.

• **Prosperity of.**
Am 6:2 — Pass ye unto Calneh, and see; and from thence go ye to Hamath the great: then go down to Gath of the Philistines: *be they* better than these kingdoms? or their border greater than your border?

• **David receives gifts of gold and silver from Toi, king of.**
2Sa 8:9–10; 1Ch 18:9–10
1Ch 18:3 — And David smote Hadarezer king of Zobah unto Hamath, as he went to stablish his dominion by the river Euphrates.

• **Conquest of, by Jeroboam.**
2Ki 14:25 — He restored the coast of Israel from the entering of Hamath unto the sea of the plain, according to the word of the LORD God of Israel, which he spake by the hand of his servant Jonah, the son of Amittai, the prophet, which *was* of Gath-hepher.
2Ki 14:28 — Now the rest of the acts of Jeroboam, and all that he did, and his might, how he warred, and how he recovered Damascus, and Hamath, *which belonged* to Judah, for Israel, are they not written in the book of the chronicles of the kings of Israel?

• **Conquest of, by the Chaldeans.**
2Ki 25:20–21

• **Israelites taken captive to.**
Isa 11:11 — And it shall come to pass in that day, *that* the Lord shall set his hand again the second time to recover the remnant of his people, which shall be left, from Assyria, and from Egypt, and from Pathros, and from Cush, and from Elam, and from Shinar, and from Hamath, and from the islands of the sea.

• **Prophecy concerning.**
Jer 49:23 — Concerning Damascus. Hamath is confounded, and Arpad: for they have heard evil tidings: they are fainthearted; *there is* sorrow on the sea; it cannot be quiet.

• **Solomon builds store cities in.**
2Ch 8:4 — And he built Tadmor in the wilderness, and all the store cities, which he built in Hamath.

HAMATH-ZOBAH

• **A town on the border of Palestine.**

• **Subdued by Solomon.**
2Ch 8:3 — And Solomon went to Hamath-zobah, and prevailed against it.

HAMMATH

• A fortified city of Naphtali.

Jos 19:35 — And the fenced cities *are* Ziddim, Zer, and Hammath, Rakkath, and Chinnereth,

See: Hammon

See: Hammoth-Dor

HAMMEDATHA • Father of Haman.

Est 3:1 — After these things did king Ahasuerus promote Haman the son of Hammedatha the Agagite, and advanced him, and set his seat above all the princes that *were* with him.

Est 3:10 — And the king took his ring from his hand, and gave it unto Haman the son of Hammedatha the Agagite, the Jews' enemy.

Est 8:5 — And said, If it please the king, and if I have found favour in his sight, and the thing *seem* right before the king, and I *be* pleasing in his eyes, let it be written to reverse the letters devised by Haman the son of Hammedatha the Agagite, which he wrote to destroy the Jews which *are* in all the king's provinces:

Est 9:10 — The ten sons of Haman the son of Hammedatha, the enemy of the Jews, slew they; but on the spoil laid they not their hand.

Est 9:24 — Because Haman the son of Hammedatha, the Agagite, the enemy of all the Jews, had devised against the Jews to destroy them, and had cast Pur, that *is*, the lot, to consume them, and to destroy them;

HAMMELECH • Name of a man, or possibly only an appellation, meaning "the king".

Jer 36:26 — But the king commanded Jerahmeel the son of Hammelech, and Seraiah the son of Azriel, and Shelemiah the son of Abdeel, to take Baruch the scribe and Jeremiah the prophet: but the LORD hid them.

Jer 38:6 — Then took they Jeremiah, and cast him into the dungeon of Malchiah the son of Hammelech, that *was* in the court of the prison: and they let down Jeremiah with cords. And in the dungeon *there was* no water, but mire: so Jeremiah sunk in the mire.

HAMMER

1Ki 6:7 — And the house, when it was in building, was built of stone made ready before it was brought thither: so that there was neither hammer nor axe *nor* any tool of iron heard in the house, while it was in building.

Isa 41:7 — So the carpenter encouraged the goldsmith, *and* he that smootheth *with* the hammer him that smote the anvil, saying, It is ready for the sodering: and he fastened it with nails, *that* it should not be moved.

Jer 10:4 — They deck it with silver and with gold; they fasten it with nails and with hammers, that it move not.

• Figurative.

Jer 23:29 — *Is* not my word like as a fire? saith the LORD; and like a hammer *that* breaketh the rock in pieces?

Jer 50:23 — How is the hammer of the whole earth cut asunder and broken! how is Babylon become a desolation among the nations!

HAMMOLEKETH • Daughter of Machir.

1Ch 7:17–18

HAMMON

• A city of Asher.

Jos 19:28 — And Hebron, and Rehob, and Hammon, and Kanah, *even* unto great Zidon;

• A Levitical city of Naphtali.

1Ch 6:76 — And out of the tribe of Naphtali; Kedesh in Galilee with her suburbs, and Hammon with her suburbs, and Kirjathaim with her suburbs.

• Possibly identical with Hammath and Hammoth-Dor.

See: Hammath

See: Hammoth-Dor

HAMMOTH-DOR

• A city of refuge of Naphtali.

Jos 21:32 — And out of the tribe of Naphtali, Kedesh in Galilee with her suburbs, *to be* a city of refuge for the slayer; and Hammoth-dor with her suburbs, and Kartan with her suburbs; three cities.

• Possibly identical with Hammath.

Jos 19:35 — And the fenced cities *are* Ziddim, Zer, and Hammath, Rakkath, and Chinnereth,

• Called Hammon.

1Ch 6:76 — And out of the tribe of Naphtali; Kedesh in Galilee with her suburbs, and Hammon with her suburbs, and Kirjathaim with her suburbs.

HAMON-GOG • Another name for Hammonah.

Eze 39:11 — And it shall come to pass in that day, *that* I will give unto Gog a place there of graves in Israel, the valley of the passengers on the east of the sea: and it shall stop the *noses* of the passengers: and there shall they bury Gog and all his multitude: and they shall call *it* The valley of Hamon-gog.

Eze 39:15 — And the passengers *that* pass through the land, when *any* seeth a man's bone, then shall he set up a sign by it, till the buriers have buried it in the valley of Hamon-gog.

HAMONAH • Burial place of the multitudes of Gog.

Eze 39:16 — And also the name of the city *shall be* Hamonah. Thus shall they cleanse the land.

HAMOR

• Father of Shechem.

• Jacob buys ground from.

Ge 33:19 — And he bought a parcel of a field, where he had spread his tent, at the hand of the children of Hamor, Shechem's father, for an hundred pieces of money.

Jos 24:32 — And the bones of Joseph, which the children of Israel brought up out of Egypt, buried they in Shechem, in a parcel of ground which Jacob bought of the sons of Hamor the father of Shechem for an hundred pieces of silver: and it became the inheritance of the children of Joseph.

Jgs 9:28 — And Gaal the son of Ebed said, Who *is* Abimelech, and who *is* Shechem, that we should serve him? *is* not *he* the son of Jerubbaal? and Zebul his officer? serve the men of Hamor the father of Shechem: for why should we serve him?

• Murdered by the sons of Jacob.

Ge 34:26 — And they slew Hamor and Shechem his son with the edge of the sword, and took Dinah out of Shechem's house, and went out.

Ge 49:6 — O my soul, come not thou into their secret; unto their assembly, mine honour, be not thou united: for in their anger they slew a man, and in their selfwill they digged down a wall.

• Called Emmor.

Ac 7:16 — And were carried over into Sychem, and laid in the sepulchre that Abraham bought for a sum of money of the sons of Emmor *the father* of Sychem.

HAMUEL • A Simeonite.

1Ch 4:26 — And the sons of Mishma; Hamuel his son, Zacchur his son, Shimei his son.

HAMUL • Son of Pharez.

Ge 46:12 — And the sons of Judah; Er, and Onan, and Shelah, and Pharez, and Zarah: but Er and Onan died in the land of Canaan. And the sons of Pharez were Hezron and Hamul.

Nu 26:21 — And the sons of Pharez were; of Hezron, the family of the Hezronites: of Hamul, the family of the Hamulites.

1Ch 2:5 — The sons of Pharez; Hezron, and Hamul.

HAMUTAL • Mother of Jehoahaz and Zedekiah.

2Ki 23:31 — Jehoahaz *was* twenty and three years old when he began to reign; and he reigned three months in Jerusalem. And his mother's name *was* Hamutal, the daughter of Jeremiah of Libnah.

2Ki 24:18 — Zedekiah *was* twenty and one years old when he began to reign, and he reigned eleven years in Jerusalem. And his mother's name *was* Hamutal, the daughter of Jeremiah of Libnah.

Jer 52:1 — Zedekiah was one and twenty years old when he began to reign, and he reigned eleven years in Jerusalem. And his mother's name *was* Hamutal the daughter of Jeremiah of Libnah.

HANAMEEL • Cousin to Jeremiah, to whom he sold a field in Anathoth.

Jer 32:7–12

HANAN

• Son of Shashak.

1Ch 8:23 — And Abdon, and Zichri, and Hanan,

• Son of Azel.

1Ch 8:38 — And Azel had six sons, whose names *are* these, Azrikam, Bocheru, and Ishmael, and Sheariah, and Obadiah, and Hanan. All these *were* the sons of Azel.

1Ch 9:44 — And Azel had six sons, whose names *are* these, Azrikam, Bocheru, and Ishmael, and Sheariah, and Obadiah, and Hanan: these *were* the sons of Azel.

• One of David's mighty men.

1Ch 11:43 — Hanan the son of Maachah, and Joshaphat the Mithnite,

• One of the Nethinim.

Ezr 2:46 — The children of Hagab, the children of Shalmai, the children of Hanan,

Ne 7:49 — The children of Hanan, the children of Giddel, the children of Gahar,

• A Levite.

Ne 8:7 — Also Jeshua, and Bani, and Sherebiah, Jamin, Akkub, Shabbethai, Hodijah, Maaseiah, Kelita, Azariah, Jozabad, Hanan, Pelaiah, and the Levites, caused the people to understand the law: and the people *stood* in their place.

Ne 10:10 — And their brethren, Shebaniah, Hodijah, Kelita, Pelaiah, Hanan,

• Probably identical with the one mentioned in Ne 13:13.

Ne 13:13 — And I made treasurers over the treasuries, Shelemiah the priest, and Zadok the scribe, and of the Levites, Pedaiah: and next to them *was* Hanan the son of Zaccur, the son of Mattaniah: for they were counted faithful, and their office *was* to distribute unto their brethren.

• A chief who sealed the covenant with Nehemiah.

Ne 10:22 — Pelatiah, Hanan, Anaiah,

Ne 10:26 — And Ahijah, Hanan, Anan,

• An officer in the temple.

Jer 35:2–10

HANANEEL • Name of a tower forming part of the wall of Jerusalem.

Ne 3:1 — Then Eliashib the high priest rose up with his brethren the priests, and they builded the sheep gate; they sanctified it, and set up the doors of it; even unto the tower of Meah they sanctified it, unto the tower of Hananeel.

Ne 12:39 — And from above the gate of Ephraim, and above the old gate, and above the fish gate, and the tower of Hananeel, and the tower of Meah, even unto the sheep gate: and they stood still in the prison gate.

Jer 31:38 — Behold, the days come, saith the LORD, that the city shall be built to the LORD from the tower of Hananeel unto the gate of the corner.

Zec 14:10 — All the land shall be turned as a plain from Geba to Rimmon south of Jerusalem: and it shall be lifted up, and inhabited in her place, from Benjamin's gate unto the place of the first gate, unto the corner gate, and *from* the tower of Hananeel unto the king's winepresses.

HANANI

• Son of Heman.

1Ch 25:4 — Of Heman: the sons of Heman; Bukkiah, Mattaniah, Uzziel, Shebuel, and Jerimoth, Hananiah, Hanani, Eliathah, Giddalti, and Romamti-ezer, Joshbekashah, Mallothi, Hothir, *and* Mahazioth:

1Ch 25:25 — The eighteenth to Hanani, *he,* his sons, and his brethren, *were* twelve:

• A prophet who rebuked Asa, king of Judah.

2Ch 16:7 — And at that time Hanani the seer came to Asa king of Judah, and said unto him, Because thou hast relied on the king of Syria, and not relied on the LORD thy God, therefore is the host of the king of Syria escaped out of thine hand.

• Father of Jehu the prophet.

1Ki 16:1 — Then the word of the LORD came to Jehu the son of Hanani against Baasha, saying,

1Ki 16:7 — And also by the hand of the prophet Jehu the son of Hanani came the word of the LORD against Baasha, and against his house, even for all the evil that he did in the sight of the LORD, in provoking him to anger with the work of his hands, in being like the house of Jeroboam; and because he killed him.

2Ch 19:2 — And Jehu the son of Hanani the seer went out to meet him, and said to king Jehoshaphat, Shouldest thou help the ungodly, and love them that hate the LORD? therefore is wrath upon thee from before the LORD.

2Ch 20:34 — Now the rest of the acts of Jehoshaphat, first and last, behold, they *are* written in the book of Jehu the son of Hanani, who is mentioned in the book of the kings of Israel.

• Possibly identical with a prophet who rebuked Asa, king of Jedah.

• A priest.

Ezr 10:20 — And of the sons of Immer; Hanani, and Zebadiah.

• A brother of Nehemiah and keeper of the gates of Jerusalem.

Ne 1:2 — That Hanani, one of my brethren, came, he and *certain* men of Judah; and I asked them concerning the Jews that had escaped, which were left of the captivity, and concerning Jerusalem.

Ne 7:2 — That I gave my brother Hanani, and Hananiah the ruler of the palace, charge over Jerusalem: for he *was* a faithful man, and feared God above many.

• A priest and musician.

Ne 12:36 — And his brethren, Shemaiah, and Azarael, Milalai, Gilalai, Maai, Nethaneel, and Judah, Hanani, with the musical instruments of David the man of God, and Ezra the scribe before them.

HANANIAH

• Son of Heman.

1Ch 25:4 — Of Heman: the sons of Heman; Bukkiah, Mattaniah, Uzziel, Shebuel, and Jerimoth, Hananiah, Hanani, Eliathah, Giddalti, and Romamti-ezer, Joshbekashah, Mallothi, Hothir, *and* Mahazioth:

1Ch 25:23 — The sixteenth to Hananiah, *he,* his sons, and his brethren, *were* twelve:

• A captain of Uzziah's army.

2Ch 26:11 — Moreover Uzziah had an host of fighting men, that went out to war by bands, according to the number of their account by the hand of Jeiel the scribe and Maaseiah the ruler, under the hand of Hananiah, *one* of the king's captains.

• Father of Zedekiah.

Jer 36:12 — Then he went down into the king's house, into the scribe's chamber: and, lo, all the princes sat there, *even* Elishama the scribe, and Delaiah the son of Shemaiah, and Elnathan the son of Achbor, and Gemariah the son of Shaphan, and Zedekiah the son of Hananiah, and all the princes.

• A prophet of Gibeon who uttered false prophecies in the temple during the reign of Zedekiah.

Jer 28:1–17

• Grandfather of Irijah.

Jer 37:13 — And when he was in the gate of Benjamin, a captain of the ward *was* there, whose name *was* Irijah, the son of Shelemiah, the son of Hananiah; and he took Jeremiah the prophet, saying, Thou fallest away to the Chaldeans.

• Son of Shashak.

1Ch 8:24 — And Hananiah, and Elam, and Antothijah,

• Hebrew name of Shadrach.

See: Shadrach

• Son of Zerubbabel.

1Ch 3:19 — And the sons of Pedaiah *were,* Zerubbabel, and Shimei: and the sons of Zerubbabel; Meshullam, and Hananiah, and Shelomith their sister:

1Ch 3:21 — And the sons of Hananiah; Pelatiah, and Jesaiah: the sons of Rephaiah, the sons of Arnan, the sons of Obadiah, the sons of Shechaniah.

• Son of Bebai.

Ezr 10:28 — Of the sons also of Bebai; Jehohanan, Hananiah, Zabbai, *and* Athlai.

• An apothecary and priest.

Ne 3:8 — Next unto him repaired Uzziel the son of Harhaiah, of the goldsmiths. Next unto him also repaired Hananiah the son of *one of* the apothecaries, and they fortified Jerusalem unto the broad wall.

• Son of Shelemiah.

Ne 3:30 — After him repaired Hananiah the son of Shelemiah, and Hanun the sixth son of Zalaph, another piece. After him repaired Meshullam the son of Berechiah over against his chamber.

• A keeper of the gates of Jerusalem.

Ne 7:2 — That I gave my brother Hanani, and Hananiah the ruler of the palace, charge over Jerusalem: for he *was* a faithful man, and feared God above many.

• One who sealed the covenant.

Ne 10:23 — Hoshea, Hananiah, Hashub,

• **A priest in time of Jehoiakim.**

Ne 12:12 — And in the days of Joiakim were priests, the chief of the fathers: of Seraiah, Meraiah; of Jeremiah, Hananiah;

Ne 12:41 — And the priests; Eliakim, Maaseiah, Miniamin, Michaiah, Elioenai, Zechariah, *and* Hananiah, with trumpets;

HAND

• **Imposition of hands.**

Heb 6:2 — Of the doctrine of baptisms, and of laying on of hands, and of resurrection of the dead, and of eternal judgment.

• **In consecration.**

Ge 48:14 — And Israel stretched out his right hand, and laid it upon Ephraim's head, who *was* the younger, and his left hand upon Manasseh's head, guiding his hands wittingly; for Manasseh *was* the firstborn.

Ex 29:10 — And thou shalt cause a bullock to be brought before the tabernacle of the congregation: and Aaron and his sons shall put their hands upon the head of the bullock.

Ex 29:15 — Thou shalt also take one ram; and Aaron and his sons shall put their hands upon the head of the ram.

Ex 29:19 — And thou shalt take the other ram; and Aaron and his sons shall put their hands upon the head of the ram.

Le 1:4 — And he shall put his hand upon the head of the burnt offering; and it shall be accepted for him to make atonement for him.

Le 3:2 — And he shall lay his hand upon the head of his offering, and kill it *at* the door of the tabernacle of the congregation: and Aaron's sons the priests shall sprinkle the blood upon the altar round about.

Le 3:8 — And he shall lay his hand upon the head of his offering, and kill it before the tabernacle of the congregation: and Aaron's sons shall sprinkle the blood thereof round about upon the altar.

Le 3:13 — And he shall lay his hand upon the head of it, and kill it before the tabernacle of the congregation: and the sons of Aaron shall sprinkle the blood thereof upon the altar round about.

Le 4:15 — And the elders of the congregation shall lay their hands upon the head of the bullock before the LORD: and the bullock shall be killed before the LORD.

Le 4:24 — And he shall lay his hand upon the head of the goat, and kill it in the place where they kill the burnt offering before the LORD: it *is* a sin offering.

Le 4:33 — And he shall lay his hand upon the head of the sin offering, and slay it for a sin offering in the place where they kill the burnt offering

Le 16:21 — And Aaron shall lay both his hands upon the head of the live goat, and confess over him all the iniquities of the children of Israel, and all their transgressions in all their sins, putting them upon the head of the goat, and shall send *him* away by the hand of a fit man into the wilderness:

• **In ordaining the Levites.**

Nu 8:10–11

• **Joshua.**

Nu 27:18–23

Dt 34:9 — And Joshua the son of Nun was full of the spirit of wisdom; for Moses had laid his hands upon him: and the children of Israel hearkened unto him, and did as the LORD commanded Moses.

• **Timothy.**

1Ti 4:14 — Neglect not the gift that is in thee, which was given thee by prophecy, with the laying on of the hands of the presbytery.

2Ti 1:6 — Wherefore I put thee in remembrance that thou stir up the gift of God, which is in thee by the putting on of my hands.

• **In healing.**

Mk 6:5 — And he could there do no mighty work, save that he laid his hands upon a few sick folk, and healed *them.*

Mk 7:32 — And they bring unto him one that was deaf, and had an impediment in his speech; and they beseech him to put his hand upon him.

Mk 16:18 — They shall take up serpents; and if they drink any deadly thing, it shall not hurt them; they shall lay hands on the sick, and they shall recover.

Lk 4:40 — Now when the sun was setting, all they that had any sick with divers diseases brought them unto him; and he laid his hands on every one of them, and healed them.

Ac 19:6 — And when Paul had laid *his* hands upon them, the Holy Ghost came on them; and they spake with tongues, and prophesied.

Ac 19:11 — And God wrought special miracles by the hands of Paul:

• **In blessing children.**

Mt 19:13 — Then were there brought unto him little children, that he should put *his* hands on them, and pray: and the disciples rebuked them.

Mk 10:16 — And he took them up in his arms, put *his* hands upon them, and blessed them.

• **In solemnizing testimony.**

Le 24:14 — Bring forth him that hath cursed without the camp; and let all that heard *him* lay their hands upon his head, and let all the congregation stone him.

• **Lifted up in benediction.**

Le 9:22 — And Aaron lifted up his hand toward the people, and blessed them, and came down from offering of the sin offering, and the burnt offering, and peace offerings.

Lk 24:50 — And he led them out as far as to Bethany, and he lifted up his hands, and blessed them.

• **In prayer.**

➔See: Prayer, miscellany of minor subtopics; attitudes in

• **Ceremonial washing of.**

Mk 7:2–5

Mt 15:2 — Why do thy disciples transgress the tradition of the elders? for they wash not their hands when they eat bread.

➔See: Ablution

➔See: Cleanliness

• **Symbolic of righteousness.**

Job 17:9 — The righteous also shall hold on his way, and he that hath clean hands shall be stronger and stronger.

• **Washing of, a symbol of innocency.**

Dt 21:6 — And all the elders of that city, *that are* next unto the slain *man,* shall wash their hands over the heifer that is beheaded in the valley:

Mt 27:24 — When Pilate saw that he could prevail nothing, but *that* rather a tumult was made, he took water, and washed *his* hands before the multitude, saying, I am innocent of the blood of this just person: see ye *to it.*

• **Clasping of, in token of contract.**

Ezr 10:19 — And they gave their hands that they would put away their wives; and *being* guilty, *they offered* a ram of the flock for their trespass.

Pr 6:1 — My son, if thou be surety for thy friend, *if* thou hast stricken thy hand with a stranger,

Pr 17:18 — A man void of understanding striketh hands, *and* becometh surety in the presence of his friend.

La 5:6 — We have given the hand *to* the Egyptians, *and to* the Assyrians, to be satisfied with bread.

Eze 17:18 — Seeing he despised the oath by breaking the covenant, when, lo, he had given his hand, and hath done all these *things,* he shall not escape.

• **Clasping of, of friendship.**

2Ki 10:15 — And when he was departed thence, he lighted on Jehonadab the son of Rechab *coming* to meet him: and he saluted him, and said to him, Is thine heart right, as my heart *is* with thy heart? And Jehonadab answered, It is. If it be, give *me* thine hand. And he gave *him* his hand; and he took him up to him into the chariot.

Job 17:3 — Lay down now, put me in a surety with thee; who *is* he *that* will strike hands with me?

• **Right hand lifted up in swearing.**

Ge 14:22 — And Abram said to the king of Sodom, I have lift up mine hand unto the LORD, the most high God, the possessor of heaven and earth,

Ps 106:26 — Therefore he lifted up his hand against them, to overthrow them in the wilderness:

Isa 62:8 — The LORD hath sworn by his right hand, and by the arm of his strength, Surely I will no more give thy corn *to be* meat for thine enemies; and the sons of the stranger shall not drink thy wine, for the which thou hast laboured:

• **Clasping of, symbol of power.**

Isa 23:11 — He stretched out his hand over the sea, he shook the kingdoms: the LORD hath given a commandment against the merchant *city,* to destroy the strong holds thereof.

Isa 41:10 — Fear thou not; for I *am* with thee: be not dismayed; for I *am* thy God: I will strengthen thee; yea, I will help thee; yea, I will uphold thee with the right hand of my righteousness.

• **Clasping of, place of honor.**

Ps 45:9 — Kings' daughters *were* among thy honourable women: upon thy right hand did stand the queen in gold of Ophir.

Ps 80:17 — Let thy hand be upon the man of thy right hand, upon the son of man *whom* thou madest strong for thyself.

• **Figurative.**

Mt 5:30 — And if thy right hand offend thee, cut if off, and cast it from thee: for it is profitable for thee that one of thy members should perish, and not *that* thy whole body should be cast into hell.

Mt 18:8 — Wherefore if thy hand or thy foot offend thee, cut them off, and cast *them* from thee: it is better for thee to enter into life halt or maimed, rather than having two hands or two feet to be cast into everlasting fire.

Mk 9:43 — And if thy hand offend thee, cut it off: it is better for thee to enter into life maimed, than having two hands to go into hell, into the fire that never shall be quenched:

• **Anthropomorphic use of.**

• **Hand of the Lord waxed short.**

Nu 11:23 — And the LORD said unto Moses, Is the LORD'S hand waxed short? thou shalt see now whether my word shall come to pass unto thee or not.

• **Hand of the Lord is mighty.**

Jos 4:24 — That all the people of the earth might know the hand of the LORD, that it *is* mighty: that ye might fear the LORD your God for ever.

• **Hand of the Lord was heavy.**

1Sa 5:6 — But the hand of the LORD was heavy upon them of Ashdod, and he destroyed them, and smote them with emerods, *even* Ashdod and the coasts thereof.

• **Hand of the Lord against the Philistines.**

1Sa 7:13 — So the Philistines were subdued, and they came no more into the coast of Israel: and the hand of the LORD was against the Philistines all the days of Samuel.

• **Hand of the Lord on Elijah.**

1Ki 18:46 — And the hand of the LORD was on Elijah; and he girded up his loins, and ran before Ahab to the entrance of Jezreel.

• **Hand of the Lord not shortened.**

Isa 59:1 — Behold, the LORD'S hand is not shortened, that it cannot save; neither his ear heavy, that it cannot hear:

• **Hand of the Lord was with the early Christians.**

Ac 11:21 — And the hand of the Lord was with them: and a great number believed, and turned unto the Lord.

• **For extended anthropomorphisms consult concordances under the word hand.**

See: Anthropomorphisms

HANDBREADTH

• A measure, about four inches.

Ex 25:25 — And thou shalt make unto it a border of an hand breadth round about, and thou shalt make a golden crown to the border thereof round about.

1Ki 7:26 — And it *was* an hand breadth thick, and the brim thereof was wrought like the brim of a cup, with flowers of lilies: it contained two thousand baths.

2Ch 4:5 — And the thickness of it *was* an handbreadth, and the brim of it like the work of the brim of a cup, with flowers of lilies; *and* it received and held three thousand baths.

Ps 39:5 — Behold, thou hast made my days *as* an handbreadth; and mine age *is* as nothing before thee: verily every man at his best state *is* altogether vanity. Selah.

Isa 48:13 — Mine hand also hath laid the foundation of the earth, and my right hand hath spanned the heavens: *when* I call unto them, they stand up together.

Jer 52:21 — And *concerning* the pillars, the height of one pillar *was* eighteen cubits; and a fillet of twelve cubits did compass it; and the thickness thereof *was* four fingers: *it was* hollow.

Eze 40:5 — And behold a wall on the outside of the house round about, and in the man's hand a measuring reed of six cubits *long* by the cubit and an hand breadth: so he measured the breadth of the building, one reed; and the height, one reed.

Eze 40:43 — And within *were* hooks, an hand broad, fastened round about: and upon the tables *was* the flesh of the offering.

⇒See: Fingerbreadth

⇒See: Span

HANDKERCHIEF

Ac 19:12 — So that from his body were brought unto the sick handkerchiefs or aprons, and the diseases departed from them, and the evil spirits went out of them.

HANES • A place in Egypt.

Isa 30:4 — For his princes were at Zoan, and his ambassadors came to Hanes.

HANGING

• Capital punishment by.

Ge 40:19–22

Jos 8:29 — And the king of Ai he hanged on a tree until eventide: and as soon as the sun was down, Joshua commanded that they should take his carcase down from the tree, and cast it at the entering of the gate of the city, and raise thereon a great heap of stones, *that remaineth* unto this day.

2Sa 4:12 — And David commanded his young men, and they slew them, and cut off their hands and their feet, and hanged *them* up over the pool in Hebron. But they took the head of Ish-bosheth, and buried *it* in the sepulchre of Abner in Hebron.

Est 7:10 — So they hanged Haman on the gallows that he had prepared for Mordecai. Then was the king's wrath pacified.

• The curse of death by.

Dt 21:22–23

Gal 3:13 — Christ hath redeemed us from the curse of the law, being made a curse for us: for it is written, Cursed *is* every one that hangeth on a tree:

⇒See: Punishment

HANGINGS ⇒See: Curtains

HANNAH

• Mother of Samuel.

• Her trials and prayer, and promise.

1Sa 1:1–18

• Samuel born to; dedicates him to God; leaves him at the temple.

1Sa 1:19–28

• Her hymn of praise.

1Sa 2:1–10

• Visits Samuel at the temple from year to year.

1Sa 2:18–19

• Children of.

1Sa 2:20–21

HANNATHON • A city of Zebulun.

Jos 19:14 — And the border compasseth it on the north side to Hannathon: and the outgoings thereof are in the valley of Jiphthah-el:

HANNIEL

• A son of Ephod.

• Appointed by Moses to divide the land among the several tribes.

Nu 34:23 — The prince of the children of Joseph, for the tribe of the children of Manasseh, Hanniel the son of Ephod.

• A son of Ulla. Called Haniel.

1Ch 7:39 — And the sons of Ulla; Arah, and Haniel, and Rezia.

HANOCH

• Son of Midian.

Ge 25:4 — And the sons of Midian; Ephah, and Epher, and Hanoch, and Abidah, and Eldaah. All these *were* the children of Keturah.

• Called Henoch.

1Ch 1:33 — And the sons of Midian; Ephah, and Epher, and Henoch, and Abida, and Eldaah. All these *are* the sons of Keturah.

• Eldest son of Reuben.

Ge 46:9 — And the sons of Reuben; Hanoch, and Phallu, and Hezron, and Carmi.

Ex 6:14 — These *be* the heads of their fathers' houses: The sons of Reuben the firstborn of Israel; Hanoch, and Pallu, Hezron, and Carmi: these *be* the families of Reuben.

Nu 26:5 — Reuben, the eldest son of Israel: the children of Reuben; Hanoch, *of whom cometh* the family of the Hanochites: of Pallu, the family of the Palluites:

1Ch 5:3 — The sons, *I say,* of Reuben the firstborn of Israel *were,* Hanoch, and Pallu, Hezron, and Carmi.

HANUN • Successor of Nahash as king of Ammon. Dishonors David's ambassadors.

2Sa 10:1–19; 1Ch 19:1–19

HAPHRAIM • A city of Issachar.

Jos 19:19 — And Haphraim, and Shihon, and Anaharath,

HAPPINESS

- **Of the wicked.**
  - **Limited to this life.**

Ps 17:14 — From men *which are* thy hand, O LORD, from men of the world, *which have* their portion in *this* life, and whose belly thou fillest with thy hid *treasure:* they are full of children, and leave the rest of their *substance* to their babes.

Lk 16:25 — But Abraham said, Son, remember that thou in thy lifetime receivedst thy good things, and likewise Lazarus evil things: but now he is comforted, and thou art tormented.

  - **Short.**

Job 20:5 — That the triumphing of the wicked *is* short, and the joy of the hypocrite *but* for a moment?

  - **Uncertain.**

Lk 12:20 — But God said unto him, *Thou* fool, this night thy soul shall be required of thee: then whose shall those things be, which thou hast provided?

  - **Vain.**

Ecc 2:1 — I said in mine heart, Go to now, I will prove thee with mirth, therefore enjoy pleasure: and, behold, this also *is* vanity.

Ecc 7:6 — For as the crackling of thorns under a pot, so *is* the laughter of the fool: this also *is* vanity.

- **Is derived from.**
  - **Their wealth.**

Job 21:13 — They spend their days in wealth, and in a moment go down to the grave.

Ps 52:7 — Lo, *this is* the man *that* made not God his strength; but trusted in the abundance of his riches, *and* strengthened himself in his wickedness.

  - **Their power.**

Job 21:7 — Wherefore do the wicked live, become old, yea, are mighty in power?

Ps 37:35 — I have seen the wicked in great power, and spreading himself like a green bay tree.

  - **Their worldly prosperity.**

Ps 37:3–4

Ps 17:14 — From men *which are* thy hand, O LORD, from men of the world, *which have* their portion in *this* life, and whose belly thou fillest with thy hid *treasure:* they are full of children, and leave the rest of their *substance* to their babes.

Ps 37:7 — Rest in the LORD, and wait patiently for him: fret not thyself because of him who prospereth in his way, because of the man who bringeth wicked devices to pass.

  - **Their gluttony.**

Isa 22:13 — And behold joy and gladness, slaying oxen, and killing sheep, eating flesh, and drinking wine: let us eat and drink; for to morrow we shall die.

Hab 1:16 — Therefore they sacrifice unto their net, and burn incense unto their drag; because by them their portion *is* fat, and their meat plenteous.

  - **Drunkenness.**

Isa 5:11 — Woe unto them that rise up early in the morning, *that* they may follow strong drink; that continue until night, *till* wine inflame them!

Isa 56:12 — Come ye, *say they,* I will fetch wine, and we will fill ourselves with strong drink; and to morrow shall be as this day, *and* much more abundant.

  - **Vain pleasure.**

Job 21:12 — They take the timbrel and harp, and rejoice at the sound of the organ.

Isa 5:12 — And the harp, and the viol, the tabret, and pipe, and wine, are in their feasts: but they regard not the work of the LORD, neither consider the operation of his hands.

  - **Successful oppression.**

Hab 1:15 — They take up all of them with the angle, they catch them in their net, and gather them in their drag: therefore they rejoice and are glad.

- **Marred by jealousy.**

Est 5:13 — Yet all this availeth me nothing, so long as I see Mordecai the Jew sitting at the king's gate.

- **Often interrupted by judgments.**

Ps 73:18–20; Jer 25:10–11

Nu 11:33 — And while the flesh *was* yet between their teeth, ere it was chewed, the wrath of the LORD was kindled against the people, and the LORD smote the people with a very great plague.

Job 15:21 — A dreadful sound *is* in his ears: in prosperity the destroyer shall come upon him.

- **Leads to sorrow.**

Pr 14:13 — Even in laughter the heart is sorrowful; and the end of that mirth *is* heaviness.

- **Leads to recklessness.**

Isa 22:12 — And in that day did the Lord GOD of hosts call to weeping, and to mourning, and to baldness, and to girding with sackcloth:

- **Sometimes a stumbling-block to saints.**

Ps 73:3 — For I was envious at the foolish, *when* I saw the prosperity of the wicked.

Ps 73:16 — When I thought to know this, it *was* too painful for me;

Jer 12:1 — Righteous *art* thou, O LORD, when I plead with thee: yet let me talk with thee of *thy* judgments: Wherefore doth the way of the wicked prosper? *wherefore* are all they happy that deal very treacherously?

Hab 1:13 — *Thou art* of purer eyes than to behold evil, and canst not look on iniquity: wherefore lookest thou upon them that deal treacherously, *and* holdest thy tongue when the wicked devoureth *the man that is* more righteous than he?

- **Saints often permitted to see the end of.**

Ps 73:17–20

- **Envy not.**

Ps 37:1 — Fret not thyself because of evildoers, neither be thou envious against the workers of iniquity.

- **Woe against.**

Am 6:1 — Woe to them *that are* at ease in Zion, and trust in the mountain of Samaria, *which are* named chief of the nations, to whom the house of Israel came!

Lk 6:25 — Woe unto you that are full! for ye shall hunger. Woe unto you that laugh now! for ye shall mourn and weep.

- **Illustrated.**

Ps 37:35–36; Lk 12:16–20; 16:19–25

- **Exemplified.**
  - Israel.

Nu 11:33 — And while the flesh *was* yet between their teeth, ere it was chewed, the wrath of the LORD was kindled against the people, and the LORD smote the people with a very great plague.

  - **Haman.**

Est 5:9–11

  - **Belshazzar.**

Da 5:1 — Belshazzar the king made a great feast to a thousand of his lords, and drank wine before the thousand.

  - **Herod.**

Ac 12:21–23

- **Of the righteous.**

Job 5:17–27; Ps 128:1–2; Pr 3:13–18; Ecc 2:24–26; 3:12–13; Isa 12:2–3; Mt 5:3–12; 1Pe 4:12–13

Dt 33:29 — Happy *art* thou, O Israel: who *is* like unto thee, O people saved by the LORD, the shield of thy help, and who *is* the sword of thy excellency! and thine enemies shall be found liars unto thee; and thou shalt tread upon their high places.

Ps 36:8 — They shall be abundantly satisfied with the fatness of thy house; and thou shalt make them drink of the river of thy pleasures.

Ps 40:8 — I delight to do thy will, O my God: yea, thy law *is* within my heart.

Ps 63:5 — My soul shall be satisfied as *with* marrow and fatness; and my mouth shall praise *thee* with joyful lips:

Ps 133:1 — Behold, how good and how pleasant *it is* for brethren to dwell together in unity!

Ps 144:15 — Happy *is that* people, that is in such a case: *yea,* happy *is that* people, whose God *is* the LORD.

Ps 146:5 — Happy *is he* that *hath* the God of Jacob for his help, whose hope *is* in the LORD his God:

Pr 14:21 — He that despiseth his neighbour sinneth: but he that hath mercy on the poor, happy *is* he.

Pr 16:20 — He that handleth a matter wisely shall find good: and whoso trusteth in the LORD, happy *is* he.

Pr 28:14 — Happy *is* the man that feareth alway: but he that hardeneth his heart shall fall into mischief.

Pr 29:18 — Where *there is* no vision, the people perish: but he that keepeth the law, happy *is* he.

Ecc 3:22 — Wherefore I perceive that *there is* nothing better, than that a man should rejoice in his own works; for that *is* his portion: for who shall bring him to see what shall be after him?

Ro 5:2 — By whom also we have access by faith into this grace wherein we stand, and rejoice in hope of the glory of God.

2Co 12:10 — Therefore I take pleasure in infirmities, in reproaches, in necessities, in persecutions, in distresses for Christ's sake: for when I am weak, then am I strong.

Php 4:7 — And the peace of God, which passeth all understanding, shall keep your hearts and minds through Christ Jesus.

1Pe 3:14 — But and if ye suffer for righteousness' sake, happy *are ye:* and be not afraid of their terror, neither be troubled;

See: Joy

See: Peace

See: Praise

HAPPY

Ne 2:2–3; Ecc 3:1–13

Ps 42:11 — Why art thou cast down, O my soul? and why art thou disquieted within me? hope thou in God: for I shall yet praise him, *who is* the health of my countenance, and my God.

Pr 15:13 — A merry heart maketh a cheerful countenance: but by sorrow of the heart the spirit is broken.

Pr 17:22 — A merry heart doeth good *like* a medicine: but a broken spirit drieth the bones.

Ecc 7:3 — Sorrow *is* better than laughter: for by the sadness of the countenance the heart is made better.

Mt 6:16 — Moreover when ye fast, be not, as the hypocrites, of a sad countenance: for they disfigure their faces, that they may appear unto men to fast. Verily I say unto you, They have their reward.

Php 4:4 — Rejoice in the Lord alway: *and* again I say, Rejoice.

HARA

- **A place in Assyria.**
- **Israelitish captives carried to.**

1Ch 5:26 — And the God of Israel stirred up the spirit of Pul king of Assyria, and the spirit of Tilgath-pilneser king of Assyria, and he carried them away, even the Reubenites, and the Gadites, and the half tribe of Manasseh, and brought them unto Halah, and Habor, and Hara, and to the river Gozan, unto this day.

HARADAH • One of the camps of Israel.

Nu 33:24–25

HARAN

• Father of Lot and brother of Abraham.

Ge 11:26–31

• Son of Caleb.

1Ch 2:46 — And Ephah, Caleb's concubine, bare Haran, and Moza, and Gazez: and Haran begat Gazez.

• A Levite.

1Ch 23:9 — The sons of Shimei; Shelomith, and Haziel, and Haran, three. These *were* the chief of the fathers of Laadan.

• A place in Mesopotamia to which Terah and Abraham migrated.

Ge 12:4–5

Ge 11:31 — And Terah took Abram his son, and Lot the son of Haran his son's son, and Sarai his daughter in law, his son Abram's wife; and they went forth with them from Ur of the Chaldees, to go into the land of Canaan; and they came unto Haran, and dwelt there.

• Called also Charran.

Ac 7:4 — Then came he out of the land of the Chaldaeans, and dwelt in Charran: and from thence, when his father was dead, he removed him into this land, wherein ye now dwell.

• Death of Terah at.

Ge 11:32 — And the days of Terah were two hundred and five years: and Terah died in Haran.

• Abraham leaves, by divine command.

Ge 12:1–5

• Jacob flees to.

Ge 29:1–35

Ge 27:43 — Now therefore, my son, obey my voice; and arise, flee thou to Laban my brother to Haran;

Ge 28:7 — And that Jacob obeyed his father and his mother, and was gone to Padan-aram;

• Jacob returns from with Rachel and Leah.

Ge 31:17–21

• Conquest of, by king of Assyria.

2Ki 19:12 — Have the gods of the nations delivered them which my fathers have destroyed; *as* Gozan, and Haran, and Rezeph, and the children of Eden which *were* in Thelasar?

• Merchants of.

Eze 27:23 — Haran, and Canneh, and Eden, the merchants of Sheba, Asshur, *and* Chilmad, *were* thy merchants.

• Idolatry in.

Jos 24:2 — And Joshua said unto all the people, Thus saith the LORD God of Israel, Your fathers dwelt on the other side of the flood in old time, *even* Terah, the father of Abraham, and the father of Nachor: and they served other gods.

Jos 24:14 — Now therefore fear the LORD, and serve him in sincerity and in truth: and put away the gods which your fathers served on the other side of the flood, and in Egypt; and serve ye the LORD.

Isa 37:12 — Have the gods of the nations delivered them which my fathers have destroyed, *as* Gozan, and Haran, and Rezeph, and the children of Eden which *were* in Telassar?

HARBONA

• Called also Harbonah.

• A chamberlain of Ahasuerus.

Est 1:10 — On the seventh day, when the heart of the king was merry with wine, he commanded Mehuman, Biztha, Harbona, Bigtha, and Abagtha, Zethar, and Carcas, the seven chamberlains that served in the presence of Ahasuerus the king,

Est 7:9 — And Harbonah, one of the chamberlains, said before the king, Behold also, the gallows fifty cubits high, which Haman had made for Mordecai, who had spoken good for the king, standeth in the house of Haman. Then the king said, Hang him thereon.

HARE

• Forbidden as food.

Le 11:6 — And the hare, because he cheweth the cud, but divideth not the hoof; he *is* unclean unto you.

Dt 14:7 — Nevertheless these ye shall not eat of them that chew the cud, or of them that divide the cloven hoof; *as* the camel, and the hare, and the coney: for they chew the cud, but divide not the hoof; *therefore* they *are* unclean unto you.

HAREM

Est 2:13–14

Est 2:3 — And let the king appoint officers in all the provinces of his kingdom, that they may gather together all the fair young virgins unto Shushan the palace, to the house of the women unto the custody of Hege the king's chamberlain, keeper of the women; and let their things for purification be given *them:*

HAREPH • Son of Caleb.

1Ch 2:51 — Salma the father of Bethlehem, Hareph the father of Beth-gader.

HARETH • A forest in which David found refuge from Saul.

1Sa 22:5 — And the prophet Gad said unto David, Abide not in the hold; depart, and get thee into the land of Judah. Then David departed, and came into the forest of Hareth.

HARHAIAH • Father of Uzziel.

Ne 3:8 — Next unto him repaired Uzziel the son of Harhaiah, of the goldsmiths. Next unto him also repaired Hananiah the son of *one of* the apothecaries, and they fortified Jerusalem unto the broad wall.

HARHAS

• Grandfather of the husband of Huldah, the prophetess.

2Ki 22:14 — So Hilkiah the priest, and Ahikam, and Achbor, and Shaphan, and Asahiah, went unto Huldah the prophetess, the wife of Shallum the son of Tikvah, the son of Harhas, keeper of the wardrobe; (now she dwelt in Jerusalem in the college;) and they communed with her.

- **Called Hasrah.**

2Ch 34:22 — And Hilkiah, and *they* that the king *had appointed,* went to Huldah the prophetess, the wife of Shallum the son of Tikvath, the son of Hasrah, keeper of the wardrobe; (now she dwelt in Jerusalem in the college:) and they spake to her to that *effect.*

HARHUR • One of the Nethinim.

Ezr 2:51 — The children of Bakbuk, the children of Hakupha, the children of Harhur,

Ne 7:53 — The children of Bakbuk, the children of Hakupha, the children of Harhur,

HARIM

- **A priest.**

1Ch 24:8 — The third to Harim, the fourth to Seorim,

- **An Israelite whose descendants returned from Babylon.**

Ezr 2:32 — The children of Harim, three hundred and twenty.

Ezr 2:39 — The children of Harim, a thousand and seventeen.

Ezr 10:31 — And *of* the sons of Harim; Eliezer, Ishijah, Malchiah, Shemaiah, Shimeon,

Ne 7:35 — The children of Harim, three hundred and twenty.

Ne 7:42 — The children of Harim, a thousand and seventeen.

- **The men who sealed the covenant.**

Ne 10:5 — Harim, Meremoth, Obadiah,

Ne 10:27 — Malluch, Harim, Baanah.

Ne 12:15 — Of Harim, Adna; of Meraioth, Helkai;

HARIPH

- **One of the exiles.**

Ne 7:24 — The children of Hariph, an hundred and twelve.

  - **Probably the same with Jorah.**

  Ezr 2:18 — The children of Jorah, an hundred and twelve.

- **One who sealed the covenant.**

Ne 10:19 — Hariph, Anathoth, Nebai,

HARLOT

- **Shamelessness of.**

Pr 7:11–27; 9:13–18

Pr 2:16 — To deliver thee from the strange woman, *even* from the stranger *which* flattereth with her words;

- **Machinations of.**

Pr 9:14–17; Isa 23:15–16

Pr 7:10 — And, behold, there met him a woman *with* the attire of an harlot, and subtil of heart.

Hos 2:13 — And I will visit upon her the days of Baalim, wherein she burned incense to them, and she decked herself with her earrings and her jewels, and she went after her lovers, and forgat me, saith the LORD.

- **To be shunned.**

Pr 5:3–20; 7:25–27

- **Hire of, not to be received at the temple.**

Dt 23:18 — Thou shalt not bring the hire of a whore, or the price of a dog, into the house of the LORD thy God for any vow: for even both these *are* abomination unto the LORD thy God.

- **Rahab.**

Jos 2:3–6

Jos 6:17 — And the city shall be accursed, *even* it, and all that *are* therein, to the LORD: only Rahab the harlot shall live, she and all that *are* with her in the house, because she hid the messengers that we sent.

Jos 6:23 — And the young men that were spies went in, and brought Rahab, and her father, and her mother, and her brethren, and all that she had; and they brought out all her kindred, and left them without the camp of Israel.

Jos 6:25 — And Joshua saved Rahab the harlot alive, and her father's household, and all that she had; and she dwelleth in Israel *even* unto this day; because she hid the messengers, which Joshua sent to spy out Jericho.

Heb 11:31 — By faith the harlot Rahab perished not with them that believed not, when she had received the spies with peace.

See: Adultery

See: Harlotry

HARLOTRY

- **Forbidden.**

Le 19:29 — Do not prostitute thy daughter, to cause her to be a whore; lest the land fall to whoredom, and the land become full of wickedness.

Dt 23:17 — There shall be no whore of the daughters of Israel, nor a sodomite of the sons of Israel.

- **Punishment of.**

Le 21:9 — And the daughter of any priest, if she profane herself by playing the whore, she profaneth her father: she shall be burnt with fire.

See: Adultery

See: Whoredom

HAROD • A spring or well by which Gideon and his army camped.

Jgs 7:1 — Then Jerubbaal, who *is* Gideon, and all the people that *were* with him, rose up early, and pitched beside the well of Harod: so that the host of the Midianites were on the north side of them, by the hill of Moreh, in the valley.

HAROEH

- **Called also Reaiah.**
- **Son of Shobal.**

1Ch 2:52 — And Shobal the father of Kirjath-jearim had sons; Haroeh, *and* half of the Manahethites.

1Ch 4:2 — And Reaiah the son of Shobal begat Jahath; and Jahath begat Ahumai and Lahad. These *are* the families of the Zorathites.

HAROSHETH

• A town of Galilee.

• The home of Sisera.

Jgs 4:2 — And the LORD sold them into the hand of Jabin king of Canaan, that reigned in Hazor; the captain of whose host *was* Sisera, which dwelt in Harosheth of the Gentiles.

Jgs 4:13 — And Sisera gathered together all his chariots, *even* nine hundred chariots of iron, and all the people that *were* with him, from Harosheth of the Gentiles unto the river of Kishon.

Jgs 4:16 — But Barak pursued after the chariots, and after the host, unto Harosheth of the Gentiles: and all the host of Sisera fell upon the edge of the sword; *and* there was not a man left.

HARP

• A stringed instrument of music.

Isa 38:20 — The LORD *was ready* to save me: therefore we will sing my songs to the stringed instruments all the days of our life in the house of the LORD.

Eze 33:32 — And, lo, thou *art* unto them as a very lovely song of one that hath a pleasant voice, and can play well on an instrument: for they hear thy words, but they do them not.

Hab 3:19 — The LORD God *is* my strength, and he will make my feet like hinds' *feet,* and he will make me to walk upon mine high places. To the chief singer on my stringed instruments.

• With three strings.

1Sa 18:6 — And it came to pass as they came, when David was returned from the slaughter of the Philistine, that the women came out of all cities of Israel, singing and dancing, to meet king Saul, with tabrets, with joy, and with instruments of musick.

• With ten strings.

Ps 33:2 — Praise the LORD with harp: sing unto him with the psaltery *and* an instrument of ten strings.

Ps 92:3 — Upon an instrument of ten strings, and upon the psaltery; upon the harp with a solemn sound.

Ps 144:9 — I will sing a new song unto thee, O God: upon a psaltery *and* an instrument of ten strings will I sing praises unto thee.

Ps 150:4 — Praise him with the timbrel and dance: praise him with stringed instruments and organs.

• Originated with Jubal.

Ge 4:21 — And his brother's name *was* Jubal: he was the father of all such as handle the harp and organ.

• Made of almug wood.

1Ki 10:12 — And the king made of the almug trees pillars for the house of the LORD, and for the king's house, harps also and psalteries for singers: there came no such almug trees, nor were seen unto this day.

• David skillful in manipulating.

1Sa 16:16 — Let our lord now command thy servants, *which are* before thee, to seek out a man, *who is* a cunning player on an harp: and it shall come to pass, when the evil spirit from God is upon thee, that he shall play with his hand, and thou shalt be well.

1Sa 16:23 — And it came to pass, when the *evil* spirit from God was upon Saul, that David took an harp, and played with his hand: so Saul was refreshed, and was well, and the evil spirit departed from him.

• Used in worship.

1Ch 25:1–7; 2Ch 5:12–13

1Sa 10:5 — After that thou shalt come to the hill of God, where *is* the garrison of the Philistines: and it shall come to pass, when thou art come thither to the city, that thou shalt meet a company of prophets coming down from the high place with a psaltery, and a tabret, and a pipe, and a harp, before them; and they shall prophesy:

1Ch 16:5 — Asaph the chief, and next to him Zechariah, Jeiel, and Shemiramoth, and Jehiel, and Mattithiah, and Eliab, and Benaiah, and Obed-edom: and Jeiel with psalteries and with harps; but Asaph made a sound with cymbals;

2Ch 29:25 — And he set the Levites in the house of the LORD with cymbals, with psalteries, and with harps, according to the commandment of David, and of Gad the king's seer, and Nathan the prophet: for *so was* the commandment of the LORD by his prophets.

Ps 33:2 — Praise the LORD with harp: sing unto him with the psaltery *and* an instrument of ten strings.

Ps 43:4 — Then will I go unto the altar of God, unto God my exceeding joy: yea, upon the harp will I praise thee, O God my God.

Ps 49:4 — I will incline mine ear to a parable: I will open my dark saying upon the harp.

Ps 57:8 — Awake up, my glory; awake, psaltery and harp: I *myself* will awake early.

Ps 71:22 — I will also praise thee with the psaltery, *even* thy truth, O my God: unto thee will I sing with the harp, O thou Holy One of Israel.

Ps 81:2 — Take a Psalm, and bring hither the timbrel, the pleasant harp with the psaltery.

Ps 92:3 — Upon an instrument of ten strings, and upon the psaltery; upon the harp with a solemn sound.

Ps 98:5 — Sing unto the LORD with the harp; with the harp, and the voice of a Psalm.

Ps 108:2 — Awake, psaltery and harp: I *myself* will awake early.

Ps 147:7 — Sing unto the LORD with thanksgiving; sing praise upon the harp unto our God:

Ps 149:3 — Let them praise his name in the dance: let them sing praises unto him with the timbrel and harp.

Ps 150:3 — Praise him with the sound of the trumpet: praise him with the psaltery and harp.

• Used, in national jubilees, after the triumph over Goliath.

1Sa 18:6 — And it came to pass as they came, when David was returned from the slaughter of the Philistine, that the women came out of all cities of Israel, singing and dancing, to meet king Saul, with tabrets, with joy, and with instruments of musick.

• Used, in national jubilees, after the triumph over the armies of Ammon and Moab.

2Ch 20:20–29

• Used when the new walls of Jerusalem were dedicated.

Ne 12:27 — And at the dedication of the wall of Jerusalem they sought the Levites out of all their places, to bring them to Jerusalem, to keep the dedication with gladness, both with thanksgivings, and with singing, *with* cymbals, psalteries, and with harps.

Ne 12:36 — And his brethren, Shemaiah, and Azarael, Milalai, Gilalai, Maai, Nethaneel, and Judah, Hanani, with the musical instruments of David the man of God, and Ezra the scribe before them.

• Used in festivities.

Job 21:11–12

Ge 31:27 — Wherefore didst thou flee away secretly, and steal away from me; and didst not tell me, that I might have sent thee away with mirth, and with songs, with tabret, and with harp?

Isa 5:12 — And the harp, and the viol, the tabret, and pipe, and wine, are in their feasts: but they regard not the work of the LORD, neither consider the operation of his hands.

Isa 23:16 — Take an harp, go about the city, thou harlot that hast been forgotten; make sweet melody, sing many songs, that thou mayest be remembered.

Isa 24:8 — The mirth of tabrets ceaseth, the noise of them that rejoice endeth, the joy of the harp ceaseth.

Isa 30:32 — And *in* every place where the grounded staff shall pass, which the LORD shall lay upon him, *it* shall be with tabrets and harps: and in battles of shaking will he fight with it.

Eze 26:13 — And I will cause the noise of thy songs to cease; and the sound of thy harps shall be no more heard.

Rev 18:22 — And the voice of harpers, and musicians, and of pipers, and trumpeters, shall be heard no more at all in thee; and no craftsman, of whatsoever craft *he be,* shall be found any more in thee; and the sound of a millstone shall be heard no more at all in thee;

• Used in mourning.

Job 30:31 — My harp also is *turned* to mourning, and my organ into the voice of them that weep.

• Discordant.

1Co 14:7 — And even things without life giving sound, whether pipe or harp, except they give a distinction in the sounds, how shall it be known what is piped or harped?

• Hung on the willows by the captive Jews.

Ps 137:2 — We hanged our harps upon the willows in the midst thereof.

• Heard in heaven, in John's apocalyptic vision.

Rev 5:8 — And when he had taken the book, the four beasts and four *and* twenty elders fell down before the Lamb, having every one of them harps, and golden vials full of odours, which are the prayers of saints.

Rev 14:2 — And I heard a voice from heaven, as the voice of many waters, and as the voice of a great thunder: and I heard the voice of harpers harping with their harps:

Rev 15:2 — And I saw as it were a sea of glass mingled with fire: and them that had gotten the victory over the beast, and over his image, and over his mark, *and* over the number of his name, stand on the sea of glass, having the harps of God.

• Symbol used to indicate when the harp was to be introduced in the music was Neginoth.

Ps 4:1 — [To the chief Musician on Neginoth, A Psalm of David.] Hear me when I call, O God of my righteousness: thou hast enlarged me *when I was* in distress; have mercy upon me, and hear my prayer.

Ps 6:1 — [To the chief Musician on Neginoth upon Sheminith, A Psalm of David.] O LORD, rebuke me not in thine anger, neither chasten me in thy hot displeasure.

Ps 54:1 — [To the chief Musician on Neginoth, Maschil, A Psalm of David, when the Ziphims came and said to Saul, Doth not David hide himself with us?] Save me, O God, by thy name, and judge me by thy strength.

Ps 55:1 — [To the chief Musician on Neginoth, Maschil, A Psalm of David.] Give ear to my prayer, O God; and hide not thyself from my supplication.

Ps 61:1 — [To the chief Musician upon Neginah, A Psalm of David.] Hear my cry, O God; attend unto my prayer.

Ps 67:1 — [To the chief Musician on Neginoth, A Psalm or Song.] God be merciful unto us, and bless us; *and* cause his face to shine upon us; Selah.

Ps 76:1 — [To the chief Musician on Neginoth, A Psalm or Song of Asaph.] In Judah *is* God known: his name *is* great in Israel.

See: Music; instruments of

HARROW • An agricultural implement used as an instrument of torture.

2Sa 12:31 — And he brought forth the people that *were* therein, and put *them* under saws, and under harrows of iron, and under axes of iron, and made them pass through the brickkiln: and thus did he unto all the cities of the children of Ammon. So David and all the people returned unto Jerusalem.

1Ch 20:3 — And he brought out the people that *were* in it, and cut *them* with saws, and with harrows of iron, and with axes. Even so dealt David with all the cities of the children of Ammon. And David and all the people returned to Jerusalem.

HARSHA • One of the Nethinim.

Ezr 2:52 — The children of Bazluth, the children of Mehida, the children of Harsha,

Ne 7:54 — The children of Bazlith, the children of Mehida, the children of Harsha,

HART ⇾See: Deer

HARUM • A descendant of Judah.

1Ch 4:8 — And Coz begat Anub, and Zobebah, and the families of Aharhel the son of Harum.

HARUMAPH • Father of Jedaiah.

Ne 3:10 — And next unto them repaired Jedaiah the son of Harumaph, even over against his house. And next unto him repaired Hattush the son of Hashabniah.

HARUZ • Father-in-law of King Manasseh.

2Ki 21:19 — Amon *was* twenty and two years old when he began to reign, and he reigned two years in Jerusalem. And his mother's name *was* Meshullemeth, the daughter of Haruz of Jotbah.

HARVEST

• Sabbath to be observed in.

Ex 34:21 — Six days thou shalt work, but on the seventh day thou shalt rest: in earing time and in harvest thou shalt rest.

• Sabbath desecrated in.

Ne 13:15–22

• Of wheat at Pentecost, in Palestine.

Le 23:15–17

Ex 34:22 — And thou shalt observe the feast of weeks, of the firstfruits of wheat harvest, and the feast of ingathering at the year's end.

• Of wheat at Pentecost, and before vintage.

Le 26:5 — And your threshing shall reach unto the vintage, and the vintage shall reach unto the sowing time: and ye shall eat your bread to the full, and dwell in your land safely.

• Of barley, before wheat.

Ex 9:31–32

• Celebrated with joy.

Jgs 9:27 — And they went out into the fields, and gathered their vineyards, and trode *the grapes,* and made merry, and went into the house of their god, and did eat and drink, and cursed Abimelech.

Isa 9:3 — Thou hast multiplied the nation, *and* not increased the joy: they joy before thee according to the joy in harvest, *and* as *men* rejoice when they divide the spoil.

Isa 16:10 — And gladness is taken away, and joy out of the plentiful field; and in the vineyards there shall be no singing, neither shall there be shouting: the treaders shall tread out no wine in *their* presses; I have made *their vintage* shouting to cease.

Jer 48:33 — And joy and gladness is taken from the plentiful field, and from the land of Moab; and I have caused wine to fail from the winepresses: none shall tread with shouting; *their* shouting *shall be* no shouting.

• Promises of plentiful.

Joel 2:23–24

Ge 8:22 — While the earth remaineth, seedtime and harvest, and cold and heat, and summer and winter, and day and night shall not cease.

Jer 5:24 — Neither say they in their heart, Let us now fear the LORD our God, that giveth rain, both the former and the latter, in his season: he reserveth unto us the appointed weeks of the harvest.

• Figurative.

Job 24:6 — They reap *every one* his corn in the field: and they gather the vintage of the wicked.

Pr 10:5 — He that gathereth in summer *is* a wise son: *but* he that sleepeth in harvest *is* a son that causeth shame.

Jer 8:20 — The harvest is past, the summer is ended, and we are not saved.

Joel 3:13 — Put ye in the sickle, for the harvest is ripe: come, get you down; for the press is full, the fats overflow; for their wickedness *is* great.

Mt 9:37 — Then saith he unto his disciples, The harvest truly *is* plenteous, but the labourers *are* few;

Mt 13:39 — The enemy that sowed them is the devil; the harvest is the end of the world; and the reapers are the angels.

Lk 10:2 — Therefore said he unto them, The harvest truly *is* great, but the labourers *are* few: pray ye therefore the Lord of the harvest, that he would send forth labourers into his harvest.

Rev 14:15 — And another angel came out of the temple, crying with a loud voice to him that sat on the cloud, Thrust in thy sickle, and reap: for the time is come for thee to reap; for the harvest of the earth is ripe.

⇾See: First Fruits

⇾See: Gleaning

⇾See: Pentecost

⇾See: Reaping

⇾See: Tabernacles, Feast of

HASADIAH • Son of Zerubbabel.

1Ch 3:20 — And Hashubah, and Ohel, and Berechiah, and Hasadiah, Jushab-hesed, five.

HASENUAH • A Benjamite.

1Ch 9:7 — And of the sons of Benjamin; Sallu the son of Meshullam, the son of Hodaviah, the son of Hasenuah,

HASHABIAH

• Son of Amaziah, a Levite.

1Ch 6:45 — The son of Hashabiah, the son of Amaziah, the son of Hilkiah,

• Son of Jeduthun, a Levite.

1Ch 25:3 — Of Jeduthun: the sons of Jeduthun; Gedaliah, and Zeri, and Jeshaiah, Hashabiah, and Mattithiah, six, under the hands of their father Jeduthun, who prophesied with a harp, to give thanks and to praise the LORD.

1Ch 25:19 — The twelfth to Hashabiah, *he,* his sons, and his brethren, *were* twelve:

• **Son of Kemuel.**

1Ch 26:30 — *And* of the Hebronites, Hashabiah and his brethren, men of valour, a thousand and seven hundred, *were* officers among them of Israel on this side Jordan westward in all the business of the LORD, and in the service of the king.

1Ch 27:17 — Of the Levites, Hashabiah the son of Kemuel: of the Aaronites, Zadok:

• **A chief Levite.**

2Ch 35:9 — Conaniah also, and Shemaiah and Nethaneel, his brethren, and Hashabiah and Jeiel and Jozabad, chief of the Levites, gave unto the Levites for passover offerings five thousand *small cattle,* and five hundred oxen.

• **Son of Bunni.**

1Ch 9:14 — And of the Levites; Shemaiah the son of Hasshub, the son of Azrikam, the son of Hashabiah, of the sons of Merari;

Ne 11:15 — Also of the Levites: Shemaiah the son of Hashub, the son of Azrikam, the son of Hashabiah, the son of Bunni;

• **Son of Mattaniah, a Levite.**

Ne 11:22 — The overseer also of the Levites at Jerusalem *was* Uzzi the son of Bani, the son of Hashabiah, the son of Mattaniah, the son of Micha. Of the sons of Asaph, the singers *were* over the business of the house of God.

• **A chief priest who had charge of the bullion and other valuables of the temple, at Jerusalem.**

Ezr 8:24 — Then I separated twelve of the chief of the priests, Sherebiah, Hashabiah, and ten of their brethren with them,

• **Probably identical with the one mentioned in Ne 12:21.**

Ne 12:21 — Of Hilkiah, Hashabiah; of Jedaiah, Nethaneel.

• **A Merarite Levite.**

Ezr 8:19 — And Hashabiah, and with him Jeshaiah of the sons of Merari, his brethren and their sons, twenty;

• **A chief of the Levites.**

Ne 3:17 — After him repaired the Levites, Rehum the son of Bani. Next unto him repaired Hashabiah, the ruler of the half part of Keilah, in his part.

Ne 10:11 — Micha, Rehob, Hashabiah,

Ne 12:24 — And the chief of the Levites: Hashabiah, Sherebiah, and Jeshua the son of Kadmiel, with their brethren over against them, to praise *and* to give thanks, according to the commandment of David the man of God, ward over against ward.

HASHABNAH • One who sealed the covenant.

Ne 10:25 — Rehum, Hashabnah, Maaseiah,

HASHABNIAH

• **Father of Hattush.**

Ne 3:10 — And next unto them repaired Jedaiah the son of Harumaph, even over against his house. And next unto him repaired Hattush the son of Hashabniah.

• **A Levite.**

Ne 9:5 — Then the Levites, Jeshua, and Kadmiel, Bani, Hashabniah, Sherebiah, Hodijah, Shebaniah, *and* Pethahiah, said, Stand up *and* bless the LORD your God for ever and ever: and blessed be thy glorious name, which is exalted above all blessing and praise.

HASHBADANA • A companion of Ezra.

Ne 8:4 — And Ezra the scribe stood upon a pulpit of wood, which they had made for the purpose; and beside him stood Mattithiah, and Shema, and Anaiah, and Urijah, and Hilkiah, and Maaseiah, on his right hand; and on his left hand, Pedaiah, and Mishael, and Malchiah, and Hashum, and Hashbadana, Zechariah, *and* Meshullam.

HASHEM • Father of several members of David's guard.

1Ch 11:34 — The sons of Hashem the Gizonite, Jonathan the son of Shage the Hararite,

HASHMONAH • A camp of the Israelites.

Nu 33:29–30

HASHUB

• **Son of Pahath-moab.**

Ne 3:11 — Malchijah the son of Harim, and Hashub the son of Pahath-moab, repaired the other piece, and the tower of the furnaces.

• **One of the captivity who assisted in repairing the wall of Jerusalem.**

Ne 3:23 — After him repaired Benjamin and Hashub over against their house. After him repaired Azariah the son of Maaseiah the son of Ananiah by his house.

• **Head of a family.**

Ne 10:23 — Hoshea, Hananiah, Hashub,

• **Called also Hasshub a Levite.**

1Ch 9:14 — And of the Levites; Shemaiah the son of Hasshub, the son of Azrikam, the son of Hashabiah, of the sons of Merari;

Ne 11:15 — Also of the Levites: Shemaiah the son of Hashub, the son of Azrikam, the son of Hashabiah, the son of Bunni;

HASHUBAH • A descendant of King Jehoiakim.

1Ch 3:20 — And Hashubah, and Ohel, and Berechiah, and Hasadiah, Jushab-hesed, five.

HASHUM

• **Ancestor of certain Jews who returned from the captivity.**

Ezr 2:19 — The children of Hashum, two hundred twenty and three.

Ezr 10:33 — Of the sons of Hashum; Mattenai, Mattathah, Zabad, Eliphelet, Jeremai, Manasseh, *and* Shimei.

Ne 7:22 — The children of Hashum, three hundred twenty and eight.

• A priest.

Ne 8:4 — And Ezra the scribe stood upon a pulpit of wood, which they had made for the purpose; and beside him stood Mattithiah, and Shema, and Anaiah, and Urijah, and Hilkiah, and Maaseiah, on his right hand; and on his left hand, Pedaiah, and Mishael, and Malchiah, and Hashum, and Hashbadana, Zechariah, *and* Meshullam.

• A head of a family.

Ne 10:18 — Hodijah, Hashum, Bezai,

HASHUPHA ✢See: Hasupha

HASRAH ✢See: Harhas

HASTE

• In judgment, by Moses and the Israelites.

Nu 32:1–19; Jos 22:10–34

✢See: Rashness

HASUPHA

• Called also Hashupha.

• A Nethinim family.

Ezr 2:43 — The Nethinims: the children of Ziha, the children of Hasupha, the children of Tabbaoth,

Ne 7:46 — The Nethinims: the children of Ziha, the children of Hashupha, the children of Tabbaoth,

HAT ✢See: Dress

HATACH • A chamberlain in the court of Ahasuerus.

Est 4:5–6, 9–10

HATHATH • A son of Othniel.

1Ch 4:13 — And the sons of Kenaz; Othniel, and Seraiah: and the sons of Othniel; Hathath.

HATIPHA • One of the Nethinim.

Ezr 2:54 — The children of Neziah, the children of Hatipha.

Ne 7:56 — The children of Neziah, the children of Hatipha.

HATITA • A porter of the temple.

Ezr 2:42 — The children of the porters: the children of Shallum, the children of Ater, the children of Talmon, the children of Akkub, the children of Hatita, the children of Shobai, *in* all an hundred thirty and nine.

Ne 7:45 — The porters: the children of Shallum, the children of Ater, the children of Talmon, the children of Akkub, the children of Hatita, the children of Shobai, an hundred thirty and eight.

HATRED

• Against iniquity, justified.

Ps 139:21–22

Ps 97:10 — Ye that love the LORD, hate evil: he preserveth the souls of his saints; he delivereth them out of the hand of the wicked.

Ps 101:3 — I will set no wicked thing before mine eyes: I hate the work of them that turn aside; *it* shall not cleave to me.

Ps 119:104 — Through thy precepts I get understanding: therefore I hate every false way.

Ps 119:128 — Therefore I esteem all *thy* precepts *concerning* all *things to be* right; *and* I hate every false way.

Ps 119:163 — I hate and abhor lying: *but* thy law do I love.

• Of God.

Ps 5:5 — The foolish shall not stand in thy sight: thou hatest all workers of iniquity.

Ps 45:7 — Thou lovest righteousness, and hatest wickedness: therefore God, thy God, hath anointed thee with the oil of gladness above thy fellows.

Mal 2:16 — For the LORD, the God of Israel, saith that he hateth putting away: for *one* covereth violence with his garment, saith the LORD of hosts: therefore take heed to your spirit, that ye deal not treacherously.

• Scriptures relating to.

Pr 26:24–26; Mt 5:43–44; Jn 15:18–19, 23–25; Gal 5:19–20; 1Jn 3:13–15

Le 19:17 — Thou shalt not hate thy brother in thine heart: thou shalt in any wise rebuke thy neighbour, and not suffer sin upon him.

Ps 25:19 — Consider mine enemies; for they are many; and they hate me with cruel hatred.

Ps 35:19 — Let not them that are mine enemies wrongfully rejoice over me: *neither* let them wink with the eye that hate me without a cause.

Pr 10:12 — Hatred stirreth up strifes: but love covereth all sins.

Pr 10:18 — He that hideth hatred *with* lying lips, and he that uttereth a slander, *is* a fool.

Pr 15:17 — Better *is* a dinner of herbs where love is, than a stalled ox and hatred therewith.

Mt 6:15 — But if ye forgive not men their trespasses, neither will your Father forgive your trespasses.

Mt 10:22 — And ye shall be hated of all *men* for my name's sake: but he that endureth to the end shall be saved.

Jn 17:14 — I have given them thy word; and the world hath hated them, because they are not of the world, even as I am not of the world.

Eph 4:31 — Let all bitterness, and wrath, and anger, and clamour, and evil speaking, be put away from you, with all malice:

Col 3:8 — But now ye also put off all these; anger, wrath, malice, blasphemy, filthy communication out of your mouth.

1Jn 2:9 — He that saith he is in the light, and hateth his brother, is in darkness even until now.

1Jn 2:11 — But he that hateth his brother is in darkness, and walketh in darkness, and knoweth not whither he goeth, because that darkness hath blinded his eyes.

1Jn 3:10 — In this the children of God are manifest, and the children of the devil: whosoever doeth not righteousness is not of God, neither he that loveth not his brother.

1Jn 4:20 — If a man say, I love God, and hateth his brother, he is a liar: for he that loveth not his brother whom he hath seen, how can he love God whom he hath not seen?

See: Envy

See: Jealousy

See: Malice

See: Revenge

HATTIL • A returned exile.

Ezr 2:57 — The children of Shephatiah, the children of Hattil, the children of Pochereth of Zebaim, the children of Ami.

Ne 7:59 — The children of Shephatiah, the children of Hattil, the children of Pochereth of Zebaim, the children of Amon.

HATTUSH

• Son of Shemaiah.

1Ch 3:22 — And the sons of Shechaniah; Shemaiah; and the sons of Shemaiah; Hattush, and Igeal, and Bariah, and Neariah, and Shaphat, six.

• A descendant of David.

Ezr 8:2 — Of the sons of Phinehas; Gershom: of the sons of Ithamar; Daniel: of the sons of David; Hattush.

Ne 3:10 — And next unto them repaired Jedaiah the son of Harumaph, even over against his house. And next unto him repaired Hattush the son of Hashabniah.

Ne 10:4 — Hattush, Shebaniah, Malluch,

Ne 12:2 — Amariah, Malluch, Hattush,

• A priest.

Ne 12:2 — Amariah, Malluch, Hattush,

HAUGHTINESS See: Pride

HAURAN • A district probably south of Damascus and east of the Jordan.

Eze 47:16 — Hamath, Berothah, Sibraim, which *is* between the border of Damascus and the border of Hamath; Hazar-hatticon, which is by the coast of Hauran.

Eze 47:18 — And the east side ye shall measure from Hauran, and from Damascus, and from Gilead, and from the land of Israel by Jordan, from the border unto the east sea. And *this is* the east side.

HAVILAH

• Son of Cush.

Ge 10:7 — And the sons of Cush; Seba, and Havilah, and Sabtah, and Raamah, and Sabtechah: and the sons of Raamah; Sheba, and Dedan.

1Ch 1:9 — And the sons of Cush; Seba, and Havilah, and Sabta, and Raamah, and Sabtecha. And the sons of Raamah; Sheba, and Dedan.

• A son of Joktan.

Ge 10:29 — And Ophir, and Havilah, and Jobab: all these *were* the sons of Joktan.

1Ch 1:23 — And Ophir, and Havilah, and Jobab. All these *were* the sons of Joktan.

• An unknown region.

Ge 2:11 — The name of the first *is* Pison: that *is* it which compasseth the whole land of Havilah, where *there is* gold;

• A district east of Amalek.

Ge 25:18 — And they dwelt from Havilah unto Shur, that *is* before Egypt, as thou goest toward Assyria: *and* he died in the presence of all his brethren.

1Sa 15:7 — And Saul smote the Amalekites from Havilah *until* thou comest to Shur, that *is* over against Egypt.

HAVOTH-JAIR

• Called also Bashan-Havoth-Jair.

Dt 3:14 — Jair the son of Manasseh took all the country of Argob unto the coasts of Geshuri and Maachathi; and called them after his own name, Bashan-havoth-jair, unto this day.

• Certain villages east of the Jordan.

Nu 32:41 — And Jair the son of Manasseh went and took the small towns thereof, and called them Havoth-jair.

Jgs 10:4 — And he had thirty sons that rode on thirty ass colts, and they had thirty cities, which are called Havoth-jair unto this day, which *are* in the land of Gilead.

HAWK • A carnivorous and unclean bird.

Le 11:16 — And the owl, and the night hawk, and the cuckow, and the hawk after his kind,

Dt 14:15 — And the owl, and the night hawk, and the cuckow, and the hawk after his kind,

Job 39:26 — Doth the hawk fly by thy wisdom, *and* stretch her wings toward the south?

HAY

Pr 27:25 — The hay appeareth, and the tender grass sheweth itself, and herbs of the mountains are gathered.

Isa 15:6 — For the waters of Nimrim shall be desolate: for the hay is withered away, the grass faileth, there is no green thing.

1Co 3:12 — Now if any man build upon this foundation gold, silver, precious stones, wood, hay, stubble;

HAZAEL

• King of Syria.

• Anointed king by Elijah.

1Ki 19:15 — And the LORD said unto him, Go, return on thy way to the wilderness of Damascus: and when thou comest, anoint Hazael *to be* king over Syria:

• Conquests by.

2Ki 8:28–29; 10:32–33; 12:17–18; 2Ch 22:5–6

2Ki 9:14 — So Jehu the son of Jehoshaphat the son of Nimshi conspired against Joram. (Now Joram had kept Ramoth-gilead, he and all Israel, because of Hazael king of Syria.

2Ki 13:3 — And the anger of the LORD was kindled against Israel, and he delivered them into the hand of Hazael king of Syria, and into the hand of Ben-hadad the son of Hazael, all *their* days.

2Ki 13:22 — But Hazael king of Syria oppressed Israel all the days of Jehoahaz.

• Conspires against, murders, and succeeds to the throne of Ben-hadad.

2Ki 8:8–15

• Death of.

2Ki 13:24 — So Hazael king of Syria died; and Ben-hadad his son reigned in his stead.

HAZAIAH • A man of Judah.

Ne 11:5 — And Maaseiah the son of Baruch, the son of Col-hozeh, the son of Hazaiah, the son of Adaiah, the son of Joiarib, the son of Zechariah, the son of Shiloni.

HAZAR-ADDAR

• Called also Adar.

• A place on the southern boundary of Canaan.

Nu 34:4 — And your border shall turn from the south to the ascent of Akrabbim, and pass on to Zin: and the going forth thereof shall be from the south to Kadesh-barnea, and shall go on to Hazar-addar, and pass on to Azmon:

Jos 15:3 — And it went out to the south side to Maaleh-acrabbim, and passed along to Zin, and ascended up on the south side unto Kadesh-barnea, and passed along to Hezron, and went up to Adar, and fetched a compass to Karkaa:

HAZAR-ENAN • The northeast boundary point of the promised land.

Nu 34:9–10

Eze 47:17 — And the border from the sea shall be Hazar-enan, the border of Damascus, and the north northward, and the border of Hamath. And *this is* the north side.

Eze 48:1 — Now these *are* the names of the tribes. From the north end to the coast of the way of Hethlon, as one goeth to Hamath, Hazar-enan, the border of Damascus northward, to the coast of Hamath; for these are his sides east *and* west; a *portion for* Dan.

HAZAR-GADDAH • A town in the southern district of Judah.

Jos 15:27 — And Hazar-gaddah, and Heshmon, and Beth-palet,

HAZAR-HATTICON • A place on the boundary of Hauran, probably east of Damascus.

Eze 47:16 — Hamath, Berothah, Sibraim, which *is* between the border of Damascus and the border of Hamath; Hazar-hatticon, which is by the coast of Hauran.

HAZAR-SHUAL • A town in the south of Judah.

Jos 15:28 — And Hazar-shual, and Beer-sheba, and Bizjothjah,

Jos 19:3 — And Hazar-shual, and Balah, and Azem,

1Ch 4:28 — And they dwelt at Beer-sheba, and Moladah, and Hazar-shual,

Ne 11:27 — And at Hazar-shual, and at Beer-sheba, and *in* the villages thereof,

HAZAR-SUSAH

• Called also Hazar-Susim.

• A city of Judah.

Jos 19:5 — And Ziklag, and Beth-marcaboth, and Hazar-susah,

1Ch 4:31 — And at Beth-marcaboth, and Hazar-susim, and at Beth-birei, and at Shaaraim. These *were* their cities unto the reign of David.

HAZARMAVETH • Son of Joktan.

Ge 10:26 — And Joktan begat Almodad, and Sheleph, and Hazar-maveth, and Jerah,

1Ch 1:20 — And Joktan begat Almodad, and Sheleph, and Hazarmaveth, and Jerah,

HAZEL

Ge 30:37 — And Jacob took him rods of green poplar, and of the hazel and chesnut tree; and pilled white strakes in them, and made the white appear which *was* in the rods.

HAZELELPONI • Daughter of Etam.

1Ch 4:3 — And these *were of* the father of Etam; Jezreel, and Ishma, and Idbash: and the name of their sister *was* Hazelelponi:

HAZERIM • A district in the south of Canaan.

Dt 2:23 — And the Avims which dwelt in Hazerim, *even* unto Azzah, the Caphtorims, which came forth out of Caphtor, destroyed them, and dwelt in their stead.)

HAZEROTH • A station in the journeyings of the children of Israel.

Nu 33:17–18

Nu 11:35 — *And* the people journeyed from Kibroth-hattaavah unto Hazeroth; and abode at Hazeroth.

Nu 12:16 — And afterward the people removed from Hazeroth, and pitched in the wilderness of Paran.

Dt 1:1 — These *be* the words which Moses spake unto all Israel on this side Jordan in the wilderness, in the plain over against the Red *sea,* between Paran, and Tophel, and Laban, and Hazeroth, and Dizahab.

HAZEZON-TAMAR

• Called also Hazazon-Tamar.

• Ancient name of En-gedi.

Ge 14:7 — And they returned, and came to En-mishpat, which *is* Kadesh, and smote all the country of the Amalekites, and also the Amorites that dwelt in Hazezon-tamar.

2Ch 20:2 — Then there came some that told Jehoshaphat, saying, There cometh a great multitude against thee from beyond the sea on this side Syria; and, behold, they *be* Hazazon-tamar, which *is* En-gedi.

HAZIEL • A Levite.

1Ch 23:9 — The sons of Shimei; Shelomith, and Haziel, and Haran, three. These *were* the chief of the fathers of Laadan.

HAZO • A son of Nahor.

Ge 22:22 — And Chesed, and Hazo, and Pildash, and Jidlaph, and Bethuel.

HAZOR

• A fortified city of Naphtali.

Jos 11:10–11

Jos 11:1 — And it came to pass, when Jabin king of Hazor had heard *those things,* that he sent to Jobab king of Madon, and to the king of Shimron, and to the king of Achshaph,

Jos 11:13 — But *as for* the cities that stood still in their strength, Israel burned none of them, save Hazor only; *that* did Joshua burn.

Jos 12:19 — The king of Madon, one; the king of Hazor, one;

Jos 19:36 — And Adamah, and Ramah, and Hazor,

Jgs 4:2 — And the LORD sold them into the hand of Jabin king of Canaan, that reigned in Hazor; the captain of whose host *was* Sisera, which dwelt in Harosheth of the Gentiles.

Jgs 4:17 — Howbeit Sisera fled away on his feet to the tent of Jael the wife of Heber the Kenite: for *there was* peace between Jabin the king of Hazor and the house of Heber the Kenite.

1Sa 12:9 — And when they forgat the LORD their God, he sold them into the hand of Sisera, captain of the host of Hazor, and into the hand of the Philistines, and into the hand of the king of Moab, and they fought against them.

2Ki 15:29 — In the days of Pekah king of Israel came Tiglath-pileser king of Assyria, and took Ijon, and Abel-beth-maachah, and Janoah, and Kedesh, and Hazor, and Gilead, and Galilee, all the land of Naphtali, and carried them captive to Assyria.

Ne 11:33 — Hazor, Ramah, Gittaim,

• A city in the south of Judah.

Jos 15:23 — And Kedesh, and Hazor, and Ithnan,

1Ki 9:15 — And this *is* the reason of the levy which king Solomon raised; for to build the house of the LORD, and his own house, and Millo, and the wall of Jerusalem, and Hazor, and Megiddo, and Gezer.

• A place north of Jerusalem.

Ne 11:33 — Hazor, Ramah, Gittaim,

HAZOR-HADATTAH • A city of Judah.

Jos 15:25 — And Hazor, Hadattah, and Kerioth, *and* Hezron, which *is* Hazor,

HEAD

• Shaven when vows were taken.

Ac 21:24 — Them take, and purify thyself with them, and be at charges with them, that they may shave *their* heads: and all may know that those things, whereof they were informed concerning thee, are nothing; but *that* thou thyself also walkest orderly, and keepest the law.

• Diseases of.

Isa 3:17 — Therefore the LORD will smite with a scab the crown of the head of the daughters of Zion, and the LORD will discover their secret parts.

• Anointed.

Le 14:18 — And the remnant of the oil that *is* in the priest's hand he shall pour upon the head of him that is to be cleansed: and the priest shall make an atonement for him before the LORD.

Le 14:29 — And the rest of the oil that *is* in the priest's hand he shall put upon the head of him that is to be cleansed, to make an atonement for him before the LORD.

HEADBANDS

Isa 3:20 — The bonnets, and the ornaments of the legs, and the headbands, and the tablets, and the earrings,

HEALING

Jn 9:1–7; Jas 5:14–20

Ac 10:38 — How God anointed Jesus of Nazareth with the Holy Ghost and with power: who went about doing good, and healing all that were oppressed of the devil; for God was with him.

1Co 12:9 — To another faith by the same Spirit; to another the gifts of healing by the same Spirit;

1Co 12:30 — Have all the gifts of healing? do all speak with tongues? do all interpret?

HEALTH

Ac 27:34 — Wherefore I pray you to take *some* meat: for this is for your health: for there shall not an hair fall from the head of any of you.

Ro 12:1 — I beseech you therefore, brethren, by the mercies of God, that ye present your bodies a living sacrifice, holy, acceptable unto God, *which is* your reasonable service.

1Co 3:16 — Know ye not that ye are the temple of God, and *that* the Spirit of God dwelleth in you?

Eph 5:29 — For no man ever yet hated his own flesh; but nourisheth and cherisheth it, even as the Lord the church:

1Ti 4:8 — For bodily exercise profiteth little: but godliness is profitable unto all things, having promise of the life that now is, and of that which is to come.

3Jn 1:2 — Beloved, I wish above all things that thou mayest prosper and be in health, even as thy soul prospereth.

HEARERS

Eze 33:30–32; Mt 7:24–27; 13:14–15, 19–23; Lk 8:11–15; Jas 1:22–25

Lk 6:49 — But he that heareth, and doeth not, is like a man that without a foundation built an house upon the earth; against which the stream did beat vehemently, and immediately it fell; and the ruin of that house was great.

Ro 2:13 — (For not the hearers of the law *are* just before God, but the doers of the law shall be justified.

Jas 1:19 — Wherefore, my beloved brethren, let every man be swift to hear, slow to speak, slow to wrath:

HEART

• Seat of the affections.

• Renewed.

Dt 30:6 — And the LORD thy God will circumcise thine heart, and the heart of thy seed, to love the LORD thy God with all thine heart, and with all thy soul, that thou mayest live.

Ps 51:10 — Create in me a clean heart, O God; and renew a right spirit within me.

Eze 11:19 — And I will give them one heart, and I will put a new spirit within you; and I will take the stony heart out of their flesh, and will give them an heart of flesh:

Eze 18:31 — Cast away from you all your transgressions, whereby ye have transgressed; and make you a new heart and a new spirit: for why will ye die, O house of Israel?

Eze 36:26 — A new heart also will I give you, and a new spirit will I put within you: and I will take away the stony heart out of your flesh, and I will give you an heart of flesh.

Ro 2:29 — But he *is* a Jew, which is one inwardly; and circumcision *is that* of the heart, in the spirit, *and* not in the letter; whose praise *is* not of men, but of God.

Eph 4:23 — And be renewed in the spirit of your mind;

Col 3:10 — And have put on the new *man,* which is renewed in knowledge after the image of him that created him:

• Regenerated.

Jn 3:3 — Jesus answered and said unto him, Verily, verily, I say unto thee, Except a man be born again, he cannot see the kingdom of God.

Jn 3:7 — Marvel not that I said unto thee, Ye must be born again.

• Graciously affected of God.

1Sa 10:26 — And Saul also went home to Gibeah; and there went with him a band of men, whose hearts God had touched.

1Ch 29:18 — O LORD God of Abraham, Isaac, and of Israel, our fathers, keep this for ever in the imagination of the thoughts of the heart of thy people, and prepare their heart unto thee:

Ezr 6:22 — And kept the feast of unleavened bread seven days with joy: for the LORD had made them joyful, and turned the heart of the king of Assyria unto them, to strengthen their hands in the work of the house of God, the God of Israel.

Ezr 7:27 — Blessed *be* the LORD God of our fathers, which hath put *such a thing* as this in the king's heart, to beautify the house of the LORD which *is* in Jerusalem:

Pr 16:1 — The preparations of the heart in man, and the answer of the tongue, *is* from the LORD.

Pr 21:1 — The king's heart *is* in the hand of the LORD, *as* the rivers of water: he turneth it whithersoever he will.

Jer 20:9 — Then I said, I will not make mention of him, nor speak any more in his name. But *his word* was in mine heart as a burning fire shut up in my bones, and I was weary with forbearing, and I could not *stay.*

Ac 16:14 — And a certain woman named Lydia, a seller of purple, of the city of Thyatira, which worshipped God, heard *us:* whose heart the Lord opened, that she attended unto the things which were spoken of Paul.

• Strengthened.

Ps 27:14 — Wait on the LORD: be of good courage, and he shall strengthen thine heart: wait, I say, on the LORD.

Ps 112:8 — His heart *is* established, he shall not be afraid, until he see *his desire* upon his enemies.

1Th 3:13 — To the end he may stablish your hearts unblameable in holiness before God, even our Father, at the coming of our Lord Jesus Christ with all his saints.

• Enlightened.

2Co 4:6 — For God, who commanded the light to shine out of darkness, hath shined in our hearts, to *give* the light of the knowledge of the glory of God in the face of Jesus Christ.

• Tried.

1Ch 29:17 — I know also, my God, that thou triest the heart, and hast pleasure in uprightness. As for me, in the uprightness of mine heart I have willingly offered all these things: and now have I seen with joy thy people, which are present here, to offer willingly unto thee.

Ps 7:9 — Oh let the wickedness of the wicked come to an end; but establish the just: for the righteous God trieth the hearts and reins.

Ps 26:2 — Examine me, O LORD, and prove me; try my reins and my heart.

Pr 17:3 — The fining pot *is* for silver, and the furnace for gold: but the LORD trieth the hearts.

Jer 11:20 — But, O LORD of hosts, that judgest righteously, that triest the reins and the heart, let me see thy vengeance on them: for unto thee have I revealed my cause.

Jer 12:3 — But thou, O LORD, knowest me: thou hast seen me, and tried mine heart toward thee: pull them out like sheep for the slaughter, and prepare them for the day of slaughter.

Jer 20:12 — But, O LORD of hosts, that triest the righteous, *and* seest the reins and the heart, let me see thy vengeance on them: for unto thee have I opened my cause.

1Th 2:4 — But as we were allowed of God to be put in trust with the gospel, even so we speak; not as pleasing men, but God, which trieth our hearts.

Heb 11:17 — By faith Abraham, when he was tried, offered up Isaac: and he that had received the promises offered up his only begotten *son,*

Rev 2:2 — I know thy works, and thy labour, and thy patience, and how thou canst not bear them which are evil: and thou hast tried them which say they are apostles, and are not, and hast found them liars:

Rev 2:10 — Fear none of those things which thou shalt suffer: behold, the devil shall cast *some* of you into prison, that ye may be tried; and ye shall have tribulation ten days: be thou faithful unto death, and I will give thee a crown of life.

• It should render to God obedience.

Dt 10:12 — And now, Israel, what doth the LORD thy God require of thee, but to fear the LORD thy God, to walk in all his ways, and to love him, and to serve the LORD thy God with all thy heart and with all thy soul,

Dt 11:13 — And it shall come to pass, if ye shall hearken diligently unto my commandments which I command you this day, to love the LORD your God, and to serve him with all your heart and with all your soul,

Dt 26:16 — This day the LORD thy God hath commanded thee to do these statutes and judgments: thou shalt therefore keep and do them with all thine heart, and with all thy soul.

1Ki 2:4 — That the LORD may continue his word which he spake concerning me, saying, If thy children take heed to their way, to walk before me in truth with all their heart and with all their soul, there shall not fail thee (said he) a man on the throne of Israel.

Ps 119:1 — Blessed *are* the undefiled in the way, who walk in the law of the LORD.

Ps 119:12 — Blessed *art* thou, O LORD: teach me thy statutes.

Eph 6:6 — Not with eyeservice, as menpleasers; but as the servants of Christ, doing the will of God from the heart;

• It should render to God faith.

Ps 27:3 — Though an host should encamp against me, my heart shall not fear: though war should rise against me, in this *will* I *be* confident.

Ps 112:7 — He shall not be afraid of evil tidings: his heart is fixed, trusting in the LORD.

Ac 8:37 — And Philip said, If thou believest with all thine heart, thou mayest. And he answered and said, I believe that Jesus Christ is the Son of God.

Ro 6:17 — But God be thanked, that ye were the servants of sin, but ye have obeyed from the heart that form of doctrine which was delivered you.

Ro 10:10 — For with the heart man believeth unto righteousness; and with the mouth confession is made unto salvation.

• It should render to God trust.

Pr 3:5 — Trust in the LORD with all thine heart; and lean not unto thine own understanding.

• It should render to God love.

Mt 22:37 — Jesus said unto him, Thou shalt love the Lord thy God with all thy heart, and with all thy soul, and with all thy mind.

• It should render to God fear.

Ps 119:161 — Princes have persecuted me without a cause: but my heart standeth in awe of thy word.

Jer 32:40 — And I will make an everlasting covenant with them, that I will not turn away from them, to do them good; but I will put my fear in their hearts, that they shall not depart from me.

• It should render to God fidelity.

Ne 9:8 — And foundest his heart faithful before thee, and madest a covenant with him to give the land of the Canaanites, the Hittites, the Amorites, and the Perizzites, and the Jebusites, and the Girgashites, to give *it, I say,* to his seed, and hast performed thy words; for thou *art* righteous:

• It should render to God zeal.

2Ch 17:16 — And next him *was* Amasiah the son of Zichri, who willingly offered himself unto the LORD; and with him two hundred thousand mighty men of valour.

Jer 20:9 — Then I said, I will not make mention of him, nor speak any more in his name. But *his word* was in mine heart as a burning fire shut up in my bones, and I was weary with forbearing, and I could not *stay.*

• It should seek God.

2Ch 19:3 — Nevertheless there are good things found in thee, in that thou hast taken away the groves out of the land, and hast prepared thine heart to seek God.

2Ch 30:19 — *That* prepareth his heart to seek God, the LORD God of his fathers, though *he be* not *cleansed* according to the purification of the sanctuary.

Ezr 7:10 — For Ezra had prepared his heart to seek the law of the LORD, and to do *it,* and to teach in Israel statutes and judgments.

Ps 10:17 — LORD, thou hast heard the desire of the humble: thou wilt prepare their heart, thou wilt cause thine ear to hear:

Ps 84:2 — My soul longeth, yea, even fainteth for the courts of the LORD: my heart and my flesh crieth out for the living God.

• It should be joyful.

1Sa 2:1 — And Hannah prayed, and said, My heart rejoiceth in the LORD, mine horn is exalted in the LORD: my mouth is enlarged over mine enemies; because I rejoice in thy salvation.

Ps 4:7 — Thou hast put gladness in my heart, more than in the time *that* their corn and their wine increased.

Ps 97:11 — Light is sown for the righteous, and gladness for the upright in heart.

Isa 65:14 — Behold, my servants shall sing for joy of heart, but ye shall cry for sorrow of heart, and shall howl for vexation of spirit.

Zec 10:7 — And *they of* Ephraim shall be like a mighty *man,* and their heart shall rejoice as through wine: yea, their children shall see *it,* and be glad; their heart shall rejoice in the LORD.

• It should be perfect.

1Ki 8:61 — Let your heart therefore be perfect with the LORD our God, to walk in his statutes, and to keep his commandments, as at this day.

Ps 101:2 — I will behave myself wisely in a perfect way. O when wilt thou come unto me? I will walk within my house with a perfect heart.

• It should be upright.

Ps 97:11 — Light is sown for the righteous, and gladness for the upright in heart.

Ps 125:4 — Do good, O LORD, unto *those that be* good, and *to them that are* upright in their hearts.

• It should be clean.

Ps 51:10 — Create in me a clean heart, O God; and renew a right spirit within me.

Ps 73:1 — Truly God *is* good to Israel, *even* to such as are of a clean heart.

• It should be pure.

Ps 24:4 — He that hath clean hands, and a pure heart; who hath not lifted up his soul unto vanity, nor sworn deceitfully.

Pr 22:11 — He that loveth pureness of heart, *for* the grace of his lips the king *shall be* his friend.

Mt 5:8 — Blessed *are* the pure in heart: for they shall see God.

1Ti 1:5 — Now the end of the commandment is charity out of a pure heart, and *of* a good conscience, and *of* faith unfeigned:

2Ti 2:22 — Flee also youthful lusts: but follow righteousness, faith, charity, peace, with them that call on the Lord out of a pure heart.

Jas 4:8 — Draw nigh to God, and he will draw nigh to you. Cleanse *your* hands, *ye* sinners; and purify *your* hearts, *ye* double minded.

1Pe 1:22 — Seeing ye have purified your souls in obeying the truth through the Spirit unto unfeigned love of the brethren, *see that ye* love one another with a pure heart fervently:

• It should be sincere.

Lk 8:15 — But that on the good ground are they, which in an honest and good heart, having heard the word, keep *it*, and bring forth fruit with patience.

Ac 2:46 — And they, continuing daily with one accord in the temple, and breaking bread from house to house, did eat their meat with gladness and singleness of heart,

Eph 6:5 — Servants, be obedient to them that are *your* masters according to the flesh, with fear and trembling, in singleness of your heart, as unto Christ;

Col 3:22 — Servants, obey in all things *your* masters according to the flesh; not with eyeservice, as menpleasers; but in singleness of heart, fearing God:

Heb 10:22 — Let us draw near with a true heart in full assurance of faith, having our hearts sprinkled from an evil conscience, and our bodies washed with pure water.

• It should be repentant.

Dt 30:2 — And shalt return unto the LORD thy God, and shalt obey his voice according to all that I command thee this day, thou and thy children, with all thine heart, and with all thy soul;

Ps 34:18 — The LORD *is* nigh unto them that are of a broken heart; and saveth such as be of a contrite spirit.

Ps 51:17 — The sacrifices of God *are* a broken spirit: a broken and a contrite heart, O God, thou wilt not despise.

• It should be devout.

1Sa 1:13 — Now Hannah, she spake in her heart; only her lips moved, but her voice was not heard: therefore Eli thought she had been drunken.

Ps 4:4 — Stand in awe, and sin not: commune with your own heart upon your bed, and be still. Selah.

Ps 9:1 — I will praise *thee*, O LORD, with my whole heart; I will shew forth all thy marvellous works.

Ps 27:8 — *When thou saidst,* Seek ye my face; my heart said unto thee, Thy face, LORD, will I seek.

Ps 77:6 — I call to remembrance my song in the night: I commune with mine own heart: and my spirit made diligent search.

Ps 119:10 — With my whole heart have I sought thee: O let me not wander from thy commandments.

Ps 119:69 — The proud have forged a lie against me: *but* I will keep thy precepts with *my* whole heart.

Ps 119:145 — I cried with *my* whole heart; hear me, O LORD: I will keep thy statutes.

• It should be wise.

1Ki 3:9 — Give therefore thy servant an understanding heart to judge thy people, that I may discern between good and bad: for who is able to judge this thy so great a people?

1Ki 3:12 — Behold, I have done according to thy words: lo, I have given thee a wise and an understanding heart; so that there was none like thee before thee, neither after thee shall any arise like unto thee.

1Ki 4:29 — And God gave Solomon wisdom and understanding exceeding much, and largeness of heart, even as the sand that *is* on the sea shore.

Job 9:4 — *He is* wise in heart, and mighty in strength: who hath hardened *himself* against him, and hath prospered?

Pr 8:10 — Receive my instruction, and not silver; and knowledge rather than choice gold.

Pr 10:8 — The wise in heart will receive commandments: but a prating fool shall fall.

Pr 11:29 — He that troubleth his own house shall inherit the wind: and the fool *shall be* servant to the wise of heart.

Pr 14:33 — Wisdom resteth in the heart of him that hath understanding: but *that which is* in the midst of fools is made known.

Pr 23:15 — My son, if thine heart be wise, my heart shall rejoice, even mine.

• It should be tender.

1Sa 24:5 — And it came to pass afterward, that David's heart smote him, because he had cut off Saul's skirt.

2Ki 22:19 — Because thine heart was tender, and thou hast humbled thyself before the LORD, when thou heardest what I spake against this place, and against the inhabitants thereof, that they should become a desolation and a curse, and hast rent thy clothes, and wept before me; I also have heard *thee,* saith the LORD.

Job 23:16 — For God maketh my heart soft, and the Almighty troubleth me:

Ps 22:14 — I am poured out like water, and all my bones are out of joint: my heart is like wax; it is melted in the midst of my bowels.

Eph 4:32 — And be ye kind one to another, tenderhearted, forgiving one another, even as God for Christ's sake hath forgiven you.

• It should be holy.

Ps 66:18 — If I regard iniquity in my heart, the Lord will not hear *me:*

1Pe 3:15 — But sanctify the Lord God in your hearts: and *be* ready always to *give* an answer to every man that asketh you a reason of the hope that is in you with meekness and fear:

• It should be compassionate.

Jer 4:19 — My bowels, my bowels! I am pained at my very heart; my heart maketh a noise in me; I cannot hold my peace, because thou hast heard, O my soul, the sound of the trump, the alarm of war.

La 3:51 — Mine eye affecteth mine heart because of all the daughters of my city.

• It should be lowly.

Mt 11:29 — Take my yoke upon you, and learn of me; for I am meek and lowly in heart: and ye shall find rest unto your souls.

• The unregenerate.

• Is full of iniquity.

Ge 6:5 — And GOD saw that the wickedness of man *was* great in the earth, and *that* every imagination of the thoughts of his heart *was* only evil continually.

Ge 8:21 — And the LORD smelled a sweet savour; and the LORD said in his heart, I will not again curse the ground any more for man's sake; for the imagination of man's heart *is* evil from his youth; neither will I again smite any more every thing living, as I have done.

1Sa 17:28 — And Eliab his eldest brother heard when he spake unto the men; and Eliab's anger was kindled against David, and he said, Why camest thou down hither? and with whom hast thou left those few sheep in the wilderness? I know thy pride, and the naughtiness of thine heart; for thou art come down that thou mightest see the battle.

Pr 6:14 — Frowardness *is* in his heart, he deviseth mischief continually; he soweth discord.

Pr 6:18 — An heart that deviseth wicked imaginations, feet that be swift in running to mischief,

Pr 11:20 — They that are of a froward heart *are* abomination to the LORD: but *such as are* upright in *their* way *are* his delight.

Ecc 8:11 — Because sentence against an evil work is not executed speedily, therefore the heart of the sons of men is fully set in them to do evil.

Ecc 9:3 — This *is* an evil among all *things* that are done under the sun, that *there is* one event unto all: yea, also the heart of the sons of men is full of evil, and madness is in their heart while they live, and after that *they go* to the dead.

Jer 4:14 — O Jerusalem, wash thine heart from wickedness, that thou mayest be saved. How long shall thy vain thoughts lodge within thee?

Jer 4:18 — Thy way and thy doings have procured these *things* unto thee; this *is* thy wickedness, because it is bitter, because it reacheth unto thine heart.

Jer 17:9 — The heart *is* deceitful above all *things,* and desperately wicked: who can know it?

Ro 1:21 — Because that, when they knew God, they glorified *him* not as God, neither were thankful; but became vain in their imaginations, and their foolish heart was darkened.

• Loves evil.

Dt 29:18 — Lest there should be among you man, or woman, or family, or tribe, whose heart turneth away this day from the LORD our God, to go *and* serve the gods of these nations; lest there should be among you a root that beareth gall and wormwood;

Ps 95:10 — Forty years long was I grieved with *this* generation, and said, It *is* a people that do err in their heart, and they have not known my ways:

Jer 17:5 — Thus saith the LORD; Cursed be the man that trusteth in man, and maketh flesh his arm, and whose heart departeth from the LORD.

• Is a fountain of evil.

Mt 12:34–35

Mk 7:21 — For from within, out of the heart of men, proceed evil thoughts, adulteries, fornications, murders,

See: Depravity of Man

• Is wayward.

2Ch 12:14 — And he did evil, because he prepared not his heart to seek the LORD.

Ps 101:4 — A froward heart shall depart from me: I will not know a wicked *person.*

Pr 6:14 — Frowardness *is* in his heart, he deviseth mischief continually; he soweth discord.

Pr 11:20 — They that are of a froward heart *are* abomination to the LORD: but *such as are* upright in *their* way *are* his delight.

Pr 12:8 — A man shall be commended according to his wisdom: but he that is of a perverse heart shall be despised.

Pr 17:20 — He that hath a froward heart findeth no good: and he that hath a perverse tongue falleth into mischief.

Jer 5:23 — But this people hath a revolting and a rebellious heart; they are revolted and gone.

Heb 3:10 — Wherefore I was grieved with that generation, and said, They do alway err in *their* heart; and they have not known my ways.

• Is blind.

Ro 1:21 — Because that, when they knew God, they glorified *him* not as God, neither were thankful; but became vain in their imaginations, and their foolish heart was darkened.

Eph 4:18 — Having the understanding darkened, being alienated from the life of God through the ignorance that is in them, because of the blindness of their heart:

✦See: Blindness; spiritual

• Is double.

1Ch 12:33 — Of Zebulun, such as went forth to battle, expert in war, with all instruments of war, fifty thousand, which could keep rank: *they were* not of double heart.

Ps 12:2 — They speak vanity every one with his neighbour: *with* flattering lips *and* with a double heart do they speak.

Pr 28:14 — Happy *is* the man that feareth alway: but he that hardeneth his heart shall fall into mischief.

Isa 9:9 — And all the people shall know, *even* Ephraim and the inhabitant of Samaria, that say in the pride and stoutness of heart,

Isa 10:12 — Wherefore it shall come to pass, *that* when the Lord hath performed his whole work upon mount Zion and on Jerusalem, I will punish the fruit of the stout heart of the king of Assyria, and the glory of his high looks.

Isa 46:12 — Hearken unto me, ye stouthearted, that *are* far from righteousness:

Hos 10:2 — Their heart is divided; now shall they be found faulty: he shall break down their altars, he shall spoil their images.

Jas 1:6 — But let him ask in faith, nothing wavering. For he that wavereth is like a wave of the sea driven with the wind and tossed.

Jas 1:8 — A double minded man *is* unstable in all his ways.

✦See: Instability

• Is hard.

Ps 76:5 — The stouthearted are spoiled, they have slept their sleep: and none of the men of might have found their hands.

Eze 2:4 — For *they are* impudent children and stiffhearted. I do send thee unto them; and thou shalt say unto them, Thus saith the Lord GOD.

Eze 3:7 — But the house of Israel will not hearken unto thee; for they will not hearken unto me: for all the house of Israel *are* impudent and hardhearted.

Eze 11:19 — And I will give them one heart, and I will put a new spirit within you; and I will take the stony heart out of their flesh, and will give them an heart of flesh:

Eze 36:26 — A new heart also will I give you, and a new spirit will I put within you: and I will take away the stony heart out of your flesh, and I will give you an heart of flesh.

Mk 6:52 — For they considered not *the miracle* of the loaves: for their heart was hardened.

Mk 10:5 — And Jesus answered and said unto them, For the hardness of your heart he wrote you this precept.

Mk 16:14 — Afterward he appeared unto the eleven as they sat at meat, and upbraided them with their unbelief and hardness of heart, because they believed not them which had seen him after he was risen.

Jn 12:40 — He hath blinded their eyes, and hardened their heart; that they should not see with *their* eyes, nor understand with *their* heart, and be converted, and I should heal them.

Ro 1:21 — Because that, when they knew God, they glorified *him* not as God, neither were thankful; but became vain in their imaginations, and their foolish heart was darkened.

Ro 2:5 — But after thy hardness and impenitent heart treasurest up unto thyself wrath against the day of wrath and revelation of the righteous judgment of God;

✦See: Impenitence

✦See: Obduracy

• Is deceitful.

Jer 17:9 — The heart *is* deceitful above all *things*, and desperately wicked: who can know it?

• Is proud.

2Ki 14:10 — Thou hast indeed smitten Edom, and thine heart hath lifted thee up: glory *of this,* and tarry at home: for why shouldest thou meddle to *thy* hurt, that thou shouldest fall, *even* thou, and Judah with thee?

2Ch 25:19 — Thou sayest, Lo, thou hast smitten the Edomites; and thine heart lifteth thee up to boast: abide now at home; why shouldest thou meddle to *thine* hurt, that thou shouldest fall, *even* thou, and Judah with thee?

Ps 101:5 — Whoso privily slandereth his neighbour, him will I cut off: him that hath an high look and a proud heart will not I suffer.

Pr 18:12 — Before destruction the heart of man is haughty, and before honour *is* humility.

Pr 28:25 — He that is of a proud heart stirreth up strife: but he that putteth his trust in the LORD shall be made fat.

Jer 48:29 — We have heard the pride of Moab, (he is exceeding proud) his loftiness, and his arrogancy, and his pride, and the haughtiness of his heart.

Jer 49:16 — Thy terribleness hath deceived thee, *and* the pride of thine heart, O thou that dwellest in the clefts of the rock, that holdest the height of the hill: though thou shouldest make thy nest as high as the eagle, I will bring thee down from thence, saith the LORD.

✦See: Pride

• Is subtle.

Pr 7:10 — And, behold, there met him a woman *with* the attire of an harlot, and subtil of heart.

✦See: Hypocrisy

• Is sensual.

Eze 6:9 — And they that escape of you shall remember me among the nations whither they shall be carried captives, because I am broken with their whorish heart, which hath departed from me, and with their eyes, which go a whoring after their idols: and they shall lothe themselves for the evils which they have committed in all their abominations.

Hos 13:6 — According to their pasture, so were they filled; they were filled, and their heart was exalted; therefore have they forgotten me.

Ro 8:7 — Because the carnal mind *is* enmity against God: for it is not subject to the law of God, neither indeed can be.

See: Lasciviousness

- **Is worldly.**

Ac 8:21–22

2Ch 26:16 — But when he was strong, his heart was lifted up to *his* destruction: for he transgressed against the LORD his God, and went into the temple of the LORD to burn incense upon the altar of incense.

Da 5:20 — But when his heart was lifted up, and his mind hardened in pride, he was deposed from his kingly throne, and they took his glory from him:

- **Is judicially hardened.**

Ac 28:26–27

Ex 4:21 — And the LORD said unto Moses, When thou goest to return into Egypt, see that thou do all those wonders before Pharaoh, which I have put in thine hand: but I will harden his heart, that he shall not let the people go.

Jos 11:20 — For it was of the LORD to harden their hearts, that they should come against Israel in battle, that he might destroy them utterly, *and* that they might have no favour, but that he might destroy them, as the LORD commanded Moses.

Isa 6:10 — Make the heart of this people fat, and make their ears heavy, and shut their eyes; lest they see with their eyes, and hear with their ears, and understand with their heart, and convert, and be healed.

- **Is malicious.**

Ps 28:3 — Draw me not away with the wicked, and with the workers of iniquity, which speak peace to their neighbours, but mischief *is* in their hearts.

Ps 140:2 — Which imagine mischiefs in *their* heart; continually are they gathered together *for* war.

Pr 24:2 — For their heart studieth destruction, and their lips talk of mischief.

Ecc 7:26 — And I find more bitter than death the woman, whose heart *is* snares and nets, *and* her hands *as* bands: whoso pleaseth God shall escape from her; but the sinner shall be taken by her.

Eze 25:15 — Thus saith the Lord GOD; Because the Philistines have dealt by revenge, and have taken vengeance with a despiteful heart, to destroy *it* for the old hatred;

See: Malice

- **Is impenitent.**

Ro 2:5 — But after thy hardness and impenitent heart treasurest up unto thyself wrath against the day of wrath and revelation of the righteous judgment of God;

See: Impenitence

- **Is diabolical.**

Jn 13:2 — And supper being ended, the devil having now put into the heart of Judas Iscariot, Simon's *son,* to betray him;

Ac 5:3 — But Peter said, Ananias, why hath Satan filled thine heart to lie to the Holy Ghost, and to keep back *part* of the price of the land?

- **Is covetous.**

Jer 22:17 — But thine eyes and thine heart *are* not but for thy covetousness, and for to shed innocent blood, and for oppression, and for violence, to do *it.*

2Pe 2:14 — Having eyes full of adultery, and that cannot cease from sin; beguiling unstable souls: an heart they have exercised with covetous practices; cursed children:

See: Covetousness

- **Is foolish.**

Pr 12:23 — A prudent man concealeth knowledge: but the heart of fools proclaimeth foolishness.

Pr 22:15 — Foolishness *is* bound in the heart of a child; *but* the rod of correction shall drive it far from him.

Ecc 9:3 — This *is* an evil among all *things* that are done under the sun, that *there is* one event unto all: yea, also the heart of the sons of men is full of evil, and madness is in their heart while they live, and after that *they go* to the dead.

- **Unclassified scriptures descriptive of the seat of the affections.**

Dt 6:5–6; Pr 15:13–15; Jer 17:9–10; Mt 15:18–20; Ro 2:14–16

Dt 5:29 — O that there were such an heart in them, that they would fear me, and keep all my commandments always, that it might be well with them, and with their children for ever!

1Sa 16:7 — But the LORD said unto Samuel, Look not on his countenance, or on the height of his stature; because I have refused him: for *the LORD seeth* not as man seeth; for man looketh on the outward appearance, but the LORD looketh on the heart.

1Ch 28:9 — And thou, Solomon my son, know thou the God of thy father, and serve him with a perfect heart and with a willing mind: for the LORD searcheth all hearts, and understandeth all the imaginations of the thoughts: if thou seek him, he will be found of thee; but if thou forsake him, he will cast thee off for ever.

2Ch 12:14 — And he did evil, because he prepared not his heart to seek the LORD.

Ps 22:26 — The meek shall eat and be satisfied: they shall praise the LORD that seek him: your heart shall live for ever.

Ps 34:18 — The LORD *is* nigh unto them that are of a broken heart; and saveth such as be of a contrite spirit.

Ps 51:10 — Create in me a clean heart, O God; and renew a right spirit within me.

Ps 51:17 — The sacrifices of God *are* a broken spirit: a broken and a contrite heart, O God, thou wilt not despise.

Ps 57:7 — My heart is fixed, O God, my heart is fixed: I will sing and give praise.

Ps 112:7 — He shall not be afraid of evil tidings: his heart is fixed, trusting in the LORD.

Pr 4:23 — Keep thy heart with all diligence; for out of it *are* the issues of life.

Pr 14:30 — A sound heart *is* the life of the flesh: but envy the rottenness of the bones.

Pr 16:1 — The preparations of the heart in man, and the answer of the tongue, *is* from the LORD.

Pr 20:9 — Who can say, I have made my heart clean, I am pure from my sin?

Jer 17:1 — The sin of Judah *is* written with a pen of iron, *and* with the point of a diamond: *it is* graven upon the table of their heart, and upon the horns of your altars;

Mt 5:8 — Blessed *are* the pure in heart: for they shall see God.

Mt 9:4 — And Jesus knowing their thoughts said, Wherefore think ye evil in your hearts?

Mt 12:33 — Either make the tree good, and his fruit good; or else make the tree corrupt, and his fruit corrupt: for the tree is known by *his* fruit.

Mt 23:26 — *Thou* blind Pharisee, cleanse first that which is within the cup and platter, that the outside of them may be clean also.

Mk 7:21 — For from within, out of the heart of men, proceed evil thoughts, adulteries, fornications, murders,

Ac 8:22 — Repent therefore of this thy wickedness, and pray God, if perhaps the thought of thine heart may be forgiven thee.

Ro 2:5 — But after thy hardness and impenitent heart treasurest up unto thyself wrath against the day of wrath and revelation of the righteous judgment of God;

Heb 3:8 — Harden not your hearts, as in the provocation, in the day of temptation in the wilderness:

Heb 3:15 — While it is said, To day if ye will hear his voice, harden not your hearts, as in the provocation.

- **Instances of hardened hearts.**
  - **Pharoah.**

    Ex 4:21; 7:3, 13, 22; 8:15, 32; 9:12; 9:34–10:1; 10:20, 27; 11:9–10; 14:4, 8, 17
  - **Sihon.**

    Dt 2:30
  - **King of Canaan.**

    Jos 11:20
  - **Others.**

    1Sa 6:6

- **Known to God.**

Ps 139:1–12; Eze 11:19–21; 36:25–26

Dt 31:21 — And it shall come to pass, when many evils and troubles are befallen them, that this song shall testify against them as a witness; for it shall not be forgotten out of the mouths of their seed: for I know their imagination which they go about, even now, before I have brought them into the land which I sware.

1Sa 16:7 — But the LORD said unto Samuel, Look not on his countenance, or on the height of his stature; because I have refused him: for *the LORD seeth* not as man seeth; for man looketh on the outward appearance, but the LORD looketh on the heart.

2Sa 7:20 — And what can David say more unto thee? for thou, Lord GOD, knowest thy servant.

1Ki 8:39 — Then hear thou in heaven thy dwelling place, and forgive, and do, and give to every man according to his ways, whose heart thou knowest; (for thou, *even* thou only, knowest the hearts of all the children of men;)

1Ch 28:9 — And thou, Solomon my son, know thou the God of thy father, and serve him with a perfect heart and with a willing mind: for the LORD searcheth all hearts, and understandeth all the imaginations of the thoughts: if thou seek him, he will be found of thee; but if thou forsake him, he will cast thee off for ever.

Job 11:11 — For he knoweth vain men: he seeth wickedness also; will he not then consider *it?*

Job 16:19 — Also now, behold, my witness *is* in heaven, and my record *is* on high.

Job 31:4 — Doth not he see my ways, and count all my steps?

Ps 1:6 — For the LORD knoweth the way of the righteous: but the way of the ungodly shall perish.

Ps 44:21 — Shall not God search this out? for he knoweth the secrets of the heart.

Ps 51:10 — Create in me a clean heart, O God; and renew a right spirit within me.

Ps 94:11 — The LORD knoweth the thoughts of man, that they *are* vanity.

Pr 5:21 — For the ways of man *are* before the eyes of the LORD, and he pondereth all his goings.

Pr 16:2 — All the ways of a man *are* clean in his own eyes; but the LORD weigheth the spirits.

Pr 21:2 — Every way of a man *is* right in his own eyes: but the LORD pondereth the hearts.

Isa 66:18 — For I *know* their works and their thoughts: it shall come, that I will gather all nations and tongues; and they shall come, and see my glory.

Jer 12:3 — But thou, O LORD, knowest me: thou hast seen me, and tried mine heart toward thee: pull them out like sheep for the slaughter, and prepare them for the day of slaughter.

Jer 17:10 — I the LORD search the heart, *I* try the reins, even to give every man according to his ways, *and* according to the fruit of his doings.

Eze 11:5 — And the Spirit of the LORD fell upon me, and said unto me, Speak; Thus saith the LORD; Thus have ye said, O house of Israel: for I know the things that come into your mind, *every one of* them.

Lk 16:15 — And he said unto them, Ye are they which justify yourselves before men; but God knoweth your hearts: for that which is highly esteemed among men is abomination in the sight of God.

Ac 1:24 — And they prayed, and said, Thou, Lord, which knowest the hearts of all *men,* shew whether of these two thou hast chosen,

Ac 15:8 — And God, which knoweth the hearts, bare them witness, giving them the Holy Ghost, even as *he did* unto us;

Ro 8:27 — And he that searcheth the hearts knoweth what *is* the mind of the Spirit, because he maketh intercession for the saints according to *the will of* God.

1Co 3:20 — And again, The Lord knoweth the thoughts of the wise, that they are vain.

Heb 4:12 — For the word of God *is* quick, and powerful, and sharper than any twoedged sword, piercing even to the dividing asunder of soul and spirit, and of the joints and marrow, and *is* a discerner of the thoughts and intents of the heart.

Rev 2:23 — And I will kill her children with death; and all the churches shall know that I am he which searcheth the reins and hearts: and I will give unto every one of you according to your works.

- **Change of.**
  - **Instances of.**
    - **Saul.**
      1Sa 10:9 — And it was *so,* that when he had turned his back to go from Samuel, God gave him another heart: and all those signs came to pass that day.
    - **Solomon.**
      1Ki 3:11–12
    - **Saul of Tarsus.**
      Ac 9:1–18
  - **See: Regeneration**
  - **See: Sanctification**

HEARTH

Jer 36:22–23

Ge 18:6 — And Abraham hastened into the tent unto Sarah, and said, Make ready quickly three measures of fine meal, knead *it,* and make cakes upon the hearth.

Isa 30:14 — And he shall break it as the breaking of the potters' vessel that is broken in pieces; he shall not spare: so that there shall not be found in the bursting of it a sherd to take fire from the hearth, or to take water *withal* out of the pit.

- **See: Brazier**

HEAT

- **Jonah overcome with.**
  Jnh 4:8 — And it came to pass, when the sun did arise, that God prepared a vehement east wind; and the sun beat upon the head of Jonah, that he fainted, and wished in himself to die, and said, *It is* better for me to die than to live.
  - **See: Sunstroke**

HEATH

Jer 17:6 — For he shall be like the heath in the desert, and shall not see when good cometh; but shall inhabit the parched places in the wilderness, *in* a salt land and not inhabited.

Jer 48:6 — Flee, save your lives, and be like the heath in the wilderness.

HEATHEN

- **Under this head are grouped all who are not embraced under the Abrahamic covenant.**
  Le 18:24–25
- **Cast out of Canaan.**
  Ps 44:2 — *How* thou didst drive out the heathen with thy hand, and plantedst them; *how* thou didst afflict the people, and cast them out.
- **Their land given to Israel.**
  Ps 136:21–22; Isa 54:1–3
  Ps 78:55 — He cast out the heathen also before them, and divided them an inheritance by line, and made the tribes of Israel to dwell in their tents.
  Ps 105:44 — And gave them the lands of the heathen: and they inherited the labour of the people;
  Ps 135:12 — And gave their land *for* an heritage, an heritage unto Israel his people.
- **Excluded from the temple.**
  La 1:10 — The adversary hath spread out his hand upon all her pleasant things: for she hath seen *that* the heathen entered into her sanctuary, whom thou didst command *that* they should not enter into thy congregation.
- **Wicked practices of.**
  - **See: Idolatry**
- **Divine revelations given to.**
  - **Abimelech.**
    Ge 20:3–7
  - **Pharaoh.**
    Ge 41:1–28
  - **Balaam.**
    Nu 22:1–41
  - **Nebuchadnezzar.**
    Da 4:1–18
  - **Belshazzar.**
    Da 5:24–29
    Da 5:5 — In the same hour came forth fingers of a man's hand, and wrote over against the candlestick upon the plaister of the wall of the king's palace: and the king saw the part of the hand that wrote.
  - **Cyrus.**
    Ezr 1:1–4
    2Ch 36:23 — Thus saith Cyrus king of Persia, All the kingdoms of the earth hath the LORD God of heaven given me; and he hath charged me to build him an house in Jerusalem, which *is* in Judah. Who *is there* among you of all his people? The LORD his God *be* with him, and let him go up.
  - **The Magi.**
    Mt 2:1–11
  - **The centurion.**
    Mt 8:5–13; Lk 7:2–9
  - **Cornelius.**
    Ac 10:1–7

- **Pious people among.**

Isa 65:5 — Which say, Stand by thyself, come not near to me; for I am holier than thou. *These* are a smoke in my nose, a fire that burneth all the day.

Ac 10:35 — But in every nation he that feareth him, and worketh righteousness, is accepted with him.

- **Instances of.**
  - **Melchizedek.**
    Ge 14:18–20
  - **Abimelech.**
    Ge 20:1–18
  - **Balaam.**
    Nu 22:1–41
  - **Jethro.**
    Ex 18:1–27
  - **Cyrus.**
    Ezr 1:1–3
  - **Eliphaz.**
    Job 4:1–21
  - **Bildad.**
    Job 8:1–22
  - **Zophar.**
    Job 11:1–20
  - **Elihu.**
    Job 32:1–22
  - **Nebuchadnezzar, after his restoration.**
    Da 4:1–37
  - **The Ninevites.**
    Jnh 3:5–10
  - **The Magi.**
    Mt 2:1–12
  - **The centurion of Capernaum.**
    Mt 8:5–13; Lk 7:2–9
  - **The centurion of Caesarea.**
    Ac 10:1–48

See: **Gentiles**

HEAVE OFFERING

See: **Offerings**

HEAVEN

- **God's dwelling place.**

Mt 10:32–33; Mk 11:25–26; Rev 12:7–9; 21:22–22:21

Dt 26:15 — Look down from thy holy habitation, from heaven, and bless thy people Israel, and the land which thou hast given us, as thou swarest unto our fathers, a land that floweth with milk and honey.

1Ki 8:30 — And hearken thou to the supplication of thy servant, and of thy people Israel, when they shall pray toward this place: and hear thou in heaven thy dwelling place: and when thou hearest, forgive.

1Ki 8:39 — Then hear thou in heaven thy dwelling place, and forgive, and do, and give to every man according to his ways, whose heart thou knowest; (for thou, *even* thou only, knowest the hearts of all the children of men;)

1Ki 8:43 — Hear thou in heaven thy dwelling place, and do according to all that the stranger calleth to thee for: that all people of the earth may know thy name, to fear thee, as *do* thy people Israel; and that they may know that this house, which I have builded, is called by thy name.

1Ki 8:49 — Then hear thou their prayer and their supplication in heaven thy dwelling place, and maintain their cause,

1Ch 16:31 — Let the heavens be glad, and let the earth rejoice: and let *men* say among the nations, The LORD reigneth.

1Ch 21:26 — And David built there an altar unto the LORD, and offered burnt offerings and peace offerings, and called upon the LORD; and he answered him from heaven by fire upon the altar of burnt offering.

2Ch 2:6 — But who is able to build him an house, seeing the heaven and heaven of heavens cannot contain him? who *am* I then, that I should build him an house, save only to burn sacrifice before him?

2Ch 6:18 — But will God in very deed dwell with men on the earth? behold, heaven and the heaven of heavens cannot contain thee; how much less this house which I have built!

2Ch 6:21 — Hearken therefore unto the supplications of thy servant, and of thy people Israel, which they shall make toward this place: hear thou from thy dwelling place, *even* from heaven; and when thou hearest, forgive.

2Ch 6:27 — Then hear thou from heaven, and forgive the sin of thy servants, and of thy people Israel, when thou hast taught them the good way, wherein they should walk; and send rain upon thy land, which thou hast given unto thy people for an inheritance.

2Ch 6:30 — Then hear thou from heaven thy dwelling place, and forgive, and render unto every man according unto all his ways, whose heart thou knowest; (for thou only knowest the hearts of the children of men:)

2Ch 6:33 — Then hear thou from the heavens, *even* from thy dwelling place, and do according to all that the stranger calleth to thee for; that all people of the earth may know thy name, and fear thee, as *doth* thy people Israel, and may know that this house which I have built is called by thy name.

2Ch 6:35 — Then hear thou from the heavens their prayer and their supplication, and maintain their cause.

2Ch 6:39 — Then hear thou from the heavens, *even* from thy dwelling place, their prayer and their supplications, and maintain their cause, and forgive thy people which have sinned against thee.

2Ch 7:14 — If my people, which are called by my name, shall humble themselves, and pray, and seek my face, and turn from their wicked ways; then will I hear from heaven, and will forgive their sin, and will heal their land.

2Ch 30:27 — Then the priests the Levites arose and blessed the people: and their voice was heard, and their prayer came *up* to his holy dwelling place, *even* unto heaven.

Ne 9:27 — Therefore thou deliveredst them into the hand of their enemies, who vexed them: and in the time of their trouble, when they cried unto thee, thou heardest *them* from heaven; and according to thy manifold mercies thou gavest them saviours, who saved them out of the hand of their enemies.

Job 22:12 — *Is* not God in the height of heaven? and behold the height of the stars, how high they are!

Job 22:14 — Thick clouds *are* a covering to him, that he seeth not; and he walketh in the circuit of heaven.

Ps 2:4 — He that sitteth in the heavens shall laugh: the Lord shall have them in derision.

Ps 11:4 — The LORD *is* in his holy temple, the LORD'S throne *is* in heaven: his eyes behold, his eyelids try, the children of men.

Ps 20:6 — Now know I that the LORD saveth his anointed; he will hear him from his holy heaven with the saving strength of his right hand.

Ps 33:13 — The LORD looketh from heaven; he beholdeth all the sons of men.

Ps 102:19 — For he hath looked down from the height of his sanctuary; from heaven did the LORD behold the earth;

Ps 113:5 — Who *is* like unto the LORD our God, who dwelleth on high,

Ps 123:1 — Unto thee lift I up mine eyes, O thou that dwellest in the heavens.

Ps 135:6 — Whatsoever the LORD pleased, *that* did he in heaven, and in earth, in the seas, and all deep places.

Ecc 5:2 — Be not rash with thy mouth, and let not thine heart be hasty to utter *any* thing before God: for God *is* in heaven, and thou upon earth: therefore let thy words be few.

Isa 55:1 — Ho, every one that thirsteth, come ye to the waters, and he that hath no money; come ye, buy, and eat; yea, come, buy wine and milk without money and without price.

Isa 57:15 — For thus saith the high and lofty One that inhabiteth eternity, whose name *is* Holy; I dwell in the high and holy *place,* with him also *that is* of a contrite and humble spirit, to revive the spirit of the humble, and to revive the heart of the contrite ones.

Isa 63:15 — Look down from heaven, and behold from the habitation of thy holiness and of thy glory: where *is* thy zeal and thy strength, the sounding of thy bowels and of thy mercies toward me? are they restrained?

Jer 23:24 — Can any hide himself in secret places that I shall not see him? saith the LORD. Do not I fill heaven and earth? saith the LORD.

La 3:41 — Let us lift up our heart with *our* hands unto God in the heavens.

Da 4:35 — And all the inhabitants of the earth *are* reputed as nothing: and he doeth according to his will in the army of heaven, and *among* the inhabitants of the earth: and none can stay his hand, or say unto him, What doest thou?

Da 5:23 — But hast lifted up thyself against the Lord of heaven; and they have brought the vessels of his house before thee, and thou, and thy lords, thy wives, and thy concubines, have drunk wine in them; and thou hast praised the gods of silver, and gold, of brass, iron, wood, and stone, which see not, nor hear, nor know: and the God in whose hand thy breath *is,* and whose *are* all thy ways, hast thou not glorified:

Zec 2:13 — Be silent, O all flesh, before the LORD: for he is raised up out of his holy habitation.

Mt 5:34 — But I say unto you, Swear not at all; neither by heaven; for it is God's throne:

Mt 5:45 — That ye may be the children of your Father which is in heaven: for he maketh his sun to rise on the evil and on the good, and sendeth rain on the just and on the unjust.

Mt 6:9 — After this manner therefore pray ye: Our Father which art in heaven, Hallowed be thy name.

Mt 11:25 — At that time Jesus answered and said, I thank thee, O Father, Lord of heaven and earth, because thou hast hid these things from the wise and prudent, and hast revealed them unto babes.

Mt 12:50 — For whosoever shall do the will of my Father which is in heaven, the same is my brother, and sister, and mother.

Mt 16:17 — And Jesus answered and said unto him, Blessed art thou, Simon Barjona: for flesh and blood hath not revealed *it* unto thee, but my Father which is in heaven.

Mt 18:10 — Take heed that ye despise not one of these little ones; for I say unto you, That in heaven their angels do always behold the face of my Father which is in heaven.

Mt 18:14 — Even so it is not the will of your Father which is in heaven, that one of these little ones should perish.

Mk 16:19 — So then after the Lord had spoken unto them, he was received up into heaven, and sat on the right hand of God.

Ac 7:49 — Heaven *is* my throne, and earth *is* my footstool: what house will ye build me? saith the Lord: or what *is* the place of my rest?

Ro 1:18 — For the wrath of God is revealed from heaven against all ungodliness and unrighteousness of men, who hold the truth in unrighteousness;

Heb 8:1 — Now of the things which we have spoken *this is* the sum: We have such an high priest, who is set on the right hand of the throne of the Majesty in the heavens;

Rev 8:1 — And when he had opened the seventh seal, there was silence in heaven about the space of half an hour.

• The future dwelling place of the righteous.

• Called a Garner.

Mt 3:12 — Whose fan *is* in his hand, and he will throughly purge his floor, and gather his wheat into the garner; but he will burn up the chaff with unquenchable fire.

• The Kingdom of Christ and of God.

Eph 5:5 — For this ye know, that no whoremonger, nor unclean person, nor covetous man, who is an idolater, hath any inheritance in the kingdom of Christ and of God.

• The Father's House.

Jn 14:2 — In my Father's house are many mansions: if *it were* not so, I would have told you. I go to prepare a place for you.

• A Heavenly Country.

Heb 11:16 — But now they desire a better *country*, that is, an heavenly: wherefore God is not ashamed to be called their God: for he hath prepared for them a city.

• A Rest.

Heb 4:9 — There remaineth therefore a rest to the people of God.

Rev 14:13 — And I heard a voice from heaven saying unto me, Write, Blessed *are* the dead which die in the Lord from henceforth: Yea, saith the Spirit, that they may rest from their labours; and their works do follow them.

• Paradise.

2Co 12:2 — I knew a man in Christ above fourteen years ago, (whether in the body, I cannot tell; or whether out of the body, I cannot tell: God knoweth;) such an one caught up to the third heaven.

2Co 12:4 — How that he was caught up into paradise, and heard unspeakable words, which it is not lawful for a man to utter.

• The wicked excluded from.

Gal 5:21 — Envyings, murders, drunkenness, revellings, and such like: of the which I tell you before, as I have also told *you* in time past, that they which do such things shall not inherit the kingdom of God.

Eph 5:5 — For this ye know, that no whoremonger, nor unclean person, nor covetous man, who is an idolater, hath any inheritance in the kingdom of Christ and of God.

Rev 22:15 — For without *are* dogs, and sorcerers, and whoremongers, and murderers, and idolaters, and whosoever loveth and maketh a lie.

• Unclassified scriptures relating to.

Isa 49:9–10; Lk 12:32–33; 15:6–7; 20:34–36; 22:29–30; Jn 5:28–29; 14:2–3; Ac 7:55–56; 2Co 12:2–4; Col 1:5–6; Heb 12:22–24; Rev 7:13–17; 14:1–3; 21:1–5, 9–11, 18–19, 21–25; 21:27–22:5

2Ki 2:11 — And it came to pass, as they still went on, and talked, that, behold, *there appeared* a chariot of fire, and horses of fire, and parted them both asunder; and Elijah went up by a whirlwind into heaven.

Job 3:17 — There the wicked cease *from* troubling; and there the weary be at rest.

Ps 16:11 — Thou wilt shew me the path of life: in thy presence *is* fulness of joy; at thy right hand *there are* pleasures for evermore.

Ps 17:15 — As for me, I will behold thy face in righteousness: I shall be satisfied, when I awake, with thy likeness.

Ps 23:6 — Surely goodness and mercy shall follow me all the days of my life: and I will dwell in the house of the LORD for ever.

Ps 24:3 — Who shall ascend into the hill of the LORD? or who shall stand in his holy place?

Ps 24:7 — Lift up your heads, O ye gates; and be ye lift up, ye everlasting doors; and the King of glory shall come in.

Ps 73:24 — Thou shalt guide me with thy counsel, and afterward receive me *to* glory.

Isa 33:17 — Thine eyes shall see the king in his beauty: they shall behold the land that is very far off.

Da 12:3 — And they that be wise shall shine as the brightness of the firmament; and they that turn many to righteousness as the stars for ever and ever.

Mal 3:17 — And they shall be mine, saith the LORD of hosts, in that day when I make up my jewels; and I will spare them, as a man spareth his own son that serveth him.

Mt 3:12 — Whose fan *is* in his hand, and he will throughly purge his floor, and gather his wheat into the garner; but he will burn up the chaff with unquenchable fire.

Mt 5:3 — Blessed *are* the poor in spirit: for theirs is the kingdom of heaven.

Mt 5:8 — Blessed *are* the pure in heart: for they shall see God.

Mt 5:12 — Rejoice, and be exceeding glad: for great *is* your reward in heaven: for so persecuted they the prophets which were before you.

Mt 5:20 — For I say unto you, That except your righteousness shall exceed *the righteousness* of the scribes and Pharisees, ye shall in no case enter into the kingdom of heaven.

Mt 6:20 — But lay up for yourselves treasures in heaven, where neither moth nor rust doth corrupt, and where thieves do not break through nor steal:

Mt 8:11 — And I say unto you, That many shall come from the east and west, and shall sit down with Abraham, and Isaac, and Jacob, in the kingdom of heaven.

Mt 13:30 — Let both grow together until the harvest: and in the time of harvest I will say to the reapers, Gather ye together first the tares, and bind them in bundles to burn them: but gather the wheat into my barn.

Mt 13:43 — Then shall the righteous shine forth as the sun in the kingdom of their Father. Who hath ears to hear, let him hear.

Mt 13:49 — So shall it be at the end of the world: the angels shall come forth, and sever the wicked from among the just,

Mt 18:10 — Take heed that ye despise not one of these little ones; for I say unto you, That in heaven their angels do always behold the face of my Father which is in heaven.

Mt 19:21 — Jesus said unto him, If thou wilt be perfect, go *and* sell that thou hast, and give to the poor, and thou shalt have treasure in heaven: and come *and* follow me.

Mt 22:30 — For in the resurrection they neither marry, nor are given in marriage, but are as the angels of God in heaven.

Mt 25:34 — Then shall the King say unto them on his right hand, Come, ye blessed of my Father, inherit the kingdom prepared for you from the foundation of the world:

Mt 25:46 — And these shall go away into everlasting punishment: but the righteous into life eternal.

Lk 10:20 — Notwithstanding in this rejoice not, that the spirits are subject unto you; but rather rejoice, because your names are written in heaven.

Lk 12:8 — Also I say unto you, Whosoever shall confess me before men, him shall the Son of man also confess before the angels of God:

Lk 15:10 — Likewise, I say unto you, there is joy in the presence of the angels of God over one sinner that repenteth.

Lk 15:32 — It was meet that we should make merry, and be glad: for this thy brother was dead, and is alive again; and was lost, and is found.

Lk 16:22 — And it came to pass, that the beggar died, and was carried by the angels into Abraham's bosom: the rich man also died, and was buried;

Lk 23:43 — And Jesus said unto him, Verily I say unto thee, To day shalt thou be with me in paradise.

Jn 10:28 — And I give unto them eternal life; and they shall never perish, neither shall any *man* pluck them out of my hand.

Jn 12:26 — If any man serve me, let him follow me; and where I am, there shall also my servant be: if any man serve me, him will *my* Father honour.

Jn 13:36 — Simon Peter said unto him, Lord, whither goest thou? Jesus answered him, Whither I go, thou canst not follow me now; but thou shalt follow me afterwards.

Jn 17:22 — And the glory which thou gavest me I have given them; that they may be one, even as we are one:

Jn 17:24 — Father, I will that they also, whom thou hast given me, be with me where I am; that they may behold my glory, which thou hast given me: for thou lovedst me before the foundation of the world.

Ro 5:17 — For if by one man's offence death reigned by one; much more they which receive abundance of grace and of the gift of righteousness shall reign in life by one, Jesus Christ.)

2Co 5:1 — For we know that if our earthly house of *this* tabernacle were dissolved, we have a building of God, an house not made with hands, eternal in the heavens.

Eph 1:18 — The eyes of your understanding being enlightened; that ye may know what is the hope of his calling, and what the riches of the glory of his inheritance in the saints,

Col 1:12 — Giving thanks unto the Father, which hath made us meet to be partakers of the inheritance of the saints in light:

Col 3:4 — When Christ, *who is* our life, shall appear, then shall ye also appear with him in glory.

1Th 2:12 — That ye would walk worthy of God, who hath called you unto his kingdom and glory.

1Th 4:17 — Then we which are alive *and* remain shall be caught up together with them in the clouds, to meet the Lord in the air: and so shall we ever be with the Lord.

2Th 1:7 — And to you who are troubled rest with us, when the Lord Jesus shall be revealed from heaven with his mighty angels,

2Th 2:14 — Whereunto he called you by our gospel, to the obtaining of the glory of our Lord Jesus Christ.

Heb 10:34 — For ye had compassion of me in my bonds, and took joyfully the spoiling of your goods, knowing in yourselves that ye have in heaven a better and an enduring substance.

Heb 11:10 — For he looked for a city which hath foundations, whose builder and maker *is* God.

Heb 11:16 — But now they desire a better *country*, that is, an heavenly: wherefore God is not ashamed to be called their God: for he hath prepared for them a city.

Heb 12:28 — Wherefore we receiving a kingdom which cannot be moved, let us have grace, whereby we may serve God acceptably with reverence and godly fear:

Heb 13:14 — For here have we no continuing city, but we seek one to come.

1Pe 1:4 — To an inheritance incorruptible, and undefiled, and that fadeth not away, reserved in heaven for you,

2Pe 1:11 — For so an entrance shall be ministered unto you abundantly into the everlasting kingdom of our Lord and Saviour Jesus Christ.

2Pe 3:13 — Nevertheless we, according to his promise, look for new heavens and a new earth, wherein dwelleth righteousness.

Rev 2:7 — He that hath an ear, let him hear what the Spirit saith unto the churches; To him that overcometh will I give to eat of the tree of life, which is in the midst of the paradise of God.

Rev 3:21 — To him that overcometh will I grant to sit with me in my throne, even as I also overcame, and am set down with my Father in his throne.

Rev 4:4 — And round about the throne *were* four and twenty seats: and upon the seats I saw four and twenty elders sitting, clothed in white raiment; and they had on their heads crowns of gold.

Rev 5:9 — And they sung a new song, saying, Thou art worthy to take the book, and to open the seals thereof: for thou wast slain, and hast redeemed us to God by thy blood out of every kindred, and tongue, and people, and nation;

Rev 7:9 — After this I beheld, and, lo, a great multitude, which no man could number, of all nations, and kindreds, and people, and tongues, stood before the throne, and before the Lamb, clothed with white robes, and palms in their hands;

Rev 15:2 — And I saw as it were a sea of glass mingled with fire: and them that had gotten the victory over the beast, and over his image, and over his mark, *and* over the number of his name, stand on the sea of glass, having the harps of God.

See: Righteous; promises to, expressed or implied

• **The physical heavens.**

Mt 24:29–30; Ac 2:19–20

Ge 1:1 — In the beginning God created the heaven and the earth.

Job 37:18 — Hast thou with him spread out the sky, *which is* strong, *and* as a molten looking glass?

Ps 19:1 — The heavens declare the glory of God; and the firmament sheweth his handywork.

Ps 33:6 — By the word of the LORD were the heavens made; and all the host of them by the breath of his mouth.

Ps 50:6 — And the heavens shall declare his righteousness: for God *is* judge himself. Selah.

Ps 68:33 — To him that rideth upon the heavens of heavens, *which were* of old; lo, he doth send out his voice, *and that* a mighty voice.

Ps 89:29 — His seed also will I make *to endure* for ever, and his throne as the days of heaven.

Ps 97:6 — The heavens declare his righteousness, and all the people see his glory.

Ps 103:11 — For as the heaven is high above the earth, *so* great is his mercy toward them that fear him.

Ps 113:4 — The LORD *is* high above all nations, *and* his glory above the heavens.

Ps 115:16 — The heaven, *even* the heavens, *are* the LORD'S: but the earth hath he given to the children of men.

Ps 136:5 — To him that by wisdom made the heavens: for his mercy *endureth* for ever.

Jer 10:12 — He hath made the earth by his power, he hath established the world by his wisdom, and hath stretched out the heavens by his discretion.

Jer 31:37 — Thus saith the LORD; If heaven above can be measured, and the foundations of the earth searched out beneath, I will also cast off all the seed of Israel for all that they have done, saith the LORD.

Eze 1:1 — Now it came to pass in the thirtieth year, in the fourth *month,* in the fifth *day* of the month, as I *was* among the captives by the river of Chebar, *that* the heavens were opened, and I saw visions of God.

• Physical heavens, creation of.

Ps 148:4–6

Ge 1:1 — In the beginning God created the heaven and the earth.

Ge 2:1 — Thus the heavens and the earth were finished, and all the host of them.

1Ch 16:26 — For all the gods of the people *are* idols: but the LORD made the heavens.

2Ch 2:12 — Huram said moreover, Blessed *be* the LORD God of Israel, that made heaven and earth, who hath given to David the king a wise son, endued with prudence and understanding, that might build an house for the LORD, and an house for his kingdom.

Ne 9:6 — Thou, *even* thou, *art* LORD alone; thou hast made heaven, the heaven of heavens, with all their host, the earth, and all *things* that *are* therein, the seas, and all that *is* therein, and thou preservest them all; and the host of heaven worshippeth thee.

Job 9:8 — Which alone spreadeth out the heavens, and treadeth upon the waves of the sea.

Ps 8:3 — When I consider thy heavens, the work of thy fingers, the moon and the stars, which thou hast ordained;

Ps 19:1 — The heavens declare the glory of God; and the firmament sheweth his handywork.

Ps 33:6 — By the word of the LORD were the heavens made; and all the host of them by the breath of his mouth.

Ps 33:9 — For he spake, and it was *done;* he commanded, and it stood fast.

Pr 8:27 — When he prepared the heavens, I *was* there: when he set a compass upon the face of the depth:

Isa 37:16 — O LORD of hosts, God of Israel, that dwellest *between* the cherubims, thou *art* the God, *even* thou alone, of all the kingdoms of the earth: thou hast made heaven and earth.

Isa 40:22 — *It is* he that sitteth upon the circle of the earth, and the inhabitants thereof *are* as grasshoppers; that stretcheth out the heavens as a curtain, and spreadeth them out as a tent to dwell in:

Isa 42:5 — Thus saith God the LORD, he that created the heavens, and stretched them out; he that spread forth the earth, and that which cometh out of it; he that giveth breath unto the people upon it, and spirit to them that walk therein:

Isa 45:12 — I have made the earth, and created man upon it: I, *even* my hands, have stretched out the heavens, and all their host have I commanded.

Jer 10:12 — He hath made the earth by his power, he hath established the world by his wisdom, and hath stretched out the heavens by his discretion.

Jer 32:17 — Ah Lord GOD! behold, thou hast made the heaven and the earth by thy great power and stretched out arm, *and* there is nothing too hard for thee:

Jer 51:15 — He hath made the earth by his power, he hath established the world by his wisdom, and hath stretched out the heaven by his understanding.

Ac 4:24 — And when they heard that, they lifted up their voice to God with one accord, and said, Lord, thou *art* God, which hast made heaven, and earth, and the sea, and all that in them is:

Ac 14:15 — And saying, Sirs, why do ye these things? We also are men of like passions with you, and preach unto you that ye should turn from these vanities unto the living God, which made heaven, and earth, and the sea, and all things that are therein:

Heb 1:10 — And, Thou, Lord, in the beginning hast laid the foundation of the earth; and the heavens are the works of thine hands:

Rev 10:6 — And sware by him that liveth for ever and ever, who created heaven, and the things that therein are, and the earth, and the things that therein are, and the sea, and the things which are therein, that there should be time no longer:

Rev 14:7 — Saying with a loud voice, Fear God, and give glory to him; for the hour of his judgment is come: and worship him that made heaven, and earth, and the sea, and the fountains of waters.

See: Creation

See: God, Creator

See: Heaven; new heavens

• Physical heavens, destruction of.

Ps 102:25–26; Heb 1:10–12; Rev 6:12–14

Job 14:12 — So man lieth down, and riseth not: till the heavens *be* no more, they shall not awake, nor be raised out of their sleep.

Isa 34:4 — And all the host of heaven shall be dissolved, and the heavens shall be rolled together as a scroll: and all their host shall fall down, as the leaf falleth off from the vine, and as a falling *fig* from the fig tree.

Isa 51:6 — Lift up your eyes to the heavens, and look upon the earth beneath: for the heavens shall vanish away like smoke, and the earth shall wax old like a garment, and they that dwell therein shall die in like manner: but my salvation shall be for ever, and my righteousness shall not be abolished.

Mt 5:18 — For verily I say unto you, Till heaven and earth pass, one jot or one tittle shall in no wise pass from the law, till all be fulfilled.

Mt 24:35 — Heaven and earth shall pass away, but my words shall not pass away.

2Pe 3:10 — But the day of the Lord will come as a thief in the night; in the which the heavens shall pass away with a great noise, and the elements shall melt with fervent heat, the earth also and the works that are therein shall be burned up.

2Pe 3:12 — Looking for and hasting unto the coming of the day of God, wherein the heavens being on fire shall be dissolved, and the elements shall melt with fervent heat?

Rev 20:11 — And I saw a great white throne, and him that sat on it, from whose face the earth and the heaven fled away; and there was found no place for them.

Rev 21:1 — And I saw a new heaven and a new earth: for the first heaven and the first earth were passed away; and there was no more sea.

Rev 21:4 — And God shall wipe away all tears from their eyes; and there shall be no more death, neither sorrow, nor crying, neither shall there be any more pain: for the former things are passed away.

- **New heavens.**

Rev 21:1–4

Isa 65:17 — For, behold, I create new heavens and a new earth: and the former shall not be remembered, nor come into mind.

Isa 66:22 — For as the new heavens and the new earth, which I will make, shall remain before me, saith the LORD, so shall your seed and your name remain.

2Pe 3:13 — Nevertheless we, according to his promise, look for new heavens and a new earth, wherein dwelleth righteousness.

HEBER

- **Head of a family in the tribe of Gad.**

1Ch 5:13 — And their brethren of the house of their fathers *were,* Michael, and Meshullam, and Sheba, and Jorai, and Jachan, and Zia, and Heber, seven.

- **A Benjamite.**

1Ch 8:22 — And Ishpan, and Heber, and Eliel,

- **A son of Beriah.**

1Ch 7:31–32

Ge 46:17 — And the sons of Asher; Jimnah, and Ishuah, and Isui, and Beriah, and Serah their sister: and the sons of Beriah; Heber, and Malchiel.

Nu 26:45 — Of the sons of Beriah: of Heber, the family of the Heberites: of Malchiel, the family of the Malchielites.

Lk 3:35 — Which was *the son* of Saruch, which was *the son* of Ragau, which was *the son* of Phalec, which was *the son* of Heber, which was *the son* of Sala,

- **Husband of Jael.**

Jgs 4:11 — Now Heber the Kenite, *which was* of the children of Hobab the father in law of Moses, had severed himself from the Kenites, and pitched his tent unto the plain of Zaanaim, which *is* by Kedesh.

Jgs 4:17 — Howbeit Sisera fled away on his feet to the tent of Jael the wife of Heber the Kenite: for *there was* peace between Jabin the king of Hazor and the house of Heber the Kenite.

Jgs 4:21 — Then Jael Heber's wife took a nail of the tent, and took an hammer in her hand, and went softly unto him, and smote the nail into his temples, and fastened it into the ground: for he was fast asleep and weary. So he died.

Jgs 5:24 — Blessed above women shall Jael the wife of Heber the Kenite be, blessed shall she be above women in the tent.

- **Son of Ezra.**

1Ch 4:18 — And his wife Jehudijah bare Jered the father of Gedor, and Heber the father of Socho, and Jekuthiel the father of Zanoah. And these *are* the sons of Bithiah the daughter of Pharaoh, which Mered took.

- **A Benjamite.**

1Ch 8:17 — And Zebadiah, and Meshullam, and Hezeki, and Heber,

HEBREW

- **A word supposed to be a corruption of the name of Eber, who was an ancestor of Abraham.**

Ge 11:14–26

Ge 10:24 — And Arphaxad begat Salah; and Salah begat Eber.

See: Genealogy

- **Applied to Abraham.**

Ge 14:13 — And there came one that had escaped, and told Abram the Hebrew; for he dwelt in the plain of Mamre the Amorite, brother of Eshcol, and brother of Aner: and these *were* confederate with Abram.

- **Applied to Abraham's descendants.**

Ge 39:14 — That she called unto the men of her house, and spake unto them, saying, See, he hath brought in an Hebrew unto us to mock us; he came in unto me to lie with me, and I cried with a loud voice:

Ge 40:15 — For indeed I was stolen away out of the land of the Hebrews: and here also have I done nothing that they should put me into the dungeon.

Ge 43:32 — And they set on for him by himself, and for them by themselves, and for the Egyptians, which did eat with him, by themselves: because the Egyptians might not eat bread with the Hebrews; for that *is* an abomination unto the Egyptians.

Ex 2:6 — And when she had opened *it,* she saw the child: and, behold, the babe wept. And she had compassion on him, and said, This *is one* of the Hebrews' children.

Dt 15:12 — *And* if thy brother, an Hebrew man, or an Hebrew woman, be sold unto thee, and serve thee six years; then in the seventh year thou shalt let him go free from thee.

1Sa 4:9 — Be strong, and quit yourselves like men, O ye Philistines, that ye be not servants unto the Hebrews, as they have been to you: quit yourselves like men, and fight.

1Sa 29:3 — Then said the princes of the Philistines, What *do* these Hebrews *here?* And Achish said unto the princes of the Philistines, *Is* not this David, the servant of Saul the king of Israel, which hath been with me these days, or these years, and I have found no fault in him since he fell *unto me* unto this day?

Jnh 1:9 — And he said unto them, I *am* an Hebrew; and I fear the LORD, the God of heaven, which hath made the sea and the dry *land.*

Ac 6:1 — And in those days, when the number of the disciples was multiplied, there arose a murmuring of the Grecians against the Hebrews, because their widows were neglected in the daily ministration.

2Co 11:22 — Are they Hebrews? so *am* I. Are they Israelites? so *am* I. Are they the seed of Abraham? so *am* I.

Php 3:5 — Circumcised the eighth day, of the stock of Israel, *of* the tribe of Benjamin, an Hebrew of the Hebrews; as touching the law, a Pharisee;

• Used to denote the language of the Jews.

Jn 5:2 — Now there is at Jerusalem by the sheep *market* a pool, which is called in the Hebrew tongue Bethesda, having five porches.

Jn 19:20 — This title then read many of the Jews: for the place where Jesus was crucified was nigh to the city: and it was written in Hebrew, *and* Greek, *and* Latin.

Ac 21:40 — And when he had given him licence, Paul stood on the stairs, and beckoned with the hand unto the people. And when there was made a great silence, he spake unto *them* in the Hebrew tongue, saying,

Ac 22:2 — (And when they heard that he spake in the Hebrew tongue to them, they kept the more silence: and he saith,)

Ac 26:14 — And when we were all fallen to the earth, I heard a voice speaking unto me, and saying in the Hebrew tongue, Saul, Saul, why persecutest thou me? *it is* hard for thee to kick against the pricks.

Rev 9:11 — And they had a king over them, *which is* the angel of the bottomless pit, whose name in the Hebrew tongue *is* Abaddon, but in the Greek tongue hath *his* name Apollyon.

See: Israelites

See: Jews

HEBRON

• A city of Asher.

Jos 19:28 — And Hebron, and Rehob, and Hammon, and Kanah, *even* unto great Zidon;

• A city of Judah, south of Jerusalem.

• When built.

Nu 13:22 — And they ascended by the south, and came unto Hebron; where Ahiman, Sheshai, and Talmai, the children of Anak, *were.* (Now Hebron was built seven years before Zoan in Egypt.)

• Fortified.

2Ch 11:10 — And Zorah, and Aijalon, and Hebron, which *are* in Judah and in Benjamin fenced cities.

• Called Kirjath-Arba.

Ge 23:1–20

• Called Arba.

Ge 35:27 — And Jacob came unto Isaac his father unto Mamre, unto the city of Arbah, which *is* Hebron, where Abraham and Isaac sojourned.

Jos 15:13 — And unto Caleb the son of Jephunneh he gave a part among the children of Judah, according to the commandment of the LORD to Joshua, *even* the city of Arba the father of Anak, which *city is* Hebron.

• Abraham dwells and Sarah dies at.

Ge 23:2 — And Sarah died in Kirjath-arba; the same *is* Hebron in the land of Canaan: and Abraham came to mourn for Sarah, and to weep for her.

• Hoham, king of, confederated with other kings of the Canaanites against Joshua.

Jos 10:3–39

• Children of Anakim dwell at.

Nu 13:22 — And they ascended by the south, and came unto Hebron; where Ahiman, Sheshai, and Talmai, the children of Anak, *were.* (Now Hebron was built seven years before Zoan in Egypt.)

Jos 11:21 — And at that time came Joshua, and cut off the Anakims from the mountains, from Hebron, from Debir, from Anab, and from all the mountains of Judah, and from all the mountains of Israel: Joshua destroyed them utterly with their cities.

• Conquest of, by Caleb.

Jos 14:6–15

Jgs 1:10 — And Judah went against the Canaanites that dwelt in Hebron: (now the name of Hebron before *was* Kirjath-arba:) and they slew Sheshai, and Ahiman, and Talmai.

Jgs 1:20 — And they gave Hebron unto Caleb, as Moses said: and he expelled thence the three sons of Anak.

• A city of refuge.

Jos 20:7 — And they appointed Kedesh in Galilee in mount Naphtali, and Shechem in mount Ephraim, and Kirjath-arba, which *is* Hebron, in the mountain of Judah.

Jos 21:11 — And they gave them the city of Arba the father of Anak, which *city is* Hebron, in the hill *country* of Judah, with the suburbs thereof round about it.

Jos 21:13 — Thus they gave to the children of Aaron the priest Hebron with her suburbs, *to be* a city of refuge for the slayer; and Libnah with her suburbs,

- **David crowned king of Judah at.**
  2Sa 2:1–11; 3:1–39
- **A city of Israel.**
  2Sa 5:1–5
- **The burial place of Sarah.**
  Ge 23:2 — And Sarah died in Kirjath-arba; the same *is* Hebron in the land of Canaan: and Abraham came to mourn for Sarah, and to weep for her.
- **The burial place of Abner.**
  2Sa 3:32 — And they buried Abner in Hebron: and the king lifted up his voice, and wept at the grave of Abner; and all the people wept.
- **The burial place of Ish-bosheth.**
  2Sa 4:12 — And David commanded his young men, and they slew them, and cut off their hands and their feet, and hanged *them* up over the pool in Hebron. But they took the head of Ish-bosheth, and buried *it* in the sepulchre of Abner in Hebron.
- **The conspirators against Ish-bosheth hanged at.**
  2Sa 4:12 — And David commanded his young men, and they slew them, and cut off their hands and their feet, and hanged *them* up over the pool in Hebron. But they took the head of Ish-bosheth, and buried *it* in the sepulchre of Abner in Hebron.
- **Absalom made king at.**
  2Sa 15:9–10
- **Jews of the Babylonian captivity dwell at.**
  Ne 11:25 — And for the villages, with their fields, *some* of the children of Judah dwelt at Kirjath-arba, and *in* the villages thereof, and at Dibon, and in the villages thereof, and at Jekabzeel, and *in* the villages thereof,
- **Pool of.**
  2Sa 4:12 — And David commanded his young men, and they slew them, and cut off their hands and their feet, and hanged *them* up over the pool in Hebron. But they took the head of Ish-bosheth, and buried *it* in the sepulchre of Abner in Hebron.

- **Son of Kohath.**
  Ex 6:18 — And the sons of Kohath; Amram, and Izhar, and Hebron, and Uzziel: and the years of the life of Kohath *were* an hundred thirty and three years.
  Nu 3:19 — And the sons of Kohath by their families; Amram, and Izehar, Hebron, and Uzziel.
  1Ch 6:2 — And the sons of Kohath; Amram, Izhar, and Hebron, and Uzziel.
  1Ch 6:18 — And the sons of Kohath *were*, Amram, and Izhar, and Hebron, and Uzziel.
  1Ch 23:12 — The sons of Kohath; Amram, Izhar, Hebron, and Uzziel, four.
  1Ch 23:19 — Of the sons of Hebron; Jeriah the first, Amariah the second, Jahaziel the third, and Jekameam the fourth.
- **The patronymic of Mareshah.**
  1Ch 2:42–43
  1Ch 15:9 — Of the sons of Hebron; Eliel the chief, and his brethren fourscore:

HEDGE

- **A fence.**
  Job 1:10 — Hast not thou made an hedge about him, and about his house, and about all that he hath on every side? thou hast blessed the work of his hands, and his substance is increased in the land.
  Isa 5:5 — And now go to; I will tell you what I will do to my vineyard: I will take away the hedge thereof, and it shall be eaten up; *and* break down the wall thereof, and it shall be trodden down:
  Jer 49:3 — Howl, O Heshbon, for Ai is spoiled: cry, ye daughters of Rabbah, gird you with sackcloth; lament, and run to and fro by the hedges; for their king shall go into captivity, *and* his priests and his princes together.
  La 3:7 — He hath hedged me about, that I cannot get out: he hath made my chain heavy.
  Eze 13:5 — Ye have not gone up into the gaps, neither made up the hedge for the house of Israel to stand in the battle in the day of the LORD.
  Eze 22:30 — And I sought for a man among them, that should make up the hedge, and stand in the gap before me for the land, that I should not destroy it: but I found none.
  Hos 2:6 — Therefore, behold, I will hedge up thy way with thorns, and make a wall, that she shall not find her paths.
  Mic 7:4 — The best of them *is* as a brier: the most upright *is sharper* than a thorn hedge: the day of thy watchmen *and* thy visitation cometh; now shall be their perplexity.
  Mk 12:1 — And he began to speak unto them by parables. A *certain* man planted a vineyard, and set an hedge about *it*, and digged *a place for* the winefat, and built a tower, and let it out to husbandmen, and went into a far country.
- **Of thorns.**
  Pr 15:19 — The way of the slothful *man is* as an hedge of thorns: but the way of the righteous *is* made plain.
- **People sheltered in.**
  Lk 14:23 — And the lord said unto the servant, Go out into the highways and hedges, and compel *them* to come in, that my house may be filled.

→See: Fence

HEGAI • Chamberlain of Ahasuerus.

Est 2:3 — And let the king appoint officers in all the provinces of his kingdom, that they may gather together all the fair young virgins unto Shushan the palace, to the house of the women unto the custody of Hege the king's chamberlain, keeper of the women; and let their things for purification be given *them:*

Est 2:8 — So it came to pass, when the king's commandment and his decree was heard, and when many maidens were gathered together unto Shushan the palace, to the custody of Hegai, that Esther was brought also unto the king's house, to the custody of Hegai, keeper of the women.

Est 2:15 — Now when the turn of Esther, the daughter of Abihail the uncle of Mordecai, who had taken her for his daughter, was come to go in unto the king, she required nothing but what Hegai the king's chamberlain, the keeper of the women, appointed. And Esther obtained favour in the sight of all them that looked upon her.

HEGIRA ⇜See: Exodus

HEIFER

• When used as sacrifice, must be without blemish and must not have come under the yoke.

Nu 19:2 — This *is* the ordinance of the law which the LORD hath commanded, saying, Speak unto the children of Israel, that they bring thee a red heifer without spot, wherein *is* no blemish, *and* upon which never came yoke:

Dt 21:3 — And it shall be, *that* the city *which is* next unto the slain man, even the elders of that city shall take an heifer, which hath not been wrought with, *and* which hath not drawn in the yoke;

• An atonement for murder.

Dt 21:1–9

• The red heifer used for the water of separation.

Nu 19:1–22

Heb 9:13 — For if the blood of bulls and of goats, and the ashes of an heifer sprinkling the unclean, sanctifieth to the purifying of the flesh:

• Used for draught.

Jgs 14:18 — And the men of the city said unto him on the seventh day before the sun went down, What *is* sweeter than honey? and what *is* stronger than a lion? And he said unto them, If ye had not plowed with my heifer, ye had not found out my riddle.

• Used for treading out wheat.

Hos 10:11 — And Ephraim *is as* an heifer *that is* taught, *and* loveth to tread out *the corn;* but I passed over upon her fair neck: I will make Ephraim to ride; Judah shall plow, *and* Jacob shall break his clods.

• Tractable.

Hos 10:11 — And Ephraim *is as* an heifer *that is* taught, *and* loveth to tread out *the corn;* but I passed over upon her fair neck: I will make Ephraim to ride; Judah shall plow, *and* Jacob shall break his clods.

• Intractable.

Hos 4:16 — For Israel slideth back as a backsliding heifer: now the LORD will feed them as a lamb in a large place.

⇜See: Kine

⇜See: Offerings

• Figurative.

• Of backsliders.

Hos 4:16 — For Israel slideth back as a backsliding heifer: now the LORD will feed them as a lamb in a large place.

• Of the obedient.

Hos 10:11 — And Ephraim *is as* an heifer *that is* taught, *and* loveth to tread out *the corn;* but I passed over upon her fair neck: I will make Ephraim to ride; Judah shall plow, *and* Jacob shall break his clods.

HEIR

Ge 25:5–6; Le 25:45–46; Nu 27:8–11; 36:1–8; Dt 21:15–17; Jos 17:3–6; Ru 4:1–12; Ecc 2:18–19; Gal 4:1–2

Ge 15:3 — And Abram said, Behold, to me thou hast given no seed: and, lo, one born in my house is mine heir.

Ge 21:10 — Wherefore she said unto Abraham, Cast out this bondwoman and her son: for the son of this bondwoman shall not be heir with my son, *even* with Isaac.

Gal 4:30 — Nevertheless what saith the scripture? Cast out the bondwoman and her son: for the son of the bondwoman shall not be heir with the son of the free woman.

⇜See: Birthright

⇜See: Firstborn

⇜See: Inheritance

⇜See: Orphan

⇜See: Will

• Figurative.

Ro 8:14–17; Gal 4:6–7

Gal 3:29 — And if ye *be* Christ's, then are ye Abraham's seed, and heirs according to the promise.

Tit 3:7 — That being justified by his grace, we should be made heirs according to the hope of eternal life.

Jas 2:5 — Hearken, my beloved brethren, Hath not God chosen the poor of this world rich in faith, and heirs of the kingdom which he hath promised to them that love him?

⇜See: Adoption

HELAH • A wife of Asher.

1Ch 4:5 — And Ashur the father of Tekoa had two wives, Helah and Naarah.

HELAM • A place east of the Jordan.

2Sa 10:16–17

HELBAH • A town of Asher.

Jgs 1:31 — Neither did Asher drive out the inhabitants of Accho, nor the inhabitants of Zidon, nor of Ahlab, nor of Achzib, nor of Helbah, nor of Aphik, nor of Rehob:

HELBON

• A village near Damascus.

• Noted for fine wines.

Eze 27:18 — Damascus *was* thy merchant in the multitude of the wares of thy making, for the multitude of all riches; in the wine of Helbon, and white wool.

HELDAI

• The Netophathite. One of David's heroes.

1Ch 27:15 — The twelfth *captain* for the twelfth month *was* Heldai the Netophathite, of Othniel: and in his course *were* twenty and four thousand.

• Called Heled.

1Ch 11:30 — Maharai the Netophathite, Heled the son of Baanah the Netophathite,

• Called Heleb.

2Sa 23:29 — Heleb the son of Baanah, a Netophathite, Ittai the son of Ribai out of Gibeah of the children of Benjamin,

• An Israelite.

Zec 6:10 — Take of *them of* the captivity, *even* of Heldai, of Tobijah, and of Jedaiah, which are come from Babylon, and come thou the same day, and go into the house of Josiah the son of Zephaniah;

HELEB *See: Heldai

HELEK • Son of Gilead.

Nu 26:30 — These *are* the sons of Gilead: *of* Jeezer, the family of the Jeezerites: of Helek, the family of the Helekites:

Jos 17:2 — There was also *a lot* for the rest of the children of Manasseh by their families; for the children of Abiezer, and for the children of Helek, and for the children of Asriel, and for the children of Shechem, and for the children of Hepher, and for the children of Shemida: these *were* the male children of Manasseh the son of Joseph by their families.

HELEM

• A descendant of Asher.

1Ch 7:35 — And the sons of his brother Helem; Zophah, and Imna, and Shelesh, and Amal.

• Probably same as Heldai.

Zec 6:10 — Take of *them of* the captivity, *even* of Heldai, of Tobijah, and of Jedaiah, which are come from Babylon, and come thou the same day, and go into the house of Josiah the son of Zephaniah;

Zec 6:14 — And the crowns shall be to Helem, and to Tobijah, and to Jedaiah, and to Hen the son of Zephaniah, for a memorial in the temple of the LORD.

HELEPH • Town of Naphtali.

Jos 19:33 — And their coast was from Heleph, from Allon to Zaanannim, and Adami, Nekeb, and Jabneel, unto Lakum; and the outgoings thereof were at Jordan:

HELEZ

• One of David's mighty men.

2Sa 23:26 — Helez the Paltite, Ira the son of Ikkesh the Tekoite,

1Ch 11:27 — Shammoth the Harorite, Helez the Pelonite,

1Ch 27:10 — The seventh *captain* for the seventh month *was* Helez the Pelonite, of the children of Ephraim: and in his course *were* twenty and four thousand.

• A man of Judah.

1Ch 2:39 — And Azariah begat Helez, and Helez begat Eleasah,

HELI • Father of Joseph.

Lk 3:23 — And Jesus himself began to be about thirty years of age, being (as was supposed) the son of Joseph, which was *the son* of Heli,

HELKAI • A priest.

Ne 12:15 — Of Harim, Adna; of Meraioth, Helkai;

HELKATH

• Called also Hukok.

• A Levitical town.

Jos 19:25 — And their border was Helkath, and Hali, and Beten, and Achshaph,

Jos 21:31 — Helkath with her suburbs, and Rehob with her suburbs; four cities.

1Ch 6:75 — And Hukok with her suburbs, and Rehob with her suburbs:

HELKATH-HAZZURIM • A battle ground.

2Sa 2:16 — And they caught every one his fellow by the head, and *thrust* his sword in his fellow's side; so they fell down together: wherefore that place was called Helkath-hazzurim, which *is* in Gibeon.

HELL

• The word used in the KJV of the O.T. from the Hebrew word sheol, the unseen state.

Eze 31:16–17

Dt 32:22 — For a fire is kindled in mine anger, and shall burn unto the lowest hell, and shall consume the earth with her increase, and set on fire the foundations of the mountains.

2Sa 22:6 — The sorrows of hell compassed me about; the snares of death prevented me;

Job 11:8 — *It is* as high as heaven; what canst thou do? deeper than hell; what canst thou know?

Job 26:6 — Hell *is* naked before him, and destruction hath no covering.

Ps 9:17 — The wicked shall be turned into hell, *and* all the nations that forget God.

Ps 16:10 — For thou wilt not leave my soul in hell; neither wilt thou suffer thine Holy One to see corruption.

Ps 18:5 — The sorrows of hell compassed me about: the snares of death prevented me.

Ps 55:15 — Let death seize upon them, *and* let them go down quick into hell: for wickedness is in their dwellings, *and* among them.

Ps 86:13 — For great *is* thy mercy toward me: and thou hast delivered my soul from the lowest hell.

Ps 116:3 — The sorrows of death compassed me, and the pains of hell gat hold upon me: I found trouble and sorrow.

Ps 139:8 — If I ascend up into heaven, thou *art* there: if I make my bed in hell, behold, thou *art there.*

Pr 5:5 — Her feet go down to death; her steps take hold on hell.

Pr 7:27 — Her house *is* the way to hell, going down to the chambers of death.

Pr 9:18 — But he knoweth not that the dead *are* there; *and that* her guests *are* in the depths of hell.

Pr 15:11 — Hell and destruction *are* before the LORD: how much more then the hearts of the children of men?

Pr 15:24 — The way of life *is* above to the wise, that he may depart from hell beneath.

Pr 23:14 — Thou shalt beat him with the rod, and shalt deliver his soul from hell.

Pr 27:20 — Hell and destruction are never full; so the eyes of man are never satisfied.

Isa 5:14 — Therefore hell hath enlarged herself, and opened her mouth without measure: and their glory, and their multitude, and their pomp, and he that rejoiceth, shall descend into it.

Isa 14:9 — Hell from beneath is moved for thee to meet *thee* at thy coming: it stirreth up the dead for thee, *even* all the chief ones of the earth; it hath raised up from their thrones all the kings of the nations.

Isa 14:15 — Yet thou shalt be brought down to hell, to the sides of the pit.

Isa 28:15 — Because ye have said, We have made a covenant with death, and with hell are we at agreement; when the overflowing scourge shall pass through, it shall not come unto us: for we have made lies our refuge, and under falsehood have we hid ourselves:

Isa 28:18 — And your covenant with death shall be disannulled, and your agreement with hell shall not stand; when the overflowing scourge shall pass through, then ye shall be trodden down by it.

Isa 57:9 — And thou wentest to the king with ointment, and didst increase thy perfumes, and didst send thy messengers far off, and didst debase *thyself even* unto hell.

Eze 32:21 — The strong among the mighty shall speak to him out of the midst of hell with them that help him: they are gone down, they lie uncircumcised, slain by the sword.

Eze 32:27 — And they shall not lie with the mighty *that are* fallen of the uncircumcised, which are gone down to hell with their weapons of war: and they have laid their swords under their heads, but their iniquities shall be upon their bones, though *they were* the terror of the mighty in the land of the living.

Am 9:2 — Though they dig into hell, thence shall mine hand take them; though they climb up to heaven, thence will I bring them down:

Jnh 2:2 — And said, I cried by reason of mine affliction unto the LORD, and he heard me; out of the belly of hell cried I, *and* thou heardest my voice.

Hab 2:5 — Yea also, because he transgresseth by wine, *he is* a proud man, neither keepeth at home, who enlargeth his desire as hell, and *is* as death, and cannot be satisfied, but gathereth unto him all nations, and heapeth unto him all people:

• Translation of the Greek word hades in N.T. of the KJV, the unseen world.

Rev 20:13–14

Mt 11:23 — And thou, Capernaum, which art exalted unto heaven, shalt be brought down to hell: for if the mighty works, which have been done in thee, had been done in Sodom, it would have remained until this day.

Mt 16:18 — And I say also unto thee, That thou art Peter, and upon this rock I will build my church; and the gates of hell shall not prevail against it.

Lk 10:15 — And thou, Capernaum, which art exalted to heaven, shalt be thrust down to hell.

Lk 16:23 — And in hell he lift up his eyes, being in torments, and seeth Abraham afar off, and Lazarus in his bosom.

Ac 2:27 — Because thou wilt not leave my soul in hell, neither wilt thou suffer thine Holy One to see corruption.

Ac 2:31 — He seeing this before spake of the resurrection of Christ, that his soul was not left in hell, neither his flesh did see corruption.

Rev 1:18 — *I am* he that liveth, and was dead; and, behold, I am alive for evermore, Amen; and have the keys of hell and of death.

Rev 6:8 — And I looked, and behold a pale horse: and his name that sat on him was Death, and Hell followed with him. And power was given unto them over the fourth part of the earth, to kill with sword, and with hunger, and with death, and with the beasts of the earth.

• Translation of the Greek word gehenna, signifying the place of torment.

Mt 5:29–30

Mt 5:22 — But I say unto you, That whosoever is angry with his brother without a cause shall be in danger of the judgment: and whosoever shall say to his brother, Raca, shall be in danger of the council: but whosoever shall say, Thou fool, shall be in danger of hell fire.

Mt 10:28 — And fear not them which kill the body, but are not able to kill the soul: but rather fear him which is able to destroy both soul and body in hell.

Mt 18:9 — And if thine eye offend thee, pluck it out, and cast *it* from thee: it is better for thee to enter into life with one eye, rather than having two eyes to be cast into hell fire.

Mt 23:15 — Woe unto you, scribes and Pharisees, hypocrites! for ye compass sea and land to make one proselyte, and when he is made, ye make him twofold more the child of hell than yourselves.

Mt 23:33 — *Ye* serpents, *ye* generation of vipers, how can ye escape the damnation of hell?

Mk 9:43 — And if thy hand offend thee, cut it off: it is better for thee to enter into life maimed, than having two hands to go into hell, into the fire that never shall be quenched:

Mk 9:45 — And if thy foot offend thee, cut it off: it is better for thee to enter halt into life, than having two feet to be cast into hell, into the fire that never shall be quenched:

Mk 9:47 — And if thine eye offend thee, pluck it out: it is better for thee to enter into the kingdom of God with one eye, than having two eyes to be cast into hell fire:

Lk 12:5 — But I will forewarn you whom ye shall fear: Fear him, which after he hath killed hath power to cast into hell; yea, I say unto you, Fear him.

Jas 3:6 — And the tongue *is* a fire, a world of iniquity: so is the tongue among our members, that it defileth the whole body, and setteth on fire the course of nature; and it is set on fire of hell.

- **Translation of the Greek word tartarus, signifying the infernal region.**

2Pe 2:4 — For if God spared not the angels that sinned, but cast *them* down to hell, and delivered *them* into chains of darkness, to be reserved unto judgment;

- **Sheol is also translated grave in KJV.**

Ps 49:14–15

Ge 37:35 — And all his sons and all his daughters rose up to comfort him; but he refused to be comforted; and he said, For I will go down into the grave unto my son mourning. Thus his father wept for him.

Ge 42:38 — And he said, My son shall not go down with you; for his brother is dead, and he is left alone: if mischief befall him by the way in the which ye go, then shall ye bring down my gray hairs with sorrow to the grave.

Ge 44:29 — And if ye take this also from me, and mischief befall him, ye shall bring down my gray hairs with sorrow to the grave.

Ge 44:31 — It shall come to pass, when he seeth that the lad *is* not *with us,* that he will die: and thy servants shall bring down the gray hairs of thy servant our father with sorrow to the grave.

1Sa 2:6 — The LORD killeth, and maketh alive: he bringeth down to the grave, and bringeth up.

1Ki 2:6 — Do therefore according to thy wisdom, and let not his hoar head go down to the grave in peace.

1Ki 2:9 — Now therefore hold him not guiltless: for thou *art* a wise man, and knowest what thou oughtest to do unto him; but his hoar head bring thou down to the grave with blood.

Job 7:9 — *As* the cloud is consumed and vanisheth away: so he that goeth down to the grave shall come up no *more.*

Job 14:13 — Oh that thou wouldest hide me in the grave, that thou wouldest keep me secret, until thy wrath be past, that thou wouldest appoint me a set time, and remember me!

Job 17:13 — If I wait, the grave *is* mine house: I have made my bed in the darkness.

Job 21:13 — They spend their days in wealth, and in a moment go down to the grave.

Job 24:19 — Drought and heat consume the snow waters: *so doth* the grave *those which* have sinned.

Ps 6:5 — For in death *there is* no remembrance of thee: in the grave who shall give thee thanks?

Ps 30:3 — O LORD, thou hast brought up my soul from the grave: thou hast kept me alive, that I should not go down to the pit.

Ps 31:17 — Let me not be ashamed, O LORD; for I have called upon thee: let the wicked be ashamed, *and* let them be silent in the grave.

Ps 88:3 — For my soul is full of troubles: and my life draweth nigh unto the grave.

Ps 89:48 — What man *is he that* liveth, and shall not see death? shall he deliver his soul from the hand of the grave? Selah.

Ps 141:7 — Our bones are scattered at the grave's mouth, as when one cutteth and cleaveth *wood* upon the earth.

Pr 1:12 — Let us swallow them up alive as the grave; and whole, as those that go down into the pit:

Pr 30:16 — The grave; and the barren womb; the earth *that* is not filled with water; and the fire *that* saith not, *It is* enough.

Ecc 9:10 — Whatsoever thy hand findeth to do, do *it* with thy might; for *there is* no work, nor device, nor knowledge, nor wisdom, in the grave, whither thou goest.

SS 8:6 — Set me as a seal upon thine heart, as a seal upon thine arm: for love *is* strong as death; jealousy *is* cruel as the grave: the coals thereof *are* coals of fire, *which hath a* most vehement flame.

Isa 14:11 — Thy pomp is brought down to the grave, *and* the noise of thy viols: the worm is spread under thee, and the worms cover thee.

Isa 38:10 — I said in the cutting off of my days, I shall go to the gates of the grave: I am deprived of the residue of my years.

Isa 38:18 — For the grave cannot praise thee, death can *not* celebrate thee: they that go down into the pit cannot hope for thy truth.

Eze 31:15 — Thus saith the Lord GOD; In the day when he went down to the grave I caused a mourning: I covered the deep for him, and I restrained the floods thereof, and the great waters were stayed: and I caused Lebanon to mourn for him, and all the trees of the field fainted for him.

Hos 13:14 — I will ransom them from the power of the grave; I will redeem them from death: O death, I will be thy plagues; O grave, I will be thy destruction: repentance shall be hid from mine eyes.

- **Sheol is also translated pit.**

Nu 16:30 — But if the LORD make a new thing, and the earth open her mouth, and swallow them up, with all that *appertain* unto them, and they go down quick into the pit; then ye shall understand that these men have provoked the LORD.

Nu 16:33 — They, and all that *appertained* to them, went down alive into the pit, and the earth closed upon them: and they perished from among the congregation.

Job 17:16 — They shall go down to the bars of the pit, when *our* rest together *is* in the dust.

- **The British revisers.**
  - **Insert the Hebrew word sheol in places where hell, grave, and pit were used in the KJV.**
    - **Except in the prophetical books and in.**

Dt 32:22 — For a fire is kindled in mine anger, and shall burn unto the lowest hell, and shall consume the earth with her increase, and set on fire the foundations of the mountains.

Ps 55:15 — Let death seize upon them, *and* let them go down quick into hell: for wickedness is in their dwellings, *and* among them.

Ps 86:13 — For great *is* thy mercy toward me: and thou hast delivered my soul from the lowest hell.

• The American revisers use Sheol where it occurs in the original.

• The future abode of the wicked.

Pr 9:13–18; 23:13–14; Mt 5:29–30; 7:13–14; 8:11–12; 13:38–42, 49–50; 18:8–9, 34–35; 25:28–30; Mk 9:43–48; Lk 16:23–26; Rev 9:1–2; 14:10–11

Ps 9:17 — The wicked shall be turned into hell, *and* all the nations that forget God.

Pr 5:5 — Her feet go down to death; her steps take hold on hell.

Pr 15:24 — The way of life *is* above to the wise, that he may depart from hell beneath.

Isa 30:33 — For Tophet *is* ordained of old; yea, for the king it is prepared; he hath made *it* deep *and* large: the pile thereof *is* fire and much wood; the breath of the LORD, like a stream of brimstone, doth kindle it.

Isa 33:14 — The sinners in Zion are afraid; fearfulness hath surprised the hypocrites. Who among us shall dwell with the devouring fire? who among us shall dwell with everlasting burnings?

Mt 3:12 — Whose fan *is* in his hand, and he will throughly purge his floor, and gather his wheat into the garner; but he will burn up the chaff with unquenchable fire.

Mt 10:28 — And fear not them which kill the body, but are not able to kill the soul: but rather fear him which is able to destroy both soul and body in hell.

Mt 13:30 — Let both grow together until the harvest: and in the time of harvest I will say to the reapers, Gather ye together first the tares, and bind them in bundles to burn them: but gather the wheat into my barn.

Mt 16:18 — And I say also unto thee, That thou art Peter, and upon this rock I will build my church; and the gates of hell shall not prevail against it.

Mt 22:13 — Then said the king to the servants, Bind him hand and foot, and take him away, and cast *him* into outer darkness; there shall be weeping and gnashing of teeth.

Mt 25:41 — Then shall he say also unto them on the left hand, Depart from me, ye cursed, into everlasting fire, prepared for the devil and his angels:

Mt 25:46 — And these shall go away into everlasting punishment: but the righteous into life eternal.

Lk 3:17 — Whose fan *is* in his hand, and he will throughly purge his floor, and will gather the wheat into his garner; but the chaff he will burn with fire unquenchable.

Lk 16:28 — For I have five brethren; that he may testify unto them, lest they also come into this place of torment.

Ac 1:25 — That he may take part of this ministry and apostleship, from which Judas by transgression fell, that he might go to his own place.

2Th 1:9 — Who shall be punished with everlasting destruction from the presence of the Lord, and from the glory of his power;

2Pe 2:4 — For if God spared not the angels that sinned, but cast *them* down to hell, and delivered *them* into chains of darkness, to be reserved unto judgment;

Jude 1:6 — And the angels which kept not their first estate, but left their own habitation, he hath reserved in everlasting chains under darkness unto the judgment of the great day.

Jude 1:23 — And others save with fear, pulling *them* out of the fire; hating even the garment spotted by the flesh.

Rev 2:11 — He that hath an ear, let him hear what the Spirit saith unto the churches; He that overcometh shall not be hurt of the second death.

Rev 11:7 — And when they shall have finished their testimony, the beast that ascendeth out of the bottomless pit shall make war against them, and shall overcome them, and kill them.

Rev 19:20 — And the beast was taken, and with him the false prophet that wrought miracles before him, with which he deceived them that had received the mark of the beast, and them that worshipped his image. These both were cast alive into a lake of fire burning with brimstone.

Rev 20:10 — And the devil that deceived them was cast into the lake of fire and brimstone, where the beast and the false prophet *are,* and shall be tormented day and night for ever and ever.

Rev 20:15 — And whosoever was not found written in the book of life was cast into the lake of fire.

Rev 21:8 — But the fearful, and unbelieving, and the abominable, and murderers, and whoremongers, and sorcerers, and idolaters, and all liars, shall have their part in the lake which burneth with fire and brimstone: which is the second death.

See: Wicked; punishment of

HELM

Ac 27:40 — And when they had taken up the anchors, they committed *themselves* unto the sea, and loosed the rudder bands, and hoisted up the mainsail to the wind, and made toward shore.

Jas 3:4 — Behold also the ships, which though *they be* so great, and *are* driven of fierce winds, yet are they turned about with a very small helm, whithersoever the governor listeth.

HELMET

• A defensive headgear worn by soldiers.

1Sa 17:5 — And *he had* an helmet of brass upon his head, and he *was* armed with a coat of mail; and the weight of the coat *was* five thousand shekels of brass.

1Sa 17:38 — And Saul armed David with his armour, and he put an helmet of brass upon his head; also he armed him with a coat of mail.

2Ch 26:14 — And Uzziah prepared for them throughout all the host shields, and spears, and helmets, and habergeons, and bows, and slings *to cast* stones.

Jer 46:4 — Harness the horses; and get up, ye horsemen, and stand forth with *your* helmets; furbish the spears, *and* put on the brigandines.

Eze 23:24 — And they shall come against thee with chariots, wagons, and wheels, and with an assembly of people, *which* shall set against thee buckler and shield and helmet round about: and I will set judgment before them, and they shall judge thee according to their judgments.

• Figurative.

Isa 59:17 — For he put on righteousness as a breastplate, and an helmet of salvation upon his head; and he put on the garments of vengeance *for* clothing, and was clad with zeal as a cloke.

Eph 6:17 — And take the helmet of salvation, and the sword of the Spirit, which is the word of God:

1Th 5:8 — But let us, who are of the day, be sober, putting on the breastplate of faith and love; and for an helmet, the hope of salvation.

HELON • Father of Eliab.

Nu 1:9 — Of Zebulun; Eliab the son of Helon.

Nu 2:7 — *Then* the tribe of Zebulun: and Eliab the son of Helon *shall be* captain of the children of Zebulun.

Nu 7:24 — On the third day Eliab the son of Helon, prince of the children of Zebulun, *did offer:*

Nu 7:29 — And for a sacrifice of peace offerings, two oxen, five rams, five he goats, five lambs of the first year: this *was* the offering of Eliab the son of Helon.

Nu 10:16 — And over the host of the tribe of the children of Zebulun *was* Eliab the son of Helon.

HELP

Ps 34:1–8; Lk 7:19–30

Ps 34:17 — *The righteous* cry, and the LORD heareth, and delivereth them out of all their troubles.

Heb 4:16 — Let us therefore come boldly unto the throne of grace, that we may obtain mercy, and find grace to help in time of need.

HELPS

1Co 12:28 — And God hath set some in the church, first apostles, secondarily prophets, thirdly teachers, after that miracles, then gifts of healings, helps, governments, diversities of tongues.

Gal 6:10 — As we have therefore opportunity, let us do good unto all *men,* especially unto them who are of the household of faith.

HEMAM

• A son of Lotan.

Ge 36:22 — And the children of Lotan were Hori and Hemam; and Lotan's sister *was* Timna.

• Called Homam.

1Ch 1:39 — And the sons of Lotan; Hori, and Homam: and Timna *was* Lotan's sister.

HEMAN

• A man noted for wisdom, to whom Solomon is compared.

1Ki 4:31 — For he was wiser than all men; than Ethan the Ezrahite, and Heman, and Chalcol, and Darda, the sons of Mahol: and his fame was in all nations round about.

1Ch 2:6 — And the sons of Zerah; Zimri, and Ethan, and Heman, and Calcol, and Dara: five of them in all.

• "The singer," a chief Levite, and musician.

1Ch 6:33 — And these *are* they that waited with their children. Of the sons of the Kohathites: Heman a singer, the son of Joel, the son of Shemuel,

1Ch 15:17 — So the Levites appointed Heman the son of Joel; and of his brethren, Asaph the son of Berechiah; and of the sons of Merari their brethren, Ethan the son of Kushaiah;

1Ch 15:19 — So the singers, Heman, Asaph, and Ethan, *were appointed* to sound with cymbals of brass;

1Ch 16:41 — And with them Heman and Jeduthun, and the rest that were chosen, who were expressed by name, to give thanks to the LORD, because his mercy *endureth* for ever;

• The king's seer.

1Ch 25:5 — All these *were* the sons of Heman the king's seer in the words of God, to lift up the horn. And God gave to Heman fourteen sons and three daughters.

• His sons and daughters temple musicians.

1Ch 25:1–6

1Ch 6:33 — And these *are* they that waited with their children. Of the sons of the Kohathites: Heman a singer, the son of Joel, the son of Shemuel,

• "Maschil of".

Ps 88:1 — [A song *or* Psalm for the sons of Korah, to the chief Musician upon Mahalath Leannoth, Maschil of Heman the Ezrahite.] O LORD God of my salvation, I have cried day *and* night before thee:

HEMATH

• Another form for Hamath.

Am 6:14 — But, behold, I will raise up against you a nation, O house of Israel, saith the LORD the God of hosts; and they shall afflict you from the entering in of Hemath unto the river of the wilderness.

• An unknown person or place.

1Ch 2:55 — And the families of the scribes which dwelt at Jabez; the Tirathites, the Shimeathites, *and* Suchathites. These *are* the Kenites that came of Hemath, the father of the house of Rechab.

HEMDAN • Son of Dishon.

Ge 36:26 — And these *are* the children of Dishon; Hemdan, and Eshban, and Ithran, and Cheran.

HEMLOCK

• A poisonous and bitter plant.

Hos 10:4 — They have spoken words, swearing falsely in making a covenant: thus judgment springeth up as hemlock in the furrows of the field.

Am 6:12 — Shall horses run upon the rock? will *one* plow *there* with oxen? for ye have turned judgment into gall, and the fruit of righteousness into hemlock:

See: Gall

HEMORRHAGE

• Menstruation.

Le 15:19 — And if a woman have an issue, *and* her issue in her flesh be blood, she shall be put apart seven days: and whosoever toucheth her shall be unclean until the even.

Mt 9:20 — And, behold, a woman, which was diseased with an issue of blood twelve years, came behind *him,* and touched the hem of his garment:

Lk 8:43 — And a woman having an issue of blood twelve years, which had spent all her living upon physicians, neither could be healed of any,

• A woman suffers twelve years.

Mk 5:25–29

See: Menstruation

HEMORRHOIDS

• A disease with which the Philistines were afflicted.

1Sa 5:11–12

Dt 28:27 — The LORD will smite thee with the botch of Egypt, and with the emerods, and with the scab, and with the itch, whereof thou canst not be healed.

1Sa 5:6 — But the hand of the LORD was heavy upon them of Ashdod, and he destroyed them, and smote them with emerods, *even* Ashdod and the coasts thereof.

1Sa 6:4 — Then said they, What *shall be* the trespass offering which we shall return to him? They answered, Five golden emerods, and five golden mice, *according to* the number of the lords of the Philistines: for one plague was on you all, and on your lords.

See: Disease

See: Tumor

HEN • Figurative.

Mt 23:37 — O Jerusalem, Jerusalem, *thou* that killest the prophets, and stonest them which are sent unto thee, how often would I have gathered thy children together, even as a hen gathereth her chickens under *her* wings, and ye would not!

Lk 13:34 — O Jerusalem, Jerusalem, which killest the prophets, and stonest them that are sent unto thee; how often would I have gathered thy children together, as a hen *doth gather* her brood under *her* wings, and ye would not!

HENA • A city on the Euphrates.

2Ki 18:34 — Where *are* the gods of Hamath, and of Arpad? where *are* the gods of Sepharvaim, Hena, and Ivah? have they delivered Samaria out of mine hand?

2Ki 19:13 — Where *is* the king of Hamath, and the king of Arpad, and the king of the city of Sepharvaim, of Hena, and Ivah?

Isa 37:13 — Where *is* the king of Hamath, and the king of Arphad, and the king of the city of Sepharvaim, Hena, and Ivah?

HENADAD • A Levite.

Ezr 3:9 — Then stood Jeshua *with* his sons and his brethren, Kadmiel and his sons, the sons of Judah, together, to set forward the workmen in the house of God: the sons of Henadad, *with* their sons and their brethren the Levites.

Ne 3:18 — After him repaired their brethren, Bavai the son of Henadad, the ruler of the half part of Keilah.

Ne 3:24 — After him repaired Binnui the son of Henadad another piece, from the house of Azariah unto the turning *of the wall,* even unto the corner.

Ne 10:9 — And the Levites: both Jeshua the son of Azaniah, Binnui of the sons of Henadad, Kadmiel;

HEPHER

• Son of Gilead, and ancestor of Zelophehad.

Nu 26:32–33; Jos 17:2–3

Nu 27:1 — Then came the daughters of Zelophehad, the son of Hepher, the son of Gilead, the son of Machir, the son of Manasseh, of the families of Manasseh the son of Joseph: and these are the names of his daughters; Mahlah, Noah, and Hoglah, and Milcah, and Tirzah.

• Son of Naarah.

1Ch 4:6 — And Naarah bare him Ahuzam, and Hepher, and Temeni, and Haahashtari. These *were* the sons of Naarah.

• One of David's heroes.

1Ch 11:36 — Hepher the Mecherathite, Ahijah the Pelonite,

• A city west of the Jordan.

Jos 12:17 — The king of Tappuah, one; the king of Hepher, one;

1Ki 4:10 — The son of Hesed, in Aruboth; to him *pertained* Sochoh, and all the land of Hepher:

HEPHZI-BAH

• Wife of Hezekiah.

2Ki 21:1 — Manasseh *was* twelve years old when he began to reign, and reigned fifty and five years in Jerusalem. And his mother's name *was* Hephzi-bah.

• A prophetic name of Jerusalem.

Isa 62:4 — Thou shalt no more be termed Forsaken; neither shall thy land any more be termed Desolate: but thou shalt be called Hephzi-bah, and thy land Beulah: for the LORD delighteth in thee, and thy land shall be married.

HERALD

Isa 40:3 — The voice of him that crieth in the wilderness, Prepare ye the way of the LORD, make straight in the desert a highway for our God.

Da 3:4 — Then an herald cried aloud, To you it is commanded, O people, nations, and languages,

• Signified by the word preacher.

1Ti 2:7 — Whereunto I am ordained a preacher, and an apostle, (I speak the truth in Christ, *and* lie not;) a teacher of the Gentiles in faith and verity.

2Ti 1:11 — Whereunto I am appointed a preacher, and an apostle, and a teacher of the Gentiles.

2Pe 2:5 — And spared not the old world, but saved Noah the eighth *person,* a preacher of righteousness, bringing in the flood upon the world of the ungodly;

HERBS

• Given for food.

Ge 1:29–30

Pr 15:17 — Better *is* a dinner of herbs where love is, than a stalled ox and hatred therewith.

→See: Vegetation

HEREDITY

Ex 20:5–6; Isa 14:20–21; 65:6–7; Jer 31:29–30; Eze 18:19–20; Jn 3:6–7

Ge 5:3 — And Adam lived an hundred and thirty years, and begat *a son* in his own likeness, after his image; and called his name Seth:

Ex 34:7 — Keeping mercy for thousands, forgiving iniquity and transgression and sin, and that will by no means clear *the guilty;* visiting the iniquity of the fathers upon the children, and upon the children's children, unto the third and to the fourth *generation.*

Nu 14:18 — The LORD *is* longsuffering, and of great mercy, forgiving iniquity and transgression, and by no means clearing *the guilty,* visiting the iniquity of the fathers upon the children unto the third and fourth *generation.*

Nu 14:33 — And your children shall wander in the wilderness forty years, and bear your whoredoms, until your carcases be wasted in the wilderness.

Job 14:4 — Who can bring a clean *thing* out of an unclean? not one.

Job 21:19 — God layeth up his iniquity for his children: he rewardeth him, and he shall know *it.*

Ps 37:28 — For the LORD loveth judgment, and forsaketh not his saints; they are preserved for ever: but the seed of the wicked shall be cut off.

Ps 51:5 — Behold, I was shapen in iniquity; and in sin did my mother conceive me.

Ps 58:3 — The wicked are estranged from the womb: they go astray as soon as they be born, speaking lies.

Isa 48:8 — Yea, thou heardest not; yea, thou knewest not; yea, from that time *that* thine ear was not opened: for I knew that thou wouldest deal very treacherously, and wast called a transgressor from the womb.

Jer 32:18 — Thou shewest lovingkindness unto thousands, and recompensest the iniquity of the fathers into the bosom of their children after them: the Great, the Mighty God, the LORD of hosts, *is* his name,

Eze 18:2 — What mean ye, that ye use this proverb concerning the land of Israel, saying, The fathers have eaten sour grapes, and the children's teeth are set on edge?

Mt 3:9 — And think not to say within yourselves, We have Abraham to *our* father: for I say unto you, that God is able of these stones to raise up children unto Abraham.

Jn 9:2 — And his disciples asked him, saying, Master, who did sin, this man, or his parents, that he was born blind?

Ro 5:12 — Wherefore, as by one man sin entered into the world, and death by sin; and so death passed upon all men, for that all have sinned:

1Co 15:22 — For as in Adam all die, even so in Christ shall all be made alive.

Eph 2:3 — Among whom also we all had our conversation in times past in the lusts of our flesh, fulfilling the desires of the flesh and of the mind; and were by nature the children of wrath, even as others.

HERES • A mountain.

Jgs 1:35 — But the Amorites would dwell in mount Heres in Aijalon, and in Shaalbim: yet the hand of the house of Joseph prevailed, so that they became tributaries.

HERESH • A Levite.

1Ch 9:15 — And Bakbakkar, Heresh, and Galal, and Mattaniah the son of Micah, the son of Zichri, the son of Asaph;

HERESY

• Propagandism of, forbidden under severe penalties.

Dt 13:1–18; Tit 3:10–11; 2Jn 1:10–11

• Teachers of, among early Christians.

2Pe 2:1–22; Jude 1:3–16

Ac 15:24 — Forasmuch as we have heard, that certain which went out from us have troubled you with words, subverting your souls, saying, *Ye must* be circumcised, and keep the law: to whom we gave no *such* commandment:

2Co 11:4 — For if he that cometh preacheth another Jesus, whom we have not preached, or *if* ye receive another spirit, which ye have not received, or another gospel, which ye have not accepted, ye might well bear with *him.*

Gal 1:7 — Which is not another; but there be some that trouble you, and would pervert the gospel of Christ.

Gal 2:4 — And that because of false brethren unawares brought in, who came in privily to spy out our liberty which we have in Christ Jesus, that they might bring us into bondage:

Rev 2:2 — I know thy works, and thy labour, and thy patience, and how thou canst not bear them which are evil: and thou hast tried them which say they are apostles, and are not, and hast found them liars:

• Paul and Silas accused of.

Ac 16:20–21

Ac 16:23 — And when they had laid many stripes upon them, they cast *them* into prison, charging the jailer to keep them safely:

- **Paul accused of.**

Ac 18:13 — Saying, This *fellow* persuadeth men to worship God contrary to the law.

- **Disavowed by Paul.**

Ac 24:13–16

⇝See: Teachers; false

HERMAS • A Christian at Rome.

Ro 16:14 — Salute Asyncritus, Phlegon, Hermas, Patrobas, Hermes, and the brethren which are with them.

HERMES • A Greek Christian.

Ro 16:14 — Salute Asyncritus, Phlegon, Hermas, Patrobas, Hermes, and the brethren which are with them.

HERMOGENES • A Christian who deserted Paul.

2Ti 1:15 — This thou knowest, that all they which are in Asia be turned away from me; of whom are Phygellus and Hermogenes.

HERMON

- **A mountain in the north of Palestine.**
- **Called Sirion.**

Dt 3:8–9

Ps 29:6 — He maketh them also to skip like a calf; Lebanon and Sirion like a young unicorn.

- **Called Sion.**

Dt 4:48 — From Aroer, which *is* by the bank of the river Arnon, even unto mount Sion, which *is* Hermon,

Ps 133:3 — As the dew of Hermon, *and as the dew* that descended upon the mountains of Zion: for there the LORD commanded the blessing, *even* life for evermore.

- **Called Shenir.**

Dt 3:9 — (*Which* Hermon the Sidonians call Sirion; and the Amorites call it Shenir;)

1Ch 5:23 — And the children of the half tribe of Manasseh dwelt in the land: they increased from Bashan unto Baal-hermon and Senir, and unto mount Hermon.

SS 4:8 — Come with me from Lebanon, *my* spouse, with me from Lebanon: look from the top of Amana, from the top of Shenir and Hermon, from the lions' dens, from the mountains of the leopards.

HEROD

- **King of Judah.**

Mt 2:1–23

- **Tetrarch of Galilee.**

Lk 3:1 — Now in the fifteenth year of the reign of Tiberius Caesar, Pontius Pilate being governor of Judaea, and Herod being tetrarch of Galilee, and his brother Philip tetrarch of Ituraea and of the region of Trachonitis, and Lysanias the tetrarch of Abilene,

Lk 23:7 — And as soon as he knew that he belonged unto Herod's jurisdiction, he sent him to Herod, who himself also was at Jerusalem at that time.

- **Incest of.**

Mt 14:3–4; Mk 6:17–19

- **Beheads John the Baptist.**

Mt 14:3–11; Mk 6:16–28

- **Desires to see Jesus.**

Lk 9:7 — Now Herod the tetrarch heard of all that was done by him: and he was perplexed, because that it was said of some, that John was risen from the dead;

Lk 9:9 — And Herod said, John have I beheaded: but who is this, of whom I hear such things? And he desired to see him.

Lk 23:8 — And when Herod saw Jesus, he was exceeding glad: for he was desirous to see him of a long *season,* because he had heard many things of him; and he hoped to have seen some miracle done by him.

- **Tyranny of.**

Lk 13:31–32

- **Jesus tried by.**

Lk 23:6–12

Lk 23:15 — No, nor yet Herod: for I sent you to him; and, lo, nothing worthy of death is done unto him.

Ac 4:27 — For of a truth against thy holy child Jesus, whom thou hast anointed, both Herod, and Pontius Pilate, with the Gentiles, and the people of Israel, were gathered together,

- **Son of Aristobulus.**

Ac 12:1–23

HERODIANS

- **A Jewish faction.**
- **Seek to entangle Jesus.**

Mt 22:16 — And they sent out unto him their disciples with the Herodians, saying, Master, we know that thou art true, and teachest the way of God in truth, neither carest thou for any *man:* for thou regardest not the person of men.

Mk 12:13 — And they send unto him certain of the Pharisees and of the Herodians, to catch him in *his* words.

- **Conspire to slay Jesus.**

Mk 3:6 — And the Pharisees went forth, and straightway took counsel with the Herodians against him, how they might destroy him.

Mk 12:13 — And they send unto him certain of the Pharisees and of the Herodians, to catch him in *his* words.

HERODIAS • Daughter of Aristobulus.

Mt 14:3 — For Herod had laid hold on John, and bound him, and put *him* in prison for Herodias' sake, his brother Philip's wife.

Mt 14:6 — But when Herod's birthday was kept, the daughter of Herodias danced before them, and pleased Herod.

Mk 6:17 — For Herod himself had sent forth and laid hold upon John, and bound him in prison for Herodias' sake, his brother Philip's wife: for he had married her.

Mk 6:19 — Therefore Herodias had a quarrel against him, and would have killed him; but she could not:

Mk 6:22 — And when the daughter of the said Herodias came in, and danced, and pleased Herod and them that sat with him, the king said unto the damsel, Ask of me whatsoever thou wilt, and I will give *it* thee.

Lk 3:19 — But Herod the tetrarch, being reproved by him for Herodias his brother Philip's wife, and for all the evils which Herod had done,

HERODION • A Roman Christian.

Ro 16:11 — Salute Herodion my kinsman. Greet them that be of the *household* of Narcissus, which are in the Lord.

HEROES

Heb 11:32–40

HERON

Le 11:19 — And the stork, the heron after her kind, and the lapwing, and the bat.

Dt 14:18 — And the stork, and the heron after her kind, and the lapwing, and the bat.

HESED • Father of one of Solomon's officers.

1Ki 4:10 — The son of Hesed, in Aruboth; to him *pertained* Sochoh, and all the land of Hepher:

HESHBON

• A city of the Amorites.

Nu 21:25–35

Dt 1:4 — After he had slain Sihon the king of the Amorites, which dwelt in Heshbon, and Og the king of Bashan, which dwelt at Astaroth in Edrei:

• Built by Reuben.

Nu 32:37 — And the children of Reuben built Heshbon, and Elealeh, and Kirjathaim,

• Allotted to Gad.

Jos 21:38–39

• Fish-pools at.

SS 7:4 — Thy neck *is* as a tower of ivory; thine eyes *like* the fishpools in Heshbon, by the gate of Bath-rabbim: thy nose *is* as the tower of Lebanon which looketh toward Damascus.

• Prophecy concerning.

Jer 48:34–35; 49:1–3

Isa 16:8 — For the fields of Heshbon languish, *and* the vine of Sibmah: the lords of the heathen have broken down the principal plants thereof, they are come *even* unto Jazer, they wandered *through* the wilderness: her branches are stretched out, they are gone over the sea.

Jer 48:2 — There shall be no more praise of Moab: in Heshbon they have devised evil against it; come, and let us cut it off from being a nation. Also thou shalt be cut down, O Madmen; the sword shall pursue thee.

HESHMON • A town in the south of Judah.

Jos 15:27 — And Hazar-gaddah, and Heshmon, and Beth-palet,

HETH

• Son of Canaan, and ancestor of the Hittites.

Ge 10:15 — And Canaan begat Sidon his firstborn, and Heth,

Ge 23:3 — And Abraham stood up from before his dead, and spake unto the sons of Heth, saying,

Ge 23:5 — And the children of Heth answered Abraham, saying unto him,

Ge 23:7 — And Abraham stood up, and bowed himself to the people of the land, *even* to the children of Heth.

Ge 23:10 — And Ephron dwelt among the children of Heth: and Ephron the Hittite answered Abraham in the audience of the children of Heth, *even* of all that went in at the gate of his city, saying,

Ge 23:16 — And Abraham hearkened unto Ephron; and Abraham weighed to Ephron the silver, which he had named in the audience of the sons of Heth, four hundred shekels of silver, current *money* with the merchant.

Ge 23:18 — Unto Abraham for a possession in the presence of the children of Heth, before all that went in at the gate of his city.

Ge 27:46 — And Rebekah said to Isaac, I am weary of my life because of the daughters of Heth: if Jacob take a wife of the daughters of Heth, such as these *which are* of the daughters of the land, what good shall my life do me?

Ge 49:32 — The purchase of the field and of the cave that *is* therein *was* from the children of Heth.

1Ch 1:13 — And Canaan begat Zidon his firstborn, and Heth,

✦See: Hittites

HETHLON • A place on the northern frontier of Palestine.

Eze 47:15 — And this *shall be* the border of the land toward the north side, from the great sea, the way of Hethlon, as men go to Zedad;

Eze 48:1 — Now these *are* the names of the tribes. From the north end to the coast of the way of Hethlon, as one goeth to Hamath, Hazar-enan, the border of Damascus northward, to the coast of Hamath; for these are his sides east *and* west; a *portion for* Dan.

HEZEKI • A Benjamite.

1Ch 8:17 — And Zebadiah, and Meshullam, and Hezeki, and Heber,

HEZEKIAH

• King of Judah.

2Ki 18:1–2

2Ki 16:20 — And Ahaz slept with his fathers, and was buried with his fathers in the city of David: and Hezekiah his son reigned in his stead.

1Ch 3:13 — Ahaz his son, Hezekiah his son, Manasseh his son,

2Ch 29:1 — Hezekiah began to reign *when he was* five and twenty years old, and he reigned nine and twenty years in Jerusalem. And his mother's name *was* Abijah, the daughter of Zechariah.

Mt 1:9 — And Ozias begat Joatham; and Joatham begat Achaz; and Achaz begat Ezekias;

- **Religious zeal of.**

2Ch 29:1–31:21

- **Purges the nation of idolatry.**

2Ki 18:4 — He removed the high places, and brake the images, and cut down the groves, and brake in pieces the brasen serpent that Moses had made: for unto those days the children of Israel did burn incense to it: and he called it Nehushtan.

2Ch 31:1 — Now when all this was finished, all Israel that were present went out to the cities of Judah, and brake the images in pieces, and cut down the groves, and threw down the high places and the altars out of all Judah and Benjamin, in Ephraim also and Manasseh, until they had utterly destroyed them all. Then all the children of Israel returned, every man to his possession, into their own cities.

2Ch 33:3 — For he built again the high places which Hezekiah his father had broken down, and he reared up altars for Baalim, and made groves, and worshipped all the host of heaven, and served them.

- **Restores the true forms of worship.**

2Ch 31:2–21

- **His piety.**

2Ki 18:5–6; 2Ch 31:20–21

2Ki 18:3 — And he did *that which was* right in the sight of the LORD, according to all that David his father did.

2Ch 29:2 — And he did *that which was* right in the sight of the LORD, according to all that David his father had done.

2Ch 32:32 — Now the rest of the acts of Hezekiah, and his goodness, behold, they *are* written in the vision of Isaiah the prophet, the son of Amoz, *and* in the book of the kings of Judah and Israel.

Jer 26:19 — Did Hezekiah king of Judah and all Judah put him at all to death? did he not fear the LORD, and besought the LORD, and the LORD repented him of the evil which he had pronounced against them? Thus might we procure great evil against our souls.

- **Military operations of.**

1Ch 4:39–43; 2Ch 32:1–33; Isa 36:1–37:38

2Ki 18:19 — And Rab-shakeh said unto them, Speak ye now to Hezekiah, Thus saith the great king, the king of Assyria, What confidence is this wherein thou trustest?

- **Sickness and restoration of.**

2Ki 20:1–11; Isa 38:1–8

2Ch 32:24 — In those days Hezekiah was sick to the death, and prayed unto the LORD: and he spake unto him, and he gave him a sign.

- **His psalm of thanksgiving.**

Isa 38:9–22

- **His lack of wisdom in showing his resources to commissioners of Babylon.**

2Ki 20:12–19; 2Ch 32:25–26; Isa 39:1–8

2Ch 32:31 — Howbeit in *the business of* the ambassadors of the princes of Babylon, who sent unto him to enquire of the wonder that was *done* in the land, God left him, to try him, that he might know all *that was* in his heart.

- **Prospered of God.**

2Ch 32:27–30

2Ki 18:7 — And the LORD was with him; *and* he prospered whithersoever he went forth: and he rebelled against the king of Assyria, and served him not.

- **Conducts the brook Gihon into Jerusalem.**

Ne 2:13–15; Isa 22:9–11

2Ki 18:17 — And the king of Assyria sent Tartan and Rabsaris and Rab-shakeh from Lachish to king Hezekiah with a great host against Jerusalem. And they went up and came to Jerusalem. And when they were come up, they came and stood by the conduit of the upper pool, which is in the highway of the fuller's field.

2Ki 20:20 — And the rest of the acts of Hezekiah, and all his might, and how he made a pool, and a conduit, and brought water into the city, *are* they not written in the book of the chronicles of the kings of Judah?

2Ch 32:4 — So there was gathered much people together, who stopped all the fountains, and the brook that ran through the midst of the land, saying, Why should the kings of Assyria come, and find much water?

2Ch 32:30 — This same Hezekiah also stopped the upper watercourse of Gihon, and brought it straight down to the west side of the city of David. And Hezekiah prospered in all his works.

2Ch 33:14 — Now after this he built a wall without the city of David, on the west side of Gihon, in the valley, even to the entering in at the fish gate, and compassed about Ophel, and raised it up a very great height, and put captains of war in all the fenced cities of Judah.

Ne 3:13 — The valley gate repaired Hanun, and the inhabitants of Zanoah; they built it, and set up the doors thereof, the locks thereof, and the bars thereof, and a thousand cubits on the wall unto the dung gate.

Ne 3:16 — After him repaired Nehemiah the son of Azbuk, the ruler of the half part of Beth-zur, unto *the place* over against the sepulchres of David, and to the pool that was made, and unto the house of the mighty.

Isa 7:3 — Then said the LORD unto Isaiah, Go forth now to meet Ahaz, thou, and Shear-jashub thy son, at the end of the conduit of the upper pool in the highway of the fuller's field;

Isa 36:2 — And the king of Assyria sent Rabshakeh from Lachish to Jerusalem unto king Hezekiah with a great army. And he stood by the conduit of the upper pool in the highway of the fuller's field.

• **Scribes of.**

Pr 25:1 — These *are* also proverbs of Solomon, which the men of Hezekiah king of Judah copied out.

• **Death and burial of.**

2Ki 20:21 — And Hezekiah slept with his fathers: and Manasseh his son reigned in his stead.

2Ch 32:33 — And Hezekiah slept with his fathers, and they buried him in the chiefest of the sepulchres of the sons of David: and all Judah and the inhabitants of Jerusalem did him honour at his death. And Manasseh his son reigned in his stead.

• **Prophecies concerning.**

2Ki 19:20–34; 20:5–6, 16–18; Isa 38:5–8; 39:5–7; Jer 26:18–19

• **Son of Neariah.**

1Ch 3:23 — And the sons of Neariah; Elioenai, and Hezekiah, and Azrikam, three.

• **One of the exiles.**

Ezr 2:16 — The children of Ater of Hezekiah, ninety and eight.

Ne 7:21 — The children of Ater of Hezekiah, ninety and eight.

• **Called Hizkijah.**

Ne 10:17 — Ater, Hizkijah, Azzur,

HEZION • Grandfather of Ben-hadad.

1Ki 15:18 — Then Asa took all the silver and the gold *that were* left in the treasures of the house of the LORD, and the treasures of the king's house, and delivered them into the hand of his servants: and king Asa sent them to Ben-hadad, the son of Tabrimon, the son of Hezion, king of Syria, that dwelt at Damascus, saying,

HEZIR

• **A Levite.**

1Ch 24:15 — The seventeenth to Hezir, the eighteenth to Aphses,

• **A prince of Judah.**

Ne 10:20 — Magpiash, Meshullam, Hezir,

HEZRAI

• **Called also Hezro.**

• **A Carmelite.**

2Sa 23:35 — Hezrai the Carmelite, Paarai the Arbite,

1Ch 11:37 — Hezro the Carmelite, Naarai the son of Ezbai,

HEZRO • See: Hezrai

HEZRON

• **Son of Pharez.**

Ge 46:12 — And the sons of Judah; Er, and Onan, and Shelah, and Pharez, and Zarah: but Er and Onan died in the land of Canaan. And the sons of Pharez were Hezron and Hamul.

• **Ancestor of the Hezronites.**

Nu 26:6 — Of Hezron, the family of the Hezronites: of Carmi, the family of the Carmites.

Nu 26:21 — And the sons of Pharez were; of Hezron, the family of the Hezronites: of Hamul, the family of the Hamulites.

1Ch 2:5 — The sons of Pharez; Hezron, and Hamul.

1Ch 2:9 — The sons also of Hezron, that were born unto him; Jerahmeel, and Ram, and Chelubai.

1Ch 2:18 — And Caleb the son of Hezron begat *children* of Azubah *his* wife, and of Jerioth: her sons *are* these; Jesher, and Shobab, and Ardon.

1Ch 2:21 — And afterward Hezron went in to the daughter of Machir the father of Gilead, whom he married when he *was* threescore years old; and she bare him Segub.

1Ch 2:24 — And after that Hezron was dead in Caleb-ephratah, then Abiah Hezron's wife bare him Ashur the father of Tekoa.

• **A son of Reuben.**

Ge 46:9 — And the sons of Reuben; Hanoch, and Phallu, and Hezron, and Carmi.

Ex 6:14 — These *be* the heads of their fathers' houses: The sons of Reuben the firstborn of Israel; Hanoch, and Pallu, Hezron, and Carmi: these *be* the families of Reuben.

1Ch 4:1 — The sons of Judah; Pharez, Hezron, and Carmi, and Hur, and Shobal.

1Ch 5:3 — The sons, *I say*, of Reuben the firstborn of Israel *were*, Hanoch, and Pallu, Hezron, and Carmi.

• **Descendants of, called Hezronites.**

Nu 26:6 — Of Hezron, the family of the Hezronites: of Carmi, the family of the Carmites.

HIDDAI

• **One of David's heroes.**

2Sa 23:30 — Benaiah the Pirathonite, Hiddai of the brooks of Gaash,

• **Called Hurai.**

1Ch 11:32 — Hurai of the brooks of Gaash, Abiel the Arbathite,

HIDDEKEL • Ancient name of the River Tigris.

Ge 2:14 — And the name of the third river *is* Hiddekel: that *is* it which goeth toward the east of Assyria. And the fourth river *is* Euphrates.

Da 10:4 — And in the four and twentieth day of the first month, as I was by the side of the great river, which *is* Hiddekel;

HIEL

• **Rebuilder of Jericho.**

1Ki 16:34 — In his days did Hiel the Bethelite build Jericho: he laid the foundation thereof in Abiram his firstborn, and set up the gates thereof in his youngest *son* Segub, according to the word of the LORD, which he spake by Joshua the son of Nun.

• In him was fulfilled the curse pronounced by Joshua.

Jos 6:26 — And Joshua adjured *them* at that time, saying, Cursed *be* the man before the LORD, that riseth up and buildeth this city Jericho: he shall lay the foundation thereof in his firstborn, and in his youngest *son* shall he set up the gates of it.

HIERAPOLIS • A city of Phrygia.

Col 4:13 — For I bear him record, that he hath a great zeal for you, and them *that are* in Laodicea, and them in Hierapolis.

HIGGAION ✧See: Music

HIGH PLACES

• A term used to describe places of worship.

Ge 12:8 — And he removed from thence unto a mountain on the east of Bethel, and pitched his tent, *having* Bethel on the west, and Hai on the east: and there he builded an altar unto the LORD, and called upon the name of the LORD.

Ge 22:2 — And he said, Take now thy son, thine only *son* Isaac, whom thou lovest, and get thee into the land of Moriah; and offer him there for a burnt offering upon one of the mountains which I will tell thee of.

Ge 22:14 — And Abraham called the name of that place Jehovah-jireh: as it is said *to* this day, In the mount of the LORD it shall be seen.

Ge 31:54 — Then Jacob offered sacrifice upon the mount, and called his brethren to eat bread: and they did eat bread, and tarried all night in the mount.

1Sa 9:12 — And they answered them, and said, He is; behold, *he is* before you: make haste now, for he came to day to the city; for *there is* a sacrifice of the people to day in the high place:

2Sa 24:25 — And David built there an altar unto the LORD, and offered burnt offerings and peace offerings. So the LORD was intreated for the land, and the plague was stayed from Israel.

1Ki 3:2 — Only the people sacrificed in high places, because there was no house built unto the name of the LORD, until those days.

1Ki 3:4 — And the king went to Gibeon to sacrifice there; for that *was* the great high place: a thousand burnt offerings did Solomon offer upon that altar.

1Ki 18:30 — And Elijah said unto all the people, Come near unto me. And all the people came near unto him. And he repaired the altar of the LORD *that was* broken down.

1Ki 18:38 — Then the fire of the LORD fell, and consumed the burnt sacrifice, and the wood, and the stones, and the dust, and licked up the water that *was* in the trench.

1Ch 16:39 — And Zadok the priest, and his brethren the priests, before the tabernacle of the LORD in the high place that *was* at Gibeon,

2Ch 1:3 — So Solomon, and all the congregation with him, went to the high place that *was* at Gibeon; for there was the tabernacle of the congregation of God, which Moses the servant of the LORD had made in the wilderness.

2Ch 33:17 — Nevertheless the people did sacrifice still in the high places, yet unto the LORD their God only.

• Signify a place of idolatrous worship.

Nu 22:41 — And it came to pass on the morrow, that Balak took Balaam, and brought him up into the high places of Baal, that thence he might see the utmost *part* of the people.

1Ki 11:7 — Then did Solomon build an high place for Chemosh, the abomination of Moab, in the hill that *is* before Jerusalem, and for Molech, the abomination of the children of Ammon.

1Ki 12:31 — And he made an house of high places, and made priests of the lowest of the people, which were not of the sons of Levi.

1Ki 14:23 — For they also built them high places, and images, and groves, on every high hill, and under every green tree.

1Ki 15:14 — But the high places were not removed: nevertheless Asa's heart was perfect with the LORD all his days.

1Ki 22:43 — And he walked in all the ways of Asa his father; he turned not aside from it, doing *that which was* right in the eyes of the LORD: nevertheless the high places were not taken away; *for* the people offered and burnt incense yet in the high places.

2Ki 17:9 — And the children of Israel did secretly *those* things that *were* not right against the LORD their God, and they built them high places in all their cities, from the tower of the watchmen to the fenced city.

2Ki 17:29 — Howbeit every nation made gods of their own, and put *them* in the houses of the high places which the Samaritans had made, every nation in their cities wherein they dwelt.

Jer 7:31 — And they have built the high places of Tophet, which is in the valley of the son of Hinnom, to burn their sons and their daughters in the fire; which I commanded *them* not, neither came it into my heart.

• Licentious practices at.

Eze 16:24–43

• The idolatrous, to be destroyed.

Le 26:30 — And I will destroy your high places, and cut down your images, and cast your carcases upon the carcases of your idols, and my soul shall abhor you.

Nu 33:52 — Then ye shall drive out all the inhabitants of the land from before you, and destroy all their pictures, and destroy all their molten images, and quite pluck down all their high places:

• Asa destroys.

2Ch 14:3 — For he took away the altars of the strange *gods,* and the high places, and brake down the images, and cut down the groves:

• **Jehoshaphat.**

2Ch 17:6 — And his heart was lifted up in the ways of the LORD: moreover he took away the high places and groves out of Judah.

• **Hezekiah.**

2Ki 18:4 — He removed the high places, and brake the images, and cut down the groves, and brake in pieces the brasen serpent that Moses had made: for unto those days the children of Israel did burn incense to it: and he called it Nehushtan.

• **Josiah.**

2Ki 23:8 — And he brought all the priests out of the cities of Judah, and defiled the high places where the priests had burned incense, from Geba to Beer-sheba, and brake down the high places of the gates that *were* in the entering in of the gate of Joshua the governor of the city, which *were* on a man's left hand at the gate of the city.

See: Groves

See: Idolatry

HIGH PRIEST **See: Priest, High**

HIGHWAYS

• **Figurative.**

Isa 35:8–10; 40:3–4; Mt 7:13–14

Pr 16:17 — The highway of the upright *is* to depart from evil: he that keepeth his way preserveth his soul.

Isa 11:16 — And there shall be an highway for the remnant of his people, which shall be left, from Assyria; like as it was to Israel in the day that he came up out of the land of Egypt.

Mt 3:3 — For this is he that was spoken of by the prophet Esaias, saying, The voice of one crying in the wilderness, Prepare ye the way of the Lord, make his paths straight.

See: Roads

See: Way

HILEN

• **A city of Judah.**

• **Assigned to the priests.**

1Ch 6:58 — And Hilen with her suburbs, Debir with her suburbs,

• **Called Holon.**

Jos 15:51 — And Goshen, and Holon, and Giloh; eleven cities with their villages:

Jos 21:15 — And Holon with her suburbs, and Debir with her suburbs,

HILKIAH

• **Officer of Hezekiah.**

2Ki 18:18 — And when they had called to the king, there came out to them Eliakim the son of Hilkiah, which *was* over the household, and Shebna the scribe, and Joah the son of Asaph the recorder.

2Ki 18:26 — Then said Eliakim the son of Hilkiah, and Shebna, and Joah, unto Rab-shakeh, Speak, I pray thee, to thy servants in the Syrian language; for we understand *it:* and talk not with us in the Jews' language in the ears of the people that *are* on the wall.

2Ki 18:37 — Then came Eliakim the son of Hilkiah, which *was* over the household, and Shebna the scribe, and Joah the son of Asaph the recorder, to Hezekiah with *their* clothes rent, and told him the words of Rab-shakeh.

Isa 22:20 — And it shall come to pass in that day, that I will call my servant Eliakim the son of Hilkiah:

Isa 36:3 — Then came forth unto him Eliakim, Hilkiah's son, which was over the house, and Shebna the scribe, and Joah, Asaph's son, the recorder.

Isa 36:22 — Then came Eliakim, the son of Hilkiah, that *was* over the household, and Shebna the scribe, and Joah, the son of Asaph, the recorder, to Hezekiah with *their* clothes rent, and told him the words of Rabshakeh.

• **High priest.**

2Ch 34:14–15

2Ki 22:4 — Go up to Hilkiah the high priest, that he may sum the silver which is brought into the house of the LORD, which the keepers of the door have gathered of the people:

2Ki 22:8 — And Hilkiah the high priest said unto Shaphan the scribe, I have found the book of the law in the house of the LORD. And Hilkiah gave the book to Shaphan, and he read it.

2Ki 22:10 — And Shaphan the scribe shewed the king, saying, Hilkiah the priest hath delivered me a book. And Shaphan read it before the king.

2Ki 22:12 — And the king commanded Hilkiah the priest, and Ahikam the son of Shaphan, and Achbor the son of Michaiah, and Shaphan the scribe, and Asahiah a servant of the king's, saying,

2Ki 22:14 — So Hilkiah the priest, and Ahikam, and Achbor, and Shaphan, and Asahiah, went unto Huldah the prophetess, the wife of Shallum the son of Tikvah, the son of Harhas, keeper of the wardrobe; (now she dwelt in Jerusalem in the college;) and they communed with her.

2Ki 23:4 — And the king commanded Hilkiah the high priest, and the priests of the second order, and the keepers of the door, to bring forth out of the temple of the LORD all the vessels that were made for Baal, and for the grove, and for all the host of heaven: and he burned them without Jerusalem in the fields of Kidron, and carried the ashes of them unto Bethel.

2Ki 23:24 — Moreover the *workers with* familiar spirits, and the wizards, and the images, and the idols, and all the abominations that were spied in the land of Judah and in Jerusalem, did Josiah put away, that he might perform the words of the law which were written in the book that Hilkiah the priest found in the house of the LORD.

1Ch 6:13 — And Shallum begat Hilkiah, and Hilkiah begat Azariah,

1Ch 9:11 — And Azariah the son of Hilkiah, the son of Meshullam, the son of Zadok, the son of Meraioth, the son of Ahitub, the ruler of the house of God;

2Ch 34:9 — And when they came to Hilkiah the high priest, they delivered the money that was brought into the house of God, which the Levites that kept the doors had gathered of the hand of Manasseh and Ephraim, and of all the remnant of Israel, and of all Judah and Benjamin; and they returned to Jerusalem.

2Ch 34:18 — Then Shaphan the scribe told the king, saying, Hilkiah the priest hath given me a book. And Shaphan read it before the king.

2Ch 34:20 — And the king commanded Hilkiah, and Ahikam the son of Shaphan, and Abdon the son of Micah, and Shaphan the scribe, and Asaiah a servant of the king's, saying,

2Ch 34:22 — And Hilkiah, and *they* that the king *had appointed,* went to Huldah the prophetess, the wife of Shallum the son of Tikvath, the son of Hasrah, keeper of the wardrobe; (now she dwelt in Jerusalem in the college:) and they spake to her to that *effect.*

Ezr 7:1 — Now after these things, in the reign of Artaxerxes king of Persia, Ezra the son of Seraiah, the son of Azariah, the son of Hilkiah,

Jer 29:3 — By the hand of Elasah the son of Shaphan, and Gemariah the son of Hilkiah, (whom Zedekiah king of Judah sent unto Babylon to Nebuchadnezzar king of Babylon) saying,

• Name of two Levites.

1Ch 6:45 — The son of Hashabiah, the son of Amaziah, the son of Hilkiah,

1Ch 26:11 — Hilkiah the second, Tebaliah the third, Zechariah the fourth: all the sons and brethren of Hosah *were* thirteen.

• Two priests.

Ne 8:4 — And Ezra the scribe stood upon a pulpit of wood, which they had made for the purpose; and beside him stood Mattithiah, and Shema, and Anaiah, and Urijah, and Hilkiah, and Maaseiah, on his right hand; and on his left hand, Pedaiah, and Mishael, and Malchiah, and Hashum, and Hashbadana, Zechariah, *and* Meshullam.

Ne 12:7 — Sallu, Amok, Hilkiah, Jedaiah. These *were* the chief of the priests and of their brethren in the days of Jeshua.

Ne 12:21 — Of Hilkiah, Hashabiah; of Jedaiah, Nethaneel.

Jer 1:1 — The words of Jeremiah the son of Hilkiah, of the priests that *were* in Anathoth in the land of Benjamin:

HILLEL • Father of Abdon.

Jgs 12:13 — And after him Abdon the son of Hillel, a Pirathonite, judged Israel.

Jgs 12:15 — And Abdon the son of Hillel the Pirathonite died, and was buried in Pirathon in the land of Ephraim, in the mount of the Amalekites.

HILLS

• Perpetual.

Ge 49:26 — The blessings of thy father have prevailed above the blessings of my progenitors unto the utmost bound of the everlasting hills: they shall be on the head of Joseph, and on the crown of the head of him that was separate from his brethren.

Hab 3:6 — He stood, and measured the earth: he beheld, and drove asunder the nations; and the everlasting mountains were scattered, the perpetual hills did bow: his ways *are* everlasting.

HIN

• A measure for liquids, and containing one-sixth or one-seventh of a bath.

• Probably equivalent to about 1 gallon 1 quart, or 1 gallon 1 1/2 quarts.

Ex 29:40 — And with the one lamb a tenth deal of flour mingled with the fourth part of an hin of beaten oil; and the fourth part of an hin of wine *for* a drink offering.

Le 19:36 — Just balances, just weights, a just ephah, and a just hin, shall ye have: I *am* the LORD your God, which brought you out of the land of Egypt.

Le 23:13 — And the meat offering thereof *shall be* two tenth deals of fine flour mingled with oil, an offering made by fire unto the LORD *for* a sweet savour: and the drink offering thereof *shall be* of wine, the fourth *part* of an hin.

HIND →See: Deer

HINNOM

• A valley west and southwest of Jerusalem.

Jos 15:8 — And the border went up by the valley of the son of Hinnom unto the south side of the Jebusite; the same *is* Jerusalem: and the border went up to the top of the mountain that *lieth* before the valley of Hinnom westward, which *is* at the end of the valley of the giants northward:

Jos 18:16 — And the border came down to the end of the mountain that *lieth* before the valley of the son of Hinnom, *and* which *is* in the valley of the giants on the north, and descended to the valley of Hinnom, to the side of Jebusi on the south, and descended to Enrogel,

2Ki 23:10 — And he defiled Topheth, which *is* in the valley of the children of Hinnom, that no man might make his son or his daughter to pass through the fire to Molech.

Ne 11:30 — Zanoah, Adullam, and *in* their villages, at Lachish, and the fields thereof, at Azekah, and *in* the villages thereof. And they dwelt from Beer-sheba unto the valley of Hinnom.

• Children offered in sacrifice in.

Jer 7:31–32

2Ch 28:3 — Moreover he burnt incense in the valley of the son of Hinnom, and burnt his children in the fire, after the abominations of the heathen whom the LORD had cast out before the children of Israel.

2Ch 33:6 — And he caused his children to pass through the fire in the valley of the son of Hinnom: also he observed times, and used enchantments, and used witchcraft, and dealt with a familiar spirit, and with wizards: he wrought much evil in the sight of the LORD, to provoke him to anger.

Jer 19:2 — And go forth unto the valley of the son of Hinnom, which *is* by the entry of the east gate, and proclaim there the words that I shall tell thee,

Jer 19:4 — Because they have forsaken me, and have estranged this place, and have burned incense in it unto other gods, whom neither they nor their fathers have known, nor the kings of Judah, and have filled this place with the blood of innocents;

Jer 19:6 — Therefore, behold, the days come, saith the LORD, that this place shall no more be called Tophet, nor The valley of the son of Hinnom, but The valley of slaughter.

Jer 32:35 — And they built the high places of Baal, which *are* in the valley of the son of Hinnom, to cause their sons and their daughters to pass through *the fire* unto Molech; which I commanded them not, neither came it into my mind, that they should do this abomination, to cause Judah to sin.

• Possibly valley of vision identical with.

Isa 22:1 — The burden of the valley of vision. What aileth thee now, that thou art wholly gone up to the housetops?

Isa 22:5 — For *it is* a day of trouble, and of treading down, and of perplexity by the Lord GOD of hosts in the valley of vision, breaking down the walls, and of crying to the mountains.

→See: Tophet

HIRAH • An Adullamite.

Ge 38:1 — And it came to pass at that time, that Judah went down from his brethren, and turned in to a certain Adullamite, whose name *was* Hirah.

Ge 38:12 — And in process of time the daughter of Shuah Judah's wife died; and Judah was comforted, and went up unto his sheepshearers to Timnath, he and his friend Hirah the Adullamite.

HIRAM

• King of Tyre.

• Builds a house for David.

2Sa 5:11 — And Hiram king of Tyre sent messengers to David, and cedar trees, and carpenters, and masons: and they built David an house.

1Ch 14:1 — Now Hiram king of Tyre sent messengers to David, and timber of cedars, with masons and carpenters, to build him an house.

• Called also Huram.

2Ch 2:3 — And Solomon sent to Huram the king of Tyre, saying, As thou didst deal with David my father, and didst send him cedars to build him an house to dwell therein, *even so deal with me.*

• Aids Solomon in building the temple.

1Ki 5:1–18; 2Ch 2:3–16

• Dissatisfied with cities given by Solomon.

1Ki 9:11–13

• Makes presents of gold and seamen to Solomon.

1Ki 9:26–28

1Ki 9:14 — And Hiram sent to the king sixscore talents of gold.

1Ki 10:11 — And the navy also of Hiram, that brought gold from Ophir, brought in from Ophir great plenty of almug trees, and precious stones.

• An artificer sent by King Hiram to execute the artistic work of the interior of the temple.

1Ki 7:13–45; 2Ch 4:11–16

• Called also Huram.

2Ch 2:13 — And now I have sent a cunning man, endued with understanding, of Huram my father's,

HIRE

• Law concerning hired property.

Ex 22:14–15

→See: Employer

→See: Master

→See: Servant

→See: Wages

HIRELING

• Not to be oppressed.

Mal 3:5 — And I will come near to you to judgment; and I will be a swift witness against the sorcerers, and against the adulterers, and against false swearers, and against those that oppress the hireling in *his* wages, the widow, and the fatherless, and that turn aside the stranger *from his right,* and fear not me, saith the LORD of hosts.

→See: Servant

HITTITES

• A tribe of Canaanites.

• Children of Heth.

Ge 10:15 — And Canaan begat Sidon his firstborn, and Heth,

Ge 23:10 — And Ephron dwelt among the children of Heth: and Ephron the Hittite answered Abraham in the audience of the children of Heth, *even* of all that went in at the gate of his city, saying,

• Sell a burying-ground to Abraham.

Ge 23:1–20

• Esau intermarries with.

Ge 26:34 — And Esau was forty years old when he took to wife Judith the daughter of Beeri the Hittite, and Bashemath the daughter of Elon the Hittite:

Ge 36:2 — Esau took his wives of the daughters of Canaan; Adah the daughter of Elon the Hittite, and Aholibamah the daughter of Anah the daughter of Zibeon the Hivite;

• Dwelling place of.

Ge 23:17–20

Nu 13:29 — The Amalekites dwell in the land of the south: and the Hittites, and the Jebusites, and the Amorites, dwell in the mountains: and the Canaanites dwell by the sea, and by the coast of Jordan.

Jos 1:4 — From the wilderness and this Lebanon even unto the great river, the river Euphrates, all the land of the Hittites, and unto the great sea toward the going down of the sun, shall be your coast.

Jgs 1:26 — And the man went into the land of the Hittites, and built a city, and called the name thereof Luz: which *is* the name thereof unto this day.

• **Their land given to the Israelites.**

Ex 3:8 — And I am come down to deliver them out of the hand of the Egyptians, and to bring them up out of that land unto a good land and a large, unto a land flowing with milk and honey; unto the place of the Canaanites, and the Hittites, and the Amorites, and the Perizzites, and the Hivites, and the Jebusites.

Dt 7:1 — When the LORD thy God shall bring thee into the land whither thou goest to possess it, and hath cast out many nations before thee, the Hittites, and the Girgashites, and the Amorites, and the Canaanites, and the Perizzites, and the Hivites, and the Jebusites, seven nations greater and mightier than thou;

Jos 1:4 — From the wilderness and this Lebanon even unto the great river, the river Euphrates, all the land of the Hittites, and unto the great sea toward the going down of the sun, shall be your coast.

• **Conquered by Joshua.**

Jos 9:1–2; 10:1–12:24

Jos 24:11 — And ye went over Jordan, and came unto Jericho: and the men of Jericho fought against you, the Amorites, and the Perizzites, and the Canaanites, and the Hittites, and the Girgashites, the Hivites, and the Jebusites; and I delivered them into your hand.

• **Intermarry with Israelites.**

Jgs 3:5–7

Ezr 9:1 — Now when these things were done, the princes came to me, saying, The people of Israel, and the priests, and the Levites, have not separated themselves from the people of the lands, *doing* according to their abominations, *even* of the Canaanites, the Hittites, the Perizzites, the Jebusites, the Ammonites, the Moabites, the Egyptians, and the Amorites.

• **Solomon intermarries with.**

2Ch 8:7–8

1Ki 11:1 — But king Solomon loved many strange women, together with the daughter of Pharaoh, women of the Moabites, Ammonites, Edomites, Zidonians, *and* Hittites;

Ne 13:26 — Did not Solomon king of Israel sin by these things? yet among many nations was there no king like him, who was beloved of his God, and God made him king over all Israel: nevertheless even him did outlandish women cause to sin.

• **Pay tribute to Solomon.**

1Ki 9:20–21

• **Retain their own kings.**

1Ki 10:29 — And a chariot came up and went out of Egypt for six hundred *shekels* of silver, and an horse for an hundred and fifty: and so for all the kings of the Hittites, and for the kings of Syria, did they bring *them* out by their means.

2Ki 7:6 — For the Lord had made the host of the Syrians to hear a noise of chariots, and a noise of horses, *even* the noise of a great host: and they said one to another, Lo, the king of Israel hath hired against us the kings of the Hittites, and the kings of the Egyptians, to come upon us.

2Ch 1:17 — And they fetched up, and brought forth out of Egypt a chariot for six hundred *shekels* of silver, and an horse for an hundred and fifty: and so brought they out *horses* for all the kings of the Hittites, and for the kings of Syria, by their means.

• **Officers from, in David's army.**

1Sa 26:6 — Then answered David and said to Ahimelech the Hittite, and to Abishai the son of Zeruiah, brother to Joab, saying, Who will go down with me to Saul to the camp? And Abishai said, I will go down with thee.

2Sa 11:3 — And David sent and enquired after the woman. And *one* said, *Is* not this Bath-sheba, the daughter of Eliam, the wife of Uriah the Hittite?

2Sa 23:39 — Uriah the Hittite: thirty and seven in all.

HIVITES

• **A tribe of Canaanites.**

Ge 10:17 — And the Hivite, and the Arkite, and the Sinite,

1Ch 1:15 — And the Hivite, and the Arkite, and the Sinite,

• **Shechemites and Gibeonites were families of.**

Ge 34:2 — And when Shechem the son of Hamor the Hivite, prince of the country, saw her, he took her, and lay with her, and defiled her.

Jos 9:7 — And the men of Israel said unto the Hivites, Peradventure ye dwell among us; and how shall we make a league with you?

Jos 11:19 — There was not a city that made peace with the children of Israel, save the Hivites the inhabitants of Gibeon: all *other* they took in battle.

• **Esau intermarries with.**

Ge 26:34 — And Esau was forty years old when he took to wife Judith the daughter of Beeri the Hittite, and Bashemath the daughter of Elon the Hittite:

Ge 36:2 — Esau took his wives of the daughters of Canaan; Adah the daughter of Elon the Hittite, and Aholibamah the daughter of Anah the daughter of Zibeon the Hivite;

• **Dwelling place of.**

Jos 11:3 — *And to* the Canaanite on the east and on the west, and *to* the Amorite, and the Hittite, and the Perizzite, and the Jebusite in the mountains, and *to* the Hivite under Hermon in the land of Mizpeh.

Jgs 3:3 — *Namely,* five lords of the Philistines, and all the Canaanites, and the Sidonians, and the Hivites that dwelt in mount Lebanon, from mount Baal-hermon unto the entering in of Hamath.

2Sa 24:7 — And came to the strong hold of Tyre, and to all the cities of the Hivites, and of the Canaanites: and they went out to the south of Judah, *even* to Beer-sheba.

• **Their land given to the Israelites.**

Ex 23:23 — For mine Angel shall go before thee, and bring thee in unto the Amorites, and the Hittites, and the Perizzites, and the Canaanites, and the Hivites, and the Jebusites: and I will cut them off.

Ex 23:28 — And I will send hornets before thee, which shall drive out the Hivite, the Canaanite, and the Hittite, from before thee.

Dt 20:17 — But thou shalt utterly destroy them; *namely,* the Hittites, and the Amorites, the Canaanites, and the Perizzites, the Hivites, and the Jebusites; as the LORD thy God hath commanded thee:

Jgs 3:5 — And the children of Israel dwelt among the Canaanites, Hittites, and Amorites, and Perizzites, and Hivites, and Jebusites:

• Conquered by Joshua.

Jos 9:1 — And it came to pass, when all the kings which *were* on this side Jordan, in the hills, and in the valleys, and in all the coasts of the great sea over against Lebanon, the Hittite, and the Amorite, the Canaanite, the Perizzite, the Hivite, and the Jebusite, heard *thereof;*

Jos 12:8 — In the mountains, and in the valleys, and in the plains, and in the springs, and in the wilderness, and in the south country; the Hittites, the Amorites, and the Canaanites, the Perizzites, the Hivites, and the Jebusites:

Jos 24:11 — And ye went over Jordan, and came unto Jericho: and the men of Jericho fought against you, the Amorites, and the Perizzites, and the Canaanites, and the Hittites, and the Girgashites, the Hivites, and the Jebusites; and I delivered them into your hand.

• Pay tribute to Solomon.

1Ki 9:21 — Their children that were left after them in the land, whom the children of Israel also were not able utterly to destroy, upon those did Solomon levy a tribute of bondservice unto this day.

2Ch 8:8 — *But* of their children, who were left after them in the land, whom the children of Israel consumed not, them did Solomon make to pay tribute until this day.

HIZKIAH • An ancestor of Zephaniah.

Zep 1:1 — The word of the LORD which came unto Zephaniah the son of Cushi, the son of Gedaliah, the son of Amariah, the son of Hizkiah, in the days of Josiah the son of Amon, king of Judah.

HIZKIJAH

• Probably identical with Hezekiah, the exile.

See: Hezekiah; one of the exiles

HOBAB • Son of Raguel.

Nu 10:29 — And Moses said unto Hobab, the son of Raguel the Midianite, Moses' father in law, We are journeying unto the place of which the LORD said, I will give it you: come thou with us, and we will do thee good: for the LORD hath spoken good concerning Israel.

Jgs 4:11 — Now Heber the Kenite, *which was* of the children of Hobab the father in law of Moses, had severed himself from the Kenites, and pitched his tent unto the plain of Zaanaim, which *is* by Kedesh.

HOBAH • A place north of Damascus.

Ge 14:15 — And he divided himself against them, he and his servants, by night, and smote them, and pursued them unto Hobah, which *is* on the left hand of Damascus.

HOD • A son of Zophah.

1Ch 7:37 — Bezer, and Hod, and Shamma and Shilshah, and Ithran, and Beera.

HODAIAH • Son of Elioenai.

1Ch 3:24 — And the sons of Elioenai *were,* Hodaiah, and Eliashib, and Pelaiah, and Akkub, and Johanan, and Dalaiah, and Anani, seven.

HODAVIAH

• A chief of the half tribe of Manasseh, whose inheritance was east of the Jordan.

1Ch 5:24 — And these *were* the heads of the house of their fathers, even Epher, and Ishi, and Eliel, and Azriel, and Jeremiah, and Hodaviah, and Jahdiel, mighty men of valour, famous men, *and* heads of the house of their fathers.

• A Benjamite.

1Ch 9:7 — And of the sons of Benjamin; Sallu the son of Meshullam, the son of Hodaviah, the son of Hasenuah,

• A Levite.

Ezr 2:40 — The Levites: the children of Jeshua and Kadmiel, of the children of Hodaviah, seventy and four.

HODESH • Wife of Shaharaim.

1Ch 8:9 — And he begat of Hodesh his wife, Jobab, and Zibia, and Mesha, and Malcham,

HODEVAH • A Levite.

Ne 7:43 — The Levites: the children of Jeshua, of Kadmiel, *and* of the children of Hodevah, seventy and four.

HODIAH

• Called also Hodijah.

• Wife of Ezra.

1Ch 4:19 — And the sons of *his* wife Hodiah the sister of Naham, the father of Keilah the Garmite, and Eshtemoa the Maachathite.

• A Levite.

Ne 8:7 — Also Jeshua, and Bani, and Sherebiah, Jamin, Akkub, Shabbethai, Hodijah, Maaseiah, Kelita, Azariah, Jozabad, Hanan, Pelaiah, and the Levites, caused the people to understand the law: and the people *stood* in their place.

Ne 9:5 — Then the Levites, Jeshua, and Kadmiel, Bani, Hashabniah, Sherebiah, Hodijah, Shebaniah, *and* Pethahiah, said, Stand up *and* bless the LORD your God for ever and ever: and blessed be thy glorious name, which is exalted above all blessing and praise.

Ne 10:10 — And their brethren, Shebaniah, Hodijah, Kelita, Pelaiah, Hanan,

Ne 10:13 — Hodijah, Bani, Beninu.

• **An Israelitish chief.**

Ne 10:18 — Hodijah, Hashum, Bezai,

HOGLAH • A daughter of Zelophehad.

Nu 26:33 — And Zelophehad the son of Hepher had no sons, but daughters: and the names of the daughters of Zelophehad *were* Mahlah, and Noah, Hoglah, Milcah, and Tirzah.

Nu 27:1 — Then came the daughters of Zelophehad, the son of Hepher, the son of Gilead, the son of Machir, the son of Manasseh, of the families of Manasseh the son of Joseph: and these are the names of his daughters; Mahlah, Noah, and Hoglah, and Milcah, and Tirzah.

Nu 36:11 — For Mahlah, Tirzah, and Hoglah, and Milcah, and Noah, the daughters of Zelophehad, were married unto their father's brothers' sons:

Jos 17:3 — But Zelophehad, the son of Hepher, the son of Gilead, the son of Machir, the son of Manasseh, had no sons, but daughters: and these *are* the names of his daughters, Mahlah, and Noah, Hoglah, Milcah, and Tirzah.

HOHAM • King of Hebron.

Jos 10:3 — Wherefore Adoni-zedek king of Jerusalem sent unto Hoham king of Hebron, and unto Piram king of Jarmuth, and unto Japhia king of Lachish, and unto Debir king of Eglon, saying,

HOLIDAY

• **For rest.**

See: Sabbath

• **One year in seven.**

Le 25:2–7

See: Jubilee

HOLINESS

Le 10:8–10; 11:44–45; Jos 7:12–13; Ps 15:1–5; 24:3–5; 119:1–3; Isa 26:8–9; 61:9–11; Zec 14:20–21; Mt 5:29–30; Mk 9:49–50; Lk 1:74–75; Ro 2:28–29; 6:1–23; 12:1–2; 13:12–14; 1Co 3:16–17; 6:12–13, 19–20; 10:31–32; 2Co 6:14–17; 13:7–8; Gal 5:22–25; Eph 1:13–14; 2:21–22; 4:20–24; 5:8–11; Php 1:10–11; Col 3:5–10, 12–15; 1Th 4:3–4; 5:22–23; 1Ti 6:11–12; 2Ti 2:16–17, 21–22; Tit 2:9–10; Heb 12:14–15; 1Pe 1:14–16; 2:11–12; 4:1–2, 6–7; 2Pe 1:2–8; 3:11–12; 1Jn 1:6–7; 3:6–10; 5:4–5; Rev 14:4–5

Ge 17:1 — And when Abram was ninety years old and nine, the LORD appeared to Abram, and said unto him, I *am* the Almighty God; walk before me, and be thou perfect.

Ge 35:2 — Then Jacob said unto his household, and to all that *were* with him, Put away the strange gods that *are* among you, and be clean, and change your garments:

Ex 19:6 — And ye shall be unto me a kingdom of priests, and an holy nation. These *are* the words which thou shalt speak unto the children of Israel.

Ex 22:31 — And ye shall be holy men unto me: neither shall ye eat *any* flesh *that is* torn of beasts in the field; ye shall cast it to the dogs.

Ex 28:36 — And thou shalt make a plate *of* pure gold, and grave upon it, *like* the engravings of a signet, HOLINESS TO THE LORD.

Ex 39:30 — And they made the plate of the holy crown *of* pure gold, and wrote upon it a writing, *like to* the engravings of a signet, HOLINESS TO THE LORD.

Le 11:47 — To make a difference between the unclean and the clean, and between the beast that may be eaten and the beast that may not be eaten.

Le 19:2 — Speak unto all the congregation of the children of Israel, and say unto them, Ye shall be holy: for I the LORD your God *am* holy.

Le 20:7 — Sanctify yourselves therefore, and be ye holy: for I *am* the LORD your God.

Le 20:26 — And ye shall be holy unto me: for I the LORD *am* holy, and have severed you from *other* people, that ye should be mine.

Dt 13:17 — And there shall cleave nought of the cursed thing to thine hand: that the LORD may turn from the fierceness of his anger, and shew thee mercy, and have compassion upon thee, and multiply thee, as he hath sworn unto thy fathers;

Dt 14:2 — for thou *art* an holy people unto the LORD thy God, and the LORD hath chosen thee to be a peculiar people unto himself, above all the nations that *are* upon the earth.

Dt 18:13 — Thou shalt be perfect with the LORD thy God.

Dt 26:19 — And to make thee high above all nations which he hath made, in praise, and in name, and in honour; and that thou mayest be an holy people unto the LORD thy God, as he hath spoken.

Dt 28:9 — The LORD shall establish thee an holy people unto himself, as he hath sworn unto thee, if thou shalt keep the commandments of the LORD thy God, and walk in his ways.

Dt 30:2 — And shalt return unto the LORD thy God, and shalt obey his voice according to all that I command thee this day, thou and thy children, with all thine heart, and with all thy soul;

Dt 30:10 — If thou shalt hearken unto the voice of the LORD thy God, to keep his commandments and his statutes which are written in this book of the law, *and* if thou turn unto the LORD thy God with all thine heart, and with all thy soul.

Job 5:24 — And thou shalt know that thy tabernacle *shall be* in peace; and thou shalt visit thy habitation, and shalt not sin.

Job 28:28 — And unto man he said, Behold, the fear of the Lord, that *is* wisdom; and to depart from evil *is* understanding.

Job 36:21 — Take heed, regard not iniquity: for this hast thou chosen rather than affliction.

Ps 4:4 — Stand in awe, and sin not: commune with your own heart upon your bed, and be still. Selah.

Ps 32:2 — Blessed *is* the man unto whom the LORD imputeth not iniquity, and in whose spirit *there is* no guile.

Ps 34:14 — Depart from evil, and do good; seek peace, and pursue it.

Ps 37:27 — Depart from evil, and do good; and dwell for evermore.

Ps 68:13 — Though ye have lien among the pots, *yet shall ye be as* the wings of a dove covered with silver, and her feathers with yellow gold.

Ps 73:1 — Truly God *is* good to Israel, *even* to such as are of a clean heart.

Ps 85:13 — Righteousness shall go before him; and shall set *us* in the way of his steps.

Ps 94:15 — But judgment shall return unto righteousness: and all the upright in heart shall follow it.

Ps 97:10 — Ye that love the LORD, hate evil: he preserveth the souls of his saints; he delivereth them out of the hand of the wicked.

Pr 11:23 — The desire of the righteous *is* only good: *but* the expectation of the wicked *is* wrath.

Pr 12:5 — The thoughts of the righteous *are* right: *but* the counsels of the wicked *are* deceit.

Pr 16:17 — The highway of the upright *is* to depart from evil: he that keepeth his way preserveth his soul.

Pr 21:8 — The way of man *is* froward and strange: but *as for* the pure, his work *is* right.

Pr 21:15 — *It is* joy to the just to do judgment: but destruction *shall be* to the workers of iniquity.

Pr 21:29 — A wicked man hardeneth his face: but *as for* the upright, he directeth his way.

Pr 22:1 — A *good* name *is* rather to be chosen than great riches, *and* loving favour rather than silver and gold.

Ecc 7:1 — A good name *is* better than precious ointment; and the day of death than the day of one's birth.

Isa 4:3 — And it shall come to pass, *that he that is* left in Zion, and *he that* remaineth in Jerusalem, shall be called holy, *even* every one that is written among the living in Jerusalem:

Isa 26:2 — Open ye the gates, that the righteous nation which keepeth the truth may enter in.

Isa 32:17 — And the work of righteousness shall be peace; and the effect of righteousness quietness and assurance for ever.

Isa 35:8 — And an highway shall be there, and a way, and it shall be called The way of holiness; the unclean shall not pass over it; but it *shall be* for those: the wayfaring men, though fools, shall not err *therein*.

Isa 51:7 — Hearken unto me, ye that know righteousness, the people in whose heart *is* my law; fear ye not the reproach of men, neither be ye afraid of their revilings.

Isa 52:1 — Awake, awake; put on thy strength, O Zion; put on thy beautiful garments, O Jerusalem, the holy city: for henceforth there shall no more come into thee the uncircumcised and the unclean.

Isa 52:11 — Depart ye, depart ye, go ye out from thence, touch no unclean *thing;* go ye out of the midst of her; be ye clean, that bear the vessels of the LORD.

Isa 57:2 — He shall enter into peace: they shall rest in their beds, *each one* walking *in* his uprightness.

Isa 60:1 — Arise, shine; for thy light is come, and the glory of the LORD is risen upon thee.

Isa 60:21 — Thy people also *shall be* all righteous: they shall inherit the land for ever, the branch of my planting, the work of my hands, that I may be glorified.

Isa 61:3 — To appoint unto them that mourn in Zion, to give unto them beauty for ashes, the oil of joy for mourning, the garment of praise for the spirit of heaviness; that they might be called trees of righteousness, the planting of the LORD, that he might be glorified.

Mic 6:8 — He hath shewed thee, O man, what *is* good; and what doth the LORD require of thee, but to do justly, and to love mercy, and to walk humbly with thy God?

Zep 2:3 — Seek ye the LORD, all ye meek of the earth, which have wrought his judgment; seek righteousness, seek meekness: it may be ye shall be hid in the day of the LORD's anger.

Zec 8:3 — Thus saith the LORD; I am returned unto Zion, and will dwell in the midst of Jerusalem: and Jerusalem shall be called a city of truth; and the mountain of the LORD of hosts the holy mountain.

Mt 5:6 — Blessed *are* they which do hunger and thirst after righteousness: for they shall be filled.

Mt 5:8 — Blessed *are* the pure in heart: for they shall see God.

Mt 5:48 — Be ye therefore perfect, even as your Father which is in heaven is perfect.

Mt 12:33 — Either make the tree good, and his fruit good; or else make the tree corrupt, and his fruit corrupt: for the tree is known by *his* fruit.

Lk 6:45 — A good man out of the good treasure of his heart bringeth forth that which is good; and an evil man out of the evil treasure of his heart bringeth forth that which is evil: for of the abundance of the heart his mouth speaketh.

Jn 1:47 — Jesus saw Nathanael coming to him, and saith of him, Behold an Israelite indeed, in whom is no guile!

Jn 4:14 — But whosoever drinketh of the water that I shall give him shall never thirst; but the water that I shall give him shall be in him a well of water springing up into everlasting life.

Jn 5:14 — Afterward Jesus findeth him in the temple, and said unto him, Behold, thou art made whole: sin no more, lest a worse thing come unto thee.

Jn 6:35 — And Jesus said unto them, I am the bread of life: he that cometh to me shall never hunger; and he that believeth on me shall never thirst.

Jn 15:19 — If ye were of the world, the world would love his own: but because ye are not of the world, but I have chosen you out of the world, therefore the world hateth you.

Jn 17:23 — I in them, and thou in me, that they may be made perfect in one; and that the world may know that thou hast sent me, and hast loved them, as thou hast loved me.

Ac 24:16 — And herein do I exercise myself, to have always a conscience void of offence toward God, and *toward* men.

Ro 7:4 — Wherefore, my brethren, ye also are become dead to the law by the body of Christ; that ye should be married to another, *even* to him who is raised from the dead, that we should bring forth fruit unto God.

Ro 7:6 — But now we are delivered from the law, that being dead wherein we were held; that we should serve in newness of spirit, and not *in* the oldness of the letter.

Ro 8:1 — *There is* therefore now no condemnation to them which are in Christ Jesus, who walk not after the flesh, but after the Spirit.

Ro 8:4 — That the righteousness of the law might be fulfilled in us, who walk not after the flesh, but after the Spirit.

Ro 8:12 — Therefore, brethren, we are debtors, not to the flesh, to live after the flesh.

Ro 11:16 — For if the firstfruit *be* holy, the lump *is* also *holy:* and if the root *be* holy, so *are* the branches.

Ro 12:9 — *Let* love be without dissimulation. Abhor that which is evil; cleave to that which is good.

Ro 14:17 — For the kingdom of God is not meat and drink; but righteousness, and peace, and joy in the Holy Ghost.

Ro 16:19 — For your obedience is come abroad unto all *men.* I am glad therefore on your behalf: but yet I would have you wise unto that which is good, and simple concerning evil.

1Co 5:7 — Purge out therefore the old leaven, that ye may be a new lump, as ye are unleavened. For even Christ our passover is sacrificed for us:

1Co 7:23 — Ye are bought with a price; be not ye the servants of men.

1Co 8:12 — But when ye sin so against the brethren, and wound their weak conscience, ye sin against Christ.

1Co 10:21 — Ye cannot drink the cup of the Lord, and the cup of devils: ye cannot be partakers of the Lord's table, and of the table of devils.

1Co 12:31 — But covet earnestly the best gifts: and yet shew I unto you a more excellent way.

1Co 15:34 — Awake to righteousness, and sin not; for some have not the knowledge of God: I speak *this* to your shame.

2Co 7:1 — Having therefore these promises, dearly beloved, let us cleanse ourselves from all filthiness of the flesh and spirit, perfecting holiness in the fear of God.

2Co 10:3 — For though we walk in the flesh, we do not war after the flesh:

2Co 10:5 — Casting down imaginations, and every high thing that exalteth itself against the knowledge of God, and bringing into captivity every thought to the obedience of Christ;

2Co 11:2 — For I am jealous over you with godly jealousy: for I have espoused you to one husband, that I may present *you as* a chaste virgin to Christ.

Gal 2:17 — But if, while we seek to be justified by Christ, we ourselves also are found sinners, *is* therefore Christ the minister of sin? God forbid.

Gal 6:15 — For in Christ Jesus neither circumcision availeth any thing, nor uncircumcision, but a new creature.

Eph 1:4 — According as he hath chosen us in him before the foundation of the world, that we should be holy and without blame before him in love:

Eph 5:1 — Be ye therefore followers of God, as dear children;

Eph 5:3 — But fornication, and all uncleanness, or covetousness, let it not be once named among you, as becometh saints;

Php 2:15 — That ye may be blameless and harmless, the sons of God, without rebuke, in the midst of a crooked and perverse nation, among whom ye shine as lights in the world;

Php 4:8 — Finally, brethren, whatsoever things are true, whatsoever things *are* honest, whatsoever things *are* just, whatsoever things *are* pure, whatsoever things *are* lovely, whatsoever things *are* of good report; if *there be* any virtue, and if *there be* any praise, think on these things.

Col 1:22 — In the body of his flesh through death, to present you holy and unblameable and unreproveable in his sight:

1Th 2:12 — That ye would walk worthy of God, who hath called you unto his kingdom and glory.

1Th 3:13 — To the end he may stablish your hearts unblameable in holiness before God, even our Father, at the coming of our Lord Jesus Christ with all his saints.

1Th 4:7 — For God hath not called us unto uncleanness, but unto holiness.

1Th 5:5 — Ye are all the children of light, and the children of the day: we are not of the night, nor of darkness.

2Th 2:13 — But we are bound to give thanks alway to God for you, brethren beloved of the Lord, because God hath from the beginning chosen you to salvation through sanctification of the Spirit and belief of the truth:

1Ti 1:5 — Now the end of the commandment is charity out of a pure heart, and *of* a good conscience, and *of* faith unfeigned:

1Ti 4:8 — For bodily exercise profiteth little: but godliness is profitable unto all things, having promise of the life that now is, and of that which is to come.

1Ti 4:12 — Let no man despise thy youth; but be thou an example of the believers, in word, in conversation, in charity, in spirit, in faith, in purity.

1Ti 5:22 — Lay hands suddenly on no man, neither be partaker of other men's sins: keep thyself pure.

1Ti 6:6 — But godliness with contentment is great gain.

2Ti 2:19 — Nevertheless the foundation of God standeth sure, having this seal, The Lord knoweth them that are his. And, Let every one that nameth the name of Christ depart from iniquity.

2Ti 3:17 — That the man of God may be perfect, thoroughly furnished unto all good works.

Tit 1:15 — Unto the pure all things *are* pure: but unto them that are defiled and unbelieving *is* nothing pure; but even their mind and conscience is defiled.

Tit 2:12 — Teaching us that, denying ungodliness and worldly lusts, we should live soberly, righteously, and godly, in this present world;

Heb 4:3 — For we which have believed do enter into rest, as he said, As I have sworn in my wrath, if they shall enter into my rest: although the works were finished from the foundation of the world.

Heb 4:9 — There remaineth therefore a rest to the people of God.

Heb 10:22 — Let us draw near with a true heart in full assurance of faith, having our hearts sprinkled from an evil conscience, and our bodies washed with pure water.

Heb 12:1 — Wherefore seeing we also are compassed about with so great a cloud of witnesses, let us lay aside every weight, and the sin which doth so easily beset us, and let us run with patience the race that is set before us,

Heb 12:10 — For they verily for a few days chastened *us* after their own pleasure; but he for *our* profit, that *we* might be partakers of his holiness.

Heb 13:9 — Be not carried about with divers and strange doctrines. For *it is* a good thing that the heart be established with grace; not with meats, which have not profited them that have been occupied therein.

Jas 1:21 — Wherefore lay apart all filthiness and superfluity of naughtiness, and receive with meekness the engrafted word, which is able to save your souls.

Jas 1:27 — Pure religion and undefiled before God and the Father is this, To visit the fatherless and widows in their affliction, *and* to keep himself unspotted from the world.

Jas 3:17 — But the wisdom that is from above is first pure, then peaceable, gentle, *and* easy to be intreated, full of mercy and good fruits, without partiality, and without hypocrisy.

Jas 4:4 — Ye adulterers and adulteresses, know ye not that the friendship of the world is enmity with God? whosoever therefore will be a friend of the world is the enemy of God.

1Pe 2:1 — Wherefore laying aside all malice, and all guile, and hypocrisies, and envies, and all evil speakings,

1Pe 2:5 — Ye also, as lively stones, are built up a spiritual house, an holy priesthood, to offer up spiritual sacrifices, acceptable to God by Jesus Christ.

1Pe 2:9 — But ye *are* a chosen generation, a royal priesthood, an holy nation, a peculiar people; that ye should shew forth the praises of him who hath called you out of darkness into his marvellous light:

1Pe 2:24 — Who his own self bare our sins in his own body on the tree, that we, being dead to sins, should live unto righteousness: by whose stripes ye were healed.

1Pe 3:11 — Let him eschew evil, and do good; let him seek peace, and ensue it.

2Pe 3:14 — Wherefore, beloved, seeing that ye look for such things, be diligent that ye may be found of him in peace, without spot, and blameless.

1Jn 2:1 — My little children, these things write I unto you, that ye sin not. And if any man sin, we have an advocate with the Father, Jesus Christ the righteous:

1Jn 2:5 — But whoso keepeth his word, in him verily is the love of God perfected: hereby know we that we are in him.

1Jn 2:29 — If ye know that he is righteous, ye know that every one that doeth righteousness is born of him.

1Jn 3:3 — And every man that hath this hope in him purifieth himself, even as he is pure.

1Jn 5:18 — We know that whosoever is born of God sinneth not; but he that is begotten of God keepeth himself, and that wicked one toucheth him not.

1Jn 5:21 — Little children, keep yourselves from idols. Amen.

2Jn 1:4 — I rejoiced greatly that I found of thy children walking in truth, as we have received a commandment from the Father.

3Jn 1:11 — Beloved, follow not that which is evil, but that which is good. He that doeth good is of God: but he that doeth evil hath not seen God.

Rev 18:4 — And I heard another voice from heaven, saying, Come out of her, my people, that ye be not partakers of her sins, and that ye receive not of her plagues.

Rev 19:8 — And to her was granted that she should be arrayed in fine linen, clean and white: for the fine linen is the righteousness of saints.

See: Desire; spiritual
See: God, Holiness of
See: Righteousness
See: Sanctification
See: Sinlessness

HOLM • A tree.

Isa 44:14 — He heweth him down cedars, and taketh the cypress and the oak, which he strengtheneth for himself among the trees of the forest: he planteth an ash, and the rain doth nourish *it*.

HOLY DAY See: Holiday

HOLY KISS

2Co 12:1–13:14

Ro 16:6 — Greet Mary, who bestowed much labour on us.

1Co 16:20 — All the brethren greet you. Greet ye one another with an holy kiss.

1Th 5:26— Greet all the brethren with an holy kiss.

HOLY PLACE

See: Tabernacle
See: Temple

HOLY SPIRIT

Ps 51:11–12; Isa 44:3–4; 63:10–11; Joel 2:28–29; Zec 4:1–7; Mt 3:16–4:1; Lk 2:25–27; Jn 1:32–33; 3:5–6; 7:38–39; 14:16–17; 16:7–14; Ac 2:2–4; 5:3–4; 8:15–19; 10:19–20, 44–47; 11:15–17; 16:6–7; 19:2–6; Ro 5:3–5; 8:1–27; 11:33–34; 15:18–19; 1Co 2:10–14; 12:3–11; 2Co 3:17–18; Gal 3:2–3; 5:16–18, 22–23; Eph 1:12–14; 4:3–4; 6:17–18; 1Th 1:5–6; 4:8–9; Tit 3:5–6; Heb 10:1–39; 1Pe 1:11–12; 1Jn 5:6–8; Jude 1:19–20

Ge 1:2 — And the earth was without form, and void; and darkness *was* upon the face of the deep. And the Spirit of God moved upon the face of the waters.

Ge 6:3 — And the LORD said, My spirit shall not always strive with man, for that he also *is* flesh: yet his days shall be an hundred and twenty years.

Ge 41:38 — And Pharaoh said unto his servants, Can we find *such a one* as this *is,* a man in whom the Spirit of God is?

Ex 31:3 — And I have filled him with the spirit of God, in wisdom, and in understanding, and in knowledge, and in all manner of workmanship,

Ex 35:31 — And he hath filled him with the spirit of God, in wisdom, in understanding, and in knowledge, and in all manner of workmanship;

Nu 27:18 — And the LORD said unto Moses, Take thee Joshua the son of Nun, a man in whom *is* the spirit, and lay thine hand upon him;

Ne 9:20 — Thou gavest also thy good spirit to instruct them, and withheldest not thy manna from their mouth, and gavest them water for their thirst.

Job 16:19 — Also now, behold, my witness *is* in heaven, and my record *is* on high.

Job 32:8 — But *there is* a spirit in man: and the inspiration of the Almighty giveth them understanding.

Job 33:4 — The Spirit of God hath made me, and the breath of the Almighty hath given me life.

Ps 103:9 — He will not always chide: neither will he keep *his anger* for ever.

Ps 139:7 — Whither shall I go from thy spirit? or whither shall I flee from thy presence?

Isa 4:4 — When the Lord shall have washed away the filth of the daughters of Zion, and shall have purged the blood of Jerusalem from the midst thereof by the spirit of judgment, and by the spirit of burning.

Isa 6:8 — Also I heard the voice of the Lord, saying, Whom shall I send, and who will go for us? Then said I, Here *am* I; send me.

Isa 11:2 — And the spirit of the LORD shall rest upon him, the spirit of wisdom and understanding, the spirit of counsel and might, the spirit of knowledge and of the fear of the LORD;

Isa 28:6 — And for a spirit of judgment to him that sitteth in judgment, and for strength to them that turn the battle to the gate.

Isa 30:1 — Woe to the rebellious children, saith the LORD, that take counsel, but not of me; and that cover with a covering, but not of my spirit, that they may add sin to sin:

Isa 32:15 — Until the spirit be poured upon us from on high, and the wilderness be a fruitful field, and the fruitful field be counted for a forest.

Isa 40:13 — Who hath directed the Spirit of the LORD, or *being* his counsellor hath taught him?

Isa 42:1 — Behold my servant, whom I uphold; mine elect, *in whom* my soul delighteth; I have put my spirit upon him: he shall bring forth judgment to the Gentiles.

Isa 48:16 — Come ye near unto me, hear ye this; I have not spoken in secret from the beginning; from the time that it was, there *am* I: and now the Lord GOD, and his Spirit, hath sent me.

Isa 51:12 — I, *even* I, *am* he that comforteth you: who *art* thou, that thou shouldest be afraid of a man *that* shall die, and of the son of man *which* shall be made as grass;

Isa 54:13 — And all thy children *shall be* taught of the LORD; and great *shall be* the peace of thy children.

Isa 59:19 — So shall they fear the name of the LORD from the west, and his glory from the rising of the sun. When the enemy shall come in like a flood, the Spirit of the LORD shall lift up a standard against him.

Isa 59:21 — As for me, this *is* my covenant with them, saith the LORD; My spirit that *is* upon thee, and my words which I have put in thy mouth, shall not depart out of thy mouth, nor out of the mouth of thy seed, nor out of the mouth of thy seed's seed, saith the LORD, from henceforth and for ever.

Isa 61:1 — The Spirit of the Lord GOD *is* upon me; because the LORD hath anointed me to preach good tidings unto the meek; he hath sent me to bind up the brokenhearted, to proclaim liberty to the captives, and the opening of the prison to *them that are* bound;

Isa 63:14 — As a beast goeth down into the valley, the Spirit of the LORD caused him to rest: so didst thou lead thy people, to make thyself a glorious name.

Eze 36:27 — And I will put my spirit within you, and cause you to walk in my statutes, and ye shall keep my judgments, and do *them*.

Eze 37:9 — Then said he unto me, Prophesy unto the wind, prophesy, son of man, and say to the wind, Thus saith the Lord GOD; Come from the four winds, O breath, and breathe upon these slain, that they may live.

Eze 37:14 — And shall put my spirit in you, and ye shall live, and I shall place you in your own land: then shall ye know that I the LORD have spoken *it*, and performed *it*, saith the LORD.

Eze 39:29 — Neither will I hide my face any more from them: for I have poured out my spirit upon the house of Israel, saith the Lord GOD.

Mic 2:7 — O *thou that art* named the house of Jacob, is the spirit of the LORD straitened? *are* these his doings? do not my words do good to him that walketh uprightly?

Mic 3:8 — But truly I am full of power by the spirit of the LORD, and of judgment, and of might, to declare unto Jacob his transgression, and to Israel his sin.

Hag 2:5 — *According to* the word that I covenanted with you when ye came out of Egypt, so my spirit remaineth among you: fear ye not.

Zec 12:10 — And I will pour upon the house of David, and upon the inhabitants of Jerusalem, the spirit of grace and of supplications: and they shall look upon me whom they have pierced, and they shall mourn for him, as one mourneth for *his* only *son*, and shall be in bitterness for him, as one that is in bitterness for *his* firstborn.

Mt 1:18 — Now the birth of Jesus Christ was on this wise: When as his mother Mary was espoused to Joseph, before they came together, she was found with child of the Holy Ghost.

Mt 1:20 — But while he thought on these things, behold, the angel of the Lord appeared unto him in a dream, saying, Joseph, thou son of David, fear not to take unto thee Mary thy wife: for that which is conceived in her is of the Holy Ghost.

Mt 3:11 — I indeed baptize you with water unto repentance: but he that cometh after me is mightier than I, whose shoes I am not worthy to bear: he shall baptize you with the Holy Ghost, and *with* fire:

Mt 10:20 — For it is not ye that speak, but the Spirit of your Father which speaketh in you.

Mt 12:28 — But if I cast out devils by the Spirit of God, then the kingdom of God is come unto you.

Mt 28:19 — Go ye therefore, and teach all nations, baptizing them in the name of the Father, and of the Son, and of the Holy Ghost:

Mk 1:10 — And straightway coming up out of the water, he saw the heavens opened, and the Spirit like a dove descending upon him:

Mk 12:36 — For David himself said by the Holy Ghost, The Lord said to my Lord, Sit thou on my right hand, till I make thine enemies thy footstool.

Mk 13:11 — But when they shall lead *you,* and deliver you up, take no thought beforehand what ye shall speak, neither do ye premeditate: but whatsoever shall be given you in that hour, that speak ye: for it is not ye that speak, but the Holy Ghost.

Lk 1:15 — For he shall be great in the sight of the Lord, and shall drink neither wine nor strong drink; and he shall be filled with the Holy Ghost, even from his mother's womb.

Lk 1:35 — And the angel answered and said unto her, The Holy Ghost shall come upon thee, and the power of the Highest shall overshadow thee: therefore also that holy thing which shall be born of thee shall be called the Son of God.

Lk 1:67 — And his father Zacharias was filled with the Holy Ghost, and prophesied, saying,

Lk 3:22 — And the Holy Ghost descended in a bodily shape like a dove upon him, and a voice came from heaven, which said, Thou art my beloved Son; in thee I am well pleased.

Lk 4:18 — The Spirit of the Lord is upon me, because he hath anointed me to preach the gospel to the poor; he hath sent me to heal the brokenhearted, to preach deliverance to the captives, and recovering of sight to the blind, to set at liberty them that are bruised,

Lk 11:13 — If ye then, being evil, know how to give good gifts unto your children: how much more shall *your* heavenly Father give the Holy Spirit to them that ask him?

Lk 12:12 — For the Holy Ghost shall teach you in the same hour what ye ought to say.

Lk 24:49 — And, behold, I send the promise of my Father upon you: but tarry ye in the city of Jerusalem, until ye be endued with power from on high.

Jn 1:9 — *That* was the true Light, which lighteth every man that cometh into the world.

Jn 3:34 — For he whom God hath sent speaketh the words of God: for God giveth not the Spirit by measure *unto him.*

Jn 4:14 — But whosoever drinketh of the water that I shall give him shall never thirst; but the water that I shall give him shall be in him a well of water springing up into everlasting life.

Jn 6:45 — It is written in the prophets, And they shall be all taught of God. Every man therefore that hath heard, and hath learned of the Father, cometh unto me.

Jn 6:63 — It is the spirit that quickeneth; the flesh profiteth nothing: the words that I speak unto you, *they* are spirit, and *they* are life.

Jn 14:26 — But the Comforter, *which is* the Holy Ghost, whom the Father will send in my name, he shall teach you all things, and bring all things to your remembrance, whatsoever I have said unto you.

Jn 15:26 — But when the Comforter is come, whom I will send unto you from the Father, *even* the Spirit of truth, which proceedeth from the Father, he shall testify of me:

Jn 20:22 — And when he had said this, he breathed on *them,* and saith unto them, Receive ye the Holy Ghost:

Ac 1:2 — Until the day in which he was taken up, after that he through the Holy Ghost had given commandments unto the apostles whom he had chosen:

Ac 1:5 — For John truly baptized with water; but ye shall be baptized with the Holy Ghost not many days hence.

Ac 1:8 — But ye shall receive power, after that the Holy Ghost is come upon you: and ye shall be witnesses unto me both in Jerusalem, and in all Judaea, and in Samaria, and unto the uttermost part of the earth.

Ac 1:16 — Men *and* brethren, this scripture must needs have been fulfilled, which the Holy Ghost by the mouth of David spake before concerning Judas, which was guide to them that took Jesus.

Ac 2:33 — Therefore being by the right hand of God exalted, and having received of the Father the promise of the Holy Ghost, he hath shed forth this, which ye now see and hear.

Ac 2:38 — Then Peter said unto them, Repent, and be baptized every one of you in the name of Jesus Christ for the remission of sins, and ye shall receive the gift of the Holy Ghost.

Ac 4:8 — Then Peter, filled with the Holy Ghost, said unto them, Ye rulers of the people, and elders of Israel,

Ac 4:31 — And when they had prayed, the place was shaken where they were assembled together; and they were all filled with the Holy Ghost, and they spake the word of God with boldness.

Ac 5:9 — Then Peter said unto her, How is it that ye have agreed together to tempt the Spirit of the Lord? behold, the feet of them which have buried thy husband *are* at the door, and shall carry thee out.

Ac 5:32 — And we are his witnesses of these things; and *so is* also the Holy Ghost, whom God hath given to them that obey him.

Ac 6:5 — And the saying pleased the whole multitude: and they chose Stephen, a man full of faith and of the Holy Ghost, and Philip, and Prochorus, and Nicanor, and Timon, and Parmenas, and Nicolas a proselyte of Antioch:

Ac 7:51 — Ye stiffnecked and uncircumcised in heart and ears, ye do always resist the Holy Ghost: as your fathers *did,* so *do* ye.

Ac 9:31 — Then had the churches rest throughout all Judaea and Galilee and Samaria, and were edified; and walking in the fear of the Lord, and in the comfort of the Holy Ghost, were multiplied.

Ac 11:24 — For he was a good man, and full of the Holy Ghost and of faith: and much people was added unto the Lord.

Ac 13:2 — As they ministered to the Lord, and fasted, the Holy Ghost said, Separate me Barnabas and Saul for the work whereunto I have called them.

Ac 13:4 — So they, being sent forth by the Holy Ghost, departed unto Seleucia; and from thence they sailed to Cyprus.

Ac 13:9 — Then Saul, (who also *is called* Paul,) filled with the Holy Ghost, set his eyes on him,

Ac 13:52 — And the disciples were filled with joy, and with the Holy Ghost.

Ac 15:8 — And God, which knoweth the hearts, bare them witness, giving them the Holy Ghost, even as *he did* unto us;

Ac 15:28 — For it seemed good to the Holy Ghost, and to us, to lay upon you no greater burden than these necessary things;

Ac 20:28 — Take heed therefore unto yourselves, and to all the flock, over the which the Holy Ghost hath made you overseers, to feed the church of God, which he hath purchased with his own blood.

Ro 1:4 — And declared *to be* the Son of God with power, according to the spirit of holiness, by the resurrection from the dead:

Ro 9:1 — I say the truth in Christ, I lie not, my conscience also bearing me witness in the Holy Ghost,

Ro 14:17 — For the kingdom of God is not meat and drink; but righteousness, and peace, and joy in the Holy Ghost.

Ro 15:13 — Now the God of hope fill you with all joy and peace in believing, that ye may abound in hope, through the power of the Holy Ghost.

Ro 15:16 — That I should be the minister of Jesus Christ to the Gentiles, ministering the gospel of God, that the offering up of the Gentiles might be acceptable, being sanctified by the Holy Ghost.

Ro 15:30 — Now I beseech you, brethren, for the Lord Jesus Christ's sake, and for the love of the Spirit, that ye strive together with me in *your* prayers to God for me;

1Co 2:4 — And my speech and my preaching *was* not with enticing words of man's wisdom, but in demonstration of the Spirit and of power:

1Co 3:16 — Know ye not that ye are the temple of God, and *that* the Spirit of God dwelleth in you?

1Co 6:11 — And such were some of you: but ye are washed, but ye are sanctified, but ye are justified in the name of the Lord Jesus, and by the Spirit of our God.

1Co 6:19 — What? know ye not that your body is the temple of the Holy Ghost *which is* in you, which ye have of God, and ye are not your own?

2Co 1:22 — Who hath also sealed us, and given the earnest of the Spirit in our hearts.

2Co 3:3 — *Forasmuch as ye are* manifestly declared to be the epistle of Christ ministered by us, written not with ink, but with the Spirit of the living God; not in tables of stone, but in fleshy tables of the heart.

2Co 3:6 — Who also hath made us able ministers of the new testament; not of the letter, but of the spirit: for the letter killeth, but the spirit giveth life.

2Co 3:8 — How shall not the ministration of the spirit be rather glorious?

2Co 5:5 — Now he that hath wrought us for the selfsame thing *is* God, who also hath given unto us the earnest of the Spirit.

2Co 6:4 — But in all *things* approving ourselves as the ministers of God, in much patience, in afflictions, in necessities, in distresses,

2Co 6:6 — By pureness, by knowledge, by longsuffering, by kindness, by the Holy Ghost, by love unfeigned,

2Co 13:14 — The grace of the Lord Jesus Christ, and the love of God, and the communion of the Holy Ghost, *be* with you all. Amen.

Gal 3:14 — That the blessing of Abraham might come on the Gentiles through Jesus Christ; that we might receive the promise of the Spirit through faith.

Gal 4:6 — And because ye are sons, God hath sent forth the Spirit of his Son into your hearts, crying, Abba, Father.

Gal 5:5 — For we through the Spirit wait for the hope of righteousness by faith.

Gal 5:25 — If we live in the Spirit, let us also walk in the Spirit.

Gal 6:8 — For he that soweth to his flesh shall of the flesh reap corruption; but he that soweth to the Spirit shall of the Spirit reap life everlasting.

Eph 1:17 — That the God of our Lord Jesus Christ, the Father of glory, may give unto you the spirit of wisdom and revelation in the knowledge of him:

Eph 2:18 — For through him we both have access by one Spirit unto the Father.

Eph 2:22 — In whom ye also are builded together for an habitation of God through the Spirit.

Eph 3:5 — Which in other ages was not made known unto the sons of men, as it is now revealed unto his holy apostles and prophets by the Spirit;

Eph 3:16 — That he would grant you, according to the riches of his glory, to be strengthened with might by his Spirit in the inner man;

Eph 4:30 — And grieve not the holy Spirit of God, whereby ye are sealed unto the day of redemption.

Eph 5:9 — (For the fruit of the Spirit is in all goodness and righteousness and truth;)

Eph 5:18 — And be not drunk with wine, wherein is excess; but be filled with the Spirit;

Php 1:19 — For I know that this shall turn to my salvation through your prayer, and the supply of the Spirit of Jesus Christ,

Php 2:1 — If *there be* therefore any consolation in Christ, if any comfort of love, if any fellowship of the Spirit, if any bowels and mercies,

Col 1:8 — Who also declared unto us your love in the Spirit.

1Th 5:19 — Quench not the Spirit.

2Th 2:13 — But we are bound to give thanks alway to God for you, brethren beloved of the Lord, because God hath from the beginning chosen you to salvation through sanctification of the Spirit and belief of the truth:

1Ti 4:1 — Now the Spirit speaketh expressly, that in the latter times some shall depart from the faith, giving heed to seducing spirits, and doctrines of devils;

2Ti 1:7 — For God hath not given us the spirit of fear; but of power, and of love, and of a sound mind.

2Ti 1:14 — That good thing which was committed unto thee keep by the Holy Ghost which dwelleth in us.

Heb 2:4 — God also bearing *them* witness, both with signs and wonders, and with divers miracles, and gifts of the Holy Ghost, according to his own will?

Heb 3:7 — Wherefore (as the Holy Ghost saith, To day if ye will hear his voice,

Heb 6:4 — For *it is* impossible for those who were once enlightened, and have tasted of the heavenly gift, and were made partakers of the Holy Ghost,

Heb 9:14 — How much more shall the blood of Christ, who through the eternal Spirit offered himself without spot to God, purge your conscience from dead works to serve the living God?

1Pe 1:2 — Elect according to the foreknowledge of God the Father, through sanctification of the Spirit, unto obedience and sprinkling of the blood of Jesus Christ: Grace unto you, and peace, be multiplied.

1Pe 1:22 — Seeing ye have purified your souls in obeying the truth through the Spirit unto unfeigned love of the brethren, *see that ye* love one another with a pure heart fervently:

1Pe 3:18 — For Christ also hath once suffered for sins, the just for the unjust, that he might bring us to God, being put to death in the flesh, but quickened by the Spirit:

1Pe 4:14 — If ye be reproached for the name of Christ, happy *are ye;* for the spirit of glory and of God resteth upon you: on their part he is evil spoken of, but on your part he is glorified.

2Pe 1:21 — For the prophecy came not in old time by the will of man: but holy men of God spake *as they were* moved by the Holy Ghost.

1Jn 2:20 — But ye have an unction from the Holy One, and ye know all things.

1Jn 3:24 — And he that keepeth his commandments dwelleth in him, and he in him. And hereby we know that he abideth in us, by the Spirit which he hath given us.

1Jn 4:2 — Hereby know ye the Spirit of God: Every spirit that confesseth that Jesus Christ is come in the flesh is of God:

1Jn 4:13 — Hereby know we that we dwell in him, and he in us, because he hath given us of his Spirit.

Rev 1:4 — John to the seven churches which are in Asia: Grace *be* unto you, and peace, from him which is, and which was, and which is to come; and from the seven Spirits which are before his throne;

Rev 2:7 — <u>He that hath an ear, let him hear what the Spirit saith unto the churches; To him that overcometh will I give to eat of the tree of life, which is in the midst of the paradise of God.</u>

Rev 2:11 — <u>He that hath an ear, let him hear what the Spirit saith unto the churches; He that overcometh shall not be hurt of the second death.</u>

Rev 2:29 — <u>He that hath an ear, let him hear what the Spirit saith unto the churches.</u>

Rev 4:5 — And out of the throne proceeded lightnings and thunderings and voices: and *there were* seven lamps of fire burning before the throne, which are the seven Spirits of God.

Rev 5:6 — And I beheld, and, lo, in the midst of the throne and of the four beasts, and in the midst of the elders, stood a Lamb as it had been slain, having seven horns and seven eyes, which are the seven Spirits of God sent forth into all the earth.

Rev 11:11 — And after three days and an half the Spirit of life from God entered into them, and they stood upon their feet; and great fear fell upon them which saw them.

Rev 14:13 — And I heard a voice from heaven saying unto me, Write, Blessed *are* the dead which die in the Lord from henceforth: Yea, saith the Spirit, that they may rest from their labours; and their works do follow them.

Rev 19:10 — And I fell at his feet to worship him. And he said unto me, See *thou do it* not: I am thy fellowservant, and of thy brethren that have the testimony of Jesus: worship God: for the testimony of Jesus is the spirit of prophecy.

Rev 22:17 — And the Spirit and the bride say, Come. And let him that heareth say, Come. And let him that is athirst come. And whosoever will, let him take the water of life freely.

See: God, a Spirit

See: Inspiration

See: Word of God; inspiration of

• Inspiration of.

• Instances of.

• Joseph.

Ge 41:38 — And Pharaoh said unto his servants, Can we find *such a one* as this *is,* a man in whom the Spirit of God is?

• Bezaleel.

Ex 31:3 — And I have filled him with the spirit of God, in wisdom, and in understanding, and in knowledge, and in all manner of workmanship,

Ex 35:31 — And he hath filled him with the spirit of God, in wisdom, in understanding, and in knowledge, and in all manner of workmanship;

• The seventy elders.

Nu 11:17 — And I will come down and talk with thee there: and I will take of the spirit which *is* upon thee, and will put *it* upon them; and they shall bear the burden of the people with thee, that thou bear it not thyself alone.

• Balaam.

Nu 24:2 — And Balaam lifted up his eyes, and he saw Israel abiding *in his tents* according to their tribes; and the spirit of God came upon him.

• Joshua.

Nu 27:18 — And the LORD said unto Moses, Take thee Joshua the son of Nun, a man in whom *is* the spirit, and lay thine hand upon him;

• The judges.

• Othniel.

Jgs 3:10 — And the Spirit of the LORD came upon him, and he judged Israel, and went out to war: and the LORD delivered Chushan-rishathaim king of Mesopotamia into his hand; and his hand prevailed against Chushan-rishathaim.

• Gideon.

Jgs 6:34 — But the Spirit of the LORD came upon Gideon, and he blew a trumpet; and Abi-ezer was gathered after him.

• Jephthah.

Jgs 11:29 — Then the Spirit of the LORD came upon Jephthah, and he passed over Gilead, and Manasseh, and passed over Mizpeh of Gilead, and from Mizpeh of Gilead he passed over *unto* the children of Ammon.

• **Sampson.**

Jgs 13:25 — And the Spirit of the LORD began to move him at times in the camp of Dan between Zorah and Eshtaol.

Jgs 14:6 — And the Spirit of the LORD came mightily upon him, and he rent him as he would have rent a kid, and *he had* nothing in his hand: but he told not his father or his mother what he had done.

Jgs 14:19 — And the Spirit of the LORD came upon him, and he went down to Ashkelon, and slew thirty men of them, and took their spoil, and gave change of garments unto them which expounded the riddle. And his anger was kindled, and he went up to his father's house.

• **King David.**

1Ch 28:11–12

• **The prophets.**

• **Azariah.**

2Ch 15:1 — And the Spirit of God came upon Azariah the son of Oded:

• **Zechariah.**

2Ch 1:1 — And Solomon the son of David was strengthened in his kingdom, and the LORD his God *was* with him, and magnified him exceedingly.

2Ch 24:20 — And the Spirit of God came upon Zechariah the son of Jehoiada the priest, which stood above the people, and said unto them, Thus saith God, Why transgress ye the commandments of the LORD, that ye cannot prosper? because ye have forsaken the LORD, he hath also forsaken you.

• **Ezekiel.**

Eze 8:3 — And he put forth the form of an hand, and took me by a lock of mine head; and the spirit lifted me up between the earth and the heaven, and brought me in the visions of God to Jerusalem, to the door of the inner gate that looketh toward the north; where *was* the seat of the image of jealousy, which provoketh to jealousy.

Eze 11:1 — Moreover the spirit lifted me up, and brought me unto the east gate of the LORD's house, which looketh eastward: and behold at the door of the gate five and twenty men; among whom I saw Jaazaniah the son of Azur, and Pelatiah the son of Benaiah, the princes of the people.

Eze 11:5 — And the Spirit of the LORD fell upon me, and said unto me, Speak; Thus saith the LORD; Thus have ye said, O house of Israel: for I know the things that come into your mind, *every one of* them.

Eze 11:24 — Afterwards the spirit took me up, and brought me in a vision by the Spirit of God into Chaldea, to them of the captivity. So the vision that I had seen went up from me.

• **Daniel.**

Da 4:8 — But at the last Daniel came in before me, whose name *was* Belteshazzar, according to the name of my god, and in whom is the spirit of the holy gods: and before him I told the dream, *saying,*

• **Zacharias.**

Lk 1:67 — And his father Zacharias was filled with the Holy Ghost, and prophesied, saying,

• **Elisabeth.**

Lk 1:41 — And it came to pass, that, when Elisabeth heard the salutation of Mary, the babe leaped in her womb; and Elisabeth was filled with the Holy Ghost:

• **Simeon.**

Lk 2:25–26

• **The disciples.**

Ac 6:3 — Wherefore, brethren, look ye out among you seven men of honest report, full of the Holy Ghost and wisdom, whom we may appoint over this business.

Ac 7:55 — But he, being full of the Holy Ghost, looked up stedfastly into heaven, and saw the glory of God, and Jesus standing on the right hand of God,

Ac 8:29 — Then the Spirit said unto Philip, Go near, and join thyself to this chariot.

Ac 9:17 — And Ananias went his way, and entered into the house; and putting his hands on him said, Brother Saul, the Lord, *even* Jesus, that appeared unto thee in the way as thou camest, hath sent me, that thou mightest receive thy sight, and be filled with the Holy Ghost.

Ac 10:45 — And they of the circumcision which believed were astonished, as many as came with Peter, because that on the Gentiles also was poured out the gift of the Holy Ghost.

See: Inspiration

• **Sin against.**

Mt 12:31–32; Ac 8:18–22

Isa 63:10 — But they rebelled, and vexed his holy Spirit: therefore he was turned to be their enemy, *and* he fought against them.

Mk 3:29 — But he that shall blaspheme against the Holy Ghost hath never forgiveness, but is in danger of eternal damnation:

Lk 2:10 — And the angel said unto them, Fear not: for, behold, I bring you good tidings of great joy, which shall be to all people.

Lk 12:10 — And whosoever shall speak a word against the Son of man, it shall be forgiven him: but unto him that blasphemeth against the Holy Ghost it shall not be forgiven.

Ac 5:3 — But Peter said, Ananias, why hath Satan filled thine heart to lie to the Holy Ghost, and to keep back *part* of the price of the land?

Ac 5:9 — Then Peter said unto her, How is it that ye have agreed together to tempt the Spirit of the Lord?

behold, the feet of them which have buried thy husband *are* at the door, and shall carry thee out.

Ac 7:51 — Ye stiffnecked and uncircumcised in heart and ears, ye do always resist the Holy Ghost: as your fathers *did,* so *do* ye.

Eph 4:30 — And grieve not the holy Spirit of God, whereby ye are sealed unto the day of redemption.

Heb 10:29 — Of how much sorer punishment, suppose ye, shall he be thought worthy, who hath trodden under foot the Son of God, and hath counted the blood of the covenant, wherewith he was sanctified, an unholy thing, and hath done despite unto the Spirit of grace?

1Jn 5:16 — If any man see his brother sin a sin *which is* not unto death, he shall ask, and he shall give him life for them that sin not unto death. There is a sin unto death: I do not say that he shall pray for it.

- **Withdrawn from incorrigible sinners.**

Pr 1:24–28; Hos 4:17–18

Ge 6:3 — And the LORD said, My spirit shall not always strive with man, for that he also *is* flesh: yet his days shall be an hundred and twenty years.

Dt 32:30 — How should one chase a thousand, and two put ten thousand to flight, except their Rock had sold them, and the LORD had shut them up?

Ps 51:11 — Cast me not away from thy presence; and take not thy holy spirit from me.

Jer 7:29 — Cut off thine hair, *O Jerusalem,* and cast *it* away, and take up a lamentation on high places; for the LORD hath rejected and forsaken the generation of his wrath.

Hos 5:6 — They shall go with their flocks and with their herds to seek the LORD; but they shall not find *him;* he hath withdrawn himself from them.

Hos 9:12 — Though they bring up their children, yet will I bereave them, *that there shall* not *be* a man *left:* yea, woe also to them when I depart from them!

Mt 15:14 — Let them alone: they be blind leaders of the blind. And if the blind lead the blind, both shall fall into the ditch.

Lk 13:7 — Then said he unto the dresser of his vineyard, Behold, these three years I come seeking fruit on this fig tree, and find none: cut it down; why cumbereth it the ground?

Ro 1:24 — Wherefore God also gave them up to uncleanness through the lusts of their own hearts, to dishonour their own bodies between themselves:

Ro 1:26 — For this cause God gave them up unto vile affections: for even their women did change the natural use into that which is against nature:

Ro 1:28 — And even as they did not like to retain God in *their* knowledge, God gave them over to a reprobate mind, to do those things which are not convenient;

↞**See: Reprobacy**

- **Instances of.**
  - **Antediluvians.**
    Ge 6:3–7
  - **People of Sodom.**
    Ge 19:13, 24–25
  - **Israelites.**
    Nu 14:26–45; Dt 1:42; 28:15–68; 31:17–18
  - **Samson.**
    Jgs 16:20
  - **Saul.**
    1Sa 16:14; 18:10–12; 19:9–11; 20:30–33; 22:7–19; 28:15–16; 2Sa 7:15

HOMAGE

- **Refused by Peter.**

Ac 10:26 — But Peter took him up, saying, Stand up; I myself also am a man.

- **Refused by Paul and Barnabas.**

Ac 14:11–18

- **By the angel seen by John in his vision.**

Rev 22:8–9

Rev 19:10 — And I fell at his feet to worship him. And he said unto me, See *thou do it* not: I am thy fellowservant, and of thy brethren that have the testimony of Jesus: worship God: for the testimony of Jesus is the spirit of prophecy.

↞**See: Worship**

- **Rendered to kings.**

1Ki 1:16 — And Bath-sheba bowed, and did obeisance unto the king. And the king said, What wouldest thou?

1Ki 1:23 — And they told the king, saying, Behold Nathan the prophet. And when he was come in before the king, he bowed himself before the king with his face to the ground.

1Ki 1:31 — Then Bath-sheba bowed with *her* face to the earth, and did reverence to the king, and said, Let my lord king David live for ever.

- **Rendered to princes.**

Est 3:2 — And all the king's servants, that *were* in the king's gate, bowed, and reverenced Haman: for the king had so commanded concerning him. But Mordecai bowed not, nor did *him* reverence.

Est 3:5 — And when Haman saw that Mordecai bowed not, nor did him reverence, then was Haman full of wrath.

HOMAM

- **Called also Heman.**
- **An Edomite.**

Ge 36:22 — And the children of Lotan were Hori and Hemam; and Lotan's sister *was* Timna.

1Ch 1:39 — And the sons of Lotan; Hori, and Homam: and Timna *was* Lotan's sister.

HOME ↞See: Family

HOMER

- **A measure.**

↞**See: Measure**

HOMESTEAD

- **Mortgaged.**

Ne 5:3 — *Some* also there were that said, We have mortgaged our lands, vineyards, and houses, that we might buy corn, because of the dearth.

• When alienable, and when inalienable.
Le 25:25–34

See: Land

HOMICIDE

• Accidental.
Ex 21:28–32; Nu 35:11–15, 22–28; Dt 4:41–43; 19:2–10; Jos 20:1–9

Ex 21:13 — And if a man lie not in wait, but God deliver *him* into his hand; then I will appoint thee a place whither he shall flee.

Nu 35:32 — And ye shall take no satisfaction for him that is fled to the city of his refuge, that he should come again to dwell in the land, until the death of the priest.

• Felonious, or murder.
Ge 4:9–12; 9:5–6; Ex 21:29–32; Nu 35:16–22, 30–31; Dt 21:1–9; 27:24–25; Job 24:1–25; Ps 26:9–10; Pr 1:11–12, 15–16; 6:16–17; Jer 7:9–10; Hos 4:1–3; Mt 5:21–22; Gal 5:19–21

Ge 49:7 — Cursed *be* their anger, for *it was* fierce; and their wrath, for it was cruel: I will divide them in Jacob, and scatter them in Israel.

Ex 20:13 — Thou shalt not kill.

Dt 5:17 — Thou shalt not kill.

Dt 17:6 — At the mouth of two witnesses, or three witnesses, shall he that is worthy of death be put to death; *but* at the mouth of one witness he shall not be put to death.

Dt 22:8 — When thou buildest a new house, then thou shalt make a battlement for thy roof, that thou bring not blood upon thine house, if any man fall from thence.

1Ki 21:19 — And thou shalt speak unto him, saying, Thus saith the LORD, Hast thou killed, and also taken possession? And thou shalt speak unto him, saying, Thus saith the LORD, In the place where dogs licked the blood of Naboth shall dogs lick thy blood, even thine.

2Ch 24:22 — Thus Joash the king remembered not the kindness which Jehoiada his father had done to him, but slew his son. And when he died, he said, The LORD look upon *it*, and require *it*.

Ps 5:6 — Thou shalt destroy them that speak leasing: the LORD will abhor the bloody and deceitful man.

Ps 9:12 — When he maketh inquisition for blood, he remembereth them: he forgetteth not the cry of the humble.

Ps 10:2 — The wicked in *his* pride doth persecute the poor: let them be taken in the devices that they have imagined.

Ps 10:8 — He sitteth in the lurking places of the villages: in the secret places doth he murder the innocent: his eyes are privily set against the poor.

Ps 37:32 — The wicked watcheth the righteous, and seeketh to slay him.

Ps 38:12 — They also that seek after my life lay snares *for me:* and they that seek my hurt speak mischievous things, and imagine deceits all the day long.

Ps 55:23 — But thou, O God, shalt bring them down into the pit of destruction: bloody and deceitful men shall not live out half their days; but I will trust in thee.

Ps 94:3 — LORD, how long shall the wicked, how long shall the wicked triumph?

Ps 94:6 — They slay the widow and the stranger, and murder the fatherless.

Pr 12:6 — The words of the wicked *are* to lie in wait for blood: but the mouth of the upright shall deliver them.

Pr 28:17 — A man that doeth violence to the blood of *any* person shall flee to the pit; let no man stay him.

Isa 26:21 — For, behold, the LORD cometh out of his place to punish the inhabitants of the earth for their iniquity: the earth also shall disclose her blood, and shall no more cover her slain.

Isa 59:3 — For your hands are defiled with blood, and your fingers with iniquity; your lips have spoken lies, your tongue hath muttered perverseness.

Isa 59:7 — Their feet run to evil, and they make haste to shed innocent blood: their thoughts *are* thoughts of iniquity; wasting and destruction *are* in their paths.

Jer 2:34 — Also in thy skirts is found the blood of the souls of the poor innocents: I have not found it by secret search, but upon all these.

Jer 19:4 — Because they have forsaken me, and have estranged this place, and have burned incense in it unto other gods, whom neither they nor their fathers have known, nor the kings of Judah, and have filled this place with the blood of innocents;

Jer 22:3 — Thus saith the LORD; Execute ye judgment and righteousness, and deliver the spoiled out of the hand of the oppressor: and do no wrong, do no violence to the stranger, the fatherless, nor the widow, neither shed innocent blood in this place.

Eze 22:9 — In thee are men that carry tales to shed blood: and in thee they eat upon the mountains: in the midst of thee they commit lewdness.

Eze 35:6 — Therefore, *as* I live, saith the Lord GOD, I will prepare thee unto blood, and blood shall pursue thee: sith thou hast not hated blood, even blood shall pursue thee.

Hos 1:4 — And the LORD said unto him, Call his name Jezreel; for yet a little *while,* and I will avenge the blood of Jezreel upon the house of Jehu, and will cause to cease the kingdom of the house of Israel.

Hab 2:10 — Thou hast consulted shame to thy house by cutting off many people, and hast sinned *against* thy soul.

Hab 2:12 — Woe to him that buildeth a town with blood, and stablisheth a city by iniquity!

Mt 15:19 — For out of the heart proceed evil thoughts, murders, adulteries, fornications, thefts, false witness, blasphemies:

Mt 19:18 — He saith unto him, Which? Jesus said, Thou shalt do no murder, Thou shalt not commit adultery, Thou shalt not steal, Thou shalt not bear false witness,

Mk 7:21 — For from within, out of the heart of men, proceed evil thoughts, adulteries, fornications, murders,

Mk 10:19 — Thou knowest the commandments, Do not commit adultery, Do not kill, Do not steal, Do not bear false witness, Defraud not, Honour thy father and mother.

Lk 18:20 — Thou knowest the commandments, Do not commit adultery, Do not kill, Do not steal, Do not bear false witness, Honour thy father and thy mother.

Ro 13:9 — For this, Thou shalt not commit adultery, Thou shalt not kill, Thou shalt not steal, Thou shalt not bear false witness, Thou shalt not covet; and if *there be* any other commandment, it is briefly comprehended in this saying, namely, Thou shalt love thy neighbour as thyself.

1Ti 1:9 — Knowing this, that the law is not made for a righteous man, but for the lawless and disobedient, for the ungodly and for sinners, for unholy and profane, for murderers of fathers and murderers of mothers, for manslayers,

Jas 2:11 — For he that said, Do not commit adultery, said also, Do not kill. Now if thou commit no adultery, yet if thou kill, thou art become a transgressor of the law.

1Pe 4:15 — But let none of you suffer as a murderer, or *as* a thief, or *as* an evildoer, or as a busybody in other men's matters.

1Jn 3:12 — Not as Cain, *who* was of that wicked one, and slew his brother. And wherefore slew he him? Because his own works were evil, and his brother's righteous.

1Jn 3:15 — Whosoever hateth his brother is a murderer: and ye know that no murderer hath eternal life abiding in him.

Rev 9:21 — Neither repented they of their murders, nor of their sorceries, nor of their fornication, nor of their thefts.

Rev 21:8 — But the fearful, and unbelieving, and the abominable, and murderers, and whoremongers, and sorcerers, and idolaters, and all liars, shall have their part in the lake which burneth with fire and brimstone: which is the second death.

Rev 22:15 — For without *are* dogs, and sorcerers, and whoremongers, and murderers, and idolaters, and whosoever loveth and maketh a lie.

See: Conspiracy

See: Fratricide

See: Parricide

See: Patricide

See: Regicide

See: Suicide

• David's repentance for, and confession of, the murder of Uriah.

Ps 51:1–17

• Instances of felonious.

• By Cain.
Ge 4:8

• Lamech.
Ge 4:23–24

• Simeon and Levi.
Ge 34:25–31

• Pharaoh.
Ex 1:16, 22

• Moses.
Ex 2:12

• Ehud.
Jgs 3:16–23

• Jael.
Jgs 4:21

• Abimelech.
Jgs 9:5, 18, 56

• An Amalekite.
2Sa 1:16

• Abner.
2Sa 2:18–24

• Joab.
2Sa 3:24–27; 20:9–10; 1Ki 2:5

• Solomon.
1Ki 2:23–46

• Rechab and Baanah.
2Sa 4:5–8

• David.
2Sa 11:14–17; 12:9; Ps 51:14

• Of Amon.
2Ki 21:23

• Absalom.
2Sa 13:22–29

• Baasha.
1Ki 15:27–29

• Zimri.
1Ki 16:9–11

• Ahab and Jezebel.
1Ki 21:10–24; 2Ki 6:32

• Hazael.
2Ki 8:15

• Jehu.
2Ki 9:24–10:25

• Athaliah.
2Ki 11:1

• Of Joash by his servants.
2Ki 12:20–21

• Menahem.
2Ki 15:16

• Of Sennacherib.
2Ki 19:37; Isa 37:38

• Manasseh.
2Ki 21:16; 24:4

• Jehoram.
2Ch 21:4

• Joash.
2Ch 24:21

• Amaziah's soldiers.
2Ch 25:12

• Nebuchadnezzar.
Jer 39:6

• Ishmael.
Jer 41:1–7

• Ammonites.
Am 1:13–15

- **Herod I.**
  Mt 2:16
- **Herod II.**
  Mt 14:10; Mk 6:27
- **Barabbas.**
  Mk 15:7; Ac 3:14
- **Sanhedrin and Pilate.**
  Mt 26:1–27:66
- **Sanhedrin.**
  Ac 7:54–60
- **Herod.**
  Ac 12:2, 19
- **By raping.**
  Jgs 19:25–28

• **Punishment of.**

Ge 4:13–15; 9:5–6; 27:43–45; Nu 35:16–21, 30–33; Dt 19:11–13; 2Sa 12:9–12

Ex 21:12 — He that smiteth a man, so that he die, shall be surely put to death.

Ex 21:14 — But if a man come presumptuously upon his neighbour, to slay him with guile; thou shalt take him from mine altar, that he may die.

Le 24:17 — And he that killeth any man shall surely be put to death.

• **Instances of the punishment of murderers.**

- **Cain.**
  Ge 4:11–15
- **David.**
  2Sa 12:9–10
- **Joab.**
  1Ki 2:31–34
- **Haman.**
  Est 7:10 — So they hanged Haman on the gallows that he had prepared for Mordecai. Then was the king's wrath pacified.

• **The murderer of Saul.**

2Sa 1:15–16

• **The murderer of Ish-bosheth.**

2Sa 4:11–12

• **The murderers of Joash.**

2Ki 14:5 — And it came to pass, as soon as the kingdom was confirmed in his hand, that he slew his servants which had slain the king his father.

HOMOSEXUALITY

Le 18:22–24; 20:13–16; Ro 1:24–32; 1Co 6:9–11; 1Ti 1:8–11

HONESTY

Le 19:35–36; Dt 25:13–16; Ps 7:3–4; Isa 33:15–16; Lk 3:12–13; 2Co 4:1–2; Col 3:1–25; 1Th 4:11–12

Dt 16:20 — That which is altogether just shalt thou follow, that thou mayest live, and inherit the land which the LORD thy God giveth thee.

Job 27:6 — My righteousness I hold fast, and will not let it go: my heart shall not reproach *me* so long as I live.

Ps 15:5 — *He that* putteth not out his money to usury, nor taketh reward against the innocent. He that doeth these *things* shall never be moved.

Ps 24:4 — He that hath clean hands, and a pure heart; who hath not lifted up his soul unto vanity, nor sworn deceitfully.

Pr 4:25 — Let thine eyes look right on, and let thine eyelids look straight before thee.

Pr 11:1 — A false balance *is* abomination to the LORD: but a just weight *is* his delight.

Pr 12:22 — Lying lips *are* abomination to the LORD: but they that deal truly *are* his delight.

Pr 16:11 — A just weight and balance *are* the LORD's: all the weights of the bag *are* his work.

Pr 20:10 — Divers weights, *and* divers measures, both of them *are* alike abomination to the LORD.

Pr 20:23 — Divers weights *are* an abomination unto the LORD; and a false balance *is* not good.

Eze 45:10 — Ye shall have just balances, and a just ephah, and a just bath.

Mt 7:12 — Therefore all things whatsoever ye would that men should do to you, do ye even so to them: for this is the law and the prophets.

Mk 10:19 — Thou knowest the commandments, Do not commit adultery, Do not kill, Do not steal, Do not bear false witness, Defraud not, Honour thy father and mother.

Lk 6:31 — And as ye would that men should do to you, do ye also to them likewise.

Ac 24:16 — And herein do I exercise myself, to have always a conscience void of offence toward God, and *toward* men.

2Co 7:2 — Receive us; we have wronged no man, we have corrupted no man, we have defrauded no man.

2Co 8:21 — Providing for honest things, not only in the sight of the Lord, but also in the sight of men.

Php 4:8 — Finally, brethren, whatsoever things are true, whatsoever things *are* honest, whatsoever things *are* just, whatsoever things *are* pure, whatsoever things *are* lovely, whatsoever things *are* of good report; if *there be* any virtue, and if *there be* any praise, think on these things.

Heb 13:18 — Pray for us: for we trust we have a good conscience, in all things willing to live honestly.

1Pe 2:12 — Having your conversation honest among the Gentiles: that, whereas they speak against you as evildoers, they may by *your* good works, which they shall behold, glorify God in the day of visitation.

• **Instances of.**

- **Jacob, returning money placed in the sacks.**
  Ge 43:12
- **The overseers of the temple repairs.**
  2Ki 12:15; 22:4–7
- **Treasures of the temple.**
  Ne 13:13

➜**See: Dishonesty**

➜**See: Integrity**

➜**See: Righteousness**

HONEY

Ex 16:31 — And the house of Israel called the name thereof Manna: and it *was* like coriander seed, white; and the taste of it *was* like wafers *made* with honey.

2Sa 17:29 — And honey, and butter, and sheep, and cheese of kine, for David, and for the people that *were* with him, to eat: for they said, The people *is* hungry, and weary, and thirsty, in the wilderness.

Pr 25:27 — *It is* not good to eat much honey: so *for men* to search their own glory *is not* glory.

SS 4:11 — Thy lips, O *my* spouse, drop *as* the honeycomb: honey and milk *are* under thy tongue; and the smell of thy garments *is* like the smell of Lebanon.

Isa 7:15 — Butter and honey shall he eat, that he may know to refuse the evil, and choose the good.

Mt 3:4 — And the same John had his raiment of camel's hair, and a leathern girdle about his loins; and his meat was locusts and wild honey.

Lk 24:42 — And they gave him a piece of a broiled fish, and of an honeycomb.

• Not to be offered with sacrifices.

Le 2:11 — No meat offering, which ye shall bring unto the LORD, shall be made with leaven: for ye shall burn no leaven, nor any honey, in any offering of the LORD made by fire.

• Found in rocks.

Dt 32:13 — He made him ride on the high places of the earth, that he might eat the increase of the fields; and he made him to suck honey out of the rock, and oil out of the flinty rock;

Ps 81:16 — He should have fed them also with the finest of the wheat: and with honey out of the rock should I have satisfied thee.

• Found upon the ground.

1Sa 14:25 — And all *they of* the land came to a wood; and there was honey upon the ground.

• Samson's riddle concerning.

Jgs 14:14 — And he said unto them, Out of the eater came forth meat, and out of the strong came forth sweetness. And they could not in three days expound the riddle.

• Sent as a present by Jacob to Egypt.

Ge 43:11 — And their father Israel said unto them, If *it must be* so now, do this; take of the best fruits in the land in your vessels, and carry down the man a present, a little balm, and a little honey, spices, and myrrh, nuts, and almonds:

• Plentiful in Palestine.

Ex 3:8 — And I am come down to deliver them out of the hand of the Egyptians, and to bring them up out of that land unto a good land and a large, unto a land flowing with milk and honey; unto the place of the Canaanites, and the Hittites, and the Amorites, and the Perizzites, and the Hivites, and the Jebusites.

Le 20:24 — But I have said unto you, Ye shall inherit their land, and I will give it unto you to possess it, a land that floweth with milk and honey: I *am* the LORD your God, which have separated you from *other* people.

Dt 8:8 — A land of wheat, and barley, and vines, and fig trees, and pomegranates; a land of oil olive, and honey;

Eze 20:6 — In the day *that* I lifted up mine hand unto them, to bring them forth of the land of Egypt into a land that I had espied for them, flowing with milk and honey, which *is* the glory of all lands:

• Plentiful in Assyria.

2Ki 18:32 — Until I come and take you away to a land like your own land, a land of corn and wine, a land of bread and vineyards, a land of oil olive and of honey, that ye may live, and not die: and hearken not unto Hezekiah, when he persuadeth you, saying, The LORD will deliver us.

• An article of merchandise from Palestine.

Eze 27:17 — Judah, and the land of Israel, they *were* thy merchants: they traded in thy market wheat of Minnith, and Pannag, and honey, and oil, and balm.

HOOD

Isa 3:23 — The glasses, and the fine linen, and the hoods, and the vails.

See: Dress

HOOF

• Parting of, one of the physical marks used for distinguishing clean and unclean animals.

Le 11:3–8; Dt 14:3–8

HOOKS

• For tabernacle, made of gold.

Ex 26:32 — And thou shalt hang it upon four pillars of shittim *wood* overlaid with gold: their hooks *shall be of* gold, upon the four sockets of silver.

Ex 26:37 — And thou shalt make for the hanging five pillars *of* shittim *wood*, and overlay them with gold, *and* their hooks *shall be of* gold: and thou shalt cast five sockets of brass for them.

Ex 36:36 — And he made thereunto four pillars *of* shittim *wood*, and overlaid them with gold: their hooks *were of* gold; and he cast for them four sockets of silver.

• For tabernacle, made of silver.

Ex 38:10–12

Ex 27:10 — And the twenty pillars thereof and their twenty sockets *shall be of* brass; the hooks of the pillars and their fillets *shall be of* silver.

Ex 38:17 — And the sockets for the pillars *were of* brass; the hooks of the pillars and their fillets *of* silver; and the overlaying of their chapiters *of* silver; and all the pillars of the court *were* filleted with silver.

Ex 38:19 — And their pillars *were* four, and their sockets *of* brass four; their hooks *of* silver, and the overlaying of their chapiters and their fillets *of* silver.

• In the temple, seen in Ezekiel's vision.

Eze 40:43 — And within *were* hooks, an hand broad, fastened round about: and upon the tables *was* the flesh of the offering.

- **Used for catching fish.**

Eze 29:4 — But I will put hooks in thy jaws, and I will cause the fish of thy rivers to stick unto thy scales, and I will bring thee up out of the midst of thy rivers, and all the fish of thy rivers shall stick unto thy scales.

- **For pruning.**

Isa 2:4 — And he shall judge among the nations, and shall rebuke many people: and they shall beat their swords into plowshares, and their spears into pruninghooks: nation shall not lift up sword against nation, neither shall they learn war any more.

Isa 18:5 — For afore the harvest, when the bud is perfect, and the sour grape is ripening in the flower, he shall both cut off the sprigs with pruninghooks, and take away *and* cut down the branches.

Joel 3:10 — Beat your plowshares into swords, and your pruninghooks into spears: let the weak say, I *am* strong.

➜**See: Fleshhook**

- **Figurative.**

Eze 38:4 — And I will turn thee back, and put hooks into thy jaws, and I will bring thee forth, and all thine army, horses and horsemen, all of them clothed with all sorts *of armour, even* a great company *with* bucklers and shields, all of them handling swords:

HOPE

Ps 78:5–7; Ac 24:14–15; 26:6–7; Ro 5:2–5; 8:24–25; Heb 6:18–19

Ps 9:18 — For the needy shall not alway be forgotten: the expectation of the poor shall *not* perish for ever.

Ps 16:9 — Therefore my heart is glad, and my glory rejoiceth: my flesh also shall rest in hope.

Ps 31:24 — Be of good courage, and he shall strengthen your heart, all ye that hope in the LORD.

Ps 33:18 — Behold, the eye of the LORD *is* upon them that fear him, upon them that hope in his mercy;

Ps 33:22 — Let thy mercy, O LORD, be upon us, according as we hope in thee.

Ps 38:15 — For in thee, O LORD, do I hope: thou wilt hear, O Lord my God.

Ps 39:7 — And now, Lord, what wait I for? my hope *is* in thee.

Ps 43:5 — Why art thou cast down, O my soul? and why art thou disquieted within me? hope in God: for I shall yet praise him, *who is* the health of my countenance, and my God.

Ps 71:5 — For thou *art* my hope, O Lord GOD: *thou art* my trust from my youth.

Ps 71:14 — But I will hope continually, and will yet praise thee more and more.

Ps 119:74 — They that fear thee will be glad when they see me; because I have hoped in thy word.

Ps 119:81 — My soul fainteth for thy salvation: *but* I hope in thy word.

Ps 119:116 — Uphold me according unto thy word, that I may live: and let me not be ashamed of my hope.

Ps 119:166 — LORD, I have hoped for thy salvation, and done thy commandments.

Ps 130:7 — Let Israel hope in the LORD: for with the LORD *there is* mercy, and with him *is* plenteous redemption.

Ps 146:5 — Happy *is he* that *hath* the God of Jacob for his help, whose hope *is* in the LORD his God:

Pr 10:28 — The hope of the righteous *shall be* gladness: but the expectation of the wicked shall perish.

Pr 13:12 — Hope deferred maketh the heart sick: but *when* the desire cometh, *it is* a tree of life.

Pr 14:32 — The wicked is driven away in his wickedness: but the righteous hath hope in his death.

Pr 23:18 — For surely there is an end; and thine expectation shall not be cut off.

Pr 24:14 — So *shall* the knowledge of wisdom *be* unto thy soul: when thou hast found *it*, then there shall be a reward, and thy expectation shall not be cut off.

Isa 38:18 — For the grave cannot praise thee, death can *not* celebrate thee: they that go down into the pit cannot hope for thy truth.

Jer 17:7 — Blessed *is* the man that trusteth in the LORD, and whose hope the LORD is.

La 3:21 — This I recall to my mind, therefore have I hope.

La 3:24 — The LORD *is* my portion, saith my soul; therefore will I hope in him.

La 3:26 — *It is* good that *a man* should both hope and quietly wait for the salvation of the LORD.

Hos 2:15 — And I will give her her vineyards from thence, and the valley of Achor for a door of hope: and she shall sing there, as in the days of her youth, and as in the day when she came up out of the land of Egypt.

Joel 3:16 — The LORD also shall roar out of Zion, and utter his voice from Jerusalem; and the heavens and the earth shall shake: but the LORD *will be* the hope of his people, and the strength of the children of Israel.

Zec 9:12 — Turn you to the strong hold, ye prisoners of hope: even to day do I declare *that* I will render double unto thee;

Ac 23:6 — But when Paul perceived that the one part were Sadducees, and the other Pharisees, he cried out in the council, Men *and* brethren, I am a Pharisee, the son of a Pharisee: of the hope and resurrection of the dead I am called in question.

Ac 28:20 — For this cause therefore have I called for you, to see *you*, and to speak with *you*: because that for the hope of Israel I am bound with this chain.

Ro 4:18 — Who against hope believed in hope, that he might become the father of many nations; according to that which was spoken, So shall thy seed be.

Ro 12:12 — Rejoicing in hope; patient in tribulation; continuing instant in prayer;

Ro 15:4 — For whatsoever things were written aforetime were written for our learning, that we through patience and comfort of the scriptures might have hope.

Ro 15:13 — Now the God of hope fill you with all joy and peace in believing, that ye may abound in hope, through the power of the Holy Ghost.

1Co 13:13 — And now abideth faith, hope, charity, these three; but the greatest of these *is* charity.

1Co 15:19 — If in this life only we have hope in Christ, we are of all men most miserable.

2Co 3:12 — Seeing then that we have such hope, we use great plainness of speech:

Gal 5:5 — For we through the Spirit wait for the hope of righteousness by faith.

Eph 1:18 — The eyes of your understanding being enlightened; that ye may know what is the hope of his calling, and what the riches of the glory of his inheritance in the saints,

Eph 4:4 — *There is* one body, and one Spirit, even as ye are called in one hope of your calling;

Eph 6:17 — And take the helmet of salvation, and the sword of the Spirit, which is the word of God:

Php 1:20 — According to my earnest expectation and *my* hope, that in nothing I shall be ashamed, but *that* with all boldness, as always, *so* now also Christ shall be magnified in my body, whether *it be* by life, or by death.

Col 1:5 — For the hope which is laid up for you in heaven, whereof ye heard before in the word of the truth of the gospel;

Col 1:23 — If ye continue in the faith grounded and settled, and *be* not moved away from the hope of the gospel, which ye have heard, *and* which was preached to every creature which is under heaven; whereof I Paul am made a minister;

Col 1:27 — To whom God would make known what *is* the riches of the glory of this mystery among the Gentiles; which is Christ in you, the hope of glory:

1Th 1:3 — Remembering without ceasing your work of faith, and labour of love, and patience of hope in our Lord Jesus Christ, in the sight of God and our Father;

1Th 5:8 — But let us, who are of the day, be sober, putting on the breastplate of faith and love; and for an helmet, the hope of salvation.

2Th 2:16 — Now our Lord Jesus Christ himself, and God, even our Father, which hath loved us, and hath given *us* everlasting consolation and good hope through grace,

1Ti 1:1 — Paul, an apostle of Jesus Christ by the commandment of God our Saviour, and Lord Jesus Christ, *which is* our hope;

Tit 1:2 — In hope of eternal life, which God, that cannot lie, promised before the world began;

Tit 2:13 — Looking for that blessed hope, and the glorious appearing of the great God and our Saviour Jesus Christ;

Tit 3:7 — That being justified by his grace, we should be made heirs according to the hope of eternal life.

Heb 3:6 — But Christ as a son over his own house; whose house are we, if we hold fast the confidence and the rejoicing of the hope firm unto the end.

Heb 6:11 — And we desire that every one of you do shew the same diligence to the full assurance of hope unto the end:

Heb 11:1 — Now faith is the substance of things hoped for, the evidence of things not seen.

1Pe 1:3 — Blessed *be* the God and Father of our Lord Jesus Christ, which according to his abundant mercy hath begotten us again unto a lively hope by the resurrection of Jesus Christ from the dead,

1Pe 1:13 — Wherefore gird up the loins of your mind, be sober, and hope to the end for the grace that is to be brought unto you at the revelation of Jesus Christ;

1Pe 1:21 — Who by him do believe in God, that raised him up from the dead, and gave him glory; that your faith and hope might be in God.

1Pe 3:15 — But sanctify the Lord God in your hearts: and *be* ready always to *give* an answer to every man that asketh you a reason of the hope that is in you with meekness and fear:

1Jn 3:3 — And every man that hath this hope in him purifieth himself, even as he is pure.

See: Faith

• Of the wicked.

Job 8:13 — So *are* the paths of all that forget God; and the hypocrite's hope shall perish:

Job 11:20 — But the eyes of the wicked shall fail, and they shall not escape, and their hope *shall be as* the giving up of the ghost.

Job 27:8 — For what *is* the hope of the hypocrite, though he hath gained, when God taketh away his soul?

Job 31:24 — If I have made gold my hope, or have said to the fine gold, *Thou art* my confidence;

Job 31:28 — This also *were* an iniquity *to be punished by* the judge: for I should have denied the God *that is* above.

Pr 10:28 — The hope of the righteous *shall be* gladness: but the expectation of the wicked shall perish.

Zec 9:5 — Ashkelon shall see *it,* and fear; Gaza also *shall see it,* and be very sorrowful, and Ekron; for her expectation shall be ashamed; and the king shall perish from Gaza, and Ashkelon shall not be inhabited.

Eph 2:12 — That at that time ye were without Christ, being aliens from the commonwealth of Israel, and strangers from the covenants of promise, having no hope, and without God in the world:

HOPHNI

• Son of Eli.

1Sa 1:3 — And this man went up out of his city yearly to worship and to sacrifice unto the LORD of hosts in Shiloh. And the two sons of Eli, Hophni and Phinehas, the priests of the LORD, *were* there.

• Sin of.

1Sa 2:12–36; 3:11–14

• Death of.

1Sa 4:4 — So the people sent to Shiloh, that they might bring from thence the ark of the covenant of the LORD of hosts, which dwelleth *between* the cherubims: and the two sons of Eli, Hophni and Phinehas, *were* there with the ark of the covenant of God.

1Sa 4:11 — And the ark of God was taken; and the two sons of Eli, Hophni and Phinehas, were slain.

1Sa 4:17 — And the messenger answered and said, Israel is fled before the Philistines, and there hath been also a great slaughter among the people, and thy two sons also, Hophni and Phinehas, are dead, and the ark of God is taken.

HOR

• Mountain on which Aaron died.

Nu 20:22–29; 33:38–39; 34:7–8

Nu 21:4 — And they journeyed from mount Hor by the way of the Red sea, to compass the land of Edom: and the soul of the people was much discouraged because of the way.

Dt 32:50 — And die in the mount whither thou goest up, and be gathered unto thy people; as Aaron thy brother died in mount Hor, and was gathered unto his people:

HOR-HAGIDGAD • One of the stations of the Israelites in the wilderness.

Nu 33:32–33

HORAM • King of Gezer.

Jos 10:33 — Then Horam king of Gezer came up to help Lachish; and Joshua smote him and his people, until he had left him none remaining.

HOREB • A range of mountains of which Sinai is chief.

1Ki 19:1–21

Ex 3:1 — Now Moses kept the flock of Jethro his father in law, the priest of Midian: and he led the flock to the backside of the desert, and came to the mountain of God, *even* to Horeb.

Ex 17:6 — Behold, I will stand before thee there upon the rock in Horeb; and thou shalt smite the rock, and there shall come water out of it, that the people may drink. And Moses did so in the sight of the elders of Israel.

Ex 33:6 — And the children of Israel stripped themselves of their ornaments by the mount Horeb.

Dt 1:2 — (*There are* eleven days' *journey* from Horeb by the way of mount Seir unto Kadesh-barnea.)

Dt 1:6 — The LORD our God spake unto us in Horeb, saying, Ye have dwelt long enough in this mount:

Dt 1:19 — And when we departed from Horeb, we went through all that great and terrible wilderness, which ye saw by the way of the mountain of the Amorites, as the LORD our God commanded us; and we came to Kadesh-barnea.

Dt 4:10 — *Specially* the day that thou stoodest before the LORD thy God in Horeb, when the LORD said unto me, Gather me the people together, and I will make them hear my words, that they may learn to fear me all the days that they shall live upon the earth, and *that* they may teach their children.

Dt 4:15 — Take ye therefore good heed unto yourselves; for ye saw no manner of similitude on the day *that* the LORD spake unto you in Horeb out of the midst of the fire:

Dt 5:2 — The LORD our God made a covenant with us in Horeb.

Dt 9:8 — Also in Horeb ye provoked the LORD to wrath, so that the LORD was angry with you to have destroyed you.

Dt 29:1 — These *are* the words of the covenant, which the LORD commanded Moses to make with the children of Israel in the land of Moab, beside the covenant which he made with them in Horeb.

1Ki 8:9 — *There was* nothing in the ark save the two tables of stone, which Moses put there at Horeb, when the LORD made *a covenant* with the children of Israel, when they came out of the land of Egypt.

2Ch 5:10 — *There was* nothing in the ark save the two tables which Moses put *therein* at Horeb, when the LORD made *a covenant* with the children of Israel, when they came out of Egypt.

Ps 106:19 — They made a calf in Horeb, and worshipped the molten image.

Mal 4:4 — Remember ye the law of Moses my servant, which I commanded unto him in Horeb for all Israel, *with* the statutes and judgments.

See: Sinai

HOREM • A fortification in Naphtali.

Jos 19:38 — And Iron, and Migdal-el, Horem, and Beth-anath, and Beth-shemesh; nineteen cities with their villages.

HORI

• Son of Lotan.

Ge 36:22 — And the children of Lotan were Hori and Hemam; and Lotan's sister *was* Timna.

Ge 36:30— Duke Dishon, duke Ezer, duke Dishan: these *are* the dukes *that came* of Hori, among their dukes in the land of Seir.

1Ch 1:39 — And the sons of Lotan; Hori, and Homam: and Timna *was* Lotan's sister.

• A Simeonite.

Nu 13:5 — Of the tribe of Simeon, Shaphat the son of Hori.

HORMAH

• A city southwest of the Dead Sea.

Nu 21:1–3

Nu 14:45 — Then the Amalekites came down, and the Canaanites which dwelt in that hill, and smote them, and discomfited them, *even* unto Hormah.

Dt 1:44 — And the Amorites, which dwelt in that mountain, came out against you, and chased you, as bees do, and destroyed you in Seir, *even* unto Hormah.

• Taken by Judah and Simeon.

Jos 12:14 — The king of Hormah, one; the king of Arad, one;

Jgs 1:17 — And Judah went with Simeon his brother, and they slew the Canaanites that inhabited Zephath, and utterly destroyed it. And the name of the city was called Hormah.

• Allotted to Simeon.

Jos 19:4 — And Eltolad, and Bethul, and Hormah,

1Ch 4:30 — And at Bethuel, and at Hormah, and at Ziklag,

• Within the territory allotted to Judah.

Jos 15:30 — And Eltolad, and Chesil, and Hormah,

1Sa 30:30 — And to *them* which *were* in Hormah, and to *them* which *were* in Chor-ashan, and to *them* which *were* in Athach,

HORN

• Used to hold the anointing oil.

1Sa 16:1 — And the LORD said unto Samuel, How long wilt thou mourn for Saul, seeing I have rejected him from reigning over Israel? fill thine horn with oil, and go, I will send thee to Jesse the Bethlehemite: for I have provided me a king among his sons.

1Ki 1:39 — And Zadok the priest took an horn of oil out of the tabernacle, and anointed Solomon. And they blew the trumpet; and all the people said, God save king Solomon.

- **Used for a trumpet.**

  See: Trumpet

- **Figurative.**
  - **Of divine protection.**

    2Sa 22:3 — The God of my rock; in him will I trust: *he is* my shield, and the horn of my salvation, my high tower, and my refuge, my saviour; thou savest me from violence.

  - **Of power.**

    1Ki 22:11 — And Zedekiah the son of Chenaanah made him horns of iron: and he said, Thus saith the LORD, With these shalt thou push the Syrians, until thou have consumed them.

    Ps 89:24 — But my faithfulness and my mercy *shall be* with him: and in my name shall his horn be exalted.

    Ps 92:10 — But my horn shalt thou exalt like *the horn of* an unicorn: I shall be anointed with fresh oil.

    Ps 132:17 — There will I make the horn of David to bud: I have ordained a lamp for mine anointed.

- **Symbolic.**

  Da 7:7–24; 8:3–9; Zec 1:18–21; Rev 17:3–16

  Da 8:20 — The ram which thou sawest having *two* horns *are* the kings of Media and Persia.

  Am 6:13 — Ye which rejoice in a thing of nought, which say, Have we not taken to us horns by our own strength?

  Mic 4:13 — Arise and thresh, O daughter of Zion: for I will make thine horn iron, and I will make thy hoofs brass: and thou shalt beat in pieces many people: and I will consecrate their gain unto the LORD, and their substance unto the Lord of the whole earth.

  Hab 3:4 — And *his* brightness was as the light; he had horns *coming* out of his hand: and there *was* the hiding of his power.

  Rev 5:6 — And I beheld, and, lo, in the midst of the throne and of the four beasts, and in the midst of the elders, stood a Lamb as it had been slain, having seven horns and seven eyes, which are the seven Spirits of God sent forth into all the earth.

  Rev 12:3 — And there appeared another wonder in heaven; and behold a great red dragon, having seven heads and ten horns, and seven crowns upon his heads.

  Rev 13:1 — And I stood upon the sand of the sea, and saw a beast rise up out of the sea, having seven heads and ten horns, and upon his horns ten crowns, and upon his heads the name of blasphemy.

  Rev 13:11 — And I beheld another beast coming up out of the earth; and he had two horns like a lamb, and he spake as a dragon.

- **Horns of the altar.**

  See: Altar

HORNET

- **Or wasp.**

  Ex 23:28 — And I will send hornets before thee, which shall drive out the Hivite, the Canaanite, and the Hittite, from before thee.

  Dt 7:20 — Moreover the LORD thy God will send the hornet among them, until they that are left, and hide themselves from thee, be destroyed.

  Jos 24:12 — And I sent the hornet before you, which drave them out from before you, *even* the two kings of the Amorites; *but* not with thy sword, nor with thy bow.

HORONAIM • A town of Moab.

Isa 15:5 — My heart shall cry out for Moab; his fugitives *shall flee* unto Zoar, an heifer of three years old: for by the mounting up of Luhith with weeping shall they go it up; for in the way of Horonaim they shall raise up a cry of destruction.

Jer 48:3 — A voice of crying *shall be* from Horonaim, spoiling and great destruction.

Jer 48:5 — For in the going up of Luhith continual weeping shall go up; for in the going down of Horonaim the enemies have heard a cry of destruction.

Jer 48:34 — From the cry of Heshbon *even* unto Elealeh, *and even* unto Jahaz, have they uttered their voice, from Zoar *even* unto Horonaim, *as* an heifer of three years old: for the waters also of Nimrim shall be desolate.

HORONITE

- **Sanballat.**

  Ne 2:10 — When Sanballat the Horonite, and Tobiah the servant, the Ammonite, heard *of it,* it grieved them exceedingly that there was come a man to seek the welfare of the children of Israel.

  Ne 2:19 — But when Sanballat the Horonite, and Tobiah the servant, the Ammonite, and Geshem the Arabian, heard *it,* they laughed us to scorn, and despised us, and said, What *is* this thing that ye do? will ye rebel against the king?

  Ne 13:28— And *one* of the sons of Joiada, the son of Eliashib the high priest, *was* son in law to Sanballat the Horonite: therefore I chased him from me.

HORSE

- **Description of.**
  - **Great strength.**

    Job 39:19–25

  - **Swifter than eagles.**

    Jer 4:13 — Behold, he shall come up as clouds, and his chariots *shall be* as a whirlwind: his horses are swifter than eagles. Woe unto us! for we are spoiled.

  - **Snorting and neighing of.**

    Isa 5:28 — Whose arrows *are* sharp, and all their bows bent, their horses' hoofs shall be counted like flint, and their wheels like a whirlwind:

    Jer 8:16 — The snorting of his horses was heard from Dan: the whole land trembled at the sound of the neighing of his strong ones; for they are come, and have devoured the land, and all that is in it; the city, and those that dwell therein.

- **A vain thing for safety.**
  Ps 33:17 — An horse *is* a vain thing for safety: neither shall he deliver *any* by his great strength.
  Pr 21:31 — The horse *is* prepared against the day of battle: but safety *is* of the LORD.

- **Used by the Egyptians in war.**
  Ex 14:9 — But the Egyptians pursued after them, all the horses *and* chariots of Pharaoh, and his horsemen, and his army, and overtook them encamping by the sea, beside Pi-hahiroth, before Baal-zephon.
  Ex 15:19 — For the horse of Pharaoh went in with his chariots and with his horsemen into the sea, and the LORD brought again the waters of the sea upon them; but the children of Israel went on dry *land* in the midst of the sea.

- **Used by the Israelites.**
  1Ki 22:4 — And he said unto Jehoshaphat, Wilt thou go with me to battle to Ramoth-gilead? And Jehoshaphat said to the king of Israel, I *am* as thou *art,* my people as thy people, my horses as thy horses.

- **Used for cavalry.**
  2Ki 18:23 — Now therefore, I pray thee, give pledges to my lord the king of Assyria, and I will deliver thee two thousand horses, if thou be able on thy part to set riders upon them.
  Jer 47:3 — At the noise of the stamping of the hoofs of his strong *horses,* at the rushing of his chariots, *and at* the rumbling of his wheels, the fathers shall not look back to *their* children for feebleness of hands;
  Jer 51:21 — And with thee will I break in pieces the horse and his rider; and with thee will I break in pieces the chariot and his rider;

- **Egypt famous for.**
  Isa 31:1 — Woe to them that go down to Egypt for help; and stay on horses, and trust in chariots, because *they are* many; and in horsemen, because they are very strong; but they look not unto the Holy One of Israel, neither seek the LORD!

- **Forbidden to kings of Israel.**
  Dt 17:16 — But he shall not multiply horses to himself, nor cause the people to return to Egypt, to the end that he should multiply horses: forasmuch as the LORD hath said unto you, Ye shall henceforth return no more that way.

- **Hamstrung by Joshua.**
  Jos 11:6 — And the LORD said unto Joshua, Be not afraid because of them: for to morrow about this time will I deliver them up all slain before Israel: thou shalt hough their horses, and burn their chariots with fire.
  Jos 11:9 — And Joshua did unto them as the LORD bade him: he houghed their horses, and burnt their chariots with fire.

- **Hamstrung by David.**
  2Sa 8:4 — And David took from him a thousand *chariots,* and seven hundred horsemen, and twenty thousand footmen: and David houghed all the chariot *horses,* but reserved of them *for* an hundred chariots.

- **Israel reproved for keeping.**
  Isa 2:7 — Their land also is full of silver and gold, neither *is there any* end of their treasures; their land is also full of horses, neither *is there any* end of their chariots:
  Isa 31:1 — Woe to them that go down to Egypt for help; and stay on horses, and trust in chariots, because *they are* many; and in horsemen, because they are very strong; but they look not unto the Holy One of Israel, neither seek the LORD!
  Eze 17:15 — But he rebelled against him in sending his ambassadors into Egypt, that they might give him horses and much people. Shall he prosper? shall he escape that doeth such *things?* or shall he break the covenant, and be delivered?
  Hos 14:3 — Asshur shall not save us; we will not ride upon horses: neither will we say any more to the work of our hands, *Ye are* our gods: for in thee the fatherless findeth mercy.

- **Exported from Egypt.**
  1Ki 10:28–29
  2Ch 9:25 — And Solomon had four thousand stalls for horses and chariots, and twelve thousand horsemen; whom he bestowed in the chariot cities, and with the king at Jerusalem.
  2Ch 9:28 — And they brought unto Solomon horses out of Egypt, and out of all lands.

- **Exported from Babylon.**
  Ezr 2:66 — Their horses *were* seven hundred thirty and six; their mules, two hundred forty and five;
  Ne 7:68 — Their horses, seven hundred thirty and six: their mules, two hundred forty and five:

- **Bits for.**
  Jas 3:3 — Behold, we put bits in the horses' mouths, that they may obey us; and we turn about their whole body.

- **Bells for.**
  Zec 14:20 — In that day shall there be upon the bells of the horses, HOLINESS UNTO THE LORD; and the pots in the LORD's house shall be like the bowls before the altar.

- **Harness for.**
  Jer 46:4 — Harness the horses; and get up, ye horsemen, and stand forth with *your* helmets; furbish the spears, *and* put on the brigandines.

- **Color of.**
  Zec 1:8 — I saw by night, and behold a man riding upon a red horse, and he stood among the myrtle trees that *were* in the bottom; and behind him *were there* red horses, speckled, and white.

- **Commerce in.**
  Rev 18:13 — And cinnamon, and odours, and ointments, and frankincense, and wine, and oil, and

fine flour, and wheat, and beasts, and sheep, and horses, and chariots, and slaves, and souls of men.

✧See: Horse; description of; exported from Babylon

✧See: Horse; description of; exported from Egypt

• Dedicated to religious uses.

2Ki 23:11 — And he took away the horses that the kings of Judah had given to the sun, at the entering in of the house of the LORD, by the chamber of Nathan-melech the chamberlain, which *was* in the suburbs, and burned the chariots of the sun with fire.

• Symbolic.

Rev 6:2–8; 19:11–21

Zec 1:8 — I saw by night, and behold a man riding upon a red horse, and he stood among the myrtle trees that *were* in the bottom; and behind him *were there* red horses, speckled, and white.

Rev 9:17 — And thus I saw the horses in the vision, and them that sat on them, having breastplates of fire, and of jacinth, and brimstone: and the heads of the horses *were* as the heads of lions; and out of their mouths issued fire and smoke and brimstone.

HORSELEACH

Pr 30:15 — The horseleach hath two daughters, *crying,* Give, give. There are three *things that are* never satisfied, *yea,* four *things* say not, *It is* enough:

HORTICULTURE

• Encouraged.

Le 19:23–25; Dt 20:19–20

✧See: Agriculture

✧See: Grafting

✧See: Pruning

HOSAH

• A city of Asher.

Jos 19:29 — And *then* the coast turneth to Ramah, and to the strong city Tyre; and the coast turneth to Hosah; and the outgoings thereof are at the sea from the coast to Achzib:

• A Levite.

1Ch 26:10–11

1Ch 16:38 — And Obed-edom with their brethren, threescore and eight; Obed-edom also the son of Jeduthun and Hosah *to be* porters:

HOSANNA • A form of Jewish acclamation.

Mk 11:9–10

Mt 21:9 — And the multitudes that went before, and that followed, cried, saying, Hosanna to the Son of David: Blessed *is* he that cometh in the name of the Lord; Hosanna in the highest.

Mt 21:15 — And when the chief priests and scribes saw the wonderful things that he did, and the children crying in the temple, and saying, Hosanna to the Son of David; they were sore displeased,

Jn 12:13 — Took branches of palm trees, and went forth to meet him, and cried, Hosanna: Blessed *is* the King of Israel that cometh in the name of the Lord.

HOSEA

• One of the minor prophets.

Hos 9:1–17

• Called Osee.

Ro 9:25 — As he saith also in Osee, I will call them my people, which were not my people; and her beloved, which was not beloved.

HOSHAIAH

• One of the returned exiles.

Ne 12:32 — And after them went Hoshaiah, and half of the princes of Judah,

• A distinguished Jewish captive.

Jer 42:1 — Then all the captains of the forces, and Johanan the son of Kareah, and Jezaniah the son of Hoshaiah, and all the people from the least even unto the greatest, came near,

Jer 43:2 — Then spake Azariah the son of Hoshaiah, and Johanan the son of Kareah, and all the proud men, saying unto Jeremiah, Thou speakest falsely: the LORD our God hath not sent thee to say, Go not into Egypt to sojourn there:

HOSHAMA • Son of Jeconiah, king of Judah.

1Ch 3:18 — Malchiram also, and Pedaiah, and Shenazar, Jecamiah, Hoshama, and Nedabiah.

HOSHEA

• The original name of Joshua.

Nu 13:8 — Of the tribe of Ephraim, Oshea the son of Nun.

Dt 32:44 — And Moses came and spake all the words of this song in the ears of the people, he, and Hoshea the son of Nun.

• Called also Oshea.

Nu 13:16 — These *are* the names of the men which Moses sent to spy out the land. And Moses called Oshea the son of Nun Jehoshua.

• A chief of Ephraim.

1Ch 27:20 — Of the children of Ephraim, Hoshea the son of Azaziah: of the half tribe of Manasseh, Joel the son of Pedaiah:

• King of Israel.

• Assassinates Pekah and usurps the throne.

2Ki 15:30 — And Hoshea the son of Elah made a conspiracy against Pekah the son of Remaliah, and smote him, and slew him, and reigned in his stead, in the twentieth year of Jotham the son of Uzziah.

• Evil reign of.

2Ki 17:1–2

- **Becomes subject to Assyria.**
  2Ki 17:3 — Against him came up Shalmaneser king of Assyria; and Hoshea became his servant, and gave him presents.
- **Conspires against Assyria and is imprisoned.**
  2Ki 17:4 — And the king of Assyria found conspiracy in Hoshea: for he had sent messengers to So king of Egypt, and brought no present to the king of Assyria, as *he had done* year by year: therefore the king of Assyria shut him up, and bound him in prison.
- **Last king to Israel.**
  2Ki 18:9–12
  2Ki 17:6 — In the ninth year of Hoshea the king of Assyria took Samaria, and carried Israel away into Assyria, and placed them in Halah and in Habor *by* the river of Gozan, and in the cities of the Medes.
  Hos 10:3 — For now they shall say, We have no king, because we feared not the LORD; what then should a king do to us?
  Hos 10:7 — *As for* Samaria, her king is cut off as the foam upon the water.

• **A Jewish exile.**
Ne 10:23 — Hoshea, Hananiah, Hashub,

HOSPITALITY

Le 19:33–34; Dt 10:18–19; 26:12–13; Pr 9:1–5; 23:6–8; Isa 58:6–7; Mt 22:2–10; 25:34–46; Lk 14:12–14; Ro 16:1–2; Tit 1:7–8; 1Pe 4:9–11; 3Jn 1:5–8

Ex 22:21 — Thou shalt neither vex a stranger, nor oppress him: for ye were strangers in the land of Egypt.

Ex 23:9 — Also thou shalt not oppress a stranger: for ye know the heart of a stranger, seeing ye were strangers in the land of Egypt.

Le 19:10 — And thou shalt not glean thy vineyard, neither shalt thou gather *every* grape of thy vineyard; thou shalt leave them for the poor and stranger: I *am* the LORD your God.

Le 24:22 — Ye shall have one manner of law, as well for the stranger, as for one of your own country: for I *am* the LORD your God.

Dt 27:19 — Cursed *be* he that perverteth the judgment of the stranger, fatherless, and widow. And all the people shall say, Amen.

Ro 12:13 — Distributing to the necessity of saints; given to hospitality.

1Ti 3:2 — A bishop then must be blameless, the husband of one wife, vigilant, sober, of good behaviour, given to hospitality, apt to teach;

1Ti 5:10 — Well reported of for good works; if she have brought up children, if she have lodged strangers, if she have washed the saints' feet, if she have relieved the afflicted, if she have diligently followed every good work.

Heb 13:2 — Be not forgetful to entertain strangers: for thereby some have entertained angels unawares.

See: Guest

See: Strangers

• **Instances of.**
- **Pharaoh to Abraham.**
  Ge 12:16
- **Melchizedek to Abraham.**
  Ge 14:18
- **Abraham to the angels.**
  Ge 18:1–8
- **Lot to the angel.**
  Ge 19:1–11
- **Abimelech to Abraham.**
  Ge 20:14–15
- **Sons of Heth to Abraham.**
  Ge 23:6, 11
- **Laban to Abraham's servant.**
  Ge 24:31
- **Laban to Jacob.**
  Ge 29:13–14
- **Isaac to Abimelech.**
  Ge 26:30
- **Joseph to his brethren.**
  Ge 43:31–34
- **Pharaoh to Jacob.**
  Ge 45:16–20; 47:7–12
- **Jethro to Moses.**
  Ex 2:20
- **Rahab to the spies.**
  Jos 2:1–16
- **Man of Gibeah to the Levite.**
  Jgs 19:16–21
- **Pharaoh to Hadad.**
  1Ki 11:17, 22
- **David to Mephibosheth.**
  2Sa 9:7–13
- **The widow of Zarephath to Elijah.**
  1Ki 17:10–24
- **The Shunammite to Elisha.**
  2Ki 4:8
- **Elisha to the Syrian spies.**
  2Ki 6:22
- **Job to strangers.**
  Job 31:32
- **Martha to Jesus.**
  Lk 10:38; Jn 12:1–2
- **Pharisees to Jesus.**
  Lk 11:37–38
- **Zaccheus to Jesus.**
  Lk 19:1–10
- **The tanner to Peter.**
  Ac 10:6, 23
- **Lydia to Paul and Silas.**
  Ac 16:15
- **Publius to Paul.**
  Ac 28:7
- **Phebe to Paul.**
  Ro 16:2
- **Onesiphorus to Paul.**
  2Ti 1:16
- **Gaius.**
  3Jn 1:5–8

- **Rewarded.**
  - **Instances of.**
    - **Rahab's.**

      Jos 6:22–25

      Jos 6:17 — And the city shall be accursed, *even* it, and all that *are* therein, to the LORD: only Rahab the harlot shall live, she and all that *are* with her in the house, because she hid the messengers that we sent.
    - **Widow of Zarephath's.**

      1Ki 17:10–24

See: **Feasts**

See: **Strangers**

HOSTAGE

2Ki 14:14 — And he took all the gold and silver, and all the vessels that were found in the house of the LORD, and in the treasures of the king's house, and hostages, and returned to Samaria.

2Ch 25:24 — And *he took* all the gold and the silver, and all the vessels that were found in the house of God with Obed-edom, and the treasures of the king's house, the hostages also, and returned to Samaria.

HOT SPRINGS

Ge 36:24 — And these *are* the children of Zibeon; both Ajah, and Anah: this *was that* Anah that found the mules in the wilderness, as he fed the asses of Zibeon his father.

HOTHAM • Son of Heber.

1Ch 7:32 — And Heber begat Japhlet, and Shomer, and Hotham, and Shua their sister.

HOTHAN • An Aroerite.

1Ch 11:44 — Uzzia the Ashterathite, Shama and Jehiel the sons of Hothan the Aroerite,

HOTHIR • Son of Heman.

1Ch 25:4 — Of Heman: the sons of Heman; Bukkiah, Mattaniah, Uzziel, Shebuel, and Jerimoth, Hananiah, Hanani, Eliathah, Giddalti, and Romamti-ezer, Joshbekashah, Mallothi, Hothir, *and* Mahazioth:

1Ch 25:28 — The one and twentieth to Hothir, *he,* his sons, and his brethren, *were* twelve:

HOUGHING

- **Of horses.**

  Jos 11:6 — And the LORD said unto Joshua, Be not afraid because of them: for to morrow about this time will I deliver them up all slain before Israel: thou shalt hough their horses, and burn their chariots with fire.

  Jos 11:9 — And Joshua did unto them as the LORD bade him: he houghed their horses, and burnt their chariots with fire.

  2Sa 8:4 — And David took from him a thousand *chariots,* and seven hundred horsemen, and twenty thousand footmen: and David houghed all the chariot *horses,* but reserved of them *for* an hundred chariots.

  1Ch 18:4 — And David took from him a thousand chariots, and seven thousand horsemen, and twenty thousand footmen: David also houghed all the chariot *horses,* but reserved of them an hundred chariots.

HOURS

- **A division of time.**

  Mt 20:3–12; 27:45–46
- **Twelve, in the day.**

  Jn 11:9 — Jesus answered, Are there not twelve hours in the day? If any man walk in the day, he stumbleth not, because he seeth the light of this world.
- **Twelve, in the night.**

  Ac 23:23 — And he called unto *him* two centurions, saying, Make ready two hundred soldiers to go to Caesarea, and horsemen threescore and ten, and spearmen two hundred, at the third hour of the night;
- **Symbolic.**

  Rev 8:1 — And when he had opened the seventh seal, there was silence in heaven about the space of half an hour.

  Rev 9:15 — And the four angels were loosed, which were prepared for an hour, and a day, and a month, and a year, for to slay the third part of men.

HOUSE

- **Built of stone.**

  Le 14:40–45

  Isa 9:10 — The bricks are fallen down, but we will build with hewn stones: the sycomores are cut down, but we will change *them into* cedars.

  Am 5:11 — Forasmuch therefore as your treading *is* upon the poor, and ye take from him burdens of wheat: ye have built houses of hewn stone, but ye shall not dwell in them; ye have planted pleasant vineyards, but ye shall not drink wine of them.
- **Built of brick.**

  Ex 1:11–14

  Ge 11:3 — And they said one to another, Go to, let us make brick, and burn them throughly. And they had brick for stone, and slime had they for morter.

  Isa 9:10 — The bricks are fallen down, but we will build with hewn stones: the sycomores are cut down, but we will change *them into* cedars.
- **Built of wood.**

  SS 1:17 — The beams of our house *are* cedar, *and* our rafters of fir.

  Isa 9:10 — The bricks are fallen down, but we will build with hewn stones: the sycomores are cut down, but we will change *them into* cedars.
- **Built into city walls.**

  Jos 2:15 — Then she let them down by a cord through the window: for her house *was* upon the town wall, and she dwelt upon the wall.
- **Used for worship.**

  Ac 1:13–14

  Ac 12:12 — And when he had considered *the thing,* he came to the house of Mary the mother of John, whose surname was Mark; where many were gathered together praying.

Ro 16:5 — Likewise *greet* the church that is in their house. Salute my wellbeloved Epaenetus, who is the firstfruits of Achaia unto Christ.

1Co 16:19 — The churches of Asia salute you. Aquila and Priscilla salute you much in the Lord, with the church that is in their house.

Col 4:15 — Salute the brethren which are in Laodicea, and Nymphas, and the church which is in his house.

Phm 1:2 — And to *our* beloved Apphia, and Archippus our fellowsoldier, and to the church in thy house:

• "A man's castle".

Dt 24:10–11

• Architecture of.

• Foundations of stone.

1Ki 5:17 — And the king commanded, and they brought great stones, costly stones, *and* hewed stones, to lay the foundation of the house.

1Ki 7:9 — All these *were of* costly stones, according to the measures of hewed stones, sawed with saws, within and without, even from the foundation unto the coping, and so on the outside toward the great court.

Ezr 6:3 — In the first year of Cyrus the king *the same* Cyrus the king made a decree *concerning* the house of God at Jerusalem, Let the house be builded, the place where they offered sacrifices, and let the foundations thereof be strongly laid; the height thereof threescore cubits, *and* the breadth thereof threescore cubits;

Jer 51:26 — And they shall not take of thee a stone for a corner, nor a stone for foundations; but thou shalt be desolate for ever, saith the LORD.

• Figurative.

Ps 87:1 — His foundation *is* in the holy mountains.

Isa 28:16 — Therefore thus saith the Lord GOD, Behold, I lay in Zion for a foundation a stone, a tried stone, a precious corner *stone,* a sure foundation: he that believeth shall not make haste.

Isa 48:13 — Mine hand also hath laid the foundation of the earth, and my right hand hath spanned the heavens: *when* I call unto them, they stand up together.

Ro 15:20 — Yea, so have I strived to preach the gospel, not where Christ was named, lest I should build upon another man's foundation:

1Co 3:11 — For other foundation can no man lay than that is laid, which is Jesus Christ.

Eph 2:20 — And are built upon the foundation of the apostles and prophets, Jesus Christ himself being the chief corner *stone;*

1Ti 6:19 — Laying up in store for themselves a good foundation against the time to come, that they may lay hold on eternal life.

Heb 6:1 — Therefore leaving the principles of the doctrine of Christ, let us go on unto perfection; not laying again the foundation of repentance from dead works, and of faith toward God,

Rev 21:14 — And the wall of the city had twelve foundations, and in them the names of the twelve apostles of the Lamb.

• Corner stone.

Job 38:6 — Whereupon are the foundations thereof fastened? or who laid the corner stone thereof;

Ps 144:12 — That our sons *may be* as plants grown up in their youth; *that* our daughters *may be* as corner stones, polished *after* the similitude of a palace:

• Figurative.

Ps 118:22 — The stone *which* the builders refused is become the head *stone* of the corner.

Isa 28:16 — Therefore thus saith the Lord GOD, Behold, I lay in Zion for a foundation a stone, a tried stone, a precious corner *stone,* a sure foundation: he that believeth shall not make haste.

Eph 2:20 — And are built upon the foundation of the apostles and prophets, Jesus Christ himself being the chief corner *stone;*

1Pe 2:6 — Wherefore also it is contained in the scripture, Behold, I lay in Sion a chief corner stone, elect, precious: and he that believeth on him shall not be confounded.

• Porches.

1Ki 7:6–7

Jgs 3:23 — Then Ehud went forth through the porch, and shut the doors of the parlour upon him, and locked them.

• Courts.

Est 1:5 — And when these days were expired, the king made a feast unto all the people that were present in Shushan the palace, both unto great and small, seven days, in the court of the garden of the king's palace;

• Summer apartment.

Jgs 3:20 — And Ehud came unto him; and he was sitting in a summer parlour, which he had for himself alone. And Ehud said, I have a message from God unto thee. And he arose out of *his* seat.

1Ki 17:19 — And he said unto her, Give me thy son. And he took him out of her bosom, and carried him up into a loft, where he abode, and laid him upon his own bed.

Am 3:15 — And I will smite the winter house with the summer house; and the houses of ivory shall perish, and the great houses shall have an end, saith the LORD.

• Inner chamber.

1Ki 22:25 — And Micaiah said, Behold, thou shalt see in that day, when thou shalt go into an inner chamber to hide thyself.

• Chambers.

Ge 43:30 — And Joseph made haste; for his bowels did yearn upon his brother: and he sought *where* to weep; and he entered into *his* chamber, and wept there.

2Sa 18:33 — And the king was much moved, and went up to the chamber over the gate, and wept: and as he went, thus he said, O my son Absalom, my son, my son Absalom! would God I had died for thee, O Absalom, my son, my son!

2Ki 1:2 — And Ahaziah fell down through a lattice in his upper chamber that *was* in Samaria, and was sick: and he sent messengers, and said unto them, Go, enquire of Baal-zebub the god of Ekron whether I shall recover of this disease.

2Ki 4:10 — Let us make a little chamber, I pray thee, on the wall; and let us set for him there a bed, and a table, and a stool, and a candlestick: and it shall be, when he cometh to us, that he shall turn in thither.

Ac 1:13 — And when they were come in, they went up into an upper room, where abode both Peter, and James, and John, and Andrew, Philip, and Thomas, Bartholomew, and Matthew, James *the son* of Alphaeus, and Simon Zelotes, and Judas *the brother* of James.

Ac 9:37 — And it came to pass in those days, that she was sick, and died: whom when they had washed, they laid *her* in an upper chamber.

Ac 20:8 — And there were many lights in the upper chamber, where they were gathered together.

• Guest chamber.

Mk 14:14 — And wheresoever he shall go in, say ye to the goodman of the house, The Master saith, Where is the guestchamber, where I shall eat the passover with my disciples?

• Pillars.

Pr 9:1 — Wisdom hath builded her house, she hath hewn out her seven pillars:

• With courts.

Ne 8:16 — So the people went forth, and brought *them*, and made themselves booths, every one upon the roof of his house, and in their courts, and in the courts of the house of God, and in the street of the water gate, and in the street of the gate of Ephraim.

• Lattice.

Jgs 5:28 — The mother of Sisera looked out at a window, and cried through the lattice, Why is his chariot *so* long in coming? why tarry the wheels of his chariots?

• Windows.

Jgs 5:28 — The mother of Sisera looked out at a window, and cried through the lattice, Why is his chariot *so* long in coming? why tarry the wheels of his chariots?

Pr 7:6 — For at the window of my house I looked through my casement,

• Ceiled and plastered.

Da 5:5 — In the same hour came forth fingers of a man's hand, and wrote over against the candlestick upon the plaister of the wall of the king's palace: and the king saw the part of the hand that wrote.

• Hinges.

Pr 26:14 — *As* the door turneth upon his hinges, so *doth* the slothful upon his bed.

• Roofs, flat.

Jos 2:6 — But she had brought them up to the roof of the house, and hid them with the stalks of flax, which she had laid in order upon the roof.

Jgs 16:27 — Now the house was full of men and women; and all the lords of the Philistines *were* there; and *there were* upon the roof about three thousand men and women, that beheld while Samson made sport.

1Sa 9:25 — And when they were come down from the high place into the city, *Samuel* communed with Saul upon the top of the house.

2Sa 11:2 — And it came to pass in an eveningtide, that David arose from off his bed, and walked upon the roof of the king's house: and from the roof he saw a woman washing herself; and the woman *was* very beautiful to look upon.

2Sa 16:22 — So they spread Absalom a tent upon the top of the house; and Absalom went in unto his father's concubines in the sight of all Israel.

Isa 15:3 — In their streets they shall gird themselves with sackcloth: on the tops of their houses, and in their streets, every one shall howl, weeping abundantly.

Isa 22:1 — The burden of the valley of vision. What aileth thee now, that thou art wholly gone up to the housetops?

Mt 24:17 — Let him which is on the housetop not come down to take any thing out of his house:

Lk 12:3 — Therefore whatsoever ye have spoken in darkness shall be heard in the light; and that which ye have spoken in the ear in closets shall be proclaimed upon the housetops.

• Battlements required in Mosaic law.

Dt 22:8 — When thou buildest a new house, then thou shalt make a battlement for thy roof, that thou bring not blood upon thine house, if any man fall from thence.

• Prayer on.

Ac 10:9 — On the morrow, as they went on their journey, and drew nigh unto the city, Peter went up upon the housetop to pray about the sixth hour:

• Altars on.

2Ki 23:12 — And the altars that *were* on the top of the upper chamber of Ahaz, which the kings of Judah had made, and the altars which Manasseh had made in the two courts of the house of the LORD, did the king beat down, and brake *them* down from thence, and cast the dust of them into the brook Kidron.

Jer 19:13 — And the houses of Jerusalem, and the houses of the kings of Judah, shall be defiled as the place of Tophet, because of all the houses upon whose roofs they have burned incense unto all the host of heaven, and have poured out drink offerings unto other gods.

Jer 32:29 — And the Chaldeans, that fight against this city, shall come and set fire on this city, and burn it with the houses, upon whose roofs they have offered incense unto Baal, and poured out drink offerings unto other gods, to provoke me to anger.

Zep 1:5 — And them that worship the host of heaven upon the housetops; and them that worship *and* that swear by the LORD, and that swear by Malcham;

• Booths on.

Ne 8:16 — So the people went forth, and brought *them*, and made themselves booths, every one upon the roof of his house, and in their courts, and in the courts of the house of God, and in the street of the water gate, and in the street of the gate of Ephraim.

• Used as place to sleep.

Jos 2:8 — And before they were laid down, she came up unto them upon the roof;

Ac 10:9 — On the morrow, as they went on their journey, and drew nigh unto the city, Peter went up upon the housetop to pray about the sixth hour:

• Used as dwelling place.

Pr 21:9 — *It is* better to dwell in a corner of the housetop, than with a brawling woman in a wide house.

Pr 25:24 — *It is* better to dwell in the corner of the housetop, than with a brawling woman and in a wide house.

• Painted.

Jer 22:14 — That saith, I will build me a wide house and large chambers, and cutteth him out windows; and *it is* cieled with cedar, and painted with vermilion.

Eze 8:10 — So I went in and saw; and behold every form of creeping things, and abominable beasts, and all the idols of the house of Israel, pourtrayed upon the wall round about.

Eze 8:12 — Then said he unto me, Son of man, hast thou seen what the ancients of the house of Israel do in the dark, every man in the chambers of his imagery? for they say, The LORD seeth us not; the LORD hath forsaken the earth.

• Chimneys of.

Hos 13:3 — Therefore they shall be as the morning cloud, and as the early dew that passeth away, as the chaff *that* is driven with the whirlwind out of the floor, and as the smoke out of the chimney.

• Texts of scripture on doorposts of.

Dt 6:9 — And thou shalt write them upon the posts of thy house, and on thy gates.

• Laws regarding sale of.

Le 25:29–33

Ne 5:3 — *Some* also there were that said, We have mortgaged our lands, vineyards, and houses, that we might buy corn, because of the dearth.

• Dedicated.

Ps 30:1–12

Dt 20:5 — And the officers shall speak unto the people, saying, What man *is there* that hath built a new house, and hath not dedicated it? let him go and return to his house, lest he die in the battle, and another man dedicate it.

• Figurative.

2Sa 7:18 — Then went king David in, and sat before the LORD, and he said, Who *am* I, O Lord GOD? and what *is* my house, that thou hast brought me hitherto?

Ps 23:6 — Surely goodness and mercy shall follow me all the days of my life: and I will dwell in the house of the LORD for ever.

Ps 36:8 — They shall be abundantly satisfied with the fatness of thy house; and thou shalt make them drink of the river of thy pleasures.

Jn 14:2 — In my Father's house are many mansions: if *it were* not so, I would have told you. I go to prepare a place for you.

2Co 5:1 — For we know that if our earthly house of *this* tabernacle were dissolved, we have a building of God, an house not made with hands, eternal in the heavens.

1Ti 3:15 — But if I tarry long, that thou mayest know how thou oughtest to behave thyself in the house of God, which is the church of the living God, the pillar and ground of the truth.

Heb 3:2 — Who was faithful to him that appointed him, as also Moses *was faithful* in all his house.

HOUSE OF GOD

• A place of prayer.

Mt 21:13 — And said unto them, It is written, My house shall be called the house of prayer; but ye have made it a den of thieves.

Mk 11:17 — And he taught, saying unto them, Is it not written, My house shall be called of all nations the house of prayer? but ye have made it a den of thieves.

Lk 19:46 — Saying unto them, It is written, My house is the house of prayer: but ye have made it a den of thieves.

• Holy.

Ecc 5:1 — Keep thy foot when thou goest to the house of God, and be more ready to hear, than to give the sacrifice of fools: for they consider not that they do evil.

Isa 62:9 — But they that have gathered it shall eat it, and praise the LORD; and they that have brought it together shall drink it in the courts of my holiness.

Eze 43:12 — This *is* the law of the house; Upon the top of the mountain the whole limit thereof round about *shall be* most holy. Behold, this *is* the law of the house.

1Co 3:17 — If any man defile the temple of God, him shall God destroy; for the temple of God is holy, which *temple* ye are.

See: Synagogue

See: Tabernacle

See: Temple

HUKKOK • A place on the boundary line of Naphtali.

Jos 19:34 — And *then* the coast turneth westward to Aznoth-tabor, and goeth out from thence to Hukkok, and reacheth to Zebulun on the south side, and reacheth to Asher on the west side, and to Judah upon Jordan toward the sunrising.

HUKOK See: Helkath

HUL • Son of Aram.

Ge 10:23 — And the children of Aram; Uz, and Hul, and Gether, and Mash.

1Ch 1:17 — The sons of Shem; Elam, and Asshur, and Arphaxad, and Lud, and Aram, and Uz, and Hul, and Gether, and Meshech.

HULDAH

- **A prophetess.**
- **Foretells the destruction of Jerusalem.**

2Ki 22:14–20; 2Ch 34:22–28

HUMAN SACRIFICE ⇜See: Offerings; human sacrifices

HUMILIATION AND SELF-AFFLICTION

- **Enjoined.**

Le 16:29–31; 23:26–32; Ezr 8:21–23

2Ch 7:14 — If my people, which are called by my name, shall humble themselves, and pray, and seek my face, and turn from their wicked ways; then will I hear from heaven, and will forgive their sin, and will heal their land.

⇜**See: Fasting**

⇜**See: Humility**

HUMILITY

Dt 9:4–29; Job 25:5–6; Ps 131:1–2; Pr 25:6–7; Zep 3:11–12; Mt 18:2–4; 20:26–27; Mk 9:33–37; 10:43–44; Lk 9:46–48; 14:10–11; 18:13–14; 22:24–27; Jn 13:14–16; 1Co 1:28–29; 2:1–3; 2Co 12:5–12; Php 2:3–11; Jas 1:9–10; 1Pe 5:5–6

Dt 15:15 — And thou shalt remember that thou wast a bondman in the land of Egypt, and the LORD thy God redeemed thee: therefore I command thee this thing to day.

Dt 32:7 — Remember the days of old, consider the years of many generations: ask thy father, and he will shew thee; thy elders, and they will tell thee.

Job 5:11 — To set up on high those that be low; that those which mourn may be exalted to safety.

Job 22:29 — When *men* are cast down, then thou shalt say, *There is* lifting up; and he shall save the humble person.

Ps 9:12 — When he maketh inquisition for blood, he remembereth them: he forgetteth not the cry of the humble.

Ps 10:17 — LORD, thou hast heard the desire of the humble: thou wilt prepare their heart, thou wilt cause thine ear to hear:

Ps 22:6 — But I *am* a worm, and no man; a reproach of men, and despised of the people.

Ps 22:26 — The meek shall eat and be satisfied: they shall praise the LORD that seek him: your heart shall live for ever.

Ps 25:9 — The meek will he guide in judgment: and the meek will he teach his way.

Ps 37:11 — But the meek shall inherit the earth; and shall delight themselves in the abundance of peace.

Ps 69:32 — The humble shall see *this, and* be glad: and your heart shall live that seek God.

Ps 86:1 — Bow down thine ear, O LORD, hear me: for I *am* poor and needy.

Ps 138:6 — Though the LORD *be* high, yet hath he respect unto the lowly: but the proud he knoweth afar off.

Ps 147:6 — The LORD lifteth up the meek: he casteth the wicked down to the ground.

Ps 149:4 — For the LORD taketh pleasure in his people: he will beautify the meek with salvation.

Pr 3:34 — Surely he scorneth the scorners: but he giveth grace unto the lowly.

Pr 10:8 — The wise in heart will receive commandments: but a prating fool shall fall.

Pr 11:2 — *When* pride cometh, then cometh shame: but with the lowly *is* wisdom.

Pr 12:15 — The way of a fool *is* right in his own eyes: but he that hearkeneth unto counsel *is* wise.

Pr 15:33 — The fear of the LORD *is* the instruction of wisdom; and before honour *is* humility.

Pr 16:19 — Better *it is to be* of an humble spirit with the lowly, than to divide the spoil with the proud.

Pr 18:12 — Before destruction the heart of man is haughty, and before honour *is* humility.

Pr 22:4 — By humility *and* the fear of the LORD *are* riches, and honour, and life.

Pr 27:2 — Let another man praise thee, and not thine own mouth; a stranger, and not thine own lips.

Pr 29:23 — A man's pride shall bring him low: but honour shall uphold the humble in spirit.

Pr 30:32 — If thou hast done foolishly in lifting up thyself, or if thou hast thought evil, *lay* thine hand upon thy mouth.

Ecc 5:2 — Be not rash with thy mouth, and let not thine heart be hasty to utter *any* thing before God: for God *is* in heaven, and thou upon earth: therefore let thy words be few.

Isa 29:19 — The meek also shall increase *their* joy in the LORD, and the poor among men shall rejoice in the Holy One of Israel.

Isa 51:1 — Hearken to me, ye that follow after righteousness, ye that seek the LORD: look unto the rock *whence* ye are hewn, and to the hole of the pit *whence* ye are digged.

Isa 57:15 — For thus saith the high and lofty One that inhabiteth eternity, whose name *is* Holy; I dwell in the high and holy *place,* with him also *that is* of a contrite and humble spirit, to revive the spirit of the humble, and to revive the heart of the contrite ones.

Isa 66:2 — For all those *things* hath mine hand made, and all those *things* have been, saith the LORD: but to this *man* will I look, *even* to *him that is* poor and of a contrite spirit, and trembleth at my word.

Jer 45:5 — And seekest thou great things for thyself? seek *them* not: for, behold, I will bring evil upon all flesh, saith the LORD: but thy life will I give unto thee for a prey in all places whither thou goest.

Eze 16:63 — That thou mayest remember, and be confounded, and never open thy mouth any more because of thy shame, when I am pacified toward thee for all that thou hast done, saith the Lord GOD.

Mic 6:8 — He hath shewed thee, O man, what *is* good; and what doth the LORD require of thee, but to do justly, and to love mercy, and to walk humbly with thy God?

Mt 5:3 — Blessed *are* the poor in spirit: for theirs is the kingdom of heaven.

Mt 11:29 — Take my yoke upon you, and learn of me; for I am meek and lowly in heart: and ye shall find rest unto your souls.

Mt 23:12 — And whosoever shall exalt himself shall be abased; and he that shall humble himself shall be exalted.

Lk 1:52 — He hath put down the mighty from *their* seats, and exalted them of low degree.

Lk 6:20 — And he lifted up his eyes on his disciples, and said, Blessed *be ye* poor: for yours is the kingdom of God.

Lk 10:21 — In that hour Jesus rejoiced in spirit, and said, I thank thee, O Father, Lord of heaven and earth, that thou hast hid these things from the wise and prudent, and hast revealed them unto babes: even so, Father; for so it seemed good in thy sight.

Lk 17:10 — So likewise ye, when ye shall have done all those things which are commanded you, say, We are unprofitable servants: we have done that which was our duty to do.

Ro 11:18 — Boast not against the branches. But if thou boast, thou bearest not the root, but the root thee.

Ro 11:20 — Well; because of unbelief they were broken off, and thou standest by faith. Be not highminded, but fear:

Ro 11:25 — For I would not, brethren, that ye should be ignorant of this mystery, lest ye should be wise in your own conceits; that blindness in part is happened to Israel, until the fulness of the Gentiles be come in.

Ro 12:3 — For I say, through the grace given unto me, to every man that is among you, not to think *of himself* more highly than he ought to think; but to think soberly, according as God hath dealt to every man the measure of faith.

Ro 12:10 — *Be* kindly affectioned one to another with brotherly love; in honour preferring one another;

Ro 12:16 — *Be* of the same mind one toward another. Mind not high things, but condescend to men of low estate. Be not wise in your own conceits.

1Co 3:18 — Let no man deceive himself. If any man among you seemeth to be wise in this world, let him become a fool, that he may be wise.

1Co 10:12 — Wherefore let him that thinketh he standeth take heed lest he fall.

1Co 13:4 — Charity suffereth long, *and* is kind; charity envieth not; charity vaunteth not itself, is not puffed up,

2Co 11:30 — If I must needs glory, I will glory of the things which concern mine infirmities.

Gal 5:26 — Let us not be desirous of vain glory, provoking one another, envying one another.

Gal 6:14 — But God forbid that I should glory, save in the cross of our Lord Jesus Christ, by whom the world is crucified unto me, and I unto the world.

Eph 4:2 — With all lowliness and meekness, with longsuffering, forbearing one another in love;

Eph 5:21 — Submitting yourselves one to another in the fear of God.

Col 3:12 — Put on therefore, as the elect of God, holy and beloved, bowels of mercies, kindness, humbleness of mind, meekness, longsuffering;

Jas 1:19 — Wherefore, my beloved brethren, let every man be swift to hear, slow to speak, slow to wrath:

Jas 3:1 — My brethren, be not many masters, knowing that we shall receive the greater condemnation.

Jas 4:6 — But he giveth more grace. Wherefore he saith, God resisteth the proud, but giveth grace unto the humble.

Jas 4:10 — Humble yourselves in the sight of the Lord, and he shall lift you up.

1Pe 5:3 — Neither as being lords over *God's* heritage, but being ensamples to the flock.

• Exemplified.

2Sa 7:18–19; Job 7:17–18; 9:14–15; 40:4–5; 42:4–6; Ps 8:3–4; 131:1–2; 144:3–4; Pr 30:2–3; Jer 10:23–24; Mt 25:37–40; Lk 7:6–7; Jn 3:29–30; 1Co 15:9–10; Php 3:12–13

Ge 18:27 — And Abraham answered and said, Behold now, I have taken upon me to speak unto the Lord, which *am but* dust and ashes:

Ge 18:32 — And he said, Oh let not the Lord be angry, and I will speak yet but this once: Peradventure ten shall be found there. And he said, I will not destroy *it* for ten's sake.

Ge 32:10 — I am not worthy of the least of all the mercies, and of all the truth, which thou hast shewed unto thy servant; for with my staff I passed over this Jordan; and now I am become two bands.

Ge 41:16 — And Joseph answered Pharaoh, saying, *It is* not in me: God shall give Pharaoh an answer of peace.

Ex 3:11 — And Moses said unto God, Who *am* I, that I should go unto Pharaoh, and that I should bring forth the children of Israel out of Egypt?

Ex 4:10 — And Moses said unto the LORD, O my Lord, I *am* not eloquent, neither heretofore, nor since thou hast spoken unto thy servant: but I *am* slow of speech, and of a slow tongue.

1Ki 3:7 — And now, O LORD my God, thou hast made thy servant king instead of David my father: and I *am but* a little child: I know not *how* to go out or come in.

1Ch 17:17 — And *yet* this was a small thing in thine eyes, O God; for thou hast *also* spoken of thy servant's house for a great while to come, and hast regarded me according to the estate of a man of high degree, O LORD God.

1Ch 29:14 — But who *am* I, and what *is* my people, that we should be able to offer so willingly after this sort? for all things *come* of thee, and of thine own have we given thee.

2Ch 1:10 — Give me now wisdom and knowledge, that I may go out and come in before this people: for who can judge this thy people, *that is so* great?

2Ch 2:6 — But who is able to build him an house, seeing the heaven and heaven of heavens cannot contain him? who *am* I then, that I should build him an house, save only to burn sacrifice before him?

Ezr 9:13 — And after all that is come upon us for our evil deeds, and for our great trespass, seeing that thou our God hast punished us less than our iniquities *deserve,* and hast given us *such* deliverance as this;

Job 10:15 — If I be wicked, woe unto me; and *if* I be righteous, *yet* will I not lift up my head. *I am* full of confusion; therefore see thou mine affliction;

Job 33:6 — Behold, I *am* according to thy wish in God's stead: I also am formed out of the clay.

Ps 73:22 — So foolish *was* I, and ignorant: I was *as* a beast before thee.

Ps 141:5 — Let the righteous smite me; *it shall be* a kindness: and let him reprove me; *it shall be* an excellent oil, *which* shall not break my head: for yet my prayer also *shall be* in their calamities.

Isa 6:5 — Then said I, Woe *is* me! for I am undone; because I *am* a man of unclean lips, and I dwell in the midst of a people of unclean lips: for mine eyes have seen the King, the LORD of hosts.

Isa 38:15 — What shall I say? he hath both spoken unto me, and himself hath done *it:* I shall go softly all my years in the bitterness of my soul.

Jer 1:6 — Then said I, Ah, Lord GOD! behold, I cannot speak: for I *am* a child.

Da 2:30 — But as for me, this secret is not revealed to me for *any* wisdom that I have more than any living, but for *their* sakes that shall make known the interpretation to the king, and that thou mightest know the thoughts of thy heart.

Mt 3:14 — But John forbad him, saying, I have need to be baptized of thee, and comest thou to me?

Mt 8:8 — The centurion answered and said, Lord, I am not worthy that thou shouldest come under my roof: but speak the word only, and my servant shall be healed.

Mt 15:27 — And she said, Truth, Lord: yet the dogs eat of the crumbs which fall from their masters' table.

Jn 1:27 — He it is, who coming after me is preferred before me, whose shoe's latchet I am not worthy to unloose.

Ac 3:12 — And when Peter saw *it,* he answered unto the people, Ye men of Israel, why marvel ye at this? or why look ye so earnestly on us, as though by our own power or holiness we had made this man to walk?

Ro 7:18 — For I know that in me (that is, in my flesh,) dwelleth no good thing: for to will is present with me; but *how* to perform that which is good I find not.

2Co 3:5 — Not that we are sufficient of ourselves to think any thing as of ourselves; but our sufficiency *is* of God;

2Co 12:7 — And lest I should be exalted above measure through the abundance of the revelations, there was given to me a thorn in the flesh, the messenger of Satan to buffet me, lest I should be exalted above measure.

Eph 3:8 — Unto me, who am less than the least of all saints, is this grace given, that I should preach among the Gentiles the unsearchable riches of Christ;

Php 4:12 — I know both how to be abased, and I know how to abound: every where and in all things I am instructed both to be full and to be hungry, both to abound and to suffer need.

1Ti 1:15 — This *is* a faithful saying, and worthy of all acceptation, that Christ Jesus came into the world to save sinners; of whom I am chief.

Rev 4:10 — The four and twenty elders fall down before him that sat on the throne, and worship him that liveth for ever and ever, and cast their crowns before the throne, saying,

• Instances of.

• Joseph.
Ge 41:16

• David.
1Sa 18:18–23; 24:14; 26:20; 2Sa 7:18–29; 1Ch 17:16–27

• Mephibosheth.
2Sa 9:8

• Ahab.
1Ki 21:29

• Josiah.
2Ch 34:27

• Elihu.
Job 32:4–7

• Isaiah.
Isa 6:5

• Elisabeth.
Lk 1:43

• John the Baptist.
Mk 1:7; Lk 3:16

• Cornelius.
Ac 10:33

• Paul.
Ro 1:12; 16:7

• Peter.
Lk 5:8; 1Pe 5:1

• John.
Rev 1:9

HUMTAH • A city of Judah.

Jos 15:54 — And Humtah, and Kirjath-arba, which *is* Hebron, and Zior; nine cities with their villages:

HUNGER

• Of Jesus.

Mt 4:2–4; Lk 4:2–4

Mt 21:18 — Now in the morning as he returned into the city, he hungered.

Mk 11:12 — And on the morrow, when they were come from Bethany, he was hungry:

Jn 4:8 — (For his disciples were gone away unto the city to buy meat.)

• A stimulus to work.

Pr 16:26 — He that laboureth laboureth for himself; for his mouth craveth it of him.

• No hunger in heaven.

Rev 7:16–17

See: Famine

• Spiritual.

Pr 2:3–5; Isa 55:1–2; Am 8:11–12

Mt 5:6 — Blessed *are* they which do hunger and thirst after righteousness: for they shall be filled.

Lk 6:21 — Blessed *are ye* that hunger now: for ye shall be filled. Blessed *are ye* that weep now: for ye shall laugh.

1Pe 2:2 — As newborn babes, desire the sincere milk of the word, that ye may grow thereby:

See: Desire; spiritual

See: Thirst

HUNTING

• Authorized in the Mosaic law.

Le 17:13 — And whatsoever man *there be* of the children of Israel, or of the strangers that sojourn among you, which hunteth and catcheth any beast or fowl that may be eaten; he shall even pour out the blood thereof, and cover it with dust.

• By Nimrod.

Ge 10:9 — He was a mighty hunter before the LORD: wherefore it is said, Even as Nimrod the mighty hunter before the LORD.

• By Esau.

Ge 27:3 — Now therefore take, I pray thee, thy weapons, thy quiver and thy bow, and go out to the field, and take me *some* venison;

Ge 27:5 — And Rebekah heard when Isaac spake to Esau his son. And Esau went to the field to hunt *for* venison, *and* to bring *it*.

Ge 27:30 — And it came to pass, as soon as Isaac had made an end of blessing Jacob, and Jacob was yet scarce gone out from the presence of Isaac his father, that Esau his brother came in from his hunting.

Ge 27:33 — And Isaac trembled very exceedingly, and said, Who? where *is* he that hath taken venison, and brought *it* me, and I have eaten of all before thou camest, and have blessed him? yea, *and* he shall be blessed.

• By Ishmael.

Ge 21:20 — And God was with the lad; and he grew, and dwelt in the wilderness, and became an archer.

• Of lion.

Job 10:16 — For it increaseth. Thou huntest me as a fierce lion: and again thou shewest thyself marvellous upon me.

• Fowling.

Ps 141:9–10

1Sa 26:20 — Now therefore, let not my blood fall to the earth before the face of the LORD: for the king of Israel is come out to seek a flea, as when one doth hunt a partridge in the mountains.

Ps 140:5 — The proud have hid a snare for me, and cords; they have spread a net by the wayside; they have set gins for me. Selah.

Pr 1:17 — Surely in vain the net is spread in the sight of any bird.

Ecc 9:12 — For man also knoweth not his time: as the fishes that are taken in an evil net, and as the birds that are caught in the snare; so *are* the sons of men snared in an evil time, when it falleth suddenly upon them.

La 3:52 — Mine enemies chased me sore, like a bird, without cause.

Am 3:5 — Can a bird fall in a snare upon the earth, where no gin *is* for him? shall *one* take up a snare from the earth, and have taken nothing at all?

• Figurative.

Jer 16:16 — Behold, I will send for many fishers, saith the LORD, and they shall fish them; and after will I send for many hunters, and they shall hunt them from every mountain, and from every hill, and out of the holes of the rocks.

HUPHAM • A Benjamite.

Nu 26:39 — Of Shupham, the family of the Shuphamites: of Hupham, the family of the Huphamites.

HUPPAH • A priest.

1Ch 24:13 — The thirteenth to Huppah, the fourteenth to Jeshebeab,

HUPPIM • A Benjamite.

Ge 46:21 — And the sons of Benjamin were Belah, and Becher, and Ashbel, Gera, and Naaman, Ehi, and Rosh, Muppim, and Huppim, and Ard.

1Ch 7:12 — Shuppim also, and Huppim, the children of Ir, *and* Hushim, the sons of Aher.

1Ch 7:15 — And Machir took to wife *the sister* of Huppim and Shuppim, whose sister's name *was* Maachah;) and the name of the second *was* Zelophehad: and Zelophehad had daughters.

HUR

• An Israelite who assisted in supporting Moses' hands during battle.

Ex 17:10 — So Joshua did as Moses had said to him, and fought with Amalek: and Moses, Aaron, and Hur went up to the top of the hill.

Ex 17:12 — But Moses' hands *were* heavy; and they took a stone, and put *it* under him, and he sat thereon; and Aaron and Hur stayed up his hands, the one on the one side, and the other on the other side; and his hands were steady until the going down of the sun.

Ex 24:14 — And he said unto the elders, Tarry ye here for us, until we come again unto you: and, behold, Aaron and Hur *are* with you: if any man have any matters to do, let him come unto them.

• A son of Caleb.

1Ch 2:19–20

Ex 31:2 — See, I have called by name Bezaleel the son of Uri, the son of Hur, of the tribe of Judah:

Ex 35:30 — And Moses said unto the children of Israel, See, the LORD hath called by name Bezaleel the son of Uri, the son of Hur, of the tribe of Judah;

Ex 38:22 — And Bezaleel the son of Uri, the son of Hur, of the tribe of Judah, made all that the LORD commanded Moses.

2Ch 1:5 — Moreover the brasen altar, that Bezaleel the son of Uri, the son of Hur, had made, he put before the tabernacle of the LORD: and Solomon and the congregation sought unto it.

- **A king of Midian.**

Nu 31:8 — And they slew the kings of Midian, beside the rest of them that were slain; *namely,* Evi, and Rekem, and Zur, and Hur, and Reba, five kings of Midian: Balaam also the son of Beor they slew with the sword.

Jos 13:21 — And all the cities of the plain, and all the kingdom of Sihon king of the Amorites, which reigned in Heshbon, whom Moses smote with the princes of Midian, Evi, and Rekem, and Zur, and Hur, and Reba, *which were* dukes of Sihon, dwelling in the country.

- **Called Ben Hur, an officer of Solomon's commissary.**

1Ki 4:8 — And these *are* their names: The son of Hur, in mount Ephraim:

- **Father of Caleb.**

1Ch 2:50 — These were the sons of Caleb the son of Hur, the firstborn of Ephratah; Shobal the father of Kirjath-jearim,

1Ch 4:4 — And Penuel the father of Gedor and Ezer the father of Hushah. These *are* the sons of Hur, the firstborn of Ephratah, the father of Bethlehem.

- **A son of Judah.**

1Ch 4:1 — The sons of Judah; Pharez, Hezron, and Carmi, and Hur, and Shobal.

- **A ruler.**

Ne 3:9 — And next unto them repaired Rephaiah the son of Hur, the ruler of the half part of Jerusalem.

HURAI • One of David's guards.

1Ch 11:32 — Hurai of the brooks of Gaash, Abiel the Arbathite,

HURAM

- **Son of Bela.**

1Ch 8:5 — And Gera, and Shephuphan, and Huram.

- **King of Tyre.**

➜**See: Hiram**

HURI • Father of Abihail.

1Ch 5:14 — These *are* the children of Abihail the son of Huri, the son of Jaroah, the son of Gilead, the son of Michael, the son of Jeshishai, the son of Jahdo, the son of Buz;

HUSBAND

Ge 2:23–24; Nu 5:11–31; Dt 22:13–21; Pr 5:15–19; Mal 2:14–16; Eph 5:22–33; Col 3:18–19

Dt 24:5 — When a man hath taken a new wife, he shall not go out to war, neither shall he be charged with any business: *but* he shall be free at home one year, and shall cheer up his wife which he hath taken.

Ecc 9:9 — Live joyfully with the wife whom thou lovest all the days of the life of thy vanity, which he hath given thee under the sun, all the days of thy vanity: for that *is* thy portion in *this* life, and in thy labour which thou takest under the sun.

Mt 19:5 — And said, For this cause shall a man leave father and mother, and shall cleave to his wife: and they twain shall be one flesh?

Mk 10:7 — For this cause shall a man leave his father and mother, and cleave to his wife;

1Co 7:3 — Let the husband render unto the wife due benevolence: and likewise also the wife unto the husband.

1Co 7:5 — Defraud ye not one the other, except *it be* with consent for a time, that ye may give yourselves to fasting and prayer; and come together again, that Satan tempt you not for your incontinency.

1Co 7:14 — For the unbelieving husband is sanctified by the wife, and the unbelieving wife is sanctified by the husband: else were your children unclean; but now are they holy.

1Co 7:16 — For what knowest thou, O wife, whether thou shalt save *thy* husband? or how knowest thou, O man, whether thou shalt save *thy* wife?

1Co 7:33 — But he that is married careth for the things that are of the world, how he may please *his* wife.

1Co 11:3 — But I would have you know, that the head of every man is Christ; and the head of the woman *is* the man; and the head of Christ *is* God.

1Ti 5:8 — But if any provide not for his own, and specially for those of his own house, he hath denied the faith, and is worse than an infidel.

1Pe 3:7 — Likewise, ye husbands, dwell with *them* according to knowledge, giving honour unto the wife, as unto the weaker vessel, and as being heirs together of the grace of life; that your prayers be not hindered.

- **Faithful.**
  - **Instances of.**
    - **Isaac.**

Ge 24:67 — And Isaac brought her into his mother Sarah's tent, and took Rebekah, and she became his wife; and he loved her: and Isaac was comforted after his mother's *death.*

- **Joseph.**

Mt 1:19 — Then Joseph her husband, being a just *man,* and not willing to make her a publick example, was minded to put her away privily.

- **Unreasonable and oppressive.**
  - **Ahasuerus.**

Est 1:10–22

- **Figurative.**

Isa 54:5–6; Hos 2:19–20

Jer 3:14 — Turn, O backsliding children, saith the LORD; for I am married unto you: and I will take you one of a city, and two of a family, and I will bring you to Zion:

Jer 31:32 — Not according to the covenant that I made with their fathers in the day *that* I took them by the hand to bring them out of the land of Egypt; which my covenant they brake, although I was an husband unto them, saith the LORD:

HUSBANDMAN

- **An agriculturist.**

Mt 21:33–46; Mk 12:1–9

Jn 15:1 — I am the true vine, and my Father is the husbandman.

1Co 3:9 — For we are labourers together with God: ye are God's husbandry, *ye are* God's building.

→See: Agriculture

HUSBANDRY

→See: Agriculture
→See: Animals
→See: Husbandman

HUSHAH

• Son of Ezer.

1Ch 4:4 — And Penuel the father of Gedor and Ezer the father of Hushah. These *are* the sons of Hur, the firstborn of Ephratah, the father of Bethlehem.

• Probably called Shuah.

1Ch 4:11 — And Chelub the brother of Shuah begat Mehir, which *was* the father of Eshton.

HUSHAI • David's friend.

2Sa 15:32–37; 16:16–19; 17:1–29

1Ch 27:33 — And Ahithophel *was* the king's counsellor: and Hushai the Archite *was* the king's companion:

HUSHAM • A Temanite.

Ge 36:34–35; 1Ch 1:45–46

HUSHIM

• Son of Dan.

Ge 46:23 — And the sons of Dan; Hushim.

• Called Shuham.

Nu 26:42 — These *are* the sons of Dan after their families: of Shuham, the family of the Shuhamites. These *are* the families of Dan after their families.

• A Benjamite.

1Ch 7:12 — Shuppim also, and Huppim, the children of Ir, *and* Hushim, the sons of Aher.

• Wife of Shaharaim.

1Ch 8:8 — And Shaharaim begat *children* in the country of Moab, after he had sent them away; Hushim and Baara *were* his wives.

1Ch 8:11 — And of Hushim he begat Abitub, and Elpaal.

HUSK

• A pod.

Nu 6:4 — All the days of his separation shall he eat nothing that is made of the vine tree, from the kernels even to the husk.

2Ki 4:42 — And there came a man from Baal-shalisha, and brought the man of God bread of the firstfruits, twenty loaves of barley, and full ears of corn in the husk thereof. And he said, Give unto the people, that they may eat.

• Eaten by the prodigal son.

Lk 15:16 — And he would fain have filled his belly with the husks that the swine did eat: and no man gave unto him.

HUZ →See: Uz

HUZZAB • Probably a region east of the Tigris.

Na 2:7 — And Huzzab shall be led away captive, she shall be brought up, and her maids shall lead *her* as with the voice of doves, tabering upon their breasts.

HYBRIDIZING

• Forbidden.

Le 19:19 — Ye shall keep my statutes. Thou shalt not let thy cattle gender with a diverse kind: thou shalt not sow thy field with mingled seed: neither shall a garment mingled of linen and woollen come upon thee.

HYGIENE

1Co 6:18 — Flee fornication. Every sin that a man doeth is without the body; but he that committeth fornication sinneth against his own body.

1Co 9:25 — And every man that striveth for the mastery is temperate in all things. Now they *do it* to obtain a corruptible crown; but we an incorruptible.

→See: Sanitation

HYMENAEUS • A false teacher.

1Ti 1:20 — Of whom is Hymenaeus and Alexander; whom I have delivered unto Satan, that they may learn not to blaspheme.

2Ti 2:17 — And their word will eat as doth a canker: of whom is Hymenaeus and Philetus;

HYMN

→See: Psalms
→See: Song

HYPOCRISY

Job 8:13–15; 15:33–34; 20:4–18; 27:8–10, 13–18; 31:33–34; 36:13–14; Ps 50:16–17; 55:12–14, 20–21; 78:34–37; Pr 7:10–21; 23:6–8; 26:18–19, 23–26; Isa 1:11–15; 29:15–16; 32:5–6; 48:1–2; 58:2–5; 66:3–5; Jer 3:10–11; 7:8–10; 42:20–22; Eze 14:7–8; 33:30–32; Hos 8:2–3; Am 5:21–27; Zec 7:5–6; Mal 1:6–14; Mt 3:7–8; 6:1–2; 7:21–23; 15:7–9; 21:28–32; 22:12–13; 23:2–33; 24:50–51; 25:41–45; Mk 7:6–8; 12:38–40; Lk 11:39–52; 12:1–2, 54–56; 13:13–17, 26–27; 14:34–35; 18:11–12; 20:46–47; Ro 2:17–29; 9:6–7; Php 3:18–19; Jas 1:22–26; 2:14–26; 2Pe 2:1–3; Jude 1:12–13

Job 13:16 — He also *shall be* my salvation: for an hypocrite shall not come before him.

Job 15:31 — Let not him that is deceived trust in vanity: for vanity shall be his recompence.

Job 17:8 — Upright *men* shall be astonied at this, and the innocent shall stir up himself against the hypocrite.

Job 34:30 — That the hypocrite reign not, lest the people be ensnared.

Ps 5:9 — For *there is* no faithfulness in their mouth; their inward part *is* very wickedness; their throat *is* an open sepulchre; they flatter with their tongue.

Ps 52:4 — Thou lovest all devouring words, O *thou* deceitful tongue.

Ps 55:23 — But thou, O God, shalt bring them down into the pit of destruction: bloody and deceitful men shall not live out half their days; but I will trust in thee.

Ps 101:7 — He that worketh deceit shall not dwell within my house: he that telleth lies shall not tarry in my sight.

Pr 11:9 — An hypocrite with *his* mouth destroyeth his neighbour: but through knowledge shall the just be delivered.

Pr 14:8 — The wisdom of the prudent *is* to understand his way: but the folly of fools *is* deceit.

Pr 15:8 — The sacrifice of the wicked *is* an abomination to the LORD: but the prayer of the upright *is* his delight.

Pr 20:14 — *It is* naught, *it is* naught, saith the buyer: but when he is gone his way, then he boasteth.

Pr 21:27 — The sacrifice of the wicked *is* abomination: how much more, *when* he bringeth it with a wicked mind?

Pr 25:19 — Confidence in an unfaithful man in time of trouble *is like* a broken tooth, and a foot out of joint.

Isa 9:17 — Therefore the Lord shall have no joy in their young men, neither shall have mercy on their fatherless and widows: for every one is an hypocrite and an evildoer, and every mouth speaketh folly. For all this his anger is not turned away, but his hand *is* stretched out still.

Isa 10:6 — I will send him against an hypocritical nation, and against the people of my wrath will I give him a charge, to take the spoil, and to take the prey, and to tread them down like the mire of the streets.

Isa 29:13 — Wherefore the Lord said, Forasmuch as this people draw near *me* with their mouth, and with their lips do honour me, but have removed their heart far from me, and their fear toward me is taught by the precept of men:

Isa 33:14 — The sinners in Zion are afraid; fearfulness hath surprised the hypocrites. Who among us shall dwell with the devouring fire? who among us shall dwell with everlasting burnings?

Isa 61:8 — For I the LORD love judgment, I hate robbery for burnt offering; and I will direct their work in truth, and I will make an everlasting covenant with them.

Isa 65:5 — Which say, Stand by thyself, come not near to me; for I am holier than thou. *These* are a smoke in my nose, a fire that burneth all the day.

Jer 5:2 — And though they say, The LORD liveth; surely they swear falsely.

Jer 6:20 — To what purpose cometh there to me incense from Sheba, and the sweet cane from a far country? your burnt offerings *are* not acceptable, nor your sacrifices sweet unto me.

Jer 7:4 — Trust ye not in lying words, saying, The temple of the LORD, The temple of the LORD, The temple of the LORD, *are* these.

Jer 9:4 — Take ye heed every one of his neighbour, and trust ye not in any brother: for every brother will utterly supplant, and every neighbour will walk with slanders.

Jer 9:8 — Their tongue *is as* an arrow shot out; it speaketh deceit: *one* speaketh peaceably to his neighbour with his mouth, but in heart he layeth his wait.

Jer 12:2 — Thou hast planted them, yea, they have taken root: they grow, yea, they bring forth fruit: thou *art* near in their mouth, and far from their reins.

Jer 17:9 — The heart *is* deceitful above all *things*, and desperately wicked: who can know it?

La 1:2 — She weepeth sore in the night, and her tears *are* on her cheeks: among all her lovers she hath none to comfort *her*: all her friends have dealt treacherously with her, they are become her enemies.

Eze 5:11 — Wherefore, *as* I live, saith the Lord GOD; Surely, because thou hast defiled my sanctuary with all thy detestable things, and with all thine abominations, therefore will I also diminish *thee;* neither shall mine eye spare, neither will I have any pity.

Eze 14:4 — Therefore speak unto them, and say unto them, Thus saith the Lord GOD; Every man of the house of Israel that setteth up his idols in his heart, and putteth the stumblingblock of his iniquity before his face, and cometh to the prophet; I the LORD will answer him that cometh according to the multitude of his idols;

Eze 20:39 — As for you, O house of Israel, thus saith the Lord GOD; Go ye, serve ye every one his idols, and hereafter *also*, if ye will not hearken unto me: but pollute ye my holy name no more with your gifts, and with your idols.

Hos 6:4 — O Ephraim, what shall I do unto thee? O Judah, what shall I do unto thee? for your goodness *is* as a morning cloud, and as the early dew it goeth away.

Hos 7:14 — And they have not cried unto me with their heart, when they howled upon their beds: they assemble themselves for corn and wine, *and* they rebel against me.

Hos 7:16 — They return, *but* not to the most High: they are like a deceitful bow: their princes shall fall by the sword for the rage of their tongue: this *shall be* their derision in the land of Egypt.

Hos 8:13 — They sacrifice flesh *for* the sacrifices of mine offerings, and *eat it;* but the LORD accepteth them not; now will he remember their iniquity, and visit their sins: they shall return to Egypt.

Hos 9:4 — They shall not offer wine *offerings* to the LORD, neither shall they be pleasing unto him: their sacrifices *shall be* unto them as the bread of mourners; all that eat thereof shall be polluted: for their bread for their soul shall not come into the house of the LORD.

Hos 10:1 — Israel *is* an empty vine, he bringeth forth fruit unto himself: according to the multitude of his fruit he hath increased the altars; according to the goodness of his land they have made goodly images.

Hos 10:4 — They have spoken words, swearing falsely in making a covenant: thus judgment springeth up as hemlock in the furrows of the field.

Hos 11:12 — Ephraim compasseth me about with lies, and the house of Israel with deceit: but Judah yet ruleth with God, and is faithful with the saints.

Ob 1:7 — All the men of thy confederacy have brought thee *even* to the border: the men that were at peace with thee have deceived thee, *and* prevailed against thee; *they that eat* thy bread have laid a wound under thee: *there is* none understanding in him.

Mic 3:11 — The heads thereof judge for reward, and the priests thereof teach for hire, and the prophets thereof divine for money: yet will they lean upon the LORD, and say, *Is* not the LORD among us? none evil can come upon us.

Mic 7:5 — Trust ye not in a friend, put ye not confidence in a guide: keep the doors of thy mouth from her that lieth in thy bosom.

Zec 13:6 — And *one* shall say unto him, What *are* these wounds in thine hands? Then he shall answer, *Those* with which I was wounded *in* the house of my friends.

Mal 2:13 — And this have ye done again, covering the altar of the LORD with tears, with weeping, and with crying out, insomuch that he regardeth not the offering any more, or receiveth *it* with good will at your hand.

Mal 3:14 — Ye have said, It *is* vain to serve God: and what profit *is it* that we have kept his ordinance, and that we have walked mournfully before the LORD of hosts?

Mt 6:5 — And when thou prayest, thou shalt not be as the hypocrites *are:* for they love to pray standing in the synagogues and in the corners of the streets, that they may be seen of men. Verily I say unto you, They have their reward.

Mt 6:16 — Moreover when ye fast, be not, as the hypocrites, of a sad countenance: for they disfigure their faces, that they may appear unto men to fast. Verily I say unto you, They have their reward.

Mt 6:24 — No man can serve two masters: for either he will hate the one, and love the other; or else he will hold to the one, and despise the other. Ye cannot serve God and mammon.

Mt 7:5 — Thou hypocrite, first cast out the beam out of thine own eye; and then shalt thou see clearly to cast out the mote out of thy brother's eye.

Mt 7:15 — Beware of false prophets, which come to you in sheep's clothing, but inwardly they are ravening wolves.

Mt 9:13 — But go ye and learn what *that* meaneth, I will have mercy, and not sacrifice: for I am not come to call the righteous, but sinners to repentance.

Mt 16:3 — And in the morning, *It will be* foul weather to day: for the sky is red and lowring. O *ye* hypocrites, ye can discern the face of the sky; but can ye not *discern* the signs of the times?

Mt 16:6 — Then Jesus said unto them, Take heed and beware of the leaven of the Pharisees and of the Sadducees.

Mt 16:12 — Then understood they how that he bade *them* not beware of the leaven of bread, but of the doctrine of the Pharisees and of the Sadducees.

Mt 22:18 — But Jesus perceived their wickedness, and said, Why tempt ye me, *ye* hypocrites?

Mt 25:3 — They that *were* foolish took their lamps, and took no oil with them:

Mk 8:15 — And he charged them, saying, Take heed, beware of the leaven of the Pharisees, and *of* the leaven of Herod.

Mk 9:50 — Salt *is* good: but if the salt have lost his saltness, wherewith will ye season it? Have salt in yourselves, and have peace one with another.

Lk 6:46 — And why call ye me, Lord, Lord, and do not the things which I say?

Lk 8:18 — Take heed therefore how ye hear: for whosoever hath, to him shall be given; and whosoever hath not, from him shall be taken even that which he seemeth to have.

Lk 16:13 — No servant can serve two masters: for either he will hate the one, and love the other; or else he will hold to the one, and despise the other. Ye cannot serve God and mammon.

Lk 16:15 — And he said unto them, Ye are they which justify yourselves before men; but God knoweth your hearts: for that which is highly esteemed among men is abomination in the sight of God.

Lk 21:16 — And ye shall be betrayed both by parents, and brethren, and kinsfolks, and friends; and *some* of you shall they cause to be put to death.

Jn 6:26 — Jesus answered them and said, Verily, verily, I say unto you, Ye seek me, not because ye saw the miracles, but because ye did eat of the loaves, and were filled.

Jn 6:70 — Jesus answered them, Have not I chosen you twelve, and one of you is a devil?

Jn 7:19 — Did not Moses give you the law, and *yet* none of you keepeth the law? Why go ye about to kill me?

Jn 15:2 — Every branch in me that beareth not fruit he taketh away: and every *branch* that beareth fruit, he purgeth it, that it may bring forth more fruit.

Jn 15:6 — If a man abide not in me, he is cast forth as a branch, and is withered; and men gather them, and cast *them* into the fire, and they are burned.

Ro 1:18 — For the wrath of God is revealed from heaven against all ungodliness and unrighteousness of men, who hold the truth in unrighteousness;

Ro 2:1 — Therefore thou art inexcusable, O man, whosoever thou art that judgest: for wherein thou judgest another, thou condemnest thyself; for thou that judgest doest the same things.

Ro 2:3 — And thinkest thou this, O man, that judgest them which do such things, and doest the same, that thou shalt escape the judgment of God?

Ro 16:18 — For they that are such serve not our Lord Jesus Christ, but their own belly; and by good words and fair speeches deceive the hearts of the simple.

1Co 13:1 — Though I speak with the tongues of men and of angels, and have not charity, I am become *as* sounding brass, or a tinkling cymbal.

2Co 4:2 — But have renounced the hidden things of dishonesty, not walking in craftiness, nor handling the word of God deceitfully; but by manifestation of the truth commending ourselves to every man's conscience in the sight of God.

2Co 5:12 — For we commend not ourselves again unto you, but give you occasion to glory on our behalf, that ye may have somewhat to *answer* them which glory in appearance, and not in heart.

Gal 6:3 — For if a man think himself to be something, when he is nothing, he deceiveth himself.

Php 3:2 — Beware of dogs, beware of evil workers, beware of the concision.

1Ti 4:2 — Speaking lies in hypocrisy; having their conscience seared with a hot iron;

2Ti 3:5 — Having a form of godliness, but denying the power thereof: from such turn away.

2Ti 3:13 — But evil men and seducers shall wax worse and worse, deceiving, and being deceived.

Tit 1:16 — They profess that they know God; but in works they deny *him,* being abominable, and disobedient, and unto every good work reprobate.

Jas 1:8 — A double minded man *is* unstable in all his ways.

Jas 3:17 — But the wisdom that is from above is first pure, then peaceable, gentle, *and* easy to be intreated, full of mercy and good fruits, without partiality, and without hypocrisy.

Jas 4:8 — Draw nigh to God, and he will draw nigh to you. Cleanse *your* hands, *ye* sinners; and purify *your* hearts, *ye* double minded.

1Pe 2:1 — Wherefore laying aside all malice, and all guile, and hypocrisies, and envies, and all evil speakings,

1Pe 2:16 — As free, and not using *your* liberty for a cloke of maliciousness, but as the servants of God.

2Pe 2:17 — These are wells without water, clouds that are carried with a tempest; to whom the mist of darkness is reserved for ever.

2Pe 2:19 — While they promise them liberty, they themselves are the servants of corruption: for of whom a man is overcome, of the same is he brought in bondage.

1Jn 1:6 — If we say that we have fellowship with him, and walk in darkness, we lie, and do not the truth:

1Jn 1:10 — If we say that we have not sinned, we make him a liar, and his word is not in us.

1Jn 2:4 — He that saith, I know him, and keepeth not his commandments, is a liar, and the truth is not in him.

1Jn 2:9 — He that saith he is in the light, and hateth his brother, is in darkness even until now.

1Jn 2:19 — They went out from us, but they were not of us; for if they had been of us, they would *no doubt* have continued with us: but *they went out,* that they might be made manifest that they were not all of us.

1Jn 4:20 — If a man say, I love God, and hateth his brother, he is a liar: for he that loveth not his brother whom he hath seen, how can he love God whom he hath not seen?

Rev 2:9 — I know thy works, and tribulation, and poverty, (but thou art rich) and *I know* the blasphemy of them which say they are Jews, and are not, but *are* the synagogue of Satan.

Rev 3:1 — And unto the angel of the church in Sardis write; These things saith he that hath the seven Spirits of God, and the seven stars; I know thy works, that thou hast a name that thou livest, and art dead.

Rev 3:9 — Behold, I will make them of the synagogue of Satan, which say they are Jews, and are not, but do lie; behold, I will make them to come and worship before thy feet, and to know that I have loved thee.

See: Deceit

See: Deception

- **Instances of.**
  - **Jacob, in impersonating Esau and deceiving his father.**
    Ge 27:1–46
  - **Jacob's sons, in deception of their father concerning Joseph.**
    Ge 37:29–35
  - **Joseph's deception of his brethren.**
    Ge 42:1–44:34
  - **Pharaoh.**
    Ex 8:15, 28–29, 32; 9:27–35; 10:8–29
  - **Balaam.**
    Nu 22:1–24:25; Jude 1:11
  - **Delilah, the wife of Samson.**
    Jgs 16:1–31
  - **Jael.**
    Jgs 4:8–21
  - **Ehud.**
    Jgs 3:15–25
  - **Rabshakeh.**
    2Ki 18:17–37
  - **Ahaz.**
    Isa 7:12, 17–25
  - **Johanan.**
    Jer 42:1–12, 20, 22
  - **Ishmael.**
    Jer 41:6–7
  - **The false prophets.**
    Eze 13:1–23
  - **Herod.**
    Mt 2:8
  - **Judas.**
    Mt 26:25, 48; Jn 12:5–6
  - **Pilate.**
    Mt 27:24
  - **Pharisees.**
    Mt 15:1–9; 22:18; Mk 12:13–14; Jn 8:4–9; 9:24; 19:15
  - **The ruler.**
    Lk 13:14–17
  - **Spies sent to entrap Jesus.**
    Lk 20:21
  - **Priests and Levites.**
    Lk 10:31–32
  - **Chief priests.**
    Jn 18:28
  - **Ananias and Sapphira.**
    Ac 5:1–10
  - **Simon Magus.**
    Ac 8:18–23
  - **Peter and other Christians at Antioch.**
    Gal 2:11–14
  - **Judaizing Christians in Galatia.**
    Gal 6:13
  - **False teachers at Ephesus.**
    Rev 2:2

See: Conspiracy

See: Treachery

HYSSOP

- **An indigenous plant to western Asia and northern Africa.**

1Ki 4:33 — And he spake of trees, from the cedar tree that *is* in Lebanon even unto the hyssop that springeth out of the wall: he spake also of beasts, and of fowl, and of creeping things, and of fishes.

• The Israelites used, in sprinkling the blood of the paschal lamb upon the lintels of their doors.

Ex 12:22 — And ye shall take a bunch of hyssop, and dip *it* in the blood that *is* in the bason, and strike the lintel and the two side posts with the blood that *is* in the bason; and none of you shall go out at the door of his house until the morning.

• The Israelites used, in sprinkling blood in purifications.

Le 14:51–52

Le 14:4 — Then shall the priest command to take for him that is to be cleansed two birds alive *and* clean, and cedar wood, and scarlet, and hyssop:

Le 14:6 — As for the living bird, he shall take it, and the cedar wood, and the scarlet, and the hyssop, and shall dip them and the living bird in the blood of the bird *that was* killed over the running water:

Heb 9:19 — For when Moses had spoken every precept to all the people according to the law, he took the blood of calves and of goats, with water, and scarlet wool, and hyssop, and sprinkled both the book, and all the people,

• Used in the sacrifices of separation.

Nu 19:6 — And the priest shall take cedar wood, and hyssop, and scarlet, and cast *it* into the midst of the burning of the heifer.

• Used in giving Jesus vinegar on the cross.

Jn 19:29 — Now there was set a vessel full of vinegar: and they filled a spunge with vinegar, and put *it* upon hyssop, and put *it* to his mouth.

• Figurative.

• Of spiritual cleansing.

Ps 51:7 — Purge me with hyssop, and I shall be clean: wash me, and I shall be whiter than snow.

I

I AM THAT I AM

• A name of deity.

Ex 3:14 — And God said unto Moses, I AM THAT I AM: and he said, Thus shalt thou say unto the children of Israel, I AM hath sent me unto you.

Rev 1:4 — John to the seven churches which are in Asia: Grace *be* unto you, and peace, from him which is, and which was, and which is to come; and from the seven Spirits which are before his throne;

Rev 1:11 — Saying, I am Alpha and Omega, the first and the last: and, What thou seest, write in a book, and send *it* unto the seven churches which are in Asia; unto Ephesus, and unto Smyrna, and unto Pergamos, and unto Thyatira, and unto Sardis, and unto Philadelphia, and unto Laodicea.

Rev 1:17 — And when I saw him, I fell at his feet as dead. And he laid his right hand upon me, saying unto me, Fear not; I am the first and the last:

I-CHABOD • Son of Phinehas, and grandson of Eli.

1Sa 4:21 — And she named the child I-chabod, saying, The glory is departed from Israel: because the ark of God was taken, and because of her father in law and her husband.

1Sa 14:3 — And Ahiah, the son of Ahitub, I-chabod's brother, the son of Phinehas, the son of Eli, the LORD'S priest in Shiloh, wearing an ephod. And the people knew not that Jonathan was gone.

IBHAR • Son of David.

2Sa 5:15 — Ibhar also, and Elishua, and Nepheg, and Japhia,

1Ch 3:6 — Ibhar also, and Elishama, and Eliphelet,

1Ch 14:5 — And Ibhar, and Elishua, and Elpalet,

IBLEAM • A city of Manasseh.

Jos 17:11 — And Manasseh had in Issachar and in Asher Beth-shean and her towns, and Ibleam and her towns, and the inhabitants of Dor and her towns, and the inhabitants of Endor and her towns, and the inhabitants of Taanach and her towns, and the inhabitants of Megiddo and her towns, *even* three countries.

Jgs 1:27 — Neither did Manasseh drive out *the inhabitants of* Beth-shean and her towns, nor Taanach and her towns, nor the inhabitants of Dor and her towns, nor the inhabitants of Ibleam and her towns, nor the inhabitants of Megiddo and her towns: but the Canaanites would dwell in that land.

2Ki 9:27 — But when Ahaziah the king of Judah saw *this*, he fled by the way of the garden house. And Jehu followed after him, and said, Smite him also in the chariot. *And they did so* at the going up to Gur, which *is* by Ibleam. And he fled to Megiddo, and died there.

IBNEIAH • A Benjamite.

1Ch 9:8 — And Ibneiah the son of Jeroham, and Elah the son of Uzzi, the son of Michri, and Meshullam the son of Shephatiah, the son of Reuel, the son of Ibnijah;

IBNIJAH • A Benjamite.

1Ch 9:8 — And Ibneiah the son of Jeroham, and Elah the son of Uzzi, the son of Michri, and Meshullam the son of Shephatiah, the son of Reuel, the son of Ibnijah;

IBRI • A Levite.

1Ch 24:27 — The sons of Merari by Jaaziah; Beno, and Shoham, and Zaccur, and Ibri.

IBZAN • A Bethlehemite and judge of Israel.

Jgs 12:8–10

ICE

Job 6:16 — Which are blackish by reason of the ice, *and* wherein the snow is hid:

Job 38:29 — Out of whose womb came the ice? and the hoary frost of heaven, who hath gendered it?

Ps 147:17 — He casteth forth his ice like morsels: who can stand before his cold?

Pr 25:13 — As the cold of snow in the time of harvest, *so is* a faithful messenger to them that send him: for he refresheth the soul of his masters.

ICONIUM

• A city of Asia Minor.

• Paul preaches.

Ac 14:21–22

Ac 13:51 — But they shook off the dust of their feet against them, and came unto Iconium.

Ac 16:2 — Which was well reported of by the brethren that were at Lystra and Iconium.

• Paul is persecuted by the people of.

Ac 14:1–6

2Ti 3:11 — Persecutions, afflictions, which came unto me at Antioch, at Iconium, at Lystra; what persecutions I endured: but out of *them* all the Lord delivered me.

ICONOCLASM

• Idols to be destroyed.

Dt 7:25–26; 12:1–4

Ex 23:24 — Thou shalt not bow down to their gods, nor serve them, nor do after their works: but thou shalt utterly overthrow them, and quite break down their images.

Ex 34:13 — But ye shall destroy their altars, break their images, and cut down their groves:

Nu 33:52 — Then ye shall drive out all the inhabitants of the land from before you, and destroy all their pictures, and destroy all their molten images, and quite pluck down all their high places:

Dt 7:5 — But thus shall ye deal with them; ye shall destroy their altars, and break down their images, and cut down their groves, and burn their graven images with fire.

Jgs 2:2 — And ye shall make no league with the inhabitants of this land; ye shall throw down their altars: but ye have not obeyed my voice: why have ye done this?

Jer 50:2 — Declare ye among the nations, and publish, and set up a standard; publish, *and* conceal not: say, Babylon is taken, Bel is confounded, Merodach is broken in pieces; her idols are confounded, her images are broken in pieces.

• Destroyed by.

• Jacob.

Ge 35:2–4

• Moses.

Ex 32:19–20

• Gideon.

Jgs 6:28–32

• David.

2Sa 5:21 — And there they left their images, and David and his men burned them.

1Ch 14:12 — And when they had left their gods there, David gave a commandment, and they were burned with fire.

• Jehu.

2Ki 10:26–28

• Jehoiada.

2Ki 11:18 — And all the people of the land went into the house of Baal, and brake it down; his altars and his images brake they in pieces thoroughly, and slew Mattan the priest of Baal before the altars. And the priest appointed officers over the house of the LORD.

• Hezekiah.

2Ki 18:3–6

• Josiah.

2Ki 23:4–20

• Asa.

2Ch 14:3–5; 15:8–16

• Jehoshaphat.

2Ch 17:6 — And his heart was lifted up in the ways of the LORD: moreover he took away the high places and groves out of Judah.

2Ch 19:3 — Nevertheless there are good things found in thee, in that thou hast taken away the groves out of the land, and hast prepared thine heart to seek God.

• Jews.

2Ch 30:14 — And they arose and took away the altars that *were* in Jerusalem, and all the altars for incense took they away, and cast *them* into the brook Kidron.

• Manasseh.

2Ch 33:15 — And he took away the strange gods, and the idol out of the house of the LORD, and all the altars that he had built in the mount of the house of the LORD, and in Jerusalem, and cast *them* out of the city.

See: Idolatry

IDALAH • A town of Zebulun.

Jos 19:15 — And Kattath, and Nahallal, and Shimron, and Idalah, and Bethlehem: twelve cities with their villages.

IDBASH • A descendant of Judah.

1Ch 4:3 — And these *were of* the father of Etam; Jezreel, and Ishma, and Idbash: and the name of their sister *was* Hazelelponi:

IDDO

• Father of Ahinadab.

1Ki 4:14 — Ahinadab the son of Iddo *had* Mahanaim:

• A descendant of Gershom.

1Ch 6:21 — Joah his son, Iddo his son, Zerah his son, Jeaterai his son.

• A son of Zechariah.

1Ch 27:21 — Of the half *tribe* of Manasseh in Gilead, Iddo the son of Zechariah: of Benjamin, Jaasiel the son of Abner:

• A prophet.

2Ch 9:29 — Now the rest of the acts of Solomon, first and last, *are* they not written in the book of Nathan the prophet, and in the prophecy of Ahijah the Shilonite, and in the visions of Iddo the seer against Jeroboam the son of Nebat?

2Ch 12:15 — Now the acts of Rehoboam, first and last, *are* they not written in the book of Shemaiah the prophet, and of Iddo the seer concerning genealogies? And *there were* wars between Rehoboam and Jeroboam continually.

2Ch 13:22 — And the rest of the acts of Abijah, and his ways, and his sayings, *are* written in the story of the prophet Iddo.

• Ancestor of Zechariah.

Ezr 5:1 — Then the prophets, Hag the prophet, and Zechariah the son of Iddo, prophesied unto the Jews that *were* in Judah and Jerusalem in the name of the God of Israel, *even* unto them.

Ezr 6:14 — And the elders of the Jews builded, and they prospered through the prophesying of Hag the prophet and Zechariah the son of Iddo. And they builded, and finished *it,* according to the commandment of the God of Israel, and according to the commandment of Cyrus, and Darius, and Artaxerxes king of Persia.

Zec 1:1 — In the eighth month, in the second year of Darius, came the word of the LORD unto Zechariah, the son of Berechiah, the son of Iddo the prophet, saying,

Zec 1:7 — Upon the four and twentieth day of the eleventh month, which *is* the month Sebat, in the second year of Darius, came the word of the LORD unto Zechariah, the son of Berechiah, the son of Iddo the prophet, saying,

• A priest.

Ne 12:4 — Iddo, Ginnetho, Abijah,

Ne 12:16 — Of Iddo, Zechariah; of Ginnethon, Meshullam;

• The chief of the Jews established at Casiphia.

Ezr 8:17 — And I sent them with commandment unto Iddo the chief at the place Casiphia, and I told them what they should say unto Iddo, *and* to his brethren the Nethinims, at the place Casiphia, that they should bring unto us ministers for the house of our God.

IDLENESS

Pr 6:9–11; 10:4–5; 21:25–26; 24:30–31, 33–34; 26:13–16; Mt 20:6–7; Lk 19:20–25; 2Th 3:10–11

Pr 6:6 — Go to the ant, thou sluggard; consider her ways, and be wise:

Pr 10:26 — As vinegar to the teeth, and as smoke to the eyes, so *is* the sluggard to them that send him.

Pr 12:9 — *He that is* despised, and hath a servant, *is* better than he that honoureth himself, and lacketh bread.

Pr 12:24 — The hand of the diligent shall bear rule: but the slothful shall be under tribute.

Pr 12:27 — The slothful *man* roasteth not that which he took in hunting: but the substance of a diligent man *is* precious.

Pr 13:4 — The soul of the sluggard desireth, and *hath* nothing: but the soul of the diligent shall be made fat.

Pr 14:23 — In all labour there is profit: but the talk of the lips *tendeth* only to penury.

Pr 15:19 — The way of the slothful *man is* as an hedge of thorns: but the way of the righteous *is* made plain.

Pr 18:9 — He also that is slothful in his work is brother to him that is a great waster.

Pr 19:15 — Slothfulness casteth into a deep sleep; and an idle soul shall suffer hunger.

Pr 19:24 — A slothful *man* hideth his hand in *his* bosom, and will not so much as bring it to his mouth again.

Pr 20:4 — The sluggard will not plow by reason of the cold; *therefore* shall he beg in harvest, and *have* nothing.

Pr 20:13 — Love not sleep, lest thou come to poverty; open thine eyes, *and* thou shalt be satisfied with bread.

Pr 22:13 — The slothful *man* saith, *There is* a lion without, I shall be slain in the streets.

Pr 23:21 — For the drunkard and the glutton shall come to poverty: and drowsiness shall clothe *a man* with rags.

Ecc 4:5 — The fool foldeth his hands together, and eateth his own flesh.

Ecc 10:18 — By much slothfulness the building decayeth; and through idleness of the hands the house droppeth through.

Isa 56:10 — His watchmen *are* blind: they are all ignorant, they *are* all dumb dogs, they cannot bark; sleeping, lying down, loving to slumber.

Eze 16:49 — Behold, this was the iniquity of thy sister Sodom, pride, fulness of bread, and abundance of idleness was in her and in her daughters, neither did she strengthen the hand of the poor and needy.

Ac 17:21 — (For all the Athenians and strangers which were there spent their time in nothing else, but either to tell, or to hear some new thing.)

1Ti 5:13 — And withal they learn *to be* idle, wandering about from house to house; and not only idle, but tattlers also and busybodies, speaking things which they ought not.

See: Industry

See: Slothfulness

IDOL

• Manufacture of.

Isa 40:19–20; 44:9–12; Ac 19:24–25

Ex 20:4 — Thou shalt not make unto thee any graven image, or any likeness *of any thing* that *is* in heaven above, or that *is* in the earth beneath, or that *is* in the water under the earth:

Ex 32:4 — And he received *them* at their hand, and fashioned it with a graving tool, after he had made it a molten calf: and they said, These *be* thy gods, O Israel, which brought thee up out of the land of Egypt.

Ex 32:20 — And he took the calf which they had made, and burnt *it* in the fire, and ground *it* to powder, and strawed *it* upon the water, and made the children of Israel drink *of it*.

Dt 4:23 — Take heed unto yourselves, lest ye forget the covenant of the LORD your God, which he made with you, and make you a graven image, *or* the likeness of any *thing*, which the LORD thy God hath forbidden thee.

Isa 44:17 — And the residue thereof he maketh a god, *even* his graven image: he falleth down unto it, and worshippeth *it*, and prayeth unto it, and saith, Deliver me; for thou *art* my god.

Hab 2:18 — What profiteth the graven image that the maker thereof hath graven it; the molten image, and a teacher of lies, that the maker of his work trusteth therein, to make dumb idols?

• Manufacture of, forbidden.

Ex 20:4 — Thou shalt not make unto thee any graven image, or any likeness *of any thing* that *is* in heaven above, or that *is* in the earth beneath, or that *is* in the water under the earth:

Ex 34:17 — Thou shalt make thee no molten gods.

• Made of gold.

Ex 32:3–4; Ps 115:4–7; 135:15–17

Isa 2:20 — In that day a man shall cast his idols of silver, and his idols of gold, which they made *each one* for himself to worship, to the moles and to the bats;

Isa 30:22 — Ye shall defile also the covering of thy graven images of silver, and the ornament of thy molten images of gold: thou shalt cast them away as a menstruous cloth; thou shalt say unto it, Get thee hence.

Isa 31:7 — For in that day every man shall cast away his idols of silver, and his idols of gold, which your own hands have made unto you *for* a sin.

Hos 8:4 — They have set up kings, but not by me: they have made princes, and I knew *it* not: of their silver and their gold have they made them idols, that they may be cut off.

• Made of silver.

Isa 2:20 — In that day a man shall cast his idols of silver, and his idols of gold, which they made *each one* for himself to worship, to the moles and to the bats;

Isa 30:22 — Ye shall defile also the covering of thy graven images of silver, and the ornament of thy molten images of gold: thou shalt cast them away as a menstruous cloth; thou shalt say unto it, Get thee hence.

Isa 31:7 — For in that day every man shall cast away his idols of silver, and his idols of gold, which your own hands have made unto you *for* a sin.

Hos 8:4 — They have set up kings, but not by me: they have made princes, and I knew *it* not: of their silver and their gold have they made them idols, that they may be cut off.

• Made of wood and stone.

Isa 44:13–19

Le 26:1 — Ye shall make you no idols nor graven image, neither rear you up a standing image, neither shall ye set up *any* image of stone in your land, to bow down unto it: for I *am* the LORD your God.

Dt 4:28 — And there ye shall serve gods, the work of men's hands, wood and stone, which neither see, nor hear, nor eat, nor smell.

2Ki 19:18 — And have cast their gods into the fire: for they *were* no gods, but the work of men's hands, wood and stone: therefore they have destroyed them.

Isa 37:19 — And have cast their gods into the fire: for they *were* no gods, but the work of men's hands, wood and stone: therefore they have destroyed them.

Isa 41:6 — They helped every one his neighbour; and *every one* said to his brother, Be of good courage.

Eze 20:32 — And that which cometh into your mind shall not be at all, that ye say, We will be as the heathen, as the families of the countries, to serve wood and stone.

• Coverings of.

Isa 30:22 — Ye shall defile also the covering of thy graven images of silver, and the ornament of thy molten images of gold: thou shalt cast them away as a menstruous cloth; thou shalt say unto it, Get thee hence.

• Prayer to, unanswered.

1Ki 18:25–29

Isa 16:12 — And it shall come to pass, when it is seen that Moab is weary on the high place, that he shall come to his sanctuary to pray; but he shall not prevail.

• Things offered to, not to be eaten.

Ex 34:15 — Lest thou make a covenant with the inhabitants of the land, and they go a whoring after their gods, and do sacrifice unto their gods, and *one* call thee, and thou eat of his sacrifice;

➜See: Iconoclasm

IDOLATRY

• Wicked practices of.

• Human sacrifices.

Le 20:2–5; 2Ki 3:26–27; 17:17–18; Ps 106:37–38; Jer 19:4–7; Eze 16:20–21

Le 18:21 — And thou shalt not let any of thy seed pass through *the fire* to Molech, neither shalt thou profane the name of thy God: I *am* the LORD.

Dt 12:31 — Thou shalt not do so unto the LORD thy God: for every abomination to the LORD, which he hateth, have they done unto their gods; for even their sons and their daughters they have burnt in the fire to their gods.

Dt 18:10 — There shall not be found among you *any one* that maketh his son or his daughter to pass through the fire, or that useth divination, *or* an observer of times, or an enchanter, or a witch,

2Ki 16:3 — But he walked in the way of the kings of Israel, yea, and made his son to pass through the fire, according to the abominations of the heathen, whom the LORD cast out from before the children of Israel.

2Ki 21:6 — And he made his son pass through the fire, and observed times, and used enchantments, and dealt with familiar spirits and wizards: he wrought much wickedness in the sight of the LORD, to provoke *him* to anger.

2Ki 23:10 — And he defiled Topheth, which *is* in the valley of the children of Hinnom, that no man might make his son or his daughter to pass through the fire to Molech.

2Ch 28:3 — Moreover he burnt incense in the valley of the son of Hinnom, and burnt his children in the fire, after the abominations of the heathen whom the LORD had cast out before the children of Israel.

2Ch 33:6 — And he caused his children to pass through the fire in the valley of the son of Hinnom: also he observed times, and used enchantments, and used witchcraft, and dealt with a familiar spirit, and with wizards: he wrought much evil in the sight of the LORD, to provoke him to anger.

Isa 57:5 — Enflaming yourselves with idols under every green tree, slaying the children in the valleys under the clifts of the rocks?

Jer 7:31 — And they have built the high places of Tophet, which is in the valley of the son of Hinnom, to burn their sons and their daughters in the fire; which I commanded *them* not, neither came it into my heart.

Jer 32:35 — And they built the high places of Baal, which *are* in the valley of the son of Hinnom, to cause their sons and their daughters to pass through *the fire* unto Molech; which I commanded them not, neither came it into my mind, that they should do this abomination, to cause Judah to sin.

Eze 20:26 — And I polluted them in their own gifts, in that they caused to pass through *the fire* all that openeth the womb, that I might make them desolate, to the end that they might know that I *am* the LORD.

Eze 20:31 — For when ye offer your gifts, when ye make your sons to pass through the fire, ye pollute yourselves with all your idols, even unto this day: and shall I be enquired of by you, O house of Israel? *As* I live, saith the Lord GOD, I will not be enquired of by you.

Eze 23:37 — That they have committed adultery, and blood is in their hands, and with their idols have they committed adultery, and have also caused their sons, whom they bare unto me, to pass for them through *the fire,* to devour *them.*

Eze 23:39 — For when they had slain their children to their idols, then they came the same day into my sanctuary to profane it; and, lo, thus have they done in the midst of mine house.

Mic 6:7 — Will the LORD be pleased with thousands of rams, *or* with ten thousands of rivers of oil? shall I give my firstborn *for* my transgression, the fruit of my body *for* the sin of my soul?

• Practices of, relating to the dead.

Dt 14:1 — Ye *are* the children of the LORD your God: ye shall not cut yourselves, nor make any baldness between your eyes for the dead.

• Licentiousness of.

Nu 25:1–3; Eze 23:1–44; Hos 4:12–14; Ro 1:26–27; 1Co 10:7–8; 1Pe 4:3–4; Rev 2:20–22; 9:20–21; 17:1–6

Ex 32:6 — And they rose up early on the morrow, and offered burnt offerings, and brought peace offerings; and the people sat down to eat and to drink, and rose up to play.

Ex 32:25 — And when Moses saw that the people *were* naked; (for Aaron had made them naked unto *their* shame among their enemies:)

1Ki 14:24 — And there were also sodomites in the land: *and* they did according to all the abominations of the nations which the LORD cast out before the children of Israel.

1Ki 15:12 — And he took away the sodomites out of the land, and removed all the idols that his fathers had made.

2Ki 17:30 — And the men of Babylon made Succoth-benoth, and the men of Cuth made Nergal, and the men of Hamath made Ashima,

2Ki 23:7 — And he brake down the houses of the sodomites, that *were* by the house of the LORD, where the women wove hangings for the grove.

Eze 16:17 — Thou hast also taken thy fair jewels of my gold and of my silver, which I had given thee, and madest to thyself images of men, and didst commit whoredom with them,

Am 2:8 — And they lay *themselves* down upon clothes laid to pledge by every altar, and they drink the wine of the condemned in the house of their god.

Mic 1:7 — And all the graven images thereof shall be beaten to pieces, and all the hires thereof shall be burned with the fire, and all the idols thereof will I lay desolate: for she gathered *it* of the hire of an harlot, and they shall return to the hire of an harlot.

Ro 1:24 — Wherefore God also gave them up to uncleanness through the lusts of their own hearts, to dishonour their own bodies between themselves:

Rev 2:14 — But I have a few things against thee, because thou hast there them that hold the doctrine of Balaam, who taught Balac to cast a stumblingblock before the children of Israel, to eat things sacrificed unto idols, and to commit fornication.

Rev 14:8 — And there followed another angel, saying, Babylon is fallen, is fallen, that great city, because she made all nations drink of the wine of the wrath of her fornication.

• Other customs of.

• Offered burnt offerings.

Ex 32:6 — And they rose up early on the morrow, and offered burnt offerings, and brought peace offerings; and the people sat down to eat and to drink, and rose up to play.

1Ki 18:26 — And they took the bullock which was given them, and they dressed *it,* and called on the name of Baal from morning even until noon, saying, O Baal, hear us. But *there was* no voice, nor any that answered. And they leaped upon the altar which was made.

Ac 14:13 — Then the priest of Jupiter, which was before their city, brought oxen and garlands unto the gates, and would have done sacrifice with the people.

• Offered libations.

Isa 57:6 — Among the smooth *stones* of the stream *is* thy portion; they, they *are* thy lot: even to them hast thou poured a drink offering, thou hast offered a meat offering. Should I receive comfort in these?

Isa 65:11 — But ye *are* they that forsake the LORD, that forget my holy mountain, that prepare a table for that troop, and that furnish the drink offering unto that number.

Jer 7:18 — The children gather wood, and the fathers kindle the fire, and the women knead *their* dough, to make cakes to the queen of heaven, and to pour out drink offerings unto other gods, that they may provoke me to anger.

Jer 19:13 — And the houses of Jerusalem, and the houses of the kings of Judah, shall be defiled as the place of Tophet, because of all the houses upon whose roofs they have burned incense unto all the host of heaven, and have poured out drink offerings unto other gods.

Jer 32:29 — And the Chaldeans, that fight against this city, shall come and set fire on this city, and burn it with the houses, upon whose roofs they have offered incense unto Baal, and poured out drink offerings unto other gods, to provoke me to anger.

Jer 44:17 — But we will certainly do whatsoever thing goeth forth out of our own mouth, to burn incense unto the queen of heaven, and to pour out drink offerings unto her, as we have done, we, and our fathers, our kings, and our princes, in the cities of Judah, and in the streets of Jerusalem: for *then* had we plenty of victuals, and were well, and saw no evil.

Jer 44:19 — And when we burned incense to the queen of heaven, and poured out drink offerings unto her, did we make her cakes to worship her, and pour out drink offerings unto her, without our men?

Jer 44:25 — Thus saith the LORD of hosts, the God of Israel, saying; Ye and your wives have both spoken with your mouths, and fulfilled with your hand, saying, We will surely perform our vows that we have vowed, to burn incense to the queen of heaven, and to pour out drink offerings unto her: ye will surely accomplish your vows, and surely perform your vows.

Eze 20:28 — *For* when I had brought them into the land, *for* the which I lifted up mine hand to give it to them, then they saw every high hill, and all the thick trees, and they offered there their sacrifices, and there they presented the provocation of their offering: there also they made their sweet savour, and poured out there their drink offerings.

• Offered libations of wine.

Dt 32:38 — Which did eat the fat of their sacrifices, *and* drank the wine of their drink offerings? let them rise up and help you, *and* be your protection.

• Offered libations of blood.

Ps 16:4 — Their sorrows shall be multiplied *that* hasten *after* another *god:* their drink offerings of blood will I not offer, nor take up their names into my lips.

Zec 9:7 — And I will take away his blood out of his mouth, and his abominations from between his teeth: but he that remaineth, even he, *shall be* for our God, and he shall be as a governor in Judah, and Ekron as a Jebusite.

• Offered meat offerings.

Isa 57:6 — Among the smooth *stones* of the stream *is* thy portion; they, they *are* thy lot: even to them hast thou poured a drink offering, thou hast offered a meat offering. Should I receive comfort in these?

Jer 7:18 — The children gather wood, and the fathers kindle the fire, and the women knead *their* dough, to make cakes to the queen of heaven, and to pour out drink offerings unto other gods, that they may provoke me to anger.

Jer 44:17 — But we will certainly do whatsoever thing goeth forth out of our own mouth, to burn incense unto the queen of heaven, and to pour out drink offerings unto her, as we have done, we, and our fathers, our kings, and our princes, in the cities of Judah, and in the streets of Jerusalem: for *then* had we plenty of victuals, and were well, and saw no evil.

Eze 16:19 — My meat also which I gave thee, fine flour, and oil, and honey, *wherewith* I fed thee, thou hast even set it before them for a sweet savour: and *thus* it was, saith the Lord GOD.

• Offered peace offerings.

Ex 32:6 — And they rose up early on the morrow, and offered burnt offerings, and brought peace offerings; and the people sat down to eat and to drink, and rose up to play.

• Incense burned on altars.

1Ki 12:33 — So he offered upon the altar which he had made in Bethel the fifteenth day of the eighth month, *even* in the month which he had devised of his own heart; and ordained a feast unto the children of Israel: and he offered upon the altar, and burnt incense.

2Ch 30:14 — And they arose and took away the altars that *were* in Jerusalem, and all the altars for incense took they away, and cast *them* into the brook Kidron.

2Ch 34:25 — Because they have forsaken me, and have burned incense unto other gods, that they might provoke me to anger with all the works of their hands; therefore my wrath shall be poured out upon this place, and shall not be quenched.

Isa 65:3 — A people that provoketh me to anger continually to my face; that sacrificeth in gardens, and burneth incense upon altars of brick;

Jer 1:16 — And I will utter my judgments against them touching all their wickedness, who have forsaken me, and have burned incense unto other gods, and worshipped the works of their own hands.

Jer 11:12 — Then shall the cities of Judah and inhabitants of Jerusalem go, and cry unto the gods unto whom they offer incense: but they shall not save them at all in the time of their trouble.

Jer 11:17 — For the LORD of hosts, that planted thee, hath pronounced evil against thee, for the evil of the house of Israel and of the house of Judah, which they have done against themselves to provoke me to anger in offering incense unto Baal.

Jer 44:3 — Because of their wickedness which they have committed to provoke me to anger, in that they went to burn incense, *and* to serve other gods, whom they knew not, *neither* they, ye, nor your fathers.

Jer 48:35 — Moreover I will cause to cease in Moab, saith the LORD, him that offereth in the high places, and him that burneth incense to his gods.

Eze 16:18 — And tookest thy broidered garments, and coveredst them: and thou hast set mine oil and mine incense before them.

Eze 23:41 — And satest upon a stately bed, and a table prepared before it, whereupon thou hast set mine incense and mine oil.

Hos 11:2 — *As* they called them, so they went from them: they sacrificed unto Baalim, and burned incense to graven images.

• Prayers to idols.

Jgs 10:14 — Go and cry unto the gods which ye have chosen; let them deliver you in the time of your tribulation.

Isa 44:17 — And the residue thereof he maketh a god, *even* his graven image: he falleth down unto it, and worshippeth *it,* and prayeth unto it, and saith, Deliver me; for thou *art* my god.

Isa 45:20 — Assemble yourselves and come; draw near together, ye *that are* escaped of the nations: they have no knowledge that set up the wood of their graven image, and pray unto a god *that* cannot save.

Isa 46:7 — They bear him upon the shoulder, they carry him, and set him in his place, and he standeth; from his place shall he not remove: yea, *one* shall cry unto him, yet can he not answer, nor save him out of his trouble.

Jnh 1:5 — Then the mariners were afraid, and cried every man unto his god, and cast forth the wares that *were* in the ship into the sea, to lighten *it* of them. But Jonah was gone down into the sides of the ship; and he lay, and was fast asleep.

- **Praise.**

Jgs 16:24 — And when the people saw him, they praised their god: for they said, Our god hath delivered into our hands our enemy, and the destroyer of our country, which slew many of us.

Da 5:4 — They drank wine, and praised the gods of gold, and of silver, of brass, of iron, of wood, and of stone.

- **Singing and dancing.**

Ex 32:18–19

- **Music.**

Da 3:5–7

- **Cutting the flesh.**

1Ki 18:28 — And they cried aloud, and cut themselves after their manner with knives and lancets, till the blood gushed out upon them.

Jer 41:5 — That there came certain from Shechem, from Shiloh, and from Samaria, *even* fourscore men, having their beards shaven, and their clothes rent, and having cut themselves, with offerings and incense in their hand, to bring *them* to the house of the LORD.

- **Kissing.**

1Ki 19:18 — Yet I have left *me* seven thousand in Israel, all the knees which have not bowed unto Baal, and every mouth which hath not kissed him.

Job 31:27 — And my heart hath been secretly enticed, or my mouth hath kissed my hand:

Hos 13:2 — And now they sin more and more, and have made them molten images of their silver, *and* idols according to their own understanding, all of it the work of the craftsmen: they say of them, Let the men that sacrifice kiss the calves.

- **Bowing.**

1Ki 19:18 — Yet I have left *me* seven thousand in Israel, all the knees which have not bowed unto Baal, and every mouth which hath not kissed him.

2Ki 5:18 — In this thing the LORD pardon thy servant, *that* when my master goeth into the house of Rimmon to worship there, and he leaneth on my hand, and I bow myself in the house of Rimmon: when I bow down myself in the house of Rimmon, the LORD pardon thy servant in this thing.

- **Tithes and gifts.**

Am 4:4–5

2Ki 23:11 — And he took away the horses that the kings of Judah had given to the sun, at the entering in of the house of the LORD, by the chamber of Nathanmelech the chamberlain, which *was* in the suburbs, and burned the chariots of the sun with fire.

Da 11:38 — But in his estate shall he honour the God of forces: and a god whom his fathers knew not shall he honour with gold, and silver, and with precious stones, and pleasant things.

- **Annual feasts.**

Eze 18:11–12; Da 3:2–3

1Ki 12:32 — And Jeroboam ordained a feast in the eighth month, on the fifteenth day of the month, like unto the feast that *is* in Judah, and he offered upon the altar. So did he in Bethel, sacrificing unto the calves that he had made: and he placed in Bethel the priests of the high places which he had made.

Eze 18:6 — *And* hath not eaten upon the mountains, neither hath lifted up his eyes to the idols of the house of Israel, neither hath defiled his neighbour's wife, neither hath come near to a menstruous woman,

Eze 18:15 — *That* hath not eaten upon the mountains, neither hath lifted up his eyes to the idols of the house of Israel, hath not defiled his neighbour's wife,

Eze 22:9 — In thee are men that carry tales to shed blood: and in thee they eat upon the mountains: in the midst of thee they commit lewdness.

- **Objects of.**
  - **Sun, moon, and stars.**

Job 31:26–28; Jer 7:17–20; Eze 8:15–16; Zep 1:4–5

Dt 4:19 — And lest thou lift up thine eyes unto heaven, and when thou seest the sun, and the moon, and the stars, *even* all the host of heaven, shouldest be driven to worship them, and serve them, which the LORD thy God hath divided unto all nations under the whole heaven.

2Ki 17:16 — And they left all the commandments of the LORD their God, and made them molten images, *even* two calves, and made a grove, and worshipped all the host of heaven, and served Baal.

2Ki 21:3 — For he built up again the high places which Hezekiah his father had destroyed; and he reared up altars for Baal, and made a grove, as did Ahab king of Israel; and worshipped all the host of heaven, and served them.

2Ki 21:5 — And he built altars for all the host of heaven in the two courts of the house of the LORD.

2Ch 33:3 — For he built again the high places which Hezekiah his father had broken down, and he reared up altars for Baalim, and made groves, and worshipped all the host of heaven, and served them.

2Ch 33:5 — And he built altars for all the host of heaven in the two courts of the house of the LORD.

Jer 8:2 — And they shall spread them before the sun, and the moon, and all the host of heaven, whom they have loved, and whom they have served, and after whom they have walked, and whom they have sought, and whom they have worshipped: they shall not be gathered, nor be buried; they shall be for dung upon the face of the earth.

Ac 7:42 — Then God turned, and gave them up to worship the host of heaven; as it is written in the book of the prophets, O ye house of Israel, have ye offered to me slain beasts and sacrifices *by the space of* forty years in the wilderness?

• Images of angels.

Col 2:18 — Let no man beguile you of your reward in a voluntary humility and worshipping of angels, intruding into those things which he hath not seen, vainly puffed up by his fleshly mind,

• Images of animals.

Ro 1:23 — And changed the glory of the uncorruptible God into an image made like to corruptible man, and to birds, and fourfooted beasts, and creeping things.

• Gods of Egypt.

Ex 12:12 — For I will pass through the land of Egypt this night, and will smite all the firstborn in the land of Egypt, both man and beast; and against all the gods of Egypt I will execute judgment: I *am* the LORD.

• Golden calf.

Ex 32:4 — And he received *them* at their hand, and fashioned it with a graving tool, after he had made it a molten calf: and they said, These *be* thy gods, O Israel, which brought thee up out of the land of Egypt.

• Brazen serpent.

2Ki 18:4 — He removed the high places, and brake the images, and cut down the groves, and brake in pieces the brasen serpent that Moses had made: for unto those days the children of Israel did burn incense to it: and he called it Nehushtan.

• Net and drag.

Hab 1:16 — Therefore they sacrifice unto their net, and burn incense unto their drag; because by them their portion *is* fat, and their meat plenteous.

• Pictures.

Nu 33:52 — Then ye shall drive out all the inhabitants of the land from before you, and destroy all their pictures, and destroy all their molten images, and quite pluck down all their high places:

Isa 2:16 — And upon all the ships of Tarshish, and upon all pleasant pictures.

• Pictures on walls.

Eze 8:10 — So I went in and saw; and behold every form of creeping things, and abominable beasts, and all the idols of the house of Israel, pourtrayed upon the wall round about.

• Earrings.

Ge 35:4 — And they gave unto Jacob all the strange gods which *were* in their hand, and *all their* earrings which *were* in their ears; and Jacob hid them under the oak which *was* by Shechem.

See: Shrine

• Denunciations against.

Ex 20:3–6; Dt 4:15–23, 25–28; 5:7–9; 11:16–17; 16:21–22; 28:15–68; 30:17–18; 31:16–21; 32:15–26; 1Ki 9:6–9; Job 31:26–28; Ps 44:20–21; 1Co 6:9–10; 8:1–13; 10:20–22

Ge 35:2 — Then Jacob said unto his household, and to all that *were* with him, Put away the strange gods that *are* among you, and be clean, and change your garments:

Ex 20:23 — Ye shall not make with me gods of silver, neither shall ye make unto you gods of gold.

Ex 23:13 — And in all *things* that I have said unto you be circumspect: and make no mention of the name of other gods, neither let it be heard out of thy mouth.

Ex 34:17 — Thou shalt make thee no molten gods.

Le 19:4 — Turn ye not unto idols, nor make to yourselves molten gods: I *am* the LORD your God.

Le 26:1 — Ye shall make you no idols nor graven image, neither rear you up a standing image, neither shall ye set up *any* image of stone in your land, to bow down unto it: for I *am* the LORD your God.

Le 26:30 — And I will destroy your high places, and cut down your images, and cast your carcases upon the carcases of your idols, and my soul shall abhor you.

Dt 11:28 — And a curse, if ye will not obey the commandments of the LORD your God, but turn aside out of the way which I command you this day, to go after other gods, which ye have not known.

Dt 12:31 — Thou shalt not do so unto the LORD thy God: for every abomination to the LORD, which he hateth, have they done unto their gods; for even their sons and their daughters they have burnt in the fire to their gods.

Dt 27:15 — Cursed *be* the man that maketh *any* graven or molten image, an abomination unto the LORD, the work of the hands of the craftsman, and putteth *it* in *a* secret *place.* And all the people shall answer and say, Amen.

Dt 31:29 — For I know that after my death ye will utterly corrupt *yourselves,* and turn aside from the way which I have commanded you; and evil will befall you in the latter days; because ye will do evil in the sight of the LORD, to provoke him to anger through the work of your hands.

1Sa 15:23 — For rebellion *is as* the sin of witchcraft, and stubbornness *is as* iniquity and idolatry. Because thou hast rejected the word of the LORD, he hath also rejected thee from *being* king.

Ps 16:4 — Their sorrows shall be multiplied *that* hasten *after* another *god:* their drink offerings of blood will I not offer, nor take up their names into my lips.

Ps 59:8 — But thou, O LORD, shalt laugh at them; thou shalt have all the heathen in derision.

Ps 79:6 — Pour out thy wrath upon the heathen that have not known thee, and upon the kingdoms that have not called upon thy name.

Ps 81:9 — There shall no strange god be in thee; neither shalt thou worship any strange god.

Ps 97:7 — Confounded be all they that serve graven images, that boast themselves of idols: worship him, all *ye* gods.

Isa 42:17 — They shall be turned back, they shall be greatly ashamed, that trust in graven images, that say to the molten images, Ye *are* our gods.

Isa 45:16 — They shall be ashamed, and also confounded, all of them: they shall go to confusion together *that are* makers of idols.

Joel 3:12 — Let the heathen be wakened, and come up to the valley of Jehoshaphat: for there will I sit to judge all the heathen round about.

Jnh 2:8 — They that observe lying vanities forsake their own mercy.

Mic 5:15 — And I will execute vengeance in anger and fury upon the heathen, such as they have not heard.

Hab 1:16 — Therefore they sacrifice unto their net, and burn incense unto their drag; because by them their portion *is* fat, and their meat plenteous.

Ac 15:20 — But that we write unto them, that they abstain from pollutions of idols, and *from* fornication, and *from* things strangled, and *from* blood.

Ac 15:29 — That ye abstain from meats offered to idols, and from blood, and from things strangled, and from fornication: from which if ye keep yourselves, ye shall do well. Fare ye well.

Ac 17:16 — Now while Paul waited for them at Athens, his spirit was stirred in him, when he saw the city wholly given to idolatry.

Ro 1:25 — Who changed the truth of God into a lie, and worshipped and served the creature more than the Creator, who is blessed for ever. Amen.

1Co 10:7 — Neither be ye idolaters, as *were* some of them; as it is written, The people sat down to eat and drink, and rose up to play.

1Co 10:14 — Wherefore, my dearly beloved, flee from idolatry.

1Jn 5:21 — Little children, keep yourselves from idols. Amen.

Rev 21:8 — But the fearful, and unbelieving, and the abominable, and murderers, and whoremongers, and sorcerers, and idolaters, and all liars, shall have their part in the lake which burneth with fire and brimstone: which is the second death.

Rev 22:15 — For without *are* dogs, and sorcerers, and whoremongers, and murderers, and idolaters, and whosoever loveth and maketh a lie.

See: Iconoclasm

• Warnings against, and punishments of.

Dt 17:2–5; Ne 9:27–37; Ps 78:58–64; 106:34–42; Isa 1:29–31; 2:6–22; 57:3–13; 65:3–4; Jer 1:15–16; 3:1–11; 5:1–17; 7:1–8:2; 13:9–27; 16:1–17:6; 18:13–15; 19:1–15; 44:1–30; Eze 6:1–14; 8:5–9:11; 14:1–14; 16:1–63; 20:1–49; 23:1–49; 44:10–12; Hos 2:2–5; 4:12–5:3; 8:5–14; 10:1–15; 12:11–13:4; Am 4:4–5; Mic 1:1–9; 5:12–14; Zep 1:1–18; Mal 2:11–13

2Ch 28:23 — For he sacrificed unto the gods of Damascus, which smote him: and he said, Because the gods of the kings of Syria help them, *therefore* will I sacrifice to them, that they may help me. But they were the ruin of him, and of all Israel.

Isa 30:22 — Ye shall defile also the covering of thy graven images of silver, and the ornament of thy molten images of gold: thou shalt cast them away as a menstruous cloth; thou shalt say unto it, Get thee hence.

Jer 8:19 — Behold the voice of the cry of the daughter of my people because of them that dwell in a far country: *Is* not the LORD in Zion? *is* not her king in her? Why have they provoked me to anger with their graven images, *and* with strange vanities?

Jer 22:9 — Then they shall answer, Because they have forsaken the covenant of the LORD their God, and worshipped other gods, and served them.

Jer 32:35 — And they built the high places of Baal, which *are* in the valley of the son of Hinnom, to cause their sons and their daughters to pass through *the fire* unto Molech; which I commanded them not, neither came it into my mind, that they should do this abomination, to cause Judah to sin.

Jer 48:8 — And the spoiler shall come upon every city, and no city shall escape: the valley also shall perish, and the plain shall be destroyed, as the LORD hath spoken.

Eze 7:19 — They shall cast their silver in the streets, and their gold shall be removed: their silver and their gold shall not be able to deliver them in the day of the wrath of the LORD: they shall not satisfy their souls, neither fill their bowels: because it is the stumblingblock of their iniquity.

Eze 22:4 — Thou art become guilty in thy blood that thou hast shed; and hast defiled thyself in thine idols which thou hast made; and thou hast caused thy days to draw near, and art come *even* unto thy years: therefore have I made thee a reproach unto the heathen, and a mocking to all countries.

Hos 1:2 — The beginning of the word of the LORD by Hosea. And the LORD said to Hosea, Go, take unto thee a wife of whoredoms and children of whoredoms: for the land hath committed great whoredom, *departing* from the LORD.

Hos 9:10 — I found Israel like grapes in the wilderness; I saw your fathers as the firstripe in the fig tree at her first time: *but* they went to Baal-peor, and separated themselves unto *that* shame; and *their* abominations were according as they loved.

Hos 11:2 — *As* they called them, so they went from them: they sacrificed unto Baalim, and burned incense to graven images.

Hos 14:8 — Ephraim *shall say,* What have I to do any more with idols? I have heard *him,* and observed him: I *am* like a green fir tree. From me is thy fruit found.

Am 3:14 — That in the day that I shall visit the transgressions of Israel upon him I will also visit the altars of Bethel: and the horns of the altar shall be cut off, and fall to the ground.

Am 5:5 — But seek not Bethel, nor enter into Gilgal, and pass not to Beer-sheba: for Gilgal shall surely go into captivity, and Bethel shall come to nought.

Mic 6:16 — For the statutes of Omri are kept, and all the works of the house of Ahab, and ye walk in their counsels; that I should make thee a desolation, and the inhabitants thereof an hissing: therefore ye shall bear the reproach of my people.

• Prophecies relating to.

Isa 17:7–8; Eze 43:7–9

Ex 12:12 — For I will pass through the land of Egypt this night, and will smite all the firstborn in the land of Egypt, both man and beast; and against all the gods of Egypt I will execute judgment: I *am* the LORD.

Nu 33:4 — For the Egyptians buried all *their* firstborn, which the LORD had smitten among them: upon their gods also the LORD executed judgments.

Isa 2:18 — And the idols he shall utterly abolish.

Isa 2:20 — In that day a man shall cast his idols of silver, and his idols of gold, which they made *each one* for himself to worship, to the moles and to the bats;

Isa 19:1 — The burden of Egypt. Behold, the LORD rideth upon a swift cloud, and shall come into Egypt: and the idols of Egypt shall be moved at his presence, and the heart of Egypt shall melt in the midst of it.

Isa 21:9 — And, behold, here cometh a chariot of men, *with* a couple of horsemen. And he answered and said, Babylon is fallen, is fallen; and all the graven images of her gods he hath broken unto the ground.

Isa 27:9 — By this therefore shall the iniquity of Jacob be purged; and this is all the fruit to take away his sin; when he maketh all the stones of the altar as chalkstones that are beaten in sunder, the groves and images shall not stand up.

Isa 31:7 — For in that day every man shall cast away his idols of silver, and his idols of gold, which your own hands have made unto you *for* a sin.

Jer 10:11 — Thus shall ye say unto them, The gods that have not made the heavens and the earth, *even* they shall perish from the earth, and from under these heavens.

Jer 10:15 — They *are* vanity, *and* the work of errors: in the time of their visitation they shall perish.

Jer 51:44 — And I will punish Bel in Babylon, and I will bring forth out of his mouth that which he hath swallowed up: and the nations shall not flow together any more unto him: yea, the wall of Babylon shall fall.

Jer 51:47 — Therefore, behold, the days come, that I will do judgment upon the graven images of Babylon: and her whole land shall be confounded, and all her slain shall fall in the midst of her.

Jer 51:52 — Wherefore, behold, the days come, saith the LORD, that I will do judgment upon her graven images: and through all her land the wounded shall groan.

Hos 10:2 — Their heart is divided; now shall they be found faulty: he shall break down their altars, he shall spoil their images.

Mic 5:13 — Thy graven images also will I cut off, and thy standing images out of the midst of thee; and thou shalt no more worship the work of thine hands.

Zep 2:11 — The LORD *will be* terrible unto them: for he will famish all the gods of the earth; and *men* shall worship him, every one from his place, *even* all the isles of the heathen.

Zec 13:2 — And it shall come to pass in that day, saith the LORD of hosts, *that* I will cut off the names of the idols out of the land, and they shall no more be remembered: and also I will cause the prophets and the unclean spirit to pass out of the land.

• Folly of.

Dt 32:37–38; 1Sa 5:3–4; 2Ch 28:22–23; Ps 115:4–5; 135:15–18; Isa 40:12–26; 41:23–24, 26–29; 44:9–20; 46:1–2, 6–7; 47:12–15; Jer 10:3–16; 16:19–20; Hos 8:5–6; Hab 2:18–19; Ac 17:22–23; Ro 1:22–23; 1Co 8:4–5

Ex 32:20 — And he took the calf which they had made, and burnt *it* in the fire, and ground *it* to powder, and strawed *it* upon the water, and made the children of Israel drink *of it.*

Dt 4:28 — And there ye shall serve gods, the work of men's hands, wood and stone, which neither see, nor hear, nor eat, nor smell.

Jgs 6:31 — And Joash said unto all that stood against him, Will ye plead for Baal? will ye save him? he that will plead for him, let him be put to death whilst *it is yet* morning: if he *be* a god, let him plead for himself, because *one* hath cast down his altar.

Jgs 10:14 — Go and cry unto the gods which ye have chosen; let them deliver you in the time of your tribulation.

1Sa 12:21 — And turn ye not aside: for *then should ye go* after vain *things,* which cannot profit nor deliver; for they *are* vain.

1Ki 18:27 — And it came to pass at noon, that Elijah mocked them, and said, Cry aloud: for he *is* a god; either he is talking, or he is pursuing, or he is in a journey, *or* peradventure he sleepeth, and must be awaked.

2Ki 3:13 — And Elisha said unto the king of Israel, What have I to do with thee? get thee to the prophets of thy father, and to the prophets of thy mother. And the king of Israel said unto him, Nay: for the LORD hath called these three kings together, to deliver them into the hand of Moab.

2Ki 19:18 — And have cast their gods into the fire: for they *were* no gods, but the work of men's hands, wood and stone: therefore they have destroyed them.

2Ch 25:15 — Wherefore the anger of the LORD was kindled against Amaziah, and he sent unto him a prophet, which said unto him, Why hast thou sought after the gods of the people, which could not deliver their own people out of thine hand?

Ps 96:5 — For all the gods of the nations *are* idols: but the LORD made the heavens.

Ps 106:20 — Thus they changed their glory into the similitude of an ox that eateth grass.

Ps 115:8 — They that make them are like unto them; *so is* every one that trusteth in them.

Isa 2:8 — Their land also is full of idols; they worship the work of their own hands, that which their own fingers have made:

Isa 16:12 — And it shall come to pass, when it is seen that Moab is weary on the high place, that he shall come to his sanctuary to pray; but he shall not prevail.

Isa 36:18 — *Beware* lest Hezekiah persuade you, saying, The LORD will deliver us. Hath any of the gods of the nations delivered his land out of the hand of the king of Assyria?

Isa 37:19 — And have cast their gods into the fire: for they *were* no gods, but the work of men's hands, wood and stone: therefore they have destroyed them.

Isa 43:9 — Let all the nations be gathered together, and let the people be assembled: who among them can declare this, and shew us former things? let them bring forth their witnesses, that they may be justified: or let them hear, and say, *It is* truth.

Isa 45:20 — Assemble yourselves and come; draw near together, ye *that are* escaped of the nations: they have no knowledge that set up the wood of their graven image, and pray unto a god *that* cannot save.

Isa 57:13 — When thou criest, let thy companies deliver thee; but the wind shall carry them all away; vanity shall take *them:* but he that putteth his trust in me shall possess the land, and shall inherit my holy mountain;

Jer 2:28 — But where *are* thy gods that thou hast made thee? let them arise, if they can save thee in the time of thy trouble: for *according to* the number of thy cities are thy gods, O Judah.

Jer 11:12 — Then shall the cities of Judah and inhabitants of Jerusalem go, and cry unto the gods unto whom they offer incense: but they shall not save them at all in the time of their trouble.

Jer 14:22 — Are there *any* among the vanities of the Gentiles that can cause rain? or can the heavens give showers? *art* not thou he, O LORD our God? therefore we will wait upon thee: for thou hast made all these *things.*

Jer 48:13 — And Moab shall be ashamed of Chemosh, as the house of Israel was ashamed of Bethel their confidence.

Jer 51:17 — Every man is brutish by *his* knowledge; every founder is confounded by the graven image: for his molten image *is* falsehood, and *there is* no breath in them.

Da 5:23 — But hast lifted up thyself against the Lord of heaven; and they have brought the vessels of his house before thee, and thou, and thy lords, thy wives, and thy concubines, have drunk wine in them; and thou hast praised the gods of silver, and gold, of brass, iron, wood, and stone, which see not, nor hear, nor know: and the God in whose hand thy breath *is,* and whose *are* all thy ways, hast thou not glorified:

Zec 10:2 — For the idols have spoken vanity, and the diviners have seen a lie, and have told false dreams; they comfort in vain: therefore they went their way as a flock, they were troubled, because *there was* no shepherd.

Ac 14:15 — And saying, Sirs, why do ye these things? We also are men of like passions with you, and preach unto you that ye should turn from these vanities unto the living God, which made heaven, and earth, and the sea, and all things that are therein:

Ac 17:29 — Forasmuch then as we are the offspring of God, we ought not to think that the Godhead is like unto gold, or silver, or stone, graven by art and man's device.

1Co 10:19 — What say I then? that the idol is any thing, or that which is offered in sacrifice to idols is any thing?

1Co 12:2 — Ye know that ye were Gentiles, carried away unto these dumb idols, even as ye were led.

Gal 4:8 — Howbeit then, when ye knew not God, ye did service unto them which by nature are no gods.

Rev 9:20 — And the rest of the men which were not killed by these plagues yet repented not of the works of their hands, that they should not worship devils, and idols of gold, and silver, and brass, and stone, and of wood: which neither can see, nor hear, nor walk:

IDUMEA ↞See: Edom

IFS

• Of the Bible.

↞See: Blessing; divine, contingent upon obedience

IGAL

• One of the spies sent to Canaan.

Nu 13:7 — Of the tribe of Issachar, Igal the son of Joseph.

• One of David's guards.

2Sa 23:36 — Igal the son of Nathan of Zobah, Bani the Gadite,

• Called also Joel.

1Ch 11:38 — Joel the brother of Nathan, Mibhar the son of Haggeri,

IGDALIAH • Father of Hanan.

Jer 35:4 — And I brought them into the house of the LORD, into the chamber of the sons of Hanan, the son of Igdaliah, a man of God, which *was* by the chamber of the princes, which *was* above the chamber of Maaseiah the son of Shallum, the keeper of the door:

IGEAL • Son of Shemaiah.

1Ch 3:22 — And the sons of Shechaniah; Shemaiah; and the sons of Shemaiah; Hattush, and Igeal, and Bariah, and Neariah, and Shaphat, six.

IGNORANCE

Job 11:7–8; 28:12–13, 20–21; 37:15–16; 38:1–39:30; Pr 7:6–23; 9:14–18; Ecc 6:11–12; 7:23–24; 8:6–7; Ro 8:24–26; 1Co 2:7–10; Jas 1:5–6

Job 8:9 — (For we *are but of* yesterday, and know nothing, because our days upon earth *are* a shadow:)

Job 11:12 — For vain man would be wise, though man be born *like* a wild ass's colt.

Job 36:26 — Behold, God *is* great, and we know *him* not, neither can the number of his years be searched out.

Job 36:29 — Also can *any* understand the spreadings of the clouds, *or* the noise of his tabernacle?

Job 37:5 — God thundereth marvellously with his voice; great things doeth he, which we cannot comprehend.

Job 37:19 — Teach us what we shall say unto him; *for* we cannot order *our speech* by reason of darkness.

Job 37:23 — *Touching* the Almighty, we cannot find him out: *he is* excellent in power, and in judgment, and in plenty of justice: he will not afflict.

Ps 139:6 — *Such* knowledge *is* too wonderful for me; it is high, I cannot *attain* unto it.

Pr 8:5 — O ye simple, understand wisdom: and, ye fools, be ye of an understanding heart.

Pr 19:2 — Also, *that* the soul *be* without knowledge, *it is* not good; and he that hasteth with *his* feet sinneth.

Pr 20:24 — Man's goings *are* of the LORD; how can a man then understand his own way?

Pr 22:3 — A prudent *man* foreseeth the evil, and hideth himself: but the simple pass on, and are punished.

Pr 27:1 — Boast not thyself of to morrow; for thou knowest not what a day may bring forth.

Pr 27:12 — A prudent *man* foreseeth the evil, *and* hideth himself; *but* the simple pass on, *and* are punished.

Pr 30:4 — Who hath ascended up into heaven, or descended? who hath gathered the wind in his fists? who hath bound the waters in a garment? who hath established all the ends of the earth? what *is* his name, and what *is* his son's name, if thou canst tell?

Ecc 3:11 — He hath made every *thing* beautiful in his time: also he hath set the world in their heart, so that no man can find out the work that God maketh from the beginning to the end.

Ecc 8:17 — Then I beheld all the work of God, that a man cannot find out the work that is done under the sun: because though a man labour to seek *it* out, yet he shall not find *it;* yea further; though a wise *man* think to know *it,* yet shall he not be able to find *it.*

Ecc 9:12 — For man also knoweth not his time: as the fishes that are taken in an evil net, and as the birds that are caught in the snare; so *are* the sons of men snared in an evil time, when it falleth suddenly upon them.

Ecc 11:5 — As thou knowest not what *is* the way of the spirit, *nor* how the bones *do grow* in the womb of her that is with child: even so thou knowest not the works of God who maketh all.

Jer 10:23 — O LORD, I know that the way of man *is* not in himself: *it is* not in man that walketh to direct his steps.

Jn 13:7 — Jesus answered and said unto him, What I do thou knowest not now; but thou shalt know hereafter.

Ac 1:7 — And he said unto them, It is not for you to know the times or the seasons, which the Father hath put in his own power.

Ac 17:23 — For as I passed by, and beheld your devotions, I found an altar with this inscription, TO THE UNKNOWN GOD. Whom therefore ye ignorantly worship, him declare I unto you.

Ac 17:30 — And the times of this ignorance God winked at; but now commandeth all men every where to repent:

1Co 3:19 — For the wisdom of this world is foolishness with God. For it is written, He taketh the wise in their own craftiness.

1Co 13:9 — For we know in part, and we prophesy in part.

1Co 13:12 — For now we see through a glass, darkly; but then face to face: now I know in part; but then shall I know even as also I am known.

See: Knowledge

See: Wisdom

- **Sins of.**

Ge 20:1–7; Le 4:1–35; 5:4–19; Nu 15:22–29; Ac 3:14–15; Gal 1:13–16; Eph 4:18–19; 1Ti 1:12–13

Le 22:14 — And if a man eat *of* the holy thing unwittingly, then he shall put the fifth *part* thereof unto it, and shall give *it* unto the priest with the holy thing.

Eze 3:18 — When I say unto the wicked, Thou shalt surely die; and thou givest him not warning, nor speakest to warn the wicked from his wicked way, to save his life; the same wicked *man* shall die in his iniquity; but his blood will I require at thine hand.

Eze 33:6 — But if the watchman see the sword come, and blow not the trumpet, and the people be not warned; if the sword come, and take *any* person from among them, he is taken away in his iniquity; but his blood will I require at the watchman's hand.

Eze 33:8 — When I say unto the wicked, O wicked *man,* thou shalt surely die; if thou dost not speak to warn the wicked from his way, that wicked *man* shall die in his iniquity; but his blood will I require at thine hand.

Eze 45:20 — And so thou shalt do the seventh *day* of the month for every one that erreth, and for *him that is* simple: so shall ye reconcile the house.

Hos 4:6 — My people are destroyed for lack of knowledge: because thou hast rejected knowledge, I will also reject thee, that thou shalt be no priest to me: seeing thou hast forgotten the law of thy God, I will also forget thy children.

Lk 12:48 — But he that knew not, and did commit things worthy of stripes, shall be beaten with few *stripes.* For unto whomsoever much is given, of him shall be much required: and to whom men have committed much, of him they will ask the more.

Lk 23:34 — Then said Jesus, Father, forgive them; for they know not what they do. And they parted his raiment, and cast lots.

Jn 16:2 — They shall put you out of the synagogues: yea, the time cometh, that whosoever killeth you will think that he doeth God service.

Ac 3:17 — And now, brethren, I wot that through ignorance ye did *it,* as *did* also your rulers.

1Co 2:8 — Which none of the princes of this world knew: for had they known *it,* they would not have crucified the Lord of glory.

- **Instances of punishment of sins of ignorance.**
  - **Pharaoh.**

    Ge 12:11–17
  - **Abimelech.**

    Ge 20:1–18

IIM

• An encampment of the Israelites.

Nu 33:45 — And they departed from Iim, and pitched in Dibon-gad.

• A town in the extreme south of Judah.

Jos 15:29 — Baalah, and Iim, and Azem,

IJE-ABARIM • One of the later halting places of Israel.

Nu 21:11 — And they journeyed from Oboth, and pitched at Ije-abarim, in the wilderness which *is* before Moab, toward the sunrising.

Nu 33:44 — And they departed from Oboth, and pitched in Ije-abarim, in the border of Moab.

IJON • A town of Naphtali.

1Ki 15:20 — So Ben-hadad hearkened unto king Asa, and sent the captains of the hosts which he had against the cities of Israel, and smote Ijon, and Dan, and Abel-beth-maachah, and all Cinneroth, with all the land of Naphtali.

2Ki 15:29 — In the days of Pekah king of Israel came Tiglath-pileser king of Assyria, and took Ijon, and Abel-beth-maachah, and Janoah, and Kedesh, and Hazor, and Gilead, and Galilee, all the land of Naphtali, and carried them captive to Assyria.

2Ch 16:4 — And Ben-hadad hearkened unto king Asa, and sent the captains of his armies against the cities of Israel; and they smote Ijon, and Dan, and Abel-maim, and all the store cities of Naphtali.

IKKESH • Father of Ira.

2Sa 23:26 — Helez the Paltite, Ira the son of Ikkesh the Tekoite,

1Ch 11:28 — Ira the son of Ikkesh the Tekoite, Abiezer the Antothite,

1Ch 27:9 — The sixth *captain* for the sixth month *was* Ira the son of Ikkesh the Tekoite: and in his course *were* twenty and four thousand.

ILAI • An Ahohite.

1Ch 11:29 — Sibbecai the Hushathite, Ilai the Ahohite,

ILLYRICUM

• Called also Dalmatia.

• Visited by Paul.

Ro 15:19 — Through mighty signs and wonders, by the power of the Spirit of God; so that from Jerusalem, and round about unto Illyricum, I have fully preached the gospel of Christ.

• Visited by Titus.

2Ti 4:10 — For Demas hath forsaken me, having loved this present world, and is departed unto Thessalonica; Crescens to Galatia, Titus unto Dalmatia.

IMAGE

• For idols.

See: Idolatry

• Figurative.

• Man created in, of God.

Ge 1:26–27

Ge 5:1 — This *is* the book of the generations of Adam. In the day that God created man, in the likeness of God made he him;

Ge 9:6 — Whoso sheddeth man's blood, by man shall his blood be shed: for in the image of God made he man.

Jas 3:9 — Therewith bless we God, even the Father; and therewith curse we men, which are made after the similitude of God.

• Regenerated into.

1Jn 3:1–3

Ps 17:15 — As for me, I will behold thy face in righteousness: I shall be satisfied, when I awake, with thy likeness.

Ro 8:29 — For whom he did foreknow, he also did predestinate *to be* conformed to the image of his Son, that he might be the firstborn among many brethren.

2Co 3:18 — But we all, with open face beholding as in a glass the glory of the Lord, are changed into the same image from glory to glory, *even* as by the Spirit of the Lord.

Eph 4:24 — And that ye put on the new man, which after God is created in righteousness and true holiness.

Col 3:10 — And have put on the new *man*, which is renewed in knowledge after the image of him that created him:

• Christ, of God.

Col 1:15 — Who is the image of the invisible God, the firstborn of every creature:

Heb 1:3 — Who being the brightness of *his* glory, and the express image of his person, and upholding all things by the word of his power, when he had by himself purged our sins, sat down on the right hand of the Majesty on high;

• Of jealousy.

Eze 8:3 — And he put forth the form of an hand, and took me by a lock of mine head; and the spirit lifted me up between the earth and the heaven, and brought me in the visions of God to Jerusalem, to the door of the inner gate that looketh toward the north; where *was* the seat of the image of jealousy, which provoketh to jealousy.

Eze 8:5 — Then said he unto me, Son of man, lift up thine eyes now the way toward the north. So I lifted up mine eyes the way toward the north, and behold northward at the gate of the altar this image of jealousy in the entry.

See: Idol

See: Idolatry

IMAGINATION

Dt 29:19–20; Pr 6:16–18

Ge 6:5 — And GOD saw that the wickedness of man *was* great in the earth, and *that* every imagination of the thoughts of his heart *was* only evil continually.

Ge 8:21 — And the LORD smelled a sweet savour; and the LORD said in his heart, I will not again curse the ground any more for man's sake; for the imagination of man's heart *is* evil from his youth; neither will I again smite any more every thing living, as I have done.

1Ch 28:9 — And thou, Solomon my son, know thou the God of thy father, and serve him with a perfect heart and with a willing mind: for the LORD searcheth all hearts, and understandeth all the imaginations of the thoughts: if thou seek him, he will be found of thee; but if thou forsake him, he will cast thee off for ever.

Mt 5:28 — But I say unto you, That whosoever looketh on a woman to lust after her hath committed adultery with her already in his heart.

Ro 1:21 — Because that, when they knew God, they glorified *him* not as God, neither were thankful; but became vain in their imaginations, and their foolish heart was darkened.

2Co 10:3 — For though we walk in the flesh, we do not war after the flesh:

IMLA

• Called also Imlah.

• Father of Michaiah the prophet.

2Ch 18:7–8

IMMANUEL

• A name of Jesus.

Isa 7:14 — Therefore the Lord himself shall give you a sign; Behold, a virgin shall conceive, and bear a son, and shall call his name Immanuel.

• Called Emmanuel.

Mt 1:23 — Behold, a virgin shall be with child, and shall bring forth a son, and they shall call his name Emmanuel, which being interpreted is, God with us.

See: Jesus, Names, Appellations, and Titles of

IMMER

• A family of priests.

1Ch 9:12 — And Adaiah the son of Jeroham, the son of Pashur, the son of Malchijah, and Maasiai the son of Adiel, the son of Jahzerah, the son of Meshullam, the son of Meshillemith, the son of Immer;

Ezr 2:37 — The children of Immer, a thousand fifty and two.

Ezr 10:20 — And of the sons of Immer; Hanani, and Zebadiah.

Ne 7:40 — The children of Immer, a thousand fifty and two.

Ne 11:13 — And his brethren, chief of the fathers, two hundred forty and two: and Amashai the son of Azareel, the son of Ahasai, the son of Meshillemoth, the son of Immer,

• Head of a division of priests.

1Ch 24:14 — The fifteenth to Bilgah, the sixteenth to Immer,

• Name of a man or town.

Ezr 2:59 — And these *were* they which went up from Tel-melah, Tel-harsa, Cherub, Addan, *and* Immer: but they could not shew their father's house, and their seed, whether they *were* of Israel:

Ne 7:61 — And these *were* they which went up *also* from Telmelah, Telharesha, Cherub, Addon, and Immer: but they could not shew their father's house, nor their seed, whether they *were* of Israel.

• Father of Zadok.

Ne 3:29 — After them repaired Zadok the son of Immer over against his house. After him repaired also Shemaiah the son of Shechaniah, the keeper of the east gate.

• Father of Pashur.

Jer 20:1–2

IMMORTALITY

Job 4:17–21; Ps 16:10–11; 49:7–9, 14–15; 102:24–28; 145:1–2; Isa 38:18–19; Da 12:2–3; Mt 19:16–17; Mk 12:26–27; Lk 10:25–28; 20:36–38; Jn 3:14–16; 5:39–40; 6:39–40, 50–51, 53–54; 11:25–26; 17:2–3; Ac 23:8–9; 26:7–8; Ro 6:22–23; 1Co 15:12–55; Col 1:5–6; 1Th 4:13–18; 2Th 1:7–9; 2Ti 1:9–10; Heb 11:13–16; 1Pe 1:3–5

Ge 5:24 — And Enoch walked with God: and he *was* not; for God took him.

2Sa 12:23 — But now he is dead, wherefore should I fast? can I bring him back again? I shall go to him, but he shall not return to me.

2Ki 2:11 — And it came to pass, as they still went on, and talked, that, behold, *there appeared* a chariot of fire, and horses of fire, and parted them both asunder; and Elijah went up by a whirlwind into heaven.

Ne 9:5 — Then the Levites, Jeshua, and Kadmiel, Bani, Hashabniah, Sherebiah, Hodijah, Shebaniah, *and* Pethahiah, said, Stand up *and* bless the LORD your God for ever and ever: and blessed be thy glorious name, which is exalted above all blessing and praise.

Job 14:13 — Oh that thou wouldest hide me in the grave, that thou wouldest keep me secret, until thy wrath be past, that thou wouldest appoint me a set time, and remember me!

Ps 21:4 — He asked life of thee, *and* thou gavest *it* him, *even* length of days for ever and ever.

Ps 22:26 — The meek shall eat and be satisfied: they shall praise the LORD that seek him: your heart shall live for ever.

Ps 23:6 — Surely goodness and mercy shall follow me all the days of my life: and I will dwell in the house of the LORD for ever.

Ps 31:5 — Into thine hand I commit my spirit: thou hast redeemed me, O LORD God of truth.

Ps 36:9 — For with thee *is* the fountain of life: in thy light shall we see light.

Ps 37:18 — The LORD knoweth the days of the upright: and their inheritance shall be for ever.

Ps 37:27 — Depart from evil, and do good; and dwell for evermore.

Ps 73:26 — My flesh and my heart faileth: *but* God *is* the strength of my heart, and my portion for ever.

Ps 86:12 — I will praise thee, O Lord my God, with all my heart: and I will glorify thy name for evermore.

Ps 121:8 — The LORD shall preserve thy going out and thy coming in from this time forth, and even for evermore.

Ps 133:3 — As the dew of Hermon, *and as the dew* that descended upon the mountains of Zion: for there the LORD commanded the blessing, *even* life for evermore.

Pr 14:32 — The wicked is driven away in his wickedness: but the righteous hath hope in his death.

Ecc 3:21 — Who knoweth the spirit of man that goeth upward, and the spirit of the beast that goeth downward to the earth?

Ecc 12:7 — Then shall the dust return to the earth as it was: and the spirit shall return unto God who gave it.

Isa 14:9 — Hell from beneath is moved for thee to meet *thee* at thy coming: it stirreth up the dead for thee, *even* all the chief ones of the earth; it hath raised up from their thrones all the kings of the nations.

Isa 25:8 — He will swallow up death in victory; and the Lord GOD will wipe away tears from off all faces; and the rebuke of his people shall he take away from off all the earth: for the LORD hath spoken *it.*

Isa 26:19 — Thy dead *men* shall live, *together with* my dead body shall they arise. Awake and sing, ye that dwell in dust: for thy dew *is as* the dew of herbs, and the earth shall cast out the dead.

Eze 32:31 — Pharaoh shall see them, and shall be comforted over all his multitude, *even* Pharaoh and all his army slain by the sword, saith the Lord GOD.

Mt 10:28 — And fear not them which kill the body, but are not able to kill the soul: but rather fear him which is able to destroy both soul and body in hell.

Mt 16:26 — For what is a man profited, if he shall gain the whole world, and lose his own soul? or what shall a man give in exchange for his soul?

Mt 25:46 — And these shall go away into everlasting punishment: but the righteous into life eternal.

Mk 10:30 — But he shall receive an hundredfold now in this time, houses, and brethren, and sisters, and mothers, and children, and lands, with persecutions; and in the world to come eternal life.

Lk 9:25 — For what is a man advantaged, if he gain the whole world, and lose himself, or be cast away?

Jn 3:36 — He that believeth on the Son hath everlasting life: and he that believeth not the Son shall not see life; but the wrath of God abideth on him.

Jn 6:44 — No man can come to me, except the Father which hath sent me draw him: and I will raise him up at the last day.

Jn 6:47 — Verily, verily, I say unto you, He that believeth on me hath everlasting life.

Jn 6:58 — This is that bread which came down from heaven: not as your fathers did eat manna, and are dead: he that eateth of this bread shall live for ever.

Jn 10:28 — And I give unto them eternal life; and they shall never perish, neither shall any *man* pluck them out of my hand.

Jn 14:19 — Yet a little while, and the world seeth me no more; but ye see me: because I live, ye shall live also.

Ac 20:32 — And now, brethren, I commend you to God, and to the word of his grace, which is able to build you up, and to give you an inheritance among all them which are sanctified.

Ac 26:18 — To open their eyes, *and* to turn *them* from darkness to light, and *from* the power of Satan unto God, that they may receive forgiveness of sins, and inheritance among them which are sanctified by faith that is in me.

Ro 2:7 — To them who by patient continuance in well doing seek for glory and honour and immortality, eternal life:

Gal 6:8 — For he that soweth to his flesh shall of the flesh reap corruption; but he that soweth to the Spirit shall of the Spirit reap life everlasting.

1Th 5:10 — Who died for us, that, whether we wake or sleep, we should live together with him.

2Th 2:16 — Now our Lord Jesus Christ himself, and God, even our Father, which hath loved us, and hath given *us* everlasting consolation and good hope through grace,

1Ti 4:8 — For bodily exercise profiteth little: but godliness is profitable unto all things, having promise of the life that now is, and of that which is to come.

1Ti 6:12 — Fight the good fight of faith, lay hold on eternal life, whereunto thou art also called, and hast professed a good profession before many witnesses.

1Ti 6:19 — Laying up in store for themselves a good foundation against the time to come, that they may lay hold on eternal life.

Tit 1:2 — In hope of eternal life, which God, that cannot lie, promised before the world began;

Tit 3:7 — That being justified by his grace, we should be made heirs according to the hope of eternal life.

Heb 9:15 — And for this cause he is the mediator of the new testament, that by means of death, for the redemption of the transgressions *that were* under the first testament, they which are called might receive the promise of eternal inheritance.

Heb 10:34 — For ye had compassion of me in my bonds, and took joyfully the spoiling of your goods, knowing in yourselves that ye have in heaven a better and an enduring substance.

Heb 11:5 — By faith Enoch was translated that he should not see death; and was not found, because God had translated him: for before his translation he had this testimony, that he pleased God.

Heb 11:10 — For he looked for a city which hath foundations, whose builder and maker *is* God.

1Jn 2:17 — And the world passeth away, and the lust thereof: but he that doeth the will of God abideth for ever.

1Jn 2:25 — And this is the promise that he hath promised us, *even* eternal life.

1Jn 5:13 — These things have I written unto you that believe on the name of the Son of God; that ye may know that ye have eternal life, and that ye may believe on the name of the Son of God.

Jude 1:21 — Keep yourselves in the love of God, looking for the mercy of our Lord Jesus Christ unto eternal life.

Rev 1:7 — Behold, he cometh with clouds; and every eye shall see him, and they *also* which pierced him: and all kindreds of the earth shall wail because of him. Even so, Amen.

Rev 3:4 — Thou hast a few names even in Sardis which have not defiled their garments; and they shall walk with me in white: for they are worthy.

Rev 22:5 — And there shall be no night there; and they need no candle, neither light of the sun; for the Lord God giveth them light: and they shall reign for ever and ever.

See: Resurrection

See: Righteous; promises to, expressed or implied

See: Wicked; punishment of

IMMUTABLE

Ps 102:25–27

Mal 3:6 — For I *am* the LORD, I change not; therefore ye sons of Jacob are not consumed.

IMNA • Son of Helem.

1Ch 7:35 — And the sons of his brother Helem; Zophah, and Imna, and Shelesh, and Amal.

IMNAH

• Firstborn of Asher.

1Ch 7:30 — The sons of Asher; Imnah, and Isuah, and Ishuai, and Beriah, and Serah their sister.

• A Levite.

2Ch 31:14 — And Kore the son of Imnah the Levite, the porter toward the east, *was* over the freewill offerings of God, to distribute the oblations of the LORD, and the most holy things.

IMPENITENCE

Le 23:26–29; 26:21–24; Dt 29:19–21; Ps 7:11–13; 58:3–5; 81:11–12; 106:24–25; 107:11–12; Pr 1:24–31; 28:13–14; Isa 32:9–11; 42:22–25; 46:12–13; Jer 3:7–10; 5:21–24; 6:16–17; 7:13–34; 8:4–22; 13:27–14:16; 15:6–7; 26:4–6; 35:14–17; 44:16–17; Eze 2:4–5; 3:1–11; 33:4–5; Zec 7:4–14; Mt 11:16–24; 23:37–38; 24:38–39, 48–51; Lk 13:1–3; Ro 2:4–5; Rev 2:21–22; 9:20–21

1Sa 15:23 — For rebellion *is as* the sin of witchcraft, and stubbornness *is as* iniquity and idolatry. Because thou hast rejected the word of the LORD, he hath also rejected thee from *being* king.

Job 9:2 — I know *it is* so of a truth: but how should man be just with God?

Job 9:4 — *He is* wise in heart, and mighty in strength: who hath hardened *himself* against him, and hath prospered?

Job 24:13 — They are of those that rebel against the light; they know not the ways thereof, nor abide in the paths thereof.

Job 33:14 — For God speaketh once, yea twice, *yet man* perceiveth it not.

Ps 10:3 — For the wicked boasteth of his heart's desire, and blesseth the covetous, *whom* the LORD abhorreth.

Ps 32:9 — Be ye not as the horse, *or* as the mule, *which* have no understanding: whose mouth must be held in with bit and bridle, lest they come near unto thee.

Ps 50:17 — Seeing thou hatest instruction, and castest my words behind thee.

Ps 50:21 — These *things* hast thou done, and I kept silence; thou thoughtest that I was altogether *such an one* as thyself: *but* I will reprove thee, and set *them* in order before thine eyes.

Ps 52:1 — Why boastest thou thyself in mischief, O mighty man? the goodness of God *endureth* continually.

Ps 52:7 — Lo, *this is* the man *that* made not God his strength; but trusted in the abundance of his riches, *and* strengthened himself in his wickedness.

Ps 68:21 — But God shall wound the head of his enemies, *and* the hairy scalp of such an one as goeth on still in his trespasses.

Ps 78:8 — And might not be as their fathers, a stubborn and rebellious generation; a generation *that* set not their heart aright, and whose spirit was not stedfast with God.

Ps 82:5 — They know not, neither will they understand; they walk on in darkness: all the foundations of the earth are out of course.

Ps 95:8 — Harden not your heart, as in the provocation, *and as in* the day of temptation in the wilderness:

Pr 11:3 — The integrity of the upright shall guide them: but the perverseness of transgressors shall destroy them.

Pr 15:10 — Correction *is* grievous unto him that forsaketh the way: *and* he that hateth reproof shall die.

Pr 15:32 — He that refuseth instruction despiseth his own soul: but he that heareth reproof getteth understanding.

Pr 19:16 — He that keepeth the commandment keepeth his own soul; *but* he that despiseth his ways shall die.

Pr 21:29 — A wicked man hardeneth his face: but *as for* the upright, he directeth his way.

Pr 26:11 — As a dog returneth to his vomit, *so* a fool returneth to his folly.

Pr 29:1 — He, that being often reproved hardeneth *his* neck, shall suddenly be destroyed, and that without remedy.

Ecc 8:11 — Because sentence against an evil work is not executed speedily, therefore the heart of the sons of men is fully set in them to do evil.

Ecc 8:13 — But it shall not be well with the wicked, neither shall he prolong *his* days, *which are* as a shadow; because he feareth not before God.

Isa 26:10 — Let favour be shewed to the wicked, *yet* will he not learn righteousness: in the land of uprightness will he deal unjustly, and will not behold the majesty of the LORD.

Isa 28:12 — To whom he said, This *is* the rest *wherewith* ye may cause the weary to rest; and this *is* the refreshing: yet they would not hear.

Isa 48:4 — Because I knew that thou *art* obstinate, and thy neck *is* an iron sinew, and thy brow brass;

Isa 48:8 — Yea, thou heardest not; yea, thou knewest not; yea, from that time *that* thine ear was not opened: for I knew that thou wouldest deal very treacherously, and wast called a transgressor from the womb.

Isa 57:11 — And of whom hast thou been afraid or feared, that thou hast lied, and hast not remembered me, nor laid *it* to thy heart? have not I held my peace even of old, and thou fearest me not?

Isa 65:12 — Therefore will I number you to the sword, and ye shall all bow down to the slaughter: because when I called, ye did not answer; when I spake, ye did not hear; but did evil before mine eyes, and did choose *that* wherein I delighted not.

Isa 65:15 — And ye shall leave your name for a curse unto my chosen: for the Lord GOD shall slay thee, and call his servants by another name:

Isa 66:4 — I also will choose their delusions, and will bring their fears upon them; because when I called, none did answer; when I spake, they did not hear: but they did evil before mine eyes, and chose *that* in which I delighted not.

Jer 2:25 — Withhold thy foot from being unshod, and thy throat from thirst: but thou saidst, There is no hope: no; for I have loved strangers, and after them will I go.

Jer 6:10 — To whom shall I speak, and give warning, that they may hear? behold, their ear *is* uncircumcised, and they cannot hearken: behold, the word of the LORD is unto them a reproach; they have no delight in it.

Jer 6:19 — Hear, O earth: behold, I will bring evil upon this people, *even* the fruit of their thoughts, because they have not hearkened unto my words, nor to my law, but rejected it.

Jer 11:8 — Yet they obeyed not, nor inclined their ear, but walked every one in the imagination of their evil heart: therefore I will bring upon them all the words of this covenant, which I commanded *them* to do; but they did *them* not.

Jer 12:11 — They have made it desolate, *and being* desolate it mourneth unto me; the whole land is made desolate, because no man layeth *it* to heart.

Jer 13:15 — Hear ye, and give ear; be not proud: for the LORD hath spoken.

Jer 13:17 — But if ye will not hear it, my soul shall weep in secret places for *your* pride; and mine eye shall weep sore, and run down with tears, because the LORD'S flock is carried away captive.

Jer 16:12 — And ye have done worse than your fathers; for, behold, ye walk every one after the imagination of his evil heart, that they may not hearken unto me:

Jer 17:23 — But they obeyed not, neither inclined their ear, but made their neck stiff, that they might not hear, nor receive instruction.

Jer 18:12 — And they said, There is no hope: but we will walk after our own devices, and we will every one do the imagination of his evil heart.

Jer 19:15 — Thus saith the LORD of hosts, the God of Israel; Behold, I will bring upon this city and upon all her towns all the evil that I have pronounced against it, because they have hardened their necks, that they might not hear my words.

Jer 22:21 — I spake unto thee in thy prosperity; *but* thou saidst, I will not hear. This *hath been* thy manner from thy youth, that thou obeyedst not my voice.

Jer 25:4 — And the LORD hath sent unto you all his servants the prophets, rising early and sending *them;* but ye have not hearkened, nor inclined your ear to hear.

Jer 29:19 — Because they have not hearkened to my words, saith the LORD, which I sent unto them by my servants the prophets, rising up early and sending *them;* but ye would not hear, saith the LORD.

Jer 32:33 — And they have turned unto me the back, and not the face: though I taught them, rising up early and teaching *them,* yet they have not hearkened to receive instruction.

Jer 44:10 — They are not humbled *even* unto this day, neither have they feared, nor walked in my law, nor in my statutes, that I set before you and before your fathers.

Eze 3:19 — Yet if thou warn the wicked, and he turn not from his wickedness, nor from his wicked way, he shall die in his iniquity; but thou hast delivered thy soul.

Eze 3:26 — And I will make thy tongue cleave to the roof of thy mouth, that thou shalt be dumb, and shalt not be to them a reprover: for they *are* a rebellious house.

Eze 12:2 — Son of man, thou dwellest in the midst of a rebellious house, which have eyes to see, and see not; they have ears to hear, and hear not: for they *are* a rebellious house.

Eze 20:8 — But they rebelled against me, and would not hearken unto me: they did not every man cast away the abominations of their eyes, neither did they forsake the idols of Egypt: then I said, I will pour out my fury upon them to accomplish my anger against them in the midst of the land of Egypt.

Eze 20:13 — But the house of Israel rebelled against me in the wilderness: they walked not in my statutes, and they despised my judgments, which *if* a man do, he shall even live in them; and my sabbaths they greatly polluted: then I said, I would pour out my fury upon them in the wilderness, to consume them.

Eze 20:21 — Notwithstanding the children rebelled against me: they walked not in my statutes, neither kept my judgments to do them, which *if* a man do, he shall even live in them; they polluted my sabbaths: then I said, I would pour out my fury upon them, to accomplish my anger against them in the wilderness.

Eze 33:9 — Nevertheless, if thou warn the wicked of his way to turn from it; if he do not turn from his way, he shall die in his iniquity; but thou hast delivered thy soul.

Da 9:13 — As *it is* written in the law of Moses, all this evil is come upon us: yet made we not our prayer before the LORD our God, that we might turn from our iniquities, and understand thy truth.

Hos 4:17 — Ephraim *is* joined to idols: let him alone.

Hos 5:4 — They will not frame their doings to turn unto their God: for the spirit of whoredoms *is* in the midst of them, and they have not known the LORD.

Hos 7:13 — Woe unto them! for they have fled from me: destruction unto them! because they have transgressed against me: though I have redeemed them, yet they have spoken lies against me.

Hos 7:15 — Though I have bound *and* strengthened their arms, yet do they imagine mischief against me.

Hos 11:2 — *As* they called them, so they went from them: they sacrificed unto Baalim, and burned incense to graven images.

Hos 11:7 — And my people are bent to backsliding from me: though they called them to the most High, none at all would exalt *him.*

Zec 1:4 — Be ye not as your fathers, unto whom the former prophets have cried, saying, Thus saith the LORD of hosts; Turn ye now from your evil ways, and *from* your evil doings: but they did not hear, nor hearken unto me, saith the LORD.

Mal 2:2 — If ye will not hear, and if ye will not lay *it* to heart, to give glory unto my name, saith the LORD of hosts, I will even send a curse upon you, and I will curse your blessings: yea, I have cursed them already, because ye do not lay *it* to heart.

Mal 2:17 — Ye have wearied the LORD with your words. Yet ye say, Wherein have we wearied *him?* When ye say, Every one that doeth evil *is* good in the sight of the LORD, and he delighteth in them; or, Where *is* the God of judgment?

Mt 12:42 — The queen of the south shall rise up in the judgment with this generation, and shall condemn it: for she came from the uttermost parts of the earth to hear the wisdom of Solomon; and, behold, a greater than Solomon *is* here.

Mt 12:44 — Then he saith, I will return into my house from whence I came out; and when he is come, he findeth *it* empty, swept, and garnished.

Mt 13:15 — For this people's heart is waxed gross, and *their* ears are dull of hearing, and their eyes they have closed; lest at any time they should see with *their* eyes, and hear with *their* ears, and should understand with *their* heart, and should be converted, and I should heal them.

Mt 27:4 — Saying, I have sinned in that I have betrayed the innocent blood. And they said, What *is that* to us? see thou *to that.*

Mt 27:25 — Then answered all the people, and said, His blood *be* on us, and on our children.

Mk 3:5 — And when he had looked round about on them with anger, being grieved for the hardness of their hearts, he saith unto the man, Stretch forth thine hand. And he stretched *it* out: and his hand was restored whole as the other.

Lk 7:35 — But wisdom is justified of all her children.

Lk 10:13 — Woe unto thee, Chorazin! woe unto thee, Bethsaida! for if the mighty works had been done in Tyre and Sidon, which have been done in you, they had a great while ago repented, sitting in sackcloth and ashes.

Lk 13:5 — I tell you, Nay: but, except ye repent, ye shall all likewise perish.

Lk 13:34 — O Jerusalem, Jerusalem, which killest the prophets, and stonest them that are sent unto thee; how often would I have gathered thy children together, as a hen *doth gather* her brood under *her* wings, and ye would not!

Lk 16:31 — And he said unto him, If they hear not Moses and the prophets, neither will they be persuaded, though one rose from the dead.

Ac 7:51 — Ye stiffnecked and uncircumcised in heart and ears, ye do always resist the Holy Ghost: as your fathers *did,* so *do* ye.

2Co 12:21 — *And* lest, when I come again, my God will humble me among you, and *that* I shall bewail many which have sinned already, and have not repented of the uncleanness and fornication and lasciviousness which they have committed.

Heb 3:8 — Harden not your hearts, as in the provocation, in the day of temptation in the wilderness:

Heb 12:17 — For ye know how that afterward, when he would have inherited the blessing, he was rejected: for he found no place of repentance, though he sought it carefully with tears.

Rev 2:5 — Remember therefore from whence thou art fallen, and repent, and do the first works; or else I will come unto thee quickly, and will remove thy candlestick out of his place, except thou repent.

Rev 3:3 — Remember therefore how thou hast received and heard, and hold fast, and repent. If therefore thou shalt not watch, I will come on thee as a thief, and thou shalt not know what hour I will come upon thee.

Rev 16:9 — And men were scorched with great heat, and blasphemed the name of God, which hath power over these plagues: and they repented not to give him glory.

Rev 16:21 — And there fell upon men a great hail out of heaven, *every stone* about the weight of a talent: and men blasphemed God because of the plague of the hail; for the plague thereof was exceeding great.

See: Afflictions; obduracy in

See: Backsliders

See: Blindness; spiritual

See: Infidelity

See: Obduracy

See: Unbelief

- **Instances of.**
  - **Pharaoh.**
    Ex 9:30, 34; 10:27; 14:5–9
  - **Israelites.**
    Nu 14:22–23; 2Ki 17:14; 2Ch 24:19; 36:16–17; Ne 9:16–17, 29–30; Jer 36:31
  - **Eli's sons.**
    1Sa 2:25
  - **Amaziah.**
    2Ch 25:16
  - **Manasseh.**
    2Ch 33:10
  - **Amon.**
    2Ch 33:23
  - **Zedekiah.**
    2Ch 36:12–13; Jer 37:2
  - **Jehoiakim and his servants.**
    Jer 36:22–24
  - **Belshazzar.**
    Da 5:22–23
  - **The rich young man.**
    Mt 19:22

IMPORTS

- **Of Egypt.**
  - **Spices.**
    Ge 37:25 — And they sat down to eat bread: and they lifted up their eyes and looked, and, behold, a company of Ishmeelites came from Gilead with their camels bearing spicery and balm and myrrh, going to carry *it* down to Egypt.
- **Of Jerusalem.**
  - **Horses, chariots, and linen.**
    1Ki 10:28–29

2Ch 1:16 — And Solomon had horses brought out of Egypt, and linen yarn: the king's merchants received the linen yarn at a price.

- **Gold, ivory, apes, peacocks.**

2Ch 9:21 — For the king's ships went to Tarshish with the servants of Huram: every three years once came the ships of Tarshish bringing gold, and silver, ivory, and apes, and peacocks.

- **Of Tyre.**

Eze 27:12–25

See: Commerce

See: Exports

See: Tribute

IMPORTUNITY See: Prayer

IMPOSITION OF HANDS See: Hand; imposition of hands

IMPRECATION

- **Instances of.**
  - **Ruth.** Ru 1:17
  - **Samuel.** 1Sa 3:17
  - **David.** 2Sa 1:21; 3:28–29
  - **Shimei.** 2Sa 16:5, 13

See: Prayer, miscellany of minor subtopics; imprecatory

IMPRESSION

Eph 6:1–4

2Ti 1:5 — When I call to remembrance the unfeigned faith that is in thee, which dwelt first in thy grandmother Lois, and thy mother Eunice; and I am persuaded that in thee also.

IMPRISONMENT

- **Of Joseph.**

Ge 39:20 — And Joseph's master took him, and put him into the prison, a place where the king's prisoners *were* bound: and he was there in the prison.

- **Jeremiah.**

Jer 38:6 — Then took they Jeremiah, and cast him into the dungeon of Malchiah the son of Hammelech, that *was* in the court of the prison: and they let down Jeremiah with cords. And in the dungeon *there was* no water, but mire: so Jeremiah sunk in the mire.

- **John the Baptist.**

Mt 11:2 — Now when John had heard in the prison the works of Christ, he sent two of his disciples,

Mt 14:3 — For Herod had laid hold on John, and bound him, and put *him* in prison for Herodias' sake, his brother Philip's wife.

- **Apostles.**

Ac 5:18 — And laid their hands on the apostles, and put them in the common prison.

- **Paul and Silas.**

Ac 16:24 — Who, having received such a charge, thrust them into the inner prison, and made their feet fast in the stocks.

- **Peter.**

Ac 12:4 — And when he had apprehended him, he put *him* in prison, and delivered *him* to four quaternions of soldiers to keep him; intending after Easter to bring him forth to the people.

- **Of debtors.**

Mt 5:26 — Verily I say unto thee, Thou shalt by no means come out thence, till thou hast paid the uttermost farthing.

Mt 18:30 — And he would not: but went and cast him into prison, till he should pay the debt.

See: Prison

See: Prisoners

See: Punishment

IMRAH • A chief of the tribe of Asher.

1Ch 7:36 — The sons of Zophah; Suah, and Harnepher, and Shual, and Beri, and Imrah,

IMRI

- **A man of Judah.**

1Ch 9:4 — Uthai the son of Ammihud, the son of Omri, the son of Imri, the son of Bani, of the children of Pharez the son of Judah.

- **Father of Zaccur.**

Ne 3:2 — And next unto him builded the men of Jericho. And next to them builded Zaccur the son of Imri.

INCARNATION See: Jesus, Incarnation of

INCENDIARISM See: Arson

INCENSE

- **Formula for compounding.**

Ex 30:34–35

- **Uses of.**

Ex 30:36–38

Le 16:12 — And he shall take a censer full of burning coals of fire from off the altar before the LORD, and his hands full of sweet incense beaten small, and bring *it* within the vail:

Nu 16:17 — And take every man his censer, and put incense in them, and bring ye before the LORD every man his censer, two hundred and fifty censers; thou also, and Aaron, each *of you* his censer.

Nu 16:40 — *To be* a memorial unto the children of Israel, that no stranger, which is not of the seed of Aaron, come near to offer incense before the LORD; that he be not as Korah, and as his company: as the LORD said to him by the hand of Moses.

Nu 16:46 — And Moses said unto Aaron, Take a censer, and put fire therein from off the altar, and put on incense, and go quickly unto the congregation, and make an atonement for them: for there is wrath gone out from the LORD; the plague is begun.

Dt 33:10 — They shall teach Jacob thy judgments, and Israel thy law: they shall put incense before thee, and whole burnt sacrifice upon thine altar.

• Compounded by Bezaleel.

Ex 37:29 — And he made the holy anointing oil, and the pure incense of sweet spices, according to the work of the apothecary.

• Compounded by priests.

1Ch 9:30 — And *some* of the sons of the priests made the ointment of the spices.

• Offered morning and evening.

Ex 30:7–8

2Ch 13:11 — And they burn unto the LORD every morning and every evening burnt sacrifices and sweet incense: the shewbread also *set they in order* upon the pure table; and the candlestick of gold with the lamps thereof, to burn every evening: for we keep the charge of the LORD our God; but ye have forsaken him.

• Offered on the golden altar.

Ex 30:1–7

Ex 40:5 — And thou shalt set the altar of gold for the incense before the ark of the testimony, and put the hanging of the door to the tabernacle.

Ex 40:27 — And he burnt sweet incense thereon; as the LORD commanded Moses.

2Ch 2:4 — Behold, I build an house to the name of the LORD my God, to dedicate *it* to him, *and* to burn before him sweet incense, and for the continual shewbread, and for the burnt offerings morning and evening, on the sabbaths, and on the new moons, and on the solemn feasts of the LORD our God. This *is an ordinance* for ever to Israel.

2Ch 32:12 — Hath not the same Hezekiah taken away his high places and his altars, and commanded Judah and Jerusalem, saying, Ye shall worship before one altar, and burn incense upon it?

• Offered in making atonement.

Le 16:12–13; Nu 16:46–47

Lk 1:10 — And the whole multitude of the people were praying without at the time of incense.

• Unlawfully offered by.

• Nadab and Abihu.

Le 10:1–2

• Korah, Dathan, and Abiram.

Nu 16:16–35

• Uzziah.

2Ch 26:16–21

• Offered in idolatrous worship.

1Ki 12:33 — So he offered upon the altar which he had made in Bethel the fifteenth day of the eighth month, *even* in the month which he had devised of his own heart; and ordained a feast unto the children of Israel: and he offered upon the altar, and burnt incense.

Jer 41:5 — That there came certain from Shechem, from Shiloh, and from Samaria, *even* fourscore men, having their beards shaven, and their clothes rent, and having cut themselves, with offerings and incense in their hand, to bring *them* to the house of the LORD.

Eze 8:11 — And there stood before them seventy men of the ancients of the house of Israel, and in the midst of them stood Jaazaniah the son of Shaphan, with every man his censer in his hand; and a thick cloud of incense went up.

• Presented by the wise men to Jesus.

Mt 2:11 — And when they were come into the house, they saw the young child with Mary his mother, and fell down, and worshipped him: and when they had opened their treasures, they presented unto him gifts; gold, and frankincense, and myrrh.

→See: Altar; of incense

• Figurative.

• Of prayer.

Ps 141:2 — Let my prayer be set forth before thee *as* incense; *and* the lifting up of my hands *as* the evening sacrifice.

• Of praise.

Mal 1:11 — For from the rising of the sun even unto the going down of the same my name *shall be* great among the Gentiles; and in every place incense *shall be* offered unto my name, and a pure offering: for my name *shall be* great among the heathen, saith the LORD of hosts.

• Of acceptable sacrifice.

Eph 5:2 — And walk in love, as Christ also hath loved us, and hath given himself for us an offering and a sacrifice to God for a sweetsmelling savour.

• Symbolic.

• Of the prayers of saints.

Rev 8:3–4

Rev 5:8 — And when he had taken the book, the four beasts and four *and* twenty elders fell down before the Lamb, having every one of them harps, and golden vials full of odours, which are the prayers of saints.

INCEST

• Defined and forbidden.

Le 18:6–18; 20:11–12, 19–21; Dt 27:22–23

Le 20:17 — And if a man shall take his sister, his father's daughter, or his mother's daughter, and see her nakedness, and she see his nakedness; it *is* a wicked thing; and they shall be cut off in the sight of their people: he hath uncovered his sister's nakedness; he shall bear his iniquity.

Dt 22:30 — A man shall not take his father's wife, nor discover his father's skirt.

Dt 27:20 — Cursed *be* he that lieth with his father's wife; because he uncovereth his father's skirt. And all the people shall say, Amen.

Eze 22:11 — And one hath committed abomination with his neighbour's wife; and another hath lewdly defiled his daughter in law; and another in thee hath humbled his sister, his father's daughter.

1Co 5:1 — It is reported commonly *that there is* fornication among you, and such fornication as is not so much as named among the Gentiles, that one should have his father's wife.

- **Instances of.**
  - **Lot with his daughters.**
    Ge 19:31–36
  - **Abraham.**
    Ge 20:12–13
  - **Nahor.**
    Ge 11:29
  - **Reuben.**
    Ge 35:22; 49:4
  - **Amram.**
    Ex 6:20
  - **Judah.**
    Ge 38:16–18; 1Ch 2:4
  - **Amnon.**
    2Sa 13:14
  - **Absalom.**
    2Sa 16:21–22
  - **Herod.**
    Mt 14:3–4; Mk 6:17–18; Lk 3:19
  - **Israel.**
    Am 2:7
- **Instances of marriage to near kin.**
  - **Isaac with Rebekah.**
    Ge 24:15, 67
  - **Jacob with Leah and Rachel.**
    Ge 29:23, 30
  - **Rehoboam.**
    2Ch 11:18

INCINERATION ✦See: Cremation

INCONSISTENCY

Mt 7:3–5; 23:3–4; Ro 2:21–23

Ro 2:1 — Therefore thou art inexcusable, O man, whosoever thou art that judgest: for wherein thou judgest another, thou condemnest thyself; for thou that judgest doest the same things.

✦**See: Deceit**

✦**See: Deception**

✦**See: Hypocrisy**

- **Instances of.**
  - **Jehu.**
    2Ki 10:16–31
  - **The Jews**
    - **In oppressing the poor.**
      Ne 5:9
    - **In accusing Jesus of violating the Sabbath.**
      Jn 7:22–23

INDECISION

1Ki 18:21 — And Elijah came unto all the people, and said, How long halt ye between two opinions? if the LORD *be* God, follow him: but if Baal, *then* follow him. And the people answered him not a word.

Hos 10:2 — Their heart is divided; now shall they be found faulty: he shall break down their altars, he shall spoil their images.

Mt 6:24 — No man can serve two masters: for either he will hate the one, and love the other; or else he will hold to the one, and despise the other. Ye cannot serve God and mammon.

Mt 26:41 — Watch and pray, that ye enter not into temptation: the spirit indeed *is* willing, but the flesh *is* weak.

Jas 1:8 — A double minded man *is* unstable in all his ways.

Jas 4:17 — Therefore to him that knoweth to do good, and doeth *it* not, to him it is sin.

✦**See: Decision**

✦**See: Instability**

✦**See: Lukewarmness**

- **Instances of.**
  - **Moses at the Red Sea.**
    Ex 14:15
  - **Joshua at Ai.**
    Jos 7:10
  - **Esther.**
    Est 5:8
  - **Rulers, who believed in Jesus.**
    Jn 12:42
  - **Felix.**
    Ac 24:25

INDIA• Probably the eastern limit of the kingdom of Ahasuerus.

Est 1:1 — Now it came to pass in the days of Ahasuerus, (this *is* Ahasuerus which reigned, from India even unto Ethiopia, *over* an hundred and seven and twenty provinces:)

Est 8:9 — Then were the king's scribes called at that time in the third month, that *is*, the month Sivan, on the three and twentieth *day* thereof; and it was written according to all that Mordecai commanded unto the Jews, and to the lieutenants, and the deputies and rulers of the provinces which *are* from India unto Ethiopia, an hundred twenty and seven provinces, unto every province according to the writing thereof, and unto every people after their language, and to the Jews according to their writing, and according to their language.

INDICTMENTS

- **Instances of.**
  - **Naboth on charge of blasphemy.**
    1Ki 21:1–16
  - **Jeremiah of treasonable prophecy, but of which he was acquitted.**
    Jer 26:1–24
  - **Jeremiah, a second indictment.**
    Jer 37:13–15
  - **Three Hebrew captives on the charge of contumacy.**
    Da 3:1–28

• **Daniel of contumacy.**
Da 6:1–24

• **Jesus, under two charges, first, of blasphemy.**
Mt 26:61, 63–65; Mk 14:58, 61–64; Lk 22:67–71; Jn 19:7

• **Jesus, under two charges, second, of treason.**
Mt 27:11, 37; Mk 15:2, 26; Lk 23:2–3, 38; Jn 18:30, 33; 19:12, 19–22

• **Stephen for blasphemy.**
Ac 6:11 — Then they suborned men, which said, We have heard him speak blasphemous words against Moses, and *against* God.
Ac 6:13 — And set up false witnesses, which said, This man ceaseth not to speak blasphemous words against this holy place, and the law:

• **Paul.**
Ac 25:18–19, 26–27
Ac 17:7 — Whom Jason hath received: and these all do contrary to the decrees of Caesar, saying that there is another king, *one* Jesus.
Ac 18:13 — Saying, This *fellow* persuadeth men to worship God contrary to the law.
Ac 24:5 — For we have found this man *a* pestilent *fellow,* and a mover of sedition among all the Jews throughout the world, and a ringleader of the sect of the Nazarenes:

• **Paul and Silas.**
Ac 16:20–21

• **Indictment quashed.**
Ac 18:14–16

INDUSTRY

Pr 10:4–5; 27:23–27; 30:25–28; 31:13–27; Ecc 2:10–11, 17–22; 1Th 4:11–12; 2Th 3:10–12
Ge 2:15 — And the LORD God took the man, and put him into the garden of Eden to dress it and to keep it.
Ex 23:12 — Six days thou shalt do thy work, and on the seventh day thou shalt rest: that thine ox and thine ass may rest, and the son of thy handmaid, and the stranger, may be refreshed.
Ex 35:2 — Six days shall work be done, but on the seventh day there shall be to you an holy day, a sabbath of rest to the LORD: whosoever doeth work therein shall be put to death.
Dt 5:13 — Six days thou shalt labour, and do all thy work:
Pr 12:11 — He that tilleth his land shall be satisfied with bread: but he that followeth vain *persons is* void of understanding.
Pr 12:24 — The hand of the diligent shall bear rule: but the slothful shall be under tribute.
Pr 12:27 — The slothful *man* roasteth not that which he took in hunting: but the substance of a diligent man *is* precious.
Pr 13:4 — The soul of the sluggard desireth, and *hath* nothing: but the soul of the diligent shall be made fat.
Pr 13:11 — Wealth *gotten* by vanity shall be diminished: but he that gathereth by labour shall increase.
Pr 13:23 — Much food *is in* the tillage of the poor: but there is *that is* destroyed for want of judgment.
Pr 14:4 — Where no oxen *are,* the crib *is* clean: but much increase *is* by the strength of the ox.
Pr 14:23 — In all labour there is profit: but the talk of the lips *tendeth* only to penury.
Pr 16:26 — He that laboureth laboureth for himself; for his mouth craveth it of him.
Pr 20:13 — Love not sleep, lest thou come to poverty; open thine eyes, *and* thou shalt be satisfied with bread.
Pr 21:5 — The thoughts of the diligent *tend* only to plenteousness; but of every one *that is* hasty only to want.
Pr 22:29 — Seest thou a man diligent in his business? he shall stand before kings; he shall not stand before mean *men.*
Pr 28:19 — He that tilleth his land shall have plenty of bread: but he that followeth after vain *persons* shall have poverty enough.
Ecc 1:3 — What profit hath a man of all his labour which he taketh under the sun?
Ecc 9:10 — Whatsoever thy hand findeth to do, do *it* with thy might; for *there is* no work, nor device, nor knowledge, nor wisdom, in the grave, whither thou goest.
Ecc 11:4 — He that observeth the wind shall not sow; and he that regardeth the clouds shall not reap.
Ecc 11:6 — In the morning sow thy seed, and in the evening withhold not thine hand: for thou knowest not whether shall prosper, either this or that, or whether they both *shall be* alike good.
Ro 12:11 — Not slothful in business; fervent in spirit; serving the Lord;
Eph 4:28 — Let him that stole steal no more: but rather let him labour, working with *his* hands the thing which is good, that he may have to give to him that needeth.
1Ti 5:8 — But if any provide not for his own, and specially for those of his own house, he hath denied the faith, and is worse than an infidel.

See: Frugality
See: Idleness
See: Slothfulness

• **Instances of.**

• **Jeroboam.**
1Ki 11:28

• **Paul.**
Ac 18:3; 20:33–34; 2Th 3:8

INFANTICIDE

Ex 1:15–16; Mt 2:16–18
Ac 7:19 — The same dealt subtilly with our kindred, and evil entreated our fathers, so that they cast out their young children, to the end they might not live.

INFANTS See: Children

INFIDELITY

Ex 14:11–12; Nu 14:27–34; 15:30–31; Dt 29:19–21; 2Ki 2:23–24; 2Ch 32:15–19; Job 15:25–26; 21:14–15; 22:13–14; 34:17–19; Ps 12:3–4; 78:19–22; 94:7–9; 106:24–25; 107:11–12; Isa 5:18–19, 24–25; 28:9–10, 14–15;, 17–22; 29:15–16; 45:9–10; 47:10–11; 57:4–11; Eze 9:9–10; Da 11:36–37; Am 7:16–17; Mal 3:13–14; Mt 25:24–27; 27:39–44; Ro 9:20–21; 2Pe 3:3–5; Jude 1:18–19

Ge 3:1 — Now the serpent was more subtil than any beast of the field which the LORD God had made. And he said unto the woman, Yea, hath God said, Ye shall not eat of every tree of the garden?

Ge 3:4 — And the serpent said unto the woman, Ye shall not surely die:

Ex 5:2 — And Pharaoh said, Who *is* the LORD, that I should obey his voice to let Israel go? I know not the LORD, neither will I let Israel go.

Ex 16:3 — And the children of Israel said unto them, Would to God we had died by the hand of the LORD in the land of Egypt, when we sat by the flesh pots, *and* when we did eat bread to the full; for ye have brought us forth into this wilderness, to kill this whole assembly with hunger.

Ex 16:7 — And in the morning, then ye shall see the glory of the LORD; for that he heareth your murmurings against the LORD: and what *are* we, that ye murmur against us?

Ex 17:7 — And he called the name of the place Massah, and Meribah, because of the chiding of the children of Israel, and because they tempted the LORD, saying, Is the LORD among us, or not?

Nu 16:41 — But on the morrow all the congregation of the children of Israel murmured against Moses and against Aaron, saying, Ye have killed the people of the LORD.

Nu 21:5 — And the people spake against God, and against Moses, Wherefore have ye brought us up out of Egypt to die in the wilderness? for *there is* no bread, neither *is there any* water; and our soul loatheth this light bread.

Dt 32:15 — But Jeshurun waxed fat, and kicked: thou art waxen fat, thou art grown thick, thou art covered *with fatness;* then he forsook God *which* made him, and lightly esteemed the Rock of his salvation.

1Ki 20:28 — And there came a man of God, and spake unto the king of Israel, and said, Thus saith the LORD, Because the Syrians have said, The LORD *is* God of the hills, but he *is* not God of the valleys, therefore will I deliver all this great multitude into thine hand, and ye shall know that I *am* the LORD.

1Ki 22:24 — But Zedekiah the son of Chenaanah went near, and smote Micaiah on the cheek, and said, Which way went the Spirit of the LORD from me to speak unto thee?

2Ch 30:6 — So the posts went with the letters from the king and his princes throughout all Israel and Judah, and according to the commandment of the king, saying, Ye children of Israel, turn again unto the LORD God of Abraham, Isaac, and Israel, and he will return to the remnant of you, that are escaped out of the hand of the kings of Assyria.

2Ch 30:10 — So the posts passed from city to city through the country of Ephraim and Manasseh even unto Zebulun: but they laughed them to scorn, and mocked them.

2Ch 36:16 — But they mocked the messengers of God, and despised his words, and misused his prophets, until the wrath of the LORD arose against his people, till *there was* no remedy.

Job 22:17 — Which said unto God, Depart from us: and what can the Almighty do for them?

Job 34:7 — What man *is* like Job, *who* drinketh up scorning like water?

Job 34:9 — For he hath said, It profiteth a man nothing that he should delight himself with God.

Job 34:33 — *Should it be* according to thy mind? he will recompense it, whether thou refuse, or whether thou choose; and not I: therefore speak what thou knowest.

Job 35:3 — For thou saidst, What advantage will it be unto thee? *and,* What profit shall I have, *if I be cleansed* from my sin?

Job 36:23 — Who hath enjoined him his way? or who can say, Thou hast wrought iniquity?

Ps 1:1 — Blessed *is* the man that walketh not in the counsel of the ungodly, nor standeth in the way of sinners, nor sitteth in the seat of the scornful.

Ps 3:2 — Many *there be* which say of my soul, *There is* no help for him in God. Selah.

Ps 4:6 — *There be* many that say, Who will shew us *any* good? LORD, lift thou up the light of thy countenance upon us.

Ps 10:11 — He hath said in his heart, God hath forgotten: he hideth his face; he will never see *it.*

Ps 10:13 — Wherefore doth the wicked contemn God? he hath said in his heart, Thou wilt not require *it.*

Ps 14:1 — The fool hath said in his heart, *There is* no God. They are corrupt, they have done abominable works, *there is* none that doeth good.

Ps 14:6 — Ye have shamed the counsel of the poor, because the LORD *is* his refuge.

Ps 42:3 — My tears have been my meat day and night, while they continually say unto me, Where *is* thy God?

Ps 50:21 — These *things* hast thou done, and I kept silence; thou thoughtest that I was altogether *such an one* as thyself: *but* I will reprove thee, and set *them* in order before thine eyes.

Ps 53:1 — The fool hath said in his heart, *There is* no God. Corrupt are they, and have done abominable iniquity: *there is* none that doeth good.

Ps 59:7 — Behold, they belch out with their mouth: swords *are* in their lips: for who, *say they,* doth hear?

Ps 64:5 — They encourage themselves *in* an evil matter: they commune of laying snares privily; they say, Who shall see them?

Ps 73:11 — And they say, How doth God know? and is there knowledge in the most High?

Pr 1:22 — How long, ye simple ones, will ye love simplicity? and the scorners delight in their scorning, and fools hate knowledge?

Pr 3:34 — Surely he scorneth the scorners: but he giveth grace unto the lowly.

Pr 9:12 — If thou be wise, thou shalt be wise for thyself: but *if* thou scornest, thou alone shalt bear *it.*

Pr 14:6 — A scorner seeketh wisdom, and *findeth it* not: but knowledge *is* easy unto him that understandeth.

Pr 14:9 — Fools make a mock at sin: but among the righteous *there is* favour.

Pr 19:29 — Judgments are prepared for scorners, and stripes for the back of fools.

Pr 24:9 — The thought of foolishness *is* sin: and the scorner *is* an abomination to men.

Isa 3:8 — For Jerusalem is ruined, and Judah is fallen: because their tongue and their doings *are* against the LORD, to provoke the eyes of his glory.

Isa 10:15 — Shall the axe boast itself against him that heweth therewith? *or* shall the saw magnify itself against him that shaketh it? as if the rod should shake *itself* against them that lift it up, *or* as if the staff should lift up *itself, as if it were* no wood.

Isa 29:20 — For the terrible one is brought to nought, and the scorner is consumed, and all that watch for iniquity are cut off:

Jer 2:31 — O generation, see ye the word of the LORD. Have I been a wilderness unto Israel? a land of darkness? wherefore say my people, We are lords; we will come no more unto thee?

Jer 5:12 — They have belied the LORD, and said, *It is* not he; neither shall evil come upon us; neither shall we see sword nor famine:

Jer 5:14 — Wherefore thus saith the LORD God of hosts, Because ye speak this word, behold, I will make my words in thy mouth fire, and this people wood, and it shall devour them.

Jer 17:15 — Behold, they say unto me, Where *is* the word of the LORD? let it come now.

Jer 43:2 — Then spake Azariah the son of Hoshaiah, and Johanan the son of Kareah, and all the proud men, saying unto Jeremiah, Thou speakest falsely: the LORD our God hath not sent thee to say, Go not into Egypt to sojourn there:

Jer 48:26 — Make ye him drunken: for he magnified *himself* against the LORD: Moab also shall wallow in his vomit, and he also shall be in derision.

Jer 48:42 — And Moab shall be destroyed from *being* a people, because he hath magnified *himself* against the LORD.

Jer 50:24 — I have laid a snare for thee, and thou art also taken, O Babylon, and thou wast not aware: thou art found, and also caught, because thou hast striven against the LORD.

Jer 50:29 — Call together the archers against Babylon: all ye that bend the bow, camp against it round about; let none thereof escape: recompense her according to her work; according to all that she hath done, do unto her: for she hath been proud against the LORD, against the Holy One of Israel.

La 1:7 — Jerusalem remembered in the days of her affliction and of her miseries all her pleasant things that she had in the days of old, when her people fell into the hand of the enemy, and none did help her: the adversaries saw her, *and* did mock at her sabbaths.

Eze 8:12 — Then said he unto me, Son of man, hast thou seen what the ancients of the house of Israel do in the dark, every man in the chambers of his imagery? for they say, The LORD seeth us not; the LORD hath forsaken the earth.

Eze 11:3 — Which say, *It is* not near; let us build houses: this *city is* the caldron, and we *be* the flesh.

Eze 12:22 — Son of man, what *is* that proverb *that* ye have in the land of Israel, saying, The days are prolonged, and every vision faileth?

Eze 18:2 — What mean ye, that ye use this proverb concerning the land of Israel, saying, The fathers have eaten sour grapes, and the children's teeth are set on edge?

Eze 18:29 — Yet saith the house of Israel, The way of the Lord is not equal. O house of Israel, are not my ways equal? are not your ways unequal?

Eze 20:49 — Then said I, Ah Lord GOD! they say of me, Doth he not speak parables?

Eze 33:17 — Yet the children of thy people say, The way of the Lord is not equal: but as for them, their way is not equal.

Eze 33:20 — Yet ye say, The way of the Lord is not equal. O ye house of Israel, I will judge you every one after his ways.

Eze 33:30 — Also, thou son of man, the children of thy people still are talking against thee by the walls and in the doors of the houses, and speak one to another, every one to his brother, saying, Come, I pray you, and hear what is the word that cometh forth from the LORD.

Eze 36:2 — Thus saith the Lord GOD; Because the enemy hath said against you, Aha, even the ancient high places are ours in possession:

Da 3:15 — Now if ye be ready that at what time ye hear the sound of the cornet, flute, harp, sackbut, psaltery, and dulcimer, and all kinds of musick, ye fall down and worship the image which I have made; *well:* but if ye worship not, ye shall be cast the same hour into the midst of a burning fiery furnace; and who *is* that God that shall deliver you out of my hands?

Da 7:25 — And he shall speak *great* words against the most High, and shall wear out the saints of the most High, and think to change times and laws: and they shall be given into his hand until a time and times and the dividing of time.

Da 8:10 — And it waxed great, *even* to the host of heaven; and it cast down *some* of the host and of the stars to the ground, and stamped upon them.

Da 8:25 — And through his policy also he shall cause craft to prosper in his hand; and he shall magnify *himself* in his heart, and by peace shall destroy many: he shall also stand up against the Prince of princes; but he shall be broken without hand.

Hos 7:5 — In the day of our king the princes have made *him* sick with bottles of wine; he stretched out his hand with scorners.

Hos 7:13 — Woe unto them! for they have fled from me: destruction unto them! because they have transgressed against me: though I have redeemed them, yet they have spoken lies against me.

Hos 7:15 — Though I have bound *and* strengthened their arms, yet do they imagine mischief against me.

Am 5:18 — Woe unto you that desire the day of the LORD! to what end *is* it for you? the day of the LORD *is* darkness, and not light.

Mic 7:10 — Then *she that is* mine enemy shall see *it,* and shame shall cover her which said unto me, Where is the LORD thy God? mine eyes shall behold her: now shall she be trodden down as the mire of the streets.

Zep 1:12 — And it shall come to pass at that time, *that* I will search Jerusalem with candles, and punish the men that are settled on their lees: that say in their heart, The LORD will not do good, neither will he do evil.

Mal 1:7 — Ye offer polluted bread upon mine altar; and ye say, Wherein have we polluted thee? In that ye say, The table of the LORD *is* contemptible.

Mt 12:24 — But when the Pharisees heard *it,* they said, This *fellow* doth not cast out devils, but by Beelzebub the prince of the devils.

Mt 22:23 — The same day came to him the Sadducees, which say that there is no resurrection, and asked him,

Mk 3:22 — And the scribes which came down from Jerusalem said, He hath Beelzebub, and by the prince of the devils casteth he out devils.

Lk 4:23 — And he said unto them, Ye will surely say unto me this proverb, Physician, heal thyself: whatsoever we have heard done in Capernaum, do also here in thy country.

Lk 11:15 — But some of them said, He casteth out devils through Beelzebub the chief of the devils.

Lk 16:14 — And the Pharisees also, who were covetous, heard all these things: and they derided him.

Lk 19:14 — But his citizens hated him, and sent a message after him, saying, We will not have *this* man to reign over us.

Lk 19:27 — But those mine enemies, which would not that I should reign over them, bring hither, and slay *them* before me.

Ac 2:13 — Others mocking said, These men are full of new wine.

Ac 13:45 — But when the Jews saw the multitudes, they were filled with envy, and spake against those things which were spoken by Paul, contradicting and blaspheming.

Ac 17:18 — Then certain philosophers of the Epicureans, and of the Stoicks, encountered him. And some said, What will this babbler say? other some, He seemeth to be a setter forth of strange gods: because he preached unto them Jesus, and the resurrection.

Ac 17:32 — And when they heard of the resurrection of the dead, some mocked: and others said, We will hear thee again of this *matter.*

Ac 23:8 — For the Sadducees say that there is no resurrection, neither angel, nor spirit: but the Pharisees confess both.

Ro 3:5 — But if our unrighteousness commend the righteousness of God, what shall we say? *Is* God unrighteous who taketh vengeance? (I speak as a man)

Heb 10:29 — Of how much sorer punishment, suppose ye, shall he be thought worthy, who hath trodden under foot the Son of God, and hath counted the blood of the covenant, wherewith he was sanctified, an unholy thing, and hath done despite unto the Spirit of grace?

2Pe 2:1 — But there were false prophets also among the people, even as there shall be false teachers among you, who privily shall bring in damnable heresies, even denying the Lord that bought them, and bring upon themselves swift destruction.

Jude 1:4 — For there are certain men crept in unawares, who were before of old ordained to this condemnation, ungodly men, turning the grace of our God into lasciviousness, and denying the only Lord God, and our Lord Jesus Christ.

Jude 1:15 — To execute judgment upon all, and to convince all that are ungodly among them of all their ungodly deeds which they have ungodly committed, and of all their hard *speeches* which ungodly sinners have spoken against him.

See: Presumption
See: Skepticism
See: Unbelief

INFIRMITY

• Physical.

• Moses exempt from.

Dt 34:7 — And Moses *was* an hundred and twenty years old when he died: his eye was not dim, nor his natural force abated.

• Caleb.

Jos 14:11 — As yet I *am as* strong this day as *I was* in the day that Moses sent me: as my strength *was* then, even so *is* my strength now, for war, both to go out, and to come in.

See: Afflictions
See: Blindness
See: Deafness
See: Lameness
See: Old Age
See: Taste

INFLUENCE

• Evil.

1Ki 11:3–4; 15:25–26; 22:51–53; 2Ki 8:16–18, 25–27; 17:21–22; 2Ch 21:5–6; 22:3–5; Pr 22:24–25; Jer 17:1–2; Mt 13:24–25; 1Co 5:6–8; Gal 5:7–9; 2Ti 2:17–18

1Ki 21:25 — But there was none like unto Ahab, which did sell himself to work wickedness in the sight of the LORD, whom Jezebel his wife stirred up.

2Ki 21:9 — But they hearkened not: and Manasseh seduced them to do more evil than did the nations whom the LORD destroyed before the children of Israel.

2Ch 33:9 — So Manasseh made Judah and the inhabitants of Jerusalem to err, *and* to do worse than the heathen, whom the LORD had destroyed before the children of Israel.

Pr 29:12 — If a ruler hearken to lies, all his servants *are* wicked.

Hos 4:9 — And there shall be, like people, like priest: and I will punish them for their ways, and reward them their doings.

Lk 12:1 — In the mean time, when there were gathered together an innumerable multitude of people, insomuch that they trode one upon another, he began to say unto his disciples first of all, Beware ye of the leaven of the Pharisees, which is hypocrisy.

Gal 3:1 — O foolish Galatians, who hath bewitched you, that ye should not obey the truth, before whose eyes Jesus Christ hath been evidently set forth, crucified among you?

2Ti 2:14 — Of these things put *them* in remembrance, charging *them* before the Lord that they strive not about words to no profit, *but* to the subverting of the hearers.

Heb 12:15 — Looking diligently lest any man fail of the grace of God; lest any root of bitterness springing up trouble *you,* and thereby many be defiled;

✧See: Example

- **Instances of.**
  - **Satan over Adam and Eve.**
    Ge 3:1–5
  - **Eve over Adam.**
    Ge 3:6
- **Good.**

1Sa 19:1–6; 20:4–9; 1Ki 22:42–43; 2Ki 15:1–3, 32–34; Mt 5:13–16; Mk 4:21–22; Lk 11:33–36; 1Th 1:7–8; 1Pe 2:11–12; 3:1–2, 15–16

Jn 7:38 — He that believeth on me, as the scripture hath said, out of his belly shall flow rivers of living water.

1Co 7:16 — For what knowest thou, O wife, whether thou shalt save *thy* husband? or how knowest thou, O man, whether thou shalt save *thy* wife?

Php 2:15 — That ye may be blameless and harmless, the sons of God, without rebuke, in the midst of a crooked and perverse nation, among whom ye shine as lights in the world;

1Ti 6:1 — Let as many servants as are under the yoke count their own masters worthy of all honour, that the name of God and *his* doctrine be not blasphemed.

Heb 11:4 — By faith Abel offered unto God a more excellent sacrifice than Cain, by which he obtained witness that he was righteous, God testifying of his gifts: and by it he being dead yet speaketh.

✧See: Example

- **Instances of.**
  - **Ezra.**
    Ezr 9:1–10:1
  - **Nehemiah.**
    Ne 4:1–5:19
  - **Hezekiah.**
    2Ch 29:1–31:21
  - **Josiah.**
    2Ki 22:1–23:37; 2Ch 34:1–35:27
  - **Manasseh.**
    2Ch 33:12–19
- **Political.**

1Ki 2:13–18; 2Ki 4:12–13; Ne 6:17–19; Da 5:10–12; Mt 20:20–24

Pr 19:6 — Many will intreat the favour of the prince: and every man *is* a friend to him that giveth gifts.

Pr 29:26 — Many seek the ruler's favour; but *every* man's judgment *cometh* from the LORD.

Ac 12:20 — And Herod was highly displeased with them of Tyre and Sidon: but they came with one accord to him, and, having made Blastus the king's chamberlain their friend, desired peace; because their country was nourished by the king's *country.*

✧See: Politics, Statecraft

INGATHERING

- **Feast of.**

✧See: Tabernacles, Feast of

INGRAFTING ✧See: Grafting

INGRATITUDE

- **Of man to God.**

Nu 16:9–10; Dt 6:11–12; 8:12–14; 28:47–48; Jgs 2:10–12; 8:34–35; 10:13–14; 1Sa 8:7–8; 2Sa 12:7–9; 1Ki 16:1–3; 2Ch 26:15–16; Ps 78:16–17, 27–32; Jer 2:6–7; Eze 16:17–22; Da 5:20–21; Hos 2:8–9; Am 3:1–2; Mic 6:3–4; Lk 17:17–18

Dt 31:16 — And the LORD said unto Moses, Behold, thou shalt sleep with thy fathers; and this people will rise up, and go a whoring after the gods of the strangers of the land, whither they go *to be* among them, and will forsake me, and break my covenant which I have made with them.

Dt 32:6 — Do ye thus requite the LORD, O foolish people and unwise? *is* not he thy father *that* hath bought thee? hath he not made thee, and established thee?

Dt 32:13 — He made him ride on the high places of the earth, that he might eat the increase of the fields; and he made him to suck honey out of the rock, and oil out of the flinty rock;

Dt 32:15 — But Jeshurun waxed fat, and kicked: thou art waxen fat, thou art grown thick, thou art covered *with fatness;* then he forsook God *which* made him, and lightly esteemed the Rock of his salvation.

Dt 32:18 — Of the Rock *that* begat thee thou art unmindful, and hast forgotten God that formed thee.

Jgs 10:11 — And the LORD said unto the children of Israel, *Did* not *I deliver you* from the Egyptians, and from the Amorites, from the children of Ammon, and from the Philistines?

1Sa 10:19 — And ye have this day rejected your God, who himself saved you out of all your adversities and your tribulations; and ye have said unto him, *Nay,* but set a king over us. Now therefore present yourselves before the LORD by your tribes, and by your thousands.

1Sa 15:17 — And Samuel said, When thou *wast* little in thine own sight, *wast* thou not *made* the head of the tribes of Israel, and the LORD anointed thee king over Israel?

1Sa 15:19 — Wherefore then didst thou not obey the voice of the LORD, but didst fly upon the spoil, and didst evil in the sight of the LORD?

2Ch 12:1 — And it came to pass, when Rehoboam had established the kingdom, and had strengthened himself, he forsook the law of the LORD, and all Israel with him.

2Ch 32:25 — But Hezekiah rendered not again according to the benefit *done* unto him; for his heart was lifted up: therefore there was wrath upon him, and upon Judah and Jerusalem.

Ne 9:25 — And they took strong cities, and a fat land, and possessed houses full of all goods, wells digged, vineyards, and oliveyards, and fruit trees in abundance: so they did eat, and were filled, and became fat, and delighted themselves in thy great goodness.

Ne 9:35 — For they have not served thee in their kingdom, and in thy great goodness that thou gavest them, and in the large and fat land which thou gavest before them, neither turned they from their wicked works.

Ps 106:7 — Our fathers understood not thy wonders in Egypt; they remembered not the multitude of thy mercies; but provoked *him* at the sea, *even* at the Red sea.

Ps 106:21 — They forgat God their saviour, which had done great things in Egypt;

Isa 1:2 — Hear, O heavens, and give ear, O earth: for the LORD hath spoken, I have nourished and brought up children, and they have rebelled against me.

Jer 2:17 — Hast thou not procured this unto thyself, in that thou hast forsaken the LORD thy God, when he led thee by the way?

Jer 2:31 — O generation, see ye the word of the LORD. Have I been a wilderness unto Israel? a land of darkness? wherefore say my people, We are lords; we will come no more unto thee?

Jer 5:7 — How shall I pardon thee for this? thy children have forsaken me, and sworn by *them that are* no gods: when I had fed them to the full, they then committed adultery, and assembled themselves by troops in the harlots' houses.

Jer 5:9 — Shall I not visit for these *things?* saith the LORD: and shall not my soul be avenged on such a nation as this?

Jer 5:24 — Neither say they in their heart, Let us now fear the LORD our God, that giveth rain, both the former and the latter, in his season: he reserveth unto us the appointed weeks of the harvest.

Da 5:18 — O thou king, the most high God gave Nebuchadnezzar thy father a kingdom, and majesty, and glory, and honour:

Hos 4:7 — As they were increased, so they sinned against me: *therefore* will I change their glory into shame.

Hos 7:13 — Woe unto them! for they have fled from me: destruction unto them! because they have transgressed against me: though I have redeemed them, yet they have spoken lies against me.

Hos 7:15 — Though I have bound *and* strengthened their arms, yet do they imagine mischief against me.

Hos 11:1 — When Israel *was* a child, then I loved him, and called my son out of Egypt.

Hos 11:3 — I taught Ephraim also to go, taking them by their arms; but they knew not that I healed them.

Hos 13:6 — According to their pasture, so were they filled; they were filled, and their heart was exalted; therefore have they forgotten me.

Jn 1:11 — He came unto his own, and his own received him not.

Ro 1:21 — Because that, when they knew God, they glorified *him* not as God, neither were thankful; but became vain in their imaginations, and their foolish heart was darkened.

2Ti 3:2 — For men shall be lovers of their own selves, covetous, boasters, proud, blasphemers, disobedient to parents, unthankful, unholy,

• Of man to man.

Pr 17:13 — Whoso rewardeth evil for good, evil shall not depart from his house.

2Ti 3:2 — For men shall be lovers of their own selves, covetous, boasters, proud, blasphemers, disobedient to parents, unthankful, unholy,

• Instances of.

• Laban to Jacob.

Ge 31:1–55

• Pharaoh's butler to Joseph.

Ge 40:23 — Yet did not the chief butler remember Joseph, but forgat him.

• Israelites to Moses.

Ex 17:2–4; Nu 16:12–14

Ex 16:3 — And the children of Israel said unto them, Would to God we had died by the hand of the LORD in the land of Egypt, when we sat by the flesh pots, *and* when we did eat bread to the full; for ye have brought us forth into this wilderness, to kill this whole assembly with hunger.

• Israelites to Gideon.

Jgs 8:35 — Neither shewed they kindness to the house of Jerubbaal, *namely,* Gideon, according to all the goodness which he had shewed unto Israel.

• Shechemites.

Jgs 9:17–18

• Men of Keilah to David.

1Sa 23:5–12

• Saul to David.

1Sa 24:1–22

• Nabal.

1Sa 25:21 — Now David had said, Surely in vain have I kept all that this *fellow* hath in the wilderness, so that nothing was missed of all that *pertained* unto him: and he hath requited me evil for good.

• David to Joab.

1Ki 2:5–6

• David with the history of Joab's services to David.

⇒See: Joab

• David to Uriah.

2Sa 11:6–17

• David's companions to David.

Ps 35:11–16; 109:4–5

Ps 38:20 — They also that render evil for good are mine adversaries; because I follow *the thing that* good *is.*

Ps 41:9 — Yea, mine own familiar friend, in whom I trusted, which did eat of my bread, hath lifted up *his* heel against me.

• Citizens.

Ecc 9:14–16

• **Joash.**

2Ch 24:22 — Thus Joash the king remembered not the kindness which Jehoiada his father had done to him, but slew his son. And when he died, he said, The LORD look upon *it,* and require *it.*

• **Jeremiah's enemies.**

Jer 18:20 — Shall evil be recompensed for good? for they have digged a pit for my soul. Remember that I stood before thee to speak good for them, *and* to turn away thy wrath from them.

INHERITANCE

• **Provisions for inheritance under Levirate marriages.**

Ge 38:7–11; Nu 36:6–9; Dt 25:5–10; Ru 3:1–8; 4:7–17

• **Unclassified scripture relating to.**

Ge 21:9–11; 25:5–6; 48:21–22; Nu 27:6–11; Dt 21:15–17; Ecc 2:18–19; Jer 32:6–8; Eze 46:16–18; Lk 15:25–31; Heb 9:16–17

Ge 15:3 — And Abram said, Behold, to me thou hast given no seed: and, lo, one born in my house is mine heir.

Ge 24:36 — And Sarah my master's wife bare a son to my master when she was old: and unto him hath he given all that he hath.

1Ki 21:3 — And Naboth said to Ahab, The LORD forbid it me, that I should give the inheritance of my fathers unto thee.

2Ch 21:3 — And their father gave them great gifts of silver, and of gold, and of precious things, with fenced cities in Judah: but the kingdom gave he to Jehoram; because he *was* the firstborn.

Job 42:15 — And in all the land were no women found *so* fair as the daughters of Job: and their father gave them inheritance among their brethren.

Pr 17:2 — A wise servant shall have rule over a son that causeth shame, and shall have part of the inheritance among the brethren.

Pr 20:21 — An inheritance *may be* gotten hastily at the beginning; but the end thereof shall not be blessed.

Lk 15:12 — And the younger of them said to *his* father, Father, give me the portion of goods that falleth *to me.* And he divided unto them *his* living.

Gal 3:15 — Brethren, I speak after the manner of men; Though *it be* but a man's covenant, yet *if it be* confirmed, no man disannulleth, or addeth thereto.

See: Heir

See: Will

• **Figurative.**

Ro 8:16–17; Eph 1:11–14

Ps 37:29 — The righteous shall inherit the land, and dwell therein for ever.

Ac 20:32 — And now, brethren, I commend you to God, and to the word of his grace, which is able to build you up, and to give you an inheritance among all them which are sanctified.

Ac 26:18 — To open their eyes, *and* to turn *them* from darkness to light, and *from* the power of Satan unto God, that they may receive forgiveness of sins, and inheritance among them which are sanctified by faith that is in me.

Tit 3:7 — That being justified by his grace, we should be made heirs according to the hope of eternal life.

Heb 1:14 — Are they not all ministering spirits, sent forth to minister for them who shall be heirs of salvation?

See: Firstborn

See: Heir

See: Will

INHOSPITABLENESS

• **Instances of.**

• **Toward the Israelites.**

• **Edom.**

Nu 20:18–21

• **Sihon.**

Nu 21:22–23

• **Ammonites and Moabites.**

Dt 23:3–6

• **Men of Gibeah toward a Levite.**

Jgs 19:15 — And they turned aside thither, to go in *and* to lodge in Gibeah: and when he went in, he sat him down in a street of the city: for *there was* no man that took them into his house to lodging.

• **Nabal toward David.**

1Sa 25:10–17

• **Samaritans toward Jesus.**

Lk 9:53 — And they did not receive him, because his face was as though he would go to Jerusalem.

See: Hospitality

INJUSTICE

Ex 22:21–22; 23:1–3, 6–7; Le 19:35–36; Dt 16:19–20; 24:17–18; Job 16:16–17; Job 31:13–15; Pr 31:4–5; Jer 22:3–5; La 3:34–36; Am 5:11–12

Le 19:15 — Ye shall do no unrighteousness in judgment: thou shalt not respect the person of the poor, nor honour the person of the mighty: *but* in righteousness shalt thou judge thy neighbour.

Dt 27:19 — Cursed *be* he that perverteth the judgment of the stranger, fatherless, and widow. And all the people shall say, Amen.

Ps 12:5 — For the oppression of the poor, for the sighing of the needy, now will I arise, saith the LORD; I will set *him* in safety *from him that* puffeth at him.

Ps 43:1 — Judge me, O God, and plead my cause against an ungodly nation: O deliver me from the deceitful and unjust man.

Ps 82:2 — How long will ye judge unjustly, and accept the persons of the wicked? Selah.

Pr 11:7 — When a wicked man dieth, *his* expectation shall perish: and the hope of unjust *men* perisheth.

Pr 17:15 — He that justifieth the wicked, and he that condemneth the just, even they both *are* abomination to the LORD.

Pr 28:8 — He that by usury and unjust gain increaseth his substance, he shall gather it for him that will pity the poor.

Pr 29:27 — An unjust man *is* an abomination to the just: and *he that is* upright in the way *is* abomination to the wicked.

Ecc 3:16 — And moreover I saw under the sun the place of judgment, *that* wickedness *was* there; and the place of righteousness, *that* iniquity *was* there.

Ecc 5:8 — If thou seest the oppression of the poor, and violent perverting of judgment and justice in a province, marvel not at the matter: for *he that is* higher than the highest regardeth; and *there be* higher than they.

Isa 26:10 — Let favour be shewed to the wicked, *yet* will he not learn righteousness: in the land of uprightness will he deal unjustly, and will not behold the majesty of the LORD.

Zep 3:5 — The just LORD *is* in the midst thereof; he will not do iniquity: every morning doth he bring his judgment to light, he faileth not; but the unjust knoweth no shame.

Lk 3:14 — And the soldiers likewise demanded of him, saying, And what shall we do? And he said unto them, Do violence to no man, neither accuse *any* falsely; and be content with your wages.

Lk 16:10 — He that is faithful in that which is least is faithful also in much: and he that is unjust in the least is unjust also in much.

1Th 4:7 — For God hath not called us unto uncleanness, but unto holiness.

Rev 22:11 — He that is unjust, let him be unjust still: and he which is filthy, let him be filthy still: and he that is righteous, let him be righteous still: and he that is holy, let him be holy still.

See: Court

See: Dishonesty

See: Fraud

See: Justice

INK

Jer 36:18 — Then Baruch answered them, He pronounced all these words unto me with his mouth, and I wrote *them* with ink in the book.

2Co 3:3 — *Forasmuch as ye are* manifestly declared to be the epistle of Christ ministered by us, written not with ink, but with the Spirit of the living God; not in tables of stone, but in fleshy tables of the heart.

2Jn 1:12 — Having many things to write unto you, I would not *write* with paper and ink: but I trust to come unto you, and speak face to face, that our joy may be full.

3Jn 1:13 — I had many things to write, but I will not with ink and pen write unto thee:

INKHORN

Eze 9:2–3

Eze 9:11 — And, behold, the man clothed with linen, which *had* the inkhorn by his side, reported the matter, saying, I have done as thou hast commanded me.

INN

Ge 42:27 — And as one of them opened his sack to give his ass provender in the inn, he espied his money; for, behold, it *was* in his sack's mouth.

Ge 43:21 — And it came to pass, when we came to the inn, that we opened our sacks, and, behold, *every* man's money *was* in the mouth of his sack, our money in full weight: and we have brought it again in our hand.

Ex 4:24 — And it came to pass by the way in the inn, that the LORD met him, and sought to kill him.

Lk 2:7 — And she brought forth her firstborn son, and wrapped him in swaddling clothes, and laid him in a manger; because there was no room for them in the inn.

Lk 10:34 — And went to *him,* and bound up his wounds, pouring in oil and wine, and set him on his own beast, and brought him to an inn, and took care of him.

INNOCENCY

• Signified by washing the hands.

Dt 21:6 — And all the elders of that city, *that are* next unto the slain *man,* shall wash their hands over the heifer that is beheaded in the valley:

Ps 26:6 — I will wash mine hands in innocency: so will I compass thine altar, O LORD:

Mt 27:24 — When Pilate saw that he could prevail nothing, but *that* rather a tumult was made, he took water, and washed *his* hands before the multitude, saying, I am innocent of the blood of this just person: see ye *to it.*

• Found in Daniel.

Da 6:22 — My God hath sent his angel, and hath shut the lions' mouths, that they have not hurt me: forasmuch as before him innocency was found in me; and also before thee, O king, have I done no hurt.

• Found in Jeremiah.

Jer 2:35 — Yet thou sayest, Because I am innocent, surely his anger shall turn from me. Behold, I will plead with thee, because thou sayest, I have not sinned.

• Professed by Pilate.

Mt 27:24 — When Pilate saw that he could prevail nothing, but *that* rather a tumult was made, he took water, and washed *his* hands before the multitude, saying, I am innocent of the blood of this just person: see ye *to it.*

• Contrasted with guilt, compare.

Ge 3:7–11

Ge 2:25 — And they were both naked, the man and his wife, and were not ashamed.

INNUENDO

Ps 35:19 — Let not them that are mine enemies wrongfully rejoice over me: *neither* let them wink with the eye that hate me without a cause.

Pr 6:13 — He winketh with his eyes, he speaketh with his feet, he teacheth with his fingers;

Pr 10:10 — He that winketh with the eye causeth sorrow: but a prating fool shall fall.

See: Accusation, False

INQUEST

Dt 21:1–9

INSANITY

Pr 26:18 — As a mad *man* who casteth firebrands, arrows, and death,

• Feigned by David.

1Sa 21:13–15

• Sent as a judgment from God.

Dt 28:28 — The LORD shall smite thee with madness, and blindness, and astonishment of heart:

Zec 12:4 — In that day, saith the LORD, I will smite every horse with astonishment, and his rider with madness: and I will open mine eyes upon the house of Judah, and will smite every horse of the people with blindness.

• Nebuchadnezzar's.

Da 4:32–34

• Jesus accused of.

Mk 3:21 — And when his friends heard *of it,* they went out to lay hold on him: for they said, He is beside himself.

Jn 10:20 — And many of them said, He hath a devil, and is mad; why hear ye him?

• Paul.

Ac 26:24–25

• Cured by Jesus.

Mt 4:24 — And his fame went throughout all Syria: and they brought unto him all sick people that were taken with divers diseases and torments, and those which were possessed with devils, and those which were lunatick, and those that had the palsy; and he healed them.

Mt 17:15 — Lord, have mercy on my son: for he is lunatick, and sore vexed: for ofttimes he falleth into the fire, and oft into the water.

• Demoniacal: Saul.

1Sa 16:14 — But the Spirit of the LORD departed from Saul, and an evil spirit from the LORD troubled him.

1Sa 18:10 — And it came to pass on the morrow, that the evil spirit from God came upon Saul, and he prophesied in the midst of the house: and David played with his hand, as at other times: and *there was* a javelin in Saul's hand.

See: Demons; possession by, instances of

INSCRIPTIONS

• On gravestones.

2Ki 23:17 — Then he said, What title *is* that that I see? And the men of the city told him, *It is* the sepulchre of the man of God, which came from Judah, and proclaimed these things that thou hast done against the altar of Bethel.

• Over Jesus at the crucifixion.

Mt 27:37 — And set up over his head his accusation written, THIS IS JESUS THE KING OF THE JEWS.

Mk 15:26 — And the superscription of his accusation was written over, THE KING OF THE JEWS.

Lk 23:38 — And a superscription also was written over him in letters of Greek, and Latin, and Hebrew, THIS IS THE KING OF THE JEWS.

Jn 19:19 — And Pilate wrote a title, and put *it* on the cross. And the writing was, JESUS OF NAZARETH THE KING OF THE JEWS.

INSECTS

• Clean and unclean.

Le 11:21–25

Dt 14:19 — And every creeping thing that flieth *is* unclean unto you: they shall not be eaten.

See: Ant

See: Bee

See: Beetle

See: Cankerworm

See: Caterpillar

See: Flea

See: Flies

See: Grasshopper

See: Hornet

See: Horse-Leech

See: Lice

See: Locust

See: Moth

See: Palmer-Worm

See: Scorpion

See: Snail

See: Spider

See: Worm

INSINCERITY **See: Hypocrisy**

INSINUATION **See: Innuendo**

INSOMNIA

• Instances of.

• Ahasuerus.

Est 6:1

• Nebuchadnezzar.

Da 6:18

INSPIRATION

Ex 25:21–22; Nu 11:16–29; Lk 12:11–12; 21:14–15; Rev 1:10–11

Ex 19:6 — And ye shall be unto me a kingdom of priests, and an holy nation. These *are* the words which thou shalt speak unto the children of Israel.

Ex 28:3 — And thou shalt speak unto all *that are* wise hearted, whom I have filled with the spirit of wisdom, that they may make Aaron's garments to consecrate him, that he may minister unto me in the priest's office.

Ex 31:3 — And I have filled him with the spirit of God, in wisdom, and in understanding, and in knowledge, and in all manner of workmanship,

Ex 31:6 — And I, behold, I have given with him Aholiab, the son of Ahisamach, of the tribe of Dan: and in the hearts of all that are wise hearted I have put wisdom, that they may make all that I have commanded thee;

Ex 35:31 — And he hath filled him with the spirit of God, in wisdom, in understanding, and in knowledge, and in all manner of workmanship;

Ex 36:1 — Then wrought Bezaleel and Aholiab, and every wise hearted man, in whom the LORD put wisdom and understanding to know how to work all manner of work for the service of the sanctuary, according to all that the LORD had commanded.

Dt 5:31 — But as for thee, stand thou here by me, and I will speak unto thee all the commandments, and the statutes, and the judgments, which thou shalt teach them, that they may do *them* in the land which I give them to possess it.

Dt 34:9 — And Joshua the son of Nun was full of the spirit of wisdom; for Moses had laid his hands upon him: and the children of Israel hearkened unto him, and did as the LORD commanded Moses.

Job 32:8 — But *there is* a spirit in man: and the inspiration of the Almighty giveth them understanding.

Isa 51:16 — And I have put my words in thy mouth, and I have covered thee in the shadow of mine hand, that I may plant the heavens, and lay the foundations of the earth, and say unto Zion, Thou *art* my people.

Jer 1:9 — Then the LORD put forth his hand, and touched my mouth. And the LORD said unto me, Behold, I have put my words in thy mouth.

Mt 10:19 — But when they deliver you up, take no thought how or what ye shall speak: for it shall be given you in that same hour what ye shall speak.

Mk 13:11 — But when they shall lead *you*, and deliver you up, take no thought beforehand what ye shall speak, neither do ye premeditate: but whatsoever shall be given you in that hour, that speak ye: for it is not ye that speak, but the Holy Ghost.

Lk 1:15 — For he shall be great in the sight of the Lord, and shall drink neither wine nor strong drink; and he shall be filled with the Holy Ghost, even from his mother's womb.

2Ti 3:16 — All scripture *is* given by inspiration of God, and *is* profitable for doctrine, for reproof, for correction, for instruction in righteousness:

See: Prophecy

See: Prophets

See: Revelation

See: Word of God; inspiration of

INSTABILITY

Ge 49:3–4; Ex 10:8–11, 16–20; 32:8–10; Ps 106:12–13; Pr 24:21–22; Hos 6:4–5; Mt 8:19–20; 13:20–21; Mk 4:14–19; Lk 8:13–14; 9:57–62; Gal 4:9–11; Jas 1:6–8; Rev 3:15–16

Ex 8:15 — But when Pharaoh saw that there was respite, he hardened his heart, and hearkened not unto them; as the LORD had said.

Ex 8:32 — And Pharaoh hardened his heart at this time also, neither would he let the people go.

Ex 9:34 — And when Pharaoh saw that the rain and the hail and the thunders were ceased, he sinned yet more, and hardened his heart, he and his servants.

Ex 14:5 — And it was told the king of Egypt that the people fled: and the heart of Pharaoh and of his servants was turned against the people, and they said, Why have we done this, that we have let Israel go from serving us?

Ex 19:8 — And all the people answered together, and said, All that the LORD hath spoken we will do. And Moses returned the words of the people unto the LORD.

Ex 24:3 — And Moses came and told the people all the words of the LORD, and all the judgments: and all the people answered with one voice, and said, All the words which the LORD hath said will we do.

Ex 24:7 — And he took the book of the covenant, and read in the audience of the people: and they said, All that the LORD hath said will we do, and be obedient.

Jgs 2:17 — And yet they would not hearken unto their judges, but they went a whoring after other gods, and bowed themselves unto them: they turned quickly out of the way which their fathers walked in, obeying the commandments of the LORD; *but* they did not so.

1Ki 18:21 — And Elijah came unto all the people, and said, How long halt ye between two opinions? if the LORD *be* God, follow him: but if Baal, *then* follow him. And the people answered him not a word.

Pr 27:8 — As a bird that wandereth from her nest, so *is* a man that wandereth from his place.

Jer 2:36 — Why gaddest thou about so much to change thy way? thou also shalt be ashamed of Egypt, as thou wast ashamed of Assyria.

Mt 6:24 — No man can serve two masters: for either he will hate the one, and love the other; or else he will hold to the one, and despise the other. Ye cannot serve God and mammon.

Mt 12:25 — And Jesus knew their thoughts, and said unto them, Every kingdom divided against itself is brought to desolation; and every city or house divided against itself shall not stand:

Lk 17:32 — Remember Lot's wife.

Jn 5:35 — He was a burning and a shining light: and ye were willing for a season to rejoice in his light.

Gal 1:6 — I marvel that ye are so soon removed from him that called you into the grace of Christ unto another gospel:

Eph 4:14 — That we *henceforth* be no more children, tossed to and fro, and carried about with every wind of doctrine, by the sleight of men, *and* cunning craftiness, whereby they lie in wait to deceive;

Heb 13:9 — Be not carried about with divers and strange doctrines. For *it is* a good thing that the heart be established with grace; not with meats, which have not profited them that have been occupied therein.

Jas 4:8 — Draw nigh to God, and he will draw nigh to you. Cleanse *your* hands, *ye* sinners; and purify *your* hearts, *ye* double minded.

2Pe 2:14 — Having eyes full of adultery, and that cannot cease from sin; beguiling unstable souls: an heart they have exercised with covetous practices; cursed children:

Rev 2:4 — Nevertheless I have *somewhat* against thee, because thou hast left thy first love.

Rev 3:2 — Be watchful, and strengthen the things which remain, that are ready to die: for I have not found thy works perfect before God.

- **See: Backsliders**
- **See: Hypocrisy**
- **See: Indecision**

- **Instances of.**
  - **Reuben.**
    Ge 49:4
  - **Saul, in his feelings toward David.**
    1Sa 18:19
  - **David, in yielding to lust.**
    2Sa 11:2–9
  - **Solomon, in yielding to his idolatrous wives.**
    1Ki 11:1–8
  - **Ephraim and Judah.**
    Hos 6:4
  - **Lot's wife.**
    Lk 17:32
  - **Disciples of Jesus.**
    Jn 6:66
  - **Mark.**
    Ac 15:38

INSTINCT

- **Of animals.**

Pr 1:17 — Surely in vain the net is spread in the sight of any bird.

Isa 1:3 — The ox knoweth his owner, and the ass his master's crib: *but* Israel doth not know, my people doth not consider.

- **Of birds.**

Jer 8:7 — Yea, the stork in the heaven knoweth her appointed times; and the turtle and the crane and the swallow observe the time of their coming; but my people know not the judgment of the LORD.

- **See: Animals**
- **See: Birds**

INSTRUCTION

- **From nature.**
  Pr 24:30–34; Ecc 1:13–18; 3:1–4:1; Mt 6:25–30
  - **See: Parables**
- **From the study of human nature.**
  Ecc 3:1–12:14
- **By object lessons.**
  - **The pot of manna.**

Ex 16:32 — And Moses said, This *is* the thing which the LORD commandeth, Fill an omer of it to be kept for your generations; that they may see the bread wherewith I have fed you in the wilderness, when I brought you forth from the land of Egypt.

- **The pillar of twelve stones at the fords of the Jordan.**
  Jos 4:19–24
- **Fringes on the borders of garments.**
  Nu 15:38–39
- **Symbolicly wearing sackcloth and going barefoot.**
  Isa 20:2–3
- **The linen girdle.**
  Jer 13:1–11
- **Potter's vessel.**
  Jer 19:1–12
- **Basket of figs.**
  Jer 24:1–10
- **Bonds and yokes.**
  Jer 27:2–11; 28:1–17
- **Illustrations on a tile.**
  Eze 4:1–3
- **Lying on one side in public view for a long period.**
  Eze 4:4–8
- **Eating bread mixed with dung.**

Eze 4:9 — Take thou also unto thee wheat, and barley, and beans, and lentiles, and millet, and fitches, and put them in one vessel, and make thee bread thereof, *according* to the number of the days that thou shalt lie upon thy side, three hundred and ninety days shalt thou eat thereof.

Eze 4:17 — That they may want bread and water, and be astonied one with another, and consume away for their iniquity.

- **Shaving the head.**
  Eze 5:1–17
- **Moving household goods.**
  Eze 12:3–16
- **Eating and drinking sparingly.**
  Eze 12:18–20
- **Individual responsiblity.**
  Eze 18:1–32
- **Sighing.**
  Eze 21:6–7
- **The boiling pot.**
  Eze 24:1–14
- **Widowhood.**
  Eze 24:16–27
- **Two sticks joined together.**
  Eze 37:16–22
- **By symbols and parables.**
  Pr 24:30–34

- **See: Animals; clean and unclean**
- **See: Firstborn**
- **See: Parables**
- **See: Passover**
- **See: Pillar**
- **See: Purification**
- **See: Symbols and Similitudes**

• Unclassified scripture relating to.

2Ch 17:7–9; Ps 78:2–8; 119:3–125; Pr 1:1–9, 20–30; 22:17–21; 24:30–34; Da 1:3–5, 17–20; Lk 20:1–2; 21:37–38; 1Co 12:28–29; Gal 3:24–25; 4:1–2; Eph 4:11–12

2Ch 15:3 — Now for a long season Israel *hath been* without the true God, and without a teaching priest, and without law.

Ezr 7:10 — For Ezra had prepared his heart to seek the law of the LORD, and to do *it,* and to teach in Israel statutes and judgments.

Ps 50:17 — Seeing thou hatest instruction, and castest my words behind thee.

Ps 143:8 — Cause me to hear thy lovingkindness in the morning; for in thee do I trust: cause me to know the way wherein I should walk; for I lift up my soul unto thee.

Ps 143:10 — Teach me to do thy will; for thou *art* my God: thy spirit *is* good; lead me into the land of uprightness.

Pr 23:12 — Apply thine heart unto instruction, and thine ears to the words of knowledge.

Pr 23:23 — Buy the truth, and sell *it* not; *also* wisdom, and instruction, and understanding.

Jer 32:33 — And they have turned unto me the back, and not the face: though I taught them, rising up early and teaching *them,* yet they have not hearkened to receive instruction.

Ro 2:18 — And knowest *his* will, and approvest the things that are more excellent, being instructed out of the law;

• Of children.

Ex 12:26–27; 13:8–10, 14–16; Dt 4:9–10; 6:4–10; 11:18–21; 31:9–13; Ps 78:5–8

Ex 10:2 — And that thou mayest tell in the ears of thy son, and of thy son's son, what things I have wrought in Egypt, and my signs which I have done among them; that ye may know how that I *am* the LORD.

Jos 8:35 — There was not a word of all that Moses commanded, which Joshua read not before all the congregation of Israel, with the women, and the little ones, and the strangers that were conversant among them.

Ps 34:11 — Come, ye children, hearken unto me: I will teach you the fear of the LORD.

Pr 20:7 — The just *man* walketh in his integrity: his children *are* blessed after him.

Pr 22:6 — Train up a child in the way he should go: and when he is old, he will not depart from it.

Isa 38:19 — The living, the living, he shall praise thee, as I *do* this day: the father to the children shall make known thy truth.

Ac 22:3 — I am verily a man *which am* a Jew, born in Tarsus, a city in Cilicia, yet brought up in this city at the feet of Gamaliel, *and* taught according to the perfect manner of the law of the fathers, and was zealous toward God, as ye all are this day.

Eph 6:4 — And, ye fathers, provoke not your children to wrath: but bring them up in the nurture and admonition of the Lord.

Col 3:20 — Children, obey *your* parents in all things: for this is well pleasing unto the Lord.

2Ti 3:15 — And that from a child thou hast known the holy scriptures, which are able to make thee wise unto salvation through faith which is in Christ Jesus.

See: Children

• In religion.

Ex 13:11–16; Le 11:44–47; Nu 15:38–39; Dt 27:1–26; 32:1–47; Jos 4:1–11; 2Ch 17:7–9; Ne 8:7–8; Isa 28:9–10; Mt 5:1–7:29; Lk 4:16–21; 20:1–18; Ro 2:19–20

Dt 31:19 — Now therefore write ye this song for you, and teach it the children of Israel: put it in their mouths, that this song may be a witness for me against the children of Israel.

Mk 12:35 — And Jesus answered and said, while he taught in the temple, How say the scribes that Christ is the Son of David?

Lk 19:47 — And he taught daily in the temple. But the chief priests and the scribes and the chief of the people sought to destroy him,

Lk 24:27 — And beginning at Moses and all the prophets, he expounded unto them in all the scriptures the things concerning himself.

Jn 7:14 — Now about the midst of the feast Jesus went up into the temple, and taught.

Jn 8:2 — And early in the morning he came again into the temple, and all the people came unto him; and he sat down, and taught them.

Gal 6:6 — Let him that is taught in the word communicate unto him that teacheth in all good things.

Jas 5:16 — Confess *your* faults one to another, and pray one for another, that ye may be healed. The effectual fervent prayer of a righteous man availeth much.

See: Children, Commandments to; instruction of

See: Jesus, History of

See: Minister, a sacred teacher; duties of

See: School

See: Teachers

• In music.

See: Music

INSTRUMENTALITY **See: Agency**

INSTRUMENTS

• Musical.

See: Music

INSURGENTS

• Army of David's.

1Sa 22:1–2

INSURRECTION

Ps 64:2 — Hide me from the secret counsel of the wicked; from the insurrection of the workers of iniquity:

- **Described by David in.**
  Ps 55:1–23
- **Led by**
  - **Bichri.**
    2Sa 20:1–26
  - **Absalom.**
  - **See: Absalom**
  - **Barabbas.**
    Mk 15:7 — And there was *one* named Barabbas, *which lay* bound with them that had made insurrection with him, who had committed murder in the insurrection.

INTEGRITY

Dt 16:19–20; Job 27:4–6; 31:1–40; Ps 7:3–5; 15:1–5; 24:3–5; 26:1–3; 33:15–16; 73:2–22; Pr 3:3–4; 4:25–27; Eze 18:7–9; Lk 3:13–14; Col 3:22–23; Tit 1:7–8

Ge 18:19 — For I know him, that he will command his children and his household after him, and they shall keep the way of the LORD, to do justice and judgment; that the LORD may bring upon Abraham that which he hath spoken of him.

Ex 18:21 — Moreover thou shalt provide out of all the people able men, such as fear God, men of truth, hating covetousness; and place *such* over them, *to be* rulers of thousands, *and* rulers of hundreds, rulers of fifties, and rulers of tens:

2Sa 22:21 — The LORD rewarded me according to my righteousness: according to the cleanness of my hands hath he recompensed me.

Job 10:7 — Thou knowest that I am not wicked; and *there is* none that can deliver out of thine hand.

Job 13:15 — Though he slay me, yet will I trust in him: but I will maintain mine own ways before him.

Job 13:18 — Behold now, I have ordered *my* cause; I know that I shall be justified.

Job 16:17 — Not for *any* injustice in mine hands: also my prayer *is* pure.

Job 29:14 — I put on righteousness, and it clothed me: my judgment *was* as a robe and a diadem.

Ps 7:8 — The LORD shall judge the people: judge me, O LORD, according to my righteousness, and according to mine integrity *that is* in me.

Ps 17:3 — Thou hast proved mine heart; thou hast visited *me* in the night; thou hast tried me, *and* shalt find nothing; I am purposed *that* my mouth shall not transgress.

Ps 18:20 — The LORD rewarded me according to my righteousness; according to the cleanness of my hands hath he recompensed me.

Ps 26:7 — That I may publish with the voice of thanksgiving, and tell of all thy wondrous works.

Ps 56:1 — Be merciful unto me, O God: for man would swallow me up; he fighting daily oppresseth me.

Ps 69:4 — They that hate me without a cause are more than the hairs of mine head: they that would destroy me, *being* mine enemies wrongfully, are mighty: then I restored *that* which I took not away.

Ps 119:121 — I have done judgment and justice: leave me not to mine oppressors.

Pr 1:3 — To receive the instruction of wisdom, justice, and judgment, and equity;

Pr 2:2 — So that thou incline thine ear unto wisdom, *and* apply thine heart to understanding;

Pr 2:5 — Then shalt thou understand the fear of the LORD, and find the knowledge of God.

Pr 2:9 — Then shalt thou understand righteousness, and judgment, and equity; *yea,* every good path.

Pr 10:9 — He that walketh uprightly walketh surely: but he that perverteth his ways shall be known.

Pr 11:3 — The integrity of the upright shall guide them: but the perverseness of transgressors shall destroy them.

Pr 11:5 — The righteousness of the perfect shall direct his way: but the wicked shall fall by his own wickedness.

Pr 12:22 — Lying lips *are* abomination to the LORD: but they that deal truly *are* his delight.

Pr 14:30 — A sound heart *is* the life of the flesh: but envy the rottenness of the bones.

Pr 15:21 — Folly *is* joy to *him that is* destitute of wisdom: but a man of understanding walketh uprightly.

Pr 16:11 — A just weight and balance *are* the LORD'S: all the weights of the bag *are* his work.

Pr 19:1 — Better *is* the poor that walketh in his integrity, than *he that is* perverse in his lips, and is a fool.

Pr 20:7 — The just *man* walketh in his integrity: his children *are* blessed after him.

Pr 21:3 — To do justice and judgment *is* more acceptable to the LORD than sacrifice.

Pr 21:15 — *It is* joy to the just to do judgment: but destruction *shall be* to the workers of iniquity.

Pr 22:11 — He that loveth pureness of heart, *for* the grace of his lips the king *shall be* his friend.

Pr 28:6 — Better *is* the poor that walketh in his uprightness, than *he that is* perverse *in his* ways, though he *be* rich.

Pr 28:20 — A faithful man shall abound with blessings: but he that maketh haste to be rich shall not be innocent.

Jer 7:5 — For if ye throughly amend your ways and your doings; if ye throughly execute judgment between a man and his neighbour;

Jer 7:7 — Then will I cause you to dwell in this place, in the land that I gave to your fathers, for ever and ever.

Eze 18:5 — But if a man be just, and do that which is lawful and right,

Mic 6:8 — He hath shewed thee, O man, what *is* good; and what doth the LORD require of thee, but to do justly, and to love mercy, and to walk humbly with thy God?

Zec 7:9 — Thus speaketh the LORD of hosts, saying, Execute true judgment, and shew mercy and compassions every man to his brother:

Mal 2:6 — The law of truth was in his mouth, and iniquity was not found in his lips: he walked with me in peace and equity, and did turn many away from iniquity.

Lk 6:31 — And as ye would that men should do to you, do ye also to them likewise.

Lk 11:42 — But woe unto you, Pharisees! for ye tithe mint and rue and all manner of herbs, and pass over judgment and the love of God: these ought ye to have done, and not to leave the other undone.

Lk 16:10 — He that is faithful in that which is least is faithful also in much: and he that is unjust in the least is unjust also in much.
Ac 23:1 — And Paul, earnestly beholding the council, said, Men *and* brethren, I have lived in all good conscience before God until this day.
Ac 24:16 — And herein do I exercise myself, to have always a conscience void of offence toward God, and *toward* men.
Ro 9:1 — I say the truth in Christ, I lie not, my conscience also bearing me witness in the Holy Ghost,
Ro 13:5 — Wherefore *ye* must needs be subject, not only for wrath, but also for conscience sake.
Ro 14:5 — One man esteemeth one day above another: another esteemeth every day *alike*. Let every man be fully persuaded in his own mind.
Ro 14:14 — I know, and am persuaded by the Lord Jesus, that *there is* nothing unclean of itself: but to him that esteemeth any thing to be unclean, to him *it is* unclean.
Ro 14:22 — Hast thou faith? have *it* to thyself before God. Happy *is* he that condemneth not himself in that thing which he alloweth.
2Co 4:2 — But have renounced the hidden things of dishonesty, not walking in craftiness, nor handling the word of God deceitfully; but by manifestation of the truth commending ourselves to every man's conscience in the sight of God.
2Co 5:11 — Knowing therefore the terror of the Lord, we persuade men; but we are made manifest unto God; and I trust also are made manifest in your consciences.
2Co 7:2 — Receive us; we have wronged no man, we have corrupted no man, we have defrauded no man.
2Co 8:21 — Providing for honest things, not only in the sight of the Lord, but also in the sight of men.
Eph 6:6 — Not with eyeservice, as menpleasers; but as the servants of Christ, doing the will of God from the heart;
Php 4:8 — Finally, brethren, whatsoever things are true, whatsoever things *are* honest, whatsoever things *are* just, whatsoever things *are* pure, whatsoever things *are* lovely, whatsoever things *are* of good report; if *there be* any virtue, and if *there be* any praise, think on these things.
1Th 2:4 — But as we were allowed of God to be put in trust with the gospel, even so we speak; not as pleasing men, but God, which trieth our hearts.
1Ti 1:5 — Now the end of the commandment is charity out of a pure heart, and *of* a good conscience, and *of* faith unfeigned:
1Ti 3:9 — Holding the mystery of the faith in a pure conscience.
Heb 13:18 — Pray for us: for we trust we have a good conscience, in all things willing to live honestly.
1Pe 2:12 — Having your conversation honest among the Gentiles: that, whereas they speak against you as evildoers, they may by *your* good works, which they shall behold, glorify God in the day of visitation.
1Pe 3:16 — Having a good conscience; that, whereas they speak evil of you, as of evildoers, they may be ashamed that falsely accuse your good conversation in Christ.

See: Character of Saints
See: Dishonesty
See: Fraud
See: Honesty
See: Justice
See: Righteousness

- **Instances of.**
  - **Pharaoh, when he learned that Sarah was Abraham's wife.**
    Ge 12:18
  - **Abimelech, when warned of God that the woman he had taken into his household was Abraham's wife.**
    Ge 26:9–11
  - **Jacob, in the care of Laban's property.**
    Ge 31:39
  - **Joseph, in resisting Potiphar's wife.**
    Ge 39:8–12
  - **Joseph, innocent of the charge on which he was cast into the dungeon.**
    Ge 40:15
  - **Jacob's sons, when accused by Joseph of robbery.**
    Ge 43:15–22; 44:7–16
  - **The Egyptian midwives, when commanded to destroy the newborn babes of the Israelites.**
    Ex 1:17–21
  - **Moses, in taking nothing from the Israelites in consideration of his services.**
    Nu 16:15
  - **Samuel, in exacting nothing from the people on account of services.**
    1Sa 12:4
  - **David, in self-reproach for the cutting of Saul's skirt.**
    1Sa 24:5
  - **David, in preventing foraging by his insurgent forces.**
    1Sa 25:15
  - **David, in his conduct while in refuge with the Philistines.**
    1Sa 29:1–11
  - **Workmen, who repaired the temple.**
    2Ki 12:15; 22:7
  - **Joab, when ordered by David to number the military forces of Israel.**
    1Ch 21:6
  - **Priests, who received the offerings of gold and other gifts for the renewing of the temple under Ezra.**
    Ezr 8:24–30
  - **Nehemiah, reforming the civil service, and receiving no compensation for his own services.**
    Ne 5:14–19

- **The Rechabites, in keeping the Nazarite vows.**
  Jer 35:12–17
- **Daniel, in his abstemiousness.**
  Da 1:8–20
- **Daniel, in maintaining uprightness of character and consistent devoutness.**
  Da 6:4
- **Joseph, the husband of Mary, in not jealously accusing her of immorality.**
  Mt 1:19
- **Zacchaeus, in the administration of his wealth.**
  Lk 19:8
- **Nathanael, in whom was no guile.**
  Jn 1:47
- **Joseph, a counselor.**
  Lk 23:50–51
- **Peter, when offered money by Simon Magus.**
  Ac 8:18–23
- **Paul and Barnabas, people of Lystra desired to deify them.**
  Ac 14:12–15

INTEMPERANCE

- See: Abstinence, Total
- See: Drunkard
- See: Drunkenness
- See: Temperance
- See: Wine

INTERCESSION

- **Of man with man.**

1Sa 2:25 — If one man sin against another, the judge shall judge him: but if a man sin against the LORD, who shall intreat for him? Notwithstanding they hearkened not unto the voice of their father, because the LORD would slay them.

- **Instances of.**
  - **Reuben for Joseph.**
    Ge 37:21–22
  - **Judah for Joseph.**
    Ge 37:26–27
  - **Pharaoh's chief baker for Joseph.**
    Ge 40:14; 41:9–13
  - **Jonathan for David.**
    1Sa 19:1–7
  - **Abigail for Nabal.**
    1Sa 25:23–35
  - **Joab for Absalom.**
    2Sa 14:1–24
  - **Bath-sheba for Solomon.**
    1Ki 1:15–31
  - **Bath-sheba for Adonijah.**
    1Ki 2:13–25
  - **Ebed-melech for Jeremiah.**
    Jer 38:7–13
  - **Elisha offers to see the king for the Shunammite.**
    2Ki 4:13
  - **The king of Syria for Naaman.**
    2Ki 5:6–8
  - **Paul for Onesimus.**
    Phm 1:10–21

- **Of man with God.**

Ex 28:29–30; 32:9–14; Nu 6:23–26; 14:11–21; 16:46–50; Dt 9:25–29; 1Sa 7:5–8; 15:24–26; Job 9:32–33; 42:8–10; Isa 62:6–7; Mt 8:5–13; Mk 6:55–56; 1Ti 2:1–2; Jas 5:14–20

Ge 20:7 — Now therefore restore the man *his* wife; for he *is* a prophet, and he shall pray for thee, and thou shalt live: and if thou restore *her* not, know thou that thou shalt surely die, thou, and all that *are* thine.

Ex 28:12 — And thou shalt put the two stones upon the shoulders of the ephod *for* stones of memorial unto the children of Israel: and Aaron shall bear their names before the LORD upon his two shoulders for a memorial.

Ex 28:38 — And it shall be upon Aaron's forehead, that Aaron may bear the iniquity of the holy things, which the children of Israel shall hallow in all their holy gifts; and it shall be always upon his forehead, that they may be accepted before the LORD.

Dt 5:5 — (I stood between the LORD and you at that time, to shew you the word of the LORD: for ye were afraid by reason of the fire, and went not up into the mount;) saying,

Dt 7:9 — Know therefore that the LORD thy God, he *is* God, the faithful God, which keepeth covenant and mercy with them that love him and keep his commandments to a thousand generations;

Dt 9:18 — And I fell down before the LORD, as at the first, forty days and forty nights: I did neither eat bread, nor drink water, because of all your sins which ye sinned, in doing wickedly in the sight of the LORD, to provoke him to anger.

Dt 9:20 — And the LORD was very angry with Aaron to have destroyed him: and I prayed for Aaron also the same time.

1Sa 12:23 — Moreover as for me, God forbid that I should sin against the LORD in ceasing to pray for you: but I will teach you the good and the right way:

1Sa 15:30 — Then he said, I have sinned: *yet* honour me now, I pray thee, before the elders of my people, and before Israel, and turn again with me, that I may worship the LORD thy God.

Job 1:5 — And it was so, when the days of *their* feasting were gone about, that Job sent and sanctified them, and rose up early in the morning, and offered burnt offerings *according* to the number of them all: for Job said, It may be that my sons have sinned, and cursed God in their hearts. Thus did Job continually.

Job 16:21 — Oh that one might plead for a man with God, as a man *pleadeth* for his neighbour!

Ps 122:6 — Pray for the peace of Jerusalem: they shall prosper that love thee.

Isa 65:8 — Thus saith the LORD, As the new wine is found in the cluster, and *one* saith, Destroy it not; for a blessing *is* in it: so will I do for my servants' sakes, that I may not destroy them all.

Jer 5:1 — Run ye to and fro through the streets of Jerusalem, and see now, and know, and seek in the broad places thereof, if ye can find a man, if there be *any* that executeth judgment, that seeketh the truth; and I will pardon it.

Jer 7:16 — Therefore pray not thou for this people, neither lift up cry nor prayer for them, neither make intercession to me: for I will not hear thee.

Jer 11:14 — Therefore pray not thou for this people, neither lift up a cry or prayer for them: for I will not hear *them* in the time that they cry unto me for their trouble.

Jer 14:11 — Then said the LORD unto me, Pray not for this people for *their* good.

Jer 15:1 — Then said the LORD unto me, Though Moses and Samuel stood before me, *yet* my mind *could* not *be* toward this people: cast *them* out of my sight, and let them go forth.

Jer 29:7 — And seek the peace of the city whither I have caused you to be carried away captives, and pray unto the LORD for it: for in the peace thereof shall ye have peace.

Eze 22:30 — And I sought for a man among them, that should make up the hedge, and stand in the gap before me for the land, that I should not destroy it: but I found none.

Eph 6:18 — Praying always with all prayer and supplication in the Spirit, and watching thereunto with all perseverance and supplication for all saints;

Heb 13:18 — Pray for us: for we trust we have a good conscience, in all things willing to live honestly.

1Pe 2:5 — Ye also, as lively stones, are built up a spiritual house, an holy priesthood, to offer up spiritual sacrifices, acceptable to God by Jesus Christ.

1Pe 2:9 — But ye *are* a chosen generation, a royal priesthood, an holy nation, a peculiar people; that ye should shew forth the praises of him who hath called you out of darkness into his marvellous light:

1Jn 5:16 — If any man see his brother sin a sin *which is* not unto death, he shall ask, and he shall give him life for them that sin not unto death. There is a sin unto death: I do not say that he shall pray for it.

• **Exemplified.**

Ge 48:15–20; Ex 32:31–32; Nu 10:35–36; 27:16–17; Jos 7:7–26; 1Ki 8:38–39, 44–45; 1Ch 29:18–19; 2Ch 6:40–41; Ps 20:1–4; 80:1–2, 14–15; 122:7–8; 132:8–10; Isa 63:17–19; 64:8–12; Da 9:3–19; Eph 1:15–19; 3:14–19; Php 1:3–5, 9–10; Col 1:3–4; 2:1–2; 1Th 3:12–13; 2Th 2:16–17; Heb 13:20–21

Ex 34:9 — And he said, If now I have found grace in thy sight, O Lord, let my Lord, I pray thee, go among us; for it *is* a stiffnecked people; and pardon our iniquity and our sin, and take us for thine inheritance.

Jgs 5:31 — So let all thine enemies perish, O LORD: but *let* them that love him *be* as the sun when he goeth forth in his might. And the land had rest forty years.

Ru 2:12 — The LORD recompense thy work, and a full reward be given thee of the LORD God of Israel, under whose wings thou art come to trust.

1Sa 1:17 — Then Eli answered and said, Go in peace: and the God of Israel grant *thee* thy petition that thou hast asked of him.

1Sa 12:23 — Moreover as for me, God forbid that I should sin against the LORD in ceasing to pray for you: but I will teach you the good and the right way:

2Sa 24:17 — And David spake unto the LORD when he saw the angel that smote the people, and said, Lo, I have sinned, and I have done wickedly: but these sheep, what have they done? let thine hand, I pray thee, be against me, and against my father's house.

1Ki 8:29 — That thine eyes may be open toward this house night and day, *even* toward the place of which thou hast said, My name shall be there: that thou mayest hearken unto the prayer which thy servant shall make toward this place.

2Ch 30:18 — For a multitude of the people, *even* many of Ephraim, and Manasseh, Issachar, and Zebulun, had not cleansed themselves, yet did they eat the passover otherwise than it was written. But Hezekiah prayed for them, saying, The good LORD pardon every one

Ps 7:9 — Oh let the wickedness of the wicked come to an end; but establish the just: for the righteous God trieth the hearts and reins.

Ps 12:1 — Help, LORD; for the godly man ceaseth; for the faithful fail from among the children of men.

Ps 25:22 — Redeem Israel, O God, out of all his troubles.

Ps 28:9 — Save thy people, and bless thine inheritance: feed them also, and lift them up for ever.

Ps 36:10 — O continue thy lovingkindness unto them that know thee; and thy righteousness to the upright in heart.

Ps 51:18 — Do good in thy good pleasure unto Zion: build thou the walls of Jerusalem.

Ps 80:17 — Let thy hand be upon the man of thy right hand, upon the son of man *whom* thou madest strong for thyself.

Ps 80:19 — Turn us again, O LORD God of hosts, cause thy face to shine; and we shall be saved.

Ps 125:4 — Do good, O LORD, unto *those that be* good, and *to them that are* upright in their hearts.

Ps 134:3 — The LORD that made heaven and earth bless thee out of Zion.

Ps 141:5 — Let the righteous smite me; *it shall be* a kindness: and let him reprove me; *it shall be* an excellent oil, *which* shall not break my head: for yet my prayer also *shall be* in their calamities.

Isa 62:1 — For Zion's sake will I not hold my peace, and for Jerusalem's sake I will not rest, until the righteousness thereof go forth as brightness, and the salvation thereof as a lamp *that* burneth.

Jer 18:20 — Shall evil be recompensed for good? for they have digged a pit for my soul. Remember that I stood before thee to speak good for them, *and* to turn away thy wrath from them.

Eze 9:8 — And it came to pass, while they were slaying them, and I was left, that I fell upon my face, and cried, and said, Ah Lord GOD! wilt thou destroy all the residue of Israel in thy pouring out of thy fury upon Jerusalem?

Eze 11:13 — And it came to pass, when I prophesied, that Pelatiah the son of Benaiah died. Then fell I down upon my face, and cried with a loud voice, and said, Ah Lord GOD! wilt thou make a full end of the remnant of Israel?

Joel 2:17 — Let the priests, the ministers of the LORD, weep between the porch and the altar, and let them say, Spare thy people, O LORD, and give not thine heritage to reproach, that the heathen should rule over them: wherefore should they say among the people, Where *is* their God?

Mic 7:14 — Feed thy people with thy rod, the flock of thine heritage, which dwell solitarily *in* the wood, in the midst of Carmel: let them feed *in* Bashan and Gilead, as in the days of old.

Mt 5:44 — But I say unto you, Love your enemies, bless them that curse you, do good to them that hate you, and pray for them which despitefully use you, and persecute you;

Mt 6:10 — Thy kingdom come. Thy will be done in earth, as *it is* in heaven.

Ac 7:60 — And he kneeled down, and cried with a loud voice, Lord, lay not this sin to their charge. And when he had said this, he fell asleep.

Ac 8:15 — Who, when they were come down, prayed for them, that they might receive the Holy Ghost:

Ro 1:9 — For God is my witness, whom I serve with my spirit in the gospel of his Son, that without ceasing I make mention of you always in my prayers;

Ro 10:1 — Brethren, my heart's desire and prayer to God for Israel is, that they might be saved.

1Co 1:3 — Grace *be* unto you, and peace, from God our Father, and *from* the Lord Jesus Christ.

2Co 9:10 — Now he that ministereth seed to the sower both minister bread for *your* food, and multiply your seed sown, and increase the fruits of your righteousness;)

2Co 9:14 — And by their prayer for you, which long after you for the exceeding grace of God in you.

2Co 13:7 — Now I pray to God that ye do no evil; not that we should appear approved, but that ye should do that which is honest, though we be as reprobates.

Gal 1:3 — Grace *be* to you and peace from God the Father, and *from* our Lord Jesus Christ,

Gal 6:16 — And as many as walk according to this rule, peace *be* on them, and mercy, and upon the Israel of God.

Col 1:9 — For this cause we also, since the day we heard *it,* do not cease to pray for you, and to desire that ye might be filled with the knowledge of his will in all wisdom and spiritual understanding;

Col 4:12 — Epaphras, who is *one* of you, a servant of Christ, saluteth you, always labouring fervently for you in prayers, that ye may stand perfect and complete in all the will of God.

1Th 1:2 — We give thanks to God always for you all, making mention of you in our prayers;

1Th 3:10 — Night and day praying exceedingly that we might see your face, and might perfect that which is lacking in your faith?

1Th 5:23 — And the very God of peace sanctify you wholly; and *I pray God* your whole spirit and soul and body be preserved blameless unto the coming of our Lord Jesus Christ.

2Th 1:11 — Wherefore also we pray always for you, that our God would count you worthy of *this* calling, and fulfil all the good pleasure of *his* goodness, and the work of faith with power:

2Th 3:5 — And the Lord direct your hearts into the love of God, and into the patient waiting for Christ.

2Th 3:16 — Now the Lord of peace himself give you peace always by all means. The Lord *be* with you all.

2Ti 1:3 — I thank God, whom I serve from *my* forefathers with pure conscience, that without ceasing I have remembrance of thee in my prayers night and day;

2Ti 1:18 — The Lord grant unto him that he may find mercy of the Lord in that day: and in how many things he ministered unto me at Ephesus, thou knowest very well.

2Ti 2:7 — Consider what I say; and the Lord give thee understanding in all things.

2Ti 4:16 — At my first answer no man stood with me, but all *men* forsook me: *I pray God* that it may not be laid to their charge.

Phm 1:4 — I thank my God, making mention of thee always in my prayers,

Phm 1:6 — That the communication of thy faith may become effectual by the acknowledging of every good thing which is in you in Christ Jesus.

1Pe 5:10 — But the God of all grace, who hath called us unto his eternal glory by Christ Jesus, after that ye have suffered a while, make you perfect, stablish, strengthen, settle *you.*

See: Prayer; intercessory

- **Additional instances of.**
  - **Abraham, in behalf of Sodom.**
    Ge 18:23–32
  - **Abraham, in behalf of Abimelech.**
    Ge 20:17–18
  - **Abraham's servant, in behalf of his master.**
    Ge 24:12 — And he said, O LORD God of my master Abraham, I pray thee, send me good speed this day, and shew kindness unto my master Abraham.
  - **Jacob, in behalf of his children.**
    Ge 49:1–33
  - **Moses, in behalf of Pharaoh.**
    Ex 8:12–13, 30–31; 10:18–19
    Ex 9:33 — And Moses went out of the city from Pharaoh, and spread abroad his hands unto the LORD: and the thunders and hail ceased, and the rain was not poured upon the earth.
  - **Moses, for Israel.**
    Nu 16:20–22; Dt 33:6–17
    Nu 21:7 — Therefore the people came to Moses, and said, We have sinned, for we have spoken

against the LORD, and against thee; pray unto the LORD, that he take away the serpents from us. And Moses prayed for the people.

Ps 106:23 — Therefore he said that he would destroy them, had not Moses his chosen stood before him in the breach, to turn away his wrath, lest he should destroy *them.*

• Moses, for Miriam.

Nu 12:13–15

• David, for Israel.

2Sa 24:17 — And David spake unto the LORD when he saw the angel that smote the people, and said, Lo, I have sinned, and I have done wickedly: but these sheep, what have they done? let thine hand, I pray thee, be against me, and against my father's house.

• Solomon, for Israel.

1Ki 8:29–53

• Ezra, for Israel.

Ezr 9:5–15

• Nehemiah, in behalf of Judah and Jerusalem.

Ne 1:4–9

• Asaph, for the church.

Ps 80:1–19; 83:1–18

• Korah, for the church.

Ps 85:1–7

• Jeremiah, for Israel.

Jer 14:7–22

• Amos, for Israel.

Am 7:2–6

• Syrophenician woman, for her daughter.

Mt 15:22 — And, behold, a woman of Canaan came out of the same coasts, and cried unto him, saying, Have mercy on me, O Lord, *thou* Son of David; my daughter is grievously vexed with a devil.

• Disciples, in behalf of Peter's wife's mother.

Lk 4:38–39

• Parents, for lunatic son.

Mk 9:17–27

Mt 17:15 — Lord, have mercy on my son: for he is lunatick, and sore vexed: for ofttimes he falleth into the fire, and oft into the water.

• Others, who sought Jesus in behalf of the afflicted.

Mt 17:14–18; Lk 5:18–20

Mt 12:22 — Then was brought unto him one possessed with a devil, blind, and dumb: and he healed him, insomuch that the blind and dumb both spake and saw.

Mt 15:22 — And, behold, a woman of Canaan came out of the same coasts, and cried unto him, saying, Have mercy on me, O Lord, *thou* Son of David; my daughter is grievously vexed with a devil.

Mt 15:30 — And great multitudes came unto him, having with them *those that were* lame, blind, dumb, maimed, and many others, and cast them down at Jesus' feet; and he healed them:

Mk 1:32 — And at even, when the sun did set, they brought unto him all that were diseased, and them that were possessed with devils.

Mk 2:3 — And they come unto him, bringing one sick of the palsy, which was borne of four.

Jn 4:47 — When he heard that Jesus was come out of Judaea into Galilee, he went unto him, and besought him that he would come down, and heal his son: for he was at the point of death.

Jn 4:49 — The nobleman saith unto him, Sir, come down ere my child die.

• Paul, for the church.

Ac 20:32 — And now, brethren, I commend you to God, and to the word of his grace, which is able to build you up, and to give you an inheritance among all them which are sanctified.

• Onesiphorus.

2Ti 1:16 — The Lord give mercy unto the house of Onesiphorus; for he oft refreshed me, and was not ashamed of my chain:

2Ti 1:18 — The Lord grant unto him that he may find mercy of the Lord in that day: and in how many things he ministered unto me at Ephesus, thou knowest very well.

• For Paul, by the churches.

Ac 14:26 — And thence sailed to Antioch, from whence they had been recommended to the grace of God for the work which they fulfilled.

Ac 15:40 — And Paul chose Silas, and departed, being recommended by the brethren unto the grace of God.

• Solicited.

• Instances of.

• By Pharaoh, of Moses.

Ex 8:8 — Then Pharaoh called for Moses and Aaron, and said, Intreat the LORD, that he may take away the frogs from me, and from my people; and I will let the people go, that they may do sacrifice unto the LORD.

Ex 8:28 — And Pharaoh said, I will let you go, that ye may sacrifice to the LORD your God in the wilderness; only ye shall not go very far away: intreat for me.

Ex 9:28 — Intreat the LORD (for *it is* enough) that there be no *more* mighty thunderings and hail; and I will let you go, and ye shall stay no longer.

Ex 10:17 — Now therefore forgive, I pray thee, my sin only this once, and intreat the LORD your God, that he may take away from me this death only.

Ex 12:32 — Also take your flocks and your herds, as ye have said, and be gone; and bless me also.

• By Paraoh, and by the Israelites.

Nu 21:7 — Therefore the people came to Moses, and said, We have sinned, for we have spoken against the LORD, and against thee; pray unto the LORD, that he take away the serpents from us. And Moses prayed for the people.

- **By Israel, of Samuel.**

1Sa 12:19 — And all the people said unto Samuel, Pray for thy servants unto the LORD thy God, that we die not: for we have added unto all our sins *this* evil, to ask us a king.

- **By Jeroboam, of a prophet.**

1Ki 13:6 — And the king answered and said unto the man of God, Intreat now the face of the LORD thy God, and pray for me, that my hand may be restored me again. And the man of God besought the LORD, and the king's hand was restored him again, and became as *it was* before.

- **By Hezekiah, of Isaiah.**

2Ki 19:1–4

- **By Zedekiah, of Jeremiah.**

Jer 37:3 — And Zedekiah the king sent Jehucal the son of Shelemiah and Zephaniah the son of Maaseiah the priest to the prophet Jeremiah, saying, Pray now unto the LORD our God for us.

- **By Zedekiah, and by Johanan.**

Jer 42:1–6

- **By Daniel, of Shadrach, Meshach and Abed-nego.**

Da 2:17–18

- **By Darius, of the Jews.**

Ezr 6:10 — That they may offer sacrifices of sweet savours unto the God of heaven, and pray for the life of the king, and of his sons.

- **By Simon Magus, of Peter.**

Ac 8:24 — Then answered Simon, and said, Pray ye to the Lord for me, that none of these things which ye have spoken come upon me.

- **By Paul, of the churches.**

Ro 15:30–32; Eph 6:19–20

2Co 1:11 — Ye also helping together by prayer for us, that for the gift *bestowed* upon us by the means of many persons thanks may be given by many on our behalf.

1Th 5:25 — Brethren, pray for us.

2Th 3:1 — Finally, brethren, pray for us, that the word of the Lord may have *free* course, and be glorified, even as *it is* with you:

Heb 13:18 — Pray for us: for we trust we have a good conscience, in all things willing to live honestly.

- **Answered.**
  - **Instances of.**
    - **Moses, in behalf of Pharaoh, for the plague of frogs to be abated.**

Ex 8:12 — And Moses and Aaron went out from Pharaoh: and Moses cried unto the LORD because of the frogs which he had brought against Pharaoh.

Ex 8:15 — But when Pharaoh saw that there was respite, he hardened his heart, and hearkened not unto them; as the LORD had said.

- **Moses, in behalf of Pharaoh, for the plague of flies.**

Ex 8:30–32

- **Moses, in behalf of Pharaoh, for the plague of rain, thunder, and hail.**

Ex 9:27–35

- **Moses, in behalf of Pharaoh, for the plague of locusts.**

Ex 10:16–20

- **Moses, in behalf of Pharaoh, for the plague of darkness.**

Ex 10:21–23

- **Moses, for the Israelites, during the battle with the Amalekites.**

Ex 17:11–14

- **Moses, after the Israelites had made the golden calf.**

Ex 32:11–14, 31–34; Dt 9:18–29

Dt 10:10 — And I stayed in the mount, according to the first time, forty days and forty nights; and the LORD hearkened unto me at that time also, *and* the LORD would not destroy thee.

Ps 106:23 — Therefore he said that he would destroy them, had not Moses his chosen stood before him in the breach, to turn away his wrath, lest he should destroy *them.*

- **Moses, after the murmuring of the people.**

Ex 33:15–17

- **Moses, when the fire of the Lord consumed the people.**

Nu 11:1–2

- **Moses, when the people murmured on account of the report of the spies.**

Nu 14:11–20

- **Moses, that the fiery serpents might be abated.**

Nu 21:4–9

- **Moses, that Miriam's leprosy might be healed.**

Nu 12:13 — And Moses cried unto the LORD, saying, Heal her now, O God, I beseech thee.

- **Moses, in behalf of Aaron, on account of his sin in making the golden calf.**

Dt 9:20 — And the LORD was very angry with Aaron to have destroyed him: and I prayed for Aaron also the same time.

- **Samuel, for deliverance from the oppressions of the Philistines.**

1Sa 7:5–14

- **The prophet of Israel, for the restoration of Jeroboam's withered hand.**

1Ki 13:1–6

- **Elijah, for the raising from the dead the son of the hospitable widow.**

1Ki 17:20–23

- **Elisha, for the raising from the dead the son of the Shunammite woman.**

2Ki 4:33–36

- **Isaiah, in behalf of Hezekiah and the people, to be delivered from Sennacherib.**
2Ki 19:1–37

- **Intercessional influence of the righteous.**

Ge 18:29–30; 26:4–5; 1Ki 11:12–13; Ps 103:17–18; Ro 11:27–28; Rev 8:3–4

Ge 18:26 — And the LORD said, If I find in Sodom fifty righteous within the city, then I will spare all the place for their sakes.

Ge 18:32 — And he said, Oh let not the Lord be angry, and I will speak yet but this once: Peradventure ten shall be found there. And he said, I will not destroy *it* for ten's sake.

Ge 19:22 — Haste thee, escape thither; for I cannot do any thing till thou be come thither. Therefore the name of the city was called Zoar.

Ge 26:24 — And the LORD appeared unto him the same night, and said, I *am* the God of Abraham thy father: fear not, for I *am* with thee, and will bless thee, and multiply thy seed for my servant Abraham's sake.

1Ki 11:34 — Howbeit I will not take the whole kingdom out of his hand: but I will make him prince all the days of his life for David my servant's sake, whom I chose, because he kept my commandments and my statutes:

1Ki 15:4 — Nevertheless for David's sake did the LORD his God give him a lamp in Jerusalem, to set up his son after him, and to establish Jerusalem:

2Ki 8:19 — Yet the LORD would not destroy Judah for David his servant's sake, as he promised him to give him alway a light, *and* to his children.

2Ch 21:7 — Howbeit the LORD would not destroy the house of David, because of the covenant that he had made with David, and as he promised to give a light to him and to his sons for ever.

Isa 37:35 — For I will defend this city to save it for mine own sake, and for my servant David's sake.

Jer 5:1 — Run ye to and fro through the streets of Jerusalem, and see now, and know, and seek in the broad places thereof, if ye can find a man, if there be *any* that executeth judgment, that seeketh the truth; and I will pardon it.

Eze 14:14 — Though these three men, Noah, Daniel, and Job, were in it, they should deliver *but* their own souls by their righteousness, saith the Lord GOD.

Eze 14:16 — *Though* these three men *were* in it, *as* I live, saith the Lord GOD, they shall deliver neither sons nor daughters; they only shall be delivered, but the land shall be desolate.

Eze 14:18 — Though these three men *were* in it, *as* I live, saith the Lord GOD, they shall deliver neither sons nor daughters, but they only shall be delivered themselves.

Eze 14:20 — Though Noah, Daniel, and Job, *were* in it, *as* I live, saith the Lord GOD, they shall deliver neither son nor daughter; they shall *but* deliver their own souls by their righteousness.

Mt 24:22 — <u>And except those days should be shortened, there should no flesh be saved: but for the elect's sake those days shall be shortened.</u>

Rev 5:8 — And when he had taken the book, the four beasts and four *and* twenty elders fell down before the Lamb, having every one of them harps, and golden vials full of odours, which are the prayers of saints.

See: Children, Commandments to; of the righteous, blessed of God

See: Jesus, Mediation of

INTEREST

- **Income from loaning money, usually called usury, but not signifying unjust rates.**

Le 25:36–37; Dt 23:19–20; Ne 5:1–13; Eze 18:8–9

Ex 22:25 — If thou lend money to *any of* my people *that is* poor by thee, thou shalt not be to him as an usurer, neither shalt thou lay upon him usury.

Ps 15:5 — *He that* putteth not out his money to usury, nor taketh reward against the innocent. He that doeth these *things* shall never be moved.

Pr 28:8 — He that by usury and unjust gain increaseth his substance, he shall gather it for him that will pity the poor.

Isa 24:2 — And it shall be, as with the people, so with the priest; as with the servant, so with his master; as with the maid, so with her mistress; as with the buyer, so with the seller; as with the lender, so with the borrower; as with the taker of usury, so with the giver of usury to him.

Eze 18:13 — Hath given forth upon usury, and hath taken increase: shall he then live? he shall not live: he hath done all these abominations; he shall surely die; his blood shall be upon him.

Eze 18:17 — *That* hath taken off his hand from the poor, *that* hath not received usury nor increase, hath executed my judgments, hath walked in my statutes; he shall not die for the iniquity of his father, he shall surely live.

Eze 22:12 — In thee have they taken gifts to shed blood; thou hast taken usury and increase, and thou hast greedily gained of thy neighbours by extortion, and hast forgotten me, saith the Lord GOD.

See: Borrowing

See: Debt

See: Debtor

See: Lending

See: Money

INTERPRETATION

- **Of dreams.**

See: Dream

- **Of foreign tongues.**

1Co 14:9–19

See: Tongues

INTERPRETER

- **Of dreams.**

Da 2:18–30

Ge 40:8 — And they said unto him, We have dreamed a dream, and *there is* no interpreter of it. And Joseph said unto them, *Do* not interpretations *belong* to God? tell me *them,* I pray you.

Ge 41:16 — And Joseph answered Pharaoh, saying, *It is* not in me: God shall give Pharaoh an answer of peace.

• Of languages.

Ge 42:23 — And they knew not that Joseph understood *them;* for he spake unto them by an interpreter.

2Ch 32:31 — Howbeit in *the business of* the ambassadors of the princes of Babylon, who sent unto him to enquire of the wonder that was *done* in the land, God left him, to try him, that he might know all *that was* in his heart.

Ne 8:8 — So they read in the book in the law of God distinctly, and gave the sense, and caused *them* to understand the reading.

Job 33:23 — If there be a messenger with him, an interpreter, one among a thousand, to shew unto man his uprightness:

• In Christian churches.

1Co 14:26–28

1Co 12:10 — To another the working of miracles; to another prophecy; to another discerning of spirits; to another *divers* kinds of tongues; to another the interpretation of tongues:

1Co 12:30 — Have all the gifts of healing? do all speak with tongues? do all interpret?

1Co 14:5 — I would that ye all spake with tongues, but rather that ye prophesied: for greater *is* he that prophesieth than he that speaketh with tongues, except he interpret, that the church may receive edifying.

1Co 14:13 — Wherefore let him that speaketh in an *unknown* tongue pray that he may interpret.

• Figurative.

Job 33:23 — If there be a messenger with him, an interpreter, one among a thousand, to shew unto man his uprightness:

INTOLERANCE, Religious

• Of idolatrous religions, taught by Moses.

Dt 13:1–18; 17:1–7

Ex 22:20 — He that sacrificeth unto *any* god, save unto the LORD only, he shall be utterly destroyed.

• Exemplified by.

• Cain.

Ge 4:8 — And Cain talked with Abel his brother: and it came to pass, when they were in the field, that Cain rose up against Abel his brother, and slew him.

• Joshua.

Nu 11:24 — And Moses went out, and told the people the words of the LORD, and gathered the seventy men of the elders of the people, and set them round about the tabernacle.

Nu 11:28 — And Joshua the son of Nun, the servant of Moses, *one* of his young men, answered and said, My lord Moses, forbid them.

• James and John.

Mk 9:38–39

Lk 9:49 — And John answered and said, Master, we saw one casting out devils in thy name; and we forbad him, because he followeth not with us.

• The Jews

• At the time of the religious revival under the leadership of Azariah.

2Ch 15:12–13

• In persecuting Jesus.

See: Jesus, History of

• In persecuting the disciples.

Ac 4:1–3, 15–21

Ac 17:13 — But when the Jews of Thessalonica had knowledge that the word of God was preached of Paul at Berea, they came thither also, and stirred up the people.

• In persecuting Stephen.

Ac 6:9–15; 7:57–59; 8:1–3

• In persecuting Paul.

Ac 21:28–31; 22:22–23

Ac 13:50 — But the Jews stirred up the devout and honourable women, and the chief men of the city, and raised persecution against Paul and Barnabas, and expelled them out of their coasts.

Ac 17:5 — But the Jews which believed not, moved with envy, took unto them certain lewd fellows of the baser sort, and gathered a company, and set all the city on an uproar, and assaulted the house of Jason, and sought to bring them out to the people.

Ac 18:13 — Saying, This *fellow* persuadeth men to worship God contrary to the law.

Ac 23:2 — And the high priest Ananias commanded them that stood by him to smite him on the mouth.

• Elijah.

1Ki 18:40 — And Elijah said unto them, Take the prophets of Baal; let not one of them escape. And they took them: and Elijah brought them down to the brook Kishon, and slew them there.

• Jehu.

2Ki 10:18–31

See: Persecution

INTOXICANTS See: Wine

INTOXICATION

See: Abstinence, Total

See: Drunkenness

INTRIGUE See: Conspiracy

INVECTIVE See: Satire

INVENTION

Pr 8:12 — I wisdom dwell with prudence, and find out knowledge of witty inventions.

- **Of musical instruments.**
  - **By Jubal.**

Ge 4:21 — And his brother's name *was* Jubal: he was the father of all such as handle the harp and organ.

  - **By David.**

1Ch 23:5 — Moreover four thousand *were* porters; and four thousand praised the LORD with the instruments which I made, *said David,* to praise *therewith.*

2Ch 7:6 — And the priests waited on their offices: the Levites also with instruments of musick of the LORD, which David the king had made to praise the LORD, because his mercy *endureth* for ever, when David praised by their ministry; and the priests sounded trumpets before them, and all Israel stood.

2Ch 29:26 — And the Levites stood with the instruments of David, and the priests with the trumpets.

Am 6:5 — That chant to the sound of the viol, *and* invent to themselves instruments of musick, like David;

- **The use of metals.**

Ge 4:22 — And Zillah, she also bare Tubal-cain, an instructer of every artificer in brass and iron: and the sister of Tubal-cain *was* Naamah.

- **Engines of war.**

2Ch 26:15 — And he made in Jerusalem engines, invented by cunning men, to be on the towers and upon the bulwarks, to shoot arrows and great stones withal. And his name spread far abroad; for he was marvellously helped, till he was strong.

INVESTIGATION

Ecc 1:13–2:12; 12:9–14

IPHEDEIAH • A Benjamite.

1Ch 8:25 — And Iphedeiah, and Penuel, the sons of Shashak;

IR • A Benjamite.

1Ch 7:12 — Shuppim also, and Huppim, the children of Ir, *and* Hushim, the sons of Aher.

IR-NAHASH • Whether a reference to a man or a town is not clear.

1Ch 4:12 — And Eshton begat Beth-rapha, and Paseah, and Tehinnah the father of Ir-nahash. These *are* the men of Rechah.

IR-SHEMESH • A city of Dan.

Jos 19:41 — And the coast of their inheritance was Zorah, and Eshtaol, and Ir-shemesh,

IRA

- **A priest.**

2Sa 20:26 — And Ira also the Jairite was a chief ruler about David.

- **The Ithrite. One of David's heroes.**

2Sa 23:38 — Ira an Ithrite, Gareb an Ithrite,

1Ch 11:40 — Ira the Ithrite, Gareb the Ithrite,

- **A Tekoite. One of David's heroes.**

2Sa 23:26 — Helez the Paltite, Ira the son of Ikkesh the Tekoite,

1Ch 11:28 — Ira the son of Ikkesh the Tekoite, Abiezer the Antothite,

1Ch 27:9 — The sixth *captain* for the sixth month *was* Ira the son of Ikkesh the Tekoite: and in his course *were* twenty and four thousand.

IRAD • Son of Enoch.

Ge 4:18 — And unto Enoch was born Irad: and Irad begat Mehujael: and Mehujael begat Methusael: and Methusael begat Lamech.

IRAM • A duke of Edom.

Ge 36:43 — Duke Magdiel, duke Iram: these *be* the dukes of Edom, according to their habitations in the land of their possession: he *is* Esau the father of the Edomites.

1Ch 1:54 — Duke Magdiel, duke Iram. These *are* the dukes of Edom.

IRI • A son of Bela.

1Ch 7:7 — And the sons of Bela; Ezbon, and Uzzi, and Uzziel, and Jerimoth, and Iri, five; heads of the house of *their* fathers, mighty men of valour; and were reckoned by their genealogies twenty and two thousand and thirty and four.

IRIJAH • A captain of the guard who imprisoned the prophet Jeremiah.

Jer 37:13–14

IRON

- **First recorded use of.**

Ge 4:22 — And Zillah, she also bare Tubal-cain, an instructer of every artificer in brass and iron: and the sister of Tubal-cain *was* Naamah.

  - **Ore of.**

Dt 8:9 — A land wherein thou shalt eat bread without scarceness, thou shalt not lack any *thing* in it; a land whose stones are iron, and out of whose hills thou mayest dig brass.

Job 28:2 — Iron is taken out of the earth, and brass *is* molten *out of* the stone.

  - **Melted.**

Eze 22:20 — *As* they gather silver, and brass, and iron, and lead, and tin, into the midst of the furnace, to blow the fire upon it, to melt *it;* so will I gather *you* in mine anger and in my fury, and I will leave *you there,* and melt you.

  - **Used in the temple.**

1Ch 22:3 — And David prepared iron in abundance for the nails for the doors of the gates, and for the joinings; and brass in abundance without weight;

1Ch 29:2 — Now I have prepared with all my might for the house of my God the gold for *things to be made* of gold, and the silver for *things* of silver, and the brass for *things* of brass, the iron for *things* of iron, and wood for *things* of wood; onyx stones, and *stones* to be set, glistering stones, and of divers colours, and all manner of precious stones, and marble stones in abundance.

1Ch 29:7 — And gave for the service of the house of God of gold five thousand talents and ten thousand drams, and of silver ten thousand talents, and of brass eighteen thousand talents, and one hundred thousand talents of iron.

- **Articles made of.**
  - **Ax.**

2Ki 6:6 — And the man of God said, Where fell it? And he shewed him the place. And he cut down a stick, and cast *it* in thither; and the iron did swim.

2Ch 18:10 — And Zedekiah the son of Chenaanah had made him horns of iron, and said, Thus saith the LORD, With these thou shalt push Syria until they be consumed.

Ecc 10:10 — If the iron be blunt, and he do not whet the edge, then must he put to more strength: but wisdom *is* profitable to direct.

Isa 10:34 — And he shall cut down the thickets of the forest with iron, and Lebanon shall fall by a mighty one.

- **Bedstead.**

Dt 3:11 — For only Og king of Bashan remained of the remnant of giants; behold, his bedstead *was* a bedstead of iron; is it not in Rabbath of the children of Ammon? nine cubits was the length thereof, and four cubits the breadth of it, after the cubit of a man.

- **Breastplate.**

Rev 9:9 — And they had breastplates, as it were breastplates of iron; and the sound of their wings *was* as the sound of chariots of many horses running to battle.

- **Chariot.**

Jos 17:16 — And the children of Joseph said, The hill is not enough for us: and all the Canaanites that dwell in the land of the valley have chariots of iron, *both they* who *are* of Beth-shean and her towns, and *they* who *are* of the valley of Jezreel.

Jos 17:18 — But the mountain shall be thine; for it *is* a wood, and thou shalt cut it down: and the outgoings of it shall be thine: for thou shalt drive out the Canaanites, though they have iron chariots, *and* though they *be* strong.

Jgs 1:19 — And the LORD was with Judah; and he drave out the inhabitants of the mountain; but could not drive out *the inhabitants of* the valley, because they had chariots of iron.

Jgs 4:3 — And the children of Israel cried unto the LORD: for he had nine hundred chariots of iron; and twenty years he mightily oppressed the children of Israel.

- **Fetters.**

Ps 105:18 — Whose feet they hurt with fetters: he was laid in iron:

Ps 107:10 — Such as sit in darkness and in the shadow of death, *being* bound in affliction and iron;

Ps 107:16 — For he hath broken the gates of brass, and cut the bars of iron in sunder.

Ps 149:8 — To bind their kings with chains, and their nobles with fetters of iron;

- **File.**

Pr 27:17 — Iron sharpeneth iron; so a man sharpeneth the countenance of his friend.

- **Furnace.**

Dt 4:20 — But the LORD hath taken you, and brought you forth out of the iron furnace, *even* out of Egypt, to be unto him a people of inheritance, as *ye are* this day.

1Ki 8:51 — For they *be* thy people, and thine inheritance, which thou broughtest forth out of Egypt, from the midst of the furnace of iron:

Jer 11:4 — Which I commanded your fathers in the day *that* I brought them forth out of the land of Egypt, from the iron furnace, saying, Obey my voice, and do them, according to all which I command you: so shall ye be my people, and I will be your God:

- **Gate.**

Ac 12:10 — When they were past the first and the second ward, they came unto the iron gate that leadeth unto the city; which opened to them of his own accord: and they went out, and passed on through one street; and forthwith the angel departed from him.

- **Harrow.**

2Sa 12:31 — And he brought forth the people that *were* therein, and put *them* under saws, and under harrows of iron, and under axes of iron, and made them pass through the brick-kiln: and thus did he unto all the cities of the children of Ammon. So David and all the people returned unto Jerusalem.

- **Horn.**

1Ki 22:11 — And Zedekiah the son of Chenaanah made him horns of iron: and he said, Thus saith the LORD, With these shalt thou push the Syrians, until thou have consumed them.

2Ch 18:10 — And Zedekiah the son of Chenaanah had made him horns of iron, and said, Thus saith the LORD, With these thou shalt push Syria until they be consumed.

Mic 4:13 — Arise and thresh, O daughter of Zion: for I will make thine horn iron, and I will make thy hoofs brass: and thou shalt beat in pieces many people: and I will consecrate their gain unto the LORD, and their substance unto the Lord of the whole earth.

- **Idols.**

Da 2:33 — His legs of iron, his feet part of iron and part of clay.

Da 5:4 — They drank wine, and praised the gods of gold, and of silver, of brass, of iron, of wood, and of stone.

Da 5:23 — But hast lifted up thyself against the Lord of heaven; and they have brought the vessels of his house before thee, and thou, and thy lords, thy wives, and thy concubines, have drunk wine in them; and thou hast praised the gods of silver, and gold, of brass, iron, wood, and stone, which see not, nor hear, nor know: and the God in whose hand thy breath *is,* and whose *are* all thy ways, hast thou not glorified:

- **Pans.**

Eze 4:3 — Moreover take thou unto thee an iron pan, and set it for a wall of iron between thee and the city: and set thy face against it, and it shall be besieged, and thou shalt lay siege against it. This *shall be* a sign to the house of Israel.

Eze 27:19 — Dan also and Javan going to and fro occupied in thy fairs: bright iron, cassia, and calamus, were in thy market.

- **Pen.**

Job 19:24 — That they were graven with an iron pen and lead in the rock for ever!

Jer 17:1 — The sin of Judah *is* written with a pen of iron, *and* with the point of a diamond: *it is* graven upon the table of their heart, and upon the horns of your altars;

- **Pillars.**

Jer 1:18 — For, behold, I have made thee this day a defenced city, and an iron pillar, and brasen walls against the whole land, against the kings of Judah, against the princes thereof, against the priests thereof, and against the people of the land.

- **Rods for scourging.**

Ps 2:9 — Thou shalt break them with a rod of iron; thou shalt dash them in pieces like a potter's vessel.

Rev 2:27 — And he shall rule them with a rod of iron; as the vessels of a potter shall they be broken to shivers: even as I received of my Father.

Rev 12:5 — And she brought forth a man child, who was to rule all nations with a rod of iron: and her child was caught up unto God, and *to* his throne.

Rev 19:15 — And out of his mouth goeth a sharp sword, that with it he should smite the nations: and he shall rule them with a rod of iron: and he treadeth the winepress of the fierceness and wrath of Almighty God.

- **Threshing instruments.**

Am 1:3 — Thus saith the LORD; For three transgressions of Damascus, and for four, I will not turn away *the punishment* thereof; because they have threshed Gilead with threshing instruments of iron:

- **Tools.**

1Ki 6:7 — And the house, when it was in building, was built of stone made ready before it was brought thither: so that there was neither hammer nor axe *nor* any tool of iron heard in the house, while it was in building.

- **Vessels.**

Jos 6:24 — And they burnt the city with fire, and all that *was* therein: only the silver, and the gold, and the vessels of brass and of iron, they put into the treasury of the house of the LORD.

- **Weapons.**

Nu 35:16 — And if he smite him with an instrument of iron, so that he die, he *is* a murderer: the murderer shall surely be put to death.

1Sa 17:7 — And the staff of his spear *was* like a weaver's beam; and his spear's head *weighed* six hundred shekels of iron: and one bearing a shield went before him.

Job 20:24 — He shall flee from the iron weapon, *and* the bow of steel shall strike him through.

Job 41:7 — Canst thou fill his skin with barbed irons? or his head with fish spears?

- **Yokes.**

Jer 28:13–14

Dt 28:48 — Therefore shalt thou serve thine enemies which the LORD shall send against thee, in hunger, and in thirst, and in nakedness, and in want of all *things:* and he shall put a yoke of iron upon thy neck, until he have destroyed thee.

- **Stones of.**

Dt 8:9 — A land wherein thou shalt eat bread without scarceness, thou shalt not lack any *thing* in it; a land whose stones are iron, and out of whose hills thou mayest dig brass.

Job 28:2 — Iron is taken out of the earth, and brass *is* molten *out of* the stone.

Isa 60:17 — For brass I will bring gold, and for iron I will bring silver, and for wood brass, and for stones iron: I will also make thy officers peace, and thine exactors righteousness.

See: Steel

- **Figurative.**

2Sa 23:7 — But the man *that* shall touch them must be fenced with iron and the staff of a spear; and they shall be utterly burned with fire in the *same* place.

Jer 15:12 — Shall iron break the northern iron and the steel?

1Ti 4:2 — Speaking lies in hypocrisy; having their conscience seared with a hot iron;

- **A city of Naphtali.**

Jos 19:38 — And Iron, and Migdal-el, Horem, and Beth-anath, and Beth-shemesh; nineteen cities with their villages.

IRONY

- **Instances of.**
  - **Michal to David.**

    2Sa 6:20
  - **Elijah to the priests of Baal.**

    1Ki 18:27
  - **Job to his accusers.**

    Job 12:2

- **Ezekiel to the prince of Tyre.**
  Eze 28:3–5
- **Micaiah.**
  1Ki 22:15
- **Amos to the Samaritans.**
  Am 4:4
- **Jesus to Pharisees.**
  Mk 2:17
- **Pharisees and Herodians to Jesus.**
  Mt 22:16
- **Roman soldiers to Jesus.**
  Mt 27:29; Mk 15:17–19; Lk 23:11; Jn 19:2–3
- **Pilate, calling Jesus king.**
  Mk 15:19; Jn 19:15
- **Superscription of Pilate over Jesus.**
  Mt 27:37; Mk 15:26; Lk 23:38; Jn 19:19
- **Agrippa to Paul.**
  Ac 26:28

See: Sarcasm

See: Satire

IRPEEL • A city of Benjamin.

Jos 18:27 — And Rekem, and Irpeel, and Taralah,

IRRIGATION

Dt 11:10 — For the land, whither thou goest in to possess it, *is* not as the land of Egypt, from whence ye came out, where thou sowedst thy seed, and wateredst *it* with thy foot, as a garden of herbs:

Pr 21:1 — The king's heart *is* in the hand of the LORD, *as* the rivers of water: he turneth it whithersoever he will.

Ecc 2:6 — I made me pools of water, to water therewith the wood that bringeth forth trees:

Isa 58:11 — And the LORD shall guide thee continually, and satisfy thy soul in drought, and make fat thy bones: and thou shalt be like a watered garden, and like a spring of water, whose waters fail not.

- **Figurative.**
  1Co 3:6 — I have planted, Apollos watered; but God gave the increase.
  1Co 3:8 — Now he that planteth and he that watereth are one: and every man shall receive his own reward according to his own labour.

IRU • Eldest son of Caleb.

1Ch 4:15 — And the sons of Caleb the son of Jephunneh; Iru, Elah, and Naam: and the sons of Elah, even Kenaz.

ISAAC

- **Miraculous son of Abraham.**
  Ge 17:15–19; 18:1–15; 21:1–8
  Jos 24:3 — And I took your father Abraham from the other side of the flood, and led him throughout all the land of Canaan, and multiplied his seed, and gave him Isaac.
  1Ch 1:28 — The sons of Abraham; Isaac, and Ishmael.
  Gal 4:28 — Now we, brethren, as Isaac was, are the children of promise.
  Heb 11:11 — Through faith also Sara herself received strength to conceive seed, and was delivered of a child when she was past age, because she judged him faithful who had promised.
- **Ancestor of Jesus.**
  Mt 1:2 — Abraham begat Isaac; and Isaac begat Jacob; and Jacob begat Judas and his brethren;
- **Offered in sacrifice by his father.**
  Ge 22:1–19
  Heb 11:17 — By faith Abraham, when he was tried, offered up Isaac: and he that had received the promises offered up his only begotten *son,*
  Jas 2:21 — Was not Abraham our father justified by works, when he had offered Isaac his son upon the altar?
- **Is provided a wife from among his kindred.**
  Ge 24:1–67
  Ge 25:20 — And Isaac was forty years old when he took Rebekah to wife, the daughter of Bethuel the Syrian of Padan-aram, the sister to Laban the Syrian.
- **Abrahamic covenant confirmed in.**
  Ge 26:2–5; 1Ch 16:15–19
- **Dwells in the south country at the well Lahai-roi.**
  Ge 24:62 — And Isaac came from the way of the well Lahai-roi; for he dwelt in the south country.
  Ge 25:11 — And it came to pass after the death of Abraham, that God blessed his son Isaac; and Isaac dwelt by the well Lahai-roi.
- **With Ishmael, buries his father in the cave of Machpelah.**
  Ge 25:9 — And his sons Isaac and Ishmael buried him in the cave of Machpelah, in the field of Ephron the son of Zohar the Hittite, which *is* before Mamre;
- **Esau and Jacob born to.**
  Ge 25:19–26
  Jos 24:4 — And I gave unto Isaac Jacob and Esau: and I gave unto Esau mount Seir, to possess it; but Jacob and his children went down into Egypt.
  1Ch 1:34 — And Abraham begat Isaac. The sons of Isaac; Esau and Israel.
- **Dwells in Gerar.**
  Ge 26:7–11
- **Prospers.**
  Ge 26:12–14
- **Possesses large flocks and herds.**
  Ge 26:14 — For he had possession of flocks, and possession of herds, and great store of servants: and the Philistines envied him.
- **Digs wells, and is defrauded of them by the herdsmen of Abimelech.**
  Ge 26:15 — For all the wells which his father's servants had digged in the days of Abraham his father, the Philistines had stopped them, and filled them with earth.
  Ge 26:21 — And they digged another well, and strove for that also: and he called the name of it Sitnah.

• Removes to the valley of Gerar, afterward called Beer-sheba.

Ge 26:22–33

• His old age; last blessing upon his sons.

Ge 27:18–40

• Death and burial of.

Ge 35:27–29

Ge 49:31 — There they buried Abraham and Sarah his wife; there they buried Isaac and Rebekah his wife; and there I buried Leah.

• His filial obedience.

Ge 22:9 — And they came to the place which God had told him of; and Abraham built an altar there, and laid the wood in order, and bound Isaac his son, and laid him on the altar upon the wood.

• His peaceableness.

Ge 26:14–22

• Was a prophet.

Ge 27:28–29

Ge 27:38 — And Esau said unto his father, Hast thou but one blessing, my father? bless me, *even* me also, O my father. And Esau lifted up his voice, and wept.

Ge 27:40 — And by thy sword shalt thou live, and shalt serve thy brother; and it shall come to pass when thou shalt have the dominion, that thou shalt break his yoke from off thy neck.

Heb 11:20 — By faith Isaac blessed Jacob and Esau concerning things to come.

• His devoutness.

Ge 24:63 — And Isaac went out to meditate in the field at the eventide: and he lifted up his eyes, and saw, and, behold, the camels *were* coming.

Ge 25:21 — And Isaac intreated the LORD for his wife, because she *was* barren: and the LORD was intreated of him, and Rebekah his wife conceived.

Ge 26:25 — And he builded an altar there, and called upon the name of the LORD and pitched his tent there: and there Isaac's servants digged a well.

Mt 8:11 — And I say unto you, That many shall come from the east and west, and shall sit down with Abraham, and Isaac, and Jacob, in the kingdom of heaven.

Lk 13:28 — There shall be weeping and gnashing of teeth, when ye shall see Abraham, and Isaac, and Jacob, and all the prophets, in the kingdom of God, and you *yourselves* thrust out.

• Prophecies concerning.

Ge 17:16–21; 18:10–14; 26:2–5

Ge 21:12 — And God said unto Abraham, Let it not be grievous in thy sight because of the lad, and because of thy bondwoman; in all that Sarah hath said unto thee, hearken unto her voice; for in Isaac shall thy seed be called.

Ge 26:24 — And the LORD appeared unto him the same night, and said, I *am* the God of Abraham thy father: fear not, for I *am* with thee, and will bless thee, and multiply thy seed for my servant Abraham's sake.

Ex 32:13 — Remember Abraham, Isaac, and Israel, thy servants, to whom thou swarest by thine own self, and saidst unto them, I will multiply your seed as the stars of heaven, and all this land that I have spoken of will I give unto your seed, and they shall inherit *it* for ever.

1Ch 16:16 — *Even of the covenant* which he made with Abraham, and of his oath unto Isaac;

Ro 9:7 — Neither, because they are the seed of Abraham, *are they* all children: but, In Isaac shall thy seed be called.

• A designation of the ten tribes.

Am 7:9 — And the high places of Isaac shall be desolate, and the sanctuaries of Israel shall be laid waste; and I will rise against the house of Jeroboam with the sword.

ISAIAH

• Called also Esaias.

• Son of Amos.

Isa 1:1 — The vision of Isaiah the son of Amoz, which he saw concerning Judah and Jerusalem in the days of Uzziah, Jotham, Ahaz, *and* Hezekiah, kings of Judah.

• Prophesies in the days of Uzziah, Jotham, Ahaz, and Hezekiah, kings of Judah.

Isa 1:1 — The vision of Isaiah the son of Amoz, which he saw concerning Judah and Jerusalem in the days of Uzziah, Jotham, Ahaz, *and* Hezekiah, kings of Judah.

Isa 6:1 — In the year that king Uzziah died I saw also the Lord sitting upon a throne, high and lifted up, and his train filled the temple.

Isa 7:1 — And it came to pass in the days of Ahaz the son of Jotham, the son of Uzziah, king of Judah, *that* Rezin the king of Syria, and Pekah the son of Remaliah, king of Israel, went up toward Jerusalem to war against it, but could not prevail against it.

Isa 7:3 — Then said the LORD unto Isaiah, Go forth now to meet Ahaz, thou, and Shear-jashub thy son, at the end of the conduit of the upper pool in the highway of the fuller's field;

Isa 14:27 — For the LORD of hosts hath purposed, and who shall disannul *it?* and his hand *is* stretched out, and who shall turn it back?

Isa 20:1 — In the year that Tartan came unto Ashdod, (when Sargon the king of Assyria sent him,) and fought against Ashdod, and took it;

Isa 36:1 — Now it came to pass in the fourteenth year of king Hezekiah, *that* Sennacherib king of Assyria came up against all the defenced cities of Judah, and took them.

Isa 38:1 — In those days was Hezekiah sick unto death. And Isaiah the prophet the son of Amoz came unto him, and said unto him, Thus saith the LORD, Set thine house in order: for thou shalt die, and not live.

Isa 39:1 — At that time Merodach-baladan, the son of Baladan, king of Babylon, sent letters and a present to Hezekiah: for he had heard that he had been sick, and was recovered.

• Prophesies at the time of the invasion by Tartan, of Assyria.

Isa 20:1 — In the year that Tartan came unto Ashdod, (when Sargon the king of Assyria sent him,) and fought against Ashdod, and took it;

• Symbolicly wears sacklcoth, and walks barefoot, as a sign to Israel.

Isa 20:2–3

• Comforts and encourages Hezekiah and the people in the siege of Jerusalem by Rab-shakeh.

2Ki 18:1–19:37; Isa 37:6–7

• Comforts Hezekiah in his affliction.

2Ki 20:1–11; Isa 38:1–22

• Performs the miracle of the returning shadow to confirm Hezekiah's faith.

2Ki 20:8–11

• Reproves Hezekiah's folly in exhibiting his resources to the commissioners from Babylon.

2Ki 20:12–19; Isa 39:1–8

• Is chronicler of the times of Uzziah and Hezekiah.

2Ch 26:22 — Now the rest of the acts of Uzziah, first and last, did Isaiah the prophet, the son of Amoz, write.

2Ch 32:32 — Now the rest of the acts of Hezekiah, and his goodness, behold, they *are* written in the vision of Isaiah the prophet, the son of Amoz, *and* in the book of the kings of Judah and Israel.

• Prophecies, reproofs, and exhortations of.

• Foretells punishment of the Jews for idolatry, and reproves self-confidence and distrust of God.

Isa 2:6–20

• Foretells the destruction of the Jews.

Isa 3:1–26

• Promises to the remnant restoration of divine favour.

Isa 4:2–6; 6:1–13

• Delineates in the parable of the vineyard the ingratitude of the Jews, and reproves it.

Isa 5:1–10

• Denounces existing corruptions.

Isa 5:8–30

• Foretells the ill success of the plot of the Israelites and Syrians against Judah.

Isa 7:1–16

• Denounces calamities against Israel and Judah.

Isa 7:16–25; 9:2–6

• Foretells prosperity under Hezekiah, and the manifestation of the Messiah.

Isa 9:1–7

• Denounces vengeance upon the enemies of Israel.

Isa 9:8–12

• Denounces the wickedness of Israel, and foretells the judgments of God.

Isa 9:13–21

• Denounces judgments against false prophets.

Isa 10:1–4

• Foretells the destruction of Sennacherib's armies.

Isa 10:5–34

• Foretells the restoration of Israel and the triumph of the Messiah's kingdom.

Isa 11:1–16

• The burden of Babylon.

Isa 13:1–14:28

• Denunciation against the Philistines.

Isa 14:9–32

• Burden of Moab.

Isa 15:1–16:14

• Burden of Damascus.

Isa 17:1–14

• Obscure prophecy. Authorities disagree who directed at: Assyrians, Egyptians, or Ethiopians.

Isa 18:1–7

• The burden of Egypt.

Isa 19:1–20:6

• Denunciations against Babylon.

Isa 21:1–10

• Prophecy concerning Seir.

Isa 21:11–12

• Prophecy concerning Arabia.

Isa 21:13–17

• Prophecy concerning the conquest of Jerusalem, the captivity of Shebna, and the promotion of Eliakim.

Isa 22:1–22

• Prophecy concerning the overthrow of Tyre.

Isa 23:1–18

• Prophecy concerning the judgments upon the land, but that a remnant of the Jews would be saved.

Isa 25:1–27:13

• Reproves Ephraim for his wickedness, and foretells the destruction by Shalmaneser.

Isa 28:1–5

• Declares the glory of God upon the remnant who are saved.

Isa 28:5–6

• Exposes the corruptions in Jerusalem and exhorts to repentance.

Isa 28:7–29

• Foretells the invasion of Sennacherib, the distress of the Jews, and the destruction of the Assyrian army.

Isa 29:1–8

• Denounces the hypocrisy of the Jews.

Isa 29:9–17

• Promises a reformation.

Isa 29:18–24

• Reproves the people for their confidence in Egypt, and their contempt of God.

Isa 30:1–17; 31:1–6

• Declares the goodness and long-suffering of God toward them.

Isa 30:18–26; 32:1–35:10

• Reproves the Jews for their spiritual blindness and infidelity.

Isa 42:18–25

• Promises ultimate restoration of the Jews.

Isa 43:1–13

• Foretells the ultimate destruction of Babylon.

Isa 43:14–17; 47:1–15

• Exhorts the people to repent.

Isa 43:22–28

• Comforts the church with promises.

Isa 44:1–45:5

Isa 48:20 — Go ye forth of Babylon, flee ye from the Chaldeans, with a voice of singing declare ye, tell this, utter it *even* to the end of the earth; say ye, The LORD hath redeemed his servant Jacob.

• Foretells the conversion of the Gentiles, and triumph of the gospel.

Isa 45:5–25

• Denounces the evils of idolatry.

Isa 46:1–13

• Reproves the Jews for their idolatries and other wickedness.

Isa 48:1–22

• Exhorts to sanctification.

Isa 56:1–8

• Foretells calamities to Judah.

Isa 57:1–59:21

• Foreshadows the person and the kingdom of the Messiah.

Isa 32:1–35:10; 42:1–25; 45:1–25; 49:1–56:12; 59:15–66:24

ISCAH • Daughter of Haran and sister of Lot.

Ge 11:29 — And Abram and Nahor took them wives: the name of Abram's wife *was* Sarai; and the name of Nahor's wife, Milcah, the daughter of Haran, the father of Milcah, and the father of Iscah.

ISCARIOT ✧See: Judas

ISH-BOSHETH

• Son of Saul.

• Called Esh-Baal.

1Ch 8:33 — And Ner begat Kish, and Kish begat Saul, and Saul begat Jonathan, and Malchi-shua, and Abinadab, and Esh-baal.

1Ch 9:39 — And Ner begat Kish; and Kish begat Saul; and Saul begat Jonathan, and Malchi-shua, and Abinadab, and Esh-baal.

• Made king by Abner.

2Sa 2:8–10

• Deserted by Abner.

2Sa 3:6–12

• Restores Michal, David's wife, to David.

2Sa 3:14–16

• Assassinated.

2Sa 4:5–8

• Avenged by David.

2Sa 4:9–12

ISH-TOB

• A small state of Aram.

2Sa 10:6 — And when the children of Ammon saw that they stank before David, the children of Ammon sent and hired the Syrians of Beth-rehob, and the Syrians of Zoba, twenty thousand footmen, and of king Maacah a thousand men, and of Ish-tob twelve thousand men.

2Sa 10:8 — And the children of Ammon came out, and put the battle in array at the entering in of the gate: and the Syrians of Zoba, and of Rehob, and Ish-tob, and Maacah, *were* by themselves in the field.

✧See: Tob

ISHBAH • Father of Eshtemoa.

1Ch 4:17 — And the sons of Ezra *were,* Jether, and Mered, and Epher, and Jalon: and she bare Miriam, and Shammai, and Ishbah the father of Eshtemoa.

ISHBAK • Son of Abraham and Keturah.

Ge 25:2 — And she bare him Zimran, and Jokshan, and Medan, and Midian, and Ishbak, and Shuah.

1Ch 1:32 — Now the sons of Keturah, Abraham's concubine: she bare Zimran, and Jokshan, and Medan, and Midian, and Ishbak, and Shuah. And the sons of Jokshan; Sheba, and Dedan.

ISHBI-BENOB • A giant warrior slain by Abishai.

2Sa 21:16 — And Ishbi-benob, which *was* of the sons of the giant, the weight of whose spear *weighed* three hundred *shekels* of brass in weight, he being girded with a new *sword,* thought to have slain David.

ISHI

• A name of deity.

Hos 2:16 — And it shall be at that day, saith the LORD, *that* thou shalt call me Ishi; and shalt call me no more Baali.

• A son of Appaim.

1Ch 2:31 — And the sons of Appaim; Ishi. And the sons of Ishi; Sheshan. And the children of Sheshan; Ahlai.

• A descendant of Judah.

1Ch 4:20 — And the sons of Shimon *were,* Amnon, and Rinnah, Ben-hanan, and Tilon. And the sons of Ishi *were,* Zoheth, and Ben-zoheth.

• A Simeonite.

1Ch 4:42 — And *some* of them, *even* of the sons of Simeon, five hundred men, went to mount Seir, having for their captains Pelatiah, and Neariah, and Rephaiah, and Uzziel, the sons of Ishi.

• One of the heads of Manasseh.

1Ch 5:24 — And these *were* the heads of the house of their fathers, even Epher, and Ishi, and Eliel, and Azriel, and Jeremiah, and Hodaviah, and Jahdiel, mighty men of valour, famous men, *and* heads of the house of their fathers.

ISHIAH • One of the heads of Issachar.

1Ch 7:3 — And the sons of Uzzi; Izrahiah: and the sons of Izrahiah; Michael, and Obadiah, and Joel, Ishiah, five: all of them chief men.

1Ch 24:21 — Concerning Rehabiah: of the sons of Rehabiah, the first *was* Isshiah.

1Ch 24:25 — The brother of Michah *was* Isshiah: of the sons of Isshiah; Zechariah.

ISHIJAH • One of the sons of Harim.

Ezr 10:31 — And *of* the sons of Harim; Eliezer, Ishijah, Malchiah, Shemaiah, Shimeon,

ISHMA • A descendant of Judah.

1Ch 4:3 — And these *were of* the father of Etam; Jezreel, and Ishma, and Idbash: and the name of their sister *was* Hazelelponi:

ISHMAEL

• Son of Abraham.

Ge 16:15–16

Ge 16:11 — And the angel of the LORD said unto her, Behold, thou *art* with child, and shalt bear a son, and shalt call his name Ishmael; because the LORD hath heard thy affliction.

1Ch 1:28 — The sons of Abraham; Isaac, and Ishmael.

• Prayer of Abraham for.

Ge 17:18 — And Abraham said unto God, O that Ishmael might live before thee!

Ge 17:20 — And as for Ishmael, I have heard thee: Behold, I have blessed him, and will make him fruitful, and will multiply him exceedingly; twelve princes shall he beget, and I will make him a great nation.

• Circumcised.

Ge 17:23–26

• Promised to be the father of a nation.

Ge 16:11–12; 21:12–13

Ge 17:20 — And as for Ishmael, I have heard thee: Behold, I have blessed him, and will make him fruitful, and will multiply him exceedingly; twelve princes shall he beget, and I will make him a great nation.

Ge 21:18 — Arise, lift up the lad, and hold him in thine hand; for I will make him a great nation.

• Sent away by Abraham.

Ge 21:6–21

• With Isaac buries his father.

Ge 25:9 — And his sons Isaac and Ishmael buried him in the cave of Machpelah, in the field of Ephron the son of Zohar the Hittite, which *is* before Mamre;

• Children of.

Ge 25:12–18; 1Ch 1:29–31

• Daughter of, marries Esau.

Ge 36:2–3

Ge 28:9 — Then went Esau unto Ishmael, and took unto the wives which he had Mahalath the daughter of Ishmael Abraham's son, the sister of Nebajoth, to be his wife.

• Death of.

Ge 25:17–18

• Father of Zebadiah.

2Ch 19:11 — And, behold, Amariah the chief priest is over you in all matters of the LORD; and Zebadiah the son of Ishmael, the ruler of the house of Judah, for all the king's matters: also the Levites *shall be* officers before you. Deal courageously, and the LORD shall be with the good.

• A son of Azel.

1Ch 8:38 — And Azel had six sons, whose names *are* these, Azrikam, Bocheru, and Ishmael, and Sheariah, and Obadiah, and Hanan. All these *were* the sons of Azel.

1Ch 9:44 — And Azel had six sons, whose names *are* these, Azrikam, Bocheru, and Ishmael, and Sheariah, and Obadiah, and Hanan: these *were* the sons of Azel.

• One of the captains of hundreds.

2Ch 23:1 — And in the seventh year Jehoiada strengthened himself, and took the captains of hundreds, Azariah the son of Jeroham, and Ishmael the son of Jehohanan, and Azariah the son of Obed, and Maaseiah the son of Adaiah, and Elishaphat the son of Zichri, into covenant with him.

• A priest of the exile.

Ezr 10:22 — And of the sons of Pashur; Elioenai, Maaseiah, Ishmael, Nethaneel, Jozabad, and Elasah.

• A son of Nethaniah. Assassinated Gedaliah, governor of Judah; takes captive many Jews.

2Ki 25:23–25; Jer 40:8–41:11

• Defeated by Johanan, and put to flight.

Jer 41:12–15

ISHMAELITES

- **Region occupied by.**

Ge 25:18 — And they dwelt from Havilah unto Shur, that *is* before Egypt, as thou goest toward Assyria: *and* he died in the presence of all his brethren.

- **Merchants of, buy Joseph.**

Ge 37:25–36

Ge 39:1 — And Joseph was brought down to Egypt; and Potiphar, an officer of Pharaoh, captain of the guard, an Egyptian, bought him of the hands of the Ishmeelites, which had brought him down thither.

- **Called Midianites.**

Ge 37:28 — Then there passed by Midianites merchantmen; and they drew and lifted up Joseph out of the pit, and sold Joseph to the Ishmeelites for twenty *pieces* of silver: and they brought Joseph into Egypt.

Ge 37:36 — And the Midianites sold him into Egypt unto Potiphar, an officer of Pharaoh's, *and* captain of the guard.

Jgs 8:24 — And Gideon said unto them, I would desire a request of you, that ye would give me every man the earrings of his prey. (For they had golden earrings, because they *were* Ishmaelites.)

Jgs 8:26 — And the weight of the golden earrings that he requested was a thousand and seven hundred *shekels* of gold; beside ornaments, and collars, and purple raiment that *was* on the kings of Midian, and beside the chains that *were* about their camels' necks.

- **Enemies to Israel.**

Ps 83:6 — The tabernacles of Edom, and the Ishmaelites; of Moab, and the Hagarenes;

➜See: Ishmael

ISHMAIAH • A prince of Zebulun.

1Ch 27:19 — Of Zebulun, Ishmaiah the son of Obadiah: of Naphtali, Jerimoth the son of Azriel:

ISHMERAI • A chief Benjamite.

1Ch 8:18 — Ishmerai also, and Jezliah, and Jobab, the sons of Elpaal;

ISHOD • One of the tribe of Manasseh.

1Ch 7:18 — And his sister Hammoleketh bare Ishod, and Abiezer, and Mahalah.

ISHPAN • A chief Benjamite.

1Ch 8:22 — And Ishpan, and Heber, and Eliel,

ISHUAH

- **Called also Isuah.**
- **Son of Asher.**

Ge 46:17 — And the sons of Asher; Jimnah, and Ishuah, and Isui, and Beriah, and Serah their sister: and the sons of Beriah; Heber, and Malchiel.

1Ch 7:30 — The sons of Asher; Imnah, and Isuah, and Ishuai, and Beriah, and Serah their sister.

ISHUI

- **Called also Ishuai, Isui, and Jesui.**
- **Son of Asher.**

Ge 46:17 — And the sons of Asher; Jimnah, and Ishuah, and Isui, and Beriah, and Serah their sister: and the sons of Beriah; Heber, and Malchiel.

Nu 26:44 — *Of* the children of Asher after their families: of Jimna, the family of the Jimnites: of Jesui, the family of the Jesuites: of Beriah, the family of the Beriites.

1Ch 7:30 — The sons of Asher; Imnah, and Isuah, and Ishuai, and Beriah, and Serah their sister.

- **Son of Saul.**

1Sa 14:49 — Now the sons of Saul were Jonathan, and Ishui, and Melchi-shua: and the names of his two daughters *were these;* the name of the firstborn Merab, and the name of the younger Michal:

ISLAND

- **Prophecies concerning.**

Ps 97:1 — The LORD reigneth; let the earth rejoice; let the multitude of isles be glad *thereof.*

Isa 11:11 — And it shall come to pass in that day, *that* the Lord shall set his hand again the second time to recover the remnant of his people, which shall be left, from Assyria, and from Egypt, and from Pathros, and from Cush, and from Elam, and from Shinar, and from Hamath, and from the islands of the sea.

Isa 41:1 — Keep silence before me, O islands; and let the people renew *their* strength: let them come near; then let them speak: let us come near together to judgment.

Isa 41:5 — The isles saw *it,* and feared; the ends of the earth were afraid, drew near, and came.

Isa 49:1 — Listen, O isles, unto me; and hearken, ye people, from far; The LORD hath called me from the womb; from the bowels of my mother hath he made mention of my name.

Zep 2:11 — The LORD *will be* terrible unto them: for he will famish all the gods of the earth; and *men* shall worship him, every one from his place, *even* all the isles of the heathen.

Rev 16:20 — And every island fled away, and the mountains were not found.

ISMACHIAH • A Levite.

2Ch 31:13 — And Jehiel, and Azaziah, and Nahath, and Asahel, and Jerimoth, and Jozabad, and Eliel, and Ismachiah, and Mahath, and Benaiah, *were* overseers under the hand of Cononiah and Shimei his brother, at the commandment of Hezekiah the king, and Azariah the ruler of the house of God.

ISMAIAH • A Gibeonite who joined David at Ziklag.

1Ch 12:4 — And Ismaiah the Gibeonite, a mighty man among the thirty, and over the thirty; and Jeremiah, and Jahaziel, and Johanan, and Josabad the Gederathite,

ISPAH • A chief Benjamite.

1Ch 8:16 — And Michael, and Ispah, and Joha, the sons of Beriah;

ISRAEL

• First sacrifice offered by, under the law.

Le 8:14–36; 9:8–24

• Second passover observed.

Nu 9:1–5

• March out of the wilderness.

Nu 10:11–36

• For itinerary of march out of wilderness.

Nu 33:1–56

• Order of camp and march.

Nu 2:1–34

• Arrive at the border of Canaan.

Nu 12:16 — And afterward the people removed from Hazeroth, and pitched in the wilderness of Paran.

• Send twelve spies to view the land.

Nu 13:1–33

Nu 32:8 — Thus did your fathers, when I sent them from Kadesh-barnea to see the land.

Dt 1:22 — And ye came near unto me every one of you, and said, We will send men before us, and they shall search us out the land, and bring us word again by what way we must go up, and into what cities we shall come.

Dt 1:25 — And they took of the fruit of the land in their hands, and brought *it* down unto us, and brought us word again, and said, *It is* a good land which the LORD our God doth give us.

Jos 14:7 — Forty years old *was* I when Moses the servant of the LORD sent me from Kadesh-barnea to espy out the land; and I brought him word again as *it was* in mine heart.

• Return with a majority and minority report.

Nu 13:26–33; 14:6–10

• Murmuring over the report.

Nu 14:1–5

• The judgment of God upon them in consequence of their unbelief and murmuring.

Nu 14:13–39

• Reaction, and their purpose to enter the land; are defeated by the Amalekites.

Nu 14:40–45; Dt 1:41–45

• Abide at Kadesh.

Dt 1:46 — So ye abode in Kadesh many days, according unto the days that ye abode *there.*

• Return to the wilderness, where they remain thirty-eight years, and all die except Joshua and Caleb.

Nu 14:20–39

• Rebellion of Korah, Dathan, and Abiram.

Nu 16:1–40

Dt 11:6 — And what he did unto Dathan and Abiram, the sons of Eliab, the son of Reuben: how the earth opened her mouth, and swallowed them up, and their households, and their tents, and all the substance that *was* in their possession, in the midst of all Israel:

• Murmur against Moses and Aaron; are plagued; fourteen thousand seven hundred die; plague stayed.

Nu 16:41–50

• Murmur for want of water in Meribah; the rock is smitten.

Nu 20:1–13

• Are refused passage through the country of Edom.

Nu 20:14–21

• The death of Aaron.

Nu 33:38–39

Nu 20:22 — And the children of Israel, *even* the whole congregation, journeyed from Kadesh, and came unto mount Hor.

Nu 20:29 — And when all the congregation saw that Aaron was dead, they mourned for Aaron thirty days, *even* all the house of Israel.

Dt 10:6 — And the children of Israel took their journey from Beeroth of the children of Jaakan to Mosera: there Aaron died, and there he was buried; and Eleazar his son ministered in the priest's office in his stead.

• Defeat the Canaanites.

Nu 21:1–3

• Are scourged with serpents.

Nu 21:4–9

• Defeat the Amorites.

Nu 21:21–32; Dt 2:24–35

• Defeat the king of Baasha.

Nu 21:33–35; Dt 3:1–17

• Arrive in the plains of Moab, at the fords of the Jordan.

Nu 33:48–49

Nu 22:1 — And the children of Israel set forward, and pitched in the plains of Moab on this side Jordan *by* Jericho.

• Commit idolatry with the people of Moab.

Nu 25:1–5

• Visited by a plague in consequence; twenty-four thousand die.

Nu 25:6–15

Nu 26:1 — And it came to pass after the plague, that the LORD spake unto Moses and unto Eleazar the son of Aaron the priest, saying,

• The people numbered for the allotment of the land.

Nu 26:1–65

• The daughters of Zelophehad sue for an inheritance.

Nu 27:1–11; Jos 17:3–6

• Conquest of the Midianites.

Nu 31:1–54

• **Nations dread.**
Dt 2:25 — This day will I begin to put the dread of thee and the fear of thee upon the nations *that are* under the whole heaven, who shall hear report of thee, and shall tremble, and be in anguish because of thee.

• **Renew the covenant.**
Dt 29:1–29

• **Moses dies, and people mourn.**
Dt 34:1–12

• **Joshua appointed leader.**
Nu 27:18–23
Dt 31:23 — And he gave Joshua the son of Nun a charge, and said, Be strong and of a good courage: for thou shalt bring the children of Israel into the land which I sware unto them: and I will be with thee.

See: Joshua

• **All who were numbered at Sinai perished in the wilderness except Caleb and Joshua.**
Dt 2:14–16
Nu 26:63 — These *are* they that were numbered by Moses and Eleazar the priest, who numbered the children of Israel in the plains of Moab by Jordan *near* Jericho.
Nu 26:65 — For the LORD had said of them, They shall surely die in the wilderness. And there was not left a man of them, save Caleb the son of Jephunneh, and Joshua the son of Nun.

• **Piety of those who entered Canaan.**
Jgs 2:7–10; Jer 2:2–3
Jos 23:8 — But cleave unto the LORD your God, as ye have done unto this day.

• **Men chosen to allot the lands of Canaan among the tribes and families.**
Nu 34:17–29

• **Remove from Shittim to Jordan.**
Jos 3:1 — And Joshua rose early in the morning; and they removed from Shittim, and came to Jordan, he and all the children of Israel, and lodged there before they passed over.

• **Cross Jordan.**
Jos 4:1–24

• **Circumcision observed and passover celebrated.**
Jos 5:1–15

• **Jericho taken.**
Jos 6:1–27

• **Ai taken.**
Jos 7:1–8:35

• **Make a league with the Gibeonites.**
Jos 9:1–27

• **Defeat the five Amoritish kings.**
Jos 10:1–43

• **Conquest of the land.**
Jos 21:43–45; Jgs 1:1–36

• **The land allotted.**
Jos 15:1–21:45

• **Two and one-half tribes erect a memorial to signify the unity of the tribes; misunderstood.**
Jos 22:1–34

• **Joshua's exhortation immediately before his death.**
Jos 23:1–16

• **Covenant renewed, death of Joshua.**
Jos 24:1–33; Jgs 2:8–9

• **Religious fidelity during the life of Joshua.**
Jos 24:31 — And Israel served the LORD all the days of Joshua, and all the days of the elders that overlived Joshua, and which had known all the works of the LORD, that he had done for Israel.
Jgs 2:7 — And the people served the LORD all the days of Joshua, and all the days of the elders that outlived Joshua, who had seen all the great works of the LORD, that he did for Israel.

ISRAEL, a Name Given to Jacob

Ge 32:24–32; Hos 12:3–4
2Ki 17:34 — Unto this day they do after the former manners: they fear not the LORD, neither do they after their statutes, or after their ordinances, or after the law and commandment which the LORD commanded the children of Jacob, whom he named Israel;

ISRAEL, Christ in Prophecy, a Name Given to

Isa 49:3 — And said unto me, Thou *art* my servant, O Israel, in whom I will be glorified.

ISRAEL, Exodus

Ex 1:1–2:25; 5:1–23; Ac 7:18–21

• **Their groaning heard of God.**
Ex 2:23–25

• **Moses commissioned as deliverer.**
Ex 3:2–4:17

• **The land of Egypt plagued on their account.**

See: Egypt

• **Exempt from the plagues.**
Ex 8:22–23; 9:4–6
Ex 9:26 — Only in the land of Goshen, where the children of Israel *were,* was there no hail.
Ex 10:23 — They saw not one another, neither rose any from his place for three days: but all the children of Israel had light in their dwellings.
Ex 11:7 — But against any of the children of Israel shall not a dog move his tongue, against man or beast: that ye may know how that the LORD doth put a difference between the Egyptians and Israel.
Ex 12:13 — And the blood shall be to you for a token upon the houses where ye *are:* and when I see the blood, I will pass over you, and the plague shall not be upon you to destroy *you,* when I smite the land of Egypt.

- **Children were spared when the firstborn of the Egyptians were slain.**
  Ex 12:13 — And the blood shall be to you for a token upon the houses where ye *are:* and when I see the blood, I will pass over you, and the plague shall not be upon you to destroy *you,* when I smite the land of Egypt.
  Ex 12:23 — For the LORD will pass through to smite the Egyptians; and when he seeth the blood upon the lintel, and on the two side posts, the LORD will pass over the door, and will not suffer the destroyer to come in unto your houses to smite *you.*
- **Instituted the passover.**
  Ex 12:1–28
- **Borrowed jewels from the Egyptians.**
  Ex 11:2–3; 12:35–36
  Ps 105:37 — He brought them forth also with silver and gold: and *there was* not one feeble *person* among their tribes.
- **Urged by the Egyptians to depart.**
  Ex 12:31–39
- **Journey from Rameses to Succoth.**
  Ex 12:37–39
- **Made the journey by night.**
  Ex 12:42 — It *is* a night to be much observed unto the LORD for bringing them out from the land of Egypt: this *is* that night of the LORD to be observed of all the children of Israel in their generations.
- **The day of their deliverance to be a memorial.**
  Ex 13:3–16
  Ex 12:42 — It *is* a night to be much observed unto the LORD for bringing them out from the land of Egypt: this *is* that night of the LORD to be observed of all the children of Israel in their generations.
- **Led of God.**
  Ex 13:21–22
  Ex 13:18 — But God led the people about, *through* the way of the wilderness of the Red sea: and the children of Israel went up harnessed out of the land of Egypt.
- **Providentially cared for.**
  Dt 8:3–4; 29:5–6
  Dt 34:7 — And Moses *was* an hundred and twenty years old when he died: his eye was not dim, nor his natural force abated.
  Ne 9:21 — Yea, forty years didst thou sustain them in the wilderness, *so that* they lacked nothing; their clothes waxed not old, and their feet swelled not.
  Ps 105:37 — He brought them forth also with silver and gold: and *there was* not one feeble *person* among their tribes.
  See: Cloud; pillar of
  See: Manna
- **Journey from Succoth to Etham.**
  Ex 13:20 — And they took their journey from Succoth, and encamped in Etham, in the edge of the wilderness.
- **Journey from Succoth to Pi-hahiroth.**
  Nu 33:5–7
  Ex 14:2 — Speak unto the children of Israel, that they turn and encamp before Pi-hahiroth, between Migdol and the sea, over against Baal-zephon: before it shall ye encamp by the sea.
- **Pursued by the Egyptians.**
  Ex 14:5–31
- **Pass through the Red Sea.**
  Ex 14:19–22; Ps 78:1–72; 105:1–107:43; 136:1–26
  Dt 11:4 — And what he did unto the army of Egypt, unto their horses, and to their chariots; how he made the water of the Red sea to overflow them as they pursued after you, and *how* the LORD hath destroyed them unto this day;
- **Order of march.**
  Nu 2:1–34
- **Journey to Marah.**
  Ex 15:23 — And when they came to Marah, they could not drink of the waters of Marah, for they *were* bitter: therefore the name of it was called Marah.
  Nu 33:8 — And they departed from before Pi-hahiroth, and passed through the midst of the sea into the wilderness, and went three days' journey in the wilderness of Etham, and pitched in Marah.
- **Murmur on account of the bitter water.**
  Ex 15:23–25
- **Murmur on account of the water of, sweetened.**
  Ex 15:25 — And he cried unto the LORD; and the LORD shewed him a tree, *which* when he had cast into the waters, the waters were made sweet: there he made for them a statute and an ordinance, and there he proved them,
- **Journey to Elim.**
  Ex 15:27 — And they came to Elim, where *were* twelve wells of water, and threescore and ten palm trees: and they encamped there by the waters.
  Nu 33:9 — And they removed from Marah, and came unto Elim: and in Elim *were* twelve fountains of water, and threescore and ten palm trees; and they pitched there.
- **For the itinerary.**
  Nu 33:1–56
- **Murmured for food.**
  Ex 16:2–3
- **Provided with manna and quails.**
  Ex 16:4–36
- **Murmured for want of water at Rephidim.**
  Ex 17:2–7
- **Murmured for want of water and water miraculously supplied from the rock at Meribah.**
  Ex 17:5–7
- **Defeat the Amalekites.**
  Dt 25:17–18
  Ex 17:13 — And Joshua discomfited Amalek and his people with the edge of the sword.

• Arrive at Sinai.

Ex 19:1 — In the third month, when the children of Israel were gone forth out of the land of Egypt, the same day came they *into* the wilderness of Sinai.

Nu 33:15 — And they departed from Rephidim, and pitched in the wilderness of Sinai.

• At the suggestion of Jethro, Moses' father-in-law, they organize a system of government.

Dt 1:9–17

Ex 18:25 — And Moses chose able men out of all Israel, and made them heads over the people, rulers of thousands, rulers of hundreds, rulers of fifties, and rulers of tens.

• The message of God to them, and their reply.

Ex 19:3–8

• Sanctify themselves for receiving the law.

Ex 19:10–15

• The law delivered to.

Ex 20:1–24:4; 25:1–31:18; Le 1:1–25:55; 27:1–34; Dt 5:1–33; 15:1–16:22

• The people receive it and covenant obedience to it.

Ex 24:3 — And Moses came and told the people all the words of the LORD, and all the judgments: and all the people answered with one voice, and said, All the words which the LORD hath said will we do.

Ex 24:7 — And he took the book of the covenant, and read in the audience of the people: and they said, All that the LORD hath said will we do, and be obedient.

• Idolatry of.

Ex 32:1–35; Dt 9:17–21

• The anger of the Lord in consequence.

Ex 32:9–14

• Moses' indignation; breaks tables of stone; commands the Levites; three thousand slain.

Ex 32:19–35

• Visited by a plague.

Ex 32:35 — And the LORD plagued the people, because they made the calf, which Aaron made.

• Obduracy of.

Dt 9:12–29

Ex 33:3 — Unto a land flowing with milk and honey: for I will not go up in the midst of thee; for thou *art* a stiffnecked people: lest I consume thee in the way.

Ex 34:9 — And he said, If now I have found grace in thy sight, O Lord, let my Lord, I pray thee, go among us; for it *is* a stiffnecked people; and pardon our iniquity and our sin, and take us for thine inheritance.

• God withdraws his presence.

Ex 33:1–3

• The mourning of, when God refused to lead them.

Ex 33:4–10

• Tables renewed.

Ex 34:1–35

• Pattern for the tabernacle and the appurtenances, and forms of worship to be observed.

Ex 25:1–31:18

• Gifts consecrated for the creation of the tabernacle.

Ex 35:1–36:7; Nu 7:1–89

• The erection of the tabernacle.

• The manufacture of the appurtenances.

• Including the garments of the priests and their sanctification.

Ex 36:8–40:38

ISRAEL, Judah

• The nation composed of the tribes of Judah and Benjamin. Called Judah.

Isa 11:12–13

Jer 4:3 — For thus saith the LORD to the men of Judah and Jerusalem, Break up your fallow ground, and sow not among thorns.

• Called Jews. Ruled by the descendants of David.

• In the historical books of Kings and Chronicles the nation is called Judah.

• In the prophecies it is frequently referred to as Israel.

Isa 8:14 — And he shall be for a sanctuary; but for a stone of stumbling and for a rock of offence to both the houses of Israel, for a gin and for a snare to the inhabitants of Jerusalem.

Isa 49:7 — Thus saith the LORD, the Redeemer of Israel, *and* his Holy One, to him whom man despiseth, to him whom the nation abhorreth, to a servant of rulers, Kings shall see and arise, princes also shall worship, because of the LORD that is faithful, *and* the Holy One of Israel, and he shall choose thee.

See: Jews

• List of rulers and periods of time over which they reigned.

See: Rehoboam (seventeen years)

See: Abijam (three years)

See: Asa (forty-one years)

See: Jehoshaphat (twenty-five years)

See: Jehoram (eight years)

See: Ahaziah (one year)

See: Athaliah (six years)

See: Joash; called also Jehoash (forty years)

See: Amaziah (twenty-nine years)

See: Uzziah; Called Azariah. King of Judah (fifty-two years)

See: Jotham (sixteen years)

See: Ahaz (sixteen years)

- See: **Hezekiah (twenty-nine years)**
- See: **Manasseh (fifty-five years)**
- See: **Amon (two years)**
- See: **Josiah (thirty-one years)**
- See: **Jehoahaz (three months)**
- See: **Jehoiakim (eleven years)**
- See: **Jehoiachin (three months)**
- See: **Zedekiah (eleven years)**

• Rehoboam succeeds Solomon; in consequence of his arbitrary policy ten tribes rebel.

1Ki 12:1–33

• Other circumstances of Rehoboam's reign.

1Ki 14:21–31; 2Ch 10:1–12:16

• Death of Rehoboam.

1Ki 14:31 — And Rehoboam slept with his fathers, and was buried with his fathers in the city of David. And his mother's name *was* Naamah an Ammonitess. And Abijam his son reigned in his stead.

• Abijam's wicked reign.

1Ki 15:1–8; 2Ch 13:1–22

• Asa's good reign.

1Ki 15:9–24; 2Ch 14:1–16:14

• Asa makes a league with Ben-hadad, king of Syria, to make war against Israel.

1Ki 15:16–24

• Jehoshaphat succeeds Asa.

2Ch 17:1–21:1

1Ki 15:24 — And Asa slept with his fathers, and was buried with his fathers in the city of David his father: and Jehoshaphat his son reigned in his stead.

• Jehoshaphat joins Ahab against the king of Syria.

1Ki 22:1–53

- See: **Jehoshaphat**

• Jehoram, called also Joram. Reigns in the stead of his father, Jehoshaphat.

2Ki 8:16–24; 2Ch 21:1–20

• Edom revolts.

2Ki 8:20–22

• Ahaziah, called also Azariah.

2Ch 22:6 — And he returned to be healed in Jezreel because of the wounds which were given him at Ramah, when he fought with Hazael king of Syria. And Azariah the son of Jehoram king of Judah went down to see Jehoram the son of Ahab at Jezreel, because he was sick.

• Ahaziah, called also Jehoahaz.

2Ch 21:17 — And they came up into Judah, and brake into it, and carried away all the substance that was found in the king's house, and his sons also, and his wives; so that there was never a son left him, save Jehoahaz, the youngest of his sons.

2Ch 25:23 — And Joash the king of Israel took Amaziah king of Judah, the son of Joash, the son of Jehoahaz, at Beth-shemesh, and brought him to Jerusalem, and brake down the wall of Jerusalem from the gate of Ephraim to the corner gate, four hundred cubits.

• Ahaziah succeeds Jehoram.

2Ki 8:24–29; 2Ch 22:1–12

• Ahaziah slain by Jehu.

2Ki 9:27–29; 2Ch 22:8–9

• Athaliah, his mother, succeeds him.

2Ki 11:1–16; 2Ch 22:10–23:15

• Jehoash, called also Joash; succeeds Athaliah.

2Ki 11:21–12:21; 2Ch 24:1–27

• The temple repaired.

2Ki 12:1–21

• Amaziah reigns; Judah is invaded by the king of Israel.

• Jerusalem is taken and the sacred things of the temple carried away.

2Ki 14:1–20; 2Ch 25:1–28

• Azariah, called also Uzziah; succeeds him.

2Ki 14:21–22; 15:1–7; 2Ch 26:1–23

• Jotham succeeds Uzziah.

2Ki 15:32–38; 2Ch 27:1–9

2Ki 15:7 — So Azariah slept with his fathers; and they buried him with his fathers in the city of David: and Jotham his son reigned in his stead.

• Rezin, king of Syria, invades Judah.

2Ki 15:37 — In those days the LORD began to send against Judah Rezin the king of Syria, and Pekah the son of Remaliah.

• Jotham is succeeded by Ahaz.

2Ch 28:1–27

2Ki 16:1 — In the seventeenth year of Pekah the son of Remaliah Ahaz the son of Jotham king of Judah began to reign.

• Judah is invaded by kings of Samaria and Syria.

2Ki 16:5–9

• Ahaz changes the fashion of the altar in the temple.

2Ki 16:10–18

• Hezekiah succeeds Ahaz.

2Ki 16:19–20; 2Ch 29:1–32:33

• His good reign.

2Ki 18:1–8

• He revolts from the sovereignty of the king of Assyria.

2Ki 18:7 — And the LORD was with him; *and* he prospered whithersoever he went forth: and he rebelled against the king of Assyria, and served him not.

• King of Assyria invades Judah, and blasphemes the God of Judah; his army overthrown.

2Ki 18:9–19:37

• Hezekiah's sickness and miraculous restoration.
2Ki 20:1–21

• Succeeded by Manasseh.
2Ch 33:1–20
2Ki 20:21 — And Hezekiah slept with his fathers: and Manasseh his son reigned in his stead.

• Manasseh's wicked reign.
2Ki 21:1–18

• Amon succeeds Manasseh on the throne.
2Ki 21:18–26; 2Ch 33:20–25

• Josiah succeeds Amon; temple repaired; book of law recovered; revival follows.
2Ki 22:1–23:30; 2Ch 34:1–35:27

• Josiah succeeded by Jehoahaz, 3 months; dethroned by king of Egypt; land under tribute.
2Ki 23:30–35; 2Ch 36:1–3

• Jehoiakim is elevated to the throne; becomes tributary to Nebuchadnezzar 3 years; rebels; is conquered.
2Ki 24:1–6; 2Ch 36:4–8

• Jehoiachin is made king; suffers invasion and is carried to Babylon.
2Ki 24:8–16; 2Ch 36:9–10

• King Zedekiah rebels; Nebuchadnezzar invades Judah, Jerusalem; takes people to Babylon.
2Ki 24:17–25:30; 2Ch 36:11–21

• The poorest of the people were left to occupy the country, and were joined by fragments of the army of Judah.
2Ki 25:22–23; Jer 40:7–12
2Ki 25:12 — But the captain of the guard left of the poor of the land *to be* vinedressers and husbandmen.
Jer 39:10 — But Nebuzar-adan the captain of the guard left of the poor of the people, which had nothing, in the land of Judah, and gave them vineyards and fields at the same time.
Jer 52:16 — But Nebuzar-adan the captain of the guard left *certain* of the poor of the land for vinedressers and for husbandmen.

• Gedaliah appointed governor over.
2Ki 25:22 — And *as for* the people that remained in the land of Judah, whom Nebuchadnezzar king of Babylon had left, even over them he made Gedaliah the son of Ahikam, the son of Shaphan, ruler.

• His administration favorable to the people.
2Ki 25:23–24; Jer 40:7–12

• Conspired against and slain by Ishmael.
Jer 40:13–41:3
2Ki 25:25 — But it came to pass in the seventh month, that Ishmael the son of Nethaniah, the son of Elishama, of the seed royal, came, and ten men with him, and smote Gedaliah, that he died, and the Jews and the Chaldees that were with him at Mizpah.

• Ishmael seeks to betray the people to the Ammonites.
Jer 41:1–18

• The people, in fear, take refuge in Egypt.
Jer 41:14–18; 42:13–18
2Ki 25:26 — And all the people, both small and great, and the captains of the armies, arose, and came to Egypt: for they were afraid of the Chaldees.

• Captivity of.

• Great wickedness the cause of their adversity.
Eze 5:1–7:27; 16:1–63; 23:22–44

• Dwell in Babylon.
Jer 52:28–30
Da 5:13 — Then was Daniel brought in before the king. *And* the king spake and said unto Daniel, *Art* thou that Daniel, which *art* of the children of the captivity of Judah, whom the king my father brought out of Jewry?
Da 6:13 — Then answered they and said before the king, That Daniel, which *is* of the children of the captivity of Judah, regardeth not thee, O king, nor the decree that thou hast signed, but maketh his petition three times a day.

• Dwell by the river Chebor.
Eze 1:1 — Now it came to pass in the thirtieth year, in the fourth *month,* in the fifth *day* of the month, as I *was* among the captives by the river of Chebar, *that* the heavens were opened, and I saw visions of God.
Eze 10:15 — And the cherubims were lifted up. This *is* the living creature that I saw by the river of Chebar.

• Patriotism of.
Ps 137:1–9

• Plotted against, by Haman.
Est 3:1–15

• Are saved by Esther.
Est 4:1–9:32

• Cyrus decrees their restoration.
2Ch 36:22–23; Ezr 1:1–4

• Cyrus directs the rebuilding of the temple, and the restoration of the vessels which had been carried to Babylon.
Ezr 1:3–11
2Ch 36:23 — Thus saith Cyrus king of Persia, All the kingdoms of the earth hath the LORD God of heaven given me; and he hath charged me to build him an house in Jerusalem, which *is* in Judah. Who *is there* among you of all his people? The LORD his God *be* with him, and let him go up.

• Proclamation renewed by Darius and Artaxerxes.
Ezr 6:1–14

• Ezra returns with seventeen hundred and fifty-four of the captivity to Jerusalem.
Ezr 2:1–70

• Temple rebuilt and dedicated.
Ezr 3:1–6:22

- **Artaxerxes issues proclamation to restore the temple service.**
  Ezr 7:1–28
- **Priests and Levites authorized to return.**
  Ezr 8:1–36
- **Corruptions among the returned captives; their reform.**
  Ezr 9:1–10:44

• Nehemiah is commissioned to lead the remainder of the captivity back to Canaan.
Ne 2:1–20; 7:5–67; Ps 85:1–13; 87:1–7; 107:1–43; 126:1–6

• Wall of Jerusalem rebuilt and dedicated.
Ne 2:1–6:19; 12:1–47

• The law read and expounded.
Ne 8:1–18

• Solemn feast is kept; priests are purified; and the covenant sealed.
Ne 8:1–10:39

• One tenth of people will dwell in Jerusalem; other nine parts dwell in other cities.
Ne 11:1–36

• Catalogue of the priests and Levites who came up with Zerubbabel.
Ne 12:1–47

• Nehemiah reforms various abuses.
Ne 13:1–31

• Expect a Messiah.
Lk 3:15 — And as the people were in expectation, and all men mused in their hearts of John, whether he were the Christ, or not;

• Many accept Jesus as the Christ.
Jn 2:23 — Now when he was in Jerusalem at the passover, in the feast *day,* many believed in his name, when they saw the miracles which he did.

Jn 10:42 — And many believed on him there.

Jn 11:45 — Then many of the Jews which came to Mary, and had seen the things which Jesus did, believed on him.

Jn 12:11 — Because that by reason of him many of the Jews went away, and believed on Jesus.

Ac 21:20 — And when they heard *it,* they glorified the Lord, and said unto him, Thou seest, brother, how many thousands of Jews there are which believe; and they are all zealous of the law:

• Reject Jesus.
→See: Jesus, Rejected

• Rejected of God.
Mt 21:43 — <u>Therefore say I unto you, The kingdom of God shall be taken from you, and given to a nation bringing forth the fruits thereof.</u>

Lk 20:16 — <u>He shall come and destroy these husbandmen, and shall give the vineyard to others.</u> And when they heard *it,* they said, God forbid.

• Prophecies concerning.

- **Of their rejection of the Messiah.**
  Isa 8:14–15; 53:1–3; Zec 11:1–17; 13:1–9

  Isa 49:5 — And now, saith the LORD that formed me from the womb *to be* his servant, to bring Jacob again to him, Though Israel be not gathered, yet shall I be glorious in the eyes of the LORD, and my God shall be my strength.

  Isa 49:7 — Thus saith the LORD, the Redeemer of Israel, *and* his Holy One, to him whom man despiseth, to him whom the nation abhorreth, to a servant of rulers, Kings shall see and arise, princes also shall worship, because of the LORD that is faithful, *and* the Holy One of Israel, and he shall choose thee.

  Isa 52:14 — As many were astonied at thee; his visage was so marred more than any man, and his form more than the sons of men:

  Mt 21:33 — <u>Hear another parable: There was a certain householder, which planted a vineyard, and hedged it round about, and digged a winepress in it, and built a tower, and let it out to husbandmen, and went into a far country:</u>

  Mt 22:1 — And Jesus answered and spake unto them again by parables, and said,

- **Of war and other judgments.**
  Dt 28:49–57; 2Ki 20:17–18; 21:12–15; 22:16–17; 23:26–27; Isa 1:1–24; 3:1–4:1; 5:1–30; 6:9–13; 7:17–25; 8:14–9:21; 22:1–14; 28:14–22; 29:1–10; 30:1–17; 31:1–3; 32:9–14; Jer 1:11–16; 4:5–31; 6:1–30; 7:8–8:22; 9:9–26; 10:17–22; 11:9–23; 13:9–27; 14:14–18; 15:1–14; 16:1–17:4; 18:15–17; 19:1–15; 21:4–7; 22:24–30; 25:8–38; 28:1–17; 34:1–22; 37:1–38:3; 42:13–45:5; Eze 4:1–5:17; 11:7–12; 12:1–28; 15:1–17:24; 19:1–14; 22:13–22; 23:22–35; 24:1–27; 33:21–29; Da 9:26–27; Joel 2:1–17; Am 2:4–5; Mic 3:1–12; 4:8–10; Hab 1:6–11; Zep 1:1–18; Zec 11:1–17; 14:1–21; Mt 21:33–34; 23:35–38; 24:14–42; Mk 13:1–13; Lk 13:34–35; 19:43–44; 21:5–25; 23:28–31

  Isa 10:12 — Wherefore it shall come to pass, *that* when the Lord hath performed his whole work upon mount Zion and on Jerusalem, I will punish the fruit of the stout heart of the king of Assyria, and the glory of his high looks.

  Jer 20:5 — Moreover I will deliver all the strength of this city, and all the labours thereof, and all the precious things thereof, and all the treasures of the kings of Judah will I give into the hand of their enemies, which shall spoil them, and take them, and carry them to Babylon.

  La 5:6 — We have given the hand *to* the Egyptians, *and to* the Assyrians, to be satisfied with bread.

  Mic 2:10 — Arise ye, and depart; for this *is* not *your* rest: because it is polluted, it shall destroy *you,* even with a sore destruction.

  Mal 4:1 — For, behold, the day cometh, that shall burn as an oven; and all the proud, yea, and all that do wickedly, shall be stubble: and the day that cometh shall burn them up, saith the LORD of hosts, that it shall leave them neither root nor branch.

  Mt 24:2 — And Jesus said unto them, <u>See ye not all these things? verily I say unto you, There shall not be left here one stone upon another, that shall not be thrown down.</u>

Rev 1:7 — Behold, he cometh with clouds; and every eye shall see him, and they *also* which pierced him: and all kindreds of the earth shall wail because of him. Even so, Amen.

• Dispersion of.

Isa 24:1 — Behold, the LORD maketh the earth empty, and maketh it waste, and turneth it upside down, and scattereth abroad the inhabitants thereof.

Jer 9:16 — I will scatter them also among the heathen, whom neither they nor their fathers have known: and I will send a sword after them, till I have consumed them.

Eze 4:13 — And the LORD said, Even thus shall the children of Israel eat their defiled bread among the Gentiles, whither I will drive them.

Eze 5:10 — Therefore the fathers shall eat the sons in the midst of thee, and the sons shall eat their fathers; and I will execute judgments in thee, and the whole remnant of thee will I scatter into all the winds.

Eze 5:12 — A third part of thee shall die with the pestilence, and with famine shall they be consumed in the midst of thee: and a third part shall fall by the sword round about thee and I will scatter a third part into all the winds, and I will draw out a sword after them.

Eze 20:23 — I lifted up mine hand unto them also in the wilderness, that I would scatter them among the heathen, and disperse them through the countries;

Eze 36:19 — And I scattered them among the heathen, and they were dispersed through the countries: according to their way and according to their doings I judged them.

Da 9:7 — O Lord, righteousness *belongeth* unto thee, but unto us confusion of faces, as at this day; to the men of Judah, and to the inhabitants of Jerusalem, and unto all Israel, *that are* near, and *that are* far off, through all the countries whither thou hast driven them, because of their trespass that they have trespassed against thee.

Hos 9:17 — My God will cast them away, because they did not hearken unto him: and they shall be wanderers among the nations.

Joel 3:6 — The children also of Judah and the children of Jerusalem have ye sold unto the Grecians, that ye might remove them far from their border.

Joel 3:20 — But Judah shall dwell for ever, and Jerusalem from generation to generation.

Am 9:9 — For, lo, I will command, and I will sift the house of Israel among all nations, like as *corn* is sifted in a sieve, yet shall not the least grain fall upon the earth.

Jn 7:35 — Then said the Jews among themselves, Whither will he go, that we shall not find him? will he go unto the dispersed among the Gentiles, and teach the Gentiles?

Ac 2:5 — And there were dwelling at Jerusalem Jews, devout men, out of every nation under heaven.

• Of blessing and restoration.

Isa 1:25–27; 2:1–5; 4:2–6; 11:11–13; 25:1–26:2; 26:12–19; 29:18–24; 30:18–26; 32:15–20; 33:13–24; 35:1–10; 37:31–32; 44:1–28; 49:13–23; 51:1–52:12; 60:1–22; 61:4–9; 62:1–12; 66:5–22; Jer 3:14–18; 4:3–18; 12:14–16; 24:1–7; 29:1–14; 30:3–22; 32:36–33:26; Eze 14:22–23; 16:60–63; 20:40–41; 36:1–38; Da 11:30–12:1; Joel 3:1–21; Am 9:9–15; Ob 1:17–21; Mic 2:12–13; Zec 1:14–2:13; 8:1–23; 10:5–12; 12:1–13:9; 14:3–21; Ro 11:1–36

Isa 27:13 — And it shall come to pass in that day, *that* the great trumpet shall be blown, and they shall come which were ready to perish in the land of Assyria, and the outcasts in the land of Egypt, and shall worship the LORD in the holy mount at Jerusalem.

Isa 40:2 — Speak ye comfortably to Jerusalem, and cry unto her, that her warfare is accomplished, that her iniquity is pardoned: for she hath received of the LORD'S hand double for all her sins.

Isa 40:9 — O Zion, that bringest good tidings, get thee up into the high mountain; O Jerusalem, that bringest good tidings, lift up thy voice with strength; lift *it* up, be not afraid; say unto the cities of Judah, Behold your God!

Isa 41:27 — The first *shall say* to Zion, Behold, behold them: and I will give to Jerusalem one that bringeth good tidings.

Jer 23:3 — And I will gather the remnant of my flock out of all countries whither I have driven them, and will bring them again to their folds; and they shall be fruitful and increase.

Jer 44:28 — Yet a small number that escape the sword shall return out of the land of Egypt into the land of Judah, and all the remnant of Judah, that are gone into the land of Egypt to sojourn there, shall know whose words shall stand, mine, or theirs.

Eze 37:12 — Therefore prophesy and say unto them, Thus saith the Lord GOD; Behold, O my people, I will open your graves, and cause you to come up out of your graves, and bring you into the land of Israel.

Eze 37:21 — And say unto them, Thus saith the Lord GOD; Behold, I will take the children of Israel from among the heathen, whither they be gone, and will gather them on every side, and bring them into their own land:

Mic 5:3 — Therefore will he give them up, until the time *that* she which travaileth hath brought forth: then the remnant of his brethren shall return unto the children of Israel.

Zep 2:7 — And the coast shall be for the remnant of the house of Judah; they shall feed thereupon: in the houses of Ashkelon shall they lie down in the evening: for the LORD their God shall visit them, and turn away their captivity.

Mal 3:4 — Then shall the offering of Judah and Jerusalem be pleasant unto the LORD, as in the days of old, and as in former years.

2Co 3:16 — Nevertheless when it shall turn to the Lord, the vail shall be taken away.

Rev 7:5 — Of the tribe of Juda *were* sealed twelve thousand. Of the tribe of Reuben *were* sealed twelve thousand. Of the tribe of Gad *were* sealed twelve thousand.

ISRAEL, Name Given to Descendants of Jacob

• Called also Israelites and Hebrews.

Ge 43:32 — And they set on for him by himself, and for them by themselves, and for the Egyptians, which did eat with him, by themselves: because the Egyptians might not eat bread with the Hebrews; for that *is* an abomination unto the Egyptians.

Ex 1:15 — And the king of Egypt spake to the Hebrew midwives, of which the name of the one *was* Shiphrah, and the name of the other Puah:

Ex 9:7 — And Pharaoh sent, and, behold, there was not one of the cattle of the Israelites dead. And the heart of Pharaoh was hardened, and he did not let the people go.

Ex 10:3 — And Moses and Aaron came in unto Pharaoh, and said unto him, Thus saith the LORD God of the Hebrews, How long wilt thou refuse to humble thyself before me? let my people go, that they may serve me.

Ex 21:2 — If thou buy an Hebrew servant, six years he shall serve: and in the seventh he shall go out free for nothing.

Le 23:42 — Ye shall dwell in booths seven days; all that are Israelites born shall dwell in booths:

Jos 13:6 — All the inhabitants of the hill country from Lebanon unto Misrephoth-maim, *and* all the Sidonians, them will I drive out from before the children of Israel: only divide thou it by lot unto the Israelites for an inheritance, as I have commanded thee.

1Sa 4:6 — And when the Philistines heard the noise of the shout, they said, What *meaneth* the noise of this great shout in the camp of the Hebrews? And they understood that the ark of the LORD was come into the camp.

1Sa 13:3 — And Jonathan smote the garrison of the Philistines that *was* in Geba, and the Philistines heard *of it.* And Saul blew the trumpet throughout all the land, saying, Let the Hebrews hear.

1Sa 13:19 — Now there was no smith found throughout all the land of Israel: for the Philistines said, Lest the Hebrews make *them* swords or spears:

1Sa 14:11 — And both of them discovered themselves unto the garrison of the Philistines: and the Philistines said, Behold, the Hebrews come forth out of the holes where they had hid themselves.

1Sa 14:21 — Moreover the Hebrews *that* were with the Philistines before that time, which went up with them into the camp *from the country* round about, even they also *turned* to be with the Israelites that *were* with Saul and Jonathan.

Php 3:5 — Circumcised the eighth day, of the stock of Israel, *of* the tribe of Benjamin, an Hebrew of the Hebrews; as touching the law, a Pharisee;

• Tribes of Israel were named after the sons of Jacob.

• In lists usually the names Levi and Joseph, two sons of Jacob, do not appear.

• The descendants of Levi were consecrated to the rites of religions.

• The two sons of Joseph, Ephraim and Manasseh, were adopted by Jacob in Joseph's stead.

Ge 48:5 — And now thy two sons, Ephraim and Manasseh, which were born unto thee in the land of Egypt before I came unto thee into Egypt, *are* mine; as Reuben and Simeon, they shall be mine.

Jos 14:4 — For the children of Joseph were two tribes, Manasseh and Ephraim: therefore they gave no part unto the Levites in the land, save cities to dwell *in,* with their suburbs for their cattle and for their substance.

• Ephraim and Manasseh appear in the tribes instead of those of Levi and Joseph, as follows.

- **Asher.**
- **Benjamin.**
- **Dan.**
- **Ephraim.**
- **Gad.**
- **Issachar.**
- **Judah.**
- **Manasseh.**
- **Naphtali.**
- **Reuben.**
- **Simeon.**
- **Zebulun.**

• Names of, seen in John's vision, on the gates of the New Jerusalem.

Rev 21:12 — And had a wall great and high, *and* had twelve gates, and at the gates twelve angels, and names written thereon, which are *the names* of the twelve tribes of the children of Israel:

• Prophecies concerning.

Ge 27:28–29; 49:1–33; Dt 33:1–29

Ge 15:5 — And he brought him forth abroad, and said, Look now toward heaven, and tell the stars, if thou be able to number them: and he said unto him, So shall thy seed be.

Ge 15:13 — And he said unto Abram, Know of a surety that thy seed shall be a stranger in a land *that is* not theirs, and shall serve them; and they shall afflict them four hundred years;

Ge 25:23 — And the LORD said unto her, Two nations *are* in thy womb, and two manner of people shall be separated from thy bowels; and *the one* people shall be stronger than *the other* people; and the elder shall serve the younger.

Ge 26:4 — And I will make thy seed to multiply as the stars of heaven, and will give unto thy seed all these countries; and in thy seed shall all the nations of the earth be blessed;

Ge 27:40 — And by thy sword shalt thou live, and shalt serve thy brother; and it shall come to pass when thou shalt have the dominion, that thou shalt break his yoke from off thy neck.

Ge 48:19 — And his father refused, and said, I know *it,* my son, I know *it:* he also shall become a people, and he also shall be great: but truly his younger brother shall be greater than he, and his seed shall become a multitude of nations.

• Prophecies concerning the multitude of.

Ge 13:16 — And I will make thy seed as the dust of the earth: so that if a man can number the dust of the earth, *then* shall thy seed also be numbered.

Ge 15:5 — And he brought him forth abroad, and said, Look now toward heaven, and tell the stars, if thou be able to number them: and he said unto him, So shall thy seed be.

Ge 22:17 — That in blessing I will bless thee, and in multiplying I will multiply thy seed as the stars of the heaven, and as the sand which *is* upon the sea shore; and thy seed shall possess the gate of his enemies;

Ge 26:4 — And I will make thy seed to multiply as the stars of heaven, and will give unto thy seed all these countries; and in thy seed shall all the nations of the earth be blessed;

Ge 28:14 — And thy seed shall be as the dust of the earth, and thou shalt spread abroad to the west, and to the east, and to the north, and to the south: and in thee and in thy seed shall all the families of the earth be blessed.

• Prophecies concerning their captivity in Egypt.

Ge 15:13–14; Ac 7:6–7

• Divided into families, each of which had a chief.

Nu 26:1–65; 1Ch 4:1–8:40

Nu 25:14 — Now the name of the Israelite that was slain, *even* that was slain with the Midianitish woman, *was* Zimri, the son of Salu, a prince of a chief house among the Simeonites.

Nu 36:1 — And the chief fathers of the families of the children of Gilead, the son of Machir, the son of Manasseh, of the families of the sons of Joseph, came near, and spake before Moses, and before the princes, the chief fathers of the children of Israel:

Jos 7:14 — In the morning therefore ye shall be brought according to your tribes: and it shall be, *that* the tribe which the LORD taketh shall come according to the families *thereof;* and the family which the LORD shall take shall come by households; and the household which the LORD shall take shall come man by man.

• Number of descendants.

• Who went into Egypt.

Ge 46:8–27

Ex 1:5 — And all the souls that came out of the loins of Jacob were seventy souls: for Joseph was in Egypt *already.*

Dt 10:22 — Thy fathers went down into Egypt with threescore and ten persons; and now the LORD thy God hath made thee as the stars of heaven for multitude.

Ac 7:14 — Then sent Joseph, and called his father Jacob to *him,* and all his kindred, threescore and fifteen souls.

• At the time of the Exodus

Ex 1:7–20; 12:37–38

Ge 47:27 — And Israel dwelt in the land of Egypt, in the country of Goshen; and they had possessions therein, and grew, and multiplied exceedingly.

Ps 105:24 — And he increased his people greatly; and made them stronger than their enemies.

Ac 7:17 — But when the time of the promise drew nigh, which God had sworn to Abraham, the people grew and multiplied in Egypt,

• Fit for military service when they left Egypt.

Ex 12:37 — And the children of Israel journeyed from Rameses to Succoth, about six hundred thousand on foot *that were* men, beside children.

• At Sinai, by tribes.

Nu 1:1–50

• After the plague.

Nu 26:1–65

• When David numbered.

2Sa 24:1–9; 1Ch 21:5–6; 27:23–24

• After the captivity.

Ne 7:66–67

Ezr 2:64 — The whole congregation together *was* forty and two thousand three hundred *and* threescore,

• In John's apocalyptic vision.

Rev 7:1–8

• Dwelt in Goshen.

Ge 46:28–34; 47:4–10, 27–28

• Dwelt in Egypt four hundred and thirty years.

Ex 12:40–41

Ge 15:13 — And he said unto Abram, Know of a surety that thy seed shall be a stranger in a land *that is* not theirs, and shall serve them; and they shall afflict them four hundred years;

Ac 7:6 — And God spake on this wise, That his seed should sojourn in a strange land; and that they should bring them into bondage, and entreat *them* evil four hundred years.

Gal 3:17 — And this I say, *that* the covenant, that was confirmed before of God in Christ, the law, which was four hundred and thirty years after, cannot disannul, that it should make the promise of none effect.

• Were enslaved and oppressed by the Egyptians.

ISRAEL, the Revolt of the Ten Tribes

• Foreshadowing circumstances indicating the separation.

• Disagreement after Saul's death.

2Sa 2:1–32; 1Ch 12:23–13:14

• Lukewarmness of the ten tribes, and zeal of Judah for David in Absalom's rebellion.

2Sa 19:41–43

- **The rebellion of Sheba.**
  2Sa 20:1–26
- **The two factions are distinguished as Israel and Judah during David's reign.**
  2Sa 21:2 — And the king called the Gibeonites, and said unto them; (now the Gibeonites *were* not of the children of Israel, but of the remnant of the Amorites; and the children of Israel had sworn unto them: and Saul sought to slay them in his zeal to the children of Israel and Judah.)
- **Providential.**
  Zec 11:14 — Then I cut asunder mine other staff, *even* Bands, that I might break the brotherhood between Judah and Israel.

• Revolt consummated under Rehoboam, son and successor of Solomon.
1Ki 12:1–33

• The ten tribes that revolted from the house of David, AKA Jacob.
Hos 12:2 — The LORD hath also a controversy with Judah, and will punish Jacob according to his ways; according to his doings will he recompense him.

• The kings of Israel, and the period of time in which they reigned.
- **See: Jeroboam (twenty-two years)**
- **See: Nadab (about two years)**
- **See: Baasha (twenty-four years)**
- **See: Elah (two years)**
- **See: Zimri (seven days)**
- **See: Omri (twelve years)**
- **See: Ahab (twenty-two years)**
- **See: Ahaziah (two years)**
- **See: Jehoram (twelve years)**
- **See: Jehu (twenty-eight years)**
- **See: Jehoahaz (seventeen years)**
- **See: Jehoash (sixteen years)**
- **See: Jeroboam; King of Israel. Successor to Jehoash (forty-one years)**
- **See: Zachariah (six months)**
- **See: Shallum (one month)**
- **See: Menahem (ten years)**
- **See: Pekahiah (two years)**
- **See: Pekah (twenty years)**
- **See: Hoshea (nine years)**
- **The ten tribes carried captive to Assyria.**

• History of.
- **War continued between the two kingdoms all the days of Rehoboam and Jeroboam.**
  1Ki 14:30 — And there was war between Rehoboam and Jeroboam all *their* days.
- **War continued between the two kingdoms all the days of Jeroboam and Abijam.**
  1Ki 15:7 — Now the rest of the acts of Abijam, and all that he did, *are* they not written in the book of the chronicles of the kings of Judah? And there was war between Abijam and Jeroboam.
- **War continued between the two kingdoms all the days of Baasha and Asa.**
  1Ki 15:16 — And there was war between Asa and Baasha king of Israel all their days.
  1Ki 15:32 — And there was war between Asa and Baasha king of Israel all their days.
- **Famine prevails in the reign of Ahab.**
  1Ki 18:1–6
- **Israel, called also Samaria. Invaded by, but defeats, Ben-hadad, king of Syria.**
  1Ki 20:1–43
- **Moab rebels.**
  2Ki 3:1–27
  2Ki 1:1 — Then Moab rebelled against Israel after the death of Ahab.
- **Army of Syria invades Israel, but peacefully withdraws through the tact of the prophet Elisha.**
  2Ki 6:8–23
- **Samaria besieged.**
  2Ki 6:24–7:20
- **Samaria, city of, taken, and the people carried to Assyria.**
  2Ki 17:1–41
- **The land repeopled.**
  2Ki 17:24 — And the king of Assyria brought *men* from Babylon, and from Cuthah, and from Ava, and from Hamath, and from Sepharvaim, and placed *them* in the cities of Samaria instead of the children of Israel: and they possessed Samaria, and dwelt in the cities thereof.
- **The remnant that remained after the able-bodied were carried into captivity affiliated with the kingdom of Judah.**
  2Ch 30:18–26
  2Ch 34:6 — And *so did he* in the cities of Manasseh, and Ephraim, and Simeon, even unto Naphtali, with their mattocks round about.
  2Ch 35:18 — And there was no passover like to that kept in Israel from the days of Samuel the prophet; neither did all the kings of Israel keep such a passover as Josiah kept, and the priests, and the Levites, and all Judah and Israel that were present, and the inhabitants of Jerusalem.

• Prophecies concerning.
- **Of captivity, famine, and judgments.**
  1Ki 14:15–16; 20:13–28; 2Ki 7:1–2; Isa 8:4–7; 9:8–21; 17:3–11; 28:1–8; Hos 1:1–9; 2:1–13; 4:1–19; 8:1–10:15; 11:5–6; 12:7–13:16; Am 2:6–9:15
  1Ki 17:1 — And Elijah the Tishbite, *who was* of the inhabitants of Gilead, said unto Ahab, *As* the LORD God of Israel liveth, before whom I stand, there

shall not be dew nor rain these years, but according to my word.

2Ki 7:17 — And the king appointed the lord on whose hand he leaned to have the charge of the gate: and the people trode upon him in the gate, and he died, as the man of God had said, who spake when the king came down to him.

2Ki 8:1 — Then spake Elisha unto the woman, whose son he had restored to life, saying, Arise, and go thou and thine household, and sojourn wheresoever thou canst sojourn: for the LORD hath called for a famine; and it shall also come upon the land seven years.

Isa 7:8 — For the head of Syria *is* Damascus, and the head of Damascus *is* Rezin; and within threescore and five years shall Ephraim be broken, that it be not a people.

• Of restoration.

Hos 2:14–23; 11:9–11; 13:13–14

Hos 14:8 — Ephraim *shall say,* What have I to do any more with idols? I have heard *him,* and observed him: I *am* like a green fir tree. From me is thy fruit found.

• Of the reunion of the ten tribes and Judah.

Eze 37:16–22

Jer 3:18 — In those days the house of Judah shall walk with the house of Israel, and they shall come together out of the land of the north to the land that I have given for an inheritance unto your fathers.

ISRAEL, under Judges

• Public affairs administered four hundred and fifty years by the judges.

Jgs 2:16–19

Ac 13:20 — And after that he gave *unto them* judges about the space of four hundred and fifty years, until Samuel the prophet.

• The original inhabitants not fully expelled.

Jgs 1:27–36; 3:1–7

• Reproved by an angel for not casting out the original inhabitants.

Jgs 2:1–5

• People turn to idolatry.

Jgs 2:10–23

• Delivered for their idolatry to the king of Mesopotamia during eight years; their repentance and deliverance.

Jgs 3:8–11

• Renew idolatry; put under king of Moab 18 years; repent; delivered; 8 years of peace follow.

Jgs 3:12–30

• Shamgar resists a foray of the Philistines and delivers Israel.

Jgs 3:31 — And after him was Shamgar the son of Anath, which slew of the Philistines six hundred men with an ox goad: and he also delivered Israel.

• People again do evil and are put under bonds for twenty years to the king of Syria.

Jgs 4:1–3

• Delivered by Deborah, a prophetess, and judged.

Jgs 4:1–5:31

• Seven years of bondage to the Midianites; delivered by Gideon.

Jgs 6:1–8:28

→See: Gideon

• Return to idolatry.

Jgs 8:33–34

• Abimelech foments an inter-tribal war.

Jgs 9:1–57

• Judged by Tola twenty-three years.

Jgs 10:1–2

• Judged by Jair twenty-two years.

Jgs 10:3–4

• Backslide; given over to the Philistines for chastisement 18 years; repent; delivered by Jephthah.

Jgs 10:6–11:40

• Ephraimites go to war against other tribes; defeated by Jephthah.

Jgs 12:1–7

• Judged by Ibzan seven years.

Jgs 12:8–10

• Judged by Elon ten years.

Jgs 12:11–12

• Judged by Abdon eight years.

Jgs 12:13–15

• Backslide again and are chastised by the Philistines forty years.

Jgs 13:1 — And the children of Israel did evil again in the sight of the LORD; and the LORD delivered them into the hand of the Philistines forty years.

• Judged by Samson twenty years.

Jgs 13:1–16:31

• Scandal of the Bethlehemite's concubine, and the consequent war between the Benjamites and the other tribes.

Jgs 19:1–21:25

• Judged by Eli forty years.

1Sa 1:1–4:22

• Smitten by the Philistines at Ebewn-ezer.

1Sa 4:1–2, 10–11

• Demand a king.

1Sa 8:5–20

Hos 13:10 — I will be thy king: where *is any other* that may save thee in all thy cities? and thy judges of whom thou saidst, Give me a king and princes?

ISRAEL, under Kings before the Separation into Two Kingdoms

• Saul anointed king.

1Sa 10:1–27; 11:12–15

1Sa 12:13 — Now therefore behold the king whom ye have chosen, *and* whom ye have desired! and, behold, the LORD hath set a king over you.

• Ammonites invade Israel, are defeated.

1Sa 11:1–15

• Philistines smitten.

1Sa 14:1–52

• Amalekites defeated.

1Sa 15:1–35

• David anointed king.

1Sa 16:11–13

• Goliath slain.

1Sa 17:1–58

• Israel defeated by the Philistines, and Saul and his sons slain.

1Sa 31:1–13

See: Saul

• David defeats the Amalekites.

1Sa 30:1–31

2Sa 1:1 — Now it came to pass after the death of Saul, when David was returned from the slaughter of the Amalekites, and David had abode two days in Ziklag;

• David made king.

2Sa 2:4 — And the men of Judah came, and there they anointed David king over the house of Judah. And they told David, saying, *That* the men of Jabesh-gilead *were they* that buried Saul.

2Sa 2:11 — And the time that David was king in Hebron over the house of Judah was seven years and six months.

• Ishbosheth made king.

2Sa 2:8–10

• The conflict between the two political factions.

2Sa 2:12–3:1

• David made king over all Israel.

2Sa 5:1–5

• Conquests of David.

2Sa 8:1–18

• Absalom's rebellion.

2Sa 15:1–18:33

See: David

• Solomon anointed king.

1Ki 1:32–40

• Temple built.

1Ki 6:1–38

• Solomon's palace built.

1Ki 7:1–51

• Solomon's death.

1Ki 11:41–43

See: Solomon

ISRAELITES See: Israel

ISSACHAR

• Son of Jacob.

Ge 30:18 — And Leah said, God hath given me my hire, because I have given my maiden to my husband: and she called his name Issachar.

Ex 1:3 — Issachar, Zebulun, and Benjamin,

1Ch 2:1 — These *are* the sons of Israel; Reuben, Simeon, Levi, and Judah, Issachar, and Zebulun,

• Jacob's prophetic benedictions upon.

Ge 49:14–15

• In the time of David.

1Ch 7:2 — And the sons of Tola; Uzzi, and Rephaiah, and Jeriel, and Jahmai, and Jibsam, and Shemuel, heads of their father's house, *to wit,* of Tola: *they were* valiant men of might in their generations; whose number *was* in the days of David two and twenty thousand and six hundred.

1Ch 7:5 — And their brethren among all the families of Issachar *were* valiant men of might, reckoned in all by their genealogies fourscore and seven thousand.

See: Issachar; tribe of

• Tribe of.

• Military forces of, taken at Sinai.

Nu 1:28–29

Nu 2:6 — And his host, and those that were numbered thereof, *were* fifty and four thousand and four hundred.

• Military forces on the plains of Moab.

Nu 26:25 — These *are* the families of Issachar according to those that were numbered of them, threescore and four thousand and three hundred.

• Moses' blessing upon.

Dt 33:18–19

• Place in march and camp.

Nu 10:14–15

Nu 2:3 — And on the east side toward the rising of the sun shall they of the standard of the camp of Judah pitch throughout their armies: and Nahshon the son of Amminadab *shall be* captain of the children of Judah.

Nu 2:5 — And those that do pitch next unto him *shall be* the tribe of Issachar: and Nethaneel the son of Zuar *shall be* captain of the children of Issachar.

• Parts of Canaan allotted to.

Jos 17:10–11; 19:17–23

• Join Deborah and Barak in war against Sisera.

Jgs 5:15 — And the princes of Issachar *were* with Deborah; even Issachar, and also Barak: he was sent on foot into the valley. For the divisions of Reuben *there were* great thoughts of heart.

• Insurgents from, joined David.

1Ch 12:32 — And of the children of Issachar, *which were men* that had understanding of the times, to know what Israel ought to do; the heads of them *were* two hundred; and all their brethren *were* at their commandment.

1Ch 12:40 — Moreover they that were nigh them, *even* unto Issachar and Zebulun and Naphtali, brought bread on asses, and on camels, and on mules, and on oxen, *and* meat, meal, cakes of figs, and bunches of raisins, and wine, and oil, and oxen, and sheep abundantly: for *there was* joy in Israel.

• Join with the kingdom of Judah after the conquest of the land by.

2Ch 30:18 — For a multitude of the people, *even* many of Ephraim, and Manasseh, Issachar, and Zebulun, had not cleansed themselves, yet did they eat the passover otherwise than it was written. But Hezekiah prayed for them, saying, The good LORD pardon every one

• For things common to all the tribes.

⇜See: Israel, name given to descendants of Jacob; tribes of Israel were named after the sons of Jacob

ISSUE OF BLOOD

Mt 9:20 — And, behold, a woman, which was diseased with an issue of blood twelve years, came behind *him,* and touched the hem of his garment:

Mk 5:25 — And a certain woman, which had an issue of blood twelve years,

Lk 8:43 — And a woman having an issue of blood twelve years, which had spent all her living upon physicians, neither could be healed of any,

⇜See: Hemorrhage

ITALY

Ac 27:2 — And entering into a ship of Adramyttium, we launched, meaning to sail by the coasts of Asia; *one* Aristarchus, a Macedonian of Thessalonica, being with us.

Heb 13:24 — Salute all them that have the rule over you, and all the saints. They of Italy salute you.

• Aquila and Priscilla expelled from.

Ac 18:2 — And found a certain Jew named Aquila, born in Pontus, lately come from Italy, with his wife Priscilla; (because that Claudius had commanded all Jews to depart from Rome:) and came unto them.

ITCH

Dt 28:27 — The LORD will smite thee with the botch of Egypt, and with the emerods, and with the scab, and with the itch, whereof thou canst not be healed.

ITHAI

• Called also Ittai.

• One of David's valiant men.

2Sa 23:29 — Heleb the son of Baanah, a Netophathite, Ittai the son of Ribai out of Gibeah of the children of Benjamin,

1Ch 11:31 — Ithai the son of Ribai of Gibeah, *that pertained* to the children of Benjamin, Benaiah the Pirathonite,

ITHAMAR

• Son of Aaron.

Ex 6:23 — And Aaron took him Elisheba, daughter of Amminadab, sister of Naashon, to wife; and she bare him Nadab, and Abihu, Eleazar, and Ithamar.

Ex 28:1 — And take thou unto thee Aaron thy brother, and his sons with him, from among the children of Israel, that he may minister unto me in the priest's office, *even* Aaron, Nadab and Abihu, Eleazar and Ithamar, Aaron's sons.

1Ch 6:3 — And the children of Amram; Aaron, and Moses, and Miriam. The sons also of Aaron; Nadab, and Abihu, Eleazar, and Ithamar.

• Intrusted with moneys of the tabernacle.

Ex 38:21 — This is the sum of the tabernacle, *even* of the tabernacle of testimony, as it was counted, according to the commandment of Moses, *for* the service of the Levites, by the hand of Ithamar, son to Aaron the priest.

• Charged with duties of the tabernacle.

Nu 4:28 — This is the service of the families of the sons of Gershon in the tabernacle of the congregation: and their charge *shall be* under the hand of Ithamar the son of Aaron the priest.

Nu 7:8 — And four wagons and eight oxen he gave unto the sons of Merari, according unto their service, under the hand of Ithamar the son of Aaron the priest.

• Forbidden to lament the death of his brothers, Nadab and Abihu.

Le 10:6–7

• Descendants of.

1Ch 24:1–19

ITHIEL

• A Benjamite.

Ne 11:7 — And these *are* the sons of Benjamin; Sallu the son of Meshullam, the son of Joed, the son of Pedaiah, the son of Kolaiah, the son of Maaseiah, the son of Ithiel, the son of Jesaiah.

• An unidentified person.

Pr 30:1 — The words of Agur the son of Jakeh, *even* the prophecy: the man spake unto Ithiel, even unto Ithiel and Ucal,

ITHMAH • A Moabite.

1Ch 11:46 — Eliel the Mahavite, and Jeribai, and Joshaviah, the sons of Elnaam, and Ithmah the Moabite,

ITHNAN • A town in the extreme south of Judah.

Jos 15:23 — And Kedesh, and Hazor, and Ithnan,

ITHRA

• Called also Jether.

• Father of Amasa.

2Sa 17:25 — And Absalom made Amasa captain of the host instead of Joab: which Amasa was a man's son, whose name *was* Ithra an Israelite, that went in to Abigail the daughter of Nahash, sister to Zeruiah Joab's mother.

1Ch 2:17 — And Abigail bare Amasa: and the father of Amasa *was* Jether the Ishmeelite.

ITHRAN

• Son of Dishon.

Ge 36:26 — And these *are* the children of Dishon; Hemdan, and Eshban, and Ithran, and Cheran.

1Ch 1:41 — The sons of Anah; Dishon. And the sons of Dishon; Amram, and Eshban, and Ithran, and Cheran.

• Son of Zophah.

1Ch 7:37 — Bezer, and Hod, and Shamma and Shilshah, and Ithran, and Beera.

ITHREAM • Son of David.

2Sa 3:5 — And the sixth, Ithream, by Eglah David's wife. These were born to David in Hebron.

1Ch 3:3 — The fifth, Shephatiah of Abital: the sixth, Ithream by Eglah his wife.

ITHRITES • Patronymic of the family of Jether.

2Sa 23:38 — Ira an Ithrite, Gareb an Ithrite,

1Ch 2:53 — And the families of Kirjath-jearim; the Ithrites, and the Puhites, and the Shumathites, and the Mishraites; of them came the Zareathites, and the Eshtaulites.

ITINERARY

• Of the Israelites.

Nu 33:1–56; Dt 10:6–7

See: Israel

ITTAH-KAZIN • A landmark in the boundary line of Zebulun.

Jos 19:13 — And from thence passeth on along on the east to Gittah-hepher, to Ittah-kazin, and goeth out to Remmon-methoar to Neah;

ITTAI

• A chief of David.

2Sa 18:2 — And David sent forth a third part of the people under the hand of Joab, and a third part under the hand of Abishai the son of Zeruiah, Joab's brother, and a third part under the hand of Ittai the Gittite. And the king said unto the people, I will surely go forth with you myself also.

1Ch 11:31 — Ithai the son of Ribai of Gibeah, *that pertained* to the children of Benjamin, Benaiah the Pirathonite,

• Supports David against Absalom.

2Sa 15:19–22

2Sa 18:2 — And David sent forth a third part of the people under the hand of Joab, and a third part under the hand of Abishai the son of Zeruiah, Joab's brother, and a third part under the hand of Ittai the Gittite. And the king said unto the people, I will surely go forth with you myself also.

2Sa 18:5 — And the king commanded Joab and Abishai and Ittai, saying, *Deal* gently for my sake with the young man, *even* with Absalom. And all the people heard when the king gave all the captains charge concerning Absalom.

ITURAEA • Small province in the northwest of Palestine.

1Ch 1:31 — Jetur, Naphish, and Kedemah. These are the sons of Ishmael.

1Ch 5:19 — And they made war with the Hagarites, with Jetur, and Nephish, and Nodab.

Lk 3:1 — Now in the fifteenth year of the reign of Tiberius Caesar, Pontius Pilate being governor of Judaea, and Herod being tetrarch of Galilee, and his brother Philip tetrarch of Ituraea and of the region of Trachonitis, and Lysanias the tetrarch of Abilene,

IVAH • A district in Babylon conquered by the Assyrians.

2Ki 18:34 — Where *are* the gods of Hamath, and of Arpad? where *are* the gods of Sepharvaim, Hena, and Ivah? have they delivered Samaria out of mine hand?

2Ki 19:13 — Where *is* the king of Hamath, and the king of Arpad, and the king of the city of Sepharvaim, of Hena, and Ivah?

Isa 37:13 — Where *is* the king of Hamath, and the king of Arphad, and the king of the city of Sepharvaim, Hena, and Ivah?

IVORY

SS 5:14 — His hands *are as* gold rings set with the beryl: his belly *is as* bright ivory overlaid *with* sapphires.

SS 7:4 — Thy neck *is* as a tower of ivory; thine eyes *like* the fishpools in Heshbon, by the gate of Bath-rabbim: thy nose *is* as the tower of Lebanon which looketh toward Damascus.

Eze 27:15 — The men of Dedan *were* thy merchants; many isles *were* the merchandise of thine hand: they brought thee *for* a present horns of ivory and ebony.

• Exported from Tarshish.

1Ki 10:22 — For the king had at sea a navy of Tharshish with the navy of Hiram: once in three years came the navy of Tharshish, bringing gold, and silver, ivory, and apes, and peacocks.

2Ch 9:21 — For the king's ships went to Tarshish with the servants of Huram: every three years once came the ships of Tarshish bringing gold, and silver, ivory, and apes, and peacocks.

• Exported from Chittim.

Eze 27:6 — *Of* the oaks of Bashan have they made thine oars; the company of the Ashurites have made thy benches *of* ivory, *brought* out of the isles of Chittim.

• Ahab's palace made of.

1Ki 22:39 — Now the rest of the acts of Ahab, and all that he did, and the ivory house which he made, and all the cities that he built, *are* they not written in the book of the chronicles of the kings of Israel?

- **Other houses made of.**

Ps 45:8 — All thy garments *smell* of myrrh, and aloes, *and* cassia, out of the ivory palaces, whereby they have made thee glad.

Am 3:15 — And I will smite the winter house with the summer house; and the houses of ivory shall perish, and the great houses shall have an end, saith the LORD.

- **Other articles made of.**
  - **Stringed instruments.**

Ps 45:8 — All thy garments *smell* of myrrh, and aloes, *and* cassia, out of the ivory palaces, whereby they have made thee glad.

  - **Thrones.**

1Ki 10:18 — Moreover the king made a great throne of ivory, and overlaid it with the best gold.

2Ch 9:17 — Moreover the king made a great throne of ivory, and overlaid it with pure gold.

  - **Benches.**

Eze 27:6 — *Of* the oaks of Bashan have they made thine oars; the company of the Ashurites have made thy benches *of* ivory, *brought* out of the isles of Chittim.

  - **Beds.**

Am 6:4 — That lie upon beds of ivory, and stretch themselves upon their couches, and eat the lambs out of the flock, and the calves out of the midst of the stall;

  - **Vessels.**

Rev 18:12 — The merchandise of gold, and silver, and precious stones, and of pearls, and fine linen, and purple, and silk, and scarlet, and all thyine wood, and all manner vessels of ivory, and all manner vessels of most precious wood, and of brass, and iron, and marble,

IZHAR • Son of Kohath.

Ex 6:18 — And the sons of Kohath; Amram, and Izhar, and Hebron, and Uzziel: and the years of the life of Kohath *were* an hundred thirty and three years.

Ex 6:21 — And the sons of Izhar; Korah, and Nepheg, and Zichri.

1Ch 6:2 — And the sons of Kohath; Amram, Izhar, and Hebron, and Uzziel.

1Ch 6:18 — And the sons of Kohath *were,* Amram, and Izhar, and Hebron, and Uzziel.

1Ch 6:38 — The son of Izhar, the son of Kohath, the son of Levi, the son of Israel.

1Ch 23:12 — The sons of Kohath; Amram, Izhar, Hebron, and Uzziel, four.

1Ch 23:18 — Of the sons of Izhar; Shelomith the chief.

IZRAHIAH • Grandson of Tola.

1Ch 7:3 — And the sons of Uzzi; Izrahiah: and the sons of Izrahiah; Michael, and Obadiah, and Joel, Ishiah, five: all of them chief men.

IZRI, perhaps the same as Zeri • Leader of the fourth division of Levitical singers.

1Ch 25:11 — The fourth to Izri, *he,* his sons, and his brethren, *were* twelve:

J

JAAKAN

• Called also Akan and Jakan.

• Son of Ezer.

Ge 36:27 — The children of Ezer *are* these; Bilhan, and Zaavan, and Akan.

Dt 10:6 — And the children of Israel took their journey from Beeroth of the children of Jaakan to Mosera: there Aaron died, and there he was buried; and Eleazar his son ministered in the priest's office in his stead.

1Ch 1:42 — The sons of Ezer; Bilhan, and Zavan, *and* Jakan. The sons of Dishan; Uz, and Aran.

JAAKOBAH • Descendant of Simeon.

1Ch 4:36 — And Elioenai, and Jaakobah, and Jeshohaiah, and Asaiah, and Adiel, and Jesimiel, and Benaiah,

JAALA

• Called also Jaalah.

• One of the servants of Solomon returned from exile.

Ezr 2:56 — The children of Jaalah, the children of Darkon, the children of Giddel,

Ne 7:58 — The children of Jaala, the children of Darkon, the children of Giddel,

JAALAM • Son of Esau.

Ge 36:5 — And Aholibamah bare Jeush, and Jaalam, and Korah: these *are* the sons of Esau, which were born unto him in the land of Canaan.

Ge 36:14 — And these were the sons of Aholibamah, the daughter of Anah the daughter of Zibeon, Esau's wife: and she bare to Esau Jeush, and Jaalam, and Korah.

Ge 36:18 — And these *are* the sons of Aholibamah Esau's wife; duke Jeush, duke Jaalam, duke Korah: these *were* the dukes *that came* of Aholibamah the daughter of Anah, Esau's wife.

1Ch 1:35 — The sons of Esau; Eliphaz, Reuel, and Jeush, and Jaalam, and Korah.

JAANAI • A Gadite chief.

1Ch 5:12 — Joel the chief, and Shapham the next, and Jaanai, and Shaphat in Bashan.

JAARE-OREGIM • Father of Elhanan.

2Sa 21:19 — And there was again a battle in Gob with the Philistines, where Elhanan the son of Jaare-oregim, a Bethlehemite, slew *the brother of* Goliath the Gittite, the staff of whose spear *was* like a weaver's beam.

JAASAU • Of the family of Bani.

Ezr 10:37 — Mattaniah, Mattenai, and Jaasau,

JAASIEL • Son of Abner.

1Ch 27:21 — Of the half *tribe* of Manasseh in Gilead, Iddo the son of Zechariah: of Benjamin, Jaasiel the son of Abner:

JAAZANIAH

• A captain who joined Gedaliah at Mizpah.

2Ki 25:23 — And when all the captains of the armies, they and their men, heard that the king of Babylon had made Gedaliah governor, there came to Gedaliah to Mizpah, even Ishmael the son of Nethaniah, and Johanan the son of Careah, and Seraiah the son of Tanhumeth the Netophathite, and Jaazaniah the son of a Maachathite, they and their men.

• Called also Jezaniah.

Jer 40:8 — Then they came to Gedaliah to Mizpah, even Ishmael the son of Nethaniah, and Johanan and Jonathan the sons of Kareah, and Seraiah the son of Tanhumeth, and the sons of Ephai the Netophathite, and Jezaniah the son of a Maachathite, they and their men.

Jer 42:1 — Then all the captains of the forces, and Johanan the son of Kareah, and Jezaniah the son of Hoshaiah, and all the people from the least even unto the greatest, came near,

• A Rechabite.

Jer 35:3 — Then I took Jaazaniah the son of Jeremiah, the son of Habaziniah, and his brethren, and all his sons, and the whole house of the Rechabites;

• An idolatrous zealot.

Eze 8:11 — And there stood before them seventy men of the ancients of the house of Israel, and in the midst of them stood Jaazaniah the son of Shaphan, with every man his censer in his hand; and a thick cloud of incense went up.

• A wicked prince of Judah.

Eze 11:1–13

JAAZER

• Called also Jazer.

• A Levitical city of refuge in Gilead.

Allotted to Gad, and given to the Levites.

Nu 21:32 — And Moses sent to spy out Jaazer, and they took the villages thereof, and drove out the Amorites that *were* there.

Nu 32:1 — Now the children of Reuben and the children of Gad had a very great multitude of cattle: and when they saw the land of Jazer, and the land of Gilead, that, behold, the place *was* a place for cattle;

Nu 32:3 — Ataroth, and Dibon, and Jazer, and Nimrah, and Heshbon, and Elealeh, and Shebam, and Nebo, and Beon,

Nu 32:35 — And Atroth, Shophan, and Jaazer, and Jogbehah,

Jos 13:25 — And their coast was Jazer, and all the cities of Gilead, and half the land of the children of Ammon, unto Aroer that *is* before Rabbah;

Jos 21:39 — Heshbon with her suburbs, Jazer with her suburbs; four cities in all.

JAAZIAH • A descendant of Merari.

1Ch 24:26–27

JAAZIEL • A Levite musician.

1Ch 15:18 — And with them their brethren of the second *degree,* Zechariah, Ben, and Jaaziel, and Shemiramoth, and Jehiel, and Unni, Eliab, and Benaiah, and Maaseiah, and Mattithiah, and Eli-pheleh, and Mikneiah, and Obed-edom, and Jeiel, the porters.

JABAL

• Son of Lamech.

• A shepherd.

Ge 4:20 — And Adah bare Jabal: he was the father of such as dwell in tents, and *of such as have* cattle.

JABBOK

• A stream on the east of the Jordan.

• The northern boundary of the possessions of the Ammonites.

Nu 21:24 — And Israel smote him with the edge of the sword, and possessed his land from Arnon unto Jabbok, even unto the children of Ammon: for the border of the children of Ammon *was* strong.

Jgs 11:13 — And the king of the children of Ammon answered unto the messengers of Jephthah, Because Israel took away my land, when they came up out of Egypt, from Arnon even unto Jabbok, and unto Jordan: now therefore restore those *lands* again peaceably.

• The northern boundary of the possessions of the Reubenites and the Gadites.

Dt 3:16 — And unto the Reubenites and unto the Gadites I gave from Gilead even unto the river Arnon half the valley, and the border even unto the river Jabbok, *which is* the border of the children of Ammon;

Jos 12:2 — Sihon king of the Amorites, who dwelt in Heshbon, *and* ruled from Aroer, which *is* upon the bank of the river Arnon, and from the middle of the river, and from half Gilead, even unto the river Jabbok, *which is* the border of the children of Ammon;

• The northern boundary of the Amorites.

Jgs 11:22 — And they possessed all the coasts of the Amorites, from Arnon even unto Jabbok, and from the wilderness even unto Jordan.

JABESH-GILEAD

• A city east of the Jordan.

Jgs 21:8–15

• Besieged by the Ammonites.

1Sa 11:1–11

• Saul and his sons buried at.

1Sa 31:11–13; 1Ch 10:11–12

2Sa 2:4 — And the men of Judah came, and there they anointed David king over the house of Judah. And they told David, saying, *That* the men of Jabesh-gilead *were they* that buried Saul.

• Bones of Saul and his son removed from, by David, and buried at Zelah.

2Sa 21:12–14

JABEZ

• A city of Judah.

1Ch 2:55 — And the families of the scribes which dwelt at Jabez; the Tirathites, the Shimeathites, *and* Suchathites. These *are* the Kenites that came of Hemath, the father of the house of Rechab.

• The head of a family.

1Ch 4:9–10

JABIN

• Names of two kings of Hazor.

Jos 11:1–14; Jgs 4:23–24

Jgs 4:2 — And the LORD sold them into the hand of Jabin king of Canaan, that reigned in Hazor; the captain of whose host *was* Sisera, which dwelt in Harosheth of the Gentiles.

Jgs 4:7 — And I will draw unto thee to the river Kishon Sisera, the captain of Jabin's army, with his chariots and his multitude; and I will deliver him into thine hand.

Jgs 4:17 — Howbeit Sisera fled away on his feet to the tent of Jael the wife of Heber the Kenite: for *there was* peace between Jabin the king of Hazor and the house of Heber the Kenite.

Ps 83:9 — Do unto them as *unto* the Midianites; as *to* Sisera, as *to* Jabin, at the brook of Kison:

JABNEEL

• A city in Judah.

Jos 15:11 — And the border went out unto the side of Ekron northward: and the border was drawn to Shicron, and passed along to mount Baalah, and went out unto Jabneel; and the goings out of the border were at the sea.

• A city of Naphtali.

Jos 19:33 — And their coast was from Heleph, from Allon to Zaanannim, and Adami, Nekeb, and Jabneel, unto Lakum; and the outgoings thereof were at Jordan:

JABNEH • A Philistine city.

2Ch 26:6 — And he went forth and warred against the Philistines, and brake down the wall of Gath, and the wall of Jabneh, and the wall of Ashdod, and built cities about Ashdod, and among the Philistines.

JACHAN • A Gadite.

1Ch 5:13 — And their brethren of the house of their fathers *were,* Michael, and Meshullam, and Sheba, and Jorai, and Jachan, and Zia, and Heber, seven.

JACHIN

• Son of Simeon.

Ge 46:10 — And the sons of Simeon; Jemuel, and Jamin, and Ohad, and Jachin, and Zohar, and Shaul the son of a Canaanitish woman.

Ex 6:15 — And the sons of Simeon; Jemuel, and Jamin, and Ohad, and Jachin, and Zohar, and Shaul the son of a Canaanitish woman: these *are* the families of Simeon.

Nu 26:12 — The sons of Simeon after their families: of Nemuel, the family of the Nemuelites: of Jamin, the family of the Jaminites: of Jachin, the family of the Jachinites:

• Called Jarib.

1Ch 4:24 — The sons of Simeon *were*, Nemuel, and Jamin, Jarib, Zerah, *and* Shaul:

• Name of a pillar.

1Ki 7:21 — And he set up the pillars in the porch of the temple: and he set up the right pillar, and called the name thereof Jachin: and he set up the left pillar, and he called the name thereof Boaz.

2Ch 3:17 — And he reared up the pillars before the temple, one on the right hand, and the other on the left; and called the name of that on the right hand Jachin, and the name of that on the left Boaz.

See: Boaz

• A priest, who returned from exile to Jerusalem.

1Ch 9:10 — And of the priests; Jedaiah, and Jehoiarib, and Jachin,

Ne 11:10 — Of the priests: Jedaiah the son of Joiarib, Jachin.

• A priest and head of one of the courses.

1Ch 24:17 — The one and twentieth to Jachin, the two and twentieth to Gamul,

JACINTH • A precious stone.

Rev 9:17 — And thus I saw the horses in the vision, and them that sat on them, having breastplates of fire, and of jacinth, and brimstone: and the heads of the horses *were* as the heads of lions; and out of their mouths issued fire and smoke and brimstone.

Rev 21:20 — The fifth, sardonyx; the sixth, sardius; the seventh, chrysolite; the eighth, beryl; the ninth, a topaz; the tenth, a chrysoprasus; the eleventh, a jacinth; the twelfth, an amethyst.

JACKAL • A carnivorous animal.

Mal 1:3 — And I hated Esau, and laid his mountains and his heritage waste for the dragons of the wilderness.

JACOB

• Son of Isaac, and twin brother of Esau.

Ge 25:24–26

Jos 24:4 — And I gave unto Isaac Jacob and Esau: and I gave unto Esau mount Seir, to possess it; but Jacob and his children went down into Egypt.

1Ch 1:34 — And Abraham begat Isaac. The sons of Isaac; Esau and Israel.

Ac 7:8 — And he gave him the covenant of circumcision: and so *Abraham* begat Isaac, and circumcised him the eighth day; and Isaac *begat* Jacob; and Jacob *begat* the twelve patriarchs.

• Ancestor of Jesus.

Mt 1:2 — Abraham begat Isaac; and Isaac begat Jacob; and Jacob begat Judas and his brethren;

• Given in answer to prayer.

Ge 25:21 — And Isaac intreated the LORD for his wife, because she *was* barren: and the LORD was intreated of him, and Rebekah his wife conceived.

• Obtains Esau's birthright for a mess of pottage.

Ge 25:29–34

Heb 12:16 — Lest there *be* any fornicator, or profane person, as Esau, who for one morsel of meat sold his birthright.

• Fraudulently obtains his father's blessing.

Ge 27:1–29

Heb 11:20 — By faith Isaac blessed Jacob and Esau concerning things to come.

• Esau seeks to slay, escapes to Padanaram.

Ge 27:41–28:5

Hos 12:12 — And Jacob fled into the country of Syria, and Israel served for a wife, and for a wife he kept *sheep.*

• His vision of the ladder.

Ge 28:10–22

• God confirms the covenant of Abraham to.

Ge 28:13–22; 35:9–15; 1Ch 16:13–18

• Sojourns in Haran with his uncle, Laban.

Ge 29:1–30:43

Hos 12:12 — And Jacob fled into the country of Syria, and Israel served for a wife, and for a wife he kept *sheep.*

• Serves fourteen years for Leah and Rachel.

Ge 29:15–30

Hos 12:12 — And Jacob fled into the country of Syria, and Israel served for a wife, and for a wife he kept *sheep.*

• Sharp practice of, with the flocks and herds of Laban.

Ge 30:32–43

• Dissatisfied with Laban's treatment and returns to the land of Canaan.

Ge 31:1–55

• Meets angels of God on the journey, and calls the place Mahanaim.

Ge 32:1–2

• Dreads to meet Esau; sends him presents; wrestles with an angel.

Ge 32:1–32

• Name of, changed to Israel.

Ge 32:28 — And he said, Thy name shall be called no more Jacob, but Israel: for as a prince hast thou power with God and with men, and hast prevailed.

Ge 35:10 — And God said unto him, Thy name *is* Jacob: thy name shall not be called any more Jacob, but Israel shall be thy name: and he called his name Israel.

• Reconciliation of, with Esau.

Ge 33:4 — And Esau ran to meet him, and embraced him, and fell on his neck, and kissed him: and they wept.

• Journeys to Succoth.

Ge 33:17 — And Jacob journeyed to Succoth, and built him an house, and made booths for his cattle: therefore the name of the place is called Succoth.

• Journeys to Shalem, where he purchases a parcel of ground from Hamor, and erects an altar.

Ge 33:18–20

• His daughter, Dinah, humbled.

Ge 34:1–31

• Returns to Bethel, where he builds an altar, and erects and dedicates a pillar.

Ge 35:1–7

• Deborah, Rebekah's nurse, dies, and is buried at Bethel.

Ge 35:8 — But Deborah Rebekah's nurse died, and she was buried beneath Bethel under an oak: and the name of it was called Allon-bachuth.

• Journeys to Ephrath.

Ge 35:16 — And they journeyed from Bethel; and there was but a little way to come to Ephrath: and Rachel travailed, and she had hard labour.

• Benjamin is born to.

Ge 35:17–18

• Rachel dies, and is "buried in the way to Ephrath, which is Bethlehem".

Ge 35:18–19

Ge 48:7 — And as for me, when I came from Padan, Rachel died by me in the land of Canaan in the way, when yet *there was* but a little way to come unto Ephrath: and I buried her there in the way of Ephrath; the same is Bethlehem.

• Erects a monument at Rachel's grave.

Ge 35:20 — And Jacob set a pillar upon her grave: that *is* the pillar of Rachel's grave unto this day.

• The incest of his son, Reuben, and his concubine, Bilhah.

Ge 35:22 — And it came to pass, when Israel dwelt in that land, that Reuben went and lay with Bilhah his father's concubine: and Israel heard *it*. Now the sons of Jacob were twelve:

• List of the names of his twelve sons.

Ge 35:23–26

• Returns to Arbah, the city of his father.

Ge 35:27 — And Jacob came unto Isaac his father unto Mamre, unto the city of Arbah, which *is* Hebron, where Abraham and Isaac sojourned.

• Dwells in the land of Canaan.

Ge 37:1 — And Jacob dwelt in the land wherein his father was a stranger, in the land of Canaan.

• His partiality for his son, Joseph, and the consequent jealousy of his other sons.

Ge 37:3–4

• Joseph's prophetic dream concerning.

Ge 37:9–11

• His grief over the loss of Joseph.

Ge 37:34–35

• Sends into Egypt to buy corn.

Ge 42:1–2; 43:1–14

• His grief over the detention of Simeon, and the demand for Benjamin to be taken into Egypt.

Ge 42:36 — And Jacob their father said unto them, Me have ye bereaved *of my children:* Joseph *is* not, and Simeon *is* not, and ye will take Benjamin *away:* all these things are against me.

• His love for Benjamin.

Ge 43:14 — And God Almighty give you mercy before the man, that he may send away your other brother, and Benjamin. If I be bereaved *of my children,* I am bereaved.

Ge 44:29 — And if ye take this also from me, and mischief befall him, ye shall bring down my gray hairs with sorrow to the grave.

• Hears that Joseph still lives.

Ge 45:26–28

• Removes to Egypt.

Ge 46:1–7; Ac 7:14–15

1Sa 12:8 — When Jacob was come into Egypt, and your fathers cried unto the LORD, then the LORD sent Moses and Aaron, which brought forth your fathers out of Egypt, and made them dwell in this place.

Ps 105:23 — Israel also came into Egypt; and Jacob sojourned in the land of Ham.

• List of his children and grandchildren who went down into Egypt.

Ge 46:8–27

• Meets Joseph.

Ge 46:28–34

• Pharaoh receives him, and is blessed by Jacob.

Ge 47:1–10

• The land of Goshen assigned to.

Ge 47:11–12

Ge 47:27 — And Israel dwelt in the land of Egypt, in the country of Goshen; and they had possessions therein, and grew, and multiplied exceedingly.

• Dwells in Egypt seventeen years.

Ge 47:28 — And Jacob lived in the land of Egypt seventeen years: so the whole age of Jacob was an hundred forty and seven years.

• Exacts a promise from Joseph to bury him with his fathers.

Ge 47:29–31

• His benediction upon Joseph and his two sons.

Ge 48:15–22

• Gives the land of the Amorites to Joseph.

Ge 48:22 — Moreover I have given to thee one portion above thy brethren, which I took out of the hand of the Amorite with my sword and with my bow.

Jn 4:5 — Then cometh he to a city of Samaria, which is called Sychar, near to the parcel of ground that Jacob gave to his son Joseph.

• His final prophetic benedictions upon his sons.

• Upon Reuben.

Ge 49:3–4

• Upon Simeon and Levi.

Ge 49:5–7

• Upon Judah.

Ge 49:8–12

• Upon Zebulun.

Ge 49:13 — Zebulun shall dwell at the haven of the sea; and he *shall be* for an haven of ships; and his border *shall be* unto Zidon.

• Upon Issachar.

Ge 49:14–15

• Upon Dan.

Ge 49:16–18

• Upon Gad.

Ge 49:19 — Gad, a troop shall overcome him: but he shall overcome at the last.

• Upon Asher.

Ge 49:20 — Out of Asher his bread *shall be* fat, and he shall yield royal dainties.

• Upon Naphtali.

Ge 49:21 — Naphtali *is* a hind let loose: he giveth goodly words.

• Upon Joseph.

Ge 49:22–26

• Upon Benjamin.

Ge 49:27 — Benjamin shall ravin *as* a wolf: in the morning he shall devour the prey, and at night he shall divide the spoil.

• Charges his sons to bury him in the field of Machpelah.

Ge 49:29–30

• Death of.

Ge 49:33 — And when Jacob had made an end of commanding his sons, he gathered up his feet into the bed, and yielded up the ghost, and was gathered unto his people.

• Body of, embalmed.

Ge 50:2 — And Joseph commanded his servants the physicians to embalm his father: and the physicians embalmed Israel.

• Forty days mourning for.

Ge 50:3 — And forty days were fulfilled for him; for so are fulfilled the days of those which are embalmed: and the Egyptians mourned for him threescore and ten days.

• Burial of.

Ge 50:4–13

• Descendants of.

Ge 29:31–30:24; 35:22–26; 46:8–27; Ex 1:1–5; 1Ch 2:1–9:44

Ge 35:18 — And it came to pass, as her soul was in departing, (for she died) that she called his name Ben-oni: but his father called him Benjamin.

• Prophecies concerning himself and descendants.

Ge 27:28–29; 28:10–15; 35:9–13; Ps 105:10–11

Ge 25:23 — And the LORD said unto her, Two nations *are* in thy womb, and two manner of people shall be separated from thy bowels; and *the one* people shall be stronger than *the other* people; and the elder shall serve the younger.

Ge 31:3 — And the LORD said unto Jacob, Return unto the land of thy fathers, and to thy kindred; and I will be with thee.

Ge 46:3 — And he said, I *am* God, the God of thy father: fear not to go down into Egypt; for I will there make of thee a great nation:

Dt 1:8 — Behold, I have set the land before you: go in and possess the land which the LORD sware unto your fathers, Abraham, Isaac, and Jacob, to give unto them and to their seed after them.

• His wealth.

Ge 36:6–7

• Well of.

Jn 4:5–30

JAEL • Wife of Heber, and slayer of Sisera.

Jgs 4:17–22

Jgs 5:6 — In the days of Shamgar the son of Anath, in the days of Jael, the highways were unoccupied, and the travelers walked through byways.

Jgs 5:24 — Blessed above women shall Jael the wife of Heber the Kenite be, blessed shall she be above women in the tent.

JAGUR • A town of Judah.

Jos 15:21 — And the uttermost cities of the tribe of the children of Judah toward the coast of Edom southward were Kabzeel, and Eder, and Jagur,

JAHATH • Name of four Levites.

1Ch 23:10–11

1Ch 4:2 — And Reaiah the son of Shobal begat Jahath; and Jahath begat Ahumai and Lahad. These *are* the families of the Zorathites.

1Ch 24:22 — Of the Izharites; Shelomoth: of the sons of Shelomoth; Jahath.

2Ch 34:12 — And the men did the work faithfully: and the overseers of them *were* Jahath and Obadiah, the Levites, of the sons of Merari; and Zechariah and Meshullam, of the sons of the Kohathites, to set *it* forward; and *other of* the Levites, all that could skill of instruments of musick.

JAHAZ

• Called also Jahaza, Jahazah, and Jahzah.

• Taken from the Moabites.

• A Levitical city in Reuben.

Jos 13:18 — And Jahaza, and Kedemoth, and Mephaath,

Jos 21:36 — And out of the tribe of Reuben, Bezer with her suburbs, and Jahazah with her suburbs,

Isa 15:4 — And Heshbon shall cry, and Elealeh: their voice shall be heard *even* unto Jahaz: therefore the armed soldiers of Moab shall cry out; his life shall be grievous unto him.

Jer 48:21 — And judgment is come upon the plain country; upon Holon, and upon Jahazah, and upon Mephaath,

• Sihon defeated at.

Nu 21:23 — And Sihon would not suffer Israel to pass through his border: but Sihon gathered all his people together, and went out against Israel into the wilderness: and he came to Jahaz, and fought against Israel.

Dt 2:32 — Then Sihon came out against us, he and all his people, to fight at Jahaz.

Jgs 11:20 — But Sihon trusted not Israel to pass through his coast: but Sihon gathered all his people together, and pitched in Jahaz, and fought against Israel.

JAHAZIAH • A returned exile.

Ezr 10:15 — Only Jonathan the son of Asahel and Jahaziah the son of Tikvah were employed about this *matter:* and Meshullam and Shabbethai the Levite helped them.

JAHAZIEL

• A disaffected Israelite who joined David at Ziklag.

1Ch 12:4 — And Ismaiah the Gibeonite, a mighty man among the thirty, and over the thirty; and Jeremiah, and Jahaziel, and Johanan, and Josabad the Gederathite,

• A priest.

1Ch 16:6 — Benaiah also and Jahaziel the priests with trumpets continually before the ark of the covenant of God.

• Son of Hebron.

1Ch 23:19 — Of the sons of Hebron; Jeriah the first, Amariah the second, Jahaziel the third, and Jekameam the fourth.

1Ch 24:23 — And the sons *of Hebron;* Jeriah *the first,* Amariah the second, Jahaziel the third, Jekameam the fourth.

• A Levite, and prophet.

2Ch 20:14 — Then upon Jahaziel the son of Zechariah, the son of Benaiah, the son of Jeiel, the son of Mattaniah, a Levite of the sons of Asaph, came the Spirit of the LORD in the midst of the congregation;

• A chief, or the father of a chief, among the exiles, who returned from Babylon.

Ezr 8:5 — Of the sons of Shechaniah; the son of Jahaziel, and with him three hundred males.

JAHDAI • A descendant of Caleb.

1Ch 2:47 — And the sons of Jahdai; Regem, and Jotham, and Gesham, and Pelet, and Ephah, and Shaaph.

JAHDIEL • Head of a family of Manasseh.

1Ch 5:24 — And these *were* the heads of the house of their fathers, even Epher, and Ishi, and Eliel, and Azriel, and Jeremiah, and Hodaviah, and Jahdiel, mighty men of valour, famous men, *and* heads of the house of their fathers.

JAHDO • Son of Buz.

1Ch 5:14 — These *are* the children of Abihail the son of Huri, the son of Jaroah, the son of Gilead, the son of Michael, the son of Jeshishai, the son of Jahdo, the son of Buz;

JAHLEEL • Son of Zebulun.

Ge 46:14 — And the sons of Zebulun; Sered, and Elon, and Jahleel.

Nu 26:26 — *Of* the sons of Zebulun after their families: of Sered, the family of the Sardites: of Elon, the family of the Elonites: of Jahleel, the family of the Jahleelites.

JAHMAI • Son of Tola.

1Ch 7:2 — And the sons of Tola; Uzzi, and Rephaiah, and Jeriel, and Jahmai, and Jibsam, and Shemuel, heads of their father's house, *to wit,* of Tola: *they were* valiant men of might in their generations; whose number *was* in the days of David two and twenty thousand and six hundred.

JAHZAH

• A city of Reuben.

1Ch 6:78 — And on the other side Jordan by Jericho, on the east side of Jordan, *were given them* out of the tribe of Reuben, Bezer in the wilderness with her suburbs, and Jahzah with her suburbs,

See: Jahaz

JAHZEEL

• Called also Jahziel.

• A son of Naphtali.

Ge 46:24 — And the sons of Naphtali; Jahzeel, and Guni, and Jezer, and Shillem.

Nu 26:48 — *Of* the sons of Naphtali after their families: of Jahzeel, the family of the Jahzeelites: of Guni, the family of the Gunites:

1Ch 7:13 — The sons of Naphtali; Jahziel, and Guni, and Jezer, and Shallum, the sons of Bilhah.

JAHZERAH • A priest.

1Ch 9:12 — And Adaiah the son of Jeroham, the son of Pashur, the son of Malchijah, and Maasiai the son of Adiel, the son of Jahzerah, the son of Meshullam, the son of Meshillemith, the son of Immer;

JAHZIEL

1Ch 7:13 — The sons of Naphtali; Jahziel, and Guni, and Jezer, and Shallum, the sons of Bilhah.

See: Jahzeel

JAILER

• Of Philippi, converted.

Ac 16:27–34

JAIR

• Son of Manasseh. Founder of twenty-three cities in Gilead.

1Ch 2:22–23

Nu 32:41 — And Jair the son of Manasseh went and took the small towns thereof, and called them Havoth-jair.

Dt 3:14 — Jair the son of Manasseh took all the country of Argob unto the coasts of Geshuri and Maachathi; and called them after his own name, Bashan-havoth-jair, unto this day.

Jos 13:30 — And their coast was from Mahanaim, all Bashan, all the kingdom of Og king of Bashan, and all the towns of Jair, which are in Bashan, threescore cities:

1Ki 4:13 — The son of Geber, in Ramoth-gilead; to him *pertained* the towns of Jair the son of Manasseh, which *are* in Gilead; to him *also pertained* the region of Argob, which is in Bashan, threescore great cities with walls and brasen bars:

• A judge of Israel.

Jgs 10:3–5

• A Benjamite.

Est 2:5 — *Now* in Shushan the palace there was a certain Jew, whose name *was* Mordecai, the son of Jair, the son of Shimei, the son of Kish, a Benjamite;

• Father of Elhanan.

1Ch 20:5 — And there was war again with the Philistines; and Elhanan the son of Jair slew Lahmi the brother of Goliath the Gittite, whose spear staff *was* like a weaver's beam.

JAIRUS

• A ruler of the synagogue in Capernaum.

Mt 9:18 — While he spake these things unto them, behold, there came a certain ruler, and worshipped him, saying, My daughter is even now dead: but come and lay thy hand upon her, and she shall live.

• Daughter of, restored to life.

Mt 9:23–26; Mk 5:22–43; Lk 8:41–56

Mt 9:18 — While he spake these things unto them, behold, there came a certain ruler, and worshipped him, saying, My daughter is even now dead: but come and lay thy hand upon her, and she shall live.

JAKAN ↞See: Jaakan

JAKEH • Father of Agur.

Pr 30:1 — The words of Agur the son of Jakeh, *even* the prophecy: the man spake unto Ithiel, even unto Ithiel and Ucal,

JAKIM

• A Benjamite.

1Ch 8:19 — And Jakim, and Zichri, and Zabdi,

• Head of a sacerdotal division in the tabernacle service.

1Ch 24:12 — The eleventh to Eliashib, the twelfth to Jakim,

JALON • Son of Ezra.

1Ch 4:17 — And the sons of Ezra *were*, Jether, and Mered, and Epher, and Jalon: and she bare Miriam, and Shammai, and Ishbah the father of Eshtemoa.

JAMBRES • An Egyptian magician.

Ex 7:11 — Then Pharaoh also called the wise men and the sorcerers: now the magicians of Egypt, they also did in like manner with their enchantments.

2Ti 3:8 — Now as Jannes and Jambres withstood Moses, so do these also resist the truth: men of corrupt minds, reprobate concerning the faith.

JAMES

• An apostle.

• Son of Zebedee and Salome.

Mt 4:21 — And going on from thence, he saw other two brethren, James *the son* of Zebedee, and John his brother, in a ship with Zebedee their father, mending their nets; and he called them.

Mt 27:56 — Among which was Mary Magdalene, and Mary the mother of James and Joses, and the mother of Zebedee's children.

Mk 15:40 — There were also women looking on afar off: among whom was Mary Magdalene, and Mary the mother of James the less and of Joses, and Salome;

Mk 16:1 — And when the sabbath was past, Mary Magdalene, and Mary the *mother* of James, and Salome, had bought sweet spices, that they might come and anoint him.

↞See: Salome

• Brother of John, and a fisherman.

Lk 5:10 — And so *was* also James, and John, the sons of Zebedee, which were partners with Simon. And Jesus said unto Simon, Fear not; from henceforth thou shalt catch men.

• Called to be an apostle.

Mt 4:21–22; Mk 1:19–20

Mt 10:2 — Now the names of the twelve apostles are these; The first, Simon, who is called Peter, and Andrew his brother; James *the son* of Zebedee, and John his brother;

Lk 6:14 — Simon, (whom he also named Peter,) and Andrew his brother, James and John, Philip and Bartholomew,

Ac 1:13 — And when they were come in, they went up into an upper room, where abode both Peter, and James, and John, and Andrew, Philip, and Thomas, Bartholomew, and Matthew, James *the son* of Alphaeus, and Simon Zelotes, and Judas *the brother* of James.

• Surnamed Boanerges by Jesus.

Mk 3:17 — And James the *son* of Zebedee, and John the brother of James; and he surnamed them Boanerges, which is, The sons of thunder:

• An intimate companion of Jesus, and present with him.

• At the great draught of fishes.

Lk 5:10 — And so *was* also James, and John, the sons of Zebedee, which were partners with Simon. And Jesus said unto Simon, Fear not; from henceforth thou shalt catch men.

• At the healing of Peter's mother-in-law.

Mk 1:29 — And forthwith, when they were come out of the synagogue, they entered into the house of Simon and Andrew, with James and John.

• At the raising of the daughter of Jairus.

Mk 5:37 — And he suffered no man to follow him, save Peter, and James, and John the brother of James.

Lk 8:51 — And when he came into the house, he suffered no man to go in, save Peter, and James, and John, and the father and the mother of the maiden.

• At the transfiguration of Jesus.

Mt 17:1 — And after six days Jesus taketh Peter, James, and John his brother, and bringeth them up into an high mountain apart,

Mk 9:2 — And after six days Jesus taketh *with him* Peter, and James, and John, and leadeth them up into an high mountain apart by themselves: and he was transfigured before them.

Lk 9:28 — And it came to pass about an eight days after these sayings, he took Peter and John and James, and went up into a mountain to pray.

• In Gethsemane.

Mt 26:37 — And he took with him Peter and the two sons of Zebedee, and began to be sorrowful and very heavy.

Mk 14:33 — And he taketh with him Peter and James and John, and began to be sore amazed, and to be very heavy;

• Asks Jesus concerning his second coming.

Mk 13:3 — And as he sat upon the mount of Olives over against the temple, Peter and James and John and Andrew asked him privately,

• Bigotry of.

Lk 9:54 — And when his disciples James and John saw *this,* they said, Lord, wilt thou that we command fire to come down from heaven, and consume them, even as Elias did?

• Civil ambitions of.

Mt 20:20–23; Mk 10:35–41

• Present at the sea of Tiberias when Jesus revealed himself to the disciples after his resurrection.

Jn 21:2 — There were together Simon Peter, and Thomas called Didymus, and Nathanael of Cana in Galilee, and the *sons* of Zebedee, and two other of his disciples.

1Co 15:7 — After that, he was seen of James; then of all the apostles.

• Martyred.

Ac 12:2 — And he killed James the brother of John with the sword.

• An apostle.

Ac 12:17 — But he, beckoning unto them with the hand to hold their peace, declared unto them how the Lord had brought him out of the prison. And he said, Go shew these things unto James, and to the brethren. And he departed, and went into another place.

• Son of Alphaeus.

Mt 10:3 — Philip, and Bartholomew; Thomas, and Matthew the publican; James *the son* of Alphaeus, and Lebbaeus, whose surname was Thaddaeus;

Mk 3:18 — And Andrew, and Philip, and Bartholomew, and Matthew, and Thomas, and James the *son* of Alphaeus, and Thaddaeus, and Simon the Canaanite,

Lk 6:15 — Matthew and Thomas, James the *son* of Alphaeus, and Simon called Zelotes,

Ac 1:13 — And when they were come in, they went up into an upper room, where abode both Peter, and James, and John, and Andrew, Philip, and Thomas, Bartholomew, and Matthew, James *the son* of Alphaeus, and Simon Zelotes, and Judas *the brother* of James.

• Brother of Jesus.

Mt 13:55 — Is not this the carpenter's son? is not his mother called Mary? and his brethren, James, and Joses, and Simon, and Judas?

Mt 27:56 — Among which was Mary Magdalene, and Mary the mother of James and Joses, and the mother of Zebedee's children.

Mk 6:3 — Is not this the carpenter, the son of Mary, the brother of James, and Joses, and of Juda, and Simon? and are not his sisters here with us? And they were offended at him.

Lk 24:10 — It was Mary Magdalene, and Joanna, and Mary *the mother* of James, and other *women that were* with them, which told these things unto the apostles.

Gal 1:19 — But other of the apostles saw I none, save James the Lord's brother.

Gal 2:9 — And when James, Cephas, and John, who seemed to be pillars, perceived the grace that was given unto me, they gave to me and Barnabas the right hands of fellowship; that we *should go* unto the heathen, and they unto the circumcision.

Gal 2:12 — For before that certain came from James, he did eat with the Gentiles: but when they were come, he withdrew and separated himself, fearing them which were of the circumcision.

• The brother of Judas.

Lk 6:16 — And Judas *the brother* of James, and Judas Iscariot, which also was the traitor.

Jude 1:1 — Jude, the servant of Jesus Christ, and brother of James, to them that are sanctified by God the Father, and preserved in Jesus Christ, *and* called:

- **The brother of Joses.**

Mk 15:40 — There were also women looking on afar off: among whom was Mary Magdalene, and Mary the mother of James the less and of Joses, and Salome;

- **Witness of Christ's resurrection.**

1Co 15:7 — After that, he was seen of James; then of all the apostles.

- **Addresses the council at Jerusalem in favor of liberty for the Gentile converts.**

Ac 15:13–21

- **Disciples sent by, to Antioch.**

Gal 2:12 — For before that certain came from James, he did eat with the Gentiles: but when they were come, he withdrew and separated himself, fearing them which were of the circumcision.

- **Hears of the success attending Paul's ministry.**

Ac 21:18–19

- **Epistle of.**

Jas 1:1 — James, a servant of God and of the Lord Jesus Christ, to the twelve tribes which are scattered abroad, greeting.

- **Brother of Jesus.**

Mt 13:55 — Is not this the carpenter's son? is not his mother called Mary? and his brethren, James, and Joses, and Simon, and Judas?

Mk 6:3 — Is not this the carpenter, the son of Mary, the brother of James, and Joses, and of Juda, and Simon? and are not his sisters here with us? And they were offended at him.

Gal 1:19 — But other of the apostles saw I none, save James the Lord's brother.

JAMIN

- **Son of Simeon.**

Ge 46:10 — And the sons of Simeon; Jemuel, and Jamin, and Ohad, and Jachin, and Zohar, and Shaul the son of a Canaanitish woman.

Ex 6:15 — And the sons of Simeon; Jemuel, and Jamin, and Ohad, and Jachin, and Zohar, and Shaul the son of a Canaanitish woman: these *are* the families of Simeon.

Nu 26:12 — The sons of Simeon after their families: of Nemuel, the family of the Nemuelites: of Jamin, the family of the Jaminites: of Jachin, the family of the Jachinites:

1Ch 4:24 — The sons of Simeon *were,* Nemuel, and Jamin, Jarib, Zerah, *and* Shaul:

- **Descendant of Hezron.**

1Ch 2:27 — And the sons of Ram the firstborn of Jerahmeel were, Maaz, and Jamin, and Eker.

- **A priest who expounded the law to the exiles who returned to Jerusalem.**

Ne 8:7 — Also Jeshua, and Bani, and Sherebiah, Jamin, Akkub, Shabbethai, Hodijah, Maaseiah, Kelita, Azariah, Jozabad, Hanan, Pelaiah, and the Levites, caused the people to understand the law: and the people *stood* in their place.

JAMLECH • Descendant of Simeon.

1Ch 4:34 — And Meshobab, and Jamlech, and Joshah the son of Amaziah,

JANNA • Ancestor of Joseph.

Lk 3:24 — Which was *the son* of Matthat, which was *the son* of Levi, which was *the son* of Melchi, which was *the son* of Janna, which was *the son* of Joseph,

JANNES • An Egyptian magician.

Ex 7:11 — Then Pharaoh also called the wise men and the sorcerers: now the magicians of Egypt, they also did in like manner with their enchantments.

2Ti 3:8 — Now as Jannes and Jambres withstood Moses, so do these also resist the truth: men of corrupt minds, reprobate concerning the faith.

JANOAH • A city of Naphtali.

2Ki 15:29 — In the days of Pekah king of Israel came Tiglath-pileser king of Assyria, and took Ijon, and Abel-beth-maachah, and Janoah, and Kedesh, and Hazor, and Gilead, and Galilee, all the land of Naphtali, and carried them captive to Assyria.

JANOHAH • A city on the border of Ephraim.

Jos 16:6–7

JANUM • A city of Judah.

Jos 15:53 — And Janum, and Beth-tappuah, and Aphekah,

JAPHETH

- **Son of Noah.**

Ge 5:32 — And Noah was five hundred years old: and Noah begat Shem, Ham, and Japheth.

Ge 6:10 — And Noah begat three sons, Shem, Ham, and Japheth.

Ge 9:18 — And the sons of Noah, that went forth of the ark, were Shem, and Ham, and Japheth: and Ham is the father of Canaan.

Ge 10:21 — Unto Shem also, the father of all the children of Eber, the brother of Japheth the elder, even to him were *children* born.

- **His life preserved at the time of the flood.**

Ge 7:13 — In the selfsame day entered Noah, and Shem, and Ham, and Japheth, the sons of Noah, and Noah's wife, and the three wives of his sons with them, into the ark;

Ge 9:18 — And the sons of Noah, that went forth of the ark, were Shem, and Ham, and Japheth: and Ham is the father of Canaan.

- **Prudence of, on the occasion of Noah's drunkenness.**

Ge 9:23 — And Shem and Japheth took a garment, and laid *it* upon both their shoulders, and went backward, and covered the nakedness of their father; and their faces *were* backward, and they saw not their father's nakedness.

Ge 9:27 — God shall enlarge Japheth, and he shall dwell in the tents of Shem; and Canaan shall be his servant.

- **Descendants of.**
  Ge 10:2–5; 1Ch 1:5–7

JAPHIA
- **King of Lachish.**
  Jos 10:3 — Wherefore Adoni-zedek king of Jerusalem sent unto Hoham king of Hebron, and unto Piram king of Jarmuth, and unto Japhia king of Lachish, and unto Debir king of Eglon, saying,
- **A town of Zebulun.**
  Jos 19:12 — And turned from Sarid eastward toward the sunrising unto the border of Chisloth-tabor, and then goeth out to Daberath, and goeth up to Japhia,
- **A son of David.**
  2Sa 5:15 — Ibhar also, and Elishua, and Nepheg, and Japhia,
  1Ch 3:7 — And Nogah, and Nepheg, and Japhia,
  1Ch 14:6 — And Nogah, and Nepheg, and Japhia,

JAPHLET • Grandson of Beriah.
1Ch 7:33 — And the sons of Japhlet; Pasach, and Bimhal, and Ashvath. These *are* the children of Japhlet.

JAPHLETI • A place whose situation is unknown.
Jos 16:3 — And goeth down westward to the coast of Japhleti, unto the coast of Beth-horon the nether, and to Gezer: and the goings out thereof are at the sea.

JAPHO • A city of Dan.
Jos 19:46 — And Me-jarkon, and Rakkon, with the border before Japho.

JARAH • Son of Ahaz.
1Ch 9:42 — And Ahaz begat Jarah; and Jarah begat Alemeth, and Azmaveth, and Zimri; and Zimri begat Moza;

JAREB • King of Asshur.
Hos 5:13 — When Ephraim saw his sickness, and Judah *saw* his wound, then went Ephraim to the Assyrian, and sent to king Jareb: yet could he not heal you, nor cure you of your wound.
Hos 10:6 — It shall be also carried unto Assyria *for* a present to king Jareb: Ephraim shall receive shame, and Israel shall be ashamed of his own counsel.

JARED
- **A descendant of Seth.**
  Ge 5:15–16, 18–20
  - **Called also Jered.**
    1Ch 1:2 — Kenan, Mahalaleel, Jered,
- **An ancestor of Jesus.**
  Lk 3:37 — Which was *the son* of Mathusala, which was *the son* of Enoch, which was *the son* of Jared, which was *the son* of Maleleel, which was *the son* of Cainan,

JARESIAH • Son of Jeroham.
1Ch 8:27 — And Jaresiah, and Eliah, and Zichri, the sons of Jeroham.

JARHA • An Egyptian.
1Ch 2:34–35

JARIB
- **Son of Simeon.**
  1Ch 4:24 — The sons of Simeon *were,* Nemuel, and Jamin, Jarib, Zerah, *and* Shaul:
- **A chief among the captivity.**
  Ezr 8:16 — Then sent I for Eliezer, for Ariel, for Shemaiah, and for Elnathan, and for Jarib, and for Elnathan, and for Nathan, and for Zechariah, and for Meshullam, chief men; also for Joiarib, and for Elnathan, men of understanding.
- **A priest who married an idolatrous wife.**
  Ezr 10:18 — And among the sons of the priests there were found that had taken strange wives: *namely,* of the sons of Jeshua the son of Jozadak, and his brethren; Maaseiah, and Eliezer, and Jarib, and Gedaliah.

JARMUTH
- **A city in Judah.**
  Jos 10:3 — Wherefore Adoni-zedek king of Jerusalem sent unto Hoham king of Hebron, and unto Piram king of Jarmuth, and unto Japhia king of Lachish, and unto Debir king of Eglon, saying,
  Jos 10:5 — Therefore the five kings of the Amorites, the king of Jerusalem, the king of Hebron, the king of Jarmuth, the king of Lachish, the king of Eglon, gathered themselves together, and went up, they and all their hosts, and encamped before Gibeon, and made war against it.
  Jos 10:23 — And they did so, and brought forth those five kings unto him out of the cave, the king of Jerusalem, the king of Hebron, the king of Jarmuth, the king of Lachish, *and* the king of Eglon.
  Jos 12:11 — The king of Jarmuth, one; the king of Lachish, one;
  Jos 15:35 — Jarmuth, and Adullam, Socoh, and Azekah,
  Ne 11:29 — And at En-rimmon, and at Zareah, and at Jarmuth,
- **A Levitical city in Issachar.**
  Jos 21:29 — Jarmuth with her suburbs, En-gannim with her suburbs; four cities.

JAROAH • A descendant of Gad.
1Ch 5:14 — These *are* the children of Abihail the son of Huri, the son of Jaroah, the son of Gilead, the son of Michael, the son of Jeshishai, the son of Jahdo, the son of Buz;

JASHEN • Father of one of David's heroes.

2Sa 23:32 — Eliahba the Shaalbonite, of the sons of Jashen, Jonathan,

JASHOBEAM

• One of David's warriors.

2Sa 23:8 — These *be* the names of the mighty men whom David had: The Tachmonite that sat in the seat, chief among the captains; the same *was* Adino the Eznite: *he lift up his spear* against eight hundred, whom he slew at one time.

1Ch 11:11 — And this *is* the number of the mighty men whom David had; Jashobeam, and Hachmonite, the chief of the captains: he lifted up his spear against three hundred slain *by him* at one time.

1Ch 27:2 — Over the first course for the first month *was* Jashobeam the son of Zabdiel: and in his course *were* twenty and four thousand.

• A Korhite Levite.

1Ch 12:6 — Elkanah, and Jesiah, and Azareel, and Joezer, and Jashobeam, the Korhites,

JASHUB

• Son of Issachar.

Nu 26:24 — Of Jashub, the family of the Jashubites: of Shimron, the family of the Shimronites.

1Ch 7:1 — Now the sons of Issachar *were,* Tola, and Puah, Jashub, and Shimron, four.

• Called Job.

Ge 46:13 — And the sons of Issachar; Tola, and Phuvah, and Job, and Shimron.

• Of the family of Bani.

Ezr 10:29 — And of the sons of Bani; Meshullam, Malluch, and Adaiah, Jashub, and Sheal, and Ramoth.

JASHUBI-LEHEM • A descendant of Shelah.

1Ch 4:22 — And Jokim, and the men of Chozeba, and Joash, and Saraph, who had the dominion in Moab, and Jashubi-lehem. And *these are* ancient things.

JASIEL • One of David's warriors.

1Ch 11:47 — Eliel, and Obed, and Jasiel the Mesobaite.

JASON

• A Christian at Thessalonica.

Ac 17:5–7

Ac 17:9 — And when they had taken security of Jason, and of the other, they let them go.

• Probably Paul's kinsman.

Ro 16:21 — Timotheus my workfellow, and Lucius, and Jason, and Sosipater, my kinsmen, salute you.

JASPER

• A precious stone set in the high priest's breastplate.

Rev 21:18–19

Ex 28:20 — And the fourth row a beryl, and an onyx, and a jasper: they shall be set in gold in their inclosings.

Ex 39:13 — And the fourth row, a beryl, an onyx, and a jasper: *they were* inclosed in ouches of gold in their inclosings.

Eze 28:13 — Thou hast been in Eden the garden of God; every precious stone *was* thy covering, the sardius, topaz, and the diamond, the beryl, the onyx, and the jasper, the sapphire, the emerald, and the carbuncle, and gold: the workmanship of thy tabrets and of thy pipes was prepared in thee in the day that thou wast created.

Rev 4:3 — And he that sat was to look upon like a jasper and a sardine stone: and *there was* a rainbow round about the throne, in sight like unto an emerald.

Rev 21:11 — Having the glory of God: and her light *was* like unto a stone most precious, even like a jasper stone, clear as crystal;

JATHNIEL • Son of Meshelemiah.

1Ch 26:2 — And the sons of Meshelemiah *were,* Zechariah the firstborn, Jediael the second, Zebadiah the third, Jathniel the fourth,

JATTIR • A Levitical city.

Jos 15:48 — And in the mountains, Shamir, and Jattir, and Socoh,

Jos 21:14 — And Jattir with her suburbs, and Eshtemoa with her suburbs,

1Sa 30:27 — To *them* which *were* in Bethel, and to *them* which *were* in south Ramoth, and to *them* which *were* in Jattir,

1Ch 6:57 — And to the sons of Aaron they gave the cities of Judah, *namely,* Hebron, *the city* of refuge, and Libnah with her suburbs, and Jattir, and Eshtemoa, with their suburbs,

JAVAN • Son of Japheth.

Ge 10:2 — The sons of Japheth; Gomer, and Magog, and Madai, and Javan, and Tubal, and Meshech, and Tiras.

Ge 10:4 — And the sons of Javan; Elishah, and Tarshish, Kittim, and Dodanim.

1Ch 1:5 — The sons of Japheth; Gomer, and Magog, and Madai, and Javan, and Tubal, and Meshech, and Tiras.

1Ch 1:7 — And the sons of Javan; Elishah, and Tarshish, Kittim, and Dodanim.

• A city in Arabia in which the Phenicians traded.

Eze 27:13 — Javan, Tubal, and Meshech, they *were* thy merchants: they traded the persons of men and vessels of brass in thy market.

Eze 27:19 — Dan also and Javan going to and fro occupied in thy fairs: bright iron, cassia, and calamus, were in thy market.

JAVELIN

• A heavy lance.

Eze 39:9 — And they that dwell in the cities of Israel shall go forth, and shall set on fire and burn the weapons, both the shields and the bucklers, the bows and the arrows, and the handstaves, and the spears, and they shall burn them with fire seven years:

• Used by Goliath.

1Sa 17:6 — And *he had* greaves of brass upon his legs, and a target of brass between his shoulders.

• Used by Saul.

1Sa 19:9–10

1Sa 18:11 — And Saul cast the javelin; for he said, I will smite David even to the wall *with it.* And David avoided out of his presence twice.

JAZER

• A city of refuge east of the Jordan.

Jos 21:39 — Heshbon with her suburbs, Jazer with her suburbs; four cities in all.

• Taken from the Amorites.

Nu 21:32 — And Moses sent to spy out Jaazer, and they took the villages thereof, and drove out the Amorites that *were* there.

Nu 32:1 — Now the children of Reuben and the children of Gad had a very great multitude of cattle: and when they saw the land of Jazer, and the land of Gilead, that, behold, the place *was* a place for cattle;

Nu 32:3 — Ataroth, and Dibon, and Jazer, and Nimrah, and Heshbon, and Elealeh, and Shebam, and Nebo, and Beon,

Nu 32:35 — And Atroth, Shophan, and Jaazer, and Jogbehah,

Jos 13:25 — And their coast was Jazer, and all the cities of Gilead, and half the land of the children of Ammon, unto Aroer that *is* before Rabbah;

• Sea of.

Jer 48:32 — O vine of Sibmah, I will weep for thee with the weeping of Jazer: thy plants are gone over the sea, they reach *even* to the sea of Jazer: the spoiler is fallen upon thy summer fruits and upon thy vintage.

JAZIZ • A shepherd.

1Ch 27:31 — And over the flocks *was* Jaziz the Hagerite. All these *were* the rulers of the substance which *was* king David's.

JEALOUSY

Pr 6:34 — For jealousy *is* the rage of a man: therefore he will not spare in the day of vengeance.

Pr 27:4 — Wrath *is* cruel, and anger *is* outrageous; but who *is* able to stand before envy?

Ecc 4:4 — Again, I considered all travail, and every right work, that for this a man is envied of his neighbour. This *is* also vanity and vexation of spirit.

SS 8:6 — Set me as a seal upon thine heart, as a seal upon thine arm: for love *is* strong as death; jealousy *is* cruel as the grave: the coals thereof *are* coals of fire, *which hath a* most vehement flame.

• Law concerning, when husband is jealous of his wife.

Nu 5:12–31

• Image of.

Eze 8:3–4

• Forbidden.

Ro 13:13 — Let us walk honestly, as in the day; not in rioting and drunkenness, not in chambering and wantonness, not in strife and envying.

• Attributed to God.

Ex 34:13–14; Isa 30:1–2; Eze 36:5–6

Ex 20:5 — Thou shalt not bow down thyself to them, nor serve them: for I the LORD thy God *am* a jealous God, visiting the iniquity of the fathers upon the children unto the third and fourth *generation* of them that hate me;

Nu 25:11 — Phinehas, the son of Eleazar, the son of Aaron the priest, hath turned my wrath away from the children of Israel, while he was zealous for my sake among them, that I consumed not the children of Israel in my jealousy.

Dt 29:20 — The LORD will not spare him, but then the anger of the LORD and his jealousy shall smoke against that man, and all the curses that are written in this book shall lie upon him, and the LORD shall blot out his name from under heaven.

Dt 32:16 — They provoked him to jealousy with strange *gods,* with abominations provoked they him to anger.

Dt 32:21 — They have moved me to jealousy with *that which is* not God; they have provoked me to anger with their vanities: and I will move them to jealousy with *those which are* not a people; I will provoke them to anger with a foolish nation.

1Ki 14:22 — And Judah did evil in the sight of the LORD, and they provoked him to jealousy with their sins which they had committed, above all that their fathers had done.

Ps 78:58 — For they provoked him to anger with their high places, and moved him to jealousy with their graven images.

Ps 79:5 — How long, LORD? wilt thou be angry for ever? shall thy jealousy burn like fire?

Isa 31:1 — Woe to them that go down to Egypt for help; and stay on horses, and trust in chariots, because *they are* many; and in horsemen, because they are very strong; but they look not unto the Holy One of Israel, neither seek the LORD!

Isa 31:3 — Now the Egyptians *are* men, and not God; and their horses flesh, and not spirit. When the LORD shall stretch out his hand, both he that helpeth shall fall, and he that is holpen shall fall down, and they all shall fail together.

Eze 16:42 — So will I make my fury toward thee to rest, and my jealousy shall depart from thee, and I will be quiet, and will be no more angry.

Eze 23:25 — And I will set my jealousy against thee, and they shall deal furiously with thee: they shall take away thy nose and thine ears; and thy remnant shall fall by the sword: they shall take thy sons and thy daughters; and thy residue shall be devoured by the fire.

Eze 38:19 — For in my jealousy *and* in the fire of my wrath have I spoken, Surely in that day there shall be a great shaking in the land of Israel;

Zep 1:18 — Neither their silver nor their gold shall be able to deliver them in the day of the LORD's wrath; but the whole land shall be devoured by the fire of his jealousy: for he shall make even a speedy riddance of all them that dwell in the land.

Zep 3:8 — Therefore wait ye upon me, saith the LORD, until the day that I rise up to the prey: for my determination *is* to gather the nations, that I may assemble the kingdoms, to pour upon them mine indignation, *even* all my fierce anger: for all the earth shall be devoured with the fire of my jealousy.

Zec 1:14 — So the angel that communed with me said unto me, Cry thou, saying, Thus saith the LORD of hosts; I am jealous for Jerusalem and for Zion with a great jealousy.

Zec 8:2 — Thus saith the LORD of hosts; I was jealous for Zion with great jealousy, and I was jealous for her with great fury.

1Co 10:22 — Do we provoke the Lord to jealousy? are we stronger than he?

See: Anthropomorphisms

• A spirit of emulation.

Ro 10:19 — But I say, Did not Israel know? First Moses saith, I will provoke you to jealousy by *them that are* no people, *and* by a foolish nation I will anger you.

Ro 11:11 — I say then, Have they stumbled that they should fall? God forbid: but *rather* through their fall salvation *is come* unto the Gentiles, for to provoke them to jealousy.

See: Emulation

See: Envy

• Figurative.

2Co 11:2 — For I am jealous over you with godly jealousy: for I have espoused you to one husband, that I may present *you as* a chaste virgin to Christ.

• Instances of.

• Cain, of Abel.

Ge 4:5–6, 8

• Sarah, of Hagar.

Ge 16:5

• Joseph's brethren, of Joseph.

Ge 37:4–11, 18–28

• Saul, of David.

1Sa 18:8–30; 19:8–24; 20:24–34

• Joab, of Abner.

2Sa 3:24–27

• Nathan, of Adonijah.

1Ki 1:24–26

• Ephraimites, of Gideon.

Jgs 8:1

• Ephraimites, of Jephthah.

Jgs 12:1

• The brother of the prodigal son.

Lk 15:25–32

• Sectional, between Israel and the tribe of Judah.

2Sa 19:41–43

JEATERAI • Descendant of Gershom.

1Ch 6:21 — Joah his son, Iddo his son, Zerah his son, Jeaterai his son.

JEBERECHIAH • Father of Zechariah.

Isa 8:2 — And I took unto me faithful witnesses to record, Uriah the priest, and Zechariah the son of Jeberechiah.

JEBUS

• Called also Jebusi.

See: Jerusalem

JEBUSITES

• One of the tribes of Canaan.

Dt 7:1 — When the LORD thy God shall bring thee into the land whither thou goest to possess it, and hath cast out many nations before thee, the Hittites, and the Girgashites, and the Amorites, and the Canaanites, and the Perizzites, and the Hivites, and the Jebusites, seven nations greater and mightier than thou;

• Land of, given to Abraham and his descendants.

Ex 23:23–24; 34:10–11

Ge 15:21 — And the Amorites, and the Canaanites, and the Girgashites, and the Jebusites.

Ex 3:8 — And I am come down to deliver them out of the hand of the Egyptians, and to bring them up out of that land unto a good land and a large, unto a land flowing with milk and honey; unto the place of the Canaanites, and the Hittites, and the Amorites, and the Perizzites, and the Hivites, and the Jebusites.

Ex 3:17 — And I have said, I will bring you up out of the affliction of Egypt unto the land of the Canaanites, and the Hittites, and the Amorites, and the Perizzites, and the Hivites, and the Jebusites, unto a land flowing with milk and honey.

Ex 33:2 — And I will send an angel before thee; and I will drive out the Canaanite, the Amorite, and the Hittite, and the Perizzite, the Hivite, and the Jebusite:

Dt 20:17 — But thou shalt utterly destroy them; *namely,* the Hittites, and the Amorites, the Canaanites, and the Perizzites, the Hivites, and the Jebusites; as the LORD thy God hath commanded thee:

• Conquered by Joshua.

Jos 10:1–12:24

Jos 24:11 — And ye went over Jordan, and came unto Jericho: and the men of Jericho fought against you, the Amorites, and the Perizzites, and the Canaanites, and the Hittites, and the Girgashites, the Hivites, and the Jebusites; and I delivered them into your hand.

• Conquered by David.

2Sa 5:6–9

• Jerusalem within the territory of.

Jos 18:28 — And Zelah, Eleph, and Jebusi, which *is* Jerusalem, Gibeath, *and* Kirjath; fourteen cities with their villages. This *is* the inheritance of the children of Benjamin according to their families.

• Not exterminated, but intermarry with the Israelites.

Jgs 3:5–6; Ezr 9:1–2; 10:18–44

• Pay tribute to Solomon.

1Ki 9:20–21

JECAMIAH • Son of Jeconiah.

1Ch 3:18 — Malchiram also, and Pedaiah, and Shenazar, Jecamiah, Hoshama, and Nedabiah.

JECHOLIAH

• Called also Jecoliah.

• Mother of Azariah.

2Ki 15:2 — Sixteen years old was he when he began to reign, and he reigned two and fifty years in Jerusalem. And his mother's name *was* Jecholiah of Jerusalem.

2Ch 26:3 — Sixteen years old *was* Uzziah when he began to reign, and he reigned fifty and two years in Jerusalem. His mother's name also was Jecoliah of Jerusalem.

JECONIAH •See: Jehoiachin

JEDAIAH

• Descendant of Simeon.

1Ch 4:37 — And Ziza the son of Shiphi, the son of Allon, the son of Jedaiah, the son of Shimri, the son of Shemaiah;

• A returned exile.

Ne 3:10 — And next unto them repaired Jedaiah the son of Harumaph, even over against his house. And next unto him repaired Hattush the son of Hashabniah.

• A priest of the captivity.

1Ch 9:10 — And of the priests; Jedaiah, and Jehoiarib, and Jachin,

1Ch 24:7 — Now the first lot came forth to Jehoiarib, the second to Jedaiah,

Ezr 2:36 — The priests: the children of Jedaiah, of the house of Jeshua, nine hundred seventy and three.

Ne 7:39 — The priests: the children of Jedaiah, of the house of Jeshua, nine hundred seventy and three.

• A priest who dwelt at Jerusalem after the return of the captivity.

Ne 11:10 — Of the priests: Jedaiah the son of Joiarib, Jachin.

Ne 12:6 — Shemaiah, and Joiarib, Jedaiah,

Ne 12:19 — And of Joiarib, Mattenai; of Jedaiah, Uzzi;

Zec 6:10 — Take of *them of* the captivity, *even* of Heldai, of Tobijah, and of Jedaiah, which are come from Babylon, and come thou the same day, and go into the house of Josiah the son of Zephaniah;

Zec 6:14 — And the crowns shall be to Helem, and to Tobijah, and to Jedaiah, and to Hen the son of Zephaniah, for a memorial in the temple of the LORD.

• Another priest, who returned from Babylon with Nehemiah.

Ne 12:7 — Sallu, Amok, Hilkiah, Jedaiah. These *were* the chief of the priests and of their brethren in the days of Jeshua.

Ne 12:21 — Of Hilkiah, Hashabiah; of Jedaiah, Nethaneel.

JEDIAEL

• Son of Benjamin.

1Ch 7:10–11

1Ch 7:6 — *The sons* of Benjamin; Bela, and Becher, and Jediael, three.

• Son of Shimri.

1Ch 11:45 — Jediael the son of Shimri, and Joha his brother, the Tizite,

• A Manassite chief, who joined David at Ziklag.

1Ch 12:20 — As he went to Ziklag, there fell to him of Manasseh, Adnah, and Jozabad, and Jediael, and Michael, and Jozabad, and Elihu, and Zilthai, captains of the thousands that *were* of Manasseh.

• Son of Meshelemiah.

1Ch 26:2 — And the sons of Meshelemiah *were*, Zechariah the firstborn, Jediael the second, Zebadiah the third, Jathniel the fourth,

JEDIDAH • Wife of Amon.

2Ki 22:1 — Josiah *was* eight years old when he began to reign, and he reigned thirty and one years in Jerusalem. And his mother's name *was* Jedidah, the daughter of Adaiah of Boscath.

JEDIDIAH • A name given to Solomon.

2Sa 12:25 — And he sent by the hand of Nathan the prophet; and he called his name Jedidiah, because of the LORD.

JEDUTHUN

• A musician of the temple.

1Ch 16:41 — And with them Heman and Jeduthun, and the rest that were chosen, who were expressed by name, to give thanks to the LORD, because his mercy *endureth* for ever;

1Ch 25:1 — Moreover David and the captains of the host separated to the service of the sons of Asaph, and of Heman, and of Jeduthun, who should prophesy with harps, with psalteries, and with cymbals: and the number of the workmen according to their service was:

Ps 39:1 — [To the chief Musician, even to Jeduthun, A Psalm of David.] I said, I will take heed to my ways, that I sin not with my tongue: I will keep my mouth with a bridle, while the wicked is before me.

Ps 62:1 — [To the chief Musician, to Jeduthun, A Psalm of David.] Truly my soul waiteth upon God: from him *cometh* my salvation.

Ps 77:1 — [To the chief Musician, to Jeduthun, A Psalm of Asaph.] I cried unto God with my voice, *even* unto God with my voice; and he gave ear unto me.

• Called Ethan.

1Ch 6:44 — And their brethren the sons of Merari *stood* on the left hand: Ethan the son of Kishi, the son of Abdi, the son of Malluch,

1Ch 15:17 — So the Levites appointed Heman the son of Joel; and of his brethren, Asaph the son of Berechiah; and of the sons of Merari their brethren, Ethan the son of Kushaiah;

JEGAR-SAHADUTHA

• Called also Galeed.

• A heap of stones on Mount Gilead.

Ge 31:47–48

JEHALELEEL • Descendant of Judah.

1Ch 4:16 — And the sons of Jehaleleel; Ziph, and Ziphah, Tiria, and Asareel.

JEHALELEL • A descendant of Merari.

2Ch 29:12 — Then the Levites arose, Mahath the son of Amasai, and Joel the son of Azariah, of the sons of the Kohathites: and of the sons of Merari, Kish the son of Abdi, and Azariah the son of Jehalelel: and of the Gershonites; Joah the son of Zimmah, and Eden the son of Joah:

JEHDEIAH

• Son of Shubael.

1Ch 24:20 — And the rest of the sons of Levi *were these:* Of the sons of Amram; Shubael: of the sons of Shubael; Jehdeiah.

• One of David's overseers.

1Ch 27:30 — Over the camels also was Obil the Ishmaelite: and over the asses *was* Jehdeiah the Meronothite:

JEHEZEKEL • A priest, and head of the twentieth division in the tabernacle service.

1Ch 24:16 — The nineteenth to Pethahiah, the twentieth to Jehezekel,

JEHIAH • A Levite, and doorkeeper of the ark.

1Ch 15:24 — And Shebaniah, and Jehoshaphat, and Nethaneel, and Amasai, and Zechariah, and Benaiah, and Eliezer, the priests, did blow with the trumpets before the ark of God: and Obed-edom and Jehiah *were* doorkeepers for the ark.

JEHIEL

• A Levite porter.

1Ch 15:18 — And with them their brethren of the second *degree,* Zechariah, Ben, and Jaaziel, and Shemiramoth, and Jehiel, and Unni, Eliab, and Benaiah, and Maaseiah, and Mattithiah, and Elipheleh, and Mikneiah, and Obed-edom, and Jeiel, the porters.

• Probably identical with Jehiah.

1Chr. 15:24 — And Shebaniah, and Jehoshaphat, and Nethaneel, and Amasai, and Zechariah, and Benaiah, and Eliezer, the priests, did blow with the trumpets before the ark of God: and Obededom and Jehiah *were* doorkeepers for the ark.

• A Gershonite Levite.

1Ch 23:8 — The sons of Laadan; the chief *was* Jehiel, and Zetham, and Joel, three.

1Ch 29:8 — And they with whom *precious* stones were found gave *them* to the treasure of the house of the LORD, by the hand of Jehiel the Gershonite.

• A companion of David's sons.

1Ch 27:32 — Also Jonathan David's uncle was a counsellor, a wise man, and a scribe: and Jehiel the son of Hachmoni *was* with the king's sons:

• Son of Jehoshaphat.

2Ch 21:2 — And he had brethren the sons of Jehoshaphat, Azariah, and Jehiel, and Zechariah, and Azariah, and Michael, and Shephatiah: all these *were* the sons of Jehoshaphat king of Israel.

• Son of Heman.

2Ch 29:14 — And of the sons of Heman; Jehiel, and Shimei: and of the sons of Jeduthun; Shemaiah, and Uzziel.

• A Levite overseer in the temple.

2Ch 31:13 — And Jehiel, and Azaziah, and Nahath, and Asahel, and Jerimoth, and Jozabad, and Eliel, and Ismachiah, and Mahath, and Benaiah, *were* overseers under the hand of Cononiah and Shimei his brother, at the commandment of Hezekiah the king, and Azariah the ruler of the house of God.

• A priest who gave extraordinary offerings for the passover.

2Ch 35:8 — And his princes gave willingly unto the people, to the priests, and to the Levites: Hilkiah and Zechariah and Jehiel, rulers of the house of God, gave unto the priests for the passover offerings two thousand and six hundred *small cattle,* and three hundred oxen.

• Father of Obadiah.

Ezr 8:9 — Of the sons of Joab; Obadiah the son of Jehiel, and with him two hundred and eighteen males.

• Father of Shechaniah.

Ezr 10:2 — And Shechaniah the son of Jehiel, *one* of the sons of Elam, answered and said unto Ezra, We have trespassed against our God, and have taken strange wives of the people of the land: yet now there is hope in Israel concerning this thing.

• Name of two priests who married idolatrous wives.

Ezr 10:21 — And of the sons of Harim; Maaseiah, and Elijah, and Shemaiah, and Jehiel, and Uzziah.

Ezr 10:26 — And of the sons of Elam; Mattaniah, Zechariah, and Jehiel, and Abdi, and Jeremoth, and Eliah.

JEHIELI • Son of Laadan.

1Ch 26:21–22

JEHIZKIAH • Son of Shallum.

2Ch 28:12 — Then certain of the heads of the children of Ephraim, Azariah the son of Johanan,

Berechiah the son of Meshillemoth, and Jehizkiah the son of Shallum, and Amasa the son of Hadlai, stood up against them that came from the war,

JEHOADAH • Son of Ahaz.

1Ch 8:36 — And Ahaz begat Jehoadah; and Jehoadah begat Alemeth, and Azmaveth, and Zimri; and Zimri begat Moza,

JEHOADDAN • Mother of Amaziah.

2Ki 14:2 — He was twenty and five years old when he began to reign, and reigned twenty and nine years in Jerusalem. And his mother's name *was* Jehoaddan of Jerusalem.

2Ch 25:1 — Amaziah *was* twenty and five years old *when* he began to reign, and he reigned twenty and nine years in Jerusalem. And his mother's name *was* Jehoaddan of Jerusalem.

JEHOAHAZ

• Son of Jehu, and king of Israel.

2Ki 13:1–9

2Ki 10:35 — And Jehu slept with his fathers: and they buried him in Samaria. And Jehoahaz his son reigned in his stead.

• Son of Jehoram, king of Judah.

2Ch 21:17 — And they came up into Judah, and brake into it, and carried away all the substance that was found in the king's house, and his sons also, and his wives; so that there was never a son left him, save Jehoahaz, the youngest of his sons.

See: Ahaziah

• Called also Shallum; king of Judah, and successor of Josiah.

2Ki 23:30–31

1Ch 3:15 — And the sons of Josiah *were,* the firstborn Johanan, the second Jehoiakim, the third Zedekiah, the fourth Shallum.

2Ch 36:1 — Then the people of the land took Jehoahaz the son of Josiah, and made him king in his father's stead in Jerusalem.

Jer 22:11 — For thus saith the LORD touching Shallum the son of Josiah king of Judah, which reigned instead of Josiah his father, which went forth out of this place; He shall not return thither any more:

• Wicked reign of.

2Ki 23:32 — And he did *that which was* evil in the sight of the LORD, according to all that his fathers had done.

• Pharaoh-nechoh, king of Egypt, invades the kingdom of, defeats him, and takes him captive to Egypt.

2Ki 23:33–35; 2Ch 36:3–4

• Prophecies concerning.

Jer 22:10–12

JEHOASH

• Called also Joash; successor of Jehoahaz.

2Ki 13:10–25

• Defeats Amaziah.

2Ki 14:8–15; 2Ch 25:17–24

2Ki 13:12 — And the rest of the acts of Joash, and all that he did, and his might wherewith he fought against Amaziah king of Judah, *are* they not written in the book of the chronicles of the kings of Israel?

• Death of.

2Ki 13:13 — And Joash slept with his fathers; and Jeroboam sat upon his throne: and Joash was buried in Samaria with the kings of Israel.

2Ki 14:16 — And Jehoash slept with his fathers, and was buried in Samaria with the kings of Israel; and Jeroboam his son reigned in his stead.

• King of Judah.

See: Joash

JEHOHANAN

• A porter of the tabernacle.

1Ch 26:3 — Elam the fifth, Jehohanan the sixth, Elioenai the seventh.

• A military chief under Jehoshaphat, whose corps consisted of two hundred and eighty thousand men.

2Ch 17:15 — And next to him *was* Jehohanan the captain, and with him two hundred and fourscore thousand.

• Probably identical with a captain of a hundred.

2Ch 23:1 — And in the seventh year Jehoiada strengthened himself, and took the captains of hundreds, Azariah the son of Jeroham, and Ishmael the son of Jehohanan, and Azariah the son of Obed, and Maaseiah the son of Adaiah, and Elishaphat the son of Zichri, into covenant with him.

• Son of Bebai.

Ezr 10:28 — Of the sons also of Bebai; Jehohanan, Hananiah, Zabbai, *and* Athlai.

• A priest among the exiles who returned from Babylon.

Ne 12:13 — Of Ezra, Meshullam; of Amariah, Jehohanan;

• A chorister in the temple.

Ne 12:42 — And Maaseiah, and Shemaiah, and Eleazar, and Uzzi, and Jehohanan, and Malchijah, and Elam, and Ezer. And the singers sang loud, with Jezrahiah *their* overseer.

JEHOIACHIN

• King of Judah and successor to Jehoiakim.

2Ki 24:6–8; 2Ch 36:8–9

• Called Jeconiah.

1Ch 3:16 — And the sons of Jehoiakim: Jeconiah his son, Zedekiah his son.

Jer 24:1 — The LORD shewed me, and, behold, two baskets of figs *were* set before the temple of the LORD, after that Nebuchadrezzar king of Babylon had carried away captive Jeconiah the son of Jehoiakim king of Judah, and the princes of Judah, with the carpenters and smiths, from Jerusalem, and had brought them to Babylon.

• Called Coniah.

Jer 22:24 — *As* I live, saith the LORD, though Coniah the son of Jehoiakim king of Judah were the signet upon my right hand, yet would I pluck thee thence;

Jer 37:1 — And king Zedekiah the son of Josiah reigned instead of Coniah the son of Jehoiakim, whom Nebuchadrezzar king of Babylon made king in the land of Judah.

• Wicked reign of.

2Ki 24:9 — And he did *that which was* evil in the sight of the LORD, according to all that his father had done.

2Ch 36:9 — Jehoiachin *was* eight years old when he began to reign, and he reigned three months and ten days in Jerusalem: and he did *that which was* evil in the sight of the LORD.

• Nebuchadnezzar invades his kingdom; takes him captive to Babylon.

2Ki 24:10–16; Jer 29:1–2

2Ch 36:10 — And when the year was expired, king Nebuchadnezzar sent, and brought him to Babylon, with the goodly vessels of the house of the LORD, and made Zedekiah his brother king over Judah and Jerusalem.

Est 2:6 — Who had been carried away from Jerusalem with the captivity which had been carried away with Jeconiah king of Judah, whom Nebuchadnezzar the king of Babylon had carried away.

Jer 27:20 — Which Nebuchadnezzar king of Babylon took not, when he carried away captive Jeconiah the son of Jehoiakim king of Judah from Jerusalem to Babylon, and all the nobles of Judah and Jerusalem;

Eze 1:2 — In the fifth *day* of the month, which *was* the fifth year of king Jehoiachin's captivity,

• Confined in prison thirty-seven years.

2Ki 25:27 — And it came to pass in the seven and thirtieth year of the captivity of Jehoiachin king of Judah, in the twelfth month, on the seven and twentieth *day* of the month, *that* Evil-merodach king of Babylon in the year that he began to reign did lift up the head of Jehoiachin king of Judah out of prison;

• Released from prison by Evilmerodach; promoted above other kings; honored until death.

2Ki 25:27–30; Jer 52:31–34

• Prophecies concerning.

Jer 22:24–30

Jer 28:4 — And I will bring again to this place Jeconiah the son of Jehoiakim king of Judah, with all the captives of Judah, that went into Babylon, saith the LORD: for I will break the yoke of the king of Babylon.

• Sons of.

1Ch 3:17–18

• Ancestor of Jesus.

Mt 1:12 — And after they were brought to Babylon, Jechonias begat Salathiel; and Salathiel begat Zorobabel;

JEHOIADA

• Father of Benaiah, one of David's officers.

2Sa 8:18 — And Benaiah the son of Jehoiada *was over* both the Cherethites and the Pelethites; and David's sons were chief rulers.

• A high priest. Overthrows Athaliah, the Queen of Judah; establishes Jehoash upon the throne.

2Ki 11:1–21; 2Ch 23:1–21

• Salutary influence of, over Jehoash.

2Ki 12:2 — And Jehoash did *that which was* right in the sight of the LORD all his days wherein Jehoiada the priest instructed him.

2Ch 24:2 — And Joash did *that which was* right in the sight of the LORD all the days of Jehoiada the priest.

2Ch 24:22 — Thus Joash the king remembered not the kindness which Jehoiada his father had done to him, but slew his son. And when he died, he said, The LORD look upon *it,* and require *it.*

• Directs the repairs of the temple.

2Ki 12:4–16; 2Ch 24:4–14

• Death of.

2Ch 24:15–16

• A priest who led three thousand seven hundred priests armed for war.

1Ch 12:27 — And Jehoiada *was* the leader of the Aaronites, and with him *were* three thousand and seven hundred;

• Son of Banaiah.

1Ch 27:34 — And after Ahithophel *was* Jehoiada the son of Benaiah, and Abiathar: and the general of the king's army *was* Joab.

• A returned exile.

Ne 3:6 — Moreover the old gate repaired Jehoiada the son of Paseah, and Meshullam the son of Besodeiah; they laid the beams thereof, and set up the doors thereof, and the locks thereof, and the bars thereof.

• A priest mentioned in Jeremiah's letter to the captive Jews.

Jer 29:26 — The LORD hath made thee priest in the stead of Jehoiada the priest, that ye should be officers in the house of the LORD, for every man *that is* mad, and maketh himself a prophet, that thou shouldest put him in prison, and in the stocks.

JEHOIAKIM

• Called also Eliakim.

• King of Judah.

1Ch 3:15 — And the sons of Josiah *were,* the firstborn Johanan, the second Jehoiakim, the third Zedekiah, the fourth Shallum.

• Ancestor of Jesus.

Mt 1:11 — And Josias begat Jechonias and his brethren, about the time they were carried away to Babylon:

• Wicked reign and final overthrow of.

2Ki 23:34–24:6; 2Ch 36:4–8; Jer 22:13–19; 26:22–23; 36:1–32; Da 1:1–2

• Dies, and is succeeded by his son, Jehoiachin.

2Ki 24:6 — So Jehoiakim slept with his fathers: and Jehoiachin his son reigned in his stead.

JEHOIARIB

• Two priests bearing the same name.

1Ch 9:10 — And of the priests; Jedaiah, and Jehoiarib, and Jachin,

1Ch 24:7 — Now the first lot came forth to Jehoiarib, the second to Jedaiah,

Ne 11:10 — Of the priests: Jedaiah the son of Joiarib, Jachin.

JEHONADAB ✦See: Jonadab

JEHONATHAN

• An overseer of David's storehouses.

1Ch 27:25 — And over the king's treasures *was* Azmaveth the son of Adiel: and over the storehouses in the fields, in the cities, and in the villages, and in the castles, *was* Jehonathan the son of Uzziah:

• A Levite sent to instruct the people in the law.

2Ch 17:8 — And with them *he sent* Levites, *even* Shemaiah, and Nethaniah, and Zebadiah, and Asahel, and Shemiramoth, and Jehonathan, and Adonijah, and Tobijah, and Tob-adonijah, Levites; and with them Elishama and Jehoram, priests.

• An obscure priest.

Ne 12:18 — Of Bilgah, Shammua; of Shemaiah, Jehonathan;

JEHORAM

• King of Judah.

1Ki 22:50 — And Jehoshaphat slept with his fathers, and was buried with his fathers in the city of David his father: and Jehoram his son reigned in his stead.

2Ki 8:16 — And in the fifth year of Joram the son of Ahab king of Israel, Jehoshaphat *being* then king of Judah, Jehoram the son of Jehoshaphat king of Judah began to reign.

1Ch 3:11 — Joram his son, Ahaziah his son, Joash his son,

2Ch 21:5 — Jehoram *was* thirty and two years old when he began to reign, and he reigned eight years in Jerusalem.

• Ancestor of Jesus.

Mt 1:8 — And Asa begat Josaphat; and Josaphat begat Joram; and Joram begat Ozias;

• Marries Athaliah, whose wicked counsels influence his reign for evil.

2Ki 8:18–19; 2Ch 21:6–13

• Slays his brothers to strengthen himself in his sovereignty.

2Ch 21:4 — Now when Jehoram was risen up to the kingdom of his father, he strengthened himself, and slew all his brethren with the sword, and *divers* also of the princes of Israel.

2Ch 21:13 — But hast walked in the way of the kings of Israel, and hast made Judah and the inhabitants of Jerusalem to go a whoring, like to the whoredoms of the house of Ahab, and also hast slain thy brethren of thy father's house, *which were* better than thyself:

• Edom revolts from.

2Ki 8:20–22; 2Ch 21:8–10

• Philistines and Arabians invade his territory.

2Ch 21:16–17

• Death of.

2Ch 21:18–20

2Ki 8:24 — And Joram slept with his fathers, and was buried with his fathers in the city of David: and Ahaziah his son reigned in his stead.

• Prophecy concerning.

2Ch 21:12–15

• A son of Ahab.

✦See: Joram

• A priest commissioned to go through Israel and instruct the people in the law.

2Ch 17:8 — And with them *he sent* Levites, *even* Shemaiah, and Nethaniah, and Zebadiah, and Asahel, and Shemiramoth, and Jehonathan, and Adonijah, and Tobijah, and Tob-adonijah, Levites; and with them Elishama and Jehoram, priests.

JEHOSHABEATH ✦See: Jehosheba

JEHOSHAPHAT

• David's recorder.

2Sa 8:16 — And Joab the son of Zeruiah *was* over the host; and Jehoshaphat the son of Ahilud *was* recorder;

2Sa 20:24 — And Adoram *was* over the tribute: and Jehoshaphat the son of Ahilud *was* recorder:

1Ki 4:3 — Elihoreph and Ahiah, the sons of Shisha, scribes; Jehoshaphat the son of Ahilud, the recorder.

1Ch 18:15 — And Joab the son Zeruiah was over the host; and Jehoshaphat the son of Ahilud, recorder.

• One of Solomon's commissariat officers.

1Ki 4:17 — Jehoshaphat the son of Paruah, in Issachar:

• King of Judah; succeeds Asa.

1Ki 15:24 — And Asa slept with his fathers, and was buried with his fathers in the city of David his father: and Jehoshaphat his son reigned in his stead.

1Ki 22:41 — And Jehoshaphat the son of Asa began to reign over Judah in the fourth year of Ahab king of Israel.

1Ch 3:10 — And Solomon's son *was* Rehoboam, Abia his son, Asa his son, Jehoshaphat his son,

2Ch 17:1 — And Jehoshaphat his son reigned in his stead, and strengthened himself against Israel.

Mt 1:8 — And Asa begat Josaphat; and Josaphat begat Joram; and Joram begat Ozias;

• Strengthens himself against Israel.

2Ch 17:2 — And he placed forces in all the fenced cities of Judah, and set garrisons in the land of

Judah, and in the cities of Ephraim, which Asa his father had taken.

• Inaugurates a system of public instruction in the law.

2Ch 17:7–9

• His wise reign.

2Ch 17:7–9; 19:3–11

1Ki 22:43 — And he walked in all the ways of Asa his father; he turned not aside from it, doing *that which was* right in the eyes of the LORD: nevertheless the high places were not taken away; *for* the people offered and burnt incense yet in the high places.

• His system of tribute.

2Ch 17:11 — Also *some* of the Philistines brought Jehoshaphat presents, and tribute silver; and the Arabians brought him flocks, seven thousand and seven hundred rams, and seven thousand and seven hundred he goats.

• His military forces and armament.

2Ch 17:12–19

• Joins Ahab in an invasion of Ramoth-gilead.

1Ki 22:1–53; 2Ch 18:1–34

• Rebuked by the prophet Jehu.

2Ch 19:2 — And Jehu the son of Hanani the seer went out to meet him, and said to king Jehoshaphat, Shouldest thou help the ungodly, and love them that hate the LORD? therefore is wrath upon thee from before the LORD.

• The allied forces of the Amorites, Moabites, and other tribes invade his territory, and are defeated by.

2Ch 20:1–37

• Builds ships for commerce with Tarshish; ships are destroyed.

1Ki 22:48–49; 2Ch 20:35–37

• Joins Jehoram, king of Israel, in an invasion of the land of Moab, defeats the Moabites.

2Ki 3:1–27

• Makes valuable gifts to the temple.

2Ki 12:18 — And Jehoash king of Judah took all the hallowed things that Jehoshaphat, and Jehoram, and Ahaziah, his fathers, kings of Judah, had dedicated, and his own hallowed things, and all the gold *that was* found in the treasures of the house of the LORD, and in the king's house, and sent *it* to Hazael king of Syria: and he went away from Jerusalem.

• Death of.

1Ki 22:50 — And Jehoshaphat slept with his fathers, and was buried with his fathers in the city of David his father: and Jehoram his son reigned in his stead.

2Ch 21:1 — Now Jehoshaphat slept with his fathers, and was buried with his fathers in the city of David. And Jehoram his son reigned in his stead.

• Religious zeal of.

2Ch 17:1–9; 19:1–20:32

1Ki 22:43 — And he walked in all the ways of Asa his father; he turned not aside from it, doing *that which was* right in the eyes of the LORD: nevertheless the high places were not taken away; *for* the people offered and burnt incense yet in the high places.

1Ki 22:46 — And the remnant of the sodomites, which remained in the days of his father Asa, he took out of the land.

2Ch 22:9 — And he sought Ahaziah: and they caught him, (for he was hid in Samaria,) and brought him to Jehu: and when they had slain him, they buried him: Because, said they, he *is* the son of Jehoshaphat, who sought the LORD with all his heart. So the house of Ahaziah had no power to keep still the kingdom.

• Prosperity of.

2Ch 17:1–20:37

1Ki 22:45 — Now the rest of the acts of Jehoshaphat, and his might that he shewed, and how he warred, *are* they not written in the book of the chronicles of the kings of Judah?

1Ki 22:48 — Jehoshaphat made ships of Tharshish to go to Ophir for gold: but they went not; for the ships were broken at Ezion-geber.

• Bequests of, to his children.

2Ch 21:2–3

• Father of Jehu.

2Ki 9:2 — And when thou comest thither, look out there Jehu the son of Jehoshaphat the son of Nimshi, and go in, and make him arise up from among his brethren, and carry him to an inner chamber;

2Ki 9:14 — So Jehu the son of Jehoshaphat the son of Nimshi conspired against Joram. (Now Joram had kept Ramoth-gilead, he and all Israel, because of Hazael king of Syria.

• A priest who assisted in bringing the ark from Obed-edom.

1Ch 15:24 — And Shebaniah, and Jehoshaphat, and Nethaneel, and Amasai, and Zechariah, and Benaiah, and Eliezer, the priests, did blow with the trumpets before the ark of God: and Obed-edom and Jehiah *were* doorkeepers for the ark.

• A valley.

Joel 3:2 — I will also gather all nations, and will bring them down into the valley of Jehoshaphat, and will plead with them there for my people and *for* my heritage Israel, whom they have scattered among the nations, and parted my land.

Joel 3:12 — Let the heathen be wakened, and come up to the valley of Jehoshaphat: for there will I sit to judge all the heathen round about.

• Called Valley of Decision.

Joel 3:14 — Multitudes, multitudes in the valley of decision: for the day of the LORD *is* near in the valley of decision.

JEHOSHEBA

• Called also Jehoshabeath.

• Daughter of Joram.

2Ki 11:2 — But Jehosheba, the daughter of king Joram, sister of Ahaziah, took Joash the son of Ahaziah and stole him from among the king's sons *which were* slain; and they hid him, *even* him and his nurse, in the bedchamber from Athaliah, so that he was not slain.

JEHOSHUA • A name sometimes given to one of the Joshuas.

Nu 13:16 — These *are* the names of the men which Moses sent to spy out the land. And Moses called Oshea the son of Nun Jehoshua.

JEHOSHUAH • A name of one of the Joshuas.

1Ch 7:27 — Non his son, Jehoshuah his son.

JEHOVAH-JIREH

• Mount Moriah, in Jerusalem.

• The place where Abraham offered Isaac.

Ge 22:14 — And Abraham called the name of that place Jehovah-jireh: as it is said *to* this day, In the mount of the LORD it shall be seen.

JEHOVAH-NISSI • An altar.

Ex 17:15 — And Moses built an altar, and called the name of it Jehovah-nissi:

JEHOVAH-SHALOM • An altar built by Gideon.

Jgs 6:24 — Then Gideon built an altar there unto the LORD, and called it Jehovah-shalom: unto this day it is yet in Ophrah of the Abi-ezrites.

JEHOZABAD

• Son of Shomer, and one of the assassins of King Jehoash.

2Ki 12:21 — For Jozachar the son of Shimeath, and Jehozabad the son of Shomer, his servants, smote him, and he died; and they buried him with his fathers in the city of David: and Amaziah his son reigned in his stead.

2Ch 24:26 — And these are they that conspired against him; Zabad the son of Shimeath an Ammonitess, and Jehozabad the son of Shimrith a Moabitess.

• Son of Obed-edom.

1Ch 26:4 — Moreover the sons of Obed-edom *were,* Shemaiah the firstborn, Jehozabad the second, Joah the third, and Sacar the fourth, and Nethaneel the fifth,

• A Benjamite chief who commanded one hundred and eighty thousand men.

2Ch 17:18 — And next him *was* Jehozabad, and with him an hundred and fourscore thousand ready prepared for the war.

JEHOZADAK

• Called also Josedech and Jozadak.

• A priest of the exile.

1Ch 6:14–15

Ezr 3:2 — Then stood up Jeshua the son of Jozadak, and his brethren the priests, and Zerubbabel the son of Shealtiel, and his brethren, and builded the altar of the God of Israel, to offer burnt offerings thereon, as *it is* written in the law of Moses the man of God.

Ezr 3:8 — Now in the second year of their coming unto the house of God at Jerusalem, in the second month, began Zerubbabel the son of Shealtiel, and Jeshua the son of Jozadak, and the remnant of their brethren the priests and the Levites, and all they that were come out of the captivity unto Jerusalem; and appointed the Levites, from twenty years old and upward, to set forward the work of the house of the LORD.

Ezr 5:2 — Then rose up Zerubbabel the son of Shealtiel, and Jeshua the son of Jozadak, and began to build the house of God which *is* at Jerusalem: and with them *were* the prophets of God helping them.

Ezr 10:18 — And among the sons of the priests there were found that had taken strange wives: *namely,* of the sons of Jeshua the son of Jozadak, and his brethren; Maaseiah, and Eliezer, and Jarib, and Gedaliah.

Ne 12:26 — These *were* in the days of Joiakim the son of Jeshua, the son of Jozadak, and in the days of Nehemiah the governor, and of Ezra the priest, the scribe.

Hag 1:1 — In the second year of Darius the king, in the sixth month, in the first day of the month, came the word of the LORD by Haggai the prophet unto Zerubbabel the son of Shealtiel, governor of Judah, and to Joshua the son of Josedech, the high priest, saying,

Hag 1:12 — Then Zerubbabel the son of Shealtiel, and Joshua the son of Josedech, the high priest, with all the remnant of the people, obeyed the voice of the LORD their God, and the words of Haggai the prophet, as the LORD their God had sent him, and the people did fear before the LORD.

Hag 1:14 — And the LORD stirred up the spirit of Zerubbabel the son of Shealtiel, governor of Judah, and the spirit of Joshua the son of Josedech, the high priest, and the spirit of all the remnant of the people; and they came and did work in the house of the LORD of hosts, their God,

Hag 2:2 — Speak now to Zerubbabel the son of Shealtiel, governor of Judah, and to Joshua the son of Josedech, the high priest, and to the residue of the people, saying,

Hag 2:4 — Yet now be strong, O Zerubbabel, saith the LORD; and be strong, O Joshua, son of Josedech, the high priest; and be strong, all ye people of the land, saith the LORD, and work: for *I am* with you, saith the LORD of hosts:

Zec 6:11 — Then take silver and gold, and make crowns, and set *them* upon the head of Joshua the son of Josedech, the high priest;

JEHU

• The prophet who announced the wrath of Jehovah against Baasha, king of Israel.

1Ki 16:1 — Then the word of the LORD came to Jehu the son of Hanani against Baasha, saying,

1Ki 16:7 — And also by the hand of the prophet Jehu the son of Hanani came the word of the LORD against Baasha, and against his house, even for all the evil that he did in the sight of the LORD, in provoking him to anger with the work of his hands, in being like the house of Jeroboam; and because he killed him.

1Ki 16:12 — Thus did Zimri destroy all the house of Baasha, according to the word of the LORD, which he spake against Baasha by Jehu the prophet,

2Ch 19:2 — And Jehu the son of Hanani the seer went out to meet him, and said to king Jehoshaphat, Shouldest thou help the ungodly, and love them that hate the LORD? therefore is wrath upon thee from before the LORD.

2Ch 20:34 — Now the rest of the acts of Jehoshaphat, first and last, behold, they *are* written in the book of Jehu the son of Hanani, who is mentioned in the book of the kings of Israel.

• Son of Nimshi, king of Israel.

2Ki 9:1–14

1Ki 19:16 — And Jehu the son of Nimshi shalt thou anoint *to be* king over Israel: and Elisha the son of Shaphat of Abel-meholah shalt thou anoint *to be* prophet in thy room.

• Religious zeal of, in slaying idolaters.

2Ki 9:14–10:28; 2Ch 22:8–9

• His territory invaded by Hazael, king of Syria.

2Ki 10:32–33

• Prophecies concerning.

1Ki 19:17 — And it shall come to pass, *that* him that escapeth the sword of Hazael shall Jehu slay: and him that escapeth from the sword of Jehu shall Elisha slay.

2Ki 10:30 — And the LORD said unto Jehu, Because thou hast done well in executing *that which is* right in mine eyes, *and* hast done unto the house of Ahab according to all that *was* in mine heart, thy children of the fourth *generation* shall sit on the throne of Israel.

2Ki 15:12 — This *was* the word of the LORD which he spake unto Jehu, saying, Thy sons shall sit on the throne of Israel unto the fourth *generation.* And so it came to pass.

Hos 1:4 — And the LORD said unto him, Call his name Jezreel; for yet a little *while,* and I will avenge the blood of Jezreel upon the house of Jehu, and will cause to cease the kingdom of the house of Israel.

• Death of.

2Ki 10:35 — And Jehu slept with his fathers: and they buried him in Samaria. And Jehoahaz his son reigned in his stead.

• Son of Obed.

1Ch 2:38 — And Obed begat Jehu, and Jehu begat Azariah,

• Son of Josibiah.

1Ch 4:35 — And Joel, and Jehu the son of Josibiah, the son of Seraiah, the son of Asiel,

• A Benjamite.

1Ch 12:3 — The chief *was* Ahiezer, then Joash, the sons of Shemaah the Gibeathite; and Jeziel, and Pelet, the sons of Azmaveth; and Berachah, and Jehu the Antothite,

JEHUBBAH • An Asherite.

1Ch 7:34 — And the sons of Shamer; Ahi, and Rohgah, Jehubbah, and Aram.

JEHUCAL

• Called also Jucal.

• Son of Shelemiah.

Jer 37:3 — And Zedekiah the king sent Jehucal the son of Shelemiah and Zephaniah the son of Maaseiah the priest to the prophet Jeremiah, saying, Pray now unto the LORD our God for us.

Jer 38:1 — Then Shephatiah the son of Mattan, and Gedaliah the son of Pashur, and Jucal the son of Shelemiah, and Pashur the son of Malchiah, heard the words that Jeremiah had spoken unto all the people, saying,

Jer 38:4 — Therefore the princes said unto the king, We beseech thee, let this man be put to death: for thus he weakeneth the hands of the men of war that remain in this city, and the hands of all the people, in speaking such words unto them: for this man seeketh not the welfare of this people, but the hurt.

JEHUD • A city of Dan.

Jos 19:45 — And Jehud, and Bene-berak, and Gath-rimmon,

JEHUDI • A Jew.

Jer 36:14 — Therefore all the princes sent Jehudi the son of Nethaniah, the son of Shelemiah, the son of Cushi, unto Baruch, saying, Take in thine hand the roll wherein thou hast read in the ears of the people, and come. So Baruch the son of Neriah took the roll in his hand, and came unto them.

Jer 36:21 — So the king sent Jehudi to fetch the roll: and he took it out of Elishama the scribe's chamber. And Jehudi read it in the ears of the king, and in the ears of all the princes which stood beside the king.

Jer 36:23 — And it came to pass, *that* when Jehudi had read three or four leaves, he cut it with the penknife, and cast *it* into the fire that *was* on the hearth, until all the roll was consumed in the fire that *was* on the hearth.

JEHUDIJAH • Wife of Ezra.

1Ch 4:18 — And his wife Jehudijah bare Jered the father of Gedor, and Heber the father of Socho, and Jekuthiel the father of Zanoah. And these *are* the sons of Bithiah the daughter of Pharaoh, which Mered took.

JEHUSH • A Benjamite.

1Ch 8:39 — And the sons of Eshek his brother *were,* Ulam his firstborn, Jehush the second, and Eliphelet the third.

JEIEL

• A Reubenite, also known as Jehiel.

1Ch 5:7 — And his brethren by their families, when the genealogy of their generations was reckoned, *were* the chief, Jeiel, and Zechariah,

• A Benjamite.

1Ch 9:35 — And in Gibeon dwelt the father of Gibeon, Jehiel, whose wife's name *was* Maachah:

• One of David's heroes.

1Ch 11:44 — Uzzia the Ashterathite, Shama and Jehiel the sons of Hothan the Aroerite,

• A Levite, and chorister in the tabernacle service.

1Ch 15:18 — And with them their brethren of the second *degree,* Zechariah, Ben, and Jaaziel, and Shemiramoth, and Jehiel, and Unni, Eliab, and Benaiah, and Maaseiah, and Mattithiah, and Eli-pheleh, and Mikneiah, and Obed-edom, and Jeiel, the porters.

1Ch 15:21 — And Mattithiah, and Elipheleh, and Mikneiah, and Obed-edom, and Jeiel, and Azaziah, with harps on the Sheminith to excel.

1Ch 16:5 — Asaph the chief, and next to him Zechariah, Jeiel, and Shemiramoth, and Jehiel, and Mattithiah, and Eliab, and Benaiah, and Obed-edom: and Jeiel with psalteries and with harps; but Asaph made a sound with cymbals;

• A Levite; ancestor of Jehaziel, who encouraged Judah against their enemies.

2Ch 20:14 — Then upon Jahaziel the son of Zechariah, the son of Benaiah, the son of Jeiel, the son of Mattaniah, a Levite of the sons of Asaph, came the Spirit of the LORD in the midst of the congregation;

• A scribe during the reign of Uzziah.

2Ch 26:11 — Moreover Uzziah had an host of fighting men, that went out to war by bands, according to the number of their account by the hand of Jeiel the scribe and Maaseiah the ruler, under the hand of Hananiah, *one* of the king's captains.

• A Levite who cleansed the temple.

2Ch 29:13 — And of the sons of Elizaphan; Shimri, and Jeiel: and of the sons of Asaph; Zechariah, and Mattaniah:

• A chief of the Levites who gave, with other chiefs, 5000 "small cattle" for sacrifice.

2Ch 35:9 — Conaniah also, and Shemaiah and Nethaneel, his brethren, and Hashabiah and Jeiel and Jozabad, chief of the Levites, gave unto the Levites for passover offerings five thousand *small cattle,* and five hundred oxen.

• A son of Adonikam, an exile who returned to Jerusalem with Ezra.

Ezr 8:13 — And of the last sons of Adonikam, whose names *are* these, Eliphelet, Jeiel, and Shemaiah, and with them threescore males.

• A priest who was defiled by marriage to an idolatrous woman.

Ezr 10:43 — Of the sons of Nebo; Jeiel, Mattithiah, Zabad, Zebina, Jadau, and Joel, Benaiah.

JEKABZEEL • A city in the south of Judah.

Ne 11:25 — And for the villages, with their fields, *some* of the children of Judah dwelt at Kirjath-arba, and *in* the villages thereof, and at Dibon, and in the villages thereof, and at Jekabzeel, and *in* the villages thereof,

JEKAMEAM • Son of Hebron.

1Ch 23:19 — Of the sons of Hebron; Jeriah the first, Amariah the second, Jahaziel the third, and Jekameam the fourth.

1Ch 24:23 — And the sons *of Hebron;* Jeriah *the first,* Amariah the second, Jahaziel the third, Jekameam the fourth.

JEKAMIAH • A descendant of Jerahmeel.

1Ch 2:41 — And Shallum begat Jekamiah, and Jekamiah begat Elishama.

JEKUTHIEL • Son of Ezra.

1Ch 4:18 — And his wife Jehudijah bare Jered the father of Gedor, and Heber the father of Socho, and Jekuthiel the father of Zanoah. And these *are* the sons of Bithiah the daughter of Pharaoh, which Mered took.

JEMIMA • Job's daughter.

Job 42:14 — And he called the name of the first, Jemima; and the name of the second, Kezia; and the name of the third, Keren-happuch.

JEMUEL • Son of Simeon.

Ge 46:10 — And the sons of Simeon; Jemuel, and Jamin, and Ohad, and Jachin, and Zohar, and Shaul the son of a Canaanitish woman.

Ex 6:15 — And the sons of Simeon; Jemuel, and Jamin, and Ohad, and Jachin, and Zohar, and Shaul the son of a Canaanitish woman: these *are* the families of Simeon.

JEPHTHAH

• A judge of Israel.

• Illegitimate, and therefore not entitled to inherit his father's property.

Jgs 11:1–2

• Escapes the violence of his half-brothers, dwells in the land of Tob.

Jgs 11:3 — Then Jephthah fled from his brethren, and dwelt in the land of Tob: and there were gathered vain men to Jephthah, and went out with him.

• Recalled from the land of Tob by the elders of Gilead.

Jgs 11:5 — And it was so, that when the children of Ammon made war against Israel, the elders of Gilead went to fetch Jephthah out of the land of Tob:

• Made captain of the host.

Jgs 11:5–11

• Made head of the land of Gilead.

Jgs 11:7–11

• His message to the king of the Ammonites.

Jgs 11:12–28

• Leads the host of Israel against the Ammonites.

Jgs 11:29–33

• His rash vow concerning his daughter.

Jgs 11:34–40

Jgs 11:31 — Then it shall be, that whatsoever cometh forth of the doors of my house to meet me, when I return in peace from the children of Ammon, shall surely be the LORD'S, and I will offer it up for a burnt offering.

• Falsely accused by the Ephraimites.

Jgs 12:1 — And the men of Ephraim gathered themselves together, and went northward, and said unto Jephthah, Wherefore passedst thou over to fight against the children of Ammon, and didst not call us to go with thee? we will burn thine house upon thee with fire.

• Leads the army of the Gileadites against the Ephraimites.

Jgs 12:4 — Then Jephthah gathered together all the men of Gilead, and fought with Ephraim: and the men of Gilead smote Ephraim, because they said, Ye Gileadites *are* fugitives of Ephraim among the Ephraimites, *and* among the Manassites.

• Judges Israel six years, dies, and is buried in Gilead.

Jgs 12:7 — And Jephthah judged Israel six years. Then died Jephthah the Gileadite, and was buried in *one of* the cities of Gilead.

• Faith of.

Heb 11:32 — And what shall I more say? for the time would fail me to tell of Gedeon, and *of* Barak, and *of* Samson, and *of* Jephthae; *of* David also, and Samuel, and *of* the prophets:

JEPHUNNEH

• Father of Caleb.

Nu 13:6 — Of the tribe of Judah, Caleb the son of Jephunneh

• An Asherite.

1Ch 7:38 — And the sons of Jether; Jephunneh, and Pispah, and Ara.

JERAH • Son of Joktan.

Ge 10:26 — And Joktan begat Almodad, and Sheleph, and Hazar-maveth, and Jerah,

1Ch 1:20 — And Joktan begat Almodad, and Sheleph, and Hazarmaveth, and Jerah,

JERAHMEEL

• Son of Hezron.

1Ch 2:9 — The sons also of Hezron, that were born unto him; Jerahmeel, and Ram, and Chelubai.

• Son of Kish.

1Ch 24:29 — Concerning Kish: the son of Kish *was* Jerahmeel.

• An officer of Jehoiakim, king of Judah.

Jer 36:26 — But the king commanded Jerahmeel the son of Hammelech, and Seraiah the son of Azriel, and Shelemiah the son of Abdeel, to take Baruch the scribe and Jeremiah the prophet: but the LORD hid them.

JERED • Son of Ezra.

1Ch 4:18 — And his wife Jehudijah bare Jered the father of Gedor, and Heber the father of Socho, and Jekuthiel the father of Zanoah. And these *are* the sons of Bithiah the daughter of Pharaoh, which Mered took.

JEREMAI • Of the family of Hashum.

Ezr 10:33 — Of the sons of Hashum; Mattenai, Mattathah, Zabad, Eliphelet, Jeremai, Manasseh, *and* Shimei.

JEREMIAH

• Of Libnah, grandfather of Jehoahaz.

2Ki 23:31 — Jehoahaz *was* twenty and three years old when he began to reign; and he reigned three months in Jerusalem. And his mother's name *was* Hamutal, the daughter of Jeremiah of Libnah.

2Ki 24:18 — Zedekiah *was* twenty and one years old when he began to reign, and he reigned eleven years in Jerusalem. And his mother's name *was* Hamutal, the daughter of Jeremiah of Libnah.

Jer 52:1 — Zedekiah was one and twenty years old when he began to reign, and he reigned eleven years in Jerusalem. And his mother's name *was* Hamutal the daughter of Jeremiah of Libnah.

• A chief of Manasseh.

1Ch 5:24 — And these *were* the heads of the house of their fathers, even Epher, and Ishi, and Eliel, and Azriel, and Jeremiah, and Hodaviah, and Jahdiel, mighty men of valour, famous men, *and* heads of the house of their fathers.

• An Israelite who joined David at Ziklag.

1Ch 12:4 — And Ismaiah the Gibeonite, a mighty man among the thirty, and over the thirty; and Jeremiah, and Jahaziel, and Johanan, and Josabad the Gederathite,

• Two Gadites who joined David at Ziklag.

1Ch 12:10 — Mishmannah the fourth, Jeremiah the fifth,

1Ch 12:13 — Jeremiah the tenth, Machbanai the eleventh.

• The prophet.

Jer 1:1 — The words of Jeremiah the son of Hilkiah, of the priests that *were* in Anathoth in the land of Benjamin:

- **A Rechabite.**

  Jer 35:3 — Then I took Jaazaniah the son of Jeremiah, the son of Habaziniah, and his brethren, and all his sons, and the whole house of the Rechabites;

- **A priest.**

  Jer 1:1 — The words of Jeremiah the son of Hilkiah, of the priests that *were* in Anathoth in the land of Benjamin:

- **Call of.**

  Jer 1:4–19

- **Time of his prophecies.**

  Jer 25:1–3

  Jer 3:6 — The LORD said also unto me in the days of Josiah the king, Hast thou seen *that* which backsliding Israel hath done? she is gone up upon every high mountain and under every green tree, and there hath played the harlot.

  Jer 21:1 — The word which came unto Jeremiah from the LORD, when king Zedekiah sent unto him Pashur the son of Melchiah, and Zephaniah the son of Maaseiah the priest, saying,

  Jer 24:1 — The LORD shewed me, and, behold, two baskets of figs *were* set before the temple of the LORD, after that Nebuchadrezzar king of Babylon had carried away captive Jeconiah the son of Jehoiakim king of Judah, and the princes of Judah, with the carpenters and smiths, from Jerusalem, and had brought them to Babylon.

  Jer 26:1 — In the beginning of the reign of Jehoiakim the son of Josiah king of Judah came this word from the LORD, saying,

  Jer 28:1 — And it came to pass the same year, in the beginning of the reign of Zedekiah king of Judah, in the fourth year, *and* in the fifth month, *that* Hananiah the son of Azur the prophet, which *was* of Gibeon, spake unto me in the house of the LORD, in the presence of the priests and of all the people, saying,

  Jer 32:1 — The word that came to Jeremiah from the LORD in the tenth year of Zedekiah king of Judah, which *was* the eighteenth year of Nebuchadrezzar.

  Jer 34:1 — The word which came unto Jeremiah from the LORD, when Nebuchadnezzar king of Babylon, and all his army, and all the kingdoms of the earth of his dominion, and all the people, fought against Jerusalem, and against all the cities thereof, saying,

  Jer 45:1 — The word that Jeremiah the prophet spake unto Baruch the son of Neriah, when he had written these words in a book at the mouth of Jeremiah, in the fourth year of Jehoiakim the son of Josiah king of Judah, saying,

  Jer 49:34 — The word of the LORD that came to Jeremiah the prophet against Elam in the beginning of the reign of Zedekiah king of Judah, saying,

- **Letter to the captives in Babylon.**

  Jer 29:1–32

- **Sorrow of, under persecution.**

  Jer 17:15–18

  Jer 15:10 — Woe is me, my mother, that thou hast borne me a man of strife and a man of contention to the whole earth! I have neither lent on usury, nor men have lent to me on usury; *yet* every one of them doth curse me.

  Jer 15:15 — O LORD, thou knowest: remember me, and visit me, and revenge me of my persecutors; take me not away in thy longsuffering: know that for thy sake I have suffered rebuke.

- **Conspiracy against.**

  Jer 11:21–23; 18:18–23

- **Foretells the desolation of Jerusalem.**

  Jer 19:1–15

- **Pashur, the governor of the temple, scourges and casts him into prison.**

  Jer 20:1–3

- **Denounces Pashur.**

  Jer 20:3–6

- **His melancholy and murmuring against God, in consequence of persecution.**

  Jer 20:7–18

- **Imprisoned by Zedekiah.**

  Jer 32:1–33:1; 37:15–21; 38:6–13; 39:15–18; La 3:53–55

- **Nebuchadnezzar directs the release of.**

  Jer 39:11–14; 40:1–4

- **Has a friend in Ahikam.**

  Jer 26:24 — Nevertheless the hand of Ahikam the son of Shaphan was with Jeremiah, that they should not give him into the hand of the people to put him to death.

- **Ebed-melech, the Egyptian, intercedes with the king for him, and secures his release.**

  Jer 38:7–13

- **Prophecies of, written by Baruch.**

  Jer 36:1–7

  Jer 36:32 — Then took Jeremiah another roll, and gave it to Baruch the scribe, the son of Neriah; who wrote therein from the mouth of Jeremiah all the words of the book which Jehoiakim king of Judah had burned in the fire: and there were added besides unto them many like words.

  Jer 45:1 — The word that Jeremiah the prophet spake unto Baruch the son of Neriah, when he had written these words in a book at the mouth of Jeremiah, in the fourth year of Jehoiakim the son of Josiah king of Judah, saying,

- **Prophecies of, destroyed by Jehoiakim.**

  Jer 36:8–32

- **Book of the prophecies of, delivered to Seriah, with a charge from Jeremiah.**

  Jer 51:59–64

- **Zedekiah seeks counsel from God by.**

  Jer 21:1–2

  Jer 37:3 — And Zedekiah the king sent Jehucal the son of Shelemiah and Zephaniah the son of Maaseiah the priest to the prophet Jeremiah, saying, Pray now unto the LORD our God for us.

Jer 38:14 — Then Zedekiah the king sent, and took Jeremiah the prophet unto him into the third entry that *is* in the house of the LORD: and the king said unto Jeremiah, I will ask thee a thing; hide nothing from me.

- **His intercession asked.**
  - **By Johanan and all the people.**

    Jer 42:1–6
  - **By Zedekiah.**

    Jer 37:3 — And Zedekiah the king sent Jehucal the son of Shelemiah and Zephaniah the son of Maaseiah the priest to the prophet Jeremiah, saying, Pray now unto the LORD our God for us.
- **Johanan carries Jeremiah into Egypt.**

  Jer 43:1–7
- **Foretells the conquest of Egypt by Babylon.**

  Jer 43:8–12
- **Prophecies of, studied by Daniel.**

  Da 9:2 — In the first year of his reign I Daniel understood by books the number of the years, whereof the word of the LORD came to Jeremiah the prophet, that he would accomplish seventy years in the desolations of Jerusalem.
- **Celibacy of.**

  Jer 16:2 — Thou shalt not take thee a wife, neither shalt thou have sons or daughters in this place.
- **Purchases a field.**

  Jer 32:7–10
- **Lamentations of.**
  - **Over Josiah.**

    2Ch 35:25 — And Jeremiah lamented for Josiah: and all the singing men and the singing women spake of Josiah in their lamentations to this day, and made them an ordinance in Israel: and, behold, they *are* written in the lamentations.
  - **Over the prosperity of the wicked.**

    Jer 12:1–6
  - **Over the desolation of God's heritage.**

    Jer 12:7–13
  - **Over Jerusalem.**

    Jer 4:14–18; 8:1–9:1; 10:19–22; La 1:1–5:22

    Jer 18:11 — Now therefore go to, speak to the men of Judah, and to the inhabitants of Jerusalem, saying, Thus saith the LORD; Behold, I frame evil against you, and devise a device against you: return ye now every one from his evil way, and make your ways and your doings good.
- **Dwells at Mizpah.**

  Jer 40:6 — Then went Jeremiah unto Gedaliah the son of Ahikam to Mizpah; and dwelt with him among the people that were left in the land.
- **Prayers of.**

  Jer 14:7–9; 32:17–25
- **Zeal of.**

  Jer 15:16 — Thy words were found, and I did eat them; and thy word was unto me the joy and rejoicing of mine heart: for I am called by thy name, O LORD God of hosts.

JEREMOTH

- **A Benjamite.**

  1Ch 8:14 — And Ahio, Shashak, and Jeremoth,
- **One of the sons of Elam.**

  Ezr 10:26 — And of the sons of Elam; Mattaniah, Zechariah, and Jehiel, and Abdi, and Jeremoth, and Eliah.
- **One of the family of Zattu.**

  Ezr 10:27 — And of the sons of Zattu; Elioenai, Eliashib, Mattaniah, and Jeremoth, and Zabad, and Aziza.

JERIAH

- **Called also Jerijah.**
- **A descendant of Hebron.**

  1Ch 23:19 — Of the sons of Hebron; Jeriah the first, Amariah the second, Jahaziel the third, and Jekameam the fourth.

  1Ch 24:23 — And the sons *of Hebron;* Jeriah *the first,* Amariah the second, Jahaziel the third, Jekameam the fourth.

  1Ch 26:31 — Among the Hebronites *was* Jerijah the chief, *even* among the Hebronites, according to the generations of his fathers. In the fortieth year of the reign of David they were sought for, and there were found among them mighty men of valour at Jazer of Gilead.

JERIBAI • A valiant man of David's guard.

1Ch 11:46 — Eliel the Mahavite, and Jeribai, and Joshaviah, the sons of Elnaam, and Ithmah the Moabite,

JERICHO

- **A city east of Jerusalem and near the Jordan.**

  Nu 22:1 — And the children of Israel set forward, and pitched in the plains of Moab on this side Jordan *by* Jericho.

  Nu 26:3 — And Moses and Eleazar the priest spake with them in the plains of Moab by Jordan *near* Jericho, saying,

  Dt 34:1 — And Moses went up from the plains of Moab unto the mountain of Nebo, to the top of Pisgah, that *is* over against Jericho. And the LORD shewed him all the land of Gilead, unto Dan,
  - **Called the City of Palm Trees.**

    Dt 34:3 — And the south, and the plain of the valley of Jericho, the city of palm trees, unto Zoar.
  - **Situation of, pleasant.**

    2Ki 2:19 — And the men of the city said unto Elisha, Behold, I pray thee, the situation of this city *is* pleasant, as my lord seeth: but the water *is* naught, and the ground barren.
  - **Rahab the harlot lived in.**

    Jos 2:1–24

    Heb 11:31 — By faith the harlot Rahab perished not with them that believed not, when she had received the spies with peace.

• Joshua sees the "captain of the host" of the Lord near.

Jos 5:13–15

• Besieged by Joshua seven days; fall and destruction of.

Jos 6:1–27

Jos 24:11 — And ye went over Jordan, and came unto Jericho: and the men of Jericho fought against you, the Amorites, and the Perizzites, and the Canaanites, and the Hittites, and the Girgashites, the Hivites, and the Jebusites; and I delivered them into your hand.

• Situated within the territory allotted to Benjamin.

Jos 18:12 — And their border on the north side was from Jordan; and the border went up to the side of Jericho on the north side, and went up through the mountains westward; and the goings out thereof were at the wilderness of Beth-aven.

Jos 18:21 — Now the cities of the tribe of the children of Benjamin according to their families were Jericho, and Beth-hoglah, and the valley of Keziz,

• The Kenites dwelt at.

Jgs 1:16 — And the children of the Kenite, Moses' father in law, went up out of the city of palm trees with the children of Judah into the wilderness of Judah, which *lieth* in the south of Arad; and they went and dwelt among the people.

• King of Moab makes conquest of, and establishes his capital at.

Jgs 3:13 — And he gathered unto him the children of Ammon and Amalek, and went and smote Israel, and possessed the city of palm trees.

• Rebuilt by Hiel.

1Ki 16:34 — In his days did Hiel the Bethelite build Jericho: he laid the foundation thereof in Abiram his firstborn, and set up the gates thereof in his youngest *son* Segub, according to the word of the LORD, which he spake by Joshua the son of Nun.

• Company of "the sons of the prophets" dwelt at.

2Ki 2:4–5

2Ki 2:15 — And when the sons of the prophets which *were* to view at Jericho saw him, they said, The spirit of Elijah doth rest on Elisha. And they came to meet him, and bowed themselves to the ground before him.

2Ki 2:18 — And when they came again to him, (for he tarried at Jericho,) he said unto them, Did I not say unto you, Go not?

• Captives of Judah, taken by the king of Israel, released at, on account of the denunciation of the prophet Oded.

2Ch 28:7–15

• Inhabitants of, taken captive to Babylon, return to, with Ezra and Nehemiah.

Ezr 2:34 — The children of Jericho, three hundred forty and five.

Ne 7:36 — The children of Jericho, three hundred forty and five.

• Inhabitants of, assist in repairing the walls of Jerusalem.

Ne 3:2 — And next unto him builded the men of Jericho. And next to them builded Zaccur the son of Imri.

• Blind men healed at, by Jesus.

Mt 20:29–34

Mk 10:46 — And they came to Jericho: and as he went out of Jericho with his disciples and a great number of people, blind Bartimaeus, the son of Timaeus, sat by the highway side begging.

Lk 18:35 — And it came to pass, that as he was come nigh unto Jericho, a certain blind man sat by the way side begging:

• Zacchaeus dwelt at.

Lk 19:1–10

• Plain of.

2Ki 25:5 — And the army of the Chaldees pursued after the king, and overtook him in the plains of Jericho: and all his army were scattered from him.

Jer 52:8 — But the army of the Chaldeans pursued after the king, and overtook Zedekiah in the plains of Jericho; and all his army was scattered from him.

• Waters of.

Jos 16:1 — And the lot of the children of Joseph fell from Jordan by Jericho, unto the water of Jericho on the east, to the wilderness that goeth up from Jericho throughout mount Bethel,

• Purified by Elisha.

2Ki 2:18–22

JERIEL • Son of Tola.

1Ch 7:2 — And the sons of Tola; Uzzi, and Rephaiah, and Jeriel, and Jahmai, and Jibsam, and Shemuel, heads of their father's house, *to wit,* of Tola: *they were* valiant men of might in their generations; whose number *was* in the days of David two and twenty thousand and six hundred.

JERIMOTH

• Called also Jeremoth .

• Son of Bela.

1Ch 7:7 — And the sons of Bela; Ezbon, and Uzzi, and Uzziel, and Jerimoth, and Iri, five; heads of the house of *their* fathers, mighty men of valour; and were reckoned by their genealogies twenty and two thousand and thirty and four.

• Son of Becher.

1Ch 7:8 — And the sons of Becher; Zemira, and Joash, and Eliezer, and Elioenai, and Omri, and Jerimoth, and Abiah, and Anathoth, and Alameth. All these *are* the sons of Becher.

• A disaffected Israelite, who denounced Saul and joined David at Ziklag.

1Ch 12:5 — Eluzai, and Jerimoth, and Bealiah, and Shemariah, and Shephatiah the Haruphite,

- **Son of Mushi.**

1Ch 23:23 — The sons of Mushi; Mahli, and Eder, and Jeremoth, three.

1Ch 24:30 — The sons also of Mushi; Mahli, and Eder, and Jerimoth. These *were* the sons of the Levites after the house of their fathers.

- **Son of Heman.**

1Ch 25:4 — Of Heman: the sons of Heman; Bukkiah, Mattaniah, Uzziel, Shebuel, and Jerimoth, Hananiah, Hanani, Eliathah, Giddalti, and Romamti-ezer, Joshbekashah, Mallothi, Hothir, *and* Mahazioth:

- **A ruler of the tribe of Naphtali.**

1Ch 27:19 — Of Zebulun, Ishmaiah the son of Obadiah: of Naphtali, Jerimoth the son of Azriel:

- **A son of David.**

2Ch 11:18 — And Rehoboam took him Mahalath the daughter of Jerimoth the son of David to wife, *and* Abihail the daughter of Eliab the son of Jesse;

JERIOTH

- **Wife of Caleb.**
- **Probably identical with Azubah.**

1Ch 2:18 — And Caleb the son of Hezron begat *children* of Azubah *his* wife, and of Jerioth: her sons *are* these; Jesher, and Shobab, and Ardon.

JEROBOAM

- **First king of Israel after the revolt. Promoted by Solomon.**

1Ki 11:28 — And the man Jeroboam *was* a mighty man of valour: and Solomon seeing the young man that he was industrious, he made him ruler over all the charge of the house of Joseph.

- **Ahijah's prophecy concerning.**

1Ki 11:29–39; 14:5–16

- **Flees to Egypt to escape from Solomon.**

1Ki 11:26–40

- **Recalled from Egypt by the ten tribes on account of disaffection toward Rehoboam, and made king.**

1Ki 12:1–20; 2Ch 10:12–19

- **Subverts the religion of Moses.**

1Ki 12:25–33; 13:33–34; 2Ch 13:8–9

1Ki 14:9 — But hast done evil above all that were before thee: for thou hast gone and made thee other gods, and molten images, to provoke me to anger, and hast cast me behind thy back:

1Ki 14:16 — And he shall give Israel up because of the sins of Jeroboam, who did sin, and who made Israel to sin.

1Ki 16:2 — Forasmuch as I exalted thee out of the dust, and made thee prince over my people Israel; and thou hast walked in the way of Jeroboam, and hast made my people Israel to sin, to provoke me to anger with their sins;

1Ki 16:26 — For he walked in all the way of Jeroboam the son of Nebat, and in his sin wherewith he made Israel to sin, to provoke the LORD God of Israel to anger with their vanities.

1Ki 16:31 — And it came to pass, as if it had been a light thing for him to walk in the sins of Jeroboam the son of Nebat, that he took to wife Jezebel the daughter of Ethbaal king of the Zidonians, and went and served Baal, and worshipped him.

2Ch 11:14 — For the Levites left their suburbs and their possession, and came to Judah and Jerusalem: for Jeroboam and his sons had cast them off from executing the priest's office unto the LORD:

- **Hand of, paralyzed.**

1Ki 13:1–10

- **His wife sent to consult the prophet Ahijah concerning her child.**

1Ki 14:1–18

- **His wars with Rehoboam.**

2Ch 11:1–4

1Ki 14:19 — And the rest of the acts of Jeroboam, how he warred, and how he reigned, behold, they *are* written in the book of the chronicles of the kings of Israel.

1Ki 14:30 — And there was war between Rehoboam and Jeroboam all *their* days.

1Ki 15:6 — And there was war between Rehoboam and Jeroboam all the days of his life.

- **His war with Abijah.**

2Ch 13:1–22

1Ki 15:7 — Now the rest of the acts of Abijam, and all that he did, *are* they not written in the book of the chronicles of the kings of Judah? And there was war between Abijam and Jeroboam.

- **Death of.**

1Ki 14:20 — And the days which Jeroboam reigned *were* two and twenty years: and he slept with his fathers, and Nadab his son reigned in his stead.

2Ch 13:20 — Neither did Jeroboam recover strength again in the days of Abijah: and the LORD struck him, and he died.

- **King of Israel.**

2Ki 14:23 — In the fifteenth year of Amaziah the son of Joash king of Judah Jeroboam the son of Joash king of Israel began to reign in Samaria, *and reigned* forty and one years.

- **Successor to Jehoash.**

2Ki 14:16 — And Jehoash slept with his fathers, and was buried in Samaria with the kings of Israel; and Jeroboam his son reigned in his stead.

- **Makes conquest of Hamath and Damascus.**

2Ki 14:25–28

- **Wicked reign of.**

2Ki 14:24 — And he did *that which was* evil in the sight of the LORD: he departed not from all the sins of Jeroboam the son of Nebat, who made Israel to sin.

- **Prophecies concerning.**

Am 7:7–13

- **Death of.**

2Ki 14:29 — And Jeroboam slept with his fathers, *even* with the kings of Israel; and Zachariah his son reigned in his stead.

• Genealogies written during his reign.

1Ch 5:17 — All these were reckoned by genealogies in the days of Jotham king of Judah, and in the days of Jeroboam king of Israel.

JEROHAM

• A Levite, and grandfather of Samuel.

1Sa 1:1 — Now there was a certain man of Ramathaim-zophim, of mount Ephraim, and his name was Elkanah, the son of Jeroham, the son of Elihu, the son of Tohu, the son of Zuph, an Ephrathite:

1Ch 6:27 — Eliab his son, Jeroham his son, Elkanah his son.

1Ch 6:34 — The son of Elkanah, the son of Jeroham, the son of Eliel, the son of Toah,

• A chief of the tribe of Benjamin.

1Ch 8:27 — And Jaresiah, and Eliah, and Zichri, the sons of Jeroham.

• A descendant of Benjamin.

1Ch 9:8 — And Ibneiah the son of Jeroham, and Elah the son of Uzzi, the son of Michri, and Meshullam the son of Shephatiah, the son of Reuel, the son of Ibnijah;

• A priest, and father of Adaiah, who dwelt in Jerusalem after the exile.

1Ch 9:12 — And Adaiah the son of Jeroham, the son of Pashur, the son of Malchijah, and Maasiai the son of Adiel, the son of Jahzerah, the son of Meshullam, the son of Meshillemith, the son of Immer;

Ne 11:12 — And their brethren that did the work of the house *were* eight hundred twenty and two: and Adaiah the son of Jeroham, the son of Pelaliah, the son of Amzi, the son of Zechariah, the son of Pashur, the son of Malchiah,

• Father of two Israelites who joined David at Ziklag.

1Ch 12:7 — And Joelah, and Zebadiah, the sons of Jeroham of Gedor.

• The father of Azareel.

1Ch 27:22 — Of Dan, Azareel the son of Jeroham. These *were* the princes of the tribes of Israel.

• Father of Azariah.

2Ch 23:1 — And in the seventh year Jehoiada strengthened himself, and took the captains of hundreds, Azariah the son of Jeroham, and Ishmael the son of Jehohanan, and Azariah the son of Obed, and Maaseiah the son of Adaiah, and Elishaphat the son of Zichri, into covenant with him.

JERUBBAAL ⇐See: Gideon

JERUEL • A wilderness in the south of Judah.

2Ch 20:16 — To morrow go ye down against them: behold, they come up by the cliff of Ziz; and ye shall find them at the end of the brook, before the wilderness of Jeruel.

JERUSALEM

• The capital of David's kingdom by divine appointment.

1Ki 15:4 — Nevertheless for David's sake did the LORD his God give him a lamp in Jerusalem, to set up his son after him, and to establish Jerusalem:

2Ki 19:34 — For I will defend this city, to save it, for mine own sake, and for my servant David's sake.

2Ch 6:6 — But I have chosen Jerusalem, that my name might be there; and have chosen David to be over my people Israel.

2Ch 12:13 — So king Rehoboam strengthened himself in Jerusalem, and reigned: for Rehoboam *was* one and forty years old when he began to reign, and he reigned seventeen years in Jerusalem, the city which the LORD had chosen out of all the tribes of Israel, to put his name there. And his mother's name *was* Naamah an Ammonitess.

• To be called God's throne.

Jer 3:17 — At that time they shall call Jerusalem the throne of the LORD; and all the nations shall be gathered unto it, to the name of the LORD, to Jerusalem: neither shall they walk any more after the imagination of their evil heart.

• The chief Levites dwelt in.

1Ch 9:34 — These chief fathers of the Levites *were* chief throughout their generations; these dwelt at Jerusalem.

• The high priest dwelt at.

Jn 18:15 — And Simon Peter followed Jesus, and *so did* another disciple: that disciple was known unto the high priest, and went in with Jesus into the palace of the high priest.

• Annual feasts kept at.

Ps 122:3–5; Jn 7:1–14

Dt 16:16 — Three times in a year shall all thy males appear before the LORD thy God in the place which he shall choose; in the feast of unleavened bread, and in the feast of weeks, and in the feast of tabernacles: and they shall not appear before the LORD empty:

Eze 36:38 — As the holy flock, as the flock of Jerusalem in her solemn feasts; so shall the waste cities be filled with flocks of men: and they shall know that I *am* the LORD.

Lk 2:41 — Now his parents went to Jerusalem every year at the feast of the passover.

Jn 4:20 — Our fathers worshipped in this mountain; and ye say, that in Jerusalem is the place where men ought to worship.

Jn 5:1 — After this there was a feast of the Jews; and Jesus went up to Jerusalem.

Jn 12:20 — And there were certain Greeks among them that came up to worship at the feast:

Ac 18:21 — But bade them farewell, saying, I must by all means keep this feast that cometh in Jerusalem: but I will return again unto you, if God will. And he sailed from Ephesus.

• Prayers of the Israelites made toward.

1Ki 8:38 — What prayer and supplication soever be *made* by any man, *or* by all thy people Israel, which shall know every man the plague of his own heart, and spread forth his hands toward this house:

Da 6:10 — Now when Daniel knew that the writing was signed, he went into his house; and his windows being open in his chamber toward Jerusalem, he kneeled upon his knees three times a day, and prayed, and gave thanks before his God, as he did aforetime.

• Beloved.

Ps 137:1–7; Isa 62:1–7

Ps 122:6 — Pray for the peace of Jerusalem: they shall prosper that love thee.

See: Country; love of

See: Patriotism

• Oaths taken in the name of.

Mt 5:35 — Nor by the earth; for it is his footstool: neither by Jerusalem; for it is the city of the great King.

• Melchizedek ancient king and priest of.

Ge 14:18 — And Melchizedek king of Salem brought forth bread and wine: and he *was* the priest of the most high God.

• King of, confederated with the four other kings of the Amorites, against Joshua and the hosts of Israel.

Jos 10:1–5

• Confederated kings defeated, and the king of Jerusalem slain by Joshua.

Jos 10:15–26

• Falls to Benjamin in the allotment of the land of Canaan.

Jos 18:28 — And Zelah, Eleph, and Jebusi, which *is* Jerusalem, Gibeath, *and* Kirjath; fourteen cities with their villages. This *is* the inheritance of the children of Benjamin according to their families.

• Conquest of, made by David.

2Sa 5:7 — Nevertheless David took the strong hold of Zion: the same *is* the city of David.

• The inhabitants of, not expelled.

Jos 15:63 — As for the Jebusites the inhabitants of Jerusalem, the children of Judah could not drive them out: but the Jebusites dwell with the children of Judah at Jerusalem unto this day.

Jgs 1:21 — And the children of Benjamin did not drive out the Jebusites that inhabited Jerusalem; but the Jebusites dwell with the children of Benjamin in Jerusalem unto this day.

• Conquest of Mount Zion in, made by David.

1Ch 11:4–6

• The citadel of Mount Zion, occupied by David, and called the City of David.

2Sa 5:5–9

1Ch 11:7 — And David dwelt in the castle; therefore they called it the city of David.

• Ark brought to, by David.

2Sa 6:12–19

• The threshing floor of Araunah within the citadel of.

2Sa 24:16 — And when the angel stretched out his hand upon Jerusalem to destroy it, the LORD repented him of the evil, and said to the angel that destroyed the people, It is enough: stay now thine hand. And the angel of the LORD was by the threshingplace of Araunah the Jebusite.

• David purchases and erects an altar upon it.

2Sa 24:16–25

• The city built around the citadel.

1Ch 11:8 — And he built the city round about, even from Millo round about: and Joab repaired the rest of the city.

• Fortified by Solomon.

1Ki 3:1 — And Solomon made affinity with Pharaoh king of Egypt, and took Pharaoh's daughter, and brought her into the city of David, until he had made an end of building his own house, and the house of the LORD, and the wall of Jerusalem round about.

1Ki 9:15 — And this *is* the reason of the levy which king Solomon raised; for to build the house of the LORD, and his own house, and Millo, and the wall of Jerusalem, and Hazor, and Megiddo, and Gezer.

• The temple built within the citadel.

See: Temple

• Captured and pillaged by.

• Shishak, king of Egypt.

1Ki 14:25–26

2Ch 12:9 — So Shishak king of Egypt came up against Jerusalem, and took away the treasures of the house of the LORD, and the treasures of the king's house; he took all: he carried away also the shields of gold which Solomon had made.

• Jehoash, king of Israel.

2Ki 14:13–14; 2Ch 25:23–24

• Nebuchadnezzar, king of Babylon.

2Ki 24:8–16; 25:1–17; 2Ch 36:17–21; Jer 39:1–18; 52:4–7, 12–24; La 1:5–8

Jer 1:3 — It came also in the days of Jehoiakim the son of Josiah king of Judah, unto the end of the eleventh year of Zedekiah the son of Josiah king of Judah, unto the carrying away of Jerusalem captive in the fifth month.

Jer 32:2 — For then the king of Babylon's army besieged Jerusalem: and Jeremiah the prophet was shut up in the court of the prison, which *was* in the king of Judah's house.

• Walls of, restored and fortified.

• By Uzziah.

2Ch 26:9–10

• By Jotham.

2Ch 27:3 — He built the high gate of the house of the LORD, and on the wall of Ophel he built much.

• By Manasseh.

2Ch 33:14 — Now after this he built a wall without the city of David, on the west side of Gihon, in the valley, even to the entering in at the fish gate, and compassed about Ophel, and raised it up a very great height, and put captains of war in all the fenced cities of Judah.

• Water supply brought in from the Gihon by Hezekiah.

2Ch 32:3–4; Ne 2:13–15; Isa 22:9–11

2Ki 18:17 — And the king of Assyria sent Tartan and Rabsaris and Rab-shakeh from Lachish to king Hezekiah with a great host against Jerusalem. And they went up and came to Jerusalem. And when they were come up, they came and stood by the conduit of the upper pool, which is in the highway of the fuller's field.

2Ki 20:20 — And the rest of the acts of Hezekiah, and all his might, and how he made a pool, and a conduit, and brought water into the city, *are* they not written in the book of the chronicles of the kings of Judah?

2Ch 32:30 — This same Hezekiah also stopped the upper watercourse of Gihon, and brought it straight down to the west side of the city of David. And Hezekiah prospered in all his works.

Isa 7:3 — Then said the LORD unto Isaiah, Go forth now to meet Ahaz, thou, and Shear-jashub thy son, at the end of the conduit of the upper pool in the highway of the fuller's field;

Isa 36:2 — And the king of Assyria sent Rabshakeh from Lachish to Jerusalem unto king Hezekiah with a great army. And he stood by the conduit of the upper pool in the highway of the fuller's field.

• Besieged.

• By Pekah.

2Ki 16:5 — Then Rezin king of Syria and Pekah son of Remaliah king of Israel came up to Jerusalem to war: and they besieged Ahaz, but could not overcome *him.*

• By the Philistines.

2Ch 21:16–17

• By Sennacherib.

2Ki 18:13–37; 19:20–37; 2Ch 32:1–33

• Rebuilding of, ordered by proclamation of Cyrus.

Ezr 1:1–4

2Ch 36:23 — Thus saith Cyrus king of Persia, All the kingdoms of the earth hath the LORD God of heaven given me; and he hath charged me to build him an house in Jerusalem, which *is* in Judah. Who *is there* among you of all his people? The LORD his God *be* with him, and let him go up.

• Rebuilt by Nehemiah under the direction of Artaxerxes.

Ne 2:1–6:19

• Wall of, dedicated.

Ne 12:27–43

• Temple restored.

✦See: Temple

• Roman rulers resided at.

• Herod I.

Mt 2:3 — When Herod the king had heard *these things,* he was troubled, and all Jerusalem with him.

• Pontius Pilate.

Lk 23:1–7; Jn 18:28–29

Mt 27:2 — And when they had bound him, they led *him* away, and delivered him to Pontius Pilate the governor.

Mk 15:1 — And straightway in the morning the chief priests held a consultation with the elders and scribes and the whole council, and bound Jesus, and carried *him* away, and delivered *him* to Pilate.

• Herod III.

Ac 12:1–23

• Life and miracles of Jesus connected with.

✦See: Jesus, History of

• Gospel first preached at.

Mic 4:2 — And many nations shall come, and say, Come, and let us go up to the mountain of the LORD, and to the house of the God of Jacob; and he will teach us of his ways, and we will walk in his paths: for the law shall go forth of Zion, and the word of the LORD from Jerusalem.

Lk 24:47 — And that repentance and remission of sins should be preached in his name among all nations, beginning at Jerusalem.

Ac 1:4 — And, being assembled together with *them,* commanded them that they should not depart from Jerusalem, but wait for the promise of the Father, which, *saith he,* ye have heard of me.

Ac 2:14 — But Peter, standing up with the eleven, lifted up his voice, and said unto them, Ye men of Judaea, and all *ye* that dwell at Jerusalem, be this known unto you, and hearken to my words:

• Pentecostal revival occurs at.

Ac 2:1–47

• Stephen martyred at.

Ac 6:8–7:60

• Disciples persecuted and dispersed from.

Ac 8:1–4; 11:19–21

• For personal incidents occurring therein see biographies of individuals.

✦See: Disciple

✦See: Herod; king of Judah

✦See: Herod; son of Aristobulus

✦See: Israelites

✦See: Pilate, Pontius

✦See: Stephen

• Wickedness of.

Lk 13:33–34

• Catalogue of abominations in.

Eze 22:3–12, 25–30; 23:1–49; 33:25–26

- **Led Judah to sin.**
  Mic 1:5 — For the transgression of Jacob *is* all this, and for the sins of the house of Israel. What *is* the transgression of Jacob? *is it* not Samaria? and what *are* the high places of Judah? *are they* not Jerusalem?
- **Prophecies against.**
  Isa 3:1–8
  Jer 9:11 — And I will make Jerusalem heaps, *and* a den of dragons; and I will make the cities of Judah desolate, without an inhabitant.
  Jer 19:6 — Therefore, behold, the days come, saith the LORD, that this place shall no more be called Tophet, nor The valley of the son of Hinnom, but The valley of slaughter.
  Jer 19:15 — Thus saith the LORD of hosts, the God of Israel; Behold, I will bring upon this city and upon all her towns all the evil that I have pronounced against it, because they have hardened their necks, that they might not hear my words.
  Jer 21:10 — For I have set my face against this city for evil, and not for good, saith the LORD: it shall be given into the hand of the king of Babylon, and he shall burn it with fire.
  Jer 26:9 — Why hast thou prophesied in the name of the LORD, saying, This house shall be like Shiloh, and this city shall be desolate without an inhabitant? And all the people were gathered against Jeremiah in the house of the LORD.
  Jer 26:11 — Then spake the priests and the prophets unto the princes and to all the people, saying, This man *is* worthy to die; for he hath prophesied against this city, as ye have heard with your ears.
  Da 9:2 — In the first year of his reign I Daniel understood by books the number of the years, whereof the word of the LORD came to Jeremiah the prophet, that he would accomplish seventy years in the desolations of Jerusalem.
  Da 9:27 — And he shall confirm the covenant with many for one week: and in the midst of the week he shall cause the sacrifice and the oblation to cease, and for the overspreading of abominations he shall make *it* desolate, even until the consummation, and that determined shall be poured upon the desolate.
  Mic 1:1 — The word of the LORD that came to Micah the Morasthite in the days of Jotham, Ahaz, *and* Hezekiah, kings of Judah, which he saw concerning Samaria and Jerusalem.
  Mic 3:12 — Therefore shall Zion for your sake be plowed *as* a field, and Jerusalem shall become heaps, and the mountain of the house as the high places of the forest.
- **Prophecies of pestilence, famine, and war in.**
  Joel 3:2–3
  Jer 34:2 — Thus saith the LORD, the God of Israel; Go and speak to Zedekiah king of Judah, and tell him, Thus saith the LORD; Behold, I will give this city into the hand of the king of Babylon, and he shall burn it with fire:
  Eze 5:12 — A third part of thee shall die with the pestilence, and with famine shall they be consumed in the midst of thee: and a third part shall fall by the sword round about thee and I will scatter a third part into all the winds, and I will draw out a sword after them.
  Am 2:5 — But I will send a fire upon Judah, and it shall devour the palaces of Jerusalem.
- **Prophecies of the destruction of.**
  Jer 7:32–34; 32:31–32; Da 9:24–27
  Jer 26:18 — Micah the Morasthite prophesied in the days of Hezekiah king of Judah, and spake to all the people of Judah, saying, Thus saith the LORD of hosts; Zion shall be plowed *like* a field, and Jerusalem shall become heaps, and the mountain of the house as the high places of a forest.
  Jer 32:29 — And the Chaldeans, that fight against this city, shall come and set fire on this city, and burn it with the houses, upon whose roofs they have offered incense unto Baal, and poured out drink offerings unto other gods, to provoke me to anger.
- **Destruction of, foretold by Jesus.**
  Mt 23:37–38; Mk 13:14–23; Lk 17:26–37; 19:41–44; 21:20–24
  Mt 24:15 — When ye therefore shall see the abomination of desolation, spoken of by Daniel the prophet, stand in the holy place, (whoso readeth, let him understand:)
  Lk 13:35 — Behold, your house is left unto you desolate: and verily I say unto you, Ye shall not see me, until *the time* come when ye shall say, Blessed *is* he that cometh in the name of the Lord.
- **Prophecies of the rebuilding of.**
  Jer 31:38–40; Eze 48:15–22; Zec 14:8–11
  Isa 44:28 — That saith of Cyrus, *He is* my shepherd, and shall perform all my pleasure: even saying to Jerusalem, Thou shalt be built; and to the temple, Thy foundation shall be laid.
  Da 9:25 — Know therefore and understand, *that* from the going forth of the commandment to restore and to build Jerusalem unto the Messiah the Prince *shall be* seven weeks, and threescore and two weeks: the street shall be built again, and the wall, even in troublous times.
- **Of final restoration of.**
  Joel 3:20–21; Zec 2:2–5; 8:1–23
- **Historical notices of.**
  - **Melchizedek was ancient king of.**
    Ge 14:18 — And Melchizedek king of Salem brought forth bread and wine: and he *was* the priest of the most high God.

JERUSALEM, Names

- **Called Jebus.**
  Jos 18:28 — And Zelah, Eleph, and Jebusi, which *is* Jerusalem, Gibeath, *and* Kirjath; fourteen cities with their villages. This *is* the inheritance of the children of Benjamin according to their families.
  Jgs 19:10 — But the man would not tarry that night, but he rose up and departed, and came over against Jebus, which is Jerusalem; and *there were* with him two asses saddled, his concubine also *was* with him.

- **Called Zion.**

1Ki 8:1 — Then Solomon assembled the elders of Israel, and all the heads of the tribes, the chief of the fathers of the children of Israel, unto king Solomon in Jerusalem, that they might bring up the ark of the covenant of the LORD out of the city of David, which *is* Zion.

Zec 9:13 — When I have bent Judah for me, filled the bow with Ephraim, and raised up thy sons, O Zion, against thy sons, O Greece, and made thee as the sword of a mighty man.

- **Called City of David.**

2Sa 5:7 — Nevertheless David took the strong hold of Zion: the same *is* the city of David.

Isa 22:9 — Ye have seen also the breaches of the city of David, that they are many: and ye gathered together the waters of the lower pool.

- **Called Salem.**

Ge 14:18 — And Melchizedek king of Salem brought forth bread and wine: and he *was* the priest of the most high God.

Ps 76:2 — In Salem also is his tabernacle, and his dwelling place in Zion.

- **Called Ariel.**

Isa 29:1 — Woe to Ariel, to Ariel, the city *where* David dwelt! add ye year to year; let them kill sacrifices.

- **Called City of God.**

Ps 46:4 — *There is* a river, the streams whereof shall make glad the city of God, the holy *place* of the tabernacles of the most High.

- **Called City of the Great King.**

Ps 48:2 — Beautiful for situation, the joy of the whole earth, *is* mount Zion, *on* the sides of the north, the city of the great King.

- **Called City of Judah.**

2Ch 25:28 — And they brought him upon horses, and buried him with his fathers in the city of Judah.

- **Called the Perfection of Beauty, the Joy of the Whole Earth.**

La 2:15 — All that pass by clap *their* hands at thee; they hiss and wag their head at the daughter of Jerusalem, *saying, Is* this the city that *men* call The perfection of beauty, The joy of the whole earth?

- **Called the Throne of the Lord.**

Jer 3:17 — At that time they shall call Jerusalem the throne of the LORD; and all the nations shall be gathered unto it, to the name of the LORD, to Jerusalem: neither shall they walk any more after the imagination of their evil heart.

- **Called Holy Mountain.**

Da 9:16 — O Lord, according to all thy righteousness, I beseech thee, let thine anger and thy fury be turned away from thy city Jerusalem, thy holy mountain: because for our sins, and for the iniquities of our fathers, Jerusalem and thy people *are become* a reproach to all *that are* about us.

Da 9:20 — And whiles I *was* speaking, and praying, and confessing my sin and the sin of my people Israel, and presenting my supplication before the LORD my God for the holy mountain of my God;

- **Called Holy City.**

Ne 11:1 — And the rulers of the people dwelt at Jerusalem: the rest of the people also cast lots, to bring one of ten to dwell in Jerusalem the holy city, and nine parts *to dwell* in *other* cities.

Ne 11:18 — All the Levites in the holy city *were* two hundred fourscore and four.

Mt 4:5 — Then the devil taketh him up into the holy city, and setteth him on a pinnacle of the temple,

- **Called City of Solemnities.**

Isa 33:20 — Look upon Zion, the city of our solemnities: thine eyes shall see Jerusalem a quiet habitation, a tabernacle *that* shall not be taken down; not one of the stakes thereof shall ever be removed, neither shall any of the cords thereof be broken.

- **Called City of Truth.**

Zec 8:3 — Thus saith the LORD; I am returned unto Zion, and will dwell in the midst of Jerusalem: and Jerusalem shall be called a city of truth; and the mountain of the LORD of hosts the holy mountain.

- **To be called "The Lord our Righteousness".**

Jer 33:16 — In those days shall Judah be saved, and Jerusalem shall dwell safely: and this *is the name* wherewith she shall be called, The LORD our righteousness.

- **Called Jehovah-Shammah.**

Eze 48:35 — *It was* round about eighteen thousand *measures:* and the name of the city from *that* day *shall be,* The LORD *is* there.

- **Called New Jerusalem.**

Rev 21:10–27

Rev 21:2 — And I John saw the holy city, new Jerusalem, coming down from God out of heaven, prepared as a bride adorned for her husband.

JERUSALEM, Situation and Appearance of

Ps 122:3 — Jerusalem is builded as a city that is compact together:

Ps 125:2 — As the mountains *are* round about Jerusalem, so the LORD *is* round about his people from henceforth even for ever.

SS 6:4 — Thou *art* beautiful, O my love, as Tirzah, comely as Jerusalem, terrible as *an army* with banners.

Mic 4:8 — And thou, O tower of the flock, the strong hold of the daughter of Zion, unto thee shall it come, even the first dominion; the kingdom shall come to the daughter of Jerusalem.

- **Walls of.**

Jer 39:4 — And it came to pass, *that* when Zedekiah the king of Judah saw them, and all the men of war, then they fled, and went forth out of the city by night, by the way of the king's garden, by the gate betwixt the two walls: and he went out the way of the plain.

- **Gates of.**
  - **Old gate; fish gate; sheep gate; prison gate.**

Ne 3:1 — Then Eliashib the high priest rose up with his brethren the priests, and they builded the sheep gate; they sanctified it, and set up the doors of it; even unto the tower of Meah they sanctified it, unto the tower of Hananeel.

Ne 3:3 — But the fish gate did the sons of Hassenaah build, who *also* laid the beams thereof, and set up the doors thereof, the locks thereof, and the bars thereof.

Ne 3:32 — And between the going up of the corner unto the sheep gate repaired the goldsmiths and the merchants.

Ne 12:39 — And from above the gate of Ephraim, and above the old gate, and above the fish gate, and the tower of Hananeel, and the tower of Meah, even unto the sheep gate: and they stood still in the prison gate.

- **Gate of Ephraim.**

2Ch 25:23 — And Joash the king of Israel took Amaziah king of Judah, the son of Joash, the son of Jehoahaz, at Beth-shemesh, and brought him to Jerusalem, and brake down the wall of Jerusalem from the gate of Ephraim to the corner gate, four hundred cubits.

Ne 12:39 — And from above the gate of Ephraim, and above the old gate, and above the fish gate, and the tower of Hananeel, and the tower of Meah, even unto the sheep gate: and they stood still in the prison gate.

- **Gate of Benjamin.**

Jer 37:13 — And when he was in the gate of Benjamin, a captain of the ward *was* there, whose name *was* Irijah, the son of Shelemiah, the son of Hananiah; and he took Jeremiah the prophet, saying, Thou fallest away to the Chaldeans.

Zec 14:10 — All the land shall be turned as a plain from Geba to Rimmon south of Jerusalem: and it shall be lifted up, and inhabited in her place, from Benjamin's gate unto the place of the first gate, unto the corner gate, and *from* the tower of Hananeel unto the king's winepresses.

- **Gate of Joshua.**

2Ki 23:8 — And he brought all the priests out of the cities of Judah, and defiled the high places where the priests had burned incense, from Geba to Beer-sheba, and brake down the high places of the gates that *were* in the entering in of the gate of Joshua the governor of the city, which *were* on a man's left hand at the gate of the city.

- **Old gate.**

Ne 3:6 — Moreover the old gate repaired Jehoiada the son of Paseah, and Meshullam the son of Besodeiah; they laid the beams thereof, and set up the doors thereof, and the locks thereof, and the bars thereof.

Ne 12:39 — And from above the gate of Ephraim, and above the old gate, and above the fish gate, and the tower of Hananeel, and the tower of Meah, even unto the sheep gate: and they stood still in the prison gate.

- **Corner gate.**

Zec 14:10 — All the land shall be turned as a plain from Geba to Rimmon south of Jerusalem: and it shall be lifted up, and inhabited in her place, from Benjamin's gate unto the place of the first gate, unto the corner gate, and *from* the tower of Hananeel unto the king's winepresses.

- **Valley gate.**

Ne 2:13 — And I went out by night by the gate of the valley, even before the dragon well, and to the dung port, and viewed the walls of Jerusalem, which were broken down, and the gates thereof were consumed with fire.

Ne 3:13 — The valley gate repaired Hanun, and the inhabitants of Zanoah; they built it, and set up the doors thereof, the locks thereof, and the bars thereof, and a thousand cubits on the wall unto the dung gate.

- **Dung gate.**

Ne 2:13 — And I went out by night by the gate of the valley, even before the dragon well, and to the dung port, and viewed the walls of Jerusalem, which were broken down, and the gates thereof were consumed with fire.

Ne 3:13 — The valley gate repaired Hanun, and the inhabitants of Zanoah; they built it, and set up the doors thereof, the locks thereof, and the bars thereof, and a thousand cubits on the wall unto the dung gate.

Ne 12:31 — Then I brought up the princes of Judah upon the wall, and appointed two great *companies of them that gave* thanks, *whereof one* went on the right hand upon the wall toward the dung gate:

- **Gate of the fountain.**

Ne 2:14 — Then I went on to the gate of the fountain, and to the king's pool: but *there was* no place for the beast *that was* under me to pass.

Ne 3:15 — But the gate of the fountain repaired Shallun the son of Col-hozeh, the ruler of part of Mizpah; he built it, and covered it, and set up the doors thereof, the locks thereof, and the bars thereof, and the wall of the pool of Siloah by the king's garden, and unto the stairs that go down from the city of David.

Ne 12:37 — And at the fountain gate, which was over against them, they went up by the stairs of the city of David, at the going up of the wall, above the house of David, even unto the water gate eastward.

- **Water gate.**

Ne 3:26 — Moreover the Nethinims dwelt in Ophel, unto *the place* over against the water gate toward the east, and the tower that lieth out.

Ne 8:1 — And all the people gathered themselves together as one man into the street that *was* before the water gate; and they spake unto Ezra the scribe to bring the book of the law of Moses, which the LORD had commanded to Israel.

Ne 12:37 — And at the fountain gate, which was over against them, they went up by the stairs of the city of David, at the going up of the wall, above the house of David, even unto the water gate eastward.

• **Horse gate.**

Ne 3:28 — From above the horse gate repaired the priests, every one over against his house.

• **King's gate.**

1Ch 9:18 — Who hitherto *waited* in the king's gate eastward: they were porters in the companies of the children of Levi.

• **Shallecheth.**

1Ch 26:16 — To Shuppim and Hosah *the lot came forth* westward, with the gate Shallecheth, by the causeway of the going up, ward against ward.

• **High gate.**

2Ch 23:20 — And he took the captains of hundreds, and the nobles, and the governors of the people, and all the people of the land, and brought down the king from the house of the LORD: and they came through the high gate into the king's house, and set the king upon the throne of the kingdom.

• **East gate.**

Ne 3:29 — After them repaired Zadok the son of Immer over against his house. After him repaired also Shemaiah the son of Shechaniah, the keeper of the east gate.

• **Miphkad.**

Ne 3:31 — After him repaired Malchiah the goldsmith's son unto the place of the Nethinims, and of the merchants, over against the gate Miphkad, and to the going up of the corner.

• **Middle gate.**

Jer 39:3 — And all the princes of the king of Babylon came in, and sat in the middle gate, *even* Nergal-sharezer, Samgar-nebo, Sarsechim, Rabsaris, Nergal-sharezer, Rabmag, with all the residue of the princes of the king of Babylon.

• **First gate.**

Zec 14:10 — All the land shall be turned as a plain from Geba to Rimmon south of Jerusalem: and it shall be lifted up, and inhabited in her place, from Benjamin's gate unto the place of the first gate, unto the corner gate, and *from* the tower of Hananeel unto the king's winepresses.

• **Buildings.**

• **High priest's palace.**

Jn 18:15 — And Simon Peter followed Jesus, and *so did* another disciple: that disciple was known unto the high priest, and went in with Jesus into the palace of the high priest.

• **Castle.**

Ac 21:34 — And some cried one thing, some another, among the multitude: and when he could not know the certainty for the tumult, he commanded him to be carried into the castle.

• **Stairs.**

Ne 3:15 — But the gate of the fountain repaired Shallun the son of Col-hozeh, the ruler of part of Mizpah; he built it, and covered it, and set up the doors thereof, the locks thereof, and the bars thereof, and the wall of the pool of Siloah by the king's garden, and unto the stairs that go down from the city of David.

• **Streets.**

• **East street.**

2Ch 29:4 — And he brought in the priests and the Levites, and gathered them together into the east street,

• **Street of the house of God.**

Ezr 10:9 — Then all the men of Judah and Benjamin gathered themselves together unto Jerusalem within three days. It *was* the ninth month, on the twentieth *day* of the month; and all the people sat in the street of the house of God, trembling because of *this* matter, and for the great rain.

• **Street of the Water gate of Ephraim gate.**

Ne 8:16 — So the people went forth, and brought *them,* and made themselves booths, every one upon the roof of his house, and in their courts, and in the courts of the house of God, and in the street of the water gate, and in the street of the gate of Ephraim.

• **Baker's street.**

Jer 37:21 — Then Zedekiah the king commanded that they should commit Jeremiah into the court of the prison, and that they should give him daily a piece of bread out of the bakers' street, until all the bread in the city were spent. Thus Jeremiah remained in the court of the prison.

• **Towers of.**

→See: **Hananeel**

→See: **Meah**

→See: **Millo**

→See: **Ophel**

→See: **Siloam**

• **Places in and around.**

• **Moriah.**

2Ch 3:1 — Then Solomon began to build the house of the LORD at Jerusalem in mount Moriah, where *the LORD* appeared unto David his father, in the place that David had prepared in the threshingfloor of Ornan the Jebusite.

• **The sepulchre of Jesus.**

Jn 19:41 — Now in the place where he was crucified there was a garden; and in the garden a new sepulchre, wherein was never man yet laid.

→See: **Calvary**

→See: **Gethsemane**

→See: **Jehoshaphat; a valley**

→See: **Olives, Mount of**

→See: **Tophet**

• **Measurement of, in Ezekiel's vision.**

Eze 45:6 — And ye shall appoint the possession of the city five thousand broad, and five and twenty thousand long, over against the oblation of the holy *portion:* it shall be for the whole house of Israel.

• **Names of the gates of, in Ezekiel's vision.**

Eze 48:31–34

JERUSHA • Daughter of Zadok.

2Ki 15:33 — Five and twenty years old was he when he began to reign, and he reigned sixteen years in Jerusalem. And his mother's name *was* Jerusha, the daughter of Zadok.

2Ch 27:1 — Jotham *was* twenty and five years old when he began to reign, and he reigned sixteen years in Jerusalem. His mother's name also *was* Jerushah, the daughter of Zadok.

JESAIAH

• Called also Jeshaiah.

• Grandson of Zerubbabel.

1Ch 3:21 — And the sons of Hananiah; Pelatiah, and Jesaiah: the sons of Rephaiah, the sons of Arnan, the sons of Obadiah, the sons of Shechaniah.

• Son of Jeduthun.

1Ch 25:3 — Of Jeduthun: the sons of Jeduthun; Gedaliah, and Zeri, and Jeshaiah, Hashabiah, and Mattithiah, six, under the hands of their father Jeduthun, who prophesied with a harp, to give thanks and to praise the LORD.

1Ch 25:15 — The eighth to Jeshaiah, *he*, his sons, and his brethren, *were* twelve:

• Grandson of Eliezer.

1Ch 26:25 — And his brethren by Eliezer; Rehabiah his son, and Jeshaiah his son, and Joram his son, and Zichri his son, and Shelomith his son.

• A Jew of the family of Elam, who returned from exile.

Ezr 8:7 — And of the sons of Elam; Jeshaiah the son of Athaliah, and with him seventy males.

• A Levite who joined Ezra to return to Jerusalem.

Ezr 8:19 — And Hashabiah, and with him Jeshaiah of the sons of Merari, his brethren and their sons, twenty;

• A Benjamite. Detailed by Lot to dwell in Jerusalem after the exile.

Ne 11:7 — And these *are* the sons of Benjamin; Sallu the son of Meshullam, the son of Joed, the son of Pedaiah, the son of Kolaiah, the son of Maaseiah, the son of Ithiel, the son of Jesaiah.

JESHANAH • A city in the north of Benjamin.

2Ch 13:19 — And Abijah pursued after Jeroboam, and took cities from him, Bethel with the towns thereof, and Jeshanah with the towns thereof, and Ephrain with the towns thereof.

JESHARELAH • A Levite, choral leader.

1Ch 25:14 — The seventh to Jesharelah, *he*, his sons, and his brethren, *were* twelve:

JESHEBEAB • A priest, and head of the fourteenth course.

1Ch 24:13 — The thirteenth to Huppah, the fourteenth to Jeshebeab,

JESHER • Son of Caleb.

1Ch 2:18 — And Caleb the son of Hezron begat *children* of Azubah *his* wife, and of Jerioth: her sons *are* these; Jesher, and Shobab, and Ardon.

JESHIMON

• A place in the Sinaitic peninsula, east of the Jordan.

Nu 21:20 — And from Bamoth *in* the valley, that *is* in the country of Moab, to the top of Pisgah, which looketh toward Jeshimon.

Nu 23:28 — And Balak brought Balaam unto the top of Peor, that looketh toward Jeshimon.

• A place in the desert of Judah.

1Sa 23:24 — And they arose, and went to Ziph before Saul: but David and his men *were* in the wilderness of Maon, in the plain on the south of Jeshimon.

1Sa 26:1 — And the Ziphites came unto Saul to Gibeah, saying, Doth not David hide himself in the hill of Hachilah, *which is* before Jeshimon?

JESHISHAI • A Gadite.

1Ch 5:14 — These *are* the children of Abihail the son of Huri, the son of Jaroah, the son of Gilead, the son of Michael, the son of Jeshishai, the son of Jahdo, the son of Buz;

JESHOHAIAH • A descendant of Simeon.

1Ch 4:36 — And Elioenai, and Jaakobah, and Jeshohaiah, and Asaiah, and Adiel, and Jesimiel, and Benaiah,

JESHUA

• A priest, head of the ninth course.

1Ch 24:11 — The ninth to Jeshua, the tenth to Shecaniah,

• Nine hundred and seventy-three of his descendants returned from Babylon.

Ezr 2:36 — The priests: the children of Jedaiah, of the house of Jeshua, nine hundred seventy and three.

Ne 7:39 — The priests: the children of Jedaiah, of the house of Jeshua, nine hundred seventy and three.

• A Levite, who had charge of the tithes.

2Ch 31:15 — And next him *were* Eden, and Miniamin, and Jeshua, and Shemaiah, Amariah, and Shecaniah, in the cities of the priests, in *their* set office, to give to their brethren by courses, as well to the great as to the small:

• His descendants returned with Ezra from Babylon.

Ezr 2:40 — The Levites: the children of Jeshua and Kadmiel, of the children of Hodaviah, seventy and four.

Ne 7:43 — The Levites: the children of Jeshua, of Kadmiel, *and* of the children of Hodevah, seventy and four.

- **A priest who accompanied Zerubbabel from Babylon.**

  Ezr 2:2 — Which came with Zerubbabel: Jeshua, Nehemiah, Seraiah, Reelaiah, Mordecai, Bilshan, Mizpar, Bigvai, Rehum, Baanah. The number of the men of the people of Israel:

  Ne 7:7 — Who came with Zerubbabel, Jeshua, Nehemiah, Azariah, Raamiah, Nahamani, Mordecai, Bilshan, Mispereth, Bigvai, Nehum, Baanah. The number, *I say,* of the men of the people of Israel *was this;*

  Ne 12:1 — Now these *are* the priests and the Levites that went up with Zerubbabel the son of Shealtiel, and Jeshua: Seraiah, Jeremiah, Ezra,

  - **Descendants of.**

    Ne 12:10 — And Jeshua begat Joiakim, Joiakim also begat Eliashib, and Eliashib begat Joiada,

  - **He rebuilt the altar.**

    Ezr 3:2 — Then stood up Jeshua the son of Jozadak, and his brethren the priests, and Zerubbabel the son of Shealtiel, and his brethren, and builded the altar of the God of Israel, to offer burnt offerings thereon, as *it is* written in the law of Moses the man of God.

  - **Rebuilt the temple.**

    Ezr 3:8–13

  - **Contends with those who sought to defeat the rebuilding.**

    Ezr 4:1–3; 5:1–2

- **Father of Jozabad.**

  Ezr 8:33 — Now on the fourth day was the silver and the gold and the vessels weighed in the house of our God by the hand of Meremoth the son of Uriah the priest; and with him *was* Eleazar the son of Phinehas; and with them *was* Jozabad the son of Jeshua, and Noadiah the son of Binnui, Levites;

- **Son of Pahath-moab.**

  Ezr 2:6 — The children of Pahath-moab, of the children of Jeshua *and* Joab, two thousand eight hundred and twelve.

  Ne 7:11 — The children of Pahath-moab, of the children of Jeshua and Joab, two thousand and eight hundred *and* eighteen.

- **Father of Ezer.**

  Ne 3:19 — And next to him repaired Ezer the son of Jeshua, the ruler of Mizpah, another piece over against the going up to the armoury at the turning *of the wall.*

- **A Levite who explained the law to the people when Ezra read it.**

  Ne 8:7 — Also Jeshua, and Bani, and Sherebiah, Jamin, Akkub, Shabbethai, Hodijah, Maaseiah, Kelita, Azariah, Jozabad, Hanan, Pelaiah, and the Levites, caused the people to understand the law: and the people *stood* in their place.

  Ne 12:8 — Moreover the Levites: Jeshua, Binnui, Kadmiel, Sherebiah, Judah, *and* Mattaniah, *which was* over the thanksgiving, he and his brethren.

- **A Levite who sealed Nehemiah's covenant.**

  Ne 10:9 — And the Levites: both Jeshua the son of Azaniah, Binnui of the sons of Henadad, Kadmiel;

- **A city of Judah.**

  Ne 11:26 — And at Jeshua, and at Moladah, and at Beth-phelet,

- **Joshua called.**

  Ne 8:17 — And all the congregation of them that were come again out of the captivity made booths, and sat under the booths: for since the days of Jeshua the son of Nun unto that day had not the children of Israel done so. And there was very great gladness.

- **Symbolic.**

  - **Prophecies concerning.**

    Zec 3:1–10; 6:9–15

  See: Joshua

JESHURUN • A name used poetically for Israel.

Dt 32:15 — But Jeshurun waxed fat, and kicked: thou art waxen fat, thou art grown thick, thou art covered *with fatness;* then he forsook God *which* made him, and lightly esteemed the Rock of his salvation.

Dt 33:5 — And he was king in Jeshurun, when the heads of the people *and* the tribes of Israel were gathered together.

Dt 33:26 — *There is* none like unto the God of Jeshurun, *who* rideth upon the heaven in thy help, and in his excellency on the sky.

Isa 44:2 — Thus saith the LORD that made thee, and formed thee from the womb, *which* will help thee; Fear not, O Jacob, my servant; and thou, Jesurun, whom I have chosen.

JESIAH

- **A disaffected Israelite who joined David at Ziklag.**

  1Ch 12:6 — Elkanah, and Jesiah, and Azareel, and Joezer, and Jashobeam, the Korhites,

- **A Kohathite Levite.**

  1Ch 23:20 — Of the sons of Uzziel; Micah the first, and Jesiah the second.

JESIMIEL • A descendant of Simeon.

1Ch 4:36 — And Elioenai, and Jaakobah, and Jeshohaiah, and Asaiah, and Adiel, and Jesimiel, and Benaiah,

JESSE

- **Father of David.**

  Ru 4:17 — And the women her neighbours gave it a name, saying, There is a son born to Naomi; and they called his name Obed: he *is* the father of Jesse, the father of David.

  1Sa 17:12 — Now David *was* the son of that Ephrathite of Bethlehemjudah, whose name *was* Jesse; and he had eight sons: and the man went among men *for* an old man in the days of Saul.

- **Ancestor of Jesus.**

  Mt 1:5–6

- **Samuel visits, under divine command, to select from his sons a successor to Saul.**

  1Sa 16:1–13

- **Saul asks, to send David to become a member of his court.**
  1Sa 16:19–23
- **Sons in Saul's army.**
  1Sa 17:13–28
- **Dwells with David in Moab.**
  1Sa 22:3–4
- **Descendants of.**
  1Ch 2:13–17

JESTING

- **Foolish, forbidden.**
  Mt 12:36 — But I say unto you, That every idle word that men shall speak, they shall give account thereof in the day of judgment.
  Eph 5:4 — Neither filthiness, nor foolish talking, nor jesting, which are not convenient: but rather giving of thanks.

JESUI • A descendant of Asher.

Nu 26:44 — *Of* the children of Asher after their families: of Jimna, the family of the Jimnites: of Jesui, the family of the Jesuites: of Beriah, the family of the Beriites.

JESUS, an Example

Mk 10:43–45; Lk 22:26–27; Jn 13:13–15; 17:21–22; Ro 15:2–3; Php 2:5–8; Col 3:10–11; Heb 12:2–4; 1Pe 1:15–16; 2:21–24; 3:17–18; 1Jn 3:1–3

Mt 11:29 — Take my yoke upon you, and learn of me; for I am meek and lowly in heart: and ye shall find rest unto your souls.

Mt 20:28 — Even as the Son of man came not to be ministered unto, but to minister, and to give his life a ransom for many.

Jn 10:4 — And when he putteth forth his own sheep, he goeth before them, and the sheep follow him: for they know his voice.

Jn 13:34 — A new commandment I give unto you, That ye love one another; as I have loved you, that ye also love one another.

Jn 17:14 — I have given them thy word; and the world hath hated them, because they are not of the world, even as I am not of the world.

Jn 17:18 — As thou hast sent me into the world, even so have I also sent them into the world.

Ro 8:29 — For whom he did foreknow, he also did predestinate *to be* conformed to the image of his Son, that he might be the firstborn among many brethren.

Ro 13:14 — But put ye on the Lord Jesus Christ, and make not provision for the flesh, to *fulfil* the lusts *thereof.*

Ro 15:5 — Now the God of patience and consolation grant you to be likeminded one toward another according to Christ Jesus:

Ro 15:7 — Wherefore receive ye one another, as Christ also received us to the glory of God.

2Co 4:10 — Always bearing about in the body the dying of the Lord Jesus, that the life also of Jesus might be made manifest in our body.

2Co 8:9 — For ye know the grace of our Lord Jesus Christ, that, though he was rich, yet for your sakes he became poor, that ye through his poverty might be rich.

2Co 10:1 — Now I Paul myself beseech you by the meekness and gentleness of Christ, who in presence *am* base among you, but being absent am bold toward you:

Gal 3:27 — For as many of you as have been baptized into Christ have put on Christ.

Gal 6:2 — Bear ye one another's burdens, and so fulfil the law of Christ.

Eph 4:13 — Till we all come in the unity of the faith, and of the knowledge of the Son of God, unto a perfect man, unto the measure of the stature of the fulness of Christ:

Eph 4:15 — But speaking the truth in love, may grow up into him in all things, which is the head, *even* Christ:

Eph 4:24 — And that ye put on the new man, which after God is created in righteousness and true holiness.

Eph 4:32 — And be ye kind one to another, tenderhearted, forgiving one another, even as God for Christ's sake hath forgiven you.

Eph 5:2 — And walk in love, as Christ also hath loved us, and hath given himself for us an offering and a sacrifice to God for a sweetsmelling savour.

Eph 6:9 — And, ye masters, do the same things unto them, forbearing threatening: knowing that your Master also is in heaven; neither is there respect of persons with him.

Col 3:13 — Forbearing one another, and forgiving one another, if any man have a quarrel against any: even as Christ forgave you, so also *do* ye.

1Th 1:6 — And ye became followers of us, and of the Lord, having received the word in much affliction, with joy of the Holy Ghost:

Heb 3:1 — Wherefore, holy brethren, partakers of the heavenly calling, consider the Apostle and High Priest of our profession, Christ Jesus;

1Jn 2:6 — He that saith he abideth in him ought himself also so to walk, even as he walked.

1Jn 3:16 — Hereby perceive we the love *of God,* because he laid down his life for us: and we ought to lay down *our* lives for the brethren.

1Jn 4:17 — Herein is our love made perfect, that we may have boldness in the day of judgment: because as he is, so are we in this world.

Rev 3:21 — To him that overcometh will I grant to sit with me in my throne, even as I also overcame, and am set down with my Father in his throne.

Rev 14:4 — These are they which were not defiled with women; for they are virgins. These are they which follow the Lamb whithersoever he goeth. These were redeemed from among men, *being* the firstfruits unto God and to the Lamb.

JESUS, Ascension of

Lk 24:50–51; Jn 7:33–34; 14:2–4; Eph 4:8–10

Ps 47:5 — God is gone up with a shout, the LORD with the sound of a trumpet.

Ps 68:18 — Thou hast ascended on high, thou hast led captivity captive: thou hast received gifts for men; yea, *for* the rebellious also, that the LORD God might dwell *among them.*

Mk 16:19 — So then after the Lord had spoken unto them, he was received up into heaven, and sat on the right hand of God.

Lk 24:26 — Ought not Christ to have suffered these things, and to enter into his glory?

Jn 1:51 — And he saith unto him, Verily, verily, I say unto you, Hereafter ye shall see heaven open, and the angels of God ascending and descending upon the Son of man.

Jn 6:62 — *What* and if ye shall see the Son of man ascend up where he was before?

Jn 7:39 — (But this spake he of the Spirit, which they that believe on him should receive: for the Holy Ghost was not yet *given;* because that Jesus was not yet glorified.)

Jn 14:12 — Verily, verily, I say unto you, He that believeth on me, the works that I do shall he do also; and greater *works* than these shall he do; because I go unto my Father.

Jn 14:28 — Ye have heard how I said unto you, I go away, and come *again* unto you. If ye loved me, ye would rejoice, because I said, I go unto the Father: for my Father is greater than I.

Jn 16:5 — But now I go my way to him that sent me; and none of you asketh me, Whither goest thou?

Jn 16:7 — Nevertheless I tell you the truth; It is expedient for you that I go away: for if I go not away, the Comforter will not come unto you; but if I depart, I will send him unto you.

Jn 16:10 — Of righteousness, because I go to my Father, and ye see me no more;

Jn 16:16 — A little while, and ye shall not see me: and again, a little while, and ye shall see me, because I go to the Father.

Jn 16:25 — These things have I spoken unto you in proverbs: but the time cometh, when I shall no more speak unto you in proverbs, but I shall shew you plainly of the Father.

Jn 16:28 — I came forth from the Father, and am come into the world: again, I leave the world, and go to the Father.

Jn 17:5 — And now, O Father, glorify thou me with thine own self with the glory which I had with thee before the world was.

Jn 17:13 — And now come I to thee; and these things I speak in the world, that they might have my joy fulfilled in themselves.

Jn 20:17 — Jesus saith unto her, Touch me not; for I am not yet ascended to my Father: but go to my brethren, and say unto them, I ascend unto my Father, and your Father; and *to* my God, and your God.

Ac 1:9 — And when he had spoken these things, while they beheld, he was taken up; and a cloud received him out of their sight.

Ac 3:21 — Whom the heaven must receive until the times of restitution of all things, which God hath spoken by the mouth of all his holy prophets since the world began.

Eph 1:20 — Which he wrought in Christ, when he raised him from the dead, and set *him* at his own right hand in the heavenly *places,*

1Ti 3:16 — And without controversy great is the mystery of godliness: God was manifest in the flesh, justified in the Spirit, seen of angels, preached unto the Gentiles, believed on in the world, received up into glory.

Heb 1:3 — Who being the brightness of *his* glory, and the express image of his person, and upholding all things by the word of his power, when he had by himself purged our sins, sat down on the right hand of the Majesty on high;

Heb 4:14 — Seeing then that we have a great high priest, that is passed into the heavens, Jesus the Son of God, let us hold fast *our* profession.

Heb 9:24 — For Christ is not entered into the holy places made with hands, *which are* the figures of the true; but into heaven itself, now to appear in the presence of God for us:

See: Exaltation

JESUS, Atonement by **See: Atonement**

JESUS, Attributes of (See by name below)

JESUS, Birth of **See: Jesus, Incarnation of**

JESUS, Compassion of

Isa 63:7–9; Mt 8:16–17; 18:11–13; Mk 8:2–3; Lk 19:41–42; Jn 11:34–38; 18:8–9

Isa 40:11 — He shall feed his flock like a shepherd: he shall gather the lambs with his arm, and carry *them* in his bosom, *and* shall gently lead those that are with young.

Isa 42:3 — A bruised reed shall he not break, and the smoking flax shall he not quench: he shall bring forth judgment unto truth.

Isa 53:4 — Surely he hath borne our griefs, and carried our sorrows: yet we did esteem him stricken, smitten of God, and afflicted.

Mt 8:3 — And Jesus put forth *his* hand, and touched him, saying, I will; be thou clean. And immediately his leprosy was cleansed.

Mt 9:36 — But when he saw the multitudes, he was moved with compassion on them, because they fainted, and were scattered abroad, as sheep having no shepherd.

Mt 14:14 — And Jesus went forth, and saw a great multitude, and was moved with compassion toward them, and he healed their sick.

Mt 15:32 — Then Jesus called his disciples *unto him,* and said, I have compassion on the multitude, because they continue with me now three days, and have nothing to eat: and I will not send them away fasting, lest they faint in the way.

Mt 20:34 — So Jesus had compassion *on them,* and touched their eyes: and immediately their eyes received sight, and they followed him.

Mt 23:37 — O Jerusalem, Jerusalem, *thou* that killest the prophets, and stonest them which are sent unto thee, how often would I have gathered thy children together, even as a hen gathereth her chickens under *her* wings, and ye would not!

Mk 6:34 — And Jesus, when he came out, saw much people, and was moved with compassion toward them, because they were as sheep not having a shepherd: and he began to teach them many things.

Lk 7:13 — And when the Lord saw her, he had compassion on her, and said unto her, Weep not.

2Co 8:9 — For ye know the grace of our Lord Jesus Christ, that, though he was rich, yet for your sakes he became poor, that ye through his poverty might be rich.

Heb 4:15 — For we have not an high priest which cannot be touched with the feeling of our infirmities; but was in all points tempted like as *we are, yet* without sin.

✦See: Jesus, Love of

JESUS, Confessing

✦See: Confession; of Christ
✦See: Testimony; religious

JESUS, Creator

Col 1:16–17

Jn 1:3 — All things were made by him; and without him was not any thing made that was made.

Jn 1:10 — He was in the world, and the world was made by him, and the world knew him not.

1Co 8:6 — But to us *there is but* one God, the Father, of whom *are* all things, and we in him; and one Lord Jesus Christ, by whom *are* all things, and we by him.

Eph 3:9 — And to make all *men* see what *is* the fellowship of the mystery, which from the beginning of the world hath been hid in God, who created all things by Jesus Christ:

Heb 1:2 — Hath in these last days spoken unto us by *his* Son, whom he hath appointed heir of all things, by whom also he made the worlds;

Heb 1:10 — And, Thou, Lord, in the beginning hast laid the foundation of the earth; and the heavens are the works of thine hands:

Rev 3:14 — And unto the angel of the church of the Laodiceans write; These things saith the Amen, the faithful and true witness, the beginning of the creation of God;

✦See: Jesus, Preexistence of

JESUS, Death of

Ps 25:1–22; 109:1–31; Isa 53:7–12; Zec 12:9–10; 13:6–7; Mt 17:12–13, 22–23; 20:17–19; 21:33–39; Mk 10:32–34; Lk 2:34–35; 18:31–33; Jn 10:17–18; 12:32–34; 13:18–19; 19:23–24, 28–30; Ac 26:22–23; 1Co 1:17–18, 23–24; 15:3–4; 2Co 4:10–11

Ge 3:15 — And I will put enmity between thee and the woman, and between thy seed and her seed; it shall bruise thy head, and thou shalt bruise his heel.

Ps 22:1 — My God, my God, why hast thou forsaken me? *why art thou so* far from helping me, *and from* the words of my roaring?

Ps 22:13 — They gaped upon me *with* their mouths, *as* a ravening and a roaring lion.

Ps 22:16 — For dogs have compassed me: the assembly of the wicked have inclosed me: they pierced my hands and my feet.

Ps 22:18 — They part my garments among them, and cast lots upon my vesture.

Ps 34:20 — He keepeth all his bones: not one of them is broken.

Ps 69:21 — They gave me also gall for my meat; and in my thirst they gave me vinegar to drink.

Ps 69:26 — For they persecute *him* whom thou hast smitten; and they talk to the grief of those whom thou hast wounded.

Isa 52:14 — As many were astonied at thee; his visage was so marred more than any man, and his form more than the sons of men:

Da 9:26 — And after threescore and two weeks shall Messiah be cut off, but not for himself: and the people of the prince that shall come shall destroy the city and the sanctuary; and the end thereof *shall be* with a flood, and unto the end of the war desolations are determined.

Mt 12:40 — For as Jonas was three days and three nights in the whale's belly; so shall the Son of man be three days and three nights in the heart of the earth.

Mt 16:4 — A wicked and adulterous generation seeketh after a sign; and there shall no sign be given unto it, but the sign of the prophet Jonas. And he left them, and departed.

Mt 16:21 — From that time forth began Jesus to shew unto his disciples, how that he must go unto Jerusalem, and suffer many things of the elders and chief priests and scribes, and be killed, and be raised again the third day.

Mt 26:2 — Ye know that after two days is *the feast of* the passover, and the Son of man is betrayed to be crucified.

Mt 26:12 — For in that she hath poured this ointment on my body, she did *it* for my burial.

Mt 26:18 — And he said, Go into the city to such a man, and say unto him, The Master saith, My time is at hand; I will keep the passover at thy house with my disciples.

Mt 26:21 — And as they did eat, he said, Verily I say unto you, that one of you shall betray me.

Mt 27:34 — They gave him vinegar to drink mingled with gall: and when he had tasted *thereof,* he would not drink.

Mt 27:39 — And they that passed by reviled him, wagging their heads,

Mt 27:46 — And about the ninth hour Jesus cried with a loud voice, saying, Eli, Eli, lama sabachthani? that is to say, My God, my God, why hast thou forsaken me?

Mk 8:31 — And he began to teach them, that the Son of man must suffer many things, and be rejected of the elders, and *of* the chief priests, and scribes, and be killed, and after three days rise again.

Mk 9:31 — For he taught his disciples, and said unto them, The Son of man is delivered into the hands of men, and they shall kill him; and after that he is killed, he shall rise the third day.

Mk 14:9 — Verily I say unto you, Wheresoever this gospel shall be preached throughout the whole world, *this* also that she hath done shall be spoken of for a memorial of her.

Mk 14:18 — And as they sat and did eat, Jesus said, Verily I say unto you, One of you which eateth with me shall betray me.

Mk 15:23 — And they gave him to drink wine mingled with myrrh: but he received *it* not.

Mk 15:28 — And the scripture was fulfilled, which saith, And he was numbered with the transgressors.

Lk 9:22 — Saying, The Son of man must suffer many things, and be rejected of the elders and chief priests and scribes, and be slain, and be raised the third day.

Lk 9:44 — Let these sayings sink down into your ears: for the Son of man shall be delivered into the hands of men.

Lk 11:30 — For as Jonas was a sign unto the Ninevites, so shall also the Son of man be to this generation.

Lk 12:50 — But I have a baptism to be baptized with; and how am I straitened till it be accomplished!

Lk 17:25 — But first must he suffer many things, and be rejected of this generation.

Lk 22:15 — And he said unto them, With desire I have desired to eat this passover with you before I suffer:

Lk 22:21 — But, behold, the hand of him that betrayeth me *is* with me on the table.

Lk 22:37 — For I say unto you, that this that is written must yet be accomplished in me, And he was reckoned among the transgressors: for the things concerning me have an end.

Lk 23:34 — Then said Jesus, Father, forgive them; for they know not what they do. And they parted his raiment, and cast lots.

Jn 10:11 — I am the good shepherd: the good shepherd giveth his life for the sheep.

Jn 10:15 — As the Father knoweth me, even so know I the Father: and I lay down my life for the sheep.

Jn 12:7 — Then said Jesus, Let her alone: against the day of my burying hath she kept this.

Jn 13:21 — When Jesus had thus said, he was troubled in spirit, and testified, and said, Verily, verily, I say unto you, that one of you shall betray me.

Jn 14:19 — Yet a little while, and the world seeth me no more; but ye see me: because I live, ye shall live also.

Jn 15:13 — Greater love hath no man than this, that a man lay down his life for his friends.

Jn 16:20 — Verily, verily, I say unto you, That ye shall weep and lament, but the world shall rejoice: and ye shall be sorrowful, but your sorrow shall be turned into joy.

Jn 18:11 — Then said Jesus unto Peter, Put up thy sword into the sheath: the cup which my Father hath given me, shall I not drink it?

Jn 19:36 — For these things were done, that the scripture should be fulfilled, A bone of him shall not be broken.

1Co 2:2 — For I determined not to know any thing among you, save Jesus Christ, and him crucified.

1Th 4:14 — For if we believe that Jesus died and rose again, even so them also which sleep in Jesus will God bring with him.

Heb 2:14 — Forasmuch then as the children are partakers of flesh and blood, he also himself likewise took part of the same; that through death he might destroy him that had the power of death, that is, the devil;

Rev 5:12 — Saying with a loud voice, Worthy is the Lamb that was slain to receive power, and riches, and wisdom, and strength, and honour, and glory, and blessing.

Rev 13:8 — And all that dwell upon the earth shall worship him, whose names are not written in the book of life of the Lamb slain from the foundation of the world.

➔See: Jesus, History of

• Design of his death.

Isa 53:1–12; Lk 22:19–20; Jn 3:14–17; 11:49–52; 12:31–33; Ac 5:30–31; Ro 3:24–25; 5:6–11; 6:3–5, 9–10; 2Co 5:14–15; Gal 4:4–5; Eph 1:6–7; 2:13–16; 5:25–27; Col 1:20–22; 2:14–15; 1Th 5:9–10; Heb 2:9–10, 14–15; 9:12–17, 25–26; 10:17–20; 13:11–12; 1Pe 1:18–21; Rev 7:14–15

Ge 3:15 — And I will put enmity between thee and the woman, and between thy seed and her seed; it shall bruise thy head, and thou shalt bruise his heel.

Da 9:24 — Seventy weeks are determined upon thy people and upon thy holy city, to finish the transgression, and to make an end of sins, and to make reconciliation for iniquity, and to bring in everlasting righteousness, and to seal up the vision and prophecy, and to anoint the most Holy.

Zec 9:11 — As for thee also, by the blood of thy covenant I have sent forth thy prisoners out of the pit wherein *is* no water.

Zec 13:1 — In that day there shall be a fountain opened to the house of David and to the inhabitants of Jerusalem for sin and for uncleanness.

Mt 20:28 — Even as the Son of man came not to be ministered unto, but to minister, and to give his life a ransom for many.

Mt 26:28 — For this is my blood of the new testament, which is shed for many for the remission of sins.

Mk 10:45 — For even the Son of man came not to be ministered unto, but to minister, and to give his life a ransom for many.

Mk 14:24 — And he said unto them, This is my blood of the new testament, which is shed for many.

Lk 24:26 — Ought not Christ to have suffered these things, and to enter into his glory?

Jn 1:29 — The next day John seeth Jesus coming unto him, and saith, Behold the Lamb of God, which taketh away the sin of the world.

Jn 6:51 — I am the living bread which came down from heaven: if any man eat of this bread, he shall live for ever: and the bread that I will give is my flesh, which I will give for the life of the world.

Jn 10:11 — I am the good shepherd: the good shepherd giveth his life for the sheep.

Jn 10:15 — As the Father knoweth me, even so know I the Father: and I lay down my life for the sheep.

Jn 10:17 — Therefore doth my Father love me, because I lay down my life, that I might take it again.

Jn 12:24 — Verily, verily, I say unto you, Except a corn of wheat fall into the ground and die, it abideth alone: but if it die, it bringeth forth much fruit.

Jn 14:19 — Yet a little while, and the world seeth me no more; but ye see me: because I live, ye shall live also.

Jn 15:13 — Greater love hath no man than this, that a man lay down his life for his friends.

Ac 20:28 — Take heed therefore unto yourselves, and to all the flock, over the which the Holy Ghost hath made you overseers, to feed the church of God, which he hath purchased with his own blood.

Ac 26:23 — That Christ should suffer, *and* that he should be the first that should rise from the dead, and should shew light unto the people, and to the Gentiles.

Ro 4:25 — Who was delivered for our offences, and was raised again for our justification.

Ro 8:3 — For what the law could not do, in that it was weak through the flesh, God sending his own Son in the likeness of sinful flesh, and for sin, condemned sin in the flesh:

Ro 8:32 — He that spared not his own Son, but delivered him up for us all, how shall he not with him also freely give us all things?

Ro 8:34 — Who *is* he that condemneth? *It is* Christ that died, yea rather, that is risen again, who is even at the right hand of God, who also maketh intercession for us.

Ro 8:39 — Nor height, nor depth, nor any other creature, shall be able to separate us from the love of God, which is in Christ Jesus our Lord.

Ro 14:9 — For to this end Christ both died, and rose, and revived, that he might be Lord both of the dead and living.

Ro 14:15 — But if thy brother be grieved with *thy* meat, now walkest thou not charitably. Destroy not him with thy meat, for whom Christ died.

1Co 5:7 — Purge out therefore the old leaven, that ye may be a new lump, as ye are unleavened. For even Christ our passover is sacrificed for us:

1Co 6:20 — For ye are bought with a price: therefore glorify God in your body, and in your spirit, which are God's.

1Co 8:11 — And through thy knowledge shall the weak brother perish, for whom Christ died?

1Co 15:3 — For I delivered unto you first of all that which I also received, how that Christ died for our sins according to the scriptures;

2Co 5:19 — To wit, that God was in Christ, reconciling the world unto himself, not imputing their trespasses unto them; and hath committed unto us the word of reconciliation.

2Co 5:21 — For he hath made him *to be* sin for us, who knew no sin; that we might be made the righteousness of God in him.

2Co 8:9 — For ye know the grace of our Lord Jesus Christ, that, though he was rich, yet for your sakes he became poor, that ye through his poverty might be rich.

Gal 1:4 — Who gave himself for our sins, that he might deliver us from this present evil world, according to the will of God and our Father:

Gal 2:20 — I am crucified with Christ: nevertheless I live; yet not I, but Christ liveth in me: and the life which I now live in the flesh I live by the faith of the Son of God, who loved me, and gave himself for me.

Gal 3:13 — Christ hath redeemed us from the curse of the law, being made a curse for us: for it is written, Cursed *is* every one that hangeth on a tree:

Eph 5:2 — And walk in love, as Christ also hath loved us, and hath given himself for us an offering and a sacrifice to God for a sweetsmelling savour.

Col 1:14 — In whom we have redemption through his blood, *even* the forgiveness of sins:

1Th 1:10 — And to wait for his Son from heaven, whom he raised from the dead, *even* Jesus, which delivered us from the wrath to come.

1Ti 2:6 — Who gave himself a ransom for all, to be testified in due time.

Tit 2:14 — Who gave himself for us, that he might redeem us from all iniquity, and purify unto himself a peculiar people, zealous of good works.

Heb 1:3 — Who being the brightness of *his* glory, and the express image of his person, and upholding all things by the word of his power, when he had by himself purged our sins, sat down on the right hand of the Majesty on high;

Heb 2:18 — For in that he himself hath suffered being tempted, he is able to succour them that are tempted.

Heb 7:27 — Who needeth not daily, as those high priests, to offer up sacrifice, first for his own sins, and then for the people's: for this he did once, when he offered up himself.

Heb 9:28 — So Christ was once offered to bear the sins of many; and unto them that look for him shall he appear the second time without sin unto salvation.

Heb 10:10 — By the which will we are sanctified through the offering of the body of Jesus Christ once *for all.*

Heb 10:12 — But this man, after he had offered one sacrifice for sins for ever, sat down on the right hand of God;

Heb 10:14 — For by one offering he hath perfected for ever them that are sanctified.

Heb 12:2 — Looking unto Jesus the author and finisher of *our* faith; who for the joy that was set before him endured the cross, despising the shame, and is set down at the right hand of the throne of God.

Heb 12:24 — And to Jesus the mediator of the new covenant, and to the blood of sprinkling, that speaketh better things than *that of* Abel.

1Pe 1:2 — Elect according to the foreknowledge of God the Father, through sanctification of the Spirit, unto obedience and sprinkling of the blood of Jesus Christ: Grace unto you, and peace, be multiplied.

1Pe 2:21 — For even hereunto were ye called: because Christ also suffered for us, leaving us an example, that ye should follow his steps:

1Pe 2:24 — Who his own self bare our sins in his own body on the tree, that we, being dead to sins, should live unto righteousness: by whose stripes ye were healed.

1Pe 3:18 — For Christ also hath once suffered for sins, the just for the unjust, that he might bring us to God, being put to death in the flesh, but quickened by the Spirit:

1Pe 4:1 — Forasmuch then as Christ hath suffered for us in the flesh, arm yourselves likewise with the same mind: for he that hath suffered in the flesh hath ceased from sin;

1Jn 1:7 — But if we walk in the light, as he is in the light, we have fellowship one with another, and the blood of Jesus Christ his Son cleanseth us from all sin.

1Jn 2:2 — And he is the propitiation for our sins: and not for ours only, but also for *the sins of* the whole world.

1Jn 3:16 — Hereby perceive we the love *of God,* because he laid down his life for us: and we ought to lay down *our* lives for the brethren.

1Jn 4:10 — Herein is love, not that we loved God, but that he loved us, and sent his Son *to be* the propitiation for our sins.

Rev 1:5 — And from Jesus Christ, *who is* the faithful witness, *and* the first begotten of the dead, and the prince of the kings of the earth. Unto him that loved us, and washed us from our sins in his own blood,

Rev 5:9 — And they sung a new song, saying, Thou art worthy to take the book, and to open the seals thereof: for thou wast slain, and hast redeemed us to God by thy blood out of every kindred, and tongue, and people, and nation;

Rev 13:8 — And all that dwell upon the earth shall worship him, whose names are not written in the book of life of the Lamb slain from the foundation of the world.

See: Atonement

See: Reconciliation

See: Satan; kingdom of, to be destroyed

• Death of, voluntary.

Mt 26:53–54; Jn 10:17–18

Isa 50:6 — I gave my back to the smiters, and my cheeks to them that plucked off the hair: I hid not my face from shame and spitting.

Isa 53:12 — Therefore will I divide him *a portion* with the great, and he shall divide the spoil with the strong; because he hath poured out his soul unto death: and he was numbered with the transgressors; and he bare the sin of many, and made intercession for the transgressors.

Mt 26:24 — The Son of man goeth as it is written of him: but woe unto that man by whom the Son of man is betrayed! it had been good for that man if he had not been born.

Mt 26:39 — And he went a little farther, and fell on his face, and prayed, saying, O my Father, if it be possible, let this cup pass from me: nevertheless not as I will, but as thou *wilt.*

Mt 26:42 — He went away again the second time, and prayed, saying, O my Father, if this cup may not pass away from me, except I drink it, thy will be done.

Mk 14:36 — And he said, Abba, Father, all things *are* possible unto thee; take away this cup from me: nevertheless not what I will, but what thou wilt.

Mk 14:39 — And again he went away, and prayed, and spake the same words.

Lk 9:51 — And it came to pass, when the time was come that he should be received up, he stedfastly set his face to go to Jerusalem,

Lk 12:50 — But I have a baptism to be baptized with; and how am I straitened till it be accomplished!

Lk 22:15 — And he said unto them, With desire I have desired to eat this passover with you before I suffer:

Lk 22:42 — Saying, Father, if thou be willing, remove this cup from me: nevertheless not my will, but thine, be done.

Jn 18:5 — They answered him, Jesus of Nazareth. Jesus saith unto them, I am *he.* And Judas also, which betrayed him, stood with them.

Jn 18:8 — Jesus answered, I have told you that I am *he:* if therefore ye seek me, let these go their way:

Jn 18:11 — Then said Jesus unto Peter, Put up thy sword into the sheath: the cup which my Father hath given me, shall I not drink it?

Jn 19:11 — Jesus answered, Thou couldest have no power *at all* against me, except it were given thee from above: therefore he that delivered me unto thee hath the greater sin.

Php 2:8 — And being found in fashion as a man, he humbled himself, and became obedient unto death, even the death of the cross.

Heb 7:27 — Who needeth not daily, as those high priests, to offer up sacrifice, first for his own sins, and then for the people's: for this he did once, when he offered up himself.

Heb 9:26 — For then must he often have suffered since the foundation of the world: but now once in the end of the world hath he appeared to put away sin by the sacrifice of himself.

JESUS, Denial of See: Jesus, Rejected

JESUS, Divinity of

• As Jehovah.

Isa 40:3 — The voice of him that crieth in the wilderness, Prepare ye the way of the LORD, make straight in the desert a highway for our God.

Mt 3:3 — For this is he that was spoken of by the prophet Esaias, saying, The voice of one crying in the wilderness, Prepare ye the way of the Lord, make his paths straight.

• Jehovah of glory.

Ps 24:7 — Lift up your heads, O ye gates; and be ye lift up, ye everlasting doors; and the King of glory shall come in.

Ps 24:10 — Who is this King of glory? The LORD of hosts, he *is* the King of glory. Selah.

1Co 2:8 — Which none of the princes of this world knew: for had they known *it,* they would not have crucified the Lord of glory.

Jas 2:1 — My brethren, have not the faith of our Lord Jesus Christ, *the Lord* of glory, with respect of persons.

• Jehovah our righteousness.

Jer 23:5–6

1Co 1:30 — But of him are ye in Christ Jesus, who of God is made unto us wisdom, and righteousness, and sanctification, and redemption:

- **Jehovah above all.**

Ps 97:9 — For thou, LORD, *art* high above all the earth: thou art exalted far above all gods.

Jn 3:31 — He that cometh from above is above all: he that is of the earth is earthly, and speaketh of the earth: he that cometh from heaven is above all.

- **Jehovah the first and the last.**
  - **1.**

    Rev 1:1–20

    Isa 44:6 — Thus saith the LORD the King of Israel, and his redeemer the LORD of hosts; I *am* the first, and I *am* the last; and beside me *there is* no God.
  - **2.**

    Isa 48:12–16

    Rev 22:13 — I am Alpha and Omega, the beginning and the end, the first and the last.

- **Jehovah's fellow and equal.**

Zec 13:7 — Awake, O sword, against my shepherd, and against the man *that is* my fellow, saith the LORD of hosts: smite the shepherd, and the sheep shall be scattered: and I will turn mine hand upon the little ones.

Php 2:6 — Who, being in the form of God, thought it not robbery to be equal with God:

- **Jehovah of hosts.**
  - **1.**

    Isa 6:1–3; Jn 12:1–50
  - **2.**

    Isa 8:13–14

    1Pe 2:8 — And a stone of stumbling, and a rock of offence, *even to them* which stumble at the word, being disobedient: whereunto also they were appointed.

- **Jehovah.**

Mt 22:42–45

Ps 110:1 — The LORD said unto my Lord, Sit thou at my right hand, until I make thine enemies thy footstool.

- **Jehovah the shepherd.**

Isa 40:10–11

Heb 13:20 — Now the God of peace, that brought again from the dead our Lord Jesus, that great shepherd of the sheep, through the blood of the everlasting covenant,

- **Jehovah, for whose glory all things were created.**

Pr 16:4 — The LORD hath made all *things* for himself: yea, even the wicked for the day of evil.

Col 1:16 — For by him were all things created, that are in heaven, and that are in earth, visible and invisible, whether *they be* thrones, or dominions, or principalities, or powers: all things were created by him, and for him:

- **Jehovah the messenger of the covenant.**

Mal 3:1 — Behold, I will send my messenger, and he shall prepare the way before me: and the Lord, whom ye seek, shall suddenly come to his temple, even the messenger of the covenant, whom ye delight in: behold, he shall come, saith the LORD of hosts.

Lk 2:27 — And he came by the Spirit into the temple: and when the parents brought in the child Jesus, to do for him after the custom of the law,

- **Invoked as Jehovah.**

Joel 2:32 — And it shall come to pass, *that* whosoever shall call on the name of the LORD shall be delivered: for in mount Zion and in Jerusalem shall be deliverance, as the LORD hath said, and in the remnant whom the LORD shall call.

1Co 1:2 — Unto the church of God which is at Corinth, to them that are sanctified in Christ Jesus, called *to be* saints, with all that in every place call upon the name of Jesus Christ our Lord, both theirs and ours:

- **Invoked as the eternal God and Creator.**

Ps 102:24–27; Heb 1:10–12

Heb 1:8 — But unto the Son *he saith,* Thy throne, O God, *is* for ever and ever: a sceptre of righteousness *is* the sceptre of thy kingdom.

- **Invoked as the mighty God.**

Isa 9:6 — For unto us a child is born, unto us a son is given: and the government shall be upon his shoulder: and his name shall be called Wonderful, Counsellor, The mighty God, The everlasting Father, The Prince of Peace.

- **Invoked as the great God and Saviour.**

Hos 1:7 — But I will have mercy upon the house of Judah, and will save them by the LORD their God, and will not save them by bow, nor by sword, nor by battle, by horses, nor by horsemen.

Tit 2:13 — Looking for that blessed hope, and the glorious appearing of the great God and our Saviour Jesus Christ;

- **Invoked as God over all.**

Ro 9:5 — Whose *are* the fathers, and of whom as concerning the flesh Christ *came,* who is over all, God blessed for ever. Amen.

- **Invoked as God the Judge.**

Ecc 12:14 — For God shall bring every work into judgment, with every secret thing, whether *it be* good, or whether *it be* evil.

1Co 4:5 — Therefore judge nothing before the time, until the Lord come, who both will bring to light the hidden things of darkness, and will make manifest the counsels of the hearts: and then shall every man have praise of God.

2Co 5:10 — For we must all appear before the judgment seat of Christ; that every one may receive the things *done* in *his* body, according to that he hath done, whether *it be* good or bad.

2Ti 4:1 — I charge *thee* therefore before God, and the Lord Jesus Christ, who shall judge the quick and the dead at his appearing and his kingdom;

- **Invoked as Emmanuel.**

Isa 7:14 — Therefore the Lord himself shall give you a sign; Behold, a virgin shall conceive, and bear a son, and shall call his name Immanuel.

Mt 1:23 — Behold, a virgin shall be with child, and shall bring forth a son, and they shall call his name Emmanuel, which being interpreted is, God with us.

• Invoked as King of kings and Lord of lords.

Da 10:17 — For how can the servant of this my lord talk with this my lord? for as for me, straightway there remained no strength in me, neither is there breath left in me.

Rev 1:5 — And from Jesus Christ, *who is* the faithful witness, *and* the first begotten of the dead, and the prince of the kings of the earth. Unto him that loved us, and washed us from our sins in his own blood,

Rev 17:14 — These shall make war with the Lamb, and the Lamb shall overcome them: for he is Lord of lords, and King of kings: and they that are with him *are* called, and chosen, and faithful.

• Invoked as the Holy One.

1Sa 2:2 — *There is* none holy as the LORD: for *there is* none beside thee: neither *is there* any rock like our God.

Ac 3:14 — But ye denied the Holy One and the Just, and desired a murderer to be granted unto you;

• Invoked as the Lord from heaven.

1Co 15:47 — The first man *is* of the earth, earthy: the second man *is* the Lord from heaven.

• Invoked as Lord of the Sabbath.

Ge 2:3 — And God blessed the seventh day, and sanctified it: because that in it he had rested from all his work which God created and made.

Mt 12:8 — For the Son of man is Lord even of the sabbath day.

• Invoked as Lord of all.

Ro 10:11–13

Ac 10:36 — The word which *God* sent unto the children of Israel, preaching peace by Jesus Christ: (he is Lord of all:)

• Invoked as Son of God.

Mt 26:63–67

• Invoked as the only begotten Son of the Father.

Jn 1:14 — And the Word was made flesh, and dwelt among us, (and we beheld his glory, the glory as of the only begotten of the Father,) full of grace and truth.

Jn 1:18 — No man hath seen God at any time; the only begotten Son, which is in the bosom of the Father, he hath declared *him.*

Jn 3:16 — For God so loved the world, that he gave his only begotten Son, that whosoever believeth in him should not perish, but have everlasting life.

Jn 3:18 — He that believeth on him is not condemned: but he that believeth not is condemned already, because he hath not believed in the name of the only begotten Son of God.

1Jn 4:9 — In this was manifested the love of God toward us, because that God sent his only begotten Son into the world, that we might live through him.

• His blood is called the blood of God.

Ac 20:28 — Take heed therefore unto yourselves, and to all the flock, over the which the Holy Ghost hath made you overseers, to feed the church of God, which he hath purchased with his own blood.

• One with the Father.

Jn 14:7–10

Jn 10:30 — I and *my* Father are one.

Jn 10:38 — But if I do, though ye believe not me, believe the works: that ye may know, and believe, that the Father is in me, and I in him.

Jn 12:45 — And he that seeth me seeth him that sent me.

Jn 17:10 — And all mine are thine, and thine are mine; and I am glorified in them.

• As sending the Spirit equally with the Father.

Jn 14:16 — And I will pray the Father, and he shall give you another Comforter, that he may abide with you for ever;

Jn 15:26 — But when the Comforter is come, whom I will send unto you from the Father, *even* the Spirit of truth, which proceedeth from the Father, he shall testify of me:

• As unsearchable equally with the Father.

Pr 30:4 — Who hath ascended up into heaven, or descended? who hath gathered the wind in his fists? who hath bound the waters in a garment? who hath established all the ends of the earth? what *is* his name, and what *is* his son's name, if thou canst tell?

Mt 11:27 — All things are delivered unto me of my Father: and no man knoweth the Son, but the Father; neither knoweth any man the Father, save the Son, and *he* to whomsoever the Son will reveal *him.*

• As Creator of all things.

Isa 40:28 — Hast thou not known? hast thou not heard, *that* the everlasting God, the LORD, the Creator of the ends of the earth, fainteth not, neither is weary? *there is* no searching of his understanding.

Jn 1:3 — All things were made by him; and without him was not any thing made that was made.

Col 1:16 — For by him were all things created, that are in heaven, and that are in earth, visible and invisible, whether *they be* thrones, or dominions, or principalities, or powers: all things were created by him, and for him:

• As supporter and preserver of all things.

Ne 9:6 — Thou, *even* thou, *art* LORD alone; thou hast made heaven, the heaven of heavens, with all their host, the earth, and all *things* that *are* therein, the seas, and all that *is* therein, and thou preservest them all; and the host of heaven worshippeth thee.

Col 1:17 — And he is before all things, and by him all things consist.

Heb 1:3 — Who being the brightness of *his* glory, and the express image of his person, and upholding all things by the word of his power, when he had by himself purged our sins, sat down on the right hand of the Majesty on high;

• Acknowledged by Old Testament saints.

Ge 32:24–30; 48:15–16; Jgs 6:22–24; 13:21–22; Job 19:25–27; Hos 12:3–5

Ge 17:1 — And when Abram was ninety years old and nine, the LORD appeared to Abram, and said unto him, I *am* the Almighty God; walk before me, and be thou perfect.

• Unclassified scripture relating to the divinity of.

Ex 23:20–21; Ps 45:6–7; 102:1–14, 24–27; Isa 8:13–14; 40:9–10; Mt 22:43–45; 28:17–18; Mk 5:6–7; Lk 4:33–34; 9:43–44; Jn 1:1–2; 5:17–18, 21–23; 10:30–33; Ac 7:37–39; Eph 6:23–24; Php 2:5–11; 2Th 1:1–2; 2:16–17

Ge 1:1 — In the beginning God created the heaven and the earth.

Nu 21:6 — And the LORD sent fiery serpents among the people, and they bit the people; and much people of Israel died.

Ps 24:10 — Who is this King of glory? The LORD of hosts, he *is* the King of glory. Selah.

Ps 110:1 — The LORD said unto my Lord, Sit thou at my right hand, until I make thine enemies thy footstool.

Isa 6:1 — In the year that king Uzziah died I saw also the Lord sitting upon a throne, high and lifted up, and his train filled the temple.

Isa 7:14 — Therefore the Lord himself shall give you a sign; Behold, a virgin shall conceive, and bear a son, and shall call his name Immanuel.

Isa 9:6 — For unto us a child is born, unto us a son is given: and the government shall be upon his shoulder: and his name shall be called Wonderful, Counsellor, The mighty God, The everlasting Father, The Prince of Peace.

Isa 40:3 — The voice of him that crieth in the wilderness, Prepare ye the way of the LORD, make straight in the desert a highway for our God.

Mal 3:1 — Behold, I will send my messenger, and he shall prepare the way before me: and the Lord, whom ye seek, shall suddenly come to his temple, even the messenger of the covenant, whom ye delight in: behold, he shall come, saith the LORD of hosts.

Mt 1:23 — Behold, a virgin shall be with child, and shall bring forth a son, and they shall call his name Emmanuel, which being interpreted is, God with us.

Mt 3:3 — For this is he that was spoken of by the prophet Esaias, saying, The voice of one crying in the wilderness, Prepare ye the way of the Lord, make his paths straight.

Mt 8:29 — And, behold, they cried out, saying, What have we to do with thee, Jesus, thou Son of God? art thou come hither to torment us before the time?

Mt 9:6 — But that ye may know that the Son of man hath power on earth to forgive sins, (then saith he to the sick of the palsy,) Arise, take up thy bed, and go unto thine house.

Mt 11:10 — For this is *he*, of whom it is written, Behold, I send my messenger before thy face, which shall prepare thy way before thee.

Lk 4:12 — And Jesus answering said unto him, It is said, Thou shalt not tempt the Lord thy God.

Lk 8:28 — When he saw Jesus, he cried out, and fell down before him, and with a loud voice said, What have I to do with thee, Jesus, *thou* Son of God most high? I beseech thee, torment me not.

Jn 12:41 — These things said Esaias, when he saw his glory, and spake of him.

Jn 12:45 — And he that seeth me seeth him that sent me.

Jn 20:28 — And Thomas answered and said unto him, My Lord and my God.

Ac 20:28 — Take heed therefore unto yourselves, and to all the flock, over the which the Holy Ghost hath made you overseers, to feed the church of God, which he hath purchased with his own blood.

Ro 1:7 — To all that be in Rome, beloved of God, called *to be* saints: Grace to you and peace from God our Father, and the Lord Jesus Christ.

Ro 9:5 — Whose *are* the fathers, and of whom as concerning the flesh Christ *came,* who is over all, God blessed for ever. Amen.

1Co 1:3 — Grace *be* unto you, and peace, from God our Father, and *from* the Lord Jesus Christ.

1Co 2:8 — Which none of the princes of this world knew: for had they known *it,* they would not have crucified the Lord of glory.

1Co 8:6 — But to us *there is but* one God, the Father, of whom *are* all things, and we in him; and one Lord Jesus Christ, by whom *are* all things, and we by him.

1Co 10:9 — Neither let us tempt Christ, as some of them also tempted, and were destroyed of serpents.

1Co 15:47 — The first man *is* of the earth, earthy: the second man *is* the Lord from heaven.

2Co 1:2 — Grace be to you and peace from God our Father, and *from* the Lord Jesus Christ.

Gal 1:1 — Paul, an apostle, (not of men, neither by man, but by Jesus Christ, and God the Father, who raised him from the dead;)

Gal 1:3 — Grace *be* to you and peace from God the Father, and *from* our Lord Jesus Christ,

Eph 1:2 — Grace *be* to you, and peace, from God our Father, and *from* the Lord Jesus Christ.

Php 1:2 — Grace *be* unto you, and peace, from God our Father, and *from* the Lord Jesus Christ.

Col 1:2 — To the saints and faithful brethren in Christ which are at Colosse: Grace *be* unto you, and peace, from God our Father and the Lord Jesus Christ.

1Th 1:1 — Paul, and Silvanus, and Timotheus, unto the church of the Thessalonians *which is* in God the Father and *in* the Lord Jesus Christ: Grace *be* unto you, and peace, from God our Father, and the Lord Jesus Christ.

1Th 3:11 — Now God himself and our Father, and our Lord Jesus Christ, direct our way unto you.

1Ti 3:16 — And without controversy great is the mystery of godliness: God was manifest in the flesh, justified in the Spirit, seen of angels, preached unto the Gentiles, believed on in the world, received up into glory.

2Ti 1:2 — To Timothy, *my* dearly beloved son: Grace, mercy, *and* peace, from God the Father and Christ Jesus our Lord.

Tit 2:13 — Looking for that blessed hope, and the glorious appearing of the great God and our Saviour Jesus Christ;

Heb 1:8 — But unto the Son *he saith,* Thy throne, O God, *is* for ever and ever: a sceptre of righteousness *is* the sceptre of thy kingdom.

Heb 1:10 — And, Thou, Lord, in the beginning hast laid the foundation of the earth; and the heavens are the works of thine hands:

1Pe 2:8 — And a stone of stumbling, and a rock of offence, *even to them* which stumble at the word, being disobedient: whereunto also they were appointed.

1Jn 5:20 — *And* we know that the Son of God is come, and hath given us an understanding, that we may know him that is true, and we are in him that is true, *even* in his Son Jesus Christ. This is the true God, and eternal life.

See: Jesus, Creator
See: Jesus, Son of God
See: Jesus, Son of Man
See: Judgment
See: Trinity

JESUS, Eternity of

Ps 102:24–27; Pr 8:22–25; Mk 12:36–37; Jn 1:1–2; 17:24–25; Heb 1:10–12; 7:24–25; 1Jn 1:1–2; 2:13–14; Rev 1:17–18; 5:13–14

Isa 9:6 — For unto us a child is born, unto us a son is given: and the government shall be upon his shoulder: and his name shall be called Wonderful, Counsellor, The mighty God, The everlasting Father, The Prince of Peace.

Mic 5:2 — But thou, Bethlehem Ephratah, *though* thou be little among the thousands of Judah, *yet* out of thee shall he come forth unto me *that is* to be ruler in Israel; whose goings forth *have been* from of old, from everlasting.

Jn 1:4 — In him was life; and the life was the light of men.

Jn 1:15 — John bare witness of him, and cried, saying, This was he of whom I spake, He that cometh after me is preferred before me: for he was before me.

Jn 6:62 — *What* and if ye shall see the Son of man ascend up where he was before?

Jn 8:23 — And he said unto them, Ye are from beneath; I am from above: ye are of this world; I am not of this world.

Jn 8:58 — Jesus said unto them, Verily, verily, I say unto you, Before Abraham was, I am.

Jn 12:41 — These things said Esaias, when he saw his glory, and spake of him.

Jn 17:5 — And now, O Father, glorify thou me with thine own self with the glory which I had with thee before the world was.

Eph 3:21 — Unto him *be* glory in the church by Christ Jesus throughout all ages, world without end. Amen.

Eph 4:10 — He that descended is the same also that ascended up far above all heavens, that he might fill all things.)

Col 1:17 — And he is before all things, and by him all things consist.

2Ti 1:9 — Who hath saved us, and called *us* with an holy calling, not according to our works, but according to his own purpose and grace, which was given us in Christ Jesus before the world began,

Heb 6:20 — Whither the forerunner is for us entered, *even* Jesus, made an high priest for ever after the order of Melchisedec.

Heb 7:16 — Who is made, not after the law of a carnal commandment, but after the power of an endless life.

Heb 13:8 — Jesus Christ the same yesterday, and to day, and for ever.

1Pe 1:20 — Who verily was foreordained before the foundation of the world, but was manifest in these last times for you,

Rev 1:8 — I am Alpha and Omega, the beginning and the ending, saith the Lord, which is, and which was, and which is to come, the Almighty.

Rev 1:11 — Saying, I am Alpha and Omega, the first and the last: and, What thou seest, write in a book, and send *it* unto the seven churches which are in Asia; unto Ephesus, and unto Smyrna, and unto Pergamos, and unto Thyatira, and unto Sardis, and unto Philadelphia, and unto Laodicea.

See: Jesus, Preexistence of

JESUS, Exaltation of

Ps 2:8–9; 24:7–10; Jn 13:31–32; Ac 2:33–34; 3:20–21; 7:55–56; Php 2:9–11; Heb 10:12–13

Ps 68:18 — Thou hast ascended on high, thou hast led captivity captive: thou hast received gifts for men; yea, *for* the rebellious also, that the LORD God might dwell *among them.*

Mk 16:19 — So then after the Lord had spoken unto them, he was received up into heaven, and sat on the right hand of God.

Lk 22:69 — Hereafter shall the Son of man sit on the right hand of the power of God.

Lk 24:26 — Ought not Christ to have suffered these things, and to enter into his glory?

Jn 7:39 — (But this spake he of the Spirit, which they that believe on him should receive: for the Holy Ghost was not yet *given;* because that Jesus was not yet glorified.)

Jn 17:5 — And now, O Father, glorify thou me with thine own self with the glory which I had with thee before the world was.

Ac 5:31 — Him hath God exalted with his right hand *to be* a Prince and a Saviour, for to give repentance to Israel, and forgiveness of sins.

Ro 8:17 — And if children, then heirs; heirs of God, and joint-heirs with Christ; if so be that we suffer with *him,* that we may be also glorified together.

Ro 8:34 — Who *is* he that condemneth? *It is* Christ that died, yea rather, that is risen again, who is even at the right hand of God, who also maketh intercession for us.

Eph 1:20 — Which he wrought in Christ, when he raised him from the dead, and set *him* at his own right hand in the heavenly *places,*

Eph 4:8 — Wherefore he saith, When he ascended up on high, he led captivity captive, and gave gifts unto men.

Eph 4:10 — He that descended is the same also that ascended up far above all heavens, that he might fill all things.)

Col 2:15 — *And* having spoiled principalities and powers, he made a shew of them openly, triumphing over them in it.

Col 3:1 — If ye then be risen with Christ, seek those things which are above, where Christ sitteth on the right hand of God.

1Ti 3:16 — And without controversy great is the mystery of godliness: God was manifest in the flesh, justified in the Spirit, seen of angels, preached unto the Gentiles, believed on in the world, received up into glory.

Heb 1:3 — Who being the brightness of *his* glory, and the express image of his person, and upholding all things by the word of his power, when he had by himself purged our sins, sat down on the right hand of the Majesty on high;

Heb 2:9 — But we see Jesus, who was made a little lower than the angels for the suffering of death, crowned with glory and honour; that he by the grace of God should taste death for every man.

Heb 4:10 — For he that is entered into his rest, he also hath ceased from his own works, as God *did* from his.

Heb 4:14 — Seeing then that we have a great high priest, that is passed into the heavens, Jesus the Son of God, let us hold fast *our* profession.

Heb 6:20 — Whither the forerunner is for us entered, *even* Jesus, made an high priest for ever after the order of Melchisedec.

Heb 7:26 — For such an high priest became us, *who is* holy, harmless, undefiled, separate from sinners, and made higher than the heavens;

Heb 8:1 — Now of the things which we have spoken *this is* the sum: We have such an high priest, who is set on the right hand of the throne of the Majesty in the heavens;

Heb 9:12 — Neither by the blood of goats and calves, but by his own blood he entered in once into the holy place, having obtained eternal redemption *for us.*

Heb 9:24 — For Christ is not entered into the holy places made with hands, *which are* the figures of the true; but into heaven itself, now to appear in the presence of God for us:

Heb 12:2 — Looking unto Jesus the author and finisher of *our* faith; who for the joy that was set before him endured the cross, despising the shame, and is set down at the right hand of the throne of God.

1Pe 3:22 — Who is gone into heaven, and is on the right hand of God; angels and authorities and powers being made subject unto him.

JESUS, Faith in

*See: **Faith**

*See: **Salvation; conditions of**

JESUS, Genealogy of *See: Jesus, History of

JESUS, Healing by *See: Miracles, of Jesus

JESUS, History of

- **Genealogy of.**
  Mt 1:1–17; Lk 3:23–38

- **Facts before the birth of.**
  - **The angel Gabriel appears to Mary (Nazareth).**
    Lk 1:26–38
  - **Mary visits Elisabeth (Hebron).**
    Lk 1:39–56
  - **Mary's magnificat (Hebron).**
    Lk 1:46–55
  - **An angel appears to Joseph concerning Mary.**
    Mt 1:18–25

- **Birth of (Bethlehem).**
  Lk 2:1–7

- **Angels appear to the shepherds.**
  Lk 2:8–20

- **Magi visit (Bethlehem).**
  Mt 2:1–12

- **Circumcision of (Bethlehem).**
  Lk 2:21 — And when eight days were accomplished for the circumcising of the child, his name was called JESUS, which was so named of the angel before he was conceived in the womb.

- **Is presented in the temple (Jerusalem).**
  Lk 2:21–38

- **Flight into, and return from, Egypt.**
  Mt 2:13–23

- **Disputes with the doctors in the temple (Jerusalem).**
  Lk 2:41–52

- **Is baptized by Jn (Jordan).**
  Mt 3:13–17; Mk 1:9–11; Lk 3:21–23

- **Temptation of (Desert of Judaea).**
  Mt 4:1–11; Mk 1:12–13; Lk 4:1–13

- **John's testimony concerning him.**
  Jn 1:1–18

- **Testimony of John the Baptist concerning (Bethabara).**
  Jn 1:19–34

- **Disciples adhere to.**
  Jn 1:35–51

- **Miracle at Cana of Galilee.**
  Jn 2:1–12

- **Drives the money changers from the temple (Jerusalem).**
  Jn 2:13–25

- **Nicodemus comes to (Jerusalem).**
  Jn 3:1–21

- **Baptizes (Aenon).**
  Jn 3:22 — After these things came Jesus and his disciples into the land of Judaea; and there he tarried with them, and baptized.

  Jn 4:2 — (Though Jesus himself baptized not, but his disciples,)

- **Returns to Galilee.**
  Jn 4:1–3

  Mt 4:12 — Now when Jesus had heard that John was cast into prison, he departed into Galilee;

Mk 1:14 — Now after that John was put in prison, Jesus came into Galilee, preaching the gospel of the kingdom of God,

Lk 4:14 — And Jesus returned in the power of the Spirit into Galilee: and there went out a fame of him through all the region round about.

• Visits Sychar, and teaches the Samaritan woman.

Jn 4:4–42

• Teaches in Galilee.

Mk 1:14–15; Lk 4:14–15; Jn 4:43–45

Mt 4:17 — From that time Jesus began to preach, and to say, Repent: for the kingdom of heaven is at hand.

• Heals a nobleman's son of Capernaum (Cana of Galilee).

Jn 4:46–54

• Is rejected by the people of Nazareth; dwells at Capernaum.

Mt 4:13–16; Lk 4:16–31

• Chooses Peter, Andrew, James, and John as disciples; miracle of the draught of fishes (Capernaum).

Mt 4:18–22; Mk 1:16–20; Lk 5:1–11

• Preaches throughout Galilee.

Mt 4:23–25; Mk 1:35–39; Lk 4:42–44

• Heals a demoniac (Capernaum).

Mk 1:21–28; Lk 4:31–37

• Heals Peter's mother-in-law (Capernaum).

Mt 8:14–17; Mk 1:29–34; Lk 4:38–41

• Heals a leper in Galilee.

Mt 8:2–4; Mk 1:40–45; Lk 5:12–16

• Heals a paralytic (Capernaum).

Mt 9:2–8; Mk 2:1–12; Lk 5:17–26

• Calls Matthew (Capernaum).

Mk 2:13–14; Lk 5:27–28

Mt 9:9 — And as Jesus passed forth from thence, he saw a man, named Matthew, sitting at the receipt of custom: and he saith unto him, Follow me. And he arose, and followed him.

• Heals an impotent man on the Sabbath day, is persecuted, and makes his defense.

Jn 5:1–47

• Defines the law of the Sabbath on the occasion of his disciples plucking the ears of corn (Capernaum).

Mt 12:1–8; Mk 2:23–28; Lk 6:1–5

• Heals a man having a withered hand (Capernaum).

Mt 12:9–14; Mk 3:1–6; Lk 6:6–11

• Withdraws from Capernaum to the Sea of Galilee, where he heals many.

Mt 12:15–21; Mk 3:7–12

• Goes up into a mountain, and calls and ordains twelve disciples (Galilee).

Mt 10:2–4; Mk 3:13–19; Lk 6:12–19

• Delivers the "Sermon on the Mount" (Galilee).

Mt 5:1–7:29; Lk 6:20–49

• Heals the servant of the centurion (near Capernaum).

Mt 8:5–13; Lk 7:1–10

• Raises from the dead the son of the widow of Nain.

Lk 7:11–17

• Receives the message from John the Baptist (Galilee).

Mt 11:2–19; Lk 7:18–35

• Upbraids the unbelieving cities about Capernaum.

Mt 11:20–30

• Anointed by a sinful woman (Capernaum).

Lk 7:36–50

• Preaches in the cities of Galilee.

Lk 8:1–3

• Heals a demoniac, and denounces the scribes and Pharisees (Galilee).

Mt 12:22–37; Mk 3:19–30; Lk 11:14–26

• Replies to the scribes and Pharisees who seek a sign from him (Galilee).

Mt 12:38–45; Lk 11:16–36

• Denounces the Pharisees and other hypocrites (Galilee).

Lk 11:37–54

• Discourses to his disciples (Galilee).

Lk 12:1–59

• Parable of the barren fig tree (Galilee).

Lk 13:6–9

• Parable of the sower (Sea of Galilee).

Mt 13:1–23; Mk 4:1–25; Lk 8:4–18

• Parable of the tares, and other teachings (Galilee).

Mk 4:26–34; 13:24–35

• Crosses the Sea of Galilee, and stills the tempest.

Mt 8:18–27; Mk 4:35–41; Lk 8:22–25

• Miracle of the swine (Gadara).

Mt 8:28–33; Mk 5:1–21; Lk 8:26–40

• Returns to Capernaum.

Mt 9:1 — And he entered into a ship, and passed over, and came into his own city.

Mk 5:21 — And when Jesus was passed over again by ship unto the other side, much people gathered unto him: and he was nigh unto the sea.

Lk 8:40 — And it came to pass, that, when Jesus was returned, the people *gladly* received him: for they were all waiting for him.

• Eats with publicans and sinners, and discourses on fasting (Capernaum).

Mt 9:10–17; Mk 2:15–22; Lk 5:29–39

• Raises to life daughter of Jairus; heals the woman who has issue of blood (Capernaum).
Mt 9:18–26; Mk 5:22–43; Lk 8:41–56

• Heals two blind men, and casts out a dumb spirit (Capernaum).
Mt 9:27–34

• Returns to Nazareth.
Mt 13:53–58; Mk 6:1–6

• Teaches in various cities in Galilee.
Mt 9:35–38

• Instructs his disciples, and empowers them to heal diseases and cast out unclean spirits.
Mt 10:1–42; Mk 6:6–13; Lk 9:1–6

• Herod falsely supposes him to be John, whom he had beheaded.
Mt 14:1–2, 6–12; Mk 6:14–16, 21–29; Lk 9:7–9

• The 12 return; goes to the desert; multitudes follow; feeds 5000 (Sea of Galilee).
Mt 14:13–21; Mk 6:30–44; Lk 9:10–17; Jn 6:1–14

• Walks on the sea (Galilee).
Mt 14:22–36; Mk 6:45–56; Jn 6:15–21

• Teaches in the synagogue in Capernaum.
Jn 6:22–65

• Disciples forsake him (Capernaum).
Jn 6:66–71

• He justifies his disciples in eating without washing their hands (Capernaum).
Mt 15:1–20; Mk 7:1–23

• Heals the daughter of the Syrophenician woman (Tyre and Sidon).
Mt 15:21–28; Mk 7:24–30

• Heals a dumb man (Decapolis).
Mt 15:29–31; Mk 7:31–37

• Feeds four thousand.
Mt 15:32–39; Mk 8:1–9

• Refuses to give a sign to the Pharisees (region of Magdala).
Mt 16:1–4; Mk 8:10–12

• Cautions his disciples against the leaven of hypocrisy (Sea of Galilee).
Mt 16:4–12; Mk 8:13–21

• Heals a blind man (Bethsaida).
Mk 8:22–26

• Foretells his death and resurrection (near Caesarea Philippi).
Mt 16:21–28; Mk 8:31–9:1; Lk 9:22–27

• Is transfigured.
Mt 17:1–13; Mk 9:2–13; Lk 9:28–36

• Heals a demoniac (Caesarea Philippi).
Mt 17:14–21; Mk 9:14–29; Lk 9:37–43

• Foretells his death and resurrection (Galilee).
Mt 17:22–23; Mk 9:30–32; Lk 9:43–45

• Miracle of tribute money in the fish's mouth.
Mt 17:24–27

• Reproves the ambition of his disciples (Capernaum).
Mt 18:1–35; Mk 9:33–50; Lk 9:46–50

• Reproves the intolerance of his disciples.
Mk 9:38–39; Lk 9:49–50

• Journeys to Jerusalem to attend the Feast of Tabernacles, passing through Samaria.
Lk 9:51–62; Jn 7:2–11

• Commissions the seventy (Samaria).
Lk 10:1–16

• Heals ten lepers.
Lk 17:11–19

• Teaches in Jerusalem at the Feast of Tabernacles.
Jn 7:14–8:59

• Answers a lawyer, with the parable of the good Samaritan (Jerusalem).
Lk 10:25–37

• Hears the report of the seventy (Jerusalem).
Lk 10:17–24

• Teaches in the house of Mary, Martha, and Lazarus, in Bethany.
Lk 10:38–42

• Teaches his disciples to pray.
Lk 11:1–13

• Heals a blind man, who, because of his faith in Jesus, was excommunicated.
Jn 9:1–41

• Teaches in Jerusalem.
Jn 9:39–10:21

• Teaches in the temple at Jerusalem, at the Feast of Dedication.
Jn 10:22–39

• Goes to Bethabara to escape violence from the rulers (east of the Jordan).
Jn 10:40–42; 11:3–16

• Returns to Bethany, and raises Lazarus from the dead.
Jn 11:1–46

• Escapes to the city of Ephraim from the conspiracy led by Caiaphas, the high priest (Judaea).
Jn 11:47–54

• Journeys toward Jerusalem to attend the passover; heals and teaches (Peraea).
Mt 19:1–2; Lk 13:10–35

Mk 10:1 — And he arose from thence, and cometh into the coasts of Judaea by the farther side of Jordan: and the people resort unto him again; and, as he was wont, he taught them again.

• Dines with a Pharisee on the Sabbath (Peraea).
Lk 14:1–24

• Teaches the multitude the conditions of discipleship (Peraea).
Lk 14:25–35

• Parables: lost sheep, lost piece of silver, prodigal son, unjust steward (Peraea).
Lk 15:1–16:13

• Reproves the hypocrisy of the Pharisees (Peraea).
Lk 16:1–31

• Enunciates the parable of the rich man and Lazarus (Peraea).
Lk 16:19–31

• Teaches his disciples concerning offenses, meekness, and humility (Peraea).
Lk 17:1–10

• Teaches the Pharisees concerning the coming of his kingdom (Peraea).
Lk 17:20–37

• Enunciates the parables of the unjust judge, and the Pharisee and publican praying in the temple (Peraea).
Lk 18:1–14

• Interprets the law concerning marriage and divorce (Peraea).
Mt 19:3–12; Mk 10:2–12

• Blesses little children (Peraea).
Mt 19:13–15; Mk 10:13–16; Lk 18:15–17

• Receives the rich young ruler, who asks what he shall do to inherit eternal life (Peraea).
Mt 19:16–22; Mk 10:17–22; Lk 18:18–24

• Enunciates the parable of the vineyard (Peraea).
Mt 20:1–16

• Foretells his death and resurrection (Peraea).
Mt 20:17–19; Mk 10:32–34; Lk 18:31–34

• Listens to the mother of James and John in behalf of her sons (Peraea).
Mt 20:20–28; Mk 10:35–45

• Heals two blind men at Jericho.
Mt 20:29–34; Mk 10:46–50; Lk 18:35–43

• Visits Zacchaeus.
Lk 19:1–10

• Enunciates the parable of the pounds (Jericho).
Lk 19:11–28

• Goes to Bethany six days before the passover.
Jn 12:1–9

• Triumphal entry into Jerusalem, while the people throw palm branches in the way.
Mt 21:1–11; Mk 11:1–11; Lk 19:29–44; Jn 12:12–19

• Enters the temple.
Mt 21:12 — And Jesus went into the temple of God, and cast out all them that sold and bought in the temple, and overthrew the tables of the money-changers, and the seats of them that sold doves,
Mk 11:11 — And Jesus entered into Jerusalem, and into the temple: and when he had looked round about upon all things, and now the eventide was come, he went out unto Bethany with the twelve.
Lk 19:45 — And he went into the temple, and began to cast out them that sold therein, and them that bought;

• Drives the money changers out of the temple.
Mt 21:12–13; Lk 19:45–46

• Heals the infirm in the temple.
Mt 21:14 — And the blind and the lame came to him in the temple; and he healed them.

• Teaches daily in the temple.
Lk 19:47–48

• Performs the miracle of causing the barren fig tree to wither.
Mt 21:17–22; Mk 11:12–14, 20–22

• Enunciates the parable of the two sons.
Mt 21:28–31

• Enunciates the parable of the wicked husbandmen.
Mt 21:33–46; Mk 12:1–12; Lk 20:9–19

• Enunciates the parable of the marriage.
Mt 22:1–14; Lk 14:16–24

• Tested by the Pharisees and Herodians, and enunciates the duty of the citizen to his government.
Mt 22:15–22; Mk 12:13–17; Lk 20:20–26

• Tried by the Sadducees concerning the resurrection of the dead.
Mt 22:23–33; Mk 12:18–27; Lk 20:27–40

• Tried by a lawyer.
Mt 22:34–40; Mk 12:28–34

• Exposes the hypocrisies of the scribes and Pharisees.
Mt 23:1–39; Mk 12:38–40; Lk 20:45–47

• Extols the widow who casts two mites into the treasury.
Mk 12:41–44; Lk 21:1–4

• Verifies the prophecy of Isaiah concerning the unbelieving Jews.
Jn 12:37–50

• Foretells the destruction of the temple, and of Jerusalem.
Mt 24:1–51; Mk 13:1–37; Lk 21:5–36

• Laments over Jerusalem.
Lk 19:41–44

Mt 23:37 — O Jerusalem, Jerusalem, *thou* that killest the prophets, and stonest them which are sent unto thee, how often would I have gathered thy children together, even as a hen gathereth her chickens under *her* wings, and ye would not!

• Enunciates the parables of the ten virgins and of the talents.

Mt 25:1–30

• Foretells the scenes of the day of judgment (Mount of Olives).

Mt 25:31–46

• Anointed with the box of precious ointment (Bethany).

Mt 26:6–13; Mk 14:3–9; Jn 12:1–8

• Last passover, and institution of the sacrament of the holy eucharist.

Mt 26:17–30; Mk 14:12–25; Lk 22:7–20

• Washes the disciples' feet.

Jn 13:1–17

• Foretells his betrayal.

Mk 14:18–21

Mt 26:23 — And he answered and said, He that dippeth *his* hand with me in the dish, the same shall betray me.

Lk 22:21 — But, behold, the hand of him that betrayeth me *is* with me on the table.

Jn 13:18 — I speak not of you all: I know whom I have chosen: but that the scripture may be fulfilled, He that eateth bread with me hath lifted up his heel against me.

• Accuses Judas of his betrayal.

Mt 26:21–25; Mk 14:18–21; Lk 22:21–23; Jn 13:21–30

• Teaches his disciples, and comforts them with promises, and promises the gift of the Holy Spirit.

Jn 14:1–16:33

• Last prayer (Jerusalem).

Jn 17:1–26

• Repairs to Gethsemane (Mount of Olives).

Mt 26:36–46; Mk 14:32–42; Lk 22:39–46

Mt 26:30 — And when they had sung an hymn, they went out into the mount of Olives.

Mk 14:26 — And when they had sung an hymn, they went out into the mount of Olives.

Jn 18:1 — When Jesus had spoken these words, he went forth with his disciples over the brook Cedron, where was a garden, into the which he entered, and his disciples.

• Is betrayed and apprehended (Gethsemane).

Mt 26:47–56; Mk 14:43–54, 66–72; Lk 22:47–53; Jn 18:2–12

• Trial of, before Caiaphas (Jerusalem).

Mt 26:57–58, 69–75; Mk 14:53–54, 66–72; Lk 22:54–62; Jn 18:13–18, 25–27

• Tried by the council.

Mt 26:59–68; Mk 14:55–65; Lk 22:63–71; Jn 18:19–21

• Led by the council to Pilate.

Mt 27:1–2, 11–14; Mk 15:1–5; Lk 23:1–5; Jn 18:28–38

• Arraigned before Herod.

Lk 23:6–12

• Tried before Pilate.

Mt 27:15–26; Mk 15:6–15; Lk 23:13–25; Jn 18:39–19:16

• Mocked by the soldiers.

Mt 27:27–31; Mk 15:16–20

• Is led away to be crucified.

Mt 27:31–34; Mk 15:20–23; Lk 23:26–32; Jn 19:16–17

• Crucified.

Mt 27:35–56; Mk 15:24–41; Lk 23:33–49; Jn 19:18–30

• Taken from the cross and buried.

Mt 27:57–66; Mk 15:42–47; Lk 23:50–56; Jn 19:31–42

• Arises from the dead.

Mt 28:2–15; Mk 16:1–11; Lk 24:1–12; Jn 20:1–18

• Is seen by Mary Magdalene.

Mt 28:1–10; Jn 20:11–17

Mk 16:9 — Now when *Jesus* was risen early the first *day* of the week, he appeared first to Mary Magdalene, out of whom he had cast seven devils.

• Is seen by Peter.

Lk 24:34 — Saying, The Lord is risen indeed, and hath appeared to Simon.

1Co 15:5 — And that he was seen of Cephas, then of the twelve:

• Appears to two disciples who journey to Emmaus.

Mk 16:12–13; Lk 24:13–35

• Appears in the midst of the disciples, when Thomas is absent (Jerusalem).

Mk 16:14–18; Lk 24:36–49; Jn 20:19–23

• Appears in the midst of the disciples, when Thomas was present (Jerusalem).

Jn 20:26–29

• Appears in the midst of the disciples, at the Sea of Galilee.

Jn 21:1–2

Mt 28:16 — Then the eleven disciples went away into Galilee, into a mountain where Jesus had appointed them.

• Appears to the apostles and upwards of five hundred brethren on a mountain in Galilee.

Mt 28:16–20; Ac 10:40–42; 1Co 15:6–7

Ac 13:31 — And he was seen many days of them which came up with him from Galilee to Jerusalem, who are his witnesses unto the people.

• Appears to James, and also to all the apostles (Jerusalem).

Ac 1:3–8

1Co 15:7 — After that, he was seen of James; then of all the apostles.

• Ascends to heaven (Bethany).

Mk 16:19–20; Lk 24:50–53; Ac 1:9–12

• Appears to Paul.

Ac 9:3–17

Ac 18:9 — Then spake the Lord to Paul in the night by a vision, Be not afraid, but speak, and hold not thy peace:

Ac 22:14 — And he said, The God of our fathers hath chosen thee, that thou shouldest know his will, and see that Just One, and shouldest hear the voice of his mouth.

Ac 22:18 — And saw him saying unto me, Make haste, and get thee quickly out of Jerusalem: for they will not receive thy testimony concerning me.

Ac 23:11 — And the night following the Lord stood by him, and said, Be of good cheer, Paul: for as thou hast testified of me in Jerusalem, so must thou bear witness also at Rome.

Ac 26:16 — But rise, and stand upon thy feet: for I have appeared unto thee for this purpose, to make thee a minister and a witness both of these things which thou hast seen, and of those things in the which I will appear unto thee;

1Co 9:1 — Am I not an apostle? am I not free? have I not seen Jesus Christ our Lord? are not ye my work in the Lord?

1Co 15:8 — And last of all he was seen of me also, as of one born out of due time.

- **Stephen's vision of.**

Ac 7:55–56

- **Appears to John on Patmos.**

Rev 1:10–18

JESUS, Holiness of

Isa 11:4–5; Lk 23:40–41; Heb 7:26–28

Ps 45:7 — Thou lovest righteousness, and hatest wickedness: therefore God, thy God, hath anointed thee with the oil of gladness above thy fellows.

Ps 89:19 — Then thou spakest in vision to thy holy one, and saidst, I have laid help upon *one that is* mighty; I have exalted *one* chosen out of the people.

Isa 32:1 — Behold, a king shall reign in righteousness, and princes shall rule in judgment.

Isa 42:21 — The LORD is well pleased for his righteousness' sake; he will magnify the law, and make *it* honourable.

Isa 49:7 — Thus saith the LORD, the Redeemer of Israel, *and* his Holy One, to him whom man despiseth, to him whom the nation abhorreth, to a servant of rulers, Kings shall see and arise, princes also shall worship, because of the LORD that is faithful, *and* the Holy One of Israel, and he shall choose thee.

Isa 50:5 — The Lord GOD hath opened mine ear, and I was not rebellious, neither turned away back.

Isa 53:9 — And he made his grave with the wicked, and with the rich in his death; because he had done no violence, neither *was any* deceit in his mouth.

Isa 59:17 — For he put on righteousness as a breastplate, and an helmet of salvation upon his head; and he put on the garments of vengeance *for* clothing, and was clad with zeal as a cloke.

Jer 23:5 — Behold, the days come, saith the LORD, that I will raise unto David a righteous Branch, and a King shall reign and prosper, and shall execute judgment and justice in the earth.

Zec 9:9 — Rejoice greatly, O daughter of Zion; shout, O daughter of Jerusalem: behold, thy King cometh unto thee: he *is* just, and having salvation; lowly, and riding upon an ass, and upon a colt the foal of an ass.

Mk 1:24 — Saying, Let *us* alone; what have we to do with thee, thou Jesus of Nazareth? art thou come to destroy us? I know thee who thou art, the Holy One of God.

Lk 1:35 — And the angel answered and said unto her, The Holy Ghost shall come upon thee, and the power of the Highest shall overshadow thee: therefore also that holy thing which shall be born of thee shall be called the Son of God.

Lk 4:34 — Saying, Let *us* alone; what have we to do with thee, *thou* Jesus of Nazareth? art thou come to destroy us? I know thee who thou art; the Holy One of God.

Lk 23:47 — Now when the centurion saw what was done, he glorified God, saying, Certainly this was a righteous man.

Jn 5:30 — I can of mine own self do nothing: as I hear, I judge: and my judgment is just; because I seek not mine own will, but the will of the Father which hath sent me.

Jn 7:18 — He that speaketh of himself seeketh his own glory: but he that seeketh his glory that sent him, the same is true, and no unrighteousness is in him.

Jn 8:46 — Which of you convinceth me of sin? And if I say the truth, why do ye not believe me?

Jn 14:30 — Hereafter I will not talk much with you: for the prince of this world cometh, and hath nothing in me.

Jn 16:10 — Of righteousness, because I go to my Father, and ye see me no more;

Ac 3:14 — But ye denied the Holy One and the Just, and desired a murderer to be granted unto you;

Ac 4:27 — For of a truth against thy holy child Jesus, whom thou hast anointed, both Herod, and Pontius Pilate, with the Gentiles, and the people of Israel, were gathered together,

Ac 4:30 — By stretching forth thine hand to heal; and that signs and wonders may be done by the name of thy holy child Jesus.

Ac 13:28 — And though they found no cause of death *in him,* yet desired they Pilate that he should be slain.

Ac 13:35 — Wherefore he saith also in another *Psalm,* Thou shalt not suffer thine Holy One to see corruption.

2Co 4:4 — In whom the god of this world hath blinded the minds of them which believe not, lest the light of the glorious gospel of Christ, who is the image of God, should shine unto them.

2Co 5:21 — For he hath made him *to be* sin for us, who knew no sin; that we might be made the righteousness of God in him.

Heb 1:9 — Thou hast loved righteousness, and hated iniquity; therefore God, *even* thy God, hath anointed thee with the oil of gladness above thy fellows.

Heb 4:15 — For we have not an high priest which cannot be touched with the feeling of our infirmities; but was in all points tempted like as *we are, yet* without sin.

Heb 9:14 — How much more shall the blood of Christ, who through the eternal Spirit offered himself without spot to God, purge your conscience from dead works to serve the living God?

1Pe 1:19 — But with the precious blood of Christ, as of a lamb without blemish and without spot:

1Pe 2:22 — Who did no sin, neither was guile found in his mouth:
1Jn 2:29 — If ye know that he is righteous, ye know that every one that doeth righteousness is born of him.
1Jn 3:5 — And ye know that he was manifested to take away our sins; and in him is no sin.
Rev 3:7 — And to the angel of the church in Philadelphia write; These things saith he that is holy, he that is true, he that hath the key of David, he that openeth, and no man shutteth; and shutteth, and no man openeth;

JESUS, Humanity of

Dt 18:15–19; Mt 16:27–28; 20:30–31; 26:26–28, 36–45; Lk 2:11–14; Php 2:7–8; Heb 2:9–10, 14–18; 1Jn 4:2–3
Ge 3:15 — And I will put enmity between thee and the woman, and between thy seed and her seed; it shall bruise thy head, and thou shalt bruise his heel.
Ps 22:22 — I will declare thy name unto my brethren: in the midst of the congregation will I praise thee.
Isa 8:18 — Behold, I and the children whom the LORD hath given me *are* for signs and for wonders in Israel from the LORD of hosts, which dwelleth in mount Zion.
Isa 9:6 — For unto us a child is born, unto us a son is given: and the government shall be upon his shoulder: and his name shall be called Wonderful, Counsellor, The mighty God, The everlasting Father, The Prince of Peace.
Da 7:13 — I saw in the night visions, and, behold, *one* like the Son of man came with the clouds of heaven, and came to the Ancient of days, and they brought him near before him.
Mt 18:11 — For the Son of man is come to save that which was lost.
Mt 20:28 — Even as the Son of man came not to be ministered unto, but to minister, and to give his life a ransom for many.
Mt 21:9 — And the multitudes that went before, and that followed, cried, saying, Hosanna to the Son of David: Blessed *is* he that cometh in the name of the Lord; Hosanna in the highest.
Mt 26:2 — Ye know that after two days is *the feast of* the passover, and the Son of man is betrayed to be crucified.
Mk 2:28 — Therefore the Son of man is Lord also of the sabbath.
Mk 9:9 — And as they came down from the mountain, he charged them that they should tell no man what things they had seen, till the Son of man were risen from the dead.
Mk 9:12 — And he answered and told them, Elias verily cometh first, and restoreth all things; and how it is written of the Son of man, that he must suffer many things, and be set at nought.
Mk 10:33 — *Saying,* Behold, we go up to Jerusalem; and the Son of man shall be delivered unto the chief priests, and unto the scribes; and they shall condemn him to death, and shall deliver him to the Gentiles:
Mk 10:45 — For even the Son of man came not to be ministered unto, but to minister, and to give his life a ransom for many.
Mk 14:21 — The Son of man indeed goeth, as it is written of him: but woe to that man by whom the Son of man is betrayed! good were it for that man if he had never been born.
Mk 14:34 — And saith unto them, My soul is exceeding sorrowful unto death: tarry ye here, and watch.
Mk 14:42 — Rise up, let us go; lo, he that betrayeth me is at hand.
Mk 14:62 — And Jesus said, I am: and ye shall see the Son of man sitting on the right hand of power, and coming in the clouds of heaven.
Mk 14:64 — Ye have heard the blasphemy: what think ye? And they all condemned him to be guilty of death.
Lk 5:24 — But that ye may know that the Son of man hath power upon earth to forgive sins, (he said unto the sick of the palsy,) I say unto thee, Arise, and take up thy couch, and go into thine house.
Lk 17:22 — And he said unto the disciples, The days will come, when ye shall desire to see one of the days of the Son of man, and ye shall not see *it.*
Lk 17:24 — For as the lightning, that lighteneth out of the one *part* under heaven, shineth unto the other *part* under heaven; so shall also the Son of man be in his day.
Lk 18:31 — Then he took *unto him* the twelve, and said unto them, Behold, we go up to Jerusalem, and all things that are written by the prophets concerning the Son of man shall be accomplished.
Lk 19:10 — For the Son of man is come to seek and to save that which was lost.
Lk 21:36 — Watch ye therefore, and pray always, that ye may be accounted worthy to escape all these things that shall come to pass, and to stand before the Son of man.
Lk 22:48 — But Jesus said unto him, Judas, betrayest thou the Son of man with a kiss?
Lk 22:69 — Hereafter shall the Son of man sit on the right hand of the power of God.
Jn 1:14 — And the Word was made flesh, and dwelt among us, (and we beheld his glory, the glory as of the only begotten of the Father,) full of grace and truth.
Jn 5:27 — And hath given him authority to execute judgment also, because he is the Son of man.
Jn 12:34 — The people answered him, We have heard out of the law that Christ abideth for ever: and how sayest thou, The Son of man must be lifted up? who is this Son of man?
Jn 13:31 — Therefore, when he was gone out, Jesus said, Now is the Son of man glorified, and God is glorified in him.
Ac 7:56 — And said, Behold, I see the heavens opened, and the Son of man standing on the right hand of God.
Ac 17:31 — Because he hath appointed a day, in the which he will judge the world in righteousness by *that* man whom he hath ordained; *whereof* he hath given assurance unto all *men,* in that he hath raised him from the dead.
Gal 4:4 — But when the fulness of the time was come, God sent forth his Son, made of a woman, made under the law,
1Ti 2:5 — For *there is* one God, and one mediator between God and men, the man Christ Jesus;
Heb 10:12 — But this man, after he had offered one sacrifice for sins for ever, sat down on the right hand of God;

2Jn 1:7 — For many deceivers are entered into the world, who confess not that Jesus Christ is come in the flesh. This is a deceiver and an antichrist.

Rev 1:13 — And in the midst of the seven candlesticks *one* like unto the Son of man, clothed with a garment down to the foot, and girt about the paps with a golden girdle.

Rev 14:14 — And I looked, and behold a white cloud, and upon the cloud *one* sat like unto the Son of man, having on his head a golden crown, and in his hand a sharp sickle.

✢See: Jesus, History of

✢See: Jesus, Incarnation of

✢See: Jesus, Prophecies Concerning; coming of

✢See: Jesus, Relation of, to the Father

JESUS, Humility of

Lk 5:27–28; Ac 8:32–33; Php 2:7–8

Zec 9:9 — Rejoice greatly, O daughter of Zion; shout, O daughter of Jerusalem: behold, thy King cometh unto thee: he *is* just, and having salvation; lowly, and riding upon an ass, and upon a colt the foal of an ass.

Mt 9:10 — And it came to pass, as Jesus sat at meat in the house, behold, many publicans and sinners came and sat down with him and his disciples.

Mt 21:5 — Tell ye the daughter of Sion, Behold, thy King cometh unto thee, meek, and sitting upon an ass, and a colt the foal of an ass.

Mk 2:14 — And as he passed by, he saw Levi the *son* of Alphaeus sitting at the receipt of custom, and said unto him, Follow me. And he arose and followed him.

Lk 22:27 — For whether *is* greater, he that sitteth at meat, or he that serveth? *is* not he that sitteth at meat? but I am among you as he that serveth.

Jn 13:5 — After that he poureth water into a bason, and began to wash the disciples' feet, and to wipe *them* with the towel wherewith he was girded.

Jn 13:14 — If I then, *your* Lord and Master, have washed your feet; ye also ought to wash one another's feet.

2Co 8:9 — For ye know the grace of our Lord Jesus Christ, that, though he was rich, yet for your sakes he became poor, that ye through his poverty might be rich.

2Co 10:1 — Now I Paul myself beseech you by the meekness and gentleness of Christ, who in presence *am* base among you, but being absent am bold toward you:

✢See: Jesus, Meekness of

✢See: Meekness

JESUS, Impeccability of

✢See: Jesus, Holiness of

✢See: Jesus, Temptation of

JESUS, in His Name

1Co 6:11 — And such were some of you: but ye are washed, but ye are sanctified, but ye are justified in the name of the Lord Jesus, and by the Spirit of our God.

Php 2:9 — Wherefore God also hath highly exalted him, and given him a name which is above every name:

Col 3:17 — And whatsoever ye do in word or deed, *do* all in the name of the Lord Jesus, giving thanks to God and the Father by him.

Rev 19:16 — And he hath on *his* vesture and on his thigh a name written, KING OF KINGS, AND LORD OF LORDS.

• To be confessed.

2Ti 2:19 — Nevertheless the foundation of God standeth sure, having this seal, The Lord knoweth them that are his. And, Let every one that nameth the name of Christ depart from iniquity.

• Prayer.

Jn 16:23–24

Jn 14:13 — And whatsoever ye shall ask in my name, that will I do, that the Father may be glorified in the Son.

Jn 16:26 — At that day ye shall ask in my name: and I say not unto you, that I will pray the Father for you:

Eph 5:20 — Giving thanks always for all things unto God and the Father in the name of our Lord Jesus Christ;

Col 3:17 — And whatsoever ye do in word or deed, *do* all in the name of the Lord Jesus, giving thanks to God and the Father by him.

Heb 13:15 — By him therefore let us offer the sacrifice of praise to God continually, that is, the fruit of *our* lips giving thanks to his name.

• Miracles performed.

Ac 3:6 — Then Peter said, Silver and gold have I none; but such as I have give I thee: In the name of Jesus Christ of Nazareth rise up and walk.

Ac 4:10 — Be it known unto you all, and to all the people of Israel, that by the name of Jesus Christ of Nazareth, whom ye crucified, whom God raised from the dead, *even* by him doth this man stand here before you whole.

Ac 19:13 — Then certain of the vagabond Jews, exorcists, took upon them to call over them which had evil spirits the name of the Lord Jesus, saying, We adjure you by Jesus whom Paul preacheth.

• Baptism.

Mt 28:19 — Go ye therefore, and teach all nations, baptizing them in the name of the Father, and of the Son, and of the Holy Ghost:

Ac 2:38 — Then Peter said unto them, Repent, and be baptized every one of you in the name of Jesus Christ for the remission of sins, and ye shall receive the gift of the Holy Ghost.

• Preaching.

Lk 24:47 — And that repentance and remission of sins should be preached in his name among all nations, beginning at Jerusalem.

• Faith.

Mt 12:21 — And in his name shall the Gentiles trust.

Jn 1:12 — But as many as received him, to them gave he power to become the sons of God, *even* to them that believe on his name:

Jn 2:23 — Now when he was in Jerusalem at the passover, in the feast *day,* many believed in his name, when they saw the miracles which he did.

• Remission of sins.

Lk 24:47 — <u>And that repentance and remission of sins should be preached in his name among all nations, beginning at Jerusalem.</u>

Ac 10:43 — To him give all the prophets witness, that through his name whosoever believeth in him shall receive remission of sins.

1Jn 2:12 — I write unto you, little children, because your sins are forgiven you for his name's sake.

• Life.

Jn 20:31 — But these are written, that ye might believe that Jesus is the Christ, the Son of God; and that believing ye might have life through his name.

• Salvation.

Ac 4:12 — Neither is there salvation in any other: for there is none other name under heaven given among men, whereby we must be saved.

Ac 10:43 — To him give all the prophets witness, that through his name whosoever believeth in him shall receive remission of sins.

✧See: Jesus, Intercession of

✧See: Jesus, Priesthood of

JESUS, Incarnation of

Dt 18:15–19; Ps 40:7–8; 89:35–36; Isa 7:14–16; Mic 5:2–3; Mt 1:16–18; 2:5–6; 13:55–56; Lk 1:26–35, 38–56; 2:1–21; 3:23–38; Php 2:7–8; Heb 2:9–17; 1Jn 1:1–3; 4:2–3

Ge 3:15 — And I will put enmity between thee and the woman, and between thy seed and her seed; it shall bruise thy head, and thou shalt bruise his heel.

Ge 12:3 — And I will bless them that bless thee, and curse him that curseth thee: and in thee shall all families of the earth be blessed.

Ge 17:7 — And I will establish my covenant between me and thee and thy seed after thee in their generations for an everlasting covenant, to be a God unto thee, and to thy seed after thee.

Ge 22:18 — And in thy seed shall all the nations of the earth be blessed; because thou hast obeyed my voice.

2Sa 7:12 — And when thy days be fulfilled, and thou shalt sleep with thy fathers, I will set up thy seed after thee, which shall proceed out of thy bowels, and I will establish his kingdom.

1Ch 5:2 — For Judah prevailed above his brethren, and of him *came* the chief ruler; but the birthright *was* Joseph's:)

Ps 2:7 — I will declare the decree: the LORD hath said unto me, Thou *art* my Son; this day have I begotten thee.

Ps 80:17 — Let thy hand be upon the man of thy right hand, upon the son of man *whom* thou madest strong for thyself.

Ps 89:19 — Then thou spakest in vision to thy holy one, and saidst, I have laid help upon *one that is* mighty; I have exalted *one* chosen out of the people.

Isa 9:6 — For unto us a child is born, unto us a son is given: and the government shall be upon his shoulder: and his name shall be called Wonderful, Counsellor, The mighty God, The everlasting Father, The Prince of Peace.

Isa 11:1 — And there shall come forth a rod out of the stem of Jesse, and a Branch shall grow out of his roots:

Isa 32:2 — And a man shall be as an hiding place from the wind, and a covert from the tempest; as rivers of water in a dry place, as the shadow of a great rock in a weary land.

Isa 49:1 — Listen, O isles, unto me; and hearken, ye people, from far; The LORD hath called me from the womb; from the bowels of my mother hath he made mention of my name.

Isa 49:5 — And now, saith the LORD that formed me from the womb *to be* his servant, to bring Jacob again to him, Though Israel be not gathered, yet shall I be glorious in the eyes of the LORD, and my God shall be my strength.

Jer 23:5 — Behold, the days come, saith the LORD, that I will raise unto David a righteous Branch, and a King shall reign and prosper, and shall execute judgment and justice in the earth.

Mt 1:1 — The book of the generation of Jesus Christ, the son of David, the son of Abraham.

Mt 1:23 — Behold, a virgin shall be with child, and shall bring forth a son, and they shall call his name Emmanuel, which being interpreted is, God with us.

Mt 8:20 — And Jesus saith unto him, <u>The foxes have holes, and the birds of the air *have* nests; but the Son of man hath not where to lay *his* head.</u>

Mt 22:45 — <u>If David then call him Lord, how is he his son?</u>

Lk 24:39 — <u>Behold my hands and my feet, that it is I myself: handle me, and see; for a spirit hath not flesh and bones, as ye see me have.</u>

Jn 1:14 — And the Word was made flesh, and dwelt among us, (and we beheld his glory, the glory as of the only begotten of the Father,) full of grace and truth.

Jn 7:42 — Hath not the scripture said, That Christ cometh of the seed of David, and out of the town of Bethlehem, where David was?

Jn 20:27 — Then saith he to Thomas, <u>reach hither thy finger, and behold my hands; and reach hither thy hand, and thrust *it* into my side: and be not faithless, but believing.</u>

Ac 2:30 — Therefore being a prophet, and knowing that God had sworn with an oath to him, that of the fruit of his loins, according to the flesh, he would raise up Christ to sit on his throne;

Ac 3:22 — For Moses truly said unto the fathers, A prophet shall the Lord your God raise up unto you of your brethren, like unto me; him shall ye hear in all things whatsoever he shall say unto you.

Ac 13:23 — Of this man's seed hath God according to *his* promise raised unto Israel a Saviour, Jesus:

Ac 13:33 — God hath fulfilled the same unto us their children, in that he hath raised up Jesus again; as it is also written in the second Psalm, Thou art my Son, this day have I begotten thee.

Ro 1:3 — Concerning his Son Jesus Christ our Lord, which was made of the seed of David according to the flesh;

Ro 8:3 — For what the law could not do, in that it was weak through the flesh, God sending his own Son in the likeness of sinful flesh, and for sin, condemned sin in the flesh:

Ro 9:5 — Whose *are* the fathers, and of whom as concerning the flesh Christ *came,* who is over all, God blessed for ever. Amen.

1Co 15:47 — The first man *is* of the earth, earthy: the second man *is* the Lord from heaven.

2Co 5:16 — Wherefore henceforth know we no man after the flesh: yea, though we have known Christ after the flesh, yet now henceforth know we *him* no more.

Gal 3:16 — Now to Abraham and his seed were the promises made. He saith not, And to seeds, as of many; but as of one, And to thy seed, which is Christ.

Gal 4:4 — But when the fulness of the time was come, God sent forth his Son, made of a woman, made under the law,

Col 1:15 — Who is the image of the invisible God, the firstborn of every creature:

1Ti 3:16 — And without controversy great is the mystery of godliness: God was manifest in the flesh, justified in the Spirit, seen of angels, preached unto the Gentiles, believed on in the world, received up into glory.

Heb 1:3 — Who being the brightness of *his* glory, and the express image of his person, and upholding all things by the word of his power, when he had by himself purged our sins, sat down on the right hand of the Majesty on high;

Heb 1:6 — And again, when he bringeth in the firstbegotten into the world, he saith, And let all the angels of God worship him.

Heb 7:14 — For *it is* evident that our Lord sprang out of Juda; of which tribe Moses spake nothing concerning priesthood.

Heb 10:5 — Wherefore when he cometh into the world, he saith, Sacrifice and offering thou wouldest not, but a body hast thou prepared me:

2Jn 1:7 — For many deceivers are entered into the world, who confess not that Jesus Christ is come in the flesh. This is a deceiver and an antichrist.

Rev 22:16 — I Jesus have sent mine angel to testify unto you these things in the churches. I am the root and the offspring of David, *and* the bright and morning star.

See: Jesus, Humanity of

See: Jesus, Relation of, to the Father

JESUS, Intercession of **See: Jesus, Mediation of**

JESUS, Judge

Isa 11:3–4; Mal 3:2–3; Mt 25:31–34; 1Co 4:4–5

Ps 72:2 — He shall judge thy people with righteousness, and thy poor with judgment.

Ps 72:4 — He shall judge the poor of the people, he shall save the children of the needy, and shall break in pieces the oppressor.

Ps 75:2 — When I shall receive the congregation I will judge uprightly.

Ps 96:13 — Before the LORD: for he cometh, for he cometh to judge the earth: he shall judge the world with righteousness, and the people with his truth.

Ps 110:6 — He shall judge among the heathen, he shall fill *the places* with the dead bodies; he shall wound the heads over many countries.

Isa 2:4 — And he shall judge among the nations, and shall rebuke many people: and they shall beat their swords into plowshares, and their spears into pruninghooks: nation shall not lift up sword against nation, neither shall they learn war any more.

Mic 4:3 — And he shall judge among many people, and rebuke strong nations afar off; and they shall beat their swords into plowshares, and their spears into pruninghooks: nation shall not lift up a sword against nation, neither shall they learn war any more.

Mic 5:1 — Now gather thyself in troops, O daughter of troops: he hath laid siege against us: they shall smite the judge of Israel with a rod upon the cheek.

Mt 3:12 — Whose fan *is* in his hand, and he will throughly purge his floor, and gather his wheat into the garner; but he will burn up the chaff with unquenchable fire.

Mt 19:28 — And Jesus said unto them, Verily I say unto you, That ye which have followed me, in the regeneration when the Son of man shall sit in the throne of his glory, ye also shall sit upon twelve thrones, judging the twelve tribes of Israel.

Lk 3:17 — Whose fan *is* in his hand, and he will throughly purge his floor, and will gather the wheat into his garner; but the chaff he will burn with fire unquenchable.

Ac 10:42 — And he commanded us to preach unto the people, and to testify that it is he which was ordained of God *to be* the Judge of quick and dead.

Ac 17:31 — Because he hath appointed a day, in the which he will judge the world in righteousness by *that* man whom he hath ordained; *whereof* he hath given assurance unto all *men,* in that he hath raised him from the dead.

Ro 2:16 — In the day when God shall judge the secrets of men by Jesus Christ according to my gospel.

Ro 14:10 — But why dost thou judge thy brother? or why dost thou set at nought thy brother? for we shall all stand before the judgment seat of Christ.

2Co 5:10 — For we must all appear before the judgment seat of Christ; that every one may receive the things *done* in *his* body, according to that he hath done, whether *it be* good or bad.

2Ti 4:1 — I charge *thee* therefore before God, and the Lord Jesus Christ, who shall judge the quick and the dead at his appearing and his kingdom;

2Ti 4:8 — Henceforth there is laid up for me a crown of righteousness, which the Lord, the righteous judge, shall give me at that day: and not to me only, but unto all them also that love his appearing.

Jas 5:9 — Grudge not one against another, brethren, lest ye be condemned: behold, the judge standeth before the door.

Rev 2:23 — And I will kill her children with death; and all the churches shall know that I am he which searcheth the reins and hearts: and I will give unto every one of you according to your works.

See: God, Judge, and His Justice

JESUS, Justice of

2Sa 23:3 — The God of Israel said, the Rock of Israel spake to me, He that ruleth over men *must be* just, ruling in the fear of God.

Zec 9:9 — Rejoice greatly, O daughter of Zion; shout, O daughter of Jerusalem: behold, thy King cometh unto thee: he *is* just, and having salvation; lowly, and riding upon an ass, and upon a colt the foal of an ass.

Mt 27:19 — When he was set down on the judgment seat, his wife sent unto him, saying, Have thou nothing to do with that just man: for I have suffered many things this day in a dream because of him.

Jn 5:30 — I can of mine own self do nothing: as I hear, I judge: and my judgment is just; because I seek not mine own will, but the will of the Father which hath sent me.

Ac 3:14 — But ye denied the Holy One and the Just, and desired a murderer to be granted unto you;

Ac 22:14 — And he said, The God of our fathers hath chosen thee, that thou shouldest know his will, and see that Just One, and shouldest hear the voice of his mouth.

See: Jesus, Holiness of

See: Jesus, Judge

JESUS, King

Ps 18:43–44; 24:7–10; 45:3–7; 89:3–4, 19–21, 36–37; 110:1–2; 132:17–18; Isa 6:1–3; 9:6–7; Jer 23:5–6; Eze 37:24–25; Da 7:13–14; Zec 9:9–10; Mt 25:31–34; Lk 1:32–33; 22:29–30; Jn 18:36–37; 1Co 15:23–28; Eph 1:20–22; Php 2:9–11; 1Ti 6:15–16; Heb 2:7–8; 10:12–13; Rev 1:5–7; 6:15–17; 19:11–12, 15–16

Ge 49:10 — The sceptre shall not depart from Judah, nor a lawgiver from between his feet, until Shiloh come; and unto him *shall* the gathering of the people *be.*

Nu 24:17 — I shall see him, but not now: I shall behold him, but not nigh: there shall come a Star out of Jacob, and a Sceptre shall rise out of Israel, and shall smite the corners of Moab, and destroy all the children of Sheth.

1Sa 2:10 — The adversaries of the LORD shall be broken to pieces; out of heaven shall he thunder upon them: the LORD shall judge the ends of the earth; and he shall give strength unto his king, and exalt the horn of his anointed.

Ps 2:6 — Yet have I set my king upon my holy hill of Zion.

Ps 72:5 — They shall fear thee as long as the sun and moon endure, throughout all generations.

Ps 72:8 — He shall have dominion also from sea to sea, and from the river unto the ends of the earth.

Ps 72:11 — Yea, all kings shall fall down before him: all nations shall serve him.

Ps 89:23 — And I will beat down his foes before his face, and plague them that hate him.

Ps 89:27 — Also I will make him *my* firstborn, higher than the kings of the earth.

Ps 89:29 — His seed also will I make *to endure* for ever, and his throne as the days of heaven.

Ps 132:11 — The LORD hath sworn *in* truth unto David; he will not turn from it; Of the fruit of thy body will I set upon thy throne.

SS 1:4 — Draw me, we will run after thee: the king hath brought me into his chambers: we will be glad and rejoice in thee, we will remember thy love more than wine: the upright love thee.

SS 1:12 — While the king *sitteth* at his table, my spikenard sendeth forth the smell thereof.

Isa 11:10 — And in that day there shall be a root of Jesse, which shall stand for an ensign of the people; to it shall the Gentiles seek: and his rest shall be glorious.

Isa 22:22 — And the key of the house of David will I lay upon his shoulder; so he shall open, and none shall shut; and he shall shut, and none shall open.

Isa 32:1 — Behold, a king shall reign in righteousness, and princes shall rule in judgment.

Isa 33:17 — Thine eyes shall see the king in his beauty: they shall behold the land that is very far off.

Isa 40:10 — Behold, the Lord GOD will come with strong *hand,* and his arm shall rule for him: behold, his reward *is* with him, and his work before him.

Isa 52:7 — How beautiful upon the mountains are the feet of him that bringeth good tidings, that publisheth peace; that bringeth good tidings of good, that publisheth salvation; that saith unto Zion, Thy God reigneth!

Isa 52:13 — Behold, my servant shall deal prudently, he shall be exalted and extolled, and be very high.

Jer 30:9 — But they shall serve the LORD their God, and David their king, whom I will raise up unto them.

Jer 33:17 — For thus saith the LORD; David shall never want a man to sit upon the throne of the house of Israel;

Da 2:35 — Then was the iron, the clay, the brass, the silver, and the gold, broken to pieces together, and became like the chaff of the summer threshingfloors; and the wind carried them away, that no place was found for them: and the stone that smote the image became a great mountain, and filled the whole earth.

Da 2:44 — And in the days of these kings shall the God of heaven set up a kingdom, which shall never be destroyed: and the kingdom shall not be left to other people, *but* it shall break in pieces and consume all these kingdoms, and it shall stand for ever.

Da 8:23 — And in the latter time of their kingdom, when the transgressors are come to the full, a king of fierce countenance, and understanding dark sentences, shall stand up.

Da 8:25 — And through his policy also he shall cause craft to prosper in his hand; and he shall magnify *himself* in his heart, and by peace shall destroy many: he shall also stand up against the Prince of princes; but he shall be broken without hand.

Da 9:25 — Know therefore and understand, *that* from the going forth of the commandment to restore and to build Jerusalem unto the Messiah the Prince *shall be* seven weeks, and threescore and two weeks: the street shall be built again, and the wall, even in troublous times.

Hos 3:5 — Afterward shall the children of Israel return, and seek the LORD their God, and David their king; and shall fear the LORD and his goodness in the latter days.

Mic 5:2 — But thou, Bethlehem Ephratah, *though* thou be little among the thousands of Judah, *yet* out of thee shall he come forth unto me *that is* to be ruler in Israel; whose goings forth *have been* from of old, from everlasting.

Mic 5:4 — And he shall stand and feed in the strength of the LORD, in the majesty of the name of the LORD his God; and they shall abide: for now shall he be great unto the ends of the earth.

Zec 6:13 — Even he shall build the temple of the LORD; and he shall bear the glory, and shall sit and rule upon his throne; and he shall be a priest upon his throne: and the counsel of peace shall be between them both.

Mt 2:2 — Saying, Where is he that is born King of the Jews? for we have seen his star in the east, and are come to worship him.

Mt 2:6 — And thou Bethlehem, in the land of Juda, art not the least among the princes of Juda: for out of thee shall come a Governor, that shall rule my people Israel.

Mt 3:12 — Whose fan *is* in his hand, and he will throughly purge his floor, and gather his wheat into the garner; but he will burn up the chaff with unquenchable fire.

Mt 11:27 — All things are delivered unto me of my Father: and no man knoweth the Son, but the Father; neither knoweth any man the Father, save the Son, and *he* to whomsoever the Son will reveal *him.*

Mt 12:6 — But I say unto you, That in this place is *one* greater than the temple.

Mt 13:41 — The Son of man shall send forth his angels, and they shall gather out of his kingdom all things that offend, and them which do iniquity;

Mt 19:28 — And Jesus said unto them, Verily I say unto you, That ye which have followed me, in the regeneration when the Son of man shall sit in the throne of his glory, ye also shall sit upon twelve thrones, judging the twelve tribes of Israel.

Mt 21:5 — Tell ye the daughter of Sion, Behold, thy King cometh unto thee, meek, and sitting upon an ass, and a colt the foal of an ass.

Mt 26:64 — Jesus saith unto him, Thou hast said: nevertheless I say unto you, Hereafter shall ye see the Son of man sitting on the right hand of power, and coming in the clouds of heaven.

Mt 27:11 — And Jesus stood before the governor: and the governor asked him, saying, Art thou the King of the Jews? And Jesus said unto him, Thou sayest.

Mt 28:18 — And Jesus came and spake unto them, saying, All power is given unto me in heaven and in earth.

Mk 14:62 — And Jesus said, I am: and ye shall see the Son of man sitting on the right hand of power, and coming in the clouds of heaven.

Lk 2:11 — For unto you is born this day in the city of David a Saviour, which is Christ the Lord.

Lk 3:17 — Whose fan *is* in his hand, and he will throughly purge his floor, and will gather the wheat into his garner; but the chaff he will burn with fire unquenchable.

Lk 10:22 — All things are delivered to me of my Father: and no man knoweth who the Son is, but the Father; and who the Father is, but the Son, and *he* to whom the Son will reveal *him.*

Lk 19:27 — But those mine enemies, which would not that I should reign over them, bring hither, and slay *them* before me.

Lk 19:38 — Saying, Blessed *be* the King that cometh in the name of the Lord: peace in heaven, and glory in the highest.

Lk 22:69 — Hereafter shall the Son of man sit on the right hand of the power of God.

Lk 23:42 — And he said unto Jesus, Lord, remember me when thou comest into thy kingdom.

Jn 1:49 — Nathanael answered and saith unto him, Rabbi, thou art the Son of God; thou art the King of Israel.

Jn 3:31 — He that cometh from above is above all: he that is of the earth is earthly, and speaketh of the earth: he that cometh from heaven is above all.

Jn 12:13 — Took branches of palm trees, and went forth to meet him, and cried, Hosanna: Blessed *is* the King of Israel that cometh in the name of the Lord.

Jn 12:15 — Fear not, daughter of Sion: behold, thy King cometh, sitting on an ass's colt.

Jn 12:41 — These things said Esaias, when he saw his glory, and spake of him.

Jn 13:3 — Jesus knowing that the Father had given all things into his hands, and that he was come from God, and went to God;

Jn 19:19 — And Pilate wrote a title, and put *it* on the cross. And the writing was, JESUS OF NAZARETH THE KING OF THE JEWS.

Ac 2:30 — Therefore being a prophet, and knowing that God had sworn with an oath to him, that of the fruit of his loins, according to the flesh, he would raise up Christ to sit on his throne;

Ac 3:15 — And killed the Prince of life, whom God hath raised from the dead; whereof we are witnesses.

Ac 5:31 — Him hath God exalted with his right hand *to be* a Prince and a Saviour, for to give repentance to Israel, and forgiveness of sins.

Ac 10:36 — The word which *God* sent unto the children of Israel, preaching peace by Jesus Christ: (he is Lord of all:)

Ro 9:5 — Whose *are* the fathers, and of whom as concerning the flesh Christ *came,* who is over all, God blessed for ever. Amen.

Ro 14:9 — For to this end Christ both died, and rose, and revived, that he might be Lord both of the dead and living.

2Ti 4:8 — Henceforth there is laid up for me a crown of righteousness, which the Lord, the righteous judge, shall give me at that day: and not to me only, but unto all them also that love his appearing.

1Pe 3:22 — Who is gone into heaven, and is on the right hand of God; angels and authorities and powers being made subject unto him.

Rev 1:18 — I *am* he that liveth, and was dead; and, behold, I am alive for evermore, Amen; and have the keys of hell and of death.

Rev 3:7 — And to the angel of the church in Philadelphia write; These things saith he that is holy, he that is true, he that hath the key of David, he that openeth, and no man shutteth; and shutteth, and no man openeth;

Rev 3:14 — And unto the angel of the church of the Laodiceans write; These things saith the Amen, the faithful and true witness, the beginning of the creation of God;

Rev 3:21 — To him that overcometh will I grant to sit with me in my throne, even as I also overcame, and am set down with my Father in his throne.

Rev 5:5 — And one of the elders saith unto me, Weep not: behold, the Lion of the tribe of Juda, the Root of David, hath prevailed to open the book, and to loose the seven seals thereof.

Rev 5:12 — Saying with a loud voice, Worthy is the Lamb that was slain to receive power, and riches, and wisdom, and strength, and honour, and glory, and blessing.

Rev 6:2 — And I saw, and behold a white horse: and he that sat on him had a bow; and a crown was given unto him: and he went forth conquering, and to conquer.

Rev 11:15 — And the seventh angel sounded; and there were great voices in heaven, saying, The kingdoms of this world are become *the kingdoms* of our Lord, and of his Christ; and he shall reign for ever and ever.

Rev 12:10 — And I heard a loud voice saying in heaven, Now is come salvation, and strength, and the kingdom of our God, and the power of his Christ: for the accuser of our brethren is cast down, which accused them before our God day and night.

Rev 14:14 — And I looked, and behold a white cloud, and upon the cloud *one* sat like unto the Son of man, having on his head a golden crown, and in his hand a sharp sickle.

Rev 17:14 — These shall make war with the Lamb, and the Lamb shall overcome them: for he is Lord of lords, and King of kings: and they that are with him *are* called, and chosen, and faithful.

Rev 20:4 — And I saw thrones, and they sat upon them, and judgment was given unto them: and *I saw* the souls of them that were beheaded for the witness of Jesus, and for the word of God, and which had not worshipped the beast, neither his image, neither had received *his* mark upon their foreheads, or in their hands; and they lived and reigned with Christ a thousand years.

Rev 20:6 — Blessed and holy *is* he that hath part in the first resurrection: on such the second death hath no power, but they shall be priests of God and of Christ, and shall reign with him a thousand years.

➜See: Church; prophecies concerning prosperity of

➜See: God, Judge, and His Justice

JESUS, Kingdom of

• Its nature (See below, unclassified prophecies concerning).

Mt 13:24–51; 18:3–4; Jn 18:36–37; 2Co 5:16–17; 10:3–5

Lk 17:21 — Neither shall they say, Lo here! or, lo there! for, behold, the kingdom of God is within you.

Jn 8:23 — And he said unto them, Ye are from beneath; I am from above: ye are of this world; I am not of this world.

➜See: Church; prophecies concerning prosperity of

• Prophecies concerning universality of the kingdom of.

Ps 22:27–31; 68:31–32; 72:8–11, 16–17; 85:10–12; 87:1–5; 89:1–37; 96:1–13; 102:13–16; 110:1–6; 138:4–5; 145:10–11; Isa 2:2–5; 4:2–3; 9:1–7; 11:1–10; 25:6–8; 29:18–19; 32:15–17; 35:1–2; 40:4–11; 42:3–4; 45:23–24; 49:1–26; 53:10–54:3; 55:10–13; 56:3–8; 59:19–60:5; 60:7–9; 66:7–23; Jer 16:19–21; Eze 17:22–23; 47:1–12; Da 7:13–14; Joel 2:28–29; Mic 4:1–4; Hag 2:7–9; Zec 2:10–11; 8:20–9:1; 14:8–9, 20–21; Mt 13:31–33; Jn 12:31–32; Ac 2:34–35; 1Co 15:24–28; Php 2:10–11; Heb 12:23–24, 27–28; Rev 5:9–10, 13–14; 19:11–20:3

Ge 12:3 — And I will bless them that bless thee, and curse him that curseth thee: and in thee shall all families of the earth be blessed.

Ge 49:10 — The sceptre shall not depart from Judah, nor a lawgiver from between his feet, until Shiloh come; and unto him *shall* the gathering of the people *be.*

Dt 32:21 — They have moved me to jealousy with *that which is* not God; they have provoked me to anger with their vanities: and I will move them to jealousy with *those which are* not a people; I will provoke them to anger with a foolish nation.

Ps 2:8 — Ask of me, and I shall give *thee* the heathen *for* thine inheritance, and the uttermost parts of the earth *for* thy possession.

Ps 47:8 — God reigneth over the heathen: God sitteth upon the throne of his holiness.

Ps 65:2 — O thou that hearest prayer, unto thee shall all flesh come.

Ps 66:4 — All the earth shall worship thee, and shall sing unto thee; they shall sing *to* thy name. Selah.

Ps 72:5 — They shall fear thee as long as the sun and moon endure, throughout all generations.

Ps 72:19 — And blessed *be* his glorious name for ever: and let the whole earth be filled *with* his glory; Amen, and Amen.

Ps 86:9 — All nations whom thou hast made shall come and worship before thee, O Lord; and shall glorify thy name.

Ps 113:3 — From the rising of the sun unto the going down of the same the LORD's name *is* to be praised.

Isa 24:16 — From the uttermost part of the earth have we heard songs, *even* glory to the righteous. But I said, My leanness, my leanness, woe unto me! the treacherous dealers have dealt treacherously; yea, the treacherous dealers have dealt very treacherously.

Isa 45:8 — Drop down, ye heavens, from above, and let the skies pour down righteousness: let the earth open, and let them bring forth salvation, and let righteousness spring up together; I the LORD have created it.

Isa 51:6 — Lift up your eyes to the heavens, and look upon the earth beneath: for the heavens shall vanish away like smoke, and the earth shall wax old like a garment, and they that dwell therein shall die in like manner: but my salvation shall be for ever, and my righteousness shall not be abolished.

Isa 51:8 — For the moth shall eat them up like a garment, and the worm shall eat them like wool: but my righteousness shall be for ever, and my salvation from generation to generation.

Isa 55:5 — Behold, thou shalt call a nation *that* thou knowest not, and nations *that* knew not thee shall run unto thee because of the LORD thy God, and for the Holy One of Israel; for he hath glorified thee.

Jer 3:17 — At that time they shall call Jerusalem the throne of the LORD; and all the nations shall be gathered unto it, to the name of the LORD, to Jerusalem:

neither shall they walk any more after the imagination of their evil heart.

Jer 4:2 — And thou shalt swear, The LORD liveth, in truth, in judgment, and in righteousness; and the nations shall bless themselves in him, and in him shall they glory.

Jer 31:34 — And they shall teach no more every man his neighbour, and every man his brother, saying, Know the LORD: for they shall all know me, from the least of them unto the greatest of them, saith the LORD; for I will forgive their iniquity, and I will remember their sin no more.

Jer 33:22 — As the host of heaven cannot be numbered, neither the sand of the sea measured: so will I multiply the seed of David my servant, and the Levites that minister unto me.

Da 2:35 — Then was the iron, the clay, the brass, the silver, and the gold, broken to pieces together, and became like the chaff of the summer threshingfloors; and the wind carried them away, that no place was found for them: and the stone that smote the image became a great mountain, and filled the whole earth.

Da 2:44 — And in the days of these kings shall the God of heaven set up a kingdom, which shall never be destroyed: and the kingdom shall not be left to other people, *but* it shall break in pieces and consume all these kingdoms, and it shall stand for ever.

Da 7:18 — But the saints of the most High shall take the kingdom, and possess the kingdom for ever, even for ever and ever.

Da 7:22 — Until the Ancient of days came, and judgment was given to the saints of the most High; and the time came that the saints possessed the kingdom.

Da 7:27 — And the kingdom and dominion, and the greatness of the kingdom under the whole heaven, shall be given to the people of the saints of the most High, whose kingdom *is* an everlasting kingdom, and all dominions shall serve and obey him.

Da 12:4 — But thou, O Daniel, shut up the words, and seal the book, *even* to the time of the end: many shall run to and fro, and knowledge shall be increased.

Hab 2:14 — For the earth shall be filled with the knowledge of the glory of the LORD, as the waters cover the sea.

Zep 2:11 — The LORD *will be* terrible unto them: for he will famish all the gods of the earth; and *men* shall worship him, every one from his place, *even* all the isles of the heathen.

Zep 3:9 — For then will I turn to the people a pure language, that they may all call upon the name of the LORD, to serve him with one consent.

Zec 4:10 — For who hath despised the day of small things? for they shall rejoice, and shall see the plummet in the hand of Zerubbabel *with* those seven; they *are* the eyes of the LORD, which run to and fro through the whole earth.

Zec 6:15 — And they *that are* far off shall come and build in the temple of the LORD, and ye shall know that the LORD of hosts hath sent me unto you. And *this* shall come to pass, if ye will diligently obey the voice of the LORD your God.

Zec 9:10 — And I will cut off the chariot from Ephraim, and the horse from Jerusalem, and the battle bow shall be cut off: and he shall speak peace unto the heathen: and his dominion *shall be* from sea *even* to sea, and from river *even* to the ends of the earth.

Zec 14:16 — And it shall come to pass, *that* every one that is left of all the nations which came against Jerusalem shall even go up from year to year to worship the King, the LORD of hosts, and to keep the feast of tabernacles.

Mal 1:11 — For from the rising of the sun even unto the going down of the same my name *shall be* great among the Gentiles; and in every place incense *shall be* offered unto my name, and a pure offering: for my name *shall be* great among the heathen, saith the LORD of hosts.

Mt 8:11 — And I say unto you, That many shall come from the east and west, and shall sit down with Abraham, and Isaac, and Jacob, in the kingdom of heaven.

Mk 13:10 — And the gospel must first be published among all nations.

Lk 1:33 — And he shall reign over the house of Jacob for ever; and of his kingdom there shall be no end.

Lk 2:10 — And the angel said unto them, Fear not: for, behold, I bring you good tidings of great joy, which shall be to all people.

Jn 3:30 — He must increase, but I *must* decrease.

Jn 10:16 — And other sheep I have, which are not of this fold: them also I must bring, and they shall hear my voice; and there shall be one fold, *and* one shepherd.

Eph 1:10 — That in the dispensation of the fulness of times he might gather together in one all things in Christ, both which are in heaven, and which are on earth; *even* in him:

Heb 8:11 — And they shall not teach every man his neighbour, and every man his brother, saying, Know the Lord: for all shall know me, from the least to the greatest.

Heb 10:13 — From henceforth expecting till his enemies be made his footstool.

Rev 6:2 — And I saw, and behold a white horse: and he that sat on him had a bow; and a crown was given unto him: and he went forth conquering, and to conquer.

Rev 11:15 — And the seventh angel sounded; and there were great voices in heaven, saying, The kingdoms of this world are become *the kingdoms* of our Lord, and of his Christ; and he shall reign for ever and ever.

Rev 12:10 — And I heard a loud voice saying in heaven, Now is come salvation, and strength, and the kingdom of our God, and the power of his Christ: for the accuser of our brethren is cast down, which accused them before our God day and night.

Rev 14:6 — And I saw another angel fly in the midst of heaven, having the everlasting gospel to preach unto them that dwell on the earth, and to every nation, and kindred, and tongue, and people,

Rev 15:4 — Who shall not fear thee, O Lord, and glorify thy name? for *thou* only *art* holy: for all nations shall come and worship before thee; for thy judgments are made manifest.

Rev 17:14 — These shall make war with the Lamb, and the Lamb shall overcome them: for he is Lord of lords, and King of kings: and they that are with him *are* called, and chosen, and faithful.

Rev 19:6 — And I heard as it were the voice of a great multitude, and as the voice of many waters, and as the voice of mighty thunderings, saying, Alleluia: for the Lord God omnipotent reigneth.

• Unclassified prophecies concerning kingdom of.

Ps 67:1–7; Isa 2:2–4; 11:1–13; 35:1–10; 42:1–7, 18–21; 49:18–23; 55:1–13; 65:17–25; Jer 3:14–19; Da 7:9–14; Am 9:11–12; Mic 4:1–7; Zec 8:20–23; 11:12–13; Mt 12:18–21; 21:4–5; 27:3–10; Lk 1:32–33; 22:29–30

Ge 22:18 — And in thy seed shall all the nations of the earth be blessed; because thou hast obeyed my voice.

Ge 49:10 — The sceptre shall not depart from Judah, nor a lawgiver from between his feet, until Shiloh come; and unto him *shall* the gathering of the people *be*.

Ps 2:9 — Thou shalt break them with a rod of iron; thou shalt dash them in pieces like a potter's vessel.

Ps 46:9 — He maketh wars to cease unto the end of the earth; he breaketh the bow, and cutteth the spear in sunder; he burneth the chariot in the fire.

Ps 72:12 — For he shall deliver the needy when he crieth; the poor also, and *him* that hath no helper.

Isa 9:5 — For every battle of the warrior *is* with confused noise, and garments rolled in blood; but *this* shall be with burning *and* fuel of fire.

Isa 25:6 — And in this mountain shall the LORD of hosts make unto all people a feast of fat things, a feast of wines on the lees, of fat things full of marrow, of wines on the lees well refined.

Isa 45:14 — Thus saith the LORD, The labour of Egypt, and merchandise of Ethiopia and of the Sabeans, men of stature, shall come over unto thee, and they shall be thine: they shall come after thee; in chains they shall come over, and they shall fall down unto thee, they shall make supplication unto thee, *saying*, Surely God *is* in thee; and *there is* none else, *there is* no God.

Isa 49:5 — And now, saith the LORD that formed me from the womb *to be* his servant, to bring Jacob again to him, Though Israel be not gathered, yet shall I be glorious in the eyes of the LORD, and my God shall be my strength.

Isa 62:11 — Behold, the LORD hath proclaimed unto the end of the world, Say ye to the daughter of Zion, Behold, thy salvation cometh; behold, his reward *is* with him, and his work before him.

Isa 66:19 — And I will set a sign among them, and I will send those that escape of them unto the nations, *to* Tarshish, Pul, and Lud, that draw the bow, *to* Tubal, and Javan, *to* the isles afar off, that have not heard my fame, neither have seen my glory; and they shall declare my glory among the Gentiles.

Da 2:44 — And in the days of these kings shall the God of heaven set up a kingdom, which shall never be destroyed: and the kingdom shall not be left to other people, *but* it shall break in pieces and consume all these kingdoms, and it shall stand for ever.

Da 7:27 — And the kingdom and dominion, and the greatness of the kingdom under the whole heaven, shall be given to the people of the saints of the most High, whose kingdom *is* an everlasting kingdom, and all dominions shall serve and obey him.

Hos 2:18 — And in that day will I make a covenant for them with the beasts of the field, and with the fowls of heaven, and *with* the creeping things of the ground: and I will break the bow and the sword and the battle out of the earth, and will make them to lie down safely.

Hos 2:23 — And I will sow her unto me in the earth; and I will have mercy upon her that had not obtained mercy; and I will say to *them which were* not my people, Thou *art* my people; and they shall say, *Thou art* my God.

Zec 9:9 — Rejoice greatly, O daughter of Zion; shout, O daughter of Jerusalem: behold, thy King cometh unto thee: he *is* just, and having salvation; lowly, and riding upon an ass, and upon a colt the foal of an ass.

Zec 13:7 — Awake, O sword, against my shepherd, and against the man *that is* my fellow, saith the LORD of hosts: smite the shepherd, and the sheep shall be scattered: and I will turn mine hand upon the little ones.

Mal 3:1 — Behold, I will send my messenger, and he shall prepare the way before me: and the Lord, whom ye seek, shall suddenly come to his temple, even the messenger of the covenant, whom ye delight in: behold, he shall come, saith the LORD of hosts.

Mt 11:5 — The blind receive their sight, and the lame walk, the lepers are cleansed, and the deaf hear, the dead are raised up, and the poor have the gospel preached to them.

Mt 11:10 — For this is *he*, of whom it is written, Behold, I send my messenger before thy face, which shall prepare thy way before thee.

Mt 12:29 — Or else how can one enter into a strong man's house, and spoil his goods, except he first bind the strong man? and then he will spoil his house.

Mt 16:28 — Verily I say unto you, There be some standing here, which shall not taste of death, till they see the Son of man coming in his kingdom.

Mt 26:15 — And said *unto them,* What will ye give me, and I will deliver him unto you? And they covenanted with him for thirty pieces of silver.

Mt 26:31 — Then saith Jesus unto them, All ye shall be offended because of me this night: for it is written, I will smite the shepherd, and the sheep of the flock shall be scattered abroad.

Mt 28:18 — And Jesus came and spake unto them, saying, All power is given unto me in heaven and in earth.

Heb 1:8 — But unto the Son *he saith,* Thy throne, O God, *is* for ever and ever: a sceptre of righteousness *is* the sceptre of thy kingdom.

2Pe 1:11 — For so an entrance shall be ministered unto you abundantly into the everlasting kingdom of our Lord and Saviour Jesus Christ.

See: Jesus, Messiah

See: Psalms; messianic

• Secular notions concerning the kingdom of.

Mt 18:1–3; 20:20–23; Mk 10:35–40; 11:9–10; Lk 9:46–48; Ac 1:6–7

Jn 6:15 — When Jesus therefore perceived that they would come and take him by force, to make him a king, he departed again into a mountain himself alone.

JESUS, Love of

Isa 63:7–9; Mt 12:49–50; 18:2–6, 10–13; 19:13–15; Mk 3:31–35; 9:36–37; 10:13–14; Lk 8:19–21; 18:15–16; 22:31–32; 24:38–40; Jn 10:3–4, 14–16; 11:33–36; 14:1–3; 15:9–13; 18:8–9; 19:26–27; 21:15–17; Ac 9:4–5; Ro 8:37–39; 2Co 5:13–14; Eph 3:17–19; 5:29–30

Ps 69:9 — For the zeal of thine house hath eaten me up; and the reproaches of them that reproached thee are fallen upon me.

Ps 72:14 — He shall redeem their soul from deceit and violence: and precious shall their blood be in his sight.

Pr 8:17 — I love them that love me; and those that seek me early shall find me.

Pr 8:31 — Rejoicing in the habitable part of his earth; and my delights *were* with the sons of men.

Isa 40:11 — He shall feed his flock like a shepherd: he shall gather the lambs with his arm, and carry *them* in his bosom, *and* shall gently lead those that are with young.

Isa 42:3 — A bruised reed shall he not break, and the smoking flax shall he not quench: he shall bring forth judgment unto truth.

Isa 53:4 — Surely he hath borne our griefs, and carried our sorrows: yet we did esteem him stricken, smitten of God, and afflicted.

Mic 5:4 — And he shall stand and feed in the strength of the LORD, in the majesty of the name of the LORD his God; and they shall abide: for now shall he be great unto the ends of the earth.

Mt 8:17 — That it might be fulfilled which was spoken by Esaias the prophet, saying, Himself took our infirmities, and bare *our* sicknesses.

Mt 9:36 — But when he saw the multitudes, he was moved with compassion on them, because they fainted, and were scattered abroad, as sheep having no shepherd.

Mt 14:14 — And Jesus went forth, and saw a great multitude, and was moved with compassion toward them, and he healed their sick.

Mt 15:32 — Then Jesus called his disciples *unto him,* and said, I have compassion on the multitude, because they continue with me now three days, and have nothing to eat: and I will not send them away fasting, lest they faint in the way.

Mt 23:37 — O Jerusalem, Jerusalem, *thou* that killest the prophets, and stonest them which are sent unto thee, how often would I have gathered thy children together, even as a hen gathereth her chickens under *her* wings, and ye would not!

Mt 28:10 — Then said Jesus unto them, Be not afraid: go tell my brethren that they go into Galilee, and there shall they see me.

Mk 8:12 — And he sighed deeply in his spirit, and saith, Why doth this generation seek after a sign? verily I say unto you, There shall no sign be given unto this generation.

Mk 9:42 — And whosoever shall offend one of *these* little ones that believe in me, it is better for him that a millstone were hanged about his neck, and he were cast into the sea.

Mk 10:16 — And he took them up in his arms, put *his* hands upon them, and blessed them.

Mk 10:21 — Then Jesus beholding him loved him, and said unto him, One thing thou lackest: go thy way, sell whatsoever thou hast, and give to the poor, and thou shalt have treasure in heaven: and come, take up the cross, and follow me.

Lk 7:13 — And when the Lord saw her, he had compassion on her, and said unto her, Weep not.

Lk 9:48 — And said unto them, Whosoever shall receive this child in my name receiveth me: and whosoever shall receive me receiveth him that sent me: for he that is least among you all, the same shall be great.

Lk 23:28 — But Jesus turning unto them said, Daughters of Jerusalem, weep not for me, but weep for yourselves, and for your children.

Jn 10:11 — I am the good shepherd: the good shepherd giveth his life for the sheep.

Jn 11:5 — Now Jesus loved Martha, and her sister, and Lazarus.

Jn 13:1 — Now before the feast of the passover, when Jesus knew that his hour was come that he should depart out of this world unto the Father, having loved his own which were in the world, he loved them unto the end.

Jn 13:23 — Now there was leaning on Jesus' bosom one of his disciples, whom Jesus loved.

Jn 13:34 — A new commandment I give unto you, That ye love one another; as I have loved you, that ye also love one another.

Jn 14:18 — I will not leave you comfortless: I will come to you.

Jn 14:21 — He that hath my commandments, and keepeth them, he it is that loveth me: and he that loveth me shall be loved of my Father, and I will love him, and will manifest myself to him.

Jn 14:27 — Peace I leave with you, my peace I give unto you: not as the world giveth, give I unto you. Let not your heart be troubled, neither let it be afraid.

Jn 15:15 — Henceforth I call you not servants; for the servant knoweth not what his lord doeth: but I have called you friends; for all things that I have heard of my Father I have made known unto you.

Jn 17:12 — While I was with them in the world, I kept them in thy name: those that thou gavest me I have kept, and none of them is lost, but the son of perdition; that the scripture might be fulfilled.

Jn 17:15 — I pray not that thou shouldest take them out of the world, but that thou shouldest keep them from the evil.

Jn 17:19 — And for their sakes I sanctify myself, that they also might be sanctified through the truth.

Jn 20:17 — Jesus saith unto her, Touch me not; for I am not yet ascended to my Father: but go to my brethren, and say unto them, I ascend unto my Father, and your Father; and *to* my God, and your God.

Jn 20:27 — Then saith he to Thomas, reach hither thy finger, and behold my hands; and reach hither thy hand, and thrust *it* into my side: and be not faithless, but believing.

Ac 10:38 — How God anointed Jesus of Nazareth with the Holy Ghost and with power: who went about doing good, and healing all that were oppressed of the devil; for God was with him.

Ro 8:35 — Who shall separate us from the love of Christ? *shall* tribulation, or distress, or persecution, or famine, or nakedness, or peril, or sword?

Ro 15:3 — For even Christ pleased not himself; but, as it is written, The reproaches of them that reproached thee fell on me.

2Co 8:9 — For ye know the grace of our Lord Jesus Christ, that, though he was rich, yet for your sakes he became poor, that ye through his poverty might be rich.

Gal 2:20 — I am crucified with Christ: nevertheless I live; yet not I, but Christ liveth in me: and the life which I now live in the flesh I live by the faith of the Son of God, who loved me, and gave himself for me.

Eph 5:2 — And walk in love, as Christ also hath loved us, and hath given himself for us an offering and a sacrifice to God for a sweetsmelling savour.

Eph 5:25 — Husbands, love your wives, even as Christ also loved the church, and gave himself for it;

2Th 2:13 — But we are bound to give thanks alway to God for you, brethren beloved of the Lord, because God hath from the beginning chosen you to salvation through sanctification of the Spirit and belief of the truth:

Heb 2:11 — For both he that sanctifieth and they who are sanctified *are* all of one: for which cause he is not ashamed to call them brethren,

Heb 2:18 — For in that he himself hath suffered being tempted, he is able to succour them that are tempted.

Heb 4:15 — For we have not an high priest which cannot be touched with the feeling of our infirmities; but was in all points tempted like as *we are, yet* without sin.

1Jn 3:16 — Hereby perceive we the love *of God,* because he laid down his life for us: and we ought to lay down *our* lives for the brethren.

Rev 1:5 — And from Jesus Christ, *who is* the faithful witness, *and* the first begotten of the dead, and the prince of the kings of the earth. Unto him that loved us, and washed us from our sins in his own blood,

Rev 3:9 — Behold, I will make them of the synagogue of Satan, which say they are Jews, and are not, but do lie; behold, I will make them to come and worship before thy feet, and to know that I have loved thee.

Rev 3:19 — As many as I love, I rebuke and chasten: be zealous therefore, and repent.

See: Jesus, Compassion of

JESUS, Mediation of

Isa 53:10–12; Da 9:17–19; Zec 1:12–13; Lk 22:31–32; 23:33–34; Jn 14:13–14; 16:23–24; 17:1–26; Ro 5:1–2; Eph 2:13–18; Heb 3:1–2; 4:14–15; 5:5–6; 6:19–7:1; 7:24–8:2; 9:11–10:21; 1Jn 2:1–2; Rev 8:3–4

Dt 18:18 — I will raise them up a Prophet from among their brethren, like unto thee, and will put my words in his mouth; and he shall speak unto them all that I shall command him.

Ps 110:4 — The LORD hath sworn, and will not repent, Thou *art* a priest for ever after the order of Melchizedek.

Zec 6:13 — Even he shall build the temple of the LORD; and he shall bear the glory, and shall sit and rule upon his throne; and he shall be a priest upon his throne: and the counsel of peace shall be between them both.

Mt 18:20 — For where two or three are gathered together in my name, there am I in the midst of them.

Jn 14:6 — Jesus saith unto him, I am the way, the truth, and the life: no man cometh unto the Father, but by me.

Jn 14:16 — And I will pray the Father, and he shall give you another Comforter, that he may abide with you for ever;

Jn 16:26 — At that day ye shall ask in my name: and I say not unto you, that I will pray the Father for you:

Jn 20:31 — But these are written, that ye might believe that Jesus is the Christ, the Son of God; and that believing ye might have life through his name.

Ro 1:8 — First, I thank my God through Jesus Christ for you all, that your faith is spoken of throughout the whole world.

Ro 6:23 — For the wages of sin *is* death; but the gift of God *is* eternal life through Jesus Christ our Lord.

Ro 8:34 — Who *is* he that condemneth? *It is* Christ that died, yea rather, that is risen again, who is even at the right hand of God, who also maketh intercession for us.

Ro 16:27 — To God only wise, *be* glory through Jesus Christ for ever. Amen.

1Co 6:11 — And such were some of you: but ye are washed, but ye are sanctified, but ye are justified in the name of the Lord Jesus, and by the Spirit of our God.

1Co 15:57 — But thanks *be* to God, which giveth us the victory through our Lord Jesus Christ.

2Co 1:20 — For all the promises of God in him *are* yea, and in him Amen, unto the glory of God by us.

Gal 4:7 — Wherefore thou art no more a servant, but a son; and if a son, then an heir of God through Christ.

Eph 3:12 — In whom we have boldness and access with confidence by the faith of him.

Eph 4:32 — And be ye kind one to another, tenderhearted, forgiving one another, even as God for Christ's sake hath forgiven you.

Eph 5:20 — Giving thanks always for all things unto God and the Father in the name of our Lord Jesus Christ;

Col 3:17 — And whatsoever ye do in word or deed, *do* all in the name of the Lord Jesus, giving thanks to God and the Father by him.

1Ti 2:1 — I exhort therefore, that, first of all, supplications, prayers, intercessions, *and* giving of thanks, be made for all men;

1Ti 2:3 — For this *is* good and acceptable in the sight of God our Saviour;

1Ti 2:5 — For *there is* one God, and one mediator between God and men, the man Christ Jesus;

Heb 2:17 — Wherefore in all things it behoved him to be made like unto *his* brethren, that he might be a merciful and faithful high priest in things *pertaining* to God, to make reconciliation for the sins of the people.

Heb 5:10 — Called of God an high priest after the order of Melchisedec.

Heb 7:3 — Without father, without mother, without descent, having neither beginning of days, nor end of life; but made like unto the Son of God; abideth a priest continually.

Heb 7:19 — For the law made nothing perfect, but the bringing in of a better hope *did;* by the which we draw nigh unto God.

Heb 7:21 — (For those priests were made without an oath; but this with an oath by him that said unto him, The Lord sware and will not repent, Thou *art* a priest for ever after the order of Melchisedec:)

Heb 8:6 — But now hath he obtained a more excellent ministry, by how much also he is the mediator of a better covenant, which was established upon better promises.

Heb 12:24 — And to Jesus the mediator of the new covenant, and to the blood of sprinkling, that speaketh better things than *that of* Abel.

Heb 13:15 — By him therefore let us offer the sacrifice of praise to God continually, that is, the fruit of *our* lips giving thanks to his name.

1Pe 2:5 — Ye also, as lively stones, are built up a spiritual house, an holy priesthood, to offer up spiritual sacrifices, acceptable to God by Jesus Christ.

1Jn 2:12 — I write unto you, little children, because your sins are forgiven you for his name's sake.

- **Typified.**
  - **Moses.**

    Dt 5:5 — (I stood between the LORD and you at that time, to shew you the word of the LORD: for ye were afraid by reason of the fire, and went not up into the mount;) saying,

    Gal 3:19 — Wherefore then *serveth* the law? It was added because of transgressions, till the seed should come to whom the promise was made; *and it was* ordained by angels in the hand of a mediator.
  - **Aaron.**

    Nu 16:48 — And he stood between the dead and the living; and the plague was stayed.

  See: Intercession

JESUS, Meekness of

Isa 50:5–6; Mt 12:19–20; 26:49–63; 27:12–14; Mk 2:6–11; Jn 8:48–50; Php 2:7–8; Heb 12:2–3

Ps 45:4 — And in thy majesty ride prosperously because of truth and meekness *and* righteousness; and thy right hand shall teach thee terrible things.

Isa 42:2 — He shall not cry, nor lift up, nor cause his voice to be heard in the street.

Isa 52:13 — Behold, my servant shall deal prudently, he shall be exalted and extolled, and be very high.

Isa 53:7 — He was oppressed, and he was afflicted, yet he opened not his mouth: he is brought as a lamb to the slaughter, and as a sheep before her shearers is dumb, so he openeth not his mouth.

Mt 11:29 — Take my yoke upon you, and learn of me; for I am meek and lowly in heart: and ye shall find rest unto your souls.

Mt 21:5 — Tell ye the daughter of Sion, Behold, thy King cometh unto thee, meek, and sitting upon an ass, and a colt the foal of an ass.

Lk 22:27 — For whether *is* greater, he that sitteth at meat, or he that serveth? *is* not he that sitteth at meat? but I am among you as he that serveth.

Lk 23:34 — Then said Jesus, Father, forgive them; for they know not what they do. And they parted his raiment, and cast lots.

Jn 13:5 — After that he poureth water into a bason, and began to wash the disciples' feet, and to wipe *them* with the towel wherewith he was girded.

Jn 13:14 — If I then, *your* Lord and Master, have washed your feet; ye also ought to wash one another's feet.

Ac 8:32 — The place of the scripture which he read was this, He was led as a sheep to the slaughter; and like a lamb dumb before his shearer, so opened he not his mouth:

2Co 10:1 — Now I Paul myself beseech you by the meekness and gentleness of Christ, who in presence *am* base among you, but being absent am bold toward you:

1Pe 2:23 — Who, when he was reviled, reviled not again; when he suffered, he threatened not; but committed *himself* to him that judgeth righteously:

See: Jesus, Humility of

See: Meekness

JESUS, Messiah

- **Messianic psalms.**

  Ps 2:1–12; 16:7–11; 67:1–7; 68:28–69:36; 72:1–19; 93:1–5; 96:1–99:9; 110:1–7; 118:19–29
- **Other scriptures relating to his messiahship.**

  Da 9:25–26; Mt 11:3–6; 16:15–16; 22:42–45; 26:63–64; Mk 12:35–37; Lk 2:28–32; 20:41–44; 24:25–27; Jn 4:25–26; 5:36–37; 8:17–18; Ac 4:26–27; 17:2–3; 26:6–7, 22–23; Ro 1:1–3; 1Pe 1:10–11; 2Pe 1:16–18; 1Jn 5:6–9

  Ps 2:2 — The kings of the earth set themselves, and the rulers take counsel together, against the LORD, and against his anointed, *saying,*

  Lk 2:38 — And she coming in that instant gave thanks likewise unto the Lord, and spake of him to all them that looked for redemption in Jerusalem.

  Jn 1:41 — He first findeth his own brother Simon, and saith unto him, We have found the Messias, which is, being interpreted, the Christ.

  Jn 1:45 — Philip findeth Nathanael, and saith unto him, We have found him, of whom Moses in the law, and the prophets, did write, Jesus of Nazareth, the son of Joseph.

  Jn 4:29 — Come, see a man, which told me all things that ever I did: is not this the Christ?

  Jn 4:42 — And said unto the woman, Now we believe, not because of thy saying: for we have heard *him* ourselves, and know that this is indeed the Christ, the Saviour of the world.

Jn 5:33 — Ye sent unto John, and he bare witness unto the truth.

Jn 5:39 — Search the scriptures; for in them ye think ye have eternal life: and they are they which testify of me.

Jn 5:46 — For had ye believed Moses, ye would have believed me: for he wrote of me.

Jn 6:27 — Labour not for the meat which perisheth, but for that meat which endureth unto everlasting life, which the Son of man shall give unto you: for him hath God the Father sealed.

Jn 8:14 — Jesus answered and said unto them, Though I bear record of myself, *yet* my record is true: for I know whence I came, and whither I go; but ye cannot tell whence I come, and whither I go.

Jn 8:25 — Then said they unto him, Who art thou? And Jesus saith unto them, Even *the same* that I said unto you from the beginning.

Jn 8:28 — Then said Jesus unto them, When ye have lifted up the Son of man, then shall ye know that I am *he*, and *that* I do nothing of myself; but as my Father hath taught me, I speak these things.

Jn 8:56 — Your father Abraham rejoiced to see my day: and he saw *it*, and was glad.

Jn 13:19 — Now I tell you before it come, that, when it is come to pass, ye may believe that I am *he*.

Ac 3:18 — But those things, which God before had shewed by the mouth of all his prophets, that Christ should suffer, he hath so fulfilled.

Ac 3:20 — And he shall send Jesus Christ, which before was preached unto you:

Ac 3:24 — Yea, and all the prophets from Samuel and those that follow after, as many as have spoken, have likewise foretold of these days.

Ac 9:22 — But Saul increased the more in strength, and confounded the Jews which dwelt at Damascus, proving that this is very Christ.

Ac 13:27 — For they that dwell at Jerusalem, and their rulers, because they knew him not, nor yet the voices of the prophets which are read every sabbath day, they have fulfilled *them* in condemning *him*.

Ac 28:23 — And when they had appointed him a day, there came many to him into *his* lodging; to whom he expounded and testified the kingdom of God, persuading them concerning Jesus, both out of the law of Moses, and *out of* the prophets, from morning till evening.

1Co 15:3 — For I delivered unto you first of all that which I also received, how that Christ died for our sins according to the scriptures;

See: Jesus, Divinity of

See: Jesus, King

JESUS, Miracles of

- **Water made wine.**
  Jn 2:1–11
- **Heals the nobleman's son.**
  Jn 4:46–54
- **First miraculous draught of fishes.**
  Lk 5:1–11
- **Demoniac in the synagogue healed.**
  Mk 1:23–26; Lk 4:33–36
- **Heals Simon's wife's mother.**
  Mt 8:14–15; Mk 1:29–31; Lk 4:38–39
- **Heals diseases in Galilee.**
  Mt 4:23–24
  Mk 1:34 — And he healed many that were sick of divers diseases, and cast out many devils; and suffered not the devils to speak, because they knew him.
- **Miracles at Jerusalem.**
  Jn 2:23 — Now when he was in Jerusalem at the passover, in the feast *day*, many believed in his name, when they saw the miracles which he did.
- **Cleanses the leper.**
  Mt 8:1–4; Mk 1:40–45; Lk 5:12–16
- **Heals the paralytic.**
  Mt 9:1–8; Mk 2:1–12; Lk 5:17–26
- **Heals the impotent man.**
  Jn 5:1–16
- **Restores the withered hand.**
  Mt 12:9–13; Mk 3:1–5; Lk 6:6–11
- **Heals multitudes from Judah, Jerusalem, and coasts of Tyre and Sidon.**
  Lk 6:17–19
- **Heals the centurion's servant.**
  Mt 8:5–13; Lk 7:1–10
- **Heals deominacs.**
  Mt 8:16–17; Lk 4:40–41
- **Raises the widow's son.**
  Lk 7:11–16
- **Heals in Galilee.**
  Lk 7:21–22
- **Heals a demoniac.**
  Mt 12:22–37; Mk 3:19–30; Lk 11:14–15, 17–23
- **Stills the tempest.**
  Mt 8:23–27; Mk 4:35–41; Lk 8:22–25
  Mt 14:32 — And when they were come into the ship, the wind ceased.
- **Healing of the diseased in the land of Gennesaret.**
  Mt 14:34–36
- **The demoniacs in Gadara healed.**
  Mt 8:28–34; Mk 5:1–20; Lk 8:26–39
- **Raises Jairus's daughter.**
  Mt 9:18–19, 23–26; Mk 5:22–24, 35–43; Lk 8:41–42, 49–56
- **Heals the woman with the issue of blood.**
  Mt 9:20–22; Mk 5:25–34; Lk 8:43–48
- **Opens the eyes of two blind men in the house.**
  Mt 9:27–31
- **A devil cast out and a dumb man cured.**
  Mt 9:32–33
- **Five thousand fed.**
  Mt 14:15–21; Mk 6:35–44; Lk 9:12–17; Jn 6:5–14

• **Heals sick in Galilee.**

Mt 14:14 — And Jesus went forth, and saw a great multitude, and was moved with compassion toward them, and he healed their sick.

• **Walking on the sea.**

Mt 14:22–33; Mk 6:45–52; Jn 6:14–21

• **The daughter of the Syrophenician healed.**

Mt 15:21–28; Mk 7:24–30

• **Healing of lame, blind, dumb, and maimed, near the Sea of Galilee.**

Mt 15:30 — And great multitudes came unto him, having with them *those that were* lame, blind, dumb, maimed, and many others, and cast them down at Jesus' feet; and he healed them:

• **Four thousand fed.**

Mt 15:32–39; Mk 8:1–9

• **One deaf and dumb cured.**

Mk 7:31–37

• **One blind cured.**

Mk 8:22–36

• **Lunatic child healed.**

Mt 17:14–21; Mk 9:14–29; Lk 9:37–43

• **Piece of money in the fish's mouth.**

Mt 17:24–27

• **The ten lepers cured.**

Lk 17:11–19

• **Opening the eyes of one born blind.**

Jn 9:1–41

• **Raising of Lazarus.**

Jn 11:1–54

• **Woman with the spirit of infirmity cured.**

Lk 13:10–17

• **The dropsy cured.**

Lk 14:1–6

• **Two blind men cured near Jericho.**

Mt 20:29–34; Mk 10:46–52; Lk 18:35–43

• **The fig tree blighted.**

Mt 21:17–22; Mk 11:12–14, 20–24

• **Healing of Malchus's ear.**

Lk 22:49–51

• **Second draught of fishes.**

Jn 21:6 — And he said unto them, Cast the net on the right side of the ship, and ye shall find. They cast therefore, and now they were not able to draw it for the multitude of fishes.

• **Not particularly described.**

Mt 4:23–24; Lk 6:17–19; 7:21–22

Mt 14:14 — And Jesus went forth, and saw a great multitude, and was moved with compassion toward them, and he healed their sick.

Mt 15:30 — And great multitudes came unto him, having with them *those that were* lame, blind, dumb, maimed, and many others, and cast them down at Jesus' feet; and he healed them:

Mk 1:34 — And he healed many that were sick of divers diseases, and cast out many devils; and suffered not the devils to speak, because they knew him.

Jn 2:23 — Now when he was in Jerusalem at the passover, in the feast *day,* many believed in his name, when they saw the miracles which he did.

Jn 3:2 — The same came to Jesus by night, and said unto him, Rabbi, we know that thou art a teacher come from God: for no man can do these miracles that thou doest, except God be with him.

• **Resurrection.**

Jn 20:1–18

Mt 28:6 — He is not here: for he is risen, as he said. Come, see the place where the Lord lay.

Mk 16:6 — And he saith unto them, Be not affrighted: Ye seek Jesus of Nazareth, which was crucified: he is risen; he is not here: behold the place where they laid him.

Lk 24:6 — He is not here, but is risen: remember how he spake unto you when he was yet in Galilee,

• **Holds the vision of his disciples, that they should not recognize him.**

Lk 24:16 — But their eyes were holden that they should not know him.

Lk 24:31 — And their eyes were opened, and they knew him; and he vanished out of their sight.

Lk 24:35 — And they told what things *were done* in the way, and how he was known of them in breaking of bread.

• **His appearances and disappearances.**

Lk 24:36–45

Lk 24:15 — And it came to pass, that, while they communed *together* and reasoned, Jesus himself drew near, and went with them.

Lk 24:31 — And their eyes were opened, and they knew him; and he vanished out of their sight.

Jn 20:19 — Then the same day at evening, being the first *day* of the week, when the doors were shut where the disciples were assembled for fear of the Jews, came Jesus and stood in the midst, and saith unto them, Peace *be* unto you.

Jn 20:26 — And after eight days again his disciples were within, and Thomas with them: *then* came Jesus, the doors being shut, and stood in the midst, and said, Peace *be* unto you.

• **Opening the understanding of his disciples.**

Lk 24:45 — Then opened he their understanding, that they might understand the scriptures,

• **His ascension.**

Lk 24:51 — And it came to pass, while he blessed them, he was parted from them, and carried up into heaven.

Ac 1:9 — And when he had spoken these things, while they beheld, he was taken up; and a cloud received him out of their sight.

See: Miracles, of Jesus

JESUS, Miscellaneous Facts Concerning

• **Brethren of.**

Mt 13:55 — Is not this the carpenter's son? is not his mother called Mary? and his brethren, James, and Joses, and Simon, and Judas?

Mk 6:3 — Is not this the carpenter, the son of Mary, the brother of James, and Joses, and of Juda, and Simon? and are not his sisters here with us? And they were offended at him.

1Co 9:5 — Have we not power to lead about a sister, a wife, as well as other apostles, and *as* the brethren of the Lord, and Cephas?

Gal 1:19 — But other of the apostles saw I none, save James the Lord's brother.

• Sisters of.

Mt 13:56 — And his sisters, are they not all with us? Whence then hath this *man* all these things?

Mk 6:3 — Is not this the carpenter, the son of Mary, the brother of James, and Joses, and of Juda, and Simon? and are not his sisters here with us? And they were offended at him.

• Was with the Israelites in the wilderness.

1Co 10:4 — And did all drink the same spiritual drink: for they drank of that spiritual Rock that followed them: and that Rock was Christ.

1Co 10:9 — Neither let us tempt Christ, as some of them also tempted, and were destroyed of serpents.

Heb 11:26 — Esteeming the reproach of Christ greater riches than the treasures in Egypt: for he had respect unto the recompence of the reward.

Jude 1:5 — I will therefore put you in remembrance, though ye once knew this, how that the Lord, having saved the people out of the land of Egypt, afterward destroyed them that believed not.

JESUS, Mission of

2Sa 23:3–4; Isa 42:6–7; 61:1–3; Mal 3:2–3; Mt 3:11–12; 10:34–36; 18:11–14; Mk 2:15–22; Lk 1:78–79; 2:30–32, 34–35; 4:18–19; 5:30–32; 12:49–53; 15:3–7; 22:35–38; 24:46–47; Jn 3:13–17; 11:50–52; 12:46–47; Ro 5:6–8; 8:3–4; 15:8–9; 2Co 5:14–15; Gal 1:3–4; 4:4–5; Heb 2:14–15

Da 9:24 — Seventy weeks are determined upon thy people and upon thy holy city, to finish the transgression, and to make an end of sins, and to make reconciliation for iniquity, and to bring in everlasting righteousness, and to seal up the vision and prophecy, and to anoint the most Holy.

Da 9:27 — And he shall confirm the covenant with many for one week: and in the midst of the week he shall cause the sacrifice and the oblation to cease, and for the overspreading of abominations he shall make *it* desolate, even until the consummation, and that determined shall be poured upon the desolate.

Mic 5:2 — But thou, Bethlehem Ephratah, *though* thou be little among the thousands of Judah, *yet* out of thee shall he come forth unto me *that is* to be ruler in Israel; whose goings forth *have been* from of old, from everlasting.

Mic 7:6 — For the son dishonoureth the father, the daughter riseth up against her mother, the daughter in law against her mother in law; a man's enemies *are* the men of his own house.

Zec 13:1 — In that day there shall be a fountain opened to the house of David and to the inhabitants of Jerusalem for sin and for uncleanness.

Mt 1:21 — And she shall bring forth a son, and thou shalt call his name Jesus: for he shall save his people from their sins.

Mt 4:23 — And Jesus went about all Galilee, teaching in their synagogues, and preaching the gospel of the kingdom, and healing all manner of sickness and all manner of disease among the people.

Mt 5:17 — Think not that I am come to destroy the law, or the prophets: I am not come to destroy, but to fulfil.

Mt 9:13 — But go ye and learn what *that* meaneth, I will have mercy, and not sacrifice: for I am not come to call the righteous, but sinners to repentance.

Mt 15:24 — But he answered and said, I am not sent but unto the lost sheep of the house of Israel.

Mt 20:28 — Even as the Son of man came not to be ministered unto, but to minister, and to give his life a ransom for many.

Mk 1:38 — And he said unto them, Let us go into the next towns, that I may preach there also: for therefore came I forth.

Mk 10:45 — For even the Son of man came not to be ministered unto, but to minister, and to give his life a ransom for many.

Lk 2:38 — And she coming in that instant gave thanks likewise unto the Lord, and spake of him to all them that looked for redemption in Jerusalem.

Lk 4:43 — And he said unto them, I must preach the kingdom of God to other cities also: for therefore am I sent.

Lk 8:1 — And it came to pass afterward, that he went throughout every city and village, preaching and shewing the glad tidings of the kingdom of God: and the twelve *were* with him,

Lk 9:56 — For the Son of man is not come to destroy men's lives, but to save *them*. And they went to another village.

Lk 19:10 — For the Son of man is come to seek and to save that which was lost.

Lk 24:26 — Ought not Christ to have suffered these things, and to enter into his glory?

Jn 4:25 — The woman saith unto him, I know that Messias cometh, which is called Christ: when he is come, he will tell us all things.

Jn 4:34 — Jesus saith unto them, My meat is to do the will of him that sent me, and to finish his work.

Jn 6:51 — I am the living bread which came down from heaven: if any man eat of this bread, he shall live for ever: and the bread that I will give is my flesh, which I will give for the life of the world.

Jn 8:12 — Then spake Jesus again unto them, saying, I am the light of the world: he that followeth me shall not walk in darkness, but shall have the light of life.

Jn 9:39 — And Jesus said, For judgment I am come into this world, that they which see not might see; and that they which see might be made blind.

Jn 10:10 — The thief cometh not, but for to steal, and to kill, and to destroy: I am come that they might have life, and that they might have *it* more abundantly.

Jn 12:27 — Now is my soul troubled; and what shall I say? Father, save me from this hour: but for this cause came I unto this hour.

Jn 18:37 — Pilate therefore said unto him, Art thou a king then? Jesus answered, Thou sayest that I am a king. To this end was I born, and for this cause came I into the world, that I should bear witness unto the truth. Every one that is of the truth heareth my voice.

Ac 5:31 — Him hath God exalted with his right hand *to be* a Prince and a Saviour, for to give repentance to Israel, and forgiveness of sins.

Ac 10:43 — To him give all the prophets witness, that through his name whosoever believeth in him shall receive remission of sins.

Ac 26:23 — That Christ should suffer, *and* that he should be the first that should rise from the dead, and should shew light unto the people, and to the Gentiles.

Ro 4:25 — Who was delivered for our offences, and was raised again for our justification.

Ro 10:4 — For Christ *is* the end of the law for righteousness to every one that believeth.

Ro 14:9 — For to this end Christ both died, and rose, and revived, that he might be Lord both of the dead and living.

Ro 14:15 — But if thy brother be grieved with *thy* meat, now walkest thou not charitably. Destroy not him with thy meat, for whom Christ died.

Eph 4:10 — He that descended is the same also that ascended up far above all heavens, that he might fill all things.)

1Ti 1:15 — This *is* a faithful saying, and worthy of all acceptation, that Christ Jesus came into the world to save sinners; of whom I am chief.

Heb 2:9 — But we see Jesus, who was made a little lower than the angels for the suffering of death, crowned with glory and honour; that he by the grace of God should taste death for every man.

Heb 2:18 — For in that he himself hath suffered being tempted, he is able to succour them that are tempted.

Heb 9:26 — For then must he often have suffered since the foundation of the world: but now once in the end of the world hath he appeared to put away sin by the sacrifice of himself.

1Jn 3:5 — And ye know that he was manifested to take away our sins; and in him is no sin.

1Jn 3:8 — He that committeth sin is of the devil; for the devil sinneth from the beginning. For this purpose the Son of God was manifested, that he might destroy the works of the devil.

1Jn 4:10 — Herein is love, not that we loved God, but that he loved us, and sent his Son *to be* the propitiation for our sins.

JESUS, Names, Appellations, and Titles of

• Adam.

1Co 15:45 — And so it is written, The first man Adam was made a living soul; the last Adam *was made* a quickening spirit.

• Advocate.

1Jn 2:1 — My little children, these things write I unto you, that ye sin not. And if any man sin, we have an advocate with the Father, Jesus Christ the righteous:

• Almighty.

Rev 1:8 — I am Alpha and Omega, the beginning and the ending, saith the Lord, which is, and which was, and which is to come, the Almighty.

• Alpha and Omega.

Rev 1:8 — I am Alpha and Omega, the beginning and the ending, saith the Lord, which is, and which was, and which is to come, the Almighty.

• Amen.

Rev 3:14 — And unto the angel of the church of the Laodiceans write; These things saith the Amen, the faithful and true witness, the beginning of the creation of God;

• Angel.

Ex 23:20–21

Ge 48:16 — The Angel which redeemed me from all evil, bless the lads; and let my name be named on them, and the name of my fathers Abraham and Isaac; and let them grow into a multitude in the midst of the earth.

• Angel of his presence.

Isa 63:9 — In all their affliction he was afflicted, and the angel of his presence saved them: in his love and in his pity he redeemed them; and he bare them, and carried them all the days of old.

• Anointed.

Ps 2:2 — The kings of the earth set themselves, and the rulers take counsel together, against the LORD, and against his anointed, *saying,*

• Apostle.

Heb 3:1 — Wherefore, holy brethren, partakers of the heavenly calling, consider the Apostle and High Priest of our profession, Christ Jesus;

• Arm of the Lord.

Isa 51:9–10

• Author and finisher of our faith.

Heb 12:2 — Looking unto Jesus the author and finisher of *our* faith; who for the joy that was set before him endured the cross, despising the shame, and is set down at the right hand of the throne of God.

• Beginning and end of the creation of God.

Rev 3:14 — And unto the angel of the church of the Laodiceans write; These things saith the Amen, the faithful and true witness, the beginning of the creation of God;

Rev 22:13 — I am Alpha and Omega, the beginning and the end, the first and the last.

• Beloved.

Eph 1:6 — To the praise of the glory of his grace, wherein he hath made us accepted in the beloved.

• Bishop.

1Pe 2:25 — For ye were as sheep going astray; but are now returned unto the Shepherd and Bishop of your souls.

• Blessed and only Potentate.

1Ti 6:15 — Which in his times he shall shew, *who is* the blessed and only Potentate, the King of kings, and Lord of lords;

• Branch.

Jer 23:5 — Behold, the days come, saith the LORD, that I will raise unto David a righteous Branch, and a King shall reign and prosper, and shall execute judgment and justice in the earth.

Zec 3:8 — Hear now, O Joshua the high priest, thou, and thy fellows that sit before thee: for they *are* men wondered at: for, behold, I will bring forth my servant the BRANCH.

• Bread of life.

Jn 6:48 — I am that bread of life.

• Bridegroom.

Mt 9:15 — And Jesus said unto them, Can the children of the bridechamber mourn, as long as the bridegroom is with them? but the days will come, when the bridegroom shall be taken from them, and then shall they fast.

• Bright and morning star.

Rev 22:16 — I Jesus have sent mine angel to testify unto you these things in the churches. I am the root and the offspring of David, *and* the bright and morning star.

• Brightness of the Father's glory.

Heb 1:3 — Who being the brightness of *his* glory, and the express image of his person, and upholding all things by the word of his power, when he had by himself purged our sins, sat down on the right hand of the Majesty on high;

• Captain of the Lord's host.

Jos 5:14 — And he said, Nay; but *as* captain of the host of the LORD am I now come. And Joshua fell on his face to the earth, and did worship, and said unto him, What saith my lord unto his servant?

• Captain of salvation.

Heb 2:10 — For it became him, for whom *are* all things, and by whom *are* all things, in bringing many sons unto glory, to make the captain of their salvation perfect through sufferings.

• Carpenter.

Mk 6:3 — Is not this the carpenter, the son of Mary, the brother of James, and Joses, and of Juda, and Simon? and are not his sisters here with us? And they were offended at him.

• Carpenter's son.

Mt 13:55 — Is not this the carpenter's son? is not his mother called Mary? and his brethren, James, and Joses, and Simon, and Judas?

• Chief Shepherd.

1Pe 5:4 — And when the chief Shepherd shall appear, ye shall receive a crown of glory that fadeth not away.

• Chief corner stone.

1Pe 2:6 — Wherefore also it is contained in the scripture, Behold, I lay in Sion a chief corner stone, elect, precious: and he that believeth on him shall not be confounded.

• Chiefest among ten thousand.

SS 5:10 — My beloved *is* white and ruddy, the chiefest among ten thousand.

• Child.

Isa 9:6 — For unto us a child is born, unto us a son is given: and the government shall be upon his shoulder: and his name shall be called Wonderful, Counsellor, The mighty God, The everlasting Father, The Prince of Peace.

Lk 2:27 — And he came by the Spirit into the temple: and when the parents brought in the child Jesus, to do for him after the custom of the law,

Lk 2:43 — And when they had fulfilled the days, as they returned, the child Jesus tarried behind in Jerusalem; and Joseph and his mother knew not *of it.*

• Chosen of God.

1Pe 2:4 — To whom coming, *as unto* a living stone, disallowed indeed of men, but chosen of God, *and* precious,

• Christ.

Mt 1:16 — And Jacob begat Joseph the husband of Mary, of whom was born Jesus, who is called Christ.

Lk 9:20 — He said unto them, But whom say ye that I am? Peter answering said, The Christ of God.

• The Christ.

Mt 16:20 — Then charged he his disciples that they should tell no man that he was Jesus the Christ.

Mk 14:61 — But he held his peace, and answered nothing. Again the high priest asked him, and said unto him, Art thou the Christ, the Son of the Blessed?

• Christ, a King.

Lk 23:2 — And they began to accuse him, saying, We found this *fellow* perverting the nation, and forbidding to give tribute to Caesar, saying that he himself is Christ a King.

• Christ Jesus.

Ac 19:4 — Then said Paul, John verily baptized with the baptism of repentance, saying unto the people, that they should believe on him which should come after him, that is, on Christ Jesus.

Ro 3:24 — Being justified freely by his grace through the redemption that is in Christ Jesus:

Ro 8:1 — *There is* therefore now no condemnation to them which are in Christ Jesus, who walk not after the flesh, but after the Spirit.

1Co 1:2 — Unto the church of God which is at Corinth, to them that are sanctified in Christ Jesus, called *to be* saints, with all that in every place call upon the name of Jesus Christ our Lord, both theirs and ours:

1Co 1:30 — But of him are ye in Christ Jesus, who of God is made unto us wisdom, and righteousness, and sanctification, and redemption:

Heb 3:1 — Wherefore, holy brethren, partakers of the heavenly calling, consider the Apostle and High Priest of our profession, Christ Jesus;

1Pe 5:10 — But the God of all grace, who hath called us unto his eternal glory by Christ Jesus, after that ye have suffered a while, make you perfect, stablish, strengthen, settle *you.*

1Pe 5:14 — Greet ye one another with a kiss of charity. Peace *be* with you all that are in Christ Jesus. Amen.

• **Christ Jesus our Lord.**

Ro 8:39 — Nor height, nor depth, nor any other creature, shall be able to separate us from the love of God, which is in Christ Jesus our Lord.

1Ti 1:12 — And I thank Christ Jesus our Lord, who hath enabled me, for that he counted me faithful, putting me into the ministry;

• **Christ of God.**

Lk 9:20 — He said unto them, But whom say ye that I am? Peter answering said, The Christ of God.

• **Christ, the chosen of God.**

Lk 23:35 — And the people stood beholding. And the rulers also with them derided *him,* saying, He saved others; let him save himself, if he be Christ, the chosen of God.

• **Christ the Lord.**

Lk 2:11 — For unto you is born this day in the city of David a Saviour, which is Christ the Lord.

• **Christ the power of God.**

1Co 1:24 — But unto them which are called, both Jews and Greeks, Christ the power of God, and the wisdom of God.

• **Christ the wisdom of God.**

1Co 1:24 — But unto them which are called, both Jews and Greeks, Christ the power of God, and the wisdom of God.

• **Christ, the Son of God.**

Ac 9:20 — And straightway he preached Christ in the synagogues, that he is the Son of God.

• **Christ, Son of the Blessed.**

Mk 14:61 — But he held his peace, and answered nothing. Again the high priest asked him, and said unto him, Art thou the Christ, the Son of the Blessed?

• **Commander.**

Isa 55:4 — Behold, I have given him *for* a witness to the people, a leader and commander to the people.

• **Consolation of Israel.**

Lk 2:25 — And, behold, there was a man in Jerusalem, whose name *was* Simeon; and the same man *was* just and devout, waiting for the consolation of Israel: and the Holy Ghost was upon him.

• **Corner stone.**

Eph 2:20 — And are built upon the foundation of the apostles and prophets, Jesus Christ himself being the chief corner *stone;*

• **Counsellor.**

Isa 9:6 — For unto us a child is born, unto us a son is given: and the government shall be upon his shoulder: and his name shall be called Wonderful, Counsellor, The mighty God, The everlasting Father, The Prince of Peace.

• **Covenant of the people.**

Isa 42:6 — I the LORD have called thee in righteousness, and will hold thine hand, and will keep thee, and give thee for a covenant of the people, for a light of the Gentiles;

• **David.**

Jer 30:9 — But they shall serve the LORD their God, and David their king, whom I will raise up unto them.

• **Daysman.**

Job 9:33 — Neither is there any daysman betwixt us, *that* might lay his hand upon us both.

• **Dayspring.**

Lk 1:78 — Through the tender mercy of our God; whereby the dayspring from on high hath visited us,

• **Day star.**

2Pe 1:19 — We have also a more sure word of prophecy; whereunto ye do well that ye take heed, as unto a light that shineth in a dark place, until the day dawn, and the day star arise in your hearts:

• **Deliverer.**

Ro 11:26 — And so all Israel shall be saved: as it is written, There shall come out of Sion the Deliverer, and shall turn away ungodliness from Jacob:

• **Desire of all nations.**

Hag 2:7 — And I will shake all nations, and the desire of all nations shall come: and I will fill this house with glory, saith the LORD of hosts.

• **Door.**

Jn 10:7 — Then said Jesus unto them again, Verily, verily, I say unto you, I am the door of the sheep.

• **Elect.**

Isa 42:1 — Behold my servant, whom I uphold; mine elect, *in whom* my soul delighteth; I have put my spirit upon him: he shall bring forth judgment to the Gentiles.

• **Emmanuel.**

Isa 7:14 — Therefore the Lord himself shall give you a sign; Behold, a virgin shall conceive, and bear a son, and shall call his name Immanuel.

• **Ensign.**

Isa 11:10 — And in that day there shall be a root of Jesse, which shall stand for an ensign of the people; to it shall the Gentiles seek: and his rest shall be glorious.

• **Eternal life.**

1Jn 5:20 — *And* we know that the Son of God is come, and hath given us an understanding, that we may know him that is true, and we are in him that is true, *even* in his Son Jesus Christ. This is the true God, and eternal life.

• **Everlasting Father.**

Isa 9:6 — For unto us a child is born, unto us a son is given: and the government shall be upon his shoulder: and his name shall be called Wonderful, Counsellor, The mighty God, The everlasting Father, The Prince of Peace.

• **Faithful and True.**

Rev 19:11 — And I saw heaven opened, and behold a white horse; and he that sat upon him *was* called Faithful and True, and in righteousness he doth judge and make war.

• **Faithful witness.**

Rev 1:5 — And from Jesus Christ, *who is* the faithful witness, *and* the first begotten of the dead, and the prince of the kings of the earth. Unto him that loved us, and washed us from our sins in his own blood,

• **Faithful and true witness.**

Rev 3:14 — And unto the angel of the church of the Laodiceans write; These things saith the Amen, the faithful and true witness, the beginning of the creation of God;

• **Finisher of faith.**

Heb 12:2 — Looking unto Jesus the author and finisher of *our* faith; who for the joy that was set before him endured the cross, despising the shame, and is set down at the right hand of the throne of God.

• **First and last.**

Rev 1:17 — And when I saw him, I fell at his feet as dead. And he laid his right hand upon me, saying unto me, Fear not; I am the first and the last:

Rev 2:8 — And unto the angel of the church in Smyrna write; These things saith the first and the last, which was dead, and is alive;

Rev 22:13 — I am Alpha and Omega, the beginning and the end, the first and the last.

• **First begotten.**

Heb 1:6 — And again, when he bringeth in the firstbegotten into the world, he saith, And let all the angels of God worship him.

• **First begotten of the dead.**

Rev 1:5 — And from Jesus Christ, *who is* the faithful witness, *and* the first begotten of the dead, and the prince of the kings of the earth. Unto him that loved us, and washed us from our sins in his own blood,

• **Firstborn.**

Ps 89:27 — Also I will make him *my* firstborn, higher than the kings of the earth.

• **Foundation.**

Isa 28:16 — Therefore thus saith the Lord GOD, Behold, I lay in Zion for a foundation a stone, a tried stone, a precious corner *stone,* a sure foundation: he that believeth shall not make haste.

• **Fountain.**

Zec 13:1 — In that day there shall be a fountain opened to the house of David and to the inhabitants of Jerusalem for sin and for uncleanness.

• **Forerunner.**

Heb 6:20 — Whither the forerunner is for us entered, *even* Jesus, made an high priest for ever after the order of Melchisedec.

• **Friend of sinners.**

Mt 11:19 — The Son of man came eating and drinking, and they say, Behold a man gluttonous, and a winebibber, a friend of publicans and sinners. But wisdom is justified of her children.

• **Gift of God.**

Jn 4:10 — Jesus answered and said unto her, If thou knewest the gift of God, and who it is that saith to thee, Give me to drink; thou wouldest have asked of him, and he would have given thee living water.

• **Glory of Israel.**

Lk 2:32 — A light to lighten the Gentiles, and the glory of thy people Israel.

• **God.**

Jn 1:1 — In the beginning was the Word, and the Word was with God, and the Word was God.

• **God blessed forever.**

Ro 9:5 — Whose *are* the fathers, and of whom as concerning the flesh Christ *came,* who is over all, God blessed for ever. Amen.

• **God manifest in the flesh.**

1Ti 3:16 — And without controversy great is the mystery of godliness: God was manifest in the flesh, justified in the Spirit, seen of angels, preached unto the Gentiles, believed on in the world, received up into glory.

• **God of Israel, the Saviour.**

Isa 45:15 — Verily thou *art* a God that hidest thyself, O God of Israel, the Saviour.

• **God of the whole earth.**

Isa 54:5— For thy Maker *is* thine husband; the LORD of hosts *is* his name; and thy Redeemer the Holy One of Israel; The God of the whole earth shall he be called.

• **God our Saviour.**

1Ti 2:3 — For this *is* good and acceptable in the sight of God our Saviour;

• **God's dear Son.**

Col 1:13 — Who hath delivered us from the power of darkness, and hath translated *us* into the kingdom of his dear Son:

• **God with us.**

Mt 1:23 — Behold, a virgin shall be with child, and shall bring forth a son, and they shall call his name Emmanuel, which being interpreted is, God with us.

• **Good Master.**

Mt 19:16 — And, behold, one came and said unto him, Good Master, what good thing shall I do, that I may have eternal life?

• **Governor.**

Mt 2:6 — And thou Bethlehem, in the land of Juda, art not the least among the princes of Juda: for out of thee shall come a Governor, that shall rule my people Israel.

• **Great shepherd of the sheep.**

Heb 13:20 — Now the God of peace, that brought again from the dead our Lord Jesus, that great shepherd of the sheep, through the blood of the everlasting covenant,

• **Head of the church.**

Eph 5:23 — For the husband is the head of the wife, even as Christ is the head of the church: and he is the saviour of the body.

• **Heir of all things.**

Heb 1:2 — Hath in these last days spoken unto us by *his* Son, whom he hath appointed heir of all things, by whom also he made the worlds;

• High priest.

Heb 4:14 — Seeing then that we have a great high priest, that is passed into the heavens, Jesus the Son of God, let us hold fast *our* profession.

• Head of every man.

1Co 11:3 — But I would have you know, that the head of every man is Christ; and the head of the woman *is* the man; and the head of Christ *is* God.

• Head of the church.

Col 1:18 — And he is the head of the body, the church: who is the beginning, the firstborn from the dead; that in all *things* he might have the preeminence.

• Head of the corner.

Mt 21:42 — Jesus saith unto them, Did ye never read in the scriptures, The stone which the builders rejected, the same is become the head of the corner: this is the Lord's doing, and it is marvellous in our eyes?

• Holy child Jesus.

Ac 4:30 — By stretching forth thine hand to heal; and that signs and wonders may be done by the name of thy holy child Jesus.

• Holy one.

Ps 16:10 — For thou wilt not leave my soul in hell; neither wilt thou suffer thine Holy One to see corruption.

Ac 3:14 — But ye denied the Holy One and the Just, and desired a murderer to be granted unto you;

• Holy one of God.

Mk 1:24 — Saying, Let *us* alone; what have we to do with thee, thou Jesus of Nazareth? art thou come to destroy us? I know thee who thou art, the Holy One of God.

• Holy one of Israel.

Isa 41:14 — Fear not, thou worm Jacob, *and* ye men of Israel; I will help thee, saith the LORD, and thy redeemer, the Holy One of Israel.

Isa 54:5 — For thy Maker *is* thine husband; the LORD of hosts *is* his name; and thy Redeemer the Holy One of Israel; The God of the whole earth shall he be called.

• Holy thing.

Lk 1:35 — And the angel answered and said unto her, The Holy Ghost shall come upon thee, and the power of the Highest shall overshadow thee: therefore also that holy thing which shall be born of thee shall be called the Son of God.

• Hope (our).

1Ti 1:1 — Paul, an apostle of Jesus Christ by the commandment of God our Saviour, and Lord Jesus Christ, *which is* our hope;

• Horn of salvation.

Lk 1:69 — And hath raised up an horn of salvation for us in the house of his servant David;

• I Am.

Jn 8:58 — Jesus said unto them, Verily, verily, I say unto you, Before Abraham was, I am.

• Image of God.

Heb 1:3 — Who being the brightness of *his* glory, and the express image of his person, and upholding all things by the word of his power, when he had by himself purged our sins, sat down on the right hand of the Majesty on high;

• Israel.

Isa 49:3 — And said unto me, Thou *art* my servant, O Israel, in whom I will be glorified.

• Jehovah.

Isa 40:3 — The voice of him that crieth in the wilderness, Prepare ye the way of the LORD, make straight in the desert a highway for our God.

• Jehovah's fellow.

Zec 13:7 — Awake, O sword, against my shepherd, and against the man *that is* my fellow, saith the LORD of hosts: smite the shepherd, and the sheep shall be scattered: and I will turn mine hand upon the little ones.

• Jesus.

Mt 1:21 — And she shall bring forth a son, and thou shalt call his name JESUS: for he shall save his people from their sins.

• Jesus Christ.

Mt 1:1 — The book of the generation of Jesus Christ, the son of David, the son of Abraham.

Jn 1:17 — For the law was given by Moses, *but* grace and truth came by Jesus Christ.

Jn 17:3 — And this is life eternal, that they might know thee the only true God, and Jesus Christ, whom thou hast sent.

Ac 2:38 — Then Peter said unto them, Repent, and be baptized every one of you in the name of Jesus Christ for the remission of sins, and ye shall receive the gift of the Holy Ghost.

Ac 4:10 — Be it known unto you all, and to all the people of Israel, that by the name of Jesus Christ of Nazareth, whom ye crucified, whom God raised from the dead, *even* by him doth this man stand here before you whole.

Ac 9:34 — And Peter said unto him, Aeneas, Jesus Christ maketh thee whole: arise, and make thy bed. And he arose immediately.

Ac 10:36 — The word which *God* sent unto the children of Israel, preaching peace by Jesus Christ: (he is Lord of all:)

Ac 16:18 — And this did she many days. But Paul, being grieved, turned and said to the spirit, I command thee in the name of Jesus Christ to come out of her. And he came out the same hour.

Ro 1:1 — Paul, a servant of Jesus Christ, called *to be* an apostle, separated unto the gospel of God,

Ro 1:3 — Concerning his Son Jesus Christ our Lord, which was made of the seed of David according to the flesh;

Ro 1:6 — Among whom are ye also the called of Jesus Christ:

Ro 2:16 — In the day when God shall judge the secrets of men by Jesus Christ according to my gospel.

Ro 5:15 — But not as the offence, so also *is* the free gift. For if through the offence of one many be dead, much more the grace of God, and the gift by grace, *which is* by one man, Jesus Christ, hath abounded unto many.

Ro 5:17 — For if by one man's offence death reigned by one; much more they which receive abundance of grace and of the gift of righteousness shall reign in life by one, Jesus Christ.)

Ro 6:3 — Know ye not, that so many of us as were baptized into Jesus Christ were baptized into his death?

1Co 1:1 — Paul, called *to be* an apostle of Jesus Christ through the will of God, and Sosthenes *our* brother,

1Co 1:4 — I thank my God always on your behalf, for the grace of God which is given you by Jesus Christ;

1Co 2:2 — For I determined not to know any thing among you, save Jesus Christ, and him crucified.

2Co 1:19 — For the Son of God, Jesus Christ, who was preached among you by us, *even* by me and Silvanus and Timotheus, was not yea and nay, but in him was yea.

2Co 4:6 — For God, who commanded the light to shine out of darkness, hath shined in our hearts, to *give* the light of the knowledge of the glory of God in the face of Jesus Christ.

2Co 13:5 — Examine yourselves, whether ye be in the faith; prove your own selves. Know ye not your own selves, how that Jesus Christ is in you, except ye be reprobates?

Gal 2:16 — Knowing that a man is not justified by the works of the law, but by the faith of Jesus Christ, even we have believed in Jesus Christ, that we might be justified by the faith of Christ, and not by the works of the law: for by the works of the law shall no flesh be justified.

Php 1:8 — For God is my record, how greatly I long after you all in the bowels of Jesus Christ.

Php 2:11 — And *that* every tongue should confess that Jesus Christ *is* Lord, to the glory of God the Father.

1Ti 1:15 — This *is* a faithful saying, and worthy of all acceptation, that Christ Jesus came into the world to save sinners; of whom I am chief.

Heb 13:8 — Jesus Christ the same yesterday, and to day, and for ever.

1Jn 1:7 — But if we walk in the light, as he is in the light, we have fellowship one with another, and the blood of Jesus Christ his Son cleanseth us from all sin.

1Jn 2:1 — My little children, these things write I unto you, that ye sin not. And if any man sin, we have an advocate with the Father, Jesus Christ the righteous:

• Jesus Christ our Lord.

Ro 1:3 — Concerning his Son Jesus Christ our Lord, which was made of the seed of David according to the flesh;

Ro 6:11 — Likewise reckon ye also yourselves to be dead indeed unto sin, but alive unto God through Jesus Christ our Lord.

Ro 6:23 — For the wages of sin *is* death; but the gift of God *is* eternal life through Jesus Christ our Lord.

1Co 1:9 — God *is* faithful, by whom ye were called unto the fellowship of his Son Jesus Christ our Lord.

1Co 7:25 — Now concerning virgins I have no commandment of the Lord: yet I give my judgment, as one that hath obtained mercy of the Lord to be faithful.

• Jesus Christ our Saviour.

Tit 3:6 — Which he shed on us abundantly through Jesus Christ our Saviour;

• Jesus of Nazareth.

Mk 1:24 — Saying, Let *us* alone; what have we to do with thee, thou Jesus of Nazareth? art thou come to destroy us? I know thee who thou art, the Holy One of God.

Lk 24:19 — And he said unto them, What things? And they said unto him, Concerning Jesus of Nazareth, which was a prophet mighty in deed and word before God and all the people:

• Jesus of Nazareth, King of the Jews.

Jn 19:19 — And Pilate wrote a title, and put *it* on the cross. And the writing was, JESUS OF NAZARETH THE KING OF THE JEWS.

• Jesus, the King of the Jews.

Mt 27:37 — And set up over his head his accusation written, THIS IS JESUS THE KING OF THE JEWS.

• Jesus, the Son of God.

Heb 4:14 — Seeing then that we have a great high priest, that is passed into the heavens, Jesus the Son of God, let us hold fast *our* profession.

• Jesus, the Son of Joseph.

Jn 6:42 — And they said, Is not this Jesus, the son of Joseph, whose father and mother we know? how is it then that he saith, I came down from heaven?

• Judge.

Ac 10:42 — And he commanded us to preach unto the people, and to testify that it is he which was ordained of God *to be* the Judge of quick and dead.

• Just man.

Mt 27:19 — When he was set down on the judgment seat, his wife sent unto him, saying, Have thou nothing to do with that just man: for I have suffered many things this day in a dream because of him.

• Just one.

Ac 3:14 — But ye denied the Holy One and the Just, and desired a murderer to be granted unto you;

Ac 7:52 — Which of the prophets have not your fathers persecuted? and they have slain them which shewed before of the coming of the Just One; of whom ye have been now the betrayers and murderers:

Ac 22:14 — And he said, The God of our fathers hath chosen thee, that thou shouldest know his will, and see that Just One, and shouldest hear the voice of his mouth.

• Just person.

Mt 27:24 — When Pilate saw that he could prevail nothing, but *that* rather a tumult was made, he took water, and washed *his* hands before the multitude, saying, I am innocent of the blood of this just person: see ye *to it*.

• King.

Mt 21:5 — Tell ye the daughter of Sion, Behold, thy King cometh unto thee, meek, and sitting upon an ass, and a colt the foal of an ass.

- **King of Israel.**

Jn 1:49 — Nathanael answered and saith unto him, Rabbi, thou art the Son of God; thou art the King of Israel.

- **King of the Jews.**

Mt 2:2 — Saying, Where is he that is born King of the Jews? for we have seen his star in the east, and are come to worship him.

- **King of saints.**

Rev 15:3 — And they sing the song of Moses the servant of God, and the song of the Lamb, saying, Great and marvellous *are* thy works, Lord God Almighty; just and true *are* thy ways, thou King of saints.

- **King of kings.**

1Ti 6:15 — Which in his times he shall shew, *who is* the blessed and only Potentate, the King of kings, and Lord of lords;

Rev 17:14 — These shall make war with the Lamb, and the Lamb shall overcome them: for he is Lord of lords, and King of kings: and they that are with him *are* called, and chosen, and faithful.

- **King of glory.**

Ps 24:7–10

- **King of Zion.**

Mt 21:5 — Tell ye the daughter of Sion, Behold, thy King cometh unto thee, meek, and sitting upon an ass, and a colt the foal of an ass.

- **King over all the earth.**

Zec 14:9 — And the LORD shall be king over all the earth: in that day shall there be one LORD, and his name one.

- **Lamb.**

Rev 7:9–10; 21:22–23

Rev 5:6 — And I beheld, and, lo, in the midst of the throne and of the four beasts, and in the midst of the elders, stood a Lamb as it had been slain, having seven horns and seven eyes, which are the seven Spirits of God sent forth into all the earth.

Rev 5:8 — And when he had taken the book, the four beasts and four *and* twenty elders fell down before the Lamb, having every one of them harps, and golden vials full of odours, which are the prayers of saints.

Rev 6:16 — And said to the mountains and rocks, Fall on us, and hide us from the face of him that sitteth on the throne, and from the wrath of the Lamb:

Rev 7:17 — For the Lamb which is in the midst of the throne shall feed them, and shall lead them unto living fountains of waters: and God shall wipe away all tears from their eyes.

Rev 12:11 — And they overcame him by the blood of the Lamb, and by the word of their testimony; and they loved not their lives unto the death.

Rev 13:8 — And all that dwell upon the earth shall worship him, whose names are not written in the book of life of the Lamb slain from the foundation of the world.

Rev 13:11 — And I beheld another beast coming up out of the earth; and he had two horns like a lamb, and he spake as a dragon.

Rev 14:1 — And I looked, and, lo, a Lamb stood on the mount Sion, and with him an hundred forty *and* four thousand, having his Father's name written in their foreheads.

Rev 14:4 — These are they which were not defiled with women; for they are virgins. These are they which follow the Lamb whithersoever he goeth. These were redeemed from among men, *being* the firstfruits unto God and to the Lamb.

Rev 15:3 — And they sing the song of Moses the servant of God, and the song of the Lamb, saying, Great and marvellous *are* thy works, Lord God Almighty; just and true *are* thy ways, thou King of saints.

Rev 17:14 — These shall make war with the Lamb, and the Lamb shall overcome them: for he is Lord of lords, and King of kings: and they that are with him *are* called, and chosen, and faithful.

Rev 19:7 — Let us be glad and rejoice, and give honour to him: for the marriage of the Lamb is come, and his wife hath made herself ready.

Rev 19:9 — And he saith unto me, Write, Blessed *are* they which are called unto the marriage supper of the Lamb. And he saith unto me, These are the true sayings of God.

Rev 21:9 — And there came unto me one of the seven angels which had the seven vials full of the seven last plagues, and talked with me, saying, Come hither, I will shew thee the bride, the Lamb's wife.

Rev 21:14 — And the wall of the city had twelve foundations, and in them the names of the twelve apostles of the Lamb.

Rev 21:27 — And there shall in no wise enter into it any thing that defileth, neither *whatsoever* worketh abomination, or *maketh* a lie: but they which are written in the Lamb's book of life.

- **Lamb of God.**

Jn 1:29 — The next day John seeth Jesus coming unto him, and saith, Behold the Lamb of God, which taketh away the sin of the world.

- **Lawgiver.**

Isa 33:22 — For the LORD *is* our judge, the LORD *is* our lawgiver, the LORD *is* our king; he will save us.

- **Leader.**

Isa 55:4 — Behold, I have given him *for* a witness to the people, a leader and commander to the people.

- **Life.**

Jn 14:6 — Jesus saith unto him, <u>I am the way, the truth, and the life: no man cometh unto the Father, but by me.</u>

- **Light.**

Jn 8:12 — Then spake Jesus again unto them, saying, <u>I am the light of the world: he that followeth me shall not walk in darkness, but shall have the light of life.</u>

- **Light, everlasting.**

Isa 60:20 — Thy sun shall no more go down; neither shall thy moon withdraw itself: for the LORD shall be thine everlasting light, and the days of thy mourning shall be ended.

• **Light of the world.**

Jn 8:12 — Then spake Jesus again unto them, saying, I am the light of the world: he that followeth me shall not walk in darkness, but shall have the light of life.

• **Light to the Gentiles.**

Isa 42:6 — I the LORD have called thee in righteousness, and will hold thine hand, and will keep thee, and give thee for a covenant of the people, for a light of the Gentiles;

• **Light, true.**

Jn 1:9 — *That* was the true Light, which lighteth every man that cometh into the world.

• **Living bread.**

Jn 6:51 — I am the living bread which came down from heaven: if any man eat of this bread, he shall live for ever: and the bread that I will give is my flesh, which I will give for the life of the world.

• **Living stone.**

1Pe 2:4 — To whom coming, *as unto* a living stone, disallowed indeed of men, but chosen of God, *and* precious,

• **Lion of the tribe of Judah.**

Rev 5:5 — And one of the elders saith unto me, Weep not: behold, the Lion of the tribe of Juda, the Root of David, hath prevailed to open the book, and to loose the seven seals thereof.

• **Lord.**

Ro 1:3 — Concerning his Son Jesus Christ our Lord, which was made of the seed of David according to the flesh;

• **Lord of lords.**

Rev 17:14 — These shall make war with the Lamb, and the Lamb shall overcome them: for he is Lord of lords, and King of kings: and they that are with him *are* called, and chosen, and faithful.

Rev 19:16 — And he hath on *his* vesture and on his thigh a name written, KING OF KINGS, AND LORD OF LORDS.

• **Lord of all.**

Ac 10:36 — The word which *God* sent unto the children of Israel, preaching peace by Jesus Christ: (he is Lord of all:)

• **Lord our righteousness.**

Jer 23:6 — In his days Judah shall be saved, and Israel shall dwell safely: and this *is* his name whereby he shall be called, THE LORD OUR RIGHTEOUSNESS.

• **Lord God Almighty.**

Rev 15:3 — And they sing the song of Moses the servant of God, and the song of the Lamb, saying, Great and marvellous *are* thy works, Lord God Almighty; just and true *are* thy ways, thou King of saints.

• **Lord from heaven.**

1Co 15:47 — The first man *is* of the earth, earthy: the second man *is* the Lord from heaven.

• **Lord and Saviour Jesus Christ.**

2Pe 1:11 — For so an entrance shall be ministered unto you abundantly into the everlasting kingdom of our Lord and Saviour Jesus Christ.

2Pe 3:18 — But grow in grace, and *in* the knowledge of our Lord and Saviour Jesus Christ. To him *be* glory both now and for ever. Amen.

• **Lord Christ.**

Col 3:24 — Knowing that of the Lord ye shall receive the reward of the inheritance: for ye serve the Lord Christ.

• **Lord Jesus.**

Ac 7:59 — And they stoned Stephen, calling upon *God,* and saying, Lord Jesus, receive my spirit.

Col 3:17 — And whatsoever ye do in word or deed, *do* all in the name of the Lord Jesus, giving thanks to God and the Father by him.

1Th 4:12 — That ye may walk honestly toward them that are without, and *that* ye may have lack of nothing.

• **Lord Jesus Christ.**

Ac 11:17 — Forasmuch then as God gave them the like gift as *he did* unto us, who believed on the Lord Jesus Christ; what was I, that I could withstand God?

Ac 16:31 — And they said, Believe on the Lord Jesus Christ, and thou shalt be saved, and thy house.

Ac 20:21 — Testifying both to the Jews, and also to the Greeks, repentance toward God, and faith toward our Lord Jesus Christ.

Ro 5:1 — Therefore being justified by faith, we have peace with God through our Lord Jesus Christ:

Ro 5:11 — And not only *so,* but we also joy in God through our Lord Jesus Christ, by whom we have now received the atonement.

Ro 13:14 — But put ye on the Lord Jesus Christ, and make not provision for the flesh, to *fulfil* the lusts *thereof.*

• **Lord Jesus Christ our Saviour.**

Tit 1:4 — To Titus, *mine* own son after the common faith: Grace, mercy, *and* peace, from God the Father and the Lord Jesus Christ our Saviour.

• **Lord of glory.**

Jas 2:1 — My brethren, have not the faith of our Lord Jesus Christ, *the Lord* of glory, with respect of persons.

• **Lord of Hosts.**

Isa 44:6 — Thus saith the LORD the King of Israel, and his redeemer the LORD of hosts; I *am* the first, and I *am* the last; and beside me *there is* no God.

• **Lord, mighty in battle.**

Ps 24:8 — Who *is* this King of glory? The LORD strong and mighty, the LORD mighty in battle.

• **Lord the dead and living.**

Ro 14:9 — For to this end Christ both died, and rose, and revived, that he might be Lord both of the dead and living.

• **Lord of the Sabbath.**

Mk 2:28 — Therefore the Son of man is Lord also of the sabbath.

• **Lord over all.**

Ro 10:12 — For there is no difference between the Jew and the Greek: for the same Lord over all is rich unto all that call upon him.

• Lord's Christ.
Lk 2:26 — And it was revealed unto him by the Holy Ghost, that he should not see death, before he had seen the Lord's Christ.

• Lord, strong and mighty.
Ps 24:8 — Who *is* this King of glory? The LORD strong and mighty, the LORD mighty in battle.

• Lord, the, our righteousness.
Jer 23:6 — In his days Judah shall be saved, and Israel shall dwell safely: and this *is* his name whereby he shall be called, THE LORD OUR RIGHTEOUSNESS.

• Lord, your holy one.
Isa 43:15 — I *am* the LORD, your Holy One, the creator of Israel, your King.

• Lord, your redeemer.
Isa 43:14 — Thus saith the LORD, your redeemer, the Holy One of Israel; For your sake I have sent to Babylon, and have brought down all their nobles, and the Chaldeans, whose cry *is* in the ships.

• Man Christ Jesus.
1Ti 2:5 — For *there is* one God, and one mediator between God and men, the man Christ Jesus;

• Man of sorrows.
Isa 53:3 — He is despised and rejected of men; a man of sorrows, and acquainted with grief: and we hid as it were *our* faces from him; he was despised, and we esteemed him not.

• Master.
Mt 23:8 — But be not ye called Rabbi: for one is your Master, *even* Christ; and all ye are brethren.

• Mediator.
1Ti 2:5 — For *there is* one God, and one mediator between God and men, the man Christ Jesus;

• Messenger of the covenant.
Mal 3:1 — Behold, I will send my messenger, and he shall prepare the way before me: and the Lord, whom ye seek, shall suddenly come to his temple, even the messenger of the covenant, whom ye delight in: behold, he shall come, saith the LORD of hosts.

• Messiah.
Jn 1:41 — He first findeth his own brother Simon, and saith unto him, We have found the Messias, which is, being interpreted, the Christ.

• Messiah the Prince.
Da 9:25 — Know therefore and understand, *that* from the going forth of the commandment to restore and to build Jerusalem unto the Messiah the Prince *shall be* seven weeks, and threescore and two weeks: the street shall be built again, and the wall, even in troublous times.

• Mighty God.
Isa 9:6 — For unto us a child is born, unto us a son is given: and the government shall be upon his shoulder: and his name shall be called Wonderful, Counsellor, The mighty God, The everlasting Father, The Prince of Peace.

• Mighty one of Israel.
Isa 30:29 — Ye shall have a song, as in the night *when* a holy solemnity is kept; and gladness of heart, as when one goeth with a pipe to come into the mountain of the LORD, to the mighty One of Israel.

• Mighty one of Jacob.
Isa 49:26 — And I will feed them that oppress thee with their own flesh; and they shall be drunken with their own blood, as with sweet wine: and all flesh shall know that I the LORD *am* thy Saviour and thy Redeemer, the mighty One of Jacob.

• Mighty to save.
Isa 63:1 — Who *is* this that cometh from Edom, with dyed garments from Bozrah? this *that is* glorious in his apparel, travelling in the greatness of his strength? I that speak in righteousness, mighty to save.

• Minister of the sanctuary.
Heb 8:2 — A minister of the sanctuary, and of the true tabernacle, which the Lord pitched, and not man.

• Morning star.
Rev 22:16 — I Jesus have sent mine angel to testify unto you these things in the churches. I am the root and the offspring of David, *and* the bright and morning star.

• Most holy.
Da 9:24 — Seventy weeks are determined upon thy people and upon thy holy city, to finish the transgression, and to make an end of sins, and to make reconciliation for iniquity, and to bring in everlasting righteousness, and to seal up the vision and prophecy, and to anoint the most Holy.

• Most mighty.
Ps 45:3 — Gird thy sword upon *thy* thigh, O *most* mighty, with thy glory and thy majesty.

• Nazarene.
Mt 2:23 — And he came and dwelt in a city called Nazareth: that it might be fulfilled which was spoken by the prophets, He shall be called a Nazarene.

• Offspring of David.
Rev 22:16 — I Jesus have sent mine angel to testify unto you these things in the churches. I am the root and the offspring of David, *and* the bright and morning star.

• Only begotten.
Jn 1:14 — And the Word was made flesh, and dwelt among us, (and we beheld his glory, the glory as of the only begotten of the Father,) full of grace and truth.

• Only begotten of the Father.
Jn 1:14 — And the Word was made flesh, and dwelt among us, (and we beheld his glory, the glory as of the only begotten of the Father,) full of grace and truth.

• Only begotten Son.
Jn 1:18 — No man hath seen God at any time; the only begotten Son, which is in the bosom of the Father, he hath declared *him*.

• Only wise God, our Saviour.
Jude 1:25 — To the only wise God our Saviour, *be* glory and majesty, dominion and power, both now and ever. Amen.

• **Passover.**

1Co 5:7 — Purge out therefore the old leaven, that ye may be a new lump, as ye are unleavened. For even Christ our passover is sacrificed for us:

• **Plant of renown.**

Eze 34:29 — And I will raise up for them a plant of renown, and they shall be no more consumed with hunger in the land, neither bear the shame of the heathen any more.

• **Potentate.**

1Ti 6:15 — Which in his times he shall shew, *who is* the blessed and only Potentate, the King of kings, and Lord of lords;

• **Power of God.**

1Co 1:24 — But unto them which are called, both Jews and Greeks, Christ the power of God, and the wisdom of God.

• **Physician.**

Mt 9:12 — But when Jesus heard *that,* he said unto them, They that be whole need not a physician, but they that are sick.

• **Precious corner stone.**

Isa 28:16 — Therefore thus saith the Lord GOD, Behold, I lay in Zion for a foundation a stone, a tried stone, a precious corner *stone,* a sure foundation: he that believeth shall not make haste.

• **Priest.**

Heb 7:17 — For he testifieth, Thou *art* a priest for ever after the order of Melchisedec.

• **Prince.**

Ac 5:31 — Him hath God exalted with his right hand *to be* a Prince and a Saviour, for to give repentance to Israel, and forgiveness of sins.

• **Prince of life.**

Ac 3:15 — And killed the Prince of life, whom God hath raised from the dead; whereof we are witnesses.

• **Prince of peace.**

Isa 9:6 — For unto us a child is born, unto us a son is given: and the government shall be upon his shoulder: and his name shall be called Wonderful, Counsellor, The mighty God, The everlasting Father, The Prince of Peace.

• **Prince of the kings of the earth.**

Rev 1:5 — And from Jesus Christ, *who is* the faithful witness, *and* the first begotten of the dead, and the prince of the kings of the earth. Unto him that loved us, and washed us from our sins in his own blood,

• **Prophet.**

Dt 18:15 — The LORD thy God will raise up unto thee a Prophet from the midst of thee, of thy brethren, like unto me; unto him ye shall hearken;

Dt 18:18 — I will raise them up a Prophet from among their brethren, like unto thee, and will put my words in his mouth; and he shall speak unto them all that I shall command him.

Mt 21:11 — And the multitude said, This is Jesus the prophet of Nazareth of Galilee.

Lk 24:19 — And he said unto them, What things? And they said unto him, Concerning Jesus of Nazareth, which was a prophet mighty in deed and word before God and all the people:

• **Propitiation.**

1Jn 2:2 — And he is the propitiation for our sins: and not for ours only, but also for *the sins of* the whole world.

• **Rabbi.**

Jn 1:49 — Nathanael answered and saith unto him, Rabbi, thou art the Son of God; thou art the King of Israel.

• **Rabboni.**

Jn 20:16 — Jesus saith unto her, Mary. She turned herself, and saith unto him, Rabboni; which is to say, Master.

• **Ransom.**

1Ti 2:6 — Who gave himself a ransom for all, to be testified in due time.

• **Redeemer.**

Isa 59:20 — And the Redeemer shall come to Zion, and unto them that turn from transgression in Jacob, saith the LORD.

• **Resurrection and life.**

Jn 11:25 — Jesus said unto her, I am the resurrection, and the life: he that believeth in me, though he were dead, yet shall he live:

• **Redemption.**

1Co 1:30 — But of him are ye in Christ Jesus, who of God is made unto us wisdom, and righteousness, and sanctification, and redemption:

• **Righteous branch.**

Jer 23:5 — Behold, the days come, saith the LORD, that I will raise unto David a righteous Branch, and a King shall reign and prosper, and shall execute judgment and justice in the earth.

• **Righteous judge.**

2Ti 4:8— Henceforth there is laid up for me a crown of righteousness, which the Lord, the righteous judge, shall give me at that day: and not to me only, but unto all them also that love his appearing.

• **Righteous servant.**

Isa 53:11 — He shall see of the travail of his soul, *and* shall be satisfied: by his knowledge shall my righteous servant justify many; for he shall bear their iniquities.

• **Righteousness.**

1Co 1:30 — But of him are ye in Christ Jesus, who of God is made unto us wisdom, and righteousness, and sanctification, and redemption:

• **Rock.**

1Co 10:4 — And did all drink the same spiritual drink: for they drank of that spiritual Rock that followed them: and that Rock was Christ.

• **Rock of offence.**

1Pe 2:8 — And a stone of stumbling, and a rock of offence, *even to them* which stumble at the word, being disobedient: whereunto also they were appointed.

• **Root of David.**

Rev 5:5 — And one of the elders saith unto me, Weep not: behold, the Lion of the tribe of Juda, the Root of

David, hath prevailed to open the book, and to loose the seven seals thereof.

Rev 22:16 — I Jesus have sent mine angel to testify unto you these things in the churches. I am the root and the offspring of David, *and* the bright and morning star.

- **Root of Jesse.**

Isa 11:10 — And in that day there shall be a root of Jesse, which shall stand for an ensign of the people; to it shall the Gentiles seek: and his rest shall be glorious.

- **Rose of Sharon.**

SS 2:1 — I *am* the rose of Sharon, *and* the lily of the valleys.

- **Ruler in Israel.**

Mic 5:2 — But thou, Bethlehem Ephratah, *though* thou be little among the thousands of Judah, *yet* out of thee shall he come forth unto me *that is* to be ruler in Israel; whose goings forth *have been* from of old, from everlasting.

- **Salvation.**

Lk 2:30 — For mine eyes have seen thy salvation,

- **Sanctification.**

1Co 1:30 — But of him are ye in Christ Jesus, who of God is made unto us wisdom, and righteousness, and sanctification, and redemption:

- **Sanctuary.**

Isa 8:14 — And he shall be for a sanctuary; but for a stone of stumbling and for a rock of offence to both the houses of Israel, for a gin and for a snare to the inhabitants of Jerusalem.

- **Saviour.**

Lk 2:11 — For unto you is born this day in the city of David a Saviour, which is Christ the Lord.

- **Saviour, Jesus Christ.**

2Ti 1:10 — But is now made manifest by the appearing of our Saviour Jesus Christ, who hath abolished death, and hath brought life and immortality to light through the gospel:

Tit 2:13 — Looking for that blessed hope, and the glorious appearing of the great God and our Saviour Jesus Christ;

2Pe 1:1 — Simon Peter, a servant and an apostle of Jesus Christ, to them that have obtained like precious faith with us through the righteousness of God and our Saviour Jesus Christ:

- **Saviour of the body.**

Eph 5:23 — For the husband is the head of the wife, even as Christ is the head of the church: and he is the saviour of the body.

- **Saviour of the world.**

1Jn 4:14 — And we have seen and do testify that the Father sent the Son *to be* the Saviour of the world.

- **Sceptre.**

Nu 24:17 — I shall see him, but not now: I shall behold him, but not nigh: there shall come a Star out of Jacob, and a Sceptre shall rise out of Israel, and shall smite the corners of Moab, and destroy all the children of Sheth.

- **Second man.**

1Co 15:47 — The first man *is* of the earth, earthy: the second man *is* the Lord from heaven.

- **Seed of David.**

2Ti 2:8 — Remember that Jesus Christ of the seed of David was raised from the dead according to my gospel:

- **Seed of the woman.**

Ge 3:15 — And I will put enmity between thee and the woman, and between thy seed and her seed; it shall bruise thy head, and thou shalt bruise his heel.

- **Servant.**

Isa 42:1 — Behold my servant, whom I uphold; mine elect, *in whom* my soul delighteth; I have put my spirit upon him: he shall bring forth judgment to the Gentiles.

- **Servant of rulers.**

Isa 49:7 — Thus saith the LORD, the Redeemer of Israel, *and* his Holy One, to him whom man despiseth, to him whom the nation abhorreth, to a servant of rulers, Kings shall see and arise, princes also shall worship, because of the LORD that is faithful, *and* the Holy One of Israel, and he shall choose thee.

- **Shepherd.**

Mk 14:27 — And Jesus saith unto them, All ye shall be offended because of me this night: for it is written, I will smite the shepherd, and the sheep shall be scattered.

- **Shepherd and bishop of souls.**

1Pe 2:25 — For ye were as sheep going astray; but are now returned unto the Shepherd and Bishop of your souls.

- **Shepherd, chief.**

1Pe 5:4 — And when the chief Shepherd shall appear, ye shall receive a crown of glory that fadeth not away.

- **Shepherd, good.**

Jn 10:11 — I am the good shepherd: the good shepherd giveth his life for the sheep.

- **Shepherd, great.**

Heb 13:20 — Now the God of peace, that brought again from the dead our Lord Jesus, that great shepherd of the sheep, through the blood of the everlasting covenant,

- **Shepherd of Israel.**

Ps 80:1 — Give ear, O Shepherd of Israel, thou that leadest Joseph like a flock; thou that dwellest *between* the cherubims, shine forth.

- **Shiloh.**

Ge 49:10 — The sceptre shall not depart from Judah, nor a lawgiver from between his feet, until Shiloh come; and unto him *shall* the gathering of the people *be*.

- **Son of the Father.**

2Jn 1:3 — Grace be with you, mercy, *and* peace, from God the Father, and from the Lord Jesus Christ, the Son of the Father, in truth and love.

- **Son of God.**

→See: **Jesus, Son of God**

• **Son of Man.**

  ➜**See: Jesus, Son of Man**

• **Son of the blessed.**

Mk 14:61 — But he held his peace, and answered nothing. Again the high priest asked him, and said unto him, Art thou the Christ, the Son of the Blessed?

• **Son of the highest.**

Lk 1:32 — He shall be great, and shall be called the Son of the Highest: and the Lord God shall give unto him the throne of his father David:

• **Son of David.**

Mt 9:27 — And when Jesus departed thence, two blind men followed him, crying, and saying, *Thou* Son of David, have mercy on us.

• **Star.**

Nu 24:17 — I shall see him, but not now: I shall behold him, but not nigh: there shall come a Star out of Jacob, and a Sceptre shall rise out of Israel, and shall smite the corners of Moab, and destroy all the children of Sheth.

• **Sun of righteousness.**

Mal 4:2 — But unto you that fear my name shall the Sun of righteousness arise with healing in his wings; and ye shall go forth, and grow up as calves of the stall.

• **Stone of stumbling.**

1Pe 2:8 — And a stone of stumbling, and a rock of offence, *even to them* which stumble at the word, being disobedient: whereunto also they were appointed.

• **Sure foundation.**

Isa 28:16 — Therefore thus saith the Lord GOD, Behold, I lay in Zion for a foundation a stone, a tried stone, a precious corner *stone,* a sure foundation: he that believeth shall not make haste.

• **Teacher.**

Jn 3:2 — The same came to Jesus by night, and said unto him, Rabbi, we know that thou art a teacher come from God: for no man can do these miracles that thou doest, except God be with him.

• **True God.**

1Jn 5:20 — *And* we know that the Son of God is come, and hath given us an understanding, that we may know him that is true, and we are in him that is true, *even* in his Son Jesus Christ. This is the true God, and eternal life.

• **True vine.**

Jn 15:1 — I am the true vine, and my Father is the husbandman.

• **Truth.**

Jn 14:6 — Jesus saith unto him, I am the way, the truth, and the life: no man cometh unto the Father, but by me.

• **Unspeakable gift.**

2Co 9:15 — Thanks *be* unto God for his unspeakable gift.

• **Very Christ.**

Ac 9:22 — But Saul increased the more in strength, and confounded the Jews which dwelt at Damascus, proving that this is very Christ.

• **Vine.**

Jn 15:1 — I am the true vine, and my Father is the husbandman.

• **Way.**

Jn 14:6 — Jesus saith unto him, I am the way, the truth, and the life: no man cometh unto the Father, but by me.

• **Which is, which was, which is to come.**

Rev 1:4 — John to the seven churches which are in Asia: Grace *be* unto you, and peace, from him which is, and which was, and which is to come; and from the seven Spirits which are before his throne;

• **Wisdom.**

Pr 8:12 — I wisdom dwell with prudence, and find out knowledge of witty inventions.

• **Wisdom of God.**

1Co 1:24 — But unto them which are called, both Jews and Greeks, Christ the power of God, and the wisdom of God.

• **Witness.**

Isa 55:4 — Behold, I have given him *for* a witness to the people, a leader and commander to the people.

Rev 1:5 — And from Jesus Christ, *who is* the faithful witness, *and* the first begotten of the dead, and the prince of the kings of the earth. Unto him that loved us, and washed us from our sins in his own blood,

• **Wonderful.**

Isa 9:6 — For unto us a child is born, unto us a son is given: and the government shall be upon his shoulder: and his name shall be called Wonderful, Counsellor, The mighty God, The everlasting Father, The Prince of Peace.

• **Word.**

Jn 1:1 — In the beginning was the Word, and the Word was with God, and the Word was God.

• **Word of God.**

Rev 19:13 — And he *was* clothed with a vesture dipped in blood: and his name is called The Word of God.

• **Word of life.**

1Jn 1:1 — That which was from the beginning, which we have heard, which we have seen with our eyes, which we have looked upon, and our hands have handled, of the Word of life;

  ➜**See: God; name of**

• **Those who use his name must depart from evil.**

2Ti 2:19 — Nevertheless the foundation of God standeth sure, having this seal, The Lord knoweth them that are his. And, Let every one that nameth the name of Christ depart from iniquity.

JESUS, Obedience of

Isa 50:5-6; Heb 10:7-9

Ps 40:8 — I delight to do thy will, O my God: yea, thy law *is* within my heart.

Isa 11:5 — And righteousness shall be the girdle of his loins, and faithfulness the girdle of his reins.

Isa 42:21 — The LORD is well pleased for his righteousness' sake; he will magnify the law, and make *it* honourable.

Mt 3:15 — And Jesus answering said unto him, Suffer *it to be so* now: for thus it becometh us to fulfil all righteousness. Then he suffered him.

Mt 26:39 — And he went a little farther, and fell on his face, and prayed, saying, O my Father, if it be possible, let this cup pass from me: nevertheless not as I will, but as thou *wilt.*

Mt 26:42 — He went away again the second time, and prayed, saying, O my Father, if this cup may not pass away from me, except I drink it, thy will be done.

Mk 14:36 — And he said, Abba, Father, all things *are* possible unto thee; take away this cup from me: nevertheless not what I will, but what thou wilt.

Lk 2:49 — And he said unto them, How is it that ye sought me? wist ye not that I must be about my Father's business?

Lk 22:42 — Saying, Father, if thou be willing, remove this cup from me: nevertheless not my will, but thine, be done.

Jn 4:34 — Jesus saith unto them, My meat is to do the will of him that sent me, and to finish his work.

Jn 5:30 — I can of mine own self do nothing: as I hear, I judge: and my judgment is just; because I seek not mine own will, but the will of the Father which hath sent me.

Jn 5:36 — But I have greater witness than *that* of John: for the works which the Father hath given me to finish, the same works that I do, bear witness of me, that the Father hath sent me.

Jn 6:38 — For I came down from heaven, not to do mine own will, but the will of him that sent me.

Jn 7:18 — He that speaketh of himself seeketh his own glory: but he that seeketh his glory that sent him, the same is true, and no unrighteousness is in him.

Jn 8:29 — And he that sent me is with me: the Father hath not left me alone; for I do always those things that please him.

Jn 8:46 — Which of you convinceth me of sin? And if I say the truth, why do ye not believe me?

Jn 8:55 — Yet ye have not known him; but I know him: and if I should say, I know him not, I shall be a liar like unto you: but I know him, and keep his saying.

Jn 9:4 — I must work the works of him that sent me, while it is day: the night cometh, when no man can work.

Jn 14:31 — But that the world may know that I love the Father; and as the Father gave me commandment, even so I do. Arise, let us go hence.

Jn 15:10 — If ye keep my commandments, ye shall abide in my love; even as I have kept my Father's commandments, and abide in his love.

Jn 17:4 — I have glorified thee on the earth: I have finished the work which thou gavest me to do.

Jn 19:30 — When Jesus therefore had received the vinegar, he said, It is finished: and he bowed his head, and gave up the ghost.

Php 2:8 — And being found in fashion as a man, he humbled himself, and became obedient unto death, even the death of the cross.

Heb 5:8 — Though he were a Son, yet learned he obedience by the things which he suffered;

JESUS, Omnipotence of

Ps 45:3–5; Isa 50:2–4; Mt 12:28–29; Lk 11:20–22; Jn 5:28–29; 10:17–18; 17:1–2; Php 3:20–21

Ps 110:3 — Thy people *shall be* willing in the day of thy power, in the beauties of holiness from the womb of the morning: thou hast the dew of thy youth.

Isa 9:6 — For unto us a child is born, unto us a son is given: and the government shall be upon his shoulder: and his name shall be called Wonderful, Counsellor, The mighty God, The everlasting Father, The Prince of Peace.

Isa 40:10 — Behold, the Lord GOD will come with strong *hand,* and his arm shall rule for him: behold, his reward *is* with him, and his work before him.

Isa 63:1 — Who *is* this that cometh from Edom, with dyed garments from Bozrah? this *that is* glorious in his apparel, travelling in the greatness of his strength? I that speak in righteousness, mighty to save.

Mt 8:3 — And Jesus put forth *his* hand, and touched him, saying, I will; be thou clean. And immediately his leprosy was cleansed.

Mt 8:16 — When the even was come, they brought unto him many that were possessed with devils: and he cast out the spirits with *his* word, and healed all that were sick:

Mt 8:27 — But the men marvelled, saying, What manner of man is this, that even the winds and the sea obey him!

Mt 10:1 — And when he had called unto *him* his twelve disciples, he gave them power *against* unclean spirits, to cast them out, and to heal all manner of sickness and all manner of disease.

Mt 12:13 — Then saith he to the man, Stretch forth thine hand. And he stretched *it* forth; and it was restored whole, like as the other.

Mt 28:18 — And Jesus came and spake unto them, saying, All power is given unto me in heaven and in earth.

Mk 3:27 — No man can enter into a strong man's house, and spoil his goods, except he will first bind the strong man; and then he will spoil his house.

Mk 6:7 — And he called *unto him* the twelve, and began to send them forth by two and two; and gave them power over unclean spirits;

Lk 5:17 — And it came to pass on a certain day, as he was teaching, that there were Pharisees and doctors of the law sitting by, which were come out of every town of Galilee, and Judaea, and Jerusalem: and the power of the Lord was *present* to heal them.

Lk 9:1 — Then he called his twelve disciples together, and gave them power and authority over all devils, and to cure diseases.

Jn 2:19 — Jesus answered and said unto them, Destroy this temple, and in three days I will raise it up.

Jn 5:21 — For as the Father raiseth up the dead, and quickeneth *them;* even so the Son quickeneth whom he will.

Jn 10:28 — And I give unto them eternal life; and they shall never perish, neither shall any *man* pluck them out of my hand.

Col 1:17 — And he is before all things, and by him all things consist.

2Th 1:9 — Who shall be punished with everlasting destruction from the presence of the Lord, and from the glory of his power;

1Ti 6:16 — Who only hath immortality, dwelling in the light which no man can approach unto; whom no man hath seen, nor can see: to whom *be* honour and power everlasting. Amen.

Heb 1:3 — Who being the brightness of *his* glory, and the express image of his person, and upholding all things by the word of his power, when he had by himself purged our sins, sat down on the right hand of the Majesty on high;

Heb 7:25 — Wherefore he is able also to save them to the uttermost that come unto God by him, seeing he ever liveth to make intercession for them.

2Pe 1:16 — For we have not followed cunningly devised fables, when we made known unto you the power and coming of our Lord Jesus Christ, but were eyewitnesses of his majesty.

Rev 1:8 — I am Alpha and Omega, the beginning and the ending, saith the Lord, which is, and which was, and which is to come, the Almighty.

Rev 3:7 — And to the angel of the church in Philadelphia write; These things saith he that is holy, he that is true, he that hath the key of David, he that openeth, and no man shutteth; and shutteth, and no man openeth;

Rev 5:12 — Saying with a loud voice, Worthy is the Lamb that was slain to receive power, and riches, and wisdom, and strength, and honour, and glory, and blessing.

+See: Jesus, Miracles of

JESUS, Omnipresence of

Mt 18:20 — For where two or three are gathered together in my name, there am I in the midst of them.

Mt 28:20 — Teaching them to observe all things whatsoever I have commanded you: and, lo, I am with you alway, *even* unto the end of the world. Amen.

Jn 3:13 — And no man hath ascended up to heaven, but he that came down from heaven, *even* the Son of man which is in heaven.

Eph 1:23 — Which is his body, the fulness of him that filleth all in all.

JESUS, Omniscience of

Pr 8:14–16; Isa 11:2–3; Mk 14:13–15; Lk 9:46–48; 22:10–13; Jn 2:24–25; 4:16–19, 28–29; 13:10–11

Isa 50:4 — The Lord GOD hath given me the tongue of the learned, that I should know how to speak a word in season to *him that is* weary: he wakeneth morning by morning, he wakeneth mine ear to hear as the learned.

Mt 9:4 — And Jesus knowing their thoughts said, Wherefore think ye evil in your hearts?

Mt 11:27 — All things are delivered unto me of my Father: and no man knoweth the Son, but the Father; neither knoweth any man the Father, save the Son, and *he* to whomsoever the Son will reveal *him.*

Mt 12:25 — And Jesus knew their thoughts, and said unto them, Every kingdom divided against itself is brought to desolation; and every city or house divided against itself shall not stand:

Mt 13:54 — And when he was come into his own country, he taught them in their synagogue, insomuch that they were astonished, and said, Whence hath this *man* this wisdom, and *these* mighty works?

Mt 22:18 — But Jesus perceived their wickedness, and said, Why tempt ye me, *ye* hypocrites?

Mt 24:25 — Behold, I have told you before.

Mt 26:46 — Rise, let us be going: behold, he is at hand that doth betray me.

Mk 2:8 — And immediately when Jesus perceived in his spirit that they so reasoned within themselves, he said unto them, Why reason ye these things in your hearts?

Mk 5:30 — And Jesus, immediately knowing in himself that virtue had gone out of him, turned him about in the press, and said, Who touched my clothes?

Mk 14:42 — Rise up, let us go; lo, he that betrayeth me is at hand.

Lk 2:40 — And the child grew, and waxed strong in spirit, filled with wisdom: and the grace of God was upon him.

Lk 2:47 — And all that heard him were astonished at his understanding and answers.

Lk 2:52 — And Jesus increased in wisdom and stature, and in favour with God and man.

Lk 5:22 — But when Jesus perceived their thoughts, he answering said unto them, What reason ye in your hearts?

Lk 6:8 — But he knew their thoughts, and said to the man which had the withered hand, Rise up, and stand forth in the midst. And he arose and stood forth.

Jn 1:48 — Nathanael saith unto him, Whence knowest thou me? Jesus answered and said unto him, Before that Philip called thee, when thou wast under the fig tree, I saw thee.

Jn 3:32 — And what he hath seen and heard, that he testifieth; and no man receiveth his testimony.

Jn 5:30 — I can of mine own self do nothing: as I hear, I judge: and my judgment is just; because I seek not mine own will, but the will of the Father which hath sent me.

Jn 5:42 — But I know you, that ye have not the love of God in you.

Jn 6:64 — But there are some of you that believe not. For Jesus knew from the beginning who they were that believed not, and who should betray him.

Jn 8:16 — And yet if I judge, my judgment is true: for I am not alone, but I and the Father that sent me.

Jn 13:1 — Now before the feast of the passover, when Jesus knew that his hour was come that he should depart out of this world unto the Father, having loved his own which were in the world, he loved them unto the end.

Jn 13:3 — Jesus knowing that the Father had given all things into his hands, and that he was come from God, and went to God;

Jn 16:30 — Now are we sure that thou knowest all things, and needest not that any man should ask thee: by this we believe that thou camest forth from God.

Jn 16:32 — Behold, the hour cometh, yea, is now come, that ye shall be scattered, every man to his own, and shall leave me alone: and yet I am not alone, because the Father is with me.

Jn 17:1 — These words spake Jesus, and lifted up his eyes to heaven, and said, Father, the hour is come; glorify thy Son, that thy Son also may glorify thee:

Jn 18:4 — Jesus therefore, knowing all things that should come upon him, went forth, and said unto them, Whom seek ye?

Jn 21:17 — He saith unto him the third time, Simon, *son* of Jonas, lovest thou me? Peter was grieved because he said unto him the third time, Lovest thou me? And he said unto him, Lord, thou knowest all things; thou knowest that I love thee. Jesus saith unto him, Feed my sheep.

Ac 1:24 — And they prayed, and said, Thou, Lord, which knowest the hearts of all *men*, shew whether of these two thou hast chosen,

Col 2:3 — In whom are hid all the treasures of wisdom and knowledge.

Rev 2:18 — And unto the angel of the church in Thyatira write; These things saith the Son of God, who hath his eyes like unto a flame of fire, and his feet *are* like fine brass;

Rev 2:23 — And I will kill her children with death; and all the churches shall know that I am he which searcheth the reins and hearts: and I will give unto every one of you according to your works.

Rev 5:5 — And one of the elders saith unto me, Weep not: behold, the Lion of the tribe of Juda, the Root of David, hath prevailed to open the book, and to loose the seven seals thereof.

Rev 5:12 — Saying with a loud voice, Worthy is the Lamb that was slain to receive power, and riches, and wisdom, and strength, and honour, and glory, and blessing.

JESUS, Parables of

- **The wise and foolish builders.**
  Mt 7:24–27
  Lk 6:47 — Whosoever cometh to me, and heareth my sayings, and doeth them, I will shew you to whom he is like:
  Lk 6:49 — But he that heareth, and doeth not, is like a man that without a foundation built an house upon the earth; against which the stream did beat vehemently, and immediately it fell; and the ruin of that house was great.
- **Two debtors.**
  Lk 7:41–47
- **The rich fool.**
  Lk 12:16–21
- **The servants waiting for their Lord.**
  Lk 12:35–40
- **Barren fig tree.**
  Lk 13:6–9
- **The sower.**
  Mt 13:3–9, 18–23; Mk 4:1–9, 14–20; Lk 8:5–8, 11–15
- **The tares.**
  Mt 13:24–30, 36–43
- **Seed growing secretly.**
  Mk 4:26–29
- **Mustard seed.**
  Mt 13:31–32; Mk 4:30–32; Lk 13:18–19
- **Leaven.**
  Lk 13:20–21
  Mt 13:33 — Another parable spake he unto them; The kingdom of heaven is like unto leaven, which a woman took, and hid in three measures of meal, till the whole was leavened.
- **Hid treasure.**
  Mt 13:44 — Again, the kingdom of heaven is like unto treasure hid in a field; the which when a man hath found, he hideth, and for joy thereof goeth and selleth all that he hath, and buyeth that field.
- **Pearl of great price.**
  Mt 13:45–46
- **Drawnet.**
  Mt 13:47–50
- **Unmerciful servant.**
  Mt 18:23–35
- **Good Samaritan.**
  Lk 10:30–37
- **Friend at midnight.**
  Lk 11:5–8
- **Good shepherd.**
  Jn 10:1–16
- **Great supper.**
  Lk 14:15–24
- **Lost sheep.**
  Mt 18:12–14; Lk 15:3–7
- **Lost piece of money.**
  Lk 15:8–10
- **The prodigal and his brother.**
  Lk 15:11–32
- **The unjust steward.**
  Lk 16:1–9
- **Rich man and Lazarus.**
  Lk 16:19–31
- **Importunate widow.**
  Lk 18:1–8
- **Pharisee and publican.**
  Lk 18:9–14
- **Laborers in the vineyard.**
  Mt 20:1–16
- **The pounds.**
  Lk 19:11–27
- **The two sons.**
  Mt 21:28–32
- **Wicked husbandmen.**
  Mt 21:33–44; Mk 12:1–12; Lk 20:9–18
- **Marriage of the king's son.**
  Mt 22:1–14
- **Fig tree leafing.**
  Mk 13:28–29
  Mt 24:32 — Now learn a parable of the fig tree; When his branch is yet tender, and putteth forth leaves, ye know that summer is nigh:
- **Man taking a far journey.**
  Mk 13:34–37

- **Ten virgins.**
  Mt 25:1–13
- **Talents.**
  Mt 25:14–30
- **The vine.**
  Jn 15:1–5

JESUS, Passion of ⇒See: Jesus, Sufferings of

JESUS, Peccability of ⇒See: Jesus, Temptation of

JESUS, Perfections of

- **Not classified under foregoing topics.**
  Mt 12:41–42; 27:3–4; Mk 1:7–8

Ps 45:2 — Thou art fairer than the children of men: grace is poured into thy lips: therefore God hath blessed thee for ever.

Isa 11:5 — And righteousness shall be the girdle of his loins, and faithfulness the girdle of his reins.

Isa 49:2 — And he hath made my mouth like a sharp sword; in the shadow of his hand hath he hid me, and made me a polished shaft; in his quiver hath he hid me;

Isa 53:9 — And he made his grave with the wicked, and with the rich in his death; because he had done no violence, neither *was any* deceit in his mouth.

Eze 34:29 — And I will raise up for them a plant of renown, and they shall be no more consumed with hunger in the land, neither bear the shame of the heathen any more.

Mic 5:4 — And he shall stand and feed in the strength of the LORD, in the majesty of the name of the LORD his God; and they shall abide: for now shall he be great unto the ends of the earth.

Hag 2:7 — And I will shake all nations, and the desire of all nations shall come: and I will fill this house with glory, saith the LORD of hosts.

Mt 3:11 — I indeed baptize you with water unto repentance: but he that cometh after me is mightier than I, whose shoes I am not worthy to bear: he shall baptize you with the Holy Ghost, and *with* fire:

Lk 3:16 — John answered, saying unto *them* all, I indeed baptize you with water; but one mightier than I cometh, the latchet of whose shoes I am not worthy to unloose: he shall baptize you with the Holy Ghost and with fire:

Lk 23:41 — And we indeed justly; for we receive the due reward of our deeds: but this man hath done nothing amiss.

Jn 1:14 — And the Word was made flesh, and dwelt among us, (and we beheld his glory, the glory as of the only begotten of the Father,) full of grace and truth.

Jn 1:18 — No man hath seen God at any time; the only begotten Son, which is in the bosom of the Father, he hath declared *him*.

Jn 5:30 — I can of mine own self do nothing: as I hear, I judge: and my judgment is just; because I seek not mine own will, but the will of the Father which hath sent me.

Jn 5:34 — But I receive not testimony from man: but these things I say, that ye might be saved.

Jn 5:41 — I receive not honour from men.

Jn 7:18 — He that speaketh of himself seeketh his own glory: but he that seeketh his glory that sent him, the same is true, and no unrighteousness is in him.

Ac 13:28 — And though they found no cause of death *in him*, yet desired they Pilate that he should be slain.

1Co 1:24 — But unto them which are called, both Jews and Greeks, Christ the power of God, and the wisdom of God.

1Co 15:45 — And so it is written, The first man Adam was made a living soul; the last Adam *was made* a quickening spirit.

1Co 15:47 — The first man *is* of the earth, earthy: the second man *is* the Lord from heaven.

2Co 1:19 — For the Son of God, Jesus Christ, who was preached among you by us, *even* by me and Silvanus and Timotheus, was not yea and nay, but in him was yea.

2Co 4:4 — In whom the god of this world hath blinded the minds of them which believe not, lest the light of the glorious gospel of Christ, who is the image of God, should shine unto them.

2Co 5:21 — For he hath made him *to be* sin for us, who knew no sin; that we might be made the righteousness of God in him.

2Co 9:15 — Thanks *be* unto God for his unspeakable gift.

Eph 3:8 — Unto me, who am less than the least of all saints, is this grace given, that I should preach among the Gentiles the unsearchable riches of Christ;

Col 1:19 — For it pleased *the Father* that in him should all fulness dwell;

2Th 3:3 — But the Lord is faithful, who shall stablish you, and keep *you* from evil.

2Ti 2:13 — If we believe not, *yet* he abideth faithful: he cannot deny himself.

Heb 1:3 — Who being the brightness of *his* glory, and the express image of his person, and upholding all things by the word of his power, when he had by himself purged our sins, sat down on the right hand of the Majesty on high;

Heb 2:10 — For it became him, for whom *are* all things, and by whom *are* all things, in bringing many sons unto glory, to make the captain of their salvation perfect through sufferings.

Heb 3:2 — Who was faithful to him that appointed him, as also Moses *was faithful* in all his house.

JESUS, Persecutions of ⇒See: Persecution

JESUS, Power of, to Forgive Sins

Lk 7:47–50

Mt 9:2 — And, behold, they brought to him a man sick of the palsy, lying on a bed: and Jesus seeing their faith said unto the sick of the palsy; Son, be of good cheer; thy sins be forgiven thee.

Mt 9:6 — But that ye may know that the Son of man hath power on earth to forgive sins, (then saith he to the sick of the palsy,) Arise, take up thy bed, and go unto thine house.

Mk 2:5 — When Jesus saw their faith, he said unto the sick of the palsy, Son, thy sins be forgiven thee.

Mk 2:10 — But that ye may know that the Son of man hath power on earth to forgive sins, (he saith to the sick of the palsy,)

Lk 5:20 — And when he saw their faith, he said unto him, Man, thy sins are forgiven thee.

Lk 5:24 — But that ye may know that the Son of man hath power upon earth to forgive sins, (he said unto the sick of the palsy,) I say unto thee, Arise, and take up thy couch, and go into thine house.

Ac 5:31 — Him hath God exalted with his right hand *to be* a Prince and a Saviour, for to give repentance to Israel, and forgiveness of sins.

Col 3:13 — Forbearing one another, and forgiving one another, if any man have a quarrel against any: even as Christ forgave you, so also *do* ye.

See: Divinity

JESUS, Prayers of

Mt 11:25–26; 26:26–27; Mk 14:32–39; Lk 9:28–29; 22:41–44; Jn 11:41–42; 12:27–28; 17:1–26

Mt 14:23 — And when he had sent the multitudes away, he went up into a mountain apart to pray: and when the evening was come, he was there alone.

Mt 15:36 — And he took the seven loaves and the fishes, and gave thanks, and brake *them,* and gave to his disciples, and the disciples to the multitude.

Mt 19:13 — Then were there brought unto him little children, that he should put *his* hands on them, and pray: and the disciples rebuked them.

Mt 26:36 — Then cometh Jesus with them unto a place called Gethsemane, and saith unto the disciples, Sit ye here, while I go and pray yonder.

Mt 26:39 — And he went a little farther, and fell on his face, and prayed, saying, O my Father, if it be possible, let this cup pass from me: nevertheless not as I will, but as thou *wilt.*

Mt 26:42 — He went away again the second time, and prayed, saying, O my Father, if this cup may not pass away from me, except I drink it, thy will be done.

Mt 26:44 — And he left them, and went away again, and prayed the third time, saying the same words.

Mt 27:46 — And about the ninth hour Jesus cried with a loud voice, saying, Eli, Eli, lama sabachthani? that is to say, My God, my God, why hast thou forsaken me?

Mk 1:35 — And in the morning, rising up a great while before day, he went out, and departed into a solitary place, and there prayed.

Mk 6:41 — And when he had taken the five loaves and the two fishes, he looked up to heaven, and blessed, and brake the loaves, and gave *them* to his disciples to set before them; and the two fishes divided he among them all.

Mk 6:46 — And when he had sent them away, he departed into a mountain to pray.

Lk 3:21 — Now when all the people were baptized, it came to pass, that Jesus also being baptized, and praying, the heaven was opened,

Lk 5:16 — And he withdrew himself into the wilderness, and prayed.

Lk 6:12 — And it came to pass in those days, that he went out into a mountain to pray, and continued all night in prayer to God.

Lk 9:18 — And it came to pass, as he was alone praying, his disciples were with him: and he asked them, saying, Whom say the people that I am?

Lk 11:1 — And it came to pass, that, as he was praying in a certain place, when he ceased, one of his disciples said unto him, Lord, teach us to pray, as John also taught his disciples.

Lk 22:32 — But I have prayed for thee, that thy faith fail not: and when thou art converted, strengthen thy brethren.

Lk 23:34 — Then said Jesus, Father, forgive them; for they know not what they do. And they parted his raiment, and cast lots.

Lk 23:46 — And when Jesus had cried with a loud voice, he said, Father, into thy hands I commend my spirit: and having said thus, he gave up the ghost.

1Co 11:24 — And when he had given thanks, he brake *it,* and said, Take, eat: this is my body, which is broken for you: this do in remembrance of me.

Heb 5:7 — Who in the days of his flesh, when he had offered up prayers and supplications with strong crying and tears unto him that was able to save him from death, and was heard in that he feared;

See: Christ

See: High Priest

See: Jesus, Mediation of

JESUS, Preexistence of

Ps 102:25–27; Pr 8:22–36; Jn 1:1–3; 8:56–58; Php 2:5–7; Col 1:15–17; Heb 1:1–2, 8–12; 2:14–16

Ge 1:26 — And God said, Let us make man in our image, after our likeness: and let them have dominion over the fish of the sea, and over the fowl of the air, and over the cattle, and over all the earth, and over every creeping thing that creepeth upon the earth.

Jn 3:13 — And no man hath ascended up to heaven, but he that came down from heaven, *even* the Son of man which is in heaven.

Jn 6:62 — *What* and if ye shall see the Son of man ascend up where he was before?

Jn 17:5 — And now, O Father, glorify thou me with thine own self with the glory which I had with thee before the world was.

Ro 11:36 — For of him, and through him, and to him, *are* all things: to whom *be* glory for ever. Amen.

1Co 8:6 — But to us *there is but* one God, the Father, of whom *are* all things, and we in him; and one Lord Jesus Christ, by whom *are* all things, and we by him.

Heb 2:9 — But we see Jesus, who was made a little lower than the angels for the suffering of death, crowned with glory and honour; that he by the grace of God should taste death for every man.

Heb 4:8 — For if Jesus had given them rest, then would he not afterward have spoken of another day.

Rev 4:11 — Thou art worthy, O Lord, to receive glory and honour and power: for thou hast created all things, and for thy pleasure they are and were created.

See: Jesus, Creator

See: Jesus, Eternity of

See: Jesus, Incarnation of

See: Jesus, Omnipotence of

See: Jesus, Omnipresence of

See: Jesus, Omniscience of

JESUS, Prescience of See: Jesus, Omniscience of

JESUS, Priesthood of

• Appointed and called by God.

Heb 3:1–2; 5:4–5

• Appointed and called by God after the order of Melchizedek.

Ps 110:4 — The LORD hath sworn, and will not repent, Thou *art* a priest for ever after the order of Melchizedek.

Heb 5:6 — As he saith also in another *place,* Thou *art* a priest for ever after the order of Melchisedec.

Heb 6:20 — Whither the forerunner is for us entered, *even* Jesus, made an high priest for ever after the order of Melchisedec.

Heb 7:15 — And it is yet far more evident: for that after the similitude of Melchisedec there ariseth another priest,

Heb 7:17 — For he testifieth, Thou *art* a priest for ever after the order of Melchisedec.

• Superior to Aaron and the Levitical priests.

Heb 8:1–2

Heb 7:11 — If therefore perfection were by the Levitical priesthood, (for under it the people received the law,) what further need *was there* that another priest should rise after the order of Melchisedec, and not be called after the order of Aaron?

Heb 7:16 — Who is made, not after the law of a carnal commandment, but after the power of an endless life.

Heb 7:22 — By so much was Jesus made a surety of a better testament.

Heb 8:6 — But now hath he obtained a more excellent ministry, by how much also he is the mediator of a better covenant, which was established upon better promises.

• Consecrated with an oath.

Heb 7:20–21

• Has an unchangeable priesthood.

Heb 7:23 — And they truly were many priests, because they were not suffered to continue by reason of death:

Heb 7:28 — For the law maketh men high priests which have infirmity; but the word of the oath, which was since the law, *maketh* the Son, who is consecrated for evermore.

• Is of unblemished purity.

Heb 7:26 — For such an high priest became us, *who is* holy, harmless, undefiled, separate from sinners, and made higher than the heavens;

Heb 7:28 — For the law maketh men high priests which have infirmity; but the word of the oath, which was since the law, *maketh* the Son, who is consecrated for evermore.

• Is faithful.

Heb 3:2 — Who was faithful to him that appointed him, as also Moses *was faithful* in all his house.

• Needed no sacrifice for himself.

Heb 7:27 — Who needeth not daily, as those high priests, to offer up sacrifice, first for his own sins, and then for the people's: for this he did once, when he offered up himself.

• Offered himself a sacrifice.

Heb 9:14 — How much more shall the blood of Christ, who through the eternal Spirit offered himself without spot to God, purge your conscience from dead works to serve the living God?

Heb 9:26 — For then must he often have suffered since the foundation of the world: but now once in the end of the world hath he appeared to put away sin by the sacrifice of himself.

• His sacrifice superior to all others.

Heb 9:13–14

Heb 9:23 — *It was* therefore necessary that the patterns of things in the heavens should be purified with these; but the heavenly things themselves with better sacrifices than these.

• Offered sacrifice but once.

Heb 7:27 — Who needeth not daily, as those high priests, to offer up sacrifice, first for his own sins, and then for the people's: for this he did once, when he offered up himself.

• Made reconciliation.

Heb 2:17 — Wherefore in all things it behoved him to be made like unto *his* brethren, that he might be a merciful and faithful high priest in things *pertaining* to God, to make reconciliation for the sins of the people.

• Obtained redemption for us.

Heb 9:12 — Neither by the blood of goats and calves, but by his own blood he entered in once into the holy place, having obtained eternal redemption *for us.*

• Entered into heaven.

Heb 4:14 — Seeing then that we have a great high priest, that is passed into the heavens, Jesus the Son of God, let us hold fast *our* profession.

Heb 10:12 — But this man, after he had offered one sacrifice for sins for ever, sat down on the right hand of God;

• Sympathizes with saints.

Heb 2:18 — For in that he himself hath suffered being tempted, he is able to succour them that are tempted.

Heb 4:15 — For we have not an high priest which cannot be touched with the feeling of our infirmities; but was in all points tempted like as *we are, yet* without sin.

- **Intercedes.**

Heb 7:25 — Wherefore he is able also to save them to the uttermost that come unto God by him, seeing he ever liveth to make intercession for them.

Heb 9:24 — For Christ is not entered into the holy places made with hands, *which are* the figures of the true; but into heaven itself, now to appear in the presence of God for us:

- **Blesses.**

Nu 6:23–26

Ac 3:26 — Unto you first God, having raised up his Son Jesus, sent him to bless you, in turning away every one of you from his iniquities.

- **On his throne.**

Zec 6:13 — Even he shall build the temple of the LORD; and he shall bear the glory, and shall sit and rule upon his throne; and he shall be a priest upon his throne: and the counsel of peace shall be between them both.

- **Appointment of, and encouragement to steadfastness.**

Heb 4:14 — Seeing then that we have a great high priest, that is passed into the heavens, Jesus the Son of God, let us hold fast *our* profession.

- **Typified.**
  - **Melchizedek.**

    Ge 14:18–20
  - **Aaron and his sons.**

    Ex 40:12–15

JESUS, Promises of

- **Prophetic.**

Mt 19:28–29; Mk 10:29–30; Lk 5:25–29; 18:29–30; 22:29–30; Jn 6:57–58; 12:25–26; 15:26–27; 16:7–16, 20–26; Ac 1:4–8

Lk 23:43 — And Jesus said unto him, Verily I say unto thee, To day shalt thou be with me in paradise.

Lk 24:49 — And, behold, I send the promise of my Father upon you: but tarry ye in the city of Jerusalem, until ye be endued with power from on high.

Jn 6:54 — Whoso eateth my flesh, and drinketh my blood, hath eternal life; and I will raise him up at the last day.

Jn 7:39 — (But this spake he of the Spirit, which they that believe on him should receive: for the Holy Ghost was not yet *given;* because that Jesus was not yet glorified.)

Jn 14:16 — And I will pray the Father, and he shall give you another Comforter, that he may abide with you for ever;

Jn 14:26 — But the Comforter, *which is* the Holy Ghost, whom the Father will send in my name, he shall teach you all things, and bring all things to your remembrance, whatsoever I have said unto you.

Jn 16:33 — These things I have spoken unto you, that in me ye might have peace. In the world ye shall have tribulation: but be of good cheer; I have overcome the world.

JESUS, Prophecies Concerning

- **Coming of.**

Ps 21:5–7; 40:6–10; 118:22–24; Isa 11:1–16; 42:1–4; 49:1–26; 53:1–12; 55:3–5; 59:16–18; 62:10–11; Jer 23:5–6; 33:15–18; Da 7:13–14; 9:24–27; Mal 3:1–3; Mt 1:20–23; Lk 1:26–37, 41–45; 2:31–32, 34–35; Ac 3:22–24; Ro 1:2–3

Ge 3:15 — And I will put enmity between thee and the woman, and between thy seed and her seed; it shall bruise thy head, and thou shalt bruise his heel.

Ge 12:3 — And I will bless them that bless thee, and curse him that curseth thee: and in thee shall all families of the earth be blessed.

Ge 49:10 — The sceptre shall not depart from Judah, nor a lawgiver from between his feet, until Shiloh come; and unto him *shall* the gathering of the people *be.*

Dt 32:18 — Of the Rock *that* begat thee thou art unmindful, and hast forgotten God that formed thee.

1Sa 2:10 — The adversaries of the LORD shall be broken to pieces; out of heaven shall he thunder upon them: the LORD shall judge the ends of the earth; and he shall give strength unto his king, and exalt the horn of his anointed.

Job 19:25 — For I know *that* my redeemer liveth, and *that* he shall stand at the latter *day* upon the earth:

Ps 68:18 — Thou hast ascended on high, thou hast led captivity captive: thou hast received gifts for men; yea, *for* the rebellious also, that the LORD God might dwell *among them.*

Ps 118:26 — Blessed *be* he that cometh in the name of the LORD: we have blessed you out of the house of the LORD.

Isa 28:16 — Therefore thus saith the Lord GOD, Behold, I lay in Zion for a foundation a stone, a tried stone, a precious corner *stone,* a sure foundation: he that believeth shall not make haste.

Isa 40:3 — The voice of him that crieth in the wilderness, Prepare ye the way of the LORD, make straight in the desert a highway for our God.

Isa 40:11 — He shall feed his flock like a shepherd: he shall gather the lambs with his arm, and carry *them* in his bosom, *and* shall gently lead those that are with young.

Isa 56:1 — Thus saith the LORD, Keep ye judgment, and do justice: for my salvation *is* near to come, and my righteousness to be revealed.

Isa 59:20 — And the Redeemer shall come to Zion, and unto them that turn from transgression in Jacob, saith the LORD.

Hag 2:7 — And I will shake all nations, and the desire of all nations shall come: and I will fill this house with glory, saith the LORD of hosts.

Zec 3:8 — Hear now, O Joshua the high priest, thou, and thy fellows that sit before thee: for they *are* men wondered at: for, behold, I will bring forth my servant the BRANCH.

Zec 9:9 — Rejoice greatly, O daughter of Zion; shout, O daughter of Jerusalem: behold, thy King cometh unto thee: he *is* just, and having salvation; lowly, and riding upon an ass, and upon a colt the foal of an ass.

Zec 13:1 — In that day there shall be a fountain opened to the house of David and to the inhabitants of Jerusalem for sin and for uncleanness.

Mal 4:2 — But unto you that fear my name shall the Sun of righteousness arise with healing in his wings; and ye shall go forth, and grow up as calves of the stall.

Lk 2:26 — And it was revealed unto him by the Holy Ghost, that he should not see death, before he had seen the Lord's Christ.

Lk 2:38 — And she coming in that instant gave thanks likewise unto the Lord, and spake of him to all them that looked for redemption in Jerusalem.

Lk 3:4 — As it is written in the book of the words of Esaias the prophet, saying, The voice of one crying in the wilderness, Prepare ye the way of the Lord, make his paths straight.

Jn 8:56 — Your father Abraham rejoiced to see my day: and he saw *it*, and was glad.

Ro 15:12 — And again, Esaias saith, There shall be a root of Jesse, and he that shall rise to reign over the Gentiles; in him shall the Gentiles trust.

Heb 7:16 — Who is made, not after the law of a carnal commandment, but after the power of an endless life.

Heb 10:9 — Then said he, Lo, I come to do thy will, O God. He taketh away the first, that he may establish the second.

See: Church; prophecies concerning prosperity of

See: Jesus, Kingdom of

See: Jesus, Prophecies Concerning

• Prophecies concerning the future glory and power of.

Jude 1:14–15; Rev 1:5–7; 6:16–17; 7:9–17; 19:11–12, 15–16

Isa 22:22 — And the key of the house of David will I lay upon his shoulder; so he shall open, and none shall shut; and he shall shut, and none shall open.

Mk 14:62 — And Jesus said, I am: and ye shall see the Son of man sitting on the right hand of power, and coming in the clouds of heaven.

1Pe 3:22 — Who is gone into heaven, and is on the right hand of God; angels and authorities and powers being made subject unto him.

Rev 1:18 — I *am* he that liveth, and was dead; and, behold, I am alive for evermore, Amen; and have the keys of hell and of death.

Rev 2:23 — And I will kill her children with death; and all the churches shall know that I am he which searcheth the reins and hearts: and I will give unto every one of you according to your works.

Rev 3:7 — And to the angel of the church in Philadelphia write; These things saith he that is holy, he that is true, he that hath the key of David, he that openeth, and no man shutteth; and shutteth, and no man openeth;

Rev 3:14 — And unto the angel of the church of the Laodiceans write; These things saith the Amen, the faithful and true witness, the beginning of the creation of God;

Rev 3:21 — To him that overcometh will I grant to sit with me in my throne, even as I also overcame, and am set down with my Father in his throne.

Rev 5:5 — And one of the elders saith unto me, Weep not: behold, the Lion of the tribe of Juda, the Root of David, hath prevailed to open the book, and to loose the seven seals thereof.

Rev 5:12 — Saying with a loud voice, Worthy is the Lamb that was slain to receive power, and riches, and wisdom, and strength, and honour, and glory, and blessing.

Rev 11:15 — And the seventh angel sounded; and there were great voices in heaven, saying, The kingdoms of this world are become *the kingdoms* of our Lord, and of his Christ; and he shall reign for ever and ever.

Rev 12:10 — And I heard a loud voice saying in heaven, Now is come salvation, and strength, and the kingdom of our God, and the power of his Christ: for the accuser of our brethren is cast down, which accused them before our God day and night.

Rev 14:14 — And I looked, and behold a white cloud, and upon the cloud *one* sat like unto the Son of man, having on his head a golden crown, and in his hand a sharp sickle.

Rev 17:14 — These shall make war with the Lamb, and the Lamb shall overcome them: for he is Lord of lords, and King of kings: and they that are with him *are* called, and chosen, and faithful.

Rev 20:4 — And I saw thrones, and they sat upon them, and judgment was given unto them: and *I saw* the souls of them that were beheaded for the witness of Jesus, and for the word of God, and which had not worshipped the beast, neither his image, neither had received *his* mark upon their foreheads, or in their hands; and they lived and reigned with Christ a thousand years.

Rev 20:6 — Blessed and holy *is* he that hath part in the first resurrection: on such the second death hath no power, but they shall be priests of God and of Christ, and shall reign with him a thousand years.

See: Jesus, Exaltation of

See: Jesus, Kingdom of

JESUS, Prophet

• Foretold.

Isa 52:7 — How beautiful upon the mountains are the feet of him that bringeth good tidings, that publisheth peace; that bringeth good tidings of good, that publisheth salvation; that saith unto Zion, Thy God reigneth!

Na 1:15 — Behold upon the mountains the feet of him that bringeth good tidings, that publisheth peace! O Judah, keep thy solemn feasts, perform thy vows: for the wicked shall no more pass through thee; he is utterly cut off.

• Anointed with the Holy Ghost.

Isa 42:1 — Behold my servant, whom I uphold; mine elect, *in whom* my soul delighteth; I have put my spirit upon him: he shall bring forth judgment to the Gentiles.

Isa 61:1 — The Spirit of the Lord GOD *is* upon me; because the LORD hath anointed me to preach good tidings unto the meek; he hath sent me to bind up the brokenhearted, to proclaim liberty to the captives, and the opening of the prison to *them that are* bound;

Lk 4:18 — The Spirit of the Lord is upon me, because he hath anointed me to preach the gospel to the poor; he hath sent me to heal the brokenhearted, to preach deliverance to the captives, and recovering of sight to the blind, to set at liberty them that are bruised,

Jn 3:34 — For he whom God hath sent speaketh the words of God: for God giveth not the Spirit by measure *unto him.*

• Reveals God.

Heb 1:1–2

Mt 11:27 — All things are delivered unto me of my Father: and no man knoweth the Son, but the Father; neither knoweth any man the Father, save the Son, and *he* to whomsoever the Son will reveal *him.*

Jn 3:2 — The same came to Jesus by night, and said unto him, Rabbi, we know that thou art a teacher come from God: for no man can do these miracles that thou doest, except God be with him.

Jn 3:13 — And no man hath ascended up to heaven, but he that came down from heaven, *even* the Son of man which is in heaven.

Jn 3:34 — For he whom God hath sent speaketh the words of God: for God giveth not the Spirit by measure *unto him.*

Jn 17:6 — I have manifested thy name unto the men which thou gavest me out of the world: thine they were, and thou gavest them me; and they have kept thy word.

Jn 17:14 — I have given them thy word; and the world hath hated them, because they are not of the world, even as I am not of the world.

Jn 17:26 — And I have declared unto them thy name, and will declare *it:* that the love wherewith thou hast loved me may be in them, and I in them.

• Declared his doctrine to be that of the Father.

Jn 12:49–50

Jn 8:26 — I have many things to say and to judge of you: but he that sent me is true; and I speak to the world those things which I have heard of him.

Jn 8:28 — Then said Jesus unto them, When ye have lifted up the Son of man, then shall ye know that I am *he,* and *that* I do nothing of myself; but as my Father hath taught me, I speak these things.

Jn 14:10 — Believest thou not that I am in the Father, and the Father in me? the words that I speak unto you I speak not of myself: but the Father that dwelleth in me, he doeth the works.

Jn 14:24 — He that loveth me not keepeth not my sayings: and the word which ye hear is not mine, but the Father's which sent me.

Jn 15:15 — Henceforth I call you not servants; for the servant knoweth not what his lord doeth: but I have called you friends; for all things that I have heard of my Father I have made known unto you.

Jn 17:8 — For I have given unto them the words which thou gavest me; and they have received *them,* and have known surely that I came out from thee, and they have believed that thou didst send me.

Jn 17:26 — And I have declared unto them thy name, and will declare *it:* that the love wherewith thou hast loved me may be in them, and I in them.

• Foretold things to come.

Mt 24:3–35; Lk 19:41–44

• Faithful.

Lk 4:43 — And he said unto them, I must preach the kingdom of God to other cities also: for therefore am I sent.

Jn 17:8 — For I have given unto them the words which thou gavest me; and they have received *them,* and have known surely that I came out from thee, and they have believed that thou didst send me.

Heb 3:2 — Who was faithful to him that appointed him, as also Moses *was faithful* in all his house.

Rev 1:5 — And from Jesus Christ, *who is* the faithful witness, *and* the first begotten of the dead, and the prince of the kings of the earth. Unto him that loved us, and washed us from our sins in his own blood,

Rev 3:14 — And unto the angel of the church of the Laodiceans write; These things saith the Amen, the faithful and true witness, the beginning of the creation of God;

• Abounded in wisdom.

Lk 2:40 — And the child grew, and waxed strong in spirit, filled with wisdom: and the grace of God was upon him.

Lk 2:47 — And all that heard him were astonished at his understanding and answers.

Lk 2:52 — And Jesus increased in wisdom and stature, and in favour with God and man.

Col 2:3 — In whom are hid all the treasures of wisdom and knowledge.

• Mighty in deed and word.

Mt 13:54 — And when he was come into his own country, he taught them in their synagogue, insomuch that they were astonished, and said, Whence hath this *man* this wisdom, and *these* mighty works?

Mk 1:27 — And they were all amazed, insomuch that they questioned among themselves, saying, What thing is this? what new doctrine *is* this? for with authority commandeth he even the unclean spirits, and they do obey him.

Lk 4:32 — And they were astonished at his doctrine: for his word was with power.

Jn 7:46 — The officers answered, Never man spake like this man.

• Unostentatious in his teaching.

Mt 12:17–20

Isa 42:2 — He shall not cry, nor lift up, nor cause his voice to be heard in the street.

• God commands us to hear.

Dt 18:15 — The LORD thy God will raise up unto thee a Prophet from the midst of thee, of thy brethren, like unto me; unto him ye shall hearken;

Ac 3:22 — For Moses truly said unto the fathers, A prophet shall the Lord your God raise up unto you of your brethren, like unto me; him shall ye hear in all things whatsoever he shall say unto you.

• God will severely visit neglect of.

Ac 3:22–23

Dt 18:10 — There shall not be found among you *any one* that maketh his son or his daughter to pass through the fire, or that useth divination, *or* an observer of times, or an enchanter, or a witch,

Dt 18:15 — The LORD thy God will raise up unto thee a Prophet from the midst of thee, of thy brethren, like unto me; unto him ye shall hearken;

Dt 18:18 — I will raise them up a Prophet from among their brethren, like unto thee, and will put my words in his mouth; and he shall speak unto them all that I shall command him.

Mt 21:11 — And the multitude said, This is Jesus the prophet of Nazareth of Galilee.

Mt 21:46 — But when they sought to lay hands on him, they feared the multitude, because they took him for a prophet.

Lk 7:16 — And there came a fear on all: and they glorified God, saying, That a great prophet is risen up among us; and, That God hath visited his people.

Lk 7:39 — Now when the Pharisee which had bidden him saw *it,* he spake within himself, saying, This man, if he were a prophet, would have known who and what manner of woman *this is* that toucheth him: for she is a sinner.

Lk 13:33 — Nevertheless I must walk to day, and to morrow, and the *day* following: for it cannot be that a prophet perish out of Jerusalem.

Lk 24:19 — And he said unto them, What things? And they said unto him, Concerning Jesus of Nazareth, which was a prophet mighty in deed and word before God and all the people:

Jn 3:2 — The same came to Jesus by night, and said unto him, Rabbi, we know that thou art a teacher come from God: for no man can do these miracles that thou doest, except God be with him.

Jn 4:19 — The woman saith unto him, Sir, I perceive that thou art a prophet.

Jn 6:14 — Then those men, when they had seen the miracle that Jesus did, said, This is of a truth that prophet that should come into the world.

Jn 7:40 — Many of the people therefore, when they heard this saying, said, Of a truth this is the Prophet.

Jn 9:17 — They say unto the blind man again, What sayest thou of him, that he hath opened thine eyes? He said, He is a prophet.

Ac 7:37 — This is that Moses, which said unto the children of Israel, A prophet shall the Lord your God raise up unto you of your brethren, like unto me; him shall ye hear.

Heb 2:3 — How shall we escape, if we neglect so great salvation; which at the first began to be spoken by the Lord, and was confirmed unto us by them that heard *him;*

JESUS, Received

Mt 4:24–25; 7:28–8:1; 19:1–2; 21:8–11; Mk 3:20–21; 6:51–52, 55–56; 11:8–10; Lk 4:14–15, 36–37; 6:17–18; 7:16–18; 19:36–38, 47–48; Jn 7:40–44; 9:24–25, 29–30; 10:41–42; 11:45–48; 12:11–13, 18–21

Mt 9:8 — But when the multitudes saw *it,* they marvelled, and glorified God, which had given such power unto men.

Mt 9:27 — And when Jesus departed thence, two blind men followed him, crying, and saying, *Thou* Son of David, have mercy on us.

Mt 9:33 — And when the devil was cast out, the dumb spake: and the multitudes marvelled, saying, It was never so seen in Israel.

Mt 12:23 — And all the people were amazed, and said, Is not this the son of David?

Mt 12:38 — Then certain of the scribes and of the Pharisees answered, saying, Master, we would see a sign from thee.

Mt 13:2 — And great multitudes were gathered together unto him, so that he went into a ship, and sat; and the whole multitude stood on the shore.

Mt 13:54 — And when he was come into his own country, he taught them in their synagogue, insomuch that they were astonished, and said, Whence hath this *man* this wisdom, and *these* mighty works?

Mt 14:13 — When Jesus heard *of it,* he departed thence by ship into a desert place apart: and when the people had heard *thereof,* they followed him on foot out of the cities.

Mt 14:33 — Then they that were in the ship came and worshipped him, saying, Of a truth thou art the Son of God.

Mt 14:35 — And when the men of that place had knowledge of him, they sent out into all that country round about, and brought unto him all that were diseased;

Mt 15:31 — Insomuch that the multitude wondered, when they saw the dumb to speak, the maimed to be whole, the lame to walk, and the blind to see: and they glorified the God of Israel.

Mt 16:1 — The Pharisees also with the Sadducees came, and tempting desired him that he would shew them a sign from heaven.

Mt 16:14 — And they said, Some *say that thou art* John the Baptist: some, Elias; and others, Jeremias, or one of the prophets.

Mt 21:15 — And when the chief priests and scribes saw the wonderful things that he did, and the children crying in the temple, and saying, Hosanna to the Son of David; they were sore displeased,

Mt 27:54 — Now when the centurion, and they that were with him, watching Jesus, saw the earthquake, and those things that were done, they feared greatly, saying, Truly this was the Son of God.

Mk 1:22 — And they were astonished at his doctrine: for he taught them as one that had authority, and not as the scribes.

Mk 1:27 — And they were all amazed, insomuch that they questioned among themselves, saying, What thing is this? what new doctrine *is* this? for with authority commandeth he even the unclean spirits, and they do obey him.

Mk 1:33 — And all the city was gathered together at the door.

Mk 1:37 — And when they had found him, they said unto him, All *men* seek for thee.

Mk 1:45 — But he went out, and began to publish *it* much, and to blaze abroad the matter, insomuch that Jesus could no more openly enter into the city, but was without in desert places: and they came to him from every quarter.

Mk 2:2 — And straightway many were gathered together, insomuch that there was no room to receive *them,* no, not so much as about the door: and he preached the word unto them.

Mk 2:12 — And immediately he arose, took up the bed, and went forth before them all; insomuch that they were all amazed, and glorified God, saying, We never saw it on this fashion.

Mk 2:15 — And it came to pass, that, as Jesus sat at meat in his house, many publicans and sinners sat also together with Jesus and his disciples: for there were many, and they followed him.

Mk 3:7 — But Jesus withdrew himself with his disciples to the sea: and a great multitude from Galilee followed him, and from Judaea,

Mk 4:1 — And he began again to teach by the sea side: and there was gathered unto him a great multitude, so that he entered into a ship, and sat in the sea; and the whole multitude was by the sea on the land.

Mk 5:21 — And when Jesus was passed over again by ship unto the other side, much people gathered unto him: and he was nigh unto the sea.

Mk 5:42 — And straightway the damsel arose, and walked; for she was *of the age* of twelve years. And they were astonished with a great astonishment.

Mk 6:2 — And when the sabbath day was come, he began to teach in the synagogue: and many hearing *him* were astonished, saying, From whence hath this *man* these things? and what wisdom *is* this which is given unto him, that even such mighty works are wrought by his hands?

Mk 6:33 — And the people saw them departing, and many knew him, and ran afoot thither out of all cities, and outwent them, and came together unto him.

Mk 7:37 — And were beyond measure astonished, saying, He hath done all things well: he maketh both the deaf to hear, and the dumb to speak.

Mk 8:11 — And the Pharisees came forth, and began to question with him, seeking of him a sign from heaven, tempting him.

Mk 8:28 — And they answered, John the Baptist: but some *say,* Elias; and others, One of the prophets.

Mk 10:1 — And he arose from thence, and cometh into the coasts of Judaea by the farther side of Jordan: and the people resort unto him again; and, as he was wont, he taught them again.

Mk 11:18 — And the scribes and chief priests heard *it,* and sought how they might destroy him: for they feared him, because all the people was astonished at his doctrine.

Mk 12:37 — David therefore himself calleth him Lord; and whence is he *then* his son? And the common people heard him gladly.

Mk 15:39 — And when the centurion, which stood over against him, saw that he so cried out, and gave up the ghost, he said, Truly this man was the Son of God.

Lk 4:22 — And all bare him witness, and wondered at the gracious words which proceeded out of his mouth. And they said, Is not this Joseph's son?

Lk 4:32 — And they were astonished at his doctrine: for his word was with power.

Lk 4:42 — And when it was day, he departed and went into a desert place: and the people sought him, and came unto him, and stayed him, that he should not depart from them.

Lk 5:1 — And it came to pass, that, as the people pressed upon him to hear the word of God, he stood by the lake of Gennesaret,

Lk 5:17 — And it came to pass on a certain day, as he was teaching, that there were Pharisees and doctors of the law sitting by, which were come out of every town of Galilee, and Judaea, and Jerusalem: and the power of the Lord was *present* to heal them.

Lk 5:19 — And when they could not find by what *way* they might bring him in because of the multitude, they went upon the housetop, and let him down through the tiling with *his* couch into the midst before Jesus.

Lk 5:26 — And they were all amazed, and they glorified God, and were filled with fear, saying, We have seen strange things to day.

Lk 7:29 — And all the people that heard *him,* and the publicans, justified God, being baptized with the baptism of John.

Lk 8:56 — And her parents were astonished: but he charged them that they should tell no man what was done.

Lk 9:11 — And the people, when they knew *it,* followed him: and he received them, and spake unto them of the kingdom of God, and healed them that had need of healing.

Lk 9:19 — They answering said, John the Baptist; but some *say,* Elias; and others *say,* that one of the old prophets is risen again.

Lk 11:16 — And others, tempting *him,* sought of him a sign from heaven.

Lk 12:1 — In the mean time, when there were gathered together an innumerable multitude of people, insomuch that they trode one upon another, he began to say unto his disciples first of all, Beware ye of the leaven of the Pharisees, which is hypocrisy.

Lk 13:17 — And when he had said these things, all his adversaries were ashamed: and all the people rejoiced for all the glorious things that were done by him.

Lk 18:43 — And immediately he received his sight, and followed him, glorifying God: and all the people, when they saw *it,* gave praise unto God.

Lk 21:38 — And all the people came early in the morning to him in the temple, for to hear him.

Lk 23:27 — And there followed him a great company of people, and of women, which also bewailed and lamented him.

Lk 23:47 — Now when the centurion saw what was done, he glorified God, saying, Certainly this was a righteous man.

Jn 2:11 — This beginning of miracles did Jesus in Cana of Galilee, and manifested forth his glory; and his disciples believed on him.

Jn 2:23 — Now when he was in Jerusalem at the passover, in the feast *day,* many believed in his name, when they saw the miracles which he did.

Jn 6:2 — And a great multitude followed him, because they saw his miracles which he did on them that were diseased.

Jn 7:31 — And many of the people believed on him, and said, When Christ cometh, will he do more miracles than these which this *man* hath done?

Jn 7:46 — The officers answered, Never man spake like this man.

Jn 8:2 — And early in the morning he came again into the temple, and all the people came unto him; and he sat down, and taught them.

Jn 8:30 — As he spake these words, many believed on him.

Jn 9:17 — They say unto the blind man again, What sayest thou of him, that he hath opened thine eyes? He said, He is a prophet.

Jn 9:33 — If this man were not of God, he could do nothing.

Jn 11:37 — And some of them said, Could not this man, which opened the eyes of the blind, have caused that even this man should not have died?

Jn 12:9 — Much people of the Jews therefore knew that he was there: and they came not for Jesus' sake only, but that they might see Lazarus also, whom he had raised from the dead.

Jn 12:34 — The people answered him, We have heard out of the law that Christ abideth for ever: and how sayest thou, The Son of man must be lifted up? who is this Son of man?

Jn 12:42 — Nevertheless among the chief rulers also many believed on him; but because of the Pharisees they did not confess *him,* lest they should be put out of the synagogue:

- **Instances of.**
  - **By Matthew.**
    Mt 9:9–10
  - **By Peter and other disciples.**
    Mk 1:16–20; Lk 5:3–11
  - **By Zacchaeus.**
    Lk 19:1–10
  - **By Philip.**
    Jn 1:43, 45
  - **Nathanael.**
    Jn 1:45–50
  - **Three thousand at Pentecost.**
    Ac 2:41; 4:4
  - **The eunuch.**
    Ac 8:27–39

See: Faith in Christ; instances of

JESUS, Redeemer

See: Jesus, Saviour
See: Redemption

JESUS, Rejected

Ps 2:1–3; Isa 6:9–10; 50:1–11; 53:1–4; Mt 7:26–27; 10:14–15; 11:16–19; 12:38–45; 13:3–14; 21:38–45; 22:2–13; 26:31–35, 69–75; Mk 6:3–6; 12:1–12; 14:27–31, 66–72; Lk 6:46–49; 7:30–35; 11:23–26; 14:16–24; 20:9–18; 22:31–34, 54–62; 24:15–25, 37–39; Jn 3:11–12, 18–19; 6:60–68; 7:3–5, 12–13, 25–27; 8:21–22, 24–30, 45–47; 9:16–17; 10:20–21; 11:46–48; 18:15–27; Ac 18:5–6; 28:24–25; Ro 9:31–32; 1Pe 2:7–8; 1Jn 2:22–23

Ps 118:22 — The stone *which* the builders refused is become the head *stone* of the corner.

Isa 8:14 — And he shall be for a sanctuary; but for a stone of stumbling and for a rock of offence to both the houses of Israel, for a gin and for a snare to the inhabitants of Jerusalem.

Isa 49:4 — Then I said, I have laboured in vain, I have spent my strength for nought, and in vain: *yet* surely my judgment *is* with the LORD, and my work with my God.

Mt 8:12 — But the children of the kingdom shall be cast out into outer darkness: there shall be weeping and gnashing of teeth.

Mt 8:34 — And, behold, the whole city came out to meet Jesus: and when they saw him, they besought *him* that he would depart out of their coasts.

Mt 10:33 — But whosoever shall deny me before men, him will I also deny before my Father which is in heaven.

Mt 13:58 — And he did not many mighty works there because of their unbelief.

Mt 17:17 — Then Jesus answered and said, O faithless and perverse generation, how long shall I be with you? how long shall I suffer you? bring him hither to me.

Mt 21:32 — For John came unto you in the way of righteousness, and ye believed him not: but the publicans and the harlots believed him: and ye, when ye had seen *it,* repented not afterward, that ye might believe him.

Mk 5:17 — And they began to pray him to depart out of their coasts.

Mk 16:16 — He that believeth and is baptized shall be saved; but he that believeth not shall be damned.

Lk 8:37 — Then the whole multitude of the country of the Gadarenes round about besought him to depart from them; for they were taken with great fear: and he went up into the ship, and returned back again.

Lk 10:16 — He that heareth you heareth me; and he that despiseth you despiseth me; and he that despiseth me despiseth him that sent me.

Lk 13:34 — O Jerusalem, Jerusalem, which killest the prophets, and stonest them that are sent unto thee; how often would I have gathered thy children together, as a hen *doth gather* her brood under *her* wings, and ye would not!

Lk 17:25 — But first must he suffer many things, and be rejected of this generation.

Lk 19:42 — Saying, If thou hadst known, even thou, at least in this thy day, the things *which belong* unto thy peace! but now they are hid from thine eyes.

Lk 22:67 — Art thou the Christ? tell us. And he said unto them, If I tell you, ye will not believe:
Lk 24:11 — And their words seemed to them as idle tales, and they believed them not.
Jn 1:11 — He came unto his own, and his own received him not.
Jn 3:32 — And what he hath seen and heard, that he testifieth; and no man receiveth his testimony.
Jn 5:38 — And ye have not his word abiding in you: for whom he hath sent, him ye believe not.
Jn 5:40 — And ye will not come to me, that ye might have life.
Jn 5:43 — I am come in my Father's name, and ye receive me not: if another shall come in his own name, him ye will receive.
Jn 6:36 — But I said unto you, That ye also have seen me, and believe not.
Jn 7:15 — And the Jews marvelled, saying, How knoweth this man letters, having never learned?
Jn 8:13 — The Pharisees therefore said unto him, Thou bearest record of thyself; thy record is not true.
Jn 8:53 — Art thou greater than our father Abraham, which is dead? and the prophets are dead: whom makest thou thyself?
Jn 9:24 — Then again called they the man that was blind, and said unto him, Give God the praise: we know that this man is a sinner.
Jn 10:24 — Then came the Jews round about him, and said unto him, How long dost thou make us to doubt? If thou be the Christ, tell us plainly.
Jn 10:33 — The Jews answered him, saying, For a good work we stone thee not; but for blasphemy; and because that thou, being a man, makest thyself God.
Jn 12:37 — But though he had done so many miracles before them, yet they believed not on him:
Jn 12:48 — He that rejecteth me, and receiveth not my words, hath one that judgeth him: the word that I have spoken, the same shall judge him in the last day.
Jn 15:18 — If the world hate you, ye know that *it hated* me before it hated you.
Jn 15:20 — Remember the word that I said unto you, The servant is not greater than his lord. If they have persecuted me, they will also persecute you; if they have kept my saying, they will keep yours also.
Jn 15:24 — If I had not done among them the works which none other man did, they had not had sin: but now have they both seen and hated both me and my Father.
Ac 13:46 — Then Paul and Barnabas waxed bold, and said, It was necessary that the word of God should first have been spoken to you: but seeing ye put it from you, and judge yourselves unworthy of everlasting life, lo, we turn to the Gentiles.
Ac 22:18 — And saw him saying unto me, Make haste, and get thee quickly out of Jerusalem: for they will not receive thy testimony concerning me.
Ac 28:27 — For the heart of this people is waxed gross, and their ears are dull of hearing, and their eyes have they closed; lest they should see with *their* eyes, and hear with *their* ears, and understand with *their* heart, and should be converted, and I should heal them.
Ro 3:3 — For what if some did not believe? shall their unbelief make the faith of God without effect?
Ro 10:16 — But they have not all obeyed the gospel. For Esaias saith, Lord, who hath believed our report?
Ro 10:21 — But to Israel he saith, All day long I have stretched forth my hands unto a disobedient and gainsaying people.
1Co 1:18 — For the preaching of the cross is to them that perish foolishness; but unto us which are saved it is the power of God.
1Co 1:23 — But we preach Christ crucified, unto the Jews a stumblingblock, and unto the Greeks foolishness;
2Ti 2:12 — If we suffer, we shall also reign with *him:* if we deny *him,* he also will deny us:
Heb 6:6 — If they shall fall away, to renew them again unto repentance; seeing they crucify to themselves the Son of God afresh, and put *him* to an open shame.
Heb 10:29 — Of how much sorer punishment, suppose ye, shall he be thought worthy, who hath trodden under foot the Son of God, and hath counted the blood of the covenant, wherewith he was sanctified, an unholy thing, and hath done despite unto the Spirit of grace?
1Pe 2:4 — To whom coming, *as unto* a living stone, disallowed indeed of men, but chosen of God, *and* precious,
2Pe 2:1 — But there were false prophets also among the people, even as there shall be false teachers among you, who privily shall bring in damnable heresies, even denying the Lord that bought them, and bring upon themselves swift destruction.
2Jn 1:7 — For many deceivers are entered into the world, who confess not that Jesus Christ is come in the flesh. This is a deceiver and an antichrist.
Jude 1:4 — For there are certain men crept in unawares, who were before of old ordained to this condemnation, ungodly men, turning the grace of our God into lasciviousness, and denying the only Lord God, and our Lord Jesus Christ.

JESUS, Relation of, to the Father

Isa 49:5–6; Jn 1:1–2; 3:34–35; 5:19–31; 6:32–33, 38–40, 44–46; 7:28–29; 8:28–29, 54–55; 10:29–30, 32–33, 36–38; 11:41–42; 12:49–50; 14:9–14; 15:9–10, 23–26; 16:27–28; 17:1–26; 1Co 15:27–28; Eph 1:20–22; Heb 1:2–3; 5:5–9; 1Jn 4:9–10
Ps 110:1 — The LORD said unto my Lord, Sit thou at my right hand, until I make thine enemies thy footstool.
Isa 42:1 — Behold my servant, whom I uphold; mine elect, *in whom* my soul delighteth; I have put my spirit upon him: he shall bring forth judgment to the Gentiles.
Isa 61:1 — The Spirit of the Lord GOD *is* upon me; because the LORD hath anointed me to preach good tidings unto the meek; he hath sent me to bind up the brokenhearted, to proclaim liberty to the captives, and the opening of the prison to *them that are* bound;
Mic 5:4 — And he shall stand and feed in the strength of the LORD, in the majesty of the name of the LORD his God; and they shall abide: for now shall he be great unto the ends of the earth.
Mt 20:23 — And he saith unto them, Ye shall drink indeed of my cup, and be baptized with the baptism that I am baptized with: but to sit on my right hand, and

on my left, is not mine to give, but *it shall be given to them* for whom it is prepared of my Father.

Mt 26:39 — And he went a little farther, and fell on his face, and prayed, saying, O my Father, if it be possible, let this cup pass from me: nevertheless not as I will, but as thou *wilt.*

Mk 10:40 — But to sit on my right hand and on my left hand is not mine to give; but *it shall be given to them* for whom it is prepared.

Mk 13:32 — But of that day and *that* hour knoweth no man, no, not the angels which are in heaven, neither the Son, but the Father.

Jn 1:14 — And the Word was made flesh, and dwelt among us, (and we beheld his glory, the glory as of the only begotten of the Father,) full of grace and truth.

Jn 4:34 — Jesus saith unto them, My meat is to do the will of him that sent me, and to finish his work.

Jn 5:37 — And the Father himself, which hath sent me, hath borne witness of me. Ye have neither heard his voice at any time, nor seen his shape.

Jn 5:45 — Do not think that I will accuse you to the Father: there is *one* that accuseth you, *even* Moses, in whom ye trust.

Jn 7:16 — Jesus answered them, and said, My doctrine is not mine, but his that sent me.

Jn 7:33 — Then said Jesus unto them, Yet a little while am I with you, and *then* I go unto him that sent me.

Jn 8:16 — And yet if I judge, my judgment is true: for I am not alone, but I and the Father that sent me.

Jn 8:19 — Then said they unto him, Where is thy Father? Jesus answered, Ye neither know me, nor my Father: if ye had known me, ye should have known my Father also.

Jn 8:38 — I speak that which I have seen with my Father: and ye do that which ye have seen with your father.

Jn 8:40 — But now ye seek to kill me, a man that hath told you the truth, which I have heard of God: this did not Abraham.

Jn 8:42 — Jesus said unto them, If God were your Father, ye would love me: for I proceeded forth and came from God; neither came I of myself, but he sent me.

Jn 8:49 — Jesus answered, I have not a devil; but I honour my Father, and ye do dishonour me.

Jn 9:4 — I must work the works of him that sent me, while it is day: the night cometh, when no man can work.

Jn 10:15 — As the Father knoweth me, even so know I the Father: and I lay down my life for the sheep.

Jn 10:18 — No man taketh it from me, but I lay it down of myself. I have power to lay it down, and I have power to take it again. This commandment have I received of my Father.

Jn 10:25 — Jesus answered them, I told you, and ye believed not: the works that I do in my Father's name, they bear witness of me.

Jn 12:44 — Jesus cried and said, He that believeth on me, believeth not on me, but on him that sent me.

Jn 14:7 — If ye had known me, ye should have known my Father also: and from henceforth ye know him, and have seen him.

Jn 14:20 — At that day ye shall know that I *am* in my Father, and ye in me, and I in you.

Jn 14:24 — He that loveth me not keepeth not my sayings: and the word which ye hear is not mine, but the Father's which sent me.

Jn 14:28 — Ye have heard how I said unto you, I go away, and come *again* unto you. If ye loved me, ye would rejoice, because I said, I go unto the Father: for my Father is greater than I.

Jn 14:31 — But that the world may know that I love the Father; and as the Father gave me commandment, even so I do. Arise, let us go hence.

Jn 15:15 — Henceforth I call you not servants; for the servant knoweth not what his lord doeth: but I have called you friends; for all things that I have heard of my Father I have made known unto you.

Jn 16:5 — But now I go my way to him that sent me; and none of you asketh me, Whither goest thou?

Jn 16:10 — Of righteousness, because I go to my Father, and ye see me no more;

Jn 16:15 — All things that the Father hath are mine: therefore said I, that he shall take of mine, and shall shew *it* unto you.

Jn 16:23 — And in that day ye shall ask me nothing. Verily, verily, I say unto you, Whatsoever ye shall ask the Father in my name, he will give *it* you.

Jn 16:25 — These things have I spoken unto you in proverbs: but the time cometh, when I shall no more speak unto you in proverbs, but I shall shew you plainly of the Father.

Jn 16:32 — Behold, the hour cometh, yea, is now come, that ye shall be scattered, every man to his own, and shall leave me alone: and yet I am not alone, because the Father is with me.

Ac 2:33 — Therefore being by the right hand of God exalted, and having received of the Father the promise of the Holy Ghost, he hath shed forth this, which ye now see and hear.

Ac 2:36 — Therefore let all the house of Israel know assuredly, that God hath made that same Jesus, whom ye have crucified, both Lord and Christ.

Ac 10:38 — How God anointed Jesus of Nazareth with the Holy Ghost and with power: who went about doing good, and healing all that were oppressed of the devil; for God was with him.

Ac 13:37 — But he, whom God raised again, saw no corruption.

Ro 1:4 — And declared *to be* the Son of God with power, according to the spirit of holiness, by the resurrection from the dead:

Ro 8:32 — He that spared not his own Son, but delivered him up for us all, how shall he not with him also freely give us all things?

1Co 1:30 — But of him are ye in Christ Jesus, who of God is made unto us wisdom, and righteousness, and sanctification, and redemption:

1Co 3:23 — And ye are Christ's; and Christ *is* God's.

1Co 11:3 — But I would have you know, that the head of every man is Christ; and the head of the woman *is* the man; and the head of Christ *is* God.

1Co 15:24 — Then *cometh* the end, when he shall have delivered up the kingdom to God, even the Father; when he shall have put down all rule and all authority and power.

2Co 4:4 — In whom the god of this world hath blinded the minds of them which believe not, lest the light of the glorious gospel of Christ, who is the image of God, should shine unto them.

2Co 4:6 — For God, who commanded the light to shine out of darkness, hath shined in our hearts, to *give* the light of the knowledge of the glory of God in the face of Jesus Christ.

Eph 1:17 — That the God of our Lord Jesus Christ, the Father of glory, may give unto you the spirit of wisdom and revelation in the knowledge of him:

Php 2:6 — Who, being in the form of God, thought it not robbery to be equal with God:

Php 2:11 — And *that* every tongue should confess that Jesus Christ *is* Lord, to the glory of God the Father.

Col 1:15 — Who is the image of the invisible God, the firstborn of every creature:

Col 1:19 — For it pleased *the Father* that in him should all fulness dwell;

1Th 5:18 — In every thing give thanks: for this is the will of God in Christ Jesus concerning you.

Heb 2:9 — But we see Jesus, who was made a little lower than the angels for the suffering of death, crowned with glory and honour; that he by the grace of God should taste death for every man.

Heb 3:2 — Who was faithful to him that appointed him, as also Moses *was faithful* in all his house.

1Pe 1:21 — Who by him do believe in God, that raised him up from the dead, and gave him glory; that your faith and hope might be in God.

1Pe 2:4 — To whom coming, *as unto* a living stone, disallowed indeed of men, but chosen of God, *and* precious,

1Pe 2:23 — Who, when he was reviled, reviled not again; when he suffered, he threatened not; but committed *himself* to him that judgeth righteously:

2Pe 1:17 — For he received from God the Father honour and glory, when there came such a voice to him from the excellent glory, This is my beloved Son, in whom I am well pleased.

1Jn 4:14 — And we have seen and do testify that the Father sent the Son *to be* the Saviour of the world.

Rev 2:27 — And he shall rule them with a rod of iron; as the vessels of a potter shall they be broken to shivers: even as I received of my Father.

Rev 3:12 — Him that overcometh will I make a pillar in the temple of my God, and he shall go no more out: and I will write upon him the name of my God, and the name of the city of my God, *which is* new Jerusalem, which cometh down out of heaven from my God: and *I will write upon him* my new name.

Rev 3:21 — To him that overcometh will I grant to sit with me in my throne, even as I also overcame, and am set down with my Father in his throne.

See: Jesus, Divinity of

See: Jesus, Humanity of

See: Jesus, Son of God

JESUS, Resurrection of

Ps 16:9–10; Mt 27:52–53; 28:6–7; Mk 9:9–10; 16:6–7; Lk 24:5–7; Jn 2:21–22; 20:1–18; Ac 2:31–32; 5:30–32; 10:40–41; 13:30–34; 17:2–3; Ro 4:24–25; 6:4–5, 9–10; 1Co 15:3–8, 12–23; 2Co 4:10–11

Ps 2:7 — I will declare the decree: the LORD hath said unto me, Thou *art* my Son; this day have I begotten thee.

Isa 26:19 — Thy dead *men* shall live, *together with* my dead body shall they arise. Awake and sing, ye that dwell in dust: for thy dew *is as* the dew of herbs, and the earth shall cast out the dead.

Mt 12:40 — For as Jonas was three days and three nights in the whale's belly; so shall the Son of man be three days and three nights in the heart of the earth.

Mt 16:4 — A wicked and adulterous generation seeketh after a sign; and there shall no sign be given unto it, but the sign of the prophet Jonas. And he left them, and departed.

Mt 16:21 — From that time forth began Jesus to shew unto his disciples, how that he must go unto Jerusalem, and suffer many things of the elders and chief priests and scribes, and be killed, and be raised again the third day.

Mt 17:23 — And they shall kill him, and the third day he shall be raised again. And they were exceeding sorry.

Mt 20:19 — And shall deliver him to the Gentiles to mock, and to scourge, and to *crucify him:* and the third day he shall rise again.

Mt 26:32 — But after I am risen again, I will go before you into Galilee.

Mt 27:63 — Saying, Sir, we remember that that deceiver said, while he was yet alive, After three days I will rise again.

Mk 8:31 — And he began to teach them, that the Son of man must suffer many things, and be rejected of the elders, and *of* the chief priests, and scribes, and be killed, and after three days rise again.

Mk 10:34 — And they shall mock him, and shall scourge him, and shall spit upon him, and shall kill him: and the third day he shall rise again.

Mk 14:28 — But after that I am risen, I will go before you into Galilee.

Mk 14:58 — We heard him say, I will destroy this temple that is made with hands, and within three days I will build another made without hands.

Lk 9:22 — Saying, The Son of man must suffer many things, and be rejected of the elders and chief priests and scribes, and be slain, and be raised the third day.

Lk 9:31 — Who appeared in glory, and spake of his decease which he should accomplish at Jerusalem.

Lk 18:33 — And they shall scourge *him,* and put him to death: and the third day he shall rise again.

Lk 24:46 — And said unto them, Thus it is written, and thus it behoved Christ to suffer, and to rise from the dead the third day:

Jn 2:19 — Jesus answered and said unto them, Destroy this temple, and in three days I will raise it up.

Jn 12:23 — And Jesus answered them, saying, The hour is come, that the Son of man should be glorified.

Jn 16:16 — A little while, and ye shall not see me: and again, a little while, and ye shall see me, because I go to the Father.

Jn 16:22 — And ye now therefore have sorrow: but I will see you again, and your heart shall rejoice, and your joy no man taketh from you.

Ac 1:3 — To whom also he shewed himself alive after his passion by many infallible proofs, being seen of them forty days, and speaking of the things pertaining to the kingdom of God:

Ac 1:22 — Beginning from the baptism of John, unto that same day that he was taken up from us, must one be ordained to be a witness with us of his resurrection.

Ac 2:24 — Whom God hath raised up, having loosed the pains of death: because it was not possible that he should be holden of it.

Ac 3:15 — And killed the Prince of life, whom God hath raised from the dead; whereof we are witnesses.

Ac 4:10 — Be it known unto you all, and to all the people of Israel, that by the name of Jesus Christ of Nazareth, whom ye crucified, whom God raised from the dead, *even* by him doth this man stand here before you whole.

Ac 4:33 — And with great power gave the apostles witness of the resurrection of the Lord Jesus: and great grace was upon them all.

Ac 17:31 — Because he hath appointed a day, in the which he will judge the world in righteousness by *that* man whom he hath ordained; *whereof* he hath given assurance unto all *men,* in that he hath raised him from the dead.

Ac 26:23 — That Christ should suffer, *and* that he should be the first that should rise from the dead, and should shew light unto the people, and to the Gentiles.

Ac 26:26 — For the king knoweth of these things, before whom also I speak freely: for I am persuaded that none of these things are hidden from him; for this thing was not done in a corner.

Ro 1:4 — And declared *to be* the Son of God with power, according to the spirit of holiness, by the resurrection from the dead:

Ro 5:10 — For if, when we were enemies, we were reconciled to God by the death of his Son, much more, being reconciled, we shall be saved by his life.

Ro 8:11 — But if the Spirit of him that raised up Jesus from the dead dwell in you, he that raised up Christ from the dead shall also quicken your mortal bodies by his Spirit that dwelleth in you.

Ro 8:34 — Who *is* he that condemneth? *It is* Christ that died, yea rather, that is risen again, who is even at the right hand of God, who also maketh intercession for us.

Ro 10:9 — That if thou shalt confess with thy mouth the Lord Jesus, and shalt believe in thine heart that God hath raised him from the dead, thou shalt be saved.

1Co 6:14 — And God hath both raised up the Lord, and will also raise up us by his own power.

2Co 4:14 — Knowing that he which raised up the Lord Jesus shall raise up us also by Jesus, and shall present *us* with you.

2Co 5:15 — And *that* he died for all, that they which live should not henceforth live unto themselves, but unto him which died for them, and rose again.

2Co 13:4 — For though he was crucified through weakness, yet he liveth by the power of God. For we also are weak in him, but we shall live with him by the power of God toward you.

Gal 1:1 — Paul, an apostle, (not of men, neither by man, but by Jesus Christ, and God the Father, who raised him from the dead;)

Eph 1:20 — Which he wrought in Christ, when he raised him from the dead, and set *him* at his own right hand in the heavenly *places,*

Php 3:10 — That I may know him, and the power of his resurrection, and the fellowship of his sufferings, being made conformable unto his death;

Col 1:18 — And he is the head of the body, the church: who is the beginning, the firstborn from the dead; that in all *things* he might have the preeminence.

Col 2:12 — Buried with him in baptism, wherein also ye are risen with *him* through the faith of the operation of God, who hath raised him from the dead.

1Th 1:10 — And to wait for his Son from heaven, whom he raised from the dead, *even* Jesus, which delivered us from the wrath to come.

1Th 4:14 — For if we believe that Jesus died and rose again, even so them also which sleep in Jesus will God bring with him.

2Ti 2:8 — Remember that Jesus Christ of the seed of David was raised from the dead according to my gospel:

Heb 13:20 — Now the God of peace, that brought again from the dead our Lord Jesus, that great shepherd of the sheep, through the blood of the everlasting covenant,

1Pe 1:3 — Blessed *be* the God and Father of our Lord Jesus Christ, which according to his abundant mercy hath begotten us again unto a lively hope by the resurrection of Jesus Christ from the dead,

1Pe 1:21 — Who by him do believe in God, that raised him up from the dead, and gave him glory; that your faith and hope might be in God.

1Pe 3:18 — For Christ also hath once suffered for sins, the just for the unjust, that he might bring us to God, being put to death in the flesh, but quickened by the Spirit:

1Pe 3:21 — The like figure whereunto *even* baptism doth also now save us (not the putting away of the filth of the flesh, but the answer of a good conscience toward God,) by the resurrection of Jesus Christ:

Rev 1:5 — And from Jesus Christ, *who is* the faithful witness, *and* the first begotten of the dead, and the prince of the kings of the earth. Unto him that loved us, and washed us from our sins in his own blood,

Rev 1:18 — <u>*I am* he that liveth, and was dead; and, behold, I am alive for evermore, Amen; and have the keys of hell and of death.</u>

See: Resurrection

JESUS, Revelations by

• Concerning his kingdom.

Mt 8:11–12; 13:24–50; 21:43–44; Mk 16:17–18; Lk 12:40–53; 13:24–35; 17:20–37; Jn 5:25–29

Mt 10:23 — <u>But when they persecute you in this city, flee ye into another: for verily I say unto you, Ye shall not have gone over the cities of Israel, till the Son of man be come.</u>

Mt 10:34 — <u>Think not that I am come to send peace on earth: I came not to send peace, but a sword.</u>

Mt 16:18 — <u>And I say also unto thee, That thou art Peter, and upon this rock I will build my church: and the gates of hell shall not prevail against it.</u>

Mt 16:28 — Verily I say unto you, There be some standing here, which shall not taste of death, till they see the Son of man coming in his kingdom.

Mt 24:14 — And this gospel of the kingdom shall be preached in all the world for a witness unto all nations; and then shall the end come.

Mk 9:1 — And he said unto them, Verily I say unto you, That there be some of them that stand here, which shall not taste of death, till they have seen the kingdom of God come with power.

Lk 9:27 — But I tell you of a truth, there be some standing here, which shall not taste of death, till they see the kingdom of God.

Jn 4:21 — Jesus saith unto her, Woman, believe me, the hour cometh, when ye shall neither in this mountain, nor yet at Jerusalem, worship the Father.

Jn 4:23 — But the hour cometh, and now is, when the true worshippers shall worship the Father in spirit and in truth: for the Father seeketh such to worship him.

Jn 6:39 — And this is the Father's will which hath sent me, that of all which he hath given me I should lose nothing, but should raise it up again at the last day.

Jn 6:54 — Whoso eateth my flesh, and drinketh my blood, hath eternal life; and I will raise him up at the last day.

Jn 12:35 — Then Jesus said unto them, Yet a little while is the light with you. Walk while ye have the light, lest darkness come upon you: for he that walketh in darkness knoweth not whither he goeth.

Jn 13:19 — Now I tell you before it come, that, when it is come to pass, ye may believe that I am *he.*

Jn 14:29 — And now I have told you before it come to pass, that, when it is come to pass, ye might believe.

Jn 16:4 — But these things have I told you, that when the time shall come, ye may remember that I told you of them. And these things I said not unto you at the beginning, because I was with you.

• Concerning his rejection by the Jews.

Mt 21:33–44

Lk 17:25 — But first must he suffer many things, and be rejected of this generation.

• Concerning his betrayal.

Mt 26:23–25

Mt 26:21 — And as they did eat, he said, Verily I say unto you, that one of you shall betray me.

• Concerning crucifixion.

Jn 3:14 — And as Moses lifted up the serpent in the wilderness, even so must the Son of man be lifted up:

Jn 8:28 — Then said Jesus unto them, When ye have lifted up the Son of man, then shall ye know that I am *he,* and *that* I do nothing of myself; but as my Father hath taught me, I speak these things.

Jn 12:32 — And I, if I be lifted up from the earth, will draw all *men* unto me.

• Concerning judgments upon the Jews.

Mt 23:37–39; 25:1–46; Mk 11:12–14; Lk 23:28–31

• Concerning the destruction of the temple, and Jerusalem.

Mt 24:1–51; Mk 13:1–37; Lk 19:41–48

• Concerning the destruction of Capernaum.

Mt 11:23 — And thou, Capernaum, which art exalted unto heaven, shalt be brought down to hell: for if the mighty works, which have been done in thee, had been done in Sodom, it would have remained until this day.

Lk 10:15 — And thou, Capernaum, which art exalted to heaven, shalt be thrust down to hell.

• Concerning persecutions of Christians.

Mt 23:34–36

• Concerning his being forsaken by his disciples.

Jn 16:32 — Behold, the hour cometh, yea, is now come, that ye shall be scattered, every man to his own, and shall leave me alone: and yet I am not alone, because the Father is with me.

• Concerning Lazarus.

Jn 11:4 — When Jesus heard *that,* he said, This sickness is not unto death, but for the glory of God, that the Son of God might be glorified thereby.

Jn 11:11 — These things said he: and after that he saith unto them, Our friend Lazarus sleepeth; but I go, that I may awake him out of sleep.

Jn 11:23 — Jesus saith unto her, Thy brother shall rise again.

Jn 11:40 — Jesus saith unto her, Said I not unto thee, that, if thou wouldest believe, thou shouldest see the glory of God?

• Concerning Peter.

Jn 21:18–23

• Concerning fame of the woman who anointed his head.

Mk 14:8–9

Mt 26:13 — Verily I say unto you, Wheresoever this gospel shall be preached in the whole world, *there* shall also this, that this woman hath done, be told for a memorial of her.

• Antichrist.

Mt 24:4–5, 23–26; Mk 13:5–6, 21–23; Lk 17:23–24; Ac 5:36–37

Lk 21:8 — And he said, Take heed that ye be not deceived: for many shall come in my name, saying, I am *Christ;* and the time draweth near: go ye not therefore after them.

• Concerning his death and resurrection.

Mt 12:39–40; 17:22–23; 20:18–19; 26:23–24, 45–46; Mk 10:32–34; Lk 9:22–24; 18:31–33; Jn 13:18–27, 36–38

Mt 16:21 — From that time forth began Jesus to shew unto his disciples, how that he must go unto Jerusalem, and suffer many things of the elders and chief priests and scribes, and be killed, and be raised again the third day.

Mt 26:2 — Ye know that after two days is *the feast of* the passover, and the Son of man is betrayed to be crucified.

Mt 26:21 — And as they did eat, he said, Verily I say unto you, that one of you shall betray me.

Mk 8:31 — And he began to teach them, that the Son of man must suffer many things, and be rejected of the elders, and *of* the chief priests, and scribes, and be killed, and after three days rise again.

Mk 9:31 — For he taught his disciples, and said unto them, The Son of man is delivered into the hands of men, and they shall kill him; and after that he is killed, he shall rise the third day.

Jn 2:19 — Jesus answered and said unto them, Destroy this temple, and in three days I will raise it up.

Jn 12:7 — Then said Jesus, Let her alone: against the day of my burying hath she kept this.

Jn 12:23 — And Jesus answered them, saying, The hour is come, that the Son of man should be glorified.

Jn 16:32 — Behold, the hour cometh, yea, is now come, that ye shall be scattered, every man to his own, and shall leave me alone: and yet I am not alone, because the Father is with me.

• Concerning ascension.

Jn 7:33–34

Jn 8:21 — Then said Jesus again unto them, I go my way, and ye shall seek me, and shall die in your sins: whither I go, ye cannot come.

Jn 12:8 — For the poor always ye have with you; but me ye have not always.

Jn 13:33 — Little children, yet a little while I am with you. Ye shall seek me: and as I said unto the Jews, Whither I go, ye cannot come; so now I say to you.

Jn 16:10 — Of righteousness, because I go to my Father, and ye see me no more;

Jn 16:16 — A little while, and ye shall not see me: and again, a little while, and ye shall see me, because I go to the Father.

JESUS, Righteousness of *See:* Jesus, Holiness of

JESUS, Salvation by *See:* Jesus, Saviour

JESUS, Saviour

2Sa 23:6–7; Job 33:23–24; Ps 72:12–14; Isa 40:10–11; 42:6–7; 49:8–9; 50:8–9; 53:10–11; 59:16–17; 61:1–3; 63:8–9; Jer 23:5–6; 33:15–16; Mt 9:12–13; 18:11–13; Lk 1:68–77; 2:30–32; 5:31–32; 15:1–10; Jn 3:16–17; 5:33–34; 6:32–33, 53–58; 7:37–39; 10:9–11, 14–16, 27–28; 11:25–27; 17:2–3; Ac 13:38–39; Ro 3:24–26; 4:25–5:1; 5:8–11; 5:17–19, 7–9; 1Co 10:3–4; 2Co 5:18–19; Gal 1:3–4; Eph 1:10–11; 2:13–18; 5:25–26; Col 1:12–14, 27–28; 3:3–4; 1Th 5:9–10; 2Ti 1:9–10; Tit 2:13–14; 1Pe 1:18–19; 2:4–7; 1Jn 4:9–10; 5:11–13; Rev 5:5–14; 21:27–22:2

Ge 12:3 — And I will bless them that bless thee, and curse him that curseth thee: and in thee shall all families of the earth be blessed.

Ge 49:18 — I have waited for thy salvation, O LORD.

Ps 14:7 — Oh that the salvation of Israel *were come* out of Zion! when the LORD bringeth back the captivity of his people, Jacob shall rejoice, *and* Israel shall be glad.

Ps 72:4 — He shall judge the poor of the people, he shall save the children of the needy, and shall break in pieces the oppressor.

Ps 72:17 — His name shall endure for ever: his name shall be continued as long as the sun: and *men* shall be blessed in him: all nations shall call him blessed.

Ps 80:17 — Let thy hand be upon the man of thy right hand, upon the son of man *whom* thou madest strong for thyself.

Ps 89:19 — Then thou spakest in vision to thy holy one, and saidst, I have laid help upon *one that is* mighty; I have exalted *one* chosen out of the people.

Isa 8:14 — And he shall be for a sanctuary; but for a stone of stumbling and for a rock of offence to both the houses of Israel, for a gin and for a snare to the inhabitants of Jerusalem.

Isa 28:16 — Therefore thus saith the Lord GOD, Behold, I lay in Zion for a foundation a stone, a tried stone, a precious corner *stone,* a sure foundation: he that believeth shall not make haste.

Isa 32:2 — And a man shall be as an hiding place from the wind, and a covert from the tempest; as rivers of water in a dry place, as the shadow of a great rock in a weary land.

Isa 49:6 — And he said, It is a light thing that thou shouldest be my servant to raise up the tribes of Jacob, and to restore the preserved of Israel: I will also give thee for a light to the Gentiles, that thou mayest be my salvation unto the end of the earth.

Isa 50:2 — Wherefore, when I came, *was there* no man? when I called, *was there* none to answer? Is my hand shortened at all, that it cannot redeem? or have I no power to deliver? behold, at my rebuke I dry up the sea, I make the rivers a wilderness: their fish stinketh, because *there is* no water, and dieth for thirst.

Isa 59:20 — And the Redeemer shall come to Zion, and unto them that turn from transgression in Jacob, saith the LORD.

Isa 62:11 — Behold, the LORD hath proclaimed unto the end of the world, Say ye to the daughter of Zion, Behold, thy salvation cometh; behold, his reward *is* with him, and his work before him.

Isa 63:1 — Who *is* this that cometh from Edom, with dyed garments from Bozrah? this *that is* glorious in his apparel, travelling in the greatness of his strength? I that speak in righteousness, mighty to save.

Isa 63:5 — And I looked, and *there was* none to help; and I wondered that *there was* none to uphold: therefore mine own arm brought salvation unto me; and my fury, it upheld me.

Eze 34:23 — And I will set up one shepherd over them, and he shall feed them, *even* my servant David; he shall feed them, and he shall be their shepherd.

Hag 2:7 — And I will shake all nations, and the desire of all nations shall come: and I will fill this house with glory, saith the LORD of hosts.

Zec 4:7 — Who *art* thou, O great mountain? before Zerubbabel *thou shalt become* a plain: and he shall bring forth the headstone *thereof with* shoutings, *crying,* Grace, grace unto it.

Zec 9:9 — Rejoice greatly, O daughter of Zion; shout, O daughter of Jerusalem: behold, thy King cometh unto thee: he *is* just, and having salvation; lowly, and riding upon an ass, and upon a colt the foal of an ass.

Mal 4:2 — But unto you that fear my name shall the Sun of righteousness arise with healing in his wings; and ye shall go forth, and grow up as calves of the stall.

Mt 1:21 — And she shall bring forth a son, and thou shalt call his name JESUS: for he shall save his people from their sins.

Mt 15:24 — But he answered and said, I am not sent but unto the lost sheep of the house of Israel.

Lk 2:11 — For unto you is born this day in the city of David a Saviour, which is Christ the Lord.

Lk 2:34 — And Simeon blessed them, and said unto Mary his mother, Behold, this *child* is set for the fall and rising again of many in Israel; and for a sign which shall be spoken against;

Lk 9:56 — For the Son of man is not come to destroy men's lives, but to save *them.* And they went to another village.

Lk 19:10 — For the Son of man is come to seek and to save that which was lost.

Jn 1:9 — *That* was the true Light, which lighteth every man that cometh into the world.

Jn 1:29 — The next day John seeth Jesus coming unto him, and saith, Behold the Lamb of God, which taketh away the sin of the world.

Jn 4:14 — But whosoever drinketh of the water that I shall give him shall never thirst; but the water that I shall give him shall be in him a well of water springing up into everlasting life.

Jn 4:42 — And said unto the woman, Now we believe, not because of thy saying: for we have heard *him* ourselves, and know that this is indeed the Christ, the Saviour of the world.

Jn 5:26 — For as the Father hath life in himself; so hath he given to the Son to have life in himself;

Jn 6:27 — Labour not for the meat which perisheth, but for that meat which endureth unto everlasting life, which the Son of man shall give unto you: for him hath God the Father sealed.

Jn 6:35 — And Jesus said unto them, I am the bread of life: he that cometh to me shall never hunger; and he that believeth on me shall never thirst.

Jn 6:37 — All that the Father giveth me shall come to me; and him that cometh to me I will in no wise cast out.

Jn 6:39 — And this is the Father's will which hath sent me, that of all which he hath given me I should lose nothing, but should raise it up again at the last day.

Jn 6:51 — I am the living bread which came down from heaven: if any man eat of this bread, he shall live for ever: and the bread that I will give is my flesh, which I will give for the life of the world.

Jn 6:68 — Then Simon Peter answered him, Lord, to whom shall we go? thou hast the words of eternal life.

Jn 8:12 — Then spake Jesus again unto them, saying, I am the light of the world: he that followeth me shall not walk in darkness, but shall have the light of life.

Jn 9:5 — As long as I am in the world, I am the light of the world.

Jn 9:39 — And Jesus said, For judgment I am come into this world, that they which see not might see; and that they which see might be made blind.

Jn 10:7 — Then said Jesus unto them again, Verily, verily, I say unto you, I am the door of the sheep.

Jn 12:47 — And if any man hear my words, and believe not, I judge him not: for I came not to judge the world, but to save the world.

Jn 14:6 — Jesus saith unto him, I am the way, the truth, and the life: no man cometh unto the Father, but by me.

Jn 14:19 — Yet a little while, and the world seeth me no more; but ye see me: because I live, ye shall live also.

Jn 16:33 — These things I have spoken unto you, that in me ye might have peace. In the world ye shall have tribulation: but be of good cheer; I have overcome the world.

Ac 3:26 — Unto you first God, having raised up his Son Jesus, sent him to bless you, in turning away every one of you from his iniquities.

Ac 4:12 — Neither is there salvation in any other: for there is none other name under heaven given among men, whereby we must be saved.

Ac 5:31 — Him hath God exalted with his right hand *to be* a Prince and a Saviour, for to give repentance to Israel, and forgiveness of sins.

Ac 13:23 — Of this man's seed hath God according to *his* promise raised unto Israel a Saviour, Jesus:

Ac 13:47 — For so hath the Lord commanded us, *saying,* I have set thee to be a light of the Gentiles, that thou shouldest be for salvation unto the ends of the earth.

Ac 15:11 — But we believe that through the grace of the Lord Jesus Christ we shall be saved, even as they.

Ac 16:31 — And they said, Believe on the Lord Jesus Christ, and thou shalt be saved, and thy house.

Ro 5:6 — For when we were yet without strength, in due time Christ died for the ungodly.

Ro 5:15 — But not as the offence, so also *is* the free gift. For if through the offence of one many be dead, much more the grace of God, and the gift by grace, *which is* by one man, Jesus Christ, hath abounded unto many.

Ro 5:21 — That as sin hath reigned unto death, even so might grace reign through righteousness unto eternal life by Jesus Christ our Lord.

Ro 6:23 — For the wages of sin *is* death; but the gift of God *is* eternal life through Jesus Christ our Lord.

Ro 8:2 — For the law of the Spirit of life in Christ Jesus hath made me free from the law of sin and death.

Ro 10:9 — That if thou shalt confess with thy mouth the Lord Jesus, and shalt believe in thine heart that God hath raised him from the dead, thou shalt be saved.

Ro 10:11 — For the scripture saith, Whosoever believeth on him shall not be ashamed.

1Co 1:30 — But of him are ye in Christ Jesus, who of God is made unto us wisdom, and righteousness, and sanctification, and redemption:

1Co 3:11 — For other foundation can no man lay than that is laid, which is Jesus Christ.

1Co 6:11 — And such were some of you: but ye are washed, but ye are sanctified, but ye are justified in the name of the Lord Jesus, and by the Spirit of our God.

1Co 15:17 — And if Christ be not raised, your faith *is* vain; ye are yet in your sins.

1Co 15:57 — But thanks *be* to God, which giveth us the victory through our Lord Jesus Christ.

2Co 5:21 — For he hath made him *to be* sin for us, who knew no sin; that we might be made the righteousness of God in him.

Gal 2:20 — I am crucified with Christ: nevertheless I live; yet not I, but Christ liveth in me: and the life which I now live in the flesh I live by the faith of the Son of God, who loved me, and gave himself for me.

Gal 4:7 — Wherefore thou art no more a servant, but a son; and if a son, then an heir of God through Christ.

Eph 2:7 — That in the ages to come he might shew the exceeding riches of his grace in *his* kindness toward us through Christ Jesus.

Eph 2:20 — And are built upon the foundation of the apostles and prophets, Jesus Christ himself being the chief corner *stone;*

Eph 4:8 — Wherefore he saith, When he ascended up on high, he led captivity captive, and gave gifts unto men.

Eph 5:2 — And walk in love, as Christ also hath loved us, and hath given himself for us an offering and a sacrifice to God for a sweetsmelling savour.

Eph 5:14 — Wherefore he saith, Awake thou that sleepest, and arise from the dead, and Christ shall give thee light.

Eph 5:23 — For the husband is the head of the wife, even as Christ is the head of the church: and he is the saviour of the body.

Php 3:20 — For our conversation is in heaven; from whence also we look for the Saviour, the Lord Jesus Christ:

Col 2:8 — Beware lest any man spoil you through philosophy and vain deceit, after the tradition of men, after the rudiments of the world, and not after Christ.

Col 2:10 — And ye are complete in him, which is the head of all principality and power:

Col 3:11 — Where there is neither Greek nor Jew, circumcision nor uncircumcision, Barbarian, Scythian, bond *nor* free: but Christ *is* all, and in all.

1Th 1:10 — And to wait for his Son from heaven, whom he raised from the dead, *even* Jesus, which delivered us from the wrath to come.

2Th 1:12 — That the name of our Lord Jesus Christ may be glorified in you, and ye in him, according to the grace of our God and the Lord Jesus Christ.

1Ti 1:1 — Paul, an apostle of Jesus Christ by the commandment of God our Saviour, and Lord Jesus Christ, *which is* our hope;

1Ti 1:15 — This *is* a faithful saying, and worthy of all acceptation, that Christ Jesus came into the world to save sinners; of whom I am chief.

2Ti 1:1 — Paul, an apostle of Jesus Christ by the will of God, according to the promise of life which is in Christ Jesus,

2Ti 1:12 — For the which cause I also suffer these things: nevertheless I am not ashamed: for I know whom I have believed, and am persuaded that he is able to keep that which I have committed unto him against that day.

2Ti 2:10 — Therefore I endure all things for the elect's sakes, that they may also obtain the salvation which is in Christ Jesus with eternal glory.

2Ti 3:15 — And that from a child thou hast known the holy scriptures, which are able to make thee wise unto salvation through faith which is in Christ Jesus.

Tit 1:4 — To Titus, *mine* own son after the common faith: Grace, mercy, *and* peace, from God the Father and the Lord Jesus Christ our Saviour.

Heb 2:3 — How shall we escape, if we neglect so great salvation; which at the first began to be spoken by the Lord, and was confirmed unto us by them that heard *him;*

Heb 2:17 — Wherefore in all things it behoved him to be made like unto *his* brethren, that he might be a merciful and faithful high priest in things *pertaining* to God, to make reconciliation for the sins of the people.

Heb 5:9 — And being made perfect, he became the author of eternal salvation unto all them that obey him;

Heb 7:22 — By so much was Jesus made a surety of a better testament.

Heb 7:25 — Wherefore he is able also to save them to the uttermost that come unto God by him, seeing he ever liveth to make intercession for them.

Heb 13:10 — We have an altar, whereof they have no right to eat which serve the tabernacle.

Heb 13:20 — Now the God of peace, that brought again from the dead our Lord Jesus, that great shepherd of the sheep, through the blood of the everlasting covenant,

1Pe 1:3 — Blessed *be* the God and Father of our Lord Jesus Christ, which according to his abundant mercy hath begotten us again unto a lively hope by the resurrection of Jesus Christ from the dead,

1Pe 2:25 — For ye were as sheep going astray; but are now returned unto the Shepherd and Bishop of your souls.

1Pe 3:18 — For Christ also hath once suffered for sins, the just for the unjust, that he might bring us to God, being put to death in the flesh, but quickened by the Spirit:

1Pe 3:21 — The like figure whereunto *even* baptism doth also now save us (not the putting away of the filth of the flesh, but the answer of a good conscience toward God,) by the resurrection of Jesus Christ:

1Pe 5:10 — But the God of all grace, who hath called us unto his eternal glory by Christ Jesus, after that ye have suffered a while, make you perfect, stablish, strengthen, settle *you.*

2Pe 1:3 — According as his divine power hath given unto us all things that *pertain* unto life and godliness, through the knowledge of him that hath called us to glory and virtue:

2Pe 1:11 — For so an entrance shall be ministered unto you abundantly into the everlasting kingdom of our Lord and Saviour Jesus Christ.

2Pe 2:20 — For if after they have escaped the pollutions of the world through the knowledge of the Lord and Saviour Jesus Christ, they are again entangled therein, and overcome, the latter end is worse with them than the beginning.

1Jn 3:5 — And ye know that he was manifested to take away our sins; and in him is no sin.

1Jn 3:8 — He that committeth sin is of the devil; for the devil sinneth from the beginning. For this purpose the Son of God was manifested, that he might destroy the works of the devil.

1Jn 4:14 — And we have seen and do testify that the Father sent the Son *to be* the Saviour of the world.

1Jn 5:20 — *And* we know that the Son of God is come, and hath given us an understanding, that we may know him that is true, and we are in him that is true, *even* in his Son Jesus Christ. This is the true God, and eternal life.

Jude 1:1 — Jude, the servant of Jesus Christ, and brother of James, to them that are sanctified by God the Father, and preserved in Jesus Christ, *and* called:

Rev 2:7 — He that hath an ear, let him hear what the Spirit saith unto the churches; To him that overcometh will I give to eat of the tree of life, which is in the midst of the paradise of God.

Rev 3:18 — I counsel thee to buy of me gold tried in the fire, that thou mayest be rich; and white raiment, that thou mayest be clothed, and *that* the shame of thy nakedness do not appear; and anoint thine eyes with eyesalve, that thou mayest see.

Rev 7:10 — And cried with a loud voice, saying, Salvation to our God which sitteth upon the throne, and unto the Lamb.

Rev 14:4 — These are they which were not defiled with women; for they are virgins. These are they which follow the Lamb whithersoever he goeth. These were redeemed from among men, *being* the firstfruits unto God and to the Lamb.

✧See: Jesus, Ascension of

✧See: Jesus, Death of; design of his death

✧See: Jesus, Faith in

JESUS, Second Coming of

Job 19:25–26; Mt 16:27–28; 23:39–25:13; 25:31–46; Mk 8:38–9:1; 13:1–37; Lk 9:26–27; 12:37–40; 17:22–37; 19:12–13; 21:5–36; Jn 14:28–29; Ac 3:20–21; 1Co 1:7–8; Php 3:20–21; 1Th 4:15–17; 5:2–3; 2Th 1:7–10; 2:1–3; 1Ti 6:14–15; Jas 5:7–9; 2Pe 3:3–4, 8–14; Jude 1:14–15

Mt 25:19 — After a long time the lord of those servants cometh, and reckoneth with them.

Mt 26:64 — Jesus saith unto him, Thou hast said: nevertheless I say unto you, Hereafter shall ye see the Son of man sitting on the right hand of power, and coming in the clouds of heaven.

Mk 14:62 — And Jesus said, I am: and ye shall see the Son of man sitting on the right hand of power, and coming in the clouds of heaven.

Lk 18:8 — I tell you that he will avenge them speedily. Nevertheless when the Son of man cometh, shall he find faith on the earth?

Lk 19:15 — And it came to pass, that when he was returned, having received the kingdom, then he commanded these servants to be called unto him, to whom he had given the money, that he might know how much every man had gained by trading.

Jn 14:3 — And if I go and prepare a place for you, I will come again, and receive you unto myself; that where I am, *there* ye may be also.

Jn 14:18 — I will not leave you comfortless: I will come to you.

Ac 1:11 — Which also said, Ye men of Galilee, why stand ye gazing up into heaven? this same Jesus, which is taken up from you into heaven, shall so come in like manner as ye have seen him go into heaven.

1Co 4:5 — Therefore judge nothing before the time, until the Lord come, who both will bring to light the hidden things of darkness, and will make manifest the counsels of the hearts: and then shall every man have praise of God.

1Co 11:26 — For as often as ye eat this bread, and drink *this* cup, ye do shew the Lord's death till he come.

1Co 15:23 — But every man in his own order: Christ the firstfruits; afterward they that are Christ's at his coming.

Php 4:5 — Let your moderation be known unto all men. The Lord *is* at hand.

Col 3:4 — When Christ, *who is* our life, shall appear, then shall ye also appear with him in glory.

1Th 1:10 — And to wait for his Son from heaven, whom he raised from the dead, *even* Jesus, which delivered us from the wrath to come.

1Th 2:19 — For what *is* our hope, or joy, or crown of rejoicing? *Are* not even ye in the presence of our Lord Jesus Christ at his coming?

1Th 3:13 — To the end he may stablish your hearts unblameable in holiness before God, even our Father, at the coming of our Lord Jesus Christ with all his saints.

1Th 5:23 — And the very God of peace sanctify you wholly; and *I pray God* your whole spirit and soul and body be preserved blameless unto the coming of our Lord Jesus Christ.

2Th 2:5 — Remember ye not, that, when I was yet with you, I told you these things?

2Th 2:8 — And then shall that Wicked be revealed, whom the Lord shall consume with the spirit of his mouth, and shall destroy with the brightness of his coming:

2Th 3:5 — And the Lord direct your hearts into the love of God, and into the patient waiting for Christ.

2Ti 4:1 — I charge *thee* therefore before God, and the Lord Jesus Christ, who shall judge the quick and the dead at his appearing and his kingdom;

2Ti 4:8 — Henceforth there is laid up for me a crown of righteousness, which the Lord, the righteous judge, shall give me at that day: and not to me only, but unto all them also that love his appearing.

Tit 2:13 — Looking for that blessed hope, and the glorious appearing of the great God and our Saviour Jesus Christ;

Heb 9:28 — So Christ was once offered to bear the sins of many; and unto them that look for him shall he appear the second time without sin unto salvation.

1Pe 1:7 — That the trial of your faith, being much more precious than of gold that perisheth, though it be tried with fire, might be found unto praise and honour and glory at the appearing of Jesus Christ:

1Pe 1:13 — Wherefore gird up the loins of your mind, be sober, and hope to the end for the grace that is to be brought unto you at the revelation of Jesus Christ;

1Pe 4:13 — But rejoice, inasmuch as ye are partakers of Christ's sufferings; that, when his glory shall be revealed, ye may be glad also with exceeding joy.

1Pe 5:4 — And when the chief Shepherd shall appear, ye shall receive a crown of glory that fadeth not away.

2Pe 1:16 — For we have not followed cunningly devised fables, when we made known unto you the power and coming of our Lord Jesus Christ, but were eyewitnesses of his majesty.

1Jn 2:28 — And now, little children, abide in him; that, when he shall appear, we may have confidence, and not be ashamed before him at his coming.

1Jn 3:2 — Beloved, now are we the sons of God, and it doth not yet appear what we shall be: but we know that, when he shall appear, we shall be like him; for we shall see him as he is.

Rev 1:7 — Behold, he cometh with clouds; and every eye shall see him, and they *also* which pierced him: and all kindreds of the earth shall wail because of him. Even so, Amen.

Rev 3:11 — Behold, I come quickly: hold that fast which thou hast, that no man take thy crown.

Rev 16:15 — Behold, I come as a thief. Blessed *is* he that watcheth, and keepeth his garments, lest he walk naked, and they see his shame.

Rev 22:12 — And, behold, I come quickly; and my reward *is* with me, to give every man according as his work shall be.

Rev 22:20 — He which testifieth these things saith, Surely I come quickly. Amen. Even so, come, Lord Jesus.

See: Millennium

JESUS, Shepherd

- **Jesus the True.**
  - **Foretold.**

Ge 49:24 — But his bow abode in strength, and the arms of his hands were made strong by the hands of the mighty *God* of Jacob; (from thence *is* the shepherd, the stone of Israel:)

Isa 40:11 — He shall feed his flock like a shepherd: he shall gather the lambs with his arm, and carry *them* in his bosom, *and* shall gently lead those that are with young.

Eze 34:23 — And I will set up one shepherd over them, and he shall feed them, *even* my servant David; he shall feed them, and he shall be their shepherd.

Eze 37:24 — And David my servant *shall be* king over them; and they all shall have one shepherd: they shall also walk in my judgments, and observe my statutes, and do them.

- **The chief.**

1Pe 5:4 — And when the chief Shepherd shall appear, ye shall receive a crown of glory that fadeth not away.

- **The good.**

Jn 10:11 — I am the good shepherd: the good shepherd giveth his life for the sheep.

Jn 10:14 — I am the good shepherd, and know my *sheep*, and am known of mine.

- **The great.**

Mic 5:4 — And he shall stand and feed in the strength of the LORD, in the majesty of the name of the LORD his God; and they shall abide: for now shall he be great unto the ends of the earth.

Heb 13:20 — Now the God of peace, that brought again from the dead our Lord Jesus, that great shepherd of the sheep, through the blood of the everlasting covenant,

- **His sheep he knows.**

Jn 10:14 — I am the good shepherd, and know my *sheep*, and am known of mine.

Jn 10:27 — My sheep hear my voice, and I know them, and they follow me:

- **He calls.**

Jn 10:3 — To him the porter openeth; and the sheep hear his voice: and he calleth his own sheep by name, and leadeth them out.

- **He gathers.**

Isa 40:11 — He shall feed his flock like a shepherd: he shall gather the lambs with his arm, and carry *them* in his bosom, *and* shall gently lead those that are with young.

Jn 10:16 — And other sheep I have, which are not of this fold: them also I must bring, and they shall hear my voice; and there shall be one fold, *and* one shepherd.

- **He guides.**

Jn 10:3–4

Ps 23:3 — He restoreth my soul: he leadeth me in the paths of righteousness for his name's sake.

- **He feeds.**

Ps 23:1–2

Jn 10:9 — I am the door: by me if any man enter in, he shall be saved, and shall go in and out, and find pasture.

- **He cherishes tenderly.**

Isa 40:11 — He shall feed his flock like a shepherd: he shall gather the lambs with his arm, and carry *them* in his bosom, *and* shall gently lead those that are with young.

- **He protects and preserves.**

Jer 31:10 — Hear the word of the LORD, O ye nations, and declare *it* in the isles afar off, and say, He that scattered Israel will gather him, and keep him, as a shepherd *doth* his flock.

Eze 34:10 — Thus saith the Lord GOD; Behold, I *am* against the shepherds; and I will require my flock at their hand, and cause them to cease from feeding the flock; neither shall the shepherds feed themselves any more; for I will deliver my flock from their mouth, that they may not be meat for them.

Zec 9:16 — And the LORD their God shall save them in that day as the flock of his people: for they *shall be as* the stones of a crown, lifted up as an ensign upon his land.

Jn 10:28 — And I give unto them eternal life; and they shall never perish, neither shall any *man* pluck them out of my hand.

- **He laid down his life for.**

Zec 13:7 — Awake, O sword, against my shepherd, and against the man *that is* my fellow, saith the LORD of hosts: smite the shepherd, and the sheep shall be scattered: and I will turn mine hand upon the little ones.

Mt 26:31 — Then saith Jesus unto them, All ye shall be offended because of me this night: for it is written, I will smite the shepherd, and the sheep of the flock shall be scattered abroad.

Jn 10:11 — I am the good shepherd: the good shepherd giveth his life for the sheep.

Jn 10:15 — As the Father knoweth me, even so know I the Father: and I lay down my life for the sheep.

Ac 20:28 — Take heed therefore unto yourselves, and to all the flock, over the which the Holy Ghost hath made you overseers, to feed the church of God, which he hath purchased with his own blood.

- **He gives eternal life to.**

Jn 10:28 — And I give unto them eternal life; and they shall never perish, neither shall any *man* pluck them out of my hand.

- **Typified.**
  - **David.**

1Sa 16:11 — And Samuel said unto Jesse, Are here all *thy* children? And he said, There remaineth yet the youngest, and, behold, he keepeth the sheep. And Samuel said unto Jesse, Send and fetch him: for we will not sit down till he come hither.

JESUS, Son of God

Ps 89:26–27; Mt 16:15–17; 26:63–64; Mk 14:61–62; Jn 1:1–2, 49–50; 3:16–18, 34–36; 5:19–21, 26–27, 36–37; 7:28–29; 8:26–29; 9:35–37; 10:17–18, 29–30, 36–38; 12:49–50; 14:9–11; 14:31–15:1; 15:8–10, 23–24; 16:27–28; 17:1–26; Ro 1:3–4; 1Co 15:27–28; Heb 1:1–3; 1Jn 2:22–24; 4:9–10; 5:9–10

Ps 2:7 — I will declare the decree: the LORD hath said unto me, Thou *art* my Son; this day have I begotten thee.

Mt 3:17 — And lo a voice from heaven, saying, This is my beloved Son, in whom I am well pleased.

Mt 4:3 — And when the tempter came to him, he said, If thou be the Son of God, command that these stones be made bread.

Mt 4:6 — And saith unto him, If thou be the Son of God, cast thyself down: for it is written, He shall give his angels charge concerning thee: and in *their* hands they shall bear thee up, lest at any time thou dash thy foot against a stone.

Mt 10:40 — He that receiveth you receiveth me, and he that receiveth me receiveth him that sent me.

Mt 11:27 — All things are delivered unto me of my Father: and no man knoweth the Son, but the Father; neither knoweth any man the Father, save the Son, and *he* to whomsoever the Son will reveal *him.*

Mt 14:33 — Then they that were in the ship came and worshipped him, saying, Of a truth thou art the Son of God.

Mt 15:13 — But he answered and said, Every plant, which my heavenly Father hath not planted, shall be rooted up.

Mt 17:5 — While he yet spake, behold, a bright cloud overshadowed them: and behold a voice out of the cloud, which said, This is my beloved Son, in whom I am well pleased; hear ye him.

Mt 18:10 — Take heed that ye despise not one of these little ones; for I say unto you, That in heaven their angels do always behold the face of my Father which is in heaven.

Mt 18:19 — Again I say unto you, That if two of you shall agree on earth as touching any thing that they shall ask, it shall be done for them of my Father which is in heaven.

Mt 20:23 — And he saith unto them, Ye shall drink indeed of my cup, and be baptized with the baptism that I am baptized with: but to sit on my right hand, and on my left, is not mine to give, but *it shall be given to them* for whom it is prepared of my Father.

Mt 21:37 — But last of all he sent unto them his son, saying, They will reverence my son.

Mt 26:53 — Thinkest thou that I cannot now pray to my Father, and he shall presently give me more than twelve legions of angels?

Mt 27:43 — He trusted in God; let him deliver him now, if he will have him: for he said, I am the Son of God.

Mt 27:54 — Now when the centurion, and they that were with him, watching Jesus, saw the earthquake, and those things that were done, they feared greatly, saying, Truly this was the Son of God.

Mk 1:1 — The beginning of the gospel of Jesus Christ, the Son of God;

Mk 1:11 — And there came a voice from heaven, *saying,* Thou art my beloved Son, in whom I am well pleased.

Mk 3:11 — And unclean spirits, when they saw him, fell down before him, and cried, saying, Thou art the Son of God.

Mk 5:7 — And cried with a loud voice, and said, What have I to do with thee, Jesus, *thou* Son of the most high God? I adjure thee by God, that thou torment me not.

Mk 9:7 — And there was a cloud that overshadowed them: and a voice came out of the cloud, saying, This is my beloved Son: hear him.

Mk 15:39 — And when the centurion, which stood over against him, saw that he so cried out, and gave up the ghost, he said, Truly this man was the Son of God.

Lk 1:32 — He shall be great, and shall be called the Son of the Highest: and the Lord God shall give unto him the throne of his father David:

Lk 1:35 — And the angel answered and said unto her, The Holy Ghost shall come upon thee, and the power of the Highest shall overshadow thee: therefore also that holy thing which shall be born of thee shall be called the Son of God.

Lk 3:22 — And the Holy Ghost descended in a bodily shape like a dove upon him, and a voice came from heaven, which said, Thou art my beloved Son; in thee I am well pleased.

Lk 4:3 — And the devil said unto him, If thou be the Son of God, command this stone that it be made bread.

Lk 4:9 — And he brought him to Jerusalem, and set him on a pinnacle of the temple, and said unto him, If thou be the Son of God, cast thyself down from hence:

Lk 4:41 — And devils also came out of many, crying out, and saying, Thou art Christ the Son of God. And he rebuking *them* suffered them not to speak: for they knew that he was Christ.

Lk 8:28 — When he saw Jesus, he cried out, and fell down before him, and with a loud voice said, What have I to do with thee, Jesus, *thou* Son of God most high? I beseech thee, torment me not.

Lk 9:35 — And there came a voice out of the cloud, saying, This is my beloved Son: hear him.

Lk 10:22 — All things are delivered to me of my Father: and no man knoweth who the Son is, but the Father; and who the Father is, but the Son, and *he* to whom the Son will reveal *him.*

Lk 20:13 — Then said the lord of the vineyard, What shall I do? I will send my beloved son: it may be they will reverence *him* when they see him.

Lk 22:29 — And I appoint unto you a kingdom, as my Father hath appointed unto me;

Lk 22:70 — Then said they all, Art thou then the Son of God? And he said unto them, Ye say that I am.

Jn 1:14 — And the Word was made flesh, and dwelt among us, (and we beheld his glory, the glory as of the only begotten of the Father,) full of grace and truth.

Jn 1:18 — No man hath seen God at any time; the only begotten Son, which is in the bosom of the Father, he hath declared *him.*

Jn 1:34 — And I saw, and bare record that this is the Son of God.

Jn 5:23 — That all *men* should honour the Son, even as they honour the Father. He that honoureth not the Son honoureth not the Father which hath sent him.

Jn 5:30 — I can of mine own self do nothing: as I hear, I judge: and my judgment is just; because I seek not mine own will, but the will of the Father which hath sent me.

Jn 5:32 — There is another that beareth witness of me; and I know that the witness which he witnesseth of me is true.

Jn 6:27 — Labour not for the meat which perisheth, but for that meat which endureth unto everlasting life, which the Son of man shall give unto you: for him hath God the Father sealed.

Jn 6:38 — For I came down from heaven, not to do mine own will, but the will of him that sent me.

Jn 6:40 — And this is the will of him that sent me, that every one which seeth the Son, and believeth on him, may have everlasting life: and I will raise him up at the last day.

Jn 6:46 — Not that any man hath seen the Father, save he which is of God, he hath seen the Father.

Jn 6:57 — As the living Father hath sent me, and I live by the Father: so he that eateth me, even he shall live by me.

Jn 6:69 — And we believe and are sure that thou art that Christ, the Son of the living God.

Jn 7:16 — Jesus answered them, and said, My doctrine is not mine, but his that sent me.

Jn 8:16 — And yet if I judge, my judgment is true: for I am not alone, but I and the Father that sent me.

Jn 8:19 — Then said they unto him, Where is thy Father? Jesus answered, Ye neither know me, nor my Father: if ye had known me, ye should have known my Father also.

Jn 8:38 — I speak that which I have seen with my Father: and ye do that which ye have seen with your father.

Jn 8:40 — But now ye seek to kill me, a man that hath told you the truth, which I have heard of God: this did not Abraham.

Jn 8:42 — Jesus said unto them, If God were your Father, ye would love me: for I proceeded forth and came from God; neither came I of myself, but he sent me.

Jn 8:49 — Jesus answered, I have not a devil; but I honour my Father, and ye do dishonour me.

Jn 8:54 — Jesus answered, If I honour myself, my honour is nothing: it is my Father that honoureth me; of whom ye say, that he is your God:

Jn 10:15 — As the Father knoweth me, even so know I the Father: and I lay down my life for the sheep.

Jn 11:4 — When Jesus heard *that,* he said, This sickness is not unto death, but for the glory of God, that the Son of God might be glorified thereby.

Jn 11:27 — She saith unto him, Yea, Lord: I believe that thou art the Christ, the Son of God, which should come into the world.

Jn 11:41 — Then they took away the stone *from the place* where the dead was laid. And Jesus lifted up *his* eyes, and said, Father, I thank thee that thou hast heard me.

Jn 13:3 — Jesus knowing that the Father had given all things into his hands, and that he was come from God, and went to God;

Jn 14:7 — If ye had known me, ye should have known my Father also: and from henceforth ye know him, and have seen him.

Jn 14:13 — And whatsoever ye shall ask in my name, that will I do, that the Father may be glorified in the Son.

Jn 14:16 — And I will pray the Father, and he shall give you another Comforter, that he may abide with you for ever;

Jn 14:20 — At that day ye shall know that I *am* in my Father, and ye in me, and I in you.

Jn 14:24 — He that loveth me not keepeth not my sayings: and the word which ye hear is not mine, but the Father's which sent me.

Jn 14:28 — Ye have heard how I said unto you, I go away, and come *again* unto you. If ye loved me, ye would rejoice, because I said, I go unto the Father: for my Father is greater than I.

Jn 16:5 — But now I go my way to him that sent me; and none of you asketh me, Whither goest thou?

Jn 16:15 — All things that the Father hath are mine: therefore said I, that he shall take of mine, and shall shew *it* unto you.

Jn 16:32 — Behold, the hour cometh, yea, is now come, that ye shall be scattered, every man to his own, and shall leave me alone: and yet I am not alone, because the Father is with me.

Jn 19:7 — The Jews answered him, We have a law, and by our law he ought to die, because he made himself the Son of God.

Jn 20:17 — Jesus saith unto her, Touch me not; for I am not yet ascended to my Father: but go to my brethren, and say unto them, I ascend unto my Father, and your Father; and *to* my God, and your God.

Jn 20:21 — Then said Jesus to them again, Peace *be* unto you: as *my* Father hath sent me, even so send I you.

Jn 20:31 — But these are written, that ye might believe that Jesus is the Christ, the Son of God; and that believing ye might have life through his name.

Ac 3:13 — The God of Abraham, and of Isaac, and of Jacob, the God of our fathers, hath glorified his Son Jesus; whom ye delivered up, and denied him in the presence of Pilate, when he was determined to let *him* go.

Ac 13:33 — God hath fulfilled the same unto us their children, in that he hath raised up Jesus again; as it is also written in the second Psalm, Thou art my Son, this day have I begotten thee.

Ro 1:9 — For God is my witness, whom I serve with my spirit in the gospel of his Son, that without ceasing I make mention of you always in my prayers;

Ro 8:3 — For what the law could not do, in that it was weak through the flesh, God sending his own Son in the likeness of sinful flesh, and for sin, condemned sin in the flesh:

Ro 8:29 — For whom he did foreknow, he also did predestinate *to be* conformed to the image of his Son, that he might be the firstborn among many brethren.

Ro 8:32 — He that spared not his own Son, but delivered him up for us all, how shall he not with him also freely give us all things?

1Co 1:9 — God *is* faithful, by whom ye were called unto the fellowship of his Son Jesus Christ our Lord.

1Co 15:24 — Then *cometh* the end, when he shall have delivered up the kingdom to God, even the Father; when he shall have put down all rule and all authority and power.

2Co 1:3 — Blessed *be* God, even the Father of our Lord Jesus Christ, the Father of mercies, and the God of all comfort;

2Co 1:19 — For the Son of God, Jesus Christ, who was preached among you by us, *even* by me and Silvanus and Timotheus, was not yea and nay, but in him was yea.

Gal 1:16 — To reveal his Son in me, that I might preach him among the heathen; immediately I conferred not with flesh and blood:

Gal 4:4 — But when the fulness of the time was come, God sent forth his Son, made of a woman, made under the law,

Eph 1:3 — Blessed *be* the God and Father of our Lord Jesus Christ, who hath blessed us with all spiritual blessings in heavenly *places* in Christ:

Eph 3:14 — For this cause I bow my knees unto the Father of our Lord Jesus Christ,

Col 1:3 — We give thanks to God and the Father of our Lord Jesus Christ, praying always for you,

Col 1:15 — Who is the image of the invisible God, the firstborn of every creature:

Col 1:19 — For it pleased *the Father* that in him should all fulness dwell;

Col 3:17 — And whatsoever ye do in word or deed, *do* all in the name of the Lord Jesus, giving thanks to God and the Father by him.

1Th 1:10 — And to wait for his Son from heaven, whom he raised from the dead, *even* Jesus, which delivered us from the wrath to come.

Heb 1:5 — For unto which of the angels said he at any time, Thou art my Son, this day have I begotten thee? And again, I will be to him a Father, and he shall be to me a Son?

Heb 4:14 — Seeing then that we have a great high priest, that is passed into the heavens, Jesus the Son of God, let us hold fast *our* profession.

Heb 5:5 — So also Christ glorified not himself to be made an high priest; but he that said unto him, Thou art my Son, to day have I begotten thee.

Heb 5:8 — Though he were a Son, yet learned he obedience by the things which he suffered;

Heb 5:10 — Called of God an high priest after the order of Melchisedec.

Heb 6:6 — If they shall fall away, to renew them again unto repentance; seeing they crucify to themselves the Son of God afresh, and put *him* to an open shame.

Heb 7:3 — Without father, without mother, without descent, having neither beginning of days, nor end of life; but made like unto the Son of God; abideth a priest continually.

Heb 10:29 — Of how much sorer punishment, suppose ye, shall he be thought worthy, who hath trodden under foot the Son of God, and hath counted the blood of the covenant, wherewith he was sanctified, an unholy thing, and hath done despite unto the Spirit of grace?

2Pe 1:17 — For he received from God the Father honour and glory, when there came such a voice to him from the excellent glory, This is my beloved Son, in whom I am well pleased.

1Jn 1:7 — But if we walk in the light, as he is in the light, we have fellowship one with another, and the blood of Jesus Christ his Son cleanseth us from all sin.

1Jn 3:8 — He that committeth sin is of the devil; for the devil sinneth from the beginning. For this purpose the Son of God was manifested, that he might destroy the works of the devil.

1Jn 3:23 — And this is his commandment, That we should believe on the name of his Son Jesus Christ, and love one another, as he gave us commandment.

1Jn 4:14 — And we have seen and do testify that the Father sent the Son *to be* the Saviour of the world.

1Jn 5:5 — Who is he that overcometh the world, but he that believeth that Jesus is the Son of God?

1Jn 5:13 — These things have I written unto you that believe on the name of the Son of God; that ye may know that ye have eternal life, and that ye may believe on the name of the Son of God.

1Jn 5:20 — *And* we know that the Son of God is come, and hath given us an understanding, that we may know him that is true, and we are in him that is true, *even* in his Son Jesus Christ. This is the true God, and eternal life.

2Jn 1:3 — Grace be with you, mercy, *and* peace, from God the Father, and from the Lord Jesus Christ, the Son of the Father, in truth and love.

Rev 2:18 — And unto the angel of the church in Thyatira write; These things saith the Son of God, who hath his eyes like unto a flame of fire, and his feet *are* like fine brass;

See: Jesus, Divinity of

See: Jesus, Relation of, to the Father

JESUS, Son of Man ✦See: Jesus, Humanity of

JESUS, Sovereignty of

✦See: Jesus, King

✦See: Jesus, Sufferings of

JESUS, Sufferings of

Mt 26:38–45; 27:24–50; Mk 14:1–15:47; Lk 4:28–29; Jn 18:1–19:42; Php 2:7–8; Heb 5:7–8; 12:2–3; 1Pe 2:21–23

Lk 2:34 — And Simeon blessed them, and said unto Mary his mother, Behold, this *child* is set for the fall and rising again of many in Israel; and for a sign which shall be spoken against;

Lk 22:23 — And they began to enquire among themselves, which of them it was that should do this thing.

Lk 22:44 — And being in an agony he prayed more earnestly: and his sweat was as it were great drops of blood falling down to the ground.

Lk 24:46 — And said unto them, Thus it is written, and thus it behoved Christ to suffer, and to rise from the dead the third day:

Jn 4:6 — Now Jacob's well was there. Jesus therefore, being wearied with *his* journey, sat thus on the well: *and* it was about the sixth hour.

Jn 11:33 — When Jesus therefore saw her weeping, and the Jews also weeping which came with her, he groaned in the spirit, and was troubled,

Jn 11:35 — Jesus wept.

Jn 12:27 — Now is my soul troubled; and what shall I say? Father, save me from this hour: but for this cause came I unto this hour.

Ac 3:18 — But those things, which God before had shewed by the mouth of all his prophets, that Christ should suffer, he hath so fulfilled.

Ac 17:3 — Opening and alleging, that Christ must needs have suffered, and risen again from the dead; and that this Jesus, whom I preach unto you, is Christ.

2Co 1:5 — For as the sufferings of Christ abound in us, so our consolation also aboundeth by Christ.

Php 3:10 — That I may know him, and the power of his resurrection, and the fellowship of his sufferings, being made conformable unto his death;

Heb 2:9 — But we see Jesus, who was made a little lower than the angels for the suffering of death, crowned with glory and honour; that he by the grace of God should taste death for every man.

Heb 4:15 — For we have not an high priest which cannot be touched with the feeling of our infirmities; but was in all points tempted like as *we are, yet* without sin.

1Pe 1:11 — Searching what, or what manner of time the Spirit of Christ which was in them did signify, when it testified beforehand the sufferings of Christ, and the glory that should follow.

1Pe 4:1 — Forasmuch then as Christ hath suffered for us in the flesh, arm yourselves likewise with the same mind: for he that hath suffered in the flesh hath ceased from sin;

Rev 5:6 — And I beheld, and, lo, in the midst of the throne and of the four beasts, and in the midst of the elders, stood a Lamb as it had been slain, having seven horns and seven eyes, which are the seven Spirits of God sent forth into all the earth.

Rev 19:13 — And he *was* clothed with a vesture dipped in blood: and his name is called The Word of God.

✦See: Jesus, Death of

✦See: Persecution

• Prophecies concerning.

Ps 22:6–8, 11–13, 17–21; 69:7–9; Isa 52:13–14; 53:1–12; Zec 11:12–13; 13:6–7; Mt 17:22–23; 20:17–19; Mk 10:1–52; Lk 2:34–35; 18:31–33

Ps 69:20 — Reproach hath broken my heart; and I am full of heaviness: and I looked *for some* to take pity, but *there was* none; and for comforters, but I found none.

Ps 109:25 — I became also a reproach unto them: *when* they looked upon me they shaked their heads.

Isa 50:6 — I gave my back to the smiters, and my cheeks to them that plucked off the hair: I hid not my face from shame and spitting.

Mic 5:1 — Now gather thyself in troops, O daughter of troops: he hath laid siege against us: they shall smite the judge of Israel with a rod upon the cheek.

Mt 16:21 — From that time forth began Jesus to shew unto his disciples, how that he must go unto Jerusalem, and suffer many things of the elders and chief priests and scribes, and be killed, and be raised again the third day.

Mt 17:12 — But I say unto you, That Elias is come already, and they knew him not, but have done unto him whatsoever they listed. Likewise shall also the Son of man suffer of them.

Mt 27:35 — And they crucified him, and parted his garments, casting lots: that it might be fulfilled which was spoken by the prophet, They parted my garments among them, and upon my vesture did they cast lots.

Mk 8:31 — And he began to teach them, that the Son of man must suffer many things, and be rejected of the elders, and *of* the chief priests, and scribes, and be killed, and after three days rise again.

Mk 15:24 — And when they had crucified him, they parted his garments, casting lots upon them, what every man should take.

Lk 9:22 — Saying, The Son of man must suffer many things, and be rejected of the elders and chief priests and scribes, and be slain, and be raised the third day.

Lk 22:37 — For I say unto you, that this that is written must yet be accomplished in me, And he was reckoned among the transgressors: for the things concerning me have an end.

Lk 23:34 — Then said Jesus, Father, forgive them; for they know not what they do. And they parted his raiment, and cast lots.

Jn 12:38 — That the saying of Esaias the prophet might be fulfilled, which he spake, Lord, who hath believed our report? and to whom hath the arm of the Lord been revealed?

Jn 19:23 — Then the soldiers, when they had crucified Jesus, took his garments, and made four parts, to every soldier a part; and also *his* coat: now the coat was without seam, woven from the top throughout.

1Pe 1:11 — Searching what, or what manner of time the Spirit of Christ which was in them did signify, when it testified beforehand the sufferings of Christ, and the glory that should follow.

JESUS, Sympathy of

See: Jesus, Compassion of

See: Jesus, Love of

JESUS, Teacher

Mt 4:23 — And Jesus went about all Galilee, teaching in their synagogues, and preaching the gospel of the kingdom, and healing all manner of sickness and all manner of disease among the people.

Mt 5:1 — And seeing the multitudes, he went up into a mountain: and when he was set, his disciples came unto him:

Mt 7:29 — For he taught them as *one* having authority, and not as the scribes.

Mt 11:1 — And it came to pass, when Jesus had made an end of commanding his twelve disciples, he departed thence to teach and to preach in their cities.

Mt 21:23 — And when he was come into the temple, the chief priests and the elders of the people came unto him as he was teaching, and said, By what authority doest thou these things? and who gave thee this authority?

Mt 22:16 — And they sent out unto him their disciples with the Herodians, saying, Master, we know that thou art true, and teachest the way of God in truth, neither carest thou for any *man:* for thou regardest not the person of men.

Mt 23:8 — But be not ye called Rabbi: for one is your Master, *even* Christ; and all ye are brethren.

Mt 26:55 — In that same hour said Jesus to the multitudes, Are ye come out as against a thief with swords and staves for to take me? I sat daily with you teaching in the temple, and ye laid no hold on me.

Mk 4:1 — And he began again to teach by the sea side: and there was gathered unto him a great multitude, so that he entered into a ship, and sat in the sea; and the whole multitude was by the sea on the land.

Mk 12:14 — And when they were come, they say unto him, Master, we know that thou art true, and carest for no man: for thou regardest not the person of men, but teachest the way of God in truth: Is it lawful to give tribute to Caesar, or not?

Lk 4:15 — And he taught in their synagogues, being glorified of all.

Lk 6:6 — And it came to pass also on another sabbath, that he entered into the synagogue and taught: and there was a man whose right hand was withered.

Lk 20:21 — And they asked him, saying, Master, we know that thou sayest and teachest rightly, neither acceptest thou the person *of any,* but teachest the way of God truly:

Lk 23:5 — And they were the more fierce, saying, He stirreth up the people, teaching throughout all Jewry, beginning from Galilee to this place.

Jn 3:2 — The same came to Jesus by night, and said unto him, Rabbi, we know that thou art a teacher come from God: for no man can do these miracles that thou doest, except God be with him.

Ac 1:1 — The former treatise have I made, O Theophilus, of all that Jesus began both to do and teach,

JESUS, Temptation of

Mt 4:1–11; Mk 1:12–13; Lk 4:1–13

Isa 7:16 — For before the child shall know to refuse the evil, and choose the good, the land that thou abhorrest shall be forsaken of both her kings.

Lk 22:28 — Ye are they which have continued with me in my temptations.

Jn 14:30 — Hereafter I will not talk much with you: for the prince of this world cometh, and hath nothing in me.

Heb 2:18 — For in that he himself hath suffered being tempted, he is able to succour them that are tempted.

Heb 4:15 — For we have not an high priest which cannot be touched with the feeling of our infirmities; but was in all points tempted like as *we are, yet* without sin.

JESUS, Types of See: Types

JESUS, Unchangeable

Heb 13:8 — Jesus Christ the same yesterday, and to day, and for ever.

JESUS, Unclassified Scriptures Relating to

Jn 6:50–51, 53–58; 10:9–11; 15:5–7

Jn 6:35 — And Jesus said unto them, I am the bread of life: he that cometh to me shall never hunger; and he that believeth on me shall never thirst.

Jn 6:41 — The Jews then murmured at him, because he said, I am the bread which came down from heaven.

Jn 6:48 — I am that bread of life.

Jn 8:12 — Then spake Jesus again unto them, saying, I am the light of the world: he that followeth me shall not walk in darkness, but shall have the light of life.

Jn 10:14 — I am the good shepherd, and know my *sheep,* and am known of mine.

Jn 11:25 — Jesus said unto her, I am the resurrection, and the life: he that believeth in me, though he were dead, yet shall he live:

Jn 14:6 — Jesus saith unto him, I am the way, the truth, and the life: no man cometh unto the Father, but by me.

Jn 15:1 — I am the true vine, and my Father is the husbandman.

Col 3:4 — When Christ, *who is* our life, shall appear, then shall ye also appear with him in glory.

2Ti 1:10 — But is now made manifest by the appearing of our Saviour Jesus Christ, who hath abolished death, and hath brought life and immortality to light through the gospel:

Rev 1:18 — I *am* he that liveth, and was dead; and, behold, I am alive for evermore, Amen; and have the keys of hell and of death.

Rev 22:13 — I am Alpha and Omega, the beginning and the end, the first and the last.

JESUS, Union of, with the Righteous

See: Righteous; promises to, expressed or implied; unity of, with Christ

JESUS, Wisdom of ⇜See: Jesus, Omniscience of

JESUS, Worship of

Jos 5:14–15; Mt 28:16–17; Mk 5:6–7; 11:9–10; Ac 7:59–60; 2Co 12:8–9; Php 2:10–11; Rev 5:8–9, 12–14

Ps 45:11 — So shall the king greatly desire thy beauty: for he *is* thy Lord; and worship thou him.

Ps 45:17 — I will make thy name to be remembered in all generations: therefore shall the people praise thee for ever and ever.

Ps 72:15 — And he shall live, and to him shall be given of the gold of Sheba: prayer also shall be made for him continually; *and* daily shall he be praised.

Mt 2:2 — Saying, Where is he that is born King of the Jews? for we have seen his star in the east, and are come to worship him.

Mt 2:11 — And when they were come into the house, they saw the young child with Mary his mother, and fell down, and worshipped him: and when they had opened their treasures, they presented unto him gifts; gold, and frankincense, and myrrh.

Mt 9:18 — While he spake these things unto them, behold, there came a certain ruler, and worshipped him, saying, My daughter is even now dead: but come and lay thy hand upon her, and she shall live.

Mt 14:33 — Then they that were in the ship came and worshipped him, saying, Of a truth thou art the Son of God.

Mt 15:25 — Then came she and worshipped him, saying, Lord, help me.

Mt 20:20 — Then came to him the mother of Zebedee's children with her sons, worshipping *him,* and desiring a certain thing of him.

Mt 21:9 — And the multitudes that went before, and that followed, cried, saying, Hosanna to the Son of David: Blessed *is* he that cometh in the name of the Lord; Hosanna in the highest.

Mt 28:9 — And as they went to tell his disciples, behold, Jesus met them, saying, <u>All hail.</u> And they came and held him by the feet, and worshipped him.

Mk 3:11 — And unclean spirits, when they saw him, fell down before him, and cried, saying, Thou art the Son of God.

Lk 4:41 — And devils also came out of many, crying out, and saying, Thou art Christ the Son of God. And he rebuking *them* suffered them not to speak: for they knew that he was Christ.

Lk 5:8 — When Simon Peter saw *it,* he fell down at Jesus' knees, saying, Depart from me; for I am a sinful man, O Lord.

Lk 23:42 — And he said unto Jesus, Lord, remember me when thou comest into thy kingdom.

Lk 24:52 — And they worshipped him, and returned to Jerusalem with great joy:

Jn 5:23 — <u>That all *men* should honour the Son, even as they honour the Father. He that honoureth not the Son honoureth not the Father which hath sent him.</u>

Jn 9:38 — And he said, Lord, I believe. And he worshipped him.

Jn 12:13 — Took branches of palm trees, and went forth to meet him, and cried, Hosanna: Blessed *is* the King of Israel that cometh in the name of the Lord.

Ac 1:24 — And they prayed, and said, Thou, Lord, which knowest the hearts of all *men,* shew whether of these two thou hast chosen,

1Co 1:2 — Unto the church of God which is at Corinth, to them that are sanctified in Christ Jesus, called *to be* saints, with all that in every place call upon the name of Jesus Christ our Lord, both theirs and ours:

1Ti 1:12 — And I thank Christ Jesus our Lord, who hath enabled me, for that he counted me faithful, putting me into the ministry;

Heb 1:6 — And again, when he bringeth in the firstbegotten into the world, he saith, And let all the angels of God worship him.

2Pe 3:18 — But grow in grace, and *in* the knowledge of our Lord and Saviour Jesus Christ. To him *be* glory both now and for ever. Amen.

Rev 7:10 — And cried with a loud voice, saying, Salvation to our God which sitteth upon the throne, and unto the Lamb.

JESUS, Zeal of

Mk 3:20–21; Lk 13:32–33

Ps 69:9 — For the zeal of thine house hath eaten me up; and the reproaches of them that reproached thee are fallen upon me.

Isa 59:17 — For he put on righteousness as a breastplate, and an helmet of salvation upon his head; and he put on the garments of vengeance *for* clothing, and was clad with zeal as a cloke.

Mt 4:23 — And Jesus went about all Galilee, teaching in their synagogues, and preaching the gospel of the kingdom, and healing all manner of sickness and all manner of disease among the people.

Mt 9:35 — And Jesus went about all the cities and villages, teaching in their synagogues, and preaching the gospel of the kingdom, and healing every sickness and every disease among the people.

Mk 1:38 — And he said unto them, <u>Let us go into the next towns, that I may preach there also: for therefore came I forth.</u>

Mk 6:6 — And he marvelled because of their unbelief. And he went round about the villages, teaching.

Lk 2:49 — And he said unto them, <u>How is it that ye sought me? wist ye not that I must be about my Father's business?</u>

Lk 4:43 — And he said unto them, <u>I must preach the kingdom of God to other cities also: for therefore am I sent.</u>

Lk 8:1 — And it came to pass afterward, that he went throughout every city and village, preaching and shewing the glad tidings of the kingdom of God: and the twelve *were* with him,

Lk 9:51 — And it came to pass, when the time was come that he should be received up, he stedfastly set his face to go to Jerusalem,

Lk 12:50 — <u>But I have a baptism to be baptized with; and how am I straitened till it be accomplished!</u>

Jn 2:17 — And his disciples remembered that it was written, The zeal of thine house hath eaten me up.

Jn 4:32 — But he said unto them, I have meat to eat that ye know not of.

Jn 4:34 — Jesus saith unto them, My meat is to do the will of him that sent me, and to finish his work.

Jn 9:4 — I must work the works of him that sent me, while it is day: the night cometh, when no man can work.

Ac 10:38 — How God anointed Jesus of Nazareth with the Holy Ghost and with power: who went about doing good, and healing all that were oppressed of the devil; for God was with him.

Ro 15:3 — For even Christ pleased not himself; but, as it is written, The reproaches of them that reproached thee fell on me.

1Ti 6:13 — I give thee charge in the sight of God, who quickeneth all things, and *before* Christ Jesus, who before Pontius Pilate witnessed a good confession;

JETHER

• Son of Gideon.

• Feared to slay the Midianitish kings.

Jgs 8:20 — And he said unto Jether his firstborn, Up, *and* slay them. But the youth drew not his sword: for he feared, because he *was* yet a youth.

• An Ishmaelite who married David's sister.

1Ki 2:5 — Moreover thou knowest also what Joab the son of Zeruiah did to me, *and* what he did to the two captains of the hosts of Israel, unto Abner the son of Ner, and unto Amasa the son of Jether, whom he slew, and shed the blood of war in peace, and put the blood of war upon his girdle that *was* about his loins, and in his shoes that *were* on his feet.

1Ki 2:32 — And the LORD shall return his blood upon his own head, who fell upon two men more righteous and better than he, and slew them with the sword, my father David not knowing *thereof, to wit,* Abner the son of Ner, captain of the host of Israel, and Amasa the son of Jether, captain of the host of Judah.

1Ch 2:17 — And Abigail bare Amasa: and the father of Amasa *was* Jether the Ishmeelite.

• Called Ithra.

2Sa 17:25 — And Absalom made Amasa captain of the host instead of Joab: which Amasa was a man's son, whose name *was* Ithra an Israelite, that went in to Abigail the daughter of Nahash, sister to Zeruiah Joab's mother.

• A son of Jada.

1Ch 2:32 — And the sons of Jada the brother of Shammai; Jether and Jonathan: and Jether died without children.

• A son of Ezra.

1Ch 4:17 — And the sons of Ezra *were,* Jether, and Mered, and Epher, and Jalon: and she bare Miriam, and Shammai, and Ishbah the father of Eshtemoa.

• A chief of the line of Asher.

1Ch 7:38 — And the sons of Jether; Jephunneh, and Pispah, and Ara.

JETHETH • A duke of Esau.

Ge 36:40 — And these *are* the names of the dukes *that came* of Esau, according to their families, after their places, by their names; duke Timnah, duke Alvah, duke Jetheth,

1Ch 1:51 — Hadad died also. And the dukes of Edom were; duke Timnah, duke Aliah, duke Jetheth,

JETHLAH • A city of Dan.

Jos 19:42 — And Shaalabbin, and Ajalon, and Jethlah,

JETHRO

• A priest of Midian.

Ex 3:1 — Now Moses kept the flock of Jethro his father in law, the priest of Midian: and he led the flock to the backside of the desert, and came to the mountain of God, *even* to Horeb.

• Moses spent forty years of exile with, and married his daughter.

Ex 2:15–22

Ex 4:18 — And Moses went and returned to Jethro his father in law, and said unto him, Let me go, I pray thee, and return unto my brethren which *are* in Egypt, and see whether they be yet alive. And Jethro said to Moses, Go in peace.

• Called also Raguel and Reuel.

Nu 10:29 — And Moses said unto Hobab, the son of Raguel the Midianite, Moses' father in law, We are journeying unto the place of which the LORD said, I will give it you: come thou with us, and we will do thee good: for the LORD hath spoken good concerning Israel.

JETUR • Son of Ishmael.

Ge 25:15 — Hadar, and Tema, Jetur, Naphish, and Kedemah:

1Ch 1:31 — Jetur, Naphish, and Kedemah. These are the sons of Ishmael.

JEUEL • A descendant of Zerah.

1Ch 9:6 — And of the sons of Zerah; Jeuel, and their brethren, six hundred and ninety.

JEUSH

• Son of Esau.

Ge 36:5 — And Aholibamah bare Jeush, and Jaalam, and Korah: these *are* the sons of Esau, which were born unto him in the land of Canaan.

Ge 36:14 — And these were the sons of Aholibamah, the daughter of Anah the daughter of Zibeon, Esau's wife: and she bare to Esau Jeush, and Jaalam, and Korah.

Ge 36:18 — And these *are* the sons of Aholibamah Esau's wife; duke Jeush, duke Jaalam, duke Korah: these *were* the dukes *that came* of Aholibamah the daughter of Anah, Esau's wife.

1Ch 1:35 — The sons of Esau; Eliphaz, Reuel, and Jeush, and Jaalam, and Korah.

• A Benjamite.

1Ch 7:10 — The sons also of Jediael; Bilhan: and the sons of Bilhan; Jeush, and Benjamin, and Ehud, and

Chenaanah, and Zethan, and Tharshish, and Ahishahar.

• A Gershonite Levite.

1Ch 23:10–11

• Son of Rehoboam.

2Ch 11:19 — Which bare him children; Jeush, and Shamariah, and Zaham.

JEUZ • Head of a Benjamite family.

1Ch 8:10 — And Jeuz, and Shachia, and Mirma. These *were* his sons, heads of the fathers.

JEWELS

• Betrothal presents of.

Ge 24:53 — And the servant brought forth jewels of silver, and jewels of gold, and raiment, and gave *them* to Rebekah: he gave also to her brother and to her mother precious things.

• Borrowed from Egyptians by Israelites.

Ex 3:22 — But every woman shall borrow of her neighbour, and of her that sojourneth in her house, jewels of silver, and jewels of gold, and raiment: and ye shall put *them* upon your sons, and upon your daughters; and ye shall spoil the Egyptians.

Ex 11:2 — Speak now in the ears of the people, and let every man borrow of his neighbour, and every woman of her neighbour, jewels of silver, and jewels of gold.

Ex 12:35 — And the children of Israel did according to the word of Moses; and they borrowed of the Egyptians jewels of silver, and jewels of gold, and raiment:

• Dedicated to the tabernacle.

Nu 31:50–52

Ex 35:22 — And they came, both men and women, as many as were willing hearted, *and* brought bracelets, and earrings, and rings, and tablets, all jewels of gold: and every man that offered *offered* an offering of gold unto the LORD.

• Regarded by Jacob as obnoxious to holiness.

Ex 33:4–6; Isa 3:18–21

Ge 35:4 — And they gave unto Jacob all the strange gods which *were* in their hand, and *all their* earrings which *were* in their ears; and Jacob hid them under the oak which *was* by Shechem.

• Tokens of love.

Eze 16:11–13

• Worn by men.

Eze 23:42 — And a voice of a multitude being at ease *was* with her: and with the men of the common sort *were* brought Sabeans from the wilderness, which put bracelets upon their hands, and beautiful crowns upon their heads.

• Figurative.

Pr 20:15 — There is gold, and a multitude of rubies: but the lips of knowledge *are* a precious jewel.

Mal 3:17 — And they shall be mine, saith the LORD of hosts, in that day when I make up my jewels; and I will spare them, as a man spareth his own son that serveth him.

See: Bracelet
See: Chains
See: Ear-Ring
See: Muffler
See: Pearl
See: Ring
See: Seal
See: Stones; precious

JEWS

• A corrupted form, doubtless, of Judah, and applied to the people of the kingdom of Judah and Benjamin.

2Ki 16:6 — At that time Rezin king of Syria recovered Elath to Syria, and drave the Jews from Elath: and the Syrians came to Elath, and dwelt there unto this day.

2Ki 25:25 — But it came to pass in the seventh month, that Ishmael the son of Nethaniah, the son of Elishama, of the seed royal, came, and ten men with him, and smote Gedaliah, that he died, and the Jews and the Chaldees that were with him at Mizpah.

2Ch 32:18 — Then they cried with a loud voice in the Jews' speech unto the people of Jerusalem that *were* on the wall, to affright them, and to trouble them; that they might take the city.

• After the dissolution Israel the name was applied to all Israelites, including the two tribes.

See: Israel

JEZANIAH See: Jaazaniah

JEZEBEL

• Daughter of Ethbaal, a Zidonian, and wife of Ahab.

1Ki 16:31 — And it came to pass, as if it had been a light thing for him to walk in the sins of Jeroboam the son of Nebat, that he took to wife Jezebel the daughter of Ethbaal king of the Zidonians, and went and served Baal, and worshipped him.

• Was an idolatress and persecuted the prophets of God.

1Ki 18:4 — For it was *so,* when Jezebel cut off the prophets of the LORD, that Obadiah took an hundred prophets, and hid them by fifty in a cave, and fed them with bread and water.)

1Ki 18:13 — Was it not told my lord what I did when Jezebel slew the prophets of the LORD, how I hid an hundred men of the LORD's prophets by fifty in a cave, and fed them with bread and water?

1Ki 18:19 — Now therefore send, *and* gather to me all Israel unto mount Carmel, and the prophets of Baal four hundred and fifty, and the prophets of the groves four hundred, which eat at Jezebel's table.

2Ki 3:2 — And he wrought evil in the sight of the LORD; but not like his father, and like his mother: for he put away the image of Baal that his father had made.

2Ki 3:13 — And Elisha said unto the king of Israel, What have I to do with thee? get thee to the prophets of thy father, and to the prophets of thy mother. And the king of Israel said unto him, Nay: for the LORD hath called these three kings together, to deliver them into the hand of Moab.

2Ki 9:7 — And thou shalt smite the house of Ahab thy master, that I may avenge the blood of my servants the prophets, and the blood of all the servants of the LORD, at the hand of Jezebel.

2Ki 9:22 — And it came to pass, when Joram saw Jehu, that he said, *Is it* peace, Jehu? And he answered, What peace, so long as the whoredoms of thy mother Jezebel and her witchcrafts *are so* many?

• Vowed to kill Elijah.

1Ki 19:1–3

• Wickedly accomplishes the death of Naboth.

1Ki 21:5–16

• Death of, foretold.

1Ki 21:23 — And of Jezebel also spake the LORD, saying, The dogs shall eat Jezebel by the wall of Jezreel.

2Ki 9:10 — And the dogs shall eat Jezebel in the portion of Jezreel, and *there shall be* none to bury *her*. And he opened the door, and fled.

• Death of, at the hand of Jehu.

2Ki 9:30–37

• Figurative.

Rev 2:20 — Notwithstanding I have a few things against thee, because thou sufferest that woman Jezebel, which calleth herself a prophetess, to teach and to seduce my servants to commit fornication, and to eat things sacrificed unto idols.

JEZER • Son of Naphtali.

Ge 46:24 — And the sons of Naphtali; Jahzeel, and Guni, and Jezer, and Shillem.

Nu 26:49 — Of Jezer, the family of the Jezerites: of Shillem, the family of the Shillemites.

1Ch 7:13 — The sons of Naphtali; Jahziel, and Guni, and Jezer, and Shallum, the sons of Bilhah.

JEZIAH • An Israelite who married an idolatrous wife.

Ezr 10:25 — Moreover of Israel: of the sons of Parosh; Ramiah, and Jeziah, and Malchiah, and Miamin, and Eleazar, and Malchijah, and Benaiah.

JEZIEL • A disaffected Israelite who joined David at Ziklag.

1Ch 12:3 — The chief *was* Ahiezer, then Joash, the sons of Shemaah the Gibeathite; and Jeziel, and Pelet, the sons of Azmaveth; and Berachah, and Jehu the Antothite,

JEZLIAH • A Benjamite.

1Ch 8:18 — Ishmerai also, and Jezliah, and Jobab, the sons of Elpaal;

JEZOAR • Son of Helah.

1Ch 4:7 — And the sons of Helah *were*, Zereth, and Jezoar, and Ethnan.

JEZRAHIAH • A leader of the choir.

Ne 12:42 — And Maaseiah, and Shemaiah, and Eleazar, and Uzzi, and Jehohanan, and Malchijah, and Elam, and Ezer. And the singers sang loud, with Jezrahiah *their* overseer.

JEZREEL

• A city in the south of Judah.

Jos 15:56 — And Jezreel, and Jokdeam, and Zanoah,

1Sa 25:43 — David also took Ahinoam of Jezreel; and they were also both of them his wives.

1Sa 27:3 — And David dwelt with Achish at Gath, he and his men, every man with his household, *even* David with his two wives, Ahinoam the Jezreelitess, and Abigail the Carmelitess, Nabal's wife.

1Sa 29:1 — Now the Philistines gathered together all their armies to Aphek: and the Israelites pitched by a fountain which *is* in Jezreel.

1Sa 29:11 — So David and his men rose up early to depart in the morning, to return into the land of the Philistines. And the Philistines went up to Jezreel.

• A city of Issachar.

Jos 19:18 — And their border was toward Jezreel, and Chesulloth, and Shunem,

2Sa 2:9 — And made him king over Gilead, and over the Ashurites, and over Jezreel, and over Ephraim, and over Benjamin, and over all Israel.

• Ahab's residence in.

1Ki 18:45–46

1Ki 21:1 — And it came to pass after these things, *that* Naboth the Jezreelite had a vineyard, which *was* in Jezreel, hard by the palace of Ahab king of Samaria.

• Naboth's vineyard in.

1Ki 21:1 — And it came to pass after these things, *that* Naboth the Jezreelite had a vineyard, which *was* in Jezreel, hard by the palace of Ahab king of Samaria.

• Joram's residence in.

2Ki 8:29 — And king Joram went back to be healed in Jezreel of the wounds which the Syrians had given him at Ramah, when he fought against Hazael king of Syria. And Ahaziah the son of Jehoram king of Judah went down to see Joram the son of Ahab in Jezreel, because he was sick.

• Jehu kills King Ahab, his wife, and friends at.

2Ki 9:15–37

2Ki 10:11 — So Jehu slew all that remained of the house of Ahab in Jezreel, and all his great men, and his kinsfolks, and his priests, until he left him none remaining.

• Prophecies concerning.

Hos 1:4–5

Hos 1:11 — Then shall the children of Judah and the children of Israel be gathered together, and appoint themselves one head, and they shall come up out of the land: for great *shall be* the day of Jezreel.

• A valley.

Jos 17:16 — And the children of Joseph said, The hill is not enough for us: and all the Canaanites that dwell in the land of the valley have chariots of iron, *both they* who *are* of Beth-shean and her towns, and *they* who *are* of the valley of Jezreel.

• Place of Gideon's battle with the Midianites.

Jgs 6:33 — Then all the Midianites and the Amalekites and the children of the east were gathered together, and went over, and pitched in the valley of Jezreel.

• Place of the defeat of the Israelites under Saul and Jonathan.

1Sa 31:1–6

1Sa 29:1 — Now the Philistines gathered together all their armies to Aphek: and the Israelites pitched by a fountain which *is* in Jezreel.

1Sa 29:11 — So David and his men rose up early to depart in the morning, to return into the land of the Philistines. And the Philistines went up to Jezreel.

2Sa 4:4 — And Jonathan, Saul's son, had a son *that was* lame of *his* feet. He was five years old when the tidings came of Saul and Jonathan out of Jezreel, and his nurse took him up, and fled: and it came to pass, as she made haste to flee, that he fell, and became lame. And his name *was* Mephibosheth.

• A descendant of Etam.

1Ch 4:3 — And these *were of* the father of Etam; Jezreel, and Ishma, and Idbash: and the name of their sister *was* Hazelelponi:

• Figurative of Israel.

Hos 1:4–5

Hos 1:11 — Then shall the children of Judah and the children of Israel be gathered together, and appoint themselves one head, and they shall come up out of the land: for great *shall be* the day of Jezreel.

JIBSAM • Son of Tola.

1Ch 7:2 — And the sons of Tola; Uzzi, and Rephaiah, and Jeriel, and Jahmai, and Jibsam, and Shemuel, heads of their father's house, *to wit,* of Tola: *they were* valiant men of might in their generations; whose number *was* in the days of David two and twenty thousand and six hundred.

JIDLAPH • Son of Nahor.

Ge 22:22 — And Chesed, and Hazo, and Pildash, and Jidlaph, and Bethuel.

JIMNAH

• Called also Jimna.

• Son of Asher.

Ge 46:17 — And the sons of Asher; Jimnah, and Ishuah, and Isui, and Beriah, and Serah their sister: and the sons of Beriah; Heber, and Malchiel.

Nu 26:44 — *Of* the children of Asher after their families: of Jimna, the family of the Jimnites: of Jesui, the family of the Jesuites: of Beriah, the family of the Beriites.

JIPHTAH • A city of Judah.

Jos 15:43 — And Jiphtah, and Ashnah, and Nezib,

JIPHTHAH-EL • A valley in Zebulun.

Jos 19:14 — And the border compasseth it on the north side to Hannathon: and the outgoings thereof are in the valley of Jiphthah-el:

Jos 19:27 — And turneth toward the sunrising to Beth-dagon, and reacheth to Zebulun, and to the valley of Jiphthah-el toward the north side of Beth-emek, and Neiel, and goeth out to Cabul on the left hand,

JOAB

• Son of David's sister.

1Ch 2:16 — Whose sisters *were* Zeruiah, and Abigail. And the sons of Zeruiah; Abishai, and Joab, and Asahel, three.

• Commander of David's army.

2Sa 8:16 — And Joab the son of Zeruiah *was* over the host; and Jehoshaphat the son of Ahilud *was* recorder;

2Sa 20:23 — Now Joab *was* over all the host of Israel: and Benaiah the son of Jehoiada *was* over the Cherethites and over the Pelethites:

1Ch 11:6 — And David said, Whosoever smiteth the Jebusites first shall be chief and captain. So Joab the son of Zeruiah went first up, and was chief.

1Ch 18:15 — And Joab the son Zeruiah was over the host; and Jehoshaphat the son of Ahilud, recorder.

1Ch 27:34 — And after Ahithophel *was* Jehoiada the son of Benaiah, and Abiathar: and the general of the king's army *was* Joab.

• Dedicated spoils of his battles.

1Ch 26:28 — And all that Samuel the seer, and Saul the son of Kish, and Abner the son of Ner, and Joab the son of Zeruiah, had dedicated; *and* whosoever had dedicated *any thing, it was* under the hand of Shelomith, and of his brethren.

• Defeated the Jebusites.

1Ch 11:6 — And David said, Whosoever smiteth the Jebusites first shall be chief and captain. So Joab the son of Zeruiah went first up, and was chief.

• Defeats and slays Abner.

2Sa 2:13–32

2Sa 3:27 — And when Abner was returned to Hebron, Joab took him aside in the gate to speak with him quietly, and smote him there under the fifth *rib,* that he died, for the blood of Asahel his brother.

1Ki 2:5 — Moreover thou knowest also what Joab the son of Zeruiah did to me, *and* what he did to the two captains of the hosts of Israel, unto Abner the son of Ner, and unto Amasa the son of Jether, whom he slew, and shed the blood of war in peace, and put the blood of war upon his girdle that *was* about his loins, and in his shoes that *were* on his feet.

• Destroys all the males in Edom.

1Ki 11:16 — (For six months did Joab remain there with all Israel, until he had cut off every male in Edom:)

Ps 60:1 — [To the chief Musician upon Shushan-eduth, Michtam of David, to teach; when he strove with Aram-naharaim and with Aram-zobah, when Joab returned, and smote of Edom in the valley of salt twelve thousand.] O God, thou hast cast us off, thou hast scattered us, thou hast been displeased; O turn thyself to us again.

• Defeats the Ammonites.

2Sa 10:7–14; 1Ch 19:6–15

• Captures Rabbah.

2Sa 11:15–25; 12:26–29; 1Ch 20:1–2

2Sa 11:1 — And it came to pass, after the year was expired, at the time when kings go forth *to battle,* that David sent Joab, and his servants with him, and all Israel; and they destroyed the children of Ammon, and besieged Rabbah. But David tarried still at Jerusalem.

• Procures the return of Absalom to Jerusalem.

2Sa 14:1–24

• Barley field of, burned by Absalom.

2Sa 14:29–33

• Pursues and kills Absalom.

2Sa 18:1–33

• Censures David for lamenting the death of Absalom.

2Sa 19:1–8

• Replaced by Amasa as commander of David's army.

2Sa 17:25 — And Absalom made Amasa captain of the host instead of Joab: which Amasa was a man's son, whose name *was* Ithra an Israelite, that went in to Abigail the daughter of Nahash, sister to Zeruiah Joab's mother.

2Sa 19:13 — And say ye to Amasa, *Art* thou not of my bone, and of my flesh? God do so to me, and more also, if thou be not captain of the host before me continually in the room of Joab.

• Kills Amasa.

2Sa 20:8–13

1Ki 2:5 — Moreover thou knowest also what Joab the son of Zeruiah did to me, *and* what he did to the two captains of the hosts of Israel, unto Abner the son of Ner, and unto Amasa the son of Jether, whom he slew, and shed the blood of war in peace, and put the blood of war upon his girdle that *was* about his loins, and in his shoes that *were* on his feet.

• Causes Sheba to be put to death.

2Sa 20:16–22

• Opposes the numbering of the people.

2Sa 24:3 — And Joab said unto the king, Now the LORD thy God add unto the people, how many soever they be, an hundredfold, and that the eyes of my lord the king may see *it:* but why doth my lord the king delight in this thing?

1Ch 21:3 — And Joab answered, The LORD make his people an hundred times so many more as they *be:* but, my lord the king, *are* they not all my lord's servants? why then doth my lord require this thing? why will he be a cause of trespass to Israel?

• Numbering the people.

2Sa 24:4–9; 1Ch 21:4–5; 27:23–24

• Supports Adonijah as successor to David.

1Ki 1:7 — And he conferred with Joab the son of Zeruiah, and with Abiathar the priest: and they following Adonijah helped *him.*

1Ki 2:28 — Then tidings came to Joab: for Joab had turned after Adonijah, though he turned not after Absalom. And Joab fled unto the tabernacle of the LORD, and caught hold on the horns of the altar.

• Slain by Benaiah, under Solomon's order.

1Ki 2:29–34

• A grandson of Kenaz.

1Ch 4:14 — And Meonothai begat Ophrah: and Seraiah begat Joab, the father of the valley of Charashim; for they were craftsmen.

• An Israelite (or the name of two Israelites whose descendants returned from Babylon to Jerusalem).

Ezr 2:6 — The children of Pahath-moab, of the children of Jeshua *and* Joab, two thousand eight hundred and twelve.

Ezr 8:9 — Of the sons of Joab; Obadiah the son of Jehiel, and with him two hundred and eighteen males.

Ne 7:11 — The children of Pahath-moab, of the children of Jeshua and Joab, two thousand and eight hundred *and* eighteen.

• "House of Joab" (Probably identical with Son of David's sister).

1Ch 2:54 — The sons of Salma; Bethlehem, and the Netophathites, Ataroth, the house of Joab, and half of the Manahethites, the Zorites.

JOAH

• Son of Asaph.

2Ki 18:18 — And when they had called to the king, there came out to them Eliakim the son of Hilkiah, which *was* over the household, and Shebna the scribe, and Joah the son of Asaph the recorder.

2Ki 18:26 — Then said Eliakim the son of Hilkiah, and Shebna, and Joah, unto Rab-shakeh, Speak, I pray thee, to thy servants in the Syrian language; for we understand *it:* and talk not with us in the Jews' language in the ears of the people that *are* on the wall.

Isa 36:3 — Then came forth unto him Eliakim, Hilkiah's son, which was over the house, and Shebna the scribe, and Joah, Asaph's son, the recorder.

Isa 36:11 — Then said Eliakim and Shebna and Joah unto Rabshakeh, Speak, I pray thee, unto thy servants in the Syrian language; for we understand *it:* and speak not to us in the Jews' language, in the ears of the people that *are* on the wall.

Isa 36:22 — Then came Eliakim, the son of Hilkiah, that *was* over the household, and Shebna the scribe, and Joah, the son of Asaph, the recorder, to Hezekiah with *their* clothes rent, and told him the words of Rabshakeh.

• A descendant of Gershom.

1Ch 6:21 — Joah his son, Iddo his son, Zerah his son, Jeaterai his son.

2Ch 29:12 — Then the Levites arose, Mahath the son of Amasai, and Joel the son of Azariah, of the sons of the Kohathites: and of the sons of Merari, Kish the son of Abdi, and Azariah the son of Jehalelel: and of the Gershonites; Joah the son of Zimmah, and Eden the son of Joah:

• A son of Obed-edom.

1Ch 26:4 — Moreover the sons of Obed-edom *were,* Shemaiah the firstborn, Jehozabad the second, Joah the third, and Sacar the fourth, and Nethaneel the fifth,

• A Levite, who repaired the temple.

2Ch 34:8 — Now in the eighteenth year of his reign, when he had purged the land, and the house, he sent Shaphan the son of Azaliah, and Maaseiah the governor of the city, and Joah the son of Joahaz the recorder, to repair the house of the LORD his God.

JOAHAZ • Father of Joah.

2Ch 34:8 — Now in the eighteenth year of his reign, when he had purged the land, and the house, he sent Shaphan the son of Azaliah, and Maaseiah the governor of the city, and Joah the son of Joahaz the recorder, to repair the house of the LORD his God.

JOANNA

• Wife of Chuza, the steward of Herod Agrippa, and a disciple of Jesus.

Lk 8:3 — And Joanna the wife of Chuza Herod's steward, and Susanna, and many others, which ministered unto him of their substance.

Lk 24:10 — It was Mary Magdalene, and Joanna, and Mary *the mother* of James, and other *women that were* with them, which told these things unto the apostles.

• An ancestor or Jesus.

Lk 3:27 — Which was *the son* of Joanna, which was *the son* of Rhesa, which was *the son* of Zorobabel, which was *the son* of Salathiel, which was *the son* of Neri,

JOASH

• Son of Becher.

1Ch 7:8 — And the sons of Becher; Zemira, and Joash, and Eliezer, and Elioenai, and Omri, and Jerimoth, and Abiah, and Anathoth, and Alameth. All these *are* the sons of Becher.

• Keeper of the stores of oil.

1Ch 27:28 — And over the olive trees and the sycomore trees that *were* in the low plains *was* Baal-hanan the Gederite: and over the cellars of oil *was* Joash:

• Father of Gideon.

Jgs 8:29–32

Jgs 6:11 — And there came an angel of the LORD, and sat under an oak which *was* in Ophrah, that *pertained* unto Joash the Abi-ezrite: and his son Gideon threshed wheat by the winepress, to hide *it* from the Midianites.

Jgs 6:29 — And they said one to another, Who hath done this thing? And when they enquired and asked, they said, Gideon the son of Joash hath done this thing.

Jgs 6:31 — And Joash said unto all that stood against him, Will ye plead for Baal? will ye save him? he that will plead for him, let him be put to death whilst *it is yet* morning: if he *be* a god, let him plead for himself, because *one* hath cast down his altar.

Jgs 7:14 — And his fellow answered and said, This *is* nothing else save the sword of Gideon the son of Joash, a man of Israel: *for* into his hand hath God delivered Midian, and all the host.

Jgs 8:13 — And Gideon the son of Joash returned from battle before the sun *was up,*

• Son of Ahab, king of Israel.

1Ki 22:26 — And the king of Israel said, Take Micaiah, and carry him back unto Amon the governor of the city, and to Joash the king's son;

2Ch 18:25 — Then the king of Israel said, Take ye Micaiah, and carry him back to Amon the governor of the city, and to Joash the king's son;

• Son of Ahaziah and king of Judah; called also Jehoash.

• Hidden for six years.

2Ki 11:1–3; 2Ch 22:11–12

• Anointed king by the priest, Jehoiada.

2Ki 11:12–21; 2Ch 23:1–21

• Righteousness of, under influence of Jehoiada.

2Ki 12:2 — And Jehoash did *that which was* right in the sight of the LORD all his days wherein Jehoiada the priest instructed him.

2Ch 24:2 — And Joash did *that which was* right in the sight of the LORD all the days of Jehoiada the priest.

• Repaired the temple.

2Ki 12:4–16; 2Ch 24:4–14

2Ch 24:27 — Now *concerning* his sons, and the greatness of the burdens *laid* upon him, and the repairing of the house of God, behold, they *are* written in the story of the book of the kings. And Amaziah his son reigned in his stead.

• Wickedness of, after Jehoiada's death.

2Ch 24:17–22

• **Procured peace from Hazael, king of Syria, by gift of dedicated treasures from the temple.**
2Ki 12:17–18; 2Ch 24:23–24

• **Prophecy against.**
2Ch 24:19–20

• **Put Jehoiada's son to death.**
2Ch 24:20–22

Mt 23:35 — That upon you may come all the righteous blood shed upon the earth, from the blood of righteous Abel unto the blood of Zacharias son of Barachias, whom ye slew between the temple and the altar.

• **Diseases of.**
2Ch 24:25 — And when they were departed from him, (for they left him in great diseases,) his own servants conspired against him for the blood of the sons of Jehoiada the priest, and slew him on his bed, and he died: and they buried him in the city of David, but they buried him not in the sepulchres of the kings.

• **Conspired against and slain.**
2Ki 12:20–21; 2Ch 24:25–26

• **A king of Israel.**
See: Jehoahaz

• **A descendant of Shelah.**
1Ch 4:22 — And Jokim, and the men of Chozeba, and Joash, and Saraph, who had the dominion in Moab, and Jashubi-lehem. And *these are* ancient things.

• **One of David's officers.**
1Ch 12:3 — The chief *was* Ahiezer, then Joash, the sons of Shemaah the Gibeathite; and Jeziel, and Pelet, the sons of Azmaveth; and Berachah, and Jehu the Antothite,

JOB

• **A man who dwelt in Uz.**
Job 1:1 — There was a man in the land of Uz, whose name *was* Job; and that man was perfect and upright, and one that feared God, and eschewed evil.

• **Righteousness of.**
Job 1:1 — There was a man in the land of Uz, whose name *was* Job; and that man was perfect and upright, and one that feared God, and eschewed evil.

Job 1:5 — And it was so, when the days of *their* feasting were gone about, that Job sent and sanctified them, and rose up early in the morning, and offered burnt offerings *according* to the number of them all: for Job said, It may be that my sons have sinned, and cursed God in their hearts. Thus did Job continually.

Job 1:8 — And the LORD said unto Satan, Hast thou considered my servant Job, that *there is* none like him in the earth, a perfect and an upright man, one that feareth God, and escheweth evil?

Job 2:3 — And the LORD said unto Satan, Hast thou considered my servant Job, that *there is* none like him in the earth, a perfect and an upright man, one that feareth God, and escheweth evil? and still he holdeth fast his integrity, although thou movedst me against him, to destroy him without cause.

Eze 14:14 — Though these three men, Noah, Daniel, and Job, were in it, they should deliver *but* their own souls by their righteousness, saith the Lord GOD.

Eze 14:20 — Though Noah, Daniel, and Job, *were* in it, *as* I live, saith the Lord GOD, they shall deliver neither son nor daughter; they shall *but* deliver their own souls by their righteousness.

• **Riches of.**
Job 1:3 — His substance also was seven thousand sheep, and three thousand camels, and five hundred yoke of oxen, and five hundred she asses, and a very great household; so that this man was the greatest of all the men of the east.

• **Trial of, by affliction of Satan.**
Job 1:13–19; 2:7–10

• **Fortitude of.**
Job 1:20–22

Job 2:10 — But he said unto her, Thou speakest as one of the foolish women speaketh. What? shall we receive good at the hand of God, and shall we not receive evil? In all this did not Job sin with his lips.

Jas 5:11 — Behold, we count them happy which endure. Ye have heard of the patience of Job, and have seen the end of the Lord; that the Lord is very pitiful, and of tender mercy.

• **Visited by Eliphaz, Bildad, and Zophar as comforters.**
Job 2:11–13

• **Complaints of, and replies by his three friends to.**
Job 3:1–37:24

• **Replied to by God.**
Job 38:1–41:34

• **Submission of, to God.**
Job 40:3–5; 42:1–6

• **Later blessings and riches of.**
Job 42:10–16

• **Death of.**
Job 42:16–17

See: Jashub

JOBAB

• **Son of Joktan.**
Ge 10:29 — And Ophir, and Havilah, and Jobab: all these *were* the sons of Joktan.

1Ch 1:23 — And Ophir, and Havilah, and Jobab. All these *were* the sons of Joktan.

• **A king of Edom.**
Ge 36:33–34; 1Ch 1:44–45

• **A king of Madon.**
Jos 11:1 — And it came to pass, when Jabin king of Hazor had heard *those things,* that he sent to Jobab king of Madon, and to the king of Shimron, and to the king of Achshaph,

• Name of two Benjamites of whom little is known.

1Ch 8:9 — And he begat of Hodesh his wife, Jobab, and Zibia, and Mesha, and Malcham,

1Ch 8:18 — Ishmerai also, and Jezliah, and Jobab, the sons of Elpaal;

JOCHEBED

• Mother of Miriam, Aaron, and Moses.

Ex 6:20 — And Amram took him Jochebed his father's sister to wife; and she bare him Aaron and Moses: and the years of the life of Amram *were* an hundred and thirty and seven years.

Nu 26:59 — And the name of Amram's wife *was* Jochebed, the daughter of Levi, whom *her mother* bare to Levi in Egypt: and she bare unto Amram Aaron and Moses, and Miriam their sister.

• Nurses Moses when he is adopted by Pharaoh's daughter.

Ex 2:1–9

JOED • A Benjamite.

Ne 11:7 — And these *are* the sons of Benjamin; Sallu the son of Meshullam, the son of Joed, the son of Pedaiah, the son of Kolaiah, the son of Maaseiah, the son of Ithiel, the son of Jesaiah.

JOEL

• Son of Samuel.

1Sa 8:2 — Now the name of his firstborn was Joel; and the name of his second, Abiah: *they were* judges in Beer-sheba.

1Ch 6:33 — And these *are* they that waited with their children. Of the sons of the Kohathites: Heman a singer, the son of Joel, the son of Shemuel,

1Ch 15:17 — So the Levites appointed Heman the son of Joel; and of his brethren, Asaph the son of Berechiah; and of the sons of Merari their brethren, Ethan the son of Kushaiah;

• Called Vashni.

1Ch 6:28 — And the sons of Samuel; the firstborn Vashni, and Abiah.

• A Simeonite.

1Ch 4:35 — And Joel, and Jehu the son of Josibiah, the son of Seraiah, the son of Asiel,

• A Reubenite.

1Ch 5:4 — The sons of Joel; Shemaiah his son, Gog his son, Shimei his son,

1Ch 5:8 — And Bela the son of Azaz, the son of Shema, the son of Joel, who dwelt in Aroer, even unto Nebo and Baal-meon:

• A Gadite.

1Ch 5:12 — Joel the chief, and Shapham the next, and Jaanai, and Shaphat in Bashan.

• A Kohathite Levite.

1Ch 6:36 — The son of Elkanah, the son of Joel, the son of Azariah, the son of Zephaniah,

• Descendant of Issachar.

1Ch 7:3 — And the sons of Uzzi; Izrahiah: and the sons of Izrahiah; Michael, and Obadiah, and Joel, Ishiah, five: all of them chief men.

• One of David's valiant men.

1Ch 11:38 — Joel the brother of Nathan, Mibhar the son of Haggeri,

• Called "Igal, son of Nathan".

2Sa 23:36 — Igal the son of Nathan of Zobah, Bani the Gadite,

• Name of two Gershonites.

1Ch 15:7 — Of the sons of Gershom; Joel the chief, and his brethren an hundred and thirty:

1Ch 15:11 — And David called for Zadok and Abiathar the priests, and for the Levites, for Uriel, Asaiah, and Joel, Shemaiah, and Eliel, and Amminadab,

1Ch 23:8 — The sons of Laadan; the chief *was* Jehiel, and Zetham, and Joel, three.

1Ch 26:22 — The sons of Jehieli; Zetham, and Joel his brother, *which were* over the treasures of the house of the LORD.

• Prince of Manasseh.

1Ch 27:20 — Of the children of Ephraim, Hoshea the son of Azaziah: of the half tribe of Manasseh, Joel the son of Pedaiah:

• A Kohathite who assisted in the cleansing of the temple.

2Ch 29:12 — Then the Levites arose, Mahath the son of Amasai, and Joel the son of Azariah, of the sons of the Kohathites: and of the sons of Merari, Kish the son of Abdi, and Azariah the son of Jehalelel: and of the Gershonites; Joah the son of Zimmah, and Eden the son of Joah:

• One of Nebo's family.

Ezr 10:43 — Of the sons of Nebo; Jeiel, Mattithiah, Zabad, Zebina, Jadau, and Joel, Benaiah.

• Son of Zichri.

Ne 11:9 — And Joel the son of Zichri *was* their overseer: and Judah the son of Senuah *was* second over the city.

• One of the twelve minor prophets, probably lived in the days of Uzziah.

Joel 1:1 — The word of the LORD that came to Joel the son of Pethuel.

Ac 2:16 — But this is that which was spoken by the prophet Joel;

• Declares the terribleness of God's judgments.

Joel 1:1–2:11

• Exhorts to repentance.

Joel 2:12–32

• Denounces judgments against the enemies of God.

Joel 3:1–17

• Sets forth the blessings of the church.

Joel 3:18–21

JOELAH • Son of Jeroham.

1Ch 12:7 — And Joelah, and Zebadiah, the sons of Jeroham of Gedor.

JOEZER • A Korhite, who joined David at Ziklag.

1Ch 12:6 — Elkanah, and Jesiah, and Azareel, and Joezer, and Jashobeam, the Korhites,

JOGBEHAH • A place in Gad.

Nu 32:35 — And Atroth, Shophan, and Jaazer, and Jogbehah,

Jgs 8:11 — And Gideon went up by the way of them that dwelt in tents on the east of Nobah and Jogbehah, and smote the host: for the host was secure.

JOGLI • A prince of Dan.

Nu 34:22 — And the prince of the tribe of the children of Dan, Bukki the son of Jogli.

JOHA

• A Benjamite.

1Ch 8:16 — And Michael, and Ispah, and Joha, the sons of Beriah;

• One of David's valiant men.

1Ch 11:45 — Jediael the son of Shimri, and Joha his brother, the Tizite,

JOHANAN

• A Jewish captain.

2Ki 25:22–24

• Warns Gedaliah against Ishmael.

Jer 40:13–16

• Ishmael defeated by.

Jer 41:11–15

• Sought prayers of Jeremiah.

Jer 42:2–3

• Disobeyed Jeremiah and took him to Egypt.

Jer 43:1–7

• Son of Josiah.

1Ch 3:15 — And the sons of Josiah *were,* the firstborn Johanan, the second Jehoiakim, the third Zedekiah, the fourth Shallum.

• A son of Elioenai.

1Ch 3:24 — And the sons of Elioenai *were,* Hodaiah, and Eliashib, and Pelaiah, and Akkub, and Johanan, and Dalaiah, and Anani, seven.

• A Levite.

1Ch 6:9–10

• Two Israelites who joined David at Ziklag.

1Ch 12:4 — And Ismaiah the Gibeonite, a mighty man among the thirty, and over the thirty; and Jeremiah, and Jahaziel, and Johanan, and Josabad the Gederathite,

1Ch 12:12 — Johanan the eighth, Elzabad the ninth,

• An Ephraimite.

2Ch 28:12 — Then certain of the heads of the children of Ephraim, Azariah the son of Johanan, Berechiah the son of Meshillemoth, and Jehizkiah the son of Shallum, and Amasa the son of Hadlai, stood up against them that came from the war,

• A returned exile.

Ezr 8:12 — And of the sons of Azgad; Johanan the son of Hakkatan, and with him an hundred and ten males.

• A priest.

Ne 12:22–23

Ezr 10:6 — Then Ezra rose up from before the house of God, and went into the chamber of Johanan the son of Eliashib: and *when* he came thither, he did eat no bread, nor drink water: for he mourned because of the transgression of them that had been carried away.

• Probably identical with Jonathan.

Ne 12:11 — And Joiada begat Jonathan, and Jonathan begat Jaddua.

• Son of Tobiah the Ammonite.

Ne 6:18 — For *there were* many in Judah sworn unto him, because he *was* the son in law of Shechaniah the son of Arah; and his son Johanan had taken the daughter of Meshullam the son of Berechiah.

JOHN, other

• A kinsman of Annas the high priest.

Ac 4:6 — And Annas the high priest, and Caiaphas, and John, and Alexander, and as many as were of the kindred of the high priest, were gathered together at Jerusalem.

• Whose surname was Mark.

See: Mark

JOHN, the Apostle

• Intimately associated with Jesus.

Jn 13:23–26

Jn 21:20 — Then Peter, turning about, seeth the disciple whom Jesus loved following; which also leaned on his breast at supper, and said, Lord, which is he that betrayeth thee?

• Is present when Jesus performs the following miracles.

• Healing of Peter's mother-in-law.

Mt 8:14–15; Mk 1:30–31; Lk 4:38–39

• Raising of the daughter of Jairus.

Mk 5:37 — And he suffered no man to follow him, save Peter, and James, and John the brother of James.

Lk 8:51 — And when he came into the house, he suffered no man to go in, save Peter, and James, and John, and the father and the mother of the maiden.

• The two draughts of fishes.

Jn 21:1–7

Lk 5:10 — And so *was* also James, and John, the sons of Zebedee, which were partners with Simon. And Jesus said unto Simon, Fear not; from henceforth thou shalt catch men.

• Transfiguration.

Mt 17:1 — And after six days Jesus taketh Peter, James, and John his brother, and bringeth them up into an high mountain apart,

Mk 9:2 — And after six days Jesus taketh *with him* Peter, and James, and John, and leadeth them up into an high mountain apart by themselves: and he was transfigured before them.

Lk 9:28 — And it came to pass about an eight days after these sayings, he took Peter and John and James, and went up into a mountain to pray.

• Is present with Jesus in the garden.

Mt 26:37 — And he took with him Peter and the two sons of Zebedee, and began to be sorrowful and very heavy.

Mk 14:33 — And he taketh with him Peter and James and John, and began to be sore amazed, and to be very heavy;

Lk 22:39 — And he came out, and went, as he was wont, to the mount of Olives; and his disciples also followed him.

• Intolerance of.

Lk 9:49–50, 54–56

Mk 9:38 — And John answered him, saying, Master, we saw one casting out devils in thy name, and he followeth not us: and we forbad him, because he followeth not us.

• Civil ambitions of.

Mt 20:20–24; Mk 10:35–41

• Prepares the passover.

Mt 26:18–19; Mk 14:13–16; Lk 22:8–13

• Present at the trial of Jesus before the high priest.

Jn 18:15–16

• Present at the crucifixion.

Jn 19:26–27

• Present at the sepulchre.

Jn 20:2–8

• Present when Jesus manifested himself at the Sea of Galilee.

Jn 21:1–25

• Present with Peter in the temple.

Ac 3:1–11

• Dwells in Jerusalem.

Ac 1:13 — And when they were come in, they went up into an upper room, where abode both Peter, and James, and John, and Andrew, Philip, and Thomas, Bartholomew, and Matthew, James *the son* of Alphaeus, and Simon Zelotes, and Judas *the brother* of James.

• Is intrusted with the care of Mary, mother of Jesus.

Jn 19:26 — When Jesus therefore saw his mother, and the disciple standing by, whom he loved, he saith unto his mother, Woman, behold thy son!

• Imprisoned by the rulers of the Jews.

Ac 4:1–19

• Sent by the church with the commission to Samaria.

Ac 8:14–17

• A pillar of the church.

Gal 2:9 — And when James, Cephas, and John, who seemed to be pillars, perceived the grace that was given unto me, they gave to me and Barnabas the right hands of fellowship; that we *should go* unto the heathen, and they unto the circumcision.

• Writes to the churches.

1 John; 2 John; 3 John

• Writes his apocalyptic vision from Patmos.

Rev 1:9 — I John, who also am your brother, and companion in tribulation, and in the kingdom and patience of Jesus Christ, was in the isle that is called Patmos, for the word of God, and for the testimony of Jesus Christ.

• Prophecy concerning.

Rev 10:11 — And he said unto me, Thou must prophesy again before many peoples, and nations, and tongues, and kings.

JOHN, the Baptist

• Prophecies concerning.

Mal 4:5–6; Lk 1:11–17

Isa 40:3 — The voice of him that crieth in the wilderness, Prepare ye the way of the LORD, make straight in the desert a highway for our God.

• Miraculous birth of.

Lk 1:11–20, 57–65

• Dwells in the desert.

Lk 3:2–3

Mt 3:1 — In those days came John the Baptist, preaching in the wilderness of Judaea,

Mk 1:4 — John did baptize in the wilderness, and preach the baptism of repentance for the remission of sins.

Lk 1:80 — And the child grew, and waxed strong in spirit, and was in the deserts till the day of his shewing unto Israel.

• Mission of.

Mk 1:2–8; Lk 1:15–17, 76–79; 3:4–6; Jn 1:7–8, 22–28, 31–34; 5:32–35; Ac 13:24–25

Mt 17:11 — And Jesus answered and said unto them, Elias truly shall first come, and restore all things.

Jn 1:15 — John bare witness of him, and cried, saying, This was he of whom I spake, He that cometh after me is preferred before me: for he was before me.

Ac 19:4 — Then said Paul, John verily baptized with the baptism of repentance, saying unto the people, that they should believe on him which should come after him, that is, on Christ Jesus.

• Ministry of.

Mt 3:1–3; Lk 3:2–3; Jn 1:6–8

Mk 1:4 — John did baptize in the wilderness, and preach the baptism of repentance for the remission of sins.

• His influence upon the public mind.

Mt 3:5–6; Jn 1:35–40

Mt 14:5 — And when he would have put him to death, he feared the multitude, because they counted him as a prophet.

Mt 21:32 — For John came unto you in the way of righteousness, and ye believed him not: but the publicans and the harlots believed him: and ye, when ye had seen *it,* repented not afterward, that ye might believe him.

Mk 1:5 — And there went out unto him all the land of Judaea, and they of Jerusalem, and were all baptized of him in the river of Jordan, confessing their sins.

Mk 11:32 — But if we shall say, Of men; they feared the people: for all *men* counted John, that he was a prophet indeed.

Lk 3:7 — Then said he to the multitude that came forth to be baptized of him, O generation of vipers, who hath warned you to flee from the wrath to come?

Lk 3:15 — And as the people were in expectation, and all men mused in their hearts of John, whether he were the Christ, or not;

Lk 20:6 — But and if we say, Of men; all the people will stone us: for they be persuaded that John was a prophet.

• Testifies to the messiahship of Jesus.

Mt 3:11–12; Mk 1:7–8; Lk 3:16–17; Jn 1:26–36; 3:23–36; 5:32–33

Jn 1:15 — John bare witness of him, and cried, saying, This was he of whom I spake, He that cometh after me is preferred before me: for he was before me.

Jn 10:41 — And many resorted unto him, and said, John did no miracle: but all things that John spake of this man were true.

Ac 13:25 — And as John fulfilled his course, he said, Whom think ye that I am? I am not *he.* But, behold, there cometh one after me, whose shoes of *his* feet I am not worthy to loose.

• Teaches his disciples to pray.

Lk 11:1 — And it came to pass, that, as he was praying in a certain place, when he ceased, one of his disciples said unto him, Lord, teach us to pray, as John also taught his disciples.

• Teaches his disciples to fast.

Lk 5:33 — And they said unto him, Why do the disciples of John fast often, and make prayers, and likewise *the disciples* of the Pharisees; but thine eat and drink?

• The baptism which he taught.

See: Baptism

• Baptizes Jesus.

Mt 3:13–16; Mk 1:9–11; Lk 3:21–22

Jn 1:32 — And John bare record, saying, I saw the Spirit descending from heaven like a dove, and it abode upon him.

• The testimony of Jesus concerning.

Mt 17:12–13; Jn 5:32–35

Mt 21:32 — For John came unto you in the way of righteousness, and ye believed him not: but the publicans and the harlots believed him: and ye, when ye had seen *it,* repented not afterward, that ye might believe him.

Mk 9:13 — But I say unto you, That Elias is indeed come, and they have done unto him whatsoever they listed, as it is written of him.

See: John, the Baptist; Jesus discourses upon

• His ministry not attested by miracles.

Jn 10:41 — And many resorted unto him, and said, John did no miracle: but all things that John spake of this man were true.

• Reproves Herod on account of his incest; Herod imprisons him, beheads him.

Mt 14:1–12; Mk 6:16–29; Lk 3:18–20

Mt 4:12 — Now when Jesus had heard that John was cast into prison, he departed into Galilee;

Mk 9:13 — But I say unto you, That Elias is indeed come, and they have done unto him whatsoever they listed, as it is written of him.

• Sends two disciples to Jesus.

Mt 11:2–6; Lk 7:18–23

• Herod falsely supposes Jesus to be.

Mt 14:1–2

Mt 16:14 — And they said, Some *say that thou art* John the Baptist: some, Elias; and others, Jeremias, or one of the prophets.

Mk 6:14 — And king Herod heard *of him;* (for his name was spread abroad:) and he said, That John the Baptist was risen from the dead, and therefore mighty works do shew forth themselves in him.

Mk 6:16 — But when Herod heard *thereof,* he said, It is John, whom I beheaded: he is risen from the dead.

Lk 9:19 — They answering said, John the Baptist; but some *say,* Elias; and others *say,* that one of the old prophets is risen again.

• Character of.

Mk 6:20 — For Herod feared John, knowing that he was a just man and an holy, and observed him; and when he heard him, he did many things, and heard him gladly.

Jn 5:35 — He was a burning and a shining light: and ye were willing for a season to rejoice in his light.

• Jesus discourses upon.

Mt 11:7–19; Lk 7:24–33

• Affected probably by the doctrines of the stoics.

Mt 11:18 — For John came neither eating nor drinking, and they say, He hath a devil.

Mk 1:6 — And John was clothed with camel's hair, and with a girdle of a skin about his loins; and he did eat locusts and wild honey;

Lk 1:80 — And the child grew, and waxed strong in spirit, and was in the deserts till the day of his shewing unto Israel.

• A Nazarite.

Mt 11:18 — For John came neither eating nor drinking, and they say, He hath a devil.

Lk 1:15 — For he shall be great in the sight of the Lord, and shall drink neither wine nor strong drink; and he shall be filled with the Holy Ghost, even from his mother's womb.

Lk 7:33 — For John the Baptist came neither eating bread nor drinking wine; and ye say, He hath a devil.

JOIADA • Son and successor of Eliashib in the high priesthood.

Ne 12:10–11

Ne 12:22 — The Levites in the days of Eliashib, Joiada, and Johanan, and Jaddua, *were* recorded chief of the fathers: also the priests, to the reign of Darius the Persian.

Ne 13:28 — And *one* of the sons of Joiada, the son of Eliashib the high priest, *was* son in law to Sanballat the Horonite: therefore I chased him from me.

JOIAKIM • A high priest.

Ne 12:10 — And Jeshua begat Joiakim, Joiakim also begat Eliashib, and Eliashib begat Joiada,

Ne 12:12 — And in the days of Joiakim were priests, the chief of the fathers: of Seraiah, Meraiah; of Jeremiah, Hananiah;

Ne 12:26 — These *were* in the days of Joiakim the son of Jeshua, the son of Jozadak, and in the days of Nehemiah the governor, and of Ezra the priest, the scribe.

JOIARIB

• A returned exile.

Ezr 8:16 — Then sent I for Eliezer, for Ariel, for Shemaiah, and for Elnathan, and for Jarib, and for Elnathan, and for Nathan, and for Zechariah, and for Meshullam, chief men; also for Joiarib, and for Elnathan, men of understanding.

• A descendant of Judah.

Ne 11:5 — And Maaseiah the son of Baruch, the son of Col-hozeh, the son of Hazaiah, the son of Adaiah, the son of Joiarib, the son of Zechariah, the son of Shiloni.

• A priest who returned from Babylon.

Ne 12:6 — Shemaiah, and Joiarib, Jedaiah,

Ne 12:19 — And of Joiarib, Mattenai; of Jedaiah, Uzzi;

See: Jehoiarib

JOKDEAM • A city of Judah.

Jos 15:56 — And Jezreel, and Jokdeam, and Zanoah,

JOKIM • A descendant of Shelah.

1Ch 4:22 — And Jokim, and the men of Chozeba, and Joash, and Saraph, who had the dominion in Moab, and Jashubi-lehem. And *these are* ancient things.

JOKMEAM • A Levitical city of Ephraim.

1Ch 6:68 — And Jokmeam with her suburbs, and Beth-horon with her suburbs,

JOKNEAM

• A Levitical city of Zebulun.

Jos 12:22 — The king of Kedesh, one; the king of Jokneam of Carmel, one;

Jos 19:11 — And their border went up toward the sea, and Maralah, and reached to Dabbasheth, and reached to the river that *is* before Jokneam;

Jos 21:34 — And unto the families of the children of Merari, the rest of the Levites, out of the tribe of Zebulun, Jokneam with her suburbs, and Kartah with her suburbs,

See: Jokmeam

JOKSHAN • Son of Abraham, by Keturah.

Ge 25:2–3

Ge 25:6 — But unto the sons of the concubines, which Abraham had, Abraham gave gifts, and sent them away from Isaac his son, while he yet lived, eastward, unto the east country.

1Ch 1:32 — Now the sons of Keturah, Abraham's concubine: she bare Zimran, and Jokshan, and Medan, and Midian, and Ishbak, and Shuah. And the sons of Jokshan; Sheba, and Dedan.

JOKTAN • Son of Eber.

Ge 10:25–26; 1Ch 1:19–20

Ge 10:29 — And Ophir, and Havilah, and Jobab: all these *were* the sons of Joktan.

1Ch 1:23 — And Ophir, and Havilah, and Jobab. All these *were* the sons of Joktan.

JOKTHEEL

• A city of Judah.

Jos 15:38 — And Dilean, and Mizpeh, and Joktheel,

• A name given by Amaziah to Selah, a stronghold of Edom.

2Ch 25:11–12

2Ki 14:7 — He slew of Edom in the valley of salt ten thousand, and took Selah by war, and called the name of it Joktheel unto this day.

• Called rock.

Jgs 1:36 — And the coast of the Amorites *was* from the going up to Akrabbim, from the rock, and upward.

JONADAB

• Nephew of David.

• His complicity with Amnon in his rape of Tamar.

2Sa 13:3–5

• Comforts David on death of Amnon.

2Sa 13:32–35

• A Rechabite and companion of Jehu.

• Called also Jehonadab.

2Ki 10:15–23

• His sons refuse to drink wine in obedience to his command.

Jer 35:5–10, 16–19

See: Rechabites

JONAH

• Called also Jonas.

• A prophet of Israel.

2Ki 14:25 — He restored the coast of Israel from the entering of Hamath unto the sea of the plain, according to the word of the LORD God of Israel, which he spake by the hand of his servant Jonah, the son of Amittai, the prophet, which *was* of Gath-hepher.

- **Sent by God to warn Nineveh.**
  Jnh 1:1–2
- **Disobedience and punishment of.**
  Jnh 1:3–17
- **Repentance and deliverance of.**
  Jnh 2:1–10
  Mt 12:40 — For as Jonas was three days and three nights in the whale's belly; so shall the Son of man be three days and three nights in the heart of the earth.
- **Brought Ninevites to repentance.**
  Jnh 3:1–10
  Mt 12:41 — The men of Nineveh shall rise in judgment with this generation, and shall condemn it: because they repented at the preaching of Jonas; and, behold, a greater than Jonas *is* here.
- **Displeased with God's mercy to Nineveh; reproved.**
  Jnh 4:1–11
- **Is a sign.**
  Lk 11:29–30
  Mt 16:4 — A wicked and adulterous generation seeketh after a sign; and there shall no sign be given unto it, but the sign of the prophet Jonas. And he left them, and departed.

JONAN • An ancestor of Christ.

Lk 3:30 — Which was *the son* of Simeon, which was *the son* of Juda, which was *the son* of Joseph, which was *the son* of Jonan, which was *the son* of Eliakim,

JONAS

See: Jonah

- **Father of Peter.**
  Jn 21:15–17
  - **Called Jona.**
    Jn 1:42 — And he brought him to Jesus. And when Jesus beheld him, he said, Thou art Simon the son of Jona: thou shalt be called Cephas, which is by interpretation, A stone.

JONATHAN

- **A Levite of Bethlehem, who becomes a priest for Micah; accepts idolatry; joins the Danites.**
  Jgs 17:7–18:30
- **Son of Saul.**
  1Sa 14:49 — Now the sons of Saul were Jonathan, and Ishui, and Melchi-shua: and the names of his two daughters *were these;* the name of the firstborn Merab, and the name of the younger Michal:
  - **Victory of, over the Philistine garrison of Geba.**
    1Sa 13:3–4
    1Sa 13:16 — And Saul, and Jonathan his son, and the people *that were* present with them, abode in Gibeah of Benjamin: but the Philistines encamped in Michmash.
  - **Victory of, over Philistines at Michmash.**
    1Sa 14:1–18
  - **Under Saul's curse pronounced against any who might take food before he was avenged of his enemies.**
    1Sa 14:24–30
    1Sa 14:43 — Then Saul said to Jonathan, Tell me what thou hast done. And Jonathan told him, and said, I did but taste a little honey with the end of the rod that *was* in mine hand, *and,* lo, I must die.
  - **Rescued by the people.**
    1Sa 14:43–45
  - **Love of, for David.**
    1Sa 18:1–4; 19:1–7; 20:1–42; 23:16–18
  - **Killed in battle with Philistines.**
    2Sa 21:12–14
    1Sa 31:2 — And the Philistines followed hard upon Saul and upon his sons; and the Philistines slew Jonathan, and Abinadab, and Melchi-shua, Saul's sons.
    1Sa 31:6 — So Saul died, and his three sons, and his armourbearer, and all his men, that same day together.
    1Ch 10:2 — And the Philistines followed hard after Saul, and after his sons; and the Philistines slew Jonathan, and Abinadab, and Malchi-shua, the sons of Saul.
  - **Buried by inhabitants of Jabesh-gilead.**
    1Sa 31:11–13
  - **Mourned by David.**
    2Sa 1:17–27
    2Sa 1:12 — And they mourned, and wept, and fasted until even, for Saul, and for Jonathan his son, and for the people of the LORD, and for the house of Israel; because they were fallen by the sword.
  - **Son of, cared for by David.**
    2Sa 9:1–13
    2Sa 4:4 — And Jonathan, Saul's son, had a son *that was* lame of *his* feet. He was five years old when the tidings came of Saul and Jonathan out of Jezreel, and his nurse took him up, and fled: and it came to pass, as she made haste to flee, that he fell, and became lame. And his name *was* Mephibosheth.
    1Ch 8:34 — And the son of Jonathan *was* Merib-baal; and Merib-baal begat Micah.
- **Son of Abiathar.**
  2Sa 15:27 — The king said also unto Zadok the priest, *Art not* thou a seer? return into the city in peace, and your two sons with you, Ahimaaz thy son, and Jonathan the son of Abiathar.
  - **Acts as spy for David.**
    2Sa 15:27–28; 17:17–22
  - **Informs Adonijah of Solomon's succession to David.**
    1Ki 1:42–48
- **Nephew of David, slays a giant, and becomes one of David's chief warriors.**
  2Sa 21:21 — And when he defied Israel, Jonathan the son of Shimeah the brother of David slew him.

1Ch 20:7 — But when he defied Israel, Jonathan the son of Shimea David's brother slew him.

- **One of David's heroes.**

2Sa 23:32 — Eliahba the Shaalbonite, of the sons of Jashen, Jonathan,

1Ch 11:34 — The sons of Hashem the Gizonite, Jonathan the son of Shage the Hararite,

- **A son of Jada.**

1Ch 2:32–33

- **Secretary of the cabinet of David.**

1Ch 27:32 — Also Jonathan David's uncle was a counsellor, a wise man, and a scribe: and Jehiel the son of Hachmoni *was* with the king's sons:

- **Father of Ebed.**

Ezr 8:6 — Of the sons also of Adin; Ebed the son of Jonathan, and with him fifty males.

- **Son of Asahel.**

Ezr 10:15 — Only Jonathan the son of Asahel and Jahaziah the son of Tikvah were employed about this *matter:* and Meshullam and Shabbethai the Levite helped them.

- **A descendant of Jeshua.**

Ne 12:11 — And Joiada begat Jonathan, and Jonathan begat Jaddua.

- **Called also Johanan.**

Ne 12:22 — The Levites in the days of Eliashib, Joiada, and Johanan, and Jaddua, *were* recorded chief of the fathers: also the priests, to the reign of Darius the Persian.

- **Name of two priests.**

Ne 12:14 — Of Melicu, Jonathan; of Shebaniah, Joseph;

Ne 12:35 — And *certain* of the priests' sons with trumpets; *namely,* Zechariah the son of Jonathan, the son of Shemaiah, the son of Mattaniah, the son of Michaiah, the son of Zaccur, the son of Asaph:

- **A scribe.**

Jer 37:15 — Wherefore the princes were wroth with Jeremiah, and smote him, and put him in prison in the house of Jonathan the scribe: for they had made that the prison.

Jer 37:20 — Therefore hear now, I pray thee, O my lord the king: let my supplication, I pray thee, be accepted before thee; that thou cause me not to return to the house of Jonathan the scribe, lest I die there.

Jer 38:26 — Then thou shalt say unto them, I presented my supplication before the king, that he would not cause me to return to Jonathan's house, to die there.

- **Son of Kareah.**

Jer 40:8 — Then they came to Gedaliah to Mizpah, even Ishmael the son of Nethaniah, and Johanan and Jonathan the sons of Kareah, and Seraiah the son of Tanhumeth, and the sons of Ephai the Netophathite, and Jezaniah the son of a Maachathite, they and their men.

JOPPA

- **A seaport.**

Jos 19:46 — And Me-jarkon, and Rakkon, with the border before Japho.

- **Exports from.**

2Ch 2:16 — And we will cut wood out of Lebanon, as much as thou shalt need: and we will bring it to thee in flotes by sea to Joppa; and thou shall carry it up to Jerusalem.

Ezr 3:7 — They gave money also unto the masons, and to the carpenters; and meat, and drink, and oil, unto them of Zidon, and to them of Tyre, to bring cedar trees from Lebanon to the sea of Joppa, according to the grant that they had of Cyrus king of Persia.

- **Passenger traffic from.**

Jnh 1:3 — But Jonah rose up to flee unto Tarshish from the presence of the LORD, and went down to Joppa; and he found a ship going to Tarshish: so he paid the fare thereof, and went down into it, to go with them unto Tarshish from the presence of the LORD.

- **Peter performs a miracle at.**

Ac 9:36–43

- **Peter has a vision of a sheet let down from heaven at.**

Ac 10:9–18

JORAH • A returned exile.

Ezr 2:18 — The children of Jorah, an hundred and twelve.

JORAI • A Gadite.

1Ch 5:13 — And their brethren of the house of their fathers *were,* Michael, and Meshullam, and Sheba, and Jorai, and Jachan, and Zia, and Heber, seven.

JORAM

- **A son of Toi.**

2Sa 8:9–10

- **Called Hadoram.**

1Ch 18:10 — He sent Hadoram his son to king David, to enquire of his welfare, and to congratulate him, because he had fought against Hadarezer, and smitten him; (for Hadarezer had war with Tou;) and *with him* all manner of vessels of gold and silver and brass.

- **King of Israel.**

- **Called also Jehoram.**

2Ki 1:17 — So he died according to the word of the LORD which Elijah had spoken. And Jehoram reigned in his stead in the second year of Jehoram the son of Jehoshaphat king of Judah; because he had no son.

2Ki 3:1 — Now Jehoram the son of Ahab began to reign over Israel in Samaria the eighteenth year of Jehoshaphat king of Judah, and reigned twelve years.

• **King of Syria sends Naaman to, that he may be healed of his leprosy.**
2Ki 5:1–27

• **Has war with the king of Syria.**
2Ki 6:8–23; 7:1–20; 8:28–29; 2Ch 22:5–6

• **Inquires for the particulars concerning Elisha's miracles.**
2Ki 8:4–5

• **Slain by Jehu.**
2Ki 9:14–26

JORDAN

• **A river in Palestine.**

• **Empties into the Dead Sea.**

Jos 15:5 — And the east border *was* the salt sea, *even* unto the end of Jordan. And *their* border in the north quarter *was* from the bay of the sea at the uttermost part of Jordan:

• **Fords of.**

Jgs 12:5–6

Ge 32:10 — I am not worthy of the least of all the mercies, and of all the truth, which thou hast shewed unto thy servant; for with my staff I passed over this Jordan; and now I am become two bands.

Jos 2:7 — And the men pursued after them the way to Jordan unto the fords: and as soon as they which pursued after them were gone out, they shut the gate.

Jgs 3:28 — And he said unto them, Follow after me: for the LORD hath delivered your enemies the Moabites into your hand. And they went down after him, and took the fords of Jordan toward Moab, and suffered not a man to pass over.

Jgs 7:24 — And Gideon sent messengers throughout all mount Ephraim, saying, Come down against the Midianites, and take before them the waters unto Beth-barah and Jordan. Then all the men of Ephraim gathered themselves together, and took the waters unto Beth-barah and Jordan.

Jgs 8:4 — And Gideon came to Jordan, *and* passed over, he, and the three hundred men that *were* with him, faint, yet pursuing *them*.

Jgs 10:9 — Moreover the children of Ammon passed over Jordan to fight also against Judah, and against Benjamin, and against the house of Ephraim; so that Israel was sore distressed.

2Sa 2:29 — And Abner and his men walked all that night through the plain, and passed over Jordan, and went through all Bithron, and they came to Mahanaim.

2Sa 17:22 — Then David arose, and all the people that *were* with him, and they passed over Jordan: by the morning light there lacked not one of them that was not gone over Jordan.

2Sa 17:24 — Then David came to Mahanaim. And Absalom passed over Jordan, he and all the men of Israel with him.

2Sa 19:15 — So the king returned, and came to Jordan. And Judah came to Gilgal, to go to meet the king, to conduct the king over Jordan.

2Sa 19:31 — And Barzillai the Gileadite came down from Rogelim, and went over Jordan with the king, to conduct him over Jordan.

1Ch 19:17 — And it was told David; and he gathered all Israel, and passed over Jordan, and came upon them, and set *the battle* in array against them. So when David had put the battle in array against the Syrians, they fought with him.

• **Swelling of, at harvest time.**

Jos 3:15 — And as they that bare the ark were come unto Jordan, and the feet of the priests that bare the ark were dipped in the brim of the water, (for Jordan overfloweth all his banks all the time of harvest,)

Jer 12:5 — If thou hast run with the footmen, and they have wearied thee, then how canst thou contend with horses? and *if* in the land of peace, *wherein* thou trustedst, *they wearied thee,* then how wilt thou do in the swelling of Jordan?

• **Swelling of, in the early spring.**

1Ch 12:15 — These *are* they that went over Jordan in the first month, when it had overflown all his banks; and they put to flight all *them* of the valleys, *both* toward the east, and toward the west.

• **The waters of, miraculously separated for the passage of the Israelites.**

Jos 3:1–5:1

Ps 114:3 — The sea saw *it,* and fled: Jordan was driven back.

• **The waters of, miraculously separated for the passage of Elijah.**

2Ki 2:6–8

• **The waters of, miraculously separated for the passage of Elisha.**

2Ki 2:14 — And he took the mantle of Elijah that fell from him, and smote the waters, and said, Where *is* the LORD God of Elijah? and when he also had smitten the waters, they parted hither and thither: and Elisha went over.

• **Crossed by a ferryboat.**

2Sa 19:18 — And there went over a ferry boat to carry over the king's household, and to do what he thought good. And Shimei the son of Gera fell down before the king, as he was come over Jordan;

• **Naaman washes in, for the healing of his leprosy.**

2Ki 5:10–14

• **John the Baptist baptizes in.**

Mt 3:6 — And were baptized of him in Jordan, confessing their sins.

Mk 1:5 — And there went out unto him all the land of Judaea, and they of Jerusalem, and were all baptized of him in the river of Jordan, confessing their sins.

• **John the Baptist baptizes Jesus in.**

Mt 3:13 — Then cometh Jesus from Galilee to Jordan unto John, to be baptized of him.

Mk 1:9 — And it came to pass in those days, that Jesus came from Nazareth of Galilee, and was baptized of John in Jordan.

• Plain of.

Ge 13:10–12

• Israelites camped in.

Nu 22:1 — And the children of Israel set forward, and pitched in the plains of Moab on this side Jordan *by* Jericho.

Nu 26:3 — And Moses and Eleazar the priest spake with them in the plains of Moab by Jordan *near* Jericho, saying,

Nu 26:63 — These *are* they that were numbered by Moses and Eleazar the priest, who numbered the children of Israel in the plains of Moab by Jordan *near* Jericho.

• Solomon's foundry in.

1Ki 7:46 — In the plain of Jordan did the king cast them, in the clay ground between Succoth and Zarthan.

2Ch 4:17 — In the plain of Jordan did the king cast them, in the clay ground between Succoth and Zeredathah.

JORIM • An ancestor of Jesus.

Lk 3:29 — Which was *the son* of Jose, which was *the son* of Eliezer, which was *the son* of Jorim, which was *the son* of Matthat, which was *the son* of Levi,

JORKOAM • Descendant of Caleb.

1Ch 2:44 — And Shema begat Raham, the father of Jorkoam: and Rekem begat Shammai.

JOSABAD • A famous archer who joined David at Ziklag.

1Ch 12:4 — And Ismaiah the Gibeonite, a mighty man among the thirty, and over the thirty; and Jeremiah, and Jahaziel, and Johanan, and Josabad the Gederathite,

JOSAPHAT ✦See: Jehoshaphat

JOSE • An ancestor of Jesus.

Lk 3:29 — Which was *the son* of Jose, which was *the son* of Eliezer, which was *the son* of Jorim, which was *the son* of Matthat, which was *the son* of Levi,

JOSEDECH ✦See: Jehozadak

JOSEPH, Husband of Mary

Mt 1:18–25

Mt 13:55 — Is not this the carpenter's son? is not his mother called Mary? and his brethren, James, and Joses, and Simon, and Judas?

Mk 6:3 — Is not this the carpenter, the son of Mary, the brother of James, and Joses, and of Juda, and Simon? and are not his sisters here with us? And they were offended at him.

Lk 1:27 — To a virgin espoused to a man whose name was Joseph, of the house of David; and the virgin's name *was* Mary.

• His genealogy.

Mt 1:1–16; Lk 3:23–38

• An angel appears and testifies to the innocency of his betrothed.

Mt 1:19–24

• Dwells at Nazareth.

Lk 2:4 — And Joseph also went up from Galilee, out of the city of Nazareth, into Judaea, unto the city of David, which is called Bethlehem; (because he was of the house and lineage of David:)

• Belongs to the city of Bethlehem.

Lk 2:4 — And Joseph also went up from Galilee, out of the city of Nazareth, into Judaea, unto the city of David, which is called Bethlehem; (because he was of the house and lineage of David:)

• Goes to Bethlehem to be enrolled.

Lk 2:1–4

• Jesus born to.

Mt 1:25 — And knew her not till she had brought forth her firstborn son: and he called his name JESUS.

Lk 2:7 — And she brought forth her firstborn son, and wrapped him in swaddling clothes, and laid him in a manger; because there was no room for them in the inn.

• Presents Jesus in the temple.

Lk 2:22–39

• Returns to Nazareth.

Lk 2:39 — And when they had performed all things according to the law of the Lord, they returned into Galilee, to their own city Nazareth.

• Warned in a dream to escape to Egypt in order to save the child's life.

Mt 2:13–15

• Warned in a dream to return to Nazareth.

Mt 2:19–23

• Attends the annual feast at Jerusalem with his family.

Lk 2:42–51

JOSEPH, Other

• Father of Igal the spy.

Nu 13:7 — Of the tribe of Issachar, Igal the son of Joseph.

• Of the sons of Asaph.

1Ch 25:2 — Of the sons of Asaph; Zaccur, and Joseph, and Nethaniah, and Asarelah, the sons of Asaph under the hands of Asaph, which prophesied according to the order of the king.

1Ch 25:9 — Now the first lot came forth for Asaph to Joseph: the second to Gedaliah, who with his brethren and sons *were* twelve:

• A priest.

Ne 12:14 — Of Melicu, Jonathan; of Shebaniah, Joseph;

• Of Arimathaea.

• Begs the body of Jesus for burial in his own tomb.

Mt 27:57–60; Mk 15:42–47; Lk 23:50–56; Jn 19:38–42

• Three ancestors of Joseph.

Lk 3:24 — Which was *the son* of Matthat, which was *the son* of Levi, which was *the son* of Melchi, which was *the son* of Janna, which was *the son* of Joseph,

Lk 3:26 — Which was *the son* of Maath, which was *the son* of Mattathias, which was *the son* of Semei, which was *the son* of Joseph, which was *the son* of Juda,

Lk 3:30 — Which was *the son* of Simeon, which was *the son* of Juda, which was *the son* of Joseph, which was *the son* of Jonan, which was *the son* of Eliakim,

• Called also Barsabas, surnamed Justus.

• One of the two persons nominated to replace Judas.

Ac 1:21–23

• A designation of the ten tribes of Israel.

Am 5:6 — Seek the LORD, and ye shall live; lest he break out like fire in the house of Joseph, and devour *it,* and *there be* none to quench *it* in Bethel.

JOSEPH, Son of Jacob

Ge 30:24 — And she called his name Joseph; and said, The LORD shall add to me another son.

• Personal appearance of.

Ge 39:6 — And he left all that he had in Joseph's hand; and he knew not ought he had, save the bread which he did eat. And Joseph was *a* goodly *person,* and well favoured.

• His father's favorite child.

Ge 37:3–4

Ge 33:2 — And he put the handmaids and their children foremost, and Leah and her children after, and Rachel and Joseph hindermost.

Ge 37:35 — And all his sons and all his daughters rose up to comfort him; but he refused to be comforted; and he said, For I will go down into the grave unto my son mourning. Thus his father wept for him.

Ge 48:22 — Moreover I have given to thee one portion above thy brethren, which I took out of the hand of the Amorite with my sword and with my bow.

1Ch 5:2 — For Judah prevailed above his brethren, and of him *came* the chief ruler; but the birthright *was* Joseph's:)

Jn 4:5 — Then cometh he to a city of Samaria, which is called Sychar, near to the parcel of ground that Jacob gave to his son Joseph.

• His father's partiality for, excites the jealousy of his brethren.

Ge 37:18–28

Ge 37:4 — And when his brethren saw that their father loved him more than all his brethren, they hated him, and could not speak peaceably unto him.

Ge 37:11 — And his brethren envied him; but his father observed the saying.

Ps 105:17 — He sent a man before them, *even* Joseph, *who* was sold for a servant:

Ac 7:9 — And the patriarchs, moved with envy, sold Joseph into Egypt: but God was with him,

• His prophetic dreams of his fortunes in Egypt.

Ge 37:5–11

• Sold into Egypt.

Ge 37:27–28

• Is falsely reported to his father as killed by wild beasts.

Ge 37:29–35

• Is bought by Potiphar, an officer of Pharaoh.

Ge 37:36 — And the Midianites sold him into Egypt unto Potiphar, an officer of Pharaoh's, *and* captain of the guard.

• Is prospered of God.

Ge 39:2–5

Ge 39:21 — But the LORD was with Joseph, and shewed him mercy, and gave him favour in the sight of the keeper of the prison.

Ge 39:23 — The keeper of the prison looked not to any thing *that was* under his hand; because the LORD was with him, and *that* which he did, the LORD made *it* to prosper.

• Is falsely accused, and cast into prison; is delivered by the friendship of another prisoner.

Ge 39:1–40:23

Ps 105:18 — Whose feet they hurt with fetters: he was laid in iron:

• Is an interpreter of dreams.

• Of the two prisoners.

Ge 40:5–23

• Of Pharaoh.

Ge 41:1–37

• His name is changed to Zaphnath-paaneah.

Ge 41:45 — And Pharaoh called Joseph's name Zaphnath-paaneah; and he gave him to wife Asenath the daughter of Poti-pherah priest of On. And Joseph went out over *all* the land of Egypt.

• Is promoted to authority next to Pharaoh at thirty years of age.

Ge 41:37–46; Ps 105:19–22

• Takes to wife the daughter of the priest of On.

Ge 41:45 — And Pharaoh called Joseph's name Zaphnath-paaneah; and he gave him to wife Asenath the daughter of Poti-pherah priest of On. And Joseph went out over *all* the land of Egypt.

• Provides against the years of famine.

Ge 41:46–57

• Exports the produce of Egypt to other countries.

Ge 41:57 — And all countries came into Egypt to Joseph for to buy *corn;* because that the famine was so sore in all lands.

• Sells stores of food to people of Egypt, exacting their money, flocks, herds, lands, lives.

Ge 47:13–26

• Exempts the priests from the exactions.

Ge 47:22 — Only the land of the priests bought he not; for the priests had a portion *assigned them* of

Pharaoh, and did eat their portion which Pharaoh gave them: wherefore they sold not their lands.

Ge 47:26 — And Joseph made it a law over the land of Egypt unto this day, *that* Pharaoh should have the fifth *part;* except the land of the priests only, *which* became not Pharaoh's.

• His father sends down into Egypt to buy corn.

Ge 42:1–44:34

• Reveals himself; sends for his father; provides the land and sustains them during the famine.

Ge 45:1–47:12

• His two sons.

Ge 41:50 — And unto Joseph were born two sons before the years of famine came, which Asenath the daughter of Poti-pherah priest of On bare unto him.

Ge 41:52 — And the name of the second called he Ephraim: For God hath caused me to be fruitful in the land of my affliction.

See: Ephraim

See: Manasseh

• Mourns the death of his father.

Ge 50:1–14

• Exacts a pledge from his brethren to convey his remains to Canaan.

Ge 50:24–25

Ex 13:19 — And Moses took the bones of Joseph with him: for he had straitly sworn the children of Israel, saying, God will surely visit you; and ye shall carry up my bones away hence with you.

Jos 24:32 — And the bones of Joseph, which the children of Israel brought up out of Egypt, buried they in Shechem, in a parcel of ground which Jacob bought of the sons of Hamor the father of Shechem for an hundred pieces of silver: and it became the inheritance of the children of Joseph.

Ac 7:16 — And were carried over into Sychem, and laid in the sepulchre that Abraham bought for a sum of money of the sons of Emmor *the father* of Sychem.

Heb 11:22 — By faith Joseph, when he died, made mention of the departing of the children of Israel; and gave commandment concerning his bones.

• Death of.

Ge 50:22–26

• Kindness of heart.

Ge 40:7–8

• His integrity.

Ge 39:7–12

• His humility.

Ge 45:7–9

Ge 41:16 — And Joseph answered Pharaoh, saying, *It is* not in me: God shall give Pharaoh an answer of peace.

• His wisdom.

Ge 41:33–57

• His piety.

Ge 41:51–52

• His faith.

Ge 45:5–8

• Was a prophet.

Ge 41:38–39

Ge 50:25 — And Joseph took an oath of the children of Israel, saying, God will surely visit you, and ye shall carry up my bones from hence.

Ex 13:19 — And Moses took the bones of Joseph with him: for he had straitly sworn the children of Israel, saying, God will surely visit you; and ye shall carry up my bones away hence with you.

• God's providence with.

Ge 39:2–5; Ps 105:17–22

• His sons conjointly called Joseph.

Dt 33:13–17

• Descendants of.

Nu 26:28–37

Ge 46:20 — And unto Joseph in the land of Egypt were born Manasseh and Ephraim, which Asenath the daughter of Poti-pherah priest of On bare unto him.

JOSES

• One of the brethren of Jesus.

Mt 13:55 — Is not this the carpenter's son? is not his mother called Mary? and his brethren, James, and Joses, and Simon, and Judas?

Mt 27:56 — Among which was Mary Magdalene, and Mary the mother of James and Joses, and the mother of Zebedee's children.

Mk 6:3 — Is not this the carpenter, the son of Mary, the brother of James, and Joses, and of Juda, and Simon? and are not his sisters here with us? And they were offended at him.

Mk 15:40 — There were also women looking on afar off: among whom was Mary Magdalene, and Mary the mother of James the less and of Joses, and Salome;

Mk 15:47 — And Mary Magdalene and Mary *the mother* of Joses beheld where he was laid.

• A Levite. Surnamed Barnabas by the apostles.

Ac 4:36 — And Joses, who by the apostles was surnamed Barnabas, (which is, being interpreted, The son of consolation,) a Levite, *and* of the country of Cyprus,

JOSHAH • A descendant of Simeon.

1Ch 4:34 — And Meshobab, and Jamlech, and Joshah the son of Amaziah,

JOSHAPHAT • One of David's valiant men.

1Ch 11:43 — Hanan the son of Maachah, and Joshaphat the Mithnite,

JOSHAVIAH • One of David's bodyguards.

1Ch 11:46 — Eliel the Mahavite, and Jeribai, and Joshaviah, the sons of Elnaam, and Ithmah the Moabite,

JOSHBEKASHAH • Son of Heman.

1Ch 25:4 — Of Heman: the sons of Heman; Bukkiah, Mattaniah, Uzziel, Shebuel, and Jerimoth, Hananiah, Hanani, Eliathah, Giddalti, and Romamti-ezer, Joshbekashah, Mallothi, Hothir, *and* Mahazioth:

1Ch 25:24 — The seventeenth to Joshbekashah, *he*, his sons, and his brethren, *were* twelve:

JOSHUA

• Called also Jehoshua, and Jehoshuah, and Oshea. Son of Nun.

Nu 13:8 — Of the tribe of Ephraim, Oshea the son of Nun.

1Ch 7:27 — Non his son, Jehoshuah his son.

• Intimately associated with Moses.

Ex 24:13 — And Moses rose up, and his minister Joshua: and Moses went up into the mount of God.

Ex 32:17 — And when Joshua heard the noise of the people as they shouted, he said unto Moses, *There is* a noise of war in the camp.

Ex 33:11 — And the LORD spake unto Moses face to face, as a man speaketh unto his friend. And he turned again into the camp: but his servant Joshua, the son of Nun, a young man, departed not out of the tabernacle.

• A religious zealot.

Nu 11:28 — And Joshua the son of Nun, the servant of Moses, *one* of his young men, answered and said, My lord Moses, forbid them.

• Sent with others to view the promised land.

Nu 13:8 — Of the tribe of Ephraim, Oshea the son of Nun.

• Makes favorable report.

Nu 14:6–10

• Rewarded for his courage and fidelity.

Nu 14:30 — Doubtless ye shall not come into the land, *concerning* which I sware to make you dwell therein, save Caleb the son of Jephunneh, and Joshua the son of Nun.

Nu 14:38 — But Joshua the son of Nun, and Caleb the son of Jephunneh, *which were* of the men that went to search the land, lived *still*.

Nu 32:12 — Save Caleb the son of Jephunneh the Kenezite, and Joshua the son of Nun: for they have wholly followed the LORD.

• Commissioned, ordained, and charged with the responsibilities of Moses' office.

Nu 27:18–23

Dt 1:38 — *But* Joshua the son of Nun, which standeth before thee, he shall go in thither: encourage him: for he shall cause Israel to inherit it.

Dt 3:28 — But charge Joshua, and encourage him, and strengthen him: for he shall go over before this people, and he shall cause them to inherit the land which thou shalt see.

Dt 31:3 — The LORD thy God, he will go over before thee, *and* he will destroy these nations from before thee, and thou shalt possess them: *and* Joshua, he shall go over before thee, as the LORD hath said.

Dt 31:7 — And Moses called unto Joshua, and said unto him in the sight of all Israel, Be strong and of a good courage: for thou must go with this people unto the land which the LORD hath sworn unto their fathers to give them; and thou shalt cause them to inherit it.

Dt 31:23 — And he gave Joshua the son of Nun a charge, and said, Be strong and of a good courage: for thou shalt bring the children of Israel into the land which I sware unto them: and I will be with thee.

Dt 34:9 — And Joshua the son of Nun was full of the spirit of wisdom; for Moses had laid his hands upon him: and the children of Israel hearkened unto him, and did as the LORD commanded Moses.

• Divinely inspired.

Nu 27:18 — And the LORD said unto Moses, Take thee Joshua the son of Nun, a man in whom *is* the spirit, and lay thine hand upon him;

Dt 34:9 — And Joshua the son of Nun was full of the spirit of wisdom; for Moses had laid his hands upon him: and the children of Israel hearkened unto him, and did as the LORD commanded Moses.

Jos 1:5 — There shall not any man be able to stand before thee all the days of thy life: as I was with Moses, *so* I will be with thee: I will not fail thee, nor forsake thee.

Jos 1:9 — Have not I commanded thee? Be strong and of a good courage; be not afraid, neither be thou dismayed: for the LORD thy God *is* with thee whithersoever thou goest.

Jos 3:7 — And the LORD said unto Joshua, This day will I begin to magnify thee in the sight of all Israel, that they may know that, as I was with Moses, so I will be with thee.

Jos 8:8 — And it shall be, when ye have taken the city, *that* ye shall set the city on fire: according to the commandment of the LORD shall ye do. See, I have commanded you.

• His life miraculously preserved when he made a favorable report of the land.

Nu 14:10 — But all the congregation bade stone them with stones. And the glory of the LORD appeared in the tabernacle of the congregation before all the children of Israel.

• Promises to.

Jos 1:5–9

• Leads the people into the land of Canaan.

Jos 1:1–4:24

Ac 7:45 — Which also our fathers that came after brought in with Jesus into the possession of the

Gentiles, whom God drave out before the face of our fathers, unto the days of David;

Heb 4:8 — For if Jesus had given them rest, then would he not afterward have spoken of another day.

• Renews circumcision of the children of Israel; reestablishes the passover; has a vision of the angel of God.

Jos 5:1–15

• Besieges and takes Jericho.

Jos 6:1–27

• Takes Ai.

Jos 7:1–8:35

• Makes a league with the Gibeonites.

Jos 9:3–27

• The kings of the six nations of the Canaanites confederate against him.

Jos 9:1–2

• The kings of the six nations of the Canaanites make war upon the Gibeonites; are defeated and slain.

Jos 10:1–43

• Defeats seven other kings.

Jos 10:28–43

• Makes conquest of Hazor.

Jos 11:1–23

• Completes the conquest of the whole land.

Jos 11:23 — So Joshua took the whole land, according to all that the LORD said unto Moses; and Joshua gave it for an inheritance unto Israel according to their divisions by their tribes. And the land rested from war.

• List of the kings whom Joshua smote.

Jos 12:1–24

• Allots the land.

Jos 13:1–19:51

• Sets the tabernacle up in Shiloh.

Jos 18:1 — And the whole congregation of the children of Israel assembled together at Shiloh, and set up the tabernacle of the congregation there. And the land was subdued before them.

• Sets apart cities of refuge.

Jos 20:1–9

• Sets apart forty-eight cities for the Levites.

Jos 21:1–45

• Exhortation of, before his death.

Jos 23:1–24:33

• Survives the Israelites who refused to enter Canaan.

Nu 26:63–65

• His portion of the land.

Jos 19:49–50

• Death and burial of.

Jos 24:29–30

• Esteem in which he was held.

Jos 1:16–18

• Faith of.

Jos 6:16 — And it came to pass at the seventh time, when the priests blew with the trumpets, Joshua said unto the people, Shout; for the LORD hath given you the city.

• Military genius of as exhibited.

• At the defeat of the Amalekites.

Ex 17:13 — And Joshua discomfited Amalek and his people with the edge of the sword.

• At Ai.

Jos 8:1–35

• In Gibeon.

Jos 10:1–43

• At Hazor.

Jos 11:1–23

• Age of, at death.

Jgs 2:8 — And Joshua the son of Nun, the servant of the LORD, died, *being* an hundred and ten years old.

• An Israelite.

1Sa 6:14 — And the cart came into the field of Joshua, a Beth-shemite, and stood there, where *there was* a great stone: and they clave the wood of the cart, and offered the kine a burnt offering unto the LORD.

1Sa 6:18 — And the golden mice, *according to* the number of all the cities of the Philistines *belonging* to the five lords, *both* of fenced cities, and of country villages, even unto the great *stone* of Abel, whereon they set down the ark of the LORD: *which stone remaineth* unto this day in the field of Joshua, the Beth-shemite.

• A governor of Jerusalem.

2Ki 23:8 — And he brought all the priests out of the cities of Judah, and defiled the high places where the priests had burned incense, from Geba to Beer-sheba, and brake down the high places of the gates that *were* in the entering in of the gate of Joshua the governor of the city, which *were* on a man's left hand at the gate of the city.

• The high priest of the captivity; called also Jeshuia.

Ezr 2:2 — Which came with Zerubbabel: Jeshua, Nehemiah, Seraiah, Reelaiah, Mordecai, Bilshan, Mizpar, Bigvai, Rehum, Baanah. The number of the men of the people of Israel:

• Assists Zerubbabel in restoring the temple.

Ezr 3:1–4:6; 5:1–17; Hag 1:12–14

Hag 1:1 — In the second year of Darius the king, in the sixth month, in the first day of the month, came the word of the LORD by Haggai the prophet unto Zerubbabel the son of Shealtiel, governor of Judah, and to Joshua the son of Josedech, the high priest, saying,

Hag 2:2 — Speak now to Zerubbabel the son of Shealtiel, governor of Judah, and to Joshua the son of Josedech, the high priest, and to the residue of the people, saying,

• Symbolic.

• Of the restoration of the church.

Zec 3:1–10; 6:9–15

JOSIAH

• King of Judah.

2Ki 21:24–22:1

1Ch 3:14 — Amon his son, Josiah his son.

2Ch 33:25 — But the people of the land slew all them that had conspired against king Amon; and the people of the land made Josiah his son king in his stead.

• Ancestor of Jesus.

Mt 1:10–11

• Slain in battle with Pharaoh-nechoh.

2Ki 23:29–30; 2Ch 35:20–24

• Lamentations for.

2Ch 35:25 — And Jeremiah lamented for Josiah: and all the singing men and the singing women spake of Josiah in their lamentations to this day, and made them an ordinance in Israel: and, behold, they *are* written in the lamentations.

• Piety of.

• Exemplified in his repairing the temple.

2Ki 22:3–7; 2Ch 34:1–4

• Solicitude when the copy of the law was discovered and read to him.

2Ki 22:8–20; 2Ch 34:14–33

• Solicitude in keeping a solemn passover.

2Ki 23:21–23; 2Ch 35:1–19

• Called Josias.

Mt 1:10–11

• Prophecies concerning.

1Ki 13:1–3

• Destroys the altar and high places of idolatry.

2Ki 23:3–20, 24–25

• Son of Zephaniah.

Zec 6:10 — Take of *them of* the captivity, *even* of Heldai, of Tobijah, and of Jedaiah, which are come from Babylon, and come thou the same day, and go into the house of Josiah the son of Zephaniah;

JOSIAS → See: Josiah; king of Judah

JOSIBIAH • A Simeonite.

1Ch 4:35 — And Joel, and Jehu the son of Josibiah, the son of Seraiah, the son of Asiel,

JOSIPHIAH • Father of a chief.

Ezr 8:10 — And of the sons of Shelomith; the son of Josiphiah, and with him an hundred and threescore males.

JOT • Vowel point in Hebrew.

Mt 5:18 — For verily I say unto you, Till heaven and earth pass, one jot or one tittle shall in no wise pass from the law, till all be fulfilled.

JOTBAH

• A place in Judah.

2Ki 21:19 — Amon *was* twenty and two years old when he began to reign, and he reigned two years in Jerusalem. And his mother's name *was* Meshullemeth, the daughter of Haruz of Jotbah.

• Called Jotbath.

Dt 10:7 — From thence they journeyed unto Gudgodah; and from Gudgodah to Jotbath, a land of rivers of waters.

JOTBATHAH • The twentieth encampment of Israel.

Nu 33:33–34

JOTHAM

• Son of Gideon.

Jgs 9:5 — And he went unto his father's house at Ophrah, and slew his brethren the sons of Jerubbaal, *being* threescore and ten persons, upon one stone: notwithstanding yet Jotham the youngest son of Jerubbaal was left; for he hid himself.

Jgs 9:57 — And all the evil of the men of Shechem did God render upon their heads: and upon them came the curse of Jotham the son of Jerubbaal.

• Rebukes the Shechemites in the parable of the trees.

Jgs 9:7–21

• Son of Azariah, king of Judah.

2Ki 15:5–7; 2Ch 26:21–27:9

2Ki 15:32 — In the second year of Pekah the son of Remaliah king of Israel began Jotham the son of Uzziah king of Judah to reign.

2Ki 15:38 — And Jotham slept with his fathers, and was buried with his fathers in the city of David his father: and Ahaz his son reigned in his stead.

1Ch 3:12 — Amaziah his son, Azariah his son, Jotham his son,

• Piety of.

2Ch 27:1–9

• The moral condition of Israel during his reign.

Hos 4:1–19

• Ancestor of Jesus.

Mt 1:9 — And Ozias begat Joatham; and Joatham begat Achaz; and Achaz begat Ezekias;

• Son of Jahdai.

1Ch 2:47 — And the sons of Jahdai; Regem, and Jotham, and Gesham, and Pelet, and Ephah, and Shaaph.

JOY

• Attributed to God.

Dt 28:63 — And it shall come to pass, *that* as the LORD rejoiced over you to do you good, and to multiply you; so the LORD will rejoice over you to destroy you, and to bring you to nought; and ye shall be plucked from off the land whither thou goest to possess it.

Dt 30:9 — And the LORD thy God will make thee plenteous in every work of thine hand, in the fruit of thy body, and in the fruit of thy cattle, and in the fruit of thy land, for good: for the LORD will again rejoice over thee for good, as he rejoiced over thy fathers:

Jer 32:41 — Yea, I will rejoice over them to do them good, and I will plant them in this land assuredly with my whole heart and with my whole soul.

- **In heaven.**
  Lk 15:10–32
- **Unclassified scriptures relating to.**
  Ps 16:5–6, 8–9; 30:11–12; 32:1–2; 63:5–7; 89:15–16; 97:11–12; 100:1–2; 119:1–2; 126:5–6; Isa 12:1–6; 35:1–2; 65:18–19; 66:10–12; Jer 31:12–14, 25–26; Lk 6:22–23; 15:6–8; 15:10–32; 24:52–53; Eph 5:18–19

Dt 12:18 — But thou must eat them before the LORD thy God in the place which the LORD thy God shall choose, thou, and thy son, and thy daughter, and thy manservant, and thy maidservant, and the Levite that *is* within thy gates: and thou shalt rejoice before the LORD thy God in all that thou puttest thine hands unto.

1Sa 2:1 — And Hannah prayed, and said, My heart rejoiceth in the LORD, mine horn is exalted in the LORD: my mouth is enlarged over mine enemies; because I rejoice in thy salvation.

1Ch 16:27 — Glory and honour *are* in his presence; strength and gladness *are* in his place.

2Ch 7:10 — And on the three and twentieth day of the seventh month he sent the people away into their tents, glad and merry in heart for the goodness that the LORD had shewed unto David, and to Solomon, and to Israel his people.

Ezr 6:22 — And kept the feast of unleavened bread seven days with joy: for the LORD had made them joyful, and turned the heart of the king of Assyria unto them, to strengthen their hands in the work of the house of God, the God of Israel.

Ne 8:10 — Then he said unto them, Go your way, eat the fat, and drink the sweet, and send portions unto them for whom nothing is prepared: for *this* day *is* holy unto our Lord: neither be ye sorry; for the joy of the LORD is your strength.

Ne 8:12 — And all the people went their way to eat, and to drink, and to send portions, and to make great mirth, because they had understood the words that were declared unto them.

Ne 12:43 — Also that day they offered great sacrifices, and rejoiced: for God had made them rejoice with great joy: the wives also and the children rejoiced: so that the joy of Jerusalem was heard even afar off.

Job 8:21 — Till he fill thy mouth with laughing, and thy lips with rejoicing.

Job 22:21 — Acquaint now thyself with him, and be at peace: thereby good shall come unto thee.

Job 22:26 — For then shalt thou have thy delight in the Almighty, and shalt lift up thy face unto God.

Job 33:26 — He shall pray unto God, and he will be favourable unto him: and he shall see his face with joy: for he will render unto man his righteousness.

Ps 2:11 — Serve the LORD with fear, and rejoice with trembling.

Ps 4:7 — Thou hast put gladness in my heart, more than in the time *that* their corn and their wine increased.

Ps 5:11 — But let all those that put their trust in thee rejoice: let them ever shout for joy, because thou defendest them: let them also that love thy name be joyful in thee.

Ps 9:2 — I will be glad and rejoice in thee: I will sing praise to thy name, O thou most High.

Ps 9:14 — That I may shew forth all thy praise in the gates of the daughter of Zion: I will rejoice in thy salvation.

Ps 13:5 — But I have trusted in thy mercy; my heart shall rejoice in thy salvation.

Ps 14:7 — Oh that the salvation of Israel *were come* out of Zion! when the LORD bringeth back the captivity of his people, Jacob shall rejoice, *and* Israel shall be glad.

Ps 16:11 — Thou wilt shew me the path of life: in thy presence *is* fulness of joy; at thy right hand *there are* pleasures for evermore.

Ps 17:15 — As for me, I will behold thy face in righteousness: I shall be satisfied, when I awake, with thy likeness.

Ps 19:8 — The statutes of the LORD *are* right, rejoicing the heart: the commandment of the LORD *is* pure, enlightening the eyes.

Ps 20:5 — We will rejoice in thy salvation, and in the name of our God we will set up *our* banners: the LORD fulfil all thy petitions.

Ps 21:1 — The king shall joy in thy strength, O LORD; and in thy salvation how greatly shall he rejoice!

Ps 21:6 — For thou hast made him most blessed for ever: thou hast made him exceeding glad with thy countenance.

Ps 28:7 — The LORD *is* my strength and my shield; my heart trusted in him, and I am helped: therefore my heart greatly rejoiceth; and with my song will I praise him.

Ps 30:5 — For his anger *endureth but* a moment; in his favour is life: weeping may endure for a night, but joy *cometh* in the morning.

Ps 32:11 — Be glad in the LORD, and rejoice, ye righteous: and shout for joy, all *ye that are* upright in heart.

Ps 33:21 — For our heart shall rejoice in him, because we have trusted in his holy name.

Ps 35:9 — And my soul shall be joyful in the LORD: it shall rejoice in his salvation.

Ps 36:8 — They shall be abundantly satisfied with the fatness of thy house; and thou shalt make them drink of the river of thy pleasures.

Ps 40:16 — Let all those that seek thee rejoice and be glad in thee: let such as love thy salvation say continually, The LORD be magnified.

Ps 42:4 — When I remember these *things,* I pour out my soul in me: for I had gone with the multitude, I went with them to the house of God, with the voice of joy and praise, with a multitude that kept holyday.

Ps 43:4 — Then will I go unto the altar of God, unto God my exceeding joy: yea, upon the harp will I praise thee, O God my God.

Ps 45:15 — With gladness and rejoicing shall they be brought: they shall enter into the king's palace.

Ps 46:4 — *There is* a river, the streams whereof shall make glad the city of God, the holy *place* of the tabernacles of the most High.

Ps 51:8 — Make me to hear joy and gladness; *that* the bones *which* thou hast broken may rejoice.

Ps 51:12 — Restore unto me the joy of thy salvation; and uphold me *with thy* free spirit.

Ps 53:6 — Oh that the salvation of Israel *were come* out of Zion! When God bringeth back the captivity of his people, Jacob shall rejoice, *and* Israel shall be glad.

Ps 63:11 — But the king shall rejoice in God; every one that sweareth by him shall glory: but the mouth of them that speak lies shall be stopped.

Ps 64:10 — The righteous shall be glad in the LORD, and shall trust in him; and all the upright in heart shall glory.

Ps 68:3 — But let the righteous be glad; let them rejoice before God: yea, let them exceedingly rejoice.

Ps 69:32 — The humble shall see *this, and* be glad: and your heart shall live that seek God.

Ps 70:4 — Let all those that seek thee rejoice and be glad in thee: and let such as love thy salvation say continually, Let God be magnified.

Ps 71:23 — My lips shall greatly rejoice when I sing unto thee; and my soul, which thou hast redeemed.

Ps 85:6 — Wilt thou not revive us again: that thy people may rejoice in thee?

Ps 104:34 — My meditation of him shall be sweet: I will be glad in the LORD.

Ps 105:3 — Glory ye in his holy name: let the heart of them rejoice that seek the LORD.

Ps 105:43 — And he brought forth his people with joy, *and* his chosen with gladness:

Ps 119:14 — I have rejoiced in the way of thy testimonies, as *much as* in all riches.

Ps 119:16 — I will delight myself in thy statutes: I will not forget thy word.

Ps 119:55 — I have remembered thy name, O LORD, in the night, and have kept thy law.

Ps 119:111 — Thy testimonies have I taken as an heritage for ever: for they *are* the rejoicing of my heart.

Ps 119:162 — I rejoice at thy word, as one that findeth great spoil.

Ps 119:165 — Great peace have they which love thy law: and nothing shall offend them.

Ps 132:16 — I will also clothe her priests with salvation: and her saints shall shout aloud for joy.

Ps 138:5 — Yea, they shall sing in the ways of the LORD: for great *is* the glory of the LORD.

Ps 149:2 — Let Israel rejoice in him that made him: let the children of Zion be joyful in their King.

Ps 149:5 — Let the saints be joyful in glory: let them sing aloud upon their beds.

Pr 10:28 — The hope of the righteous *shall be* gladness: but the expectation of the wicked shall perish.

Pr 13:9 — The light of the righteous rejoiceth: but the lamp of the wicked shall be put out.

Pr 19:23 — The fear of the LORD *tendeth* to life: and *he that hath it* shall abide satisfied; he shall not be visited with evil.

Pr 28:12 — When righteous *men* do rejoice, *there is* great glory: but when the wicked rise, a man is hidden.

Pr 29:6 — In the transgression of an evil man *there is* a snare: but the righteous doth sing and rejoice.

Ecc 2:26 — For *God* giveth to a man that *is* good in his sight wisdom, and knowledge, and joy: but to the sinner he giveth travail, to gather and to heap up, that he may give to *him that is* good before God. This also *is* vanity and vexation of spirit.

Isa 9:3 — Thou hast multiplied the nation, *and* not increased the joy: they joy before thee according to the joy in harvest, *and* as *men* rejoice when they divide the spoil.

Isa 25:9 — And it shall be said in that day, Lo, this *is* our God; we have waited for him, and he will save us: this *is* the LORD; we have waited for him, we will be glad and rejoice in his salvation.

Isa 29:19 — The meek also shall increase *their* joy in the LORD, and the poor among men shall rejoice in the Holy One of Israel.

Isa 30:29 — Ye shall have a song, as in the night *when* a holy solemnity is kept; and gladness of heart, as when one goeth with a pipe to come into the mountain of the LORD, to the mighty One of Israel.

Isa 35:10 — And the ransomed of the LORD shall return, and come to Zion with songs and everlasting joy upon their heads: they shall obtain joy and gladness, and sorrow and sighing shall flee away.

Isa 41:16 — Thou shalt fan them, and the wind shall carry them away, and the whirlwind shall scatter them: and thou shalt rejoice in the LORD, *and* shalt glory in the Holy One of Israel.

Isa 44:23 — Sing, O ye heavens; for the LORD hath done *it:* shout, ye lower parts of the earth: break forth into singing, ye mountains, O forest, and every tree therein: for the LORD hath redeemed Jacob, and glorified himself in Israel.

Isa 49:13 — Sing, O heavens; and be joyful, O earth; and break forth into singing, O mountains: for the LORD hath comforted his people, and will have mercy upon his afflicted.

Isa 51:11 — Therefore the redeemed of the LORD shall return, and come with singing unto Zion; and everlasting joy *shall be* upon their head: they shall obtain gladness and joy; *and* sorrow and mourning shall flee away.

Isa 52:9 — Break forth into joy, sing together, ye waste places of Jerusalem: for the LORD hath comforted his people, he hath redeemed Jerusalem.

Isa 55:12 — For ye shall go out with joy, and be led forth with peace: the mountains and the hills shall break forth before you into singing, and all the trees of the field shall clap *their* hands.

Isa 56:7 — Even them will I bring to my holy mountain, and make them joyful in my house of prayer: their burnt offerings and their sacrifices *shall be* accepted upon mine altar; for mine house shall be called an house of prayer for all people.

Isa 61:3 — To appoint unto them that mourn in Zion, to give unto them beauty for ashes, the oil of joy for mourning, the garment of praise for the spirit of heaviness; that they might be called trees of righteousness, the planting of the LORD, that he might be glorified.

Isa 61:7 — For your shame *ye shall have* double; and *for* confusion they shall rejoice in their portion: therefore in their land they shall possess the double: everlasting joy shall be unto them.

Isa 61:10 — I will greatly rejoice in the LORD, my soul shall be joyful in my God; for he hath clothed me with the garments of salvation, he hath covered me with the robe of righteousness, as a bridegroom decketh *himself* with ornaments, and as a bride adorneth *herself* with her jewels.

Isa 65:14 — Behold, my servants shall sing for joy of heart, but ye shall cry for sorrow of heart, and shall howl for vexation of spirit.

Isa 66:14 — And when ye see *this,* your heart shall rejoice, and your bones shall flourish like an herb: and the hand of the LORD shall be known toward his servants, and *his* indignation toward his enemies.

Jer 15:16 — Thy words were found, and I did eat them; and thy word was unto me the joy and rejoicing of mine heart: for I am called by thy name, O LORD God of hosts.

Jer 33:6 — Behold, I will bring it health and cure, and I will cure them, and will reveal unto them the abundance of peace and truth.

Jer 33:11 — The voice of joy, and the voice of gladness, the voice of the bridegroom, and the voice of the bride, the voice of them that shall say, Praise the LORD of hosts: for the LORD *is* good; for his mercy *endureth* for ever: *and* of them that shall bring the sacrifice of praise into the house of the LORD. For I will cause to return the captivity of the land, as at the first, saith the LORD.

Joel 2:23 — Be glad then, ye children of Zion, and rejoice in the LORD your God: for he hath given you the former rain moderately, and he will cause to come down for you the rain, the former rain, and the latter rain in the first *month.*

Na 1:15 — Behold upon the mountains the feet of him that bringeth good tidings, that publisheth peace! O Judah, keep thy solemn feasts, perform thy vows: for the wicked shall no more pass through thee; he is utterly cut off.

Hab 3:18 — Yet I will rejoice in the LORD, I will joy in the God of my salvation.

Zep 3:14 — Sing, O daughter of Zion; shout, O Israel; be glad and rejoice with all the heart, O daughter of Jerusalem.

Hag 2:9 — The glory of this latter house shall be greater than of the former, saith the LORD of hosts: and in this place will I give peace, saith the LORD of hosts.

Zec 2:10 — Sing and rejoice, O daughter of Zion: for, lo, I come, and I will dwell in the midst of thee, saith the LORD.

Zec 9:9 — Rejoice greatly, O daughter of Zion; shout, O daughter of Jerusalem: behold, thy King cometh unto thee: he *is* just, and having salvation; lowly, and riding upon an ass, and upon a colt the foal of an ass.

Zec 10:7 — And *they of* Ephraim shall be like a mighty *man,* and their heart shall rejoice as through wine: yea, their children shall see *it,* and be glad; their heart shall rejoice in the LORD.

Mt 18:13 — And if so be that he find it, verily I say unto you, he rejoiceth more of *that* sheep, than of the ninety and nine which went not astray.

Mt 25:21 — His lord said unto him, Well done, *thou* good and faithful servant: thou hast been faithful over a few things, I will make thee ruler over many things: enter thou into the joy of thy lord.

Lk 1:47 — And my spirit hath rejoiced in God my Saviour.

Lk 2:10 — And the angel said unto them, Fear not: for, behold, I bring you good tidings of great joy, which shall be to all people.

Lk 10:20 — Notwithstanding in this rejoice not, that the spirits are subject unto you; but rather rejoice, because your names are written in heaven.

Jn 16:20 — Verily, verily, I say unto you, That ye shall weep and lament, but the world shall rejoice: and ye shall be sorrowful, but your sorrow shall be turned into joy.

Jn 16:22 — And ye now therefore have sorrow: but I will see you again, and your heart shall rejoice, and your joy no man taketh from you.

Jn 16:24 — Hitherto have ye asked nothing in my name: ask, and ye shall receive, that your joy may be full.

Jn 16:33 — These things I have spoken unto you, that in me ye might have peace. In the world ye shall have tribulation: but be of good cheer; I have overcome the world.

Jn 17:13 — And now come I to thee; and these things I speak in the world, that they might have my joy fulfilled in themselves.

Ac 2:28 — Thou hast made known to me the ways of life; thou shalt make me full of joy with thy countenance.

Ac 8:8 — And there was great joy in that city.

Ac 8:39 — And when they were come up out of the water, the Spirit of the Lord caught away Philip, that the eunuch saw him no more: and he went on his way rejoicing.

Ac 13:52 — And the disciples were filled with joy, and with the Holy Ghost.

Ac 16:25 — And at midnight Paul and Silas prayed, and sang praises unto God: and the prisoners heard them.

Ac 16:34 — And when he had brought them into his house, he set meat before them, and rejoiced, believing in God with all his house.

Ro 5:2 — By whom also we have access by faith into this grace wherein we stand, and rejoice in hope of the glory of God.

Ro 5:11 — And not only *so,* but we also joy in God through our Lord Jesus Christ, by whom we have now received the atonement.

Ro 12:12 — Rejoicing in hope; patient in tribulation; continuing instant in prayer;

Ro 14:17 — For the kingdom of God is not meat and drink; but righteousness, and peace, and joy in the Holy Ghost.

Ro 15:13 — Now the God of hope fill you with all joy and peace in believing, that ye may abound in hope, through the power of the Holy Ghost.

2Co 1:12 — For our rejoicing is this, the testimony of our conscience, that in simplicity and godly sincerity, not with fleshly wisdom, but by the grace of God, we have had our conversation in the world, and more abundantly to you-ward.

2Co 1:24 — Not for that we have dominion over your faith, but are helpers of your joy: for by faith ye stand.

2Co 6:10 — As sorrowful, yet alway rejoicing; as poor, yet making many rich; as having nothing, and *yet* possessing all things.

2Co 7:4 — Great *is* my boldness of speech toward you, great *is* my glorying of you: I am filled with comfort, I am exceeding joyful in all our tribulation.

2Co 8:2 — How that in a great trial of affliction the abundance of their joy and their deep poverty abounded unto the riches of their liberality.

2Co 12:10 — Therefore I take pleasure in infirmities, in reproaches, in necessities, in persecutions, in distresses for Christ's sake: for when I am weak, then am I strong.

Gal 5:22 — But the fruit of the Spirit is love, joy, peace, longsuffering, gentleness, goodness, faith,

Php 3:3 — For we are the circumcision, which worship God in the spirit, and rejoice in Christ Jesus, and have no confidence in the flesh.

Php 4:4 — Rejoice in the Lord alway: *and* again I say, Rejoice.

Col 1:11 — Strengthened with all might, according to his glorious power, unto all patience and longsuffering with joyfulness;

1Th 1:6 — And ye became followers of us, and of the Lord, having received the word in much affliction, with joy of the Holy Ghost:

1Th 5:16 — Rejoice evermore.

Heb 10:34 — For ye had compassion of me in my bonds, and took joyfully the spoiling of your goods, knowing in yourselves that ye have in heaven a better and an enduring substance.

Jas 1:2 — My brethren, count it all joy when ye fall into divers temptations;

Jas 5:13 — Is any among you afflicted? let him pray. Is any merry? let him sing psalms.

1Pe 1:8 — Whom having not seen, ye love; in whom, though now ye see *him* not, yet believing, ye rejoice with joy unspeakable and full of glory:

1Pe 4:13 — But rejoice, inasmuch as ye are partakers of Christ's sufferings; that, when his glory shall be revealed, ye may be glad also with exceeding joy.

1Jn 1:4 — And these things write we unto you, that your joy may be full.

Jude 1:24 — Now unto him that is able to keep you from falling, and to present *you* faultless before the presence of his glory with exceeding joy,

See: Happiness

See: Praise

See: Thanksgiving

• Instances of the wicked.

Job 20:5; Pr 14:13; 15:21; Ecc 2:10; 7:6; 11:8–9; Isa 16:10; Jas 4:9

• Instances of, Old Testament.

• Moses and the Israelites, when Pharaoh and his army were destroyed.

Ex 15:1–22

• Deborah and the Israelites, when Sisera was overthrown.

Jgs 5:1–31

• Jephthah's daughter, when he returned from his victory over the Ammonites.

Jgs 11:34

• Hannah, when Samuel was born.

1Sa 2:1–11

• Naomi, when Boaz showed kindness to Ruth.

Ru 2:20; 4:14

• The Israelites.

• When Saul was presented as their king.

1Sa 10:24 — And Samuel said to all the people, See ye him whom the LORD hath chosen, that *there is* none like him among all the people? And all the people shouted, and said, God save the king.

• When David slew Goliath.

1Sa 18:6–7

• When they repaired to David to Hebron to make him king.

1Ch 12:40 — Moreover they that were nigh them, *even* unto Issachar and Zebulun and Naphtali, brought bread on asses, and on camels, and on mules, and on oxen, *and* meat, meal, cakes of figs, and bunches of raisins, and wine, and oil, and oxen, and sheep abundantly: for *there was* joy in Israel.

• When they took the ark from Kirjath-jearim.

1Ch 13:8 — And David and all Israel played before God with all *their* might, and with singing, and with harps, and with psalteries, and with timbrels, and with cymbals, and with trumpets.

• When they brought the ark from the house of Obed-edom to Jerusalem.

1Ch 15:16 — And David spake to the chief of the Levites to appoint their brethren *to be* the singers with instruments of musick, psalteries and harps and cymbals, sounding, by lifting up the voice with joy.

1Ch 15:25 — So David, and the elders of Israel, and the captains over thousands, went to bring up the ark of the covenant of the LORD out of the house of Obed-edom with joy.

1Ch 15:28 — Thus all Israel brought up the ark of the covenant of the LORD with shouting, and with sound of the cornet, and with trumpets, and with cymbals, making a noise with psalteries and harps.

• When they made gifts to the house of God.

1Ch 29:9 — Then the people rejoiced, for that they offered willingly, because with perfect heart they offered willingly to the LORD: and David the king also rejoiced with great joy.

• When they kept the dedication of the temple, and the feast of tabernacles under Ezra.

Ezr 6:16 — And the children of Israel, the priests, and the Levites, and the rest of the children of the captivity, kept the dedication of this house of God with joy,

Ezr 6:22 — And kept the feast of unleavened bread seven days with joy: for the LORD had made them joyful, and turned the heart of the king of Assyria unto them, to strengthen their hands in the work of the house of God, the God of Israel.

- **The Jews, after hearing, anew, the word of God.**
  Ne 8:9–18
- **The Jews, when they turned away from idolatry.**
  2Ch 15:14–15
  2Ch 23:18 — Also Jehoiada appointed the offices of the house of the LORD by the hand of the priests the Levites, whom David had distributed in the house of the LORD, to offer the burnt offerings of the LORD, as *it is* written in the law of Moses, with rejoicing and with singing, *as it was ordained* by David.
  2Ch 23:21 — And all the people of the land rejoiced: and the city was quiet, after that they had slain Athaliah with the sword.
  2Ch 29:30 — Moreover Hezekiah the king and the princes commanded the Levites to sing praise unto the LORD with the words of David, and of Asaph the seer. And they sang praises with gladness, and they bowed their heads and worshipped.
  2Ch 29:36 — And Hezekiah rejoiced, and all the people, that God had prepared the people: for the thing was *done* suddenly.
  2Ch 30:21 — And the children of Israel that were present at Jerusalem kept the feast of unleavened bread seven days with great gladness: and the Levites and the priests praised the LORD day by day, *singing* with loud instruments unto the LORD.
  2Ch 30:23 — And the whole assembly took counsel to keep other seven days: and they kept *other* seven days with gladness.
  2Ch 30:26 — So there was great joy in Jerusalem: for since the time of Solomon the son of David king of Israel *there was* not the like in Jerusalem.
- **The Jews, when the wall of Jerusalem was dedicated.**
  Ne 12:43 — Also that day they offered great sacrifices, and rejoiced: for God had made them rejoice with great joy: the wives also and the children rejoiced: so that the joy of Jerusalem was heard even afar off.
- **The Jews, when the foundation of the second temple was laid.**
  Ezr 3:11–13
- **David, over the offerings of the princes and people for the house of God.**
  1Ch 29:10–19
- **Jews, over the hanging of Haman.**
  Est 8:15–16
  Est 7:10 — So they hanged Haman on the gallows that he had prepared for Mordecai. Then was the king's wrath pacified.

- **Instances of, New Testament.**
  - **Elisabeth, when Mary visited her.**
    Lk 1:5–44
  - **Mary, when she visited Elisabeth.**
    Lk 1:46–56
  - **Zecharias, when John was born.**
    Lk 1:67–79
  - **Angels, when Jesus was born.**
    Lk 2:13–14
  - **The shepherds, when they saw the infant Jesus.**
    Lk 2:20
  - **The Magi.**
    Mt 2:10
  - **Simeon, when Jesus was presented in the temple.**
    Lk 2:28–32
  - **The disciples, because the devils were subject to them.**
    Lk 10:17
  - **The father, when his prodigal son returns.**
    Lk 15:20–32
  - **Angels, when sinners repent.**
    Lk 15:7; 15:10
  - **The disciples, when Jesus triumphantly entered Jerusalem.**
    Mt 21:8–9; Mk 11:8–10
  - **The women who returned from the Lord's sepulchre.**
    Mt 28:8
  - **The disciple, after the resurrection of Jesus.**
    Lk 24:41
  - **The disciples in the temple, after the ascension of Jesus.**
    Lk 24:53
  - **The disciples in the temple, because they had received the gift of the Holy Ghost.**
    Ac 2:46–47
  - **The impotent man, healed by Peter.**
    Ac 3:8
  - **Paul, when he went up to Jerusalem.**
    Ac 20:22–24
  - **Paul and Silas, in the jail at Philippi.**
    Ac 16:25
  - **Rhoda, when she heard Peter at the gate.**
    Ac 12:14
  - **The disciples at Jerusalem, when Peter told them about the conversion of Cornelius and other Gentiles.**
    Ac 11:18

• Barnabas, when he saw the success of the gospel at Antioch.
Ac 11:22–23

• Paul and the Corinthians, because the excommunicated member repented.
2Co 1:24; 2:3

• Paul and Titus, because of the hospitality of the Corinthians.
Ro 15:32; 1Co 16:18; 2Co 7:13; 8:6

• The Macedonians, when they made a contribution for the Christians at Jerusalem.
2Co 8:2

• Paul, when he prayed for the Philippians.
Php 1:4

• Thessalonians, when they believed Paul's gospel.
1Th 1:6

• Paul, rejoicing over his converts.
1Th 2:19–20; 3:9; Phm 1:7

• Early Christians, when they believed in Jesus.
1Pe 1:8–9

JOZABAD

• Two men of Manasseh.

1Ch 12:20 — As he went to Ziklag, there fell to him of Manasseh, Adnah, and Jozabad, and Jediael, and Michael, and Jozabad, and Elihu, and Zilthai, captains of the thousands that *were* of Manasseh.

• Two Levites.

2Ch 31:13 — And Jehiel, and Azaziah, and Nahath, and Asahel, and Jerimoth, and Jozabad, and Eliel, and Ismachiah, and Mahath, and Benaiah, *were* overseers under the hand of Cononiah and Shimei his brother, at the commandment of Hezekiah the king, and Azariah the ruler of the house of God.

2Ch 35:9 — Conaniah also, and Shemaiah and Nethaneel, his brethren, and Hashabiah and Jeiel and Jozabad, chief of the Levites, gave unto the Levites for passover offerings five thousand *small cattle,* and five hundred oxen.

• Son of Jeshua.

Ezr 8:33 — Now on the fourth day was the silver and the gold and the vessels weighed in the house of our God by the hand of Meremoth the son of Uriah the priest; and with him *was* Eleazar the son of Phinehas; and with them *was* Jozabad the son of Jeshua, and Noadiah the son of Binnui, Levites;

• A priest.

Ezr 10:22 — And of the sons of Pashur; Elioenai, Maaseiah, Ishmael, Nethaneel, Jozabad, and Elasah.

• Three Levites.

Ezr 10:23 — Also of the Levites; Jozabad, and Shimei, and Kelaiah, (the same *is* Kelita,) Pethahiah, Judah, and Eliezer.

Ne 8:7 — Also Jeshua, and Bani, and Sherebiah, Jamin, Akkub, Shabbethai, Hodijah, Maaseiah, Kelita, Azariah, Jozabad, Hanan, Pelaiah, and the Levites, caused the people to understand the law: and the people *stood* in their place.

Ne 11:16 — And Shabbethai and Jozabad, of the chief of the Levites, *had* the oversight of the outward business of the house of God.

• One of David's famous warriors.

1Ch 12:4 — And Ismaiah the Gibeonite, a mighty man among the thirty, and over the thirty; and Jeremiah, and Jahaziel, and Johanan, and Josabad the Gederathite,

JOZACHAR

• One of the two servants of Joash, king of Judah, who slew him in Millo.

2Ki 12:21 — For Jozachar the son of Shimeath, and Jehozabad the son of Shomer, his servants, smote him, and he died; and they buried him with his fathers in the city of David: and Amaziah his son reigned in his stead.

• Called Zabad.

2Ch 24:26 — And these are they that conspired against him; Zabad the son of Shimeath an Ammonitess, and Jehozabad the son of Shimrith a Moabitess.

JOZADAK ↞See: Jehozadak

JUBAL • Inventor of musical instruments.

Ge 4:21 — And his brother's name *was* Jubal: he was the father of all such as handle the harp and organ.

JUBILEE

• Called Acceptable Year of the Lord.

Isa 61:2 — To proclaim the acceptable year of the LORD, and the day of vengeance of our God; to comfort all that mourn;

• Called the Year of Liberty.

Eze 46:17 — But if he give a gift of his inheritance to one of his servants, then it shall be his to the year of liberty; after it shall return to the prince: but his inheritance shall be his sons' for them.

• Laws concerning.

Le 25:8–55; 27:17–24

Nu 36:4 — And when the jubile of the children of Israel shall be, then shall their inheritance be put unto the inheritance of the tribe whereunto they are received: so shall their inheritance be taken away from the inheritance of the tribe of our fathers.

↞See: Sabbatic Year

JUCAL ↞See: Jehucal

JUDAH

• Son of Jacob.

Ge 35:23 — The sons of Leah; Reuben, Jacob's firstborn, and Simeon, and Levi, and Judah, and Issachar, and Zebulun:

• Intercedes for Joseph's life when his brethren were about to slay him.
Ge 37:26–27

• Takes two wives.
Ge 38:1–6

- **Dwells at Chezib.**
  Ge 38:5 — And she yet again conceived, and bare a son; and called his name Shelah: and he was at Chezib, when she bare him.
- **His incest with his daughter-in-law.**
  Ge 38:12–26
- **Goes down into Egypt for corn.**
  Ge 43:1–10; 44:14–34
  Ge 46:28 — And he sent Judah before him unto Joseph, to direct his face unto Goshen; and they came into the land of Goshen.
- **Prophetic benediction of his father upon.**
  Ge 49:8–12
- **The ancestor of Jesus.**
  Mt 1:2–3
  Rev 5:5 — And one of the elders saith unto me, Weep not: behold, the Lion of the tribe of Juda, the Root of David, hath prevailed to open the book, and to loose the seven seals thereof.

• Tribe of.

- **Prophecies concerning.**
  Ge 49:10 — The sceptre shall not depart from Judah, nor a lawgiver from between his feet, until Shiloh come; and unto him *shall* the gathering of the people *be*.
- **Enrollment of the military forces of, at Sinai.**
  Nu 1:26–27
  Nu 2:4 — And his host, and those that were numbered of them, *were* threescore and fourteen thousand and six hundred.
- **Enrollment of the military forces of, at Bezek.**
  1Sa 11:8 — And when he numbered them in Bezek, the children of Israel were three hundred thousand, and the men of Judah thirty thousand.
  2Sa 24:9 — And Joab gave up the sum of the number of the people unto the king: and there were in Israel eight hundred thousand valiant men that drew the sword; and the men of Judah *were* five hundred thousand men.
- **Enrollment of the military forces of, in the plain of Moab.**
  Nu 26:22 — These *are* the families of Judah according to those that were numbered of them, threescore and sixteen thousand and five hundred.
- **Place of, in camp and march.**
  Nu 2:3 — And on the east side toward the rising of the sun shall they of the standard of the camp of Judah pitch throughout their armies: and Nahshon the son of Amminadab *shall be* captain of the children of Judah.
  Nu 2:9 — All that were numbered in the camp of Judah *were* an hundred thousand and fourscore thousand and six thousand and four hundred, throughout their armies. These shall first set forth.
  Nu 10:14 — In the first *place* went the standard of the camp of the children of Judah according to their armies: and over his host *was* Nahshon the son of Amminadab.
- **By whom commanded.**
  Nu 2:3 — And on the east side toward the rising of the sun shall they of the standard of the camp of Judah pitch throughout their armies: and Nahshon the son of Amminadab *shall be* captain of the children of Judah.
- **Moses' benediction upon.**
  Dt 33:7 — And this *is the blessing* of Judah: and he said, Hear, LORD, the voice of Judah, and bring him unto his people: let his hands be sufficient for him; and be thou an help *to him* from his enemies.
- **Commissioned of God to lead in the conquest of the promised land.**
  Jgs 1:1–21
- **Make David king.**
  2Sa 2:1–11; 5:4–5
- **Upbraided by David for lukewarmness toward him after Absalom's defeat.**
  2Sa 19:11–15
- **Accused by the other tribes of stealing the heart of David.**
  2Sa 19:41–43
- **Loyal to David at the time of the insurrection led by Sheba.**
  2Sa 20:1–2
- **Is accorded the birthright forfeited by Reuben.**
  1Ch 5:1–2
  1Ch 28:4 — Howbeit the LORD God of Israel chose me before all the house of my father to be king over Israel for ever: for he hath chosen Judah *to be* the ruler; and of the house of Judah, the house of my father; and among the sons of my father he liked me to make *me* king over all Israel:
  Ps 60:7 — Gilead *is* mine, and Manasseh *is* mine; Ephraim also *is* the strength of mine head; Judah *is* my lawgiver;
- **Loyal to the house of David at the time of the revolt of the ten tribes.**
  1Ki 12:20 — And it came to pass, when all Israel heard that Jeroboam was come again, that they sent and called him unto the congregation, and made him king over all Israel: there was none that followed the house of David, but the tribe of Judah only.
- **Inheritance of.**
  Jos 15:1–63
  Jos 18:5 — And they shall divide it into seven parts: Judah shall abide in their coast on the south, and the house of Joseph shall abide in their coasts on the north.
  Jos 19:1 — And the second lot came forth to Simeon, *even* for the tribe of the children of Simeon according to their families: and their inheritance was within the inheritance of the children of Judah.
  Jos 19:9 — Out of the portion of the children of Judah *was* the inheritance of the children of Simeon: for the part of the children of Judah was too much for them: therefore the children of

Simeon had their inheritance within the inheritance of them.

• **Name of two exiled priests.**

Ezr 10:23 — Also of the Levites; Jozabad, and Shimei, and Kelaiah, (the same *is* Kelita,) Pethahiah, Judah, and Eliezer.

Ne 12:8 — Moreover the Levites: Jeshua, Binnui, Kadmiel, Sherebiah, Judah, *and* Mattaniah, *which was* over the thanksgiving, he and his brethren.

• **A Benjamite.**

Ne 11:9 — And Joel the son of Zichri *was* their overseer: and Judah the son of Senuah *was* second over the city.

• **A prince or priest who assisted in the dedication of the walls of Jerusalem.**

Ne 12:34 — Judah, and Benjamin, and Shemaiah, and Jeremiah,

Ne 12:36 — And his brethren, Shemaiah, and Azarael, Milalai, Gilalai, Maai, Nethaneel, and Judah, Hanani, with the musical instruments of David the man of God, and Ezra the scribe before them.

JUDAISM

• **The religion of the Jews.**

• **To yield place to the gospel.**

Mt 3:8–9; 5:17–19, 21–44; 9:16–17

• **A corrupt form of Christianity.**

Ac 21:20–25; Gal 3:1–6:18

Ac 15:1 — And certain men which came down from Judaea taught the brethren, *and said,* Except ye be circumcised after the manner of Moses, ye cannot be saved.

See: Teachers; false

JUDAS

• **Surnamed Iscariot.**

Mt 10:4 — Simon the Canaanite, and Judas Iscariot, who also betrayed him.

Mk 3:19 — And Judas Iscariot, which also betrayed him: and they went into an house.

Lk 6:16 — And Judas *the brother* of James, and Judas Iscariot, which also was the traitor.

• **Chosen as an apostle.**

Ac 1:17 — For he was numbered with us, and had obtained part of this ministry.

• **Treasurer of the disciples.**

Jn 12:6 — This he said, not that he cared for the poor; but because he was a thief, and had the bag, and bare what was put therein.

Jn 13:29 — For some *of them* thought, because Judas had the bag, that Jesus had said unto him, Buy *those things* that we have need of against the feast; or, that he should give something to the poor.

• **His covetousness exemplified by his protest against the breaking of the box of ointment.**

Jn 12:4–6

• **His covetousness exemplified by his bargain to betray Jesus for a sum of money.**

Mt 26:14–16; Mk 14:10–11; Lk 22:3–6

Jn 13:2 — And supper being ended, the devil having now put into the heart of Judas Iscariot, Simon's *son,* to betray him;

• **His apostasy.**

Jn 17:12 — <u>While I was with them in the world, I kept them in thy name: those that thou gavest me I have kept, and none of them is lost, but the son of perdition; that the scripture might be fulfilled.</u>

• **Betrays the Lord.**

Mt 26:47–50; Mk 14:43–45; Lk 22:47–49; Jn 18:2–5; Ac 1:16–25

• **Returns the money to the rulers of the Jews.**

Mt 27:3–10

• **Hangs himself.**

Mt 27:5 — And he cast down the pieces of silver in the temple, and departed, and went and hanged himself.

Ac 1:18 — Now this man purchased a field with the reward of iniquity; and falling headlong, he burst asunder in the midst, and all his bowels gushed out.

• **Prophecies concerning.**

Zec 11:12–13; Mt 26:21–25; Mk 14:18–21; Lk 22:21–23; Jn 13:18–26

Ps 41:9 — Yea, mine own familiar friend, in whom I trusted, which did eat of my bread, hath lifted up *his* heel against me.

Ps 109:8 — Let his days be few; *and* let another take his office.

Jn 17:12 — <u>While I was with them in the world, I kept them in thy name: those that thou gavest me I have kept, and none of them is lost, but the son of perdition; that the scripture might be fulfilled.</u>

Ac 1:16 — Men *and* brethren, this scripture must needs have been fulfilled, which the Holy Ghost by the mouth of David spake before concerning Judas, which was guide to them that took Jesus.

Ac 1:20 — For it is written in the book of Psalms, Let his habitation be desolate, and let no man dwell therein: and his bishoprick let another take.

• **One of the brethren of Jesus.**

Mt 13:55 — Is not this the carpenter's son? is not his mother called Mary? and his brethren, James, and Joses, and Simon, and Judas?

Mk 6:3 — Is not this the carpenter, the son of Mary, the brother of James, and Joses, and of Juda, and Simon? and are not his sisters here with us? And they were offended at him.

• **Brother of James and writer of the Epistle of Jude.**

Lk 6:16 — And Judas *the brother* of James, and Judas Iscariot, which also was the traitor.

Ac 1:13 — And when they were come in, they went up into an upper room, where abode both Peter, and James, and John, and Andrew, Philip, and Thomas, Bartholomew, and Matthew, James *the son* of Alphaeus, and Simon Zelotes, and Judas *the brother* of James.

Jude 1:1 — Jude, the servant of Jesus Christ, and brother of James, to them that are sanctified by God the Father, and preserved in Jesus Christ, *and* called:

• An apostle; probably identical with Lebbaeus, or Thaddaeus.

Jn 14:22 — Judas saith unto him, not Iscariot, Lord, how is it that thou wilt manifest thyself unto us, and not unto the world?

• Of Galilee, who stirred up a sedition among the Jews soon after the birth of Jesus.

Ac 5:37 — After this man rose up Judas of Galilee in the days of the taxing, and drew away much people after him: he also perished; and all, *even* as many as obeyed him, were dispersed.

• A disciple who entertained Paul.

Ac 9:11 — And the Lord *said* unto him, Arise, and go into the street which is called Straight, and enquire in the house of Judas for *one* called Saul, of Tarsus: for, behold, he prayeth,

• Surnamed Barsabas. A Christian sent to Antioch with Paul and Barnabas.

Ac 15:22–32

JUDEA

• The southern division of Palestine.

• Called also Judah and Judaea.

Mt 4:25 — And there followed him great multitudes of people from Galilee, and *from* Decapolis, and *from* Jerusalem, and *from* Judaea, and *from* beyond Jordan.

Lk 5:17 — And it came to pass on a certain day, as he was teaching, that there were Pharisees and doctors of the law sitting by, which were come out of every town of Galilee, and Judaea, and Jerusalem: and the power of the Lord was *present* to heal them.

Jn 4:47 — When he heard that Jesus was come out of Judaea into Galilee, he went unto him, and besought him that he would come down, and heal his son: for he was at the point of death.

Jn 4:54 — This *is* again the second miracle *that* Jesus did, when he was come out of Judaea into Galilee.

• It extended from the Jordan and Dead Sea to the Mediterranean.

• And from Shiloh on the north to the wilderness on the south.

• Applies to all Palestine.

Lk 1:5 — There was in the days of Herod, the king of Judaea, a certain priest named Zacharias, of the course of Abia: and his wife *was* of the daughters of Aaron, and her name *was* Elisabeth.

• Applies to the territory east of Jordan.

Mt 19:1 — And it came to pass, *that* when Jesus had finished these sayings, he departed from Galilee, and came into the coasts of Judaea beyond Jordan;

Mk 10:1 — And he arose from thence, and cometh into the coasts of Judaea by the farther side of Jordan: and the people resort unto him again; and, as he was wont, he taught them again.

Lk 23:5 — And they were the more fierce, saying, He stirreth up the people, teaching throughout all Jewry, beginning from Galilee to this place.

• Wilderness of.

• Called Beth-arabah.

Jos 15:6 — And the border went up to Beth-hogla, and passed along by the north of Beth-arabah; and the border went up to the stone of Bohan the son of Reuben:

Jos 15:61 — In the wilderness, Beth-arabah, Middin, and Secacah,

• Assigned to Benjamin.

Jos 18:22 — And Beth-arabah, and Zemaraim, and Bethel,

• John the Baptist preaches in.

Mt 3:1 — In those days came John the Baptist, preaching in the wilderness of Judaea,

Lk 3:3 — And he came into all the country about Jordan, preaching the baptism of repentance for the remission of sins;

JUDGE

• Appointed by Persians.

Ezr 7:25 — And thou, Ezra, after the wisdom of thy God, that *is* in thine hand, set magistrates and judges, which may judge all the people that *are* beyond the river, all such as know the laws of thy God; and teach ye them that know *them* not.

• Kings and other rulers as.

1Ki 3:16–28; 2Ki 8:1–6; Ps 72:1–4; Mt 27:11–26; Ac 23:34–24:27; 25:11–12

2Sa 8:15 — And David reigned over all Israel; and David executed judgment and justice unto all his people.

2Sa 15:2 — And Absalom rose up early, and stood beside the way of the gate: and it was so, that when any man that had a controversy came to the king for judgment, then Absalom called unto him, and said, Of what city *art* thou? And he said, Thy servant is of one of the tribes of Israel.

1Ki 10:9 — Blessed be the LORD thy God, which delighted in thee, to set thee on the throne of Israel: because the LORD loved Israel for ever, therefore made he thee king, to do judgment and justice.

• Priests and Levites as.

Eze 44:23–24; Mt 26:57–62

Dt 17:9 — And thou shalt come unto the priests the Levites, and unto the judge that shall be in those days, and enquire; and they shall shew thee the sentence of judgment:

2Ch 19:8 — Moreover in Jerusalem did Jehoshaphat set of the Levites, and *of* the priests, and of the chief of the fathers of Israel, for the judgment of the LORD, and for controversies, when they returned to Jerusalem.

- **Women as.**
  - **Deborah.**
    Jgs 4:4 — And Deborah, a prophetess, the wife of Lapidoth, she judged Israel at that time.
- **Held circuit courts.**
  1Sa 7:16 — And he went from year to year in circuit to Bethel, and Gilgal, and Mizpeh, and judged Israel in all those places.
  - **See: Court**
  - **See: Justice**
  - **See: Witness**
- **Character of, and precepts relating to.**
  Ex 18:21–22; Dt 1:12–17; 16:18–20; 17:8–11; 19:16–19; 25:1–3; 2Ch 19:5–10; Ps 58:1–2; 72:1–2, 12–14; 82:2–4; Isa 5:22–23; 28:5–6
  Ex 22:9 — For all manner of trespass, *whether it be* for ox, for ass, for sheep, for raiment, *or* for any manner of lost thing, which *another* challengeth to be his, the cause of both parties shall come before the judges; *and* whom the judges shall condemn, he shall pay double unto his neighbour.
  Ex 22:28 — Thou shalt not revile the gods, nor curse the ruler of thy people.
  Le 19:15 — Ye shall do no unrighteousness in judgment: thou shalt not respect the person of the poor, nor honour the person of the mighty: *but* in righteousness shalt thou judge thy neighbour.
  1Sa 2:25 — If one man sin against another, the judge shall judge him: but if a man sin against the LORD, who shall intreat for him? Notwithstanding they hearkened not unto the voice of their father, because the LORD would slay them.
  1Sa 8:3 — And his sons walked not in his ways, but turned aside after lucre, and took bribes, and perverted judgment.
  1Ki 3:9 — Give therefore thy servant an understanding heart to judge thy people, that I may discern between good and bad: for who is able to judge this thy so great a people?
  Ps 72:4 — He shall judge the poor of the people, he shall save the children of the needy, and shall break in pieces the oppressor.
  Pr 24:23 — These *things* also *belong* to the wise. *It is* not good to have respect of persons in judgment.
  Eze 44:24 — And in controversy they shall stand in judgment; *and* they shall judge it according to my judgments: and they shall keep my laws and my statutes in all mine assemblies; and they shall hallow my sabbaths.
  Da 9:12 — And he hath confirmed his words, which he spake against us, and against our judges that judged us, by bringing upon us a great evil: for under the whole heaven hath not been done as hath been done upon Jerusalem.
  Mic 7:3 — That they may do evil with both hands earnestly, the prince asketh, and the judge *asketh* for a reward; and the great *man,* he uttereth his mischievous desire: so they wrap it up.
  Zep 3:3 — Her princes within her *are* roaring lions; her judges *are* evening wolves; they gnaw not the bones till the morrow.
  Jn 7:24 — Judge not according to the appearance, but judge righteous judgment.
  - **See: Court**
  - **See: Justice**
- **Corrupt.**
  - **Instances of.**
    - **Eli's sons.**
      1Sa 2:12–17, 22–25
    - **Samuel's sons.**
      1Sa 8:1–5
    - **The judges of Jezreel.**
      1Ki 21:8–13
    - **Pilate.**
      Mt 27:24; Mk 15:15, 19–24
    - **Felix.**
      Ac 24:26–27
- **God as.**
  - **See: God, Judge, and His Justice**
- **Judges of Israel.**
  - **During the time when the land was ruled by judges.**
    Jgs 2:16–19
    Ac 13:20 — And after that he gave *unto them* judges about the space of four hundred and fifty years, until Samuel the prophet.
  - **Othniel.**
    Jgs 3:9–11
  - **Ehud.**
    Jgs 3:15–30
  - **Shamgar.**
    Jgs 3:31 — And after him was Shamgar the son of Anath, which slew of the Philistines six hundred men with an ox goad: and he also delivered Israel.
  - **Deborah.**
    Jgs 4:1–5:31
  - **Gideon.**
    Jgs 6:11–8:35
  - **Abimelech.**
    Jgs 9:1–54
  - **Tola.**
    Jgs 10:1–2
  - **Jair.**
    Jgs 10:3–5
  - **Jephthah.**
    Jgs 11:1–12:7
  - **Ibzan.**
    Jgs 12:8–10
  - **Elon.**
    Jgs 12:11–12
  - **Abdon.**
    Jgs 12:13–14
  - **Samson.**
    Jgs 13:1–16:31

- **Eli judged Israel.**

1Sa 4:18 — And it came to pass, when he made mention of the ark of God, that he fell from off the seat backward by the side of the gate, and his neck brake, and he died: for he was an old man, and heavy. And he had judged Israel forty years.

- **Samuel as judge.**

1Sa 7:15–17

1Sa 7:6 — And they gathered together to Mizpeh, and drew water, and poured *it* out before the LORD, and fasted on that day, and said there, We have sinned against the LORD. And Samuel judged the children of Israel in Mizpeh.

- **The sons of Samuel.**

1Sa 8:1–5

JUDGING ↞See: Uncharitableness

JUDGMENT

- **The general.**

Job 31:13–15; Ps 50:3–6; Eze 18:20–28; Da 7:9–10; Mt 7:22–23; 12:36–37, 41–42; 13:40–43, 49–50; 22:11–13; 25:1–46; Lk 10:10–14; 11:31–32; 12:2–5; 13:24–29; 19:12–26; 20:45–47; Ac 2:19–21; Ro 2:5–10, 12–16; 14:10–12; 2Th 1:7–8; 2Pe 3:10–12; Jude 1:14–15; Rev 6:15–17; 20:11–15

1Ch 16:33 — Then shall the trees of the wood sing out at the presence of the LORD, because he cometh to judge the earth.

Job 14:17 — My transgression *is* sealed up in a bag, and thou sewest up mine iniquity.

Job 21:30 — That the wicked is reserved to the day of destruction? they shall be brought forth to the day of wrath.

Ps 9:7 — But the LORD shall endure for ever: he hath prepared his throne for judgment.

Ps 96:13 — Before the LORD: for he cometh, for he cometh to judge the earth: he shall judge the world with righteousness, and the people with his truth.

Ps 98:9 — Before the LORD; for he cometh to judge the earth: with righteousness shall he judge the world, and the people with equity.

Ecc 3:17 — I said in mine heart, God shall judge the righteous and the wicked: for *there is* a time there for every purpose and for every work.

Ecc 11:9 — Rejoice, O young man, in thy youth; and let thy heart cheer thee in the days of thy youth, and walk in the ways of thine heart, and in the sight of thine eyes: but know thou, that for all these *things* God will bring thee into judgment.

Ecc 12:14 — For God shall bring every work into judgment, with every secret thing, whether *it be* good, or whether *it be* evil.

Am 4:12 — Therefore thus will I do unto thee, O Israel: *and* because I will do this unto thee, prepare to meet thy God, O Israel.

Mt 3:12 — Whose fan *is* in his hand, and he will throughly purge his floor, and gather his wheat into the garner; but he will burn up the chaff with unquenchable fire.

Mt 8:29 — And, behold, they cried out, saying, What have we to do with thee, Jesus, thou Son of God? art thou come hither to torment us before the time?

Mt 10:15 — Verily I say unto you, It shall be more tolerable for the land of Sodom and Gomorrha in the day of judgment, than for that city.

Mt 11:22 — But I say unto you, It shall be more tolerable for Tyre and Sidon at the day of judgment, than for you.

Mt 13:30 — Let both grow together until the harvest: and in the time of harvest I will say to the reapers, Gather ye together first the tares, and bind them in bundles to burn them: but gather the wheat into my barn.

Mt 16:27 — For the Son of man shall come in the glory of his Father with his angels; and then he shall reward every man according to his works.

Mt 23:14 — Woe unto you, scribes and Pharisees, hypocrites! for ye devour widows' houses, and for a pretence make long prayer: therefore ye shall receive the greater damnation.

Mk 4:22 — For there is nothing hid, which shall not be manifested; neither was any thing kept secret, but that it should come abroad.

Mk 8:38 — Whosoever therefore shall be ashamed of me and of my words in this adulterous and sinful generation; of him also shall the Son of man be ashamed, when he cometh in the glory of his Father with the holy angels.

Mk 13:32 — But of that day and *that* hour knoweth no man, no, not the angels which are in heaven, neither the Son, but the Father.

Lk 3:17 — Whose fan *is* in his hand, and he will throughly purge his floor, and will gather the wheat into his garner; but the chaff he will burn with fire unquenchable.

Jn 5:22 — For the Father judgeth no man, but hath committed all judgment unto the Son:

Jn 12:48 — He that rejecteth me, and receiveth not my words, hath one that judgeth him: the word that I have spoken, the same shall judge him in the last day.

Ac 10:42 — And he commanded us to preach unto the people, and to testify that it is he which was ordained of God *to be* the Judge of quick and dead.

Ac 17:31 — Because he hath appointed a day, in the which he will judge the world in righteousness by *that* man whom he hath ordained; *whereof* he hath given assurance unto all *men*, in that he hath raised him from the dead.

Ac 24:25 — And as he reasoned of righteousness, temperance, and judgment to come Felix trembled, and answered, Go thy way for this time; when I have a convenient season, I will call for thee.

1Co 3:13 — Every man's work shall be made manifest: for the day shall declare it, because it shall be revealed by fire; and the fire shall try every man's work of what sort it is.

1Co 4:5 — Therefore judge nothing before the time, until the Lord come, who both will bring to light the hidden things of darkness, and will make manifest the counsels of the hearts: and then shall every man have praise of God.

1Co 6:2 — Do ye not know that the saints shall judge the world? and if the world shall be judged by you, are ye unworthy to judge the smallest matters?

2Co 5:10 — For we must all appear before the judgment seat of Christ; that every one may receive the things *done* in *his* body, according to that he hath done, whether *it be* good or bad.

2Ti 4:1 — I charge *thee* therefore before God, and the Lord Jesus Christ, who shall judge the quick and the dead at his appearing and his kingdom;

2Ti 4:8 — Henceforth there is laid up for me a crown of righteousness, which the Lord, the righteous judge, shall give me at that day: and not to me only, but unto all them also that love his appearing.

Heb 6:2 — Of the doctrine of baptisms, and of laying on of hands, and of resurrection of the dead, and of eternal judgment.

Heb 9:27 — And as it is appointed unto men once to die, but after this the judgment:

Heb 10:27 — But a certain fearful looking for of judgment and fiery indignation, which shall devour the adversaries.

1Pe 4:5 — Who shall give account to him that is ready to judge the quick and the dead.

1Pe 4:7 — But the end of all things is at hand: be ye therefore sober, and watch unto prayer.

2Pe 2:4 — For if God spared not the angels that sinned, but cast *them* down to hell, and delivered *them* into chains of darkness, to be reserved unto judgment;

2Pe 2:9 — The Lord knoweth how to deliver the godly out of temptations, and to reserve the unjust unto the day of judgment to be punished:

2Pe 3:7 — But the heavens and the earth, which are now, by the same word are kept in store, reserved unto fire against the day of judgment and perdition of ungodly men.

1Jn 4:17 — Herein is our love made perfect, that we may have boldness in the day of judgment: because as he is, so are we in this world.

Jude 1:6 — And the angels which kept not their first estate, but left their own habitation, he hath reserved in everlasting chains under darkness unto the judgment of the great day.

Jude 1:24 — Now unto him that is able to keep you from falling, and to present *you* faultless before the presence of his glory with exceeding joy,

Rev 1:7 — Behold, he cometh with clouds; and every eye shall see him, and they *also* which pierced him: and all kindreds of the earth shall wail because of him. Even so, Amen.

Rev 11:18 — And the nations were angry, and thy wrath is come, and the time of the dead, that they should be judged, and that thou shouldest give reward unto thy servants the prophets, and to the saints, and them that fear thy name, small and great; and shouldest destroy them which destroy the earth.

Rev 22:12 — And, behold, I come quickly; and my reward *is* with me, to give every man according as his work shall be.

• According to opportunity and works.

Pr 24:11–12; Isa 3:10–11; 5:15–16; Jer 17:10–11; Eze 7:3–4; 9:4–6; 18:4–9, 19–32; 33:18–20; Mt 10:14–15; Lk 10:12–15; 11:49–51; 12:47–48; 13:6–9; 19:12–27; 20:47–21:4; Jn 3:19–20; Ro 2:5–12; 1Co 3:12–15; 2Co 2:15–16; Gal 6:5–10; Eph 6:7–8; Heb 2:2–3; 10:26–30; Jas 2:12–13; 2Pe 2:20–21; Rev 20:12–13

Ge 4:7 — If thou doest well, shalt thou not be accepted? and if thou doest not well, sin lieth at the door. And unto thee *shall be* his desire, and thou shalt rule over him.

Job 34:11 — For the work of a man shall he render unto him, and cause every man to find according to *his* ways.

Ps 62:12 — Also unto thee, O Lord, *belongeth* mercy: for thou renderest to every man according to his work.

Pr 11:31 — Behold, the righteous shall be recompensed in the earth: much more the wicked and the sinner.

Pr 12:14 — A man shall be satisfied with good by the fruit of *his* mouth: and the recompense of a man's hands shall be rendered unto him.

Isa 24:2 — And it shall be, as with the people, so with the priest; as with the servant, so with his master; as with the maid, so with her mistress; as with the buyer, so with the seller; as with the lender, so with the borrower; as with the taker of usury, so with the giver of usury to him.

Isa 59:18 — According to *their* deeds, accordingly he will repay, fury to his adversaries, recompence to his enemies; to the islands he will repay recompence.

Jer 32:19 — Great in counsel, and mighty in work: for thine eyes *are* open upon all the ways of the sons of men: to give every one according to his ways, and according to the fruit of his doings:

Eze 7:27 — The king shall mourn, and the prince shall be clothed with desolation, and the hands of the people of the land shall be troubled: I will do unto them after their way, and according to their deserts will I judge them; and they shall know that I *am* the LORD.

Eze 16:59 — For thus saith the Lord GOD; I will even deal with thee as thou hast done, which hast despised the oath in breaking the covenant.

Eze 39:24 — According to their uncleanness and according to their transgressions have I done unto them, and hid my face from them.

Hos 4:9 — And there shall be, like people, like priest: and I will punish them for their ways, and reward them their doings.

Hos 12:2 — The LORD hath also a controversy with Judah, and will punish Jacob according to his ways; according to his doings will he recompense him.

Am 3:2 — You only have I known of all the families of the earth: therefore I will punish you for all your iniquities.

Zec 1:6 — But my words and my statutes, which I commanded my servants the prophets, did they not take hold of your fathers? and they returned and said, Like as the LORD of hosts thought to do unto us, according to our ways, and according to our doings, so hath he dealt with us.

Mt 11:24 — But I say unto you, That it shall be more tolerable for the land of Sodom in the day of judgment, than for thee.

Mt 12:37 — For by thy words thou shalt be justified, and by thy words thou shalt be condemned.

Mt 23:14 — Woe unto you, scribes and Pharisees, hypocrites! for ye devour widows' houses, and for a pretence make long prayer: therefore ye shall receive the greater damnation.

Mk 6:11 — And whosoever shall not receive you, nor hear you, when ye depart thence, shake off the dust under your feet for a testimony against them. Verily I say unto you, It shall be more tolerable for Sodom and Gomorrha in the day of judgment, than for that city.

Mk 14:21 — The Son of man indeed goeth, as it is written of him: but woe to that man by whom the Son of man is betrayed! good were it for that man if he had never been born.

Lk 9:5 — And whosoever will not receive you, when ye go out of that city, shake off the very dust from your feet for a testimony against them.

Jn 5:45 — Do not think that I will accuse you to the Father: there is *one* that accuseth you, *even* Moses, in whom ye trust.

Jn 9:41 — Jesus said unto them, If ye were blind, ye should have no sin: but now ye say, We see; therefore your sin remaineth.

Jn 12:48 — He that rejecteth me, and receiveth not my words, hath one that judgeth him: the word that I have spoken, the same shall judge him in the last day.

Jn 15:22 — If I had not come and spoken unto them, they had not had sin: but now they have no cloke for their sin.

Jn 15:24 — If I had not done among them the works which none other man did, they had not had sin: but now have they both seen and hated both me and my Father.

Ro 2:27 — And shall not uncircumcision which is by nature, if it fulfil the law, judge thee, who by the letter and circumcision dost transgress the law?

1Co 3:8 — Now he that planteth and he that watereth are one: and every man shall receive his own reward according to his own labour.

1Co 4:5 — Therefore judge nothing before the time, until the Lord come, who both will bring to light the hidden things of darkness, and will make manifest the counsels of the hearts: and then shall every man have praise of God.

2Co 11:15 — Therefore *it is* no great thing if his ministers also be transformed as the ministers of righteousness; whose end shall be according to their works.

Col 3:25 — But he that doeth wrong shall receive for the wrong which he hath done: and there is no respect of persons.

1Ti 1:13 — Who was before a blasphemer, and a persecutor, and injurious: but I obtained mercy, because I did *it* ignorantly in unbelief.

2Ti 4:14 — Alexander the coppersmith did me much evil: the Lord reward him according to his works:

Heb 12:25 — See that ye refuse not him that speaketh. For if they escaped not who refused him that spake on earth, much more *shall not* we *escape,* if we turn away from him that *speaketh* from heaven:

1Pe 1:17 — And if ye call on the Father, who without respect of persons judgeth according to every man's work, pass the time of your sojourning *here* in fear:

Rev 2:23 — And I will kill her children with death; and all the churches shall know that I am he which searcheth the reins and hearts: and I will give unto every one of you according to your works.

- **Parables.**
  Lk 12:47–48
  - **Parable of the vineyard.**
    Isa 5:1–6
  - **Parable of the husbandman.**
    Isa 28:24–28
  - **Parable of the wicked husbandmen.**
    Mt 21:33–36
  - **Parable of the talents.**
    Mt 25:14–30

See: God, Judge, and His Justice

See: Jesus, Judge

See: Punishment; according to deeds

JUDGMENT-HALL See: Pretorium

JUDGMENT SEAT

Mt 27:19 — When he was set down on the judgment seat, his wife sent unto him, saying, Have thou nothing to do with that just man: for I have suffered many things this day in a dream because of him.

Ac 18:12 — And when Gallio was the deputy of Achaia, the Jews made insurrection with one accord against Paul, and brought him to the judgment seat,

Ac 25:10 — Then said Paul, I stand at Caesar's judgment seat, where I ought to be judged: to the Jews have I done no wrong, as thou very well knowest.

- **Of Christ.**
  Ro 14:10 — But why dost thou judge thy brother? or why dost thou set at nought thy brother? for we shall all stand before the judgment seat of Christ.

JUDGMENTS

- **On the serpent.**
  Ge 3:14–15
- **On Eve.**
  Ge 3:16 — Unto the woman he said, I will greatly multiply thy sorrow and thy conception; in sorrow thou shalt bring forth children; and thy desire *shall be* to thy husband, and he shall rule over thee.
- **On Adam.**
  Ge 3:17–19
- **On Cain.**
  Ge 4:11–15
- **On the Antediluvians.**
  Ge 6:1–22
- **On Sodomites.**
  Ge 19:23–25

- **On Egyptians, the plagues and overthrow.**
  Ex 7:1–14:31
- **On Nadab and Abihu.**
  Le 10:1–3
- **On Miriam.**
  Nu 12:1–15
- **Upon the Israelites.**
  - **For worshiping Aaron's calf.**
    Ex 32:35 — And the LORD plagued the people, because they made the calf, which Aaron made.
  - **For murmuring.**
    Nu 11:33–34; 14:22–23, 35–37; 25:4–5
    Nu 11:1 — And *when* the people complained, it displeased the LORD: and the LORD heard *it;* and his anger was kindled; and the fire of the LORD burnt among them, and consumed *them that were* in the uttermost parts of the camp.
    Nu 14:32 — But *as for* you, your carcases, they shall fall in this wilderness.
    Nu 21:6 — And the LORD sent fiery serpents among the people, and they bit the people; and much people of Israel died.
    Nu 25:9 — And those that died in the plague were twenty and four thousand.
  - **The forty years' wandering a judgment.**
    Nu 14:26–39; 26:63–65; Dt 2:14–17
  - **Delivered into the hands of the Assyrians.**
    2Ki 17:6–41
  - **Delivered into the hands of the Chaldeans.**
    2Ch 26:14–21
- **Upon the Canaanites.**
  Dt 7:1–26; 12:29–32
  Le 18:25 — And the land is defiled: therefore I do visit the iniquity thereof upon it, and the land itself vomiteth out her inhabitants.
- **Upon the Canaanites, with the conquest of, by Joshua.**
  See: Canaanites
- **Upon Abimelech.**
  Jgs 9:52–57
- **Upon Uzzah.**
  2Sa 6:7 — And the anger of the LORD was kindled against Uzzah; and God smote him there for *his* error; and there he died by the ark of God.
- **Upon Hananiah, the false prophet.**
  Jer 28:15–17
- **Upon Eli's house.**
  1Sa 2:27–36; 4:10–22
- **Upon the prophet of Judah, for disobedience.**
  1Ki 13:1–24
- **Upon Zimri.**
  1Ki 16:18–19
- **Upon Gehazi.**
  2Ki 5:27 — The leprosy therefore of Naaman shall cleave unto thee, and unto thy seed for ever. And he went out from his presence a leper *as white* as snow.
- **Upon Sennacherib.**
  2Ki 19:35–37
- **Denounced against Solomon.**
  1Ki 11:9–14
  1Ki 11:23 — And God stirred him up *another* adversary, Rezon the son of Eliadah, which fled from his lord Hadadezer king of Zobah:
- **Denounced against Jeroboam.**
  1Ki 14:7–15
- **Denounced against Ahab and Jezebel.**
  1Ki 21:19–24
- **Denounced against Ahaziah.**
  2Ch 22:7–9
- **Denounced against Manasseh.**
  2Ch 33:11 — Wherefore the LORD brought upon them the captains of the host of the king of Assyria, which took Manasseh among the thorns, and bound him with fetters, and carried him to Babylon.
- **Denounced against disobedience.**
  Le 26:14–39; Dt 28:15–29:29; 32:19–43
- **Misunderstood.**
  Jer 16:10 — And it shall come to pass, when thou shalt shew this people all these words, and they shall say unto thee, Wherefore hath the LORD pronounced all this great evil against us? or what *is* our iniquity? or what *is* our sin that we have committed against the LORD our God?
  Joel 2:17 — Let the priests, the ministers of the LORD, weep between the porch and the altar, and let them say, Spare thy people, O LORD, and give not thine heritage to reproach, that the heathen should rule over them: wherefore should they say among the people, Where *is* their God?
- **No escape from.**
  Isa 2:12–19; Eze 14:13–14; Am 5:16–20; 9:1–4; Heb 2:1–3; 10:28–29; Rev 6:16–17
  Ex 20:7 — Thou shalt not take the name of the LORD thy God in vain; for the LORD will not hold him guiltless that taketh his name in vain.
  Ex 34:7 — Keeping mercy for thousands, forgiving iniquity and transgression and sin, and that will by no means clear *the guilty;* visiting the iniquity of the fathers upon the children, and upon the children's children, unto the third and to the fourth *generation.*
  Isa 2:10 — Enter into the rock, and hide thee in the dust, for fear of the LORD, and for the glory of his majesty.
  Isa 2:21 — To go into the clefts of the rocks, and into the tops of the ragged rocks, for fear of the LORD, and for the glory of his majesty, when he ariseth to shake terribly the earth.
  Mt 23:33 — *Ye* serpents, *ye* generation of vipers, how can ye escape the damnation of hell?
  Heb 12:25 — See that ye refuse not him that speaketh. For if they escaped not who refused him that spake on earth, much more *shall not* we *escape,* if we turn away from him that *speaketh* from heaven:
  See: Escape

- **Executed by human instrumentality.**

Jer 51:2 — And will send unto Babylon fanners, that shall fan her, and shall empty her land: for in the day of trouble they shall be against her round about.

- **Delayed.**

Ps 10:6 — He hath said in his heart, I shall not be moved: for *I shall* never *be* in adversity.

Ps 50:21 — These *things* hast thou done, and I kept silence; thou thoughtest that I was altogether *such an one* as thyself: *but* I will reprove thee, and set *them* in order before thine eyes.

Ps 55:19 — God shall hear, and afflict them, even he that abideth of old. Selah. Because they have no changes, therefore they fear not God.

See: Chastisement

See: Punishment

See: Punishment; delayed

See: Sin; punishment of

- **Design of.**

Ex 14:17–18; Dt 29:22–28; Ps 83:16–18; Isa 64:1–2; Eze 11:10–12; 14:7–8; 21:3–5; 30:25–26; 38:22–23; Da 4:24–26

Ex 14:31 — And Israel saw that great work which the LORD did upon the Egyptians: and the people feared the LORD, and believed the LORD, and his servant Moses.

Le 10:3 — Then Moses said unto Aaron, This *is it* that the LORD spake, saying, I will be sanctified in them that come nigh me, and before all the people I will be glorified. And Aaron held his peace.

Ps 9:16 — The LORD is known *by* the judgment *which* he executeth: the wicked is snared in the work of his own hands. Higgaion. Selah.

Ps 9:20 — Put them in fear, O LORD: *that* the nations may know themselves *to be but* men. Selah.

Ps 59:13 — Consume *them* in wrath, consume *them,* that they *may* not *be:* and let them know that God ruleth in Jacob unto the ends of the earth. Selah.

Isa 26:9 — With my soul have I desired thee in the night; yea, with my spirit within me will I seek thee early: for when thy judgments *are* in the earth, the inhabitants of the world will learn righteousness.

Eze 12:16 — But I will leave a few men of them from the sword, from the famine, and from the pestilence; that they may declare all their abominations among the heathen whither they come; and they shall know that I *am* the LORD.

Eze 25:5 — And I will make Rabbah a stable for camels, and the Ammonites a couchingplace for flocks: and ye shall know that I *am* the LORD.

Eze 25:7 — Behold, therefore I will stretch out mine hand upon thee, and will deliver thee for a spoil to the heathen; and I will cut thee off from the people, and I will cause thee to perish out of the countries: I will destroy thee; and thou shalt know that I *am* the LORD.

Eze 25:11 — And I will execute judgments upon Moab; and they shall know that I *am* the LORD.

Eze 26:6 — And her daughters which *are* in the field shall be slain by the sword; and they shall know that I *am* the LORD.

Eze 29:9 — And the land of Egypt shall be desolate and waste; and they shall know that I *am* the LORD: because he hath said, The river *is* mine, and I have made *it.*

Eze 29:16 — And it shall be no more the confidence of the house of Israel, which bringeth *their* iniquity to remembrance, when they shall look after them: but they shall know that I *am* the Lord GOD.

Eze 30:8 — And they shall know that I *am* the LORD, when I have set a fire in Egypt, and *when* all her helpers shall be destroyed.

Eze 33:29 — Then shall they know that I *am* the LORD, when I have laid the land most desolate because of all their abominations which they have committed.

Da 4:17 — This matter *is* by the decree of the watchers, and the demand by the word of the holy ones: to the intent that the living may know that the most High ruleth in the kingdom of men, and giveth it to whomsoever he will, and setteth up over it the basest of men.

Da 4:34 — And at the end of the days I Nebuchadnezzar lifted up mine eyes unto heaven, and mine understanding returned unto me, and I blessed the most High, and I praised and honoured him that liveth for ever, whose dominion *is* an everlasting dominion, and his kingdom *is* from generation to generation:

Ro 9:17 — For the scripture saith unto Pharaoh, Even for this same purpose have I raised thee up, that I might shew my power in thee, and that my name might be declared throughout all the earth.

Ro 9:22 — *What* if God, willing to shew *his* wrath, and to make his power known, endured with much longsuffering the vessels of wrath fitted to destruction:

1Co 10:6 — Now these things were our examples, to the intent we should not lust after evil things, as they also lusted.

1Co 10:11 — Now all these things happened unto them for ensamples: and they are written for our admonition, upon whom the ends of the world are come.

Rev 2:23 — And I will kill her children with death; and all the churches shall know that I am he which searcheth the reins and hearts: and I will give unto every one of you according to your works.

See: Afflictions; design of

See: Chastisement

See: Punishment

See: Sin; punishment of

JUDITH

- **A wife of Esau.**

Ge 26:34 — And Esau was forty years old when he took to wife Judith the daughter of Beeri the Hittite, and Bashemath the daughter of Elon the Hittite:

- **Called Aholibamah.**

Ge 36:2 — Esau took his wives of the daughters of Canaan; Adah the daughter of Elon the Hittite, and Aholibamah the daughter of Anah the daughter of Zibeon the Hivite;

JULIA • A Christian woman in Rome.

Ro 16:15 — Salute Philologus, and Julia, Nereus, and his sister, and Olympas, and all the saints which are with them.

JULIUS • A centurion.

Ac 27:1 — And when it was determined that we should sail into Italy, they delivered Paul and certain other prisoners unto *one* named Julius, a centurion of Augustus' band.

Ac 27:3 — And the next *day* we touched at Sidon. And Julius courteously entreated Paul, and gave *him* liberty to go unto his friends to refresh himself.

Ac 27:43 — But the centurion, willing to save Paul, kept them from *their* purpose; and commanded that they which could swim should cast *themselves* first *into the sea,* and get to land:

JUNIA • A kinsman of Paul.

Ro 16:7 — Salute Andronicus and Junia, my kinsmen, and my fellowprisoners, who are of note among the apostles, who also were in Christ before me.

JUNIPER • A tree.

1Ki 19:4–5

Job 30:4 — Who cut up mallows by the bushes, and juniper roots *for* their meat.

Ps 120:4 — Sharp arrows of the mighty, with coals of juniper.

JUPITER • A Greek and Roman deity.

Ac 14:12–13

Ac 19:35 — And when the townclerk had appeased the people, he said, *Ye* men of Ephesus, what man is there that knoweth not how that the city of the Ephesians is a worshipper of the great goddess Diana, and of the *image* which fell down from Jupiter?

JURY

• Of ten men.

Ru 4:2 — And he took ten men of the elders of the city, and said, Sit ye down here. And they sat down.

• Of seventy men, elders (senators).

Nu 11:16–17, 24–25

JUSHAB-HESED • Son of Zerubbabel.

1Ch 3:20 — And Hashubah, and Ohel, and Berechiah, and Hasadiah, Jushab-hesed, five.

JUSTICE

Ex 23:1–3, 6–8; Le 19:13–15; Dt 16:18–20; 25:1–4; Ps 72:1–2; 82:2–4; Ecc 3:16–17; Isa 59:14–15; Jer 22:1–4; La 3:35–36; Am 5:11–12; Mt 5:23–24

Ezr 7:26 — And whosoever will not do the law of thy God, and the law of the king, let judgment be executed speedily upon him, whether *it be* unto death, or to banishment, or to confiscation of goods, or to imprisonment.

Pr 17:15 — He that justifieth the wicked, and he that condemneth the just, even they both *are* abomination to the LORD.

Pr 17:26 — Also to punish the just *is* not good, *nor* to strike princes for equity.

Pr 18:5 — *It is* not good to accept the person of the wicked, to overthrow the righteous in judgment.

Pr 18:17 — *He that is* first in his own cause *seemeth* just; but his neighbour cometh and searcheth him.

Pr 20:8 — A king that sitteth in the throne of judgment scattereth away all evil with his eyes.

Pr 22:27 — If thou hast nothing to pay, why should he take away thy bed from under thee?

Pr 24:23 — These *things* also *belong* to the wise. *It is* not good to have respect of persons in judgment.

Pr 28:21 — To have respect of persons *is* not good: for for a piece of bread *that* man will transgress.

Pr 29:26 — Many seek the ruler's favour; but *every* man's judgment *cometh* from the LORD.

Ecc 5:8 — If thou seest the oppression of the poor, and violent perverting of judgment and justice in a province, marvel not at the matter: for *he that is* higher than the highest regardeth; and *there be* higher than they.

Ecc 7:7 — Surely oppression maketh a wise man mad; and a gift destroyeth the heart.

Isa 1:17 — Learn to do well; seek judgment, relieve the oppressed, judge the fatherless, plead for the widow.

Isa 56:1 — Thus saith the LORD, Keep ye judgment, and do justice: for my salvation *is* near to come, and my righteousness to be revealed.

Am 5:7 — Ye who turn judgment to wormwood, and leave off righteousness in the earth,

Mic 7:3 — That they may do evil with both hands earnestly, the prince asketh, and the judge *asketh* for a reward; and the great *man,* he uttereth his mischievous desire: so they wrap it up.

Hab 1:4 — Therefore the law is slacked, and judgment doth never go forth: for the wicked doth compass about the righteous; therefore wrong judgment proceedeth.

Zec 8:16 — These *are* the things that ye shall do; Speak ye every man the truth to his neighbour; execute the judgment of truth and peace in your gates:

Mt 12:7 — <u>But if ye had known what *this* meaneth, I will have mercy, and not sacrifice, ye would not have condemned the guiltless.</u>

Jn 7:24 — <u>Judge not according to the appearance, but judge righteous judgment.</u>

Jn 7:51 — Doth our law judge *any* man, before it hear him, and know what he doeth?

1Co 13:6 — Rejoiceth not in iniquity, but rejoiceth in the truth;

See: Court

See: Judge

See: Lawyer

See: Witness

JUSTIFICATION

Isa 45:24–25; 46:12–13; 51:5–6; Ro 1:16–17; 3:21–22, 24–26; 4:5–5:1; 5:11–21; 7:1–8:1; 8:30–31, 33–34; 9:30–32; 10:1–21; Gal 2:14–21; 3:8–9, 21–24; 4:21–31; 5:4–6; Php 3:8–9; Col 2:13–14; Jas 2:20–23

Ge 15:6 — And he believed in the LORD; and he counted it to him for righteousness.

Ps 32:2 — Blessed *is* the man unto whom the LORD imputeth not iniquity, and in whose spirit *there is* no guile.

Ps 71:16 — I will go in the strength of the Lord GOD: I will make mention of thy righteousness, *even* of thine only.

Ps 89:16 — In thy name shall they rejoice all the day: and in thy righteousness shall they be exalted.

Isa 42:21 — The LORD is well pleased for his righteousness' sake; he will magnify the law, and make *it* honourable.

Isa 50:8 — *He is* near that justifieth me; who will contend with me? let us stand together: who *is* mine adversary? let him come near to me.

Isa 53:11 — He shall see of the travail of his soul, *and* shall be satisfied: by his knowledge shall my righteous servant justify many; for he shall bear their iniquities.

Isa 54:17 — No weapon that is formed against thee shall prosper; and every tongue *that* shall rise against thee in judgment thou shalt condemn. This *is* the heritage of the servants of the LORD, and their righteousness *is* of me, saith the LORD.

Isa 56:1 — Thus saith the LORD, Keep ye judgment, and do justice: for my salvation *is* near to come, and my righteousness to be revealed.

Isa 61:10 — I will greatly rejoice in the LORD, my soul shall be joyful in my God; for he hath clothed me with the garments of salvation, he hath covered me with the robe of righteousness, as a bridegroom decketh *himself* with ornaments, and as a bride adorneth *herself* with her jewels.

Jer 23:6 — In his days Judah shall be saved, and Israel shall dwell safely: and this *is* his name whereby he shall be called, THE LORD OUR RIGHTEOUSNESS.

Hab 2:4 — Behold, his soul *which* is lifted up is not upright in him: but the just shall live by his faith.

Zec 3:4 — And he answered and spake unto those that stood before him, saying, Take away the filthy garments from him. And unto him he said, Behold, I have caused thine iniquity to pass from thee, and I will clothe thee with change of raiment.

Jn 5:24 — Verily, verily, I say unto you, He that heareth my word, and believeth on him that sent me, hath everlasting life, and shall not come into condemnation; but is passed from death unto life.

Ac 13:39 — And by him all that believe are justified from all things, from which ye could not be justified by the law of Moses.

Ro 2:13 — (For not the hearers of the law *are* just before God, but the doers of the law shall be justified.

Ro 3:28 — Therefore we conclude that a man is justified by faith without the deeds of the law.

Ro 3:30 — Seeing *it is* one God, which shall justify the circumcision by faith, and uncircumcision through faith.

Ro 4:3 — For what saith the scripture? Abraham believed God, and it was counted unto him for righteousness.

Ro 5:9 — Much more then, being now justified by his blood, we shall be saved from wrath through him.

Ro 6:22 — But now being made free from sin, and become servants to God, ye have your fruit unto holiness, and the end everlasting life.

1Co 1:30 — But of him are ye in Christ Jesus, who of God is made unto us wisdom, and righteousness, and sanctification, and redemption:

1Co 6:11 — And such were some of you: but ye are washed, but ye are sanctified, but ye are justified in the name of the Lord Jesus, and by the Spirit of our God.

2Co 5:19 — To wit, that God was in Christ, reconciling the world unto himself, not imputing their trespasses unto them; and hath committed unto us the word of reconciliation.

2Co 5:21 — For he hath made him *to be* sin for us, who knew no sin; that we might be made the righteousness of God in him.

Gal 3:6 — Even as Abraham believed God, and it was accounted to him for righteousness.

Gal 3:11 — But that no man is justified by the law in the sight of God, *it is* evident: for, The just shall live by faith.

Eph 6:14 — Stand therefore, having your loins girt about with truth, and having on the breastplate of righteousness;

Tit 3:7 — That being justified by his grace, we should be made heirs according to the hope of eternal life.

Heb 11:4 — By faith Abel offered unto God a more excellent sacrifice than Cain, by which he obtained witness that he was righteous, God testifying of his gifts: and by it he being dead yet speaketh.

Heb 11:7 — By faith Noah, being warned of God of things not seen as yet, moved with fear, prepared an ark to the saving of his house; by the which he condemned the world, and became heir of the righteousness which is by faith.

Jas 2:26 — For as the body without the spirit is dead, so faith without works is dead also.

• Kindred subjects to.

See: Adoption

See: Forgiveness

See: Regeneration

See: Sanctification

See: Sin; confession of

See: Sin; forgiveness of

JUSTUS

• A disciple nominated with Matthias to succeed Judas Iscariot.

Ac 1:23 — And they appointed two, Joseph called Barsabas, who was surnamed Justus, and Matthias.

• A believer in Corinth.

Ac 18:7 — And he departed thence, and entered into a certain *man's* house, named Justus, *one* that worshipped God, whose house joined hard to the synagogue.

• A disciple in Rome.

• Called also Jesus.

Col 4:11 — And Jesus, which is called Justus, who are of the circumcision. These only *are my* fellow workers unto the kingdom of God, which have been a comfort unto me.

JUTTAH • A Levitical city in Judah.

Jos 15:55 — Maon, Carmel, and Ziph, and Juttah,

Jos 21:16 — And Ain with her suburbs, and Juttah with her suburbs, *and* Beth-shemesh with her suburbs; nine cities out of those two tribes.

K

KABZEEL • A city of Judah.

Jos 15:21 — And the uttermost cities of the tribe of the children of Judah toward the coast of Edom southward were Kabzeel, and Eder, and Jagur,

2Sa 23:20 — And Benaiah the son of Jehoiada, the son of a valiant man, of Kabzeel, who had done many acts, he slew two lionlike men of Moab: he went down also and slew a lion in the midst of a pit in time of snow:

1Ch 11:22 — Benaiah the son of Jehoiada, the son of a valiant man of Kabzeel, who had done many acts; he slew two lionlike men of Moab: also he went down and slew a lion in a pit in a snowy day.

KADESH

• Called also Kadesh-Barnea.

• A city on the southern boundary of Palestine.

Jos 15:3 — And it went out to the south side to Maaleh-acrabbim, and passed along to Zin, and ascended up on the south side unto Kadesh-barnea, and passed along to Hezron, and went up to Adar, and fetched a compass to Karkaa:

• Smitten by Chedorlaomer.

Ge 14:7 — And they returned, and came to En-mishpat, which *is* Kadesh, and smote all the country of the Amalekites, and also the Amorites that dwelt in Hazezon-tamar.

• Abraham dwells by the wells near.

Ge 14:7 — And they returned, and came to En-mishpat, which *is* Kadesh, and smote all the country of the Amalekites, and also the Amorites that dwelt in Hazezon-tamar.

Ge 16:14 — Wherefore the well was called Beer-lahai-roi; behold, *it is* between Kadesh and Bered.

Ge 20:1 — And Abraham journeyed from thence toward the south country, and dwelled between Kadesh and Shur, and sojourned in Gerar.

• Israel encamps at.

Nu 12:16 — And afterward the people removed from Hazeroth, and pitched in the wilderness of Paran.

Nu 13:26 — And they went and came to Moses, and to Aaron, and to all the congregation of the children of Israel, unto the wilderness of Paran, to Kadesh; and brought back word unto them, and unto all the congregation, and shewed them the fruit of the land.

Nu 20:1 — Then came the children of Israel, *even* the whole congregation, into the desert of Zin in the first month: and the people abode in Kadesh; and Miriam died there, and was buried there.

Nu 33:36 — And they removed from Ezion-gaber, and pitched in the wilderness of Zin, which *is* Kadesh.

• Canaanites defeated at.

Jos 10:41 — And Joshua smote them from Kadesh-barnea even unto Gaza, and all the country of Goshen, even unto Gibeon.

KADMIEL

• A Levite.

Ezr 2:40 — The Levites: the children of Jeshua and Kadmiel, of the children of Hodaviah, seventy and four.

Ezr 3:9 — Then stood Jeshua *with* his sons and his brethren, Kadmiel and his sons, the sons of Judah, together, to set forward the workmen in the house of God: the sons of Henadad, *with* their sons and their brethren the Levites.

Ne 7:43 — The Levites: the children of Jeshua, of Kadmiel, *and* of the children of Hodevah, seventy and four.

Ne 12:8 — Moreover the Levites: Jeshua, Binnui, Kadmiel, Sherebiah, Judah, *and* Mattaniah, *which was* over the thanksgiving, he and his brethren.

Ne 12:24 — And the chief of the Levites: Hashabiah, Sherebiah, and Jeshua the son of Kadmiel, with their brethren over against them, to praise *and* to give thanks, according to the commandment of David the man of God, ward over against ward.

• A Levite who assisted in leading the devotions of the people.

Ne 9:4–5

Ne 10:9 — And the Levites: both Jeshua the son of Azaniah, Binnui of the sons of Henadad, Kadmiel;

KALLAI • A priest.

Ne 12:20 — Of Sallai, Kallai; of Amok, Eber;

KANAH

• A brook dividing Ephraim from Manasseh.

Jos 16:8 — The border went out from Tappuah westward unto the river Kanah; and the goings out thereof were at the sea. This *is* the inheritance of the tribe of the children of Ephraim by their families.

Jos 17:9 — And the coast descended unto the river Kanah, southward of the river: these cities of Ephraim *are* among the cities of Manasseh: the coast of Manasseh also *was* on the north side of the river, and the outgoings of it were at the sea:

• A town in Asher.

Jos 19:28 — And Hebron, and Rehob, and Hammon, and Kanah, *even* unto great Zidon;

KAREAH

• Called also Careah.

• Father of Johanan.

Jer 41:13–14

2Ki 25:23 — And when all the captains of the armies, they and their men, heard that the king of Babylon had made Gedaliah governor, there came to Gedaliah to Mizpah, even Ishmael the son of Nethaniah, and Johanan the son of Careah, and Seraiah the son of Tanhumeth the Netophathite, and Jaazaniah the son of a Maachathite, they and their men.

Jer 40:8 — Then they came to Gedaliah to Mizpah, even Ishmael the son of Nethaniah, and Johanan and Jonathan the sons of Kareah, and Seraiah the son of Tanhumeth, and the sons of Ephai the Netophathite, and Jezaniah the son of a Maachathite, they and their men.

Jer 40:13 — Moreover Johanan the son of Kareah, and all the captains of the forces that *were* in the fields, came to Gedaliah to Mizpah,

Jer 41:11 — But when Johanan the son of Kareah, and all the captains of the forces that *were* with him, heard of all the evil that Ishmael the son of Nethaniah had done,

Jer 41:16 — Then took Johanan the son of Kareah, and all the captains of the forces that *were* with him, all the remnant of the people whom he had recovered from Ishmael the son of Nethaniah, from Mizpah, after *that* he had slain Gedaliah the son of Ahikam, *even* mighty men of war, and the women, and the children, and the eunuchs, whom he had brought again from Gibeon:

KARKAA • A city of Judah.

Jos 15:3 — And it went out to the south side to Maaleh-acrabbim, and passed along to Zin, and ascended up on the south side unto Kadesh-barnea, and passed along to Hezron, and went up to Adar, and fetched a compass to Karkaa:

KARKOR • A city in Gad.

Jgs 8:10 — Now Zebah and Zalmunna *were* in Karkor, and their hosts with them, about fifteen thousand *men,* all that were left of all the hosts of the children of the east: for there fell an hundred and twenty thousand men that drew sword.

KARTAH • A city of Zebulun.

Jos 21:34 — And unto the families of the children of Merari, the rest of the Levites, out of the tribe of Zebulun, Jokneam with her suburbs, and Kartah with her suburbs,

KARTAN • A Levitical city in Naphtali.

Jos 21:32 — And out of the tribe of Naphtali, Kedesh in Galilee with her suburbs, *to be* a city of refuge for the slayer; and Hammoth-dor with her suburbs, and Kartan with her suburbs; three cities.

KATTATH • A city in Zebulun.

Jos 19:15 — And Kattath, and Nahallal, and Shimron, and Idalah, and Bethlehem: twelve cities with their villages.

KEDAR

• Son of Ishmael.

Ge 25:13 — And these *are* the names of the sons of Ishmael, by their names, according to their generations: the firstborn of Ishmael, Nebajoth; and Kedar, and Adbeel, and Mibsam,

1Ch 1:29 — These *are* their generations: The firstborn of Ishmael, Nebaioth; then Kedar, and Adbeel, and Mibsam,

• A nomadic clan of the Ishmaelites.

Ps 120:5 — Woe is me, that I sojourn in Mesech, *that* I dwell in the tents of Kedar!

SS 1:5 — I *am* black, but comely, O ye daughters of Jerusalem, as the tents of Kedar, as the curtains of Solomon.

Isa 21:16 — For thus hath the Lord said unto me, Within a year, according to the years of an hireling, and all the glory of Kedar shall fail:

Isa 42:11 — Let the wilderness and the cities thereof lift up *their voice,* the villages *that* Kedar doth inhabit: let the inhabitants of the rock sing, let them shout from the top of the mountains.

Isa 60:7 — All the flocks of Kedar shall be gathered together unto thee, the rams of Nebaioth shall minister unto thee: they shall come up with acceptance on mine altar, and I will glorify the house of my glory.

Jer 49:28 — Concerning Kedar, and concerning the kingdoms of Hazor, which Nebuchadrezzar king of Babylon shall smite, thus saith the LORD; Arise ye, go up to Kedar, and spoil the men of the east.

• Flocks of.

Isa 60:7 — All the flocks of Kedar shall be gathered together unto thee, the rams of Nebaioth shall minister unto thee: they shall come up with acceptance on mine altar, and I will glorify the house of my glory.

Jer 49:28 — Concerning Kedar, and concerning the kingdoms of Hazor, which Nebuchadrezzar king of Babylon shall smite, thus saith the LORD; Arise ye, go up to Kedar, and spoil the men of the east.

• Princes and commerce of.

Eze 27:21 — Arabia, and all the princes of Kedar, they occupied with thee in lambs, and rams, and goats: in these *were they* thy merchants.

KEDEMAH • Son of Ishmael.

Ge 25:15 — Hadar, and Tema, Jetur, Naphish, and Kedemah:

1Ch 1:31 — Jetur, Naphish, and Kedemah. These are the sons of Ishmael.

KEDEMOTH

• A city of Moab.

• Allotted to Reuben and the Merarite Levites.

Jos 13:18 — And Jahaza, and Kedemoth, and Mephaath,

1Ch 6:79 — Kedemoth also with her suburbs, and Mephaath with her suburbs:

• Encircled by a wilderness of same name.

Dt 2:26 — And I sent messengers out of the wilderness of Kedemoth unto Sihon king of Heshbon with words of peace, saying,

KEDESH

• A city of Judah.

Jos 15:23 — And Kedesh, and Hazor, and Ithnan,

• Possibly identical with Kadesh-Barnea.

• A Canaanite city taken by Joshua.

Jos 12:22 — The king of Kedesh, one; the king of Jokneam of Carmel, one;

1Ch 6:72 — And out of the tribe of Issachar; Kedesh with her suburbs, Daberath with her suburbs,

• Called also Kishion and Kishon.

Jos 19:20 — And Rabbith, and Kishion, and Abez,

Jos 21:28 — And out of the tribe of Issachar, Kishon with her suburbs, Dabareh with her suburbs,

• A city of refuge.

Jos 20:7 — And they appointed Kedesh in Galilee in mount Naphtali, and Shechem in mount Ephraim, and Kirjath-arba, which *is* Hebron, in the mountain of Judah.

Jos 21:32 — And out of the tribe of Naphtali, Kedesh in Galilee with her suburbs, *to be* a city of refuge for the slayer; and Hammoth-dor with her suburbs, and Kartan with her suburbs; three cities.

• Called also Kedesh-Naphtali. A city of refuge.

Judg. 4:6 And she sent and called Barak the son of Abinoam out of Kedeshnaphtali, and said unto him, Hath not the LORD God of Israel commanded, *saying,* Go and draw toward mount Tabor, and take with thee ten thousand men of the children of Naphtali and of the children of Zebulun?

• Home of Barak and Heber.

Jgs 4:6 — And she sent and called Barak the son of Abinoam out of Kedesh-naphtali, and said unto him, Hath not the LORD God of Israel commanded, *saying,* Go and draw toward mount Tabor, and take with thee ten thousand men of the children of Naphtali and of the children of Zebulun?

Jgs 4:9 — And she said, I will surely go with thee: notwithstanding the journey that thou takest shall not be for thine honour; for the LORD shall sell Sisera into the hand of a woman. And Deborah arose, and went with Barak to Kedesh.

Jgs 4:11 — Now Heber the Kenite, *which was* of the children of Hobab the father in law of Moses, had severed himself from the Kenites, and pitched his tent unto the plain of Zaanaim, which *is* by Kedesh.

• Captured by Tiglath-pileser.

2Ki 15:29 — In the days of Pekah king of Israel came Tiglath-pileser king of Assyria, and took Ijon, and Abel-beth-maachah, and Janoah, and Kedesh, and Hazor, and Gilead, and Galilee, all the land of Naphtali, and carried them captive to Assyria.

KEHELATHAH • An encampment of Israel.

Nu 33:22–23

KEILAH

• One of a group of nine cities in the southern part of Palestine allotted to Judah.

Jos 15:44 — And Keilah, and Achzib, and Mareshah; nine cities with their villages:

• Philistines make a predatory excursion against, after harvest.

1Sa 23:1 — Then they told David, saying, Behold, the Philistines fight against Keilah, and they rob the threshingfloors.

• David rescues.

1Sa 23:2–13

• Rulers of, aid in restoring the wall of Jerusalem after the captivity.

Ne 3:17–18

• A descendant of Caleb.

1Ch 4:19 — And the sons of *his* wife Hodiah the sister of Naham, the father of Keilah the Garmite, and Eshtemoa the Maachathite.

KELAIAH

• Called also Kelita.

• A Levite who divorced his Gentile wife after the captivity, and assisted Ezra in expounding the law.

Ezr 10:23 — Also of the Levites; Jozabad, and Shimei, and Kelaiah, (the same *is* Kelita,) Pethahiah, Judah, and Eliezer.

Ne 8:7 — Also Jeshua, and Bani, and Sherebiah, Jamin, Akkub, Shabbethai, Hodijah, Maaseiah, Kelita, Azariah, Jozabad, Hanan, Pelaiah, and the Levites, caused the people to understand the law: and the people *stood* in their place.

Ne 10:10 — And their brethren, Shebaniah, Hodijah, Kelita, Pelaiah, Hanan,

KEMUEL

• Son of Nahor.

Ge 22:21 — Huz his firstborn, and Buz his brother, and Kemuel the father of Aram,

• A prince of Ephraim.

Nu 34:24 — And the prince of the tribe of the children of Ephraim, Kemuel the son of Shiphtan.

• A Levite.

1Ch 27:17 — Of the Levites, Hashabiah the son of Kemuel: of the Aronites, Zadok:

KENAN • See: Cainan

KENATH

• Called also Nobah.

• A city of Gilead.

Nu 32:42 — And Nobah went and took Kenath, and the villages thereof, and called it Nobah, after his own name.

1Ch 2:23 — And he took Geshur, and Aram, with the towns of Jair, from them, with Kenath, and the towns thereof, *even* threescore cities. All these *belonged to* the sons of Machir the father of Gilead.

KENAZ

• Grandson of Esau.

Ge 36:11 — And the sons of Eliphaz were Teman, Omar, Zepho, and Gatam, and Kenaz.

Ge 36:15 — These *were* dukes of the sons of Esau: the sons of Eliphaz the firstborn *son* of Esau; duke Teman, duke Omar, duke Zepho, duke Kenaz,

1Ch 1:36 — The sons of Eliphaz; Teman, and Omar, Zephi, and Gatam, Kenaz, and Timna, and Amalek.

• A duke of Edom.

Ge 36:42 — Duke Kenaz, duke Teman, duke Mibzar,

1Ch 1:53 — Duke Kenaz, duke Teman, duke Mibzar,

• Brother of Caleb.

Jos 15:17 — And Othniel the son of Kenaz, the brother of Caleb, took it: and he gave him Achsah his daughter to wife.

Jgs 1:13 — And Othniel the son of Kenaz, Caleb's younger brother, took it: and he gave him Achsah his daughter to wife.

Jgs 3:9 — And when the children of Israel cried unto the LORD, the LORD raised up a deliverer to the children of Israel, who delivered them, *even* Othniel the son of Kenaz, Caleb's younger brother.

Jgs 3:11 — And the land had rest forty years. And Othniel the son of Kenaz died.

1Ch 4:13 — And the sons of Kenaz; Othniel, and Seraiah: and the sons of Othniel; Hathath.

• Grandson of Caleb.

1Ch 4:15 — And the sons of Caleb the son of Jephunneh; Iru, Elah, and Naam: and the sons of Elah, even Kenaz.

KENITES

• A Canaanitish tribe whose country was given to Abraham.

Nu 24:21–23

Ge 15:19 — The Kenites, and the Kenizzites, and the Kadmonites,

• The descendants of Jethro, a Midianite, father-in-law of Moses.

Jgs 1:16 — And the children of the Kenite, Moses' father in law, went up out of the city of palm trees with the children of Judah into the wilderness of Judah, which *lieth* in the south of Arad; and they went and dwelt among the people.

Jgs 4:11 — Now Heber the Kenite, *which was* of the children of Hobab the father in law of Moses, had severed himself from the Kenites, and pitched his tent unto the plain of Zaanaim, which *is* by Kedesh.

1Ch 2:55 — And the families of the scribes which dwelt at Jabez; the Tirathites, the Shimeathites, *and* Suchathites. These *are* the Kenites that came of Hemath, the father of the house of Rechab.

• Join the Israelites and dwell later in the wilderness of Judah.

Jgs 1:16–17

• Jael, one of the, betrays and slays Sisera.

Jgs 4:17–21

KENIZZITES • An Edomitish tribe whose land was promised to Abraham.

Ge 15:19 — The Kenites, and the Kenizzites, and the Kadmonites,

KERCHIEF ✧See: Handkerchief

KEREN-HAPPUCH • Youngest daughter of Job.

Job 42:14 — And he called the name of the first, Jemima; and the name of the second, Kezia; and the name of the third, Keren-happuch.

KERIOTH

• A city of Judah.

Jos 15:25 — And Hazor, Hadattah, and Kerioth, *and* Hezron, which *is* Hazor,

• Called also Kirioth. A city of Moab.

Jer 48:24 — And upon Kerioth, and upon Bozrah, and upon all the cities of the land of Moab, far or near.

Jer 48:41 — Kerioth is taken, and the strong holds are surprised, and the mighty men's hearts in Moab at that day shall be as the heart of a woman in her pangs.

Am 2:2 — But I will send a fire upon Moab, and it shall devour the palaces of Kirioth: and Moab shall die with tumult, with shouting, *and* with the sound of the trumpet:

KETURAH • Wife or concubine of Abraham.

Ge 25:1–4

1Ch 1:32 — Now the sons of Keturah, Abraham's concubine: she bare Zimran, and Jokshan, and Medan, and Midian, and Ishbak, and Shuah. And the sons of Jokshan; Sheba, and Dedan.

KEY

Jgs 3:25 — And they tarried till they were ashamed: and, behold, he opened not the doors of the parlour; therefore they took a key, and opened *them:* and, behold, their lord *was* fallen down dead on the earth.

• A symbol of authority.

Isa 22:22 — And the key of the house of David will I lay upon his shoulder; so he shall open, and none shall shut; and he shall shut, and none shall open.

Mt 16:19 — And I will give unto thee the keys of the kingdom of heaven: and whatsoever thou shalt bind on earth shall be bound in heaven: and whatsoever thou shalt loose on earth shall be loosed in heaven.

Rev 1:18 — I *am* he that liveth, and was dead; and, behold, I am alive for evermore, Amen; and have the keys of hell and of death.

Rev 3:7 — And to the angel of the church in Philadelphia write; These things saith he that is holy, he that is true, he that hath the key of David, he that openeth, and no man shutteth; and shutteth, and no man openeth;

Rev 9:1 — And the fifth angel sounded, and I saw a star fall from heaven unto the earth: and to him was given the key of the bottomless pit.

Rev 20:1 — And I saw an angel come down from heaven, having the key of the bottomless pit and a great chain in his hand.

• Figurative.

Lk 11:52 — Woe unto you, lawyers! for ye have taken away the key of knowledge: ye entered not in yourselves, and them that were entering in ye hindered.

KEZIA • Second daughter of Job.

Job 42:14 — And he called the name of the first, Jemima; and the name of the second, Kezia; and the name of the third, Keren-happuch.

KEZIZ • A valley and city of Benjamin.

Jos 18:21 — Now the cities of the tribe of the children of Benjamin according to their families were Jericho, and Beth-hoglah, and the valley of Keziz,

KIBROTH-HATTAAVAH • A station where the Israelites were miraculously fed with quails.

Nu 11:31–35; 33:16–17

Dt 9:22 — And at Taberah, and at Massah, and at Kibroth-hattaavah, ye provoked the LORD to wrath.

KIBZAIM • A Levitical city in Ephraim.

Jos 21:22 — And Kibzaim with her suburbs, and Beth-horon with her suburbs; four cities.

KIDNAPPING

• Forbidden.

Ex 21:16 — And he that stealeth a man, and selleth him, or if he be found in his hand, he shall surely be put to death.

Dt 24:7 — If a man be found stealing any of his brethren of the children of Israel, and maketh merchandise of him, or selleth him; then that thief shall die; and thou shalt put evil away from among you.

• Instances of.

Jgs 21:20–23

KIDNEY

• Burnt offering of the.

Le 3:1–17; 4:9–10; 7:4–5

Ex 29:13 — And thou shalt take all the fat that covereth the inwards, and the caul *that is* above the liver, and the two kidneys, and the fat that is upon them, and burn *them* upon the altar.

Ex 29:22 — Also thou shalt take of the ram the fat and the rump, and the fat that covereth the inwards, and the *caul* above the liver, and the two kidneys, and the fat that *is* upon them, and the right shoulder; for it *is* a ram of consecration:

Le 8:16 — And he took all the fat that *was* upon the inwards, and caul *above* the liver, and the two kidneys, and their fat, and Moses burned *it* upon the altar.

Le 9:10 — But the fat, and the kidneys, and the caul above the liver of the sin offering, he burnt upon the altar; as the LORD commanded Moses.

Dt 32:14 — Butter of kine, and milk of sheep, with fat of lambs, and rams of the breed of Bashan, and goats, with the fat of kidneys of wheat; and thou didst drink the pure blood of the grape.

KIDRON

• Called also Cedron.

• A valley and stream between Jerusalem and the Mount of Olives.

1Ki 2:37 — For it shall be, *that* on the day thou goest out, and passest over the brook Kidron, thou shalt know for certain that thou shalt surely die: thy blood shall be upon thine own head.

Ne 2:15 — Then went I up in the night by the brook, and viewed the wall, and turned back, and entered by the gate of the valley, and *so* returned.

Jer 31:40 — And the whole valley of the dead bodies, and of the ashes, and all the fields unto the brook of Kidron, unto the corner of the horse gate toward the east, *shall be* holy unto the LORD; it shall not be plucked up, nor thrown down any more for ever.

• David flees from Absalom across.

2Sa 15:23 — And all the country wept with a loud voice, and all the people passed over: the king also himself passed over the brook Kidron, and all the people passed over, toward the way of the wilderness.

• Destruction of idols at, by Asa, Josiah, and the Levites.

1Ki 15:13 — And also Maachah his mother, even her he removed from *being* queen, because she had made an idol in a grove; and Asa destroyed her idol, and burnt *it* by the brook Kidron.

2Ki 23:6 — And he brought out the grove from the house of the LORD, without Jerusalem, unto the brook Kidron, and burned it at the brook Kidron, and stamped *it* small to powder, and cast the powder thereof upon the graves of the children of the people.

2Ki 23:12 — And the altars that *were* on the top of the upper chamber of Ahaz, which the kings of Judah had made, and the altars which Manasseh had made in the two courts of the house of the LORD, did the king beat down, and brake *them* down from thence, and cast the dust of them into the brook Kidron.

2Ch 29:16 — And the priests went into the inner part of the house of the LORD, to cleanse *it,* and brought out all the uncleanness that they found in the temple of the LORD into the court of the house of the LORD. And the Levites took *it,* to carry *it* out abroad into the brook Kidron.

- **Source of, closed by Hezekiah.**

2Ch 32:4 — So there was gathered much people together, who stopped all the fountains, and the brook that ran through the midst of the land, saying, Why should the kings of Assyria come, and find much water?

- **Jesus crossed, on the night of his agony.**

Jn 18:1 — When Jesus had spoken these words, he went forth with his disciples over the brook Cedron, where was a garden, into the which he entered, and his disciples.

KILLING *See:* Homicide

KINAH • A city of Judah.

Jos 15:22 — And Kinah, and Dimonah, and Adadah,

KINDNESS

Dt 22:1–4; Zec 7:9–10; Mt 25:34–36; Lk 6:34–35; Ro 15:1–2; 1Co 13:4–7; Gal 6:1–2; 1Ti 5:1–25; 1Pe 3:8–9; 1Jn 3:17–18

Le 19:34 — *But* the stranger that dwelleth with you shall be unto you as one born among you, and thou shalt love him as thyself; for ye were strangers in the land of Egypt: I *am* the LORD your God.

Ps 112:5 — A good man sheweth favour, and lendeth: he will guide his affairs with discretion.

Pr 14:21 — He that despiseth his neighbour sinneth: but he that hath mercy on the poor, happy *is* he.

Pr 19:22 — The desire of a man *is* his kindness: and a poor man *is* better than a liar.

Pr 31:26 — She openeth her mouth with wisdom; and in her tongue *is* the law of kindness.

Isa 11:13 — The envy also of Ephraim shall depart, and the adversaries of Judah shall be cut off: Ephraim shall not envy Judah, and Judah shall not vex Ephraim.

Mt 5:7 — Blessed *are* the merciful: for they shall obtain mercy.

Mt 5:42 — Give to him that asketh thee, and from him that would borrow of thee turn not thou away.

Lk 6:30 — Give to every man that asketh of thee; and of him that taketh away thy goods ask *them* not again.

Ac 20:35 — I have shewed you all things, how that so labouring ye ought to support the weak, and to remember the words of the Lord Jesus, how he said, It is more blessed to give than to receive.

Ro 12:15 — Rejoice with them that do rejoice, and weep with them that weep.

Ro 15:5 — Now the God of patience and consolation grant you to be likeminded one toward another according to Christ Jesus:

Gal 6:10 — As we have therefore opportunity, let us do good unto all *men,* especially unto them who are of the household of faith.

Eph 4:32 — And be ye kind one to another, tenderhearted, forgiving one another, even as God for Christ's sake hath forgiven you.

Col 3:12 — Put on therefore, as the elect of God, holy and beloved, bowels of mercies, kindness, humbleness of mind, meekness, longsuffering;

Col 3:14 — And above all these things *put on* charity, which is the bond of perfectness.

Heb 5:2 — Who can have compassion on the ignorant, and on them that are out of the way; for that he himself also is compassed with infirmity.

1Pe 4:8 — And above all things have fervent charity among yourselves: for charity shall cover the multitude of sins.

2Pe 1:7 — And to godliness brotherly kindness; and to brotherly kindness charity.

- **Instances of.**
  - **Pharaoh to Jacob.** Ge 45:16–20; 47:5–6
  - **Pharaoh's daughter to Moses.** Ex 2:6–10
  - **Rahab to the spies.** Jos 2:6–16
  - **David to Mephibosheth.** 2Sa 9:1–13
  - **Joab to Absalom.** 2Sa 14:1–24
  - **Ahab to Ben-hadad.** 1Ki 20:32–34
  - **Elisha to the woman whose son he restored to life.** 2Ki 8:1
  - **Evil-merodach to Jehoiachin.** 2Ki 25:28–30
  - **Jehoshabeath to Joash.** 2Ch 22:11
  - **Jews to the people.** Ne 5:8–19
  - **Mordecai to Esther.** Est 2:7
  - **Nebuchadnezzar to Jeremiah.** Jer 39:11–12
  - **Joseph to Mary.** Mt 1:19
  - **Centurion to his servant.** Lk 7:2–6
  - **Jews to Mary and Martha.** Jn 11:19, 33
  - **John to Mary.** Jn 19:27
  - **Felix to Paul.** Ac 24:23
  - **Julius to Paul.** Ac 27:3, 43
  - **Onesiphorus to Paul.** 2Ti 1:16–18

KINE

- **Pharaoh's dream of.**

Ge 41:2–7, 26–30

See: Cattle, of the bovine species

- **Figurative.**

Am 4:1 — Hear this word, ye kine of Bashan, that *are* in the mountain of Samaria, which oppress the poor, which crush the needy, which say to their masters, Bring, and let us drink.

KING

• Called King of Kings.

Ezr 7:12 — Artaxerxes, king of kings, unto Ezra the priest, a scribe of the law of the God of heaven, perfect *peace,* and at such a time.

Eze 26:7 — For thus saith the Lord GOD; Behold, I will bring upon Tyrus Nebuchadrezzar king of Babylon, a king of kings, from the north, with horses, and with chariots, and with horsemen, and companies, and much people.

Da 2:37 — Thou, O king, *art* a king of kings: for the God of heaven hath given thee a kingdom, power, and strength, and glory.

• Divinely authorized.

1Sa 9:16–17; 2Ch 2:11–12

Dt 17:15 — Thou shalt in any wise set *him* king over thee, whom the LORD thy God shall choose: *one* from among thy brethren shalt thou set king over thee: thou mayest not set a stranger over thee, which *is* not thy brother.

1Sa 16:12 — And he sent, and brought him in. Now he *was* ruddy, *and* withal of a beautiful countenance, and goodly to look to. And the LORD said, Arise, anoint him: for this *is* he.

1Ch 22:10 — He shall build an house for my name; and he shall be my son, and I *will be* his father; and I will establish the throne of his kingdom over Israel for ever.

Pr 8:15 — By me kings reign, and princes decree justice.

Da 2:21 — And he changeth the times and the seasons: he removeth kings, and setteth up kings: he giveth wisdom unto the wise, and knowledge to them that know understanding:

Da 2:37 — Thou, O king, *art* a king of kings: for the God of heaven hath given thee a kingdom, power, and strength, and glory.

Da 4:17 — This matter *is* by the decree of the watchers, and the demand by the word of the holy ones: to the intent that the living may know that the most High ruleth in the kingdom of men, and giveth it to whomsoever he will, and setteth up over it the basest of men.

Da 5:20 — But when his heart was lifted up, and his mind hardened in pride, he was deposed from his kingly throne, and they took his glory from him:

Hos 8:4 — They have set up kings, but not by me: they have made princes, and I knew *it* not: of their silver and their gold have they made them idols, that they may be cut off.

Hos 13:11 — I gave thee a king in mine anger, and took *him* away in my wrath.

• How chosen.

• By divine appointment: Saul.

1Sa 10:1 — Then Samuel took a vial of oil, and poured *it* upon his head, and kissed him, and said, *Is it* not because the LORD hath anointed thee *to be* captain over his inheritance?

• David and the Davidic dynasty.

1Sa 16:1–13

• Hereditary succession.

2Sa 7:12–16; 1Ki 1:28–30; 2Ch 21:3–4; Ps 89:35–37

See: Israel, Judah; list of rulers

• Not hereditary.

1Ch 1:43–51

See: Israel, The Revolt of the Ten Tribes; the kings of Israel

• By lot.

1Sa 10:20–21

• Modes of induction into office.

• By anointing.

See: Anointing

• By proclamation.

1Ki 1:33–34

2Sa 15:10 — But Absalom sent spies throughout all the tribes of Israel, saying, As soon as ye hear the sound of the trumpet, then ye shall say, Absalom reigneth in Hebron.

2Ki 9:13 — Then they hasted, and took every man his garment, and put *it* under him on the top of the stairs, and blew with trumpets, saying, Jehu is king.

2Ki 11:12 — And he brought forth the king's son, and put the crown upon him, and *gave him* the testimony; and they made him king, and anointed him; and they clapped their hands, and said, God save the king.

• By an oath.

2Ki 11:4 — And the seventh year Jehoiada sent and fetched the rulers over hundreds, with the captains and the guard, and brought them to him into the house of the LORD, and made a covenant with them, and took an oath of them in the house of the LORD, and shewed them the king's son.

• Ceremonial recognition of.

• Prostration.

1Sa 25:41 — And she arose, and bowed herself on *her* face to the earth, and said, Behold, *let* thine handmaid *be* a servant to wash the feet of the servants of my lord.

2Sa 9:6 — Now when Mephibosheth, the son of Jonathan, the son of Saul, was come unto David, he fell on his face, and did reverence. And David said, Mephibosheth. And he answered, Behold thy servant!

2Sa 9:8 — And he bowed himself, and said, What is thy servant, that thou shouldest look upon such a dead dog as I *am?*

1Ki 1:23 — And they told the king, saying, Behold Nathan the prophet. And when he was come in before the king, he bowed himself before the king with his face to the ground.

1Ki 1:31 — Then Bath-sheba bowed with *her* face to the earth, and did reverence to the king, and said, Let my lord king David live for ever.

1Ki 1:47 — And moreover the king's servants came to bless our lord king David, saying, God make the name of Solomon better than thy name, and make his throne greater than thy throne. And the king bowed himself upon the bed.

- **Obeisance.**
  1Ki 1:16 — And Bath-sheba bowed, and did obeisance unto the king. And the king said, What wouldest thou?
- **Kneeling before.**
  Mt 27:29 — And when they had platted a crown of thorns, they put *it* upon his head, and a reed in his right hand: and they bowed the knee before him, and mocked him, saying, Hail, King of the Jews!
- **Salutation to, "O king, live forever".**
  Da 2:4 — Then spake the Chaldeans to the king in Syriack, O king, live for ever: tell thy servants the dream, and we will shew the interpretation.
  Da 6:6 — Then these presidents and princes assembled together to the king, and said thus unto him, King Darius, live for ever.
  Da 6:21 — Then said Daniel unto the king, O king, live for ever.

- **Acts as judge.**
  2Ki 8:1–6; Ps 72:1–4; Ac 25:11–12
  2Sa 8:15 — And David reigned over all Israel; and David executed judgment and justice unto all his people.
  2Sa 15:2 — And Absalom rose up early, and stood beside the way of the gate: and it was so, that when any man that had a controversy came to the king for judgment, then Absalom called unto him, and said, Of what city *art* thou? And he said, Thy servant is of one of the tribes of Israel.
  1Ki 10:9 — Blessed be the LORD thy God, which delighted in thee, to set thee on the throne of Israel: because the LORD loved Israel for ever, therefore made he thee king, to do judgment and justice.
  Ps 122:5 — For there are set thrones of judgment, the thrones of the house of David.
  Ac 25:20 — And because I doubted of such manner of questions, I asked *him* whether he would go to Jerusalem, and there be judged of these matters.
- **Precepts concerning.**
  Dt 17:14–19; Pr 31:4–5; Eze 46:16–18
- **Obedience to, enjoined.**
  Ecc 8:2–5
- **Rights and duties of.**
  Pr 25:5–6
  Pr 25:2 — *It is* the glory of God to conceal a thing: but the honour of kings *is* to search out a matter.
  Pr 25:15 — By long forbearing is a prince persuaded, and a soft tongue breaketh the bone.
  Pr 29:4 — The king by judgment establisheth the land: but he that receiveth gifts overthroweth it.
  Pr 29:12 — If a ruler hearken to lies, all his servants *are* wicked.
  Pr 29:14 — The king that faithfully judgeth the poor, his throne shall be established for ever.
  Jer 21:12 — O house of David, thus saith the LORD; Execute judgment in the morning, and deliver *him that is* spoiled out of the hand of the oppressor, lest my fury go out like fire, and burn that none can quench *it*, because of the evil of your doings.
- **Exercise executive clemency.**
  1Sa 11:13 — And Saul said, There shall not a man be put to death this day: for to day the LORD hath wrought salvation in Israel.
- **Constitutional restrictions of.**
  Dt 17:18–20; 1Sa 10:24–25; Jer 34:8–11; Da 6:12–15
  2Sa 5:3 — So all the elders of Israel came to the king to Hebron; and king David made a league with them in Hebron before the LORD: and they anointed David king over Israel.
  2Ki 11:12 — And he brought forth the king's son, and put the crown upon him, and *gave him* the testimony; and they made him king, and anointed him; and they clapped their hands, and said, God save the king.
  2Ki 11:17 — And Jehoiada made a covenant between the LORD and the king and the people that they should be the LORD'S people; between the king also and the people.
  2Ch 23:11 — Then they brought out the king's son, and put upon him the crown, and *gave him* the testimony, and made him king. And Jehoiada and his sons anointed him, and said, God save the king.
- **Influenced by popular opinion.**
  - **Saul.**
    1Sa 14:45 — And the people said unto Saul, Shall Jonathan die, who hath wrought this great salvation in Israel? God forbid: *as* the LORD liveth, there shall not one hair of his head fall to the ground; for he hath wrought with God this day. So the people rescued Jonathan, that he died not.
    1Sa 15:24 — And Saul said unto Samuel, I have sinned: for I have transgressed the commandment of the LORD, and thy words: because I feared the people, and obeyed their voice.
  - **David.**
    2Ch 20:21 — And when he had consulted with the people, he appointed singers unto the LORD, and that should praise the beauty of holiness, as they went out before the army, and to say, Praise the LORD; for his mercy *endureth* for ever.
  - **Hezekiah.**
    2Ch 30:2 — For the king had taken counsel, and his princes, and all the congregation in Jerusalem, to keep the passover in the second month.
  - **Zedekiah.**
    Jer 38:24–27
    Jer 38:19 — And Zedekiah the king said unto Jeremiah, I am afraid of the Jews that are fallen to the Chaldeans, lest they deliver me into their hand, and they mock me.
  - **Herod.**
    Ac 12:2–3
    Mt 14:5 — And when he would have put him to death, he feared the multitude, because they counted him as a prophet.
  - **Pilate.**
    Jn 19:6–13

• **Religious duties of.**
Eze 45:9–25; 46:4–8
Eze 46:2 — And the prince shall enter by the way of the porch of *that* gate without, and shall stand by the post of the gate, and the priests shall prepare his burnt offering and his peace offerings, and he shall worship at the threshold of the gate: then he shall go forth; but the gate shall not be shut until the evening.

• **Deification of.**
Eze 28:2 — Son of man, say unto the prince of Tyrus, Thus saith the Lord GOD; Because thine heart *is* lifted up, and thou hast said, I *am* a God, I sit *in* the seat of God, in the midst of the seas; yet thou *art* a man, and not God, though thou set thine heart as the heart of God:
Eze 28:9 — Wilt thou yet say before him that slayeth thee, I *am* God? but thou *shalt be* a man, and no God, in the hand of him that slayeth thee.

• **Loyalty to, enjoined.**
Pr 16:14–15
Ecc 10:20 — Curse not the king, no not in thy thought; and curse not the rich in thy bedchamber: for a bird of the air shall carry the voice, and that which hath wings shall tell the matter.

• **Influence of queens over.**

• **Bath-sheba.**
1Ki 1:28–34

• **Jezebel.**
1Ki 19:1–3; 21:5–16
1Ki 18:4 — For it was *so,* when Jezebel cut off the prophets of the LORD, that Obadiah took an hundred prophets, and hid them by fifty in a cave, and fed them with bread and water.)
1Ki 18:13 — Was it not told my lord what I did when Jezebel slew the prophets of the LORD, how I hid an hundred men of the LORD'S prophets by fifty in a cave, and fed them with bread and water?

• **Esther.**
Est 5:1–8

• **Respect due to.**
Job 34:18 — *Is it fit* to say to a king, *Thou art* wicked? *and* to princes, *Ye are* ungodly?
Isa 8:21 — And they shall pass through it, hardly bestead and hungry: and it shall come to pass, that when they shall be hungry, they shall fret themselves, and curse their king and their God, and look upward.
Mt 22:21 — They say unto him, Caesar's. Then saith he unto them, Render therefore unto Caesar the things which are Caesar's; and unto God the things that are God's.
Mk 12:17 — And Jesus answering said unto them, Render to Caesar the things that are Caesar's, and to God the things that are God's. And they marvelled at him.

• **Emoluments of.**

• **Confiscations of property.**
1Ki 21:1–16
2Sa 16:4 — Then said the king to Ziba, Behold, thine *are* all that *pertained* unto Mephibosheth. And Ziba said, I humbly beseech thee *that* I may find grace in thy sight, my lord, O king.

• **Spoils.**
2Sa 12:30 — And he took their king's crown from off his head, the weight whereof *was* a talent of gold with the precious stones: and it was *set* on David's head. And he brought forth the spoil of the city in great abundance.
1Ch 26:27 — Out of the spoils won in battles did they dedicate to maintain the house of the LORD.
2Ch 24:23 — And it came to pass at the end of the year, *that* the host of Syria came up against him: and they came to Judah and Jerusalem, and destroyed all the princes of the people from among the people, and sent all the spoil of them unto the king of Damascus.

• **Tariff on imports, and internal revenue on merchandise.**
1Ki 10:15–29

• **Tribute.**
2Sa 20:24 — And Adoram *was* over the tribute: and Jehoshaphat the son of Ahilud *was* recorder:
1Ki 12:18 — Then king Rehoboam sent Adoram, who *was* over the tribute; and all Israel stoned him with stones, that he died. Therefore king Rehoboam made speed to get him up to his chariot, to flee to Jerusalem.
2Ch 17:11 — Also *some* of the Philistines brought Jehoshaphat presents, and tribute silver; and the Arabians brought him flocks, seven thousand and seven hundred rams, and seven thousand and seven hundred he goats.

• **Poll tax.**
Mt 17:24–27

• **Presents.**
1Sa 10:27 — But the children of Belial said, How shall this man save us? And they despised him, and brought him no presents. But he held his peace.
1Sa 16:20 — And Jesse took an ass *laden* with bread, and a bottle of wine, and a kid, and sent *them* by David his son unto Saul.
2Sa 8:2 — And he smote Moab, and measured them with a line, casting them down to the ground; even with two lines measured he to put to death, and with one full line to keep alive. And so the Moabites became David's servants, *and* brought gifts.
1Ki 10:2 — And she came to Jerusalem with a very great train, with camels that bare spices, and very much gold, and precious stones: and when she was come to Solomon, she communed with him of all that was in her heart.
1Ki 10:10 — And she gave the king an hundred and twenty talents of gold, and of spices very great store, and precious stones: there came no more such abundance of spices as these which the queen of Sheba gave to king Solomon.
1Ki 10:25 — And they brought every man his present, vessels of silver, and vessels of gold, and garments,

and armour, and spices, horses, and mules, a rate year by year.

2Ch 9:24 — And they brought every man his present, vessels of silver, and vessels of gold, and raiment, harness, and spices, horses, and mules, a rate year by year.

Ps 72:10 — The kings of Tarshish and of the isles shall bring presents: the kings of Sheba and Seba shall offer gifts.

• Commissary of.

1Ki 4:7–19, 27–28; 1Ch 27:25–31; 2Ch 32:28–29

2Ch 26:10 — Also he built towers in the desert, and digged many wells: for he had much cattle, both in the low country, and in the plains: husbandmen *also,* and vine dressers in the mountains, and in Carmel: for he loved husbandry.

• Extensive studs of.

2Ch 9:24–25

Jgs 12:14 — And he had forty sons and thirty nephews, that rode on threescore and ten ass colts: and he judged Israel eight years.

1Ki 1:33 — The king also said unto them, Take with you the servants of your lord, and cause Solomon my son to ride upon mine own mule, and bring him down to Gihon:

1Ki 4:26 — And Solomon had forty thousand stalls of horses for his chariots, and twelve thousand horsemen.

1Ki 10:25 — And they brought every man his present, vessels of silver, and vessels of gold, and garments, and armour, and spices, horses, and mules, a rate year by year.

Est 6:8 — Let the royal apparel be brought which the king *useth* to wear, and the horse that the king rideth upon, and the crown royal which is set upon his head:

• Chief officers of.

• Captain of the host.

2Sa 8:16 — And Joab the son of Zeruiah *was* over the host; and Jehoshaphat the son of Ahilud *was* recorder;

1Ki 4:4 — And Benaiah the son of Jehoiada *was* over the host: and Zadok and Abiathar *were* the priests:

• Recorder.

2Sa 8:16 — And Joab the son of Zeruiah *was* over the host; and Jehoshaphat the son of Ahilud *was* recorder;

2Sa 20:24 — And Adoram *was* over the tribute: and Jehoshaphat the son of Ahilud *was* recorder:

1Ki 4:3 — Elihoreph and Ahiah, the sons of Shisha, scribes; Jehoshaphat the son of Ahilud, the recorder.

• Scribe.

2Sa 8:17 — And Zadok the son of Ahitub, and Ahimelech the son of Abiathar, *were* the priests; and Seraiah *was* the scribe;

2Sa 20:25 — And Sheva *was* scribe: and Zadok and Abiathar *were* the priests:

1Ki 4:3 — Elihoreph and Ahiah, the sons of Shisha, scribes; Jehoshaphat the son of Ahilud, the recorder.

• Chief priests.

2Sa 8:17 — And Zadok the son of Ahitub, and Ahimelech the son of Abiathar, *were* the priests; and Seraiah *was* the scribe;

2Sa 20:25 — And Sheva *was* scribe: and Zadok and Abiathar *were* the priests:

1Ki 4:2 — And these *were* the princes which he had; Azariah the son of Zadok the priest,

• Chief of the bodyguard.

2Sa 8:18 — And Benaiah the son of Jehoiada *was over* both the Cherethites and the Pelethites; and David's sons were chief rulers.

2Sa 15:18 — And all his servants passed on beside him; and all the Cherethites, and all the Pelethites, and all the Gittites, six hundred men which came after him from Gath, passed on before the king.

2Sa 20:23 — Now Joab *was* over all the host of Israel: and Benaiah the son of Jehoiada *was* over the Cherethites and over the Pelethites:

1Ch 11:25 — Behold, he was honourable among the thirty, but attained not to the *first* three: and David set him over his guard.

• Collector of tribute.

2Sa 20:24 — And Adoram *was* over the tribute: and Jehoshaphat the son of Ahilud *was* recorder:

• Chief ruler.

Est 3:1–2; 8:1–2

2Sa 20:26 — And Ira also the Jairite was a chief ruler about David.

1Ki 4:5 — And Azariah the son of Nathan *was* over the officers: and Zabud the son of Nathan *was* principal officer, *and* the king's friend:

Est 8:15 — And Mordecai went out from the presence of the king in royal apparel of blue and white, and with a great crown of gold, and with a garment of fine linen and purple: and the city of Shushan rejoiced and was glad.

Est 10:3 — For Mordecai the Jew *was* next unto king Ahasuerus, and great among the Jews, and accepted of the multitude of his brethren, seeking the wealth of his people, and speaking peace to all his seed.

• Counselor.

1Ki 4:5 — And Azariah the son of Nathan *was* over the officers: and Zabud the son of Nathan *was* principal officer, *and* the king's friend:

• Provincial governors.

Da 6:1–3

• Subordinate officers of.

• Governor of the household.

1Ki 4:6 — And Ahishar *was* over the household: and Adoniram the son of Abda *was* over the tribute.

2Ch 28:7 — And Zichri, a mighty man of Ephraim, slew Maaseiah the king's son, and Azrikam the governor of the house, and Elkanah *that was* next to the king.

- **Keeper of the wardrobe.**

2Ki 22:14 — So Hilkiah the priest, and Ahikam, and Achbor, and Shaphan, and Asahiah, went unto Huldah the prophetess, the wife of Shallum the son of Tikvah, the son of Harhas, keeper of the wardrobe; (now she dwelt in Jerusalem in the college;) and they communed with her.

2Ch 34:22 — And Hilkiah, and *they* that the king *had appointed,* went to Huldah the prophetess, the wife of Shallum the son of Tikvath, the son of Hasrah, keeper of the wardrobe; (now she dwelt in Jerusalem in the college:) and they spake to her to that *effect.*

- **Drunkenness of, forbidden.**

Pr 31:4–5

- **Drunken, instances of.**

Hos 7:5 — In the day of our king the princes have made *him* sick with bottles of wine; he stretched out his hand with scorners.

- **Baasha.**

1Ki 16:9 — And his servant Zimri, captain of half *his* chariots, conspired against him, as he was in Tirzah, drinking himself drunk in the house of Arza steward of *his* house in Tirzah.

- **Ben-hadad.**

1Ki 20:16 — And they went out at noon. But Ben-hadad *was* drinking himself drunk in the pavilions, he and the kings, the thirty and two kings that helped him.

- **Belshazzar.**

Da 5:1–4

Da 5:23 — But hast lifted up thyself against the Lord of heaven; and they have brought the vessels of his house before thee, and thou, and thy lords, thy wives, and thy concubines, have drunk wine in them; and thou hast praised the gods of silver, and gold, of brass, iron, wood, and stone, which see not, nor hear, nor know: and the God in whose hand thy breath *is,* and whose *are* all thy ways, hast thou not glorified:

- **Ahasuerus.**

Est 1:7 — And they gave *them* drink in vessels of gold, (the vessels being diverse one from another,) and royal wine in abundance, according to the state of the king.

Est 1:10 — On the seventh day, when the heart of the king was merry with wine, he commanded Mehuman, Biztha, Harbona, Bigtha, and Abagtha, Zethar, and Carcas, the seven chamberlains that served in the presence of Ahasuerus the king,

Est 5:6 — And the king said unto Esther at the banquet of wine, What *is* thy petition? and it shall be granted thee: and what *is* thy request? even to the half of the kingdom it shall be performed.

Est 7:2 — And the king said again unto Esther on the second day at the banquet of wine, What *is* thy petition, queen Esther? and it shall be granted thee: and what *is* thy request? and it shall be performed, *even* to the half of the kingdom.

- **Prayer for.**

Ezr 6:10 — That they may offer sacrifices of sweet savours unto the God of heaven, and pray for the life of the king, and of his sons.

- **Prayer for, enjoined.**

1Ti 2:1–2

- **Decrees of, irrevocable.**

Da 6:8–9, 12–15

Est 8:8 — Write ye also for the Jews, as it liketh you, in the king's name, and seal *it* with the king's ring: for the writing which is written in the king's name, and sealed with the king's ring, may no man reverse.

- **Chronicles of, kept.**

1Ki 11:41 — And the rest of the acts of Solomon, and all that he did, and his wisdom, *are* they not written in the book of the acts of Solomon?

1Ki 14:19 — And the rest of the acts of Jeroboam, how he warred, and how he reigned, behold, they *are* written in the book of the chronicles of the kings of Israel.

2Ki 21:25 — Now the rest of the acts of Amon which he did, *are* they not written in the book of the chronicles of the kings of Judah?

1Ch 9:1 — So all Israel were reckoned by genealogies; and, behold, they *were* written in the book of the kings of Israel and Judah, *who* were carried away to Babylon for their transgression.

1Ch 27:24 — Joab the son of Zeruiah began to number, but he finished not, because there fell wrath for it against Israel; neither was the number put in the account of the chronicles of king David.

1Ch 29:29 — Now the acts of David the king, first and last, behold, they *are* written in the book of Samuel the seer, and in the book of Nathan the prophet, and in the book of Gad the seer,

2Ch 9:29 — Now the rest of the acts of Solomon, first and last, *are* they not written in the book of Nathan the prophet, and in the prophecy of Ahijah the Shilonite, and in the visions of Iddo the seer against Jeroboam the son of Nebat?

2Ch 12:15 — Now the acts of Rehoboam, first and last, *are* they not written in the book of Shemaiah the prophet, and of Iddo the seer concerning genealogies? And *there were* wars between Rehoboam and Jeroboam continually.

2Ch 20:34 — Now the rest of the acts of Jehoshaphat, first and last, behold, they *are* written in the book of Jehu the son of Hanani, who is mentioned in the book of the kings of Israel.

2Ch 26:22 — Now the rest of the acts of Uzziah, first and last, did Isaiah the prophet, the son of Amoz, write.

2Ch 32:32 — Now the rest of the acts of Hezekiah, and his goodness, behold, they *are* written in the vision of Isaiah the prophet, the son of Amoz, *and* in the book of the kings of Judah and Israel.

Ezr 5:17 — Now therefore, if *it seem* good to the king, let there be search made in the king's treasure house, which *is* there at Babylon, whether it be *so,* that a decree was made of Cyrus the king to build this house of God at Jerusalem, and let the king send his pleasure to us concerning this matter.

Est 6:1 — On that night could not the king sleep, and he commanded to bring the book of records of the chronicles; and they were read before the king.

See: Government

See: Rulers

- **For the kings of Israel, before and after the revolt of the ten tribes.**

See: Israel

KING'S DALE

Ge 14:17 — And the king of Sodom went out to meet him after his return from the slaughter of Chedorlaomer, and of the kings that *were* with him, at the valley of Shaveh, which *is* the king's dale.

2Sa 18:18 — Now Absalom in his lifetime had taken and reared up for himself a pillar, which *is* in the king's dale: for he said, I have no son to keep my name in remembrance: and he called the pillar after his own name: and it is called unto this day, Absalom's place.

KINGDOM OF HEAVEN

- **Likened to a man who sowed good seed.**

Mt 13:24–30, 38–43; Mk 4:26–29

- **Likened to a grain of mustard seed.**

Mt 13:31–32; Mk 4:30–31; Lk 13:18–19

- **Likened to leaven.**

Mt 13:33 — Another parable spake he unto them; The kingdom of heaven is like unto leaven, which a woman took, and hid in three measures of meal, till the whole was leavened.

Lk 13:21 — It is like leaven, which a woman took and hid in three measures of meal, till the whole was leavened.

- **Likened to a treasure.**

Mt 13:44 — Again, the kingdom of heaven is like unto treasure hid in a field; the which when a man hath found, he hideth, and for joy thereof goeth and selleth all that he hath, and buyeth that field.

- **Likened to a pearl.**

Mt 13:45 — Again, the kingdom of heaven is like unto a merchant man, seeking goodly pearls:

- **Likened to a net.**

Mt 13:47–50

- **Likened to a king who called his servants to a reckoning.**

Mt 18:23–35

- **Likened to a householder.**

Mt 20:1–16

- **Likened to a king who made a marriage feast for his son.**

Mt 22:2–14; Lk 14:16–24

- **Likened to ten virgins.**

Mt 25:1–13

- **Likened to a man traveling into a far country, who called his servants, and delivered to them his goods.**

Mt 25:14–30; Lk 19:12–27

- **"My kingdom is not of this world".**

Jn 18:36 — Jesus answered, My kingdom is not of this world: if my kingdom were of this world, then would my servants fight, that I should not be delivered to the Jews: but now is my kingdom not from hence.

- **Children of the.**

Mt 18:3 — And said, Verily I say unto you, Except ye be converted, and become as little children, ye shall not enter into the kingdom of heaven.

Mt 19:14 — But Jesus said, Suffer little children, and forbid them not, to come unto me: for of such is the kingdom of heaven.

Mk 10:14 — But when Jesus saw *it,* he was much displeased, and said unto them, Suffer the little children to come unto me, and forbid them not: for of such is the kingdom of God.

Lk 18:16 — But Jesus called them *unto him,* and said, Suffer little children to come unto me, and forbid them not: for of such is the kingdom of God.

- **Rich cannot enter.**

Mt 19:23–24; Mk 10:23–25; Lk 18:24–25, 29–30

- **Keys of.**

Mt 16:19 — And I will give unto thee the keys of the kingdom of heaven: and whatsoever thou shalt bind on earth shall be bound in heaven: and whatsoever thou shalt loose on earth shall be loosed in heaven.

- **Glad tidings of.**

Lk 8:1 — And it came to pass afterward, that he went throughout every city and village, preaching and shewing the glad tidings of the kingdom of God: and the twelve *were* with him,

- **Mysteries of.**

Lk 8:10 — And he said, Unto you it is given to know the mysteries of the kingdom of God: but to others in parables; that seeing they might not see, and hearing they might not understand.

- **Is not me and drink.**

Ro 14:17 — For the kingdom of God is not meat and drink; but righteousness, and peace, and joy in the Holy Ghost.

See: Church

See: Jesus, Kingdom of

KINGDOM OF SATAN

Mt 12:26 — And if Satan cast out Satan, he is divided against himself; how shall then his kingdom stand?

KIR

- **The inhabitants of Damascus carried into captivity to, by the king of Assyria.**

2Ki 16:9 — And the king of Assyria hearkened unto him: for the king of Assyria went up against Damascus, and took it, and carried *the people of* it captive to Kir, and slew Rezin.

• Prophecies concerning.

Isa 22:6 — And Elam bare the quiver with chariots of men *and* horsemen, and Kir uncovered the shield.

Am 1:5 — I will break also the bar of Damascus, and cut off the inhabitant from the plain of Aven, and him that holdeth the sceptre from the house of Eden: and the people of Syria shall go into captivity unto Kir, saith the LORD.

Am 9:7 — *Are* ye not as children of the Ethiopians unto me, O children of Israel? saith the LORD. Have not I brought up Israel out of the land of Egypt? and the Philistines from Caphtor, and the Syrians from Kir?

KIR-HARASETH

• Called also Kirharesh, Kir-Hareseth, and Kir-Heres.

• A city of Moab.

2Ki 3:25 — And they beat down the cities, and on every good piece of land cast every man his stone, and filled it; and they stopped all the wells of water, and felled all the good trees: only in Kir-haraseth left they the stones thereof; howbeit the slingers went about *it,* and smote it.

Isa 16:7 — Therefore shall Moab howl for Moab, every one shall howl: for the foundations of Kir-hareseth shall ye mourn; surely *they are* stricken.

Isa 16:11 — Wherefore my bowels shall sound like an harp for Moab, and mine inward parts for Kir-haresh.

Jer 48:31 — Therefore will I howl for Moab, and I will cry out for all Moab; *mine heart* shall mourn for the men of Kir-heres.

Jer 48:36 — Therefore mine heart shall sound for Moab like pipes, and mine heart shall sound like pipes for the men of Kir-heres: because the riches *that* he hath gotten are perished.

• Called Kir of Moab.

Isa 15:1 — The burden of Moab. Because in the night Ar of Moab is laid waste, *and* brought to silence; because in the night Kir of Moab is laid waste, *and* brought to silence;

KIRIATHAIM ↞See: Kirjathaim

KIRJATH-ARBA • An early name of Hebron.

Ge 23:2 — And Sarah died in Kirjath-arba; the same *is* Hebron in the land of Canaan: and Abraham came to mourn for Sarah, and to weep for her.

Jos 14:15 — And the name of Hebron before *was* Kirjath-arba; *which Arba was* a great man among the Anakims. And the land had rest from war.

Jgs 1:10 — And Judah went against the Canaanites that dwelt in Hebron: (now the name of Hebron before *was* Kirjath-arba:) and they slew Sheshai, and Ahiman, and Talmai.

KIRJATH-HUZOTH • A residence of Balak.

Nu 22:39 — And Balaam went with Balak, and they came unto Kirjath-huzoth.

KIRJATH-JEARIM

• Called also Baalah, one of the four cities of the Gibeonites.

• Inhabitants of not smitten, on account of covenant made by Israelites with Gibeonites.

Jos 9:3–27

• In the territory allotted to Judah.

Jos 15:9 — And the border was drawn from the top of the hill unto the fountain of the water of Nephtoah, and went out to the cities of mount Ephron; and the border was drawn to Baalah, which *is* Kirjath-jearim:

Jos 15:60 — Kirjath-baal, which *is* Kirjath-jearim, and Rabbah; two cities with their villages:

Jos 18:14 — And the border was drawn *thence,* and compassed the corner of the sea southward, from the hill that *lieth* before Beth-horon southward; and the goings out thereof were at Kirjath-baal, which *is* Kirjath-jearim, a city of the children of Judah: this *was* the west quarter.

• The Philistines bring the ark to.

1Sa 6:1–21

• Ark remains twenty years at.

1Sa 7:1–2; 1Ch 13:5–6

• David brings the ark from.

2Sa 6:1–11; 1Ch 13:5–8

2Ch 1:4 — But the ark of God had David brought up from Kirjath-jearim to *the place which* David had prepared for it: for he had pitched a tent for it at Jerusalem.

• Inhabitants of, who were taken into captivity to Babylon, returned.

Ezr 2:25 — The children of Kirjath-arim, Chephirah, and Beeroth, seven hundred and forty and three.

Ne 7:29 — The men of Kirjath-jearim, Chephirah, and Beeroth, seven hundred forty and three.

• Urijah, the prophet, an inhabitant of.

Jer 26:20 — And there was also a man that prophesied in the name of the LORD, Urijah the son of Shemaiah of Kirjath-jearim, who prophesied against this city and against this land according to all the words of Jeremiah:

KIRJATH-SANNAH

• A city of Judah.

Jos 15:49 — And Dannah, and Kirjath-sannah, which *is* Debir,

↞See: Debir

KIRJATH-SEPHER

Jos 15:15–16

↞See: Debir

KIRJATHAIM

• Called also Kiriathaim.

• A city of Reuben.

Nu 32:37 — And the children of Reuben built Heshbon, and Elealeh, and Kirjathaim,

Jos 13:19 — And Kirjathaim, and Sibmah, and Zareth-shahar in the mount of the valley,

• **Prophecies concerning.**

Jer 48:1 — Against Moab thus saith the LORD of hosts, the God of Israel; Woe unto Nebo! for it is spoiled: Kiriathaim is confounded *and* taken: Misgab is confounded and dismayed.

Jer 48:23 — And upon Kiriathaim, and upon Beth-gamul, and upon Beth-meon,

Eze 25:9 — Therefore, behold, I will open the side of Moab from the cities, from his cities *which are* on his frontiers, the glory of the country, Beth-jeshimoth, Baal-meon, and Kiriathaim,

• **A Levitical city in Naphtali.**

1Ch 6:76 — And out of the tribe of Naphtali; Kedesh in Galilee with her suburbs, and Hammon with her suburbs, and Kirjathaim with her suburbs.

KISH

• **Father of Saul.**

1Sa 9:1–3

1Sa 10:21 — When he had caused the tribe of Benjamin to come near by their families, the family of Matri was taken, and Saul the son of Kish was taken: and when they sought him, he could not be found.

2Sa 21:14 — And the bones of Saul and Jonathan his son buried they in the country of Benjamin in Zelah, in the sepulchre of Kish his father: and they performed all that the king commanded. And after that God was intreated for the land.

• **Called Cis.**

Ac 13:21 — And afterward they desired a king: and God gave unto them Saul the son of Cis, a man of the tribe of Benjamin, by the space of forty years.

• **A Benjamite.**

1Ch 8:30 — And his firstborn son Abdon, and Zur, and Kish, and Baal, and Nadab,

1Ch 9:36 — And his firstborn son Abdon, then Zur, and Kish, and Baal, and Ner, and Nadab,

• **A Levite.**

1Ch 23:21–22

1Ch 24:29 — Concerning Kish: the son of Kish was Jerahmeel.

• **A Levite.**

2Ch 29:12 — Then the Levites arose, Mahath the son of Amasai, and Joel the son of Azariah, of the sons of the Kohathites: and of the sons of Merari, Kish the son of Abdi, and Azariah the son of Jehalelel: and of the Gershonites; Joah the son of Zimmah, and Eden the son of Joah:

• **Great-grandfather of Mordecai.**

Est 2:5 — *Now* in Shushan the palace there was a certain Jew, whose name *was* Mordecai, the son of Jair, the son of Shimei, the son of Kish, a Benjamite;

KISHI

• **Called also Kushaiah.**

• **Father of Ethan, a chief assistant in the temple music.**

1Ch 6:44 — And their brethren the sons of Merari *stood* on the left hand: Ethan the son of Kishi, the son of Abdi, the son of Malluch,

1Ch 15:17 — So the Levites appointed Heman the son of Joel; and of his brethren, Asaph the son of Berechiah; and of the sons of Merari their brethren, Ethan the son of Kushaiah;

KISHION →See: Kedesh

KISHON

• **Called also Kison.**

• **A river of Palestine emptying into the Mediterranean near northern base of Mount Carmel.**

• **Sisera defeated at, and his army destroyed in.**

Jgs 4:7 — And I will draw unto thee to the river Kishon Sisera, the captain of Jabin's army, with his chariots and his multitude; and I will deliver him into thine hand.

Jgs 4:13 — And Sisera gathered together all his chariots, *even* nine hundred chariots of iron, and all the people that *were* with him, from Harosheth of the Gentiles unto the river of Kishon.

Jgs 5:21 — The river of Kishon swept them away, that ancient river, the river Kishon. O my soul, thou hast trodden down strength.

Ps 83:9 — Do unto them as *unto* the Midianites; as *to* Sisera, as *to* Jabin, at the brook of Kison:

• **Prophets of Baal destroyed by Elijah at.**

1Ki 18:40 — And Elijah said unto them, Take the prophets of Baal; let not one of them escape. And they took them: and Elijah brought them down to the brook Kishon, and slew them there.

KISS

• **Of affection.**

Ge 27:26–27; 2Sa 19:1–43

Ge 31:55 — And early in the morning Laban rose up, and kissed his sons and his daughters, and blessed them: and Laban departed, and returned unto his place.

Ge 33:4 — And Esau ran to meet him, and embraced him, and fell on his neck, and kissed him: and they wept.

Ge 48:10 — Now the eyes of Israel were dim for age, *so that* he could not see. And he brought them near unto him; and he kissed them, and embraced them.

Ge 50:1 — And Joseph fell upon his father's face, and wept upon him, and kissed him.

Ex 18:7 — And Moses went out to meet his father in law, and did obeisance, and kissed him; and they asked each other of *their* welfare; and they came into the tent.

Ru 1:14 — And they lifted up their voice, and wept again: and Orpah kissed her mother in law; but Ruth clave unto her.

2Sa 14:33 — So Joab came to the king, and told him: and when he had called for Absalom, he came to the king, and bowed himself on his face to the ground before the king: and the king kissed Absalom.

Lk 15:20 — And he arose, and came to his father. But when he was yet a great way off, his father saw him, and had compassion, and ran, and fell on his neck, and kissed him.

Ac 20:37 — And they all wept sore, and fell on Paul's neck, and kissed him,

• The feet of Jesus kissed by the penitent woman.

Lk 7:38 — And stood at his feet behind *him* weeping, and began to wash his feet with tears, and did wipe *them* with the hairs of her head, and kissed his feet, and anointed *them* with the ointment.

• Deceitful.

Pr 27:6 — Faithful *are* the wounds of a friend; but the kisses of an enemy *are* deceitful.

• Deceitful of Joab, when he slew Amasa.

2Sa 20:9–10

• Deceitful of Judas, when he betrayed Jesus.

Mt 26:48 — Now he that betrayed him gave them a sign, saying, Whomsoever I shall kiss, that same is he: hold him fast.

Lk 22:48 — But Jesus said unto him, Judas, betrayest thou the Son of man with a kiss?

• Holy.

Ro 16:16 — Salute one another with an holy kiss. The churches of Christ salute you.

2Co 13:12 — Greet one another with an holy kiss.

1Th 5:26 — Greet all the brethren with an holy kiss.

1Pe 5:14 — Greet ye one another with a kiss of charity. Peace *be* with you all that are in Christ Jesus. Amen.

KITE • A bird forbidden as food.

Le 11:14 — And the vulture, and the kite after his kind;

Dt 14:13 — And the glede, and the kite, and the vulture after his kind,

KITHLISH • A city of Judah.

Jos 15:40 — And Cabbon, and Lahmam, and Kithlish,

KITRON • A city of Zebulun.

Jgs 1:30 — Neither did Zebulun drive out the inhabitants of Kitron, nor the inhabitants of Nahalol; but the Canaanites dwelt among them, and became tributaries.

KITTIM ➜See: Chittim

KNEADING-TROUGH

Ex 8:3 — And the river shall bring forth frogs abundantly, which shall go up and come into thine house, and into thy bedchamber, and upon thy bed, and into the house of thy servants, and upon thy people, and into thine ovens, and into thy kneadingtroughs:

Ex 12:34 — And the people took their dough before it was leavened, their kneadingtroughs being bound up in their clothes upon their shoulders.

Dt 28:5 — Blessed *shall be* thy basket and thy store.

Dt 28:17 — Cursed *shall be* thy basket and thy store.

KNIFE

• An edged tool used by Abraham in offering Isaac.

Ge 22:6 — And Abraham took the wood of the burnt offering, and laid *it* upon Isaac his son; and he took the fire in his hand, and a knife; and they went both of them together.

• Of the temple, returned fromn Babylon.

Ezr 1:9 — And this *is* the number of them: thirty chargers of gold, a thousand chargers of silver, nine and twenty knives,

• Used for sharpening pens.

Jer 36:23 — And it came to pass, *that* when Jehudi had read three or four leaves, he cut it with the penknife, and cast *it* into the fire that *was* on the hearth, until all the roll was consumed in the fire that *was* on the hearth.

• Self-flagellation with, in idolatrous worship.

1Ki 18:28 — And they cried aloud, and cut themselves after their manner with knives and lancets, till the blood gushed out upon them.

KNOWLEDGE

• Of good and evil.

Ge 2:9 — And out of the ground made the LORD God to grow every tree that is pleasant to the sight, and good for food; the tree of life also in the midst of the garden, and the tree of knowledge of good and evil.

Ge 2:17 — But of the tree of the knowledge of good and evil, thou shalt not eat of it: for in the day that thou eatest thereof thou shalt surely die.

Ge 3:22 — And the LORD God said, Behold, the man is become as one of us, to know good and evil: and now, lest he put forth his hand, and take also of the tree of life, and eat, and live for ever:

• Is power.

Pr 3:20 — By his knowledge the depths are broken up, and the clouds drop down the dew.

Pr 24:5 — A wise man *is* strong; yea, a man of knowledge increaseth strength.

• Desire for.

Pr 2:1–3:35

1Ki 3:9 — Give therefore thy servant an understanding heart to judge thy people, that I may discern between good and bad: for who is able to judge this thy so great a people?

Ps 119:66 — Teach me good judgment and knowledge: for I have believed thy commandments.

Pr 12:1 — Whoso loveth instruction loveth knowledge: but he that hateth reproof *is* brutish.

Pr 15:14 — The heart of him that hath understanding seeketh knowledge: but the mouth of fools feedeth on foolishness.

Pr 18:15 — The heart of the prudent getteth knowledge; and the ear of the wise seeketh knowledge.

• Rejected.

Hos 4:6 — My people are destroyed for lack of knowledge: because thou hast rejected knowledge, I will also reject thee, that thou shalt be no priest to me: seeing thou hast forgotten the law of thy God, I will also forget thy children.

• Those who reject are destroyed.

Hos 4:6 — My people are destroyed for lack of knowledge: because thou hast rejected knowledge, I will also reject thee, that thou shalt be no priest to me: seeing thou hast forgotten the law of thy God, I will also forget thy children.

• Fools hate.

Pr 1:22 — How long, ye simple ones, will ye love simplicity? and the scorners delight in their scorning, and fools hate knowledge?

Pr 1:29 — For that they hated knowledge, and did not choose the fear of the LORD:

• A divine gift.

1Co 12:8 — For to one is given by the Spirit the word of wisdom; to another the word of knowledge by the same Spirit;

• Is pleasant.

Pr 2:10 — When wisdom entereth into thine heart, and knowledge is pleasant unto thy soul;

• Shall be increased.

Da 12:4 — But thou, O Daniel, shut up the words, and seal the book, *even* to the time of the end: many shall run to and fro, and knowledge shall be increased.

• The earth shall be full of.

Isa 11:9 — They shall not hurt nor destroy in all my holy mountain: for the earth shall be full of the knowledge of the LORD, as the waters cover the sea.

• Fear of the Lord is the beginning of.

Pr 1:7 — The fear of the LORD *is* the beginning of knowledge: *but* fools despise wisdom and instruction.

• Of more value than gold.

Pr 8:10 — Receive my instruction, and not silver; and knowledge rather than choice gold.

• The priest's lips should keep.

Mal 2:7 — For the priest's lips should keep knowledge, and they should seek the law at his mouth: for he *is* the messenger of the LORD of hosts.

• Of salvation.

Lk 1:77 — To give knowledge of salvation unto his people by the remission of their sins,

• Key of.

Lk 11:52 — Woe unto you, lawyers! for ye have taken away the key of knowledge: ye entered not in yourselves, and them that were entering in ye hindered.

• Now we know in part.

1Co 13:9–12

• Of God more than burnt offering.

Hos 6:6 — For I desired mercy, and not sacrifice; and the knowledge of God more than burnt offerings.

• Of Christ.

Php 3:8 — Yea doubtless, and I count all things *but* loss for the excellency of the knowledge of Christ Jesus my Lord: for whom I have suffered the loss of all things, and do count them *but* dung, that I may win Christ,

See: Wisdom

KOA • A symbolic term.

Eze 23:23 — The Babylonians, and all the Chaldeans, Pekod, and Shoa, and Koa, *and* all the Assyrians with them: all of them desirable young men, captains and rulers, great lords and renowned, all of them riding upon horses.

KOHATH

• Son of Levi.

Ge 46:11 — And the sons of Levi; Gershon, Kohath, and Merari.

Ex 6:16 — And these *are* the names of the sons of Levi according to their generations; Gershon, and Kohath, and Merari: and the years of the life of Levi *were* an hundred thirty and seven years.

• Grandfather of Moses, Aaron, and Miriam.

Nu 26:58–59

• Father of the Kohathites, one of the divisions of the Levites.

Ex 6:18 — And the sons of Kohath; Amram, and Izhar, and Hebron, and Uzziel: and the years of the life of Kohath *were* an hundred thirty and three years.

Nu 3:19 — And the sons of Kohath by their families; Amram, and Izehar, Hebron, and Uzziel.

Nu 3:27 — And of Kohath *was* the family of the Amramites, and the family of the Izeharites, and the family of the Hebronites, and the family of the Uzzielites: these *are* the families of the Kohathites.

See: Levites

KOLAIAH

• A Benjamite and ancestor of Sallu.

Ne 11:7 — And these *are* the sons of Benjamin; Sallu the son of Meshullam, the son of Joed, the son of Pedaiah, the son of Kolaiah, the son of Maaseiah, the son of Ithiel, the son of Jesaiah.

• Father of the false prophet Ahab.

Jer 29:21 — Thus saith the LORD of hosts, the God of Israel, of Ahab the son of Kolaiah, and of Zedekiah the son of Maaseiah, which prophesy a lie unto you in my name; Behold, I will deliver them into the hand of Nebuchadrezzar king of Babylon; and he shall slay them before your eyes;

KORAH

• A son of Esau.

Ge 36:5 — And Aholibamah bare Jeush, and Jaalam, and Korah: these *are* the sons of Esau, which were born unto him in the land of Canaan.

Ge 36:14 — And these were the sons of Aholibamah, the daughter of Anah the daughter of Zibeon, Esau's wife: and she bare to Esau Jeush, and Jaalam, and Korah.

Ge 36:18 — And these *are* the sons of Aholibamah Esau's wife; duke Jeush, duke Jaalam, duke Korah: these *were* the dukes *that came* of Aholibamah the daughter of Anah, Esau's wife.

• A Korhite Levite.

Ex 6:18 — And the sons of Kohath; Amram, and Izhar, and Hebron, and Uzziel: and the years of the life of Kohath *were* an hundred thirty and three years.

Ex 6:21 — And the sons of Izhar; Korah, and Nepheg, and Zichri.

Ex 6:24 — And the sons of Korah; Assir, and Elkanah, and Abiasaph: these *are* the families of the Korhites.

• Jealous of Moses; leads 250 princes in an insurrection; is swallowed by the earth.

Nu 16:1–50; 26:9–10

Dt 11:6 — And what he did unto Dathan and Abiram, the sons of Eliab, the son of Reuben: how the earth opened her mouth, and swallowed them up, and their households, and their tents, and all the substance that *was* in their possession, in the midst of all Israel:

Ps 106:17 — The earth opened and swallowed up Dathan, and covered the company of Abiram.

Jude 1:11 — Woe unto them! for they have gone in the way of Cain, and ran greedily after the error of Balaam for reward, and perished in the gainsaying of Core.

• Son of Hebron.

1Ch 2:43 — And the sons of Hebron; Korah, and Tappuah, and Rekem, and Shema.

• Son of Kohath and head of the family of sacred musicians among the Levites.

1Ch 6:22 — The sons of Kohath; Amminadab his son, Korah his son, Assir his son,

Ps 42:1 — [To the chief Musician, Maschil, for the sons of Korah.] As the hart panteth after the water brooks, so panteth my soul after thee, O God.

Ps 45:1 — [To the chief Musician upon Shoshannim, for the sons of Korah, Maschil, A song of loves.] My heart is inditing a good matter: I speak of the things which I have made touching the king: my tongue *is* the pen of a ready writer.

Ps 46:1 — [To the chief Musician for the sons of Korah, A song upon Alamoth.] God *is* our refuge and strength, a very present help in trouble.

Ps 47:1 — [To the chief Musician, A Psalm for the sons of Korah.] O clap your hands, all ye people; shout unto God with the voice of triumph.

Ps 48:1 — [A song *and* Psalm for the sons of Korah.] Great *is* the LORD, and greatly to be praised in the city of our God, *in* the mountain of his holiness.

Ps 87:1 — [A Psalm *or* song for the sons of Korah.] His foundation *is* in the holy mountains.

Ps 88:1 — [A song *or* Psalm for the sons of Korah, to the chief Musician upon Mahalath Leannoth, Maschil of Heman the Ezrahite.] O LORD God of my salvation, I have cried day *and* night before thee:

KORE

• A Korahite.

1Ch 9:19 — And Shallum the son of Kore, the son of Ebiasaph, the son of Korah, and his brethren, of the house of his father, the Korahites, *were* over the work of the service, keepers of the gates of the tabernacle: and their fathers, *being* over the host of the LORD, *were* keepers of the entry.

1Ch 26:1 — Concerning the divisions of the porters: Of the Korhites *was* Meshelemiah the son of Kore, of the sons of Asaph.

• A Levite; keeper of the east gate.

2Ch 31:14 — And Kore the son of Imnah the Levite, the porter toward the east, *was* over the freewill offerings of God, to distribute the oblations of the LORD, and the most holy things.

KORHITES

• A division of the Levites.

See: Levites

KOZ

• Called also Hakkoz.

• Head of the seventh division priests.

1Ch 24:10 — The seventh to Hakkoz, the eighth to Abijah,

• Descendants of, excluded from priesthood because of defective genealogies.

Ezr 2:61 — And of the children of the priests: the children of Habaiah, the children of Koz, the children of Barzillai; which took a wife of the daughters of Barzillai the Gileadite, and was called after their name:

Ne 7:63 — And of the priests: the children of Habaiah, the children of Koz, the children of Barzillai, which took *one* of the daughters of Barzillai the Gileadite to wife, and was called after their name.

• Repair walls of Jerusalem.

Ne 3:4 — And next unto them repaired Meremoth the son of Urijah, the son of Koz. And next unto them repaired Meshullam the son of Berechiah, the son of Meshezabeel. And next unto them repaired Zadok the son of Baana.

Ne 3:21 — After him repaired Meremoth the son of Urijah the son of Koz another piece, from the door of the house of Eliashib even to the end of the house of Eliashib.

KUSHAIAH **See: Kishi**

L

LAADAH • Son of Shelah.

1Ch 4:21 — The sons of Shelah the son of Judah *were,* Er the father of Lecah, and Laadah the father of Mareshah, and the families of the house of them that wrought fine linen, of the house of Ashbea,

LAADAN

• A descendant of Ephraim.

1Ch 7:26 — Laadan his son, Ammihud his son, Elishama his son,

• A Levite. Called also Libni.

1Ch 23:7–9

1Ch 6:17 — And these *be* the names of the sons of Gershom; Libni, and Shimei.

1Ch 26:21 — *As concerning* the sons of Laadan; the sons of the Gershonite Laadan, chief fathers, *even* of Laadan the Gershonite, *were* Jehieli.

LABAN

• Son of Bethuel.

Ge 28:5 — And Isaac sent away Jacob: and he went to Padan-aram unto Laban, son of Bethuel the Syrian, the brother of Rebekah, Jacob's and Esau's mother.

• Brother of Rebekah.

Ge 22:23 — And Bethuel begat Rebekah: these eight Milcah did bear to Nahor, Abraham's brother.

Ge 24:15 — And it came to pass, before he had done speaking, that, behold, Rebekah came out, who was born to Bethuel, son of Milcah, the wife of Nahor, Abraham's brother, with her pitcher upon her shoulder.

Ge 24:29 — And Rebekah had a brother, and his name *was* Laban: and Laban ran out unto the man, unto the well.

• Receives the servant of Abraham.

Ge 24:29–33

• Receives Jacob, and gives him his daughters in marriage.

Ge 29:12–30

• Jacob becomes his servant.

Ge 29:15–20; 30:27–43

Ge 29:27 — Fulfil her week, and we will give thee this also for the service which thou shalt serve with me yet seven other years.

• Outwitted by Jacob.

Ge 30:37–31:21

• Pursues Jacob, overtakes him at Mount Gilead, and covenants with him.

Ge 31:22–55

LABOR

Ex 20:9–11; Dt 24:14–15; Mt 20:1–15; 1Th 4:11–12; 2Th 3:7–13

Ge 3:19 — In the sweat of thy face shalt thou eat bread, till thou return unto the ground; for out of it wast thou taken: for dust thou *art,* and unto dust shalt thou return.

Ex 23:12 — Six days thou shalt do thy work, and on the seventh day thou shalt rest: that thine ox and thine ass may rest, and the son of thy handmaid, and the stranger, may be refreshed.

Ex 34:21 — Six days thou shalt work, but on the seventh day thou shalt rest: in earing time and in harvest thou shalt rest.

Le 19:13 — Thou shalt not defraud thy neighbour, neither rob *him:* the wages of him that is hired shall not abide with thee all night until the morning.

Le 23:3 — Six days shall work be done: but the seventh day *is* the sabbath of rest, an holy convocation; ye shall do no work *therein:* it *is* the sabbath of the LORD in all your dwellings.

Dt 25:4 — Thou shalt not muzzle the ox when he treadeth out *the corn.*

Ecc 5:12 — The sleep of a labouring man *is* sweet, whether he eat little or much: but the abundance of the rich will not suffer him to sleep.

Jer 22:13 — Woe unto him that buildeth his house by unrighteousness, and his chambers by wrong; *that* useth his neighbour's service without wages, and giveth him not for his work;

Mal 3:5 — And I will come near to you to judgment; and I will be a swift witness against the sorcerers, and against the adulterers, and against false swearers, and against those that oppress the hireling in *his* wages, the widow, and the fatherless, and that turn aside the stranger *from his right,* and fear not me, saith the LORD of hosts.

Lk 10:7 — And in the same house remain, eating and drinking such things as they give: for the labourer is worthy of his hire. Go not from house to house.

Ac 20:35 — I have shewed you all things, how that so labouring ye ought to support the weak, and to remember the words of the Lord Jesus, how he said, It is more blessed to give than to receive.

1Co 9:9 — For it is written in the law of Moses, Thou shalt not muzzle the mouth of the ox that treadeth out the corn. Doth God take care for oxen?

Eph 4:28 — Let him that stole steal no more: but rather let him labour, working with *his* hands the thing which is good, that he may have to give to him that needeth.

1Ti 5:18 — For the scripture saith, Thou shalt not muzzle the ox that treadeth out the corn. And, The labourer *is* worthy of his reward.

Jas 5:4 — Behold, the hire of the labourers who have reaped down your fields, which is of you kept back by fraud, crieth: and the cries of them which have reaped are entered into the ears of the Lord of sabaoth.

See: Employee

See: Employer

See: Idleness

↞See: Industry
↞See: Master
↞See: Servant

LACE

Ex 39:31 — And they tied unto it a lace of blue, to fasten *it* on high upon the mitre; as the LORD commanded Moses.

LACHISH

- **A city.**
- **King of, besieges Gibeon.**

Jos 10:5 — Therefore the five kings of the Amorites, the king of Jerusalem, the king of Hebron, the king of Jarmuth, the king of Lachish, the king of Eglon, gathered themselves together, and went up, they and all their hosts, and encamped before Gibeon, and made war against it.

- **Captured by Joshua.**

Jos 10:31–32

- **Allotted to Judah.**

Jos 15:39 — Lachish, and Bozkath, and Eglon,

- **Fortified by Rehoboam.**

2Ch 11:9 — And Adoraim, and Lachish, and Azekah,

- **Assassination of Amaziah at.**

2Ki 14:19 — Now they made a conspiracy against him in Jerusalem: and he fled to Lachish; but they sent after him to Lachish, and slew him there.

- **Besieged by Sennacherib.**

2Ki 18:13–17

2Ki 19:8 — So Rab-shakeh returned, and found the king of Assyria warring against Libnah: for he had heard that he was departed from Lachish.

2Ch 32:9 — After this did Sennacherib king of Assyria send his servants to Jerusalem, (but he *himself laid siege* against Lachish, and all his power with him,) unto Hezekiah king of Judah, and unto all Judah that *were* at Jerusalem, saying,

- **Besieged by Nebuchadnezzar.**

Jer 34:7 — When the king of Babylon's army fought against Jerusalem, and against all the cities of Judah that were left, against Lachish, and against Azekah: for these defenced cities remained of the cities of Judah.

- **Prophecy concerning.**

Mic 1:13 — O thou inhabitant of Lachish, bind the chariot to the swift beast: she *is* the beginning of the sin to the daughter of Zion: for the transgressions of Israel were found in thee.

LACHRYMATORY

Ps 56:8 — Thou tellest my wanderings: put thou my tears into thy bottle: *are they* not in thy book?

LADDER

- **In Jacob's vision.**

Ge 28:12 — And he dreamed, and behold a ladder set up on the earth, and the top of it reached to heaven: and behold the angels of God ascending and descending on it.

LAHAD • A descendant of Judah.

1Ch 4:2 — And Reaiah the son of Shobal begat Jahath; and Jahath begat Ahumai and Lahad. These *are* the families of the Zorathites.

LAHAI-ROI

- **Called also Beer-Lahairoi.**
- **A well near Kadesh, where Hagar fled to.**

Ge 16:7–14

- **Isaac dwells at.**

Ge 24:62 — And Isaac came from the way of the well Lahai-roi; for he dwelt in the south country.

Ge 25:11 — And it came to pass after the death of Abraham, that God blessed his son Isaac; and Isaac dwelt by the well Lahai-roi.

LAHMAM • A city of Judah.

Jos 15:40 — And Cabbon, and Lahmam, and Kithlish,

LAHMI

- **Brother of Goliath.**
- **Slain by Elhanan.**

2Sa 21:19 — And there was again a battle in Gob with the Philistines, where Elhanan the son of Jaare-oregim, a Bethlehemite, slew *the brother of* Goliath the Gittite, the staff of whose spear *was* like a weaver's beam.

1Ch 20:5 — And there was war again with the Philistines; and Elhanan the son of Jair slew Lahmi the brother of Goliath the Gittite, whose spear staff *was* like a weaver's beam.

LAISH

- **Called also Leshem.**

↞See: Dan

- **A native of Gallim.**

1Sa 25:44 — But Saul had given Michal his daughter, David's wife, to Phalti the son of Laish, which *was* of Gallim.

2Sa 3:15 — And Ish-bosheth sent, and took her from *her* husband, *even* from Phaltiel the son of Laish.

- **A town near Jerusalem.**

Isa 10:30 — Lift up thy voice, O daughter of Gallim: cause it to be heard unto Laish, O poor Anathoth.

LAKE

- **Of fire.**

Rev 20:14–15

Rev 19:20 — And the beast was taken, and with him the false prophet that wrought miracles before him, with which he deceived them that had received the mark of the beast, and them that worshipped his image. These both were cast alive into a lake of fire burning with brimstone.

Rev 20:10 — And the devil that deceived them was cast into the lake of fire and brimstone, where the beast and the false prophet *are,* and shall be tormented day and night for ever and ever.

Rev 21:8 — But the fearful, and unbelieving, and the abominable, and murderers, and whoremongers, and sorcerers, and idolaters, and all liars, shall have their part in the lake which burneth with fire and brimstone: which is the second death.

LAKUM • A city in Naphtali.

Jos 19:33 — And their coast was from Heleph, from Allon to Zaanannim, and Adami, Nekeb, and Jabneel, unto Lakum; and the outgoings thereof were at Jordan:

LAMA SABACHTHANI • The dying wail of Jesus.

Ps 22:1 — My God, my God, why hast thou forsaken me? *why art thou so* far from helping me, *and from* the words of my roaring?

Mt 27:46 — And about the ninth hour Jesus cried with a loud voice, saying, Eli, Eli, lama sabachthani? that is to say, My God, my God, why hast thou forsaken me?

Mk 15:34 — And at the ninth hour Jesus cried with a loud voice, saying, Eloi, Eloi, lama sabachthani? which is, being interpreted, My God, my God, why hast thou forsaken me?

LAMB

• Offering of.

Ex 29:38–41; Nu 28:3–8

Le 3:7 — If he offer a lamb for his offering, then shall he offer it before the LORD.

Le 4:32 — And if he bring a lamb for a sin offering, he shall bring it a female without blemish.

Le 5:6 — And he shall bring his trespass offering unto the LORD for his sin which he hath sinned, a female from the flock, a lamb or a kid of the goats, for a sin offering; and the priest shall make an atonement for him concerning his sin.

Le 22:23 — Either a bullock or a lamb that hath any thing superfluous or lacking in his parts, that mayest thou offer *for* a freewill offering; but for a vow it shall not be accepted.

Le 23:12 — And ye shall offer that day when ye wave the sheaf an he lamb without blemish of the first year for a burnt offering unto the LORD.

Nu 6:12 — And he shall consecrate unto the LORD the days of his separation, and shall bring a lamb of the first year for a trespass offering: but the days that were before shall be lost, because his separation was defiled.

Nu 7:15 — One young bullock, one ram, one lamb of the first year, for a burnt offering:

Nu 7:21 — One young bullock, one ram, one lamb of the first year, for a burnt offering:

• Not to be seethed in its mother's milk.

Ex 23:19 — The first of the firstfruits of thy land thou shalt bring into the house of the LORD thy God. Thou shalt not seethe a kid in his mother's milk.

LAMB OF GOD

• An appellation of Jesus.

Rev 7:9–10; 21:22–23; 21:27–22:1

Jn 1:29 — The next day John seeth Jesus coming unto him, and saith, Behold the Lamb of God, which taketh away the sin of the world.

Rev 6:16 — And said to the mountains and rocks, Fall on us, and hide us from the face of him that sitteth on the throne, and from the wrath of the Lamb:

Rev 7:14 — And I said unto him, Sir, thou knowest. And he said to me, These are they which came out of great tribulation, and have washed their robes, and made them white in the blood of the Lamb.

Rev 7:17 — For the Lamb which is in the midst of the throne shall feed them, and shall lead them unto living fountains of waters: and God shall wipe away all tears from their eyes.

Rev 12:11 — And they overcame him by the blood of the Lamb, and by the word of their testimony; and they loved not their lives unto the death.

Rev 13:8 — And all that dwell upon the earth shall worship him, whose names are not written in the book of life of the Lamb slain from the foundation of the world.

Rev 14:1 — And I looked, and, lo, a Lamb stood on the mount Sion, and with him an hundred forty *and* four thousand, having his Father's name written in their foreheads.

Rev 14:4 — These are they which were not defiled with women; for they are virgins. These are they which follow the Lamb whithersoever he goeth. These were redeemed from among men, *being* the firstfruits unto God and to the Lamb.

Rev 15:3 — And they sing the song of Moses the servant of God, and the song of the Lamb, saying, Great and marvellous *are* thy works, Lord God Almighty; just and true *are* thy ways, thou King of saints.

Rev 17:14 — These shall make war with the Lamb, and the Lamb shall overcome them: for he is Lord of lords, and King of kings: and they that are with him *are* called, and chosen, and faithful.

Rev 19:7 — Let us be glad and rejoice, and give honour to him: for the marriage of the Lamb is come, and his wife hath made herself ready.

Rev 21:9 — And there came unto me one of the seven angels which had the seven vials full of the seven last plagues, and talked with me, saying, Come hither, I will shew thee the bride, the Lamb's wife.

Rev 21:14 — And the wall of the city had twelve foundations, and in them the names of the twelve apostles of the Lamb.

Rev 22:3 — And there shall be no more curse: but the throne of God and of the Lamb shall be in it; and his servants shall serve him:

LAMECH

• Father of Jabal, Jubal, and Tubal-cain.

Ge 4:18–24

• Son of Methuselah, and father of Noah. Lived 777 years.

Ge 5:25–31

1Ch 1:3 — Henoch, Methuselah, Lamech,

• **Ancestor of Jesus.**

Lk 3:36 — Which was *the son* of Cainan, which was *the son* of Arphaxad, which was *the son* of Sem, which was *the son* of Noe, which was *the son* of Lamech,

LAMENESS

• **Disqualified priests from exercising the priestly office.**

Le 21:18 — For whatsoever man *he be* that hath a blemish, he shall not approach: a blind man, or a lame, or he that hath a flat nose, or any thing superfluous,

• **Disqualified animals for sacrificial uses.**

Dt 15:21 — And if there be *any* blemish therein, *as if it be* lame, or blind, *or have* any ill blemish, thou shalt not sacrifice it unto the LORD thy God.

• **Hated by David.**

2Sa 5:8 — And David said on that day, Whosoever getteth up to the gutter, and smiteth the Jebusites, and the lame and the blind, *that are* hated of David's soul, *he shall be chief and captain.* Wherefore they said, The blind and the lame shall not come into the house.

• **Healed by Jesus.**

Mt 11:5 — The blind receive their sight, and the lame walk, the lepers are cleansed, and the deaf hear, the dead are raised up, and the poor have the gospel preached to them.

Mt 15:31 — Insomuch that the multitude wondered, when they saw the dumb to speak, the maimed to be whole, the lame to walk, and the blind to see: and they glorified the God of Israel.

Mt 21:14 — And the blind and the lame came to him in the temple; and he healed them.

Lk 7:22 — Then Jesus answering said unto them, Go your way, and tell John what things ye have seen and heard; how that the blind see, the lame walk, the lepers are cleansed, the deaf hear, the dead are raised, to the poor the gospel is preached.

• **Healed by Peter.**

Ac 3:2–11

• **Figurative.**

Heb 12:13 — And make straight paths for your feet, lest that which is lame be turned out of the way; but let it rather be healed.

LAMENTATIONS

• **Of David.**

Ps 60:1–3

• **Of Jeremiah.**

Lamentations 1–5

• **Of Ezekiel.**

Eze 19:1–14; 28:12–19

See: Elegy

LAMP

• **Miraculously appeared at Abraham's sacrifice.**

Ge 15:17 — And it came to pass, that, when the sun went down, and it was dark, behold a smoking furnace, and a burning lamp that passed between those pieces.

• **For the tabernacle.**

Ex 25:31–40; 37:17–22

• **Kept burning at night in the tabernacle and cared for by priests.**

Ex 27:20–21; Le 24:2–4

• **Figurative.**

Job 18:6 — The light shall be dark in his tabernacle, and his candle shall be put out with him.

Ps 119:105 — Thy word *is* a lamp unto my feet, and a light unto my path.

Pr 13:9 — The light of the righteous rejoiceth: but the lamp of the wicked shall be put out.

Pr 20:20 — Whoso curseth his father or his mother, his lamp shall be put out in obscure darkness.

Isa 62:1 — For Zion's sake will I not hold my peace, and for Jerusalem's sake I will not rest, until the righteousness thereof go forth as brightness, and the salvation thereof as a lamp *that* burneth.

Jer 25:10 — Moreover I will take from them the voice of mirth, and the voice of gladness, the voice of the bridegroom, and the voice of the bride, the sound of the millstones, and the light of the candle.

Zep 1:12 — And it shall come to pass at that time, *that* I will search Jerusalem with candles, and punish the men that are settled on their lees: that say in their heart, The LORD will not do good, neither will he do evil.

Mt 6:22 — The light of the body is the eye: if therefore thine eye be single, thy whole body shall be full of light.

2Pe 1:19 — We have also a more sure word of prophecy; whereunto ye do well that ye take heed, as unto a light that shineth in a dark place, until the day dawn, and the day star arise in your hearts:

Rev 21:23 — And the city had no need of the sun, neither of the moon, to shine in it: for the glory of God did lighten it, and the Lamb *is* the light thereof.

• **Symbolic.**

Rev 4:5 — And out of the throne proceeded lightnings and thunderings and voices: and *there were* seven lamps of fire burning before the throne, which are the seven Spirits of God.

Rev 8:10 — And the third angel sounded, and there fell a great star from heaven, burning as it were a lamp, and it fell upon the third part of the rivers, and upon the fountains of waters;

See: Candlestick

LANCE

See: Javelin

See: Spear

LAND

• Appeared on third creative day.

Ge 1:9 — And God said, Let the waters under the heaven be gathered together unto one place, and let the dry *land* appear: and it was so.

• Original title to, from God.

Ge 13:14–17

Ge 15:7 — And he said unto him, I *am* the LORD that brought thee out of Ur of the Chaldees, to give thee this land to inherit it.

Ex 23:31 — And I will set thy bounds from the Red sea even unto the sea of the Philistines, and from the desert unto the river: for I will deliver the inhabitants of the land into your hand; and thou shalt drive them out before thee.

Le 25:23 — The land shall not be sold for ever: for the land *is* mine; for ye *are* strangers and sojourners with me.

• Bought and sold.

Ge 23:3–18; Ac 5:1–8

Ge 33:19 — And he bought a parcel of a field, where he had spread his tent, at the hand of the children of Hamor, Shechem's father, for an hundred pieces of money.

Ac 4:34 — Neither was there any among them that lacked: for as many as were possessors of lands or houses sold them, and brought the prices of the things that were sold,

• Sale and redemption of, laws concerning.

Le 25:15–16, 23–33; 27:17–24; Jer 32:7–16

Nu 36:4 — And when the jubile of the children of Israel shall be, then shall their inheritance be put unto the inheritance of the tribe whereunto they are received: so shall their inheritance be taken away from the inheritance of the tribe of our fathers.

Jer 32:25 — And thou hast said unto me, O Lord GOD, Buy thee the field for money, and take witnesses; for the city is given into the hand of the Chaldeans.

Jer 32:44 — Men shall buy fields for money, and subscribe evidences, and seal *them,* and take witnesses in the land of Benjamin, and in the places about Jerusalem, and in the cities of Judah, and in the cities of the mountains, and in the cities of the valley, and in the cities of the south: for I will cause their captivity to return, saith the LORD.

Eze 46:18 — Moreover the prince shall not take of the people's inheritance by oppression, to thrust them out of their possession; *but* he shall give his sons inheritance out of his own possession: that my people be not scattered every man from his possession.

• Conveyance of, by written deeds and other forms.

Ge 23:3–20; Ru 4:3–8; Jer 32:9–14

Ru 4:11 — And all the people that *were* in the gate, and the elders, said, *We are* witnesses. The LORD make the woman that is come into thine house like Rachel and like Leah, which two did build the house of Israel: and do thou worthily in Ephratah, and be famous in Bethlehem:

• Conveyance of, witnessed.

Ge 23:10–11; Ru 4:9–11; Jer 32:9–14

• Sold for debt.

Ne 5:3–5

• Rights in, alienated.

2Ki 8:1–6

• Leased.

Mt 21:33–41; Lk 20:9–16

• Priests' part in.

Ge 47:22 — Only the land of the priests bought he not; for the priests had a portion *assigned them* of Pharaoh, and did eat their portion which Pharaoh gave them: wherefore they sold not their lands.

Eze 48:10 — And for them, *even* for the priests, shall be *this* holy oblation; toward the north five and twenty thousand *in length,* and toward the west ten thousand in breadth, and toward the east ten thousand in breadth, and toward the south five and twenty thousand in length: and the sanctuary of the LORD shall be in the midst thereof.

• King's part in.

Eze 48:21 — And the residue *shall be* for the prince, on the one side and on the other of the holy oblation, and of the possession of the city, over against the five and twenty thousand of the oblation toward the east border, and westward over against the five and twenty thousand toward the west border, over against the portions for the prince: and it shall be the holy oblation; and the sanctuary of the house *shall be* in the midst thereof.

• Widow's dower in.

Ru 4:3–9

• Unmarried woman's rights in.

Nu 27:1–11; 36:1–11

• Rest every seventh year for benefit of poor.

Ex 23:11 — But the seventh *year* thou shalt let it rest and lie still; that the poor of thy people may eat: and what they leave the beasts of the field shall eat. In like manner thou shalt deal with thy vineyard, *and* with thy oliveyard.

• Products of, for all.

Ecc 5:9 — Moreover the profit of the earth is for all: the king *himself* is served by the field.

• Monopoly of.

Ge 47:20–26; Mic 2:1–2

Isa 5:8 — Woe unto them that join house to house, *that* lay field to field, till *there be* no place, that they may be placed alone in the midst of the earth!

See: Mortgage

• Rules for apportioning Canaan among the tribes.

Eze 47:22 — And it shall come to pass, *that* ye shall divide it by lot for an inheritance unto you, and to the strangers that sojourn among you, which shall beget children among you: and they shall be unto you as born in the country among the children of Israel; they shall have inheritance with you among the tribes of Israel.

See: Canaan

LANDMARKS

• Protected from fraudulent removal.

Dt 19:14 — Thou shalt not remove thy neighbour's landmark, which they of old time have set in thine inheritance, which thou shalt inherit in the land that the LORD thy God giveth thee to possess it.

Dt 27:17 — Cursed *be* he that removeth his neighbour's landmark. And all the people shall say, Amen.

Job 24:2 — *Some* remove the landmarks; they violently take away flocks, and feed *thereof.*

Pr 22:28 — Remove not the ancient landmark, which thy fathers have set.

Pr 23:10 — Remove not the old landmark; and enter not into the fields of the fatherless:

Hos 5:10 — The princes of Judah were like them that remove the bound: *therefore* I will pour out my wrath upon them like water.

LANGUAGE

• Unity of.

Ge 11:1 — And the whole earth was of one language, and of one speech.

Ge 11:6 — And the LORD said, Behold, the people *is* one, and they have all one language; and this they begin to do: and now nothing will be restrained from them, which they have imagined to do.

• Confusion of.

Ge 11:1–9

Ge 10:5 — By these were the isles of the Gentiles divided in their lands; every one after his tongue, after their families, in their nations.

Ge 10:20 — These *are* the sons of Ham, after their families, after their tongues, in their countries, *and* in their nations.

Ge 10:31 — These *are* the sons of Shem, after their families, after their tongues, in their lands, after their nations.

• Dialects of the Jews.

Jgs 12:6 — Then said they unto him, Say now Shibboleth: and he said Sibboleth: for he could not frame to pronounce *it* right. Then they took him, and slew him at the passages of Jordan: and there fell at that time of the Ephraimites forty and two thousand.

Mt 26:73 — And after a while came unto *him* they that stood by, and said to Peter, Surely thou also art *one* of them; for thy speech bewrayeth thee.

• Many spoken at Jerusalem.

Ac 2:8–11

Jn 19:20 — This title then read many of the Jews: for the place where Jesus was crucified was nigh to the city: and it was written in Hebrew, *and* Greek, *and* Latin.

• Speaking in unknown, in religious assemblies, forbidden.

1Co 14:2–28

• Gift of.

Ac 2:7–8; 1Co 14:1–40

Mk 16:17 — And these signs shall follow them that believe; In my name shall they cast out devils; they shall speak with new tongues;

Ac 10:46 — For they heard them speak with tongues, and magnify God. Then answered Peter,

Ac 19:6 — And when Paul had laid *his* hands upon them, the Holy Ghost came on them; and they spake with tongues, and prophesied.

1Co 12:10 — To another the working of miracles; to another prophecy; to another discerning of spirits; to another *divers* kinds of tongues; to another the interpretation of tongues:

• Mentioned in Scripture.

• Of Ashdod.

Ne 13:24 — And their children spake half in the speech of Ashdod, and could not speak in the Jews' language, but according to the language of each people.

• Of Chaldee.

Da 1:4 — Children in whom *was* no blemish, but well favoured, and skilful in all wisdom, and cunning in knowledge, and understanding science, and such as *had* ability in them to stand in the king's palace, and whom they might teach the learning and the tongue of the Chaldeans.

• Of Egyptian.

Ps 114:1 — When Israel went out of Egypt, the house of Jacob from a people of strange language;

Ac 2:10 — Phrygia, and Pamphylia, in Egypt, and in the parts of Libya about Cyrene, and strangers of Rome, Jews and proselytes,

• Of Greek.

Lk 23:38 — And a superscription also was written over him in letters of Greek, and Latin, and Hebrew, THIS IS THE KING OF THE JEWS.

Ac 21:37 — And as Paul was to be led into the castle, he said unto the chief captain, May I speak unto thee? Who said, Canst thou speak Greek?

• Of Latin.

Lk 23:38 — And a superscription also was written over him in letters of Greek, and Latin, and Hebrew, THIS IS THE KING OF THE JEWS.

Jn 19:20 — This title then read many of the Jews: for the place where Jesus was crucified was nigh to the city: and it was written in Hebrew, *and* Greek, *and* Latin.

• Of Lycaonia.

Ac 14:11 — And when the people saw what Paul had done, they lifted up their voices, saying in the speech of Lycaonia, The gods are come down to us in the likeness of men.

• Of Parthia and other lands.

Ac 2:9 — Parthians, and Medes, and Elamites, and the dwellers in Mesopotamia, and in Judaea, and Cappadocia, in Pontus, and Asia,

Ac 2:11 — Cretes and Arabians, we do hear them speak in our tongues the wonderful works of God.

• Of Syria.

2Ki 18:26 — Then said Eliakim the son of Hilkiah, and Shebna, and Joah, unto Rab-shakeh, Speak, I pray thee, to thy servants in the Syrian language; for we understand *it:* and talk not with us in the Jews' language in the ears of the people that *are* on the wall.

Ezr 4:7 — And in the days of Artaxerxes wrote Bishlam, Mithredath, Tabeel, and the rest of their companions, unto Artaxerxes king of Persia; and the writing of the letter *was* written in the Syrian tongue, and interpreted in the Syrian tongue.

Da 2:4 — Then spake the Chaldeans to the king in Syriack, O king, live for ever: tell thy servants the dream, and we will shew the interpretation.

LANTERN

Jn 18:3 — Judas then, having received a band *of men* and officers from the chief priests and Pharisees, cometh thither with lanterns and torches and weapons.

LAODICEA

• A Phrygian city.

• Paul's concern for.

Col 2:1 — For I would that ye knew what great conflict I have for you, and *for* them at Laodicea, and *for* as many as have not seen my face in the flesh;

• Epaphras's zeal for.

Col 4:13 — For I bear him record, that he hath a great zeal for you, and them *that are* in Laodicea, and them in Hierapolis.

• Epistle to the Colossians to be read in.

Col 4:15–16

• Message to, through John.

Rev 3:14–22

Rev 1:11 — Saying, I am Alpha and Omega, the first and the last: and, What thou seest, write in a book, and send *it* unto the seven churches which are in Asia; unto Ephesus, and unto Smyrna, and unto Pergamos, and unto Thyatira, and unto Sardis, and unto Philadelphia, and unto Laodicea.

LAPIDARY • One who cuts precious stones.

Ex 31:5 — And in cutting of stones, to set *them,* and in carving of timber, to work in all manner of workmanship.

Ex 35:33 — And in the cutting of stones, to set *them,* and in carving of wood, to make any manner of cunning work.

LAPIDOTH • Husband of Deborah.

Jgs 4:4 — And Deborah, a prophetess, the wife of Lapidoth, she judged Israel at that time.

LAPWING • A bird forbidden as food.

Le 11:19 — And the stork, the heron after her kind, and the lapwing, and the bat.

Dt 14:18 — And the stork, and the heron after her kind, and the lapwing, and the bat.

LARCENY ✦See: Theft and Thieves

LASCIVIOUSNESS

Pr 2:16–18; 5:3–5, 8–13; 7:6–27; 9:13–18; 30:18–20; Mk 7:21–23; Ro 1:22–29; 1Co 6:9–10, 15–18; Gal 5:19–21; Eph 4:17–19; 1Pe 4:2–3

Ex 32:6 — And they rose up early on the morrow, and offered burnt offerings, and brought peace offerings; and the people sat down to eat and to drink, and rose up to play.

Pr 20:16 — Take his garment that is surety *for* a stranger: and take a pledge of him for a strange woman.

Joel 3:3 — And they have cast lots for my people; and have given a boy for an harlot, and sold a girl for wine, that they might drink.

Ro 7:8 — But sin, taking occasion by the commandment, wrought in me all manner of concupiscence. For without the law sin *was* dead.

Ro 13:13 — Let us walk honestly, as in the day; not in rioting and drunkenness, not in chambering and wantonness, not in strife and envying.

1Co 6:13 — Meats for the belly, and the belly for meats: but God shall destroy both it and them. Now the body *is* not for fornication, but for the Lord; and the Lord for the body.

1Co 9:27 — But I keep under my body, and bring *it* into subjection: lest that by any means, when I have preached to others, I myself should be a castaway.

2Co 12:21 — *And* lest, when I come again, my God will humble me among you, and *that* I shall bewail many which have sinned already, and have not repented of the uncleanness and fornication and lasciviousness which they have committed.

Eph 5:5 — For this ye know, that no whoremonger, nor unclean person, nor covetous man, who is an idolater, hath any inheritance in the kingdom of Christ and of God.

Col 3:5 — Mortify therefore your members which are upon the earth; fornication, uncleanness, inordinate affection, evil concupiscence, and covetousness, which is idolatry:

1Th 4:5 — Not in the lust of concupiscence, even as the Gentiles which know not God:

2Ti 3:6 — For of this sort are they which creep into houses, and lead captive silly women laden with sins, led away with divers lusts,

Jude 1:4 — For there are certain men crept in unawares, who were before of old ordained to this condemnation, ungodly men, turning the grace of our God into lasciviousness, and denying the only Lord God, and our Lord Jesus Christ.

Jude 1:7 — Even as Sodom and Gomorrha, and the cities about them in like manner, giving themselves over to fornication, and going after strange flesh, are set forth for an example, suffering the vengeance of eternal fire.

✦See: Adultery

✦See: Idolatry; wicked practices of; licentiousness of

✦See: Incest

✦See: Lust

- ✦See: Rape
- ✦See: Sensuality
- ✦See: Sodomy
- ✦See: Whore
- ✦See: Whoredom

• Figurative.
Eze 16:15–59
✦See: Whoredom

• Instances of.

• Sodomites.
Ge 19:5

• Lot's daughters.
Ge 19:30–38

• Judah.
Ge 38:15–16

• The Gibeahites.
Jgs 19:22–25

• Eli's sons.
1Sa 2:22

• David.
2Sa 5:13; 11:2–27

• Amnon.
2Sa 13:1–14

• Solomon.
1Ki 11:1–3

• Rehoboam.
2Ch 11:21–23

• Persian kings.
Est 2:3, 13–14, 19

LASEA • A city of Crete.

Ac 27:8 — And, hardly passing it, came unto a place which is called The fair havens; nigh whereunto was the city *of* Lasea.

LASHA • A place at the southern extremity of Canaan.

Ge 10:19 — And the border of the Canaanites was from Sidon, as thou comest to Gerar, unto Gaza; as thou goest, unto Sodom, and Gomorrah, and Admah, and Zeboim, even unto Lasha.

LASHARON • King of, killed by Joshua.

Jos 12:18 — The king of Aphek, one; the king of Lasharon, one;

LATIN

Lk 23:38 — And a superscription also was written over him in letters of Greek, and Latin, and Hebrew, THIS IS THE KING OF THE JEWS.

Jn 19:20 — This title then read many of the Jews: for the place where Jesus was crucified was nigh to the city: and it was written in Hebrew, *and* Greek, *and* Latin.

LAUGHTER

• A time for.
Ecc 3:4 — A time to weep, and a time to laugh; a time to mourn, and a time to dance;

• Attributed to God.
Ps 37:13 — The Lord shall laugh at him: for he seeth that his day is coming.

Ps 59:8 — But thou, O LORD, shalt laugh at them; thou shalt have all the heathen in derision.

Pr 1:26 — I also will laugh at your calamity; I will mock when your fear cometh;

✦See: Happiness
✦See: Joy

LAVER

• Directions for making.
Ex 30:18–20

• Situation of, in the tabernacle, tent of the congregation, and the altar.
Ex 40:7 — And thou shalt set the laver between the tent of the congregation and the altar, and shalt put water therein.

• Sanctified.
Ex 30:28 — And the altar of burnt offering with all his vessels, and the laver and his foot.

Ex 40:11 — And thou shalt anoint the laver and his foot, and sanctify it.

Le 8:11 — And he sprinkled thereof upon the altar seven times, and anointed the altar and all his vessels, both the laver and his foot, to sanctify them.

• Used for washing.
Ex 40:30–32

• Brazen, made by Solomon for the temple.
1Ki 7:23–26, 38–39; 2Ch 4:2–14

1Ki 7:30 — And every base had four brasen wheels, and plates of brass: and the four corners thereof had undersetters: under the laver *were* undersetters molten, at the side of every addition.

• Altered by Ahaz.
2Ki 16:17 — And king Ahaz cut off the borders of the bases, and removed the laver from off them; and took down the sea from off the brasen oxen that *were* under it, and put it upon a pavement of stones.

• Broken and carried to Babylon by the Chaldeans.
2Ki 25:13 — And the pillars of brass that *were* in the house of the LORD, and the bases, and the brasen sea that *was* in the house of the LORD, did the Chaldees break in pieces, and carried the brass of them to Babylon.

2Ki 25:16 — The two pillars, one sea, and the bases which Solomon had made for the house of the LORD; the brass of all these vessels was without weight.

Jer 52:17 — Also the pillars of brass that *were* in the house of the LORD, and the bases, and the brasen sea that *was* in the house of the LORD, the Chaldeans brake, and carried all the brass of them to Babylon.

Jer 52:20 — The two pillars, one sea, and twelve brasen bulls that *were* under the bases, which king Solomon had made in the house of the LORD: the brass of all these vessels was without weight.

• **Figurative.**

Rev 4:6 — And before the throne *there was* a sea of glass like unto crystal: and in the midst of the throne, and round about the throne, *were* four beasts full of eyes before and behind.

Rev 15:2 — And I saw as it were a sea of glass mingled with fire: and them that had gotten the victory over the beast, and over his image, and over his mark, *and* over the number of his name, stand on the sea of glass, having the harps of God.

• **In connection with.**

Ex 38:8 — And he made the laver *of* brass, and the foot of it *of* brass, of the lookingglasses of *the women* assembling, which assembled *at* the door of the tabernacle of the congregation.

1Ki 7:23 — And he made a molten sea, ten cubits from the one brim to the other: *it was* round all about, and his height *was* five cubits: and a line of thirty cubits did compass it round about.

LAW

Ps 19:7–9; 119:1–8; Pr 28:4–5; Lk 20:22–25; Ro 2:14–15; 1Ti 1:8–10

Mt 22:21 — They say unto him, Caesar's. Then saith he unto them, Render therefore unto Caesar the things which are Caesar's; and unto God the things that are God's.

Lk 16:17 — And it is easier for heaven and earth to pass, than one tittle of the law to fail.

Ro 7:7 — What shall we say then? *Is* the law sin? God forbid. Nay, I had not known sin, but by the law: for I had not known lust, except the law had said, Thou shalt not covet.

Ro 7:12 — Wherefore the law *is* holy, and the commandment holy, and just, and good.

Ro 7:14 — For we know that the law is spiritual: but I am carnal, sold under sin.

Ro 13:10 — Love worketh no ill to his neighbour: therefore love *is* the fulfilling of the law.

1Ti 1:5 — Now the end of the commandment is charity out of a pure heart, and *of* a good conscience, and *of* faith unfeigned:

Jas 1:25 — But whoso looketh into the perfect law of liberty, and continueth *therein*, he being not a forgetful hearer, but a doer of the work, this man shall be blessed in his deed.

1Jn 3:4 — Whosoever committeth sin transgresseth also the law: for sin is the transgression of the law.

1Jn 5:3 — For this is the love of God, that we keep his commandments: and his commandments are not grievous.

See: Commandments

See: Duty; of man to God

See: Litigation

• **Of Moses.**

• **Contained in the books (Given at Sinai).**

Ex 1:1; Dt 34:12

Hab 3:3 — God came from Teman, and the Holy One from mount Paran. Selah. His glory covered the heavens, and the earth was full of his praise.

• **Received by the disposition of angels.**

Dt 33:2 — And he said, The LORD came from Sinai, and rose up from Seir unto them; he shined forth from mount Paran, and he came with ten thousands of saints: from his right hand *went* a fiery law for them.

Ps 68:17 — The chariots of God *are* twenty thousand, *even* thousands of angels: the Lord *is* among them, *as in* Sinai, in the holy *place*.

Ac 7:53 — Who have received the law by the disposition of angels, and have not kept *it*.

Gal 3:19 — Wherefore then *serveth* the law? It was added because of transgressions, till the seed should come to whom the promise was made; *and it was* ordained by angels in the hand of a mediator.

Heb 2:2 — For if the word spoken by angels was stedfast, and every transgression and disobedience received a just recompence of reward;

• **Was given because of transgressions until the Messiah came.**

Gal 3:19 — Wherefore then *serveth* the law? It was added because of transgressions, till the seed should come to whom the promise was made; *and it was* ordained by angels in the hand of a mediator.

• **Engraved on stone.**

Ex 20:3–17; Dt 5:4–22

Ex 24:12 — And the LORD said unto Moses, Come up to me into the mount, and be there: and I will give thee tables of stone, and a law, and commandments which I have written; that thou mayest teach them.

Ex 31:18 — And he gave unto Moses, when he had made an end of communing with him upon mount Sinai, two tables of testimony, tables of stone, written with the finger of God.

Ex 32:16 — And the tables *were* the work of God, and the writing *was* the writing of God, graven upon the tables.

Ex 34:29 — And it came to pass, when Moses came down from mount Sinai with the two tables of testimony in Moses' hand, when he came down from the mount, that Moses wist not that the skin of his face shone while he talked with him.

Ex 40:20 — And he took and put the testimony into the ark, and set the staves on the ark, and put the mercy seat above upon the ark:

Dt 4:13 — And he declared unto you his covenant, which he commanded you to perform, *even* ten commandments; and he wrote them upon two tables of stone.

Dt 9:10 — And the LORD delivered unto me two tables of stone written with the finger of God; and on them *was written* according to all the words, which the LORD spake with you in the mount out of the midst of the fire in the day of the assembly.

See: Commandments

See: Table

- **Preserved in the ark of the covenant.**

Ex 25:16 — And thou shalt put into the ark the testimony which I shall give thee.

Dt 31:9 — And Moses wrote this law, and delivered it unto the priests the sons of Levi, which bare the ark of the covenant of the LORD, and unto all the elders of Israel.

Dt 31:26 — Take this book of the law, and put it in the side of the ark of the covenant of the LORD your God, that it may be there for a witness against thee.

- **Found by Hilkiah in the house of the Lord.**

2Ki 22:8 — And Hilkiah the high priest said unto Shaphan the scribe, I have found the book of the law in the house of the LORD. And Hilkiah gave the book to Shaphan, and he read it.

- **Engraved upon monuments.**

Dt 27:2–8; Jos 8:30–35

- **To be written on doorposts.**

Dt 6:9 — And thou shalt write them upon the posts of thy house, and on thy gates.

Dt 11:20 — And thou shalt write them upon the door posts of thine house, and upon thy gates:

- **To be written on frontlets for the forehead, and parchment for the hand.**

Dt 6:4–9; 11:18–21

Ex 13:9 — And it shall be for a sign unto thee upon thine hand, and for a memorial between thine eyes, that the LORD's law may be in thy mouth: for with a strong hand hath the LORD brought thee out of Egypt.

Ex 13:16 — And it shall be for a token upon thine hand, and for frontlets between thine eyes: for by strength of hand the LORD brought us forth out of Egypt.

- **Children instructed in.**

See: Children

See: Instruction

- **Expounded by the priests and Levites.**

Le 10:11 — And that ye may teach the children of Israel all the statutes which the LORD hath spoken unto them by the hand of Moses.

Dt 33:10 — They shall teach Jacob thy judgments, and Israel thy law: they shall put incense before thee, and whole burnt sacrifice upon thine altar.

2Ch 35:3 — And said unto the Levites that taught all Israel, which were holy unto the LORD, Put the holy ark in the house which Solomon the son of David king of Israel did build; *it shall* not *be* a burden upon *your* shoulders: serve now the LORD your God, and his people Israel,

- **Expounded by princes, priests, and Levites publicly taught.**

Ne 8:1–18

Ezr 7:10 — For Ezra had prepared his heart to seek the law of the LORD, and to do *it,* and to teach in Israel statutes and judgments.

- **Expounded from city to city.**

2Ch 17:7–10

- **Expounded in synagogues.**

Ac 13:14–14:1; 17:1–3

Lk 4:16 — And he came to Nazareth, where he had been brought up: and, as his custom was, he went into the synagogue on the sabbath day, and stood up for to read.

Lk 4:32 — And they were astonished at his doctrine: for his word was with power.

Ac 9:20 — And straightway he preached Christ in the synagogues, that he is the Son of God.

Ac 15:21 — For Moses of old time hath in every city them that preach him, being read in the synagogues every sabbath day.

Ac 18:4 — And he reasoned in the synagogue every sabbath, and persuaded the Jews and the Greeks.

Ac 18:26 — And he began to speak boldly in the synagogue: whom when Aquila and Priscilla had heard, they took him unto *them,* and expounded unto him the way of God more perfectly.

- **Expounded to the assembled nation at the Feast of Tabernacles in the sabbatic year.**

Dt 31:10–13

- **Renewed by Moses.**

Dt 4:44–46

- **Curses of, responsively read by Levites and people at Ebal and Gerizim.**

Dt 27:12–26; Jos 8:33–35

- **Formed a constitution on which the civil government of the Israelites was founded.**

Dt 17:18–20

2Ki 11:12 — And he brought forth the king's son, and put the crown upon him, and *gave him* the testimony; and they made him king, and anointed him; and they clapped their hands, and said, God save the king.

2Ch 23:11 — Then they brought out the king's son, and put upon him the crown, and *gave him* the testimony, and made him king. And Jehoiada and his sons anointed him, and said, God save the king.

See: Government; constitutional

- **Divine authority for.**

Ex 19:16–24; 20:1–17; 24:12–18; 32:15–16; 34:1–4, 27–28; Dt 4:10–13; 5:1–22; 10:1–5; 33:2–4; Heb 9:18–21

Ex 31:18 — And he gave unto Moses, when he had made an end of communing with him upon mount Sinai, two tables of testimony, tables of stone, written with the finger of God.

Le 26:46 — These *are* the statutes and judgments and laws, which the LORD made between him and the children of Israel in mount Sinai by the hand of Moses.

Dt 4:36 — Out of heaven he made thee to hear his voice, that he might instruct thee: and upon earth he shewed thee his great fire; and thou heardest his words out of the midst of the fire.

Dt 9:10 — And the LORD delivered unto me two tables of stone written with the finger of God; and on them *was written* according to all the words, which the

LORD spake with you in the mount out of the midst of the fire in the day of the assembly.

1Ki 8:9 — *There was* nothing in the ark save the two tables of stone, which Moses put there at Horeb, when the LORD made *a covenant* with the children of Israel, when they came out of the land of Egypt.

Ezr 7:6 — This Ezra went up from Babylon; and he *was* a ready scribe in the law of Moses, which the LORD God of Israel had given: and the king granted him all his request, according to the hand of the LORD his God upon him.

Ne 1:7 — We have dealt very corruptly against thee, and have not kept the commandments, nor the statutes, nor the judgments, which thou commandedst thy servant Moses.

Ne 8:1 — And all the people gathered themselves together as one man into the street that *was* before the water gate; and they spake unto Ezra the scribe to bring the book of the law of Moses, which the LORD had commanded to Israel.

Ne 9:14 — And madest known unto them thy holy sabbath, and commandedst them precepts, statutes, and laws, by the hand of Moses thy servant:

Ps 78:5 — For he established a testimony in Jacob, and appointed a law in Israel, which he commanded our fathers, that they should make them known to their children:

Ps 103:7 — He made known his ways unto Moses, his acts unto the children of Israel.

Isa 33:22 — For the LORD *is* our judge, the LORD *is* our lawgiver, the LORD *is* our king; he will save us.

Mal 4:4 — Remember ye the law of Moses my servant, which I commanded unto him in Horeb for all Israel, *with* the statutes and judgments.

Ac 7:38 — This is he, that was in the church in the wilderness with the angel which spake to him in the mount Sina, and *with* our fathers: who received the lively oracles to give unto us:

Ac 7:53 — Who have received the law by the disposition of angels, and have not kept *it*.

Gal 3:19 — Wherefore then *serveth* the law? It was added because of transgressions, till the seed should come to whom the promise was made; *and it was* ordained by angels in the hand of a mediator.

• Prophecies in, of the Messiah.

Ac 26:22–23; Ro 3:21–22

Lk 24:44 — And he said unto them, These *are* the words which I spake unto you, while I was yet with you, that all things must be fulfilled, which were written in the law of Moses, and *in* the prophets, and *in* the Psalms, concerning me.

Jn 1:45 — Philip findeth Nathanael, and saith unto him, We have found him, of whom Moses in the law, and the prophets, did write, Jesus of Nazareth, the son of Joseph.

Jn 5:46 — For had ye believed Moses, ye would have believed me: for he wrote of me.

Jn 12:34 — The people answered him, We have heard out of the law that Christ abideth for ever: and how sayest thou, The Son of man must be lifted up? who is this Son of man?

Ac 28:23 — And when they had appointed him a day, there came many to him into *his* lodging; to whom he expounded and testified the kingdom of God, persuading them concerning Jesus, both out of the law of Moses, and *out of* the prophets, from morning till evening.

➔See: Jesus, Prophecies Concerning

• Epitomized by Jesus.

Mk 12:29–33

Mt 22:40 — On these two commandments hang all the law and the prophets.

Lk 10:27 — And he answering said, Thou shalt love the Lord thy God with all thy heart, and with all thy soul, and with all thy strength, and with all thy mind; and thy neighbour as thyself.

• Book of found by Hilkiah in the temple.

2Ki 22:8 — And Hilkiah the high priest said unto Shaphan the scribe, I have found the book of the law in the house of the LORD. And Hilkiah gave the book to Shaphan, and he read it.

2Ch 34:14 — And when they brought out the money that was brought into the house of the LORD, Hilkiah the priest found a book of the law of the LORD *given* by Moses.

• Temporary.

Mt 5:17–45; Lk 16:16–17; Jn 4:20–24; Ac 15:1–29; 21:20–25; Ro 3:1–2; 7:1–6; 2Co 3:7–14; Gal 2:3–9; 4:30–31; Col 2:14–23; Heb 8:4–13; 9:8–24; 10:1–18; 12:18–19

Jer 3:16 — And it shall come to pass, when ye be multiplied and increased in the land, in those days, saith the LORD, they shall say no more, The ark of the covenant of the LORD: neither shall it come to mind: neither shall they remember it; neither shall they visit *it;* neither shall *that* be done any more.

Da 9:27 — And he shall confirm the covenant with many for one week: and in the midst of the week he shall cause the sacrifice and the oblation to cease, and for the overspreading of abominations he shall make *it* desolate, even until the consummation, and that determined shall be poured upon the desolate.

Jn 1:17 — For the law was given by Moses, *but* grace and truth came by Jesus Christ.

Jn 8:35 — And the servant abideth not in the house for ever: *but* the Son abideth ever.

Ac 6:14 — For we have heard him say, that this Jesus of Nazareth shall destroy this place, and shall change the customs which Moses delivered us.

Ac 10:28 — And he said unto them, Ye know how that it is an unlawful thing for a man that is a Jew to keep company, or come unto one of another nation; but God hath shewed me that I should not call any man common or unclean.

Ac 13:39 — And by him all that believe are justified from all things, from which ye could not be justified by the law of Moses.

Ro 8:3 — For what the law could not do, in that it was weak through the flesh, God sending his own Son in the likeness of sinful flesh, and for sin, condemned sin in the flesh:

Ro 10:4 — For Christ *is* the end of the law for righteousness to every one that believeth.

Eph 2:15 — Having abolished in his flesh the enmity, *even* the law of commandments *contained* in ordinances; for to make in himself of twain one new man, *so* making peace;

Heb 11:40 — God having provided some better thing for us, that they without us should not be made perfect.

Heb 12:27 — And this *word,* Yet once more, signifieth the removing of those things that are shaken, as of things that are made, that those things which cannot be shaken may remain.

LAWSUITS

• To be avoided.

Pr 25:8–10; Mt 5:25–26; 1Co 6:1–8

See: Actions at Law

See: Adjudication at Law

See: Arbitration

See: Compromise

See: Court

See: Justice

LAWYER

• One versed in the Mosaic law.

Lk 10:25–37

• Tested Jesus with questions.

Mt 22:35 — Then one of them, *which was* a lawyer, asked *him a question,* tempting him, and saying,

• Jesus' satire against.

Lk 11:45–52

• Zenas.

Tit 3:13 — Bring Zenas the lawyer and Apollos on their journey diligently, that nothing be wanting unto them.

See: Litigation

LAYING ON OF HANDS See: Hand; imposition of hands

LAZARUS

• Brother of Mary and Martha.

• Sickness and death of.

Jn 11:1–14

• Resurrection of.

Jn 11:38–44; 12:17–18

• Supped with Jesus.

Jn 12:1–2

Jn 12:9 — Much people of the Jews therefore knew that he was there: and they came not for Jesus' sake only, but that they might see Lazarus also, whom he had raised from the dead.

• Plotted against by the chief priests.

Jn 12:10–11

LAZINESS See: Slothfulness

LEAD

• A mineral.

Ex 15:10 — Thou didst blow with thy wind, the sea covered them: they sank as lead in the mighty waters.

• Purified by fire.

Nu 31:22 — Only the gold, and the silver, the brass, the iron, the tin, and the lead,

Jer 6:29 — The bellows are burned, the lead is consumed of the fire; the founder melteth in vain: for the wicked are not plucked away.

Eze 22:18 — Son of man, the house of Israel is to me become dross: all they *are* brass, and tin, and iron, and lead, in the midst of the furnace; they are *even* the dross of silver.

Eze 22:20 — *As* they gather silver, and brass, and iron, and lead, and tin, into the midst of the furnace, to blow the fire upon it, to melt *it;* so will I gather *you* in mine anger and in my fury, and I will leave *you there,* and melt you.

• Used in making inscriptions on stone.

Job 19:24 — That they were graven with an iron pen and lead in the rock for ever!

• Lead-founder.

Jer 6:29 — The bellows are burned, the lead is consumed of the fire; the founder melteth in vain: for the wicked are not plucked away.

Eze 22:18 — Son of man, the house of Israel is to me become dross: all they *are* brass, and tin, and iron, and lead, in the midst of the furnace; they are *even* the dross of silver.

Eze 22:20 — *As* they gather silver, and brass, and iron, and lead, and tin, into the midst of the furnace, to blow the fire upon it, to melt *it;* so will I gather *you* in mine anger and in my fury, and I will leave *you there,* and melt you.

• Trade in.

Eze 27:12 — Tarshish *was* thy merchant by reason of the multitude of all *kind of* riches; with silver, iron, tin, and lead, they traded in thy fairs.

• Used for weighing.

Zec 5:7–8

LEADERSHIP

• Instances of.

See: Abraham

See: Deborah

See: Gideon

See: Joshua

See: Moses

LEAGUE

See: Alliances

See: Treaty

LEAH

• Daughter of Laban.

Ge 29:16 — And Laban had two daughters: the name of the elder *was* Leah, and the name of the younger *was* Rachel.

• Married to Jacob.

Ge 29:23–26

• Children of.

Ge 29:31–35; 30:9–13, 17–21

• Flees with Jacob.

Ge 33:2–7

Ge 31:4 — And Jacob sent and called Rachel and Leah to the field unto his flock,

Ge 31:14 — And Rachel and Leah answered and said unto him, *Is there* yet any portion or inheritance for us in our father's house?

Ge 31:17 — Then Jacob rose up, and set his sons and his wives upon camels;

• "Builder of the house of Israel".

Ru 4:11 — And all the people that *were* in the gate, and the elders, said, *We are* witnesses. The LORD make the woman that is come into thine house like Rachel and like Leah, which two did build the house of Israel: and do thou worthily in Ephratah, and be famous in Bethlehem:

LEARNING

See: Instruction

See: Knowledge

LEASE

• Of real estate.

Mt 21:33–41; Mk 12:1–9; Lk 20:9–16

See: Land

LEASING

• Falsifying.

Ps 4:2 — O ye sons of men, how long *will ye turn* my glory into shame? *how long* will ye love vanity, *and* seek after leasing? Selah.

LEATHER

• Girdles of.

2Ki 1:8 — And they answered him, *He was* an hairy man, and girt with a girdle of leather about his loins. And he said, It *is* Elijah the Tishbite.

Mt 3:4 — And the same John had his raiment of camel's hair, and a leathern girdle about his loins; and his meat was locusts and wild honey.

• Tanning of.

Ac 10:5–6

Ac 9:43 — And it came to pass, that he tarried many days in Joppa with one Simon a tanner.

• Called skin.

Ge 3:21 — Unto Adam also and to his wife did the LORD God make coats of skins, and clothed them.

Mk 1:6 — And John was clothed with camel's hair, and with a girdle of a skin about his loins; and he did eat locusts and wild honey;

• Hide.

Le 8:17 — But the bullock, and his hide, his flesh, and his dung, he burnt with fire without the camp; as the LORD commanded Moses.

LEAVEN

• For bread.

Ex 12:34 — And the people took their dough before it was leavened, their kneadingtroughs being bound up in their clothes upon their shoulders.

Ex 12:39 — And they baked unleavened cakes of the dough which they brought forth out of Egypt, for it was not leavened; because they were thrust out of Egypt, and could not tarry, neither had they prepared for themselves any victual.

Hos 7:4 — They *are* all adulterers, as an oven heated by the baker, *who* ceaseth from raising after he hath kneaded the dough, until it be leavened.

Mt 13:33 — Another parable spake he unto them; The kingdom of heaven is like unto leaven, which a woman took, and hid in three measures of meal, till the whole was leavened.

• Leavened bread used with peace offering.

Le 7:13 — Besides the cakes, he shall offer *for* his offering leavened bread with the sacrifice of thanksgiving of his peace offerings.

Am 4:5 — And offer a sacrifice of thanksgiving with leaven, and proclaim *and* publish the free offerings: for this liketh you, O ye children of Israel, saith the Lord GOD.

• With wave offering.

Le 23:15–17

• Leavened bread forbidden with meat offerings.

Ex 23:18 — Thou shalt not offer the blood of my sacrifice with leavened bread; neither shall the fat of my sacrifice remain until the morning.

Ex 34:25 — Thou shalt not offer the blood of my sacrifice with leaven; neither shall the sacrifice of the feast of the passover be left unto the morning.

Le 2:11 — No meat offering, which ye shall bring unto the LORD, shall be made with leaven: for ye shall burn no leaven, nor any honey, in any offering of the LORD made by fire.

Le 6:17 — It shall not be baken with leaven. I have given it *unto them for* their portion of my offerings made by fire; it *is* most holy, as *is* the sin offering, and as the trespass offering.

Le 10:12 — And Moses spake unto Aaron, and unto Eleazar and unto Ithamar, his sons that were left, Take the meat offering that remaineth of the offerings of the LORD made by fire, and eat it without leaven beside the altar: for it *is* most holy:

• Leavened bread at the passover.

Ex 12:19–20; 13:3–4

Ex 13:7 — Unleavened bread shall be eaten seven days; and there shall no leavened bread be seen with thee, neither shall there be leaven seen with thee in all thy quarters.

Ex 23:18 — Thou shalt not offer the blood of my sacrifice with leavened bread; neither shall the fat of my sacrifice remain until the morning.

- **Leavened bread with blood.**

Ex 23:18 — Thou shalt not offer the blood of my sacrifice with leavened bread; neither shall the fat of my sacrifice remain until the morning.

Ex 34:25 — Thou shalt not offer the blood of my sacrifice with leaven; neither shall the sacrifice of the feast of the passover be left unto the morning.

- **A type of sin.**

1Co 5:6–8

- **Figurative.**
  - **Of the hypocrisy of the Pharisees.**

Mt 16:6–12

Mk 8:15 — And he charged them, saying, Take heed, beware of the leaven of the Pharisees, and *of* the leaven of Herod.

Lk 12:1 — In the mean time, when there were gathered together an innumerable multitude of people, insomuch that they trode one upon another, he began to say unto his disciples first of all, Beware ye of the leaven of the Pharisees, which is hypocrisy.

- **Of other evils.**

1Co 5:6–8

Gal 5:9 — A little leaven leaveneth the whole lump.

- **Parable of.**

Mt 13:33 — Another parable spake he unto them; The kingdom of heaven is like unto leaven, which a woman took, and hid in three measures of meal, till the whole was leavened.

Lk 13:21 — It is like leaven, which a woman took and hid in three measures of meal, till the whole was leavened.

LEBANAH

- **Called also Lebana.**
- **One of the Nethinim.**

Ezr 2:45 — The children of Lebanah, the children of Hagabah, the children of Akkub,

Ne 7:48 — The children of Lebana, the children of Hagaba, the children of Shalmai,

LEBANON

- **A mountain range.**
- **Northern boundary of the land of Canaan.**

Dt 1:7 — Turn you, and take your journey, and go to the mount of the Amorites, and unto all *the places* nigh thereunto, in the plain, in the hills, and in the vale, and in the south, and by the sea side, to the land of the Canaanites, and unto Lebanon, unto the great river, the river Euphrates.

Dt 3:25 — I pray thee, let me go over, and see the good land that *is* beyond Jordan, that goodly mountain, and Lebanon.

Dt 11:24 — Every place whereon the soles of your feet shall tread shall be yours: from the wilderness and Lebanon, from the river, the river Euphrates, even unto the uttermost sea shall your coast be.

Jos 1:4 — From the wilderness and this Lebanon even unto the great river, the river Euphrates, all the land of the Hittites, and unto the great sea toward the going down of the sun, shall be your coast.

Jos 9:1 — And it came to pass, when all the kings which *were* on this side Jordan, in the hills, and in the valleys, and in all the coasts of the great sea over against Lebanon, the Hittite, and the Amorite, the Canaanite, the Perizzite, the Hivite, and the Jebusite, heard *thereof;*

- **Early inhabitants of.**

Jgs 3:3 — *Namely,* five lords of the Philistines, and all the Canaanites, and the Sidonians, and the Hivites that dwelt in mount Lebanon, from mount Baal-hermon unto the entering in of Hamath.

- **Snow of.**

Jer 18:14 — Will *a man* leave the snow of Lebanon *which cometh* from the rock of the field? *or* shall the cold flowing waters that come from another place be forsaken?

- **Streams of.**

SS 4:15 — A fountain of gardens, a well of living waters, and streams from Lebanon.

- **Cedars of.**

Jgs 9:15 — And the bramble said unto the trees, If in truth ye anoint me king over you, *then* come *and* put your trust in my shadow: and if not, let fire come out of the bramble, and devour the cedars of Lebanon.

2Ki 19:23 — By the messengers thou hast reproached the Lord, and hast said, With the multitude of my chariots I am come up to the height of the mountains, to the sides of Lebanon, and will cut down the tall cedar trees thereof, *and* the choice fir trees thereof: and I will enter into the lodgings of his borders, *and into* the forest of his Carmel.

2Ch 2:8 — Send me also cedar trees, fir trees, and algum trees, out of Lebanon: for I know that thy servants can skill to cut timber in Lebanon; and, behold, my servants *shall be* with thy servants,

Ps 29:5 — The voice of the LORD breaketh the cedars; yea, the LORD breaketh the cedars of Lebanon.

Ps 104:16 — The trees of the LORD are full *of sap;* the cedars of Lebanon, which he hath planted;

Isa 2:13 — And upon all the cedars of Lebanon, *that are* high and lifted up, and upon all the oaks of Bashan,

Isa 14:8 — Yea, the fir trees rejoice at thee, *and* the cedars of Lebanon, *saying,* Since thou art laid down, no feller is come up against us.

Eze 27:5 — They have made all thy *ship* boards of fir trees of Senir: they have taken cedars from Lebanon to make masts for thee.

- **Other trees of.**

2Ki 19:23 — By the messengers thou hast reproached the Lord, and hast said, With the multitude of my chariots I am come up to the height of the mountains, to the sides of Lebanon, and will cut down the tall cedar trees thereof, *and* the choice fir trees thereof: and I will enter into the lodgings of his borders, *and into* the forest of his Carmel.

2Ch 2:8 — Send me also cedar trees, fir trees, and algum trees, out of Lebanon: for I know that thy servants can skill to cut timber in Lebanon; and, behold, my servants *shall be* with thy servants,

• Flower of.

Na 1:4 — He rebuketh the sea, and maketh it dry, and drieth up all the rivers: Bashan languisheth, and Carmel, and the flower of Lebanon languisheth.

• Beasts of.

Isa 40:16 — And Lebanon *is* not sufficient to burn, nor the beasts thereof sufficient for a burnt offering.

• Fertility and productiveness of.

Hos 14:5–7

• "House of the forest of".

1Ki 7:2–5

• Valley of.

Jos 11:17 — *Even* from the mount Halak, that goeth up to Seir, even unto Baal-gad in the valley of Lebanon under mount Hermon: and all their kings he took, and smote them, and slew them.

Jos 12:7 — And these *are* the kings of the country which Joshua and the children of Israel smote on this side Jordan on the west, from Baal-gad in the valley of Lebanon even unto the mount Halak, that goeth up to Seir; which Joshua gave unto the tribes of Israel *for* a possession according to their divisions;

• Tower of.

SS 7:4 — Thy neck *is* as a tower of ivory; thine eyes *like* the fishpools in Heshbon, by the gate of Bath-rabbim: thy nose *is* as the tower of Lebanon which looketh toward Damascus.

• Solomon had cities of store in.

1Ki 9:19 — And all the cities of store that Solomon had, and cities for his chariots, and cities for his horsemen, and that which Solomon desired to build in Jerusalem, and in Lebanon, and in all the land of his dominion.

• Figurative.

Isa 29:17 — *Is* it not yet a very little while, and Lebanon shall be turned into a fruitful field, and the fruitful field shall be esteemed as a forest?

Jer 22:6 — For thus saith the LORD unto the king's house of Judah; Thou *art* Gilead unto me, *and* the head of Lebanon: *yet* surely I will make thee a wilderness, *and* cities *which* are not inhabited.

LEBAOTH

• A city of Simeon.

Jos 15:32 — And Lebaoth, and Shilhim, and Ain, and Rimmon: all the cities *are* twenty and nine, with their villages:

↞See: Beth-Lebaoth

LEBBAEUS

• Surnamed Thaddaeus.

• One of the twelve apostles.

Mt 10:3 — Philip, and Bartholomew; Thomas, and Matthew the publican; James *the son* of Alphaeus, and Lebbaeus, whose surname was Thaddaeus;

LEBONAH • A city on the highway from Bethel to Shechem.

Jgs 21:19 — Then they said, Behold, *there is* a feast of the LORD in Shiloh yearly *in a place* which *is* on the north side of Bethel, on the east side of the highway that goeth up from Bethel to Shechem, and on the south of Lebonah.

LECAH • A town or person in Judah.

1Ch 4:21 — The sons of Shelah the son of Judah *were*, Er the father of Lecah, and Laadah the father of Mareshah, and the families of the house of them that wrought fine linen, of the house of Ashbea,

LEEK

Nu 11:5 — We remember the fish, which we did eat in Egypt freely; the cucumbers, and the melons, and the leeks, and the onions, and the garlick:

LEES • Settlings of wine.

Ps 75:8 — For in the hand of the LORD *there is* a cup, and the wine is red; it is full of mixture; and he poureth out of the same: but the dregs thereof, all the wicked of the earth shall wring *them* out, *and* drink *them*.

Isa 25:6 — And in this mountain shall the LORD of hosts make unto all people a feast of fat things, a feast of wines on the lees, of fat things full of marrow, of wines on the lees well refined.

Jer 48:11 — Moab hath been at ease from his youth, and he hath settled on his lees, and hath not been emptied from vessel to vessel, neither hath he gone into captivity: therefore his taste remained in him, and his scent is not changed.

Zep 1:12 — And it shall come to pass at that time, *that* I will search Jerusalem with candles, and punish the men that are settled on their lees: that say in their heart, The LORD will not do good, neither will he do evil.

LEFT-HANDED

Jgs 3:15 — But when the children of Israel cried unto the LORD, the LORD raised them up a deliverer, Ehud the son of Gera, a Benjamite, a man lefthanded: and by him the children of Israel sent a present unto Eglon the king of Moab.

Jgs 20:16 — Among all this people *there were* seven hundred chosen men lefthanded; every one could sling stones at an hair *breadth*, and not miss.

LEGALISM

Mk 2:24 — And the Pharisees said unto him, Behold, why do they on the sabbath day that which is not lawful?

Ac 15:5 — But there rose up certain of the sect of the Pharisees which believed, saying, That it was needful to circumcise them, and to command *them* to keep the law of Moses.

Ro 10:2 — For I bear them record that they have a zeal of God, but not according to knowledge.

Gal 1:14 — And profited in the Jews' religion above many my equals in mine own nation, being more exceedingly zealous of the traditions of my fathers.

LEGENDS

• "Holiness to the Lord," engraved on the high priest's mitre.

Ex 28:36 — And thou shalt make a plate *of* pure gold, and grave upon it, *like* the engravings of a signet, HOLINESS TO THE LORD.

Ex 39:30 — And they made the plate of the holy crown *of* pure gold, and wrote upon it a writing, *like to* the engravings of a signet, HOLINESS TO THE LORD.

• "Holiness to the Lord," engraved on bells of horses, on pots and bowls.

Zec 14:20 — In that day shall there be upon the bells of the horses, HOLINESS UNTO THE LORD; and the pots in the LORD'S house shall be like the bowls before the altar.

• "This is Jesus, the King of the Jews".

Mt 27:37 — And set up over his head his accusation written, THIS IS JESUS THE KING OF THE JEWS.

• Precepts written on doorposts and gates, and worn on the hand and forehead.

Dt 6:6–9; 11:18–20

Isa 57:8 — Behind the doors also and the posts hast thou set up thy remembrance: for thou hast discovered *thyself to another* than me, and art gone up; thou hast enlarged thy bed, and made thee *a covenant* with them; thou lovedst their bed where thou sawest *it.*

LEGION

• Of angels.

Mt 26:53 — Thinkest thou that I cannot now pray to my Father, and he shall presently give me more than twelve legions of angels?

• Devils.

Mk 5:9 — And he asked him, What *is* thy name? And he answered, saying, My name *is* Legion: for we are many.

Mk 5:15 — And they come to Jesus, and see him that was possessed with the devil, and had the legion, sitting, and clothed, and in his right mind: and they were afraid.

LEGISLATION

• Class, forbidden.

Ex 12:49 — One law shall be to him that is homeborn, and unto the stranger that sojourneth among you.

Le 24:22 — Ye shall have one manner of law, as well for the stranger, as for one of your own country: for I *am* the LORD your God.

Nu 9:14 — And if a stranger shall sojourn among you, and will keep the passover unto the LORD; according to the ordinance of the passover, and according to the manner thereof, so shall he do: ye shall have one ordinance, both for the stranger, and for him that was born in the land.

Nu 15:15 — One ordinance *shall be both* for you of the congregation, and also for the stranger that sojourneth *with you,* an ordinance for ever in your generations: as ye *are,* so shall the stranger be before the LORD.

Nu 15:29 — Ye shall have one law for him that sinneth through ignorance, *both for* him that is born among the children of Israel, and for the stranger that sojourneth among them.

Gal 3:28 — There is neither Jew nor Greek, there is neither bond nor free, there is neither male nor female: for ye are all one in Christ Jesus.

• Supplemental, concerning Sabbath-breaking.

Nu 15:32–35

• Supplemental, inheritance.

Nu 27:1–11

See: Government

See: Law

LEGS

• Of the crucified broken.

Jn 19:31–32

LEHABIM • A Mizraite people.

Ge 10:13 — And Mizraim begat Ludim, and Anamim, and Lehabim, and Naphtuhim,

1Ch 1:11 — And Mizraim begat Ludim, and Anamim, and Lehabim, and Napthtuhim,

LEHI • A district of Judah, where Samson slew a thousand Philistines with the jawbone of an ass.

Jgs 15:9–19

LEMUEL

• A king.

• Probably refers to Solomon.

Pr 31:1 — The words of king Lemuel, the prophecy that his mother taught him.

Pr 31:4 — *It is* not for kings, O Lemuel, *it is* not for kings to drink wine; nor for princes strong drink:

LENDING

Ex 22:25–27; Le 25:35–37; Dt 15:1–11; 23:19–20; 24:10–13; Ne 5:1–13; Ps 37:25–26; Isa 24:1–2; Lk 6:34–35

Dt 24:6 — No man shall take the nether or the upper millstone to pledge: for he taketh *a man's* life to pledge.

Dt 24:17 — Thou shalt not pervert the judgment of the stranger, *nor* of the fatherless; nor take a widow's raiment to pledge:

Ps 112:5 — A good man sheweth favour, and lendeth: he will guide his affairs with discretion.

Pr 19:17 — He that hath pity upon the poor lendeth unto the LORD; and that which he hath given will he pay him again.

Pr 22:7 — The rich ruleth over the poor, and the borrower *is* servant to the lender.

Pr 28:8 — He that by usury and unjust gain increaseth his substance, he shall gather it for him that will pity the poor.

Eze 18:13 — Hath given forth upon usury, and hath taken increase: shall he then live? he shall not live: he hath done all these abominations; he shall surely die; his blood shall be upon him.

Mt 5:42 — Give to him that asketh thee, and from him that would borrow of thee turn not thou away.

See: Borrowing

See: Interest

See: Money

LENTILES

Ge 25:34 — Then Jacob gave Esau bread and pottage of lentiles; and he did eat and drink, and rose up, and went his way: thus Esau despised *his* birthright.

2Sa 17:28 — Brought beds, and basons, and earthen vessels, and wheat, and barley, and flour, and parched *corn,* and beans, and lentiles, and parched *pulse,*

2Sa 23:11 — And after him *was* Shammah the son of Agee the Hararite. And the Philistines were gathered together into a troop, where was a piece of ground full of lentiles: and the people fled from the Philistines.

Eze 4:9 — Take thou also unto thee wheat, and barley, and beans, and lentiles, and millet, and fitches, and put them in one vessel, and make thee bread thereof, *according* to the number of the days that thou shalt lie upon thy side, three hundred and ninety days shalt thou eat thereof.

LEOPARD

• A carnivorous animal.

SS 4:8 — Come with me from Lebanon, *my* spouse, with me from Lebanon: look from the top of Amana, from the top of Shenir and Hermon, from the lions' dens, from the mountains of the leopards.

• Fierceness of.

Jer 5:6 — Wherefore a lion out of the forest shall slay them, *and* a wolf of the evenings shall spoil them, a leopard shall watch over their cities: every one that goeth out thence shall be torn in pieces: because their transgressions are many, *and* their backslidings are increased.

Jer 13:23 — Can the Ethiopian change his skin, or the leopard his spots? *then* may ye also do good, that are accustomed to do evil.

Hos 13:7 — Therefore I will be unto them as a lion: as a leopard by the way will I observe *them:*

Hab 1:8 — Their horses also are swifter than the leopards, and are more fierce than the evening wolves: and their horsemen shall spread themselves, and their horsemen shall come from far; they shall fly as the eagle *that* hasteth to eat.

• Figurative.

Da 7:6 — After this I beheld, and lo another, like a leopard, which had upon the back of it four wings of a fowl; the beast had also four heads; and dominion was given to it.

• Taming of, the triumph of the gospel.

Isa 11:6 — The wolf also shall dwell with the lamb, and the leopard shall lie down with the kid; and the calf and the young lion and the fatling together; and a little child shall lead them.

LEPROSY

• Law concerning.

Le 13:1–14:57; Nu 5:1–3

Le 22:4 — What man soever of the seed of Aaron *is* a leper, or hath a running issue; he shall not eat of the holy things, until he be clean. And whoso toucheth any thing *that is* unclean *by* the dead, or a man whose seed goeth from him;

Nu 12:14 — And the LORD said unto Moses, If her father had but spit in her face, should she not be ashamed seven days? let her be shut out from the camp seven days, and after that let her be received in *again.*

Dt 24:8 — Take heed in the plague of leprosy, that thou observe diligently, and do according to all that the priests the Levites shall teach you: as I commanded them, so ye shall observe to do.

Mt 8:4 — And Jesus saith unto him, See thou tell no man; but go thy way, shew thyself to the priest, and offer the gift that Moses commanded, for a testimony unto them.

Lk 5:14 — And he charged him to tell no man: but go, and shew thyself to the priest, and offer for thy cleansing, according as Moses commanded, for a testimony unto them.

Lk 17:14 — And when he saw *them,* he said unto them, Go shew yourselves unto the priests. And it came to pass, that, as they went, they were cleansed.

• Sent as a judgment.

• On Miriam.

Nu 12:1–10

• On Gehazi.

2Ki 5:27 — The leprosy therefore of Naaman shall cleave unto thee, and unto thy seed for ever. And he went out from his presence a leper *as white* as snow.

• On Uzziah.

2Ch 26:20–21

• Entailed.

2Ki 5:27 — The leprosy therefore of Naaman shall cleave unto thee, and unto thy seed for ever. And he went out from his presence a leper *as white* as snow.

• Isolation of lepers.

Le 13:46 — All the days wherein the plague *shall be* in him he shall be defiled; he *is* unclean: he shall dwell alone; without the camp *shall* his habitation *be.*

Nu 5:2 — Command the children of Israel, that they put out of the camp every leper, and every one that hath an issue, and whosoever is defiled by the dead:

Nu 12:14 — And the LORD said unto Moses, If her father had but spit in her face, should she not be ashamed seven days? let her be shut out from the camp seven days, and after that let her be received in *again.*

2Ki 15:5 — And the LORD smote the king, so that he was a leper unto the day of his death, and dwelt in a several house. And Jotham the king's son *was* over the house, judging the people of the land.

2Ch 26:21 — And Uzziah the king was a leper unto the day of his death, and dwelt in a several house, *being* a leper; for he was cut off from the house of the LORD: and Jotham his son *was* over the king's house, judging the people of the land.

• Separate burial of.

2Ch 26:23 — So Uzziah slept with his fathers, and they buried him with his fathers in the field of the burial which *belonged* to the kings; for they said, He *is* a leper: and Jotham his son reigned in his stead.

• Instances of leprosy.

• Four lepers outside Samaria.

2Ki 7:3

• Azariah.

2Ki 15:5

• Simon.

Mk 14:3

• Healed.

• Miriam.

Nu 12:13–14

• Naaman.

2Ki 5:8–14

• By Jesus.

Mk 1:40–42; Lk 17:12–14

Mt 8:3 — And Jesus put forth *his* hand, and touched him, saying, <u>I will; be thou clean.</u> And immediately his leprosy was cleansed.

Lk 5:13 — And he put forth *his* hand, and touched him, saying, <u>I will: be thou clean.</u> And immediately the leprosy departed from him.

• Disciples empowered to heal.

Mt 10:8 — <u>Heal the sick, cleanse the lepers, raise the dead, cast out devils: freely ye have received, freely give.</u>

LESHEM

• Called also Laish.

✦See: Dan

LETTERS

• Written by David to Joab.

2Sa 11:14 — And it came to pass in the morning, that David wrote a letter to Joab, and sent *it* by the hand of Uriah.

• Written by king of Syria to king of Israel.

2Ki 5:5–6

• Written by Rabshakeh to Hezekiah.

Isa 37:9–14

• Written by King of Babylon to Hezekiah.

Isa 39:1 — At that time Merodach-baladan, the son of Baladan, king of Babylon, sent letters and a present to Hezekiah: for he had heard that he had been sick, and was recovered.

• Written by Sennacherib to Hezekiah.

2Ki 19:14 — And Hezekiah received the letter of the hand of the messengers, and read it: and Hezekiah went up into the house of the LORD, and spread it before the LORD.

• Of Artaxerxes to Nehemiah.

Ne 2:7–9

• Open letter form Sanballat to Nehemiah.

Ne 6:5 — Then sent Sanballat his servant unto me in like manner the fifth time with an open letter in his hand;

• Written by Luke to Theophilus, the books of Luke and Acts.

Ac 1:1 — The former treatise have I made, O Theophilus, of all that Jesus began both to do and teach,

• Written by Claudius Lysias to Felix.

Ac 23:25–30

• Letters of intercession by Paul and Philemon in behalf of Onesimus.

Phm 1:1 — Paul, a prisoner of Jesus Christ, and Timothy our brother, unto Philemon our dearly beloved, and fellowlabourer,

• Letters of recommendation.

2Co 3:1 — Do we begin again to commend ourselves? or need we, as some *others,* epistles of commendation to you, or *letters* of commendation from you?

LETUSHIM • A son of Dedan.

Ge 25:3 — And Jokshan begat Sheba, and Dedan. And the sons of Dedan were Asshurim, and Letushim, and Leummim.

LEUMMIM • A son of Dedan.

Ge 25:3 — And Jokshan begat Sheba, and Dedan. And the sons of Dedan were Asshurim, and Letushim, and Leummim.

LEVI

• Son of Jacob.

Ge 29:34 — And she conceived again, and bare a son; and said, Now this time will my husband be joined unto me, because I have born him three sons: therefore was his name called Levi.

Ge 35:23 — The sons of Leah; Reuben, Jacob's firstborn, and Simeon, and Levi, and Judah, and Issachar, and Zebulun:

1Ch 2:1 — These *are* the sons of Israel; Reuben, Simeon, Levi, and Judah, Issachar, and Zebulun,

• Avenges the seduction of Dinah.

Ge 34:1–31; 49:5–7

• Jacob's prophecy regarding.

Ge 49:5–7

• His age at death.

Ex 6:16 — And these *are* the names of the sons of Levi according to their generations; Gershon, and

Kohath, and Merari: and the years of the life of Levi *were* an hundred thirty and seven years.

• Descendants of, made ministers of religion.

See: Levites

LEVIATHAN

• Possibly a crocodile.

Job 41:1–34

Ps 104:26 — There go the ships: *there is* that leviathan, *whom* thou hast made to play therein.

• The crooked serpent.

Isa 27:1 — In that day the LORD with his sore and great and strong sword shall punish leviathan the piercing serpent, even leviathan that crooked serpent; and he shall slay the dragon that *is* in the sea.

• Figurative.

Ps 74:14 — Thou brakest the heads of leviathan in pieces, *and* gavest him *to be* meat to the people inhabiting the wilderness.

LEVITES

• The descendants of Levi.

• Set apart as ministers of religion.

Nu 1:47–54; 3:6–16; 26:57–62

Nu 16:9 — *Seemeth it but* a small thing unto you, that the God of Israel hath separated you from the congregation of Israel, to bring you near to himself to do the service of the tabernacle of the LORD, and to stand before the congregation to minister unto them?

Dt 10:8 — At that time the LORD separated the tribe of Levi, to bear the ark of the covenant of the LORD, to stand before the LORD to minister unto him, and to bless in his name, unto this day.

1Ch 15:2 — Then David said, None ought to carry the ark of God but the Levites: for them hath the LORD chosen to carry the ark of God, and to minister unto him for ever.

• Substituted in the place of the firstborn.

Nu 3:41–45; 8:16–18

Nu 3:12 — And I, behold, I have taken the Levites from among the children of Israel instead of all the firstborn that openeth the matrix among the children of Israel: therefore the Levites shall be mine;

Nu 8:14 — Thus shalt thou separate the Levites from among the children of Israel: and the Levites shall be mine.

Nu 18:6 — And I, behold, I have taken your brethren the Levites from among the children of Israel: to you *they are* given *as* a gift for the LORD, to do the service of the tabernacle of the congregation.

• Religious zeal of.

Ex 32:26–28; Dt 33:9–10; Mal 2:4–5

• Consecration of.

Nu 8:6–21

• Sedition among, led by Korah, Dathan, Abiram, and On, on account of jealousy toward Moses and Aaron.

Nu 4:19–20; 16:1–50

• Three divisions of, each having the name of one of its progenitors, Gershon, Kohath, and Merari.

Nu 3:17 — And these were the sons of Levi by their names; Gershon, and Kohath, and Merari.

• Gershonites and their duties.

Nu 3:18–26; 4:23–26

Nu 10:17 — And the tabernacle was taken down; and the sons of Gershon and the sons of Merari set forward, bearing the tabernacle.

• Ruling chief over the Gershonites was the second son of the ruling high priest.

Nu 4:28 — This is the service of the families of the sons of Gershon in the tabernacle of the congregation: and their charge *shall be* under the hand of Ithamar the son of Aaron the priest.

• Kohathites, consisting of the families of the Amramites, Izeharites, Hebronites, Uzzielites.

Nu 4:18–20

Nu 3:27 — And of Kohath *was* the family of the Amramites, and the family of the Izeharites, and the family of the Hebronites, and the family of the Uzzielites: these *are* the families of the Kohathites.

• Of the Amramites, Aaron and his family were set apart as priests.

Nu 8:1–14; 17:1–18:1

Ex 28:1 — And take thou unto thee Aaron thy brother, and his sons with him, from among the children of Israel, that he may minister unto me in the priest's office, *even* Aaron, Nadab and Abihu, Eleazar and Ithamar, Aaron's sons.

Ex 29:9 — And thou shalt gird them with girdles, Aaron and his sons, and put the bonnets on them: and the priest's office shall be theirs for a perpetual statute: and thou shalt consecrate Aaron and his sons.

Nu 3:38 — But those that encamp before the tabernacle toward the east, *even* before the tabernacle of the congregation eastward, *shall be* Moses, and Aaron and his sons, keeping the charge of the sanctuary for the charge of the children of Israel; and the stranger that cometh nigh shall be put to death.

• Of Amramites, remaining families appointed to take charge of certain items in temple.

Nu 3:27–32; 4:2–15

• The chief over the Kohathites was the oldest son of the ruling high priest.

Nu 3:32 — And Eleazar the son of Aaron the priest *shall be* chief over the chief of the Levites, *and have* the oversight of them that keep the charge of the sanctuary.

1Ch 9:20 — And Phinehas the son of Eleazar was the ruler over them in time past, *and* the Lord *was* with him.

• Merarites.

Nu 3:33–37; 4:31–33; 1Ch 6:29–30; 23:21–23

Nu 3:20 — And the sons of Merari by their families; Mahli, and Mushi. These *are* the families of the Levites according to the house of their fathers.

Nu 7:8 — And four wagons and eight oxen he gave unto the sons of Merari, according unto their service, under the hand of Ithamar the son of Aaron the priest.

Nu 10:17 — And the tabernacle was taken down; and the sons of Gershon and the sons of Merari set forward, bearing the tabernacle.

1Ch 6:19 — The sons of Merari; Mahli, and Mushi. And these *are* the families of the Levites according to their fathers.

• The chief over the Merarites was the second son of the ruling high priest.

Nu 4:33 — This *is* the service of the families of the sons of Merari, according to all their service, in the tabernacle of the congregation, under the hand of Ithamar the son of Aaron the priest.

• Place of, in camp and march.

Nu 1:50–53; 3:23–35

Nu 2:17 — Then the tabernacle of the congregation shall set forward with the camp of the Levites in the midst of the camp: as they encamp, so shall they set forward, every man in his place by their standards.

• Cities assigned to, in the land of Canaan.

Jos 21:1–45

• Lodged in the chambers of the temple.

1Ch 9:27 — And they lodged round about the house of God, because the charge *was* upon them, and the opening thereof every morning *pertained* to them.

1Ch 9:33 — And these *are* the singers, chief of the fathers of the Levites, *who remaining* in the chambers *were* free: for they were employed in that work day and night.

Eze 40:44 — And without the inner gate *were* the chambers of the singers in the inner court, which *was* at the side of the north gate; and their prospect *was* toward the south: one at the side of the east gate *having* the prospect toward the north.

• Resided also in villages outside of Jerusalem.

Ne 12:29 — Also from the house of Gilgal, and out of the fields of Geba and Azmaveth: for the singers had builded them villages round about Jerusalem.

• Age of, when inducted into office.

Nu 8:23–26

Nu 4:3 — From thirty years old and upward even until fifty years old, all that enter into the host, to do the work in the tabernacle of the congregation.

Nu 4:30 — From thirty years old and upward even unto fifty years old shalt thou number them, every one that entereth into the service, to do the work of the tabernacle of the congregation.

Nu 4:47 — From thirty years old and upward even unto fifty years old, every one that came to do the service of the ministry, and the service of the burden in the tabernacle of the congregation,

1Ch 23:3 — Now the Levites were numbered from the age of thirty years and upward: and their number by their polls, man by man, was thirty and eight thousand.

1Ch 23:24 — These *were* the sons of Levi after the house of their fathers; *even* the chief of the fathers, as they were counted by number of names by their polls, that did the work for the service of the house of the LORD, from the age of twenty years and upward.

1Ch 23:27 — For by the last words of David the Levites *were* numbered from twenty years old and above:

Ezr 3:8 — Now in the second year of their coming unto the house of God at Jerusalem, in the second month, began Zerubbabel the son of Shealtiel, and Jeshua the son of Jozadak, and the remnant of their brethren the priests and the Levites, and all they that were come out of the captivity unto Jerusalem; and appointed the Levites, from twenty years old and upward, to set forward the work of the house of the LORD.

• Age of, when retired from office.

Nu 8:25–26

Nu 4:3 — From thirty years old and upward even until fifty years old, all that enter into the host, to do the work in the tabernacle of the congregation.

Nu 4:47 — From thirty years old and upward even unto fifty years old, every one that came to do the service of the ministry, and the service of the burden in the tabernacle of the congregation,

• Functions of.

• Had charge of the tabernacle in camp and on the march.

Nu 1:50–53; 3:6–9, 21–37; 4:1–15, 17–49; 18:3–6

Nu 8:19 — And I have given the Levites *as* a gift to Aaron and to his sons from among the children of Israel, to do the service of the children of Israel in the tabernacle of the congregation, and to make an atonement for the children of Israel: that there be no plague among the children of Israel, when the children of Israel come nigh unto the sanctuary.

Nu 8:22 — And after that went the Levites in to do their service in the tabernacle of the congregation before Aaron, and before his sons: as the LORD had commanded Moses concerning the Levites, so did they unto them.

• Had charge of the temple.

1Ch 9:27–29; 23:2–32; Ezr 8:24–34

• Bore the ark of the covenant.

1Ch 15:26–27

Dt 10:8 — At that time the LORD separated the tribe of Levi, to bear the ark of the covenant of the LORD, to stand before the LORD to minister unto him, and to bless in his name, unto this day.

1Ch 15:2 — Then David said, None ought to carry the ark of God but the Levites: for them hath the LORD chosen to carry the ark of God, and to minister unto him for ever.

• Ministered before the ark.

1Ch 16:4 — And he appointed *certain* of the Levites to minister before the ark of the LORD, and to record, and to thank and praise the LORD God of Israel:

• Custodians and administrators of the tithes and other offerings.

1Ch 9:26–29; 2Ch 31:11–19; Ezr 8:29–30

1Ch 26:28 — And all that Samuel the seer, and Saul the son of Kish, and Abner the son of Ner, and Joab the son of Zeruiah, had dedicated; *and* whosoever had dedicated *any thing, it was* under the hand of Shelomith, and of his brethren.

1Ch 29:8 — And they with whom *precious* stones were found gave *them* to the treasure of the house of the LORD, by the hand of Jehiel the Gershonite.

2Ch 24:5 — And he gathered together the priests and the Levites, and said to them, Go out unto the cities of Judah, and gather of all Israel money to repair the house of your God from year to year, and see that ye hasten the matter. Howbeit the Levites hastened it not.

2Ch 24:11 — Now it came to pass, that at what time the chest was brought unto the king's office by the hand of the Levites, and when they saw that *there was* much money, the king's scribe and the high priest's officer came and emptied the chest, and took it, and carried it to his place again. Thus they did day by day, and gathered money in abundance.

2Ch 34:9 — And when they came to Hilkiah the high priest, they delivered the money that was brought into the house of God, which the Levites that kept the doors had gathered of the hand of Manasseh and Ephraim, and of all the remnant of Israel, and of all Judah and Benjamin; and they returned to Jerusalem.

Ezr 8:33 — Now on the fourth day was the silver and the gold and the vessels weighed in the house of our God by the hand of Meremoth the son of Uriah the priest; and with him *was* Eleazar the son of Phinehas; and with them *was* Jozabad the son of Jeshua, and Noadiah the son of Binnui, Levites;

Ne 12:44 — And at that time were some appointed over the chambers for the treasures, for the offerings, for the firstfruits, and for the tithes, to gather into them out of the fields of the cities the portions of the law for the priests and Levites: for Judah rejoiced for the priests and for the Levites that waited.

• Prepared the shewbread.

1Ch 23:28–29

• Assisted the priests in preparing the sacrifice.

2Ch 29:12–36; 35:1–18

• Killed the passover for the children of the captivity.

Ezr 6:20–21

• Teachers of the law.

2Ch 17:8–9; Ne 8:7–13; Mal 2:6–7

Dt 33:10 — They shall teach Jacob thy judgments, and Israel thy law: they shall put incense before thee, and whole burnt sacrifice upon thine altar.

2Ch 30:22 — And Hezekiah spake comfortably unto all the Levites that taught the good knowledge of the LORD: and they did eat throughout the feast seven days, offering peace offerings, and making confession to the LORD God of their fathers.

2Ch 35:3 — And said unto the Levites that taught all Israel, which were holy unto the LORD, Put the holy ark in the house which Solomon the son of David king of Israel did build; *it shall* not *be* a burden upon *your* shoulders: serve now the LORD your God, and his people Israel,

• Were judges.

2Ch 19:8–11

Dt 17:9 — And thou shalt come unto the priests the Levites, and unto the judge that shall be in those days, and enquire; and they shall shew thee the sentence of judgment:

1Ch 23:4 — Of which, twenty and four thousand *were* to set forward the work of the house of the LORD; and six thousand *were* officers and judges:

1Ch 26:29 — Of the Izharites, Chenaniah and his sons *were* for the outward business over Israel, for officers and judges.

Ne 11:16 — And Shabbethai and Jozabad, of the chief of the Levites, *had* the oversight of the outward business of the house of God.

See: Judge

• Were scribes of the sacred books.

See: Scribe

• Pronounced the blessings of the law in the responsive service at Mount Gerizim.

Dt 27:12 — These shall stand upon mount Gerizim to bless the people, when ye are come over Jordan; Simeon, and Levi, and Judah, and Issachar, and Joseph, and Benjamin:

Jos 8:33 — And all Israel, and their elders, and officers, and their judges, stood on this side the ark and on that side before the priests the Levites, which bare the ark of the covenant of the LORD, as well the stranger, as he that was born among them; half of them over against mount Gerizim, and half of them over against mount Ebal; as Moses the servant of the LORD had commanded before, that they should bless the people of Israel.

• Were porters of the doors.

See: Porters

• Were overseers in building and the repairs of the temple.

1Ch 23:2–4; Ezr 3:8–9

• Were musicians of the temple service.

See: Music

• Supervised weights and measures.

1Ch 23:29 — Both for the shewbread, and for the fine flour for meat offering, and for the unleavened cakes, and for *that which is baked in* the pan, and for that which is fried, and for all manner of measure and size;

• List of those who returned from captivity.

Ezr 2:40–63; 8:16–20; Ne 7:43–73; 12:1–47

Ezr 7:7 — And there went up *some* of the children of Israel, and of the priests, and the Levites, and the singers, and the porters, and the Nethinims, unto Jerusalem, in the seventh year of Artaxerxes the king.

• Sealed the covenant with Nehemiah.

Ne 10:9–28

• Emoluments of.

• In lieu of landed inheritance, forty-eight cities with suburbs were assigned to them.

Nu 35:2–8; Dt 12:18–19; 14:27–29; 18:1–8; 1Ch 6:54–81; Eze 34:1–5

Nu 18:24 — But the tithes of the children of Israel, which they offer *as* an heave offering unto the LORD, I have given to the Levites to inherit: therefore I have said unto them, Among the children of Israel they shall have no inheritance.

Nu 26:62 — And those that were numbered of them were twenty and three thousand, all males from a month old and upward: for they were not numbered among the children of Israel, because there was no inheritance given them among the children of Israel.

Dt 10:9 — Wherefore Levi hath no part nor inheritance with his brethren; the LORD *is* his inheritance, according as the LORD thy God promised him.

Dt 12:12 — And ye shall rejoice before the LORD your God, ye, and your sons, and your daughters, and your menservants, and your maidservants, and the Levite that *is* within your gates; forasmuch as he hath no part nor inheritance with you.

Jos 13:14 — Only unto the tribe of Levi he gave none inheritance; the sacrifices of the LORD God of Israel made by fire *are* their inheritance, as he said unto them.

Jos 14:3 — For Moses had given the inheritance of two tribes and an half tribe on the other side Jordan: but unto the Levites he gave none inheritance among them.

Jos 18:7 — But the Levites have no part among you; for the priesthood of the LORD is their inheritance: and Gad, and Reuben, and half the tribe of Manasseh, have received their inheritance beyond Jordan on the east, which Moses the servant of the LORD gave them.

1Ch 13:2 — And David said unto all the congregation of Israel, If *it seem* good unto you, and *that it be* of the LORD our God, let us send abroad unto our brethren every where, *that are* left in all the land of Israel, and with them *also* to the priests and Levites *which are* in their cities *and* suburbs, that they may gather themselves unto us:

2Ch 23:2 — And they went about in Judah, and gathered the Levites out of all the cities of Judah, and the chief of the fathers of Israel, and they came to Jerusalem.

• Assigned to, by families.

Jos 21:4–40

• Suburbs of their cities were inalienable for debt.

Le 25:32–34

• Tithes and other offerings.

Nu 18:26–32; Dt 18:1–8; 26:11–13; Ne 10:38–39

Nu 18:24 — But the tithes of the children of Israel, which they offer *as* an heave offering unto the LORD, I have given to the Levites to inherit: therefore I have said unto them, Among the children of Israel they shall have no inheritance.

Jos 13:14 — Only unto the tribe of Levi he gave none inheritance; the sacrifices of the LORD God of Israel made by fire *are* their inheritance, as he said unto them.

Ne 12:44 — And at that time were some appointed over the chambers for the treasures, for the offerings, for the firstfruits, and for the tithes, to gather into them out of the fields of the cities the portions of the law for the priests and Levites: for Judah rejoiced for the priests and for the Levites that waited.

Ne 12:47 — And all Israel in the days of Zerubbabel, and in the days of Nehemiah, gave the portions of the singers and the porters, every day his portion: and they sanctified *holy things* unto the Levites; and the Levites sanctified *them* unto the children of Aaron.

• First fruits.

Ne 12:44 — And at that time were some appointed over the chambers for the treasures, for the offerings, for the firstfruits, and for the tithes, to gather into them out of the fields of the cities the portions of the law for the priests and Levites: for Judah rejoiced for the priests and for the Levites that waited.

Ne 12:47 — And all Israel in the days of Zerubbabel, and in the days of Nehemiah, gave the portions of the singers and the porters, every day his portion: and they sanctified *holy things* unto the Levites; and the Levites sanctified *them* unto the children of Aaron.

• Spoils of war, including captives.

Nu 31:42–47

Nu 31:30 — And of the children of Israel's half, thou shalt take one portion of fifty, of the persons, of the beeves, of the asses, and of the flocks, of all manner of beasts, and give them unto the Levites, which keep the charge of the tabernacle of the LORD.

+See: Tithes

• Tithes withheld from.

Ne 13:10–13

Mal 3:10 — Bring ye all the tithes into the storehouse, that there may be meat in mine house, and prove me now herewith, saith the LORD of hosts, if I will not open you the windows of heaven, and pour you out a blessing, that *there shall* not *be room* enough *to receive it.*

• Pensioned.

2Ch 31:16–18

• Owned lands.

Dt 18:8 — They shall have like portions to eat, beside that which cometh of the sale of his patrimony.

1Ki 2:26 — And unto Abiathar the priest said the king, Get thee to Anathoth, unto thine own fields; for thou *art* worthy of death: but I will not at this time put thee to death, because thou barest the ark of the Lord

GOD before David my father, and because thou hast been afflicted in all wherein my father was afflicted.

• Land allotted to, by Ezekiel.

Eze 48:13–14

• Enrollment of, at Sinai.

Nu 1:47–49; 3:14–39; 4:2–3; 26:57–62; 1Ch 23:3–5

Nu 2:33 — But the Levites were not numbered among the children of Israel; as the LORD commanded Moses.

• Degraded from the Levitical office by Jeroboam.

2Ch 11:13–17; 13:9–11

• Loyal to the ruler.

2Ki 11:7–11

2Ch 23:7 — And the Levites shall compass the king round about, every man with his weapons in his hand; and whosoever *else* cometh into the house, he shall be put to death: but be ye with the king when he cometh in, and when he goeth out.

• Intermarry with Canaanites.

Ezr 9:1–2; 10:23–24

• Exempt from enrollment for military duty.

Nu 1:47–54

1Ch 12:26 — Of the children of Levi four thousand and six hundred.

• Subordinate to the sons of Aaron.

Nu 3:9 — And thou shalt give the Levites unto Aaron and to his sons: they *are* wholly given unto him out of the children of Israel.

Nu 8:19 — And I have given the Levites *as* a gift to Aaron and to his sons from among the children of Israel, to do the service of the children of Israel in the tabernacle of the congregation, and to make an atonement for the children of Israel: that there be no plague among the children of Israel, when the children of Israel come nigh unto the sanctuary.

Nu 18:6 — And I, behold, I have taken your brethren the Levites from among the children of Israel: to you *they are* given *as* a gift for the LORD, to do the service of the tabernacle of the congregation.

• Prophecies concerning.

Eze 44:10–14

Jer 33:18 — Neither shall the priests the Levites want a man before me to offer burnt offerings, and to kindle meat offerings, and to do sacrifice continually.

Mal 3:3 — And he shall sit *as* a refiner and purifier of silver: and he shall purify the sons of Levi, and purge them as gold and silver, that they may offer unto the LORD an offering in righteousness.

• Prophecies of their repentance of the crucifixion of the Messiah.

Zec 12:10–13

• John's vision concerning.

Rev 7:7 — Of the tribe of Simeon *were* sealed twelve thousand. Of the tribe of Levi *were* sealed twelve thousand. Of the tribe of Issachar *were* sealed twelve thousand.

LEX TALIONIS ✣See: Retaliation

LIARS

• All men liars.

Ps 116:11 — I said in my haste, All men *are* liars.

• Satan a.

Jn 8:44 — Ye are of your father the devil, and the lusts of *your* father ye will do. He was a murderer from the beginning, and abode not in the truth, because there is no truth in him. When he speaketh a lie, he speaketh of his own: for he is a liar, and the father of it.

Jn 8:55 — Yet ye have not known him; but I know him: and if I should say, I know him not, I shall be a liar like unto you: but I know him, and keep his saying.

• Prohibited the kingdom of heaven.

Rev 21:8 — But the fearful, and unbelieving, and the abominable, and murderers, and whoremongers, and sorcerers, and idolaters, and all liars, shall have their part in the lake which burneth with fire and brimstone: which is the second death.

✣See: Deceit

✣See: Deception

✣See: Falsehood

✣See: Hypocrisy

LIBERALITY

Ex 22:29–30; 25:1–8; 35:4–29; 36:3–6; Dt 12:11–12, 17–19; 14:27–29; 15:7–18; 18:1–8; 24:19–22; Ezr 1:2–4; Ps 41:1–3; 132:1–5; Pr 3:9–10; 11:24–25; Ecc 11:1–2; Hag 2:18–19; Mal 3:10–12; Mt 6:1–4; 19:21–22; 25:34–40; Lk 3:10–11; 12:33–34; 1Co 16:1–3; 2Co 8:7–9; 8:11–15; 9:6–13; 1Ti 6:17–19

Ex 13:2 — Sanctify unto me all the firstborn, whatsoever openeth the womb among the children of Israel, *both* of man and of beast: it *is* mine.

Ex 13:12 — That thou shalt set apart unto the LORD all that openeth the matrix, and every firstling that cometh of a beast which thou hast; the males *shall be* the LORD'S.

Ex 23:15 — Thou shalt keep the feast of unleavened bread: (thou shalt eat unleavened bread seven days, as I commanded thee, in the time appointed of the month Abib; for in it thou camest out from Egypt: and none shall appear before me empty:)

Ex 34:20 — But the firstling of an ass thou shalt redeem with a lamb: and if thou redeem *him* not, then shalt thou break his neck. All the firstborn of thy sons thou shalt redeem. And none shall appear before me empty.

Ex 38:8 — And he made the laver *of* brass, and the foot of it *of* brass, of the lookingglasses of *the women* assembling, which assembled *at* the door of the tabernacle of the congregation.

Le 19:5 — And if ye offer a sacrifice of peace offerings unto the LORD, ye shall offer it at your own will.

Le 22:29 — And when ye will offer a sacrifice of thanksgiving unto the LORD, offer *it* at your own will.

Nu 35:8 — And the cities which ye shall give *shall be* of the possession of the children of Israel: from *them that have* many ye shall give many; but from *them that have* few ye shall give few: every one shall give of his cities unto the Levites according to his inheritance which he inheriteth.

Dt 16:10 — And thou shalt keep the feast of weeks unto the LORD thy God with a tribute of a freewill offering of thine hand, which thou shalt give *unto the LORD thy God,* according as the LORD thy God hath blessed thee:

Dt 16:17 — Every man *shall give* as he is able, according to the blessing of the LORD thy God which he hath given thee.

2Sa 24:24 — And the king said unto Araunah, Nay; but I will surely buy *it* of thee at a price: neither will I offer burnt offerings unto the LORD my God of that which doth cost me nothing. So David bought the threshingfloor and the oxen for fifty shekels of silver.

1Ch 22:19 — Now set your heart and your soul to seek the LORD your God; arise therefore, and build ye the sanctuary of the LORD God, to bring the ark of the covenant of the LORD, and the holy vessels of God, into the house that is to be built to the name of the LORD.

1Ch 28:10 — Take heed now; for the LORD hath chosen thee to build an house for the sanctuary: be strong, and do *it.*

1Ch 28:20 — And David said to Solomon his son, Be strong and of good courage, and do *it:* fear not, nor be dismayed: for the LORD God, *even* my God, *will be* with thee; he will not fail thee, nor forsake thee, until thou hast finished all the work for the service of the house of the LORD.

1Ch 29:5 — The gold for *things* of gold, and the silver for *things* of silver, and for all manner of work *to be made* by the hands of artificers. And who *then* is willing to consecrate his service this day unto the LORD?

2Ch 15:7 — Be ye strong therefore, and let not your hands be weak: for your work shall be rewarded.

2Ch 15:18 — And he brought into the house of God the things that his father had dedicated, and that he himself had dedicated, silver, and gold, and vessels.

Ps 76:11 — Vow, and pay unto the LORD your God: let all that be round about him bring presents unto him that ought to be feared.

Ps 112:5 — A good man sheweth favour, and lendeth: he will guide his affairs with discretion.

Ps 112:9 — He hath dispersed, he hath given to the poor; his righteousness endureth for ever; his horn shall be exalted with honour.

Pr 13:7 — There is that maketh himself rich, yet *hath* nothing: *there is* that maketh himself poor, yet *hath* great riches.

Pr 14:21 — He that despiseth his neighbour sinneth: but he that hath mercy on the poor, happy *is* he.

Pr 19:6 — Many will intreat the favour of the prince: and every man *is* a friend to him that giveth gifts.

Pr 19:17 — He that hath pity upon the poor lendeth unto the LORD; and that which he hath given will he pay him again.

Pr 21:26 — He coveteth greedily all the day long: but the righteous giveth and spareth not.

Pr 22:9 — He that hath a bountiful eye shall be blessed; for he giveth of his bread to the poor.

Pr 28:27 — He that giveth unto the poor shall not lack: but he that hideth his eyes shall have many a curse.

Pr 31:20 — She stretcheth out her hand to the poor; yea, she reacheth forth her hands to the needy.

Isa 32:8 — But the liberal deviseth liberal things; and by liberal things shall he stand.

Isa 60:7 — All the flocks of Kedar shall be gathered together unto thee, the rams of Nebaioth shall minister unto thee: they shall come up with acceptance on mine altar, and I will glorify the house of my glory.

Isa 60:9 — Surely the isles shall wait for me, and the ships of Tarshish first, to bring thy sons from far, their silver and their gold with them, unto the name of the LORD thy God, and to the Holy One of Israel, because he hath glorified thee.

Isa 60:17 — For brass I will bring gold, and for iron I will bring silver, and for wood brass, and for stones iron: I will also make thy officers peace, and thine exactors righteousness.

Hag 1:8 — Go up to the mountain, and bring wood, and build the house; and I will take pleasure in it, and I will be glorified, saith the LORD.

Mt 5:42 — Give to him that asketh thee, and from him that would borrow of thee turn not thou away.

Lk 6:38 — Give, and it shall be given unto you; good measure, pressed down, and shaken together, and running over, shall men give into your bosom. For with the same measure that ye mete withal it shall be measured to you again.

Lk 11:41 — But rather give alms of such things as ye have; and, behold, all things are clean unto you.

Lk 16:9 — And I say unto you, Make to yourselves friends of the mammon of unrighteousness; that, when ye fail, they may receive you into everlasting habitations.

Ac 10:4 — And when he looked on him, he was afraid, and said, What is it, Lord? And he said unto him, Thy prayers and thine alms are come up for a memorial before God.

Ac 20:35 — I have shewed you all things, how that so labouring ye ought to support the weak, and to remember the words of the Lord Jesus, how he said, It is more blessed to give than to receive.

Ro 12:8 — Or he that exhorteth, on exhortation: he that giveth, *let him do it* with simplicity; he that ruleth, with diligence; he that sheweth mercy, with cheerfulness.

Ro 12:13 — Distributing to the necessity of saints; given to hospitality.

Ro 15:27 — It hath pleased them verily; and their debtors they are. For if the Gentiles have been made partakers of their spiritual things, their duty is also to minister unto them in carnal things.

1Co 13:3 — And though I bestow all my goods to feed *the poor,* and though I give my body to be burned, and have not charity, it profiteth me nothing.

2Co 8:24 — Wherefore shew ye to them, and before the churches, the proof of your love, and of our boasting on your behalf.

Eph 4:28 — Let him that stole steal no more: but rather let him labour, working with *his* hands the thing which is good, that he may have to give to him that needeth.

1Ti 5:16 — If any man or woman that believeth have widows, let them relieve them, and let not the church be charged; that it may relieve them that are widows indeed.

Phm 1:14 — But without thy mind would I do nothing; that thy benefit should not be as it were of necessity, but willingly.

Heb 6:10 — For God *is* not unrighteous to forget your work and labour of love, which ye have shewed toward his name, in that ye have ministered to the saints, and do minister.

Heb 13:16 — But to do good and to communicate forget not: for with such sacrifices God is well pleased.

1Jn 3:17 — But whoso hath this world's good, and seeth his brother have need, and shutteth up his bowels *of compassion* from him, how dwelleth the love of God in him?

See: Alms

See: Beneficence

See: Charitableness

See: Giving

See: Minister, a sacred teacher; emoluments of

See: Poor; duty to

See: Rich

See: Riches

See: Tithes

• Instances of.

• King of Sodom to Abraham.
Ge 14:21

• Jacob.
Ge 28:22

• Pharaoh to Joseph's people.
Ge 45:18–20

• Israelites at the erection of the tabernacle.
Ex 35:21–29; 36:3–7; 38:8; Nu 7:1–89; 31:48–54; Jos 18:1

• Reubenites.
Jos 22:24–29

• David.
2Sa 7:2; 8:11; 1Ki 7:51; 8:17–18; 1Ch 17:1; 21:24; 22:1–19; 26:26; 28:2; 29:2–5, 17; Ps 132:1–5

• Barzillai and others to David.
2Sa 17:27–29; 19:32

• Araunah for sacrifice.
2Sa 24:22–23

• Joab to David.
2Sa 12:26–28

• Israelites' offerings for the temple.
1Ch 29:6–9, 16–17

• Samuel.
1Ch 26:27–28

• Solomon.
1Ki 4:29; 5:4–5; 6:1–38; 7:51; 8:13; 2Ch 2:1–6

• Queen of Sheba to Solomon.
1Ki 10:10

• Asa and Abijam.
1Ki 15:15

• Elisha toward Elijah.
1Ki 19:21

• Jehoshaphat.
2Ki 12:18

• Joash and his people.
2Ki 12:4–14; 2Ch 24:4–14

• David.
1Ch 16:3

• Hezekiah.
2Ch 29:1–30:12; 31:1–10; 31:21

• Manasseh.
2Ch 33:16

• Josiah.
2Ki 22:3–6; 2Ch 34:8–13; 35:1–19

• Jews after the captivity.
Ezr 1:5–6; 2:68–69; 3:2–9; 5:2–6; 6:14–22; 8:25–35; Ne 3:1–32; 4:6; 6:3; 7:70–72; 10:32–39; 13:12, 31; Hag 1:12–14; 2:18–19

• Cyrus.
Ezr 1:2–4, 7–11; 3:7; 5:13–15; 6:3

• Darius.
Ezr 6:7–12

• Artaxerxes.
Ezr 7:13–27; 8:24–36

• The Magi.
Mt 2:11

• Centurion.
Lk 7:4–5

• Mary Magdalene.
Lk 8:2–3

• The good Samaritan.
Lk 10:33–35

• Poor widow.
Lk 21:2–4

• Christians in Jerusalem.
Ac 2:44–45; 4:32–37

• Christians in Antioch.
Ac 11:29

• Christians at Philippi.
Php 4:18

• Christians at Corinth.
2Co 8:19; 9:1–13

• Christians at Macedonia.
2Co 8:1–4

• People of Melita to Paul.
Ac 28:10

LIBERTINES • Freedmen.

Ac 6:9 — Then there arose certain of *the synagogue*, which is called the synagogue of the Libertines, and Cyrenians, and Alexandrians, and of them of Cilicia and of Asia, disputing with Stephen.

LIBERTY

• Proclaimed in the year of jubilee.
Jer 34:15–17

Le 25:10 — And ye shall hallow the fiftieth year, and proclaim liberty throughout *all* the land unto all the inhabitants thereof: it shall be a jubile unto you; and ye shall return every man unto his possession, and ye shall return every man unto his family.

Jer 34:8 — *This is* the word that came unto Jeremiah from the LORD, after that the king Zedekiah had made a covenant with all the people which *were* at Jerusalem, to proclaim liberty unto them;

- **Political.**

Jgs 17:6 — In those days *there was* no king in Israel, *but* every man did *that which was* right in his own eyes.

Jgs 21:25 — In those days *there was* no king in Israel: every man did *that which was* right in his own eyes.

Ac 22:28 — And the chief captain answered, With a great sum obtained I this freedom. And Paul said, But I was *free* born.

See: Jubilee

- **Figurative.**

Jn 8:32–33

Isa 61:2 — To proclaim the acceptable year of the LORD, and the day of vengeance of our God; to comfort all that mourn;

Isa 63:4 — For the day of vengeance *is* in mine heart, and the year of my redeemed is come.

Lk 4:19 — To preach the acceptable year of the Lord.

Jn 8:36 — If the Son therefore shall make you free, ye shall be free indeed.

Gal 3:28 — There is neither Jew nor Greek, there is neither bond nor free, there is neither male nor female: for ye are all one in Christ Jesus.

Eph 6:8 — Knowing that whatsoever good thing any man doeth, the same shall he receive of the Lord, whether *he be* bond or free.

Col 3:11 — Where there is neither Greek nor Jew, circumcision nor uncircumcision, Barbarian, Scythian, bond *nor* free: but Christ *is* all, and in all.

LIBNAH

- **A station of the Israelites in the desert.**

Nu 33:20 — And they departed from Rimmon-parez, and pitched in Libnah.

- **A city of Judah. Captured by Joshua.**

Jos 10:29–32

Jos 10:39 — And he took it, and the king thereof, and all the cities thereof; and they smote them with the edge of the sword, and utterly destroyed all the souls that *were* therein; he left none remaining: as he had done to Hebron, so he did to Debir, and to the king thereof; as he had done also to Libnah, and to her king.

Jos 12:15 — The king of Libnah, one; the king of Adullam, one;

- **Allotted to the priests.**

Jos 21:13 — Thus they gave to the children of Aaron the priest Hebron with her suburbs, *to be* a city of refuge for the slayer; and Libnah with her suburbs,

1Ch 6:57 — And to the sons of Aaron they gave the cities of Judah, *namely,* Hebron, *the city* of refuge, and Libnah with her suburbs, and Jattir, and Eshtemoa, with their suburbs,

- **Sennacherib besieged; his army defeated near.**

Isa 37:8–36

2Ki 19:8 — So Rab-shakeh returned, and found the king of Assyria warring against Libnah: for he had heard that he was departed from Lachish.

2Ki 19:35 — And it came to pass that night, that the angel of the LORD went out, and smote in the camp of the Assyrians an hundred fourscore and five thousand: and when they arose early in the morning, behold, they *were* all dead corpses.

LIBNI

- **Son of Gershon.**

Ex 6:17 — The sons of Gershon; Libni, and Shimi, according to their families.

Nu 3:18 — And these *are* the names of the sons of Gershon by their families; Libni, and Shimei.

1Ch 6:17 — And these *be* the names of the sons of Gershom; Libni, and Shimei.

1Ch 6:20 — Of Gershom; Libni his son, Jahath his son, Zimmah his son,

- **Descendants called Libnites.**

Nu 3:21 — Of Gershon *was* the family of the Libnites, and the family of the Shimites: these *are* the families of the Gershonites.

Nu 26:58 — These *are* the families of the Levites: the family of the Libnites, the family of the Hebronites, the family of the Mahlites, the family of the Mushites, the family of the Korathites. And Kohath begat Amram.

- **Grandson of Merari.**

1Ch 6:29 — The sons of Merari; Mahli, Libni his son, Shimei his son, Uzza his son,

LIBYA

- **Region north of Egypt.**

Eze 30:5 — Ethiopia, and Libya, and Lydia, and all the mingled people, and Chub, and the men of the land that is in league, shall fall with them by the sword.

Eze 38:5 — Persia, Ethiopia, and Libya with them; all of them with shield and helmet:

Ac 2:10 — Phrygia, and Pamphylia, in Egypt, and in the parts of Libya about Cyrene, and strangers of Rome, Jews and proselytes,

- **Called also Lubim and Phut.**

See: Lubims

See: Phut

LIBYANS

- **The inhabitants of Libya.**

Jer 46:9 — Come up, ye horses; and rage, ye chariots; and let the mighty men come forth; the Ethiopians and the Libyans, that handle the shield; and the Lydians, that handle *and* bend the bow.

Da 11:43 — But he shall have power over the treasures of gold and of silver, and over all the precious things of Egypt: and the Libyans and the Ethiopians *shall be* at his steps.

LICE

• Plague of.

Ex 8:16–19

Ps 105:31 — He spake, and there came divers sorts of flies, *and* lice in all their coasts.

LICENTIOUSNESS

See: Adultery

See: Lasciviousness

LIFE

• Miscellany of minor sub-topics.

• Breath of.

Ge 2:7 — And the LORD God formed man *of* the dust of the ground, and breathed into his nostrils the breath of life; and man became a living soul.

• Called Spirit of God.

Job 27:3 — All the while my breath *is* in me, and the spirit of God *is* in my nostrils;

• Tree of.

Ge 2:9 — And out of the ground made the LORD God to grow every tree that is pleasant to the sight, and good for food; the tree of life also in the midst of the garden, and the tree of knowledge of good and evil.

Ge 3:22 — And the LORD God said, Behold, the man is become as one of us, to know good and evil: and now, lest he put forth his hand, and take also of the tree of life, and eat, and live for ever:

Ge 3:24 — So he drove out the man; and he placed at the east of the garden of Eden Cherubim, and a flaming sword which turned every way, to keep the way of the tree of life.

Pr 3:18 — She *is* a tree of life to them that lay hold upon her: and happy *is every one* that retaineth her.

Pr 13:12 — Hope deferred maketh the heart sick: but *when* the desire cometh, *it is* a tree of life.

Rev 2:7 — He that hath an ear, let him hear what the Spirit saith unto the churches; To him that overcometh will I give to eat of the tree of life, which is in the midst of the paradise of God.

• Sacredness of, an inference from what is taught in the law concerning murder.

See: Homicide

• Long life promised to obedient children.

Ex 20:12 — Honour thy father and thy mother: that thy days may be long upon the land which the LORD thy God giveth thee.

Dt 5:16 — Honour thy father and thy mother, as the LORD thy God hath commanded thee; that thy days may be prolonged, and that it may go well with thee, in the land which the LORD thy God giveth thee.

• Long life promised to those who keep the commandments.

Dt 4:40 — Thou shalt keep therefore his statutes, and his commandments, which I command thee this day, that it may go well with thee, and with thy children after thee, and that thou mayest prolong *thy* days upon the earth, which the LORD thy God giveth thee, for ever.

Dt 22:7 — *But* thou shalt in any wise let the dam go, and take the young to thee; that it may be well with thee, and *that* thou mayest prolong *thy* days.

• Vanity of.

Ecc 1:1–7:29

• Hated.

Ecc 2:17 — Therefore I hated life; because the work that is wrought under the sun is grievous unto me: for all *is* vanity and vexation of spirit.

• To be hated for Christ's sake.

Lk 14:26 — If any *man* come to me, and hate not his father, and mother, and wife, and children, and brethren, and sisters, yea, and his own life also, he cannot be my disciple.

• What shall a man give in exchange for.

Mt 16:26 — For what is a man profited, if he shall gain the whole world, and lose his own soul? or what shall a man give in exchange for his soul?

Mk 8:37 — Or what shall a man give in exchange for his soul?

• He that loseth it shall save it.

Mt 16:25–26

Mt 10:39 — He that findeth his life shall lose it: and he that loseth his life for my sake shall find it.

Lk 9:24 — For whosoever will save his life shall lose it: but whosoever will lose his life for my sake, the same shall save it.

Jn 12:25 — He that loveth his life shall lose it; and he that hateth his life in this world shall keep it unto life eternal.

• Weary of.

• Job.

Job 3:1–26; 7:1–3; 10:18–20

• Jeremiah.

Jer 20:14–18

• Elijah.

1Ki 19:1–8

• Jonah.

Jnh 4:8–9

See: Suicide

• Life of Christ a ransom.

Mt 20:28 — Even as the Son of man came not to be ministered unto, but to minister, and to give his life a ransom for many.

Mk 10:45 — For even the Son of man came not to be ministered unto, but to minister, and to give his life a ransom for many.

1Ti 2:6 — Who gave himself a ransom for all, to be testified in due time.

See: Life; spiritual

• Brevity and uncertainty of.

Job 4:19–21; 7:6–10; 9:25–26; 10:20–21; 13:28–14:2; Ps 39:4–6; 89:47–48; 90:5–6, 9–10; 103:14–16; 144:3–4; Isa 40:6–7; Jas 1:10–11; 4:14–15

Ge 18:27 — And Abraham answered and said, Behold now, I have taken upon me to speak unto the Lord, which *am but* dust and ashes:

Ge 47:9 — And Jacob said unto Pharaoh, The days of the years of my pilgrimage *are* an hundred and thirty years: few and evil have the days of the years of my life been, and have not attained unto the days of the years of the life of my fathers in the days of their pilgrimage.

1Sa 20:3 — And David sware moreover, and said, Thy father certainly knoweth that I have found grace in thine eyes; and he saith, Let not Jonathan know this, lest he be grieved: but truly *as* the LORD liveth, and *as* thy soul liveth, *there is* but a step between me and death.

2Sa 14:14 — For we must needs die, and *are* as water spilt on the ground, which cannot be gathered up again; neither doth God respect *any* person: yet doth he devise means, that his banished be not expelled from him.

1Ch 29:15 — For we *are* strangers before thee, and sojourners, as *were* all our fathers: our days on the earth *are* as a shadow, and *there is* none abiding.

Job 7:17 — What *is* man, that thou shouldest magnify him? and that thou shouldest set thine heart upon him?

Job 8:9 — (For we *are but of* yesterday, and know nothing, because our days upon earth *are* a shadow:)

Job 10:9 — Remember, I beseech thee, that thou hast made me as the clay; and wilt thou bring me into dust again?

Job 13:12 — Your remembrances *are* like unto ashes, your bodies to bodies of clay.

Job 13:25 — Wilt thou break a leaf driven to and fro? and wilt thou pursue the dry stubble?

Job 17:1 — My breath is corrupt, my days are extinct, the graves *are ready* for me.

Ps 22:29 — All *they that be* fat upon earth shall eat and worship: all they that go down to the dust shall bow before him: and none can keep alive his own soul.

Ps 39:11 — When thou with rebukes dost correct man for iniquity, thou makest his beauty to consume away like a moth: surely every man *is* vanity. Selah.

Ps 78:39 — For he remembered that they *were but* flesh; a wind that passeth away, and cometh not again.

Ps 90:3 — Thou turnest man to destruction; and sayest, Return, ye children of men.

Ps 102:11 — My days *are* like a shadow that declineth; and I am withered like grass.

Ps 146:4 — His breath goeth forth, he returneth to his earth; in that very day his thoughts perish.

Pr 27:1 — Boast not thyself of to morrow; for thou knowest not what a day may bring forth.

Ecc 1:4 — *One* generation passeth away, and *another* generation cometh: but the earth abideth for ever.

Ecc 6:12 — For who knoweth what *is* good for man in *this* life, all the days of his vain life which he spendeth as a shadow? for who can tell a man what shall be after him under the sun?

Isa 2:22 — Cease ye from man, whose breath *is* in his nostrils: for wherein is he to be accounted of?

Isa 38:12 — Mine age is departed, and is removed from me as a shepherd's tent: I have cut off like a weaver my life: he will cut me off with pining sickness: from day *even* to night wilt thou make an end of me.

Isa 40:24 — Yea, they shall not be planted; yea, they shall not be sown: yea, their stock shall not take root in the earth: and he shall also blow upon them, and they shall wither, and the whirlwind shall take them away as stubble.

Isa 50:9 — Behold, the Lord GOD will help me; who *is* he *that* shall condemn me? lo, they all shall wax old as a garment; the moth shall eat them up.

Isa 51:8 — For the moth shall eat them up like a garment, and the worm shall eat them like wool: but my righteousness shall be for ever, and my salvation from generation to generation.

Isa 51:12 — I, *even* I, *am* he that comforteth you: who *art* thou, that thou shouldest be afraid of a man *that* shall die, and of the son of man *which* shall be made as grass;

Isa 64:6 — But we are all as an unclean *thing,* and all our righteousnesses *are* as filthy rags; and we all do fade as a leaf; and our iniquities, like the wind, have taken us away.

Lk 12:20 — But God said unto him, *Thou* fool, this night thy soul shall be required of thee: then whose shall those things be, which thou hast provided?

1Pe 1:24 — For all flesh *is* as grass, and all the glory of man as the flower of grass. The grass withereth, and the flower thereof falleth away:

See: Death

• Everlasting.

Mt 19:16–21; Jn 3:14–16; 5:24–25; 6:50–58; 10:27–28; 17:2–3; Ro 6:22–23; 1Co 15:53–54; 1Jn 5:11–13

Ps 21:4 — He asked life of thee, *and* thou gavest *it* him, *even* length of days for ever and ever.

Ps 121:8 — The LORD shall preserve thy going out and thy coming in from this time forth, and even for evermore.

Ps 133:3 — As the dew of Hermon, *and as the dew* that descended upon the mountains of Zion: for there the LORD commanded the blessing, *even* life for evermore.

Isa 25:8 — He will swallow up death in victory; and the Lord GOD will wipe away tears from off all faces; and the rebuke of his people shall he take away from off all the earth: for the LORD hath spoken *it.*

Da 12:2 — And many of them that sleep in the dust of the earth shall awake, some to everlasting life, and some to shame *and* everlasting contempt.

Mt 19:29 — And every one that hath forsaken houses, or brethren, or sisters, or father, or mother, or wife, or children, or lands, for my name's sake, shall receive an hundredfold, and shall inherit everlasting life.

Mt 25:46 — And these shall go away into everlasting punishment: but the righteous into life eternal.

Mk 10:30 — But he shall receive an hundredfold now in this time, houses, and brethren, and sisters, and mothers, and children, and lands, with persecutions; and in the world to come eternal life.

Lk 18:18 — And a certain ruler asked him, saying, Good Master, what shall I do to inherit eternal life?

Lk 18:30 — Who shall not receive manifold more in this present time, and in the world to come life everlasting.

Lk 20:36 — Neither can they die any more: for they are equal unto the angels; and are the children of God, being the children of the resurrection.

Jn 4:14 — But whosoever drinketh of the water that I shall give him shall never thirst; but the water that I shall give him shall be in him a well of water springing up into everlasting life.

Jn 5:29 — And shall come forth; they that have done good, unto the resurrection of life; and they that have done evil, unto the resurrection of damnation.

Jn 5:39 — Search the scriptures; for in them ye think ye have eternal life: and they are they which testify of me.

Jn 6:27 — Labour not for the meat which perisheth, but for that meat which endureth unto everlasting life, which the Son of man shall give unto you: for him hath God the Father sealed.

Jn 6:40 — And this is the will of him that sent me, that every one which seeth the Son, and believeth on him, may have everlasting life: and I will raise him up at the last day.

Jn 6:47 — Verily, verily, I say unto you, He that believeth on me hath everlasting life.

Jn 6:68 — Then Simon Peter answered him, Lord, to whom shall we go? thou hast the words of eternal life.

Jn 10:10 — The thief cometh not, but for to steal, and to kill, and to destroy: I am come that they might have life, and that they might have *it* more abundantly.

Jn 12:25 — He that loveth his life shall lose it; and he that hateth his life in this world shall keep it unto life eternal.

Jn 12:50 — And I know that his commandment is life everlasting: whatsoever I speak therefore, even as the Father said unto me, so I speak.

Ac 13:46 — Then Paul and Barnabas waxed bold, and said, It was necessary that the word of God should first have been spoken to you: but seeing ye put it from you, and judge yourselves unworthy of everlasting life, lo, we turn to the Gentiles.

Ac 13:48 — And when the Gentiles heard this, they were glad, and glorified the word of the Lord: and as many as were ordained to eternal life believed.

Ro 2:7 — To them who by patient continuance in well doing seek for glory and honour and immortality, eternal life:

Ro 5:21 — That as sin hath reigned unto death, even so might grace reign through righteousness unto eternal life by Jesus Christ our Lord.

2Co 5:1 — For we know that if our earthly house of *this* tabernacle were dissolved, we have a building of God, an house not made with hands, eternal in the heavens.

Gal 6:8 — For he that soweth to his flesh shall of the flesh reap corruption; but he that soweth to the Spirit shall of the Spirit reap life everlasting.

1Ti 1:16 — Howbeit for this cause I obtained mercy, that in me first Jesus Christ might shew forth all longsuffering, for a pattern to them which should hereafter believe on him to life everlasting.

1Ti 4:8 — For bodily exercise profiteth little: but godliness is profitable unto all things, having promise of the life that now is, and of that which is to come.

1Ti 6:12 — Fight the good fight of faith, lay hold on eternal life, whereunto thou art also called, and hast professed a good profession before many witnesses.

1Ti 6:19 — Laying up in store for themselves a good foundation against the time to come, that they may lay hold on eternal life.

2Ti 1:10 — But is now made manifest by the appearing of our Saviour Jesus Christ, who hath abolished death, and hath brought life and immortality to light through the gospel:

Tit 1:2 — In hope of eternal life, which God, that cannot lie, promised before the world began;

Tit 3:7 — That being justified by his grace, we should be made heirs according to the hope of eternal life.

1Jn 2:25 — And this is the promise that he hath promised us, *even* eternal life.

1Jn 3:15 — Whosoever hateth his brother is a murderer: and ye know that no murderer hath eternal life abiding in him.

1Jn 5:20 — *And* we know that the Son of God is come, and hath given us an understanding, that we may know him that is true, and we are in him that is true, *even* in his Son Jesus Christ. This is the true God, and eternal life.

Jude 1:21 — Keep yourselves in the love of God, looking for the mercy of our Lord Jesus Christ unto eternal life.

Rev 1:18 — *I am* he that liveth, and was dead; and, behold, I am alive for evermore, Amen; and have the keys of hell and of death.

See: Immortality

• From God.

Dt 32:39–40; Job 34:14–15; Isa 38:16–20; Ac 17:25–26

Ge 2:7 — And the LORD God formed man *of* the dust of the ground, and breathed into his nostrils the breath of life; and man became a living soul.

Dt 8:3 — And he humbled thee, and suffered thee to hunger, and fed thee with manna, which thou knewest not, neither did thy fathers know; that he might make thee know that man doth not live by bread only, but by every *word* that proceedeth out of the mouth of the LORD doth man live.

Dt 30:20 — That thou mayest love the LORD thy God, *and* that thou mayest obey his voice, and that thou mayest cleave unto him: for he *is* thy life, and the length of thy days: that thou mayest dwell in the land which the LORD sware unto thy fathers, to Abraham, to Isaac, and to Jacob, to give them.

1Sa 2:6 — The LORD killeth, and maketh alive: he bringeth down to the grave, and bringeth up.

Job 27:3 — All the while my breath *is* in me, and the spirit of God *is* in my nostrils;

Ps 22:29 — All *they that be* fat upon earth shall eat and worship: all they that go down to the dust shall bow before him: and none can keep alive his own soul.

Ps 30:3 — O LORD, thou hast brought up my soul from the grave: thou hast kept me alive, that I should not go down to the pit.

Ps 68:20 — *He that is* our God *is* the God of salvation; and unto God the Lord *belong* the issues from death.

Ps 104:30 — Thou sendest forth thy spirit, they are created: and thou renewest the face of the earth.

Ecc 12:7 — Then shall the dust return to the earth as it was: and the spirit shall return unto God who gave it.

Ac 17:28 — For in him we live, and move, and have our being; as certain also of your own poets have said, For we are also his offspring.

Ro 4:17 — (As it is written, I have made thee a father of many nations,) before him whom he believed, *even* God, who quickeneth the dead, and calleth those things which be not as though they were.

1Ti 6:13 — I give thee charge in the sight of God, who quickeneth all things, and *before* Christ Jesus, who before Pontius Pilate witnessed a good confession;

Jas 4:15 — For that ye *ought* to say, If the Lord will, we shall live, and do this, or that.

- **Long.**

  See: Longevity

- **Spiritual.**

Jn 3:3–16; 5:24–26; 11:25–26; 17:2–3; Ro 6:4–5, 22–23; 1Jn 1:1–2

Jn 5:40 — And ye will not come to me, that ye might have life.

Jn 6:27 — Labour not for the meat which perisheth, but for that meat which endureth unto everlasting life, which the Son of man shall give unto you: for him hath God the Father sealed.

Jn 6:33 — For the bread of God is he which cometh down from heaven, and giveth life unto the world.

Jn 6:35 — And Jesus said unto them, I am the bread of life: he that cometh to me shall never hunger; and he that believeth on me shall never thirst.

Jn 6:40 — And this is the will of him that sent me, that every one which seeth the Son, and believeth on him, may have everlasting life: and I will raise him up at the last day.

Jn 6:47 — Verily, verily, I say unto you, He that believeth on me hath everlasting life.

Jn 10:10 — The thief cometh not, but for to steal, and to kill, and to destroy: I am come that they might have life, and that they might have *it* more abundantly.

Jn 14:6 — Jesus saith unto him, I am the way, the truth, and the life: no man cometh unto the Father, but by me.

Jn 20:31 — But these are written, that ye might believe that Jesus is the Christ, the Son of God; and that believing ye might have life through his name.

Ro 6:8 — Now if we be dead with Christ, we believe that we shall also live with him:

Ro 6:11 — Likewise reckon ye also yourselves to be dead indeed unto sin, but alive unto God through Jesus Christ our Lord.

Ro 6:13 — Neither yield ye your members *as* instruments of unrighteousness unto sin: but yield yourselves unto God, as those that are alive from the dead, and your members *as* instruments of righteousness unto God.

Ro 8:10 — And if Christ *be* in you, the body *is* dead because of sin; but the Spirit *is* life because of righteousness.

LIFT HANDS

Ps 28:2 — Hear the voice of my supplications, when I cry unto thee, when I lift up my hands toward thy holy oracle.

La 2:19 — Arise, cry out in the night: in the beginning of the watches pour out thine heart like water before the face of the Lord: lift up thy hands toward him for the life of thy young children, that faint for hunger in the top of every street.

1Ti 2:8 — I will therefore that men pray every where, lifting up holy hands, without wrath and doubting.

LIGHT

- **Created.**

Ge 1:3–5

Ps 74:16 — The day *is* thine, the night also *is* thine: thou hast prepared the light and the sun.

Isa 45:7 — I form the light, and create darkness: I make peace, and create evil: I the LORD do all these *things*.

2Co 4:6 — For God, who commanded the light to shine out of darkness, hath shined in our hearts, to *give* the light of the knowledge of the glory of God in the face of Jesus Christ.

- **Miraculous.**

Mt 17:2 — And was transfigured before them: and his face did shine as the sun, and his raiment was white as the light.

Ac 9:3 — And as he journeyed, he came near Damascus: and suddenly there shined round about him a light from heaven:

- **Figurative and symbolic.**

Isa 60:19–20; Jn 1:4–5, 7–9; 3:19–21; 12:35–36

1Ki 11:36 — And unto his son will I give one tribe, that David my servant may have a light alway before me in Jerusalem, the city which I have chosen me to put my name there.

Ps 27:1 — The LORD *is* my light and my salvation; whom shall I fear? the LORD *is* the strength of my life; of whom shall I be afraid?

Ps 119:105 — Thy word *is* a lamp unto my feet, and a light unto my path.

Ps 119:130 — The entrance of thy words giveth light; it giveth understanding unto the simple.

Pr 6:23 — For the commandment *is* a lamp; and the law *is* light; and reproofs of instruction *are* the way of life:

Ecc 2:13 — Then I saw that wisdom excelleth folly, as far as light excelleth darkness.

Isa 8:20 — To the law and to the testimony: if they speak not according to this word, *it is* because *there is* no light in them.

Isa 49:6 — And he said, It is a light thing that thou shouldest be my servant to raise up the tribes of Jacob, and to restore the preserved of Israel: I will also give thee for a light to the Gentiles, that thou mayest be my salvation unto the end of the earth.

Isa 58:8 — Then shall thy light break forth as the morning, and thine health shall spring forth speedily: and thy righteousness shall go before thee; the glory of the LORD shall be thy rereward.

Mt 4:16 — The people which sat in darkness saw great light; and to them which sat in the region and shadow of death light is sprung up.

Mt 5:14 — Ye are the light of the world. A city that is set on an hill cannot be hid.

Lk 2:32 — A light to lighten the Gentiles, and the glory of thy people Israel.

Lk 11:34 — The light of the body is the eye: therefore when thine eye is single, thy whole body also is full of light; but when *thine eye* is evil, thy body also *is* full of darkness.

Lk 16:8 — And the lord commended the unjust steward, because he had done wisely: for the children of this world are in their generation wiser than the children of light.

Jn 5:35 — He was a burning and a shining light: and ye were willing for a season to rejoice in his light.

Jn 8:12 — Then spake Jesus again unto them, saying, I am the light of the world: he that followeth me shall not walk in darkness, but shall have the light of life.

Jn 9:5 — As long as I am in the world, I am the light of the world.

Ac 26:18 — To open their eyes, *and* to turn *them* from darkness to light, and *from* the power of Satan unto God, that they may receive forgiveness of sins, and inheritance among them which are sanctified by faith that is in me.

Eph 5:8 — For ye were sometimes darkness, but now *are ye* light in the Lord: walk as children of light:

Eph 5:14 — Wherefore he saith, Awake thou that sleepest, and arise from the dead, and Christ shall give thee light.

Php 2:15 — That ye may be blameless and harmless, the sons of God, without rebuke, in the midst of a crooked and perverse nation, among whom ye shine as lights in the world;

1Th 5:5 — Ye are all the children of light, and the children of the day: we are not of the night, nor of darkness.

1Ti 6:16 — Who only hath immortality, dwelling in the light which no man can approach unto; whom no man hath seen, nor can see: to whom *be* honour and power everlasting. Amen.

Jas 1:17 — Every good gift and every perfect gift is from above, and cometh down from the Father of lights, with whom is no variableness, neither shadow of turning.

1Pe 2:9 — But ye *are* a chosen generation, a royal priesthood, an holy nation, a peculiar people; that ye should shew forth the praises of him who hath called you out of darkness into his marvellous light:

2Pe 1:19 — We have also a more sure word of prophecy; whereunto ye do well that ye take heed, as unto a light that shineth in a dark place, until the day dawn, and the day star arise in your hearts:

1Jn 1:5 — This then is the message which we have heard of him, and declare unto you, that God is light, and in him is no darkness at all.

1Jn 1:7 — But if we walk in the light, as he is in the light, we have fellowship one with another, and the blood of Jesus Christ his Son cleanseth us from all sin.

Rev 21:23 — And the city had no need of the sun, neither of the moon, to shine in it: for the glory of God did lighten it, and the Lamb *is* the light thereof.

LIGHTNING

Eze 1:13–14

Job 28:26 — When he made a decree for the rain, and a way for the lightning of the thunder:

Job 37:3 — He directeth it under the whole heaven, and his lightning unto the ends of the earth.

Job 38:25 — Who hath divided a watercourse for the overflowing of waters, or a way for the lightning of thunder;

Job 38:35 — Canst thou send lightnings, that they may go, and say unto thee, Here we *are*?

Ps 18:14 — Yea, he sent out his arrows, and scattered them; and he shot out lightnings, and discomfited them.

Ps 77:18 — The voice of thy thunder *was* in the heaven: the lightnings lightened the world: the earth trembled and shook.

Ps 78:48 — He gave up their cattle also to the hail, and their flocks to hot thunderbolts.

Ps 97:4 — His lightnings enlightened the world: the earth saw, and trembled.

Ps 135:7 — He causeth the vapours to ascend from the ends of the earth; he maketh lightnings for the rain; he bringeth the wind out of his treasuries.

Ps 144:6 — Cast forth lightning, and scatter them: shoot out thine arrows, and destroy them.

Jer 10:13 — When he uttereth his voice, *there is* a multitude of waters in the heavens, and he causeth the vapors to ascend from the ends of the earth; he maketh lightnings with rain, and bringeth forth the wind out of his treasures.

Jer 51:16 — When he uttereth *his* voice, *there is* a multitude of waters in the heavens; and he causeth the vapors to ascend from the ends of the earth: he maketh lightnings with rain, and bringeth forth the wind out of his treasures.

Da 10:6 — His body also *was* like the beryl, and his face as the appearance of lightning, and his eyes as lamps of fire, and his arms and his feet like in colour to polished brass, and the voice of his words like the voice of a multitude.

Na 2:4 — The chariots shall rage in the streets, they shall justle one against another in the broad ways: they shall seem like torches, they shall run like the lightnings.

Zec 9:14 — And the LORD shall be seen over them, and his arrow shall go forth as the lightning: and the LORD GOD shall blow the trumpet, and shall go with whirlwinds of the south.

Zec 10:1 — Ask ye of the LORD rain in the time of the latter rain; *so* the LORD shall make bright clouds, and give them showers of rain, to every one grass in the field.

Mt 24:27 — For as the lightning cometh out of the east, and shineth even unto the west; so shall also the coming of the Son of man be.

Mt 28:3 — His countenance was like lightning, and his raiment white as snow:

Lk 10:18 — And he said unto them, I beheld Satan as lightning fall from heaven.

Rev 4:5 — And out of the throne proceeded lightnings and thunderings and voices: and *there were* seven lamps of fire burning before the throne, which are the seven Spirits of God.

Rev 8:5 — And the angel took the censer, and filled it with fire of the altar, and cast *it* into the earth: and there were voices, and thunderings, and lightnings, and an earthquake.

Rev 11:19 — And the temple of God was opened in heaven, and there was seen in his temple the ark of his testament: and there were lightnings, and voices, and thunderings, and an earthquake, and great hail.

Rev 16:18 — And there were voices, and thunders, and lightnings; and there was a great earthquake, such as was not since men were upon the earth, so mighty an earthquake, *and* so great.

LIGN-ALOE

• A tree.

• Not identified by naturalists.

Nu 24:6 — As the valleys are they spread forth, as gardens by the river's side, as the trees of lign aloes which the LORD hath planted, *and* as cedar trees beside the waters.

LIGURE • A precious stone.

Ex 28:19 — And the third row a ligure, an agate, and an amethyst.

Ex 39:12 — And the third row, a ligure, an agate, and an amethyst.

LILY

• The principal chapiters of the temple ornamented with carvings of.

1Ki 7:19 — And the chapiters that *were* upon the top of the pillars *were* of lily work in the porch, four cubits.

1Ki 7:22 — And upon the top of the pillars *was* lily work: so was the work of the pillars finished.

1Ki 7:26 — And it *was* an hand breadth thick, and the brim thereof was wrought like the brim of a cup, with flowers of lilies: it contained two thousand baths.

• Molded on the rim of the molten laver in the temple.

1Ki 7:26 — And it *was* an hand breadth thick, and the brim thereof was wrought like the brim of a cup, with flowers of lilies: it contained two thousand baths.

2Ch 4:5 — And the thickness of it *was* an handbreadth, and the brim of it like the work of the brim of a cup, with flowers of lilies; *and* it received and held three thousand baths.

• Lessons of trust gathered from.

Mt 6:28–30

Lk 12:27 — Consider the lilies how they grow: they toil not, they spin not; and yet I say unto you, that Solomon in all his glory was not arrayed like one of these.

• Figurative.

• Of the lips of the beloved.

SS 5:13 — His cheeks *are* as a bed of spices, *as* sweet flowers: his lips *like* lilies, dropping sweet smelling myrrh.

LIME

Isa 33:12 — And the people shall be as the burnings of lime: *as* thorns cut up shall they be burned in the fire.

Am 2:1 — Thus saith the LORD; For three transgressions of Moab, and for four, I will not turn away *the punishment* thereof; because he burned the bones of the king of Edom into lime:

LINEN

• Exported from Egypt.

1Ki 10:28 — And Solomon had horses brought out of Egypt, and linen yarn: the king's merchants received the linen yarn at a price.

Eze 27:7 — Fine linen with broidered work from Egypt was that which thou spreadest forth to be thy sail; blue and purple from the isles of Elishah was that which covered thee.

• Exported from Syria.

Eze 27:16 — Syria *was* thy merchant by reason of the multitude of the wares of thy making: they occupied in thy fairs with emeralds, purple, and broidered work, and fine linen, and coral, and agate.

• Curtains of the tabernacle made of.

Ex 26:1 — Moreover thou shalt make the tabernacle *with* ten curtains *of* fine twined linen, and blue, and purple, and scarlet: *with* cherubims of cunning work shalt thou make them.

Ex 27:9 — And thou shalt make the court of the tabernacle: for the south side southward *there shall be* hangings for the court *of* fine twined linen of an hundred cubits long for one side:

• Vestments of priests made of.

Ex 28:5–8, 39–42

Ex 28:15 — And thou shalt make the breastplate of judgment with cunning work; after the work of the ephod thou shalt make it; *of* gold, *of* blue, and *of* purple, and *of* scarlet, and *of* fine twined linen, shalt thou make it.

• Livery of royal households made of.

Ge 41:42 — And Pharaoh took off his ring from his hand, and put it upon Joseph's hand, and arrayed him in vestures of fine linen, and put a gold chain about his neck;

Est 8:15 — And Mordecai went out from the presence of the king in royal apparel of blue and white, and with a great crown of gold, and with a garment of fine linen and purple: and the city of Shushan rejoiced and was glad.

• Garments for men made of.

Ge 41:42 — And Pharaoh took off his ring from his hand, and put it upon Joseph's hand, and arrayed him in vestures of fine linen, and put a gold chain about his neck;

Eze 9:2 — And, behold, six men came from the way of the higher gate, which lieth toward the north, and every man a slaughter weapon in his hand; and one man among them *was* clothed with linen, with a writer's inkhorn by his side: and they went in, and stood beside the brasen altar.

Lk 16:19 — There was a certain rich man, which was clothed in purple and fine linen, and fared sumptuously every day:

• Garments for women made of.

Eze 16:10–13

Isa 3:23 — The glasses, and the fine linen, and the hoods, and the vails.

• Bedding made of.

Pr 7:16 — I have decked my bed with coverings of tapestry, with carved *works,* with fine linen of Egypt.

• Mosaic law forbade its being mingled with wool.

Le 19:19 — Ye shall keep my statutes. Thou shalt not let thy cattle gender with a diverse kind: thou shalt not sow thy field with mingled seed: neither shall a garment mingled of linen and woollen come upon thee.

Dt 22:11 — Thou shalt not wear a garment of divers sorts, *as* of woollen and linen together.

• The body of Jesus wrapped in.

Mk 15:46 — And he bought fine linen, and took him down, and wrapped him in the linen, and laid him in a sepulchre which was hewn out of a rock, and rolled a stone unto the door of the sepulchre.

Jn 20:5 — And he stooping down, *and looking in,* saw the linen clothes lying; yet went he not in.

• Figurative.

• Pure and white, of righteousness.

Rev 15:6 — And the seven angels came out of the temple, having the seven plagues, clothed in pure and white linen, and having their breasts girded with golden girdles.

Rev 19:8 — And to her was granted that she should be arrayed in fine linen, clean and white: for the fine linen is the righteousness of saints.

Rev 19:14 — And the armies *which were* in heaven followed him upon white horses, clothed in fine linen, white and clean.

LINUS • A Christian at Rome.

2Ti 4:21 — Do thy diligence to come before winter. Eubulus greeteth thee, and Pudens, and Linus, and Claudia, and all the brethren.

LION

• King of beasts.

Mic 5:8 — And the remnant of Jacob shall be among the Gentiles in the midst of many people as a lion among the beasts of the forest, as a young lion among the flocks of sheep: who, if he go through, both treadeth down, and teareth in pieces, and none can deliver.

• Fierceness of.

Job 4:10 — The roaring of the lion, and the voice of the fierce lion, and the teeth of the young lions, are broken.

Job 28:8 — The lion's whelps have not trodden it, nor the fierce lion passed by it.

Ps 7:2 — Lest he tear my soul like a lion, rending *it* in pieces, while *there is* none to deliver.

Pr 22:13 — The slothful *man* saith, *There is* a lion without, I shall be slain in the streets.

Jer 2:15 — The young lions roared upon him, *and* yelled, and they made his land waste: his cities are burned without inhabitant.

Jer 49:19 — Behold, he shall come up like a lion from the swelling of Jordan against the habitation of the strong: but I will suddenly make him run away from her: and who *is* a chosen *man, that* I may appoint over her? for who *is* like me? and who will appoint me the time? and who *is* that shepherd that will stand before me?

Jer 50:44 — Behold, he shall come up like a lion from the swelling of Jordan unto the habitation of the strong: but I will make them suddenly run away from her: and who *is* a chosen *man, that* I may appoint over her? for who *is* like me? and who will appoint me the time? and who *is* that shepherd that will stand before me?

Hos 13:8 — I will meet them as a bear *that is* bereaved *of her whelps,* and will rend the caul of their heart, and there will I devour them like a lion: the wild beast shall tear them.

• The roaring of.

Ps 22:13 — They gaped upon me *with* their mouths, *as* a ravening and a roaring lion.

Pr 20:2 — The fear of a king *is* as the roaring of a lion: *whoso* provoketh him to anger sinneth *against* his own soul.

• Strength of.

Pr 30:30 — A lion *which is* strongest among beasts, and turneth not away for any;

Isa 38:13 — I reckoned till morning, *that,* as a lion, so will he break all my bones: from day *even* to night wilt thou make an end of me.

Joel 1:6 — For a nation is come up upon my land, strong, and without number, whose teeth *are* the teeth of a lion, and he hath the cheek teeth of a great lion.

• Instincts of, in taking prey.

Ps 10:9 — He lieth in wait secretly as a lion in his den: he lieth in wait to catch the poor: he doth catch the poor, when he draweth him into his net.

Ps 17:12 — Like as a lion *that* is greedy of his prey, and as it were a young lion lurking in secret places.

La 3:10 — He *was* unto me *as* a bear lying in wait, *and as* a lion in secret places.

Am 3:4 — Will a lion roar in the forest, when he hath no prey? will a young lion cry out of his den, if he have taken nothing?

Na 2:12 — The lion did tear in pieces enough for his whelps, and strangled for his lionesses, and filled his holes with prey, and his dens with ravin.

• Lair of, in the jungles.

Jer 4:7 — The lion is come up from his thicket, and the destroyer of the Gentiles is on his way; he is gone forth from his place to make thy land desolate; *and* thy cities shall be laid waste, without an inhabitant.

Jer 25:38 — He hath forsaken his covert, as the lion: for their land is desolate because of the fierceness of the oppressor, and because of his fierce anger.

• The bases in the temple ornamented by mouldings of.

1Ki 7:29 — And on the borders that *were* between the ledges *were* lions, oxen, and cherubims: and upon the ledges *there was* a base above: and beneath the lions and oxen *were* certain additions made of thin work.

1Ki 7:36 — For on the plates of the ledges thereof, and on the borders thereof, he graved cherubims, lions, and palm trees, according to the proportion of every one, and additions round about.

• Twelve statues of, on the stairs leading to Solomon's throne.

1Ki 10:19–20

• Samson's riddle concerning.

Jgs 14:14 — And he said unto them, Out of the eater came forth meat, and out of the strong came forth sweetness. And they could not in three days expound the riddle.

Jgs 14:18 — And the men of the city said unto him on the seventh day before the sun went down, What *is* sweeter than honey? and what *is* stronger than a lion? And he said unto them, If ye had not plowed with my heifer, ye had not found out my riddle.

• Proverb of.

Ecc 9:4 — For to him that is joined to all the living there is hope: for a living dog is better than a dead lion.

• Parable of.

Eze 19:1–9

• Kept in captivity.

Da 6:1–28

• Sent as judgment upon the Samaritans.

2Ki 17:25–26

• Slain by.

• Samson.

Jgs 14:5–9

• David.

1Sa 17:34 — And David said unto Saul, Thy servant kept his father's sheep, and there came a lion, and a bear, and took a lamb out of the flock:

1Sa 17:36 — Thy servant slew both the lion and the bear: and this uncircumcised Philistine shall be as one of them, seeing he hath defied the armies of the living God.

• Benaiah.

2Sa 23:20 — And Benaiah the son of Jehoiada, the son of a valiant man, of Kabzeel, who had done many acts, he slew two lionlike men of Moab: he went down also and slew a lion in the midst of a pit in time of snow:

• Saints.

Heb 11:33 — Who through faith subdued kingdoms, wrought righteousness, obtained promises, stopped the mouths of lions,

• Disobedient prophet slain by.

1Ki 13:24–28

• An unnamed person slain by.

1Ki 20:36 — Then said he unto him, Because thou hast not obeyed the voice of the LORD, behold, as soon as thou art departed from me, a lion shall slay thee. And as soon as he was departed from him, a lion found him, and slew him.

• Used for the torture of criminals.

Da 6:16–24

Da 7:12 — As concerning the rest of the beasts, they had their dominion taken away: yet their lives were prolonged for a season and time.

2Ti 4:17 — Notwithstanding the Lord stood with me, and strengthened me; that by me the preaching might be fully known, and *that* all the Gentiles might hear: and I was delivered out of the mouth of the lion.

• Figurative.

• Of a ruler's wrath.

Pr 19:12 — The king's wrath *is* as the roaring of a lion; but his favour *is* as dew upon the grass.

Jer 5:6 — Wherefore a lion out of the forest shall slay them, *and* a wolf of the evenings shall spoil them, a leopard shall watch over their cities: every one that goeth out thence shall be torn in pieces: because their transgressions are many, *and* their backslidings are increased.

Jer 50:17 — Israel *is* a scattered sheep; the lions have driven *him* away: first the king of Assyria hath devoured him; and last this Nebuchadrezzar king of Babylon hath broken his bones.

Hos 5:14 — For I will *be* unto Ephraim as a lion, and as a young lion to the house of Judah: I, *even* I, will tear and go away; I will take away, and none shall rescue *him*.

• Of Satan.

1Pe 5:8 — Be sober, be vigilant; because your adversary the devil, as a roaring lion, walketh about, seeking whom he may devour:

• Of divine judgments.

Isa 15:9 — For the waters of Dimon shall be full of blood: for I will bring more upon Dimon, lions upon him that escapeth of Moab, and upon the remnant of the land.

• Symbolic.

Ge 49:9 — Judah *is* a lion's whelp: from the prey, my son, thou art gone up: he stooped down, he couched as a lion, and as an old lion; who shall rouse him up?

Isa 29:1 — Woe to Ariel, to Ariel, the city *where* David dwelt! add ye year to year; let them kill sacrifices.

Eze 1:10 — As for the likeness of their faces, they four had the face of a man, and the face of a lion, on the right side: and they four had the face of an ox on the left side; they four also had the face of an eagle.

Eze 10:14 — And every one had four faces: the first face *was* the face of a cherub, and the second face *was* the face of a man, and the third the face of a lion, and the fourth the face of an eagle.

Da 7:4 — The first *was* like a lion, and had eagle's wings: I beheld till the wings thereof were plucked, and it was lifted up from the earth, and made stand upon the feet as a man, and a man's heart was given to it.

Rev 4:7 — And the first beast *was* like a lion, and the second beast like a calf, and the third beast had a face as a man, and the fourth beast *was* like a flying eagle.

Rev 5:5 — And one of the elders saith unto me, Weep not: behold, the Lion of the tribe of Juda, the Root of David, hath prevailed to open the book, and to loose the seven seals thereof.

Rev 9:8 — And they had hair as the hair of women, and their teeth were as *the teeth* of lions.

Rev 9:17 — And thus I saw the horses in the vision, and them that sat on them, having breastplates of fire, and of jacinth, and brimstone: and the heads of the horses *were* as the heads of lions; and out of their mouths issued fire and smoke and brimstone.

Rev 13:2 — And the beast which I saw was like unto a leopard, and his feet were as *the feet* of a bear, and his mouth as the mouth of a lion: and the dragon gave him his power, and his seat, and great authority.

LISTEN

Ps 116:1–2

Jas 1:19 — Wherefore, my beloved brethren, let every man be swift to hear, slow to speak, slow to wrath:

LITIGATION

• To be avoided.

1Co 6:1–8

Mt 5:25 — Agree with thine adversary quickly, whiles thou art in the way with him; lest at any time the adversary deliver thee to the judge, and the judge deliver thee to the officer, and thou be cast into prison.

Lk 12:58 — When thou goest with thine adversary to the magistrate, *as thou art* in the way, give diligence that thou mayest be delivered from him; lest he hale thee to the judge, and the judge deliver thee to the officer, and the officer cast thee into prison.

See: Actions at Law

See: Adjudication at Law

See: Arbitration

See: Compromise

LITTER • An Oriental contrivance for carrying persons.

Isa 66:20 — And they shall bring all your brethren *for* an offering unto the LORD out of all nations upon horses, and in chariots, and in litters, and upon mules, and upon swift beasts, to my holy mountain Jerusalem, saith the LORD, as the children of Israel bring an offering in a clean vessel into the house of the LORD.

LIVER

• Burnt in sacrifice.

Le 3:5 — And Aaron's sons shall burn it on the altar upon the burnt sacrifice, which *is* upon the wood that *is* on the fire: *it is* an offering made by fire, of a sweet savour unto the LORD.

• Superstitious rites with.

Eze 21:21 — For the king of Babylon stood at the parting of the way, at the head of the two ways, to use divination: he made *his* arrows bright, he consulted with images, he looked in the liver.

LIVERY

• Of seizin.

See: Land; conveyance of, by written deeds and other forms

LIZARD

Le 11:30 — And the ferret, and the chameleon, and the lizard, and the snail, and the mole.

Pr 30:28 — The spider taketh hold with her hands, and is in kings' palaces.

LO-AMMI • A symbolic name given to a son of Hosea.

Hos 1:9 — Then said *God,* Call his name Lo-ammi: for ye *are* not my people, and I will not be your *God.*

LO-DEBAR

• A city in Manasseh.

2Sa 9:4–5

2Sa 17:27 — And it came to pass, when David was come to Mahanaim, that Shobi the son of Nahash of Rabbah of the children of Ammon, and Machir the son of Ammiel of Lo-debar, and Barzillai the Gileadite of Rogelim,

• Home of Mephibosheth, the lame son of Jonathan.

2Sa 9:3–5

LO-RUHAMAH • Hosea's daughter.

Hos 1:6–8

LOAVES

• Miracle of the five.

Mt 14:15–21; Lk 9:12–17

Mt 16:9 — Do ye not yet understand, neither remember the five loaves of the five thousand, and how many baskets ye took up?

• Miracle of the seven.

Mt 15:34–38

Mt 16:10 — Neither the seven loaves of the four thousand, and how many baskets ye took up?

See: Bread

LOBBYING

Ezr 4:4–5

See: Diplomacy

See: Influence; political

LOCK

Jgs 3:23–25; Ne 3:13–14

SS 5:5 — I rose up to open to my beloved; and my hands dropped *with* myrrh, and my fingers *with* sweet smelling myrrh, upon the handles of the lock.

LOCUST

• Authorized as food.

Le 11:22 — *Even* these of them ye may eat; the locust after his kind, and the bald locust after his kind, and the beetle after his kind, and the grasshopper after his kind.

• Used as food.

Mt 3:4 — And the same John had his raiment of camel's hair, and a leathern girdle about his loins; and his meat was locusts and wild honey.

Mk 1:6 — And John was clothed with camel's hair, and with a girdle of a skin about his loins; and he did eat locusts and wild honey;

• Plague of.

Ex 10:1–19; Ps 105:34–35

• Devastation by.

Joel 1:4–7; Rev 9:7–10

Dt 28:38 — Thou shalt carry much seed out into the field, and shalt gather *but* little in; for the locust shall consume it.

1Ki 8:37 — If there be in the land famine, if there be pestilence, blasting, mildew, locust, *or* if there be caterpiller; if their enemy besiege them in the land of their cities; whatsoever plague, whatsoever sickness *there be;*

2Ch 7:13 — If I shut up heaven that there be no rain, or if I command the locusts to devour the land, or if I send pestilence among my people;

Isa 33:4 — And your spoil shall be gathered *like* the gathering of the caterpiller: as the running to and fro of locusts shall he run upon them.

• Sun obscured by.

Joel 2:2 — A day of darkness and of gloominess, a day of clouds and of thick darkness, as the morning spread upon the mountains: a great people and a strong; there hath not been ever the like, neither shall be any more after it, *even* to the years of many generations.

Joel 2:10 — The earth shall quake before them; the heavens shall tremble: the sun and the moon shall be dark, and the stars shall withdraw their shining:

• Instincts of.

Pr 30:27 — The locusts have no king, yet go they forth all of them by bands;

• In King James Version often inaccurately translated grasshopper.

Jgs 6:5 — For they came up with their cattle and their tents, and they came as grasshoppers for multitude; *for* both they and their camels were without number: and they entered into the land to destroy it.

Jgs 7:12 — And the Midianites and the Amalekites and all the children of the east lay along in the valley like grasshoppers for multitude; and their camels *were* without number, as the sand by the sea side for multitude.

Job 39:20 — Canst thou make him afraid as a grasshopper? the glory of his nostrils *is* terrible.

Jer 46:23 — They shall cut down her forest, saith the LORD, though it cannot be searched; because they are more than the grasshoppers, and *are* innumerable.

See: Grasshopper

• Figurative.

Jer 46:23 — They shall cut down her forest, saith the LORD, though it cannot be searched; because they are more than the grasshoppers, and *are* innumerable.

• Symbolic.

Rev 9:3–10

LOD

• A city in Benjamin.

1Ch 8:12 — The sons of Elpaal; Eber, and Misham, and Shamed, who built Ono, and Lod, with the towns thereof:

Ezr 2:33 — The children of Lod, Hadid, and Ono, seven hundred twenty and five.

Ne 7:37 — The children of Lod, Hadid, and Ono, seven hundred twenty and one.

Ne 11:35 — Lod, and Ono, the valley of craftsmen.

• Called Lydda.

Ac 9:38 — And forasmuch as Lydda was nigh to Joppa, and the disciples had heard that Peter was there, they sent unto him two men, desiring *him* that he would not delay to come to them.

LOG • A measure for liquids, holding about a pint.

Le 14:10 — And on the eighth day he shall take two he lambs without blemish, and one ewe lamb of the first year without blemish, and three tenth deals of fine flour *for* a meat offering, mingled with oil, and one log of oil.

Le 14:12 — And the priest shall take one he lamb, and offer him for a trespass offering, and the log of oil, and wave them *for* a wave offering before the LORD:

Le 14:15 — And the priest shall take *some* of the log of oil, and pour *it* into the palm of his own left hand:

Le 14:24 — And the priest shall take the lamb of the trespass offering, and the log of oil, and the priest shall wave them *for* a wave offering before the LORD:

LOIS

• Grandmother of Timothy.

• Commended by Paul for her faith.

2Ti 1:5 — When I call to remembrance the unfeigned faith that is in thee, which dwelt first in thy grandmother Lois, and thy mother Eunice; and I am persuaded that in thee also.

LONG-SUFFERING

2Co 6:4–6; Eph 4:1–2; Col 3:12–13

1Co 13:4 — Charity suffereth long, *and* is kind; charity envieth not; charity vaunteth not itself, is not puffed up,

1Co 13:7 — Beareth all things, believeth all things, hopeth all things, endureth all things.

Gal 5:22 — But the fruit of the Spirit is love, joy, peace, longsuffering, gentleness, goodness, faith,

Col 1:11 — Strengthened with all might, according to his glorious power, unto all patience and longsuffering with joyfulness;

1Ti 1:16 — Howbeit for this cause I obtained mercy, that in me first Jesus Christ might shew forth all longsuffering, for a pattern to them which should hereafter believe on him to life everlasting.

2Ti 3:10 — But thou hast fully known my doctrine, manner of life, purpose, faith, longsuffering, charity, patience,

2Ti 4:2 — Preach the word; be instant in season, out of season; reprove, rebuke, exhort with all longsuffering and doctrine.

➜See: Charitableness

➜See: God, Long-Suffering of

➜See: Patience

LONGEVITY

1Ki 3:11–14; Ps 34:11–13; Pr 3:1–2; 1Pe 3:10–11

Ge 6:3 — And the LORD said, My spirit shall not always strive with man, for that he also *is* flesh: yet his days shall be an hundred and twenty years.

Ex 20:12 — Honour thy father and thy mother: that thy days may be long upon the land which the LORD thy God giveth thee.

Job 5:26 — Thou shalt come to *thy* grave in a full age, like as a shock of corn cometh in in his season.

Ps 21:4 — He asked life of thee, *and* thou gavest *it* him, *even* length of days for ever and ever.

Ps 90:10 — The days of our years *are* threescore years and ten; and if by reason of strength *they be* fourscore years, yet *is* their strength labour and sorrow; for it is soon cut off, and we fly away.

Ps 91:16 — With long life will I satisfy him, and shew him my salvation.

Pr 3:16 — Length of days *is* in her right hand; *and* in her left hand riches and honour.

Pr 9:11 — For by me thy days shall be multiplied, and the years of thy life shall be increased.

Pr 10:27 — The fear of the LORD prolongeth days: but the years of the wicked shall be shortened.

Isa 65:20 — There shall be no more thence an infant of days, nor an old man that hath not filled his days: for the child shall die an hundred years old; but the sinner *being* an hundred years old shall be accursed.

➜See: Old Age

- **Instances of.**
  - **Adam, 930 years.**
    Ge 5:5
  - **Seth, 912 years.**
    Ge 5:8
  - **Enos, 905 years.**
    Ge 5:11
  - **Cainan, 910 years.**
    Ge 5:14
  - **Mahalaleel, 895 years.**
    Ge 5:17
  - **Jared, 962 years.**
    Ge 5:20
  - **Enoch, 365 years.**
    Ge 5:23
  - **Methuselah, 969 years.**
    Ge 5:27
  - **Lamech, 777 years.**
    Ge 5:31
  - **Noah, 950 years.**
    Ge 9:29
  - **Shem.**
    Ge 11:11
  - **Arphaxad.**
    Ge 11:13
  - **Salah.**
    Ge 11:15
  - **Eber.**
    Ge 11:17
  - **Peleg.**
    Ge 11:19
  - **Reu.**
    Ge 11:21
  - **Serug.**
    Ge 11:23
  - **Nahor.**
    Ge 11:25
  - **Terah, 205 years.**
    Ge 11:32
  - **Sarah, 127 years.**
    Ge 23:1
  - **Abraham, 175 years.**
    Ge 25:7
  - **Isaac, 180 years.**
    Ge 35:28
  - **Jacob, 147 years.**
    Ge 47:28
  - **Joseph, 110 years.**
    Ge 50:26
  - **Amram, 137 years.**
    Ex 6:20
  - **Aaron, 123 years.**
    Nu 33:39
  - **Moses, 120 years.**
    Dt 31:2; 34:7
  - **Joshua, 110 years.**
    Jos 24:29
  - **Eli, 98 years.**
    1Sa 4:15
  - **Barzillai, 80 years.**
    2Sa 19:32
  - **Job.**
    Job 42:16
  - **Jehoiada, 130 years.**
    2Ch 24:15
  - **Anna.**
    Lk 2:36–37
  - **Paul.**
    Phm 1:9

LOOKING-GLASS ➜See: Mirror

LORD

• A prince.

Jos 13:3 — From Sihor, which *is* before Egypt, even unto the borders of Ekron northward, *which* is counted to the Canaanite: five lords of the Philistines; the Gazathites, and the Ashdothites, the Eshkalonites, the Gittites, and the Ekronites; also the Avites:

Jgs 3:3 — *Namely,* five lords of the Philistines, and all the Canaanites, and the Sidonians, and the Hivites that dwelt in mount Lebanon, from mount Baal-hermon unto the entering in of Hamath.

1Sa 5:8 — They sent therefore and gathered all the lords of the Philistines unto them, and said, What shall we do with the ark of the God of Israel? And they answered, Let the ark of the God of Israel be carried about unto Gath. And they carried the ark of the God of Israel about *thither.*

1Sa 6:4 — Then said they, What *shall be* the trespass offering which we shall return to him? They answered, Five golden emerods, and five golden mice, *according to* the number of the lords of the Philistines: for one plague was on you all, and on your lords.

⇜See: God

⇜See: Jesus, Names, Appellations, and Titles of; Lord

LORD'S DAY ⇜See: Sabbath

LORD'S PRAYER

Mt 6:9–13; Lk 11:2–4

LORD'S SUPPER ⇜See: Eucharist

LOST SHEEP

• Parable of.

Mt 18:12–13; Lk 15:4–7

LOST, The ⇜See: Wicked; punishment of

LOT

• Feast of.

⇜See: Purim

• The son of Haran.

• Accompanies Terah from Ur of the Chaldees to Haran.

Ge 11:31 — And Terah took Abram his son, and Lot the son of Haran his son's son, and Sarai his daughter in law, his son Abram's wife; and they went forth with them from Ur of the Chaldees, to go into the land of Canaan; and they came unto Haran, and dwelt there.

• Migrates with Abraham to the land of Canaan.

Ge 12:4 — So Abram departed, as the LORD had spoken unto him; and Lot went with him: and Abram *was* seventy and five years old when he departed out of Haran.

• Accompanies Abraham to Egypt; returns with him to Bethel.

Ge 13:1–3

• Rich in flocks, and herds, and servants; separates from Abraham, and locates in Sodom.

Ge 13:5–14

• Taken captive by Chedorlaomer; rescued by Abraham.

Ge 14:1–16

• Providentially saved from destruction in Sodom.

Ge 19:1–38; Lk 17:28–29

• Righteous.

2Pe 2:7–8

• Disobediently protests against going to the mountains, and chooses Zoar.

Ge 19:17–22

• His wife disobediently longs after Sodom, and becomes a pillar of salt.

Ge 19:26 — But his wife looked back from behind him, and she became a pillar of salt.

Lk 17:32 — Remember Lot's wife.

• Commits incest with his daughters.

Ge 19:30–38

• Descendants of.

⇜See: Ammonites

⇜See: Moabites

LOT, The

Pr 16:33 — The lot is cast into the lap; but the whole disposing thereof *is* of the LORD.

Pr 18:18 — The lot causeth contentions to cease, and parteth between the mighty.

Isa 34:17 — And he hath cast the lot for them, and his hand hath divided it unto them by line: they shall possess it for ever, from generation to generation shall they dwell therein.

Joel 3:3 — And they have cast lots for my people; and have given a boy for an harlot, and sold a girl for wine, that they might drink.

• The scapegoat chosen by.

Le 16:8–10

• The land of Canaan divided among the tribes by.

Jos 15:1–63; 21:1–45

Nu 26:55 — Notwithstanding the land shall be divided by lot: according to the names of the tribes of their fathers they shall inherit.

Jos 18:10 — And Joshua cast lots for them in Shiloh before the LORD: and there Joshua divided the land unto the children of Israel according to their divisions.

Jos 19:51 — These *are* the inheritances which Eleazar the priest, and Joshua the son of Nun, and the heads of the fathers of the tribes of the children of Israel, divided for an inheritance by lot in Shiloh before the LORD, at the door of the tabernacle of the congregation. So they made an end of dividing the country.

1Ch 6:61 — And unto the sons of Kohath, *which were* left of the family of that tribe, *were cities given* out of the half tribe, *namely, out of* the half *tribe* of Manasseh, by lot, ten cities.

1Ch 6:65 — And they gave by lot out of the tribe of the children of Judah, and out of the tribe of the children of Simeon, and out of the tribe of the children of Benjamin, these cities, which are called by *their* names.

Eze 45:1 — Moreover, when ye shall divide by lot the land for inheritance, ye shall offer an oblation unto the LORD, an holy portion of the land: the length *shall be* the length of five and twenty thousand *reeds,* and the breadth *shall be* ten thousand. This *shall be* holy in all the borders thereof round about.

Eze 47:22 — And it shall come to pass, *that* ye shall divide it by lot for an inheritance unto you, and to the strangers that sojourn among you, which shall beget children among you: and they shall be unto you as born in the country among the children of Israel; they shall have inheritance with you among the tribes of Israel.

Eze 48:29 — This *is* the land which ye shall divide by lot unto the tribes of Israel for inheritance, and these *are* their portions, saith the Lord GOD.

Mic 2:5 — Therefore thou shalt have none that shall cast a cord by lot in the congregation of the LORD.

Ac 13:19 — And when he had destroyed seven nations in the land of Chanaan, he divided their land to them by lot.

• Saul chosen king by.

1Sa 10:20–21

• Priests and Levites designated by, for sanctuary service.

1Ch 24:5–31

1Ch 26:13 — And they cast lots, as well the small as the great, according to the house of their fathers, for every gate.

Ne 10:34 — And we cast the lots among the priests, the Levites, and the people, for the wood offering, to bring *it* into the house of our God, after the houses of our fathers, at times appointed year by year, to burn upon the altar of the LORD our God, as *it is* written in the law:

Lk 1:9 — According to the custom of the priest's office, his lot was to burn incense when he went into the temple of the Lord.

• Used after the captivity.

Ne 11:1 — And the rulers of the people dwelt at Jerusalem: the rest of the people also cast lots, to bring one of ten to dwell in Jerusalem the holy city, and nine parts *to dwell* in *other* cities.

• An apostle chosen by.

Ac 1:26 — And they gave forth their lots; and the lot fell upon Matthias; and he was numbered with the eleven apostles.

• Achan's guilt ascertained by.

Jos 7:14–18

• Jonathan's guilt ascertained by.

1Sa 14:41–42

• Jonah's guilt ascertained by.

Jnh 1:7 — And they said every one to his fellow, Come, and let us cast lots, that we may know for whose cause this evil *is* upon us. So they cast lots, and the lot fell upon Jonah.

• Used to fix the time for the execution of condemned persons.

Est 3:7 — In the first month, that *is,* the month Nisan, in the twelfth year of king Ahasuerus, they cast Pur, that *is,* the lot, before Haman from day to day, and from month to month, *to* the twelfth *month,* that *is,* the month Adar.

Est 9:24 — Because Haman the son of Hammedatha, the Agagite, the enemy of all the Jews, had devised against the Jews to destroy them, and had cast Pur, that *is,* the lot, to consume them, and to destroy them;

• The garments of Jesus divided by.

Jn 19:23–24

Ps 22:18 — They part my garments among them, and cast lots upon my vesture.

Mt 27:35 — And they crucified him, and parted his garments, casting lots: that it might be fulfilled which was spoken by the prophet, They parted my garments among them, and upon my vesture did they cast lots.

Mk 15:24 — And when they had crucified him, they parted his garments, casting lots upon them, what every man should take.

LOVE

• Of children for parents.

✣See: Children

• Of God.

✣See: God, Love of

• Of man for God.

Ps 45:10–11; 63:5–6; 69:35–36; 73:25–26; Isa 56:6–7; Jer 2:2–3; Mt 22:37–38; Mk 12:29–30, 32–33; 1Jn 3:17–18; 4:16–5:3

Ex 20:6 — And shewing mercy unto thousands of them that love me, and keep my commandments.

Dt 5:10 — And shewing mercy unto thousands of them that love me and keep my commandments.

Dt 6:5 — And thou shalt love the LORD thy God with all thine heart, and with all thy soul, and with all thy might.

Dt 7:9 — Know therefore that the LORD thy God, he *is* God, the faithful God, which keepeth covenant and mercy with them that love him and keep his commandments to a thousand generations;

Dt 10:12 — And now, Israel, what doth the LORD thy God require of thee, but to fear the LORD thy God, to walk in all his ways, and to love him, and to serve the LORD thy God with all thy heart and with all thy soul,

Dt 11:1 — Therefore thou shalt love the LORD thy God, and keep his charge, and his statutes, and his judgments, and his commandments, alway.

Dt 11:13 — And it shall come to pass, if ye shall hearken diligently unto my commandments which I command you this day, to love the LORD your God, and to serve him with all your heart and with all your soul,

Dt 11:22 — For if ye shall diligently keep all these commandments which I command you, to do them, to love the LORD your God, to walk in all his ways, and to cleave unto him;

Dt 13:3 — Thou shalt not hearken unto the words of that prophet, or that dreamer of dreams: for the LORD your God proveth you, to know whether ye love the LORD your God with all your heart and with all your soul.

Dt 30:6 — And the LORD thy God will circumcise thine heart, and the heart of thy seed, to love the LORD thy God with all thine heart, and with all thy soul, that thou mayest live.

Dt 30:16 — In that I command thee this day to love the LORD thy God, to walk in his ways, and to keep his commandments and his statutes and his judgments, that thou mayest live and multiply: and the LORD thy God shall bless thee in the land whither thou goest to possess it.

Dt 30:20 — That thou mayest love the LORD thy God, *and* that thou mayest obey his voice, and that thou mayest cleave unto him: for he *is* thy life, and the length of thy days: that thou mayest dwell in the land which the LORD sware unto thy fathers, to Abraham, to Isaac, and to Jacob, to give them.

Jos 22:5 — But take diligent heed to do the commandment and the law, which Moses the servant of the LORD charged you, to love the LORD your God, and to walk in all his ways, and to keep his commandments, and to cleave unto him, and to serve him with all your heart and with all your soul.

Jos 23:11 — Take good heed therefore unto yourselves, that ye love the LORD your God.

Ps 18:1 — I will love thee, O LORD, my strength.

Ps 31:23 — O love the LORD, all ye his saints: *for* the LORD preserveth the faithful, and plentifully rewardeth the proud doer.

Ps 37:4 — Delight thyself also in the LORD; and he shall give thee the desires of thine heart.

Ps 91:14 — Because he hath set his love upon me, therefore will I deliver him: I will set him on high, because he hath known my name.

Ps 97:10 — Ye that love the LORD, hate evil: he preserveth the souls of his saints; he delivereth them out of the hand of the wicked.

Ps 116:1 — I love the LORD, because he hath heard my voice *and* my supplications.

Ps 145:20 — The LORD preserveth all them that love him: but all the wicked will he destroy.

Pr 8:17 — I love them that love me; and those that seek me early shall find me.

Pr 23:26 — My son, give me thine heart, and let thine eyes observe my ways.

Lk 11:42 — But woe unto you, Pharisees! for ye tithe mint and rue and all manner of herbs, and pass over judgment and the love of God: these ought ye to have done, and not to leave the other undone.

Jn 5:42 — But I know you, that ye have not the love of God in you.

Ro 5:5 — And hope maketh not ashamed; because the love of God is shed abroad in our hearts by the Holy Ghost which is given unto us.

Ro 8:28 — And we know that all things work together for good to them that love God, to them who are the called according to *his* purpose.

1Co 8:3 — But if any man love God, the same is known of him.

Php 1:9 — And this I pray, that your love may abound yet more and more in knowledge and *in* all judgment;

2Th 3:5 — And the Lord direct your hearts into the love of God, and into the patient waiting for Christ.

2Ti 1:7 — For God hath not given us the spirit of fear; but of power, and of love, and of a sound mind.

1Jn 2:5 — But whoso keepeth his word, in him verily is the love of God perfected: hereby know we that we are in him.

1Jn 2:15 — Love not the world, neither the things *that are* in the world. If any man love the world, the love of the Father is not in him.

1Jn 4:12 — No man hath seen God at any time. If we love one another, God dwelleth in us, and his love is perfected in us.

2Jn 1:6 — And this is love, that we walk after his commandments. This is the commandment, That, as ye have heard from the beginning, ye should walk in it.

Jude 1:21 — Keep yourselves in the love of God, looking for the mercy of our Lord Jesus Christ unto eternal life.

• Of man for Jesus.

Mt 10:37–38; 25:34–40; 27:55–61; Lk 2:29–30; 2Co 5:14–15; Eph 3:17–19; Php 1:20–21; 3:7–8

Mk 9:41 — For whosoever shall give you a cup of water to drink in my name, because ye belong to Christ, verily I say unto you, he shall not lose his reward.

Lk 7:47 — Wherefore I say unto thee, Her sins, which are many, are forgiven; for she loved much: but to whom little is forgiven, *the same* loveth little.

Jn 8:42 — Jesus said unto them, If God were your Father, ye would love me: for I proceeded forth and came from God; neither came I of myself, but he sent me.

Jn 14:15 — If ye love me, keep my commandments.

Jn 14:21 — He that hath my commandments, and keepeth them, he it is that loveth me: and he that loveth me shall be loved of my Father, and I will love him, and will manifest myself to him.

Jn 14:23 — Jesus answered and said unto him, If a man love me, he will keep my words: and my Father will love him, and we will come unto him, and make our abode with him.

Jn 14:28 — Ye have heard how I said unto you, I go away, and come *again* unto you. If ye loved me, ye would rejoice, because I said, I go unto the Father: for my Father is greater than I.

Jn 15:9 — As the Father hath loved me, so have I loved you: continue ye in my love.

Jn 16:27 — For the Father himself loveth you, because ye have loved me, and have believed that I came out from God.

Jn 17:26 — And I have declared unto them thy name, and will declare *it*: that the love wherewith thou hast loved me may be in them, and I in them.

Jn 21:17 — He saith unto him the third time, Simon, *son* of Jonas, lovest thou me? Peter was grieved because he said unto him the third time, Lovest thou me? And he said unto him, Lord, thou knowest all things; thou knowest that I love thee. Jesus saith unto him, Feed my sheep.

Ac 21:13 — Then Paul answered, What mean ye to weep and to break mine heart? for I am ready not to be bound only, but also to die at Jerusalem for the name of the Lord Jesus.

1Co 16:22 — If any man love not the Lord Jesus Christ, let him be Anathema Maranatha.

2Co 5:6 — Therefore *we are* always confident, knowing that, whilst we are at home in the body, we are absent from the Lord:

2Co 5:8 — We are confident, *I say,* and willing rather to be absent from the body, and to be present with the Lord.

Gal 5:6 — For in Jesus Christ neither circumcision availeth any thing, nor uncircumcision; but faith which worketh by love.

Gal 5:22 — But the fruit of the Spirit is love, joy, peace, longsuffering, gentleness, goodness, faith,

Gal 6:14 — But God forbid that I should glory, save in the cross of our Lord Jesus Christ, by whom the world is crucified unto me, and I unto the world.

Eph 4:15 — But speaking the truth in love, may grow up into him in all things, which is the head, *even* Christ:

Eph 6:24 — Grace *be* with all them that love our Lord Jesus Christ in sincerity. Amen.

Php 1:9 — And this I pray, that your love may abound yet more and more in knowledge and *in* all judgment;

Php 1:23 — For I am in a strait betwixt two, having a desire to depart, and to be with Christ; which is far better:

Col 1:8 — Who also declared unto us your love in the Spirit.

2Th 3:5 — And the Lord direct your hearts into the love of God, and into the patient waiting for Christ.

2Ti 1:13 — Hold fast the form of sound words, which thou hast heard of me, in faith and love which is in Christ Jesus.

2Ti 4:8 — Henceforth there is laid up for me a crown of righteousness, which the Lord, the righteous judge, shall give me at that day: and not to me only, but unto all them also that love his appearing.

Phm 1:5 — Hearing of thy love and faith, which thou hast toward the Lord Jesus, and toward all saints;

Heb 6:10 — For God *is* not unrighteous to forget your work and labour of love, which ye have shewed toward his name, in that ye have ministered to the saints, and do minister.

Jas 1:12 — Blessed *is* the man that endureth temptation: for when he is tried, he shall receive the crown of life, which the Lord hath promised to them that love him.

Jas 2:5 — Hearken, my beloved brethren, Hath not God chosen the poor of this world rich in faith, and heirs of the kingdom which he hath promised to them that love him?

1Pe 1:8 — Whom having not seen, ye love; in whom, though now ye see *him* not, yet believing, ye rejoice with joy unspeakable and full of glory:

1Pe 2:7 — Unto you therefore which believe *he is* precious: but unto them which be disobedient, the stone which the builders disallowed, the same is made the head of the corner,

Rev 2:4 — Nevertheless I have *somewhat* against thee, because thou hast left thy first love.

- **Instances of love for Jesus.**
  - **Mary.**
    Mt 26:6–13; Lk 10:39; Jn 12:3–8
  - **Peter.**
    Mt 17:4; Jn 13:37; 18:10; 20:3–6; 21:7
  - **Thomas.**
    Jn 11:16
  - **The disciples.**
    Mk 16:10; Lk 24:17–41; Jn 20:20
  - **Mary Magdalene and other disciples.**
    Mt 27:55–56, 61; 28:1–9; Lk 8:2–3; 23:27; 23:55–24:10; Jn 20:1–2, 11–18
  - **A man of Gadara out of whom Jesus cast an evil spirit.**
    Mk 5:18
  - **Joseph of Aramathaea.**
    Mt 27:57–60
  - **Nicodemus.**
    Jn 19:39–40
  - **Women of Jerusalem.**
    Lk 23:27
- **Of man for man.**

Ps 133:1–3; SS 8:6–7; Mt 5:41–47; 10:41–42; 25:34–40; Mk 12:30–33; Lk 6:31–35; 10:30–37; Jn 13:14–15, 34–35; 15:12–13; Ro 12:9–10; 13:8–10; 1Co 13:1–14:1; 2Co 8:7–8; Gal 5:13–14; Col 3:12–14; 1Pe 3:8–9; 1Jn 2:9–11; 3:16–19; 4:11–12; 4:20–5:2

Le 19:18 — Thou shalt not avenge, nor bear any grudge against the children of thy people, but thou shalt love thy neighbour as thyself: I *am* the LORD.

Le 19:34 — *But* the stranger that dwelleth with you shall be unto you as one born among you, and thou shalt love him as thyself; for ye were strangers in the land of Egypt: I *am* the LORD your God.

Dt 10:19 — Love ye therefore the stranger: for ye were strangers in the land of Egypt.

Pr 10:12 — Hatred stirreth up strifes: but love covereth all sins.

Pr 15:17 — Better *is* a dinner of herbs where love is, than a stalled ox and hatred therewith.

Pr 17:9 — He that covereth a transgression seeketh love; but he that repeateth a matter separateth *very* friends.

Pr 17:17 — A friend loveth at all times, and a brother is born for adversity.

Mt 7:12 — Therefore all things whatsoever ye would that men should do to you, do ye even so to them: for this is the law and the prophets.

Mt 19:19 — Honour thy father and *thy* mother: and, Thou shalt love thy neighbour as thyself.

Mk 9:41 — For whosoever shall give you a cup of water to drink in my name, because ye belong to Christ, verily I say unto you, he shall not lose his reward.

Jn 15:17 — These things I command you, that ye love one another.

1Co 8:1 — Now as touching things offered unto idols, we know that we all have knowledge. Knowledge puffeth up, but charity edifieth.

1Co 16:14 — Let all your things be done with charity.

Gal 5:22 — But the fruit of the Spirit is love, joy, peace, longsuffering, gentleness, goodness, faith,

Gal 5:26 — Let us not be desirous of vain glory, provoking one another, envying one another.

Eph 5:2 — And walk in love, as Christ also hath loved us, and hath given himself for us an offering and a sacrifice to God for a sweetsmelling savour.

Php 1:9 — And this I pray, that your love may abound yet more and more in knowledge and *in* all judgment;

Php 2:2 — Fulfil ye my joy, that ye be likeminded, having the same love, *being* of one accord, of one mind.

Col 2:2 — That their hearts might be comforted, being knit together in love, and unto all riches of the full assurance of understanding, to the acknowledgement of the mystery of God, and of the Father, and of Christ;

1Th 1:3 — Remembering without ceasing your work of faith, and labour of love, and patience of hope in our Lord Jesus Christ, in the sight of God and our Father;

1Th 3:12 — And the Lord make you to increase and abound in love one toward another, and toward all *men,* even as we *do* toward you:

1Th 4:9 — But as touching brotherly love ye need not that I write unto you: for ye yourselves are taught of God to love one another.

1Ti 1:5 — Now the end of the commandment is charity out of a pure heart, and *of* a good conscience, and *of* faith unfeigned:

1Ti 1:14 — And the grace of our Lord was exceeding abundant with faith and love which is in Christ Jesus.

1Ti 2:15 — Notwithstanding she shall be saved in childbearing, if they continue in faith and charity and holiness with sobriety.

1Ti 4:12 — Let no man despise thy youth; but be thou an example of the believers, in word, in conversation, in charity, in spirit, in faith, in purity.

1Ti 6:2 — And they that have believing masters, let them not despise *them,* because they are brethren; but rather do *them* service, because they are faithful and beloved, partakers of the benefit. These things teach and exhort.

1Ti 6:11 — But thou, O man of God, flee these things; and follow after righteousness, godliness, faith, love, patience, meekness.

2Ti 2:22 — Flee also youthful lusts: but follow righteousness, faith, charity, peace, with them that call on the Lord out of a pure heart.

Tit 3:15 — All that are with me salute thee. Greet them that love us in the faith. Grace *be* with you all. Amen.

Phm 1:12 — Whom I have sent again: thou therefore receive him, that is, mine own bowels:

Phm 1:16 — Not now as a servant, but above a servant, a brother beloved, specially to me, but how much more unto thee, both in the flesh, and in the Lord?

Heb 10:24 — And let us consider one another to provoke unto love and to good works:

Jas 2:8 — If ye fulfil the royal law according to the scripture, Thou shalt love thy neighbour as thyself, ye do well:

1Pe 1:22 — Seeing ye have purified your souls in obeying the truth through the Spirit unto unfeigned love of the brethren, *see that ye* love one another with a pure heart fervently:

1Pe 2:17 — Honour all *men.* Love the brotherhood. Fear God. Honour the king.

1Pe 4:8 — And above all things have fervent charity among yourselves: for charity shall cover the multitude of sins.

2Pe 1:7 — And to godliness brotherly kindness; and to brotherly kindness charity.

1Jn 3:11 — For this is the message that ye heard from the beginning, that we should love one another.

1Jn 3:14 — We know that we have passed from death unto life, because we love the brethren. He that loveth not *his* brother abideth in death.

1Jn 3:23 — And this is his commandment, That we should believe on the name of his Son Jesus Christ, and love one another, as he gave us commandment.

1Jn 4:7 — Beloved, let us love one another: for love is of God; and every one that loveth is born of God, and knoweth God.

2Jn 1:5 — And now I beseech thee, lady, not as though I wrote a new commandment unto thee, but that which we had from the beginning, that we love one another.

• Exemplification of the love of man for man.

Ex 32:31–32; Ps 133:1–3; Pr 24:17–18; Mt 5:41–42; 10:41–42; 25:34–40; Lk 10:25–37; Ac 20:26–27; Ro 9:1–3; 12:15–16; 15:1–2, 14–15; 16:1–16; 1Co 4:14–16; 2Co 1:3–6; 1:23–2:17; 6:4–6, 11–13; 7:1–4; 12:14–16, 19–21; Gal 4:11–20; 6:1–2; Php 1:3–5, 7–8, 23–26; Col 1:3–4; 1:28–2:1; 1Th 1:3–4; 2:7–8, 11–12, 17–20; 3:7–10; 1Ti 5:9–10; 2Ti 1:3–4; Phm 1:8–9, 16–21; Heb 6:9–10; 13:1–3

Mk 9:41 — For whosoever shall give you a cup of water to drink in my name, because ye belong to Christ, verily I say unto you, he shall not lose his reward.

Ac 20:31 — Therefore watch, and remember, that by the space of three years I ceased not to warn every one night and day with tears.

Ac 26:29 — And Paul said, I would to God, that not only thou, but also all that hear me this day, were both almost, and altogether such as I am, except these bonds.

Ro 1:12 — That is, that I may be comforted together with you by the mutual faith both of you and me.

Ro 5:7 — For scarcely for a righteous man will one die: yet peradventure for a good man some would even dare to die.

Ro 14:19 — Let us therefore follow after the things which make for peace, and things wherewith one may edify another.

Ro 14:21 — *It is* good neither to eat flesh, nor to drink wine, nor *any thing* whereby thy brother stumbleth, or is offended, or is made weak.

Ro 15:5 — Now the God of patience and consolation grant you to be likeminded one toward another according to Christ Jesus:

Ro 15:7 — Wherefore receive ye one another, as Christ also received us to the glory of God.

Ro 15:24 — Whensoever I take my journey into Spain, I will come to you: for I trust to see you in my journey, and to be brought on my way thitherward by you, if first I be somewhat filled with your *company.*

Ro 15:32 — That I may come unto you with joy by the will of God, and may with you be refreshed.

1Co 1:4 — I thank my God always on your behalf, for the grace of God which is given you by Jesus Christ;

1Co 8:13 — Wherefore, if meat make my brother to offend, I will eat no flesh while the world standeth, lest I make my brother to offend.

1Co 10:24 — Let no man seek his own, but every man another's *wealth.*

2Co 1:14 — As also ye have acknowledged us in part, that we are your rejoicing, even as ye also *are* ours in the day of the Lord Jesus.

2Co 3:2 — Ye are our epistle written in our hearts, known and read of all men:

2Co 4:5 — For we preach not ourselves, but Christ Jesus the Lord; and ourselves your servants for Jesus' sake.

2Co 7:7 — And not by his coming only, but by the consolation wherewith he was comforted in you, when he told us your earnest desire, your mourning, your fervent mind toward me; so that I rejoiced the more.

2Co 7:12 — Wherefore, though I wrote unto you, *I did it* not for his cause that had done the wrong, nor for his cause that suffered wrong, but that our care for you in the sight of God might appear unto you.

2Co 11:2 — For I am jealous over you with godly jealousy: for I have espoused you to one husband, that I may present *you as* a chaste virgin to Christ.

2Co 13:9 — For we are glad, when we are weak, and ye are strong: and this also we wish, *even* your perfection.

Gal 6:10 — As we have therefore opportunity, let us do good unto all *men,* especially unto them who are of the household of faith.

Eph 3:13 — Wherefore I desire that ye faint not at my tribulations for you, which is your glory.

Eph 4:2 — With all lowliness and meekness, with longsuffering, forbearing one another in love;

Eph 4:32 — And be ye kind one to another, tenderhearted, forgiving one another, even as God for Christ's sake hath forgiven you.

Eph 6:22 — Whom I have sent unto you for the same purpose, that ye might know our affairs, and *that* he might comfort your hearts.

Eph 6:24 — Grace *be* with all them that love our Lord Jesus Christ in sincerity. Amen.

Php 2:19 — But I trust in the Lord Jesus to send Timotheus shortly unto you, that I also may be of good comfort, when I know your state.

Php 3:18 — (For many walk, of whom I have told you often, and now tell you even weeping, *that they are* the enemies of the cross of Christ:

Php 4:1 — Therefore, my brethren dearly beloved and longed for, my joy and crown, so stand fast in the Lord, *my* dearly beloved.

Col 1:24 — Who now rejoice in my sufferings for you, and fill up that which is behind of the afflictions of Christ in my flesh for his body's sake, which is the church:

Col 2:5 — For though I be absent in the flesh, yet am I with you in the spirit, joying and beholding your order, and the stedfastness of your faith in Christ.

Col 4:7 — All my state shall Tychicus declare unto you, *who is* a beloved brother, and a faithful minister and fellowservant in the Lord:

1Th 3:5 — For this cause, when I could no longer forbear, I sent to know your faith, lest by some means the tempter have tempted you, and our labour be in vain.

1Th 3:12 — And the Lord make you to increase and abound in love one toward another, and toward all *men,* even as we *do* toward you:

1Th 5:8 — But let us, who are of the day, be sober, putting on the breastplate of faith and love; and for an helmet, the hope of salvation.

1Th 5:11 — Wherefore comfort yourselves together, and edify one another, even as also ye do.

1Th 5:14 — Now we exhort you, brethren, warn them that are unruly, comfort the feebleminded, support the weak, be patient toward all *men.*

2Th 1:4 — So that we ourselves glory in you in the churches of God for your patience and faith in all your persecutions and tribulations that ye endure:

1Ti 1:5 — Now the end of the commandment is charity out of a pure heart, and *of* a good conscience, and *of* faith unfeigned:

1Ti 6:2 — And they that have believing masters, let them not despise *them,* because they are brethren; but rather do *them* service, because they are faithful and beloved, partakers of the benefit. These things teach and exhort.

1Ti 6:11 — But thou, O man of God, flee these things; and follow after righteousness, godliness, faith, love, patience, meekness.

2Ti 1:8 — Be not thou therefore ashamed of the testimony of our Lord, nor of me his prisoner: but be thou partaker of the afflictions of the gospel according to the power of God;

2Ti 2:10 — Therefore I endure all things for the elect's sakes, that they may also obtain the salvation which is in Christ Jesus with eternal glory.

Phm 1:12 — Whom I have sent again: thou therefore receive him, that is, mine own bowels:

Heb 5:2 — Who can have compassion on the ignorant, and on them that are out of the way; for that he himself also is compassed with infirmity.

Heb 13:22 — And I beseech you, brethren, suffer the word of exhortation: for I have written a letter unto you in few words.

Jas 1:27 — Pure religion and undefiled before God and the Father is this, To visit the fatherless and widows in their affliction, *and* to keep himself unspotted from the world.

See: Fraternity

- **Instances of.**
  - **Abraham for Lot.**
    Ge 14:14–16
  - **Naomi, Ruth, and Boaz.**
    Ru 1:1–3:18
  - **David and Jonathan.**
    1Sa 20:1–42
  - **David's subjects.**
    2Sa 15:30; 17:27–29
  - **Obadiah for the prophets.**
    1Ki 18:4
  - **Jehoshabeath for Joash.**
    2Ch 22:11
  - **Nehemiah for Israelites.**
    Ne 5:10–15
  - **Mordecai for Esther.**
    Est 2:7
  - **Job's friends.**
    Job 42:11
  - **Centurion for his servant.**
    Lk 7:2–6
  - **Roman Christians for Paul.**
    Ac 28:15
- **Of money.**
  - **The root of evil.**
    1Ti 6:10 — For the love of money is the root of all evil: which while some coveted after, they have erred from the faith, and pierced themselves through with many sorrows.

  See: Riches
- **Of parents for children.**

  See: Brother

  See: Fraternity

  See: Friendship

  See: Parents

LOVEFEASTS • Assemblies of Christian fellowship.

2Pe 2:13 — And shall receive the reward of unrighteousness, *as* they that count it pleasure to riot in the daytime. Spots *they are* and blemishes, sporting themselves with their own deceivings while they feast with you;

Jude 1:12 — These are spots in your feasts of charity, when they feast with you, feeding themselves without fear: clouds *they are* without water, carried about of winds; trees whose fruit withereth, without fruit, twice dead, plucked up by the roots;

LOVERS

- **Instances of.**
  - **Isaac for Rebekah.**
    Ge 24:67
  - **Jacob for Rachel.**
    Ge 29:20, 30
  - **Shechem for Dinah.**
    Ge 34:3, 12
  - **Boaz for Ruth.**
    Ru 2:1–4:22

LOYALTY

- **Enjoined.**

  Ex 22:28 — Thou shalt not revile the gods, nor curse the ruler of thy people.

  Nu 27:20 — And thou shalt put some of thine honour upon him, that all the congregation of the children of Israel may be obedient.

  Ezr 6:10 — That they may offer sacrifices of sweet savours unto the God of heaven, and pray for the life of the king, and of his sons.

  Ezr 7:26 — And whosoever will not do the law of thy God, and the law of the king, let judgment be executed speedily upon him, whether *it be* unto death, or to banishment, or to confiscation of goods, or to imprisonment.

  Job 34:18 — *Is it fit* to say to a king, *Thou art* wicked? *and* to princes, *Ye are* ungodly?

  Pr 24:21 — My son, fear thou the LORD and the king: *and* meddle not with them that are given to change:

  Ecc 8:2 — I *counsel thee* to keep the king's commandment, and *that* in regard of the oath of God.

  Ecc 10:4 — If the spirit of the ruler rise up against thee, leave not thy place; for yielding pacifieth great offences.

  Ro 13:1 — Let every soul be subject unto the higher powers. For there is no power but of God: the powers that be are ordained of God.

  Tit 3:1 — Put them in mind to be subject to principalities and powers, to obey magistrates, to be ready to every good work,
- **Enforced.**

  Ezr 10:8 — And that whosoever would not come within three days, according to the counsel of the princes and the elders, all his substance should be forfeited, and himself separated from the congregation of those that had been carried away.

  Pr 17:11 — An evil *man* seeketh only rebellion: therefore a cruel messenger shall be sent against him.
- **Disloyalty.**

  2Pe 2:10 — But chiefly them that walk after the flesh in the lust of uncleanness, and despise government. Presumptuous *are they,* selfwilled, they are not afraid to speak evil of dignities.

  See: Patriotism

- **Instances of.**
  - **Israelites.**
    Jos 1:16–18; 2Sa 3:36–37; 15:23, 30; 18:3; 21:17; 1Ch 12:38
  - **David.**
    1Sa 24:6–10; 26:6–16; 2Sa 1:14
  - **Uriah.**
    2Sa 11:9
  - **Ittai.**
    2Sa 15:21
  - **Hushai.**
    2Sa 17:15–16
  - **David's soldiers.**
    2Sa 18:12–13; 23:15–16
  - **Joab.**
    2Sa 19:5–6
  - **Barzillai.**
    2Sa 19:32
  - **Jehoiada.**
    2Ki 11:4–12
  - **Mordecai.**
    Est 2:21–23

LUBIMS

- **Inhabitants of northern Africa.**

2Ch 12:3 — With twelve hundred chariots, and threescore thousand horsemen: and the people *were* without number that came with him out of Egypt; the Lubim, the Sukkiims, and the Ethiopians.

2Ch 16:8 — Were not the Ethiopians and the Lubims a huge host, with very many chariots and horsemen? yet, because thou didst rely on the LORD, he delivered them into thine hand.

- **The region they inhabited was called Phut.**

Eze 27:10 — They of Persia and of Lud and of Phut were in thine army, thy men of war: they hanged the shield and helmet in thee; they set forth thy comeliness.

Na 3:9 — Ethiopia and Egypt *were* her strength, and *it was* infinite; Put and Lubim were thy helpers.

See: Phut

- **Called Libya.**

Ac 2:10 — Phrygia, and Pamphylia, in Egypt, and in the parts of Libya about Cyrene, and strangers of Rome, Jews and proselytes,

LUCAS

- **Fellow-laborer of Paul.**
  Phm 1:1–25
- **See Luke.**
  Lk 1:1–24:53

LUCIFER

Isa 14:12 — How art thou fallen from heaven, O Lucifer, son of the morning! *how* art thou cut down to the ground, which didst weaken the nations!

LUCIUS

- **A Christian at Antioch.**

Ac 13:1 — Now there were in the church that was at Antioch certain prophets and teachers; as Barnabas, and Simeon that was called Niger, and Lucius of Cyrene, and Manaen, which had been brought up with Herod the tetrarch, and Saul.

- **A kinsman of Paul.**

Ro 16:21 — Timotheus my workfellow, and Lucius, and Jason, and Sosipater, my kinsmen, salute you.

LUD

- **A son of Shem.**

Ge 10:22 — The children of Shem; Elam, and Asshur, and Arphaxad, and Lud, and Aram.

1Ch 1:17 — The sons of Shem; Elam, and Asshur, and Arphaxad, and Lud, and Aram, and Uz, and Hul, and Gether, and Meshech.

LUDIM

- **Son of Mizraim.**

Ge 10:13 — And Mizraim begat Ludim, and Anamim, and Lehabim, and Naphtuhim,

1Ch 1:11 — And Mizraim begat Ludim, and Anamim, and Lehabim, and Napthtuhim,

- **Descendants of Ludim.**

Ge 10:13 — And Mizraim begat Ludim, and Anamim, and Lehabim, and Naphtuhim,

  - **Warriors.**

Isa 66:19 — And I will set a sign among them, and I will send those that escape of them unto the nations, *to* Tarshish, Pul, and Lud, that draw the bow, *to* Tubal, and Javan, *to* the isles afar off, that have not heard my fame, neither have seen my glory; and they shall declare my glory among the Gentiles.

Jer 46:9 — Come up, ye horses; and rage, ye chariots; and let the mighty men come forth; the Ethiopians and the Libyans, that handle the shield; and the Lydians, that handle *and* bend the bow.

Eze 27:10 — They of Persia and of Lud and of Phut were in thine army, thy men of war: they hanged the shield and helmet in thee; they set forth thy comeliness.

Eze 30:5 — Ethiopia, and Libya, and Lydia, and all the mingled people, and Chub, and the men of the land that is in league, shall fall with them by the sword.

LUHITH • A city of Moab.

Isa 15:5 — My heart shall cry out for Moab; his fugitives *shall flee* unto Zoar, an heifer of three years old: for by the mounting up of Luhith with weeping shall they go it up; for in the way of Horonaim they shall raise up a cry of destruction.

Jer 48:5 — For in the going up of Luhith continual weeping shall go up; for in the going down of Horonaim the enemies have heard a cry of destruction.

LUKE

- **A disciple.**
- **A physician.**

Col 4:14 — Luke, the beloved physician, and Demas, greet you.

- **Wrote to Theophilus.**

Lk 1:1–4; Ac 1:1–2

- **Accompanies Paul.**
  - **In his tour of Asia and Macedonia.**

    Ac 16:10–13; 20:5–6
  - **To Jerusalem.**

    Ac 21:1–18
  - **To Rome.**

    Ac 27:1–28:31

    2Ti 4:11 — Only Luke is with me. Take Mark, and bring him with thee: for he is profitable to me for the ministry.

    Phm 1:24 — Marcus, Aristarchus, Demas, Lucas, my fellowlabourers.

LUKEWARMNESS

- **Figurative.**

Hag 1:4–11; 2:15–16; Rev 3:15–16

Jer 9:3 — And they bend their tongues *like* their bow *for* lies: but they are not valiant for the truth upon the earth; for they proceed from evil to evil, and they know not me, saith the LORD.

Eze 13:5 — Ye have not gone up into the gaps, neither made up the hedge for the house of Israel to stand in the battle in the day of the LORD.

Eze 16:30 — How weak is thine heart, saith the Lord GOD, seeing thou doest all these *things,* the work of an imperious whorish woman;

Hos 6:4 — O Ephraim, what shall I do unto thee? O Judah, what shall I do unto thee? for your goodness *is* as a morning cloud, and as the early dew it goeth away.

Hos 10:2 — Their heart is divided; now shall they be found faulty: he shall break down their altars, he shall spoil their images.

Hag 1:2 — Thus speaketh the LORD of hosts, saying, This people say, The time is not come, the time that the LORD's house should be built.

Mt 26:41 — Watch and pray, that ye enter not into temptation: the spirit indeed *is* willing, but the flesh *is* weak.

Rev 2:4 — Nevertheless I have *somewhat* against thee, because thou hast left thy first love.

Rev 3:2 — Be watchful, and strengthen the things which remain, that are ready to die: for I have not found thy works perfect before God.

See: Backsliders

See: Blindness; spiritual

- **Instances of.**
  - **The Reubenites, when Deborah called on them to assist Sisera.**

    Jgs 5:16
  - **The Jews under Nehemiah.**

    Ne 3:5; 13:11
  - **The church at Pergamos.**

    Rev 2:14–16
  - **The church at Thyatira.**

    Rev 2:20–24
  - **The church at Sardis.**

    Rev 3:1–3
  - **The church at Laodicea.**

    Rev 3:14–16

LUNACY

See: Demons

See: Insanity

LUST

- **Evil desire.**

Job 31:9–12; Pr 6:24–25; 1Co 10:6–7; 2Ti 4:3–4; Jas 1:14–15; 4:1–3; 1Jn 2:16–17

Ge 3:6 — And when the woman saw that the tree *was* good for food, and that it *was* pleasant to the eyes, and a tree to be desired to make *one* wise, she took of the fruit thereof, and did eat, and gave also unto her husband with her; and he did eat.

Ex 20:17 — Thou shalt not covet thy neighbour's house, thou shalt not covet thy neighbour's wife, nor his manservant, nor his maidservant, nor his ox, nor his ass, nor any thing that *is* thy neighbour's.

Ps 81:12 — So I gave them up unto their own hearts' lust: *and* they walked in their own counsels.

Mt 5:28 — But I say unto you, That whosoever looketh on a woman to lust after her hath committed adultery with her already in his heart.

Mk 4:19 — And the cares of this world, and the deceitfulness of riches, and the lusts of other things entering in, choke the word, and it becometh unfruitful.

Jn 8:44 — Ye are of your father the devil, and the lusts of *your* father ye will do. He was a murderer from the beginning, and abode not in the truth, because there is no truth in him. When he speaketh a lie, he speaketh of his own: for he is a liar, and the father of it.

1Co 9:27 — But I keep under my body, and bring *it* into subjection: lest that by any means, when I have preached to others, I myself should be a castaway.

Eph 4:22 — That ye put off concerning the former conversation the old man, which is corrupt according to the deceitful lusts;

1Ti 6:9 — But they that will be rich fall into temptation and a snare, and *into* many foolish and hurtful lusts, which drown men in destruction and perdition.

2Ti 2:22 — Flee also youthful lusts: but follow righteousness, faith, charity, peace, with them that call on the Lord out of a pure heart.

Tit 2:12 — Teaching us that, denying ungodliness and worldly lusts, we should live soberly, righteously, and godly, in this present world;

1Pe 2:11 — Dearly beloved, I beseech *you* as strangers and pilgrims, abstain from fleshly lusts, which war against the soul;

1Pe 4:3 — For the time past of *our* life may suffice us to have wrought the will of the Gentiles, when we walked in lasciviousness, lusts, excess of wine, revellings, banquetings, and abominable idolatries:

2Pe 2:18 — For when they speak great swelling *words* of vanity, they allure through the lusts of the flesh, *through much* wantonness, those that were clean escaped from them who live in error.

2Pe 3:3 — Knowing this first, that there shall come in the last days scoffers, walking after their own lusts,

Jude 1:16 — These are murmurers, complainers, walking after their own lusts; and their mouth speaketh great swelling *words,* having men's persons in admiration because of advantage.

Jude 1:18 — How that they told you there should be mockers in the last time, who should walk after their own ungodly lusts.

See: Adultery

See: Covetousness

See: Incest

See: Lasciviousness

See: Sensuality

See: Sodomy

LYCAONIA

• A province of Asia Minor.

• Paul visits towns of.

Ac 14:6–21; 16:1–2

LYCIA

• A province of Asia Minor.

• Paul visits.

Ac 27:5 — And when we had sailed over the sea of Cilicia and Pamphylia, we came to Myra, *a city* of Lycia.

LYDDA

• Called also Lod.

• A city of Benjamin.

1Ch 8:12 — The sons of Elpaal; Eber, and Misham, and Shamed, who built Ono, and Lod, with the towns thereof:

Ezr 2:33 — The children of Lod, Hadid, and Ono, seven hundred twenty and five.

Ne 11:35 — Lod, and Ono, the valley of craftsmen.

• Peter heals Aeneas in.

Ac 9:32–35

LYDIA

• A woman of Thyatira, who with her household was converted through the preaching of Paul.

Ac 16:14–15

• Entertains Paul and Silas.

Ac 16:15 — And when she was baptized, and her household, she besought *us,* saying, If ye have judged me to be faithful to the Lord, come into my house, and abide *there.* And she constrained us.

Ac 16:40 — And they went out of the prison, and entered into *the house of* Lydia and when they had seen the brethren, they comforted them, and departed.

• Incorrectly put for Lud.

Eze 30:5 — Ethiopia, and Libya, and Lydia, and all the mingled people, and Chub, and the men of the land that is in league, shall fall with them by the sword.

LYING

• Lying spirit from God.

1Ki 22:21–23; 2Ch 18:20–22

See: Falsehood

See: Hypocrisy

LYSANIAS • A tetrarch.

Lk 3:1 — Now in the fifteenth year of the reign of Tiberius Caesar, Pontius Pilate being governor of Judaea, and Herod being tetrarch of Galilee, and his brother Philip tetrarch of Ituraea and of the region of Trachonitis, and Lysanias the tetrarch of Abilene,

LYSIAS

• Chief captain of Roman troops in Jerusalem.

Ac 24:7 — But the chief captain Lysias came *upon us,* and with great violence took *him* away out of our hands,

Ac 24:22 — And when Felix heard these things, having more perfect knowledge of *that* way, he deferred them, and said, When Lysias the chief captain shall come down, I will know the uttermost of your matter.

See: Claudius Lysius

LYSTRA

• One of two cities of Lycaonia, to which Paul and Barnabas fled from persecutions in Iconium.

Ac 14:6–23

2Ti 3:11 — Persecutions, afflictions, which came unto me at Antioch, at Iconium, at Lystra; what persecutions I endured: but out of *them* all the Lord delivered me.

• Church of, elders ordained for, by Paul and Barnabas.

Ac 14:23 — And when they had ordained them elders in every church, and had prayed with fasting, they commended them to the Lord, on whom they believed.

• Timothy a resident of.

Ac 16:1–4

M

MAACHAH

• Son of Nahor.

Ge 22:24 — And his concubine, whose name *was* Reumah, she bare also Tebah, and Gaham, and Thahash, and Maachah.

• Mother of Absalom.

1Ch 3:2 — The third, Absalom the son of Maachah the daughter of Talmai king of Geshur: the fourth, Adonijah the son of Haggith:

• Called also Maacah.

2Sa 3:3 — And his second, Chileab, of Abigail the wife of Nabal the Carmelite; and the third, Absalom the son of Maacah the daughter of Talmai king of Geshur;

• Father of Achish.

1Ki 2:39 — And it came to pass at the end of three years, that two of the servants of Shimei ran away unto Achish son of Maachah king of Gath. And they told Shimei, saying, Behold, thy servants *be* in Gath.

• Called also Maoch.

1Sa 27:2 — And David arose, and he passed over with the six hundred men that *were* with him unto Achish, the son of Maoch, king of Gath.

• Mother of Abijam and grandmother of Asa.

1Ki 15:10–13; 2Ch 11:20–23

1Ki 15:2 — Three years reigned he in Jerusalem. And his mother's name *was* Maachah, the daughter of Abishalom.

2Ch 15:16 — And also *concerning* Maachah the mother of Asa the king, he removed her from *being* queen, because she had made an idol in a grove: and Asa cut down her idol, and stamped *it*, and burnt *it* at the brook Kidron.

• Called also Michaiah.

2Ch 13:2 — He reigned three years in Jerusalem. His mother's name also *was* Michaiah the daughter of Uriel of Gibeah. And there was war between Abijah and Jeroboam.

• Wife of Machir.

1Ch 7:15–16

• Concubine of Caleb.

1Ch 2:48 — Maachah, Caleb's concubine, bare Sheber, and Tirhanah.

• Wife of Jehiel.

1Ch 8:29 — And at Gibeon dwelt the father of Gibeon; whose wife's name *was* Maachah:

1Ch 9:35 — And in Gibeon dwelt the father of Gibeon, Jehiel, whose wife's name *was* Maachah:

• Father of Hanan.

1Ch 11:43 — Hanan the son of Maachah, and Joshaphat the Mithnite,

• Father of Shephatiah.

1Ch 27:16 — Furthermore over the tribes of Israel: the ruler of the Reubenites *was* Eliezer the son of Zichri: of the Simeonites, Shephatiah the son of Maachah:

• Called also Maacah and Maachathi. A small kingdom east of Bashan.

1Ch 19:6–7

Dt 3:14 — Jair the son of Manasseh took all the country of Argob unto the coasts of Geshuri and Maachathi; and called them after his own name, Bashan-havoth-jair, unto this day.

Jos 12:5 — And reigned in mount Hermon, and in Salcah, and in all Bashan, unto the border of the Geshurites and the Maachathites, and half Gilead, the border of Sihon king of Heshbon.

2Sa 10:6 — And when the children of Ammon saw that they stank before David, the children of Ammon sent and hired the Syrians of Beth-rehob, and the Syrians of Zoba, twenty thousand footmen, and of king Maacah a thousand men, and of Ish-tob twelve thousand men.

2Sa 10:8 — And the children of Ammon came out, and put the battle in array at the entering in of the gate: and the Syrians of Zoba, and of Rehob, and Ish-tob, and Maacah, *were* by themselves in the field.

MAADAI • A returned exile.

Ezr 10:34 — Of the sons of Bani; Maadai, Amram, and Uel,

MAADIAH • A priest.

Ne 12:5 — Miamin, Maadiah, Bilgah,

MAAI • A priest.

Ne 12:36 — And his brethren, Shemaiah, and Azarael, Milalai, Gilalai, Maai, Nethaneel, and Judah, Hanani, with the musical instruments of David the man of God, and Ezra the scribe before them.

MAALEH-ACRABBIM

• An acclivity on the southern border of Judah.

Jos 15:3 — And it went out to the south side to Maaleh-acrabbim, and passed along to Zin, and ascended up on the south side unto Kadesh-barnea, and passed along to Hezron, and went up to Adar, and fetched a compass to Karkaa:

➜See: Akrabbim

MAARATH • A city of Judah.

Jos 15:59 — And Maarath, and Beth-anoth, and Eltekon; six cities with their villages:

MAASEIAH

• A Levite musician.

1Ch 15:18 — And with them their brethren of the second *degree,* Zechariah, Ben, and Jaaziel, and Shemiramoth, and Jehiel, and Unni, Eliab, and Benaiah, and Maaseiah, and Mattithiah, and Elipheleh, and Mikneiah, and Obed-edom, and Jeiel, the porters.

1Ch 15:20 — And Zechariah, and Aziel, and Shemiramoth, and Jehiel, and Unni, and Eliab, and Maaseiah, and Benaiah, with psalteries on Alamoth;

• A captain of hundreds.

2Ch 23:1 — And in the seventh year Jehoiada strengthened himself, and took the captains of hundreds, Azariah the son of Jeroham, and Ishmael the son of Jehohanan, and Azariah the son of Obed, and Maaseiah the son of Adaiah, and Elishaphat the son of Zichri, into covenant with him.

• An officer of Uzziah.

2Ch 26:11 — Moreover Uzziah had an host of fighting men, that went out to war by bands, according to the number of their account by the hand of Jeiel the scribe and Maaseiah the ruler, under the hand of Hananiah, *one* of the king's captains.

• Son of Ahaz.

• Slain by Zichri.

2Ch 28:7 — And Zichri, a mighty man of Ephraim, slew Maaseiah the king's son, and Azrikam the governor of the house, and Elkanah *that was* next to the king.

• Governor of Jerusalem.

2Ch 34:8 — Now in the eighteenth year of his reign, when he had purged the land, and the house, he sent Shaphan the son of Azaliah, and Maaseiah the governor of the city, and Joah the son of Joahaz the recorder, to repair the house of the LORD his God.

• The name of a number of priests of the exile.

Ezr 10:21–22; Ne 12:41–42

Ezr 10:18 — And among the sons of the priests there were found that had taken strange wives: *namely,* of the sons of Jeshua the son of Jozadak, and his brethren; Maaseiah, and Eliezer, and Jarib, and Gedaliah.

Ne 8:4 — And Ezra the scribe stood upon a pulpit of wood, which they had made for the purpose; and beside him stood Mattithiah, and Shema, and Anaiah, and Urijah, and Hilkiah, and Maaseiah, on his right hand; and on his left hand, Pedaiah, and Mishael, and Malchiah, and Hashum, and Hashbadana, Zechariah, *and* Meshullam.

Ne 8:7 — Also Jeshua, and Bani, and Sherebiah, Jamin, Akkub, Shabbethai, Hodijah, Maaseiah, Kelita, Azariah, Jozabad, Hanan, Pelaiah, and the Levites, caused the people to understand the law: and the people *stood* in their place.

Jer 21:1 — The word which came unto Jeremiah from the LORD, when king Zedekiah sent unto him Pashur the son of Melchiah, and Zephaniah the son of Maaseiah the priest, saying,

Jer 29:25 — Thus speaketh the LORD of hosts, the God of Israel, saying, Because thou hast sent letters in thy name unto all the people that *are* at Jerusalem, and to Zephaniah the son of Maaseiah the priest, and to all the priests, saying,

Jer 37:3 — And Zedekiah the king sent Jehucal the son of Shelemiah and Zephaniah the son of Maaseiah the priest to the prophet Jeremiah, saying, Pray now unto the LORD our God for us.

• A returned exile.

Ezr 10:30 — And of the sons of Pahath-moab; Adna, and Chelal, Benaiah, Maaseiah, Mattaniah, Bezaleel, and Binnui, and Manasseh.

• Father of Azariah.

Ne 3:23 — After him repaired Benjamin and Hashub over against their house. After him repaired Azariah the son of Maaseiah the son of Ananiah by his house.

• One who sealed the covenant.

Ne 10:25 — Rehum, Hashabnah, Maaseiah,

• A descendant of Pharez.

Ne 11:5 — And Maaseiah the son of Baruch, the son of Col-hozeh, the son of Hazaiah, the son of Adaiah, the son of Joiarib, the son of Zechariah, the son of Shiloni.

• A Benjamite.

Ne 11:7 — And these *are* the sons of Benjamin; Sallu the son of Meshullam, the son of Joed, the son of Pedaiah, the son of Kolaiah, the son of Maaseiah, the son of Ithiel, the son of Jesaiah.

• Father of a false prophet.

Jer 29:21 — Thus saith the LORD of hosts, the God of Israel, of Ahab the son of Kolaiah, and of Zedekiah the son of Maaseiah, which prophesy a lie unto you in my name; Behold, I will deliver them into the hand of Nebuchadrezzar king of Babylon; and he shall slay them before your eyes;

• An officer of the temple.

Jer 35:4 — And I brought them into the house of the LORD, into the chamber of the sons of Hanan, the son of Igdaliah, a man of God, which *was* by the chamber of the princes, which *was* above the chamber of Maaseiah the son of Shallum, the keeper of the door:

• Grandfather of Baruch.

Jer 32:12 — And I gave the evidence of the purchase unto Baruch the son of Neriah, the son of Maaseiah, in the sight of Hanameel mine uncle's *son,* and in the presence of the witnesses that subscribed the book of the purchase, before all the Jews that sat in the court of the prison.

Jer 51:59 — The word which Jeremiah the prophet commanded Seraiah the son of Neriah, the son of Maaseiah, when he went with Zedekiah the king of Judah into Babylon in the fourth year of his reign. And *this* Seraiah was a quiet prince.

MAASIAI • A priest.

1Ch 9:12 — And Adaiah the son of Jeroham, the son of Pashur, the son of Malchijah, and Maasiai the son of Adiel, the son of Jahzerah, the son of Meshullam, the son of Meshillemith, the son of Immer;

MAATH • An ancestor of Jesus.

Lk 3:26 — Which was *the son* of Maath, which was *the son* of Mattathias, which was *the son* of Semei, which was *the son* of Joseph, which was *the son* of Juda,

MAAZ • A son of Ram.

1Ch 2:27 — And the sons of Ram the firstborn of Jerahmeel were, Maaz, and Jamin, and Eker.

MAAZIAH

• A priest.

1Ch 24:18 — The three and twentieth to Delaiah, the four and twentieth to Maaziah.

• A priest who sealed the covenant with Nehemiah.

Ne 10:8 — Maaziah, Bilgai, Shemaiah: these *were* the priests.

MACEDONIA

• A country in southeastern Europe.

• Paul has a vision concerning.

Ac 16:9 — And a vision appeared to Paul in the night; There stood a man of Macedonia, and prayed him, saying, Come over into Macedonia, and help us.

• Paul preaches in, at Philippi.

Ac 16:12 — And from thence to Philippi, which is the chief city of that part of Macedonia, *and* a colony: and we were in that city abiding certain days.

• Paul revisits.

Ac 20:1–6

2Co 2:13 — I had no rest in my spirit, because I found not Titus my brother: but taking my leave of them, I went from thence into Macedonia.

2Co 7:5 — For, when we were come into Macedonia, our flesh had no rest, but we were troubled on every side; without *were* fightings, within *were* fears.

• Church at, sends contributions to the poor in Jerusalem.

2Co 8:1–5

Ro 15:26 — For it hath pleased them of Macedonia and Achaia to make a certain contribution for the poor saints which are at Jerusalem.

• Timothy visits.

Ac 19:22 — So he sent into Macedonia two of them that ministered unto him, Timotheus and Erastus; but he himself stayed in Asia for a season.

• Disciples in.

Ac 19:23 — And the same time there arose no small stir about that way.

Ac 27:2 — And entering into a ship of Adramyttium, we launched, meaning to sail by the coasts of Asia; *one* Aristarchus, a Macedonian of Thessalonica, being with us.

MACHBANAI • A Gadite warrior.

1Ch 12:13 — Jeremiah the tenth, Machbanai the eleventh.

MACHI • A Gadite.

Nu 13:15 — Of the tribe of Gad, Geuel the son of Machi.

MACHIR

• One of the sons of Manasseh.

Ge 50:23 — And Joseph saw Ephraim's children of the third *generation:* the children also of Machir the son Manasseh were brought up upon Joseph's knees.

• Father of the Machirites.

Nu 26:29 — Of the sons of Manasseh: of Machir, the family of the Machirites: and Machir begat Gilead: of Gilead *come* the family of the Gileadites.

Nu 36:1 — And the chief fathers of the families of the children of Gilead, the son of Machir, the son of Manasseh, of the families of the sons of Joseph, came near, and spake before Moses, and before the princes, the chief fathers of the children of Israel:

• The land of Gilead allotted to.

Nu 32:39–40

Dt 3:15 — And I gave Gilead unto Machir.

Jos 13:31 — And half Gilead, and Ashtaroth, and Edrei, cities of the kingdom of Og in Bashan, *were pertaining* unto the children of Machir the son of Manasseh, even to the one half of the children of Machir by their families.

• Certain cities of Bashan given to.

Jos 13:31 — And half Gilead, and Ashtaroth, and Edrei, cities of the kingdom of Og in Bashan, *were pertaining* unto the children of Machir the son of Manasseh, even to the one half of the children of Machir by their families.

Jos 17:1 — There was also a lot for the tribe of Manasseh; for he *was* the firstborn of Joseph; *to wit,* for Machir the firstborn of Manasseh, the father of Gilead: because he was a man of war, therefore he had Gilead and Bashan.

• A man of Lo-debar who took care of Jonathan's lame son, Mephibosheth.

2Sa 9:4–5

2Sa 17:27 — And it came to pass, when David was come to Mahanaim, that Shobi the son of Nahash of Rabbah of the children of Ammon, and Machir the son of Ammiel of Lo-debar, and Barzillai the Gileadite of Rogelim,

MACHNADEBAI • A Jew.

Ezr 10:40 — Machnadebai, Shashai, Sharai,

MACHPELAH • The burying place of Sarah, Abraham, Isaac, Rebekah, Leah, and Jacob.

Ge 23:17–20; 49:30–31

Ge 23:9 — That he may give me the cave of Machpelah, which he hath, which *is* in the end of his field; for as much money as it is worth he shall give it me for a possession of a buryingplace amongst you.

Ge 25:9 — And his sons Isaac and Ishmael buried him in the cave of Machpelah, in the field of Ephron the son of Zohar the Hittite, which *is* before Mamre;

Ge 50:13 — For his sons carried him into the land of Canaan, and buried him in the cave of the field of Machpelah, which Abraham bought with the field for a possession of a buryingplace of Ephron the Hittite, before Mamre.

Ac 7:16 — And were carried over into Sychem, and laid in the sepulchre that Abraham bought for a sum of money of the sons of Emmor *the father* of Sychem.

MADAI • Son of Japheth.

Ge 10:2 — The sons of Japheth; Gomer, and Magog, and Madai, and Javan, and Tubal, and Meshech, and Tiras.

1Ch 1:5 — The sons of Japheth; Gomer, and Magog, and Madai, and Javan, and Tubal, and Meshech, and Tiras.

MADMANNAH • A city of Judah.

Jos 15:31 — And Ziklag, and Madmannah, and Sansannah,

MADMENAH • A city of Benjamin.

Isa 10:31 — Madmenah is removed; the inhabitants of Gebim gather themselves to flee.

MADNESS

See: Insanity

MADON • A Canaanitish city.

Jos 11:1 — And it came to pass, when Jabin king of Hazor had heard *those things,* that he sent to Jobab king of Madon, and to the king of Shimron, and to the king of Achshaph,

Jos 12:19 — The king of Madon, one; the king of Hazor, one;

MAGDALA

• A city of Galilee.

• Christ visits.

Mt 15:39 — And he sent away the multitude, and took ship, and came into the coasts of Magdala,

MAGI • The wise men who visited Jesus.

Mt 2:1–12

MAGIC

See: Astrology

See: Magician

See: Necromancy

See: Sorcery

See: Witchcraft

MAGICIAN

• A person who claims to understand and explain mysteries by magic.

Da 1:20 — And in all matters of wisdom *and* understanding, that the king enquired of them, he found them ten times better than all the magicians *and* astrologers that *were* in all his realm.

• Failed to interpret Pharaoh's dreams.

Ge 41:8 — And it came to pass in the morning that his spirit was troubled; and he sent and called for all the magicians of Egypt, and all the wise men thereof: and Pharaoh told them his dream; but *there was* none that could interpret them unto Pharaoh.

Ge 41:24 — And the thin ears devoured the seven good ears: and I told *this* unto the magicians; but *there was* none that could declare *it* to me.

• Failed to interpret Nebuchadnezzar's dreams.

Da 2:2–13

Da 4:7 — Then came in the magicians, the astrologers, the Chaldeans, and the soothsayers: and I told the dream before them; but they did not make known unto me the interpretation thereof.

• Wrought apparent miracles.

Ex 7:11–12

Ex 7:22 — And the magicians of Egypt did so with their enchantments: and Pharaoh's heart was hardened, neither did he hearken unto them; as the LORD had said.

Ex 8:7 — And the magicians did so with their enchantments, and brought up frogs upon the land of Egypt.

Ex 8:18 — And the magicians did so with their enchantments to bring forth lice, but they could not: so there were lice upon man, and upon beast.

MAGISTRATE • An officer of civil law.

Jgs 18:7 — Then the five men departed, and came to Laish, and saw the people that *were* therein, how they dwelt careless, after the manner of the Zidonians, quiet and secure; and *there was* no magistrate in the land, that might put *them* to shame in *any* thing; and they *were* far from the Zidonians, and had no business with *any* man.

Ezr 7:25 — And thou, Ezra, after the wisdom of thy God, that *is* in thine hand, set magistrates and judges, which may judge all the people that *are* beyond the river, all such as know the laws of thy God; and teach ye them that know *them* not.

Lk 12:11 — And when they bring you unto the synagogues, and *unto* magistrates, and powers, take ye no thought how or what thing ye shall answer, or what ye shall say:

Lk 12:58 — When thou goest with thine adversary to the magistrate, *as thou art* in the way, give diligence that thou mayest be delivered from him; lest he hale thee to the judge, and the judge deliver thee to the officer, and the officer cast thee into prison.

Ac 16:20 — And brought them to the magistrates, saying, These men, being Jews, do exceedingly trouble our city,

Ac 16:22 — And the multitude rose up together against them: and the magistrates rent off their clothes, and commanded to beat *them.*

Ac 16:35 — And when it was day, the magistrates sent the serjeants, saying, Let those men go.

Ac 16:38 — And the serjeants told these words unto the magistrates: and they feared, when they heard that they were Romans.

• Obedience to, enjoined.

Tit 3:1 — Put them in mind to be subject to principalities and powers, to obey magistrates, to be ready to every good work,

See: Government

See: Rulers

MAGNA CHARTA

• Of the Israelites.

See: Constitution

MAGNANIMITY

• Instances of.

• Joshua and the elders of Israel to the Gibeonites who had deceived the Israelites.

Jos 9:3–27

• Of Moses.

See: Moses

• David to Saul.

1Sa 24:3–11

• Ahab to Benhadad.

1Ki 20:32–34

See: Charitableness

MAGNIFICAT

• Of Mary.

Lk 1:46–55

MAGOG

• Son of Japheth.

Ge 10:2 — The sons of Japheth; Gomer, and Magog, and Madai, and Javan, and Tubal, and Meshech, and Tiras.

1Ch 1:5 — The sons of Japheth; Gomer, and Magog, and Madai, and Javan, and Tubal, and Meshech, and Tiras.

• Prophecy concerning.

Eze 38:2 — Son of man, set thy face against Gog, the land of Magog, the chief prince of Meshech and Tubal, and prophesy against him,

Eze 39:6 — And I will send a fire on Magog, and among them that dwell carelessly in the isles: and they shall know that I *am* the LORD.

• Symbolic of the enemies of God.

Rev 20:8 — And shall go out to deceive the nations which are in the four quarters of the earth, Gog and Magog, to gather them together to battle: the number of whom *is* as the sand of the sea.

MAGOR-MISSABIB • A symbolic name given by Jeremiah to Pashur.

Jer 20:3–6

MAGPIASH • A person or family.

Ne 10:20 — Magpiash, Meshullam, Hezir,

MAHALAH • Grandson of Manasseh.

1Ch 7:18 — And his sister Hammoleketh bare Ishod, and Abiezer, and Mahalah.

MAHALALEEL

• Called also Maleleel.

• Son of Cainan.

Ge 5:12–17

1Ch 1:2 — Kenan, Mahalaleel, Jered,

Lk 3:37 — Which was *the son* of Mathusala, which was *the son* of Enoch, which was *the son* of Jared, which was *the son* of Maleleel, which was *the son* of Cainan,

• A man of Judah.

Ne 11:4 — And at Jerusalem dwelt *certain* of the children of Judah, and of the children of Benjamin. Of the children of Judah; Athaiah the son of Uzziah, the son of Zechariah, the son of Amariah, the son of Shephatiah, the son of Mahalaleel, of the children of Perez;

MAHALATH

• Daughter of Ishmael.

Ge 28:9 — Then went Esau unto Ishmael, and took unto the wives which he had Mahalath the daughter of Ishmael Abraham's son, the sister of Nebajoth, to be his wife.

• Called also Bashemath.

Ge 36:3 — And Bashemath Ishmael's daughter, sister of Nebajoth.

• A granddaughter of David.

2Ch 11:18 — And Rehoboam took him Mahalath the daughter of Jerimoth the son of David to wife, *and* Abihail the daughter of Eliab the son of Jesse;

See: Music

MAHANAIM

• The place where Jacob had the vision of angels.

Ge 32:2 — And when Jacob saw them, he said, This *is* God's host: and he called the name of that place Mahanaim.

• The town of, allotted to Gad.

Jos 13:26 — And from Heshbon unto Ramath-mizpeh, and Betonim; and from Mahanaim unto the border of Debir;

Jos 13:30 — And their coast was from Mahanaim, all Bashan, all the kingdom of Og king of Bashan, and all the towns of Jair, which are in Bashan, threescore cities:

• One of the Levitical cities.

Jos 21:38 — And out of the tribe of Gad, Ramoth in Gilead with her suburbs, *to be* a city of refuge for the slayer; and Mahanaim with her suburbs,

• Ishbosheth establishes himself at, when made king over Israel.

2Sa 2:8–12

• David lodges at, at the time of Absalom's rebellion.

2Sa 17:27–29

1Ki 2:8 — And, behold, *thou hast* with thee Shimei the son of Gera, a Benjamite of Bahurim, which cursed me with a grievous curse in the day when I went to Mahanaim: but he came down to meet me at Jordan, and I sware to him by the LORD, saying, I will not put thee to death with the sword.

MAHANEH-DAN • An encampment of the Danites.

Jgs 13:25 — And the Spirit of the LORD began to move him at times in the camp of Dan between Zorah and Eshtaol.

Jgs 18:12 — And they went up, and pitched in Kirjath-jearim, in Judah: wherefore they called that place Mahaneh-dan unto this day: behold, *it is* behind Kirjath-jearim.

MAHARAI • One of David's warriors.

2Sa 23:28 — Zalmon the Ahohite, Maharai the Netophathite,

1Ch 11:30 — Maharai the Netophathite, Heled the son of Baanah the Netophathite,

1Ch 27:13 — The tenth *captain* for the tenth month *was* Maharai the Netophathite, of the Zarhites: and in his course *were* twenty and four thousand.

MAHATH • Name of two descendants of Kohath.

1Ch 6:35 — The son of Zuph, the son of Elkanah, the son of Mahath, the son of Amasai,

2Ch 29:12 — Then the Levites arose, Mahath the son of Amasai, and Joel the son of Azariah, of the sons of the Kohathites: and of the sons of Merari, Kish the son of Abdi, and Azariah the son of Jehalelel: and of the Gershonites; Joah the son of Zimmah, and Eden the son of Joah:

2Ch 31:13 — And Jehiel, and Azaziah, and Nahath, and Asahel, and Jerimoth, and Jozabad, and Eliel, and Ismachiah, and Mahath, and Benaiah, *were* overseers under the hand of Cononiah and Shimei his brother, at the commandment of Hezekiah the king, and Azariah the ruler of the house of God.

MAHAZIOTH • Son of Heman.

1Ch 25:4 — Of Heman: the sons of Heman; Bukkiah, Mattaniah, Uzziel, Shebuel, and Jerimoth, Hananiah, Hanani, Eliathah, Giddalti, and Romamti-ezer, Joshbekashah, Mallothi, Hothir, *and* Mahazioth:

1Ch 25:30 — The three and twentieth to Mahazioth, *he,* his sons, and his brethren, *were* twelve:

MAHER-SHALAL-HASH-BAZ • A symbolic name.

Isa 8:1–4

MAHLAH

• One of the daughters of Zelophehad.

• Special legislation in regard to the inheritance of.

Nu 27:1–7; 36:1–12; Jos 17:3–4

Nu 26:33 — And Zelophehad the son of Hepher had no sons, but daughters: and the names of the daughters of Zelophehad *were* Mahlah, and Noah, Hoglah, Milcah, and Tirzah.

MAHLI

• Son of Merari.

Ex 6:19 — And the sons of Merari; Mahali and Mushi: these *are* the families of Levi according to their generations.

1Ch 6:19 — The sons of Merari; Mahli, and Mushi. And these *are* the families of the Levites according to their fathers.

Ezr 8:18 — And by the good hand of our God upon us they brought us a man of understanding, of the sons of Mahli, the son of Levi, the son of Israel; and Sherebiah, with his sons and his brethren, eighteen;

• Son of Mushi.

1Ch 6:47 — The son of Mahli, the son of Mushi, the son of Merari, the son of Levi.

1Ch 23:23 — The sons of Mushi; Mahli, and Eder, and Jeremoth, three.

1Ch 24:30 — The sons also of Mushi; Mahli, and Eder, and Jerimoth. These *were* the sons of the Levites after the house of their fathers.

MAHLON

• Son of Naomi.

• First husband of Ruth.

Ru 4:9–10

Ru 1:2 — And the name of the man *was* Elimelech, and the name of his wife Naomi, and the name of his two sons Mahlon and Chilion, Ephrathites of Bethlehemjudah. And they came into the country of Moab, and continued there.

Ru 1:5 — And Mahlon and Chilion died also both of them; and the woman was left of her two sons and her husband.

MAHOL • Father of Heman, Chalcol, and Darda.

1Ki 4:31 — For he was wiser than all men; than Ethan the Ezrahite, and Heman, and Chalcol, and Darda, the sons of Mahol: and his fame was in all nations round about.

MAIDEN

→See: Servant

→See: Virgin

MAIL

• Information, public or private. Carried by post.

Est 3:13 — And the letters were sent by posts into all the king's provinces, to destroy, to kill, and to cause to perish, all Jews, both young and old, little children and women, in one day, *even* upon the thirteenth *day* of the twelfth month, which *is* the month Adar, and *to take* the spoil of them for a prey.

Est 8:10 — And he wrote in the king Ahasuerus' name, and sealed it with the king's ring, and sent letters by posts on horseback, *and* riders on mules, camels, *and* young dromedaries:

• Armor.

1Sa 17:5 — And *he had* an helmet of brass upon his head, and he *was* armed with a coat of mail; and the weight of the coat *was* five thousand shekels of brass.

✠See: Armor

MAJESTY

• Name of God.

Heb 1:3 — Who being the brightness of *his* glory, and the express image of his person, and upholding all things by the word of his power, when he had by himself purged our sins, sat down on the right hand of the Majesty on high;

Heb 8:1 — Now of the things which we have spoken *this is* the sum: We have such an high priest, who is set on the right hand of the throne of the Majesty in the heavens;

✠See: God

MAJORITY AND MINORITY REPORTS

• Of the spies.

Nu 13:26–33; 14:6–10

MAKAZ • A place in Judah.

1Ki 4:9 — The son of Dekar, in Makaz, and in Shaalbim, and Beth-shemesh, and Elon-beth-hanan:

MAKHELOTH • An encampment of Israel.

Nu 33:25–26

MAKKEDAH

• A city in Judah; conquered by Joshua.

Jos 10:28 — And that day Joshua took Makkedah, and smote it with the edge of the sword, and the king thereof he utterly destroyed, them, and all the souls *that were* therein; he let none remain: and he did to the king of Makkedah as he did unto the king of Jericho.

Jos 12:16 — The king of Makkedah, one; the king of Bethel, one;

• Five kings of the Amorites hide in a cave of, and are slain by Joshua.

Jos 10:16–27

Jos 10:5 — Therefore the five kings of the Amorites, the king of Jerusalem, the king of Hebron, the king of Jarmuth, the king of Lachish, the king of Eglon, gathered themselves together, and went up, they and all their hosts, and encamped before Gibeon, and made war against it.

MAKTESH • A district where merchants traded.

Zep 1:11 — Howl, ye inhabitants of Maktesh, for all the merchant people are cut down; all they that bear silver are cut off.

MALACHI

• Last of the minor prophets.

Mal 1:1 — The burden of the word of the LORD to Israel by Malachi.

• Reproves the church for its impiety.

Mal 1:1–2:17; 3:7–15

• Foretells the coming of the Messiah.

Mal 3:1–6

• Foretells the judgments on the wicked and consolations of the righteous.

Mal 4:1–3

• Foretells the coming of the forerunner of the Messiah.

Mal 4:4–6

MALCHAM

• A Benjamite.

1Ch 8:9 — And he begat of Hodesh his wife, Jobab, and Zibia, and Mesha, and Malcham,

• An idol.

Zep 1:5 — And them that worship the host of heaven upon the housetops; and them that worship *and* that swear by the LORD, and that swear by Malcham;

MALCHIAH

• Called also Malchijah.

• A Gershonite.

1Ch 6:40 — The son of Michael, the son of Baaseiah, the son of Malchiah,

• An Aaronite.

1Ch 9:12 — And Adaiah the son of Jeroham, the son of Pashur, the son of Malchijah, and Maasiai the son of Adiel, the son of Jahzerah, the son of Meshullam, the son of Meshillemith, the son of Immer;

Ne 11:12 — And their brethren that did the work of the house *were* eight hundred twenty and two: and Adaiah the son of Jeroham, the son of Pelaliah, the son of Amzi, the son of Zechariah, the son of Pashur, the son of Malchiah,

Jer 38:1 — Then Shephatiah the son of Mattan, and Gedaliah the son of Pashur, and Jucal the son of Shelemiah, and Pashur the son of Malchiah, heard the words that Jeremiah had spoken unto all the people, saying,

• Called also Melchiah.

Jer 21:1 — The word which came unto Jeremiah from the LORD, when king Zedekiah sent unto him Pashur the son of Melchiah, and Zephaniah the son of Maaseiah the priest, saying,

• Head of a division of priests.

1Ch 24:9 — The fifth to Malchijah, the sixth to Mijamin,

• Name of three exiles.

Ezr 10:25 — Moreover of Israel: of the sons of Parosh; Ramiah, and Jeziah, and Malchiah, and Miamin, and Eleazar, and Malchijah, and Benaiah.

Ezr 10:31 — And *of* the sons of Harim; Eliezer, Ishijah, Malchiah, Shemaiah, Shimeon,

• A son of Rechab who repaired the dung gate of Jerusalem.

Ne 3:14 — But the dung gate repaired Malchiah the son of Rechab, the ruler of part of Beth-haccerem; he build it, and set up the doors thereof, the locks thereof, and the bars thereof.

• A Jew who helped repair the walls of Jerusalem.

Ne 3:31 — After him repaired Malchiah the goldsmith's son unto the place of the Nethinims, and of the merchants, over against the gate Miphkad, and to the going up of the corner.

• A Jew who stood by Ezra when he read the book of the law to the people.

Ne 8:4 — And Ezra the scribe stood upon a pulpit of wood, which they had made for the purpose; and beside him stood Mattithiah, and Shema, and Anaiah, and Urijah, and Hilkiah, and Maaseiah, on his right hand; and on his left hand, Pedaiah, and Mishael, and Malchiah, and Hashum, and Hashbadana, Zechariah, *and* Meshullam.

• A priest who sealed the covenant with Nehemiah.

Ne 10:3 — Pashur, Amariah, Malchijah,

• A priest appointed to assist in dedicating the walls of Jerusalem.

Ne 12:42 — And Maaseiah, and Shemaiah, and Eleazar, and Uzzi, and Jehohanan, and Malchijah, and Elam, and Ezer. And the singers sang loud, with Jezrahiah *their* overseer.

MALCHIEL • Son of Beriah.

Ge 46:17 — And the sons of Asher; Jimnah, and Ishuah, and Isui, and Beriah, and Serah their sister: and the sons of Beriah; Heber, and Malchiel.

Nu 26:45 — Of the sons of Beriah: of Heber, the family of the Heberites: of Malchiel, the family of the Malchielites.

1Ch 7:31 — And the sons of Beriah; Heber, and Malchiel, who *is* the father of Birzavith.

MALCHIRAM • Son of Jeconiah.

1Ch 3:18 — Malchiram also, and Pedaiah, and Shenazar, Jecamiah, Hoshama, and Nedabiah.

MALCHUS

• Servant of the high priest.

• Peter assaults in Gethsemane; healed by Jesus.

Lk 22:50–51

Mt 26:51 — And, behold, one of them which were with Jesus stretched out *his* hand, and drew his sword, and struck a servant of the high priest's, and smote off his ear.

Mk 14:47 — And one of them that stood by drew a sword, and smote a servant of the high priest, and cut off his ear.

Jn 18:10 — Then Simon Peter having a sword drew it, and smote the high priest's servant, and cut off his right ear. The servant's name was Malchus.

MALEFACTOR • Crucified with Jesus.

Mt 27:38–44; Lk 23:32–39

MALFEASANCE IN OFFICE

• Instances of.

• The lessees of the vineyard, in one of the parables of Jesus.

Mk 12:1–8; Lk 20:9–15

• The steward mentioned in one of the parables of Jesus.

Lk 16:1–7

MALICE

Le 19:17–18; Dt 27:17–18; 32:32–33; 2Ki 6:21–22; Job 31:29–30; Ps 7:14–16; 10:7–10; 22:7–8; 35:15–16, 19–21; 41:5–8; 55:10–11; 56:5–6; 59:3–4, 6–7; 62:3–4; 64:2–6; 69:10–12; 70:2–3; 71:10–11; 109:2–5, 16–18; 140:1–4; Pr 4:16–17; 6:14–16, 18–19; 24:17–18; Isa 29:20–21; 59:4–7; La 4:3–4; Eze 25:6–7; 26:2–3; Mt 5:38–41; 18:28–35; Jn 18:22–23; Ac 23:12–14; Ro 1:29–32; Gal 5:19–21; Php 1:15–16; 1Jn 3:13–15; 3Jn 1:1–14

Ge 3:15 — And I will put enmity between thee and the woman, and between thy seed and her seed; it shall bruise thy head, and thou shalt bruise his heel.

Le 19:14 — Thou shalt not curse the deaf, nor put a stumblingblock before the blind, but shalt fear thy God: I *am* the LORD.

Job 15:35 — They conceive mischief, and bring forth vanity, and their belly prepareth deceit.

Ps 4:2 — O ye sons of men, how long *will ye turn* my glory into shame? *how long* will ye love vanity, *and* seek after leasing? Selah.

Ps 10:14 — Thou hast seen *it;* for thou beholdest mischief and spite, to requite *it* with thy hand: the poor committeth himself unto thee; thou art the helper of the fatherless.

Ps 21:11 — For they intended evil against thee: they imagined a mischievous device, *which* they are not able *to perform.*

Ps 38:16 — For I said, *Hear me,* lest *otherwise* they should rejoice over me: when my foot slippeth, they magnify *themselves* against me.

Ps 38:19 — But mine enemies *are* lively, *and* they are strong: and they that hate me wrongfully are multiplied.

Ps 55:3 — Because of the voice of the enemy, because of the oppression of the wicked: for they cast iniquity upon me, and in wrath they hate me.

Ps 57:4 — My soul *is* among lions: *and* I lie *even among* them that are set on fire, *even* the sons of men, whose teeth *are* spears and arrows, and their tongue a sharp sword.

Ps 57:6 — They have prepared a net for my steps; my soul is bowed down: they have digged a pit before me, into the midst whereof they are fallen *themselves*. Selah.

Ps 69:4 — They that hate me without a cause are more than the hairs of mine head: they that would destroy me, *being* mine enemies wrongfully, are mighty: then I restored *that* which I took not away.

Ps 69:26 — For they persecute *him* whom thou hast smitten; and they talk to the grief of those whom thou hast wounded.

Ps 71:13 — Let them be confounded *and* consumed that are adversaries to my soul; let them be covered *with* reproach and dishonour that seek my hurt.

Ps 71:24 — My tongue also shall talk of thy righteousness all the day long: for they are confounded, for they are brought unto shame, that seek my hurt.

Ps 74:20 — Have respect unto the covenant: for the dark places of the earth are full of the habitations of cruelty.

Ps 86:14 — O God, the proud are risen against me, and the assemblies of violent *men* have sought after my soul; and have not set thee before them.

Ps 102:8 — Mine enemies reproach me all the day; *and* they that are mad against me are sworn against me.

Ps 119:78 — Let the proud be ashamed; for they dealt perversely with me without a cause: *but* I will meditate in thy precepts.

Ps 119:150 — They draw nigh that follow after mischief: they are far from thy law.

Pr 10:6 — Blessings *are* upon the head of the just: but violence covereth the mouth of the wicked.

Pr 10:12 — Hatred stirreth up strifes: but love covereth all sins.

Pr 11:17 — The merciful man doeth good to his own soul: but *he that is* cruel troubleth his own flesh.

Pr 12:10 — A righteous *man* regardeth the life of his beast: but the tender mercies of the wicked *are* cruel.

Pr 14:17 — *He that is* soon angry dealeth foolishly: and a man of wicked devices is hated.

Pr 14:22 — Do they not err that devise evil? but mercy and truth *shall be* to them that devise good.

Pr 15:17 — Better *is* a dinner of herbs where love is, than a stalled ox and hatred therewith.

Pr 16:30 — He shutteth his eyes to devise froward things: moving his lips he bringeth evil to pass.

Pr 17:5 — Whoso mocketh the poor reproacheth his Maker: *and* he that is glad at calamities shall not be unpunished.

Pr 20:22 — Say not thou, I will recompense evil; *but* wait on the LORD, and he shall save thee.

Pr 21:10 — The soul of the wicked desireth evil: his neighbour findeth no favour in his eyes.

Pr 24:8 — He that deviseth to do evil shall be called a mischievous person.

Pr 24:29 — Say not, I will do so to him as he hath done to me: I will render to the man according to his work.

Pr 26:2 — As the bird by wandering, as the swallow by flying, so the curse causeless shall not come.

Pr 26:27 — Whoso diggeth a pit shall fall therein: and he that rolleth a stone, it will return upon him.

Pr 28:10 — Whoso causeth the righteous to go astray in an evil way, he shall fall himself into his own pit: but the upright shall have good *things* in possession.

Pr 30:14 — *There is* a generation, whose teeth *are as* swords, and their jaw teeth *as* knives, to devour the poor from off the earth, and the needy from *among* men.

Isa 32:6 — For the vile person will speak villany, and his heart will work iniquity, to practise hypocrisy, and to utter error against the LORD, to make empty the soul of the hungry, and he will cause the drink of the thirsty to fail.

Jer 20:10 — For I heard the defaming of many, fear on every side. Report, *say they,* and we will report it. All my familiars watched for my halting, *saying,* Peradventure he will be enticed, and we shall prevail against him, and we shall take our revenge on him.

Eze 18:18 — *As for* his father, because he cruelly oppressed, spoiled his brother by violence, and did *that* which *is* not good among his people, lo, even he shall die in his iniquity.

Eze 25:3 — And say unto the Ammonites, Hear the word of the Lord GOD; Thus saith the Lord GOD; Because thou saidst, Aha, against my sanctuary, when it was profaned; and against the land of Israel, when it was desolate; and against the house of Judah, when they went into captivity;

Eze 25:12 — Thus saith the Lord GOD; Because that Edom hath dealt against the house of Judah by taking vengeance, and hath greatly offended, and revenged himself upon them;

Eze 25:15 — Thus saith the Lord GOD; Because the Philistines have dealt by revenge, and have taken vengeance with a despiteful heart, to destroy *it* for the old hatred;

Eze 25:17 — And I will execute great vengeance upon them with furious rebukes; and they shall know that I *am* the LORD, when I shall lay my vengeance upon them.

Am 1:11 — Thus saith the LORD; For three transgressions of Edom, and for four, I will not turn away *the punishment* thereof; because he did pursue his brother with the sword, and did cast off all pity, and his anger did tear perpetually, and he kept his wrath for ever:

Mic 2:1 — Woe to them that devise iniquity, and work evil upon their beds! when the morning is light, they practise it, because it is in the power of their hand.

Zec 7:10 — And oppress not the widow, nor the fatherless, the stranger, nor the poor; and let none of you imagine evil against his brother in your heart.

Zec 8:17 — And let none of you imagine evil in your hearts against his neighbour; and love no false oath: for all these *are things* that I hate, saith the LORD.

Mt 6:15 — <u>But if ye forgive not men their trespasses, neither will your Father forgive your trespasses.</u>

Mt 26:52 — Then said Jesus unto him, <u>Put up again thy sword into his place: for all they that take the sword shall perish with the sword.</u>

Mk 15:10 — For he knew that the chief priests had delivered him for envy.

Lk 6:29 — <u>And unto him that smiteth thee on the *one* cheek offer also the other; and him that taketh away thy cloke forbid not *to take thy* coat also.</u>

Jn 8:44 — <u>Ye are of your father the devil, and the lusts of *your* father ye will do. He was a murderer from the beginning, and abode not in the truth, because there is</u>

<u>no truth in him. When he speaketh a lie, he speaketh of his own: for he is a liar, and the father of it.</u>

Ro 12:19 — Dearly beloved, avenge not yourselves, but *rather* give place unto wrath: for it is written, Vengeance *is* mine; I will repay, saith the Lord.

1Co 5:8 — Therefore let us keep the feast, not with old leaven, neither with the leaven of malice and wickedness; but with the unleavened *bread* of sincerity and truth.

1Co 14:20 — Brethren, be not children in understanding: howbeit in malice be ye children, but in understanding be men.

Eph 4:31 — Let all bitterness, and wrath, and anger, and clamour, and evil speaking, be put away from you, with all malice:

Col 3:8 — But now ye also put off all these; anger, wrath, malice, blasphemy, filthy communication out of your mouth.

1Th 5:15 — See that none render evil for evil unto any *man;* but ever follow that which is good, both among yourselves, and to all *men.*

Tit 3:3 — For we ourselves also were sometimes foolish, disobedient, deceived, serving divers lusts and pleasures, living in malice and envy, hateful, *and* hating one another.

Jas 1:21 — Wherefore lay apart all filthiness and superfluity of naughtiness, and receive with meekness the engrafted word, which is able to save your souls.

Jas 2:13 — For he shall have judgment without mercy, that hath shewed no mercy; and mercy rejoiceth against judgment.

1Pe 2:1 — Wherefore laying aside all malice, and all guile, and hypocrisies, and envies, and all evil speakings,

1Pe 3:9 — Not rendering evil for evil, or railing for railing: but contrariwise blessing; knowing that ye are thereunto called, that ye should inherit a blessing.

1Jn 2:9 — He that saith he is in the light, and hateth his brother, is in darkness even until now.

1Jn 2:11 — But he that hateth his brother is in darkness, and walketh in darkness, and knoweth not whither he goeth, because that darkness hath blinded his eyes.

1Jn 3:10 — In this the children of God are manifest, and the children of the devil: whosoever doeth not righteousness is not of God, neither he that loveth not his brother.

1Jn 4:20 — If a man say, I love God, and hateth his brother, he is a liar: for he that loveth not his brother whom he hath seen, how can he love God whom he hath not seen?

See: Conspiracy

See: Hatred

See: Homicide

See: Jealousy

See: Revenge

- **Instances of.**
  - **Cain toward Abel.**
    Ge 4:8
  - **Ishmael toward Sarah.**
    Ge 21:9
  - **Sarah toward Hagar.**
    Ge 21:10
  - **Philistines toward Isaac.**
    Ge 26:1–35
  - **Esau toward Jacob.**
    Ge 27:41
  - **Joseph's brethren toward Joseph.**
    Ge 37:1–36; 42:21
  - **Potiphar's wife toward Joseph.**
    Ge 39:14–20
  - **Ammonites toward the Israelites.**
    Dt 23:3–4
  - **Saul toward David.**
    1Sa 18:8–29; 19:1–24; 20:30–33; 22:6–18; 23:7–23; 26:18
  - **David toward Michal.**
    2Sa 6:21–23
  - **David toward Joab.**
    1Ki 2:5–6
  - **David toward Shimei.**
    1Ki 2:8–9
  - **Shimei toward David.**
    2Sa 16:5–8
  - **Ahithophel toward David.**
    2Sa 17:1–3
  - **Jezebel toward Elijah.**
    1Ki 19:1–2
  - **Ahaziah toward Elijah.**
    2Ki 1:1–18
  - **Jehoram toward Elisha.**
    2Ki 6:31
  - **Samaritans toward the Jews.**
    Ezr 4:1–24; Ne 2:10; 4:1–23; 6:1–19
  - **Haman toward Mordecai.**
    Est 3:5–15; 5:9–14
  - **Jeremiah's enemies.**
    Jer 26:8–11; 38:1–28
  - **Nebuchadnezzar toward Zedekiah.**
    Jer 52:10–11
  - **Daniel's enemies.**
    Da 6:4–9
  - **Herodias toward John.**
    Mt 14:3–10; Mk 6:24–28
  - **Herod toward Jesus.**
    Lk 23:11
  - **The Jews toward Jesus.**
    Mt 27:18; Mk 12:12; 15:10; Lk 11:53–54
  - **James and John toward the Samaritans.**
    Lk 9:54
  - **Jews toward Paul.**
    Ac 17:5; 23:12; 25:3
  - **Masters of the sorcerous damsel toward Paul.**
    Ac 16:19–24

MALINGERING

• Instances of.

• David feigning madness.

1Sa 21:13–15

MALLOTHI • Son of Heman, a singer.

1Ch 25:4 — Of Heman: the sons of Heman; Bukkiah, Mattaniah, Uzziel, Shebuel, and Jerimoth, Hananiah, Hanani, Eliathah, Giddalti, and Romamti-ezer, Joshbekashah, Mallothi, Hothir, *and* Mahazioth:

1Ch 25:26 — The nineteenth to Mallothi, *he,* his sons, and his brethren, *were* twelve:

MALLOWS • A plant.

Job 30:4 — Who cut up mallows by the bushes, and juniper roots *for* their meat.

MALLUCH

• A Merarite Levite.

1Ch 6:44 — And their brethren the sons of Merari *stood* on the left hand: Ethan the son of Kishi, the son of Abdi, the son of Malluch,

• Son of Bani, who divorced his Gentile wife after the captivity.

Ezr 10:29 — And of the sons of Bani; Meshullam, Malluch, and Adaiah, Jashub, and Sheal, and Ramoth.

• One of the family of Harim, who divorced his Gentile wife after the captivity.

Ezr 10:32 — Benjamin, Malluch, *and* Shemariah.

• A priest who sealed the covenant with Nehemiah.

Ne 10:4 — Hattush, Shebaniah, Malluch,

Ne 12:2 — Amariah, Malluch, Hattush,

• A chief of the people who sealed the covenant with Nehemiah.

Ne 10:27 — Malluch, Harim, Baanah.

MAMMON

• Wealth.

Mt 6:24 — No man can serve two masters: for either he will hate the one, and love the other; or else he will hold to the one, and despise the other. Ye cannot serve God and mammon.

Lk 16:9 — And I say unto you, Make to yourselves friends of the mammon of unrighteousness; that, when ye fail, they may receive you into everlasting habitations.

Lk 16:11 — If therefore ye have not been faithful in the unrighteous mammon, who will commit to your trust the true *riches?*

Lk 16:13 — No servant can serve two masters: for either he will hate the one, and love the other; or else he will hold to the one, and despise the other. Ye cannot serve God and mammon.

→See: Rich

→See: Riches

MAMRE

• A plain near Hebron.

• Abraham resides in.

Ge 13:18 — Then Abram removed *his* tent, and came and dwelt in the plain of Mamre, which *is* in Hebron, and built there an altar unto the LORD.

Ge 14:13 — And there came one that had escaped, and told Abram the Hebrew; for he dwelt in the plain of Mamre the Amorite, brother of Eshcol, and brother of Aner: and these *were* confederate with Abram.

• Entertains three angels, and is promised a son.

Ge 18:1–15

• Isaac dwells in.

Ge 35:27 — And Jacob came unto Isaac his father unto Mamre, unto the city of Arbah, which *is* Hebron, where Abraham and Isaac sojourned.

• An Amorite and confederate of Abraham.

Ge 14:13 — And there came one that had escaped, and told Abram the Hebrew; for he dwelt in the plain of Mamre the Amorite, brother of Eshcol, and brother of Aner: and these *were* confederate with Abram.

Ge 14:24 — Save only that which the young men have eaten, and the portion of the men which went with me, Aner, Eshcol, and Mamre; let them take their portion.

MAN

• Created.

Ge 1:26–27; 5:1–2; Job 10:2–3, 8–9

Ge 2:7 — And the LORD God formed man *of* the dust of the ground, and breathed into his nostrils the breath of life; and man became a living soul.

Dt 4:32 — For ask now of the days that are past, which were before thee, since the day that God created man upon the earth, and *ask* from the one side of heaven unto the other, whether there hath been *any such thing* as this great thing *is,* or hath been heard like it?

Job 4:17 — Shall mortal man be more just than God? shall a man be more pure than his maker?

Job 31:15 — Did not he that made me in the womb make him? and did not one fashion us in the womb?

Job 33:4 — The Spirit of God hath made me, and the breath of the Almighty hath given me life.

Job 34:19 — *How much less to him* that accepteth not the persons of princes, nor regardeth the rich more than the poor? for they all *are* the work of his hands.

Job 35:10 — But none saith, Where *is* God my maker, who giveth songs in the night;

Ps 8:5 — For thou hast made him a little lower than the angels, and hast crowned him with glory and honour.

Ps 100:3 — Know ye that the LORD he *is* God: *it is* he *that* hath made us, and not we ourselves; *we are* his people, and the sheep of his pasture.

Ps 119:73 — Thy hands have made me and fashioned me: give me understanding, that I may learn thy commandments.

Ps 138:8 — The LORD will perfect *that which* concerneth me: thy mercy, O LORD, *endureth* for ever: forsake not the works of thine own hands.

Ps 139:14 — I will praise thee; for I am fearfully *and* wonderfully made: marvellous *are* thy works; and *that* my soul knoweth right well.

Ecc 7:29 — Lo, this only have I found, that God hath made man upright; but they have sought out many inventions.

Isa 17:7 — At that day shall a man look to his Maker, and his eyes shall have respect to the Holy One of Israel.

Isa 42:5 — Thus saith God the LORD, he that created the heavens, and stretched them out; he that spread forth the earth, and that which cometh out of it; he that giveth breath unto the people upon it, and spirit to them that walk therein:

Isa 43:7 — *Even* every one that is called by my name: for I have created him for my glory, I have formed him; yea, I have made him.

Isa 45:12 — I have made the earth, and created man upon it: I, *even* my hands, have stretched out the heavens, and all their host have I commanded.

Isa 64:8 — But now, O LORD, thou *art* our father; we *are* the clay, and thou our potter; and we all *are* the work of thy hand.

Jer 27:5 — I have made the earth, the man and the beast that *are* upon the ground, by my great power and by my outstretched arm, and have given it unto whom it seemed meet unto me.

Zec 12:1 — The burden of the word of the LORD for Israel, saith the LORD, which stretcheth forth the heavens, and layeth the foundation of the earth, and formeth the spirit of man within him.

Mal 2:10 — Have we not all one father? hath not one God created us? why do we deal treacherously every man against his brother, by profaning the covenant of our fathers?

Mk 10:6 — But from the beginning of the creation God made them male and female.

Heb 2:7 — Thou madest him a little lower than the angels; thou crownedst him with glory and honour, and didst set him over the works of thy hands:

See: Man; Created in the image of God

• Created in the image of God.

Ge 1:26–27; 1Co 15:48–49

Ge 9:6 — Whoso sheddeth man's blood, by man shall his blood be shed: for in the image of God made he man.

Ecc 7:29 — Lo, this only have I found, that God hath made man upright; but they have sought out many inventions.

1Co 11:7 — For a man indeed ought not to cover *his* head, forasmuch as he is the image and glory of God: but the woman is the glory of the man.

Jas 3:9 — Therewith bless we God, even the Father; and therewith curse we men, which are made after the similitude of God.

• Design of the creation of.

Ps 8:6–8

Pr 16:4 — The LORD hath made all *things* for himself: yea, even the wicked for the day of evil.

Isa 43:7 — *Even* every one that is called by my name: for I have created him for my glory, I have formed him; yea, I have made him.

• Dominion of.

Ge 2:19–20; 9:2–3; Heb 2:7–8

Ge 1:26 — And God said, Let us make man in our image, after our likeness: and let them have dominion over the fish of the sea, and over the fowl of the air, and over the cattle, and over all the earth, and over every creeping thing that creepeth upon the earth.

Ge 1:28 — And God blessed them, and God said unto them, Be fruitful, and multiply, and replenish the earth, and subdue it: and have dominion over the fish of the sea, and over the fowl of the air, and over every living thing that moveth upon the earth.

Jer 27:6 — And now have I given all these lands into the hand of Nebuchadnezzar the king of Babylon, my servant; and the beasts of the field have I given him also to serve him.

Jer 28:14 — For thus saith the LORD of hosts, the God of Israel; I have put a yoke of iron upon the neck of all these nations, that they may serve Nebuchad-nezzar king of Babylon; and they shall serve him: and I have given him the beasts of the field also.

Da 2:38 — And wheresoever the children of men dwell, the beasts of the field and the fowls of the heaven hath he given into thine hand, and hath made thee ruler over them all. Thou *art* this head of gold.

• Duty of.

See: Duty

See: Neighbor

• Equality of.

Job 31:13–15; Ps 33:13–15; Mt 20:25–28; Mk 10:42–44

Pr 22:2 — The rich and poor meet together: the LORD *is* the maker of them all.

Mt 23:8 — But be not ye called Rabbi: for one is your Master, *even* Christ; and all ye are brethren.

Mt 23:11 — But he that is greatest among you shall be your servant.

Ac 10:28 — And he said unto them, Ye know how that it is an unlawful thing for a man that is a Jew to keep company, or come unto one of another nation; but God hath shewed me that I should not call any man common or unclean.

Ac 17:26 — And hath made of one blood all nations of men for to dwell on all the face of the earth, and hath determined the times before appointed, and the bounds of their habitation;

Gal 3:28 — There is neither Jew nor Greek, there is neither bond nor free, there is neither male nor female: for ye are all one in Christ Jesus.

See: Race; human, unity of

• Ignorance of.

See: Ignorance

• **Immortal.**

→See: **Immortality**

• **Insignificance of.**

Job 4:18–19; 22:2–5; 25:4–6; 35:2–8; 38:12–13; Ps 8:3–4; 144:3–4

Job 15:14 — What *is* man, that he should be clean? and *he which is* born of a woman, that he should be righteous?

Job 38:4 — Where wast thou when I laid the foundations of the earth? declare, if thou hast understanding.

• **Little lower than the angels.**

Job 4:18–21; Heb 2:7–8

Ps 8:5 — For thou hast made him a little lower than the angels, and hast crowned him with glory and honour.

• **Mortal.**

Ecc 2:14–15; 1Co 15:21–22

Job 4:17 — Shall mortal man be more just than God? shall a man be more pure than his maker?

Ecc 3:20 — All go unto one place; all are of the dust, and all turn to dust again.

Heb 9:27 — And as it is appointed unto men once to die, but after this the judgment:

→See: **Death**

• **Spirit.**

Jn 3:3–8; Ro 7:14–25; 2Co 4:6–7; 5:1–9

Job 4:19 — How much less *in* them that dwell in houses of clay, whose foundation *is* in the dust, *which* are crushed before the moth?

Job 32:8 — But *there is* a spirit in man: and the inspiration of the Almighty giveth them understanding.

Ps 31:5 — Into thine hand I commit my spirit: thou hast redeemed me, O LORD God of truth.

Pr 20:27 — The spirit of man *is* the candle of the LORD, searching all the inward parts of the belly.

Ecc 1:8 — All things *are* full of labour; man cannot utter *it:* the eye is not satisfied with seeing, nor the ear filled with hearing.

Ecc 3:21 — Who knoweth the spirit of man that goeth upward, and the spirit of the beast that goeth downward to the earth?

Ecc 12:7 — Then shall the dust return to the earth as it was: and the spirit shall return unto God who gave it.

Isa 26:9 — With my soul have I desired thee in the night; yea, with my spirit within me will I seek thee early: for when thy judgments *are* in the earth, the inhabitants of the world will learn righteousness.

Zec 12:1 — The burden of the word of the LORD for Israel, saith the LORD, which stretcheth forth the heavens, and layeth the foundation of the earth, and formeth the spirit of man within him.

Mt 4:4 — But he answered and said, It is written, Man shall not live by bread alone, but by every word that proceedeth out of the mouth of God.

Mt 10:28 — And fear not them which kill the body, but are not able to kill the soul: but rather fear him which is able to destroy both soul and body in hell.

Mt 26:41 — Watch and pray, that ye enter not into temptation: the spirit indeed *is* willing, but the flesh *is* weak.

Mk 14:38 — Watch ye and pray, lest ye enter into temptation. The spirit truly *is* ready, but the flesh *is* weak.

Lk 22:40 — And when he was at the place, he said unto them, Pray that ye enter not into temptation.

Lk 23:46 — And when Jesus had cried with a loud voice, he said, Father, into thy hands I commend my spirit: and having said thus, he gave up the ghost.

Lk 24:39 — Behold my hands and my feet, that it is I myself: handle me, and see; for a spirit hath not flesh and bones, as ye see me have.

Jn 4:24 — God *is* a Spirit: and they that worship him must worship *him* in spirit and in truth.

Ac 7:59 — And they stoned Stephen, calling upon *God,* and saying, Lord Jesus, receive my spirit.

Ro 1:9 — For God is my witness, whom I serve with my spirit in the gospel of his Son, that without ceasing I make mention of you always in my prayers;

Ro 2:29 — But he *is* a Jew, which is one inwardly; and circumcision *is that* of the heart, in the spirit, *and* not in the letter; whose praise *is* not of men, but of God.

1Co 2:11 — For what man knoweth the things of a man, save the spirit of man which is in him? even so the things of God knoweth no man, but the Spirit of God.

1Co 6:20 — For ye are bought with a price: therefore glorify God in your body, and in your spirit, which are God's.

1Co 7:34 — There is difference *also* between a wife and a virgin. The unmarried woman careth for the things of the Lord, that she may be holy both in body and in spirit: but she that is married careth for the things of the world, how she may please *her* husband.

1Co 14:14 — For if I pray in an *unknown* tongue, my spirit prayeth, but my understanding is unfruitful.

2Co 4:16 — For which cause we faint not; but though our outward man perish, yet the inward *man* is renewed day by day.

Eph 3:16 — That he would grant you, according to the riches of his glory, to be strengthened with might by his Spirit in the inner man;

Eph 4:4 — *There is* one body, and one Spirit, even as ye are called in one hope of your calling;

1Th 5:23 — And the very God of peace sanctify you wholly; and *I pray God* your whole spirit and soul and body be preserved blameless unto the coming of our Lord Jesus Christ.

Heb 4:12 — For the word of God *is* quick, and powerful, and sharper than any twoedged sword, piercing even to the dividing asunder of soul and spirit, and of the joints and marrow, and *is* a discerner of the thoughts and intents of the heart.

Jas 2:26 — For as the body without the spirit is dead, so faith without works is dead also.

• **State of, after the fall.**

→See: **Depravity of Man**

• **State of, before the fall.**

→See: **Man; created in the image of God**

• **Young Men.**

→See: **Young Men**

MANAEN • An associate of Herod in his youth, and a Christian teacher.

Ac 13:1 — Now there were in the church that was at Antioch certain prophets and teachers; as Barnabas, and Simeon that was called Niger, and Lucius of Cyrene, and Manaen, which had been brought up with Herod the tetrarch, and Saul.

MANAHATH

• **Son of Shobal.**

Ge 36:23 — And the children of Shobal *were* these; Alvan, and Manahath, and Ebal, Shepho, and Onam.

1Ch 1:40 — The sons of Shobal; Alian, and Manahath, and Ebal, Shephi, and Onam. And the sons of Zibeon; Aiah, and Anah.

• **A city in Benjamin.**

1Ch 8:6 — And these *are* the sons of Ehud: these are the heads of the fathers of the inhabitants of Geba, and they removed them to Manahath:

MANASSEH

• **Son of Joseph and Asenath.**

Ge 41:50–51

Ge 46:20 — And unto Joseph in the land of Egypt were born Manasseh and Ephraim, which Asenath the daughter of Poti-pherah priest of On bare unto him.

• **Adopted by Jacob on his deathbed.**

Ge 48:5–20

Ge 48:1 — And it came to pass after these things, that *one* told Joseph, Behold, thy father *is* sick: and he took with him his two sons, Manasseh and Ephraim.

• **Called Manasses.**

Rev 7:6 — Of the tribe of Aser *were* sealed twelve thousand. Of the tribe of Nepthalim *were* sealed twelve thousand. Of the tribe of Manasses *were* sealed twelve thousand.

• **Tribe.**

• **Descendants of Joseph.**

• **Ephraim and Manasseh were reckoned among primogenitors of the twelve tribes; adopted by Jacob.**

Ge 48:5 — And now thy two sons, Ephraim and Manasseh, which were born unto thee in the land of Egypt before I came unto thee into Egypt, *are* mine; as Reuben and Simeon, they shall be mine.

• **Prophecy concerning.**

Ge 49:25–26

• **Enumeration of.**

Nu 1:34–35; 26:29–34

• **Place of, in camp and march.**

Nu 10:22–23

Nu 2:18 — On the west side *shall be* the standard of the camp of Ephraim according to their armies: and the captain of the sons of Ephraim *shall be* Elishama the son of Ammihud.

Nu 2:20 — And by him *shall be* the tribe of Manasseh: and the captain of the children of Manasseh *shall be* Gamaliel the son of Pedahzur.

• **Blessing of Moses on.**

Dt 33:13–17

• **Inheritance of one-half of tribe east of Jordan.**

Nu 32:39–42

Nu 32:33 — And Moses gave unto them, *even* to the children of Gad, and to the children of Reuben, and unto half the tribe of Manasseh the son of Joseph, the kingdom of Sihon king of the Amorites, and the kingdom of Og king of Bashan, the land, with the cities thereof in the coasts, *even* the cities of the country round about.

• **One-half of tribe west of Jordan.**

Jos 17:5–11

Jos 16:9 — And the separate cities for the children of Ephraim *were* among the inheritance of the children of Manasseh, all the cities with their villages.

• **The eastern half assists in the conquest of the country west of the Jordan.**

Dt 3:18–20; Jos 1:12–15; 4:12–13

• **Join other eastern tribes in erecting a monument to the unity of Israel; misunderstood.**

Jos 22:1–34

• **Join Gideon in war with the Midianites.**

Jgs 6:1–40

• **Malcontents of, join David.**

1Ch 12:19 — And there fell *some* of Manasseh to David, when he came with the Philistines against Saul to battle: but they helped them not: for the lords of the Philistines upon advisement sent him away, saying, He will fall to his master Saul to *the jeopardy of* our heads.

1Ch 12:31 — And of the half tribe of Manasseh eighteen thousand, which were expressed by name, to come and make David king.

• **Smitten by Hazael.**

2Ki 10:33 — From Jordan eastward, all the land of Gilead, the Gadites, and the Reubenites, and the Manassites, from Aroer, which is by the river Arnon, even Gilead and Bashan.

• **Return from captivity.**

1Ch 9:3 — And in Jerusalem dwelt of the children of Judah, and of the children of Benjamin, and of the children of Ephraim, and Manasseh;

• **Reallotment of territory to, by Ezekiel.**

Eze 48:4 — And by the border of Naphtali, from the east side unto the west side, a *portion for* Manasseh.

• **Affiliate with the Jews in the reign of Hezekiah.**

2Ch 30:1–27

- **Incorporated into kingdom of Judah.**

  2Ch 34:6–7

  2Ch 15:9 — And he gathered all Judah and Benjamin, and the strangers with them out of Ephraim and Manasseh, and out of Simeon: for they fell to him out of Israel in abundance, when they saw that the LORD his God *was* with him.

  See: Israel, name given to descendants of Jacob; tribes of Israel were named after the sons of Jacob

- **Father of Gershom.**

  Jgs 18:30 — And the children of Dan set up the graven image: and Jonathan, the son of Gershom, the son of Manasseh, he and his sons were priests to the tribe of Dan until the day of the captivity of the land.

- **King of Judah, history of.**

  2Ki 21:1–18; 2Ch 33:1–20

- **Two Jews who put away their Gentile wives after the captivity.**

  Ezr 10:30 — And of the sons of Pahath-moab; Adna, and Chelal, Benaiah, Maaseiah, Mattaniah, Bezaleel, and Binnui, and Manasseh.

  Ezr 10:33 — Of the sons of Hashum; Mattenai, Mattathah, Zabad, Eliphelet, Jeremai, Manasseh, *and* Shimei.

MANDRAKE

Ge 30:14–16

SS 7:13 — The mandrakes give a smell, and at our gates *are* all manner of pleasant *fruits,* new and old, *which* I have laid up for thee, O my beloved.

MANEH

- **A weight.**
- **Rendered pound.**

  Ne 7:71–72

  1Ki 10:17 — And he made three hundred shields of beaten gold; three pound of gold went to one shield: and the king put them in the house of the forest of Lebanon.

  Ezr 2:69 — They gave after their ability unto the treasure of the work threescore and one thousand drams of gold, and five thousand pound of silver, and one hundred priests' garments.

- **Equal to one hundred shekels.**

  1Ki 10:17 — And he made three hundred shields of beaten gold; three pound of gold went to one shield: and the king put them in the house of the forest of Lebanon.

  2Ch 9:16 — And three hundred shields *made he of* beaten gold: three hundred *shekels* of gold went to one shield. And the king put them in the house of the forest of Lebanon.

  See: Weights

MANGER

Lk 2:7 — And she brought forth her firstborn son, and wrapped him in swaddling clothes, and laid him in a manger; because there was no room for them in the inn.

Lk 2:12 — And this *shall be* a sign unto you; Ye shall find the babe wrapped in swaddling clothes, lying in a manger.

Lk 2:16 — And they came with haste, and found Mary, and Joseph, and the babe lying in a manger.

- **Rendered stall.**

  Lk 13:15 — The Lord then answered him, and said, *Thou* hypocrite, doth not each one of you on the sabbath loose his ox or *his* ass from the stall, and lead *him* away to watering?

MANNA

Ex 16:4–35; Nu 11:6–10

Dt 8:3 — And he humbled thee, and suffered thee to hunger, and fed thee with manna, which thou knewest not, neither did thy fathers know; that he might make thee know that man doth not live by bread only, but by every *word* that proceedeth out of the mouth of the LORD doth man live.

Dt 8:16 — Who fed thee in the wilderness with manna, which thy fathers knew not, that he might humble thee, and that he might prove thee, to do thee good at thy latter end;

Jos 5:12 — And the manna ceased on the morrow after they had eaten of the old corn of the land; neither had the children of Israel manna any more; but they did eat of the fruit of the land of Canaan that year.

Ne 9:20 — Thou gavest also thy good spirit to instruct them, and withheldest not thy manna from their mouth, and gavest them water for their thirst.

Ps 78:24 — And had rained down manna upon them to eat, and had given them of the corn of heaven.

Jn 6:31 — Our fathers did eat manna in the desert; as it is written, He gave them bread from heaven to eat.

Jn 6:49 — Your fathers did eat manna in the wilderness, and are dead.

Jn 6:58 — This is that bread which came down from heaven: not as your fathers did eat manna, and are dead: he that eateth of this bread shall live for ever.

- **Preserved in the ark of the testimony.**

  Ex 16:33 — And Moses said unto Aaron, Take a pot, and put an omer full of manna therein, and lay it up before the LORD, to be kept for your generations.

  Heb 9:4 — Which had the golden censer, and the ark of the covenant overlaid round about with gold, wherein *was* the golden pot that had manna, and Aaron's rod that budded, and the tables of the covenant;

- **Figurative.**

  Jn 6:48–51

  1Co 10:3 — And did all eat the same spiritual meat;

  Rev 2:17 — He that hath an ear, let him hear what the Spirit saith unto the churches; To him that overcometh will I give to eat of the hidden manna, and will give him a white stone, and in the stone a new name written, which no man knoweth saving he that receiveth *it.*

MANNERS

• Social customs.

• Obeisance to strangers.

Ge 18:2 — And he lift up his eyes and looked, and, lo, three men stood by him: and when he saw *them,* he ran to meet them from the tent door, and bowed himself toward the ground,

Ge 19:1 — And there came two angels to Sodom at even; and Lot sat in the gate of Sodom: and Lot seeing *them* rose up to meet them; and he bowed himself with his face toward the ground;

• Standing while guests eat.

Ge 18:8 — And he took butter, and milk, and the calf which he had dressed, and set *it* before them; and he stood by them under the tree, and they did eat.

• Standing in presence of superiors.

Ge 31:35 — And she said to her father, Let it not displease my lord that I cannot rise up before thee; for the custom of women is upon me. And he searched, but found not the images.

Job 29:8 — The young men saw me, and hid themselves: and the aged arose, *and* stood up.

• Standing of the aged.

Le 19:32 — Thou shalt rise up before the hoary head, and honour the face of the old man, and fear thy God: I *am* the LORD.

• Courteousness enjoined.

1Pe 3:8 — Finally, *be ye* all of one mind, having compassion one of another, love as brethren, *be* pitiful, *be* courteous:

• Rules for guests.

Pr 23:1–2

1Co 10:27 — If any of them that believe not bid you *to a feast,* and ye be disposed to go; whatsoever is set before you, eat, asking no question for conscience sake.

See: Salutations

MANOAH • A Danite of Zorah and father of Samson.

Jgs 13:2–24

MANSERVANT **See: Servant**

MANSION

• Figurative.

Jn 14:2 — In my Father's house are many mansions: if *it were* not so, I would have told you. I go to prepare a place for you.

MANSLAUGHTER

See: Fratricide
See: Homicide
See: Regicide

MANSLAYER

See: Cities of Refuge
See: Homicide

MANTLE

• Rent in token of grief.

Ezr 9:3 — And when I heard this thing, I rent my garment and my mantle, and plucked off the hair of my head and of my beard, and sat down astonied.

Job 1:20 — Then Job arose, and rent his mantle, and shaved his head, and fell down upon the ground, and worshipped,

Job 2:12 — And when they lifted up their eyes afar off, and knew him not, they lifted up their voice, and wept; and they rent every one his mantle, and sprinkled dust upon their heads toward heaven.

• Of Elijah.

2Ki 2:13–14

1Ki 19:19 — So he departed thence, and found Elisha the son of Shaphat, who *was* plowing *with* twelve yoke *of oxen* before him, and he with the twelfth: and Elijah passed by him, and cast his mantle upon him.

2Ki 2:8 — And Elijah took his mantle, and wrapped *it* together, and smote the waters, and they were divided hither and thither, so that they two went over on dry ground.

See: Dress

MANURE

• Used as fertilizer.

Lk 14:34–35

Isa 25:10 — For in this mountain shall the hand of the LORD rest, and Moab shall be trodden down under him, even as straw is trodden down for the dunghill.

Lk 13:8 — And he answering said unto him, Lord, let it alone this year also, till I shall dig about it, and dung *it:*

MAON

• A city allotted to Judah.

Jos 15:55 — Maon, Carmel, and Ziph, and Juttah,

• Dwelling place of Nabal.

1Sa 25:2 — And *there was* a man in Maon, whose possessions *were* in Carmel; and the man *was* very great, and he had three thousand sheep, and a thousand goats: and he was shearing his sheep in Carmel.

• David with his insurgents encamps near.

1Sa 23:24–25

• Uzziah engages in war against the people of, called Mehunims.

2Ch 26:7 — And God helped him against the Philistines, and against the Arabians that dwelt in Gurbaal, and the Mehunims.

MARAH • The first station of the Israelites, where Moses made the bitter waters sweet.

Ex 15:22–25; Nu 33:8–9

MARALAH • A landmark on the boundary of Zebulun.

Jos 19:11 — And their border went up toward the sea, and Maralah, and reached to Dabbasheth, and reached to the river that *is* before Jokneam;

MARBLE

• In the temple.

1Ch 29:2 — Now I have prepared with all my might for the house of my God the gold for *things to be made* of gold, and the silver for *things* of silver, and the brass for *things* of brass, the iron for *things* of iron, and wood for *things* of wood; onyx stones, and *stones* to be set, glistering stones, and of divers colours, and all manner of precious stones, and marble stones in abundance.

• Pillars of.

Est 1:6 — *Where were* white, green, and blue, *hangings,* fastened with cords of fine linen and purple to silver rings and pillars of marble: the beds *were of* gold and silver, upon a pavement of red, and blue, and white, and black, marble.

SS 5:15 — His legs *are as* pillars of marble, set upon sockets of fine gold: his countenance *is* as Lebanon, excellent as the cedars.

• Merchandise of.

Rev 18:12 — The merchandise of gold, and silver, and precious stones, and of pearls, and fine linen, and purple, and silk, and scarlet, and all thyine wood, and all manner vessels of ivory, and all manner vessels of most precious wood, and of brass, and iron, and marble,

• Mosaics of.

Est 1:6 — *Where were* white, green, and blue, *hangings,* fastened with cords of fine linen and purple to silver rings and pillars of marble: the beds *were of* gold and silver, upon a pavement of red, and blue, and white, and black, marble.

MARESHAH

• A city of Judah.

2Ch 14:9–10

Jos 15:44 — And Keilah, and Achzib, and Mareshah; nine cities with their villages:

2Ch 11:8 — And Gath, and Mareshah, and Ziph,

• Birthplace of Eliezer the prophet.

2Ch 20:37 — Then Eliezer the son of Dodavah of Mareshah prophesied against Jehoshaphat, saying, Because thou hast joined thyself with Ahaziah, the LORD hath broken thy works. And the ships were broken, that they were not able to go to Tarshish.

• Prophecy concerning.

Mic 1:15 — Yet will I bring an heir unto thee, O inhabitant of Mareshah: he shall come unto Adullam the glory of Israel.

• Father of Hebron.

1Ch 2:42 — Now the sons of Caleb the brother of Jerahmeel *were,* Mesha his firstborn, which was the father of Ziph; and the sons of Mareshah the father of Hebron.

• A son of, or possibly a city founded by, Laadah.

1Ch 4:21 — The sons of Shelah the son of Judah *were,* Er the father of Lecah, and Laadah the father of Mareshah, and the families of the house of them that wrought fine linen, of the house of Ashbea,

MARINER

1Ki 9:27 — And Hiram sent in the navy his servants, shipmen that had knowledge of the sea, with the servants of Solomon.

2Ch 8:18 — And Huram sent him by the hands of his servants ships, and servants that had knowledge of the sea; and they went with the servants of Solomon to Ophir, and took thence four hundred and fifty talents of gold, and brought *them* to king Solomon.

Isa 42:10 — Sing unto the LORD a new song, *and* his praise from the end of the earth, ye that go down to the sea, and all that is therein; the isles, and the inhabitants thereof.

Eze 27:27 — Thy riches, and thy fairs, thy merchandise, thy mariners, and thy pilots, thy calkers, and the occupiers of thy merchandise, and all thy men of war, that *are* in thee, and in all thy company which *is* in the midst of thee, shall fall into the midst of the seas in the day of thy ruin.

• Perils of.

Ps 107:23–30; Ac 27:17–44

Jnh 1:5 — Then the mariners were afraid, and cried every man unto his god, and cast forth the wares that *were* in the ship into the sea, to lighten *it* of them. But Jonah was gone down into the sides of the ship; and he lay, and was fast asleep.

• Cowardice of.

Ac 27:30 — And as the shipmen were about to flee out of the ship, when they had let down the boat into the sea, under colour as though they would have cast anchors out of the foreship,

See: Commerce

See: Ship

MARK

• A nephew of Barnabas.

Col 4:10 — Aristarchus my fellowprisoner saluteth you, and Marcus, sister's son to Barnabas, (touching whom ye received commandments: if he come unto you, receive him;)

• A disciple of Jesus.

Ac 12:12 — And when he had considered *the thing,* he came to the house of Mary the mother of John, whose surname was Mark; where many were gathered together praying.

Ac 12:25 — And Barnabas and Saul returned from Jerusalem, when they had fulfilled *their* ministry, and took with them John, whose surname was Mark.

Ac 13:5 — And when they were at Salamis, they preached the word of God in the synagogues of the Jews: and they had also John to *their* minister.

Ac 13:13 — Now when Paul and his company loosed from Paphos, they came to Perga in Pamphylia: and John departing from them returned to Jerusalem.

• Paul and Barnabas contend concerning.

Ac 15:36–39

• A convert of Peter.

1Pe 5:13 — The *church that is* at Babylon, elected together with *you,* saluteth you; and *so doth* Marcus my son.

• Fellow-worker with Paul at Rome.

Col 4:10–11

2Ti 4:11 — Only Luke is with me. Take Mark, and bring him with thee: for he is profitable to me for the ministry.

Phm 1:24 — Marcus, Aristarchus, Demas, Lucas, my fellowlabourers.

MARKET

• A place for general merchandise.

• Hell at gates.

✦See: Gates

• Judgment seat at.

Ac 16:19 — And when her masters saw that the hope of their gains was gone, they caught Paul and Silas, and drew *them* into the marketplace unto the rulers,

• Traffic of, in Tyre, consisted of.

Eze 27:13–25

• horses.
• horsemen.
• mules.
• horns.
• ivory and ebony.
• emeralds.
• purple.
• broidered wares and linen and costly apparel.
• coral.
• agate.
• honey.
• balm.
• wine.
• wool.
• oil.
• cassia.
• calamus.
• charioteers' clothing.
• lambs, rams, goats.
• precious stones and gold.
• spices.

MAROTH

• A city of Judah.

Mic 1:12 — For the inhabitant of Maroth waited carefully for good: but evil came down from the LORD unto the gate of Jerusalem.

MARRIAGE

• Consanguineous, Abraham and Sarah.

Ge 20:9–16

Ge 11:29 — And Abram and Nahor took them wives: the name of Abram's wife *was* Sarai; and the name of Nahor's wife, Milcah, the daughter of Haran, the father of Milcah, and the father of Iscah.

Ge 12:13 — Say, I pray thee, thou *art* my sister: that it may be well with me for thy sake; and my soul shall live because of thee.

Ge 20:3 — But God came to Abimelech in a dream by night, and said to him, Behold, thou *art but* a dead man, for the woman which thou hast taken; for she *is* a man's wife.

• Isaac and Rebekah.

Ge 24:3–4

Ge 24:67 — And Isaac brought her into his mother Sarah's tent, and took Rebekah, and she became his wife; and he loved her: and Isaac was comforted after his mother's *death.*

Ge 28:2 — Arise, go to Padan-aram, to the house of Bethuel thy mother's father; and take thee a wife from thence of the daughters of Laban thy mother's brother.

• Jacob and his wives.

Ge 29:15–30

• Levirate, the brother required to marry a brother's widow.

Dt 25:5–10; Mk 12:19–23

Ge 38:8 — And Judah said unto Onan, Go in unto thy brother's wife, and marry her, and raise up seed to thy brother.

Ge 38:11 — Then said Judah to Tamar his daughter in law, Remain a widow at thy father's house, till Shelah my son be grown: for he said, Lest peradventure he die also, as his brethren *did.* And Tamar went and dwelt in her father's house.

Ru 4:5 — Then said Boaz, What day thou buyest the field of the hand of Naomi, thou must buy *it* also of Ruth the Moabitess, the wife of the dead, to raise up the name of the dead upon his inheritance.

Mt 22:24 — Saying, Master, Moses said, If a man die, having no children, his brother shall marry his wife, and raise up seed unto his brother.

Lk 20:28 — Saying, Master, Moses wrote unto us, If any man's brother die, having a wife, and he die without children, that his brother should take his wife, and raise up seed unto his brother.

• Parents contract for their children.

• Hagar selects a wife for Ishmael.

Ge 21:21 — And he dwelt in the wilderness of Paran: and his mother took him a wife out of the land of Egypt.

• Abraham for Isaac.

Ge 24:1–67

• Laban arranges for his daughters' marriage.

Ge 29:1–35

• Samson asks his parents to procure him a wife.

Jgs 14:2 — And he came up, and told his father and his mother, and said, I have seen a woman in Timnath of the daughters of the Philistines: now therefore get her for me to wife.

• Parents' consent required in the Mosaic law.

Ex 22:17 — If her father utterly refuse to give her unto him, he shall pay money according to the dowry of virgins.

• Presents given to parents to secure their favor.

Ge 24:53 — And the servant brought forth jewels of silver, and jewels of gold, and raiment, and gave *them* to Rebekah: he gave also to her brother and to her mother precious things.

Ge 34:12 — Ask me never so much dowry and gift, and I will give according as ye shall say unto me: but give me the damsel to wife.

Dt 22:29 — Then the man that lay with her shall give unto the damsel's father fifty *shekels* of silver, and she shall be his wife; because he hath humbled her, he may not put her away all his days.

1Sa 18:25 — And Saul said, Thus shall ye say to David, The king desireth not any dowry, but an hundred foreskins of the Philistines, to be avenged of the king's enemies. But Saul thought to make David fall by the hand of the Philistines.

Hos 3:2 — So I bought her to me for fifteen *pieces* of silver, and *for* an homer of barley, and an half homer of barley:

• Nuptial feasts.

Mt 22:11–12

Ge 29:22 — And Laban gathered together all the men of the place, and made a feast.

Jgs 14:12 — And Samson said unto them, I will now put forth a riddle unto you: if ye can certainly declare it me within the seven days of the feast, and find *it* out, then I will give you thirty sheets and thirty change of garments:

Est 2:18 — Then the king made a great feast unto all his princes and his servants, *even* Esther's feast; and he made a release to the provinces, and gave gifts, according to the state of the king.

• Jesus present at.

Jn 2:1–5

• Ceremony attested by witnesses.

Ru 4:1–11; Isa 8:1–3

• Bridegroom exempt one year from military duty.

Dt 24:5 — When a man hath taken a new wife, he shall not go out to war, neither shall he be charged with any business: *but* he shall be free at home one year, and shall cheer up his wife which he hath taken.

• Bridal ornaments.

Isa 49:18 — Lift up thine eyes round about, and behold: all these gather themselves together, *and* come to thee. *As* I live, saith the LORD, thou shalt surely clothe thee with them all, as with an ornament, and bind them *on thee,* as a bride *doeth.*

Jer 2:32 — Can a maid forget her ornaments, *or* a bride her attire? yet my people have forgotten me days without number.

• Bridal presents.

Ge 24:53 — And the servant brought forth jewels of silver, and jewels of gold, and raiment, and gave *them* to Rebekah: he gave also to her brother and to her mother precious things.

Ps 45:12 — And the daughter of Tyre *shall be there* with a gift; *even* the rich among the people shall intreat thy favour.

• Herald preceded the bridegroom.

Mt 25:6 — And at midnight there was a cry made, Behold, the bridegroom cometh; go ye out to meet him.

• Wedding robes adorned with jewels.

Isa 61:10 — I will greatly rejoice in the LORD, my soul shall be joyful in my God; for he hath clothed me with the garments of salvation, he hath covered me with the robe of righteousness, as a bridegroom decketh *himself* with ornaments, and as a bride adorneth *herself* with her jewels.

• Wives obtained by purchase.

Ge 29:20 — And Jacob served seven years for Rachel; and they seemed unto him *but* a few days, for the love he had to her.

Ru 4:10 — Moreover Ruth the Moabitess, the wife of Mahlon, have I purchased to be my wife, to raise up the name of the dead upon his inheritance, that the name of the dead be not cut off from among his brethren, and from the gate of his place: ye *are* witnesses this day.

Hos 3:2 — So I bought her to me for fifteen *pieces* of silver, and *for* an homer of barley, and an half homer of barley:

Hos 12:12 — And Jacob fled into the country of Syria, and Israel served for a wife, and for a wife he kept *sheep.*

• Wives obtained by kidnapping.

Jgs 21:21–23

• Given by Kings.

1Sa 17:25 — And the men of Israel said, Have ye seen this man that is come up? surely to defy Israel is he come up: and it shall be, *that* the man who killeth him, the king will enrich him with great riches, and will give him his daughter, and make his father's house free in Israel.

1Sa 18:17 — And Saul said to David, Behold my elder daughter Merab, her will I give thee to wife: only be thou valiant for me, and fight the LORD's battles. For Saul said, Let not mine hand be upon him, but let the hand of the Philistines be upon him.

1Sa 18:21 — And Saul said, I will give him her, that she may be a snare to him, and that the hand of the Philistines may be against him. Wherefore Saul said to David, Thou shalt this day be my son in law in *the one of* the twain.

• Daughters given in, as rewards of valor.

Jgs 1:12 — And Caleb said, He that smiteth Kirjath-sepher, and taketh it, to him will I give Achsah my daughter to wife.

1Sa 17:25 — And the men of Israel said, Have ye seen this man that is come up? surely to defy Israel is he come up: and it shall be, *that* the man who killeth him, the king will enrich him with great riches, and will give him his daughter, and make his father's house free in Israel.

1Sa 18:27 — Wherefore David arose and went, he and his men, and slew of the Philistines two hundred men; and David brought their foreskins, and they gave them in full tale to the king, that he might be the king's son in law. And Saul gave him Michal his daughter to wife.

• Wives taken by edict.

Est 2:2–4, 8–14

• David gave one hundred Philistine foreskins for a wife.

2Sa 3:14 — And David sent messengers to Ish-bosheth Saul's son, saying, Deliver *me* my wife Michal, which I espoused to me for an hundred foreskins of the Philistines.

• Wives among the Israelites must be Israelites.

Dt 7:3–4; Ezr 9:1–2; Ne 13:26–27

Ex 34:16 — And thou take of their daughters unto thy sons, and their daughters go a whoring after their gods, and make thy sons go a whoring after their gods.

1Ch 23:22 — And Eleazar died, and had no sons, but daughters: and their brethren the sons of Kish took them.

Ezr 9:12 — Now therefore give not your daughters unto their sons, neither take their daughters unto your sons, nor seek their peace or their wealth for ever: that ye may be strong, and eat the good of the land, and leave *it* for an inheritance to your children for ever.

Ne 10:30 — And that we would not give our daughters unto the people of the land, nor take their daughters for our sons:

Mal 2:11 — Judah hath dealt treacherously, and an abomination is committed in Israel and in Jerusalem; for Judah hath profaned the holiness of the LORD which he loved, and hath married the daughter of a strange god.

1Co 7:39 — The wife is bound by the law as long as her husband liveth; but if her husband be dead, she is at liberty to be married to whom she will; only in the Lord.

2Co 6:14 — Be ye not unequally yoked together with unbelievers: for what fellowship hath righteousness with unrighteousness? and what communion hath light with darkness?

• Betrothal a quasi-marriage.

Mt 1:18 — Now the birth of Jesus Christ was on this wise: When as his mother Mary was espoused to Joseph, before they came together, she was found with child of the Holy Ghost.

Lk 1:27 — To a virgin espoused to a man whose name was Joseph, of the house of David; and the virgin's name *was* Mary.

• Betrothal made with the spirit.

Eze 16:8 — Now when I passed by thee, and looked upon thee, behold, thy time *was* the time of love; and I spread my skirt over thee, and covered thy nakedness: yea, I sware unto thee, and entered into a covenant with thee, saith the Lord GOD, and thou becamest mine.

• Celibacy deplored.

Jgs 11:38 — And he said, Go. And he sent her away *for* two months: and she went with her companions, and bewailed her virginity upon the mountains.

Isa 4:1 — And in that day seven women shall take hold of one man, saying, We will eat our own bread, and wear our own apparel: only let us be called by thy name, to take away our reproach.

Jer 16:9 — For thus saith the LORD of hosts, the God of Israel; Behold, I will cause to cease out of this place in your eyes, and in your days, the voice of mirth, and the voice of gladness, the voice of the bridegroom, and the voice of the bride.

• Celibacy advised.

1Co 7:7–8, 24–40

• Obligations under, inferior to duty to God.

Dt 13:6–10

Mt 19:29 — And every one that hath forsaken houses, or brethren, or sisters, or father, or mother, or wife, or children, or lands, for my name's sake, shall receive an hundredfold, and shall inherit everlasting life.

Lk 14:26 — If any *man* come to me, and hate not his father, and mother, and wife, and children, and brethren, and sisters, yea, and his own life also, he cannot be my disciple.

• Not binding after death.

Mt 22:29–30; Mk 12:24–25

See: Bride

See: Bridegroom

• Unclassified scripture relating to.

Ge 2:23–24; Ex 22:16–17; Le 18:6–18; 20:19–21; 21:13–15; Dt 21:10–14; 24:1–5; Hos 2:19–20; Mal 2:13–16; Mt 5:31–32; 19:2–9; Mk 6:17–18; 10:2–12; Ro 7:1–3; 1Co 7:1–40; 11:11–12

Le 20:14 — And if a man take a wife and her mother, it *is* wickedness: they shall be burnt with fire, both he and they; that there be no wickedness among you.

Le 20:17 — And if a man shall take his sister, his father's daughter, or his mother's daughter, and see her nakedness, and she see his nakedness; it *is* a wicked thing; and they shall be cut off in the sight of their people: he hath uncovered his sister's nakedness; he shall bear his iniquity.

Le 21:1 — And the LORD said unto Moses, Speak unto the priests the sons of Aaron, and say unto them, There shall none be defiled for the dead among his people:

Le 21:7 — They shall not take a wife *that is* a whore, or profane; neither shall they take a woman put away from her husband: for he *is* holy unto his God.

Nu 36:8 — And every daughter, that possesseth an inheritance in any tribe of the children of Israel, shall be wife unto one of the family of the tribe of her father, that the children of Israel may enjoy every man the inheritance of his fathers.

Dt 22:30 — A man shall not take his father's wife, nor discover his father's skirt.

Pr 18:22 — *Whoso* findeth a wife findeth a good *thing*, and obtaineth favour of the LORD.

Pr 21:9 — *It is* better to dwell in a corner of the housetop, than with a brawling woman in a wide house.

Pr 21:19 — *It is* better to dwell in the wilderness, than with a contentious and an angry woman.

Jer 29:6 — Take ye wives, and beget sons and daughters; and take wives for your sons, and give your daughters to husbands, that they may bear sons and daughters; that ye may be increased there, and not diminished.

Lk 16:18 — Whosoever putteth away his wife, and marrieth another, committeth adultery: and whosoever marrieth her that is put away from *her* husband committeth adultery.

1Co 6:16 — What? know ye not that he which is joined to an harlot is one body? for two, saith he, shall be one flesh.

1Co 9:5 — Have we not power to lead about a sister, a wife, as well as other apostles, and *as* the brethren of the Lord, and Cephas?

1Ti 3:2 — A bishop then must be blameless, the husband of one wife, vigilant, sober, of good behaviour, given to hospitality, apt to teach;

1Ti 3:12 — Let the deacons be the husbands of one wife, ruling their children and their own houses well.

1Ti 4:1 — Now the Spirit speaketh expressly, that in the latter times some shall depart from the faith, giving heed to seducing spirits, and doctrines of devils;

1Ti 4:3 — Forbidding to marry, *and commanding* to abstain from meats, which God hath created to be received with thanksgiving of them which believe and know the truth.

1Ti 5:14 — I will therefore that the younger women marry, bear children, guide the house, give none occasion to the adversary to speak reproachfully.

Heb 13:4 — Marriage *is* honourable in all, and the bed undefiled: but whoremongers and adulterers God will judge.

- **Figurative.**

Isa 62:4–5; Hos 2:19–20; Eph 5:30–32; Rev 19:7–9

Isa 54:5 — For thy Maker *is* thine husband; the LORD of hosts *is* his name; and thy Redeemer the Holy One of Israel; The God of the whole earth shall he be called.

Jer 3:14 — Turn, O backsliding children, saith the LORD; for I am married unto you: and I will take you one of a city, and two of a family, and I will bring you to Zion:

Jer 31:32 — Not according to the covenant that I made with their fathers in the day *that* I took them by the hand to bring them out of the land of Egypt; which my covenant they brake, although I was an husband unto them, saith the LORD:

Hos 1:2 — The beginning of the word of the LORD by Hosea. And the LORD said to Hosea, Go, take unto thee a wife of whoredoms and children of whoredoms: for the land hath committed great whoredom, *departing* from the LORD.

- **Parables from.**

Mt 25:1–10

Mt 22:2 — The kingdom of heaven is like unto a certain king, which made a marriage for his son,

See: Divorce

See: Husband

See: Wife

MARS' HILL • A hill in Athens.

Ac 17:19–34

MARTHA

- **Sister of Mary and Lazarus.**

Jn 11:1 — Now a certain *man* was sick, *named* Lazarus, of Bethany, the town of Mary and her sister Martha.

- **Ministers to Jesus.**

Lk 10:38–42

Jn 12:2 — There they made him a supper; and Martha served: but Lazarus was one of them that sat at the table with him.

- **Beloved by Jesus.**

Jn 11:5 — Now Jesus loved Martha, and her sister, and Lazarus.

See: Lazarus

See: Mary

MARTYRDOM

Mt 10:21–22; 23:34–35; Lk 21:16–17; Rev 6:9–11; 11:7–12

Ps 44:22 — Yea, for thy sake are we killed all the day long; we are counted as sheep for the slaughter.

Mt 10:39 — He that findeth his life shall lose it: and he that loseth his life for my sake shall find it.

Mt 16:25 — For whosoever will save his life shall lose it: and whosoever will lose his life for my sake shall find it.

Mt 24:9 — Then shall they deliver you up to be afflicted, and shall kill you: and ye shall be hated of all nations for my name's sake.

Mk 13:12 — Now the brother shall betray the brother to death, and the father the son; and children shall rise up against *their* parents, and shall cause them to be put to death.

Lk 9:24 — For whosoever will save his life shall lose it: but whosoever will lose his life for my sake, the same shall save it.

Lk 11:50 — That the blood of all the prophets, which was shed from the foundation of the world, may be required of this generation;

Jn 12:25 — He that loveth his life shall lose it; and he that hateth his life in this world shall keep it unto life eternal.

Ro 8:36 — As it is written, For thy sake we are killed all the day long; we are accounted as sheep for the slaughter.

1Co 13:3 — And though I bestow all my goods to feed *the poor,* and though I give my body to be burned, and have not charity, it profiteth me nothing.

Rev 12:11 — And they overcame him by the blood of the Lamb, and by the word of their testimony; and they loved not their lives unto the death.

Rev 16:6 — For they have shed the blood of saints and prophets, and thou hast given them blood to drink; for they are worthy.

Rev 17:6 — And I saw the woman drunken with the blood of the saints, and with the blood of the martyrs of Jesus: and when I saw her, I wondered with great admiration.

See: Persecution

• Instances of.

• Abel.
Ge 4:3–8

• Prophets slain by Jezebel.
1Ki 18:4, 13

• Zechariah.
2Ch 24:21–22

• John the Baptist.
Mk 6:18–28

• Jesus.

See: Jesus, Death of

See: Jesus, History of

See: Jesus, Rejected

See: Jesus, Sufferings of

• Stephen.
Ac 7:58–60

• James the apostle.
Ac 12:2

• The prophets.
Mt 22:6; 23:35; Ro 11:3; 1Th 2:15; Heb 11:32–37

MARY

• The mother of Jesus.
Lk 1:26–38; 2:5–19

Mt 1:16 — And Jacob begat Joseph the husband of Mary, of whom was born Jesus, who is called Christ.

• Visits her cousin Elisabeth.
Lk 1:39–56

• Attends the feast at Jerusalem, misses Jesus, seeks and finds him in the temple.
Lk 2:48–51

• Is present with Jesus at a marriage in Cana of Galilee.
Jn 2:1–10

• Seeks Jesus when he is teaching in a house.
Mt 12:46–47

Mk 3:31 — There came then his brethren and his mother, and, standing without, sent unto him, calling him.

Lk 8:19 — Then came to him *his* mother and his brethren, and could not come at him for the press.

• Present at the cross.
Jn 19:25–27

• Is committed to the care of John.

Jn 19:27 — Then saith he to the disciple, Behold thy mother! And from that hour that disciple took her unto his own *home.*

• Dwells with the disciples in Jerusalem.

Ac 1:14 — These all continued with one accord in prayer and supplication, with the women, and Mary the mother of Jesus, and with his brethren.

• Prophecies concerning.

Isa 7:14 — Therefore the Lord himself shall give you a sign; Behold, a virgin shall conceive, and bear a son, and shall call his name Immanuel.

Lk 2:35 — (Yea, a sword shall pierce through thy own soul also,) that the thoughts of many hearts may be revealed.

• Magdalene.

• Possessed of devils; delivered by Jesus.
Lk 8:2–3

Mk 16:9 — Now when *Jesus* was risen early the first *day* of the week, he appeared first to Mary Magdalene, out of whom he had cast seven devils.

• Present at the crucifixion.

Mt 27:56 — Among which was Mary Magdalene, and Mary the mother of James and Joses, and the mother of Zebedee's children.

Mk 15:40 — There were also women looking on afar off: among whom was Mary Magdalene, and Mary the mother of James the less and of Joses, and Salome;

Jn 19:25 — Now there stood by the cross of Jesus his mother, and his mother's sister, Mary the *wife* of Cleophas, and Mary Magdalene.

• Present at the sepulchre.
Mt 28:1–7; Mk 15:47–16:7; Lk 23:55–24:7; Jn 20:11–13

Mt 27:61 — And there was Mary Magdalene, and the other Mary, sitting over against the sepulchre.

Jn 20:1 — The first *day* of the week cometh Mary Magdalene early, when it was yet dark, unto the sepulchre, and seeth the stone taken away from the sepulchre.

• Recognizes Jesus after the resurrection.
Mt 28:8–10; Jn 20:14–18

Mk 16:9 — Now when *Jesus* was risen early the first *day* of the week, he appeared first to Mary Magdalene, out of whom he had cast seven devils.

• Sister of Mary, the mother of Jesus, and wife of Cleophas.

Jn 19:25 — Now there stood by the cross of Jesus his mother, and his mother's sister, Mary the *wife* of Cleophas, and Mary Magdalene.

• Mother of James and Joses.

Mt 27:56 — Among which was Mary Magdalene, and Mary the mother of James and Joses, and the mother of Zebedee's children.

Mk 15:40 — There were also women looking on afar off: among whom was Mary Magdalene, and Mary the mother of James the less and of Joses, and Salome;

Jn 19:25 — Now there stood by the cross of Jesus his mother, and his mother's sister, Mary the *wife* of Cleophas, and Mary Magdalene.

• At the sepulchre.

Mt 27:61 — And there was Mary Magdalene, and the other Mary, sitting over against the sepulchre.

Mk 15:47 — And Mary Magdalene and Mary *the mother* of Joses beheld where he was laid.

• Assists in preparing the body of Jesus for burial.

Mt 28:1 — In the end of the sabbath, as it began to dawn toward the first *day* of the week, came Mary Magdalene and the other Mary to see the sepulchre.

Mk 16:1 — And when the sabbath was past, Mary Magdalene, and Mary the *mother* of James, and Salome, had bought sweet spices, that they might come and anoint him.

• A witness of the resurrection.

Lk 24:10 — It was Mary Magdalene, and Joanna, and Mary *the mother* of James, and other *women that were* with them, which told these things unto the apostles.

• Sister of Lazarus.

• Sits at Jesus' feet for instruction.

Lk 10:38–42

• Beloved of Jesus.

Jn 11:1 — Now a certain *man* was sick, *named* Lazarus, of Bethany, the town of Mary and her sister Martha.

Jn 11:5 — Now Jesus loved Martha, and her sister, and Lazarus.

• Anoints Jesus.

Mt 26:7–13; Mk 14:3–9

Jn 11:2 — (It was *that* Mary which anointed the Lord with ointment, and wiped his feet with her hair, whose brother Lazarus was sick.)

Jn 12:3 — Then took Mary a pound of ointment of spikenard, very costly, and anointed the feet of Jesus, and wiped his feet with her hair: and the house was filled with the odour of the ointment.

• Mother of Mark and sister of Barnabas.

Ac 12:12 — And when he had considered *the thing,* he came to the house of Mary the mother of John, whose surname was Mark; where many were gathered together praying.

Col 4:10 — Aristarchus my fellowprisoner saluteth you, and Marcus, sister's son to Barnabas, (touching whom ye received commandments: if he come unto you, receive him;)

• A Christian woman in Rome.

Ro 16:6 — Greet Mary, who bestowed much labour on us.

MASCHIL ⇒See: Music

MASH • Son of Aram.

Ge 10:23 — And the children of Aram; Uz, and Hul, and Gether, and Mash.

MASHAL

• Called also Mishal and Misheal.

• A Levitical city in Asher.

Jos 19:26 — And Alammelech, and Amad, and Misheal; and reacheth to Carmel westward, and to Shihor-libnath;

Jos 21:30 — And out of the tribe of Asher, Mishal with her suburbs, Abdon with her suburbs,

1Ch 6:74 — And out of the tribe of Asher; Mashal with her suburbs, and Abdon with her suburbs,

MASKING

• By Tamar.

Ge 38:14 — And she put her widow's garments off from her, and covered her with a vail, and wrapped herself, and sat in an open place, which *is* by the way to Timnath; for she saw that Shelah was grown, and she was not given unto him to wife.

MASON

• A trade in the time of David.

2Sa 5:11 — And Hiram king of Tyre sent messengers to David, and cedar trees, and carpenters, and masons: and they built David an house.

• A trade of later times.

2Ki 12:12 — And to masons, and hewers of stone, and to buy timber and hewed stone to repair the breaches of the house of the LORD, and for all that was laid out for the house to repair *it.*

2Ki 22:6 — Unto carpenters, and builders, and masons, and to buy timber and hewn stone to repair the house.

1Ch 14:1 — Now Hiram king of Tyre sent messengers to David, and timber of cedars, with masons and carpenters, to build him an house.

Ezr 3:7 — They gave money also unto the masons, and to the carpenters; and meat, and drink, and oil, unto them of Zidon, and to them of Tyre, to bring cedar trees from Lebanon to the sea of Joppa, according to the grant that they had of Cyrus king of Persia.

MASREKAH • A place in Edom.

Ge 36:36 — And Hadad died, and Samlah of Masrekah reigned in his stead.

1Ch 1:47 — And when Hadad was dead, Samlah of Masrekah reigned in his stead.

MASSA • Son of Ishmael.

Ge 25:14 — And Mishma, and Dumah, and Massa,

1Ch 1:30 — Mishma and Dumah, Massa, Hadad, and Tema,

MASSACRE

• Authorized by Moses.

Dt 20:13 — And when the LORD thy God hath delivered it into thine hands, thou shalt smite every male thereof with the edge of the sword:

Dt 20:16 — But of the cities of these people, which the LORD thy God doth give thee *for* an inheritance, thou shalt save alive nothing that breatheth:

- **Decree to destroy the Jews.**
  Est 3:1–15
- **Instances of.**
  - **Inhabitants of Heshbon.**
    Dt 2:34
  - **Inhabitants of Bashan.**
    Dt 3:6
  - **Inhabitants of Ai.**
    Jos 8:24–26
  - **Inhabitants of Hazor.**
    Jos 11:11–12
  - **Inhabitants of the cities of the seven kings.**
    Jos 10:28–40
  - **Midianites.**
    Nu 31:7–8
  - **Prophets of Baal.**
    1Ki 18:40
  - **Worshipers of Baal.**
    2Ki 10:18–28
  - **Sons of Ahab.**
    2Ki 10:1–8
  - **Seed royal of Athaliah.**
    2Ki 11:1
  - **Inhabitants of Tiphsah.**
    2Ki 15:16
  - **Edomites.**
    2Ki 14:7

See: Captive

MASSAH

- **An encampment of the Israelites.**

Ex 17:7 — And he called the name of the place Massah, and Meribah, because of the chiding of the children of Israel, and because they tempted the LORD, saying, Is the LORD among us, or not?

See: Meribah

MASTER

- **Jesus called.**

Jn 13:13–14

Mt 8:19 — And a certain scribe came, and said unto him, Master, I will follow thee whithersoever thou goest.

Mt 10:25 — It is enough for the disciple that he be as his master, and the servant as his lord. If they have called the master of the house Beelzebub, how much more *shall they call* them of his household?

Mt 23:8 — But be not ye called Rabbi: for one is your Master, *even* Christ; and all ye are brethren.

Mt 26:18 — And he said, Go into the city to such a man, and say unto him, The Master saith, My time is at hand; I will keep the passover at thy house with my disciples.

Mt 26:25 — Then Judas, which betrayed him, answered and said, Master, is it I? He said unto him, Thou hast said.

Mt 26:49 — And forthwith he came to Jesus, and said, Hail, master; and kissed him.

Mk 14:45 — And as soon as he was come, he goeth straightway to him, and saith, Master, master; and kissed him.

Lk 8:24 — And they came to him, and awoke him, saying, Master, master, we perish. Then he arose, and rebuked the wind and the raging of the water: and they ceased, and there was a calm.

- **Jesus prohibited the appellation.**

Mt 23:8 — But be not ye called Rabbi: for one is your Master, *even* Christ; and all ye are brethren.

- **Scriptures relating to masters of servants.**

Ex 21:20–21, 26–27; Dt 24:14–15; Job 31:13–15; Phm 1:10–16

Le 19:13 — Thou shalt not defraud thy neighbour, neither rob *him:* the wages of him that is hired shall not abide with thee all night until the morning.

Le 25:43 — Thou shalt not rule over him with rigour; but shalt fear thy God.

Dt 5:14 — But the seventh day *is* the sabbath of the LORD thy God: *in it* thou shalt not do any work, thou, nor thy son, nor thy daughter, nor thy manservant, nor thy maidservant, nor thine ox, nor thine ass, nor any of thy cattle, nor thy stranger that *is* within thy gates; that thy manservant and thy maidservant may rest as well as thou.

Pr 22:16 — He that oppresseth the poor to increase his *riches, and* he that giveth to the rich, *shall* surely *come* to want.

Pr 29:12 — If a ruler hearken to lies, all his servants *are* wicked.

Pr 29:21 — He that delicately bringeth up his servant from a child shall have him become *his* son at the length.

Jer 22:13 — Woe unto him that buildeth his house by unrighteousness, and his chambers by wrong; *that* useth his neighbour's service without wages, and giveth him not for his work;

Mal 3:5 — And I will come near to you to judgment; and I will be a swift witness against the sorcerers, and against the adulterers, and against false swearers, and against those that oppress the hireling in *his* wages, the widow, and the fatherless, and that turn aside the stranger *from his right,* and fear not me, saith the LORD of hosts.

Ro 4:4 — Now to him that worketh is the reward not reckoned of grace, but of debt.

Eph 6:9 — And, ye masters, do the same things unto them, forbearing threatening: knowing that your Master also is in heaven; neither is there respect of persons with him.

Col 4:1 — Masters, give unto *your* servants that which is just and equal; knowing that ye also have a Master in heaven.

1Ti 5:18 — For the scripture saith, Thou shalt not muzzle the ox that treadeth out the corn. And, The labourer *is* worthy of his reward.

Jas 5:4 — Behold, the hire of the labourers who have reaped down your fields, which is of you kept back by fraud, crieth: and the cries of them which have reaped are entered into the ears of the Lord of sabaoth.

↞**See: Servant**

- **Good.**
  - **Instances of.**
    - **Abraham.**

      Ge 18:19 — For I know him, that he will command his children and his household after him, and they shall keep the way of the LORD, to do justice and judgment; that the LORD may bring upon Abraham that which he hath spoken of him.
    - **Job.**

      Job 31:13–15
    - **The centurion.**

      Lk 7:2 — And a certain centurion's servant, who was dear unto him, was sick, and ready to die.
- **Unjust.**
  - **Instances of.**
    - **Sarah to Hagar.**

      Ge 16:6 — But Abram said unto Sarai, Behold, thy maid *is* in thy hand; do to her as it pleaseth thee. And when Sarai dealt hardly with her, she fled from her face.
    - **Laban to Jacob.**

      Ge 31:7 — And your father hath deceived me, and changed my wages ten times; but God suffered him not to hurt me.
    - **Potiphar's wife to Joseph.**

      Ge 39:7–20

MASTER WORKMAN

Pr 8:30 — Then I was by him, *as* one brought up *with him:* and I was daily *his* delight, rejoicing always before him;

1Co 3:10 — According to the grace of God which is given unto me, as a wise masterbuilder, I have laid the foundation, and another buildeth thereon. But let every man take heed how he buildeth thereupon.

- **Instances of.**
  - **Tubal-cain.**

    Ge 4:22
  - **Bezaleel.**

    Ex 31:2–11; 35:30–35
  - **Hiram.**

    1Ki 7:13–50; 2Ch 2:13–14; 4:11–18

↞**See: Art**

MASTERY

Ex 32:18 — And he said, *It is* not the voice of *them that* shout for mastery, neither *is it* the voice of *them that* cry for being overcome: *but* the noise of *them that* sing do I hear.

1Co 9:25 — And every man that striveth for the mastery is temperate in all things. Now they *do it* to obtain a corruptible crown; but we an incorruptible.

MATERIALISM

Ac 23:8 — For the Sadducees say that there is no resurrection, neither angel, nor spirit: but the Pharisees confess both.

↞**See: Infidelity**

MATRED • Mother of Mehetabel.

Ge 36:39 — And Baal-hanan the son of Achbor died, and Hadar reigned in his stead: and the name of his city *was* Pau; and his wife's name *was* Mehetabel, the daughter of Matred, the daughter of Mezahab.

1Ch 1:50 — And when Baal-hanan was dead, Hadad reigned in his stead: and the name of his city *was* Pai; and his wife's name *was* Mehetabel, the daughter of Matred, the daughter of Mezahab.

MATRI • A Benjamite.

1Sa 10:21 — When he had caused the tribe of Benjamin to come near by their families, the family of Matri was taken, and Saul the son of Kish was taken: and when they sought him, he could not be found.

MATTAN

- **A priest of Baal slain in the idol temple at Jerusalem.**

  2Ki 11:18 — And all the people of the land went into the house of Baal, and brake it down; his altars and his images brake they in pieces thoroughly, and slew Mattan the priest of Baal before the altars. And the priest appointed officers over the house of the LORD.

  2Ch 23:17 — Then all the people went to the house of Baal, and brake it down, and brake his altars and his images in pieces, and slew Mattan the priest of Baal before the altars.
- **Father of Shephatiah.**

  Jer 38:1 — Then Shephatiah the son of Mattan, and Gedaliah the son of Pashur, and Jucal the son of Shelemiah, and Pashur the son of Malchiah, heard the words that Jeremiah had spoken unto all the people, saying,

MATTANAH • A station of Israel.

Nu 21:18–19

MATTANIAH

- **Original name of Zedekiah, king of Judah.**

  2Ki 24:17 — And the king of Babylon made Mattaniah his father's brother king in his stead, and changed his name to Zedekiah.

  ↞**See: Zedekiah**
- **A Levite of the sons of Asaph.**

  2Ch 20:14 — Then upon Jahaziel the son of Zechariah, the son of Benaiah, the son of Jeiel, the son of Mattaniah, a Levite of the sons of Asaph, came the Spirit of the LORD in the midst of the congregation;

  Ne 12:8 — Moreover the Levites: Jeshua, Binnui, Kadmiel, Sherebiah, Judah, *and* Mattaniah, *which was* over the thanksgiving, he and his brethren.

• Son of Heman, who had charge of the ninth division of musicians.

1Ch 25:4 — Of Heman: the sons of Heman; Bukkiah, Mattaniah, Uzziel, Shebuel, and Jerimoth, Hananiah, Hanani, Eliathah, Giddalti, and Romamti-ezer, Joshbekashah, Mallothi, Hothir, *and* Mahazioth:

1Ch 25:16 — The ninth to Mattaniah, *he,* his sons, and his brethren, *were* twelve:

• Descendant of Asaph, who assisted in purifying the temple.

2Ch 29:13 — And of the sons of Elizaphan; Shimri, and Jeiel: and of the sons of Asaph; Zechariah, and Mattaniah:

• Four Israelites who divorced their Gentile wives after the captivity.

Ezr 10:26–27

Ezr 10:30 — And of the sons of Pahath-moab; Adna, and Chelal, Benaiah, Maaseiah, Mattaniah, Bezaleel, and Binnui, and Manasseh.

Ezr 10:37 — Mattaniah, Mattenai, and Jaasau,

• A Levite and father of Zaccur.

Ne 13:13 — And I made treasurers over the treasuries, Shelemiah the priest, and Zadok the scribe, and of the Levites, Pedaiah: and next to them *was* Hanan the son of Zaccur, the son of Mattaniah: for they were counted faithful, and their office *was* to distribute unto their brethren.

MATTATHA • An ancestor of Jesus.

Lk 3:31 — Which was *the son* of Melea, which was *the son* of Menan, which was *the son* of Mattatha, which was *the son* of Nathan, which was *the son* of David,

MATTATHAH • One of the family of Hashum.

Ezr 10:33 — Of the sons of Hashum; Mattenai, Mattathah, Zabad, Eliphelet, Jeremai, Manasseh, *and* Shimei.

MATTATHIAS • An ancestor of Jesus.

Lk 3:25–26

MATTENAI

• Two Israelites who put away their Gentile wives after the captivity.

Ezr 10:33 — Of the sons of Hashum; Mattenai, Mattathah, Zabad, Eliphelet, Jeremai, Manasseh, *and* Shimei.

Ezr 10:37 — Mattaniah, Mattenai, and Jaasau,

• A priest in the time of Joiakim.

Ne 12:19 — And of Joiarib, Mattenai; of Jedaiah, Uzzi;

MATTHAN • An ancestor of Jesus.

Mt 1:15 — And Eliud begat Eleazar; and Eleazar begat Matthan; and Matthan begat Jacob;

MATTHAT

• Father of Heli, and ancestor of Joseph.

Lk 3:24 — Which was *the son* of Matthat, which was *the son* of Levi, which was *the son* of Melchi, which was *the son* of Janna, which was *the son* of Joseph,

• Father of Jorim, and ancestor of Joseph.

Lk 3:29 — Which was *the son* of Jose, which was *the son* of Eliezer, which was *the son* of Jorim, which was *the son* of Matthat, which was *the son* of Levi,

MATTHEW

• Called also Levi.

• A receiver of customs.

• Becomes a disciple of Jesus.

Mt 9:9–10; Mk 2:14–15; Lk 5:27–29

Mt 10:3 — Philip, and Bartholomew; Thomas, and Matthew the publican; James *the son* of Alphaeus, and Lebbaeus, whose surname was Thaddaeus;

Mk 3:18 — And Andrew, and Philip, and Bartholomew, and Matthew, and Thomas, and James the *son* of Alphaeus, and Thaddaeus, and Simon the Canaanite,

Lk 6:15 — Matthew and Thomas, James the *son* of Alphaeus, and Simon called Zelotes,

Ac 1:13 — And when they were come in, they went up into an upper room, where abode both Peter, and James, and John, and Andrew, Philip, and Thomas, Bartholomew, and Matthew, James *the son* of Alphaeus, and Simon Zelotes, and Judas *the brother* of James.

MATTHIAS

• Surnamed Justus.

• Chosen as an apostle in the place of Judas.

Ac 1:15–26

MATTITHIAH

• A Levite who had charge of the baked offerings.

1Ch 9:31 — And Mattithiah, *one* of the Levites, who *was* the firstborn of Shallum the Korahite, had the set office over the things that were made in the pans.

• A Levite musician.

1Ch 15:18 — And with them their brethren of the second *degree,* Zechariah, Ben, and Jaaziel, and Shemiramoth, and Jehiel, and Unni, Eliab, and Benaiah, and Maaseiah, and Mattithiah, and Elipheleh, and Mikneiah, and Obed-edom, and Jeiel, the porters.

1Ch 15:21 — And Mattithiah, and Elipheleh, and Mikneiah, and Obed-edom, and Jeiel, and Azaziah, with harps on the Sheminith to excel.

1Ch 16:5 — Asaph the chief, and next to him Zechariah, Jeiel, and Shemiramoth, and Jehiel, and Mattithiah, and Eliab, and Benaiah, and Obed-edom: and Jeiel with psalteries and with harps; but Asaph made a sound with cymbals;

• A chief of the fourteenth division of temple musicians.

1Ch 25:3 — Of Jeduthun: the sons of Jeduthun; Gedaliah, and Zeri, and Jeshaiah, Hashabiah, and

Mattithiah, six, under the hands of their father Jeduthun, who prophesied with a harp, to give thanks and to praise the LORD.

1Ch 25:21 — The fourteenth to Mattithiah, *he,* his sons, and his brethren, *were* twelve:

• An Israelite who divorced his Gentile wife after the captivity.

Ezr 10:43 — Of the sons of Nebo; Jeiel, Mattithiah, Zabad, Zebina, Jadau, and Joel, Benaiah.

• A prince who stood by Ezra when he read the law to the people.

Ne 8:4 — And Ezra the scribe stood upon a pulpit of wood, which they had made for the purpose; and beside him stood Mattithiah, and Shema, and Anaiah, and Urijah, and Hilkiah, and Maaseiah, on his right hand; and on his left hand, Pedaiah, and Mishael, and Malchiah, and Hashum, and Hashbadana, Zechariah, *and* Meshullam.

MATTOCK

1Sa 13:20–21

Isa 7:25 — And *on* all hills that shall be digged with the mattock, there shall not come thither the fear of briers and thorns: but it shall be for the sending forth of oxen, and for the treading of lesser cattle.

MATURITY

Mt 13:1–30; 28:19–20; Heb 5:12–13

2Co 5:17 — Therefore if any man *be* in Christ, *he is* a new creature: old things are passed away; behold, all things are become new.

Eph 4:14 — That we *henceforth* be no more children, tossed to and fro, and carried about with every wind of doctrine, by the sleight of men, *and* cunning craftiness, whereby they lie in wait to deceive;

1Pe 2:2 — As newborn babes, desire the sincere milk of the word, that ye may grow thereby:

MAUL

Pr 25:18 — A man that beareth false witness against his neighbour *is* a maul, and a sword, and a sharp arrow.

MAZZAROTH

• Probably signs of the zodiac.

Job 38:32 — Canst thou bring forth Mazzaroth in his season? or canst thou guide Arcturus with his sons?

See: Music

ME-JARKON • A city in Dan.

Jos 19:46 — And Me-jarkon, and Rakkon, with the border before Japho.

MEAH • A tower in Jerusalem.

Ne 3:1 — Then Eliashib the high priest rose up with his brethren the priests, and they builded the sheep gate; they sanctified it, and set up the doors of it; even unto the tower of Meah they sanctified it, unto the tower of Hananeel.

Ne 12:39 — And from above the gate of Ephraim, and above the old gate, and above the fish gate, and the tower of Hananeel, and the tower of Meah, even unto the sheep gate: and they stood still in the prison gate.

MEAL

See: Eating

See: Food

MEASURE

• Equivalents of ancient measurement.

• Dry.

• Bushel, about a peck.

Mt 5:15 — Neither do men light a candle, and put it under a bushel, but on a candlestick; and it giveth light unto all that are in the house.

Mk 4:21 — And he said unto them, Is a candle brought to be put under a bushel, or under a bed? and not to be set on a candlestick?

Lk 11:33 — No man, when he hath lighted a candle, putteth *it* in a secret place, neither under a bushel, but on a candlestick, that they which come in may see the light.

• Cab, or kab, about two quarts.

2Ki 6:25 — And there was a great famine in Samaria: and, behold, they besieged it, until an ass's head was *sold* for fourscore *pieces* of silver, and the fourth part of a cab of dove's dung for five *pieces* of silver.

• Cor, equal to one homer or ten ephahs, equal to about eleven and one-ninth bushels.

1Ki 4:22 — And Solomon's provision for one day was thirty measures of fine flour, and threescore measures of meal,

1Ki 5:11 — And Solomon gave Hiram twenty thousand measures of wheat *for* food to his household, and twenty measures of pure oil: thus gave Solomon to Hiram year by year.

2Ch 2:10 — And, behold, I will give to thy servants, the hewers that cut timber, twenty thousand measures of beaten wheat, and twenty thousand measures of barley, and twenty thousand baths of wine, and twenty thousand baths of oil.

2Ch 27:5 — He fought also with the king of the Ammonites, and prevailed against them. And the children of Ammon gave him the same year an hundred talents of silver, and ten thousand measures of wheat, and ten thousand of barley. So much did the children of Ammon pay unto him, both the second year, and the third.

Ezr 7:22 — Unto an hundred talents of silver, and to an hundred measures of wheat, and to an hundred baths of wine, and to an hundred baths of oil, and salt without prescribing *how much.*

• Ephah, equal to three seah, and in liquid, to a bath, containing about a bushel and a half.

Eze 45:10–11; Zec 5:6–10

Ex 16:36 — Now an omer *is* the tenth *part* of an ephah.

Le 5:11 — But if he be not able to bring two turtledoves, or two young pigeons, then he that sinned shall bring for his offering the tenth part of an ephah of fine flour for a sin offering; he shall put no oil upon it, neither shall he put *any* frankincense thereon: for it *is* a sin offering.

Le 6:20 — This *is* the offering of Aaron and of his sons, which they shall offer unto the LORD in the day when he is anointed; the tenth part of an ephah of fine flour for a meat offering perpetual, half of it in the morning, and half thereof at night.

Le 19:36 — Just balances, just weights, a just ephah, and a just hin, shall ye have: I *am* the LORD your God, which brought you out of the land of Egypt.

Nu 5:15 — Then shall the man bring his wife unto the priest, and he shall bring her offering for her, the tenth *part* of an ephah of barley meal; he shall pour no oil upon it, nor put frankincense thereon; for it *is* an offering of jealousy, an offering of memorial, bringing iniquity to remembrance.

Nu 28:5 — And a tenth *part* of an ephah of flour for a meat offering, mingled with the fourth *part* of an hin of beaten oil.

Jgs 6:19 — And Gideon went in, and made ready a kid, and unleavened cakes of an ephah of flour: the flesh he put in a basket, and he put the broth in a pot, and brought *it* out unto him under the oak, and presented *it*.

Ru 2:17 — So she gleaned in the field until even, and beat out that she had gleaned: and it was about an ephah of barley.

1Sa 1:24 — And when she had weaned him, she took him up with her, with three bullocks, and one ephah of flour, and a bottle of wine, and brought him unto the house of the LORD in Shiloh: and the child *was* young.

1Sa 17:17 — And Jesse said unto David his son, Take now for thy brethren an ephah of this parched *corn*, and these ten loaves, and run to the camp to thy brethren;

Isa 5:10 — Yea, ten acres of vineyard shall yield one bath, and the seed of an homer shall yield an ephah.

Eze 45:13 — This *is* the oblation that ye shall offer; the sixth part of an ephah of an homer of wheat, and ye shall give the sixth part of an ephah of an homer of barley:

Eze 45:24 — And he shall prepare a meat offering of an ephah for a bullock, and an ephah for a ram, and an hin of oil for an ephah.

Eze 46:5 — And the meat offering *shall be* an ephah for a ram, and the meat offering for the lambs as he shall be able to give, and an hin of oil to an ephah.

Eze 46:7 — And he shall prepare a meat offering, an ephah for a bullock, and an ephah for a ram, and for the lambs according as his hand shall attain unto, and an hin of oil to an ephah.

Eze 46:11 — And in the feasts and in the solemnities the meat offering shall be an ephah to a bullock, and ephah to a ram, and to the lambs as he is able to give, and an hin of oil to an ephah.

Eze 46:14 — And thou shalt prepare a meat offering for it every morning, the sixth part of an ephah, and the third part of an hin of oil, to temper with the fine flour; a meat offering continually by a perpetual ordinance unto the LORD.

Am 8:5 — Saying, When will the new moon be gone, that we may sell corn? and the sabbath, that we may set forth wheat, making the ephah small, and the shekel great, and falsifying the balances by deceit?

• Half-homer, about five and a half bushels.

Hos 3:2 — So I bought her to me for fifteen *pieces* of silver, and *for* an homer of barley, and an half homer of barley:

• Homer, about eleven bushels, equal to a cor or ten ephahs.

Eze 45:11–14

Le 27:16 — And if a man shall sanctify unto the LORD *some part* of a field of his possession, then thy estimation shall be according to the seed thereof: an homer of barley seed *shall be valued* at fifty shekels of silver.

Nu 11:32 — And the people stood up all that day, and all *that* night, and all the next day, and they gathered the quails: he that gathered least gathered ten homers: and they spread *them* all abroad for themselves round about the camp.

Isa 5:10 — Yea, ten acres of vineyard shall yield one bath, and the seed of an homer shall yield an ephah.

Hos 3:2 — So I bought her to me for fifteen *pieces* of silver, and *for* an homer of barley, and an half homer of barley:

• Omer, about one bushel.

Ex 16:32–33

Ex 16:16 — This *is* the thing which the LORD hath commanded, Gather of it every man *according to* his eating, an omer for every man, according to the number of your persons; take ye every man for *them* which *are* in his tents.

Ex 16:18 — And when they did mete *it* with an omer, he that gathered much had nothing over, and he that gathered little had no lack; they gathered every man according to his eating.

Ex 16:22 — And it came to pass, *that* on the sixth day they gathered twice as much bread, two omers for one *man*: and all the rulers of the congregation came and told Moses.

Ex 16:36 — Now an omer *is* the tenth *part* of an ephah.

• Seah, about a peck and a half.

Ge 18:6 — And Abraham hastened into the tent unto Sarah, and said, Make ready quickly three measures of fine meal, knead *it*, and make cakes upon the hearth.

1Sa 25:18 — Then Abigail made haste, and took two hundred loaves, and two bottles of wine, and five sheep ready dressed, and five measures of parched *corn,* and an hundred clusters of raisins, and two hundred cakes of figs, and laid *them* on asses.

1Ki 18:32 — And with the stones he built an altar in the name of the LORD: and he made a trench about the altar, as great as would contain two measures of seed.

2Ki 7:1 — Then Elisha said, Hear ye the word of the LORD; Thus saith the LORD, To morrow about this time *shall* a measure of fine flour *be sold* for a shekel, and two measures of barley for a shekel, in the gate of Samaria.

2Ki 7:16 — And the people went out, and spoiled the tents of the Syrians. So a measure of fine flour was *sold* for a shekel, and two measures of barley for a shekel, according to the word of the LORD.

2Ki 7:18 — And it came to pass as the man of God had spoken to the king, saying, Two measures of barley for a shekel, and a measure of fine flour for a shekel, shall be to morrow about this time in the gate of Samaria:

• Tenth deal, about a gallon, equal to one-tenth of an ephah.

Nu 28:12–13, 20–21, 28–29; 29:3–4, 9–10, 14–15

Ex 29:40 — And with the one lamb a tenth deal of flour mingled with the fourth part of an hin of beaten oil; and the fourth part of an hin of wine *for* a drink offering.

Le 14:10 — And on the eighth day he shall take two he lambs without blemish, and one ewe lamb of the first year without blemish, and three tenth deals of fine flour *for* a meat offering, mingled with oil, and one log of oil.

Le 14:21 — And if he *be* poor, and cannot get so much; then he shall take one lamb *for* a trespass offering to be waved, to make an atonement for him, and one tenth deal of fine flour mingled with oil for a meat offering, and a log of oil;

Le 23:13 — And the meat offering thereof *shall be* two tenth deals of fine flour mingled with oil, an offering made by fire unto the LORD *for* a sweet savour: and the drink offering thereof *shall be* of wine, the fourth *part* of an hin.

Le 23:17 — Ye shall bring out of your habitations two wave loaves of two tenth deals: they shall be of fine flour; they shall be baken with leaven; *they are* the firstfruits unto the LORD.

Le 24:5 — And thou shalt take fine flour, and bake twelve cakes thereof: two tenth deals shall be in one cake.

Nu 15:4 — Then shall he that offereth his offering unto the LORD bring a meat offering of a tenth deal of flour mingled with the fourth *part* of an hin of oil.

Nu 15:6 — Or for a ram, thou shalt prepare *for* a meat offering two tenth deals of flour mingled with the third *part* of an hin of oil.

Nu 15:9 — Then shall he bring with a bullock a meat offering of three tenth deals of flour mingled with half an hin of oil.

Nu 28:9 — And on the sabbath day two lambs of the first year without spot, and two tenth deals of flour *for* a meat offering, mingled with oil, and the drink offering thereof:

• Liquid.

• Bath, about eight gallons and a half.

Eze 45:10–11

1Ki 7:26 — And it *was* an hand breadth thick, and the brim thereof was wrought like the brim of a cup, with flowers of lilies: it contained two thousand baths.

1Ki 7:38 — Then made he ten lavers of brass: one laver contained forty baths: *and* every laver was four cubits: *and* upon every one of the ten bases one laver.

2Ch 2:10 — And, behold, I will give to thy servants, the hewers that cut timber, twenty thousand measures of beaten wheat, and twenty thousand measures of barley, and twenty thousand baths of wine, and twenty thousand baths of oil.

2Ch 4:5 — And the thickness of it *was* an handbreadth, and the brim of it like the work of the brim of a cup, with flowers of lilies; *and* it received and held three thousand baths.

Ezr 7:22 — Unto an hundred talents of silver, and to an hundred measures of wheat, and to an hundred baths of wine, and to an hundred baths of oil, and salt without prescribing *how much.*

Isa 5:10 — Yea, ten acres of vineyard shall yield one bath, and the seed of an homer shall yield an ephah.

Eze 45:14 — Concerning the ordinance of oil, the bath of oil, *ye shall offer* the tenth part of a bath out of the cor, *which is* an homer of ten baths; for ten baths *are* an homer:

Lk 16:6 — And he said, An hundred measures of oil. And he said unto him, Take thy bill, and sit down quickly, and write fifty.

• Firkin, nearly nine gallons.

Jn 2:6 — And there were set there six waterpots of stone, after the manner of the purifying of the Jews, containing two or three firkins apiece.

• Hin, about a gallon and a half.

Nu 15:4–10

Ex 29:40 — And with the one lamb a tenth deal of flour mingled with the fourth part of an hin of beaten oil; and the fourth part of an hin of wine *for* a drink offering.

Ex 30:24 — And of cassia five hundred *shekels,* after the shekel of the sanctuary, and of oil olive an hin:

Le 19:36 — Just balances, just weights, a just ephah, and a just hin, shall ye have: I *am* the LORD your God, which brought you out of the land of Egypt.

Le 23:13 — And the meat offering thereof *shall be* two tenth deals of fine flour mingled with oil, an offering made by fire unto the LORD *for* a sweet savour: and the drink offering thereof *shall be* of wine, the fourth *part* of an hin.

Nu 28:5 — And a tenth *part* of an ephah of flour for a meat offering, mingled with the fourth *part* of an hin of beaten oil.

Nu 28:7 — And the drink offering thereof *shall be* the fourth *part* of an hin for the one lamb: in the holy *place* shalt thou cause the strong wine to be poured unto the LORD *for* a drink offering.

Nu 28:14 — And their drink offerings shall be half an hin of wine unto a bullock, and the third *part* of an hin unto a ram, and a fourth *part* of an hin unto a lamb: this *is* the burnt offering of every month throughout the months of the year.

Eze 4:11 — Thou shalt drink also water by measure, the sixth part of an hin: from time to time shalt thou drink.

Eze 45:24 — And he shall prepare a meat offering of an ephah for a bullock, and an ephah for a ram, and an hin of oil for an ephah.

Eze 46:5 — And the meat offering *shall be* an ephah for a ram, and the meat offering for the lambs as he shall be able to give, and an hin of oil to an ephah.

Eze 46:7 — And he shall prepare a meat offering, an ephah for a bullock, and an ephah for a ram, and for the lambs according as his hand shall attain unto, and an hin of oil to an ephah.

Eze 46:11 — And in the feasts and in the solemnities the meat offering shall be an ephah to a bullock, and ephah to a ram, and to the lambs as he is able to give, and an hin of oil to an ephah.

Eze 46:14 — And thou shalt prepare a meat offering for it every morning, the sixth part of an ephah, and the third part of an hin of oil, to temper with the fine flour; a meat offering continually by a perpetual ordinance unto the LORD.

• Log, about a pint, one-twelfth of a hin.

Le 14:10 — And on the eighth day he shall take two he lambs without blemish, and one ewe lamb of the first year without blemish, and three tenth deals of fine flour *for* a meat offering, mingled with oil, and one log of oil.

Le 14:12 — And the priest shall take one he lamb, and offer him for a trespass offering, and the log of oil, and wave them *for* a wave offering before the LORD:

Le 14:15 — And the priest shall take *some* of the log of oil, and pour *it* into the palm of his own left hand:

Le 14:21 — And if he *be* poor, and cannot get so much; then he shall take one lamb *for* a trespass offering to be waved, to make an atonement for him, and one tenth deal of fine flour mingled with oil for a meat offering, and a log of oil;

Le 14:24 — And the priest shall take the lamb of the trespass offering, and the log of oil, and the priest shall wave them *for* a wave offering before the LORD:

➜See: Weights

• Linear.

• Finger.

Jer 52:21 — And *concerning* the pillars, the height of one pillar *was* eighteen cubits; and a fillet of twelve cubits did compass it; and the thickness thereof *was* four fingers: *it was* hollow.

• Handbreadth.

Ex 25:25 — And thou shalt make unto it a border of an hand breadth round about, and thou shalt make a golden crown to the border thereof round about.

Ex 37:12 — Also he made thereunto a border of an handbreadth round about; and made a crown of gold for the border thereof round about.

1Ki 7:26 — And it *was* an hand breadth thick, and the brim thereof was wrought like the brim of a cup, with flowers of lilies: it contained two thousand baths.

2Ch 4:5 — And the thickness of it *was* an handbreadth, and the brim of it like the work of the brim of a cup, with flowers of lilies; *and* it received and held three thousand baths.

Ps 39:5 — Behold, thou hast made my days *as* an handbreadth; and mine age *is* as nothing before thee: verily every man at his best state *is* altogether vanity. Selah.

Eze 40:5 — And behold a wall on the outside of the house round about, and in the man's hand a measuring reed of six cubits *long* by the cubit and an hand breadth: so he measured the breadth of the building, one reed; and the height, one reed.

Eze 40:43 — And within *were* hooks, an hand broad, fastened round about: and upon the tables *was* the flesh of the offering.

Eze 43:13 — And these *are* the measures of the altar after the cubits: The cubit *is* a cubit and an hand breadth; even the bottom *shall be* a cubit, and the breadth a cubit, and the border thereof by the edge thereof round about *shall be* a span: and this *shall be* the higher place of the altar.

• Span.

Ex 28:16 — Foursquare it shall be *being* doubled; a span *shall be* the length thereof, and a span *shall be* the breadth thereof.

1Sa 17:4 — And there went out a champion out of the camp of the Philistines, named Goliath, of Gath, whose height *was* six cubits and a span.

Isa 40:12 — Who hath measured the waters in the hollow of his hand, and meted out heaven with the span, and comprehended the dust of the earth in a measure, and weighed the mountains in scales, and the hills in a balance?

Isa 48:13 — Mine hand also hath laid the foundation of the earth, and my right hand hath spanned the heavens: *when* I call unto them, they stand up together.

La 2:20 — Behold, O LORD, and consider to whom thou hast done this. Shall the women eat their fruit, *and* children of a span long? shall the priest and the prophet be slain in the sanctuary of the Lord?

Eze 43:13 — And these *are* the measures of the altar after the cubits: The cubit *is* a cubit and an hand breadth; even the bottom *shall be* a cubit, and the breadth a cubit, and the border thereof by the edge thereof round about *shall be* a span: and this *shall be* the higher place of the altar.

- **Cubit, the length of the forearm.**

See: Cubit

- **Reed, probably six cubits.**

Eze 40:5 — And behold a wall on the outside of the house round about, and in the man's hand a measuring reed of six cubits *long* by the cubit and an hand breadth: so he measured the breadth of the building, one reed; and the height, one reed.

- **Fathom.**

Ac 27:28 — And sounded, and found *it* twenty fathoms: and when they had gone a little further, they sounded again, and found *it* fifteen fathoms.

- **Pace.**

2Sa 6:13 — And it was *so,* that when they that bare the ark of the LORD had gone six paces, he sacrificed oxen and fatlings.

- **Furlong.**

Lk 24:13 — And, behold, two of them went that same day to a village called Emmaus, which was from Jerusalem *about* threescore furlongs.

- **Mile, probably nine-tenths of an English mile.**

Mt 5:41 — And whosoever shall compel thee to go a mile, go with him twain.

- **Sabbath day's journey, two thousand paces.**

Ac 1:12 — Then returned they unto Jerusalem from the mount called Olivet, which is from Jerusalem a sabbath day's journey.

- **Must be just.**

Le 19:35–36; Dt 25:13–16; Hos 12:7–9; Mic 6:10–12

Pr 11:1 — A false balance *is* abomination to the LORD: but a just weight *is* his delight.

Pr 16:11 — A just weight and balance *are* the LORD's: all the weights of the bag *are* his work.

Pr 20:10 — Divers weights, *and* divers measures, both of them *are* alike abomination to the LORD.

Pr 20:23 — Divers weights *are* an abomination unto the LORD; and a false balance *is* not good.

See: Dishonesty

See: Integrity

MEAT OFFERING • See: Offerings; meat, or meal

MEBUNNAI • One of David's guards.

2Sa 23:27 — Abiezer the Anethothite, Mebunnai the Hushathite,

MECHANIC

Pr 8:30 — Then I was by him, *as* one brought up *with him:* and I was daily *his* delight, rejoicing always before him;

1Co 3:10 — According to the grace of God which is given unto me, as a wise masterbuilder, I have laid the foundation, and another buildeth thereon. But let every man take heed how he buildeth thereupon.

- **Instances of.**
  - **Tubal-cain.**

Ge 4:22

  - **Bezaleel.**

Ex 31:2–11; 35:30–35

  - **Hiram.**

1Ki 7:13–50; 2Ch 2:13–14; 4:11–18

See: Art

MEDAD • One of the seventy elders who did not go to the tabernacle with Moses, but prophesied in the camp.

Nu 11:26–29

MEDAN • Son of Abraham and Keturah.

Ge 25:2 — And she bare him Zimran, and Jokshan, and Medan, and Midian, and Ishbak, and Shuah.

1Ch 1:32 — Now the sons of Keturah, Abraham's concubine: she bare Zimran, and Jokshan, and Medan, and Midian, and Ishbak, and Shuah. And the sons of Jokshan; Sheba, and Dedan.

MEDDLING

See: Busybody

See: Talebearer

MEDEBA

- **A city of Moab.**

Nu 21:30 — We have shot at them; Heshbon is perished even unto Dibon, and we have laid them waste even unto Nophah, which *reacheth* unto Medeba.

- **An idolatrous high place.**

Isa 15:2 — He is gone up to Bajith, and to Dibon, the high places, to weep: Moab shall howl over Nebo, and over Medeba: on all their heads *shall be* baldness, *and* every beard cut off.

- **Allotted to Reuben.**

Jos 13:9 — From Aroer, that *is* upon the bank of the river Arnon, and the city that *is* in the midst of the river, and all the plain of Medeba unto Dibon;

Jos 13:16 — And their coast was from Aroer, that *is* on the bank of the river Arnon, and the city that *is* in the midst of the river, and all the plain by Medeba;

- **David defeats army and the Ammonites at.**

1Ch 19:7–15

MEDES

- **Inhabitants of Media.**
- **Israelites distributed among, when carried to Assyria.**

2Ki 17:6 — In the ninth year of Hoshea the king of Assyria took Samaria, and carried Israel away into Assyria, and placed them in Halah and in Habor *by* the river of Gozan, and in the cities of the Medes.

2Ki 18:11 — And the king of Assyria did carry away Israel unto Assyria, and put them in Halah and in Habor *by* the river of Gozan, and in the cities of the Medes:

• **Palace in the Babylonian province of.**

Ezr 6:2 — And there was found at Achmetha, in the palace that is in the province of the Medes, a roll, and therein *was* a record thus written:

• **An essential part of the Medo-Persian empire.**

Est 1:1–19

• **Supremacy of, in the Chaldean empire.**

Da 5:28 — PERES; Thy kingdom is divided, and given to the Medes and Persians.

Da 5:31 — And Darius the Median took the kingdom, *being* about threescore and two years old.

Da 9:1 — In the first year of Darius the son of Ahasuerus, of the seed of the Medes, which was made king over the realm of the Chaldeans;

Da 11:1 — Also I in the first year of Darius the Mede, *even* I, stood to confirm and to strengthen him.

MEDIA ✦See: Medes

MEDIATION

✦**See: Intercession**

✦**See: Jesus, Mediation of**

MEDICINE

Jer 51:8–9

Pr 17:22 — A merry heart doeth good *like* a medicine: but a broken spirit drieth the bones.

Isa 1:6 — From the sole of the foot even unto the head *there is* no soundness in it; *but* wounds, and bruises, and putrifying sores: they have not been closed, neither bound up, neither mollified with ointment.

Isa 38:21 — For Isaiah had said, Let them take a lump of figs, and lay *it* for a plaister upon the boil, and he shall recover.

Jer 8:22 — *Is there* no balm in Gilead; *is there* no physician there? why then is not the health of the daughter of my people recovered?

Jer 30:13 — *There is* none to plead thy cause, that thou mayest be bound up: thou hast no healing medicines.

Jer 46:11 — Go up into Gilead, and take balm, O virgin, the daughter of Egypt: in vain shalt thou use many medicines; *for* thou shalt not be cured.

Eze 47:12 — And by the river upon the bank thereof, on this side and on that side, shall grow all trees for meat, whose leaf shall not fade, neither shall the fruit thereof be consumed: it shall bring forth new fruit according to his months, because their waters they issued out of the sanctuary: and the fruit thereof shall be for meat, and the leaf thereof for medicine.

Lk 10:34 — And went to *him*, and bound up his wounds, pouring in oil and wine, and set him on his own beast, and brought him to an inn, and took care of him.

Rev 22:2 — In the midst of the street of it, and on either side of the river, *was there* the tree of life, which bare twelve *manner* of fruits, *and* yielded her fruit every month: and the leaves of the tree *were* for the healing of the nations.

✦**See: Disease**

✦**See: Physician**

MEDITATION

Ps 63:5–6; 73:12–22; 77:10–12; 119:15–16, 97–99; 139:17–18; 1Ti 4:13–15

Jos 1:8 — This book of the law shall not depart out of thy mouth; but thou shalt meditate therein day and night, that thou mayest observe to do according to all that is written therein: for then thou shalt make thy way prosperous, and then thou shalt have good success.

Ps 1:2 — But his delight *is* in the law of the LORD; and in his law doth he meditate day and night.

Ps 4:4 — Stand in awe, and sin not: commune with your own heart upon your bed, and be still. Selah.

Ps 19:14 — Let the words of my mouth, and the meditation of my heart, be acceptable in thy sight, O LORD, my strength, and my redeemer.

Ps 39:3 — My heart was hot within me, while I was musing the fire burned: *then* spake I with my tongue,

Ps 49:3 — My mouth shall speak of wisdom; and the meditation of my heart *shall be* of understanding.

Ps 104:34 — My meditation of him shall be sweet: I will be glad in the LORD.

Ps 119:11 — Thy word have I hid in mine heart, that I might not sin against thee.

Ps 119:23 — Princes also did sit *and* speak against me: *but* thy servant did meditate in thy statutes.

Ps 119:48 — My hands also will I lift up unto thy commandments, which I have loved; and I will meditate in thy statutes.

Ps 119:55 — I have remembered thy name, O LORD, in the night, and have kept thy law.

Ps 119:59 — I thought on my ways, and turned my feet unto thy testimonies.

Ps 119:78 — Let the proud be ashamed; for they dealt perversely with me without a cause: *but* I will meditate in thy precepts.

Ps 119:148 — Mine eyes prevent the *night* watches, that I might meditate in thy word.

Ps 143:5 — I remember the days of old; I meditate on all thy works; I muse on the work of thy hands.

• **Instances of.**

• **Isaac.**

Ge 24:63

MEDITERRANEAN SEA

• **Mentioned in Scripture as the great sea.**

Nu 34:6–7

Jos 1:4 — From the wilderness and this Lebanon even unto the great river, the river Euphrates, all the land of the Hittites, and unto the great sea toward the going down of the sun, shall be your coast.

Jos 9:1 — And it came to pass, when all the kings which *were* on this side Jordan, in the hills, and in the valleys, and in all the coasts of the great sea over against Lebanon, the Hittite, and the Amorite, the Canaanite, the Perizzite, the Hivite, and the Jebusite, heard *thereof*;

Jos 15:12 — And the west border *was* to the great sea, and the coast *thereof*. This *is* the coast of the children of Judah round about according to their families.

Jos 15:47 — Ashdod with her towns and her villages, Gaza with her towns and her villages, unto the river of Egypt, and the great sea, and the border *thereof*:

Jos 23:4 — Behold, I have divided unto you by lot these nations that remain, to be an inheritance for your tribes, from Jordan, with all the nations that I have cut off, even unto the great sea westward.

Eze 47:10 — And it shall come to pass, *that* the fishers shall stand upon it from En-gedi even unto Eneglaim; they shall be a *place* to spread forth nets; their fish shall be according to their kinds, as the fish of the great sea, exceeding many.

Eze 47:15 — And this *shall be* the border of the land toward the north side, from the great sea, the way of Hethlon, as men go to Zedad;

Eze 47:20 — The west side also *shall be* the great sea from the border, till a man come over against Hamath. This *is* the west side.

Eze 48:28 — And by the border of Gad, at the south side southward, the border shall be even from Tamar *unto* the waters of strife *in* Kadesh, *and* to the river toward the great sea.

• Sea of the Philistines.

Ex 23:31 — And I will set thy bounds from the Red sea even unto the sea of the Philistines, and from the desert unto the river: for I will deliver the inhabitants of the land into your hand; and thou shalt drive them out before thee.

• Sea of Joppa.

Ezr 3:7 — They gave money also unto the masons, and to the carpenters; and meat, and drink, and oil, unto them of Zidon, and to them of Tyre, to bring cedar trees from Lebanon to the sea of Joppa, according to the grant that they had of Cyrus king of Persia.

• The hinder sea.

Zec 14:8 — And it shall be in that day, *that* living waters shall go out from Jerusalem; half of them toward the former sea, and half of them toward the hinder sea: in summer and in winter shall it be.

• The uttermost sea.

Dt 11:24 — Every place whereon the soles of your feet shall tread shall be yours: from the wilderness and Lebanon, from the river, the river Euphrates, even unto the uttermost sea shall your coast be.

• The utmost sea.

Joel 2:20 — But I will remove far off from you the northern *army*, and will drive him into a land barren and desolate, with his face toward the east sea, and his hinder part toward the utmost sea, and his stink shall come up, and his ill savour shall come up, because he hath done great things.

MEEKNESS

Ps 76:8–9; La 3:28–30; Mt 5:38–42; 27:13–14; 1Co 13:4–5; Gal 5:22–23; 5:26–6:1; Eph 4:1–2; Php 2:14–15; Col 3:12–13; 1Th 5:14–15; 1Ti 3:2–3; 6:11–12; 2Ti 2:24–25; Jas 3:17–18; 1Pe 2:18–23; 2Pe 1:5–7

Ps 22:26 — The meek shall eat and be satisfied: they shall praise the LORD that seek him: your heart shall live for ever.

Ps 25:9 — The meek will he guide in judgment: and the meek will he teach his way.

Ps 34:14 — Depart from evil, and do good; seek peace, and pursue it.

Ps 37:11 — But the meek shall inherit the earth; and shall delight themselves in the abundance of peace.

Ps 147:6 — The LORD lifteth up the meek: he casteth the wicked down to the ground.

Ps 149:4 — For the LORD taketh pleasure in his people: he will beautify the meek with salvation.

Pr 14:29 — *He that is* slow to wrath *is* of great understanding: but *he that is* hasty of spirit exalteth folly.

Pr 15:1 — A soft answer turneth away wrath: but grievous words stir up anger.

Pr 15:18 — A wrathful man stirreth up strife: but *he that is* slow to anger appeaseth strife.

Pr 16:32 — *He that is* slow to anger *is* better than the mighty; and he that ruleth his spirit than he that taketh a city.

Pr 17:1 — Better *is* a dry morsel, and quietness therewith, than an house full of sacrifices *with* strife.

Pr 19:11 — The discretion of a man deferreth his anger; and *it is* his glory to pass over a transgression.

Pr 20:3 — *It is* an honour for a man to cease from strife: but every fool will be meddling.

Pr 25:15 — By long forbearing is a prince persuaded, and a soft tongue breaketh the bone.

Pr 29:8 — Scornful men bring a city into a snare: but wise *men* turn away wrath.

Ecc 7:8 — Better *is* the end of a thing than the beginning thereof: *and* the patient in spirit *is* better than the proud in spirit.

Ecc 10:4 — If the spirit of the ruler rise up against thee, leave not thy place; for yielding pacifieth great offences.

Isa 11:4 — But with righteousness shall he judge the poor, and reprove with equity for the meek of the earth: and he shall smite the earth with the rod of his mouth, and with the breath of his lips shall he slay the wicked.

Isa 29:19 — The meek also shall increase *their* joy in the LORD, and the poor among men shall rejoice in the Holy One of Israel.

Am 3:3 — Can two walk together, except they be agreed?

Zep 2:3 — Seek ye the LORD, all ye meek of the earth, which have wrought his judgment; seek righteousness, seek meekness: it may be ye shall be hid in the day of the LORD'S anger.

Mt 5:5 — Blessed *are* the meek: for they shall inherit the earth.

Mt 5:9 — Blessed *are* the peacemakers: for they shall be called the children of God.

Mt 11:29 — Take my yoke upon you, and learn of me; for I am meek and lowly in heart: and ye shall find rest unto your souls.

Mk 9:50 — Salt *is* good: but if the salt have lost his saltness, wherewith will ye season it? Have salt in yourselves, and have peace one with another.

Lk 6:29 — And unto him that smiteth thee on the *one* cheek offer also the other; and him that taketh away thy cloke forbid not *to take thy* coat also.

Ro 12:14 — Bless them which persecute you: bless, and curse not.

Ro 12:18 — If it be possible, as much as lieth in you, live peaceably with all men.

Ro 14:19 — Let us therefore follow after the things which make for peace, and things wherewith one may edify another.

1Co 6:7 — Now therefore there is utterly a fault among you, because ye go to law one with another. Why do ye not rather take wrong? why do ye not rather *suffer yourselves to* be defrauded?

1Co 7:15 — But if the unbelieving depart, let him depart. A brother or a sister is not under bondage in such *cases:* but God hath called us to peace.

1Co 10:32 — Give none offence, neither to the Jews, nor to the Gentiles, nor to the church of God:

1Co 13:7 — Beareth all things, believeth all things, hopeth all things, endureth all things.

2Co 10:1 — Now I Paul myself beseech you by the meekness and gentleness of Christ, who in presence *am* base among you, but being absent am bold toward you:

2Co 13:11 — Finally, brethren, farewell. Be perfect, be of good comfort, be of one mind, live in peace; and the God of love and peace shall be with you.

2Th 3:5 — And the Lord direct your hearts into the love of God, and into the patient waiting for Christ.

Tit 2:2 — That the aged men be sober, grave, temperate, sound in faith, in charity, in patience.

Tit 2:9 — *Exhort* servants to be obedient unto their own masters, *and* to please *them* well in all *things;* not answering again;

Tit 3:2 — To speak evil of no man, to be no brawlers, *but* gentle, shewing all meekness unto all men.

Heb 10:36 — For ye have need of patience, that, after ye have done the will of God, ye might receive the promise.

Heb 12:14 — Follow peace with all *men,* and holiness, without which no man shall see the Lord:

Jas 1:4 — But let patience have *her* perfect work, that ye may be perfect and entire, wanting nothing.

Jas 1:19 — Wherefore, my beloved brethren, let every man be swift to hear, slow to speak, slow to wrath:

Jas 1:21 — Wherefore lay apart all filthiness and superfluity of naughtiness, and receive with meekness the engrafted word, which is able to save your souls.

Jas 3:13 — Who *is* a wise man and endued with knowledge among you? let him shew out of a good conversation his works with meekness of wisdom.

1Pe 3:4 — But *let it be* the hidden man of the heart, in that which is not corruptible, *even the ornament* of a meek and quiet spirit, which is in the sight of God of great price.

1Pe 3:11 — Let him eschew evil, and do good; let him seek peace, and ensue it.

1Pe 3:15 — But sanctify the Lord God in your hearts: and *be* ready always to *give* an answer to every man that asketh you a reason of the hope that is in you with meekness and fear:

Jude 1:9 — Yet Michael the archangel, when contending with the devil he disputed about the body of Moses, durst not bring against him a railing accusation, but said, The Lord rebuke thee.

See: Humility

See: Kindness

See: Patience

- **Instances of.**
  - **Abraham.**
    Ge 13:8
  - **Isaac.**
    Ge 26:20–22
  - **Moses.**
    Ex 2:13; 14:13–14; 15:24; 16:7–8; 17:2; Nu 12:3; 16:4–11
  - **Gideon.**
    Jgs 8:2–3
  - **Hannah.**
    1Sa 1:13–16
  - **Saul.**
    1Sa 10:27
  - **David.**
    1Sa 17:29; 2Sa 16:9–14; Ps 38:13–14; 120:5–7
  - **Paul.**
    Ac 21:20–26; 1Th 2:7; 2Ti 4:16
  - **The Thessalonians.**
    2Th 1:4
  - **Job.**
    Jas 5:11
  - **The angel.**
    Jude 1:9
  - **Meekness of Jesus.**

See: Jesus, Meekness of

- **Of Jesus.**

Isa 42:1–4; Mt 12:19–20; 26:47–54

Isa 53:7 — He was oppressed, and he was afflicted, yet he opened not his mouth: he is brought as a lamb to the slaughter, and as a sheep before her shearers is dumb, so he openeth not his mouth.

See: Jesus, Humility of

MEGIDDO

- **Called also Megiddon and probably Armageddon.**
- **A city in Issachar situated on the southern edge of the plain of Esdraelon.**

Jos 17:11 — And Manasseh had in Issachar and in Asher Beth-shean and her towns, and Ibleam and her towns, and the inhabitants of Dor and her towns, and the inhabitants of Endor and her towns, and the inhabitants of Taanach and her towns, and the inhabitants of Megiddo and her towns, *even* three countries.

1Ch 7:29 — And by the borders of the children of Manasseh, Beth-shean and her towns, Taanach and her towns, Megiddo and her towns, Dor and her towns. In these dwelt the children of Joseph the son of Israel.

- **Conquest of, by Joshua.**

Jos 12:21 — The king of Taanach, one; the king of Megiddo, one;

• Walled by Solomon.

1Ki 9:15 — And this *is* the reason of the levy which king Solomon raised; for to build the house of the LORD, and his own house, and Millo, and the wall of Jerusalem, and Hazor, and Megiddo, and Gezer.

• Included in one of Solomon's commissary districts.

1Ki 4:12 — Baana the son of Ahilud; *to him pertained* Taanach and Megiddo, and all Beth-shean, which is by Zartanah beneath Jezreel, from Beth-shean to Abel-meholah, *even* unto *the place that is* beyond Jokneam:

• Ahaziah dies at.

2Ki 9:27 — But when Ahaziah the king of Judah saw *this*, he fled by the way of the garden house. And Jehu followed after him, and said, Smite him also in the chariot. *And they did so* at the going up to Gur, which *is* by Ibleam. And he fled to Megiddo, and died there.

• Valley of, Deborah defeats Sisera in.

Jgs 5:19 — The kings came *and* fought, then fought the kings of Canaan in Taanach by the waters of Megiddo; they took no gain of money.

• Josiah slain at, by Pharaoh-nechoh.

2Ki 23:29–30; 2Ch 35:22–24

• Prophecy concerning.

Zec 12:11 — In that day shall there be a great mourning in Jerusalem, as the mourning of Hadadrimmon in the valley of Megiddon.

MEHETABEEL • A person whose grandson tried to intimidate Nehemiah.

Ne 6:10 — Afterward I came unto the house of Shemaiah the son of Delaiah the son of Mehetabeel, who *was* shut up; and he said, Let us meet together in the house of God, within the temple, and let us shut the doors of the temple: for they will come to slay thee; yea, in the night will they come to slay thee.

MEHETABEL • Wife of Hadar.

Ge 36:39 — And Baal-hanan the son of Achbor died, and Hadar reigned in his stead: and the name of his city *was* Pau; and his wife's name *was* Mehetabel, the daughter of Matred, the daughter of Mezahab.

1Ch 1:50 — And when Baal-hanan was dead, Hadad reigned in his stead: and the name of his city *was* Pai; and his wife's name *was* Mehetabel, the daughter of Matred, the daughter of Mezahab.

MEHIDA • A person whose descendants returned from Babylon.

Ezr 2:52 — The children of Bazluth, the children of Mehida, the children of Harsha,

Ne 7:54 — The children of Bazlith, the children of Mehida, the children of Harsha,

MEHIR • Son of Chelub.

1Ch 4:11 — And Chelub the brother of Shuah begat Mehir, which *was* the father of Eshton.

MEHOLATHITE • An inhabitant of a city in Issachar.

1Sa 18:19 — But it came to pass at the time when Merab Saul's daughter should have been given to David, that she was given unto Adriel the Meholathite to wife.

2Sa 21:8 — But the king took the two sons of Rizpah the daughter of Aiah, whom she bare unto Saul, Armoni and Mephibosheth; and the five sons of Michal the daughter of Saul, whom she brought up for Adriel the son of Barzillai the Meholathite:

MEHUJAEL • Son of Irad.

Ge 4:18 — And unto Enoch was born Irad: and Irad begat Mehujael: and Mehujael begat Methusael: and Methusael begat Lamech.

MEHUMAN • A chamberlain of Ahasuerus.

Est 1:10 — On the seventh day, when the heart of the king was merry with wine, he commanded Mehuman, Biztha, Harbona, Bigtha, and Abagtha, Zethar, and Carcas, the seven chamberlains that served in the presence of Ahasuerus the king,

MEHUNIM

• A person whose descendants returned from exile.

Ezr 2:50 — The children of Asnah, the children of Mehunim, the children of Nephusim,

• Called also Meunim.

Ne 7:52 — The children of Besai, the children of Meunim, the children of Nephishesim,

MEKONAH • A city in Judah.

Ne 11:28 — And at Ziklag, and at Mekonah, and in the villages thereof,

MELATIAH • A Gibeonite who assisted in repairing the wall of Jerusalem.

Ne 3:7 — And next unto them repaired Melatiah the Gibeonite, and Jadon the Meronothite, the men of Gibeon, and of Mizpah, unto the throne of the governor on this side the river.

MELCHI

• Ancestor of Jesus.

Lk 3:24 — Which was *the son* of Matthat, which was *the son* of Levi, which was *the son* of Melchi, which was *the son* of Janna, which was *the son* of Joseph,

• Remote ancestor of Jesus.

Lk 3:28 — Which was *the son* of Melchi, which was *the son* of Addi, which was *the son* of Cosam, which was *the son* of Elmodam, which was *the son* of Er,

MELCHISHUA

• Called also Malchishua.

• Son of King Saul.

1Sa 14:49 — Now the sons of Saul were Jonathan, and Ishui, and Melchi-shua: and the names of his two daughters *were these;* the name of the firstborn Merab, and the name of the younger Michal:

1Sa 31:2 — And the Philistines followed hard upon Saul and upon his sons; and the Philistines slew Jonathan, and Abinadab, and Melchi-shua, Saul's sons.

1Ch 8:33 — And Ner begat Kish, and Kish begat Saul, and Saul begat Jonathan, and Malchi-shua, and Abinadab, and Esh-baal.

1Ch 9:39 — And Ner begat Kish; and Kish begat Saul; and Saul begat Jonathan, and Malchi-shua, and Abinadab, and Esh-baal.

1Ch 10:2 — And the Philistines followed hard after Saul, and after his sons; and the Philistines slew Jonathan, and Abinadab, and Malchi-shua, the sons of Saul.

MELCHIZEDEK

• King of Salem.

Ge 14:18–20

Ps 110:4 — The LORD hath sworn, and will not repent, Thou *art* a priest for ever after the order of Melchizedek.

• A priest and type of Christ.

Heb 6:20–7:21

Heb 5:6 — As he saith also in another *place,* Thou *art* a priest for ever after the order of Melchisedec.

Heb 5:10 — Called of God an high priest after the order of Melchisedec.

MELECH • Son of Micah.

1Ch 8:35 — And the sons of Micah *were,* Pithon, and Melech, and Tarea, and Ahaz.

1Ch 9:41— And the sons of Micah *were,* Pithon, and Melech, and Tahrea, *and Ahaz.*

MELICU • A priest.

Ne 12:14 — Of Melicu, Jonathan; of Shebaniah, Joseph;

MELITA,

• An island in the Mediterranean.

• Paul shipwrecked on the coast of.

Ac 28:1–10

MELON

Nu 11:5 — We remember the fish, which we did eat in Egypt freely; the cucumbers, and the melons, and the leeks, and the onions, and the garlick:

MELZAR • The steward whom the prince of the eunuchs set over Daniel and the three Hebrew children.

Da 1:11–16

MEMORIAL

• Passover.

Ex 12:14 — And this day shall be unto you for a memorial; and ye shall keep it a feast to the LORD throughout your generations; ye shall keep it a feast by an ordinance for ever.

*See: Passover

• Firstborn set apart as a.

Ex 13:12–16

• Pot of manna.

Ex 16:32–34

• Feast of Tabernacles.

Le 23:43 — That your generations may know that I made the children of Israel to dwell in booths, when I brought them out of the land of Egypt: I *am* the LORD your God.

• Shoulder stones of the ephod.

Ex 28:12 — And thou shalt put the two stones upon the shoulders of the ephod *for* stones of memorial unto the children of Israel: and Aaron shall bear their names before the LORD upon his two shoulders for a memorial.

• Lord's Supper.

1Co 11:24–26

Lk 22:19 — And he took bread, and gave thanks, and brake *it,* and gave unto them, saying, This is my body which is given for you: this do in remembrance of me.

*See: Pillar

MEMORIES

Ps 63:6 — When I remember thee upon my bed, *and* meditate on thee in the *night* watches.

Ecc 12:1 — Remember now thy Creator in the days of thy youth, while the evil days come not, nor the years draw nigh, when thou shalt say, I have no pleasure in them;

Jnh 2:7 — When my soul fainted within me I remembered the LORD: and my prayer came in unto thee, into thine holy temple.

Zec 10:9 — And I will sow them among the people: and they shall remember me in far countries; and they shall live with their children, and turn again.

MEMORIZE

Pr 2:1–5; 3:1–2

Ps 119:11 — Thy word have I hid in mine heart, that I might not sin against thee.

Isa 55:11 — So shall my word be that goeth forth out of my mouth: it shall not return unto me void, but it shall accomplish that which I please, and it shall prosper *in the thing* whereto I sent it.

1Ti 4:13 — Till I come, give attendance to reading, to exhortation, to doctrine.

2Ti 3:15 — And that from a child thou hast known the holy scriptures, which are able to make thee wise unto salvation through faith which is in Christ Jesus.

MEMORY

1Jn 1:1–10

Ps 103:10 — He hath not dealt with us after our sins; nor rewarded us according to our iniquities.

Ps 103:12 — As far as the east is from the west, *so* far hath he removed our transgressions from us.

Mic 7:19 — He will turn again, he will have compassion upon us; he will subdue our iniquities; and thou wilt cast all their sins into the depths of the sea.

Heb 8:12 — For I will be merciful to their unrighteousness, and their sins and their iniquities will I remember no more.

MEMPHIS

• Called also Noph.

• A celebrated city of Egypt.

Hos 9:6 — For, lo, they are gone because of destruction: Egypt shall gather them up, Memphis shall bury them: the pleasant *places* for their silver, nettles shall possess them: thorns *shall be* in their tabernacles.

• Prophecies concerning.

Isa 19:13 — The princes of Zoan are become fools, the princes of Noph are deceived; they have also seduced Egypt, *even they that are* the stay of the tribes thereof.

Jer 2:16 — Also the children of Noph and Tahapanes have broken the crown of thy head.

Jer 46:14 — Declare ye in Egypt, and publish in Migdol, and publish in Noph and in Tahpanhes: say ye, Stand fast, and prepare thee; for the sword shall devour round about thee.

Jer 46:19 — O thou daughter dwelling in Egypt, furnish thyself to go into captivity: for Noph shall be waste and desolate without an inhabitant.

Eze 30:16 — And I will set fire in Egypt: Sin shall have great pain, and No shall be rent asunder, and Noph *shall have* distresses daily.

MEMUCAN • One of the seven princes of Ahasuerus who counsels the king to divorce Queen Vashti.

Est 1:14–21

MENAHEM • King of Israel.

2Ki 15:13–22

MENAN • An ancestor of Jesus.

Lk 3:31 — Which was *the son* of Melea, which was *the son* of Menan, which was *the son* of Mattatha, which was *the son* of Nathan, which was *the son* of David,

MENE

Da 5:25–26

MENSES ➜See: Menstruation

MENSTRUATION

• Law relating to.

Le 15:19–30

Le 20:18 — And if a man shall lie with a woman having her sickness, and shall uncover her nakedness; he hath discovered her fountain, and she hath uncovered the fountain of her blood: and both of them shall be cut off from among their people.

Eze 18:6 — *And* hath not eaten upon the mountains, neither hath lifted up his eyes to the idols of the house of Israel, neither hath defiled his neighbour's wife, neither hath come near to a menstruous woman,

• Cessation of, in old age.

Ge 18:11 — Now Abraham and Sarah *were* old *and* well stricken in age; *and* it ceased to be with Sarah after the manner of women.

• Immunities of women during.

Ge 31:35 — And she said to her father, Let it not displease my lord that I cannot rise up before thee; for the custom of women is upon me. And he searched, but found not the images.

• Of animals.

Jer 2:24 — A wild ass used to the wilderness, *that* snuffeth up the wind at her pleasure; in her occasion who can turn her away? all they that seek her will not weary themselves; in her month they shall find her.

• Uncleanness of.

Isa 30:22 — Ye shall defile also the covering of thy graven images of silver, and the ornament of thy molten images of gold: thou shalt cast them away as a menstruous cloth; thou shalt say unto it, Get thee hence.

• Figurative.

Isa 30:22 — Ye shall defile also the covering of thy graven images of silver, and the ornament of thy molten images of gold: thou shalt cast them away as a menstruous cloth; thou shalt say unto it, Get thee hence.

La 1:17 — Zion spreadeth forth her hands, *and there is* none to comfort her: the LORD hath commanded concerning Jacob, *that* his adversaries *should be* round about him: Jerusalem is as a menstruous woman among them.

Eze 36:17 — Son of man, when the house of Israel dwelt in their own land, they defiled it by their own way and by their doings: their way was before me as the uncleanness of a removed woman.

MEONENIM • A place in Ephraim.

Jgs 9:37 — And Gaal spake again and said, See there come people down by the middle of the land, and another company come along by the plain of Meonenim.

MEONOTHAI • Father of Ophrah.

1Ch 4:14 — And Meonothai begat Ophrah: and Seraiah begat Joab, the father of the valley of Charashim; for they were craftsmen.

MEPHAATH • A Levitical city in Reuben.

Jos 13:18 — And Jahaza, and Kedemoth, and Mephaath,

Jos 21:37 — Kedemoth with her suburbs, and Mephaath with her suburbs; four cities.

1Ch 6:79 — Kedemoth also with her suburbs, and Mephaath with her suburbs:

Jer 48:21 — And judgment is come upon the plain country; upon Holon, and upon Jahazah, and upon Mephaath,

MEPHIBOSHETH

• Son of Saul by Rizpah, whom David surrendered to the Gibeonites to be slain.

2Sa 21:8–9

• Son of Jonathan.

2Sa 4:4 — And Jonathan, Saul's son, had a son *that was* lame of *his* feet. He was five years old when the tidings came of Saul and Jonathan out of Jezreel, and his nurse took him up, and fled: and it came to pass, as she made haste to flee, that he fell, and became lame. And his name *was* Mephibosheth.

• Called Merib-baal.

1Ch 8:34 — And the son of Jonathan *was* Merib-baal; and Merib-baal begat Micah.

1Ch 9:40 — And the son of Jonathan *was* Merib-baal: and Merib-baal begat Micah.

• Was lame.

2Sa 4:4 — And Jonathan, Saul's son, had a son *that was* lame of *his* feet. He was five years old when the tidings came of Saul and Jonathan out of Jezreel, and his nurse took him up, and fled: and it came to pass, as she made haste to flee, that he fell, and became lame. And his name *was* Mephibosheth.

• David entertains him at his table.

2Sa 9:1–7

2Sa 21:7 — But the king spared Mephibosheth, the son of Jonathan the son of Saul, because of the LORD's oath that *was* between them, between David and Jonathan the son of Saul.

• Property restored to.

2Sa 9:9–10

• His ingratitude to David at the time of Absalom's usurpation.

2Sa 16:1–4; 19:24–30

• Property of, confiscated.

2Sa 19:29–30

2Sa 16:4 — Then said the king to Ziba, Behold, thine *are* all that *pertained* unto Mephibosheth. And Ziba said, I humbly beseech thee *that* I may find grace in thy sight, my lord, O king.

MERAB

• Daughter of King Saul.

1Sa 14:49 — Now the sons of Saul were Jonathan, and Ishui, and Melchi-shua: and the names of his two daughters *were these;* the name of the firstborn Merab, and the name of the younger Michal:

• Betrothed to David by Saul.

1Sa 18:17–18

• Betrothed to David but given to Adriel as wife.

1Sa 18:19 — But it came to pass at the time when Merab Saul's daughter should have been given to David, that she was given unto Adriel the Meholathite to wife.

MERAIAH • A priest.

Ne 12:12 — And in the days of Joiakim were priests, the chief of the fathers: of Seraiah, Meraiah; of Jeremiah, Hananiah;

MERAIOTH

• A high priest of the line of Eleazar.

1Ch 6:6–7

1Ch 6:52 — Meraioth his son, Amariah his son, Ahitub his son,

Ezr 7:3 — The son of Amariah, the son of Azariah, the son of Meraioth,

• Probably identical with the priest of same name.

1Ch 9:11 — And Azariah the son of Hilkiah, the son of Meshullam, the son of Zadok, the son of Meraioth, the son of Ahitub, the ruler of the house of God;

Ne 11:11 — Seraiah the son of Hilkiah, the son of Meshullam, the son of Zadok, the son of Meraioth, the son of Ahitub, *was* the ruler of the house of God.

• A priest in the time of Joiakim.

Ne 12:15 — Of Harim, Adna; of Meraioth, Helkai;

MERARI

• Son of Levi.

Ge 46:11 — And the sons of Levi; Gershon, Kohath, and Merari.

• Head of the Merarite Levites.

Nu 3:33–35

Nu 3:17 — And these were the sons of Levi by their names; Gershon, and Kohath, and Merari.

See: Levites

MERATHAIM • Probably a poetical name for Chaldea.

Jer 50:21 — Go up against the land of Merathaim, *even* against it, and against the inhabitants of Pekod: waste and utterly destroy after them, saith the LORD, and do according to all that I have commanded thee.

MERCENARIES See: Soldiers

MERCHANDISE See: Commerce

MERCHANT

Eze 27:21–36

Ge 23:16 — And Abraham hearkened unto Ephron; and Abraham weighed to Ephron the silver, which he had named in the audience of the sons of Heth, four hundred shekels of silver, current *money* with the merchant.

Ge 37:28 — Then there passed by Midianites merchantmen; and they drew and lifted up Joseph out of the pit, and sold Joseph to the Ishmeelites for twenty *pieces* of silver: and they brought Joseph into Egypt.

1Ki 10:15 — Beside *that he had* of the merchantmen, and of the traffick of the spice merchants, and of all the kings of Arabia, and of the governors of the country.

1Ki 10:28 — And Solomon had horses brought out of Egypt, and linen yarn: the king's merchants received the linen yarn at a price.

2Ch 9:14 — Beside *that which* chapmen and merchants brought. And all the kings of Arabia and governors of the country brought gold and silver to Solomon.

Ne 3:32 — And between the going up of the corner unto the sheep gate repaired the goldsmiths and the merchants.

Ne 13:20 — So the merchants and sellers of all kind of ware lodged without Jerusalem once or twice.

Job 41:6 — Shall the companions make a banquet of him? shall they part him among the merchants?

SS 3:6 — Who *is* this that cometh out of the wilderness like pillars of smoke, perfumed with myrrh and frankincense, with all powders of the merchant?

Isa 23:2 — Be still, ye inhabitants of the isle; thou whom the merchants of Zidon, that pass over the sea, have replenished.

Isa 47:15 — Thus shall they be unto thee with whom thou hast laboured, *even* thy merchants, from thy youth: they shall wander every one to his quarter; none shall save thee.

Eze 17:4 — He cropped off the top of his young twigs, and carried it into a land of traffick; he set it in a city of merchants.

Eze 27:13 — Javan, Tubal, and Meshech, they *were* thy merchants: they traded the persons of men and vessels of brass in thy market.

Eze 27:17 — Judah, and the land of Israel, they *were* thy merchants: they traded in thy market wheat of Minnith, and Pannag, and honey, and oil, and balm.

Eze 38:13 — Sheba, and Dedan, and the merchants of Tarshish, with all the young lions thereof, shall say unto thee, Art thou come to take a spoil? hast thou gathered thy company to take a prey? to carry away silver and gold, to take away cattle and goods, to take a great spoil?

Hos 12:7 — *He is* a merchant, the balances of deceit *are* in his hand: he loveth to oppress.

Na 3:16 — Thou hast multiplied thy merchants above the stars of heaven: the cankerworm spoileth, and fleeth away.

Mt 13:45 — <u>Again, the kingdom of heaven is like unto a merchant man, seeking goodly pearls:</u>

Rev 18:3 — For all nations have drunk of the wine of the wrath of her fornication, and the kings of the earth have committed fornication with her, and the merchants of the earth are waxed rich through the abundance of her delicacies.

Rev 18:11 — And the merchants of the earth shall weep and mourn over her; for no man buyeth their merchandise any more:

Rev 18:23 — And the light of a candle shall shine no more at all in thee; and the voice of the bridegroom and of the bride shall be heard no more at all in thee: for thy merchants were the great men of the earth; for by thy sorceries were all nations deceived.

→See: Commerce

MERCURIUS, Mercury

- **Paul taken for, in Lycaonia.**
  Ac 14:11–12

MERCY

Ps 37:25–26; Pr 3:3–4; 14:21–22; Col 3:12–13

2Sa 22:26 — With the merciful thou wilt shew thyself merciful, *and* with the upright man thou wilt shew thyself upright.

Ps 18:25 — With the merciful thou wilt shew thyself merciful; with an upright man thou wilt shew thyself upright;

Ps 85:10 — Mercy and truth are met together; righteousness and peace have kissed *each other.*

Pr 11:17 — The merciful man doeth good to his own soul: but *he that is* cruel troubleth his own flesh.

Pr 12:10 — A righteous *man* regardeth the life of his beast: but the tender mercies of the wicked *are* cruel.

Pr 14:31 — He that oppresseth the poor reproacheth his Maker: but he that honoureth him hath mercy on the poor.

Pr 20:28 — Mercy and truth preserve the king: and his throne is upholden by mercy.

Pr 21:21 — He that followeth after righteousness and mercy findeth life, righteousness, and honour.

Hos 4:1 — Hear the word of the LORD, ye children of Israel: for the LORD hath a controversy with the inhabitants of the land, because *there is* no truth, nor mercy, nor knowledge of God in the land.

Hos 12:6 — Therefore turn thou to thy God: keep mercy and judgment, and wait on thy God continually.

Mic 6:8 — He hath shewed thee, O man, what *is* good; and what doth the LORD require of thee, but to do justly, and to love mercy, and to walk humbly with thy God?

Mt 5:7 — <u>Blessed *are* the merciful: for they shall obtain mercy.</u>

Mt 23:23 — <u>Woe unto you, scribes and Pharisees, hypocrites! for ye pay tithe of mint and anise and cummin, and have omitted the weightier *matters* of the law, judgment, mercy, and faith: these ought ye to have done, and not to leave the other undone.</u>

Lk 6:36 — <u>Be ye therefore merciful, as your Father also is merciful.</u>

Ro 12:8 — Or he that exhorteth, on exhortation: he that giveth, *let him do it* with simplicity; he that ruleth, with diligence; he that sheweth mercy, with cheerfulness.

Jas 2:13 — For he shall have judgment without mercy, that hath shewed no mercy; and mercy rejoiceth against judgment.

→See: God, Mercy of

→See: Kindness

- **Instances of.**
  - **The prison keeper, to Joseph.**
    Ge 39:21–23
  - **Joshua to Rahab.**
    Jos 6:25
  - **The Israelites to the man of Bethel.**
    Jgs 1:23–26
  - **David to Saul.**
    1Sa 24:10–13, 17

MERCY SEAT

- **Description of.**
  Ex 25:17–22

- **Placed on the ark of the testimony.**

Ex 26:34 — And thou shalt put the mercy seat upon the ark of the testimony in the most holy *place*.

Ex 30:6 — And thou shalt put it before the vail that *is* by the ark of the testimony, before the mercy seat that *is* over the testimony, where I will meet with thee.

Ex 31:7 — The tabernacle of the congregation, and the ark of the testimony, and the mercy seat that *is* thereupon, and all the furniture of the tabernacle,

Ex 40:20 — And he took and put the testimony into the ark, and set the staves on the ark, and put the mercy seat above upon the ark:

Heb 9:5 — And over it the cherubims of glory shadowing the mercyseat; of which we cannot now speak particularly.

- **Materials of, to be a freewill offering.**

Ex 35:4–12

- **Made by Bezaleel.**

Ex 37:6–9

Ex 37:1 — And Bezaleel made the ark *of* shittim wood: two cubits and a half *was* the length of it, and a cubit and a half the breadth of it, and a cubit and a half the height of it:

- **Sprinkled with blood.**

Le 16:14–15

- **The shekinah upon.**

Ex 25:22 — And there I will meet with thee, and I will commune with thee from above the mercy seat, from between the two cherubims which *are* upon the ark of the testimony, of all *things* which I will give thee in commandment unto the children of Israel.

Ex 30:6 — And thou shalt put it before the vail that *is* by the ark of the testimony, before the mercy seat that *is* over the testimony, where I will meet with thee.

Ex 30:36 — And thou shalt beat *some* of it very small, and put of it before the testimony in the tabernacle of the congregation, where I will meet with thee: it shall be unto you most holy.

Le 16:2 — And the LORD said unto Moses, Speak unto Aaron thy brother, that he come not at all times into the holy *place* within the vail before the mercy seat, which *is* upon the ark; that he die not: for I will appear in the cloud upon the mercy seat.

Nu 7:89 — And when Moses was gone into the tabernacle of the congregation to speak with him, then he heard the voice of one speaking unto him from off the mercy seat that *was* upon the ark of testimony, from between the two cherubims: and he spake unto him.

Nu 17:4 — And thou shalt lay them up in the tabernacle of the congregation before the testimony, where I will meet with you.

1Sa 4:4 — So the people sent to Shiloh, that they might bring from thence the ark of the covenant of the LORD of hosts, which dwelleth *between* the cherubims: and the two sons of Eli, Hophni and Phinehas, *were* there with the ark of the covenant of God.

2Sa 6:2 — And David arose, and went with all the people that *were* with him from Baale of Judah, to bring up from thence the ark of God, whose name is called by the name of the LORD of hosts that dwelleth *between* the cherubims.

2Ki 19:15 — And Hezekiah prayed before the LORD, and said, O LORD God of Israel, which dwellest *between* the cherubims, thou art the God, *even* thou alone, of all the kingdoms of the earth: thou hast made heaven and earth.

1Ch 13:6 — And David went up, and all Israel, to Baalah, *that is*, to Kirjath-jearim, which *belonged* to Judah, to bring up thence the ark of God the LORD, that dwelleth *between* the cherubims, whose name is called *on it*.

Ps 80:1 — Give ear, O Shepherd of Israel, thou that leadest Joseph like a flock; thou that dwellest *between* the cherubims, shine forth.

Ps 99:1 — The LORD reigneth; let the people tremble: he sitteth *between* the cherubims; let the earth be moved.

Isa 37:16 — O LORD of hosts, God of Israel, that dwellest *between* the cherubims, thou *art* the God, *even* thou alone, of all the kingdoms of the earth: thou hast made heaven and earth.

Heb 4:16 — Let us therefore come boldly unto the throne of grace, that we may obtain mercy, and find grace to help in time of need.

- **In Solomon's temple.**

1Ch 28:11 — Then David gave to Solomon his son the pattern of the porch, and of the houses thereof, and of the treasuries thereof, and of the upper chambers thereof, and of the inner parlours thereof, and of the place of the mercy seat,

See: Tabernacle

MERED • Son of Ezra.

1Ch 4:17–18

MEREMOTH

- **A priest who was appointed to weigh and register gold and silver vessels brought to Jerusalem.**

Ezr 8:33 — Now on the fourth day was the silver and the gold and the vessels weighed in the house of our God by the hand of Meremoth the son of Uriah the priest; and with him *was* Eleazar the son of Phinehas; and with them *was* Jozabad the son of Jeshua, and Noadiah the son of Binnui, Levites;

Ne 3:4 — And next unto them repaired Meremoth the son of Urijah, the son of Koz. And next unto them repaired Meshullam the son of Berechiah, the son of Meshezabeel. And next unto them repaired Zadok the son of Baana.

Ne 3:21 — After him repaired Meremoth the son of Urijah the son of Koz another piece, from the door of the house of Eliashib even to the end of the house of Eliashib.

- **A Jew who divorced his Gentile wife after the captivity.**

Ezr 10:36 — Vaniah, Meremoth, Eliashib,

• A priest who sealed the covenant with Nehemiah.

Ne 10:5 — Harim, Meremoth, Obadiah,

Ne 12:3 — Shechaniah, Rehum, Meremoth,

MERES • One of the princes of Persia.

Est 1:14 — And the next unto him *was* Carshena, Shethar, Admatha, Tarshish, Meres, Marsena, *and* Memucan, the seven princes of Persia and Media, which saw the king's face, *and* which sat the first in the kingdom;)

MERIB-BAAL ✣See: Mephibosheth

MERIBAH

• A place in Rephidim, where Moses struck a rock and brought forth water.

Ex 17:1–7

• Meribah-kadesh, fountain in the desert of Zin.

Nu 20:13 — This *is* the water of Meribah; because the children of Israel strove with the LORD, and he was sanctified in them.

Nu 20:24 — Aaron shall be gathered unto his people: for he shall not enter into the land which I have given unto the children of Israel, because ye rebelled against my word at the water of Meribah.

MERIT

• Personal.

✣See: Grace of God

MERODACH • A Babylonian idol.

Jer 50:2 — Declare ye among the nations, and publish, and set up a standard; publish, *and* conceal not: say, Babylon is taken, Bel is confounded, Merodach is broken in pieces; her idols are confounded, her images are broken in pieces.

MERODACH-BALADAN

• Called also Berodach-Baladan, king of Persia.

• Sends congratulatory letters and a present to Hezekiah.

2Ki 20:12 — At that time Berodach-baladan, the son of Baladan, king of Babylon, sent letters and a present unto Hezekiah: for he had heard that Hezekiah had been sick.

Isa 39:1 — At that time Merodach-baladan, the son of Baladan, king of Babylon, sent letters and a present to Hezekiah: for he had heard that he had been sick, and was recovered.

MEROM

• The district near the springs of Jordan.

• Joshua conquered the confederacy of kings under Jabin, king of Hazor, near.

Jos 11:5–7

MEROZ

• A place north of Mount Tabor.

• Deborah and Barak curse the inhabitants of, in their song of triumph.

Jgs 5:23 — Curse ye Meroz, said the angel of the LORD, curse ye bitterly the inhabitants thereof; because they came not to the help of the LORD, to the help of the LORD against the mighty.

MESHA

• King of Moab; tributary to Ahab.

2Ki 3:4–5

• Son of Caleb.

1Ch 2:42 — Now the sons of Caleb the brother of Jerahmeel *were,* Mesha his firstborn, which was the father of Ziph; and the sons of Mareshah the father of Hebron.

• A place in possession of the Joktanites.

Ge 10:30 — And their dwelling was from Mesha, as thou goest unto Sephar a mount of the east.

• A Benjamite.

1Ch 8:9 — And he begat of Hodesh his wife, Jobab, and Zibia, and Mesha, and Malcham,

MESHACH • A name given by the chief eunuch to Mishael, one of the three Hebrew children.

Da 3:12–30

Da 1:7 — Unto whom the prince of the eunuchs gave names: for he gave unto Daniel *the name* of Belteshazzar; and to Hananiah, of Shadrach; and to Mishael, of Meshach; and to Azariah, of Abed-nego.

Da 2:49 — Then Daniel requested of the king, and he set Shadrach, Meshach, and Abed-nego, over the affairs of the province of Babylon: but Daniel *sat* in the gate of the king.

MESHECH

• Son of Japheth.

Ge 10:2 — The sons of Japheth; Gomer, and Magog, and Madai, and Javan, and Tubal, and Meshech, and Tiras.

1Ch 1:5 — The sons of Japheth; Gomer, and Magog, and Madai, and Javan, and Tubal, and Meshech, and Tiras.

• Son of Shem.

1Ch 1:17 — The sons of Shem; Elam, and Asshur, and Arphaxad, and Lud, and Aram, and Uz, and Hul, and Gether, and Meshech.

• A tribe.

Ps 120:5 — Woe is me, that I sojourn in Mesech, *that* I dwell in the tents of Kedar!

• The Moschi.

Eze 38:2–3

Eze 27:13 — Javan, Tubal, and Meshech, they *were* thy merchants: they traded the persons of men and vessels of brass in thy market.

Eze 32:26 — There *is* Meshech, Tubal, and all her multitude: her graves *are* round about him: all of them uncircumcised, slain by the sword, though they caused their terror in the land of the living.

MESHELEMIAH • A gatekeeper of the temple.

1Ch 26:1–2

1Ch 9:21 — *And* Zechariah the son of Meshelemiah *was* porter of the door of the tabernacle of the congregation.

1Ch 26:9 — And Meshelemiah had sons and brethren, strong men, eighteen.

MESHEZABEEL

• Ancestor of Meshullam.

Ne 3:4 — And next unto them repaired Meremoth the son of Urijah, the son of Koz. And next unto them repaired Meshullam the son of Berechiah, the son of Meshezabeel. And next unto them repaired Zadok the son of Baana.

• A person who sealed the covenant.

Ne 10:21 — Meshezabeel, Zadok, Jaddua,

Ne 11:24 — And Pethahiah the son of Meshezabeel, of the children of Zerah the son of Judah, *was* at the king's hand in all matters concerning the people.

MESHILLEMITH • A priest.

1Ch 9:12 — And Adaiah the son of Jeroham, the son of Pashur, the son of Malchijah, and Maasiai the son of Adiel, the son of Jahzerah, the son of Meshullam, the son of Meshillemith, the son of Immer;

MESHILLEMOTH

• Father of an Ephraimite who protested against the attempt of the Israelites to enslave their captive brethren.

2Ch 28:12–13

• A priest.

Ne 11:13 — And his brethren, chief of the fathers, two hundred forty and two: and Amashai the son of Azareel, the son of Ahasai, the son of Meshillemoth, the son of Immer,

MESHOBAB • A Simeonite.

1Ch 4:34 — And Meshobab, and Jamlech, and Joshah the son of Amaziah,

MESHULLAM

• Grandfather of Shaphan.

2Ki 22:3 — And it came to pass in the eighteenth year of king Josiah, *that* the king sent Shaphan the son of Azaliah, the son of Meshullam, the scribe, to the house of the LORD, saying,

• A son of Zerubbabel.

1Ch 3:19 — And the sons of Pedaiah *were,* Zerub-babel, and Shimei: and the sons of Zerub-babel; Meshullam, and Hananiah, and Shelomith their sister:

• A Gadite of Bashan.

1Ch 5:13 — And their brethren of the house of their fathers *were,* Michael, and Meshullam, and Sheba, and Jorai, and Jachan, and Zia, and Heber, seven.

• Three Benjamites.

1Ch 9:7–8

1Ch 8:17 — And Zebadiah, and Meshullam, and Hezeki, and Heber,

• An Aaronite.

1Ch 9:11 — And Azariah the son of Hilkiah, the son of Meshullam, the son of Zadok, the son of Meraioth, the son of Ahitub, the ruler of the house of God;

Ne 11:11 — Seraiah the son of Hilkiah, the son of Meshullam, the son of Zadok, the son of Meraioth, the son of Ahitub, *was* the ruler of the house of God.

• A priest.

1Ch 9:12 — And Adaiah the son of Jeroham, the son of Pashur, the son of Malchijah, and Maasiai the son of Adiel, the son of Jahzerah, the son of Meshullam, the son of Meshillemith, the son of Immer;

• A Kohathite and overseer of the temple repairs.

2Ch 34:12 — And the men did the work faithfully: and the overseers of them *were* Jahath and Obadiah, the Levites, of the sons of Merari; and Zechariah and Meshullam, of the sons of the Kohathites, to set *it* forward; and *other of* the Levites, all that could skill of instruments of musick.

• A chief who returned with Ezra.

Ezr 8:16 — Then sent I for Eliezer, for Ariel, for Shemaiah, and for Elnathan, and for Jarib, and for Elnathan, and for Nathan, and for Zechariah, and for Meshullam, chief men; also for Joiarib, and for Elnathan, men of understanding.

• A returned exile.

Ezr 10:15 — Only Jonathan the son of Asahel and Jahaziah the son of Tikvah were employed about this *matter:* and Meshullam and Shabbethai the Levite helped them.

• Son of Bani who divorced his Gentile wife.

Ezr 10:29 — And of the sons of Bani; Meshullam, Malluch, and Adaiah, Jashub, and Sheal, and Ramoth.

• Two persons who rebuilt portions of the wall.

Ne 3:4 — And next unto them repaired Meremoth the son of Urijah, the son of Koz. And next unto them repaired Meshullam the son of Berechiah, the son of Meshezabeel. And next unto them repaired Zadok the son of Baana.

Ne 3:6 — Moreover the old gate repaired Jehoiada the son of Paseah, and Meshullam the son of Besodeiah; they laid the beams thereof, and set up the doors thereof, and the locks thereof, and the bars thereof.

Ne 3:30 — After him repaired Hananiah the son of Shelemiah, and Hanun the sixth son of Zalaph, another piece. After him repaired Meshullam the son of Berechiah over against his chamber.

• A prince who stood by Ezra when he read the law to the people.

Ne 8:4 — And Ezra the scribe stood upon a pulpit of wood, which they had made for the purpose; and beside him stood Mattithiah, and Shema, and Anaiah, and Urijah, and Hilkiah, and Maaseiah, on his right hand; and on his left hand, Pedaiah, and Mishael, and Malchiah, and Hashum, and Hashbadana, Zechariah, *and* Meshullam.

• Two priests who signed the covenant.

Ne 10:7 — Meshullam, Abijah, Mijamin,

Ne 10:20 — Magpiash, Meshullam, Hezir,

• A Benjamite.

Ne 11:7 — And these *are* the sons of Benjamin; Sallu the son of Meshullam, the son of Joed, the son of Pedaiah, the son of Kolaiah, the son of Maaseiah, the son of Ithiel, the son of Jesaiah.

• Two priests who returned with Zerubbabel from Babylon.

Ne 12:13 — Of Ezra, Meshullam; of Amariah, Jehohanan;

Ne 12:16 — Of Iddo, Zechariah; of Ginnethon, Meshullam;

Ne 12:33 — And Azariah, Ezra, and Meshullam,

• A Levite.

Ne 12:25 — Mattaniah, and Bakbukiah, Obadiah, Meshullam, Talmon, Akkub, *were* porters keeping the ward at the thresholds of the gates.

MESHULLEMETH • Wife of Manasseh and mother of Amon.

2Ki 21:19 — Amon *was* twenty and two years old when he began to reign, and he reigned two years in Jerusalem. And his mother's name *was* Meshullemeth, the daughter of Haruz of Jotbah.

MESOPOTAMIA

• The country between the Tigris and the Euphrates.

• Abraham a native of.

Ac 7:2 — And he said, Men, brethren, and fathers, hearken; The God of glory appeared unto our father Abraham, when he was in Mesopotamia, before he dwelt in Charran,

• Nahor dwelt in.

Ge 24:10 — And the servant took ten camels of the camels of his master, and departed; for all the goods of his master *were* in his hand: and he arose, and went to Mesopotamia, unto the city of Nahor.

• People who dwelt in, called Syrians.

Ge 25:20 — And Isaac was forty years old when he took Rebekah to wife, the daughter of Bethuel the Syrian of Padan-aram, the sister to Laban the Syrian.

• Balaam from.

Dt 23:4 — Because they met you not with bread and with water in the way, when ye came forth out of Egypt; and because they hired against thee Balaam the son of Beor of Pethor of Mesopotamia, to curse thee.

• The children of Israel subjected to, eight years under the judgments of God.

Jgs 3:8 — Therefore the anger of the LORD was hot against Israel, and he sold them into the hand of Chushan-rishathaim king of Mesopotamia: and the children of Israel served Chushan-rishathaim eight years.

• The children of Israel delivered from, by Othniel.

Jgs 3:9–10

• Chariots hired from, by the Ammonites.

1Ch 19:6–7

• People of, present at Pentecost.

Ac 2:9 — Parthians, and Medes, and Elamites, and the dwellers in Mesopotamia, and in Judaea, and Cappadocia, in Pontus, and Asia,

See: Babylon

See: Chaldea

MESSENGER

• Figurative.

Mal 4:5–6

Hag 1:13 — Then spake Haggai the LORD's messenger in the LORD's message unto the people, saying, I *am* with you, saith the LORD.

Mal 2:7 — For the priest's lips should keep knowledge, and they should seek the law at his mouth: for he *is* the messenger of the LORD of hosts.

Mal 3:1 — Behold, I will send my messenger, and he shall prepare the way before me: and the Lord, whom ye seek, shall suddenly come to his temple, even the messenger of the covenant, whom ye delight in: behold, he shall come, saith the LORD of hosts.

Mt 11:10 — For this is *he*, of whom it is written, Behold, I send my messenger before thy face, which shall prepare thy way before thee.

Mk 1:2 — As it is written in the prophets, Behold, I send my messenger before thy face, which shall prepare thy way before thee.

Lk 7:27 — This is *he*, of whom it is written, Behold, I send my messenger before thy face, which shall prepare thy way before thee.

• Of Satan.

2Co 12:7 — And lest I should be exalted above measure through the abundance of the revelations, there was given to me a thorn in the flesh, the messenger of Satan to buffet me, lest I should be exalted above measure.

MESSIAH See: Jesus, Names, Appellations, and Titles of; Messiah

METAL

See: Brass, or more probably copper

See: Gold

See: Iron

See: Lead

See: Silver

See: Tin

METAPHOR

• Jesus spoke in.

Mk 4:11 — And he said unto them, Unto you it is given to know the mystery of the kingdom of God: but unto them that are without, all these *things* are done in parables:

See: Parables

METEOROLOGY AND CELESTIAL PHENOMENA

Ge 2:5–6; Job 26:7–8; 27:20–21; 28:24–27; 36:27–33; 37:6–22; 38:8–11, 24–29, 31–35; Ps 18:8–15; 19:2–6; 29:3–10; 65:8–12; 104:2–3, 19–20; 147:7–8; 148:7–8; Ecc 1:6–7; Isa 5:5–6; Jer 4:11–12; Joel 2:30–31; Mt 8:24–27; 16:2–3; Lk 8:24–25; 12:54–56; 23:44–45; Ac 2:19–20; Jas 5:17–18; Rev 6:12–14; 9:1–2

Ge 27:39 — And Isaac his father answered and said unto him, Behold, thy dwelling shall be the fatness of the earth, and of the dew of heaven from above;

Job 9:7 — Which commandeth the sun, and it riseth not; and sealeth up the stars.

Job 26:11 — The pillars of heaven tremble and are astonished at his reproof.

Job 29:19 — My root *was* spread out by the waters, and the dew lay all night upon my branch.

Job 38:22 — Hast thou entered into the treasures of the snow? or hast thou seen the treasures of the hail,

Job 38:37 — Who can number the clouds in wisdom? or who can stay the bottles of heaven,

Ps 104:7 — At thy rebuke they fled; at the voice of thy thunder they hasted away.

Ps 104:13 — He watereth the hills from his chambers: the earth is satisfied with the fruit of thy works.

Pr 25:23 — The north wind driveth away rain: so *doth* an angry countenance a backbiting tongue.

Pr 26:1 — As snow in summer, and as rain in harvest, so honour is not seemly for a fool.

Pr 30:4 — Who hath ascended up into heaven, or descended? who hath gathered the wind in his fists? who hath bound the waters in a garment? who hath established all the ends of the earth? what *is* his name, and what *is* his son's name, if thou canst tell?

Ecc 11:3 — If the clouds be full of rain, they empty *themselves* upon the earth: and if the tree fall toward the south, or toward the north, in the place where the tree falleth, there it shall be.

Isa 13:13 — Therefore I will shake the heavens, and the earth shall remove out of her place, in the wrath of the LORD of hosts, and in the day of his fierce anger.

Isa 24:18 — And it shall come to pass, *that* he who fleeth from the noise of the fear shall fall into the pit; and he that cometh up out of the midst of the pit shall be taken in the snare: for the windows from on high are open, and the foundations of the earth do shake.

Isa 50:3 — I clothe the heavens with blackness, and I make sackcloth their covering.

Jer 10:13 — When he uttereth his voice, *there is* a multitude of waters in the heavens, and he causeth the vapors to ascend from the ends of the earth; he maketh lightnings with rain, and bringeth forth the wind out of his treasures.

Jer 51:16 — When he uttereth *his* voice, *there is* a multitude of waters in the heavens; and he causeth the vapors to ascend from the ends of the earth: he maketh lightnings with rain, and bringeth forth the wind out of his treasures.

Da 2:21 — And he changeth the times and the seasons: he removeth kings, and setteth up kings: he giveth wisdom unto the wise, and knowledge to them that know understanding:

Hos 6:4 — O Ephraim, what shall I do unto thee? O Judah, what shall I do unto thee? for your goodness *is* as a morning cloud, and as the early dew it goeth away.

Hos 8:7 — For they have sown the wind, and they shall reap the whirlwind: it hath no stalk: the bud shall yield no meal: if so be it yield, the strangers shall swallow it up.

Hos 13:15 — Though he be fruitful among *his* brethren, an east wind shall come, the wind of the LORD shall come up from the wilderness, and his spring shall become dry, and his fountain shall be dried up: he shall spoil the treasure of all pleasant vessels.

Am 9:6 — *It is* he that buildeth his stories in the heaven, and hath founded his troop in the earth; he that calleth for the waters of the sea, and poureth them out upon the face of the earth: The LORD *is* his name.

Na 1:3 — The LORD *is* slow to anger, and great in power, and will not at all acquit *the wicked:* the LORD hath his way in the whirlwind and in the storm, and the clouds *are* the dust of his feet.

Mt 24:27 — For as the lightning cometh out of the east, and shineth even unto the west; so shall also the coming of the Son of man be.

Mt 24:29 — Immediately after the tribulation of those days shall the sun be darkened, and the moon shall not give her light, and the stars shall fall from heaven, and the powers of the heavens shall be shaken:

Mt 27:45 — Now from the sixth hour there was darkness over all the land unto the ninth hour.

Lk 21:25 — And there shall be signs in the sun, and in the moon, and in the stars; and upon the earth distress of nations, with perplexity; the sea and the waves roaring;

Jn 3:8 — The wind bloweth where it listeth, and thou hearest the sound thereof, but canst not tell whence it cometh, and whither it goeth: so is every one that is born of the Spirit.

2Pe 2:17 — These are wells without water, clouds that are carried with a tempest; to whom the mist of darkness is reserved for ever.

Jude 1:12 — These are spots in your feasts of charity, when they feast with you, feeding themselves without fear: clouds *they are* without water, carried about of winds; trees whose fruit withereth, without fruit, twice dead, plucked up by the roots;

Rev 7:1 — And after these things I saw four angels standing on the four corners of the earth, holding the four winds of the earth, that the wind should not blow on the earth, nor on the sea, nor on any tree.

Rev 8:5 — And the angel took the censer, and filled it with fire of the altar, and cast *it* into the earth: and there were voices, and thunderings, and lightnings, and an earthquake.

Rev 8:7 — The first angel sounded, and there followed hail and fire mingled with blood, and they were cast upon the earth: and the third part of trees was burnt up, and all green grass was burnt up.

Rev 8:10 — And the third angel sounded, and there fell a great star from heaven, burning as it were a lamp, and it fell upon the third part of the rivers, and upon the fountains of waters;

Rev 8:12 — And the fourth angel sounded, and the third part of the sun was smitten, and the third part of the moon, and the third part of the stars; so as the third part of them was darkened, and the day shone not for a third part of it, and the night likewise.

Rev 11:6 — These have power to shut heaven, that it rain not in the days of their prophecy: and have power over waters to turn them to blood, and to smite the earth with all plagues, as often as they will.

Rev 16:21 — And there fell upon men a great hail out of heaven, *every stone* about the weight of a talent: and men blasphemed God because of the plague of the hail; for the plague thereof was exceeding great.

• Phenomena of.

• The deluge.

Ge 7:8 — Of clean beasts, and of beasts that *are* not clean, and of fowls, and of every thing that creepeth upon the earth,

• Fire from heaven on the cities of the plain.

Ge 19:24–25

• Plagues of hail, thunder, and lightning in Egypt.

Ex 9:22–29; Ps 78:17–23

• Plagues of darkness.

Ex 10:22–23

• East wind that divided the Red Sea.

Ex 14:21 — And Moses stretched out his hand over the sea; and the LORD caused the sea to go *back* by a strong east wind all that night, and made the sea dry *land,* and the waters were divided.

• East wind that brought the quails.

Nu 11:31–32; Ps 78:26–28

• Pillar of cloud and fire.

See: Pillar

• Sun stood still.

Jos 10:12–13

• Dew on Gideon's fleece.

Jgs 6:36–40

• Stars in their courses fought against Sisera.

Jgs 5:20 — They fought from heaven; the stars in their courses fought against Sisera.

• Stones from heaven.

Jos 10:11 — And it came to pass, as they fled from before Israel, *and* were in the going down to Bethhoron, that the LORD cast down great stones from heaven upon them unto Azekah, and they died: *they were* more which died with hailstones than they whom the children of Israel slew with the sword.

• Fire from heaven at Elijah's command.

2Ki 1:10–14

• The whirlwind which carried Elijah to heaven.

2Ki 2:1 — And it came to pass, when the LORD would take up Elijah into heaven by a whirlwind, that Elijah went with Elisha from Gilgal.

2Ki 2:11 — And it came to pass, as they still went on, and talked, that, behold, *there appeared* a chariot of fire, and horses of fire, and parted them both asunder; and Elijah went up by a whirlwind into heaven.

• Wind under God's control.

Ps 107:25 — For he commandeth, and raiseth the stormy wind, which lifteth up the waves thereof.

• East wind.

Ps 48:7 — Thou breakest the ships of Tarshish with an east wind.

• Rain, formation of.

Ps 135:6–7

• Dew, copiuos.

Ps 133:3 — As the dew of Hermon, *and as the dew* that descended upon the mountains of Zion: for there the LORD commanded the blessing, *even* life for evermore.

• Rain in answer to Samuel's prayer.

1Sa 12:16–18

• Elijah's prayer.

1Ki 18:41–45

• Rain discomfits the Philistine army.

1Sa 7:10 — And as Samuel was offering up the burnt offering, the Philistines drew near to battle against Israel: but the LORD thundered with a great thunder on that day upon the Philistines, and discomfited them; and they were smitten before Israel.

• Wind destroyed Job's children.

Job 1:18–19

• Darkness at the crucifixion.

Lk 23:44–45

Mt 27:45 — Now from the sixth hour there was darkness over all the land unto the ninth hour.

• The autumnal weather on the Mediterranean.

Ac 27:9–14

Ac 27:20 — And when neither sun nor stars in many days appeared, and no small tempest lay on *us,* all hope that we should be saved was then taken away.

See: Astronomy

See: Dew

See: Hail

See: Rain

• Symbolic.

• Used in the revelation of John.

Rev 6:12–14; 8:3–12; 9:1–2, 17–19; 10:1–6; 12:1–4, 7–9; 14:1–15:4; 16:17–21; 19:11–18

Rev 7:1 — And after these things I saw four angels standing on the four corners of the earth, holding the four winds of the earth, that the wind should not blow on the earth, nor on the sea, nor on any tree.

Rev 11:6 — These have power to shut heaven, that it rain not in the days of their prophecy: and have power over waters to turn them to blood, and to smite the earth with all plagues, as often as they will.

Rev 16:8 — And the fourth angel poured out his vial upon the sun; and power was given unto him to scorch men with fire.

Rev 20:11 — And I saw a great white throne, and him that sat on it, from whose face the earth and the heaven fled away; and there was found no place for them.

Rev 21:1 — And I saw a new heaven and a new earth: for the first heaven and the first earth were passed away; and there was no more sea.

METHEG-AMMAH • A place in Philistia.

2Sa 8:1 — And after this it came to pass, that David smote the Philistines, and subdued them: and David took Metheg-ammah out of the hand of the Philistines.

METHODS

1Co 9:22 — To the weak became I as weak, that I might gain the weak: I am made all things to all *men,* that I might by all means save some.

METHUSAEL • Father of Lamech.

Ge 4:18 — And unto Enoch was born Irad: and Irad begat Mehujael: and Mehujael begat Methusael: and Methusael begat Lamech.

METHUSELAH • Son of Enoch and grandfather of Noah.

Ge 5:21–27

1Ch 1:3 — Henoch, Methuselah, Lamech,

MEZAHAB • Grandfather of Mehetabel.

Ge 36:39 — And Baal-hanan the son of Achbor died, and Hadar reigned in his stead: and the name of his city *was* Pau; and his wife's name *was* Mehetabel, the daughter of Matred, the daughter of Mezahab.

1Ch 1:50 — And when Baal-hanan was dead, Hadad reigned in his stead: and the name of his city *was* Pai; and his wife's name *was* Mehetabel, the daughter of Matred, the daughter of Mezahab.

MIAMIN

• A Jew who divorced his Gentile wife after the captivity.

Ezr 10:25 — Moreover of Israel: of the sons of Parosh; Ramiah, and Jeziah, and Malchiah, and Miamin, and Eleazar, and Malchijah, and Benaiah.

• A priest who returned with Zerubbabel from Babylon.

Ne 12:5 — Miamin, Maadiah, Bilgah,

MIBHAR • One of David's valiant men.

1Ch 11:38 — Joel the brother of Nathan, Mibhar the son of Haggeri,

MIBSAM

• Son of Ishmael.

Ge 25:13 — And these *are* the names of the sons of Ishmael, by their names, according to their generations: the firstborn of Ishmael, Nebajoth; and Kedar, and Adbeel, and Mibsam,

1Ch 1:29 — These *are* their generations: The firstborn of Ishmael, Nebaioth; then Kedar, and Adbeel, and Mibsam,

• Son of Shallum.

1Ch 4:25 — Shallum his son, Mibsam his son, Mishma his son.

MIBZAR • Chief of Edom.

Ge 36:42 — Duke Kenaz, duke Teman, duke Mibzar,

1Ch 1:53 — Duke Kenaz, duke Teman, duke Mibzar,

MICAH

• An Ephraimite.

• His robbery and idolatry.

Jgs 17:1–18:31

• Head of a family of Reuben.

1Ch 5:5 — Micah his son, Reaia his son, Baal his son,

• Son of Mephibosheth.

1Ch 8:34–35; 9:40–41

• Called also Micha.

2Sa 9:12 — And Mephibosheth had a young son, whose name *was* Micha. And all that dwelt in the house of Ziba *were* servants unto Mephibosheth.

• A Kohathite.

• Called also Michah.

1Ch 24:24–25

1Ch 23:20 — Of the sons of Uzziel; Michah the first, and Jesiah the second.

• Father of Abdon.

2Ch 34:20 — And the king commanded Hilkiah, and Ahikam the son of Shaphan, and Abdon the son of Micah, and Shaphan the scribe, and Asaiah a servant of the king's, saying,

• One of the minor prophets.

Jer 26:18–19; Mic 1:14–15

Mic 1:1 — The word of the LORD that came to Micah the Morasthite in the days of Jotham, Ahaz, *and* Hezekiah, kings of Judah, which he saw concerning Samaria and Jerusalem.

• Denounces the idolatry of his times.

Mic 1:1–16

• Denounces the oppressions of the covetous.

Mic 2:1–11

• Foretells the restoration of Israel.

Mic 2:12–13

• Foretells the injustice of judges and falsehoods of false prophets.

Mic 3:1–12

• **Prophesies the coming of the Messiah.**
Mic 4:1–5:15

• **Denounces the oppressions, frauds, and other abominations.**
Mic 6:1–16

• **Laments the state of Zion, and foretells the triumphs, righteousness, and the mercies of God.**
Mic 7:1–20

MICAIAH • A prophet who reproved King Ahab.

1Ki 22:8–28; 2Ch 18:4–27

MICE ✦See: Mouse

MICHA

✦**See: Micah; Called also Micha. Son of Mephibosheth**

• **A Levite.**

Ne 10:11 — Micha, Rehob, Hashabiah,

Ne 11:17 — And Mattaniah the son of Micha, the son of Zabdi, the son of Asaph, *was* the principal to begin the thanksgiving in prayer: and Bakbukiah the second among his brethren, and Abda the son of Shammua, the son of Galal, the son of Jeduthun.

Ne 11:22 — The overseer also of the Levites at Jerusalem *was* Uzzi the son of Bani, the son of Hashabiah, the son of Mattaniah, the son of Micha. Of the sons of Asaph, the singers *were* over the business of the house of God.

MICHAEL

• **An Asherite.**

Nu 13:13 — Of the tribe of Asher, Sethur the son of Michael.

• **Two Gadites.**
1Ch 5:13–14

• **A Gershonite Levite.**

1Ch 6:40 — The son of Michael, the son of Baaseiah, the son of Malchiah,

• **A descendant of Issachar.**

1Ch 7:3 — And the sons of Uzzi; Izrahiah: and the sons of Izrahiah; Michael, and Obadiah, and Joel, Ishiah, five: all of them chief men.

• **A Benjamite.**

1Ch 8:16 — And Michael, and Ispah, and Joha, the sons of Beriah;

• **A captain of the thousands of Manasseh who joined David at Ziklag.**

1Ch 12:20 — As he went to Ziklag, there fell to him of Manasseh, Adnah, and Jozabad, and Jediael, and Michael, and Jozabad, and Elihu, and Zilthai, captains of the thousands that *were* of Manasseh.

• **Father of Omri.**

1Ch 27:18 — Of Judah, Elihu, *one* of the brethren of David: of Issachar, Omri the son of Michael:

• **Son of Jehoshaphat.**

• **Slain by his brother, Jehoram.**
2Ch 21:2–4

• **Father of Zebadiah.**

Ezr 8:8 — And of the sons of Shephatiah; Zebadiah the son of Michael, and with him fourscore males.

• **The Archangel.**

• **His message to Daniel.**

Da 10:13 — But the prince of the kingdom of Persia withstood me one and twenty days: but, lo, Michael, one of the chief princes, came to help me; and I remained there with the kings of Persia.

Da 10:21 — But I will shew thee that which is noted in the scripture of truth: and *there is* none that holdeth with me in these things, but Michael your prince.

Da 12:1 — And at that time shall Michael stand up, the great prince which standeth for the children of thy people: and there shall be a time of trouble, such as never was since there was a nation *even* to that same time: and at that time thy people shall be delivered, every one that shall be found written in the book.

• **Contention with the devil.**

Jude 1:9 — Yet Michael the archangel, when contending with the devil he disputed about the body of Moses, durst not bring against him a railing accusation, but said, The Lord rebuke thee.

• **Fights with the dragon.**

Rev 12:7 — And there was war in heaven: Michael and his angels fought against the dragon; and the dragon fought and his angels,

MICHAIAH

• **Father of Achbor.**

2Ki 22:12 — And the king commanded Hilkiah the priest, and Ahikam the son of Shaphan, and Achbor the son of Michaiah, and Shaphan the scribe, and Asahiah a servant of the king's, saying,

✦**See: Maachah; called also Michaiah.**

Mother of Abijam and grandmother of Asa

• **A prince sent by Jehoshaphat to teach the law in the cities of Judah.**

2Ch 17:7 — Also in the third year of his reign he sent to his princes, *even* to Ben-hail, and to Obadiah, and to Zechariah, and to Nethaneel, and to Michaiah, to teach in the cities of Judah.

• **A priest of the family of Asaph.**

Ne 12:35 — And *certain* of the priests' sons with trumpets; *namely,* Zechariah the son of Jonathan, the son of Shemaiah, the son of Mattaniah, the son of Michaiah, the son of Zaccur, the son of Asaph:

Ne 12:41 — And the priests; Eliakim, Maaseiah, Miniamin, Michaiah, Elioenai, Zechariah, *and* Hananiah, with trumpets;

• Son of Gemariah, who expounds to the princes the prophecies of Jeremiah read by Baruch to the people.

Jer 36:11–14

MICHAL

• Daughter of Saul.

• Given to David as a reward for slaying Goliath.

1Sa 18:22–28

• Rescues David from death.

1Sa 19:9–17

• Saul forcibly separates them and she is given in marriage to Phalti.

1Sa 25:44 — But Saul had given Michal his daughter, David's wife, to Phalti the son of Laish, which *was* of Gallim.

• David recovers, to himself.

2Sa 3:13–16

• Ridicules David on account of his religious zeal.

2Sa 6:20–23

2Sa 6:16 — And as the ark of the LORD came into the city of David, Michal Saul's daughter looked through a window, and saw king David leaping and dancing before the LORD; and she despised him in her heart.

MICHMAS ✧See: Michmash

MICHMASH

• A city of Benjamin.

1Sa 13:5 — And the Philistines gathered themselves together to fight with Israel, thirty thousand chariots, and six thousand horsemen, and people as the sand which *is* on the sea shore in multitude: and they came up, and pitched in Michmash, eastward from Beth-aven.

• People of the captivity return to, and dwell in.

Ezr 2:27 — The men of Michmas, an hundred twenty and two.

Ne 11:31 — The children also of Benjamin from Geba *dwelt* at Michmash, and Aija, and Bethel, and *in* their villages,

• Prophecy concerning the king of Assyria storing his baggage at.

Isa 10:28 — He is come to Aiath, he is passed to Migron; at Michmash he hath laid up his carriages:

• Is garrisoned by Saul.

1Sa 13:2 — Saul chose him three thousand *men* of Israel; *whereof* two thousand were with Saul in Michmash and in mount Bethel, and a thousand were with Jonathan in Gibeah of Benjamin: and the rest of the people he sent every man to his tent.

• Philistines smitten at, by Jonathan.

1Sa 14:31 — And they smote the Philistines that day from Michmash to Aijalon: and the people were very faint.

MICHMETHAH • A city between Ephraim and Manasseh.

Jos 16:6 — And the border went out toward the sea to Michmethah on the north side; and the border went about eastward unto Taanath-shiloh, and passed by it on the east to Janohah;

Jos 17:7 — And the coast of Manasseh was from Asher to Michmethah, that *lieth* before Shechem; and the border went along on the right hand unto the inhabitants of En-tappuah.

MICHRI • A Benjamite.

1Ch 9:8 — And Ibneiah the son of Jeroham, and Elah the son of Uzzi, the son of Michri, and Meshullam the son of Shephatiah, the son of Reuel, the son of Ibnijah;

MICHTAM ✧See: Music

MIDDIN • A city of Judah.

Jos 15:61 — In the wilderness, Beth-arabah, Middin, and Secacah,

MIDIAN • Son of Abraham by Keturah.

1Ch 1:32–33

Ge 25:2 — And she bare him Zimran, and Jokshan, and Medan, and Midian, and Ishbak, and Shuah.

Ge 25:4 — And the sons of Midian; Ephah, and Epher, and Hanoch, and Abidah, and Eldaah. All these *were* the children of Keturah.

MIDIANITES

• Descendants of Midian, son of Abraham by Keturah.

Ge 25:1–2; 1Ch 1:32–33

Ge 25:4 — And the sons of Midian; Ephah, and Epher, and Hanoch, and Abidah, and Eldaah. All these *were* the children of Keturah.

• Called Ishmaelites.

Ge 37:25 — And they sat down to eat bread: and they lifted up their eyes and looked, and, behold, a company of Ishmeelites came from Gilead with their camels bearing spicery and balm and myrrh, going to carry *it* down to Egypt.

Ge 37:28 — Then there passed by Midianites merchantmen; and they drew and lifted up Joseph out of the pit, and sold Joseph to the Ishmeelites for twenty *pieces* of silver: and they brought Joseph into Egypt.

Jgs 8:24 — And Gideon said unto them, I would desire a request of you, that ye would give me every man the earrings of his prey. (For they had golden earrings, because they *were* Ishmaelites.)

• Were merchantmen.

Ge 37:28 — Then there passed by Midianites merchantmen; and they drew and lifted up Joseph out of the pit, and sold Joseph to the Ishmeelites for twenty *pieces* of silver: and they brought Joseph into Egypt.

• Buy Joseph and sell him to Potiphar.

Ge 37:28 — Then there passed by Midianites merchantmen; and they drew and lifted up Joseph out of the pit, and sold Joseph to the Ishmeelites for twenty *pieces* of silver: and they brought Joseph into Egypt.

Ge 37:36 — And the Midianites sold him into Egypt unto Potiphar, an officer of Pharaoh's, *and* captain of the guard.

• Defeated by Israelites under Phinehas, 5 kings slain, women taken captive.

Nu 31:1–54

• Defeated by Gideon.

Jgs 6:1–8:35

• Owned multitudes of camels, and dromedaries, and large quantities of gold.

Isa 60:6 — The multitude of camels shall cover thee, the dromedaries of Midian and Ephah; all they from Sheba shall come: they shall bring gold and incense; and they shall shew forth the praises of the LORD.

• A snare to the Israelites.

Nu 25:16–18

• Prophecies concerning.

Isa 60:6 — The multitude of camels shall cover thee, the dromedaries of Midian and Ephah; all they from Sheba shall come: they shall bring gold and incense; and they shall shew forth the praises of the LORD.

Hab 3:7 — I saw the tents of Cushan in affliction: *and* the curtains of the land of Midian did tremble.

MIDWIFERY

Ex 1:15–21

Ge 35:17 — And it came to pass, when she was in hard labour, that the midwife said unto her, Fear not; thou shalt have this son also.

Eze 16:4 — And *as for* thy nativity, in the day thou wast born thy navel was not cut, neither wast thou washed in water to supple *thee;* thou wast not salted at all, nor swaddled at all.

MIGDAL-EL • A city of Naphtali.

Jos 19:38 — And Iron, and Migdal-el, Horem, and Beth-anath, and Beth-shemesh; nineteen cities with their villages.

MIGDAL-GAD • A city of Judah.

Jos 15:37 — Zenan, and Hadashah, and Migdal-gad,

MIGDOL

• A place near the Red Sea where the Israelites encamped.

Nu 33:7–8

Ex 14:2 — Speak unto the children of Israel, that they turn and encamp before Pi-hahiroth, between Migdol and the sea, over against Baal-zephon: before it shall ye encamp by the sea.

• A city on the northeastern border of lower Egypt.

Jer 44:1 — The word that came to Jeremiah concerning all the Jews which dwell in the land of Egypt, which dwell at Migdol, and at Tahpanhes, and at Noph, and in the country of Pathros, saying,

Jer 46:14 — Declare ye in Egypt, and publish in Migdol, and publish in Noph and in Tahpanhes: say ye, Stand fast, and prepare thee; for the sword shall devour round about thee.

MIGRON

• A city in Benjamin.

• Saul encamps near, under a pomegranate tree.

1Sa 14:2 — And Saul tarried in the uttermost part of Gibeah under a pomegranate tree which is in Migron: and the people that *were* with him *were* about six hundred men;

• Prophecy concerning.

Isa 10:28 — He is come to Aiath, he is passed to Migron; at Michmash he hath laid up his carriages:

MIJAMIN

• A priest in the time of David.

1Ch 24:9 — The fifth to Malchijah, the sixth to Mijamin,

• A priest who sealed the covenant with Nehemiah.

Ne 10:7 — Meshullam, Abijah, Mijamin,

MIKLOTH

• A Benjamite of Jerusalem.

1Ch 9:37–38

1Ch 8:32 — And Mikloth begat Shimeah. And these also dwelt with their brethren in Jerusalem, over against them.

• A ruler in the reign of David.

1Ch 27:4 — And over the course of the second month *was* Dodai an Ahohite, and of his course *was* Mikloth also the ruler: in his course likewise *were* twenty and four thousand.

MIKNEIAH • A doorkeeper of the temple, and musician.

1Ch 15:18 — And with them their brethren of the second *degree,* Zechariah, Ben, and Jaaziel, and Shemiramoth, and Jehiel, and Unni, Eliab, and Benaiah, and Maaseiah, and Mattithiah, and Elipheleh, and Mikneiah, and Obed-edom, and Jeiel, the porters.

1Ch 15:21 — And Mattithiah, and Elipheleh, and Mikneiah, and Obed-edom, and Jeiel, and Azaziah, with harps on the Sheminith to excel.

MILALAI • A priest who took part in the dedication of the walls of Jerusalem.

Ne 12:36 — And his brethren, Shemaiah, and Azarael, Milalai, Gilalai, Maai, Nethaneel, and Judah, Hanani, with the musical instruments of David the man of God, and Ezra the scribe before them.

MILCAH

• Wife of Naher and mother of Bethuel.

Ge 22:20–23

Ge 11:29 — And Abram and Nahor took them wives: the name of Abram's wife *was* Sarai; and the name of Nahor's wife, Milcah, the daughter of Haran, the father of Milcah, and the father of Iscah.

Ge 24:15 — And it came to pass, before he had done speaking, that, behold, Rebekah came out, who was born to Bethuel, son of Milcah, the wife of Nahor,

Abraham's brother, with her pitcher upon her shoulder.

Ge 24:24 — And she said unto him, I *am* the daughter of Bethuel the son of Milcah, which she bare unto Nahor.

Ge 24:47 — And I asked her, and said, Whose daughter *art* thou? And she said, The daughter of Bethuel, Nahor's son, whom Milcah bare unto him: and I put the earring upon her face, and the bracelets upon her hands.

• Daughter of Zelophehad. Special legislation in regard to the inheritance of.

Nu 27:1–7; 36:1–12; Jos 17:3–4

Nu 26:33 — And Zelophehad the son of Hepher had no sons, but daughters: and the names of the daughters of Zelophehad *were* Mahlah, and Noah, Hoglah, Milcah, and Tirzah.

MILCOM ↞See: Molech

MILDEW

Dt 28:22 — The LORD shall smite thee with a consumption, and with a fever, and with an inflammation, and with an extreme burning, and with the sword, and with blasting, and with mildew; and they shall pursue thee until thou perish.

Am 4:9 — I have smitten you with blasting and mildew: when your gardens and your vineyards and your fig trees and your olive trees increased, the palmerworm devoured *them:* yet have ye not returned unto me, saith the LORD.

Hag 2:17 — I smote you with blasting and with mildew and with hail in all the labours of your hands; yet ye *turned* not to me, saith the LORD.

MILE

Mt 5:41 — And whosoever shall compel thee to go a mile, go with him twain.

MILETUS

• Called also Miletum.

• A seaport in Asia Minor that Paul visits.

Ac 20:15 — And we sailed thence, and came the next *day* over against Chios; and the next *day* we arrived at Samos, and tarried at Trogyllium; and the next *day* we came to Miletus.

• Paul sends to Ephesus for the elders of the church, and addresses them at.

Ac 20:17–38

• Trophimus left sick at.

2Ti 4:20 — Erastus abode at Corinth: but Trophimus have I left at Miletum sick.

MILITARY INSTRUCTION

• Of children.

2Sa 1:18 — (Also he bade them teach the children of Judah *the use of* the bow: behold, it is written in the book of Jasher.)

↞**See: Armies**

MILK

• Used for food.

Ge 18:8 — And he took butter, and milk, and the calf which he had dressed, and set *it* before them; and he stood by them under the tree, and they did eat.

Jgs 4:19 — And he said unto her, Give me, I pray thee, a little water to drink; for I am thirsty. And she opened a bottle of milk, and gave him drink, and covered him.

SS 5:1 — I am come into my garden, my sister, *my* spouse: I have gathered my myrrh with my spice; I have eaten my honeycomb with my honey; I have drunk my wine with my milk: eat, O friends; drink, yea, drink abundantly, O beloved.

Eze 25:4 — Behold, therefore I will deliver thee to the men of the east for a possession, and they shall set their palaces in thee, and make their dwellings in thee: they shall eat thy fruit, and they shall drink thy milk.

1Co 9:7 — Who goeth a warfare any time at his own charges? who planteth a vineyard, and eateth not of the fruit thereof? or who feedeth a flock, and eateth not of the milk of the flock?

• Of goats.

Pr 27:27 — And *thou shalt have* goats' milk enough for thy food, for the food of thy household, and *for* the maintenance for thy maidens.

• Of sheep.

Isa 7:21–22

Dt 32:14 — Butter of kine, and milk of sheep, with fat of lambs, and rams of the breed of Bashan, and goats, with the fat of kidneys of wheat; and thou didst drink the pure blood of the grape.

• Of camels.

Ge 32:15 — Thirty milch camels with their colts, forty kine, and ten bulls, twenty she asses, and ten foals.

• Of cows.

Dt 32:14 — Butter of kine, and milk of sheep, with fat of lambs, and rams of the breed of Bashan, and goats, with the fat of kidneys of wheat; and thou didst drink the pure blood of the grape.

1Sa 6:7 — Now therefore make a new cart, and take two milch kine, on which there hath come no yoke, and tie the kine to the cart, and bring their calves home from them:

1Sa 6:10 — And the men did so; and took two milch kine, and tied them to the cart, and shut up their calves at home:

• Churned.

Pr 30:33 — Surely the churning of milk bringeth forth butter, and the wringing of the nose bringeth forth blood: so the forcing of wrath bringeth forth strife.

• Kid not to be seethed in its mother's.

Ex 23:19 — The first of the firstfruits of thy land thou shalt bring into the house of the LORD thy God. Thou shalt not seethe a kid in his mother's milk.

Dt 14:21 — Ye shall not eat *of* any thing that dieth of itself: thou shalt give it unto the stranger that *is* in thy gates, that he may eat it; or thou mayest sell it unto an alien: for thou *art* an holy people unto the

Lord thy God. Thou shalt not seethe a kid in his mother's milk.

- **Figurative.**

Heb 5:12–13

Ex 3:8 — And I am come down to deliver them out of the hand of the Egyptians, and to bring them up out of that land unto a good land and a large, unto a land flowing with milk and honey; unto the place of the Canaanites, and the Hittites, and the Amorites, and the Perizzites, and the Hivites, and the Jebusites.

Ex 3:17 — And I have said, I will bring you up out of the affliction of Egypt unto the land of the Canaanites, and the Hittites, and the Amorites, and the Perizzites, and the Hivites, and the Jebusites, unto a land flowing with milk and honey.

Ex 13:5 — And it shall be when the Lord shall bring thee into the land of the Canaanites, and the Hittites, and the Amorites, and the Hivites, and the Jebusites, which he sware unto thy fathers to give thee, a land flowing with milk and honey, that thou shalt keep this service in this month.

Ex 33:3 — Unto a land flowing with milk and honey: for I will not go up in the midst of thee; for thou *art* a stiffnecked people: lest I consume thee in the way.

Nu 13:27 — And they told him, and said, We came unto the land whither thou sentest us, and surely it floweth with milk and honey; and this *is* the fruit of it.

Dt 26:9 — And he hath brought us into this place, and hath given us this land, *even* a land that floweth with milk and honey.

Dt 26:15 — Look down from thy holy habitation, from heaven, and bless thy people Israel, and the land which thou hast given us, as thou swarest unto our fathers, a land that floweth with milk and honey.

Isa 55:1 — Ho, every one that thirsteth, come ye to the waters, and he that hath no money; come ye, buy, and eat; yea, come, buy wine and milk without money and without price.

Isa 60:16 — Thou shalt also suck the milk of the Gentiles, and shalt suck the breast of kings: and thou shalt know that I the Lord *am* thy Saviour and thy Redeemer, the mighty One of Jacob.

Jer 11:5 — That I may perform the oath which I have sworn unto your fathers, to give them a land flowing with milk and honey, as *it is* this day. Then answered I, and said, So be it, O Lord.

Jer 32:22 — And hast given them this land, which thou didst swear to their fathers to give them, a land flowing with milk and honey;

Eze 20:6 — In the day *that* I lifted up mine hand unto them, to bring them forth of the land of Egypt into a land that I had espied for them, flowing with milk and honey, which *is* the glory of all lands:

Joel 3:18 — And it shall come to pass in that day, *that* the mountains shall drop down new wine, and the hills shall flow with milk, and all the rivers of Judah shall flow with waters, and a fountain shall come forth of the house of the Lord, and shall water the valley of Shittim.

1Co 3:2 — I have fed you with milk, and not with meat: for hitherto ye were not able *to bear it,* neither yet now are ye able.

1Pe 2:2 — As newborn babes, desire the sincere milk of the word, that ye may grow thereby:

MILL

Jer 25:10 — Moreover I will take from them the voice of mirth, and the voice of gladness, the voice of the bridegroom, and the voice of the bride, the sound of the millstones, and the light of the candle.

- **Upper and nether stones of.**

Dt 24:6 — No man shall take the nether or the upper millstone to pledge: for he taketh *a man's* life to pledge.

Job 41:24 — His heart is as firm as a stone; yea, as hard as a piece of the nether *millstone.*

Isa 47:2 — Take the millstones, and grind meal: uncover thy locks, make bare the leg, uncover the thigh, pass over the rivers.

- **Used in Egypt.**

Ex 11:5 — And all the firstborn in the land of Egypt shall die, from the firstborn of Pharaoh that sitteth upon his throne, even unto the firstborn of the maidservant that *is* behind the mill; and all the firstborn of beasts.

- **Operated by women.**

Mt 24:41 — Two *women shall be* grinding at the mill; the one shall be taken, and the other left.

- **Operated by captives.**

Jgs 16:21 — But the Philistines took him, and put out his eyes, and brought him down to Gaza, and bound him with fetters of brass; and he did grind in the prison house.

La 5:13 — They took the young men to grind, and the children fell under the wood.

- **Manna ground in.**

Nu 11:8 — *And* the people went about, and gathered *it,* and ground *it* in mills, or beat *it* in a mortar, and baked *it* in pans, and made cakes of it: and the taste of it was as the taste of fresh oil.

- **Sound of, to cease.**

Rev 18:22 — And the voice of harpers, and musicians, and of pipers, and trumpeters, shall be heard no more at all in thee; and no craftsman, of whatsoever craft *he be,* shall be found any more in thee; and the sound of a millstone shall be heard no more at all in thee;

See: Millstone

MILLENNIUM

Isa 65:17–25; Zep 3:11–13; Zec 9:9–10; 14:16–21; Mt 16:18–19; Rev 20:1–15

Mt 26:29 — But I say unto you, I will not drink henceforth of this fruit of the vine, until that day when I drink it new with you in my Father's kingdom.

Mk 14:25 — Verily I say unto you, I will drink no more of the fruit of the vine, until that day that I drink it new in the kingdom of God.

Heb 8:11 — And they shall not teach every man his neighbour, and every man his brother, saying, Know the Lord: for all shall know me, from the least to the greatest.

Rev 14:6 — And I saw another angel fly in the midst of heaven, having the everlasting gospel to preach unto them that dwell on the earth, and to every nation, and kindred, and tongue, and people,

See: Church; prophecies concerning prosperity of

See: Jesus, Kingdom of

See: Jesus, Second Coming of

MILLET

Eze 4:9 — Take thou also unto thee wheat, and barley, and beans, and lentiles, and millet, and fitches, and put them in one vessel, and make thee bread thereof, *according* to the number of the days that thou shalt lie upon thy side, three hundred and ninety days shalt thou eat thereof.

MILLO

• The house of Millo, possibly a clan at Shechem.

Jgs 9:6 — And all the men of Shechem gathered together, and all the house of Millo, and went, and made Abimelech king, by the plain of the pillar that *was* in Shechem.

Jgs 9:20 — But if not, let fire come out from Abimelech, and devour the men of Shechem, and the house of Millo; and let fire come out from the men of Shechem, and from the house of Millo, and devour Abimelech.

• A name given to part of the citadel of Jerusalem.

2Sa 5:9 — So David dwelt in the fort, and called it the city of David. And David built round about from Millo and inward.

1Ch 11:8 — And he built the city round about, even from Millo round about: and Joab repaired the rest of the city.

• King Solomon raises a levy to repair.

1Ki 9:15 — And this *is* the reason of the levy which king Solomon raised; for to build the house of the LORD, and his own house, and Millo, and the wall of Jerusalem, and Hazor, and Megiddo, and Gezer.

1Ki 9:24 — But Pharaoh's daughter came up out of the city of David unto her house which *Solomon* had built for her: then did he build Millo.

1Ki 11:27 — And this *was* the cause that he lifted up *his* hand against the king: Solomon built Millo, *and* repaired the breaches of the city of David his father.

• Repaired by King Hezekiah.

2Ch 32:5 — Also he strengthened himself, and built up all the wall that was broken, and raised *it* up to the towers, and another wall without, and repaired Millo *in* the city of David, and made darts and shields in abundance.

• King Joash murdered at.

2Ki 12:20 — And his servants arose, and made a conspiracy, and slew Joash in the house of Millo, which goeth down to Silla.

MILLSTONE

• Not to be taken in pledge.

Dt 24:6 — No man shall take the nether or the upper millstone to pledge: for he taketh *a man's* life to pledge.

• Probably used in executions by drowning.

Mt 18:6 — But whoso shall offend one of these little ones which believe in me, it were better for him that a millstone were hanged about his neck, and *that* he were drowned in the depth of the sea.

Mk 9:42 — And whosoever shall offend one of *these* little ones that believe in me, it is better for him that a millstone were hanged about his neck, and he were cast into the sea.

Lk 17:2 — It were better for him that a millstone were hanged about his neck, and he cast into the sea, than that he should offend one of these little ones.

• Abimelech killed by one being hurled upon him.

Jgs 9:53 — And a certain woman cast a piece of a millstone upon Abimelech's head, and all to brake his skull.

• Figurative of the hard heart.

Job 41:24 — His heart is as firm as a stone; yea, as hard as a piece of the nether *millstone*.

MINCING

Isa 3:16 — Moreover the LORD saith, Because the daughters of Zion are haughty, and walk with stretched forth necks and wanton eyes, walking and mincing *as* they go, and making a tinkling with their feet:

MINERALS

See: Adamant

See: Agate

See: Alabaster

See: Amethyst

See: Beryl

See: Brimstone

See: Chalcedony

See: Chalk

See: Chrysolyte

See: Chrysoprasus

See: Copper

See: Coral

See: Diamond

See: Flint

See: Gold

See: Iron

See: Jacinth

See: Jasper

See: Lead

See: Lime

See: Marble

- **See: Nitre**
- **See: Pitch**
- **See: Salt**
- **See: Sapphire**
- **See: Sardius**
- **See: Sardonyx**
- **See: Silver**
- **See: Slime**
- **See: Stones**
- **See: Stones; precious**
- **See: Tin**
- **See: Topaz**

MINIAMIN

• A Levite who assisted in the distribution of the sacred offerings in the time of Hezekiah.

2Ch 31:15 — And next him *were* Eden, and Miniamin, and Jeshua, and Shemaiah, Amariah, and Shecaniah, in the cities of the priests, in *their* set office, to give to their brethren by courses, as well to the great as to the small:

• A priest who came from Babylon with Zerubbabel.

Ne 12:17 — Of Abijah, Zichri; of Miniamin, of Moadiah, Piltai;

Ne 12:41 — And the priests; Eliakim, Maaseiah, Miniamin, Michaiah, Elioenai, Zechariah, *and* Hananiah, with trumpets;

MINISTER, a sacred teacher

• Called.

• Ambassadors for Christ.

2Co 5:20 — Now then we are ambassadors for Christ, as though God did beseech *you* by us: we pray *you* in Christ's stead, be ye reconciled to God.

• Angels of the Church.

Rev 1:20–2:1

• Apostles.

Lk 6:13 — And when it was day, he called *unto him* his disciples: and of them he chose twelve, whom also he named apostles;

Rev 18:20 — Rejoice over her, *thou* heaven, and *ye* holy apostles and prophets; for God hath avenged you on her.

• Apostles of Jesus Christ.

Tit 1:1 — Paul, a servant of God, and an apostle of Jesus Christ, according to the faith of God's elect, and the acknowledging of the truth which is after godliness;

• Defenders of the Faith.

Php 1:7 — Even as it is meet for me to think this of you all, because I have you in my heart; inasmuch as both in my bonds, and in the defence and confirmation of the gospel, ye all are partakers of my grace.

• Elders.

1Ti 5:17 — Let the elders that rule well be counted worthy of double honour, especially they who labour in the word and doctrine.

1Pe 5:1 — The elders which are among you I exhort, who am also an elder, and a witness of the sufferings of Christ, and also a partaker of the glory that shall be revealed:

• Evangelists.

Eph 4:11 — And he gave some, apostles; and some, prophets; and some, evangelists; and some, pastors and teachers;

2Ti 4:5 — But watch thou in all things, endure afflictions, do the work of an evangelist, make full proof of thy ministry.

• Fishers of Men.

Mt 4:19 — And he saith unto them, Follow me, and I will make you fishers of men.

Mk 1:17 — And Jesus said unto them, Come ye after me, and I will make you to become fishers of men.

• Laborers.

Mt 9:38 — Pray ye therefore the Lord of the harvest, that he will send forth labourers into his harvest.

Phm 1:1 — Paul, a prisoner of Jesus Christ, and Timothy our brother, unto Philemon our dearly beloved, and fellowlabourer,

• Laborers in the Gospel of Christ.

1Th 3:2 — And sent Timotheus, our brother, and minister of God, and our fellowlabourer in the gospel of Christ, to establish you, and to comfort you concerning your faith:

• Lights.

Jn 5:35 — He was a burning and a shining light: and ye were willing for a season to rejoice in his light.

• Men of God.

Dt 33:1 — And this *is* the blessing, wherewith Moses the man of God blessed the children of Israel before his death.

1Ti 6:11 — But thou, O man of God, flee these things; and follow after righteousness, godliness, faith, love, patience, meekness.

• Messengers of the Church.

2Co 8:23 — Whether *any do enquire* of Titus, *he is* my partner and fellowhelper concerning you: or our brethren *be enquired of, they are* the messengers of the churches, *and* the glory of Christ.

• Messengers of the Lord of Hosts.

Mal 2:7 — For the priest's lips should keep knowledge, and they should seek the law at his mouth: for he *is* the messenger of the LORD of hosts.

• Ministers of God.

Isa 61:6 — But ye shall be named the Priests of the LORD: *men* shall call you the Ministers of our God: ye shall eat the riches of the Gentiles, and in their glory shall ye boast yourselves.

2Co 6:4 — But in all *things* approving ourselves as the ministers of God, in much patience, in afflictions, in necessities, in distresses,

- **Ministers of the Lord.**

Joel 2:17 — Let the priests, the ministers of the LORD, weep between the porch and the altar, and let them say, Spare thy people, O LORD, and give not thine heritage to reproach, that the heathen should rule over them: wherefore should they say among the people, Where *is* their God?

- **Ministers of Christ.**

Ro 15:16 — That I should be the minister of Jesus Christ to the Gentiles, ministering the gospel of God, that the offering up of the Gentiles might be acceptable, being sanctified by the Holy Ghost.

1Co 4:1 — Let a man so account of us, as of the ministers of Christ, and stewards of the mysteries of God.

- **Ministers of the Sanctuary.**

Eze 45:4 — The holy *portion* of the land shall be for the priests the ministers of the sanctuary, which shall come near to minister unto the LORD: and it shall be a place for their houses, and an holy place for the sanctuary.

- **Ministers of the Gospel.**

Eph 3:7 — Whereof I was made a minister, according to the gift of the grace of God given unto me by the effectual working of his power.

Col 1:23 — If ye continue in the faith grounded and settled, and *be* not moved away from the hope of the gospel, which ye have heard, *and* which was preached to every creature which is under heaven; whereof I Paul am made a minister;

- **Ministers of the Word.**

Lk 1:2 — Even as they delivered them unto us, which from the beginning were eyewitnesses, and ministers of the word;

- **Ministers of the New Testament.**

2Co 3:6 — Who also hath made us able ministers of the new testament; not of the letter, but of the spirit: for the letter killeth, but the spirit giveth life.

- **Ministers of the Church.**

Col 1:24–25

- **Ministers of Righteousness.**

2Co 11:15 — Therefore *it is* no great thing if his ministers also be transformed as the ministers of righteousness; whose end shall be according to their works.

- **Overseers.**

Ac 20:28 — Take heed therefore unto yourselves, and to all the flock, over the which the Holy Ghost hath made you overseers, to feed the church of God, which he hath purchased with his own blood.

- **Pastors.**

Jn 21:16–18

Jer 3:15 — And I will give you pastors according to mine heart, which shall feed you with knowledge and understanding.

Eph 4:11 — And he gave some, apostles; and some, prophets; and some, evangelists; and some, pastors and teachers;

- **Preachers.**

Ro 10:14 — How then shall they call on him in whom they have not believed? and how shall they believe in him of whom they have not heard? and how shall they hear without a preacher?

1Ti 2:7 — Whereunto I am ordained a preacher, and an apostle, (I speak the truth in Christ, *and* lie not;) a teacher of the Gentiles in faith and verity.

- **Preachers of Righteousness.**

2Pe 2:5 — And spared not the old world, but saved Noah the eighth *person,* a preacher of righteousness, bringing in the flood upon the world of the ungodly;

- **Servants of God.**

Tit 1:1 — Paul, a servant of God, and an apostle of Jesus Christ, according to the faith of God's elect, and the acknowledging of the truth which is after godliness;

Jas 1:1 — James, a servant of God and of the Lord Jesus Christ, to the twelve tribes which are scattered abroad, greeting.

- **Servants of the Lord.**

2Ti 2:24 — And the servant of the Lord must not strive; but be gentle unto all *men,* apt to teach, patient,

- **Servants of Jesus Christ.**

Php 1:1 — Paul and Timotheus, the servants of Jesus Christ, to all the saints in Christ Jesus which are at Philippi, with the bishops and deacons:

Jude 1:1 — Jude, the servant of Jesus Christ, and brother of James, to them that are sanctified by God the Father, and preserved in Jesus Christ, *and* called:

- **Servants of the Church.**

2Co 4:5 — For we preach not ourselves, but Christ Jesus the Lord; and ourselves your servants for Jesus' sake.

- **Shepherds.**

Jer 23:4 — And I will set up shepherds over them which shall feed them: and they shall fear no more, nor be dismayed, neither shall they be lacking, saith the LORD.

- **Soldiers of Christ.**

2Ti 2:3–4

Php 2:25 — Yet I supposed it necessary to send to you Epaphroditus, my brother, and companion in labour, and fellow soldier, but your messenger, and he that ministered to my wants.

- **Stars.**

Rev 1:20–2:1

- **Stewards of God.**

Tit 1:7 — For a bishop must be blameless, as the steward of God; not selfwilled, not soon angry, not given to wine, no striker, not given to filthy lucre;

• **Stewards of the Grace of God.**

1Pe 4:10 — As every man hath received the gift, *even so* minister the same one to another, as good stewards of the manifold grace of God.

• **Stewards of the Mysteries of God.**

1Co 4:1 — Let a man so account of us, as of the ministers of Christ, and stewards of the mysteries of God.

• **Teachers.**

Isa 30:20 — And *though* the Lord give you the bread of adversity, and the water of affliction, yet shall not thy teachers be removed into a corner any more, but thine eyes shall see thy teachers:

Eph 4:11 — And he gave some, apostles; and some, prophets; and some, evangelists; and some, pastors and teachers;

• **Watchmen.**

Isa 62:6 — I have set watchmen upon thy walls, O Jerusalem, *which* shall never hold their peace day nor night: ye that make mention of the LORD, keep not silence,

Eze 33:7 — So thou, O son of man, I have set thee a watchman unto the house of Israel; therefore thou shalt hear the word at my mouth, and warn them from me.

• **Witnesses.**

Ac 1:8 — But ye shall receive power, after that the Holy Ghost is come upon you: and ye shall be witnesses unto me both in Jerusalem, and in all Judaea, and in Samaria, and unto the uttermost part of the earth.

Ac 5:32 — And we are his witnesses of these things; and *so is* also the Holy Ghost, whom God hath given to them that obey him.

Ac 26:16 — But rise, and stand upon thy feet: for I have appeared unto thee for this purpose, to make thee a minister and a witness both of these things which thou hast seen, and of those things in the which I will appear unto thee;

• **Workers Together with God.**

2Co 6:1 — We then, *as* workers together *with him,* beseech *you* also that ye receive not the grace of God in vain.

• **Likened to sowers.**

Mt 13:3–8; Mk 4:3–20; Lk 8:5–8

Ps 126:6 — He that goeth forth and weepeth, bearing precious seed, shall doubtless come again with rejoicing, bringing his sheaves *with him.*

• **Call of.**

Nu 3:5–13; 1Sa 3:4–10; Isa 6:8–10; Jnh 1:1–2; 3:1–2; Mt 4:18–22; Mk 1:17–20; Lk 10:1–2; Ac 13:2–3; 22:12–15; 26:14–18; Ro 10:14–15; 1Co 1:27–28; 9:16–19; 2Co 5:18–20; Gal 1:15–16; Eph 3:7–8; 4:11–12; Col 1:25–29; 1Ti 1:12–14

Ex 28:1 — And take thou unto thee Aaron thy brother, and his sons with him, from among the children of Israel, that he may minister unto me in the priest's office, *even* Aaron, Nadab and Abihu, Eleazar and Ithamar, Aaron's sons.

1Ki 19:16 — And Jehu the son of Nimshi shalt thou anoint *to be* king over Israel: and Elisha the son of Shaphat of Abel-meholah shalt thou anoint *to be* prophet in thy room.

1Ki 19:19 — So he departed thence, and found Elisha the son of Shaphat, who *was* plowing *with* twelve yoke *of oxen* before him, and he with the twelfth: and Elijah passed by him, and cast his mantle upon him.

1Ch 23:13 — The sons of Amram; Aaron and Moses: and Aaron was separated, that he should sanctify the most holy things, he and his sons for ever, to burn incense before the LORD, to minister unto him, and to bless in his name for ever.

Jer 1:5 — Before I formed thee in the belly I knew thee; and before thou camest forth out of the womb I sanctified thee, *and* I ordained thee a prophet unto the nations.

Am 2:11 — And I raised up of your sons for prophets, and of your young men for Nazarites. *Is it* not even thus, O ye children of Israel? saith the LORD.

Mt 9:9 — And as Jesus passed forth from thence, he saw a man, named Matthew, sitting at the receipt of custom: and he saith unto him, Follow me. And he arose, and followed him.

Mk 2:14 — And as he passed by, he saw Levi the *son* of Alphaeus sitting at the receipt of custom, and said unto him, Follow me. And he arose and followed him.

Jn 1:43 — The day following Jesus would go forth into Galilee, and findeth Philip, and saith unto him, Follow me.

Ac 20:24 — But none of these things move me, neither count I my life dear unto myself, so that I might finish my course with joy, and the ministry, which I have received of the Lord Jesus, to testify the gospel of the grace of God.

Ro 1:1 — Paul, a servant of Jesus Christ, called *to be* an apostle, separated unto the gospel of God,

1Co 1:1 — Paul, called *to be* an apostle of Jesus Christ through the will of God, and Sosthenes *our* brother,

2Co 1:1 — Paul, an apostle of Jesus Christ by the will of God, and Timothy *our* brother, unto the church of God which is at Corinth, with all the saints which are in all Achaia:

Col 1:1 — Paul, an apostle of Jesus Christ by the will of God, and Timotheus *our* brother,

Col 4:17 — And say to Archippus, Take heed to the ministry which thou hast received in the Lord, that thou fulfil it.

1Ti 2:7 — Whereunto I am ordained a preacher, and an apostle, (I speak the truth in Christ, *and* lie not;) a teacher of the Gentiles in faith and verity.

2Ti 1:11 — Whereunto I am appointed a preacher, and an apostle, and a teacher of the Gentiles.

Tit 1:3 — But hath in due times manifested his word through preaching, which is committed unto me according to the commandment of God our Saviour;

Heb 5:4 — And no man taketh this honour unto himself, but he that is called of God, as *was* Aaron.

See: Call, Personal

See: Excuses

See: Levites

↞See: Priest, Duties of

↞See: Priest, High

↞See: Priest, Miscellaneous Facts Concerning

• Character and qualifications of.

Le 10:3–11; Nu 16:9–10; Dt 32:1–3; Isa 6:5–8; Jer 1:7–8; Eze 34:1–31; Mal 2:6–7; Mt 10:16–20, 22–24; 11:25–26; 13:51–52; 20:25–28; 23:8–11; Lk 12:42–44; Jn 4:36–38; 10:2–5, 11–15; 13:13–17; 15:20–21; 17:16–18; Ac 6:3–4; 20:22–24; Ro 2:21–23; 1Co 1:27–30; 3:7–10; 4:10–13; 9:16–23; 2Co 2:15–17; 3:6–10; 4:1–10; 5:18–20; 6:3–7; 10:1–2; 1Th 2:3–12; 1Ti 1:1–20; 3:1–13; 6:13–14, 20–21; 2Ti 1:1–2:7; 2:14–16, 20–26; 3:16–17; Tit 1:1–3:15; Heb 5:1–3, 12–14; 13:6–7; Jas 3:16–18; 1Pe 4:10–11

Le 21:6 — They shall be holy unto their God, and not profane the name of their God: for the offerings of the LORD made by fire, *and* the bread of their God, they do offer: therefore they shall be holy.

1Sa 2:35 — And I will raise me up a faithful priest, *that* shall do according to *that* which *is* in mine heart and in my mind: and I will build him a sure house; and he shall walk before mine anointed for ever.

1Sa 12:7 — Now therefore stand still, that I may reason with you before the LORD of all the righteous acts of the LORD, which he did to you and to your fathers.

2Ch 6:41 — Now therefore arise, O LORD God, into thy resting place, thou, and the ark of thy strength: let thy priests, O LORD God, be clothed with salvation, and let thy saints rejoice in goodness.

2Ch 29:11 — My sons, be not now negligent: for the LORD hath chosen you to stand before him, to serve him, and that ye should minister unto him, and burn incense.

Ezr 7:10 — For Ezra had prepared his heart to seek the law of the LORD, and to do *it,* and to teach in Israel statutes and judgments.

Ps 68:11 — The Lord gave the word: great *was* the company of those that published *it.*

Pr 11:30 — The fruit of the righteous *is* a tree of life; and he that winneth souls *is* wise.

Isa 32:20 — Blessed *are* ye that sow beside all waters, that send forth *thither* the feet of the ox and the ass.

Isa 52:11 — Depart ye, depart ye, go ye out from thence, touch no unclean *thing;* go ye out of the midst of her; be ye clean, that bear the vessels of the LORD.

Jer 3:15 — And I will give you pastors according to mine heart, which shall feed you with knowledge and understanding.

Jer 20:9 — Then I said, I will not make mention of him, nor speak any more in his name. But *his word* was in mine heart as a burning fire shut up in my bones, and I was weary with forbearing, and I could not *stay.*

Mt 24:45 — Who then is a faithful and wise servant, whom his lord hath made ruler over his household, to give them meat in due season?

Lk 6:39 — And he spake a parable unto them, Can the blind lead the blind? shall they not both fall into the ditch?

Lk 10:21 — In that hour Jesus rejoiced in spirit, and said, I thank thee, O Father, Lord of heaven and earth, that thou hast hid these things from the wise and prudent, and hast revealed them unto babes: even so, Father; for so it seemed good in thy sight.

Lk 22:27 — For whether *is* greater, he that sitteth at meat, or he that serveth? *is* not he that sitteth at meat? but I am among you as he that serveth.

Lk 24:49 — And, behold, I send the promise of my Father upon you: but tarry ye in the city of Jerusalem, until ye be endued with power from on high.

Jn 3:27 — John answered and said, A man can receive nothing, except it be given him from heaven.

Jn 3:34 — For he whom God hath sent speaketh the words of God: for God giveth not the Spirit by measure *unto him.*

Jn 17:20 — Neither pray I for these alone, but for them also which shall believe on me through their word;

Ac 1:8 — But ye shall receive power, after that the Holy Ghost is come upon you: and ye shall be witnesses unto me both in Jerusalem, and in all Judaea, and in Samaria, and unto the uttermost part of the earth.

Ac 4:8 — Then Peter, filled with the Holy Ghost, said unto them, Ye rulers of the people, and elders of Israel,

Ac 4:31 — And when they had prayed, the place was shaken where they were assembled together; and they were all filled with the Holy Ghost, and they spake the word of God with boldness.

1Co 1:23 — But we preach Christ crucified, unto the Jews a stumblingblock, and unto the Greeks foolishness;

1Co 2:2 — For I determined not to know any thing among you, save Jesus Christ, and him crucified.

1Co 9:27 — But I keep under my body, and bring *it* into subjection: lest that by any means, when I have preached to others, I myself should be a castaway.

1Co 15:10 — But by the grace of God I am what I am: and his grace *which was bestowed* upon me was not in vain; but I laboured more abundantly than they all: yet not I, but the grace of God which was with me.

2Co 5:11 — Knowing therefore the terror of the Lord, we persuade men; but we are made manifest unto God; and I trust also are made manifest in your consciences.

2Co 10:8 — For though I should boast somewhat more of our authority, which the Lord hath given us for edification, and not for your destruction, I should not be ashamed:

2Co 13:10 — Therefore I write these things being absent, lest being present I should use sharpness, according to the power which the Lord hath given me to edification, and not to destruction.

Gal 2:8 — (For he that wrought effectually in Peter to the apostleship of the circumcision, the same was mighty in me toward the Gentiles:)

Gal 6:17 — From henceforth let no man trouble me: for I bear in my body the marks of the Lord Jesus.

Php 3:17 — Brethren, be followers together of me, and mark them which walk so as ye have us for an ensample.

1Ti 3:15 — But if I tarry long, that thou mayest know how thou oughtest to behave thyself in the house of God, which is the church of the living God, the pillar and ground of the truth.

1Ti 5:17 — Let the elders that rule well be counted worthy of double honour, especially they who labour in the word and doctrine.

1Ti 5:21 — I charge *thee* before God, and the Lord Jesus Christ, and the elect angels, that thou observe these things without preferring one before another, doing nothing by partiality.

1Ti 6:11 — But thou, O man of God, flee these things; and follow after righteousness, godliness, faith, love, patience, meekness.

2Ti 3:14 — But continue thou in the things which thou hast learned and hast been assured of, knowing of whom thou hast learned *them;*

Heb 13:9 — Be not carried about with divers and strange doctrines. For *it is* a good thing that the heart be established with grace; not with meats, which have not profited them that have been occupied therein.

Heb 13:17 — Obey them that have the rule over you, and submit yourselves: for they watch for your souls, as they that must give account, that they may do it with joy, and not with grief: for that *is* unprofitable for you.

Jas 3:1 — My brethren, be not many masters, knowing that we shall receive the greater condemnation.

Jas 3:13 — Who *is* a wise man and endued with knowledge among you? let him shew out of a good conversation his works with meekness of wisdom.

• Charge delivered to.

Nu 18:1–7; 27:18–23; Dt 31:7–8, 14–23; Jos 1:1–9; Mt 10:5–42; Lk 10:1–16; 1Ti 1:18–5:22; 6:1–21; 2Ti 1:6–13; 2:1–4:8

Eze 3:4 — And he said unto me, Son of man, go, get thee unto the house of Israel, and speak with my words unto them.

Mk 6:11 — <u>And whosoever shall not receive you, nor hear you, when ye depart thence, shake off the dust under your feet for a testimony against them. Verily I say unto you, It shall be more tolerable for Sodom and Gomorrha in the day of judgment, than for that city.</u>

• Courage of.

↞See: Courage

↞See: Reproof; faithfulness in

• Duties of.

Le 10:8–11; 2Ki 17:27–28; Isa 40:1–3; 62:6–7; Jer 1:7–8, 17–19; 15:19–21; Eze 2:6–8; 3:8–10, 17–21; 33:1–9; 34:2–31; Joel 1:13–15; Mt 10:11–13, 27–28; 18:5–6; 20:25–28; 28:19–20; Mk 10:43–45; Jn 4:35–38; 21:15–17; Ac 1:21–22; 18:9–10; 26:16–18; Ro 1:14–15; 12:3–8; 1Co 4:1–2; 9:16–17; 2Co 4:1–2; 6:3–10; 7:4–9; Eph 3:8–10; 4:11–12; 1Th 2:4–8, 10–12; 1Ti 1:3–4, 18–19; 4:6–7; 4:12–5:3; 5:7–11, 19–22; 6:3–4, 10–14, 17–21; 2Ti 1:6–8; 2:2–7, 14–16, 23–25; 4:1–2; 1Pe 5:1–4; 2Pe 1:12–16

Ex 4:12 — Now therefore go, and I will be with thy mouth, and teach thee what thou shalt say.

Jos 1:8 — This book of the law shall not depart out of thy mouth; but thou shalt meditate therein day and night, that thou mayest observe to do according to all that is written therein: for then thou shalt make thy way prosperous, and then thou shalt have good success.

2Ch 29:11 — My sons, be not now negligent: for the LORD hath chosen you to stand before him, to serve him, and that ye should minister unto him, and burn incense.

Isa 40:9 — O Zion, that bringest good tidings, get thee up into the high mountain; O Jerusalem, that bringest good tidings, lift up thy voice with strength; lift *it* up, be not afraid; say unto the cities of Judah, Behold your God!

Isa 40:11 — He shall feed his flock like a shepherd: he shall gather the lambs with his arm, and carry *them* in his bosom, *and* shall gently lead those that are with young.

Isa 52:11 — Depart ye, depart ye, go ye out from thence, touch no unclean *thing;* go ye out of the midst of her; be ye clean, that bear the vessels of the LORD.

Isa 57:14 — And shall say, Cast ye up, cast ye up, prepare the way, take up the stumblingblock out of the way of my people.

Isa 58:1 — Cry aloud, spare not, lift up thy voice like a trumpet, and shew my people their transgression, and the house of Jacob their sins.

Jer 4:15 — For a voice declareth from Dan, and publisheth affliction from mount Ephraim.

Jer 6:27 — I have set thee *for* a tower *and* a fortress among my people, that thou mayest know and try their way.

Jer 23:4 — And I will set up shepherds over them which shall feed them: and they shall fear no more, nor be dismayed, neither shall they be lacking, saith the LORD.

Jer 23:22 — But if they had stood in my counsel, and had caused my people to hear my words, then they should have turned them from their evil way, and from the evil of their doings.

Jer 23:28 — The prophet that hath a dream, let him tell a dream; and he that hath my word, let him speak my word faithfully. What *is* the chaff to the wheat? saith the LORD.

Jer 26:2 — Thus saith the LORD; Stand in the court of the LORD's house, and speak unto all the cities of Judah, which come to worship in the LORD's house, all the words that I command thee to speak unto them; diminish not a word:

Eze 3:27 — But when I speak with thee, I will open thy mouth, and thou shalt say unto them, Thus saith the Lord GOD; He that heareth, let him hear; and he that forbeareth, let him forbear: for they *are* a rebellious house.

Eze 6:11 — Thus saith the Lord GOD; Smite with thine hand, and stamp with thy foot, and say, Alas for all the evil abominations of the house of Israel! for they shall fall by the sword, by the famine, and by the pestilence.

Eze 44:23 — And they shall teach my people *the difference* between the holy and profane, and cause them to discern between the unclean and the clean.

Joel 2:17 — Let the priests, the ministers of the LORD, weep between the porch and the altar, and let them say, Spare thy people, O LORD, and give not thine heritage to reproach, that the heathen should rule over them: wherefore should they say among the people, Where *is* their God?

Jnh 1:2 — Arise, go to Nineveh, that great city, and cry against it; for their wickedness is come up before me.

Na 1:15 — Behold upon the mountains the feet of him that bringeth good tidings, that publisheth peace! O Judah, keep thy solemn feasts, perform thy vows: for the wicked shall no more pass through thee; he is utterly cut off.

Hab 2:2 — And the LORD answered me, and said, Write the vision, and make *it* plain upon tables, that he may run that readeth it.

Mal 2:7 — For the priest's lips should keep knowledge, and they should seek the law at his mouth: for he *is* the messenger of the LORD of hosts.

Mt 7:6 — Give not that which is holy unto the dogs, neither cast ye your pearls before swine, lest they trample them under their feet, and turn again and rend you.

Mt 10:7 — And as ye go, preach, saying, The kingdom of heaven is at hand.

Mt 10:16 — Behold, I send you forth as sheep in the midst of wolves: be ye therefore wise as serpents, and harmless as doves.

Mt 10:25 — It is enough for the disciple that he be as his master, and the servant as his lord. If they have called the master of the house Beelzebub, how much more *shall they call* them of his household?

Mt 16:19 — And I will give unto thee the keys of the kingdom of heaven: and whatsoever thou shalt bind on earth shall be bound in heaven: and whatsoever thou shalt loose on earth shall be loosed in heaven.

Mt 18:18 — Verily I say unto you, Whatsoever ye shall bind on earth shall be bound in heaven: and whatsoever ye shall loose on earth shall be loosed in heaven.

Lk 9:48 — And said unto them, Whosoever shall receive this child in my name receiveth me: and whosoever shall receive me receiveth him that sent me: for he that is least among you all, the same shall be great.

Lk 22:32 — But I have prayed for thee, that thy faith fail not: and when thou art converted, strengthen thy brethren.

Lk 24:48 — And ye are witnesses of these things.

Jn 3:34 — For he whom God hath sent speaketh the words of God: for God giveth not the Spirit by measure *unto him.*

Jn 15:27 — And ye also shall bear witness, because ye have been with me from the beginning.

Jn 20:23 — Whose soever sins ye remit, they are remitted unto them; *and* whose soever *sins* ye retain, they are retained.

Ac 5:20 — Go, stand and speak in the temple to the people all the words of this life.

Ac 6:2 — Then the twelve called the multitude of the disciples *unto them,* and said, It is not reason that we should leave the word of God, and serve tables.

Ac 6:4 — But we will give ourselves continually to prayer, and to the ministry of the word.

Ac 10:42 — And he commanded us to preach unto the people, and to testify that it is he which was ordained of God *to be* the Judge of quick and dead.

Ac 16:4 — And as they went through the cities, they delivered them the decrees for to keep, that were ordained of the apostles and elders which were at Jerusalem.

Ac 20:28 — Take heed therefore unto yourselves, and to all the flock, over the which the Holy Ghost hath made you overseers, to feed the church of God, which he hath purchased with his own blood.

Ac 22:15 — For thou shalt be his witness unto all men of what thou hast seen and heard.

1Co 1:16 — And I baptized also the household of Stephanas: besides, I know not whether I baptized any other.

1Co 4:21 — What will ye? shall I come unto you with a rod, or in love, and *in* the spirit of meekness?

2Co 1:24 — Not for that we have dominion over your faith, but are helpers of your joy: for by faith ye stand.

2Co 4:5 — For we preach not ourselves, but Christ Jesus the Lord; and ourselves your servants for Jesus' sake.

2Co 5:14 — For the love of Christ constraineth us; because we thus judge, that if one died for all, then were all dead:

2Co 5:18 — And all things *are* of God, who hath reconciled us to himself by Jesus Christ, and hath given to us the ministry of reconciliation;

2Co 5:20 — Now then we are ambassadors for Christ, as though God did beseech *you* by us: we pray *you* in Christ's stead, be ye reconciled to God.

2Co 7:12 — Wherefore, though I wrote unto you, *I did it* not for his cause that had done the wrong, nor for his cause that suffered wrong, but that our care for you in the sight of God might appear unto you.

2Co 7:15 — And his inward affection is more abundant toward you, whilst he remembereth the obedience of you all, how with fear and trembling ye received him.

2Co 8:23 — Whether *any do enquire* of Titus, *he is* my partner and fellowhelper concerning you: or our brethren *be enquired of, they are* the messengers of the churches, *and* the glory of Christ.

2Co 10:8 — For though I should boast somewhat more of our authority, which the Lord hath given us for edification, and not for your destruction, I should not be ashamed:

2Co 12:15 — And I will very gladly spend and be spent for you; though the more abundantly I love you, the less I be loved.

2Co 12:19 — Again, think ye that we excuse ourselves unto you? we speak before God in Christ: but *we do* all things, dearly beloved, for your edifying.

2Co 13:2 — I told you before, and foretell you, as if I were present, the second time; and being absent now I write to them which heretofore have sinned, and to all other, that, if I come again, I will not spare:

2Co 13:10 — Therefore I write these things being absent, lest being present I should use sharpness, according to the power which the Lord hath given me to edification, and not to destruction.

Gal 1:10 — For do I now persuade men, or God? or do I seek to please men? for if I yet pleased men, I should not be the servant of Christ.

Eph 6:20 — For which I am an ambassador in bonds: that therein I may speak boldly, as I ought to speak.

Col 4:17 — And say to Archippus, Take heed to the ministry which thou hast received in the Lord, that thou fulfil it.

1Th 3:2 — And sent Timotheus, our brother, and minister of God, and our fellowlabourer in the gospel of Christ, to establish you, and to comfort you concerning your faith:

1Th 5:12 — And we beseech you, brethren, to know them which labour among you, and are over you in the Lord, and admonish you;

2Th 3:4 — And we have confidence in the Lord touching you, that ye both do and will do the things which we command you.

1Ti 1:11 — According to the glorious gospel of the blessed God, which was committed to my trust.

1Ti 2:7 — Whereunto I am ordained a preacher, and an apostle, (I speak the truth in Christ, *and* lie not;) a teacher of the Gentiles in faith and verity.

2Ti 4:5 — But watch thou in all things, endure afflictions, do the work of an evangelist, make full proof of thy ministry.

➜See: Minister, a sacred teacher; charge delivered to

• Duties of the church to.

1Co 11:1–2; 16:15–16; 1Th 5:12–13; Heb 13:17–18

Dt 1:38 — *But* Joshua the son of Nun, which standeth before thee, he shall go in thither: encourage him: for he shall cause Israel to inherit it.

Dt 3:28 — But charge Joshua, and encourage him, and strengthen him: for he shall go over before this people, and he shall cause them to inherit the land which thou shalt see.

Dt 12:19 — Take heed to thyself that thou forsake not the Levite as long as thou livest upon the earth.

Dt 31:7 — And Moses called unto Joshua, and said unto him in the sight of all Israel, Be strong and of a good courage: for thou must go with this people unto the land which the LORD hath sworn unto their fathers to give them; and thou shalt cause them to inherit it.

Mal 2:7 — For the priest's lips should keep knowledge, and they should seek the law at his mouth: for he *is* the messenger of the LORD of hosts.

Php 3:17 — Brethren, be followers together of me, and mark them which walk so as ye have us for an ensample.

Col 4:10 — Aristarchus my fellowprisoner saluteth you, and Marcus, sister's son to Barnabas, (touching whom ye received commandments: if he come unto you, receive him;)

Heb 13:7 — Remember them which have the rule over you, who have spoken unto you the word of God: whose faith follow, considering the end of *their* conversation.

➜See: Church; duty of, to ministers

• Emoluments of.

Dt 18:1–2; Mt 10:9–10; Lk 10:7–8; 22:35–36; Ac 20:33–34; 1Co 9:1–23; 2Co 1:14–15; 11:7–9; 12:13–18; Php 4:10–18; 1Th 2:5–6; 2Th 3:7–9

Nu 18:20 — And the LORD spake unto Aaron, Thou shalt have no inheritance in their land, neither shalt thou have any part among them: I *am* thy part and thine inheritance among the children of Israel.

Dt 10:9 — Wherefore Levi hath no part nor inheritance with his brethren; the LORD *is* his inheritance, according as the LORD thy God promised him.

Dt 14:27 — And the Levite that *is* within thy gates; thou shalt not forsake him; for he hath no part nor inheritance with thee.

Jos 13:14 — Only unto the tribe of Levi he gave none inheritance; the sacrifices of the LORD God of Israel made by fire *are* their inheritance, as he said unto them.

Jos 13:33 — But unto the tribe of Levi Moses gave not *any* inheritance: the LORD God of Israel *was* their inheritance, as he said unto them.

Jos 18:7 — But the Levites have no part among you; for the priesthood of the LORD is their inheritance: and Gad, and Reuben, and half the tribe of Manasseh, have received their inheritance beyond Jordan on the east, which Moses the servant of the LORD gave them.

Jer 31:14 — And I will satiate the soul of the priests with fatness, and my people shall be satisfied with my goodness, saith the LORD.

Eze 44:28 — And it shall be unto them for an inheritance: I *am* their inheritance: and ye shall give them no possession in Israel: I *am* their possession.

Mk 6:8 — And commanded them that they should take nothing for *their* journey, save a staff only; no scrip, no bread, no money in *their* purse:

Jn 4:36 — And he that reapeth receiveth wages, and gathereth fruit unto life eternal: that both he that soweth and he that reapeth may rejoice together.

Gal 6:6 — Let him that is taught in the word communicate unto him that teacheth in all good things.

1Th 2:9 — For ye remember, brethren, our labour and travail: for labouring night and day, because we would not be chargeable unto any of you, we preached unto you the gospel of God.

1Ti 5:18 — For the scripture saith, Thou shalt not muzzle the ox that treadeth out the corn. And, The labourer *is* worthy of his reward.

3Jn 1:7 — Because that for his name's sake they went forth, taking nothing of the Gentiles.

+See: Levites

+See: Minister, a sacred teacher; emoluments of

+See: Priest, Emoluments of

- **Hospitality to.**
  - **Woman of Zarephath to Elijah.**
    1Ki 17:10–16
  - **The Shunammite to Elisha.**
    2Ki 4:8–10
  - **The barbarians to Paul.**
    Ac 28:1–10
  - **Simon the tanner to Peter.**
    Ac 9:43 — And it came to pass, that he tarried many days in Joppa with one Simon a tanner.
  - **The Philippian jailer.**
    Ac 16:33–34
  - **Aquila and Priscilla to Paul.**
    Ac 18:3 — And because he was of the same craft, he abode with them, and wrought: for by their occupation they were tentmakers.
  - **Aquila and Priscilla to Apollos.**
    Ac 18:26 — And he began to speak boldly in the synagogue: whom when Aquila and Priscilla had heard, they took him unto *them,* and expounded unto him the way of God more perfectly.
  - **Justus to Paul.**
    Ac 18:7 — And he departed thence, and entered into a certain *man's* house, named Justus, *one* that worshipped God, whose house joined hard to the synagogue.
  - **Philip the evangelist to Paul.**
    Ac 21:8–10
- **Ordination of.**
  - **Matthias.**
    Ac 1:26 — And they gave forth their lots; and the lot fell upon Matthias; and he was numbered with the eleven apostles.
  - **Seven deacons.**
    Ac 6:5–6
  - **Paul and Barnabas.**
    Ac 13:3 — And when they had fasted and prayed, and laid *their* hands on them, they sent *them* away.
  - **Paul and Timothy.**
    1Ti 4:14 — Neglect not the gift that is in thee, which was given thee by prophecy, with the laying on of the hands of the presbytery.

  +See: Levites

- **Prayer for, enjoined.**
  Mt 9:37–38; Ro 15:30–32; Eph 6:18–20; Col 4:2–4; 2Th 3:1–2; Heb 13:18–19
  Lk 10:2 — Therefore said he unto them, <u>The harvest truly *is* great, but the labourers *are* few: pray ye therefore the Lord of the harvest, that he would send forth labourers into his harvest.</u>
  2Co 1:11 — Ye also helping together by prayer for us, that for the gift *bestowed* upon us by the means of many persons thanks may be given by many on our behalf.
  Php 1:19 — For I know that this shall turn to my salvation through your prayer, and the supply of the Spirit of Jesus Christ,
  1Th 5:25 — Brethren, pray for us.
  Phm 1:22 — But withal prepare me also a lodging: for I trust that through your prayers I shall be given unto you.
- **Prayer for, exemplified.**
  Ac 1:24–25
  2Ch 6:41 — Now therefore arise, O LORD God, into thy resting place, thou, and the ark of thy strength: let thy priests, O LORD God, be clothed with salvation, and let thy saints rejoice in goodness.
  Ps 132:9 — Let thy priests be clothed with righteousness; and let thy saints shout for joy.
  Ac 4:29 — And now, Lord, behold their threatenings: and grant unto thy servants, that with all boldness they may speak thy word,
  Ac 6:6 — Whom they set before the apostles: and when they had prayed, they laid *their* hands on them.
  Ac 12:5 — Peter therefore was kept in prison: but prayer was made without ceasing of the church unto God for him.
  Ac 14:23 — And when they had ordained them elders in every church, and had prayed with fasting, they commended them to the Lord, on whom they believed.
- **Promises to, and joys of.**
  2Sa 23:6–7; Ps 126:5–6; Jer 1:7–10, 17–19; Mt 10:28–31; Lk 12:11–12; Jn 4:36–38; Ac 1:4–5; 1Co 9:9–10; 2Co 2:14–16; 7:6–7; 1Th 2:19–20; 3:8–9
  Jer 20:11 — But the LORD *is* with me as a mighty terrible one: therefore my persecutors shall stumble, and they shall not prevail: they shall be greatly ashamed; for they shall not prosper: *their* everlasting confusion shall never be forgotten.
  Da 12:3 — And they that be wise shall shine as the brightness of the firmament; and they that turn many to righteousness as the stars for ever and ever.
  Mt 28:20 — <u>Teaching them to observe all things whatsoever I have commanded you: and, lo, I am with you alway, *even* unto the end of the world. Amen.</u>
  Lk 24:49 — <u>And, behold, I send the promise of my Father upon you: but tarry ye in the city of Jerusalem, until ye be endued with power from on high.</u>
  Ac 1:8 — <u>But ye shall receive power, after that the Holy Ghost is come upon you: and ye shall be witnesses unto me both in Jerusalem, and in all Judaea, and in Samaria, and unto the uttermost part of the earth.</u>
  Php 2:16 — Holding forth the word of life; that I may rejoice in the day of Christ, that I have not run in vain, neither laboured in vain.
  1Th 2:13 — For this cause also thank we God without ceasing, because, when ye received the word of God which ye heard of us, ye received *it* not *as* the word of men, but as it is in truth, the word of God, which effectually worketh also in you that believe.

3Jn 1:4 — I have no greater joy than to hear that my children walk in truth.

↞See: Righteous; promises to, expressed or implied

- **Success attending.**
  - **Jonah.**
    Jnh 1:5–6; 3:4–9
    Jnh 1:9 — And he said unto them, I *am* an Hebrew; and I fear the LORD, the God of heaven, which hath made the sea and the dry *land.*
    Jnh 1:14 — Wherefore they cried unto the LORD, and said, We beseech thee, O LORD, we beseech thee, let us not perish for this man's life, and lay not upon us innocent blood: for thou, O LORD, hast done as it pleased thee.
    Jnh 1:16 — Then the men feared the LORD exceedingly, and offered a sacrifice unto the LORD, and made vows.
  - **Apostles.**
    Ac 2:1–4
    Ac 2:41 — Then they that gladly received his word were baptized: and the same day there were added *unto them* about three thousand souls.
  - **Philip.**
    Ac 8:6 — And the people with one accord gave heed unto those things which Philip spake, hearing and seeing the miracles which he did.
    Ac 8:8 — And there was great joy in that city.
    Ac 8:12 — But when they believed Philip preaching the things concerning the kingdom of God, and the name of Jesus Christ, they were baptized, both men and women.
  - **Peter.**
    Ac 9:32–35
  - **Paul.**
    Ac 13:16–43; 2Co 3:2–3
    1Co 4:15 — For though ye have ten thousand instructers in Christ, yet *have ye* not many fathers: for in Christ Jesus I have begotten you through the gospel.
    1Co 9:2 — If I be not an apostle unto others, yet doubtless I am to you: for the seal of mine apostleship are ye in the Lord.
    1Co 15:11 — Therefore whether *it were* I or they, so we preach, and so ye believed.
    2Co 12:12 — Truly the signs of an apostle were wrought among you in all patience, in signs, and wonders, and mighty deeds.
    2Co 13:4 — For though he was crucified through weakness, yet he liveth by the power of God. For we also are weak in him, but we shall live with him by the power of God toward you.
    Php 2:16 — Holding forth the word of life; that I may rejoice in the day of Christ, that I have not run in vain, neither laboured in vain.
    1Th 1:5 — For our gospel came not unto you in word only, but also in power, and in the Holy Ghost, and in much assurance; as ye know what manner of men we were among you for your sake.
  - **Apollos.**
    Ac 18:24–28

↞See: Revivals

- **Trials and persecutions of.**
  1Ki 19:1–10; Isa 20:2–3; Eze 24:15–18; Am 7:10–17; Mt 10:16–27; 1Co 2:1–4; 4:9–13; 2Co 6:4–10; 11:23–33; 12:7–12; Gal 4:13–14
  Hos 1:2 — The beginning of the word of the LORD by Hosea. And the LORD said to Hosea, Go, take unto thee a wife of whoredoms and children of whoredoms: for the land hath committed great whoredom, *departing* from the LORD.
  Am 5:10 — They hate him that rebuketh in the gate, and they abhor him that speaketh uprightly.
  Mt 23:34 — Wherefore, behold, I send unto you prophets, and wise men, and scribes: and *some* of them ye shall kill and crucify; and *some* of them shall ye scourge in your synagogues, and persecute *them* from city to city:
  Jn 13:16 — Verily, verily, I say unto you, The servant is not greater than his lord; neither he that is sent greater than he that sent him.
  2Co 7:5 — For, when we were come into Macedonia, our flesh had no rest, but we were troubled on every side; without *were* fightings, within *were* fears.
  Eph 3:1 — For this cause I Paul, the prisoner of Jesus Christ for you Gentiles,
- **Falsely accused.**

↞See: Accusation, False

↞See: Persecution

- **Instances of persecution.**
  - **Micaiah.**
    1Ki 22:24–27
  - **Hanani.**
    2Ch 16:10
  - **Zechariah.**
    2Ch 24:20–21
  - **The apostles.**
    Ac 5:17–42
  - **Peter.**
    Ac 12:3–19
  - **Paul.**
    Ac 9:23–25, 29–30; 14:6–20; 16:11–17:13; 20:3; 21:27–40; 22:18, 21, 24–30; 23:11–26:32; 2Co 11:31–33; Gal 1:21–24; 2Ti 1:8, 16; 2:9; 4:16–17

↞See: Elijah

↞See: Jeremiah

- **Zealous.**
  - **Titus.**
    2Co 8:16–17
  - **Epaphroditus.**
    Php 2:25–30
  - **Epaphras.**
    Col 4:12–13
  - **Tychicus.**
    Col 4:7 — All my state shall Tychicus declare unto you, *who is* a beloved brother, and a faithful minister and fellowservant in the Lord:

- **John, in his vision.**
  Rev 5:4–5

  See: Zeal, Religious

MINISTER, an officer in civil government

- **Joseph.**
  Ge 41:40–44
- **Ira.**
  2Sa 20:26 — And Ira also the Jairite was a chief ruler about David.
- **Zabud.**
  1Ki 4:5 — And Azariah the son of Nathan *was* over the officers: and Zabud the son of Nathan *was* principal officer, *and* the king's friend:
- **Ahithophel.**
  1Ch 27:33 — And Ahithophel *was* the king's counsellor: and Hushai the Archite *was* the king's companion:
- **Zebadiah.**
  2Ch 19:11 — And, behold, Amariah the chief priest is over you in all matters of the LORD; and Zebadiah the son of Ishmael, the ruler of the house of Judah, for all the king's matters: also the Levites *shall be* officers before you. Deal courageously, and the LORD shall be with the good.
- **Elkanah.**
  2Ch 28:7 — And Zichri, a mighty man of Ephraim, slew Maaseiah the king's son, and Azrikam the governor of the house, and Elkanah *that was* next to the king.
- **Haman.**
  Est 3:1 — After these things did king Ahasuerus promote Haman the son of Hammedatha the Agagite, and advanced him, and set his seat above all the princes that *were* with him.
- **Mordecai.**
  Est 8:1–9:32
  Est 10:3 — For Mordecai the Jew *was* next unto king Ahasuerus, and great among the Jews, and accepted of the multitude of his brethren, seeking the wealth of his people, and speaking peace to all his seed.
- **Daniel.**
  Da 6:1–3
  Da 2:48 — Then the king made Daniel a great man, and gave him many great gifts, and made him ruler over the whole province of Babylon, and chief of the governors over all the wise *men* of Babylon.

  See: Cabinet

MINISTER, Faithful

- **Instances of.**
  - **Moses.**
    Dt 4:26; 30:19; Heb 3:2, 5
  - **Micaiah.**
    2Ch 18:12–13
  - **Azariah.**
    2Ch 26:16–20
  - **Balaam.**
    Nu 22:18, 38; 23:8, 12; 24:12–14
  - **Nathan.**
    2Sa 12:1–14
  - **Isaiah.**
    Isa 22:4–5; 39:3–7
  - **Jeremiah.**
    Jer 17:16; 26:1–15; 28:1–17; 37:9–10, 16–18
  - **John the Baptist.**
    Mt 3:2–12; Mk 6:18–28; Lk 3:7–9, 19
  - **Peter.**
    Ac 8:18–23
  - **Paul.**
    Ac 20:26–27; Col 1:7
  - **The apostles.**
    Ac 3:12–26; 4:9–13, 19–20, 31; 5:21, 29–32

MINISTER, False and Corrupt

Dt 13:1–5; 18:20–22; Isa 8:19–20; 9:14–16; 29:10–11; 43:27–28; 56:10–12; Jer 5:13–14; 6:13–14; 8:10–11; 14:13–16; 23:1–2, 14–16, 25–39; 27:9–18; La 4:13–14; Eze 13:1–23; 14:9–10; 22:25–26; 34:1–31; Hos 4:8–13; 9:7–8; Am 2:11–12; Mic 3:5–7; Zec 11:4–5, 16–17; 13:2–5; Mal 1:6–10; 2:1–3, 8–9; Mt 7:22–23; 15:13–14; 20:20–27; 23:3–4; 24:4–5, 48–51; Mk 9:33–35; 10:35–37; 13:21–22; Lk 11:46–52; 12:45–46; Jn 10:12–13; Ac 20:29–30; Ro 2:19–25; 16:17–18; 1Co 3:1–4, 10–16; 11:18–19; 2Co 11:1–33; Gal 1:6–8; Php 1:15–16; Col 2:18–19; 1Ti 1:3–7; 4:1–3; 6:3–5, 20–21; 2Ti 2:14–18; 3:6–9; Tit 1:10–14; 3:10–11; 2Pe 2:1–22; 1Jn 4:1–3; 2Jn 1:10–11; Rev 2:1–2, 14–15, 20–23

1Ki 12:31 — And he made an house of high places, and made priests of the lowest of the people, which were not of the sons of Levi.

2Ch 29:34 — But the priests were too few, so that they could not flay all the burnt offerings: wherefore their brethren the Levites did help them, till the work was ended, and until the *other* priests had sanctified themselves: for the Levites *were* more upright in heart to sanctify themselves than the priests.

2Ch 30:15 — Then they killed the passover on the fourteenth *day* of the second month: and the priests and the Levites were ashamed, and sanctified themselves, and brought in the burnt offerings into the house of the LORD.

Ne 13:29 — Remember them, O my God, because they have defiled the priesthood, and the covenant of the priesthood, and of the Levites.

Pr 19:27 — Cease, my son, to hear the instruction *that causeth* to err from the words of knowledge.

Isa 3:12 — *As for* my people, children *are* their oppressors, and women rule over them. O my people, they which lead thee cause *thee* to err, and destroy the way of thy paths.

Isa 5:20 — Woe unto them that call evil good, and good evil; that put darkness for light, and light for darkness; that put bitter for sweet, and sweet for bitter!

Isa 28:7 — But they also have erred through wine, and through strong drink are out of the way; the priest and the prophet have erred through strong drink, they are swallowed up of wine, they are out of the way through strong drink; they err in vision, they stumble *in* judgment.

Isa 30:10 — Which say to the seers, See not; and to the prophets, Prophesy not unto us right things, speak unto us smooth things, prophesy deceits:

Isa 44:20 — He feedeth on ashes: a deceived heart hath turned him aside, that he cannot deliver his soul, nor say, *Is there* not a lie in my right hand?

Jer 2:8 — The priests said not, Where *is* the LORD? and they that handle the law knew me not: the pastors also transgressed against me, and the prophets prophesied by Baal, and walked after *things that* do not profit.

Jer 5:30 — A wonderful and horrible thing is committed in the land;

Jer 10:21 — For the pastors are become brutish, and have not sought the LORD: therefore they shall not prosper, and all their flocks shall be scattered.

Jer 12:10 — Many pastors have destroyed my vineyard, they have trodden my portion under foot, they have made my pleasant portion a desolate wilderness.

Jer 13:20 — Lift up your eyes, and behold them that come from the north: where *is* the flock *that* was given thee, thy beautiful flock?

Jer 23:11 — For both prophet and priest are profane; yea, in my house have I found their wickedness, saith the LORD.

Jer 48:10 — Cursed *be* he that doeth the work of the LORD deceitfully, and cursed *be* he that keepeth back his sword from blood.

Jer 50:6 — My people hath been lost sheep: their shepherds have caused them to go astray, they have turned them away *on* the mountains: they have gone from mountain to hill, they have forgotten their restingplace.

La 2:14 — Thy prophets have seen vain and foolish things for thee: and they have not discovered thine iniquity, to turn away thy captivity; but have seen for thee false burdens and causes of banishment.

Eze 22:28 — And her prophets have daubed them with untempered *morter,* seeing vanity, and divining lies unto them, saying, Thus saith the Lord GOD, when the LORD hath not spoken.

Eze 44:8 — And ye have not kept the charge of mine holy things: but ye have set keepers of my charge in my sanctuary for yourselves.

Eze 44:10 — And the Levites that are gone away far from me, when Israel went astray, which went astray away from me after their idols; they shall even bear their iniquity.

Hos 4:6 — My people are destroyed for lack of knowledge: because thou hast rejected knowledge, I will also reject thee, that thou shalt be no priest to me: seeing thou hast forgotten the law of thy God, I will also forget thy children.

Hos 5:1 — Hear ye this, O priests; and hearken, ye house of Israel; and give ye ear, O house of the king; for judgment *is* toward you, because ye have been a snare on Mizpah, and a net spread upon Tabor.

Hos 6:9 — And as troops of robbers wait for a man, *so* the company of priests murder in the way by consent: for they commit lewdness.

Mic 2:11 — If a man walking in the spirit and falsehood do lie, *saying,* I will prophesy unto thee of wine and of strong drink; he shall even be the prophet of this people.

Mic 3:11 — The heads thereof judge for reward, and the priests thereof teach for hire, and the prophets thereof divine for money: yet will they lean upon the LORD, and say, *Is* not the LORD among us? none evil can come upon us.

Zep 3:4 — Her prophets *are* light *and* treacherous persons: her priests have polluted the sanctuary, they have done violence to the law.

Zec 10:3 — Mine anger was kindled against the shepherds, and I punished the goats: for the LORD of hosts hath visited his flock the house of Judah, and hath made them as his goodly horse in the battle.

Mt 5:19 — Whosoever therefore shall break one of these least commandments, and shall teach men so, he shall be called the least in the kingdom of heaven: but whosoever shall do and teach *them,* the same shall be called great in the kingdom of heaven.

Mt 7:15 — Beware of false prophets, which come to you in sheep's clothing, but inwardly they are ravening wolves.

Mt 15:9 — But in vain they do worship me, teaching *for* doctrines the commandments of men.

Mt 23:13 — But woe unto you, scribes and Pharisees, hypocrites! for ye shut up the kingdom of heaven against men: for ye neither go in *yourselves,* neither suffer ye them that are entering to go in.

Mt 24:11 — And many false prophets shall rise, and shall deceive many.

Mt 24:24 — For there shall arise false Christs, and false prophets, and shall shew great signs and wonders; insomuch that, if *it were* possible, they shall deceive the very elect.

Mt 24:26 — Wherefore if they shall say unto you, Behold, he is in the desert; go not forth: behold, *he is* in the secret chambers; believe *it* not.

Lk 6:39 — And he spake a parable unto them, Can the blind lead the blind? shall they not both fall into the ditch?

Lk 9:46 — Then there arose a reasoning among them, which of them should be greatest.

Lk 11:35 — Take heed therefore that the light which is in thee be not darkness.

Lk 21:8 — And he said, Take heed that ye be not deceived: for many shall come in my name, saying, I am *Christ;* and the time draweth near: go ye not therefore after them.

Lk 22:24 — And there was also a strife among them, which of them should be accounted the greatest.

Jn 3:10 — Jesus answered and said unto him, Art thou a master of Israel, and knowest not these things?

Jn 5:43 — I am come in my Father's name, and ye receive me not: if another shall come in his own name, him ye will receive.

Jn 10:1 — Verily, verily, I say unto you, He that entereth not by the door into the sheepfold, but climbeth up some other way, the same is a thief and a robber.

Jn 10:5 — And a stranger will they not follow, but will flee from him: for they know not the voice of strangers.

Jn 10:8 — All that ever came before me are thieves and robbers: but the sheep did not hear them.

Jn 10:10 — The thief cometh not, but for to steal, and to kill, and to destroy: I am come that they might have life, and that they might have *it* more abundantly.

1Co 3:21 — Therefore let no man glory in men. For all things are yours;

2Co 2:17 — For we are not as many, which corrupt the word of God: but as of sincerity, but as of God, in the sight of God speak we in Christ.

Gal 5:10 — I have confidence in you through the Lord, that ye will be none otherwise minded: but he that troubleth you shall bear his judgment, whosoever he be.

Eph 4:14 — That we *henceforth* be no more children, tossed to and fro, and carried about with every wind of doctrine, by the sleight of men, *and* cunning craftiness, whereby they lie in wait to deceive;

Php 3:2 — Beware of dogs, beware of evil workers, beware of the concision.

Col 2:4 — And this I say, lest any man should beguile you with enticing words.

Col 2:8 — Beware lest any man spoil you through philosophy and vain deceit, after the tradition of men, after the rudiments of the world, and not after Christ.

1Ti 1:19 — Holding faith, and a good conscience; which some having put away concerning faith have made shipwreck:

1Ti 4:7 — But refuse profane and old wives' fables, and exercise thyself *rather* unto godliness.

2Ti 3:13 — But evil men and seducers shall wax worse and worse, deceiving, and being deceived.

2Ti 4:3 — For the time will come when they will not endure sound doctrine; but after their own lusts shall they heap to themselves teachers, having itching ears;

Heb 13:9 — Be not carried about with divers and strange doctrines. For *it is* a good thing that the heart be established with grace; not with meats, which have not profited them that have been occupied therein.

2Pe 3:16 — As also in all *his* epistles, speaking in them of these things; in which are some things hard to be understood, which they that are unlearned and unstable wrest, as *they do* also the other scriptures, unto their own destruction.

1Jn 2:18 — Little children, it is the last time: and as ye have heard that antichrist shall come, even now are there many antichrists; whereby we know that it is the last time.

1Jn 2:26 — These *things* have I written unto you concerning them that seduce you.

1Jn 4:5 — They are of the world: therefore speak they of the world, and the world heareth them.

2Jn 1:7 — For many deceivers are entered into the world, who confess not that Jesus Christ is come in the flesh. This is a deceiver and an antichrist.

3Jn 1:10 — Wherefore, if I come, I will remember his deeds which he doeth, prating against us with malicious words: and not content therewith, neither doth he himself receive the brethren, and forbiddeth them that would, and casteth *them* out of the church.

Jude 1:4 — For there are certain men crept in unawares, who were before of old ordained to this condemnation, ungodly men, turning the grace of our God into lasciviousness, and denying the only Lord God, and our Lord Jesus Christ.

Jude 1:11 — Woe unto them! for they have gone in the way of Cain, and ran greedily after the error of Balaam for reward, and perished in the gainsaying of Core.

Rev 2:12 — And to the angel of the church in Pergamos write; These things saith he which hath the sharp sword with two edges;

Rev 2:18 — And unto the angel of the church in Thyatira write; These things saith the Son of God, who hath his eyes like unto a flame of fire, and his feet *are* like fine brass;

- **Instances of.**
  - **Aaron.**
    Nu 12:1–12
  - **Nadab and Abihu.**
    Le 10:1–2
  - **Korah, Dathan, and Abiram.**
    Nu 16:1–50
  - **Eli's sons.**
    1Sa 2:12–17, 22, 25, 28–29
  - **Samuel's sons.**
    1Sa 8:1–3; 1Ch 6:28
  - **The old prophet of Bethel.**
    1Ki 13:11–32
  - **Jonathan.**
    Jgs 17:7–18:31
  - **Noadiah.**
    Ne 6:14
  - **Priests under Jehoash.**
    2Ki 12:7; 2Ch 24:5–6
  - **Hezekiah.**
    2Ch 30:3, 5
  - **Priests and Levites.**
    Ezr 2:61–62; 9:1–2; 10:18–24; Ne 13:4–13, 28–29; Zec 7:5–6
  - **Hananiah.**
    Jer 28:1–17
  - **Jonah.**
    Jnh 1:1–6
  - **Rulers in the temple.**
    Mt 16:6–12; 23:16; Lk 12:1
  - **Caiaphas.**
    Mt 26:2–3, 57, 63–65; Jn 11:49–51; 18:14
  - **Judas.**
    Mt 26:14–16, 21–25, 47–50; 27:3–5; Jn 12:4–6; Ac 1:18
  - **Simon the sorcerer.**
    Ac 8:9–11
  - **Judaizing Christians.**
    Ac 15:1; Gal 3:1–6:18
  - **Diotrephes.**
    3Jn 1:9
  - **Elymas.**
    Ac 13:6–11
  - **Hymenaeus.**
    1Ti 1:20; 2Ti 2:17
  - **Philetus.**
    2Ti 2:17–18

MINISTER, Miscellany of Minor Sub-Topics

• Teachers of schools.

2Ch 17:7-9

1Sa 19:20 — And Saul sent messengers to take David: and when they saw the company of the prophets prophesying, and Samuel standing *as* appointed over them, the Spirit of God was upon the messengers of Saul, and they also prophesied.

2Ki 2:3 — And the sons of the prophets that *were* at Bethel came forth to Elisha, and said unto him, Knowest thou that the LORD will take away thy master from thy head to day? And he said, Yea, I know *it;* hold ye your peace.

2Ki 2:5 — And the sons of the prophets that *were* at Jericho came to Elisha, and said unto him, Knowest thou that the LORD will take away thy master from thy head to day? And he answered, Yea, I know *it;* hold ye your peace.

2Ki 2:15 — And when the sons of the prophets which *were* to view at Jericho saw him, they said, The spirit of Elijah doth rest on Elisha. And they came to meet him, and bowed themselves to the ground before him.

2Ki 4:38 — And Elisha came again to Gilgal: and *there was* a dearth in the land; and the sons of the prophets *were* sitting before him: and he said unto his servant, Set on the great pot, and seethe pottage for the sons of the prophets.

2Ch 15:3 — Now for a long season Israel *hath been* without the true God, and without a teaching priest, and without law.

Ac 13:1 — Now there were in the church that was at Antioch certain prophets and teachers; as Barnabas, and Simeon that was called Niger, and Lucius of Cyrene, and Manaen, which had been brought up with Herod the tetrarch, and Saul.

• Hired.

Jgs 18:4 — And he said unto them, Thus and thus dealeth Micah with me, and hath hired me, and I am his priest.

• Exempt from taxation.

Ezr 7:24 — Also we certify you, that touching any of the priests and Levites, singers, porters, Nethinims, or ministers of this house of God, it shall not be lawful to impose toll, tribute, or custom, upon them.

• Non-partisan in politics.

2Sa 15:24-27

• Influential in public affairs.

• Designate kings.

1Sa 9:15-16; 16:1-13

1Sa 10:1 — Then Samuel took a vial of oil, and poured *it* upon his head, and kissed him, and said, *Is it* not because the LORD hath anointed thee *to be* captain over his inheritance?

• Recommend civil and military appointments.

2Ki 4:13 — And he said unto him, Say now unto her, Behold, thou hast been careful for us with all this care; what *is* to be done for thee? wouldest thou be spoken for to the king, or to the captain of the host? And she answered, I dwell among mine own people.

• Expostulate with rulers.

• Samuel with Saul.

1Sa 13:11-14; 15:10-31

• Nathan with David.

2Sa 12:1-14

• Elijah with Ahab.

1Ki 18:17-18

• Tact of.

1Co 9:20-23; 10:28-33

1Co 10:23 — All things are lawful for me, but all things are not expedient: all things are lawful for me, but all things edify not.

2Co 12:16 — But be it so, I did not burden you: nevertheless, being crafty, I caught you with guile.

• Recreations for.

Mk 6:31-32

Mk 6:45 — And straightway he constrained his disciples to get into the ship, and to go to the other side before unto Bethsaida, while he sent away the people.

• Take leave of congregations.

Ac 20:17-38

• Personal bearing of.

Tit 2:7-8

• Preach without ecclesiastical authority.

Gal 1:15-2:9

• Patience of.

Jas 5:10 — Take, my brethren, the prophets, who have spoken in the name of the Lord, for an example of suffering affliction, and of patience.

• Work of, will be tried.

1Co 3:12-15

• Responsibility of.

Eze 3:17-21; Mt 10:14-40; Ac 20:26-27

Eze 33:8 — When I say unto the wicked, O wicked *man,* thou shalt surely die; if thou dost not speak to warn the wicked from his way, that wicked *man* shall die in his iniquity; but his blood will I require at thine hand.

Ac 18:6 — And when they opposed themselves, and blasphemed, he shook *his* raiment, and said unto them, Your blood *be* upon your own heads; I *am* clean: from henceforth I will go unto the Gentiles.

• Speaking evil of, forbidden.

Jude 1:8-10

• Marriage of.

Le 21:7-15; Tit 1:5-7

Mt 8:14 — And when Jesus was come into Peter's house, he saw his wife's mother laid, and sick of a fever.

1Co 9:5 — Have we not power to lead about a sister, a wife, as well as other apostles, and *as* the brethren of the Lord, and Cephas?

1Ti 3:2 — A bishop then must be blameless, the husband of one wife, vigilant, sober, of good behaviour, given to hospitality, apt to teach;

1Ti 3:12 — Let the deacons be the husbands of one wife, ruling their children and their own houses well.

• Incorruptible.

• Balaam.

Nu 22:37–38; 24:12–14; 2Pe 2:15–16

Nu 22:18 — And Balaam answered and said unto the servants of Balak, If Balak would give me his house full of silver and gold, I cannot go beyond the word of the LORD my God, to do less or more.

Nu 23:8 — How shall I curse, whom God hath not cursed? or how shall I defy, *whom* the LORD hath not defied?

Nu 23:12 — And he answered and said, Must I not take heed to speak that which the LORD hath put in my mouth?

• Micaiah.

1Ki 22:13–14

• Peter.

Ac 8:18–23

• Love of, for the church, exemplified by Paul.

1Th 1:2–4

Php 1:7 — Even as it is meet for me to think this of you all, because I have you in my heart; inasmuch as both in my bonds, and in the defence and confirmation of the gospel, ye all are partakers of my grace.

1Th 2:8 — So being affectionately desirous of you, we were willing to have imparted unto you, not the gospel of God only, but also our own souls, because ye were dear unto us.

1Th 2:11 — As ye know how we exhorted and comforted and charged every one of you, as a father *doth* his children,

• Kindness to.

• Ebed-melech to Jeremiah.

Jer 38:7–13

• Fear of.

1Sa 16:4 — And Samuel did that which the LORD spake, and came to Bethlehem. And the elders of the town trembled at his coming, and said, Comest thou peaceably?

• Examples to the flock.

Php 3:17 — Brethren, be followers together of me, and mark them which walk so as ye have us for an ensample.

2Th 3:9 — Not because we have not power, but to make ourselves an ensample unto you to follow us.

1Ti 4:12 — Let no man despise thy youth; but be thou an example of the believers, in word, in conversation, in charity, in spirit, in faith, in purity.

1Pe 5:3 — Neither as being lords over *God's* heritage, but being ensamples to the flock.

• Intolerance of.

Mt 15:23 — But he answered her not a word. And his disciples came and besought him, saying, Send her away; for she crieth after us.

Mt 19:13 — Then were there brought unto him little children, that he should put *his* hands on them, and pray: and the disciples rebuked them.

Mk 10:13 — And they brought young children to him, that he should touch them: and *his* disciples rebuked those that brought *them*.

Lk 18:15 — And they brought unto him also infants, that he would touch them: but when *his* disciples saw *it*, they rebuked them.

• Message of, rejected.

Eze 33:30–33

• Inconsistent.

Mt 27:3–7

• God's care of.

1Ki 17:1–16; 19:1–18; Mt 10:29–31; Lk 12:6–7

Isa 30:20 — And *though* the Lord give you the bread of adversity, and the water of affliction, yet shall not thy teachers be removed into a corner any more, but thine eyes shall see thy teachers:

• Their calling glorious.

2Co 3:7–11

• Discouragements of.

Eze 3:8–9; Hab 1:2–3; Mk 6:3–4

Isa 53:1 — Who hath believed our report? and to whom is the arm of the LORD revealed?

Eze 3:14 — So the spirit lifted me up, and took me away, and I went in bitterness, in the heat of my spirit; but the hand of the LORD was strong upon me.

Mt 13:57 — And they were offended in him. But Jesus said unto them, A prophet is not without honour, save in his own country, and in his own house.

Lk 4:24 — And he said, Verily I say unto you, No prophet is accepted in his own country.

Jn 4:44 — For Jesus himself testified, that a prophet hath no honour in his own country.

• Defended.

Jer 26:16–19

• Beloved.

Ac 20:37–38; 21:5–6

• Sent forth two and two.

• Disciples.

Mk 6:7 — And he called *unto him* the twelve, and began to send them forth by two and two; and gave them power over unclean spirits;

• Paul and Barnabas.

Ac 13:2–3

• Judas and Silas.

Ac 15:27 — We have sent therefore Judas and Silas, who shall also tell *you* the same things by mouth.

• Barnabas and Mark.

Ac 15:37 — And Barnabas determined to take with them John, whose surname was Mark.

Ac 15:39 — And the contention was so sharp between them, that they departed asunder one from the other: and so Barnabas took Mark, and sailed unto Cyprus;

• Paul and Silas.

Ac 15:40 — And Paul chose Silas, and departed, being recommended by the brethren unto the grace of God.

• Paul and Timothy.

Ac 16:1–4

• **Paul and Titus.**

2Co 8:19 — And not *that* only, but who was also chosen of the churches to travel with us with this grace, which is administered by us to the glory of the same Lord, and *declaration of* your ready mind:

2Co 8:23 — Whether *any do enquire* of Titus, *he is* my partner and fellowhelper concerning you: or our brethren *be enquired of, they are* the messengers of the churches, *and* the glory of Christ.

• **Timothy and Erastus.**

Ac 19:22 — So he sent into Macedonia two of them that ministered unto him, Timotheus and Erastus; but he himself stayed in Asia for a season.

• **Titus and a companion.**

2Co 12:18 — I desired Titus, and with *him* I sent a brother. Did Titus make a gain of you? walked we not in the same spirit? *walked we* not in the same steps?

➔See: Minister, a sacred teacher; trials and persecutions of

MINNI • A district of Armenia.

Jer 51:27 — Set ye up a standard in the land, blow the trumpet among the nations, prepare the nations against her, call together against her the kingdoms of Ararat, Minni, and Ashchenaz; appoint a captain against her; cause the horses to come up as the rough caterpillers.

MINNITH • A place east of the Jordan.

Jgs 11:33 — And he smote them from Aroer, even till thou come to Minnith, *even* twenty cities, and unto the plain of the vineyards, with a very great slaughter. Thus the children of Ammon were subdued before the children of Israel.

Eze 27:17 — Judah, and the land of Israel, they *were* thy merchants: they traded in thy market wheat of Minnith, and Pannag, and honey, and oil, and balm.

MINORITY REPORT ➔See: Reports

MINORS

• **Legal status of.**

Gal 4:1–2

➔See: Orphan

➔See: Young Men

MINT

Mt 23:23 — Woe unto you, scribes and Pharisees, hypocrites! for ye pay tithe of mint and anise and cummin, and have omitted the weightier *matters* of the law, judgment, mercy, and faith: these ought ye to have done, and not to leave the other undone.

Lk 11:42 — But woe unto you, Pharisees! for ye tithe mint and rue and all manner of herbs, and pass over judgment and the love of God: these ought ye to have done, and not to leave the other undone.

MIRACLES of the Disciples

• **By the seventy.**

Lk 10:17–20

• **By other disciples.**

Mk 9:39 — But Jesus said, Forbid him not: for there is no man which shall do a miracle in my name, that can lightly speak evil of me.

Jn 14:12 — Verily, verily, I say unto you, He that believeth on me, the works that I do shall he do also; and greater *works* than these shall he do; because I go unto my Father.

• **By the apostles.**

Ac 3:12–13; 9:34–35

Ac 3:6 — Then Peter said, Silver and gold have I none; but such as I have give I thee: In the name of Jesus Christ of Nazareth rise up and walk.

Ac 3:16 — And his name through faith in his name hath made this man strong, whom ye see and know: yea, the faith which is by him hath given him this perfect soundness in the presence of you all.

Ac 4:10 — Be it known unto you all, and to all the people of Israel, that by the name of Jesus Christ of Nazareth, whom ye crucified, whom God raised from the dead, *even* by him doth this man stand here before you whole.

Ac 4:30 — By stretching forth thine hand to heal; and that signs and wonders may be done by the name of thy holy child Jesus.

Ac 16:18 — And this did she many days. But Paul, being grieved, turned and said to the spirit, I command thee in the name of Jesus Christ to come out of her. And he came out the same hour.

• **Peter cures the sick.**

Ac 5:15–16

• **Peter cures Aeneas.**

Ac 9:34 — And Peter said unto him, Aeneas, Jesus Christ maketh thee whole: arise, and make thy bed. And he arose immediately.

• **Peter raises Dorcas.**

Ac 9:40 — But Peter put them all forth, and kneeled down, and prayed; and turning *him* to the body said, Tabitha, arise. And she opened her eyes: and when she saw Peter, she sat up.

• **Peter causes the death of Ananias and Sapphira.**

Ac 5:5 — And Ananias hearing these words fell down, and gave up the ghost: and great fear came on all them that heard these things.

Ac 5:10 — Then fell she down straightway at his feet, and yielded up the ghost: and the young men came in, and found her dead, and, carrying *her* forth, buried *her* by her husband.

• **Peter and John cure a lame man.**

Ac 3:2–11

• **Peter and other apostles delivered from prison.**

Ac 5:19–23; 12:6–11

Ac 16:26 — And suddenly there was a great earthquake, so that the foundations of the prison were shaken: and immediately all the doors were opened, and every one's bands were loosed.

• Philip carried away by the Spirit.

Ac 8:39 — And when they were come up out of the water, the Spirit of the Lord caught away Philip, that the eunuch saw him no more: and he went on his way rejoicing.

• Paul strikes Elymas with blindness.

Ac 13:11 — And now, behold, the hand of the Lord *is* upon thee, and thou shalt be blind, not seeing the sun for a season. And immediately there fell on him a mist and a darkness; and he went about seeking some to lead him by the hand.

• Paul heals a cripple.

Ac 14:10 — Said with a loud voice, Stand upright on thy feet. And he leaped and walked.

• Paul casts out evil spirits, and cures sick.

Ac 19:11–12; 28:8–9

Ac 16:18 — And this did she many days. But Paul, being grieved, turned and said to the spirit, I command thee in the name of Jesus Christ to come out of her. And he came out the same hour.

• Paul raises Eutychus to life.

Ac 20:9–12

• Paul shakes a viper off his hand.

Ac 28:5 — And he shook off the beast into the fire, and felt no harm.

• Paul cured of blindness.

Ac 9:3–6, 17–18

MIRACLES, Genesis-Deuteronomy

• Catalogue of, and supernatural events.

• Creation.

Ge 1:1–31

• Flood.

Ge 7:1–8:22

• Confusion of tongues.

Ge 11:1–9

• Fire on Abraham's sacrifice.

Ge 15:17 — And it came to pass, that, when the sun went down, and it was dark, behold a smoking furnace, and a burning lamp that passed between those pieces.

• Conception of Isaac.

Ge 17:17 — Then Abraham fell upon his face, and laughed, and said in his heart, Shall *a child* be born unto him that is an hundred years old? and shall Sarah, that is ninety years old, bear?

Ge 18:12 — Therefore Sarah laughed within herself, saying, After I am waxed old shall I have pleasure, my lord being old also?

Ge 21:2 — For Sarah conceived, and bare Abraham a son in his old age, at the set time of which God had spoken to him.

• Destruction of Sodom.

Ge 19:1–38

• Lot's wife turned to salt.

Ge 19:26 — But his wife looked back from behind him, and she became a pillar of salt.

• Closing of the wombs of Abimelech's household.

Ge 20:17–18

• Opening of Hagar's eyes.

Ge 21:19 — And God opened her eyes, and she saw a well of water; and she went, and filled the bottle with water, and gave the lad drink.

• Conception of Jacob and Esau.

Ge 25:21 — And Isaac intreated the LORD for his wife, because she *was* barren: and the LORD was intreated of him, and Rebekah his wife conceived.

• Opening of Rachel's womb.

Ge 30:22 — And God remembered Rachel, and God hearkened to her, and opened her womb.

• Flaming bush.

Ex 3:2 — And the angel of the LORD appeared unto him in a flame of fire out of the midst of a bush: and he looked, and, behold, the bush burned with fire, and the bush *was* not consumed.

• Transformation of Moses' rod into a serpent.

Ex 4:3–4

Ex 4:30 — And Aaron spake all the words which the LORD had spoken unto Moses, and did the signs in the sight of the people.

Ex 7:10 — And Moses and Aaron went in unto Pharaoh, and they did so as the LORD had commanded: and Aaron cast down his rod before Pharaoh, and before his servants, and it became a serpent.

Ex 7:12 — For they cast down every man his rod, and they became serpents: but Aaron's rod swallowed up their rods.

• Moses' leprosy.

Ex 4:6–7

Ex 4:30 — And Aaron spake all the words which the LORD had spoken unto Moses, and did the signs in the sight of the people.

• Plagues in Egypt.

See: Plague

• Pillar of cloud and fire.

Ex 13:21–22; 14:19–20

• Passage of the Red Sea.

Ex 14:22 — And the children of Israel went into the midst of the sea upon the dry *ground:* and the waters *were* a wall unto them on their right hand, and on their left.

• Destruction of Pharaoh and his army.

Ex 14:23–30

• Sweetening the waters of Marah.

Ex 15:25 — And he cried unto the LORD; and the LORD shewed him a tree, *which* when he had cast into the waters, the waters were made sweet: there he made for them a statute and an ordinance, and there he proved them,

• Manna.

Ex 16:4–31

- **Quails.**
  Ex 16:13 — And it came to pass, that at even the quails came up, and covered the camp: and in the morning the dew lay round about the host.
- **Defeat of Amalek.**
  Ex 17:9–13
- **Transfiguration of the face of Moses.**
  Ex 34:29–35
- **Water from the rock.**
  Ex 17:5 — And the LORD said unto Moses, Go on before the people, and take with thee of the elders of Israel; and thy rod, wherewith thou smotest the river, take in thine hand, and go.
  Ex 17:7 — And he called the name of the place Massah, and Meribah, because of the chiding of the children of Israel, and because they tempted the LORD, saying, Is the LORD among us, or not?
- **Thundering and lightning on Sinai.**
  Ex 19:16–20; 24:15–17
  Ex 24:10 — And they saw the God of Israel: and *there was* under his feet as it were a paved work of a sapphire stone, and as it were the body of heaven in *his* clearness.
  Dt 4:33 — Did *ever* people hear the voice of God speaking out of the midst of the fire, as thou hast heard, and live?
- **Miriam's leprosy.**
  Nu 12:10–15
- **Judgment by fire.**
  Nu 11:1–3
- **Destruction of Korah.**
  Nu 16:31–35; Dt 11:6–7
- **Plague.**
  Nu 16:46–50
- **Aaron's rod buds.**
  Nu 17:1–9
- **Waters from the rock in Kadesh.**
  Nu 20:8–11
- **Scourge of serpents.**
  Nu 21:6–9
- **Destruction of Nadab and Abihu.**
  Le 10:1–2
- **Balaam's ass speaks.**
  Nu 22:23–30
- **Preservation of Moses.**
  Dt 34:7 — And Moses *was* an hundred and twenty years old when he died: his eye was not dim, nor his natural force abated.

MIRACLES, Joshua-Jonah

- **Jordan divided.**
  Jos 3:14–17; 4:16–18
- **Fall of Jericho.**
  Jos 6:20 — So the people shouted when *the priests* blew with the trumpets: and it came to pass, when the people heard the sound of the trumpet, and the people shouted with a great shout, that the wall fell down flat, so that the people went up into the city, every man straight before him, and they took the city.
- **Midianites destroyed.**
  Jgs 7:16–22
- **Hail on the confederated kings.**
  Jos 10:11 — And it came to pass, as they fled from before Israel, *and* were in the going down to Beth-horon, that the LORD cast down great stones from heaven upon them unto Azekah, and they died: *they were* more which died with hailstones than they whom the children of Israel slew with the sword.
- **Sun and moon stand still.**
  Jos 10:12–14
- **Dew on Gideon's fleece.**
  Jgs 6:37–40
- **Samson's strength.**
  Jgs 16:29–30
  Jgs 14:6 — And the Spirit of the LORD came mightily upon him, and he rent him as he would have rent a kid, and *he had* nothing in his hand: but he told not his father or his mother what he had done.
  Jgs 16:3 — And Samson lay till midnight, and arose at midnight, and took the doors of the gate of the city, and the two posts, and went away with them, bar and all, and put *them* upon his shoulders, and carried them up to the top of an hill that is before Hebron.
- **Samson supplied with water.**
  Jgs 15:19 — But God clave an hollow place that *was* in the jaw, and there came water thereout; and when he had drunk, his spirit came again, and he revived: wherefore he called the name thereof En-hakkore, which *is* in Lehi unto this day.
- **Fall of Dagon.**
  1Sa 5:1–4
- **Cows return the ark.**
  1Sa 6:7–14
- **Hemorrhoids.**
  1Sa 5:9–6:18
- **Destruction of the people of Beth-shemesh.**
  1Sa 6:19–20
- **Thunder.**
  1Sa 12:16–18
- **Destruction of Uzzah.**
  2Sa 6:1–8
- **Plague in Israel.**
  1Ch 21:14–26
- **Fire on the sacrifices of Aaron.**
  Le 9:24 — And there came a fire out from before the LORD, and consumed upon the altar the burnt offering and the fat: *which* when all the people saw, they shouted, and fell on their faces.
- **Fire on the sacrifices of Gideon.**
  Jgs 6:21 — Then the angel of the LORD put forth the end of the staff that *was* in his hand, and touched the flesh and the unleavened cakes; and there rose up fire out of the rock, and consumed the flesh and the unleavened cakes. Then the angel of the LORD departed out of his sight.
- **Fire on the sacrifices of Manoah.**
  Jgs 13:19–20

• **Fire on the sacrifices of Solomon.**
2Ch 7:1 — Now when Solomon had made an end of praying, the fire came down from heaven, and consumed the burnt offering and the sacrifices; and the glory of the LORD filled the house.

• **Fire on the sacrifices of Elijah.**
1Ki 18:38 — Then the fire of the LORD fell, and consumed the burnt sacrifice, and the wood, and the stones, and the dust, and licked up the water that *was* in the trench.

• **Jeroboam's hand withered.**
1Ki 13:3–6

• **Appearance of blood.**
2Ki 3:20–22

• **Panic of the Syrians.**
2Ki 7:6–7

• **Elijah is fed by ravens.**
1Ki 17:6 — And the ravens brought him bread and flesh in the morning, and bread and flesh in the evening; and he drank of the brook.

• **Elijah is fed by an angel.**
1Ki 19:1–8

• **Elijah increases the widow's meal and oil.**
1Ki 17:9–16
Lk 4:26 — But unto none of them was Elias sent, save unto Sarepta, *a city* of Sidon, unto a woman *that was* a widow.

• **Elijah raises the widow's son.**
1Ki 17:17–24

• **Rain in answer to Elijah's prayer.**
1Ki 18:41–45

• **Elijah brings fire on Ahaziah's army.**
2Ki 1:10–12

• **Elijah divides Jordan.**
2Ki 2:8 — And Elijah took his mantle, and wrapped *it* together, and smote the waters, and they were divided hither and thither, so that they two went over on dry ground.

• **Elijah's translation.**
2Ki 2:11 — And it came to pass, as they still went on, and talked, that, behold, *there appeared* a chariot of fire, and horses of fire, and parted them both asunder; and Elijah went up by a whirlwind into heaven.

• **Elisha divides Jordan.**
2Ki 2:14 — And he took the mantle of Elijah that fell from him, and smote the waters, and said, Where *is* the LORD God of Elijah? and when he also had smitten the waters, they parted hither and thither: and Elisha went over.

• **Elisha sweetens the waters of Jericho.**
2Ki 2:19–22

• **Elisha increases a widow's oil.**
2Ki 4:1–7

• **Elisha raises the Shunammite's child.**
2Ki 4:18–37

• **Elisha renders harmless the poisoned pottage.**
2Ki 4:38–41

• **Elisha feeds one hundred men.**
2Ki 4:42–44

• **Elisha cures Naaman.**
2Ki 5:1–19

• **Elisha smites Gehazi with leprosy.**
2Ki 5:26–27

• **Elisha causes the ax to float.**
2Ki 6:6 — And the man of God said, Where fell it? And he shewed him the place. And he cut down a stick, and cast *it* in thither; and the iron did swim.

• **Elisha reveals the counsel of the king of Syria.**
2Ki 6:12 — And one of his servants said, None, my lord, O king: but Elisha, the prophet that *is* in Israel, telleth the king of Israel the words that thou speakest in thy bedchamber.

• **Elisha causes the eyes of his servant to be opened.**
2Ki 6:17 — And Elisha prayed, and said, LORD, I pray thee, open his eyes, that he may see. And the LORD opened the eyes of the young man; and he saw: and, behold, the mountain *was* full of horses and chariots of fire round about Elisha.

• **Elisha smites with blindness the army of the king of Syria.**
2Ki 6:18 — And when they came down to him, Elisha prayed unto the LORD, and said, Smite this people, I pray thee, with blindness. And he smote them with blindness according to the word of Elisha.

• **Elisha restores the dead man to life.**
2Ki 13:21 — And it came to pass, as they were burying a man, that, behold, they spied a band *of men;* and they cast the man into the sepulchre of Elisha: and when the man was let down, and touched the bones of Elisha, he revived, and stood up on his feet.

• **Destruction of Sennacherib's army.**
2Ki 19:35 — And it came to pass that night, that the angel of the LORD went out, and smote in the camp of the Assyrians an hundred fourscore and five thousand: and when they arose early in the morning, behold, they *were* all dead corpses.
Isa 37:36 — Then the angel of the LORD went forth, and smote in the camp of the Assyrians a hundred and fourscore and five thousand: and when they arose early in the morning, behold, they *were* all dead corpses.

• **Return of the shadow on the sun dial.**
2Ki 20:9–11

• **Hezekiah's cure.**
Isa 38:21 — For Isaiah had said, Let them take a lump of figs, and lay *it* for a plaister upon the boil, and he shall recover.

• **Deliverance of Shadrach, Meshach, and Abed-nego.**
Da 3:23–27

• **Deliverance of Daniel.**
Da 6:22 — My God hath sent his angel, and hath shut the lions' mouths, that they have not hurt me: foras-

much as before him innocency was found in me; and also before thee, O king, have I done no hurt.

- **The sea calmed on Jonah being cast into it.**
  Jnh 1:15 — So they took up Jonah, and cast him forth into the sea: and the sea ceased from her raging.
- **Jonah in the fish's belly.**
  Jnh 1:17 — Now the LORD had prepared a great fish to swallow up Jonah. And Jonah was in the belly of the fish three days and three nights.
  Jnh 2:10 — And the LORD spake unto the fish, and it vomited out Jonah upon the dry *land.*
- **Jonah and his gourd.**
  Jnh 4:6–7

MIRACLES, of Jesus, in chronological order

- **Water made wine.**
  Jn 2:1–11
- **Heals the nobleman's son.**
  Jn 4:46–54
- **Draught of fishes.**
  Lk 5:1–11
- **Heals the demoniac.**
  Mk 1:23–26; Lk 4:33–36
- **Heals Peter's mother-in-law.**
  Mt 8:14–17; Mk 1:29–31; Lk 4:38–39
- **Cleanses the leper.**
  Mt 8:1–4; Mk 1:40–45; Lk 5:12–16
- **Heals the paralytic.**
  Mt 9:1–8; Mk 2:1–12; Lk 5:17–26
- **Healing of the impotent man.**
  Jn 5:1–16
- **Restoring the withered hand.**
  Mt 12:9–13; Mk 3:1–5; Lk 6:6–11
- **Restores the centurion's servant.**
  Mt 8:5–13; Lk 7:1–10
- **Raises the widow's son to life.**
  Lk 7:11–16
- **Heals a demoniac.**
  Mt 12:22–37; Lk 11:14–15
  Mk 3:11 — And unclean spirits, when they saw him, fell down before him, and cried, saying, Thou art the Son of God.
- **Stills the tempest.**
  Mt 8:23–27; Mk 4:35–41; Lk 8:22–25
  Mt 14:32 — And when they were come into the ship, the wind ceased.
- **Casts devils out of two men of Gadara.**
  Mt 8:28–34; Mk 5:1–20; Lk 8:26–39
- **Raises from the dead the daughter of Jairus.**
  Mt 9:18–19, 23–26; Mk 5:22–24, 35–43; Lk 8:41–42, 49–56
- **Cures the woman with the issue of blood.**
  Mt 9:20–22; Mk 5:25–34; Lk 8:43–48
- **Restores two blind men to sight.**
  Mt 9:27–31
- **Heals a demoniac.**
  Mt 9:32–33
- **Feeds five thousand people.**
  Mt 14:15–21; Mk 6:35–44; Lk 9:12–17; Jn 6:5–14
- **Walks on the sea.**
  Mt 14:22–33; Mk 6:45–52; Jn 6:16–21
- **Heals the daughter of the Syrophenician woman.**
  Mt 15:21–28; Mk 7:24–30
- **Feeds four thousand people.**
  Mt 15:32–39; Mk 8:1–9
- **Restores one deaf and dumb.**
  Mk 7:31–37
- **Restores a blind man.**
  Mk 8:22–26
- **Restores lunatic child.**
  Mt 17:14–21; Mk 9:14–29; Lk 9:37–43
- **Tribute money obtained from a fish's mouth.**
  Mt 17:24–27
- **Restores ten lepers.**
  Lk 17:11–19
- **Opens the eyes of a man born blind.**
  Jn 9:1–41
- **Raises Lazarus from the dead.**
  Jn 11:1–46
- **Heals the woman with the spirit of infirmity.**
  Lk 13:10–17
- **Cures a man with dropsy.**
  Lk 14:1–6
- **Restores two blind men near Jericho.**
  Mt 20:29–34; Mk 10:46–52; Lk 18:35–43
- **Curses a fig tree.**
  Mt 21:17–22; Mk 11:12–14, 20–24
- **Heals the ear of Malchus.**
  Lk 22:49–51
- **Second draught of fishes.**
  Jn 21:6 — And he said unto them, Cast the net on the right side of the ship, and ye shall find. They cast therefore, and now they were not able to draw it for the multitude of fishes.

MIRACLES, Other

- **Miracles surrounding Christ's birth.**
  - **Conception by Elisabeth.**
    Lk 1:24–25
    Lk 1:18 — And Zacharias said unto the angel, Whereby shall I know this? for I am an old man, and my wife well stricken in years.
  - **The incarnation of Jesus.**
    Mt 1:18–25; Lk 1:26–80
  - **The appearance of the star of Bethlehem.**
    Mt 2:1–9
  - **The deliverance of Jesus.**
    Mt 2:13–23

• **Convincing effect of.**

Ex 4:28–31; 10:16–17; 12:31–33; Jgs 6:17–22, 36–7:1; Da 3:28–29; 4:2–3; Lk 5:4–11; Jn 2:22–23; 4:48–53; 11:43–45; 12:10–11; 20:30–31; Ac 9:32–42; 13:8–12; 19:13–18; Ro 15:18–19

Ex 10:7 — And Pharaoh's servants said unto him, How long shall this man be a snare unto us? let the men go, that they may serve the LORD their God: knowest thou not yet that Egypt is destroyed?

Ex 14:25 — And took off their chariot wheels, that they drave them heavily: so that the Egyptians said, Let us flee from the face of Israel; for the LORD fighteth for them against the Egyptians.

Ex 14:31 — And Israel saw that great work which the LORD did upon the Egyptians: and the people feared the LORD, and believed the LORD, and his servant Moses.

Jn 2:11 — This beginning of miracles did Jesus in Cana of Galilee, and manifested forth his glory; and his disciples believed on him.

Jn 7:31 — And many of the people believed on him, and said, When Christ cometh, will he do more miracles than these which this *man* hath done?

Ac 8:6 — And the people with one accord gave heed unto those things which Philip spake, hearing and seeing the miracles which he did.

See: Miracles, Other; design of

• **Design of.**

Ex 3:19–20; 4:2–9; 8:8–10; 9:14–16; 10:1–2, 16–17; 11:7–9; 12:29–33; 14:24–25; 16:4–6; 19:4–5; Nu 16:28–35; 17:1–12; Dt 4:33–35; 11:1–8; 29:1–9; Jos 2:9–11; 3:10–11; 4:23–5:1; 1Sa 6:6–18; 12:17–18; 1Ki 18:37–39; 2Ki 5:14–15; 2Ch 7:1–3; Ps 78:10–32; 106:9–12; Da 3:28–29; 6:20–27; Jnh 1:14–16; Mt 11:3–5; Mk 2:9–12; Lk 18:42–43; Jn 11:40–42; Ac 3:1–10; 4:21–22

Ex 7:5 — And the Egyptians shall know that I *am* the LORD, when I stretch forth mine hand upon Egypt, and bring out the children of Israel from among them.

Ex 7:17 — Thus saith the LORD, In this thou shalt know that I *am* the LORD: behold, I will smite with the rod that *is* in mine hand upon the waters which *are* in the river, and they shall be turned to blood.

Ex 8:22 — And I will sever in that day the land of Goshen, in which my people dwell, that no swarms *of flies* shall be there; to the end thou mayest know that I *am* the LORD in the midst of the earth.

Ex 9:29 — And Moses said unto him, As soon as I am gone out of the city, I will spread abroad my hands unto the LORD; *and* the thunder shall cease, neither shall there be any more hail; that thou mayest know how that the earth *is* the LORD'S.

Ex 11:1 — And the LORD said unto Moses, Yet will I bring one plague *more* upon Pharaoh, and upon Egypt; afterwards he will let you go hence: when he shall let *you* go, he shall surely thrust you out hence altogether.

Ex 14:4 — And I will harden Pharaoh's heart, that he shall follow after them; and I will be honoured upon Pharaoh, and upon all his host; that the Egyptians may know that I *am* the LORD. And they did so.

Ex 14:18 — And the Egyptians shall know that I *am* the LORD, when I have gotten me honour upon Pharaoh, upon his chariots, and upon his horsemen.

Ex 14:31 — And Israel saw that great work which the LORD did upon the Egyptians: and the people feared the LORD, and believed the LORD, and his servant Moses.

Ex 19:9 — And the LORD said unto Moses, Lo, I come unto thee in a thick cloud, that the people may hear when I speak with thee, and believe thee for ever. And Moses told the words of the people unto the LORD.

Nu 14:11 — And the LORD said unto Moses, How long will this people provoke me? and how long will it be ere they believe me, for all the signs which I have shewed among them?

Jgs 2:7 — And the people served the LORD all the days of Joshua, and all the days of the elders that outlived Joshua, who had seen all the great works of the LORD, that he did for Israel.

1Ki 18:24 — And call ye on the name of your gods, and I will call on the name of the LORD: and the God that answereth by fire, let him be God. And all the people answered and said, It is well spoken.

Jer 32:20 — Which hast set signs and wonders in the land of Egypt, *even* unto this day, and in Israel, and among *other* men; and hast made thee a name, as at this day;

Da 2:47 — The king answered unto Daniel, and said, Of a truth *it is*, that your God is a God of gods, and a Lord of kings, and a revealer of secrets, seeing thou couldst reveal this secret.

Zec 2:9 — For, behold, I will shake mine hand upon them, and they shall be a spoil to their servants: and ye shall know that the LORD of hosts hath sent me.

Mt 4:3 — And when the tempter came to him, he said, If thou be the Son of God, command that these stones be made bread.

Lk 3:4 — As it is written in the book of the words of Esaias the prophet, saying, The voice of one crying in the wilderness, Prepare ye the way of the Lord, make his paths straight.

Lk 3:6 — And all flesh shall see the salvation of God.

Lk 5:26 — And they were all amazed, and they glorified God, and were filled with fear, saying, We have seen strange things to day.

Jn 2:11 — This beginning of miracles did Jesus in Cana of Galilee, and manifested forth his glory; and his disciples believed on him.

Jn 4:48 — Then said Jesus unto him, Except ye see signs and wonders, ye will not believe.

Jn 5:36 — But I have greater witness than *that* of John: for the works which the Father hath given me to finish, the same works that I do, bear witness of me, that the Father hath sent me.

Jn 9:3 — Jesus answered, Neither hath this man sinned, nor his parents: but that the works of God should be made manifest in him.

Jn 11:4 — When Jesus heard *that,* he said, This sickness is not unto death, but for the glory of God, that the Son of God might be glorified thereby.

Ac 2:22 — Ye men of Israel, hear these words; Jesus of Nazareth, a man approved of God among you by miracles and wonders and signs, which God did by him in the midst of you, as ye yourselves also know:

1Co 1:22 — For the Jews require a sign, and the Greeks seek after wisdom:

• Miraculous gifts of the Holy Ghost.

• Foretold.

Isa 35:4–6; Joel 2:28–29

• Of different kinds.

1Co 12:4–6

• Enumerated.

1Co 12:8–10

1Co 12:28 — And God hath set some in the church, first apostles, secondarily prophets, thirdly teachers, after that miracles, then gifts of healings, helps, governments, diversities of tongues.

• Christ was endued with.

Mt 12:28 — But if I cast out devils by the Spirit of God, then the kingdom of God is come unto you.

• Poured out on Pentecost.

Ac 2:1–4

• Communicated on preaching the gospel.

Ac 10:44–46

• Communicated by laying on of the apostles' hands.

Ac 8:17–18

Ac 19:6 — And when Paul had laid *his* hands upon them, the Holy Ghost came on them; and they spake with tongues, and prophesied.

• Communicated for the confirmation of the gospel.

Mk 16:20 — And they went forth, and preached every where, the Lord working with *them,* and confirming the word with signs following. Amen.

Ac 14:3 — Long time therefore abode they speaking boldly in the Lord, which gave testimony unto the word of his grace, and granted signs and wonders to be done by their hands.

Ro 15:19 — Through mighty signs and wonders, by the power of the Spirit of God; so that from Jerusalem, and round about unto Illyricum, I have fully preached the gospel of Christ.

Heb 2:4 — God also bearing *them* witness, both with signs and wonders, and with divers miracles, and gifts of the Holy Ghost, according to his own will?

• Communicated for the edification of the church.

1Co 14:12–13

1Co 12:7 — But the manifestation of the Spirit is given to every man to profit withal.

• To be sought after.

1Co 12:31 — But covet earnestly the best gifts: and yet shew I unto you a more excellent way.

1Co 14:1 — Follow after charity, and desire spiritual *gifts,* but rather that ye may prophesy.

• Temporary nature of.

1Co 13:8 — Charity never faileth: but whether *there be* prophecies, they shall fail; whether *there be* tongues, they shall cease; whether *there be* knowledge, it shall vanish away.

• Not to be neglected.

1Ti 4:14 — Neglect not the gift that is in thee, which was given thee by prophecy, with the laying on of the hands of the presbytery.

2Ti 1:6 — Wherefore I put thee in remembrance that thou stir up the gift of God, which is in thee by the putting on of my hands.

• Not to be despised.

1Th 5:20 — Despise not prophesyings.

• Not to be purchased.

Ac 8:20 — But Peter said unto him, Thy money perish with thee, because thou hast thought that the gift of God may be purchased with money.

• Miscellany of minor sub-topics.

• Called Marvelous Things.

Ps 78:12 — Marvellous things did he in the sight of their fathers, in the land of Egypt, *in* the field of Zoan.

• Called Marvelous Works.

Ps 105:5 — Remember his marvellous works that he hath done; his wonders, and the judgments of his mouth;

Isa 29:14 — Therefore, behold, I will proceed to do a marvellous work among this people, *even* a marvellous work and a wonder: for the wisdom of their wise *men* shall perish, and the understanding of their prudent *men* shall be hid.

• Called Signs and Wonders.

Jer 32:21 — And hast brought forth thy people Israel out of the land of Egypt with signs, and with wonders, and with a strong hand, and with a stretched out arm, and with great terror;

Jn 4:48 — Then said Jesus unto him, Except ye see signs and wonders, ye will not believe.

2Co 12:12 — Truly the signs of an apostle were wrought among you in all patience, in signs, and wonders, and mighty deeds.

• Performed through the power of God.

Jn 3:2 — The same came to Jesus by night, and said unto him, Rabbi, we know that thou art a teacher come from God: for no man can do these miracles that thou doest, except God be with him.

Ac 14:3 — Long time therefore abode they speaking boldly in the Lord, which gave testimony unto the word of his grace, and granted signs and wonders to be done by their hands.

Ac 15:12 — Then all the multitude kept silence, and gave audience to Barnabas and Paul, declaring what miracles and wonders God had wrought among the Gentiles by them.

Ac 19:11 — And God wrought special miracles by the hands of Paul:

• Performed through the power of the Holy Ghost.

1Co 12:9–10

Mt 12:28 — But if I cast out devils by the Spirit of God, then the kingdom of God is come unto you.

Ro 15:19 — Through mighty signs and wonders, by the power of the Spirit of God; so that from Jerusalem, and round about unto Illyricum, I have fully preached the gospel of Christ.

1Co 12:28 — And God hath set some in the church, first apostles, secondarily prophets, thirdly teachers, after that miracles, then gifts of healings, helps, governments, diversities of tongues.

1Co 12:30 — Have all the gifts of healing? do all speak with tongues? do all interpret?

• Performed in the name of Christ.

Mk 16:17 — And these signs shall follow them that believe; In my name shall they cast out devils; they shall speak with new tongues;

Ac 3:16 — And his name through faith in his name hath made this man strong, whom ye see and know: yea, the faith which is by him hath given him this perfect soundness in the presence of you all.

Ac 4:30 — By stretching forth thine hand to heal; and that signs and wonders may be done by the name of thy holy child Jesus.

• Faith required in those who perform.

Mt 17:20 — And Jesus said unto them, Because of your unbelief: for verily I say unto you, If ye have faith as a grain of mustard seed, ye shall say unto this mountain, Remove hence to yonder place; and it shall remove; and nothing shall be impossible unto you.

Mt 21:21 — Jesus answered and said unto them, Verily I say unto you, If ye have faith, and doubt not, ye shall not only do this *which is done* to the fig tree, but also if ye shall say unto this mountain, Be thou removed, and be thou cast into the sea; it shall be done.

Jn 14:12 — Verily, verily, I say unto you, He that believeth on me, the works that I do shall he do also; and greater *works* than these shall he do; because I go unto my Father.

Ac 3:16 — And his name through faith in his name hath made this man strong, whom ye see and know: yea, the faith which is by him hath given him this perfect soundness in the presence of you all.

Ac 6:8 — And Stephen, full of faith and power, did great wonders and miracles among the people.

• Faith required in those for whom they were performed.

Mk 9:22–24

Mt 9:28 — And when he was come into the house, the blind men came to him: and Jesus saith unto them, Believe ye that I am able to do this? They said unto him, Yea, Lord.

Ac 14:9 — The same heard Paul speak: who stedfastly beholding him, and perceiving that he had faith to be healed,

• Power to work, given the disciples.

Mk 3:14–15; 16:17–18

Mk 16:20 — And they went forth, and preached every where, the Lord working with *them,* and confirming the word with signs following. Amen.

• Demanded by unbelievers.

Mt 12:38–39

Mt 16:1 — The Pharisees also with the Sadducees came, and tempting desired him that he would shew them a sign from heaven.

Lk 11:16 — And others, tempting *him,* sought of him a sign from heaven.

Lk 11:29 — And when the people were gathered thick together, he began to say, This is an evil generation: they seek a sign; and there shall no sign be given it, but the sign of Jonas the prophet.

Lk 23:8 — And when Herod saw Jesus, he was exceeding glad: for he was desirous to see him of a long *season,* because he had heard many things of him; and he hoped to have seen some miracle done by him.

• Alleged miracles performed by magicians.

Ex 7:10–12

Ex 7:22 — And the magicians of Egypt did so with their enchantments: and Pharaoh's heart was hardened, neither did he hearken unto them; as the LORD had said.

Ex 8:7 — And the magicians did so with their enchantments, and brought up frogs upon the land of Egypt.

• Alleged miracles performed by other imposters.

Mt 7:22 — Many will say to me in that day, Lord, Lord, have we not prophesied in thy name? and in thy name have cast out devils? and in thy name done many wonderful works?

• Performed through the powers of evil.

2Th 2:9 — *Even him,* whose coming is after the working of Satan with all power and signs and lying wonders,

Rev 16:14 — For they are the spirits of devils, working miracles, *which* go forth unto the kings of the earth and of the whole world, to gather them to the battle of that great day of God Almighty.

• Wrought in support of false religions.

Dt 13:1–2

• Wrought by false Christs.

Mt 24:24 — For there shall arise false Christs, and false prophets, and shall shew great signs and wonders; insomuch that, if *it were* possible, they shall deceive the very elect.

• Wrought by false prophets.

Mt 24:24 — For there shall arise false Christs, and false prophets, and shall shew great signs and wonders; insomuch that, if *it were* possible, they shall deceive the very elect.

Rev 19:20 — And the beast was taken, and with him the false prophet that wrought miracles before him, with which he deceived them that had received the mark of the beast, and them that worshipped his image. These both were cast alive into a lake of fire burning with brimstone.

- **Wrought by the Witch of En-dor.**
  1Sa 28:7–14
- **Wrought by Simon Magus.**
  Ac 8:9–11
- **Not to be regarded.**
  Dt 13:3 — Thou shalt not hearken unto the words of that prophet, or that dreamer of dreams: for the LORD your God proveth you, to know whether ye love the LORD your God with all your heart and with all your soul.
- **Deceive the ungodly.**
  2Th 2:10–12
  Rev 13:14 — And deceiveth them that dwell on the earth by *the means of* those miracles which he had power to do in the sight of the beast; saying to them that dwell on the earth, that they should make an image to the beast, which had the wound by a sword, and did live.
  Rev 19:20 — And the beast was taken, and with him the false prophet that wrought miracles before him, with which he deceived them that had received the mark of the beast, and them that worshipped his image. These both were cast alive into a lake of fire burning with brimstone.
- **A mark of apostasy.**
  2Th 2:3 — Let no man deceive you by any means: for *that day shall not come,* except there come a falling away first, and that man of sin be revealed, the son of perdition;
  2Th 2:9 — *Even him,* whose coming is after the working of Satan with all power and signs and lying wonders,
  Rev 13:13 — And he doeth great wonders, so that he maketh fire come down from heaven on the earth in the sight of men,

MIRE

- **Figurative.**
  Ps 40:2 — He brought me up also out of an horrible pit, out of the miry clay, and set my feet upon a rock, *and* established my goings.
  Ps 69:2 — I sink in deep mire, where *there is* no standing: I am come into deep waters, where the floods overflow me.

MIRIAM, sister of Moses

- **Watches over Moses when he is in the ark.**
  Ex 2:4–8
- **Song of, after the destruction of Pharaoh and his army.**
  Ex 15:20–21
  Mic 6:4 — For I brought thee up out of the land of Egypt, and redeemed thee out of the house of servants; and I sent before thee Moses, Aaron, and Miriam.
- **Jealous of Moses; stricken with leprosy; healed on account of the intercession of Moses.**
  Nu 12:1–16
  Dt 24:9 — Remember what the LORD thy God did unto Miriam by the way, after that ye were come forth out of Egypt.
- **Dies and is buried at Kadesh.**
  Nu 20:1 — Then came the children of Israel, *even* the whole congregation, into the desert of Zin in the first month: and the people abode in Kadesh; and Miriam died there, and was buried there.

MIRMA • A Benjamite.

1Ch 8:10 — And Jeuz, and Shachia, and Mirma. These *were* his sons, heads of the fathers.

MIRROR

- **Of brass.**
  Job 37:18 — Hast thou with him spread out the sky, *which is* strong, *and* as a molten looking glass?
- **Given by the Israelitish women to be melted for the laver.**
  Ex 38:8 — And he made the laver *of* brass, and the foot of it *of* brass, of the lookingglasses of *the women* assembling, which assembled *at* the door of the tabernacle of the congregation.
- **Figurative.**
  Jas 1:23–24
  1Co 13:12 — For now we see through a glass, darkly; but then face to face: now I know in part; but then shall I know even as also I am known.
  2Co 3:18 — But we all, with open face beholding as in a glass the glory of the Lord, are changed into the same image from glory to glory, *even* as by the Spirit of the Lord.

MISCEGENATION

- **Forbidden by.**
  - **Abraham.**
    Ge 24:3 — And I will make thee swear by the LORD, the God of heaven, and the God of the earth, that thou shalt not take a wife unto my son of the daughters of the Canaanites, among whom I dwell:
  - **Jacob.**
    Ge 28:1 — And Isaac called Jacob, and blessed him, and charged him, and said unto him, Thou shalt not take a wife of the daughters of Canaan.
  - **Moses.**
    Ex 34:12–16; Dt 7:3–4
  - **Joshua.**
    Jos 23:12 — Else if ye do in any wise go back, and cleave unto the remnant of these nations, *even* these that remain among you, and shall make marriages with them, and go in unto them, and they to you:
- **Reasons for prohibition.**
  Jos 23:12–13
  Ex 34:16 — And thou take of their daughters unto thy sons, and their daughters go a whoring after their

gods, and make thy sons go a whoring after their gods.

Dt 7:4 — For they will turn away thy son from following me, that they may serve other gods: so will the anger of the LORD be kindled against you, and destroy thee suddenly.

• Results of.

Jgs 3:6–7

• Instances of.

• Moses.

Nu 12:1

• Esau.

Ge 26:34–35

• Israel.

Nu 25:1, 6–8; Jgs 3:5–8

MISER

Ecc 4:7–8

MISGAB • An unknown place.

Jer 48:1 — Against Moab thus saith the LORD of hosts, the God of Israel; Woe unto Nebo! for it is spoiled: Kiriathaim is confounded *and* taken: Misgab is confounded and dismayed.

MISHAEL

• A son of Uzziel.

Ex 6:22 — And the sons of Uzziel; Mishael, and Elzaphan, and Zithri.

• Helps carry the bodies of Nadab and Abihu out of the camp.

Le 10:4 — And Moses called Mishael and Elzaphan, the sons of Uzziel the uncle of Aaron, and said unto them, Come near, carry your brethren from before the sanctuary out of the camp.

• A Jew who stood by Ezra when he read the law to the people.

Ne 8:4 — And Ezra the scribe stood upon a pulpit of wood, which they had made for the purpose; and beside him stood Mattithiah, and Shema, and Anaiah, and Urijah, and Hilkiah, and Maaseiah, on his right hand; and on his left hand, Pedaiah, and Mishael, and Malchiah, and Hashum, and Hashbadana, Zechariah, *and* Meshullam.

• Called also Meshach. One of three Hebrew children trained with Daniel at the court of Babylon.

Da 1:6–7, 11–20

• Assists Daniel in interpreting Nebuchadnezzar's dream.

Da 2:17–23

• Cast into the fiery furnace.

Da 3:13–30

MISHAM • A Benjamite.

1Ch 8:12 — The sons of Elpaal; Eber, and Misham, and Shamed, who built Ono, and Lod, with the towns thereof:

MISHEAL

• Called also Mishal.

• A Levitical city.

Jos 19:26 — And Alammelech, and Amad, and Misheal; and reacheth to Carmel westward, and to Shihor-libnath;

Jos 21:30 — And out of the tribe of Asher, Mishal with her suburbs, Abdon with her suburbs,

MISHMA

• Son of Ishmael.

Ge 25:14 — And Mishma, and Dumah, and Massa,

1Ch 1:30 — Mishma and Dumah, Massa, Hadad, and Tema,

• Of the tribe of Simeon.

1Ch 4:25–26

MISHMANNAH • A Gadite who joined David at Ziklag.

1Ch 12:10 — Mishmannah the fourth, Jeremiah the fifth,

MISJUDGMENT

• Instances of.

• Of the Reubenites and Gadites.

Nu 32:1–33; Jos 22:11–31

• Of Hannah.

1Sa 1:14–17

See: Accusation, False

See: Uncharitableness

MISPAR See: Mispereth

MISPERETH

• Called also Mizpar.

• A Jew who returned with Zerubbabel from Babylon.

Ezr 2:2 — Which came with Zerubbabel: Jeshua, Nehemiah, Seraiah, Reelaiah, Mordecai, Bilshan, Mizpar, Bigvai, Rehum, Baanah. The number of the men of the people of Israel:

Ne 7:7 — Who came with Zerubbabel, Jeshua, Nehemiah, Azariah, Raamiah, Nahamani, Mordecai, Bilshan, Mispereth, Bigvai, Nehum, Baanah. The number, *I say,* of the men of the people of Israel *was this;*

MISREPHOTH-MAIM • A city of eastern Zidon.

Jos 11:8 — And the LORD delivered them into the hand of Israel, who smote them, and chased them unto great Zidon, and unto Misrephoth-maim, and unto the valley of Mizpeh eastward; and they smote them, until they left them none remaining.

Jos 13:6 — All the inhabitants of the hill country from Lebanon unto Misrephoth-maim, *and* all the Sidonians, them will I drive out from before the children of Israel: only divide thou it by lot unto the Israelites for an inheritance, as I have commanded thee.

MISSIONS

2Ki 17:27–28; 1Ch 16:23–24; Isa 43:6–7; Jnh 1:1–3:9; Lk 24:47–48; Ac 10:9–20; 13:2–4; 26:14–18; Rev 14:6–7

Ps 18:49 — Therefore will I give thanks unto thee, O LORD, among the heathen, and sing praises unto thy name.

Ps 96:3 — Declare his glory among the heathen, his wonders among all people.

Ps 96:10 — Say among the heathen *that* the LORD reigneth: the world also shall be established that it shall not be moved: he shall judge the people righteously.

Mt 24:14 — And this gospel of the kingdom shall be preached in all the world for a witness unto all nations; and then shall the end come.

Mt 28:19 — Go ye therefore, and teach all nations, baptizing them in the name of the Father, and of the Son, and of the Holy Ghost:

Mk 13:10 — And the gospel must first be published among all nations.

Mk 16:15 — And he said unto them, Go ye into all the world, and preach the gospel to every creature.

Ac 13:47 — For so hath the Lord commanded us, *saying*, I have set thee to be a light of the Gentiles, that thou shouldest be for salvation unto the ends of the earth.

1Co 16:9 — For a great door and effectual is opened unto me, and *there are* many adversaries.

• Missionary hymn.

Ps 96:1–13

• The first to do homage to the Messiah were heathen.

Mt 2:11 — And when they were come into the house, they saw the young child with Mary his mother, and fell down, and worshipped him: and when they had opened their treasures, they presented unto him gifts; gold, and frankincense, and myrrh.

See: Gentiles; conversion of

See: Heathen

See: Jesus, King

See: Jesus, Kingdom of; prophecies concerning

MIST

Ge 2:6 — But there went up a mist from the earth, and watered the whole face of the ground.

2Pe 2:17 — These are wells without water, clouds that are carried with a tempest; to whom the mist of darkness is reserved for ever.

MITE

• About one-fifth of a cent.

Mk 12:42 — And there came a certain poor widow, and she threw in two mites, which make a farthing.

• Widow's.

Lk 21:2 — And he saw also a certain poor widow casting in thither two mites.

MITER

Ex 28:36–39; 39:28–31

Ex 28:4 — And these *are* the garments which they shall make; a breastplate, and an ephod, and a robe, and a broidered coat, a mitre, and a girdle: and they shall make holy garments for Aaron thy brother, and his sons, that he may minister unto me in the priest's office.

Eze 21:26 — Thus saith the Lord GOD; Remove the diadem, and take off the crown: this *shall* not *be* the same: exalt *him that is* low, and abase *him that is* high.

MITHCAH • An encampment of the Israelites.

Nu 33:28–29

MITHREDATH

• Treasurer of Cyrus.

Ezr 1:8 — Even those did Cyrus king of Persia bring forth by the hand of Mithredath the treasurer, and numbered them unto Sheshbazzar, the prince of Judah.

• A Persian officer who joined in writing a letter inimical to the Jews.

Ezr 4:7 — And in the days of Artaxerxes wrote Bishlam, Mithredath, Tabeel, and the rest of their companions, unto Artaxerxes king of Persia; and the writing of the letter *was* written in the Syrian tongue, and interpreted in the Syrian tongue.

MITYLENE, capital of Lesbos

• Paul visits.

Ac 20:14–15

MIZAR • A hill.

Ps 42:6 — O my God, my soul is cast down within me: therefore will I remember thee from the land of Jordan, and of the Hermonites, from the hill Mizar.

MIZPAH

• A city allotted to Benjamin.

Jos 18:26 — And Mizpeh, and Chephirah, and Mozah,

• The Israelites assemble at.

Jgs 20:1–3

• The Israelites decree the penalty to be visited upon the Benjamites for their maltreatment of the Levite's concubine.

Jgs 20:10 — And we will take ten men of an hundred throughout all the tribes of Israel, and an hundred of a thousand, and a thousand out of ten thousand, to fetch victual for the people, that they may do, when they come to Gibeah of Benjamin, according to all the folly that they have wrought in Israel.

• Assembled by Samuel that he might reprove them for their idolatry.

1Sa 7:5 — And Samuel said, Gather all Israel to Mizpeh, and I will pray for you unto the LORD.

• Crown Saul king of Israel at.

1Sa 10:17–25

• A judgment seat of Samuel.

1Sa 7:16 — And he went from year to year in circuit to Bethel, and Gilgal, and Mizpeh, and judged Israel in all those places.

• Walled by Asa.

1Ki 15:22 — Then king Asa made a proclamation throughout all Judah; none *was* exempted: and they took away the stones of Ramah, and the timber thereof, wherewith Baasha had builded; and king Asa built with them Geba of Benjamin, and Mizpah.

2Ch 16:6 — Then Asa the king took all Judah; and they carried away the stones of Ramah, and the timber thereof, wherewith Baasha was building; and he built therewith Geba and Mizpah.

• Temporarily the capital of the country after the children of Israel had been carried away captive.

Jer 40:6–15; 41:1–14

2Ki 25:23 — And when all the captains of the armies, they and their men, heard that the king of Babylon had made Gedaliah governor, there came to Gedaliah to Mizpah, even Ishmael the son of Nethaniah, and Johanan the son of Careah, and Seraiah the son of Tanhumeth the Netophathite, and Jaazaniah the son of a Maachathite, they and their men.

2Ki 25:25 — But it came to pass in the seventh month, that Ishmael the son of Nethaniah, the son of Elishama, of the seed royal, came, and ten men with him, and smote Gedaliah, that he died, and the Jews and the Chaldees that were with him at Mizpah.

• Captivity returned to.

Ne 3:7 — And next unto them repaired Melatiah the Gibeonite, and Jadon the Meronothite, the men of Gibeon, and of Mizpah, unto the throne of the governor on this side the river.

Ne 3:15 — But the gate of the fountain repaired Shallun the son of Col-hozeh, the ruler of part of Mizpah; he built it, and covered it, and set up the doors thereof, the locks thereof, and the bars thereof, and the wall of the pool of Siloah by the king's garden, and unto the stairs that go down from the city of David.

Ne 3:19 — And next to him repaired Ezer the son of Jeshua, the ruler of Mizpah, another piece over against the going up to the armoury at the turning *of the wall*.

• A valley near Lebanon.

Jos 11:3 — *And to* the Canaanite on the east and on the west, and *to* the Amorite, and the Hittite, and the Perizzite, and the Jebusite in the mountains, and *to* the Hivite under Hermon in the land of Mizpeh.

Jos 11:8 — And the LORD delivered them into the hand of Israel, who smote them, and chased them unto great Zidon, and unto Misrephoth-maim, and unto the valley of Mizpeh eastward; and they smote them, until they left them none remaining.

• A city in Moab.

• David gives his parents to the care of the king of.

1Sa 22:3–4

• A city in the lowland of Judah.

Jos 15:38 — And Dilean, and Mizpeh, and Joktheel,

MIZRAIM • Son of Ham.

Ge 10:6 — And the sons of Ham; Cush, and Mizraim, and Phut, and Canaan.

Ge 10:13 — And Mizraim begat Ludim, and Anamim, and Lehabim, and Naphtuhim,

1Ch 1:8 — The sons of Ham; Cush, and Mizraim, Put, and Canaan.

1Ch 1:11 — And Mizraim begat Ludim, and Anamim, and Lehabim, and Napthtuhim,

MIZZAH • Son of Reuel.

Ge 36:13 — And these *are* the sons of Reuel; Nahath, and Zerah, Shammah, and Mizzah: these were the sons of Bashemath Esau's wife.

Ge 36:17 — And these *are* the sons of Reuel Esau's son; duke Nahath, duke Zerah, duke Shammah, duke Mizzah: these *are* the dukes *that came* of Reuel in the land of Edom; these *are* the sons of Bashemath Esau's wife.

1Ch 1:37 — The sons of Reuel; Nahath, Zerah, Shammah, and Mizzah.

MNASON • A native and Christian of Cyprus who entertained Paul.

Ac 21:16 — There went with us also *certain* of the disciples of Caesarea, and brought with them one Mnason of Cyprus, an old disciple, with whom we should lodge.

MOAB

• Son of Lot.

Ge 19:37 — And the firstborn bare a son, and called his name Moab: the same *is* the father of the Moabites unto this day.

• Plains of.

• Israelites come in.

Dt 2:17–18

• Military forces numbered in.

Nu 26:3 — And Moses and Eleazar the priest spake with them in the plains of Moab by Jordan *near* Jericho, saying,

Nu 26:63 — These *are* they that were numbered by Moses and Eleazar the priest, who numbered the children of Israel in the plains of Moab by Jordan *near* Jericho.

• The law rehearsed in, by Moses.

Nu 35:1–36:13; Dt 29:1–33:29

• The Israelites renew their covenant in.

Dt 29:1 — These *are* the words of the covenant, which the LORD commanded Moses to make with the children of Israel in the land of Moab, beside the covenant which he made with them in Horeb.

• The land of promise allotted in.

Jos 13:32 — These *are the countries* which Moses did distribute for inheritance in the plains of Moab, on the other side Jordan, by Jericho, eastward.

MOABITES

• Descendants of Lot through his son Moab.

Ge 19:37 — And the firstborn bare a son, and called his name Moab: the same *is* the father of the Moabites unto this day.

• Called the people of Chemosh.

Nu 21:29 — Woe to thee, Moab! thou art undone, O people of Chemosh: he hath given his sons that escaped, and his daughters, into captivity unto Sihon king of the Amorites.

• The territory east of Jordan, bounded on the north by the river Arnon.

Nu 21:13 — From thence they removed, and pitched on the other side of Arnon, which *is* in the wilderness that cometh out of the coasts of the Amorites: for Arnon *is* the border of Moab, between Moab and the Amorites.

Jgs 11:18 — Then they went along through the wilderness, and compassed the land of Edom, and the land of Moab, and came by the east side of the land of Moab, and pitched on the other side of Arnon, but came not within the border of Moab: for Arnon *was* the border of Moab.

• Children of Israel commanded not to distress the Moabites.

Dt 2:9 — And the LORD said unto me, Distress not the Moabites, neither contend with them in battle: for I will not give thee of their land *for* a possession; because I have given Ar unto the children of Lot *for* a possession.

• Refuse passage of Jephthah's army through their territory.

Jgs 11:17–18

• Balak was king of.

Nu 22:4 — And Moab said unto the elders of Midian, Now shall this company lick up all *that are* round about us, as the ox licketh up the grass of the field. And Balak the son of Zippor *was* king of the Moabites at that time.

• Balak calls for Baalam to curse Israel.

Nu 22:1–24:25

Jos 24:9 — Then Balak the son of Zippor, king of Moab, arose and warred against Israel, and sent and called Balaam the son of Beor to curse you:

Mic 6:5 — O my people, remember now what Balak king of Moab consulted, and what Balaam the son of Beor answered him from Shittim unto Gilgal; that ye may know the righteousness of the LORD.

• Are a snare to the Israelites.

Nu 25:1–3; Ezr 9:1–2

Ru 1:4 — And they took them wives of the women of Moab; the name of the one *was* Orpah, and the name of the other Ruth: and they dwelled there about ten years.

1Ki 11:1 — But king Solomon loved many strange women, together with the daughter of Pharaoh, women of the Moabites, Ammonites, Edomites, Zidonians, *and* Hittites;

1Ch 8:8 — And Shaharaim begat *children* in the country of Moab, after he had sent them away; Hushim and Baara *were* his wives.

Ne 13:23 — In those days also saw I Jews *that* had married wives of Ashdod, of Ammon, *and* of Moab:

• Land of, not given to the Israelites as a possession.

Dt 2:9 — And the LORD said unto me, Distress not the Moabites, neither contend with them in battle: for I will not give thee of their land *for* a possession; because I have given Ar unto the children of Lot *for* a possession.

Dt 2:29 — (As the children of Esau which dwell in Seir, and the Moabites which dwell in Ar, did unto me;) until I shall pass over Jordan into the land which the LORD our God giveth us.

• David takes refuge among, from Saul.

1Sa 22:3–4

• David conquers.

1Ch 18:2–11

2Sa 8:2 — And he smote Moab, and measured them with a line, casting them down to the ground; even with two lines measured he to put to death, and with one full line to keep alive. And so the Moabites became David's servants, *and* brought gifts.

2Sa 23:20 — And Benaiah the son of Jehoiada, the son of a valiant man, of Kabzeel, who had done many acts, he slew two lionlike men of Moab: he went down also and slew a lion in the midst of a pit in time of snow:

1Ch 11:22 — Benaiah the son of Jehoiada, the son of a valiant man of Kabzeel, who had done many acts; he slew two lionlike men of Moab: also he went down and slew a lion in a pit in a snowy day.

• Israelites had war with.

2Ki 3:5–27; 2Ch 20:1–37

2Ki 13:20 — And Elisha died, and they buried him. And the bands of the Moabites invaded the land at the coming in of the year.

2Ki 24:2 — And the LORD sent against him bands of the Chaldees, and bands of the Syrians, and bands of the Moabites, and bands of the children of Ammon, and sent them against Judah to destroy it, according to the word of the LORD, which he spake by his servants the prophets.

• Prophecies concerning judgments upon.

Jer 48:1–47

MOADIAH • A priest.

Ne 12:17 — Of Abijah, Zichri; of Miniamin, of Moadiah, Piltai;

MOB

• At Thessalonica.

Ac 17:5 — But the Jews which believed not, moved with envy, took unto them certain lewd fellows of the baser sort, and gathered a company, and set all the city on an uproar, and assaulted the house of Jason, and sought to bring them out to the people.

- **At Jerusalem.**
  Ac 21:28 — Crying out, Men of Israel, help: This is the man, that teacheth all *men* every where against the people, and the law, and this place: and further brought Greeks also into the temple, and hath polluted this holy place.
  Ac 21:30 — And all the city was moved, and the people ran together: and they took Paul, and drew him out of the temple: and forthwith the doors were shut.
- **At Ephesus.**
  Ac 19:29–40

MOCKING

- **Ishmael mocks Sarah.**
  Ge 21:9 — And Sarah saw the son of Hagar the Egyptian, which she had born unto Abraham, mocking.
- **Elijah mocks the priests of Baal.**
  1Ki 18:27 — And it came to pass at noon, that Elijah mocked them, and said, Cry aloud: for he *is* a god; either he is talking, or he is pursuing, or he is in a journey, *or* peradventure he sleepeth, and must be awaked.
- **Zedekiah mocks Micaiah.**
  1Ki 22:24 — But Zedekiah the son of Chenaanah went near, and smote Micaiah on the cheek, and said, Which way went the Spirit of the LORD from me to speak unto thee?
- **Children mock Elisha.**
  2Ki 2:23 — And he went up from thence unto Bethel: and as he was going up by the way, there came forth little children out of the city, and mocked him, and said unto him, Go up, thou bald head; go up, thou bald head.
- **The tormentors of Job mock.**
  Job 15:12 — Why doth thine heart carry thee away? and what do thy eyes wink at,
  Job 30:1 — But now *they that are* younger than I have me in derision, whose fathers I would have disdained to have set with the dogs of my flock.
- **The persecutors of Jesus mock him.**
  Mt 26:67–68; 27:28–31, 39–44; Mk 15:17–20, 29–32; Lk 23:1–56; Jn 19:2–3
  Mk 10:34 — And they shall mock him, and shall scourge him, and shall spit upon him, and shall kill him: and the third day he shall rise again.
  Mk 14:65 — And some began to spit on him, and to cover his face, and to buffet him, and to say unto him, Prophesy: and the servants did strike him with the palms of their hands.
  Jn 19:5 — Then came Jesus forth, wearing the crown of thorns, and the purple robe. And *Pilate* saith unto them, Behold the man!
  1Pe 2:23 — Who, when he was reviled, reviled not again; when he suffered, he threatened not; but committed *himself* to him that judgeth righteously:
- **The Ammonites mock God.**
  Eze 25:3 — And say unto the Ammonites, Hear the word of the Lord GOD; Thus saith the Lord GOD; Because thou saidst, Aha, against my sanctuary, when it was profaned; and against the land of Israel, when it was desolate; and against the house of Judah, when they went into captivity;
- **Tyre mocks Jerusalem.**
  Eze 26:2 — Son of man, because that Tyrus hath said against Jerusalem, Aha, she is broken *that was* the gates of the people: she is turned unto me: I shall be replenished, *now* she is laid waste:
- **The obdurately wicked mock.**
  Isa 28:15 — Because ye have said, We have made a covenant with death, and with hell are we at agreement; when the overflowing scourge shall pass through, it shall not come unto us: for we have made lies our refuge, and under falsehood have we hid ourselves:
  Isa 28:22 — Now therefore be ye not mockers, lest your bands be made strong: for I have heard from the Lord GOD of hosts a consumption, even determined upon the whole earth.
  2Pe 3:3 — Knowing this first, that there shall come in the last days scoffers, walking after their own lusts,
  See: Scoffing
- **Figurative.**
  Pr 1:26 — I also will laugh at your calamity; I will mock when your fear cometh;

MODESTY

- **Of women.**
  1Ti 2:9 — In like manner also, that women adorn themselves in modest apparel, with shamefacedness and sobriety; not with broided hair, or gold, or pearls, or costly array;
- **Instances of.**
  - **Saul.**
    1Sa 9:21
  - **Vashti.**
    Est 1:11–12
  - **Elihu.**
    Job 32:4–7

  See: Humility

MOLDING

Job 28:2 — Iron is taken out of the earth, and brass *is* molten *out of* the stone.
Eze 24:11 — Then set it empty upon the coals thereof, that the brass of it may be hot, and may burn, and *that* the filthiness of it may be molten in it, *that* the scum of it may be consumed.

- **Of images.**
  Ex 32:4 — And he received *them* at their hand, and fashioned it with a graving tool, after he had made it a molten calf: and they said, These *be* thy gods, O Israel, which brought thee up out of the land of Egypt.
  Ex 32:8 — They have turned aside quickly out of the way which I commanded them: they have made them a molten calf, and have worshipped it, and have sacrificed thereunto, and said, These *be* thy gods, O Israel, which have brought thee up out of the land of Egypt.

Ex 34:17 — Thou shalt make thee no molten gods.

Le 19:4 — Turn ye not unto idols, nor make to yourselves molten gods: I *am* the LORD your God.

Dt 9:12 — And the LORD said unto me, Arise, get thee down quickly from hence; for thy people which thou hast brought forth out of Egypt have corrupted *themselves;* they are quickly turned aside out of the way which I commanded them; they have made them a molten image.

• Pillars.

1Ki 7:15 — For he cast two pillars of brass, of eighteen cubits high apiece: and a line of twelve cubits did compass either of them about.

• Laver.

1Ki 7:23 — And he made a molten sea, ten cubits from the one brim to the other: *it was* round all about, and his height *was* five cubits: and a line of thirty cubits did compass it round about.

• Done in the plain of Jordan.

1Ki 7:46 — In the plain of Jordan did the king cast them, in the clay ground between Succoth and Zarthan.

2Ch 4:17 — In the plain of Jordan did the king cast them, in the clay ground between Succoth and Zeredathah.

• Mirrors.

Job 37:18 — Hast thou with him spread out the sky, *which is* strong, *and* as a molten looking glass?

MOLE

Le 11:30 — And the ferret, and the chameleon, and the lizard, and the snail, and the mole.

Isa 2:20 — In that day a man shall cast his idols of silver, and his idols of gold, which they made *each one* for himself to worship, to the moles and to the bats;

MOLECH

• Called also Moloch and Milcom.

• An idol of the Ammonites.

Ac 7:43 — Yea, ye took up the tabernacle of Moloch, and the star of your god Remphan, figures which ye made to worship them: and I will carry you away beyond Babylon.

• Worshiped by the wives of Solomon, and by Solomon.

1Ki 11:1–8

• Children sacrificed to.

Le 20:2–5; Eze 16:20–21

Le 18:21 — And thou shalt not let any of thy seed pass through *the fire* to Molech, neither shalt thou profane the name of thy God: I *am* the LORD.

2Ki 16:3 — But he walked in the way of the kings of Israel, yea, and made his son to pass through the fire, according to the abominations of the heathen, whom the LORD cast out from before the children of Israel.

2Ki 21:6 — And he made his son pass through the fire, and observed times, and used enchantments, and dealt with familiar spirits and wizards: he wrought much wickedness in the sight of the LORD, to provoke *him* to anger.

2Ki 23:10 — And he defiled Topheth, which *is* in the valley of the children of Hinnom, that no man might make his son or his daughter to pass through the fire to Molech.

2Ch 28:3 — Moreover he burnt incense in the valley of the son of Hinnom, and burnt his children in the fire, after the abominations of the heathen whom the LORD had cast out before the children of Israel.

Isa 57:5 — Enflaming yourselves with idols under every green tree, slaying the children in the valleys under the clifts of the rocks?

Jer 7:31 — And they have built the high places of Tophet, which is in the valley of the son of Hinnom, to burn their sons and their daughters in the fire; which I commanded *them* not, neither came it into my heart.

Jer 32:35 — And they built the high places of Baal, which *are* in the valley of the son of Hinnom, to cause their sons and their daughters to pass through *the fire* unto Molech; which I commanded them not, neither came it into my mind, that they should do this abomination, to cause Judah to sin.

Eze 20:26 — And I polluted them in their own gifts, in that they caused to pass through *the fire* all that openeth the womb, that I might make them desolate, to the end that they might know that I *am* the LORD.

Eze 20:31 — For when ye offer your gifts, when ye make your sons to pass through the fire, ye pollute yourselves with all your idols, even unto this day: and shall I be enquired of by you, O house of Israel? *As* I live, saith the Lord GOD, I will not be enquired of by you.

Eze 23:37 — That they have committed adultery, and blood is in their hands, and with their idols have they committed adultery, and have also caused their sons, whom they bare unto me, to pass for them through *the fire,* to devour *them.*

Eze 23:39 — For when they had slain their children to their idols, then they came the same day into my sanctuary to profane it; and, lo, thus have they done in the midst of mine house.

MONARCHY

• Described by Samuel.

1Sa 8:11–18

See: **Government**

See: **King**

MONEY

• Silver used as.

Ge 17:12–13; 42:25–35; 43:12–23; 44:1–8; 47:14–18; Ex 21:34–35; Nu 3:48–51; Dt 14:25–26; 2Ki 12:7–16; Ne 5:10–11; Isa 55:1–2; Jer 32:9–10

Ge 17:23 — And Abraham took Ishmael his son, and all that were born in his house, and all that were bought with his money, every male among the men of Abraham's house; and circumcised the flesh of their foreskin in the selfsame day, as God had said unto him.

Ge 17:27 — And all the men of his house, born in the house, and bought with money of the stranger, were circumcised with him.

Ge 20:16 — And unto Sarah he said, Behold, I have given thy brother a thousand *pieces* of silver: behold, he *is* to thee a covering of the eyes, unto all that *are* with thee, and with all *other:* thus she was reproved.

Ge 23:9 — That he may give me the cave of Machpelah, which he hath, which *is* in the end of his field; for as much money as it is worth he shall give it me for a possession of a buryingplace amongst you.

Ge 23:13 — And he spake unto Ephron in the audience of the people of the land, saying, But if thou *wilt give it,* I pray thee, hear me: I will give thee money for the field; take *it* of me, and I will bury my dead there.

Ge 31:15 — Are we not counted of him strangers? for he hath sold us, and hath quite devoured also our money.

Ge 37:28 — Then there passed by Midianites merchantmen; and they drew and lifted up Joseph out of the pit, and sold Joseph to the Ishmeelites for twenty *pieces* of silver: and they brought Joseph into Egypt.

Ex 12:44 — But every man's servant that is bought for money, when thou hast circumcised him, then shall he eat thereof.

Ex 21:11 — And if he do not these three unto her, then shall she go out free without money.

Ex 21:21 — Notwithstanding, if he continue a day or two, he shall not be punished: for he *is* his money.

Ex 22:7 — If a man shall deliver unto his neighbour money or stuff to keep, and it be stolen out of the man's house; if the thief be found, let him pay double.

Ex 22:17 — If her father utterly refuse to give her unto him, he shall pay money according to the dowry of virgins.

Ex 22:25 — If thou lend money to *any of* my people *that is* poor by thee, thou shalt not be to him as an usurer, neither shalt thou lay upon him usury.

Ex 30:16 — And thou shalt take the atonement money of the children of Israel, and shalt appoint it for the service of the tabernacle of the congregation; that it may be a memorial unto the children of Israel before the LORD, to make an atonement for your souls.

Le 22:11 — But if the priest buy *any* soul with his money, he shall eat of it, and he that is born in his house: they shall eat of his meat.

Le 25:37 — Thou shalt not give him thy money upon usury, nor lend him thy victuals for increase.

Le 25:51 — If *there be* yet many years *behind,* according unto them he shall give again the price of his redemption out of the money that he was bought for.

Le 27:15 — And if he that sanctified it will redeem his house, then he shall add the fifth *part* of the money of thy estimation unto it, and it shall be his.

Le 27:18 — But if he sanctify his field after the jubile, then the priest shall reckon unto him the money according to the years that remain, even unto the year of the jubile, and it shall be abated from thy estimation.

Nu 18:16 — And those that are to be redeemed from a month old shalt thou redeem, according to thine estimation, for the money of five shekels, after the shekel of the sanctuary, which *is* twenty gerahs.

Dt 2:6 — Ye shall buy meat of them for money, that ye may eat; and ye shall also buy water of them for money, that ye may drink.

Dt 2:28 — Thou shalt sell me meat for money, that I may eat; and give me water for money, that I may drink: only I will pass through on my feet;

Dt 21:14 — And it shall be, if thou have no delight in her, then thou shalt let her go whither she will; but thou shalt not sell her at all for money, thou shalt not make merchandise of her, because thou hast humbled her.

Dt 23:19 — Thou shalt not lend upon usury to thy brother; usury of money, usury of victuals, usury of any thing that is lent upon usury:

Jgs 5:19 — The kings came *and* fought, then fought the kings of Canaan in Taanach by the waters of Megiddo; they took no gain of money.

Jgs 16:18 — And when Delilah saw that he had told her all his heart, she sent and called for the lords of the Philistines, saying, Come up this once, for he hath shewed me all his heart. Then the lords of the Philistines came up unto her, and brought money in their hand.

Jgs 17:4 — Yet he restored the money unto his mother; and his mother took two hundred *shekels* of silver, and gave them to the founder, who made thereof a graven image and a molten image: and they were in the house of Micah.

1Ki 21:2 — And Ahab spake unto Naboth, saying, Give me thy vineyard, that I may have it for a garden of herbs, because it *is* near unto my house: and I will give thee for it a better vineyard than it; *or,* if it seem good to thee, I will give thee the worth of it in money.

1Ki 21:6 — And he said unto her, Because I spake unto Naboth the Jezreelite, and said unto him, Give me thy vineyard for money; or else, if it please thee, I will give thee *another* vineyard for it: and he answered, I will not give thee my vineyard.

1Ki 21:15 — And it came to pass, when Jezebel heard that Naboth was stoned, and was dead, that Jezebel said to Ahab, Arise, take possession of the vineyard of Naboth the Jezreelite, which he refused to give thee for money: for Naboth is not alive, but dead.

2Ki 5:26 — And he said unto him, Went not mine heart *with thee,* when the man turned again from his chariot to meet thee? *Is it* a time to receive money, and to receive garments, and oliveyards, and vineyards, and sheep, and oxen, and menservants, and maidservants?

2Ki 12:4 — And Jehoash said to the priests, All the money of the dedicated things that is brought into the house of the LORD, *even* the money of every one that passeth *the account,* the money that every man is set at, *and* all the money that cometh into any man's heart to bring into the house of the LORD,

2Ki 15:20 — And Menahem exacted the money of Israel, *even* of all the mighty men of wealth, of each man fifty shekels of silver, to give to the king of

Assyria. So the king of Assyria turned back, and stayed not there in the land.

2Ki 22:7 — Howbeit there was no reckoning made with them of the money that was delivered into their hand, because they dealt faithfully.

2Ki 22:9 — And Shaphan the scribe came to the king, and brought the king word again, and said, Thy servants have gathered the money that was found in the house, and have delivered it into the hand of them that do the work, that have the oversight of the house of the LORD.

2Ki 23:35 — And Jehoiakim gave the silver and the gold to Pharaoh; but he taxed the land to give the money according to the commandment of Pharaoh: he exacted the silver and the gold of the people of the land, of every one according to his taxation, to give *it* unto Pharaoh-nechoh.

2Ch 24:5 — And he gathered together the priests and the Levites, and said to them, Go out unto the cities of Judah, and gather of all Israel money to repair the house of your God from year to year, and see that ye hasten the matter. Howbeit the Levites hastened it not.

2Ch 24:11 — Now it came to pass, that at what time the chest was brought unto the king's office by the hand of the Levites, and when they saw that *there was* much money, the king's scribe and the high priest's officer came and emptied the chest, and took it, and carried it to his place again. Thus they did day by day, and gathered money in abundance.

2Ch 24:14 — And when they had finished *it,* they brought the rest of the money before the king and Jehoiada, whereof were made vessels for the house of the LORD, *even* vessels to minister, and to offer *withal,* and spoons, and vessels of gold and silver. And they offered burnt offerings in the house of the LORD continually all the days of Jehoiada.

2Ch 34:9 — And when they came to Hilkiah the high priest, they delivered the money that was brought into the house of God, which the Levites that kept the doors had gathered of the hand of Manasseh and Ephraim, and of all the remnant of Israel, and of all Judah and Benjamin; and they returned to Jerusalem.

2Ch 34:14 — And when they brought out the money that was brought into the house of the LORD, Hilkiah the priest found a book of the law of the LORD *given* by Moses.

2Ch 34:17 — And they have gathered together the money that was found in the house of the LORD, and have delivered it into the hand of the overseers, and to the hand of the workmen.

Ezr 3:7 — They gave money also unto the masons, and to the carpenters; and meat, and drink, and oil, unto them of Zidon, and to them of Tyre, to bring cedar trees from Lebanon to the sea of Joppa, according to the grant that they had of Cyrus king of Persia.

Ezr 7:17 — That thou mayest buy speedily with this money bullocks, rams, lambs, with their meat offerings and their drink offerings, and offer them upon the altar of the house of your God which *is* in Jerusalem.

Ne 5:4 — There were also that said, We have borrowed money for the king's tribute, *and that upon* our lands and vineyards.

Est 4:7 — And Mordecai told him of all that had happened unto him, and of the sum of the money that Haman had promised to pay to the king's treasuries for the Jews, to destroy them.

Job 31:39 — If I have eaten the fruits thereof without money, or have caused the owners thereof to lose their life:

Ps 15:5 — *He that* putteth not out his money to usury, nor taketh reward against the innocent. He that doeth these *things* shall never be moved.

Pr 7:20 — He hath taken a bag of money with him, *and* will come home at the day appointed.

Ecc 7:12 — For wisdom *is* a defence, *and* money *is* a defence: but the excellency of knowledge *is, that* wisdom giveth life to them that have it.

Ecc 10:19 — A feast is made for laughter, and wine maketh merry: but money answereth all *things.*

Isa 43:24 — Thou hast bought me no sweet cane with money, neither hast thou filled me with the fat of thy sacrifices: but thou hast made me to serve with thy sins, thou hast wearied me with thine iniquities.

Isa 52:3 — For thus saith the LORD, Ye have sold yourselves for nought; and ye shall be redeemed without money.

Jer 32:25 — And thou hast said unto me, O Lord GOD, Buy thee the field for money, and take witnesses; for the city is given into the hand of the Chaldeans.

Jer 32:44 — Men shall buy fields for money, and subscribe evidences, and seal *them,* and take witnesses in the land of Benjamin, and in the places about Jerusalem, and in the cities of Judah, and in the cities of the mountains, and in the cities of the valley, and in the cities of the south: for I will cause their captivity to return, saith the LORD.

La 5:4 — We have drunken our water for money; our wood is sold unto us.

Mic 3:11 — The heads thereof judge for reward, and the priests thereof teach for hire, and the prophets thereof divine for money: yet will they lean upon the LORD, and say, *Is* not the LORD among us? none evil can come upon us.

Mt 25:18 — But he that had received one went and digged in the earth, and hid his lord's money.

Mt 25:27 — Thou oughtest therefore to have put my money to the exchangers, and *then* at my coming I should have received mine own with usury.

Mt 28:12 — And when they were assembled with the elders, and had taken counsel, they gave large money unto the soldiers,

Mt 28:15 — So they took the money, and did as they were taught: and this saying is commonly reported among the Jews until this day.

Mk 14:11 — And when they heard *it,* they were glad, and promised to give him money. And he sought how he might conveniently betray him.

Lk 9:3 — And he said unto them, Take nothing for *your* journey, neither staves, nor scrip, neither bread, neither money; neither have two coats apiece.

Lk 19:15 — And it came to pass, that when he was returned, having received the kingdom, then he commanded these servants to be called unto him, to whom he had given the money, that he might know how much every man had gained by trading.

Lk 19:23 — Wherefore then gavest not thou my money into the bank, that at my coming I might have required mine own with usury?

Lk 22:5 — And they were glad, and covenanted to give him money.

Ac 7:16 — And were carried over into Sychem, and laid in the sepulchre that Abraham bought for a sum of money of the sons of Emmor *the father* of Sychem.

Ac 8:20 — But Peter said unto him, Thy money perish with thee, because thou hast thought that the gift of God may be purchased with money.

- **Argurion, Greek.**

Mt 25:18 — But he that had received one went and digged in the earth, and hid his lord's money.

Mt 25:27 — Thou oughtest therefore to have put my money to the exchangers, and *then* at my coming I should have received mine own with usury.

- **Gold used as.**

Ezr 8:25–27

Ge 13:2 — And Abram *was* very rich in cattle, in silver, and in gold.

Ge 24:35 — And the LORD hath blessed my master greatly; and he is become great: and he hath given him flocks, and herds, and silver, and gold, and menservants, and maidservants, and camels, and asses.

Ge 44:1 — And he commanded the steward of his house, saying, Fill the men's sacks *with* food, as much as they can carry, and put every man's money in his sack's mouth.

Ge 44:8 — Behold, the money, which we found in our sacks' mouths, we brought again unto thee out of the land of Canaan: how then should we steal out of thy lord's house silver or gold?

1Ch 21:25 — So David gave to Ornan for the place six hundred shekels of gold by weight.

Isa 13:17 — Behold, I will stir up the Medes against them, which shall not regard silver; and *as for* gold, they shall not delight in it.

Isa 46:6 — They lavish gold out of the bag, and weigh silver in the balance, *and* hire a goldsmith; and he maketh it a god: they fall down, yea, they worship.

Isa 60:9 — Surely the isles shall wait for me, and the ships of Tarshish first, to bring thy sons from far, their silver and their gold with them, unto the name of the LORD thy God, and to the Holy One of Israel, because he hath glorified thee.

Eze 7:19 — They shall cast their silver in the streets, and their gold shall be removed: their silver and their gold shall not be able to deliver them in the day of the wrath of the LORD: they shall not satisfy their souls, neither fill their bowels: because it is the stumblingblock of their iniquity.

Eze 28:4 — With thy wisdom and with thine understanding thou hast gotten thee riches, and hast gotten gold and silver into thy treasures:

Mt 2:11 — And when they were come into the house, they saw the young child with Mary his mother, and fell down, and worshipped him: and when they had opened their treasures, they presented unto him gifts; gold, and frankincense, and myrrh.

Mt 10:9 — Provide neither gold, nor silver, nor brass in your purses,

Ac 3:6 — Then Peter said, Silver and gold have I none; but such as I have give I thee: In the name of Jesus Christ of Nazareth rise up and walk.

Ac 20:33 — I have coveted no man's silver, or gold, or apparel.

1Pe 1:18 — Forasmuch as ye know that ye were not redeemed with corruptible things, *as* silver and gold, from your vain conversation *received* by tradition from your fathers;

- **Copper used as.**

Mk 6:8 — And commanded them that they should take nothing for *their* journey, save a staff only; no scrip, no bread, no money in *their* purse:

Mk 12:41 — And Jesus sat over against the treasury, and beheld how the people cast money into the treasury: and many that were rich cast in much.

- **Weighed.**

Jer 32:9–10

Ge 23:16 — And Abraham hearkened unto Ephron; and Abraham weighed to Ephron the silver, which he had named in the audience of the sons of Heth, four hundred shekels of silver, current *money* with the merchant.

Ge 43:21 — And it came to pass, when we came to the inn, that we opened our sacks, and, behold, *every* man's money *was* in the mouth of his sack, our money in full weight: and we have brought it again in our hand.

Job 28:15 — It cannot be gotten for gold, neither shall silver be weighed *for* the price thereof.

Zec 11:12 — And I said unto them, If ye think good, give *me* my price; and if not, forbear. So they weighed for my price thirty *pieces* of silver.

- **Image on.**

Mt 22:20–21

- **Conscience.**

Jgs 17:2 — And he said unto his mother, The eleven hundred *shekels* of silver that were taken from thee, about which thou cursedst, and spakest of also in mine ears, behold, the silver is with me; I took it. And his mother said, Blessed *be thou* of the LORD, my son.

Mt 27:3 — Then Judas, which had betrayeth him, when he saw that he was condemned, repented himself, and brought again the thirty pieces of silver to the chief priests and elders,

Mt 27:5 — And he cast down the pieces of silver in the temple, and departed, and went and hanged himself.

- **Atonement.**

Ex 30:12–16; Le 5:15–16

• **Sin.**

2Ki 12:16 — The trespass money and sin money was not brought into the house of the LORD: it was the priests'.

• **Value of, varied corruptly.**

Am 8:5 — Saying, When will the new moon be gone, that we may sell corn? and the sabbath, that we may set forth wheat, making the ephah small, and the shekel great, and falsifying the balances by deceit?

• **Love of, the root of evil.**

1Ti 6:10 — For the love of money is the root of all evil: which while some coveted after, they have erred from the faith, and pierced themselves through with many sorrows.

→See: **Farthing**
→See: **Gerah**
→See: **Mite**
→See: **Penny**
→See: **Pound**
→See: **Shekel**
→See: **Silver**
→See: **Talent**

MONEY CHANGERS

Mt 21:12 — And Jesus went into the temple of God, and cast out all them that sold and bought in the temple, and overthrew the tables of the moneychangers, and the seats of them that sold doves,

Mk 11:15 — And they come to Jerusalem: and Jesus went into the temple, and began to cast out them that sold and bought in the temple, and overthrew the tables of the moneychangers, and the seats of them that sold doves;

Jn 2:15 — And when he had made a scourge of small cords, he drove them all out of the temple, and the sheep, and the oxen; and poured out the changers' money, and overthrew the tables;

MONOPOLY

• **Of lands.**

Isa 5:8 — Woe unto them that join house to house, *that* lay field to field, till *there be* no place, that they may be placed alone in the midst of the earth!

Mic 2:2 — And they covet fields, and take *them* by violence; and houses, and take *them* away: so they oppress a man and his house, even a man and his heritage.

• **By Pharaoh.**

Ge 47:19–26

• **Of food.**

Pr 11:26 — He that withholdeth corn, the people shall curse him: but blessing *shall be* upon the head of him that selleth *it.*

MONTH

• **Ancient use of.**

Ge 7:11 — In the six hundredth year of Noah's life, in the second month, the seventeenth day of the month, the same day were all the fountains of the great deep broken up, and the windows of heaven were opened.

Ge 8:4 — And the ark rested in the seventh month, on the seventeenth day of the month, upon the mountains of Ararat.

• **Twelve months reckoned to a year.**

1Ch 27:1–15

• **Abib, or April.**

Ex 13:4 — This day came ye out in the month Abib.

Dt 16:1 — Observe the month of Abib, and keep the passover unto the LORD thy God: for in the month of Abib the LORD thy God brought thee forth out of Egypt by night.

• **The Jewish calendar began with.**

Ex 12:2 — This month *shall be* unto you the beginning of months: it *shall be* the first month of the year to you.

• **Passover instituted and celebrated in.**

Ex 12:1–28

Ex 23:15 — Thou shalt keep the feast of unleavened bread: (thou shalt eat unleavened bread seven days, as I commanded thee, in the time appointed of the month Abib; for in it thou camest out from Egypt: and none shall appear before me empty:)

• **Israelites left Egypt in.**

Ex 13:4 — This day came ye out in the month Abib.

• **Tabernacle set up in.**

Ex 40:2 — On the first day of the first month shalt thou set up the tabernacle of the tent of the congregation.

Ex 40:17 — And it came to pass in the first month in the second year, on the first *day* of the month, *that* the tabernacle was reared up.

• **Israelites arrive at Zin in.**

Nu 20:1 — Then came the children of Israel, *even* the whole congregation, into the desert of Zin in the first month: and the people abode in Kadesh; and Miriam died there, and was buried there.

• **Cross Jordan in.**

Jos 4:19 — And the people came up out of Jordan on the tenth *day* of the first month, and encamped in Gilgal, in the east border of Jericho.

• **Jordan overflows in.**

1Ch 12:15 — These *are* they that went over Jordan in the first month, when it had overflown all his banks; and they put to flight all *them* of the valleys, *both* toward the east, and toward the west.

• **Decree to put the Jews to death in.**

Est 3:12 — Then were the king's scribes called on the thirteenth day of the first month, and there was written according to all that Haman had commanded unto the king's lieutenants, and to the governors that *were* over every province, and to the rulers of every people of every province according to the writing thereof, and *to* every people after their language; in the name of king Ahasuerus was it written, and sealed with the king's ring.

- **The death of Jesus in.**
  Mt 26:1–27:66
- **After the captivity called Nisan.**
  Ne 2:1 — And it came to pass in the month Nisan, in the twentieth year of Artaxerxes the king, *that* wine *was* before him: and I took up the wine, and gave *it* unto the king. Now I had not been *beforetime* sad in his presence.
  Est 3:7 — In the first month, that *is,* the month Nisan, in the twelfth year of king Ahasuerus, they cast Pur, that *is,* the lot, before Haman from day to day, and from month to month, *to* the twelfth *month,* that *is,* the month Adar.

- **Zif, or May.**
  1Ki 6:1 — And it came to pass in the four hundred and eightieth year after the children of Israel were come out of the land of Egypt, in the fourth year of Solomon's reign over Israel, in the month Zif, which *is* the second month, that he began to build the house of the LORD.
  1Ki 6:37 — In the fourth year was the foundation of the house of the LORD laid, in the month Zif:
  - **Israel numbered in.**
    Nu 1:1 — And the LORD spake unto Moses in the wilderness of Sinai, in the tabernacle of the congregation, on the first *day* of the second month, in the second year after they were come out of the land of Egypt, saying,
    Nu 1:18 — And they assembled all the congregation together on the first *day* of the second month, and they declared their pedigrees after their families, by the house of their fathers, according to the number of the names, from twenty years old and upward, by their polls.
  - **Passover to be observed in, by the unclean and others who could not observe it in the first month.**
    Nu 9:10–11
  - **Israel departed from the wilderness of Zin in.**
    Nu 10:11 — And it came to pass on the twentieth *day* of the second month, in the second year, that the cloud was taken up from off the tabernacle of the testimony.
  - **Temple begun in.**
    1Ki 6:1 — And it came to pass in the four hundred and eightieth year after the children of Israel were come out of the land of Egypt, in the fourth year of Solomon's reign over Israel, in the month Zif, which *is* the second month, that he began to build the house of the LORD.
    2Ch 3:2 — And he began to build in the second *day* of the second month, in the fourth year of his reign.
  - **An irregular passover celebrated in.**
    2Ch 30:1–27
  - **Rebuilding of the temple begun in.**
    Ezr 3:8 — Now in the second year of their coming unto the house of God at Jerusalem, in the second month, began Zerubbabel the son of Shealtiel, and Jeshua the son of Jozadak, and the remnant of their brethren the priests and the Levites, and all they that were come out of the captivity unto Jerusalem; and appointed the Levites, from twenty years old and upward, to set forward the work of the house of the LORD.

- **Sivan, or June.**
  Est 8:9 — Then were the king's scribes called at that time in the third month, that *is,* the month Sivan, on the three and twentieth *day* thereof; and it was written according to all that Mordecai commanded unto the Jews, and to the lieutenants, and the deputies and rulers of the provinces which *are* from India unto Ethiopia, an hundred twenty and seven provinces, unto every province according to the writing thereof, and unto every people after their language, and to the Jews according to their writing, and according to their language.
  - **Asa renews the covenant of himself and people in.**
    2Ch 15:10 — So they gathered themselves together at Jerusalem in the third month, in the fifteenth year of the reign of Asa.

- **Tammuz, or July. Referred to by number only in the Bible.**
  - **Jerusalem taken by Nebuchadnezzar in.**
    Jer 52:6–7
    Jer 39:2 — *And* in the eleventh year of Zedekiah, in the fourth month, the ninth *day* of the month, the city was broken up.

- **Ab, or August. Referred to by number only in the Bible.**
  - **Aaron died on the first day of.**
    Nu 33:38 — And Aaron the priest went up into mount Hor at the commandment of the LORD, and died there, in the fortieth year after the children of Israel were come out of the land of Egypt, in the first *day* of the fifth month.
  - **Temple destroyed in.**
    2Ki 25:8–10; Jer 52:12–30
    Jer 1:3 — It came also in the days of Jehoiakim the son of Josiah king of Judah, unto the end of the eleventh year of Zedekiah the son of Josiah king of Judah, unto the carrying away of Jerusalem captive in the fifth month.
  - **Ezra arrived at Jerusalem in.**
    Ezr 7:8–9

- **Elul, or September.**
  - **Wall of Jerusalem finished in.**
    Ne 6:15 — So the wall was finished in the twenty and fifth *day* of *the month* Elul, in fifty and two days.
  - **Temple built in.**
    Hag 1:14–15

- **Ethanim, or October.**
  1Ki 8:2 — And all the men of Israel assembled themselves unto king Solomon at the feast in the month Ethanim, which *is* the seventh month.

• **Feasts held in.**
Ne 8:13–15
Le 23:24 — Speak unto the children of Israel, saying, In the seventh month, in the first *day* of the month, shall ye have a sabbath, a memorial of blowing of trumpets, an holy convocation.
Le 23:27 — Also on the tenth *day* of this seventh month *there shall be* a day of atonement: it shall be an holy convocation unto you; and ye shall afflict your souls, and offer an offering made by fire unto the LORD.

• **Jubilee proclaimed in.**
Le 25:9 — Then shalt thou cause the trumpet of the jubile to sound on the tenth *day* of the seventh month, in the day of atonement shall ye make the trumpet sound throughout all your land.

• **Solomon's temple dedicated in.**
1Ki 8:2 — And all the men of Israel assembled themselves unto king Solomon at the feast in the month Ethanim, which *is* the seventh month.

• **Altar rebuilt and offerings renewed in.**
Ezr 3:1 — And when the seventh month was come, and the children of Israel *were* in the cities, the people gathered themselves together as one man to Jerusalem.
Ezr 3:6 — From the first day of the seventh month began they to offer burnt offerings unto the LORD. But the foundation of the temple of the LORD was not *yet* laid.

• **Bul, or November.**

• **The temple finished in.**
1Ki 6:38 — And in the eleventh year, in the month Bul, which *is* the eigh88th month, was the house finished throughout all the parts thereof, and according to all the fashion of it. So was he seven years in building it.

• **Jeroboam's idolatrous feast in.**
1Ki 12:32–33
1Ch 27:11 — The eighth *captain* for the eighth month *was* Sibbecai the Hushathite, of the Zarhites: and in his course *were* twenty and four thousand.

• **Chisleu, or December.**
Ezr 10:9 — Then all the men of Judah and Benjamin gathered themselves together unto Jerusalem within three days. It *was* the ninth month, on the twentieth *day* of the month; and all the people sat in the street of the house of God, trembling because of *this* matter, and for the great rain.
Jer 36:9 — And it came to pass in the fifth year of Jehoiakim the son of Josiah king of Judah, in the ninth month, *that* they proclaimed a fast before the LORD to all the people in Jerusalem, and to all the people that came from the cities of Judah unto Jerusalem.
Jer 36:22 — Now the king sat in the winterhouse in the ninth month: and *there was a fire* on the hearth burning before him.
Zec 7:1 — And it came to pass in the fourth year of king Darius, *that* the word of the LORD came unto Zechariah in the fourth *day* of the ninth month, *even* in Chisleu;

• **Tebeth, or January.**
Est 2:16 — So Esther was taken unto king Ahasuerus into his house royal in the tenth month, which *is* the month Tebeth, in the seventh year of his reign.

• **Nebuchadnezzar besieges Jerusalem in.**
2Ki 25:1 — And it came to pass in the ninth year of his reign, in the tenth month, in the tenth *day* of the month, *that* Nebuchadnezzar king of Babylon came, he, and all his host, against Jerusalem, and pitched against it; and they built forts against it round about.
Jer 52:4 — And it came to pass in the ninth year of his reign, in the tenth month, in the tenth day of the month, *that* Nebuchadrezzar king of Babylon came, he and all his army, against Jerusalem, and pitched against it, and built forts against it round about.

• **Sebat, or February.**
Zec 1:7 — Upon the four and twentieth day of the eleventh month, which *is* the month Sebat, in the second year of Darius, came the word of the LORD unto Zechariah, the son of Berechiah, the son of Iddo the prophet, saying,

• **Moses probably died in.**
Dt 1:3 — And it came to pass in the fortieth year, in the eleventh month, on the first *day* of the month, *that* Moses spake unto the children of Israel, according unto all that the LORD had given him in commandment unto them;

• **Adar, or March.**
Est 3:7 — In the first month, that *is*, the month Nisan, in the twelfth year of king Ahasuerus, they cast Pur, that *is*, the lot, before Haman from day to day, and from month to month, *to* the twelfth *month*, that *is*, the month Adar.

• **Second temple finished in.**
Ezr 6:15 — And this house was finished on the third day of the month Adar, which was in the sixth year of the reign of Darius the king.

• **Feast of Purim in.**
Est 9:1–26

• **Months in prophecy.**
Rev 11:2 — But the court which is without the temple leave out, and measure it not; for it is given unto the Gentiles: and the holy city shall they tread under foot forty *and* two months.

MONUMENT

✢See: Pillar

MOON

• **Created by God.**
Ps 136:7–9
Ge 1:16 — And God made two great lights; the greater light to rule the day, and the lesser light to rule the night: *he made* the stars also.

Ps 8:3 — When I consider thy heavens, the work of thy fingers, the moon and the stars, which thou hast ordained;

- **Its light.**

Job 31:26 — If I beheld the sun when it shined, or the moon walking *in* brightness;

Ecc 12:2 — While the sun, or the light, or the moon, or the stars, be not darkened, nor the clouds return after the rain:

SS 6:10 — Who *is she that* looketh forth as the morning, fair as the moon, clear as the sun, *and* terrible as *an army* with banners?

Jer 31:35 — Thus saith the LORD, which giveth the sun for a light by day, *and* the ordinances of the moon and of the stars for a light by night, which divideth the sea when the waves thereof roar; The LORD of hosts *is* his name:

1Co 15:41 — *There is* one glory of the sun, and another glory of the moon, and another glory of the stars: for *one* star differeth from *another* star in glory.

- **Its influences.**

Dt 33:14 — And for the precious fruits *brought forth* by the sun, and for the precious things put forth by the moon,

Ps 121:6 — The sun shall not smite thee by day, nor the moon by night.

- **Seasons of (months).**

Ps 104:19 — He appointed the moon for seasons: the sun knoweth his going down.

- **Joseph's dream concerning.**

Ge 37:9 — And he dreamed yet another dream, and told it his brethren, and said, Behold, I have dreamed a dream more; and, behold, the sun and the moon and the eleven stars made obeisance to me.

- **Stands still.**

Jos 10:12–13

Hab 3:11 — The sun *and* moon stood still in their habitation: at the light of thine arrows they went, *and* at the shining of thy glittering spear.

- **Worship of, forbidden.**

Dt 4:19 — And lest thou lift up thine eyes unto heaven, and when thou seest the sun, and the moon, and the stars, *even* all the host of heaven, shouldest be driven to worship them, and serve them, which the LORD thy God hath divided unto all nations under the whole heaven.

Dt 17:3 — And hath gone and served other gods, and worshipped them, either the sun, or moon, or any of the host of heaven, which I have not commanded;

- **Worshiped.**

Job 31:26–27; Jer 44:17–19

2Ki 23:5 — And he put down the idolatrous priests, whom the kings of Judah had ordained to burn incense in the high places in the cities of Judah, and in the places round about Jerusalem; them also that burned incense unto Baal, to the sun, and to the moon, and to the planets, and to all the host of heaven.

Jer 7:18 — The children gather wood, and the fathers kindle the fire, and the women knead *their* dough, to make cakes to the queen of heaven, and to pour out drink offerings unto other gods, that they may provoke me to anger.

Jer 8:2 — And they shall spread them before the sun, and the moon, and all the host of heaven, whom they have loved, and whom they have served, and after whom they have walked, and whom they have sought, and whom they have worshipped: they shall not be gathered, nor be buried; they shall be for dung upon the face of the earth.

Jer 44:25 — Thus saith the LORD of hosts, the God of Israel, saying; Ye and your wives have both spoken with your mouths, and fulfilled with your hand, saying, We will surely perform our vows that we have vowed, to burn incense to the queen of heaven, and to pour out drink offerings unto her: ye will surely accomplish your vows, and surely perform your vows.

- **No light of, in heaven.**

Rev 21:23 — And the city had no need of the sun, neither of the moon, to shine in it: for the glory of God did lighten it, and the Lamb *is* the light thereof.

- **Darkening of.**

Job 25:5 — Behold even to the moon, and it shineth not; yea, the stars are not pure in his sight.

Isa 13:10 — For the stars of heaven and the constellations thereof shall not give their light: the sun shall be darkened in his going forth, and the moon shall not cause her light to shine.

Isa 24:23 — Then the moon shall be confounded, and the sun ashamed, when the LORD of hosts shall reign in mount Zion, and in Jerusalem, and before his ancients gloriously.

Eze 32:7 — And when I shall put thee out, I will cover the heaven, and make the stars thereof dark; I will cover the sun with a cloud, and the moon shall not give her light.

Joel 2:10 — The earth shall quake before them; the heavens shall tremble: the sun and the moon shall be dark, and the stars shall withdraw their shining:

Joel 2:31 — The sun shall be turned into darkness, and the moon into blood, before the great and the terrible day of the LORD come.

Joel 3:15 — The sun and the moon shall be darkened, and the stars shall withdraw their shining.

Mt 24:29 — Immediately after the tribulation of those days shall the sun be darkened, and the moon shall not give her light, and the stars shall fall from heaven, and the powers of the heavens shall be shaken:

Mk 13:24 — But in those days, after that tribulation, the sun shall be darkened, and the moon shall not give her light,

Lk 21:25 — And there shall be signs in the sun, and in the moon, and in the stars; and upon the earth distress of nations, with perplexity; the sea and the waves roaring;

Ac 2:20 — The sun shall be turned into darkness, and the moon into blood, before that great and notable day of the Lord come:

Rev 6:12 — And I beheld when he had opened the sixth seal, and, lo, there was a great earthquake; and the sun became black as sackcloth of hair, and the moon became as blood;

Rev 8:12 — And the fourth angel sounded, and the third part of the sun was smitten, and the third part of the moon, and the third part of the stars; so as the third part of them was darkened, and the day shone not for a third part of it, and the night likewise.

• Figurative.

• Shining of.

Isa 30:26 — Moreover the light of the moon shall be as the light of the sun, and the light of the sun shall be sevenfold, as the light of seven days, in the day that the LORD bindeth up the breach of his people, and healeth the stroke of their wound.

Isa 60:19 — The sun shall be no more thy light by day; neither for brightness shall the moon give light unto thee: but the LORD shall be unto thee an everlasting light, and thy God thy glory.

Rev 21:23 — And the city had no need of the sun, neither of the moon, to shine in it: for the glory of God did lighten it, and the Lamb *is* the light thereof.

• Symbolic.

Rev 12:1 — And there appeared a great wonder in heaven; a woman clothed with the sun, and the moon under her feet, and upon her head a crown of twelve stars:

• Feast of the New Moon.

Nu 28:11–15

Nu 10:10 — Also in the day of your gladness, and in your solemn days, and in the beginnings of your months, ye shall blow with the trumpets over your burnt offerings, and over the sacrifices of your peace offerings; that they may be to you for a memorial before your God: I *am* the LORD your God.

1Ch 23:31 — And to offer all burnt sacrifices unto the LORD in the sabbaths, in the new moons, and on the set feasts, by number, according to the order commanded unto them, continually before the LORD:

2Ch 31:3 — *He appointed* also the king's portion of his substance for the burnt offerings, *to wit,* for the morning and evening burnt offerings, and the burnt offerings for the sabbaths, and for the new moons, and for the set feasts, as *it is* written in the law of the LORD.

Ezr 3:5 — And afterward *offered* the continual burnt offering, both of the new moons, and of all the set feasts of the LORD that were consecrated, and of every one that willingly offered a freewill offering unto the LORD.

• Traffic at time of, prohibited.

Am 8:5 — Saying, When will the new moon be gone, that we may sell corn? and the sabbath, that we may set forth wheat, making the ephah small, and the shekel great, and falsifying the balances by deceit?

MORAL AGENCY ⇜See: Contingencies

MORAL LAW ⇜See: Law

MORALITY

⇜See: Duty; of man to man

⇜See: Integrity

⇜See: Neighbor

MORDECAI

• A Jewish captive in Persia.

Est 2:5–6

• Foster father of Esther.

Est 2:7 — And he brought up Hadassah, that *is,* Esther, his uncle's daughter: for she had neither father nor mother, and the maid *was* fair and beautiful; whom Mordecai, when her father and mother were dead, took for his own daughter.

• Informs Ahasuerus of a conspiracy against his life, and is rewarded.

Est 2:21–23; 6:1–11

• Promoted in Haman's place.

Est 8:1–2; 10:1–3

Est 8:15 — And Mordecai went out from the presence of the king in royal apparel of blue and white, and with a great crown of gold, and with a garment of fine linen and purple: and the city of Shushan rejoiced and was glad.

• Intercedes with Ahasuerus for the Jews; establishes the festival of Purim in commemoration of their deliverance.

Est 8:1–9:32

MOREH

• A plain near Shechem and Gilgal.

Ge 12:6 — And Abram passed through the land unto the place of Sichem, unto the plain of Moreh. And the Canaanite *was* then in the land.

Dt 11:30 — *Are* they not on the other side Jordan, by the way where the sun goeth down, in the land of the Canaanites, which dwell in the champaign over against Gilgal, beside the plains of Moreh?

• A hill in the plain of Jezreel where the Midianites encamped.

Jgs 7:1 — Then Jerubbaal, who *is* Gideon, and all the people that *were* with him, rose up early, and pitched beside the well of Harod: so that the host of the Midianites were on the north side of them, by the hill of Moreh, in the valley.

Jgs 7:12 — And the Midianites and the Amalekites and all the children of the east lay along in the valley like grasshoppers for multitude; and their camels *were* without number, as the sand by the sea side for multitude.

MORIAH

• The land of.

Ge 22:2 — And he said, Take now thy son, thine only *son* Isaac, whom thou lovest, and get thee into the land of Moriah; and offer him there for a burnt offering upon one of the mountains which I will tell thee of.

2Ch 3:1 — Then Solomon began to build the house of the LORD at Jerusalem in mount Moriah, where *the LORD* appeared unto David his father, in the place that David had prepared in the threshingfloor of Ornan the Jebusite.

MORTAR

• An instrument for pulverizing grains.

Nu 11:8 — *And* the people went about, and gathered *it,* and ground *it* in mills, or beat *it* in a mortar, and baked *it* in pans, and made cakes of it: and the taste of it was as the taste of fresh oil.

Pr 27:22 — Though thou shouldest bray a fool in a mortar among wheat with a pestle, *yet* will not his foolishness depart from him.

✧See: Grinding

✧See: Mill

• A cement.

Ex 1:14 — And they made their lives bitter with hard bondage, in morter, and in brick, and in all manner of service in the field: all their service, wherein they made them serve, *was* with rigour.

• Slime used as, in building tower of Babel.

Ge 11:3 — And they said one to another, Go to, let us make brick, and burn them throughly. And they had brick for stone, and slime had they for morter.

• Used to plaster houses.

Le 14:42 — And they shall take other stones, and put *them* in the place of those stones; and he shall take other morter, and shall plaister the house.

Le 14:45 — And he shall break down the house, the stones of it, and the timber thereof, and all the morter of the house; and he shall carry *them* forth out of the city into an unclean place.

• Untempered, not enduring.

Eze 13:10–15

Eze 22:28 — And her prophets have daubed them with untempered *morter,* seeing vanity, and divining lies unto them, saying, Thus saith the Lord GOD, when the LORD hath not spoken.

• To be trodden to make firm.

Na 3:14 — Draw thee waters for the siege, fortify thy strong holds: go into clay, and tread the morter, make strong the brickkiln.

• Figurative.

Isa 41:25 — I have raised up *one* from the north, and he shall come: from the rising of the sun shall he call upon my name: and he shall come upon princes as *upon* morter, and as the potter treadeth clay.

MORTGAGE

• On land.

Ne 5:3 — *Some* also there were that said, We have mortgaged our lands, vineyards, and houses, that we might buy corn, because of the dearth.

✧See: Land

MORTIFICATION

• Instances of.

• David's ambassadors, sent to Hanun.

2Sa 10:1–5

• Judas.

Mt 27:3–5

✧See: Humility

MOSAIC LAW ✧See: Law

MOSERA

• An encampment of the Israelites where Aaron died.

Dt 10:6 — And the children of Israel took their journey from Beeroth of the children of Jaakan to Mosera: there Aaron died, and there he was buried; and Eleazar his son ministered in the priest's office in his stead.

• Probably identical with Moseroth.

✧See: Moseroth

MOSEROTH • An encampment of the Israelites.

Nu 33:30–31

MOSES

• A Levite and son of Amram.

Ex 2:1–4

Ex 6:20 — And Amram took him Jochebed his father's sister to wife; and she bare him Aaron and Moses: and the years of the life of Amram *were* an hundred and thirty and seven years.

Ac 7:20 — In which time Moses was born, and was exceeding fair, and nourished up in his father's house three months:

Heb 11:23 — By faith Moses, when he was born, was hid three months of his parents, because they saw *he was* a proper child; and they were not afraid of the king's commandment.

• Hidden in an ark.

Ex 2:3 — And when she could not longer hide him, she took for him an ark of bulrushes, and daubed it with slime and with pitch, and put the child therein; and she laid *it* in the flags by the river's brink.

• Discovered and adopted by the daughter of Pharaoh.

Ex 2:5–10

• Learned in all the wisdom of Egypt.

Ac 7:22 — And Moses was learned in all the wisdom of the Egyptians, and was mighty in words and in deeds.

• His loyalty to his race.

Heb 11:24–26

• Takes the life of an Egyptian; flees from Egypt; finds refuge among the Midianites.

Ex 2:11–22; Ac 7:24–29

• Joins himself to Jethro, priest of Midian; marries his daughter Zipporah; has two sons.

Ex 2:15–22; 18:3–4

• Is herdman for Jethro in the desert of Horeb.

Ex 3:1 — Now Moses kept the flock of Jethro his father in law, the priest of Midian: and he led the flock to the backside of the desert, and came to the mountain of God, *even* to Horeb.

• Has the vision of the burning bush.

Ex 3:2–6

• God reveals to him his purpose to deliver the Israelites and bring them into the land of Canaan.

Ex 3:7–10

• Commissioned as leader of the Israelites.

Ex 3:10–22

Ex 6:13 — And the LORD spake unto Moses and unto Aaron, and gave them a charge unto the children of Israel, and unto Pharaoh king of Egypt, to bring the children of Israel out of the land of Egypt.

• His rod miraculously turned into a serpent, and his hand made leprous, and each restored.

Ex 4:1–9

Ex 4:28 — And Moses told Aaron all the words of the LORD who had sent him, and all the signs which he had commanded him.

• With his wife and sons leaves Jethro to perform his mission.

Ex 4:18–20

• His controversy with his wife on account of circumcision.

Ex 4:20–26

• Meets Aaron in the wilderness.

Ex 4:27–28

• With Aaron assembles the leaders of Israel.

Ex 4:29–31

• With Aaron goes before Pharaoh; in the name of Jehovah demands the liberties of his people.

Ex 5:1 — And afterward Moses and Aaron went in, and told Pharaoh, Thus saith the LORD God of Israel, Let my people go, that they may hold a feast unto me in the wilderness.

• Rejected by Pharaoh; hardships of the Israelites increased.

Ex 5:1–23

• People murmur against Moses and Aaron.

Ex 5:20–21; 16:2–3; 17:2–3; Nu 14:2–4; 20:2–5; 21:4–6; Dt 1:26–28

Ex 15:24 — And the people murmured against Moses, saying, What shall we drink?

Nu 16:41 — But on the morrow all the congregation of the children of Israel murmured against Moses and against Aaron, saying, Ye have killed the people of the LORD.

Dt 1:12 — How can I myself alone bear your cumbrance, and your burden, and your strife?

See: Israel

• Receives comfort and assurance from the Lord.

Ex 6:1–8

• Unbelief of the people.

Ex 6:9 — And Moses spake so unto the children of Israel: but they hearkened not unto Moses for anguish of spirit, and for cruel bondage.

• Renews his appeal to Pharaoh.

Ex 6:11 — Go in, speak unto Pharaoh king of Egypt, that he let the children of Israel go out of his land.

• Under divine direction brings plagues upon the land of Egypt.

Ex 7:1–12:51

• Secures the deliverance of the people and leads them out of Egypt.

Ex 13:1–22

• Crosses the Red Sea; Pharaoh and his army are destroyed.

Ex 14:1–31

• Composes a song for the children of Israel on their deliverance from Pharaoh.

Ex 15:1–27

• Joined by his family in the wilderness.

Ex 18:1–12

• Institutes a system of government.

Ex 18:13–26; Nu 11:16–30; Dt 1:9–18

• Receives the law and ordains divers statutes.

See: Law; of Moses

• Face of, transfigured.

Ex 34:29–35

2Co 3:13 — And not as Moses, *which* put a vail over his face, that the children of Israel could not stedfastly look to the end of that which is abolished:

• Sets up the tabernacle.

See: Tabernacle

• Reproves Aaron for making the golden calf.

Ex 32:22–23

• Reproves Aaron for irregularity in the offerings.

Le 10:16–20

• Jealousy of Aaron and Miriam toward.

Nu 12:1–16

• Rebellion of Korah, Dathan, and Abiram against.

Nu 16:1–50

• Appoints Joshua as his successor.

Nu 27:22–23; Dt 31:7–8

Dt 31:14 — And the LORD said unto Moses, Behold, thy days approach that thou must die: call Joshua, and present yourselves in the tabernacle of the congregation, that I may give him a charge. And Moses and Joshua went, and presented themselves in the tabernacle of the congregation.

Dt 31:23 — And he gave Joshua the son of Nun a charge, and said, Be strong and of a good courage: for thou shalt bring the children of Israel into the land which I sware unto them: and I will be with thee.

Dt 34:9 — And Joshua the son of Nun was full of the spirit of wisdom; for Moses had laid his hands upon him: and the children of Israel hearkened unto him, and did as the LORD commanded Moses.

• Not permitted to enter Canaan, but views the land from Mount Pisgah.

Nu 27:12–14; Dt 3:23–29; 32:48–52; 34:1–8

Dt 1:37 — Also the LORD was angry with me for your sakes, saying, Thou also shalt not go in thither.

• Death and burial of.

Dt 34:1–6

Nu 31:2 — Avenge the children of Israel of the Midianites: afterward shalt thou be gathered unto thy people.

Dt 32:50 — And die in the mount whither thou goest up, and be gathered unto thy people; as Aaron thy brother died in mount Hor, and was gathered unto his people:

• Body of, disputed over.

Jude 1:9 — Yet Michael the archangel, when contending with the devil he disputed about the body of Moses, durst not bring against him a railing accusation, but said, The Lord rebuke thee.

• One hundred and twenty years old at death.

Dt 31:2 — And he said unto them, I *am* an hundred and twenty years old this day; I can no more go out and come in: also the LORD hath said unto me, Thou shalt not go over this Jordan.

• Mourning for, thirty days in the plains of Moab.

Dt 34:8 — And the children of Israel wept for Moses in the plains of Moab thirty days: so the days of weeping *and* mourning for Moses were ended.

• His virility.

Dt 31:2 — And he said unto them, I *am* an hundred and twenty years old this day; I can no more go out and come in: also the LORD hath said unto me, Thou shalt not go over this Jordan.

Dt 34:7 — And Moses *was* an hundred and twenty years old when he died: his eye was not dim, nor his natural force abated.

• Present with Jesus on the mount of transfiguration.

Mt 17:3–4

Mk 9:4 — And there appeared unto them Elias with Moses: and they were talking with Jesus.

Lk 9:30 — And, behold, there talked with him two men, which were Moses and Elias:

• Type of Christ.

Dt 18:15–18

Ac 3:22 — For Moses truly said unto the fathers, A prophet shall the Lord your God raise up unto you of your brethren, like unto me; him shall ye hear in all things whatsoever he shall say unto you.

Ac 7:37 — This is that Moses, which said unto the children of Israel, A prophet shall the Lord your God raise up unto you of your brethren, like unto me; him shall ye hear.

• Benedictions of.

• Upon the people.

Nu 10:35–36

Le 9:23 — And Moses and Aaron went into the tabernacle of the congregation, and came out, and blessed the people: and the glory of the LORD appeared unto all the people.

Dt 1:11 — (The LORD God of your fathers make you a thousand times so many more as ye *are,* and bless you, as he hath promised you!)

• Last benediction upon the twelve tribes.

Dt 33:1–29

• Character of.

• Murmurings of.

Ex 5:22–23; Nu 11:10–15

• Impatience of.

Ex 5:22–23; Nu 11:10–15

Ex 6:12 — And Moses spake before the LORD, saying, Behold, the children of Israel have not hearkened unto me; how then shall Pharaoh hear me, who *am* of uncircumcised lips?

Ex 32:19 — And it came to pass, as soon as he came nigh unto the camp, that he saw the calf, and the dancing: and Moses' anger waxed hot, and he cast the tables out of his hands, and brake them beneath the mount.

Nu 16:15 — And Moses was very wroth, and said unto the LORD, Respect not thou their offering: I have not taken one ass from them, neither have I hurt one of them.

Nu 20:10 — And Moses and Aaron gathered the congregation together before the rock, and he said unto them, Hear now, ye rebels; must we fetch you water out of this rock?

Nu 31:14 — And Moses was wroth with the officers of the host, *with* the captains over thousands, and captains over hundreds, which came from the battle.

• Respected and feared.

Ex 33:8 — And it came to pass, when Moses went out unto the tabernacle, *that* all the people rose up, and stood every man *at* his tent door, and looked after Moses, until he was gone into the tabernacle.

• Faith of.

Dt 9:1–3; Heb 11:23–28

Nu 10:29 — And Moses said unto Hobab, the son of Raguel the Midianite, Moses' father in law, We are journeying unto the place of which the LORD said, I will give it you: come thou with us, and we will do thee good: for the LORD hath spoken good concerning Israel.

• **Called the man of God.**

Dt 33:1 — And this *is* the blessing, wherewith Moses the man of God blessed the children of Israel before his death.

• **God spake to, as a man to his friend.**

Ex 33:11 — And the LORD spake unto Moses face to face, as a man speaketh unto his friend. And he turned again into the camp: but his servant Joshua, the son of Nun, a young man, departed not out of the tabernacle.

• **Magnified of God.**

Nu 14:12–20; Dt 9:13–29

Ex 19:9 — And the LORD said unto Moses, Lo, I come unto thee in a thick cloud, that the people may hear when I speak with thee, and believe thee for ever. And Moses told the words of the people unto the LORD.

Ex 32:30 — And it came to pass on the morrow, that Moses said unto the people, Ye have sinned a great sin: and now I will go up unto the LORD; peradventure I shall make an atonement for your sin.

• **Magnanimity of, toward Eldad and Medad.**

Nu 11:29 — And Moses said unto him, Enviest thou for my sake? would God that all the LORD'S people were prophets, *and* that the LORD would put his spirit upon them!

• **Meekness of.**

Ex 14:13–14; 15:24–25; 16:2–3, 7–8; Nu 16:4–11

Nu 12:3 — (Now the man Moses *was* very meek, above all the men which *were* upon the face of the earth.)

• **Obedience of.**

Ex 7:6 — And Moses and Aaron did as the LORD commanded them, so did they.

Ex 40:16 — Thus did Moses: according to all that the LORD commanded him, so did he.

Ex 40:19 — And he spread abroad the tent over the tabernacle, and put the covering of the tent above upon it; as the LORD commanded Moses.

Ex 40:21 — And he brought the ark into the tabernacle, and set up the vail of the covering, and covered the ark of the testimony; as the LORD commanded Moses.

• **Unaspiring.**

Nu 14:12–20; Dt 9:13–29

Ex 32:30 — And it came to pass on the morrow, that Moses said unto the people, Ye have sinned a great sin: and now I will go up unto the LORD; peradventure I shall make an atonement for your sin.

• **Intercessory prayers of.**

✣See: Intercession; additional instances of

✣See: Intercession; solicited; instances of

✣See: Prayer; answered; instances of

• **Miracles of.**

✣See: Miracles, Genesis-Deuteronomy

• **Prophecies of.**

Ex 4:11–12; 19:3–9; Nu 12:7–8; Mk 7:9–10; Ac 7:37–38

Ex 3:10 — Come now therefore, and I will send thee unto Pharaoh, that thou mayest bring forth my people the children of Israel out of Egypt.

Ex 4:5 — That they may believe that the LORD God of their fathers, the God of Abraham, the God of Isaac, and the God of Jacob, hath appeared unto thee.

Ex 6:13 — And the LORD spake unto Moses and unto Aaron, and gave them a charge unto the children of Israel, and unto Pharaoh king of Egypt, to bring the children of Israel out of the land of Egypt.

Ex 7:2 — Thou shalt speak all that I command thee: and Aaron thy brother shall speak unto Pharaoh, that he send the children of Israel out of his land.

Ex 17:16 — For he said, Because the LORD hath sworn *that* the LORD *will have* war with Amalek from generation to generation.

Ex 33:11 — And the LORD spake unto Moses face to face, as a man speaketh unto his friend. And he turned again into the camp: but his servant Joshua, the son of Nun, a young man, departed not out of the tabernacle.

Nu 11:17 — And I will come down and talk with thee there: and I will take of the spirit which *is* upon thee, and will put *it* upon them; and they shall bear the burden of the people with thee, that thou bear it not thyself alone.

Nu 36:13 — These *are* the commandments and the judgments, which the LORD commanded by the hand of Moses unto the children of Israel in the plains of Moab by Jordan *near* Jericho.

Dt 1:3 — And it came to pass in the fortieth year, in the eleventh month, on the first *day* of the month, *that* Moses spake unto the children of Israel, according unto all that the LORD had given him in commandment unto them;

Dt 5:31 — But as for thee, stand thou here by me, and I will speak unto thee all the commandments, and the statutes, and the judgments, which thou shalt teach them, that they may do *them* in the land which I give them to possess it.

Dt 18:15 — The LORD thy God will raise up unto thee a Prophet from the midst of thee, of thy brethren, like unto me; unto him ye shall hearken;

Dt 18:18 — I will raise them up a Prophet from among their brethren, like unto thee, and will put my words in his mouth; and he shall speak unto them all that I shall command him.

Dt 34:10 — And there arose not a prophet since in Israel like unto Moses, whom the LORD knew face to face,

Dt 34:12 — And in all that mighty hand, and in all the great terror which Moses shewed in the sight of all Israel.

Hos 12:13 — And by a prophet the LORD brought Israel out of Egypt, and by a prophet was he preserved.

MOTE • A small particle.

Mt 7:3–5; Lk 6:41–42

MOTH

• An insect.

Job 4:19 — How much less *in* them that dwell in houses of clay, whose foundation *is* in the dust, *which* are crushed before the moth?

Job 27:18 — He buildeth his house as a moth, and as a booth *that* the keeper maketh.

Ps 39:11 — When thou with rebukes dost correct man for iniquity, thou makest his beauty to consume away like a moth: surely every man *is* vanity. Selah.

• Destructive of garments.

Job 13:28 — And he, as a rotten thing, consumeth, as a garment that is moth eaten.

Isa 50:9 — Behold, the Lord God will help me; who *is* he *that* shall condemn me? lo, they all shall wax old as a garment; the moth shall eat them up.

Isa 51:8 — For the moth shall eat them up like a garment, and the worm shall eat them like wool: but my righteousness shall be for ever, and my salvation from generation to generation.

Hos 5:12 — Therefore *will* I *be* unto Ephraim as a moth, and to the house of Judah as rottenness.

• Figurative.

Mt 6:19–20

Jas 5:2 — Your riches are corrupted, and your garments are motheaten.

MOTHER

Pr 23:22–25; Mt 15:4–6; Mk 7:10–12

Ex 20:12 — Honour thy father and thy mother: that thy days may be long upon the land which the Lord thy God giveth thee.

Ex 21:15 — And he that smiteth his father, or his mother, shall be surely put to death.

Ex 21:17 — And he that curseth his father, or his mother, shall surely be put to death.

Le 18:7 — The nakedness of thy father, or the nakedness of thy mother, shalt thou not uncover: she is thy mother; thou shalt not uncover her nakedness.

Le 19:3 — Ye shall fear every man his mother, and his father, and keep my sabbaths: I *am* the Lord your God.

Le 20:9 — For every one that curseth his father or his mother shall be surely put to death: he hath cursed his father or his mother; his blood *shall be* upon him.

Dt 5:16 — Honour thy father and thy mother, as the Lord thy God hath commanded thee; that thy days may be prolonged, and that it may go well with thee, in the land which the Lord thy God giveth thee.

1Ki 19:20 — And he left the oxen, and ran after Elijah, and said, Let me, I pray thee, kiss my father and my mother, and *then* I will follow thee. And he said unto him, Go back again: for what have I done to thee?

Pr 1:8 — My son, hear the instruction of thy father, and forsake not the law of thy mother:

Pr 6:20 — My son, keep thy father's commandment, and forsake not the law of thy mother:

Pr 10:1 — The proverbs of Solomon. A wise son maketh a glad father: but a foolish son *is* the heaviness of his mother.

Pr 15:20 — A wise son maketh a glad father: but a foolish man despiseth his mother.

Pr 19:26 — He that wasteth *his* father, *and* chaseth away *his* mother, *is* a son that causeth shame, and bringeth reproach.

Pr 20:20 — Whoso curseth his father or his mother, his lamp shall be put out in obscure darkness.

Pr 28:24 — Whoso robbeth his father or his mother, and saith, *It is* no transgression; the same *is* the companion of a destroyer.

Pr 29:15 — The rod and reproof give wisdom: but a child left *to himself* bringeth his mother to shame.

Pr 30:11 — *There is* a generation *that* curseth their father, and doth not bless their mother.

Pr 30:17 — The eye *that* mocketh at *his* father, and despiseth to obey *his* mother, the ravens of the valley shall pick it out, and the young eagles shall eat it.

Mt 10:37 — He that loveth father or mother more than me is not worthy of me: and he that loveth son or daughter more than me is not worthy of me.

Mt 19:19 — Honour thy father and *thy* mother: and, Thou shalt love thy neighbour as thyself.

Mk 10:19 — Thou knowest the commandments, Do not commit adultery, Do not kill, Do not steal, Do not bear false witness, Defraud not, Honour thy father and mother.

Lk 18:20 — Thou knowest the commandments, Do not commit adultery, Do not kill, Do not steal, Do not bear false witness, Honour thy father and thy mother.

Eph 6:2 — Honour thy father and mother; (which is the first commandment with promise;)

2Ti 1:5 — When I call to remembrance the unfeigned faith that is in thee, which dwelt first in thy grandmother Lois, and thy mother Eunice; and I am persuaded that in thee also.

See: Parents

MOTHER-IN-LAW

Mt 10:35 — For I am come to set a man at variance against his father, and the daughter against her mother, and the daughter in law against her mother in law.

• Not to be defiled.

Le 18:17 — Thou shalt not uncover the nakedness of a woman and her daughter, neither shalt thou take her son's daughter, or her daughter's daughter, to uncover her nakedness; *for* they *are* her near kinswomen: it *is* wickedness.

Le 20:14 — And if a man take a wife and her mother, it *is* wickedness: they shall be burnt with fire, both he and they; that there be no wickedness among you.

Dt 27:23 — Cursed *be* he that lieth with his mother in law. And all the people shall say, Amen.

• Beloved by Ruth.

Ru 1:14–17

• Peter's, healed by Jesus.

Mk 1:30–31

MOTIVATE

2Ti 1:1–18

Ro 12:18 — If it be possible, as much as lieth in you, live peaceably with all men.

1Co 12:25 — That there should be no schism in the body; but *that* the members should have the same care one for another.

1Pe 1:22 — Seeing ye have purified your souls in obeying the truth through the Spirit unto unfeigned love of the brethren, *see that ye* love one another with a pure heart fervently:

2Pe 1:13 — Yea, I think it meet, as long as I am in this tabernacle, to stir you up by putting *you* in remembrance;

2Pe 3:1 — This second epistle, beloved, I now write unto you; in *both* which I stir up your pure minds by way of remembrance:

MOTIVATION

Pr 23:7 — For as he thinketh in his heart, so *is* he: Eat and drink, saith he to thee; but his heart *is* not with thee.

Ac 17:6 — And when they found them not, they drew Jason and certain brethren unto the rulers of the city, crying, These that have turned the world upside down are come hither also;

Ro 1:8 — First, I thank my God through Jesus Christ for you all, that your faith is spoken of throughout the whole world.

Php 4:8 — Finally, brethren, whatsoever things are true, whatsoever things *are* honest, whatsoever things *are* just, whatsoever things *are* pure, whatsoever things *are* lovely, whatsoever things *are* of good report; if *there be* any virtue, and if *there be* any praise, think on these things.

MOTIVE

• Ascribed to God.

Eze 36:21–22

Ps 106:8 — Nevertheless he saved them for his name's sake, that he might make his mighty power to be known.

Eze 36:32 — Not for your sakes do I *this,* saith the Lord GOD, be it known unto you: be ashamed and confounded for your own ways, O house of Israel.

• Right, required.

Mt 6:1–18

• Sinful, illustrated by Cain.

Ge 4:7 — If thou doest well, shalt thou not be accepted? and if thou doest not well, sin lieth at the door. And unto thee *shall be* his desire, and thou shalt rule over him.

1Jn 3:12 — Not as Cain, *who* was of that wicked one, and slew his brother. And wherefore slew he him? Because his own works were evil, and his brother's righteous.

• Misunderstood.

• The tribes of Reuben and Gad, in asking inheritance east of Jordan.

Nu 32:1–33

• The tribes of Reuben and Gad, when they built the memorial.

Jos 22:9–34

• David's, by King Hanun.

2Sa 10:2–3; 1Ch 19:3–4

• The king of Syria's, in sending presents to the king of Israel by Naaman.

2Ki 5:5–7

• Job's, in his righteousness.

Job 1:9–11; 2:4–5

MOTTO See: Legends

MOUNTAIN

• Melted.

Isa 64:1–3

Dt 4:11 — And ye came near and stood under the mountain; and the mountain burned with fire unto the midst of heaven, with darkness, clouds, and thick darkness.

Dt 5:23 — And it came to pass, when ye heard the voice out of the midst of the darkness, (for the mountain did burn with fire,) that ye came near unto me, *even* all the heads of your tribes, and your elders;

Jgs 5:5 — The mountains melted from before the LORD, *even* that Sinai from before the LORD God of Israel.

Ps 97:5 — The hills melted like wax at the presence of the LORD, at the presence of the Lord of the whole earth.

Mic 1:4 — And the mountains shall be molten under him, and the valleys shall be cleft, as wax before the fire, *and* as the waters *that are* poured down a steep place.

Na 1:5 — The mountains quake at him, and the hills melt, and the earth is burned at his presence, yea, the world, and all that dwell therein.

• Overturning and removing of.

Job 9:5 — Which removeth the mountains, and they know not: which overturneth them in his anger.

Job 14:18 — And surely the mountain falling cometh to nought, and the rock is removed out of his place.

Job 28:9 — He putteth forth his hand upon the rock; he overturneth the mountains by the roots.

Eze 38:20 — So that the fishes of the sea, and the fowls of the heaven, and the beasts of the field, and all creeping things that creep upon the earth, and all the men that *are* upon the face of the earth, shall shake at my presence, and the mountains shall be thrown down, and the steep places shall fall, and every wall shall fall to the ground.

• Abraham offers Isaac upon Mount Moriah, afterward called Mount Zion, the site of the temple.

Ge 22:2 — And he said, Take now thy son, thine only *son* Isaac, whom thou lovest, and get thee into the land of Moriah; and offer him there for a burnt offering upon one of the mountains which I will tell thee of.

See: Zion

- **Horeb appointed as a place for the Israelites to worship.**

Ex 3:12 — And he said, Certainly I will be with thee; and this *shall be* a token unto thee, that I have sent thee: When thou hast brought forth the people out of Egypt, ye shall serve God upon this mountain.

- **Used for idolatrous worship.**

Dt 12:2 — Ye shall utterly destroy all the places, wherein the nations which ye shall possess served their gods, upon the high mountains, and upon the hills, and under every green tree:

1Sa 10:5 — After that thou shalt come to the hill of God, where *is* the garrison of the Philistines: and it shall come to pass, when thou art come thither to the city, that thou shalt meet a company of prophets coming down from the high place with a psaltery, and a tabret, and a pipe, and a harp, before them; and they shall prophesy:

1Ki 14:23 — For they also built them high places, and images, and groves, on every high hill, and under every green tree.

Jer 3:6 — The LORD said also unto me in the days of Josiah the king, Hast thou seen *that* which backsliding Israel hath done? she is gone up upon every high mountain and under every green tree, and there hath played the harlot.

Hos 4:13 — They sacrifice upon the tops of the mountains, and burn incense upon the hills, under oaks and poplars and elms, because the shadow thereof *is* good: therefore your daughters shall commit whoredom, and your spouses shall commit adultery.

- **Jesus tempted upon.**

Mt 4:8 — Again, the devil taketh him up into an exceeding high mountain, and sheweth him all the kingdoms of the world, and the glory of them;

Lk 4:5 — And the devil, taking him up into an high mountain, shewed unto him all the kingdoms of the world in a moment of time.

- **Jesus preaches from.**

Mt 5:1 — And seeing the multitudes, he went up into a mountain: and when he was set, his disciples came unto him:

- **Jesus goes up into, for prayer.**

Mt 14:23 — And when he had sent the multitudes away, he went up into a mountain apart to pray: and when the evening was come, he was there alone.

Lk 6:12 — And it came to pass in those days, that he went out into a mountain to pray, and continued all night in prayer to God.

Lk 9:28 — And it came to pass about an eight days after these sayings, he took Peter and John and James, and went up into a mountain to pray.

- **Jesus is transfigured upon.**

Mt 17:1–9; Mk 9:2–10; Lk 9:28–36

- **Jesus meets his disciples on, after his resurrection.**

Mt 28:16–17

- **Signals from.**

Isa 28:16–17

Isa 13:2 — Lift ye up a banner upon the high mountain, exalt the voice unto them, shake the hand, that they may go into the gates of the nobles.

Isa 18:3 — All ye inhabitants of the world, and dwellers on the earth, see ye, when he lifteth up an ensign on the mountains; and when he bloweth a trumpet, hear ye.

Isa 30:17 — One thousand *shall flee* at the rebuke of one; at the rebuke of five shall ye flee: till ye be left as a beacon upon the top of a mountain, and as an ensign on an hill.

- **Removed by faith.**

Mt 17:20 — And Jesus said unto them, Because of your unbelief: for verily I say unto you, If ye have faith as a grain of mustard seed, ye shall say unto this mountain, Remove hence to yonder place; and it shall remove; and nothing shall be impossible unto you.

Mt 21:21 — Jesus answered and said unto them, Verily I say unto you, If ye have faith, and doubt not, ye shall not only do this *which is done* to the fig tree, but also if ye shall say unto this mountain, Be thou removed, and be thou cast into the sea; it shall be done.

Mk 11:23 — For verily I say unto you, That whosoever shall say unto this mountain, Be thou removed, and be thou cast into the sea; and shall not doubt in his heart, but shall believe that those things which he saith shall come to pass; he shall have whatsoever he saith.

- **Burning mountains.**

See: Volcanoes

MOURNING

- **For the dead.**
  - **Head uncovered.**

Le 10:6 — And Moses said unto Aaron, and unto Eleazar and unto Ithamar, his sons, Uncover not your heads, neither rend your clothes; lest ye die, and lest wrath come upon all the people: but let your brethren, the whole house of Israel, bewail the burning which the LORD hath kindled.

Le 21:10 — And *he that is* the high priest among his brethren, upon whose head the anointing oil was poured, and that is consecrated to put on the garments, shall not uncover his head, nor rend his clothes;

  - **Lying on ground.**

2Sa 14:2 — And Joab sent to Tekoah, and fetched thence a wise woman, and said unto her, I pray thee, feign thyself to be a mourner, and put on now mourning apparel, and anoint not thyself with oil, but be as a woman that had a long time mourned for the dead:

  - **Personal appearance neglected.**

2Sa 12:16 — David therefore besought God for the child; and David fasted, and went in, and lay all night upon the earth.

  - **Cutting the flesh.**

Le 21:1–5; Jer 16:6–7

Le 19:28 — Ye shall not make any cuttings in your flesh for the dead, nor print any marks upon you: I *am* the LORD.

Dt 14:1 — Ye *are* the children of the LORD your God: ye shall not cut yourselves, nor make any baldness between your eyes for the dead.

Jer 41:5 — That there came certain from Shechem, from Shiloh, and from Samaria, *even* fourscore men, having their beards shaven, and their clothes rent, and having cut themselves, with offerings and incense in their hand, to bring *them* to the house of the LORD.

- **Lamentations.**

Mt 2:17–18

Ge 50:10 — And they came to the threshingfloor of Atad, which *is* beyond Jordan, and there they mourned with a great and very sore lamentation: and he made a mourning for his father seven days.

Ex 12:30 — And Pharaoh rose up in the night, he, and all his servants, and all the Egyptians; and there was a great cry in Egypt; for *there was* not a house where *there was* not one dead.

1Sa 30:4 — Then David and the people that *were* with him lifted up their voice and wept, until they had no more power to weep.

Jer 22:18 — Therefore thus saith the LORD concerning Jehoiakim the son of Josiah king of Judah; They shall not lament for him, *saying,* Ah my brother! or, Ah sister! they shall not lament for him, *saying,* Ah lord! or, Ah his glory!

- **Fasting.**

1Sa 31:13 — And they took their bones, and buried *them* under a tree at Jabesh, and fasted seven days.

2Sa 1:12 — And they mourned, and wept, and fasted until even, for Saul, and for Jonathan his son, and for the people of the LORD, and for the house of Israel; because they were fallen by the sword.

2Sa 3:35 — And when all the people came to cause David to eat meat while it was yet day, David sware, saying, So do God to me, and more also, if I taste bread, or ought else, till the sun be down.

- **Priests prohibited, except for nearest of kin.**

Le 21:1–11

- **For Nadab and Abihu forbidden.**

Le 10:6 — And Moses said unto Aaron, and unto Eleazar and unto Ithamar, his sons, Uncover not your heads, neither rend your clothes; lest ye die, and lest wrath come upon all the people: but let your brethren, the whole house of Israel, bewail the burning which the LORD hath kindled.

- **Sexes separated in.**

Zec 12:12 — And the land shall mourn, every family apart; the family of the house of David apart, and their wives apart; the family of the house of Nathan apart, and their wives apart;

Zec 12:14 — All the families that remain, every family apart, and their wives apart.

- **Hired mourners.**

2Ch 35:25 — And Jeremiah lamented for Josiah: and all the singing men and the singing women spake of Josiah in their lamentations to this day, and made them an ordinance in Israel: and, behold, they *are* written in the lamentations.

Ecc 12:5 — Also *when* they shall be afraid of *that which is* high, and fears *shall be* in the way, and the almond tree shall flourish, and the grasshopper shall be a burden, and desire shall fail: because man goeth to his long home, and the mourners go about the streets:

Jer 9:17 — Thus saith the LORD of hosts, Consider ye, and call for the mourning women, that they may come; and send for cunning *women,* that they may come:

Mt 9:23 — And when Jesus came into the ruler's house, and saw the minstrels and the people making a noise,

- **Abraham mourned for Sarah.**

Ge 23:2 — And Sarah died in Kirjath-arba; the same *is* Hebron in the land of Canaan: and Abraham came to mourn for Sarah, and to weep for her.

- **Egyptians mourned for Jacob seventy days.**

Ge 50:1–3

- **Israelites mourned for Aaron thirty days.**

Nu 20:29 — And when all the congregation saw that Aaron was dead, they mourned for Aaron thirty days, *even* all the house of Israel.

- **David's lamentations.**
  - **Over the death of Saul and his sons.**

  2Sa 1:17–27

  - **Over the death of Abner.**

  2Sa 3:33–34

  - **Over the death of Absalom.**

  2Sa 18:33 — And the king was much moved, and went up to the chamber over the gate, and wept: and as he went, thus he said, O my son Absalom, my son, my son Absalom! would God I had died for thee, O Absalom, my son, my son!

- **Jeremiah and the singing men and singing women lament for Josiah.**

2Ch 35:25 — And Jeremiah lamented for Josiah: and all the singing men and the singing women spake of Josiah in their lamentations to this day, and made them an ordinance in Israel: and, behold, they *are* written in the lamentations.

- **For calamities and other sorrows.**
  - **Rending the garments.**

  Ge 37:29 — And Reuben returned unto the pit; and, behold, Joseph *was* not in the pit; and he rent his clothes.

  Ge 37:34 — And Jacob rent his clothes, and put sackcloth upon his loins, and mourned for his son many days.

  Ge 44:13 — Then they rent their clothes, and laded every man his ass, and returned to the city.

Nu 14:6 — And Joshua the son of Nun, and Caleb the son of Jephunneh, *which were* of them that searched the land, rent their clothes:

Jgs 11:35 — And it came to pass, when he saw her, that he rent his clothes, and said, Alas, my daughter! thou hast brought me very low, and thou art one of them that trouble me: for I have opened my mouth unto the LORD, and I cannot go back.

2Sa 1:2 — It came even to pass on the third day, that, behold, a man came out of the camp from Saul with his clothes rent, and earth upon his head: and *so* it was, when he came to David, that he fell to the earth, and did obeisance.

2Sa 1:11 — Then David took hold on his clothes, and rent them; and likewise all the men that *were* with him:

2Sa 3:31 — And David said to Joab, and to all the people that *were* with him, Rend your clothes, and gird you with sackcloth, and mourn before Abner. And king David *himself* followed the bier.

2Sa 13:19 — And Tamar put ashes on her head, and rent her garment of divers colours that *was* on her, and laid her hand on her head, and went on crying.

2Sa 13:31 — Then the king arose, and tare his garments, and lay on the earth; and all his servants stood by with their clothes rent.

2Sa 15:32 — And it came to pass, that *when* David was come to the top *of the mount,* where he worshipped God, behold, Hushai the Archite came to meet him with his coat rent, and earth upon his head:

2Ki 2:12 — And Elisha saw *it,* and he cried, My father, my father, the chariot of Israel, and the horsemen thereof. And he saw him no more: and he took hold of his own clothes, and rent them in two pieces.

2Ki 5:8 — And it was *so,* when Elisha the man of God had heard that the king of Israel had rent his clothes, that he sent to the king, saying, Wherefore hast thou rent thy clothes? let him come now to me, and he shall know that there is a prophet in Israel.

2Ki 6:30 — And it came to pass, when the king heard the words of the woman, that he rent his clothes; and he passed by upon the wall, and the people looked, and, behold, *he had* sackcloth within upon his flesh.

2Ki 11:14 — And when she looked, behold, the king stood by a pillar, as the manner *was,* and the princes and the trumpeters by the king, and all the people of the land rejoiced, and blew with trumpets: and Athaliah rent her clothes, and cried, Treason, Treason.

2Ki 19:1 — And it came to pass, when king Hezekiah heard *it,* that he rent his clothes, and covered himself with sackcloth, and went into the house of the LORD.

2Ki 22:11 — And it came to pass, when the king had heard the words of the book of the law, that he rent his clothes.

2Ki 22:19 — Because thine heart was tender, and thou hast humbled thyself before the LORD, when thou heardest what I spake against this place, and against the inhabitants thereof, that they should become a desolation and a curse, and hast rent thy clothes, and wept before me; I also have heard *thee,* saith the LORD.

Ezr 9:3 — And when I heard this thing, I rent my garment and my mantle, and plucked off the hair of my head and of my beard, and sat down astonied.

Ezr 9:5 — And at the evening sacrifice I arose up from my heaviness; and having rent my garment and my mantle, I fell upon my knees, and spread out my hands unto the LORD my God.

Job 1:20 — Then Job arose, and rent his mantle, and shaved his head, and fell down upon the ground, and worshipped,

Job 2:12 — And when they lifted up their eyes afar off, and knew him not, they lifted up their voice, and wept; and they rent every one his mantle, and sprinkled dust upon their heads toward heaven.

Isa 37:1 — And it came to pass, when king Hezekiah heard *it,* that he rent his clothes, and covered himself with sackcloth, and went into the house of the LORD.

Jer 41:5 — That there came certain from Shechem, from Shiloh, and from Samaria, *even* fourscore men, having their beards shaven, and their clothes rent, and having cut themselves, with offerings and incense in their hand, to bring *them* to the house of the LORD.

Mt 26:65 — Then the high priest rent his clothes, saying, He hath spoken blasphemy; what further need have we of witnesses? behold, now ye have heard his blasphemy.

Ac 14:14 — *Which* when the apostles, Barnabas and Paul, heard *of,* they rent their clothes, and ran in among the people, crying out,

• Wearing mourning dress.

Ge 38:14 — And she put her widow's garments off from her, and covered her with a vail, and wrapped herself, and sat in an open place, which *is* by the way to Timnath; for she saw that Shelah was grown, and she was not given unto him to wife.

2Sa 14:2 — And Joab sent to Tekoah, and fetched thence a wise woman, and said unto her, I pray thee, feign thyself to be a mourner, and put on now mourning apparel, and anoint not thyself with oil, but be as a woman that had a long time mourned for the dead:

See: Sackcloth

• Cutting or plucking off the hair and beard.

Ezr 9:3 — And when I heard this thing, I rent my garment and my mantle, and plucked off the hair of my head and of my beard, and sat down astonied.

Jer 7:29 — Cut off thine hair, *O Jerusalem,* and cast *it* away, and take up a lamentation on high places; for the LORD hath rejected and forsaken the generation of his wrath.

See: Baldness

• Covering the head and face.

Jer 14:3–4

2Sa 15:30 — And David went up by the ascent of *mount* Olivet, and wept as he went up, and had his head covered, and he went barefoot: and all the people that *was* with him covered every man his head, and they went up, weeping as they went up.

2Sa 19:4 — But the king covered his face, and the king cried with a loud voice, O my son Absalom, O Absalom, my son, my son!

Est 6:12 — And Mordecai came again to the king's gate. But Haman hasted to his house mourning, and having his head covered.

• Covering the upper lip.

Le 13:45 — And the leper in whom the plague *is,* his clothes shall be rent, and his head bare, and he shall put a covering upon his upper lip, and shall cry, Unclean, unclean.

Eze 24:17 — Forbear to cry, make no mourning for the dead, bind the tire of thine head upon thee, and put on thy shoes upon thy feet, and cover not *thy* lips, and eat not the bread of men.

Eze 24:22 — And ye shall do as I have done: ye shall not cover *your* lips, nor eat the bread of men.

Mic 3:7 — Then shall the seers be ashamed, and the diviners confounded: yea, they shall all cover their lips; for *there is* no answer of God.

• Laying aside ornaments.

Ex 33:4 — And when the people heard these evil tidings, they mourned: and no man did put on him his ornaments.

Ex 33:6 — And the children of Israel stripped themselves of their ornaments by the mount Horeb.

• Walking barefoot.

2Sa 15:30 — And David went up by the ascent of *mount* Olivet, and wept as he went up, and had his head covered, and he went barefoot: and all the people that *was* with him covered every man his head, and they went up, weeping as they went up.

Isa 20:2 — At the same time spake the LORD by Isaiah the son of Amoz, saying, Go and loose the sackcloth from off thy loins, and put off thy shoe from thy foot. And he did so, walking naked and barefoot.

• Laying the hand on the head.

2Sa 13:19 — And Tamar put ashes on her head, and rent her garment of divers colours that *was* on her, and laid her hand on her head, and went on crying.

Jer 2:37 — Yea, thou shalt go forth from him, and thine hands upon thine head: for the LORD hath rejected thy confidences, and thou shalt not prosper in them.

• Ashes put on the head.

Eze 27:30 — And shall cause their voice to be heard against thee, and shall cry bitterly, and shall cast up dust upon their heads, they shall wallow themselves in the ashes:

• Dust on the head.

Jos 7:6 — And Joshua rent his clothes, and fell to the earth upon his face before the ark of the LORD until the eventide, he and the elders of Israel, and put dust upon their heads.

• Dressing in black.

Jer 14:2 — Judah mourneth, and the gates thereof languish; they are black unto the ground; and the cry of Jerusalem is gone up.

• Sitting on the ground.

Isa 3:26 — And her gates shall lament and mourn; and she *being* desolate shall sit upon the ground.

• Caused ceremonial defilement.

Nu 19:11–16

Le 21:1 — And the LORD said unto Moses, Speak unto the priests the sons of Aaron, and say unto them, There shall none be defiled for the dead among his people:

Nu 31:19 — And do ye abide without the camp seven days: whosoever hath killed any person, and whosoever hath touched any slain, purify *both* yourselves and your captives on the third day, and on the seventh day.

• Prevented offerings from being accepted.

Dt 26:14 — I have not eaten thereof in my mourning, neither have I taken away *ought* thereof for *any* unclean *use,* nor given *ought* thereof for the dead: *but* I have hearkened to the voice of the LORD my God, *and* have done according to all that thou hast commanded me.

Hos 9:4 — They shall not offer wine *offerings* to the LORD, neither shall they be pleasing unto him: their sacrifices *shall be* unto them as the bread of mourners; all that eat thereof shall be polluted: for their bread for their soul shall not come into the house of the LORD.

→See: Elegy

MOUSE

• Forbidden as food.

Le 11:29 — These also *shall be* unclean unto you among the creeping things that creep upon the earth; the weasel, and the mouse, and the tortoise after his kind,

• Used as food.

Isa 66:17 — They that sanctify themselves, and purify themselves in the gardens behind one *tree* in the midst, eating swine's flesh, and the abomination, and the mouse, shall be consumed together, saith the LORD.

• Images of.

1Sa 6:4–5

1Sa 6:11 — And they laid the ark of the LORD upon the cart, and the coffer with the mice of gold and the images of their emerods.

1Sa 6:18 — And the golden mice, *according to* the number of all the cities of the Philistines *belonging* to the five lords, *both* of fenced cities, and of country villages, even unto the great *stone* of Abel, whereon they set down the ark of the LORD: *which stone remaineth* unto this day in the field of Joshua, the Beth-shemite.

MOWING

Ps 72:6 — He shall come down like rain upon the mown grass: as showers *that* water the earth.

Ps 90:6 — In the morning it flourisheth, and groweth up; in the evening it is cut down, and withereth.

Ps 129:7 — Wherewith the mower filleth not his hand; nor he that bindeth sheaves his bosom.

Am 7:1 — Thus hath the Lord GOD shewed unto me; and, behold, he formed grasshoppers in the beginning of the shooting up of the latter growth; and, lo, *it was* the latter growth after the king's mowings.

MOZA

• A son of Caleb.

1Ch 2:46 — And Ephah, Caleb's concubine, bare Haran, and Moza, and Gazez: and Haran begat Gazez.

• A Benjamite.

1Ch 8:36–37; 9:42–43

MOZAH • A city of Benjamin.

Jos 18:26 — And Mizpeh, and Chephirah, and Mozah,

MUFFLER

Isa 3:19 — The chains, and the bracelets, and the mufflers,

MULBERRY TREE

2Sa 5:23–24

Ps 84:6 — *Who* passing through the valley of Baca make it a well; the rain also filleth the pools.

MULE

• Uses of.

• For royal riders.

2Sa 13:29 — And the servants of Absalom did unto Amnon as Absalom had commanded. Then all the king's sons arose, and every man gat him up upon his mule, and fled.

2Sa 18:9 — And Absalom met the servants of David. And Absalom rode upon a mule, and the mule went under the thick boughs of a great oak, and his head caught hold of the oak, and he was taken up between the heaven and the earth; and the mule that *was* under him went away.

1Ki 1:33 — The king also said unto them, Take with you the servants of your lord, and cause Solomon my son to ride upon mine own mule, and bring him down to Gihon:

1Ki 1:38 — So Zadok the priest, and Nathan the prophet, and Benaiah the son of Jehoiada, and the Cherethites, and the Pelethites, went down, and caused Solomon to ride upon king David's mule, and brought him to Gihon.

• Ridden by posts.

Est 8:10 — And he wrote in the king Ahasuerus' name, and sealed it with the king's ring, and sent letters by posts on horseback, *and* riders on mules, camels, *and* young dromedaries:

Est 8:14 — *So* the posts that rode upon mules *and* camels went out, being hastened and pressed on by the king's commandment. And the decree was given at Shushan the palace.

• Ridden by saints in Isaiah's prophetic vsion of the kingdom of Christ.

Isa 66:20 — And they shall bring all your brethren *for* an offering unto the LORD out of all nations upon horses, and in chariots, and in litters, and upon mules, and upon swift beasts, to my holy mountain Jerusalem, saith the LORD, as the children of Israel bring an offering in a clean vessel into the house of the LORD.

• Ridden as pack animals.

2Ki 5:17 — And Naaman said, Shall there not then, I pray thee, be given to thy servant two mules' burden of earth? for thy servant will henceforth offer neither burnt offering nor sacrifice unto other gods, but unto the LORD.

1Ch 12:40 — Moreover they that were nigh them, *even* unto Issachar and Zebulun and Naphtali, brought bread on asses, and on camels, and on mules, and on oxen, *and* meat, meal, cakes of figs, and bunches of raisins, and wine, and oil, and oxen, and sheep abundantly: for *there was* joy in Israel.

• Tribute paid in.

1Ki 10:25 — And they brought every man his present, vessels of silver, and vessels of gold, and garments, and armour, and spices, horses, and mules, a rate year by year.

• Used in barter.

Eze 27:14 — They of the house of Togarmah traded in thy fairs with horses and horsemen and mules.

• Used by the captivity in returning from Babylon.

Ezr 2:66 — Their horses *were* seven hundred thirty and six; their mules, two hundred forty and five;

Ne 7:68 — Their horses, seven hundred thirty and six: their mules, two hundred forty and five:

• Used in war.

Zec 14:15 — And so shall be the plague of the horse, of the mule, of the camel, and of the ass, and of all the beasts that shall be in these tents, as this plague.

MUNITIONS

• Fortifications.

Na 2:1 — He that dasheth in pieces is come up before thy face: keep the munition, watch the way, make *thy* loins strong, fortify *thy* power mightily.

MUPPIM • Son of Benjamin.

Ge 46:21 — And the sons of Benjamin were Belah, and Becher, and Ashbel, Gera, and Naaman, Ehi, and Rosh, Muppim, and Huppim, and Ard.

MURDER ✦See: Homicide

MURMURING

• Of Israelites against Moses.

Ex 16:2–3; Nu 16:2–3, 13–14; 20:2–4

Ex 5:21 — And they said unto them, The LORD look upon you, and judge; because ye have made our savour to be abhorred in the eyes of Pharaoh, and in the eyes of his servants, to put a sword in their hand to slay us.

Ex 15:24 — And the people murmured against Moses, saying, What shall we drink?

Nu 16:41 — But on the morrow all the congregation of the children of Israel murmured against Moses and against Aaron, saying, Ye have killed the people of the LORD.

- **Against God.**

Ex 5:22–23; Nu 14:26–37; 17:10–11; Job 15:11–12; 33:12–13; Ps 44:9–26; 73:13–22; 78:17–21; Ro 9:19–20

Ex 16:8 — And Moses said, *This shall be,* when the LORD shall give you in the evening flesh to eat, and in the morning bread to the full; for that the LORD heareth your murmurings which ye murmur against him: and what *are* we? your murmurings *are* not against us, but against the LORD.

Ex 16:12 — I have heard the murmurings of the children of Israel: speak unto them, saying, At even ye shall eat flesh, and in the morning ye shall be filled with bread; and ye shall know that I *am* the LORD your God.

Job 34:37 — For he addeth rebellion unto his sin, he clappeth *his hands* among us, and multiplieth his words against God.

Ps 37:1 — Fret not thyself because of evildoers, neither be thou envious against the workers of iniquity.

Pr 19:3 — The foolishness of man perverteth his way: and his heart fretteth against the LORD.

Ecc 7:10 — Say not thou, What is *the cause* that the former days were better than these? for thou dost not enquire wisely concerning this.

Jer 15:10 — Woe is me, my mother, that thou hast borne me a man of strife and a man of contention to the whole earth! I have neither lent on usury, nor men have lent to me on usury; *yet* every one of them doth curse me.

La 3:39 — Wherefore doth a living man complain, a man for the punishment of his sins?

Mal 3:14 — Ye have said, It *is* vain to serve God: and what profit *is it* that we have kept his ordinance, and that we have walked mournfully before the LORD of hosts?

Lk 10:40 — But Martha was cumbered about much serving, and came to him, and said, Lord, dost thou not care that my sister hath left me to serve alone? bid her therefore that she help me.

1Co 10:10 — Neither murmur ye, as some of them also murmured, and were destroyed of the destroyer.

Php 2:14 — Do all things without murmurings and disputings:

Jas 5:9 — Grudge not one against another, brethren, lest ye be condemned: behold, the judge standeth before the door.

Jude 1:16 — These are murmurers, complainers, walking after their own lusts; and their mouth speaketh great swelling *words,* having men's persons in admiration because of advantage.

- **Instances of.**
  - **Cain.**
    Ge 4:13–14
  - **Rachel.**
    Ge 30:1
  - **Moses.**
    Ex 5:22–23; Nu 11:11–15
  - **Israelites.**
    Ex 5:21; 14:11–12; 15:23–24; 16:2–3; 17:2–3; Nu 11:1–10, 33; 14:1–45; 16:41; 20:2–5; 21:5–6; Dt 1:27–28; Ps 106:24–26
  - **Korah.**
    Nu 16:8–11
  - **Job.**
    Job 3:1–26; 6:1–7:21; 9:1–10:22; 13:1–28; 19:1–29; 23:1–17; 30:1–31
  - **David.**
    2Sa 6:8; Ps 116:10–11
  - **Asaph.**
    Ps 73:3
  - **Elijah.**
    1Ki 19:4, 10
  - **Solomon.**
    Ecc 2:17–18
  - **Hezekiah.**
    Isa 38:10–18
  - **Jeremiah.**
    Jer 20:14–18; La 3:1–66
  - **Jonah.**
    Jnh 4:1–11
  - **Jews, against Jesus.**
    Jn 6:41–43, 52

See: Contentment
See: Doubting
See: Envy
See: Ingratitude
See: Resignation

MURRAIN • A plague of Egypt.

Ex 9:3 — Behold, the hand of the LORD is upon thy cattle which *is* in the field, upon the horses, upon the asses, upon the camels, upon the oxen, and upon the sheep: *there shall be* a very grievous murrain.

Ex 9:6 — And the LORD did that thing on the morrow, and all the cattle of Egypt died: but of the cattle of the children of Israel died not one.

Ps 78:50 — He made a way to his anger; he spared not their soul from death, but gave their life over to the pestilence;

MUSHI • Of the sons of Merari.

Ex 6:19 — And the sons of Merari; Mahali and Mushi: these *are* the families of Levi according to their generations.

1Ch 6:19 — The sons of Merari; Mahli, and Mushi. And these *are* the families of the Levites according to their fathers.

1Ch 6:47 — The son of Mahli, the son of Mushi, the son of Merari, the son of Levi.

MUSIC

- **Teachers of.**

1Ch 25:7–8

1Ch 15:22 — And Chenaniah, chief of the Levites, *was* for song: he instructed about the song, because he *was* skilful.

2Ch 23:13 — And she looked, and, behold, the king stood at his pillar at the entering in, and the princes and the trumpets by the king: and all the people of the land rejoiced, and sounded with trumpets, also the singers with instruments of musick, and such as taught to sing praise. Then Athaliah rent her clothes, and said, Treason, Treason.

- **Physical effect of, on man.**

1Sa 16:15–16

1Sa 16:23 — And it came to pass, when the *evil* spirit from God was upon Saul, that David took an harp, and played with his hand: so Saul was refreshed, and was well, and the evil spirit departed from him.

- **Discoursed during the offering of sacrifices.**

2Ch 29:27–28

- **Precentor.**

Ne 12:42 — And Maaseiah, and Shemaiah, and Eleazar, and Uzzi, and Jehohanan, and Malchijah, and Elam, and Ezer. And the singers sang loud, with Jezrahiah *their* overseer.

- **Chief musician.**

Ne 12:42 — And Maaseiah, and Shemaiah, and Eleazar, and Uzzi, and Jehohanan, and Malchijah, and Elam, and Ezer. And the singers sang loud, with Jezrahiah *their* overseer.

Hab 3:19 — The LORD God *is* my strength, and he will make my feet like hinds' *feet,* and he will make me to walk upon mine high places. To the chief singer on my stringed instruments.

- **Chambers for musicians in the temple, in Ezekiel's vision.**

Eze 40:44 — And without the inner gate *were* the chambers of the singers in the inner court, which *was* at the side of the north gate; and their prospect *was* toward the south: one at the side of the east gate *having* the prospect toward the north.

- **In heaven.**

Rev 5:8–9; 14:2–3; 15:2–3

- **Instruments of.**
  - **Invented by Jubal.**

  Ge 4:21 — And his brother's name *was* Jubal: he was the father of all such as handle the harp and organ.

  - **Invented by David.**

  1Ch 23:5 — Moreover four thousand *were* porters; and four thousand praised the LORD with the instruments which I made, *said David,* to praise *therewith.*

  2Ch 7:6 — And the priests waited on their offices: the Levites also with instruments of musick of the LORD, which David the king had made to praise the LORD, because his mercy *endureth* for ever, when David praised by their ministry; and the priests sounded trumpets before them, and all Israel stood.

  2Ch 29:26 — And the Levites stood with the instruments of David, and the priests with the trumpets.

  Am 6:5 — That chant to the sound of the viol, *and* invent to themselves instruments of musick, like David;

- **Made by Solomon.**

1Ki 10:12 — And the king made of the almug trees pillars for the house of the LORD, and for the king's house, harps also and psalteries for singers: there came no such almug trees, nor were seen unto this day.

2Ch 9:11 — And the king made *of* the algum trees terraces to the house of the LORD, and to the king's palace, and harps and psalteries for singers: and there were none such seen before in the land of Judah.

Ecc 2:8 — I gathered me also silver and gold, and the peculiar treasure of kings and of the provinces: I gat me men singers and women singers, and the delights of the sons of men, *as* musical instruments, and that of all sorts.

- **Made by Tyrians.**

Eze 28:13 — Thou hast been in Eden the garden of God; every precious stone *was* thy covering, the sardius, topaz, and the diamond, the beryl, the onyx, and the jasper, the sapphire, the emerald, and the carbuncle, and gold: the workmanship of thy tabrets and of thy pipes was prepared in thee in the day that thou wast created.

- **Cornet.**

Da 3:5 — *That* at what time ye hear the sound of the cornet, flute, harp, sackbut, psaltery, dulcimer, and all kinds of musick, ye fall down and worship the golden image that Nebuchadnezzar the king hath set up:

Da 3:7 — Therefore at that time, when all the people heard the sound of the cornet, flute, harp, sackbut, psaltery, and all kinds of musick, all the people, the nations, and the languages, fell down *and* worshipped the golden image that Nebuchadnezzar the king had set up.

Da 3:10 — Thou, O king, hast made a decree, that every man that shall hear the sound of the cornet, flute, harp, sackbut, psaltery, and dulcimer, and all kinds of musick, shall fall down and worship the golden image:

See: Trumpet

- **Cymbal.**

See: Cymbal

- **Dulcimer, a double pipe.**

Da 3:5 — *That* at what time ye hear the sound of the cornet, flute, harp, sackbut, psaltery, dulcimer, and all kinds of musick, ye fall down and worship the golden image that Nebuchadnezzar the king hath set up:

Da 3:10 — Thou, O king, hast made a decree, that every man that shall hear the sound of the cornet, flute, harp, sackbut, psaltery, and dulcimer, and all kinds of musick, shall fall down and worship the golden image:

Da 3:15 — Now if ye be ready that at what time ye hear the sound of the cornet, flute, harp, sackbut, psaltery, and dulcimer, and all kinds of musick, ye fall down and worship the image which I have made; *well:* but if ye worship not, ye shall be cast the same hour into the midst of a burning fiery furnace; and who *is* that God that shall deliver you out of my hands?

• Flute.

Da 3:5 — *That* at what time ye hear the sound of the cornet, flute, harp, sackbut, psaltery, dulcimer, and all kinds of musick, ye fall down and worship the golden image that Nebuchadnezzar the king hath set up:

Da 3:7 — Therefore at that time, when all the people heard the sound of the cornet, flute, harp, sackbut, psaltery, and all kinds of musick, all the people, the nations, and the languages, fell down *and* worshipped the golden image that Nebuchadnezzar the king had set up.

Da 3:10 — Thou, O king, hast made a decree, that every man that shall hear the sound of the cornet, flute, harp, sackbut, psaltery, and dulcimer, and all kinds of musick, shall fall down and worship the golden image:

Da 3:15 — Now if ye be ready that at what time ye hear the sound of the cornet, flute, harp, sackbut, psaltery, and dulcimer, and all kinds of musick, ye fall down and worship the image which I have made; *well:* but if ye worship not, ye shall be cast the same hour into the midst of a burning fiery furnace; and who *is* that God that shall deliver you out of my hands?

• Gittith, a stringed instrument.

Ps 8:1–9; 81:1–16; 84:1–12

• Harp.

↞See: Harp

• Organ, probably composed of pipes furnishing a number of notes.

Ge 4:21 — And his brother's name *was* Jubal: he was the father of all such as handle the harp and organ.

Job 21:12 — They take the timbrel and harp, and rejoice at the sound of the organ.

Job 30:31 — My harp also is *turned* to mourning, and my organ into the voice of them that weep.

Ps 150:4 — Praise him with the timbrel and dance: praise him with stringed instruments and organs.

• Pipe.

↞See: Pipe

• Psaltery.

↞See: Psaltery

• Sackbut, a harp.

Da 3:5 — *That* at what time ye hear the sound of the cornet, flute, harp, sackbut, psaltery, dulcimer, and all kinds of musick, ye fall down and worship the golden image that Nebuchadnezzar the king hath set up:

Da 3:7 — Therefore at that time, when all the people heard the sound of the cornet, flute, harp, sackbut, psaltery, and all kinds of musick, all the people, the nations, and the languages, fell down *and* worshipped the golden image that Nebuchadnezzar the king had set up.

Da 3:10 — Thou, O king, hast made a decree, that every man that shall hear the sound of the cornet, flute, harp, sackbut, psaltery, and dulcimer, and all kinds of musick, shall fall down and worship the golden image:

Da 3:15 — Now if ye be ready that at what time ye hear the sound of the cornet, flute, harp, sackbut, psaltery, and dulcimer, and all kinds of musick, ye fall down and worship the image which I have made; *well:* but if ye worship not, ye shall be cast the same hour into the midst of a burning fiery furnace; and who *is* that God that shall deliver you out of my hands?

• Tabret.

↞See: Timbrel

• Timbrel, a tambourine.

↞See: Timbrel

• Trumpet.

↞See: Trumpet

• Viol, a lyre.

Isa 5:12 — And the harp, and the viol, the tabret, and pipe, and wine, are in their feasts: but they regard not the work of the LORD, neither consider the operation of his hands.

Isa 14:11 — Thy pomp is brought down to the grave, *and* the noise of thy viols: the worm is spread under thee, and the worms cover thee.

Am 5:23 — Take thou away from me the noise of thy songs; for I will not hear the melody of thy viols.

Am 6:5 — That chant to the sound of the viol, *and* invent to themselves instruments of musick, like David;

• Symbols used in.

• Alamoth [literally "virgins"].

• A term that seems to indicate rendering of song by female voices, possibly soprano.

Ps 46:1–11

1Ch 15:20 — And Zechariah, and Aziel, and Shemiramoth, and Jehiel, and Unni, and Eliab, and Maaseiah, and Benaiah, with psalteries on Alamoth;

• Al-Taschith.

• Seems to indicate the kind of ode or melody in which the ode should be sung.

Ps 57:1 — [To the chief Musician, Altaschith, Michtam of David, when he fled from Saul in the cave.] Be merciful unto me, O God, be merciful unto me: for my soul trusteth in thee: yea, in the shadow of thy wings will I make my refuge, until *these* calamities be overpast.

Ps 58:1 — [To the chief Musician, Altaschith, Michtam of David.] Do ye indeed speak righteousness, O congregation? do ye judge uprightly, O ye sons of men?

Ps 59:1 — [To the chief Musician, Altaschith, Michtam of David; when Saul sent, and they watched the house to kill him.] Deliver me from mine enemies, O my God: defend me from them that rise up against me.

Ps 75:1 — [To the chief Musician, Altaschith, A Psalm *or* song of Asaph.] Unto thee, O God, do we give thanks, *unto thee* do we give thanks: for *that* thy name is near thy wondrous works declare.

- **Higgaion.**
  - **According to Gesenius, the murmuring tone of a harp, should be rendered in plaintive manner.**

Ps 92:3 — Upon an instrument of ten strings, and upon the psaltery; upon the harp with a solemn sound.

  - **Combined with "Selah".**
  - **May have been for a pause in the vocal music while the instruments rendered an interlude.**

Ps 9:16 — The LORD is known *by* the judgment *which* he executeth: the wicked is snared in the work of his own hands. Higgaion. Selah.

  - **Mendelssohn translates it "meditation, thought".**
    - **Music was to be rendered in a mode to promote devout meditation.**

Ps 19:14 — Let the words of my mouth, and the meditation of my heart, be acceptable in thy sight, O LORD, my strength, and my redeemer.

- **Mahalath, Maschil, Leannoth.**
  - **Use uncertain. May indicate instruments to be played or melody to be sung.**

Ps 53:1 — [To the chief Musician upon Mahalath, Maschil, A *Psalm* of David.] The fool hath said in his heart, *There is* no God. Corrupt are they, and have done abominable iniquity: *there is* none that doeth good.

Ps 88:1 — [A song *or* Psalm for the sons of Korah, to the chief Musician upon Mahalath Leannoth, Maschil of Heman the Ezrahite.] O LORD God of my salvation, I have cried day *and* night before thee:

- **Maschil [Meaning unknown].**
  - **Where it occurs elsewhere it is equivalent to the English words, to become wise by instruction.**

Ps 32:1 — [A *Psalm* of David, Maschil.] Blessed *is he whose* transgression *is* forgiven, *whose* sin *is* covered.

Ps 42:1 — [To the chief Musician, Maschil, for the sons of Korah.] As the hart panteth after the water brooks, so panteth my soul after thee, O God.

Ps 44:1 — [To the chief Musician for the sons of Korah, Maschil.] We have heard with our ears, O God, our fathers have told us, *what* work thou didst in their days, in the times of old.

Ps 45:1 — [To the chief Musician upon Shoshannim, for the sons of Korah, Maschil, A song of loves.] My heart is inditing a good matter: I speak of the things which I have made touching the king: my tongue *is* the pen of a ready writer.

Ps 52:1 — [To the chief Musician, Maschil, A *Psalm* of David, when Doeg the Edomite came and told Saul, and said unto him, David is come to the house of Ahimelech.] Why boastest thou thyself in mischief, O mighty man? the goodness of God *endureth* continually.

Ps 53:1 — [To the chief Musician upon Mahalath, Maschil, A *Psalm* of David.] The fool hath said in his heart, *There is* no God. Corrupt are they, and have done abominable iniquity: *there is* none that doeth good.

Ps 54:1 — [To the chief Musician on Neginoth, Maschil, A *Psalm* of David, when the Ziphims came and said to Saul, Doth not David hide himself with us?] Save me, O God, by thy name, and judge me by thy strength.

Ps 55:1 — [To the chief Musician on Neginoth, Maschil, A *Psalm* of David.] Give ear to my prayer, O God; and hide not thyself from my supplication.

Ps 74:1 — [Maschil of Asaph.] O God, why hast thou cast us off for ever? *why* doth thine anger smoke against the sheep of thy pasture?

Ps 78:1 — [Maschil of Asaph.] Give ear, O my people, *to* my law: incline your ears to the words of my mouth.

Ps 88:1 — [A song *or* Psalm for the sons of Korah, to the chief Musician upon Mahalath Leannoth, Maschil of Heman the Ezrahite.] O LORD God of my salvation, I have cried day *and* night before thee:

Ps 89:1 — [Maschil of Ethan the Ezrahite.] I will sing of the mercies of the LORD for ever: with my mouth will I make known thy faithfulness to all generations.

Ps 142:1 — [Maschil of David; A Prayer when he was in the cave.] I cried unto the LORD with my voice; with my voice unto the LORD did I make my supplication.

- **Michtam.**
  - **A musical term Luther interprets as "golden," or precious.**
  - **Ewald interprets it as signifying a plaintive manner.**

Ps 16:1 — [Michtam of David.} Preserve me, O God: for in thee do I put my trust.

Ps 56:1 — [To the chief Musician upon Jonathelemrechokim, Michtam of David, when the Philistines took him in Gath.] Be merciful unto me, O God: for man would swallow me up; he fighting daily oppresseth me.

Ps 57:1 — [To the chief Musician, Altaschith, Michtam of David, when he fled from Saul in the cave.] Be merciful unto me, O God, be merciful unto me: for my soul trusteth in thee: yea, in the shadow of thy wings will I make my refuge, until *these* calamities be overpast.

Ps 58:1 — [To the chief Musician, Altaschith, Michtam of David.] Do ye indeed speak righteousness, O congregation? do ye judge uprightly, O ye sons of men?

Ps 59:1 — [To the chief Musician, Altaschith, Michtam of David; when Saul sent, and they watched the house to kill him.] Deliver me from mine enemies, O my God: defend me from them that rise up against me.

Ps 60:1 — [To the chief Musician upon Shushan-eduth, Michtam of David, to teach; when he strove with Aram-naharaim and with Aram-zobah, when Joab returned, and smote of Edom in the valley of salt twelve thousand.] O God, thou hast cast us off, thou hast scattered us, thou hast been displeased; O turn thyself to us again.

• **Muthlabben.**

• **Authorities, ancient and modern, differ as to the probable signification.**

• **Gesenius and De Wette interpret it, "with the voice of virgins, by boys".**

• **Others derive the word from a different Hebrew root, and interpret it as a funeral ode.**

Ps 9:1 — [To the chief Musician upon Muthlabben, A Psalm of David.] I will praise *thee,* O LORD, with my whole heart; I will shew forth all thy marvellous works.

• **Neginah and Neginoth.**

• **Seems to indicate that the song should be accompanied by stringed instruments.**

Ps 4:1 — [To the chief Musician on Neginoth, A Psalm of David.] Hear me when I call, O God of my righteousness: thou hast enlarged me *when I was* in distress; have mercy upon me, and hear my prayer.

Ps 54:1 — [To the chief Musician on Neginoth, Maschil, A *Psalm* of David, when the Ziphims came and said to Saul, Doth not David hide himself with us?] Save me, O God, by thy name, and judge me by thy strength.

Ps 55:1 — [To the chief Musician on Neginoth, Maschil, A *Psalm* of David.] Give ear to my prayer, O God; and hide not thyself from my supplication.

Ps 61:1 — [To the chief Musician upon Neginah, A *Psalm* of David.] Hear my cry, O God; attend unto my prayer.

Ps 67:1 — [To the chief Musician on Neginoth, A Psalm *or* song.] God be merciful unto us, and bless us; *and* cause his face to shine upon us; Selah.

Hab 3:19 — The LORD God *is* my strength, and he will make my feet like hinds' *feet,* and he will make me to walk upon mine high places. To the chief singer on my stringed instruments.

• **Nehiloth.**

• **Seems to indicate that when this Psalm was sung it was to be accompanied by wind instruments.**

Ps 5:1 — [To the chief Musician upon Nehiloth, A Psalm of David.] Give ear to my words, O LORD, consider my meditation.

• **Selah.**

• **Appears frequently in the Psalms.**

• **Purpose uncertain. Maybe a pause in vocal music while an instrumental interlude or finale is rendered.**

• **Sheminity, translated "eighth".**

• **Probably indicates the measure, movement, or pitch.**

Ps 6:1 — [To the chief Musician on Neginoth upon Sheminith, A Psalm of David.] O LORD, rebuke me not in thine anger, neither chasten me in thy hot displeasure.

Ps 12:1 — [To the chief Musician upon Sheminith, A Psalm of David.] Help, LORD; for the godly man ceaseth; for the faithful fail from among the children of men.

• **Shiggaion, called also Shigionoth.**

• **Supposed to have been musical terms to guide in rendering the song.**

• **At the close of the chapter the author refers the ode "to the chief musician, stringed instruments".**

• **The term may suggest the movement in interpreting the music set to it.**

Hab 3:1–19

Ps 7:1 — [Shiggaion of David, which he sang unto the LORD, concerning the words of Cush the Benjamite.] O Lord my God, in thee do I put my trust: save me from all them that persecute me, and deliver me:

• **Shoshannim and Shushan-Eduth.**

• **Seems to indicate the manner in which these Psalms were to be rendered.**

• **Kimchi, Tremellius, and Eichhorn render it "hexachorda" singing with six stringed instruments.**

Ps 45:1 — [To the chief Musician upon Shoshannim, for the sons of Korah, Maschil, A song of loves.] My heart is inditing a good matter: I speak of the things which I have made touching the king: my tongue *is* the pen of a ready writer.

Ps 60:1 — [To the chief Musician upon Shushan-eduth, Michtam of David, to teach; when he strove with Aram-naharaim and with Aram-zobah, when Joab returned, and smote of Edom in the valley of salt twelve thousand.] O God, thou hast cast us off, thou hast scattered us, thou hast been displeased; O turn thyself to us again.

Ps 69:1 — [To chief Musician upon Shoshannim, A *Psalm* of David.] Save me, O God; for the waters are come in unto *my* soul.

Ps 80:1 — [To the chief Musician upon Shoshannim-Eduth, A Psalm of Asaph.] Give ear, O Shepherd of Israel, thou that leadest Joseph like a flock; thou that dwellest *between* the cherubims, shine forth.

• Unclassified scripture relating to.

Ex 15:1–27; Nu 21:17–20; Jgs 5:1–31; 1Sa 18:6–7; 1Ch 6:31–32; 15:16–22, 27–28; 16:4–39, 41–42; 23:5–6; 25:1–31; 2Ch 5:12–13; 20:21–22; 29:25–28; Ezr 2:64–65; 3:10–11; Ne 12:27–47; Ps 33:1–4; 68:1–35; 81:1–3; 92:1–3; 95:1–2; 98:1–8; 135:1–3; 137:1–6; 149:1–3; 150:1–6; Isa 24:8–9; Da 3:4–7, 10–16; Rev 14:2–3

Ge 31:27 — Wherefore didst thou flee away secretly, and steal away from me; and didst not tell me, that I might have sent thee away with mirth, and with songs, with tabret, and with harp?

Jgs 11:34 — And Jephthah came to Mizpeh unto his house, and, behold, his daughter came out to meet him with timbrels and with dances: and she *was his* only child; beside her he had neither son nor daughter.

2Sa 19:35 — I *am* this day fourscore years old: *and* can I discern between good and evil? can thy servant taste what I eat or what I drink? can I hear any more the voice of singing men and singing women? wherefore then should thy servant be yet a burden unto my lord the king?

1Ki 1:40 — And all the people came up after him, and the people piped with pipes, and rejoiced with great joy, so that the earth rent with the sound of them.

1Ch 15:24 — And Shebaniah, and Jehoshaphat, and Nethaneel, and Amasai, and Zechariah, and Benaiah, and Eliezer, the priests, did blow with the trumpets before the ark of God: and Obed-edom and Jehiah *were* doorkeepers for the ark.

1Ch 23:3 — Now the Levites were numbered from the age of thirty years and upward: and their number by their polls, man by man, was thirty and eight thousand.

1Ch 23:27 — For by the last words of David the Levites *were* numbered from twenty years old and above:

1Ch 23:30 — And to stand every morning to thank and praise the LORD, and likewise at even;

2Ch 20:19 — And the Levites, of the children of the Kohathites, and of the children of the Korhites, stood up to praise the LORD God of Israel with a loud voice on high.

2Ch 20:28 — And they came to Jerusalem with psalteries and harps and trumpets unto the house of the LORD.

2Ch 23:13 — And she looked, and, behold, the king stood at his pillar at the entering in, and the princes and the trumpets by the king: and all the people of the land rejoiced, and sounded with trumpets, also the singers with instruments of musick, and such as taught to sing praise. Then Athaliah rent her clothes, and said, Treason, Treason.

2Ch 23:18 — Also Jehoiada appointed the offices of the house of the LORD by the hand of the priests the Levites, whom David had distributed in the house of the LORD, to offer the burnt offerings of the LORD, as *it is* written in the law of Moses, with rejoicing and with singing, *as it was ordained* by David.

2Ch 31:2 — And Hezekiah appointed the courses of the priests and the Levites after their courses, every man according to his service, the priests and Levites for burnt offerings and for peace offerings, to minister, and to give thanks, and to praise in the gates of the tents of the LORD.

2Ch 35:15 — And the singers the sons of Asaph *were* in their place, according to the commandment of David, and Asaph, and Heman, and Jeduthun the king's seer; and the porters *waited* at every gate; they might not depart from their service; for their brethren the Levites prepared for them.

2Ch 35:25 — And Jeremiah lamented for Josiah: and all the singing men and the singing women spake of Josiah in their lamentations to this day, and made them an ordinance in Israel: and, behold, they *are* written in the lamentations.

Ne 12:24 — And the chief of the Levites: Hashabiah, Sherebiah, and Jeshua the son of Kadmiel, with their brethren over against them, to praise *and* to give thanks, according to the commandment of David the man of God, ward over against ward.

Job 21:12 — They take the timbrel and harp, and rejoice at the sound of the organ.

Job 30:31 — My harp also is *turned* to mourning, and my organ into the voice of them that weep.

Ps 87:7 — As well the singers as the players on instruments *shall be there:* all my springs *are* in thee.

Ps 104:33 — I will sing unto the LORD as long as I live: I will sing praise to my God while I have my being.

Ps 105:2 — Sing unto him, sing psalms unto him: talk ye of all his wondrous works.

Ps 144:9 — I will sing a new song unto thee, O God: upon a psaltery *and* an instrument of ten strings will I sing praises unto thee.

Ps 149:6 — *Let* the high *praises* of God *be* in their mouth, and a twoedged sword in their hand;

Pr 25:20 — *As* he that taketh away a garment in cold weather, *and as* vinegar upon nitre, so *is* he that singeth songs to an heavy heart.

Ecc 2:8 — I gathered me also silver and gold, and the peculiar treasure of kings and of the provinces: I gat me men singers and women singers, and the delights of the sons of men, *as* musical instruments, and that of all sorts.

Isa 5:12 — And the harp, and the viol, the tabret, and pipe, and wine, are in their feasts: but they regard not the work of the LORD, neither consider the operation of his hands.

Isa 14:11 — Thy pomp is brought down to the grave, *and* the noise of thy viols: the worm is spread under thee, and the worms cover thee.

Isa 16:10 — And gladness is taken away, and joy out of the plentiful field; and in the vineyards there shall be no singing, neither shall there be shouting: the treaders shall tread out no wine in *their* presses; I have made *their vintage* shouting to cease.

Isa 23:16 — Take an harp, go about the city, thou harlot that hast been forgotten; make sweet melody, sing many songs, that thou mayest be remembered.

Isa 30:29 — Ye shall have a song, as in the night *when* a holy solemnity is kept; and gladness of heart, as when one goeth with a pipe to come into the mountain of the LORD, to the mighty One of Israel.

Isa 30:32 — And *in* every place where the grounded staff shall pass, which the LORD shall lay upon him, *it* shall be with tabrets and harps: and in battles of shaking will he fight with it.

Jer 31:4 — Again I will build thee, and thou shalt be built, O virgin of Israel: thou shalt again be adorned with thy tabrets, and shalt go forth in the dances of them that make merry.

Eze 26:13 — And I will cause the noise of thy songs to cease; and the sound of thy harps shall be no more heard.

Eze 33:32 — And, lo, thou *art* unto them as a very lovely song of one that hath a pleasant voice, and can play well on an instrument: for they hear thy words, but they do them not.

Am 6:5 — That chant to the sound of the viol, *and* invent to themselves instruments of musick, like David;

Am 8:10 — And I will turn your feasts into mourning, and all your songs into lamentation; and I will bring up sackcloth upon all loins, and baldness upon every head; and I will make it as the mourning of an only *son,* and the end thereof as a bitter day.

Mt 9:23 — And when Jesus came into the ruler's house, and saw the minstrels and the people making a noise,

Mt 11:17 — And saying, We have piped unto you, and ye have not danced; we have mourned unto you, and ye have not lamented.

Mk 14:26 — And when they had sung an hymn, they went out into the mount of Olives.

1Co 14:15 — What is it then? I will pray with the spirit, and I will pray with the understanding also: I will sing with the spirit, and I will sing with the understanding also.

Eph 5:19 — Speaking to yourselves in psalms and hymns and spiritual songs, singing and making melody in your heart to the Lord;

Col 3:16 — Let the word of Christ dwell in you richly in all wisdom; teaching and admonishing one another in psalms and hymns and spiritual songs, singing with grace in your hearts to the Lord.

Heb 2:12 — Saying, I will declare thy name unto my brethren, in the midst of the church will I sing praise unto thee.

Rev 18:22 — And the voice of harpers, and musicians, and of pipers, and trumpeters, shall be heard no more at all in thee; and no craftsman, of whatsoever craft *he be,* shall be found any more in thee; and the sound of a millstone shall be heard no more at all in thee;

See: Praise

See: Psalms

MUSTARD

Mt 13:31–32; Mk 4:30–33

Mt 17:20 — And Jesus said unto them, Because of your unbelief: for verily I say unto you, If ye have faith as a grain of mustard seed, ye shall say unto this mountain, Remove hence to yonder place; and it shall remove; and nothing shall be impossible unto you.

Lk 13:19 — It is like a grain of mustard seed, which a man took, and cast into his garden; and it grew, and waxed a great tree; and the fowls of the air lodged in the branches of it.

MUSTER

- **Of troops.**

1Sa 14:17 — Then said Saul unto the people that *were* with him, Number now, and see who is gone from us. And when they had numbered, behold, Jonathan and his armourbearer *were* not *there.*

2Sa 20:4 — Then said the king to Amasa, Assemble me the men of Judah within three days, and be thou here present.

1Ki 20:26 — And it came to pass at the return of the year, that Ben-hadad numbered the Syrians, and went up to Aphek, to fight against Israel.

2Ki 25:19 — And out of the city he took an officer that was set over the men of war, and five men of them that were in the king's presence, which were found in the city, and the principal scribe of the host, which mustered the people of the land, and threescore men of the people of the land *that were* found in the city:

Isa 13:4 — The noise of a multitude in the mountains, like as of a great people; a tumultuous noise of the kingdoms of nations gathered together: the LORD of hosts mustereth the host of the battle.

See: Armies

MUTH-LABBEN **See: Music**

MUTINY

- **Israelites against Moses.**

Nu 14:4 — And they said one to another, Let us make a captain, and let us return into Egypt.

See: Conspiracy

MYRA

- **A city of Lycia.**
- **Paul visits.**

Ac 27:5–6

MYRRH

- **A fragrant gum.**
- **A product of the land of Canaan.**

SS 4:6 — Until the day break, and the shadows flee away, I will get me to the mountain of myrrh, and to the hill of frankincense.

SS 4:14 — Spikenard and saffron; calamus and cinnamon, with all trees of frankincense; myrrh and aloes, with all the chief spices:

SS 5:1 — I am come into my garden, my sister, *my* spouse: I have gathered my myrrh with my spice; I have eaten my honeycomb with my honey; I have drunk my wine with my milk: eat, O friends; drink, yea, drink abundantly, O beloved.

• One of the compounds in the sacred anointing oil.

Ex 30:23 — Take thou also unto thee principal spices, of pure myrrh five hundred *shekels,* and of sweet cinnamon half so much, *even* two hundred and fifty *shekels,* and of sweet calamus two hundred and fifty *shekels,*

• Used as a perfume.

Est 2:12 — Now when every maid's turn was come to go in to king Ahasuerus, after that she had been twelve months, according to the manner of the women, (for so were the days of their purifications accomplished, *to wit,* six months with oil of myrrh, and six months with sweet odours, and with *other* things for the purifying of the women;)

Ps 45:8 — All thy garments *smell* of myrrh, and aloes, *and* cassia, out of the ivory palaces, whereby they have made thee glad.

Pr 7:17 — I have perfumed my bed with myrrh, aloes, and cinnamon.

SS 3:6 — Who *is* this that cometh out of the wilderness like pillars of smoke, perfumed with myrrh and frankincense, with all powders of the merchant?

SS 5:13 — His cheeks *are* as a bed of spices, *as* sweet flowers: his lips *like* lilies, dropping sweet smelling myrrh.

• Brought by wise men as a present to Jesus.

Mt 2:11 — And when they were come into the house, they saw the young child with Mary his mother, and fell down, and worshipped him: and when they had opened their treasures, they presented unto him gifts; gold, and frankincense, and myrrh.

• Offered to Jesus on the cross.

Mk 15:23 — And they gave him to drink wine mingled with myrrh: but he received *it* not.

• Used for embalming.

Jn 19:39 — And there came also Nicodemus, which at the first came to Jesus by night, and brought a mixture of myrrh and aloes, about an hundred pound *weight.*

• Traffic in.

Ge 37:25 — And they sat down to eat bread: and they lifted up their eyes and looked, and, behold, a company of Ishmeelites came from Gilead with their camels bearing spicery and balm and myrrh, going to carry *it* down to Egypt.

Ge 43:11 — And their father Israel said unto them, If *it must be* so now, do this; take of the best fruits in the land in your vessels, and carry down the man a present, a little balm, and a little honey, spices, and myrrh, nuts, and almonds:

MYRTLE

Ne 8:15 — And that they should publish and proclaim in all their cities, and in Jerusalem, saying, Go forth unto the mount, and fetch olive branches, and pine branches, and myrtle branches, and palm branches, and branches of thick trees, to make booths, as *it is* written.

Isa 41:19 — I will plant in the wilderness the cedar, the shittah tree, and the myrtle, and the oil tree; I will set in the desert the fir tree, *and* the pine, and the box tree together:

Isa 55:13 — Instead of the thorn shall come up the fir tree, and instead of the brier shall come up the myrtle tree: and it shall be to the LORD for a name, for an everlasting sign *that* shall not be cut off.

Zec 1:8 — I saw by night, and behold a man riding upon a red horse, and he stood among the myrtle trees that *were* in the bottom; and behind him *were there* red horses, speckled, and white.

MYSIA

• A province of Asia Minor.

• Paul visits.

Ac 16:7–8

MYSTERIES

• Of redemption.

Jn 3:8–12; Ro 16:25–26; 1Co 2:7–10; 2Co 3:12–18; Eph 1:9–10; 3:3–5, 18–19; Col 1:25–27; 4:3–4; 1Pe 1:10–12

Dt 29:29 — The secret *things belong* unto the LORD our God: but *those things which* are revealed *belong* unto us and to our children for ever, that *we* may do all the words of this law.

Job 15:8 — Hast thou heard the secret of God? and dost thou restrain wisdom to thyself?

Ps 25:14 — The secret of the LORD *is* with them that fear him; and he will shew them his covenant.

Pr 3:32 — For the froward *is* abomination to the LORD: but his secret *is* with the righteous.

Am 3:7 — Surely the Lord GOD will do nothing, but he revealeth his secret unto his servants the prophets.

Mt 11:25 — At that time Jesus answered and said, I thank thee, O Father, Lord of heaven and earth, because thou hast hid these things from the wise and prudent, and hast revealed them unto babes.

Mt 13:11 — He answered and said unto them, Because it is given unto you to know the mysteries of the kingdom of heaven, but to them it is not given.

Mt 13:35 — That it might be fulfilled which was spoken by the prophet, saying, I will open my mouth in parables; I will utter things which have been kept secret from the foundation of the world.

Mk 4:11 — And he said unto them, Unto you it is given to know the mystery of the kingdom of God: but unto them that are without, all these *things* are done in parables:

Lk 8:10 — And he said, Unto you it is given to know the mysteries of the kingdom of God: but to others in parables; that seeing they might not see, and hearing they might not understand.

Eph 3:9 — And to make all *men* see what *is* the fellowship of the mystery, which from the beginning of the world hath been hid in God, who created all things by Jesus Christ:

Eph 6:19 — And for me, that utterance may be given unto me, that I may open my mouth boldly, to make known the mystery of the gospel,

Col 2:2 — That their hearts might be comforted, being knit together in love, and unto all riches of the full assurance of understanding, to the acknowledgement of the mystery of God, and of the Father, and of Christ;

2Th 2:7 — For the mystery of iniquity doth already work: only he who now letteth *will let,* until he be taken out of the way.

1Ti 3:9 — Holding the mystery of the faith in a pure conscience.

1Ti 3:16 — And without controversy great is the mystery of godliness: God was manifest in the flesh, justified in the Spirit, seen of angels, preached unto the Gentiles, believed on in the world, received up into glory.

Heb 5:11 — Of whom we have many things to say, and hard to be uttered, seeing ye are dull of hearing.

Rev 10:7 — But in the days of the voice of the seventh angel, when he shall begin to sound, the mystery of God should be finished, as he hath declared to his servants the prophets.

See: Salvation; plan of

MYTHS

1Ti 1:4 — Neither give heed to fables and endless genealogies, which minister questions, rather than godly edifying which is in faith: *so do.*

1Ti 4:7 — But refuse profane and old wives' fables, and exercise thyself *rather* unto godliness.

2Ti 4:4 — And they shall turn away *their* ears from the truth, and shall be turned unto fables.

Tit 1:14 — Not giving heed to Jewish fables, and commandments of men, that turn from the truth.

N

NAAM • Son of Caleb.

1Ch 4:15 — And the sons of Caleb the son of Jephunneh; Iru, Elah, and Naam: and the sons of Elah, even Kenaz.

NAAMAH

• Sister of Tubal-cain.

Ge 4:22 — And Zillah, she also bare Tubal-cain, an instructer of every artificer in brass and iron: and the sister of Tubal-cain *was* Naamah.

• A wife of Solomon and mother of King Rehoboam.

1Ki 14:21 — And Rehoboam the son of Solomon reigned in Judah. Rehoboam *was* forty and one years old when he began to reign, and he reigned seventeen years in Jerusalem, the city which the LORD did choose out of all the tribes of Israel, to put his name there. And his mother's name *was* Naamah an Ammonitess.

1Ki 14:31 — And Rehoboam slept with his fathers, and was buried with his fathers in the city of David. And his mother's name *was* Naamah an Ammonitess. And Abijam his son reigned in his stead.

2Ch 12:13 — So king Rehoboam strengthened himself in Jerusalem, and reigned: for Rehoboam *was* one and forty years old when he began to reign, and he reigned seventeen years in Jerusalem, the city which the LORD had chosen out of all the tribes of Israel, to put his name there. And his mother's name *was* Naamah an Ammonitess.

• A city of Judah.

Jos 15:41 — And Gederoth, Beth-dagon, and Naamah, and Makkedah; sixteen cities with their villages:

NAAMAN

• Son of Benjamin.

Ge 46:21 — And the sons of Benjamin were Belah, and Becher, and Ashbel, Gera, and Naaman, Ehi, and Rosh, Muppim, and Huppim, and Ard.

• Son of Bela.

Nu 26:40 — And the sons of Bela were Ard and Naaman: *of Ard,* the family of the Ardites: *and* of Naaman, the family of the Naamites.

1Ch 8:4 — And Abishua, and Naaman, and Ahoah,

• Son of Ehud.

1Ch 8:7 — And Naaman, and Ahiah, and Gera, he removed them, and begat Uzza, and Ahihud.

• A Syrian general.

• Healed of leprosy by Elisha.

2Ki 5:1–23

Lk 4:27 — And many lepers were in Israel in the time of Eliseus the prophet; and none of them was cleansed, saving Naaman the Syrian.

NAARAH • A wife of Ashur.

1Ch 4:5–6

NAARAI

• Called also Paarai.

• One of David's heroes.

1Ch 11:37 — Hezro the Carmelite, Naarai the son of Ezbai,

NAARAN • A city in the eastern limits of Ephraim.

1Ch 7:28 — And their possessions and habitations *were,* Bethel and the towns thereof, and eastward Naaran, and westward Gezer, with the towns thereof; Shechem also and the towns thereof, unto Gaza and the towns thereof:

NAARATH • A city on the southern boundary of Ephraim.

Jos 16:7 — And it went down from Janohah to Ataroth, and to Naarath, and came to Jericho, and went out at Jordan.

NAASHON

• Called also Naasson and Nahshon.

• A captain of Judah's host.

Ex 6:23 — And Aaron took him Elisheba, daughter of Amminadab, sister of Naashon, to wife; and she bare him Nadab, and Abihu, Eleazar, and Ithamar.

Nu 1:7 — Of Judah; Nahshon the son of Amminadab.

Nu 2:3 — And on the east side toward the rising of the sun shall they of the standard of the camp of Judah pitch throughout their armies: and Nahshon the son of Amminadab *shall be* captain of the children of Judah.

Nu 7:12 — And he that offered his offering the first day was Nahshon the son of Amminadab, of the tribe of Judah:

Nu 7:17 — And for a sacrifice of peace offerings, two oxen, five rams, five he goats, five lambs of the first year: this *was* the offering of Nahshon the son of Amminadab.

Nu 10:14 — In the first *place* went the standard of the camp of the children of Judah according to their armies: and over his host *was* Nahshon the son of Amminadab.

• In the lineage of Christ.

Mt 1:4 — And Aram begat Aminadab; and Aminadab begat Naasson; and Naasson begat Salmon;

Lk 3:32 — Which was *the son* of Jesse, which was *the son* of Obed, which was *the son* of Booz, which was *the son* of Salmon, which was *the son* of Naasson,

NABAL, husband of Abigail

• History of.
1Sa 25:2–38

NABOTH

• A Jezreelite.
• His vineyard forcibly taken by Ahab; stoned at the instigation of Jezebel.
1Ki 21:1–19

• His murder avenged.
2Ki 9:21–36

NACHON

• Called also Chidon.
• Uzzah slain at the threshing floor of.
2Sa 6:6–7
1Ch 13:9 — And when they came unto the threshingfloor of Chidon, Uzza put forth his hand to hold the ark; for the oxen stumbled.

NACHOR • An ancestor of Jesus.

Lk 3:34 — Which was *the son* of Jacob, which was *the son* of Isaac, which was *the son* of Abraham, which was *the son* of Thara, which was *the son* of Nachor,

NADAB

• Son of Aaron.
Ex 6:23 — And Aaron took him Elisheba, daughter of Amminadab, sister of Naashon, to wife; and she bare him Nadab, and Abihu, Eleazar, and Ithamar.

• Called to Mount Sinai with Moses and Aaron to worship.
Ex 24:9–10
Ex 24:1 — And he said unto Moses, Come up unto the LORD, thou, and Aaron, Nadab, and Abihu, and seventy of the elders of Israel; and worship ye afar off.

• Set apart to priesthood.
Ex 28:40–43
Ex 28:1 — And take thou unto thee Aaron thy brother, and his sons with him, from among the children of Israel, that he may minister unto me in the priest's office, *even* Aaron, Nadab and Abihu, Eleazar and Ithamar, Aaron's sons.
Ex 28:4 — And these *are* the garments which they shall make; a breastplate, and an ephod, and a robe, and a broidered coat, a mitre, and a girdle: and they shall make holy garments for Aaron thy brother, and his sons, that he may minister unto me in the priest's office.

• Offers strange fire to God, and is destroyed.
Le 10:1–2
Nu 3:4 — And Nadab and Abihu died before the LORD, when they offered strange fire before the LORD, in the wilderness of Sinai, and they had no children: and Eleazar and Ithamar ministered in the priest's office in the sight of Aaron their father.
Nu 26:61 — And Nadab and Abihu died, when they offered strange fire before the LORD.

• Is buried.
Le 10:4–5

• His father and brothers forbidden to mourn.
Le 10:6–7

• Son and successor of Jeroboam.
1Ki 14:20 — And the days which Jeroboam reigned *were* two and twenty years: and he slept with his fathers, and Nadab his son reigned in his stead.

• His wicked reign; murdered by Baasha.
1Ki 15:25–31

• Great-grandson of Jerahmeel.
1Ch 2:28 — And the sons of Onam were, Shammai, and Jada. And the sons of Shammai; Nadab, and Abishur.
1Ch 2:30 — And the sons of Nadab; Seled, and Appaim: but Seled died without children.

• A Benjamite.
1Ch 8:30 — And his firstborn son Abdon, and Zur, and Kish, and Baal, and Nadab,
1Ch 9:36 — And his firstborn son Abdon, then Zur, and Kish, and Baal, and Ner, and Nadab,

NAGGE • An ancestor of Jesus.

Lk 3:25 — Which was *the son* of Mattathias, which was *the son* of Amos, which was *the son* of Naum, which was *the son* of Esli, which was *the son* of Nagge,

NAHALIEL • A station of the Israelites.

Nu 21:19 — And from Mattanah to Nahaliel: and from Nahaliel to Bamoth:

NAHALLAL

• Called also Nahalal and Nahalol.
• A Levitical city.
Jos 19:15 — And Kattath, and Nahallal, and Shimron, and Idalah, and Bethlehem: twelve cities with their villages.
Jos 21:35 — Dimnah with her suburbs, Nahalal with her suburbs; four cities.
Jgs 1:30 — Neither did Zebulun drive out the inhabitants of Kitron, nor the inhabitants of Nahalol; but the Canaanites dwelt among them, and became tributaries.

NAHAM • Brother of Hodiah.

1Ch 4:19 — And the sons of *his* wife Hodiah the sister of Naham, the father of Keilah the Garmite, and Eshtemoa the Maachathite.

NAHAMANI • A Jewish exile.

Ne 7:7 — Who came with Zerubbabel, Jeshua, Nehemiah, Azariah, Raamiah, Nahamani, Mordecai, Bilshan, Mispereth, Bigvai, Nehum, Baanah. The number, *I say,* of the men of the people of Israel *was this;*

NAHARAI

• Called also Nahari.

• One of David's heroes.

2Sa 23:37 — Zelek the Ammonite, Nahari the Beerothite, armourbearer to Joab the son of Zeruiah,

1Ch 11:39 — Zelek the Ammonite, Naharai the Berothite, the armourbearer of Joab the son of Zeruiah,

NAHASH

• An Ammonite king. Defeated by Saul at Jabesh-gilead.

1Sa 11:1–11

• Kindness of, to David, and death.

2Sa 10:1–2; 1Ch 19:1–2

• Probably identical with Jesse.

2Sa 17:25 — And Absalom made Amasa captain of the host instead of Joab: which Amasa was a man's son, whose name *was* Ithra an Israelite, that went in to Abigail the daughter of Nahash, sister to Zeruiah Joab's mother.

NAHATH

• Son of Reuel.

Ge 36:13 — And these *are* the sons of Reuel; Nahath, and Zerah, Shammah, and Mizzah: these were the sons of Bashemath Esau's wife.

Ge 36:17 — And these *are* the sons of Reuel Esau's son; duke Nahath, duke Zerah, duke Shammah, duke Mizzah: these *are* the dukes *that came* of Reuel in the land of Edom; these *are* the sons of Bashemath Esau's wife.

1Ch 1:37 — The sons of Reuel; Nahath, Zerah, Shammah, and Mizzah.

• A Levite.

1Ch 6:26 — *As for* Elkanah: the sons of Elkanah; Zophai his son, and Nahath his son,

• Called also Toah and Tohu.

1Sa 1:1 — Now there was a certain man of Ramathaim-zophim, of mount Ephraim, and his name was Elkanah, the son of Jeroham, the son of Elihu, the son of Tohu, the son of Zuph, an Ephrathite:

1Ch 6:34 — The son of Elkanah, the son of Jeroham, the son of Eliel, the son of Toah,

• A Levite and overseer of the sacred offerings.

2Ch 31:13 — And Jehiel, and Azaziah, and Nahath, and Asahel, and Jerimoth, and Jozabad, and Eliel, and Ismachiah, and Mahath, and Benaiah, *were* overseers under the hand of Cononiah and Shimei his brother, at the commandment of Hezekiah the king, and Azariah the ruler of the house of God.

NAHBI • A prince of Naphtali, and one of the twelve spies.

Nu 13:14 — Of the tribe of Naphtali, Nahbi the son of Vophsi.

NAHOR

• Grandfather of Abraham.

Ge 11:22–26

1Ch 1:26 — Serug, Nahor, Terah,

• In the lineage of Christ.

Lk 3:34 — Which was *the son* of Jacob, which was *the son* of Isaac, which was *the son* of Abraham, which was *the son* of Thara, which was *the son* of Nachor,

• Brother of Abraham.

Ge 11:26 — And Terah lived seventy years, and begat Abram, Nahor, and Haran.

Jos 24:2 — And Joshua said unto all the people, Thus saith the LORD God of Israel, Your fathers dwelt on the other side of the flood in old time, *even* Terah, the father of Abraham, and the father of Nachor: and they served other gods.

• Marriage and descendants of.

Ge 22:20–24

Ge 11:27 — Now these *are* the generations of Terah: Terah begat Abram, Nahor, and Haran; and Haran begat Lot.

Ge 11:29 — And Abram and Nahor took them wives: the name of Abram's wife *was* Sarai; and the name of Nahor's wife, Milcah, the daughter of Haran, the father of Milcah, and the father of Iscah.

Ge 24:15 — And it came to pass, before he had done speaking, that, behold, Rebekah came out, who was born to Bethuel, son of Milcah, the wife of Nahor, Abraham's brother, with her pitcher upon her shoulder.

Ge 24:24 — And she said unto him, I *am* the daughter of Bethuel the son of Milcah, which she bare unto Nahor.

NAHSHON

• Son of Amminadab.

Ex 6:23 — And Aaron took him Elisheba, daughter of Amminadab, sister of Naashon, to wife; and she bare him Nadab, and Abihu, Eleazar, and Ithamar.

Nu 1:7 — Of Judah; Nahshon the son of Amminadab.

1Ch 2:10 — And Ram begat Amminadab; and Amminadab begat Nahshon, prince of the children of Judah;

• Captain of the host of Judah.

Nu 2:3 — And on the east side toward the rising of the sun shall they of the standard of the camp of Judah pitch throughout their armies: and Nahshon the son of Amminadab *shall be* captain of the children of Judah.

Nu 10:14 — In the first *place* went the standard of the camp of the children of Judah according to their armies: and over his host *was* Nahshon the son of Amminadab.

1Ch 2:10 — And Ram begat Amminadab; and Amminadab begat Nahshon, prince of the children of Judah;

• **Liberality of.**

Nu 7:12 — And he that offered his offering the first day was Nahshon the son of Amminadab, of the tribe of Judah:

Nu 7:17 — And for a sacrifice of peace offerings, two oxen, five rams, five he goats, five lambs of the first year: this *was* the offering of Nahshon the son of Amminadab.

NAHUM

• **One of the minor prophets.**

• **Prophesies against the Assyrians; declares the majesty of God and his care for his people.**

Na 1:1–15

• **Foretells the destruction of Nineveh.**

Na 2:1–3:19

NAIL

Isa 41:7 — So the carpenter encouraged the goldsmith, *and* he that smootheth *with* the hammer him that smote the anvil, saying, It is ready for the sodering: and he fastened it with nails, *that* it should not be moved.

Jer 10:4 — They deck it with silver and with gold; they fasten it with nails and with hammers, that it move not.

• **Made of iron.**

1Ch 22:3 — And David prepared iron in abundance for the nails for the doors of the gates, and for the joinings; and brass in abundance without weight;

• **Made of gold.**

2Ch 3:9 — And the weight of the nails *was* fifty shekels of gold. And he overlaid the upper chambers with gold.

• **Jael kills Sisera with.**

Jgs 4:21 — Then Jael Heber's wife took a nail of the tent, and took an hammer in her hand, and went softly unto him, and smote the nail into his temples, and fastened it into the ground: for he was fast asleep and weary. So he died.

• **Figurative.**

Ezr 9:8 — And now for a little space grace hath been *shewed* from the LORD our God, to leave us a remnant to escape, and to give us a nail in his holy place, that our God may lighten our eyes, and give us a little reviving in our bondage.

Isa 22:23 — And I will fasten him as a nail in a sure place; and he shall be for a glorious throne to his father's house.

Isa 22:25 — In that day, saith the LORD of hosts, shall the nail that is fastened in the sure place be removed, and be cut down, and fall; and the burden that *was* upon it shall be cut off: for the LORD hath spoken *it*.

Zec 10:4 — Out of him came forth the corner, out of him the nail, out of him the battle bow, out of him every oppressor together.

NAIN

• **A city in Galilee.**

• **Jesus restores to life a widow's son in.**

Lk 7:11 — And it came to pass the day after, that he went into a city called Nain; and many of his disciples went with him, and much people.

NAIOTH • A place in Ramah.

1Sa 19:18–19

1Sa 19:22 — Then went he also to Ramah, and came to a great well that *is* in Sechu: and he asked and said, Where *are* Samuel and David? And *one* said, Behold, *they be* at Naioth in Ramah.

1Sa 20:1 — And David fled from Naioth in Ramah, and came and said before Jonathan, What have I done? what *is* mine iniquity? and what *is* my sin before thy father, that he seeketh my life?

NAME

• **Value of a good.**

Pr 22:1 — A *good* name *is* rather to be chosen than great riches, *and* loving favour rather than silver and gold.

Ecc 7:1 — A good name *is* better than precious ointment; and the day of death than the day of one's birth.

• **A new name given to persons who have spiritual adoption.**

Isa 62:2 — And the Gentiles shall see thy righteousness, and all kings thy glory: and thou shalt be called by a new name, which the mouth of the LORD shall name.

• **To Abraham.**

Ge 17:5 — Neither shall thy name any more be called Abram, but thy name shall be Abraham; for a father of many nations have I made thee.

• **To Sarah.**

Ge 17:15 — And God said unto Abraham, As for Sarai thy wife, thou shalt not call her name Sarai, but Sarah *shall* her name *be.*

• **To Jacob.**

Ge 32:28 — And he said, Thy name shall be called no more Jacob, but Israel: for as a prince hast thou power with God and with men, and hast prevailed.

• **To Paul.**

Ac 13:9 — Then Saul, (who also *is called* Paul,) filled with the Holy Ghost, set his eyes on him,

• **Intercessional influence of the name of Jesus.**

→**See: Jesus, in His Name**

• **Symbolic.**

Hos 1:3–4

Hos 1:6 — And she conceived again, and bare a daughter. And *God* said unto him, Call her name Loruhamah: for I will no more have mercy upon the house of Israel; but I will utterly take them away.

Hos 1:9 — Then said *God,* Call his name Lo-ammi: for ye *are* not my people, and I will not be your *God.*

Hos 2:1 — Say ye unto your brethren, Ammi; and to your sisters, Ru-hamah.

NAMES OF GOD ⇒See: God; name of

NAMES OF JESUS ⇒See: Jesus, Names, Appellations, and Titles of

NAOMI

• Wife of Elimelech, mother-in-law of Ruth, kinswoman of Boaz.

• Dwelt in Moab.

Ru 1:1–4:22

NAPHISH

• Called also Nephish.

• A son of Ishmael.

Ge 25:15 — Hadar, and Tema, Jetur, Naphish, and Kedemah:

1Ch 1:31 — Jetur, Naphish, and Kedemah. These are the sons of Ishmael.

NAPHTALI

• Son of Jacob and Bilhah.

Ge 30:7–8

Ge 35:25 — And the sons of Bilhah, Rachel's handmaid; Dan, and Naphtali:

• Jacob blesses.

Ge 49:21 — Naphtali *is* a hind let loose: he giveth goodly words.

• Sons of.

Ge 46:24 — And the sons of Naphtali; Jahzeel, and Guni, and Jezer, and Shillem.

1Ch 7:13 — The sons of Naphtali; Jahziel, and Guni, and Jezer, and Shallum, the sons of Bilhah.

• Tribe, census of.

Nu 1:42–43; 26:48–50

• Position assigned to, in camp and march.

Nu 2:25–31; 10:25–27

• Moses' benediction on.

Dt 33:23 — And of Naphtali he said, O Naphtali, satisfied with favour, and full with the blessing of the LORD: possess thou the west and the south.

• Inheritance of.

Jos 19:32–39

Jgs 1:33 — Neither did Naphtali drive out the inhabitants of Beth-shemesh, nor the inhabitants of Beth-anath; but he dwelt among the Canaanites, the inhabitants of the land: nevertheless the inhabitants of Beth-shemesh and of Beth-anath became tributaries unto them.

Eze 48:3 — And by the border of Asher, from the east side even unto the west side, a *portion for* Naphtali.

• Defeat Sisera.

Jgs 4:6 — And she sent and called Barak the son of Abinoam out of Kedesh-naphtali, and said unto him, Hath not the LORD God of Israel commanded, *saying,* Go and draw toward mount Tabor, and take with thee ten thousand men of the children of Naphtali and of the children of Zebulun?

Jgs 4:10 — And Barak called Zebulun and Naphtali to Kedesh; and he went up with ten thousand men at his feet: and Deborah went up with him.

Jgs 5:18 — Zebulun and Naphtali *were* a people *that* jeoparded their lives unto the death in the high places of the field.

• Follow Gideon.

Jgs 6:35 — And he sent messengers throughout all Manasseh; who also was gathered after him: and he sent messengers unto Asher, and unto Zebulun, and unto Naphtali; and they came up to meet them.

Jgs 7:23 — And the men of Israel gathered themselves together out of Naphtali, and out of Asher, and out of all Manasseh, and pursued after the Midianites.

• Aid in conveying the ark to Jerusalem.

Ps 68:27 — There *is* little Benjamin *with* their ruler, the princes of Judah *and* their council, the princes of Zebulun, *and* the princes of Naphtali.

• Military operations of.

1Ch 12:34 — And of Naphtali a thousand captains, and with them with shield and spear thirty and seven thousand.

1Ch 12:40 — Moreover they that were nigh them, *even* unto Issachar and Zebulun and Naphtali, brought bread on asses, and on camels, and on mules, and on oxen, *and* meat, meal, cakes of figs, and bunches of raisins, and wine, and oil, and oxen, and sheep abundantly: for *there was* joy in Israel.

• Military operations against.

1Ki 15:20 — So Ben-hadad hearkened unto king Asa, and sent the captains of the hosts which he had against the cities of Israel, and smote Ijon, and Dan, and Abel-beth-maachah, and all Cinneroth, with all the land of Naphtali.

2Ki 15:29 — In the days of Pekah king of Israel came Tiglath-pileser king of Assyria, and took Ijon, and Abel-beth-maachah, and Janoah, and Kedesh, and Hazor, and Gilead, and Galilee, all the land of Naphtali, and carried them captive to Assyria.

2Ch 16:4 — And Ben-hadad hearkened unto king Asa, and sent the captains of his armies against the cities of Israel; and they smote Ijon, and Dan, and Abel-maim, and all the store cities of Naphtali.

• Prophecies concerning.

Isa 9:1–2

Rev 7:6 — Of the tribe of Aser *were* sealed twelve thousand. Of the tribe of Nepthalim *were* sealed twelve thousand. Of the tribe of Manasses *were* sealed twelve thousand.

NAPHTUHIM • The inhabitants of central Egypt.

Ge 10:13 — And Mizraim begat Ludim, and Anamim, and Lehabim, and Naphtuhim,

1Ch 1:11 — And Mizraim begat Ludim, and Anamim, and Lehabim, and Napthtuhim,

NARCISSUS • A believer at Rome.

Ro 16:11 — Salute Herodion my kinsman. Greet them that be of the *household* of Narcissus, which are in the Lord.

NATHAN

• Son of David and Bath-sheba.

2Sa 5:14 — And these *be* the names of those that were born unto him in Jerusalem; Shammuah, and Shobab, and Nathan, and Solomon,

1Ch 3:5 — And these were born unto him in Jerusalem; Shimea, and Shobab, and Nathan, and Solomon, four, of Bath-shua the daughter of Ammiel:

1Ch 14:4 — Now these *are* the names of *his* children which he had in Jerusalem; Shammua, and Shobab, Nathan, and Solomon,

• A prophet in the time of David.

• His message to David concerning the building of a temple.

2Sa 7:1–17; 1Ch 17:1–15

• Reproves David for his adultery with Bath-sheba and his murder of Uriah.

2Sa 12:1–15

• Gives Solomon the name Jedidiah.

2Sa 12:25 — And he sent by the hand of Nathan the prophet; and he called his name Jedidiah, because of the LORD.

• Assists Bath-sheba in securing to Solomon, her son, the succession to the throne.

1Ki 1:10–14, 22–27

• Assists in anointing Solomon.

1Ki 1:32–45

• Kept the chronicles.

1Ch 29:29 — Now the acts of David the king, first and last, behold, they *are* written in the book of Samuel the seer, and in the book of Nathan the prophet, and in the book of Gad the seer,

2Ch 9:29 — Now the rest of the acts of Solomon, first and last, *are* they not written in the book of Nathan the prophet, and in the prophecy of Ahijah the Shilonite, and in the visions of Iddo the seer against Jeroboam the son of Nebat?

• Assists David in the organization of the tabernacle.

2Ch 29:25 — And he set the Levites in the house of the LORD with cymbals, with psalteries, and with harps, according to the commandment of David, and of Gad the king's seer, and Nathan the prophet: for *so was* the commandment of the LORD by his prophets.

NATHAN-MELECH • An idolatrous chamberlain.

2Ki 23:11 — And he took away the horses that the kings of Judah had given to the sun, at the entering in of the house of the LORD, by the chamber of Nathan-melech the chamberlain, which *was* in the suburbs, and burned the chariots of the sun with fire.

NATHANAEL

• Becomes a disciple of Jesus.

Jn 1:45–49

Jn 21:2 — There were together Simon Peter, and Thomas called Didymus, and Nathanael of Cana in Galilee, and the *sons* of Zebedee, and two other of his disciples.

NATION

• Sins of.

Isa 30:1–2

• Chastised.

Isa 14:26–27; Jer 18:6–10; 25:12–33; Eze 2:3–5; 39:23–24; Da 7:9–12; 9:3–16; Joel 1:1–20

Jer 5:29 — Shall I not visit for these *things?* saith the LORD: shall not my soul be avenged on such a nation as this?

Hos 7:12 — When they shall go, I will spread my net upon them; I will bring them down as the fowls of the heaven; I will chastise them, as their congregation hath heard.

Am 9:9 — For, lo, I will command, and I will sift the house of Israel among all nations, like as *corn* is sifted in a sieve, yet shall not the least grain fall upon the earth.

Zep 3:6 — I have cut off the nations: their towers are desolate; I made their streets waste, that none passeth by: their cities are destroyed, so that there is no man, that there is none inhabitant.

Zep 3:8 — Therefore wait ye upon me, saith the LORD, until the day that I rise up to the prey: for my determination *is* to gather the nations, that I may assemble the kingdoms, to pour upon them mine indignation, *even* all my fierce anger: for all the earth shall be devoured with the fire of my jealousy.

• Perish.

Ps 9:17 — The wicked shall be turned into hell, *and* all the nations that forget God.

Isa 60:12 — For the nation and kingdom that will not serve thee shall perish; yea, *those* nations shall be utterly wasted.

• National adversity, prayer in.

Jgs 21:2–4; 2Ch 7:13–14; Ps 74:1–23

Joel 2:12 — Therefore also now, saith the LORD, turn ye *even* to me with all your heart, and with fasting, and with weeping, and with mourning:

• National adversity lamented.

Ezr 9:1–15; Ne 1:4–11; Jer 8:20–21; 9:1–2

Jer 6:14 — They have healed also the hurt *of the daughter* of my people slightly, saying, Peace, peace; when *there is* no peace.

Jer 8:11 — For they have healed the hurt of the daughter of my people slightly, saying, Peace, peace; when *there is* no peace.

➜See: Sin; national, punishment of

• Prayer for.

Ps 85:1–7; La 2:20–22; 5:1–22; Da 9:3–21

• Involved in sins of rulers.

2Sa 24:10–17; 1Ch 21:7–17

Ge 20:4 — But Abimelech had not come near her: and he said, Lord, wilt thou slay also a righteous nation?

Ge 20:9 — Then Abimelech called Abraham, and said unto him, What hast thou done unto us? and what have I offended thee, that thou hast brought on me and on my kingdom a great sin? thou hast done deeds unto me that ought not to be done.

• Involved in sins of other individuals, as Achan.

Jos 7:11–26

Jos 7:1 — But the children of Israel committed a trespass in the accursed thing: for Achan, the son of Carmi, the son of Zabdi, the son of Zerah, of the tribe of Judah, took of the accursed thing: and the anger of the LORD was kindled against the children of Israel.

• Peace of.

Ps 89:15–18

Job 34:29 — When he giveth quietness, who then can make trouble? and when he hideth *his* face, who then can behold him? whether *it be done* against a nation, or against a man only:

Ps 33:12 — Blessed *is* the nation whose God *is* the LORD: *and* the people *whom* he hath chosen for his own inheritance.

• Promises of peace to.

Isa 14:4–7; 60:17–18; Eze 34:25–28; Mic 4:3–4; Zec 8:4–5

Le 26:6 — And I will give peace in the land, and ye shall lie down, and none shall make *you* afraid: and I will rid evil beasts out of the land, neither shall the sword go through your land.

1Ki 2:33 — Their blood shall therefore return upon the head of Joab, and upon the head of his seed for ever: but upon David, and upon his seed, and upon his house, and upon his throne, shall there be peace for ever from the LORD.

2Ki 20:19 — Then said Hezekiah unto Isaiah, Good is the word of the LORD which thou hast spoken. And he said, *Is it* not *good,* if peace and truth be in my days?

1Ch 22:9 — Behold, a son shall be born to thee, who shall be a man of rest; and I will give him rest from all his enemies round about: for his name shall be Solomon, and I will give peace and quietness unto Israel in his days.

Ps 29:11 — The LORD will give strength unto his people; the LORD will bless his people with peace.

Ps 46:9 — He maketh wars to cease unto the end of the earth; he breaketh the bow, and cutteth the spear in sunder; he burneth the chariot in the fire.

Ps 72:3 — The mountains shall bring peace to the people, and the little hills, by righteousness.

Ps 72:7 — In his days shall the righteous flourish; and abundance of peace so long as the moon endureth.

Ps 128:6 — Yea, thou shalt see thy children's children, *and* peace upon Israel.

Isa 2:4 — And he shall judge among the nations, and shall rebuke many people: and they shall beat their swords into plowshares, and their spears into pruninghooks: nation shall not lift up sword against nation, neither shall they learn war any more.

Isa 65:25 — The wolf and the lamb shall feed together, and the lion shall eat straw like the bullock: and dust *shall be* the serpent's meat. They shall not hurt nor destroy in all my holy mountain, saith the LORD.

Jer 30:10 — Therefore fear thou not, O my servant Jacob, saith the LORD; neither be dismayed, O Israel: for, lo, I will save thee from afar, and thy seed from the land of their captivity; and Jacob shall return, and shall be in rest, and be quiet, and none shall make *him* afraid.

Jer 50:34 — Their Redeemer *is* strong; the LORD of hosts *is* his name: he shall throughly plead their cause, that he may give rest to the land, and disquiet the inhabitants of Babylon.

Hos 2:18 — And in that day will I make a covenant for them with the beasts of the field, and with the fowls of heaven, and *with* the creeping things of the ground: and I will break the bow and the sword and the battle out of the earth, and will make them to lie down safely.

Zec 1:11 — And they answered the angel of the LORD that stood among the myrtle trees, and said, We have walked to and fro through the earth, and, behold, all the earth sitteth still, and is at rest.

Zec 3:10 — In that day, saith the LORD of hosts, shall ye call every man his neighbour under the vine and under the fig tree.

Zec 9:10 — And I will cut off the chariot from Ephraim, and the horse from Jerusalem, and the battle bow shall be cut off: and he shall speak peace unto the heathen: and his dominion *shall be* from sea *even* to sea, and from river *even* to the ends of the earth.

Zec 14:11 — And *men* shall dwell in it, and there shall be no more utter destruction; but Jerusalem shall be safely inhabited.

• Prayer for peace.

1Ti 2:1–2

Jer 29:7 — And seek the peace of the city whither I have caused you to be carried away captives, and pray unto the LORD for it: for in the peace thereof shall ye have peace.

• Peace given by God.

Ps 147:13–14

Jos 21:44 — And the LORD gave them rest round about, according to all that he sware unto their fathers: and there stood not a man of all their enemies before them; the LORD delivered all their enemies into their hand.

1Ch 22:18 — *Is* not the LORD your God with you? and hath he *not* given you rest on every side? for he hath given the inhabitants of the land into mine hand; and the land is subdued before the LORD, and before his people.

1Ch 23:25 — For David said, The LORD God of Israel hath given rest unto his people, that they may dwell in Jerusalem for ever:

Ecc 3:8 — A time to love, and a time to hate; a time of war, and a time of peace.

Isa 45:7 — I form the light, and create darkness: I make peace, and create evil: I the LORD do all these *things.*

- **Instances of national peace.**

Jos 14:15; Jgs 3:11, 30; 1Ki 4:24–25

See: War

- **Righteousness exalteth.**

Pr 14:34 — Righteousness exalteth a nation: but sin *is* a reproach to any people.

See: Government

See: King

See: Rulers

NATURAL RELIGION See: Religion; natural

NATURALIZATION

Ac 22:28 — And the chief captain answered, With a great sum obtained I this freedom. And Paul said, But I was *free* born.

Eph 2:12 — That at that time ye were without Christ, being aliens from the commonwealth of Israel, and strangers from the covenants of promise, having no hope, and without God in the world:

Eph 2:19 — Now therefore ye are no more strangers and foreigners, but fellowcitizens with the saints, and of the household of God;

NAUM • An ancestor of Jesus.

Lk 3:25 — Which was *the son* of Mattathias, which was *the son* of Amos, which was *the son* of Naum, which was *the son* of Esli, which was *the son* of Nagge,

NAVEL

- **Treatment of, at birth.**

Eze 16:4 — And *as for* thy nativity, in the day thou wast born thy navel was not cut, neither wast thou washed in water to supple *thee;* thou wast not salted at all, nor swaddled at all.

NAVIGATION

- **Sounding in.**

Ac 27:28 — And sounded, and found *it* twenty fathoms: and when they had gone a little further, they sounded again, and found *it* fifteen fathoms.

See: Commerce

See: Mariner

See: Navy

NAVY

- **Solomon's.**

1Ki 9:26 — And king Solomon made a navy of ships in Ezion-geber, which is beside Eloth, on the shore of the Red sea, in the land of Edom.

- **Hiram's.**

1Ki 10:11 — And the navy also of Hiram, that brought gold from Ophir, brought in from Ophir great plenty of almug trees, and precious stones.

- **Of Chittim.**

Da 11:30 — For the ships of Chittim shall come against him: therefore he shall be grieved, and return, and have indignation against the holy covenant: so shall he do; he shall even return, and have intelligence with them that forsake the holy covenant.

Da 11:40 — And at the time of the end shall the king of the south push at him: and the king of the north shall come against him like a whirlwind, with chariots, and with horsemen, and with many ships; and he shall enter into the countries, and shall overflow and pass over.

See: Commerce

See: Mariner

See: Navigation

NAZARENE See: Nazareth

NAZARETH

- **A village in Galilee.**
- **Joseph and Mary dwell at.**

Lk 1:26–27

Mt 2:23 — And he came and dwelt in a city called Nazareth: that it might be fulfilled which was spoken by the prophets, He shall be called a Nazarene.

Lk 1:56 — And Mary abode with her about three months, and returned to her own house.

Lk 2:4 — And Joseph also went up from Galilee, out of the city of Nazareth, into Judaea, unto the city of David, which is called Bethlehem; (because he was of the house and lineage of David:)

Lk 2:39 — And when they had performed all things according to the law of the Lord, they returned into Galilee, to their own city Nazareth.

Lk 2:51 — And he went down with them, and came to Nazareth, and was subject unto them: but his mother kept all these sayings in her heart.

- **Jesus from.**

Mt 21:11 — And the multitude said, This is Jesus the prophet of Nazareth of Galilee.

Mk 1:24 — Saying, Let *us* alone; what have we to do with thee, thou Jesus of Nazareth? art thou come to destroy us? I know thee who thou art, the Holy One of God.

Mk 10:47 — And when he heard that it was Jesus of Nazareth, he began to cry out, and say, Jesus, *thou* Son of David, have mercy on me.

Lk 4:34 — Saying, Let *us* alone; what have we to do with thee, *thou* Jesus of Nazareth? art thou come to destroy us? I know thee who thou art; the Holy One of God.

Lk 18:37 — And they told him, that Jesus of Nazareth passeth by.

Lk 24:19 — And he said unto them, What things? And they said unto him, Concerning Jesus of Nazareth, which was a prophet mighty in deed and word before God and all the people:

- **People of, reject Jesus.**

Lk 4:16–30

• Its name opprobrious.

Jn 1:46 — And Nathanael said unto him, Can there any good thing come out of Nazareth? Philip saith unto him, Come and see.

NAZARITE

• Law concerning.

Nu 6:1–21

Jgs 13:5 — For, lo, thou shalt conceive, and bear a son; and no razor shall come on his head: for the child shall be a Nazarite unto God from the womb: and he shall begin to deliver Israel out of the hand of the Philistines.

• Character of.

Am 2:11–12

La 4:7 — Her Nazarites were purer than snow, they were whiter than milk, they were more ruddy in body than rubies, their polishing *was* of sapphire:

• Instances of.

• Samson.

Jgs 13:5, 7; 16:17

• Samuel.

1Sa 1:11

• Rechabites.

Jer 35:1–19

• John the Baptist.

Mt 11:18; Lk 1:15; 7:33

NEAH • A city in Zebulun.

Jos 19:13 — And from thence passeth on along on the east to Gittah-hepher, to Ittah-kazin, and goeth out to Remmon-methoar to Neah;

NEAPOLIS

• A seaport of Macedonia.

• Paul visits.

Ac 16:11 — Therefore loosing from Troas, we came with a straight course to Samothracia, and the next day to Neapolis;

NEARIAH

• Son of Shemaiah.

1Ch 3:22–23

• A Simeonite captain.

1Ch 4:42 — And *some* of them, *even* of the sons of Simeon, five hundred men, went to mount Seir, having for their captains Pelatiah, and Neariah, and Rephaiah, and Uzziel, the sons of Ishi.

NEBAIOTH

• Called also Nebajoth.

• Son of Ishmael.

Ge 25:13 — And these *are* the names of the sons of Ishmael, by their names, according to their generations: the firstborn of Ishmael, Nebajoth; and Kedar, and Adbeel, and Mibsam,

Ge 28:9 — Then went Esau unto Ishmael, and took unto the wives which he had Mahalath the daughter of Ishmael Abraham's son, the sister of Nebajoth, to be his wife.

Ge 36:3 — And Bashemath Ishmael's daughter, sister of Nebajoth.

1Ch 1:29 — These *are* their generations: The firstborn of Ishmael, Nebaioth; then Kedar, and Adbeel, and Mibsam,

• Prophecies concerning.

Isa 60:7 — All the flocks of Kedar shall be gathered together unto thee, the rams of Nebaioth shall minister unto thee: they shall come up with acceptance on mine altar, and I will glorify the house of my glory.

NEBALLAT • A town occupied by the Benjamites after the captivity.

Ne 11:34 — Hadid, Zeboim, Neballat,

NEBAT • Father of Jeroboam.

1Ki 11:26 — And Jeroboam the son of Nebat, an Ephrathite of Zereda, Solomon's servant, whose mother's name *was* Zeruah, a widow woman, even he lifted up *his* hand against the king.

1Ki 12:2 — And it came to pass, when Jeroboam the son of Nebat, who was yet in Egypt, heard *of it,* (for he was fled from the presence of king Solomon, and Jeroboam dwelt in Egypt;)

NEBO

• A city allotted to Reuben.

Nu 32:3 — Ataroth, and Dibon, and Jazer, and Nimrah, and Heshbon, and Elealeh, and Shebam, and Nebo, and Beon,

Nu 32:38 — And Nebo, and Baal-meon, (their names being changed,) and Shibmah: and gave other names unto the cities which they builded.

1Ch 5:8 — And Bela the son of Azaz, the son of Shema, the son of Joel, who dwelt in Aroer, even unto Nebo and Baal-meon:

• Prophecies concerning.

Isa 15:2 — He is gone up to Bajith, and to Dibon, the high places, to weep: Moab shall howl over Nebo, and over Medeba: on all their heads *shall be* baldness, *and* every beard cut off.

Jer 48:1 — Against Moab thus saith the LORD of hosts, the God of Israel; Woe unto Nebo! for it is spoiled: Kiriathaim is confounded *and* taken: Misgab is confounded and dismayed.

Jer 48:22 — And upon Dibon, and upon Nebo, and upon Beth-diblathaim,

• A mountain range east of the Jordan.

• Moses views Canaan from.

Dt 32:49–50

• A mountain range east of the Jordan.

• Moses dies on.

Dt 34:1 — And Moses went up from the plains of Moab unto the mountain of Nebo, to the top of Pisgah, that *is* over against Jericho. And the LORD shewed him all the land of Gilead, unto Dan,

• A city in Judah.

Ezr 2:29 — The children of Nebo, fifty and two.

Ne 7:33 — The men of the other Nebo, fifty and two.

• The ancestor of certain Jews.

Ezr 10:43 — Of the sons of Nebo; Jeiel, Mattithiah, Zabad, Zebina, Jadau, and Joel, Benaiah.

• A Babylonian idol.

Isa 46:1 — Bel boweth down, Nebo stoopeth, their idols were upon the beasts, and upon the cattle: your carriages *were* heavy loaden; *they are* a burden to the weary *beast*.

NEBUCHADNEZZAR

• Called also Nebuchadrezzar.

• King of Babylon.

Jer 21:2 — Enquire, I pray thee, of the LORD for us; for Nebuchadrezzar king of Babylon maketh war against us; if so be that the LORD will deal with us according to all his wondrous works, that he may go up from us.

• Empire of.

***See: Babylon**

• His administration.

Da 1:1–4:37

• Conquests of.

• Of Jerusalem.

2Ki 24:1–25:30; 2Ch 36:5–21; Jer 39:1–18

1Ch 6:15 — And Jehozadak went *into captivity*, when the LORD carried away Judah and Jerusalem by the hand of Nebuchadnezzar.

Ezr 1:7 — Also Cyrus the king brought forth the vessels of the house of the LORD, which Nebuchadnezzar had brought forth out of Jerusalem, and had put them in the house of his gods;

• Of Egypt.

2Ki 24:7 — And the king of Egypt came not again any more out of his land: for the king of Babylon had taken from the river of Egypt unto the river Euphrates all that pertained to the king of Egypt.

Jer 46:2 — Against Egypt, against the army of Pharaoh-necho king of Egypt, which was by the river Euphrates in Carchemish, which Nebuchadrezzar king of Babylon smote in the fourth year of Jehoiakim the son of Josiah king of Judah.

• Of Tyre.

Eze 29:18 — Son of man, Nebuchadrezzar king of Babylon caused his army to serve a great service against Tyrus: every head *was* made bald, and every shoulder *was* peeled: yet had he no wages, nor his army, for Tyrus, for the service that he had served against it:

• An instrument of God's judgments.

Jer 27:8 — And it shall come to pass, *that* the nation and kingdom which will not serve the same Nebuchadnezzar the king of Babylon, and that will not put their neck under the yoke of the king of Babylon, that nation will I punish, saith the LORD, with the sword, and with the famine, and with the pestilence, until I have consumed them by his hand.

• Prophecies concerning.

Jer 27:6–9; 49:30–33; Eze 26:7–12

Jer 21:7 — And afterward, saith the LORD, I will deliver Zedekiah king of Judah, and his servants, and the people, and such as are left in this city from the pestilence, from the sword, and from the famine, into the hand of Nebuchadrezzar king of Babylon, and into the hand of their enemies, and into the hand of those that seek their life: and he shall smite them with the edge of the sword; he shall not spare them, neither have pity, nor have mercy.

Jer 21:10 — For I have set my face against this city for evil, and not for good, saith the LORD: it shall be given into the hand of the king of Babylon, and he shall burn it with fire.

Jer 22:25 — And I will give thee into the hand of them that seek thy life, and into the hand *of them* whose face thou fearest, even into the hand of Nebuchadrezzar king of Babylon, and into the hand of the Chaldeans.

Jer 25:9 — Behold, I will send and take all the families of the north, saith the LORD, and Nebuchadrezzar the king of Babylon, my servant, and will bring them against this land, and against the inhabitants thereof, and against all these nations round about, and will utterly destroy them, and make them an astonishment, and an hissing, and perpetual desolations.

Jer 32:28 — Therefore thus saith the LORD; Behold, I will give this city into the hand of the Chaldeans, and into the hand of Nebuchadrezzar king of Babylon, and he shall take it:

Jer 43:10 — And say unto them, Thus saith the LORD of hosts, the God of Israel; Behold, I will send and take Nebuchadrezzar the king of Babylon, my servant, and will set his throne upon these stones that I have hid; and he shall spread his royal pavilion over them.

Jer 46:13 — The word that the LORD spake to Jeremiah the prophet, how Nebuchadrezzar king of Babylon should come *and* smite the land of Egypt.

NEBUSHASBAN • A prince of Nebuchadnezzar.

Jer 39:13 — So Nebuzar-adan the captain of the guard sent, and Nebushasban, Rab-saris, and Nergal-sharezer, Rabmag, and all the king of Babylon's princes;

NEBUZAR-ADAN

• Captain of the guard of King Nebuchadnezzar

• Commands the Assyrian army which besieged Jerusalem and carried the inhabitants to Babylon.

2Ki 25:8–21; Jer 39:9–10; 52:12–30

Jer 43:6 — *Even* men, and women, and children, and the king's daughters, and every person that Nebuzar-adan the captain of the guard had left with Gedaliah the son of Ahikam the son of Shaphan, and Jeremiah the prophet, and Baruch the son of Neriah.

• Protects Jeremiah.

Jer 39:11–14; 40:1–5

NECHO • King of Egypt.

2Ch 35:20 — After all this, when Josiah had prepared the temple, Necho king of Egypt came up to fight against Charchemish by Euphrates: and Josiah went out against him.

2Ch 35:22 — Nevertheless Josiah would not turn his face from him, but disguised himself, that he might fight with him, and hearkened not unto the words of Necho from the mouth of God, and came to fight in the valley of Megiddo.

2Ch 36:4 — And the king of Egypt made Eliakim his brother king over Judah and Jerusalem, and turned his name to Jehoiakim. And Necho took Jehoahaz his brother, and carried him to Egypt.

NECKLACE

• King James Version, tablets.

Ex 35:22 — And they came, both men and women, as many as were willing hearted, *and* brought bracelets, and earrings, and rings, and tablets, all jewels of gold: and every man that offered *offered* an offering of gold unto the LORD.

Nu 31:50 — We have therefore brought an oblation for the LORD, what every man hath gotten, of jewels of gold, chains, and bracelets, rings, earrings, and tablets, to make an atonement for our souls before the LORD.

NECROMANCY

Dt 18:11 — Or a charmer, or a consulter with familiar spirits, or a wizard, or a necromancer.

Dt 26:14 — I have not eaten thereof in my mourning, neither have I taken away *ought* thereof for *any* unclean *use,* nor given *ought* thereof for the dead: *but* I have hearkened to the voice of the LORD my God, *and* have done according to all that thou hast commanded me.

Isa 8:19 — And when they shall say unto you, Seek unto them that have familiar spirits, and unto wizards that peep, and that mutter: should not a people seek unto their God? for the living to the dead?

Isa 29:4 — And thou shalt be brought down, *and* shalt speak out of the ground, and thy speech shall be low out of the dust, and thy voice shall be, as of one that hath a familiar spirit, out of the ground, and thy speech shall whisper out of the dust.

• Instances of.

• The witch of En-dor.

1Sa 28:7–19

⇜See: Familiar spirits

⇜See: Sorcery

⇜See: Witchcraft

NEDABIAH • Son of Jeconiah.

1Ch 3:18 — Malchiram also, and Pedaiah, and Shenazar, Jecamiah, Hoshama, and Nedabiah.

NEEDLE

Mt 19:24 — <u>And again I say unto you, It is easier for a camel to go through the eye of a needle, than for a rich man to enter into the kingdom of God.</u>

Mk 10:25 — <u>It is easier for a camel to go through the eye of a needle, than for a rich man to enter into the kingdom of God.</u>

Lk 18:25 — <u>For it is easier for a camel to go through a needle's eye, than for a rich man to enter into the kingdom of God.</u>

NEEDLEWORK ⇜See: Embroidery

NEEDS SUPPLIED

Mt 6:8 — <u>Be not ye therefore like unto them: for your Father knoweth what things ye have need of, before ye ask him.</u>

Heb 4:16 — Let us therefore come boldly unto the throne of grace, that we may obtain mercy, and find grace to help in time of need.

NEGINOTH ⇜See: Music

NEHEMIAH

• Son of Hachaliah.

Ne 1:1 — The words of Nehemiah the son of Hachaliah. And it came to pass in the month Chisleu, in the twentieth year, as I was in Shushan the palace,

• Cupbearer of Artaxerxes.

Ne 1:11–2:1

• Is grieved over the desolation of his country.

Ne 1:1–11

• Is sent by the king to rebuild Jerusalem.

Ne 2:1–8

• Register of the people whom he led from Babylon.

Ne 7:1–73

• Register of the priests and Levites.

Ne 12:1–22

• Rebuilds Jerusalem.

Ne 2:1–6:19

• His administration as ruler of the people.

Ne 5:1–6:19; 8:1–11:36; 13:1–31

• Two Jews who returned to Jerusalem from exile.

Ezr 2:2 — Which came with Zerubbabel: Jeshua, Nehemiah, Seraiah, Reelaiah, Mordecai, Bilshan, Mizpar, Bigvai, Rehum, Baanah. The number of the men of the people of Israel:

Ne 3:16 — After him repaired Nehemiah the son of Azbuk, the ruler of the half part of Beth-zur, unto *the place* over against the sepulchres of David, and to the pool that was made, and unto the house of the mighty.

Ne 7:7 — Who came with Zerubbabel, Jeshua, Nehemiah, Azariah, Raamiah, Nahamani, Mordecai, Bilshan, Mispereth, Bigvai, Nehum, Baanah. The number, *I say,* of the men of the people of Israel *was this;*

NEHILOTH ⇜See: Music

NEHUM • A chief exile.

Ne 7:7 — Who came with Zerubbabel, Jeshua, Nehemiah, Azariah, Raamiah, Nahamani, Mordecai, Bilshan, Mispereth, Bigvai, Nehum, Baanah. The number, *I say,* of the men of the people of Israel *was this;*

NEHUSHTA • Wife of Jehoiakim, king of Judah, and mother of Jehoiachin.

2Ki 24:6 — So Jehoiakim slept with his fathers: and Jehoiachin his son reigned in his stead.

2Ki 24:8 — Jehoiachin *was* eighteen years old when he began to reign, and he reigned in Jerusalem three months. And his mother's name *was* Nehushta, the daughter of Elnathan of Jerusalem.

NEHUSHTAN • The brazen serpent.

2Ki 18:4 — He removed the high places, and brake the images, and cut down the groves, and brake in pieces the brasen serpent that Moses had made: for unto those days the children of Israel did burn incense to it: and he called it Nehushtan.

NEIEL • A landmark on the boundary of Asher.

Jos 19:27 — And turneth toward the sunrising to Beth-dagon, and reacheth to Zebulun, and to the valley of Jiphthah-el toward the north side of Beth-emek, and Neiel, and goeth out to Cabul on the left hand,

NEIGHBOR

Ex 23:4–5; Le 6:2–5; 19:16–18; Dt 22:1–4; Ps 15:1–3; Pr 3:28–29; Isa 58:6–14; Zec 8:16–17; Mt 25:34–46; Lk 10:25–37; Ro 13:9–10; Jas 2:8–9

Ex 20:16 — Thou shalt not bear false witness against thy neighbour.

Le 19:13 — Thou shalt not defraud thy neighbour, neither rob *him:* the wages of him that is hired shall not abide with thee all night until the morning.

Jer 22:13 — Woe unto him that buildeth his house by unrighteousness, and his chambers by wrong; *that* useth his neighbour's service without wages, and giveth him not for his work;

Mt 7:12 — Therefore all things whatsoever ye would that men should do to you, do ye even so to them: for this is the law and the prophets.

Mt 19:19 — Honour thy father and *thy* mother: and, Thou shalt love thy neighbour as thyself.

Mt 22:39 — And the second *is* like unto it, Thou shalt love thy neighbour as thyself.

Mk 12:31 — And the second *is* like, *namely* this, Thou shalt love thy neighbour as thyself. There is none other commandment greater than these.

Ro 15:2 — Let every one of us please *his* neighbour for *his* good to edification.

Gal 5:14 — For all the law is fulfilled in one word, *even* in this; Thou shalt love thy neighbour as thyself.

Gal 6:10 — As we have therefore opportunity, let us do good unto all *men,* especially unto them who are of the household of faith.

Heb 13:3 — Remember them that are in bonds, as bound with them; *and* them which suffer adversity, as being yourselves also in the body.

See: Duty

See: Man

NEKEB • A city in Naphtali.

Jos 19:33 — And their coast was from Heleph, from Allon to Zaanannim, and Adami, Nekeb, and Jabneel, unto Lakum; and the outgoings thereof were at Jordan:

NEKODA • Name of two Jewish exiles.

Ezr 2:48 — The children of Rezin, the children of Nekoda, the children of Gazzam,

Ezr 2:60 — The children of Delaiah, the children of Tobiah, the children of Nekoda, six hundred fifty and two.

Ne 7:50 — The children of Reaiah, the children of Rezin, the children of Nekoda,

Ne 7:62 — The children of Delaiah, the children of Tobiah, the children of Nekoda, six hundred forty and two.

NEMUEL

• A Reubenite.

Nu 26:9 — And the sons of Eliab; Nemuel, and Dathan, and Abiram. This *is that* Dathan and Abiram, *which were* famous in the congregation, who strove against Moses and against Aaron in the company of Korah, when they strove against the LORD:

• A son of Simeon.

Nu 26:12 — The sons of Simeon after their families: of Nemuel, the family of the Nemuelites: of Jamin, the family of the Jaminites: of Jachin, the family of the Jachinites:

1Ch 4:24 — The sons of Simeon *were,* Nemuel, and Jamin, Jarib, Zerah, *and* Shaul:

NEOPHYTES

1Co 3:1–2

Mk 4:33 — And with many such parables spake he the word unto them, as they were able to hear *it.*

Jn 16:4 — But these things have I told you, that when the time shall come, ye may remember that I told you of them. And these things I said not unto you at the beginning, because I was with you.

Jn 16:12 — I have yet many things to say unto you, but ye cannot bear them now.

1Co 8:9 — But take heed lest by any means this liberty of yours become a stumblingblock to them that are weak.

NEPHEG

• Son of Izhar.

Ex 6:21 — And the sons of Izhar; Korah, and Nepheg, and Zichri.

• A son of David.

2Sa 5:15 — Ibhar also, and Elishua, and Nepheg, and Japhia,

1Ch 3:7 — And Nogah, and Nepheg, and Japhia,

1Ch 14:6 — And Nogah, and Nepheg, and Japhia,

NEPHISHESIM • A family of the Nephinim.

Ne 7:52 — The children of Besai, the children of Meunim, the children of Nephishesim,

NEPHTOAH • A stream between Judah and Benjamin.

Jos 15:9 — And the border was drawn from the top of the hill unto the fountain of the water of Nephtoah, and went out to the cities of mount Ephron; and the border was drawn to Baalah, which *is* Kirjath-jearim:

Jos 18:15 — And the south quarter *was* from the end of Kirjath-jearim, and the border went out on the west, and went out to the well of waters of Nephtoah:

NEPOTISM

• Of Joseph.

Ge 47:11–12

• Of Saul.

1Sa 14:50 — And the name of Saul's wife *was* Ahinoam, the daughter of Ahimaaz: and the name of the captain of his host *was* Abner, the son of Ner, Saul's uncle.

• Of David.

2Sa 8:16 — And Joab the son of Zeruiah *was* over the host; and Jehoshaphat the son of Ahilud *was* recorder;

2Sa 19:13 — And say ye to Amasa, *Art* thou not of my bone, and of my flesh? God do so to me, and more also, if thou be not captain of the host before me continually in the room of Joab.

• Of Nehemiah.

Ne 7:2 — That I gave my brother Hanani, and Hananiah the ruler of the palace, charge over Jerusalem: for he *was* a faithful man, and feared God above many.

NER

• Father of Abner.

1Sa 14:50 — And the name of Saul's wife *was* Ahinoam, the daughter of Ahimaaz: and the name of the captain of his host *was* Abner, the son of Ner, Saul's uncle.

• Father of Kish.

1Ch 8:33 — And Ner begat Kish, and Kish begat Saul, and Saul begat Jonathan, and Malchi-shua, and Abinadab, and Esh-baal.

1Ch 9:39 — And Ner begat Kish; and Kish begat Saul; and Saul begat Jonathan, and Malchi-shua, and Abinadab, and Esh-baal.

NEREUS • A Christian at Rome.

Ro 16:15 — Salute Philologus, and Julia, Nereus, and his sister, and Olympas, and all the saints which are with them.

NERGAL • An idol.

2Ki 17:30 — And the men of Babylon made Succoth-benoth, and the men of Cuth made Nergal, and the men of Hamath made Ashima,

NERGAL-SHAREZER • The name of princes of Babylon.

Jer 39:3 — And all the princes of the king of Babylon came in, and sat in the middle gate, *even* Nergal-sharezer, Samgar-nebo, Sarsechim, Rab-saris, Nergal-sharezer, Rabmag, with all the residue of the princes of the king of Babylon.

Jer 39:13 — So Nebuzar-adan the captain of the guard sent, and Nebushasban, Rab-saris, and Nergal-sharezer, Rabmag, and all the king of Babylon's princes;

NERI • An ancestor of Jesus.

Lk 3:27 — Which was *the son* of Joanna, which was *the son* of Rhesa, which was *the son* of Zorobabel, which was *the son* of Salathiel, which was *the son* of Neri,

NERIAH • Father of Baruch.

Jer 32:12 — And I gave the evidence of the purchase unto Baruch the son of Neriah, the son of Maaseiah, in the sight of Hanameel mine uncle's *son,* and in the presence of the witnesses that subscribed the book of the purchase, before all the Jews that sat in the court of the prison.

NEST

• Bird's in a rock.

Nu 24:21 — And he looked on the Kenites, and took up his parable, and said, Strong is thy dwellingplace, and thou puttest thy nest in a rock.

Mt 8:20 — And Jesus saith unto him, The foxes have holes, and the birds of the air *have* nests; but the Son of man hath not where to lay *his* head.

• Birds stir.

Dt 32:11 — As an eagle stirreth up her nest, fluttereth over her young, spreadeth abroad her wings, taketh them, beareth them on her wings:

NET

• Of checker work.

1Ki 7:17 — *And* nets of checker work, and wreaths of chain work, for the chapiters which *were* upon the top of the pillars; seven for the one chapiter, and seven for the other chapiter.

• Hidden in a pit.

Ps 35:7–8

• Set for birds.

Pr 1:17 — Surely in vain the net is spread in the sight of any bird.

• Set for wild animals.

Isa 51:20 — Thy sons have fainted, they lie at the head of all the streets, as a wild bull in a net: they are full of the fury of the LORD, the rebuke of thy God.

• Fish caught in.

Mt 4:18–21; Jn 21:6–11

Mt 13:47 — Again, the kingdom of heaven is like unto a net, that was cast into the sea, and gathered of every kind:

Lk 5:4 — Now when he had left speaking, he said unto Simon, Launch out into the deep, and let down your nets for a draught.

➔See: Snare

• Figurative.

Ps 35:7–8

Job 18:8 — For he is cast into a net by his own feet, and he walketh upon a snare.

Job 19:6 — Know now that God hath overthrown me, and hath compassed me with his net.

Ps 9:15 — The heathen are sunk down in the pit *that* they made: in the net which they hid is their own foot taken.

Ps 10:9 — He lieth in wait secretly as a lion in his den: he lieth in wait to catch the poor: he doth catch the poor, when he draweth him into his net.

Ps 25:15 — Mine eyes *are* ever toward the LORD; for he shall pluck my feet out of the net.

Ps 31:4 — Pull me out of the net that they have laid privily for me: for thou *art* my strength.

Ps 57:6 — They have prepared a net for my steps; my soul is bowed down: they have digged a pit before me, into the midst whereof they are fallen *themselves.* Selah.

Ps 66:11 — Thou broughtest us into the net; thou laidst affliction upon our loins.

Ps 140:5 — The proud have hid a snare for me, and cords; they have spread a net by the wayside; they have set gins for me. Selah.

Ps 141:10 — Let the wicked fall into their own nets, whilst that I withal escape.

Pr 12:12 — The wicked desireth the net of evil *men:* but the root of the righteous yieldeth *fruit.*

Pr 29:5 — A man that flattereth his neighbour spreadeth a net for his feet.

Ecc 7:26 — And I find more bitter than death the woman, whose heart *is* snares and nets, *and* her hands *as* bands: whoso pleaseth God shall escape from her; but the sinner shall be taken by her.

Ecc 9:12 — For man also knoweth not his time: as the fishes that are taken in an evil net, and as the birds that are caught in the snare; so *are* the sons of men snared in an evil time, when it falleth suddenly upon them.

Isa 19:8 — The fishers also shall mourn, and all they that cast angle into the brooks shall lament, and they that spread nets upon the waters shall languish.

Eze 26:5 — It shall be *a place for* the spreading of nets in the midst of the sea: for I have spoken *it,* saith the Lord GOD: and it shall become a spoil to the nations.

Eze 26:14 — And I will make thee like the top of a rock: thou shalt be *a place* to spread nets upon; thou shalt be built no more: for I the LORD have spoken *it,* saith the Lord GOD.

Eze 47:10 — And it shall come to pass, *that* the fishers shall stand upon it from En-gedi even unto En-eglaim; they shall be a *place* to spread forth nets; their fish shall be according to their kinds, as the fish of the great sea, exceeding many.

Hos 7:12 — When they shall go, I will spread my net upon them; I will bring them down as the fowls of the heaven; I will chastise them, as their congregation hath heard.

NETHANEEL

• The prince of Issachar.

• Numbers the tribe.

Nu 1:8 — Of Issachar; Nethaneel the son of Zuar.

• Captain of the host of Issachar.

Nu 2:5 — And those that do pitch next unto him *shall be* the tribe of Issachar: and Nethaneel the son of Zuar *shall be* captain of the children of Issachar.

Nu 10:15 — And over the host of the tribe of the children of Issachar *was* Nethaneel the son of Zuar.

• Liberality of, for the tabernacle.

Nu 7:18–23

• A priest and doorkeeper for the ark.

1Ch 15:24 — And Shebaniah, and Jehoshaphat, and Nethaneel, and Amasai, and Zechariah, and Benaiah, and Eliezer, the priests, did blow with the trumpets before the ark of God: and Obed-edom and Jehiah *were* doorkeepers for the ark.

• A Levite.

1Ch 24:6 — And Shemaiah the son of Nethaneel the scribe, *one* of the Levites, wrote them before the king, and the princes, and Zadok the priest, and Ahimelech the son of Abiathar, and *before* the chief of the fathers of the priests and Levites: one principal household being taken for Eleazar, and *one* taken for Ithamar.

• Son of Obed-edom, and porter of the temple.

1Ch 26:4 — Moreover the sons of Obed-edom *were,* Shemaiah the firstborn, Jehozabad the second, Joah the third, and Sacar the fourth, and Nethaneel the fifth,

• A prince sent by Jehoshaphat to teach the law in the cities of Judah.

2Ch 17:7 — Also in the third year of his reign he sent to his princes, *even* to Ben-hail, and to Obadiah, and to Zechariah, and to Nethaneel, and to Michaiah, to teach in the cities of Judah.

• A Levite.

2Ch 35:9 — Conaniah also, and Shemaiah and Nethaneel, his brethren, and Hashabiah and Jeiel and Jozabad, chief of the Levites, gave unto the Levites for passover offerings five thousand *small cattle,* and five hundred oxen.

• A priest who divorced his Gentile wife.

Ezr 10:22 — And of the sons of Pashur; Elioenai, Maaseiah, Ishmael, Nethaneel, Jozabad, and Elasah.

• A priest.

Ne 12:21 — Of Hilkiah, Hashabiah; of Jedaiah, Nethaneel.

• A Levite and musician.

Ne 12:36 — And his brethren, Shemaiah, and Azarael, Milalai, Gilalai, Maai, Nethaneel, and Judah, Hanani, with the musical instruments of David the man of God, and Ezra the scribe before them.

NETHANIAH

• Father of Ishmael.

Jer 40:14–15; 41:1–2, 6–7, 9–12

2Ki 25:23 — And when all the captains of the armies, they and their men, heard that the king of Babylon had made Gedaliah governor, there came to Gedaliah to Mizpah, even Ishmael the son of Nethaniah, and Johanan the son of Careah, and Seraiah the son of Tanhumeth the Netophathite, and Jaazaniah the son of a Maachathite, they and their men.

2Ki 25:25 — But it came to pass in the seventh month, that Ishmael the son of Nethaniah, the son of Elishama, of the seed royal, came, and ten men with him, and smote Gedaliah, that he died, and the Jews and the Chaldees that were with him at Mizpah.

Jer 40:8 — Then they came to Gedaliah to Mizpah, even Ishmael the son of Nethaniah, and Johanan and Jonathan the sons of Kareah, and Seraiah the son of Tanhumeth, and the sons of Ephai the Netophathite, and Jezaniah the son of a Maachathite, they and their men.

• A singer, and chief of the temple musicians.

1Ch 25:2 — Of the sons of Asaph; Zaccur, and Joseph, and Nethaniah, and Asarelah, the sons of Asaph under the hands of Asaph, which prophesied according to the order of the king.

1Ch 25:12 — The fifth to Nethaniah, *he,* his sons, and his brethren, *were* twelve:

• A Levite appointed by Jehoshaphat to accompany the princes who were to teach the law in Judah.

2Ch 17:8 — And with them *he sent* Levites, *even* Shemaiah, and Nethaniah, and Zebadiah, and Asahel, and Shemiramoth, and Jehonathan, and Adonijah, and Tobijah, and Tob-adonijah, Levites; and with them Elishama and Jehoram, priests.

• Father of Jehudi.

Jer 36:14 — Therefore all the princes sent Jehudi the son of Nethaniah, the son of Shelemiah, the son of Cushi, unto Baruch, saying, Take in thine hand the roll wherein thou hast read in the ears of the people, and come. So Baruch the son of Neriah took the roll in his hand, and came unto them.

NETHINIM

• Servants of the Levites.

Ezr 8:20 — Also of the Nethinims, whom David and the princes had appointed for the service of the Levites, two hundred and twenty Nethinims: all of them were expressed by name.

• Return from the captivity.

1Ch 9:2 — Now the first inhabitants that *dwelt* in their possessions in their cities *were,* the Israelites, the priests, Levites, and the Nethinims.

Ezr 2:43 — The Nethinims: the children of Ziha, the children of Hasupha, the children of Tabbaoth,

Ezr 2:58 — All the Nethinims, and the children of Solomon's servants, *were* three hundred ninety and two.

Ezr 2:70 — So the priests, and the Levites, and *some* of the people, and the singers, and the porters, and the Nethinims, dwelt in their cities, and all Israel in their cities.

Ezr 7:7 — And there went up *some* of the children of Israel, and of the priests, and the Levites, and the singers, and the porters, and the Nethinims, unto Jerusalem, in the seventh year of Artaxerxes the king.

Ezr 7:24 — Also we certify you, that touching any of the priests and Levites, singers, porters, Nethinims, or ministers of this house of God, it shall not be lawful to impose toll, tribute, or custom, upon them.

Ezr 8:17 — And I sent them with commandment unto Iddo the chief at the place Casiphia, and I told them what they should say unto Iddo, *and* to his brethren the Nethinims, at the place Casiphia, that they should bring unto us ministers for the house of our God.

Ne 3:26 — Moreover the Nethinims dwelt in Ophel, unto *the place* over against the water gate toward the east, and the tower that lieth out.

Ne 3:31 — After him repaired Malchiah the goldsmith's son unto the place of the Nethinims, and of the merchants, over against the gate Miphkad, and to the going up of the corner.

Ne 7:46 — The Nethinims: the children of Ziha, the children of Hashupha, the children of Tabbaoth,

Ne 7:60 — All the Nethinims, and the children of Solomon's servants, *were* three hundred ninety and two.

Ne 7:73 — So the priests, and the Levites, and the porters, and the singers, and *some* of the people, and the Nethinims, and all Israel, dwelt in their cities; and when the seventh month came, the children of Israel *were* in their cities.

Ne 10:28 — And the rest of the people, the priests, the Levites, the porters, the singers, the Nethinims, and all they that had separated themselves from the people of the lands unto the law of God, their wives, their sons, and their daughters, every one having knowledge, and having understanding;

Ne 11:3 — Now these *are* the chief of the province that dwelt in Jerusalem: but in the cities of Judah dwelt every one in his possession in their cities, *to wit,* Israel, the priests, and the Levites, and the Nethinims, and the children of Solomon's servants.

Ne 11:21 — But the Nethinims dwelt in Ophel: and Ziha and Gispa *were* over the Nethinims.

NETOPHAH • A city in Judah.

Ezr 2:22 — The men of Netophah, fifty and six.

Ne 7:26 — The men of Bethlehem and Netophah, an hundred fourscore and eight.

NETTLES

• An obnoxious plant.

Pr 24:31 — And, lo, it was all grown over with thorns, *and* nettles had covered the face thereof, and the stone wall thereof was broken down.

Isa 34:13 — And thorns shall come up in her palaces, nettles and brambles in the fortresses thereof: and it shall be an habitation of dragons, *and* a court for owls.

• Figurative.

Job 30:7 — Among the bushes they brayed; under the nettles they were gathered together.

Hos 9:6 — For, lo, they are gone because of destruction: Egypt shall gather them up, Memphis shall bury them: the pleasant *places* for their silver, nettles shall possess them: thorns *shall be* in their tabernacles.

Zep 2:9 — Therefore *as* I live, saith the LORD of hosts, the God of Israel, Surely Moab shall be as Sodom, and the children of Ammon as Gomorrah, *even* the breeding of nettles, and saltpits, and a perpetual desolation: the residue of my people shall spoil them, and the remnant of my people shall possess them.

NEW AGE

Dt 18:9–14; Jn 1:1–3

Jer 14:14 — Then the LORD said unto me, The prophets prophesy lies in my name: I sent them not, neither have I commanded them, neither spake unto them: they prophesy unto you a false vision and divination, and a thing of nought, and the deceit of their heart.

Lk 22:69 — Hereafter shall the Son of man sit on the right hand of the power of God.

Jn 10:30 — I and *my* Father are one.

Jn 14:9 — Jesus saith unto him, Have I been so long time with you, and yet hast thou not known me, Philip? he that hath seen me hath seen the Father; and how sayest thou *then,* Shew us the Father?

Heb 9:27 — And as it is appointed unto men once to die, but after this the judgment:

NEW CREATURE
See: Regeneration

NEW MOON

• Feast of.

Nu 28:11–15

Nu 10:10 — Also in the day of your gladness, and in your solemn days, and in the beginnings of your months, ye shall blow with the trumpets over your burnt offerings, and over the sacrifices of your peace offerings; that they may be to you for a memorial before your God: I *am* the LORD your God.

1Ch 23:31 — And to offer all burnt sacrifices unto the LORD in the sabbaths, in the new moons, and on the set feasts, by number, according to the order commanded unto them, continually before the LORD:

2Ch 31:3 — *He appointed* also the king's portion of his substance for the burnt offerings, *to wit,* for the morning and evening burnt offerings, and the burnt offerings for the sabbaths, and for the new moons, and for the set feasts, as *it is* written in the law of the LORD.

• Traffic at time of, suspended.

Am 8:5 — Saying, When will the new moon be gone, that we may sell corn? and the sabbath, that we may set forth wheat, making the ephah small, and the shekel great, and falsifying the balances by deceit?

NEZIAH • One of the Nethinim.

Ezr 2:54 — The children of Neziah, the children of Hatipha.

Ne 7:56 — The children of Neziah, the children of Hatipha.

NEZIB • A city in Judah.

Jos 15:43 — And Jiphtah, and Ashnah, and Nezib,

NIBHAZ • An idol.

2Ki 17:31 — And the Avites made Nibhaz and Tartak, and the Sepharvites burnt their children in fire to Adrammelech and Anammelech, the gods of Sepharvaim.

NIBSHAN • A city of Judah.

Jos 15:62 — And Nibshan, and the city of Salt, and En-gedi; six cities with their villages.

NICANOR • A deacon of the church at Jerusalem.

Ac 6:5 — And the saying pleased the whole multitude: and they chose Stephen, a man full of faith and of the Holy Ghost, and Philip, and Prochorus, and Nicanor, and Timon, and Parmenas, and Nicolas a proselyte of Antioch:

NICODEMUS

• A Jewish rabbi.

• Becomes a disciple of Jesus.

Jn 3:1–10; 7:50–53; 19:39–42

NICOLAITANES

Rev 2:6 — But this thou hast, that thou hatest the deeds of the Nicolaitanes, which I also hate.

Rev 2:15 — So hast thou also them that hold the doctrine of the Nicolaitanes, which thing I hate.

NICOLAS • A proselyte of Antioch, and deacon of the church at Jerusalem.

Ac 6:5–6

NICOPOLIS

• A city of Thrace.

• Paul lives in.

Tit 3:12 — When I shall send Artemas unto thee, or Tychicus, be diligent to come unto me to Nicopolis: for I have determined there to winter.

NIGER • Surname of Simeon.

Ac 13:1 — Now there were in the church that was at Antioch certain prophets and teachers; as Barnabas, and Simeon that was called Niger, and Lucius of Cyrene, and Manaen, which had been brought up with Herod the tetrarch, and Saul.

NIGHT

Ge 1:5 — And God called the light Day, and the darkness he called Night. And the evening and the morning were the first day.

Ge 1:16 — And God made two great lights; the greater light to rule the day, and the lesser light to rule the night: *he made* the stars also.

Ge 1:18 — And to rule over the day and over the night, and to divide the light from the darkness: and God saw that *it was* good.

• Meditations in.

Ps 19:2 — Day unto day uttereth speech, and night unto night sheweth knowledge.

Ps 77:6 — I call to remembrance my song in the night: I commune with mine own heart: and my spirit made diligent search.

Ps 119:148 — Mine eyes prevent the *night* watches, that I might meditate in thy word.

Ps 139:11 — If I say, Surely the darkness shall cover me; even the night shall be light about me.

• Worship in.

Ps 134:1 — Behold, bless ye the LORD, all *ye* servants of the LORD, which by night stand in the house of the LORD.

• Jesus prays all night.

Lk 6:12 — And it came to pass in those days, that he went out into a mountain to pray, and continued all night in prayer to God.

• No night in heaven.

Rev 21:25 — And the gates of it shall not be shut at all by day: for there shall be no night there.

Rev 22:5 — And there shall be no night there; and they need no candle, neither light of the sun; for the Lord God giveth them light: and they shall reign for ever and ever.

• Divided into watches.

Ex 14:24 — And it came to pass, that in the morning watch the LORD looked unto the host of the Egyptians through the pillar of fire and of the cloud, and troubled the host of the Egyptians,

Jgs 7:19 — So Gideon, and the hundred men that *were* with him, came unto the outside of the camp in the beginning of the middle watch; and they had but newly set the watch: and they blew the trumpets, and brake the pitchers that *were* in their hands.

1Sa 11:11 — And it was *so* on the morrow, that Saul put the people in three companies; and they came into the midst of the host in the morning watch, and slew the Ammonites until the heat of the day: and it came to pass, that they which remained were scattered, so that two of them were not left together.

Ne 12:9 — Also Bakbukiah and Unni, their brethren, *were* over against them in the watches.

Ps 63:6 — When I remember thee upon my bed, *and* meditate on thee in the *night* watches.

Ps 119:148 — Mine eyes prevent the *night* watches, that I might meditate in thy word.

La 2:19 — Arise, cry out in the night: in the beginning of the watches pour out thine heart like water before the face of the Lord: lift up thy hands toward him for the life of thy young children, that faint for hunger in the top of every street.

Mt 14:25 — And in the fourth watch of the night Jesus went unto them, walking on the sea.

Lk 12:38 — And if he shall come in the second watch, or come in the third watch, and find *them* so, blessed are those servants.

• Divided into hours.

Ac 23:23 — And he called unto *him* two centurions, saying, Make ready two hundred soldiers to go to Caesarea, and horsemen threescore and ten, and spearmen two hundred, at the third hour of the night;

• Used figuratively.

Isa 21:11–12

Isa 15:1 — The burden of Moab. Because in the night Ar of Moab is laid waste, *and* brought to silence; because in the night Kir of Moab is laid waste, *and* brought to silence;

Jn 9:4 — I must work the works of him that sent me, while it is day: the night cometh, when no man can work.

Ro 13:12 — The night is far spent, the day is at hand: let us therefore cast off the works of darkness, and let us put on the armour of light.

1Th 5:5 — Ye are all the children of light, and the children of the day: we are not of the night, nor of darkness.

NIGHT HAWK

• Forbidden as food.

Le 11:16 — And the owl, and the night hawk, and the cuckow, and the hawk after his kind,

Dt 14:15 — And the owl, and the night hawk, and the cuckow, and the hawk after his kind,

NILE

• Called the River.

Isa 19:5–10

Isa 11:15 — And the LORD shall utterly destroy the tongue of the Egyptian sea; and with his mighty wind shall he shake his hand over the river, and shall smite it in the seven streams, and make *men* go over dryshod.

Eze 29:4 — But I will put hooks in thy jaws, and I will cause the fish of thy rivers to stick unto thy scales, and I will bring thee up out of the midst of thy rivers, and all the fish of thy rivers shall stick unto thy scales.

Am 8:8 — Shall not the land tremble for this, and every one mourn that dwelleth therein? and it shall rise up wholly as a flood; and it shall be cast out and drowned, as *by* the flood of Egypt.

• Called Sihor.

Isa 23:3 — And by great waters the seed of Sihor, the harvest of the river, *is* her revenue; and she is a mart of nations.

Jer 2:18 — And now what hast thou to do in the way of Egypt, to drink the waters of Sihor? or what hast thou to do in the way of Assyria, to drink the waters of the river?

NIMRAH • A city in Gad.

Nu 32:3 — Ataroth, and Dibon, and Jazer, and Nimrah, and Heshbon, and Elealeh, and Shebam, and Nebo, and Beon,

NIMRIM • Waters on the borders of Gad and Moab.

Isa 15:6 — For the waters of Nimrim shall be desolate: for the hay is withered away, the grass faileth, there is no green thing.

Jer 48:34 — From the cry of Heshbon *even* unto Elealeh, *and even* unto Jahaz, have they uttered their voice, from Zoar *even* unto Horonaim, *as* an heifer of three years old: for the waters also of Nimrim shall be desolate.

NIMROD

• Son of Cush.

• "A mighty hunter before the Lord".

Ge 10:8–9

1Ch 1:10 — And Cush begat Nimrod: he began to be mighty upon the earth.

• Founder of Babylon.

⇜See: Babylon

NIMSHI • Father of Jehu.

2Ki 9:2 — And when thou comest thither, look out there Jehu the son of Jehoshaphat the son of Nimshi, and go in, and make him arise up from among his brethren, and carry him to an inner chamber;

2Ki 9:20 — And the watchman told, saying, He came even unto them, and cometh not again: and the driving is like the driving of Jehu the son of Nimshi; for he driveth furiously.

NINEVEH

• Capital of the Assyrian empire.

Ge 10:11–12

• Contained a population of upwards of one hundred and twenty thousand when Jonah preached.

Jnh 4:11 — And should not I spare Nineveh, that great city, wherein are more than sixscore thousand persons that cannot discern between their right hand and their left hand; and *also* much cattle?

• Extent of.

Jnh 3:4 — And Jonah began to enter into the city a day's journey, and he cried, and said, Yet forty days, and Nineveh shall be overthrown.

• Sennacherib in.

2Ki 19:36–37; Isa 37:37–38

• Jonah preaches to.

Jnh 1:1–2; 3:1–10

• Nahum prophesies against.

Na 1:1–3:19

• Zephaniah foretells the desolation of.

Zep 2:13–15

NISAN

• The first month in the Jewish calendar.

⇜See: Month

NISROCH • An idol.

2Ki 19:36–37; Isa 37:37–38

NITRE • A chemical.

Pr 25:20 — *As* he that taketh away a garment in cold weather, *and as* vinegar upon nitre, so *is* he that singeth songs to an heavy heart.

Jer 2:22 — For though thou wash thee with nitre, and take thee much sope, *yet* thine iniquity is marked before me, saith the Lord GOD.

NO • A city on the Nile.

Eze 30:14–16

Jer 46:25 — The LORD of hosts, the God of Israel, saith; Behold, I will punish the multitude of No, and Pharaoh, and Egypt, with their gods, and their kings; even Pharaoh, and *all* them that trust in him:

Na 3:8 — Art thou better than populous No, that was situate among the rivers, *that had* the waters round about it, whose rampart *was* the sea, *and* her wall *was* from the sea?

NOADIAH

• A Levite who assisted in weighing the silver, gold, and vessels of the temple brought back from Babylon.

Ezr 8:33 — Now on the fourth day was the silver and the gold and the vessels weighed in the house of our God by the hand of Meremoth the son of Uriah the priest; and with him *was* Eleazar the son of Phinehas; and with them *was* Jozabad the son of Jeshua, and Noadiah the son of Binnui, Levites;

• A false prophetess.

Ne 6:14 — My God, think thou upon Tobiah and Sanballat according to these their works, and on the prophetess Noadiah, and the rest of the prophets, that would have put me in fear.

NOAH

• Son of Lamech.

Ge 5:28–29

• Builds an ark and saves his family from the flood.

Ge 6:14–22

Ge 7:8 — Of clean beasts, and of beasts that *are* not clean, and of fowls, and of every thing that creepeth upon the earth,

Mt 24:38 — For as in the days that were before the flood they were eating and drinking, marrying and giving in marriage, until the day that Noe entered into the ark,

Lk 17:27 — They did eat, they drank, they married wives, they were given in marriage, until the day that Noe entered into the ark, and the flood came, and destroyed them all.

Heb 11:7 — By faith Noah, being warned of God of things not seen as yet, moved with fear, prepared an ark to the saving of his house; by the which he condemned the world, and became heir of the righteousness which is by faith.

1Pe 3:20 — Which sometime were disobedient, when once the longsuffering of God waited in the days of Noah, while the ark was a preparing, wherein few, that is, eight souls were saved by water.

• Builds an altar and offers sacrifices.

Ge 8:20–21

• Receives the covenant from God that no flood should again visit the earth; rainbow instituted as a token of the covenant.

Ge 9:9–17

Ge 8:20 — And Noah builded an altar unto the LORD; and took of every clean beast, and of every clean fowl, and offered burnt offerings on the altar.

Ge 8:22 — While the earth remaineth, seedtime and harvest, and cold and heat, and summer and winter, and day and night shall not cease.

• Intoxication of, and his curse upon Canaan.

Ge 9:20–27

• His blessing upon Shem and Japheth.

Ge 9:26–27

• Dies at the age of nine hundred and fifty years.

Ge 9:28–29

• A daughter of Zelophehad.

• Special legislation in regard to the inheritance of.

Nu 27:1–7; 36:1–13; Jos 17:3–7

Nu 26:33 — And Zelophehad the son of Hepher had no sons, but daughters: and the names of the daughters of Zelophehad *were* Mahlah, and Noah, Hoglah, Milcah, and Tirzah.

NOB

• A city of Benjamin.

Ne 11:31–32

• Called "the city of the priests".

1Sa 22:19 — And Nob, the city of the priests, smote he with the edge of the sword, both men and women, children and sucklings, and oxen, and asses, and sheep, with the edge of the sword.

• Abode of Ahimelech, the priest.

1Sa 21:1 — Then came David to Nob to Ahimelech the priest: and Ahimelech was afraid at the meeting of David, and said unto him, Why *art* thou alone, and no man with thee?

1Sa 22:11 — Then the king sent to call Ahimelech the priest, the son of Ahitub, and all his father's house, the priests that *were* in Nob: and they came all of them to the king.

• Probable seat of the tabernacle in Saul's time.

1Sa 21:4 — And the priest answered David, and said, *There is* no common bread under mine hand, but there is hallowed bread; if the young men have kept themselves at least from women.

1Sa 21:6 — So the priest gave him hallowed *bread:* for there was no bread there but the shewbread, that was taken from before the LORD, to put hot bread in the day when it was taken away.

1Sa 21:9 — And the priest said, The sword of Goliath the Philistine, whom thou slewest in the valley of Elah, behold, it *is here* wrapped in a cloth behind the ephod: if thou wilt take that, take *it:* for *there is* no other save that here. And David said, *There is* none like that; give it me.

• David flees to, and is aided by Ahimelech.

1Sa 21:1–9; 22:9–10

• Destroyed by Saul.

2Sa 22:9 — There went up a smoke out of his nostrils, and fire out of his mouth devoured: coals were kindled by it.

• Prophecy concerning.

Isa 10:32 — As yet shall he remain at Nob that day: he shall shake his hand *against* the mount of the daughter of Zion, the hill of Jerusalem.

NOBAH • An Israelite.

Nu 32:42 — And Nobah went and took Kenath, and the villages thereof, and called it Nobah, after his own name.

NOBLEMAN

Jn 4:46–53

NOD

• Cain dwelt in.

Ge 4:16 — And Cain went out from the presence of the LORD, and dwelt in the land of Nod, on the east of Eden.

NOGAH • Son of David.

1Ch 3:7 — And Nogah, and Nepheg, and Japhia,

1Ch 14:6 — And Nogah, and Nepheg, and Japhia,

NOHAH • Son of Benjamin.

1Ch 8:2 — Nohah the fourth, and Rapha the fifth.

NOLLE PROSEQUI

• Of the complaint against Paul.

Ac 18:12–17

NONCONFORMITY

See: Church and State

See: Form

See: Form; formalism

NOPH

• A city of Egypt.

Jer 2:16 — Also the children of Noph and Tahapanes have broken the crown of thy head.

• Prophecy against Jews in.

Jer 44:1–30

• Prophecies against.

Jer 46:13–19; Eze 30:13–16

Isa 19:13 — The princes of Zoan are become fools, the princes of Noph are deceived; they have also seduced Egypt, *even they that are* the stay of the tribes thereof.

NOPHAH • A city of Sihon.

Nu 21:30 — We have shot at them; Heshbon is perished even unto Dibon, and we have laid them waste even unto Nophah, which *reacheth* unto Medeba.

NOSE

• Jewels for.

Pr 11:22 — *As* a jewel of gold in a swine's snout, *so is* a fair woman which is without discretion.

Isa 3:21 — The rings, and nose jewels,

Eze 16:12 — And I put a jewel on thy forehead, and earrings in thine ears, and a beautiful crown upon thine head.

• Mutilated.

Eze 23:25 — And I will set my jealousy against thee, and they shall deal furiously with thee: they shall take away thy nose and thine ears; and thy remnant shall fall by the sword: they shall take thy sons and thy daughters; and thy residue shall be devoured by the fire.

NURSE

Ge 24:59 — And they sent away Rebekah their sister, and her nurse, and Abraham's servant, and his men.

Ge 35:8 — But Deborah Rebekah's nurse died, and she was buried beneath Bethel under an oak: and the name of it was called Allon-bachuth.

Ex 2:7 — Then said his sister to Pharaoh's daughter, Shall I go and call to thee a nurse of the Hebrew women, that she may nurse the child for thee?

Ru 4:16 — And Naomi took the child, and laid it in her bosom, and became nurse unto it.

2Ki 11:2 — But Jehosheba, the daughter of king Joram, sister of Ahaziah, took Joash the son of Ahaziah and stole him from among the king's sons *which were* slain; and they hid him, *even* him and his nurse, in the bedchamber from Athaliah, so that he was not slain.

Isa 60:4 — Lift up thine eyes round about, and see: all they gather themselves together, they come to thee: thy sons shall come from far, and thy daughters shall be nursed at *thy* side.

1Th 2:7 — But we were gentle among you, even as a nurse cherisheth her children:

• Careless.

2Sa 4:4 — And Jonathan, Saul's son, had a son *that was* lame of *his* feet. He was five years old when the tidings came of Saul and Jonathan out of Jezreel, and his nurse took him up, and fled: and it came to pass, as she made haste to flee, that he fell, and became lame. And his name *was* Mephibosheth.

NUT

Ge 43:11 — And their father Israel said unto them, If *it must be* so now, do this; take of the best fruits in the land in your vessels, and carry down the man a present, a little balm, and a little honey, spices, and myrrh, nuts, and almonds:

SS 6:11 — I went down into the garden of nuts to see the fruits of the valley, *and* to see whether the vine flourished, *and* the pomegranates budded.

NUTRITION

Ps 51:1–13; Heb 5:12–13

Isa 50:4 — The Lord GOD hath given me the tongue of the learned, that I should know how to speak a word in season to *him that is* weary: he wakeneth morning by morning, he wakeneth mine ear to hear as the learned.

1Pe 2:2 — As newborn babes, desire the sincere milk of the word, that ye may grow thereby:

NYMPHAS

• A Christian of Laodicea.

• House of, used as a place of worship.

Col 4:15 — Salute the brethren which are in Laodicea, and Nymphas, and the church which is in his house.

O

OAK

• A tree.

• Grew in Palestine.

Ge 35:4 — And they gave unto Jacob all the strange gods which *were* in their hand, and *all their* earrings which *were* in their ears; and Jacob hid them under the oak which *was* by Shechem.

• Absalom hung in the boughs of.

2Sa 18:9 — And Absalom met the servants of David. And Absalom rode upon a mule, and the mule went under the thick boughs of a great oak, and his head caught hold of the oak, and he was taken up between the heaven and the earth; and the mule that *was* under him went away.

2Sa 18:14 — Then said Joab, I may not tarry thus with thee. And he took three darts in his hand, and thrust them through the heart of Absalom, while he *was* yet alive in the midst of the oak.

• Deborah buried under.

Ge 35:8 — But Deborah Rebekah's nurse died, and she was buried beneath Bethel under an oak: and the name of it was called Allon-bachuth.

• Oars made of.

Eze 27:6 — *Of* the oaks of Bashan have they made thine oars; the company of the Ashurites have made thy benches *of* ivory, *brought* out of the isles of Chittim.

• Figurative.

Am 2:9 — Yet destroyed I the Amorite before them, whose height *was* like the height of the cedars, and he *was* strong as the oaks; yet I destroyed his fruit from above, and his roots from beneath.

OAR

Isa 33:21 — But there the glorious LORD *will be* unto us a place of broad rivers *and* streams; wherein shall go no galley with oars, neither shall gallant ship pass thereby.

Eze 27:6 — *Of* the oaks of Bashan have they made thine oars; the company of the Ashurites have made thy benches *of* ivory, *brought* out of the isles of Chittim.

Eze 27:29 — And all that handle the oar, the mariners, *and* all the pilots of the sea, shall come down from their ships, they shall stand upon the land;

OATH

• A solemn qualification.

• Used in solemnizing covenants.

• Between Abraham and the king of Sodom.

Ge 14:22–23

• Between Abraham and Abimelech.

Ge 21:22–23

• Between Isaac and Abimelech.

Ge 26:26–29

Ge 26:31 — And they rose up betimes in the morning, and sware one to another: and Isaac sent them away, and they departed from him in peace.

• Abraham requires oath of his servant Eliezer.

Ge 24:2–3

Ge 24:9 — And the servant put his hand under the thigh of Abraham his master, and sware to him concerning that matter.

• Esau confirms the sale of his birthright by.

Ge 25:33 — And Jacob said, Swear to me this day; and he sware unto him: and he sold his birthright unto Jacob.

• Jacob confirms the covenant between him and Laban by.

Ge 31:53 — The God of Abraham, and the God of Nahor, the God of their father, judge betwixt us. And Jacob sware by the fear of his father Isaac.

• Jacob requires Joseph to swear that he would bury him with his fathers.

Ge 47:28–31

• Joseph requires a like oath.

Ge 50:25 — And Joseph took an oath of the children of Israel, saying, God will surely visit you, and ye shall carry up my bones from hence.

• Rahab requires an oath from the spies.

Jos 2:12–14

Jos 6:22 — But Joshua had said unto the two men that had spied out the country, Go into the harlot's house, and bring out thence the woman, and all that she hath, as ye sware unto her.

• The Israelites confirm the covenant with the Hivites.

Jos 9:3–20

• Moses covenants with Caleb by.

Jos 14:9 — And Moses sware on that day, saying, Surely the land whereon thy feet have trodden shall be thine inheritance, and thy children's for ever, because thou hast wholly followed the LORD my God.

• The elders of Gilead confirm their pledge to Jephthah by.

Jgs 11:10 — And the elders of Gilead said unto Jephthah, The LORD be witness between us, if we do not so according to thy words.

• The Israelites swear in Mizpeh.

Jgs 21:5 — And the children of Israel said, Who *is there* among all the tribes of Israel that came not up with the congregation unto the LORD? For they had made a great oath concerning him that came not up to the LORD to Mizpeh, saying, He shall surely be put to death.

• Ruth swears to Naomi.

Ru 1:17 — Where thou diest, will I die, and there will I be buried: the LORD do so to me, and more also, *if ought* but death part thee and me.

• Boaz swears to Ruth.

Ru 3:13 — Tarry this night, and it shall be in the morning, *that* if he will perform unto thee the part of a kinsman, well; let him do the kinsman's part: but if he will not do the part of a kinsman to thee, then will I do the part of a kinsman to thee, *as* the LORD liveth: lie down until the morning.

• Saul swears to Jonathan.

1Sa 19:6 — And Saul hearkened unto the voice of Jonathan: and Saul sware, *As* the LORD liveth, he shall not be slain.

• Jonathan and David confirm a covenant by.

1Sa 20:13–17

1Sa 20:3 — And David sware moreover, and said, Thy father certainly knoweth that I have found grace in thine eyes; and he saith, Let not Jonathan know this, lest he be grieved: but truly *as* the LORD liveth, and *as* thy soul liveth, *there is* but a step between me and death.

• David swears to Saul.

1Sa 24:21–22

2Sa 21:7 — But the king spared Mephibosheth, the son of Jonathan the son of Saul, because of the LORD'S oath that *was* between them, between David and Jonathan the son of Saul.

• Saul swears to the witch of En-dor.

1Sa 28:10 — And Saul sware to her by the LORD, saying, *As* the LORD liveth, there shall no punishment happen to thee for this thing.

• David swears not to eat until the sun goes down.

2Sa 3:35 — And when all the people came to cause David to eat meat while it was yet day, David sware, saying, So do God to me, and more also, if I taste bread, or ought else, till the sun be down.

• Joab confirms his word by.

2Sa 19:7 — Now therefore arise, go forth, and speak comfortably unto thy servants: for I swear by the LORD, if thou go not forth, there will not tarry one with thee this night: and that will be worse unto thee than all the evil that befell thee from thy youth until now.

• David swears to Bath-sheba that Solomon shall be king.

1Ki 1:28–29

• Solomon confirms his word by.

1Ki 2:23 — Then king Solomon sware by the LORD, saying, God do so to me, and more also, if Adonijah have not spoken this word against his own life.

• Shimei confirms his word by.

1Ki 2:42 — And the king sent and called for Shimei, and said unto him, Did I not make thee to swear by the LORD, and protested unto thee, saying, Know for a certain, on the day thou goest out, and walkest abroad any whither, that thou shalt surely die? and thou saidst unto me, The word *that* I have heard *is* good.

• Elisha seals his vow to follow Elijah by.

2Ki 2:2 — And Elijah said unto Elisha, Tarry here, I pray thee; for the LORD hath sent me to Bethel. And Elisha said *unto him, As* the LORD liveth, and as thy soul liveth, I will not leave thee. So they went down to Bethel.

• King of Samaria confirms his word with an.

2Ki 6:31 — Then he said, God do so and more also to me, if the head of Elisha the son of Shaphat shall stand on him this day.

• Gehazi confirms his lie by.

2Ki 5:20 — But Gehazi, the servant of Elisha the man of God, said, Behold, my master hath spared Naaman this Syrian, in not receiving at his hands that which he brought: but, *as* the LORD liveth, I will run after him, and take somewhat of him.

• Jehoida requires an oath from the rulers.

2Ki 11:4 — And the seventh year Jehoiada sent and fetched the rulers over hundreds, with the captains and the guard, and brought them to him into the house of the LORD, and made a covenant with them, and took an oath of them in the house of the LORD, and shewed them the king's son.

• Zedekiah violates.

2Ch 36:13 — And he also rebelled against king Nebuchadnezzar, who had made him swear by God: but he stiffened his neck, and hardened his heart from turning unto the LORD God of Israel.

• Ezra requires, of the priests and Levites.

Ezr 10:5 — Then arose Ezra, and made the chief priests, the Levites, and all Israel, to swear that they should do according to this word. And they sware.

Ezr 10:19 — And they gave their hands that they would put away their wives; and *being* guilty, *they offered* a ram of the flock for their trespass.

• Nehemiah requires, of the priests and Levites.

Ne 5:12–13

• Zedekiah swears to Jeremiah.

Jer 38:16 — So Zedekiah the king sware secretly unto Jeremiah, saying, *As* the LORD liveth, that made us this soul, I will not put thee to death, neither will I give thee into the hand of these men that seek thy life.

• Gedaliah confirms his word by.

Jer 40:9 — And Gedaliah the son of Ahikam the son of Shaphan sware unto them and to their men, saying, Fear not to serve the Chaldeans: dwell in the land, and serve the king of Babylon, and it shall be well with you.

• Peter confirms his denial of Jesus by.

Mk 14:71 — But he began to curse and to swear, *saying,* I know not this man of whom ye speak.

• Attributed to God.

Heb 6:13–14

Ge 22:16 — And said, By myself have I sworn, saith the LORD, for because thou hast done this thing, and hast not withheld thy son, thine only *son:*

Ps 89:35 — Once have I sworn by my holiness that I will not lie unto David.

Ps 95:11 — Unto whom I sware in my wrath that they should not enter into my rest.

Ps 105:9 — Which *covenant* he made with Abraham, and his oath unto Isaac;

Ps 132:11 — The LORD hath sworn *in* truth unto David; he will not turn from it; Of the fruit of thy body will I set upon thy throne.

Isa 14:24 — The LORD of hosts hath sworn, saying, Surely as I have thought, so shall it come to pass; and as I have purposed, *so* shall it stand:

Isa 45:23 — I have sworn by myself, the word is gone out of my mouth *in* righteousness, and shall not return, That unto me every knee shall bow, every tongue shall swear.

Jer 11:5 — That I may perform the oath which I have sworn unto your fathers, to give them a land flowing with milk and honey, as *it is* this day. Then answered I, and said, So be it, O LORD.

Jer 22:5 — But if ye will not hear these words, I swear by myself, saith the LORD, that this house shall become a desolation.

Jer 49:13 — For I have sworn by myself, saith the LORD, that Bozrah shall become a desolation, a reproach, a waste, and a curse; and all the cities thereof shall be perpetual wastes.

Jer 51:14 — The LORD of hosts hath sworn by himself, *saying,* Surely I will fill thee with men, as with caterpillers; and they shall lift up a shout against thee.

Lk 1:73 — The oath which he sware to our father Abraham,

Heb 3:11 — So I sware in my wrath, They shall not enter into my rest.)

Heb 3:18 — And to whom sware he that they should not enter into his rest, but to them that believed not?

Heb 4:3 — For we which have believed do enter into rest, as he said, As I have sworn in my wrath, if they shall enter into my rest: although the works were finished from the foundation of the world.

Heb 6:17 — Wherein God, willing more abundantly to shew unto the heirs of promise the immutability of his counsel, confirmed *it* by an oath:

Heb 7:21 — (For those priests were made without an oath; but this with an oath by him that said unto him, The Lord sware and will not repent, Thou *art* a priest for ever after the order of Melchisedec:)

Heb 7:28 — For the law maketh men high priests which have infirmity; but the word of the oath, which was since the law, *maketh* the Son, who is consecrated for evermore.

Rev 10:6 — And sware by him that liveth for ever and ever, who created heaven, and the things that therein are, and the earth, and the things that therein are, and the sea, and the things which are therein, that there should be time no longer:

• Unclassified scripture relating to.

Ex 22:10–11; Le 6:2–5; Nu 5:19–24; 1Ki 8:31–32; Ps 15:1–2; Jer 7:8–9; Mt 5:33–37; 14:3–12; 23:18–22; Ac 23:12–14; Rev 10:5–6

Ex 20:7 — Thou shalt not take the name of the LORD thy God in vain; for the LORD will not hold him guiltless that taketh his name in vain.

Ex 23:1 — Thou shalt not raise a false report: put not thine hand with the wicked to be an unrighteous witness.

Le 19:12 — And ye shall not swear by my name falsely, neither shalt thou profane the name of thy God: I *am* the LORD.

Dt 5:11 — Thou shalt not take the name of the LORD thy God in vain: for the LORD will not hold *him* guiltless that taketh his name in vain.

Dt 6:13 — Thou shalt fear the LORD thy God, and serve him, and shalt swear by his name.

Ps 15:4 — In whose eyes a vile person is contemned; but he honoureth them that fear the LORD. *He that* sweareth to *his own* hurt, and changeth not.

Ecc 8:2 — I *counsel thee* to keep the king's commandment, and *that* in regard of the oath of God.

Isa 48:1 — Hear ye this, O house of Jacob, which are called by the name of Israel, and are come forth out of the waters of Judah, which swear by the name of the LORD, and make mention of the God of Israel, *but* not in truth, nor in righteousness.

Jer 4:2 — And thou shalt swear, The LORD liveth, in truth, in judgment, and in righteousness; and the nations shall bless themselves in him, and in him shall they glory.

Jer 5:2 — And though they say, The LORD liveth; surely they swear falsely.

Jer 5:7 — How shall I pardon thee for this? thy children have forsaken me, and sworn by *them that are* no gods: when I had fed them to the full, they then committed adultery, and assembled themselves by troops in the harlots' houses.

Jer 12:16 — And it shall come to pass, if they will diligently learn the ways of my people, to swear by my name, The LORD liveth; as they taught my people to swear by Baal; then shall they be built in the midst of my people.

Da 9:11 — Yea, all Israel have transgressed thy law, even by departing, that they might not obey thy voice; therefore the curse is poured upon us, and the oath that *is* written in the law of Moses the servant of God, because we have sinned against him.

Da 12:7 — And I heard the man clothed in linen, which *was* upon the waters of the river, when he held up his right hand and his left hand unto heaven, and sware by him that liveth for ever that *it shall be* for a time, times, and an half; and when he shall have accomplished to scatter the power of the holy people, all these *things* shall be finished.

Hos 4:15 — Though thou, Israel, play the harlot, *yet* let not Judah offend; and come not ye unto Gilgal, neither go ye up to Beth-aven, nor swear, The LORD liveth.

Mt 26:63 — But Jesus held his peace. And the high priest answered and said unto him, I adjure thee by the living God, that thou tell us whether thou be the Christ, the Son of God.

Mk 6:26 — And the king was exceeding sorry; *yet* for his oath's sake, and for their sakes which sat with him, he would not reject her.

2Co 1:23 — Moreover I call God for a record upon my soul, that to spare you I came not as yet unto Corinth.

Gal 1:20 — Now the things which I write unto you, behold, before God, I lie not.

Heb 6:16 — For men verily swear by the greater: and an oath for confirmation *is* to them an end of all strife.

Jas 5:12 — But above all things, my brethren, swear not, neither by heaven, neither by the earth, neither by any other oath: but let your yea be yea; and *your* nay, nay; lest ye fall into condemnation.

See: Covenant

See: Falsehood, False Witness

See: God; name of; profaned

See: Perjury

OBADIAH

• The governor of Ahab's house.

• Conceals in a cave one hundred prophets persecuted by Jezebel.

1Ki 18:3–4

• Meets Elijah and receives a commission from him.

1Ki 18:3–16

• Head of a family.

1Ch 3:21 — And the sons of Hananiah; Pelatiah, and Jesaiah: the sons of Rephaiah, the sons of Arnan, the sons of Obadiah, the sons of Shechaniah.

• A descendant of Tola.

1Ch 7:3 — And the sons of Uzzi; Izrahiah: and the sons of Izrahiah; Michael, and Obadiah, and Joel, Ishiah, five: all of them chief men.

• Son of Azel.

1Ch 8:38 — And Azel had six sons, whose names *are* these, Azrikam, Bocheru, and Ishmael, and Sheariah, and Obadiah, and Hanan. All these *were* the sons of Azel.

1Ch 9:44 — And Azel had six sons, whose names *are* these, Azrikam, Bocheru, and Ishmael, and Sheariah, and Obadiah, and Hanan: these *were* the sons of Azel.

• A Levite.

1Ch 9:16 — And Obadiah the son of Shemaiah, the son of Galal, the son of Jeduthun, and Berechiah the son of Asa, the son of Elkanah, that dwelt in the villages of the Netophathites.

• A Gadite warrior who joined David at Ziklag.

1Ch 12:9 — Ezer the first, Obadiah the second, Eliab the third,

• Father of Ishmaiah.

1Ch 27:19 — Of Zebulun, Ishmaiah the son of Obadiah: of Naphtali, Jerimoth the son of Azriel:

• A prince of Judah who instructed the people in the law.

2Ch 17:7–9

• A Levite.

• One of the overseers in the repairing of the temple by Josiah.

2Ch 34:12 — And the men did the work faithfully: and the overseers of them *were* Jahath and Obadiah, the Levites, of the sons of Merari; and Zechariah and Meshullam, of the sons of the Kohathites, to set *it* forward; and *other of* the Levites, all that could skill of instruments of musick.

• A descendant of Joab who returned from Babylon.

Ezr 8:9 — Of the sons of Joab; Obadiah the son of Jehiel, and with him two hundred and eighteen males.

• A priest who sealed with Nehemiah a covenant to observe God's law.

Ne 10:5 — Harim, Meremoth, Obadiah,

• A gatekeeper of Jerusalem, under Nehemiah.

Ne 12:25 — Mattaniah, and Bakbukiah, Obadiah, Meshullam, Talmon, Akkub, *were* porters keeping the ward at the thresholds of the gates.

• A prophet who prophesied the destruction of Edom.

Ob 1:1–21

OBAL

• Called also Ebal.

• A son of Joktan.

Ge 10:28 — And Obal, and Abimael, and Sheba,

1Ch 1:22 — And Ebal, and Abimael, and Sheba,

OBDURACY

2Ch 36:15–16; Ps 95:8–11; Pr 1:24–31; Rev 9:20–21

Pr 29:1 — He, that being often reproved hardeneth *his* neck, shall suddenly be destroyed, and that without remedy.

Heb 3:8 — Harden not your hearts, as in the provocation, in the day of temptation in the wilderness:

Heb 3:15 — While it is said, To day if ye will hear his voice, harden not your hearts, as in the provocation.

Heb 4:7 — Again, he limiteth a certain day, saying in David, To day, after so long a time; as it is said, To day if ye will hear his voice, harden not your hearts.

See: Afflictions; obduracy in

See: Impenitence

See: Reprobacy

• Instances of.

• The antediluvians.

Ge 6:3, 5, 7

• **Sodomites.**
Ge 19:9, 14

• **Pharaoh.**
Ex 7:14, 22–23; 8:15, 19, 32; 9:7, 12, 35; 10:20, 28

• **Israelites.**
Nu 14:22

• **Sons of Eli.**
1Sa 2:22–25

OBED

• **Son of Boaz and grandfather of David.**
Ru 4:17–22
1Ch 2:12 — And Boaz begat Obed, and Obed begat Jesse,
Mt 1:5 — And Salmon begat Booz of Rachab; and Booz begat Obed of Ruth; and Obed begat Jesse;
Lk 3:32 — Which was *the son* of Jesse, which was *the son* of Obed, which was *the son* of Booz, which was *the son* of Salmon, which was *the son* of Naasson,

• **Son of Ephlal and grandson of Zabad.**
1Ch 2:37–38

• **One of David's heroes.**
1Ch 11:47 — Eliel, and Obed, and Jasiel the Mesobaite.

• **Son of Shemaiah. A gatekeeper of the temple.**
1Ch 26:7 — The sons of Shemaiah; Othni, and Rephael, and Obed, Elzabad, whose brethren *were* strong men, Elihu, and Semachiah.

• **Father of Azariah.**
2Ch 23:1 — And in the seventh year Jehoiada strengthened himself, and took the captains of hundreds, Azariah the son of Jeroham, and Ishmael the son of Jehohanan, and Azariah the son of Obed, and Maaseiah the son of Adaiah, and Elishaphat the son of Zichri, into covenant with him.

OBED-EDOM

• **A Korhite Levite.**
1Ch 26:4–8
1Ch 15:18 — And with them their brethren of the second *degree,* Zechariah, Ben, and Jaaziel, and Shemiramoth, and Jehiel, and Unni, Eliab, and Benaiah, and Maaseiah, and Mattithiah, and Elipheleh, and Mikneiah, and Obed-edom, and Jeiel, the porters.

• **Doorkeeper of the ark.**
1Ch 15:24 — And Shebaniah, and Jehoshaphat, and Nethaneel, and Amasai, and Zechariah, and Benaiah, and Eliezer, the priests, did blow with the trumpets before the ark of God: and Obed-edom and Jehiah *were* doorkeepers for the ark.

• **David leaves ark with.**
1Ch 13:13–14
2Sa 6:10 — So David would not remove the ark of the LORD unto him into the city of David: but David carried it aside into the house of Obed-edom the Gittite.

• **Ark removed from.**
2Sa 6:12 — And it was told king David, saying, The LORD hath blessed the house of Obed-edom, and all that *pertaineth* unto him, because of the ark of God. So David went and brought up the ark of God from the house of Obed-edom into the city of David with gladness.
1Ch 15:25 — So David, and the elders of Israel, and the captains over thousands, went to bring up the ark of the covenant of the LORD out of the house of Obed-edom with joy.

• **Appointed to sound with harps.**
1Ch 15:21 — And Mattithiah, and Elipheleh, and Mikneiah, and Obed-edom, and Jeiel, and Azaziah, with harps on the Sheminith to excel.

• **Appointed to minister before the ark.**
1Ch 16:4–5, 37–38

• **A doorkeeper of the temple.**
1Ch 16:38 — And Obed-edom with their brethren, threescore and eight; Obed-edom also the son of Jeduthun and Hosah *to be* porters:

• **A conservator of the vessels of the temple in time of Amaziah.**
2Ch 25:24 — And *he took* all the gold and the silver, and all the vessels that were found in the house of God with Obed-edom, and the treasures of the king's house, the hostages also, and returned to Samaria.

OBEDIENCE

Jos 14:6–14; Ps 103:17–18, 20–21; 111:10–112:1; 119:4–6, 15–16, 30–31, 44–45, 55–56, 59–60, 100–102, 104–106, 166–168; Eze 33:14–16; Mt 25:20–23; Lk 6:46–48; 12:37–38; Jas 2:10–12; 1Jn 2:3–6; 5:2–3
Ge 18:19 — For I know him, that he will command his children and his household after him, and they shall keep the way of the LORD, to do justice and judgment; that the LORD may bring upon Abraham that which he hath spoken of him.
Ex 19:5 — Now therefore, if ye will obey my voice indeed, and keep my covenant, then ye shall be a peculiar treasure unto me above all people: for all the earth *is* mine:
Ex 20:6 — And shewing mercy unto thousands of them that love me, and keep my commandments.
Ex 24:7 — And he took the book of the covenant, and read in the audience of the people: and they said, All that the LORD hath said will we do, and be obedient.
Nu 9:23 — At the commandment of the LORD they rested in the tents, and at the commandment of the LORD they journeyed: they kept the charge of the LORD, at the commandment of the LORD by the hand of Moses.
Nu 14:24 — But my servant Caleb, because he had another spirit with him, and hath followed me fully, him will I bring into the land whereinto he went; and his seed shall possess it.
Dt 5:10 — And shewing mercy unto thousands of them that love me and keep my commandments.
Jos 22:2 — And said unto them, Ye have kept all that Moses the servant of the LORD commanded you, and have obeyed my voice in all that I commanded you:
Jos 24:24 — And the people said unto Joshua, The LORD our God will we serve, and his voice will we obey.

1Ki 3:14 — And if thou wilt walk in my ways, to keep my statutes and my commandments, as thy father David did walk, then I will lengthen thy days.

2Ki 18:6 — For he clave to the LORD, *and* departed not from following him, but kept his commandments, which the LORD commanded Moses.

2Ki 21:8 — Neither will I make the feet of Israel move any more out of the land which I gave their fathers; only if they will observe to do according to all that I have commanded them, and according to all the law that my servant Moses commanded them.

Ne 1:5 — And said, I beseech thee, O LORD God of heaven, the great and terrible God, that keepeth covenant and mercy for them that love him and observe his commandments:

Ps 1:2 — But his delight *is* in the law of the LORD; and in his law doth he meditate day and night.

Ps 18:44 — As soon as they hear of me, they shall obey me: the strangers shall submit themselves unto me.

Ps 25:10 — All the paths of the LORD *are* mercy and truth unto such as keep his covenant and his testimonies.

Ps 99:7 — He spake unto them in the cloudy pillar: they kept his testimonies, and the ordinance *that* he gave them.

Ps 119:2 — Blessed *are* they that keep his testimonies, *and that* seek him with the whole heart.

Ps 119:8 — I will keep thy statutes: O forsake me not utterly.

Ps 119:10 — With my whole heart have I sought thee: O let me not wander from thy commandments.

Ps 119:22 — Remove from me reproach and contempt; for I have kept thy testimonies.

Ps 119:33 — Teach me, O LORD, the way of thy statutes; and I shall keep it *unto* the end.

Ps 119:72 — The law of thy mouth *is* better unto me than thousands of gold and silver.

Ps 119:77 — Let thy tender mercies come unto me, that I may live: for thy law *is* my delight.

Ps 119:87 — They had almost consumed me upon earth; but I forsook not thy precepts.

Ps 119:97 — O how love I thy law! it *is* my meditation all the day.

Ps 119:109 — My soul *is* continually in my hand: yet do I not forget thy law.

Ps 119:112 — I have inclined mine heart to perform thy statutes alway, *even unto* the end.

Ps 119:129 — Thy testimonies *are* wonderful: therefore doth my soul keep them.

Ps 143:10 — Teach me to do thy will; for thou *art* my God: thy spirit *is* good; lead me into the land of uprightness.

Pr 1:33 — But whoso hearkeneth unto me shall dwell safely, and shall be quiet from fear of evil.

Pr 19:16 — He that keepeth the commandment keepeth his own soul; *but* he that despiseth his ways shall die.

Pr 28:7 — Whoso keepeth the law *is* a wise son: but he that is a companion of riotous *men* shameth his father.

Isa 1:19 — If ye be willing and obedient, ye shall eat the good of the land:

Jer 7:23 — But this thing commanded I them, saying, Obey my voice, and I will be your God, and ye shall be my people: and walk ye in all the ways that I have commanded you, that it may be well unto you.

Eze 18:19 — Yet say ye, Why? doth not the son bear the iniquity of the father? When the son hath done that which is lawful and right, *and* hath kept all my statutes, and hath done them, he shall surely live.

Da 7:27 — And the kingdom and dominion, and the greatness of the kingdom under the whole heaven, shall be given to the people of the saints of the most High, whose kingdom *is* an everlasting kingdom, and all dominions shall serve and obey him.

Mt 5:19 — Whosoever therefore shall break one of these least commandments, and shall teach men so, he shall be called the least in the kingdom of heaven: but whosoever shall do and teach *them,* the same shall be called great in the kingdom of heaven.

Mt 6:24 — No man can serve two masters: for either he will hate the one, and love the other; or else he will hold to the one, and despise the other. Ye cannot serve God and mammon.

Mt 9:9 — And as Jesus passed forth from thence, he saw a man, named Matthew, sitting at the receipt of custom: and he saith unto him, Follow me. And he arose, and followed him.

Mt 12:50 — For whosoever shall do the will of my Father which is in heaven, the same is my brother, and sister, and mother.

Mt 13:8 — But other fell into good ground, and brought forth fruit, some an hundredfold, some sixtyfold, some thirtyfold.

Mt 13:23 — But he that received seed into the good ground is he that heareth the word, and understandeth *it;* which also beareth fruit, and bringeth forth, some an hundredfold, some sixty, some thirty.

Mk 2:14 — And as he passed by, he saw Levi the *son* of Alphaeus sitting at the receipt of custom, and said unto him, Follow me. And he arose and followed him.

Mk 3:35 — For whosoever shall do the will of God, the same is my brother, and my sister, and mother.

Mk 4:20 — And these are they which are sown on good ground; such as hear the word, and receive *it,* and bring forth fruit, some thirtyfold, some sixty, and some an hundred.

Lk 1:6 — And they were both righteous before God, walking in all the commandments and ordinances of the Lord blameless.

Lk 8:15 — But that on the good ground are they, which in an honest and good heart, having heard the word, keep *it,* and bring forth fruit with patience.

Lk 8:21 — And he answered and said unto them, My mother and my brethren are these which hear the word of God, and do it.

Lk 11:2 — And he said unto them, When ye pray, say, Our Father which art in heaven, Hallowed be thy name. Thy kingdom come. Thy will be done, as in heaven, so in earth.

Lk 11:28 — But he said, Yea rather, blessed *are* they that hear the word of God, and keep it.

Jn 8:28 — Then said Jesus unto them, When ye have lifted up the Son of man, then shall ye know that I am *he,* and *that* I do nothing of myself; but as my Father hath taught me, I speak these things.

Jn 8:51 — Verily, verily, I say unto you, If a man keep my saying, he shall never see death.

Jn 9:4 — I must work the works of him that sent me, while it is day: the night cometh, when no man can work.

Jn 10:27 — My sheep hear my voice, and I know them, and they follow me:

Jn 14:15 — If ye love me, keep my commandments.

Jn 14:23 — Jesus answered and said unto him, If a man love me, he will keep my words: and my Father will love him, and we will come unto him, and make our abode with him.

Jn 14:31 — But that the world may know that I love the Father; and as the Father gave me commandment, even so I do. Arise, let us go hence.

Jn 15:10 — If ye keep my commandments, ye shall abide in my love; even as I have kept my Father's commandments, and abide in his love.

Jn 15:14 — Ye are my friends, if ye do whatsoever I command you.

Jn 15:16 — Ye have not chosen me, but I have chosen you, and ordained you, that ye should go and bring forth fruit, and *that* your fruit should remain: that whatsoever ye shall ask of the Father in my name, he may give it you.

Ac 4:19 — But Peter and John answered and said unto them, Whether it be right in the sight of God to hearken unto you more than unto God, judge ye.

Ac 5:29 — Then Peter and the *other* apostles answered and said, We ought to obey God rather than men.

Ro 6:17 — But God be thanked, that ye were the servants of sin, but ye have obeyed from the heart that form of doctrine which was delivered you.

Eph 2:10 — For we are his workmanship, created in Christ Jesus unto good works, which God hath before ordained that we should walk in them.

Php 2:12 — Wherefore, my beloved, as ye have always obeyed, not as in my presence only, but now much more in my absence, work out your own salvation with fear and trembling.

Heb 10:7 — Then said I, Lo, I come (in the volume of the book it is written of me,) to do thy will, O God.

1Pe 1:2 — Elect according to the foreknowledge of God the Father, through sanctification of the Spirit, unto obedience and sprinkling of the blood of Jesus Christ: Grace unto you, and peace, be multiplied.

1Pe 1:14 — As obedient children, not fashioning yourselves according to the former lusts in your ignorance:

1Jn 2:17 — And the world passeth away, and the lust thereof: but he that doeth the will of God abideth for ever.

1Jn 3:22 — And whatsoever we ask, we receive of him, because we keep his commandments, and do those things that are pleasing in his sight.

1Jn 3:24 — And he that keepeth his commandments dwelleth in him, and he in him. And hereby we know that he abideth in us, by the Spirit which he hath given us.

2Jn 1:6 — And this is love, that we walk after his commandments. This is the commandment, That, as ye have heard from the beginning, ye should walk in it.

2Jn 1:9 — Whosoever transgresseth, and abideth not in the doctrine of Christ, hath not God. He that abideth in the doctrine of Christ, he hath both the Father and the Son.

Rev 12:17 — And the dragon was wroth with the woman, and went to make war with the remnant of her seed, which keep the commandments of God, and have the testimony of Jesus Christ.

Rev 22:7 — Behold, I come quickly: blessed is he that keepeth the sayings of the prophecy of this book.

Rev 22:14 — Blessed *are* they that do his commandments, that they may have right to the tree of life, and may enter in through the gates into the city.

See: Blessing; divine, contingent upon obedience

• **Enjoined.**

Le 19:36–37; 26:3–13; Nu 15:38–40; Dt 4:1–40; 5:1–6:25; 8:1–6, 11–14, 16–20; 10:12–13; 11:1–3, 8–9, 13–28; 26:16–18; 27:1–10; 28:1–68; Jos 23:6–7; 24:14–15; 2Ki 17:37–38; 1Ch 28:9–10; Eph 6:6–8; Jas 1:22–25

Ge 17:9 — And God said unto Abraham, Thou shalt keep my covenant therefore, thou, and thy seed after thee in their generations.

Ex 23:22 — But if thou shalt indeed obey his voice, and do all that I speak; then I will be an enemy unto thine enemies, and an adversary unto thine adversaries.

Le 19:19 — Ye shall keep my statutes. Thou shalt not let thy cattle gender with a diverse kind: thou shalt not sow thy field with mingled seed: neither shall a garment mingled of linen and woollen come upon thee.

Le 20:8 — And ye shall keep my statutes, and do them: I *am* the LORD which sanctify you.

Le 20:22 — Ye shall therefore keep all my statutes, and all my judgments, and do them: that the land, whither I bring you to dwell therein, spue you not out.

Le 22:31 — Therefore shall ye keep my commandments, and do them: I *am* the LORD.

Dt 11:32 — And ye shall observe to do all the statutes and judgments which I set before you this day.

Dt 13:4 — Ye shall walk after the LORD your God, and fear him, and keep his commandments, and obey his voice, and ye shall serve him, and cleave unto him.

Dt 32:46 — And he said unto them, Set your hearts unto all the words which I testify among you this day, which ye shall command your children to observe to do, all the words of this law.

Jos 22:5 — But take diligent heed to do the commandment and the law, which Moses the servant of the LORD charged you, to love the LORD your God, and to walk in all his ways, and to keep his commandments, and to cleave unto him, and to serve him with all your heart and with all your soul.

1Sa 12:24 — Only fear the LORD, and serve him in truth with all your heart: for consider how great *things* he hath done for you.

1Sa 15:22 — And Samuel said, Hath the LORD *as great* delight in burnt offerings and sacrifices, as in obeying the voice of the LORD? Behold, to obey *is* better than sacrifice, *and* to hearken than the fat of rams.

1Ch 16:15 — Be ye mindful always of his covenant; the word *which* he commanded to a thousand generations;

1Ch 28:20 — And David said to Solomon his son, Be strong and of good courage, and do *it:* fear not, nor be dismayed: for the LORD God, *even* my God, *will be* with thee; he will not fail thee, nor forsake thee, until thou hast finished all the work for the service of the house of the LORD.

Ezr 7:10 — For Ezra had prepared his heart to seek the law of the LORD, and to do *it,* and to teach in Israel statutes and judgments.

Ezr 7:23 — Whatsoever is commanded by the God of heaven, let it be diligently done for the house of the God of heaven: for why should there be wrath against the realm of the king and his sons?

Ps 76:11 — Vow, and pay unto the LORD your God: let all that be round about him bring presents unto him that ought to be feared.

Ecc 12:13 — Let us hear the conclusion of the whole matter: Fear God, and keep his commandments: for this *is* the whole *duty* of man.

Jer 26:13 — Therefore now amend your ways and your doings, and obey the voice of the LORD your God; and the LORD will repent him of the evil that he hath pronounced against you.

Jer 38:20 — But Jeremiah said, They shall not deliver *thee.* Obey, I beseech thee, the voice of the LORD, which I speak unto thee: so it shall be well unto thee, and thy soul shall live.

Mal 4:4 — Remember ye the law of Moses my servant, which I commanded unto him in Horeb for all Israel, *with* the statutes and judgments.

Mt 9:9 — And as Jesus passed forth from thence, he saw a man, named Matthew, sitting at the receipt of custom: and he saith unto him, Follow me. And he arose, and followed him.

Mt 19:17 — And he said unto him, Why callest thou me good? *there is* none good but one, *that is,* God: but if thou wilt enter into life, keep the commandments.

Mt 19:29 — And every one that hath forsaken houses, or brethren, or sisters, or father, or mother, or wife, or children, or lands, for my name's sake, shall receive an hundredfold, and shall inherit everlasting life.

Mk 2:14 — And as he passed by, he saw Levi the *son* of Alphaeus sitting at the receipt of custom, and said unto him, Follow me. And he arose and followed him.

Jn 12:26 — If any man serve me, let him follow me; and where I am, there shall also my servant be: if any man serve me, him will *my* Father honour.

Jn 13:17 — If ye know these things, happy are ye if ye do them.

Jn 14:15 — If ye love me, keep my commandments.

Jn 14:21 — He that hath my commandments, and keepeth them, he it is that loveth me: and he that loveth me shall be loved of my Father, and I will love him, and will manifest myself to him.

Gal 3:10 — For as many as are of the works of the law are under the curse: for it is written, Cursed *is* every one that continueth not in all things which are written in the book of the law to do them.

Gal 3:12 — And the law is not of faith: but, The man that doeth them shall live in them.

Gal 5:3 — For I testify again to every man that is circumcised, that he is a debtor to do the whole law.

Eph 4:1 — I therefore, the prisoner of the Lord, beseech you that ye walk worthy of the vocation wherewith ye are called,

Eph 4:17 — This I say therefore, and testify in the Lord, that ye henceforth walk not as other Gentiles walk, in the vanity of their mind,

Php 2:12 — Wherefore, my beloved, as ye have always obeyed, not as in my presence only, but now much more in my absence, work out your own salvation with fear and trembling.

1Ti 6:14 — That thou keep *this* commandment without spot, unrebukeable, until the appearing of our Lord Jesus Christ:

1Ti 6:18 — That they do good, that they be rich in good works, ready to distribute, willing to communicate;

Heb 13:16 — But to do good and to communicate forget not: for with such sacrifices God is well pleased.

See: Commandments

See: Duty

See: Law

• Exemplified.

Jos 14:6–14; 2Ch 31:20–21; Ps 26:3–6; 101:2–3; 106:30–31; 119:30–31, 44–45, 47–48, 54–56, 59–60, 100–102, 105–106, 166–168; 2Co 6:3–4; Php 3:7–14; Rev 14:4–5

Ge 6:9 — These *are* the generations of Noah: Noah was a just man *and* perfect in his generations, *and* Noah walked with God.

Nu 9:23 — At the commandment of the LORD they rested in the tents, and at the commandment of the LORD they journeyed: they kept the charge of the LORD, at the commandment of the LORD by the hand of Moses.

Nu 14:24 — But my servant Caleb, because he had another spirit with him, and hath followed me fully, him will I bring into the land whereinto he went; and his seed shall possess it.

2Ki 18:6 — For he clave to the LORD, *and* departed not from following him, but kept his commandments, which the LORD commanded Moses.

2Ki 20:3 — I beseech thee, O LORD, remember now how I have walked before thee in truth and with a perfect heart, and have done *that which is* good in thy sight. And Hezekiah wept sore.

2Ch 24:16 — And they buried him in the city of David among the kings, because he had done good in Israel, both toward God, and toward his house.

Ezr 7:10 — For Ezra had prepared his heart to seek the law of the LORD, and to do *it,* and to teach in Israel statutes and judgments.

Ne 7:2 — That I gave my brother Hanani, and Hananiah the ruler of the palace, charge over Jerusalem: for he *was* a faithful man, and feared God above many.

Job 1:8 — And the LORD said unto Satan, Hast thou considered my servant Job, that *there is* none like him in the earth, a perfect and an upright man, one that feareth God, and escheweth evil?

Ps 17:3 — Thou hast proved mine heart; thou hast visited *me* in the night; thou hast tried me, *and* shalt find nothing; I am purposed *that* my mouth shall not transgress.

Ps 99:7 — He spake unto them in the cloudy pillar: they kept his testimonies, and the ordinance *that* he gave them.

Ps 119:40 — Behold, I have longed after thy precepts: quicken me in thy righteousness.

Ps 119:51 — The proud have had me greatly in derision: *yet* have I not declined from thy law.

Ps 119:67 — Before I was afflicted I went astray: but now have I kept thy word.

Ps 119:69 — The proud have forged a lie against me: *but* I will keep thy precepts with *my* whole heart.

Ps 119:110 — The wicked have laid a snare for me: yet I erred not from thy precepts.

Ps 119:112 — I have inclined mine heart to perform thy statutes alway, *even unto* the end.

Ac 23:1 — And Paul, earnestly beholding the council, said, Men *and* brethren, I have lived in all good conscience before God until this day.

Ac 24:16 — And herein do I exercise myself, to have always a conscience void of offence toward God, and *toward* men.

Ro 6:17 — But God be thanked, that ye were the servants of sin, but ye have obeyed from the heart that form of doctrine which was delivered you.

2Co 1:12 — For our rejoicing is this, the testimony of our conscience, that in simplicity and godly sincerity, not with fleshly wisdom, but by the grace of God, we have had our conversation in the world, and more abundantly to you-ward.

1Th 1:9 — For they themselves shew of us what manner of entering in we had unto you, and how ye turned to God from idols to serve the living and true God;

1Th 2:10 — Ye *are* witnesses, and God *also,* how holily and justly and unblameably we behaved ourselves among you that believe:

2Ti 1:3 — I thank God, whom I serve from *my* forefathers with pure conscience, that without ceasing I have remembrance of thee in my prayers night and day;

Rev 2:19 — I know thy works, and charity, and service, and faith, and thy patience, and thy works; and the last *to be* more than the first.

Rev 3:4 — Thou hast a few names even in Sardis which have not defiled their garments; and they shall walk with me in white: for they are worthy.

→See: Blessing; divine, contingent upon obedience

→See: Commandments

• Filial.

→See: Children

• Instances of.

• Noah.
Ge 6:9, 22; 7:5; Heb 11:7

• Abraham.
Ge 12:1–4; 17:23; 21:4; 22:12; Ne 9:8; Ac 7:3–8; Heb 11:8–17; Jas 2:21

• Bethuel and Laban.
Ge 24:50

• Jacob.
Ge 35:1, 7

• Moses.
Nu 27:12–22; Heb 3:2–3

• Moses and Aaron.
Ex 7:6; 40:16, 21, 23, 32

• Israelites.
Ex 12:28; 32:25–29; 39:42–43; Nu 9:20–21; Dt 33:9; Jgs 2:7; Ps 99:7

• Under the preaching of Haggai.
Hag 1:12

• Caleb.
Dt 1:36

• Joshua.
Jos 10:40; 11:15

• Reubenites.
Jos 22:2–3

• Gideon.
Jgs 6:25–28

• David.
1Sa 18:14; 25:28; 1Ki 11:6, 34; 15:5; 2Ch 29:2; Ac 13:22

• Elisha.
1Ki 19:19–21

• Hezekiah.
2Ki 18:6; 2Ch 31:20–21; Isa 38:3

• Josiah.
2Ki 22:2; 23:24–25

• Asa.
2Ch 14:2

• Jehoshaphat.
2Ch 17:3–6; 20:32; 22:9

• Jehoiada.
2Ch 24:16

• Uzziah.
2Ch 26:4–5

• Jotham.
2Ch 27:2

• Levites.
2Ch 29:34

• Cyrus.
2Ch 36:22–23; Ezr 1:1–4

• Ezra.
Ezr 7:10

• Hanani.
Ne 7:2

• Job.
Job 1:8

• Daniel.
Da 6:10

- **Three Hebrews.**
  Da 3:1–30
- **Jonah.**
  Jnh 3:3
- **Ninevites.**
  Jnh 3:5–10
- **Zacharias.**
  Lk 1:6
- **Simeon.**
  Lk 2:25
- **Joseph.**
  Mt 1:24; 2:14
- **Mary.**
  Lk 1:38
- **Jesus.**
  Mt 3:15; 26:39, 42; Lk 22:42; Jn 4:32, 34; 5:30; 12:49–50; 14:31; 17:4; Heb 3:2
- **John the Baptist.**
  Mt 3:15
- **John and James.**
  Mk 1:19–20
- **Mathew.**
  Mt 9:9
- **Simon and Andrew.**
  Mk 1:16–18
- **Levi.**
  Mk 2:14
- **Nathanael.**
  Jn 1:47
- **The rich young man.**
  Mt 19:20; Mk 10:19–20; Lk 18:21
- **The disciples.**
  Jn 17:6
- **Cornelius.**
  Ac 10:2
- **Paul.**
  Ac 23:1; 26:4–5; 2Ti 1:3

• To civil law.
  See: Citizens

OBIL

• An Ishmaelite.

• Camel keeper for David.

1Ch 27:30 — Over the camels also was Obil the Ishmaelite: and over the asses *was* Jehdeiah the Meronothite:

OBJECT TEACHING **See: Instruction**

OBLATION **See: Offerings**

OBLIGATION

• A motive of obedience.

Dt 4:32–40; 6:1–11:32

Dt 26:16 — This day the LORD thy God hath commanded thee to do these statutes and judgments: thou shalt therefore keep and do them with all thine heart, and with all thy soul.

Dt 32:6 — Do ye thus requite the LORD, O foolish people and unwise? *is* not he thy father *that* hath bought thee? hath he not made thee, and established thee?

1Sa 12:24 — Only fear the LORD, and serve him in truth with all your heart: for consider how great *things* he hath done for you.

1Ch 16:12 — Remember his marvellous works that he hath done, his wonders, and the judgments of his mouth;

Ro 2:4 — Or despisest thou the riches of his goodness and forbearance and longsuffering; not knowing that the goodness of God leadeth thee to repentance?

2Co 5:15 — And *that* he died for all, that they which live should not henceforth live unto themselves, but unto him which died for them, and rose again.

• Acknowledgment of.

Ps 116:12–14

Ps 116:17 — I will offer to thee the sacrifice of thanksgiving, and will call upon the name of the LORD.

See: Duty

OBLIQUITY, moral **See: Depravity of Man**

OBOTH • A camping place of Israel in the forty years' wandering.

Nu 21:10–11; 33:43–44

OBSEQUIOUSNESS

• Instances of.

- **Abigail.**
  1Sa 25:23–31, 41
- **Mephibosheth.**
  2Sa 9:8
- **The woman of Tekoah.**
  2Sa 14:4–20

OBSTETRICS

Eze 16:4 — And *as for* thy nativity, in the day thou wast born thy navel was not cut, neither wast thou washed in water to supple *thee;* thou wast not salted at all, nor swaddled at all.

See: Midwifery

OCCULT SCIENCE **See: Sorcery**

OCRAN • An Asherite and the father of Pagiel who numbers Israel.

Nu 1:13 — Of Asher; Pagiel the son of Ocran.

Nu 2:27 — And those that encamp by him *shall be* the tribe of Asher: and the captain of the children of Asher *shall be* Pagiel the son of Ocran.

Nu 10:26 — And over the host of the tribe of the children of Asher *was* Pagiel the son of Ocran.

ODED

• A prophet in Samaria.

2Ch 28:9 — But a prophet of the LORD was there, whose name *was* Oded: and he went out before the host that came to Samaria, and said unto them,

Behold, because the LORD God of your fathers was wroth with Judah, he hath delivered them into your hand, and ye have slain them in a rage *that* reacheth up unto heaven.

• Father of the prophet Azariah.

2Ch 15:1 — And the Spirit of God came upon Azariah the son of Oded:

ODOR

See: Incense

See: Perfume

OFFENSES See: Temptation

OFFERINGS

• Offered at the door of the tabernacle.

Le 17:8–9

Le 1:3 — If his offering *be* a burnt sacrifice of the herd, let him offer a male without blemish: he shall offer it of his own voluntary will at the door of the tabernacle of the congregation before the LORD.

Le 3:2 — And he shall lay his hand upon the head of his offering, and kill it *at* the door of the tabernacle of the congregation: and Aaron's sons the priests shall sprinkle the blood upon the altar round about.

Le 17:4 — And bringeth it not unto the door of the tabernacle of the congregation, to offer an offering unto the LORD before the tabernacle of the LORD; blood shall be imputed unto that man; he hath shed blood; and that man shall be cut off from among his people:

• Offered at the door of the temple.

1Ki 8:62 — And the king, and all Israel with him, offered sacrifice before the LORD.

1Ki 12:27 — If this people go up to do sacrifice in the house of the LORD at Jerusalem, then shall the heart of this people turn again unto their lord, *even* unto Rehoboam king of Judah, and they shall kill me, and go again to Rehoboam king of Judah.

2Ch 7:12 — And the LORD appeared to Solomon by night, and said unto him, I have heard thy prayer, and have chosen this place to myself for an house of sacrifice.

• All animal sacrifices must be eight days old or over.

Le 22:27 — When a bullock, or a sheep, or a goat, is brought forth, then it shall be seven days under the dam; and from the eighth day and thenceforth it shall be accepted for an offering made by fire unto the LORD.

• Must be salted.

Le 2:13 — And every oblation of thy meat offering shalt thou season with salt; neither shalt thou suffer the salt of the covenant of thy God to be lacking from thy meat offering: with all thine offerings thou shalt offer salt.

Eze 43:24 — And thou shalt offer them before the LORD, and the priests shall cast salt upon them, and they shall offer them up *for* a burnt offering unto the LORD.

Mk 9:49 — For every one shall be salted with fire, and every sacrifice shall be salted with salt.

• Must be accompanied with leaven.

Le 7:13 — Besides the cakes, he shall offer *for* his offering leavened bread with the sacrifice of thanksgiving of his peace offerings.

Am 4:5 — And offer a sacrifice of thanksgiving with leaven, and proclaim *and* publish the free offerings: for this liketh you, O ye children of Israel, saith the Lord GOD.

• Must be without leaven.

Ex 23:18 — Thou shalt not offer the blood of my sacrifice with leavened bread; neither shall the fat of my sacrifice remain until the morning.

Ex 34:25 — Thou shalt not offer the blood of my sacrifice with leaven; neither shall the sacrifice of the feast of the passover be left unto the morning.

• Eaten.

1Sa 9:13 — As soon as ye be come into the city, ye shall straightway find him, before he go up to the high place to eat: for the people will not eat until he come, because he doth bless the sacrifice; *and* afterwards they eat that be bidden. Now therefore get you up; for about this time ye shall find him.

• Ordinance relating to scapegoat.

Le 16:7–26

• Atonement for sin made by.

See: Atonement

• Figurative.

Ps 51:17 — The sacrifices of God *are* a broken spirit: a broken and a contrite heart, O God, thou wilt not despise.

Jer 33:11 — The voice of joy, and the voice of gladness, the voice of the bridegroom, and the voice of the bride, the voice of them that shall say, Praise the LORD of hosts: for the LORD *is* good; for his mercy *endureth* for ever: *and* of them that shall bring the sacrifice of praise into the house of the LORD. For I will cause to return the captivity of the land, as at the first, saith the LORD.

Ro 12:1 — I beseech you therefore, brethren, by the mercies of God, that ye present your bodies a living sacrifice, holy, acceptable unto God, *which is* your reasonable service.

Php 4:18 — But I have all, and abound: I am full, having received of Epaphroditus the things *which were sent* from you, an odour of a sweet smell, a sacrifice acceptable, wellpleasing to God.

Heb 13:15 — By him therefore let us offer the sacrifice of praise to God continually, that is, the fruit of *our* lips giving thanks to his name.

• Animal sacrifices.

• A type of Christ.

Ps 40:6–8; Isa 53:11–12; Heb 9:19–10:14; 13:11–13

Le 16:21 — And Aaron shall lay both his hands upon the head of the live goat, and confess over him all the iniquities of the children of Israel, and all their transgressions in all their sins, putting them upon the head of the goat, and shall send *him* away by the hand of a fit man into the wilderness:

Jn 1:29 — The next day John seeth Jesus coming unto him, and saith, Behold the Lamb of God, which taketh away the sin of the world.

1Co 5:7 — Purge out therefore the old leaven, that ye may be a new lump, as ye are unleavened. For even Christ our passover is sacrificed for us:

2Co 5:21 — For he hath made him *to be* sin for us, who knew no sin; that we might be made the righteousness of God in him.

Eph 5:2 — And walk in love, as Christ also hath loved us, and hath given himself for us an offering and a sacrifice to God for a sweetsmelling savour.

Rev 5:6 — And I beheld, and, lo, in the midst of the throne and of the four beasts, and in the midst of the elders, stood a Lamb as it had been slain, having seven horns and seven eyes, which are the seven Spirits of God sent forth into all the earth.

• Burnt.

Le 9:2 — And he said unto Aaron, Take thee a young calf for a sin offering, and a ram for a burnt offering, without blemish, and offer *them* before the LORD.

• Its purpose was to make an atonement for sin.

Le 7:1–38

Le 1:4 — And he shall put his hand upon the head of the burnt offering; and it shall be accepted for him to make atonement for him.

• Ordinances concerning.

Ex 29:15–18; Le 1:1–17; 5:7–10; 6:9–13; 17:8–9; 23:26–37; Nu 15:24–25; 28:26–29:40

Le 23:18 — And ye shall offer with the bread seven lambs without blemish of the first year, and one young bullock, and two rams: they shall be *for* a burnt offering unto the LORD, with their meat offering, and their drink offerings, *even* an offering made by fire, of sweet savour unto the LORD.

Nu 19:9 — And a man *that is* clean shall gather up the ashes of the heifer, and lay *them* up without the camp in a clean place, and it shall be kept for the congregation of the children of Israel for a water of separation: it *is* a purification for sin.

• Accompanied by other offerings.

Nu 15:3–16

• Skins of, belonged to priests.

Le 7:8 — And the priest that offereth any man's burnt offering, *even* the priest shall have to himself the skin of the burnt offering which he hath offered.

• Offered daily, morning and evening.

Ex 29:38–42; Nu 28:1–31; Eze 46:13–15

Ge 15:17 — And it came to pass, that, when the sun went down, and it was dark, behold a smoking furnace, and a burning lamp that passed between those pieces.

Le 6:20 — This *is* the offering of Aaron and of his sons, which they shall offer unto the LORD in the day when he is anointed; the tenth part of an ephah of fine flour for a meat offering perpetual, half of it in the morning, and half thereof at night.

Nu 29:6 — Beside the burnt offering of the month, and his meat offering, and the daily burnt offering, and his meat offering, and their drink offerings, according unto their manner, for a sweet savour, a sacrifice made by fire unto the LORD.

1Ch 16:40 — To offer burnt offerings unto the LORD upon the altar of the burnt offering continually morning and evening, and *to do* according to all that is written in the law of the LORD, which he commanded Israel;

2Ch 2:4 — Behold, I build an house to the name of the LORD my God, to dedicate *it* to him, *and* to burn before him sweet incense, and for the continual shewbread, and for the burnt offerings morning and evening, on the sabbaths, and on the new moons, and on the solemn feasts of the LORD our God. This *is an ordinance* for ever to Israel.

2Ch 13:11 — And they burn unto the LORD every morning and every evening burnt sacrifices and sweet incense: the shewbread also *set they in order* upon the pure table; and the candlestick of gold with the lamps thereof, to burn every evening: for we keep the charge of the LORD our God; but ye have forsaken him.

Ezr 3:3 — And they set the altar upon his bases; for fear *was* upon them because of the people of those countries: and they offered burnt offerings thereon unto the LORD, *even* burnt offerings morning and evening.

• Music with.

Nu 10:10 — Also in the day of your gladness, and in your solemn days, and in the beginnings of your months, ye shall blow with the trumpets over your burnt offerings, and over the sacrifices of your peace offerings; that they may be to you for a memorial before your God: I *am* the LORD your God.

• Drink.

• Libations of wine offered with the sacrifices.

Ex 29:40–41; Nu 28:5–15, 24–31; 29:6–11, 18–40

Ge 35:14 — And Jacob set up a pillar in the place where he talked with him, *even* a pillar of stone: and he poured a drink offering thereon, and he poured oil thereon.

Ex 30:9 — Ye shall offer no strange incense thereon, nor burnt sacrifice, nor meat offering; neither shall ye pour drink offering thereon.

Le 23:13 — And the meat offering thereof *shall be* two tenth deals of fine flour mingled with oil, an offering made by fire unto the LORD *for* a sweet savour: and the drink offering thereof *shall be* of wine, the fourth *part* of an hin.

Le 23:18 — And ye shall offer with the bread seven lambs without blemish of the first year, and one young bullock, and two rams: they shall be *for* a burnt offering unto the LORD, with their meat offering, and their drink offerings, *even* an offering made by fire, of sweet savour unto the LORD.

Nu 6:17 — And he shall offer the ram *for* a sacrifice of peace offerings unto the LORD, with the basket of unleavened bread: the priest shall offer also his meat offering, and his drink offering.

Nu 15:24 — Then it shall be, if *ought* be committed by ignorance without the knowledge of the congregation, that all the congregation shall offer one young bullock for a burnt offering, for a sweet savour unto the LORD, with his meat offering, and his drink offering, according to the manner, and one kid of the goats for a sin offering.

2Ki 16:13 — and he burnt his burnt offering and his meat offering, and poured his drink offering, and sprinkled the blood of his peace offerings, upon the altar.

1Ch 29:21 — And they sacrificed sacrifices unto the LORD, and offered burnt offerings unto the LORD, on the morrow after that day, *even* a thousand bullocks, a thousand rams, *and* a thousand lambs, with their drink offerings, and sacrifices in abundance for all Israel:

2Ch 29:35 — And also the burnt offerings *were* in abundance, with the fat of the peace offerings, and the drink offerings for *every* burnt offering. So the service of the house of the LORD was set in order.

Ezr 7:17 — That thou mayest buy speedily with this money bullocks, rams, lambs, with their meat offerings and their drink offerings, and offer them upon the altar of the house of your God which *is* in Jerusalem.

- **Free will.**
  - **Must be perfect.**
    Le 22:17–25
  - **To be eaten by priests.**
    Le 7:11–18
  - **With meat and drink offerings.**
    Nu 15:1–16
  - **Obligatory when signified in a vow.**
    Dt 16:10 — And thou shalt keep the feast of weeks unto the LORD thy God with a tribute of a freewill offering of thine hand, which thou shalt give *unto the LORD thy God,* according as the LORD thy God hath blessed thee:

    Dt 23:23 — That which is gone out of thy lips thou shalt keep and perform; *even* a freewill offering, according as thou hast vowed unto the LORD thy God, which thou hast promised with thy mouth.
- **Heave.**
  - **Given to the priests' families as part of their emoluments.**
    Nu 18:10–19

    Le 10:14 — And the wave breast and heave shoulder shall ye eat in a clean place; thou, and thy sons, and thy daughters with thee: for *they be* thy due, and thy sons' due, *which* are given out of the sacrifices of peace offerings of the children of Israel.

    Nu 5:9 — And every offering of all the holy things of the children of Israel, which they bring unto the priest, shall be his.

    Nu 18:24 — But the tithes of the children of Israel, which they offer *as* an heave offering unto the LORD, I have given to the Levites to inherit: therefore I have said unto them, Among the children of Israel they shall have no inheritance.
  - **Consecrated by being elevated by the priest.**
    Ex 29:27 — And thou shalt sanctify the breast of the wave offering, and the shoulder of the heave offering, which is waved, and which is heaved up, of the ram of the consecration, *even* of *that* which *is* for Aaron, and of *that* which is for his sons:
  - **Consisted of the right thigh or hind quarter.**
    Ex 29:27–28; Le 7:12–14

    Le 7:32 — And the right shoulder shall ye give unto the priest *for* an heave offering of the sacrifices of your peace offerings.

    Le 7:34 — For the wave breast and the heave shoulder have I taken of the children of Israel from off the sacrifices of their peace offerings, and have given them unto Aaron the priest and unto his sons by a statute for ever from among the children of Israel.

    Le 10:15 — The heave shoulder and the wave breast shall they bring with the offerings made by fire of the fat, to wave *it for* a wave offering before the LORD; and it shall be thine, and thy sons' with thee, by a statute for ever; as the LORD hath commanded.
  - **Consisted of spoils, including captives and other articles of war.**
    Nu 31:29 — Take *it* of their half, and give *it* unto Eleazar the priest, *for* an heave offering of the LORD.

    Nu 31:41 — And Moses gave the tribute, *which was* the LORD's heave offering, unto Eleazar the priest, as the LORD commanded Moses.
  - **When offered.**
    Le 7:12–14; Nu 15:19–21

    Nu 6:20 — And the priest shall wave them *for* a wave offering before the LORD: this *is* holy for the priest, with the wave breast and heave shoulder: and after that the Nazarite may drink wine.
  - **In certain instances this offering was brought to the tabernacle, or temple.**
    Dt 12:17–18

    Dt 12:6 — And thither ye shall bring your burnt offerings, and your sacrifices, and your tithes, and heave offerings of your hand, and your vows, and your freewill offerings, and the firstlings of your herds and of your flocks:

    Dt 12:11 — Then there shall be a place which the LORD your God shall choose to cause his name to dwell there; thither shall ye bring all that I command you; your burnt offerings, and your sacrifices, your tithes, and the heave offering of your hand, and all your choice vows which ye vow unto the LORD:

- **To be offered on taking possession of the land of Canaan.**
  Nu 15:18–21

- **Human sacrifices.**
  - **Forbidden.**
    Le 20:2–5
    Le 18:21 — And thou shalt not let any of thy seed pass through *the fire* to Molech, neither shalt thou profane the name of thy God: I *am* the LORD.
    Dt 12:31 — Thou shalt not do so unto the LORD thy God: for every abomination to the LORD, which he hateth, have they done unto their gods; for even their sons and their daughters they have burnt in the fire to their gods.
  - **Abraham.**
    Ge 22:1–19; Heb 11:17–19
  - **Caananites.**
    Dt 12:31 — Thou shalt not do so unto the LORD thy God: for every abomination to the LORD, which he hateth, have they done unto their gods; for even their sons and their daughters they have burnt in the fire to their gods.
  - **Moabites.**
    2Ki 3:27 — Then he took his eldest son that should have reigned in his stead, and offered him *for* a burnt offering upon the wall. And there was great indignation against Israel: and they departed from him, and returned to *their own* land.
  - **Israelites.**
    Eze 16:20–21
    2Ki 16:3 — But he walked in the way of the kings of Israel, yea, and made his son to pass through the fire, according to the abominations of the heathen, whom the LORD cast out from before the children of Israel.
    2Ki 23:10 — And he defiled Topheth, which *is* in the valley of the children of Hinnom, that no man might make his son or his daughter to pass through the fire to Molech.
    2Ch 28:3 — Moreover he burnt incense in the valley of the son of Hinnom, and burnt his children in the fire, after the abominations of the heathen whom the LORD had cast out before the children of Israel.
    Isa 57:5 — Enflaming yourselves with idols under every green tree, slaying the children in the valleys under the clifts of the rocks?
    Jer 7:31 — And they have built the high places of Tophet, which is in the valley of the son of Hinnom, to burn their sons and their daughters in the fire; which I commanded *them* not, neither came it into my heart.
    Jer 19:5 — They have built also the high places of Baal, to burn their sons with fire *for* burnt offerings unto Baal, which I commanded not, nor spake *it,* neither came *it* into my mind:
    Jer 32:35 — And they built the high places of Baal, which *are* in the valley of the son of Hinnom, to cause their sons and their daughters to pass through *the fire* unto Molech; which I commanded them not, neither came it into my mind, that they should do this abomination, to cause Judah to sin.
    Eze 20:26 — And I polluted them in their own gifts, in that they caused to pass through *the fire* all that openeth the womb, that I might make them desolate, to the end that they might know that I *am* the LORD.
    Eze 20:31 — For when ye offer your gifts, when ye make your sons to pass through the fire, ye pollute yourselves with all your idols, even unto this day: and shall I be enquired of by you, O house of Israel? *As* I live, saith the Lord GOD, I will not be enquired of by you.
    Eze 23:37 — That they have committed adultery, and blood is in their hands, and with their idols have they committed adultery, and have also caused their sons, whom they bare unto me, to pass for them through *the fire,* to devour *them.*
    Eze 23:39 — For when they had slain their children to their idols, then they came the same day into my sanctuary to profane it; and, lo, thus have they done in the midst of mine house.
  - **By the Sepharvites to idols.**
    2Ki 17:31 — And the Avites made Nibhaz and Tartak, and the Sepharvites burnt their children in fire to Adrammelech and Anammelech, the gods of Sepharvaim.
  - **To demons.**
    Ps 106:37–38
  - **To Baal.**
    Jer 19:5–6

- **Insufficiency of.**
  Heb 8:7–9:15; 10:1–12, 18–20

  *See: Ordinance

- **Meat, or meal.**
  - **Ordinances concerning.**
    Ex 29:40–41; Le 2:1–16; 5:11–12; 6:14–23; 7:9–13; 23:16–17; Nu 5:25–26; 15:3–16; 28:12–13, 20–21, 26–31; 29:3–4
    Ex 30:9 — Ye shall offer no strange incense thereon, nor burnt sacrifice, nor meat offering; neither shall ye pour drink offering thereon.
    Ex 40:29 — And he put the altar of burnt offering *by* the door of the tabernacle of the tent of the congregation, and offered upon it the burnt offering and the meat offering; as the LORD commanded Moses.
    Le 7:37 — This *is* the law of the burnt offering, of the meat offering, and of the sin offering, and of the trespass offering, and of the consecrations, and of the sacrifice of the peace offerings;
    Le 9:17 — And he brought the meat offering, and took an handful thereof, and burnt *it* upon the altar, beside the burnt sacrifice of the morning.
    Le 23:13 — And the meat offering thereof *shall be* two tenth deals of fine flour mingled with oil, an offering made by fire unto the LORD *for* a sweet savour: and the drink offering thereof *shall be* of wine, the fourth *part* of an hin.

Nu 4:16 — And to the office of Eleazar the son of Aaron the priest *pertaineth* the oil for the light, and the sweet incense, and the daily meat offering, and the anointing oil, *and* the oversight of all the tabernacle, and of all that therein *is,* in the sanctuary, and in the vessels thereof.

Nu 5:15 — Then shall the man bring his wife unto the priest, and he shall bring her offering for her, the tenth *part* of an ephah of barley meal; he shall pour no oil upon it, nor put frankincense thereon; for it *is* an offering of jealousy, an offering of memorial, bringing iniquity to remembrance.

Nu 5:18 — And the priest shall set the woman before the LORD, and uncover the woman's head, and put the offering of memorial in her hands, which *is* the jealousy offering: and the priest shall have in his hand the bitter water that causeth the curse:

Nu 8:8 — Then let them take a young bullock with his meat offering, *even* fine flour mingled with oil, and another young bullock shalt thou take for a sin offering.

Nu 15:24 — Then it shall be, if *ought* be committed by ignorance without the knowledge of the congregation, that all the congregation shall offer one young bullock for a burnt offering, for a sweet savour unto the LORD, with his meat offering, and his drink offering, according to the manner, and one kid of the goats for a sin offering.

Nu 18:9 — This shall be thine of the most holy things, *reserved* from the fire: every oblation of theirs, every meat offering of theirs, and every sin offering of theirs, and every trespass offering of theirs, which they shall render unto me, *shall be* most holy for thee and for thy sons.

Nu 28:5 — And a tenth *part* of an ephah of flour for a meat offering, mingled with the fourth *part* of an hin of beaten oil.

Nu 28:9 — And on the sabbath day two lambs of the first year without spot, and two tenth deals of flour *for* a meat offering, mingled with oil, and the drink offering thereof:

Nu 29:14 — And their meat offering *shall be of* flour mingled with oil, three tenth deals unto every bullock of the thirteen bullocks, two tenth deals to each ram of the two rams,

• To be eaten in the Holy Place.

Nu 18:9–10

Le 10:13 — And ye shall eat it in the holy place, because it *is* thy due, and thy sons' due, of the sacrifices of the LORD made by fire: for so I am commanded.

• Offered with the sacrifices.

Nu 15:3–16

• Not mixed with leaven.

Le 6:14–18; 10:12–13

Le 2:4 — And if thou bring an oblation of a meat offering baken in the oven, *it shall be* unleavened cakes of fine flour mingled with oil, or unleavened wafers anointed with oil.

Le 2:11 — No meat offering, which ye shall bring unto the LORD, shall be made with leaven: for ye shall burn no leaven, nor any honey, in any offering of the LORD made by fire.

Nu 6:15 — And a basket of unleavened bread, cakes of fine flour mingled with oil, and wafers of unleavened bread anointed with oil, and their meat offering, and their drink offerings.

Nu 6:17 — And he shall offer the ram *for* a sacrifice of peace offerings unto the LORD, with the basket of unleavened bread: the priest shall offer also his meat offering, and his drink offering.

• Storerooms for, in the temple reconstructed by Ezra.

Ne 13:5–6

Ne 12:44 — And at that time were some appointed over the chambers for the treasures, for the offerings, for the firstfruits, and for the tithes, to gather into them out of the fields of the cities the portions of the law for the priests and Levites: for Judah rejoiced for the priests and for the Levites that waited.

• Storerooms for, provided for in the vision of Ezekiel.

Eze 42:13 — Then said he unto me, The north chambers *and* the south chambers, which *are* before the separate place, they *be* holy chambers, where the priests that approach unto the LORD shall eat the most holy things: there shall they lay the most holy things, and the meat offering, and the sin offering, and the trespass offering; for the place *is* holy.

• Peace.

• Laws concerning.

Ex 29:19–22; Le 7:11–15; 9:3–4, 15–21

Ex 29:31 — And thou shalt take the ram of the consecration, and seethe his flesh in the holy place.

Le 7:18 — And if *any* of the flesh of the sacrifice of his peace offerings be eaten at all on the third day, it shall not be accepted, neither shall it be imputed unto him that offereth it: it shall be an abomination, and the soul that eateth of it shall bear his iniquity.

Le 23:19 — Then ye shall sacrifice one kid of the goats for a sin offering, and two lambs of the first year for a sacrifice of peace offerings.

Nu 6:14 — And he shall offer his offering unto the LORD, one he lamb of the first year without blemish for a burnt offering, and one ewe lamb of the first year without blemish for a sin offering, and one ram without blemish for peace offerings,

Nu 10:10 — Also in the day of your gladness, and in your solemn days, and in the beginnings of your months, ye shall blow with the trumpets over your burnt offerings, and over the sacrifices of your peace offerings; that they may be to you for a memorial before your God: I *am* the LORD your God.

- **Sin.**
  - **Ordinances concerning.**

Ex 29:10–14; Le 4:1–6:7, 26–30; 9:1–21; 12:6–8; Nu 6:10–11; 28:22–24; 29:5–6, 16–38; Heb 13:11–13

Le 14:19 — And the priest shall offer the sin offering, and make an atonement for him that is to be cleansed from his uncleanness; and afterward he shall kill the burnt offering:

Le 14:22 — And two turtledoves, or two young pigeons, such as he is able to get; and the one shall be a sin offering, and the other a burnt offering.

Le 14:31 — *Even* such as he is able to get, the one *for* a sin offering, and the other *for* a burnt offering, with the meat offering: and the priest shall make an atonement for him that is to be cleansed before the LORD.

Le 15:30 — And the priest shall offer the one *for* a sin offering, and the other *for* a burnt offering; and the priest shall make an atonement for her before the LORD for the issue of her uncleanness.

Le 23:19 — Then ye shall sacrifice one kid of the goats for a sin offering, and two lambs of the first year for a sacrifice of peace offerings.

Nu 6:14 — And he shall offer his offering unto the LORD, one he lamb of the first year without blemish for a burnt offering, and one ewe lamb of the first year without blemish for a sin offering, and one ram without blemish for peace offerings,

Nu 6:16 — And the priest shall bring *them* before the LORD, and shall offer his sin offering, and his burnt offering:

Nu 8:8 — Then let them take a young bullock with his meat offering, *even* fine flour mingled with oil, and another young bullock shalt thou take for a sin offering.

Nu 8:12 — And the Levites shall lay their hands upon the heads of the bullocks: and thou shalt offer the one *for* a sin offering, and the other *for* a burnt offering, unto the LORD, to make an atonement for the Levites.

Nu 15:27 — And if any soul sin through ignorance, then he shall bring a she goat of the first year for a sin offering.

Nu 28:15 — And one kid of the goats for a sin offering unto the LORD shall be offered, beside the continual burnt offering, and his drink offering.

Nu 28:30 — *And* one kid of the goats, to make an atonement for you.

Nu 29:11 — One kid of the goats *for* a sin offering; beside the sin offering of atonement, and the continual burnt offering, and the meat offering of it, and their drink offerings.

  - **Temporary.**

Heb 9:1–10:39

Da 11:31 — And arms shall stand on his part, and they shall pollute the sanctuary of strength, and shall take away the daily *sacrifice,* and they shall place the abomination that maketh desolate.

- **Special sacrifices.**
  - **In consecration of the altar.**

⇛See: Altar

  - **In consecration of priests.**

⇛See: Priest, Emoluments of

⇛See: Priest, Mosaic

  - **In consecration of the temple.**

⇛See: Temple, Solomon's; facts about; dedication of

  - **In consecration for leprosy.**

⇛See: Leprosy

  - **In consecration for defilement.**

⇛See: Defilement

- **Thank.**
  - **Ordinances concerning.**

Le 7:11–15; Dt 12:11–12

Le 22:29 — And when ye will offer a sacrifice of thanksgiving unto the LORD, offer *it* at your own will.

- **Trespass.**
  - **Ordinances concerning.**

Le 5:1–6:7; 7:1–7; 14:10–22; 15:29–30; 19:21–22

Le 15:15 — And the priest shall offer them, the one *for* a sin offering, and the other *for* a burnt offering; and the priest shall make an atonement for him before the LORD for his issue.

Nu 6:12 — And he shall consecrate unto the LORD the days of his separation, and shall bring a lamb of the first year for a trespass offering: but the days that were before shall be lost, because his separation was defiled.

Ezr 10:19 — And they gave their hands that they would put away their wives; and *being* guilty, *they offered* a ram of the flock for their trespass.

  - **To be eaten by the priests.**

Le 7:6–7; Nu 18:9–10

Le 14:13 — And he shall slay the lamb in the place where he shall kill the sin offering and the burnt offering, in the holy place: for as the sin offering *is* the priest's, *so is* the trespass offering: it *is* most holy:

  - **Offered by idolaters.**

1Sa 6:17–18

1Sa 6:3 — And they said, If ye send away the ark of the God of Israel, send it not empty; but in any wise return him a trespass offering: then ye shall be healed, and it shall be known to you why his hand is not removed from you.

1Sa 6:8 — And take the ark of the LORD, and lay it upon the cart; and put the jewels of gold, which ye return him *for* a trespass offering, in a coffer by the side thereof; and send it away, that it may go.

⇛See: Offerings; sin

- **Unavailing when not accompanied by piety.**

Ps 50:8–14; 51:16–17; Isa 1:11–14; Jer 7:21–23; Am 5:21–24; Mic 6:6–8

1Sa 15:22 — And Samuel said, Hath the LORD *as great* delight in burnt offerings and sacrifices, as in obeying the voice of the LORD? Behold, to obey *is* better than sacrifice, *and* to hearken than the fat of rams.

Ps 40:6 — Sacrifice and offering thou didst not desire; mine ears hast thou opened: burnt offering and sin offering hast thou not required.

Pr 21:3 — To do justice and judgment *is* more acceptable to the LORD than sacrifice.

Pr 21:27 — The sacrifice of the wicked *is* abomination: how much more, *when* he bringeth it with a wicked mind?

Isa 40:16 — And Lebanon *is* not sufficient to burn, nor the beasts thereof sufficient for a burnt offering.

Isa 66:3 — He that killeth an ox *is as if* he slew a man; he that sacrificeth a lamb, *as if* he cut off a dog's neck; he that offereth an oblation, *as if he offered* swine's blood; he that burneth incense, *as if* he blessed an idol. Yea, they have chosen their own ways, and their soul delighteth in their abominations.

Jer 6:20 — To what purpose cometh there to me incense from Sheba, and the sweet cane from a far country? your burnt offerings *are* not acceptable, nor your sacrifices sweet unto me.

Jer 14:12 — When they fast, I will not hear their cry; and when they offer burnt offering and an oblation, I will not accept them: but I will consume them by the sword, and by the famine, and by the pestilence.

Hos 6:6 — For I desired mercy, and not sacrifice; and the knowledge of God more than burnt offerings.

Hos 8:13 — They sacrifice flesh *for* the sacrifices of mine offerings, and *eat it;* but the LORD accepteth them not; now will he remember their iniquity, and visit their sins: they shall return to Egypt.

Mk 12:33 — And to love him with all the heart, and with all the understanding, and with all the soul, and with all the strength, and to love *his* neighbour as himself, is more than all whole burnt offerings and sacrifices.

• Vow.

Le 7:16–17; 22:17–25; Dt 23:21–23

• Wave.

• Ordinances concerning.

Ex 29:26–28; Le 7:29–34; 8:25–29; 9:19–21; 10:14–15; 23:10–11, 17–20; Nu 6:19–20

Ex 29:22 — Also thou shalt take of the ram the fat and the rump, and the fat that covereth the inwards, and the *caul* above the liver, and the two kidneys, and the fat that *is* upon them, and the right shoulder; for it *is* a ram of consecration:

Nu 5:25 — Then the priest shall take the jealousy offering out of the woman's hand, and shall wave the offering before the LORD, and offer it upon the altar:

• Belonged to the priests.

Ex 29:26–28

Le 7:31 — And the priest shall burn the fat upon the altar: but the breast shall be Aaron's and his sons'.

Le 7:34 — For the wave breast and the heave shoulder have I taken of the children of Israel from off the sacrifices of their peace offerings, and have given them unto Aaron the priest and unto his sons by a statute for ever from among the children of Israel.

Le 8:29 — And Moses took the breast, and waved it *for* a wave offering before the LORD: *for* of the ram of consecration it was Moses' part; as the LORD commanded Moses.

Le 9:21 — And the breasts and the right shoulder Aaron waved *for* a wave offering before the LORD; as Moses commanded.

Le 23:20 — And the priest shall wave them with the bread of the first fruits *for* a wave offering before the LORD, with the two lambs: they shall be holy to the LORD for the priest.

Nu 18:11 — And this *is* thine; the heave offering of their gift, with all the wave offerings of the children of Israel: I have given them unto thee, and to thy sons and to thy daughters with thee, by a statute for ever: every one that is clean in thy house shall eat of it.

Nu 18:18 — And the flesh of them shall be thine, as the wave breast and as the right shoulder are thine.

• To be eaten.

Le 10:14–15; Nu 18:18–19

Nu 18:11 — And this *is* thine; the heave offering of their gift, with all the wave offerings of the children of Israel: I have given them unto thee, and to thy sons and to thy daughters with thee, by a statute for ever: every one that is clean in thy house shall eat of it.

Nu 18:31 — And ye shall eat it in every place, ye and your households: for it *is* your reward for your service in the tabernacle of the congregation.

• Wood.

• Fuel for the temple.

Ne 10:34 — And we cast the lots among the priests, the Levites, and the people, for the wood offering, to bring *it* into the house of our God, after the houses of our fathers, at times appointed year by year, to burn upon the altar of the LORD our God, as *it is* written in the law:

Ne 13:31 — And for the wood offering, at times appointed, and for the firstfruits. Remember me, O my God, for good.

OFFICER

• Civil.

• Chosen by the people.

Dt 1:13–16

• Appointed by kings.

2Sa 8:16–18; 20:23–26; 1Ki 4:1–19

1Ki 9:22 — But of the children of Israel did Solomon make no bondmen: but they *were* men of war, and his servants, and his princes, and his captains, and rulers of his chariots, and his horsemen.

Ezr 7:25 — And thou, Ezra, after the wisdom of thy God, that *is* in thine hand, set magistrates and judges, which may judge all the people that *are* beyond the river, all such as know the laws of thy God; and teach ye them that know *them* not.

✦See: Government

✦See: **Judge**
✦See: **Rulers**

• **Ecclesiastical.**

✦See: **Apostle**
✦See: **Deacon**
✦See: **Elder**
✦See: **Levites**
✦See: **Minister, Miscellany of Minor Sub-Topics**
✦See: **Priest, High**

OG, king of Bashan

• **A man of gigantic stature.**

Nu 21:33 — And they turned and went up by the way of Bashan: and Og the king of Bashan went out against them, he, and all his people, to the battle at Edrei.

Dt 3:11 — For only Og king of Bashan remained of the remnant of giants; behold, his bedstead *was* a bedstead of iron; is it not in Rabbath of the children of Ammon? nine cubits was the length thereof, and four cubits the breadth of it, after the cubit of a man.

Jos 12:4 — And the coast of Og king of Bashan, *which was* of the remnant of the giants, that dwelt at Ashtaroth and at Edrei,

Jos 13:12 — All the kingdom of Og in Bashan, which reigned in Ashtaroth and in Edrei, who remained of the remnant of the giants: for these did Moses smite, and cast them out.

• **Defeated and slain by Moses.**

Nu 21:33–35; Dt 3:1–7; Ps 135:10–11; 136:18–20

Dt 1:4 — After he had slain Sihon the king of the Amorites, which dwelt in Heshbon, and Og the king of Bashan, which dwelt at Astaroth in Edrei:

Dt 29:7 — And when ye came unto this place, Sihon the king of Heshbon, and Og the king of Bashan, came out against us unto battle, and we smote them:

Dt 31:4 — And the LORD shall do unto them as he did to Sihon and to Og, kings of the Amorites, and unto the land of them, whom he destroyed.

Jos 2:10 — For we have heard how the LORD dried up the water of the Red sea for you, when ye came out of Egypt; and what ye did unto the two kings of the Amorites, that *were* on the other side Jordan, Sihon and Og, whom ye utterly destroyed.

Jos 9:10 — And all that he did to the two kings of the Amorites, that *were* beyond Jordan, to Sihon king of Heshbon, and to Og king of Bashan, which *was* at Ashtaroth.

• **Land of, given to Gad, Reuben, and Manasseh.**

Dt 3:8–17; 4:47–49; 29:7–8; Jos 12:4–6; 13:30–31; Ps 136:20–21

Nu 32:33 — And Moses gave unto them, *even* to the children of Gad, and to the children of Reuben, and unto half the tribe of Manasseh the son of Joseph, the kingdom of Sihon king of the Amorites, and the kingdom of Og king of Bashan, the land, with the cities thereof in the coasts, *even* the cities of the country round about.

Jos 13:12 — All the kingdom of Og in Bashan, which reigned in Ashtaroth and in Edrei, who remained of the remnant of the giants: for these did Moses smite, and cast them out.

1Ki 4:19 — Geber the son of Uri *was* in the country of Gilead, *in* the country of Sihon king of the Amorites, and of Og king of Bashan; and *he was* the only officer which *was* in the land.

Ne 9:22 — Moreover thou gavest them kingdoms and nations, and didst divide them into corners: so they possessed the land of Sihon, and the land of the king of Heshbon, and the land of Og king of Bashan.

OHAD • Son of Simeon.

Ge 46:10 — And the sons of Simeon; Jemuel, and Jamin, and Ohad, and Jachin, and Zohar, and Shaul the son of a Canaanitish woman.

Ex 6:15 — And the sons of Simeon; Jemuel, and Jamin, and Ohad, and Jachin, and Zohar, and Shaul the son of a Canaanitish woman: these *are* the families of Simeon.

OHEL • Son of Zerubabbel.

1Ch 3:20 — And Hashubah, and Ohel, and Berechiah, and Hasadiah, Jushab-hesed, five.

OIL

• **Sacred.**

Ex 30:23–25

Ex 31:11 — And the anointing oil, and sweet incense for the holy *place:* according to all that I have commanded thee shall they do.

Ex 35:8 — And oil for the light, and spices for anointing oil, and for the sweet incense,

Ex 35:15 — And the incense altar, and his staves, and the anointing oil, and the sweet incense, and the hanging for the door at the entering in of the tabernacle,

Ex 35:28 — And spice, and oil for the light, and for the anointing oil, and for the sweet incense.

Ex 37:29 — And he made the holy anointing oil, and the pure incense of sweet spices, according to the work of the apothecary.

Ex 39:38 — And the golden altar, and the anointing oil, and the sweet incense, and the hanging for the tabernacle door,

Nu 4:16 — And to the office of Eleazar the son of Aaron the priest *pertaineth* the oil for the light, and the sweet incense, and the daily meat offering, and the anointing oil, *and* the oversight of all the tabernacle, and of all that therein *is,* in the sanctuary, and in the vessels thereof.

1Ch 9:30 — And *some* of the sons of the priests made the ointment of the spices.

• **Punishment for profaning.**

Ex 30:31–33

• **Used for idols.**

Eze 23:41 — And satest upon a stately bed, and a table prepared before it, whereupon thou hast set mine incense and mine oil.

• **Illuminating, for tabernacle.**

Le 24:2–4

Ex 25:6 — Oil for the light, spices for anointing oil, and for sweet incense,

Ex 27:20 — And thou shalt command the children of Israel, that they bring thee pure oil olive beaten for the light, to cause the lamp to burn always.

• **For domestic use.**

Mt 25:3 — They that *were* foolish took their lamps, and took no oil with them:

• **Used for food.**

Le 2:4–5; 1Ki 17:12–16

Le 14:10 — And on the eighth day he shall take two he lambs without blemish, and one ewe lamb of the first year without blemish, and three tenth deals of fine flour *for* a meat offering, mingled with oil, and one log of oil.

Le 14:21 — And if he *be* poor, and cannot get so much; then he shall take one lamb *for* a trespass offering to be waved, to make an atonement for him, and one tenth deal of fine flour mingled with oil for a meat offering, and a log of oil;

Dt 12:17 — Thou mayest not eat within thy gates the tithe of thy corn, or of thy wine, or of thy oil, or the firstlings of thy herds or of thy flock, nor any of thy vows which thou vowest, nor thy freewill offerings, or heave offering of thine hand:

Pr 21:17 — He that loveth pleasure *shall be* a poor man: he that loveth wine and oil shall not be rich.

Eze 16:13 — Thus wast thou decked with gold and silver; and thy raiment *was of* fine linen, and silk, and broidered work; thou didst eat fine flour, and honey, and oil: and thou wast exceeding beautiful, and thou didst prosper into a kingdom.

Hos 2:5 — For their mother hath played the harlot: she that conceived them hath done shamefully: for she said, I will go after my lovers, that give *me* my bread and my water, my wool and my flax, mine oil and my drink.

• **For the head.**

Ps 23:5 — Thou preparest a table before me in the presence of mine enemies: thou anointest my head with oil; my cup runneth over.

Ps 105:15 — *Saying,* Touch not mine anointed, and do my prophets no harm.

Lk 7:46 — My head with oil thou didst not anoint: but this woman hath anointed my feet with ointment.

• **For anointing kings.**

1Sa 10:1 — Then Samuel took a vial of oil, and poured *it* upon his head, and kissed him, and said, *Is it* not because the LORD hath anointed thee *to be* captain over his inheritance?

1Sa 16:1 — And the LORD said unto Samuel, How long wilt thou mourn for Saul, seeing I have rejected him from reigning over Israel? fill thine horn with oil, and go, I will send thee to Jesse the Bethlehemite: for I have provided me a king among his sons.

1Sa 16:13 — Then Samuel took the horn of oil, and anointed him in the midst of his brethren: and the Spirit of the LORD came upon David from that day forward. So Samuel rose up, and went to Ramah.

1Ki 1:39 — And Zadok the priest took an horn of oil out of the tabernacle, and anointed Solomon. And they blew the trumpet; and all the people said, God save king Solomon.

• **Tribute paid in.**

Hos 12:1 — Ephraim feedeth on wind, and followeth after the east wind: he daily increaseth lies and desolation; and they do make a covenant with the Assyrians, and oil is carried into Egypt.

• **Commerce in.**

2Ki 4:1–7

• **Petroleum.**

Job 29:6 — When I washed my steps with butter, and the rock poured me out rivers of oil;

See: Anointing

See: Ointment

OINTMENT

• **Not sacred.**

Mk 14:3–5; Jn 12:3–5

2Ki 20:13 — And Hezekiah hearkened unto them, and shewed them all the house of his precious things, the silver, and the gold, and the spices, and the precious ointment, and *all* the house of his armour, and all that was found in his treasures: there was nothing in his house, nor in all his dominion, that Hezekiah shewed them not.

Est 2:12 — Now when every maid's turn was come to go in to king Ahasuerus, after that she had been twelve months, according to the manner of the women, (for so were the days of their purifications accomplished, *to wit,* six months with oil of myrrh, and six months with sweet odours, and with *other* things for the purifying of the women;)

Ecc 7:1 — A good name *is* better than precious ointment; and the day of death than the day of one's birth.

Ecc 10:1 — Dead flies cause the ointment of the apothecary to send forth a stinking savour: *so doth* a little folly him that is in reputation for wisdom *and* honour.

SS 1:3 — Because of the savour of thy good ointments thy name *is as* ointment poured forth, therefore do the virgins love thee.

SS 4:10 — How fair is thy love, my sister, *my* spouse! how much better is thy love than wine! and the smell of thine ointments than all spices!

Am 6:6 — That drink wine in bowls, and anoint themselves with the chief ointments: but they are not grieved for the affliction of Joseph.

• **The alabaster box of.**

Mt 26:7 — There came unto him a woman having an alabaster box of very precious ointment, and poured it on his head, as he sat *at meat.*

• **Sacred.**

• **Formula for.**

Ex 30:23–25

• **Uses of.**

Ex 30:26–33

• **Compounded by Bezaleel.**

Ex 37:1 — And Bezaleel made the ark *of* shittim wood: two cubits and a half *was* the length of it, and a cubit and a half the breadth of it, and a cubit and a half the height of it:

Ex 37:29 — And he made the holy anointing oil, and the pure incense of sweet spices, according to the work of the apothecary.

➻See: Oil; sacred

OLD AGE

2Sa 19:34–37; Job 32:4–9; Ps 148:12–13; Ecc 12:1–7; Tit 2:2–3

Ge 15:15 — And thou shalt go to thy fathers in peace; thou shalt be buried in a good old age.

Ge 34:7 — And the sons of Jacob came out of the field when they heard *it:* and the men were grieved, and they were very wroth, because he had wrought folly in Israel in lying with Jacob's daughter; which thing ought not to be done.

Ge 47:9 — And Jacob said unto Pharaoh, The days of the years of my pilgrimage *are* an hundred and thirty years: few and evil have the days of the years of my life been, and have not attained unto the days of the years of the life of my fathers in the days of their pilgrimage.

1Ch 29:28 — And he died in a good old age, full of days, riches, and honour: and Solomon his son reigned in his stead.

Job 5:26 — Thou shalt come to *thy* grave in a full age, like as a shock of corn cometh in in his season.

Job 11:17 — And *thine* age shall be clearer than the noonday; thou shalt shine forth, thou shalt be as the morning.

Job 12:12 — With the ancient *is* wisdom; and in length of days understanding.

Job 42:17 — So Job died, *being* old and full of days.

Ps 71:9 — Cast me not off in the time of old age; forsake me not when my strength faileth.

Ps 71:18 — Now also when I am old and greyheaded, O God, forsake me not; until I have shewed thy strength unto *this* generation, *and* thy power to every one *that* is to come.

Ps 90:10 — The days of our years *are* threescore years and ten; and if by reason of strength *they be* fourscore years, yet *is* their strength labour and sorrow; for it is soon cut off, and we fly away.

Ps 92:14 — They shall still bring forth fruit in old age; they shall be fat and flourishing;

Pr 16:31 — The hoary head *is* a crown of glory, *if* it be found in the way of righteousness.

Ecc 6:3 — If a man beget an hundred *children,* and live many years, so that the days of his years be many, and his soul be not filled with good, and also *that* he have no burial; I say, *that* an untimely birth *is* better than he.

Ecc 6:6 — Yea, though he live a thousand years twice *told,* yet hath he seen no good: do not all go to one place?

Isa 46:4 — And *even* to *your* old age I *am* he; and *even* to hoar hairs will I carry *you:* I have made, and I will bear; even I will carry, and will deliver *you.*

Lk 2:37 — And she *was* a widow of about fourscore and four years, which departed not from the temple, but served *God* with fastings and prayers night and day.

Phm 1:9 — Yet for love's sake I rather beseech *thee,* being such an one as Paul the aged, and now also a prisoner of Jesus Christ.

➻See: Infirmity

➻See: Longevity

OLIVE

• **A fruit tree.**

• **Branch of, brought by the dove to Noah's ark.**

Ge 8:11 — And the dove came in to him in the evening; and, lo, in her mouth *was* an olive leaf pluckt off: so Noah knew that the waters were abated from off the earth.

• **Common to the land of Canaan.**

Ex 23:11 — But the seventh *year* thou shalt let it rest and lie still; that the poor of thy people may eat: and what they leave the beasts of the field shall eat. In like manner thou shalt deal with thy vineyard, *and* with thy oliveyard.

Dt 6:11 — And houses full of all good *things,* which thou filledst not, and wells digged, which thou diggedst not, vineyards and olive trees, which thou plantedst not; when thou shalt have eaten and be full;

Dt 8:8 — A land of wheat, and barley, and vines, and fig trees, and pomegranates; a land of oil olive, and honey;

• **Israelites commanded to cultivate in the land of promise.**

Dt 28:40 — Thou shalt have olive trees throughout all thy coasts, but thou shalt not anoint *thyself* with the oil; for thine olive shall cast *his fruit.*

• **Branches of, used for booths.**

Ne 8:15 — And that they should publish and proclaim in all their cities, and in Jerusalem, saying, Go forth unto the mount, and fetch olive branches, and pine branches, and myrtle branches, and palm branches, and branches of thick trees, to make booths, as *it is* written.

• **Bears flowers.**

Job 15:33 — He shall shake off his unripe grape as the vine, and shall cast off his flower as the olive.

• **Precepts concerning gleaning the fruit of.**

Dt 24:20 — When thou beatest thine olive tree, thou shalt not go over the boughs again: it shall be for the stranger, for the fatherless, and for the widow.

Isa 17:6 — Yet gleaning grapes shall be left in it, as the shaking of an olive tree, two *or* three berries in the top of the uppermost bough, four *or* five in the outmost fruitful branches thereof, saith the LORD God of Israel.

• **Cherubim made of the wood of.**

1Ki 6:31–33

1Ki 6:23 — And within the oracle he made two cherubims *of* olive tree, *each* ten cubits high.

• Fable of.

Jgs 9:8 — The trees went forth *on a time* to anoint a king over them; and they said unto the olive tree, Reign thou over us.

• Figurative.

• Of prosperity.

Ps 128:3 — Thy wife *shall be* as a fruitful vine by the sides of thine house: thy children like olive plants round about thy table.

• The wild, a figure of the Gentiles; the cultivated, of the Jews.

Ro 11:17–21

Ro 11:24 — For if thou wert cut out of the olive tree which is wild by nature, and wert graffed contrary to nature into a good olive tree: how much more shall these, which be the natural *branches,* be graffed into their own olive tree?

• Symbolic.

Zec 4:2–12

Rev 11:4 — These are the two olive trees, and the two candlesticks standing before the God of the earth.

• Fruit of.

• Oil extracted from, used as illuminating oil in the tabernacle.

Ex 39:37 — The pure candlestick, *with* the lamps thereof, *even with* the lamps to be set in order, and all the vessels thereof, and the oil for light,

Le 24:2 — Command the children of Israel, that they bring unto thee pure oil olive beaten for the light, to cause the lamps to burn continually.

Zec 4:12 — And I answered again, and said unto him, What *be these* two olive branches which through the two golden pipes empty the golden *oil* out of themselves?

⇜See: Oil

OLIVES, MOUNT OF

• Called Mount of Corruption.

2Ki 23:13 — And the high places that *were* before Jerusalem, which *were* on the right hand of the mount of corruption, which Solomon the king of Israel had builded for Ashtoreth the abomination of the Zidonians, and for Chemosh the abomination of the Moabites, and for Milcom the abomination of the children of Ammon, did the king defile.

• East of Jerusalem; the highway to and from the east passed over it.

2Sa 15:30 — And David went up by the ascent of *mount* Olivet, and wept as he went up, and had his head covered, and he went barefoot: and all the people that *was* with him covered every man his head, and they went up, weeping as they went up.

• Jesus' triumphant entry into Jerusalem by way of.

Mt 21:1 — And when they drew nigh unto Jerusalem, and were come to Bethphage, unto the mount of Olives, then sent Jesus two disciples,

Mk 11:1 — And when they came nigh to Jerusalem, unto Bethphage and Bethany, at the mount of Olives, he sendeth forth two of his disciples,

Lk 19:29 — And it came to pass, when he was come nigh to Bethphage and Bethany, at the mount called *the mount* of Olives, he sent two of his disciples,

Lk 19:37 — And when he was come nigh, even now at the descent of the mount of Olives, the whole multitude of the disciples began to rejoice and praise God with a loud voice for all the mighty works that they had seen;

• Jesus repairs to.

Mt 24:3 — And as he sat upon the mount of Olives, the disciples came unto him privately, saying, Tell us, when shall these things be? and what *shall be* the sign of thy coming, and of the end of the world?

Mt 26:30 — And when they had sung an hymn, they went out into the mount of Olives.

Mk 13:3 — And as he sat upon the mount of Olives over against the temple, Peter and James and John and Andrew asked him privately,

Mk 14:26 — And when they had sung an hymn, they went out into the mount of Olives.

Lk 21:37 — And in the day time he was teaching in the temple; and at night he went out, and abode in the mount that is called *the mount* of Olives.

Lk 22:39 — And he came out, and went, as he was wont, to the mount of Olives; and his disciples also followed him.

• Jesus makes his ascension from.

Ac 1:12 — Then returned they unto Jerusalem from the mount called Olivet, which is from Jerusalem a sabbath day's journey.

OLIVET ⇜See: Olives, Mount of

OLYMPAS • A believer at Rome.

Ro 16:15 — Salute Philologus, and Julia, Nereus, and his sister, and Olympas, and all the saints which are with them.

OMAR • Son of Eliphaz, grandson of Esau.

Ge 36:11 — And the sons of Eliphaz were Teman, Omar, Zepho, and Gatam, and Kenaz.

Ge 36:15 — These *were* dukes of the sons of Esau: the sons of Eliphaz the firstborn *son* of Esau; duke Teman, duke Omar, duke Zepho, duke Kenaz,

1Ch 1:36 — The sons of Eliphaz; Teman, and Omar, Zephi, and Gatam, Kenaz, and Timna, and Amalek.

OMEGA

• Alpha and Omega, the all-comprehensiveness of Christ.

Rev 1:8 — I am Alpha and Omega, the beginning and the ending, saith the Lord, which is, and which was, and which is to come, the Almighty.

Rev 1:11 — Saying, I am Alpha and Omega, the first and the last: and, What thou seest, write in a book, and send *it* unto the seven churches which are in Asia; unto Ephesus, and unto Smyrna, and unto

Pergamos, and unto Thyatira, and unto Sardis, and unto Philadelphia, and unto Laodicea.

Rev 21:6 — And he said unto me, It is done. I am Alpha and Omega, the beginning and the end. I will give unto him that is athirst of the fountain of the water of life freely.

Rev 22:13 — I am Alpha and Omega, the beginning and the end, the first and the last.

OMER, one-tenth part of an ephah

• A dry measure containing two or three and a half quarts.

Ex 16:16–18

Ex 16:36 — Now an omer *is* the tenth *part* of an ephah.

OMNIPOTENCE

See: God, Omnipotent

See: Jesus, Omnipotence of

OMNISCIENCE

See: God, Omniscient

See: Jesus, Omniscience of

OMRI

• King of Israel.

• Commander of army of Israel; proclaimed king by army upon news of assassination of King Elah.

1Ki 16:16 — And the people *that were* encamped heard say, Zimri hath conspired, and hath also slain the king: wherefore all Israel made Omri, the captain of the host, king over Israel that day in the camp.

• Defeats his rival, Tibni, and establishes himself.

1Ki 16:17–22

• Surrenders cities to king of Syria.

1Ki 20:34 — And *Ben-hadad* said unto him, The cities, which my father took from thy father, I will restore; and thou shalt make streets for thee in Damascus, as my father made in Samaria. Then *said Ahab,* I will send thee away with this covenant. So he made a covenant with him, and sent him away.

• Wicked reign and death of.

1Ki 16:23–28

• Denounced by Micah.

Mic 6:16 — For the statutes of Omri are kept, and all the works of the house of Ahab, and ye walk in their counsels; that I should make thee a desolation, and the inhabitants thereof an hissing: therefore ye shall bear the reproach of my people.

• A son of Becher, grandson of Benjamin.

1Ch 7:8 — And the sons of Becher; Zemira, and Joash, and Eliezer, and Elioenai, and Omri, and Jerimoth, and Abiah, and Anathoth, and Alameth. All these *are* the sons of Becher.

• A descendant of Pharez.

1Ch 9:4 — Uthai the son of Ammihud, the son of Omri, the son of Imri, the son of Bani, of the children of Pharez the son of Judah.

• Son of Michael, and ruler of tribe of Issachar in time of David.

1Ch 27:18 — Of Judah, Elihu, *one* of the brethren of David: of Issachar, Omri the son of Michael:

ON

• Capital of lower Egypt.

Ge 41:45 — And Pharaoh called Joseph's name Zaphnath-paaneah; and he gave him to wife Asenath the daughter of Poti-pherah priest of On. And Joseph went out over *all* the land of Egypt.

Ge 46:20 — And unto Joseph in the land of Egypt were born Manasseh and Ephraim, which Asenath the daughter of Poti-pherah priest of On bare unto him.

• A leader of the Reubenites who rebelled against Moses.

Nu 16:1 — Now Korah, the son of Izhar, the son of Kohath, the son of Levi, and Dathan and Abiram, the sons of Eliab, and On, the son of Peleth, sons of Reuben, took *men:*

ONAM

• A son of Shobal.

Ge 36:23 — And the children of Shobal *were* these; Alvan, and Manahath, and Ebal, Shepho, and Onam.

1Ch 1:40 — The sons of Shobal; Alian, and Manahath, and Ebal, Shephi, and Onam. And the sons of Zibeon; Aiah, and Anah.

• Son of Jerahmeel.

1Ch 2:26 — Jerahmeel had also another wife, whose name *was* Atarah; she *was* the mother of Onam.

1Ch 2:28 — And the sons of Onam were, Shammai, and Jada. And the sons of Shammai; Nadab, and Abishur.

ONAN

• Son of Judah.

• Slain for his refusal to raise seed to his brother.

Ge 38:8–10

Ge 38:4 — And she conceived again, and bare a son; and she called his name Onan.

Ge 46:12 — And the sons of Judah; Er, and Onan, and Shelah, and Pharez, and Zarah: but Er and Onan died in the land of Canaan. And the sons of Pharez were Hezron and Hamul.

Nu 26:19 — The sons of Judah *were* Er and Onan: and Er and Onan died in the land of Canaan.

1Ch 2:3 — The sons of Judah; Er, and Onan, and Shelah: *which* three were born unto him of the daughter of Shua the Canaanitess. And Er, the first-born of Judah, was evil in the sight of the LORD; and he slew him.

ONESIMUS • A fugitive slave and convert of Paul.

Col 4:9 — With Onesimus, a faithful and beloved brother, who is *one* of you. They shall make known unto you all things which *are done* here.

Phm 1:10 — I beseech thee for my son Onesimus, whom I have begotten in my bonds:

ONESIPHORUS • A Christian of Ephesus.

2Ti 1:16–17

2Ti 4:19 — Salute Prisca and Aquila, and the household of Onesiphorus.

ONION

Nu 11:5 — We remember the fish, which we did eat in Egypt freely; the cucumbers, and the melons, and the leeks, and the onions, and the garlick:

ONO • A town of Benjamim.

1Ch 8:12 — The sons of Elpaal; Eber, and Misham, and Shamed, who built Ono, and Lod, with the towns thereof:

Ne 6:2 — That Sanballat and Geshem sent unto me, saying, Come, let us meet together in *some one of* the villages in the plain of Ono. But they thought to do me mischief.

Ne 11:35 — Lod, and Ono, the valley of craftsmen.

ONYCHA

• A component of the sacred ointment.

• Made from the shells of a species of mussel, possessing an odor.

Ex 30:34 — And the LORD said unto Moses, Take unto thee sweet spices, stacte, and onycha, and galbanum; *these* sweet spices with pure frankincense: of each shall there be a like *weight:*

ONYX

• Precious stone.

Job 28:16 — It cannot be valued with the gold of Ophir, with the precious onyx, or the sapphire.

Eze 28:13 — Thou hast been in Eden the garden of God; every precious stone *was* thy covering, the sardius, topaz, and the diamond, the beryl, the onyx, and the jasper, the sapphire, the emerald, and the carbuncle, and gold: the workmanship of thy tabrets and of thy pipes was prepared in thee in the day that thou wast created.

• Used in erecting the temple.

1Ch 29:2 — Now I have prepared with all my might for the house of my God the gold for *things to be made* of gold, and the silver for *things* of silver, and the brass for *things* of brass, the iron for *things* of iron, and wood for *things* of wood; onyx stones, and *stones* to be set, glistering stones, and of divers colours, and all manner of precious stones, and marble stones in abundance.

• Seen in the foundations of the city of the New Jerusalem in John's apocalyptic vision.

Rev 21:20 — The fifth, sardonyx; the sixth, sardius; the seventh, chrysolite; the eighth, beryl; the ninth, a topaz; the tenth, a chrysoprasus; the eleventh, a jacinth; the twelfth, an amethyst.

• Exported from Havilah.

Ge 2:12 — And the gold of that land *is* good: there *is* bdellium and the onyx stone.

• Used in the breastplate.

Ex 28:9–12

Ex 28:20 — And the fourth row a beryl, and an onyx, and a jasper: they shall be set in gold in their inclosings.

Ex 39:6 — And they wrought onyx stones inclosed in ouches of gold, graven, as signets are graven, with the names of the children of Israel.

Ex 39:13 — And the fourth row, a beryl, an onyx, and a jasper: *they were* inclosed in ouches of gold in their inclosings.

• Contributed by Israelites for the priests' garments.

Ex 25:7 — Onyx stones, and stones to be set in the ephod, and in the breastplate.

Ex 35:9 — And onyx stones, and stones to be set for the ephod, and for the breastplate.

OPHEL

• A gate in the wall of the city and the temple.

Ne 3:26–27

2Ch 27:3 — He built the high gate of the house of the LORD, and on the wall of Ophel he built much.

2Ch 33:14 — Now after this he built a wall without the city of David, on the west side of Gihon, in the valley, even to the entering in at the fish gate, and compassed about Ophel, and raised it up a very great height, and put captains of war in all the fenced cities of Judah.

OPHIR

• Son of Joktan.

Ge 10:29 — And Ophir, and Havilah, and Jobab: all these *were* the sons of Joktan.

1Ch 1:23 — And Ophir, and Havilah, and Jobab. All these *were* the sons of Joktan.

• A country celebrated for its gold and other valuable merchandise.

• Products of, used by Solomon and Hiram.

1Ki 9:28 — And they came to Ophir, and fetched from thence gold, four hundred and twenty talents, and brought *it* to king Solomon.

1Ki 10:11 — And the navy also of Hiram, that brought gold from Ophir, brought in from Ophir great plenty of almug trees, and precious stones.

2Ch 8:18 — And Huram sent him by the hands of his servants ships, and servants that had knowledge of the sea; and they went with the servants of Solomon to Ophir, and took thence four hundred and fifty talents of gold, and brought *them* to king Solomon.

2Ch 9:10 — And the servants also of Huram, and the servants of Solomon, which brought gold from Ophir, brought algum trees and precious stones.

• Jehoshaphat sends ships to, which are wrecked.

1Ki 22:48 — Jehoshaphat made ships of Tharshish to go to Ophir for gold: but they went not; for the ships were broken at Ezion-geber.

• Gold of, proverbial for its fineness.

1Ch 29:4 — *Even* three thousand talents of gold, of the gold of Ophir, and seven thousand talents of refined silver, to overlay the walls of the houses *withal:*

Job 22:24 — Then shalt thou lay up gold as dust, and the *gold* of Ophir as the stones of the brooks.

Job 28:16 — It cannot be valued with the gold of Ophir, with the precious onyx, or the sapphire.

Ps 45:9 — Kings' daughters *were* among thy honourable women: upon thy right hand did stand the queen in gold of Ophir.

Isa 13:12 — I will make a man more precious than fine gold; even a man than the golden wedge of Ophir.

OPHNI • A town of the Benjamites.

Jos 18:24 — And Chephar-haammonai, and Ophni, and Gaba; twelve cities with their villages:

OPHRAH

• A city in Benjamin.

Jos 18:23 — And Avim, and Parah, and Ophrah,

1Sa 13:17 — And the spoilers came out of the camp of the Philistines in three companies: one company turned unto the way *that leadeth to* Ophrah, unto the land of Shual:

• Possibly identical with Ephrain.

2Ch 13:19 — And Abijah pursued after Jeroboam, and took cities from him, Bethel with the towns thereof, and Jeshanah with the towns thereof, and Ephrain with the towns thereof.

• Possibly identical with Ephraim.

Jn 11:54 — Jesus therefore walked no more openly among the Jews; but went thence unto a country near to the wilderness, into a city called Ephraim, and there continued with his disciples.

• A city in Manasseh, home of Gideon.

Jgs 6:11 — And there came an angel of the LORD, and sat under an oak which *was* in Ophrah, that *pertained* unto Joash the Abi-ezrite: and his son Gideon threshed wheat by the winepress, to hide *it* from the Midianites.

Jgs 6:24 — Then Gideon built an altar there unto the LORD, and called it Jehovah-shalom: unto this day it is yet in Ophrah of the Abi-ezrites.

Jgs 8:27 — And Gideon made an ephod thereof, and put it in his city, *even* in Ophrah: and all Israel went thither a whoring after it: which thing became a snare unto Gideon, and to his house.

Jgs 8:32 — And Gideon the son of Joash died in a good old age, and was buried in the sepulchre of Joash his father, in Ophrah of the Abi-ezrites.

Jgs 9:5 — And he went unto his father's house at Ophrah, and slew his brethren the sons of Jerubbaal, *being* threescore and ten persons, upon one stone: notwithstanding yet Jotham the youngest son of Jerubbaal was left; for he hid himself.

• Son of Meonothai.

1Ch 4:14 — And Meonothai begat Ophrah: and Seraiah begat Joab, the father of the valley of Charashim; for they were craftsmen.

OPINION, PUBLIC

• Kings influenced by.

See: King

• Jesus inquires about.

Mt 16:13 — When Jesus came into the coasts of Caesarea Philippi, he asked his disciples, saying, Whom do men say that I the Son of man am?

Lk 9:18 — And it came to pass, as he was alone praying, his disciples were with him: and he asked them, saying, Whom say the people that I am?

• Feared by.

• Nicodemus.

Jn 3:2 — The same came to Jesus by night, and said unto him, Rabbi, we know that thou art a teacher come from God: for no man can do these miracles that thou doest, except God be with him.

• Joseph of Arimathaea.

Jn 19:38 — And after this Joseph of Arimathaea, being a disciple of Jesus, but secretly for fear of the Jews, besought Pilate that he might take away the body of Jesus: and Pilate gave *him* leave. He came therefore, and took the body of Jesus.

• The parents of the man who was born blind.

Jn 9:21–22

• Rulers, who believed in Jesus, but feared the Pharisees.

Jn 12:42–43

• Chief priests, who feared to answer the questions of Jesus.

Mt 21:26 — But if we shall say, Of men; we fear the people; for all hold John as a prophet.

Mk 11:18 — And the scribes and chief priests heard *it,* and sought how they might destroy him: for they feared him, because all the people was astonished at his doctrine.

Mk 11:32 — But if we shall say, Of men; they feared the people: for all *men* counted John, that he was a prophet indeed.

Mk 12:12 — And they sought to lay hold on him, but feared the people: for they knew that he had spoken the parable against them: and they left him, and went their way.

• **Chief priests, who feared to further persecute the disciples.**

Ac 4:21 — So when they had further threatened them, they let them go, finding nothing how they might punish them, because of the people: for all *men* glorified God for that which was done.

Ac 5:26 — Then went the captain with the officers, and brought them without violence: for they feared the people, lest they should have been stoned.

• **Concessions to.**

• **By Paul, in circumcising Timothy.**

Ac 16:3 — Him would Paul have to go forth with him; and took and circumcised him because of the Jews which were in those quarters: for they knew all that his father was a Greek.

• **James and the Christian elders, who required Paul to observe certain rites.**

Ac 21:18–26

• **Disciples, who urged circumcision.**

Gal 6:12 — As many as desire to make a fair shew in the flesh, they constrain you to be circumcised; only lest they should suffer persecution for the cross of Christ.

• **Peter and Barnabas with others.**

Gal 2:11–14

See: Prudence

• **Corrupt yielding to.**

• **By Herod, in the case of John the Baptist.**

Mk 6:26 — And the king was exceeding sorry; *yet* for his oath's sake, and for their sakes which sat with him, he would not reject her.

• **By Herod, in the case of Peter.**

Ac 12:3 — And because he saw it pleased the Jews, he proceeded further to take Peter also. (Then were the days of unleavened bread.)

• **By Peter, concerning Jesus.**

Mt 26:69–75

• **By Pilate.**

Mt 27:23–27; Lk 23:13–25; Jn 18:38–39; 19:4–16

Mk 15:15 — And *so* Pilate, willing to content the people, released Barabbas unto them, and delivered Jesus, when he had scourged *him*, to be crucified.

• **By Felix and Festus, concerning Paul.**

Ac 24:27 — But after two years Porcius Festus came into Felix' room: and Felix, willing to shew the Jews a pleasure, left Paul bound.

Ac 25:9 — But Festus, willing to do the Jews a pleasure, answered Paul, and said, Wilt thou go up to Jerusalem, and there be judged of these things before me?

OPINIONS

2Ti 4:3 — For the time will come when they will not endure sound doctrine; but after their own lusts shall they heap to themselves teachers, having itching ears;

Tit 1:9 — Holding fast the faithful word as he hath been taught, that he may be able by sound doctrine both to exhort and to convince the gainsayers.

OPPORTUNITY

• **The measure of responsibility.**

Pr 1:24–32; Eze 33:1–17; Mt 10:14–15; 11:20–24; 23:34–38; 25:1–46; Lk 13:25–28; 14:16–24; 19:12–27

Jer 8:20 — The harvest is past, the summer is ended, and we are not saved.

Eze 3:19 — Yet if thou warn the wicked, and he turn not from his wickedness, nor from his wicked way, he shall die in his iniquity; but thou hast delivered thy soul.

Hos 5:6 — They shall go with their flocks and with their herds to seek the LORD; but they shall not find *him;* he hath withdrawn himself from them.

Lk 12:47 — And that servant, which knew his lord's will, and prepared not *himself,* neither did according to his will, shall be beaten with many *stripes.*

See: Judgment; according to opportunity and works

See: Responsibility

OPPRESSION

• **God is a refuge from.**

Ps 9:9 — The LORD also will be a refuge for the oppressed, a refuge in times of trouble.

• **Prayers against.**

Ps 17:9 — From the wicked that oppress me, *from* my deadly enemies, *who* compass me about.

Ps 44:24 — Wherefore hidest thou thy face, *and* forgettest our affliction and our oppression?

Ps 119:121 — I have done judgment and justice: leave me not to mine oppressors.

Ps 119:134 — Deliver me from the oppression of man: so will I keep thy precepts.

Isa 38:14 — Like a crane *or* a swallow, so did I chatter: I did mourn as a dove: mine eyes fail *with looking* upward: O LORD, I am oppressed; undertake for me.

• **God's aid promised against.**

Ps 12:5 — For the oppression of the poor, for the sighing of the needy, now will I arise, saith the LORD; I will set *him* in safety *from him that* puffeth at him.

Ps 72:4 — He shall judge the poor of the people, he shall save the children of the needy, and shall break in pieces the oppressor.

Ps 72:14 — He shall redeem their soul from deceit and violence: and precious shall their blood be in his sight.

Jer 50:34 — Their Redeemer *is* strong; the LORD of hosts *is* his name: he shall throughly plead their cause, that he may give rest to the land, and disquiet the inhabitants of Babylon.

• **God will judge.**

Isa 10:1–34; Mal 3:1–18

Ps 103:6 — The LORD executeth righteousness and judgment for all that are oppressed.

Ecc 5:8 — If thou seest the oppression of the poor, and violent perverting of judgment and justice in a province, marvel not at the matter: for *he that is* higher than the highest regardeth; and *there be* higher than they.

Jer 22:17 — But thine eyes and thine heart *are* not but for thy covetousness, and for to shed innocent blood, and for oppression, and for violence, to do *it*.

Eze 22:7 — In thee have they set light by father and mother: in the midst of thee have they dealt by oppression with the stranger: in thee have they vexed the fatherless and the widow.

Am 4:1 — Hear this word, ye kine of Bashan, that *are* in the mountain of Samaria, which oppress the poor, which crush the needy, which say to their masters, Bring, and let us drink.

Mic 2:2 — And they covet fields, and take *them* by violence; and houses, and take *them* away: so they oppress a man and his house, even a man and his heritage.

Jas 5:4 — Behold, the hire of the labourers who have reaped down your fields, which is of you kept back by fraud, crieth: and the cries of them which have reaped are entered into the ears of the Lord of sabaoth.

• National, God judges.

Ac 7:7 — And the nation to whom they shall be in bondage will I judge, said God: and after that shall they come forth, and serve me in this place.

• National, relieved.

Jgs 6:1–8:35; 10:1–18; 2Ki 13:1–25

Ex 3:9 — Now therefore, behold, the cry of the children of Israel is come unto me: and I have also seen the oppression wherewith the Egyptians oppress them.

Dt 26:7 — And when we cried unto the LORD God of our fathers, the LORD heard our voice, and looked on our affliction, and our labour, and our oppression:

Jgs 2:14 — And the anger of the LORD was hot against Israel, and he delivered them into the hands of spoilers that spoiled them, and he sold them into the hands of their enemies round about, so that they could not any longer stand before their enemies.

Isa 52:4 — For thus saith the Lord GOD, My people went down aforetime into Egypt to sojourn there; and the Assyrian oppressed them without cause.

• Instances of.

• Hagar, by Sarah.

Ge 16:6

• Israelites, by Egyptians.

Ex 1:10–22; 5:1–23

• Rehoboam resolves to oppress the Israelites.

1Ki 12:14

• Unclassified scripture relating to.

Ex 22:21–24; Dt 23:15–16; 24:14–15; Job 27:13–23; Ps 10:17–18; Isa 33:15–16; Am 5:11–12; 8:4–6; Mic 2:1–3; Hab 2:5–11; Mt 23:2–4

Ps 9:9 — The LORD also will be a refuge for the oppressed, a refuge in times of trouble.

Ps 12:5 — For the oppression of the poor, for the sighing of the needy, now will I arise, saith the LORD; I will set *him* in safety *from him that* puffeth at him.

Ps 62:10 — Trust not in oppression, and become not vain in robbery: if riches increase, set not your heart *upon them*.

Ps 74:21 — O let not the oppressed return ashamed: let the poor and needy praise thy name.

Ps 119:134 — Deliver me from the oppression of man: so will I keep thy precepts.

Pr 3:31 — Envy thou not the oppressor, and choose none of his ways.

Pr 14:31 — He that oppresseth the poor reproacheth his Maker: but he that honoureth him hath mercy on the poor.

Pr 22:16 — He that oppresseth the poor to increase his *riches, and* he that giveth to the rich, *shall* surely *come* to want.

Pr 22:22 — Rob not the poor, because he *is* poor: neither oppress the afflicted in the gate:

Pr 28:3 — A poor man that oppresseth the poor *is like* a sweeping rain which leaveth no food.

Pr 30:14 — *There is* a generation, whose teeth *are as* swords, and their jaw teeth *as* knives, to devour the poor from off the earth, and the needy from *among* men.

Ecc 4:1 — So I returned, and considered all the oppressions that are done under the sun: and behold the tears of *such as were* oppressed, and they had no comforter; and on the side of their oppressors *there was* power; but they had no comforter.

Ecc 5:8 — If thou seest the oppression of the poor, and violent perverting of judgment and justice in a province, marvel not at the matter: for *he that is* higher than the highest regardeth; and *there be* higher than they.

Ecc 7:7 — Surely oppression maketh a wise man mad; and a gift destroyeth the heart.

Isa 1:17 — Learn to do well; seek judgment, relieve the oppressed, judge the fatherless, plead for the widow.

Isa 5:8 — Woe unto them that join house to house, *that* lay field to field, till *there be* no place, that they may be placed alone in the midst of the earth!

Isa 58:6 — *Is* not this the fast that I have chosen? to loose the bands of wickedness, to undo the heavy burdens, and to let the oppressed go free, and that ye break every yoke?

Jer 21:12 — O house of David, thus saith the LORD; Execute judgment in the morning, and deliver *him that is* spoiled out of the hand of the oppressor, lest my fury go out like fire, and burn that none can quench *it*, because of the evil of your doings.

Eze 22:29 — The people of the land have used oppression, and exercised robbery, and have vexed the poor and needy: yea, they have oppressed the stranger wrongfully.

Eze 45:9 — Thus saith the Lord GOD; Let it suffice you, O princes of Israel: remove violence and spoil, and execute judgment and justice, take away your exactions from my people, saith the Lord GOD.

Zec 7:10 — And oppress not the widow, nor the fatherless, the stranger, nor the poor; and let none of you imagine evil against his brother in your heart.

Jas 2:6 — But ye have despised the poor. Do not rich men oppress you, and draw you before the judgment seats?

ORACLE

• The Holy Place.

1Ki 6:5 — And against the wall of the house he built chambers round about, *against* the walls of the house round about, *both* of the temple and of the oracle: and he made chambers round about:

Ps 28:2 — Hear the voice of my supplications, when I cry unto thee, when I lift up my hands toward thy holy oracle.

• The scriptures called oracles.

Ac 7:38 — This is he, that was in the church in the wilderness with the angel which spake to him in the mount Sina, and *with* our fathers: who received the lively oracles to give unto us:

Ro 3:2 — Much every way: chiefly, because that unto them were committed the oracles of God.

Heb 5:12 — For when for the time ye ought to be teachers, ye have need that one teach you again which *be* the first principles of the oracles of God; and are become such as have need of milk, and not of strong meat.

1Pe 4:11 — If any man speak, *let him speak* as the oracles of God; if any man minister, *let him do it* as of the ability which God giveth: that God in all things may be glorified through Jesus Christ, to whom be praise and dominion for ever and ever. Amen.

See: Tabernacle

ORATOR

Isa 3:3 — The captain of fifty, and the honourable man, and the counsellor, and the cunning artificer, and the eloquent orator.

• Instances of.

• Jonah.

Jnh 3:4–10

• The apostles.

Ac 2:1–41

• Tertullus.

Ac 24:1

• Apollos.

Ac 18:24–28

ORDINANCE

• A decree.

Ex 12:14 — And this day shall be unto you for a memorial; and ye shall keep it a feast to the LORD throughout your generations; ye shall keep it a feast by an ordinance for ever.

Ex 12:24 — And ye shall observe this thing for an ordinance to thee and to thy sons for ever.

Ex 12:43 — And the LORD said unto Moses and Aaron, This *is* the ordinance of the passover: There shall no stranger eat thereof:

Ex 13:10 — Thou shalt therefore keep this ordinance in his season from year to year.

Ex 15:25 — And he cried unto the LORD; and the LORD shewed him a tree, *which* when he had cast into the waters, the waters were made sweet: there he made for them a statute and an ordinance, and there he proved them,

Nu 9:14 — And if a stranger shall sojourn among you, and will keep the passover unto the LORD; according to the ordinance of the passover, and according to the manner thereof, so shall he do: ye shall have one ordinance, both for the stranger, and for him that was born in the land.

Nu 10:8 — And the sons of Aaron, the priests, shall blow with the trumpets; and they shall be to you for an ordinance for ever throughout your generations.

Nu 15:15 — One ordinance *shall be both* for you of the congregation, and also for the stranger that sojourneth *with you,* an ordinance for ever in your generations: as ye *are,* so shall the stranger be before the LORD.

Nu 18:8 — And the LORD spake unto Aaron, Behold, I also have given thee the charge of mine heave offerings of all the hallowed things of the children of Israel; unto thee have I given them by reason of the anointing, and to thy sons, by an ordinance for ever.

Isa 24:5 — The earth also is defiled under the inhabitants thereof; because they have transgressed the laws, changed the ordinance, broken the everlasting covenant.

Mal 4:4 — Remember ye the law of Moses my servant, which I commanded unto him in Horeb for all Israel, *with* the statutes and judgments.

Ro 13:2 — Whosoever therefore resisteth the power, resisteth the ordinance of God: and they that resist shall receive to themselves damnation.

1Pe 2:13 — Submit yourselves to every ordinance of man for the Lord's sake: whether it be to the king, as supreme;

• Insufficiency of, for salvation.

Isa 1:10–17; Col 2:20–23; Heb 9:8–10

Gal 5:6 — For in Jesus Christ neither circumcision availeth any thing, nor uncircumcision; but faith which worketh by love.

Gal 6:15 — For in Christ Jesus neither circumcision availeth any thing, nor uncircumcision, but a new creature.

Eph 2:15 — Having abolished in his flesh the enmity, *even* the law of commandments *contained* in ordinances; for to make in himself of twain one new man, *so* making peace;

Col 2:14 — Blotting out the handwriting of ordinances that was against us, which was contrary to us, and took it out of the way, nailing it to his cross;

Heb 9:1 — Then verily the first *covenant* had also ordinances of divine service, and a worldly sanctuary.

See: Form

See: Form; formalism

ORDINATION

• Of priests.

See: Priest, Emoluments of

See: Priest, High

See: Priest, Miscellaneous Facts Concerning

↠See: Priest, Mosaic

- **Of ministers.**

↠See: Minister, a Sacred Teacher

OREB

- **A prince of Midian.**
  - **Overcome by Gideon and killed by the Ephraimites.**

Jgs 7:25 — And they took two princes of the Midianites, Oreb and Zeeb; and they slew Oreb upon the rock Oreb, and Zeeb they slew at the winepress of Zeeb, and pursued Midian, and brought the heads of Oreb and Zeeb to Gideon on the other side Jordan.

Jgs 8:3 — God hath delivered into your hands the princes of Midian, Oreb and Zeeb: and what was I able to do in comparison of you? Then their anger was abated toward him, when he had said that.

Ps 83:11 — Make their nobles like Oreb, and like Zeeb: yea, all their princes as Zebah, and as Zalmunna:

- **A rock east of the Jordan, where Oreb was slain.**

Jgs 7:25 — And they took two princes of the Midianites, Oreb and Zeeb; and they slew Oreb upon the rock Oreb, and Zeeb they slew at the winepress of Zeeb, and pursued Midian, and brought the heads of Oreb and Zeeb to Gideon on the other side Jordan.

Isa 10:26 — And the LORD of hosts shall stir up a scourge for him according to the slaughter of Midian at the rock of Oreb: and *as* his rod *was* upon the sea, so shall he lift it up after the manner of Egypt.

OREN • Son of Jerahmeel.

1Ch 2:25 — And the sons of Jerahmeel the firstborn of Hezron were, Ram the firstborn, and Bunah, and Oren, and Ozem, *and* Ahijah.

ORGAN ↠See: Music; instruments of

ORGANIZE

1Co 14:20 — Brethren, be not children in understanding: howbeit in malice be ye children, but in understanding be men.

ORION • The constellation of.

Job 9:9 — Which maketh Arcturus, Orion, and Pleiades, and the chambers of the south.

Job 38:31 — Canst thou bind the sweet influences of Pleiades, or loose the bands of Orion?

Isa 13:10 — For the stars of heaven and the constellations thereof shall not give their light: the sun shall be darkened in his going forth, and the moon shall not cause her light to shine.

Am 5:8 — *Seek him* that maketh the seven stars and Orion, and turneth the shadow of death into the morning, and maketh the day dark with night: that calleth for the waters of the sea, and poureth them out upon the face of the earth: The LORD *is* his name:

ORNAN

- **A Jebusite.**

1Ch 21:15–25

1Ch 21:28 — At that time when David saw that the LORD had answered him in the threshingfloor of Ornan the Jebusite, then he sacrificed there.

2Ch 3:1 — Then Solomon began to build the house of the LORD at Jerusalem in mount Moriah, where *the LORD* appeared unto David his father, in the place that David had prepared in the threshingfloor of Ornan the Jebusite.

- **Called Araunah.**

2Sa 24:16–25

ORPAH • Daughter-in-law of Naomi.

Ru 1:4 — And they took them wives of the women of Moab; the name of the one *was* Orpah, and the name of the other Ruth: and they dwelled there about ten years.

Ru 1:14 — And they lifted up their voice, and wept again: and Orpah kissed her mother in law; but Ruth clave unto her.

ORPHAN

Ex 22:22–24; Dt 14:28–29; 24:17–22; 26:12–13; Job 29:12–13; 31:16–18; Ps 10:17–18; Isa 10:1–2; Jer 7:6–7

Dt 10:18 — He doth execute the judgment of the fatherless and widow, and loveth the stranger, in giving him food and raiment.

Dt 16:11 — And thou shalt rejoice before the LORD thy God, thou, and thy son, and thy daughter, and thy manservant, and thy maidservant, and the Levite that *is* within thy gates, and the stranger, and the fatherless, and the widow, that *are* among you, in the place which the LORD thy God hath chosen to place his name there.

Dt 16:14 — And thou shalt rejoice in thy feast, thou, and thy son, and thy daughter, and thy manservant, and thy maidservant, and the Levite, the stranger, and the fatherless, and the widow, that *are* within thy gates.

Dt 27:19 — Cursed *be* he that perverteth the judgment of the stranger, fatherless, and widow. And all the people shall say, Amen.

Job 6:27 — Yea, ye overwhelm the fatherless, and ye dig *a pit* for your friend.

Job 22:9 — Thou hast sent widows away empty, and the arms of the fatherless have been broken.

Job 24:3 — They drive away the ass of the fatherless, they take the widow's ox for a pledge.

Job 24:9 — They pluck the fatherless from the breast, and take a pledge of the poor.

Job 31:21 — If I have lifted up my hand against the fatherless, when I saw my help in the gate:

Ps 10:14 — Thou hast seen *it;* for thou beholdest mischief and spite, to requite *it* with thy hand: the poor committeth himself unto thee; thou art the helper of the fatherless.

Ps 27:10 — When my father and my mother forsake me, then the LORD will take me up.

Ps 68:5 — A father of the fatherless, and a judge of the widows, *is* God in his holy habitation.

Ps 82:3 — Defend the poor and fatherless: do justice to the afflicted and needy.

Ps 94:6 — They slay the widow and the stranger, and murder the fatherless.

Ps 146:9 — The LORD preserveth the strangers; he relieveth the fatherless and widow: but the way of the wicked he turneth upside down.

Pr 23:10 — Remove not the old landmark; and enter not into the fields of the fatherless:

Isa 1:17 — Learn to do well; seek judgment, relieve the oppressed, judge the fatherless, plead for the widow.

Isa 1:23 — Thy princes *are* rebellious, and companions of thieves: every one loveth gifts, and followeth after rewards: they judge not the fatherless, neither doth the cause of the widow come unto them.

Jer 5:28 — They are waxen fat, they shine: yea, they overpass the deeds of the wicked: they judge not the cause, the cause of the fatherless, yet they prosper; and the right of the needy do they not judge.

Jer 22:3 — Thus saith the LORD; Execute ye judgment and righteousness, and deliver the spoiled out of the hand of the oppressor: and do no wrong, do no violence to the stranger, the fatherless, nor the widow, neither shed innocent blood in this place.

Jer 49:11 — Leave thy fatherless children, I will preserve *them* alive; and let thy widows trust in me.

Hos 14:3 — Asshur shall not save us; we will not ride upon horses: neither will we say any more to the work of our hands, *Ye are* our gods: for in thee the fatherless findeth mercy.

Mal 3:5 — And I will come near to you to judgment; and I will be a swift witness against the sorcerers, and against the adulterers, and against false swearers, and against those that oppress the hireling in *his* wages, the widow, and the fatherless, and that turn aside the stranger *from his right*, and fear not me, saith the LORD of hosts.

Jas 1:27 — Pure religion and undefiled before God and the Father is this, To visit the fatherless and widows in their affliction, *and* to keep himself unspotted from the world.

➾See: Adoption

➾See: Children

➾See: Widow

• Instances of.

• Lot.

Ge 11:27–28

• Daughters of Zelophehad.

Nu 27:1–5

• Jotham.

Jgs 9:16–21

• Mephibosheth.

2Sa 9:3

• Joash.

2Ki 11:1–12

• Esther.

Est 2:7

• A type of Zion in affliction.

La 5:3

OSEE • Hosea, so called.

Ro 9:25 — As he saith also in Osee, I will call them my people, which were not my people; and her beloved, which was not beloved.

OSPRAY

• A carnivorous bird.

• Forbidden as food.

Le 11:13 — And these *are they which ye* shall have in abomination among the fowls; they shall not be eaten, they *are* an abomination: the eagle, and the ossifrage, and the ospray,

Dt 14:12 — But these *are they* of which ye shall not eat: the eagle, and ossifrage, and the ospray,

OSSIFRAGE

• A carnivorous bird.

• Forbidden as food.

Le 11:13 — And these *are they which ye* shall have in abomination among the fowls; they shall not be eaten, they *are* an abomination: the eagle, and the ossifrage, and the ospray,

Dt 14:12 — But these *are they* of which ye shall not eat: the eagle, and ossifrage, and the ospray,

OSTENTATION

• In prayer and almsgiving.

Pr 25:14 — Whoso boasteth himself of a false gift *is like* clouds and wind without rain.

Pr 27:2 — Let another man praise thee, and not thine own mouth; a stranger, and not thine own lips.

Mt 6:1 — Take heed that ye do not your alms before men, to be seen of them: otherwise ye have no reward of your Father which is in heaven.

OSTRICHES

Job 39:13–18

Isa 13:21 — But wild beasts of the desert shall lie there; and their houses shall be full of doleful creatures; and owls shall dwell there, and satyrs shall dance there.

Isa 34:13 — And thorns shall come up in her palaces, nettles and brambles in the fortresses thereof: and it shall be an habitation of dragons, *and* a court for owls.

Isa 43:20 — The beast of the field shall honour me, the dragons and the owls: because I give waters in the wilderness, *and* rivers in the desert, to give drink to my people, my chosen.

La 4:3 — Even the sea monsters draw out the breast, they give suck to their young ones: the daughter of my people *is become* cruel, like the ostriches in the wilderness.

• The cry of.

Mic 1:8 — Therefore I will wail and howl, I will go stripped and naked: I will make a wailing like the dragons, and mourning as the owls.

• In King James Version occurs the word owl.

Le 11:16 — And the owl, and the night hawk, and the cuckow, and the hawk after his kind,

Dt 14:15 — And the owl, and the night hawk, and the cuckow, and the hawk after his kind,

Job 30:29 — I am a brother to dragons, and a companion to owls.

Isa 43:20 — The beast of the field shall honour me, the dragons and the owls: because I give waters in the wilderness, *and* rivers in the desert, to give drink to my people, my chosen.

Jer 50:39 — Therefore the wild beasts of the desert with the wild beasts of the islands shall dwell *there*, and the owls shall dwell therein: and it shall be no more inhabited for ever; neither shall it be dwelt in from generation to generation.

Mic 1:8 — Therefore I will wail and howl, I will go stripped and naked: I will make a wailing like the dragons, and mourning as the owls.

OTHNI • Son of Shemaiah.

1Ch 26:7 — The sons of Shemaiah; Othni, and Rephael, and Obed, Elzabad, whose brethren *were* strong men, Elihu, and Semachiah.

OTHNIEL

• Son of Kenaz and nephew of Caleb.

• Conquers Kirjath-sepher, and as reward secures Caleb's daughter to wife.

Jos 15:16–20; Jgs 1:12–13

• Becomes deliverer and judge of Israel.

Jgs 3:8–11

• Death of.

Jgs 3:11 — And the land had rest forty years. And Othniel the son of Kenaz died.

• Descendants of.

1Ch 4:13–14

OUCHES • Sockets.

Ex 28:11 — With the work of an engraver in stone, *like* the engravings of a signet, shalt thou engrave the two stones with the names of the children of Israel: thou shalt make them to be set in ouches of gold.

OVEN

• For baking.

Ex 8:3 — And the river shall bring forth frogs abundantly, which shall go up and come into thine house, and into thy bedchamber, and upon thy bed, and into the house of thy servants, and upon thy people, and into thine ovens, and into thy kneadingtroughs:

Le 2:4 — And if thou bring an oblation of a meat offering baken in the oven, *it shall be* unleavened cakes of fine flour mingled with oil, or unleavened wafers anointed with oil.

Le 7:9 — And all the meat offering that is baken in the oven, and all that is dressed in the fryingpan, and in the pan, shall be the priest's that offereth it.

Le 11:35 — And every *thing* whereupon *any part* of their carcase falleth shall be unclean; *whether it be* oven, or ranges for pots, they shall be broken down: *for* they *are* unclean, and shall be unclean unto you.

Le 26:26 — *And* when I have broken the staff of your bread, ten women shall bake your bread in one oven, and they shall deliver *you* your bread again by weight: and ye shall eat, and not be satisfied.

See: Bread

• Figurative.

Hos 7:6–7

Ps 21:9 — Thou shalt make them as a fiery oven in the time of thine anger: the LORD shall swallow them up in his wrath, and the fire shall devour them.

Hos 7:4 — They *are* all adulterers, as an oven heated by the baker, *who* ceaseth from raising after he hath kneaded the dough, until it be leavened.

Mal 4:1 — For, behold, the day cometh, that shall burn as an oven; and all the proud, yea, and all that do wickedly, shall be stubble: and the day that cometh shall burn them up, saith the LORD of hosts, that it shall leave them neither root nor branch.

Mt 6:30 — Wherefore, if God so clothe the grass of the field, which to day is, and to morrow is cast into the oven, *shall he* not much more *clothe* you, O ye of little faith?

Lk 12:28 — If then God so clothe the grass, which is to day in the field, and to morrow is cast into the oven; how much more *will he clothe* you, O ye of little faith?

OVERCOMING **See: Perseverance**

OVERSEER

Mt 24:48–49

See: Bishop

OWL

• A carnivorous bird.

• Unclean.

Le 11:16–17

Dt 14:16 — The little owl, and the great owl, and the swan,

• Ostrich is substituted in some versions.

Le 11:16 — And the owl, and the night hawk, and the cuckow, and the hawk after his kind,

Dt 14:15 — And the owl, and the night hawk, and the cuckow, and the hawk after his kind,

Job 30:29 — I am a brother to dragons, and a companion to owls.

Isa 13:21 — But wild beasts of the desert shall lie there; and their houses shall be full of doleful creatures; and owls shall dwell there, and satyrs shall dance there.

Isa 34:11 — But the cormorant and the bittern shall possess it; the owl also and the raven shall dwell in it: and he shall stretch out upon it the line of confusion, and the stones of emptiness.

Isa 34:13 — And thorns shall come up in her palaces, nettles and brambles in the fortresses thereof: and it shall be an habitation of dragons, *and* a court for owls.

Isa 43:20 — The beast of the field shall honour me, the dragons and the owls: because I give waters in the wilderness, *and* rivers in the desert, to give drink to my people, my chosen.

Jer 50:39 — Therefore the wild beasts of the desert with the wild beasts of the islands shall dwell *there*, and the owls shall dwell therein: and it shall be no more inhabited for ever; neither shall it be dwelt in from generation to generation.

Mic 1:8 — Therefore I will wail and howl, I will go stripped and naked: I will make a wailing like the dragons, and mourning as the owls.

OX

See: Bullock, or Ox

See: Cattle, of the Bovine Species

OZEM

• Son of Jesse.

1Ch 2:15 — Ozem the sixth, David the seventh:

• Son of Jerahmeel.

1Ch 2:25 — And the sons of Jerahmeel the firstborn of Hezron were, Ram the firstborn, and Bunah, and Oren, and Ozem, *and* Ahijah.

OZIAS

• A form given to the name of King Uzziah.

Mt 1:8–9

See: Uzziah

OZNI • Son of Gad.

Nu 26:16 — Of Ozni, the family of the Oznites: of Eri, the family of the Erites:

P

PAARAI

• One of David's valiant men.

2Sa 23:35 — Hezrai the Carmelite, Paarai the Arbite,

• Called Naarai.

1Ch 11:37 — Hezro the Carmelite, Naarai the son of Ezbai,

PACIFISM

Mt 26:52 — Then said Jesus unto him, Put up again thy sword into his place: for all they that take the sword shall perish with the sword.

PACK ANIMALS

• Used for transporting army supplies.

1Ch 12:40 — Moreover they that were nigh them, *even* unto Issachar and Zebulun and Naphtali, brought bread on asses, and on camels, and on mules, and on oxen, *and* meat, meal, cakes of figs, and bunches of raisins, and wine, and oil, and oxen, and sheep abundantly: for *there was* joy in Israel.

PADAN-ARAM ↞See: Mesopotamia

PADON • One of the Nethinim.

Ezr 2:44 — The children of Keros, the children of Siaha, the children of Padon,

Ne 7:47 — The children of Keros, the children of Sia, the children of Padon,

PAGIEL

• Son of Ocran.

• A leader of the tribe of Asher at time of Exodus.

Nu 1:13 — Of Asher; Pagiel the son of Ocran.

Nu 2:27 — And those that encamp by him *shall be* the tribe of Asher: and the captain of the children of Asher *shall be* Pagiel the son of Ocran.

Nu 7:72 — On the eleventh day Pagiel the son of Ocran, prince of the children of Asher, *offered:*

Nu 7:77 — And for a sacrifice of peace offerings, two oxen, five rams, five he goats, five lambs of the first year: this *was* the offering of Pagiel the son of Ocran.

Nu 10:26 — And over the host of the tribe of the children of Asher *was* Pagiel the son of Ocran.

PAHATH-MOAB • The ancestor of an influential family of Judah, which returned to Jerusalem from the captivity.

Ezr 2:6 — The children of Pahath-moab, of the children of Jeshua *and* Joab, two thousand eight hundred and twelve.

Ezr 10:30 — And of the sons of Pahath-moab; Adna, and Chelal, Benaiah, Maaseiah, Mattaniah, Bezaleel, and Binnui, and Manasseh.

Ne 3:11 — Malchijah the son of Harim, and Hashub the son of Pahath-moab, repaired the other piece, and the tower of the furnaces.

Ne 7:11 — The children of Pahath-moab, of the children of Jeshua and Joab, two thousand and eight hundred *and* eighteen.

PAI

• A city in Edom.

1Ch 1:50 — And when Baal-hanan was dead, Hadad reigned in his stead: and the name of his city *was* Pai; and his wife's name *was* Mehetabel, the daughter of Matred, the daughter of Mezahab.

• Called Pau.

Ge 36:39 — And Baal-hanan the son of Achbor died, and Hadar reigned in his stead: and the name of his city *was* Pau; and his wife's name *was* Mehetabel, the daughter of Matred, the daughter of Mezahab.

PAIN

Job 30:17–18

Job 14:22 — But his flesh upon him shall have pain, and his soul within him shall mourn.

Job 33:19 — He is chastened also with pain upon his bed, and the multitude of his bones with strong *pain:*

La 3:5 — He hath builded against me, and compassed *me* with gall and travail.

Rev 16:10 — And the fifth angel poured out his vial upon the seat of the beast; and his kingdom was full of darkness; and they gnawed their tongues for pain,

Rev 21:4 — And God shall wipe away all tears from their eyes; and there shall be no more death, neither sorrow, nor crying, neither shall there be any more pain: for the former things are passed away.

↞See: Afflictions

PAINTING

• Around the eyes, to enlarge their appearance.

2Ki 9:30 — And when Jehu was come to Jezreel, Jezebel heard *of it;* and she painted her face, and tired her head, and looked out at a window.

Jer 4:30 — And *when* thou *art* spoiled, what wilt thou do? Though thou clothest thyself with crimson, though thou deckest thee with ornaments of gold, though thou rentest thy face with painting, in vain shalt thou make thyself fair; *thy* lovers will despise thee, they will seek thy life.

Eze 23:40 — And furthermore, that ye have sent for men to come from far, unto whom a messenger *was* sent; and, lo, they came: for whom thou didst wash thyself, paintedst thy eyes, and deckedst thyself with ornaments,

• Of rooms.

Jer 22:14 — That saith, I will build me a wide house and large chambers, and cutteth him out windows; and *it is* cieled with cedar, and painted with vermilion.

• Of portraits.

Eze 23:14 — And *that* she increased her whoredoms: for when she saw men pourtrayed upon the wall, the images of the Chaldeans pourtrayed with vermilion,

See: Picture

PALACE

• For kings.

1Ki 21:1 — And it came to pass after these things, *that* Naboth the Jezreelite had a vineyard, which *was* in Jezreel, hard by the palace of Ahab king of Samaria.

2Ki 15:25 — But Pekah the son of Remaliah, a captain of his, conspired against him, and smote him in Samaria, in the palace of the king's house, with Argob and Arieh, and with him fifty men of the Gileadites: and he killed him, and reigned in his room.

Jer 49:27 — And I will kindle a fire in the wall of Damascus, and it shall consume the palaces of Benhadad.

Am 1:12 — But I will send a fire upon Teman, which shall devour the palaces of Bozrah.

Na 2:6 — The gates of the rivers shall be opened, and the palace shall be dissolved.

• Of David.

2Sa 7:2 — That the king said unto Nathan the prophet, See now, I dwell in an house of cedar, but the ark of God dwelleth within curtains.

• Of Solomon.

1Ki 7:1–12

• At Babylon.

Da 4:29 — At the end of twelve months he walked in the palace of the kingdom of Babylon.

Da 5:5 — In the same hour came forth fingers of a man's hand, and wrote over against the candlestick upon the plaister of the wall of the king's palace: and the king saw the part of the hand that wrote.

Da 6:18 — Then the king went to his palace, and passed the night fasting: neither were instruments of musick brought before him: and his sleep went from him.

• At Shushan.

Ne 1:1 — The words of Nehemiah the son of Hachaliah. And it came to pass in the month Chisleu, in the twentieth year, as I was in Shushan the palace,

Est 1:2 — *That* in those days, when the king Ahasuerus sat on the throne of his kingdom, which *was* in Shushan the palace,

Est 7:7 — And the king arising from the banquet of wine in his wrath *went* into the palace garden: and Haman stood up to make request for his life to Esther the queen; for he saw that there was evil determined against him by the king.

Da 8:2 — And I saw in a vision; and it came to pass, when I saw, that I *was* at Shushan *in* the palace, which *is* in the province of Elam; and I saw in a vision, and I was by the river of Ulai.

• Archives kept in.

Ezr 6:2 — And there was found at Achmetha, in the palace that is in the province of the Medes, a roll, and therein *was* a record thus written:

• Proclamations issued from.

Am 3:9 — Publish in the palaces at Ashdod, and in the palaces in the land of Egypt, and say, Assemble yourselves upon the mountains of Samaria, and behold the great tumults in the midst thereof, and the oppressed in the midst thereof.

• Figurative.

• Of a government.

Am 1:12 — But I will send a fire upon Teman, which shall devour the palaces of Bozrah.

Am 2:2 — But I will send a fire upon Moab, and it shall devour the palaces of Kirioth: and Moab shall die with tumult, with shouting, *and* with the sound of the trumpet:

Na 2:6 — The gates of the rivers shall be opened, and the palace shall be dissolved.

PALAL

• Son of Uzai.

• One of the workmen in rebuilding the walls of Jerusalem.

Ne 3:25 — Palal the son of Uzai, over against the turning *of the wall,* and the tower which lieth out from the king's high house, that *was* by the court of the prison. After him Pedaiah the son of Parosh.

PALE HORSE • Symbol of death.

Rev 6:8 — And I looked, and behold a pale horse: and his name that sat on him was Death, and Hell followed with him. And power was given unto them over the fourth part of the earth, to kill with sword, and with hunger, and with death, and with the beasts of the earth.

PALESTINE See: Canaan

PALLU

• Called also Phallu.

• Son of Reuben.

Ge 46:9 — And the sons of Reuben; Hanoch, and Phallu, and Hezron, and Carmi.

Ex 6:14 — These *be* the heads of their fathers' houses: The sons of Reuben the firstborn of Israel; Hanoch, and Pallu, Hezron, and Carmi: these *be* the families of Reuben.

Nu 26:5 — Reuben, the eldest son of Israel: the children of Reuben; Hanoch, *of whom cometh* the family of the Hanochites: of Pallu, the family of the Palluites:

Nu 26:8 — And the sons of Pallu; Eliab.

1Ch 5:3 — The sons, *I say,* of Reuben the firstborn of Israel *were,* Hanoch, and Pallu, Hezron, and Carmi.

PALM TREE

• Deborah judged Israel under.

Jgs 4:5 — And she dwelt under the palm tree of Deborah between Ramah and Bethel in mount Ephraim: and the children of Israel came up to her for judgment.

• Wood of, used in the temple.

1Ki 6:29 — And he carved all the walls of the house round about with carved figures of cherubims and palm trees and open flowers, within and without.

1Ki 6:32 — The two doors also *were of* olive tree; and he carved upon them carvings of cherubims and palm trees and open flowers, and overlaid *them* with gold, and spread gold upon the cherubims, and upon the palm trees.

1Ki 6:35 — And he carved *thereon* cherubims and palm trees and open flowers: and covered *them* with gold fitted upon the carved work.

2Ch 3:5 — And the greater house he cieled with fir tree, which he overlaid with fine gold, and set thereon palm trees and chains.

• In the temple seen in the vision of Ezekiel.

Eze 40:16 — And *there were* narrow windows to the little chambers, and to their posts within the gate round about, and likewise to the arches: and windows *were* round about inward: and upon *each* post *were* palm trees.

Eze 41:18 — And *it was* made with cherubims and palm trees, so that a palm tree *was* between a cherub and a cherub; and *every* cherub had two faces;

• Branches of, thrown in the way when Jesus made his triumphal entry into Jerusalem.

Jn 12:13 — Took branches of palm trees, and went forth to meet him, and cried, Hosanna: Blessed *is* the King of Israel that cometh in the name of the Lord.

• Jericho was called the City of Palm Trees.

Dt 34:3 — And the south, and the plain of the valley of Jericho, the city of palm trees, unto Zoar.

• Figurative.

• Of the prosperity of the righteous.

Ps 92:12 — The righteous shall flourish like the palm tree: he shall grow like a cedar in Lebanon.

• Used as a symbol of victory.

Rev 7:9 — After this I beheld, and, lo, a great multitude, which no man could number, of all nations, and kindreds, and people, and tongues, stood before the throne, and before the Lamb, clothed with white robes, and palms in their hands;

PALMER-WORM

Joel 1:4 — That which the palmerworm hath left hath the locust eaten; and that which the locust hath left hath the cankerworm eaten; and that which the cankerworm hath left hath the caterpiller eaten.

Joel 2:25 — And I will restore to you the years that the locust hath eaten, the cankerworm, and the caterpiller, and the palmerworm, my great army which I sent among you.

Am 4:9 — I have smitten you with blasting and mildew: when your gardens and your vineyards and your fig trees and your olive trees increased, the palmerworm devoured *them:* yet have ye not returned unto me, saith the LORD.

PALSY →See: Paralysis

PALTI • A chief Benjamite and one of the twelve spies sent into Canaan.

Nu 13:9 — Of the tribe of Benjamin, Palti the son of Raphu.

PALTIEL

• A chief of Issachar.

• One of the committee of twelve appointed to divide Canaan among the tribes.

Nu 34:26 — And the prince of the tribe of the children of Issachar, Paltiel the son of Azzan.

PAMPHYLIA

• A province in Asia Minor.

• Men of, in Jerusalem.

Ac 2:10 — Phrygia, and Pamphylia, in Egypt, and in the parts of Libya about Cyrene, and strangers of Rome, Jews and proselytes,

• Paul goes to.

Ac 13:13–14

Ac 14:24 — And after they had passed throughout Pisidia, they came to Pamphylia.

• John, surnamed Mark, in.

Ac 13:13 — Now when Paul and his company loosed from Paphos, they came to Perga in Pamphylia: and John departing from them returned to Jerusalem.

Ac 15:38 — But Paul thought not good to take him with them, who departed from them from Pamphylia, and went not with them to the work.

• Sea of.

Ac 27:5 — And when we had sailed over the sea of Cilicia and Pamphylia, we came to Myra, *a city* of Lycia.

PANENTHEISM

Ac 17:28 — For in him we live, and move, and have our being; as certain also of your own poets have said, For we are also his offspring.

PANIC

• In armies.

Le 26:17 — And I will set my face against you, and ye shall be slain before your enemies: they that hate you shall reign over you; and ye shall flee when none pursueth you.

Dt 32:30 — How should one chase a thousand, and two put ten thousand to flight, except their Rock had sold them, and the LORD had shut them up?

Jos 23:10 — One man of you shall chase a thousand: for the LORD your God, he *it is* that fighteth for you, as he hath promised you.

Ps 35:5 — Let them be as chaff before the wind: and let the angel of the LORD chase *them.*

• **From God.**
Ex 15:14–16; 1Sa 14:15–20; 2Ki 7:6–7; 2Ch 20:22–23
Ge 35:5 — And they journeyed: and the terror of God was upon the cities that *were* round about them, and they did not pursue after the sons of Jacob.
Jgs 7:22 — And the three hundred blew the trumpets, and the LORD set every man's sword against his fellow, even throughout all the host: and the host fled to Beth-shittah in Zererath, *and* to the border of Abel-meholah, unto Tabbath.
See: Armies

PANTOMIME

• **By Isaiah.**
Isa 20:2–3

• **By Ezekial.**
Eze 4:1–8
Eze 12:18 — Son of man, eat thy bread with quaking, and drink thy water with trembling and with carefulness;

• **By Agabus.**
Ac 21:11 — And when he was come unto us, he took Paul's girdle, and bound his own hands and feet, and said, Thus saith the Holy Ghost, So shall the Jews at Jerusalem bind the man that owneth this girdle, and shall deliver *him* into the hands of the Gentiles.

PAPER

2Jn 1:12 — Having many things to write unto you, I would not *write* with paper and ink: but I trust to come unto you, and speak face to face, that our joy may be full.
See: Parchment

PAPHOS

• **A city of Cyprus.**

• **Paul blinds a sorcerer in.**
Ac 13:6–13

PAPYRUS

Ex 2:3 — And when she could not longer hide him, she took for him an ark of bulrushes, and daubed it with slime and with pitch, and put the child therein; and she laid *it* in the flags by the river's brink.

PARABLES

• **Of the trees.**
Jgs 9:8–15

• **Of the lamb.**
2Sa 12:1–6

• **Of the woman of Tekoa.**
2Sa 14:5–12

• **Of the garment rent in pieces.**
1Ki 11:30–32

• **Of the prisoner of war.**
1Ki 20:39–42

• **Of the thistle and cedar.**
2Ki 14:9 — And Jehoash the king of Israel sent to Amaziah king of Judah, saying, The thistle that *was* in Lebanon sent to the cedar that *was* in Lebanon, saying, Give thy daughter to my son to wife: and there passed by a wild beast that *was* in Lebanon, and trode down the thistle.

• **Of a vine of Egypt.**
Ps 80:8–16

• **Of the vineyard.**
Isa 5:1–7; 27:2–3

• **Of the husbandman.**
Isa 28:23–29

• **Of the skins filled with wine.**
Jer 13:12–14

• **Of the vine.**
Eze 15:1–8; 17:5–10; 19:10–14

• **Of the two eagles.**
Eze 17:1–24

• **Of lions' whelps.**
Eze 19:1–9

• **Of Aholah and Aholibah.**
Eze 23:1–49

• **The boiling pot.**
Eze 24:3–5

• **The gourd.**
Jnh 4:10–11

• **The sheet let down from heaven in Peter's vision.**
Ac 10:10–16

• **The two covenants.**
Gal 4:22–31

• **The mercenary soldier.**
2Ti 2:3–4

• **Husbandman.**
2Ti 2:6 — The husbandman that laboureth must be first partaker of the fruits.

• **Furnished house.**
2Ti 2:20–21

• **The athlete.**
2Ti 2:5 — And if a man also strive for masteries, *yet* is he not crowned, except he strive lawfully.

• **Looking-glass.**
Jas 1:23–25
See: Jesus, Parables of
See: Symbols and Similitudes
See: Types

PARADISE

• **The place of the glorified spirits.**
Lk 23:43 — And Jesus said unto him, Verily I say unto thee, To day shalt thou be with me in paradise.
2Co 12:4 — How that he was caught up into paradise, and heard unspeakable words, which it is not lawful for a man to utter.
Rev 2:7 — He that hath an ear, let him hear what the Spirit saith unto the churches; To him that overcometh will I give to eat of the tree of life, which is in the midst of the paradise of God.
See: Eden

PARADOX

2Co 6:8–10; 12:10–11; Eph 3:17–19

Pr 13:7 — There is that maketh himself rich, yet *hath* nothing: *there is* that maketh himself poor, yet *hath* great riches.

Mt 10:39 — He that findeth his life shall lose it: and he that loseth his life for my sake shall find it.

Mt 16:25 — For whosoever will save his life shall lose it: and whosoever will lose his life for my sake shall find it.

Mk 8:35 — For whosoever will save his life shall lose it; but whosoever shall lose his life for my sake and the gospel's, the same shall save it.

Lk 17:33 — Whosoever shall seek to save his life shall lose it; and whosoever shall lose his life shall preserve it.

Jn 12:25 — He that loveth his life shall lose it; and he that hateth his life in this world shall keep it unto life eternal.

1Co 3:18 — Let no man deceive himself. If any man among you seemeth to be wise in this world, let him become a fool, that he may be wise.

2Co 6:4 — But in all *things* approving ourselves as the ministers of God, in much patience, in afflictions, in necessities, in distresses,

2Co 12:4 — How that he was caught up into paradise, and heard unspeakable words, which it is not lawful for a man to utter.

Php 3:7 — But what things were gain to me, those I counted loss for Christ.

Rev 21:18 — And the building of the wall of it was *of* jasper: and the city *was* pure gold, like unto clear glass.

Rev 21:21 — And the twelve gates *were* twelve pearls; every several gate was of one pearl: and the street of the city *was* pure gold, as it were transparent glass.

PARAH • A city in Benjamin.

Jos 18:23 — And Avim, and Parah, and Ophrah,

PARALYSIS

• Cured by Jesus.

Mt 4:24 — And his fame went throughout all Syria: and they brought unto him all sick people that were taken with divers diseases and torments, and those which were possessed with devils, and those which were lunatick, and those that had the palsy; and he healed them.

Mt 8:6 — And saying, Lord, my servant lieth at home sick of the palsy, grievously tormented.

Mt 8:13 — And Jesus said unto the centurion, Go thy way; and as thou hast believed, so be it done unto thee. And his servant was healed in the selfsame hour.

Mt 9:2 — And, behold, they brought to him a man sick of the palsy, lying on a bed: and Jesus seeing their faith said unto the sick of the palsy; Son, be of good cheer; thy sins be forgiven thee.

Mt 9:6 — But that ye may know that the Son of man hath power on earth to forgive sins, (then saith he to the sick of the palsy,) Arise, take up thy bed, and go unto thine house.

• Cured by Philip.

Ac 8:7 — For unclean spirits, crying with loud voice, came out of many that were possessed *with them:* and many taken with palsies, and that were lame, were healed.

• Cured by Peter.

Ac 9:33–34

PARAN

• Desert or wilderness of.

Ge 21:21 — And he dwelt in the wilderness of Paran: and his mother took him a wife out of the land of Egypt.

Nu 10:12 — And the children of Israel took their journeys out of the wilderness of Sinai; and the cloud rested in the wilderness of Paran.

Nu 12:16 — And afterward the people removed from Hazeroth, and pitched in the wilderness of Paran.

Nu 13:3 — And Moses by the commandment of the LORD sent them from the wilderness of Paran: all those men *were* heads of the children of Israel.

Nu 13:26 — And they went and came to Moses, and to Aaron, and to all the congregation of the children of Israel, unto the wilderness of Paran, to Kadesh; and brought back word unto them, and unto all the congregation, and shewed them the fruit of the land.

Dt 1:1 — These *be* the words which Moses spake unto all Israel on this side Jordan in the wilderness, in the plain over against the Red *sea,* between Paran, and Tophel, and Laban, and Hazeroth, and Dizahab.

• Mountains of.

Dt 33:2 — And he said, The LORD came from Sinai, and rose up from Seir unto them; he shined forth from mount Paran, and he came with ten thousands of saints: from his right hand *went* a fiery law for them.

Hab 3:3 — God came from Teman, and the Holy One from mount Paran. Selah. His glory covered the heavens, and the earth was full of his praise.

• Israelites encamp in.

Nu 12:16 — And afterward the people removed from Hazeroth, and pitched in the wilderness of Paran.

• David takes refuge in.

1Sa 25:1 — And Samuel died; and all the Israelites were gathered together, and lamented him, and buried him in his house at Ramah. And David arose, and went down to the wilderness of Paran.

• Hadad flees to.

1Ki 11:17–18

PARCHMENT

2Ti 4:13 — The cloke that I left at Troas with Carpus, when thou comest, bring *with thee,* and the books, *but* especially the parchments.

PARDON

• Of sin.

→See: Sin; forgiveness of

PARENTS

• Covenant benefits of, entailed on children.

Ge 6:18 — But with thee will I establish my covenant; and thou shalt come into the ark, thou, and thy sons, and thy wife, and thy sons' wives with thee.

Ex 20:6 — And shewing mercy unto thousands of them that love me, and keep my commandments.

Ps 103:17 — But the mercy of the LORD *is* from everlasting to everlasting upon them that fear him, and his righteousness unto children's children;

- **Curses entailed.**

Eze 16:44–45

Ex 20:5 — Thou shalt not bow down thyself to them, nor serve them: for I the LORD thy God *am* a jealous God, visiting the iniquity of the fathers upon the children unto the third and fourth *generation* of them that hate me;

Le 20:5 — Then I will set my face against that man, and against his family, and will cut him off, and all that go a whoring after him, to commit whoredom with Molech, from among their people.

Isa 14:20 — Thou shalt not be joined with them in burial, because thou hast destroyed thy land, *and* slain thy people: the seed of evildoers shall never be renowned.

Jer 9:14 — But have walked after the imagination of their own heart, and after Baalim, which their fathers taught them:

La 5:7 — Our fathers have sinned, *and are* not; and we have borne their iniquities.

- **Involved in children's wickedness.**

1Sa 2:27–36; 4:10–22

- **Partiality of.**
  - **Isaac for Esau.**

    Ge 25:28 — And Isaac loved Esau, because he did eat of *his* venison: but Rebekah loved Jacob.

  - **Rebekah for Jacob.**

    Ge 27:6–17

    Ge 25:28 — And Isaac loved Esau, because he did eat of *his* venison: but Rebekah loved Jacob.

  - **Jacob for Joseph.**

    Ge 33:2 — And he put the handmaids and their children foremost, and Leah and her children after, and Rachel and Joseph hindermost.

    Ge 37:3 — Now Israel loved Joseph more than all his children, because he *was* the son of his old age: and he made him a coat of *many* colours.

    Ge 48:22 — Moreover I have given to thee one portion above thy brethren, which I took out of the hand of the Amorite with my sword and with my bow.

  - **Jacob for Benjamin.**

    Ge 42:4 — But Benjamin, Joseph's brother, Jacob sent not with his brethren; for he said, Lest peradventure mischief befall him.

  See: Partiality

- **Parental affection exemplified.**
  - **By Hagar.**

    Ge 21:15–16

  - **Rebekah's mother.**

    Ge 24:55 — And her brother and her mother said, Let the damsel abide with us *a few* days, at the least ten; after that she shall go.

  - **Isaac and Rebekah.**

    Ge 25:28 — And Isaac loved Esau, because he did eat of *his* venison: but Rebekah loved Jacob.

  - **Isaac.**

    Ge 27:26–27

  - **Laban.**

    Ge 31:26–28

  - **Jacob.**

    Ge 37:3–4; 43:13–14; 45:26–28; 48:10–11

    Ge 42:4 — But Benjamin, Joseph's brother, Jacob sent not with his brethren; for he said, Lest peradventure mischief befall him.

    Ge 42:38 — And he said, My son shall not go down with you; for his brother is dead, and he is left alone: if mischief befall him by the way in the which ye go, then shall ye bring down my gray hairs with sorrow to the grave.

  - **Moses' mother.**

    Ex 2:1–25

  - **Naomi.**

    Ru 1:8–9

  - **Hannah.**

    1Sa 2:19 — Moreover his mother made him a little coat, and brought *it* to him from year to year, when she came up with her husband to offer the yearly sacrifice.

  - **David.**

    2Sa 12:18–23; 13:38–14:1; 18:12–13; 18:33–19:6

    2Sa 14:33 — So Joab came to the king, and told him: and when he had called for Absalom, he came to the king, and bowed himself on his face to the ground before the king: and the king kissed Absalom.

    2Sa 18:5 — And the king commanded Joab and Abishai and Ittai, saying, *Deal* gently for my sake with the young man, *even* with Absalom. And all the people heard when the king gave all the captains charge concerning Absalom.

  - **Rizpah.**

    2Sa 21:10 — And Rizpah the daughter of Aiah took sackcloth, and spread it for her upon the rock, from the beginning of harvest until water dropped upon them out of heaven, and suffered neither the birds of the air to rest on them by day, nor the beasts of the field by night.

  - **The mother of the infant brought to Solomon by the harlots.**

    1Ki 3:22–28

  - **Mary.**

    Mt 12:46 — While he yet talked to the people, behold, *his* mother and his brethren stood without, desiring to speak with him.

    Lk 2:48 — And when they saw him, they were amazed: and his mother said unto him, Son, why hast thou thus dealt with us? behold, thy father and I have sought thee sorrowing.

    Jn 2:5 — His mother saith unto the servants, Whatsoever he saith unto you, do *it*.

Jn 19:25 — Now there stood by the cross of Jesus his mother, and his mother's sister, Mary the *wife* of Cleophas, and Mary Magdalene.

- **Jairus.**

Mk 5:23 — And besought him greatly, saying, My little daughter lieth at the point of death: *I pray thee,* come and lay thy hands on her, that she may be healed; and she shall live.

- **Father of demoniac.**

Mk 9:24 — And straightway the father of the child cried out, and said with tears, Lord, I believe; help thou mine unbelief.

- **Nobleman.**

Jn 4:49 — The nobleman saith unto him, Sir, come down ere my child die.

• Indulgent.

- **Eli.**

1Sa 2:27–36; 3:13–14

- **David.**

1Ki 1:6 — And his father had not displeased him at any time in saying, Why hast thou done so? and he also *was a* very goodly *man;* and *his mother* bare him after Absalom.

• Paternal blessings.

- **Of Noah.**

Ge 9:24–27

- **Of Abraham.**

Ge 17:18 — And Abraham said unto God, O that Ishmael might live before thee!

- **Of Isaac.**

Ge 27:10–40; 28:3–4

- **Of Jacob.**

Ge 48:15–20; 49:1–28

• Prayers in behalf of children.

- **Of Hannah.**

1Sa 1:27 — For this child I prayed; and the LORD hath given me my petition which I asked of him:

- **Of David.**

2Sa 7:25–29; 1Ch 17:16–27

2Sa 12:16 — David therefore besought God for the child; and David fasted, and went in, and lay all night upon the earth.

1Ch 22:12 — Only the LORD give thee wisdom and understanding, and give thee charge concerning Israel, that thou mayest keep the law of the LORD thy God.

1Ch 29:19 — And give unto Solomon my son a perfect heart, to keep thy commandments, thy testimonies, and thy statutes, and to do all *these things,* and to build the palace, for the which I have made provision.

- **Of Job.**

Job 1:5 — And it was so, when the days of *their* feasting were gone about, that Job sent and sanctified them, and rose up early in the morning, and offered burnt offerings *according* to the number of them all: for Job said, It may be that my sons have sinned, and cursed God in their hearts. Thus did Job continually.

• Paternal reproaches.

Ge 9:24–25; 49:3–7

• Influence of.

See: Influence

• Unclassified scriptures relating to.

Ex 12:26–27; Dt 4:9–10; 6:20–24; 11:18–21; Ps 78:5–6; Pr 23:13–14; Lk 11:11–13; Col 3:12–15; 1Ti 3:4–5

Ge 18:19 — For I know him, that he will command his children and his household after him, and they shall keep the way of the LORD, to do justice and judgment; that the LORD may bring upon Abraham that which he hath spoken of him.

Ex 10:2 — And that thou mayest tell in the ears of thy son, and of thy son's son, what things I have wrought in Egypt, and my signs which I have done among them; that ye may know how that I *am* the LORD.

Ex 13:8 — And thou shalt shew thy son in that day, saying, *This is done* because of that *which* the LORD did unto me when I came forth out of Egypt.

Ex 13:14 — And it shall be when thy son asketh thee in time to come, saying, What *is* this? that thou shalt say unto him, By strength of hand the LORD brought us out from Egypt, from the house of bondage:

Ex 20:5 — Thou shalt not bow down thyself to them, nor serve them: for I the LORD thy God *am* a jealous God, visiting the iniquity of the fathers upon the children unto the third and fourth *generation* of them that hate me;

Ex 20:10 — But the seventh day *is* the sabbath of the LORD thy God: *in it* thou shalt not do any work, thou, nor thy son, nor thy daughter, thy manservant, nor thy maidservant, nor thy cattle, nor thy stranger that *is* within thy gates:

Ex 21:17 — And he that curseth his father, or his mother, shall surely be put to death.

Le 20:9 — For every one that curseth his father or his mother shall be surely put to death: he hath cursed his father or his mother; his blood *shall be* upon him.

Le 23:3 — Six days shall work be done: but the seventh day *is* the sabbath of rest, an holy convocation; ye shall do no work *therein:* it *is* the sabbath of the LORD in all your dwellings.

Dt 6:7 — And thou shalt teach them diligently unto thy children, and shalt talk of them when thou sittest in thine house, and when thou walkest by the way, and when thou liest down, and when thou risest up.

Dt 32:46 — And he said unto them, Set your hearts unto all the words which I testify among you this day, which ye shall command your children to observe to do, all the words of this law.

Ps 103:13 — Like as a father pitieth *his* children, *so* the LORD pitieth them that fear him.

Pr 3:12 — For whom the LORD loveth he correcteth; even as a father the son *in whom* he delighteth.

Pr 13:22 — A good *man* leaveth an inheritance to his children's children: and the wealth of the sinner is laid up for the just.

Pr 13:24 — He that spareth his rod hateth his son: but he that loveth him chasteneth him betimes.

Pr 19:18 — Chasten thy son while there is hope, and let not thy soul spare for his crying.

Pr 22:6 — Train up a child in the way he should go: and when he is old, he will not depart from it.

Pr 22:15 — Foolishness *is* bound in the heart of a child; *but* the rod of correction shall drive it far from him.

Pr 27:11 — My son, be wise, and make my heart glad, that I may answer him that reproacheth me.

Pr 29:15 — The rod and reproof give wisdom: but a child left *to himself* bringeth his mother to shame.

Pr 29:17 — Correct thy son, and he shall give thee rest; yea, he shall give delight unto thy soul.

Pr 31:28 — Her children arise up, and call her blessed; her husband *also,* and he praiseth her.

Isa 38:19 — The living, the living, he shall praise thee, as I *do* this day: the father to the children shall make known thy truth.

Isa 49:15 — Can a woman forget her sucking child, that she should not have compassion on the son of her womb? yea, they may forget, yet will I not forget thee.

Isa 66:13 — As one whom his mother comforteth, so will I comfort you; and ye shall be comforted in Jerusalem.

Jer 31:1 — At the same time, saith the LORD, will I be the God of all the families of Israel, and they shall be my people.

Jer 49:11 — Leave thy fatherless children, I will preserve *them* alive; and let thy widows trust in me.

La 5:7 — Our fathers have sinned, *and are* not; and we have borne their iniquities.

Joel 1:3 — Tell ye your children of it, and *let* your children *tell* their children, and their children another generation.

Mal 4:6 — And he shall turn the heart of the fathers to the children, and the heart of the children to their fathers, lest I come and smite the earth with a curse.

Mt 10:37 — He that loveth father or mother more than me is not worthy of me: and he that loveth son or daughter more than me is not worthy of me.

Ro 12:10 — *Be* kindly affectioned one to another with brotherly love; in honour preferring one another;

1Co 4:15 — For though ye have ten thousand instructers in Christ, yet *have ye* not many fathers: for in Christ Jesus I have begotten you through the gospel.

2Co 12:14 — Behold, the third time I am ready to come to you; and I will not be burdensome to you: for I seek not yours, but you: for the children ought not to lay up for the parents, but the parents for the children.

Eph 6:4 — And, ye fathers, provoke not your children to wrath: but bring them up in the nurture and admonition of the Lord.

Php 1:8 — For God is my record, how greatly I long after you all in the bowels of Jesus Christ.

Col 3:21 — Fathers, provoke not your children *to anger,* lest they be discouraged.

1Th 2:11 — As ye know how we exhorted and comforted and charged every one of you, as a father *doth* his children,

1Ti 3:12 — Let the deacons be the husbands of one wife, ruling their children and their own houses well.

1Ti 5:8 — But if any provide not for his own, and specially for those of his own house, he hath denied the faith, and is worse than an infidel.

Tit 1:6 — If any be blameless, the husband of one wife, having faithful children not accused of riot or unruly.

Tit 2:4 — That they may teach the young women to be sober, to love their husbands, to love their children,

Heb 12:7 — If ye endure chastening, God dealeth with you as with sons; for what son is he whom the father chasteneth not?

1Jn 3:7 — Little children, let no man deceive you: he that doeth righteousness is righteous, even as he is righteous.

See: Children

See: Instruction

PARLOR

1Sa 9:22 — And Samuel took Saul and his servant, and brought them into the parlour, and made them sit in the chiefest place among them that were bidden, which *were* about thirty persons.

PARMASHTA • Son of Haman.

Est 9:9 — And Parmashta, and Arisai, and Aridai, and Vajezatha,

PARMENAS • One of the disciples.

Ac 6:5 — And the saying pleased the whole multitude: and they chose Stephen, a man full of faith and of the Holy Ghost, and Philip, and Prochorus, and Nicanor, and Timon, and Parmenas, and Nicolas a proselyte of Antioch:

PARNACH • Father of Elizaphan.

Nu 34:25 — And the prince of the tribe of the children of Zebulun, Elizaphan the son of Parnach.

PAROSH

• Called also Pharosh.

• The ancestor of one of the families which returned to Jerusalem from captivity in Babylon.

Ezr 2:3 — The children of Parosh, two thousand an hundred seventy and two.

Ezr 8:3 — Of the sons of Shechaniah, of the sons of Pharosh; Zechariah: and with him were reckoned by genealogy of the males an hundred and fifty.

Ezr 10:25 — Moreover of Israel: of the sons of Parosh; Ramiah, and Jeziah, and Malchiah, and Miamin, and Eleazar, and Malchijah, and Benaiah.

Ne 7:8 — The children of Parosh, two thousand an hundred seventy and two.

Ne 10:14 — The chief of the people; Parosh, Pahath-moab, Elam, Zatthu, Bani,

PARRICIDE

2Ki 19:37 — And it came to pass, as he was worshipping in the house of Nisroch his god, that Adrammelech and Sharezer his sons smote him with the sword: and they escaped into the land of Armenia. And Esar-haddon his son reigned in his stead.

2Ch 32:21 — And the LORD sent an angel, which cut off all the mighty men of valour, and the leaders and captains in the camp of the king of Assyria. So he returned with shame of face to his own land. And when he was come into the house of his god, they that came forth of his own bowels slew him there with the sword.

Isa 37:38 — And it came to pass, as he was worshipping in the house of Nisroch his god, that Adrammelech and Sharezer his sons smote him with the sword; and they escaped into the land of Armenia: and Esar-haddon his son reigned in his stead.

PARSHANDATHA • Son of Haman.

Est 9:7 — And Parshandatha, and Dalphon, and Aspatha,

PARSIMONY

• Of the Jews toward the temple.

Hag 1:2 — Thus speaketh the LORD of hosts, saying, This people say, The time is not come, the time that the LORD'S house should be built.

Hag 1:4 — *Is it* time for you, O ye, to dwell in your cieled houses, and this house *lie* waste?

Hag 1:6 — Ye have sown much, and bring in little; ye eat, but ye have not enough; ye drink, but ye are not filled with drink; ye clothe you, but there is none warm; and he that earneth wages earneth wages *to put it* into a bag with holes.

Hag 1:9 — Ye looked for much, and, lo, *it came* to little; and when ye brought *it* home, I did blow upon it. Why? saith the LORD of hosts. Because of mine house that *is* waste, and ye run every man unto his own house.

• Of the Jews toward God.

Mal 3:8–9

• Of the disciples, when the ointment was poured on Jesus.

Mt 26:8–9; Jn 12:4–5

• Punishment of.

Hag 1:9–11

See: Liberality

PARTHIANS • The inhabitants of Parthia, a country northwest of Persia.

Ac 2:9 — Parthians, and Medes, and Elamites, and the dwellers in Mesopotamia, and in Judaea, and Cappadocia, in Pontus, and Asia,

PARTIALITY

• Among brethren forbidden.

1Ti 5:21 — I charge *thee* before God, and the Lord Jesus Christ, and the elect angels, that thou observe these things without preferring one before another, doing nothing by partiality.

• Of parents for particular children.

See: Parents

• Its effect on other children.

Ge 37:4 — And when his brethren saw that their father loved him more than all his brethren, they hated him, and could not speak peaceably unto him.

PARTICEPS CRIMINIS

2Jn 1:11 — For he that biddeth him God speed is partaker of his evil deeds.

See: Collusion

PARTNERSHIP

• With God.

1Co 3:7 — So then neither is he that planteth any thing, neither he that watereth; but God that giveth the increase.

1Co 3:9 — For we are labourers together with God: ye are God's husbandry, *ye are* God's building.

2Co 6:1 — We then, *as* workers together *with him*, beseech *you* also that ye receive not the grace of God in vain.

Php 2:13 — For it is God which worketh in you both to will and to do of *his* good pleasure.

See: Providence

PARTRIDGE

1Sa 26:20 — Now therefore, let not my blood fall to the earth before the face of the LORD: for the king of Israel is come out to seek a flea, as when one doth hunt a partridge in the mountains.

Jer 17:11 — As the partridge sitteth *on eggs*, and hatcheth *them* not; *so* he that getteth riches, and not by right, shall leave them in the midst of his days, and at his end shall be a fool.

PARUAH • Father of Jehoshaphat.

1Ki 4:17 — Jehoshaphat the son of Paruah, in Issachar:

PARVAIM • An unknown gold region.

2Ch 3:6 — And he garnished the house with precious stones for beauty: and the gold *was* gold of Parvaim.

PAS-DAMMIM

• A battle between David and the Philistines, fought at.

1Ch 11:13 — He was with David at Pas-dammim, and there the Philistines were gathered together to battle, where was a parcel of ground full of barley; and the people fled from before the Philistines.

• Called Ephes-Dammim.

1Sa 17:1 — Now the Philistines gathered together their armies to battle, and were gathered together at Shochoh, which *belongeth* to Judah, and pitched between Shochoh and Azekah, in Ephes-dammim.

PASACH • Son of Japhlet.

1Ch 7:33 — And the sons of Japhlet; Pasach, and Bimhal, and Ashvath. These *are* the children of Japhlet.

PASCHAL LAMB ⇝See: Passover

PASEAH

• A son of Eshton.

1Ch 4:12 — And Eshton begat Beth-rapha, and Paseah, and Tehinnah the father of Ir-nahash. These *are* the men of Rechah.

• Called also Phaseah.

Neh. 7:51 — The children of Gazzam, the children of Uzza, the children of Phaseah,

• Ancestor of a family which returned to Jerusalem from captivity in Babylon.

Ezr 2:49 — The children of Uzza, the children of Paseah, the children of Besai,

Ne 7:51 — The children of Gazzam, the children of Uzza, the children of Phaseah,

• Father of Jehoiada. Probably identical with preceding.

Ne 3:6 — Moreover the old gate repaired Jehoiada the son of Paseah, and Meshullam the son of Besodeiah; they laid the beams thereof, and set up the doors thereof, and the locks thereof, and the bars thereof.

PASHUR

• A priest.

• Son of Malchijah.

1Ch 9:12 — And Adaiah the son of Jeroham, the son of Pashur, the son of Malchijah, and Maasiai the son of Adiel, the son of Jahzerah, the son of Meshullam, the son of Meshillemith, the son of Immer;

• An influential man, and ancestor of an influential family.

Ezr 2:38 — The children of Pashur, a thousand two hundred forty and seven.

Ezr 10:22 — And of the sons of Pashur; Elioenai, Maaseiah, Ishmael, Nethaneel, Jozabad, and Elasah.

Ne 7:41 — The children of Pashur, a thousand two hundred forty and seven.

Ne 10:3 — Pashur, Amariah, Malchijah,

Ne 11:12 — And their brethren that did the work of the house *were* eight hundred twenty and two: and Adaiah the son of Jeroham, the son of Pelaliah, the son of Amzi, the son of Zechariah, the son of Pashur, the son of Malchiah,

Jer 21:1 — The word which came unto Jeremiah from the LORD, when king Zedekiah sent unto him Pashur the son of Melchiah, and Zephaniah the son of Maaseiah the priest, saying,

Jer 38:1 — Then Shephatiah the son of Mattan, and Gedaliah the son of Pashur, and Jucal the son of Shelemiah, and Pashur the son of Malchiah, heard the words that Jeremiah had spoken unto all the people, saying,

• Son of Immer and governor of the temple.

• Beats and imprisons Jeremiah.

Jer 20:1–6

• Father of Gedaliah, who persecuted Jeremiah.

Jer 38:1 — Then Shephatiah the son of Mattan, and Gedaliah the son of Pashur, and Jucal the son of Shelemiah, and Pashur the son of Malchiah, heard the words that Jeremiah had spoken unto all the people, saying,

PASSENGER ⇝See: Commerce

PASSION

Ac 1:3 — To whom also he shewed himself alive after his passion by many infallible proofs, being seen of them forty days, and speaking of the things pertaining to the kingdom of God:

⇝See: Jesus, Sufferings of

PASSOVER

• Institution of.

Ex 12:3–49; 23:15–18; Le 23:4–8; Nu 9:2–5, 13–14; 28:16–25; Dt 16:1–8

Ex 34:18 — The feast of unleavened bread shalt thou keep. Seven days thou shalt eat unleavened bread, as I commanded thee, in the time of the month Abib: for in the month Abib thou camest out from Egypt.

Dt 16:16 — Three times in a year shall all thy males appear before the LORD thy God in the place which he shall choose; in the feast of unleavened bread, and in the feast of weeks, and in the feast of tabernacles: and they shall not appear before the LORD empty:

Ps 81:3 — Blow up the trumpet in the new moon, in the time appointed, on our solemn feast day.

Ps 81:5 — This he ordained in Joseph *for* a testimony, when he went out through the land of Egypt: *where* I heard a language *that* I understood not.

• Design of.

Ex 12:21–28

• Special passover, for those who were unclean, or on journey, to be held in second month.

Nu 9:6–12; 2Ch 30:2–4

• Lamb killed by Levites, for those who were ceremonially unclean.

2Ch 35:3–11

2Ch 30:17 — For *there were* many in the congregation that were not sanctified: therefore the Levites had the charge of the killing of the passovers for every one *that was* not clean, to sanctify *them* unto the LORD.

Ezr 6:20 — For the priests and the Levites were purified together, all of them *were* pure, and killed the passover for all the children of the captivity, and for their brethren the priests, and for themselves.

• Strangers authorized to celebrate.

Ex 12:48–49

Nu 9:14 — And if a stranger shall sojourn among you, and will keep the passover unto the LORD; according to the ordinance of the passover, and according to the manner thereof, so shall he do: ye shall have one ordinance, both for the stranger, and for him that was born in the land.

- **Observed at place designated by God.**

Dt 16:5–7

- **Observed with unleavened bread.**

Ex 12:15–20; Dt 16:3–4

Ex 12:8 — And they shall eat the flesh in that night, roast with fire, and unleavened bread; *and* with bitter *herbs* they shall eat it.

Ex 13:3 — And Moses said unto the people, Remember this day, in which ye came out from Egypt, out of the house of bondage; for by strength of hand the LORD brought you out from this *place:* there shall no leavened bread be eaten.

Ex 13:6 — Seven days thou shalt eat unleavened bread, and in the seventh day *shall be* a feast to the LORD.

Ex 23:15 — Thou shalt keep the feast of unleavened bread: (thou shalt eat unleavened bread seven days, as I commanded thee, in the time appointed of the month Abib; for in it thou camest out from Egypt: and none shall appear before me empty:)

Le 23:6 — And on the fifteenth day of the same month *is* the feast of unleavened bread unto the LORD: seven days ye must eat unleavened bread.

Nu 9:11 — The fourteenth day of the second month at even they shall keep it, *and* eat it with unleavened bread and bitter *herbs.*

Nu 28:17 — And in the fifteenth day of this month *is* the feast: seven days shall unleavened bread be eaten.

Mk 14:12 — And the first day of unleavened bread, when they killed the passover, his disciples said unto him, Where wilt thou that we go and prepare that thou mayest eat the passover?

Lk 22:7 — Then came the day of unleavened bread, when the passover must be killed.

Ac 12:3 — And because he saw it pleased the Jews, he proceeded further to take Peter also. (Then were the days of unleavened bread.)

1Co 5:8 — Therefore let us keep the feast, not with old leaven, neither with the leaven of malice and wickedness; but with the unleavened *bread* of sincerity and truth.

- **Penalty for neglecting to observe.**

Nu 9:13 — But the man that *is* clean, and is not in a journey, and forbeareth to keep the passover, even the same soul shall be cut off from among his people: because he brought not the offering of the LORD in his appointed season, that man shall bear his sin.

- **Reinstituted by Ezekiel.**

Eze 45:21–24

- **Observation of, renewed by the Israelites on entering Canaan.**

Jos 5:10–11

- **Observation of, renewed by Hezekiah.**

2Ch 30:1 — And Hezekiah sent to all Israel and Judah, and wrote letters also to Ephraim and Manasseh, that they should come to the house of the LORD at Jerusalem, to keep the passover unto the LORD God of Israel.

- **Observation of, renewed by Josiah.**

2Ki 23:22–23

2Ch 35:1 — Moreover Josiah kept a passover unto the LORD in Jerusalem: and they killed the passover on the fourteenth *day* of the first month.

2Ch 35:18 — And there was no passover like to that kept in Israel from the days of Samuel the prophet; neither did all the kings of Israel keep such a passover as Josiah kept, and the priests, and the Levites, and all Judah and Israel that were present, and the inhabitants of Jerusalem.

- **Observation of, after return from captivity.**

Ezr 6:19–20

- **Observed by Jesus.**

Mt 26:17–20; Jn 13:1–38

Lk 22:15 — And he said unto them, With desire I have desired to eat this passover with you before I suffer:

Jn 2:13 — And the Jews' passover was at hand, and Jesus went up to Jerusalem,

Jn 2:23 — Now when he was in Jerusalem at the passover, in the feast *day,* many believed in his name, when they saw the miracles which he did.

- **Jesus in the temple at time of.**

Lk 2:41–50

- **Jesus crucified at time of.**

Mk 14:1–2

Mt 26:2 — Ye know that after two days is *the feast of* the passover, and the Son of man is betrayed to be crucified.

Jn 18:28 — Then led they Jesus from Caiaphas unto the hall of judgment: and it was early; and they themselves went not into the judgment hall, lest they should be defiled; but that they might eat the passover.

- **The lamb of, a type of Christ.**

1Co 5:7 — Purge out therefore the old leaven, that ye may be a new lump, as ye are unleavened. For even Christ our passover is sacrificed for us:

- **Lord's Supper ordained at.**

Mt 26:26–28; Mk 14:12–25; Lk 22:7–20

- **Prisoner released at, by the Romans.**

Lk 23:16–17

Mt 27:15 — Now at *that* feast the governor was wont to release unto the people a prisoner, whom they would.

Mk 15:6 — Now at *that* feast he released unto them one prisoner, whomsoever they desired.

Jn 18:39 — But ye have a custom, that I should release unto you one at the passover: will ye therefore that I release unto you the King of the Jews?

- **Peter imprisoned at time of.**

Ac 12:3 — And because he saw it pleased the Jews, he proceeded further to take Peter also. (Then were the days of unleavened bread.)

- **Christ called our passover.**

1Co 5:7 — Purge out therefore the old leaven, that ye may be a new lump, as ye are unleavened. For even Christ our passover is sacrificed for us:

See: Feasts

PASSPORTS

- **Given to Nehemiah.**

Ne 2:7–9

PASTOR

Jer 22:22 — The wind shall eat up all thy pastors, and thy lovers shall go into captivity: surely then shalt thou be ashamed and confounded for all thy wickedness.

See: Shepherd

PASTORING

Ac 20:29 — For I know this, that after my departing shall grievous wolves enter in among you, not sparing the flock.

Eph 4:11 — And he gave some, apostles; and some, prophets; and some, evangelists; and some, pastors and teachers;

1Pe 5:2 — Feed the flock of God which is among you, taking the oversight *thereof,* not by constraint, but willingly; not for filthy lucre, but of a ready mind;

PATARA

- **A Lycian city in Asia Minor.**
- **Visited by Paul.**

Ac 21:1–2

PATHROS

- **A part of Upper Egypt.**
- **Jewish captives in.**

Isa 11:11 — And it shall come to pass in that day, *that* the Lord shall set his hand again the second time to recover the remnant of his people, which shall be left, from Assyria, and from Egypt, and from Pathros, and from Cush, and from Elam, and from Shinar, and from Hamath, and from the islands of the sea.

Jer 44:1 — The word that came to Jeremiah concerning all the Jews which dwell in the land of Egypt, which dwell at Migdol, and at Tahpanhes, and at Noph, and in the country of Pathros, saying,

Jer 44:15 — Then all the men which knew that their wives had burned incense unto other gods, and all the women that stood by, a great multitude, even all the people that dwelt in the land of Egypt, in Pathros, answered Jeremiah, saying,

Eze 29:14 — And I will bring again the captivity of Egypt, and will cause them to return *into* the land of Pathros, into the land of their habitation; and they shall be there a base kingdom.

- **Prophecy against.**

Eze 30:14 — And I will make Pathros desolate, and will set fire in Zoan, and will execute judgments in No.

PATHRUSIM

- **A descendant of Mizraim.**
- **Ancestor of the Philistines.**

Ge 10:14 — And Pathrusim, and Casluhim, (out of whom came Philistim,) and Caphtorim.

1Ch 1:12 — And Pathrusim, and Casluhim, (of whom came the Philistines,) and Caphthorim.

PATIENCE

Ps 37:7–9; Ecc 7:8–9; La 3:26–27; Ro 5:3–4; 15:4–5; 1Co 13:4–5; 2Co 6:4–6; Eph 4:1–2; Col 1:10–11; 3:12–13; 1Ti 3:2–3; 2Ti 2:24–25; Tit 2:1–2; Jas 1:3–4; 5:7–8; 1Pe 2:19–23; 2Pe 1:5–6

Pr 15:18 — A wrathful man stirreth up strife: but *he that is* slow to anger appeaseth strife.

Lk 8:15 — But that on the good ground are they, which in an honest and good heart, having heard the word, keep *it,* and bring forth fruit with patience.

Lk 21:19 — In your patience possess ye your souls.

Ro 2:7 — To them who by patient continuance in well doing seek for glory and honour and immortality, eternal life:

Ro 8:25 — But if we hope for that we see not, *then* do we with patience wait for *it.*

Ro 12:12 — Rejoicing in hope; patient in tribulation; continuing instant in prayer;

2Co 12:12 — Truly the signs of an apostle were wrought among you in all patience, in signs, and wonders, and mighty deeds.

Gal 6:9 — And let us not be weary in well doing: for in due season we shall reap, if we faint not.

1Th 1:3 — Remembering without ceasing your work of faith, and labour of love, and patience of hope in our Lord Jesus Christ, in the sight of God and our Father;

1Th 5:14 — Now we exhort you, brethren, warn them that are unruly, comfort the feebleminded, support the weak, be patient toward all *men.*

2Th 3:5 — And the Lord direct your hearts into the love of God, and into the patient waiting for Christ.

1Ti 6:11 — But thou, O man of God, flee these things; and follow after righteousness, godliness, faith, love, patience, meekness.

Tit 2:9 — *Exhort* servants to be obedient unto their own masters, *and* to please *them* well in all *things;* not answering again;

Heb 6:12 — That ye be not slothful, but followers of them who through faith and patience inherit the promises.

Heb 6:15 — And so, after he had patiently endured, he obtained the promise.

Heb 10:36 — For ye have need of patience, that, after ye have done the will of God, ye might receive the promise.

Heb 12:1 — Wherefore seeing we also are compassed about with so great a cloud of witnesses, let us lay aside every weight, and the sin which doth so easily beset us, and let us run with patience the race that is set before us,

Jas 1:19 — Wherefore, my beloved brethren, let every man be swift to hear, slow to speak, slow to wrath:

Rev 1:9 — I John, who also am your brother, and companion in tribulation, and in the kingdom and patience of Jesus Christ, was in the isle that is called Patmos, for the word of God, and for the testimony of Jesus Christ.

Rev 13:10 — He that leadeth into captivity shall go into captivity: he that killeth with the sword must be killed with the sword. Here is the patience and the faith of the saints.

Rev 14:12 — Here is the patience of the saints: here *are* they that keep the commandments of God, and the faith of Jesus.

See: Long-Suffering

See: Meekness

- **Instances of.**
  - **Isaac toward the people of Gerar.** Ge 26:15–22
  - **Moses.** Ex 16:7–8
  - **Job.** Job 1:21; Jas 5:11
  - **David.** Ps 40:1
  - **Simeon.** Lk 2:25
  - **Paul.** 2Ti 3:10
  - **Prophets.** Jas 5:10
  - **The Thessalonians.** 2Th 1:4
  - **The church at Ephesus.** Rev 2:2–3
  - **The church at Thyatira.** Rev 2:19
  - **John.** Rev 1:9

PATMOS

- **An island in the Aegean Sea.**
- **John an exile on.**

Rev 1:9 — I John, who also am your brother, and companion in tribulation, and in the kingdom and patience of Jesus Christ, was in the isle that is called Patmos, for the word of God, and for the testimony of Jesus Christ.

PATRIARCH • Head of a family.

Ac 7:9 — And the patriarchs, moved with envy, sold Joseph into Egypt: but God was with him,

PATRIARCHAL GOVERNMENT **See: Government**

PATRICIDE

- **Of Sennacherib.**

2Ki 19:37 — And it came to pass, as he was worshipping in the house of Nisroch his god, that Adrammelech and Sharezer his sons smote him with the sword: and they escaped into the land of Armenia. And Esar-haddon his son reigned in his stead.

Isa 37:38 — And it came to pass, as he was worshipping in the house of Nisroch his god, that Adrammelech and Sharezer his sons smote him with the sword; and they escaped into the land of Armenia: and Esar-haddon his son reigned in his stead.

PATRIOTISM

Dt 26:1–11; Jgs 5:1–31; Ps 85:1–13; 122:6–7; 128:5–6; 137:1–6; Jer 8:21–9:2; La 5:1–22

Ps 51:18 — Do good in thy good pleasure unto Zion: build thou the walls of Jerusalem.

Isa 62:1 — For Zion's sake will I not hold my peace, and for Jerusalem's sake I will not rest, until the righteousness thereof go forth as brightness, and the salvation thereof as a lamp *that* burneth.

Jer 8:11 — For they have healed the hurt of the daughter of my people slightly, saying, Peace, peace; when *there is* no peace.

See: Country; love of

- **Instances of.**
  - **Moses.** Heb 11:24–26
  - **Deborah.** Jgs 4:1–5:31
  - **The tribes of Zebulun and Naphtali.** Jgs 5:18–20
  - **Eli.** 1Sa 4:17–18
  - **Phinehas' wife.** 1Sa 4:19–22
  - **Joab.** 2Sa 10:12
  - **Uriah.** 2Sa 11:11
  - **Hadad.** 1Ki 11:21–22
  - **The lepers of Samaria.** 2Ki 7:9
  - **Nehemiah.** Ne 1:2, 4–11; 2:3
- **Wanting in.**
  - **The tribes of Reuben, Asher, and Dan.** Jgs 5:15–17
  - **Inhabitants of Meroz.**

    Jgs 5:23 — Curse ye Meroz, said the angel of the LORD, curse ye bitterly the inhabitants thereof; because they came not to the help of the LORD, to the help of the LORD against the mighty.
  - **Inhabitants of Succoth and Penuel.** Jgs 8:4–17

PATROBAS • A believer at Rome.

Ro 16:14 — Salute Asyncritus, Phlegon, Hermas, Patrobas, Hermes, and the brethren which are with them.

PATTERN

- **Of the tabernacle.**

Heb 8:5 — Who serve unto the example and shadow of heavenly things, as Moses was admonished of God when he was about to make the tabernacle: for, See, saith he, *that* thou make all things according to the pattern shewed to thee in the mount.

Heb 9:23 — *It was* therefore necessary that the patterns of things in the heavens should be purified with these; but the heavenly things themselves with better sacrifices than these.

See: Tabernacle

PAU

• Called also Pai.

• A city of Edom.

Ge 36:39 — And Baal-hanan the son of Achbor died, and Hadar reigned in his stead: and the name of his city *was* Pau; and his wife's name *was* Mehetabel, the daughter of Matred, the daughter of Mezahab.

1Ch 1:50 — And when Baal-hanan was dead, Hadad reigned in his stead: and the name of his city *was* Pai; and his wife's name *was* Mehetabel, the daughter of Matred, the daughter of Mezahab.

PAUL, Ministry, Ac 16–28

• Makes his second tour of the churches.

Ac 15:36

• Chooses Silas as his companion, and passes through Syria and Cilicia, confirming the churches.

Ac 15:36–41

• Visits Lystra; circumcises Timothy.

Ac 16:1–5

• Goes through Phrygia and Galatia; forbidden by the Holy Ghost to preach in Asia.

Ac 16:6–7

• Visits Mysia; essays to go to Bithynia, but is restrained by the Spirit.

Ac 16:8 — And they passing by Mysia came down to Troas.

• Goes to Troas, where he has a vision; immediately proceeds to Macedonia.

Ac 16:9–10

• Visits Samothracia and Neopolis; comes to Philippi, the chief city of Macedonia.

Ac 16:11–12

• Visits a place of prayer at the river side; preaches the word.

Ac 16:13 — And on the sabbath we went out of the city by a river side, where prayer was wont to be made; and we sat down, and spake unto the women which resorted *thither.*

• Merchant, Lydia, of Thyatira, is converted and baptized.

Ac 16:14–15

• Reproves soothsayer; causes evil spirit to come out of damsel who practices divination.

Ac 16:16–18

• Persecuted, beaten, and cast into prison with Silas.

Ac 16:19–24

• Sings songs of praise in the prison; an earthquake shakes the prison.

Ac 16:25–26

• Preaches to the alarmed jailer, who believes, and is baptized with his household.

Ac 16:27–34

• Is released by the civil authorities on the ground of his being a Roman citizen.

Ac 16:35–39

2Co 6:5 — In stripes, in imprisonments, in tumults, in labours, in watchings, in fastings;

2Co 11:25 — Thrice was I beaten with rods, once was I stoned, thrice I suffered shipwreck, a night and a day I have been in the deep;

1Th 2:2 — But even after that we had suffered before, and were shamefully entreated, as ye know, at Philippi, we were bold in our God to speak unto you the gospel of God with much contention.

• Is received at the house of Lydia.

Ac 16:40 — And they went out of the prison, and entered into *the house of* Lydia and when they had seen the brethren, they comforted them, and departed.

• Visits Amphipolis, and Apollonia, and Thessalonica; preaches in the synagogue.

Ac 17:1–4

• Is persecuted.

Ac 17:5–9; 2Th 1:1–4

• Escapes to Berea by night; preaches in synagogue; many honorable women and men believe.

Ac 17:10–12

• Persecuted by the Jews who come from Thessalonica; is conducted by the brethren to Athens.

Ac 17:13–15

• Disputes on Mars' Hill with Grecians.

Ac 17:16–34

• Visits Corinth.

Ac 18:1 — After these things Paul departed from Athens, and came to Corinth;

• Dwells with Aquila and his wife, Priscilla, who were tentmakers; joins in their handicraft.

Ac 18:2–3

• Reasons in the synagogue every Sabbath; is rejected of the Jews; turns to the Gentiles.

Ac 18:4–6

• Makes his abode with Justus; stays there one year and six months, teaching the word of God.

Ac 18:7–11

• Persecuted by Jews; drawn before the deputy; charged with wicked lewdness; accusation dismissed.

• Takes his leave after many days, and sails unto Syria, accompanied by Aquila and Priscilla.

Ac 18:12–18

• Visits Ephesus, where he leaves Aquila and Priscilla.

Ac 18:19 — And he came to Ephesus, and left them there: but he himself entered into the synagogue, and reasoned with the Jews.

• Enters into a synagogue, where he reasons with the Jews.

Ac 18:19–20

• Starts on his return journey to Jerusalem; visits Caesarea.

Ac 18:22 — And when he had landed at Caesarea, and gone up, and saluted the church, he went down to Antioch.

• Goes over the country of Galatia and Phrygia, in order, strengthening the disciples.

Ac 18:23 — And after he had spent some time *there,* he departed, and went over *all* the country of Galatia and Phrygia in order, strengthening all the disciples.

• Returns to Ephesus; baptizes in the name of the Lord Jesus.

Ac 19:1 — And it came to pass, that, while Apollos was at Corinth, Paul having passed through the upper coasts came to Ephesus: and finding certain disciples,

• Lays his hands upon the disciples, who are baptized with the Holy Ghost.

Ac 19:1–7

• Preaches in the synagogue; remains in Ephesus for the space of two years; heals the sick.

Ac 19:8–12

• Casts out evil spirit; many believe and bring books of sorcery to be burned.

Ac 19:13–20; 1Co 16:8–9

• Sends Timothy and Erastus into Macedonia, but remains himself in Asia for a season.

Ac 19:21–22

• Spread of gospel interferes with makers of idols; persecuted; accusations against Paul dismissed.

Ac 19:23–41

2Co 1:8 — For we would not, brethren, have you ignorant of our trouble which came to us in Asia, that we were pressed out of measure, above strength, insomuch that we despaired even of life:

2Ti 4:14 — Alexander the coppersmith did me much evil: the Lord reward him according to his works:

• Proceeds to Macedonia after confirming the churches in those parts.

Ac 20:1–2

• Comes into Greece and abides three months; returns through Macedonia.

Ac 20:2–6

• Visits Troas; preaches until daybreak; restores to life young man who fell from window.

Ac 20:6–12

• Visits Assos, Mitylene, Chios, Samos, Trogyllium, and Miletus; hastens to Jerusalem for Pentecost.

Ac 20:13–16

• Sends for the elders of the church of Ephesus; testifies repentance toward God.

Ac 20:17–21

• Declares he was going bound in spirit to Jerusalem.

Ac 20:24 — But none of these things move me, neither count I my life dear unto myself, so that I might finish my course with joy, and the ministry, which I have received of the Lord Jesus, to testify the gospel of the grace of God.

• Exhorts them to take heed to themselves and flock over whom Holy Ghost made them overseers.

Ac 20:25–35

• Kneels down and prays and takes his departure.

Ac 20:36–38

• Visits Coos, Rhodes, Patara; takes ship for Tyre; tarries at Tyre seven days.

Ac 21:1–3

• Brought on his way by the disciples to the outskirts of the city.

Ac 21:4–5

• Kneels down and prays; comes to Ptolemais; salutes the brethren, and abides one day.

Ac 21:5–7

• Departs for Caesarea; is admonished by Agabus not to go to Jerusalem; proceeds to Jerusalem.

Ac 21:8–16

• Is received by brethren gladly; talks of his ministry among the Gentiles.

Ac 21:17–26

• Enters the temple; the people are stirred against him by Jews from Asia.

Ac 21:27–29

• An uproar is created; he is thrust out of the temple; the chief captain interposes and arrests him.

Ac 21:30–33

• His defense.

Ac 21:33–22:21

- **Is confined in the castle.**
  Ac 22:24–30
- **Is brought before the council; his defense.**
  Ac 22:30–23:5
- **Is returned to the castle.**
  Ac 23:10 — And when there arose a great dissension, the chief captain, fearing lest Paul should have been pulled in pieces of them, commanded the soldiers to go down, and to take him by force from among them, and to bring *him* into the castle.
- **Is cheered by a vision, promising him that he shall bear witness in Rome.**
  Ac 23:11 — And the night following the Lord stood by him, and said, <u>Be of good cheer, Paul: for as thou hast testified of me in Jerusalem, so must thou bear witness also at Rome.</u>
- **Jews conspire against his life.**
  Ac 23:12–15
- **Thwarted by his nephew.**
  Ac 23:16–22
- **Is escorted to Caesarea by a military guard.**
  Ac 23:23–33
- **Is confined in Herod's judgment hall in Caesarea.**
  Ac 23:35 — I will hear thee, said he, when thine accusers are also come. And he commanded him to be kept in Herod's judgment hall.
- **His trial before Felix.**
  Ac 24:1–27
- **Remains in custody for two years.**
  Ac 24:27 — But after two years Porcius Festus came into Felix' room: and Felix, willing to shew the Jews a pleasure, left Paul bound.
- **His trial before Festus.**
  Ac 25:1–12
- **Appeals to Caesar.**
  Ac 25:10–12
- **His examination before Agrippa.**
  Ac 25:13–26:32
- **Is taken to Rome in custody of Julius, a centurion, and guard of soldiers.**
  Ac 27:1–5
- **Transferred to ship of Alexandria; sails by way of Cnidus, Crete, Salamis, and Fair Havens.**
  Ac 27:6–8
- **Predicts misfortune to the ship; his counsel not heeded, and the voyage resumed.**
  Ac 27:9–13
- **The ship encounters a tempest; Paul encourages and comforts the officers and crew.**
  Ac 27:14–41
- **Soldiers advise putting prisoners to death; centurion interferes; all on board, 276, reach safety.**
  Ac 27:42–44
- **Kind treatment by the inhabitants of the island.**
  Ac 28:1–2
- **Is bitten by a viper and miraculously preserved.**
  Ac 28:3–6
- **Heals the ruler's father and others.**
  Ac 28:7–10
- **Is delayed in Melita; proceeds; delays at Syracuse; sails by Rhegium and Puteoli.**
  Ac 28:11–13
- **Meets brethren who accompany him to Rome from Appii forum; arrives at Rome.**
  Ac 28:14–15
- **Permitted to dwell by himself in custody of a soldier.**
  Ac 28:16 — And when we came to Rome, the centurion delivered the prisoners to the captain of the guard: but Paul was suffered to dwell by himself with a soldier that kept him.
- **Calls the chief Jews together; is kindly received; testifies to the kingdom of heaven.**
  Ac 28:17–29
- **Dwells two years in his own hired house, preaching and teaching.**
  Ac 28:30–31

PAUL, Ministry, Ac 9–15

- **Preaches in Damascus.**
  Ac 9:20
  Ac 9:22 — But Saul increased the more in strength, and confounded the Jews which dwelt at Damascus, proving that this is very Christ.
- **Is persecuted by the Jews.**
  Ac 9:23–24
- **Escapes by being let down from the wall in a basket; goes to Arabia.**
  Gal 1:17 — Neither went I up to Jerusalem to them which were apostles before me; but I went into Arabia, and returned again unto Damascus.
- **Goes to Jerusalem.**
  Ac 9:25–26; Gal 1:18–19
- **Received by the disciples in Jerusalem.**
  Ac 9:26–29
- **Goes to Caesarea.**
  Ac 9:30 — *Which* when the brethren knew, they brought him down to Caesarea, and sent him forth to Tarsus.
  Ac 18:22 — And when he had landed at Caesarea, and gone up, and saluted the church, he went down to Antioch.
- **Sent unto the Gentiles.**
  Ac 13:2–3, 47–48; 22:17–21; Gal 1:15–24

Ro 11:13 — For I speak to you Gentiles, inasmuch as I am the apostle of the Gentiles, I magnify mine office:

Ro 15:16 — That I should be the minister of Jesus Christ to the Gentiles, ministering the gospel of God, that the offering up of the Gentiles might be acceptable, being sanctified by the Holy Ghost.

• Has Barnabas as his companion.

Ac 11:25–26

• Teaches at Antioch one year.

Ac 11:26 — And when he had found him, he brought him unto Antioch. And it came to pass, that a whole year they assembled themselves with the church, and taught much people. And the disciples were called Christians first in Antioch.

• Conveys the contributions of the Christians in Antioch to the Christians in Jerusalem.

Ac 11:27–30

• Returns with John to Antioch.

Ac 12:25 — And Barnabas and Saul returned from Jerusalem, when they had fulfilled *their* ministry, and took with them John, whose surname was Mark.

• Visits Seleucia.

Ac 13:4 — So they, being sent forth by the Holy Ghost, departed unto Seleucia; and from thence they sailed to Cyprus.

• Visits Cyprus.

Ac 13:4 — So they, being sent forth by the Holy Ghost, departed unto Seleucia; and from thence they sailed to Cyprus.

• Preaches at Salamis.

Ac 13:5 — And when they were at Salamis, they preached the word of God in the synagogues of the Jews: and they had also John to *their* minister.

• Preaches at Paphos.

Ac 13:6 — And when they had gone through the isle unto Paphos, they found a certain sorcerer, a false prophet, a Jew, whose name *was* Bar-jesus:

• Sergius Paulus, deputy of the country, is a convert of.

Ac 13:7–12

• Contends with Elymas the sorcerer.

Ac 13:6–12

• Visits Perga in Pamphylia.

Ac 13:13 — Now when Paul and his company loosed from Paphos, they came to Perga in Pamphylia: and John departing from them returned to Jerusalem.

• John, a companion of, departs for Jerusalem.

Ac 13:13 — Now when Paul and his company loosed from Paphos, they came to Perga in Pamphylia: and John departing from them returned to Jerusalem.

• Visits Antioch in Pisidia, and preaches in the synagogue.

Ac 13:14–41

• His message received gladly by the Gentiles.

Ac 13:42 — And when the Jews were gone out of the synagogue, the Gentiles besought that these words might be preached to them the next sabbath.

Ac 13:49 — And the word of the Lord was published throughout all the region.

• Persecuted and expelled.

Ac 13:50–51

• Visits Iconium; preaches to Jews and Greeks; persecuted; escapes to Lystra; goes to Derbe.

Ac 14:1–6

• Heals an impotent man.

Ac 14:8–10

• The people attempt to worship him.

Ac 14:11–18

• Is persecuted by certain Jews from Antioch and Iconium, and is stoned.

Ac 14:19 — And there came thither *certain* Jews from Antioch and Iconium, who persuaded the people, and, having stoned Paul, drew *him* out of the city, supposing he had been dead.

2Co 11:25 — Thrice was I beaten with rods, once was I stoned, thrice I suffered shipwreck, a night and a day I have been in the deep;

2Ti 3:11 — Persecutions, afflictions, which came unto me at Antioch, at Iconium, at Lystra; what persecutions I endured: but out of *them* all the Lord delivered me.

• Escapes to Derbe, where he preaches the gospel, and returns to Lystra, Iconium, Antioch.

Ac 14:19–20

• Confirms the souls of the disciples, exhorts them to continue in the faith, and ordains elders.

Ac 14:21–23

• Revisits Pisidia, Pamphylia, Perga, Attalia, and Antioch, in Syria, where he abode.

Ac 14:24–28

• Contends with the Judaizing Christians against circumcision.

Ac 15:1–2

• Refers the question as to circumcision to the apostles and elders at Jerusalem.

Ac 15:2 — When therefore Paul and Barnabas had no small dissension and disputation with them, they determined that Paul and Barnabas, and certain other of them, should go up to Jerusalem unto the apostles and elders about this question.

Ac 15:4 — And when they were come to Jerusalem, they were received of the church, and *of* the apostles and elders, and they declared all things that God had done with them.

• He declares to the apostles at Jerusalem the miracles and wonders God had wrought among the Gentiles by them.

Ac 15:12 — Then all the multitude kept silence, and gave audience to Barnabas and Paul, declaring what miracles and wonders God had wrought among the Gentiles by them.

• Returns to Antioch, accompanied by Barnabas, Judas, and Silas, with letters to the Gentiles.

Ac 15:22 — Then pleased it the apostles and elders, with the whole church, to send chosen men of their own company to Antioch with Paul and Barnabas; *namely,* Judas surnamed Barsabas, and Silas, chief men among the brethren:

Ac 15:25 — It seemed good unto us, being assembled with one accord, to send chosen men unto you with our beloved Barnabas and Paul,

PAUL, Miscellaneous

• Supports himself.

Ac 20:33–35

Ac 18:3 — And because he was of the same craft, he abode with them, and wrought: for by their occupation they were tentmakers.

• Sickness of, in Asia.

2Co 1:8–11

• His resolute determination to go to Jerusalem against the repeated admonition of the Holy Ghost.

Ac 20:22–23; 21:10–14

Ac 21:4 — And finding disciples, we tarried there seven days: who said to Paul through the Spirit, that he should not go up to Jerusalem.

• Caught up to the third heavens.

2Co 12:1–4

• Has "a thorn in the flesh".

2Co 12:7–9; Gal 4:13–14

• His independence of character.

1Th 2:9 — For ye remember, brethren, our labour and travail: for labouring night and day, because we would not be chargeable unto any of you, we preached unto you the gospel of God.

2Th 3:8 — Neither did we eat any man's bread for nought; but wrought with labour and travail night and day, that we might not be chargeable to any of you:

• Persecutions of.

1Th 2:2 — But even after that we had suffered before, and were shamefully entreated, as ye know, at Philippi, we were bold in our God to speak unto you the gospel of God with much contention.

Heb 10:34 — For ye had compassion of me in my bonds, and took joyfully the spoiling of your goods, knowing in yourselves that ye have in heaven a better and an enduring substance.

• Zeal of.

See: Zeal, Religious; exemplified by Paul

• Persecutions endured by.

Ac 9:23–25; 16:19–25; 20:22–24; 21:27–33; 22:22–24; 23:12–15; Ro 8:35–37; 1Co 4:11–13; 2Co 1:8–10; 4:8–12; 6:4–5, 8–10; 11:23–27, 32–33; Php 2:17–18; 1Th 2:14–15; 2Ti 2:9–10; 3:11–12; 4:16–17

Ac 2:24 — Whom God hath raised up, having loosed the pains of death: because it was not possible that he should be holden of it.

Ac 9:16 — For I will shew him how great things he must suffer for my name's sake.

Ac 9:29 — And he spake boldly in the name of the Lord Jesus, and disputed against the Grecians: but they went about to slay him.

Ac 21:13 — Then Paul answered, What mean ye to weep and to break mine heart? for I am ready not to be bound only, but also to die at Jerusalem for the name of the Lord Jesus.

Ac 23:10 — And when there arose a great dissension, the chief captain, fearing lest Paul should have been pulled in pieces of them, commanded the soldiers to go down, and to take him by force from among them, and to bring *him* into the castle.

1Co 4:9 — For I think that God hath set forth us the apostles last, as it were appointed to death: for we are made a spectacle unto the world, and to angels, and to men.

2Co 12:10 — Therefore I take pleasure in infirmities, in reproaches, in necessities, in persecutions, in distresses for Christ's sake: for when I am weak, then am I strong.

Gal 5:11 — And I, brethren, if I yet preach circumcision, why do I yet suffer persecution? then is the offence of the cross ceased.

Gal 6:17 — From henceforth let no man trouble me: for I bear in my body the marks of the Lord Jesus.

Php 1:30 — Having the same conflict which ye saw in me, and now hear *to be* in me.

Col 1:24 — Who now rejoice in my sufferings for you, and fill up that which is behind of the afflictions of Christ in my flesh for his body's sake, which is the church:

1Th 2:2 — But even after that we had suffered before, and were shamefully entreated, as ye know, at Philippi, we were bold in our God to speak unto you the gospel of God with much contention.

1Th 3:4 — For verily, when we were with you, we told you before that we should suffer tribulation; even as it came to pass, and ye know.

2Ti 1:12 — For the which cause I also suffer these things: nevertheless I am not ashamed: for I know whom I have believed, and am persuaded that he is able to keep that which I have committed unto him against that day.

PAUL, through Conversion

• Called also Saul.

Ac 8:1 — And Saul was consenting unto his death. And at that time there was a great persecution against the church which was at Jerusalem; and they were all scattered abroad throughout the regions of Judaea and Samaria, except the apostles.

Ac 9:1 — And Saul, yet breathing out threatenings and slaughter against the disciples of the Lord, went unto the high priest,

Ac 13:9 — Then Saul, (who also *is called* Paul,) filled with the Holy Ghost, set his eyes on him,

• Of the tribe of Benjamin.

Ro 11:1 — I say then, Hath God cast away his people? God forbid. For I also am an Israelite, of the seed of Abraham, *of* the tribe of Benjamin.

Php 3:5 — Circumcised the eighth day, of the stock of Israel, *of* the tribe of Benjamin, an Hebrew of the Hebrews; as touching the law, a Pharisee;

• Personal appearance of.

2Co 10:1 — Now I Paul myself beseech you by the meekness and gentleness of Christ, who in presence *am* base among you, but being absent am bold toward you:

2Co 10:10 — For *his* letters, say they, *are* weighty and powerful; but *his* bodily presence *is* weak, and *his* speech contemptible.

2Co 11:6 — But though *I be* rude in speech, yet not in knowledge; but we have been throughly made manifest among you in all things.

• Born in Tarsus.

Ac 9:11 — And the Lord *said* unto him, Arise, and go into the street which is called Straight, and enquire in the house of Judas for *one* called Saul, of Tarsus: for, behold, he prayeth,

Ac 21:39 — But Paul said, I am a man *which am* a Jew of Tarsus, *a city* in Cilicia, a citizen of no mean city: and, I beseech thee, suffer me to speak unto the people.

Ac 22:3 — I am verily a man *which am* a Jew, born in Tarsus, a city in Cilicia, yet brought up in this city at the feet of Gamaliel, *and* taught according to the perfect manner of the law of the fathers, and was zealous toward God, as ye all are this day.

• Educated at Jerusalem in the school of Gamaliel.

Ac 22:3 — I am verily a man *which am* a Jew, born in Tarsus, a city in Cilicia, yet brought up in this city at the feet of Gamaliel, *and* taught according to the perfect manner of the law of the fathers, and was zealous toward God, as ye all are this day.

Ac 26:4 — My manner of life from my youth, which was at the first among mine own nation at Jerusalem, know all the Jews;

• A zealous Pharisee.

Ac 22:3 — I am verily a man *which am* a Jew, born in Tarsus, a city in Cilicia, yet brought up in this city at the feet of Gamaliel, *and* taught according to the perfect manner of the law of the fathers, and was zealous toward God, as ye all are this day.

Ac 23:6 — But when Paul perceived that the one part were Sadducees, and the other Pharisees, he cried out in the council, Men *and* brethren, I am a Pharisee, the son of a Pharisee: of the hope and resurrection of the dead I am called in question.

Ac 26:5 — Which knew me from the beginning, if they would testify, that after the most straitest sect of our religion I lived a Pharisee.

2Co 11:22 — Are they Hebrews? so *am* I. Are they Israelites? so *am* I. Are they the seed of Abraham? so *am* I.

Gal 1:14 — And profited in the Jews' religion above many my equals in mine own nation, being more exceedingly zealous of the traditions of my fathers.

Php 3:5 — Circumcised the eighth day, of the stock of Israel, *of* the tribe of Benjamin, an Hebrew of the Hebrews; as touching the law, a Pharisee;

• A Roman.

Ac 22:25–28

Ac 16:37 — But Paul said unto them, They have beaten us openly uncondemned, being Romans, and have cast *us* into prison; and now do they thrust us out privily? nay verily; but let them come themselves and fetch us out.

• Persecutes the Christians; present at, and gives consent to, the stoning of Stephen.

Ac 7:58 — And cast *him* out of the city, and stoned *him:* and the witnesses laid down their clothes at a young man's feet, whose name was Saul.

Ac 8:1 — And Saul was consenting unto his death. And at that time there was a great persecution against the church which was at Jerusalem; and they were all scattered abroad throughout the regions of Judaea and Samaria, except the apostles.

Ac 8:3 — As for Saul, he made havock of the church, entering into every house, and haling men and women committed *them* to prison.

Ac 9:1 — And Saul, yet breathing out threatenings and slaughter against the disciples of the Lord, went unto the high priest,

Ac 22:4 — And I persecuted this way unto the death, binding and delivering into prisons both men and women.

• Sent to Damascus with letters for the arrest and return to Jerusalem of Christians.

Ac 9:1–2

• His vision and conversion.

Ac 9:3–22; 22:4–19; 26:9–15; 1Ti 1:12–13

1Co 9:1 — Am I not an apostle? am I not free? have I not seen Jesus Christ our Lord? are not ye my work in the Lord?

1Co 15:8 — And last of all he was seen of me also, as of one born out of due time.

Gal 1:13 — For ye have heard of my conversation in time past in the Jews' religion, how that beyond measure I persecuted the church of God, and wasted it:

• Is baptized.

Ac 9:18 — And immediately there fell from his eyes as it had been scales: and he received sight forthwith, and arose, and was baptized.

Ac 22:16 — And now why tarriest thou? arise, and be baptized, and wash away thy sins, calling on the name of the Lord.

• Called to be an apostle.

Ac 22:14–21; 26:16–18; 1Co 9:1–2; Gal 1:15–16

Ro 1:1 — Paul, a servant of Jesus Christ, called *to be* an apostle, separated unto the gospel of God,

1Co 1:1 — Paul, called *to be* an apostle of Jesus Christ through the will of God, and Sosthenes *our* brother,

1Co 15:9 — For I am the least of the apostles, that am not meet to be called an apostle, because I persecuted the church of God.

Gal 1:1 — Paul, an apostle, (not of men, neither by man, but by Jesus Christ, and God the Father, who raised him from the dead;)

Eph 1:1 — Paul, an apostle of Jesus Christ by the will of God, to the saints which are at Ephesus, and to the faithful in Christ Jesus:

Col 1:1 — Paul, an apostle of Jesus Christ by the will of God, and Timotheus *our* brother,

1Ti 1:1 — Paul, an apostle of Jesus Christ by the commandment of God our Saviour, and Lord Jesus Christ, *which is* our hope;

1Ti 2:7 — Whereunto I am ordained a preacher, and an apostle, (I speak the truth in Christ, *and* lie not;) a teacher of the Gentiles in faith and verity.

2Ti 1:1 — Paul, an apostle of Jesus Christ by the will of God, according to the promise of life which is in Christ Jesus,

2Ti 1:11 — Whereunto I am appointed a preacher, and an apostle, and a teacher of the Gentiles.

Tit 1:1 — Paul, a servant of God, and an apostle of Jesus Christ, according to the faith of God's elect, and the acknowledging of the truth which is after godliness;

Tit 1:3 — But hath in due times manifested his word through preaching, which is committed unto me according to the commandment of God our Saviour;

PAVILION ↞See: Tabernacle

PAWN

Dt 24:10–13

Ex 22:26 — If thou at all take thy neighbour's raiment to pledge, thou shalt deliver it unto him by that the sun goeth down:

Dt 24:17 — Thou shalt not pervert the judgment of the stranger, *nor* of the fatherless; nor take a widow's raiment to pledge:

Job 24:3 — They drive away the ass of the fatherless, they take the widow's ox for a pledge.

Pr 22:27 — If thou hast nothing to pay, why should he take away thy bed from under thee?

Eze 18:5 — But if a man be just, and do that which is lawful and right,

Eze 18:7 — And hath not oppressed any, *but* hath restored to the debtor his pledge, hath spoiled none by violence, hath given his bread to the hungry, and hath covered the naked with a garment;

Eze 18:12 — Hath oppressed the poor and needy, hath spoiled by violence, hath not restored the pledge, and hath lifted up his eyes to the idols, hath committed abomination,

Eze 33:15 — *If* the wicked restore the pledge, give again that he had robbed, walk in the statutes of life, without committing iniquity; he shall surely live, he shall not die.

Am 2:8 — And they lay *themselves* down upon clothes laid to pledge by every altar, and they drink the wine of the condemned in the house of their god.

↞**See: Surety**

PAY

Mt 10:9–15; 1Ti 5:17–18

Dt 25:4 — Thou shalt not muzzle the ox when he treadeth out *the corn.*

Lk 10:7 — And in the same house remain, eating and drinking such things as they give: for the labourer is worthy of his hire. Go not from house to house.

1Co 9:9 — For it is written in the law of Moses, Thou shalt not muzzle the mouth of the ox that treadeth out the corn. Doth God take care for oxen?

PEACE

- **Exemplified.**

↞**See: Charitableness**

↞**See: Nation; peace of**

- **By Abraham.**

Ge 13:8–9

- **By Abimelech.**

Ge 26:29 — That thou wilt do us no hurt, as we have not touched thee, and as we have done unto thee nothing but good, and have sent thee away in peace: thou *art* now the blessed of the LORD.

- **By Mordecai.**

Est 10:3 — For Mordecai the Jew *was* next unto king Ahasuerus, and great among the Jews, and accepted of the multitude of his brethren, seeking the wealth of his people, and speaking peace to all his seed.

- **By David.**

Ps 120:7 — I *am for* peace: but when I speak, they *are* for war.

- **Social.**

Job 5:23–24; Ps 120:6–7; Mt 10:21–22, 34–36; Ac 7:26–29; 17:7–9; Jas 3:17–18; 1Pe 3:10–11

Ge 45:24 — So he sent his brethren away, and they departed: and he said unto them, See that ye fall not out by the way.

Le 26:6 — And I will give peace in the land, and ye shall lie down, and none shall make *you* afraid: and I will rid evil beasts out of the land, neither shall the sword go through your land.

Ps 34:14 — Depart from evil, and do good; seek peace, and pursue it.

Ps 133:1 — Behold, how good and how pleasant *it is* for brethren to dwell together in unity!

Pr 12:20 — Deceit *is* in the heart of them that imagine evil: but to the counsellors of peace *is* joy.

Pr 15:17 — Better *is* a dinner of herbs where love is, than a stalled ox and hatred therewith.

Pr 16:7 — When a man's ways please the LORD, he maketh even his enemies to be at peace with him.

Pr 17:1 — Better *is* a dry morsel, and quietness therewith, than an house full of sacrifices *with* strife.

Pr 17:14 — The beginning of strife *is as* when one letteth out water: therefore leave off contention, before it be meddled with.

Pr 20:3 — *It is* an honour for a man to cease from strife: but every fool will be meddling.

Ecc 4:6 — Better *is* an handful *with* quietness, than both the hands full *with* travail and vexation of spirit.

Isa 2:4 — And he shall judge among the nations, and shall rebuke many people: and they shall beat their swords into plowshares, and their spears into pruninghooks: nation shall not lift up sword against nation, neither shall they learn war any more.

Isa 45:7 — I form the light, and create darkness: I make peace, and create evil: I the LORD do all these *things.*

Jer 29:7 — And seek the peace of the city whither I have caused you to be carried away captives, and pray unto the LORD for it: for in the peace thereof shall ye have peace.

Hos 2:18 — And in that day will I make a covenant for them with the beasts of the field, and with the fowls of heaven, and *with* the creeping things of the ground: and I will break the bow and the sword and the battle out of the earth, and will make them to lie down safely.

Zec 8:19 — Thus saith the LORD of hosts; The fast of the fourth *month,* and the fast of the fifth, and the fast of the seventh, and the fast of the tenth, shall be to the house of Judah joy and gladness, and cheerful feasts; therefore love the truth and peace.

Mt 5:9 — Blessed *are* the peacemakers: for they shall be called the children of God.

Mk 9:50 — Salt *is* good: but if the salt have lost his saltness, wherewith will ye season it? Have salt in yourselves, and have peace one with another.

Lk 2:14 — Glory to God in the highest, and on earth peace, good will toward men.

Ro 12:18 — If it be possible, as much as lieth in you, live peaceably with all men.

Ro 14:19 — Let us therefore follow after the things which make for peace, and things wherewith one may edify another.

1Co 14:33 — For God is not *the author* of confusion, but of peace, as in all churches of the saints.

2Co 13:11 — Finally, brethren, farewell. Be perfect, be of good comfort, be of one mind, live in peace; and the God of love and peace shall be with you.

Eph 4:3 — Endeavouring to keep the unity of the Spirit in the bond of peace.

1Th 5:13 — And to esteem them very highly in love for their work's sake. *And* be at peace among yourselves.

1Ti 2:2 — For kings, and *for* all that are in authority; that we may lead a quiet and peaceable life in all godliness and honesty.

2Ti 2:22 — Flee also youthful lusts: but follow righteousness, faith, charity, peace, with them that call on the Lord out of a pure heart.

Heb 12:14 — Follow peace with all *men,* and holiness, without which no man shall see the Lord:

• Spiritual.

Ps 1:1–2; 25:12–13; 73:25–26; Pr 3:13–18; Isa 11:6–9; 12:1–2; 25:7–8; 32:17–18; 57:1–2; Eph 2:14–17

Job 22:21 — Acquaint now thyself with him, and be at peace: thereby good shall come unto thee.

Job 22:26 — For then shalt thou have thy delight in the Almighty, and shalt lift up thy face unto God.

Job 34:29 — When he giveth quietness, who then can make trouble? and when he hideth *his* face, who then can behold him? whether *it be done* against a nation, or against a man only:

Ps 4:8 — I will both lay me down in peace, and sleep: for thou, LORD, only makest me dwell in safety.

Ps 17:15 — As for me, I will behold thy face in righteousness: I shall be satisfied, when I awake, with thy likeness.

Ps 29:11 — The LORD will give strength unto his people; the LORD will bless his people with peace.

Ps 37:4 — Delight thyself also in the LORD; and he shall give thee the desires of thine heart.

Ps 37:11 — But the meek shall inherit the earth; and shall delight themselves in the abundance of peace.

Ps 37:37 — Mark the perfect *man,* and behold the upright: for the end of *that* man *is* peace.

Ps 85:8 — I will hear what God the LORD will speak: for he will speak peace unto his people, and to his saints: but let them not turn again to folly.

Ps 119:165 — Great peace have they which love thy law: and nothing shall offend them.

Ps 125:1 — They that trust in the LORD *shall be* as mount Zion, *which* cannot be removed, *but* abideth for ever.

Ps 125:5 — As for such as turn aside unto their crooked ways, the LORD shall lead them forth with the workers of iniquity: *but* peace *shall be* upon Israel.

Pr 3:24 — When thou liest down, thou shalt not be afraid: yea, thou shalt lie down, and thy sleep shall be sweet.

Pr 14:14 — The backslider in heart shall be filled with his own ways: and a good man *shall be satisfied* from himself.

Isa 9:6 — For unto us a child is born, unto us a son is given: and the government shall be upon his shoulder: and his name shall be called Wonderful, Counsellor, The mighty God, The everlasting Father, The Prince of Peace.

Isa 11:13 — The envy also of Ephraim shall depart, and the adversaries of Judah shall be cut off: Ephraim shall not envy Judah, and Judah shall not vex Ephraim.

Isa 26:3 — Thou wilt keep *him* in perfect peace, *whose* mind *is* stayed *on thee:* because he trusteth in thee.

Isa 26:12 — LORD, thou wilt ordain peace for us: for thou also hast wrought all our works in us.

Isa 27:5 — Or let him take hold of my strength, *that* he may make peace with me; *and* he shall make peace with me.

Isa 28:12 — To whom he said, This *is* the rest *wherewith* ye may cause the weary to rest; and this *is* the refreshing: yet they would not hear.

Isa 30:26 — Moreover the light of the moon shall be as the light of the sun, and the light of the sun shall be sevenfold, as the light of seven days, in the day that the LORD bindeth up the breach of his people, and healeth the stroke of their wound.

Isa 32:2 — And a man shall be as an hiding place from the wind, and a covert from the tempest; as rivers of water in a dry place, as the shadow of a great rock in a weary land.

Isa 48:18 — O that thou hadst hearkened to my commandments! then had thy peace been as a river, and thy righteousness as the waves of the sea:

Isa 53:5 — But he *was* wounded for our transgressions, *he was* bruised for our iniquities: the chastisement of our peace *was* upon him; and with his stripes we are healed.

Isa 54:1 — Sing, O barren, thou *that* didst not bear; break forth into singing, and cry aloud, thou *that* didst not travail with child: for more *are* the children of the desolate than the children of the married wife, saith the LORD.

Isa 54:10 — For the mountains shall depart, and the hills be removed; but my kindness shall not depart from thee, neither shall the covenant of my peace be removed, saith the LORD that hath mercy on thee.

Isa 54:13 — And all thy children *shall be* taught of the LORD; and great *shall be* the peace of thy children.

Isa 55:2 — Wherefore do ye spend money for *that which is* not bread? and your labour for *that which* satisfieth not? hearken diligently unto me, and eat ye *that which is* good, and let your soul delight itself in fatness.

Isa 55:12 — For ye shall go out with joy, and be led forth with peace: the mountains and the hills shall break forth before you into singing, and all the trees of the field shall clap *their* hands.

Isa 57:19 — I create the fruit of the lips; Peace, peace to *him that is* far off, and to *him that is* near, saith the LORD; and I will heal him.

Isa 60:20 — Thy sun shall no more go down; neither shall thy moon withdraw itself: for the LORD shall be thine everlasting light, and the days of thy mourning shall be ended.

Jer 33:6 — Behold, I will bring it health and cure, and I will cure them, and will reveal unto them the abundance of peace and truth.

Eze 34:25 — And I will make with them a covenant of peace, and will cause the evil beasts to cease out of the land: and they shall dwell safely in the wilderness, and sleep in the woods.

Hag 2:9 — The glory of this latter house shall be greater than of the former, saith the LORD of hosts: and in this place will I give peace, saith the LORD of hosts.

Mal 2:5 — My covenant was with him of life and peace; and I gave them to him *for* the fear wherewith he feared me, and was afraid before my name.

Lk 1:79 — To give light to them that sit in darkness and *in* the shadow of death, to guide our feet into the way of peace.

Lk 2:14 — Glory to God in the highest, and on earth peace, good will toward men.

Lk 2:29 — Lord, now lettest thou thy servant depart in peace, according to thy word:

Jn 7:38 — He that believeth on me, as the scripture hath said, out of his belly shall flow rivers of living water.

Jn 14:27 — Peace I leave with you, my peace I give unto you: not as the world giveth, give I unto you. Let not your heart be troubled, neither let it be afraid.

Jn 16:33 — These things I have spoken unto you, that in me ye might have peace. In the world ye shall have tribulation: but be of good cheer; I have overcome the world.

Jn 20:19 — Then the same day at evening, being the first *day* of the week, when the doors were shut where the disciples were assembled for fear of the Jews, came Jesus and stood in the midst, and saith unto them, Peace *be* unto you.

Ac 10:36 — The word which *God* sent unto the children of Israel, preaching peace by Jesus Christ: (he is Lord of all:)

Ro 2:10 — But glory, honour, and peace, to every man that worketh good, to the Jew first, and also to the Gentile:

Ro 5:1 — Therefore being justified by faith, we have peace with God through our Lord Jesus Christ:

Ro 8:6 — For to be carnally minded *is* death; but to be spiritually minded *is* life and peace.

Ro 10:15 — And how shall they preach, except they be sent? as it is written, How beautiful are the feet of them that preach the gospel of peace, and bring glad tidings of good things!

Ro 14:17 — For the kingdom of God is not meat and drink; but righteousness, and peace, and joy in the Holy Ghost.

Ro 15:13 — Now the God of hope fill you with all joy and peace in believing, that ye may abound in hope, through the power of the Holy Ghost.

Ro 15:33 — Now the God of peace *be* with you all. Amen.

1Co 1:3 — Grace *be* unto you, and peace, from God our Father, and *from* the Lord Jesus Christ.

2Co 1:2 — Grace be to you and peace from God our Father, and *from* the Lord Jesus Christ.

Gal 1:3 — Grace *be* to you and peace from God the Father, and *from* our Lord Jesus Christ,

Gal 5:22 — But the fruit of the Spirit is love, joy, peace, longsuffering, gentleness, goodness, faith,

Php 4:7 — And the peace of God, which passeth all understanding, shall keep your hearts and minds through Christ Jesus.

Php 4:9 — Those things, which ye have both learned, and received, and heard, and seen in me, do: and the God of peace shall be with you.

Col 1:20 — And, having made peace through the blood of his cross, by him to reconcile all things unto himself; by him, *I say,* whether *they be* things in earth, or things in heaven.

Col 3:15 — And let the peace of God rule in your hearts, to the which also ye are called in one body; and be ye thankful.

1Th 1:1 — Paul, and Silvanus, and Timotheus, unto the church of the Thessalonians *which is* in God the

Father and *in* the Lord Jesus Christ: Grace *be* unto you, and peace, from God our Father, and the Lord Jesus Christ.

2Th 3:16 — Now the Lord of peace himself give you peace always by all means. The Lord *be* with you all.

1Ti 1:2 — Unto Timothy, *my* own son in the faith: Grace, mercy, *and* peace, from God our Father and Jesus Christ our Lord.

2Ti 1:2 — To Timothy, *my* dearly beloved son: Grace, mercy, *and* peace, from God the Father and Christ Jesus our Lord.

Tit 1:4 — To Titus, *mine* own son after the common faith: Grace, mercy, *and* peace, from God the Father and the Lord Jesus Christ our Saviour.

Phm 1:3 — Grace to you, and peace, from God our Father and the Lord Jesus Christ.

Rev 1:4 — John to the seven churches which are in Asia: Grace *be* unto you, and peace, from him which is, and which was, and which is to come; and from the seven Spirits which are before his throne;

See: Charitableness

See: Joy

See: Praise

PEACE OFFERINGS

Ex 20:24 — An altar of earth thou shalt make unto me, and shalt sacrifice thereon thy burnt offerings, and thy peace offerings, thy sheep, and thine oxen: in all places where I record my name I will come unto thee, and I will bless thee.

Ex 24:5 — And he sent young men of the children of Israel, which offered burnt offerings, and sacrificed peace offerings of oxen unto the LORD.

Le 3:6 — And if his offering for a sacrifice of peace offering unto the LORD *be* of the flock; male or female, he shall offer it without blemish.

Le 7:11 — And this *is* the law of the sacrifice of peace offerings, which he shall offer unto the LORD.

Le 19:5 — And if ye offer a sacrifice of peace offerings unto the LORD, ye shall offer it at your own will.

• Offered by.

• The princes.

Nu 7:17 — And for a sacrifice of peace offerings, two oxen, five rams, five he goats, five lambs of the first year: this *was* the offering of Nahshon the son of Amminadab.

• Joshua.

Jos 8:31 — As Moses the servant of the LORD commanded the children of Israel, as it is written in the book of the law of Moses, an altar of whole stones, over which no man hath lift up *any* iron: and they offered thereon burnt offerings unto the LORD, and sacrificed peace offerings.

• David.

2Sa 6:17 — And they brought in the ark of the LORD, and set it in his place, in the midst of the tabernacle that David had pitched for it: and David offered burnt offerings and peace offerings before the LORD.

2Sa 24:25 — And David built there an altar unto the LORD, and offered burnt offerings and peace offerings. So the LORD was intreated for the land, and the plague was stayed from Israel.

See: Offerings

PEACOCK

1Ki 10:22 — For the king had at sea a navy of Tharshish with the navy of Hiram: once in three years came the navy of Tharshish, bringing gold, and silver, ivory, and apes, and peacocks.

2Ch 9:21 — For the king's ships went to Tarshish with the servants of Huram: every three years once came the ships of Tarshish bringing gold, and silver, ivory, and apes, and peacocks.

Job 39:13 — *Gavest thou* the goodly wings unto the peacocks? or wings and feathers unto the ostrich?

PEARL

Job 28:18 — No mention shall be made of coral, or of pearls: for the price of wisdom *is* above rubies.

Rev 17:4 — And the woman was arrayed in purple and scarlet colour, and decked with gold and precious stones and pearls, having a golden cup in her hand full of abominations and filthiness of her fornication:

Rev 18:12 — The merchandise of gold, and silver, and precious stones, and of pearls, and fine linen, and purple, and silk, and scarlet, and all thyine wood, and all manner vessels of ivory, and all manner vessels of most precious wood, and of brass, and iron, and marble,

Rev 18:16 — And saying, Alas, alas, that great city, that was clothed in fine linen, and purple, and scarlet, and decked with gold, and precious stones, and pearls!

• "Pearl of great price".

Mt 13:46 — Who, when he had found one pearl of great price, went and sold all that he had, and bought it.

• Ornaments made of.

1Ti 2:9 — In like manner also, that women adorn themselves in modest apparel, with shamefacedness and sobriety; not with broided hair, or gold, or pearls, or costly array;

• Figurative.

Mt 7:6 — Give not that which is holy unto the dogs, neither cast ye your pearls before swine, lest they trample them under their feet, and turn again and rend you.

• Symbolic.

Rev 21:21 — And the twelve gates *were* twelve pearls; every several gate was of one pearl: and the street of the city *was* pure gold, as it were transparent glass.

PEDAHEL • Chief of Naphtali.

Nu 34:28 — And the prince of the tribe of the children of Naphtali, Pedahel the son of Ammihud.

PEDAHZUR • Father of Gamaliel.

Nu 1:10 — Of the children of Joseph: of Ephraim; Elishama the son of Ammihud: of Manasseh; Gamaliel the son of Pedahzur.

Nu 2:20 — And by him *shall be* the tribe of Manasseh: and the captain of the children of Manasseh *shall be* Gamaliel the son of Pedahzur.

Nu 7:54 — On the eighth day *offered* Gamaliel the son of Pedahzur, prince of the children of Manasseh:

Nu 7:59 — And for a sacrifice of peace offerings, two oxen, five rams, five he goats, five lambs of the first year: this *was* the offering of Gamaliel the son of Pedahzur.

Nu 10:23 — And over the host of the tribe of the children of Manasseh *was* Gamaliel the son of Pedahzur.

PEDAIAH

• Grandfather of King Josiah.

2Ki 23:36 — Jehoiakim *was* twenty and five years old when he began to reign; and he reigned eleven years in Jerusalem. And his mother's name *was* Zebudah, the daughter of Pedaiah of Rumah.

• Father of Zerubbabel.

1Ch 3:18–19

• Father of Joel.

1Ch 27:20 — Of the children of Ephraim, Hoshea the son of Azaziah: of the half tribe of Manasseh, Joel the son of Pedaiah:

• Son of Parosh.

Ne 3:25 — Palal the son of Uzai, over against the turning *of the wall,* and the tower which lieth out from the king's high house, that *was* by the court of the prison. After him Pedaiah the son of Parosh.

• A Levite appointed as treasurer by Nehemiah.

Ne 8:4 — And Ezra the scribe stood upon a pulpit of wood, which they had made for the purpose; and beside him stood Mattithiah, and Shema, and Anaiah, and Urijah, and Hilkiah, and Maaseiah, on his right hand; and on his left hand, Pedaiah, and Mishael, and Malchiah, and Hashum, and Hashbadana, Zechariah, *and* Meshullam.

Ne 13:13 — And I made treasurers over the treasuries, Shelemiah the priest, and Zadok the scribe, and of the Levites, Pedaiah: and next to them *was* Hanan the son of Zaccur, the son of Mattaniah: for they were counted faithful, and their office *was* to distribute unto their brethren.

• A Benjamite.

Ne 11:7 — And these *are* the sons of Benjamin; Sallu the son of Meshullam, the son of Joed, the son of Pedaiah, the son of Kolaiah, the son of Maaseiah, the son of Ithiel, the son of Jesaiah.

PEDDLING

2Co 2:17 — For we are not as many, which corrupt the word of God: but as of sincerity, but as of God, in the sight of God speak we in Christ.

PEKAH

• Son of Remaliah.

• Captain of the army of Israel.

2Ki 15:25 — But Pekah the son of Remaliah, a captain of his, conspired against him, and smote him in Samaria, in the palace of the king's house, with Argob and Arieh, and with him fifty men of the Gileadites: and he killed him, and reigned in his room.

• Conspires against and assassinates King Pekahiah.

2Ki 15:25 — But Pekah the son of Remaliah, a captain of his, conspired against him, and smote him in Samaria, in the palace of the king's house, with Argob and Arieh, and with him fifty men of the Gileadites: and he killed him, and reigned in his room.

• Is made king of Israel.

2Ki 15:27 — In the two and fiftieth year of Azariah king of Judah Pekah the son of Remaliah began to reign over Israel in Samaria, *and reigned* twenty years.

• Victorious in war with Judah.

2Ch 28:5–6

• Is plotted against and slain by Hoshea.

2Ki 15:30–31

• Prophecies against.

Isa 7:1–16; 8:4–10

PEKAHIAH

• Son of Menahem.

• King of Israel.

2Ki 15:22–26

• Plotted against and slain by Pekah.

2Ki 15:25 — But Pekah the son of Remaliah, a captain of his, conspired against him, and smote him in Samaria, in the palace of the king's house, with Argob and Arieh, and with him fifty men of the Gileadites: and he killed him, and reigned in his room.

PEKOD • Name for Chaldea.

Jer 50:21 — Go up against the land of Merathaim, *even* against it, and against the inhabitants of Pekod: waste and utterly destroy after them, saith the LORD, and do according to all that I have commanded thee.

Eze 23:23 — The Babylonians, and all the Chaldeans, Pekod, and Shoa, and Koa, *and* all the Assyrians with them: all of them desirable young men, captains and rulers, great lords and renowned, all of them riding upon horses.

PELAIAH

• Son of Elioenai.

1Ch 3:24 — And the sons of Elioenai *were,* Hodaiah, and Eliashib, and Pelaiah, and Akkub, and Johanan, and Dalaiah, and Anani, seven.

• A Levite who assisted Ezra in instructing the people in the law.

Ne 8:7 — Also Jeshua, and Bani, and Sherebiah, Jamin, Akkub, Shabbethai, Hodijah, Maaseiah, Kelita, Azariah, Jozabad, Hanan, Pelaiah, and the Levites, caused the people to understand the law: and the people *stood* in their place.

Ne 10:10 — And their brethren, Shebaniah, Hodijah, Kelita, Pelaiah, Hanan,

PELALIAH • A priest.

Ne 11:12 — And their brethren that did the work of the house *were* eight hundred twenty and two: and Adaiah the son of Jeroham, the son of Pelaliah, the son of Amzi, the son of Zechariah, the son of Pashur, the son of Malchiah,

PELATIAH

• A son of Hananiah, of the family of David.

1Ch 3:21 — And the sons of Hananiah; Pelatiah, and Jesaiah: the sons of Rephaiah, the sons of Arnan, the sons of Obadiah, the sons of Shechaniah.

• A Simeonite who was captain in an expedition against the Amalekites.

1Ch 4:42–43

• One of those who signed the covenant with Nehemiah.

Ne 10:22 — Pelatiah, Hanan, Anaiah,

• A prince against whom Ezekiel prophesied, and who fell dead at the close of the prophecy.

Eze 11:1–13

PELEG

• Son of Eber.

Ge 11:16–19

Ge 10:25 — And unto Eber were born two sons: the name of one *was* Peleg; for in his days was the earth divided; and his brother's name *was* Joktan.

1Ch 1:19 — And unto Eber were born two sons: the name of the one *was* Peleg; because in his days the earth was divided: and his brother's name *was* Joktan.

1Ch 1:25 — Eber, Peleg, Reu,

PELET

• Son of Jahdai.

1Ch 2:47 — And the sons of Jahdai; Regem, and Jotham, and Gesham, and Pelet, and Ephah, and Shaaph.

• Son of Azmaveth.

1Ch 12:3 — The chief *was* Ahiezer, then Joash, the sons of Shemaah the Gibeathite; and Jeziel, and Pelet, the sons of Azmaveth; and Berachah, and Jehu the Antothite,

PELETH

• A Reubenite.

Nu 16:1 — Now Korah, the son of Izhar, the son of Kohath, the son of Levi, and Dathan and Abiram, the sons of Eliab, and On, the son of Peleth, sons of Reuben, took *men:*

• Son of Jonathan.

1Ch 2:33 — And the sons of Jonathan; Peleth, and Zaza. These were the sons of Jerahmeel.

PELETHITES

• A part of David's bodyguard.

2Sa 8:18 — And Benaiah the son of Jehoiada *was over* both the Cherethites and the Pelethites; and David's sons were chief rulers.

2Sa 20:7 — And there went out after him Joab's men, and the Cherethites, and the Pelethites, and all the mighty men: and they went out of Jerusalem, to pursue after Sheba the son of Bichri.

2Sa 20:23 — Now Joab *was* over all the host of Israel: and Benaiah the son of Jehoiada *was* over the Cherethites and over the Pelethites:

1Ki 1:38 — So Zadok the priest, and Nathan the prophet, and Benaiah the son of Jehoiada, and the Cherethites, and the Pelethites, went down, and caused Solomon to ride upon king David's mule, and brought him to Gihon.

1Ch 18:17 — And Benaiah the son of Jehoiada *was* over the Cherethites and the Pelethites; and the sons of David *were* chief about the king.

• Absalom's escort.

2Sa 15:18 — And all his servants passed on beside him; and all the Cherethites, and all the Pelethites, and all the Gittites, six hundred men which came after him from Gath, passed on before the king.

PELICAN

Le 11:18 — And the swan, and the pelican, and the gier eagle,

Dt 14:17 — And the pelican, and the gier eagle, and the cormorant,

Ps 102:6 — I am like a pelican of the wilderness: I am like an owl of the desert.

PELONITE

• An Ephraimite.

1Ch 11:27 — Shammoth the Harorite, Helez the Pelonite,

1Ch 27:10 — The seventh *captain* for the seventh month *was* Helez the Pelonite, of the children of Ephraim: and in his course *were* twenty and four thousand.

• An appellation of Ahijah the prophet.

1Ch 11:36 — Hepher the Mecherathite, Ahijah the Pelonite,

PEN

Jgs 5:14 — Out of Ephraim *was there* a root of them against Amalek; after thee, Benjamin, among thy people; out of Machir came down governors, and out of Zebulun they that handle the pen of the writer.

Ps 45:1 — My heart is inditing a good matter: I speak of the things which I have made touching the king: my tongue *is* the pen of a ready writer.

Isa 8:1 — Moreover the LORD said unto me, Take thee a great roll, and write in it with a man's pen concerning Maher-shalal-hash-baz.

Jer 8:8 — How do ye say, We *are* wise, and the law of the LORD *is* with us? Lo, certainly in vain made he *it;* the pen of the scribes *is* in vain.

3Jn 1:13 — I had many things to write, but I will not with ink and pen write unto thee:

• **Made of iron.**

Job 19:24 — That they were graven with an iron pen and lead in the rock for ever!

Jer 17:1 — The sin of Judah *is* written with a pen of iron, *and* with the point of a diamond: *it is* graven upon the table of their heart, and upon the horns of your altars;

PENALTY

See: Judgments

See: Punishment

See: Sin; punishment of

See: Wicked; punishment of

PENIEL • See: Penuel

PENINNAH • One of the wives of Elkanah.

1Sa 1:2 — And he had two wives; the name of the one *was* Hannah, and the name of the other Peninnah: and Peninnah had children, but Hannah had no children.

PENITENCE

See: Repentance

See: Sin; confession of

PENITENT

• **Promises to.**

Le 26:40–42; Nu 5:6–7; Dt 4:29–31; 30:1–10; Job 22:23–29; 33:26–28; Ps 6:8–9; 24:3–6; 32:5–6; 90:14–15; 145:18–19; Eze 18:21–23; 33:10–16; Mt 6:14–15; 7:7–11; 11:28–30; 18:11–14; Lk 11:9–13; 15:4–32; 18:10–14; Ac 13:38–39; Ro 10:9–13

Dt 5:29 — O that there were such an heart in them, that they would fear me, and keep all my commandments always, that it might be well with them, and with their children for ever!

2Ki 22:19 — Because thine heart was tender, and thou hast humbled thyself before the LORD, when thou heardest what I spake against this place, and against the inhabitants thereof, that they should become a desolation and a curse, and hast rent thy clothes, and wept before me; I also have heard *thee*, saith the LORD.

1Ch 28:9 — And thou, Solomon my son, know thou the God of thy father, and serve him with a perfect heart and with a willing mind: for the LORD searcheth all hearts, and understandeth all the imaginations of the thoughts: if thou seek him, he will be found of thee; but if thou forsake him, he will cast thee off for ever.

Job 23:6 — Will he plead against me with *his* great power? No; but he would put *strength* in me.

Ps 9:10 — And they that know thy name will put their trust in thee: for thou, LORD, hast not forsaken them that seek thee.

Ps 22:26 — The meek shall eat and be satisfied: they shall praise the LORD that seek him: your heart shall live for ever.

Ps 34:18 — The LORD *is* nigh unto them that are of a broken heart; and saveth such as be of a contrite spirit.

Ps 51:17 — The sacrifices of God *are* a broken spirit: a broken and a contrite heart, O God, thou wilt not despise.

Ps 70:4 — Let all those that seek thee rejoice and be glad in thee: and let such as love thy salvation say continually, Let God be magnified.

Ps 147:3 — He healeth the broken in heart, and bindeth up their wounds.

Isa 27:5 — Or let him take hold of my strength, *that* he may make peace with me; *and* he shall make peace with me.

Mt 5:4 — Blessed *are* they that mourn: for they shall be comforted.

Mt 12:20 — A bruised reed shall he not break, and smoking flax shall he not quench, till he send forth judgment unto victory.

Mt 12:31 — Wherefore I say unto you, All manner of sin and blasphemy shall be forgiven unto men: but the blasphemy *against* the *Holy* Ghost shall not be forgiven unto men.

Lk 4:18 — The Spirit of the Lord is upon me, because he hath anointed me to preach the gospel to the poor; he hath sent me to heal the brokenhearted, to preach deliverance to the captives, and recovering of sight to the blind, to set at liberty them that are bruised,

Lk 6:37 — Judge not, and ye shall not be judged: condemn not, and ye shall not be condemned: forgive, and ye shall be forgiven:

Lk 12:10 — And whosoever shall speak a word against the Son of man, it shall be forgiven him: but unto him that blasphemeth against the Holy Ghost it shall not be forgiven.

Lk 19:10 — For the Son of man is come to seek and to save that which was lost.

Jn 6:37 — All that the Father giveth me shall come to me; and him that cometh to me I will in no wise cast out.

Jn 10:9 — I am the door: by me if any man enter in, he shall be saved, and shall go in and out, and find pasture.

1Jn 1:9 — If we confess our sins, he is faithful and just to forgive us *our* sins, and to cleanse us from all unrighteousness.

See: Forgiveness

See: Obduracy

See: Repentance

See: Reprobacy

See: Sin; confession of

PENKNIFE

Jer 36:23 — And it came to pass, *that* when Jehudi had read three or four leaves, he cut it with the penknife, and cast *it* into the fire that *was* on the hearth, until all the roll was consumed in the fire that *was* on the hearth.

PENNY

• About seventeen cents, later fifteen cents.

Mt 18:28 — But the same servant went out, and found one of his fellowservants, which owed him an hundred pence: and he laid hands on him, and took *him* by the throat, saying, Pay me that thou owest.

Mk 6:37 — He answered and said unto them, Give ye them to eat. And they say unto him, Shall we go and buy two hundred pennyworth of bread, and give them to eat?

Mk 14:5 — For it might have been sold for more than three hundred pence, and have been given to the poor. And they murmured against her.

Lk 7:41 — There was a certain creditor which had two debtors: the one owed five hundred pence, and the other fifty.

Lk 10:35 — And on the morrow when he departed, he took out two pence, and gave *them* to the host, and said unto him, Take care of him; and whatsoever thou spendest more, when I come again, I will repay thee.

• Roman, bore Caesar's image.

Mt 22:19–21

• A day's wages.

Mt 20:2–14

PENSION

• Of Levites.

2Ch 31:16–18

PENTECOST

• Called Feast of Weeks.

Ex 34:22 — And thou shalt observe the feast of weeks, of the firstfruits of wheat harvest, and the feast of ingathering at the year's end.

Dt 16:10 — And thou shalt keep the feast of weeks unto the LORD thy God with a tribute of a freewill offering of thine hand, which thou shalt give *unto the LORD thy God,* according as the LORD thy God hath blessed thee:

• Called Feast of Harvest.

Ex 23:16 — And the feast of harvest, the firstfruits of thy labours, which thou hast sown in the field: and the feast of ingathering, *which is* in the end of the year, when thou hast gathered in thy labours out of the field.

• Called Day of First Fruits.

Nu 28:26 — Also in the day of the firstfruits, when ye bring a new meat offering unto the LORD, after your weeks *be out,* ye shall have an holy convocation; ye shall do no servile work:

• Called Day of Pentecost.

Ac 2:1 — And when the day of Pentecost was fully come, they were all with one accord in one place.

Ac 20:16 — For Paul had determined to sail by Ephesus, because he would not spend the time in Asia: for he hasted, if it were possible for him, to be at Jerusalem the day of Pentecost.

1Co 16:8 — But I will tarry at Ephesus until Pentecost.

• Institution of.

Le 23:15–21; Nu 28:26–31; Dt 16:9–12

Ex 23:16 — And the feast of harvest, the firstfruits of thy labours, which thou hast sown in the field: and the feast of ingathering, *which is* in the end of the year, when thou hast gathered in thy labours out of the field.

Ex 34:22 — And thou shalt observe the feast of weeks, of the firstfruits of wheat harvest, and the feast of ingathering at the year's end.

Dt 16:16 — Three times in a year shall all thy males appear before the LORD thy God in the place which he shall choose; in the feast of unleavened bread, and in the feast of weeks, and in the feast of tabernacles: and they shall not appear before the LORD empty:

• Holy Ghost given to the apostles on the first day of.

Ac 2:1–47

See: Feasts

PENUEL

• City built where Jacob wrestled with the angel.

Jgs 8:8–9

Ge 32:31 — And as he passed over Penuel the sun rose upon him, and he halted upon his thigh.

Jgs 8:17 — And he beat down the tower of Penuel, and slew the men of the city.

1Ki 12:25 — Then Jeroboam built Shechem in mount Ephraim, and dwelt therein; and went out from thence, and built Penuel.

• Called also Peniel.

Gen. 32:30 — And Jacob called the name of the place Peniel: for I have seen God face to face, and my life is preserved.

• Chief of Gedor.

1Ch 4:4 — And Penuel the father of Gedor and Ezer the father of Hushah. These *are* the sons of Hur, the firstborn of Ephratah, the father of Bethlehem.

• A Benjamite.

1Ch 8:25 — And Iphedeiah, and Penuel, the sons of Shashak;

PENURIOUSNESS See: Parsimony

PEOPLE, common

• Heard Jesus gladly.

Mt 7:28 — And it came to pass, when Jesus had ended these sayings, the people were astonished at his doctrine:

Mt 9:8 — But when the multitudes saw *it,* they marvelled, and glorified God, which had given such power unto men.

Mt 9:33 — And when the devil was cast out, the dumb spake: and the multitudes marvelled, saying, It was never so seen in Israel.

Mt 13:54 — And when he was come into his own country, he taught them in their synagogue, insomuch that they were astonished, and said, Whence hath this *man* this wisdom, and *these* mighty works?

Mk 6:2 — And when the sabbath day was come, he began to teach in the synagogue: and many hearing *him* were astonished, saying, From whence hath this *man* these things? and what wisdom *is* this which is given unto him, that even such mighty works are wrought by his hands?

PEOR

• A mountain in Moab.

• Balak builds altars on.

Nu 23:28–30

PERESH • Son of Machir.

1Ch 7:16 — And Maachah the wife of Machir bare a son, and she called his name Peresh; and the name of his brother *was* Sheresh; and his sons *were* Ulam and Rakem.

PEREZ • See: Pharez

PEREZ-UZZA • Place where the Lord smote Uzzah.

2Sa 6:8 — And David was displeased, because the LORD had made a breach upon Uzzah: and he called the name of the place Perez-uzzah to this day.

1Ch 13:11 — And David was displeased, because the LORD had made a breach upon Uzza: wherefore that place is called Perez-uzza to this day.

PERFECTION

• Ascribed to Noah.

Ge 6:8–9

• Ascribed to Jacob.

Nu 23:21 — He hath not beheld iniquity in Jacob, neither hath he seen perverseness in Israel: the LORD his God *is* with him, and the shout of a king *is* among them.

• Ascribed to David.

1Ki 11:4 — For it came to pass, when Solomon was old, *that* his wives turned away his heart after other gods: and his heart was not perfect with the LORD his God, as *was* the heart of David his father.

1Ki 11:6 — And Solomon did evil in the sight of the LORD, and went not fully after the LORD, as *did* David his father.

• Ascribed to Asa.

1Ki 15:14 — But the high places were not removed: nevertheless Asa's heart was perfect with the LORD all his days.

• Ascribed to Job.

Job 1:1 — There was a man in the land of Uz, whose name *was* Job; and that man was perfect and upright, and one that feared God, and eschewed evil.

• Ascribed to Zacharias and Elisabeth.

Lk 1:6 — And they were both righteous before God, walking in all the commandments and ordinances of the Lord blameless.

• Ascribed to Nathanael.

Jn 1:47 — Jesus saw Nathanael coming to him, and saith of him, Behold an Israelite indeed, in whom is no guile!

• Unclassified scripture relating to.

Job 9:20–21; Ps 119:1–3; Eph 4:1–32; Php 3:12–15; Col 1:21–22; 2:9–11; Heb 13:20–21; 1Jn 3:6–10

Ge 17:1 — And when Abram was ninety years old and nine, the LORD appeared to Abram, and said unto him, I *am* the Almighty God; walk before me, and be thou perfect.

Dt 5:32 — Ye shall observe to do therefore as the LORD your God hath commanded you: ye shall not turn aside to the right hand or to the left.

Dt 18:13 — Thou shalt be perfect with the LORD thy God.

Jos 23:6 — Be ye therefore very courageous to keep and to do all that is written in the book of the law of Moses, that ye turn not aside therefrom *to* the right hand or *to* the left;

1Ki 8:61 — Let your heart therefore be perfect with the LORD our God, to walk in his statutes, and to keep his commandments, as at this day.

1Ch 28:9 — And thou, Solomon my son, know thou the God of thy father, and serve him with a perfect heart and with a willing mind: for the LORD searcheth all hearts, and understandeth all the imaginations of the thoughts: if thou seek him, he will be found of thee; but if thou forsake him, he will cast thee off for ever.

1Ch 29:19 — And give unto Solomon my son a perfect heart, to keep thy commandments, thy testimonies, and thy statutes, and to do all *these things,* and to build the palace, for the which I have made provision.

2Ch 6:36 — If they sin against thee, (for *there is* no man which sinneth not,) and thou be angry with them, and deliver them over before *their* enemies, and they carry them away captives unto a land far off or near;

Ps 18:32 — *It is* God that girdeth me with strength, and maketh my way perfect.

Ps 37:31 — The law of his God *is* in his heart; none of his steps shall slide.

Ps 37:37 — Mark the perfect *man,* and behold the upright: for the end of *that* man *is* peace.

Ps 101:2 — I will behave myself wisely in a perfect way. O when wilt thou come unto me? I will walk within my house with a perfect heart.

Ps 106:3 — Blessed *are* they that keep judgment, *and* he that doeth righteousness at all times.

Ps 119:6 — Then shall I not be ashamed, when I have respect unto all thy commandments.

Ps 119:96 — I have seen an end of all perfection: *but* thy commandment *is* exceeding broad.

Pr 2:21 — For the upright shall dwell in the land, and the perfect shall remain in it.

Ecc 7:20 — For *there is* not a just man upon earth, that doeth good, and sinneth not.

Mt 5:6 — Blessed *are* they which do hunger and thirst after righteousness: for they shall be filled.

Mt 5:48 — Be ye therefore perfect, even as your Father which is in heaven is perfect.

Mt 19:21 — Jesus said unto him, If thou wilt be perfect, go *and* sell that thou hast, and give to the poor, and thou shalt have treasure in heaven: and come *and* follow me.

Lk 6:40 — The disciple is not above his master: but every one that is perfect shall be as his master.

1Co 2:6 — Howbeit we speak wisdom among them that are perfect: yet not the wisdom of this world, nor of the princes of this world, that come to nought:

2Co 7:1 — Having therefore these promises, dearly beloved, let us cleanse ourselves from all filthiness of the flesh and spirit, perfecting holiness in the fear of God.

2Co 13:9 — For we are glad, when we are weak, and ye are strong: and this also we wish, *even* your perfection.

2Co 13:11 — Finally, brethren, farewell. Be perfect, be of good comfort, be of one mind, live in peace; and the God of love and peace shall be with you.

Php 1:10 — That ye may approve things that are excellent; that ye may be sincere and without offence till the day of Christ;

Php 2:15 — That ye may be blameless and harmless, the sons of God, without rebuke, in the midst of a crooked and perverse nation, among whom ye shine as lights in the world;

Col 1:28 — Whom we preach, warning every man, and teaching every man in all wisdom; that we may present every man perfect in Christ Jesus:

Col 3:14 — And above all these things *put on* charity, which is the bond of perfectness.

Col 4:12 — Epaphras, who is *one* of you, a servant of Christ, saluteth you, always labouring fervently for you in prayers, that ye may stand perfect and complete in all the will of God.

1Th 3:10 — Night and day praying exceedingly that we might see your face, and might perfect that which is lacking in your faith?

1Th 3:13 — To the end he may stablish your hearts unblameable in holiness before God, even our Father, at the coming of our Lord Jesus Christ with all his saints.

2Ti 2:1 — Thou therefore, my son, be strong in the grace that is in Christ Jesus.

2Ti 3:17 — That the man of God may be perfect, thoroughly furnished unto all good works.

Heb 6:1 — Therefore leaving the principles of the doctrine of Christ, let us go on unto perfection; not laying again the foundation of repentance from dead works, and of faith toward God,

Heb 10:14 — For by one offering he hath perfected for ever them that are sanctified.

Jas 1:4 — But let patience have *her* perfect work, that ye may be perfect and entire, wanting nothing.

Jas 1:25 — But whoso looketh into the perfect law of liberty, and continueth *therein,* he being not a forgetful hearer, but a doer of the work, this man shall be blessed in his deed.

Jas 3:2 — For in many things we offend all. If any man offend not in word, the same *is* a perfect man, *and* able also to bridle the whole body.

1Pe 5:10 — But the God of all grace, who hath called us unto his eternal glory by Christ Jesus, after that ye have suffered a while, make you perfect, stablish, strengthen, settle *you.*

1Jn 2:5 — But whoso keepeth his word, in him verily is the love of God perfected: hereby know we that we are in him.

1Jn 4:12 — No man hath seen God at any time. If we love one another, God dwelleth in us, and his love is perfected in us.

1Jn 5:18 — We know that whosoever is born of God sinneth not; but he that is begotten of God keepeth himself, and that wicked one toucheth him not.

See: God, Perfection of

See: Holiness

See: Sanctification

PERFIDY

See: Conspiracy

See: Hypocrisy

See: Treachery

PERFUME

Pr 27:9 — Ointment and perfume rejoice the heart: so *doth* the sweetness of a man's friend by hearty counsel.

SS 3:6 — Who *is* this that cometh out of the wilderness like pillars of smoke, perfumed with myrrh and frankincense, with all powders of the merchant?

Isa 57:9 — And thou wentest to the king with ointment, and didst increase thy perfumes, and didst send thy messengers far off, and didst debase *thyself even* unto hell.

• Used in the tabernacle.

Ex 30:7 — And Aaron shall burn thereon sweet incense every morning: when he dresseth the lamps, he shall burn incense upon it.

Ex 35:28 — And spice, and oil for the light, and for the anointing oil, and for the sweet incense.

• Beds perfumed with myrrh.

Pr 7:17 — I have perfumed my bed with myrrh, aloes, and cinnamon.

• Smelling bottles, translated "tablets" in King James Version.

Isa 3:20 — The bonnets, and the ornaments of the legs, and the headbands, and the tablets, and the earrings,

PERGA

• The capital of Pamphylia.

• Paul preaches in.

Ac 13:13–14

Ac 14:25 — And when they had preached the word in Perga, they went down into Attalia:

PERGAMOS

• A city of Mysia.

• One of the "seven churches" in.

Rev 2:12–17

Rev 1:11 — Saying, I am Alpha and Omega, the first and the last: and, What thou seest, write in a book, and send *it* unto the seven churches which are in

Asia; unto Ephesus, and unto Smyrna, and unto Pergamos, and unto Thyatira, and unto Sardis, and unto Philadelphia, and unto Laodicea.

PERIDA

• One of the servants of Solomon.

• Descendants of, returned to Jerusalem from captivity in Babylon.

Ne 7:57 — The children of Solomon's servants: the children of Sotai, the children of Sophereth, the children of Perida,

• Called Peruda.

Ezr 2:55 — The children of Solomon's servants: the children of Sotai, the children of Sophereth, the children of Peruda,

PERIZZITES

• One of the seven nations in the land of Canaan.

Ge 13:7 — And there was a strife between the herdmen of Abram's cattle and the herdmen of Lot's cattle: and the Canaanite and the Perizzite dwelled then in the land.

• Territory of, given to Abraham.

Ge 15:20 — And the Hittites, and the Perizzites, and the Rephaims,

Ex 3:8 — And I am come down to deliver them out of the hand of the Egyptians, and to bring them up out of that land unto a good land and a large, unto a land flowing with milk and honey; unto the place of the Canaanites, and the Hittites, and the Amorites, and the Perizzites, and the Hivites, and the Jebusites.

Ex 23:23 — For mine Angel shall go before thee, and bring thee in unto the Amorites, and the Hittites, and the Perizzites, and the Canaanites, and the Hivites, and the Jebusites: and I will cut them off.

• Doomed to destruction.

Dt 20:17 — But thou shalt utterly destroy them; *namely,* the Hittites, and the Amorites, the Canaanites, and the Perizzites, the Hivites, and the Jebusites; as the LORD thy God hath commanded thee:

• Not all destroyed; Israelites marry among.

Jgs 3:5–7; Ezr 9:1–2

→See: Canaanites

PERJURY

Le 6:2–7; 1Ti 1:9–10

Le 19:12 — And ye shall not swear by my name falsely, neither shalt thou profane the name of thy God: I *am* the LORD.

Isa 48:1 — Hear ye this, O house of Jacob, which are called by the name of Israel, and are come forth out of the waters of Judah, which swear by the name of the LORD, and make mention of the God of Israel, *but* not in truth, nor in righteousness.

Jer 5:2 — And though they say, The LORD liveth; surely they swear falsely.

Jer 7:9 — Will ye steal, murder, and commit adultery, and swear falsely, and burn incense unto Baal, and walk after other gods whom ye know not;

Hos 10:4 — They have spoken words, swearing falsely in making a covenant: thus judgment springeth up as hemlock in the furrows of the field.

Zec 5:4 — I will bring it forth, saith the LORD of hosts, and it shall enter into the house of the thief, and into the house of him that sweareth falsely by my name: and it shall remain in the midst of his house, and shall consume it with the timber thereof and the stones thereof.

Zec 8:17 — And let none of you imagine evil in your hearts against his neighbour; and love no false oath: for all these *are things* that I hate, saith the LORD.

Mal 3:5 — And I will come near to you to judgment; and I will be a swift witness against the sorcerers, and against the adulterers, and against false swearers, and against those that oppress the hireling in *his* wages, the widow, and the fatherless, and that turn aside the stranger *from his right,* and fear not me, saith the LORD of hosts.

Mt 5:33 — Again, ye have heard that it hath been said by them of old time, Thou shalt not forswear thyself, but shalt perform unto the Lord thine oaths:

→See: Falsehood

→See: Falsehood, False Witness

→See: Oath

• Instances of.

• Zedekiah.

2Ch 36:13

• Witnesses against Naboth.

1Ki 21:8–13

• Witnesses against David.

Ps 35:11

• Witnesses against Jesus.

Mt 26:59; Mk 14:56–57

• Witnesses against Stephen.

Ac 6:11, 13–14

• Witnesses against Peter, when he denied Jesus with an oath.

Mt 26:74; Mk 14:71

PERSECUTION

• Of Jesus.

Ps 2:1–5; 22:1–2, 6–8, 11–21; 69:1–21; Isa 53:2–5, 7–10; Mt 26:3–4, 14–16; 27:25–30, 39–44; Mk 3:21–22; 15:1–47; Lk 4:28–29; 11:53–54; 22:2–5, 52–53, 63–65; Jn 7:19–20; 15:20–21, 24–25; 18:22–23, 29–30; 19:1–42; Ac 3:13–15; 13:27–29; Heb 12:2–3

Ge 3:15 — And I will put enmity between thee and the woman, and between thy seed and her seed; it shall bruise thy head, and thou shalt bruise his heel.

Ps 69:26 — For they persecute *him* whom thou hast smitten; and they talk to the grief of those whom thou hast wounded.

Ps 109:25 — I became also a reproach unto them: *when* they looked upon me they shaked their heads.

Isa 49:7 — Thus saith the LORD, the Redeemer of Israel, *and* his Holy One, to him whom man despiseth, to him whom the nation abhorreth, to a servant of rulers, Kings shall see and arise, princes also shall worship, because of the LORD that is faithful, *and* the Holy One of Israel, and he shall choose thee.

Isa 50:6 — I gave my back to the smiters, and my cheeks to them that plucked off the hair: I hid not my face from shame and spitting.

Isa 52:14 — As many were astonied at thee; his visage was so marred more than any man, and his form more than the sons of men:

Mic 5:1 — Now gather thyself in troops, O daughter of troops: he hath laid siege against us: they shall smite the judge of Israel with a rod upon the cheek.

Mt 2:13 — And when they were departed, behold, the angel of the Lord appeareth to Joseph in a dream, saying, Arise, and take the young child and his mother, and flee into Egypt, and be thou there until I bring thee word: for Herod will seek the young child to destroy him.

Mt 11:19 — The Son of man came eating and drinking, and they say, Behold a man gluttonous, and a winebibber, a friend of publicans and sinners. But wisdom is justified of her children.

Mt 12:14 — Then the Pharisees went out, and held a council against him, how they might destroy him.

Mt 12:24 — But when the Pharisees heard *it,* they said, This *fellow* doth not cast out devils, but by Beelzebub the prince of the devils.

Mt 16:1 — The Pharisees also with the Sadducees came, and tempting desired him that he would shew them a sign from heaven.

Mt 20:22 — But Jesus answered and said, Ye know not what ye ask. Are ye able to drink of the cup that I shall drink of, and to be baptized with the baptism that I am baptized with? They say unto him, We are able.

Mt 22:15 — Then went the Pharisees, and took counsel how they might entangle him in *his* talk.

Mt 26:59 — Now the chief priests, and elders, and all the council, sought false witness against Jesus, to put him to death;

Mt 26:67 — Then did they spit in his face, and buffeted him; and others smote *him* with the palms of their hands,

Mk 3:6 — And the Pharisees went forth, and straightway took counsel with the Herodians against him, how they might destroy him.

Mk 11:18 — And the scribes and chief priests heard *it,* and sought how they might destroy him: for they feared him, because all the people was astonished at his doctrine.

Mk 12:13 — And they send unto him certain of the Pharisees and of the Herodians, to catch him in *his* words.

Mk 14:1 — After two days was *the feast of* the passover, and of unleavened bread: and the chief priests and the scribes sought how they might take him by craft, and put *him* to death.

Mk 14:48 — And Jesus answered and said unto them, Are ye come out, as against a thief, with swords and *with* staves to take me?

Mk 14:65 — And some began to spit on him, and to cover his face, and to buffet him, and to say unto him, Prophesy: and the servants did strike him with the palms of their hands.

Mk 16:17 — And these signs shall follow them that believe; In my name shall they cast out devils; they shall speak with new tongues;

Lk 6:11 — And they were filled with madness; and communed one with another what they might do to Jesus.

Lk 7:34 — The Son of man is come eating and drinking; and ye say, Behold a gluttonous man, and a winebibber, a friend of publicans and sinners!

Lk 11:15 — But some of them said, He casteth out devils through Beelzebub the chief of the devils.

Lk 12:50 — But I have a baptism to be baptized with; and how am I straitened till it be accomplished!

Lk 13:31 — The same day there came certain of the Pharisees, saying unto him, Get thee out, and depart hence: for Herod will kill thee.

Lk 19:14 — But his citizens hated him, and sent a message after him, saying, We will not have this *man* to reign over us.

Lk 19:47 — And he taught daily in the temple. But the chief priests and the scribes and the chief of the people sought to destroy him,

Lk 20:20 — And they watched *him,* and sent forth spies, which should feign themselves just men, that they might take hold of his words, that so they might deliver him unto the power and authority of the governor.

Lk 23:11 — And Herod with his men of war set him at nought, and mocked *him,* and arrayed him in a gorgeous robe, and sent him again to Pilate.

Lk 23:23 — And they were instant with loud voices, requiring that he might be crucified. And the voices of them and of the chief priests prevailed.

Jn 5:16 — And therefore did the Jews persecute Jesus, and sought to slay him, because he had done these things on the sabbath day.

Jn 7:1 — After these things Jesus walked in Galilee: for he would not walk in Jewry, because the Jews sought to kill him.

Jn 7:7 — The world cannot hate you; but me it hateth, because I testify of it, that the works thereof are evil.

Jn 7:30 — Then they sought to take him: but no man laid hands on him, because his hour was not yet come.

Jn 7:32 — The Pharisees heard that the people murmured such things concerning him; and the Pharisees and the chief priests sent officers to take him.

Jn 8:37 — I know that ye are Abraham's seed; but ye seek to kill me, because my word hath no place in you.

Jn 8:40 — But now ye seek to kill me, a man that hath told you the truth, which I have heard of God: this did not Abraham.

Jn 8:48 — Then answered the Jews, and said unto him, Say we not well that thou art a Samaritan, and hast a devil?

Jn 8:52 — Then said the Jews unto him, Now we know that thou hast a devil. Abraham is dead, and the prophets; and thou sayest, If a man keep my saying, he shall never taste of death.

Jn 8:59 — Then took they up stones to cast at him: but Jesus hid himself, and went out of the temple, going through the midst of them, and so passed by.

Jn 10:20 — And many of them said, He hath a devil, and is mad; why hear ye him?

Jn 10:31 — Then the Jews took up stones again to stone him.

Jn 10:39 — Therefore they sought again to take him: but he escaped out of their hand,

Jn 11:57 — Now both the chief priests and the Pharisees had given a commandment, that, if any man knew where he were, he should shew *it,* that they might take him.

Jn 14:30 — Hereafter I will not talk much with you: for the prince of this world cometh, and hath nothing in me.

Jn 15:18 — If the world hate you, ye know that *it hated* me before it hated you.

Ac 2:23 — Him, being delivered by the determinate counsel and foreknowledge of God, ye have taken, and by wicked hands have crucified and slain:

Ac 4:27 — For of a truth against thy holy child Jesus, whom thou hast anointed, both Herod, and Pontius Pilate, with the Gentiles, and the people of Israel, were gathered together,

Ac 7:52 — Which of the prophets have not your fathers persecuted? and they have slain them which shewed before of the coming of the Just One; of whom ye have been now the betrayers and murderers:

1Pe 4:1 — Forasmuch then as Christ hath suffered for us in the flesh, arm yourselves likewise with the same mind: for he that hath suffered in the flesh hath ceased from sin;

• Of the righteous.

Job 2:4–5; 12:4–5; Ps 44:15–18; 69:10–12; 74:7–8; 119:85–87; Isa 29:20–21; 51:12–13; Jer 20:7–8; 26:11–14; Mt 5:10–12; 10:16–18, 21–23; 20:22–23; 23:34–35; 24:8–10; Mk 13:11–13; Lk 6:22–23, 26–27; 21:12–19; Jn 15:18–19; 16:1–2; Ac 4:16–20; 5:40–42; Ro 8:35–37; 1Co 4:9–13; 2Co 4:8–12; 6:4–5, 8–10; 11:23–27; Php 1:12–14, 28–29; 1Th 2:14–15; 2Ti 2:9–10; 3:2–3; 4:16–17; Heb 10:32–34; 11:25–27, 33–38; 12:3–4; 1Pe 3:16–17; 4:3–4, 12–14; Rev 6:9–11; 7:13–17

Ge 49:23 — The archers have sorely grieved him, and shot *at him,* and hated him:

Job 1:9 — Then Satan answered the LORD, and said, Doth Job fear God for nought?

Ps 11:2 — For, lo, the wicked bend *their* bow, they make ready their arrow upon the string, that they may privily shoot at the upright in heart.

Ps 37:32 — The wicked watcheth the righteous, and seeketh to slay him.

Ps 38:20 — They also that render evil for good are mine adversaries; because I follow *the thing that* good *is.*

Ps 42:3 — My tears have been my meat day and night, while they continually say unto me, Where *is* thy God?

Ps 42:10 — *As* with a sword in my bones, mine enemies reproach me; while they say daily unto me, Where *is* thy God?

Ps 44:22 — Yea, for thy sake are we killed all the day long; we are counted as sheep for the slaughter.

Ps 56:5 — Every day they wrest my words: all their thoughts *are* against me for evil.

Ps 94:5 — They break in pieces thy people, O LORD, and afflict thine heritage.

Ps 119:51 — The proud have had me greatly in derision: *yet* have I not declined from thy law.

Ps 119:61 — The bands of the wicked have robbed me: *but* I have not forgotten thy law.

Ps 119:69 — The proud have forged a lie against me: *but* I will keep thy precepts with *my* whole heart.

Ps 119:78 — Let the proud be ashamed; for they dealt perversely with me without a cause: *but* I will meditate in thy precepts.

Ps 119:95 — The wicked have waited for me to destroy me: *but* I will consider thy testimonies.

Ps 119:110 — The wicked have laid a snare for me: yet I erred not from thy precepts.

Ps 119:157 — Many *are* my persecutors and mine enemies; *yet* do I not decline from thy testimonies.

Ps 119:161 — Princes have persecuted me without a cause: but my heart standeth in awe of thy word.

Pr 29:10 — The bloodthirsty hate the upright: but the just seek his soul.

Pr 29:27 — An unjust man *is* an abomination to the just: and *he that is* upright in the way *is* abomination to the wicked.

Isa 26:20 — Come, my people, enter thou into thy chambers, and shut thy doors about thee: hide thyself as it were for a little moment, until the indignation be overpast.

Isa 59:15 — Yea, truth faileth; and he *that* departeth from evil maketh himself a prey: and the LORD saw *it,* and it displeased him that *there was* no judgment.

Jer 2:30 — In vain have I smitten your children; they received no correction: your own sword hath devoured your prophets, like a destroying lion.

Jer 11:19 — But I *was* like a lamb *or* an ox *that* is brought to the slaughter; and I knew not that they had devised devices against me, *saying,* Let us destroy the tree with the fruit thereof, and let us cut him off from the land of the living, that his name may be no more remembered.

Jer 15:10 — Woe is me, my mother, that thou hast borne me a man of strife and a man of contention to the whole earth! I have neither lent on usury, nor men have lent to me on usury; *yet* every one of them doth curse me.

Jer 18:18 — Then said they, Come, and let us devise devices against Jeremiah; for the law shall not perish from the priest, nor counsel from the wise, nor the word from the prophet. Come, and let us smite him with the tongue, and let us not give heed to any of his words.

Jer 50:7 — All that found them have devoured them: and their adversaries said, We offend not, because they have sinned against the LORD, the habitation of justice, even the LORD, the hope of their fathers.

Am 5:10 — They hate him that rebuketh in the gate, and they abhor him that speaketh uprightly.

Hab 1:13 — *Thou art* of purer eyes than to behold evil, and canst not look on iniquity: wherefore lookest thou upon them that deal treacherously, *and* holdest thy tongue when the wicked devoureth *the man that is* more righteous than he?

Mt 5:44 — But I say unto you, Love your enemies, bless them that curse you, do good to them that hate you, and pray for them which despitefully use you, and persecute you;

Mt 10:28 — And fear not them which kill the body, but are not able to kill the soul: but rather fear him which is able to destroy both soul and body in hell.

Mk 8:35 — For whosoever will save his life shall lose it; but whosoever shall lose his life for my sake and the gospel's, the same shall save it.

Mk 9:42 — And whosoever shall offend one of *these* little ones that believe in me, it is better for him that a millstone were hanged about his neck, and he were cast into the sea.

Mk 13:9 — But take heed to yourselves: for they shall deliver you up to councils; and in the synagogues ye shall be beaten: and ye shall be brought before rulers and kings for my sake, for a testimony against them.

Lk 17:33 — Whosoever shall seek to save his life shall lose it; and whosoever shall lose his life shall preserve it.

Jn 12:42 — Nevertheless among the chief rulers also many believed on him; but because of the Pharisees they did not confess *him,* lest they should be put out of the synagogue:

Jn 17:14 — I have given them thy word; and the world hath hated them, because they are not of the world, even as I am not of the world.

Ac 5:29 — Then Peter and the *other* apostles answered and said, We ought to obey God rather than men.

Ac 7:52 — Which of the prophets have not your fathers persecuted? and they have slain them which shewed before of the coming of the Just One; of whom ye have been now the betrayers and murderers:

Ac 8:4 — Therefore they that were scattered abroad went every where preaching the word.

Ac 28:22 — But we desire to hear of thee what thou thinkest: for as concerning this sect, we know that every where it is spoken against.

Ro 8:17 — And if children, then heirs; heirs of God, and joint-heirs with Christ; if so be that we suffer with *him,* that we may be also glorified together.

1Co 13:3 — And though I bestow all my goods to feed *the poor,* and though I give my body to be burned, and have not charity, it profiteth me nothing.

2Co 12:10 — Therefore I take pleasure in infirmities, in reproaches, in necessities, in persecutions, in distresses for Christ's sake: for when I am weak, then am I strong.

Gal 4:29 — But as then he that was born after the flesh persecuted him *that was born* after the Spirit, even so *it is* now.

Gal 6:12 — As many as desire to make a fair shew in the flesh, they constrain you to be circumcised; only lest they should suffer persecution for the cross of Christ.

Gal 6:17 — From henceforth let no man trouble me: for I bear in my body the marks of the Lord Jesus.

Col 1:24 — Who now rejoice in my sufferings for you, and fill up that which is behind of the afflictions of Christ in my flesh for his body's sake, which is the church:

1Th 1:6 — And ye became followers of us, and of the Lord, having received the word in much affliction, with joy of the Holy Ghost:

1Th 2:2 — But even after that we had suffered before, and were shamefully entreated, as ye know, at Philippi, we were bold in our God to speak unto you the gospel of God with much contention.

2Th 1:4 — So that we ourselves glory in you in the churches of God for your patience and faith in all your persecutions and tribulations that ye endure:

2Ti 1:8 — Be not thou therefore ashamed of the testimony of our Lord, nor of me his prisoner: but be thou partaker of the afflictions of the gospel according to the power of God;

2Ti 1:12 — For the which cause I also suffer these things: nevertheless I am not ashamed: for I know whom I have believed, and am persuaded that he is able to keep that which I have committed unto him against that day.

2Ti 2:12 — If we suffer, we shall also reign with *him:* if we deny *him,* he also will deny us:

2Ti 3:12 — Yea, and all that will live godly in Christ Jesus shall suffer persecution.

Heb 13:13 — Let us go forth therefore unto him without the camp, bearing his reproach.

Jas 2:6 — But ye have despised the poor. Do not rich men oppress you, and draw you before the judgment seats?

Jas 5:6 — Ye have condemned *and* killed the just; *and* he doth not resist you.

Jas 5:10 — Take, my brethren, the prophets, who have spoken in the name of the Lord, for an example of suffering affliction, and of patience.

1Pe 3:14 — But and if ye suffer for righteousness' sake, happy *are ye:* and be not afraid of their terror, neither be troubled;

1Pe 4:16 — Yet if *any man suffer* as a Christian, let him not be ashamed; but let him glorify God on this behalf.

1Pe 4:19 — Wherefore let them that suffer according to the will of God commit the keeping of their souls *to him* in well doing, as unto a faithful Creator.

1Jn 3:1 — Behold, what manner of love the Father hath bestowed upon us, that we should be called the sons of God: therefore the world knoweth us not, because it knew him not.

1Jn 3:13 — Marvel not, my brethren, if the world hate you.

Rev 2:3 — And hast borne, and hast patience, and for my name's sake hast laboured, and hast not fainted.

Rev 2:10 — Fear none of those things which thou shalt suffer: behold, the devil shall cast *some* of you into prison, that ye may be tried; and ye shall have tribulation ten days: be thou faithful unto death, and I will give thee a crown of life.

Rev 2:13 — I know thy works, and where thou dwellest, *even* where Satan's seat *is:* and thou holdest fast my name, and hast not denied my faith, even in those days wherein Antipas *was* my faithful martyr, who was slain among you, where Satan dwelleth.

Rev 12:11 — And they overcame him by the blood of the Lamb, and by the word of their testimony; and they loved not their lives unto the death.

Rev 17:6 — And I saw the woman drunken with the blood of the saints, and with the blood of the martyrs of Jesus: and when I saw her, I wondered with great admiration.

Rev 20:4 — And I saw thrones, and they sat upon them, and judgment was given unto them: and *I saw* the souls of them that were beheaded for the witness of Jesus, and for the word of God, and which had not worshipped the beast, neither his image, neither had received *his* mark upon their foreheads, or in their hands; and they lived and reigned with Christ a thousand years.

See: Paul, Ministry, Ac 16–28

See: Paul, Ministry, Ac 9–15

See: Paul, Miscellaneous

- **A mode of divine chastisement.**
  La 1:3
- **Diffuses the gospel.**
  Ac 11:19–21; Php 1:12–14
  Ac 8:1 — And Saul was consenting unto his death. And at that time there was a great persecution against the church which was at Jerusalem; and they were all scattered abroad throughout the regions of Judaea and Samaria, except the apostles.
  Ac 8:4 — Therefore they that were scattered abroad went every where preaching the word.
- **Prayer for deliverance from.**
  Ps 70:1–4; 83:1–18
  Ps 140:1 — Deliver me, O LORD, from the evil man: preserve me from the violent man;
  Ps 140:4 — Keep me, O LORD, from the hands of the wicked; preserve me from the violent man; who have purposed to overthrow my goings.
  Ps 142:6 — Attend unto my cry; for I am brought very low: deliver me from my persecutors; for they are stronger than I.
- **Deliverance from.**
  Ps 124:1–8; 129:1–2
- **Instances of.**
  - **Abel.**
    Ge 4:8; Mt 23:35; 1Jn 3:12
  - **Lot.**
    Ge 19:9
  - **Moses.**
    Ex 2:15; 17:4
  - **David.**
    Ps 31:13; 59:1–2
  - **Prophets martyred by Jezebel.**
    1Ki 18:4
  - **Gideon.**
    Jgs 6:28–32
  - **Elijah.**
    1Ki 18:10; 19:1–21; 2Ki 1:9; 2:23
  - **Micaiah.**
    1Ki 22:26; 2Ch 18:26
  - **Elisha.**
    2Ki 6:31
  - **Hanani.**
    2Ch 16:10
  - **Zachariah.**
    2Ch 24:21; Mt 23:35
  - **Job.**
    Job 13:4–13; 16:1–4; 17:2; 19:1–5; 30:1–10
  - **Jeremiah.**
    Jer 15:10, 15; 17:15–18; 18:18–23; 26:1–24; 32:2; 33:1; 36:26; 37:1–38:6
  - **Urijah.**
    Jer 26:23
  - **prophets.**
    Mt 21:35–36
  - **The three Hebrew children of the captivity.**
    Da 3:8–23
  - **Daniel.**
    Da 6:1–28
  - **The Jews.**
    Ezr 4:1–24; Ne 4:1–23
  - **John the Baptist.**
    Mt 14:3–12
  - **James.**
    Ac 12:2
  - **Simon.**
    Mk 15:21
  - **The disciples.**
    Jn 9:22, 34; 20:19
  - **Lazarus.**
    Jn 12:10
  - **The apostles.**
    Ac 4:3–18; 5:18–42; 12:1–19; Rev 1:9
  - **Stephen.**
    Ac 6:9–7:60
  - **The church.**
    Ac 8:1; 9:1–14; Gal 1:13
  - **Timothy.**
    Heb 13:23
  - **John.**
    Rev 1:9
  - **Antipas.**
    Rev 2:13
  - **The church of Smyrna.**
    Rev 2:8–10

PERSEVERANCE

Mk 4:3–8; Lk 22:31–32; Jn 6:39–40; 8:31–32; 10:28–29; 15:4–5; Ac 14:21–22; Ro 2:6–7; 8:33–35, 37–39; 1Co 1:8–9; 15:1–2; 2Co 1:21–22; Col 1:22–23; 2Th 2:15–17; 2Ti 1:12–13; Heb 3:5–6; 6:11–12, 17–18; 10:35–36; 12:1–13; Jas 5:10–11; 1Pe 1:4–7; 2Pe 1:10–11; 3:17–18; Rev 2:10–11, 25–28; 3:11–12; 21:7–8

1Ch 16:11 — Seek the LORD and his strength, seek his face continually.

Job 17:9 — The righteous also shall hold on his way, and he that hath clean hands shall be stronger and stronger.

Ps 37:24 — Though he fall, he shall not be utterly cast down: for the LORD upholdeth *him with* his hand.

Ps 37:28 — For the LORD loveth judgment, and forsaketh not his saints; they are preserved for ever: but the seed of the wicked shall be cut off.

Ps 73:24 — Thou shalt guide me with thy counsel, and afterward receive me *to* glory.

Ps 138:8 — The LORD will perfect *that which* concerneth me: thy mercy, O LORD, *endureth* for ever: forsake not the works of thine own hands.

Pr 4:18 — But the path of the just *is* as the shining light, that shineth more and more unto the perfect day.

Jer 32:40 — And I will make an everlasting covenant with them, that I will not turn away from them, to do them good; but I will put my fear in their hearts, that they shall not depart from me.

Hos 12:6 — Therefore turn thou to thy God: keep mercy and judgment, and wait on thy God continually.

Mt 10:22 — And ye shall be hated of all *men* for my name's sake: but he that endureth to the end shall be saved.

Mt 24:13 — But he that shall endure unto the end, the same shall be saved.

Mk 13:13 — And ye shall be hated of all *men* for my name's sake: but he that shall endure unto the end, the same shall be saved.

Lk 10:42 — But one thing is needful: and Mary hath chosen that good part, which shall not be taken away from her.

Jn 6:37 — All that the Father giveth me shall come to me; and him that cometh to me I will in no wise cast out.

Jn 15:7 — If ye abide in me, and my words abide in you, ye shall ask what ye will, and it shall be done unto you.

Jn 15:9 — As the Father hath loved me, so have I loved you: continue ye in my love.

Ac 11:23 — Who, when he came, and had seen the grace of God, was glad, and exhorted them all, that with purpose of heart they would cleave unto the Lord.

Ac 13:43 — Now when the congregation was broken up, many of the Jews and religious proselytes followed Paul and Barnabas: who, speaking to them, persuaded them to continue in the grace of God.

Ro 8:30 — Moreover whom he did predestinate, them he also called: and whom he called, them he also justified: and whom he justified, them he also glorified.

Ro 11:29 — For the gifts and calling of God *are* without repentance.

1Co 15:58 — Therefore, my beloved brethren, be ye stedfast, unmovable, always abounding in the work of the Lord, forasmuch as ye know that your labour is not in vain in the Lord.

1Co 16:13 — Watch ye, stand fast in the faith, quit you like men, be strong.

2Co 5:9 — Wherefore we labour, that, whether present or absent, we may be accepted of him.

2Co 5:15 — And *that* he died for all, that they which live should not henceforth live unto themselves, but unto him which died for them, and rose again.

Gal 5:1 — Stand fast therefore in the liberty wherewith Christ hath made us free, and be not entangled again with the yoke of bondage.

Gal 5:10 — I have confidence in you through the Lord, that ye will be none otherwise minded: but he that troubleth you shall bear his judgment, whosoever he be.

Gal 6:9 — And let us not be weary in well doing: for in due season we shall reap, if we faint not.

Eph 4:14 — That we *henceforth* be no more children, tossed to and fro, and carried about with every wind of doctrine, by the sleight of men, *and* cunning craftiness, whereby they lie in wait to deceive;

Eph 6:13 — Wherefore take unto you the whole armour of God, that ye may be able to withstand in the evil day, and having done all, to stand.

Eph 6:18 — Praying always with all prayer and supplication in the Spirit, and watching thereunto with all perseverance and supplication for all saints;

Php 1:6 — Being confident of this very thing, that he which hath begun a good work in you will perform *it* until the day of Jesus Christ:

Php 1:27 — Only let your conversation be as it becometh the gospel of Christ: that whether I come and see you, or else be absent, I may hear of your affairs, that ye stand fast in one spirit, with one mind striving together for the faith of the gospel;

Php 3:16 — Nevertheless, whereto we have already attained, let us walk by the same rule, let us mind the same thing.

Php 4:1 — Therefore, my brethren dearly beloved and longed for, my joy and crown, so stand fast in the Lord, *my* dearly beloved.

Col 1:10 — That ye might walk worthy of the Lord unto all pleasing, being fruitful in every good work, and increasing in the knowledge of God;

Col 2:7 — Rooted and built up in him, and stablished in the faith, as ye have been taught, abounding therein with thanksgiving.

1Th 3:8 — For now we live, if ye stand fast in the Lord.

1Th 3:13 — To the end he may stablish your hearts unblameable in holiness before God, even our Father, at the coming of our Lord Jesus Christ with all his saints.

1Th 5:21 — Prove all things; hold fast that which is good.

2Th 3:13 — But ye, brethren, be not weary in well doing.

2Ti 2:1 — Thou therefore, my son, be strong in the grace that is in Christ Jesus.

2Ti 2:12 — If we suffer, we shall also reign with *him:* if we deny *him,* he also will deny us:

2Ti 3:14 — But continue thou in the things which thou hast learned and hast been assured of, knowing of whom thou hast learned *them;*

2Ti 4:18 — And the Lord shall deliver me from every evil work, and will preserve *me* unto his heavenly kingdom: to whom *be* glory for ever and ever. Amen.

Tit 1:9 — Holding fast the faithful word as he hath been taught, that he may be able by sound doctrine both to exhort and to convince the gainsayers.

Heb 2:1 — Therefore we ought to give the more earnest heed to the things which we have heard, lest at any time we should let *them* slip.

Heb 3:14 — For we are made partakers of Christ, if we hold the beginning of our confidence stedfast unto the end;

Heb 4:14 — Seeing then that we have a great high priest, that is passed into the heavens, Jesus the Son of God, let us hold fast *our* profession.

Heb 6:1 — Therefore leaving the principles of the doctrine of Christ, let us go on unto perfection; not laying again the foundation of repentance from dead works, and of faith toward God,

Heb 6:15 — And so, after he had patiently endured, he obtained the promise.

Heb 10:23 — Let us hold fast the profession of *our* faith without wavering; (for he is faithful that promised;)

Heb 12:15 — Looking diligently lest any man fail of the grace of God; lest any root of bitterness springing up trouble *you,* and thereby many be defiled;

Heb 13:9 — Be not carried about with divers and strange doctrines. For *it is* a good thing that the heart be established with grace; not with meats, which have not profited them that have been occupied therein.

Heb 13:13 — Let us go forth therefore unto him without the camp, bearing his reproach.

Jas 1:4 — But let patience have *her* perfect work, that ye may be perfect and entire, wanting nothing.

Jas 1:12 — Blessed *is* the man that endureth temptation: for when he is tried, he shall receive the crown of life, which the Lord hath promised to them that love him.

Jas 1:25 — But whoso looketh into the perfect law of liberty, and continueth *therein,* he being not a forgetful hearer, but a doer of the work, this man shall be blessed in his deed.

1Pe 5:8 — Be sober, be vigilant; because your adversary the devil, as a roaring lion, walketh about, seeking whom he may devour:

1Jn 2:19 — They went out from us, but they were not of us; for if they had been of us, they would *no doubt* have continued with us: but *they went out,* that they might be made manifest that they were not all of us.

1Jn 2:27 — But the anointing which ye have received of him abideth in you, and ye need not that any man teach you: but as the same anointing teacheth you of all things, and is truth, and is no lie, and even as it hath taught you, ye shall abide in him.

Rev 2:7 — <u>He that hath an ear, let him hear what the Spirit saith unto the churches; To him that overcometh will I give to eat of the tree of life, which is in the midst of the paradise of God.</u>

Rev 2:17 — <u>He that hath an ear, let him hear what the Spirit saith unto the churches; To him that overcometh will I give to eat of the hidden manna, and will give him a white stone, and in the stone a new name written, which no man knoweth saving he that receiveth *it.*</u>

Rev 3:5 — <u>He that overcometh, the same shall be clothed in white raiment; and I will not blot out his name out of the book of life, but I will confess his name before my Father, and before his angels.</u>

Rev 3:21 — <u>To him that overcometh will I grant to sit with me in my throne, even as I also overcame, and am set down with my Father in his throne.</u>

Rev 14:12 — Here is the patience of the saints: here *are* they that keep the commandments of God, and the faith of Jesus.

Rev 16:15 — <u>Behold, I come as a thief. Blessed *is* he that watcheth, and keepeth his garments, lest he walk naked, and they see his shame.</u>

Rev 22:11 — He that is unjust, let him be unjust still: and he which is filthy, let him be filthy still: and he that is righteous, let him be righteous still: and he that is holy, let him be holy still.

See: Character of Saints

See: Instability

See: Stability

- **Instances of.**
  - **Jacob, in prayer.**
    Ge 32:24–26
  - **Caleb and Joshua, in representing the land of promise.**
    Nu 14:24, 38

PERSIA

• An empire which extended from India to Ethiopia, comprising 127 provinces.

Est 1:1 — Now it came to pass in the days of Ahasuerus, (this *is* Ahasuerus which reigned, from India even unto Ethiopia, *over* an hundred and seven and twenty provinces:)

Da 6:1 — It pleased Darius to set over the kingdom an hundred and twenty princes, which should be over the whole kingdom;

• Government of, restricted by constitutional limitations.

Da 6:8–12

Est 8:8 — Write ye also for the Jews, as it liketh you, in the king's name, and seal *it* with the king's ring: for the writing which is written in the king's name, and sealed with the king's ring, may no man reverse.

• Municipal governments in, provided with dual governors.

Ne 3:16–18

Ne 3:9 — And next unto them repaired Rephaiah the son of Hur, the ruler of the half part of Jerusalem.

Ne 3:12 — And next unto him repaired Shallum the son of Halohesh, the ruler of the half part of Jerusalem, he and his daughters.

• The princes advisory in matters of administration.

Da 6:1–7

• Status of women in; queen sat on the throne with the king.

Ne 2:6 — And the king said unto me, (the queen also sitting by him,) For how long shall thy journey be? and when wilt thou return? So it pleased the king to send me; and I set him a time.

• Vashti divorced for refusing to appear before the king's courtiers.

Est 1:10–22

Est 2:4 — And let the maiden which pleaseth the king be queen instead of Vashti. And the thing pleased the king; and he did so.

• Israel captive in.

2Ch 36:20 — And them that had escaped from the sword carried he away to Babylon; where they were servants to him and his sons until the reign of the kingdom of Persia:

• Israel's captivity foretold.

Hos 13:16 — Samaria shall become desolate; for she hath rebelled against her God: they shall fall by the sword: their infants shall be dashed in pieces, and their women with child shall be ripped up.

• Men of, in the Tyrian army.

Eze 27:10 — They of Persia and of Lud and of Phut were in thine army, thy men of war: they hanged the shield and helmet in thee; they set forth thy comeliness.

• Rulers of.

• Ahasuerus.

Est 1:3 — In the third year of his reign, he made a feast unto all his princes and his servants; the power of Persia and Media, the nobles and princes of the provinces, *being* before him:

• Darius.

Da 5:31–6:28

Da 9:1 — In the first year of Darius the son of Ahasuerus, of the seed of the Medes, which was made king over the realm of the Chaldeans;

• Artaxerxes I.

Ezr 4:7–24

• Artaxerxes II.

Ezr 7:1–28; Ne 2:1–20

Ne 5:14 — Moreover from the time that I was appointed to be their governor in the land of Judah, from the twentieth year even unto the two and thirtieth year of Artaxerxes the king, *that is,* twelve years, I and my brethren have not eaten the bread of the governor.

• Cyrus.

2Ch 36:22–23; Ezr 1:1–11; 5:13–14; Isa 41:2–3; 44:28–45:4; 48:14–15

Ezr 3:7 — They gave money also unto the masons, and to the carpenters; and meat, and drink, and oil, unto them of Zidon, and to them of Tyre, to bring cedar trees from Lebanon to the sea of Joppa, according to the grant that they had of Cyrus king of Persia.

Ezr 4:3 — But Zerubbabel, and Jeshua, and the rest of the chief of the fathers of Israel, said unto them, Ye have nothing to do with us to build an house unto our God; but we ourselves together will build unto the LORD God of Israel, as king Cyrus the king of Persia hath commanded us.

Ezr 5:17 — Now therefore, if *it seem* good to the king, let there be search made in the king's treasure house, which *is* there at Babylon, whether it be *so,* that a decree was made of Cyrus the king to build this house of God at Jerusalem, and let the king send his pleasure to us concerning this matter.

Ezr 6:3 — In the first year of Cyrus the king *the same* Cyrus the king made a decree *concerning* the house of God at Jerusalem, Let the house be builded, the place where they offered sacrifices, and let the foundations thereof be strongly laid; the height thereof threescore cubits, *and* the breadth thereof threescore cubits;

Isa 45:13 — I have raised him up in righteousness, and I will direct all his ways: he shall build my city, and he shall let go my captives, not for price nor reward, saith the LORD of hosts.

Isa 46:11 — Calling a ravenous bird from the east, the man that executeth my counsel from a far country: yea, I have spoken *it,* I will also bring it to pass; I have purposed *it,* I will also do it.

• Princes of.

Est 1:14 — And the next unto him *was* Carshena, Shethar, Admatha, Tarshish, Meres, Marsena, *and* Memucan, the seven princes of Persia and Media, which saw the king's face, *and* which sat the first in the kingdom;)

• System of justice.

Ezr 7:25 — And thou, Ezra, after the wisdom of thy God, that *is* in thine hand, set magistrates and judges, which may judge all the people that *are* beyond the river, all such as know the laws of thy God; and teach ye them that know *them* not.

• Prophecies concerning.

Isa 21:1–10; Jer 49:34–39; 51:11–64; Eze 32:24–25; Da 2:31–45; 7:1–8:27; 11:1–4

Isa 13:17 — Behold, I will stir up the Medes against them, which shall not regard silver; and *as for* gold, they shall not delight in it.

Eze 38:5 — Persia, Ethiopia, and Libya with them; all of them with shield and helmet:

Da 5:28 — PERES; Thy kingdom is divided, and given to the Medes and Persians.

See: Babylon

See: Chaldea

PERSIS • A Christian woman in Rome.

Ro 16:12 — Salute Tryphena and Tryphosa, who labour in the Lord. Salute the beloved Persis, which laboured much in the Lord.

PERSONAL CALL

See: Call, Personal

See: Minister, a sacred teacher; call of

PERSONIFICATION

• Of wisdom.

Pr 1:1–2:9; 8:1–9:18

• Of the church.

SS 1:1–8:14

See: Pantomime

PERSPECT

Ps 18:20–28; 73:1–28

Ps 25:14 — The secret of the LORD *is* with them that fear him; and he will shew them his covenant.

Mk 7:34 — And looking up to heaven, he sighed, and saith unto him, Ephphatha, that is, Be opened.

Ro 8:37 — Nay, in all these things we are more than conquerors through him that loved us.

PERUDA

• One of the servants of Solomon.

• Descendants of, return to Jerusalem from captivity in Babylon.

Ezr 2:55 — The children of Solomon's servants: the children of Sotai, the children of Sophereth, the children of Peruda,

• Called Perida.

Ne 7:57 — The children of Solomon's servants: the children of Sotai, the children of Sophereth, the children of Perida,

PESTILENCE

• Sent as a judgment.

Le 26:16 — I also will do this unto you; I will even appoint over you terror, consumption, and the burning ague, that shall consume the eyes, and cause sorrow of heart: and ye shall sow your seed in vain, for your enemies shall eat it.

Le 26:25 — And I will bring a sword upon you, that shall avenge the quarrel of *my* covenant: and when ye are gathered together within your cities, I will send the pestilence among you; and ye shall be delivered into the hand of the enemy.

• Sent upon the Egyptians.

See: Egypt

See: Plague

PETER

• Called also Simon Bar-Jona and Cephas.

Mt 16:16–19

Mk 3:16 — And Simon he surnamed Peter;

Jn 1:42 — And he brought him to Jesus. And when Jesus beheld him, he said, Thou art Simon the son of Jona: thou shalt be called Cephas, which is by interpretation, A stone.

• A fisherman.

Lk 5:1–7

Mt 4:18 — And Jesus, walking by the sea of Galilee, saw two brethren, Simon called Peter, and Andrew his brother, casting a net into the sea: for they were fishers.

Jn 21:3 — Simon Peter saith unto them, I go a fishing. They say unto him, We also go with thee. They went forth, and entered into a ship immediately; and that night they caught nothing.

• Call of.

Mt 4:18–20; Mk 1:16–18; Lk 5:1–11

• His wife's mother healed.

Mk 1:29–30

Mt 8:14 — And when Jesus was come into Peter's house, he saw his wife's mother laid, and sick of a fever.

Lk 4:38 — And he arose out of the synagogue, and entered into Simon's house. And Simon's wife's mother was taken with a great fever; and they besought him for her.

• An apostle.

Mt 16:18–19

Mt 10:2 — Now the names of the twelve apostles are these; The first, Simon, who is called Peter, and Andrew his brother; James *the son* of Zebedee, and John his brother;

Mk 3:16 — And Simon he surnamed Peter;

Lk 6:14 — Simon, (whom he also named Peter,) and Andrew his brother, James and John, Philip and Bartholomew,

Ac 1:13 — And when they were come in, they went up into an upper room, where abode both Peter, and James, and John, and Andrew, Philip, and Thomas, Bartholomew, and Matthew, James *the son* of Alphaeus, and Simon Zelotes, and Judas *the brother* of James.

• An evangelist.

Mk 1:36–37

• Confesses Jesus as Christ.

Mt 16:16–19; Jn 6:68–69

Mk 8:29 — And he saith unto them, But whom say ye that I am? And Peter answereth and saith unto him, Thou art the Christ.

Lk 9:20 — He said unto them, But whom say ye that I am? Peter answering said, The Christ of God.

• His presumption in rebuking Jesus.

Mt 16:22–23; Mk 8:32–33

• His presumption when the throng was pressing Jesus and the woman of infirmity touched him.

Lk 8:45 — And Jesus said, Who touched me? When all denied, Peter and they that were with him said, Master, the multitude throng thee and press *thee,* and sayest thou, Who touched me?

• His presumption in refusing to let Jesus wash his feet.

Jn 13:6–11

• Present at the healing of Jairus's daughter.

Mk 5:37 — And he suffered no man to follow him, save Peter, and James, and John the brother of James.

Lk 8:51 — And when he came into the house, he suffered no man to go in, save Peter, and James, and John, and the father and the mother of the maiden.

• Present at the transfiguration.

Mt 17:1–4; Mk 9:2–6; Lk 9:28–33; 2Pe 1:16–18

• Present in Gethsemane.

Mt 26:36–46; Mk 14:33–42; Lk 22:40–46

• Seeks the interpretation of the parable of the steward.

Lk 12:41 — Then Peter said unto him, Lord, speakest thou this parable unto us, or even to all?

• Seeks the interpretation of the law of forgiveness.

Mt 18:21 — Then came Peter to him, and said, Lord, how oft shall my brother sin against me, and I forgive him? till seven times?

• Seeks the interpretation of the law of defilement.

Mt 15:15 — Then answered Peter and said unto him, Declare unto us this parable.

• Seeks the interpretation of the prophecy of Jesus concerning his second coming.

Mk 13:3–4

• Walks upon the water of the Sea of Galilee.

Mt 14:28–31

• Sent with John to prepare the passover.

Lk 22:8 — And he sent Peter and John, saying, Go and prepare us the passover, that we may eat.

• Calls attention to the withered fig tree.

Mk 11:21 — And Peter calling to remembrance saith unto him, Master, behold, the fig tree which thou cursedst is withered away.

• His perfidy foretold by Jesus, and his profession of fidelity.

Mt 26:33–35; Mk 14:29–31; Lk 22:31–34; Jn 13:36–38

• Cuts off the ear of Malchus.

Mt 26:51 — And, behold, one of them which were with Jesus stretched out *his* hand, and drew his sword, and struck a servant of the high priest's, and smote off his ear.

Mk 14:47 — And one of them that stood by drew a sword, and smote a servant of the high priest, and cut off his ear.

Lk 22:50 — And one of them smote the servant of the high priest, and cut off his right ear.

• Follows Jesus to the high priest's palace.

Mt 26:58 — But Peter followed him afar off unto the high priest's palace, and went in, and sat with the servants, to see the end.

Mk 14:54 — And Peter followed him afar off, even into the palace of the high priest: and he sat with the servants, and warmed himself at the fire.

Lk 22:54 — Then took they him, and led *him*, and brought him into the high priest's house. And Peter followed afar off.

Jn 18:15 — And Simon Peter followed Jesus, and *so did* another disciple: that disciple was known unto the high priest, and went in with Jesus into the palace of the high priest.

• His denial of Jesus, and his repentance.

Mt 26:69–75; Mk 14:66–72; Lk 22:55–62; Jn 18:17–18, 25–27

• Visits the sepulchre.

Jn 20:2–6

Lk 24:12 — Then arose Peter, and ran unto the sepulchre; and stooping down, he beheld the linen clothes laid by themselves, and departed, wondering in himself at that which was come to pass.

• Jesus sends message to, after the resurrection.

Mk 16:7 — But go your way, tell his disciples and Peter that he goeth before you into Galilee: there shall ye see him, as he said unto you.

• Jesus appears to.

1Co 15:4–5

Lk 24:34 — Saying, The Lord is risen indeed, and hath appeared to Simon.

• Present at Sea of Tiberias when Jesus appeared to disciples; commissioned to feed flock of Christ.

Jn 21:1–23

• Abides in Jerusalem.

Ac 1:13 — And when they were come in, they went up into an upper room, where abode both Peter, and James, and John, and Andrew, Philip, and Thomas, Bartholomew, and Matthew, James *the son* of Alphaeus, and Simon Zelotes, and Judas *the brother* of James.

• After death of Judas, he recommends that the vacancy in the apostleship be filled.

Ac 1:15–22

• Preaches at Pentecost.

Ac 2:14–40

• Heals the impotent man in the portico of the temple.

Ac 3:1–26

• Accused by the council, his defense.

Ac 4:1–23

• Foretells the death of Ananias and Sapphira.

Ac 5:1–11

• Imprisoned and scourged, his defense before the council.

Ac 5:17–42

• Goes to Samaria.

Ac 8:14 — Now when the apostles which were at Jerusalem heard that Samaria had received the word of God, they sent unto them Peter and John:

• Prays for the baptism of the Holy Ghost.

Ac 8:15–18

• Rebukes Simon, the sorcerer, who desires to purchase like power.

Ac 8:18–24

• Returns to Jerusalem.

Ac 8:25 — And they, when they had testified and preached the word of the Lord, returned to Jerusalem, and preached the gospel in many villages of the Samaritans.

• Receives Paul.

Gal 1:18 — Then after three years I went up to Jerusalem to see Peter, and abode with him fifteen days.

Gal 2:9 — And when James, Cephas, and John, who seemed to be pillars, perceived the grace that was given unto me, they gave to me and Barnabas the right hands of fellowship; that we *should go* unto the heathen, and they unto the circumcision.

• Visits Lydda; heals Aeneas.

Ac 9:32–34

• Visits Joppa; dwells with Simon, the tanner; raises Dorcas from the dead.

Ac 9:36–43

• Has a vision of a sheet containing clean and unclean animals.

Ac 10:9–16

• Receives servant of centurion; goes to Caesarea; preaches and baptizes centurion and household.

Ac 10:1–48

• Advocates, in the council of the apostles and elders, the preaching of the gospel to the Gentiles.

Ac 11:1–18; 15:7–11

• Imprisoned and delivered by an angel.

Ac 12:3–19

• Writes two epistles.

1Pe 1:1 — Peter, an apostle of Jesus Christ, to the strangers scattered throughout Pontus, Galatia, Cappadocia, Asia, and Bithynia,

2Pe 1:1 — Simon Peter, a servant and an apostle of Jesus Christ, to them that have obtained like precious faith with us through the righteousness of God and our Saviour Jesus Christ:

• Miracles of.

⇜See: Miracles of the disciples

PETHAHIAH

• A priest in the reign of David.

1Ch 24:16 — The nineteenth to Pethahiah, the twentieth to Jehezekel,

• A Levite who divorced his Gentile wife.

Ezr 10:23 — Also of the Levites; Jozabad, and Shimei, and Kelaiah, (the same *is* Kelita,) Pethahiah, Judah, and Eliezer.

• Probably identical with the one mentioned in Ne 9:5.

Ne 9:5 — Then the Levites, Jeshua, and Kadmiel, Bani, Hashabniah, Sherebiah, Hodijah, Shebaniah, *and* Pethahiah, said, Stand up *and* bless the LORD your God for ever and ever: and blessed be thy glorious name, which is exalted above all blessing and praise.

• A counselor of Artaxerxes.

Ne 11:24 — And Pethahiah the son of Meshezabeel, of the children of Zerah the son of Judah, *was* at the king's hand in all matters concerning the people.

PETHOR

• A city in Mesopotamia.

• Home of the prophet Balaam.

Nu 22:5 — He sent messengers therefore unto Balaam the son of Beor to Pethor, which *is* by the river of the land of the children of his people, to call him, saying, Behold, there is a people come out from Egypt: behold, they cover the face of the earth, and they abide over against me:

Dt 23:4 — Because they met you not with bread and with water in the way, when ye came forth out of Egypt; and because they hired against thee Balaam the son of Beor of Pethor of Mesopotamia, to curse thee.

PETHUEL • Father of the prophet Joel.

Joel 1:1 — The word of the LORD that came to Joel the son of Pethuel.

PETITION

• Right of, recognized by Pharaoh.

Ex 5:15–18

• Right of, recognized by Israel.

Nu 27:1–5; 32:1–5; 36:1–5; Jos 21:1–2

Jos 17:4 — And they came near before Eleazar the priest, and before Joshua the son of Nun, and before the princes, saying, The LORD commanded Moses to give us an inheritance among our brethren. Therefore according to the commandment of the LORD he gave them an inheritance among the brethren of their father.

Jos 17:14 — And the children of Joseph spake unto Joshua, saying, Why hast thou given me *but* one lot and one portion to inherit, seeing I *am* a great people, forasmuch as the LORD hath blessed me hitherto?

Jos 17:16 — And the children of Joseph said, The hill is not enough for us: and all the Canaanites that dwell in the land of the valley have chariots of iron, *both they* who *are* of Beth-shean and her towns, and *they* who *are* of the valley of Jezreel.

• Right of, recognized by David.

1Ki 1:15–21

• Right of, recognized by Rehoboam.

1Ki 12:1–17; 2Ch 10:1–19

• Right of, recognized by Jehoram.

2Ki 8:3 — And it came to pass at the seven years' end, that the woman returned out of the land of the Philistines: and she went forth to cry unto the king for her house and for her land.

2Ki 8:6 — And when the king asked the woman, she told him. So the king appointed unto her a certain officer, saying, Restore all that *was* hers, and all the fruits of the field since the day that she left the land, even until now.

PETROLEUM

• Figurative.

Job 29:6 — When I washed my steps with butter, and the rock poured me out rivers of oil;

PEULTHAI • A porter of the tabernacle.

1Ch 26:5 — Ammiel the sixth, Issachar the seventh, Peulthai the eighth: for God blessed him.

PHALLU

• Called also Pallu.

• Son of Reuben.

Ge 46:9 — And the sons of Reuben; Hanoch, and Phallu, and Hezron, and Carmi.

Ex 6:14 — These *be* the heads of their fathers' houses: The sons of Reuben the firstborn of Israel; Hanoch, and Pallu, Hezron, and Carmi: these *be* the families of Reuben.

Nu 26:5 — Reuben, the eldest son of Israel: the children of Reuben; Hanoch, *of whom cometh* the family of the Hanochites: of Pallu, the family of the Palluites:

Nu 26:8 — And the sons of Pallu; Eliab.

1Ch 5:3 — The sons, *I say,* of Reuben the firstborn of Israel *were,* Hanoch, and Pallu, Hezron, and Carmi.

PHALTI

• Called also Phaltiel.

• Son-in-law of Saul.

2Sa 3:15–16

1Sa 25:44 — But Saul had given Michal his daughter, David's wife, to Phalti the son of Laish, which *was* of Gallim.

PHALTIEL ✦See: Phalti

PHARAOH

• King of Egypt at the time of Abraham.

Ge 12:14–20

Ps 105:14 — He suffered no man to do them wrong: yea, he reproved kings for their sakes;

• Ruler of Egypt at the time of the famine.

✦See: Egypt

✦See: Israelites

• Ruler of Egypt at the time of the deliverance and Exodus of the children of Israel.

✦See: Israelites

• Father-in-law of Mered.

1Ch 4:18 — And his wife Jehudijah bare Jered the father of Gedor, and Heber the father of Socho, and Jekuthiel the father of Zanoah. And these *are* the sons of Bithiah the daughter of Pharaoh, which Mered took.

• Ruler of Egypt at the time of David.

1Ki 11:17–22

• Father-in-law of Solomon.

1Ki 3:1 — And Solomon made affinity with Pharaoh king of Egypt, and took Pharaoh's daughter, and brought her into the city of David, until he had made an end of building his own house, and the house of the LORD, and the wall of Jerusalem round about.

1Ki 9:16 — *For* Pharaoh king of Egypt had gone up, and taken Gezer, and burnt it with fire, and slain the Canaanites that dwelt in the city, and given it *for* a present unto his daughter, Solomon's wife.

• At the time of Hezekiah.

2Ki 18:21 — Now, behold, thou trustest upon the staff of this bruised reed, *even* upon Egypt, on which if a man lean, it will go into his hand, and pierce it: so is Pharaoh king of Egypt unto all that trust on him.

• Pharaoh-nechoh. His invasion of Assyria, Josiah's death.

2Ki 23:29–35; 2Ch 35:20–24; 36:3–4

2Ki 24:7 — And the king of Egypt came not again any more out of his land: for the king of Babylon had taken from the river of Egypt unto the river Euphrates all that pertained to the king of Egypt.

Jer 46:2 — Against Egypt, against the army of Pharaoh-necho king of Egypt, which was by the river Euphrates in Carchemish, which Nebuchadrezzar king of Babylon smote in the fourth year of Jehoiakim the son of Josiah king of Judah.

Jer 47:1 — The word of the LORD that came to Jeremiah the prophet against the Philistines, before that Pharaoh smote Gaza.

• Pharaoh-hophra.

Jer 37:4–7; 44:1–30; Eze 17:15–17

• Prophecies concerning.

Jer 46:25–26; Eze 29:1–21; 30:21–26

Jer 44:30 — Thus saith the LORD; Behold, I will give Pharaoh-hophra king of Egypt into the hand of his enemies, and into the hand of them that seek his life; as I gave Zedekiah king of Judah into the hand of Nebuchadrezzar king of Babylon, his enemy, and that sought his life.

PHARES ✦See: Pharez

PHAREZ

• Called also Perez and Phares.

• A twin son of Judah by Tamar.

Ge 38:29 — And it came to pass, as he drew back his hand, that, behold, his brother came out: and she said, How hast thou broken forth? *this* breach *be* upon thee: therefore his name was called Pharez.

1Ch 2:4 — And Tamar his daughter in law bare him Pharez and Zerah. All the sons of Judah *were* five.

• Children of.

Nu 26:20–21

Ge 46:12 — And the sons of Judah; Er, and Onan, and Shelah, and Pharez, and Zarah: but Er and Onan died in the land of Canaan. And the sons of Pharez were Hezron and Hamul.

1Ch 2:5 — The sons of Pharez; Hezron, and Hamul.

1Ch 9:4 — Uthai the son of Ammihud, the son of Omri, the son of Imri, the son of Bani, of the children of Pharez the son of Judah.

• Children of, return from the captivity.

Ne 11:4 — And at Jerusalem dwelt *certain* of the children of Judah, and of the children of Benjamin. Of the children of Judah; Athaiah the son of Uzziah, the son of Zechariah, the son of Amariah, the son of Shephatiah, the son of Mahalaleel, of the children of Perez;

Ne 11:6 — All the sons of Perez that dwelt at Jerusalem *were* four hundred threescore and eight valiant men.

• In the lineage of Jesus.

Mt 1:3 — And Judas begat Phares and Zara of Thamar; and Phares begat Esrom; and Esrom begat Aram;

Lk 3:33 — Which was *the son* of Aminadab, which was *the son* of Aram, which was *the son* of Esrom, which was *the son* of Phares, which was *the son* of Juda,

PHARISEES

• A sect of the Jews.

Ac 15:5 — But there rose up certain of the sect of the Pharisees which believed, saying, That it was needful to circumcise them, and to command *them* to keep the law of Moses.

• Doctrines of.

Mt 15:9 — But in vain they do worship me, teaching *for* doctrines the commandments of men.

• Doctrines concerning the resurrection.

Ac 23:6 — But when Paul perceived that the one part were Sadducees, and the other Pharisees, he cried out in the council, Men *and* brethren, I am a Pharisee, the son of a Pharisee: of the hope and resurrection of the dead I am called in question.

Ac 23:8 — For the Sadducees say that there is no resurrection, neither angel, nor spirit: but the Pharisees confess both.

• Doctrines concerning association with publicans and sinners.

Mt 9:11–13

• Traditions of, in regard to fasting.

Mt 9:14 — Then came to him the disciples of John, saying, Why do we and the Pharisees fast oft, but thy disciples fast not?

Lk 18:12 — I fast twice in the week, I give tithes of all that I possess.

• Traditions of, in regard to the washing of hands.

Mt 15:1–3; Mk 7:1–15

• Traditions of, in regard to the duties of children to parents.

Mt 15:4–9

• Traditions of, in regard to the Sabbath.

Mt 12:2–8

• Hypocrisy of, reproved by John.

Mt 3:7–10

• Hypocrisy of, reproved by Jesus.

Mt 6:2–8, 16–18; 15:1–9; 16:1–12; 21:33–46; 23:2–33; Lk 11:14–12:1; 15:1–9

• Reject John.

Lk 7:30 — But the Pharisees and lawyers rejected the counsel of God against themselves, being not baptized of him.

• Reject Christ.

Mt 12:38–39

Mt 15:12 — Then came his disciples, and said unto him, Knowest thou that the Pharisees were offended, after they heard this saying?

Jn 7:48 — Have any of the rulers or of the Pharisees believed on him?

• Come to Jesus with questions.

Mt 22:15–22

Mt 19:3 — The Pharisees also came unto him, tempting him, and saying unto him, Is it lawful for a man to put away his wife for every cause?

• Minister to Jesus.

Lk 7:36 — And one of the Pharisees desired him that he would eat with him. And he went into the Pharisee's house, and sat down to meat.

Lk 11:37 — And as he spake, a certain Pharisee besought him to dine with him: and he went in, and sat down to meat.

Lk 14:1 — And it came to pass, as he went into the house of one of the chief Pharisees to eat bread on the sabbath day, that they watched him.

• Become disciples of Jesus.

Jn 3:1 — There was a man of the Pharisees, named Nicodemus, a ruler of the Jews:

Ac 15:5 — But there rose up certain of the sect of the Pharisees which believed, saying, That it was needful to circumcise them, and to command *them* to keep the law of Moses.

Ac 22:3 — I am verily a man *which am* a Jew, born in Tarsus, a city in Cilicia, yet brought up in this city at the feet of Gamaliel, *and* taught according to the perfect manner of the law of the fathers, and was zealous toward God, as ye all are this day.

• Paul a Pharisee.

Ac 23:6 — But when Paul perceived that the one part were Sadducees, and the other Pharisees, he cried out in the council, Men *and* brethren, I am a Pharisee, the son of a Pharisee: of the hope and resurrection of the dead I am called in question.

Ac 26:5 — Which knew me from the beginning, if they would testify, that after the most straitest sect of our religion I lived a Pharisee.

See: Herodians

See: Sadducees

PHAROSH

• Called also Parosh.

• The ancestor of one of the families which returned to Jerusalem from captivity in Babylon.

Ezr 2:3 — The children of Parosh, two thousand an hundred seventy and two.

Ezr 8:3 — Of the sons of Shechaniah, of the sons of Pharosh; Zechariah: and with him were reckoned by genealogy of the males an hundred and fifty.

Ezr 10:25 — Moreover of Israel: of the sons of Parosh; Ramiah, and Jeziah, and Malchiah, and Miamin, and Eleazar, and Malchijah, and Benaiah.

Ne 7:8 — The children of Parosh, two thousand an hundred seventy and two.

Ne 10:14 — The chief of the people; Parosh, Pahathmoab, Elam, Zatthu, Bani,

PHARPAR

• A river of Damascus.

• Referred to by Naaman.

2Ki 5:12 — *Are* not Abana and Pharpar, rivers of Damascus, better than all the waters of Israel? may I not wash in them, and be clean? So he turned and went away in a rage.

PHASEAH

• Called also Paseah.

• Ancestor of a family which returned to Jerusalem from the captivity.

Ezr 2:49 — The children of Uzza, the children of Paseah, the children of Besai,

Ne 3:6 — Moreover the old gate repaired Jehoiada the son of Paseah, and Meshullam the son of Besodeiah; they laid the beams thereof, and set up the doors thereof, and the locks thereof, and the bars thereof.

Ne 7:51 — The children of Gazzam, the children of Uzza, the children of Phaseah,

PHEBE • A deaconess of the church at Cenchrea.

Ro 16:1 — I commend unto you Phebe our sister, which is a servant of the church which is at Cenchrea:

PHENICE • A harbor of Crete.

Ac 27:12–13

Ac 27:21 — But after long abstinence Paul stood forth in the midst of them, and said, Sirs, ye should have hearkened unto me, and not have loosed from Crete, and to have gained this harm and loss.

PHENICIA

• Called also Phenice.

• Inhabitants of, descended from Canaan.

Ge 10:18–19

Ge 10:15 — And Canaan begat Sidon his firstborn, and Heth,

• Called Zidonians.

Jgs 18:7 — Then the five men departed, and came to Laish, and saw the people that *were* therein, how they dwelt careless, after the manner of the Zidonians, quiet and secure; and *there was* no magistrate in the land, that might put *them* to shame in *any* thing; and they *were* far from the Zidonians, and had no business with *any* man.

Eze 32:30 — There *be* the princes of the north, all of them, and all the Zidonians, which are gone down with the slain; with their terror they are ashamed of their might; and they lie uncircumcised with *them that be* slain by the sword, and bear their shame with them that go down to the pit.

• Jews from, hear Jesus.

Mk 3:8 — And from Jerusalem, and from Idumaea, and *from* beyond Jordan; and they about Tyre and Sidon, a great multitude, when they had heard what great things he did, came unto him.

• Paul visits the churches in.

Ac 21:2–4

Ac 15:3 — And being brought on their way by the church, they passed through Phenice and Samaria, declaring the conversion of the Gentiles: and they caused great joy unto all the brethren.

Ac 27:3 — And the next *day* we touched at Sidon. And Julius courteously entreated Paul, and gave *him* liberty to go unto his friends to refresh himself.

PHICHOL • Chief captain of the Philistines.

Ge 21:22 — And it came to pass at that time, that Abimelech and Phichol the chief captain of his host spake unto Abraham, saying, God *is* with thee in all that thou doest:

Ge 21:32 — Thus they made a covenant at Beersheba: then Abimelech rose up, and Phichol the chief captain of his host, and they returned into the land of the Philistines.

Ge 26:26 — Then Abimelech went to him from Gerar, and Ahuzzath one of his friends, and Phichol the chief captain of his army.

PHILADELPHIA

• A city of Lydia.

• One of the "seven churches" at.

Rev 3:7–13

Rev 1:11 — Saying, I am Alpha and Omega, the first and the last: and, What thou seest, write in a book, and send *it* unto the seven churches which are in Asia; unto Ephesus, and unto Smyrna, and unto Pergamos, and unto Thyatira, and unto Sardis, and unto Philadelphia, and unto Laodicea.

PHILANTHROPY

Isa 58:6–12

See: Alms

See: Beneficence

See: Charitableness

See: Liberality

See: Neighbour

See: Poor

PHILEMON

• A Christian in Colosse.

• Paul's letter to.

Phm 1:1–25

PHILETUS • A heretical teacher at Rome.

2Ti 2:17–18

PHILIP

• Brother of Herod and husband of Herodias.

Mt 14:3 — For Herod had laid hold on John, and bound him, and put *him* in prison for Herodias' sake, his brother Philip's wife.

Mk 6:17 — For Herod himself had sent forth and laid hold upon John, and bound him in prison for Herodias' sake, his brother Philip's wife: for he had married her.

Lk 3:19 — But Herod the tetrarch, being reproved by him for Herodias his brother Philip's wife, and for all the evils which Herod had done,

- **Tetrarch of Iturea.**

Lk 3:1 — Now in the fifteenth year of the reign of Tiberius Caesar, Pontius Pilate being governor of Judaea, and Herod being tetrarch of Galilee, and his brother Philip tetrarch of Ituraea and of the region of Trachonitis, and Lysanias the tetrarch of Abilene,

- **One of the seven deacons.**

Ac 6:5 — And the saying pleased the whole multitude: and they chose Stephen, a man full of faith and of the Holy Ghost, and Philip, and Prochorus, and Nicanor, and Timon, and Parmenas, and Nicolas a proselyte of Antioch:

- **Successfully preaches in Samaria.**

Ac 8:4–14

- **Expounds the Scriptures to the Ethiopian eunuch whom he baptizes.**

Ac 8:27–38

- **Caught away by the Spirit to Azotus, preaches in the cities, and goes to Caesarea.**

Ac 8:39–40

- **Abides at Caesarea, and entertains Paul.**

Ac 21:8 — And the next *day* we that were of Paul's company departed, and came unto Caesarea: and we entered into the house of Philip the evangelist, which was *one* of the seven; and abode with him.

- **Has four daughters, prophetesses.**

Ac 21:9–10

- **One of the twelve apostles.**

Mt 10:3 — Philip, and Bartholomew; Thomas, and Matthew the publican; James *the son* of Alphaeus, and Lebbaeus, whose surname was Thaddaeus;

Mk 3:18 — And Andrew, and Philip, and Bartholomew, and Matthew, and Thomas, and James the *son* of Alphaeus, and Thaddaeus, and Simon the Canaanite,

Lk 6:14 — Simon, (whom he also named Peter,) and Andrew his brother, James and John, Philip and Bartholomew,

Ac 1:13 — And when they were come in, they went up into an upper room, where abode both Peter, and James, and John, and Andrew, Philip, and Thomas, Bartholomew, and Matthew, James *the son* of Alphaeus, and Simon Zelotes, and Judas *the brother* of James.

- **Call of.**

Jn 1:43 — The day following Jesus would go forth into Galilee, and findeth Philip, and saith unto him, Follow me.

- **Brings Nathanael to Jesus.**

Jn 1:45–50

- **Assists in caring for the multitude whom Jesus miraculously feeds.**

Jn 6:5–7

- **Brings certain Greeks to Jesus who desire to see him.**

Jn 12:20–22

- **Asks Jesus to show the Father.**

Jn 14:8–13

PHILIPPI

- **A city of Macedonia.**
- **Paul preaches in.**

Ac 16:12–40; 20:1–6

1Th 2:2 — But even after that we had suffered before, and were shamefully entreated, as ye know, at Philippi, we were bold in our God to speak unto you the gospel of God with much contention.

- **Contributes to the maintenance of Paul.**

Php 4:10–18

- **Paul sends Epaphroditus to.**

Php 2:25 — Yet I supposed it necessary to send to you Epaphroditus, my brother, and companion in labour, and fellow soldier, but your messenger, and he that ministered to my wants.

- **Paul writes a letter to the Christians of.**

Php 1:1 — Paul and Timotheus, the servants of Jesus Christ, to all the saints in Christ Jesus which are at Philippi, with the bishops and deacons:

PHILISTIA • The sea coast in the west of Dan and Simeon.

Ps 60:8 — Moab *is* my washpot; over Edom will I cast out my shoe: Philistia, triumph thou because of me.

Ps 87:4 — I will make mention of Rahab and Babylon to them that know me: behold Philistia, and Tyre, with Ethiopia; this *man* was born there.

Ps 108:9 — Moab *is* my washpot; over Edom will I cast out my shoe; over Philistia will I triumph.

PHILISTINES • Descendants of Mizraim.

Ge 10:14 — And Pathrusim, and Casluhim, (out of whom came Philistim,) and Caphtorim.

1Ch 1:12 — And Pathrusim, and Casluhim, (of whom came the Philistines,) and Caphthorim.

Jer 47:4 — Because of the day that cometh to spoil all the Philistines, *and* to cut off from Tyrus and Zidon every helper that remaineth: for the LORD will spoil the Philistines, the remnant of the country of Caphtor.

Am 9:7 — *Are* ye not as children of the Ethiopians unto me, O children of Israel? saith the LORD. Have not I brought up Israel out of the land of Egypt? and the Philistines from Caphtor, and the Syrians from Kir?

- **Called Cherethites.**

1Sa 30:14–16

Eze 25:16 — Therefore thus saith the Lord GOD; Behold, I will stretch out mine hand upon the Philistines, and I will cut off the Cherethims, and destroy the remnant of the sea coast.

Zep 2:5 — Woe unto the inhabitants of the sea coast, the nation of the Cherethites! the word of the LORD *is* against you; O Canaan, the land of the Philistines, I will even destroy thee, that there shall be no inhabitant.

- **Called Casluhim.**

Ge 10:14 — And Pathrusim, and Casluhim, (out of whom came Philistim,) and Caphtorim.

1Ch 1:12 — And Pathrusim, and Casluhim, (of whom came the Philistines,) and Caphthorim.

• **Called Caphtorim.**

Jer 47:4 — Because of the day that cometh to spoil all the Philistines, *and* to cut off from Tyrus and Zidon every helper that remaineth: for the LORD will spoil the Philistines, the remnant of the country of Caphtor.

Am 9:7 — *Are* ye not as children of the Ethiopians unto me, O children of Israel? saith the LORD. Have not I brought up Israel out of the land of Egypt? and the Philistines from Caphtor, and the Syrians from Kir?

• **Territory of.**

Ex 13:17 — And it came to pass, when Pharaoh had let the people go, that God led them not *through* the way of the land of the Philistines, although that *was* near; for God said, Lest peradventure the people repent when they see war, and they return to Egypt:

Ex 23:31 — And I will set thy bounds from the Red sea even unto the sea of the Philistines, and from the desert unto the river: for I will deliver the inhabitants of the land into your hand; and thou shalt drive them out before thee.

Dt 2:23 — And the Avims which dwelt in Hazerim, *even* unto Azzah, the Caphtorims, which came forth out of Caphtor, destroyed them, and dwelt in their stead.)

Jos 13:3 — From Sihor, which *is* before Egypt, even unto the borders of Ekron northward, *which* is counted to the Canaanite: five lords of the Philistines; the Gazathites, and the Ashdothites, the Eshkalonites, the Gittites, and the Ekronites; also the Avites:

Jos 15:47 — Ashdod with her towns and her villages, Gaza with her towns and her villages, unto the river of Egypt, and the great sea, and the border *thereof*:

• **Lords of.**

1Sa 29:6–7

Jos 13:3 — From Sihor, which *is* before Egypt, even unto the borders of Ekron northward, *which* is counted to the Canaanite: five lords of the Philistines; the Gazathites, and the Ashdothites, the Eshkalonites, the Gittites, and the Ekronites; also the Avites:

Jgs 3:3 — *Namely,* five lords of the Philistines, and all the Canaanites, and the Sidonians, and the Hivites that dwelt in mount Lebanon, from mount Baal-hermon unto the entering in of Hamath.

Jgs 16:5 — And the lords of the Philistines came up unto her, and said unto her, Entice him, and see wherein his great strength *lieth,* and by what *means* we may prevail against him, that we may bind him to afflict him: and we will give thee every one of us eleven hundred *pieces* of silver.

Jgs 16:30 — And Samson said, Let me die with the Philistines. And he bowed himself with *all his* might; and the house fell upon the lords, and upon all the people that *were* therein. So the dead which he slew at his death were more than *they* which he slew in his life.

1Sa 5:8 — They sent therefore and gathered all the lords of the Philistines unto them, and said, What shall we do with the ark of the God of Israel? And they answered, Let the ark of the God of Israel be carried about unto Gath. And they carried the ark of the God of Israel about *thither.*

1Sa 5:11 — So they sent and gathered together all the lords of the Philistines, and said, Send away the ark of the God of Israel, and let it go again to his own place, that it slay us not, and our people: for there was a deadly destruction throughout all the city; the hand of God was very heavy there.

1Sa 6:4 — Then said they, What *shall be* the trespass offering which we shall return to him? They answered, Five golden emerods, and five golden mice, *according to* the number of the lords of the Philistines: for one plague was on you all, and on your lords.

1Sa 6:12 — And the kine took the straight way to the way of Beth-shemesh, *and* went along the highway, lowing as they went, and turned not aside *to* the right hand or *to* the left; and the lords of the Philistines went after them unto the border of Beth-shemesh.

1Sa 7:7 — And when the Philistines heard that the children of Israel were gathered together to Mizpeh, the lords of the Philistines went up against Israel. And when the children of Israel heard *it,* they were afraid of the Philistines.

1Sa 29:2 — And the lords of the Philistines passed on by hundreds, and by thousands: but David and his men passed on in the rereward with Achish.

• **Kings of.**

• **Abimelech I.**

Ge 20:1–18

• **Abimelech II.**

Ge 26:1–35

• **Achish.**

1Sa 21:10–15; 27:2–28:2; 29:1–11

• **Suffered to remain in Canaan.**

Jgs 3:3–4

• **Shamgar slays six hundred with an ox goad.**

Jgs 3:31 — And after him was Shamgar the son of Anath, which slew of the Philistines six hundred men with an ox goad: and he also delivered Israel.

• **For their history during the leadership of Samson.**

Jgs 13:1–16:31

• **Defeat the Israelites; take the ark; suffer plagues; return the ark.**

1Sa 4:1–6:21

• **Army of.**

1Sa 13:5 — And the Philistines gathered themselves together to fight with Israel, thirty thousand chariots, and six thousand horsemen, and people as the sand which *is* on the sea shore in multitude: and they came up, and pitched in Michmash, eastward from Beth-aven.

• **Defeated by Samuel.**

1Sa 7:1–17

- **Defeated by Saul and Jonathan.**
  1Sa 13:1–14:52
  1Sa 9:16 — To morrow about this time I will send thee a man out of the land of Benjamin, and thou shalt anoint him *to be* captain over my people Israel, that he may save my people out of the hand of the Philistines: for I have looked upon my people, because their cry is come unto me.
- **Their champion, Goliath, slain by David.**
  1Sa 17:1–58
- **David slays two hundred.**
  1Sa 18:22–30
- **David finds refuge among.**
  1Sa 27:1–12
- **Defeat the Israelites and slay Saul and his sons.**
  1Sa 31:1–13
  1Ch 10:1 — Now the Philistines fought against Israel; and the men of Israel fled from before the Philistines, and fell down slain in mount Gilboa.
- **Defeated by David.**
  2Sa 5:17–25; 23:9–16; 1Ch 14:8–16
- **Pay tribute to Jehoshaphat.**
  2Ch 17:11 — Also *some* of the Philistines brought Jehoshaphat presents, and tribute silver; and the Arabians brought him flocks, seven thousand and seven hundred rams, and seven thousand and seven hundred he goats.
- **Defeated by Hezekiah.**
  2Ki 18:8 — He smote the Philistines, *even* unto Gaza, and the borders thereof, from the tower of the watchmen to the fenced city.
- **Prophecies against.**
  Isa 9:11–12; 14:29–31; Jer 25:17–20; 47:1–7; Eze 25:15–17; Am 1:6–8; Zep 2:4–7; Zec 9:5–7

PHILOLOGUS • A disciple in Rome.

Ro 16:15 — Salute Philologus, and Julia, Nereus, and his sister, and Olympas, and all the saints which are with them.

PHILOSOPHY

- **The nature of things.**
  Ecc 1:1–7:29
- **A philosophical disquisition on wisdom.**
  Job 28:1–28
- **Philosophical inductions and deductions relating to God and his providence.**
  Job 5:8–20; 9:1–35; 10:2–21; 12:6–24; 33:12–30; 37:1–24
- **Reveals the mysteries of providence.**
  Ro 1:19–20
  Pr 25:2 — *It is* the glory of God to conceal a thing: but the honour of kings *is* to search out a matter.
- **Is not sufficient for an adequate knowledge of God.**
  1Co 1:21–22
- **Is not sufficient for salvation through the atonement of Jesus Christ.**
  1Co 2:6–10
- **Employment of, was not Paul's method of preaching the gospel.**
  1Co 2:1–5
  1Co 1:17 — For Christ sent me not to baptize, but to preach the gospel: not with wisdom of words, lest the cross of Christ should be made of none effect.
  1Co 1:19 — For it is written, I will destroy the wisdom of the wise, and will bring to nothing the understanding of the prudent.
  1Co 1:21 — For after that in the wisdom of God the world by wisdom knew not God, it pleased God by the foolishness of preaching to save them that believe.
  1Co 2:13 — Which things also we speak, not in the words which man's wisdom teacheth, but which the Holy Ghost teacheth; comparing spiritual things with spiritual.
- **Greek schools of.**
  Ac 17:18 — Then certain philosophers of the Epicureans, and of the Stoicks, encountered him. And some said, What will this babbler say? other some, He seemeth to be a setter forth of strange gods: because he preached unto them Jesus, and the resurrection.
- **Rabbinical.**
  Col 2:16–19
  Col 2:8 — Beware lest any man spoil you through philosophy and vain deceit, after the tradition of men, after the rudiments of the world, and not after Christ.
  1Ti 6:20 — O Timothy, keep that which is committed to thy trust, avoiding profane *and* vain babblings, and oppositions of science falsely so called:

See: God; unclassified scripture relating to
See: Reasoning

PHINEHAS

- **High priest.**
  Ex 6:25 — And Eleazar Aaron's son took him *one* of the daughters of Putiel to wife; and she bare him Phinehas: these *are* the heads of the fathers of the Levites according to their families.
  1Ch 6:4 — Eleazar begat Phinehas, Phinehas begat Abishua,
  1Ch 6:50 — And these *are* the sons of Aaron; Eleazar his son, Phinehas his son, Abishua his son,
  - **Religious zeal of, in slaying the Israelitish women who had committed abomination.**
    Nu 25:7–15
    Ps 106:30 — Then stood up Phinehas, and executed judgment: and *so* the plague was stayed.
  - **Chief of the Korahite Levites.**
    1Ch 9:19–20

• **Sent to sound the trumpets in the battle with the Midianites.**

Nu 31:6 — And Moses sent them to the war, a thousand of *every* tribe, them and Phinehas the son of Eleazar the priest, to the war, with the holy instruments, and the trumpets to blow in his hand.

• **A commissioner to the Israelites east of the Jordan.**

Jos 22:13–32

• **Inheritance allotted to.**

Jos 24:33 — And Eleazar the son of Aaron died; and they buried him in a hill *that pertained to* Phinehas his son, which was given him in mount Ephraim.

• **Mediator in behalf of the people.**

Jgs 20:28 — And Phinehas, the son of Eleazar, the son of Aaron, stood before it in those days,) saying, Shall I yet again go out to battle against the children of Benjamin my brother, or shall I cease? And the LORD said, Go up; for to morrow I will deliver them into thine hand.

• **Son of Eli.**

1Sa 1:3 — And this man went up out of his city yearly to worship and to sacrifice unto the LORD of hosts in Shiloh. And the two sons of Eli, Hophni and Phinehas, the priests of the LORD, *were* there.

• **Wickedness of.**

1Sa 2:12–17, 22–25

1Sa 2:34 — And this *shall be* a sign unto thee, that shall come upon thy two sons, on Hophni and Phinehas; in one day they shall die both of them.

• **Slain in battle.**

1Sa 4:4–11

1Sa 4:17 — And the messenger answered and said, Israel is fled before the Philistines, and there hath been also a great slaughter among the people, and thy two sons also, Hophni and Phinehas, are dead, and the ark of God is taken.

1Sa 4:19 — And his daughter in law, Phinehas' wife, was with child, *near* to be delivered: and when she heard the tidings that the ark of God was taken, and that her father in law and her husband were dead, she bowed herself and travailed; for her pains came upon her.

• **Son of.**

1Sa 14:3 — And Ahiah, the son of Ahitub, I-chabod's brother, the son of Phinehas, the son of Eli, the LORD's priest in Shiloh, wearing an ephod. And the people knew not that Jonathan was gone.

• **A priest.**

Ezr 8:33 — Now on the fourth day was the silver and the gold and the vessels weighed in the house of our God by the hand of Meremoth the son of Uriah the priest; and with him *was* Eleazar the son of Phinehas; and with them *was* Jozabad the son of Jeshua, and Noadiah the son of Binnui, Levites;

PHLEGON • A disciple in Rome.

Ro 16:14 — Salute Asyncritus, Phlegon, Hermas, Patrobas, Hermes, and the brethren which are with them.

PHRYGIA

• **An inland province of Asia Minor.**

• **People from, in Jerusalem.**

Ac 2:10 — Phrygia, and Pamphylia, in Egypt, and in the parts of Libya about Cyrene, and strangers of Rome, Jews and proselytes,

• **Paul in.**

Ac 16:6 — Now when they had gone throughout Phrygia and the region of Galatia, and were forbidden of the Holy Ghost to preach the word in Asia,

Ac 18:23 — And after he had spent some time *there,* he departed, and went over *all* the country of Galatia and Phrygia in order, strengthening all the disciples.

PHURAH • A servant of Gideon.

Jgs 7:10–11

PHUT

• **Called also Put.**

• **Son of Ham.**

Ge 10:6 — And the sons of Ham; Cush, and Mizraim, and Phut, and Canaan.

1Ch 1:8 — The sons of Ham; Cush, and Mizraim, Put, and Canaan.

• **The descendants of Phut, or the country inhabited by them.**

Jer 46:9 — Come up, ye horses; and rage, ye chariots; and let the mighty men come forth; the Ethiopians and the Libyans, that handle the shield; and the Lydians, that handle *and* bend the bow.

Eze 27:10 — They of Persia and of Lud and of Phut were in thine army, thy men of war: they hanged the shield and helmet in thee; they set forth thy comeliness.

Eze 30:5 — Ethiopia, and Libya, and Lydia, and all the mingled people, and Chub, and the men of the land that is in league, shall fall with them by the sword.

Eze 38:5 — Persia, Ethiopia, and Libya with them; all of them with shield and helmet:

Na 3:9 — Ethiopia and Egypt *were* her strength, and *it was* infinite; Put and Lubim were thy helpers.

PHUVAH

• **Called also Pua and Puah.**

• **Son of Issachar.**

Ge 46:13 — And the sons of Issachar; Tola, and Phuvah, and Job, and Shimron.

Nu 26:23 — *Of* the sons of Issachar after their families: *of* Tola, the family of the Tolaites: of Pua, the family of the Punites:

1Ch 7:1 — Now the sons of Issachar *were,* Tola, and Puah, Jashub, and Shimrom, four.

• **Descendants of.**

Nu 26:23 — *Of* the sons of Issachar after their families: *of* Tola, the family of the Tolaites: of Pua, the family of the Punites:

PHYGELLUS

• A Christian in Asia.

• Turns from Paul.

2Ti 1:15 — This thou knowest, that all they which are in Asia be turned away from me; of whom are Phygellus and Hermogenes.

PHYLACTERY

• A small box containing slips of parchment on which were written portions of the law.

Dt 6:4–9

Ex 13:9 — And it shall be for a sign unto thee upon thine hand, and for a memorial between thine eyes, that the LORD's law may be in thy mouth: for with a strong hand hath the LORD brought thee out of Egypt.

Ex 13:16 — And it shall be for a token upon thine hand, and for frontlets between thine eyes: for by strength of hand the LORD brought us forth out of Egypt.

Dt 11:18 — Therefore shall ye lay up these my words in your heart and in your soul, and bind them for a sign upon your hand, that they may be as frontlets between your eyes.

• Worn ostentatiously by the Jews, on the head and left arm.

Mt 23:5 — But all their works they do for to be seen of men: they make broad their phylacteries, and enlarge the borders of their garments,

PHYSICIAN

2Ch 16:12 — And Asa in the thirty and ninth year of his reign was diseased in his feet, until his disease *was* exceeding *great:* yet in his disease he sought not to the LORD, but to the physicians.

Mt 9:12 — But when Jesus heard *that,* he said unto them, They that be whole need not a physician, but they that are sick.

Mk 5:26 — And had suffered many things of many physicians, and had spent all that she had, and was nothing bettered, but rather grew worse,

Lk 8:43 — And a woman having an issue of blood twelve years, which had spent all her living upon physicians, neither could be healed of any,

• Proverbs about.

Mk 2:17 — When Jesus heard *it,* he saith unto them, They that are whole have no need of the physician, but they that are sick: I came not to call the righteous, but sinners to repentance.

Lk 4:23 — And he said unto them, Ye will surely say unto me this proverb, Physician, heal thyself: whatsoever we have heard done in Capernaum, do also here in thy country.

• Luke a physician.

Col 4:14 — Luke, the beloved physician, and Demas, greet you.

• Figurative.

Job 13:4 — But ye *are* forgers of lies, ye *are* all physicians of no value.

Jer 8:22 — *Is there* no balm in Gilead; *is there* no physician there? why then is not the health of the daughter of my people recovered?

Lk 5:31 — And Jesus answering said unto them, They that are whole need not a physician; but they that are sick.

PHYSIOGNOMY

• Character revealed.

Isa 3:9 — The shew of their countenance doth witness against them; and they declare their sin as Sodom, they hide *it* not. Woe unto their soul! for they have rewarded evil unto themselves.

See: Face

PHYSIOLOGY

Ps 139:14–16

Job 10:11 — Thou hast clothed me with skin and flesh, and hast fenced me with bones and sinews.

Pr 14:30 — A sound heart *is* the life of the flesh: but envy the rottenness of the bones.

See: Anatomy

See: Hygiene

• Figurative.

Eph 4:16 — From whom the whole body fitly joined together and compacted by that which every joint supplieth, according to the effectual working in the measure of every part, maketh increase of the body unto the edifying of itself in love.

Col 2:19 — And not holding the Head, from which all the body by joints and bands having nourishment ministered, and knit together, increaseth with the increase of God.

PI-BESETH

• A city in lower Egypt.

• Prophesied against by Ezekiel.

Eze 30:17 — The young men of Aven and of Pi-beseth shall fall by the sword: and these *cities* shall go into captivity.

PI-HAHIROTH • The place on the western shore of the Red Sea where Pharaoh overtook the Israelites.

Nu 33:7–8

Ex 14:2 — Speak unto the children of Israel, that they turn and encamp before Pi-hahiroth, between Migdol and the sea, over against Baal-zephon: before it shall ye encamp by the sea.

Ex 14:9 — But the Egyptians pursued after them, all the horses *and* chariots of Pharaoh, and his horsemen, and his army, and overtook them encamping by the sea, beside Pi-hahiroth, before Baal-zephon.

PICTURE

Le 26:1 — Ye shall make you no idols nor graven image, neither rear you up a standing image, neither shall ye set up *any* image of stone in your land, to bow down unto it: for I *am* the LORD your God.

Nu 33:52 — Then ye shall drive out all the inhabitants of the land from before you, and destroy all their pictures, and destroy all their molten images, and quite pluck down all their high places:

Pr 25:11 — A word fitly spoken *is like* apples of gold in pictures of silver.

Isa 2:16 — And upon all the ships of Tarshish, and upon all pleasant pictures.

PIECE OF SILVER ⇜See: Silver

PIETY ⇜See: Religion

PIGEON

• Used as sacrifice.

Ge 15:9 — And he said unto him, Take me an heifer of three years old, and a she goat of three years old, and a ram of three years old, and a turtledove, and a young pigeon.

Le 1:14 — And if the burnt sacrifice for his offering to the LORD *be* of fowls, then he shall bring his offering of turtledoves, or of young pigeons.

Le 5:7 — And if he be not able to bring a lamb, then he shall bring for his trespass, which he hath committed, two turtledoves, or two young pigeons, unto the LORD; one for a sin offering, and the other for a burnt offering.

Le 12:8 — And if she be not able to bring a lamb, then she shall bring two turtles, or two young pigeons; the one for the burnt offering, and the other for a sin offering: and the priest shall make an atonement for her, and she shall be clean.

Le 14:22 — And two turtledoves, or two young pigeons, such as he is able to get; and the one shall be a sin offering, and the other a burnt offering.

Lk 2:24 — And to offer a sacrifice according to that which is said in the law of the Lord, A pair of turtledoves, or two young pigeons.

⇜See: Dove, Turtle

PILATE, PONTIUS

• Roman governor of Judaea.

Mt 27:2 — And when they had bound him, they led *him* away, and delivered him to Pontius Pilate the governor.

Lk 3:1 — Now in the fifteenth year of the reign of Tiberius Caesar, Pontius Pilate being governor of Judaea, and Herod being tetrarch of Galilee, and his brother Philip tetrarch of Ituraea and of the region of Trachonitis, and Lysanias the tetrarch of Abilene,

• Causes slaughter of certain Galileans.

Lk 13:1 — There were present at that season some that told him of the Galilaeans, whose blood Pilate had mingled with their sacrifices.

• Tries Jesus and orders his crucifixion.

Mt 27:1–66; Mk 15:1–47; Lk 23:1–56; Jn 18:28–19:42

Ac 3:13 — The God of Abraham, and of Isaac, and of Jacob, the God of our fathers, hath glorified his Son Jesus; whom ye delivered up, and denied him in the presence of Pilate, when he was determined to let *him* go.

Ac 4:27 — For of a truth against thy holy child Jesus, whom thou hast anointed, both Herod, and Pontius Pilate, with the Gentiles, and the people of Israel, were gathered together,

Ac 13:28 — And though they found no cause of death *in him,* yet desired they Pilate that he should be slain.

1Ti 6:13 — I give thee charge in the sight of God, who quickeneth all things, and *before* Christ Jesus, who before Pontius Pilate witnessed a good confession;

• Allows Joseph of Arimathea to take Jesus' body.

Mt 27:57–58; Mk 15:43–45

Lk 23:52 — This *man* went unto Pilate, and begged the body of Jesus.

Jn 19:38 — And after this Joseph of Arimathaea, being a disciple of Jesus, but secretly for fear of the Jews, besought Pilate that he might take away the body of Jesus: and Pilate gave *him* leave. He came therefore, and took the body of Jesus.

PILDASH • Son of Nahor.

Ge 22:22 — And Chesed, and Hazo, and Pildash, and Jidlaph, and Bethuel.

PILEHA • One of those who sealed the covenant with Nehemiah.

Ne 10:24 — Hallohesh, Pileha, Shobek,

PILLAR

• Of Solomon's temple.

1Ki 7:13–22

2Ki 25:17 — The height of the one pillar *was* eighteen cubits, and the chapiter upon it *was* brass: and the height of the chapiter three cubits; and the wreathen work, and pomegranates upon the chapiter round about, all of brass: and like unto these had the second pillar with wreathen work.

• Broken and carried to Babylon.

Jer 52:20–21

2Ki 25:13 — And the pillars of brass that *were* in the house of the LORD, and the bases, and the brasen sea that *was* in the house of the LORD, did the Chaldees break in pieces, and carried the brass of them to Babylon.

Jer 52:17 — Also the pillars of brass that *were* in the house of the LORD, and the bases, and the brasen sea that *was* in the house of the LORD, the Chaldeans brake, and carried all the brass of them to Babylon.

• Of Solomon's palaces.

1Ki 7:6 — And he made a porch of pillars; the length thereof *was* fifty cubits, and the breadth thereof thirty cubits: and the porch was before them: and the *other* pillars and the thick beam *were* before them.

• Used to mark roads.

Jer 31:21 — Set thee up waymarks, make thee high heaps: set thine heart toward the highway, *even* the way *which* thou wentest: turn again, O virgin of Israel, turn again to these thy cities.

• Pillar of salt, Lot's wife turned to.

Ge 19:26 — But his wife looked back from behind him, and she became a pillar of salt.

Lk 17:32 — Remember Lot's wife.

• Monuments erected to commemorate events.

• By Jacob, his vision of angels.

Ge 28:18 — And Jacob rose up early in the morning, and took the stone that he had put *for* his pillows, and set it up *for* a pillar, and poured oil upon the top of it.

Ge 31:13 — I *am* the God of Bethel, where thou anointedst the pillar, *and* where thou vowedst a vow unto me: now arise, get thee out from this land, and return unto the land of thy kindred.

Ge 35:14 — And Jacob set up a pillar in the place where he talked with him, *even* a pillar of stone: and he poured a drink offering thereon, and he poured oil thereon.

• By Jacob, his covenant with Laban.

Ge 31:45 — And Jacob took a stone, and set it up *for* a pillar.

• By Moses, the covenant between Jehovah and Israel.

Ex 24:4 — And Moses wrote all the words of the LORD, and rose up early in the morning, and builded an altar under the hill, and twelve pillars, according to the twelve tribes of Israel.

• By Joshua, the passing over Jordan.

Dt 27:2–6; Jos 4:1–9

Jos 8:30 — Then Joshua built an altar unto the LORD God of Israel in mount Ebal,

• By Joshua, at Shechem.

Jos 24:25–27

Jgs 9:6 — And all the men of Shechem gathered together, and all the house of Millo, and went, and made Abimelech king, by the plain of the pillar that *was* in Shechem.

• By Samuel, the discomfiture of the Philistines.

1Sa 7:12 — Then Samuel took a stone, and set *it* between Mizpeh and Shen, and called the name of it Eben-ezer, saying, Hitherto hath the LORD helped us.

• By Absalom, to keep his name in remembrance.

2Sa 18:18 — Now Absalom in his lifetime had taken and reared up for himself a pillar, which *is* in the king's dale: for he said, I have no son to keep my name in remembrance: and he called the pillar after his own name: and it is called unto this day, Absalom's place.

• As a boundary.

Jos 15:6 — And the border went up to Beth-hogla, and passed along by the north of Beth-arabah; and the border went up to the stone of Bohan the son of Reuben:

Jos 18:17 — And was drawn from the north, and went forth to En-shemesh, and went forth toward Geliloth, which *is* over against the going up of Adummim, and descended to the stone of Bohan the son of Reuben,

• As a waymark.

1Sa 20:19 — And *when* thou hast stayed three days, *then* thou shalt go down quickly, and come to the place where thou didst hide thyself when the business was *in hand,* and shalt remain by the stone Ezel.

• As a landmark.

2Sa 20:8 — When they *were* at the great stone which *is* in Gibeon, Amasa went before them. And Joab's garment that he had put on was girded unto him, and upon it a girdle *with* a sword fastened upon his loins in the sheath thereof; and as he went forth it fell out.

1Ki 1:9 — And Adonijah slew sheep and oxen and fat cattle by the stone of Zoheleth, which *is* by En-rogel, and called all his brethren the king's sons, and all the men of Judah the king's servants:

• Prophecy of one in Egypt.

Isa 19:19 — In that day shall there be an altar to the LORD in the midst of the land of Egypt, and a pillar at the border thereof to the LORD.

• Monuments of idolatry, to be destroyed.

Dt 12:3 — And ye shall overthrow their altars, and break their pillars, and burn their groves with fire; and ye shall hew down the graven images of their gods, and destroy the names of them out of that place.

See: Cloud; pillar of

• Figurative.

Rev 3:12 — Him that overcometh will I make a pillar in the temple of my God, and he shall go no more out: and I will write upon him the name of my God, and the name of the city of my God, *which is* new Jerusalem, which cometh down out of heaven from my God: and *I will write upon him* my new name.

PILLOW

• A cushion.

Ge 28:11 — And he lighted upon a certain place, and tarried there all night, because the sun was set; and he took of the stones of that place, and *put* them for his pillows, and lay down in that place to sleep.

Ge 28:18 — And Jacob rose up early in the morning, and took the stone that he had put *for* his pillows, and set it up *for* a pillar, and poured oil upon the top of it.

1Sa 26:7 — So David and Abishai came to the people by night: and, behold, Saul lay sleeping within the trench, and his spear stuck in the ground at his bolster: but Abner and the people lay round about him.

1Sa 26:11 — The LORD forbid that I should stretch forth mine hand against the LORD'S anointed: but, I pray thee, take thou now the spear that *is* at his bolster, and the cruse of water, and let us go.

1Sa 26:16 — This thing *is* not good that thou hast done. *As* the LORD liveth, ye *are* worthy to die, because ye have not kept your master, the LORD'S anointed. And now see where the king's spear is, and the cruse of water that *was* at his bolster.

• A support for the head.

• Stones used for.

Ge 28:11 — And he lighted upon a certain place, and tarried there all night, because the sun was set; and he took of the stones of that place, and *put* them for his pillows, and lay down in that place to sleep.

Ge 28:18 — And Jacob rose up early in the morning, and took the stone that he had put *for* his pillows, and set it up *for* a pillar, and poured oil upon the top of it.

• Called bolster.

1Sa 26:11–12

1Sa 26:7 — So David and Abishai came to the people by night: and, behold, Saul lay sleeping within the trench, and his spear stuck in the ground at his bolster: but Abner and the people lay round about him.

1Sa 26:16 — This thing *is* not good that thou hast done. *As* the LORD liveth, ye *are* worthy to die, because ye have not kept your master, the LORD's anointed. And now see where the king's spear is, and the cruse of water that *was* at his bolster.

• Made of goats' hair.

1Sa 19:13 — And Michal took an image, and laid *it* in the bed, and put a pillow of goats' *hair* for his bolster, and covered *it* with a cloth.

1Sa 19:16 — And when the messengers were come in, behold, *there was* an image in the bed, with a pillow of goats' *hair* for his bolster.

• Jesus sleeps on.

Mk 4:38 — And he was in the hinder part of the ship, asleep on a pillow: and they awake him, and say unto him, Master, carest thou not that we perish?

• Figurative.

• Of false teachers.

Eze 13:18 — And say, Thus saith the Lord GOD; Woe to the *women* that sew pillows to all armholes, and make kerchiefs upon the head of every stature to hunt souls! Will ye hunt the souls of my people, and will ye save the souls alive *that come* unto you?

Eze 13:20 — Wherefore thus saith the Lord GOD; Behold, I *am* against your pillows, wherewith ye there hunt the souls to make *them* fly, and I will tear them from your arms, and will let the souls go, *even* the souls that ye hunt to make *them* fly.

PILOT

Eze 27:27–29

Eze 27:8 — The inhabitants of Zidon and Arvad were thy mariners: thy wise *men,* O Tyrus, *that* were in thee, were thy pilots.

PILTAI • A priest who returned to Jerusalem from captivity in Babylon.

Ne 12:17 — Of Abijah, Zichri; of Miniamin, of Moadiah, Piltai;

PIN ⇜See: Nail

PINE • A tree.

Ne 8:15 — And that they should publish and proclaim in all their cities, and in Jerusalem, saying, Go forth unto the mount, and fetch olive branches, and pine branches, and myrtle branches, and palm branches, and branches of thick trees, to make booths, as *it is* written.

Isa 41:19 — I will plant in the wilderness the cedar, the shittah tree, and the myrtle, and the oil tree; I will set in the desert the fir tree, *and* the pine, and the box tree together:

Isa 60:13 — The glory of Lebanon shall come unto thee, the fir tree, the pine tree, and the box together, to beautify the place of my sanctuary; and I will make the place of my feet glorious.

PINNACLE

• Of temple.

Mt 4:5 — Then the devil taketh him up into the holy city, and setteth him on a pinnacle of the temple,

PINON • A leader of Edom.

Ge 36:41 — Duke Aholibamah, duke Elah, duke Pinon,

1Ch 1:52 — Duke Aholibamah, duke Elah, duke Pinon,

PIPE

• A wind instrument of music.

• Used in religious services.

1Sa 10:5 — After that thou shalt come to the hill of God, where *is* the garrison of the Philistines: and it shall come to pass, when thou art come thither to the city, that thou shalt meet a company of prophets coming down from the high place with a psaltery, and a tabret, and a pipe, and a harp, before them; and they shall prophesy:

Isa 30:29 — Ye shall have a song, as in the night *when* a holy solemnity is kept; and gladness of heart, as when one goeth with a pipe to come into the mountain of the LORD, to the mighty One of Israel.

⇜See: Music; instruments of

PIRAM

• A king of the Amorites.

• Overcome and slain by Joshua.

Jos 10:16–18, 24–27

Jos 10:3 — Wherefore Adoni-zedek king of Jerusalem sent unto Hoham king of Hebron, and unto Piram king of Jarmuth, and unto Japhia king of Lachish, and unto Debir king of Eglon, saying,

PIRATHON

• A place in the land of Ephraim.

Jgs 12:15 — And Abdon the son of Hillel the Pirathonite died, and was buried in Pirathon in the land of Ephraim, in the mount of the Amalekites.

• Men of.

Jgs 12:13 — And after him Abdon the son of Hillel, a Pirathonite, judged Israel.

2Sa 23:30 — Benaiah the Pirathonite, Hiddai of the brooks of Gaash,

1Ch 11:31 — Ithai the son of Ribai of Gibeah, *that pertained* to the children of Benjamin, Benaiah the Pirathonite,

1Ch 27:14 — The eleventh *captain* for the eleventh month *was* Benaiah the Pirathonite, of the children of Ephraim: and in his course *were* twenty and four thousand.

PIRATHONITE

See: Pirathon

PISGAH

• A ridge or mountain east of the Jordan, opposite to Jericho.

• The Israelites come to.

Nu 21:20 — And from Bamoth *in* the valley, that *is* in the country of Moab, to the top of Pisgah, which looketh toward Jeshimon.

• A boundary of the country assigned to the Reubenites and Gadites.

Dt 3:17 — The plain also, and Jordan, and the coast *thereof,* from Chinnereth even unto the sea of the plain, *even* the salt sea, under Ashdoth-pisgah eastward.

Dt 4:49 — And all the plain on this side Jordan eastward, even unto the sea of the plain, under the springs of Pisgah.

Jos 12:3 — And from the plain to the sea of Chinneroth on the east, and unto the sea of the plain, *even* the salt sea on the east, the way to Beth-jeshimoth; and from the south, under Ashdoth-pisgah:

• Balaam prophesies on.

Nu 23:14–24

• Moses views Palestine from.

Dt 34:1–4

Dt 3:27 — Get thee up into the top of Pisgah, and lift up thine eyes westward, and northward, and southward, and eastward, and behold *it* with thine eyes: for thou shalt not go over this Jordan.

PISIDIA

• A province in Asia Minor.

• Paul visits.

Ac 13:14 — But when they departed from Perga, they came to Antioch in Pisidia, and went into the synagogue on the sabbath day, and sat down.

Ac 14:24 — And after they had passed throughout Pisidia, they came to Pamphylia.

PISON • One of the rivers of Eden.

Ge 2:11 — The name of the first *is* Pison: that *is* it which compasseth the whole land of Havilah, where *there is* gold;

PISPAH • An Asherite.

1Ch 7:38 — And the sons of Jether; Jephunneh, and Pispah, and Ara.

PIT

• Benaiah slays a lion in.

2Sa 23:20 — And Benaiah the son of Jehoiada, the son of a valiant man, of Kabzeel, who had done many acts, he slew two lionlike men of Moab: he went down also and slew a lion in the midst of a pit in time of snow:

• Figurative.

Ps 7:15–16; Ecc 10:1–20

Ps 40:2 — He brought me up also out of an horrible pit, out of the miry clay, and set my feet upon a rock, *and* established my goings.

Ps 57:6 — They have prepared a net for my steps; my soul is bowed down: they have digged a pit before me, into the midst whereof they are fallen *themselves.* Selah.

Ps 69:15 — Let not the waterflood overflow me, neither let the deep swallow me up, and let not the pit shut her mouth upon me.

Ps 119:85 — The proud have digged pits for me, which *are* not after thy law.

Pr 23:27 — For a whore *is* a deep ditch; and a strange woman *is* a narrow pit.

Pr 26:27 — Whoso diggeth a pit shall fall therein: and he that rolleth a stone, it will return upon him.

Pr 28:10 — Whoso causeth the righteous to go astray in an evil way, he shall fall himself into his own pit: but the upright shall have good *things* in possession.

Jer 48:44 — He that fleeth from the fear shall fall into the pit; and he that getteth up out of the pit shall be taken in the snare: for I will bring upon it, *even* upon Moab, the year of their visitation, saith the LORD.

• The bottomless pit.

Rev 9:1–2

Rev 9:11 — And they had a king over them, *which is* the angel of the bottomless pit, whose name in the Hebrew tongue *is* Abaddon, but in the Greek tongue hath *his* name Apollyon.

Rev 11:7 — And when they shall have finished their testimony, the beast that ascendeth out of the bottomless pit shall make war against them, and shall overcome them, and kill them.

Rev 17:8 — The beast that thou sawest was, and is not; and shall ascend out of the bottomless pit, and go into perdition: and they that dwell on the earth shall wonder, whose names were not written in the book of life from the foundation of the world, when they behold the beast that was, and is not, and yet is.

Rev 20:1 — And I saw an angel come down from heaven, having the key of the bottomless pit and a great chain in his hand.

Rev 20:3 — And cast him into the bottomless pit, and shut him up, and set a seal upon him, that he should deceive the nations no more, till the thousand years should be fulfilled: and after that he must be loosed a little season.

PITCH

• An opaque mineral used as a plaster and cement.

Isa 34:9 — And the streams thereof shall be turned into pitch, and the dust thereof into brimstone, and the land thereof shall become burning pitch.

• Used by Noah in the ark.

Ge 6:14 — Make thee an ark of gopher wood; rooms shalt thou make in the ark, and shalt pitch it within and without with pitch.

• In making the ark in which Moses was hidden.

Ex 2:3 — And when she could not longer hide him, she took for him an ark of bulrushes, and daubed it with slime and with pitch, and put the child therein; and she laid *it* in the flags by the river's brink.

↞See: Bitumen

PITCHER

• Earthen.

La 4:2 — The precious sons of Zion, comparable to fine gold, how are they esteemed as earthen pitchers, the work of the hands of the potter!

• Used by Gideon in his battle with the Midianites.

Jgs 7:10–20

PITHOM • A treasure city in lower Egypt.

Ex 1:11 — Therefore they did set over them taskmasters to afflict them with their burdens. And they built for Pharaoh treasure cities, Pithom and Raamses.

PITHON • Son of Micah.

1Ch 8:35 — And the sons of Micah *were,* Pithon, and Melech, and Tarea, and Ahaz.

1Ch 9:41 — And the sons of Micah *were,* Pithon, and Melech, and Tahrea, *and Ahaz.*

PITY

• Of God.

Isa 63:9 — In all their affliction he was afflicted, and the angel of his presence saved them: in his love and in his pity he redeemed them; and he bare them, and carried them all the days of old.

Jas 5:11 — Behold, we count them happy which endure. Ye have heard of the patience of Job, and have seen the end of the Lord; that the Lord is very pitiful, and of tender mercy.

• Of Jesus.

Mk 6:34 — And Jesus, when he came out, saw much people, and was moved with compassion toward them, because they were as sheep not having a shepherd: and he began to teach them many things.

↞See: Jesus, Compassion of

• Not to be shown offenders.

Dt 25:11–12

Dt 7:16 — And thou shalt consume all the people which the LORD thy God shall deliver thee; thine eye shall have no pity upon them: neither shalt thou serve their gods; for that *will be* a snare unto thee.

Dt 13:8 — Thou shalt not consent unto him, nor hearken unto him; neither shall thine eye pity him, neither shalt thou spare, neither shalt thou conceal him:

Dt 19:13 — Thine eye shall not pity him, but thou shalt put away *the guilt of* innocent blood from Israel, that it may go well with thee.

Dt 19:21 — And thine eye shall not pity; *but* life *shall go* for life, eye for eye, tooth for tooth, hand for hand, foot for foot.

↞See: Mercy

• Instances of.

• The master of the impecunious servant.

Mt 18:27

PLAGUE

• As a judgment on the Egyptians.

Ps 105:1–45; 135:8–9

Ac 7:36 — He brought them out, after that he had shewed wonders and signs in the land of Egypt, and in the Red sea, and in the wilderness forty years.

• The plague of blood.

Ex 7:14–25

• The plague of frogs.

Ex 8:1–15

• The plague of lice.

Ex 8:16–19

• The plague of flies.

Ex 8:20 — And the LORD said unto Moses, Rise up early in the morning, and stand before Pharaoh; lo, he cometh forth to the water; and say unto him, Thus saith the LORD, Let my people go, that they may serve me.

• On cattle.

Ex 9:1–7

• Of boils and blains.

Ex 9:8–12

• Of hail.

Ex 9:18–34

• Of locusts.

Ex 10:1–20

• Of darkness.

Ex 10:21–23

• Death of the firstborn.

Ex 11:4–7; 12:29–30

Ex 12:17 — And ye shall observe *the feast of* unleavened bread; for in this selfsame day have I brought your armies out of the land of Egypt: therefore shall ye observe this day in your generations by an ordinance for ever.

• On the Israelites.

• On account of idolatry.

Ex 32:35 — And the LORD plagued the people, because they made the calf, which Aaron made.

• After eating quail.

Nu 11:33 — And while the flesh *was* yet between their teeth, ere it was chewed, the wrath of the

Lord was kindled against the people, and the Lord smote the people with a very great plague.

- **After refusing to enter the promised land.**

Nu 14:37 — Even those men that did bring up the evil report upon the land, died by the plague before the Lord.

- **After murmuring on account of the destruction of Korah.**

Nu 16:41–50

- **After murmuring on account of serpents.**

Nu 21:6 — And the Lord sent fiery serpents among the people, and they bit the people; and much people of Israel died.

- **After murmuring for the sin of Peor.**

Jos 22:17 — *Is* the iniquity of Peor too little for us, from which we are not cleansed until this day, although there was a plague in the congregation of the Lord,

- **After murmuring on account of David's sin.**

2Sa 24:10–25

- **On the Philistines.**

1Sa 6:4–5

- **Denounced as a judgment.**

Le 26:21 — And if ye walk contrary unto me, and will not hearken unto me; I will bring seven times more plagues upon you according to your sins.

Dt 28:59 — Then the Lord will make thy plagues wonderful, and the plagues of thy seed, *even* great plagues, and of long continuance, and sore sicknesses, and of long continuance.

- **Foretold.**

Rev 15:6–16:21; 22:18–19

Rev 11:6 — These have power to shut heaven, that it rain not in the days of their prophecy: and have power over waters to turn them to blood, and to smite the earth with all plagues, as often as they will.

Rev 15:1 — And I saw another sign in heaven, great and marvellous, seven angels having the seven last plagues; for in them is filled up the wrath of God.

See: Judgments

See: Pestilence

PLAN OF SALVATION

See: Jesus, Mission of

See: Redemption

See: Salvation

PLANE • A tool.

Isa 44:13 — The carpenter stretcheth out *his* rule; he marketh it out with a line; he fitteth it with planes, and he marketh it out with the compass, and maketh it after the figure of a man, according to the beauty of a man; that it may remain in the house.

PLANET

See: Astronomy

See: Stars

PLANTS • See: Botany

PLASTER

Le 14:42–43

Le 14:48 — And if the priest shall come in, and look *upon it,* and, behold, the plague hath not spread in the house, after the house was plaistered: then the priest shall pronounce the house clean, because the plague is healed.

Dt 27:2 — And it shall be on the day when ye shall pass over Jordan unto the land which the Lord thy God giveth thee, that thou shalt set thee up great stones, and plaister them with plaister:

Da 5:5 — In the same hour came forth fingers of a man's hand, and wrote over against the candlestick upon the plaister of the wall of the king's palace: and the king saw the part of the hand that wrote.

PLEADING

Dt 17:8 — If there arise a matter too hard for thee in judgment, between blood and blood, between plea and plea, and between stroke and stroke, *being* matters of controversy within thy gates: then shalt thou arise, and get thee up into the place which the Lord thy God shall choose;

- **Of the guilty.**

Jos 7:19–21

- **Jesus declined to plead.**

Jn 18:33–34

Mt 26:62 — And the high priest arose, and said unto him, Answerest thou nothing? what *is it which* these witness against thee?

Mk 15:2 — And Pilate asked him, Art thou the King of the Jews? And he answering said unto him, Thou sayest *it.*

Lk 23:3 — And Pilate asked him, saying, Art thou the King of the Jews? And he answered him and said, Thou sayest *it.*

- **Prisoners required to plead.**

Ac 7:1 — Then said the high priest, Are these things so?

See: Defense

PLEASURE

- **Worldly.**

Job 20:12–16; 21:12–13; Ecc 2:1–13; Isa 5:11–12; 22:12–13; 47:8–9

Pr 9:17 — Stolen waters are sweet, and bread *eaten* in secret is pleasant.

Pr 15:21 — Folly *is* joy to *him that is* destitute of wisdom: but a man of understanding walketh uprightly.

Pr 21:17 — He that loveth pleasure *shall be* a poor man: he that loveth wine and oil shall not be rich.

Ecc 1:17 — And I gave my heart to know wisdom, and to know madness and folly: I perceived that this also is vexation of spirit.

Am 6:1 — Woe to them *that are* at ease in Zion, and trust in the mountain of Samaria, *which are* named chief of the nations, to whom the house of Israel came!

Lk 8:14 — And that which fell among thorns are they, which, when they have heard, go forth, and are choked with cares and riches and pleasures of *this* life, and bring no fruit to perfection.

Ro 1:32 — Who knowing the judgment of God, that they which commit such things are worthy of death, not only do the same, but have pleasure in them that do them.

2Th 2:12 — That they all might be damned who believed not the truth, but had pleasure in unrighteousness.

1Ti 5:6 — But she that liveth in pleasure is dead while she liveth.

2Ti 3:4 — Traitors, heady, highminded, lovers of pleasures more than lovers of God;

Tit 3:3 — For we ourselves also were sometimes foolish, disobedient, deceived, serving divers lusts and pleasures, living in malice and envy, hateful, *and* hating one another.

Heb 11:16 — But now they desire a better *country,* that is, an heavenly: wherefore God is not ashamed to be called their God: for he hath prepared for them a city.

Heb 11:25 — Choosing rather to suffer affliction with the people of God, than to enjoy the pleasures of sin for a season;

2Pe 2:13 — And shall receive the reward of unrighteousness, *as* they that count it pleasure to riot in the daytime. Spots *they are* and blemishes, sporting themselves with their own deceivings while they feast with you;

See: Happiness

See: Joy

See: Worldliness

PLEDGE

Ge 38:17–20

• Creditor must not enter the house of a debtor to take.

Dt 24:10–13

See: Pawn

See: Surety

PLEIADES

Job 9:9 — Which maketh Arcturus, Orion, and Pleiades, and the chambers of the south.

Job 38:31 — Canst thou bind the sweet influences of Pleiades, or loose the bands of Orion?

Am 5:8 — *Seek him* that maketh the seven stars and Orion, and turneth the shadow of death into the morning, and maketh the day dark with night: that calleth for the waters of the sea, and poureth them out upon the face of the earth: The LORD *is* his name:

PLOW

• Shares of, sharpened by smiths of the Philistines.

1Sa 13:20 — But all the Israelites went down to the Philistines, to sharpen every man his share, and his coulter, and his axe, and his mattock.

• Used by Elisha with twelve yoke of oxen.

1Ki 19:19 — So he departed thence, and found Elisha the son of Shaphat, who *was* plowing *with* twelve yoke *of oxen* before him, and he with the twelfth: and Elijah passed by him, and cast his mantle upon him.

• By Job's servants.

Job 1:14 — And there came a messenger unto Job, and said, The oxen were plowing, and the asses feeding beside them:

• Figurative.

• Of afflictions.

Ps 129:3 — The plowers plowed upon my back: they made long their furrows.

PLOWSHARE

Isa 2:4 — And he shall judge among the nations, and shall rebuke many people: and they shall beat their swords into plowshares, and their spears into pruninghooks: nation shall not lift up sword against nation, neither shall they learn war any more.

Joel 3:10 — Beat your plowshares into swords, and your pruninghooks into spears: let the weak say, I *am* strong.

Mic 4:3 — And he shall judge among many people, and rebuke strong nations afar off; and they shall beat their swords into plowshares, and their spears into pruninghooks: nation shall not lift up a sword against nation, neither shall they learn war any more.

PLUMMET

Am 7:7–8

Zec 4:10 — For who hath despised the day of small things? for they shall rejoice, and shall see the plummet in the hand of Zerubbabel *with* those seven; they *are* the eyes of the LORD, which run to and fro through the whole earth.

• Figurative.

Isa 28:17 — Judgment also will I lay to the line, and righteousness to the plummet: and the hail shall sweep away the refuge of lies, and the waters shall overflow the hiding place.

POCHERETH • The ancestor of a family which returned to Jerusalem from captivity in Babylon.

Ezr 2:57 — The children of Shephatiah, the children of Hattil, the children of Pochereth of Zebaim, the children of Ami.

Ne 7:59 — The children of Shephatiah, the children of Hattil, the children of Pochereth of Zebaim, the children of Amon.

POET

• Greek.

Ac 17:28 — For in him we live, and move, and have our being; as certain also of your own poets have said, For we are also his offspring.

Tit 1:12 — One of themselves, *even* a prophet of their own, said, The Cretians *are* alway liars, evil beasts, slow bellies.

See: Poetry

See: Psalms

See: Song

POETRY

• **Acrostic.**

Ps 25:1–22; 34:1–22; 37:1–40; 111:1–112:10; 119:1–176; 145:1–21; Pr 31:10–31; La 1:1–5:22

• **Didactic.**

• **Moses' song.**

Dt 32:1–52

• **The Book of Job; the Proverbs; the Song of Solomon; the books of prophecy.**

⇝See: Psalms; didactic

• **Elegy.**

• **On the death of Saul.**

2Sa 1:19–27

• **Of Abner.**

2Sa 3:33–34

⇝See: Elegy

• **Epic.**

• **Moses' song.**

Ex 15:1–19

• **Miriam's song.**

Ex 15:21 — And Miriam answered them, Sing ye to the LORD, for he hath triumphed gloriously; the horse and his rider hath he thrown into the sea.

• **Song of Deborah.**

Jgs 5:1–31

• **Lyrics, sacred.**

• **Moses' and Miriam's songs.**

Ex 15:1–27

• **Hannah's song.**

1Sa 2:1–10

• **The song of Elisabeth.**

Lk 1:42–45

• **Of Mary.**

Lk 1:46–55

• **Of Zacharias.**

Ps 1:1–6; Lk 1:68–79

POLICY ⇝See: Diplomacy

POLITICS, STATECRAFT

• **Corruption in.**

Ps 12:8 — The wicked walk on every side, when the vilest men are exalted.

• **In the court of Ahasuerus.**

Est 3:1–15

• **Of Darius.**

Da 6:4–15

• **Instances of.**

• **Absalom, electioneering for the throne.**

2Sa 15:2–6

• **Pilate, condemning Jesus to gratify popular clamor.**

Mt 27:23–27; Lk 23:13–25; Jn 18:38–39; 19:4–13

Mk 15:15 — And *so* Pilate, willing to content the people, released Barabbas unto them, and delivered Jesus, when he had scourged *him,* to be crucified.

• **Ministers in.**

• **Zadok the priest, a partisan of David.**

2Sa 15:24–29

• **Nathan, the prophet, influences the selection of David's successor.**

1Ki 1:11–40

• **Women in.**

• **The wise woman of Abel, who saved the city through diplomacy.**

2Sa 20:16–22

• **Bath-sheba, in securing the crown for Solomon.**

1Ki 1:15–21

• **Herodias, in influencing the administration of Herod.**

Mt 14:3–11; Mk 6:17–28

• **Mother of Zebedee's children, in seeking favor for her sons.**

Mt 20:20–23

• **For influence in.**

⇝See: Diplomacy

⇝See: Government

⇝See: Influence; political

POLL TAX ⇝See: Tax

POLYGAMY

• **Forbidden.**

Mal 2:14–15; Mt 19:4–5; Mk 10:2–8

Le 18:18 — Neither shalt thou take a wife to her sister, to vex *her,* to uncover her nakedness, beside the other in her life *time.*

Dt 17:17 — Neither shall he multiply wives to himself, that his heart turn not away: neither shall he greatly multiply to himself silver and gold.

1Ti 3:2 — A bishop then must be blameless, the husband of one wife, vigilant, sober, of good behaviour, given to hospitality, apt to teach;

1Ti 3:12 — Let the deacons be the husbands of one wife, ruling their children and their own houses well.

Tit 1:6 — If any be blameless, the husband of one wife, having faithful children not accused of riot or unruly.

• **Authorized.**

2Sa 12:8 — And I gave thee thy master's house, and thy master's wives into thy bosom, and gave thee the house of Israel and of Judah; and if *that had been* too little, I would moreover have given unto thee such and such things.

• **Tolerated.**

Ex 21:10 — If he take him another *wife;* her food, her raiment, and her duty of marriage, shall he not diminish.

1Sa 1:2 — And he had two wives; the name of the one *was* Hannah, and the name of the other Peninnah: and Peninnah had children, but Hannah had no children.

2Ch 24:3 — And Jehoiada took for him two wives; and he begat sons and daughters.

- **Practiced.**
  Job 27:15 — Those that remain of him shall be buried in death: and his widows shall not weep.
  - **By Lamech.**
    Ge 4:19 — And Lamech took unto him two wives: the name of the one *was* Adah, and the name of the other Zillah.
  - **By Abraham.**
    Ge 16:1–16
  - **By Esau.**
    Ge 26:34 — And Esau was forty years old when he took to wife Judith the daughter of Beeri the Hittite, and Bashemath the daughter of Elon the Hittite:
    Ge 28:9 — Then went Esau unto Ishmael, and took unto the wives which he had Mahalath the daughter of Ishmael Abraham's son, the sister of Nebajoth, to be his wife.
  - **By Jacob.**
    Ge 29:30 — And he went in also unto Rachel, and he loved also Rachel more than Leah, and served with him yet seven other years.
  - **By Ashur.**
    1Ch 4:5 — And Ashur the father of Tekoa had two wives, Helah and Naarah.
  - **By Gideon.**
    Jgs 8:30 — And Gideon had threescore and ten sons of his body begotten: for he had many wives.
  - **By Elkanah.**
    1Sa 1:2 — And he had two wives; the name of the one *was* Hannah, and the name of the other Peninnah: and Peninnah had children, but Hannah had no children.
  - **By David.**
    1Sa 25:39–44; 2Sa 3:2–5
    2Sa 5:13 — And David took *him* more concubines and wives out of Jerusalem, after he was come from Hebron: and there were yet sons and daughters born to David.
    1Ch 14:3 — And David took more wives at Jerusalem: and David begat more sons and daughters.
  - **By Solomon.**
    1Ki 11:1–8
  - **By Rehoboam.**
    2Ch 11:18–23
  - **By Abijah.**
    2Ch 13:21 — But Abijah waxed mighty, and married fourteen wives, and begat twenty and two sons, and sixteen daughters.
  - **By Jehoram.**
    2Ch 21:14 — Behold, with a great plague will the LORD smite thy people, and thy children, and thy wives, and all thy goods:
  - **By Joash.**
    2Ch 24:3 — And Jehoiada took for him two wives; and he begat sons and daughters.
  - **By Ahab.**
    2Ki 10:1 — And Ahab had seventy sons in Samaria. And Jehu wrote letters, and sent to Samaria, unto the rulers of Jezreel, to the elders, and to them that brought up Ahab's *children,* saying,
  - **By Jehoiachin.**
    2Ki 24:15 — And he carried away Jehoiachin to Babylon, and the king's mother, and the king's wives, and his officers, and the mighty of the land, *those* carried he into captivity from Jerusalem to Babylon.
  - **By Belshazzar.**
    1Ch 2:1–8:40
    Da 5:2 — Belshazzar, whiles he tasted the wine, commanded to bring the golden and silver vessels which his father Nebuchadnezzar had taken out of the temple which *was* in Jerusalem; that the king, and his princes, his wives, and his concubines, might drink therein.
  - **By Hosea.**
    Hos 3:1–2
- **Mosaic law, respecting the firstborn in.**
  Dt 21:15–17
- **Sought by women.**
  Isa 4:1 — And in that day seven women shall take hold of one man, saying, We will eat our own bread, and wear our own apparel: only let us be called by thy name, to take away our reproach.
- **The evil effects of.**
  - **Husband's favoritism in.**
    Dt 21:15–17
  - **Jacob's.**
    Ge 29:30 — And he went in also unto Rachel, and he loved also Rachel more than Leah, and served with him yet seven other years.
    Ge 30:15 — And she said unto her, *Is it* a small matter that thou hast taken my husband? and wouldest thou take away my son's mandrakes also? And Rachel said, Therefore he shall lie with thee to night for thy son's mandrakes.
  - **Elkanah's.**
    1Sa 1:5 — But unto Hannah he gave a worthy portion; for he loved Hannah: but the LORD had shut up her womb.
  - **Rehoboam's.**
    2Ch 11:21 — And Rehoboam loved Maachah the daughter of Absalom above all his wives and his concubines: (for he took eighteen wives, and threescore concubines; and begat twenty and eight sons, and threescore daughters.)
  - **Domestic infelicity.**
    - **In Abraham's family.**
      Ge 16:1–16; 21:9–16
    - **In Jacob's family.**
      Ge 29:30–34; 30:1–23
    - **In Elkanah's family.**
      1Sa 1:4–7
  - **Upon Solomon.**
    1Ki 11:4–8

See: Concubinage

See: Marriage

POLYTHEISM

Ge 31:19 — And Laban went to shear his sheep: and Rachel had stolen the images that *were* her father's.

Ge 35:2 — Then Jacob said unto his household, and to all that *were* with him, Put away the strange gods that *are* among you, and be clean, and change your garments:

Ge 35:4 — And they gave unto Jacob all the strange gods which *were* in their hand, and *all their* earrings which *were* in their ears; and Jacob hid them under the oak which *was* by Shechem.

Jos 24:2 — And Joshua said unto all the people, Thus saith the LORD God of Israel, Your fathers dwelt on the other side of the flood in old time, *even* Terah, the father of Abraham, and the father of Nachor: and they served other gods.

Jos 24:23 — Now therefore put away, *said he,* the strange gods which *are* among you, and incline your heart unto the LORD God of Israel.

Jgs 2:13 — And they forsook the LORD, and served Baal and Ashtaroth.

Jgs 3:7 — And the children of Israel did evil in the sight of the LORD, and forgat the LORD their God, and served Baalim and the groves.

Jgs 10:16 — And they put away the strange gods from among them, and served the LORD: and his soul was grieved for the misery of Israel.

Jgs 17:5 — And the man Micah had an house of gods, and made an ephod, and teraphim, and consecrated one of his sons, who became his priest.

Jer 2:28 — But where *are* thy gods that thou hast made thee? let them arise, if they can save thee in the time of thy trouble: for *according to* the number of thy cities are thy gods, O Judah.

Jer 11:13 — For *according to* the number of thy cities were thy gods, O Judah; and *according to* the number of the streets of Jerusalem have ye set up altars to *that* shameful thing, *even* altars to burn incense unto Baal.

Da 4:8 — But at the last Daniel came in before me, whose name *was* Belteshazzar, according to the name of my god, and in whom is the spirit of the holy gods: and before him I told the dream, *saying,*

1Co 8:5 — For though there be that are called gods, whether in heaven or in earth, (as there be gods many, and lords many,)

POMEGRANATE

• A fruit.

• Abounded in the land of Canaan.

1Sa 14:2 — And Saul tarried in the uttermost part of Gibeah under a pomegranate tree which is in Migron: and the people that *were* with him *were* about six hundred men;

• Brought by the spies to show the fruitfulness of the land of Canaan.

Nu 13:23 — And they came unto the brook of Eshcol, and cut down from thence a branch with one cluster of grapes, and they bare it between two upon a staff; and *they brought* of the pomegranates, and of the figs.

• Figures of the fruits of, were embroidered on the ephod.

Ex 28:33–34

Ex 39:24 — And they made upon the hems of the robe pomegranates *of* blue, and purple, and scarlet, *and* twined *linen.*

• Figures of the fruits of, were carved on the pillars of the temple.

Jer 52:22–23

1Ki 7:18 — And he made the pillars, and two rows round about upon the one network, to cover the chapiters that *were* upon the top, with pomegranates: and so did he for the other chapiter.

1Ki 7:20 — And the chapiters upon the two pillars *had pomegranates* also above, over against the belly which *was* by the network: and the pomegranates *were* two hundred in rows round about upon the other chapiter.

1Ki 7:42 — And four hundred pomegranates for the two networks, *even* two rows of pomegranates for one network, to cover the two bowls of the chapiters that *were* upon the pillars;

• Wine made of.

SS 8:2 — I would lead thee, *and* bring thee into my mother's house, *who* would instruct me: I would cause thee to drink of spiced wine of the juice of my pomegranate.

PONTIUS See: Pilate, Pontius

PONTUS

• A province of Asia Minor.

Ac 2:9 — Parthians, and Medes, and Elamites, and the dwellers in Mesopotamia, and in Judaea, and Cappadocia, in Pontus, and Asia,

1Pe 1:1 — Peter, an apostle of Jesus Christ, to the strangers scattered throughout Pontus, Galatia, Cappadocia, Asia, and Bithynia,

• Aquila lived in.

Ac 18:2 — And found a certain Jew named Aquila, born in Pontus, lately come from Italy, with his wife Priscilla; (because that Claudius had commanded all Jews to depart from Rome:) and came unto them.

POOL

• Of Samaria.

1Ki 22:38 — And *one* washed the chariot in the pool of Samaria; and the dogs licked up his blood; and they washed his armour; according unto the word of the LORD which he spake.

• Of Jerusalem, upper pool.

2Ki 18:17 — And the king of Assyria sent Tartan and Rabsaris and Rab-shakeh from Lachish to king Hezekiah with a great host against Jerusalem. And they went up and came to Jerusalem. And when they were come up, they came and stood by the conduit of the upper pool, which is in the highway of the fuller's field.

Isa 36:2 — And the king of Assyria sent Rabshakeh from Lachish to Jerusalem unto king Hezekiah with a great army. And he stood by the conduit of the upper pool in the highway of the fuller's field.

• Of Jerusalem, lower pool.

Isa 22:9 — Ye have seen also the breaches of the city of David, that they are many: and ye gathered together the waters of the lower pool.

• Of Siloah.

Ne 3:15 — But the gate of the fountain repaired Shallun the son of Col-hozeh, the ruler of part of Mizpah; he built it, and covered it, and set up the doors thereof, the locks thereof, and the bars thereof, and the wall of the pool of Siloah by the king's garden, and unto the stairs that go down from the city of David.

Jn 9:7 — And said unto him, Go, wash in the pool of Siloam, (which is by interpretation, Sent.) He went his way therefore, and washed, and came seeing.

Jn 9:11 — He answered and said, A man that is called Jesus made clay, and anointed mine eyes, and said unto me, Go to the pool of Siloam, and wash: and I went and washed, and I received sight.

• Of Heshbon.

SS 7:4 — Thy neck *is* as a tower of ivory; thine eyes *like* the fishpools in Heshbon, by the gate of Bath-rabbim: thy nose *is* as the tower of Lebanon which looketh toward Damascus.

POOR

• Atonement money of, uniform with that of the rich.

Ex 30:15 — The rich shall not give more, and the poor shall not give less than half a shekel, when *they* give an offering unto the LORD, to make an atonement for your souls.

• Inexpensive offerings of the impecunious.

Le 14:21–22

Le 5:7 — And if he be not able to bring a lamb, then he shall bring for his trespass, which he hath committed, two turtledoves, or two young pigeons, unto the LORD; one for a sin offering, and the other for a burnt offering.

Le 12:8 — And if she be not able to bring a lamb, then she shall bring two turtles, or two young pigeons; the one for the burnt offering, and the other for a sin offering: and the priest shall make an atonement for her, and she shall be clean.

See: Alms

See: Beneficence

See: Liberality

See: Orphan

See: Poverty

See: Rich

See: Riches

See: Widow

• Unclassified scripture relating to.

Job 29:11–13, 15–16; 31:15–22; Ps 82:3–4; Pr 13:7–8; 14:20–21; Ecc 9:15–16; Mk 12:43–44; Lk 6:30–35; 16:20–21; Jas 1:9–10

Ex 23:3 — Neither shalt thou countenance a poor man in his cause.

Ex 23:6 — Thou shalt not wrest the judgment of thy poor in his cause.

Le 19:15 — Ye shall do no unrighteousness in judgment: thou shalt not respect the person of the poor, nor honour the person of the mighty: *but* in righteousness shalt thou judge thy neighbour.

1Sa 2:7 — The LORD maketh poor, and maketh rich: he bringeth low, and lifteth up.

Ne 8:10 — Then he said unto them, Go your way, eat the fat, and drink the sweet, and send portions unto them for whom nothing is prepared: for *this* day *is* holy unto our Lord: neither be ye sorry; for the joy of the LORD is your strength.

Ne 8:12 — And all the people went their way to eat, and to drink, and to send portions, and to make great mirth, because they had understood the words that were declared unto them.

Job 30:25 — Did not I weep for him that was in trouble? was *not* my soul grieved for the poor?

Job 34:19 — *How much less to him* that accepteth not the persons of princes, nor regardeth the rich more than the poor? for they all *are* the work of his hands.

Ps 37:16 — A little that a righteous man hath *is* better than the riches of many wicked.

Ps 109:16 — Because that he remembered not to shew mercy, but persecuted the poor and needy man, that he might even slay the broken in heart.

Pr 10:15 — The rich man's wealth *is* his strong city: the destruction of the poor *is* their poverty.

Pr 13:23 — Much food *is in* the tillage of the poor: but there is *that is* destroyed for want of judgment.

Pr 14:31 — He that oppresseth the poor reproacheth his Maker: but he that honoureth him hath mercy on the poor.

Pr 18:23 — The poor useth intreaties; but the rich answereth roughly.

Pr 19:1 — Better *is* the poor that walketh in his integrity, than *he that is* perverse in his lips, and is a fool.

Pr 19:4 — Wealth maketh many friends; but the poor is separated from his neighbour.

Pr 19:7 — All the brethren of the poor do hate him: how much more do his friends go far from him? he pursueth *them with* words, *yet* they *are* wanting *to him.*

Pr 19:17 — He that hath pity upon the poor lendeth unto the LORD; and that which he hath given will he pay him again.

Pr 19:22 — The desire of a man *is* his kindness: and a poor man *is* better than a liar.

Pr 20:13 — Love not sleep, lest thou come to poverty; open thine eyes, *and* thou shalt be satisfied with bread.

Pr 21:13 — Whoso stoppeth his ears at the cry of the poor, he also shall cry himself, but shall not be heard.

Pr 22:2 — The rich and poor meet together: the LORD *is* the maker of them all.

Pr 22:9 — He that hath a bountiful eye shall be blessed; for he giveth of his bread to the poor.

Pr 23:21 — For the drunkard and the glutton shall come to poverty: and drowsiness shall clothe *a man* with rags.

Pr 28:6 — Better *is* the poor that walketh in his uprightness, than *he that is* perverse *in his* ways, though he *be* rich.

Pr 28:8 — He that by usury and unjust gain increaseth his substance, he shall gather it for him that will pity the poor.

Pr 28:11 — The rich man *is* wise in his own conceit; but the poor that hath understanding searcheth him out.

Pr 28:19 — He that tilleth his land shall have plenty of bread: but he that followeth after vain *persons* shall have poverty enough.

Pr 29:14 — The king that faithfully judgeth the poor, his throne shall be established for ever.

Ecc 4:6 — Better *is* an handful *with* quietness, than both the hands full *with* travail and vexation of spirit.

Ecc 4:13 — Better *is* a poor and a wise child than an old and foolish king, who will no more be admonished.

Ecc 6:8 — For what hath the wise more than the fool? what hath the poor, that knoweth to walk before the living?

Jer 22:16 — He judged the cause of the poor and needy; then *it was* well *with him: was* not this to know me? saith the LORD.

Eze 16:49 — Behold, this was the iniquity of thy sister Sodom, pride, fulness of bread, and abundance of idleness was in her and in her daughters, neither did she strengthen the hand of the poor and needy.

Mt 25:42 — For I was an hungred, and ye gave me no meat: I was thirsty, and ye gave me no drink:

Mt 25:45 — Then shall he answer them, saying, Verily I say unto you, Inasmuch as ye did *it* not to one of the least of these, ye did *it* not to me.

Mt 26:11 — For ye have the poor always with you; but me ye have not always.

Mk 14:7 — For ye have the poor with you always, and whensoever ye will ye may do them good: but me ye have not always.

Jn 12:6 — This he said, not that he cared for the poor; but because he was a thief, and had the bag, and bare what was put therein.

• Duty to.

Ex 22:25–27; Le 19:9–10; 25:25–28, 35–37, 39–43; Dt 14:28–29; 15:2–14; 24:12–21; 26:12–13; Ps 41:1–3; 112:4–5; Isa 16:3–4; Eze 18:1–32; Mt 25:35–36; Lk 14:12–14; 1Co 16:1–2; 2Co 9:1–15; 1Ti 5:9–10; Jas 2:2–9, 15–16; 1Jn 3:17–19

Ex 23:11 — But the seventh *year* thou shalt let it rest and lie still; that the poor of thy people may eat: and what they leave the beasts of the field shall eat. In like manner thou shalt deal with thy vineyard, *and* with thy oliveyard.

Le 23:22 — And when ye reap the harvest of your land, thou shalt not make clean riddance of the corners of thy field when thou reapest, neither shalt thou gather any gleaning of thy harvest: thou shalt leave them unto the poor, and to the stranger: I *am* the LORD your God.

Ne 8:10 — Then he said unto them, Go your way, eat the fat, and drink the sweet, and send portions unto them for whom nothing is prepared: for *this* day *is* holy unto our Lord: neither be ye sorry; for the joy of the LORD is your strength.

Ps 37:21 — The wicked borroweth, and payeth not again: but the righteous sheweth mercy, and giveth.

Ps 37:26 — *He is* ever merciful, and lendeth; and his seed *is* blessed.

Ps 112:9 — He hath dispersed, he hath given to the poor; his righteousness endureth for ever; his horn shall be exalted with honour.

Pr 28:27 — He that giveth unto the poor shall not lack: but he that hideth his eyes shall have many a curse.

Pr 29:7 — The righteous considereth the cause of the poor: *but* the wicked regardeth not to know *it.*

Pr 31:9 — Open thy mouth, judge righteously, and plead the cause of the poor and needy.

Pr 31:20 — She stretcheth out her hand to the poor; yea, she reacheth forth her hands to the needy.

Isa 1:17 — Learn to do well; seek judgment, relieve the oppressed, judge the fatherless, plead for the widow.

Isa 58:7 — *Is it* not to deal thy bread to the hungry, and that thou bring the poor that are cast out to thy house? when thou seest the naked, that thou cover him; and that thou hide not thyself from thine own flesh?

Isa 58:10 — And *if* thou draw out thy soul to the hungry, and satisfy the afflicted soul; then shall thy light rise in obscurity, and thy darkness *be* as the noonday:

Da 4:27 — Wherefore, O king, let my counsel be acceptable unto thee, and break off thy sins by righteousness, and thine iniquities by shewing mercy to the poor; if it may be a lengthening of thy tranquility.

Zec 7:10 — And oppress not the widow, nor the fatherless, the stranger, nor the poor; and let none of you imagine evil against his brother in your heart.

Mt 5:42 — Give to him that asketh thee, and from him that would borrow of thee turn not thou away.

Mt 19:21 — Jesus said unto him, If thou wilt be perfect, go *and* sell that thou hast, and give to the poor, and thou shalt have treasure in heaven: and come *and* follow me.

Mk 14:7 — For ye have the poor with you always, and whensoever ye will ye may do them good: but me ye have not always.

Lk 3:11 — He answereth and saith unto them, He that hath two coats, let him impart to him that hath none; and he that hath meat, let him do likewise.

Lk 6:30 — Give to every man that asketh of thee; and of him that taketh away thy goods ask *them* not again.

Lk 11:41 — But rather give alms of such things as ye have; and, behold, all things are clean unto you.

Lk 12:33 — Sell that ye have, and give alms; provide yourselves bags which wax not old, a treasure in the heavens that faileth not, where no thief approacheth, neither moth corrupteth.

Lk 18:22 — Now when Jesus heard these things, he said unto him, Yet lackest thou one thing: sell all that thou hast, and distribute unto the poor, and thou shalt have treasure in heaven: and come, follow me.

Lk 19:8 — And Zacchaeus stood, and said unto the Lord; Behold, Lord, the half of my goods I give to the poor; and if I have taken any thing from any man by false accusation, I restore *him* fourfold.

Ac 20:35 — I have shewed you all things, how that so labouring ye ought to support the weak, and to remember the words of the Lord Jesus, how he said, It is more blessed to give than to receive.

Ro 12:8 — Or he that exhorteth, on exhortation: he that giveth, *let him do it* with simplicity; he that ruleth, with diligence; he that sheweth mercy, with cheerfulness.

Ro 12:13 — Distributing to the necessity of saints; given to hospitality.

Ro 12:20 — Therefore if thine enemy hunger, feed him; if he thirst, give him drink: for in so doing thou shalt heap coals of fire on his head.

1Co 13:3 — And though I bestow all my goods to feed *the poor,* and though I give my body to be burned, and have not charity, it profiteth me nothing.

2Co 6:10 — As sorrowful, yet alway rejoicing; as poor, yet making many rich; as having nothing, and *yet* possessing all things.

2Co 8:9 — For ye know the grace of our Lord Jesus Christ, that, though he was rich, yet for your sakes he became poor, that ye through his poverty might be rich.

Gal 2:10 — Only *they would* that we should remember the poor; the same which I also was forward to do.

Gal 6:10 — As we have therefore opportunity, let us do good unto all *men,* especially unto them who are of the household of faith.

Eph 4:28 — Let him that stole steal no more: but rather let him labour, working with *his* hands the thing which is good, that he may have to give to him that needeth.

1Ti 5:16 — If any man or woman that believeth have widows, let them relieve them, and let not the church be charged; that it may relieve them that are widows indeed.

Heb 13:3 — Remember them that are in bonds, as bound with them; *and* them which suffer adversity, as being yourselves also in the body.

Jas 1:27 — Pure religion and undefiled before God and the Father is this, To visit the fatherless and widows in their affliction, *and* to keep himself unspotted from the world.

Jas 5:4 — Behold, the hire of the labourers who have reaped down your fields, which is of you kept back by fraud, crieth: and the cries of them which have reaped are entered into the ears of the Lord of sabaoth.

- **Figurative.**
  - **Poor in spirit.**

Isa 66:2 — For all those *things* hath mine hand made, and all those *things* have been, saith the LORD: but to this *man* will I look, *even* to *him that is* poor and of a contrite spirit, and trembleth at my word.

Mt 5:3 — Blessed *are* the poor in spirit: for theirs is the kingdom of heaven.

Lk 6:20 — And he lifted up his eyes on his disciples, and said, Blessed *be ye* poor: for yours is the kingdom of God.

See: Creditor

See: Debtor

See: Employee

See: Employer

See: Servant

See: Wages

- **God's care of.**

1Sa 2:7–8; Job 5:15–16; 34:18–19; Ps 72:12–14; 113:7–8; Pr 22:22–23; 29:1–27

Job 31:15 — Did not he that made me in the womb make him? and did not one fashion us in the womb?

Job 34:28 — So that they cause the cry of the poor to come unto him, and he heareth the cry of the afflicted.

Job 36:6 — He preserveth not the life of the wicked: but giveth right to the poor.

Job 36:15 — He delivereth the poor in his affliction, and openeth their ears in oppression.

Ps 9:18 — For the needy shall not alway be forgotten: the expectation of the poor shall *not* perish for ever.

Ps 10:14 — Thou hast seen *it;* for thou beholdest mischief and spite, to requite *it* with thy hand: the poor committeth himself unto thee; thou art the helper of the fatherless.

Ps 12:5 — For the oppression of the poor, for the sighing of the needy, now will I arise, saith the LORD; I will set *him* in safety *from him that* puffeth at him.

Ps 14:6 — Ye have shamed the counsel of the poor, because the LORD *is* his refuge.

Ps 34:6 — This poor man cried, and the LORD heard *him,* and saved him out of all his troubles.

Ps 35:10 — All my bones shall say, LORD, who *is* like unto thee, which deliverest the poor from him that is too strong for him, yea, the poor and the needy from him that spoileth him?

Ps 68:10 — Thy congregation hath dwelt therein: thou, O God, hast prepared of thy goodness for the poor.

Ps 69:33 — For the LORD heareth the poor, and despiseth not his prisoners.

Ps 72:2 — He shall judge thy people with righteousness, and thy poor with judgment.

Ps 72:4 — He shall judge the poor of the people, he shall save the children of the needy, and shall break in pieces the oppressor.

Ps 74:21 — O let not the oppressed return ashamed: let the poor and needy praise thy name.

Ps 102:17 — He will regard the prayer of the destitute, and not despise their prayer.

Ps 107:9 — For he satisfieth the longing soul, and filleth the hungry soul with goodness.

Ps 107:36 — And there he maketh the hungry to dwell, that they may prepare a city for habitation;

Ps 107:41 — Yet setteth he the poor on high from affliction, and maketh *him* families like a flock.

Ps 109:31 — For he shall stand at the right hand of the poor, to save *him* from those that condemn his soul.

Ps 132:15 — I will abundantly bless her provision: I will satisfy her poor with bread.

Ps 140:12 — I know that the LORD will maintain the cause of the afflicted, *and* the right of the poor.

Ps 146:5 — Happy *is he* that *hath* the God of Jacob for his help, whose hope *is* in the LORD his God:

Ps 146:7 — Which executeth judgment for the oppressed: which giveth food to the hungry. The LORD looseth the prisoners:

Pr 22:2 — The rich and poor meet together: the LORD *is* the maker of them all.

Ecc 5:8 — If thou seest the oppression of the poor, and violent perverting of judgment and justice in a province, marvel not at the matter: for *he that is* higher than the highest regardeth; and *there be* higher than they.

Isa 11:4 — But with righteousness shall he judge the poor, and reprove with equity for the meek of the earth: and he shall smite the earth with the rod of his mouth, and with the breath of his lips shall he slay the wicked.

Isa 14:30 — And the firstborn of the poor shall feed, and the needy shall lie down in safety: and I will kill thy root with famine, and he shall slay thy remnant.

Isa 14:32 — What shall *one* then answer the messengers of the nation? That the LORD hath founded Zion, and the poor of his people shall trust in it.

Isa 25:4 — For thou hast been a strength to the poor, a strength to the needy in his distress, a refuge from the storm, a shadow from the heat, when the blast of the terrible ones *is* as a storm *against* the wall.

Isa 29:19 — The meek also shall increase *their* joy in the LORD, and the poor among men shall rejoice in the Holy One of Israel.

Isa 41:17 — *When* the poor and needy seek water, and *there is* none, *and* their tongue faileth for thirst, I the LORD will hear them, *I* the God of Israel will not forsake them.

Jer 20:13 — Sing unto the LORD, praise ye the LORD: for he hath delivered the soul of the poor from the hand of evildoers.

Zep 3:12 — I will also leave in the midst of thee an afflicted and poor people, and they shall trust in the name of the LORD.

Zec 11:7 — And I will feed the flock of slaughter, *even* you, O poor of the flock. And I took unto me two staves; the one I called Beauty, and the other I called Bands; and I fed the flock.

Mt 11:5 — The blind receive their sight, and the lame walk, the lepers are cleansed, and the deaf hear, the dead are raised up, and the poor have the gospel preached to them.

Lk 4:18 — The Spirit of the Lord is upon me, because he hath anointed me to preach the gospel to the poor; he hath sent me to heal the brokenhearted, to preach deliverance to the captives, and recovering of sight to the blind, to set at liberty them that are bruised,

Lk 7:22 — Then Jesus answering said unto them, Go your way, and tell John what things ye have seen and heard; how that the blind see, the lame walk, the lepers are cleansed, the deaf hear, the dead are raised, to the poor the gospel is preached.

Lk 16:22 — And it came to pass, that the beggar died, and was carried by the angels into Abraham's bosom: the rich man also died, and was buried;

Jas 2:5 — Hearken, my beloved brethren, Hath not God chosen the poor of this world rich in faith, and heirs of the kingdom which he hath promised to them that love him?

See: God, Goodness of

See: God, Providence of

- **Kindness to.**
  - **Instances of.**
    - **To Ruth.**

      Ru 2:23 — So she kept fast by the maidens of Boaz to glean unto the end of barley harvest and of wheat harvest; and dwelt with her mother in law.
    - **To Ruth, by Boaz.**

      Ru 2:14–16
    - **To the widow of Zorephath.**

      1Ki 17:12–24
    - **Prophet's widow.**

      2Ki 4:1–7
    - **Jews.**

      Est 9:22 — As the days wherein the Jews rested from their enemies, and the month which was turned unto them from sorrow to joy, and from mourning into a good day: that they should make them days of feasting and joy, and of sending portions one to another, and gifts to the poor.
    - **By Job.**

      Job 29:11–16; 31:16–21, 38–40
    - **The Temanites.**

      Isa 21:14 — The inhabitants of the land of Tema brought water to him that was thirsty, they prevented with their bread him that fled.
    - **Nebuzar-adan.**

      Jer 39:10 — But Nebuzar-adan the captain of the guard left of the poor of the people, which had nothing, in the land of Judah, and gave them vineyards and fields at the same time.
    - **The good Samaritan.**

      Lk 10:33–35

• **Zacchaeus.**

Lk 19:8 — And Zacchaeus stood, and said unto the Lord; Behold, Lord, the half of my goods I give to the poor; and if I have taken any thing from any man by false accusation, I restore *him* fourfold.

• **Christian churches.**

Ro 15:25–26; 2Co 8:1–4

Ac 6:1 — And in those days, when the number of the disciples was multiplied, there arose a murmuring of the Grecians against the Hebrews, because their widows were neglected in the daily ministration.

Ac 11:29 — Then the disciples, every man according to his ability, determined to send relief unto the brethren which dwelt in Judaea:

• **Dorcas.**

Ac 9:36 — Now there was at Joppa a certain disciple named Tabitha, which by interpretation is called Dorcas: this woman was full of good works and almsdeeds which she did.

• **Cornelius.**

Ac 10:2 — A devout *man,* and one that feared God with all his house, which gave much alms to the people, and prayed to God alway.

Ac 10:4 — And when he looked on him, he was afraid, and said, What is it, Lord? And he said unto him, Thy prayers and thine alms are come up for a memorial before God.

• **Church at Antioch.**

Ac 11:29–30

• **Paul.**

Ro 15:25 — But now I go unto Jerusalem to minister unto the saints.

• **Churches of Macedonia and Achaia.**

2Co 8:1–5

Ro 15:26 — For it hath pleased them of Macedonia and Achaia to make a certain contribution for the poor saints which are at Jerusalem.

• Oppressions of.

Ne 5:1–13; Job 20:19–21; 22:6–7, 9–11; 24:7–10; Ps 10:8–10; Isa 3:14–15; 10:1–2; 32:6–7; Am 2:6–8; 4:1–2; 5:11–12

Job 24:4 — They turn the needy out of the way: the poor of the earth hide themselves together.

Ps 10:2 — The wicked in *his* pride doth persecute the poor: let them be taken in the devices that they have imagined.

Ps 37:14 — The wicked have drawn out the sword, and have bent their bow, to cast down the poor and needy, *and* to slay such as be of upright conversation.

Pr 14:20 — The poor is hated even of his own neighbour: but the rich *hath* many friends.

Pr 17:5 — Whoso mocketh the poor reproacheth his Maker: *and* he that is glad at calamities shall not be unpunished.

Pr 19:7 — All the brethren of the poor do hate him: how much more do his friends go far from him? he pursueth *them with* words, *yet* they *are* wanting *to him.*

Pr 22:7 — The rich ruleth over the poor, and the borrower *is* servant to the lender.

Pr 22:16 — He that oppresseth the poor to increase his *riches, and* he that giveth to the rich, *shall* surely *come* to want.

Pr 28:3 — A poor man that oppresseth the poor *is like* a sweeping rain which leaveth no food.

Pr 28:15 — *As* a roaring lion, and a ranging bear; *so is* a wicked ruler over the poor people.

Pr 30:14 — *There is* a generation, whose teeth *are as* swords, and their jaw teeth *as* knives, to devour the poor from off the earth, and the needy from *among* men.

Ecc 5:8 — If thou seest the oppression of the poor, and violent perverting of judgment and justice in a province, marvel not at the matter: for *he that is* higher than the highest regardeth; and *there be* higher than they.

Eze 18:12 — Hath oppressed the poor and needy, hath spoiled by violence, hath not restored the pledge, and hath lifted up his eyes to the idols, hath committed abomination,

Eze 22:29 — The people of the land have used oppression, and exercised robbery, and have vexed the poor and needy: yea, they have oppressed the stranger wrongfully.

Am 8:4 — Hear this, O ye that swallow up the needy, even to make the poor of the land to fail,

Am 8:6 — That we may buy the poor for silver, and the needy for a pair of shoes; *yea,* and sell the refuse of the wheat?

Hab 3:14 — Thou didst strike through with his staves the head of his villages: they came out as a whirlwind to scatter me: their rejoicing *was* as to devour the poor secretly.

Jas 2:6 — But ye have despised the poor. Do not rich men oppress you, and draw you before the judgment seats?

See: Poor; duty to

• **Instances of.**

• **The widow's son.**

2Ki 4:1–7

See: Creditor

See: Debtor

See: Servant

See: Wages

POPLAR • A tree.

Ge 30:37 — And Jacob took him rods of green poplar, and of the hazel and chesnut tree; and pilled white strakes in them, and made the white appear which *was* in the rods.

Hos 4:13 — They sacrifice upon the tops of the mountains, and burn incense upon the hills, under oaks and poplars and elms, because the shadow thereof *is* good: therefore your daughters shall commit whoredom, and your spouses shall commit adultery.

POPULAR SINS

• Laws against.

Ex 23:2 — Thou shalt not follow a multitude to *do* evil; neither shalt thou speak in a cause to decline after many to wrest *judgment:*

✧See: Sin

POPULARITY

• Instances of.

• David.

2Sa 3:36

• Absalom.

2Sa 15:2–6, 13

• Job.

Job 29:1–25

PORATHA • Son of Haman.

Est 9:8 — And Poratha, and Adalia, and Aridatha,

PORCH ✧See: Temple

PORCIUS ✧See: Festus

PORNOGRAPHY

Ps 24:3–5; Pr 7:1–27; Tit 1:15–16; 2:11–13

Job 31:1 — I made a covenant with mine eyes; why then should I think upon a maid?

Pr 14:34 — Righteousness exalteth a nation: but sin *is* a reproach to any people.

Mt 5:8 — <u>Blessed *are* the pure in heart: for they shall see God.</u>

Mt 18:6 — <u>But whoso shall offend one of these little ones which believe in me, it were better for him that a millstone were hanged about his neck, and *that* he were drowned in the depth of the sea.</u>

Mt 18:10 — <u>Take heed that ye despise not one of these little ones; for I say unto you, That in heaven their angels do always behold the face of my Father which is in heaven.</u>

Mt 18:14 — <u>Even so it is not the will of your Father which is in heaven, that one of these little ones should perish.</u>

Php 4:8 — Finally, brethren, whatsoever things are true, whatsoever things *are* honest, whatsoever things *are* just, whatsoever things *are* pure, whatsoever things *are* lovely, whatsoever things *are* of good report; if *there be* any virtue, and if *there be* any praise, think on these things.

1Ti 4:12 — Let no man despise thy youth; but be thou an example of the believers, in word, in conversation, in charity, in spirit, in faith, in purity.

2Ti 3:6 — For of this sort are they which creep into houses, and lead captive silly women laden with sins, led away with divers lusts,

PORPOISE

Ex 25:5 — And rams' skins dyed red, and badgers' skins, and shittim wood,

Ex 26:14 — And thou shalt make a covering for the tent *of* rams' skins dyed red, and a covering above *of* badgers' skins.

Ex 36:19 — And he made a covering for the tent *of* rams' skins dyed red, and a covering *of* badgers' skins above *that.*

Ex 39:34 — And the covering of rams' skins dyed red, and the covering of badgers' skins, and the vail of the covering,

PORTERS

• Guards at the city gates, the doors of the king's palace, and doors of the temple.

1Ch 9:17–32

2Ch 34:13 — Also *they were* over the bearers of burdens, and *were* overseers of all that wrought the work in any manner of service: and of the Levites *there were* scribes, and officers, and porters.

2Ch 35:15 — And the singers the sons of Asaph *were* in their place, according to the commandment of David, and Asaph, and Heman, and Jeduthun the king's seer; and the porters *waited* at every gate; they might not depart from their service; for their brethren the Levites prepared for them.

• Lodged round about the temple in order to be present for opening the doors.

1Ch 9:27 — And they lodged round about the house of God, because the charge *was* upon them, and the opening thereof every morning *pertained* to them.

• One-third were porters of the temple.

2Ch 23:4 — This *is* the thing that ye shall do; A third part of you entering on the sabbath, of the priests and of the Levites, *shall be* porters of the doors;

• One-third were porters of the king's house.

2Ch 23:5 — And a third part *shall be* at the king's house; and a third part at the gate of the foundation: and all the people *shall be* in the courts of the house of the LORD.

• One-third were porters of the gate of the foundation.

2Ch 23:5 — And a third part *shall be* at the king's house; and a third part at the gate of the foundation: and all the people *shall be* in the courts of the house of the LORD.

• They served, also, as porters of the gates of the walls.

Ne 12:25 — Mattaniah, and Bakbukiah, Obadiah, Meshullam, Talmon, Akkub, *were* porters keeping the ward at the thresholds of the gates.

• They served in twenty-four courses.

1Ch 26:13–19

• Their posts were determined by lot.

1Ch 26:13–19

1Ch 24:31 — These likewise cast lots over against their brethren the sons of Aaron in the presence of David the king, and Zadok, and Ahimelech, and the chief of the fathers of the priests and Levites, even the principal fathers over against their younger brethren.

POSITIVE

Ro 8:37–39

Ro 12:3 — For I say, through the grace given unto me, to every man that is among you, not to think *of himself* more highly than he ought to think; but to think soberly, according as God hath dealt to every man the measure of faith.

Gal 2:20 — I am crucified with Christ: nevertheless I live; yet not I, but Christ liveth in me: and the life which I now live in the flesh I live by the faith of the Son of God, who loved me, and gave himself for me.

Php 4:13 — I can do all things through Christ which strengtheneth me.

POST

• A bearer of message.

Job 9:25 — Now my days are swifter than a post: they flee away, they see no good.

Jer 51:31 — One post shall run to meet another, and one messenger to meet another, to shew the king of Babylon that his city is taken at *one* end,

• Of Hezekiah.

2Ch 30:6 — So the posts went with the letters from the king and his princes throughout all Israel and Judah, and according to the commandment of the king, saying, Ye children of Israel, turn again unto the LORD God of Abraham, Isaac, and Israel, and he will return to the remnant of you, that are escaped out of the hand of the kings of Assyria.

2Ch 30:10 — So the posts passed from city to city through the country of Ephraim and Manasseh even unto Zebulun: but they laughed them to scorn, and mocked them.

• Of Ahasuerus.

Est 3:13 — And the letters were sent by posts into all the king's provinces, to destroy, to kill, and to cause to perish, all Jews, both young and old, little children and women, in one day, *even* upon the thirteenth *day* of the twelfth month, which *is* the month Adar, and *to take* the spoil of them for a prey.

Est 3:15 — The posts went out, being hastened by the king's commandment, and the decree was given in Shushan the palace. And the king and Haman sat down to drink; but the city Shushan was perplexed.

Est 8:10 — And he wrote in the king Ahasuerus' name, and sealed it with the king's ring, and sent letters by posts on horseback, *and* riders on mules, camels, *and* young dromedaries:

Est 8:14 — *So* the posts that rode upon mules *and* camels went out, being hastened and pressed on by the king's commandment. And the decree was given at Shushan the palace.

POTI-PHERAH

• A priest of On.

• Joseph's father-in-law.

Ge 41:45 — And Pharaoh called Joseph's name Zaphnath-paaneah; and he gave him to wife Asenath the daughter of Poti-pherah priest of On. And Joseph went out over *all* the land of Egypt.

Ge 41:50 — And unto Joseph were born two sons before the years of famine came, which Asenath the daughter of Poti-pherah priest of On bare unto him.

Ge 46:20 — And unto Joseph in the land of Egypt were born Manasseh and Ephraim, which Asenath the daughter of Poti-pherah priest of On bare unto him.

POTIPHAR

• An officer of Pharaoh.

• Joseph's master.

Ge 37:36 — And the Midianites sold him into Egypt unto Potiphar, an officer of Pharaoh's, *and* captain of the guard.

Ge 39:1 — And Joseph was brought down to Egypt; and Potiphar, an officer of Pharaoh, captain of the guard, an Egyptian, bought him of the hands of the Ishmeelites, which had brought him down thither.

POTSHERD • Fragment of earthenware.

Job 2:8 — And he took him a potsherd to scrape himself withal; and he sat down among the ashes.

Isa 45:9 — Woe unto him that striveth with his Maker! *Let* the potsherd *strive* with the potsherds of the earth. Shall the clay say to him that fashioneth it, What makest thou? or thy work, He hath no hands?

POTTERY

• Clay prepared for, by treading.

Isa 41:25 — I have raised up *one* from the north, and he shall come: from the rising of the sun shall he call upon my name: and he shall come upon princes as *upon* morter, and as the potter treadeth clay.

• Vessels made of.

Jer 18:3–4

• Place for manufacture of, outside the wall of Jerusalem, bought as a burying ground for the poor.

Mt 27:7–10

• Figurative.

Isa 64:8 — But now, O LORD, thou *art* our father; we *are* the clay, and thou our potter; and we all *are* the work of thy hand.

Ro 9:21 — Hath not the potter power over the clay, of the same lump to make one vessel unto honour, and another unto dishonour?

• Of weakness, in the idol in Nebuchadnezzar's vision.

Da 2:41 — And whereas thou sawest the feet and toes, part of potters' clay, and part of iron, the kingdom shall be divided; but there shall be in it of the strength of the iron, forasmuch as thou sawest the iron mixed with miry clay.

POUND

• The Hebrew word "maneh" is translated "pound" and is equivalent to about 1lb 14oz.

Ne 7:71–72

1Ki 10:17 — And he made three hundred shields of beaten gold; three pound of gold went to one shield:

and the king put them in the house of the forest of Lebanon.

Ezr 2:69 — They gave after their ability unto the treasure of the work threescore and one thousand drams of gold, and five thousand pound of silver, and one hundred priests' garments.

- **The weight was equivalent to about twelve ounces.**

Jn 12:3 — Then took Mary a pound of ointment of spikenard, very costly, and anointed the feet of Jesus, and wiped his feet with her hair: and the house was filled with the odour of the ointment.

- **The Greek word "mina" is translated "pound," and worth approximately nineteen dollars.**

Lk 19:13–25

See: Measure

See: Weights

POVERTY

Pr 24:33–34; 30:8–9

Pr 6:11 — So shall thy poverty come as one that travelleth, and thy want as an armed man.

Pr 10:15 — The rich man's wealth *is* his strong city: the destruction of the poor *is* their poverty.

Pr 15:16 — Better *is* little with the fear of the LORD than great treasure and trouble therewith.

Pr 16:8 — Better *is* a little with righteousness than great revenues without right.

Pr 20:13 — Love not sleep, lest thou come to poverty; open thine eyes, *and* thou shalt be satisfied with bread.

Pr 23:21 — For the drunkard and the glutton shall come to poverty: and drowsiness shall clothe *a man* with rags.

Pr 28:19 — He that tilleth his land shall have plenty of bread: but he that followeth after vain *persons* shall have poverty enough.

Ecc 4:6 — Better *is* an handful *with* quietness, than both the hands full *with* travail and vexation of spirit.

See: Poor

POWER

- **Spiritual.**

Isa 40:29–31; Jn 7:38–39; Ac 2:2–4; 1Co 1:24–28; 4:19–20; Eph 1:19–20

Ge 32:28 — And he said, Thy name shall be called no more Jacob, but Israel: for as a prince hast thou power with God and with men, and hast prevailed.

Mk 9:29 — And he said unto them, This kind can come forth by nothing, but by prayer and fasting.

Lk 1:17 — And he shall go before him in the spirit and power of Elias, to turn the hearts of the fathers to the children, and the disobedient to the wisdom of the just; to make ready a people prepared for the Lord.

Lk 4:32 — And they were astonished at his doctrine: for his word was with power.

Lk 24:49 — And, behold, I send the promise of my Father upon you: but tarry ye in the city of Jerusalem, until ye be endued with power from on high.

Ac 1:8 — But ye shall receive power, after that the Holy Ghost is come upon you: and ye shall be witnesses unto me both in Jerusalem, and in all Judaea, and in Samaria, and unto the uttermost part of the earth.

Ac 6:8 — And Stephen, full of faith and power, did great wonders and miracles among the people.

2Co 12:9 — And he said unto me, My grace is sufficient for thee: for my strength is made perfect in weakness. Most gladly therefore will I rather glory in my infirmities, that the power of Christ may rest upon me.

1Th 1:5 — For our gospel came not unto you in word only, but also in power, and in the Holy Ghost, and in much assurance; as ye know what manner of men we were among you for your sake.

2Ti 1:7 — For God hath not given us the spirit of fear; but of power, and of love, and of a sound mind.

Heb 6:5 — And have tasted the good word of God, and the powers of the world to come,

See: Holy Spirit

POWER, of Christ

- **As the Son of God, is the power of God.**

Jn 5:17–19; 10:28–30

- **As man, is from the Father.**

Ac 10:38 — How God anointed Jesus of Nazareth with the Holy Ghost and with power: who went about doing good, and healing all that were oppressed of the devil; for God was with him.

- **Described as.**
  - **Supreme.**

Eph 1:20–21

1Pe 3:22 — Who is gone into heaven, and is on the right hand of God; angels and authorities and powers being made subject unto him.

  - **Unlimited.**

Mt 28:18 — And Jesus came and spake unto them, saying, All power is given unto me in heaven and in earth.

  - **Over all flesh.**

Jn 17:2 — As thou hast given him power over all flesh, that he should give eternal life to as many as thou hast given him.

  - **Over all things.**

Jn 3:35 — The Father loveth the Son, and hath given all things into his hand.

Eph 1:22 — And hath put all *things* under his feet, and gave him *to be* the head over all *things* to the church,

  - **Glorious.**

2Th 1:9 — Who shall be punished with everlasting destruction from the presence of the Lord, and from the glory of his power;

  - **Everlasting.**

1Ti 6:16 — Who only hath immortality, dwelling in the light which no man can approach unto; whom no man hath seen, nor can see: to whom *be* honour and power everlasting. Amen.

- **Is able to subdue all things.**

Php 3:21 — Who shall change our vile body, that it may be fashioned like unto his glorious body, according to the working whereby he is able even to subdue all things unto himself.

- **Exemplified in creation.**

Jn 1:3 — All things were made by him; and without him was not any thing made that was made.

Jn 1:10 — He was in the world, and the world was made by him, and the world knew him not.

Col 1:16 — For by him were all things created, that are in heaven, and that are in earth, visible and invisible, whether *they be* thrones, or dominions, or principalities, or powers: all things were created by him, and for him:

- **Upholding all things.**

Col 1:17 — And he is before all things, and by him all things consist.

Heb 1:3 — Who being the brightness of *his* glory, and the express image of his person, and upholding all things by the word of his power, when he had by himself purged our sins, sat down on the right hand of the Majesty on high;

- **Salvation.**

Isa 63:1 — Who *is* this that cometh from Edom, with dyed garments from Bozrah? this *that is* glorious in his apparel, travelling in the greatness of his strength? I that speak in righteousness, mighty to save.

Heb 7:25 — Wherefore he is able also to save them to the uttermost that come unto God by him, seeing he ever liveth to make intercession for them.

- **His teaching.**

Mt 7:28–29

Lk 4:32 — And they were astonished at his doctrine: for his word was with power.

- **Working miracles.**

Mt 8:27 — But the men marvelled, saying, What manner of man is this, that even the winds and the sea obey him!

Lk 5:17 — And it came to pass on a certain day, as he was teaching, that there were Pharisees and doctors of the law sitting by, which were come out of every town of Galilee, and Judaea, and Jerusalem: and the power of the Lord was *present* to heal them.

- **Enabling others to work miracles.**

Mk 16:17–18

Mt 10:1 — And when he had called unto *him* his twelve disciples, he gave them power *against* unclean spirits, to cast them out, and to heal all manner of sickness and all manner of disease.

Lk 10:17 — And the seventy returned again with joy, saying, Lord, even the devils are subject unto us through thy name.

- **Forgiving sins.**

Mt 9:6 — But that ye may know that the Son of man hath power on earth to forgive sins, (then saith he to the sick of the palsy,) Arise, take up thy bed, and go unto thine house.

Ac 5:31 — Him hath God exalted with his right hand *to be* a Prince and a Saviour, for to give repentance to Israel, and forgiveness of sins.

- **Giving spiritual life.**

Jn 5:25–26

Jn 5:21 — For as the Father raiseth up the dead, and quickeneth *them;* even so the Son quickeneth whom he will.

- **Giving eternal life.**

Jn 17:2 — As thou hast given him power over all flesh, that he should give eternal life to as many as thou hast given him.

- **Raising the dead.**

Jn 5:28–29

- **Rising from the dead.**

Jn 2:19 — Jesus answered and said unto them, Destroy this temple, and in three days I will raise it up.

Jn 10:18 — No man taketh it from me, but I lay it down of myself. I have power to lay it down, and I have power to take it again. This commandment have I received of my Father.

- **Overcoming the world.**

Jn 16:33 — These things I have spoken unto you, that in me ye might have peace. In the world ye shall have tribulation: but be of good cheer; I have overcome the world.

- **Overcoming Satan.**

Col 2:15 — *And* having spoiled principalities and powers, he made a shew of them openly, triumphing over them in it.

Heb 2:14 — Forasmuch then as the children are partakers of flesh and blood, he also himself likewise took part of the same; that through death he might destroy him that had the power of death, that is, the devil;

- **Destroying the works of Satan.**

1Jn 3:8 — He that committeth sin is of the devil; for the devil sinneth from the beginning. For this purpose the Son of God was manifested, that he might destroy the works of the devil.

- **Ministers should make known.**

2Pe 1:16 — For we have not followed cunningly devised fables, when we made known unto you the power and coming of our Lord Jesus Christ, but were eyewitnesses of his majesty.

- **Saints made willing by.**

Ps 110:3 — Thy people *shall be* willing in the day of thy power, in the beauties of holiness from the womb of the morning: thou hast the dew of thy youth.

- **Succored by.**

Heb 2:18 — For in that he himself hath suffered being tempted, he is able to succour them that are tempted.

- **Strengthened by.**

Php 4:13 — I can do all things through Christ which strengtheneth me.

2Ti 4:17 — Notwithstanding the Lord stood with me, and strengthened me; that by me the preaching might be fully known, and *that* all the Gentiles might hear: and I was delivered out of the mouth of the lion.

- **Preserved by.**

2Ti 1:12 — For the which cause I also suffer these things: nevertheless I am not ashamed: for I know whom I have believed, and am persuaded that he is able to keep that which I have committed unto him against that day.

2Ti 4:18 — And the Lord shall deliver me from every evil work, and will preserve *me* unto his heavenly kingdom: to whom *be* glory for ever and ever. Amen.

- **Bodies of, shall be changed by.**

Php 3:21 — Who shall change our vile body, that it may be fashioned like unto his glorious body, according to the working whereby he is able even to subdue all things unto himself.

- **Rests upon saints.**

2Co 12:9 — And he said unto me, My grace is sufficient for thee: for my strength is made perfect in weakness. Most gladly therefore will I rather glory in my infirmities, that the power of Christ may rest upon me.

- **Present in the assembly of saints.**

1Co 5:4 — In the name of our Lord Jesus Christ, when ye are gathered together, and my spirit, with the power of our Lord Jesus Christ,

- **Shall be specially manifested at his second coming.**

Mk 13:26 — And then shall they see the Son of man coming in the clouds with great power and glory.

2Pe 1:16 — For we have not followed cunningly devised fables, when we made known unto you the power and coming of our Lord Jesus Christ, but were eyewitnesses of his majesty.

- **Shall subdue all power.**

1Co 15:24 — Then *cometh* the end, when he shall have delivered up the kingdom to God, even the Father; when he shall have put down all rule and all authority and power.

- **The wicked shall be destroyed by.**

Ps 2:9 — Thou shalt break them with a rod of iron; thou shalt dash them in pieces like a potter's vessel.

Isa 11:4 — But with righteousness shall he judge the poor, and reprove with equity for the meek of the earth: and he shall smite the earth with the rod of his mouth, and with the breath of his lips shall he slay the wicked.

Isa 63:3 — I have trodden the winepress alone; and of the people *there was* none with me: for I will tread them in mine anger, and trample them in my fury; and their blood shall be sprinkled upon my garments, and I will stain all my raiment.

2Th 1:9 — Who shall be punished with everlasting destruction from the presence of the Lord, and from the glory of his power;

See: Jesus, History of

See: Jesus, Miracles of

See: Jesus, Omnipotence of

See: Jesus, Power of, to Forgive Sins

POWER, of God

- **One of his attributes.**

Ps 62:11 — God hath spoken once; twice have I heard this; that power *belongeth* unto God.

- **Expressed by.**
  - **The voice of God.**

Ps 29:3 — The voice of the LORD *is* upon the waters: the God of glory thundereth: the LORD *is* upon many waters.

Ps 29:5 — The voice of the LORD breaketh the cedars; yea, the LORD breaketh the cedars of Lebanon.

Ps 68:33 — To him that rideth upon the heavens of heavens, *which were* of old; lo, he doth send out his voice, *and that* a mighty voice.

  - **The finger of God.**

Ex 8:19 — Then the magicians said unto Pharaoh, This *is* the finger of God: and Pharaoh's heart was hardened, and he hearkened not unto them; as the LORD had said.

Ps 8:3 — When I consider thy heavens, the work of thy fingers, the moon and the stars, which thou hast ordained;

  - **The hand of God.**

Ex 9:3 — Behold, the hand of the LORD is upon thy cattle which *is* in the field, upon the horses, upon the asses, upon the camels, upon the oxen, and upon the sheep: *there shall be* a very grievous murrain.

Ex 9:15 — For now I will stretch out my hand, that I may smite thee and thy people with pestilence; and thou shalt be cut off from the earth.

Isa 48:13 — Mine hand also hath laid the foundation of the earth, and my right hand hath spanned the heavens: *when* I call unto them, they stand up together.

  - **The arm of God.**

Job 40:9 — Hast thou an arm like God? or canst thou thunder with a voice like him?

Isa 52:10 — The LORD hath made bare his holy arm in the eyes of all the nations; and all the ends of the earth shall see the salvation of our God.

  - **Thunder of his power.**

Job 26:14 — Lo, these *are* parts of his ways: but how little a portion is heard of him? but the thunder of his power who can understand?

- **Described as.**
  - **Great.**

Ps 79:11 — Let the sighing of the prisoner come before thee; according to the greatness of thy power preserve thou those that are appointed to die;

Na 1:3 — The LORD *is* slow to anger, and great in power, and will not at all acquit *the wicked:* the LORD hath his way in the whirlwind and in the storm, and the clouds *are* the dust of his feet.

  - **Strong.**

Ps 89:13 — Thou hast a mighty arm: strong is thy hand, *and* high is thy right hand.

Ps 136:12 — With a strong hand, and with a stretched out arm: for his mercy *endureth* for ever.

- **Glorious.**
  Ex 15:6 — Thy right hand, O LORD, is become glorious in power: thy right hand, O LORD, hath dashed in pieces the enemy.
  Isa 63:12 — That led *them* by the right hand of Moses with his glorious arm, dividing the water before them, to make himself an everlasting name?

- **Mighty.**
  Job 9:4 — *He is* wise in heart, and mighty in strength: who hath hardened *himself* against him, and hath prospered?
  Ps 89:13 — Thou hast a mighty arm: strong is thy hand, *and* high is thy right hand.

- **Everlasting.**
  Isa 26:4 — Trust ye in the LORD for ever: for in the LORD JEHOVAH *is* everlasting strength:
  Ro 1:20 — For the invisible things of him from the creation of the world are clearly seen, being understood by the things that are made, *even* his eternal power and Godhead; so that they are without excuse:

- **Sovereign.**
  Ro 9:21 — Hath not the potter power over the clay, of the same lump to make one vessel unto honour, and another unto dishonour?

- **Effectual.**
  Isa 43:13 — Yea, before the day *was* I *am* he; and *there is* none that can deliver out of my hand: I will work, and who shall let it?
  Eph 3:7 — Whereof I was made a minister, according to the gift of the grace of God given unto me by the effectual working of his power.

- **Irresistible.**
  Dt 32:39 — See now that I, *even* I, *am* he, and *there is* no god with me: I kill, and I make alive; I wound, and I heal: neither *is there any* that can deliver out of my hand.
  Da 4:35 — And all the inhabitants of the earth *are* reputed as nothing: and he doeth according to his will in the army of heaven, and *among* the inhabitants of the earth: and none can stay his hand, or say unto him, What doest thou?

- **Incomparable.**
  Ex 15:11–12
  Dt 3:24 — O Lord GOD, thou hast begun to shew thy servant thy greatness, and thy mighty hand: for what God *is there* in heaven or in earth, that can do according to thy works, and according to thy might?
  Job 40:9 — Hast thou an arm like God? or canst thou thunder with a voice like him?
  Ps 89:8 — O LORD God of hosts, who *is* a strong LORD like unto thee? or to thy faithfulness round about thee?

- **Unsearchable.**
  Job 5:9 — Which doeth great things and unsearchable; marvellous things without number:
  Job 9:10 — Which doeth great things past finding out; yea, and wonders without number.

- **Incomprehensible.**
  Job 26:14 — Lo, these *are* parts of his ways: but how little a portion is heard of him? but the thunder of his power who can understand?
  Ecc 3:11 — He hath made every *thing* beautiful in his time: also he hath set the world in their heart, so that no man can find out the work that God maketh from the beginning to the end.

- **All things possible to.**
  Mt 19:26 — But Jesus beheld *them,* and said unto them, With men this is impossible; but with God all things are possible.

- **Nothing too hard for.**
  Ge 18:14 — Is any thing too hard for the LORD? At the time appointed I will return unto thee, according to the time of life, and Sarah shall have a son.
  Jer 32:27 — Behold, I *am* the LORD, the God of all flesh: is there any thing too hard for me?

- **Can save by many or by few.**
  1Sa 14:6 — And Jonathan said to the young man that bare his armour, Come, and let us go over unto the garrison of these uncircumcised: it may be that the LORD will work for us: for *there is* no restraint to the LORD to save by many or by few.

- **Is the source of all strength.**
  1Ch 29:12 — Both riches and honour *come* of thee, and thou reignest over all; and in thine hand *is* power and might; and in thine hand *it is* to make great, and to give strength unto all.
  Ps 68:35 — O God, *thou art* terrible out of thy holy places: the God of Israel *is* he that giveth strength and power unto *his* people. Blessed *be* God.

- **Exemplified in.**
  - **The creation.**
    Ps 102:25 — Of old hast thou laid the foundation of the earth: and the heavens *are* the work of thy hands.
    Jer 10:12 — He hath made the earth by his power, he hath established the world by his wisdom, and hath stretched out the heavens by his discretion.
  - **Establishing and governing all things.**
    Ps 65:6 — Which by his strength setteth fast the mountains; *being* girded with power:
    Ps 66:7 — He ruleth by his power for ever; his eyes behold the nations: let not the rebellious exalt themselves. Selah.
  - **The miracles of Christ.**
    Lk 11:20 — But if I with the finger of God cast out devils, no doubt the kingdom of God is come upon you.
  - **The resurrection of Christ.**
    2Co 13:4 — For though he was crucified through weakness, yet he liveth by the power of God. For we also are weak in him, but we shall live with him by the power of God toward you.
    Col 2:12 — Buried with him in baptism, wherein also ye are risen with *him* through the faith of the operation of God, who hath raised him from the dead.

- **The resurrection of saints.**
  1Co 6:14 — And God hath both raised up the Lord, and will also raise up us by his own power.
- **Making the gospel affectual.**
  Ro 1:16 — For I am not ashamed of the gospel of Christ: for it is the power of God unto salvation to every one that believeth; to the Jew first, and also to the Greek.
  1Co 1:18 — For the preaching of the cross is to them that perish foolishness; but unto us which are saved it is the power of God.
  1Co 1:24 — But unto them which are called, both Jews and Greeks, Christ the power of God, and the wisdom of God.
- **Delivering his people.**
  Ps 106:8 — Nevertheless he saved them for his name's sake, that he might make his mighty power to be known.
- **The destruction of the wicked.**
  Ex 9:16 — And in very deed for this *cause* have I raised thee up, for to shew *in* thee my power; and that my name may be declared throughout all the earth.
  Ro 9:22 — *What* if God, willing to shew *his* wrath, and to make his power known, endured with much longsuffering the vessels of wrath fitted to destruction:

- **Saints long for exhibitions of.**
  Ps 63:1–2
- **Saints have confidence in.**
  Jer 20:11 — But the LORD *is* with me as a mighty terrible one: therefore my persecutors shall stumble, and they shall not prevail: they shall be greatly ashamed; for they shall not prosper: *their* everlasting confusion shall never be forgotten.
- **Saints receive increase of grace by.**
  2Co 9:8 — And God *is* able to make all grace abound toward you; that ye, always having all sufficiency in all *things,* may abound to every good work:
- **Saints strengthened by.**
  Eph 6:10 — Finally, my brethren, be strong in the Lord, and in the power of his might.
  Col 1:11 — Strengthened with all might, according to his glorious power, unto all patience and longsuffering with joyfulness;
- **Saints upheld by.**
  Ps 37:17 — For the arms of the wicked shall be broken: but the LORD upholdeth the righteous.
  Isa 41:10 — Fear thou not; for I *am* with thee: be not dismayed; for I *am* thy God: I will strengthen thee; yea, I will help thee; yea, I will uphold thee with the right hand of my righteousness.
- **Saints supported in affliction by.**
  2Co 6:7 — By the word of truth, by the power of God, by the armour of righteousness on the right hand and on the left,
  2Ti 1:8 — Be not thou therefore ashamed of the testimony of our Lord, nor of me his prisoner: but be thou partaker of the afflictions of the gospel according to the power of God;
- **Saints delivered by.**
  Ne 1:10 — Now these *are* thy servants and thy people, whom thou hast redeemed by thy great power, and by thy strong hand.
  Da 3:17 — If it be *so,* our God whom we serve is able to deliver us from the burning fiery furnace, and he will deliver *us* out of thine hand, O king.
- **Saints exalted by.**
  Job 36:22 — Behold, God exalteth by his power: who teacheth like him?
- **Saints kept by, unto salvation.**
  1Pe 1:5 — Who are kept by the power of God through faith unto salvation ready to be revealed in the last time.
- **Exerted in behalf of saints.**
  1Ch 16:9 — Sing unto him, sing psalms unto him, talk ye of all his wondrous works.
- **Works in and for saints.**
  2Co 13:4 — For though he was crucified through weakness, yet he liveth by the power of God. For we also are weak in him, but we shall live with him by the power of God toward you.
  Eph 1:19 — And what *is* the exceeding greatness of his power to us-ward who believe, according to the working of his mighty power,
  Eph 3:20 — Now unto him that is able to do exceeding abundantly above all that we ask or think, according to the power that worketh in us,
- **The faith of saints stands in.**
  1Co 2:5 — That your faith should not stand in the wisdom of men, but in the power of God.
- **Should be acknowledged.**
  1Ch 29:11 — Thine, O LORD, *is* the greatness, and the power, and the glory, and the victory, and the majesty: for all *that is* in the heaven and in the earth *is thine;* thine *is* the kingdom, O LORD, and thou art exalted as head above all.
  Isa 33:13 — Hear, ye *that are* far off, what I have done; and, ye *that are* near, acknowledge my might.
- **Should be pleaded in prayer.**
  Ps 79:11 — Let the sighing of the prisoner come before thee; according to the greatness of thy power preserve thou those that are appointed to die;
  Mt 6:13 — And lead us not into temptation, but deliver us from evil: For thine is the kingdom, and the power, and the glory, for ever. Amen.
- **Should be feared.**
  Jer 5:22 — Fear ye not me? saith the LORD: will ye not tremble at my presence, which have placed the sand *for* the bound of the sea by a perpetual decree, that it cannot pass it: and though the waves thereof toss themselves, yet can they not prevail; though they roar, yet can they not pass over it?
  Mt 10:28 — And fear not them which kill the body, but are not able to kill the soul: but rather fear him which is able to destroy both soul and body in hell.
- **Should be magnified.**
  Ps 21:13 — Be thou exalted, LORD, in thine own strength: *so* will we sing and praise thy power.

Jude 1:25 — To the only wise God our Saviour, *be* glory and majesty, dominion and power, both now and ever. Amen.

- **Efficiency of ministers is through.**

1Co 3:6–8

Gal 2:8 — (For he that wrought effectually in Peter to the apostleship of the circumcision, the same was mighty in me toward the Gentiles:)

Eph 3:7 — Whereof I was made a minister, according to the gift of the grace of God given unto me by the effectual working of his power.

- **Is a ground of trust.**

Isa 26:4 — Trust ye in the LORD for ever: for in the LORD JEHOVAH *is* everlasting strength:

Ro 4:21 — And being fully persuaded that, what he had promised, he was able also to perform.

- **The wicked know not.**

Mt 22:29 — Jesus answered and said unto them, Ye do err, not knowing the scriptures, nor the power of God.

- **The wicked have against them.**

Ezr 8:22 — For I was ashamed to require of the king a band of soldiers and horsemen to help us against the enemy in the way: because we had spoken unto the king, saying, The hand of our God *is* upon all them for good that seek him; but his power and his wrath *is* against all them that forsake him.

- **The wicked shall be destroyed by.**

Lk 12:5 — But I will forewarn you whom ye shall fear: Fear him, which after he hath killed hath power to cast into hell; yea, I say unto you, Fear him.

- **The heavenly host magnified.**

Rev 4:11 — Thou art worthy, O Lord, to receive glory and honour and power: for thou hast created all things, and for thy pleasure they are and were created.

Rev 5:13 — And every creature which is in heaven, and on the earth, and under the earth, and such as are in the sea, and all that are in them, heard I saying, Blessing, and honour, and glory, and power, *be* unto him that sitteth upon the throne, and unto the Lamb for ever and ever.

Rev 11:17 — Saying, We give thee thanks, O Lord God Almighty, which art, and wast, and art to come; because thou hast taken to thee thy great power, and hast reigned.

See: God, Omnipotent

See: God, Power of

POWER, of the Holy Ghost

- **Is the power of God.**

Mt 12:28 — But if I cast out devils by the Spirit of God, then the kingdom of God is come unto you.

Lk 11:20 — But if I with the finger of God cast out devils, no doubt the kingdom of God is come upon you.

- **Christ commenced his ministry in.**

Lk 4:14 — And Jesus returned in the power of the Spirit into Galilee: and there went out a fame of him through all the region round about.

- **Christ wrought his miracles by.**

Mt 12:28 — But if I cast out devils by the Spirit of God, then the kingdom of God is come unto you.

- **Exemplified in.**
  - **Creation.**

Ge 1:2 — And the earth was without form, and void; and darkness *was* upon the face of the deep. And the Spirit of God moved upon the face of the waters.

Job 26:13 — By his spirit he hath garnished the heavens; his hand hath formed the crooked serpent.

Ps 104:30 — Thou sendest forth thy spirit, they are created: and thou renewest the face of the earth.

  - **The conception of Christ.**

Lk 1:35 — And the angel answered and said unto her, The Holy Ghost shall come upon thee, and the power of the Highest shall overshadow thee: therefore also that holy thing which shall be born of thee shall be called the Son of God.

  - **Raising Christ from the dead.**

1Pe 3:18 — For Christ also hath once suffered for sins, the just for the unjust, that he might bring us to God, being put to death in the flesh, but quickened by the Spirit:

  - **Giving spiritual life.**

Eze 37:11–14

Ro 8:11 — But if the Spirit of him that raised up Jesus from the dead dwell in you, he that raised up Christ from the dead shall also quicken your mortal bodies by his Spirit that dwelleth in you.

  - **Working miracles.**

Ro 15:19 — Through mighty signs and wonders, by the power of the Spirit of God; so that from Jerusalem, and round about unto Illyricum, I have fully preached the gospel of Christ.

  - **Making the gospel efficacious.**

1Co 2:4 — And my speech and my preaching *was* not with enticing words of man's wisdom, but in demonstration of the Spirit and of power:

1Th 1:5 — For our gospel came not unto you in word only, but also in power, and in the Holy Ghost, and in much assurance; as ye know what manner of men we were among you for your sake.

  - **Overcoming all difficulties.**

Zec 4:6–7

- **Promised by the Father.**

Lk 24:49 — And, behold, I send the promise of my Father upon you: but tarry ye in the city of Jerusalem, until ye be endued with power from on high.

- **Promised by Christ.**

Ac 1:8 — But ye shall receive power, after that the Holy Ghost is come upon you: and ye shall be witnesses unto me both in Jerusalem, and in all Judaea, and in Samaria, and unto the uttermost part of the earth.

- **Saints upheld by.**

Ps 51:12 — Restore unto me the joy of thy salvation; and uphold me *with thy* free spirit.

• Saints strengthened by.

Eph 3:16 — That he would grant you, according to the riches of his glory, to be strengthened with might by his Spirit in the inner man;

• Saints enabled to speak the truth boldly by.

2Ti 1:7–8

Mic 3:8 — But truly I am full of power by the spirit of the LORD, and of judgment, and of might, to declare unto Jacob his transgression, and to Israel his sin.

Ac 6:5 — And the saying pleased the whole multitude: and they chose Stephen, a man full of faith and of the Holy Ghost, and Philip, and Prochorus, and Nicanor, and Timon, and Parmenas, and Nicolas a proselyte of Antioch:

Ac 6:10 — And they were not able to resist the wisdom and the spirit by which he spake.

• Saints helped in prayer by.

Ro 8:26 — Likewise the Spirit also helpeth our infirmities: for we know not what we should pray for as we ought: but the Spirit itself maketh intercession for us with groanings which cannot be uttered.

• Saints abound in hope by.

Ro 15:13 — Now the God of hope fill you with all joy and peace in believing, that ye may abound in hope, through the power of the Holy Ghost.

• Qualifies ministers.

Ac 1:8–9

Lk 24:49 — And, behold, I send the promise of my Father upon you: but tarry ye in the city of Jerusalem, until ye be endued with power from on high.

• God's word the instrument of.

Eph 6:17 — And take the helmet of salvation, and the sword of the Spirit, which is the word of God:

See: Holy Spirit

PRAISE

• Song of Moses, after the passage of the Red Sea.

Ex 15:1–19

• Of Miriam.

Ex 15:21 — And Miriam answered them, Sing ye to the LORD, for he hath triumphed gloriously; the horse and his rider hath he thrown into the sea.

• Of Deborah, after defeating the Canaanites.

Jgs 5:1–31

• Of Hannah.

1Sa 2:1–10

• Of David, celebrating his deliverance from the hand of Saul.

2Sa 22:1–51

• Of Hannah, on bringing the ark to Zion.

1Ch 16:8–36

• Of Hannah, at the close of his reign.

1Ch 29:10–19

• The chorus when Solomon brought the ark into the temple.

2Ch 5:13 — It came even to pass, as the trumpeters and singers *were* as one, to make one sound to be heard in praising and thanking the LORD; and when they lifted up *their* voice with the trumpets and cymbals and instruments of musick, and praised the LORD, *saying,* For *he is* good; for his mercy *endureth* for ever: that *then* the house was filled with a cloud, *even* the house of the LORD;

• Psalms of, for God's goodness to Israel.

Ps 46:1–11; 48:1–14; 65:1–66:20; 68:1–35; 76:1–12; 81:1–16; 85:1–13; 98:1–9; 105:1–45; 124:1–8; 126:1–6; 129:1–8; 135:1–136:26

• For God's goodness to righteous men.

Ps 23:1–6; 34:1–22; 36:1–12; 91:1–16; 100:1–5; 103:1–22; 107:1–43; 117:1–2; 121:1–8

• For God's goodness to individuals.

Ps 9:1–20; 18:1–50; 22:1–31; 30:1–12; 40:1–17; 75:1–10; 103:1–22; 108:1–13; 116:1–19; 118:1–29; 138:1–8; 144:1–15

• For God's attributes.

Ps 8:1–9; 19:1–14; 22:1–31; 24:1–10; 29:1–11; 33:1–22; 47:1–9; 50:1–23; 65:1–66:20; 76:1–77:20; 92:1–93:5; 95:1–99:9; 104:1–35; 111:1–10; 113:1–115:18; 134:1–3; 139:1–24; 147:1–148:14; 150:1–6

• Unclassified scriptures relating to.

Ex 15:1–2; 1Ch 16:33–34; Ne 9:5–6; Ps 22:22–23; 24:7–10; 28:6–7; 32:11–33:3; 34:1–3; 43:3–4; 47:6–7; 57:7–9; 63:3–6; 66:1–2; 67:3–4; 68:32–34; 71:14–15; 92:1–3; 95:1–2, 6–7; 96:1–4, 7–9; 98:4–6; 99:9–101:1; 103:20–22; 104:33–34; 105:1–5; 107:8–9, 31–32; 108:1–3; 113:1–2; 116:12–14; 116:17–117:2; 118:28–29; 119:171–172; 134:1–2; 135:1–3; 135:19–136:26; 138:1–2; 144:1–2; 145:1–150:6; Isa 12:1–6; 24:14–16; 38:18–19; 42:10–12; 52:7–10; Lk 1:46–55, 67–75; 17:15–16; 19:37–38; 24:52–53; Ac 2:46–47; Eph 3:20–21

Ge 14:20 — And blessed be the most high God, which hath delivered thine enemies into thy hand. And he gave him tithes of all.

Dt 10:21 — He *is* thy praise, and he *is* thy God, that hath done for thee these great and terrible things, which thine eyes have seen.

Jgs 5:3 — Hear, O ye kings; give ear, O ye princes; I, *even* I, will sing unto the LORD; I will sing *praise* to the LORD God of Israel.

2Sa 22:4 — I will call on the LORD, *who is* worthy to be praised: so shall I be saved from mine enemies.

1Ch 16:31 — Let the heavens be glad, and let the earth rejoice: and let *men* say among the nations, The LORD reigneth.

1Ch 16:36 — Blessed *be* the LORD God of Israel for ever and ever. And all the people said, Amen, and praised the LORD.

1Ch 23:30 — And to stand every morning to thank and praise the LORD, and likewise at even;

2Ch 7:3 — And when all the children of Israel saw how the fire came down, and the glory of the LORD upon the house, they bowed themselves with their faces to the ground upon the pavement, and worshipped, and praised the LORD, *saying,* For *he is* good; for his mercy *endureth* for ever.

Job 36:24 — Remember that thou magnify his work, which men behold.

Ps 7:17 — I will praise the LORD according to his righteousness: and will sing praise to the name of the LORD most high.

Ps 8:2 — Out of the mouth of babes and sucklings hast thou ordained strength because of thine enemies, that thou mightest still the enemy and the avenger.

Ps 9:11 — Sing praises to the LORD, which dwelleth in Zion: declare among the people his doings.

Ps 18:3 — I will call upon the LORD, *who is worthy* to be praised: so shall I be saved from mine enemies.

Ps 21:13 — Be thou exalted, LORD, in thine own strength: *so* will we sing and praise thy power.

Ps 22:25 — My praise *shall be* of thee in the great congregation: I will pay my vows before them that fear him.

Ps 26:12 — My foot standeth in an even place: in the congregations will I bless the LORD.

Ps 30:4 — Sing unto the LORD, O ye saints of his, and give thanks at the remembrance of his holiness.

Ps 35:18 — I will give thee thanks in the great congregation: I will praise thee among much people.

Ps 35:28 — And my tongue shall speak of thy righteousness *and* of thy praise all the day long.

Ps 41:13 — Blessed *be* the LORD God of Israel from everlasting, and to everlasting. Amen, and Amen.

Ps 42:4 — When I remember these *things,* I pour out my soul in me: for I had gone with the multitude, I went with them to the house of God, with the voice of joy and praise, with a multitude that kept holyday.

Ps 47:1 — O clap your hands, all ye people; shout unto God with the voice of triumph.

Ps 48:1 — Great *is* the LORD, and greatly to be praised in the city of our God, *in* the mountain of his holiness.

Ps 50:23 — Whoso offereth praise glorifieth me: and to him that ordereth *his* conversation *aright* will I shew the salvation of God.

Ps 51:15 — O Lord, open thou my lips; and my mouth shall shew forth thy praise.

Ps 52:9 — I will praise thee for ever, because thou hast done *it:* and I will wait on thy name; for *it is* good before thy saints.

Ps 56:10 — In God will I praise *his* word: in the LORD will I praise *his* word.

Ps 56:12 — Thy vows *are* upon me, O God: I will render praises unto thee.

Ps 61:8 — So will I sing praise unto thy name for ever, that I may daily perform my vows.

Ps 65:1 — Praise waiteth for thee, O God, in Sion: and unto thee shall the vow be performed.

Ps 66:4 — All the earth shall worship thee, and shall sing unto thee; they shall sing *to* thy name. Selah.

Ps 66:8 — O bless our God, ye people, and make the voice of his praise to be heard:

Ps 68:4 — Sing unto God, sing praises to his name: extol him that rideth upon the heavens by his name JAH, and rejoice before him.

Ps 68:26 — Bless ye God in the congregations, *even* the Lord, from the fountain of Israel.

Ps 69:30 — I will praise the name of God with a song, and will magnify him with thanksgiving.

Ps 69:34 — Let the heaven and earth praise him, the seas, and every thing that moveth therein.

Ps 70:4 — Let all those that seek thee rejoice and be glad in thee: and let such as love thy salvation say continually, Let God be magnified.

Ps 71:8 — Let my mouth be filled *with* thy praise *and with* thy honour all the day.

Ps 71:22 — I will also praise thee with the psaltery, *even* thy truth, O my God: unto thee will I sing with the harp, O thou Holy One of Israel.

Ps 75:1 — Unto thee, O God, do we give thanks, *unto thee* do we give thanks: for *that* thy name is near thy wondrous works declare.

Ps 79:13 — So we thy people and sheep of thy pasture will give thee thanks for ever: we will shew forth thy praise to all generations.

Ps 81:1 — Sing aloud unto God our strength: make a joyful noise unto the God of Jacob.

Ps 84:4 — Blessed *are* they that dwell in thy house: they will be still praising thee. Selah.

Ps 86:12 — I will praise thee, O Lord my God, with all my heart: and I will glorify thy name for evermore.

Ps 89:5 — And the heavens shall praise thy wonders, O LORD: thy faithfulness also in the congregation of the saints.

Ps 89:52 — Blessed *be* the LORD for evermore. Amen, and Amen.

Ps 97:12 — Rejoice in the LORD, ye righteous; and give thanks at the remembrance of his holiness.

Ps 99:3 — Let them praise thy great and terrible name; *for* it *is* holy.

Ps 99:5 — Exalt ye the LORD our God, and worship at his footstool; *for* he *is* holy.

Ps 106:1 — Praise ye the LORD. O give thanks unto the LORD; for *he is* good: for his mercy *endureth* for ever.

Ps 106:48 — Blessed *be* the LORD God of Israel from everlasting to everlasting: and let all the people say, Amen. Praise ye the LORD.

Ps 107:15 — Oh that *men* would praise the LORD *for* his goodness, and *for* his wonderful works to the children of men!

Ps 107:21 — Oh that *men* would praise the LORD *for* his goodness, and *for* his wonderful works to the children of men!

Ps 109:30 — I will greatly praise the LORD with my mouth; yea, I will praise him among the multitude.

Ps 111:1 — Praise ye the LORD. I will praise the LORD with *my* whole heart, in the assembly of the upright, and *in* the congregation.

Ps 111:10 — The fear of the LORD *is* the beginning of wisdom: a good understanding have all they that do *his commandments:* his praise endureth for ever.

Ps 115:18 — But we will bless the LORD from this time forth and for evermore. Praise the LORD.

Ps 118:15 — The voice of rejoicing and salvation *is* in the tabernacles of the righteous: the right hand of the LORD doeth valiantly.

Ps 119:7 — I will praise thee with uprightness of heart, when I shall have learned thy righteous judgments.

Ps 119:62 — At midnight I will rise to give thanks unto thee because of thy righteous judgments.

Ps 119:108 — Accept, I beseech thee, the freewill offerings of my mouth, O LORD, and teach me thy judgments.

Ps 119:164 — Seven times a day do I praise thee because of thy righteous judgments.

Ps 119:175 — Let my soul live, and it shall praise thee; and let thy judgments help me.

Ps 140:13 — Surely the righteous shall give thanks unto thy name: the upright shall dwell in thy presence.

Ps 144:9 — I will sing a new song unto thee, O God: upon a psaltery *and* an instrument of ten strings will I sing praises unto thee.

Isa 25:1 — O LORD, thou *art* my God; I will exalt thee, I will praise thy name; for thou hast done wonderful *things; thy* counsels of old *are* faithfulness *and* truth.

Isa 35:10 — And the ransomed of the LORD shall return, and come to Zion with songs and everlasting joy upon their heads: they shall obtain joy and gladness, and sorrow and sighing shall flee away.

Isa 43:21 — This people have I formed for myself; they shall shew forth my praise.

Isa 49:13 — Sing, O heavens; and be joyful, O earth; and break forth into singing, O mountains: for the LORD hath comforted his people, and will have mercy upon his afflicted.

Isa 51:3 — For the LORD shall comfort Zion: he will comfort all her waste places; and he will make her wilderness like Eden, and her desert like the garden of the LORD; joy and gladness shall be found therein, thanksgiving, and the voice of melody.

Isa 61:3 — To appoint unto them that mourn in Zion, to give unto them beauty for ashes, the oil of joy for mourning, the garment of praise for the spirit of heaviness; that they might be called trees of righteousness, the planting of the LORD, that he might be glorified.

Jer 31:7 — For thus saith the LORD; Sing with gladness for Jacob, and shout among the chief of the nations: publish ye, praise ye, and say, O LORD, save thy people, the remnant of Israel.

Jer 33:11 — The voice of joy, and the voice of gladness, the voice of the bridegroom, and the voice of the bride, the voice of them that shall say, Praise the LORD of hosts: for the LORD *is* good; for his mercy *endureth* for ever: *and* of them that shall bring the sacrifice of praise into the house of the LORD. For I will cause to return the captivity of the land, as at the first, saith the LORD.

Da 2:20 — Daniel answered and said, Blessed be the name of God for ever and ever: for wisdom and might are his:

Da 2:23 — I thank thee, and praise thee, O thou God of my fathers, who hast given me wisdom and might, and hast made known unto me now what we desired of thee: for thou hast *now* made known unto us the king's matter.

Da 4:37 — Now I Nebuchadnezzar praise and extol and honour the King of heaven, all whose works *are* truth, and his ways judgment: and those that walk in pride he is able to abase.

Jnh 2:9 — But I will sacrifice unto thee with the voice of thanksgiving; I will pay *that* that I have vowed. Salvation *is* of the LORD.

Mt 26:30 — And when they had sung an hymn, they went out into the mount of Olives.

Mk 14:26 — And when they had sung an hymn, they went out into the mount of Olives.

Lk 2:20 — And the shepherds returned, glorifying and praising God for all the things that they had heard and seen, as it was told unto them.

Ac 4:24 — And when they heard that, they lifted up their voice to God with one accord, and said, Lord, thou *art* God, which hast made heaven, and earth, and the sea, and all that in them is:

Ac 16:25 — And at midnight Paul and Silas prayed, and sang praises unto God: and the prisoners heard them.

Ro 11:36 — For of him, and through him, and to him, *are* all things: to whom *be* glory for ever. Amen.

Ro 16:27 — To God only wise, *be* glory through Jesus Christ for ever. Amen.

1Co 14:15 — What is it then? I will pray with the spirit, and I will pray with the understanding also: I will sing with the spirit, and I will sing with the understanding also.

1Co 15:57 — But thanks *be* to God, which giveth us the victory through our Lord Jesus Christ.

Eph 1:3 — Blessed *be* the God and Father of our Lord Jesus Christ, who hath blessed us with all spiritual blessings in heavenly *places* in Christ:

Eph 5:19 — Speaking to yourselves in psalms and hymns and spiritual songs, singing and making melody in your heart to the Lord;

Php 4:20 — Now unto God and our Father *be* glory for ever and ever. Amen.

1Ti 1:17 — Now unto the King eternal, immortal, invisible, the only wise God, *be* honour and glory for ever and ever. Amen.

Heb 2:12 — Saying, I will declare thy name unto my brethren, in the midst of the church will I sing praise unto thee.

Heb 13:15 — By him therefore let us offer the sacrifice of praise to God continually, that is, the fruit of *our* lips giving thanks to his name.

Jas 5:13 — Is any among you afflicted? let him pray. Is any merry? let him sing psalms.

1Pe 1:3 — Blessed *be* the God and Father of our Lord Jesus Christ, which according to his abundant mercy hath begotten us again unto a lively hope by the resurrection of Jesus Christ from the dead,

1Pe 2:9 — But ye *are* a chosen generation, a royal priesthood, an holy nation, a peculiar people; that ye should shew forth the praises of him who hath called you out of darkness into his marvellous light:

1Pe 4:11 — If any man speak, *let him speak* as the oracles of God; if any man minister, *let him do it* as of the ability which God giveth: that God in all things may be glorified through Jesus Christ, to whom be praise and dominion for ever and ever. Amen.

1Pe 5:11 — To him *be* glory and dominion for ever and ever. Amen.

2Pe 3:18 — But grow in grace, and *in* the knowledge of our Lord and Saviour Jesus Christ. To him *be* glory both now and for ever. Amen.

Jude 1:25 — To the only wise God our Saviour, *be* glory and majesty, dominion and power, both now and ever. Amen.

Rev 1:6 — And hath made us kings and priests unto God and his Father; to him *be* glory and dominion for ever and ever. Amen.

Rev 14:7 — Saying with a loud voice, Fear God, and give glory to him; for the hour of his judgment is come: and worship him that made heaven, and earth, and the sea, and the fountains of waters.

• In heaven.

Ps 103:20–21; Lk 2:13–14; Rev 4:8–11; 5:9–14; 7:9–12; 11:16–17; 14:2–3; 15:3–4; 19:1–7

Ne 9:6 — Thou, *even* thou, *art* LORD alone; thou hast made heaven, the heaven of heavens, with all their host, the earth, and all *things* that *are* therein, the seas, and all that *is* therein, and thou preservest them all; and the host of heaven worshippeth thee.

Job 38:7 — When the morning stars sang together, and all the sons of God shouted for joy?

Ps 148:2 — Praise ye him, all his angels: praise ye him, all his hosts.

Ps 148:4 — Praise him, ye heavens of heavens, and ye waters that *be* above the heavens.

Isa 6:3 — And one cried unto another, and said, Holy, holy, holy, *is* the LORD of hosts: the whole earth *is* full of his glory.

Eze 3:12 — Then the spirit took me up, and I heard behind me a voice of a great rushing, *saying,* Blessed *be* the glory of the LORD from his place.

Lk 15:7 — I say unto you, that likewise joy shall be in heaven over one sinner that repenteth, more than over ninety and nine just persons, which need no repentance.

Lk 15:10 — Likewise, I say unto you, there is joy in the presence of the angels of God over one sinner that repenteth.

Rev 1:6 — And hath made us kings and priests unto God and his Father; to him *be* glory and dominion for ever and ever. Amen.

PRAYER

• Unclassified scripture relating to.

Ge 32:24–28; Ps 105:3–4; Mt 6:5–13; 7:7–8; Mk 9:28–29; Lk 11:1–13; Eph 3:11–12; 6:18–19; 1Th 5:17–18; Rev 8:3–4

1Ch 16:11 — Seek the LORD and his strength, seek his face continually.

1Ch 16:35 — And say ye, Save us, O God of our salvation, and gather us together, and deliver us from the heathen, that we may give thanks to thy holy name, *and* glory in thy praise.

2Ch 7:14 — If my people, which are called by my name, shall humble themselves, and pray, and seek my face, and turn from their wicked ways; then will I hear from heaven, and will forgive their sin, and will heal their land.

Ne 4:9 — Nevertheless we made our prayer unto our God, and set a watch against them day and night, because of them.

Ps 27:8 — *When thou saidst,* Seek ye my face; my heart said unto thee, Thy face, LORD, will I seek.

Ps 145:18 — The LORD *is* nigh unto all them that call upon him, to all that call upon him in truth.

Pr 15:8 — The sacrifice of the wicked *is* an abomination to the LORD: but the prayer of the upright *is* his delight.

Ecc 5:2 — Be not rash with thy mouth, and let not thine heart be hasty to utter *any* thing before God: for God *is* in heaven, and thou upon earth: therefore let thy words be few.

Isa 55:6 — Seek ye the LORD while he may be found, call ye upon him while he is near:

La 3:41 — Let us lift up our heart with *our* hands unto God in the heavens.

Hos 12:4 — Yea, he had power over the angel, and prevailed: he wept, and made supplication unto him: he found him *in* Bethel, and there he spake with us;

Zec 12:10 — And I will pour upon the house of David, and upon the inhabitants of Jerusalem, the spirit of grace and of supplications: and they shall look upon me whom they have pierced, and they shall mourn for him, as one mourneth for *his* only *son,* and shall be in bitterness for him, as one that is in bitterness for *his* firstborn.

Mt 21:22 — And all things, whatsoever ye shall ask in prayer, believing, ye shall receive.

Mk 11:24 — Therefore I say unto you, What things soever ye desire, when ye pray, believe that ye receive *them,* and ye shall have *them.*

Lk 18:1 — And he spake a parable unto them *to this end,* that men ought always to pray, and not to faint;

Ro 8:26 — Likewise the Spirit also helpeth our infirmities: for we know not what we should pray for as we ought: but the Spirit itself maketh intercession for us with groanings which cannot be uttered.

1Co 14:15 — What is it then? I will pray with the spirit, and I will pray with the understanding also: I will sing with the spirit, and I will sing with the understanding also.

Php 4:6 — Be careful for nothing; but in every thing by prayer and supplication with thanksgiving let your requests be made known unto God.

Col 4:2 — Continue in prayer, and watch in the same with thanksgiving;

1Ti 2:8 — I will therefore that men pray every where, lifting up holy hands, without wrath and doubting.

Heb 4:16 — Let us therefore come boldly unto the throne of grace, that we may obtain mercy, and find grace to help in time of need.

Jas 5:16 — Confess *your* faults one to another, and pray one for another, that ye may be healed. The effectual fervent prayer of a righteous man availeth much.

Jude 1:20 — But ye, beloved, building up yourselves on your most holy faith, praying in the Holy Ghost,

Rev 5:8 — And when he had taken the book, the four beasts and four *and* twenty elders fell down before the Lamb, having every one of them harps, and golden vials full of odours, which are the prayers of saints.

• Answer to, promised.

Ex 33:17–20; Dt 4:29–31; 1Ki 8:22–53; 2Ch 6:1–42; 7:13–15; Job 8:5–6; Ps 37:4–5; 50:14–15; 55:16–17; 86:5–7; 102:17–20; 145:18–19; Jer 29:12–13; Joel 2:18–19; Am 5:4–6; Mt 6:5–13; 7:7–11; 18:19–20; Mk 11:24–25; Lk 11:5–13; 18:1–7; Jn 4:23–24; 14:13–14; 16:23–24, 26–27; Ro 10:12–13; Heb 10:22–23; Jas 1:5–7; 1Jn 5:14–15

Ex 6:5 — And I have also heard the groaning of the children of Israel, whom the Egyptians keep in bondage; and I have remembered my covenant.

Ex 22:23 — If thou afflict them in any wise, and they cry at all unto me, I will surely hear their cry;

Ex 22:27 — For that *is* his covering only, it *is* his raiment for his skin: wherein shall he sleep? and it shall come to pass, when he crieth unto me, that I will hear; for I *am* gracious.

Dt 4:7 — For what nation *is there so* great, who *hath* God *so* nigh unto them, as the LORD our God *is* in all *things that* we call upon him *for?*

1Ch 28:9 — And thou, Solomon my son, know thou the God of thy father, and serve him with a perfect heart and with a willing mind: for the LORD searcheth all hearts, and understandeth all the imaginations of the thoughts: if thou seek him, he will be found of thee; but if thou forsake him, he will cast thee off for ever.

Job 12:4 — I am *as* one mocked of his neighbour, who calleth upon God, and he answereth him: the just upright *man is* laughed to scorn.

Job 22:27 — Thou shalt make thy prayer unto him, and he shall hear thee, and thou shalt pay thy vows.

Job 33:26 — He shall pray unto God, and he will be favourable unto him: and he shall see his face with joy: for he will render unto man his righteousness.

Ps 9:10 — And they that know thy name will put their trust in thee: for thou, LORD, hast not forsaken them that seek thee.

Ps 9:12 — When he maketh inquisition for blood, he remembereth them: he forgetteth not the cry of the humble.

Ps 10:17 — LORD, thou hast heard the desire of the humble: thou wilt prepare their heart, thou wilt cause thine ear to hear:

Ps 18:3 — I will call upon the LORD, *who is worthy* to be praised: so shall I be saved from mine enemies.

Ps 32:6 — For this shall every one that is godly pray unto thee in a time when thou mayest be found: surely in the floods of great waters they shall not come nigh unto him.

Ps 34:15 — The eyes of the LORD *are* upon the righteous, and his ears *are open* unto their cry.

Ps 34:17 — *The righteous* cry, and the LORD heareth, and delivereth them out of all their troubles.

Ps 38:15 — For in thee, O LORD, do I hope: thou wilt hear, O Lord my God.

Ps 56:9 — When I cry *unto thee,* then shall mine enemies turn back: this I know; for God *is* for me.

Ps 65:2 — O thou that hearest prayer, unto thee shall all flesh come.

Ps 65:5 — By terrible things in righteousness wilt thou answer us, O God of our salvation; *who art* the confidence of all the ends of the earth, and of them that are afar off *upon* the sea:

Ps 69:33 — For the LORD heareth the poor, and despiseth not his prisoners.

Ps 81:10 — I *am* the LORD thy God, which brought thee out of the land of Egypt: open thy mouth wide, and I will fill it.

Ps 91:15 — He shall call upon me, and I will answer him: I *will be* with him in trouble; I will deliver him, and honour him.

Pr 2:3 — Yea, if thou criest after knowledge, *and* liftest up thy voice for understanding;

Pr 2:5 — Then shalt thou understand the fear of the LORD, and find the knowledge of God.

Pr 3:6 — In all thy ways acknowledge him, and he shall direct thy paths.

Pr 10:24 — The fear of the wicked, it shall come upon him: but the desire of the righteous shall be granted.

Pr 15:8 — The sacrifice of the wicked *is* an abomination to the LORD: but the prayer of the upright *is* his delight.

Pr 15:29 — The LORD *is* far from the wicked: but he heareth the prayer of the righteous.

Pr 16:1 — The preparations of the heart in man, and the answer of the tongue, *is* from the LORD.

Isa 19:20 — And it shall be for a sign and for a witness unto the LORD of hosts in the land of Egypt: for they shall cry unto the LORD because of the oppressors, and he shall send them a saviour, and a great one, and he shall deliver them.

Isa 30:19 — For the people shall dwell in Zion at Jerusalem: thou shalt weep no more: he will be very gracious unto thee at the voice of thy cry; when he shall hear it, he will answer thee.

Isa 55:6 — Seek ye the LORD while he may be found, call ye upon him while he is near:

Isa 58:9 — Then shalt thou call, and the LORD shall answer; thou shalt cry, and he shall say, Here I *am.* If thou take away from the midst of thee the yoke, the putting forth of the finger, and speaking vanity;

Isa 65:24 — And it shall come to pass, that before they call, I will answer; and while they are yet speaking, I will hear.

Jer 31:9 — They shall come with weeping, and with supplications will I lead them: I will cause them to walk by the rivers of waters in a straight way, wherein they shall not stumble: for I am a father to Israel, and Ephraim *is* my firstborn.

Jer 33:3 — Call unto me, and I will answer thee, and shew thee great and mighty things, which thou knowest not.

La 3:25 — The LORD *is* good unto them that wait for him, to the soul *that* seeketh him.

Eze 36:37 — Thus saith the Lord GOD; I will yet *for* this be enquired of by the house of Israel, to do *it* for them; I will increase them with men like a flock.

Joel 2:32 — And it shall come to pass, *that* whosoever shall call on the name of the LORD shall be delivered: for in mount Zion and in Jerusalem shall be deliverance, as the LORD hath said, and in the remnant whom the LORD shall call.

Zep 2:3 — Seek ye the LORD, all ye meek of the earth, which have wrought his judgment; seek righteousness, seek meekness: it may be ye shall be hid in the day of the LORD's anger.

Zec 10:1 — Ask ye of the LORD rain in the time of the latter rain; *so* the LORD shall make bright clouds, and give them showers of rain, to every one grass in the field.

Zec 10:6 — And I will strengthen the house of Judah, and I will save the house of Joseph, and I will bring them again to place them; for I have mercy upon them: and they shall be as though I had not cast them off: for I *am* the LORD their God, and will hear them.

Zec 13:9 — And I will bring the third part through the fire, and will refine them as silver is refined, and will try them as gold is tried: they shall call on my name, and I will hear them: I will say, It *is* my people: and they shall say, The LORD *is* my God.

Mt 21:22 — And all things, whatsoever ye shall ask in prayer, believing, ye shall receive.

Lk 21:36 — Watch ye therefore, and pray always, that ye may be accounted worthy to escape all these things that shall come to pass, and to stand before the Son of man.

Jn 4:10 — Jesus answered and said unto her, If thou knewest the gift of God, and who it is that saith to thee, Give me to drink; thou wouldest have asked of him, and he would have given thee living water.

Jn 9:31 — Now we know that God heareth not sinners: but if any man be a worshipper of God, and doeth his will, him he heareth.

Jn 15:7 — If ye abide in me, and my words abide in you, ye shall ask what ye will, and it shall be done unto you.

Jn 15:16 — Ye have not chosen me, but I have chosen you, and ordained you, that ye should go and bring forth fruit, and *that* your fruit should remain: that whatsoever ye shall ask of the Father in my name, he may give it you.

Ac 7:34 — I have seen, I have seen the affliction of my people which is in Egypt, and I have heard their groaning, and am come down to deliver them. And now come, I will send thee into Egypt.

Ac 22:16 — And now why tarriest thou? arise, and be baptized, and wash away thy sins, calling on the name of the Lord.

Ro 8:26 — Likewise the Spirit also helpeth our infirmities: for we know not what we should pray for as we ought: but the Spirit itself maketh intercession for us with groanings which cannot be uttered.

Eph 2:18 — For through him we both have access by one Spirit unto the Father.

Eph 3:20 — Now unto him that is able to do exceeding abundantly above all that we ask or think, according to the power that worketh in us,

Heb 4:16 — Let us therefore come boldly unto the throne of grace, that we may obtain mercy, and find grace to help in time of need.

Heb 11:6 — But without faith *it is* impossible to please *him:* for he that cometh to God must believe that he is, and *that* he is a rewarder of them that diligently seek him.

Jas 4:8 — Draw nigh to God, and he will draw nigh to you. Cleanse *your* hands, *ye* sinners; and purify *your* hearts, *ye* double minded.

Jas 4:10 — Humble yourselves in the sight of the Lord, and he shall lift you up.

Jas 5:16 — Confess *your* faults one to another, and pray one for another, that ye may be healed. The effectual fervent prayer of a righteous man availeth much.

1Jn 3:22 — And whatsoever we ask, we receive of him, because we keep his commandments, and do those things that are pleasing in his sight.

• Answered.

Ps 6:8–9; 22:4–5; 30:2–3; 34:4–6; 66:19–20; 77:1–2; 99:6–8; 107:6–7, 13–20; 116:1–2; La 3:57–58; Jnh 2:1–2; Lk 23:42–43; 2Co 12:8–9; Jas 5:17–18

Job 34:28 — So that they cause the cry of the poor to come unto him, and he heareth the cry of the afflicted.

Ps 3:4 — I cried unto the LORD with my voice, and he heard me out of his holy hill. Selah.

Ps 4:1 — Hear me when I call, O God of my righteousness: thou hast enlarged me *when I was* in distress; have mercy upon me, and hear my prayer.

Ps 18:6 — In my distress I called upon the LORD, and cried unto my God: he heard my voice out of his temple, and my cry came before him, *even* into his ears.

Ps 21:2 — Thou hast given him his heart's desire, and hast not withholden the request of his lips. Selah.

Ps 21:4 — He asked life of thee, *and* thou gavest *it* him, *even* length of days for ever and ever.

Ps 22:24 — For he hath not despised nor abhorred the affliction of the afflicted; neither hath he hid his face from him; but when he cried unto him, he heard.

Ps 28:6 — Blessed *be* the LORD, because he hath heard the voice of my supplications.

Ps 31:22 — For I said in my haste, I am cut off from before thine eyes: nevertheless thou heardest the voice of my supplications when I cried unto thee.

Ps 40:1 — I waited patiently for the LORD; and he inclined unto me, and heard my cry.

Ps 81:7 — Thou calledst in trouble, and I delivered thee; I answered thee in the secret place of thunder: I proved thee at the waters of Meribah. Selah.

Ps 106:44 — Nevertheless he regarded their affliction, when he heard their cry:

Ps 118:5 — I called upon the LORD in distress: the LORD answered me, *and set me* in a large place.

Ps 118:21 — I will praise thee: for thou hast heard me, and art become my salvation.

Ps 119:26 — I have declared my ways, and thou heardest me: teach me thy statutes.

Ps 120:1 — In my distress I cried unto the LORD, and he heard me.

Ps 138:3 — In the day when I cried thou answeredst me, *and* strengthenedst me *with* strength in my soul.

Hos 12:4 — Yea, he had power over the angel, and prevailed: he wept, and made supplication unto him: he found him *in* Bethel, and there he spake with us;

Jnh 2:7 — When my soul fainted within me I remembered the LORD: and my prayer came in unto thee, into thine holy temple.

Ac 4:31 — And when they had prayed, the place was shaken where they were assembled together; and they were all filled with the Holy Ghost, and they spake the word of God with boldness.

- **Instances of.**
  - **Cain.**
    Ge 4:13–15
  - **Abraham**
    - **For a son.**
      Ge 15:1–21
    - **Entreating for Sodom.**
      Ge 18:23–33
    - **For Ishmael.**
      Ge 17:20 — And as for Ishmael, I have heard thee: Behold, I have blessed him, and will make him fruitful, and will multiply him exceedingly; twelve princes shall he beget, and I will make him a great nation.
    - **For Abimelech.**
      Ge 20:17 — So Abraham prayed unto God: and God healed Abimelech, and his wife, and his maidservants; and they bare *children.*
  - **Hagar, for deliverance.**
    Ge 16:7–13
  - **Abraham's servant, for guidance.**
    Ge 24:12–52
  - **Rebekah, concerning her pains in pregnancy.**
    Ge 25:22–23
  - **Jacob, for deliverance from Esau.**
    Ge 32:9–33:17
  - **Moses.**
  - **For help at the Red Sea.**
    Ex 14:15–16
  - **At the waters of Marah.**
    Ex 15:25 — And he cried unto the LORD; and the LORD shewed him a tree, *which* when he had cast into the waters, the waters were made sweet: there he made for them a statute and an ordinance, and there he proved them,
  - **At Horeb.**
    Ex 17:4–6
  - **In the battle with the Amalekites.**
    Ex 17:8–14
  - **Concerning the murmuring of the Israelites for flesh.**
    Nu 11:11–35
  - **In behalf of Miriam's leprosy.**
    Nu 12:13–15
  - **Along with Aaron and Samuel.**
    Ps 99:6 — Moses and Aaron among his priests, and Samuel among them that call upon his name; they called upon the LORD, and he answered them.
  - **Israelites.**
    - **For deliverance from bondage.**
      Ex 2:23–25; 3:7–10
      Ac 7:34 — I have seen, I have seen the affliction of my people which is in Egypt, and I have heard their groaning, and am come down to deliver them. And now come, I will send thee into Egypt.
    - **From Pharaoh's army.**
      Ex 14:10–30
    - **From the king of Mesopotamis.**
      Jgs 3:9 — And when the children of Israel cried unto the LORD, the LORD raised up a deliverer to the children of Israel, who delivered them, *even* Othniel the son of Kenaz, Caleb's younger brother.
      Jgs 3:15 — But when the children of Israel cried unto the LORD, the LORD raised them up a deliverer, Ehud the son of Gera, a Benjamite, a man lefthanded: and by him the children of Israel sent a present unto Eglon the king of Moab.
    - **From the king of Sisera.**
      Jgs 4:23–24; 1Sa 12:9–11
      Jgs 4:3 — And the children of Israel cried unto the LORD: for he had nine hundred chariots of iron; and twenty years he mightily oppressed the children of Israel.
    - **From the king of Ammon.**
      Jgs 10:6–11:33
    - **For God's favor under the reproofs of Azariah.**
      1Ch 15:1–15
    - **From Babylonian bondage.**
      Ne 9:27 — Therefore thou deliveredst them into the hand of their enemies, who vexed them: and in the time of their trouble, when they cried unto thee, thou heardest *them* from heaven; and according to thy manifold mercies thou gavest them saviours, who saved them out of the hand of their enemies.
  - **Gideon, asking the token of dew.**
    Jgs 6:36–40
  - **Manoah, asking about Samson.**
    Jgs 13:8–9
  - **Samson, asking for strength.**
    Jgs 16:28–30
  - **Hannah, asking for a child.**
    1Sa 1:10–17, 19–20
  - **David.**
    - **Asking whether Keilah would be delivered into his hands.**
      1Sa 23:10–12

• **Asking whether Ziklag would be delivered into his hands.**

1Sa 30:8 — And David enquired at the LORD, saying, Shall I pursue after this troop? shall I overtake them? And he answered him, Pursue: for thou shalt surely overtake *them,* and without fail recover *all.*

• **Asking whether he should go into Judah after Saul's death.**

2Sa 2:1 — And it came to pass after this, that David enquired of the LORD, saying, Shall I go up into any of the cities of Judah? And the LORD said unto him, Go up. And David said, Whither shall I go up? And he said, Unto Hebron.

• **Asking whether he should go against the Philistines.**

2Sa 5:19–25

• **In adversity.**

Ps 118:5 — I called upon the LORD in distress: the LORD answered me, *and set me* in a large place.

Ps 138:3 — In the day when I cried thou answeredst me, *and* strengthenedst me *with* strength in my soul.

• **Solomon asks for wisdom.**

1Ki 3:1–13; 9:2–3

• **Elijah.**

• **Raising the widow's son.**

1Ki 17:22 — And the LORD heard the voice of Elijah; and the soul of the child came into him again, and he revived.

• **Asking fire on his sacrifice.**

1Ki 18:36–38

• **Asking rain on his sacrifice.**

1Ki 18:42–45

1Ki 17:1 — And Elijah the Tishbite, *who was* of the inhabitants of Gilead, said unto Ahab, *As* the LORD God of Israel liveth, before whom I stand, there shall not be dew nor rain these years, but according to my word.

1Ki 18:1 — And it came to pass *after* many days, that the word of the LORD came to Elijah in the third year, saying, Go, shew thyself unto Ahab; and I will send rain upon the earth.

Jas 5:17 — Elias was a man subject to like passions as we are, and he prayed earnestly that it might not rain: and it rained not on the earth by the space of three years and six months.

• **Elisha, leading the Syrian army.**

2Ki 6:17–20

• **Jabez, asking for prosperity.**

1Ch 4:10 — And Jabez called on the God of Israel, saying, Oh that thou wouldest bless me indeed, and enlarge my coast, and that thine hand might be with me, and that thou wouldest keep *me* from evil, that it may not grieve me! And God granted him that which he requested.

• **Abijah, for victory over Jeroboam.**

2Ch 13:14–18

• **Asa, for victory over Zerah.**

2Ch 14:11–15

• **The people of Judah.**

2Ch 15:15 — And all Judah rejoiced at the oath: for they had sworn with all their heart, and sought him with their whole desire; and he was found of them: and the LORD gave them rest round about.

• **Jehoshaphat, for victory over the Canaanites.**

2Ch 20:6–27

2Ch 18:31 — And it came to pass, when the captains of the chariots saw Jehoshaphat, that they said, It *is* the king of Israel. Therefore they compassed about him to fight: but Jehoshaphat cried out, and the LORD helped him; and God moved them *to depart* from him.

• **Jehoahaz, for victory over Hazael.**

2Ki 13:4 — And Jehoahaz besought the LORD, and the LORD hearkened unto him: for he saw the oppression of Israel, because the king of Syria oppressed them.

• **Priests and Levites, when blessing the people.**

2Ch 30:27 — Then the priests the Levites arose and blessed the people: and their voice was heard, and their prayer came *up* to his holy dwelling place, *even* unto heaven.

• **Hezekiah and Isaiah, for deliverance from Sennacherib.**

2Ki 19:14–20; 2Ch 32:20–23

• **Hezekiah and Isaiah, to save Hezekiah's life.**

2Ki 20:1–7

2Ki 20:11 — And Isaiah the prophet cried unto the LORD: and he brought the shadow ten degrees backward, by which it had gone down in the dial of Ahaz.

2Ch 32:24 — In those days Hezekiah was sick to the death, and prayed unto the LORD: and he spake unto him, and he gave him a sign.

• **Manasseh, for deliverance from the king of Babylon.**

2Ch 33:13 — And prayed unto him: and he was intreated of him, and heard his supplication, and brought him again to Jerusalem into his kingdom. Then Manasseh knew that the LORD he *was* God.

2Ch 33:19 — His prayer also, and *how God* was intreated of him, and all his sin, and his trespass, and the places wherein he built high places, and set up groves and graven images, before he was humbled: behold, they *are* written among the sayings of the seers.

• **Reubenites, for deliverance from the Hagarites.**

1Ch 5:20 — And they were helped against them, and the Hagarites were delivered into their hand, and all that *were* with them: for they cried to God in the battle, and he was intreated of them; because they put their trust in him.

- **The Jews, returning from the captivity.**

Ezr 8:21 — Then I proclaimed a fast there, at the river of Ahava, that we might afflict ourselves before our God, to seek of him a right way for us, and for our little ones, and for all our substance.

Ezr 8:23 — So we fasted and besought our God for this: and he was intreated of us.

- **Ezekiel, to have the baking of his bread of affliction changed.**

Eze 4:12–15

- **Daniel.**
  - **For the interpretation of Nebuchadnezzar's dream.**

    Da 2:19–23
  - **Interceding for the people.**

    Da 9:20–23
  - **In a vision.**

    Da 10:12 — Then said he unto me, Fear not, Daniel: for from the first day that thou didst set thine heart to understand, and to chasten thyself before thy God, thy words were heard, and I am come for thy words.

- **Zacharias, for a son.**

Lk 1:13 — But the angel said unto him, Fear not, Zacharias: for thy prayer is heard; and thy wife Elisabeth shall bear thee a son, and thou shalt call his name John.

- **The leper, for healing.**

Mt 8:2–3; Mk 1:40–43; Lk 5:12–13

- **Centurion, for his servant.**

Mt 8:5–13; Lk 7:3–10; Jn 4:50–51

- **Peter, asking that Tabitha be restored.**

Ac 9:40 — But Peter put them all forth, and kneeled down, and prayed; and turning *him* to the body said, Tabitha, arise. And she opened her eyes: and when she saw Peter, she sat up.

- **The disciples, for Peter.**

Ac 12:5–17

- **Paul, to be restored to health.**

2Co 1:9–11

• Confession in.

Nu 5:5–7; Ne 1:6–7; 9:33–35; Job 40:4–5; Ps 38:4–8; 51:3–4; 106:6–7; Isa 59:12–13; Da 9:5–15

Le 5:5 — And it shall be, when he shall be guilty in one of these *things*, that he shall confess that he hath sinned in that *thing*:

Le 26:40 — If they shall confess their iniquity, and the iniquity of their fathers, with their trespass which they trespassed against me, and that also they have walked contrary unto me;

Jgs 10:10 — And the children of Israel cried unto the LORD, saying, We have sinned against thee, both because we have forsaken our God, and also served Baalim.

Jgs 10:15 — And the children of Israel said unto the LORD, We have sinned: do thou unto us whatsoever seemeth good unto thee; deliver us only, we pray thee, this day.

1Sa 12:10 — And they cried unto the LORD, and said, We have sinned, because we have forsaken the LORD, and have served Baalim and Ashtaroth: but now deliver us out of the hand of our enemies, and we will serve thee.

1Ki 8:47 — *Yet* if they shall bethink themselves in the land whither they were carried captives, and repent, and make supplication unto thee in the land of them that carried them captives, saying, We have sinned, and have done perversely, we have committed wickedness;

Ezr 9:6 — And said, O my God, I am ashamed and blush to lift up my face to thee, my God: for our iniquities are increased over *our* head, and our trespass is grown up unto the heavens.

Ezr 9:15 — O LORD God of Israel, thou *art* righteous: for we remain yet escaped, as *it is* this day: behold, we *are* before thee in our trespasses: for we cannot stand before thee because of this.

Ne 9:2 — And the seed of Israel separated themselves from all strangers, and stood and confessed their sins, and the iniquities of their fathers.

Job 7:20 — I have sinned; what shall I do unto thee, O thou preserver of men? why hast thou set me as a mark against thee, so that I am a burden to myself?

Ps 31:10 — For my life is spent with grief, and my years with sighing: my strength faileth because of mine iniquity, and my bones are consumed.

Ps 32:3 — When I kept silence, my bones waxed old through my roaring all the day long.

Ps 32:5 — I acknowledged my sin unto thee, and mine iniquity have I not hid. I said, I will confess my transgressions unto the LORD; and thou forgavest the iniquity of my sin. Selah.

Ps 38:10 — My heart panteth, my strength faileth me: as for the light of mine eyes, it also is gone from me.

Ps 38:18 — For I will declare mine iniquity; I will be sorry for my sin.

Ps 40:12 — For innumerable evils have compassed me about: mine iniquities have taken hold upon me, so that I am not able to look up; they are more than the hairs of mine head: therefore my heart faileth me.

Ps 69:5 — O God, thou knowest my foolishness; and my sins are not hid from thee.

Ps 119:176 — I have gone astray like a lost sheep; seek thy servant; for I do not forget thy commandments.

Ps 130:3 — If thou, LORD, shouldest mark iniquities, O Lord, who shall stand?

Pr 28:13 — He that covereth his sins shall not prosper: but whoso confesseth and forsaketh *them* shall have mercy.

Isa 6:5 — Then said I, Woe *is* me! for I am undone; because I *am* a man of unclean lips, and I dwell in the midst of a people of unclean lips: for mine eyes have seen the King, the LORD of hosts.

Jer 3:13 — Only acknowledge thine iniquity, that thou hast transgressed against the LORD thy God, and hast scattered thy ways to the strangers under every green tree, and ye have not obeyed my voice, saith the LORD.

Jer 3:25 — We lie down in our shame, and our confusion covereth us: for we have sinned against the LORD our God, we and our fathers, from our youth even unto this day, and have not obeyed the voice of the LORD our God.

Jer 14:7 — O LORD, though our iniquities testify against us, do thou *it* for thy name's sake: for our backslidings are many; we have sinned against thee.

Jer 14:20 — We acknowledge, O LORD, our wickedness, *and* the iniquity of our fathers: for we have sinned against thee.

La 1:18 — The LORD is righteous; for I have rebelled against his commandment: hear, I pray you, all people, and behold my sorrow: my virgins and my young men are gone into captivity.

La 3:42 — We have transgressed and have rebelled: thou hast not pardoned.

La 5:16 — The crown is fallen *from* our head: woe unto us, that we have sinned!

• Importunity in.

Ge 18:23–32; 32:24–29; Jgs 6:36–40; 1Sa 1:10–11; 1Ki 8:22–30; Ezr 9:5–6; Ne 1:4–6; Ps 22:1–2; 28:1–2; 35:22–23; 55:1–2, 16–17; 61:1–2; 88:1–2; 102:1–2; 119:145–147; 130:1–2; 141:1–2; 142:1–2; Isa 38:2–3; Da 9:16–19; Mt 15:22–28; Mk 7:25–29; Lk 11:5–8; 18:1–7

Ex 32:32 — Yet now, if thou wilt forgive their sin—; and if not, blot me, I pray thee, out of thy book which thou hast written.

Dt 9:25 — Thus I fell down before the LORD forty days and forty nights, as I fell down *at the first;* because the LORD had said he would destroy you.

Jgs 16:28 — And Samson called unto the LORD, and said, O Lord GOD, remember me, I pray thee, and strengthen me, I pray thee, only this once, O God, that I may be at once avenged of the Philistines for my two eyes.

1Sa 12:23 — Moreover as for me, God forbid that I should sin against the LORD in ceasing to pray for you: but I will teach you the good and the right way:

Ps 17:1 — Hear the right, O LORD, attend unto my cry, give ear unto my prayer, *that goeth* not out of feigned lips.

Ps 17:6 — I have called upon thee, for thou wilt hear me, O God: incline thine ear unto me, *and hear* my speech.

Ps 22:19 — But be not thou far from me, O LORD: O my strength, haste thee to help me.

Ps 57:2 — I will cry unto God most high; unto God that performeth *all things* for me.

Ps 70:5 — But I *am* poor and needy: make haste unto me, O God: thou *art* my help and my deliverer; O LORD, make no tarrying.

Ps 86:3 — Be merciful unto me, O Lord: for I cry unto thee daily.

Ps 86:6 — Give ear, O LORD, unto my prayer; and attend to the voice of my supplications.

Ps 88:9 — Mine eye mourneth by reason of affliction: LORD, I have called daily upon thee, I have stretched out my hands unto thee.

Ps 88:13 — But unto thee have I cried, O LORD; and in the morning shall my prayer prevent thee.

Ps 119:58 — I intreated thy favour with *my* whole heart: be merciful unto me according to thy word.

Isa 62:7 — And give him no rest, till he establish, and till he make Jerusalem a praise in the earth.

Isa 64:12 — Wilt thou refrain thyself for these *things,* O LORD? wilt thou hold thy peace, and afflict us very sore?

Da 9:3 — And I set my face unto the Lord God, to seek by prayer and supplications, with fasting, and sackcloth, and ashes:

Jnh 1:14 — Wherefore they cried unto the LORD, and said, We beseech thee, O LORD, we beseech thee, let us not perish for this man's life, and lay not upon us innocent blood: for thou, O LORD, hast done as it pleased thee.

Hab 1:2 — O LORD, how long shall I cry, and thou wilt not hear! *even* cry out unto thee *of* violence, and thou wilt not save!

Lk 7:3 — And when he heard of Jesus, he sent unto him the elders of the Jews, beseeching him that he would come and heal his servant.

Lk 22:44 — And being in an agony he prayed more earnestly: and his sweat was as it were great drops of blood falling down to the ground.

Ro 8:26 — Likewise the Spirit also helpeth our infirmities: for we know not what we should pray for as we ought: but the Spirit itself maketh intercession for us with groanings which cannot be uttered.

2Co 12:8 — For this thing I besought the Lord thrice, that it might depart from me.

Eph 6:18 — Praying always with all prayer and supplication in the Spirit, and watching thereunto with all perseverance and supplication for all saints;

Heb 5:7 — Who in the days of his flesh, when he had offered up prayers and supplications with strong crying and tears unto him that was able to save him from death, and was heard in that he feared;

• Instances of.

• Jacob.

Ge 32:24–30

• Moses.

Ex 33:12–16

Ex 34:9 — And he said, If now I have found grace in thy sight, O Lord, let my Lord, I pray thee, go among us; for it *is* a stiffnecked people; and pardon our iniquity and our sin, and take us for thine inheritance.

• Elijah.

1Ki 18:24–44

• The two blind men of Jericho.

Mt 20:30–31

Mk 10:48 — And many charged him that he should hold his peace: but he cried the more a great deal, *Thou* Son of David, have mercy on me.

Lk 18:39 — And they which went before rebuked him, that he should hold his peace: but he cried so much the more, *Thou* Son of David, have mercy on me.

- **The Syrophenician woman.**
  Mt 15:22–28; Mk 7:25–30
- **The centurion.**
  Lk 7:3–4
  Mt 8:5 — And when Jesus was entered into Capernaum, there came unto him a centurion, beseeching him,

• Intercessory.

See: Intercession
See: Jesus, Mediation of

• Of the wicked not heard.

See: Wicked; prayer of

• Pleas offered in.

Ge 32:9–12; Ex 32:11–13; Nu 14:13–18; Dt 3:24–25; 9:25–29; Jos 7:8–9; 2Sa 7:25–29; 1Ki 8:25–26, 59–60; 18:36–37; 2Ki 19:15–19; Ne 1:8–9; Ps 9:19–20; 74:10–11, 20–23; 79:10–12; 83:1–2; 86:1–5; 89:49–51; 109:21–27; 115:1–2; 119:42–43, 145–146, 173–176; 143:11–12; Isa 37:15–20; 63:17–19; Jer 18:20–21; La 3:56–63

Ex 33:13 — Now therefore, I pray thee, if I have found grace in thy sight, shew me now thy way, that I may know thee, that I may find grace in thy sight: and consider that this nation *is* thy people.

Nu 16:22 — And they fell upon their faces, and said, O God, the God of the spirits of all flesh, shall one man sin, and wilt thou be wroth with all the congregation?

Dt 9:18 — And I fell down before the LORD, as at the first, forty days and forty nights: I did neither eat bread, nor drink water, because of all your sins which ye sinned, in doing wickedly in the sight of the LORD, to provoke him to anger.

2Ch 14:11 — And Asa cried unto the LORD his God, and said, LORD, *it is* nothing with thee to help, whether with many, or with them that have no power: help us, O LORD our God; for we rest on thee, and in thy name we go against this multitude. O LORD, thou *art* our God; let not man prevail against thee.

Ne 9:32 — Now therefore, our God, the great, the mighty, and the terrible God, who keepest covenant and mercy, let not all the trouble seem little before thee, that hath come upon us, on our kings, on our princes, and on our priests, and on our prophets, and on our fathers, and on all thy people, since the time of the kings of Assyria unto this day.

Ps 4:1 — Hear me when I call, O God of my righteousness: thou hast enlarged me *when I was* in distress; have mercy upon me, and hear my prayer.

Ps 25:6 — Remember, O LORD, thy tender mercies and thy lovingkindnesses; for they *have been* ever of old.

Ps 27:9 — Hide not thy face *far* from me; put not thy servant away in anger: thou hast been my help; leave me not, neither forsake me, O God of my salvation.

Ps 31:3 — For thou *art* my rock and my fortress; therefore for thy name's sake lead me, and guide me.

Ps 38:16 — For I said, *Hear me,* lest *otherwise* they should rejoice over me: when my foot slippeth, they magnify *themselves* against me.

Ps 69:6 — Let not them that wait on thee, O Lord GOD of hosts, be ashamed for my sake: let not those that seek thee be confounded for my sake, O God of Israel.

Ps 69:13 — But as for me, my prayer *is* unto thee, O LORD, *in* an acceptable time: O God, in the multitude of thy mercy hear me, in the truth of thy salvation.

Ps 69:16 — Hear me, O LORD; for thy lovingkindness *is* good: turn unto me according to the multitude of thy tender mercies.

Ps 71:18 — Now also when I am old and greyheaded, O God, forsake me not; until I have shewed thy strength unto *this* generation, *and* thy power to every one *that* is to come.

Ps 74:18 — Remember this, *that* the enemy hath reproached, O LORD, and *that* the foolish people have blasphemed thy name.

Ps 83:18 — That *men* may know that thou, whose name alone *is* JEHOVAH, *art* the most high over all the earth.

Ps 86:17 — Shew me a token for good; that they which hate me may see *it,* and be ashamed: because thou, LORD, hast holpen me, and comforted me.

Ps 106:47 — Save us, O LORD our God, and gather us from among the heathen, to give thanks unto thy holy name, *and* to triumph in thy praise.

Ps 119:38 — Stablish thy word unto thy servant, who *is devoted* to thy fear.

Ps 119:49 — Remember the word unto thy servant, upon which thou hast caused me to hope.

Ps 119:73 — Thy hands have made me and fashioned me: give me understanding, that I may learn thy commandments.

Ps 119:94 — I *am* thine, save me; for I have sought thy precepts.

Ps 119:116 — Uphold me according unto thy word, that I may live: and let me not be ashamed of my hope.

Ps 119:124 — Deal with thy servant according unto thy mercy, and teach me thy statutes.

Ps 119:149 — Hear my voice according unto thy lovingkindness: O LORD, quicken me according to thy judgment.

Ps 119:153 — Consider mine affliction, and deliver me: for I do not forget thy law.

Jer 14:21 — Do not abhor *us,* for thy name's sake, do not disgrace the throne of thy glory: remember, break not thy covenant with us.

Joel 2:17 — Let the priests, the ministers of the LORD, weep between the porch and the altar, and let them say, Spare thy people, O LORD, and give not thine heritage to reproach, that the heathen should rule over them: wherefore should they say among the people, Where *is* their God?

• Thanksgiving and, before taking food.

Mt 26:26–27; Mk 8:6–7; 14:22–23; 1Co 10:30–31; 1Ti 4:3–5

Jos 9:14 — And the men took of their victuals, and asked not *counsel* at the mouth of the LORD.

1Sa 9:13 — As soon as ye be come into the city, ye shall straightway find him, before he go up to the high place to eat: for the people will not eat until he come, because he doth bless the sacrifice; *and* afterwards they eat that be bidden. Now therefore get you up; for about this time ye shall find him.

Mt 14:19 — And he commanded the multitude to sit down on the grass, and took the five loaves, and the two fishes, and looking up to heaven, he blessed, and brake, and gave the loaves to *his* disciples, and the disciples to the multitude.

Mt 15:36 — And he took the seven loaves and the fishes, and gave thanks, and brake *them,* and gave to his disciples, and the disciples to the multitude.

Mk 6:41 — And when he had taken the five loaves and the two fishes, he looked up to heaven, and blessed, and brake the loaves, and gave *them* to his disciples to set before them; and the two fishes divided he among them all.

Lk 9:16 — Then he took the five loaves and the two fishes, and looking up to heaven, he blessed them, and brake, and gave to the disciples to set before the multitude.

Lk 22:19 — And he took bread, and gave thanks, and brake *it,* and gave unto them, saying, This is my body which is given for you: this do in remembrance of me.

Jn 6:11 — And Jesus took the loaves; and when he had given thanks, he distributed to the disciples, and the disciples to them that were set down; and likewise of the fishes as much as they would.

Jn 6:23 — (Howbeit there came other boats from Tiberias nigh unto the place where they did eat bread, after that the Lord had given thanks:)

Ac 27:35 — And when he had thus spoken, he took bread, and gave thanks to God in presence of them all: and when he had broken *it,* he began to eat.

Ro 14:6 — He that regardeth the day, regardeth *it* unto the Lord; and he that regardeth not the day, to the Lord he doth not regard *it.* He that eateth, eateth to the Lord, for he giveth God thanks; and he that eateth not, to the Lord he eateth not, and giveth God thanks.

1Co 11:24 — And when he had given thanks, he brake *it,* and said, Take, eat: this is my body, which is broken for you: this do in remembrance of me.

PRAYER, Miscellany of Minor Sub-Topics

• Attitudes in.

See: Worship

• Prayer test proposed by Elijah.

1Ki 18:24–39

• Daily in the morning.

Ps 5:3 — My voice shalt thou hear in the morning, O LORD; in the morning will I direct *my prayer* unto thee, and will look up.

Ps 88:13 — But unto thee have I cried, O LORD; and in the morning shall my prayer prevent thee.

Ps 143:8 — Cause me to hear thy lovingkindness in the morning; for in thee do I trust: cause me to know the way wherein I should walk; for I lift up my soul unto thee.

Isa 33:2 — O LORD, be gracious unto us; we have waited for thee: be thou their arm every morning, our salvation also in the time of trouble.

• Twice daily.

Ps 88:1 — O LORD God of my salvation, I have cried day *and* night before thee:

• Thrice daily.

Ps 55:17 — Evening, and morning, and at noon, will I pray, and cry aloud: and he shall hear my voice.

Da 6:10 — Now when Daniel knew that the writing was signed, he went into his house; and his windows being open in his chamber toward Jerusalem, he kneeled upon his knees three times a day, and prayed, and gave thanks before his God, as he did aforetime.

• All night.

Lk 6:12 — And it came to pass in those days, that he went out into a mountain to pray, and continued all night in prayer to God.

• Without ceasing.

1Th 5:17 — Pray without ceasing.

• Boldness in.

• Enjoined.

Heb 4:16 — Let us therefore come boldly unto the throne of grace, that we may obtain mercy, and find grace to help in time of need.

• Exemplified by Abraham in his inquiry concerning Sodom.

Ge 18:23–32

• Exemplified by Moses, supplicating for assistance in delivering Israel.

Ex 33:12 — And Moses said unto the LORD, See, thou sayest unto me, Bring up this people: and thou hast not let me know whom thou wilt send with me. Yet thou hast said, I know thee by name, and thou hast also found grace in my sight.

Ex 33:18 — And he said, I beseech thee, shew me thy glory.

• Secret.

Ge 24:63 — And Isaac went out to meditate in the field at the eventide: and he lifted up his eyes, and saw, and, behold, the camels *were* coming.

Mt 6:6 — But thou, when thou prayest, enter into thy closet, and when thou hast shut thy door, pray to thy Father which is in secret; and thy Father which seeth in secret shall reward thee openly.

• Silent.

Ps 5:1 — Give ear to my words, O LORD, consider my meditation.

• Weeping in.

Ezr 10:1 — Now when Ezra had prayed, and when he had confessed, weeping and casting himself down before the house of God, there assembled unto him out of Israel a very great congregation of men and women and children: for the people wept very sore.

• In loud voice, satirized by Elijah.

1Ki 18:27 — And it came to pass at noon, that Elijah mocked them, and said, Cry aloud: for he *is* a god; either he is talking, or he is pursuing, or he is in a journey, *or* peradventure he sleepeth, and must be awaked.

- **Long.**
  - **Of Pharisees.**

    Mt 23:14 — Woe unto you, scribes and Pharisees, hypocrites! for ye devour widows' houses, and for a pretence make long prayer: therefore ye shall receive the greater damnation.
  - **Of scribes.**

    Mk 12:40 — Which devour widows' houses, and for a pretence make long prayers: these shall receive greater damnation.

    Lk 20:47 — Which devour widows' houses, and for a shew make long prayers: the same shall receive greater damnation.
- **Profuse, to be avoided.**

  Ecc 5:2 — Be not rash with thy mouth, and let not thine heart be hasty to utter *any* thing before God: for God *is* in heaven, and thou upon earth: therefore let thy words be few.

  Mt 6:7 — But when ye pray, use not vain repetitions, as the heathen *do:* for they think that they shall be heard for their much speaking.
- **Vain repetitions of, to be avoided.**

  Mt 6:7 — But when ye pray, use not vain repetitions, as the heathen *do:* for they think that they shall be heard for their much speaking.
- **Tokens asked for, as assurance of answer.**
  - **By Abraham's servant.**

    Ge 24:14 — And let it come to pass, that the damsel to whom I shall say, Let down thy pitcher, I pray thee, that I may drink; and she shall say, Drink, and I will give thy camels drink also: *let the same be* she *that* thou hast appointed for thy servant Isaac; and thereby shall I know that thou hast shewed kindness unto my master.
  - **Gideon asks for a sign of dew on a fleece.**

    Jgs 6:36–40
- **Rebuked.**
  - **Of Moses, at the Red Sea.**

    Ex 14:15 — And the LORD said unto Moses, Wherefore criest thou unto me? speak unto the children of Israel, that they go forward:
  - **Of Moses, when he prayed to see Canaan.**

    Dt 3:23–27
  - **Of Joshua.**

    Jos 7:10 — And the LORD said unto Joshua, Get thee up; wherefore liest thou thus upon thy face?
- **Evils averted by.**

  Jer 26:19 — Did Hezekiah king of Judah and all Judah put him at all to death? did he not fear the LORD, and besought the LORD, and the LORD repented him of the evil which he had pronounced against them? Thus might we procure great evil against our souls.
- **Unbelief in.**

  Job 21:15 — What *is* the Almighty, that we should serve him? and what profit should we have, if we pray unto him?
- **"Lord's Prayer".**

  Mt 6:9–13; Lk 11:2–4
- **Answer to, withheld.**
  - **Of Balaam.**

    Dt 23:5 — Nevertheless the LORD thy God would not hearken unto Balaam; but the LORD thy God turned the curse into a blessing unto thee, because the LORD thy God loved thee.

    Jos 24:10 — But I would not hearken unto Balaam; therefore he blessed you still: so I delivered you out of his hand.
  - **Of Job.**

    Job 30:20 — I cry unto thee, and thou dost not hear me: I stand up, and thou regardest me *not.*

    Job 42:12 — So the LORD blessed the latter end of Job more than his beginning: for he had fourteen thousand sheep, and six thousand camels, and a thousand yoke of oxen, and a thousand she asses.
  - **Of the Israelites, when attacked by the Amorites.**

    Dt 1:45 — And ye returned and wept before the LORD; but the LORD would not hearken to your voice, nor give ear unto you.
  - **The prayer of Jesus, "Let this cup pass".**

    Mt 26:44–27:66

    Mt 26:39 — And he went a little farther, and fell on his face, and prayed, saying, O my Father, if it be possible, let this cup pass from me: nevertheless not as I will, but as thou *wilt.*

    Mt 26:42 — He went away again the second time, and prayed, saying, O my Father, if this cup may not pass away from me, except I drink it, thy will be done.
- **Answer to, delayed.**

  Ps 22:1–2

  Ps 40:1 — I waited patiently for the LORD; and he inclined unto me, and heard my cry.

  Ps 80:4 — O LORD God of hosts, how long wilt thou be angry against the prayer of thy people?

  Ps 88:14 — LORD, why castest thou off my soul? *why* hidest thou thy face from me?

  Jer 42:7 — And it came to pass after ten days, that the word of the LORD came unto Jeremiah.

  Hab 1:2 — O LORD, how long shall I cry, and thou wilt not hear! *even* cry out unto thee *of* violence, and thou wilt not save!

  Lk 18:7 — And shall not God avenge his own elect, which cry day and night unto him, though he bear long with them?
- **Answer to, exceeds petition.**
  - **Solomon asked wisdom; the answer included wisdom, riches, honour, and long life.**

    1Ki 3:7–14; 2Ch 1:10–12
- **The disciples prayed for Peter; the answer included Peter's deliverance.**

  Ac 12:5 — Peter therefore was kept in prison: but prayer was made without ceasing of the church unto God for him.

  Ac 12:15 — And they said unto her, Thou art mad. But she constantly affirmed that it was even so. Then said they, It is his angel.

• Answer to, different from the request.

• Moses asked to be permitted to cross Jordan; answer was permission to view the land of promise.

Dt 3:23–27

• The Israelites lusted for the fleshpots of Egypt; answer gave them flesh, but also leanness of soul.

Ps 106:14–15

• Martha and Mary asked Jesus to heal their brother Jesus; delayed, but raised Lazarus from the dead.

Jn 11:1–57

• Paul asked that the thorn in the flesh be removed; the answer was promise of grace to endure it.

2Co 12:8–9

• In behalf of nations.

See: Nation; prayer for

• Penitential.

• Of David.

Ps 51:1–17

• Of the publican.

Lk 18:13 — And the publican, standing afar off, would not lift up so much as *his* eyes unto heaven, but smote upon his breast, saying, God be merciful to me a sinner.

See: Prayer; confession in

See: Sin; confession of

• Imprecatory.

Nu 22:6–11; 23:7–8; 24:9–10; Dt 11:29–30; 27:11–13; Jos 8:33–34; 2Sa 16:10–12; Ne 4:4–5; Job 3:1–10; Ps 31:17–18; 40:14–15; 68:1–2; 69:23–24, 27–28; 70:2–3; 83:13–17; 109:9–20, 28–29; 140:9–10; Jer 18:21–23; La 3:64–66; Gal 1:8–9; 2Ti 4:14–15

Nu 16:15 — And Moses was very wroth, and said unto the LORD, Respect not thou their offering: I have not taken one ass from them, neither have I hurt one of them.

Dt 33:11 — Bless, LORD, his substance, and accept the work of his hands: smite through the loins of them that rise against him, and of them that hate him, that they rise not again.

Jgs 16:28 — And Samson called unto the LORD, and said, O Lord GOD, remember me, I pray thee, and strengthen me, I pray thee, only this once, O God, that I may be at once avenged of the Philistines for my two eyes.

Ne 5:13 — Also I shook my lap, and said, So God shake out every man from his house, and from his labour, that performeth not this promise, even thus be he shaken out, and emptied. And all the congregation said, Amen, and praised the LORD. And the people did according to this promise.

Job 27:7 — Let mine enemy be as the wicked, and he that riseth up against me as the unrighteous.

Ps 5:10 — Destroy thou them, O God; let them fall by their own counsels; cast them out in the multitude of their transgressions; for they have rebelled against thee.

Ps 6:10 — Let all mine enemies be ashamed and sore vexed: let them return *and* be ashamed suddenly.

Ps 9:20 — Put them in fear, O LORD: *that* the nations may know themselves *to be but* men. Selah.

Ps 10:2 — The wicked in *his* pride doth persecute the poor: let them be taken in the devices that they have imagined.

Ps 10:15 — Break thou the arm of the wicked and the evil *man:* seek out his wickedness *till* thou find none.

Ps 25:3 — Yea, let none that wait on thee be ashamed: let them be ashamed which transgress without cause.

Ps 28:4 — Give them according to their deeds, and according to the wickedness of their endeavours: give them after the work of their hands; render to them their desert.

Ps 35:4 — Let them be confounded and put to shame that seek after my soul: let them be turned back and brought to confusion that devise my hurt.

Ps 35:8 — Let destruction come upon him at unawares; and let his net that he hath hid catch himself: into that very destruction let him fall.

Ps 35:26 — Let them be ashamed and brought to confusion together that rejoice at mine hurt: let them be clothed with shame and dishonour that magnify *themselves* against me.

Ps 54:5 — He shall reward evil unto mine enemies: cut them off in thy truth.

Ps 55:9 — Destroy, O Lord, *and* divide their tongues: for I have seen violence and strife in the city.

Ps 55:15 — Let death seize upon them, *and* let them go down quick into hell: for wickedness is in their dwellings, *and* among them.

Ps 56:7 — Shall they escape by iniquity? in *thine* anger cast down the people, O God.

Ps 58:7 — Let them melt away as waters *which* run continually: *when* he bendeth *his bow to shoot* his arrows, let them be as cut in pieces.

Ps 59:5 — Thou therefore, O LORD God of hosts, the God of Israel, awake to visit all the heathen: be not merciful to any wicked transgressors. Selah.

Ps 59:11 — Slay them not, lest my people forget: scatter them by thy power; and bring them down, O Lord our shield.

Ps 59:15 — Let them wander up and down for meat, and grudge if they be not satisfied.

Ps 71:13 — Let them be confounded *and* consumed that are adversaries to my soul; let them be covered *with* reproach and dishonour that seek my hurt.

Ps 79:10 — Wherefore should the heathen say, Where *is* their God? let him be known among the heathen in our sight *by* the revenging of the blood of thy servants *which is* shed.

Ps 79:12 — And render unto our neighbours sevenfold into their bosom their reproach, wherewith they have reproached thee, O Lord.

Ps 94:2 — Lift up thyself, thou judge of the earth: render a reward to the proud.

Ps 109:7 — When he shall be judged, let him be condemned: and let his prayer become sin.

Ps 119:78 — Let the proud be ashamed; for they dealt perversely with me without a cause: *but* I will meditate in thy precepts.

Ps 119:84 — How many *are* the days of thy servant? when wilt thou execute judgment on them that persecute me?

Ps 129:5 — Let them all be confounded and turned back that hate Zion.

Ps 143:12 — And of thy mercy cut off mine enemies, and destroy all them that afflict my soul: for I *am* thy servant.

Ps 144:6 — Cast forth lightning, and scatter them: shoot out thine arrows, and destroy them.

Jer 11:20 — But, O LORD of hosts, that judgest righteously, that triest the reins and the heart, let me see thy vengeance on them: for unto thee have I revealed my cause.

Jer 12:3 — But thou, O LORD, knowest me: thou hast seen me, and tried mine heart toward thee: pull them out like sheep for the slaughter, and prepare them for the day of slaughter.

Jer 15:15 — O LORD, thou knowest: remember me, and visit me, and revenge me of my persecutors; take me not away in thy longsuffering: know that for thy sake I have suffered rebuke.

Jer 17:18 — Let them be confounded that persecute me, but let not me be confounded: let them be dismayed, but let not me be dismayed: bring upon them the day of evil, and destroy them with double destruction.

Jer 20:12 — But, O LORD of hosts, that triest the righteous, *and* seest the reins and the heart, let me see thy vengeance on them: for unto thee have I opened my cause.

La 1:22 — Let all their wickedness come before thee; and do unto them, as thou hast done unto me for all my transgressions: for my sighs *are* many, and my heart *is* faint.

- **Submission in.**
  - **Exemplified by Jesus.**

    Mt 26:39 — And he went a little farther, and fell on his face, and prayed, saying, O my Father, if it be possible, let this cup pass from me: nevertheless not as I will, but as thou *wilt.*

    Mk 14:36 — And he said, Abba, Father, all things *are* possible unto thee; take away this cup from me: nevertheless not what I will, but what thou wilt.

    Lk 22:42 — Saying, Father, if thou be willing, remove this cup from me: nevertheless not my will, but thine, be done.
  - **Exemplified by David.**

    2Sa 12:22–23
  - **Exemplified by Job.**

    Job 1:20–21
- **Private, enjoined.**

  Mt 6:6 — But thou, when thou prayest, enter into thy closet, and when thou hast shut thy door, pray to thy Father which is in secret; and thy Father which seeth in secret shall reward thee openly.
- **Exemplified by.**
  - **Lot.**

    Ge 19:20 — Behold now, this city is near to flee unto, and it is a little one: Oh, let me escape thither, (*is* it not a little one?) and my soul shall live.
  - **Eliezer.**

    Ge 24:12 — And he said, O LORD God of my master Abraham, I pray thee, send me good speed this day, and shew kindness unto my master Abraham.
  - **Jacob.**

    Ge 32:9–12
  - **Gideon.**

    Jgs 6:22 — And when Gideon perceived that he *was* an angel of the LORD, Gideon said, Alas, O Lord GOD! for because I have seen an angel of the LORD face to face.

    Jgs 6:36 — And Gideon said unto God, If thou wilt save Israel by mine hand, as thou hast said,

    Jgs 6:39 — And Gideon said unto God, Let not thine anger be hot against me, and I will speak but this once: let me prove, I pray thee, but this once with the fleece; let it now be dry only upon the fleece, and upon all the ground let there be dew.
  - **Hannah.**

    1Sa 1:10 — And she *was* in bitterness of soul, and prayed unto the LORD, and wept sore.
  - **David.**

    2Sa 7:18–29
  - **Hezekiah.**

    2Ki 20:2 — Then he turned his face to the wall, and prayed unto the LORD, saying,
  - **Isaiah.**

    2Ki 20:11 — And Isaiah the prophet cried unto the LORD: and he brought the shadow ten degrees backward, by which it had gone down in the dial of Ahaz.
  - **Manasseh.**

    2Ch 33:18–19
  - **Ezra.**

    Ezr 9:5–6
  - **Nehemiah.**

    Ne 2:4 — Then the king said unto me, For what dost thou make request? So I prayed to the God of heaven.
  - **Jeremiah.**

    Jer 32:16–25
  - **Daniel.**

    Da 9:3 — And I set my face unto the Lord God, to seek by prayer and supplications, with fasting, and sackcloth, and ashes:

    Da 9:19 — O Lord, hear; O Lord, forgive; O Lord, hearken and do; defer not, for thine own sake, O my God: for thy city and thy people are called by thy name.

• Jonah.

Jnh 2:1 — Then Jonah prayed unto the LORD his God out of the fish's belly,

• Habakkuk.

Hab 1:2 — O LORD, how long shall I cry, and thou wilt not hear! *even* cry out unto thee *of* violence, and thou wilt not save!

• Anna.

Lk 2:37 — And she *was* a widow of about fourscore and four years, which departed not from the temple, but served *God* with fastings and prayers night and day.

• Jesus.

Mt 14:23 — And when he had sent the multitudes away, he went up into a mountain apart to pray: and when the evening was come, he was there alone.

Mt 26:36 — Then cometh Jesus with them unto a place called Gethsemane, and saith unto the disciples, Sit ye here, while I go and pray yonder.

Mt 26:39 — And he went a little farther, and fell on his face, and prayed, saying, O my Father, if it be possible, let this cup pass from me: nevertheless not as I will, but as thou *wilt.*

Mk 1:35 — And in the morning, rising up a great while before day, he went out, and departed into a solitary place, and there prayed.

Lk 9:18 — And it came to pass, as he was alone praying, his disciples were with him: and he asked them, saying, Whom say the people that I am?

Lk 9:29 — And as he prayed, the fashion of his countenance was altered, and his raiment *was* white *and* glistering.

• Paul.

Ac 9:11 — And the Lord *said* unto him, Arise, and go into the street which is called Straight, and enquire in the house of Judas for *one* called Saul, of Tarsus: for, behold, he prayeth,

• Peter.

Ac 9:40 — But Peter put them all forth, and kneeled down, and prayed; and turning *him* to the body said, Tabitha, arise. And she opened her eyes: and when she saw Peter, she sat up.

Ac 10:9 — On the morrow, as they went on their journey, and drew nigh unto the city, Peter went up upon the housetop to pray about the sixth hour:

• Cornelius.

Ac 10:30 — And Cornelius said, Four days ago I was fasting until this hour; and at the ninth hour I prayed in my house, and, behold, a man stood before me in bright clothing,

• Family.

• By Abraham.

Ge 12:5 — And Abram took Sarai his wife, and Lot his brother's son, and all their substance that they had gathered, and the souls that they had gotten in Haran; and they went forth to go into the land of Canaan; and into the land of Canaan they came.

Ge 12:8 — And he removed from thence unto a mountain on the east of Bethel, and pitched his tent, *having* Bethel on the west, and Hai on the east: and there he builded an altar unto the LORD, and called upon the name of the LORD.

• By Jacob.

Ge 35:3 — And let us arise, and go up to Bethel; and I will make there an altar unto God, who answered me in the day of my distress, and was with me in the way which I went.

• By Cornelius.

Ac 10:2 — A devout *man,* and one that feared God with all his house, which gave much alms to the people, and prayed to God alway.

• Social.

Ac 1:13–14

Mt 18:19 — Again I say unto you, That if two of you shall agree on earth as touching any thing that they shall ask, it shall be done for them of my Father which is in heaven.

Ac 16:25 — And at midnight Paul and Silas prayed, and sang praises unto God: and the prisoners heard them.

Ac 20:36 — And when he had thus spoken, he kneeled down, and prayed with them all.

Ac 21:5 — And when we had accomplished those days, we departed and went our way; and they all brought us on our way, with wives and children, till *we were* out of the city: and we kneeled down on the shore, and prayed.

• Held in private houses.

Ac 1:13–14

Ac 12:12 — And when he had considered *the thing,* he came to the house of Mary the mother of John, whose surname was Mark; where many were gathered together praying.

• Held in the temple.

Ac 2:46 — And they, continuing daily with one accord in the temple, and breaking bread from house to house, did eat their meat with gladness and singleness of heart,

Ac 3:1 — Now Peter and John went up together into the temple at the hour of prayer, *being* the ninth *hour.*

• Of Jesus.

• In a mountain.

Mt 14:23 — And when he had sent the multitudes away, he went up into a mountain apart to pray: and when the evening was come, he was there alone.

Mk 6:46 — And when he had sent them away, he departed into a mountain to pray.

Lk 6:12 — And it came to pass in those days, that he went out into a mountain to pray, and continued all night in prayer to God.

Lk 9:28 — And it came to pass about an eight days after these sayings, he took Peter and John and James, and went up into a mountain to pray.

• **In Gethsemane.**

Mt 26:36 — Then cometh Jesus with them unto a place called Gethsemane, and saith unto the disciples, Sit ye here, while I go and pray yonder.

Mk 14:32 — And they came to a place which was named Gethsemane: and he saith to his disciples, Sit ye here, while I shall pray.

Lk 22:45 — And when he rose up from prayer, and was come to his disciples, he found them sleeping for sorrow,

• **The Lord's Prayer.**

Mt 6:9 — After this manner therefore pray ye: Our Father which art in heaven, Hallowed be thy name.

Lk 11:1 — And it came to pass, that, as he was praying in a certain place, when he ceased, one of his disciples said unto him, Lord, teach us to pray, as John also taught his disciples.

• **Before day.**

Mk 1:35 — And in the morning, rising up a great while before day, he went out, and departed into a solitary place, and there prayed.

• **In distress.**

Jn 12:27 — Now is my soul troubled; and what shall I say? Father, save me from this hour: but for this cause came I unto this hour.

Heb 5:7 — Who in the days of his flesh, when he had offered up prayers and supplications with strong crying and tears unto him that was able to save him from death, and was heard in that he feared;

• **In the wilderness.**

Lk 5:16 — And he withdrew himself into the wilderness, and prayed.

• **In behalf of Peter.**

Lk 22:31–32

• **For the Comforter.**

Jn 14:16 — And I will pray the Father, and he shall give you another Comforter, that he may abide with you for ever;

• **After the supper.**

Jn 17:1–26

• **Of the apostles.**

Ac 1:24–25

• **To idols.**

1Ki 18:26–29

PRAYERFULNESS

Ps 5:1–3; Eph 1:15–16

Ps 42:8 — *Yet* the LORD will command his lovingkindness in the daytime, and in the night his song *shall be* with me, *and* my prayer unto the God of my life.

Ps 109:4 — For my love they are my adversaries: but I *give myself unto* prayer.

Ps 116:2 — Because he hath inclined his ear unto me, therefore will I call upon *him* as long as I live.

Da 6:10 — Now when Daniel knew that the writing was signed, he went into his house; and his windows being open in his chamber toward Jerusalem, he kneeled upon his knees three times a day, and prayed, and gave thanks before his God, as he did aforetime.

Lk 2:37 — And she *was* a widow of about fourscore and four years, which departed not from the temple, but served *God* with fastings and prayers night and day.

Ac 6:4 — But we will give ourselves continually to prayer, and to the ministry of the word.

Ac 10:2 — A devout *man,* and one that feared God with all his house, which gave much alms to the people, and prayed to God alway.

Ac 10:9 — On the morrow, as they went on their journey, and drew nigh unto the city, Peter went up upon the housetop to pray about the sixth hour:

Ro 1:9 — For God is my witness, whom I serve with my spirit in the gospel of his Son, that without ceasing I make mention of you always in my prayers;

Ro 12:12 — Rejoicing in hope; patient in tribulation; continuing instant in prayer;

Col 1:9 — For this cause we also, since the day we heard *it,* do not cease to pray for you, and to desire that ye might be filled with the knowledge of his will in all wisdom and spiritual understanding;

1Th 3:10 — Night and day praying exceedingly that we might see your face, and might perfect that which is lacking in your faith?

1Th 5:17 — Pray without ceasing.

1Ti 5:5 — Now she that is a widow indeed, and desolate, trusteth in God, and continueth in supplications and prayers night and day.

2Ti 1:3 — I thank God, whom I serve from *my* forefathers with pure conscience, that without ceasing I have remembrance of thee in my prayers night and day;

PRAYERLESSNESS

Job 21:14–15

Job 15:4 — Yea, thou castest off fear, and restrainest prayer before God.

Job 27:10 — Will he delight himself in the Almighty? will he always call upon God?

Ps 14:4 — Have all the workers of iniquity no knowledge? who eat up my people *as* they eat bread, and call not upon the LORD.

Ps 53:4 — Have the workers of iniquity no knowledge? who eat up my people *as* they eat bread: they have not called upon God.

Ps 79:6 — Pour out thy wrath upon the heathen that have not known thee, and upon the kingdoms that have not called upon thy name.

Isa 43:22 — But thou hast not called upon me, O Jacob; but thou hast been weary of me, O Israel.

Isa 64:7 — And *there is* none that calleth upon thy name, that stirreth up himself to take hold of thee: for thou hast hid thy face from us, and hast consumed us, because of our iniquities.

Jer 10:21 — For the pastors are become brutish, and have not sought the LORD: therefore they shall not prosper, and all their flocks shall be scattered.

Jer 10:25 — Pour out thy fury upon the heathen that know thee not, and upon the families that call not on thy name: for they have eaten up Jacob, and devoured him, and consumed him, and have made his habitation desolate.

Da 9:13 — As *it is* written in the law of Moses, all this evil is come upon us: yet made we not our prayer before the LORD our God, that we might turn from our iniquities, and understand thy truth.

Hos 7:7 — They are all hot as an oven, and have devoured their judges; all their kings are fallen: *there is* none among them that calleth unto me.

Jnh 1:6 — So the shipmaster came to him, and said unto him, What meanest thou, O sleeper? arise, call upon thy God, if so be that God will think upon us, that we perish not.

Zep 1:6 — And them that are turned back from the LORD; and *those* that have not sought the LORD, nor enquired for him.

PREACHING

• The act of exhorting, prophesying, reproving, teaching.

• Solomon called preacher.

Ecc 1:1 — The words of the Preacher, the son of David, king in Jerusalem.

Ecc 1:12 — I the Preacher was king over Israel in Jerusalem.

• Noah called preacher.

2Pe 2:5 — And spared not the old world, but saved Noah the eighth *person,* a preacher of righteousness, bringing in the flood upon the world of the ungodly;

• Sitting while.

Mt 5:1 — And seeing the multitudes, he went up into a mountain: and when he was set, his disciples came unto him:

Lk 4:20 — And he closed the book, and he gave *it* again to the minister, and sat down. And the eyes of all them that were in the synagogue were fastened on him.

Lk 5:3 — And he entered into one of the ships, which was Simon's, and prayed him that he would thrust out a little from the land. And he sat down, and taught the people out of the ship.

• Moses, slow of speech.

Ex 4:10–12

• Repentance

• The subject of John the Baptist's.

Mt 3:2 — And saying, Repent ye: for the kingdom of heaven is at hand.

Mk 1:4 — John did baptize in the wilderness, and preach the baptism of repentance for the remission of sins.

Mk 1:15 — And saying, The time is fulfilled, and the kingdom of God is at hand: repent ye, and believe the gospel.

Lk 3:3 — And he came into all the country about Jordan, preaching the baptism of repentance for the remission of sins;

• The subject of Christ's.

Mt 4:17 — From that time Jesus began to preach, and to say, Repent: for the kingdom of heaven is at hand.

Mk 1:15 — And saying, The time is fulfilled, and the kingdom of God is at hand: repent ye, and believe the gospel.

• The subject of the apostles'.

Mk 6:12 — And they went out, and preached that men should repent.

• "The Gospel of the Kingdom of God," the subject of Christ's.

Mk 1:14–15

Mk 2:2 — And straightway many were gathered together, insomuch that there was no room to receive *them,* no, not so much as about the door: and he preached the word unto them.

Lk 8:1 — And it came to pass afterward, that he went throughout every city and village, preaching and shewing the glad tidings of the kingdom of God: and the twelve *were* with him,

• Christ crucified and risen, the burden of Paul's.

Ac 17:3 — Opening and alleging, that Christ must needs have suffered, and risen again from the dead; and that this Jesus, whom I preach unto you, is Christ.

• Effective.

• By Azariah.

2Ch 15:1–15

• By Jonah.

Jnh 3:1–10

• By Peter and other apostles.

Ac 2:14–41

• By Philip.

Ac 8:5–12; 8:27–38

• By Paul.

Ac 13:16–43

Ac 9:20 — And straightway he preached Christ in the synagogues, that he is the Son of God.

↞See: Revivals

• Impenitence under.

• Of Asa.

2Ch 16:7–10

• Of Ahab.

2Ch 18:7–26

• Of the Jews.

Ac 13:46 — Then Paul and Barnabas waxed bold, and said, It was necessary that the word of God should first have been spoken to you: but seeing ye put it from you, and judge yourselves unworthy of everlasting life, lo, we turn to the Gentiles.

↞See: Call, Personal

↞See: Minister, a sacred teacher

↞See: Minister, Miscellany of Minor Sub-Topics

↞See: Obduracy

• Unclassified scripture relating to.

Mt 11:25–26; 1Co 1:17–18, 27–29; 2:1–8, 12–13; 14:1–20, 24–25; 2Co 2:14–16; 3:12–13; Col 1:23–29; 1Th 2:3–12; 1Ti 6:20–21; 2Ti 2:15–16; Tit 3:8–9

Ps 8:2 — Out of the mouth of babes and sucklings hast thou ordained strength because of thine enemies, that thou mightest still the enemy and the avenger.

Lk 10:21 — In that hour Jesus rejoiced in spirit, and said, I thank thee, O Father, Lord of heaven and earth, that thou hast hid these things from the wise and prudent, and hast revealed them unto babes: even so, Father; for so it seemed good in thy sight.

1Co 1:21 — For after that in the wisdom of God the world by wisdom knew not God, it pleased God by the foolishness of preaching to save them that believe.

1Co 1:23 — But we preach Christ crucified, unto the Jews a stumblingblock, and unto the Greeks foolishness;

1Th 1:5 — For our gospel came not unto you in word only, but also in power, and in the Holy Ghost, and in much assurance; as ye know what manner of men we were among you for your sake.

Tit 1:3 — But hath in due times manifested his word through preaching, which is committed unto me according to the commandment of God our Saviour;

PRECEPTS

See: Commandments

See: Law

PRECIOUS STONES See: Stones

PREDESTINATION

Ge 21:12–13; Dt 7:7–8; Job 23:13–14; Ps 78:67–68, 70–72; 105:17–22; Isa 44:1–2; Jer 1:4–5; Mal 1:2–3; Mt 11:25–26; 24:40–41; Lk 4:25–27; 17:34–36; Jn 6:44–45; Ro 8:28–30; 9:7–33; 11:7–8; 1Co 1:26–29; Eph 1:4–5, 9–11; Tit 1:1–2

Ex 9:16 — And in very deed for this *cause* have I raised thee up, for to shew *in* thee my power; and that my name may be declared throughout all the earth.

Ex 33:19 — And he said, I will make all my goodness pass before thee, and I will proclaim the name of the LORD before thee; and will be gracious to whom I will be gracious, and will shew mercy on whom I will shew mercy.

Dt 4:37 — And because he loved thy fathers, therefore he chose their seed after them, and brought thee out in his sight with his mighty power out of Egypt;

Dt 10:15 — Only the LORD had a delight in thy fathers to love them, and he chose their seed after them, *even* you above all people, as *it is* this day.

Dt 32:8 — When the most High divided to the nations their inheritance, when he separated the sons of Adam, he set the bounds of the people according to the number of the children of Israel.

Jos 11:20 — For it was of the LORD to harden their hearts, that they should come against Israel in battle, that he might destroy them utterly, *and* that they might have no favour, but that he might destroy them, as the LORD commanded Moses.

1Sa 12:22 — For the LORD will not forsake his people for his great name's sake: because it hath pleased the LORD to make you his people.

1Ki 12:15 — Wherefore the king hearkened not unto the people; for the cause was from the LORD, that he might perform his saying, which the LORD spake by Ahijah the Shilonite unto Jeroboam the son of Nebat.

1Ki 20:42 — And he said unto him, Thus saith the LORD, Because thou hast let go out of *thy* hand a man whom I appointed to utter destruction, therefore thy life shall go for his life, and thy people for his people.

2Ki 19:25 — Hast thou not heard long ago *how* I have done it, *and* of ancient times that I have formed it? now have I brought it to pass, that thou shouldest be to lay waste fenced cities *into* ruinous heaps.

2Ch 6:6 — But I have chosen Jerusalem, that my name might be there; and have chosen David to be over my people Israel.

Ps 33:12 — Blessed *is* the nation whose God *is* the LORD: *and* the people *whom* he hath chosen for his own inheritance.

Ps 65:4 — Blessed *is the man whom* thou choosest, and causest to approach *unto thee, that* he may dwell in thy courts: we shall be satisfied with the goodness of thy house, *even* of thy holy temple.

Ps 135:4 — For the LORD hath chosen Jacob unto himself, *and* Israel for his peculiar treasure.

Pr 16:4 — The LORD hath made all *things* for himself: yea, even the wicked for the day of evil.

Isa 44:7 — And who, as I, shall call, and shall declare it, and set it in order for me, since I appointed the ancient people? and the things that are coming, and shall come, let them shew unto them.

Mt 20:16 — So the last shall be first, and the first last: for many be called, but few chosen.

Mt 20:23 — And he saith unto them, Ye shall drink indeed of my cup, and be baptized with the baptism that I am baptized with: but to sit on my right hand, and on my left, is not mine to give, but *it shall be given to them* for whom it is prepared of my Father.

Mt 22:14 — For many are called, but few *are* chosen.

Mt 24:22 — And except those days should be shortened, there should no flesh be saved: but for the elect's sake those days shall be shortened.

Mt 25:34 — Then shall the King say unto them on his right hand, Come, ye blessed of my Father, inherit the kingdom prepared for you from the foundation of the world:

Mt 26:24 — The Son of man goeth as it is written of him: but woe unto that man by whom the Son of man is betrayed! it had been good for that man if he had not been born.

Mk 13:20 — And except that the Lord had shortened those days, no flesh should be saved: but for the elect's sake, whom he hath chosen, he hath shortened the days.

Mk 13:22 — For false Christs and false prophets shall rise, and shall shew signs and wonders, to seduce, if *it were* possible, even the elect.

Mk 14:21 — The Son of man indeed goeth, as it is written of him: but woe to that man by whom the Son of man is betrayed! good were it for that man if he had never been born.

Lk 8:10 — And he said, Unto you it is given to know the mysteries of the kingdom of God: but to others in parables; that seeing they might not see, and hearing they might not understand.

Lk 10:20 — Notwithstanding in this rejoice not, that the spirits are subject unto you; but rather rejoice, because your names are written in heaven.

Lk 18:7 — And shall not God avenge his own elect, which cry day and night unto him, though he bear long with them?

Lk 22:22 — And truly the Son of man goeth, as it was determined: but woe unto that man by whom he is betrayed!

Jn 6:37 — All that the Father giveth me shall come to me; and him that cometh to me I will in no wise cast out.

Jn 6:39 — And this is the Father's will which hath sent me, that of all which he hath given me I should lose nothing, but should raise it up again at the last day.

Jn 15:16 — Ye have not chosen me, but I have chosen you, and ordained you, that ye should go and bring forth fruit, and *that* your fruit should remain: that whatsoever ye shall ask of the Father in my name, he may give it you.

Jn 15:19 — If ye were of the world, the world would love his own: but because ye are not of the world, but I have chosen you out of the world, therefore the world hateth you.

Jn 17:2 — As thou hast given him power over all flesh, that he should give eternal life to as many as thou hast given him.

Jn 17:6 — I have manifested thy name unto the men which thou gavest me out of the world: thine they were, and thou gavest them me; and they have kept thy word.

Jn 17:9 — I pray for them: I pray not for the world, but for them which thou hast given me; for they are thine.

Jn 21:23 — Then went this saying abroad among the brethren, that that disciple should not die: yet Jesus said not unto him, He shall not die; but, If I will that he tarry till I come, what *is that* to thee?

Ac 1:7 — And he said unto them, It is not for you to know the times or the seasons, which the Father hath put in his own power.

Ac 2:23 — Him, being delivered by the determinate counsel and foreknowledge of God, ye have taken, and by wicked hands have crucified and slain:

Ac 2:39 — For the promise is unto you, and to your children, and to all that are afar off, *even* as many as the Lord our God shall call.

Ac 2:47 — Praising God, and having favour with all the people. And the Lord added to the church daily such as should be saved.

Ac 3:18 — But those things, which God before had shewed by the mouth of all his prophets, that Christ should suffer, he hath so fulfilled.

Ac 4:28 — For to do whatsoever thy hand and thy counsel determined before to be done.

Ac 13:48 — And when the Gentiles heard this, they were glad, and glorified the word of the Lord: and as many as were ordained to eternal life believed.

Ac 17:26 — And hath made of one blood all nations of men for to dwell on all the face of the earth, and hath determined the times before appointed, and the bounds of their habitation;

Ac 22:14 — And he said, The God of our fathers hath chosen thee, that thou shouldest know his will, and see that Just One, and shouldest hear the voice of his mouth.

Ro 1:6 — Among whom are ye also the called of Jesus Christ:

Ro 8:33 — Who shall lay any thing to the charge of God's elect? *It is* God that justifieth.

Ro 11:5 — Even so then at this present time also there is a remnant according to the election of grace.

1Co 2:7 — But we speak the wisdom of God in a mystery, *even* the hidden *wisdom,* which God ordained before the world unto our glory:

Gal 1:15 — But when it pleased God, who separated me from my mother's womb, and called *me* by his grace,

Eph 2:10 — For we are his workmanship, created in Christ Jesus unto good works, which God hath before ordained that we should walk in them.

Eph 3:11 — According to the eternal purpose which he purposed in Christ Jesus our Lord:

Col 3:12 — Put on therefore, as the elect of God, holy and beloved, bowels of mercies, kindness, humbleness of mind, meekness, longsuffering;

1Th 1:4 — Knowing, brethren beloved, your election of God.

1Th 2:12 — That ye would walk worthy of God, who hath called you unto his kingdom and glory.

2Th 2:13 — But we are bound to give thanks alway to God for you, brethren beloved of the Lord, because God hath from the beginning chosen you to salvation through sanctification of the Spirit and belief of the truth:

2Ti 1:9 — Who hath saved us, and called *us* with an holy calling, not according to our works, but according to his own purpose and grace, which was given us in Christ Jesus before the world began,

Jas 1:18 — Of his own will begat he us with the word of truth, that we should be a kind of firstfruits of his creatures.

1Pe 1:2 — Elect according to the foreknowledge of God the Father, through sanctification of the Spirit, unto obedience and sprinkling of the blood of Jesus Christ: Grace unto you, and peace, be multiplied.

1Pe 1:20 — Who verily was foreordained before the foundation of the world, but was manifest in these last times for you,

2Pe 1:10 — Wherefore the rather, brethren, give diligence to make your calling and election sure: for if ye do these things, ye shall never fall:

Jude 1:4 — For there are certain men crept in unawares, who were before of old ordained to this condemnation, ungodly men, turning the grace of our God into lasciviousness, and denying the only Lord God, and our Lord Jesus Christ.

Rev 13:8 — And all that dwell upon the earth shall worship him, whose names are not written in the book of life of the Lamb slain from the foundation of the world.

PREJUDICE

Lk 9:53 — And they did not receive him, because his face was as though he would go to Jerusalem.

Jn 4:9 — Then saith the woman of Samaria unto him, How is it that thou, being a Jew, askest drink of me, which am a woman of Samaria? for the Jews have no dealings with the Samaritans.

Ac 10:28 — And he said unto them, Ye know how that it is an unlawful thing for a man that is a Jew to keep company, or come unto one of another nation; but God hath shewed me that I should not call any man common or unclean.

Ac 11:3 — Saying, Thou wentest in to men uncircumcised, and didst eat with them.

Gal 2:12 — For before that certain came from James, he did eat with the Gentiles: but when they were come, he withdrew and separated himself, fearing them which were of the circumcision.

PRESCIENCE ↞See: God, Foreknowledge of

PRESENTS

• To Abraham, by Pharaoh.

Ge 12:16 — And he entreated Abram well for her sake: and he had sheep, and oxen, and he asses, and menservants, and maidservants, and she asses, and camels.

• To Abraham, by Abimelech.

Ge 20:14 — And Abimelech took sheep, and oxen, and menservants, and womenservants, and gave *them* unto Abraham, and restored him Sarah his wife.

• To Rebekah.

Ge 24:22 — And it came to pass, as the camels had done drinking, that the man took a golden earring of half a shekel weight, and two bracelets for her hands of ten *shekels* weight of gold;

• To Esau.

Ge 32:13–15

• To prophets.

1Ki 14:3 — And take with thee ten loaves, and cracknels, and a cruse of honey, and go to him: he shall tell thee what shall become of the child.

2Ki 4:42 — And there came a man from Baal-shalisha, and brought the man of God bread of the firstfruits, twenty loaves of barley, and full ears of corn in the husk thereof. And he said, Give unto the people, that they may eat.

• To those in adversity.

Job 42:10–11

• Betrothal.

Ge 24:53 — And the servant brought forth jewels of silver, and jewels of gold, and raiment, and gave *them* to Rebekah: he gave also to her brother and to her mother precious things.

• Marriage.

Est 2:18 — Then the king made a great feast unto all his princes and his servants, *even* Esther's feast; and he made a release to the provinces, and gave gifts, according to the state of the king.

• Propitiatory.

Ge 33:8–11; 1Sa 25:27–35

Ge 32:20 — And say ye moreover, Behold, thy servant Jacob *is* behind us. For he said, I will appease him with the present that goeth before me, and afterward I will see his face; peradventure he will accept of me.

Pr 21:14 — A gift in secret pacifieth anger: and a reward in the bosom strong wrath.

• To confirm covenants.

Ge 21:28–30; 1Sa 18:3–4

• Rewards of service.

Da 5:7 — The king cried aloud to bring in the astrologers, the Chaldeans, and the soothsayers. *And* the king spake, and said to the wise *men* of Babylon, Whosoever shall read this writing, and shew me the interpretation thereof, shall be clothed with scarlet, and *have* a chain of gold about his neck, and shall be the third ruler in the kingdom.

• Kings to kings.

1Ki 15:18–19

2Sa 8:10 — Then Toi sent Joram his son unto king David, to salute him, and to bless him, because he had fought against Hadadezer, and smitten him: for Hadadezer had wars with Toi. And *Joram* brought with him vessels of silver, and vessels of gold, and vessels of brass:

1Ki 10:10 — And she gave the king an hundred and twenty talents of gold, and of spices very great store, and precious stones: there came no more such abundance of spices as these which the queen of Sheba gave to king Solomon.

1Ki 10:13 — And king Solomon gave unto the queen of Sheba all her desire, whatsoever she asked, beside *that* which Solomon gave her of his royal bounty. So she turned and went to her own country, she and her servants.

• To corrupt courts, forbidden.

Ex 23:8 — And thou shalt take no gift: for the gift blindeth the wise, and perverteth the words of the righteous.

Dt 16:19 — Thou shalt not wrest judgment; thou shalt not respect persons, neither take a gift: for a gift doth blind the eyes of the wise, and pervert the words of the righteous.

Dt 27:25 — Cursed *be* he that taketh reward to slay an innocent person. And all the people shall say, Amen.

Isa 5:23 — Which justify the wicked for reward, and take away the righteousness of the righteous from him!

↞See: Bribery

↞See: Liberality

PRESUMPTION

Ex 14:11–12; Dt 29:19–20; Pr 18:12–13; 25:6–7; Isa 5:18–25; 14:13–14; 28:14–18; 29:15–16; 45:9–10; Mt 4:5–7; Lk 4:9–11; 12:18–20; 14:7–11; 18:11–12; Ro 9:20–21; 1Co 10:9–12; 2Th 2:3–4; Jas 4:13–16; 2Pe 2:10–11

Ex 5:2 — And Pharaoh said, Who *is* the LORD, that I should obey his voice to let Israel go? I know not the LORD, neither will I let Israel go.

Ex 17:7 — And he called the name of the place Massah, and Meribah, because of the chiding of the children of

Israel, and because they tempted the LORD, saying, Is the LORD among us, or not?

Nu 15:30 — But the soul that doeth *ought* presumptuously, *whether he be* born in the land, or a stranger, the same reproacheth the LORD; and that soul shall be cut off from among his people.

Nu 16:41 — But on the morrow all the congregation of the children of Israel murmured against Moses and against Aaron, saying, Ye have killed the people of the LORD.

Nu 21:5 — And the people spake against God, and against Moses, Wherefore have ye brought us up out of Egypt to die in the wilderness? for *there is* no bread, neither *is there any* water; and our soul loatheth this light bread.

Dt 6:16 — Ye shall not tempt the LORD your God, as ye tempted *him* in Massah.

1Ki 20:28 — And there came a man of God, and spake unto the king of Israel, and said, Thus saith the LORD, Because the Syrians have said, The LORD *is* God of the hills, but he *is* not God of the valleys, therefore will I deliver all this great multitude into thine hand, and ye shall know that I *am* the LORD.

1Ki 22:24 — But Zedekiah the son of Chenaanah went near, and smote Micaiah on the cheek, and said, Which way went the Spirit of the LORD from me to speak unto thee?

Job 15:25 — For he stretcheth out his hand against God, and strengtheneth himself against the Almighty.

Ps 19:13 — Keep back thy servant also from presumptuous *sins;* let them not have dominion over me: then shall I be upright, and I shall be innocent from the great transgression.

Ps 131:1 — LORD, my heart is not haughty, nor mine eyes lofty: neither do I exercise myself in great matters, or in things too high for me.

Isa 10:15 — Shall the axe boast itself against him that heweth therewith? *or* shall the saw magnify itself against him that shaketh it? as if the rod should shake *itself* against them that lift it up, *or* as if the staff should lift up *itself, as if it were* no wood.

Isa 28:22 — Now therefore be ye not mockers, lest your bands be made strong: for I have heard from the Lord GOD of hosts a consumption, even determined upon the whole earth.

Isa 29:20 — For the terrible one is brought to nought, and the scorner is consumed, and all that watch for iniquity are cut off:

Isa 58:3 — Wherefore have we fasted, *say they,* and thou seest not? *wherefore* have we afflicted our soul, and thou takest no knowledge? Behold, in the day of your fast ye find pleasure, and exact all your labours.

Isa 65:5 — Which say, Stand by thyself, come not near to me; for I am holier than thou. *These* are a smoke in my nose, a fire that burneth all the day.

Jer 23:34 — And *as for* the prophet, and the priest, and the people, that shall say, The burden of the LORD, I will even punish that man and his house.

Ro 1:32 — Who knowing the judgment of God, that they which commit such things are worthy of death, not only do the same, but have pleasure in them that do them.

• Instances of.

• Satan, when he said to Eve, "Ye shall not surely die".
Ge 3:1–5

• Builders of Babel.
Ge 11:4

• Abraham, in questioning about Sodom.
Ge 18:23–32

• Moses, in upbraiding Jehovah.
Nu 11:11–15, 22

• Nadab and Abihu.
Le 10:1–2

• Israelites, in ascending to the top of the hill against the Amalekites.
Nu 14:44–45

• Israelites, murmuring at Meribah.
Ex 17:2, 7

• Israelites, in reviling God.
Mal 1:6–7, 12; 3:7–8, 13

• Korah, Dathan, and Abiram.
Nu 16:3

• Saul, in sacrificing.
1Sa 13:8–14

• Saul, in sparing the Amalekites.
1Sa 15:3, 9–23

• Men of Beth-shemesh.
1Sa 6:19

• Uzzah, in steadying the ark.
2Sa 6:6–7

• David's anger at Uzzah's death.
2Sa 6:8

• David, in numbering Israel.
2Sa 24:1–17

• Jeroboam.
1Ki 13:4

• Ben-hadad.
1Ki 20:10

• Uzziah.
2Ch 26:16

• Sennacherib.
2Ch 32:13–14

• Job, in cursing the day of his birth.
Job 3:1–26

• Job, reproved by Eliphaz.
Job 4:1–5:27

• Jonah.
Jnh 4:1–8

• Peter, in objecting to Jesus' statement that he must be killed.
Mt 16:21–23; Mk 8:32

• Peter, in reflecting on his knowledge when he asked, amid a throng, who touched him.
Lk 8:45

• Peter, in objecting to Jesus washing his feet.
Jn 13:8

• **Peter, in asking Jesus, "What shall this man do?".**
Jn 21:20–22

• **The disciples, in rebuking those who brought little children to Jesus.**
Mt 19:13; Mk 10:13–14; Lk 18:15

• **The disciples, in their indignation at the anointing of Jesus.**
Mt 26:8–9; Mk 14:4–5; Jn 12:5

• **Reproving Jesus.**
Jn 7:3–5

• **James and John, in desiring to call down fire on the Samaritans.**
Lk 9:54

• **Those who reviled Jesus.**
Mt 27:42–43; Mk 15:29–32

• **Theudas.**
Ac 5:36

• **Sons of Sceva.**
Ac 19:13–14

• **Diotrephes.**
3Jn 1:9

See: Blasphemy

See: Mocking

See: Pride

PRETORIUM

• **Called also Common Hall, Judgment Hall and Palace.**

Mt 27:27 — Then the soldiers of the governor took Jesus into the common hall, and gathered unto him the whole band *of soldiers.*

Mk 15:16 — And the soldiers led him away into the hall, called Praetorium; and they call together the whole band.

Jn 18:28 — Then led they Jesus from Caiaphas unto the hall of judgment: and it was early; and they themselves went not into the judgment hall, lest they should be defiled; but that they might eat the passover.

Jn 18:33 — Then Pilate entered into the judgment hall again, and called Jesus, and said unto him, Art thou the King of the Jews?

Jn 19:9 — And went again into the judgment hall, and saith unto Jesus, Whence art thou? But Jesus gave him no answer.

Ac 23:35 — I will hear thee, said he, when thine accusers are also come. And he commanded him to be kept in Herod's judgment hall.

Php 1:13 — So that my bonds in Christ are manifest in all the palace, and in all other *places;*

PRIDE

Ex 18:10–11; Dt 8:11–14, 17–20; Jgs 9:14–15; 1Sa 2:3–5; 2Ki 14:9–10; 2Ch 25:18–19; Job 12:2–3; 15:1–13; 18:3–4; 21:31–32; 32:9–13; Ps 10:2–6; 12:3–4; 73:8–9; 75:4–6; 119:69–70; Pr 6:16–17; 16:18–19; 18:11–12; 30:12–13; Isa 2:11–17; 3:16–26; 9:9–10; 10:5–16; 14:12–16; 16:6–7; 47:7–10; Jer 9:23–24; 48:14–15; 50:31–32; Eze 28:2–9; 31:10–14; Ob 1:3–4; Hab 2:4–5; Mt 20:26–27; 23:6–8, 10–12; Mk 7:21–22; 12:38–39; Lk 1:51–52; 14:8–9; 20:45–47; Ro 1:29–30; 11:17–21; 1Co 4:6–8; 8:1–2; 1Ti 6:3–4; Rev 3:17–18; 18:7–8

Le 26:19 — And I will break the pride of your power; and I will make your heaven as iron, and your earth as brass:

1Ki 20:11 — And the king of Israel answered and said, Tell *him,* Let not him that girdeth on *his harness* boast himself as he that putteth it off.

Job 11:12 — For vain man would be wise, though man be born *like* a wild ass's colt.

Job 13:2 — What ye know, *the same* do I know also: I *am* not inferior unto you.

Job 13:5 — Oh that ye would altogether hold your peace! and it should be your wisdom.

Job 37:24 — Men do therefore fear him: he respecteth not any *that are* wise of heart.

Ps 9:20 — Put them in fear, O LORD: *that* the nations may know themselves *to be but* men. Selah.

Ps 10:11 — He hath said in his heart, God hath forgotten: he hideth his face; he will never see *it.*

Ps 18:27 — For thou wilt save the afflicted people; but wilt bring down high looks.

Ps 31:23 — O love the LORD, all ye his saints: *for* the LORD preserveth the faithful, and plentifully rewardeth the proud doer.

Ps 49:11 — Their inward thought *is, that* their houses *shall continue* for ever, *and* their dwelling places to all generations; they call *their* lands after their own names.

Ps 52:7 — Lo, *this is* the man *that* made not God his strength; but trusted in the abundance of his riches, *and* strengthened himself in his wickedness.

Ps 73:6 — Therefore pride compasseth them about as a chain; violence covereth them *as* a garment.

Ps 101:5 — Whoso privily slandereth his neighbour, him will I cut off: him that hath an high look and a proud heart will not I suffer.

Ps 119:21 — Thou hast rebuked the proud *that are* cursed, which do err from thy commandments.

Ps 119:78 — Let the proud be ashamed; for they dealt perversely with me without a cause: *but* I will meditate in thy precepts.

Ps 138:6 — Though the LORD *be* high, yet hath he respect unto the lowly: but the proud he knoweth afar off.

Pr 3:34 — Surely he scorneth the scorners: but he giveth grace unto the lowly.

Pr 8:13 — The fear of the LORD *is* to hate evil: pride, and arrogancy, and the evil way, and the froward mouth, do I hate.

Pr 10:17 — He *is in* the way of life that keepeth instruction: but he that refuseth reproof erreth.

Pr 11:2 — *When* pride cometh, then cometh shame: but with the lowly *is* wisdom.

Pr 11:12 — He that is void of wisdom despiseth his neighbour: but a man of understanding holdeth his peace.

Pr 12:9 — *He that is* despised, and hath a servant, *is* better than he that honoureth himself, and lacketh bread.

Pr 12:15 — The way of a fool *is* right in his own eyes: but he that hearkeneth unto counsel *is* wise.

Pr 13:10 — Only by pride cometh contention: but with the well advised *is* wisdom.

Pr 14:21 — He that despiseth his neighbour sinneth: but he that hath mercy on the poor, happy *is* he.

Pr 15:5 — A fool despiseth his father's instruction: but he that regardeth reproof is prudent.

Pr 15:10 — Correction *is* grievous unto him that forsaketh the way: *and* he that hateth reproof shall die.

Pr 15:12 — A scorner loveth not one that reproveth him: neither will he go unto the wise.

Pr 15:25 — The LORD will destroy the house of the proud: but he will establish the border of the widow.

Pr 15:32 — He that refuseth instruction despiseth his own soul: but he that heareth reproof getteth understanding.

Pr 16:5 — Every one *that is* proud in heart *is* an abomination to the LORD: *though* hand *join* in hand, he shall not be unpunished.

Pr 17:19 — He loveth transgression that loveth strife: *and* he that exalteth his gate seeketh destruction.

Pr 20:6 — Most men will proclaim every one his own goodness: but a faithful man who can find?

Pr 21:4 — An high look, and a proud heart, *and* the plowing of the wicked, *is* sin.

Pr 21:24 — Proud *and* haughty scorner *is* his name, who dealeth in proud wrath.

Pr 25:14 — Whoso boasteth himself of a false gift *is like* clouds and wind without rain.

Pr 25:27 — *It is* not good to eat much honey: so *for men* to search their own glory *is not* glory.

Pr 26:5 — Answer a fool according to his folly, lest he be wise in his own conceit.

Pr 26:12 — Seest thou a man wise in his own conceit? *there is* more hope of a fool than of him.

Pr 26:16 — The sluggard *is* wiser in his own conceit than seven men that can render a reason.

Pr 27:2 — Let another man praise thee, and not thine own mouth; a stranger, and not thine own lips.

Pr 28:11 — The rich man *is* wise in his own conceit; but the poor that hath understanding searcheth him out.

Pr 28:25 — He that is of a proud heart stirreth up strife: but he that putteth his trust in the LORD shall be made fat.

Pr 29:8 — Scornful men bring a city into a snare: but wise *men* turn away wrath.

Pr 29:23 — A man's pride shall bring him low: but honour shall uphold the humble in spirit.

Isa 5:8 — Woe unto them that join house to house, *that* lay field to field, till *there be* no place, that they may be placed alone in the midst of the earth!

Isa 5:15 — And the mean man shall be brought down, and the mighty man shall be humbled, and the eyes of the lofty shall be humbled:

Isa 13:11 — And I will punish the world for *their* evil, and the wicked for their iniquity; and I will cause the arrogancy of the proud to cease, and will lay low the haughtiness of the terrible.

Isa 22:16 — What hast thou here? and whom hast thou here, that thou hast hewed thee out a sepulchre here, *as* he that heweth him out a sepulchre on high, *and* that graveth an habitation for himself in a rock?

Isa 22:19 — And I will drive thee from thy station, and from thy state shall he pull thee down.

Isa 23:7 — *Is* this your joyous *city*, whose antiquity *is* of ancient days? her own feet shall carry her afar off to sojourn.

Isa 23:9 — The LORD of hosts hath purposed it, to stain the pride of all glory, *and* to bring into contempt all the honourable of the earth.

Isa 24:4 — The earth mourneth *and* fadeth away, the world languisheth *and* fadeth away, the haughty people of the earth do languish.

Isa 24:21 — And it shall come to pass in that day, *that* the LORD shall punish the host of the high ones *that are* on high, and the kings of the earth upon the earth.

Isa 26:5 — For he bringeth down them that dwell on high; the lofty city, he layeth it low; he layeth it low, *even* to the ground; he bringeth it *even* to the dust.

Isa 28:3 — The crown of pride, the drunkards of Ephraim, shall be trodden under feet:

Jer 13:9 — Thus saith the LORD, After this manner will I mar the pride of Judah, and the great pride of Jerusalem.

Jer 13:15 — Hear ye, and give ear; be not proud: for the LORD hath spoken.

Jer 13:17 — But if ye will not hear it, my soul shall weep in secret places for *your* pride; and mine eye shall weep sore, and run down with tears, because the LORD'S flock is carried away captive.

Jer 48:7 — For because thou hast trusted in thy works and in thy treasures, thou shalt also be taken: and Chemosh shall go forth into captivity *with* his priests and his princes together.

Jer 48:29 — We have heard the pride of Moab, (he is exceeding proud) his loftiness, and his arrogancy, and his pride, and the haughtiness of his heart.

Jer 49:4 — Wherefore gloriest thou in the valleys, thy flowing valley, O backsliding daughter? that trusted in her treasures, *saying*, Who shall come unto me?

Jer 49:16 — Thy terribleness hath deceived thee, *and* the pride of thine heart, O thou that dwellest in the clefts of the rock, that holdest the height of the hill: though thou shouldest make thy nest as high as the eagle, I will bring thee down from thence, saith the LORD.

Eze 16:56 — For thy sister Sodom was not mentioned by thy mouth in the day of thy pride,

Eze 28:17 — Thine heart was lifted up because of thy beauty, thou hast corrupted thy wisdom by reason of thy brightness: I will cast thee to the ground, I will lay thee before kings, that they may behold thee.

Eze 30:6 — Thus saith the LORD; They also that uphold Egypt shall fall; and the pride of her power shall come down: from the tower of Syene shall they fall in it by the sword, saith the Lord GOD.

Da 4:37 — Now I Nebuchadnezzar praise and extol and honour the King of heaven, all whose works *are* truth, and his ways judgment: and those that walk in pride he is able to abase.

Da 11:45 — And he shall plant the tabernacles of his palace between the seas in the glorious holy mountain; yet he shall come to his end, and none shall help him.

Hos 5:5 — And the pride of Israel doth testify to his face: therefore shall Israel and Ephraim fall in their iniquity; Judah also shall fall with them.

Hos 7:10 — And the pride of Israel testifieth to his face: and they do not return to the LORD their God, nor seek him for all this.

Hos 10:11 — And Ephraim *is as* an heifer *that is* taught, *and* loveth to tread out *the corn;* but I passed over upon her fair neck: I will make Ephraim to ride; Judah shall plow, *and* Jacob shall break his clods.

Na 3:19 — *There is* no healing of thy bruise; thy wound is grievous: all that hear the bruit of thee shall clap the hands over thee: for upon whom hath not thy wickedness passed continually?

Hab 2:9 — Woe to him that coveteth an evil covetousness to his house, that he may set his nest on high, that he may be delivered from the power of evil!

Zep 2:10 — This shall they have for their pride, because they have reproached and magnified *themselves* against the people of the LORD of hosts.

Zep 2:15 — This *is* the rejoicing city that dwelt carelessly, that said in her heart, I *am,* and *there is* none beside me: how is she become a desolation, a place for beasts to lie down in! every one that passeth by her shall hiss, *and* wag his hand.

Zep 3:11 — In that day shalt thou not be ashamed for all thy doings, wherein thou hast transgressed against me: for then I will take away out of the midst of thee them that rejoice in thy pride, and thou shalt no more be haughty because of my holy mountain.

Mal 4:1 — For, behold, the day cometh, that shall burn as an oven; and all the proud, yea, and all that do wickedly, shall be stubble: and the day that cometh shall burn them up, saith the LORD of hosts, that it shall leave them neither root nor branch.

Mk 10:43 — But so shall it not be among you: but whosoever will be great among you, shall be your minister:

Lk 9:46 — Then there arose a reasoning among them, which of them should be greatest.

Lk 11:43 — Woe unto you, Pharisees! for ye love the uppermost seats in the synagogues, and greetings in the markets.

Lk 18:14 — I tell you, this man went down to his house justified *rather* than the other: for every one that exalteth himself shall be abased; and he that humbleth himself shall be exalted.

Ro 1:22 — Professing themselves to be wise, they became fools,

Ro 11:25 — For I would not, brethren, that ye should be ignorant of this mystery, lest ye should be wise in your own conceits; that blindness in part is happened to Israel, until the fulness of the Gentiles be come in.

Ro 12:3 — For I say, through the grace given unto me, to every man that is among you, not to think *of himself* more highly than he ought to think; but to think soberly, according as God hath dealt to every man the measure of faith.

Ro 12:16 — *Be* of the same mind one toward another. Mind not high things, but condescend to men of low estate. Be not wise in your own conceits.

1Co 1:29 — That no flesh should glory in his presence.

1Co 3:18 — Let no man deceive himself. If any man among you seemeth to be wise in this world, let him become a fool, that he may be wise.

1Co 4:10 — We *are* fools for Christ's sake, but ye *are* wise in Christ; we *are* weak, but ye *are* strong; ye *are* honourable, but we *are* despised.

1Co 5:2 — And ye are puffed up, and have not rather mourned, that he that hath done this deed might be taken away from among you.

1Co 5:6 — Your glorying *is* not good. Know ye not that a little leaven leaveneth the whole lump?

1Co 10:12 — Wherefore let him that thinketh he standeth take heed lest he fall.

1Co 13:4 — Charity suffereth long, *and* is kind; charity envieth not; charity vaunteth not itself, is not puffed up,

1Co 14:38 — But if any man be ignorant, let him be ignorant.

2Co 10:5 — Casting down imaginations, and every high thing that exalteth itself against the knowledge of God, and bringing into captivity every thought to the obedience of Christ;

2Co 10:12 — For we dare not make ourselves of the number, or compare ourselves with some that commend themselves: but they measuring themselves by themselves, and comparing themselves among themselves, are not wise.

2Co 10:18 — For not he that commendeth himself is approved, but whom the Lord commendeth.

2Co 12:7 — And lest I should be exalted above measure through the abundance of the revelations, there was given to me a thorn in the flesh, the messenger of Satan to buffet me, lest I should be exalted above measure.

Gal 6:3 — For if a man think himself to be something, when he is nothing, he deceiveth himself.

Eph 4:17 — This I say therefore, and testify in the Lord, that ye henceforth walk not as other Gentiles walk, in the vanity of their mind,

Php 2:3 — *Let* nothing *be done* through strife or vainglory; but in lowliness of mind let each esteem other better than themselves.

1Ti 2:9 — In like manner also, that women adorn themselves in modest apparel, with shamefacedness and sobriety; not with broided hair, or gold, or pearls, or costly array;

1Ti 3:6 — Not a novice, lest being lifted up with pride he fall into the condemnation of the devil.

1Ti 6:17 — Charge them that are rich in this world, that they be not highminded, nor trust in uncertain riches, but in the living God, who giveth us richly all things to enjoy;

2Ti 3:2 — For men shall be lovers of their own selves, covetous, boasters, proud, blasphemers, disobedient to parents, unthankful, unholy,

2Ti 3:4 — Traitors, heady, highminded, lovers of pleasures more than lovers of God;

Jas 3:1 — My brethren, be not many masters, knowing that we shall receive the greater condemnation.

Jas 4:6 — But he giveth more grace. Wherefore he saith, God resisteth the proud, but giveth grace unto the humble.

1Pe 5:3 — Neither as being lords over *God's* heritage, but being ensamples to the flock.

1Pe 5:5 — Likewise, ye younger, submit yourselves unto the elder. Yea, all *of you* be subject one to another, and be clothed with humility: for God resisteth the proud, and giveth grace to the humble.

1Jn 2:16 — For all that *is* in the world, the lust of the flesh, and the lust of the eyes, and the pride of life, is not of the Father, but is of the world.

⇝See: Rich

- **Instances of.**
  - **Ahithophel.**
    2Sa 17:23
  - **Naaman, refusing to wash in Jordan.**
    2Ki 5:11–13
  - **Hezekiah, in displaying his resources.**
    2Ki 20:13; 2Ch 32:31; Isa 39:2
  - **Uzziah.**
    2Ch 26:16–19
  - **Haman.**
    Est 3:5; 5:11, 13; 6:6; 7:10
  - **Kings of Tyre.**
    Eze 28:2
  - **Nebuchadnezzar.**
    Da 4:30–34; 5:20

⇝See: Ambition

PRIEST, Antemosaic

- **Melchizedek.**

Heb 5:10–11; 7:1–21

Ge 14:18 — And Melchizedek king of Salem brought forth bread and wine: and he *was* the priest of the most high God.

Heb 5:6 — As he saith also in another *place,* Thou *art* a priest for ever after the order of Melchisedec.

Heb 6:20 — Whither the forerunner is for us entered, *even* Jesus, made an high priest for ever after the order of Melchisedec.

- **Jethro.**

Ex 2:16 — Now the priest of Midian had seven daughters: and they came and drew *water,* and filled the troughs to water their father's flock.

- **Priests in Israel before the giving of the law.**

Ex 19:22 — And let the priests also, which come near to the LORD, sanctify themselves, lest the LORD break forth upon them.

Ex 19:24 — And the LORD said unto him, Away, get thee down, and thou shalt come up, thou, and Aaron with thee: but let not the priests and the people break through to come up unto the LORD, lest he break forth upon them.

- **Called angel.**

Ecc 5:6 — Suffer not thy mouth to cause thy flesh to sin; neither say thou before the angel, that it *was* an error: wherefore should God be angry at thy voice, and destroy the work of thine hands?

PRIEST, Duties of

- **To offer sacrifices.**

Le 1:4–17; 4:5–12, 25–26, 30–35; 2Ch 35:11–14

Le 2:2 — And he shall bring it to Aaron's sons the priests: and he shall take thereout his handful of the flour thereof, and of the oil thereof, with all the frankincense thereof; and the priest shall burn the memorial of it upon the altar, *to be* an offering made by fire, of a sweet savour unto the LORD:

Le 2:16 — And the priest shall burn the memorial of it, *part* of the beaten corn thereof, and *part* of the oil thereof, with all the frankincense thereof: *it is* an offering made by fire unto the LORD.

Le 3:5 — And Aaron's sons shall burn it on the altar upon the burnt sacrifice, which *is* upon the wood that *is* on the fire: *it is* an offering made by fire, of a sweet savour unto the LORD.

Le 3:11 — And the priest shall burn it upon the altar: *it is* the food of the offering made by fire unto the LORD.

Le 3:13 — And he shall lay his hand upon the head of it, and kill it before the tabernacle of the congregation: and the sons of Aaron shall sprinkle the blood thereof upon the altar round about.

Le 3:16 — And the priest shall burn them upon the altar: *it is* the food of the offering made by fire for a sweet savour: all the fat *is* the LORD'S.

Le 4:17 — And the priest shall dip his finger *in some* of the blood, and sprinkle *it* seven times before the LORD, *even* before the vail.

1Ch 16:40 — To offer burnt offerings unto the LORD upon the altar of the burnt offering continually morning and evening, and *to do* according to all that is written in the law of the LORD, which he commanded Israel;

2Ch 13:11 — And they burn unto the LORD every morning and every evening burnt sacrifices and sweet incense: the shewbread also *set they in order* upon the pure table; and the candlestick of gold with the lamps thereof, to burn every evening: for we keep the charge of the LORD our God; but ye have forsaken him.

2Ch 29:34 — But the priests were too few, so that they could not flay all the burnt offerings: wherefore their brethren the Levites did help them, till the work was ended, and until the *other* priests had sanctified themselves: for the Levites *were* more upright in heart to sanctify themselves than the priests.

Ezr 6:20 — For the priests and the Levites were purified together, all of them *were* pure, and killed the passover for all the children of the captivity, and for their brethren the priests, and for themselves.

Heb 10:11 — And every priest standeth daily ministering and offering oftentimes the same sacrifices, which can never take away sins:

⇝See: Offerings

- **To offer the first fruits.**

Le 23:10–11; Dt 26:3–4

- **Pronounce benedictions.**

Nu 6:22–27

Dt 21:5 — And the priests the sons of Levi shall come near; for them the LORD thy God hath chosen to minister unto him, and to bless in the name of the LORD; and by their word shall every controversy and every stroke be *tried:*

2Ch 30:27 — Then the priests the Levites arose and blessed the people: and their voice was heard, and their prayer came *up* to his holy dwelling place, *even* unto heaven.

• Teach the law.

Dt 31:9–13

Le 10:11 — And that ye may teach the children of Israel all the statutes which the LORD hath spoken unto them by the hand of Moses.

Dt 24:8 — Take heed in the plague of leprosy, that thou observe diligently, and do according to all that the priests the Levites shall teach you: as I commanded them, so ye shall observe to do.

Dt 27:14 — And the Levites shall speak, and say unto all the men of Israel with a loud voice,

Dt 33:10 — They shall teach Jacob thy judgments, and Israel thy law: they shall put incense before thee, and whole burnt sacrifice upon thine altar.

Jer 2:8 — The priests said not, Where *is* the LORD? and they that handle the law knew me not: the pastors also transgressed against me, and the prophets prophesied by Baal, and walked after *things that* do not profit.

Mal 2:7 — For the priest's lips should keep knowledge, and they should seek the law at his mouth: for he *is* the messenger of the LORD of hosts.

• Light the lamps in the tabernacle.

Ex 27:20–21; Le 24:3–4

2Ch 13:11 — And they burn unto the LORD every morning and every evening burnt sacrifices and sweet incense: the shewbread also *set they in order* upon the pure table; and the candlestick of gold with the lamps thereof, to burn every evening: for we keep the charge of the LORD our God; but ye have forsaken him.

• Keep the sacred fire always burning.

Le 6:12–13

• To furnish a quota of wood for the sanctuary.

Ne 10:34 — And we cast the lots among the priests, the Levites, and the people, for the wood offering, to bring *it* into the house of our God, after the houses of our fathers, at times appointed year by year, to burn upon the altar of the LORD our God, as *it is* written in the law:

• Responsible for the sanctuary.

Nu 4:5–15

Nu 18:1 — And the LORD said unto Aaron, Thou and thy sons and thy father's house with thee shall bear the iniquity of the sanctuary: and thou and thy sons with thee shall bear the iniquity of your priesthood.

Nu 18:5 — And ye shall keep the charge of the sanctuary, and the charge of the altar: that there be no wrath any more upon the children of Israel.

Nu 18:7 — Therefore thou and thy sons with thee shall keep your priest's office for every thing of the altar, and within the vail; and ye shall serve: I have given your priest's office *unto you as* a service of gift: and the stranger that cometh nigh shall be put to death.

• To act as scribes.

Ezr 7:1–6

Ne 8:9 — And Nehemiah, which *is* the Tirshatha, and Ezra the priest the scribe, and the Levites that taught the people, said unto all the people, This day *is* holy unto the LORD your God; mourn not, nor weep. For all the people wept, when they heard the words of the law.

• Be present at and supervise the tithing.

Ne 10:38 — And the priest the son of Aaron shall be with the Levites, when the Levites take tithes: and the Levites shall bring up the tithe of the tithes unto the house of our God, to the chambers, into the treasure house.

• Sound the trumpet in calling assemblies and in battle.

Nu 10:2–10; Jos 6:1–27

Nu 31:6 — And Moses sent them to the war, a thousand of *every* tribe, them and Phinehas the son of Eleazar the priest, to the war, with the holy instruments, and the trumpets to blow in his hand.

2Ch 13:12 — And, behold, God himself is with us for *our* captain, and his priests with sounding trumpets to cry alarm against you. O children of Israel, fight ye not against the LORD God of your fathers; for ye shall not prosper.

• Examine lepers.

See: Leprosy

• Purify the unclean.

Le 15:31 — Thus shall ye separate the children of Israel from their uncleanness; that they die not in their uncleanness, when they defile my tabernacle that *is* among them.

See: Defilement

• Value things devoted.

Le 27:8 — But if he be poorer than thy estimation, then he shall present himself before the priest, and the priest shall value him; according to his ability that vowed shall the priest value him.

Le 27:12 — And the priest shall value it, whether it be good or bad: as thou valuest it, *who art* the priest, so shall it be.

• Officiate in the Holy Place.

Heb 9:6 — Now when these things were thus ordained, the priests went always into the first tabernacle, accomplishing the service *of God.*

• Chiefs of Levites.

Nu 3:9 — And thou shalt give the Levites unto Aaron and to his sons: they *are* wholly given unto him out of the children of Israel.

Nu 3:32 — And Eleazar the son of Aaron the priest *shall be* chief over the chief of the Levites, *and have* the oversight of them that keep the charge of the sanctuary.

Nu 4:19 — But thus do unto them, that they may live, and not die, when they approach unto the most holy things: Aaron and his sons shall go in, and appoint them every one to his service and to his burden:

Nu 4:28 — This is the service of the families of the sons of Gershon in the tabernacle of the congregation: and their charge *shall be* under the hand of Ithamar the son of Aaron the priest.

Nu 4:33 — This *is* the service of the families of the sons of Merari, according to all their service, in the tabernacle of the congregation, under the hand of Ithamar the son of Aaron the priest.

1Ch 9:20 — And Phinehas the son of Eleazar was the ruler over them in time past, *and* the Lord *was* with him.

- **To act as magistrates.**

Nu 5:14–31; Dt 17:8–13; Eze 44:23–24

Dt 19:17 — Then both the men, between whom the controversy *is,* shall stand before the LORD, before the priests and the judges, which shall be in those days;

Dt 21:5 — And the priests the sons of Levi shall come near; for them the LORD thy God hath chosen to minister unto him, and to bless in the name of the LORD; and by their word shall every controversy and every stroke be *tried:*

2Ch 19:8 — Moreover in Jerusalem did Jehoshaphat set of the Levites, and *of* the priests, and of the chief of the fathers of Israel, for the judgment of the LORD, and for controversies, when they returned to Jerusalem.

- **To encourage the army on the eve of battle.**

Dt 20:2–4

- **Bear the ark through the Jordan.**

Jos 3:1–17; 4:15–18

- **Bear the ark in battle.**

1Sa 4:3–5

PRIEST, Emoluments of

- **Emoluments of.**
  - **No part of the land of Canaan allowed to.**

Dt 18:1–2

Nu 18:20 — And the LORD spake unto Aaron, Thou shalt have no inheritance in their land, neither shalt thou have any part among them: I *am* thy part and thine inheritance among the children of Israel.

Dt 10:9 — Wherefore Levi hath no part nor inheritance with his brethren; the LORD *is* his inheritance, according as the LORD thy God promised him.

Dt 14:27 — And the Levite that *is* within thy gates; thou shalt not forsake him; for he hath no part nor inheritance with thee.

Jos 13:14 — Only unto the tribe of Levi he gave none inheritance; the sacrifices of the LORD God of Israel made by fire *are* their inheritance, as he said unto them.

Jos 13:33 — But unto the tribe of Levi Moses gave not *any* inheritance: the LORD God of Israel *was* their inheritance, as he said unto them.

Jos 14:3 — For Moses had given the inheritance of two tribes and an half tribe on the other side Jordan: but unto the Levites he gave none inheritance among them.

Jos 18:7 — But the Levites have no part among you; for the priesthood of the LORD is their inheritance: and Gad, and Reuben, and half the tribe of Manasseh, have received their inheritance beyond Jordan on the east, which Moses the servant of the LORD gave them.

Eze 44:28 — And it shall be unto them for an inheritance: I *am* their inheritance: and ye shall give them no possession in Israel: I *am* their possession.

- **Provided with cities and suburbs.**

Le 25:32–34; Nu 35:2–8; Jos 21:1–4; 21:13–19, 41–42; 1Ch 6:57–60; Eze 45:1–6; 48:8–20

Ne 11:3 — Now these *are* the chief of the province that dwelt in Jerusalem: but in the cities of Judah dwelt every one in his possession in their cities, *to wit,* Israel, the priests, and the Levites, and the Nethinims, and the children of Solomon's servants.

Ne 11:20 — And the residue of Israel, of the priests, *and* the Levites, *were* in all the cities of Judah, every one in his inheritance.

- **Own lands sanctified to the Lord.**

Le 27:21 — But the field, when it goeth out in the jubile, shall be holy unto the LORD, as a field devoted; the possession thereof shall be the priest's.

- **Tithes of the tithes.**

Nu 18:8–18, 26–32

Ne 10:38 — And the priest the son of Aaron shall be with the Levites, when the Levites take tithes: and the Levites shall bring up the tithe of the tithes unto the house of our God, to the chambers, into the treasure house.

- **Part of the spoils of war, including captives.**

Nu 31:25–29

- **First fruits.**

Nu 18:12–13, 17–18; Dt 18:3–5

Le 23:20 — And the priest shall wave them with the bread of the first fruits *for* a wave offering before the LORD, with the two lambs: they shall be holy to the LORD for the priest.

Le 24:9 — And it shall be Aaron's and his sons'; and they shall eat it in the holy place: for it *is* most holy unto him of the offerings of the LORD made by fire by a perpetual statute.

Ne 10:36 — Also the firstborn of our sons, and of our cattle, as *it is* written in the law, and the firstlings of our herds and of our flocks, to bring to the house of our God, unto the priests that minister in the house of our God:

- **Redemption money.**

Le 27:23 — Then the priest shall reckon unto him the worth of thy estimation, *even* unto the year of the jubile: and he shall give thine estimation in that day, *as* a holy thing unto the LORD.

- **Redemption of firstborn.**

Nu 3:46–51; 18:15–16

- **Things devoted.**

Nu 5:9–10

Le 27:21 — But the field, when it goeth out in the jubile, shall be holy unto the LORD, as a field devoted; the possession thereof shall be the priest's.

Nu 18:14 — Every thing devoted in Israel shall be thine.

- **Fines.**

Le 5:16 — And he shall make amends for the harm that he hath done in the holy thing, and shall add the fifth part thereto, and give it unto the priest: and the priest shall make an atonement for him with the ram of the trespass offering, and it shall be forgiven him.

Le 22:14 — And if a man eat *of* the holy thing unwittingly, then he shall put the fifth *part* thereof unto it, and shall give *it* unto the priest with the holy thing.

Nu 5:8 — But if the man have no kinsman to recompense the trespass unto, let the trespass be recompensed unto the LORD, *even* to the priest; beside the ram of the atonement, whereby an atonement shall be made for him.

- **Trespass money and other trespass offerings.**

Nu 5:5–10

Le 5:15 — If a soul commit a trespass, and sin through ignorance, in the holy things of the LORD; then he shall bring for his trespass unto the LORD a ram without blemish out of the flocks, with thy estimation by shekels of silver, after the shekel of the sanctuary, for a trespass offering:

Le 5:18 — And he shall bring a ram without blemish out of the flock, with thy estimation, for a trespass offering, unto the priest: and the priest shall make an atonement for him concerning his ignorance wherein he erred and wist *it* not, and it shall be forgiven him.

Nu 18:9 — This shall be thine of the most holy things, *reserved* from the fire: every oblation of theirs, every meat offering of theirs, and every sin offering of theirs, and every trespass offering of theirs, which they shall render unto me, *shall be* most holy for thee and for thy sons.

2Ki 12:16 — The trespass money and sin money was not brought into the house of the LORD: it was the priests'.

- **The shewbread.**

Le 24:5–9

Ex 25:30 — And thou shalt set upon the table shewbread before me alway.

2Ch 2:4 — Behold, I build an house to the name of the LORD my God, to dedicate *it* to him, *and* to burn before him sweet incense, and for the continual shewbread, and for the burnt offerings morning and evening, on the sabbaths, and on the new moons, and on the solemn feasts of the LORD our God. This *is an ordinance* for ever to Israel.

2Ch 13:11 — And they burn unto the LORD every morning and every evening burnt sacrifices and sweet incense: the shewbread also *set they in order* upon the pure table; and the candlestick of gold with the lamps thereof, to burn every evening: for we keep the charge of the LORD our God; but ye have forsaken him.

Ne 10:33 — For the shewbread, and for the continual meat offering, and for the continual burnt offering, of the sabbaths, of the new moons, for the set feasts, and for the holy *things,* and for the sin offerings to make an atonement for Israel, and *for* all the work of the house of our God.

Mt 12:4 — How he entered into the house of God, and did eat the shewbread, which was not lawful for him to eat, neither for them which were with him, but only for the priests?

Heb 9:2 — For there was a tabernacle made; the first, wherein *was* the candlestick, and the table, and the shewbread; which is called the sanctuary.

- **Portions of sacrifices and offerings.**

Ex 29:27–34; Le 2:2–3, 9–10; 5:12–13; 6:15–18; 7:6–10, 31–34; 10:12–14; 14:12–13; Nu 6:19–20; 18:8–19; Dt 18:3–5; 1Sa 2:13–14; Eze 44:28–45:4

Le 5:16 — And he shall make amends for the harm that he hath done in the holy thing, and shall add the fifth part thereto, and give it unto the priest: and the priest shall make an atonement for him with the ram of the trespass offering, and it shall be forgiven him.

Le 6:26 — The priest that offereth it for sin shall eat it: in the holy place shall it be eaten, in the court of the tabernacle of the congregation.

1Co 9:13 — Do ye not know that they which minister about holy things live *of the things* of the temple? and they which wait at the altar are partakers with the altar?

1Co 10:18 — Behold Israel after the flesh: are not they which eat of the sacrifices partakers of the altar?

- **Regulations by Hezekiah concerning emoluments.**

2Ch 31:4–19

- **Portion of land allotted to, in redistribution in Ezekiel's vision.**

Eze 48:8–14

- **For sustenance of their families.**

Le 22:11–13

Nu 18:11 — And this *is* thine; the heave offering of their gift, with all the wave offerings of the children of Israel: I have given them unto thee, and to thy sons and to thy daughters with thee, by a statute for ever: every one that is clean in thy house shall eat of it.

Nu 18:19 — All the heave offerings of the holy things, which the children of Israel offer unto the LORD, have I given thee, and thy sons and thy daughters with thee, by a statute for ever: it is a covenant of salt for ever before the LORD unto thee and to thy seed with thee.

- **Figurative.**

Ex 19:6 — And ye shall be unto me a kingdom of priests, and an holy nation. These *are* the words which thou shalt speak unto the children of Israel.

Isa 61:6 — But ye shall be named the Priests of the LORD: *men* shall call you the Ministers of our God: ye shall eat the riches of the Gentiles, and in their glory shall ye boast yourselves.

1Pe 2:9 — But ye *are* a chosen generation, a royal priesthood, an holy nation, a peculiar people; that ye should shew forth the praises of him who hath called you out of darkness into his marvellous light:

Rev 1:6 — And hath made us kings and priests unto God and his Father; to him *be* glory and dominion for ever and ever. Amen.

Rev 5:10 — And hast made us unto our God kings and priests: and we shall reign on the earth.

Rev 20:6 — Blessed and holy *is* he that hath part in the first resurrection: on such the second death hath no power, but they shall be priests of God and of Christ, and shall reign with him a thousand years.

PRIEST, High

• Aaron's function was superior to that of other priests; title appears after institution of office.

Le 21:10–15

Nu 3:32 — And Eleazar the son of Aaron the priest *shall be* chief over the chief of the Levites, *and have* the oversight of them that keep the charge of the sanctuary.

• For qualifications, consecration, etc..

✢See: Priest, Mosaic

• Vestments of.

Ex 28:2–43; 39:1–31; Le 8:7–9

• Respect due to.

Ac 23:5 — Then said Paul, I wist not, brethren, that he was the high priest: for it is written, Thou shalt not speak evil of the ruler of thy people.

• Duties of.

• Had charge of the sanctuary and altar.

Nu 18:2 — And thy brethren also of the tribe of Levi, the tribe of thy father, bring thou with thee, that they may be joined unto thee, and minister unto thee: but thou and thy sons with thee *shall minister* before the tabernacle of witness.

Nu 18:5 — And ye shall keep the charge of the sanctuary, and the charge of the altar: that there be no wrath any more upon the children of Israel.

Nu 18:7 — Therefore thou and thy sons with thee shall keep your priest's office for every thing of the altar, and within the vail; and ye shall serve: I have given your priest's office *unto you as* a service of gift: and the stranger that cometh nigh shall be put to death.

• To offer sacrifices.

Heb 5:1 — For every high priest taken from among men is ordained for men in things *pertaining* to God, that he may offer both gifts and sacrifices for sins:

Heb 8:3 — For every high priest is ordained to offer gifts and sacrifices: wherefore *it is* of necessity that this man have somewhat also to offer.

• To designate subordinate priests for duty.

Nu 4:19 — But thus do unto them, that they may live, and not die, when they approach unto the most holy things: Aaron and his sons shall go in, and appoint them every one to his service and to his burden:

1Sa 2:36 — And it shall come to pass, *that* every one that is left in thine house shall come *and* crouch to him for a piece of silver and a morsel of bread, and shall say, Put me, I pray thee, into one of the priests' offices, that I may eat a piece of bread.

• To officiate in consecrations of Levites.

Nu 8:11–21

• To have charge of the treasury.

2Ch 24:6–14

2Ki 12:10— And it was *so,* when they saw that *there was* much money in the chest, that the king's scribe and the high priest came up, and they put up in bags, and told the money that was found in the house of the LORD.

2Ki 22:4 — Go up to Hilkiah the high priest, that he may sum the silver which is brought into the house of the LORD, which the keepers of the door have gathered of the people:

2Ch 34:9 — And when they came to Hilkiah the high priest, they delivered the money that was brought into the house of God, which the Levites that kept the doors had gathered of the hand of Manasseh and Ephraim, and of all the remnant of Israel, and of all Judah and Benjamin; and they returned to Jerusalem.

• To light the lamps of tabernacle.

Ex 27:20–21; Le 24:3–4

Ex 30:8 — And when Aaron lighteth the lamps at even, he shall burn incense upon it, a perpetual incense before the LORD throughout your generations.

Nu 8:3 — And Aaron did so; he lighted the lamps thereof over against the candlestick, as the LORD commanded Moses.

• To burn incense.

Ex 30:7–8

1Sa 2:28 — And did I choose him out of all the tribes of Israel *to be* my priest, to offer upon mine altar, to burn incense, to wear an ephod before me? and did I give unto the house of thy father all the offerings made by fire of the children of Israel?

1Ch 23:13 — The sons of Amram; Aaron and Moses: and Aaron was separated, that he should sanctify the most holy things, he and his sons for ever, to burn incense before the LORD, to minister unto him, and to bless in his name for ever.

• To place shewbread on the table every Sabbath.

Le 24:8 — Every sabbath he shall set it in order before the LORD continually, *being taken* from the children of Israel by an everlasting covenant.

• To offer for his own sins of ignorance.

Le 4:3–12

• On the day of atonement.

Le 16:1–34; Heb 9:22–23

Ex 30:10 — And Aaron shall make an atonement upon the horns of it once in a year with the blood of the sin offering of atonements: once in the year shall he make atonement upon it throughout your generations: it *is* most holy unto the LORD.

Heb 5:3 — And by reason hereof he ought, as for the people, so also for himself, to offer for sins.

Heb 9:7 — But into the second *went* the high priest alone once every year, not without blood, which he offered for himself, and *for* the errors of the people:

• Judicial.

Dt 17:8–13; Ac 5:21–28; 23:1–5

Nu 5:15 — Then shall the man bring his wife unto the priest, and he shall bring her offering for her, the tenth *part* of an ephah of barley meal; he shall pour no oil upon it, nor put frankincense thereon; for it *is* an offering of jealousy, an offering of memorial, bringing iniquity to remembrance.

1Sa 4:18 — And it came to pass, when he made mention of the ark of God, that he fell from off the seat backward by the side of the gate, and his neck brake, and he died: for he was an old man, and heavy. And he had judged Israel forty years.

Hos 4:4 — Yet let no man strive, nor reprove another: for thy people *are* as they that strive with the priest.

Mt 26:3 — Then assembled together the chief priests, and the scribes, and the elders of the people, unto the palace of the high priest, who was called Caiaphas,

Mt 26:50 — And Jesus said unto him, Friend, wherefore art thou come? Then came they, and laid hands on Jesus, and took him.

Mt 26:57 — And they that had laid hold on Jesus led *him* away to Caiaphas the high priest, where the scribes and the elders were assembled.

Mt 26:62 — And the high priest arose, and said unto him, Answerest thou nothing? what *is it which* these witness against thee?

• To number the people.

Nu 1:3 — From twenty years old and upward, all that are able to go forth to war in Israel: thou and Aaron shall number them by their armies.

• Officiate at choice of ruler.

Nu 27:18–19

Nu 27:21 — And he shall stand before Eleazar the priest, who shall ask *counsel* for him after the judgment of Urim before the LORD: at his word shall they go out, and at his word they shall come in, *both* he, and all the children of Israel with him, even all the congregation.

• Distribute spoils of war.

Nu 31:26–29

• Emoluments of.

See: **Priest, Emoluments of**

• A second priest, under the high priest.

Nu 3:32 — And Eleazar the son of Aaron the priest *shall be* chief over the chief of the Levites, *and have* the oversight of them that keep the charge of the sanctuary.

Nu 4:16 — And to the office of Eleazar the son of Aaron the priest *pertaineth* the oil for the light, and the sweet incense, and the daily meat offering, and the anointing oil, *and* the oversight of all the tabernacle, and of all that therein *is*, in the sanctuary, and in the vessels thereof.

Nu 31:6 — And Moses sent them to the war, a thousand of *every* tribe, them and Phinehas the son of Eleazar the priest, to the war, with the holy instruments, and the trumpets to blow in his hand.

2Sa 15:24 — And lo Zadok also, and all the Levites *were* with him, bearing the ark of the covenant of God: and they set down the ark of God; and Abiathar went up, until all the people had done passing out of the city.

2Ki 25:18 — And the captain of the guard took Seraiah the chief priest, and Zephaniah the second priest, and the three keepers of the door:

1Ch 9:20 — And Phinehas the son of Eleazar was the ruler over them in time past, *and* the Lord *was* with him.

Lk 3:2 — Annas and Caiaphas being the high priests, the word of God came unto John the son of Zacharias in the wilderness.

PRIEST, Miscellaneous Facts Concerning

• Loyal to Rehoboam at the time of the revolt of the ten tribes.

2Ch 11:13 — And the priests and the Levites that *were* in all Israel resorted to him out of all their coasts.

• Zeal of, in purging the temple.

2Ch 29:4–17

• Wickedness of.

2Ch 36:14 — Moreover all the chief of the priests, and the people, transgressed very much after all the abominations of the heathen; and polluted the house of the LORD which he had hallowed in Jerusalem.

• Taken with the captivity to Babylon.

Jer 29:1 — Now these *are* the words of the letter that Jeremiah the prophet sent from Jerusalem unto the residue of the elders which were carried away captives, and to the priests, and to the prophets, and to all the people whom Nebuchadnezzar had carried away captive from Jerusalem to Babylon;

• Return from the captivity.

Ezr 2:36–39; 8:24–30; Ne 7:39–42, 63–73; 10:1–8; 12:1–7

Ezr 1:5 — Then rose up the chief of the fathers of Judah and Benjamin, and the priests, and the Levites, with all *them* whose spirit God had raised, to go up to build the house of the LORD which *is* in Jerusalem.

Ezr 2:61 — And of the children of the priests: the children of Habaiah, the children of Koz, the children of Barzillai; which took a wife of the daughters of Barzillai the Gileadite, and was called after their name:

Ezr 2:70 — So the priests, and the Levites, and *some* of the people, and the singers, and the porters, and the Nethinims, dwelt in their cities, and all Israel in their cities.

Ezr 3:8 — Now in the second year of their coming unto the house of God at Jerusalem, in the second month, began Zerubbabel the son of Shealtiel, and Jeshua the son of Jozadak, and the remnant of their brethren the priests and the Levites, and all they that were come out of the captivity unto Jerusalem; and appointed the Levites, from twenty years old and upward, to set forward the work of the house of the LORD.

Ezr 7:7 — And there went up *some* of the children of Israel, and of the priests, and the Levites, and the singers, and the porters, and the Nethinims, unto Jerusalem, in the seventh year of Artaxerxes the king.

• Polluted by marrying idolatrous wives.

Ezr 9:1–2; 10:18–19

Ezr 10:5 — Then arose Ezra, and made the chief priests, the Levites, and all Israel, to swear that they should do according to this word. And they sware.

Ne 10:28 — And the rest of the people, the priests, the Levites, the porters, the singers, the Nethinims, and all they that had separated themselves from the people of the lands unto the law of God, their wives, their sons, and their daughters, every one having knowledge, and having understanding;

• Restore the altar, and offer sacrifices.

Ezr 3:1–7

• Supervise the building of the temple.

Ezr 3:8–13

• Inquire of John the Baptist whether he were the Christ.

Jn 1:19 — And this is the record of John, when the Jews sent priests and Levites from Jerusalem to ask him, Who art thou?

• Conspire to destroy Jesus.

Mt 26:3–5, 14–15; Mk 14:10–11, 43–47, 53–66; Lk 22:1–6; 22:66–23:2; Jn 19:15–16

Mt 26:47 — And while he yet spake, lo, Judas, one of the twelve, came, and with him a great multitude with swords and staves, from the chief priests and elders of the people.

Mt 26:51 — And, behold, one of them which were with Jesus stretched out *his* hand, and drew his sword, and struck a servant of the high priest's, and smote off his ear.

Mk 15:1 — And straightway in the morning the chief priests held a consultation with the elders and scribes and the whole council, and bound Jesus, and carried *him* away, and delivered *him* to Pilate.

Lk 22:50 — And one of them smote the servant of the high priest, and cut off his right ear.

Lk 22:54 — Then took they him, and led *him,* and brought him into the high priest's house. And Peter followed afar off.

Jn 11:47 — Then gathered the chief priests and the Pharisees a council, and said, What do we? for this man doeth many miracles.

Jn 19:18 — Where they crucified him, and two others with him, on either side one, and Jesus in the midst.

• Try and condemn Jesus.

Mt 26:57–68; 27:1–2; Mk 14:53–65; Lk 22:54–71; 23:13–24; Jn 18:15–32

• Incite the people to ask that Barabbas be released and Jesus destroyed.

Mt 27:20 — But the chief priests and elders persuaded the multitude that they should ask Barabbas, and destroy Jesus.

Mk 15:11 — But the chief priests moved the people, that he should rather release Barabbas unto them.

Lk 23:18 — And they cried out all at once, saying, Away with this *man,* and release unto us Barabbas:

• Persecute the disciples.

Ac 22:5 — As also the high priest doth bear me witness, and all the estate of the elders: from whom also I received letters unto the brethren, and went to Damascus, to bring them which were there bound unto Jerusalem, for to be punished.

• Reprove and threaten Peter and John.

Ac 4:6–21; 5:17–41

• Try, condemn, and stone Stephen.

Ac 6:12–7:60

• Paul brought before.

Ac 22:30–23:5

• Many converts among.

Ac 6:7 — And the word of God increased; and the number of the disciples multiplied in Jerusalem greatly; and a great company of the priests were obedient to the faith.

• Corrupt.

Jer 23:11–12

Eze 22:26 — Her priests have violated my law, and have profaned mine holy things: they have put no difference between the holy and profane, neither have they shewed *difference* between the unclean and the clean, and have hid their eyes from my sabbaths, and I am profaned among them.

Lk 10:31 — And by chance there came down a certain priest that way: and when he saw him, he passed by on the other side.

• Instances of.

• Eli's sons.

1Sa 2:12–17, 22

• Eli's sons of the captivity.

Ezr 9:1–2; 10:18–22; Ne 13:4–9, 13, 28–29

• Zealous.

1Ch 9:10–13

• Priestly office performed by prophets.

1Sa 16:5

PRIEST, Mosaic

Ex 28:1–4

Ex 29:9 — And thou shalt gird them with girdles, Aaron and his sons, and put the bonnets on them: and the priest's office shall be theirs for a perpetual statute: and thou shalt consecrate Aaron and his sons.

Ex 29:44 — And I will sanctify the tabernacle of the congregation, and the altar: I will sanctify also both Aaron and his sons, to minister to me in the priest's office.

Nu 3:10 — And thou shalt appoint Aaron and his sons, and they shall wait on their priest's office: and the stranger that cometh nigh shall be put to death.

Nu 18:7 — Therefore thou and thy sons with thee shall keep your priest's office for every thing of the altar, and within the vail; and ye shall serve: I have given your priest's office *unto you as* a service of gift: and the stranger that cometh nigh shall be put to death.

1Ch 23:13 — The sons of Amram; Aaron and Moses: and Aaron was separated, that he should sanctify the most holy things, he and his sons for ever, to burn incense before the LORD, to minister unto him, and to bless in his name for ever.

• Hereditary descent of office.

Ex 27:21 — In the tabernacle of the congregation without the vail, which *is* before the testimony, Aaron and his sons shall order it from evening to morning before the LORD: *it shall be* a statute for ever unto their generations on the behalf of the children of Israel.

Ex 28:43 — And they shall be upon Aaron, and upon his sons, when they come in unto the tabernacle of the congregation, or when they come near unto the altar to minister in the holy *place;* that they bear not iniquity, and die: *it shall be* a statute for ever unto him and his seed after him.

Ex 29:9 — And thou shalt gird them with girdles, Aaron and his sons, and put the bonnets on them: and the priest's office shall be theirs for a perpetual statute: and thou shalt consecrate Aaron and his sons.

• Consecration of.

Ex 29:1–9;, 19–35; 40:12–16; Le 6:20–23; 8:6–35

Heb 7:21 — (For those priests were made without an oath; but this with an oath by him that said unto him, The Lord sware and will not repent, Thou *art* a priest for ever after the order of Melchisedec:)

• Is holy.

Le 21:6–7

Le 22:9 — They shall therefore keep mine ordinance, lest they bear sin for it, and die therefore, if they profane it: I the LORD do sanctify them.

Le 22:16 — Or suffer them to bear the iniquity of trespass, when they eat their holy things: for I the LORD do sanctify them.

• Ablutions of.

Ex 40:30–32

Le 16:24 — And he shall wash his flesh with water in the holy place, and put on his garments, and come forth, and offer his burnt offering, and the burnt offering of the people, and make an atonement for himself, and for the people.

See: Priest, Mosaic; consecration of

• Must be without blemish.

Le 21:17–23

• Vestments of.

Ex 28:2–43; 39:1–29; Le 6:10–11; Eze 44:17–19

Le 8:13 — And Moses brought Aaron's sons, and put coats upon them, and girded them with girdles, and put bonnets upon them; as the LORD commanded Moses.

• Don vestments in temple.

Eze 42:14 — When the priests enter therein, then shall they not go out of the holy *place* into the utter court, but there they shall lay their garments wherein they minister; for they *are* holy; and shall put on other garments, and shall approach to *those things* which *are* for the people.

Eze 44:19 — And when they go forth into the utter court, *even* into the utter court to the people, they shall put off their garments wherein they ministered, and lay them in the holy chambers, and they shall put on other garments; and they shall not sanctify the people with their garments.

• Atonement for.

Le 16:6 — And Aaron shall offer his bullock of the sin offering, which *is* for himself, and make an atonement for himself, and for his house.

Le 16:24 — And he shall wash his flesh with water in the holy place, and put on his garments, and come forth, and offer his burnt offering, and the burnt offering of the people, and make an atonement for himself, and for the people.

Eze 44:27 — And in the day that he goeth into the sanctuary, unto the inner court, to minister in the sanctuary, he shall offer his sin offering, saith the Lord GOD.

• Defilement and purification of.

Eze 44:25–26

• Marriage of.

Le 21:7–15

Eze 44:22 — Neither shall they take for their wives a widow, nor her that is put away: but they shall take maidens of the seed of the house of Israel, or a widow that had a priest before.

• Chambers for, in temple.

Eze 40:45–46

• Exempt from tax.

Ezr 7:24 — Also we certify you, that touching any of the priests and Levites, singers, porters, Nethinims, or ministers of this house of God, it shall not be lawful to impose toll, tribute, or custom, upon them.

• Armed and organized for war at the time of the disaffection toward Saul.

1Ch 12:27–28

• Beard and hair of.

Eze 44:20 — Neither shall they shave their heads, nor suffer their locks to grow long; they shall only poll their heads.

• Twenty-four courses of.

1Ch 24:1–19; 2Ch 35:4–5; Ezr 2:36–39

1Ch 28:13 — Also for the courses of the priests and the Levites, and for all the work of the service of the house of the LORD, and for all the vessels of service in the house of the LORD.

1Ch 28:21 — And, behold, the courses of the priests and the Levites, *even they shall be with thee* for all the service of the house of God: and *there shall be* with thee for all manner of workmanship every willing skilful man, for any manner of service: also the princes and all the people *will be* wholly at thy commandment.

2Ch 8:14 — And he appointed, according to the order of David his father, the courses of the priests to their service, and the Levites to their charges, to praise and minister before the priests, as the duty of every day required: the porters also by their courses at every gate: for so had David the man of God commanded.

2Ch 31:2 — And Hezekiah appointed the courses of the priests and the Levites after their courses, every man according to his service, the priests and Levites for burnt offerings and for peace offerings, to minister, and to give thanks, and to praise in the gates of the tents of the LORD.

Ne 13:30 — Thus cleansed I them from all strangers, and appointed the wards of the priests and the Levites, every one in his business;

• Chosen by lot.

Lk 1:8–9

Lk 1:23 — And it came to pass, that, as soon as the days of his ministration were accomplished, he departed to his own house.

• Usurpations of office of.

Nu 16:1–50

Nu 3:10 — And thou shalt appoint Aaron and his sons, and they shall wait on their priest's office: and the stranger that cometh nigh shall be put to death.

Nu 18:7 — Therefore thou and thy sons with thee shall keep your priest's office for every thing of the altar, and within the vail; and ye shall serve: I have given your priest's office *unto you as* a service of gift: and the stranger that cometh nigh shall be put to death.

2Ch 26:18 — And they withstood Uzziah the king, and said unto him, *It appertaineth* not unto thee, Uzziah, to burn incense unto the LORD, but to the priests the sons of Aaron, that are consecrated to burn incense: go out of the sanctuary; for thou hast trespassed; neither *shall it be* for thine honour from the LORD God.

• Priests were appointed by Jeroboam who were not of the sons of Levi.

1Ki 12:31 — And he made an house of high places, and made priests of the lowest of the people, which were not of the sons of Levi.

1Ki 13:33 — After this thing Jeroboam returned not from his evil way, but made again of the lowest of the people priests of the high places: whosoever would, he consecrated him, and he became *one* of the priests of the high places.

✦See: Levites

PRIMOGENITURE

✦See: Birthright

✦See: Firstborn

PRINCE OF PEACE ✦See: Jesus, Names, Appellations, and Titles of; Prince of Peace

PRINCESSES • Taught in household duties.

2Sa 13:8–9

PRISCA • A disciple in Ephesus.

2Ti 4:19 — Salute Prisca and Aquila, and the household of Onesiphorus.

PRISCILLA

• Wife of Aquila.

• A disciple at Corinth.

Ac 18:1–3, 18–19; Ro 16:3–4

Ac 18:26 — And he began to speak boldly in the synagogue: whom when Aquila and Priscilla had heard, they took him unto *them,* and expounded unto him the way of God more perfectly.

1Co 16:19 — The churches of Asia salute you. Aquila and Priscilla salute you much in the Lord, with the church that is in their house.

2Ti 4:19 — Salute Prisca and Aquila, and the household of Onesiphorus.

PRISON

Ge 42:16–19; Ac 12:4–5

Ge 39:20 — And Joseph's master took him, and put him into the prison, a place where the king's prisoners *were* bound: and he was there in the prison.

Le 24:12 — And they put him in ward, that the mind of the LORD might be shewed them.

Nu 15:34 — And they put him in ward, because it was not declared what should be done to him.

Ezr 7:26 — And whosoever will not do the law of thy God, and the law of the king, let judgment be executed speedily upon him, whether *it be* unto death, or to banishment, or to confiscation of goods, or to imprisonment.

Jer 52:11 — Then he put out the eyes of Zedekiah; and the king of Babylon bound him in chains, and carried him to Babylon, and put him in prison till the day of his death.

Lk 23:19 — (Who for a certain sedition made in the city, and for murder, was cast into prison.)

Ac 4:3 — And they laid hands on them, and put *them* in hold unto the next day: for it was now eventide.

• Public ward of.

Ac 5:18 — And laid their hands on the apostles, and put them in the common prison.

• Cells of.

Ac 16:24 — Who, having received such a charge, thrust them into the inner prison, and made their feet fast in the stocks.

• Court of.

Jer 33:1 — Moreover the word of the LORD came unto Jeremiah the second time, while he was yet shut up in the court of the prison, saying,

• Dungeon in.

✦See: Dungeon

✦See: Imprisonment

✦See: Prisoners

PRISONERS

• Joseph.

Ge 39:20–41:44

• Jeremiah.

Jer 38:6–28

Jer 39:14 — Even they sent, and took Jeremiah out of the court of the prison, and committed him unto Gedaliah the son of Ahikam the son of Shaphan, that he should carry him home: so he dwelt among the people.

• John the Baptist.

Mt 14:3–12

Mt 11:2 — Now when John had heard in the prison the works of Christ, he sent two of his disciples,

Mk 6:17 — For Herod himself had sent forth and laid hold upon John, and bound him in prison for Herodias' sake, his brother Philip's wife: for he had married her.

Lk 3:20 — Added yet this above all, that he shut up John in prison.

• Jesus.

Mt 26:47–27:66; Mk 14:43–15:47; Lk 22:47–23:56; Jn 18:3–19:42

• Apostles.

Ac 5:17–42

• Peter.

Ac 12:3–19

• Paul.

Ac 16:19–40; 21:27–28:31

• Silas.

Ac 16:19–40

• Required to labor.

Jgs 16:21 — But the Philistines took him, and put out his eyes, and brought him down to Gaza, and bound him with fetters of brass; and he did grind in the prison house.

• Kept on bread and water of affliction.

1Ki 22:27 — And say, Thus saith the king, Put this *fellow* in the prison, and feed him with bread of affliction and with water of affliction, until I come in peace.

• Kept in chains.

Ac 12:6 — And when Herod would have brought him forth, the same night Peter was sleeping between two soldiers, bound with two chains: and the keepers before the door kept the prison.

• Kept in stocks.

Pr 7:22 — He goeth after her straightway, as an ox goeth to the slaughter, or as a fool to the correction of the stocks;

Jer 29:26 — The LORD hath made thee priest in the stead of Jehoiada the priest, that ye should be officers in the house of the LORD, for every man *that is* mad, and maketh himself a prophet, that thou shouldest put him in prison, and in the stocks.

Ac 16:24 — Who, having received such a charge, thrust them into the inner prison, and made their feet fast in the stocks.

• Confined in.

• Court of the palace.

Jer 32:2 — For then the king of Babylon's army besieged Jerusalem: and Jeremiah the prophet was shut up in the court of the prison, which *was* in the king of Judah's house.

• The house of the scribe.

Jer 37:15 — Wherefore the princes were wroth with Jeremiah, and smote him, and put him in prison in the house of Jonathan the scribe: for they had made that the prison.

• The house of captain of the guard.

Ge 40:3 — And he put them in ward in the house of the captain of the guard, into the prison, the place where Joseph *was* bound.

• Visited by friends.

Mt 11:2 — Now when John had heard in the prison the works of Christ, he sent two of his disciples,

Ac 24:23 — And he commanded a centurion to keep Paul, and to let *him* have liberty, and that he should forbid none of his acquaintance to minister or come unto him.

• Bound to soldiers.

Ac 12:6–7

• Severe hardships of, mitigated.

Jer 37:20–21

• Cruelty to.

La 3:53–54

Jer 38:6 — Then took they Jeremiah, and cast him into the dungeon of Malchiah the son of Hammelech, that *was* in the court of the prison: and they let down Jeremiah with cords. And in the dungeon *there was* no water, but mire: so Jeremiah sunk in the mire.

⇛See: Captive

• Keepers responsible for.

Ac 12:18–19

• Tortured to extort self-criminating testimony.

Ac 22:24 — The chief captain commanded him to be brought into the castle, and bade that he should be examined by scourging; that he might know wherefore they cried so against him.

• Scourged.

2Co 11:23–24

Mt 27:26 — Then released he Barabbas unto them: and when he had scourged Jesus, he delivered *him* to be crucified.

Mk 15:15 — And *so* Pilate, willing to content the people, released Barabbas unto them, and delivered Jesus, when he had scourged *him,* to be crucified.

Ac 16:23 — And when they had laid many stripes upon them, they cast *them* into prison, charging the jailer to keep them safely:

Ac 16:33 — And he took them the same hour of the night, and washed *their* stripes; and was baptized, he and all his, straightway.

2Co 6:5 — In stripes, in imprisonments, in tumults, in labours, in watchings, in fastings;

- **Permitted to make defense.**

Ac 24:10 — Then Paul, after that the governor had beckoned unto him to speak, answered, Forasmuch as I know that thou hast been of many years a judge unto this nation, I do the more cheerfully answer for myself:

Ac 25:8 — While he answered for himself, Neither against the law of the Jews, neither against the temple, nor yet against Caesar, have I offended any thing at all.

Ac 25:16 — To whom I answered, It is not the manner of the Romans to deliver any man to die, before that he which is accused have the accusers face to face, and have licence to answer for himself concerning the crime laid against him.

Ac 26:1 — Then Agrippa said unto Paul, Thou art permitted to speak for thyself. Then Paul stretched forth the hand, and answered for himself:

2Ti 4:16 — At my first answer no man stood with me, but all *men* forsook me: *I pray God* that it may not be laid to their charge.

- **Kindness to.**
  - **By the prison keeper to Jeremiah.**

Jer 38:7–28

  - **By Philippian jailer to Paul.**

Ac 16:33 — And he took them the same hour of the night, and washed *their* stripes; and was baptized, he and all his, straightway.

  - **By Felix.**

Ac 24:23 — And he commanded a centurion to keep Paul, and to let *him* have liberty, and that he should forbid none of his acquaintance to minister or come unto him.

  - **By Julius, the centurion.**

Ac 28:30–31

Ac 27:1 — And when it was determined that we should sail into Italy, they delivered Paul and certain other prisoners unto *one* named Julius, a centurion of Augustus' band.

Ac 27:3 — And the next *day* we touched at Sidon. And Julius courteously entreated Paul, and gave *him* liberty to go unto his friends to refresh himself.

Ac 28:16 — And when we came to Rome, the centurion delivered the prisoners to the captain of the guard: but Paul was suffered to dwell by himself with a soldier that kept him.

  - **To be visited and ministered to.**

Mt 25:35–46

  - **Released at feasts.**

Mt 27:15–17

Mk 15:6 — Now at *that* feast he released unto them one prisoner, whomsoever they desired.

Lk 23:17 — (For of necessity he must release one unto them at the feast.)

Jn 18:39 — But ye have a custom, that I should release unto you one at the passover: will ye therefore that I release unto you the King of the Jews?

- **Of war.**
  - **Put to death.**

Jos 10:16–27

1Sa 15:33 — And Samuel said, As thy sword hath made women childless, so shall thy mother be childless among women. And Samuel hewed Agag in pieces before the LORD in Gilgal.

1Sa 27:11 — And David saved neither man nor woman alive, to bring *tidings* to Gath, saying, Lest they should tell on us, saying, So did David, and so *will be* his manner all the while he dwelleth in the country of the Philistines.

2Sa 12:31 — And he brought forth the people that *were* therein, and put *them* under saws, and under harrows of iron, and under axes of iron, and made them pass through the brickkiln: and thus did he unto all the cities of the children of Ammon. So David and all the people returned unto Jerusalem.

2Ki 25:7 — And they slew the sons of Zedekiah before his eyes, and put out the eyes of Zedekiah, and bound him with fetters of brass, and carried him to Babylon.

1Ch 20:3 — And he brought out the people that *were* in it, and cut *them* with saws, and with harrows of iron, and with axes. Even so dealt David with all the cities of the children of Ammon. And David and all the people returned to Jerusalem.

La 3:34 — To crush under his feet all the prisoners of the earth,

Hos 13:16 — Samaria shall become desolate; for she hath rebelled against her God: they shall fall by the sword: their infants shall be dashed in pieces, and their women with child shall be ripped up.

Am 1:13 — Thus saith the LORD; For three transgressions of the children of Ammon, and for four, I will not turn away *the punishment* thereof; because they have ripped up the women with child of Gilead, that they might enlarge their border:

- **Put to death by divine command.**

Nu 31:9 — And the children of Israel took *all* the women of Midian captives, and their little ones, and took the spoil of all their cattle, and all their flocks, and all their goods.

Nu 31:17 — Now therefore kill every male among the little ones, and kill every woman that hath known man by lying with him.

- **Thumbs and toes cut off.**

Jgs 1:6–7

- **Blinded.**

2Ki 25:7 — And they slew the sons of Zedekiah before his eyes, and put out the eyes of Zedekiah, and bound him with fetters of brass, and carried him to Babylon.

See: Captive

- **Consolations for.**

Ps 102:19–20

Ps 69:33 — For the LORD heareth the poor, and despiseth not his prisoners.

Ps 79:11 — Let the sighing of the prisoner come before thee; according to the greatness of thy power preserve thou those that are appointed to die;

Ps 146:7 — Which executeth judgment for the oppressed: which giveth food to the hungry. The LORD looseth the prisoners:

See: Captive

See: Imprisonment

- **Figurative.**

Isa 61:1 — The Spirit of the Lord GOD *is* upon me; because the LORD hath anointed me to preach good tidings unto the meek; he hath sent me to bind up the brokenhearted, to proclaim liberty to the captives, and the opening of the prison to *them that are* bound;

Lk 4:18 — The Spirit of the Lord is upon me, because he hath anointed me to preach the gospel to the poor; he hath sent me to heal the brokenhearted, to preach deliverance to the captives, and recovering of sight to the blind, to set at liberty them that are bruised,

PRIVILEGE See: Judgment; according to opportunity and works

PRIZE

- **A reward of merit.**

1Co 9:24 — Know ye not that they which run in a race run all, but one receiveth the prize? So run, that ye may obtain.

- **Figurative.**

Php 3:14 — I press toward the mark for the prize of the high calling of God in Christ Jesus.

PROBATION

Ro 5:4 — And patience, experience; and experience, hope:

- **Adam on.**

Ge 2:15–17

Ge 3:3 — But of the fruit of the tree which *is* in the midst of the garden, God hath said, Ye shall not eat of it, neither shall ye touch it, lest ye die.

- **Amorites.**

Ge 15:16 — But in the fourth generation they shall come hither again: for the iniquity of the Amorites *is* not yet full.

- **Solomon.**

1Ki 9:4–9; 11:9–12

1Ki 3:14 — And if thou wilt walk in my ways, to keep my statutes and my commandments, as thy father David did walk, then I will lengthen thy days.

- **Taught in parables of the talents and pounds.**

Mt 25:14–30; Lk 19:12–27

- **Taught in the parable of the fig tree.**

Lk 13:6–9

- **Taught in the parable of the embezzling steward.**

Lk 16:1–12

- **Taught by Paul.**

Heb 6:1–20

- **None after death.**

Mt 25:10–13

Mt 12:32 — And whosoever speaketh a word against the Son of man, it shall be forgiven him: but whosoever speaketh against the Holy Ghost, it shall not be forgiven him, neither in this world, neither in the *world* to come.

Mt 26:24 — The Son of man goeth as it is written of him: but woe unto that man by whom the Son of man is betrayed! it had been good for that man if he had not been born.

See: Perseverance

PROCHORUS • An early Christian deacon.

Ac 6:5 — And the saying pleased the whole multitude: and they chose Stephen, a man full of faith and of the Holy Ghost, and Philip, and Prochorus, and Nicanor, and Timon, and Parmenas, and Nicolas a proselyte of Antioch:

PROCLAMATION

- **Imperial.**

2Ch 30:1–10; Est 8:10–14; Da 3:4–7

Est 1:22 — For he sent letters into all the king's provinces, into every province according to the writing thereof, and to every people after their language, that every man should bear rule in his own house, and that *it* should be published according to the language of every people.

Est 6:9 — And let this apparel and horse be delivered to the hand of one of the king's most noble princes, that they may array the man *withal* whom the king delighteth to honour, and bring him on horseback through the street of the city, and proclaim before him, Thus shall it be done to the man whom the king delighteth to honour.

Isa 40:3 — The voice of him that crieth in the wilderness, Prepare ye the way of the LORD, make straight in the desert a highway for our God.

Isa 40:9 — O Zion, that bringest good tidings, get thee up into the high mountain; O Jerusalem, that bringest good tidings, lift up thy voice with strength; lift *it* up, be not afraid; say unto the cities of Judah, Behold your God!

Da 4:1 — Nebuchadnezzar the king, unto all people, nations, and languages, that dwell in all the earth; Peace be multiplied unto you.

Da 5:29 — Then commanded Belshazzar, and they clothed Daniel with scarlet, and *put* a chain of gold about his neck, and made a proclamation concerning him, that he should be the third ruler in the kingdom.

- **Emancipation.**

Ezr 1:1–4

2Ch 36:23 — Thus saith Cyrus king of Persia, All the kingdoms of the earth hath the LORD God of heaven given me; and he hath charged me to build him an house in Jerusalem, which *is* in Judah. Who *is there* among you of all his people? The LORD his God *be* with him, and let him go up.

PROCRASTINATION
Eze 11:2–3; 12:27–28; Mt 24:48–51; 25:2–13; Lk 9:59–62; 1Th 5:2–3; Heb 3:7–4:7

Ex 22:29 — Thou shalt not delay *to offer* the first of thy ripe fruits, and of thy liquors: the firstborn of thy sons shalt thou give unto me.

Pr 27:1 — Boast not thyself of to morrow; for thou knowest not what a day may bring forth.

Eze 12:22 — Son of man, what *is* that proverb *that* ye have in the land of Israel, saying, The days are prolonged, and every vision faileth?

Mt 8:21 — And another of his disciples said unto him, Lord, suffer me first to go and bury my father.

Ac 24:25 — And as he reasoned of righteousness, temperance, and judgment to come Felix trembled, and answered, Go thy way for this time; when I have a convenient season, I will call for thee.

- **See: Excuses**

- **Instances of.**
  - **Pharaoh.**
    Ex 8:10
  - **Elisha.**
    1Ki 19:20–21
  - **Esther.**
    Est 5:8

PRODIGAL SON
Lk 15:11–32

PRODIGALITY
- **See: Extravagance**
- **See: Frugality**
- **See: Industry**

PROFANATION **See: Profanity**

PROFANITY
- **See: Blasphemy**
- **See: Oath**

- **Of the name of God.**
  - **See: God; name of; profaned**
- **Of the Sabbath.**
  - **See: Sabbath**

PROFESSION
- **False.**
  Pr 20:6 — Most men will proclaim every one his own goodness: but a faithful man who can find?
  Hos 8:2 — Israel shall cry unto me, My God, we know thee.
- **Of faith in Jesus.**
  - **See: Confession**
  - **See: Testimony; religious**

PROGNOSTICATION
- **By astrologers.**
  Isa 47:13 — Thou art wearied in the multitude of thy counsels. Let now the astrologers, the stargazers, the monthly prognosticators, stand up, and save thee from *these things* that shall come upon thee.
  - **See: Prophecy**
  - **See: Prophets**

PROHIBITION
- **Of the use of intoxicating liquors.**
- **To priests on duty.**
  Le 10:9 — Do not drink wine nor strong drink, thou, nor thy sons with thee, when ye go into the tabernacle of the congregation, lest ye die: *it shall be* a statute for ever throughout your generations:
- **To Nazarites.**
  Nu 6:3–4
  - **See: Abstinence, Total**
  - **See: Commandments**
  - **See: Drunkenness**

PROMISES
- **To the afflicted.**
  - **See: Assurance; saints privileged to have; comfort in affliction**
  - **See: Psalms; afflictions**
- **To backsliders.**
  - **See: Backsliders**
- **To children.**
  - **See: Children**
- **To orphans.**
  - **See: Orphan**
- **To widows.**
  - **See: Widow**
- **To penitents.**
  - **See: Penitent**
- **To the righteous.**
  - **See: Righteous**
- **To seekers.**
  - **See: Seekers**
  - **See: Blessing; spiritual, from God**
  - **See: God, Goodness of**
  - **See: Jesus, Compassion of**
  - **See: Jesus, Love of**

PROMOTION
Ps 75:6–7; 78:70–71; 113:7–8

- **As a reward of merit.**
  1Ch 11:6 — And David said, Whosoever smiteth the Jebusites first shall be chief and captain. So Joab the son of Zeruiah went first up, and was chief.
- **Instances of.**
  - **Abraham.**
    Ge 12:2
  - **Joseph, from imprisoned slave to prince.**
    Ge 41:1–45

- **Moses, from exile to lawgiver.**
  - **See: Moses**
- **Aaron, from slave to high priest.**
  - **See: Aaron**
- **Saul, from obscurity to a scepter.**
  - **See: Saul**
- **David, from shepherd to throne.**
  - **See: David**
- **Jeroboam, from slave to throne.**
  1Ki 11:26–35
- **Baasha, "out of the dust" to throne.**
  1Ki 16:1–2
- **Daniel, from captive to premier.**
  Da 2:48
  - **See: Daniel**
- **Shadrach, Meshach, and Abednego.**
  Da 3:30

PROPAGATION

- **Of species, enjoined.**
  Ge 1:11–12, 21–25
  Ge 1:28 — And God blessed them, and God said unto them, Be fruitful, and multiply, and replenish the earth, and subdue it: and have dominion over the fish of the sea, and over the fowl of the air, and over every living thing that moveth upon the earth.
  Ge 9:1 — And God blessed Noah and his sons, and said unto them, Be fruitful, and multiply, and replenish the earth.
  Ge 9:7 — And you, be ye fruitful, and multiply; bring forth abundantly in the earth, and multiply therein.
  - **See: Barrenness, sterility of women**

PROPERTY

- **In real estate.**
  Ge 23:17–18
  Ge 26:20 — And the herdmen of Gerar did strive with Isaac's herdmen, saying, The water *is* ours: and he called the name of the well Esek; because they strove with him.
  - **Rights in, violated.**
    Ge 21:25–33; 26:18–22
  - **Dedicated.**
    Le 27:16–25
  - **Dwellings.**
    - **Alienated for debt.**
      Le 25:29–30
    - **By absence.**
      2Ki 8:1–6
    - **In villages, inalienable.**
      Le 25:31–33
    - **Dedicated.**
      Le 27:14–15
  - **Confiscation of (Naboth's vineyard).**
    1Ki 21:15–16
  - **Priests exempt from taxes.**
    Ge 47:22 — Only the land of the priests bought he not; for the priests had a portion *assigned them* of Pharaoh, and did eat their portion which Pharaoh gave them: wherefore they sold not their lands.
  - **Entail of.**
    Nu 27:1–11; 36:1–9
  - **Inherited.**
    Ecc 2:21 — For there is a man whose labour *is* in wisdom, and in knowledge, and in equity; yet to a man that hath not laboured therein shall he leave it *for* his portion. This also *is* vanity and a great evil.
  - **Landmarks of, not to be removed.**
    Dt 19:14 — Thou shalt not remove thy neighbour's landmark, which they of old time have set in thine inheritance, which thou shalt inherit in the land that the LORD thy God giveth thee to possess it.
    Dt 27:17 — Cursed *be* he that removeth his neighbour's landmark. And all the people shall say, Amen.
- **Personal.**
  - **Rights in, sacred.**
    Ex 20:17 — Thou shalt not covet thy neighbour's house, thou shalt not covet thy neighbour's wife, nor his manservant, nor his maidservant, nor his ox, nor his ass, nor any thing that *is* thy neighbour's.
    Dt 5:21 — Neither shalt thou desire thy neighbour's wife, neither shalt thou covet thy neighbour's house, his field, or his manservant, or his maidservant, his ox, or his ass, or any *thing* that *is* thy neighbour's.
  - **Laws concerning trespass of, and violence to.**
    Ex 21:28–36
    Ex 22:9 — For all manner of trespass, *whether it be* for ox, for ass, for sheep, for raiment, *or* for any manner of lost thing, which *another* challengeth to be his, the cause of both parties shall come before the judges; *and* whom the judges shall condemn, he shall pay double unto his neighbour.
    Dt 23:25 — When thou comest into the standing corn of thy neighbour, then thou mayest pluck the ears with thine hand; but thou shalt not move a sickle unto thy neighbour's standing corn.
  - **Strayed, to be returned to owner.**
    Le 6:3–4; Dt 22:1–3
  - **Hired.**
    Ex 22:14–15
  - **Loaned.**
    Ex 22:10–15
  - **Sold for debt.**
    Pr 22:26–27
  - **Sold for rights of redemption of.**
    Jer 32:7 — Behold, Hanameel the son of Shallum thine uncle shall come unto thee, saying, Buy thee my field that *is* in Anathoth: for the right of redemption *is* thine to buy *it*.
  - **Dedicated to God, redemption of.**
    Le 27:9–13, 26–33

• In slaves.

Ex 21:4 — If his master have given him a wife, and she have born him sons or daughters; the wife and her children shall be her master's, and he shall go out by himself.

PROPHECY

• Concerning Jesus.

***See: Jesus, Prophecies Concerning**

• Concerning church.

***See: Church; prophecies concerning prosperity of**

• Relating to various countries, nations, and cities (Look under their respective titles).

• Respecting individuals (Look under their names).

• Inspired.

Isa 28:22 — Now therefore be ye not mockers, lest your bands be made strong: for I have heard from the Lord GOD of hosts a consumption, even determined upon the whole earth.

Lk 1:70 — As he spake by the mouth of his holy prophets, which have been since the world began:

2Ti 3:16 — All scripture *is* given by inspiration of God, and *is* profitable for doctrine, for reproof, for correction, for instruction in righteousness:

2Pe 1:21 — For the prophecy came not in old time by the will of man: but holy men of God spake *as they were* moved by the Holy Ghost.

• "The word of the Lord came unto," etc..

• Elijah.

1Ki 17:8 — And the word of the LORD came unto him, saying,

1Ki 21:17 — And the word of the LORD came to Elijah the Tishbite, saying,

1Ki 21:28 — And the word of the LORD came to Elijah the Tishbite, saying,

• Isaiah.

Isa 2:1 — The word that Isaiah the son of Amoz saw concerning Judah and Jerusalem.

Isa 8:5 — The LORD spake also unto me again, saying,

Isa 13:1 — The burden of Babylon, which Isaiah the son of Amoz did see.

Isa 14:28 — In the year that king Ahaz died was this burden.

Isa 38:4 — Then came the word of the LORD to Isaiah, saying,

• Jeremiah.

Jer 25:1–2

Jer 1:4 — Then the word of the LORD came unto me, saying,

Jer 7:1 — The word that came to Jeremiah from the LORD, saying,

Jer 11:1 — The word that came to Jeremiah from the LORD, saying,

Jer 13:8 — Then the word of the LORD came unto me, saying,

Jer 16:1 — The word of the LORD came also unto me, saying,

Jer 18:1 — The word which came to Jeremiah from the LORD, saying,

Jer 26:1 — In the beginning of the reign of Jehoiakim the son of Josiah king of Judah came this word from the LORD, saying,

Jer 27:1 — In the beginning of the reign of Jehoiakim the son of Josiah king of Judah came this word unto Jeremiah from the LORD, saying,

Jer 29:30 — Then came the word of the LORD unto Jeremiah, saying,

Jer 30:1 — The word that came to Jeremiah from the LORD, saying,

Jer 30:4 — And these *are* the words that the LORD spake concerning Israel and concerning Judah.

Jer 32:1 — The word that came to Jeremiah from the LORD in the tenth year of Zedekiah king of Judah, which *was* the eighteenth year of Nebuchadrezzar.

Jer 32:6 — And Jeremiah said, The word of the LORD came unto me, saying,

Jer 32:26 — Then came the word of the LORD unto Jeremiah, saying,

Jer 33:1 — Moreover the word of the LORD came unto Jeremiah the second time, while he was yet shut up in the court of the prison, saying,

Jer 33:19 — And the word of the LORD came unto Jeremiah, saying,

Jer 33:23 — Moreover the word of the LORD came to Jeremiah, saying,

Jer 34:12 — Therefore the word of the LORD came to Jeremiah from the LORD, saying,

Jer 35:12 — Then came the word of the LORD unto Jeremiah, saying,

Jer 36:1 — And it came to pass in the fourth year of Jehoiakim the son of Josiah king of Judah, *that* this word came unto Jeremiah from the LORD, saying,

Jer 37:6 — Then came the word of the LORD unto the prophet Jeremiah, saying,

Jer 40:1 — The word that came to Jeremiah from the LORD, after that Nebuzar-adan the captain of the guard had let him go from Ramah, when he had taken him being bound in chains among all that were carried away captive of Jerusalem and Judah, which were carried away captive unto Babylon.

Jer 43:8 — Then came the word of the LORD unto Jeremiah in Tahpanhes, saying,

Jer 44:1 — The word that came to Jeremiah concerning all the Jews which dwell in the land of Egypt, which dwell at Migdol, and at Tahpanhes, and at Noph, and in the country of Pathros, saying,

Jer 46:1 — The word of the LORD which came to Jeremiah the prophet against the Gentiles;

Jer 49:34 — The word of the LORD that came to Jeremiah the prophet against Elam in the beginning of the reign of Zedekiah king of Judah, saying,

Jer 50:1 — The word that the LORD spake against Babylon *and* against the land of the Chaldeans by Jeremiah the prophet.

- **Ezekiel.**

Eze 3:16 — And it came to pass at the end of seven days, that the word of the LORD came unto me, saying,

Eze 6:1 — And the word of the LORD came unto me, saying,

Eze 7:1 — Moreover the word of the LORD came unto me, saying,

Eze 11:14 — Again the word of the LORD came unto me, saying,

Eze 12:1 — The word of the LORD also came unto me, saying,

Eze 12:8 — And in the morning came the word of the LORD unto me, saying,

Eze 12:17 — Moreover the word of the LORD came to me, saying,

Eze 12:21 — And the word of the LORD came unto me, saying,

Eze 13:1 — And the word of the LORD came unto me, saying,

Eze 14:12 — The word of the LORD came again to me, saying,

Eze 15:1 — And the word of the LORD came unto me, saying,

Eze 16:1 — Again the word of the LORD came unto me, saying,

Eze 17:1 — And the word of the LORD came unto me, saying,

Eze 17:11 — Moreover the word of the LORD came unto me, saying,

Eze 18:1 — The word of the LORD came unto me again, saying,

Eze 20:45 — Moreover the word of the LORD came unto me, saying,

Eze 21:1 — And the word of the LORD came unto me, saying,

Eze 21:8 — Again the word of the LORD came unto me, saying,

Eze 21:18 — The word of the LORD came unto me again, saying,

Eze 22:1 — Moreover the word of the LORD came unto me, saying,

Eze 22:17 — And the word of the LORD came unto me, saying,

Eze 22:23 — And the word of the LORD came unto me, saying,

Eze 23:1 — The word of the LORD came again unto me, saying,

Eze 24:1 — Again in the ninth year, in the tenth month, in the tenth *day* of the month, the word of the LORD came unto me, saying,

Eze 24:15 — Also the word of the LORD came unto me, saying,

Eze 24:20 — Then I answered them, The word of the LORD came unto me, saying,

Eze 25:1 — The word of the LORD came again unto me, saying,

Eze 26:1 — And it came to pass in the eleventh year, in the first *day* of the month, *that* the word of the LORD came unto me, saying,

Eze 27:1 — The word of the LORD came again unto me, saying,

Eze 28:1 — The word of the LORD came again unto me, saying,

Eze 28:11 — Moreover the word of the LORD came unto me, saying,

Eze 28:20 — Again the word of the LORD came unto me, saying,

Eze 29:1 — In the tenth year, in the tenth *month,* in the twelfth *day* of the month, the word of the LORD came unto me, saying,

Eze 29:17 — And it came to pass in the seven and twentieth year, in the first *month,* in the first *day* of the month, the word of the LORD came unto me, saying,

Eze 30:1 — The word of the LORD came again unto me, saying,

Eze 30:20 — And it came to pass in the eleventh year, in the first *month,* in the seventh *day* of the month, *that* the word of the LORD came unto me, saying,

Eze 31:1 — And it came to pass in the eleventh year, in the third *month,* in the first *day* of the month, *that* the word of the LORD came unto me, saying,

Eze 32:1 — And it came to pass in the twelfth year, in the twelfth month, in the first *day* of the month, *that* the word of the LORD came unto me, saying,

Eze 32:17 — It came to pass also in the twelfth year, in the fifteenth day of the month, *that* the word of the LORD came unto me, saying,

Eze 33:1 — Again the word of the LORD came unto me, saying,

Eze 33:23 — Then the word of the LORD came unto me, saying,

Eze 34:1 — And the word of the LORD came unto me, saying,

Eze 35:1 — Moreover the word of the LORD came unto me, saying,

Eze 36:16 — Moreover the word of the LORD came unto me, saying,

Eze 37:15 — The word of the LORD came again unto me, saying,

Eze 38:1 — And the word of the LORD came unto me, saying,

- **Amos.**

Am 7:14–15

- **Jonah.**

Jnh 3:1 — And the word of the LORD came unto Jonah the second time, saying,

- **Haggai.**

Hag 2:1 — In the seventh *month,* in the one and twentieth *day* of the month, came the word of the LORD by the prophet Haggai, saying,

Hag 2:10 — In the four and twentieth *day* of the ninth *month,* in the second year of Darius, came the word of the LORD by Haggai the prophet, saying,

Hag 2:20 — And again the word of the LORD came unto Haggai in the four and twentieth *day* of the month, saying,

• **Zechariah.**

Zec 1:7 — Upon the four and twentieth day of the eleventh month, which *is* the month Sebat, in the second year of Darius, came the word of the LORD unto Zechariah, the son of Berechiah, the son of Iddo the prophet, saying,

Zec 4:8 — Moreover the word of the LORD came unto me, saying,

Zec 6:9 — And the word of the LORD came unto me, saying,

Zec 7:1 — And it came to pass in the fourth year of king Darius, *that* the word of the LORD came unto Zechariah in the fourth *day* of the ninth month, *even* in Chisleu;

Zec 7:4 — Then came the word of the LORD of hosts unto me, saying,

Zec 7:8 — And the word of the LORD came unto Zechariah, saying,

Zec 8:1 — Again the word of the LORD of hosts came *to me,* saying,

Zec 8:18 — And the word of the LORD of hosts came unto me, saying,

• **Publicly proclaimed.**

Jer 11:6 — Then the LORD said unto me, Proclaim all these words in the cities of Judah, and in the streets of Jerusalem, saying, Hear ye the words of this covenant, and do them.

• **Exemplified in pantomime.**

Eze 4:1–5:4

Ac 21:11 — And when he was come unto us, he took Paul's girdle, and bound his own hands and feet, and said, Thus saith the Holy Ghost, So shall the Jews at Jerusalem bind the man that owneth this girdle, and shall deliver *him* into the hands of the Gentiles.

• **Written by an amanuensis.**

Jer 45:1 — The word that Jeremiah the prophet spake unto Baruch the son of Neriah, when he had written these words in a book at the mouth of Jeremiah, in the fourth year of Jehoiakim the son of Josiah king of Judah, saying,

• **Written in books.**

Jer 45:1 — The word that Jeremiah the prophet spake unto Baruch the son of Neriah, when he had written these words in a book at the mouth of Jeremiah, in the fourth year of Jehoiakim the son of Josiah king of Judah, saying,

Jer 51:60 — So Jeremiah wrote in a book all the evil that should come upon Babylon, *even* all these words that are written against Babylon.

• **Proof of God's foreknowledge.**

Isa 43:9 — Let all the nations be gathered together, and let the people be assembled: who among them can declare this, and shew us former things? let them bring forth their witnesses, that they may be justified: or let them hear, and say, *It is* truth.

• **Sure fulfillment of.**

Eze 12:22–25

Eze 12:28 — Therefore say unto them, Thus saith the Lord GOD; There shall none of my words be prolonged any more, but the word which I have spoken shall be done, saith the Lord GOD.

Hab 2:3 — For the vision *is* yet for an appointed time, but at the end it shall speak, and not lie: though it tarry, wait for it; because it will surely come, it will not tarry.

Mt 5:18 — For verily I say unto you, Till heaven and earth pass, one jot or one tittle shall in no wise pass from the law, till all be fulfilled.

Mt 24:35 — Heaven and earth shall pass away, but my words shall not pass away.

Ac 13:27 — For they that dwell at Jerusalem, and their rulers, because they knew him not, nor yet the voices of the prophets which are read every sabbath day, they have fulfilled *them* in condemning *him.*

Ac 13:29 — And when they had fulfilled all that was written of him, they took *him* down from the tree, and laid *him* in a sepulchre.

• **Cessation of.**

La 2:9 — Her gates are sunk into the ground; he hath destroyed and broken her bars: her king and her princes *are* among the Gentiles: the law *is* no *more;* her prophets also find no vision from the LORD.

• **Of apostasy.**

Jude 1:17–18

1Jn 2:18 — Little children, it is the last time: and as ye have heard that antichrist shall come, even now are there many antichrists; whereby we know that it is the last time.

• **Of false teachers.**

2Pe 2:3 — And through covetousness shall they with feigned words make merchandise of you: whose judgment now of a long time lingereth not, and their damnation slumbereth not.

• **Tribulations of the righteous.**

Rev 2:10 — Fear none of those things which thou shalt suffer: behold, the devil shall cast *some* of you into prison, that ye may be tried; and ye shall have tribulation ten days: be thou faithful unto death, and I will give thee a crown of life.

PROPHECY, Concerning Messiah, and Fulfillment

• **Also quotations of.**

• **1.**

Ge 12:3 — And I will bless them that bless thee, and curse him that curseth thee: and in thee shall all families of the earth be blessed.

Ge 18:18 — Seeing that Abraham shall surely become a great and mighty nation, and all the nations of the earth shall be blessed in him?

Ge 22:18 — And in thy seed shall all the nations of the earth be blessed; because thou hast obeyed my voice.

Ac 3:25 — Ye are the children of the prophets, and of the covenant which God made with our fathers, saying unto Abraham, And in thy seed shall all the kindreds of the earth be blessed.

Gal 3:8 — And the scripture, foreseeing that God would justify the heathen through faith, preached before the gospel unto Abraham, *saying,* In thee shall all nations be blessed.

• 2.

Ge 22:16-17; Lk 1:72-74

Ge 17:7 — And I will establish my covenant between me and thee and thy seed after thee in their generations for an everlasting covenant, to be a God unto thee, and to thy seed after thee.

Ge 17:19 — And God said, Sarah thy wife shall bear thee a son indeed; and thou shalt call his name Isaac: and I will establish my covenant with him for an everlasting covenant, *and* with his seed after him.

Lk 1:55 — As he spake to our fathers, to Abraham, and to his seed for ever.

• 3.

Ac 3:22-23

Dt 18:15 — The LORD thy God will raise up unto thee a Prophet from the midst of thee, of thy brethren, like unto me; unto him ye shall hearken;

Dt 18:18 — I will raise them up a Prophet from among their brethren, like unto thee, and will put my words in his mouth; and he shall speak unto them all that I shall command him.

• 4.

Ps 2:1-2; Ac 4:25-26

• 5.

Heb 5:1-14

Ps 2:7 — I will declare the decree: the LORD hath said unto me, Thou *art* my Son; this day have I begotten thee.

Ac 13:33 — God hath fulfilled the same unto us their children, in that he hath raised up Jesus again; as it is also written in the second Psalm, Thou art my Son, this day have I begotten thee.

Heb 1:5 — For unto which of the angels said he at any time, Thou art my Son, this day have I begotten thee? And again, I will be to him a Father, and he shall be to me a Son?

• 6.

Ps 8:2 — Out of the mouth of babes and sucklings hast thou ordained strength because of thine enemies, that thou mightest still the enemy and the avenger.

Mt 21:16 — And said unto him, Hearest thou what these say? And Jesus saith unto them, Yea; have ye never read, Out of the mouth of babes and sucklings thou hast perfected praise?

• 7.

Ps 8:4-6; Heb 2:6-8

• 8.

Ps 16:8-11; Ac 2:25-28

Ac 2:31 — He seeing this before spake of the resurrection of Christ, that his soul was not left in hell, neither his flesh did see corruption.

• 9.

Ps 16:10 — For thou wilt not leave my soul in hell; neither wilt thou suffer thine Holy One to see corruption.

Ac 13:35 — Wherefore he saith also in another *Psalm,* Thou shalt not suffer thine Holy One to see corruption.

• 10.

Ps 22:1 — My God, my God, why hast thou forsaken me? *why art thou so* far from helping me, *and from* the words of my roaring?

Mt 27:46 — And about the ninth hour Jesus cried with a loud voice, saying, Eli, Eli, lama sabachthani? that is to say, My God, my God, why hast thou forsaken me?

Mk 15:34 — And at the ninth hour Jesus cried with a loud voice, saying, Eloi, Eloi, lama sabachthani? which is, being interpreted, My God, my God, why hast thou forsaken me?

• 11.

Ps 22:18 — They part my garments among them, and cast lots upon my vesture.

Mt 27:35 — And they crucified him, and parted his garments, casting lots: that it might be fulfilled which was spoken by the prophet, They parted my garments among them, and upon my vesture did they cast lots.

Mk 15:24 — And when they had crucified him, they parted his garments, casting lots upon them, what every man should take.

Lk 23:34 — Then said Jesus, Father, forgive them; for they know not what they do. And they parted his raiment, and cast lots.

Jn 19:24 — They said therefore among themselves, Let us not rend it, but cast lots for it, whose it shall be: that the scripture might be fulfilled, which saith, They parted my raiment among them, and for my vesture they did cast lots. These things therefore the soldiers did.

• 12.

Ps 22:22 — I will declare thy name unto my brethren: in the midst of the congregation will I praise thee.

Heb 2:12 — Saying, I will declare thy name unto my brethren, in the midst of the church will I sing praise unto thee.

• 13.

Ps 31:5 — Into thine hand I commit my spirit: thou hast redeemed me, O LORD God of truth.

Lk 23:46 — And when Jesus had cried with a loud voice, he said, Father, into thy hands I commend my spirit: and having said thus, he gave up the ghost.

• 14.

Ps 41:9 — Yea, mine own familiar friend, in whom I trusted, which did eat of my bread, hath lifted up *his* heel against me.

Jn 13:18 — I speak not of you all: I know whom I have chosen: but that the scripture may be fulfilled, He that eateth bread with me hath lifted up his heel against me.

Ac 1:16 — Men *and* brethren, this scripture must needs have been fulfilled, which the Holy Ghost by the mouth of David spake before concerning Judas, which was guide to them that took Jesus.

• **15.**

Ps 45:6–7; Heb 1:8–9

• **16.**

Eph 4:8-10

Ps 68:18 — Thou hast ascended on high, thou hast led captivity captive: thou hast received gifts for men; yea, *for* the rebellious also, that the LORD God might dwell *among them.*

• **17.**

Jn 19:28-29

Ps 69:21 — They gave me also gall for my meat; and in my thirst they gave me vinegar to drink.

Mt 27:48 — And straightway one of them ran, and took a sponge, and filled *it* with vinegar, and put *it* on a reed, and gave him to drink.

Mk 15:36 — And one ran and filled a sponge full of vinegar, and put *it* on a reed, and gave him to drink, saying, Let alone; let us see whether Elias will come to take him down.

Lk 23:36 — And the soldiers also mocked him, coming to him, and offering him vinegar,

• **18.**

Ps 69:25 — Let their habitation be desolate; *and* let none dwell in their tents.

Ps 109:8 — Let his days be few; *and* let another take his office.

Ac 1:20 — For it is written in the book of Psalms, Let his habitation be desolate, and let no man dwell therein: and his bishoprick let another take.

• **19.**

Ps 95:7–11; Heb 3:7–11; 4:5-7

Heb 4:3 — For we which have believed do enter into rest, as he said, As I have sworn in my wrath, if they shall enter into my rest: although the works were finished from the foundation of the world.

• **20.**

Ps 102:25–27; Heb 1:10–12

• **21.**

Ac 2:34–35

Ps 110:1 — The LORD said unto my Lord, Sit thou at my right hand, until I make thine enemies thy footstool.

Mt 22:44 — The Lord said unto my Lord, Sit thou on my right hand, till I make thine enemies thy footstool?

Mk 12:36 — For David himself said by the Holy Ghost, The Lord said to my Lord, Sit thou on my right hand, till I make thine enemies thy footstool.

Lk 20:42 — And David himself saith in the book of Psalms, The Lord said unto my Lord, Sit thou on my right hand,

Heb 1:13 — But to which of the angels said he at any times, Sit on my right hand, until I make thine enemies thy footstool?

• **22.**

Heb 5:1–14

Ps 110:4 — The LORD hath sworn, and will not repent, Thou *art* a priest for ever after the order of Melchizedek.

• **23.**

Ps 118:22–23; Mk 12:10–11

Mt 21:42 — Jesus saith unto them, Did ye never read in the scriptures, The stone which the builders rejected, the same is become the head of the corner: this is the Lord's doing, and it is marvellous in our eyes?

Lk 20:17 — And he beheld them, and said, What is this then that is written, The stone which the builders rejected, the same is become the head of the corner?

Ac 4:11 — This is the stone which was set at nought of you builders, which is become the head of the corner.

• **24.**

Ps 118:25–26

Mt 21:9 — And the multitudes that went before, and that followed, cried, saying, Hosanna to the Son of David: Blessed *is* he that cometh in the name of the Lord; Hosanna in the highest.

Mk 11:9 — And they that went before, and they that followed, cried, saying, Hosanna; Blessed *is* he that cometh in the name of the Lord:

Jn 12:13 — Took branches of palm trees, and went forth to meet him, and cried, Hosanna: Blessed *is* the King of Israel that cometh in the name of the Lord.

• **25.**

Ps 132:11 — The LORD hath sworn *in* truth unto David; he will not turn from it; Of the fruit of thy body will I set upon thy throne.

Ps 132:17 — There will I make the horn of David to bud: I have ordained a lamp for mine anointed.

Lk 1:69 — And hath raised up an horn of salvation for us in the house of his servant David;

Ac 2:30 — Therefore being a prophet, and knowing that God had sworn with an oath to him, that of the fruit of his loins, according to the flesh, he would raise up Christ to sit on his throne;

• **26.**

Isa 7:14 — Therefore the Lord himself shall give you a sign; Behold, a virgin shall conceive, and bear a son, and shall call his name Immanuel.

Mt 1:23 — Behold, a virgin shall be with child, and shall bring forth a son, and they shall call his name Emmanuel, which being interpreted is, God with us.

• **27.**

Isa 9:1–2; Mt 4:15–16

• **28.**

Lk 1:32–33

Isa 9:7 — Of the increase of *his* government and peace *there shall be* no end, upon the throne of David, and upon his kingdom, to order it, and to establish it with judgment and with justice from henceforth even for ever. The zeal of the LORD of hosts will perform this.

Da 7:14 — And there was given him dominion, and glory, and a kingdom, that all people, nations, and languages, should serve him: his dominion *is* an everlasting dominion, which shall not pass away, and his kingdom *that* which shall not be destroyed.

Da 7:27 — And the kingdom and dominion, and the greatness of the kingdom under the whole heaven, shall be given to the people of the saints of the most High, whose kingdom *is* an everlasting kingdom, and all dominions shall serve and obey him.

• 29.

Isa 11:10 — And in that day there shall be a root of Jesse, which shall stand for an ensign of the people; to it shall the Gentiles seek: and his rest shall be glorious.

Ro 15:12 — And again, Esaias saith, There shall be a root of Jesse, and he that shall rise to reign over the Gentiles; in him shall the Gentiles trust.

• 30.

Isa 25:8 — He will swallow up death in victory; and the Lord God will wipe away tears from off all faces; and the rebuke of his people shall he take away from off all the earth: for the LORD hath spoken *it.*

1Co 15:54 — So when this corruptible shall have put on incorruption, and this mortal shall have put on immortality, then shall be brought to pass the saying that is written, Death is swallowed up in victory.

• 31.

Isa 59:20–21; Ro 11:26–27

• 32.

Isa 28:16 — Therefore thus saith the Lord GOD, Behold, I lay in Zion for a foundation a stone, a tried stone, a precious corner *stone,* a sure foundation: he that believeth shall not make haste.

Ro 9:33 — As it is written, Behold, I lay in Sion a stumblingstone and rock of offence: and whosoever believeth on him shall not be ashamed.

1Pe 2:6 — Wherefore also it is contained in the scripture, Behold, I lay in Sion a chief corner stone, elect, precious: and he that believeth on him shall not be confounded.

• 33.

Isa 40:3–5; Lk 3:4–6

Mt 3:3 — For this is he that was spoken of by the prophet Esaias, saying, The voice of one crying in the wilderness, Prepare ye the way of the Lord, make his paths straight.

Mk 1:3 — The voice of one crying in the wilderness, Prepare ye the way of the Lord, make his paths straight.

• 34.

Isa 42:1–4; Mt 12:17–21

• 35.

Ac 13:47–48

Isa 49:6 — And he said, It is a light thing that thou shouldest be my servant to raise up the tribes of Jacob, and to restore the preserved of Israel: I will also give thee for a light to the Gentiles, that thou mayest be my salvation unto the end of the earth.

Lk 2:32 — A light to lighten the Gentiles, and the glory of thy people Israel.

Ac 26:23 — That Christ should suffer, *and* that he should be the first that should rise from the dead, and should shew light unto the people, and to the Gentiles.

• 36.

Isa 53:1 — Who hath believed our report? and to whom is the arm of the LORD revealed?

Jn 12:38 — That the saying of Esaias the prophet might be fulfilled, which he spake, Lord, who hath believed our report? and to whom hath the arm of the Lord been revealed?

Ro 10:16 — But they have not all obeyed the gospel. For Esaias saith, Lord, who hath believed our report?

• 37.

Isa 53:3–6; Ac 26:22–23

• 38.

Isa 53:4–6; 1Pe 2:24–25

Isa 53:11 — He shall see of the travail of his soul, *and* shall be satisfied: by his knowledge shall my righteous servant justify many; for he shall bear their iniquities.

• 39.

Isa 53:4 — Surely he hath borne our griefs, and carried our sorrows: yet we did esteem him stricken, smitten of God, and afflicted.

Mt 8:17 — That it might be fulfilled which was spoken by Esaias the prophet, saying, Himself took our infirmities, and bare *our* sicknesses.

• 40.

Isa 53:9 — And he made his grave with the wicked, and with the rich in his death; because he had done no violence, neither *was any* deceit in his mouth.

1Pe 2:22 — Who did no sin, neither was guile found in his mouth:

• 41.

Isa 53:12 — Therefore will I divide him *a portion* with the great, and he shall divide the spoil with the strong; because he hath poured out his soul unto death: and he was numbered with the transgressors; and he bare the sin of many, and made intercession for the transgressors.

Mk 15:28 — And the scripture was fulfilled, which saith, And he was numbered with the transgressors.

Lk 22:37 — For I say unto you, that this that is written must yet be accomplished in me, And he was reckoned among the transgressors: for the things concerning me have an end.

• 42.

Isa 54:13 — And all thy children *shall be* taught of the LORD; and great *shall be* the peace of thy children.

Jn 6:45 — It is written in the prophets, And they shall be all taught of God. Every man therefore that hath heard, and hath learned of the Father, cometh unto me.

• 43.

Isa 55:3 — Incline your ear, and come unto me: hear, and your soul shall live; and I will make an everlasting covenant with you, *even* the sure mercies of David.

Ac 13:34 — And as concerning that he raised him up from the dead, *now* no more to return to corruption, he said on this wise, I will give you the sure mercies of David.

• 44.

Jer 31:31–34; Heb 8:8–12; 10:16–17

• 45.

Hos 1:10 — Yet the number of the children of Israel shall be as the sand of the sea, which cannot be measured nor numbered; and it shall come to pass, *that* in the place where it was said unto them, Ye *are* not my people, *there* it shall be said unto them, *Ye are* the sons of the living God.

Ro 9:26 — And it shall come to pass, *that* in the place where it was said unto them, Ye *are* not my people; there shall they be called the children of the living God.

• 46.

Hos 2:23 — And I will sow her unto me in the earth; and I will have mercy upon her that had not obtained mercy; and I will say to *them which were* not my people, Thou *art* my people; and they shall say, *Thou art* my God.

Ro 9:25 — As he saith also in Osee, I will call them my people, which were not my people; and her beloved, which was not beloved.

1Pe 2:10 — Which in time past *were* not a people, but *are* now the people of God: which had not obtained mercy, but now have obtained mercy.

• 47.

Joel 2:28–32; Ac 2:16–21

• 48.

Am 9:11–12; Ac 15:16–17

• 49.

Mt 2:5–6

Mic 5:2 — But thou, Bethlehem Ephratah, *though* thou be little among the thousands of Judah, *yet* out of thee shall he come forth unto me *that is* to be ruler in Israel; whose goings forth *have been* from of old, from everlasting.

Jn 7:42 — Hath not the scripture said, That Christ cometh of the seed of David, and out of the town of Bethlehem, where David was?

• 50.

Ac 13:40–41

Hab 1:5 — Behold ye among the heathen, and regard, and wonder marvellously: for *I* will work a work in your days, *which* ye will not believe, though it be told *you.*

• 51.

Hag 2:6 — For thus saith the LORD of hosts; Yet once, it *is* a little while, and I will shake the heavens, and the earth, and the sea, and the dry *land;*

Heb 12:26 — Whose voice then shook the earth: but now he hath promised, saying, Yet once more I shake not the earth only, but also heaven.

• 52.

Mt 21:4–5; Jn 12:14–15

Zec 9:9 — Rejoice greatly, O daughter of Zion; shout, O daughter of Jerusalem: behold, thy King cometh unto thee: he *is* just, and having salvation; lowly, and riding upon an ass, and upon a colt the foal of an ass.

• 53.

Mt 27:9–10

Zec 11:13 — And the LORD said unto me, Cast it unto the potter: a goodly price that I was prised at of them. And I took the thirty *pieces* of silver, and cast them to the potter in the house of the LORD.

• 54.

Zec 12:10 — And I will pour upon the house of David, and upon the inhabitants of Jerusalem, the spirit of grace and of supplications: and they shall look upon me whom they have pierced, and they shall mourn for him, as one mourneth for *his* only *son,* and shall be in bitterness for him, as one that is in bitterness for *his* firstborn.

Jn 19:37 — And again another scripture saith, They shall look on him whom they pierced.

• 55.

Zec 13:7 — Awake, O sword, against my shepherd, and against the man *that is* my fellow, saith the LORD of hosts: smite the shepherd, and the sheep shall be scattered: and I will turn mine hand upon the little ones.

Mt 26:31 — Then saith Jesus unto them, All ye shall be offended because of me this night: for it is written, I will smite the shepherd, and the sheep of the flock shall be scattered abroad.

Mt 26:56 — But all this was done, that the scriptures of the prophets might be fulfilled. Then all the disciples forsook him, and fled.

Mk 14:27 — And Jesus saith unto them, All ye shall be offended because of me this night: for it is written, I will smite the shepherd, and the sheep shall be scattered.

Mk 14:50 — And they all forsook him, and fled.

• 56.

Mal 3:1 — Behold, I will send my messenger, and he shall prepare the way before me: and the Lord, whom ye seek, shall suddenly come to his temple, even the messenger of the covenant, whom ye delight in: behold, he shall come, saith the LORD of hosts.

Mt 11:10 — For this is *he,* of whom it is written, Behold, I send my messenger before thy face, which shall prepare thy way before thee.

Mk 1:2 — As it is written in the prophets, Behold, I send my messenger before thy face, which shall prepare thy way before thee.

Lk 7:27 — This is *he,* of whom it is written, Behold, I send my messenger before thy face, which shall prepare thy way before thee.

• 57.

Mal 4:5–6; Mt 11:13–14; 17:10–13; Mk 9:11–13; Lk 1:16–17

➜See: Jesus, Prophecies Concerning

→See: **Prophetesses**
→See: **Prophets**

PROPHECY, Miscellaneous, Fulfilled

• The birth and zeal of Josiah.

2Ki 23:1–20

1Ki 13:2 — And he cried against the altar in the word of the LORD, and said, O altar, altar, thus saith the LORD; Behold, a child shall be born unto the house of David, Josiah by name; and upon thee shall he offer the priests of the high places that burn incense upon thee, and men's bones shall be burnt upon thee.

• Death of the prophet of Judah.

1Ki 13:21–22, 24–30

• Extinction of Jeroboam's house.

1Ki 14:5–17

• Extinction of Baasha's house.

1Ki 16:2–3, 9–13

• Concerning the rebuilding of Jericho.

Jos 6:26 — And Joshua adjured *them* at that time, saying, Cursed *be* the man before the LORD, that riseth up and buildeth this city Jericho: he shall lay the foundation thereof in his firstborn, and in his youngest *son* shall he set up the gates of it.

1Ki 16:34 — In his days did Hiel the Bethelite build Jericho: he laid the foundation thereof in Abiram his firstborn, and set up the gates thereof in his youngest *son* Segub, according to the word of the LORD, which he spake by Joshua the son of Nun.

• The drought, foretold by Elijah.

1Ki 17:14 — For thus saith the LORD God of Israel, The barrel of meal shall not waste, neither shall the cruse of oil fail, until the day *that* the LORD sendeth rain upon the earth.

• Destruction of Ben-hadad's army.

1Ki 20:13–30

• The death of a man who refused to smite a prophet.

1Ki 20:35–36

• The death of Ahab.

1Ki 21:18–24; 22:31–38

1Ki 20:42 — And he said unto him, Thus saith the LORD, Because thou hast let go out of *thy* hand a man whom I appointed to utter destruction, therefore thy life shall go for his life, and thy people for his people.

• The death of Ahaziah.

2Ki 1:3–17

• Elijah's translation.

2Ki 2:3–11

• Cannibalism among the children of Israel.

2Ki 6:28–29

Le 26:29 — And ye shall eat the flesh of your sons, and the flesh of your daughters shall ye eat.

Dt 28:53 — And thou shalt eat the fruit of thine own body, the flesh of thy sons and of thy daughters, which the LORD thy God hath given thee, in the siege, and in the straitness, wherewith thine enemies shall distress thee:

Jer 19:9 — And I will cause them to eat the flesh of their sons and the flesh of their daughters, and they shall eat every one the flesh of his friend in the siege and straitness, wherewith their enemies, and they that seek their lives, shall straiten them.

La 4:10 — The hands of the pitiful women have sodden their own children: they were their meat in the destruction of the daughter of my people.

• The death of the Samaritan lord.

2Ki 7:19–20

2Ki 7:2 — Then a lord on whose hand the king leaned answered the man of God, and said, Behold, *if* the LORD would make windows in heaven, might this thing be? And he said, Behold, thou shalt see *it* with thine eyes, but shalt not eat thereof.

• The end of the famine in Samaria.

2Ki 7:1–18

• Jezebel's tragic death.

2Ki 9:33–37

1Ki 21:23 — And of Jezebel also spake the LORD, saying, The dogs shall eat Jezebel by the wall of Jezreel.

2Ki 9:10 — And the dogs shall eat Jezebel in the portion of Jezreel, and *there shall be* none to bury *her.* And he opened the door, and fled.

• The smiting of Syria by Joash.

2Ki 13:16–25

• The conquest of Jeroboam.

2Ki 14:25–28

• Four generations of Jehu to sit upon the throne of Israel.

2Ki 10:30 — And the LORD said unto Jehu, Because thou hast done well in executing *that which is* right in mine eyes, *and* hast done unto the house of Ahab according to all that *was* in mine heart, thy children of the fourth *generation* shall sit on the throne of Israel.

2Ki 15:12 — This *was* the word of the LORD which he spake unto Jehu, saying, Thy sons shall sit on the throne of Israel unto the fourth *generation.* And so it came to pass.

• Destruction of Sennacherib's army, and his death.

2Ki 19:6–7, 20–37

• The captivity of Judah.

2Ki 20:17–18; 24:10–16; 25:11–21

• Concerning Christ.

→See: **Jesus, Prophecies Concerning**
→See: **Prophecy, Concerning Messiah, and Fulfillment**

• Concerning John.

Mt 3:3 — For this is he that was spoken of by the prophet Esaias, saying, The voice of one crying in the wilderness, Prepare ye the way of the Lord, make his paths straight.

• Rachel weeping for her children.

Mt 2:17–18

Jer 31:15 — Thus saith the LORD; A voice was heard in Ramah, lamentation, *and* bitter weeping; Rahel weeping for her children refused to be comforted for her children, because they *were* not.

• Deliverance of Jeremiah.

Jer 39:15–18

• Invasion of Judah by the Chaldeans.

Hab 1:6–11

• Invasion of Judah by the Chaldeans fulfilled.

2Ki 25:1–30; 2Ch 36:17–21

• Betrayal of Jesus by Judas, prophecy.

Ps 41:9 — Yea, mine own familiar friend, in whom I trusted, which did eat of my bread, hath lifted up *his* heel against me.

• Betrayal of Jesus by Judas, fulfillment.

Jn 18:1–9

Jn 13:18 — I speak not of you all: I know whom I have chosen: but that the scripture may be fulfilled, He that eateth bread with me hath lifted up his heel against me.

• Judas' self-destruction.

Ps 69:25 — Let their habitation be desolate; *and* let none dwell in their tents.

Ac 1:16 — Men *and* brethren, this scripture must needs have been fulfilled, which the Holy Ghost by the mouth of David spake before concerning Judas, which was guide to them that took Jesus.

Ac 1:20 — For it is written in the book of Psalms, Let his habitation be desolate, and let no man dwell therein: and his bishoprick let another take.

• Judas' self-destruction, fulfilled.

Ac 1:16–20

Mt 27:5 — And he cast down the pieces of silver in the temple, and departed, and went and hanged himself.

• Outpouring of the Holy Spirit.

Joel 2:28–29

• Outpouring of the Holy Spirit, fulfilled.

Ac 2:16–21

• Spiritual blindness of the Jews.

Isa 6:9 — And he said, Go, and tell this people, Hear ye indeed, but understand not; and see ye indeed, but perceive not.

Isa 29:13 — Wherefore the Lord said, Forasmuch as this people draw near *me* with their mouth, and with their lips do honour me, but have removed their heart far from me, and their fear toward me is taught by the precept of men:

• Spiritual blindness of the Jews, fulfilled.

Mk 7:6–7; Ac 28:25–27

• Mission of Jesus.

Ps 68:18 — Thou hast ascended on high, thou hast led captivity captive: thou hast received gifts for men; yea, *for* the rebellious also, that the LORD God might dwell *among them.*

• Mission of Jesus, fulfilled.

Eph 4:8 — Wherefore he saith, When he ascended up on high, he led captivity captive, and gave gifts unto men.

Eph 4:10 — He that descended is the same also that ascended up far above all heavens, that he might fill all things.)

See: Jesus, Mission of

• Captivity of the Jews.

2Ki 25:1–8; Ezr 1:1–11; Jer 25:11–12; 32:3–5

Jer 29:10 — For thus saith the LORD, That after seventy years be accomplished at Babylon I will visit you, and perform my good word toward you, in causing you to return to this place.

Jer 29:14 — And I will be found of you, saith the LORD: and I will turn away your captivity, and I will gather you from all the nations, and from all the places whither I have driven you, saith the LORD; and I will bring you again into the place whence I caused you to be carried away captive.

Da 9:2 — In the first year of his reign I Daniel understood by books the number of the years, whereof the word of the LORD came to Jeremiah the prophet, that he would accomplish seventy years in the desolations of Jerusalem.

• Of the destruction of the ship in which Paul sailed.

Ac 27:18–44

Ac 27:10 — And said unto them, Sirs, I perceive that this voyage will be with hurt and much damage, not only of the lading and ship, but also of our lives.

PROPHETESSES

Joel 2:28–29

Eze 13:17 — Likewise, thou son of man, set thy face against the daughters of thy people, which prophesy out of their own heart; and prophesy thou against them,

• Miriam.

Ex 15:20 — And Miriam the prophetess, the sister of Aaron, took a timbrel in her hand; and all the women went out after her with timbrels and with dances.

• Deborah.

Jgs 4:4 — And Deborah, a prophetess, the wife of Lapidoth, she judged Israel at that time.

• Huldah.

2Ki 22:14 — So Hilkiah the priest, and Ahikam, and Achbor, and Shaphan, and Asahiah, went unto Huldah the prophetess, the wife of Shallum the son of Tikvah, the son of Harhas, keeper of the wardrobe; (now she dwelt in Jerusalem in the college;) and they communed with her.

• Noadiah.

Ne 6:14 — My God, think thou upon Tobiah and Sanballat according to these their works, and on the prophetess Noadiah, and the rest of the prophets, that would have put me in fear.

• Isaiah's wife.

Isa 8:3 — And I went unto the prophetess; and she conceived, and bare a son. Then said the LORD to me, Call his name Maher-shalal-hash-baz.

• Elisabeth.

Lk 1:41–45

• Anna.

Lk 2:36–38

• **Daughters of Philip.**

Ac 21:9 — And the same man had four daughters, virgins, which did prophesy.

• **Jezebel.**

Rev 2:20 — Notwithstanding I have a few things against thee, because thou sufferest that woman Jezebel, which calleth herself a prophetess, to teach and to seduce my servants to commit fornication, and to eat things sacrificed unto idols.

See: Women

PROPHETS

• **Called seers.**

1Sa 9:19 — And Samuel answered Saul, and said, I *am* the seer: go up before me unto the high place; for ye shall eat with me to day, and to morrow I will let thee go, and will tell thee all that *is* in thine heart.

2Sa 15:27 — The king said also unto Zadok the priest, *Art not* thou a seer? return into the city in peace, and your two sons with you, Ahimaaz thy son, and Jonathan the son of Abiathar.

2Sa 24:11 — For when David was up in the morning, the word of the LORD came unto the prophet Gad, David's seer, saying,

2Ki 17:13 — Yet the LORD testified against Israel, and against Judah, by all the prophets, *and by* all the seers, saying, Turn ye from your evil ways, and keep my commandments *and* my statutes, according to all the law which I commanded your fathers, and which I sent to you by my servants the prophets.

1Ch 9:22 — All these *which were* chosen to be porters in the gates were two hundred and twelve. These were reckoned by their genealogy in their villages, whom David and Samuel the seer did ordain in their set office.

1Ch 29:29 — Now the acts of David the king, first and last, behold, they *are* written in the book of Samuel the seer, and in the book of Nathan the prophet, and in the book of Gad the seer,

2Ch 9:29 — Now the rest of the acts of Solomon, first and last, *are* they not written in the book of Nathan the prophet, and in the prophecy of Ahijah the Shilonite, and in the visions of Iddo the seer against Jeroboam the son of Nebat?

2Ch 12:15 — Now the acts of Rehoboam, first and last, *are* they not written in the book of Shemaiah the prophet, and of Iddo the seer concerning genealogies? And *there were* wars between Rehoboam and Jeroboam continually.

2Ch 29:30 — Moreover Hezekiah the king and the princes commanded the Levites to sing praise unto the LORD with the words of David, and of Asaph the seer. And they sang praises with gladness, and they bowed their heads and worshipped.

Isa 30:10 — Which say to the seers, See not; and to the prophets, Prophesy not unto us right things, speak unto us smooth things, prophesy deceits:

Mic 3:7 — Then shall the seers be ashamed, and the diviners confounded: yea, they shall all cover their lips; for *there is* no answer of God.

• **Schools of.**

2Ki 2:3–15

1Ki 20:35 — And a certain man of the sons of the prophets said unto his neighbour in the word of the LORD, Smite me, I pray thee. And the man refused to smite him.

2Ki 4:1 — Now there cried a certain woman of the wives of the sons of the prophets unto Elisha, saying, Thy servant my husband is dead; and thou knowest that thy servant did fear the LORD: and the creditor is come to take unto him my two sons to be bondmen.

2Ki 4:38 — And Elisha came again to Gilgal: and *there was* a dearth in the land; and the sons of the prophets *were* sitting before him: and he said unto his servant, Set on the great pot, and seethe pottage for the sons of the prophets.

2Ki 9:1 — And Elisha the prophet called one of the children of the prophets, and said unto him, Gird up thy loins, and take this box of oil in thine hand, and go to Ramoth-gilead:

• **Kept the chronicles.**

1Ch 29:29 — Now the acts of David the king, first and last, behold, they *are* written in the book of Samuel the seer, and in the book of Nathan the prophet, and in the book of Gad the seer,

2Ch 9:29 — Now the rest of the acts of Solomon, first and last, *are* they not written in the book of Nathan the prophet, and in the prophecy of Ahijah the Shilonite, and in the visions of Iddo the seer against Jeroboam the son of Nebat?

2Ch 12:15 — Now the acts of Rehoboam, first and last, *are* they not written in the book of Shemaiah the prophet, and of Iddo the seer concerning genealogies? And *there were* wars between Rehoboam and Jeroboam continually.

• **Counsellors to kings.**

Isa 37:2–3

• **Not honored in their own country.**

Lk 4:24–27

Mt 13:57 — And they were offended in him. But Jesus said unto them, A prophet is not without honour, save in his own country, and in his own house.

Jn 4:44 — For Jesus himself testified, that a prophet hath no honour in his own country.

• **Inspired by angels.**

Zec 1:13–14

Zec 1:9 — Then said I, O my lord, what *are* these? And the angel that talked with me said unto me, I will shew thee what these *be*.

Zec 1:19 — And I said unto the angel that talked with me, What *be* these? And he answered me, These *are* the horns which have scattered Judah, Israel, and Jerusalem.

Ac 7:53 — Who have received the law by the disposition of angels, and have not kept *it*.

Gal 3:19 — Wherefore then *serveth* the law? It was added because of transgressions, till the seed should come to whom the promise was made; *and it was* ordained by angels in the hand of a mediator.

Heb 2:2 — For if the word spoken by angels was stedfast, and every transgression and disobedience received a just recompence of reward;

- **Persecutions of.**

2Ch 36:16 — But they mocked the messengers of God, and despised his words, and misused his prophets, until the wrath of the LORD arose against his people, till *there was* no remedy.

Am 2:12 — But ye gave the Nazarites wine to drink; and commanded the prophets, saying, Prophesy not.

- **Martyrs.**

Jer 2:30 — In vain have I smitten your children; they received no correction: your own sword hath devoured your prophets, like a destroying lion.

Mt 23:37 — O Jerusalem, Jerusalem, *thou* that killest the prophets, and stonest them which are sent unto thee, how often would I have gathered thy children together, even as a hen gathereth her chickens under *her* wings, and ye would not!

Mk 12:5 — And again he sent another; and him they killed, and many others; beating some, and killing some.

Lk 13:34 — O Jerusalem, Jerusalem, which killest the prophets, and stonest them that are sent unto thee; how often would I have gathered thy children together, as a hen *doth gather* her brood under *her* wings, and ye would not!

1Th 2:15 — Who both killed the Lord Jesus, and their own prophets, and have persecuted us; and they please not God, and are contrary to all men:

Heb 11:37 — They were stoned, they were sawn asunder, were tempted, were slain with the sword: they wandered about in sheepskins and goatskins; being destitute, afflicted, tormented;

Rev 16:6 — For they have shed the blood of saints and prophets, and thou hast given them blood to drink; for they are worthy.

- **Emoluments of.**
  - **Presents.**

1Sa 9:7–8; 2Ki 8:8–9

1Ki 14:3 — And take with thee ten loaves, and cracknels, and a cruse of honey, and go to him: he shall tell thee what shall become of the child.

2Ki 4:42 — And there came a man from Baal-shalisha, and brought the man of God bread of the firstfruits, twenty loaves of barley, and full ears of corn in the husk thereof. And he said, Give unto the people, that they may eat.

Eze 13:19 — And will ye pollute me among my people for handfuls of barley and for pieces of bread, to slay the souls that should not die, and to save the souls alive that should not live, by your lying to my people that hear *your* lies?

  - **Presents refused by.**

1Ki 13:7–8

Nu 22:18 — And Balaam answered and said unto the servants of Balak, If Balak would give me his house full of silver and gold, I cannot go beyond the word of the LORD my God, to do less or more.

2Ki 5:5 — And the king of Syria said, Go to, go, and I will send a letter unto the king of Israel. And he departed, and took with him ten talents of silver, and six thousand *pieces* of gold, and ten changes of raiment.

2Ki 5:16 — But he said, *As* the LORD liveth, before whom I stand, I will receive none. And he urged him to take *it;* but he refused.

- **False.**

Jer 23:25–27, 30–32

1Ki 13:18 — He said unto him, I *am* a prophet also as thou *art;* and an angel spake unto me by the word of the LORD, saying, Bring him back with thee into thine house, that he may eat bread and drink water. *But* he lied unto him.

Ne 6:12 — And, lo, I perceived that God had not sent him; but that he pronounced this prophecy against me: for Tobiah and Sanballat had hired him.

La 2:14 — Thy prophets have seen vain and foolish things for thee: and they have not discovered thine iniquity, to turn away thy captivity; but have seen for thee false burdens and causes of banishment.

  - **Admonitions to.**

Dt 13:1–3

  - **Denunciations against.**

Dt 18:20 — But the prophet, which shall presume to speak a word in my name, which I have not commanded him to speak, or that shall speak in the name of other gods, even that prophet shall die.

Jer 14:15 — Therefore thus saith the LORD concerning the prophets that prophesy in my name, and I sent them not, yet they say, Sword and famine shall not be in this land; By sword and famine shall those prophets be consumed.

  - **Punishment of.**

Jer 14:13–16; 28:16–17

Jer 20:6 — And thou, Pashur, and all that dwell in thine house shall go into captivity: and thou shalt come to Babylon, and there thou shalt die, and shalt be buried there, thou, and all thy friends, to whom thou hast prophesied lies.

Jer 29:32 — Therefore thus saith the LORD; Behold, I will punish Shemaiah the Nehelamite, and his seed: he shall not have a man to dwell among this people; neither shall he behold the good that I will do for my people, saith the LORD; because he hath taught rebellion against the LORD.

Zec 13:3 — And it shall come to pass, *that* when any shall yet prophesy, then his father and his mother that begat him shall say unto him, Thou shalt not live; for thou speakest lies in the name of the LORD: and his father and his mother that begat him shall thrust him through when he prophesieth.

  - **Instances of.**
    - **Noadiah.**

Ne 6:14 — My God, think thou upon Tobiah and Sanballat according to these their works, and on the prophetess Noadiah, and the rest of the prophets, that would have put me in fear.

    - **Four hundred in Samaria.**

1Ki 22:6–12

2Ch 18:5 — Therefore the king of Israel gathered together of prophets four hundred men, and said unto them, Shall we go to Ramoth-gilead to battle, or shall I forbear? And they said, Go up; for God will deliver *it* into the king's hand.

See: Minister, False and Corrupt

• Inspiration of.

Ge 41:38–39; Ex 3:14–15; Nu 9:8–10; 12:6–8; 16:28–29; 24:2–4, 15–16; Dt 1:5–6; 5:4–6; 34:9–11; Jgs 6:7–10; 1Sa 3:4–10, 19–21; 9:15–20; 10:6–7; 19:23–24; 2Sa 7:3–7; 23:2–3; 2Ki 3:11–12; 6:8–12; 1Ch 28:11–12; Ezr 5:1–2; Job 33:14–16; Isa 6:1–9; Jer 1:1–2, 4–10; 13:1–3; 26:1–2; 27:1–2; Eze 2:1–2, 4–5; 3:10–12, 16–17; 11:4–5; Da 9:1–22; 10:7–9; Hos 1:1–2; Joel 2:28–29; Am 3:7–8; 7:14–15; Jnh 3:1–2; Lk 2:25–27; Ac 2:2–4; 7:55–56; 21:10–11; Ro 1:1–2; 1Co 12:7–11; 1Pe 1:10–11

Ge 40:8 — And they said unto him, We have dreamed a dream, and *there is* no interpreter of it. And Joseph said unto them, *Do* not interpretations *belong* to God? tell me *them,* I pray you.

Ge 41:16 — And Joseph answered Pharaoh, saying, *It is* not in me: God shall give Pharaoh an answer of peace.

Ex 4:12 — Now therefore go, and I will be with thy mouth, and teach thee what thou shalt say.

Ex 4:15 — And thou shalt speak unto him, and put words in his mouth: and I will be with thy mouth, and with his mouth, and will teach you what ye shall do.

Ex 4:27 — And the LORD said to Aaron, Go into the wilderness to meet Moses. And he went, and met him in the mount of God, and kissed him.

Ex 6:13 — And the LORD spake unto Moses and unto Aaron, and gave them a charge unto the children of Israel, and unto Pharaoh king of Egypt, to bring the children of Israel out of the land of Egypt.

Ex 6:29 — That the LORD spake unto Moses, saying, I *am* the LORD: speak thou unto Pharaoh king of Egypt all that I say unto thee.

Ex 7:2 — Thou shalt speak all that I command thee: and Aaron thy brother shall speak unto Pharaoh, that he send the children of Israel out of his land.

Ex 19:3 — And Moses went up unto God, and the LORD called unto him out of the mountain, saying, Thus shalt thou say to the house of Jacob, and tell the children of Israel;

Ex 19:9 — And the LORD said unto Moses, Lo, I come unto thee in a thick cloud, that the people may hear when I speak with thee, and believe thee for ever. And Moses told the words of the people unto the LORD.

Ex 19:19 — And when the voice of the trumpet sounded long, and waxed louder and louder, Moses spake, and God answered him by a voice.

Ex 24:16 — And the glory of the LORD abode upon mount Sinai, and the cloud covered it six days: and the seventh day he called unto Moses out of the midst of the cloud.

Ex 25:9 — According to all that I shew thee, *after* the pattern of the tabernacle, and the pattern of all the instruments thereof, even so shall ye make *it.*

Ex 25:22 — And there I will meet with thee, and I will commune with thee from above the mercy seat, from between the two cherubims which *are* upon the ark of the testimony, of all *things* which I will give thee in commandment unto the children of Israel.

Ex 26:30 — And thou shalt rear up the tabernacle according to the fashion thereof which was shewed thee in the mount.

Ex 33:9 — And it came to pass, as Moses entered into the tabernacle, the cloudy pillar descended, and stood *at* the door of the tabernacle, and *the* LORD talked with Moses.

Ex 35:31 — And he hath filled him with the spirit of God, in wisdom, in understanding, and in knowledge, and in all manner of workmanship;

Ex 35:35 — Them hath he filled with wisdom of heart, to work all manner of work, of the engraver, and of the cunning workman, and of the embroiderer, in blue, and in purple, in scarlet, and in fine linen, and of the weaver, *even* of them that do any work, and of those that devise cunning work.

Le 1:1 — And the LORD called unto Moses, and spake unto him out of the tabernacle of the congregation, saying,

Nu 1:1 — And the LORD spake unto Moses in the wilderness of Sinai, in the tabernacle of the congregation, on the first *day* of the second month, in the second year after they were come out of the land of Egypt, saying,

Nu 7:89 — And when Moses was gone into the tabernacle of the congregation to speak with him, then he heard the voice of one speaking unto him from off the mercy seat that *was* upon the ark of testimony, from between the two cherubims: and he spake unto him.

Nu 11:17 — And I will come down and talk with thee there: and I will take of the spirit which *is* upon thee, and will put *it* upon them; and they shall bear the burden of the people with thee, that thou bear it not thyself alone.

Nu 11:25 — And the LORD came down in a cloud, and spake unto him, and took of the spirit that *was* upon him, and gave *it* unto the seventy elders: and it came to pass, *that,* when the spirit rested upon them, they prophesied, and did not cease.

Nu 22:18 — And Balaam answered and said unto the servants of Balak, If Balak would give me his house full of silver and gold, I cannot go beyond the word of the LORD my God, to do less or more.

Nu 22:38 — And Balaam said unto Balak, Lo, I am come unto thee: have I now any power at all to say any thing? the word that God putteth in my mouth, that shall I speak.

Nu 23:5 — And the LORD put a word in Balaam's mouth, and said, Return unto Balak, and thus thou shalt speak.

Nu 23:12 — And he answered and said, Must I not take heed to speak that which the LORD hath put in my mouth?

Nu 23:20 — Behold, I have received *commandment* to bless: and he hath blessed; and I cannot reverse it.

Nu 23:26 — But Balaam answered and said unto Balak, Told not I thee, saying, All that the LORD speaketh, that I must do?

Dt 5:31 — But as for thee, stand thou here by me, and I will speak unto thee all the commandments, and the statutes, and the judgments, which thou shalt teach them, that they may do *them* in the land which I give them to possess it.

Jos 3:7 — And the LORD said unto Joshua, This day will I begin to magnify thee in the sight of all Israel, that they may know that, as I was with Moses, so I will be with thee.

Jgs 6:34 — But the Spirit of the LORD came upon Gideon, and he blew a trumpet; and Abi-ezer was gathered after him.

Jgs 11:29 — Then the Spirit of the LORD came upon Jephthah, and he passed over Gilead, and Manasseh, and passed over Mizpeh of Gilead, and from Mizpeh of Gilead he passed over *unto* the children of Ammon.

Jgs 13:25 — And the Spirit of the LORD began to move him at times in the camp of Dan between Zorah and Eshtaol.

Jgs 14:6 — And the Spirit of the LORD came mightily upon him, and he rent him as he would have rent a kid, and *he had* nothing in his hand: but he told not his father or his mother what he had done.

Jgs 14:19 — And the Spirit of the LORD came upon him, and he went down to Ashkelon, and slew thirty men of them, and took their spoil, and gave change of garments unto them which expounded the riddle. And his anger was kindled, and he went up to his father's house.

1Sa 3:1 — And the child Samuel ministered unto the LORD before Eli. And the word of the LORD was precious in those days; *there was* no open vision.

1Sa 9:6 — And he said unto him, Behold now, *there is* in this city a man of God, and *he is* an honourable man; all that he saith cometh surely to pass: now let us go thither; peradventure he can shew us our way that we should go.

1Sa 10:10 — And when they came thither to the hill, behold, a company of prophets met him; and the Spirit of God came upon him, and he prophesied among them.

1Sa 16:13 — Then Samuel took the horn of oil, and anointed him in the midst of his brethren: and the Spirit of the LORD came upon David from that day forward. So Samuel rose up, and went to Ramah.

1Sa 19:20 — And Saul sent messengers to take David: and when they saw the company of the prophets prophesying, and Samuel standing *as* appointed over them, the Spirit of God was upon the messengers of Saul, and they also prophesied.

2Sa 12:1 — And the LORD sent Nathan unto David. And he came unto him, and said unto him, There were two men in one city; the one rich, and the other poor.

1Ki 13:20 — And it came to pass, as they sat at the table, that the word of the LORD came unto the prophet that brought him back:

1Ki 14:5 — And the LORD said unto Ahijah, Behold, the wife of Jeroboam cometh to ask a thing of thee for her son; for he is sick: thus and thus shalt thou say unto her: for it shall be, when she cometh in, that she shall feign herself *to be* another *woman.*

1Ki 17:1 — And Elijah the Tishbite, *who was* of the inhabitants of Gilead, said unto Ahab, *As* the LORD God of Israel liveth, before whom I stand, there shall not be dew nor rain these years, but according to my word.

1Ki 17:24 — And the woman said to Elijah, Now by this I know that thou *art* a man of God, *and* that the word of the LORD in thy mouth *is* truth.

1Ki 18:36 — And it came to pass at *the time of* the offering of the *evening* sacrifice, that Elijah the prophet came near, and said, LORD God of Abraham, Isaac, and of Israel, let it be known this day that thou art God in Israel, and *that* I *am* thy servant, and *that* I have done all these things at thy word.

1Ki 18:46 — And the hand of the LORD was on Elijah; and he girded up his loins, and ran before Ahab to the entrance of Jezreel.

1Ki 19:9 — And he came thither unto a cave, and lodged there; and, behold, the word of the LORD *came* to him, and he said unto him, What doest thou here, Elijah?

1Ki 22:14 — And Micaiah said, *As* the LORD liveth, what the LORD saith unto me, that will I speak.

1Ki 22:28 — And Micaiah said, If thou return at all in peace, the LORD hath not spoken by me. And he said, Hearken, O people, every one of you.

2Ki 1:12 — And Elijah answered and said unto them, If I *be* a man of God, let fire come down from heaven, and consume thee and thy fifty. And the fire of God came down from heaven, and consumed him and his fifty.

2Ki 2:9 — And it came to pass, when they were gone over, that Elijah said unto Elisha, Ask what I shall do for thee, before I be taken away from thee. And Elisha said, I pray thee, let a double portion of thy spirit be upon me.

2Ki 2:15 — And when the sons of the prophets which *were* to view at Jericho saw him, they said, The spirit of Elijah doth rest on Elisha. And they came to meet him, and bowed themselves to the ground before him.

2Ki 3:15 — But now bring me a minstrel. And it came to pass, when the minstrel played, that the hand of the LORD came upon him.

2Ki 4:27 — And when she came to the man of God to the hill, she caught him by the feet: but Gehazi came near to thrust her away. And the man of God said, Let her alone; for her soul *is* vexed within her: and the LORD hath hid *it* from me, and hath not told me.

2Ki 5:8 — And it was *so,* when Elisha the man of God had heard that the king of Israel had rent his clothes, that he sent to the king, saying, Wherefore hast thou rent thy clothes? let him come now to me, and he shall know that there is a prophet in Israel.

2Ki 6:17 — And Elisha prayed, and said, LORD, I pray thee, open his eyes, that he may see. And the LORD opened the eyes of the young man; and he saw: and, behold, the mountain *was* full of horses and chariots of fire round about Elisha.

2Ki 6:32 — But Elisha sat in his house, and the elders sat with him; and *the king* sent a man from before him: but ere the messenger came to him, he said to the elders, See ye how this son of a murderer hath sent to take away mine head? look, when the messenger cometh, shut the door, and hold him fast at the door: *is* not the sound of his master's feet behind him?

2Ki 10:10 — Know now that there shall fall unto the earth nothing of the word of the LORD, which the LORD spake concerning the house of Ahab: for the LORD hath done *that* which he spake by his servant Elijah.

1Ch 12:18 — Then the spirit came upon Amasai, *who was* chief of the captains, *and he said,* Thine *are we,* David, and on thy side, thou son of Jesse: peace, peace *be* unto thee, and peace *be* to thine helpers; for thy God helpeth thee. Then David received them, and made them captains of the band.

1Ch 21:18 — Then the angel of the LORD commanded Gad to say to David, that David should go up, and set up an altar unto the LORD in the threshingfloor of Ornan the Jebusite.

1Ch 28:19 — All *this, said David,* the LORD made me understand in writing by *his* hand upon me, *even* all the works of this pattern.

2Ch 8:14 — And he appointed, according to the order of David his father, the courses of the priests to their service, and the Levites to their charges, to praise and minister before the priests, as the duty of every day required: the porters also by their courses at every gate: for so had David the man of God commanded.

2Ch 15:1 — And the Spirit of God came upon Azariah the son of Oded:

2Ch 18:27 — And Micaiah said, If thou certainly return in peace, *then* hath not the LORD spoken by me. And he said, Hearken, all ye people.

2Ch 20:14 — Then upon Jahaziel the son of Zechariah, the son of Benaiah, the son of Jeiel, the son of Mattaniah, a Levite of the sons of Asaph, came the Spirit of the LORD in the midst of the congregation;

2Ch 24:20 — And the Spirit of God came upon Zechariah the son of Jehoiada the priest, which stood above the people, and said unto them, Thus saith God, Why transgress ye the commandments of the LORD, that ye cannot prosper? because ye have forsaken the LORD, he hath also forsaken you.

2Ch 26:5 — And he sought God in the days of Zechariah, who had understanding in the visions of God: and as long as he sought the LORD, God made him to prosper.

2Ch 33:18 — Now the rest of the acts of Manasseh, and his prayer unto his God, and the words of the seers that spake to him in the name of the LORD God of Israel, behold, they *are written* in the book of the kings of Israel.

2Ch 36:12 — And he did *that which was* evil in the sight of the LORD his God, *and* humbled not himself before Jeremiah the prophet *speaking* from the mouth of the LORD.

2Ch 36:15 — And the LORD God of their fathers sent to them by his messengers, rising up betimes, and sending; because he had compassion on his people, and on his dwelling place:

Ne 9:30 — Yet many years didst thou forbear them, and testifiedst against them by thy spirit in thy prophets: yet would they not give ear: therefore gavest thou them into the hand of the people of the lands.

Job 32:8 — But *there is* a spirit in man: and the inspiration of the Almighty giveth them understanding.

Ps 103:7 — He made known his ways unto Moses, his acts unto the children of Israel.

Isa 8:11 — For the LORD spake thus to me with a strong hand, and instructed me that I should not walk in the way of this people, saying,

Isa 44:26 — That confirmeth the word of his servant, and performeth the counsel of his messengers; that saith to Jerusalem, Thou shalt be inhabited; and to the cities of Judah, Ye shall be built, and I will raise up the decayed places thereof:

Isa 63:11 — Then he remembered the days of old, Moses, *and* his people, *saying,* Where *is* he that brought them up out of the sea with the shepherd of his flock? where *is* he that put his holy Spirit within him?

Jer 2:1 — Moreover the word of the LORD came to me, saying,

Jer 7:1 — The word that came to Jeremiah from the LORD, saying,

Jer 7:25 — Since the day that your fathers came forth out of the land of Egypt unto this day I have even sent unto you all my servants the prophets, daily rising up early and sending *them:*

Jer 11:1 — The word that came to Jeremiah from the LORD, saying,

Jer 11:18 — And the LORD hath given me knowledge *of it,* and I know *it:* then thou shewedst me their doings.

Jer 16:1 — The word of the LORD came also unto me, saying,

Jer 18:1 — The word which came to Jeremiah from the LORD, saying,

Jer 20:9 — Then I said, I will not make mention of him, nor speak any more in his name. But *his word* was in mine heart as a burning fire shut up in my bones, and I was weary with forbearing, and I could not *stay.*

Jer 23:9 — Mine heart within me is broken because of the prophets; all my bones shake; I am like a drunken man, and like a man whom wine hath overcome, because of the LORD, and because of the words of his holiness.

Jer 24:4 — Again the word of the LORD came unto me, saying,

Jer 25:3 — From the thirteenth year of Josiah the son of Amon king of Judah, even unto this day, that *is* the three and twentieth year, the word of the LORD hath come unto me, and I have spoken unto you, rising early and speaking; but ye have not hearkened.

Jer 26:12 — Then spake Jeremiah unto all the princes and to all the people, saying, The LORD sent me to prophesy against this house and against this city all the words that ye have heard.

Jer 29:30 — Then came the word of the LORD unto Jeremiah, saying,

Jer 33:1 — Moreover the word of the LORD came unto Jeremiah the second time, while he was yet shut up in the court of the prison, saying,

Jer 34:1 — The word which came unto Jeremiah from the LORD, when Nebuchadnezzar king of Babylon, and all his army, and all the kingdoms of the earth of his dominion, and all the people, fought against Jerusalem, and against all the cities thereof, saying,

Jer 42:4 — Then Jeremiah the prophet said unto them, I have heard *you;* behold, I will pray unto the LORD your God according to your words; and it shall come to pass, *that* whatsoever thing the LORD shall answer you, I will declare *it* unto you; I will keep nothing back from you.

Jer 42:7 — And it came to pass after ten days, that the word of the LORD came unto Jeremiah.

Eze 1:1 — Now it came to pass in the thirtieth year, in the fourth *month,* in the fifth *day* of the month, as I *was* among the captives by the river of Chebar, *that* the heavens were opened, and I saw visions of God.

Eze 1:3 — The word of the LORD came expressly unto Ezekiel the priest, the son of Buzi, in the land of the Chaldeans by the river Chebar; and the hand of the LORD was there upon him.

Eze 1:20 — Whithersoever the spirit was to go, they went, thither *was their* spirit to go; and the wheels were lifted up over against them: for the spirit of the living creature *was* in the wheels.

Eze 3:14 — So the spirit lifted me up, and took me away, and I went in bitterness, in the heat of my spirit; but the hand of the LORD was strong upon me.

Eze 3:22 — And the hand of the LORD was there upon me; and he said unto me, Arise, go forth into the plain, and I will there talk with thee.

Eze 3:24 — Then the spirit entered into me, and set me upon my feet, and spake with me, and said unto me, Go, shut thyself within thine house.

Eze 3:27 — But when I speak with thee, I will open thy mouth, and thou shalt say unto them, Thus saith the Lord GOD; He that heareth, let him hear; and he that forbeareth, let him forbear: for they *are* a rebellious house.

Eze 8:1 — And it came to pass in the sixth year, in the sixth *month,* in the fifth *day* of the month, *as* I sat in mine house, and the elders of Judah sat before me, that the hand of the Lord GOD fell there upon me.

Eze 11:1 — Moreover the spirit lifted me up, and brought me unto the east gate of the LORD'S house, which looketh eastward: and behold at the door of the gate five and twenty men; among whom I saw Jaazaniah the son of Azur, and Pelatiah the son of Benaiah, the princes of the people.

Eze 11:24 — Afterwards the spirit took me up, and brought me in a vision by the Spirit of God into Chaldea, to them of the captivity. So the vision that I had seen went up from me.

Eze 33:22 — Now the hand of the LORD was upon me in the evening, afore he that was escaped came; and had opened my mouth, until he came to me in the morning; and my mouth was opened, and I was no more dumb.

Eze 37:1 — The hand of the LORD was upon me, and carried me out in the spirit of the LORD, and set me down in the midst of the valley which *was* full of bones,

Eze 40:1 — In the five and twentieth year of our captivity, in the beginning of the year, in the tenth *day* of the month, in the fourteenth year after that the city was smitten, in the selfsame day the hand of the LORD was upon me, and brought me thither.

Eze 43:5 — So the spirit took me up, and brought me into the inner court; and, behold, the glory of the LORD filled the house.

Da 1:17 — As for these four children, God gave them knowledge and skill in all learning and wisdom: and Daniel had understanding in all visions and dreams.

Da 2:19 — Then was the secret revealed unto Daniel in a night vision. Then Daniel blessed the God of heaven.

Da 7:16 — I came near unto one of them that stood by, and asked him the truth of all this. So he told me, and made me know the interpretation of the things.

Da 8:16 — And I heard a man's voice between *the banks of* Ulai, which called, and said, Gabriel, make this *man* to understand the vision.

Hos 12:10 — I have also spoken by the prophets, and I have multiplied visions, and used similitudes, by the ministry of the prophets.

Am 7:7 — Thus he shewed me: and, behold, the Lord stood upon a wall *made* by a plumbline, with a plumbline in his hand.

Am 9:1 — I saw the LORD standing upon the altar: and he said, Smite the lintel of the door, that the posts may shake: and cut them in the head, all of them; and I will slay the last of them with the sword: he that fleeth of them shall not flee away, and he that escapeth of them shall not be delivered.

Ob 1:1 — The vision of Obadiah. Thus saith the Lord GOD concerning Edom; We have heard a rumour from the LORD, and an ambassador is sent among the heathen, Arise ye, and let us rise up against her in battle.

Jnh 1:1 — Now the word of the LORD came unto Jonah the son of Amittai, saying,

Mic 1:1 — The word of the LORD that came to Micah the Morasthite in the days of Jotham, Ahaz, *and* Hezekiah, kings of Judah, which he saw concerning Samaria and Jerusalem.

Mic 3:8 — But truly I am full of power by the spirit of the LORD, and of judgment, and of might, to declare unto Jacob his transgression, and to Israel his sin.

Hab 3:2 — O LORD, I have heard thy speech, *and* was afraid: O LORD, revive thy work in the midst of the years, in the midst of the years make known; in wrath remember mercy.

Hab 3:16 — When I heard, my belly trembled; my lips quivered at the voice: rottenness entered into my bones, and I trembled in myself, that I might rest in the day of trouble: when he cometh up unto the people, he will invade them with his troops.

Hag 1:13 — Then spake Haggai the LORD's messenger in the LORD's message unto the people, saying, I *am* with you, saith the LORD.

Zec 1:1 — In the eighth month, in the second year of Darius, came the word of the LORD unto Zechariah, the son of Berechiah, the son of Iddo the prophet, saying,

Zec 1:7 — Upon the four and twentieth day of the eleventh month, which *is* the month Sebat, in the second year of Darius, came the word of the LORD unto Zechariah, the son of Berechiah, the son of Iddo the prophet, saying,

Zec 2:9 — For, behold, I will shake mine hand upon them, and they shall be a spoil to their servants: and ye shall know that the LORD of hosts hath sent me.

Zec 7:12 — Yea, they made their hearts *as* an adamant stone, lest they should hear the law, and the words which the LORD of hosts hath sent in his spirit by the former prophets: therefore came a great wrath from the LORD of hosts.

Mk 12:36 — For David himself said by the Holy Ghost, The Lord said to my Lord, Sit thou on my right hand, till I make thine enemies thy footstool.

Lk 1:15 — For he shall be great in the sight of the Lord, and shall drink neither wine nor strong drink; and he shall be filled with the Holy Ghost, even from his mother's womb.

Lk 1:41 — And it came to pass, that, when Elisabeth heard the salutation of Mary, the babe leaped in her womb; and Elisabeth was filled with the Holy Ghost:

Lk 1:67 — And his father Zacharias was filled with the Holy Ghost, and prophesied, saying,

Lk 1:70 — As he spake by the mouth of his holy prophets, which have been since the world began:

Lk 3:2 — Annas and Caiaphas being the high priests, the word of God came unto John the son of Zacharias in the wilderness.

Jn 1:6 — There was a man sent from God, whose name *was* John.

Ac 2:30 — Therefore being a prophet, and knowing that God had sworn with an oath to him, that of the fruit of his loins, according to the flesh, he would raise up Christ to sit on his throne;

Ac 3:18 — But those things, which God before had shewed by the mouth of all his prophets, that Christ should suffer, he hath so fulfilled.

Ac 8:29 — Then the Spirit said unto Philip, Go near, and join thyself to this chariot.

Ac 8:39 — And when they were come up out of the water, the Spirit of the Lord caught away Philip, that the eunuch saw him no more: and he went on his way rejoicing.

Ac 11:28 — And there stood up one of them named Agabus, and signified by the spirit that there should be great dearth throughout all the world: which came to pass in the days of Claudius Caesar.

Ac 21:4 — And finding disciples, we tarried there seven days: who said to Paul through the Spirit, that he should not go up to Jerusalem.

Ac 28:25 — And when they agreed not among themselves, they departed, after that Paul had spoken one word, Well spake the Holy Ghost by Esaias the prophet unto our fathers,

1Co 14:32 — And the spirits of the prophets are subject to the prophets.

Heb 1:1 — God, who at sundry times and in divers manners spake in time past unto the fathers by the prophets,

Heb 3:5 — And Moses verily *was* faithful in all his house, as a servant, for a testimony of those things which were to be spoken after;

Jas 5:10 — Take, my brethren, the prophets, who have spoken in the name of the Lord, for an example of suffering affliction, and of patience.

2Pe 1:21 — For the prophecy came not in old time by the will of man: but holy men of God spake *as they were* moved by the Holy Ghost.

Jude 1:14 — And Enoch also, the seventh from Adam, prophesied of these, saying, Behold, the Lord cometh with ten thousands of his saints,

Rev 2:7 — He that hath an ear, let him hear what the Spirit saith unto the churches; To him that overcometh will I give to eat of the tree of life, which is in the midst of the paradise of God.

Rev 10:7 — But in the days of the voice of the seventh angel, when he shall begin to sound, the mystery of God should be finished, as he hath declared to his servants the prophets.

Rev 14:13 — And I heard a voice from heaven saying unto me, Write, Blessed *are* the dead which die in the Lord from henceforth: Yea, saith the Spirit, that they may rest from their labours; and their works do follow them.

Rev 22:6 — And he said unto me, These sayings *are* faithful and true: and the Lord God of the holy prophets sent his angel to shew unto his servants the things which must shortly be done.

Rev 22:8 — And I John saw these things, and heard *them.* And when I had heard and seen, I fell down to worship before the feet of the angel which shewed me these things.

See: Revelation

See: Word of God; inspiration of

PROPITIATION

Ro 5:10–11; 2Co 5:18–19; Col 1:20–22

Ro 3:25 — Whom God hath set forth *to be* a propitiation through faith in his blood, to declare his righteousness for the remission of sins that are past, through the forbearance of God;

Ro 5:1 — Therefore being justified by faith, we have peace with God through our Lord Jesus Christ:

Heb 9:5 — And over it the cherubims of glory shadowing the mercyseat; of which we cannot now speak particularly.

1Jn 2:2 — And he is the propitiation for our sins: and not for ours only, but also for *the sins of* the whole world.

1Jn 4:10 — Herein is love, not that we loved God, but that he loved us, and sent his Son *to be* the propitiation for our sins.

See: Atonement

PROSELYTE

Ac 9:22–30; Ro 2:9–10

Pr 29:25 — The fear of man bringeth a snare: but whoso putteth his trust in the LORD shall be safe.

Jn 7:13 — Howbeit no man spake openly of him for fear of the Jews.

Jn 19:38 — And after this Joseph of Arimathaea, being a disciple of Jesus, but secretly for fear of the Jews, besought Pilate that he might take away the body of Jesus: and Pilate gave *him* leave. He came therefore, and took the body of Jesus.

Jn 20:19 — Then the same day at evening, being the first *day* of the week, when the doors were shut where the disciples were assembled for fear of the Jews, came Jesus and stood in the midst, and saith unto them, Peace *be* unto you.

Ro 1:16 — For I am not ashamed of the gospel of Christ: for it is the power of God unto salvation to every one that believeth; to the Jew first, and also to the Greek.

PROSPERITY

• From God.

Ge 49:24–26; Ps 128:1–2

Ge 33:11 — Take, I pray thee, my blessing that is brought to thee; because God hath dealt graciously with me, and because I have enough. And he urged him, and he took *it.*

Ps 127:1 — Except the LORD build the house, they labour in vain that build it: except the LORD keep the city, the watchman waketh *but* in vain.

• Design of.

Ecc 7:14 — In the day of prosperity be joyful, but in the day of adversity consider: God also hath set the one over against the other, to the end that man should find nothing after him.

• Dangers of.

Dt 8:10–18

Dt 31:20 — For when I shall have brought them into the land which I sware unto their fathers, that floweth with milk and honey; and they shall have eaten and filled themselves, and waxen fat; then will they turn unto other gods, and serve them, and provoke me, and break my covenant.

Dt 32:15 — But Jeshurun waxed fat, and kicked: thou art waxen fat, thou art grown thick, thou art covered *with fatness;* then he forsook God *which* made him, and lightly esteemed the Rock of his salvation.

Jer 5:7 — How shall I pardon thee for this? thy children have forsaken me, and sworn by *them that are* no gods: when I had fed them to the full, they then committed adultery, and assembled themselves by troops in the harlots' houses.

Hos 13:6 — According to their pasture, so were they filled; they were filled, and their heart was exalted; therefore have they forgotten me.

• Evil effects of.

Hos 4:7 — As they were increased, so they sinned against me: *therefore* will I change their glory into shame.

• Pride in.

2Ch 32:25 — But Hezekiah rendered not again according to the benefit *done* unto him; for his heart was lifted up: therefore there was wrath upon him, and upon Judah and Jerusalem.

• Forgetfulness of God in.

2Ch 12:1 — And it came to pass, when Rehoboam had established the kingdom, and had strengthened himself, he forsook the law of the LORD, and all Israel with him.

2Ch 26:16 — But when he was strong, his heart was lifted up to *his* destruction: for he transgressed against the LORD his God, and went into the temple of the LORD to burn incense upon the altar of incense.

• The prosperous despise the unfortunate.

Job 12:5 — He that is ready to slip with *his* feet *is as* a lamp despised in the thought of him that is at ease.

• Promised to the righteous.

Job 22:23–27

• Prudence in.

• Instances of.

• Joseph and Daniel, as deduced from their general conduct.

↞See: Joseph, Son of Jacob

↞See: Daniel

↞See: Blessing; temporal, from God

↞See: Rich

↞See: Riches

PROSTITUTION, lascivious

• Forbidden.

Le 19:29 — Do not prostitute thy daughter, to cause her to be a whore; lest the land fall to whoredom, and the land become full of wickedness.

Dt 23:17 — There shall be no whore of the daughters of Israel, nor a sodomite of the sons of Israel.

↞See: Adultery

↞See: Lasciviousness

PROTECTION

Ps 62:1–12

Le 11:5 — And the coney, because he cheweth the cud, but divideth not the hoof; he *is* unclean unto you.

Dt 14:7 — Nevertheless these ye shall not eat of them that chew the cud, or of them that divide the cloven hoof; *as* the camel, and the hare, and the coney: for they chew the cud, but divide not the hoof; *therefore* they *are* unclean unto you.

Ps 9:9 — The LORD also will be a refuge for the oppressed, a refuge in times of trouble.

Ps 10:1 — Why standest thou afar off, O LORD? *why* hidest thou *thyself* in times of trouble?

Ps 27:5 — For in the time of trouble he shall hide me in his pavilion: in the secret of his tabernacle shall he hide me; he shall set me up upon a rock.

Pr 30:26 — The conies *are but* a feeble folk, yet make they their houses in the rocks;

Isa 2:10 — Enter into the rock, and hide thee in the dust, for fear of the LORD, and for the glory of his majesty.

Jer 13:4 — Take the girdle that thou hast got, which *is* upon thy loins, and arise, go to Euphrates, and hide it there in a hole of the rock.

PROTRACTED MEETINGS

2Ch 7:8–10

1Ki 8:65 — And at that time Solomon held a feast, and all Israel with him, a great congregation, from the entering in of Hamath unto the river of Egypt, before the LORD our God, seven days and seven days, *even* fourteen days.

2Ch 30:23 — And the whole assembly took counsel to keep other seven days: and they kept *other* seven days with gladness.

See: Revivals

PROUD See: Pride

PROVERBS

• Design of.

Pr 1:1–4

• Written by Solomon.

Pr 1:1 — The proverbs of Solomon the son of David, king of Israel;

Pr 25:1 — These *are* also proverbs of Solomon, which the men of Hezekiah king of Judah copied out.

• Miscellany of.

1Sa 24:13–14; Eze 12:22–23; 18:2–4

1Sa 10:12 — And one of the same place answered and said, But who *is* their father? Therefore it became a proverb, *Is* Saul also among the prophets?

2Sa 3:8 — Then was Abner very wroth for the words of Ish-bosheth, and said, *Am* I a dog's head, which against Judah do shew kindness this day unto the house of Saul thy father, to his brethren, and to his friends, and have not delivered thee into the hand of David, that thou chargest me to day with a fault concerning this woman?

2Sa 20:18 — Then she spake, saying, They were wont to speak in old time, saying, They shall surely ask *counsel* at Abel: and so they ended *the matter.*

1Ki 20:11 — And the king of Israel answered and said, Tell *him,* Let not him that girdeth on *his harness* boast himself as he that putteth it off.

Pr 1:17 — Surely in vain the net is spread in the sight of any bird.

Jer 31:29 — In those days they shall say no more, The fathers have eaten a sour grape, and the children's teeth are set on edge.

Eze 16:44 — Behold, every one that useth proverbs shall use *this* proverb against thee, saying, As is the mother, *so is* her daughter.

Hos 4:9 — And there shall be, like people, like priest: and I will punish them for their ways, and reward them their doings.

Mt 12:33 — Either make the tree good, and his fruit good; or else make the tree corrupt, and his fruit corrupt: for the tree is known by *his* fruit.

Lk 4:23 — And he said unto them, Ye will surely say unto me this proverb, Physician, heal thyself: whatsoever we have heard done in Capernaum, do also here in thy country.

Lk 6:44 — For every tree is known by his own fruit. For of thorns men do not gather figs, nor of a bramble bush gather they grapes.

Lk 14:34 — Salt *is* good: but if the salt have lost his savour, wherewith shall it be seasoned?

Jn 1:46 — And Nathanael said unto him, Can there any good thing come out of Nazareth? Philip saith unto him, Come and see.

1Co 15:33 — Be not deceived: evil communications corrupt good manners.

Gal 6:7 — Be not deceived; God is not mocked: for whatsoever a man soweth, that shall he also reap.

See: Riddle

PROVIDENCE

• Of God.

See: God, Providence of, Overruling Interpositions of the

PROXY

• In priest's service.

2Ch 30:17 — For *there were* many in the congregation that were not sanctified: therefore the Levites had the charge of the killing of the passovers for every one *that was* not clean, to sanctify *them* unto the LORD.

See: Substitution

See: Suffering; vicarious

PRUDENCE

Job 34:3–4; Pr 6:1–2; 14:15–16; 16:20–21; 18:15–16; 22:26–27; 23:1–3; 25:8–10; 26:4–5; Ecc 7:16–17; 8:2–3; Mt 5:25–26; Lk 14:28–32; 1Co 8:8–13; 10:25–33

Ps 39:1 — I said, I will take heed to my ways, that I sin not with my tongue: I will keep my mouth with a bridle, while the wicked is before me.

Ps 112:5 — A good man sheweth favour, and lendeth: he will guide his affairs with discretion.

Pr 8:12 — I wisdom dwell with prudence, and find out knowledge of witty inventions.

Pr 11:13 — A talebearer revealeth secrets: but he that is of a faithful spirit concealeth the matter.

Pr 11:15 — He that is surety for a stranger shall smart *for it:* and he that hateth suretiship is sure.

Pr 11:29 — He that troubleth his own house shall inherit the wind: and the fool *shall be* servant to the wise of heart.

Pr 12:8 — A man shall be commended according to his wisdom: but he that is of a perverse heart shall be despised.

Pr 12:16 — A fool's wrath is presently known: but a prudent *man* covereth shame.

Pr 12:23 — A prudent man concealeth knowledge: but the heart of fools proclaimeth foolishness.

Pr 13:16 — Every prudent *man* dealeth with knowledge: but a fool layeth open *his* folly.

Pr 14:8 — The wisdom of the prudent *is* to understand his way: but the folly of fools *is* deceit.

Pr 14:18 — The simple inherit folly: but the prudent are crowned with knowledge.
Pr 15:5 — A fool despiseth his father's instruction: but he that regardeth reproof is prudent.
Pr 15:22 — Without counsel purposes are disappointed: but in the multitude of counsellors they are established.
Pr 17:2 — A wise servant shall have rule over a son that causeth shame, and shall have part of the inheritance among the brethren.
Pr 17:18 — A man void of understanding striketh hands, *and* becometh surety in the presence of his friend.
Pr 19:2 — Also, *that* the soul *be* without knowledge, *it is* not good; and he that hasteth with *his* feet sinneth.
Pr 20:5 — Counsel in the heart of man *is like* deep water; but a man of understanding will draw it out.
Pr 20:16 — Take his garment that is surety *for* a stranger: and take a pledge of him for a strange woman.
Pr 20:18 — *Every* purpose is established by counsel: and with good advice make war.
Pr 21:5 — The thoughts of the diligent *tend* only to plenteousness; but of every one *that is* hasty only to want.
Pr 21:20 — *There is* treasure to be desired and oil in the dwelling of the wise; but a foolish man spendeth it up.
Pr 21:23 — Whoso keepeth his mouth and his tongue keepeth his soul from troubles.
Pr 22:3 — A prudent *man* foreseeth the evil, and hideth himself: but the simple pass on, and are punished.
Pr 22:7 — The rich ruleth over the poor, and the borrower *is* servant to the lender.
Pr 23:9 — Speak not in the ears of a fool: for he will despise the wisdom of thy words.
Pr 24:6 — For by wise counsel thou shalt make thy war: and in multitude of counsellors *there is* safety.
Pr 24:27 — Prepare thy work without, and make it fit for thyself in the field; and afterwards build thine house.
Pr 27:12 — A prudent *man* foreseeth the evil, *and* hideth himself; *but* the simple pass on, *and* are punished.
Pr 29:8 — Scornful men bring a city into a snare: but wise *men* turn away wrath.
Pr 29:11 — A fool uttereth all his mind: but a wise *man* keepeth it in till afterwards.
Ecc 10:1 — Dead flies cause the ointment of the apothecary to send forth a stinking savour: *so doth* a little folly him that is in reputation for wisdom *and* honour.
Ecc 10:10 — If the iron be blunt, and he do not whet the edge, then must he put to more strength: but wisdom *is* profitable to direct.
Hos 14:9 — Who *is* wise, and he shall understand these *things?* prudent, and he shall know them? for the ways of the LORD *are* right, and the just shall walk in them: but the transgressors shall fall therein.
Am 5:13 — Therefore the prudent shall keep silence in that time; for it *is* an evil time.
Mt 7:6 — Give not that which is holy unto the dogs, neither cast ye your pearls before swine, lest they trample them under their feet, and turn again and rend you.
Ro 14:16 — Let not then your good be evil spoken of:
1Co 6:12 — All things are lawful unto me, but all things are not expedient: all things are lawful for me, but I will not be brought under the power of any.
1Co 10:23 — All things are lawful for me, but all things are not expedient: all things are lawful for me, but all things edify not.
Col 4:5 — Walk in wisdom toward them that are without, redeeming the time.
Jas 1:19 — Wherefore, my beloved brethren, let every man be swift to hear, slow to speak, slow to wrath:

See: Diplomacy

See: Gentleness

See: Wisdom

- **Instances of.**
  - **Jacob, in his conduct toward Esau.**
    Ge 32:3–21
  - **Jacob, toward his sons, after Dinah's defilement.**
    Ge 34:5, 30
  - **Joseph, in the affairs of Egypt.**
    Ge 41:33–57
  - **Jethro's advice to Moses.**
    Ex 18:17–23
  - **The Israelites, in the threatened war with the two and one-half tribes.**
    Jos 22:10–34
  - **Saul, in not slaying the Jabesh-gileadites.**
    1Sa 11:13
  - **David, in his conduct with Saul.**
    1Sa 18:5–30
  - **David, in overthrowing Ahithophel's counsel.**
    2Sa 15:33–37
  - **Abigail, in averting David's wrath.**
    1Sa 25:18–31
  - **Achish, in dismissing David.**
    1Sa 29:1–11
  - **Elijah, in his flight from Jezebel.**
    1Ki 19:3–4
  - **Rehoboam's counsellors.**
    1Ki 12:7
  - **Jehoram, in suspecting a Syrian stratagem.**
    2Ki 7:12–13
  - **Nehemiah, in conduct of affairs at Jerusalem.**
    Ne 2:12–16; 4:13–23
  - **Daniel.**
    Da 1:8–14
  - **Certain elders of Israel.**
    Jer 26:17–23
  - **Of Jesus, in charging those who were healed not to advertise his miracles.**
    Mt 9:30; 16:20; Mk 3:12; 5:43; 7:36; 8:30; 9:9
  - **Of Jesus, going to the feast secretly.**
    Jn 7:10
  - **Jesus, in walking "no more openly".**
    Jn 11:54; 12:36
  - **Jesus, in avoiding his enemies.**
    Mt 12:14–16; Mk 3:7; Jn 11:47–54

• **Joseph, in his conduct toward Mary.**
Mt 1:19

• **Peter, in escaping Herod.**
Ac 12:17

• **Paul, in circumcising Timothy.**
Ac 16:3

• **Paul, in performing temple rites.**
Ac 21:20–26

• **Paul, in setting the Jewish sects on each other.**
Ac 23:6

• **Paul, in avoiding suspicion in administering the gifts of the churches.**
2Co 8:20

• **Paul, in his lack of, in his persistence of going to Jerusalem despite the warnings of the Spirit and his friends.**
Ac 20:22–25, 37–38; 21:10–14

• **Paul and Barnabas, in escaping persecution.**
Ac 14:6

• **Paul and Silas, in escaping from Berea.**
Ac 17:10–15

• **The town clerk of Ephesus, in averting a riot.**
Ac 19:29–41

See: Diplomacy

PRUNING

Le 25:3–4; Jn 15:2–6

Isa 5:6 — And I will lay it waste: it shall not be pruned, nor digged; but there shall come up briers and thorns: I will also command the clouds that they rain no rain upon it.

Isa 18:5 — For afore the harvest, when the bud is perfect, and the sour grape is ripening in the flower, he shall both cut off the sprigs with pruninghooks, and take away *and* cut down the branches.

• **Pruning-hook.**

Isa 2:4 — And he shall judge among the nations, and shall rebuke many people: and they shall beat their swords into plowshares, and their spears into pruninghooks: nation shall not lift up sword against nation, neither shall they learn war any more.

Isa 18:5 — For afore the harvest, when the bud is perfect, and the sour grape is ripening in the flower, he shall both cut off the sprigs with pruninghooks, and take away *and* cut down the branches.

Joel 3:10 — Beat your plowshares into swords, and your pruninghooks into spears: let the weak say, I *am* strong.

Mic 4:3 — And he shall judge among many people, and rebuke strong nations afar off; and they shall beat their swords into plowshares, and their spears into pruninghooks: nation shall not lift up a sword against nation, neither shall they learn war any more.

PSALMS

• **Of Moses, celebrating the deliverance at the Red Sea.**
Ex 15:1–19

• **Didactic songs composed by Moses, celebrating the providence, righteousness, and judgments of God.**
Dt 32:1–43; Ps 90:1–17

• **Son of Deborah, celebrating Israel's victory over Sisera.**
Jgs 5:1–31

• **Of Hannah, in thankfulness for a son.**
1Sa 2:1–10

• **Of David, celebrating his deliverance.**
2Sa 22:1–51

• **Of David, on the occasion of removing the ark.**
1Ch 16:7–36

• **Of David, at the close of his reign.**
2Sa 23:2–7; 1Ch 29:10–19

• **Of Isaiah.**
Isa 12:1–6; 25:1–26:21

• **Of Hezekiah, celebrating deliverance from death.**
Isa 38:9–20

• **Of Mary.**
Lk 1:46–55

• **Elisabeth.**
Lk 1:42–45

• **Zacharias.**
Lk 1:68–79

• **Afflictions.**
Ps 3:1–5:12; 7:1–17; 11:1–7; 13:1–6; 16:1–17:15; 22:1–31; 26:1–28:9; 31:1–24; 35:1–28; 41:1–44:26; 54:1–57:11; 59:1–64:10; 69:1–71:24; 74:1–23; 77:1–20; 79:1–80:19; 83:1–84:12; 86:1–17; 88:1–89:52; 94:1–23; 102:1–28; 109:1–31; 120:1–7; 123:1–4; 129:1–8; 137:1–9; 140:1–143:12

• **Didactic.**
Ps 1:1–6; 5:1–12; 7:1–17; 9:1–12:8; 14:1–15:5; 17:1–15; 24:1–25:22; 32:1–11; 34:1–22; 36:1–37:40; 39:1–13; 49:1–50:23; 52:1–53:6; 58:1–11; 73:1–28; 75:1–10; 82:1–8; 84:1–12; 90:1–92:15; 94:1–23; 101:1–8; 112:1–10; 119:1–176; 121:1–8; 125:1–5; 127:1–128:6; 131:1–3; 133:1–3

• **Historical.**
Ps 78:1–72; 105:1–106:48

• **Imprecatory.**

See: Prayer, miscellany of minor subtopics; imprecatory

• **Intercessional.**
Ps 20:1–9; 67:1–7; 122:1–9; 132:1–18; 144:1–15

• **Messianic.**

See: Jesus, Messiah; messianic psalms

• **Penitential.**

Ps 6:1–10; 25:1–22; 32:1–11; 38:1–22; 51:1–19; 102:1–28; 130:1–8; 143:1–12

• **Praise.**

• **For God's attributes.**

Ps 8:1–9; 19:1–14; 24:1–10; 29:1–11; 33:1–22; 47:1–9; 50:1–23; 65:1–66:20; 76:1–77:20; 93:1–5; 95:1–97:12; 99:1–9; 104:1–35; 111:1–10; 113:1–115:18; 134:1–3; 139:1–24; 147:1–148:14; 150:1–6

• **Prophetic.**

Ps 2:1–12; 16:1–11; 22:1–31; 40:1–17; 45:1–17; 68:1–69:36; 72:1–20; 87:1–7; 97:1–12; 110:1–7; 118:1–29

• **Thanksgiving.**

Ps 21:1–13; 46:1–11; 48:1–14; 65:1–66:20; 68:1–35; 76:1–12; 81:1–16; 85:1–13; 98:1–9; 105:1–45; 124:1–8; 126:1–6; 129:1–8; 135:1–136:26; 149:1–9

• **For God's goodness to good men.**

Ps 23:1–6; 34:1–22; 36:1–12; 91:1–16; 100:1–5; 103:1–22; 107:1–43; 117:1–2; 121:1–8; 145:1–146:10

• **For God's mercies to individuals.**

Ps 9:1–20; 18:1–50; 30:1–12; 34:1–22; 40:1–17; 75:1–10; 103:1–22; 108:1–13; 116:1–19; 118:1–29; 138:1–8; 144:1–15

PSALTERY

• **A harp.**

• **Used in religious services.**

1Ch 25:5–6

2Sa 6:5 — And David and all the house of Israel played before the LORD on all manner of *instruments made of* fir wood, even on harps, and on psalteries, and on timbrels, and on cornets, and on cymbals.

1Ch 13:8 — And David and all Israel played before God with all *their* might, and with singing, and with harps, and with psalteries, and with timbrels, and with cymbals, and with trumpets.

1Ch 16:5 — Asaph the chief, and next to him Zechariah, Jeiel, and Shemiramoth, and Jehiel, and Mattithiah, and Eliab, and Benaiah, and Obed-edom: and Jeiel with psalteries and with harps; but Asaph made a sound with cymbals;

1Ch 25:1 — Moreover David and the captains of the host separated to the service of the sons of Asaph, and of Heman, and of Jeduthun, who should prophesy with harps, with psalteries, and with cymbals: and the number of the workmen according to their service was:

2Ch 29:25 — And he set the Levites in the house of the LORD with cymbals, with psalteries, and with harps, according to the commandment of David, and of Gad the king's seer, and Nathan the prophet: for *so was* the commandment of the LORD by his prophets.

Ps 33:2 — Praise the LORD with harp: sing unto him with the psaltery *and* an instrument of ten strings.

Ps 57:8 — Awake up, my glory; awake, psaltery and harp: I *myself* will awake early.

Ps 71:22 — I will also praise thee with the psaltery, *even* thy truth, O my God: unto thee will I sing with the harp, O thou Holy One of Israel.

Ps 81:2 — Take a Psalm, and bring hither the timbrel, the pleasant harp with the psaltery.

Ps 92:3 — Upon an instrument of ten strings, and upon the psaltery; upon the harp with a solemn sound.

Ps 108:2 — Awake, psaltery and harp: I *myself* will awake early.

Ps 144:9 — I will sing a new song unto thee, O God: upon a psaltery *and* an instrument of ten strings will I sing praises unto thee.

Ps 150:3 — Praise him with the sound of the trumpet: praise him with the psaltery and harp.

Rev 5:8 — And when he had taken the book, the four beasts and four *and* twenty elders fell down before the Lamb, having every one of them harps, and golden vials full of odours, which are the prayers of saints.

• **At the dedication of the new wall when the captivity returned.**

Ne 12:27 — And at the dedication of the wall of Jerusalem they sought the Levites out of all their places, to bring them to Jerusalem, to keep the dedication with gladness, both with thanksgivings, and with singing, *with* cymbals, psalteries, and with harps.

• **Used in idolatrous worship.**

Da 3:5 — *That* at what time ye hear the sound of the cornet, flute, harp, sackbut, psaltery, dulcimer, and all kinds of musick, ye fall down and worship the golden image that Nebuchadnezzar the king hath set up:

Da 3:7 — Therefore at that time, when all the people heard the sound of the cornet, flute, harp, sackbut, psaltery, and all kinds of musick, all the people, the nations, and the languages, fell down *and* worshipped the golden image that Nebuchadnezzar the king had set up.

Da 3:10 — Thou, O king, hast made a decree, that every man that shall hear the sound of the cornet, flute, harp, sackbut, psaltery, and dulcimer, and all kinds of musick, shall fall down and worship the golden image:

Da 3:15 — Now if ye be ready that at what time ye hear the sound of the cornet, flute, harp, sackbut, psaltery, and dulcimer, and all kinds of musick, ye fall down and worship the image which I have made; *well:* but if ye worship not, ye shall be cast the same hour into the midst of a burning fiery furnace; and who *is* that God that shall deliver you out of my hands?

See: Music; instruments of

PTOLEMAIS

• **A seaport in Asher, formerly called Accho.**

See: Accho

• **Paul visits.**

Ac 21:7 — And when we had finished *our* course from Tyre, we came to Ptolemais, and saluted the brethren, and abode with them one day.

PUA ↞See: Phuvah

PUAH

• A Hebrew midwife.

Ex 1:15 — And the king of Egypt spake to the Hebrew midwives, of which the name of the one *was* Shiphrah, and the name of the other Puah:

• Father of Tola.

Jgs 10:1 — And after Abimelech there arose to defend Israel Tola the son of Puah, the son of Dodo, a man of Issachar; and he dwelt in Shamir in mount Ephraim.

↞See: Phuvah

PUBLICANS

• Roman tax collectors.

• Disreputable.

Mt 5:46–47

Mt 9:11 — And when the Pharisees saw *it,* they said unto his disciples, Why eateth your Master with publicans and sinners?

Mt 11:19 — The Son of man came eating and drinking, and they say, Behold a man gluttonous, and a winebibber, a friend of publicans and sinners. But wisdom is justified of her children.

Mt 18:17 — And if he shall neglect to hear them, tell *it* unto the church: but if he neglect to hear the church, let him be unto thee as an heathen man and a publican.

Mt 21:31 — Whether of them twain did the will of *his* father? They say unto him, The first. Jesus saith unto them, Verily I say unto you, That the publicans and the harlots go into the kingdom of God before you.

Lk 18:11 — The Pharisee stood and prayed thus with himself, God, I thank thee, that I am not as other men *are,* extortioners, unjust, adulterers, or even as this publican.

• Repent under the preaching of John the Baptist.

Mt 21:32 — For John came unto you in the way of righteousness, and ye believed him not: but the publicans and the harlots believed him: and ye, when ye had seen *it,* repented not afterward, that ye might believe him.

Lk 3:12 — Then came also publicans to be baptized, and said unto him, Master, what shall we do?

Lk 7:29 — And all the people that heard *him,* and the publicans, justified God, being baptized with the baptism of John.

• Matthew, the collector of Capernaum, becomes an apostle.

Mt 9:9 — And as Jesus passed forth from thence, he saw a man, named Matthew, sitting at the receipt of custom: and he saith unto him, Follow me. And he arose, and followed him.

Mt 10:3 — Philip, and Bartholomew; Thomas, and Matthew the publican; James *the son* of Alphaeus, and Lebbaeus, whose surname was Thaddaeus;

Mk 2:14 — And as he passed by, he saw Levi the *son* of Alphaeus sitting at the receipt of custom, and said unto him, Follow me. And he arose and followed him.

Lk 5:27 — And after these things he went forth, and saw a publican, named Levi, sitting at the receipt of custom: and he said unto him, Follow me.

• Parable concerning.

Lk 18:9–14

• Zacchaeus, chief among, receives Jesus into his house.

Lk 19:2–10

PUBLIUS

• Chief man in the island of Melita.

• Father of, healed by Paul.

Ac 28:7–8

PUDENS • A Christian in Rome.

2Ti 4:21 — Do thy diligence to come before winter. Eubulus greeteth thee, and Pudens, and Linus, and Claudia, and all the brethren.

PUL

• King of Assyria.

1Ch 5:26 — And the God of Israel stirred up the spirit of Pul king of Assyria, and the spirit of Tilgath-pilneser king of Assyria, and he carried them away, even the Reubenites, and the Gadites, and the half tribe of Manasseh, and brought them unto Halah, and Habor, and Hara, and to the river Gozan, unto this day.

• Forced tribute from Menahem, king of Israel.

2Ki 15:19 — *And* Pul the king of Assyria came against the land: and Menahem gave Pul a thousand talents of silver, that his hand might be with him to confirm the kingdom in his hand.

• A place or tribe in Africa.

Isa 66:19 — And I will set a sign among them, and I will send those that escape of them unto the nations, *to* Tarshish, Pul, and Lud, that draw the bow, *to* Tubal, and Javan, *to* the isles afar off, that have not heard my fame, neither have seen my glory; and they shall declare my glory among the Gentiles.

PULPIT

2Ch 6:13 — For Solomon had made a brasen scaffold, of five cubits long, and five cubits broad, and three cubits high, and had set it in the midst of the court: and upon it he stood, and kneeled down upon his knees before all the congregation of Israel, and spread forth his hands toward heaven,

Ne 8:4 — And Ezra the scribe stood upon a pulpit of wood, which they had made for the purpose; and beside him stood Mattithiah, and Shema, and Anaiah, and Urijah, and Hilkiah, and Maaseiah, on his right hand; and on his left hand, Pedaiah, and Mishael, and Malchiah, and Hashum, and Hashbadana, Zechariah, *and* Meshullam.

PULSE • A sort of food.

Da 1:12 — Prove thy servants, I beseech thee, ten days; and let them give us pulse to eat, and water to drink.

Da 1:16 — Thus Melzar took away the portion of their meat, and the wine that they should drink; and gave them pulse.

PUNISHMENT

• Capital.

Ge 9:6 — Whoso sheddeth man's blood, by man shall his blood be shed: for in the image of God made he man.

Ex 21:14 — But if a man come presumptuously upon his neighbour, to slay him with guile; thou shalt take him from mine altar, that he may die.

Le 20:10 — And the man that committeth adultery with *another* man's wife, *even he* that committeth adultery with his neighbour's wife, the adulterer and the adulteress shall surely be put to death.

Dt 13:9 — But thou shalt surely kill him; thine hand shall be first upon him to put him to death, and afterwards the hand of all the people.

• Death penalty.

• Shall not be remitted.

Nu 35:31 — Moreover ye shall take no satisfaction for the life of a murderer, which *is* guilty of death: but he shall be surely put to death.

• In the Mosaic law the death penalty was inflicted for murder.

Ge 9:5–6; Nu 35:16–21, 30–33

Dt 17:6 — At the mouth of two witnesses, or three witnesses, shall he that is worthy of death be put to death; *but* at the mouth of one witness he shall not be put to death.

• For adultery.

Le 20:10 — And the man that committeth adultery with *another* man's wife, *even he* that committeth adultery with his neighbour's wife, the adulterer and the adulteress shall surely be put to death.

Dt 22:24 — Then ye shall bring them both out unto the gate of that city, and ye shall stone them with stones that they die; the damsel, because she cried not, *being* in the city; and the man, because he hath humbled his neighbour's wife: so thou shalt put away evil from among you.

• For incest.

Le 20:11–12

Le 20:14 — And if a man take a wife and her mother, it *is* wickedness: they shall be burnt with fire, both he and they; that there be no wickedness among you.

• For bestiality.

Le 20:15–16

Ex 22:19 — Whosoever lieth with a beast shall surely be put to death.

• For sodomy.

Le 18:22 — Thou shalt not lie with mankind, as with womankind: it *is* abomination.

Le 20:13 — If a man also lie with mankind, as he lieth with a woman, both of them have committed an abomination: they shall surely be put to death; their blood *shall be* upon them.

• For incontinence.

Dt 22:21–24

• For rape of a betrothed virgin.

Dt 22:25 — But if a man find a betrothed damsel in the field, and the man force her, and lie with her: then the man only that lay with her shall die:

• For perjury.

Zec 5:4 — I will bring it forth, saith the LORD of hosts, and it shall enter into the house of the thief, and into the house of him that sweareth falsely by my name: and it shall remain in the midst of his house, and shall consume it with the timber thereof and the stones thereof.

• For kidnapping.

Ex 21:16 — And he that stealeth a man, and selleth him, or if he be found in his hand, he shall surely be put to death.

Dt 24:7 — If a man be found stealing any of his brethren of the children of Israel, and maketh merchandise of him, or selleth him; then that thief shall die; and thou shalt put evil away from among you.

• Upon a priest's daughter, who committed fornication.

Le 21:9 — And the daughter of any priest, if she profane herself by playing the whore, she profaneth her father: she shall be burnt with fire.

• For witchcraft.

Ex 22:18 — Thou shalt not suffer a witch to live.

• For offering human sacrifice.

Le 20:2–5

• For striking or cursing father or mother.

Ex 21:15 — And he that smiteth his father, or his mother, shall be surely put to death.

Ex 21:17 — And he that curseth his father, or his mother, shall surely be put to death.

Le 20:9 — For every one that curseth his father or his mother shall be surely put to death: he hath cursed his father or his mother; his blood *shall be* upon him.

• For disobedience to parents.

Dt 21:18–21

• For theft.

Zec 5:3–4

• For blasphemy.

Le 24:11–14

Le 24:16 — And he that blasphemeth the name of the LORD, he shall surely be put to death, *and* all the congregation shall certainly stone him: as well the stranger, as he that is born in the land, when he blasphemeth the name *of the LORD*, shall be put to death.

Le 24:23 — And Moses spake to the children of Israel, that they should bring forth him that had cursed out of the camp, and stone him with stones. And the children of Israel did as the LORD commanded Moses.

• **For Sabbath desecration.**

Nu 15:32–36

Ex 35:2 — Six days shall work be done, but on the seventh day there shall be to you an holy day, a sabbath of rest to the LORD: whosoever doeth work therein shall be put to death.

• **For prophesying falsely, or propagating false doctrines.**

Dt 13:1–10

• **For sacrificing to false gods.**

Ex 22:20 — He that sacrificeth unto *any* god, save unto the LORD only, he shall be utterly destroyed.

• **For refusing to abide by the decision of court.**

Dt 17:12 — And the man that will do presumptuously, and will not hearken unto the priest that standeth to minister there before the LORD thy God, or unto the judge, even that man shall die: and thou shalt put away the evil from Israel.

• **For treason.**

1Ki 2:25 — And king Solomon sent by the hand of Benaiah the son of Jehoiada; and he fell upon him that he died.

Est 2:23 — And when inquisition was made of the matter, it was found out; therefore they were both hanged on a tree: and it was written in the book of the chronicles before the king.

• **For sedition.**

Ac 5:36–37

• **Modes of execution of death penalty.**

• **Burning.**

Da 3:19–23

Ge 38:24 — And it came to pass about three months after, that it was told Judah, saying, Tamar thy daughter in law hath played the harlot; and also, behold, she *is* with child by whoredom. And Judah said, Bring her forth, and let her be burnt.

Le 20:14 — And if a man take a wife and her mother, it *is* wickedness: they shall be burnt with fire, both he and they; that there be no wickedness among you.

Le 21:9 — And the daughter of any priest, if she profane herself by playing the whore, she profaneth her father: she shall be burnt with fire.

Jer 29:22 — And of them shall be taken up a curse by all the captivity of Judah which *are* in Babylon, saying, The LORD make thee like Zedekiah and like Ahab, whom the king of Babylon roasted in the fire;

Eze 23:25 — And I will set my jealousy against thee, and they shall deal furiously with thee: they shall take away thy nose and thine ears; and thy remnant shall fall by the sword: they shall take thy sons and thy daughters; and thy residue shall be devoured by the fire.

• **Stoning.**

Nu 15:33–36

Le 20:2 — Again, thou shalt say to the children of Israel, Whosoever *he be* of the children of Israel, or of the strangers that sojourn in Israel, that giveth *any* of his seed unto Molech; he shall surely be put to death: the people of the land shall stone him with stones.

Le 20:27 — A man also or woman that hath a familiar spirit, or that is a wizard, shall surely be put to death: they shall stone them with stones: their blood *shall be* upon them.

Le 24:14 — Bring forth him that hath cursed without the camp; and let all that heard *him* lay their hands upon his head, and let all the congregation stone him.

Nu 14:10 — But all the congregation bade stone them with stones. And the glory of the LORD appeared in the tabernacle of the congregation before all the children of Israel.

Dt 13:10 — And thou shalt stone him with stones, that he die; because he hath sought to thrust thee away from the LORD thy God, which brought thee out of the land of Egypt, from the house of bondage.

Dt 17:5 — Then shalt thou bring forth that man or that woman, which have committed that wicked thing, unto thy gates, *even* that man or that woman, and shalt stone them with stones, till they die.

Dt 22:21 — Then they shall bring out the damsel to the door of her father's house, and the men of her city shall stone her with stones that she die: because she hath wrought folly in Israel, to play the whore in her father's house: so shalt thou put evil away from among you.

Dt 22:24 — Then ye shall bring them both out unto the gate of that city, and ye shall stone them with stones that they die; the damsel, because she cried not, *being* in the city; and the man, because he hath humbled his neighbour's wife: so thou shalt put away evil from among you.

Jos 7:25 — And Joshua said, Why hast thou troubled us? the LORD shall trouble thee this day. And all Israel stoned him with stones, and burned them with fire, after they had stoned them with stones.

1Ki 21:10 — And set two men, sons of Belial, before him, to bear witness against him, saying, Thou didst blaspheme God and the king. And *then* carry him out, and stone him, that he may die.

Eze 16:40 — They shall also bring up a company against thee, and they shall stone thee with stones, and thrust thee through with their swords.

• **Hanging.**

Dt 21:22–23

Ge 40:22 — But he hanged the chief baker: as Joseph had interpreted to them.

Jos 8:29 — And the king of Ai he hanged on a tree until eventide: and as soon as the sun was down, Joshua commanded that they should take his carcase down from the tree, and cast it at the entering of the gate of the city, and raise thereon a great heap of stones, *that remaineth* unto this day.

• Beheading.

Mk 6:27–28

Mt 14:10 — And he sent, and beheaded John in the prison.

Mk 6:16 — But when Herod heard *thereof,* he said, It is John, whom I beheaded: he is risen from the dead.

• Crucifixion.

Mt 27:35 — And they crucified him, and parted his garments, casting lots: that it might be fulfilled which was spoken by the prophet, They parted my garments among them, and upon my vesture did they cast lots.

Mt 27:38 — Then were there two thieves crucified with him, one on the right hand, and another on the left.

Mk 15:24 — And when they had crucified him, they parted his garments, casting lots upon them, what every man should take.

Mk 15:27 — And with him they crucify two thieves; the one on his right hand, and the other on his left.

Lk 23:33 — And when they were come to the place, which is called Calvary, there they crucified him, and the malefactors, one on the right hand, and the other on the left.

• The sword.

Ex 32:27–28

1Ki 2:25 — And king Solomon sent by the hand of Benaiah the son of Jehoiada; and he fell upon him that he died.

1Ki 2:34 — So Benaiah the son of Jehoiada went up, and fell upon him, and slew him: and he was buried in his own house in the wilderness.

1Ki 2:46 — So the king commanded Benaiah the son of Jehoiada; which went out, and fell upon him, that he died. And the kingdom was established in the hand of Solomon.

Ac 12:2 — And he killed James the brother of John with the sword.

• Executed by the witnesses.

Dt 13:9 — But thou shalt surely kill him; thine hand shall be first upon him to put him to death, and afterwards the hand of all the people.

Dt 17:7 — The hands of the witnesses shall be first upon him to put him to death, and afterward the hands of all the people. So thou shalt put the evil away from among you.

Ac 7:58 — And cast *him* out of the city, and stoned *him:* and the witnesses laid down their clothes at a young man's feet, whose name was Saul.

• Executed by the congregation.

Nu 15:35–36

Dt 13:9 — But thou shalt surely kill him; thine hand shall be first upon him to put him to death, and afterwards the hand of all the people.

• Not inflicted on testimony of less than two witnesses.

Nu 35:30 — Whoso killeth any person, the murderer shall be put to death by the mouth of witnesses: but one witness shall not testify against any person *to cause him* to die.

Dt 17:6 — At the mouth of two witnesses, or three witnesses, shall he that is worthy of death be put to death; *but* at the mouth of one witness he shall not be put to death.

Dt 19:15 — One witness shall not rise up against a man for any iniquity, or for any sin, in any sin that he sinneth: at the mouth of two witnesses, or at the mouth of three witnesses, shall the matter be established.

• Minor offenses.

• Punishable by scourging.

Dt 25:2–3

Le 19:20 — And whosoever lieth carnally with a woman, that *is* a bondmaid, betrothed to an husband, and not at all redeemed, nor freedom given her; she shall be scourged; they shall not be put to death, because she was not free.

Dt 22:18 — And the elders of that city shall take that man and chastise him;

Pr 17:10 — A reproof entereth more into a wise man than an hundred stripes into a fool.

Pr 19:29 — Judgments are prepared for scorners, and stripes for the back of fools.

Pr 20:30 — The blueness of a wound cleanseth away evil: so *do* stripes the inward parts of the belly.

Mt 27:26 — Then released he Barabbas unto them: and when he had scourged Jesus, he delivered *him* to be crucified.

Mk 15:15 — And *so* Pilate, willing to content the people, released Barabbas unto them, and delivered Jesus, when he had scourged *him,* to be crucified.

Lk 23:16 — I will therefore chastise him, and release *him.*

Jn 19:1 — Then Pilate therefore took Jesus, and scourged *him.*

Ac 22:24 — The chief captain commanded him to be brought into the castle, and bade that he should be examined by scourging; that he might know wherefore they cried so against him.

Ac 22:29 — Then straightway they departed from him which should have examined him: and the chief captain also was afraid, after he knew that he was a Roman, and because he had bound him.

• Imprisonment.

Ge 40:1–23

Ge 39:20 — And Joseph's master took him, and put him into the prison, a place where the king's prisoners *were* bound: and he was there in the prison.

See: Prison

- **Confinement within limits.**

1Ki 2:36–38

1Ki 2:26 — And unto Abiathar the priest said the king, Get thee to Anathoth, unto thine own fields; for thou *art* worthy of death: but I will not at this time put thee to death, because thou barest the ark of the Lord GOD before David my father, and because thou hast been afflicted in all wherein my father was afflicted.

- **Entailed.**
  - **On children.**

Eze 18:2–3

Ex 34:7 — Keeping mercy for thousands, forgiving iniquity and transgression and sin, and that will by no means clear *the guilty;* visiting the iniquity of the fathers upon the children, and upon the children's children, unto the third and to the fourth *generation.*

Jer 31:29 — In those days they shall say no more, The fathers have eaten a sour grape, and the children's teeth are set on edge.

La 5:7 — Our fathers have sinned, *and are* not; and we have borne their iniquities.

See: Afflictions; design of

See: Chastisement

See: Fine

See: Judgments

See: Retaliation

See: Wicked; punishment of

- **According to deeds.**

Lk 12:47–48

Job 34:11 — For the work of a man shall he render unto him, and cause every man to find according to *his* ways.

Ps 62:12 — Also unto thee, O Lord, *belongeth* mercy: for thou renderest to every man according to his work.

Pr 12:14 — A man shall be satisfied with good by the fruit of *his* mouth: and the recompense of a man's hands shall be rendered unto him.

Pr 24:12 — If thou sayest, Behold, we knew it not; doth not he that pondereth the heart consider *it?* and he that keepeth thy soul, doth *not* he know *it?* and shall *not* he render to *every* man according to his works?

Isa 59:18 — According to *their* deeds, accordingly he will repay, fury to his adversaries, recompence to his enemies; to the islands he will repay recompence.

Jer 17:10 — I the LORD search the heart, *I* try the reins, even to give every man according to his ways, *and* according to the fruit of his doings.

Eze 7:3 — Now *is* the end *come* upon thee, and I will send mine anger upon thee, and will judge thee according to thy ways, and will recompense upon thee all thine abominations.

Eze 7:27 — The king shall mourn, and the prince shall be clothed with desolation, and the hands of the people of the land shall be troubled: I will do unto them after their way, and according to their deserts will I judge them; and they shall know that I *am* the LORD.

Eze 16:59 — For thus saith the Lord GOD; I will even deal with thee as thou hast done, which hast despised the oath in breaking the covenant.

Eze 39:24 — According to their uncleanness and according to their transgressions have I done unto them, and hid my face from them.

Zec 1:6 — But my words and my statutes, which I commanded my servants the prophets, did they not take hold of your fathers? and they returned and said, Like as the LORD of hosts thought to do unto us, according to our ways, and according to our doings, so hath he dealt with us.

Mt 5:22 — <u>But I say unto you, That whosoever is angry with his brother without a cause shall be in danger of the judgment: and whosoever shall say to his brother, Raca, shall be in danger of the council: but whosoever shall say, Thou fool, shall be in danger of hell fire.</u>

Mt 16:27 — <u>For the Son of man shall come in the glory of his Father with his angels; and then he shall reward every man according to his works.</u>

Mt 23:14 — <u>Woe unto you, scribes and Pharisees, hypocrites! for ye devour widows' houses, and for a pretence make long prayer: therefore ye shall receive the greater damnation.</u>

Lk 20:47 — <u>Which devour widows' houses, and for a shew make long prayers: the same shall receive greater damnation.</u>

- **Parable of vineyard.**

Isa 5:1–7

- **Parable of husbandman.**

Mt 21:33–41

- **Parable of the talents.**

Mt 25:14–30

See: Judgment; according to opportunity and works

- **Delayed.**

Pr 1:24–30; Ecc 8:11–13; Hab 1:2–4

Ps 50:21 — These *things* hast thou done, and I kept silence; thou thoughtest that I was altogether *such an one* as thyself: *but* I will reprove thee, and set *them* in order before thine eyes.

Ps 55:19 — God shall hear, and afflict them, even he that abideth of old. Selah. Because they have no changes, therefore they fear not God.

- **Design of.**
  - **To secure obedience.**

Ex 20:3–5; Le 26:14–39; Dt 13:10–11

Ge 2:17 — But of the tree of the knowledge of good and evil, thou shalt not eat of it: for in the day that thou eatest thereof thou shalt surely die.

Dt 17:13 — And all the people shall hear, and fear, and do no more presumptuously.

Dt 19:20 — And those which remain shall hear, and fear, and shall henceforth commit no more any such evil among you.

Dt 21:21 — And all the men of his city shall stone him with stones, that he die: so shalt thou put evil away from among you; and all Israel shall hear, and fear.

Pr 19:25 — Smite a scorner, and the simple will beware: and reprove one that hath understanding, *and* he will understand knowledge.

Pr 21:11 — When the scorner is punished, the simple is made wise: and when the wise is instructed, he receiveth knowledge.

Pr 26:3 — A whip for the horse, a bridle for the ass, and a rod for the fool's back.

See: Judgments; design of

• Divine.

• No escape from.

Pr 1:24–31; Jer 25:28–29; Am 2:14–16

Job 11:20 — But the eyes of the wicked shall fail, and they shall not escape, and their hope *shall be as* the giving up of the ghost.

Pr 11:21 — *Though* hand *join* in hand, the wicked shall not be unpunished: but the seed of the righteous shall be delivered.

Pr 16:5 — Every one *that is* proud in heart *is* an abomination to the LORD: *though* hand *join* in hand, he shall not be unpunished.

Pr 29:1 — He, that being often reproved hardeneth *his* neck, shall suddenly be destroyed, and that without remedy.

Jer 11:11 — Therefore thus saith the LORD, Behold, I will bring evil upon them, which they shall not be able to escape; and though they shall cry unto me, I will not hearken unto them.

Jer 15:1 — Then said the LORD unto me, Though Moses and Samuel stood before me, *yet* my mind *could* not *be* toward this people: cast *them* out of my sight, and let them go forth.

Eze 7:19 — They shall cast their silver in the streets, and their gold shall be removed: their silver and their gold shall not be able to deliver them in the day of the wrath of the LORD: they shall not satisfy their souls, neither fill their bowels: because it is the stumblingblock of their iniquity.

Zep 1:18 — Neither their silver nor their gold shall be able to deliver them in the day of the LORD's wrath; but the whole land shall be devoured by the fire of his jealousy: for he shall make even a speedy riddance of all them that dwell in the land.

Mt 10:28 — And fear not them which kill the body, but are not able to kill the soul: but rather fear him which is able to destroy both soul and body in hell.

Mt 23:33 — *Ye* serpents, *ye* generation of vipers, how can ye escape the damnation of hell?

Ro 2:3 — And thinkest thou this, O man, that judgest them which do such things, and doest the same, that thou shalt escape the judgment of God?

Col 3:25 — But he that doeth wrong shall receive for the wrong which he hath done: and there is no respect of persons.

Heb 2:3 — How shall we escape, if we neglect so great salvation; which at the first began to be spoken by the Lord, and was confirmed unto us by them that heard *him;*

Heb 12:25 — See that ye refuse not him that speaketh. For if they escaped not who refused him that spake on earth, much more *shall not* we *escape,* if we turn away from him that *speaketh* from heaven:

• Eternal.

Isa 34:8–10; Heb 10:28–31; Rev 14:10–11

Da 12:2 — And many of them that sleep in the dust of the earth shall awake, some to everlasting life, and some to shame *and* everlasting contempt.

Mt 3:12 — Whose fan *is* in his hand, and he will throughly purge his floor, and gather his wheat into the garner; but he will burn up the chaff with unquenchable fire.

Mt 10:28 — And fear not them which kill the body, but are not able to kill the soul: but rather fear him which is able to destroy both soul and body in hell.

Mt 18:8 — Wherefore if thy hand or thy foot offend thee, cut them off, and cast *them* from thee: it is better for thee to enter into life halt or maimed, rather than having two hands or two feet to be cast into everlasting fire.

Mt 25:41 — Then shall he say also unto them on the left hand, Depart from me, ye cursed, into everlasting fire, prepared for the devil and his angels:

Mt 25:46 — And these shall go away into everlasting punishment: but the righteous into life eternal.

Mk 3:29 — But he that shall blaspheme against the Holy Ghost hath never forgiveness, but is in danger of eternal damnation:

Lk 3:17 — Whose fan *is* in his hand, and he will throughly purge his floor, and will gather the wheat into his garner; but the chaff he will burn with fire unquenchable.

Jn 5:29 — And shall come forth; they that have done good, unto the resurrection of life; and they that have done evil, unto the resurrection of damnation.

Heb 6:2 — Of the doctrine of baptisms, and of laying on of hands, and of resurrection of the dead, and of eternal judgment.

Rev 19:3 — And again they said, Alleluia. And her smoke rose up for ever and ever.

Rev 20:10 — And the devil that deceived them was cast into the lake of fire and brimstone, where the beast and the false prophet *are,* and shall be tormented day and night for ever and ever.

See: Wicked; punishment of

PUNON

• A city of Edom.

• A camping ground of the Israelites, in their forty years' wandering.

Nu 33:42–43

PUR

• The lot.

Est 3:7 — In the first month, that *is,* the month Nisan, in the twelfth year of king Ahasuerus, they cast Pur, that *is,* the lot, before Haman from day to day, and from month to month, *to* the twelfth *month,* that *is,* the month Adar.

➛See: Purim

PURIFICATION

• Sanitary and symbolic.

• For women before marriage.

Est 2:12 — Now when every maid's turn was come to go in to king Ahasuerus, after that she had been twelve months, according to the manner of the women, (for so were the days of their purifications accomplished, *to wit,* six months with oil of myrrh, and six months with sweet odours, and with *other* things for the purifying of the women;)

• For women, after childbirth.

Le 12:6–8

Lk 2:22 — And when the days of her purification according to the law of Moses were accomplished, they brought him to Jerusalem, to present *him* to the Lord;

• For women, after menstruation.

Le 15:19–33

2Sa 11:4 — And David sent messengers, and took her; and she came in unto him, and he lay with her; for she was purified from her uncleanness: and she returned unto her house.

• Of the Jews before the passover.

Jn 11:55 — And the Jews' passover was nigh at hand: and many went out of the country up to Jerusalem before the passover, to purify themselves.

• For those who have slain in battle.

Nu 31:19–24

• Of lepers.

➛See: Leprosy

• By fire, for things that resist fire.

Nu 31:23 — Every thing that may abide the fire, ye shall make *it* go through the fire, and it shall be clean: nevertheless it shall be purified with the water of separation: and all that abideth not the fire ye shall make go through the water.

• By blood.

Ex 24:5–8; Le 14:6–7; Heb 9:12–14, 19–22

• By abstaining from sexual intercourse.

Ex 19:15 — And he said unto the people, Be ready against the third day: come not at *your* wives.

• Washing in water parts of animal sacrifices.

Le 1:9 — But his inwards and his legs shall he wash in water: and the priest shall burn all on the altar, *to be* a burnt sacrifice, an offering made by fire, of a sweet savour unto the LORD.

Le 1:13 — But he shall wash the inwards and the legs with water: and the priest shall bring *it* all, and burn *it* upon the altar: it *is* a burnt sacrifice, an offering made by fire, of a sweet savour unto the LORD.

Le 9:14 — And he did wash the inwards and the legs, and burnt *them* upon the burnt offering on the altar.

2Ch 4:6 — He made also ten lavers, and put five on the right hand, and five on the left, to wash in them: such things as they offered for the burnt offering they washed in them; but the sea *was* for the priests to wash in.

• Penalty to be imposed upon those who do not observe the ordinances concerning.

Le 7:20–21

Nu 19:13 — Whosoever toucheth the dead body of any man that is dead, and purifieth not himself, defileth the tabernacle of the LORD; and that soul shall be cut off from Israel: because the water of separation was not sprinkled upon him, he shall be unclean; his uncleanness *is* yet upon him.

Nu 19:20 — But the man that shall be unclean, and shall not purify himself, that soul shall be cut off from among the congregation, because he hath defiled the sanctuary of the LORD: the water of separation hath not been sprinkled upon him; he *is* unclean.

• Water of.

Nu 19:17–21

Nu 31:23 — Every thing that may abide the fire, ye shall make *it* go through the fire, and it shall be clean: nevertheless it shall be purified with the water of separation: and all that abideth not the fire ye shall make go through the water.

• Washing hands in water, symbolic of innocency.

Dt 21:6 — And all the elders of that city, *that are* next unto the slain *man,* shall wash their hands over the heifer that is beheaded in the valley:

Ps 26:6 — I will wash mine hands in innocency: so will I compass thine altar, O LORD:

Mt 27:24 — When Pilate saw that he could prevail nothing, but *that* rather a tumult was made, he took water, and washed *his* hands before the multitude, saying, I am innocent of the blood of this just person: see ye *to it.*

• Traditions of the elders concerning.

Mk 7:2–5, 8–9

Mt 15:2 — Why do thy disciples transgress the tradition of the elders? for they wash not their hands when they eat bread.

Lk 11:38 — And when the Pharisee saw *it,* he marvelled that he had not first washed before dinner.

• Of Paul, to show his fidelity to the law.

Ac 21:24 — Them take, and purify thyself with them, and be at charges with them, that they may shave *their* heads: and all may know that those things, whereof they were informed concerning thee, are nothing; but *that* thou thyself also walkest orderly, and keepest the law.

Ac 21:26 — Then Paul took the men, and the next day purifying himself with them entered into the temple, to signify the accomplishment of the days of purification, until that an offering should be offered for every one of them.

• Figurative.

Ps 26:6 — I will wash mine hands in innocency: so will I compass thine altar, O LORD:

Ps 51:7 — Purge me with hyssop, and I shall be clean: wash me, and I shall be whiter than snow.

Eze 36:25 — Then will I sprinkle clean water upon you, and ye shall be clean: from all your filthiness, and from all your idols, will I cleanse you.

Heb 10:22 — Let us draw near with a true heart in full assurance of faith, having our hearts sprinkled from an evil conscience, and our bodies washed with pure water.

See: Ablution

See: Defilement

See: Sanitation

• Scriptures relating to.

Ex 30:18–21; 40:30–32; Le 14:8–9; 15:4–13, 16–27; Nu 8:6–7; 19:7–8; Mk 7:2–9

Ge 35:2 — Then Jacob said unto his household, and to all that *were* with him, Put away the strange gods that *are* among you, and be clean, and change your garments:

Ex 19:10 — And the LORD said unto Moses, Go unto the people, and sanctify them to day and to morrow, and let them wash their clothes,

Ex 19:14 — And Moses went down from the mount unto the people, and sanctified the people; and they washed their clothes.

Ex 29:4 — And Aaron and his sons thou shalt bring unto the door of the tabernacle of the congregation, and shalt wash them with water.

Ex 40:12 — And thou shalt bring Aaron and his sons unto the door of the tabernacle of the congregation, and wash them with water.

Le 8:6 — And Moses brought Aaron and his sons, and washed them with water.

Le 16:4 — He shall put on the holy linen coat, and he shall have the linen breeches upon his flesh, and shall be girded with a linen girdle, and with the linen mitre shall he be attired: these *are* holy garments; therefore shall he wash his flesh in water, and *so* put them on.

Le 16:24 — And he shall wash his flesh with water in the holy place, and put on his garments, and come forth, and offer his burnt offering, and the burnt offering of the people, and make an atonement for himself, and for the people.

Le 16:26 — And he that let go the goat for the scapegoat shall wash his clothes, and bathe his flesh in water, and afterward come into the camp.

Le 16:28 — And he that burneth them shall wash his clothes, and bathe his flesh in water, and afterward he shall come into the camp.

Le 17:15 — And every soul that eateth that which died *of itself,* or that which was torn *with beasts, whether it be* one of your own country, or a stranger, he shall both wash his clothes, and bathe *himself* in water, and be unclean until the even: then shall he be clean.

Le 22:3 — Say unto them, Whosoever *he be* of all your seed among your generations, that goeth unto the holy things, which the children of Israel hallow unto the LORD, having his uncleanness upon him, that soul shall be cut off from my presence: I *am* the LORD.

Nu 8:21 — And the Levites were purified, and they washed their clothes; and Aaron offered them *as* an offering before the LORD; and Aaron made an atonement for them to cleanse them.

Nu 19:19 — And the clean *person* shall sprinkle upon the unclean on the third day, and on the seventh day: and on the seventh day he shall purify himself, and wash his clothes, and bathe himself in water, and shall be clean at even.

2Ch 4:6 — He made also ten lavers, and put five on the right hand, and five on the left, to wash in them: such things as they offered for the burnt offering they washed in them; but the sea *was* for the priests to wash in.

Mt 15:2 — Why do thy disciples transgress the tradition of the elders? for they wash not their hands when they eat bread.

Heb 9:10 — *Which stood* only in meats and drinks, and divers washings, and carnal ordinances, imposed *on them* until the time of reformation.

PURIM • A feast instituted to commemorate the deliverance of the Jews from the plot of Haman.

Est 9:20–32

PURITY

• Of heart.

Ps 24:3–5; Mal 3:2–3; 2Ti 2:21–22; Heb 9:13–14

Ps 12:6 — The words of the LORD *are* pure words: *as* silver tried in a furnace of earth, purified seven times.

Ps 19:8 — The statutes of the LORD *are* right, rejoicing the heart: the commandment of the LORD *is* pure, enlightening the eyes.

Ps 51:7 — Purge me with hyssop, and I shall be clean: wash me, and I shall be whiter than snow.

Ps 65:3 — Iniquities prevail against me: *as for* our transgressions, thou shalt purge them away.

Ps 119:140 — Thy word *is* very pure: therefore thy servant loveth it.

Pr 15:26 — The thoughts of the wicked *are* an abomination to the LORD: but *the words* of the pure *are* pleasant words.

Pr 20:9 — Who can say, I have made my heart clean, I am pure from my sin?

Pr 21:8 — The way of man *is* froward and strange: but *as for* the pure, his work *is* right.

Pr 30:12 — *There is* a generation *that are* pure in their own eyes, and *yet* is not washed from their filthiness.

Isa 1:18 — Come now, and let us reason together, saith the LORD: though your sins be as scarlet, they shall be as white as snow; though they be red like crimson, they shall be as wool.

Isa 1:25 — And I will turn my hand upon thee, and purely purge away thy dross, and take away all thy tin:

Isa 6:7 — And he laid *it* upon my mouth, and said, Lo, this hath touched thy lips; and thine iniquity is taken away, and thy sin purged.

Da 12:10 — Many shall be purified, and made white, and tried; but the wicked shall do wickedly: and none of the wicked shall understand; but the wise shall understand.

Mic 6:11 — Shall I count *them* pure with the wicked balances, and with the bag of deceitful weights?

Mt 5:8 — Blessed *are* the pure in heart: for they shall see God.

Jn 15:2 — Every branch in me that beareth not fruit he taketh away: and every *branch* that beareth fruit, he purgeth it, that it may bring forth more fruit.

Php 4:8 — Finally, brethren, whatsoever things are true, whatsoever things *are* honest, whatsoever things *are* just, whatsoever things *are* pure, whatsoever things *are* lovely, whatsoever things *are* of good report; if *there be* any virtue, and if *there be* any praise, think on these things.

1Ti 1:5 — Now the end of the commandment is charity out of a pure heart, and *of* a good conscience, and *of* faith unfeigned:

1Ti 3:9 — Holding the mystery of the faith in a pure conscience.

1Ti 5:22 — Lay hands suddenly on no man, neither be partaker of other men's sins: keep thyself pure.

2Ti 1:3 — I thank God, whom I serve from *my* forefathers with pure conscience, that without ceasing I have remembrance of thee in my prayers night and day;

Tit 1:15 — Unto the pure all things *are* pure: but unto them that are defiled and unbelieving *is* nothing pure; but even their mind and conscience is defiled.

Heb 10:2 — For then would they not have ceased to be offered? because that the worshippers once purged should have had no more conscience of sins.

Jas 4:8 — Draw nigh to God, and he will draw nigh to you. Cleanse *your* hands, *ye* sinners; and purify *your* hearts, *ye* double minded.

1Pe 1:22 — Seeing ye have purified your souls in obeying the truth through the Spirit unto unfeigned love of the brethren, *see that ye* love one another with a pure heart fervently:

1Jn 3:3 — And every man that hath this hope in him purifieth himself, even as he is pure.

• For the symbolisms of purity.

See: Ablution

See: Colors; white: symbol of holiness

See: Defilement

See: Purification

PURVEYOR

• For Solomon.

1Ki 4:7–19

1Ki 4:27 — And those officers provided victual for king Solomon, and for all that came unto king Solomon's table, every man in his month: they lacked nothing.

PUT See: Phut

PUTEOLI

• A seaport of Italy.

• Paul stays a week at.

Ac 28:13–14

PUTIEL • The father-in-law of Eleazar the priest.

Ex 6:25 — And Eleazar Aaron's son took him *one* of the daughters of Putiel to wife; and she bare him Phinehas: these *are* the heads of the fathers of the Levites according to their families.

PYGARG • Probably a species of antelope.

Dt 14:5 — The hart, and the roebuck, and the fallow deer, and the wild goat, and the pygarg, and the wild ox, and the chamois.

Q

QUAIL

• Miracle of, in the wilderness of Sin.

Ex 16:13 — And it came to pass, that at even the quails came up, and covered the camp: and in the morning the dew lay round about the host.

• Miracle of, at Kibroth-hattaavah.

Nu 11:31–32

Ps 105:40 — *The people* asked, and he brought quails, and satisfied them with the bread of heaven.

QUARANTINE ↞See: Sanitation; quarantine

QUARRIES

Jgs 3:19 — But he himself turned again from the quarries that *were* by Gilgal, and said, I have a secret errand unto thee, O king: who said, Keep silence. And all that stood by him went out from him.

Jgs 3:26 — And Ehud escaped while they tarried, and passed beyond the quarries, and escaped unto Seirath.

QUARTUS • A Christian in Corinth.

Ro 16:23 — Gaius mine host, and of the whole church, saluteth you. Erastus the chamberlain of the city saluteth you, and Quartus a brother.

QUATERNION • A squad of four soldiers.

Ac 12:4 — And when he had apprehended him, he put *him* in prison, and delivered *him* to four quaternions of soldiers to keep him; intending after Easter to bring him forth to the people.

QUEEN

• The wife of a king.

1Ki 11:19 — And Hadad found great favour in the sight of Pharaoh, so that he gave him to wife the sister of his own wife, the sister of Tahpenes the queen.

• Crowned.

Est 1:11 — To bring Vashti the queen before the king with the crown royal, to shew the people and the princes her beauty: for she *was* fair to look on.

Est 2:17 — And the king loved Esther above all the women, and she obtained grace and favour in his sight more than all the virgins; so that he set the royal crown upon her head, and made her queen instead of Vashti.

• Divorced.

Est 1:10–22

• Sits on the throne with the king.

Ne 2:6 — And the king said unto me, (the queen also sitting by him,) For how long shall thy journey be? and when wilt thou return? So it pleased the king to send me; and I set him a time.

• Makes feasts for the women of the royal household.

Est 1:9 — Also Vashti the queen made a feast for the women *in* the royal house which *belonged* to king Ahasuerus.

• Exerts an evil influence in public affairs.

↞See: Jezebel

• Counsels the king.

Da 5:10–12

• Of Sheba visits Solomon.

1Ki 10:1–13

• Candace, of Ethiopia.

Ac 8:27 — And he arose and went: and, behold, a man of Ethiopia, an eunuch of great authority under Candace queen of the Ethiopians, who had the charge of all her treasure, and had come to Jerusalem for to worship,

• The reigning sovereign, Athaliah.

↞See: Athaliah

• The moon called queen of heaven.

Jer 44:7–19

Jer 7:18 — The children gather wood, and the fathers kindle the fire, and the women knead *their* dough, to make cakes to the queen of heaven, and to pour out drink offerings unto other gods, that they may provoke me to anger.

Jer 44:25 — Thus saith the LORD of hosts, the God of Israel, saying; Ye and your wives have both spoken with your mouths, and fulfilled with your hand, saying, We will surely perform our vows that we have vowed, to burn incense to the queen of heaven, and to pour out drink offerings unto her: ye will surely accomplish your vows, and surely perform your vows.

• Worshiped.

↞See: Idolatry

QUICKENING

• Of the church.

• By the Father.

Ps 71:20 — *Thou,* which hast shewed me great and sore troubles, shalt quicken me again, and shalt bring me up again from the depths of the earth.

Ps 80:18 — So will not we go back from thee: quicken us, and we will call upon thy name.

Ro 4:17 — (As it is written, I have made thee a father of many nations,) before him whom he believed, *even* God, who quickeneth the dead, and calleth those things which be not as though they were.

Ro 8:11 — But if the Spirit of him that raised up Jesus from the dead dwell in you, he that raised up Christ from the dead shall also quicken your mortal bodies by his Spirit that dwelleth in you.

Eph 2:1 — And you *hath he quickened,* who were dead in trespasses and sins;

1Ti 6:13 — I give thee charge in the sight of God, who quickeneth all things, and *before* Christ Jesus, who before Pontius Pilate witnessed a good confession;

- **By the Son.**

Jn 5:21 — For as the Father raiseth up the dead, and quickeneth *them;* even so the Son quickeneth whom he will.

1Co 15:45 — And so it is written, The first man Adam was made a living soul; the last Adam *was made* a quickening spirit.

- **By the Holy Spirit.**

Jn 6:63 — It is the spirit that quickeneth; the flesh profiteth nothing: the words that I speak unto you, *they* are spirit, and *they* are life.

Ro 8:11 — But if the Spirit of him that raised up Jesus from the dead dwell in you, he that raised up Christ from the dead shall also quicken your mortal bodies by his Spirit that dwelleth in you.

2Co 3:6 — Who also hath made us able ministers of the new testament; not of the letter, but of the spirit: for the letter killeth, but the spirit giveth life.

1Pe 3:18 — For Christ also hath once suffered for sins, the just for the unjust, that he might bring us to God, being put to death in the flesh, but quickened by the Spirit:

QUIET

Ac 7:55–60

Isa 30:15 — For thus saith the Lord God, the Holy One of Israel; In returning and rest shall ye be saved; in quietness and in confidence shall be your strength: and ye would not.

Isa 32:17 — And the work of righteousness shall be peace; and the effect of righteousness quietness and assurance for ever.

Gal 5:22 — But the fruit of the Spirit is love, joy, peace, longsuffering, gentleness, goodness, faith,

Heb 12:11 — Now no chastening for the present seemeth to be joyous, but grievous: nevertheless afterward it yieldeth the peaceable fruit of righteousness unto them which are exercised thereby.

QUIVER

- **For arrows.**

Ge 27:3 — Now therefore take, I pray thee, thy weapons, thy quiver and thy bow, and go out to the field, and take me *some* venison;

Isa 22:6 — And Elam bare the quiver with chariots of men *and* horsemen, and Kir uncovered the shield.

R

RAAMAH

• Son of Cush.

Ge 10:7 — And the sons of Cush; Seba, and Havilah, and Sabtah, and Raamah, and Sabtechah: and the sons of Raamah; Sheba, and Dedan.

1Ch 1:9 — And the sons of Cush; Seba, and Havilah, and Sabta, and Raamah, and Sabtecha. And the sons of Raamah; Sheba, and Dedan.

• A place in Arabia.

Eze 27:22 — The merchants of Sheba and Raamah, they *were* thy merchants: they occupied in thy fairs with chief of all spices, and with all precious stones, and gold.

RAAMIAH

• One of those who returned to Jerusalem from captivity in Babylon.

Ne 7:7 — Who came with Zerubbabel, Jeshua, Nehemiah, Azariah, Raamiah, Nahamani, Mordecai, Bilshan, Mispereth, Bigvai, Nehum, Baanah. The number, *I say,* of the men of the people of Israel *was this;*

• Called Reelaiah.

Ezr 2:2 — Which came with Zerubbabel: Jeshua, Nehemiah, Seraiah, Reelaiah, Mordecai, Bilshan, Mizpar, Bigvai, Rehum, Baanah. The number of the men of the people of Israel:

RAAMSES ✦See: Rameses

RABMAG • An Assyrian prince, or, possibly, a second name given to Nergalsharezer.

Jer 39:3 — And all the princes of the king of Babylon came in, and sat in the middle gate, *even* Nergalsharezer, Samgar-nebo, Sarsechim, Rab-saris, Nergalsharezer, Rabmag, with all the residue of the princes of the king of Babylon.

Jer 39:13 — So Nebuzar-adan the captain of the guard sent, and Nebushasban, Rab-saris, and Nergalsharezer, Rabmag, and all the king of Babylon's princes;

RAB-SHAKEH

• An Assyrian officer.

• Sent by Sennacherib against Jerusalem; causes disloyalty to Hezekiah and a surrender of the city.

2Ki 18:17–36; Isa 36:1–22

2Ki 19:4 — It may be the LORD thy God will hear all the words of Rab-shakeh, whom the king of Assyria his master hath sent to reproach the living God; and will reprove the words which the LORD thy God hath heard: wherefore lift up *thy* prayer for the remnant that are left.

2Ki 19:8 — So Rab-shakeh returned, and found the king of Assyria warring against Libnah: for he had heard that he was departed from Lachish.

Isa 37:4 — It may be the LORD thy God will hear the words of Rabshakeh, whom the king of Assyria his master hath sent to reproach the living God, and will reprove the words which the LORD thy God hath heard: wherefore lift up *thy* prayer for the remnant that is left.

Isa 37:8 — So Rabshakeh returned, and found the king of Assyria warring against Libnah: for he had heard that he was departed from Lachish.

RABBAH

• Called also Rabbath. A city east of the Jordan, originally belonging to the Ammonites.

Jos 13:25 — And their coast was Jazer, and all the cities of Gilead, and half the land of the children of Ammon, unto Aroer that *is* before Rabbah;

• Bedstead of the giant Og kept at.

Dt 3:11 — For only Og king of Bashan remained of the remnant of giants; behold, his bedstead *was* a bedstead of iron; is it not in Rabbath of the children of Ammon? nine cubits was the length thereof, and four cubits the breadth of it, after the cubit of a man.

• Taken by David.

2Sa 12:26–31; 1Ch 20:1–3

2Sa 11:1 — And it came to pass, after the year was expired, at the time when kings go forth *to battle,* that David sent Joab, and his servants with him, and all Israel; and they destroyed the children of Ammon, and besieged Rabbah. But David tarried still at Jerusalem.

• Possessed again by the Ammonites; prophesied against.

Jer 49:2–3

Eze 21:20 — Appoint a way, that the sword may come to Rabbath of the Ammonites, and to Judah in Jerusalem the defenced.

Eze 25:5 — And I will make Rabbah a stable for camels, and the Ammonites a couchingplace for flocks: and ye shall know that I *am* the LORD.

Am 1:14 — But I will kindle a fire in the wall of Rabbah, and it shall devour the palaces thereof, with shouting in the day of battle, with a tempest in the day of the whirlwind:

• A city in Judah.

Jos 15:60 — Kirjath-baal, which *is* Kirjath-jearim, and Rabbah; two cities with their villages:

RABBATH ✦See: Rabbah

RABBI

• The title of a teacher.

Mt 23:7–8

Jn 3:2 — The same came to Jesus by night, and said unto him, Rabbi, we know that thou art a teacher come from God: for no man can do these miracles that thou doest, except God be with him.

• Ostentatiously used by the Pharisees.

Mt 23:7 — And greetings in the markets, and to be called of men, Rabbi, Rabbi.

• Used in addressing John.

Jn 3:26 — And they came unto John, and said unto him, Rabbi, he that was with thee beyond Jordan, to whom thou barest witness, behold, the same baptizeth, and all *men* come to him.

• Used in addressing Jesus.

Mt 26:25 — Then Judas, which betrayed him, answered and said, Master, is it I? He said unto him, Thou hast said.

Mt 26:49 — And forthwith he came to Jesus, and said, Hail, master; and kissed him.

Mk 9:5 — And Peter answered and said to Jesus, Master, it is good for us to be here: and let us make three tabernacles; one for thee, and one for Moses, and one for Elias.

Mk 11:21 — And Peter calling to remembrance saith unto him, Master, behold, the fig tree which thou cursedst is withered away.

Mk 14:45 — And as soon as he was come, he goeth straightway to him, and saith, Master, master; and kissed him.

Jn 1:38 — Then Jesus turned, and saw them following, and saith unto them, What seek ye? They said unto him, Rabbi, (which is to say, being interpreted, Master,) where dwellest thou?

Jn 1:49 — Nathanael answered and saith unto him, Rabbi, thou art the Son of God; thou art the King of Israel.

Jn 3:2 — The same came to Jesus by night, and said unto him, Rabbi, we know that thou art a teacher come from God: for no man can do these miracles that thou doest, except God be with him.

Jn 4:31 — In the mean while his disciples prayed him, saying, Master, eat.

Jn 6:25 — And when they had found him on the other side of the sea, they said unto him, Rabbi, when camest thou hither?

Jn 9:2 — And his disciples asked him, saying, Master, who did sin, this man, or his parents, that he was born blind?

Jn 11:8 — *His* disciples say unto him, Master, the Jews of late sought to stone thee; and goest thou thither again?

• Jesus called Rabboni.

Mk 10:51 — And Jesus answered and said unto him, What wilt thou that I should do unto thee? The blind man said unto him, Lord, that I might receive my sight.

Jn 20:16 — Jesus saith unto her, Mary. She turned herself, and saith unto him, Rabboni; which is to say, Master.

• Forbidden by Jesus as a title to his disciples.

Mt 23:8 — But be not ye called Rabbi: for one is your Master, *even* Christ; and all ye are brethren.

RABBITH • A city in Issachar.

Jos 19:20 — And Rabbith, and Kishion, and Abez,

RABSARIS

• An Assyrian officer.

• Sent by Sennacherib against Jerusalem.

2Ki 18:17 — And the king of Assyria sent Tartan and Rabsaris and Rab-shakeh from Lachish to king Hezekiah with a great host against Jerusalem. And they went up and came to Jerusalem. And when they were come up, they came and stood by the conduit of the upper pool, which *is* in the highway of the fuller's field.

• An Assyrian prince in time of Nebuchadnezzar, or, possibly, a second name given to Nebushasban.

Jer 39:3 — And all the princes of the king of Babylon came in, and sat in the middle gate, *even* Nergal-sharezer, Samgar-nebo, Sarsechim, Rabsaris, Nergal-sharezer, Rabmag, with all the residue of the princes of the king of Babylon.

Jer 39:13 — So Nebuzar-adan the captain of the guard sent, and Nebushasban, Rabsaris, and Nergal-sharezer, Rabmag, and all the king of Babylon's princes;

RACA

Mt 5:22 — But I say unto you, That whosoever is angry with his brother without a cause shall be in danger of the judgment: and whosoever shall say to his brother, Raca, shall be in danger of the council: but whosoever shall say, Thou fool, shall be in danger of hell fire.

RACE

• Human, unity of.

Ge 3:20 — And Adam called his wife's name Eve; because she was the mother of all living.

Mal 2:10 — Have we not all one father? hath not one God created us? why do we deal treacherously every man against his brother, by profaning the covenant of our fathers?

• Foot race.

• Figurative.

Heb 12:1–2

Ps 19:5 — Which *is* as a bridegroom coming out of his chamber, *and* rejoiceth as a strong man to run a race.

Ecc 9:11 — I returned, and saw under the sun, that the race *is* not to the swift, nor the battle to the strong, neither yet bread to the wise, nor yet riches to men of understanding, nor yet favour to men of skill; but time and chance happeneth to them all.

1Co 9:24 — Know ye not that they which run in a race run all, but one receiveth the prize? So run, that ye may obtain.

Gal 5:7 — Ye did run well; who did hinder you that ye should not obey the truth?

Php 2:16 — Holding forth the word of life; that I may rejoice in the day of Christ, that I have not run in vain, neither laboured in vain.

RACHAB ✦See: Rahab

RACHAL • A city in Judah.

1Sa 30:29 — And to *them* which *were* in Rachal, and to *them* which *were* in the cities of the Jerahmeelites, and to *them* which *were* in the cities of the Kenites,

RACHEL

• Daughter of Laban and wife of Jacob.

• Meets Jacob at the well.

Ge 29:9–12

• Jacob serves Laban fourteen years to secure her for his wife.

Ge 29:15–30

• Sterility of.

Ge 29:31 — And when the LORD saw that Leah *was* hated, he opened her womb: but Rachel *was* barren.

• Her grief in consequence of her sterility; gives her maid to Jacob in order to secure children in her own name.

Ge 30:1–8, 22–34

Ge 30:15 — And she said unto her, *Is it* a small matter that thou hast taken my husband? and wouldest thou take away my son's mandrakes also? And Rachel said, Therefore he shall lie with thee to night for thy son's mandrakes.

• Later fecundity of, becomes the mother of Joseph.

Ge 30:22–25

• Later fecundity of, becomes the mother of Benjamin.

Ge 35:16–18

Ge 35:24 — The sons of Rachel; Joseph, and Benjamin:

• Steals the household images of her father.

Ge 31:14–19, 33–35

Ge 31:4 — And Jacob sent and called Rachel and Leah to the field unto his flock,

• Her death and burial.

Ge 35:18–20

Ge 48:7 — And as for me, when I came from Padan, Rachel died by me in the land of Canaan in the way, when yet *there was* but a little way to come unto Ephrath: and I buried her there in the way of Ephrath; the same is Bethlehem.

1Sa 10:2 — When thou art departed from me to day, then thou shalt find two men by Rachel's sepulchre in the border of Benjamin at Zelzah; and they will say unto thee, The asses which thou wentest to seek are found: and, lo, thy father hath left the care of the asses, and sorroweth for you, saying, What shall I do for my son?

RADDAI • Son of Jesse.

1Ch 2:14 — Nethaneel the fourth, Raddai the fifth,

RADIO

1Co 9:22 — To the weak became I as weak, that I might gain the weak: I am made all things to all *men,* that I might by all means save some.

Eph 2:2 — Wherein in time past ye walked according to the course of this world, according to the prince of the power of the air, the spirit that now worketh in the children of disobedience:

RAGAU

• Called also Reu.

• Son of Peleg and ancestor of Jesus.

Ge 11:18–21

1Ch 1:25 — Eber, Peleg, Reu,

Lk 3:35 — Which was *the son* of Saruch, which was *the son* of Ragau, which was *the son* of Phalec, which was *the son* of Heber, which was *the son* of Sala,

RAGUEL

• Called also Reuel and Jethro.

• Moses' father-in-law.

Nu 10:29 — And Moses said unto Hobab, the son of Raguel the Midianite, Moses' father in law, We are journeying unto the place of which the LORD said, I will give it you: come thou with us, and we will do thee good: for the LORD hath spoken good concerning Israel.

✦See: Jethro

RAHAB

• A woman of Jericho who assists the spies of Israel.

Jos 2:1–24

• Is spared at the taking of Jericho.

Jos 6:17–25

• Ancestor of Joseph; called also Rachab.

Mt 1:5 — And Salmon begat Booz of Rachab; and Booz begat Obed of Ruth; and Obed begat Jesse;

• Faith of, commended.

Heb 11:31 — By faith the harlot Rahab perished not with them that believed not, when she had received the spies with peace.

Jas 2:25 — Likewise also was not Rahab the harlot justified by works, when she had received the messengers, and had sent *them* out another way?

• A symbolic name applied to Egypt.

Ps 87:4 — I will make mention of Rahab and Babylon to them that know me: behold Philistia, and Tyre, with Ethiopia; this *man* was born there.

Ps 89:10 — Thou hast broken Rahab in pieces, as one that is slain; thou hast scattered thine enemies with thy strong arm.

Isa 30:7 — For the Egyptians shall help in vain, and to no purpose: therefore have I cried concerning this, Their strength *is* to sit still.

Isa 51:9 — Awake, awake, put on strength, O arm of the LORD; awake, as in the ancient days, in the generations of old. *Art* thou not it that hath cut Rahab, *and* wounded the dragon?

RAHAM • Son of Shema.

1Ch 2:44 — And Shema begat Raham, the father of Jorkoam: and Rekem begat Shammai.

RAILING

• Forbidden.

1Co 5:11 — But now I have written unto you not to keep company, if any man that is called a brother be a fornicator, or covetous, or an idolater, or a railer, or a drunkard, or an extortioner; with such an one no not to eat.

1Ti 6:4 — He is proud, knowing nothing, but doting about questions and strifes of words, whereof cometh envy, strife, railings, evil surmisings,

1Pe 3:9 — Not rendering evil for evil, or railing for railing: but contrariwise blessing; knowing that ye are thereunto called, that ye should inherit a blessing.

2Pe 2:11 — Whereas angels, which are greater in power and might, bring not railing accusation against them before the Lord.

Jude 1:9 — Yet Michael the archangel, when contending with the devil he disputed about the body of Moses, durst not bring against him a railing accusation, but said, The Lord rebuke thee.

↞See: Slander

↞See: Speaking; evil

• Instances of.

1Sa 25:14; 2Sa 16:7; Mk 15:29

RAIMENT ↞See: Dress

RAIN

• Forty days of, at the time of the flood.

Ge 7:10–12, 17–24

Ge 7:4 — For yet seven days, and I will cause it to rain upon the earth forty days and forty nights; and every living substance that I have made will I destroy from off the face of the earth.

• The plague of, upon Egypt.

Ex 9:22–26, 33–34

• Miraculously caused by Samuel.

1Sa 12:16–19

• Miraculously caused by Elijah.

1Ki 18:41–45

• David delivered by.

2Sa 5:17–21

Isa 28:21 — For the LORD shall rise up as *in* mount Perazim, he shall be wroth as *in* the valley of Gibeon, that he may do his work, his strange work; and bring to pass his act, his strange act.

• North wind unfavorable to.

Pr 25:23 — The north wind driveth away rain: so *doth* an angry countenance a backbiting tongue.

• Withheld as judgment.

Dt 11:17 — And *then* the LORD's wrath be kindled against you, and he shut up the heaven, that there be no rain, and that the land yield not her fruit; and *lest* ye perish quickly from off the good land which the LORD giveth you.

Dt 28:24 — The LORD shall make the rain of thy land powder and dust: from heaven shall it come down upon thee, until thou be destroyed.

1Ki 8:35 — When heaven is shut up, and there is no rain, because they have sinned against thee; if they pray toward this place, and confess thy name, and turn from their sin, when thou afflictest them:

2Ch 7:13 — If I shut up heaven that there be no rain, or if I command the locusts to devour the land, or if I send pestilence among my people;

Jer 3:3 — Therefore the showers have been withholden, and there hath been no latter rain; and thou hadst a whore's forehead, thou refusedst to be ashamed.

Am 4:7 — And also I have withholden the rain from you, when *there were* yet three months to the harvest: and I caused it to rain upon one city, and caused it not to rain upon another city: one piece was rained upon, and the piece whereupon it rained not withered.

Zec 14:17 — And it shall be, *that* whoso will not come up of *all* the families of the earth unto Jerusalem to worship the King, the LORD of hosts, even upon them shall be no rain.

• The earth shall no more be destroyed by.

Ge 9:8–17

• Sent by God.

Dt 11:13–14

Job 37:6 — For he saith to the snow, Be thou *on* the earth; likewise to the small rain, and to the great rain of his strength.

Isa 30:23 — Then shall he give the rain of thy seed, that thou shalt sow the ground withal; and bread of the increase of the earth, and it shall be fat and plenteous: in that day shall thy cattle feed in large pastures.

Jer 5:24 — Neither say they in their heart, Let us now fear the LORD our God, that giveth rain, both the former and the latter, in his season: he reserveth unto us the appointed weeks of the harvest.

Jer 14:22 — Are there *any* among the vanities of the Gentiles that can cause rain? or can the heavens give showers? *art* not thou he, O LORD our God? therefore we will wait upon thee: for thou hast made all these *things*.

• Contingent upon obedience.

Le 26:3–4; Dt 11:13–14

• Prayer for.

1Ki 8:35–36; 2Ch 6:26–27

• Answer to prayer for, promised.

2Ch 7:13–14

Zec 10:1 — Ask ye of the LORD rain in the time of the latter rain; *so* the LORD shall make bright clouds, and give them showers of rain, to every one grass in the field.

• Withheld, in answer to prayer.

Jas 5:17–18

• Rainy season in Palestine in the ninth month, corresponding to December.

Ezr 10:9 — Then all the men of Judah and Benjamin gathered themselves together unto Jerusalem within three days. It *was* the ninth month, on the twentieth *day* of the month; and all the people sat in the street of the house of God, trembling because of *this* matter, and for the great rain.

Ezr 10:13 — But the people *are* many, and *it is* a time of much rain, and we are not able to stand without, neither *is this* a work of one day or two: for we are many that have transgressed in this thing.

See: Meteorology and Celestial Phenomena

• Figurative.

Ps 72:6 — He shall come down like rain upon the mown grass: as showers *that* water the earth.

RAINBOW

• A token that the earth shall no more be destroyed by flood.

Ge 9:8–16

Eze 1:28 — As the appearance of the bow that is in the cloud in the day of rain, so *was* the appearance of the brightness round about. This *was* the appearance of the likeness of the glory of the LORD. And when I saw *it,* I fell upon my face, and I heard a voice of one that spake.

• Symbolic.

Rev 4:3 — And he that sat was to look upon like a jasper and a sardine stone: and *there was* a rainbow round about the throne, in sight like unto an emerald.

Rev 10:1 — And I saw another mighty angel come down from heaven, clothed with a cloud: and a rainbow *was* upon his head, and his face *was* as it were the sun, and his feet as pillars of fire:

See: Meteorology and Celestial Phenomena

RAISIN

• Preserved grape.

• Given by Abigail to David.

1Sa 25:18 — Then Abigail made haste, and took two hundred loaves, and two bottles of wine, and five sheep ready dressed, and five measures of parched *corn,* and an hundred clusters of raisins, and two hundred cakes of figs, and laid *them* on asses.

• Given to the famishing Egyptian to revive him.

1Sa 30:12 — And they gave him a piece of a cake of figs, and two clusters of raisins: and when he had eaten, his spirit came again to him: for he had eaten no bread, nor drunk *any* water, three days and three nights.

• Given by Ziba to David.

2Sa 16:1 — And when David was a little past the top *of the hill,* behold, Ziba the servant of Mephibosheth met him, with a couple of asses saddled, and upon them two hundred *loaves* of bread, and an hundred bunches of raisins, and an hundred of summer fruits, and a bottle of wine.

• Given to David at Ziklag.

1Ch 12:40 — Moreover they that were nigh them, *even* unto Issachar and Zebulun and Naphtali, brought bread on asses, and on camels, and on mules, and on oxen, *and* meat, meal, cakes of figs, and bunches of raisins, and wine, and oil, and oxen, and sheep abundantly: for *there was* joy in Israel.

RAISING

• From the dead.

See: Dead

See: Resurrection

RAKEM

• A descendant of Machir

• Son of Manasseh.

1Ch 7:16 — And Maachah the wife of Machir bare a son, and she called his name Peresh; and the name of his brother *was* Sheresh; and his sons *were* Ulam and Rakem.

RAKKATH • A city in Naphtali.

Jos 19:39 — This *is* the inheritance of the tribe of the children of Naphtali according to their families, the cities and their villages.

RAKKON • A city in Dan.

Jos 19:46 — And Me-jarkon, and Rakkon, with the border before Japho.

RAM

• Son of Hezron and an ancestor of Jesus.

1Ch 2:9–10

Ru 4:19 — And Hezron begat Ram, and Ram begat Amminadab,

• Called Aram.

Mt 1:3–4

Lk 3:33 — Which was *the son* of Aminadab, which was *the son* of Aram, which was *the son* of Esrom, which was *the son* of Phares, which was *the son* of Juda,

• Son of Jerahmeel.

1Ch 2:25 — And the sons of Jerahmeel the firstborn of Hezron were, Ram the firstborn, and Bunah, and Oren, and Ozem, *and* Ahijah.

1Ch 2:27 — And the sons of Ram the firstborn of Jerahmeel were, Maaz, and Jamin, and Eker.

• An ancestor, probably of Elihu.

Job 32:2 — Then was kindled the wrath of Elihu the son of Barachel the Buzite, of the kindred of Ram: against Job was his wrath kindled, because he justified himself rather than God.

• A sheep.

• Skins of, used for the roof of the tabernacle.

Ex 26:14 — And thou shalt make a covering for the tent *of* rams' skins dyed red, and a covering above *of* badgers' skins.

Ex 39:34 — And the covering of rams' skins dyed red, and the covering of badgers' skins, and the vail of the covering,

- **Seen in Daniel's vision.**

Da 8:3 — Then I lifted up mine eyes, and saw, and, behold, there stood before the river a ram which had *two* horns: and the *two* horns *were* high; but one *was* higher than the other, and the higher came up last.

Da 8:20 — The ram which thou sawest having *two* horns *are* the kings of Media and Persia.

- **Used in sacrifice.**

See: Offerings

- **Trumpets made of the horns of.**

See: Trumpets

RAMA See: Ramah; called Rama

RAMAH

- **Called Rama.**

Mt 2:18 — In Rama was there a voice heard, lamentation, and weeping, and great mourning, Rachel weeping *for* her children, and would not be comforted, because they are not.

- **A city allotted to Benjamin.**

Jos 18:25 — Gibeon, and Ramah, and Beeroth,

Jgs 19:13 — And he said unto his servant, Come, and let us draw near to one of these places to lodge all night, in Gibeah, or in Ramah.

- **Attempted fortification of, by King Baasha; destruction of, by Asa.**

1Ki 15:17–22; 2Ch 16:1–6

- **People of, return from the Babylonian captivity.**

Ezr 2:26 — The children of Ramah and Gaba, six hundred twenty and one.

Ne 7:30 — The men of Ramah and Gaba, six hundred twenty and one.

Ne 11:33 — Hazor, Ramah, Gittaim,

- **Jeremiah imprisoned in.**

Jer 40:1 — The word that came to Jeremiah from the LORD, after that Nebuzar-adan the captain of the guard had let him go from Ramah, when he had taken him being bound in chains among all that were carried away captive of Jerusalem and Judah, which were carried away captive unto Babylon.

- **Prophecies concerning.**

Isa 10:29 — They are gone over the passage: they have taken up their lodging at Geba; Ramah is afraid; Gibeah of Saul is fled.

Jer 31:15 — Thus saith the LORD; A voice was heard in Ramah, lamentation, *and* bitter weeping; Rahel weeping for her children refused to be comforted for her children, because they *were* not.

Hos 5:8 — Blow ye the cornet in Gibeah, *and* the trumpet in Ramah: cry aloud *at* Beth-aven, after thee, O Benjamin.

Mt 2:18 — In Rama was there a voice heard, lamentation, and weeping, and great mourning, Rachel weeping *for* her children, and would not be comforted, because they are not.

- **A city of Asher.**

Jos 19:29 — And *then* the coast turneth to Ramah, and to the strong city Tyre; and the coast turneth to Hosah; and the outgoings thereof are at the sea from the coast to Achzib:

- **A city of Naphtali.**

Jos 19:36 — And Adamah, and Ramah, and Hazor,

- **A city in Mount Ephraim.**

Jgs 4:5 — And she dwelt under the palm tree of Deborah between Ramah and Bethel in mount Ephraim: and the children of Israel came up to her for judgment.

- **Called also Ramathaim-Zophim.**

1Sa 1:1 — Now there was a certain man of Ramathaim-zophim, of mount Ephraim, and his name was Elkanah, the son of Jeroham, the son of Elihu, the son of Tohu, the son of Zuph, an Ephrathite:

- **Home of Elkanah.**

1Sa 1:1 — Now there was a certain man of Ramathaim-zophim, of mount Ephraim, and his name was Elkanah, the son of Jeroham, the son of Elihu, the son of Tohu, the son of Zuph, an Ephrathite:

1Sa 1:19 — And they rose up in the morning early, and worshipped before the LORD, and returned, and came to their house to Ramah: and Elkanah knew Hannah his wife; and the LORD remembered her.

1Sa 2:11 — And Elkanah went to Ramah to his house. And the child did minister unto the LORD before Eli the priest.

- **Home of Samuel.**

1Sa 1:19–20

1Sa 7:17 — And his return *was* to Ramah; for there *was* his house; and there he judged Israel; and there he built an altar unto the LORD.

1Sa 8:4 — Then all the elders of Israel gathered themselves together, and came to Samuel unto Ramah,

1Sa 15:34 — Then Samuel went to Ramah; and Saul went up to his house to Gibeah of Saul.

1Sa 16:13 — Then Samuel took the horn of oil, and anointed him in the midst of his brethren: and the Spirit of the LORD came upon David from that day forward. So Samuel rose up, and went to Ramah.

- **David flees to.**

1Sa 19:18 — So David fled, and escaped, and came to Samuel to Ramah, and told him all that Saul had done to him. And he and Samuel went and dwelt in Naioth.

- **Samuel dies and was buried in.**

1Sa 25:1 — And Samuel died; and all the Israelites were gathered together, and lamented him, and buried him in his house at Ramah. And David arose, and went down to the wilderness of Paran.

1Sa 28:3 — Now Samuel was dead, and all Israel had lamented him, and buried him in Ramah, even in his own city. And Saul had put away those that had familiar spirits, and the wizards, out of the land.

See: Ramoth-Gilead

RAMATH • A city of Simeon.

Jos 19:8 — And all the villages that *were* round about these cities to Baalath-beer, Ramath of the south. This is the inheritance of the tribe of the children of Simeon according to their families.

RAMATH-LEHI

• Place where Samson slew a thousand Philistines with the jawbone of an ass.

Jgs 15:17 — And it came to pass, when he had made an end of speaking, that he cast away the jawbone out of his hand, and called that place Ramath-lehi.

RAMATH-MIZPEH • A town in Gad.

Jos 13:26 — And from Heshbon unto Ramath-mizpeh, and Betonim; and from Mahanaim unto the border of Debir;

RAMATHAIM-ZOPHIM ↞See: Ramah

RAMESES

• Called also Raamses.

• The district in Egypt inhabited by the Israelites.

Ge 47:11 — And Joseph placed his father and his brethren, and gave them a possession in the land of Egypt, in the best of the land, in the land of Rameses, as Pharaoh had commanded.

Ex 1:11 — Therefore they did set over them taskmasters to afflict them with their burdens. And they built for Pharaoh treasure cities, Pithom and Raamses.

Ex 12:37 — And the children of Israel journeyed from Rameses to Succoth, about six hundred thousand on foot *that were* men, beside children.

Nu 33:3 — And they departed from Rameses in the first month, on the fifteenth day of the first month; on the morrow after the passover the children of Israel went out with an high hand in the sight of all the Egyptians.

Nu 33:5 — And the children of Israel removed from Rameses, and pitched in Succoth.

• City of, built by the Israelites as a treasure city for Pharaoh.

Ex 1:1 — Now these *are* the names of the children of Israel, which came into Egypt; every man and his household came with Jacob.

RAMIAH

• An Israelite in the time of Ezra.

• Had taken a strange wife.

Ezr 10:25 — Moreover of Israel: of the sons of Parosh; Ramiah, and Jeziah, and Malchiah, and Miamin, and Eleazar, and Malchijah, and Benaiah.

RAMOTH

• An Israelite in the time of Ezra who had taken a strange wife.

Ezr 10:29 — And of the sons of Bani; Meshullam, Malluch, and Adaiah, Jashub, and Sheal, and Ramoth.

• A place probably in the south of Simeon.

• Called Ramath of the south or south Ramoth.

Jos 19:8 — And all the villages that *were* round about these cities to Baalath-beer, Ramath of the south. This is the inheritance of the tribe of the children of Simeon according to their families.

1Sa 30:27 — To *them* which *were* in Bethel, and to *them* which *were* in south Ramoth, and to *them* which *were* in Jattir,

• A city of Issachar.

• Allotted to the Levites.

1Ch 6:73 — And Ramoth with her suburbs, and Anem with her suburbs:

• Ramoth in Gilead.

↞See: Ramoth-Gilead

RAMOTH-GILEAD

• Called also Ramah.

2Ki 8:29 — And king Joram went back to be healed in Jezreel of the wounds which the Syrians had given him at Ramah, when he fought against Hazael king of Syria. And Ahaziah the son of Jehoram king of Judah went down to see Joram the son of Ahab in Jezreel, because he was sick.

2Ch 22:6 — And he returned to be healed in Jezreel because of the wounds which were given him at Ramah, when he fought with Hazael king of Syria. And Azariah the son of Jehoram king of Judah went down to see Jehoram the son of Ahab at Jezreel, because he was sick.

• A city of Gad, and a city of refuge.

Dt 4:43 — *Namely,* Bezer in the wilderness, in the plain country, of the Reubenites; and Ramoth in Gilead, of the Gadites; and Golan in Bashan, of the Manassites.

Jos 20:8 — And on the other side Jordan by Jericho eastward, they assigned Bezer in the wilderness upon the plain out of the tribe of Reuben, and Ramoth in Gilead out of the tribe of Gad, and Golan in Bashan out of the tribe of Manasseh.

1Ch 6:80 — And out of the tribe of Gad; Ramoth in Gilead with her suburbs, and Mahanaim with her suburbs,

• One of Solomon's commissaries at.

1Ki 4:13 — The son of Geber, in Ramoth-gilead; to him *pertained* the towns of Jair the son of Manasseh, which *are* in Gilead; to him *also pertained* the region of Argob, which is in Bashan, threescore great cities with walls and brasen bars:

• In the possession of the Syrians.

1Ki 22:3 — And the king of Israel said unto his servants, Know ye that Ramoth in Gilead *is* ours, and we *be* still, *and* take it not out of the hand of the king of Syria?

• Besieged by Israel and Judah; Ahab slain at.

1Ki 22:29–36; 2Ch 18:1–34

• Recovered by Joram; Joram wounded at.

2Ki 8:28–29; 9:14–15; 2Ch 22:5–6

- **Elisha anoints Jehu king at.**
  2Ki 9:1–6

RANSOM

- **Of a man's life.**
  Ps 49:7–8
  Ex 21:30 — If there be laid on him a sum of money, then he shall give for the ransom of his life whatsoever is laid upon him.
  Ex 30:12 — When thou takest the sum of the children of Israel after their number, then shall they give every man a ransom for his soul unto the LORD, when thou numberest them; that there be no plague among them, when *thou* numberest them.
  Job 36:18 — Because *there is* wrath, *beware* lest he take thee away with *his* stroke: then a great ransom cannot deliver thee.
  Pr 6:35 — He will not regard any ransom; neither will he rest content, though thou givest many gifts.
  Pr 13:8 — The ransom of a man's life *are* his riches: but the poor heareth not rebuke.
  Hos 13:14 — I will ransom them from the power of the grave; I will redeem them from death: O death, I will be thy plagues; O grave, I will be thy destruction: repentance shall be hid from mine eyes.
- **Figurative.**
  Job 33:24 — Then he is gracious unto him, and saith, Deliver him from going down to the pit: I have found a ransom.
  Isa 35:10 — And the ransomed of the LORD shall return, and come to Zion with songs and everlasting joy upon their heads: they shall obtain joy and gladness, and sorrow and sighing shall flee away.
  Isa 51:10 — *Art* thou not it which hath dried the sea, the waters of the great deep; that hath made the depths of the sea a way for the ransomed to pass over?
  Mt 20:28 — Even as the Son of man came not to be ministered unto, but to minister, and to give his life a ransom for many.
  1Ti 2:6 — Who gave himself a ransom for all, to be testified in due time.

See: Jesus, Death of
See: Jesus, Messiah
See: Jesus, Mission of
See: Jesus, Names, Appellations, and Titles of
See: Jesus, Saviour
See: Redemption
See: Saviour

RAPE

- **Law imposes death penalty for.**
  Dt 22:25–27
- **Captives afflicted with.**
  Isa 13:16 — Their children also shall be dashed to pieces before their eyes; their houses shall be spoiled, and their wives ravished.
  La 5:11 — They ravished the women in Zion, *and* the maids in the cities of Judah.
  Zec 14:2 — For I will gather all nations against Jerusalem to battle; and the city shall be taken, and the houses rifled, and the women ravished; and half of the city shall go forth into captivity, and the residue of the people shall not be cut off from the city.
- **Instances of.**
  - **Servant of a Levite, by Benjamites; tribe of Benjamites nearly exterminated as punishment.**
    Jgs 19:22–30; 20:35
  - **Of Tamar by Amnon; avenged in the death of Amnon at the hand of Absalom, Tamar's brother.**
    2Sa 13:6–29, 32–33

RAPHA

- **Son of Benjamin.**
  1Ch 8:2 — Nohah the fourth, and Rapha the fifth.
- **A descendant of Jonathan.**
  1Ch 8:37 — And Moza begat Binea: Rapha *was* his son, Eleasah his son, Azel his son:
  - **Called also Rephaiah.**
    1Ch 9:43 — And Moza begat Binea; and Rephaiah his son, Eleasah his son, Azel his son.
- **An ancestor of certain Philistine warriors.**
  2Sa 21:16 — And Ishbi-benob, which *was* of the sons of the giant, the weight of whose spear *weighed* three hundred *shekels* of brass in weight, he being girded with a new *sword,* thought to have slain David.
  2Sa 21:20 — And there was yet a battle in Gath, where was a man of *great* stature, that had on every hand six fingers, and on every foot six toes, four and twenty in number; and he also was born to the giant.
  2Sa 21:22 — These four were born to the giant in Gath, and fell by the hand of David, and by the hand of his servants.
  1Ch 20:4 — And it came to pass after this, that there arose war at Gezer with the Philistines; at which time Sibbechai the Hushathite slew Sippai, *that was* of the children of the giant: and they were subdued.
  1Ch 20:6 — And yet again there was war at Gath, where was a man of *great* stature, whose fingers and toes *were* four and twenty, six *on each hand,* and six *on each foot:* and he also was the son of the giant.
  1Ch 20:8 — These were born unto the giant in Gath; and they fell by the hand of David, and by the hand of his servants.

RAPHU • A Benjamite.

Nu 13:9 — Of the tribe of Benjamin, Palti the son of Raphu.

RAPTURE

1Th 4:13–18

RASHNESS

Ps 116:11 — I said in my haste, All men *are* liars.
Pr 14:29 — *He that is* slow to wrath *is* of great understanding: but *he that is* hasty of spirit exalteth folly.

Pr 19:2 — Also, *that* the soul *be* without knowledge, *it is* not good; and he that hasteth with *his* feet sinneth.

Pr 21:5 — The thoughts of the diligent *tend* only to plenteousness; but of every one *that is* hasty only to want.

Pr 25:8 — Go not forth hastily to strive, lest *thou know not* what to do in the end thereof, when thy neighbour hath put thee to shame.

Pr 29:20 — Seest thou a man *that is* hasty in his words? *there is* more hope of a fool than of him.

Ecc 5:2 — Be not rash with thy mouth, and let not thine heart be hasty to utter *any* thing before God: for God *is* in heaven, and thou upon earth: therefore let thy words be few.

Ecc 7:9 — Be not hasty in thy spirit to be angry: for anger resteth in the bosom of fools.

- **Instances of.**
  - **Moses, in slaying the Egyptian.**
    Ex 2:11–12; Ac 7:24–25
  - **Moses, when he smote the rock.**
    Nu 20:10–12
  - **Jephtha's vow.**
    Jgs 11:31–39
  - **Israel's vow to destroy the Benjamites.**
    Jgs 21:1–23
  - **Uzzah, in steadying the ark.**
    2Sa 6:6–7
  - **David in his genorosity to Ziba.**
    2Sa 16:4; 19:26–29
  - **Rehoboam, in forsaking the counsel of the old men.**
    1Ki 12:8–15
  - **Josiah, in fighting against Necho.**
    2Ch 35:20–24
  - **Naaman, in refusing to wash in Jordan.**
    2Ki 5:11–12
  - **James and John, in desiring to call down fire on the Samaritans.**
    Lk 9:54
  - **Paul, in persisting in going to Jerusalem, against the repeated admonitions of the Holy Ghost.**
    Ac 21:4, 10–15
  - **The centurion, in rejecting Paul's counsel.**
    Ac 27:11

RAVEN

- **A black carnivorous bird.**

  Pr 30:17 — The eye *that* mocketh at *his* father, and despiseth to obey *his* mother, the ravens of the valley shall pick it out, and the young eagles shall eat it.

  SS 5:11 — His head *is as* the most fine gold, his locks *are* bushy, *and* black as a raven.

- **Forbidden as food.**

  Le 11:15 — Every raven after his kind;

  Dt 14:14 — And every raven after his kind,

- **Preserved by Noah in the ark.**

  Ge 8:7 — And he sent forth a raven, which went forth to and fro, until the waters were dried up from off the earth.

- **Fed Elijah.**
  1Ki 17:4–6

- **Cared for by divine providence.**

  Lk 12:24 — Consider the ravens: for they neither sow nor reap; which neither have storehouse nor barn; and God feedeth them: how much more are ye better than the fowls?

RAVISHMENT

See: Rape

RAZOR

- **Nazarite forbidden to use.**

  Nu 6:5 — All the days of the vow of his separation there shall no razor come upon his head: until the days be fulfilled, in the which he separateth *himself* unto the LORD, he shall be holy, *and* shall let the locks of the hair of his head grow.

- **Figurative.**

  Ps 52:2 — Thy tongue deviseth mischiefs; like a sharp rasor, working deceitfully.

  Isa 7:20 — In the same day shall the Lord shave with a razor that is hired, *namely,* by them beyond the river, by the king of Assyria, the head, and the hair of the feet: and it shall also consume the beard.

  Eze 5:1 — And thou, son of man, take thee a sharp knife, take thee a barber's razor, and cause *it* to pass upon thine head and upon thy beard: then take thee balances to weigh, and divide the *hair.*

READING

- **Taught.**

  Dt 6:9 — And thou shalt write them upon the posts of thy house, and on thy gates.

  Dt 11:20 — And thou shalt write them upon the door posts of thine house, and upon thy gates:

READINGS, SELECT

- **Judah's defense.**
  Ge 44:18–34
- **Joseph revealing his identity.**
  Ge 45:1–15
- **The deliverance of the Israelites from Pharaoh.**
  Ex 14:5–30
- **Song of Moses when Pharaoh and his army were overthrown.**
  Ex 15:1–19
- **David's lament over Absalom.**
  2Sa 18:19–33
- **Lights and shadows.**
  Ru 1:1–22
- **Elijah's miraculous preservation.**
  1Ki 17:1–16
- **Elisha and the widow's oil.**
  2Ki 4:1–7
- **Naaman the leper.**
  2Ki 5:1–14
- **Esther's triumph.**
  Est 4:1–17; 7:1–10

• **The brevity of life.**
Job 14:1–10

• **Nature's testimony.**
Job 28:1–28

• **God's challenge to Job.**
Job 38:1–41

• **The beasts of the field.**
Job 39:1–30

• **The righteous and the wicked in contrast.**
Ps 1:1–6

• **The triumphant king.**
Ps 2:1–12

• **Man in nature.**
Ps 8:1–9

• **Man in extremity.**
Ps 18:1–19

• **Confidence in God.**
Ps 23:1–6

• **The king of glory.**
Ps 24:1–10

• **The glory of God.**
Ps 29:1–11

• **Our refuge.**
Ps 46:1–11

• **The majesty of God.**
Ps 77:13–20

• **The joy of the righteous.**
Ps 84:1–12

• **The state of the godly.**
Ps 91:1–16

• **The new song.**
Ps 98:1–9

• **The majesty and providence of God.**
Ps 104:1–35

• **In captivity.**
Ps 137:1–9

• **The omnipresence of God.**
Ps 139:1–24

• **Old age.**
Ecc 12:1–7

• **Christ's kingdom foreshadowed.**
Isa 35:1–10

• **The omnipotence and incomparableness of God.**
Isa 40:1–31

• **The wrath of God.**
Am 9:1–6

• **The majesty of God.**
Hab 3:3–13

• **Mary's magnificat.**
Lk 1:46–56

• **The prophetic blessing of Zacharias.**
Lk 1:67–80

• **The beatitudes.**
Mt 5:1–16

• **God's providence.**
Mt 6:26–34

• **Wise and foolish builders.**
Mt 7:21–27

• **The good Samaritan.**
Lk 10:25–37

• **The prodigal son.**
Lk 15:11–32

• **The raising of Lazarus.**
Jn 11:1–3, 18–46

• **The betrayal.**
Lk 22:47–62

• **The resurrection.**
Lk 24:1–12

• **Peter at pentecost.**
Ac 2:1–36

• **Stephen's defense.**
Ac 7:1–56

• **Paul and Silas in prison.**
Ac 16:16–40

• **Paul on Mars' hill.**
Ac 17:22–31

• **Paul before Felix.**
Ac 24:1–27

• **Paul before Agrippa.**
Ac 26:1–32

• **Charity.**
1Co 13:1–13

• **The new heaven and the new earth.**
Rev 21:1–27

• **The river of life.**
Rev 22:1–21

• **For other selections.**
✦See: Elegy
✦See: Personification

REAIA • Son of Micah, a Reubenite.
1Ch 5:5 — Micah his son, Reaia his son, Baal his son,

REAIAH

• **A man of Judah.**
• **Son of Shobal.**
1Ch 4:2 — And Reaiah the son of Shobal begat Jahath; and Jahath begat Ahumai and Lahad. These *are* the families of the Zorathites.
• **Apparently called Haroeh.**
1Ch 2:52 — And Shobal the father of Kirjath-jearim had sons; Haroeh, *and* half of the Manahethites.

• **Ancestor of a family which returned to Jerusalem from captivity in Babylon.**
Ezr 2:47 — The children of Giddel, the children of Gahar, the children of Reaiah,
Ne 7:50 — The children of Reaiah, the children of Rezin, the children of Nekoda,

REAPING

Ps 129:7 — Wherewith the mower filleth not his hand; nor he that bindeth sheaves his bosom.

• The ark of the Lord returned by the Philistines at the time of.

1Sa 6:13 — And *they of* Beth-shemesh *were* reaping their wheat harvest in the valley: and they lifted up their eyes, and saw the ark, and rejoiced to see *it*.

• Laws concerning gleaning at the time of.

See: Gleaning

• Figurative.

Hos 10:12–13

Ps 126:6 — He that goeth forth and weepeth, bearing precious seed, shall doubtless come again with rejoicing, bringing his sheaves *with him*.

REASONING

• With God.

Job 13:17–28

Job 13:3 — Surely I would speak to the Almighty, and I desire to reason with God.

• God reasons with men.

Isa 5:3–4

Ex 4:11 — And the LORD said unto him, Who hath made man's mouth? or who maketh the dumb, or deaf, or the seeing, or the blind? have not I the LORD?

Ex 20:5 — Thou shalt not bow down thyself to them, nor serve them: for I the LORD thy God *am* a jealous God, visiting the iniquity of the fathers upon the children unto the third and fourth *generation* of them that hate me;

Ex 20:11 — For *in* six days the LORD made heaven and earth, the sea, and all that in them *is*, and rested the seventh day: wherefore the LORD blessed the sabbath day, and hallowed it.

Isa 1:18 — Come now, and let us reason together, saith the LORD: though your sins be as scarlet, they shall be as white as snow; though they be red like crimson, they shall be as wool.

Isa 43:26 — Put me in remembrance: let us plead together: declare thou, that thou mayest be justified.

Hos 4:1 — Hear the word of the LORD, ye children of Israel: for the LORD hath a controversy with the inhabitants of the land, because *there is* no truth, nor mercy, nor knowledge of God in the land.

Mic 6:2 — Hear ye, O mountains, the LORD'S controversy, and ye strong foundations of the earth: for the LORD hath a controversy with his people, and he will plead with Israel.

• Natural understanding.

Da 4:36 — At the same time my reason returned unto me; and for the glory of my kingdom, mine honour and brightness returned unto me; and my counsellors and my lords sought unto me; and I was established in my kingdom, and excellent majesty was added unto me.

• To be applied to religion.

1Co 10:15 — I speak as to wise men; judge ye what I say.

1Pe 3:15 — But sanctify the Lord God in your hearts: and *be* ready always to *give* an answer to every man that asketh you a reason of the hope that is in you with meekness and fear:

• Not a sufficient guide in human affairs.

Dt 12:8 — Ye shall not do after all *the things* that we do here this day, every man whatsoever *is* right in his own eyes.

Pr 3:5 — Trust in the LORD with all thine heart; and lean not unto thine own understanding.

Pr 14:12 — There is a way which seemeth right unto a man, but the end thereof *are* the ways of death.

• Of the Pharisees.

Lk 5:21–22

Lk 20:5 — And they reasoned with themselves, saying, If we shall say, From heaven; he will say, Why then believed ye him not?

• Of Paul from the Scriptures.

Ac 17:2 — And Paul, as his manner was, went in unto them, and three sabbath days reasoned with them out of the scriptures,

Ac 18:4 — And he reasoned in the synagogue every sabbath, and persuaded the Jews and the Greeks.

Ac 18:19 — And he came to Ephesus, and left them there: but he himself entered into the synagogue, and reasoned with the Jews.

Ac 24:25 — And as he reasoned of righteousness, temperance, and judgment to come Felix trembled, and answered, Go thy way for this time; when I have a convenient season, I will call for thee.

• The gospel cannot be explained by.

1Co 1:18–28; 2:1–14

See: Investigation

See: Philosophy

REBA

• A king of Midian.

• Slain by the Israelites.

Nu 31:8 — And they slew the kings of Midian, beside the rest of them that were slain; *namely*, Evi, and Rekem, and Zur, and Hur, and Reba, five kings of Midian: Balaam also the son of Beor they slew with the sword.

Jos 13:21 — And all the cities of the plain, and all the kingdom of Sihon king of the Amorites, which reigned in Heshbon, whom Moses smote with the princes of Midian, Evi, and Rekem, and Zur, and Hur, and Reba, *which were* dukes of Sihon, dwelling in the country.

REBECCA See: Rebekah

REBEKAH

• Daughter of Bethuel, grandniece of Abraham.

Ge 22:20–23

• Becomes Isaac's wife.

Ge 24:15–67

Ge 25:20 — And Isaac was forty years old when he took Rebekah to wife, the daughter of Bethuel the Syrian of Padan-aram, the sister to Laban the Syrian.

• Mother of Esau and Jacob.

Ge 25:21–28

• **Passes as Isaac's sister.**
Ge 26:6–11

• **Displeased with Esau's wives.**
Ge 26:34–35

• **Prompts Jacob to deceive Isaac.**
Ge 27:5–29

• **Sends Jacob to Laban.**
Ge 27:42–46

• **Burial place of.**
Ge 49:31 — There they buried Abraham and Sarah his wife; there they buried Isaac and Rebekah his wife; and there I buried Leah.

• **Called Rebekah.**
Ro 9:10 — And not only *this;* but when Rebecca also had conceived by one, *even* by our father Isaac;

REBELLION

• **Treasonable.**
Pr 17:11 — An evil *man* seeketh only rebellion: therefore a cruel messenger shall be sent against him.

• **Instances of.**

• **Absalom.**
2Sa 15:1–18:33

• **Sheba.**
2Sa 20:1–26

• **Revolt of the ten tribes.**
1Ki 12:16–20; 2Ch 10:1–19; 13:5–12

See: Sin

REBUKING

Mt 7:1–5

Pr 9:8 — Reprove not a scorner, lest he hate thee: rebuke a wise man, and he will love thee.

Pr 13:1 — A wise son *heareth* his father's instruction: but a scorner heareth not rebuke.

Pr 17:17 — A friend loveth at all times, and a brother is born for adversity.

Pr 27:6 — Faithful *are* the wounds of a friend; but the kisses of an enemy *are* deceitful.

Pr 28:23 — He that rebuketh a man afterwards shall find more favour than he that flattereth with the tongue.

Ecc 7:5 — *It is* better to hear the rebuke of the wise, than for a man to hear the song of fools.

RECHAB

• **Son of Rimmon.**

• **Murders Ish-bosheth, son of Saul; put to death by David.**
2Sa 4:5–12

• **Father of Jehonadab.**
2Ki 10:15 — And when he was departed thence, he lighted on Jehonadab the son of Rechab *coming* to meet him: and he saluted him, and said to him, Is thine heart right, as my heart *is* with thy heart? And Jehonadab answered, It is. If it be, give *me* thine hand. And he gave *him* his hand; and he took him up to him into the chariot.

2Ki 10:23 — And Jehu went, and Jehonadab the son of Rechab, into the house of Baal, and said unto the worshippers of Baal, Search, and look that there be here with you none of the servants of the LORD, but the worshippers of Baal only.

1Ch 2:55 — And the families of the scribes which dwelt at Jabez; the Tirathites, the Shimeathites, *and* Suchathites. These *are* the Kenites that came of Hemath, the father of the house of Rechab.

Jer 35:6 — But they said, We will drink no wine: for Jonadab the son of Rechab our father commanded us, saying, Ye shall drink no wine, *neither* ye, nor your sons for ever:

Jer 35:8 — Thus have we obeyed the voice of Jonadab the son of Rechab our father in all that he hath charged us, to drink no wine all our days, we, our wives, our sons, nor our daughters;

Jer 35:16 — Because the sons of Jonadab the son of Rechab have performed the commandment of their father, which he commanded them; but this people hath not hearkened unto me:

Jer 35:19 — Therefore thus saith the LORD of hosts, the God of Israel; Jonadab the son of Rechab shall not want a man to stand before me for ever.

• **Ancestor of the Rechabites.**
Jer 35:1–19

• **Father of Malchiah.**
Ne 3:14 — But the dung gate repaired Malchiah the son of Rechab, the ruler of part of Beth-haccerem; he build it, and set up the doors thereof, the locks thereof, and the bars thereof.

RECHABITES

• **A family of Kenites descended from Rechab, through Jonadab.**
1Ch 2:55 — And the families of the scribes which dwelt at Jabez; the Tirathites, the Shimeathites, *and* Suchathites. These *are* the Kenites that came of Hemath, the father of the house of Rechab.

Jer 35:6 — But they said, We will drink no wine: for Jonadab the son of Rechab our father commanded us, saying, Ye shall drink no wine, *neither* ye, nor your sons for ever:

• **Enjoined by Jonadab to drink no wine.**
Jer 35:6 — But they said, We will drink no wine: for Jonadab the son of Rechab our father commanded us, saying, Ye shall drink no wine, *neither* ye, nor your sons for ever:

• **Adhere to the injunction of abstinence; perpetuation of the family promised as a reward.**
Jer 35:1–19

See: Abstinence, Total
See: Nazarite

RECHAH • A city of unknown location.

1Ch 4:12 — And Eshton begat Beth-rapha, and Paseah, and Tehinnah the father of Ir-nahash. These *are* the men of Rechah.

RECIPROCITY

Ro 15:27 — It hath pleased them verily; and their debtors they are. For if the Gentiles have been made partakers of their spiritual things, their duty is also to minister unto them in carnal things.

1Co 9:11 — If we have sown unto you spiritual things, *is it* a great thing if we shall reap your carnal things?

Gal 6:6 — Let him that is taught in the word communicate unto him that teacheth in all good things.

RECONCILIATION

- **Between man and man.**

Mt 5:23–26

- **Of Esau and Jacob.**

Ge 33:4 — And Esau ran to meet him, and embraced him, and fell on his neck, and kissed him: and they wept.

Ge 33:11 — Take, I pray thee, my blessing that is brought to thee; because God hath dealt graciously with me, and because I have enough. And he urged him, and he took *it.*

- **Between Pilate and Herod.**

Lk 23:12 — And the same day Pilate and Herod were made friends together: for before they were at enmity between themselves.

- **Between God and man.**

2Co 5:18–21; Eph 2:15–18; Col 1:20–22

Le 8:15 — And he slew *it;* and Moses took the blood, and put *it* upon the horns of the altar round about with his finger, and purified the altar, and poured the blood at the bottom of the altar, and sanctified it, to make reconciliation upon it.

Eze 45:15 — And one lamb out of the flock, out of two hundred, out of the fat pastures of Israel; for a meat offering, and for a burnt offering, and for peace offerings, to make reconciliation for them, saith the Lord GOD.

Da 9:24 — Seventy weeks are determined upon thy people and upon thy holy city, to finish the transgression, and to make an end of sins, and to make reconciliation for iniquity, and to bring in everlasting righteousness, and to seal up the vision and prophecy, and to anoint the most Holy.

Ro 5:1 — Therefore being justified by faith, we have peace with God through our Lord Jesus Christ:

Ro 11:15 — For if the casting away of them *be* the reconciling of the world, what *shall* the receiving *of them be,* but life from the dead?

Heb 2:17 — Wherefore in all things it behoved him to be made like unto *his* brethren, that he might be a merciful and faithful high priest in things *pertaining* to God, to make reconciliation for the sins of the people.

See: Atonement

See: Jesus, Mission of

See: Propitiation

See: Redemption

RECONNOISSANCE

- **Of Jericho.**

Jos 2:1–24

- **Of Bethel.**

Jgs 1:23 — And the house of Joseph sent to descry Bethel. (Now the name of the city before *was* Luz.)

- **Of Laish.**

Jgs 18:2–10

RECORDER

See: Scribe

See: Secretary

RECREATION

- **Jesus takes, from the fatigues of his ministry.**

Mk 6:31–32

Mk 7:24 — And from thence he arose, and went into the borders of Tyre and Sidon, and entered into an house, and would have no man know *it:* but he could not be hid.

RED

See: Colors

RED HEIFER

- **Of purification.**

Nu 19:1–22

RED SEA

- **The locusts which devastated Egypt destroyed in.**

Ex 10:19 — And the LORD turned a mighty strong west wind, which took away the locusts, and cast them into the Red sea; there remained not one locust in all the coasts of Egypt.

- **Israelites cross; Pharaoh and his army drowned in.**

Ex 14:1–15:1; Jos 24:6–7; Ne 9:9–11; Ps 106:7–11; 136:13–15; Isa 43:16–17; 1Co 10:1–2

Ex 15:4 — Pharaoh's chariots and his host hath he cast into the sea: his chosen captains also are drowned in the Red sea.

Ex 15:11 — Who *is* like unto thee, O LORD, among the gods? who *is* like thee, glorious in holiness, fearful *in* praises, doing wonders?

Ex 15:19 — For the horse of Pharaoh went in with his chariots and with his horsemen into the sea, and the LORD brought again the waters of the sea upon them; but the children of Israel went on dry *land* in the midst of the sea.

Nu 33:8 — And they departed from before Pi-hahiroth, and passed through the midst of the sea into the wilderness, and went three days' journey in the wilderness of Etham, and pitched in Marah.

Dt 11:4 — And what he did unto the army of Egypt, unto their horses, and to their chariots; how he made the water of the Red sea to overflow them as they pursued after you, and *how* the LORD hath destroyed them unto this day;

Jos 2:10 — For we have heard how the LORD dried up the water of the Red sea for you, when ye came out of Egypt; and what ye did unto the two kings of the

Amorites, that *were* on the other side Jordan, Sihon and Og, whom ye utterly destroyed.

Jos 4:23 — For the LORD your God dried up the waters of Jordan from before you, until ye were passed over, as the LORD your God did to the Red sea, which he dried up from before us, until we were gone over:

Jgs 11:16 — But when Israel came up from Egypt, and walked through the wilderness unto the Red sea, and came to Kadesh;

2Sa 22:16 — And the channels of the sea appeared, the foundations of the world were discovered, at the rebuking of the LORD, at the blast of the breath of his nostrils.

Ps 66:6 — He turned the sea into dry *land:* they went through the flood on foot: there did we rejoice in him.

Ps 78:13 — He divided the sea, and caused them to pass through; and he made the waters to stand as an heap.

Ps 78:53 — And he led them on safely, so that they feared not: but the sea overwhelmed their enemies.

Ps 106:22 — Wondrous works in the land of Ham, *and* terrible things by the Red sea.

Ac 7:36 — He brought them out, after that he had shewed wonders and signs in the land of Egypt, and in the Red sea, and in the wilderness forty years.

Heb 11:29 — By faith they passed through the Red sea as by dry *land:* which the Egyptians assaying to do were drowned.

• Israelites camp by.

Nu 33:10–11; Dt 2:1–3

Ex 14:2 — Speak unto the children of Israel, that they turn and encamp before Pi-hahiroth, between Migdol and the sea, over against Baal-zephon: before it shall ye encamp by the sea.

Ex 14:9 — But the Egyptians pursued after them, all the horses *and* chariots of Pharaoh, and his horsemen, and his army, and overtook them encamping by the sea, beside Pi-hahiroth, before Baal-zephon.

Nu 14:25 — (Now the Amalekites and the Canaanites dwelt in the valley.) To morrow turn you, and get you into the wilderness by the way of the Red sea.

Nu 21:4 — And they journeyed from mount Hor by the way of the Red sea, to compass the land of Edom: and the soul of the people was much discouraged because of the way.

Dt 1:40 — But *as for* you, turn you, and take your journey into the wilderness by the way of the Red sea.

• Boundary of the promised land.

Ex 23:31 — And I will set thy bounds from the Red sea even unto the sea of the Philistines, and from the desert unto the river: for I will deliver the inhabitants of the land into your hand; and thou shalt drive them out before thee.

• Solomon builds ships on.

1Ki 9:26 — And king Solomon made a navy of ships in Ezion-geber, which is beside Eloth, on the shore of the Red sea, in the land of Edom.

• Wilderness of.

Ex 13:18 — But God led the people about, *through* the way of the wilderness of the Red sea: and the children of Israel went up harnessed out of the land of Egypt.

REDEMPTION

• Of persons or property.

Le 25:25–34; 27:2–33; Ru 4:3–10

• Redemption money paid to priests.

Nu 3:46–51

• Of firstborn.

➜See: Firstborn

• Of land.

➜See: Jubilee

• Of our souls.

Ro 3:24–26; Gal 4:4–5; Col 1:20–22; 1Pe 1:18–19; Rev 5:9–10

Ps 111:9 — He sent redemption unto his people: he hath commanded his covenant for ever: holy and reverend *is* his name.

Ps 130:7 — Let Israel hope in the LORD: for with the LORD *there is* mercy, and with him *is* plenteous redemption.

Mt 20:28 — <u>Even as the Son of man came not to be ministered unto, but to minister, and to give his life a ransom for many.</u>

Mk 10:45 — <u>For even the Son of man came not to be ministered unto, but to minister, and to give his life a ransom for many.</u>

Lk 2:38 — And she coming in that instant gave thanks likewise unto the Lord, and spake of him to all them that looked for redemption in Jerusalem.

Ac 20:28 — Take heed therefore unto yourselves, and to all the flock, over the which the Holy Ghost hath made you overseers, to feed the church of God, which he hath purchased with his own blood.

1Co 1:30 — But of him are ye in Christ Jesus, who of God is made unto us wisdom, and righteousness, and sanctification, and redemption:

1Co 6:20 — For ye are bought with a price: therefore glorify God in your body, and in your spirit, which are God's.

1Co 7:23 — Ye are bought with a price; be not ye the servants of men.

Gal 1:4 — Who gave himself for our sins, that he might deliver us from this present evil world, according to the will of God and our Father:

Gal 2:20 — I am crucified with Christ: nevertheless I live; yet not I, but Christ liveth in me: and the life which I now live in the flesh I live by the faith of the Son of God, who loved me, and gave himself for me.

Eph 1:7 — In whom we have redemption through his blood, the forgiveness of sins, according to the riches of his grace;

Eph 5:2 — And walk in love, as Christ also hath loved us, and hath given himself for us an offering and a sacrifice to God for a sweetsmelling savour.

Col 1:14 — In whom we have redemption through his blood, *even* the forgiveness of sins:

1Ti 2:6 — Who gave himself a ransom for all, to be testified in due time.

Tit 2:14 — Who gave himself for us, that he might redeem us from all iniquity, and purify unto himself a peculiar people, zealous of good works.

Heb 9:12 — Neither by the blood of goats and calves, but by his own blood he entered in once into the holy place, having obtained eternal redemption *for us.*

Heb 9:15 — And for this cause he is the mediator of the new testament, that by means of death, for the redemption of the transgressions *that were* under the first testament, they which are called might receive the promise of eternal inheritance.

See: Atonement

See: Ransom

REED

• A water plant.

Isa 19:6–7

Isa 35:7 — And the parched ground shall become a pool, and the thirsty land springs of water: in the habitation of dragons, where each lay, *shall be* grass with reeds and rushes.

Jer 51:32 — And that the passages are stopped, and the reeds they have burned with fire, and the men of war are affrighted.

• Used as a measuring device of six cubits.

Eze 40:3–8; 42:16–19; Rev 21:15–16

Eze 41:8 — I saw also the height of the house round about: the foundations of the side chambers *were* a full reed of six great cubits.

Eze 45:1 — Moreover, when ye shall divide by lot the land for inheritance, ye shall offer an oblation unto the LORD, an holy portion of the land: the length *shall be* the length of five and twenty thousand *reeds,* and the breadth *shall be* ten thousand. This *shall be* holy in all the borders thereof round about.

Rev 11:1 — And there was given me a reed like unto a rod: and the angel stood, saying, Rise, and measure the temple of God, and the altar, and them that worship therein.

• Mockingly given to Jesus as a symbol of royalty.

Mt 27:29 — And when they had platted a crown of thorns, they put *it* upon his head, and a reed in his right hand: and they bowed the knee before him, and mocked him, saying, Hail, King of the Jews!

• Jesus smitten with.

Mt 27:30 — And they spit upon him, and took the reed, and smote him on the head.

Mk 15:19 — And they smote him on the head with a reed, and did spit upon him, and bowing *their* knees worshipped him.

• Figurative.

• Of weakness.

1Ki 14:15 — For the LORD shall smite Israel, as a reed is shaken in the water, and he shall root up Israel out of this good land, which he gave to their fathers, and shall scatter them beyond the river, because they have made their groves, provoking the LORD to anger.

2Ki 18:21 — Now, behold, thou trustest upon the staff of this bruised reed, *even* upon Egypt, on which if a man lean, it will go into his hand, and pierce it: so is Pharaoh king of Egypt unto all that trust on him.

Isa 36:6 — Lo, thou trustest in the staff of this broken reed, on Egypt; whereon if a man lean, it will go into his hand, and pierce it: so *is* Pharaoh king of Egypt to all that trust in him.

Isa 42:3 — A bruised reed shall he not break, and the smoking flax shall he not quench: he shall bring forth judgment unto truth.

Eze 29:6 — And all the inhabitants of Egypt shall know that I *am* the LORD, because they have been a staff of reed to the house of Israel.

Mt 11:7 — And as they departed, Jesus began to say unto the multitudes concerning John, What went ye out into the wilderness to see? A reed shaken with the wind?

Mt 12:20 — A bruised reed shall he not break, and smoking flax shall he not quench, till he send forth judgment unto victory.

REELAIAH

• A returned captive from Babylon.

Ezr 2:2 — Which came with Zerubbabel: Jeshua, Nehemiah, Seraiah, Reelaiah, Mordecai, Bilshan, Mizpar, Bigvai, Rehum, Baanah. The number of the men of the people of Israel:

• Called Raamiah.

Ne 7:7 — Who came with Zerubbabel, Jeshua, Nehemiah, Azariah, Raamiah, Nahamani, Mordecai, Bilshan, Mispereth, Bigvai, Nehum, Baanah. The number, *I say,* of the men of the people of Israel *was this;*

REFINING

• The process of eliminating by fire the dross of metals.

• Of gold.

1Ch 28:18 — And for the altar of incense refined gold by weight; and gold for the pattern of the chariot of the cherubims, that spread out *their wings,* and covered the ark of the covenant of the LORD.

• Of silver.

1Ch 29:4 — *Even* three thousand talents of gold, of the gold of Ophir, and seven thousand talents of refined silver, to overlay the walls of the houses *withal:*

• Of wine.

Isa 25:6 — And in this mountain shall the LORD of hosts make unto all people a feast of fat things, a feast of wines on the lees, of fat things full of marrow, of wines on the lees well refined.

• Figurative.

• Of the corrective judgments of God.

Mal 3:2–3

Isa 1:25 — And I will turn my hand upon thee, and purely purge away thy dross, and take away all thy tin:

Isa 48:10 — Behold, I have refined thee, but not with silver; I have chosen thee in the furnace of affliction.

Jer 9:7 — Therefore thus saith the LORD of hosts, Behold, I will melt them, and try them; for how shall I do for the daughter of my people?

Zec 13:9 — And I will bring the third part through the fire, and will refine them as silver is refined, and will try them as gold is tried: they shall call on my name, and I will hear them: I will say, It *is* my people: and they shall say, The LORD *is* my God.

• **Of the purity of the word of God.**

Ps 18:30 — *As for* God, his way *is* perfect: the word of the LORD is tried: he *is* a buckler to all those that trust in him.

Ps 119:140 — Thy word *is* very pure: therefore thy servant loveth it.

REFUGE

• **Cities of.**

• **From the avenger of blood.**

Ex 21:13–14; Nu 35:11–32; Dt 4:41–43; 19:2–13; Jos 20:1–6

• **List of.**

Jos 20:7–9

• **Roads made to.**

Dt 19:3 — Thou shalt prepare thee a way, and divide the coasts of thy land, which the LORD thy God giveth thee to inherit, into three parts, that every slayer may flee thither.

• **Figurative.**

• **Of Christ.**

Heb 6:18 — That by two immutable things, in which *it was* impossible for God to lie, we might have a strong consolation, who have fled for refuge to lay hold upon the hope set before us:

REFUGEE SLAVES

• **Laws concerning.**

Dt 23:15–16

See: Servant; bond

REGEM • Son of Jahdai.

1Ch 2:47 — And the sons of Jahdai; Regem, and Jotham, and Gesham, and Pelet, and Ephah, and Shaaph.

REGEM-MELECH • A captive sent as a messenger from the Jews in Babylon to Jerusalem.

Zec 7:2 — When they had sent unto the house of God Sherezer and Regem-melech, and their men, to pray before the LORD,

REGENCY

1Ki 22:47 — *There was* then no king in Edom: a deputy *was* king.

2Ki 15:5 — And the LORD smote the king, so that he was a leper unto the day of his death, and dwelt in a several house. And Jotham the king's son *was* over the house, judging the people of the land.

REGENERATION

Isa 1:16–17; 32:3–4; 35:5–6; 44:3–5; 55:1–3; Jer 17:13–14; 31:33–34; 32:38–40; Eze 11:19–20; 36:26–27; 37:1–14; Mt 12:33–35, 43–44; Mk 4:26–29; 5:19–20; Lk 1:16–17; 8:38–39; Jn 3:3–8; 6:44–45, 50–51; 10:9–10; Ro 2:28–29; 6:3–23; 7:24–25; 8:2–6, 13–16; 1Co 2:14–16; 3:6–7; 2Co 1:21–22; Eph 2:5–6; 4:7–8, 21–24; Col 2:11–13; 3:9–10; Tit 3:5–6; Heb 4:1–12; 8:10–11; 10:16–17, 22–23; Jas 5:19–20; 1Pe 1:2–3, 22–23; 2Pe 1:3–4; 1Jn 5:4–5, 11–12

Dt 29:4 — Yet the LORD hath not given you an heart to perceive, and eyes to see, and ears to hear, unto this day.

Dt 30:6 — And the LORD thy God will circumcise thine heart, and the heart of thy seed, to love the LORD thy God with all thine heart, and with all thy soul, that thou mayest live.

1Ki 8:58 — That he may incline our hearts unto him, to walk in all his ways, and to keep his commandments, and his statutes, and his judgments, which he commanded our fathers.

Ps 36:9 — For with thee *is* the fountain of life: in thy light shall we see light.

Ps 51:2 — Wash me throughly from mine iniquity, and cleanse me from my sin.

Ps 51:7 — Purge me with hyssop, and I shall be clean: wash me, and I shall be whiter than snow.

Ps 51:10 — Create in me a clean heart, O God; and renew a right spirit within me.

Ps 65:3 — Iniquities prevail against me: *as for* our transgressions, thou shalt purge them away.

Ps 68:18 — Thou hast ascended on high, thou hast led captivity captive: thou hast received gifts for men; yea, *for* the rebellious also, that the LORD God might dwell *among them.*

Ps 87:4 — I will make mention of Rahab and Babylon to them that know me: behold Philistia, and Tyre, with Ethiopia; this *man* was born there.

Ps 87:6 — The LORD shall count, when he writeth up the people, that this man was born there. Selah.

Ps 110:3 — Thy people *shall be* willing in the day of thy power, in the beauties of holiness from the womb of the morning: thou hast the dew of thy youth.

Pr 4:23 — Keep thy heart with all diligence; for out of it *are* the issues of life.

Pr 12:28 — In the way of righteousness *is* life; and *in* the pathway *thereof there is* no death.

Pr 14:27 — The fear of the LORD *is* a fountain of life, to depart from the snares of death.

Pr 16:1 — The preparations of the heart in man, and the answer of the tongue, *is* from the LORD.

Isa 1:25 — And I will turn my hand upon thee, and purely purge away thy dross, and take away all thy tin:

Isa 4:4 — When the Lord shall have washed away the filth of the daughters of Zion, and shall have purged the blood of Jerusalem from the midst thereof by the spirit of judgment, and by the spirit of burning.

Isa 12:3 — Therefore with joy shall ye draw water out of the wells of salvation.

Isa 26:12 — LORD, thou wilt ordain peace for us: for thou also hast wrought all our works in us.

Isa 29:23 — But when he seeth his children, the work of mine hands, in the midst of him, they shall sanctify my name, and sanctify the Holy One of Jacob, and shall fear the God of Israel.

Isa 32:15 — Until the spirit be poured upon us from on high, and the wilderness be a fruitful field, and the fruitful field be counted for a forest.

Isa 32:17 — And the work of righteousness shall be peace; and the effect of righteousness quietness and assurance for ever.

Isa 42:16 — And I will bring the blind by a way *that* they knew not; I will lead them in paths *that* they have not known: I will make darkness light before them, and crooked things straight. These things will I do unto them, and not forsake them.

Isa 43:7 — *Even* every one that is called by my name: for I have created him for my glory, I have formed him; yea, I have made him.

Isa 49:9 — That thou mayest say to the prisoners, Go forth; to them that *are* in darkness, Shew yourselves. They shall feed in the ways, and their pastures *shall be* in all high places.

Jer 13:23 — Can the Ethiopian change his skin, or the leopard his spots? *then* may ye also do good, that are accustomed to do evil.

Jer 24:7 — And I will give them an heart to know me, that I *am* the LORD: and they shall be my people, and I will be their God: for they shall return unto me with their whole heart.

Jer 31:3 — The LORD hath appeared of old unto me, *saying*, Yea, I have loved thee with an everlasting love: therefore with lovingkindness have I drawn thee.

Jer 33:6 — Behold, I will bring it health and cure, and I will cure them, and will reveal unto them the abundance of peace and truth.

Eze 16:9 — Then washed I thee with water; yea, I throughly washed away thy blood from thee, and I anointed thee with oil.

Eze 18:31 — Cast away from you all your transgressions, whereby ye have transgressed; and make you a new heart and a new spirit: for why will ye die, O house of Israel?

Eze 36:29 — I will also save you from all your uncleannesses: and I will call for the corn, and will increase it, and lay no famine upon you.

Eze 44:7 — In that ye have brought *into my sanctuary* strangers, uncircumcised in heart, and uncircumcised in flesh, to be in my sanctuary, to pollute it, *even* my house, when ye offer my bread, the fat and the blood, and they have broken my covenant because of all your abominations.

Eze 44:9 — Thus saith the Lord GOD; No stranger, uncircumcised in heart, nor uncircumcised in flesh, shall enter into my sanctuary, of any stranger that *is* among the children of Israel.

Zec 12:10 — And I will pour upon the house of David, and upon the inhabitants of Jerusalem, the spirit of grace and of supplications: and they shall look upon me whom they have pierced, and they shall mourn for him, as one mourneth for *his* only *son*, and shall be in bitterness for him, as one that is in bitterness for *his* firstborn.

Mt 13:23 — But he that received seed into the good ground is he that heareth the word, and understandeth *it*; which also beareth fruit, and bringeth forth, some an hundredfold, some sixty, some thirty.

Mt 13:33 — Another parable spake he unto them; The kingdom of heaven is like unto leaven, which a woman took, and hid in three measures of meal, till the whole was leavened.

Mt 18:3 — And said, Verily I say unto you, Except ye be converted, and become as little children, ye shall not enter into the kingdom of heaven.

Mk 4:20 — And these are they which are sown on good ground; such as hear the word, and receive *it*, and bring forth fruit, some thirtyfold, some sixty, and some an hundred.

Mk 10:15 — Verily I say unto you, Whosoever shall not receive the kingdom of God as a little child, he shall not enter therein.

Lk 8:35 — Then they went out to see what was done; and came to Jesus, and found the man, out of whom the devils were departed, sitting at the feet of Jesus, clothed, and in his right mind: and they were afraid.

Lk 13:21 — It is like leaven, which a woman took and hid in three measures of meal, till the whole was leavened.

Lk 18:17 — Verily I say unto you, Whosoever shall not receive the kingdom of God as a little child shall in no wise enter therein.

Jn 1:4 — In him was life; and the life was the light of men.

Jn 1:13 — Which were born, not of blood, nor of the will of the flesh, nor of the will of man, but of God.

Jn 1:16 — And of his fulness have all we received, and grace for grace.

Jn 4:10 — Jesus answered and said unto her, If thou knewest the gift of God, and who it is that saith to thee, Give me to drink; thou wouldest have asked of him, and he would have given thee living water.

Jn 4:14 — But whosoever drinketh of the water that I shall give him shall never thirst; but the water that I shall give him shall be in him a well of water springing up into everlasting life.

Jn 5:24 — Verily, verily, I say unto you, He that heareth my word, and believeth on him that sent me, hath everlasting life, and shall not come into condemnation; but is passed from death unto life.

Jn 6:47 — Verily, verily, I say unto you, He that believeth on me hath everlasting life.

Jn 6:57 — As the living Father hath sent me, and I live by the Father: so he that eateth me, even he shall live by me.

Jn 8:12 — Then spake Jesus again unto them, saying, I am the light of the world: he that followeth me shall not walk in darkness, but shall have the light of life.

Jn 8:32 — And ye shall know the truth, and the truth shall make you free.

Jn 8:36 — If the Son therefore shall make you free, ye shall be free indeed.

Jn 13:8 — Peter saith unto him, Thou shalt never wash my feet. Jesus answered him, If I wash thee not, thou hast no part with me.

Jn 15:1 — I am the true vine, and my Father is the husbandman.

Jn 15:3 — Now ye are clean through the word which I have spoken unto you.

Jn 17:2 — As thou hast given him power over all flesh, that he should give eternal life to as many as thou hast given him.

Ac 2:38 — Then Peter said unto them, Repent, and be baptized every one of you in the name of Jesus Christ for the remission of sins, and ye shall receive the gift of the Holy Ghost.

Ac 2:47 — Praising God, and having favour with all the people. And the Lord added to the church daily such as should be saved.

Ac 3:26 — Unto you first God, having raised up his Son Jesus, sent him to bless you, in turning away every one of you from his iniquities.

Ac 11:17 — Forasmuch then as God gave them the like gift as *he did* unto us, who believed on the Lord Jesus Christ; what was I, that I could withstand God?

Ac 11:21 — And the hand of the Lord was with them: and a great number believed, and turned unto the Lord.

Ac 15:9 — And put no difference between us and them, purifying their hearts by faith.

Ac 16:14 — And a certain woman named Lydia, a seller of purple, of the city of Thyatira, which worshipped God, heard *us:* whose heart the Lord opened, that she attended unto the things which were spoken of Paul.

Ac 21:19 — And when he had saluted them, he declared particularly what things God had wrought among the Gentiles by his ministry.

Ac 26:18 — To open their eyes, *and* to turn *them* from darkness to light, and *from* the power of Satan unto God, that they may receive forgiveness of sins, and inheritance among them which are sanctified by faith that is in me.

Ro 7:6 — But now we are delivered from the law, that being dead wherein we were held; that we should serve in newness of spirit, and not *in* the oldness of the letter.

Ro 8:9 — But ye are not in the flesh, but in the Spirit, if so be that the Spirit of God dwell in you. Now if any man have not the Spirit of Christ, he is none of his.

Ro 12:2 — And be not conformed to this world: but be ye transformed by the renewing of your mind, that ye may prove what is that good, and acceptable, and perfect, will of God.

Ro 15:16 — That I should be the minister of Jesus Christ to the Gentiles, ministering the gospel of God, that the offering up of the Gentiles might be acceptable, being sanctified by the Holy Ghost.

1Co 1:9 — God *is* faithful, by whom ye were called unto the fellowship of his Son Jesus Christ our Lord.

1Co 1:24 — But unto them which are called, both Jews and Greeks, Christ the power of God, and the wisdom of God.

1Co 1:30 — But of him are ye in Christ Jesus, who of God is made unto us wisdom, and righteousness, and sanctification, and redemption:

1Co 2:12 — Now we have received, not the spirit of the world, but the spirit which is of God; that we might know the things that are freely given to us of God.

1Co 3:9 — For we are labourers together with God: ye are God's husbandry, *ye are* God's building.

1Co 6:11 — And such were some of you: but ye are washed, but ye are sanctified, but ye are justified in the name of the Lord Jesus, and by the Spirit of our God.

1Co 12:6 — And there are diversities of operations, but it is the same God which worketh all in all.

1Co 12:13 — For by one Spirit are we all baptized into one body, whether *we be* Jews or Gentiles, whether *we be* bond or free; and have been all made to drink into one Spirit.

1Co 15:10 — But by the grace of God I am what I am: and his grace *which was bestowed* upon me was not in vain; but I laboured more abundantly than they all: yet not I, but the grace of God which was with me.

2Co 3:3 — *Forasmuch as ye are* manifestly declared to be the epistle of Christ ministered by us, written not with ink, but with the Spirit of the living God; not in tables of stone, but in fleshy tables of the heart.

2Co 3:18 — But we all, with open face beholding as in a glass the glory of the Lord, are changed into the same image from glory to glory, *even* as by the Spirit of the Lord.

2Co 4:6 — For God, who commanded the light to shine out of darkness, hath shined in our hearts, to *give* the light of the knowledge of the glory of God in the face of Jesus Christ.

2Co 5:5 — Now he that hath wrought us for the selfsame thing *is* God, who also hath given unto us the earnest of the Spirit.

2Co 5:17 — Therefore if any man *be* in Christ, *he is* a new creature: old things are passed away; behold, all things are become new.

Gal 2:20 — I am crucified with Christ: nevertheless I live; yet not I, but Christ liveth in me: and the life which I now live in the flesh I live by the faith of the Son of God, who loved me, and gave himself for me.

Gal 4:29 — But as then he that was born after the flesh persecuted him *that was born* after the Spirit, even so *it is* now.

Gal 6:15 — For in Christ Jesus neither circumcision availeth any thing, nor uncircumcision, but a new creature.

Eph 2:1 — And you *hath he quickened,* who were dead in trespasses and sins;

Eph 2:8 — For by grace are ye saved through faith; and that not of yourselves: *it is* the gift of God:

Eph 2:10 — For we are his workmanship, created in Christ Jesus unto good works, which God hath before ordained that we should walk in them.

Eph 4:16 — From whom the whole body fitly joined together and compacted by that which every joint supplieth, according to the effectual working in the measure of every part, maketh increase of the body unto the edifying of itself in love.

Eph 5:14 — Wherefore he saith, Awake thou that sleepest, and arise from the dead, and Christ shall give thee light.

Php 1:6 — Being confident of this very thing, that he which hath begun a good work in you will perform *it* until the day of Jesus Christ:

2Th 2:13 — But we are bound to give thanks alway to God for you, brethren beloved of the Lord, because God hath from the beginning chosen you to salvation through sanctification of the Spirit and belief of the truth:

Jas 1:18 — Of his own will begat he us with the word of truth, that we should be a kind of firstfruits of his creatures.

1Pe 2:3 — If so be ye have tasted that the Lord *is* gracious.

1Pe 2:9 — But ye *are* a chosen generation, a royal priesthood, an holy nation, a peculiar people; that ye should shew forth the praises of him who hath called you out of darkness into his marvellous light:

1Jn 2:27 — But the anointing which ye have received of him abideth in you, and ye need not that any man teach you: but as the same anointing teacheth you of all things, and is truth, and is no lie, and even as it hath taught you, ye shall abide in him.

1Jn 2:29 — If ye know that he is righteous, ye know that every one that doeth righteousness is born of him.

1Jn 3:9 — Whosoever is born of God doth not commit sin; for his seed remaineth in him: and he cannot sin, because he is born of God.

1Jn 3:14 — We know that we have passed from death unto life, because we love the brethren. He that loveth not *his* brother abideth in death.

1Jn 4:7 — Beloved, let us love one another: for love is of God; and every one that loveth is born of God, and knoweth God.

1Jn 5:1 — Whosoever believeth that Jesus is the Christ is born of God: and every one that loveth him that begat loveth him also that is begotten of him.

1Jn 5:18 — We know that whosoever is born of God sinneth not; but he that is begotten of God keepeth himself, and that wicked one toucheth him not.

See: Atonement

See: Reconciliation

See: Redemption

See: Sanctification

See: Sin; forgiveness of

- **Instances of.**
  - **Jacob.**
    Ge 32:29
  - **Saul.**
    1Sa 10:9
  - **Saul of Tarsus.**
    Ac 9:3–18
  - **All righteous persons.**

See: Righteous

REGICIDE

- **Of Ehud.**
  Jgs 3:16–23
- **Of Saul.**
  2Sa 1:16 — And David said unto him, Thy blood *be* upon thy head; for thy mouth hath testified against thee, saying, I have slain the LORD's anointed.
- **Of Ish-bosheth.**
  2Sa 4:5–8
- **Of Nadab.**
  1Ki 15:27–29
- **Of Elah.**
  1Ki 16:9–11
- **Of Joram.**
  2Ki 9:24 — And Jehu drew a bow with his full strength, and smote Jehoram between his arms, and the arrow went out at his heart, and he sunk down in his chariot.
- **Of Ahaziah.**
  2Ki 9:27 — But when Ahaziah the king of Judah saw *this,* he fled by the way of the garden house. And Jehu followed after him, and said, Smite him also in the chariot. *And they did so* at the going up to Gur, which *is* by Ibleam. And he fled to Megiddo, and died there.
- **Of Joash.**
  2Ki 12:20–21
- **Of Amaziah.**
  2Ki 14:19–20
- **Of Zachariah.**
  2Ki 15:10 — And Shallum the son of Jabesh conspired against him, and smote him before the people, and slew him, and reigned in his stead.
- **Of Shallum.**
  2Ki 15:14 — For Menahem the son of Gadi went up from Tirzah, and came to Samaria, and smote Shallum the son of Jabesh in Samaria, and slew him, and reigned in his stead.
- **Of Pekahiah.**
  2Ki 15:25 — But Pekah the son of Remaliah, a captain of his, conspired against him, and smote him in Samaria, in the palace of the king's house, with Argob and Arieh, and with him fifty men of the Gileadites: and he killed him, and reigned in his room.
- **Of Pekah.**
  2Ki 15:30 — And Hoshea the son of Elah made a conspiracy against Pekah the son of Remaliah, and smote him, and slew him, and reigned in his stead, in the twentieth year of Jotham the son of Uzziah.
- **Of Sennacherib.**
  2Ki 19:36–37; Isa 37:37–38

See: Homicide

REGISTRATION

- **Of citizens.**
  Isa 4:3 — And it shall come to pass, *that he that is* left in Zion, and *he that* remaineth in Jerusalem, shall be called holy, *even* every one that is written among the living in Jerusalem:

See: Census

REHABIAH • Son of Eliezer.

1Ch 23:17 — And the sons of Eliezer *were,* Rehabiah the chief. And Eliezer had none other sons; but the sons of Rehabiah were very many.

1Ch 24:21 — Concerning Rehabiah: of the sons of Rehabiah, the first *was* Isshiah.

1Ch 26:25 — And his brethren by Eliezer; Rehabiah his son, and Jeshaiah his son, and Joram his son, and Zichri his son, and Shelomith his son.

REHOB

- **Father of Hadadezer, king of Zobah.**
  2Sa 8:3 — David smote also Hadadezer, the son of Rehob, king of Zobah, as he went to recover his border at the river Euphrates.

2Sa 8:12 — Of Syria, and of Moab, and of the children of Ammon, and of the Philistines, and of Amalek, and of the spoil of Hadadezer, son of Rehob, king of Zobah.

• A Levite who sealed the covenant with Nehemiah.

Ne 10:11 — Micha, Rehob, Hashabiah,

• A town in northern Palestine.

• The limit of the investigation made by the twelve spies.

Nu 13:21 — So they went up, and searched the land from the wilderness of Zin unto Rehob, as men come to Hamath.

• Possessed by the Syrians.

2Sa 10:6 — And when the children of Ammon saw that they stank before David, the children of Ammon sent and hired the Syrians of Beth-rehob, and the Syrians of Zoba, twenty thousand footmen, and of king Maacah a thousand men, and of Ish-tob twelve thousand men.

2Sa 10:8 — And the children of Ammon came out, and put the battle in array at the entering in of the gate: and the Syrians of Zoba, and of Rehob, and Ish-tob, and Maacah, *were* by themselves in the field.

• Called Beth-Rehob.

2Sa 10:6 — And when the children of Ammon saw that they stank before David, the children of Ammon sent and hired the Syrians of Beth-rehob, and the Syrians of Zoba, twenty thousand footmen, and of king Maacah a thousand men, and of Ish-tob twelve thousand men.

• An unlocated town of Asher.

Jos 19:28 — And Hebron, and Rehob, and Hammon, and Kanah, *even* unto great Zidon;

• A Levitical city of Asher.

Jos 19:30 — Ummah also, and Aphek, and Rehob: twenty and two cities with their villages.

Jos 21:31 — Helkath with her suburbs, and Rehob with her suburbs; four cities.

1Ch 6:75 — And Hukok with her suburbs, and Rehob with her suburbs:

• Canaanites not drive from.

Jgs 1:31 — Neither did Asher drive out the inhabitants of Accho, nor the inhabitants of Zidon, nor of Ahlab, nor of Achzib, nor of Helbah, nor of Aphik, nor of Rehob:

REHOBOAM

• Successor to Solomon as king.

1Ki 11:43 — And Solomon slept with his fathers, and was buried in the city of David his father: and Rehoboam his son reigned in his stead.

2Ch 9:31 — And Solomon slept with his fathers, and he was buried in the city of David his father: and Rehoboam his son reigned in his stead.

• Refuses to reform abuses.

1Ki 12:1–15; 2Ch 10:1–15

• Ten tribes, under leadership of Jeroboam, successfully revolt from.

1Ki 12:16–24; 2Ch 10:16–11:4

• Builds fortified cities; is temporarily prosperous.

2Ch 11:5–23

• Invaded by king of Egypt and despoiled.

1Ki 14:25–28; 2Ch 12:1–12

• Death of.

1Ki 14:31 — And Rehoboam slept with his fathers, and was buried with his fathers in the city of David. And his mother's name *was* Naamah an Ammonitess. And Abijam his son reigned in his stead.

2Ch 12:16 — And Rehoboam slept with his fathers, and was buried in the city of David: and Abijah his son reigned in his stead.

• Genealogy and descendants of.

1Ch 3:1–24; Mt 1:1–25

• Called Roboam.

Mt 1:7 — And Solomon begat Roboam; and Roboam begat Abia; and Abia begat Asa;

REHOBOTH

• A city built by Asshur.

Ge 10:11 — Out of that land went forth Asshur, and builded Nineveh, and the city Rehoboth, and Calah,

• A city of the Edomites.

Ge 36:37 — And Samlah died, and Saul of Rehoboth *by* the river reigned in his stead.

1Ch 1:48 — And when Samlah was dead, Shaul of Rehoboth by the river reigned in his stead.

• The name given to a well dug by Isaac.

Ge 26:22 — And he removed from thence, and digged another well; and for that they strove not: and he called the name of it Rehoboth; and he said, For now the LORD hath made room for us, and we shall be fruitful in the land.

REHUM

• A captive who returned to Jerusalem from Babylon.

Ezr 2:2 — Which came with Zerubbabel: Jeshua, Nehemiah, Seraiah, Reelaiah, Mordecai, Bilshan, Mizpar, Bigvai, Rehum, Baanah. The number of the men of the people of Israel:

• Called Nehum.

Ne 7:7 — Who came with Zerubbabel, Jeshua, Nehemiah, Azariah, Raamiah, Nahamani, Mordecai, Bilshan, Mispereth, Bigvai, Nehum, Baanah. The number, *I say,* of the men of the people of Israel *was this;*

• A chancellor who wrote a letter to Artaxerxes, influencing him against the Jews.

Ezr 4:8–9

Ezr 4:17 — *Then* sent the king an answer unto Rehum the chancellor, and *to* Shimshai the scribe, and *to* the rest of their companions that dwell in Samaria, and *unto* the rest beyond the river, Peace, and at such a time.

Ezr 4:23 — Now when the copy of king Artaxerxes' letter *was* read before Rehum, and Shimshai the scribe, and their companions, they went up in haste to Jerusalem unto the Jews, and made them to cease by force and power.

• A Levite who repaired part of the wall of Jerusalem.

Ne 3:17 — After him repaired the Levites, Rehum the son of Bani. Next unto him repaired Hashabiah, the ruler of the half part of Keilah, in his part.

• A Jew of the exile who signed the covenant with Nehemiah.

Ne 10:25 — Rehum, Hashabnah, Maaseiah,

• A priest who returned to Jerusalem from captivity in Babylon.

Ne 12:3 — Shechaniah, Rehum, Meremoth,

REI • An Israelite loyal to David at the time of the usurpation of Adonijah.

1Ki 1:8 — But Zadok the priest, and Benaiah the son of Jehoiada, and Nathan the prophet, and Shimei, and Rei, and the mighty men which *belonged* to David, were not with Adonijah.

REINCARNATION

1Jn 4:1–3

Ac 17:31 — Because he hath appointed a day, in the which he will judge the world in righteousness by *that* man whom he hath ordained; *whereof* he hath given assurance unto all *men,* in that he hath raised him from the dead.

Heb 9:27 — And as it is appointed unto men once to die, but after this the judgment:

REJECTION

• Of God.

See: God; rejected

• Of Jesus.

See: Jesus, Rejected

REKEM

• A king of the Midianites.

• Slain by the Israelites.

Nu 31:8 — And they slew the kings of Midian, beside the rest of them that were slain; *namely,* Evi, and Rekem, and Zur, and Hur, and Reba, five kings of Midian: Balaam also the son of Beor they slew with the sword.

Jos 13:21 — And all the cities of the plain, and all the kingdom of Sihon king of the Amorites, which reigned in Heshbon, whom Moses smote with the princes of Midian, Evi, and Rekem, and Zur, and Hur, and Reba, *which were* dukes of Sihon, dwelling in the country.

• A son of Hebron.

1Ch 2:43–44

• A city in Benjamin.

Jos 18:27 — And Rekem, and Irpeel, and Taralah,

RELEASE

• Year of.

See: Jubilee

RELEVANCE

1Co 9:20–27

1Co 10:33 — Even as I please all *men* in all *things,* not seeking mine own profit, but the *profit* of many, that they may be saved.

RELIGION

• False.

Dt 32:31–33

See: Idolatry

See: Intolerance, Religious

See: Teachers; false

• Family.

See: Family

• National.

• Supported by taxes.

Ex 30:11–16

Ex 38:26 — A bekah for every man, *that is,* half a shekel, after the shekel of the sanctuary, for every one that went to be numbered, from twenty years old and upward, for six hundred thousand and three thousand and five hundred and fifty *men.*

• Priests supported by the state.

2Ch 11:13–15

1Ki 18:19 — Now therefore send, *and* gather to me all Israel unto mount Carmel, and the prophets of Baal four hundred and fifty, and the prophets of the groves four hundred, which eat at Jezebel's table.

• Subverted by Jeroboam.

1Ki 12:26–33; 2Ch 11:13–15

• Established by Jeroboam.

1Ki 12:26–33

• Natural.

Job 12:7–16; 35:10–12; 37:1–24; Ps 8:1–9; 19:1–6; Ac 17:23–28; Ro 1:18–20; 10:16–18

Ac 14:17 — Nevertheless he left not himself without witness, in that he did good, and gave us rain from heaven, and fruitful seasons, filling our hearts with food and gladness.

See: Revivals

• True.

Mt 5:1–7:29; 22:36–40; Ac 10:34–35; Ro 8:1–18; 10:1–13; 12:1–21; 1Co 13:1–13; Gal 5:22–25; 1Th 5:15–23; Jas 2:8–26; 2Pe 1:5–9; Jude 1:20–21

Jas 1:27 — Pure religion and undefiled before God and the Father is this, To visit the fatherless and widows in their affliction, *and* to keep himself unspotted from the world.

See: Blessing; spiritual, from God

See: Commandments

✦See: **Duty**
✦See: **Graces**
✦See: **Regeneration**
✦See: **Repentance**
✦See: **Sanctification**
✦See: **Sin; forgiveness of**

• Instances of conspicuously religious persons.

• Abel.
Ge 4:4–8; Heb 11:4

• Noah.
Ge 6:1–9:29

• Abraham.
Ge 12:1–8; 15:1–21; 17:1–27; 18:22–33

• Jacob.
Ge 28:10–22; 32:24–32

• Moses.
Ex 3:2–22; Dt 32:33

• Jethro.
Ex 18:12

• Joshua.
Jos 1:1–18

• Gideon.
Jgs 6:1–7:25

• Samuel.
1Sa 3:1–21

• David.
✦See: **Psalms; of David**

• Solomon.
1Ki 5:3–5; 2Ch 6:1–42

• Jehu.
2Ki 10:16–30

• Hezekiah.
2Ki 18:3–7; 19:14–19

• Jehoshaphat.
2Ch 17:3–9; 19:1–20:37

• Jabez.
1Ch 4:9–10

• Asa.
2Ch 14:1–15:19

• Josiah.
2Ki 22:1–23:37

• Daniel.
Da 6:4–22

• The three Hebrews.
Da 3:1–30

• Zacharias.
Lk 1:13, 67–79

• Simeon.
Lk 2:25–35

• Anna, the prophetess.
Lk 2:36–37

• The centurion.
Lk 7:1–10

• Cornelius.
Ac 10:1–48

• Eunice and Lois.
2Ti 1:5

✦See: **John, the Apostle**
✦See: **Paul, Ministry, Ac 16–28**
✦See: **Paul, Ministry, Ac 9–15**
✦See: **Paul, Miscellaneous**
✦See: **Paul, through Conversion**
✦See: **Peter**
✦See: **Stephen**

✦See: **Apostles**
✦See: **Disciple**

REMALIAH

• Father of Pekah, king of Israel.

2Ki 15:25

2Ki 15:27 — In the two and fiftieth year of Azariah king of Judah Pekah the son of Remaliah began to reign over Israel in Samaria, *and reigned* twenty years.

2Ki 15:30 — And Hoshea the son of Elah made a conspiracy against Pekah the son of Remaliah, and smote him, and slew him, and reigned in his stead, in the twentieth year of Jotham the son of Uzziah.

2Ki 16:1 — In the seventeenth year of Pekah the son of Remaliah Ahaz the son of Jotham king of Judah began to reign.

2Ki 16:5 — Then Rezin king of Syria and Pekah son of Remaliah king of Israel came up to Jerusalem to war: and they besieged Ahaz, but could not overcome *him.*

2Ch 28:6 — For Pekah the son of Remaliah slew in Judah an hundred and twenty thousand in one day, *which were* all valiant men; because they had forsaken the LORD God of their fathers.

Isa 7:1 — And it came to pass in the days of Ahaz the son of Jotham, the son of Uzziah, king of Judah, *that* Rezin the king of Syria, and Pekah the son of Remaliah, king of Israel, went up toward Jerusalem to war against it, but could not prevail against it.

Isa 7:4 — And say unto him, Take heed, and be quiet; fear not, neither be fainthearted for the two tails of these smoking firebrands, for the fierce anger of Rezin with Syria, and of the son of Remaliah.

Isa 8:6 — Forasmuch as this people refuseth the waters of Shiloah that go softly, and rejoice in Rezin and Remaliah's son;

REMMON ✦See: Rimmon; a city south of Jerusalem

REMMON-METHOAR ✦See: Rimmon; a city of Zebulun

REMORSE

Ps 38:2–6; 51:1–4, 7–17; Pr 1:25–27; 5:7–13; Isa 57:20–21; Eze 7:16–18, 25–26

Ps 31:10 — For my life is spent with grief, and my years with sighing: my strength faileth because of mine iniquity, and my bones are consumed.

Pr 28:1 — The wicked flee when no man pursueth: but the righteous are bold as a lion.

Isa 2:19 — And they shall go into the holes of the rocks, and into the caves of the earth, for fear of the LORD, and for the glory of his majesty, when he ariseth to shake terribly the earth.

Isa 2:21 — To go into the clefts of the rocks, and into the tops of the ragged rocks, for fear of the LORD, and for the glory of his majesty, when he ariseth to shake terribly the earth.

Isa 6:5 — Then said I, Woe *is* me! for I am undone; because I *am* a man of unclean lips, and I dwell in the midst of a people of unclean lips: for mine eyes have seen the King, the LORD of hosts.

Isa 48:22 — *There is* no peace, saith the LORD, unto the wicked.

La 1:20 — Behold, O LORD; for I *am* in distress: my bowels are troubled; mine heart is turned within me; for I have grievously rebelled: abroad the sword bereaveth, at home *there is* as death.

Eze 33:10 — Therefore, O thou son of man, speak unto the house of Israel; Thus ye speak, saying, If our transgressions and our sins *be* upon us, and we pine away in them, how should we then live?

Lk 13:28 — <u>There shall be weeping and gnashing of teeth, when ye shall see Abraham, and Isaac, and Jacob, and all the prophets, in the kingdom of God, and you *yourselves* thrust out.</u>

Ac 2:37 — Now when they heard *this,* they were pricked in their heart, and said unto Peter and to the rest of the apostles, Men *and* brethren, what shall we do?

Ac 9:6 — And he trembling and astonished said, Lord, what wilt thou have me to do? And the Lord *said* unto him, <u>Arise, and go into the city, and it shall be told thee what thou must do.</u>

1Jn 3:20 — For if our heart condemn us, God is greater than our heart, and knoweth all things.

- **Instances of.**
  - **David.**
    Ps 51:1–19
  - **Peter.**
    Mt 26:75
  - **Judas.**
    Mt 27:3–5

✦See: Conviction; of sin

✦See: Penitent

✦See: Repentance

✦See: Sin; confession of

RENDING

- **Of garments, a token of affliction.**

Isa 36:22–37:1

Ge 37:29 — And Reuben returned unto the pit; and, behold, Joseph *was* not in the pit; and he rent his clothes.

Ge 37:34 — And Jacob rent his clothes, and put sackcloth upon his loins, and mourned for his son many days.

Ge 44:13 — Then they rent their clothes, and laded every man his ass, and returned to the city.

Nu 14:6 — And Joshua the son of Nun, and Caleb the son of Jephunneh, *which were* of them that searched the land, rent their clothes:

Jgs 11:35 — And it came to pass, when he saw her, that he rent his clothes, and said, Alas, my daughter! thou hast brought me very low, and thou art one of them that trouble me: for I have opened my mouth unto the LORD, and I cannot go back.

2Sa 1:2 — It came even to pass on the third day, that, behold, a man came out of the camp from Saul with his clothes rent, and earth upon his head: and *so* it was, when he came to David, that he fell to the earth, and did obeisance.

2Sa 1:11 — Then David took hold on his clothes, and rent them; and likewise all the men that *were* with him:

2Sa 3:31 — And David said to Joab, and to all the people that *were* with him, Rend your clothes, and gird you with sackcloth, and mourn before Abner. And king David *himself* followed the bier.

2Sa 13:19 — And Tamar put ashes on her head, and rent her garment of divers colours that *was* on her, and laid her hand on her head, and went on crying.

2Sa 13:31 — Then the king arose, and tare his garments, and lay on the earth; and all his servants stood by with their clothes rent.

2Sa 15:32 — And it came to pass, that *when* David was come to the top *of the mount,* where he worshipped God, behold, Hushai the Archite came to meet him with his coat rent, and earth upon his head:

2Ki 2:12 — And Elisha saw *it,* and he cried, My father, my father, the chariot of Israel, and the horsemen thereof. And he saw him no more: and he took hold of his own clothes, and rent them in two pieces.

2Ki 5:8 — And it was *so,* when Elisha the man of God had heard that the king of Israel had rent his clothes, that he sent to the king, saying, Wherefore hast thou rent thy clothes? let him come now to me, and he shall know that there is a prophet in Israel.

2Ki 6:30 — And it came to pass, when the king heard the words of the woman, that he rent his clothes; and he passed by upon the wall, and the people looked, and, behold, *he had* sackcloth within upon his flesh.

2Ki 11:14 — And when she looked, behold, the king stood by a pillar, as the manner *was,* and the princes and the trumpeters by the king, and all the people of the land rejoiced, and blew with trumpets: and Athaliah rent her clothes, and cried, Treason, Treason.

2Ki 19:1 — And it came to pass, when king Hezekiah heard *it,* that he rent his clothes, and covered himself with sackcloth, and went into the house of the LORD.

2Ki 22:11 — And it came to pass, when the king had heard the words of the book of the law, that he rent his clothes.

2Ki 22:19 — Because thine heart was tender, and thou hast humbled thyself before the LORD, when thou heardest what I spake against this place, and against the inhabitants thereof, that they should become a desolation and a curse, and hast rent thy clothes, and wept before me; I also have heard *thee,* saith the LORD.

Ezr 9:3 — And when I heard this thing, I rent my garment and my mantle, and plucked off the hair of my head and of my beard, and sat down astonied.

Ezr 9:5 — And at the evening sacrifice I arose up from my heaviness; and having rent my garment and my mantle, I fell upon my knees, and spread out my hands unto the LORD my God.

Job 1:20 — Then Job arose, and rent his mantle, and shaved his head, and fell down upon the ground, and worshipped,

Job 2:12 — And when they lifted up their eyes afar off, and knew him not, they lifted up their voice, and wept; and they rent every one his mantle, and sprinkled dust upon their heads toward heaven.

Jer 41:5 — That there came certain from Shechem, from Shiloh, and from Samaria, *even* fourscore men, having their beards shaven, and their clothes rent, and having cut themselves, with offerings and incense in their hand, to bring *them* to the house of the LORD.

Mt 26:65 — Then the high priest rent his clothes, saying, He hath spoken blasphemy; what further need have we of witnesses? behold, now ye have heard his blasphemy.

Ac 14:14 — *Which* when the apostles, Barnabas and Paul, heard *of,* they rent their clothes, and ran in among the people, crying out,

- **Figurative.**

Joel 2:13 — And rend your heart, and not your garments, and turn unto the LORD your God: for he *is* gracious and merciful, slow to anger, and of great kindness, and repenteth him of the evil.

- **Symbol of rending of a kingdom.**

1Sa 15:27–28

RENTING

- **Land.**

Mt 21:33–41; Lk 20:9–16

- **Houses.**

Ac 28:30 — And Paul dwelt two whole years in his own hired house, and received all that came in unto him,

REPENTANCE

- **Attributed to God.**

Ge 6:6–7; Jnh 3:9–10

Ex 32:14 — And the LORD repented of the evil which he thought to do unto his people.

Dt 32:36 — For the LORD shall judge his people, and repent himself for his servants, when he seeth that *their* power is gone, and *there is* none shut up, or left.

Jgs 2:18 — And when the LORD raised them up judges, then the LORD was with the judge, and delivered them out of the hand of their enemies all the days of the judge: for it repented the LORD because of their groanings by reason of them that oppressed them and vexed them.

1Sa 15:11 — It repenteth me that I have set up Saul *to be* king: for he is turned back from following me, and hath not performed my commandments. And it grieved Samuel; and he cried unto the LORD all night.

1Sa 15:29 — And also the Strength of Israel will not lie nor repent: for he *is* not a man, that he should repent.

1Sa 15:35 — And Samuel came no more to see Saul until the day of his death: nevertheless Samuel mourned for Saul: and the LORD repented that he had made Saul king over Israel.

2Sa 24:16 — And when the angel stretched out his hand upon Jerusalem to destroy it, the LORD repented him of the evil, and said to the angel that destroyed the people, It is enough: stay now thine hand. And the angel of the LORD was by the threshingplace of Araunah the Jebusite.

1Ch 21:15 — And God sent an angel unto Jerusalem to destroy it: and as he was destroying, the LORD beheld, and he repented him of the evil, and said to the angel that destroyed, It is enough, stay now thine hand. And the angel of the LORD stood by the threshingfloor of Ornan the Jebusite.

Ps 106:45 — And he remembered for them his covenant, and repented according to the multitude of his mercies.

Ps 110:4 — The LORD hath sworn, and will not repent, Thou *art* a priest for ever after the order of Melchizedek.

Ps 135:14 — For the LORD will judge his people, and he will repent himself concerning his servants.

Jer 15:6 — Thou hast forsaken me, saith the LORD, thou art gone backward: therefore will I stretch out my hand against thee, and destroy thee; I am weary with repenting.

Jer 18:8 — If that nation, against whom I have pronounced, turn from their evil, I will repent of the evil that I thought to do unto them.

Jer 18:10 — If it do evil in my sight, that it obey not my voice, then I will repent of the good, wherewith I said I would benefit them.

Jer 26:3 — If so be they will hearken, and turn every man from his evil way, that I may repent me of the evil, which I purpose to do unto them because of the evil of their doings.

Jer 42:10 — If ye will still abide in this land, then will I build you, and not pull *you* down, and I will plant you, and not pluck *you* up: for I repent me of the evil that I have done unto you.

Joel 2:13 — And rend your heart, and not your garments, and turn unto the LORD your God: for he *is* gracious and merciful, slow to anger, and of great kindness, and repenteth him of the evil.

Am 7:3 — The LORD repented for this: It shall not be, saith the LORD.

Am 7:6 — The LORD repented for this: This also shall not be, saith the Lord GOD.

- **The burden of the preaching of John the Baptist.**

Mt 3:1–17

- **The burden of the preaching of Jesus.**

Mt 4:17 — From that time Jesus began to preach, and to say, Repent: for the kingdom of heaven is at hand.

Mk 1:15 — And saying, The time is fulfilled, and the kingdom of God is at hand: repent ye, and believe the gospel.

• Exhortation to.

Pr 1:23–33; Hos 14:1–3; Am 5:4–6

Jer 7:3 — Thus saith the LORD of hosts, the God of Israel, Amend your ways and your doings, and I will cause you to dwell in this place.

Jer 7:5 — For if ye throughly amend your ways and your doings; if ye throughly execute judgment between a man and his neighbour;

Jer 26:3 — If so be they will hearken, and turn every man from his evil way, that I may repent me of the evil, which I purpose to do unto them because of the evil of their doings.

Mt 3:2 — And saying, Repent ye: for the kingdom of heaven is at hand.

• Condition of God's favor.

Le 26:40–42

2Ch 7:14 — If my people, which are called by my name, shall humble themselves, and pray, and seek my face, and turn from their wicked ways; then will I hear from heaven, and will forgive their sin, and will heal their land.

• Unavailing to Israel.

Nu 14:39–45

• Unavailing to Esau.

Heb 12:16–17

• Unclassified scripture relating to.

Le 26:40–42; Dt 4:29–31; 30:1–3, 8–10; 1Ki 8:33–50; 2Ch 6:36–39; 30:6–9; Job 11:13–15; 33:26–28; 34:31–32; Ps 95:7–8; Pr 1:22–23; Isa 55:6–7; 61:1–2; Jer 3:12–14; 4:1–4; 13:15–16; 50:4–5; Eze 11:18–20; 16:61–63; 18:21–23, 27–28, 30–32; 33:10–12, 14–16; 37:1–28; Hos 14:1–2; Joel 2:12–13, 15–18; Jnh 3:8–9; Mt 3:7–8; Lk 13:1–5; 15:1–10; 18:10–14; Jas 4:8–10; Rev 3:2–3

Dt 10:16 — Circumcise therefore the foreskin of your heart, and be no more stiffnecked.

Dt 32:29 — O that they were wise, *that* they understood this, *that* they would consider their latter end!

2Ch 7:14 — If my people, which are called by my name, shall humble themselves, and pray, and seek my face, and turn from their wicked ways; then will I hear from heaven, and will forgive their sin, and will heal their land.

Ne 1:9 — But *if* ye turn unto me, and keep my commandments, and do them; though there were of you cast out unto the uttermost part of the heaven, *yet* will I gather them from thence, and will bring them unto the place that I have chosen to set my name there.

Job 22:23 — If thou return to the Almighty, thou shalt be built up, thou shalt put away iniquity far from thy tabernacles.

Job 36:10 — He openeth also their ear to discipline, and commandeth that they return from iniquity.

Ps 22:27 — All the ends of the world shall remember and turn unto the LORD: and all the kindreds of the nations shall worship before thee.

Ps 34:14 — Depart from evil, and do good; seek peace, and pursue it.

Ps 34:18 — The LORD *is* nigh unto them that are of a broken heart; and saveth such as be of a contrite spirit.

Ps 51:17 — The sacrifices of God *are* a broken spirit: a broken and a contrite heart, O God, thou wilt not despise.

Ps 147:3 — He healeth the broken in heart, and bindeth up their wounds.

Pr 9:6 — Forsake the foolish, and live; and go in the way of understanding.

Pr 28:13 — He that covereth his sins shall not prosper: but whoso confesseth and forsaketh *them* shall have mercy.

Isa 10:21 — The remnant shall return, *even* the remnant of Jacob, unto the mighty God.

Isa 22:12 — And in that day did the Lord GOD of hosts call to weeping, and to mourning, and to baldness, and to girding with sackcloth:

Isa 31:6 — Turn ye unto *him from* whom the children of Israel have deeply revolted.

Isa 44:22 — I have blotted out, as a thick cloud, thy transgressions, and, as a cloud, thy sins: return unto me; for I have redeemed thee.

Isa 46:8 — Remember this, and shew yourselves men: bring it again to mind, O ye transgressors.

Isa 57:15 — For thus saith the high and lofty One that inhabiteth eternity, whose name *is* Holy; I dwell in the high and holy *place,* with him also *that is* of a contrite and humble spirit, to revive the spirit of the humble, and to revive the heart of the contrite ones.

Isa 59:20 — And the Redeemer shall come to Zion, and unto them that turn from transgression in Jacob, saith the LORD.

Jer 3:4 — Wilt thou not from this time cry unto me, My father, thou art the guide of my youth?

Jer 3:19 — But I said, How shall I put thee among the children, and give thee a pleasant land, a goodly heritage of the hosts of nations? and I said, Thou shalt call me, My father; and shalt not turn away from me.

Jer 4:14 — O Jerusalem, wash thine heart from wickedness, that thou mayest be saved. How long shall thy vain thoughts lodge within thee?

Jer 6:8 — Be thou instructed, O Jerusalem, lest my soul depart from thee; lest I make thee desolate, a land not inhabited.

Jer 6:16 — Thus saith the LORD, Stand ye in the ways, and see, and ask for the old paths, where is the good way, and walk therein, and ye shall find rest for your souls. But they said, We will not walk *therein.*

Jer 7:5 — For if ye throughly amend your ways and your doings; if ye throughly execute judgment between a man and his neighbour;

Jer 7:7 — Then will I cause you to dwell in this place, in the land that I gave to your fathers, for ever and ever.

Jer 18:8 — If that nation, against whom I have pronounced, turn from their evil, I will repent of the evil that I thought to do unto them.

Jer 18:11 — Now therefore go to, speak to the men of Judah, and to the inhabitants of Jerusalem, saying, Thus saith the LORD; Behold, I frame evil against you, and devise a device against you: return ye now every one from his evil way, and make your ways and your doings good.

Jer 24:7 — And I will give them an heart to know me, that I *am* the LORD: and they shall be my people, and I will be their God: for they shall return unto me with their whole heart.

Jer 25:5 — They said, Turn ye again now every one from his evil way, and from the evil of your doings, and dwell in the land that the LORD hath given unto you and to your fathers for ever and ever:

Jer 26:3 — If so be they will hearken, and turn every man from his evil way, that I may repent me of the evil, which I purpose to do unto them because of the evil of their doings.

Jer 26:13 — Therefore now amend your ways and your doings, and obey the voice of the LORD your God; and the LORD will repent him of the evil that he hath pronounced against you.

Jer 31:9 — They shall come with weeping, and with supplications will I lead them: I will cause them to walk by the rivers of waters in a straight way, wherein they shall not stumble: for I am a father to Israel, and Ephraim *is* my firstborn.

Jer 35:15 — I have sent also unto you all my servants the prophets, rising up early and sending *them,* saying, Return ye now every man from his evil way, and amend your doings, and go not after other gods to serve them, and ye shall dwell in the land which I have given to you and to your fathers: but ye have not inclined your ear, nor hearkened unto me.

Jer 36:3 — It may be that the house of Judah will hear all the evil which I purpose to do unto them; that they may return every man from his evil way; that I may forgive their iniquity and their sin.

Jer 36:7 — It may be they will present their supplication before the LORD, and will return every one from his evil way: for great *is* the anger and the fury that the LORD hath pronounced against this people.

Eze 7:16 — But they that escape of them shall escape, and shall be on the mountains like doves of the valleys, all of them mourning, every one for his iniquity.

Eze 12:3 — Therefore, thou son of man, prepare thee stuff for removing, and remove by day in their sight; and thou shalt remove from thy place to another place in their sight: it may be they will consider, though they *be* a rebellious house.

Eze 14:6 — Therefore say unto the house of Israel, Thus saith the Lord GOD; Repent, and turn *yourselves* from your idols; and turn away your faces from all your abominations.

Eze 20:43 — And there shall ye remember your ways, and all your doings, wherein ye have been defiled; and ye shall lothe yourselves in your own sight for all your evils that ye have committed.

Eze 33:19 — But if the wicked turn from his wickedness, and do that which is lawful and right, he shall live thereby.

Eze 36:31 — Then shall ye remember your own evil ways, and your doings that *were* not good, and shall lothe yourselves in your own sight for your iniquities and for your abominations.

Da 4:27 — Wherefore, O king, let my counsel be acceptable unto thee, and break off thy sins by righteousness, and thine iniquities by shewing mercy to the poor; if it may be a lengthening of thy tranquility.

Hos 2:7 — And she shall follow after her lovers, but she shall not overtake them; and she shall seek them, but shall not find *them:* then shall she say, I will go and return to my first husband; for then *was it* better with me than now.

Hos 3:5 — Afterward shall the children of Israel return, and seek the LORD their God, and David their king; and shall fear the LORD and his goodness in the latter days.

Hos 5:15 — I will go *and* return to my place, till they acknowledge their offence, and seek my face: in their affliction they will seek me early.

Hos 10:12 — Sow to yourselves in righteousness, reap in mercy; break up your fallow ground: for *it is* time to seek the LORD, till he come and rain righteousness upon you.

Hos 12:6 — Therefore turn thou to thy God: keep mercy and judgment, and wait on thy God continually.

Joel 1:14 — Sanctify ye a fast, call a solemn assembly, gather the elders *and* all the inhabitants of the land *into* the house of the LORD your God, and cry unto the LORD,

Am 4:12 — Therefore thus will I do unto thee, O Israel: *and* because I will do this unto thee, prepare to meet thy God, O Israel.

Am 5:6 — Seek the LORD, and ye shall live; lest he break out like fire in the house of Joseph, and devour *it,* and *there be* none to quench *it* in Bethel.

Am 5:15 — Hate the evil, and love the good, and establish judgment in the gate: it may be that the LORD God of hosts will be gracious unto the remnant of Joseph.

Hag 1:7 — Thus saith the LORD of hosts; Consider your ways.

Zec 1:3 — Therefore say thou unto them, Thus saith the LORD of hosts; Turn ye unto me, saith the LORD of hosts, and I will turn unto you, saith the LORD of hosts.

Zec 12:10 — And I will pour upon the house of David, and upon the inhabitants of Jerusalem, the spirit of grace and of supplications: and they shall look upon me whom they have pierced, and they shall mourn for him, as one mourneth for *his* only *son,* and shall be in bitterness for him, as one that is in bitterness for *his* firstborn.

Mal 3:7 — Even from the days of your fathers ye are gone away from mine ordinances, and have not kept *them.* Return unto me, and I will return unto you, saith the LORD of hosts. But ye said, Wherein shall we return?

Mt 3:2 — And saying, Repent ye: for the kingdom of heaven is at hand.

Mt 4:17 — From that time Jesus began to preach, and to say, Repent: for the kingdom of heaven is at hand.

Mt 5:4 — Blessed *are* they that mourn: for they shall be comforted.

Mt 9:13 — But go ye and learn what *that* meaneth, I will have mercy, and not sacrifice: for I am not come to call the righteous, but sinners to repentance.

Mk 1:4 — John did baptize in the wilderness, and preach the baptism of repentance for the remission of sins.

Mk 1:15 — And saying, The time is fulfilled, and the kingdom of God is at hand: repent ye, and believe the gospel.

Mk 2:17 — When Jesus heard *it,* he saith unto them, They that are whole have no need of the physician, but they that are sick: I came not to call the righteous, but sinners to repentance.

Mk 6:12 — And they went out, and preached that men should repent.

Lk 3:3 — And he came into all the country about Jordan, preaching the baptism of repentance for the remission of sins;

Lk 5:32 — I came not to call the righteous, but sinners to repentance.

Lk 6:21 — Blessed *are ye* that hunger now: for ye shall be filled. Blessed *are ye* that weep now: for ye shall laugh.

Lk 10:13 — Woe unto thee, Chorazin! woe unto thee, Bethsaida! for if the mighty works had been done in Tyre and Sidon, which have been done in you, they had a great while ago repented, sitting in sackcloth and ashes.

Lk 24:47 — And that repentance and remission of sins should be preached in his name among all nations, beginning at Jerusalem.

Ac 2:38 — Then Peter said unto them, Repent, and be baptized every one of you in the name of Jesus Christ for the remission of sins, and ye shall receive the gift of the Holy Ghost.

Ac 2:40 — And with many other words did he testify and exhort, saying, Save yourselves from this untoward generation.

Ac 3:19 — Repent ye therefore, and be converted, that your sins may be blotted out, when the times of refreshing shall come from the presence of the Lord;

Ac 5:31 — Him hath God exalted with his right hand *to be* a Prince and a Saviour, for to give repentance to Israel, and forgiveness of sins.

Ac 8:22 — Repent therefore of this thy wickedness, and pray God, if perhaps the thought of thine heart may be forgiven thee.

Ac 17:30 — And the times of this ignorance God winked at; but now commandeth all men every where to repent:

Ac 20:21 — Testifying both to the Jews, and also to the Greeks, repentance toward God, and faith toward our Lord Jesus Christ.

Ac 26:20 — But shewed first unto them of Damascus, and at Jerusalem, and throughout all the coasts of Judaea, and *then* to the Gentiles, that they should repent and turn to God, and do works meet for repentance.

Ro 2:4 — Or despisest thou the riches of his goodness and forbearance and longsuffering; not knowing that the goodness of God leadeth thee to repentance?

Ro 11:23 — And they also, if they abide not still in unbelief, shall be graffed in: for God is able to graff them in again.

Ro 14:11 — For it is written, *As* I live, saith the Lord, every knee shall bow to me, and every tongue shall confess to God.

Eph 5:14 — Wherefore he saith, Awake thou that sleepest, and arise from the dead, and Christ shall give thee light.

2Ti 2:25 — In meekness instructing those that oppose themselves; if God peradventure will give them repentance to the acknowledging of the truth;

Heb 6:1 — Therefore leaving the principles of the doctrine of Christ, let us go on unto perfection; not laying again the foundation of repentance from dead works, and of faith toward God,

1Jn 1:9 — If we confess our sins, he is faithful and just to forgive us *our* sins, and to cleanse us from all unrighteousness.

Rev 2:5 — Remember therefore from whence thou art fallen, and repent, and do the first works; or else I will come unto thee quickly, and will remove thy candlestick out of his place, except thou repent.

Rev 2:16 — Repent; or else I will come unto thee quickly, and will fight against them with the sword of my mouth.

Rev 3:19 — As many as I love, I rebuke and chasten: be zealous therefore, and repent.

See: Conviction

See: Penitence

See: Remorse

See: Sin; confession of

See: Sin; forgiveness of

• Instances of.

• Joseph's brethren, of their maltreatment of Joseph.
Ge 42:21; 50:17–18

• Pharaoh, of his hardness of heart.
Ex 9:27; 10:16–17

• Balaam, of his spiritual blindness.
Nu 22:24–35

• Israelites, of worshiping the golden calf.
Ex 33:3–4

• Israelites, murmuring on account of lack of bread and water; plague of serpents came.
Nu 21:4–7

• Israelites, when rebuked by an angel for not expelling the Canaanites.
Jgs 2:1–5

• Israelites, of their idolatry, when afflicted by the Philistines.
Jgs 10:6–16; 1Sa 7:3–6

• Israelites, in asking for a king.
1Sa 12:16–20

• Israelites, in the time of Asa, under the preaching of Azariah.
2Ch 15:1–15

• Israelites, under the preaching of Obed.
2Ch 28:9–15

• **Israelites, under the influence of Hezekiah.**
2Ch 30:11

• **Achan, of his theft.**
Jos 7:20

• **Saul, at the reproof of Samuel for not destroying the Amalekites.**
1Sa 15:6–31

• **David, at the rebuke of Nathan, the prophet, of his sins of adultery and murder.**
2Sa 12:7–14

See: Psalms; penitential

• **Rehoboam, when his kingdom was invaded, and Jerusalem besieged.**
2Ch 12:1–12

• **Hezekiah, at the time of his sickness.**
2Ch 32:26

• **Hezekiah, when reproved by the prophet Micah.**
Jer 26:18–19

• **Ahab, when reproved by Elijah for his idolatry.**
1Ki 21:17–29

• **Jehoahaz.**
2Ki 13:4

• **Josiah, when he heard the law which had been discovered in the temple by Hilkiah.**
2Ki 22:11–20

• **Manasseh, when he was carried captive to Babylon by the king of Assyria.**
2Ch 33:12–13

• **The Jews of the captivity, at the dedication of the temple.**
Ezr 6:21

• **The Jews of the captivity, of their idolatrous marriages.**
Ezr 10:1–44

• **The Jews of the captivity, of their oppressive usury.**
Ne 5:1–13

• **The Jews of the captivity, after hearing the law expounded by Ezra.**
Ne 8:1–12; 9:1–3

• **The Jews of the captivity, under the preaching of Haggai.**
Hag 1:1–15

• **Jonah, after his punishment.**
Jnh 2:2–9

• **The Ninevites, under the preaching of Jonah.**
Jnh 3:5–9

• **The Jews, under the preaching of John the Baptist.**
Mt 3:6

• **The woman who anointed Jesus with oil.**
Lk 7:37–48

• **The disobedient son.**
Mt 21:29

• **The prodigal son.**
Lk 15:17–21

• **Peter, of his denial of Jesus.**
Mt 26:75; Mk 14:72; Lk 22:62

• **Judas.**
Mt 27:3–5; Ac 1:16, 18

• **The Ephesians, under the preaching of Paul.**
Ac 19:18

• **Exemplified.**
Ezr 9:13–14; Ne 1:6–7; 9:16–37; Job 42:5–6; Ps 38:3–4; 51:1–4, 7–17; 73:21–22; 119:59–60; 130:1–3; Isa 59:12–15; 64:5–7; Jer 3:21–22; 31:18–19; La 3:40–41; Da 9:5–7; Lk 15:17–20; 2Co 7:9–11

Nu 21:7 — Therefore the people came to Moses, and said, We have sinned, for we have spoken against the LORD, and against thee; pray unto the LORD, that he take away the serpents from us. And Moses prayed for the people.

2Sa 24:10 — And David's heart smote him after that he had numbered the people. And David said unto the LORD, I have sinned greatly in that I have done: and now, I beseech thee, O LORD, take away the iniquity of thy servant; for I have done very foolishly.

2Sa 24:17 — And David spake unto the LORD when he saw the angel that smote the people, and said, Lo, I have sinned, and I have done wickedly: but these sheep, what have they done? let thine hand, I pray thee, be against me, and against my father's house.

1Ch 21:17 — And David said unto God, *Is it* not I *that* commanded the people to be numbered? even I it is that have sinned and done evil indeed; but *as for* these sheep, what have they done? let thine hand, I pray thee, O LORD my God, be on me, and on my father's house; but not on thy people, that they should be plagued.

2Ch 29:6 — For our fathers have trespassed, and done *that which was* evil in the eyes of the LORD our God, and have forsaken him, and have turned away their faces from the habitation of the LORD, and turned *their* backs.

Ezr 9:4 — Then were assembled unto me every one that trembled at the words of the God of Israel, because of the transgression of those that had been carried away; and I sat astonied until the evening sacrifice.

Ezr 9:6 — And said, O my God, I am ashamed and blush to lift up my face to thee, my God: for our iniquities are increased over *our* head, and our trespass is grown up unto the heavens.

Ezr 9:10 — And now, O our God, what shall we say after this? for we have forsaken thy commandments,

Job 7:20 — I have sinned; what shall I do unto thee, O thou preserver of men? why hast thou set me as a mark against thee, so that I am a burden to myself?

Job 9:20 — If I justify myself, mine own mouth shall condemn me: *if I say, I am* perfect, it shall also prove me perverse.

Job 13:23 — How many *are* mine iniquities and sins? make me to know my transgression and my sin.

Job 40:4 — Behold, I am vile; what shall I answer thee? I will lay mine hand upon my mouth.

Ps 32:5 — I acknowledged my sin unto thee, and mine iniquity have I not hid. I said, I will confess my transgressions unto the LORD; and thou forgavest the iniquity of my sin. Selah.

Ps 38:18 — For I will declare mine iniquity; I will be sorry for my sin.

Ps 40:12 — For innumerable evils have compassed me about: mine iniquities have taken hold upon me, so that I am not able to look up; they are more than the hairs of mine head: therefore my heart faileth me.

Ps 41:4 — I said, LORD, be merciful unto me: heal my soul; for I have sinned against thee.

Ps 69:5 — O God, thou knowest my foolishness; and my sins are not hid from thee.

Ps 69:10 — When I wept, *and chastened* my soul with fasting, that was to my reproach.

Ps 106:6 — We have sinned with our fathers, we have committed iniquity, we have done wickedly.

Ps 119:176 — I have gone astray like a lost sheep; seek thy servant; for I do not forget thy commandments.

Isa 6:5 — Then said I, Woe *is* me! for I am undone; because I *am* a man of unclean lips, and I dwell in the midst of a people of unclean lips: for mine eyes have seen the King, the LORD of hosts.

Isa 38:15 — What shall I say? he hath both spoken unto me, and himself hath done *it:* I shall go softly all my years in the bitterness of my soul.

Isa 38:17 — Behold, for peace I had great bitterness: but thou hast in love to my soul *delivered it* from the pit of corruption: for thou hast cast all my sins behind thy back.

Jer 3:25 — We lie down in our shame, and our confusion covereth us: for we have sinned against the LORD our God, we and our fathers, from our youth even unto this day, and have not obeyed the voice of the LORD our God.

Jer 8:14 — Why do we sit still? assemble yourselves, and let us enter into the defenced cities, and let us be silent there: for the LORD our God hath put us to silence, and given us water of gall to drink, because we have sinned against the LORD.

Jer 14:7 — O LORD, though our iniquities testify against us, do thou *it* for thy name's sake: for our backslidings are many; we have sinned against thee.

Jer 14:20 — We acknowledge, O LORD, our wickedness, *and* the iniquity of our fathers: for we have sinned against thee.

Da 10:12 — Then said he unto me, Fear not, Daniel: for from the first day that thou didst set thine heart to understand, and to chasten thyself before thy God, thy words were heard, and I am come for thy words.

Hos 6:1 — Come, and let us return unto the LORD: for he hath torn, and he will heal us; he hath smitten, and he will bind us up.

Hos 14:3 — Asshur shall not save us; we will not ride upon horses: neither will we say any more to the work of our hands, *Ye are* our gods: for in thee the fatherless findeth mercy.

Hos 14:8 — Ephraim *shall say,* What have I to do any more with idols? I have heard *him,* and observed him: I *am* like a green fir tree. From me is thy fruit found.

Jnh 3:10 — And God saw their works, that they turned from their evil way; and God repented of the evil, that he had said that he would do unto them; and he did *it* not.

Mic 7:9 — I will bear the indignation of the LORD, because I have sinned against him, until he plead my cause, and execute judgment for me: he will bring me forth to the light, *and* I shall behold his righteousness.

1Co 15:9 — For I am the least of the apostles, that am not meet to be called an apostle, because I persecuted the church of God.

1Pe 2:25 — For ye were as sheep going astray; but are now returned unto the Shepherd and Bishop of your souls.

✣See: Sin; confession of

REPETITION

• In prayers.

✣See: Prayer

REPHAEL • A porter of the temple in the time of David.

1Ch 26:7 — The sons of Shemaiah; Othni, and Rephael, and Obed, Elzabad, whose brethren *were* strong men, Elihu, and Semachiah.

REPHAH • A grandson of Ephraim.

1Ch 7:25 — And Rephah *was* his son, also Resheph, and Telah his son, and Tahan his son,

REPHAIAH

• A descendant of David.

1Ch 3:21 — And the sons of Hananiah; Pelatiah, and Jesaiah: the sons of Rephaiah, the sons of Arnan, the sons of Obadiah, the sons of Shechaniah.

• A Simeonite captain.

1Ch 4:42 — And *some* of them, *even* of the sons of Simeon, five hundred men, went to mount Seir, having for their captains Pelatiah, and Neariah, and Rephaiah, and Uzziel, the sons of Ishi.

• Son of Tola, of the tribe of Issachar.

1Ch 7:2 — And the sons of Tola; Uzzi, and Rephaiah, and Jeriel, and Jahmai, and Jibsam, and Shemuel, heads of their father's house, *to wit,* of Tola: *they were* valiant men of might in their generations; whose number *was* in the days of David two and twenty thousand and six hundred.

• A descendant of Jonathan.

1Ch 9:43 — And Moza begat Binea; and Rephaiah his son, Eleasah his son, Azel his son.

• Called Rapha.

1Ch 8:37 — And Moza begat Binea: Rapha *was* his son, Eleasah his son, Azel his son:

• **Governor over half of Jerusalem in the time of Nehemiah.**

Ne 3:9 — And next unto them repaired Rephaiah the son of Hur, the ruler of the half part of Jerusalem.

REPHAIM

• **An ancient people of great stature from Palestine.**

Ge 14:5 — And in the fourteenth year came Chedorlaomer, and the kings that *were* with him, and smote the Rephaims in Ashteroth Karnaim, and the Zuzims in Ham, and the Emims in Shaveh Kiriathaim,

Ge 15:20 — And the Hittites, and the Perizzites, and the Rephaims,

Dt 2:11 — Which also were accounted giants, as the Anakims; but the Moabites call them Emims.

Dt 2:20 — (That also was accounted a land of giants: giants dwelt therein in old time; and the Ammonites call them Zamzummims;

Dt 3:11 — For only Og king of Bashan remained of the remnant of giants; behold, his bedstead *was* a bedstead of iron; is it not in Rabbath of the children of Ammon? nine cubits was the length thereof, and four cubits the breadth of it, after the cubit of a man.

Dt 3:13 — And the rest of Gilead, and all Bashan, *being* the kingdom of Og, gave I unto the half tribe of Manasseh; all the region of Argob, with all Bashan, which was called the land of giants.

Jos 12:4 — And the coast of Og king of Bashan, *which was* of the remnant of the giants, that dwelt at Ashtaroth and at Edrei,

Jos 13:12 — All the kingdom of Og in Bashan, which reigned in Ashtaroth and in Edrei, who remained of the remnant of the giants: for these did Moses smite, and cast them out.

Jos 17:15 — And Joshua answered them, If thou *be* a great people, *then* get thee up to the wood *country*, and cut down for thyself there in the land of the Perizzites and of the giants, if mount Ephraim be too narrow for thee.

• **A valley. Boundary between Judah and Benjamin.**

Jos 15:8 — And the border went up by the valley of the son of Hinnom unto the south side of the Jebusite; the same *is* Jerusalem: and the border went up to the top of the mountain that *lieth* before the valley of Hinnom westward, which *is* at the end of the valley of the giants northward:

Jos 18:16 — And the border came down to the end of the mountain that *lieth* before the valley of the son of Hinnom, *and* which *is* in the valley of the giants on the north, and descended to the valley of Hinnom, to the side of Jebusi on the south, and descended to En-rogel,

• **Battle ground of David and the Philistines.**

2Sa 5:18 — The Philistines also came and spread themselves in the valley of Rephaim.

2Sa 5:22 — And the Philistines came up yet again, and spread themselves in the valley of Rephaim.

2Sa 23:13 — And three of the thirty chief went down, and came to David in the harvest time unto the cave of Adullam: and the troop of the Philistines pitched in the valley of Rephaim.

1Ch 11:15 — Now three of the thirty captains went down to the rock to David, into the cave of Adullam; and the host of the Philistines encamped in the valley of Rephaim.

1Ch 14:9 — And the Philistines came and spread themselves in the valley of Rephaim.

• **Productiveness of.**

Isa 17:5 — And it shall be as when the harvestman gathereth the corn, and reapeth the ears with his arm; and it shall be as he that gathereth ears in the valley of Rephaim.

REPHIDIM • A camping place of Israel in the forty years of wandering.

Nu 33:14–15

Ex 17:1 — And all the congregation of the children of Israel journeyed from the wilderness of Sin, after their journeys, according to the commandment of the LORD, and pitched in Rephidim: and *there was* no water for the people to drink.

Ex 17:8 — Then came Amalek, and fought with Israel in Rephidim.

Ex 19:2 — For they were departed from Rephidim, and were come *to* the desert of Sinai, and had pitched in the wilderness; and there Israel camped before the mount.

REPORTING

Ac 14:27 — And when they were come, and had gathered the church together, they rehearsed all that God had done with them, and how he had opened the door of faith unto the Gentiles.

1Co 1:11 — For it hath been declared unto me of you, my brethren, by them *which are of the house* of Chloe, that there are contentions among you.

1Co 5:1 — It is reported commonly *that there is* fornication among you, and such fornication as is not so much as named among the Gentiles, that one should have his father's wife.

REPORTS

• **Majority and minority.**

• **Of spies.**

Nu 13:26–33; 14:6–10

REPROBACY

Ge 6:5–7; Dt 28:15–68; 31:17–18; Ps 81:11–12; Pr 1:24–28; Isa 6:9–10; 22:12–14; 29:9–12; Mt 13:14–15; 25:8–13; Lk 13:24–28; Ro 9:21–22; 11:7–8, 17–20; 2Co 13:5–7; 2Th 2:7–12; Heb 3:10–12, 17–19; 6:4–8; 10:26–31; 12:15–17; Jude 1:4–13

Ge 19:13 — For we will destroy this place, because the cry of them is waxen great before the face of the LORD; and the LORD hath sent us to destroy it.

Isa 28:13 — But the word of the LORD was unto them precept upon precept, precept upon precept; line upon line, line upon line; here a little, *and* there a little; that they might go, and fall backward, and be broken, and snared, and taken.

Isa 65:12 — Therefore will I number you to the sword, and ye shall all bow down to the slaughter: because when I called, ye did not answer; when I spake, ye did not hear; but did evil before mine eyes, and did choose *that* wherein I delighted not.

Jer 6:30 — Reprobate silver shall *men* call them, because the LORD hath rejected them.

Jer 7:16 — Therefore pray not thou for this people, neither lift up cry nor prayer for them, neither make intercession to me: for I will not hear thee.

Jer 15:1 — Then said the LORD unto me, Though Moses and Samuel stood before me, *yet* my mind *could* not *be* toward this people: cast *them* out of my sight, and let them go forth.

Hos 5:6 — They shall go with their flocks and with their herds to seek the LORD; but they shall not find *him;* he hath withdrawn himself from them.

Mt 15:14 — Let them alone: they be blind leaders of the blind. And if the blind lead the blind, both shall fall into the ditch.

Mk 3:29 — But he that shall blaspheme against the Holy Ghost hath never forgiveness, but is in danger of eternal damnation:

Lk 14:24 — For I say unto you, That none of those men which were bidden shall taste of my supper.

Jn 10:26 — But ye believe not, because ye are not of my sheep, as I said unto you.

Jn 17:12 — While I was with them in the world, I kept them in thy name: those that thou gavest me I have kept, and none of them is lost, but the son of perdition; that the scripture might be fulfilled.

2Ti 3:8 — Now as Jannes and Jambres withstood Moses, so do these also resist the truth: men of corrupt minds, reprobate concerning the faith.

1Jn 5:16 — If any man see his brother sin a sin *which is* not unto death, he shall ask, and he shall give him life for them that sin not unto death. There is a sin unto death: I do not say that he shall pray for it.

Rev 22:11 — He that is unjust, let him be unjust still: and he which is filthy, let him be filthy still: and he that is righteous, let him be righteous still: and he that is holy, let him be holy still.

See: Obduracy

- **Instances of.**
  - **Israel.**
    Nu 14:26–45; Dt 1:42–43
  - **Eli's house.**
    1Sa 3:14
  - **Saul.**
    1Sa 15:23; 16:14; 18:12; 28:15

REPRODUCTION **See: Propagation**

REPROOF

Pr 9:7–8; 15:31–32; 27:5–6; Mt 18:15–17; Lk 17:3–4; 1Ti 5:1–2

Le 19:17 — Thou shalt not hate thy brother in thine heart: thou shalt in any wise rebuke thy neighbour, and not suffer sin upon him.

Ps 141:5 — Let the righteous smite me; *it shall be* a kindness: and let him reprove me; *it shall be* an excellent oil, *which* shall not break my head: for yet my prayer also *shall be* in their calamities.

Pr 10:17 — He *is in* the way of life that keepeth instruction: but he that refuseth reproof erreth.

Pr 12:1 — Whoso loveth instruction loveth knowledge: but he that hateth reproof *is* brutish.

Pr 13:18 — Poverty and shame *shall be to* him that refuseth instruction: but he that regardeth reproof shall be honoured.

Pr 15:5 — A fool despiseth his father's instruction: but he that regardeth reproof is prudent.

Pr 15:10 — Correction *is* grievous unto him that forsaketh the way: *and* he that hateth reproof shall die.

Pr 15:12 — A scorner loveth not one that reproveth him: neither will he go unto the wise.

Pr 17:10 — A reproof entereth more into a wise man than an hundred stripes into a fool.

Pr 19:25 — Smite a scorner, and the simple will beware: and reprove one that hath understanding, *and* he will understand knowledge.

Pr 21:11 — When the scorner is punished, the simple is made wise: and when the wise is instructed, he receiveth knowledge.

Pr 25:12 — *As* an earring of gold, and an ornament of fine gold, *so is* a wise reprover upon an obedient ear.

Pr 26:5 — Answer a fool according to his folly, lest he be wise in his own conceit.

Pr 28:23 — He that rebuketh a man afterwards shall find more favour than he that flattereth with the tongue.

Ecc 7:5 — *It is* better to hear the rebuke of the wise, than for a man to hear the song of fools.

Am 5:10 — They hate him that rebuketh in the gate, and they abhor him that speaketh uprightly.

Jn 7:7 — The world cannot hate you; but me it hateth, because I testify of it, that the works thereof are evil.

Gal 4:16 — Am I therefore become your enemy, because I tell you the truth?

Eph 4:15 — But speaking the truth in love, may grow up into him in all things, which is the head, *even* Christ:

Eph 5:11 — And have no fellowship with the unfruitful works of darkness, but rather reprove *them.*

Eph 5:13 — But all things that are reproved are made manifest by the light: for whatsoever doth make manifest is light.

Php 3:1 — Finally, my brethren, rejoice in the Lord. To write the same things to you, to me indeed *is* not grievous, but for you *it is* safe.

1Th 5:14 — Now we exhort you, brethren, warn them that are unruly, comfort the feebleminded, support the weak, be patient toward all *men.*

1Ti 5:20 — Them that sin rebuke before all, that others also may fear.

2Ti 4:2 — Preach the word; be instant in season, out of season; reprove, rebuke, exhort with all longsuffering and doctrine.

Tit 1:13 — This witness is true. Wherefore rebuke them sharply, that they may be sound in the faith;

Heb 3:13 — But exhort one another daily, while it is called To day; lest any of you be hardened through the deceitfulness of sin.

Rev 11:10 — And they that dwell upon the earth shall rejoice over them, and make merry, and shall send gifts one to another; because these two prophets tormented them that dwelt on the earth.

- **Faithfulness in.**
  - **Instances of.**
    - **Moses, of Pharaoh.**

      Ex 10:29 — And Moses said, Thou hast spoken well, I will see thy face again no more.

      Ex 11:8 — And all these thy servants shall come down unto me, and bow down themselves unto me, saying, Get thee out, and all the people that follow thee: and after that I will go out. And he went out from Pharaoh in a great anger.
    - **Moses, of the Israelites.**

      Ex 16:6–7; 32:19–30; Dt 1:26–43; 9:16–24; 29:2–4; 31:27–29; 32:15–18

      Nu 14:41 — And Moses said, Wherefore now do ye transgress the commandment of the LORD? but it shall not prosper.

      Nu 20:10 — And Moses and Aaron gathered the congregation together before the rock, and he said unto them, Hear now, ye rebels; must we fetch you water out of this rock?

      Nu 32:14 — And, behold, ye are risen up in your fathers' stead, an increase of sinful men, to augment yet the fierce anger of the LORD toward Israel.

      Dt 1:12 — How can I myself alone bear your cumbrance, and your burden, and your strife?
    - **Moses, of Eleazar.**

      Le 10:16–18
    - **Moses, of Korah.**

      Nu 16:9–11
    - **Israelites, of the two and one-half tribes.**

      Jos 22:15–20
    - **Israelites, of the tribe of Benjamin.**

      Jgs 20:12–13
    - **Samuel, of Saul.**

      1Sa 15:14–35
    - **Jonathan, of Saul.**

      1Sa 19:4–5
    - **Nathan, of David.**

      2Sa 12:1–9
    - **Joab, of David.**

      2Sa 19:1–7

      2Sa 24:3 — And Joab said unto the king, Now the LORD thy God add unto the people, how many soever they be, an hundredfold, and that the eyes of my lord the king may see *it:* but why doth my lord the king delight in this thing?

      1Ch 21:3 — And Joab answered, The LORD make his people an hundred times so many more as they *be:* but, my lord the king, *are* they not all my lord's servants? why then doth my lord require this thing? why will he be a cause of trespass to Israel?
    - **The prophet Gad, of David.**

      2Sa 24:13 — So Gad came to David, and told him, and said unto him, Shall seven years of famine come unto thee in thy land? or wilt thou flee three months before thine enemies, while they pursue thee? or that there be three days' pestilence in thy land? now advise, and see what answer I shall return to him that sent me.
    - **Shemaiah, of Rehoboam.**

      2Ch 12:5 — Then came Shemaiah the prophet to Rehoboam, and *to* the princes of Judah, that were gathered together to Jerusalem because of Shishak, and said unto them, Thus saith the LORD, Ye have forsaken me, and therefore have I also left you in the hand of Shishak.
    - **A prophet of Judah, of Jeroboam.**

      1Ki 13:1–10; 2Ch 13:8–11
    - **Elijah, of Ahab.**

      1Ki 18:18–21; 21:20–24
    - **Elijah, of Ahaziah.**

      2Ki 1:1–18
    - **Micaiah, of Ahab.**

      1Ki 22:14–28
    - **Elisha, of Jehoram.**

      2Ki 3:13–14
    - **Elisha, of Gehazi.**

      2Ki 5:26 — And he said unto him, Went not mine heart *with thee,* when the man turned again from his chariot to meet thee? *Is it* a time to receive money, and to receive garments, and oliveyards, and vineyards, and sheep, and oxen, and menservants, and maidservants?
    - **Elisha, of Hazael.**

      2Ki 8:11–13
    - **Elisha, of Jeroboam.**

      2Ki 13:19 — And the man of God was wroth with him, and said, Thou shouldest have smitten five or six times; then hadst thou smitten Syria till thou hadst consumed *it:* whereas now thou shalt smite Syria *but* thrice.
    - **Isaiah, of Hezekiah.**

      2Ki 20:17 — Behold, the days come, that all that *is* in thine house, and that which thy fathers have laid up in store unto this day, shall be carried into Babylon: nothing shall be left, saith the LORD.
    - **Jehoash, of Jehoiada.**

      2Ki 12:7 — Then king Jehoash called for Jehoiada the priest, and the *other* priests, and said unto them, Why repair ye not the breaches of the house? now therefore receive no *more* money of your acquaintance, but deliver it for the breaches of the house.
    - **Azariah, of Asa.**

      2Ch 15:2 — And he went out to meet Asa, and said unto him, Hear ye me, Asa, and all Judah and Benjamin; The LORD *is* with you, while ye be with him; and if ye seek him, he will be found of you; but if ye forsake him, he will forsake you.
    - **Azariah, of Uzziah.**

      2Ch 26:17–18
    - **Hanani, of Asa.**

      2Ch 16:7–9

- **Jehu, of Jehoshaphat.**
  2Ch 19:2 — And Jehu the son of Hanani the seer went out to meet him, and said to king Jehoshaphat, Shouldest thou help the ungodly, and love them that hate the LORD? therefore is wrath upon thee from before the LORD.
- **Zechariah, of the princes of Judah.**
  2Ch 24:20 — And the Spirit of God came upon Zechariah the son of Jehoiada the priest, which stood above the people, and said unto them, Thus saith God, Why transgress ye the commandments of the LORD, that ye cannot prosper? because ye have forsaken the LORD, he hath also forsaken you.
- **Oded, of the people of Samaria.**
  2Ch 28:9–11
- **Jeremiah, of the cities of Judah.**
  Jer 26:8–11
- **Ezra, of the men of Judah and Benjamin.**
  Ezr 10:10 — And Ezra the priest stood up, and said unto them, Ye have transgressed, and have taken strange wives, to increase the trespass of Israel.
- **Nehemiah, of the Jews.**
  Ne 5:6–13
- **Nehemiah, of the corruptions in the temple, and of the violation of the Sabbath.**
  Ne 13:1–31
- **Daniel, of Nebuchadnezzar.**
  Da 4:27 — Wherefore, O king, let my counsel be acceptable unto thee, and break off thy sins by righteousness, and thine iniquities by shewing mercy to the poor; if it may be a lengthening of thy tranquility.
- **Daniel, of Belshazzar.**
  Da 5:17–24
- **Amos, of the Israelites.**
  Am 7:12–17
- **Jesus, of the Jews; when Pharisees and Sadducees came to him desiring a sign.**
  Mt 16:1–4; Mk 8:11–12
- **Jesus, of the scribes and Pharisees.**
  Mt 23:1–39; Lk 11:37–54
- **Jesus, of the Pharisees.**
  Lk 16:1–31
- **Jesus, when they brought the woman to him who was taken in adultery.**
  Jn 8:7 — So when they continued asking him, he lifted up himself, and said unto them, He that is without sin among you, let him first cast a stone at her.
- **In his parable of the king's feast.**
  Lk 14:16–24
- **In his parable of the two sons.**
  Mt 21:28–32
- **In his parable of the vineyard.**
  Mt 21:33–46; Mk 12:1–12; Lk 20:9–20
- **In his parable of the barren fig tree.**
  Lk 13:6–9
- **In his parable of the withering of the fig tree.**
  Mt 21:17–20; Mk 11:12–14
- **John the Baptist, of the Jews.**
  Mt 3:7–12; Lk 3:7–9
- **John the Baptist, of Herod.**
  Lk 3:19–20
  Mt 14:3 — For Herod had laid hold on John, and bound him, and put *him* in prison for Herodias' sake, his brother Philip's wife.
  Mk 6:17 — For Herod himself had sent forth and laid hold upon John, and bound him in prison for Herodias' sake, his brother Philip's wife: for he had married her.
- **Peter, of Simon, the sorcerer.**
  Ac 8:20–23
- **Stephen, of the high priest.**
  Ac 7:51–53
- **Paul, of Elymas, the sorcerer.**
  Ac 13:9–11
- **Paul, of Ananias the high priest.**
  Ac 23:3 — Then said Paul unto him, God shall smite thee, *thou* whited wall: for sittest thou to judge me after the law, and commandest me to be smitten contrary to the law?
- **Paul and Silas, of the magistrates of Philippi.**
  Ac 16:37–40

• Despised.

- **By the Israelites.**
  Nu 14:9–10
  Jer 26:11 — Then spake the priests and the prophets unto the princes and to all the people, saying, This man *is* worthy to die; for he hath prophesied against this city, as ye have heard with your ears.
- **By Ahab.**
  1Ki 18:17 — And it came to pass, when Ahab saw Elijah, that Ahab said unto him, *Art* thou he that troubleth Israel?
  1Ki 21:20 — And Ahab said to Elijah, Hast thou found me, O mine enemy? And he answered, I have found *thee:* because thou hast sold thyself to work evil in the sight of the LORD.
  1Ki 22:8 — And the king of Israel said unto Jehoshaphat, *There is* yet one man, Micaiah the son of Imlah, by whom we may enquire of the LORD: but I hate him; for he doth not prophesy good concerning me, but evil. And Jehoshaphat said, Let not the king say so.
- **By Asa.**
  2Ch 16:10 — Then Asa was wroth with the seer, and put him in a prison house; for *he was* in a rage with him because of this *thing.* And Asa oppressed *some* of the people the same time.
- **By Herodias.**
  Mk 6:18–19
- **By people of Nazareth.**
  Lk 4:28–29

• **Jews.**

Ac 5:33 — When they heard *that,* they were cut *to the heart,* and took counsel to slay them.

Ac 7:54 — When they heard these things, they were cut to the heart, and they gnashed on him with *their* teeth.

See: Reprobacy

REPUTATION

• Good.

Pr 22:1 — A *good* name *is* rather to be chosen than great riches, *and* loving favour rather than silver and gold.

Ecc 7:1 — A good name *is* better than precious ointment; and the day of death than the day of one's birth.

See: Character of Saints

See: Name

RESHEPH • Grandson of Ephraim.

1Ch 7:25 — And Rephah *was* his son, also Resheph, and Telah his son, and Tahan his son,

RESIGNATION

Php 4:11–13; Heb 12:3–12; 1Pe 4:12–13

Job 5:17 — Behold, happy *is* the man whom God correcteth: therefore despise not thou the chastening of the Almighty:

Job 34:31 — Surely it is meet to be said unto God, I have borne *chastisement,* I will not offend *any more:*

Ps 4:4 — Stand in awe, and sin not: commune with your own heart upon your bed, and be still. Selah.

Ps 46:10 — Be still, and know that I *am* God: I will be exalted among the heathen, I will be exalted in the earth.

Pr 3:11 — My son, despise not the chastening of the LORD; neither be weary of his correction:

Pr 18:14 — The spirit of a man will sustain his infirmity; but a wounded spirit who can bear?

Jer 51:50 — Ye that have escaped the sword, go away, stand not still: remember the LORD afar off, and let Jerusalem come into your mind.

La 3:39 — Wherefore doth a living man complain, a man for the punishment of his sins?

Mic 6:9 — The LORD's voice crieth unto the city, and *the man of* wisdom shall see thy name: hear ye the rod, and who hath appointed it.

Mt 6:10 — Thy kingdom come. Thy will be done in earth, as *it is* in heaven.

Lk 11:2 — And he said unto them, When ye pray, say, Our Father which art in heaven, Hallowed be thy name. Thy kingdom come. Thy will be done, as in heaven, so in earth.

Lk 21:19 — In your patience possess ye your souls.

Ro 12:12 — Rejoicing in hope; patient in tribulation; continuing instant in prayer;

Php 2:14 — Do all things without murmurings and disputings:

Col 1:11 — Strengthened with all might, according to his glorious power, unto all patience and longsuffering with joyfulness;

1Th 3:3 — That no man should be moved by these afflictions: for yourselves know that we are appointed thereunto.

2Ti 2:3 — Thou therefore endure hardness, as a good soldier of Jesus Christ.

2Ti 4:5 — But watch thou in all things, endure afflictions, do the work of an evangelist, make full proof of thy ministry.

Heb 10:34 — For ye had compassion of me in my bonds, and took joyfully the spoiling of your goods, knowing in yourselves that ye have in heaven a better and an enduring substance.

Jas 1:9 — Let the brother of low degree rejoice in that he is exalted:

Jas 4:7 — Submit yourselves therefore to God. Resist the devil, and he will flee from you.

Jas 5:13 — Is any among you afflicted? let him pray. Is any merry? let him sing psalms.

1Pe 1:6 — Wherein ye greatly rejoice, though now for a season, if need be, ye are in heaviness through manifold temptations:

1Pe 4:19 — Wherefore let them that suffer according to the will of God commit the keeping of their souls *to him* in well doing, as unto a faithful Creator.

• Exemplified.

Le 10:1–3; 2Sa 16:10–11; Job 1:13–22; 2:9–10; Lk 23:40–41; Ac 7:59–60; Ro 5:3–5; 2Co 6:3–11; Php 1:20–24

Jgs 10:15 — And the children of Israel said unto the LORD, We have sinned: do thou unto us whatsoever seemeth good unto thee; deliver us only, we pray thee, this day.

1Sa 3:18 — And Samuel told him every whit, and hid nothing from him. And he said, It *is* the LORD: let him do what seemeth him good.

2Sa 12:23 — But now he is dead, wherefore should I fast? can I bring him back again? I shall go to him, but he shall not return to me.

2Sa 15:26 — But if he thus say, I have no delight in thee; behold, *here am* I, let him do to me as seemeth good unto him.

2Sa 24:14 — And David said unto Gad, I am in a great strait: let us fall now into the hand of the LORD; for his mercies *are* great: and let me not fall into the hand of man.

2Ki 4:26 — Run now, I pray thee, to meet her, and say unto her, *Is it* well with thee? *is it* well with thy husband? *is it* well with the child? And she answered, *It is* well.

2Ki 20:19 — Then said Hezekiah unto Isaiah, Good is the word of the LORD which thou hast spoken. And he said, *Is it* not *good,* if peace and truth be in my days?

Ne 9:33 — Howbeit thou *art* just in all that is brought upon us; for thou hast done right, but we have done wickedly:

Est 4:16 — Go, gather together all the Jews that are present in Shushan, and fast ye for me, and neither eat nor drink three days, night or day: I also and my maidens will fast likewise; and so will I go in unto the king, which *is* not according to the law: and if I perish, I perish.

Ps 39:9 — I was dumb, I opened not my mouth; because thou didst *it.*

Ps 103:10 — He hath not dealt with us after our sins; nor rewarded us according to our iniquities.

Ps 119:75 — I know, O LORD, that thy judgments *are* right, and that *thou* in faithfulness hast afflicted me.

Isa 39:8 — Then said Hezekiah to Isaiah, Good *is* the word of the LORD which thou hast spoken. He said moreover, For there shall be peace and truth in my days.

Jer 10:19 — Woe is me for my hurt! my wound is grievous: but I said, Truly this *is* a grief, and I must bear it.

La 1:18 — The LORD is righteous; for I have rebelled against his commandment: hear, I pray you, all people, and behold my sorrow: my virgins and my young men are gone into captivity.

Da 9:14 — Therefore hath the LORD watched upon the evil, and brought it upon us: for the LORD our God *is* righteous in all his works which he doeth: for we obeyed not his voice.

Mic 7:9 — I will bear the indignation of the LORD, because I have sinned against him, until he plead my cause, and execute judgment for me: he will bring me forth to the light, *and* I shall behold his righteousness.

Mt 26:39 — And he went a little farther, and fell on his face, and prayed, saying, O my Father, if it be possible, let this cup pass from me: nevertheless not as I will, but as thou *wilt.*

Mk 14:36 — And he said, Abba, Father, all things *are* possible unto thee; take away this cup from me: nevertheless not what I will, but what thou wilt.

Lk 22:42 — Saying, Father, if thou be willing, remove this cup from me: nevertheless not my will, but thine, be done.

Jn 18:11 — Then said Jesus unto Peter, Put up thy sword into the sheath: the cup which my Father hath given me, shall I not drink it?

Ac 21:14 — And when he would not be persuaded, we ceased, saying, The will of the Lord be done.

2Co 7:4 — Great *is* my boldness of speech toward you, great *is* my glorying of you: I am filled with comfort, I am exceeding joyful in all our tribulation.

2Th 1:4 — So that we ourselves glory in you in the churches of God for your patience and faith in all your persecutions and tribulations that ye endure:

2Ti 4:6 — For I am now ready to be offered, and the time of my departure is at hand.

Jas 5:11 — Behold, we count them happy which endure. Ye have heard of the patience of Job, and have seen the end of the Lord; that the Lord is very pitiful, and of tender mercy.

➔See: Afflictions, Benefits of

➔See: Afflictions; resignation in

RESPECT

• To the aged.

Le 19:32 — Thou shalt rise up before the hoary head, and honour the face of the old man, and fear thy God: I *am* the LORD.

• To rulers.

Pr 25:6 — Put not forth thyself in the presence of the king, and stand not in the place of great *men:*

• To a host.

Lk 14:10 — But when thou art bidden, go and sit down in the lowest room; that when he that bade thee cometh, he may say unto thee, Friend, go up higher: then shalt thou have worship in the presence of them that sit at meat with thee.

• To one another.

Ro 12:10 — *Be* kindly affectioned one to another with brotherly love; in honour preferring one another;

Php 2:3 — *Let* nothing *be done* through strife or vainglory; but in lowliness of mind let each esteem other better than themselves.

1Pe 2:17 — Honour all *men.* Love the brotherhood. Fear God. Honour the king.

RESPECT OF PERSONS

Jas 2:1–9

Pr 24:23 — These *things* also *belong* to the wise. *It is* not good to have respect of persons in judgment.

Pr 28:21 — To have respect of persons *is* not good: for for a piece of bread *that* man will transgress.

• God does not have.

Job 31:13–15; Ro 2:11–12; Eph 6:8–9

Dt 10:17 — For the LORD your God *is* God of gods, and Lord of lords, a great God, a mighty, and a terrible, which regardeth not persons, nor taketh reward:

2Ch 19:7 — Wherefore now let the fear of the LORD be upon you; take heed and do *it:* for *there is* no iniquity with the LORD our God, nor respect of persons, nor taking of gifts.

Job 34:19 — *How much less to him* that accepteth not the persons of princes, nor regardeth the rich more than the poor? for they all *are* the work of his hands.

Ac 10:34 — Then Peter opened *his* mouth, and said, Of a truth I perceive that God is no respecter of persons:

Ac 15:9 — And put no difference between us and them, purifying their hearts by faith.

Ro 10:12 — For there is no difference between the Jew and the Greek: for the same Lord over all is rich unto all that call upon him.

Col 3:25 — But he that doeth wrong shall receive for the wrong which he hath done: and there is no respect of persons.

1Pe 1:17 — And if ye call on the Father, who without respect of persons judgeth according to every man's work, pass the time of your sojourning *here* in fear:

➔See: God, Judge, and His Justice

➔See: Justice

RESPONSIBILITY

• Attempts to shift.

• Adam.

Ge 3:12–13

• Eve.

Ge 3:13 — And the LORD God said unto the woman, What *is* this *that* thou hast done? And the woman said, The serpent beguiled me, and I did eat.

• **Sarah.**

Ge 16:2 — And Sarai said unto Abram, Behold now, the LORD hath restrained me from bearing: I pray thee, go in unto my maid; it may be that I may obtain children by her. And Abram hearkened to the voice of Sarai.

Ge 16:5 — And Sarai said unto Abram, My wrong *be* upon thee: I have given my maid into thy bosom; and when she saw that she had conceived, I was despised in her eyes: the LORD judge between me and thee.

• **Esau.**

Ge 25:29–34

Ge 27:36 — And he said, Is not he rightly named Jacob? for he hath supplanted me these two times: he took away my birthright; and, behold, now he hath taken away my blessing. And he said, Hast thou not reserved a blessing for me?

• **Aaron.**

Ex 32:22–24

• **Saul.**

1Sa 15:20–21

• **Pilate.**

Mt 27:24 — When Pilate saw that he could prevail nothing, but *that* rather a tumult was made, he took water, and washed *his* hands before the multitude, saying, I am innocent of the blood of this just person: see ye *to it.*

• **Assumed by the Jews for the death of Jesus.**

Mt 27:25 — Then answered all the people, and said, His blood *be* on us, and on our children.

• **Personal.**

Jn 15:22–24; 1Co 3:13–15

Eze 18:20 — The soul that sinneth, it shall die. The son shall not bear the iniquity of the father, neither shall the father bear the iniquity of the son: the righteousness of the righteous shall be upon him, and the wickedness of the wicked shall be upon him.

Eze 18:30 — Therefore I will judge you, O house of Israel, every one according to his ways, saith the Lord GOD. Repent, and turn *yourselves* from all your transgressions; so iniquity shall not be your ruin.

Mt 12:37 — For by thy words thou shalt be justified, and by thy words thou shalt be condemned.

Jn 9:41 — Jesus said unto them, If ye were blind, ye should have no sin: but now ye say, We see; therefore your sin remaineth.

1Co 3:8 — Now he that planteth and he that watereth are one: and every man shall receive his own reward according to his own labour.

Gal 6:5 — For every man shall bear his own burden.

Rev 2:23 — And I will kill her children with death; and all the churches shall know that I am he which searcheth the reins and hearts: and I will give unto every one of you according to your works.

• **According to privilege.**

Eze 18:1–30; 33:1–19; Mt 10:11–15; 11:20–24; 12:41–42; 23:31–35; 25:14–30; Lk 10:10–15; 11:31–32; 49–51; 13:6–9; 19:12–27; 21:1–4; Jn 3:18–19; Ac 17:30–31; Ro 12:6–8

Mk 6:11 — And whosoever shall not receive you, nor hear you, when ye depart thence, shake off the dust under your feet for a testimony against them. Verily I say unto you, It shall be more tolerable for Sodom and Gomorrha in the day of judgment, than for that city.

Lk 9:5 — And whosoever will not receive you, when ye go out of that city, shake off the very dust from your feet for a testimony against them.

Jn 12:48 — He that rejecteth me, and receiveth not my words, hath one that judgeth him: the word that I have spoken, the same shall judge him in the last day.

Jn 15:22 — If I had not come and spoken unto them, they had not had sin: but now they have no cloke for their sin.

Jn 15:24 — If I had not done among them the works which none other man did, they had not had sin: but now have they both seen and hated both me and my Father.

Ro 12:3 — For I say, through the grace given unto me, to every man that is among you, not to think *of himself* more highly than he ought to think; but to think soberly, according as God hath dealt to every man the measure of faith.

Eph 4:7 — But unto every one of us is given grace according to the measure of the gift of Christ.

1Ti 6:20 — O Timothy, keep that which is committed to thy trust, avoiding profane *and* vain babblings, and oppositions of science falsely so called:

See: Judgment; according to opportunity and works

See: Privilege

RESPONSIVE RELIGIOUS SERVICE

Dt 27:14–26

RESSURECTION

1Co 15:1–58; 1Th 4:13–18

Ac 3:15 — And killed the Prince of life, whom God hath raised from the dead; whereof we are witnesses.

Ac 13:30 — But God raised him from the dead:

Ac 13:34 — And as concerning that he raised him up from the dead, *now* no more to return to corruption, he said on this wise, I will give you the sure mercies of David.

Ac 17:31 — Because he hath appointed a day, in the which he will judge the world in righteousness by *that* man whom he hath ordained; *whereof* he hath given assurance unto all *men,* in that he hath raised him from the dead.

1Th 1:10 — And to wait for his Son from heaven, whom he raised from the dead, *even* Jesus, which delivered us from the wrath to come.

2Pe 1:16 — For we have not followed cunningly devised fables, when we made known unto you the power and coming of our Lord Jesus Christ, but were eyewitnesses of his majesty.

REST

• **Divine institutions for.**

See: Sabbath

• Days of.

Ex 23:12 — Six days thou shalt do thy work, and on the seventh day thou shalt rest: that thine ox and thine ass may rest, and the son of thy handmaid, and the stranger, may be refreshed.

Ex 34:21 — Six days thou shalt work, but on the seventh day thou shalt rest: in earing time and in harvest thou shalt rest.

• The annual feasts added rest days.

Le 23:7–8, 30–31, 35–36; Nu 28:25–26

Le 23:21 — And ye shall proclaim on the selfsame day, *that* it may be an holy convocation unto you: ye shall do no servile work *therein: it shall be* a statute for ever in all your dwellings throughout your generations.

Le 23:25 — Ye shall do no servile work *therein:* but ye shall offer an offering made by fire unto the LORD.

Le 23:28 — And ye shall do no work in that same day: for it *is* a day of atonement, to make an atonement for you before the LORD your God.

Nu 28:18 — In the first day *shall be* an holy convocation; ye shall do no manner of servile work *therein:*

Nu 29:1 — And in the seventh month, on the first *day* of the month, ye shall have an holy convocation; ye shall do no servile work: it is a day of blowing the trumpets unto you.

Nu 29:7 — And ye shall have on the tenth *day* of this seventh month an holy convocation; and ye shall afflict your souls: ye shall not do any work *therein:*

Nu 29:12 — And on the fifteenth day of the seventh month ye shall have an holy convocation; ye shall do no servile work, and ye shall keep a feast unto the LORD seven days:

Nu 29:35 — On the eighth day ye shall have a solemn assembly: ye shall do no servile work *therein:*

• Recommended by Jesus.

Mk 6:31–32

Mt 8:18 — Now when Jesus saw great multitudes about him, he gave commandment to depart unto the other side.

Mt 8:24 — And, behold, there arose a great tempest in the sea, insomuch that the ship was covered with the waves: but he was asleep.

• Heavenly.

2Th 1:7 — And to you who are troubled rest with us, when the Lord Jesus shall be revealed from heaven with his mighty angels,

• Spiritual.

Heb 4:1–11

Mt 11:29 — Take my yoke upon you, and learn of me; for I am meek and lowly in heart: and ye shall find rest unto your souls.

See: Peace; spiritual

RESTITUTION

• To be made for injury to life, limb, or property.

Ex 21:30–36

Le 24:18 — And he that killeth a beast shall make it good; beast for beast.

• To be made for theft.

Ex 22:1–4; Pr 6:30–31

Eze 33:15 — *If* the wicked restore the pledge, give again that he had robbed, walk in the statutes of life, without committing iniquity; he shall surely live, he shall not die.

• To be made for dishonesty.

Le 6:2–5

Nu 5:7 — Then they shall confess their sin which they have done: and he shall recompense his trespass with the principal thereof, and add unto it the fifth *part* thereof, and give *it* unto *him* against whom he hath trespassed.

Job 20:18 — That which he laboured for shall he restore, and shall not swallow *it* down: according to *his* substance *shall* the restitution *be,* and he shall not rejoice *therein.*

Eze 33:15 — *If* the wicked restore the pledge, give again that he had robbed, walk in the statutes of life, without committing iniquity; he shall surely live, he shall not die.

Lk 19:8 — And Zacchaeus stood, and said unto the Lord; Behold, Lord, the half of my goods I give to the poor; and if I have taken any thing from any man by false accusation, I restore *him* fourfold.

RESTORATION

• Of the Jews.

See: Israelites

• Of all things.

Rev 21:1–5

Ac 3:21 — Whom the heaven must receive until the times of restitution of all things, which God hath spoken by the mouth of all his holy prophets since the world began.

RESURRECTION

Job 14:12–15; 19:25–27; Ps 16:9–10; Eze 37:1–14; Da 12:2–3; Mt 22:23–32; 25:1–13; 27:52–53; Mk 12:18–27; Lk 20:27–38; Jn 5:28–29; 6:39–40; 11:23–25; Ac 2:26–31; 24:14–15; 26:6–8; Ro 4:16–21; 8:10–11, 21–23; 1Co 15:12–32, 35–57; 2Co 5:1–5; Php 3:10–11; Rev 20:4–6

Ps 17:15 — As for me, I will behold thy face in righteousness: I shall be satisfied, when I awake, with thy likeness.

Ps 49:15 — But God will redeem my soul from the power of the grave: for he shall receive me. Selah.

Isa 25:8 — He will swallow up death in victory; and the Lord GOD will wipe away tears from off all faces; and the rebuke of his people shall he take away from off all the earth: for the LORD hath spoken *it.*

Isa 26:19 — Thy dead *men* shall live, *together with* my dead body shall they arise. Awake and sing, ye that dwell in dust: for thy dew *is as* the dew of herbs, and the earth shall cast out the dead.

Da 12:13 — But go thou thy way till the end *be:* for thou shalt rest, and stand in thy lot at the end of the days.

Hos 13:14 — I will ransom them from the power of the grave; I will redeem them from death: O death, I will be thy plagues; O grave, I will be thy destruction: repentance shall be hid from mine eyes.

Mt 24:31 — And he shall send his angels with a great sound of a trumpet, and they shall gather together his elect from the four winds, from one end of heaven to the other.

Lk 14:14 — And thou shalt be blessed; for they cannot recompense thee: for thou shalt be recompensed at the resurrection of the just.

Jn 5:21 — For as the Father raiseth up the dead, and quickeneth *them;* even so the Son quickeneth whom he will.

Jn 5:25 — Verily, verily, I say unto you, The hour is coming, and now is, when the dead shall hear the voice of the Son of God: and they that hear shall live.

Jn 6:44 — No man can come to me, except the Father which hath sent me draw him: and I will raise him up at the last day.

Jn 6:54 — Whoso eateth my flesh, and drinketh my blood, hath eternal life; and I will raise him up at the last day.

Jn 14:19 — Yet a little while, and the world seeth me no more; but ye see me: because I live, ye shall live also.

Ac 4:1 — And as they spake unto the people, the priests, and the captain of the temple, and the Sadducees, came upon them,

Ac 17:18 — Then certain philosophers of the Epicureans, and of the Stoicks, encountered him. And some said, What will this babbler say? other some, He seemeth to be a setter forth of strange gods: because he preached unto them Jesus, and the resurrection.

Ac 17:32 — And when they heard of the resurrection of the dead, some mocked: and others said, We will hear thee again of this *matter.*

Ac 23:6 — But when Paul perceived that the one part were Sadducees, and the other Pharisees, he cried out in the council, Men *and* brethren, I am a Pharisee, the son of a Pharisee: of the hope and resurrection of the dead I am called in question.

Ac 23:8 — For the Sadducees say that there is no resurrection, neither angel, nor spirit: but the Pharisees confess both.

Ro 8:19 — For the earnest expectation of the creature waiteth for the manifestation of the sons of God.

1Co 6:14 — And God hath both raised up the Lord, and will also raise up us by his own power.

2Co 4:14 — Knowing that he which raised up the Lord Jesus shall raise up us also by Jesus, and shall present *us* with you.

Php 3:21 — Who shall change our vile body, that it may be fashioned like unto his glorious body, according to the working whereby he is able even to subdue all things unto himself.

1Th 4:14 — For if we believe that Jesus died and rose again, even so them also which sleep in Jesus will God bring with him.

1Th 4:16 — For the Lord himself shall descend from heaven with a shout, with the voice of the archangel, and with the trump of God: and the dead in Christ shall rise first:

2Ti 1:10 — But is now made manifest by the appearing of our Saviour Jesus Christ, who hath abolished death, and hath brought life and immortality to light through the gospel:

2Ti 2:18 — Who concerning the truth have erred, saying that the resurrection is past already; and overthrow the faith of some.

Heb 6:2 — Of the doctrine of baptisms, and of laying on of hands, and of resurrection of the dead, and of eternal judgment.

Heb 11:19 — Accounting that God *was* able to raise *him* up, even from the dead; from whence also he received him in a figure.

Heb 11:35 — Women received their dead raised to life again: and others were tortured, not accepting deliverance; that they might obtain a better resurrection:

Rev 1:18 — I *am* he that liveth, and was dead; and, behold, I am alive for evermore, Amen; and have the keys of hell and of death.

Rev 20:13 — And the sea gave up the dead which were in it; and death and hell delivered up the dead which were in them: and they were judged every man according to their works.

See: Dead; raised to life, instances of

• Of Jesus.

See: Jesus, History of

See: Jesus, Miracles of

See: Jesus, Resurrection of

See: Jesus, Revelations by

• Figurative.

• Of regeneration.

Eph 2:5–6

Ro 6:4 — Therefore we are buried with him by baptism into death: that like as Christ was raised up from the dead by the glory of the Father, even so we also should walk in newness of life.

Eph 2:1 — And you *hath he quickened,* who were dead in trespasses and sins;

Col 2:12 — Buried with him in baptism, wherein also ye are risen with *him* through the faith of the operation of God, who hath raised him from the dead.

Col 3:1 — If ye then be risen with Christ, seek those things which are above, where Christ sitteth on the right hand of God.

• Typified.

• Isaac.

Ge 22:13 — And Abraham lifted up his eyes, and looked, and behold behind *him* a ram caught in a thicket by his horns: and Abraham went and took the ram, and offered him up for a burnt offering in the stead of his son.

Heb 11:19 — Accounting that God *was* able to raise *him* up, even from the dead; from whence also he received him in a figure.

• Jonah.

Jnh 2:10 — And the LORD spake unto the fish, and it vomited out Jonah upon the dry *land.*

Mt 12:40 — For as Jonas was three days and three nights in the whale's belly; so shall the Son of man be three days and three nights in the heart of the earth.

• **Symbolic.**
Rev 11:11 — And after three days and an half the Spirit of life from God entered into them, and they stood upon their feet; and great fear fell upon them which saw them.

RETALIATION

Ex 21:23–25; Le 24:17–22; Dt 19:19–21; Mt 5:38–44; 7:1–2; Lk 9:52–56; 1Co 6:7–8

Le 19:18 — Thou shalt not avenge, nor bear any grudge against the children of thy people, but thou shalt love thy neighbour as thyself: I *am* the LORD.

Ps 10:2 — The wicked in *his* pride doth persecute the poor: let them be taken in the devices that they have imagined.

Pr 20:22 — Say not thou, I will recompense evil; *but* wait on the LORD, and he shall save thee.

Pr 24:29 — Say not, I will do so to him as he hath done to me: I will render to the man according to his work.

Pr 26:27 — Whoso diggeth a pit shall fall therein: and he that rolleth a stone, it will return upon him.

Isa 33:1 — Woe to thee that spoilest, and thou *wast* not spoiled; and dealest treacherously, and they dealt not treacherously with thee! when thou shalt cease to spoil, thou shalt be spoiled; *and* when thou shalt make an end to deal treacherously, they shall deal treacherously with thee.

Ro 12:17 — Recompense to no man evil for evil. Provide things honest in the sight of all men.

Ro 12:19 — Dearly beloved, avenge not yourselves, but *rather* give place unto wrath: for it is written, Vengeance *is* mine; I will repay, saith the Lord.

1Th 5:15 — See that none render evil for evil unto any *man;* but ever follow that which is good, both among yourselves, and to all *men.*

1Pe 3:9 — Not rendering evil for evil, or railing for railing: but contrariwise blessing; knowing that ye are thereunto called, that ye should inherit a blessing.

See: Avenger of Blood

See: Hatred

See: Malice

See: Revenge

• **Instances of.**

• **Israelites on the Amalekites.**
Dt 25:17–19; 1Sa 15:1–9

• **Gideon on the princes of Succoth.**
Jgs 8:7, 13–16

• **Kings of Midian.**
Jgs 8:18–21

• **Penuel.**
Jgs 8:8, 17

• **Joab on Abner.**
2Sa 3:27, 30

• **David upon Michal.**
2Sa 6:21–23

• **David on Joab.**
1Ki 2:5–6

• **Shimei.**
1Ki 2:8–9

• **Jews on the Chaldeans.**
Est 9:1–32

RETRIBUTION **See: Sin; punishment of**

REU • Son of Peleg and ancestor of Abraham.

Ge 11:18–21

1Ch 1:25 — Eber, Peleg, Reu,

REUBEN

• **Son of Jacob.**

Ge 29:32 — And Leah conceived, and bare a son, and she called his name Reuben: for she said, Surely the LORD hath looked upon my affliction; now therefore my husband will love me.

1Ch 2:1 — These *are* the sons of Israel; Reuben, Simeon, Levi, and Judah, Issachar, and Zebulun,

• **Brings mandrakes to his mother.**

Ge 30:14 — And Reuben went in the days of wheat harvest, and found mandrakes in the field, and brought them unto his mother Leah. Then Rachel said to Leah, Give me, I pray thee, of thy son's mandrakes.

• **Commits incest with one of his father's concubines, and, in consequence, forfeits the birthright.**

Ge 35:22 — And it came to pass, when Israel dwelt in that land, that Reuben went and lay with Bilhah his father's concubine: and Israel heard *it.* Now the sons of Jacob were twelve:

Ge 49:4 — Unstable as water, thou shalt not excel; because thou wentest up to thy father's bed; then defiledst thou *it:* he went up to my couch.

1Ch 5:1 — Now the sons of Reuben the firstborn of Israel, (for he *was* the firstborn; but, forasmuch as he defiled his father's bed, his birthright was given unto the sons of Joseph the son of Israel: and the genealogy is not to be reckoned after the birthright.

• **Adroitly seeks to save Joseph from the conspiracy of his brethren.**

Ge 37:21–30

Ge 42:22 — And Reuben answered them, saying, Spake I not unto you, saying, Do not sin against the child; and ye would not hear? therefore, behold, also his blood is required.

• **Offers to become surety for Benjamin.**

Ge 42:37 — And Reuben spake unto his father, saying, Slay my two sons, if I bring him not to thee: deliver him into my hand, and I will bring him to thee again.

• **Jacob's prophetic benediction upon.**

Ge 49:3–4

• **His children.**

1Ch 5:3–6

Ge 46:9 — And the sons of Reuben; Hanoch, and Phallu, and Hezron, and Carmi.

Ex 6:14 — These *be* the heads of their fathers' houses: The sons of Reuben the firstborn of Israel; Hanoch, and Pallu, Hezron, and Carmi: these *be* the families of Reuben.

Nu 16:1 — Now Korah, the son of Izhar, the son of Kohath, the son of Levi, and Dathan and Abiram, the sons of Eliab, and On, the son of Peleth, sons of Reuben, took *men:*

REUBENITES

• The descendants of Reuben.

• Military enrollment of, at Sinai.

Nu 1:20–21

• Military enrollment of, in Moab.

Nu 26:7 — These *are* the families of the Reubenites: and they that were numbered of them were forty and three thousand and seven hundred and thirty.

• Place of, in camp and march.

Nu 2:10 — On the south side *shall be* the standard of the camp of Reuben according to their armies: and the captain of the children of Reuben *shall be* Elizur the son of Shedeur.

• Standard of.

Nu 10:18 — And the standard of the camp of Reuben set forward according to their armies: and over his host *was* Elizur the son of Shedeur.

• Have their inheritance east of the Jordan.

Nu 32:1–42; Dt 3:1–20; Jos 13:15–23

Jos 18:7 — But the Levites have no part among you; for the priesthood of the LORD is their inheritance: and Gad, and Reuben, and half the tribe of Manasseh, have received their inheritance beyond Jordan on the east, which Moses the servant of the LORD gave them.

• Assist the other tribes in conquest of the region west of the Jordan.

Jos 1:12–18; 22:1–6

• Unite tribes in building a monument to signify the unity of the tribes; misunderstood.

Jos 22:10–34

• Reproached by Deborah.

Jgs 5:15–16

• Taken captive into Assyria.

2Ki 15:29 — In the days of Pekah king of Israel came Tiglath-pileser king of Assyria, and took Ijon, and Abel-beth-maachah, and Janoah, and Kedesh, and Hazor, and Gilead, and Galilee, all the land of Naphtali, and carried them captive to Assyria.

1Ch 5:26 — And the God of Israel stirred up the spirit of Pul king of Assyria, and the spirit of Tilgath-pilneser king of Assyria, and he carried them away, even the Reubenites, and the Gadites, and the half tribe of Manasseh, and brought them unto Halah, and Habor, and Hara, and to the river Gozan, unto this day.

✢See: Israel

REUEL

• Son of Esau.

Ge 36:4 — And Adah bare to Esau Eliphaz; and Bashemath bare Reuel;

Ge 36:10 — These *are* the names of Esau's sons; Eliphaz the son of Adah the wife of Esau, Reuel the son of Bashemath the wife of Esau.

Ge 36:13 — And these *are* the sons of Reuel; Nahath, and Zerah, Shammah, and Mizzah: these were the sons of Bashemath Esau's wife.

Ge 36:17 — And these *are* the sons of Reuel Esau's son; duke Nahath, duke Zerah, duke Shammah, duke Mizzah: these *are* the dukes *that came* of Reuel in the land of Edom; these *are* the sons of Bashemath Esau's wife.

1Ch 1:35 — The sons of Esau; Eliphaz, Reuel, and Jeush, and Jaalam, and Korah.

1Ch 1:37 — The sons of Reuel; Nahath, Zerah, Shammah, and Mizzah.

• Father-in-law of Moses.

Ex 2:18 — And when they came to Reuel their father, he said, How *is it that* ye are come so soon to day?

• Called also Jethro and Raguel.

✢See: Jethro

• Father of Eliasaph.

Nu 2:14 — Then the tribe of Gad: and the captain of the sons of Gad *shall be* Eliasaph the son of Reuel.

• Called Deuel.

Nu 1:14 — Of Gad; Eliasaph the son of Deuel.

Nu 7:42 — On the sixth day Eliasaph the son of Deuel, prince of the children of Gad, *offered:*

Nu 7:47 — And for a sacrifice of peace offerings, two oxen, five rams, five he goats, five lambs of the first year: this *was* the offering of Eliasaph the son of Deuel.

Nu 10:20 — And over the host of the tribe of the children of Gad was Eliasaph the son of Deuel.

• A Benjamite.

1Ch 9:8 — And Ibneiah the son of Jeroham, and Elah the son of Uzzi, the son of Michri, and Meshullam the son of Shephatiah, the son of Reuel, the son of Ibnijah;

REUMAH • A concubine of Nahor.

Ge 22:24 — And his concubine, whose name *was* Reumah, she bare also Tebah, and Gaham, and Thahash, and Maachah.

REVELATION

• God reveals himself to Moses.

Ex 3:1–6; 6:1–3

Ex 3:14 — And God said unto Moses, I AM THAT I AM: and he said, Thus shalt thou say unto the children of Israel, I AM hath sent me unto you.

• The law is revealed.

Ex 20:1–35:35; Le 1:1–7:38

• The law is revealed in the pattern of the temple.

1Ch 28:11–19

• The sonship of Jesus.

Mt 3:17 — And lo a voice from heaven, saying, This is my beloved Son, in whom I am well pleased.

Mt 16:17 — And Jesus answered and said unto him, Blessed art thou, Simon Barjona: for flesh and blood hath not revealed *it* unto thee, but my Father which is in heaven.

Mt 17:5 — While he yet spake, behold, a bright cloud overshadowed them: and behold a voice out of the cloud, which said, This is my beloved Son, in whom I am well pleased; hear ye him.

See: Inspiration

See: Prophecy

See: Prophets

See: Word of God; inspiration of

REVENGE

• Forbidden.

Le 19:18 — Thou shalt not avenge, nor bear any grudge against the children of thy people, but thou shalt love thy neighbour as thyself: I *am* the LORD.

Pr 24:29 — Say not, I will do so to him as he hath done to me: I will render to the man according to his work.

Ro 12:17 — Recompense to no man evil for evil. Provide things honest in the sight of all men.

Ro 12:19 — Dearly beloved, avenge not yourselves, but *rather* give place unto wrath: for it is written, Vengeance *is* mine; I will repay, saith the Lord.

1Th 5:15 — See that none render evil for evil unto any *man;* but ever follow that which is good, both among yourselves, and to all *men.*

1Pe 3:9 — Not rendering evil for evil, or railing for railing: but contrariwise blessing; knowing that ye are thereunto called, that ye should inherit a blessing.

• Jesus an example of forbearing.

1Pe 2:23 — Who, when he was reviled, reviled not again; when he suffered, he threatened not; but committed *himself* to him that judgeth righteously:

• Rebuked by Jesus.

Lk 9:54–55

• Inconsistent with a Christian spirit.

Lk 9:55 — But he turned, and rebuked them, and said, Ye know not what manner of spirit ye are of.

• Proceeds from a spiteful heart.

Eze 25:15 — Thus saith the Lord GOD; Because the Philistines have dealt by revenge, and have taken vengeance with a despiteful heart, to destroy *it* for the old hatred;

• Punishment for.

Eze 25:15–17; Am 1:11–12

• Exemplified by.

• Simeon and Levi.

Ge 34:25 — And it came to pass on the third day, when they were sore, that two of the sons of Jacob, Simeon and Levi, Dinah's brethren, took each man his sword, and came upon the city boldly, and slew all the males.

• Samson.

Jgs 15:7–8; 16:28–30

• Joab.

2Sa 3:27 — And when Abner was returned to Hebron, Joab took him aside in the gate to speak with him quietly, and smote him there under the fifth *rib,* that he died, for the blood of Asahel his brother.

• Absalom.

2Sa 13:23–29

• Jezebel.

1Ki 19:2 — Then Jezebel sent a messenger unto Elijah, saying, So let the gods do *to me,* and more also, if I make not thy life as the life of one of them by to morrow about this time.

• Ahab.

1Ki 22:27 — And say, Thus saith the king, Put this *fellow* in the prison, and feed him with bread of affliction and with water of affliction, until I come in peace.

• Haman.

Est 3:8–15

• The Edomites.

Eze 25:12 — Thus saith the Lord GOD; Because that Edom hath dealt against the house of Judah by taking vengeance, and hath greatly offended, and revenged himself upon them;

• The Philistines.

Eze 25:15 — Thus saith the Lord GOD; Because the Philistines have dealt by revenge, and have taken vengeance with a despiteful heart, to destroy *it* for the old hatred;

• Herodias.

Mk 6:19–24

• James and John.

Lk 9:54 — And when his disciples James and John saw *this,* they said, Lord, wilt thou that we command fire to come down from heaven, and consume them, even as Elias did?

• The chief priests.

Ac 5:33 — When they heard *that,* they were cut *to the heart,* and took counsel to slay them.

• The Jews.

Ac 7:54–59

Ac 23:12 — And when it was day, certain of the Jews banded together, and bound themselves under a curse, saying that they would neither eat nor drink till they had killed Paul.

See: Retaliation

REVENUE

• Solomon's.

2Ch 9:13–14

See: Tax

REVERENCE

• For God.

Ex 19:16–24; 34:29–35

Ge 17:3 — And Abram fell on his face: and God talked with him, saying,

Ex 3:5 — And he said, Draw not nigh hither: put off thy shoes from off thy feet, for the place whereon thou standest is holy ground.

Isa 45:9 — Woe unto him that striveth with his Maker! *Let* the potsherd *strive* with the potsherds of the earth. Shall the clay say to him that fashioneth it, What makest thou? or thy work, He hath no hands?

See: Fear of God

- **For God's house.**

Le 19:30 — Ye shall keep my sabbaths, and reverence my sanctuary: I *am* the LORD.

Le 26:2 — Ye shall keep my sabbaths, and reverence my sanctuary: I *am* the LORD.

- **For ministers.**

1Th 5:12–13

1Sa 16:4 — And Samuel did that which the LORD spake, and came to Bethlehem. And the elders of the town trembled at his coming, and said, Comest thou peaceably?

Ac 28:10 — Who also honoured us with many honours; and when we departed, they laded *us* with such things as were necessary.

1Co 16:18 — For they have refreshed my spirit and yours: therefore acknowledge ye them that are such.

Php 2:29 — Receive him therefore in the Lord with all gladness; and hold such in reputation:

1Ti 5:17 — Let the elders that rule well be counted worthy of double honour, especially they who labour in the word and doctrine.

Heb 13:7 — Remember them which have the rule over you, who have spoken unto you the word of God: whose faith follow, considering the end of *their* conversation.

Heb 13:17 — Obey them that have the rule over you, and submit yourselves: for they watch for your souls, as they that must give account, that they may do it with joy, and not with grief: for that *is* unprofitable for you.

See: Minister, a sacred teacher

- **For kings.**

1Sa 24:6 — And he said unto his men, The LORD forbid that I should do this thing unto my master, the LORD'S anointed, to stretch forth mine hand against him, seeing he is the anointed of the LORD.

1Sa 26:9 — And David said to Abishai, Destroy him not: for who can stretch forth his hand against the LORD'S anointed, and be guiltless?

1Sa 26:11 — The LORD forbid that I should stretch forth mine hand against the LORD'S anointed: but, I pray thee, take thou now the spear that *is* at his bolster, and the cruse of water, and let us go.

2Sa 1:14 — And David said unto him, How wast thou not afraid to stretch forth thine hand to destroy the LORD'S anointed?

2Sa 16:21 — And Ahithophel said unto Absalom, Go in unto thy father's concubines, which he hath left to keep the house; and all Israel shall hear that thou art abhorred of thy father: then shall the hands of all that *are* with thee be strong.

Ecc 10:20 — Curse not the king, no not in thy thought; and curse not the rich in thy bedchamber: for a bird of the air shall carry the voice, and that which hath wings shall tell the matter.

1Pe 2:17 — Honour all *men.* Love the brotherhood. Fear God. Honour the king.

See: Rulers

- **For magistrates.**

Ex 22:28 — Thou shalt not revile the gods, nor curse the ruler of thy people.

2Pe 2:10 — But chiefly them that walk after the flesh in the lust of uncleanness, and despise government. Presumptuous *are they,* selfwilled, they are not afraid to speak evil of dignities.

Jude 1:8 — Likewise also these *filthy* dreamers defile the flesh, despise dominion, and speak evil of dignities.

See: Rulers

- **For parents.**

Ex 20:12 — Honour thy father and thy mother: that thy days may be long upon the land which the LORD thy God giveth thee.

Le 19:3 — Ye shall fear every man his mother, and his father, and keep my sabbaths: I *am* the LORD your God.

Isa 45:10 — Woe unto him that saith unto *his* father, What begettest thou? or to the woman, What hast thou brought forth?

See: Parents

- **For the aged.**

Job 32:4–7

Le 19:32 — Thou shalt rise up before the hoary head, and honour the face of the old man, and fear thy God: I *am* the LORD.

REVILING

- **Of Jesus.**

Mt 27:39–44

See: Mocking

REVIVALS

- **Religious.**

Zec 8:20–23

  - **Prayer for.**

Hab 3:2 — O LORD, I have heard thy speech, *and* was afraid: O LORD, revive thy work in the midst of the years, in the midst of the years make known; in wrath remember mercy.

  - **Prophecies concerning.**

Mic 4:1–8

Isa 32:15 — Until the spirit be poured upon us from on high, and the wilderness be a fruitful field, and the fruitful field be counted for a forest.

Joel 2:28 — And it shall come to pass afterward, *that* I will pour out my spirit upon all flesh; and your sons and your daughters shall prophesy, your old men shall dream dreams, your young men shall see visions:

Hab 3:2 — O LORD, I have heard thy speech, *and* was afraid: O LORD, revive thy work in the midst of the years, in the midst of the years make known; in wrath remember mercy.

- **Instances of.**

  - **Under Joshua.**

Jos 5:2–9

  - **Under Samuel.**

1Sa 7:1–6

• **Under Elijah.**
1Ki 18:17–40

• **Under Jehoash and Jehoiada.**
2Ki 11:1–12:21; 2Ch 23:1–24:27

• **Under Hezekiah.**
2Ki 18:1–7; 2Ch 29:1–31:21

• **Under Josiah.**
2Ki 22:1–23:37; 2Ch 34:1–35:27

• **Under Asa.**
2Ch 14:2–5; 15:1–14

• **Under Manasseh.**
2Ch 33:12–19

• **In Nineveh.**
Jnh 3:4–10

• **At pentecost, and post-pentecostal times.**
Ac 2:1–42, 46–47; 4:4; 5:14; 6:7; 9:35; 11:20–21; 12:24; 14:1; 19:17–20

See: Religion

REVOLT

• **Of the ten tribes.**
1Ki 12:1–24

REWARD

• **A motive to faithfulness.**
Le 25:18–19; 26:3–45; Dt 11:13–16, 18–21, 26–29; 15:9–11; 27:12–26; Isa 1:16–20; 40:10–11; Jer 17:24–26; 22:3–4; Mt 16:24–27; 20:1–16; 25:34–46; Lk 6:22–23; Eph 6:1–3; Heb 12:1–2; 1Pe 3:9–12; 2Pe 1:10–11; Rev 2:25–28; 7:14–17

Ex 20:6 — And shewing mercy unto thousands of them that love me, and keep my commandments.

Ex 20:12 — Honour thy father and thy mother: that thy days may be long upon the land which the LORD thy God giveth thee.

Dt 4:40 — Thou shalt keep therefore his statutes, and his commandments, which I command thee this day, that it may go well with thee, and with thy children after thee, and that thou mayest prolong *thy* days upon the earth, which the LORD thy God giveth thee, for ever.

Dt 6:3 — Hear therefore, O Israel, and observe to do *it;* that it may be well with thee, and that ye may increase mightily, as the LORD God of thy fathers hath promised thee, in the land that floweth with milk and honey.

Dt 6:18 — And thou shalt do *that which is* right and good in the sight of the LORD: that it may be well with thee, and that thou mayest go in and possess the good land which the LORD sware unto thy fathers,

Dt 22:7 — *But* thou shalt in any wise let the dam go, and take the young to thee; that it may be well with thee, and *that* thou mayest prolong *thy* days.

Dt 24:19 — When thou cuttest down thine harvest in thy field, and hast forgot a sheaf in the field, thou shalt not go again to fetch it: it shall be for the stranger, for the fatherless, and for the widow: that the LORD thy God may bless thee in all the work of thine hands.

Dt 25:15 — *But* thou shalt have a perfect and just weight, a perfect and just measure shalt thou have: that thy days may be lengthened in the land which the LORD thy God giveth thee.

Jos 8:33 — And all Israel, and their elders, and officers, and their judges, stood on this side the ark and on that side before the priests the Levites, which bare the ark of the covenant of the LORD, as well the stranger, as he that was born among them; half of them over against mount Gerizim, and half of them over against mount Ebal; as Moses the servant of the LORD had commanded before, that they should bless the people of Israel.

Isa 3:10 — Say ye to the righteous, that *it shall be* well *with him:* for they shall eat the fruit of their doings.

Mt 10:32 — Whosoever therefore shall confess me before men, him will I confess also before my Father which is in heaven.

Mk 10:21 — Then Jesus beholding him loved him, and said unto him, One thing thou lackest: go thy way, sell whatsoever thou hast, and give to the poor, and thou shalt have treasure in heaven: and come, take up the cross, and follow me.

Mk 13:13 — And ye shall be hated of all *men* for my name's sake: but he that shall endure unto the end, the same shall be saved.

Lk 6:35 — But love ye your enemies, and do good, and lend, hoping for nothing again; and your reward shall be great, and ye shall be the children of the Highest: for he is kind unto the unthankful and *to* the evil.

Lk 12:8 — Also I say unto you, Whosoever shall confess me before men, him shall the Son of man also confess before the angels of God:

Ac 26:18 — To open their eyes, *and* to turn *them* from darkness to light, and *from* the power of Satan unto God, that they may receive forgiveness of sins, and inheritance among them which are sanctified by faith that is in me.

Ro 2:10 — But glory, honour, and peace, to every man that worketh good, to the Jew first, and also to the Gentile:

1Co 3:8 — Now he that planteth and he that watereth are one: and every man shall receive his own reward according to his own labour.

Heb 10:34 — For ye had compassion of me in my bonds, and took joyfully the spoiling of your goods, knowing in yourselves that ye have in heaven a better and an enduring substance.

Heb 10:36 — For ye have need of patience, that, after ye have done the will of God, ye might receive the promise.

Heb 11:26 — Esteeming the reproach of Christ greater riches than the treasures in Egypt: for he had respect unto the recompence of the reward.

Heb 12:28 — Wherefore we receiving a kingdom which cannot be moved, let us have grace, whereby we may serve God acceptably with reverence and godly fear:

Rev 2:10 — Fear none of those things which thou shalt suffer: behold, the devil shall cast *some* of you into prison, that ye may be tried; and ye shall have tribulation ten days: be thou faithful unto death, and I will give thee a crown of life.

Rev 2:17 — He that hath an ear, let him hear what the Spirit saith unto the churches; To him that overcometh will I give to eat of the hidden manna, and will give him a white stone, and in the stone a new name written, which no man knoweth saving he that receiveth *it.*

Rev 22:12 — And, behold, I come quickly; and my reward *is* with me, to give every man according as his work shall be.

See: Blessing; divine, contingent upon obedience

See: Punishment

See: Righteous; promises to, expressed or implied

See: Sin; separates from God

See: Wicked; punishment of

REZEPH • A city destroyed by the Assyrians.

2Ki 19:12 — Have the gods of the nations delivered them which my fathers have destroyed; *as* Gozan, and Haran, and Rezeph, and the children of Eden which *were* in Thelasar?

Isa 37:12 — Have the gods of the nations delivered them which my fathers have destroyed, *as* Gozan, and Haran, and Rezeph, and the children of Eden which *were* in Telassar?

REZIA • An Asherite.

1Ch 7:39 — And the sons of Ulla; Arah, and Haniel, and Rezia.

REZIN

- **A king of Syria who harassed the kingdom of Judah.**

2Ki 16:5–9

2Ki 15:37 — In those days the LORD began to send against Judah Rezin the king of Syria, and Pekah the son of Remaliah.

- **Prophecy against.**

Isa 7:1–9; 8:4–8

Isa 9:11 — Therefore the LORD shall set up the adversaries of Rezin against him, and join his enemies together;

- **A returned Babylonian captive.**

Ezr 2:48 — The children of Rezin, the children of Nekoda, the children of Gazzam,

Ne 7:50 — The children of Reaiah, the children of Rezin, the children of Nekoda,

REZON, king of Damascus • An adversary of Solomon.

1Ki 11:23–25

RHEGIUM

- **A city of Italy.**
- **Touched by Paul on the way to Rome.**

Ac 28:13 — And from thence we fetched a compass, and came to Rhegium: and after one day the south wind blew, and we came the next day to Puteoli:

RHESA • An ancestor of Jesus.

Lk 3:27 — Which was *the son* of Joanna, which was *the son* of Rhesa, which was *the son* of Zorobabel, which was *the son* of Salathiel, which was *the son* of Neri,

RHODA • A Christian girl in Jerusalem.

Ac 12:13 — And as Peter knocked at the door of the gate, a damsel came to hearken, named Rhoda.

RHODES • An island visited by Paul.

Ac 21:1 — And it came to pass, that after we were gotten from them, and had launched, we came with a straight course unto Coos, and the *day* following unto Rhodes, and from thence unto Patara:

RIBAI

- **A Benjamite.**
- **Father of Ittai.**

2Sa 23:29 — Heleb the son of Baanah, a Netophathite, Ittai the son of Ribai out of Gibeah of the children of Benjamin,

1Ch 11:31 — Ithai the son of Ribai of Gibeah, *that pertained* to the children of Benjamin, Benaiah the Pirathonite,

RIBBAND

Nu 15:38 — Speak unto the children of Israel, and bid them that they make them fringes in the borders of their garments throughout their generations, and that they put upon the fringe of the borders a ribband of blue:

RIBLAH

- **A border town of the promised land.**

Nu 34:10–11

- **King Jehoahaz overthrown in, by Pharaoh.**

2Ki 23:33 — And Pharaoh-nechoh put him in bands at Riblah in the land of Hamath, that he might not reign in Jerusalem; and put the land to a tribute of an hundred talents of silver, and a talent of gold.

- **Headquarters of Nebuchadnezzar in siege of Jerusalem.**

2Ki 25:20–21; Jer 39:5–6

2Ki 25:6 — So they took the king, and brought him up to the king of Babylon to Riblah; and they gave judgment upon him.

Jer 52:9 — Then they took the king, and carried him up unto the king of Babylon to Riblah in the land of Hamath; where he gave judgment upon him.

Jer 52:26 — So Nebuzar-adan the captain of the guard took them, and brought them to the king of Babylon to Riblah.

RICH

• The.

Ne 5:1–13; Job 21:7–15; 27:13–23; 31:24–25; Ps 49:16–18; 52:1–7; 73:3–22; Ecc 5:13–14, 19–20; Jer 5:7–9, 27–29; 22:13–19; Am 6:1–6; Zep 1:1–18; Mt 19:23–24; Mk 10:17–27; Lk 6:24–25; 12:15–21; 16:13–14, 19–26; 18:22–26; 1Ti 6:17–19; Jas 1:9–11; 5:1–3

Job 31:28 — This also *were* an iniquity *to be punished by* the judge: for I should have denied the God *that is* above.

Pr 14:20 — The poor is hated even of his own neighbour: but the rich *hath* many friends.

Pr 18:11 — The rich man's wealth *is* his strong city, and as an high wall in his own conceit.

Pr 18:23 — The poor useth intreaties; but the rich answereth roughly.

Pr 28:11 — The rich man *is* wise in his own conceit; but the poor that hath understanding searcheth him out.

Jer 9:23 — Thus saith the LORD, Let not the wise *man* glory in his wisdom, neither let the mighty *man* glory in his might, let not the rich *man* glory in his riches:

Jer 17:11 — As the partridge sitteth *on eggs,* and hatcheth *them* not; *so* he that getteth riches, and not by right, shall leave them in the midst of his days, and at his end shall be a fool.

Eze 7:19 — They shall cast their silver in the streets, and their gold shall be removed: their silver and their gold shall not be able to deliver them in the day of the wrath of the LORD: they shall not satisfy their souls, neither fill their bowels: because it is the stumblingblock of their iniquity.

Eze 28:5 — By thy great wisdom *and* by thy traffick hast thou increased thy riches, and thine heart is lifted up because of thy riches:

Mic 6:12 — For the rich men thereof are full of violence, and the inhabitants thereof have spoken lies, and their tongue *is* deceitful in their mouth.

→See: Riches

• Instances of.

• Abraham.
Ge 13:2; 24:35

• Solomon.
1Ki 10:23

• Hezekiah.
2Ki 20:12–18

• Job.
Job 1:3

• Joseph of Arimathea.
Mt 27:57

• Zacchaeus.
Lk 19:2

RICHES

Dt 6:10–12; 8:10–18; Pr 13:7–8; 15:16–17; 23:4–5; 27:23–24; 30:8–9; Ecc 5:9–6:2; 7:11–12; Mt 6:19–21; 19:16–29; Mk 10:17–25; Lk 18:18–25; 1Ti 6:4–11, 17–19; Jas 2:6–7; 5:1–5

Dt 31:20 — For when I shall have brought them into the land which I sware unto their fathers, that floweth with milk and honey; and they shall have eaten and filled themselves, and waxen fat; then will they turn unto other gods, and serve them, and provoke me, and break my covenant.

Dt 32:15 — But Jeshurun waxed fat, and kicked: thou art waxen fat, thou art grown thick, thou art covered *with fatness;* then he forsook God *which* made him, and lightly esteemed the Rock of his salvation.

1Sa 2:7 — The LORD maketh poor, and maketh rich: he bringeth low, and lifteth up.

Ps 37:16 — A little that a righteous man hath *is* better than the riches of many wicked.

Pr 10:2 — Treasures of wickedness profit nothing: but righteousness delivereth from death.

Pr 10:22 — The blessing of the LORD, it maketh rich, and he addeth no sorrow with it.

Pr 11:4 — Riches profit not in the day of wrath: but righteousness delivereth from death.

Pr 11:28 — He that trusteth in his riches shall fall: but the righteous shall flourish as a branch.

Pr 14:24 — The crown of the wise is their riches: *but* the foolishness of fools *is* folly.

Pr 15:6 — In the house of the righteous *is* much treasure: but in the revenues of the wicked is trouble.

Pr 16:8 — Better *is* a little with righteousness than great revenues without right.

Pr 19:4 — Wealth maketh many friends; but the poor is separated from his neighbour.

Pr 21:6 — The getting of treasures by a lying tongue *is* a vanity tossed to and fro of them that seek death.

Pr 28:8 — He that by usury and unjust gain increaseth his substance, he shall gather it for him that will pity the poor.

Pr 28:20 — A faithful man shall abound with blessings: but he that maketh haste to be rich shall not be innocent.

Pr 28:22 — He that hasteth to be rich *hath* an evil eye, and considereth not that poverty shall come upon him.

Ecc 10:19 — A feast is made for laughter, and wine maketh merry: but money answereth all *things.*

Isa 5:8 — Woe unto them that join house to house, *that* lay field to field, till *there be* no place, that they may be placed alone in the midst of the earth!

Jer 48:36 — Therefore mine heart shall sound for Moab like pipes, and mine heart shall sound like pipes for the men of Kir-heres: because the riches *that* he hath gotten are perished.

Hos 12:8 — And Ephraim said, Yet I am become rich, I have found me out substance: *in* all my labours they shall find none iniquity in me that *were* sin.

Mt 13:22 — He also that received seed among the thorns is he that heareth the word; and the care of this world, and the deceitfulness of riches, choke the word, and he becometh unfruitful.

Mk 4:19 — And the cares of this world, and the deceitfulness of riches, and the lusts of other things entering in, choke the word, and it becometh unfruitful.

Lk 12:15 — And he said unto them, Take heed, and beware of covetousness: for a man's life consisteth not in the abundance of the things which he possesseth.

1Jn 3:17 — But whoso hath this world's good, and seeth his brother have need, and shutteth up his bowels *of compassion* from him, how dwelleth the love of God in him?

• Figurative.

Rev 3:18 — I counsel thee to buy of me gold tried in the fire, that thou mayest be rich; and white raiment, that thou mayest be clothed, and *that* the shame of thy nakedness do not appear; and anoint thine eyes with eyesalve, that thou mayest see.

See: Covetousness

See: Rich

RIDDLE

• Used as a test of wit at Samson's feast.

Jgs 14:12–18

• By Agur.

Pr 30:15–16, 18–31

See: Parables

See: Proverbs

RIGHTEOUS

• Miscellany of minor sub-topics.

• Compared with.

• The sun.

Jgs 5:31 — So let all thine enemies perish, O LORD: but *let* them that love him *be* as the sun when he goeth forth in his might. And the land had rest forty years.

Mt 13:43 — Then shall the righteous shine forth as the sun in the kingdom of their Father. Who hath ears to hear, let him hear.

• The stars.

Da 12:3 — And they that be wise shall shine as the brightness of the firmament; and they that turn many to righteousness as the stars for ever and ever.

• The lights.

Mt 5:14 — Ye are the light of the world. A city that is set on an hill cannot be hid.

Php 2:15 — That ye may be blameless and harmless, the sons of God, without rebuke, in the midst of a crooked and perverse nation, among whom ye shine as lights in the world;

• Mount Zion.

Ps 125:1–2

• Lebanon.

Hos 14:5–7

• Treasure.

Ex 19:5 — Now therefore, if ye will obey my voice indeed, and keep my covenant, then ye shall be a peculiar treasure unto me above all people: for all the earth *is* mine:

Ps 135:4 — For the LORD hath chosen Jacob unto himself, *and* Israel for his peculiar treasure.

• Jewels.

Mal 3:17 — And they shall be mine, saith the LORD of hosts, in that day when I make up my jewels; and I will spare them, as a man spareth his own son that serveth him.

• Gold.

Job 23:10 — But he knoweth the way that I take: *when* he hath tried me, I shall come forth as gold.

La 4:2 — The precious sons of Zion, comparable to fine gold, how are they esteemed as earthen pitchers, the work of the hands of the potter!

• Vessels of gold and silver.

2Ti 2:20 — But in a great house there are not only vessels of gold and of silver, but also of wood and of earth; and some to honour, and some to dishonour.

• Stones of a crown.

Zec 9:16 — And the LORD their God shall save them in that day as the flock of his people: for they *shall be as* the stones of a crown, lifted up as an ensign upon his land.

• Lively stones.

1Pe 2:5 — Ye also, as lively stones, are built up a spiritual house, an holy priesthood, to offer up spiritual sacrifices, acceptable to God by Jesus Christ.

• Babes.

Mt 11:25 — At that time Jesus answered and said, I thank thee, O Father, Lord of heaven and earth, because thou hast hid these things from the wise and prudent, and hast revealed them unto babes.

1Pe 2:2 — As newborn babes, desire the sincere milk of the word, that ye may grow thereby:

• Little children.

Mt 18:3 — And said, Verily I say unto you, Except ye be converted, and become as little children, ye shall not enter into the kingdom of heaven.

1Co 14:20 — Brethren, be not children in understanding: howbeit in malice be ye children, but in understanding be men.

• Obedient children.

1Pe 1:14 — As obedient children, not fashioning yourselves according to the former lusts in your ignorance:

• Members of the body.

1Co 12:20 — But now *are they* many members, yet but one body.

1Co 12:27 — Now ye are the body of Christ, and members in particular.

• Soldiers.

2Ti 2:3–4

• Runners in a race.

1Co 9:24 — Know ye not that they which run in a race run all, but one receiveth the prize? So run, that ye may obtain.

Heb 12:1 — Wherefore seeing we also are compassed about with so great a cloud of witnesses, let us lay aside every weight, and the sin which doth so easily beset us, and let us run with patience the race that is set before us,

• **Wrestlers.**

2Ti 2:5 — And if a man also strive for masteries, *yet* is he not crowned, except he strive lawfully.

• **Good servants.**

Mt 25:21 — His lord said unto him, Well done, *thou* good and faithful servant: thou hast been faithful over a few things, I will make thee ruler over many things: enter thou into the joy of thy lord.

• **Strangers and pilgrims.**

1Pe 2:11 — Dearly beloved, I beseech *you* as strangers and pilgrims, abstain from fleshly lusts, which war against the soul;

• **Sheep.**

Jn 10:1–42

Ps 78:52 — But made his own people to go forth like sheep, and guided them in the wilderness like a flock.

Mt 25:33 — And he shall set the sheep on his right hand, but the goats on the left.

• **Lambs.**

Isa 40:11 — He shall feed his flock like a shepherd: he shall gather the lambs with his arm, and carry *them* in his bosom, *and* shall gently lead those that are with young.

Jn 21:15 — So when they had dined, Jesus saith to Simon Peter, Simon, *son* of Jonas, lovest thou me more than these? He saith unto him, Yea, Lord; thou knowest that I love thee. He saith unto him, Feed my lambs.

• **Calves of the stall.**

Mal 4:2 — But unto you that fear my name shall the Sun of righteousness arise with healing in his wings; and ye shall go forth, and grow up as calves of the stall.

• **Lions.**

Pr 28:1 — The wicked flee when no man pursueth: but the righteous are bold as a lion.

Mic 5:8 — And the remnant of Jacob shall be among the Gentiles in the midst of many people as a lion among the beasts of the forest, as a young lion among the flocks of sheep: who, if he go through, both treadeth down, and teareth in pieces, and none can deliver.

• **Eagles.**

Ps 103:5 — Who satisfieth thy mouth with good *things; so that* thy youth is renewed like the eagle's.

Isa 40:31 — But they that wait upon the LORD shall renew *their* strength; they shall mount up with wings as eagles; they shall run, and not be weary; *and* they shall walk, and not faint.

• **Doves.**

Ps 68:13 — Though ye have lien among the pots, *yet shall ye be as* the wings of a dove covered with silver, and her feathers with yellow gold.

Isa 60:8 — Who *are* these *that* fly as a cloud, and as the doves to their windows?

• **Thirsting deer.**

Ps 42:1 — As the hart panteth after the water brooks, so panteth my soul after thee, O God.

• **Good fishes.**

Mt 13:48 — Which, when it was full, they drew to shore, and sat down, and gathered the good into vessels, but cast the bad away.

• **Dew and showers.**

Mic 5:7 — And the remnant of Jacob shall be in the midst of many people as a dew from the LORD, as the showers upon the grass, that tarrieth not for man, nor waiteth for the sons of men.

• **Watered gardens.**

Isa 58:11 — And the LORD shall guide thee continually, and satisfy thy soul in drought, and make fat thy bones: and thou shalt be like a watered garden, and like a spring of water, whose waters fail not.

• **Unfailing springs.**

Isa 58:11 — And the LORD shall guide thee continually, and satisfy thy soul in drought, and make fat thy bones: and thou shalt be like a watered garden, and like a spring of water, whose waters fail not.

• **Vines.**

SS 6:11 — I went down into the garden of nuts to see the fruits of the valley, *and* to see whether the vine flourished, *and* the pomegranates budded.

Hos 14:7 — They that dwell under his shadow shall return; they shall revive *as* the corn, and grow as the vine: the scent thereof *shall be* as the wine of Lebanon.

• **Branches of a vine.**

Jn 15:4–5

Jn 15:2 — Every branch in me that beareth not fruit he taketh away: and every *branch* that beareth fruit, he purgeth it, that it may bring forth more fruit.

• **Pomegranates.**

SS 4:13 — Thy plants *are* an orchard of pomegranates, with pleasant fruits; camphire, with spikenard,

• **Good figs.**

Jer 24:2–7

• **Lilies.**

SS 2:2 — As the lily among thorns, so *is* my love among the daughters.

Hos 14:5 — I will be as the dew unto Israel: he shall grow as the lily, and cast forth his roots as Lebanon.

• **Willows by the water courses.**

Isa 44:4 — And they shall spring up as among the grass, as willows by the water courses.

• **Trees planted by rivers.**

Ps 1:3 — And he shall be like a tree planted by the rivers of water, that bringeth forth his fruit in his season; his leaf also shall not wither; and whatsoever he doeth shall prosper.

- **Cedars in Lebanon.**
  Ps 92:12 — The righteous shall flourish like the palm tree: he shall grow like a cedar in Lebanon.
- **Palm trees.**
  Ps 92:12 — The righteous shall flourish like the palm tree: he shall grow like a cedar in Lebanon.
- **Green olive trees.**
  Ps 52:8 — But I *am* like a green olive tree in the house of God: I trust in the mercy of God for ever and ever.
  Hos 14:6 — His branches shall spread, and his beauty shall be as the olive tree, and his smell as Lebanon.
- **Fruitful trees.**
  Ps 1:3 — And he shall be like a tree planted by the rivers of water, that bringeth forth his fruit in his season; his leaf also shall not wither; and whatsoever he doeth shall prosper.
  Jer 17:8 — For he shall be as a tree planted by the waters, and *that* spreadeth out her roots by the river, and shall not see when heat cometh, but her leaf shall be green; and shall not be careful in the year of drought, neither shall cease from yielding fruit.
- **Corn.**
  Hos 14:7 — They that dwell under his shadow shall return; they shall revive *as* the corn, and grow as the vine: the scent thereof *shall be* as the wine of Lebanon.
- **Wheat.**
  Mt 13:29–30
  Mt 3:12 — Whose fan *is* in his hand, and he will throughly purge his floor, and gather his wheat into the garner; but he will burn up the chaff with unquenchable fire.
- **Salt.**
  Mt 5:13 — <u>Ye are the salt of the earth: but if the salt have lost his savour, wherewith shall it be salted? it is thenceforth good for nothing, but to be cast out, and to be trodden under foot of men.</u>

- **Access of, to God.**
  Ps 31:19–20
  Isa 12:6 — Cry out and shout, thou inhabitant of Zion: for great *is* the Holy One of Israel in the midst of thee.
- **Few.**
  Mt 7:14 — <u>Because strait *is* the gate, and narrow *is* the way, which leadeth unto life, and few there be that find it.</u>
  Mt 22:14 — <u>For many are called, but few *are* chosen.</u>
- **Relation of, to God.**
  Le 20:24–26
- **Righteous and wicked, circumstances of, contrasted.**
  Job 8:1–22; Ps 17:14–15
  - **At the judgment.**
    ↞**See: Judgment; the general**
  - **Fellowship of.**
    ↞**See: Fellowship**
  - **Hatred toward.**
    ↞**See: Persecution**
  - **Joy of.**
    ↞**See: Joy**
  - **Perseverance of.**
    ↞**See: Perseverance**
- **Contrasted with the wicked.**
  ↞**See: Wicked; contrasted with the righteous**
  ↞**See: Wicked; described**
- **Described.**
  Ps 1:1–3; 15:1–5; 24:3–5; 37:30–31; 87:5–6; 112:1–10; 119:1–3; Pr 2:9–12; Isa 33:15–16; Jer 31:12–14, 33–34; Eze 18:5–9; Zec 3:7–8; Mt 5:3–10, 13–16; 7:16–20, 24–27; Mk 10:14–15; Lk 18:16–17; Jn 8:31–32; 10:4–5; Ac 8:36–37; 11:23–24; 18:1–28; Ro 1:6–7; 6:1–23; 8:5–6, 14–16, 35–39; 1Co 1:26–27; 2:12–13; 6:9–11; 15:48–49; 2Co 4:1–2; Gal 5:22–26; Eph 1:4–7; 2:4–6, 13–14, 19–22; 3:17–19; 4:13–16, 22–32; Php 3:7–11; Col 1:9–13; 1Th 5:4–5; 2Ti 2:21–25; Phm 1:5–6; 1Pe 2:9–10; 4:1–2; 1Jn 2:5–6, 12–15; 3:2–3, 6–7, 18–19; Rev 14:4–5
  Ex 33:16 — For wherein shall it be known here that I and thy people have found grace in thy sight? *is it* not in that thou goest with us? so shall we be separated, I and thy people, from all the people that *are* upon the face of the earth.
  1Sa 13:14 — But now thy kingdom shall not continue: the LORD hath sought him a man after his own heart, and the LORD hath commanded him *to be* captain over his people, because thou hast not kept *that* which the LORD commanded thee.
  Ezr 10:3 — Now therefore let us make a covenant with our God to put away all the wives, and such as are born of them, according to the counsel of my lord, and of those that tremble at the commandment of our God; and let it be done according to the law.
  Ps 4:3 — But know that the LORD hath set apart him that is godly for himself: the LORD will hear when I call unto him.
  Ps 37:26 — *He is* ever merciful, and lendeth; and his seed *is* blessed.
  Ps 64:10 — The righteous shall be glad in the LORD, and shall trust in him; and all the upright in heart shall glory.
  Ps 84:7 — They go from strength to strength, *every one of them* in Zion appeareth before God.
  Pr 4:18 — But the path of the just *is* as the shining light, that shineth more and more unto the perfect day.
  Pr 13:5 — A righteous *man* hateth lying: but a wicked *man* is loathsome, and cometh to shame.

Pr 25:26 — A righteous man falling down before the wicked *is as* a troubled fountain, and a corrupt spring.

Isa 51:1 — Hearken to me, ye that follow after righteousness, ye that seek the LORD: look unto the rock *whence* ye are hewn, and to the hole of the pit *whence* ye are digged.

Isa 54:13 — And all thy children *shall be* taught of the LORD; and great *shall be* the peace of thy children.

Isa 60:21 — Thy people also *shall be* all righteous: they shall inherit the land for ever, the branch of my planting, the work of my hands, that I may be glorified.

Isa 62:12 — And they shall call them, The holy people, The redeemed of the LORD: and thou shalt be called, Sought out, A city not forsaken.

Isa 63:8 — For he said, Surely they *are* my people, children *that* will not lie: so he was their Saviour.

Eze 44:9 — Thus saith the Lord GOD; No stranger, uncircumcised in heart, nor uncircumcised in flesh, shall enter into my sanctuary, of any stranger that *is* among the children of Israel.

Zec 3:2 — And the LORD said unto Satan, The LORD rebuke thee, O Satan; even the LORD that hath chosen Jerusalem rebuke thee: *is* not this a brand plucked out of the fire?

Mt 12:50 — For whosoever shall do the will of my Father which is in heaven, the same is my brother, and sister, and mother.

Mt 13:23 — But he that received seed into the good ground is he that heareth the word, and understandeth *it;* which also beareth fruit, and bringeth forth, some an hundredfold, some sixty, some thirty.

Mt 13:38 — The field is the world; the good seed are the children of the kingdom; but the tares are the children of the wicked *one;*

Mt 19:14 — But Jesus said, Suffer little children, and forbid them not, to come unto me: for of such is the kingdom of heaven.

Lk 6:45 — A good man out of the good treasure of his heart bringeth forth that which is good; and an evil man out of the evil treasure of his heart bringeth forth that which is evil: for of the abundance of the heart his mouth speaketh.

Jn 3:21 — But he that doeth truth cometh to the light, that his deeds may be made manifest, that they are wrought in God.

Jn 8:39 — They answered and said unto him, Abraham is our father. Jesus saith unto them, If ye were Abraham's children, ye would do the works of Abraham.

Jn 8:42 — Jesus said unto them, If God were your Father, ye would love me: for I proceeded forth and came from God; neither came I of myself, but he sent me.

Jn 8:47 — He that is of God heareth God's words: ye therefore hear *them* not, because ye are not of God.

Jn 10:27 — My sheep hear my voice, and I know them, and they follow me:

Jn 13:35 — By this shall all *men* know that ye are my disciples, if ye have love one to another.

Jn 15:14 — Ye are my friends, if ye do whatsoever I command you.

Ac 2:38 — Then Peter said unto them, Repent, and be baptized every one of you in the name of Jesus Christ for the remission of sins, and ye shall receive the gift of the Holy Ghost.

Ac 2:47 — Praising God, and having favour with all the people. And the Lord added to the church daily such as should be saved.

Ac 10:47 — Can any man forbid water, that these should not be baptized, which have received the Holy Ghost as well as we?

Ro 8:9 — But ye are not in the flesh, but in the Spirit, if so be that the Spirit of God dwell in you. Now if any man have not the Spirit of Christ, he is none of his.

Ro 8:29 — For whom he did foreknow, he also did predestinate *to be* conformed to the image of his Son, that he might be the firstborn among many brethren.

Ro 9:8 — That is, They which are the children of the flesh, these *are* not the children of God: but the children of the promise are counted for the seed.

Ro 15:14 — And I myself also am persuaded of you, my brethren, that ye also are full of goodness, filled with all knowledge, able also to admonish one another.

Ro 16:19 — For your obedience is come abroad unto all *men.* I am glad therefore on your behalf: but yet I would have you wise unto that which is good, and simple concerning evil.

1Co 1:2 — Unto the church of God which is at Corinth, to them that are sanctified in Christ Jesus, called *to be* saints, with all that in every place call upon the name of Jesus Christ our Lord, both theirs and ours:

1Co 1:30 — But of him are ye in Christ Jesus, who of God is made unto us wisdom, and righteousness, and sanctification, and redemption:

2Co 1:12 — For our rejoicing is this, the testimony of our conscience, that in simplicity and godly sincerity, not with fleshly wisdom, but by the grace of God, we have had our conversation in the world, and more abundantly to you-ward.

2Co 5:17 — Therefore if any man *be* in Christ, *he is* a new creature: old things are passed away; behold, all things are become new.

2Co 5:21 — For he hath made him *to be* sin for us, who knew no sin; that we might be made the righteousness of God in him.

Eph 1:1 — Paul, an apostle of Jesus Christ by the will of God, to the saints which are at Ephesus, and to the faithful in Christ Jesus:

Eph 2:1 — And you *hath he quickened,* who were dead in trespasses and sins;

Eph 2:10 — For we are his workmanship, created in Christ Jesus unto good works, which God hath before ordained that we should walk in them.

Eph 5:8 — For ye were sometimes darkness, but now *are ye* light in the Lord: walk as children of light:

Php 2:15 — That ye may be blameless and harmless, the sons of God, without rebuke, in the midst of a crooked and perverse nation, among whom ye shine as lights in the world;

Php 3:3 — For we are the circumcision, which worship God in the spirit, and rejoice in Christ Jesus, and have no confidence in the flesh.

Php 4:8 — Finally, brethren, whatsoever things are true, whatsoever things *are* honest, whatsoever things *are* just, whatsoever things *are* pure, whatsoever things *are* lovely, whatsoever things *are* of good report; if *there be* any virtue, and if *there be* any praise, think on these things.

Col 2:7 — Rooted and built up in him, and stablished in the faith, as ye have been taught, abounding therein with thanksgiving.

Col 3:3 — For ye are dead, and your life is hid with Christ in God.

1Th 1:3 — Remembering without ceasing your work of faith, and labour of love, and patience of hope in our Lord Jesus Christ, in the sight of God and our Father;

1Th 5:27 — I charge you by the Lord that this epistle be read unto all the holy brethren.

2Ti 2:19 — Nevertheless the foundation of God standeth sure, having this seal, The Lord knoweth them that are his. And, Let every one that nameth the name of Christ depart from iniquity.

Heb 3:1 — Wherefore, holy brethren, partakers of the heavenly calling, consider the Apostle and High Priest of our profession, Christ Jesus;

Heb 3:6 — But Christ as a son over his own house; whose house are we, if we hold fast the confidence and the rejoicing of the hope firm unto the end.

1Pe 2:5 — Ye also, as lively stones, are built up a spiritual house, an holy priesthood, to offer up spiritual sacrifices, acceptable to God by Jesus Christ.

2Pe 1:1 — Simon Peter, a servant and an apostle of Jesus Christ, to them that have obtained like precious faith with us through the righteousness of God and our Saviour Jesus Christ:

1Jn 2:3 — And hereby we do know that we know him, if we keep his commandments.

1Jn 3:9 — Whosoever is born of God doth not commit sin; for his seed remaineth in him: and he cannot sin, because he is born of God.

1Jn 3:14 — We know that we have passed from death unto life, because we love the brethren. He that loveth not *his* brother abideth in death.

1Jn 4:7 — Beloved, let us love one another: for love is of God; and every one that loveth is born of God, and knoweth God.

1Jn 5:1 — Whosoever believeth that Jesus is the Christ is born of God: and every one that loveth him that begat loveth him also that is begotten of him.

2Jn 1:9 — Whosoever transgresseth, and abideth not in the doctrine of Christ, hath not God. He that abideth in the doctrine of Christ, he hath both the Father and the Son.

Rev 1:6 — And hath made us kings and priests unto God and his Father; to him *be* glory and dominion for ever and ever. Amen.

Rev 17:14 — These shall make war with the Lamb, and the Lamb shall overcome them: for he is Lord of lords, and King of kings: and they that are with him *are* called, and chosen, and faithful.

✦See: Wicked; described

• Promises to, expressed or implied.

Le 26:5–6; Dt 28:1–13; Job 5:11–27; 8:4–7, 20–21; 11:15–20; 22:21–30; 36:7–12; Ps 15:2–5; 25:10–14; 32:6–8; 33:18–19; 34:9–10; 37:3–5, 23–29; 41:1–2; 91:3–7, 9–12; 94:17–18; 97:10–11; 121:3–8; 125:1–3; 128:1–6; 145:18–21; Pr 3:1–10, 25–26; Isa 4:5–6; 11:6–9; 33:21–22; 40:10–11; 41:10–11; 44:2–3; 49:9–12; 50:7–9; 54:1–17; 56:2–8; 57:1–2; 58:8–14; 59:20–21; 65:13–14, 17–25; 66:13–14; Jer 17:7–8; Eze 18:5–9, 19–20; 34:11–17, 22–31; Da 12:1–3; Hag 2:4–5; Mal 3:16–18; 4:2–3; Mt 5:3–12; 7:7–8; 10:28–32; 18:10–20; 24:21–22; 25:33–34; Mk 10:29–30; 11:23–24; Lk 6:20–23; 11:9–10; 16:22–25; 18:29–30; 19:16–21; 20:35–36; 21:27–28; 22:29–30; Jn 3:15–18; 6:39–40; 10:27–29; 12:25–26; 14:1–3, 12–13, 15–21; Ro 5:9–11; 6:22–23; 8:14–18, 32–39; 10:11–13; 1Co 1:8–9; 3:21–23; 6:2–3; 13:10–12; 15:48–57; 2Co 1:20–22; 4:14–15; Gal 6:8–9; 1Th 3:12–13; 4:15–18; 5:9–11; 2Th 1:5–7; 2:13–14; 2Ti 2:10–12; Tit 2:11–14; Heb 4:15–16; 6:16–20; 10:34–36; 12:22–23; 13:5–6; 1Pe 1:2–5; 2:5–6, 9–10; 3:9–12; 5:6–7; 2Pe 1:10–11; Rev 2:10–11, 26–28; 3:4–5; 7:3–4, 9–17; 14:1–5; 20:4–6; 21:3–7; 22:4–5

Ge 15:1 — After these things the word of the LORD came unto Abram in a vision, saying, Fear not, Abram: I *am* thy shield, *and* thy exceeding great reward.

Ge 22:17 — That in blessing I will bless thee, and in multiplying I will multiply thy seed as the stars of the heaven, and as the sand which *is* upon the sea shore; and thy seed shall possess the gate of his enemies;

Ex 23:22 — But if thou shalt indeed obey his voice, and do all that I speak; then I will be an enemy unto thine enemies, and an adversary unto thine adversaries.

Le 26:10 — And ye shall eat old store, and bring forth the old because of the new.

Dt 33:27 — The eternal God *is thy* refuge, and underneath *are* the everlasting arms: and he shall thrust out the enemy from before thee; and shall say, Destroy *them*.

1Sa 2:9 — He will keep the feet of his saints, and the wicked shall be silent in darkness; for by strength shall no man prevail.

2Ch 16:9 — For the eyes of the LORD run to and fro throughout the whole earth, to shew himself strong in the behalf of *them* whose heart *is* perfect toward him. Herein thou hast done foolishly: therefore from henceforth thou shalt have wars.

Ezr 8:22 — For I was ashamed to require of the king a band of soldiers and horsemen to help us against the enemy in the way: because we had spoken unto the king, saying, The hand of our God *is* upon all them for good that seek him; but his power and his wrath *is* against all them that forsake him.

Ps 4:3 — But know that the LORD hath set apart him that is godly for himself: the LORD will hear when I call unto him.

Ps 5:12 — For thou, LORD, wilt bless the righteous; with favour wilt thou compass him as *with* a shield.

Ps 23:6 — Surely goodness and mercy shall follow me all the days of my life: and I will dwell in the house of the LORD for ever.

Ps 28:8 — The LORD *is* their strength, and he *is* the saving strength of his anointed.

Ps 29:11 — The LORD will give strength unto his people; the LORD will bless his people with peace.

Ps 32:10 — Many sorrows *shall be* to the wicked: but he that trusteth in the LORD, mercy shall compass him about.

Ps 34:15 — The eyes of the LORD *are* upon the righteous, and his ears *are open* unto their cry.

Ps 34:17 — *The righteous* cry, and the LORD heareth, and delivereth them out of all their troubles.

Ps 37:9 — For evildoers shall be cut off: but those that wait upon the LORD, they shall inherit the earth.

Ps 37:18 — The LORD knoweth the days of the upright: and their inheritance shall be for ever.

Ps 37:34 — Wait on the LORD, and keep his way, and he shall exalt thee to inherit the land: when the wicked are cut off, thou shalt see *it*.

Ps 50:15 — And call upon me in the day of trouble: I will deliver thee, and thou shalt glorify me.

Ps 55:22 — Cast thy burden upon the LORD, and he shall sustain thee: he shall never suffer the righteous to be moved.

Ps 58:11 — So that a man shall say, Verily *there is* a reward for the righteous: verily he is a God that judgeth in the earth.

Ps 62:8 — Trust in him at all times; *ye* people, pour out your heart before him: God *is* a refuge for us. Selah.

Ps 65:4 — Blessed *is the man whom* thou choosest, and causest to approach *unto thee, that* he may dwell in thy courts: we shall be satisfied with the goodness of thy house, *even* of thy holy temple.

Ps 73:24 — Thou shalt guide me with thy counsel, and afterward receive me *to* glory.

Ps 81:10 — I *am* the LORD thy God, which brought thee out of the land of Egypt: open thy mouth wide, and I will fill it.

Ps 84:11 — For the LORD God *is* a sun and shield: the LORD will give grace and glory: no good *thing* will he withhold from them that walk uprightly.

Ps 85:9 — Surely his salvation *is* nigh them that fear him; that glory may dwell in our land.

Ps 91:1 — He that dwelleth in the secret place of the most High shall abide under the shadow of the Almighty.

Ps 111:5 — He hath given meat unto them that fear him: he will ever be mindful of his covenant.

Ps 112:6 — Surely he shall not be moved for ever: the righteous shall be in everlasting remembrance.

Pr 1:33 — But whoso hearkeneth unto me shall dwell safely, and shall be quiet from fear of evil.

Pr 2:21 — For the upright shall dwell in the land, and the perfect shall remain in it.

Pr 10:3 — The LORD will not suffer the soul of the righteous to famish: but he casteth away the substance of the wicked.

Pr 12:2 — A good *man* obtaineth favour of the LORD: but a man of wicked devices will he condemn.

Pr 14:26 — In the fear of the LORD *is* strong confidence: and his children shall have a place of refuge.

Pr 15:29 — The LORD *is* far from the wicked: but he heareth the prayer of the righteous.

Pr 16:7 — When a man's ways please the LORD, he maketh even his enemies to be at peace with him.

Pr 21:21 — He that followeth after righteousness and mercy findeth life, righteousness, and honour.

Pr 28:25 — He that is of a proud heart stirreth up strife: but he that putteth his trust in the LORD shall be made fat.

Pr 29:25 — The fear of man bringeth a snare: but whoso putteth his trust in the LORD shall be safe.

Ecc 7:18 — *It is* good that thou shouldest take hold of this; yea, also from this withdraw not thine hand: for he that feareth God shall come forth of them all.

Ecc 8:5 — Whoso keepeth the commandment shall feel no evil thing: and a wise man's heart discerneth both time and judgment.

Isa 25:8 — He will swallow up death in victory; and the Lord GOD will wipe away tears from off all faces; and the rebuke of his people shall he take away from off all the earth: for the LORD hath spoken *it*.

Isa 26:3 — Thou wilt keep *him* in perfect peace, *whose* mind *is* stayed *on thee:* because he trusteth in thee.

Isa 33:16 — He shall dwell on high: his place of defence *shall be* the munitions of rocks: bread shall be given him; his waters *shall be* sure.

Isa 33:24 — And the inhabitant shall not say, I am sick: the people that dwell therein *shall be* forgiven *their* iniquity.

Isa 35:10 — And the ransomed of the LORD shall return, and come to Zion with songs and everlasting joy upon their heads: they shall obtain joy and gladness, and sorrow and sighing shall flee away.

Isa 40:29 — He giveth power to the faint; and to *them that have* no might he increaseth strength.

Isa 40:31 — But they that wait upon the LORD shall renew *their* strength; they shall mount up with wings as eagles; they shall run, and not be weary; *and* they shall walk, and not faint.

Isa 41:13 — For I the LORD thy God will hold thy right hand, saying unto thee, Fear not; I will help thee.

Isa 43:2 — When thou passest through the waters, I *will be* with thee; and through the rivers, they shall not overflow thee: when thou walkest through the fire, thou shalt not be burned; neither shall the flame kindle upon thee.

Isa 51:11 — Therefore the redeemed of the LORD shall return, and come with singing unto Zion; and everlasting joy *shall be* upon their head: they shall obtain gladness and joy; *and* sorrow and mourning shall flee away.

Isa 64:4 — For since the beginning of the world *men* have not heard, nor perceived by the ear, neither hath the eye seen, O God, beside thee, *what* he hath prepared for him that waiteth for him.

Hos 6:3 — Then shall we know, *if* we follow on to know the LORD: his going forth is prepared as the morning; and he shall come unto us as the rain, as the latter *and* former rain unto the earth.

Na 1:7 — The LORD *is* good, a strong hold in the day of trouble; and he knoweth them that trust in him.

Hag 1:13 — Then spake Haggai the LORD's messenger in the LORD's message unto the people, saying, I *am* with you, saith the LORD.

Zec 3:7 — Thus saith the LORD of hosts; If thou wilt walk in my ways, and if thou wilt keep my charge, then thou shalt also judge my house, and shalt also keep my courts, and I will give thee places to walk among these that stand by.

Mt 3:12 — Whose fan *is* in his hand, and he will throughly purge his floor, and gather his wheat into the garner; but he will burn up the chaff with unquenchable fire.

Mt 8:11 — And I say unto you, That many shall come from the east and west, and shall sit down with Abraham, and Isaac, and Jacob, in the kingdom of heaven.

Mt 13:43 — Then shall the righteous shine forth as the sun in the kingdom of their Father. Who hath ears to hear, let him hear.

Mt 19:29 — And every one that hath forsaken houses, or brethren, or sisters, or father, or mother, or wife, or children, or lands, for my name's sake, shall receive an hundredfold, and shall inherit everlasting life.

Mt 25:21 — His lord said unto him, Well done, *thou* good and faithful servant: thou hast been faithful over a few things, I will make thee ruler over many things: enter thou into the joy of thy lord.

Mt 25:46 — And these shall go away into everlasting punishment: but the righteous into life eternal.

Mt 28:20 — Teaching them to observe all things whatsoever I have commanded you: and, lo, I am with you alway, *even* unto the end of the world. Amen.

Mk 3:35 — For whosoever shall do the will of God, the same is my brother, and my sister, and mother.

Mk 8:35 — For whosoever will save his life shall lose it; but whosoever shall lose his life for my sake and the gospel's, the same shall save it.

Mk 9:41 — For whosoever shall give you a cup of water to drink in my name, because ye belong to Christ, verily I say unto you, he shall not lose his reward.

Mk 10:21 — Then Jesus beholding him loved him, and said unto him, One thing thou lackest: go thy way, sell whatsoever thou hast, and give to the poor, and thou shalt have treasure in heaven: and come, take up the cross, and follow me.

Mk 13:13 — And ye shall be hated of all *men* for my name's sake: but he that shall endure unto the end, the same shall be saved.

Mk 13:27 — And then shall he send his angels, and shall gather together his elect from the four winds, from the uttermost part of the earth to the uttermost part of heaven.

Lk 3:17 — Whose fan *is* in his hand, and he will throughly purge his floor, and will gather the wheat into his garner; but the chaff he will burn with fire unquenchable.

Lk 10:20 — Notwithstanding in this rejoice not, that the spirits are subject unto you; but rather rejoice, because your names are written in heaven.

Lk 12:7 — But even the very hairs of your head are all numbered. Fear not therefore: ye are of more value than many sparrows.

Lk 12:32 — Fear not, little flock; for it is your Father's good pleasure to give you the kingdom.

Lk 21:18 — But there shall not an hair of your head perish.

Lk 23:43 — And Jesus said unto him, Verily I say unto thee, To day shalt thou be with me in paradise.

Jn 3:36 — He that believeth on the Son hath everlasting life: and he that believeth not the Son shall not see life; but the wrath of God abideth on him.

Jn 4:14 — But whosoever drinketh of the water that I shall give him shall never thirst; but the water that I shall give him shall be in him a well of water springing up into everlasting life.

Jn 5:24 — Verily, verily, I say unto you, He that heareth my word, and believeth on him that sent me, hath everlasting life, and shall not come into condemnation; but is passed from death unto life.

Jn 5:29 — And shall come forth; they that have done good, unto the resurrection of life; and they that have done evil, unto the resurrection of damnation.

Jn 8:12 — Then spake Jesus again unto them, saying, I am the light of the world: he that followeth me shall not walk in darkness, but shall have the light of life.

Jn 8:51 — Verily, verily, I say unto you, If a man keep my saying, he shall never see death.

Jn 9:31 — Now we know that God heareth not sinners: but if any man be a worshipper of God, and doeth his will, him he heareth.

Jn 13:36 — Simon Peter said unto him, Lord, whither goest thou? Jesus answered him, Whither I go, thou canst not follow me now; but thou shalt follow me afterwards.

Jn 14:23 — Jesus answered and said unto him, If a man love me, he will keep my words: and my Father will love him, and we will come unto him, and make our abode with him.

Jn 16:33 — These things I have spoken unto you, that in me ye might have peace. In the world ye shall have tribulation: but be of good cheer; I have overcome the world.

Jn 17:2 — As thou hast given him power over all flesh, that he should give eternal life to as many as thou hast given him.

Jn 17:22 — And the glory which thou gavest me I have given them; that they may be one, even as we are one:

Jn 17:24 — Father, I will that they also, whom thou hast given me, be with me where I am; that they may behold my glory, which thou hast given me: for thou lovedst me before the foundation of the world.

Ac 10:4 — And when he looked on him, he was afraid, and said, What is it, Lord? And he said unto him, Thy prayers and thine alms are come up for a memorial before God.

Ac 10:31 — And said, Cornelius, thy prayer is heard, and thine alms are had in remembrance in the sight of God.

Ac 20:32 — And now, brethren, I commend you to God, and to the word of his grace, which is able to build you up, and to give you an inheritance among all them which are sanctified.

Ac 26:18 — To open their eyes, *and* to turn *them* from darkness to light, and *from* the power of Satan unto God, that they may receive forgiveness of sins, and inheritance among them which are sanctified by faith that is in me.

Ro 2:7 — To them who by patient continuance in well doing seek for glory and honour and immortality, eternal life:

Ro 2:10 — But glory, honour, and peace, to every man that worketh good, to the Jew first, and also to the Gentile:

Ro 5:17 — For if by one man's offence death reigned by one; much more they which receive abundance of grace and of the gift of righteousness shall reign in life by one, Jesus Christ.)

Ro 8:28 — And we know that all things work together for good to them that love God, to them who are the called according to *his* purpose.

Ro 9:33 — As it is written, Behold, I lay in Sion a stumblingstone and rock of offence: and whosoever believeth on him shall not be ashamed.

Ro 10:9 — That if thou shalt confess with thy mouth the Lord Jesus, and shalt believe in thine heart that God hath raised him from the dead, thou shalt be saved.

Ro 13:11 — And that, knowing the time, that now *it is* high time to awake out of sleep: for now *is* our salvation nearer than when we believed.

1Co 2:9 — But as it is written, Eye hath not seen, nor ear heard, neither have entered into the heart of man, the things which God hath prepared for them that love him.

1Co 8:3 — But if any man love God, the same is known of him.

2Co 4:17 — For our light affliction, which is but for a moment, worketh for us a far more exceeding *and* eternal weight of glory;

2Co 7:1 — Having therefore these promises, dearly beloved, let us cleanse ourselves from all filthiness of the flesh and spirit, perfecting holiness in the fear of God.

Gal 3:29 — And if ye *be* Christ's, then are ye Abraham's seed, and heirs according to the promise.

Eph 1:18 — The eyes of your understanding being enlightened; that ye may know what is the hope of his calling, and what the riches of the glory of his inheritance in the saints,

Eph 2:7 — That in the ages to come he might shew the exceeding riches of his grace in *his* kindness toward us through Christ Jesus.

Eph 6:8 — Knowing that whatsoever good thing any man doeth, the same shall he receive of the Lord, whether *he be* bond or free.

Php 4:7 — And the peace of God, which passeth all understanding, shall keep your hearts and minds through Christ Jesus.

Php 4:19 — But my God shall supply all your need according to his riches in glory by Christ Jesus.

Col 1:5 — For the hope which is laid up for you in heaven, whereof ye heard before in the word of the truth of the gospel;

Col 1:12 — Giving thanks unto the Father, which hath made us meet to be partakers of the inheritance of the saints in light:

Col 3:4 — When Christ, *who is* our life, shall appear, then shall ye also appear with him in glory.

Col 3:24 — Knowing that of the Lord ye shall receive the reward of the inheritance: for ye serve the Lord Christ.

1Th 2:12 — That ye would walk worthy of God, who hath called you unto his kingdom and glory.

1Ti 1:16 — Howbeit for this cause I obtained mercy, that in me first Jesus Christ might shew forth all longsuffering, for a pattern to them which should hereafter believe on him to life everlasting.

1Ti 4:8 — For bodily exercise profiteth little: but godliness is profitable unto all things, having promise of the life that now is, and of that which is to come.

2Ti 1:12 — For the which cause I also suffer these things: nevertheless I am not ashamed: for I know whom I have believed, and am persuaded that he is able to keep that which I have committed unto him against that day.

2Ti 2:19 — Nevertheless the foundation of God standeth sure, having this seal, The Lord knoweth them that are his. And, Let every one that nameth the name of Christ depart from iniquity.

2Ti 4:8 — Henceforth there is laid up for me a crown of righteousness, which the Lord, the righteous judge, shall give me at that day: and not to me only, but unto all them also that love his appearing.

Tit 3:7 — That being justified by his grace, we should be made heirs according to the hope of eternal life.

Heb 1:14 — Are they not all ministering spirits, sent forth to minister for them who shall be heirs of salvation?

Heb 2:10 — For it became him, for whom *are* all things, and by whom *are* all things, in bringing many sons unto glory, to make the captain of their salvation perfect through sufferings.

Heb 2:15 — And deliver them who through fear of death were all their lifetime subject to bondage.

Heb 4:9 — There remaineth therefore a rest to the people of God.

Heb 6:10 — For God *is* not unrighteous to forget your work and labour of love, which ye have shewed toward his name, in that ye have ministered to the saints, and do minister.

Heb 9:15 — And for this cause he is the mediator of the new testament, that by means of death, for the redemption of the transgressions *that were* under the first testament, they which are called might receive the promise of eternal inheritance.

Heb 9:28 — So Christ was once offered to bear the sins of many; and unto them that look for him shall he appear the second time without sin unto salvation.

Heb 11:16 — But now they desire a better *country*, that is, an heavenly: wherefore God is not ashamed to be called their God: for he hath prepared for them a city.

Heb 12:28 — Wherefore we receiving a kingdom which cannot be moved, let us have grace, whereby we may serve God acceptably with reverence and godly fear:

Jas 1:5 — If any of you lack wisdom, let him ask of God, that giveth to all *men* liberally, and upbraideth not; and it shall be given him.

Jas 1:12 — Blessed *is* the man that endureth temptation: for when he is tried, he shall receive the crown of life, which the Lord hath promised to them that love him.

Jas 1:25 — But whoso looketh into the perfect law of liberty, and continueth *therein,* he being not a forgetful hearer, but a doer of the work, this man shall be blessed in his deed.

Jas 2:5 — Hearken, my beloved brethren, Hath not God chosen the poor of this world rich in faith, and heirs of the kingdom which he hath promised to them that love him?

Jas 4:8 — Draw nigh to God, and he will draw nigh to you. Cleanse *your* hands, *ye* sinners; and purify *your* hearts, *ye* double minded.

1Pe 4:13 — But rejoice, inasmuch as ye are partakers of Christ's sufferings; that, when his glory shall be revealed, ye may be glad also with exceeding joy.

1Pe 5:4 — And when the chief Shepherd shall appear, ye shall receive a crown of glory that fadeth not away.

1Pe 5:10 — But the God of all grace, who hath called us unto his eternal glory by Christ Jesus, after that ye have suffered a while, make you perfect, stablish, strengthen, settle *you.*

2Pe 1:4 — Whereby are given unto us exceeding great and precious promises: that by these ye might be partakers of the divine nature, having escaped the corruption that is in the world through lust.

2Pe 2:9 — The Lord knoweth how to deliver the godly out of temptations, and to reserve the unjust unto the day of judgment to be punished:

1Jn 1:7 — But if we walk in the light, as he is in the light, we have fellowship one with another, and the blood of Jesus Christ his Son cleanseth us from all sin.

1Jn 1:9 — If we confess our sins, he is faithful and just to forgive us *our* sins, and to cleanse us from all unrighteousness.

1Jn 2:17 — And the world passeth away, and the lust thereof: but he that doeth the will of God abideth for ever.

1Jn 2:25 — And this is the promise that he hath promised us, *even* eternal life.

1Jn 2:28 — And now, little children, abide in him; that, when he shall appear, we may have confidence, and not be ashamed before him at his coming.

1Jn 3:2 — Beloved, now are we the sons of God, and it doth not yet appear what we shall be: but we know that, when he shall appear, we shall be like him; for we shall see him as he is.

1Jn 3:22 — And whatsoever we ask, we receive of him, because we keep his commandments, and do those things that are pleasing in his sight.

1Jn 5:13 — These things have I written unto you that believe on the name of the Son of God; that ye may know that ye have eternal life, and that ye may believe on the name of the Son of God.

Rev 1:6 — And hath made us kings and priests unto God and his Father; to him *be* glory and dominion for ever and ever. Amen.

Rev 2:7 — He that hath an ear, let him hear what the Spirit saith unto the churches; To him that overcometh will I give to eat of the tree of life, which is in the midst of the paradise of God.

Rev 2:17 — He that hath an ear, let him hear what the Spirit saith unto the churches; To him that overcometh will I give to eat of the hidden manna, and will give him a white stone, and in the stone a new name written, which no man knoweth saving he that receiveth *it.*

Rev 3:10 — Because thou hast kept the word of my patience, I also will keep thee from the hour of temptation, which shall come upon all the world, to try them that dwell upon the earth.

Rev 3:12 — Him that overcometh will I make a pillar in the temple of my God, and he shall go no more out: and I will write upon him the name of my God, and the name of the city of my God, *which is* new Jerusalem, which cometh down out of heaven from my God: and *I will write upon him* my new name.

Rev 3:21 — To him that overcometh will I grant to sit with me in my throne, even as I also overcame, and am set down with my Father in his throne.

Rev 11:12 — And they heard a great voice from heaven saying unto them, Come up hither. And they ascended up to heaven in a cloud; and their enemies beheld them.

Rev 11:18 — And the nations were angry, and thy wrath is come, and the time of the dead, that they should be judged, and that thou shouldest give reward unto thy servants the prophets, and to the saints, and them that fear thy name, small and great; and shouldest destroy them which destroy the earth.

Rev 14:13 — And I heard a voice from heaven saying unto me, Write, Blessed *are* the dead which die in the Lord from henceforth: Yea, saith the Spirit, that they may rest from their labours; and their works do follow them.

Rev 16:15 — Behold, I come as a thief. Blessed *is* he that watcheth, and keepeth his garments, lest he walk naked, and they see his shame.

Rev 21:24 — And the nations of them which are saved shall walk in the light of it: and the kings of the earth do bring their glory and honour into it.

Rev 22:7 — Behold, I come quickly: blessed is he that keepeth the sayings of the prophecy of this book.

Rev 22:12 — And, behold, I come quickly; and my reward *is* with me, to give every man according as his work shall be.

Rev 22:14 — Blessed *are* they that do his commandments, that they may have right to the tree of life, and may enter in through the gates into the city.

✦See: Adoption

✦See: Assurance; saints privileged to have; comfort in affliction

✣See: God, Preserver

✣See: God, Providence of

• **For promises in particular.**

✣See: Backsliders

✣See: Obedience

✣See: Penitent; promises to

• **Unity of, with Christ.**

Jn 6:51–57; 15:1–11; 17:21–23; 1Co 6:13–20; 10:16–17; 12:12–13; Col 2:6–7; Rev 19:7–9

Jn 14:20 — At that day ye shall know that I *am* in my Father, and ye in me, and I in you.

Jn 15:19 — If ye were of the world, the world would love his own: but because ye are not of the world, but I have chosen you out of the world, therefore the world hateth you.

Jn 17:26 — And I have declared unto them thy name, and will declare *it:* that the love wherewith thou hast loved me may be in them, and I in them.

Ro 8:1 — *There is* therefore now no condemnation to them which are in Christ Jesus, who walk not after the flesh, but after the Spirit.

Ro 8:10 — And if Christ *be* in you, the body *is* dead because of sin; but the Spirit *is* life because of righteousness.

Ro 12:5 — So we, *being* many, are one body in Christ, and every one members one of another.

1Co 12:27 — Now ye are the body of Christ, and members in particular.

2Co 5:17 — Therefore if any man *be* in Christ, *he is* a new creature: old things are passed away; behold, all things are become new.

2Co 5:21 — For he hath made him *to be* sin for us, who knew no sin; that we might be made the righteousness of God in him.

2Co 11:2 — For I am jealous over you with godly jealousy: for I have espoused you to one husband, that I may present *you as* a chaste virgin to Christ.

2Co 13:5 — Examine yourselves, whether ye be in the faith; prove your own selves. Know ye not your own selves, how that Jesus Christ is in you, except ye be reprobates?

Gal 2:20 — I am crucified with Christ: nevertheless I live; yet not I, but Christ liveth in me: and the life which I now live in the flesh I live by the faith of the Son of God, who loved me, and gave himself for me.

Eph 5:30 — For we are members of his body, of his flesh, and of his bones.

Eph 5:32 — This is a great mystery: but I speak concerning Christ and the church.

Col 1:27 — To whom God would make known what *is* the riches of the glory of this mystery among the Gentiles; which is Christ in you, the hope of glory:

1Pe 4:13 — But rejoice, inasmuch as ye are partakers of Christ's sufferings; that, when his glory shall be revealed, ye may be glad also with exceeding joy.

1Jn 2:6 — He that saith he abideth in him ought himself also so to walk, even as he walked.

1Jn 2:24 — Let that therefore abide in you, which ye have heard from the beginning. If that which ye have heard from the beginning shall remain in you, ye also shall continue in the Son, and in the Father.

1Jn 2:28 — And now, little children, abide in him; that, when he shall appear, we may have confidence, and not be ashamed before him at his coming.

1Jn 3:6 — Whosoever abideth in him sinneth not: whosoever sinneth hath not seen him, neither known him.

1Jn 3:24 — And he that keepeth his commandments dwelleth in him, and he in him. And hereby we know that he abideth in us, by the Spirit which he hath given us.

1Jn 4:13 — Hereby know we that we dwell in him, and he in us, because he hath given us of his Spirit.

1Jn 5:12 — He that hath the Son hath life; *and* he that hath not the Son of God hath not life.

1Jn 5:20 — *And* we know that the Son of God is come, and hath given us an understanding, that we may know him that is true, and we are in him that is true, *even* in his Son Jesus Christ. This is the true God, and eternal life.

2Jn 1:9 — Whosoever transgresseth, and abideth not in the doctrine of Christ, hath not God. He that abideth in the doctrine of Christ, he hath both the Father and the Son.

Rev 21:9 — And there came unto me one of the seven angels which had the seven vials full of the seven last plagues, and talked with me, saying, Come hither, I will shew thee the bride, the Lamb's wife.

✣See: Adoption

✣See: Communion

✣See: Fellowship

RIGHTEOUSNESS

• **By faith.**

Ge 15:6 — And he believed in the LORD; and he counted it to him for righteousness.

Ro 4:3 — For what saith the scripture? Abraham believed God, and it was counted unto him for righteousness.

Ro 4:5 — But to him that worketh not, but believeth on him that justifieth the ungodly, his faith is counted for righteousness.

Ro 4:9 — *Cometh* this blessedness then upon the circumcision *only,* or upon the uncircumcision also? for we say that faith was reckoned to Abraham for righteousness.

Ro 4:11 — And he received the sign of circumcision, a seal of the righteousness of the faith which *he had yet* being uncircumcised: that he might be the father of all them that believe, though they be not circumcised; that righteousness might be imputed unto them also:

Ro 4:13 — For the promise, that he should be the heir of the world, *was* not to Abraham, or to his seed, through the law, but through the righteousness of faith.

Ro 4:20 — He staggered not at the promise of God through unbelief; but was strong in faith, giving glory to God;

Ro 4:22 — And therefore it was imputed to him for righteousness.

Ro 4:24 — But for us also, to whom it shall be imputed, if we believe on him that raised up Jesus our Lord from the dead;

• Garment of.

Mt 22:11–14

Job 29:14 — I put on righteousness, and it clothed me: my judgment *was* as a robe and a diadem.

• Imputed on account of obedience.

Dt 6:25 — And it shall be our righteousness, if we observe to do all these commandments before the LORD our God, as he hath commanded us.

Job 33:26 — He shall pray unto God, and he will be favourable unto him: and he shall see his face with joy: for he will render unto man his righteousness.

• Fruits of.

Ps 15:1–5; 24:3–5; 101:3–4; 112:4–8; Pr 2:5–20; 11:5–6, 18–19; Isa 32:16–18; 33:15–17; 55:12–13; 58:6–14; Eze 18:5–9; Mk 3:33–35; Lk 3:10–14; Jn 14:21–24; 15:4–5; Ac 11:29–30; Ro 5:1–5; 6:19–22; 7:4–6; 8:4–6; 14:17–19; 15:1–7; 1Co 4:19–20; 13:1–13; 2Co 7:10–11; Gal 5:22–23; 6:7–8; Eph 1:13–14; Php 1:27–29; 3:12–14; 4:11–13; Col 1:12–13; 3:9–17; 1Th 1:9–10; 2Th 1:3–5; 1Ti 2:9–10; 5:9–10; 2Ti 4:6–8; Tit 2:11–12; Phm 1:5–6; Jas 2:14–26; 3:11–18; 1Pe 3:1–11; 2Pe 1:5–9; 1Jn 2:3–6, 10–11; 3:6–7, 9–11, 17–24; 4:4–5:5; Rev 2:2–3

Dt 6:25 — And it shall be our righteousness, if we observe to do all these commandments before the LORD our God, as he hath commanded us.

Jos 22:31 — And Phinehas the son of Eleazar the priest said unto the children of Reuben, and to the children of Gad, and to the children of Manasseh, This day we perceive that the LORD *is* among us, because ye have not committed this trespass against the LORD: now ye have delivered the children of Israel out of the hand of the LORD.

Ps 1:3 — And he shall be like a tree planted by the rivers of water, that bringeth forth his fruit in his season; his leaf also shall not wither; and whatsoever he doeth shall prosper.

Ps 106:3 — Blessed *are* they that keep judgment, *and* he that doeth righteousness at all times.

Pr 10:2 — Treasures of wickedness profit nothing: but righteousness delivereth from death.

Pr 10:16 — The labour of the righteous *tendeth* to life: the fruit of the wicked to sin.

Pr 11:30 — The fruit of the righteous *is* a tree of life; and he that winneth souls *is* wise.

Pr 12:28 — In the way of righteousness *is* life; and *in* the pathway *thereof there is* no death.

Pr 13:6 — Righteousness keepeth *him that is* upright in the way: but wickedness overthroweth the sinner.

Pr 14:34 — Righteousness exalteth a nation: but sin *is* a reproach to any people.

Pr 21:3 — To do justice and judgment *is* more acceptable to the LORD than sacrifice.

Pr 29:7 — The righteous considereth the cause of the poor: *but* the wicked regardeth not to know *it*.

Isa 28:17 — Judgment also will I lay to the line, and righteousness to the plummet: and the hail shall sweep away the refuge of lies, and the waters shall overflow the hiding place.

Isa 62:1 — For Zion's sake will I not hold my peace, and for Jerusalem's sake I will not rest, until the righteousness thereof go forth as brightness, and the salvation thereof as a lamp *that* burneth.

Eze 33:15 — *If* the wicked restore the pledge, give again that he had robbed, walk in the statutes of life, without committing iniquity; he shall surely live, he shall not die.

Da 12:3 — And they that be wise shall shine as the brightness of the firmament; and they that turn many to righteousness as the stars for ever and ever.

Hos 10:12 — Sow to yourselves in righteousness, reap in mercy; break up your fallow ground: for *it is* time to seek the LORD, till he come and rain righteousness upon you.

Mal 3:3 — And he shall sit *as* a refiner and purifier of silver: and he shall purify the sons of Levi, and purge them as gold and silver, that they may offer unto the LORD an offering in righteousness.

Mal 4:2 — But unto you that fear my name shall the Sun of righteousness arise with healing in his wings; and ye shall go forth, and grow up as calves of the stall.

Mt 5:20 — For I say unto you, That except your righteousness shall exceed *the righteousness* of the scribes and Pharisees, ye shall in no case enter into the kingdom of heaven.

Mt 12:35 — A good man out of the good treasure of the heart bringeth forth good things: and an evil man out of the evil treasure bringeth forth evil things.

Mt 12:50 — For whosoever shall do the will of my Father which is in heaven, the same is my brother, and sister, and mother.

Lk 8:15 — But that on the good ground are they, which in an honest and good heart, having heard the word, keep *it*, and bring forth fruit with patience.

Jn 3:21 — But he that doeth truth cometh to the light, that his deeds may be made manifest, that they are wrought in God.

Jn 3:33 — He that hath received his testimony hath set to his seal that God is true.

Jn 8:47 — He that is of God heareth God's words: ye therefore hear *them* not, because ye are not of God.

Jn 8:49 — Jesus answered, I have not a devil; but I honour my Father, and ye do dishonour me.

Jn 13:35 — By this shall all *men* know that ye are my disciples, if ye have love one to another.

Jn 15:8 — Herein is my Father glorified, that ye bear much fruit; so shall ye be my disciples.

Jn 15:12 — This is my commandment, That ye love one another, as I have loved you.

Ac 9:36 — Now there was at Joppa a certain disciple named Tabitha, which by interpretation is called

Dorcas: this woman was full of good works and almsdeeds which she did.

Ac 19:19 — Many of them also which used curious arts brought their books together, and burned them before all *men:* and they counted the price of them, and found it fifty thousand *pieces* of silver.

1Co 12:3 — Wherefore I give you to understand, that no man speaking by the Spirit of God calleth Jesus accursed: and *that* no man can say that Jesus is the Lord, but by the Holy Ghost.

2Co 5:17 — Therefore if any man *be* in Christ, *he is* a new creature: old things are passed away; behold, all things are become new.

2Co 9:10 — Now he that ministereth seed to the sower both minister bread for *your* food, and multiply your seed sown, and increase the fruits of your righteousness;)

2Co 10:5 — Casting down imaginations, and every high thing that exalteth itself against the knowledge of God, and bringing into captivity every thought to the obedience of Christ;

2Co 13:5 — Examine yourselves, whether ye be in the faith; prove your own selves. Know ye not your own selves, how that Jesus Christ is in you, except ye be reprobates?

Gal 4:6 — And because ye are sons, God hath sent forth the Spirit of his Son into your hearts, crying, Abba, Father.

Eph 5:9 — (For the fruit of the Spirit is in all goodness and righteousness and truth;)

Php 1:11 — Being filled with the fruits of righteousness, which are by Jesus Christ, unto the glory and praise of God.

Php 2:13 — For it is God which worketh in you both to will and to do of *his* good pleasure.

Col 3:3 — For ye are dead, and your life is hid with Christ in God.

Col 3:5 — Mortify therefore your members which are upon the earth; fornication, uncleanness, inordinate affection, evil concupiscence, and covetousness, which is idolatry:

1Th 1:3 — Remembering without ceasing your work of faith, and labour of love, and patience of hope in our Lord Jesus Christ, in the sight of God and our Father;

2Ti 2:22 — Flee also youthful lusts: but follow righteousness, faith, charity, peace, with them that call on the Lord out of a pure heart.

Tit 2:2 — That the aged men be sober, grave, temperate, sound in faith, in charity, in patience.

Tit 3:14 — And let ours also learn to maintain good works for necessary uses, that they be not unfruitful.

Jas 1:27 — Pure religion and undefiled before God and the Father is this, To visit the fatherless and widows in their affliction, *and* to keep himself unspotted from the world.

1Pe 3:14 — But and if ye suffer for righteousness' sake, happy *are ye:* and be not afraid of their terror, neither be troubled;

1Pe 4:2 — That he no longer should live the rest of *his* time in the flesh to the lusts of men, but to the will of God.

1Jn 2:24 — Let that therefore abide in you, which ye have heard from the beginning. If that which ye have heard from the beginning shall remain in you, ye also shall continue in the Son, and in the Father.

1Jn 2:29 — If ye know that he is righteous, ye know that every one that doeth righteousness is born of him.

1Jn 3:3 — And every man that hath this hope in him purifieth himself, even as he is pure.

1Jn 3:14 — We know that we have passed from death unto life, because we love the brethren. He that loveth not *his* brother abideth in death.

1Jn 5:10 — He that believeth on the Son of God hath the witness in himself: he that believeth not God hath made him a liar; because he believeth not the record that God gave of his Son.

1Jn 5:13 — These things have I written unto you that believe on the name of the Son of God; that ye may know that ye have eternal life, and that ye may believe on the name of the Son of God.

1Jn 5:18 — We know that whosoever is born of God sinneth not; but he that is begotten of God keepeth himself, and that wicked one toucheth him not.

2Jn 1:9 — Whosoever transgresseth, and abideth not in the doctrine of Christ, hath not God. He that abideth in the doctrine of Christ, he hath both the Father and the Son.

3Jn 1:11 — Beloved, follow not that which is evil, but that which is good. He that doeth good is of God: but he that doeth evil hath not seen God.

Rev 2:19 — I know thy works, and charity, and service, and faith, and thy patience, and thy works; and the last *to be* more than the first.

• Symbolized.

Eze 47:12 — And by the river upon the bank thereof, on this side and on that side, shall grow all trees for meat, whose leaf shall not fade, neither shall the fruit thereof be consumed: it shall bring forth new fruit according to his months, because their waters they issued out of the sanctuary: and the fruit thereof shall be for meat, and the leaf thereof for medicine.

Rev 22:2 — In the midst of the street of it, and on either side of the river, *was there* the tree of life, which bare twelve *manner* of fruits, *and* yielded her fruit every month: and the leaves of the tree *were* for the healing of the nations.

See: Sin; fruits of

See: Works; good

RIMMON

• Father of the murderers of Ish-bosheth.

2Sa 4:2 — And Saul's son had two men *that were* captains of bands: the name of the one *was* Baanah, and the name of the other Rechab, the sons of Rimmon a Beerothite, of the children of Benjamin: (for Beeroth also was reckoned to Benjamin:

2Sa 4:5 — And the sons of Rimmon the Beerothite, Rechab and Baanah, went, and came about the heat of the day to the house of Ish-bosheth, who lay on a bed at noon.

2Sa 4:9 — And David answered Rechab and Baanah his brother, the sons of Rimmon the Beerothite, and said unto them, As the LORD liveth, who hath redeemed my soul out of all adversity,

• A city south of Jerusalem.

Zec 14:10 — All the land shall be turned as a plain from Geba to Rimmon south of Jerusalem: and it shall be lifted up, and inhabited in her place, from Benjamin's gate unto the place of the first gate, unto the corner gate, and *from* the tower of Hananeel unto the king's winepresses.

• Allotted to Judah.

Jos 15:32 — And Lebaoth, and Shilhim, and Ain, and Rimmon: all the cities *are* twenty and nine, with their villages:

Ne 11:29 — And at En-rimmon, and at Zareah, and at Jarmuth,

• Allotted to Judah and afterward to Simeon.

Jos 19:7 — Ain, Remmon, and Ether, and Ashan; four cities and their villages:

1Ch 4:32 — And their villages *were,* Etam, and Ain, Rimmon, and Tochen, and Ashan, five cities:

• Called Remmon.

Jos 19:7 — Ain, Remmon, and Ether, and Ashan; four cities and their villages:

• Called En-Rimmon.

Ne 11:29 — And at En-rimmon, and at Zareah, and at Jarmuth,

• A city of Zebulun.

1Ch 6:77 — Unto the rest of the children of Merari *were given* out of the tribe of Zebulun. Rimmon with her suburbs, Tabor with her suburbs:

• Called Remmon-Methoar.

Jos 19:13 — And from thence passeth on along on the east to Gittah-hepher, to Ittah-kazin, and goeth out to Remmon-methoar to Neah;

• A rock in Benjamin.

Jgs 20:45 — And they turned and fled toward the wilderness unto the rock of Rimmon: and they gleaned of them in the highways five thousand men; and pursued hard after them unto Gidom, and slew two thousand men of them.

Jgs 20:47 — But six hundred men turned and fled to the wilderness unto the rock Rimmon, and abode in the rock Rimmon four months.

Jgs 21:13 — And the whole congregation sent *some* to speak to the children of Benjamin that *were* in the rock Rimmon, and to call peaceably unto them.

• A Syrian idol.

2Ki 5:18 — In this thing the LORD pardon thy servant, *that* when my master goeth into the house of Rimmon to worship there, and he leaneth on my hand, and I bow myself in the house of Rimmon: when I bow down myself in the house of Rimmon, the LORD pardon thy servant in this thing.

RIMMON-PAREZ • A camping place of the Israelites.

Nu 33:19–20

RING

• Of gold.

Nu 31:50 — We have therefore brought an oblation for the LORD, what every man hath gotten, of jewels of gold, chains, and bracelets, rings, earrings, and tablets, to make an atonement for our souls before the LORD.

• Worn as a badge of office.

Ge 41:42 — And Pharaoh took off his ring from his hand, and put it upon Joseph's hand, and arrayed him in vestures of fine linen, and put a gold chain about his neck;

• Given as a token.

Est 8:2–10

Est 3:10 — And the king took his ring from his hand, and gave it unto Haman the son of Hammedatha the Agagite, the Jews' enemy.

Est 3:12 — Then were the king's scribes called on the thirteenth day of the first month, and there was written according to all that Haman had commanded unto the king's lieutenants, and to the governors that *were* over every province, and to the rulers of every people of every province according to the writing thereof, and *to* every people after their language; in the name of king Ahasuerus was it written, and sealed with the king's ring.

• Worn in the nose.

Pr 11:22 — *As* a jewel of gold in a swine's snout, *so is* a fair woman which is without discretion.

Isa 3:21 — The rings, and nose jewels,

• Offerings of, to the tabernacle.

Ex 35:22 — And they came, both men and women, as many as were willing hearted, *and* brought bracelets, and earrings, and rings, and tablets, all jewels of gold: and every man that offered *offered* an offering of gold unto the LORD.

Nu 31:50 — We have therefore brought an oblation for the LORD, what every man hath gotten, of jewels of gold, chains, and bracelets, rings, earrings, and tablets, to make an atonement for our souls before the LORD.

RINNAH • A son of Shimon.

1Ch 4:20 — And the sons of Shimon *were,* Amnon, and Rinnah, Ben-hanan, and Tilon. And the sons of Ishi *were,* Zoheth, and Ben-zoheth.

RIPHATH • A son of Gomer.

Ge 10:3 — And the sons of Gomer; Ashkenaz, and Riphath, and Togarmah.

1Ch 1:6 — And the sons of Gomer; Aschenaz, and Riphath, and Togarmah.

RISING

• Early.

Pr 31:15 — She riseth also while it is yet night, and giveth meat to her household, and a portion to her maidens.

- **For devotions.**
  - Ps 5:3 — My voice shalt thou hear in the morning, O LORD; in the morning will I direct *my prayer* unto thee, and will look up.
  - Ps 59:16 — But I will sing of thy power; yea, I will sing aloud of thy mercy in the morning: for thou hast been my defence and refuge in the day of my trouble.
  - Ps 63:1 — O God, thou *art* my God; early will I seek thee: my soul thirsteth for thee, my flesh longeth for thee in a dry and thirsty land, where no water is;
  - Ps 88:13 — But unto thee have I cried, O LORD; and in the morning shall my prayer prevent thee.
  - SS 7:12 — Let us get up early to the vineyards; let us see if the vine flourish, *whether* the tender grape appear, *and* the pomegranates bud forth: there will I give thee my loves.
  - Isa 26:9 — With my soul have I desired thee in the night; yea, with my spirit within me will I seek thee early: for when thy judgments *are* in the earth, the inhabitants of the world will learn righteousness.
- **Practiced by the wicked.**
  - Pr 27:14 — He that blesseth his friend with a loud voice, rising early in the morning, it shall be counted a curse to him.
  - Mic 2:1 — Woe to them that devise iniquity, and work evil upon their beds! when the morning is light, they practise it, because it is in the power of their hand.
  - Zep 3:7 — I said, Surely thou wilt fear me, thou wilt receive instruction; so their dwelling should not be cut off, howsoever I punished them: but they rose early, *and* corrupted all their doings.
- **Practiced by drunkards.**
  - Isa 5:11 — Woe unto them that rise up early in the morning, *that* they may follow strong drink; that continue until night, *till* wine inflame them!
- **Illustrates spiritual diligence.**
  Ro 13:11–12
- **Instances of.**
  - **Lot.**
    Ge 19:23
  - **Abraham.**
    Ge 19:27; 21:14; 22:3
  - **Isaac.**
    Ge 26:31
  - **Abimelech.**
    Ge 20:8
  - **Jacob.**
    Ge 28:18; 32:31
  - **Laban.**
    Ge 31:55
  - **Moses.**
    Ex 8:20; 9:13
  - **Joshua.**
    Jos 3:1; 6:12, 15; 7:16
  - **Gideon.**
    Jgs 6:38
  - **Elkanah.**
    1Sa 1:19
  - **Samuel.**
    1Sa 15:12
  - **David.**
    1Sa 17:20
  - **Mary.**
    Mk 16:2; Lk 24:1
  - **Apostles.**
    Ac 5:21
  - **See: Industry**
- **Late.**
  - **Consequences of.**
    Pr 6:9–11; 24:33–34
  - **See: Idleness**
  - **See: Slothfulness**

RISSAH • A camping place of the Israelites.

Nu 33:21–22

RITHMAH • A camping place of the Israelites.

Nu 33:18–19

RIVER

- **Figurative.**
  - **Of salvation.**
    Eze 47:1–12; Rev 22:1–2
    - Ps 36:8 — They shall be abundantly satisfied with the fatness of thy house; and thou shalt make them drink of the river of thy pleasures.
    - Ps 46:4 — *There is* a river, the streams whereof shall make glad the city of God, the holy *place* of the tabernacles of the most High.
    - Isa 32:2 — And a man shall be as an hiding place from the wind, and a covert from the tempest; as rivers of water in a dry place, as the shadow of a great rock in a weary land.
  - **Of grief.**
    - Ps 119:136 — Rivers of waters run down mine eyes, because they keep not thy law.
    - La 3:48 — Mine eye runneth down with rivers of water for the destruction of the daughter of my people.

RIZPAH

- **Concubine of Saul.**
  - 2Sa 3:7 — And Saul had a concubine, whose name *was* Rizpah, the daughter of Aiah: and *Ish-bosheth* said to Abner, Wherefore hast thou gone in unto my father's concubine?
- **Guards the bodies of her sons hanged by command of David.**
  2Sa 21:8–11

ROADS

- **Public highways.**
  - Dt 2:27 — Let me pass through thy land: I will go along by the high way, I will neither turn unto the right hand nor to the left.

• From Gibeon to Beth-horon.

Jos 10:10 — And the LORD discomfited them before Israel, and slew them with a great slaughter at Gibeon, and chased them along the way that goeth up to Beth-horon, and smote them to Azekah, and unto Makkedah.

• From Bethel to Shechem.

Jgs 21:19 — Then they said, Behold, *there is* a feast of the LORD in Shiloh yearly *in a place* which *is* on the north side of Bethel, on the east side of the highway that goeth up from Bethel to Shechem, and on the south of Lebonah.

• From Judaea to Galilee, by way of Samaria.

Jn 4:3–5

Jn 4:43 — Now after two days he departed thence, and went into Galilee.

• To the house of God.

Jgs 20:31 — And the children of Benjamin went out against the people, *and* were drawn away from the city; and they began to smite of the people, *and* kill, as at other times, in the highways, of which one goeth up to the house of God, and the other to Gibeah in the field, about thirty men of Israel.

• To cities of refuge.

Dt 19:3 — Thou shalt prepare thee a way, and divide the coasts of thy land, which the LORD thy God giveth thee to inherit, into three parts, that every slayer may flee thither.

• Built by rulers.

Nu 20:17 — Let us pass, I pray thee, through thy country: we will not pass through the fields, or through the vineyards, neither will we drink *of* the water of the wells: we will go by the king's *high* way, we will not turn to the right hand nor to the left, until we have passed thy borders.

Nu 21:22 — Let me pass through thy land: we will not turn into the fields, or into the vineyards; we will not drink *of* the waters of the well: *but* we will go along by the king's *high* way, until we be past thy borders.

• Figurative.

See: Highways

ROBBERS

Pr 1:11–16

• Dens of.

Jer 7:11 — Is this house, which is called by my name, become a den of robbers in your eyes? Behold, even I have seen *it,* saith the LORD.

• Bands of.

Hos 6:9 — And as troops of robbers wait for a man, *so* the company of priests murder in the way by consent: for they commit lewdness.

Hos 7:1 — When I would have healed Israel, then the iniquity of Ephraim was discovered, and the wickedness of Samaria: for they commit falsehood; and the thief cometh in, *and* the troop of robbers spoileth without.

See: Robbery

See: Theft and Thieves

ROBBERY

• Forbidden.

Le 19:13 — Thou shalt not defraud thy neighbour, neither rob *him:* the wages of him that is hired shall not abide with thee all night until the morning.

Isa 61:8 — For I the LORD love judgment, I hate robbery for burnt offering; and I will direct their work in truth, and I will make an everlasting covenant with them.

• Punished with death.

Eze 18:10 — If he beget a son *that is* a robber, a shedder of blood, and *that* doeth the like to *any* one of these *things,*

Eze 18:13 — Hath given forth upon usury, and hath taken increase: shall he then live? he shall not live: he hath done all these abominations; he shall surely die; his blood shall be upon him.

• Forgiven.

Eze 33:15 — *If* the wicked restore the pledge, give again that he had robbed, walk in the statutes of life, without committing iniquity; he shall surely live, he shall not die.

• Instances of.

Jgs 9:25; Lk 10:30

See: Robbers

See: Theft and Thieves

ROBE

• Of righteousness.

2Ch 6:41 — Now therefore arise, O LORD God, into thy resting place, thou, and the ark of thy strength: let thy priests, O LORD God, be clothed with salvation, and let thy saints rejoice in goodness.

Isa 61:10 — I will greatly rejoice in the LORD, my soul shall be joyful in my God; for he hath clothed me with the garments of salvation, he hath covered me with the robe of righteousness, as a bridegroom decketh *himself* with ornaments, and as a bride adorneth *herself* with her jewels.

Rev 6:11 — And white robes were given unto every one of them; and it was said unto them, that they should rest yet for a little season, until their fellowservants also and their brethren, that should be killed as they *were,* should be fulfilled.

Rev 7:9 — After this I beheld, and, lo, a great multitude, which no man could number, of all nations, and kindreds, and people, and tongues, stood before the throne, and before the Lamb, clothed with white robes, and palms in their hands;

Rev 7:13 — And one of the elders answered, saying unto me, What are these which are arrayed in white robes? and whence came they?

• Parable of the man who was not dressed in a wedding garment.

Mt 22:11 — And when the king came in to see the guests, he saw there a man which had not on a wedding garment:

See: Dress

ROCK

• Smitten by Moses for water.

Ps 78:15–16

Dt 8:15 — Who led thee through that great and terrible wilderness, *wherein were* fiery serpents, and scorpions, and drought, where *there was* no water; who brought thee forth water out of the rock of flint;

Ps 78:20 — Behold, he smote the rock, that the waters gushed out, and the streams overflowed; can he give bread also? can he provide flesh for his people?

• Houses in.

Mt 7:24–25

Jer 49:16 — Thy terribleness hath deceived thee, *and* the pride of thine heart, O thou that dwellest in the clefts of the rock, that holdest the height of the hill: though thou shouldest make thy nest as high as the eagle, I will bring thee down from thence, saith the LORD.

Ob 1:3 — The pride of thine heart hath deceived thee, thou that dwellest in the clefts of the rock, whose habitation *is* high; that saith in his heart, Who shall bring me down to the ground?

• Oil from.

Dt 32:13 — He made him ride on the high places of the earth, that he might eat the increase of the fields; and he made him to suck honey out of the rock, and oil out of the flinty rock;

Job 29:6 — When I washed my steps with butter, and the rock poured me out rivers of oil;

• Name of deity.

Dt 32:4 — *He is* the Rock, his work *is* perfect: for all his ways *are* judgment: a God of truth and without iniquity, just and right *is* he.

• Figurative.

2Sa 22:32 — For who *is* God, save the LORD? and who *is* a rock, save our God?

2Sa 22:47 — The LORD liveth; and blessed *be* my rock; and exalted be the God of the rock of my salvation.

2Sa 23:3 — The God of Israel said, the Rock of Israel spake to me, He that ruleth over men *must be* just, ruling in the fear of God.

Ps 18:2 — The LORD *is* my rock, and my fortress, and my deliverer; my God, my strength, in whom I will trust; my buckler, and the horn of my salvation, *and* my high tower.

Ps 31:2 — Bow down thine ear to me; deliver me speedily: be thou my strong rock, for an house of defence to save me.

Ps 40:2 — He brought me up also out of an horrible pit, out of the miry clay, and set my feet upon a rock, *and* established my goings.

Isa 17:10 — Because thou hast forgotten the God of thy salvation, and hast not been mindful of the rock of thy strength, therefore shalt thou plant pleasant plants, and shalt set it with strange slips:

Isa 32:2 — And a man shall be as an hiding place from the wind, and a covert from the tempest; as rivers of water in a dry place, as the shadow of a great rock in a weary land.

Mt 16:18 — And I say also unto thee, That thou art Peter, and upon this rock I will build my church; and the gates of hell shall not prevail against it.

1Co 10:4 — And did all drink the same spiritual drink: for they drank of that spiritual Rock that followed them: and that Rock was Christ.

ROE ↞See: Deer

ROGELIM • The home of Barzillai.

2Sa 17:27 — And it came to pass, when David was come to Mahanaim, that Shobi the son of Nahash of Rabbah of the children of Ammon, and Machir the son of Ammiel of Lo-debar, and Barzillai the Gileadite of Rogelim,

2Sa 19:31 — And Barzillai the Gileadite came down from Rogelim, and went over Jordan with the king, to conduct him over Jordan.

ROHGAH • Son of Shamer.

1Ch 7:34 — And the sons of Shamer; Ahi, and Rohgah, Jehubbah, and Aram.

ROLE MODEL

Dt 6:7–9; Eze 18:1–32

Pr 22:6 — Train up a child in the way he should go: and when he is old, he will not depart from it.

1Co 4:16 — Wherefore I beseech you, be ye followers of me.

1Co 11:1 — Be ye followers of me, even as I also *am* of Christ.

Php 3:17 — Brethren, be followers together of me, and mark them which walk so as ye have us for an ensample.

2Ti 3:15 — And that from a child thou hast known the holy scriptures, which are able to make thee wise unto salvation through faith which is in Christ Jesus.

Jas 5:16 — Confess *your* faults one to another, and pray one for another, that ye may be healed. The effectual fervent prayer of a righteous man availeth much.

ROLL

• Metallic table.

Isa 8:1 — Moreover the LORD said unto me, Take thee a great roll, and write in it with a man's pen concerning Maher-shalal-hash-baz.

↞See: Book

ROMAMTI-EZER • Son of Heman.

1Ch 25:4 — Of Heman: the sons of Heman; Bukkiah, Mattaniah, Uzziel, Shebuel, and Jerimoth, Hananiah, Hanani, Eliathah, Giddalti, and Romamti-ezer, Joshbekashah, Mallothi, Hothir, *and* Mahazioth:

1Ch 25:31 — The four and twentieth to Romamti-ezer, *he,* his sons, and his brethren, *were* twelve.

ROMAN EMPIRE

• Ruled by Augustus Caesar.

Lk 2:1 — And it came to pass in those days, that there went out a decree from Caesar Augustus, that all the world should be taxed.

- **Ruled by Tiberius Caesar.**

Lk 3:1 — Now in the fifteenth year of the reign of Tiberius Caesar, Pontius Pilate being governor of Judaea, and Herod being tetrarch of Galilee, and his brother Philip tetrarch of Ituraea and of the region of Trachonitis, and Lysanias the tetrarch of Abilene,

- **Ruled by Claudius Caesar.**

Ac 18:2 — And found a certain Jew named Aquila, born in Pontus, lately come from Italy, with his wife Priscilla; (because that Claudius had commanded all Jews to depart from Rome:) and came unto them.

- **Ruled by Nero.**

Php 4:22 — All the saints salute you, chiefly they that are of Caesar's household.

- **Citizenship in, by nativity.**

Ac 22:28 — And the chief captain answered, With a great sum obtained I this freedom. And Paul said, But I was *free* born.

- **Citizenship in, by purchase.**

Ac 22:28 — And the chief captain answered, With a great sum obtained I this freedom. And Paul said, But I was *free* born.

- **Rights of citizens.**

Ac 22:25–29

Ac 16:37 — But Paul said unto them, They have beaten us openly uncondemned, being Romans, and have cast *us* into prison; and now do they thrust us out privily? nay verily; but let them come themselves and fetch us out.

- **Rights of trial.**

Ac 25:16 — To whom I answered, It is not the manner of the Romans to deliver any man to die, before that he which is accused have the accusers face to face, and have licence to answer for himself concerning the crime laid against him.

- **Rights of appeal.**

Ac 25:10 — Then said Paul, I stand at Caesar's judgment seat, where I ought to be judged: to the Jews have I done no wrong, as thou very well knowest.

Ac 25:21 — But when Paul had appealed to be reserved unto the hearing of Augustus, I commanded him to be kept till I might send him to Caesar.

ROME

- **The capital of the Roman empire.**
- **Jews excluded from, by Claudius.**

Ac 18:2 — And found a certain Jew named Aquila, born in Pontus, lately come from Italy, with his wife Priscilla; (because that Claudius had commanded all Jews to depart from Rome:) and came unto them.

- **Paul's visit to.**

See: Paul, Ministry, Ac 16–28

- **Visited by Onesiphorus.**

2Ti 1:16–17

- **Paul desires to preach in.**

Ro 1:15 — So, as much as in me is, I am ready to preach the gospel to you that are at Rome also.

- **Abominations in.**

Ro 1:18–32

- **Christians in.**

Ro 16:5–17; Php 1:12–18

Php 4:22 — All the saints salute you, chiefly they that are of Caesar's household.

2Ti 4:21 — Do thy diligence to come before winter. Eubulus greeteth thee, and Pudens, and Linus, and Claudia, and all the brethren.

- **Paul's letter to the Christians in.**

Ro 1:7 — To all that be in Rome, beloved of God, called *to be* saints: Grace to you and peace from God our Father, and the Lord Jesus Christ.

  - **Testifies to them the gospel of Christ.**

  Ro 1:16 — For I am not ashamed of the gospel of Christ: for it is the power of God unto salvation to every one that believeth; to the Jew first, and also to the Greek.

  - **The condemnation of the Gentiles.**

  Ro 1:18 — For the wrath of God is revealed from heaven against all ungodliness and unrighteousness of men, who hold the truth in unrighteousness;

  - **The condemnation of the Jews.**

  Ro 2:1–29

  - **God's judgment against all sin.**

  Ro 3:1–31

  Ro 2:6 — Who will render to every man according to his deeds:

  - **Justification by faith in Jesus Christ.**

  Ro 4:1–5:21

  Ro 3:24 — Being justified freely by his grace through the redemption that is in Christ Jesus:

  - **The faith of Abraham.**

  Ro 4:1–25

  - **The fruits of faith.**

  Ro 5:1–7:25

  - **The works of the flesh and the Spirit.**

  Ro 8:1–39

  - **God's supreme power over all.**

  Ro 9:1–33; 11:1–36

  - **The righteousness of the law and of faith.**

  Ro 10:1–21

  - **Exhorted to humility, love, and good works.**

  Ro 12:1–21

  - **Exhorted to obey magistrates.**

  Ro 13:1–14

  - **Exhorted to mutual forbearance.**

  Ro 14:1–15:33

  - **Requested to greet various brethren.**

  Ro 16:1–27

ROOF **See: House; roofs, flat**

ROPE

- **Threefold.**

Ecc 4:12 — And if one prevail against him, two shall withstand him; and a threefold cord is not quickly broken.

- **Worn on the head as an emblem of servitude.**

1Ki 20:31–32

• **Used in casting lots.**

Mic 2:5 — Therefore thou shalt have none that shall cast a cord by lot in the congregation of the LORD.

• **Figurative.**

• **Of love.**

Hos 11:4 — I drew them with cords of a man, with bands of love: and I was to them as they that take off the yoke on their jaws, and I laid meat unto them.

• **Of affliction.**

Job 36:8 — And if *they be* bound in fetters, *and* be holden in cords of affliction;

• **Of temptations.**

Ps 140:5 — The proud have hid a snare for me, and cords; they have spread a net by the wayside; they have set gins for me. Selah.

Pr 5:22 — His own iniquities shall take the wicked himself, and he shall be holden with the cords of his sins.

ROSE

SS 2:1 — I *am* the rose of Sharon, *and* the lily of the valleys.

Isa 35:1 — The wilderness and the solitary place shall be glad for them; and the desert shall rejoice, and blossom as the rose.

ROSH

• **Son of Benjamin.**

Ge 46:21 — And the sons of Benjamin were Belah, and Becher, and Ashbel, Gera, and Naaman, Ehi, and Rosh, Muppim, and Huppim, and Ard.

• **An ancient people.**

Eze 38:2–3

Eze 39:1 — Therefore, thou son of man, prophesy against Gog, and say, Thus saith the Lord GOD; Behold, I *am* against thee, O Gog, the chief prince of Meshech and Tubal:

RUBY

Job 28:18 — No mention shall be made of coral, or of pearls: for the price of wisdom *is* above rubies.

Pr 20:15 — There is gold, and a multitude of rubies: but the lips of knowledge *are* a precious jewel.

Pr 31:10 — Who can find a virtuous woman? for her price *is* far above rubies.

La 4:7 — Her Nazarites were purer than snow, they were whiter than milk, they were more ruddy in body than rubies, their polishing *was* of sapphire:

RUE

Lk 11:42 — But woe unto you, Pharisees! for ye tithe mint and rue and all manner of herbs, and pass over judgment and the love of God: these ought ye to have done, and not to leave the other undone.

RUFUS

• **Son of Simon.**

Mk 15:21 — And they compel one Simon a Cyrenian, who passed by, coming out of the country, the father of Alexander and Rufus, to bear his cross.

• **Probably identical with the Rufus.**

Ro 16:13 — Salute Rufus chosen in the Lord, and his mother and mine.

RUHAMAH • A symbolic name of Israel.

Hos 2:1 — Say ye unto your brethren, Ammi; and to your sisters, Ru-hamah.

RULERS

• **Appointed and removed by God.**

See: Government; God in

• **Chastised.**

Da 4:1–37

See: Nation

• **Monarchical.**

See: King

• **Patriarchal.**

Ge 27:29 — Let people serve thee, and nations bow down to thee: be lord over thy brethren, and let thy mother's sons bow down to thee: cursed *be* every one that curseth thee, and blessed *be* he that blesseth thee.

Ge 27:37 — And Isaac answered and said unto Esau, Behold, I have made him thy lord, and all his brethren have I given to him for servants; and with corn and wine have I sustained him: and what shall I do now unto thee, my son?

• **Instances of.**

• **Nimrod.**

Ge 10:8–10

• **Abraham.**

Ge 14:13–24; 17:6; 21:21–32

• **Melchizedek.**

Ge 14:18

• **Isaac.**

Ge 26:26–31

• **Judah.**

Ge 38:24

• **Heads of families.**

Ex 6:14

• **Ishmael.**

Ge 17:20

• **Esau, and the dukes of Edom.**

Ge 36:1–43

• **Theocratic.**

See: Government

• **Character and qualifications of.**

Ex 18:21–22; Dt 16:18–20; 2Sa 23:3–4; Ps 2:10–11; 72:1–17; Pr 16:12–13; 24:23–26; 25:2–3; 31:4–5, 8–9; Ecc 10:16–17; Isa 5:22–23; Ro 13:1–7; 1Ti 2:1–2; 1Pe 2:13–14

Ge 41:33 — Now therefore let Pharaoh look out a man discreet and wise, and set him over the land of Egypt.

Ex 23:8 — And thou shalt take no gift: for the gift blindeth the wise, and perverteth the words of the righteous.

Dt 1:13 — Take you wise men, and understanding, and known among your tribes, and I will make them rulers over you.

Dt 27:19 — Cursed *be* he that perverteth the judgment of the stranger, fatherless, and widow. And all the people shall say, Amen.

Ezr 7:25 — And thou, Ezra, after the wisdom of thy God, that *is* in thine hand, set magistrates and judges, which may judge all the people that *are* beyond the river, all such as know the laws of thy God; and teach ye them that know *them* not.

Pr 16:10 — A divine sentence *is* in the lips of the king: his mouth transgresseth not in judgment.

Pr 17:7 — Excellent speech becometh not a fool: much less do lying lips a prince.

Pr 19:12 — The king's wrath *is* as the roaring of a lion; but his favour *is* as dew upon the grass.

Pr 20:8 — A king that sitteth in the throne of judgment scattereth away all evil with his eyes.

Pr 20:26 — A wise king scattereth the wicked, and bringeth the wheel over them.

Pr 20:28 — Mercy and truth preserve the king: and his throne is upholden by mercy.

Pr 21:1 — The king's heart *is* in the hand of the LORD, *as* the rivers of water: he turneth it whithersoever he will.

Pr 25:5 — Take away the wicked *from* before the king, and his throne shall be established in righteousness.

Pr 28:2 — For the transgression of a land many *are* the princes thereof: but by a man of understanding *and* knowledge the state *thereof* shall be prolonged.

Pr 28:16 — The prince that wanteth understanding *is* also a great oppressor: *but* he that hateth covetousness shall prolong *his* days.

Pr 29:2 — When the righteous are in authority, the people rejoice: but when the wicked beareth rule, the people mourn.

Pr 29:4 — The king by judgment establisheth the land: but he that receiveth gifts overthroweth it.

Pr 29:14 — The king that faithfully judgeth the poor, his throne shall be established for ever.

Ecc 8:4 — Where the word of a king *is, there is* power: and who may say unto him, What doest thou?

Isa 16:5 — And in mercy shall the throne be established: and he shall sit upon it in truth in the tabernacle of David, judging, and seeking judgment, and hasting righteousness.

Isa 28:6 — And for a spirit of judgment to him that sitteth in judgment, and for strength to them that turn the battle to the gate.

Isa 60:17 — For brass I will bring gold, and for iron I will bring silver, and for wood brass, and for stones iron: I will also make thy officers peace, and thine exactors righteousness.

Jer 13:18 — Say unto the king and to the queen, Humble yourselves, sit down: for your principalities shall come down, *even* the crown of your glory.

Ro 12:8 — Or he that exhorteth, on exhortation: he that giveth, *let him do it* with simplicity; he that ruleth, with diligence; he that sheweth mercy, with cheerfulness.

• Duties of.

Ex 18:20–21; 23:6–7; Nu 27:16–17; Dt 1:16–17; 16:18–20; 17:16–20; 19:18–19; Jos 1:7–8; 2Ch 19:6–7; Ezr 7:25–26; Ps 82:2–4; Jer 22:1–3; Zec 7:9–10

Ex 18:16 — When they have a matter, they come unto me; and I judge between one and another, and I do make *them* know the statutes of God, and his laws.

Ex 23:3 — Neither shalt thou countenance a poor man in his cause.

Ex 23:9 — Also thou shalt not oppress a stranger: for ye know the heart of a stranger, seeing ye were strangers in the land of Egypt.

Le 19:15 — Ye shall do no unrighteousness in judgment: thou shalt not respect the person of the poor, nor honour the person of the mighty: *but* in righteousness shalt thou judge thy neighbour.

Le 24:22 — Ye shall have one manner of law, as well for the stranger, as for one of your own country: for I *am* the LORD your God.

Dt 24:16 — The fathers shall not be put to death for the children, neither shall the children be put to death for the fathers: every man shall be put to death for his own sin.

Dt 25:1 — If there be a controversy between men, and they come unto judgment, that *the judges* may judge them; then they shall justify the righteous, and condemn the wicked.

2Ch 9:8 — Blessed be the LORD thy God, which delighted in thee to set thee on his throne, *to be* king for the LORD thy God: because thy God loved Israel, to establish them for ever, therefore made he thee king over them, to do judgment and justice.

Ps 148:11 — Kings of the earth, and all people; princes, and all judges of the earth:

Ps 148:13 — Let them praise the name of the LORD: for his name alone is excellent; his glory *is* above the earth and heaven.

Isa 58:6 — *Is* not this the fast that I have chosen? to loose the bands of wickedness, to undo the heavy burdens, and to let the oppressed go free, and that ye break every yoke?

Jer 21:12 — O house of David, thus saith the LORD; Execute judgment in the morning, and deliver *him that is* spoiled out of the hand of the oppressor, lest my fury go out like fire, and burn that none can quench *it*, because of the evil of your doings.

Zec 8:16 — These *are* the things that ye shall do; Speak ye every man the truth to his neighbour; execute the judgment of truth and peace in your gates:

Ro 13:3 — For rulers are not a terror to good works, but to the evil. Wilt thou then not be afraid of the power? do that which is good, and thou shalt have praise of the same:

1Ti 2:2 — For kings, and *for* all that are in authority; that we may lead a quiet and peaceable life in all godliness and honesty.

1Pe 2:14 — Or unto governors, as unto them that are sent by him for the punishment of evildoers, and for the praise of them that do well.

RULERS, Righteous

• Instances of.

• Pharaoh, in his treatment of Abraham.

Ge 12:15–20

• Abimelech, in his treatment of Abraham.
Ge 20:1–18

• Abimelech, in his treatment of Isaac.
Ge 26:6–11

• Joseph, in his conduct of the affairs of Egypt.
Ge 41:37–57

• Pharaoh, in his treatment of Jacob and his family.
Ge 47:5–10; 50:1–6

• Moses, in his administration of the affairs of the children of Israel.
Nu 16:15

✧See: Government; Mosaic

• Samuel, in not taking reward for judgment.
1Sa 12:3–4

• Saul, after the defeat of the Ammonites.
1Sa 11:12–13

• Solomon, in his judgment between the two women who claimed the same child.
1Ki 3:16–28

• Solomon, according to the testimony of the queen of Sheba.
1Ki 10:6–9

• Asa, in abolishing sodomy and other abominations of idolatry.
1Ki 15:11–15; 2Ch 14:2–5

• Jehoshaphat, in walking in the ways of the Lord.
1Ki 22:41–46; 2Ch 17:3–10; 19:1–11; 20:3–30

• Hezekiah, in his fear of the Lord.
2Ki 18:3; 20:1–11; 2Ch 30:1–31:21

• Josiah, in repairing the temple and in other good works.
2Ki 22:1–23:37; 2Ch 34:1–35:27

• Cyrus, in emancipating the Jews.
Ezr 1:1–11

• Darius, in advancing the rebuilding of the temple.
Ezr 6:1–12

• Artaxerxes, in commissioning Ezra to restore the forms of worship at Jerusalem.
Ezr 7:1–28; Ne 2:1–20; 5:14

• Nehemiah.
Ne 4:1–5:19

• Daniel.

✧See: Daniel

• King of Nineveh, in repenting, and proclaiming a fast.
Jnh 3:6–9

RULERS, Wicked

Ge 15:13–14; 1Sa 8:10–18; Ne 5:7–9; 9:34–37; Ps 10:17–18; 58:1–2; 94:20–21; Pr 28:15–16; 30:21–22; Ecc 3:16–17; 4:13–14; 10:5–7, 16–17; Isa 3:14–15; 10:1–3; 14:4–20; 28:14–15; 29:20–21; 59:14–15; Jer 5:28–29; Eze 21:25–26; 34:2–4, 7–10; Am 3:10–11; 4:1–2; 5:11–12; 6:12–13; Mic 3:1–3; Micah 3:9–11; Micah 7:3–4; Hab 2:5–13

Ex 3:9 — Now therefore, behold, the cry of the children of Israel is come unto me: and I have also seen the oppression wherewith the Egyptians oppress them.

Dt 27:19 — Cursed *be* he that perverteth the judgment of the stranger, fatherless, and widow. And all the people shall say, Amen.

2Ch 28:19 — For the LORD brought Judah low because of Ahaz king of Israel; for he made Judah naked, and transgressed sore against the LORD.

Job 24:22 — He draweth also the mighty with his power: he riseth up, and no *man* is sure of life.

Job 24:24 — They are exalted for a little while, but are gone and brought low; they are taken out of the way as all *other,* and cut off as the tops of the ears of corn.

Job 35:9 — By reason of the multitude of oppressions they make *the oppressed* to cry: they cry out by reason of the arm of the mighty.

Ps 12:5 — For the oppression of the poor, for the sighing of the needy, now will I arise, saith the LORD; I will set *him* in safety *from him that* puffeth at him.

Ps 12:8 — The wicked walk on every side, when the vilest men are exalted.

Ps 49:20 — Man *that is* in honour, and understandeth not, is like the beasts *that* perish.

Ps 82:2 — How long will ye judge unjustly, and accept the persons of the wicked? Selah.

Ps 110:5 — The Lord at thy right hand shall strike through kings in the day of his wrath.

Pr 17:15 — He that justifieth the wicked, and he that condemneth the just, even they both *are* abomination to the LORD.

Pr 17:26 — Also to punish the just *is* not good, *nor* to strike princes for equity.

Pr 28:28 — When the wicked rise, men hide themselves: but when they perish, the righteous increase.

Pr 29:2 — When the righteous are in authority, the people rejoice: but when the wicked beareth rule, the people mourn.

Pr 29:4 — The king by judgment establisheth the land: but he that receiveth gifts overthroweth it.

Pr 29:12 — If a ruler hearken to lies, all his servants *are* wicked.

Ecc 4:1 — So I returned, and considered all the oppressions that are done under the sun: and behold the tears of *such as were* oppressed, and they had no comforter; and on the side of their oppressors *there was* power; but they had no comforter.

Ecc 5:8 — If thou seest the oppression of the poor, and violent perverting of judgment and justice in a province, marvel not at the matter: for *he that is* higher than the highest regardeth; and *there be* higher than they.

Ecc 8:9 — All this have I seen, and applied my heart unto every work that is done under the sun: *there is* a time wherein one man ruleth over another to his own hurt.

Isa 1:23 — Thy princes *are* rebellious, and companions of thieves: every one loveth gifts, and followeth after rewards: they judge not the fatherless, neither doth the cause of the widow come unto them.

Isa 3:12 — *As for* my people, children *are* their oppressors, and women rule over them. O my people, they which lead thee cause *thee* to err, and destroy the way of thy paths.

Isa 5:7 — For the vineyard of the LORD of hosts *is* the house of Israel, and the men of Judah his pleasant plant: and he looked for judgment, but behold oppression; for righteousness, but behold a cry.

Isa 30:33 — For Tophet *is* ordained of old; yea, for the king it is prepared; he hath made *it* deep *and* large: the pile thereof *is* fire and much wood; the breath of the LORD, like a stream of brimstone, doth kindle it.

Isa 33:1 — Woe to thee that spoilest, and thou *wast* not spoiled; and dealest treacherously, and they dealt not treacherously with thee! when thou shalt cease to spoil, thou shalt be spoiled; *and* when thou shalt make an end to deal treacherously, they shall deal treacherously with thee.

Isa 40:23 — That bringeth the princes to nothing; he maketh the judges of the earth as vanity.

Isa 52:5 — Now therefore, what have I here, saith the LORD, that my people is taken away for nought? they that rule over them make them to howl, saith the LORD; and my name continually every day is blasphemed.

Eze 22:6 — Behold, the princes of Israel, every one were in thee to their power to shed blood.

Eze 22:27 — Her princes in the midst thereof *are* like wolves ravening the prey, to shed blood, *and* to destroy souls, to get dishonest gain.

Eze 28:2 — Son of man, say unto the prince of Tyrus, Thus saith the Lord GOD; Because thine heart *is* lifted up, and thou hast said, I *am* a God, I sit *in* the seat of God, in the midst of the seas; yet thou *art* a man, and not God, though thou set thine heart as the heart of God:

Eze 45:9 — Thus saith the Lord GOD; Let it suffice you, O princes of Israel: remove violence and spoil, and execute judgment and justice, take away your exactions from my people, saith the Lord GOD.

Hos 5:10 — The princes of Judah were like them that remove the bound: *therefore* I will pour out my wrath upon them like water.

Hos 7:3 — They make the king glad with their wickedness, and the princes with their lies.

Hos 10:7 — *As for* Samaria, her king is cut off as the foam upon the water.

Hab 1:4 — Therefore the law is slacked, and judgment doth never go forth: for the wicked doth compass about the righteous; therefore wrong judgment proceedeth.

Zep 1:8 — And it shall come to pass in the day of the LORD's sacrifice, that I will punish the princes, and the king's children, and all such as are clothed with strange apparel.

Zep 3:3 — Her princes within her *are* roaring lions; her judges *are* evening wolves; they gnaw not the bones till the morrow.

Ac 23:3 — Then said Paul unto him, God shall smite thee, *thou* whited wall: for sittest thou to judge me after the law, and commandest me to be smitten contrary to the law?

Jas 2:6 — But ye have despised the poor. Do not rich men oppress you, and draw you before the judgment seats?

Jas 2:9 — But if ye have respect to persons, ye commit sin, and are convinced of the law as transgressors.

- **Instances of.**
  - **Potiphar, putting Joseph into prison.**
    Ge 39:20; 40:15
  - **Pharaoh, oppressing the Israelites.**
    Ex 1:1–11:10
  - **Adoni-bezek, torturing seventy kings.**
    Jgs 1:7
  - **Abimelech, slaying his seventy brothers.**
    Jgs 9:1–5
  - **Eli's sons, desecrating the sacrifices.**
    1Sa 2:12–17
  - **Eli's sons, debauching themselves and the worshipers.**
    1Sa 2:22
  - **Samuel's sons, taking bribes.**
    1Sa 8:1–5
  - **Saul, sparing Agag and the best of the booty.**
    1Sa 15:8–35
  - **Saul, in jealousy plotting against David.**
    1Sa 18:8–29
  - **Saul, seeking to slay David.**
    1Sa 19:1–24
  - **Saul, slaying Ahimelech and the priests.**
    1Sa 22:7–19
  - **Hanun, maltreating David's servants.**
    2Sa 10:4; 1Ch 19:2–5
  - **David, numbering Israel and Judah.**
    2Sa 24:1–9; 1Ch 21:1–7; 27:23–24
  - **Solomon, luxurious, and idolatrous.**
    1Ki 11:1–13
  - **Solomon, oppressing the people.**
    1Ki 4:7–23; 12:4
  - **Rehoboam, making the yoke heavy.**
    1Ki 12:8–11; 2Ch 10:1–15
  - **Jeroboam, perverting the true worship.**
    1Ki 12:26–13:5; 14:16
  - **Jeroboam, exalting debased persons to the priesthood.**
    Nu 3:10; 1Ki 12:31; 13:33; 2Ki 17:32; 2Ch 11:14–15; Eze 44:7
  - **Abijam, walking in the sins of Rehoboam.**
    1Ki 15:3
  - **Nadab, walking in the ways of Jeroboam.**
    1Ki 15:26
  - **Baasha, walking in the ways of Jeroboam.**
    1Ki 15:33–34
  - **Asa, imprisoning the seer, and oppressing the people.**
    2Ch 16:10
  - **Zimri, walking in the ways of Jeroboam.**
    1Ki 16:19
  - **Omri, walking in the ways of Jeroboam.**
    1Ki 16:25–29
  - **Ahab, serving Baal.**
    1Ki 16:30–33; 21:21–26
  - **Ahab, confiscating Naboth's vineyard.**
    1Sa 8:14; 1Ki 21:1–29; 22:38; 2Ki 9:26

• **Jehoram, cleaving to the sins of Jeroboam.**
2Ki 3:2–3

• **Hazael, committing rapine.**
2Ki 8:12; 10:32; 12:17; 13:3–7

• **Jehoram, walking in the ways of the kings of Israel.**
2Ki 8:18; 2Ch 21:13

• **Jehu, departing not from the sins of Jeroboam.**
2Ki 10:29

• **Jehoahaz, in following the sins of Jeroboam.**
2Ki 13:1–2

• **Jehoash, in following the wicked example of Jeroboam.**
2Ki 13:10–11

• **Jeroboam II, not departing from the sins of Jeroboam.**
2Ki 14:23–24

• **Zachariah, Menahem, Pekahiah, and Pekah, following the sins of Jeroboam.**
2Ki 15:9, 18, 24, 28

• **Zachariah, Menahem, Pekahiah, and Pekah, conspiring against and slaying Pekahiah.**
2Ki 15:25

• **Hoshea, who conspired against Pekah.**
2Ki 15:30

• **Hoshea, in permitting Baal worship.**
2Ki 17:1–2, 7–18

• **Ahaz, burning his children in idolatrous sacrifice.**
2Ki 16:3; 2Ch 28:2–4

• **Manasseh, who committed the abominations of the heathen.**
2Ki 21:1–17; 2Ch 33:2–7

• **Amon, who followed the evil example of Manasseh.**
2Ki 21:19–22

• **Jehoahaz, who followed in the ways of his fathers.**
2Ki 23:32

• **Jehoiakim, in walking in the ways of his father.**
2Ki 23:37

• **Jehoiakim and Jehoiachin.**
2Ki 24:9

• **Zedekiah, following the evil example of Jehoiakim.**
2Ki 24:19; 2Ch 36:12–13

• **Zedekiah, following the evil example of Jehoiakim and persecuting Jeremiah.**
Jer 38:5–6

• **Joash, slaying Zechariah.**
2Ch 24:2, 17–25

• **Ahaziah, doing evil after the house of Ahab.**
2Ch 22:1–9

• **Amaziah, worshiping the gods of Seir.**
2Ch 25:14

• **Uzziah, invading the priest's office.**
2Ch 26:16

• **Ahasuerus and Haman, decreeing the death of the Jews.**
Est 3:1–15

• **Nebuchadnezzar, commanding to destroy the wise men.**
Da 2:1–13

• **Nebuchadnezzar, committing the three Hebrews to the furnace.**
Da 3:1–23

• **Belshazzar, in drunkenness and committing sacrilege.**
Da 5:22–23

• **Darius, in deifying himself.**
Da 6:7, 9

• **The princes, conspiring against Daniel.**
Da 6:1–9

• **Herod the Great, slaying the children in Bethlehem.**
Mt 2:16–18

• **Herod Antipas, in beheading John the Baptist.**
Mt 14:1–11

• **Herod Antipas, in craftiness and tyranny.**
Lk 13:31–32; 23:6–15

• **Herod Agrippa, persecuting the church.**
Ac 12:1–19

• **Pilate, delivering Jesus for crucifixion.**
Mt 27:11–26; Mk 15:15

• **Chief priests, elders, and all the council, seeking false witness against Jesus.**
Mt 26:59

• **Ananias, commanding to smite Paul.**
Ac 23:2

See: Government

See: Judge

See: King

RUMAH

• **A city of unascertained location.**

• **Home of Jehoiakim's mother.**

2Ki 23:36 — Jehoiakim *was* twenty and five years old when he began to reign; and he reigned eleven years in Jerusalem. And his mother's name *was* Zebudah, the daughter of Pedaiah of Rumah.

RUTH

• **The daughter-in-law of Naomi.**

Ru 1:4 — And they took them wives of the women of Moab; the name of the one *was* Orpah, and the name of the other Ruth: and they dwelled there about ten years.

• **Her devotion to Naomi.**

Ru 1:6–18

- **Goes to Bethlehem.**

Ru 1:19 — So they two went until they came to Bethlehem. And it came to pass, when they were come to Bethlehem, that all the city was moved about them, and they said, *Is* this Naomi?

Ru 1:22 — So Naomi returned, and Ruth the Moabitess, her daughter in law, with her, which returned out of the country of Moab: and they came to Bethlehem in the beginning of barley harvest.

- **Gleaned in the field of Boaz.**

Ru 2:3 — And she went, and came, and gleaned in the field after the reapers: and her hap was to light on a part of the field *belonging* unto Boaz, who *was* of the kindred of Elimelech.

- **Receives kindness from Boaz.**

Ru 2:4–17

Ru 3:15 — Also he said, Bring the vail that *thou hast* upon thee, and hold it. And when she held it, he measured six *measures* of barley, and laid *it* on her: and she went into the city.

- **Under Naomi's instructions claims from Boaz the duty of a kinsman.**

Ru 3:1–9

- **Marries Boaz.**

Ru 4:9–13

- **Becomes an ancestor of Jesus.**

Ru 4:21–22

Ru 4:13 — So Boaz took Ruth, and she was his wife: and when he went in unto her, the LORD gave her conception, and she bare a son.

RYE

- **A small grain grown in Egypt.**

Ex 9:32 — But the wheat and the rie were not smitten: for they *were* not grown up.

- **Cultivated in Canaan.**

Isa 28:25 — When he hath made plain the face thereof, doth he not cast abroad the fitches, and scatter the cummin, and cast in the principal wheat and the appointed barley and rie in their place?

- **Used in bread.**

Eze 4:9 — Take thou also unto thee wheat, and barley, and beans, and lentiles, and millet, and fitches, and put them in one vessel, and make thee bread thereof, *according* to the number of the days that thou shalt lie upon thy side, three hundred and ninety days shalt thou eat thereof.

S

SABBATH

• **Signifying a rest period.**

Ge 2:2–3; Le 23:1–44; 25:1–55; 26:34–35

• **Preparations for.**

Ex 16:22 — And it came to pass, *that* on the sixth day they gathered twice as much bread, two omers for one *man:* and all the rulers of the congregation came and told Moses.

Mt 27:62 — Now the next day, that followed the day of the preparation, the chief priests and Pharisees came together unto Pilate,

Mk 15:42 — And now when the even was come, because it was the preparation, that is, the day before the sabbath,

Lk 23:54 — And that day was the preparation, and the sabbath drew on.

Jn 19:31 — The Jews therefore, because it was the preparation, that the bodies should not remain upon the cross on the sabbath day, (for that sabbath day was an high day,) besought Pilate that their legs might be broken, and *that* they might be taken away.

• **Religious usages on.**

Ge 2:3 — And God blessed the seventh day, and sanctified it: because that in it he had rested from all his work which God created and made.

Mk 6:2 — And when the sabbath day was come, he began to teach in the synagogue: and many hearing *him* were astonished, saying, From whence hath this *man* these things? and what wisdom *is* this which is given unto him, that even such mighty works are wrought by his hands?

Lk 4:16 — And he came to Nazareth, where he had been brought up: and, as his custom was, he went into the synagogue on the sabbath day, and stood up for to read.

Lk 4:31 — And came down to Capernaum, a city of Galilee, and taught them on the sabbath days.

Lk 6:6 — And it came to pass also on another sabbath, that he entered into the synagogue and taught: and there was a man whose right hand was withered.

Lk 13:10 — And he was teaching in one of the synagogues on the sabbath.

Ac 13:14 — But when they departed from Perga, they came to Antioch in Pisidia, and went into the synagogue on the sabbath day, and sat down.

• **Sacrifices on.**

Nu 28:9–10; Eze 46:4–5

• **Unclassified scripture relating to.**

Ge 2:2–3; Ex 16:23–30; 20:8–11; 31:13–17; 35:2–3; Le 16:29–31; 23:1–3, 27–32; 26:34–35; Nu 15:32–36; 28:9–10; Dt 5:12–15; Ne 9:13–14; 13:15–22; Ps 92:1–15; Isa 56:4–7; 58:13–14; Jer 17:21–22, 24–25; Eze 20:12–13, 20–21; Mt 12:1–8, 10–13; Mk 2:27–28; Lk 6:1–10; 13:10–17; 14:1–6; Jn 5:5–14; 7:21–24; 9:1–34

Ex 16:5 — And it shall come to pass, that on the sixth day they shall prepare *that* which they bring in; and it shall be twice as much as they gather daily.

Ex 23:12 — Six days thou shalt do thy work, and on the seventh day thou shalt rest: that thine ox and thine ass may rest, and the son of thy handmaid, and the stranger, may be refreshed.

Ex 34:21 — Six days thou shalt work, but on the seventh day thou shalt rest: in earing time and in harvest thou shalt rest.

Le 19:3 — Ye shall fear every man his mother, and his father, and keep my sabbaths: I *am* the LORD your God.

Le 19:30 — Ye shall keep my sabbaths, and reverence my sanctuary: I *am* the LORD.

Le 24:8 — Every sabbath he shall set it in order before the LORD continually, *being taken* from the children of Israel by an everlasting covenant.

Le 26:2 — Ye shall keep my sabbaths, and reverence my sanctuary: I *am* the LORD.

2Ki 4:23 — And he said, Wherefore wilt thou go to him to day? *it is* neither new moon, nor sabbath. And she said, *It shall be* well.

1Ch 9:32 — And *other* of their brethren, of the sons of the Kohathites, *were* over the shewbread, to prepare *it* every sabbath.

2Ch 36:21 — To fulfil the word of the LORD by the mouth of Jeremiah, until the land had enjoyed her sabbaths: *for* as long as she lay desolate she kept sabbath, to fulfil threescore and ten years.

Ne 10:31 — And *if* the people of the land bring ware or any victuals on the sabbath day to sell, *that* we would not buy it of them on the sabbath, or on the holy day: and *that* we would leave the seventh year, and the exaction of every debt.

Ps 118:24 — This *is* the day *which* the LORD hath made; we will rejoice and be glad in it.

Isa 1:13 — Bring no more vain oblations; incense is an abomination unto me; the new moons and sabbaths, the calling of assemblies, I cannot away with; *it is* iniquity, even the solemn meeting.

Isa 56:2 — Blessed *is* the man *that* doeth this, and the son of man *that* layeth hold on it; that keepeth the sabbath from polluting it, and keepeth his hand from doing any evil.

Isa 66:23 — And it shall come to pass, *that* from one new moon to another, and from one sabbath to another, shall all flesh come to worship before me, saith the LORD.

Jer 17:27 — But if ye will not hearken unto me to hallow the sabbath day, and not to bear a burden, even entering in at the gates of Jerusalem on the sabbath day; then will I kindle a fire in the gates thereof, and it shall devour the palaces of Jerusalem, and it shall not be quenched.

La 1:7 — Jerusalem remembered in the days of her affliction and of her miseries all her pleasant things that she had in the days of old, when her people fell into the hand of the enemy, and none did help her: the adversaries saw her, *and* did mock at her sabbaths.

La 2:6 — And he hath violently taken away his tabernacle, as *if it were of* a garden: he hath destroyed his places of the assembly: the LORD hath caused the solemn feasts and sabbaths to be forgotten in Zion, and hath despised in the indignation of his anger the king and the priest.

Eze 20:16 — Because they despised my judgments, and walked not in my statutes, but polluted my sabbaths: for their heart went after their idols.

Eze 20:24 — Because they had not executed my judgments, but had despised my statutes, and had polluted my sabbaths, and their eyes were after their fathers' idols.

Eze 22:8 — Thou hast despised mine holy things, and hast profaned my sabbaths.

Eze 23:38 — Moreover this they have done unto me: they have defiled my sanctuary in the same day, and have profaned my sabbaths.

Eze 44:24 — And in controversy they shall stand in judgment; *and* they shall judge it according to my judgments: and they shall keep my laws and my statutes in all mine assemblies; and they shall hallow my sabbaths.

Eze 46:1 — Thus saith the Lord GOD; The gate of the inner court that looketh toward the east shall be shut the six working days; but on the sabbath it shall be opened, and in the day of the new moon it shall be opened.

Eze 46:3 — Likewise the people of the land shall worship at the door of this gate before the LORD in the sabbaths and in the new moons.

Hos 2:11 — I will also cause all her mirth to cease, her feast days, her new moons, and her sabbaths, and all her solemn feasts.

Am 8:5 — Saying, When will the new moon be gone, that we may sell corn? and the sabbath, that we may set forth wheat, making the ephah small, and the shekel great, and falsifying the balances by deceit?

Mt 24:20 — But pray ye that your flight be not in the winter, neither on the sabbath day:

Mk 6:2 — And when the sabbath day was come, he began to teach in the synagogue: and many hearing *him* were astonished, saying, From whence hath this *man* these things? and what wisdom *is* this which is given unto him, that even such mighty works are wrought by his hands?

Mk 16:1 — And when the sabbath was past, Mary Magdalene, and Mary the *mother* of James, and Salome, had bought sweet spices, that they might come and anoint him.

Lk 4:16 — And he came to Nazareth, where he had been brought up: and, as his custom was, he went into the synagogue on the sabbath day, and stood up for to read.

Lk 4:31 — And came down to Capernaum, a city of Galilee, and taught them on the sabbath days.

Lk 23:54 — And that day was the preparation, and the sabbath drew on.

Lk 23:56 — And they returned, and prepared spices and ointments; and rested the sabbath day according to the commandment.

Jn 19:31 — The Jews therefore, because it was the preparation, that the bodies should not remain upon the cross on the sabbath day, (for that sabbath day was an high day,) besought Pilate that their legs might be broken, and *that* they might be taken away.

Ac 13:14 — But when they departed from Perga, they came to Antioch in Pisidia, and went into the synagogue on the sabbath day, and sat down.

Ac 13:27 — For they that dwell at Jerusalem, and their rulers, because they knew him not, nor yet the voices of the prophets which are read every sabbath day, they have fulfilled *them* in condemning *him.*

Ac 13:42 — And when the Jews were gone out of the synagogue, the Gentiles besought that these words might be preached to them the next sabbath.

Ac 13:44 — And the next sabbath day came almost the whole city together to hear the word of God.

Ac 15:21 — For Moses of old time hath in every city them that preach him, being read in the synagogues every sabbath day.

Ac 16:13 — And on the sabbath we went out of the city by a river side, where prayer was wont to be made; and we sat down, and spake unto the women which resorted *thither.*

Ac 17:2 — And Paul, as his manner was, went in unto them, and three sabbath days reasoned with them out of the scriptures,

Ac 18:4 — And he reasoned in the synagogue every sabbath, and persuaded the Jews and the Greeks.

Col 2:16 — Let no man therefore judge you in meat, or in drink, or in respect of an holyday, or of the new moon, or of the sabbath *days:*

Heb 4:4 — For he spake in a certain place of the seventh *day* on this wise, And God did rest the seventh day from all his works.

Heb 4:9 — There remaineth therefore a rest to the people of God.

- **Observance of.**
  - **By Moses.**

    Nu 15:32–34
  - **By Nehemiah.**

    Ne 13:15 — In those days saw I in Judah *some* treading winepresses on the sabbath, and bringing in sheaves, and lading asses; as also wine, grapes, and figs, and all *manner of* burdens, which they brought into Jerusalem on the sabbath day: and I testified *against them* in the day wherein they sold victuals.

    Ne 13:21 — Then I testified against them, and said unto them, Why lodge ye about the wall? if ye do so again, I will lay hands on you. From that time forth came they no *more* on the sabbath.

• By the women preparing to embalm the body of Jesus.

Lk 23:56 — And they returned, and prepared spices and ointments; and rested the sabbath day according to the commandment.

• By Paul.

Ac 13:14 — But when they departed from Perga, they came to Antioch in Pisidia, and went into the synagogue on the sabbath day, and sat down.

• By disciples.

Ac 16:13 — And on the sabbath we went out of the city by a river side, where prayer was wont to be made; and we sat down, and spake unto the women which resorted *thither.*

• By John.

Rev 1:10 — I was in the Spirit on the Lord's day, and heard behind me a great voice, as of a trumpet,

• Violations of.

• Instances of.

• Gathering manna.

Ex 16:27 — And it came to pass, *that* there went out *some* of the people on the seventh day for to gather, and they found none.

• Gathering sticks.

Nu 15:32 — And while the children of Israel were in the wilderness, they found a man that gathered sticks upon the sabbath day.

• Men of Tyre.

Ne 13:16 — There dwelt men of Tyre also therein, which brought fish, and all manner of ware, and sold on the sabbath unto the children of Judah, and in Jerusalem.

• Inhabitants of Jerusalem.

Jer 17:21–23

• Christian Sabbath.

• First day of the week, Sunday.

Mt 28:5–6; Jn 20:11–16

Mt 28:1 — In the end of the sabbath, as it began to dawn toward the first *day* of the week, came Mary Magdalene and the other Mary to see the sepulchre.

Mt 28:9 — And as they went to tell his disciples, behold, Jesus met them, saying, <u>All hail.</u> And they came and held him by the feet, and worshipped him.

Mk 16:9 — Now when *Jesus* was risen early the first *day* of the week, he appeared first to Mary Magdalene, out of whom he had cast seven devils.

Jn 20:1 — The first *day* of the week cometh Mary Magdalene early, when it was yet dark, unto the sepulchre, and seeth the stone taken away from the sepulchre.

Jn 20:19 — Then the same day at evening, being the first *day* of the week, when the doors were shut where the disciples were assembled for fear of the Jews, came Jesus and stood in the midst, and saith unto them, <u>Peace *be* unto you.</u>

Jn 20:26 — And after eight days again his disciples were within, and Thomas with them: *then* came Jesus, the doors being shut, and stood in the midst, and said, <u>Peace *be* unto you.</u>

Ac 20:7 — And upon the first *day* of the week, when the disciples came together to break bread, Paul preached unto them, ready to depart on the morrow; and continued his speech until midnight.

1Co 16:2 — Upon the first *day* of the week let every one of you lay by him in store, as *God* hath prospered him, that there be no gatherings when I come.

Rev 1:10 — I was in the Spirit on the Lord's day, and heard behind me a great voice, as of a trumpet,

SABBATH DAY'S JOURNEY • About two thousand paces.

Ac 1:12 — Then returned they unto Jerusalem from the mount called Olivet, which is from Jerusalem a sabbath day's journey.

SABBATIC YEAR

• A rest recurring every seventh year.

• Called Year of Release.

Dt 15:9 — Beware that there be not a thought in thy wicked heart, saying, The seventh year, the year of release, is at hand; and thine eye be evil against thy poor brother, and thou givest him nought; and he cry unto the LORD against thee, and it be sin unto thee.

Dt 31:10 — And Moses commanded them, saying, At the end of *every* seven years, in the solemnity of the year of release, in the feast of tabernacles,

• Ordinances concerning.

Ex 23:9–11; Le 25:1–55

• Israelitish bondservants set free in.

Ex 21:2 — If thou buy an Hebrew servant, six years he shall serve: and in the seventh he shall go out free for nothing.

Dt 15:12 — *And* if thy brother, an Hebrew man, or an Hebrew woman, be sold unto thee, and serve thee six years; then in the seventh year thou shalt let him go free from thee.

Jer 34:14 — At the end of seven years let ye go every man his brother an Hebrew, which hath been sold unto thee; and when he hath served thee six years, thou shalt let him go free from thee: but your fathers hearkened not unto me, neither inclined their ear.

• Creditors required to release debtors in.

Dt 15:1–6, 12–18

Ne 10:31 — And *if* the people of the land bring ware or any victuals on the sabbath day to sell, *that* we would not buy it of them on the sabbath, or on the holy day: and *that* we would leave the seventh year, and the exaction of every debt.

• Ordinances concerning instruction in the law during.

Dt 31:10–13

Ne 8:18 — Also day by day, from the first day unto the last day, he read in the book of the law of God. And they kept the feast seven days; and on the eighth day *was* a solemn assembly, according unto the manner.

• **Punishment to follow violation of the ordinances concerning.**

Le 26:32–41; Jer 34:12–22

See: Jubilee

SABEANS

• **A people who invaded the land of Uz.**

Job 1:15 — And the Sabeans fell *upon them,* and took them away; yea, they have slain the servants with the edge of the sword; and I only am escaped alone to tell thee.

Isa 43:3 — For I *am* the LORD thy God, the Holy One of Israel, thy Saviour: I gave Egypt *for* thy ransom, Ethiopia and Seba for thee.

• **Giants among.**

Isa 45:14 — Thus saith the LORD, The labour of Egypt, and merchandise of Ethiopia and of the Sabeans, men of stature, shall come over unto thee, and they shall be thine: they shall come after thee; in chains they shall come over, and they shall fall down unto thee, they shall make supplication unto thee, *saying,* Surely God *is* in thee; and *there is* none else, *there is* no God.

• **Prophecies concerning.**

Isa 43:3 — For I *am* the LORD thy God, the Holy One of Israel, thy Saviour: I gave Egypt *for* thy ransom, Ethiopia and Seba for thee.

Joel 3:8 — And I will sell your sons and your daughters into the hand of the children of Judah, and they shall sell them to the Sabeans, to a people far off: for the LORD hath spoken *it.*

• **Proverbial drunkards.**

Eze 23:42 — And a voice of a multitude being at ease *was* with her: and with the men of the common sort *were* brought Sabeans from the wilderness, which put bracelets upon their hands, and beautiful crowns upon their heads.

SABTA

• **Called also Sabtah.**

• **Son of Cush.**

Ge 10:7 — And the sons of Cush; Seba, and Havilah, and Sabtah, and Raamah, and Sabtechah: and the sons of Raamah; Sheba, and Dedan.

1Ch 1:9 — And the sons of Cush; Seba, and Havilah, and Sabta, and Raamah, and Sabtecha. And the sons of Raamah; Sheba, and Dedan.

SABTECHA • Son of Cush.

Ge 10:7 — And the sons of Cush; Seba, and Havilah, and Sabtah, and Raamah, and Sabtechah: and the sons of Raamah; Sheba, and Dedan.

1Ch 1:9 — And the sons of Cush; Seba, and Havilah, and Sabta, and Raamah, and Sabtecha. And the sons of Raamah; Sheba, and Dedan.

SACAR

• **Father of Ahiam.**

1Ch 11:35 — Ahiam the son of Sacar the Hararite, Eliphal the son of Ur,

• **Called Sharar.**

2Sa 23:33 — Shammah the Hararite, Ahiam the son of Sharar the Hararite,

• **A Korhite.**

• **Son of Obed-edom.**

1Ch 26:4 — Moreover the sons of Obed-edom *were,* Shemaiah the firstborn, Jehozabad the second, Joah the third, and Sacar the fourth, and Nethaneel the fifth,

SACKBUT

• **A stringed instrument of music.**

Da 3:5 — *That* at what time ye hear the sound of the cornet, flute, harp, sackbut, psaltery, dulcimer, and all kinds of musick, ye fall down and worship the golden image that Nebuchadnezzar the king hath set up:

Da 3:7 — Therefore at that time, when all the people heard the sound of the cornet, flute, harp, sackbut, psaltery, and all kinds of musick, all the people, the nations, and the languages, fell down *and* worshipped the golden image that Nebuchadnezzar the king had set up.

Da 3:10 — Thou, O king, hast made a decree, that every man that shall hear the sound of the cornet, flute, harp, sackbut, psaltery, and dulcimer, and all kinds of musick, shall fall down and worship the golden image:

Da 3:15 — Now if ye be ready that at what time ye hear the sound of the cornet, flute, harp, sackbut, psaltery, and dulcimer, and all kinds of musick, ye fall down and worship the image which I have made; *well:* but if ye worship not, ye shall be cast the same hour into the midst of a burning fiery furnace; and who *is* that God that shall deliver you out of my hands?

See: Music; instruments of

SACKCLOTH

• **A symbol of mourning.**

1Ki 20:31–32

Job 16:15 — I have sewed sackcloth upon my skin, and defiled my horn in the dust.

Isa 15:3 — In their streets they shall gird themselves with sackcloth: on the tops of their houses, and in their streets, every one shall howl, weeping abundantly.

Jer 4:8 — For this gird you with sackcloth, lament and howl: for the fierce anger of the LORD is not turned back from us.

Jer 6:26 — O daughter of my people, gird *thee* with sackcloth, and wallow thyself in ashes: make thee mourning, *as for* an only son, most bitter lamentation: for the spoiler shall suddenly come upon us.

Jer 49:3 — Howl, O Heshbon, for Ai is spoiled: cry, ye daughters of Rabbah, gird you with sackcloth; lament, and run to and fro by the hedges; for their king shall go into captivity, *and* his priests and his princes together.

La 2:10 — The elders of the daughter of Zion sit upon the ground, *and* keep silence: they have cast up dust upon their heads; they have girded themselves with sackcloth: the virgins of Jerusalem hang down their heads to the ground.

Eze 7:18 — They shall also gird *themselves* with sackcloth, and horror shall cover them; and shame *shall be* upon all faces, and baldness upon all their heads.

Da 9:3 — And I set my face unto the Lord God, to seek by prayer and supplications, with fasting, and sackcloth, and ashes:

Joel 1:8 — Lament like a virgin girded with sackcloth for the husband of her youth.

• Worn by Jacob when it was reported to him that Joseph had been devoured by wild beasts.

Ge 37:34 — And Jacob rent his clothes, and put sackcloth upon his loins, and mourned for his son many days.

• Animals covered with, at time of national mourning.

Jnh 3:8 — But let man and beast be covered with sackcloth, and cry mightily unto God: yea, let them turn every one from his evil way, and from the violence that *is* in their hands.

See: Mourning

SACRIFICES

• Figurative.

Zep 1:7–8

Isa 34:6 — The sword of the LORD is filled with blood, it is made fat with fatness, *and* with the blood of lambs and goats, with the fat of the kidneys of rams: for the LORD hath a sacrifice in Bozrah, and a great slaughter in the land of Idumea.

Eze 39:17 — And, thou son of man, thus saith the Lord GOD; Speak unto every feathered fowl, and to every beast of the field, Assemble yourselves, and come; gather yourselves on every side to my sacrifice that I do sacrifice for you, *even* a great sacrifice upon the mountains of Israel, that ye may eat flesh, and drink blood.

Ro 12:1 — I beseech you therefore, brethren, by the mercies of God, that ye present your bodies a living sacrifice, holy, acceptable unto God, *which is* your reasonable service.

Php 2:17 — Yea, and if I be offered upon the sacrifice and service of your faith, I joy, and rejoice with you all.

Php 4:18 — But I have all, and abound: I am full, having received of Epaphroditus the things *which were sent* from you, an odour of a sweet smell, a sacrifice acceptable, wellpleasing to God.

• Of self-denial.

Php 3:7–8

• Of praise.

Ps 116:17 — I will offer to thee the sacrifice of thanksgiving, and will call upon the name of the LORD.

Jer 33:11 — The voice of joy, and the voice of gladness, the voice of the bridegroom, and the voice of the bride, the voice of them that shall say, Praise the LORD of hosts: for the LORD *is* good; for his mercy *endureth* for ever: *and* of them that shall bring the sacrifice of praise into the house of the LORD. For I will cause to return the captivity of the land, as at the first, saith the LORD.

Hos 14:2 — Take with you words, and turn to the LORD: say unto him, Take away all iniquity, and receive *us* graciously: so will we render the calves of our lips.

Heb 13:15 — By him therefore let us offer the sacrifice of praise to God continually, that is, the fruit of *our* lips giving thanks to his name.

• Calves of the lips, signifying praise.

Hos 14:2 — Take with you words, and turn to the LORD: say unto him, Take away all iniquity, and receive *us* graciously: so will we render the calves of our lips.

See: Offerings

SACRILEGE

• Profaning holy things.

• Forbidden.

Le 19:8 — Therefore *every one* that eateth it shall bear his iniquity, because he hath profaned the hallowed thing of the LORD: and that soul shall be cut off from among his people.

1Co 3:17 — If any man defile the temple of God, him shall God destroy; for the temple of God is holy, which *temple* ye are.

Tit 1:11 — Whose mouths must be stopped, who subvert whole houses, teaching things which they ought not, for filthy lucre's sake.

1Pe 5:2 — Feed the flock of God which is among you, taking the oversight *thereof,* not by constraint, but willingly; not for filthy lucre, but of a ready mind;

• Instances of.

• Esau sells his birthright.

Ge 25:33

• Hadab and Abihu offer strange fire.

Le 10:1–7; Nu 3:4

• Uzzah.

2Sa 6:6–7

• Uzziah.

2Ch 26:16–21

• Korah and his company.

Nu 16:40

• The people of Beth-shemesh.

1Sa 6:19

• Ahaz.

2Ch 28:24

• Money changers in the temple.

Mt 21:12–13; Lk 19:45; Jn 2:14–16

• Those who profaned the holy eucharist.

1Co 11:29

SADDUCEES

• A sect of the Jews.

• Rebuked by John the Baptist.

Mt 3:7–9; Lk 3:7–9

• Reject the doctrine of the resurrection.

Mt 22:23–34; Mk 12:18–27; Lk 20:27–40; Ac 23:7–8

• **Jesus warns his disciples aginst.**
Mt 16:6–12

• **Persecute the apostles.**
Ac 4:1–3; 5:17–33

SADOC • An ancestor of Joseph.

Mt 1:14 — And Azor begat Sadoc; and Sadoc begat Achim; and Achim begat Eliud;

SAILORS ✦See: Mariner

SAINTS ✦See: Righteous

SALAH

• **Called also Sala and Shelah.**

• **Son of Arphaxad and ancestor of Joseph.**
Ge 11:12–15
Ge 10:24 — And Arphaxad begat Salah; and Salah begat Eber.
1Ch 1:18 — And Arphaxad begat Shelah, and Shelah begat Eber.
1Ch 1:24 — Shem, Arphaxad, Shelah,
Lk 3:35 — Which was *the son* of Saruch, which was *the son* of Ragau, which was *the son* of Phalec, which was *the son* of Heber, which was *the son* of Sala,

SALAMIS

• **A city of Cyprus.**

• **Paul and Barnabas preach in.**
Ac 13:4–5

SALATHIEL ✦See: Shealtiel

SALCAH

• **Called also Salchah.**

• **A city of Gad.**
Dt 3:10 — All the cities of the plain, and all Gilead, and all Bashan, unto Salchah and Edrei, cities of the kingdom of Og in Bashan.
Jos 12:5 — And reigned in mount Hermon, and in Salcah, and in all Bashan, unto the border of the Geshurites and the Maachathites, and half Gilead, the border of Sihon king of Heshbon.
Jos 13:11 — And Gilead, and the border of the Geshurites and Maachathites, and all mount Hermon, and all Bashan unto Salcah;
1Ch 5:11 — And the children of Gad dwelt over against them, in the land of Bashan unto Salchah:

SALEM ✦See: Jerusalem

SALIM • A city near to Aenon.

Jn 3:23 — And John also was baptizing in Aenon near to Salim, because there was much water there: and they came, and were baptized.

SALLAI

• **A Benjamite, dwelling in Jerusalem.**
Ne 11:8 — And after him Gabbai, Sallai, nine hundred twenty and eight.

• **A priest who returned to Jerusalem with Zerubbabel.**
Ne 12:20 — Of Sallai, Kallai; of Amok, Eber;

• **Called Sallu.**
Ne 12:7 — Sallu, Amok, Hilkiah, Jedaiah. These *were* the chief of the priests and of their brethren in the days of Jeshua.

SALLU

• **A Benjamite, dwelling in Jerusalem.**
1Ch 9:7 — And of the sons of Benjamin; Sallu the son of Meshullam, the son of Hodaviah, the son of Hasenuah,
Ne 11:7 — And these *are* the sons of Benjamin; Sallu the son of Meshullam, the son of Joed, the son of Pedaiah, the son of Kolaiah, the son of Maaseiah, the son of Ithiel, the son of Jesaiah.

✦See: Sallai; a priest who returned to Jerusalem with Zerubbabel

SALMA

• **Son of Caleb.**
1Ch 2:51 — Salma the father of Bethlehem, Hareph the father of Beth-gader.
1Ch 2:54 — The sons of Salma; Bethlehem, and the Netophathites, Ataroth, the house of Joab, and half of the Manahethites, the Zorites.

• **Father of Boaz.**
Ru 4:20–21
1Ch 2:11 — And Nahshon begat Salma, and Salma begat Boaz,

• **In the lineage of Joseph.**
Mt 1:4–5

• **Called also Salmon.**
Lk 3:32 — Which was *the son* of Jesse, which was *the son* of Obed, which was *the son* of Booz, which was *the son* of Salmon, which was *the son* of Naasson,

SALMON

• **A hill.**
Ps 68:14 — When the Almighty scattered kings in it, it was *white* as snow in Salmon.

✦See: Salma; called also Salmon. Father of Boaz

SALMONE • A promontory of Crete.

Ac 27:7 — And when we had sailed slowly many days, and scarce were come over against Cnidus, the wind not suffering us, we sailed under Crete, over against Salmone;

SALOME

• **Mother of James and John.**
Mt 27:56 — Among which was Mary Magdalene, and Mary the mother of James and Joses, and the mother of Zebedee's children.
Mk 15:40 — There were also women looking on afar off: among whom was Mary Magdalene, and Mary the mother of James the less and of Joses, and Salome;

Mk 16:1 — And when the sabbath was past, Mary Magdalene, and Mary the *mother* of James, and Salome, had bought sweet spices, that they might come and anoint him.

- **Asks Jesus to promote her sons.**

Mt 20:20–21

- **Present at the cross.**

Mk 15:40 — There were also women looking on afar off: among whom was Mary Magdalene, and Mary the mother of James the less and of Joses, and Salome;

- **Present at the sepulchre.**

Mk 16:1–2

SALT

- **Lot's wife turned into a pillar of.**

Ge 19:26 — But his wife looked back from behind him, and she became a pillar of salt.

- **The city of Salt.**

Jos 15:62 — And Nibshan, and the city of Salt, and En-gedi; six cities with their villages.

- **The valley of salt.**

2Sa 8:13 — And David gat *him* a name when he returned from smiting of the Syrians in the valley of salt, *being* eighteen thousand *men.*

2Ki 14:7 — He slew of Edom in the valley of salt ten thousand, and took Selah by war, and called the name of it Joktheel unto this day.

- **Salt sea.**

Ge 14:3 — All these were joined together in the vale of Siddim, which is the salt sea.

Nu 34:12 — And the border shall go down to Jordan, and the goings out of it shall be at the salt sea: this shall be your land with the coasts thereof round about.

Dt 3:17 — The plain also, and Jordan, and the coast *thereof,* from Chinnereth even unto the sea of the plain, *even* the salt sea, under Ashdoth-pisgah eastward.

Jos 3:16 — That the waters which came down from above stood *and* rose up upon an heap very far from the city Adam, that *is* beside Zaretan: and those that came down toward the sea of the plain, *even* the salt sea, failed, *and* were cut off: and the people passed over right against Jericho.

Jos 12:3 — And from the plain to the sea of Chinneroth on the east, and unto the sea of the plain, *even* the salt sea on the east, the way to Beth-jeshimoth; and from the south, under Ashdoth-pisgah:

Jos 15:2 — And their south border was from the shore of the salt sea, from the bay that looketh southward:

- **Salt pits.**

Zep 2:9 — Therefore *as* I live, saith the LORD of hosts, the God of Israel, Surely Moab shall be as Sodom, and the children of Ammon as Gomorrah, *even* the breeding of nettles, and saltpits, and a perpetual desolation: the residue of my people shall spoil them, and the remnant of my people shall possess them.

- **All animal sacrifices were required to be seasoned with.**

Le 2:13 — And every oblation of thy meat offering shalt thou season with salt; neither shalt thou suffer the salt of the covenant of thy God to be lacking from thy meat offering: with all thine offerings thou shalt offer salt.

Ezr 6:9 — And that which they have need of, both young bullocks, and rams, and lambs, for the burnt offerings of the God of heaven, wheat, salt, wine, and oil, according to the appointment of the priests which *are* at Jerusalem, let it be given them day by day without fail:

Eze 43:24 — And thou shalt offer them before the LORD, and the priests shall cast salt upon them, and they shall offer them up *for* a burnt offering unto the LORD.

Mk 9:49 — <u>For every one shall be salted with fire, and every sacrifice shall be salted with salt.</u>

- **Used in ratifying covenants.**

Nu 18:19 — All the heave offerings of the holy things, which the children of Israel offer unto the LORD, have I given thee, and thy sons and thy daughters with thee, by a statute for ever: it is a covenant of salt for ever before the LORD unto thee and to thy seed with thee.

2Ch 13:5 — Ought ye not to know that the LORD God of Israel gave the kingdom over Israel to David for ever, *even* to him and to his sons by a covenant of salt?

- **Elisha casts, into the pool of Jericho, to purify it.**

2Ki 2:20–21

- **Figurative.**
  - **Of the saving efficacy of the church.**

Mk 9:49–50

Mt 5:13 — <u>Ye are the salt of the earth: but if the salt have lost his savour, wherewith shall it be salted? it is thenceforth good for nothing, but to be cast out, and to be trodden under foot of men.</u>

Lk 14:34 — <u>Salt *is* good: but if the salt have lost his savour, wherewith shall it be seasoned?</u>

  - **Of wise conversation.**

Col 4:6 — Let your speech *be* alway with grace, seasoned with salt, that ye may know how ye ought to answer every man.

SALUTATIONS

- **By kissing.**

2Sa 20:9 — And Joab said to Amasa, *Art* thou in health, my brother? And Joab took Amasa by the beard with the right hand to kiss him.

Mt 26:49 — And forthwith he came to Jesus, and said, Hail, master; and kissed him.

- **By bowing.**

Ge 19:1–2

Ge 18:2 — And he lift up his eyes and looked, and, lo, three men stood by him: and when he saw *them,* he ran to meet them from the tent door, and bowed himself toward the ground,

Ge 23:7 — And Abraham stood up, and bowed himself to the people of the land, *even* to the children of Heth.

Ge 27:29 — Let people serve thee, and nations bow down to thee: be lord over thy brethren, and let thy mother's sons bow down to thee: cursed *be* every one that curseth thee, and blessed *be* he that blesseth thee.

Ge 33:3 — And he passed over before them, and bowed himself to the ground seven times, until he came near to his brother.

Ge 37:10 — And he told *it* to his father, and to his brethren: and his father rebuked him, and said unto him, What *is* this dream that thou hast dreamed? Shall I and thy mother and thy brethren indeed come to bow down ourselves to thee to the earth?

Ge 41:43 — And he made him to ride in the second chariot which he had; and they cried before him, Bow the knee: and he made him *ruler* over all the land of Egypt.

Ge 43:26 — And when Joseph came home, they brought him the present which *was* in their hand into the house, and bowed themselves to him to the earth.

Ge 43:28 — And they answered, Thy servant our father *is* in good health, he *is* yet alive. And they bowed down their heads, and made obeisance.

Ge 49:8 — Judah, thou *art he* whom thy brethren shall praise: thy hand *shall be* in the neck of thine enemies; thy father's children shall bow down before thee.

1Sa 25:23 — And when Abigail saw David, she hasted, and lighted off the ass, and fell before David on her face, and bowed herself to the ground,

2Sa 18:28 — And Ahimaaz called, and said unto the king, All is well. And he fell down to the earth upon his face before the king, and said, Blessed *be* the LORD thy God, which hath delivered up the men that lifted up their hand against my lord the king.

1Ki 1:16 — And Bath-sheba bowed, and did obeisance unto the king. And the king said, What wouldest thou?

Est 8:3 — And Esther spake yet again before the king, and fell down at his feet, and besought him with tears to put away the mischief of Haman the Agagite, and his device that he had devised against the Jews.

Mt 2:11 — And when they were come into the house, they saw the young child with Mary his mother, and fell down, and worshipped him: and when they had opened their treasures, they presented unto him gifts; gold, and frankincense, and myrrh.

Mk 5:22 — And, behold, there cometh one of the rulers of the synagogue, Jairus by name; and when he saw him, he fell at his feet,

• Addresses in.

• "My lords".

Ge 19:2 — And he said, Behold now, my lords, turn in, I pray you, into your servant's house, and tarry all night, and wash your feet, and ye shall rise up early, and go on your ways. And they said, Nay; but we will abide in the street all night.

• "God be gracious unto thee".

Ge 43:29 — And he lifted up his eyes, and saw his brother Benjamin, his mother's son, and said, *Is* this your younger brother, of whom ye spake unto me? And he said, God be gracious unto thee, my son.

• "Peace".

1Sa 25:6 — And thus shall ye say to him that liveth *in prosperity,* Peace *be* both to thee, and peace *be* to thine house, and peace *be* unto all that thou hast.

• "Art thou in health, my brother?".

2Sa 20:9 — And Joab said to Amasa, *Art* thou in health, my brother? And Joab took Amasa by the beard with the right hand to kiss him.

• "Hail, Master".

Mt 26:49 — And forthwith he came to Jesus, and said, Hail, master; and kissed him.

• "All hail".

Mt 28:9 — And as they went to tell his disciples, behold, Jesus met them, saying, All hail. And they came and held him by the feet, and worshipped him.

• "Peace to this house".

Lk 10:5 — And into whatsoever house ye enter, first say, Peace *be* to this house.

• "Peace unto you".

Jn 20:21 — Then said Jesus to them again, Peace *be* unto you: as *my* Father hath sent me, even so send I you.

• From a master to his servants, "The Lord be with you".

Ru 2:4 — And behold, Boaz came from Bethlehem, and said unto the reapers, The LORD *be* with you. And they answered him, The LORD bless thee.

• Servants to their masters, "The Lord bless thee".

Ru 2:4 — And behold, Boaz came from Bethlehem, and said unto the reapers, The LORD *be* with you. And they answered him, The LORD bless thee.

• By letter.

1Co 16:21 — The salutation of *me* Paul with mine own hand.

2Co 13:13 — All the saints salute you.

Php 4:21 — Salute every saint in Christ Jesus. The brethren which are with me greet you.

Col 4:18 — The salutation by the hand of me Paul. Remember my bonds. Grace *be* with you. Amen.

2Th 3:17 — The salutation of Paul with mine own hand, which is the token in every epistle: so I write.

2Jn 1:13 — The children of thy elect sister greet thee. Amen.

3Jn 1:14 — But I trust I shall shortly see thee, and we shall speak face to face. Peace *be* to thee. *Our* friends salute thee. Greet the friends by name.

• To rulers.

See: King

See: Manners

SALVATION

• Illustrated by.

• A horn.

Ps 18:2 — The LORD *is* my rock, and my fortress, and my deliverer; my God, my strength, in whom I will trust; my buckler, and the horn of my salvation, *and* my high tower.

Lk 1:69 — And hath raised up an horn of salvation for us in the house of his servant David;

• A tower.

2Sa 22:51 — *He is* the tower of salvation for his king: and sheweth mercy to his anointed, unto David, and to his seed for evermore.

• A helmet.

Isa 59:17 — For he put on righteousness as a breastplate, and an helmet of salvation upon his head; and he put on the garments of vengeance *for* clothing, and was clad with zeal as a cloke.

Eph 6:17 — And take the helmet of salvation, and the sword of the Spirit, which is the word of God:

• A shield.

2Sa 22:36 — Thou hast also given me the shield of thy salvation: and thy gentleness hath made me great.

• A lamp.

Isa 62:1 — For Zion's sake will I not hold my peace, and for Jerusalem's sake I will not rest, until the righteousness thereof go forth as brightness, and the salvation thereof as a lamp *that* burneth.

• A cup.

Ps 116:13 — I will take the cup of salvation, and call upon the name of the LORD.

• Clothing.

2Ch 6:41 — Now therefore arise, O LORD God, into thy resting place, thou, and the ark of thy strength: let thy priests, O LORD God, be clothed with salvation, and let thy saints rejoice in goodness.

Ps 132:16 — I will also clothe her priests with salvation: and her saints shall shout aloud for joy.

Ps 149:4 — For the LORD taketh pleasure in his people: he will beautify the meek with salvation.

Isa 61:10 — I will greatly rejoice in the LORD, my soul shall be joyful in my God; for he hath clothed me with the garments of salvation, he hath covered me with the robe of righteousness, as a bridegroom decketh *himself* with ornaments, and as a bride adorneth *herself* with her jewels.

• Wells.

Isa 12:3 — Therefore with joy shall ye draw water out of the wells of salvation.

• Walls and bulwarks.

Isa 26:1 — In that day shall this song be sung in the land of Judah; We have a strong city; salvation will *God* appoint *for* walls and bulwarks.

Isa 60:18 — Violence shall no more be heard in thy land, wasting nor destruction within thy borders; but thou shalt call thy walls Salvation, and thy gates Praise.

• Chariots.

Hab 3:8 — Was the LORD displeased against the rivers? *was* thine anger against the rivers? *was* thy wrath against the sea, that thou didst ride upon thine horses *and* thy chariots of salvation?

• A victory.

1Co 15:57 — But thanks *be* to God, which giveth us the victory through our Lord Jesus Christ.

• Typified by the brazen serpent.

Nu 21:4–9; Jn 3:14–15

See: Atonement

• Unclassified scripture relating to.

Dt 30:19–20; 1Ki 8:41–43; Ps 36:8–9; 63:5–6; 68:18–20; 98:2–3; 121:1–8; Pr 1:20–21; 8:1–5; 9:1–6; Isa 25:6–7; 29:18–19; 32:1–4; 46:12–13; 49:10–11; 51:4–5; 55:1–3, 6–7; 56:6–8; 57:18–19; 61:1–3; Mt 11:28–30; 22:9–10; Mk 16:15–16; Lk 2:31–32; 5:31–32; 13:29–30; 14:16–24; 15:4–32; Jn 3:14–17; 7:37–38; 11:51–52; 15:4–5; Ac 11:17–18; 13:38–39; 15:7–9; 16:30–31; Ro 1:16–17; 3:21–26, 28–30; 4:1–5:2; 5:15–21; 7:24–25; 9:30–33; 10:8–13; 11:1–36; 2Co 6:17–18; Gal 3:1–28; Eph 1:9–10; 2:3–5, 8–9, 14–15; Php 3:7–11; Col 1:5–6, 20–23, 26–27; 1Th 5:8–10; 2Th 2:13–14; 1Ti 1:15–16; 2:3–6; 2Ti 1:9–10; Tit 3:3–7; Heb 4:1–10; 1Pe 1:9–10; 1Jn 4:9–10; Rev 3:17–18; 7:9–10

Ge 12:1 — Now the LORD had said unto Abram, Get thee out of thy country, and from thy kindred, and from thy father's house, unto a land that I will shew thee:

Ge 12:3 — And I will bless them that bless thee, and curse him that curseth thee: and in thee shall all families of the earth be blessed.

Ex 15:2 — The LORD *is* my strength and song, and he is become my salvation: he *is* my God, and I will prepare him an habitation; my father's God, and I will exalt him.

Dt 32:15 — But Jeshurun waxed fat, and kicked: thou art waxen fat, thou art grown thick, thou art covered *with fatness;* then he forsook God *which* made him, and lightly esteemed the Rock of his salvation.

2Sa 14:14 — For we must needs die, and *are* as water spilt on the ground, which cannot be gathered up again; neither doth God respect *any* person: yet doth he devise means, that his banished be not expelled from him.

1Ch 16:35 — And say ye, Save us, O God of our salvation, and gather us together, and deliver us from the heathen, that we may give thanks to thy holy name, *and* glory in thy praise.

2Ch 6:41 — Now therefore arise, O LORD God, into thy resting place, thou, and the ark of thy strength: let thy priests, O LORD God, be clothed with salvation, and let thy saints rejoice in goodness.

Ps 3:8 — Salvation *belongeth* unto the LORD: thy blessing *is* upon thy people. Selah.

Ps 37:39 — But the salvation of the righteous *is* of the LORD: *he is* their strength in the time of trouble.

Ps 46:4 — *There is* a river, the streams whereof shall make glad the city of God, the holy *place* of the tabernacles of the most High.

Ps 65:4 — Blessed *is the man whom* thou choosest, and causest to approach *unto thee, that* he may dwell in thy courts: we shall be satisfied with the goodness of thy house, *even* of thy holy temple.

Ps 86:13 — For great *is* thy mercy toward me: and thou hast delivered my soul from the lowest hell.

Ps 90:14 — O satisfy us early with thy mercy; that we may rejoice and be glad all our days.

Ps 91:16 — With long life will I satisfy him, and shew him my salvation.

Ps 95:1 — O come, let us sing unto the LORD: let us make a joyful noise to the rock of our salvation.

Ps 106:8 — Nevertheless he saved them for his name's sake, that he might make his mighty power to be known.

Ps 107:9 — For he satisfieth the longing soul, and filleth the hungry soul with goodness.

Ps 132:16 — I will also clothe her priests with salvation: and her saints shall shout aloud for joy.

Isa 1:18 — Come now, and let us reason together, saith the LORD: though your sins be as scarlet, they shall be as white as snow; though they be red like crimson, they shall be as wool.

Isa 2:5 — O house of Jacob, come ye, and let us walk in the light of the LORD.

Isa 29:24 — They also that erred in spirit shall come to understanding, and they that murmured shall learn doctrine.

Isa 35:8 — And an highway shall be there, and a way, and it shall be called The way of holiness; the unclean shall not pass over it; but it *shall be* for those: the wayfaring men, though fools, shall not err *therein.*

Isa 44:3 — For I will pour water upon him that is thirsty, and floods upon the dry ground: I will pour my spirit upon thy seed, and my blessing upon thine offspring:

Isa 45:17 — *But* Israel shall be saved in the LORD with an everlasting salvation: ye shall not be ashamed nor confounded world without end.

Isa 50:10 — Who *is* among you that feareth the LORD, that obeyeth the voice of his servant, that walketh *in* darkness, and hath no light? let him trust in the name of the LORD, and stay upon his God.

Isa 52:10 — The LORD hath made bare his holy arm in the eyes of all the nations; and all the ends of the earth shall see the salvation of our God.

Isa 52:15 — So shall he sprinkle many nations; the kings shall shut their mouths at him: for *that* which had not been told them shall they see; and *that* which they had not heard shall they consider.

Isa 56:1 — Thus saith the LORD, Keep ye judgment, and do justice: for my salvation *is* near to come, and my righteousness to be revealed.

Isa 63:9 — In all their affliction he was afflicted, and the angel of his presence saved them: in his love and in his pity he redeemed them; and he bare them, and carried them all the days of old.

Jer 3:23 — Truly in vain *is salvation hoped for* from the hills, *and from* the multitude of mountains: truly in the LORD our God *is* the salvation of Israel.

Jer 21:8 — And unto this people thou shalt say, Thus saith the LORD; Behold, I set before you the way of life, and the way of death.

Eze 18:32 — For I have no pleasure in the death of him that dieth, saith the Lord GOD: wherefore turn *yourselves,* and live ye.

Joel 2:32 — And it shall come to pass, *that* whosoever shall call on the name of the LORD shall be delivered: for in mount Zion and in Jerusalem shall be deliverance, as the LORD hath said, and in the remnant whom the LORD shall call.

Am 5:4 — For thus saith the LORD unto the house of Israel, Seek ye me, and ye shall live:

Zec 14:8 — And it shall be in that day, *that* living waters shall go out from Jerusalem; half of them toward the former sea, and half of them toward the hinder sea: in summer and in winter shall it be.

Mal 4:2 — But unto you that fear my name shall the Sun of righteousness arise with healing in his wings; and ye shall go forth, and grow up as calves of the stall.

Mt 1:21 — And she shall bring forth a son, and thou shalt call his name JESUS: for he shall save his people from their sins.

Mt 3:9 — And think not to say within yourselves, We have Abraham to *our* father: for I say unto you, that God is able of these stones to raise up children unto Abraham.

Mt 18:14 — Even so it is not the will of your Father which is in heaven, that one of these little ones should perish.

Mt 21:31 — Whether of them twain did the will of *his* father? They say unto him, The first. Jesus saith unto them, Verily I say unto you, That the publicans and the harlots go into the kingdom of God before you.

Mt 22:14 — For many are called, but few *are* chosen.

Mt 23:37 — O Jerusalem, Jerusalem, *thou* that killest the prophets, and stonest them which are sent unto thee, how often would I have gathered thy children together, even as a hen gathereth her chickens under *her* wings, and ye would not!

Mt 24:14 — And this gospel of the kingdom shall be preached in all the world for a witness unto all nations; and then shall the end come.

Mt 28:19 — Go ye therefore, and teach all nations, baptizing them in the name of the Father, and of the Son, and of the Holy Ghost:

Mk 2:17 — When Jesus heard *it,* he saith unto them, They that are whole have no need of the physician, but they that are sick: I came not to call the righteous, but sinners to repentance.

Lk 2:10 — And the angel said unto them, Fear not: for, behold, I bring you good tidings of great joy, which shall be to all people.

Lk 3:6 — And all flesh shall see the salvation of God.

Lk 7:47 — Wherefore I say unto thee, Her sins, which are many, are forgiven; for she loved much: but to whom little is forgiven, *the same* loveth little.

Lk 15:2 — And the Pharisees and scribes murmured, saying, This man receiveth sinners, and eateth with them.

Lk 19:10 — For the Son of man is come to seek and to save that which was lost.

Lk 24:47 — And that repentance and remission of sins should be preached in his name among all nations, beginning at Jerusalem.

Jn 1:7 — The same came for a witness, to bear witness of the Light, that all *men* through him might believe.

Jn 4:14 — But whosoever drinketh of the water that I shall give him shall never thirst; but the water that I shall give him shall be in him a well of water springing up into everlasting life.

Jn 4:22 — Ye worship ye know not what: we know what we worship: for salvation is of the Jews.

Jn 5:40 — And ye will not come to me, that ye might have life.

Jn 6:35 — And Jesus said unto them, I am the bread of life: he that cometh to me shall never hunger; and he that believeth on me shall never thirst.

Jn 6:37 — All that the Father giveth me shall come to me; and him that cometh to me I will in no wise cast out.

Jn 10:16 — And other sheep I have, which are not of this fold: them also I must bring, and they shall hear my voice; and there shall be one fold, *and* one shepherd.

Jn 12:32 — And I, if I be lifted up from the earth, will draw all *men* unto me.

Ac 2:39 — For the promise is unto you, and to your children, and to all that are afar off, *even* as many as the Lord our God shall call.

Ac 4:12 — Neither is there salvation in any other: for there is none other name under heaven given among men, whereby we must be saved.

Ac 5:20 — Go, stand and speak in the temple to the people all the words of this life.

Ac 13:26 — Men *and* brethren, children of the stock of Abraham, and whosoever among you feareth God, to you is the word of this salvation sent.

Ac 13:47 — For so hath the Lord commanded us, *saying,* I have set thee to be a light of the Gentiles, that thou shouldest be for salvation unto the ends of the earth.

Ac 15:11 — But we believe that through the grace of the Lord Jesus Christ we shall be saved, even as they.

Ac 16:17 — The same followed Paul and us, and cried, saying, These men are the servants of the most high God, which shew unto us the way of salvation.

Ac 20:21 — Testifying both to the Jews, and also to the Greeks, repentance toward God, and faith toward our Lord Jesus Christ.

Ac 28:28 — Be it known therefore unto you, that the salvation of God is sent unto the Gentiles, and *that* they will hear it.

Ro 1:5 — By whom we have received grace and apostleship, for obedience to the faith among all nations, for his name:

Ro 1:14 — I am debtor both to the Greeks, and to the Barbarians; both to the wise, and to the unwise.

Ro 2:26 — Therefore if the uncircumcision keep the righteousness of the law, shall not his uncircumcision be counted for circumcision?

Ro 10:4 — For Christ *is* the end of the law for righteousness to every one that believeth.

Ro 15:9 — And that the Gentiles might glorify God for *his* mercy; as it is written, For this cause I will confess to thee among the Gentiles, and sing unto thy name.

Ro 15:16 — That I should be the minister of Jesus Christ to the Gentiles, ministering the gospel of God, that the offering up of the Gentiles might be acceptable, being sanctified by the Holy Ghost.

1Co 1:18 — For the preaching of the cross is to them that perish foolishness; but unto us which are saved it is the power of God.

1Co 6:11 — And such were some of you: but ye are washed, but ye are sanctified, but ye are justified in the name of the Lord Jesus, and by the Spirit of our God.

2Co 5:17 — Therefore if any man *be* in Christ, *he is* a new creature: old things are passed away; behold, all things are become new.

2Co 5:20 — Now then we are ambassadors for Christ, as though God did beseech *you* by us: we pray *you* in Christ's stead, be ye reconciled to God.

2Co 6:1 — We then, *as* workers together *with him,* beseech *you* also that ye receive not the grace of God in vain.

2Co 7:10 — For godly sorrow worketh repentance to salvation not to be repented of: but the sorrow of the world worketh death.

Gal 1:4 — Who gave himself for our sins, that he might deliver us from this present evil world, according to the will of God and our Father:

Gal 2:16 — Knowing that a man is not justified by the works of the law, but by the faith of Jesus Christ, even we have believed in Jesus Christ, that we might be justified by the faith of Christ, and not by the works of the law: for by the works of the law shall no flesh be justified.

Eph 1:13 — In whom ye also *trusted,* after that ye heard the word of truth, the gospel of your salvation: in whom also after that ye believed, ye were sealed with that holy Spirit of promise,

Eph 2:1 — And you *hath he quickened,* who were dead in trespasses and sins;

Eph 2:17 — And came and preached peace to you which were afar off, and to them that were nigh.

Eph 3:6 — That the Gentiles should be fellowheirs, and of the same body, and partakers of his promise in Christ by the gospel:

Eph 3:9 — And to make all *men* see what *is* the fellowship of the mystery, which from the beginning of the world hath been hid in God, who created all things by Jesus Christ:

Eph 5:14 — Wherefore he saith, Awake thou that sleepest, and arise from the dead, and Christ shall give thee light.

Php 2:12 — Wherefore, my beloved, as ye have always obeyed, not as in my presence only, but now much more in my absence, work out your own salvation with fear and trembling.

Col 3:11 — Where there is neither Greek nor Jew, circumcision nor uncircumcision, Barbarian, Scythian, bond *nor* free: but Christ *is* all, and in all.

1Ti 1:13 — Who was before a blasphemer, and a persecutor, and injurious: but I obtained mercy, because I did *it* ignorantly in unbelief.

1Ti 4:10 — For therefore we both labour and suffer reproach, because we trust in the living God, who is the Saviour of all men, specially of those that believe.

2Ti 2:10 — Therefore I endure all things for the elect's sakes, that they may also obtain the salvation which is in Christ Jesus with eternal glory.

2Ti 3:15 — And that from a child thou hast known the holy scriptures, which are able to make thee wise unto salvation through faith which is in Christ Jesus.

Tit 2:11 — For the grace of God that bringeth salvation hath appeared to all men,

Heb 1:14 — Are they not all ministering spirits, sent forth to minister for them who shall be heirs of salvation?

Heb 2:3 — How shall we escape, if we neglect so great salvation; which at the first began to be spoken by the Lord, and was confirmed unto us by them that heard *him;*

Heb 2:10 — For it became him, for whom *are* all things, and by whom *are* all things, in bringing many sons unto glory, to make the captain of their salvation perfect through sufferings.

Heb 5:9 — And being made perfect, he became the author of eternal salvation unto all them that obey him;

Heb 7:25 — Wherefore he is able also to save them to the uttermost that come unto God by him, seeing he ever liveth to make intercession for them.

Jas 1:21 — Wherefore lay apart all filthiness and superfluity of naughtiness, and receive with meekness the engrafted word, which is able to save your souls.

1Pe 1:5 — Who are kept by the power of God through faith unto salvation ready to be revealed in the last time.

2Pe 3:9 — The Lord is not slack concerning his promise, as some men count slackness; but is longsuffering to us-ward, not willing that any should perish, but that all should come to repentance.

2Pe 3:15 — And account *that* the longsuffering of our Lord *is* salvation; even as our beloved brother Paul also according to the wisdom given unto him hath written unto you;

1Jn 2:25 — And this is the promise that he hath promised us, *even* eternal life.

1Jn 5:11 — And this is the record, that God hath given to us eternal life, and this life is in his Son.

Jude 1:3 — Beloved, when I gave all diligence to write unto you of the common salvation, it was needful for me to write unto you, and exhort *you* that ye should earnestly contend for the faith which was once delivered unto the saints.

Rev 3:20 — Behold, I stand at the door, and knock: if any man hear my voice, and open the door, I will come in to him, and will sup with him, and he with me.

Rev 5:9 — And they sung a new song, saying, Thou art worthy to take the book, and to open the seals thereof: for thou wast slain, and hast redeemed us to God by thy blood out of every kindred, and tongue, and people, and nation;

Rev 14:6 — And I saw another angel fly in the midst of heaven, having the everlasting gospel to preach unto them that dwell on the earth, and to every nation, and kindred, and tongue, and people,

Rev 21:6 — And he said unto me, It is done. I am Alpha and Omega, the beginning and the end. I will give unto him that is athirst of the fountain of the water of life freely.

Rev 22:17 — And the Spirit and the bride say, Come. And let him that heareth say, Come. And let him that is athirst come. And whosoever will, let him take the water of life freely.

See: Adoption

See: Redemption

See: Regeneration

See: Sanctification

• Conditions of.

Mt 19:16–21; Lk 14:25–33; 18:18–26; Jn 3:3–12, 14–18; 6:28–29; 11:25–26

Mt 3:2 — And saying, Repent ye: for the kingdom of heaven is at hand.

Mt 18:3 — And said, Verily I say unto you, Except ye be converted, and become as little children, ye shall not enter into the kingdom of heaven.

Mt 24:13 — But he that shall endure unto the end, the same shall be saved.

Mk 1:4 — John did baptize in the wilderness, and preach the baptism of repentance for the remission of sins.

Lk 3:8 — Bring forth therefore fruits worthy of repentance, and begin not to say within yourselves, We have Abraham to *our* father: for I say unto you, That God is able of these stones to raise up children unto Abraham.

Jn 5:24 — Verily, verily, I say unto you, He that heareth my word, and believeth on him that sent me, hath everlasting life, and shall not come into condemnation; but is passed from death unto life.

Jn 6:47 — Verily, verily, I say unto you, He that believeth on me hath everlasting life.

Jn 9:35 — Jesus heard that they had cast him out; and when he had found him, he said unto him, Dost thou believe on the Son of God?

Jn 12:36 — While ye have light, believe in the light, that ye may be the children of light. These things spake Jesus, and departed, and did hide himself from them.

Jn 20:31 — But these are written, that ye might believe that Jesus is the Christ, the Son of God; and that believing ye might have life through his name.

Ac 2:38 — Then Peter said unto them, Repent, and be baptized every one of you in the name of Jesus Christ for the remission of sins, and ye shall receive the gift of the Holy Ghost.

Ac 3:19 — Repent ye therefore, and be converted, that your sins may be blotted out, when the times of refreshing shall come from the presence of the Lord;

Ac 3:23 — And it shall come to pass, *that* every soul, which will not hear that prophet, shall be destroyed from among the people.

See: Blessing; divine, contingent upon obedience

See: Faith

See: Obedience

See: Perseverance

See: Repentance

• Plan of.

Jn 6:44–45; 19:28–30; Ro 1:16–17; 10:3–9; 16:25–26; 1Co 1:21–25; 2:7–9; 2Co 5:18–19; Gal 4:4–5; Eph 1:3–23; 2:4–10; 3:1–11; Col 1:19–23, 26–27; 2Th 2:13–14; 2Ti 1:9–10; Heb 2:9–10, 14–18; 6:17–20; Rev 5:2–5

Mk 4:11 — And he said unto them, Unto you it is given to know the mystery of the kingdom of God: but unto them that are without, all these *things* are done in parables:

Jn 6:37 — All that the Father giveth me shall come to me; and him that cometh to me I will in no wise cast out.

Jn 6:65 — And he said, Therefore said I unto you, that no man can come unto me, except it were given unto him of my Father.

Jn 17:4 — I have glorified thee on the earth: I have finished the work which thou gavest me to do.

Jn 18:11 — Then said Jesus unto Peter, Put up thy sword into the sheath: the cup which my Father hath given me, shall I not drink it?

Ac 3:18 — But those things, which God before had shewed by the mouth of all his prophets, that Christ should suffer, he hath so fulfilled.

Ac 17:3 — Opening and alleging, that Christ must needs have suffered, and risen again from the dead; and that this Jesus, whom I preach unto you, is Christ.

Eph 6:19 — And for me, that utterance may be given unto me, that I may open my mouth boldly, to make known the mystery of the gospel,

1Ti 3:16 — And without controversy great is the mystery of godliness: God was manifest in the flesh, justified in the Spirit, seen of angels, preached unto the Gentiles, believed on in the world, received up into glory.

Rev 10:7 — But in the days of the voice of the seventh angel, when he shall begin to sound, the mystery of God should be finished, as he hath declared to his servants the prophets.

See: Jesus, Mission of

See: Redemption

See: Regeneration

See: Sanctification

See: Sin; forgiveness of

SAMARIA

• City of, built by Omri.

1Ki 16:24 — And he bought the hill Samaria of Shemer for two talents of silver, and built on the hill, and called the name of the city which he built, after the name of Shemer, owner of the hill, Samaria.

• Capital of the kingdom of the ten tribes.

1Ki 16:29 — And in the thirty and eighth year of Asa king of Judah began Ahab the son of Omri to reign over Israel: and Ahab the son of Omri reigned over Israel in Samaria twenty and two years.

1Ki 22:51 — Ahaziah the son of Ahab began to reign over Israel in Samaria the seventeenth year of Jehoshaphat king of Judah, and reigned two years over Israel.

2Ki 13:1 — In the three and twentieth year of Joash the son of Ahaziah king of Judah Jehoahaz the son of Jehu began to reign over Israel in Samaria, *and reigned* seventeen years.

2Ki 13:10 — In the thirty and seventh year of Joash king of Judah began Jehoash the son of Jehoahaz to reign over Israel in Samaria, *and reigned* sixteen years.

2Ki 15:8 — In the thirty and eighth year of Azariah king of Judah did Zachariah the son of Jeroboam reign over Israel in Samaria six months.

• Besieged by Ben-hadad.

1Ki 20:1–43; 2Ki 6:24–7:20

• The king of Syria is led into, by Elisha, who miraculously blinds him and his army.

2Ki 6:8–23

• Ahab ruled in.

See: Ahab

See: Jezebel

• Besieged by Shalmaneser, king of Assyria, 3 years; taken; the people carried away.

2Ki 17:5–6; 18:9–11

• Idolatry of.

1Ki 16:32 — And he reared up an altar for Baal in the house of Baal, which he had built in Samaria.

2Ki 13:6 — Nevertheless they departed not from the sins of the house of Jeroboam, who made Israel sin, *but* walked therein: and there remained the grove also in Samaria.)

• Temple of, destroyed.

2Ki 10:17–28

2Ki 23:19 — And all the houses also of the high places that *were* in the cities of Samaria, which the kings of Israel had made to provoke *the LORD* to anger, Josiah took away, and did to them according to all the acts that he had done in Bethel.

• Paul and Barnabas preach in.

Ac 15:3 — And being brought on their way by the church, they passed through Phenice and Samaria, declaring the conversion of the Gentiles: and they caused great joy unto all the brethren.

- **Visited by Philip, Peter, and John.**
  Ac 8:5–25

• Country of.

Isa 7:9 — And the head of Ephraim *is* Samaria, and the head of Samaria *is* Remaliah's son. If ye will not believe, surely ye shall not be established.

- **Foreign colonies distributed among the cities of, by the king of Assyria.**
  2Ki 17:24–41; Ezr 4:9–10
- **Roads through, from Judaea into Galilee.**
  Jn 4:3–8
  Lk 17:11 — And it came to pass, as he went to Jerusalem, that he passed through the midst of Samaria and Galilee.
- **Jesus journeys through.**
  Jn 4:1–42
- **Jesus heals lepers in.**
  Lk 17:11–19
- **The good Samaritan from.**
  Lk 10:33–35
- **No dealings between the Jews and the inhabitants of.**
  Jn 4:9 — Then saith the woman of Samaria unto him, How is it that thou, being a Jew, askest drink of me, which am a woman of Samaria? for the Jews have no dealings with the Samaritans.
- **Expect the Messiah.**
  Jn 4:25 — The woman saith unto him, I know that Messias cometh, which is called Christ: when he is come, he will tell us all things.
- **Disciples made from the inhabitants of.**
  Jn 4:39–42; Ac 8:5–8, 14–17
  Ac 8:25 — And they, when they had testified and preached the word of the Lord, returned to Jerusalem, and preached the gospel in many villages of the Samaritans.
- **Jesus forbids the apostles to preach in the cities of.**
  Mt 10:5 — These twelve Jesus sent forth, and commanded them, saying, Go not into the way of the Gentiles, and into *any* city of the Samaritans enter ye not:

SAMGAR-NEBO

• A prince of Babylon.

• At the siege of Jerusalem.

Jer 39:3 — And all the princes of the king of Babylon came in, and sat in the middle gate, *even* Nergal-sharezer, Samgar-nebo, Sarsechim, Rab-saris, Nergal-sharezer, Rabmag, with all the residue of the princes of the king of Babylon.

SAMLAH • One of the ancient kings of Edom.

Ge 36:36–37; 1Ch 1:47–48

SAMOS

• An island in the Aegean Sea.

• Paul's ship put in there.

Ac 20:15 — And we sailed thence, and came the next *day* over against Chios; and the next *day* we arrived at Samos, and tarried at Trogyllium; and the next *day* we came to Miletus.

SAMOTHRACIA

• An island in the Aegean Sea.

• Paul's ship put in there.

Ac 16:11 — Therefore loosing from Troas, we came with a straight course to Samothracia, and the next day to Neapolis;

SAMSON

• A judge of Israel.

Jgs 16:31 — Then his brethren and all the house of his father came down, and took him, and brought *him* up, and buried him between Zorah and Eshtaol in the buryingplace of Manoah his father. And he judged Israel twenty years.

• A Danite, son of Manoah. Miraculous birth of; a Nazarite from his mother's womb.

Jgs 13:2–7, 24–25

• Desires a Philistine woman for his wife; slays a lion.

Jgs 14:1–7

• His marriage feast and the riddle propounded.

Jgs 14:8–19

• Slays thirty Philistines.

Jgs 14:19 — And the Spirit of the LORD came upon him, and he went down to Ashkelon, and slew thirty men of them, and took their spoil, and gave change of garments unto them which expounded the riddle. And his anger was kindled, and he went up to his father's house.

• Wife of, estranged.

Jgs 14:20–15:2

• Is avenged for the estrangement of his wife.

Jgs 15:3–8

• His great strength.

Jgs 15:7–14

Heb 11:32 — And what shall I more say? for the time would fail me to tell of Gedeon, and *of* Barak, and *of* Samson, and *of* Jephthae; *of* David also, and Samuel, and *of* the prophets:

• Slays a thousand Philistines with the jawbone of an ass.

Jgs 15:13–17

• Miraculously supplied with water.

Jgs 15:18–19

• Cohabits with Delilah, a harlot; her machinations with the Philistines to overcome him.

Jgs 16:1–20

• Blinded by Philistines; confined to hard labor in prison; pulls down pillars of temple; dies.

Jgs 16:21–31

Heb 11:32 — And what shall I more say? for the time would fail me to tell of Gedeon, and *of* Barak, and *of* Samson, and *of* Jephthae; *of* David also, and Samuel, and *of* the prophets:

SAMUEL

• Miraculous birth of.

1Sa 1:7–20

• Consecrated to God before his birth.

1Sa 1:24–28

1Sa 1:11 — And she vowed a vow, and said, O LORD of hosts, if thou wilt indeed look on the affliction of thine handmaid, and remember me, and not forget thine handmaid, but wilt give unto thine handmaid a man child, then I will give him unto the LORD all the days of his life, and there shall no razor come upon his head.

1Sa 1:22 — But Hannah went not up; for she said unto her husband, *I will not go up* until the child be weaned, and *then* I will bring him, that he may appear before the LORD, and there abide for ever.

• His mother's song of thanksgiving.

1Sa 2:1–10

• Ministered in the house of God.

1Sa 2:18–19

1Sa 2:11 — And Elkanah went to Ramah to his house. And the child did minister unto the LORD before Eli the priest.

• Blessed of God.

1Sa 2:21 — And the LORD visited Hannah, so that she conceived, and bare three sons and two daughters. And the child Samuel grew before the LORD.

1Sa 3:19 — And Samuel grew, and the LORD was with him, and did let none of his words fall to the ground.

• His vision concerning the house of Eli.

1Sa 3:1–18

• A prophet of the Israelites.

1Sa 3:20–4:1

• A judge of Israel, his judgment seat at Bethel, Gilgal, Mizpeh, and Ramah.

1Sa 7:15–17

• Organizes the tabernacle service.

1Ch 9:22 — All these *which were* chosen to be porters in the gates were two hundred and twelve. These were reckoned by their genealogy in their villages, whom David and Samuel the seer did ordain in their set office.

1Ch 26:28 — And all that Samuel the seer, and Saul the son of Kish, and Abner the son of Ner, and Joab the son of Zeruiah, had dedicated; *and* whosoever had dedicated *any thing, it was* under the hand of Shelomith, and of his brethren.

2Ch 35:18 — And there was no passover like to that kept in Israel from the days of Samuel the prophet; neither did all the kings of Israel keep such a passover as Josiah kept, and the priests, and the Levites, and all Judah and Israel that were present, and the inhabitants of Jerusalem.

• Israelites repent under his reproofs and admonitions.

1Sa 7:4–6

• The Philistines defeated through his intercession and sacrifices.

1Sa 7:7–14

• Makes his corrupt sons judges in Israel.

1Sa 8:1–3

• People desire a king; he protests.

1Sa 8:4–22

• Anoints Saul king of Israel.

1Sa 9:1–10:27

• Renews the kingdom of Saul.

1Sa 11:12–15

• Reproves Saul; foretells that his kingdom shall not be established.

1Sa 13:11–15; 15:1–35

• Anoints David to be king.

1Sa 16:1–23

• Shelters David when escaping from Saul.

1Sa 19:18 — So David fled, and escaped, and came to Samuel to Ramah, and told him all that Saul had done to him. And he and Samuel went and dwelt in Naioth.

• Death of, the lament for him.

1Sa 25:1 — And Samuel died; and all the Israelites were gathered together, and lamented him, and buried him in his house at Ramah. And David arose, and went down to the wilderness of Paran.

• Called up by the witch of Endor.

1Sa 28:3–20

• His integrity as judge and ruler.

1Sa 12:1–5

Ps 99:6 — Moses and Aaron among his priests, and Samuel among them that call upon his name; they called upon the LORD, and he answered them.

Jer 15:1 — Then said the LORD unto me, Though Moses and Samuel stood before me, *yet* my mind *could* not *be* toward this people: cast *them* out of my sight, and let them go forth.

Heb 11:32 — And what shall I more say? for the time would fail me to tell of Gedeon, and *of* Barak, and *of* Samson, and *of* Jephthae; *of* David also, and Samuel, and *of* the prophets:

• Chronicles of.

1Ch 29:29 — Now the acts of David the king, first and last, behold, they *are* written in the book of Samuel the seer, and in the book of Nathan the prophet, and in the book of Gad the seer,

• Sons of.

1Ch 6:28 — And the sons of Samuel; the firstborn Vashni, and Abiah.

1Ch 6:33 — And these *are* they that waited with their children. Of the sons of the Kohathites: Heman a singer, the son of Joel, the son of Shemuel,

• Called Shemuel.

1Ch 6:33 — And these *are* they that waited with their children. Of the sons of the Kohathites: Heman a singer, the son of Joel, the son of Shemuel,

SANBALLAT • An enemy of the Jews in rebuilding Jerusalem after the captivity.

Ne 4:1–23; 6:1–19

Ne 2:10 — When Sanballat the Horonite, and Tobiah the servant, the Ammonite, heard *of it,* it grieved them exceedingly that there was come a man to seek the welfare of the children of Israel.

Ne 2:19 — But when Sanballat the Horonite, and Tobiah the servant, the Ammonite, and Geshem the Arabian, heard *it,* they laughed us to scorn, and despised us, and said, What *is* this thing that ye do? will ye rebel against the king?

Ne 13:28 — And *one* of the sons of Joiada, the son of Eliashib the high priest, *was* son in law to Sanballat the Horonite: therefore I chased him from me.

SANCTIFICATION

• Firstborn of Israelites sanctified.

Ex 13:2 — Sanctify unto me all the firstborn, whatsoever openeth the womb among the children of Israel, *both* of man and of beast: it *is* mine.

• All Israel sanctified.

Ex 19:10 — And the LORD said unto Moses, Go unto the people, and sanctify them to day and to morrow, and let them wash their clothes,

Ex 19:14 — And Moses went down from the mount unto the people, and sanctified the people; and they washed their clothes.

• Material things sanctified by anointing.

Ex 40:9–11

• The Lord the sanctifier.

Ex 31:13 — Speak thou also unto the children of Israel, saying, Verily my sabbaths ye shall keep: for it is a sign between me and you throughout your generations; that ye may know that I *am* the LORD that doth sanctify you.

Le 20:8 — And ye shall keep my statutes, and do them: I *am* the LORD which sanctify you.

Le 21:8 — Thou shalt sanctify him therefore; for he offereth the bread of thy God: he shall be holy unto thee: for I the LORD, which sanctify you, *am* holy.

Le 22:9 — They shall therefore keep mine ordinance, lest they bear sin for it, and die therefore, if they profane it: I the LORD do sanctify them.

• The altar sanctifies the gift.

Ex 29:37 — Seven days thou shalt make an atonement for the altar, and sanctify it; and it shall be an altar most holy: whatsoever toucheth the altar shall be holy.

Ex 30:29 — And thou shalt sanctify them, that they may be most holy: whatsoever toucheth them shall be holy.

• Tabernacle sanctified by God's presence.

Ex 40:34–35

Ex 29:43 — And there I will meet with the children of Israel, and *the tabernacle* shall be sanctified by my glory.

• Unclassified scripture relating to.

Le 21:1–23; Ac 26:17–18; 1Co 13:1–13; 2Co 1:21–22; Eph 1:3–4; 4:12–13, 15–16; 5:25–27; 1Th 4:3–4; 2Th 2:13–14; 2Pe 1:2–4

Ex 31:13 — Speak thou also unto the children of Israel, saying, Verily my sabbaths ye shall keep: for it is a sign between me and you throughout your generations; that ye may know that I *am* the LORD that doth sanctify you.

Ex 33:16 — For wherein shall it be known here that I and thy people have found grace in thy sight? *is it* not in that thou goest with us? so shall we be separated, I and thy people, from all the people that *are* upon the face of the earth.

Jer 1:5 — Before I formed thee in the belly I knew thee; and before thou camest forth out of the womb I sanctified thee, *and* I ordained thee a prophet unto the nations.

Eze 37:28 — And the heathen shall know that I the LORD do sanctify Israel, when my sanctuary shall be in the midst of them for evermore.

Jn 17:17 — Sanctify them through thy truth: thy word is truth.

Jn 17:19 — And for their sakes I sanctify myself, that they also might be sanctified through the truth.

Ro 15:16 — That I should be the minister of Jesus Christ to the Gentiles, ministering the gospel of God, that the offering up of the Gentiles might be acceptable, being sanctified by the Holy Ghost.

1Co 1:2 — Unto the church of God which is at Corinth, to them that are sanctified in Christ Jesus, called *to be* saints, with all that in every place call upon the name of Jesus Christ our Lord, both theirs and ours:

1Co 1:30 — But of him are ye in Christ Jesus, who of God is made unto us wisdom, and righteousness, and sanctification, and redemption:

1Co 6:11 — And such were some of you: but ye are washed, but ye are sanctified, but ye are justified in the name of the Lord Jesus, and by the Spirit of our God.

Gal 2:20 — I am crucified with Christ: nevertheless I live; yet not I, but Christ liveth in me: and the life which I now live in the flesh I live by the faith of the Son of God, who loved me, and gave himself for me.

Gal 6:14 — But God forbid that I should glory, save in the cross of our Lord Jesus Christ, by whom the world is crucified unto me, and I unto the world.

Eph 3:19 — And to know the love of Christ, which passeth knowledge, that ye might be filled with all the fulness of God.

Eph 4:7 — But unto every one of us is given grace according to the measure of the gift of Christ.

Col 2:11 — In whom also ye are circumcised with the circumcision made without hands, in putting off the body of the sins of the flesh by the circumcision of Christ:

1Th 5:23 — And the very God of peace sanctify you wholly; and *I pray God* your whole spirit and soul and body be preserved blameless unto the coming of our Lord Jesus Christ.

2Ti 2:11 — *It is* a faithful saying: For if we be dead with *him,* we shall also live with *him:*

2Ti 2:21 — If a man therefore purge himself from these, he shall be a vessel unto honour, sanctified, and meet for the master's use, *and* prepared unto every good work.

Heb 2:11 — For both he that sanctifieth and they who are sanctified *are* all of one: for which cause he is not ashamed to call them brethren,

Heb 9:14 — How much more shall the blood of Christ, who through the eternal Spirit offered himself without spot to God, purge your conscience from dead works to serve the living God?

Heb 10:10 — By the which will we are sanctified through the offering of the body of Jesus Christ once *for all.*

Heb 10:14 — For by one offering he hath perfected for ever them that are sanctified.

Heb 12:10 — For they verily for a few days chastened *us* after their own pleasure; but he for *our* profit, that *we* might be partakers of his holiness.

Heb 13:12 — Wherefore Jesus also, that he might sanctify the people with his own blood, suffered without the gate.

Heb 13:21 — Make you perfect in every good work to do his will, working in you that which is wellpleasing in his sight, through Jesus Christ; to whom *be* glory for ever and ever. Amen.

1Pe 1:2 — Elect according to the foreknowledge of God the Father, through sanctification of the Spirit, unto obedience and sprinkling of the blood of Jesus Christ: Grace unto you, and peace, be multiplied.

1Jn 1:9 — If we confess our sins, he is faithful and just to forgive us *our* sins, and to cleanse us from all unrighteousness.

Jude 1:1 — Jude, the servant of Jesus Christ, and brother of James, to them that are sanctified by God the Father, and preserved in Jesus Christ, *and* called:

Jude 1:24 — Now unto him that is able to keep you from falling, and to present *you* faultless before the presence of his glory with exceeding joy,

Rev 7:14 — And I said unto him, Sir, thou knowest. And he said to me, These are they which came out of great tribulation, and have washed their robes, and made them white in the blood of the Lamb.

See: Holiness

See: Redemption

See: Regeneration

See: Salvation

See: Sin; forgiveness of

SANCTUARY

• The Holy of Holies.

• In the tabernacle.

Heb 9:2 — For there was a tabernacle made; the first, wherein *was* the candlestick, and the table, and the shewbread; which is called the sanctuary.

• Divine dwelling place.

Ex 25:8 — And let them make me a sanctuary; that I may dwell among them.

• Reverence for.

Le 19:30 — Ye shall keep my sabbaths, and reverence my sanctuary: I *am* the LORD.

Le 26:2 — Ye shall keep my sabbaths, and reverence my sanctuary: I *am* the LORD.

• In charge of high priest.

Ex 27:21 — In the tabernacle of the congregation without the vail, which *is* before the testimony, Aaron and his sons shall order it from evening to morning before the LORD: *it shall be* a statute for ever unto their generations on the behalf of the children of Israel.

Le 24:3 — Without the vail of the testimony, in the tabernacle of the congregation, shall Aaron order it from the evening unto the morning before the LORD continually: *it shall be* a statute for ever in your generations.

Nu 18:5 — And ye shall keep the charge of the sanctuary, and the charge of the altar: that there be no wrath any more upon the children of Israel.

• The holy place in the temple.

La 2:7 — The Lord hath cast off his altar, he hath abhorred his sanctuary, he hath given up into the hand of the enemy the walls of her palaces; they have made a noise in the house of the LORD, as in the day of a solemn feast.

La 2:20 — Behold, O LORD, and consider to whom thou hast done this. Shall the women eat their fruit, *and* children of a span long? shall the priest and the prophet be slain in the sanctuary of the Lord?

Eze 42:20 — He measured it by the four sides: it had a wall round about, five hundred *reeds* long, and five hundred broad, to make a separation between the sanctuary and the profane place.

• Figurative.

Eze 11:16 — Therefore say, Thus saith the Lord GOD; Although I have cast them far off among the heathen, and although I have scattered them among the countries, yet will I be to them as a little sanctuary in the countries where they shall come.

• Symbolic.

Heb 8:2 — A minister of the sanctuary, and of the true tabernacle, which the Lord pitched, and not man.

Heb 8:5 — Who serve unto the example and shadow of heavenly things, as Moses was admonished of God when he was about to make the tabernacle: for, See, saith he, *that* thou make all things according to the pattern shewed to thee in the mount.

See: Tabernacle

See: Temple

SANDAL See: Shoe

SANHEDRIN ✢See: Government

SANITATION

• Carcases.

Le 10:4–5; 11:24–28, 31–40; Nu 19:11–16; Dt 21:22–23

Le 5:2 — Or if a soul touch any unclean thing, whether *it be* a carcase of an unclean beast, or a carcase of unclean cattle, or the carcase of unclean creeping things, and *if* it be hidden from him; he also shall be unclean, and guilty.

Le 22:4 — What man soever of the seed of Aaron *is* a leper, or hath a running issue; he shall not eat of the holy things, until he be clean. And whoso toucheth any thing *that is* unclean *by* the dead, or a man whose seed goeth from him;

Le 22:6 — The soul which hath touched any such shall be unclean until even, and shall not eat of the holy things, unless he wash his flesh with water.

Nu 9:6 — And there were certain men, who were defiled by the dead body of a man, that they could not keep the passover on that day: and they came before Moses and before Aaron on that day:

Nu 9:10 — Speak unto the children of Israel, saying, If any man of you or of your posterity shall be unclean by reason of a dead body, or *be* in a journey afar off, yet he shall keep the passover unto the LORD.

Nu 31:19 — And do ye abide without the camp seven days: whosoever hath killed any person, and whosoever hath touched any slain, purify *both* yourselves and your captives on the third day, and on the seventh day.

• Childbirth.

Le 12:3 — And in the eighth day the flesh of his foreskin shall be circumcised.

Eze 16:4 — And *as for* thy nativity, in the day thou wast born thy navel was not cut, neither wast thou washed in water to supple *thee;* thou wast not salted at all, nor swaddled at all.

• Circumcision.

✢See: Circumcision

• Contagion.

Le 5:2–3; 11:24–28, 31–40; 13:2–59; 14:2–3, 8–9, 34–48, 54–57; 15:2–13, 16–28, 31–33; 22:4–8; Nu 5:2–4; 19:11–16; 31:19–20; Dt 23:10–11

Le 7:19 — And the flesh that toucheth any unclean *thing* shall not be eaten; it shall be burnt with fire: and as for the flesh, all that be clean shall eat thereof.

Le 7:21 — Moreover the soul that shall touch any unclean *thing, as* the uncleanness of man, or *any* unclean beast, or any abominable unclean *thing,* and eat of the flesh of the sacrifice of peace offerings, which *pertain* unto the LORD, even that soul shall be cut off from his people.

Nu 9:6 — And there were certain men, who were defiled by the dead body of a man, that they could not keep the passover on that day: and they came before Moses and before Aaron on that day:

Nu 9:10 — Speak unto the children of Israel, saying, If any man of you or of your posterity shall be unclean by reason of a dead body, or *be* in a journey afar off, yet he shall keep the passover unto the LORD.

Nu 19:22 — And whatsoever the unclean *person* toucheth shall be unclean; and the soul that toucheth *it* shall be unclean until even.

Dt 24:8 — Take heed in the plague of leprosy, that thou observe diligently, and do according to all that the priests the Levites shall teach you: as I commanded them, so ye shall observe to do.

• Disinfection.

Le 11:24–40; 13:47–59; 14:8–9, 34–48, 54–57; 15:2–13, 16–28; Nu 31:19–20, 22–24

Le 2:13 — And every oblation of thy meat offering shalt thou season with salt; neither shalt thou suffer the salt of the covenant of thy God to be lacking from thy meat offering: with all thine offerings thou shalt offer salt.

Le 7:19 — And the flesh that toucheth any unclean *thing* shall not be eaten; it shall be burnt with fire: and as for the flesh, all that be clean shall eat thereof.

Le 13:6 — And the priest shall look on him again the seventh day: and, behold, *if* the plague *be* somewhat dark, *and* the plague spread not in the skin, the priest shall pronounce him clean: it *is but* a scab: and he shall wash his clothes, and be clean.

Le 13:34 — And in the seventh day the priest shall look on the scall: and, behold, *if* the scall be not spread in the skin, nor *be* in sight deeper than the skin; then the priest shall pronounce him clean: and he shall wash his clothes, and be clean.

✢See: Purification

• Filth, disposition of.

Le 4:11–12; 16:27–28; Dt 23:12–13

Ex 29:14 — But the flesh of the bullock, and his skin, and his dung, shalt thou burn with fire without the camp: it *is* a sin offering.

Ex 29:34 — And if ought of the flesh of the consecrations, or of the bread, remain unto the morning, then thou shalt burn the remainder with fire: it shall not be eaten, because it *is* holy.

Le 4:21 — And he shall carry forth the bullock without the camp, and burn him as he burned the first bullock: it *is* a sin offering for the congregation.

Le 6:30 — And no sin offering, whereof *any* of the blood is brought into the tabernacle of the congregation to reconcile *withal* in the holy *place,* shall be eaten: it shall be burnt in the fire.

Le 7:17 — But the remainder of the flesh of the sacrifice on the third day shall be burnt with fire.

Le 7:19 — And the flesh that toucheth any unclean *thing* shall not be eaten; it shall be burnt with fire: and as for the flesh, all that be clean shall eat thereof.

Le 8:17 — But the bullock, and his hide, his flesh, and his dung, he burnt with fire without the camp; as the LORD commanded Moses.

Le 8:32 — And that which remaineth of the flesh and of the bread shall ye burn with fire.

Le 9:11 — And the flesh and the hide he burnt with fire without the camp.

Le 19:6 — It shall be eaten the same day ye offer it, and on the morrow: and if ought remain until the third day, it shall be burnt in the fire.

Heb 13:11 — For the bodies of those beasts, whose blood is brought into the sanctuary by the high priest for sin, are burned without the camp.

• Food.

Le 7:15–19, 23–27; 11:2–23, 26–27, 29–43, 46–47; 17:10–15; 19:5–8; Dt 12:20–25; 14:3–21; 15:22–23

Le 3:17 — *It shall be* a perpetual statute for your generations throughout all your dwellings, that ye eat neither fat nor blood.

Le 19:26 — Ye shall not eat *any thing* with the blood: neither shall ye use enchantment, nor observe times.

Le 22:8 — That which dieth of itself, or is torn *with beasts,* he shall not eat to defile himself therewith: I *am* the LORD.

Dt 12:16 — Only ye shall not eat the blood; ye shall pour it upon the earth as water.

Dt 14:26 — And thou shalt bestow that money for whatsoever thy soul lusteth after, for oxen, or for sheep, or for wine, or for strong drink, or for whatsoever thy soul desireth: and thou shalt eat there before the LORD thy God, and thou shalt rejoice, thou, and thine household,

• Gluttony, disease resulting from.

Nu 11:18–20, 31–33

• Penalties concerning.

Dt 28:21–22, 59–62

Dt 28:15 — But it shall come to pass, if thou wilt not hearken unto the voice of the LORD thy God, to observe to do all his commandments and his statutes which I command thee this day; that all these curses shall come upon thee, and overtake thee:

Dt 28:27 — The LORD will smite thee with the botch of Egypt, and with the emerods, and with the scab, and with the itch, whereof thou canst not be healed.

Dt 28:35 — The LORD shall smite thee in the knees, and in the legs, with a sore botch that cannot be healed, from the sole of thy foot unto the top of thy head.

Dt 28:45 — Moreover all these curses shall come upon thee, and shall pursue thee, and overtake thee, till thou be destroyed; because thou hearkenedst not unto the voice of the LORD thy God, to keep his commandments and his statutes which he commanded thee:

• Quarantine.

Le 13:2–5, 31–33, 45–46; 14:2–3, 34–38; Nu 5:2–3; 31:11–20; Dt 23:10–11

Le 14:8 — And he that is to be cleansed shall wash his clothes, and shave off all his hair, and wash himself in water, that he may be clean: and after that he shall come into the camp, and shall tarry abroad out of his tent seven days.

Le 15:19 — And if a woman have an issue, *and* her issue in her flesh be blood, she shall be put apart seven days: and whosoever toucheth her shall be unclean until the even.

• Instances of.

Nu 12:14–15

Nu 12:10 — And the cloud departed from off the tabernacle; and, behold, Miriam *became* leprous, *white* as snow: and Aaron looked upon Miriam, and, behold, *she was* leprous.

2Ki 7:3 — And there were four leprous men at the entering in of the gate: and they said one to another, Why sit we here until we die?

2Ki 15:5 — And the LORD smote the king, so that he was a leper unto the day of his death, and dwelt in a several house. And Jotham the king's son *was* over the house, judging the people of the land.

2Ch 26:21 — And Uzziah the king was a leper unto the day of his death, and dwelt in a several house, *being* a leper; for he was cut off from the house of the LORD: and Jotham his son *was* over the king's house, judging the people of the land.

Lk 17:12 — And as he entered into a certain village, there met him ten men that were lepers, which stood afar off:

• Rest enjoined.

Ex 20:9–11; 31:13–17; 34:21–22; Le 23:3–8, 24–42; 25:2–12; Nu 9:2–3; 28:16–18, 25–26; Dt 5:12–14

Ex 35:2 — Six days shall work be done, but on the seventh day there shall be to you an holy day, a sabbath of rest to the LORD: whosoever doeth work therein shall be put to death.

Nu 29:1 — And in the seventh month, on the first *day* of the month, ye shall have an holy convocation; ye shall do no servile work: it is a day of blowing the trumpets unto you.

Nu 29:7 — And ye shall have on the tenth *day* of this seventh month an holy convocation; and ye shall afflict your souls: ye shall not do any work *therein:*

➜See: Recreation

➜See: Rest

➜See: Sabbath

➜See: Sabbatic Year

• Uncleanness.

Le 20:2–6, 10–21; Dt 27:20–23

• Venereal diseases.

Le 15:2–13, 16–28, 31–33

Le 22:4 — What man soever of the seed of Aaron *is* a leper, or hath a running issue; he shall not eat of the holy things, until he be clean. And whoso toucheth any thing *that is* unclean *by* the dead, or a man whose seed goeth from him;

Le 22:6 — The soul which hath touched any such shall be unclean until even, and shall not eat of the holy things, unless he wash his flesh with water.

• Women in childbirth.

Le 12:4–5

Le 12:2 — Speak unto the children of Israel, saying, If a woman have conceived seed, and born a man child: then she shall be unclean seven days; according to the days of the separation for her infirmity shall she be unclean.

➜See: Ablution

➜See: Defilement

➜See: Leprosy

↞See: **Purification**
↞See: **Uncleanness**

SANSANNAH • A city of Judah.

Jos 15:31 — And Ziklag, and Madmannah, and Sansannah,

SAPH

• Called also Sippai.

• A Philistine giant.

2Sa 21:18 — And it came to pass after this, that there was again a battle with the Philistines at Gob: then Sibbechai the Hushathite slew Saph, which *was* of the sons of the giant.

1Ch 20:4 — And it came to pass after this, that there arose war at Gezer with the Philistines; at which time Sibbechai the Hushathite slew Sippai, *that was* of the children of the giant: and they were subdued.

SAPHIR • A city prophesied against by Micah.

Mic 1:11 — Pass ye away, thou inhabitant of Saphir, having thy shame naked: the inhabitant of Zaanan came not forth in the mourning of Beth-ezel; he shall receive of you his standing.

SAPPHIRA

• Wife of Ananias.

• Falsehood and death of.

Ac 5:1–10

SAPPHIRE

• A precious stone.

Job 28:6 — The stones of it *are* the place of sapphires: and it hath dust of gold.

Job 28:16 — It cannot be valued with the gold of Ophir, with the precious onyx, or the sapphire.

Isa 54:11 — O thou afflicted, tossed with tempest, *and* not comforted, behold, I will lay thy stones with fair colors, and lay thy foundations with sapphires.

Eze 28:13 — Thou hast been in Eden the garden of God; every precious stone *was* thy covering, the sardius, topaz, and the diamond, the beryl, the onyx, and the jasper, the sapphire, the emerald, and the carbuncle, and gold: the workmanship of thy tabrets and of thy pipes was prepared in thee in the day that thou wast created.

• Set in the breastplate.

Ex 28:18 — And the second row *shall be* an emerald, a sapphire, and a diamond.

• The color of the firmament.

Eze 1:26 — And above the firmament that *was* over their heads *was* the likeness of a throne, as the appearance of a sapphire stone: and upon the likeness of the throne *was* the likeness as the appearance of a man above upon it.

• Seen in the foundation of the New Jerusalem in John's apocalyptic vision.

Rev 21:19 — And the foundations of the wall of the city *were* garnished with all manner of precious stones. The first foundation *was* jasper; the second, sapphire; the third, a chalcedony; the fourth, an emerald;

SARAH

• Wife of Abraham.

Ge 11:29–31

• Called also Sarai.

Ge 12:5 — And Abram took Sarai his wife, and Lot his brother's son, and all their substance that they had gathered, and the souls that they had gotten in Haran; and they went forth to go into the land of Canaan; and into the land of Canaan they came.

• Near of kin to Abraham.

Ge 12:10–20

Ge 20:12 — And yet indeed *she is* my sister; she *is* the daughter of my father, but not the daughter of my mother; and she became my wife.

• Abraham represents her as sister; king Abimelech takes her; restored to Abraham by a dream.

Ge 20:1–14

• Is sterile; gives her maid, Hagar, to Abraham as a wife.

Ge 16:1–3

• Her jealousy of Hagar.

Ge 16:4–6; 21:9–14

• Her miraculous conception of Isaac.

Ge 17:15–21; 18:9–15

• Name changed from Sarai to Sarah.

Ge 17:15 — And God said unto Abraham, As for Sarai thy wife, thou shalt not call her name Sarai, but Sarah *shall* her name *be.*

• Gives birth to Isaac.

Ge 21:6–8

Ge 21:3 — And Abraham called the name of his son that was born unto him, whom Sarah bare to him, Isaac.

• Death and burial of.

Ge 23:1–20

Ge 25:10 — The field which Abraham purchased of the sons of Heth: there was Abraham buried, and Sarah his wife.

• Character of.

1Pe 3:5–6

Heb 11:11 — Through faith also Sara herself received strength to conceive seed, and was delivered of a child when she was past age, because she judged him faithful who had promised.

↞See: **Serah**

SARAPH • A descendant of Shelah.

1Ch 4:22 — And Jokim, and the men of Chozeba, and Joash, and Saraph, who had the dominion in Moab, and Jashubi-lehem. And *these are* ancient things.

SARCASM

• Instances of.

• Cain's self-justifying argument when God asked him where Abel was.

Ge 4:9

- **Israelites reproaching Moses.**
  Ex 14:11
- **God reproaching Israel.**
  Nu 11:20; Jgs 10:14
- **Balak reproaching Balaam.**
  Nu 24:11
- **Joshua to descendants of Joseph.**
  Jos 17:15
- **By Jotham.**
  Jgs 9:7–19
- **By Samson.**
  Jgs 14:18
- **The men of Jabesh to Nahash.**
  1Sa 11:10
- **Eliab to David.**
  1Sa 17:28
- **Elijah to the priests of Baal.**
  1Ki 18:27
- **David's reply to Michal's irony.**
  2Sa 6:21
- **Ahab's reply to Ben-hadad.**
  1Ki 20:11
- **Jehoash to Amaziah.**
  2Ki 14:9–10; 2Ch 25:18–19
- **Rabshakeh to Hezekiah.**
  2Ki 18:23–24
- **Sanballat's address to the army of Samaria.**
  Ne 4:2–3
- **Zophar to Job.**
  Job 11:12
- **Job to Zophar.**
  Job 12:2–3
- **Of Solomon.**
  Pr 26:16
- **The persecutors of Jesus.**
  Mt 27:28–29; Lk 23:11; Jn 19:2–3, 5, 15
- **Paul.**
  1Ti 4:7
- **Agrippa to Paul.**
  Ac 26:28

See: Irony

See: Satire

SARDIS

- **A city in Asia.**
- **One of the seven churches in.**

Rev 3:1–4

Rev 1:11 — Saying, I am Alpha and Omega, the first and the last: and, What thou seest, write in a book, and send *it* unto the seven churches which are in Asia; unto Ephesus, and unto Smyrna, and unto Pergamos, and unto Thyatira, and unto Sardis, and unto Philadelphia, and unto Laodicea.

SARDITES

- **Family of.**

Nu 26:26 — *Of* the sons of Zebulun after their families: of Sered, the family of the Sardites: of Elon, the family of the Elonites: of Jahleel, the family of the Jahleelites.

SARDIUS

- **A precious stone.**
- **In the breastplate.**

Ex 28:17 — And thou shalt set in it settings of stones, *even* four rows of stones: *the first* row *shall be* a sardius, a topaz, and a carbuncle: *this shall be* the first row.

Ex 39:10 — And they set in it four rows of stones: *the first* row *was* a sardius, a topaz, and a carbuncle: this *was* the first row.

- **In the garden of Eden.**

Eze 28:13 — Thou hast been in Eden the garden of God; every precious stone *was* thy covering, the sardius, topaz, and the diamond, the beryl, the onyx, and the jasper, the sapphire, the emerald, and the carbuncle, and gold: the workmanship of thy tabrets and of thy pipes was prepared in thee in the day that thou wast created.

- **Seen in John's apocalyptic vision of the foundation of the New Jerusalem.**

Rev 21:20 — The fifth, sardonyx; the sixth, sardius; the seventh, chrysolite; the eighth, beryl; the ninth, a topaz; the tenth, a chrysoprasus; the eleventh, a jacinth; the twelfth, an amethyst.

- **Figurative.**

Rev 4:3 — And he that sat was to look upon like a jasper and a sardine stone: and *there was* a rainbow round about the throne, in sight like unto an emerald.

SARDONYX

- **A precious stone.**
- **Figurative.**
  - **In the foundation of the heavenly city.**

    Rev 21:20 — The fifth, sardonyx; the sixth, sardius; the seventh, chrysolite; the eighth, beryl; the ninth, a topaz; the tenth, a chrysoprasus; the eleventh, a jacinth; the twelfth, an amethyst.

SAREPTA See: Zarephath

SARGON • A king of Assyria.

Isa 20:1 — In the year that Tartan came unto Ashdod, (when Sargon the king of Assyria sent him,) and fought against Ashdod, and took it;

SARID • A city on the boundary of the tribe of Zebulun.

Jos 19:10 — And the third lot came up for the children of Zebulun according to their families: and the border of their inheritance was unto Sarid:

Jos 19:12 — And turned from Sarid eastward toward the sunrising unto the border of Chisloth-tabor, and then goeth out to Daberath, and goeth up to Japhia,

SARON ⇜See: Sharon

SARSECHIM

- **A prince of Babylon.**
- **Present at the taking of Jerusalem.**

Jer 39:3 — And all the princes of the king of Babylon came in, and sat in the middle gate, *even* Nergal-sharezer, Samgar-nebo, Sarsechim, Rab-saris, Nergal-sharezer, Rabmag, with all the residue of the princes of the king of Babylon.

SARUCH ⇜See: Serug

SATAN

- **Called Abaddon.**

Rev 9:11 — And they had a king over them, *which is* the angel of the bottomless pit, whose name in the Hebrew tongue *is* Abaddon, but in the Greek tongue hath *his* name Apollyon.

- **Called accuser of our brethren.**

Rev 12:10 — And I heard a loud voice saying in heaven, Now is come salvation, and strength, and the kingdom of our God, and the power of his Christ: for the accuser of our brethren is cast down, which accused them before our God day and night.

- **Called adversary.**

1Pe 5:8 — Be sober, be vigilant; because your adversary the devil, as a roaring lion, walketh about, seeking whom he may devour:

- **Called angel of the bottomless pit.**

Rev 9:11 — And they had a king over them, *which is* the angel of the bottomless pit, whose name in the Hebrew tongue *is* Abaddon, but in the Greek tongue hath *his* name Apollyon.

- **Called Apollyon.**

Rev 9:11 — And they had a king over them, *which is* the angel of the bottomless pit, whose name in the Hebrew tongue *is* Abaddon, but in the Greek tongue hath *his* name Apollyon.

- **Called Beelzebub.**

Mt 12:24 — But when the Pharisees heard *it,* they said, This *fellow* doth not cast out devils, but by Beelzebub the prince of the devils.

Mk 3:22 — And the scribes which came down from Jerusalem said, He hath Beelzebub, and by the prince of the devils casteth he out devils.

Lk 11:15 — But some of them said, He casteth out devils through Beelzebub the chief of the devils.

- **Called Belial.**

2Co 6:15 — And what concord hath Christ with Belial? or what part hath he that believeth with an infidel?

- **Called the devil.**

Mt 4:1 — Then was Jesus led up of the Spirit into the wilderness to be tempted of the devil.

Lk 4:2 — Being forty days tempted of the devil. And in those days he did eat nothing: and when they were ended, he afterward hungered.

Lk 4:6 — And the devil said unto him, All this power will I give thee, and the glory of them: for that is delivered unto me; and to whomsoever I will I give it.

Rev 20:2 — And he laid hold on the dragon, that old serpent, which is the Devil, and Satan, and bound him a thousand years,

- **Called enemy.**

Mt 13:39 — The enemy that sowed them is the devil; the harvest is the end of the world; and the reapers are the angels.

- **Called evil spirit.**

1Sa 16:14 — But the Spirit of the LORD departed from Saul, and an evil spirit from the LORD troubled him.

- **Called father of lies.**

Jn 8:44 — Ye are of your father the devil, and the lusts of *your* father ye will do. He was a murderer from the beginning, and abode not in the truth, because there is no truth in him. When he speaketh a lie, he speaketh of his own: for he is a liar, and the father of it.

- **Called gates of hell.**

Mt 16:18 — And I say also unto thee, That thou art Peter, and upon this rock I will build my church; and the gates of hell shall not prevail against it.

- **Called great red dragon.**

Rev 12:3 — And there appeared another wonder in heaven; and behold a great red dragon, having seven heads and ten horns, and seven crowns upon his heads.

- **Called liar.**

Jn 8:44 — Ye are of your father the devil, and the lusts of *your* father ye will do. He was a murderer from the beginning, and abode not in the truth, because there is no truth in him. When he speaketh a lie, he speaketh of his own: for he is a liar, and the father of it.

- **Called lying spirit.**

1Ki 22:22 — And the LORD said unto him, Wherewith? And he said, I will go forth, and I will be a lying spirit in the mouth of all his prophets. And he said, Thou shalt persuade *him,* and prevail also: go forth, and do so.

- **Called murderer.**

Jn 8:44 — Ye are of your father the devil, and the lusts of *your* father ye will do. He was a murderer from the beginning, and abode not in the truth, because there is no truth in him. When he speaketh a lie, he speaketh of his own: for he is a liar, and the father of it.

- **Called old serpent.**

Rev 12:9 — And the great dragon was cast out, that old serpent, called the Devil, and Satan, which deceiveth the whole world: he was cast out into the earth, and his angels were cast out with him.

Rev 20:2 — And he laid hold on the dragon, that old serpent, which is the Devil, and Satan, and bound him a thousand years,

- **Called power of darkness.**

Col 1:13 — Who hath delivered us from the power of darkness, and hath translated *us* into the kingdom of his dear Son:

• Called prince of this world.

Jn 12:31 — Now is the judgment of this world: now shall the prince of this world be cast out.

Jn 14:30 — Hereafter I will not talk much with you: for the prince of this world cometh, and hath nothing in me.

Jn 16:11 — Of judgment, because the prince of this world is judged.

• Called of devils.

Mt 12:24 — But when the Pharisees heard *it,* they said, This *fellow* doth not cast out devils, but by Beelzebub the prince of the devils.

• Called of the power of the air.

Eph 2:2 — Wherein in time past ye walked according to the course of this world, according to the prince of the power of the air, the spirit that now worketh in the children of disobedience:

• Called ruler of the darkness of this world.

Eph 6:12 — For we wrestle not against flesh and blood, but against principalities, against powers, against the rulers of the darkness of this world, against spiritual wickedness in high *places.*

• Called Satan.

1Ch 21:1 — And Satan stood up against Israel, and provoked David to number Israel.

Job 1:6 — Now there was a day when the sons of God came to present themselves before the LORD, and Satan came also among them.

Jn 13:27 — And after the sop Satan entered into him. Then said Jesus unto him, That thou doest, do quickly.

Ac 5:3 — But Peter said, Ananias, why hath Satan filled thine heart to lie to the Holy Ghost, and to keep back *part* of the price of the land?

Ac 26:18 — To open their eyes, *and* to turn *them* from darkness to light, and *from* the power of Satan unto God, that they may receive forgiveness of sins, and inheritance among them which are sanctified by faith that is in me.

Ro 16:20 — And the God of peace shall bruise Satan under your feet shortly. The grace of our Lord Jesus Christ *be* with you. Amen.

• Called serpent.

Ge 3:4 — And the serpent said unto the woman, Ye shall not surely die:

Ge 3:14 — And the LORD God said unto the serpent, Because thou hast done this, thou *art* cursed above all cattle, and above every beast of the field; upon thy belly shalt thou go, and dust shalt thou eat all the days of thy life:

2Co 11:3 — But I fear, lest by any means, as the serpent beguiled Eve through his subtilty, so your minds should be corrupted from the simplicity that is in Christ.

• Called spirit that worketh in the children of disobedience.

Eph 2:2 — Wherein in time past ye walked according to the course of this world, according to the prince of the power of the air, the spirit that now worketh in the children of disobedience:

• Called tempter.

Mt 4:3 — And when the tempter came to him, he said, If thou be the Son of God, command that these stones be made bread.

1Th 3:5 — For this cause, when I could no longer forbear, I sent to know your faith, lest by some means the tempter have tempted you, and our labour be in vain.

• Called the god of this world.

2Co 4:4 — In whom the god of this world hath blinded the minds of them which believe not, lest the light of the glorious gospel of Christ, who is the image of God, should shine unto them.

• Called unclean spirit.

Mt 12:43 — When the unclean spirit is gone out of a man, he walketh through dry places, seeking rest, and findeth none.

• Called wicked one.

Mt 13:19 — When any one heareth the word of the kingdom, and understandeth *it* not, then cometh the wicked *one,* and catcheth away that which was sown in his heart. This is he which received seed by the way side.

Mt 13:38 — The field is the world; the good seed are the children of the kingdom; but the tares are the children of the wicked *one;*

• Kingdom of, to be destroyed.

2Sa 23:6–7; Lk 11:21–22

Mt 12:29 — Or else how can one enter into a strong man's house, and spoil his goods, except he first bind the strong man? and then he will spoil his house.

Mt 13:30 — Let both grow together until the harvest: and in the time of harvest I will say to the reapers, Gather ye together first the tares, and bind them in bundles to burn them: but gather the wheat into my barn.

1Jn 3:8 — He that committeth sin is of the devil; for the devil sinneth from the beginning. For this purpose the Son of God was manifested, that he might destroy the works of the devil.

• Synagogue of.

Rev 2:9 — I know thy works, and tribulation, and poverty, (but thou art rich) and *I know* the blasphemy of them which say they are Jews, and are not, but *are* the synagogue of Satan.

Rev 3:9 — Behold, I will make them of the synagogue of Satan, which say they are Jews, and are not, but do lie; behold, I will make them to come and worship before thy feet, and to know that I have loved thee.

• Unclassified scripture relating to.

Ge 3:4–5, 14–15; Job 1:6–7, 9–12; 2:3–7; Zec 3:1–2; Mt 4:1–11; 13:38–39; Mk 3:22–26; Lk 4:1–13; 2Co 11:14–15; Eph 6:11–16; 1Ti 3:6–7; 1Pe 5:8–9; Rev 2:9–10; 12:9–12; 20:1–3, 7–8

Ge 3:1 — Now the serpent was more subtil than any beast of the field which the LORD God had made. And he said unto the woman, Yea, hath God said, Ye shall not eat of every tree of the garden?

1Ch 21:1 — And Satan stood up against Israel, and provoked David to number Israel.

Job 9:24 — The earth is given into the hand of the wicked: he covereth the faces of the judges thereof; if not, where, *and* who *is* he?

Ps 109:6 — Set thou a wicked man over him: and let Satan stand at his right hand.

Mt 9:34 — But the Pharisees said, He casteth out devils through the prince of the devils.

Mt 13:19 — When any one heareth the word of the kingdom, and understandeth *it* not, then cometh the wicked *one*, and catcheth away that which was sown in his heart. This is he which received seed by the way side.

Mt 25:41 — Then shall he say also unto them on the left hand, Depart from me, ye cursed, into everlasting fire, prepared for the devil and his angels:

Mk 1:13 — And he was there in the wilderness forty days, tempted of Satan; and was with the wild beasts; and the angels ministered unto him.

Mk 4:15 — And these are they by the way side, where the word is sown; but when they have heard, Satan cometh immediately, and taketh away the word that was sown in their hearts.

Lk 8:12 — Those by the way side are they that hear; then cometh the devil, and taketh away the word out of their hearts, lest they should believe and be saved.

Lk 10:18 — And he said unto them, I beheld Satan as lightning fall from heaven.

Lk 11:15 — But some of them said, He casteth out devils through Beelzebub the chief of the devils.

Lk 11:18 — If Satan also be divided against himself, how shall his kingdom stand? because ye say that I cast out devils through Beelzebub.

Lk 13:16 — And ought not this woman, being a daughter of Abraham, whom Satan hath bound, lo, these eighteen years, be loosed from this bond on the sabbath day?

Lk 22:31 — And the Lord said, Simon, Simon, behold, Satan hath desired *to have* you, that he may sift *you* as wheat:

Lk 22:53 — When I was daily with you in the temple, ye stretched forth no hands against me: but this is your hour, and the power of darkness.

Jn 8:38 — I speak that which I have seen with my Father: and ye do that which ye have seen with your father.

Jn 8:41 — Ye do the deeds of your father. Then said they to him, We be not born of fornication; we have one Father, *even* God.

Jn 8:44 — Ye are of your father the devil, and the lusts of *your* father ye will do. He was a murderer from the beginning, and abode not in the truth, because there is no truth in him. When he speaketh a lie, he speaketh of his own: for he is a liar, and the father of it.

Jn 12:31 — Now is the judgment of this world: now shall the prince of this world be cast out.

Jn 13:2 — And supper being ended, the devil having now put into the heart of Judas Iscariot, Simon's *son*, to betray him;

Jn 13:27 — And after the sop Satan entered into him. Then said Jesus unto him, That thou doest, do quickly.

Jn 14:30 — Hereafter I will not talk much with you: for the prince of this world cometh, and hath nothing in me.

Jn 16:11 — Of judgment, because the prince of this world is judged.

Ac 5:3 — But Peter said, Ananias, why hath Satan filled thine heart to lie to the Holy Ghost, and to keep back *part* of the price of the land?

Ac 13:10 — And said, O full of all subtilty and all mischief, *thou* child of the devil, *thou* enemy of all righteousness, wilt thou not cease to pervert the right ways of the Lord?

Ac 26:18 — To open their eyes, *and* to turn *them* from darkness to light, and *from* the power of Satan unto God, that they may receive forgiveness of sins, and inheritance among them which are sanctified by faith that is in me.

Ro 16:20 — And the God of peace shall bruise Satan under your feet shortly. The grace of our Lord Jesus Christ *be* with you. Amen.

1Co 7:5 — Defraud ye not one the other, except *it be* with consent for a time, that ye may give yourselves to fasting and prayer; and come together again, that Satan tempt you not for your incontinency.

2Co 2:11 — Lest Satan should get an advantage of us: for we are not ignorant of his devices.

2Co 4:4 — In whom the god of this world hath blinded the minds of them which believe not, lest the light of the glorious gospel of Christ, who is the image of God, should shine unto them.

2Co 11:3 — But I fear, lest by any means, as the serpent beguiled Eve through his subtilty, so your minds should be corrupted from the simplicity that is in Christ.

2Co 12:7 — And lest I should be exalted above measure through the abundance of the revelations, there was given to me a thorn in the flesh, the messenger of Satan to buffet me, lest I should be exalted above measure.

Eph 2:2 — Wherein in time past ye walked according to the course of this world, according to the prince of the power of the air, the spirit that now worketh in the children of disobedience:

Eph 4:27 — Neither give place to the devil.

Col 1:13 — Who hath delivered us from the power of darkness, and hath translated *us* into the kingdom of his dear Son:

Col 2:15 — *And* having spoiled principalities and powers, he made a shew of them openly, triumphing over them in it.

1Th 2:18 — Wherefore we would have come unto you, even I Paul, once and again; but Satan hindered us.

1Th 3:5 — For this cause, when I could no longer forbear, I sent to know your faith, lest by some means the tempter have tempted you, and our labour be in vain.

2Th 2:9 — *Even him*, whose coming is after the working of Satan with all power and signs and lying wonders,

1Ti 1:20 — Of whom is Hymenaeus and Alexander; whom I have delivered unto Satan, that they may learn not to blaspheme.

1Ti 5:15 — For some are already turned aside after Satan.

2Ti 2:26 — And *that* they may recover themselves out of the snare of the devil, who are taken captive by him at his will.

Heb 2:14 — Forasmuch then as the children are partakers of flesh and blood, he also himself likewise took part of the same; that through death he might destroy him that had the power of death, that is, the devil;

Jas 4:7 — Submit yourselves therefore to God. Resist the devil, and he will flee from you.

2Pe 2:4 — For if God spared not the angels that sinned, but cast *them* down to hell, and delivered *them* into chains of darkness, to be reserved unto judgment;

1Jn 2:13 — I write unto you, fathers, because ye have known him *that is* from the beginning. I write unto you, young men, because ye have overcome the wicked one. I write unto you, little children, because ye have known the Father.

1Jn 3:8 — He that committeth sin is of the devil; for the devil sinneth from the beginning. For this purpose the Son of God was manifested, that he might destroy the works of the devil.

1Jn 3:10 — In this the children of God are manifest, and the children of the devil: whosoever doeth not righteousness is not of God, neither he that loveth not his brother.

1Jn 3:12 — Not as Cain, *who* was of that wicked one, and slew his brother. And wherefore slew he him? Because his own works were evil, and his brother's righteous.

1Jn 5:18 — We know that whosoever is born of God sinneth not; but he that is begotten of God keepeth himself, and that wicked one toucheth him not.

Jude 1:6 — And the angels which kept not their first estate, but left their own habitation, he hath reserved in everlasting chains under darkness unto the judgment of the great day.

Jude 1:9 — Yet Michael the archangel, when contending with the devil he disputed about the body of Moses, durst not bring against him a railing accusation, but said, The Lord rebuke thee.

Rev 2:13 — I know thy works, and where thou dwellest, *even* where Satan's seat *is:* and thou holdest fast my name, and hast not denied my faith, even in those days wherein Antipas *was* my faithful martyr, who was slain among you, where Satan dwelleth.

Rev 2:24 — But unto you I say, and unto the rest in Thyatira, as many as have not this doctrine, and which have not known the depths of Satan, as they speak; I will put upon you none other burden.

Rev 3:9 — Behold, I will make them of the synagogue of Satan, which say they are Jews, and are not, but do lie; behold, I will make them to come and worship before thy feet, and to know that I have loved thee.

Rev 9:11 — And they had a king over them, *which is* the angel of the bottomless pit, whose name in the Hebrew tongue *is* Abaddon, but in the Greek tongue hath *his* name Apollyon.

Rev 20:10 — And the devil that deceived them was cast into the lake of fire and brimstone, where the beast and the false prophet *are,* and shall be tormented day and night for ever and ever.

See: Demons

SATIRE

• Hannah's song of exultation over Peninnah.

1Sa 1:5–10; 2:1–10

• Of Jesus against hypocrites.

Mt 23:2–33; Mk 12:13–40; Lk 11:39–54

See: Irony

See: Sarcasm

SATYR

• A mythological creature.

• Represented as half man and half goat.

Le 17:7 — And they shall no more offer their sacrifices unto devils, after whom they have gone a whoring. This shall be a statute for ever unto them throughout their generations.

2Ch 11:15 — And he ordained him priests for the high places, and for the devils, and for the calves which he had made.

Isa 13:21 — But wild beasts of the desert shall lie there; and their houses shall be full of doleful creatures; and owls shall dwell there, and satyrs shall dance there.

Isa 34:14 — The wild beasts of the desert shall also meet with the wild beasts of the island, and the satyr shall cry to his fellow; the screech owl also shall rest there, and find for herself a place of rest.

SAUL

• King of Edom.

Ge 36:37–38

• Called also Shaul.

1Ch 1:48–49

• King of Israel.

• A Benjamite, son of Kish.

1Sa 9:1–2

• Sons of.

1Ch 8:33 — And Ner begat Kish, and Kish begat Saul, and Saul begat Jonathan, and Malchi-shua, and Abinadab, and Esh-baal.

• His personal appearance.

1Sa 9:2 — And he had a son, whose name *was* Saul, a choice young man, and a goodly: and *there was* not among the children of Israel a goodlier person than he: from his shoulders and upward *he was* higher than any of the people.

1Sa 10:23 — And they ran and fetched him thence: and when he stood among the people, he was higher than any of the people from his shoulders and upward.

• Made king of Israel.

1Sa 9:1–10:27; 11:12–15

Hos 13:11 — I gave thee a king in mine anger, and took *him* away in my wrath.

• Dwells at Gibeah of Saul.

1Sa 14:2 — And Saul tarried in the uttermost part of Gibeah under a pomegranate tree which is in Migron: and the people that *were* with him *were* about six hundred men;

1Sa 15:34 — Then Samuel went to Ramah; and Saul went up to his house to Gibeah of Saul.

Isa 10:29 — They are gone over the passage: they have taken up their lodging at Geba; Ramah is afraid; Gibeah of Saul is fled.

• Defeats the Philistines.

1Sa 13:1–23

1Sa 14:46 — Then Saul went up from following the Philistines: and the Philistines went to their own place.

1Sa 14:52 — And there was sore war against the Philistines all the days of Saul: and when Saul saw any strong man, or any valiant man, he took him unto him.

• Smites the Amalekites.

1Sa 15:1–35

• Is reproved by Samuel for usurping the priest functions.

1Sa 13:11–14

• Is reproved by Samuel for disobedience in not slaying the Amalekites, loss of kingdom foretold.

1Sa 15:1–35

• Dedicates the spoils of war.

1Sa 15:21–25

1Ch 26:28 — And all that Samuel the seer, and Saul the son of Kish, and Abner the son of Ner, and Joab the son of Zeruiah, had dedicated; *and* whosoever had dedicated *any thing, it was* under the hand of Shelomith, and of his brethren.

• Sends messengers to Jesse, asking that David be sent to him as musician and armor-bearer.

1Sa 16:17–23

• Defeats the Philistines after Goliath is slain by David.

1Sa 17:1–58

• His jealousy of David; gives his daughter, Michal, to David to be his wife; becomes David's enemy.

1Sa 18:1–30

• Tries to slay David; Jonathan intercedes and incurs his father's displeasure.

1Sa 19:1–24

• Hears Doeg's charge against Ahimelech, and slays the priest and his family.

1Sa 22:9–19

• Pursues David to the wilderness of Ziph; the Ziphites betray David to.

1Sa 23:1–29

• Pursues David to En-gedi.

1Sa 24:1–6

• His life saved by David.

1Sa 24:5–8

• Saul's contrition for his bad faith.

1Sa 24:16–22

• David is again betrayed, by the Ziphites; Saul pursues him to the hill of Hachilah.

1Sa 26:1–25

• Slays the Gibeonites; crime avenged by the death of seven of his sons.

2Sa 21:1–9

• His kingdom invaded by Philistines; seeks counsel of the witch of En-dor, who foretells his death.

1Sa 28:3–29:1

• Is defeated, and with his sons is slain.

1Sa 31:1–13

• Is defeated; rescued by the people of Jabesh and burned; bones of buried under a tree at Jabesh.

1Sa 31:1–2Sa 2:32; 1Ch 10:1–14

• His death a judgment on account of his sins.

1Ch 10:13 — So Saul died for his transgression which he committed against the LORD, *even* against the word of the LORD, which he kept not, and also for asking *counsel* of *one that had* a familiar spirit, to enquire *of it;*

• Of Tarsus.

✣See: Paul, through Conversion

SAVIOUR ✣See: Jesus, Saviour

SAW

• Used as an instrument of torture.

2Sa 12:31 — And he brought forth the people that *were* therein, and put *them* under saws, and under harrows of iron, and under axes of iron, and made them pass through the brickkiln: and thus did he unto all the cities of the children of Ammon. So David and all the people returned unto Jerusalem.

Heb 11:37 — They were stoned, they were sawn asunder, were tempted, were slain with the sword: they wandered about in sheepskins and goatskins; being destitute, afflicted, tormented;

• Used for cutting stone.

1Ki 7:9 — All these *were of* costly stones, according to the measures of hewed stones, sawed with saws, within and without, even from the foundation unto the coping, and so on the outside toward the great court.

• Figurative.

Isa 10:15 — Shall the axe boast itself against him that heweth therewith? *or* shall the saw magnify itself against him that shaketh it? as if the rod should shake *itself* against them that lift it up, *or* as if the staff should lift up *itself, as if it were* no wood.

SCAB

• Disease of the skin.

Le 13:6–8

Le 13:2 — When a man shall have in the skin of his flesh a rising, a scab, or a bright spot, and it be in the skin of his flesh *like* the plague of leprosy; then he shall be brought unto Aaron the priest, or unto one of his sons the priests:

Le 14:56 — And for a rising, and for a scab, and for a bright spot:

Le 21:20 — Or crookbackt, or a dwarf, or that hath a blemish in his eye, or be scurvy, or scabbed, or hath his stones broken;

Le 22:22 — Blind, or broken, or maimed, or having a wen, or scurvy, or scabbed, ye shall not offer these unto the LORD, nor make an offering by fire of them upon the altar unto the LORD.

Dt 28:27 — The LORD will smite thee with the botch of Egypt, and with the emerods, and with the scab, and with the itch, whereof thou canst not be healed.

Isa 3:17 — Therefore the LORD will smite with a scab the crown of the head of the daughters of Zion, and the LORD will discover their secret parts.

➜See: Disease

➜See: Sanitation

➜See: Scurvy

SCALES

• Fell from Paul's eyes.

Ac 9:18 — And immediately there fell from his eyes as it had been scales: and he received sight forthwith, and arose, and was baptized.

• For measure.

➜See: Balances

SCALL

• A form of leprosy.

Le 13:30 — Then the priest shall see the plague: and, behold, if it *be* in sight deeper than the skin; *and there be* in it a yellow thin hair; then the priest shall pronounce him unclean: it *is* a dry scall, *even* a leprosy upon the head or beard.

➜See: Leprosy

SCAPEBIRD

Le 14:4–7

Le 14:53 — But he shall let go the living bird out of the city into the open fields, and make an atonement for the house: and it shall be clean.

SCAPEGOAT

Le 16:7–10, 20–34

SCARLET ➜See: Colors

SCEPTER

• A wand used by kings to signify favor or disfavor to those who desired audience.

Est 5:2 — And it was so, when the king saw Esther the queen standing in the court, *that* she obtained favour in his sight: and the king held out to Esther the golden sceptre that *was* in his hand. So Esther drew near, and touched the top of the sceptre.

Est 8:4 — Then the king held out the golden sceptre toward Esther. So Esther arose, and stood before the king,

• A symbol of authority.

Nu 24:17 — I shall see him, but not now: I shall behold him, but not nigh: there shall come a Star out of Jacob, and a Sceptre shall rise out of Israel, and shall smite the corners of Moab, and destroy all the children of Sheth.

Isa 14:5 — The LORD hath broken the staff of the wicked, *and* the sceptre of the rulers.

• Made of gold.

Est 4:11 — All the king's servants, and the people of the king's provinces, do know, that whosoever, whether man or woman, shall come unto the king into the inner court, who is not called, *there is* one law of his to put *him* to death, except such to whom the king shall hold out the golden sceptre, that he may live: but I have not been called to come in unto the king these thirty days.

• Made of iron.

Ps 2:9 — Thou shalt break them with a rod of iron; thou shalt dash them in pieces like a potter's vessel.

Rev 2:27 — And he shall rule them with a rod of iron; as the vessels of a potter shall they be broken to shivers: even as I received of my Father.

Rev 12:5 — And she brought forth a man child, who was to rule all nations with a rod of iron: and her child was caught up unto God, and *to* his throne.

• Figurative.

Ge 49:10 — The sceptre shall not depart from Judah, nor a lawgiver from between his feet, until Shiloh come; and unto him *shall* the gathering of the people *be.*

Nu 24:17 — I shall see him, but not now: I shall behold him, but not nigh: there shall come a Star out of Jacob, and a Sceptre shall rise out of Israel, and shall smite the corners of Moab, and destroy all the children of Sheth.

Isa 9:4 — For thou hast broken the yoke of his burden, and the staff of his shoulder, the rod of his oppressor, as in the day of Midian.

SCEVA • A Jew of Ephesus.

Ac 19:13–17

SCHOOL

• Of the prophets

• At Naioth.

1Sa 19:20 — And Saul sent messengers to take David: and when they saw the company of the prophets prophesying, and Samuel standing *as* appointed over them, the Spirit of God was upon the messengers of Saul, and they also prophesied.

• At Bethel.

2Ki 2:3 — And the sons of the prophets that *were* at Bethel came forth to Elisha, and said unto him, Knowest thou that the LORD will take away thy master from thy head to day? And he said, Yea, I know *it;* hold ye your peace.

- **At Jericho.**

2Ki 2:5 — And the sons of the prophets that *were* at Jericho came to Elisha, and said unto him, Knowest thou that the LORD will take away thy master from thy head to day? And he answered, Yea, I know *it;* hold ye your peace.

2Ki 2:15 — And when the sons of the prophets which *were* to view at Jericho saw him, they said, The spirit of Elijah doth rest on Elisha. And they came to meet him, and bowed themselves to the ground before him.

- **At Gilgal.**

2Ki 4:38 — And Elisha came again to Gilgal: and *there was* a dearth in the land; and the sons of the prophets *were* sitting before him: and he said unto his servant, Set on the great pot, and seethe pottage for the sons of the prophets.

- **At Jerusalem, probably.**

2Ki 22:14 — So Hilkiah the priest, and Ahikam, and Achbor, and Shaphan, and Asahiah, went unto Huldah the prophetess, the wife of Shallum the son of Tikvah, the son of Harhas, keeper of the wardrobe; (now she dwelt in Jerusalem in the college;) and they communed with her.

2Ch 34:22 — And Hilkiah, and *they* that the king *had appointed,* went to Huldah the prophetess, the wife of Shallum the son of Tikvath, the son of Hasrah, keeper of the wardrobe; (now she dwelt in Jerusalem in the college:) and they spake to her to that *effect.*

- **Crowded attendance at.**

2Ki 6:1 — And the sons of the prophets said unto Elisha, Behold now, the place where we dwell with thee is too strait for us.

- **In the home.**

Dt 4:9–10; 11:19–20; Ps 78:5–8

Dt 6:7 — And thou shalt teach them diligently unto thy children, and shalt talk of them when thou sittest in thine house, and when thou walkest by the way, and when thou liest down, and when thou risest up.

Dt 6:9 — And thou shalt write them upon the posts of thy house, and on thy gates.

- **Bible school.**

Dt 31:10–13

- **State.**

2Ch 17:7–9; Da 1:3–21

- **Of Gamaliel.**

Ac 5:34 — Then stood there up one in the council, a Pharisee, named Gamaliel, a doctor of the law, had in reputation among all the people, and commanded to put the apostles forth a little space;

Ac 22:3 — I am verily a man *which am* a Jew, born in Tarsus, a city in Cilicia, yet brought up in this city at the feet of Gamaliel, *and* taught according to the perfect manner of the law of the fathers, and was zealous toward God, as ye all are this day.

- **Of Tyrannus.**

Ac 19:9 — But when divers were hardened, and believed not, but spake evil of that way before the multitude, he departed from them, and separated the disciples, disputing daily in the school of one Tyrannus.

- **Schoolmaster.**

Gal 3:24–25

See: Instruction

See: Psalms; didactic

SCIENCE

- **Observations of, and deductions from, facts.**

Job 26:7–14; 28:1–28; Ecc 1:13–17

- **So-called, false.**

1Ti 6:20 — O Timothy, keep that which is committed to thy trust, avoiding profane *and* vain babblings, and oppositions of science falsely so called:

- **The key of knowledge.**

Lk 11:52 — Woe unto you, lawyers! for ye have taken away the key of knowledge: ye entered not in yourselves, and them that were entering in ye hindered.

Ro 2:20 — An instructor of the foolish, a teacher of babes, which hast the form of knowledge and of the truth in the law.

See: Astronomy

See: Geology

See: Philosophy

SCOFFING

2Ch 30:6–10; Job 21:14–15; Ps 78:19–20; 107:11–12; Isa 5:18–19, 24–25; Eze 11:2–3; 2Pe 3:3–4

2Ch 36:16 — But they mocked the messengers of God, and despised his words, and misused his prophets, until the wrath of the LORD arose against his people, till *there was* no remedy.

Job 34:7 — What man *is* like Job, *who* drinketh up scorning like water?

Ps 1:1 — Blessed *is* the man that walketh not in the counsel of the ungodly, nor standeth in the way of sinners, nor sitteth in the seat of the scornful.

Ps 42:3 — My tears have been my meat day and night, while they continually say unto me, Where *is* thy God?

Ps 42:10 — *As* with a sword in my bones, mine enemies reproach me; while they say daily unto me, Where *is* thy God?

Ps 73:11 — And they say, How doth God know? and is there knowledge in the most High?

Pr 1:22 — How long, ye simple ones, will ye love simplicity? and the scorners delight in their scorning, and fools hate knowledge?

Pr 1:25 — But ye have set at nought all my counsel, and would none of my reproof:

Pr 3:34 — Surely he scorneth the scorners: but he giveth grace unto the lowly.

Pr 9:12 — If thou be wise, thou shalt be wise for thyself: but *if* thou scornest, thou alone shalt bear *it.*

Pr 13:1 — A wise son *heareth* his father's instruction: but a scorner heareth not rebuke.

Pr 14:6 — A scorner seeketh wisdom, and *findeth it* not: but knowledge *is* easy unto him that understandeth.

Pr 14:9 — Fools make a mock at sin: but among the righteous *there is* favour.

Pr 19:29 — Judgments are prepared for scorners, and stripes for the back of fools.

Pr 21:11 — When the scorner is punished, the simple is made wise: and when the wise is instructed, he receiveth knowledge.

Pr 21:24 — Proud *and* haughty scorner *is* his name, who dealeth in proud wrath.

Pr 22:10 — Cast out the scorner, and contention shall go out; yea, strife and reproach shall cease.

Pr 24:9 — The thought of foolishness *is* sin: and the scorner *is* an abomination to men.

Isa 10:15 — Shall the axe boast itself against him that heweth therewith? *or* shall the saw magnify itself against him that shaketh it? as if the rod should shake *itself* against them that lift it up, *or* as if the staff should lift up *itself, as if it were* no wood.

Isa 29:20 — For the terrible one is brought to nought, and the scorner is consumed, and all that watch for iniquity are cut off:

Isa 57:4 — Against whom do ye sport yourselves? against whom make ye a wide mouth, *and* draw out the tongue? *are* ye not children of transgression, a seed of falsehood,

Jer 17:15 — Behold, they say unto me, Where *is* the word of the LORD? let it come now.

Jer 43:2 — Then spake Azariah the son of Hoshaiah, and Johanan the son of Kareah, and all the proud men, saying unto Jeremiah, Thou speakest falsely: the LORD our God hath not sent thee to say, Go not into Egypt to sojourn there:

La 1:7 — Jerusalem remembered in the days of her affliction and of her miseries all her pleasant things that she had in the days of old, when her people fell into the hand of the enemy, and none did help her: the adversaries saw her, *and* did mock at her sabbaths.

Eze 8:12 — Then said he unto me, Son of man, hast thou seen what the ancients of the house of Israel do in the dark, every man in the chambers of his imagery? for they say, The LORD seeth us not; the LORD hath forsaken the earth.

Eze 9:9 — Then said he unto me, The iniquity of the house of Israel and Judah *is* exceeding great, and the land is full of blood, and the city full of perverseness: for they say, The LORD hath forsaken the earth, and the LORD seeth not.

Eze 12:22 — Son of man, what *is* that proverb *that* ye have in the land of Israel, saying, The days are prolonged, and every vision faileth?

Eze 33:20 — Yet ye say, The way of the Lord is not equal. O ye house of Israel, I will judge you every one after his ways.

Hos 7:5 — In the day of our king the princes have made *him* sick with bottles of wine; he stretched out his hand with scorners.

Mt 12:24 — But when the Pharisees heard *it,* they said, This *fellow* doth not cast out devils, but by Beelzebub the prince of the devils.

Mk 3:22 — And the scribes which came down from Jerusalem said, He hath Beelzebub, and by the prince of the devils casteth he out devils.

Lk 4:23 — And he said unto them, Ye will surely say unto me this proverb, Physician, heal thyself: whatsoever we have heard done in Capernaum, do also here in thy country.

Lk 11:15 — But some of them said, He casteth out devils through Beelzebub the chief of the devils.

Lk 16:14 — And the Pharisees also, who were covetous, heard all these things: and they derided him.

Ac 2:13 — Others mocking said, These men are full of new wine.

Ac 13:45 — But when the Jews saw the multitudes, they were filled with envy, and spake against those things which were spoken by Paul, contradicting and blaspheming.

Ac 17:18 — Then certain philosophers of the Epicureans, and of the Stoicks, encountered him. And some said, What will this babbler say? other some, He seemeth to be a setter forth of strange gods: because he preached unto them Jesus, and the resurrection.

Ac 17:32 — And when they heard of the resurrection of the dead, some mocked: and others said, We will hear thee again of this *matter.*

Heb 10:29 — Of how much sorer punishment, suppose ye, shall he be thought worthy, who hath trodden under foot the Son of God, and hath counted the blood of the covenant, wherewith he was sanctified, an unholy thing, and hath done despite unto the Spirit of grace?

See: Hatred

See: Malice

See: Unbelief

- **Instances of.**
  - **Ishmael.**
    Ge 21:9
  - **Children at Bethel.**
    2Ki 2:23
  - **Ephraim and Manasseh.**
    2Ch 30:10
  - **Chiefs of Judah.**
    2Ch 36:16
  - **Sanballat.**
    Ne 4:1
  - **Enemies of Job.**
    Job 30:1, 9
  - **Enemies of David.**
    Ps 35:15–16
  - **Rulers of Israel.**
    Isa 28:14
  - **Ammonites.**
    Eze 25:3
  - **Tyrians.**
    Eze 26:2
  - **Heathen.**
    Eze 36:2–3
  - **Soldiers.**
    Mt 27:28–30; Lk 23:36

- **Chief priests.**
  Mt 27:41
- **Pharisees.**
  Lk 16:14
- **The men who held Jesus.**
  Lk 22:63–64
- **Herod.**
  Lk 23:11
- **People and rulers.**
  Lk 23:35
- **Some of the multitude.**
  Ac 2:13
- **Athenians.**
  Ac 17:32

SCORPION

- **A venomous insect common in the wilderness through which the children of Israel journeyed.**
  Dt 8:15 — Who led thee through that great and terrible wilderness, *wherein were* fiery serpents, and scorpions, and drought, where *there was* no water; who brought thee forth water out of the rock of flint;
- **Power over, given to the seventy.**
  Lk 10:19 — Behold, I give unto you power to tread on serpents and scorpions, and over all the power of the enemy: and nothing shall by any means hurt you.
- **Unfit for food.**
  Lk 11:12 — Or if he shall ask an egg, will he offer him a scorpion?
- **Sting of, in the tail.**
  Rev 9:10 — And they had tails like unto scorpions, and there were stings in their tails: and their power *was* to hurt men five months.
- **Figurative.**
  - **Of enemies.**
    Eze 2:6 — And thou, son of man, be not afraid of them, neither be afraid of their words, though briers and thorns *be* with thee, and thou dost dwell among scorpions: be not afraid of their words, nor be dismayed at their looks, though they *be* a rebellious house.
  - **Of cruelty.**
    1Ki 12:11 — And now whereas my father did lade you with a heavy yoke, I will add to your yoke: my father hath chastised you with whips, but I will chastise you with scorpions.
    1Ki 12:14 — And spake to them after the counsel of the young men, saying, My father made your yoke heavy, and I will add to your yoke: my father *also* chastised you with whips, but I will chastise you with scorpions.
- **Symbolic.**
  Rev 9:3 — And there came out of the smoke locusts upon the earth: and unto them was given power, as the scorpions of the earth have power.
  Rev 9:5 — And to them it was given that they should not kill them, but that they should be tormented five months: and their torment *was* as the torment of a scorpion, when he striketh a man.
  Rev 9:10 — And they had tails like unto scorpions, and there were stings in their tails: and their power *was* to hurt men five months.

SCOURGING

- **Corporal punishment by stripes.**
- **Prescribed in the Mosaic law for fornication.**
  Le 19:20 — And whosoever lieth carnally with a woman, that *is* a bondmaid, betrothed to an husband, and not at all redeemed, nor freedom given her; she shall be scourged; they shall not be put to death, because she was not free.
  Dt 22:18 — And the elders of that city shall take that man and chastise him;
- **Prescribed in the Mosaic law for other offenses.**
  Dt 25:2 — And it shall be, if the wicked man *be* worthy to be beaten, that the judge shall cause him to lie down, and to be beaten before his face, according to his fault, by a certain number.
- **Forty stripes the maximum limit.**
  Dt 25:3 — Forty stripes he may give him, *and* not exceed: lest, *if* he should exceed, and beat him above these with many stripes, then thy brother should seem vile unto thee.
- **Fatal.**
  Job 9:23 — If the scourge slay suddenly, he will laugh at the trial of the innocent.
- **Fatal, of servants avenged.**
  Ex 21:20 — And if a man smite his servant, or his maid, with a rod, and he die under his hand; he shall be surely punished.
- **Foretold by Jesus as a persecution of the Christians.**
  Mt 10:17 — But beware of men: for they will deliver you up to the councils, and they will scourge you in their synagogues;
- **Of children.**
  See: Children, Commandments to; correction of
  See: Punishment
- **Instances of.**
  - **Jesus.**
    Mt 20:19; 27:26; Mk 15:15; Jn 19:1
  - **Paul and Silas.**
    Ac 16:23 — And when they had laid many stripes upon them, they cast *them* into prison, charging the jailer to keep them safely:
  - **Paul.**
    2Co 11:24–25
    Ac 21:32 — Who immediately took soldiers and centurions, and ran down unto them: and when they saw the chief captain and the soldiers, they left beating of Paul.

Ac 22:24 — The chief captain commanded him to be brought into the castle, and bade that he should be examined by scourging; that he might know wherefore they cried so against him.

• Sosthenes.

Ac 18:17 — Then all the Greeks took Sosthenes, the chief ruler of the synagogue, and beat *him* before the judgment seat. And Gallio cared for none of those things.

• Figurative.

• Of the oppressions of rulers.

1Ki 12:11 — And now whereas my father did lade you with a heavy yoke, I will add to your yoke: my father hath chastised you with whips, but I will chastise you with scorpions.

• Of the evil tongue.

Job 5:21 — Thou shalt be hid from the scourge of the tongue: neither shalt thou be afraid of destruction when it cometh.

See: Assault and Battery

SCRIBE

• A writer and transcriber of the law.

2Sa 8:17 — And Zadok the son of Ahitub, and Ahimelech the son of Abiathar, *were* the priests; and Seraiah *was* the scribe;

2Sa 20:25 — And Sheva *was* scribe: and Zadok and Abiathar *were* the priests:

1Ki 4:3 — Elihoreph and Ahiah, the sons of Shisha, scribes; Jehoshaphat the son of Ahilud, the recorder.

2Ki 12:10 — And it was *so,* when they saw that *there was* much money in the chest, that the king's scribe and the high priest came up, and they put up in bags, and told the money that was found in the house of the LORD.

2Ki 18:37 — Then came Eliakim the son of Hilkiah, which *was* over the household, and Shebna the scribe, and Joah the son of Asaph the recorder, to Hezekiah with *their* clothes rent, and told him the words of Rab-shakeh.

2Ki 19:2 — And he sent Eliakim, which *was* over the household, and Shebna the scribe, and the elders of the priests, covered with sackcloth, to Isaiah the prophet the son of Amoz.

1Ch 24:6 — And Shemaiah the son of Nethaneel the scribe, *one* of the Levites, wrote them before the king, and the princes, and Zadok the priest, and Ahimelech the son of Abiathar, and *before* the chief of the fathers of the priests and Levites: one principal household being taken for Eleazar, and *one* taken for Ithamar.

1Ch 27:32 — Also Jonathan David's uncle was a counsellor, a wise man, and a scribe: and Jehiel the son of Hachmoni *was* with the king's sons:

Ne 13:13 — And I made treasurers over the treasuries, Shelemiah the priest, and Zadok the scribe, and of the Levites, Pedaiah: and next to them *was* Hanan the son of Zaccur, the son of Mattaniah: for they were counted faithful, and their office *was* to distribute unto their brethren.

Jer 36:12 — Then he went down into the king's house, into the scribe's chamber: and, lo, all the princes sat there, *even* Elishama the scribe, and Delaiah the son of Shemaiah, and Elnathan the son of Achbor, and Gemariah the son of Shaphan, and Zedekiah the son of Hananiah, and all the princes.

• King's secretary.

2Ki 12:10–12; 22:1–14

Est 3:12 — Then were the king's scribes called on the thirteenth day of the first month, and there was written according to all that Haman had commanded unto the king's lieutenants, and to the governors that *were* over every province, and to the rulers of every people of every province according to the writing thereof, and *to* every people after their language; in the name of king Ahasuerus was it written, and sealed with the king's ring.

Est 8:9 — Then were the king's scribes called at that time in the third month, that *is,* the month Sivan, on the three and twentieth *day* thereof; and it was written according to all that Mordecai commanded unto the Jews, and to the lieutenants, and the deputies and rulers of the provinces which *are* from India unto Ethiopia, an hundred twenty and seven provinces, unto every province according to the writing thereof, and unto every people after their language, and to the Jews according to their writing, and according to their language.

• Mustering officer of the army.

2Ki 25:19 — And out of the city he took an officer that was set over the men of war, and five men of them that were in the king's presence, which were found in the city, and the principal scribe of the host, which mustered the people of the land, and threescore men of the people of the land *that were* found in the city:

2Ch 26:11 — Moreover Uzziah had an host of fighting men, that went out to war by bands, according to the number of their account by the hand of Jeiel the scribe and Maaseiah the ruler, under the hand of Hananiah, *one* of the king's captains.

• Instructors in the law.

Mt 23:2–3

Mt 7:29 — For he taught them as *one* having authority, and not as the scribes.

Mt 13:52 — Then said he unto them, Therefore every scribe *which is* instructed unto the kingdom of heaven is like unto a man *that is* an householder, which bringeth forth out of his treasure *things* new and old.

Mt 17:10 — And his disciples asked him, saying, Why then say the scribes that Elias must first come?

See: Levites

• Test Jesus with questions, bringing to Jesus a woman taken in adultery.

Jn 8:3 — And the scribes and Pharisees brought unto him a woman taken in adultery; and when they had set her in the midst,

• Members of the council.

Mt 2:4 — And when he had gathered all the chief priests and scribes of the people together, he demanded of them where Christ should be born.

• **Conspire against Jesus.**

Mt 26:3 — Then assembled together the chief priests, and the scribes, and the elders of the people, unto the palace of the high priest, who was called Caiaphas,

Mt 26:57 — And they that had laid hold on Jesus led *him* away to Caiaphas the high priest, where the scribes and the elders were assembled.

Mt 27:41 — Likewise also the chief priests mocking *him,* with the scribes and elders, said,

Mk 14:1 — After two days was *the feast of* the passover, and of unleavened bread: and the chief priests and the scribes sought how they might take him by craft, and put *him* to death.

Lk 22:66 — And as soon as it was day, the elders of the people and the chief priests and the scribes came together, and led him into their council, saying,

• **Hypocrisy of, reproved by Jesus.**

Mt 5:20 — For I say unto you, That except your righteousness shall exceed *the righteousness* of the scribes and Pharisees, ye shall in no case enter into the kingdom of heaven.

Mt 9:3 — And, behold, certain of the scribes said within themselves, This *man* blasphemeth.

Mt 12:38 — Then certain of the scribes and of the Pharisees answered, saying, Master, we would see a sign from thee.

Mt 15:1 — Then came to Jesus scribes and Pharisees, which were of Jerusalem, saying,

Mt 16:21 — From that time forth began Jesus to shew unto his disciples, how that he must go unto Jerusalem, and suffer many things of the elders and chief priests and scribes, and be killed, and be raised again the third day.

Mt 20:18 — Behold, we go up to Jerusalem; and the Son of man shall be betrayed unto the chief priests and unto the scribes, and they shall condemn him to death,

Mt 21:15 — And when the chief priests and scribes saw the wonderful things that he did, and the children crying in the temple, and saying, Hosanna to the Son of David; they were sore displeased,

SCRIPTURES

• **The word of God.**

Jer 30:2 — Thus speaketh the LORD God of Israel, saying, Write thee all the words that I have spoken unto thee in a book.

• **Interpreted by doctors.**

Jn 3:10 — Jesus answered and said unto him, Art thou a master of Israel, and knowest not these things?

Jn 7:52 — They answered and said unto him, Art thou also of Galilee? Search, and look: for out of Galilee ariseth no prophet.

• **Inspired.**

2Ti 3:16 — All scripture *is* given by inspiration of God, and *is* profitable for doctrine, for reproof, for correction, for instruction in righteousness:

See: Word of God

SCURVY

Le 22:22 — Blind, or broken, or maimed, or having a wen, or scurvy, or scabbed, ye shall not offer these unto the LORD, nor make an offering by fire of them upon the altar unto the LORD.

See: Scab

SCYTHIANS

Col 3:11 — Where there is neither Greek nor Jew, circumcision nor uncircumcision, Barbarian, Scythian, bond *nor* free: but Christ *is* all, and in all.

SEA

• **Creation of.**

Ge 1:9–10; Ps 148:4–5

Ps 95:5 — The sea *is* his, and he made it: and his hands formed the dry *land.*

• **Limits of, established by God.**

Job 26:10 — He hath compassed the waters with bounds, until the day and night come to an end.

Job 38:8 — Or *who* shut up the sea with doors, when it brake forth, *as if* it had issued out of the womb?

Ps 33:7 — He gathereth the waters of the sea together as an heap: he layeth up the depth in storehouses.

Jer 5:22 — Fear ye not me? saith the LORD: will ye not tremble at my presence, which have placed the sand *for* the bound of the sea by a perpetual decree, that it cannot pass it: and though the waves thereof toss themselves, yet can they not prevail; though they roar, yet can they not pass over it?

• **Calmed by Jesus.**

Mt 8:24–26; Mk 4:37–39

• **Jesus walked on.**

Mt 14:25–31

• **Dead, to be given up by, at the resurrection.**

Rev 20:13 — And the sea gave up the dead which were in it; and death and hell delivered up the dead which were in them: and they were judged every man according to their works.

• **Symbolic.**

• **In Daniel's vision.**

Da 7:2–3

• **In John's apocalyptic vision.**

Rev 8:8–9; 10:5–6

Rev 4:6 — And before the throne *there was* a sea of glass like unto crystal: and in the midst of the throne, and round about the throne, *were* four beasts full of eyes before and behind.

Rev 10:2 — And he had in his hand a little book open: and he set his right foot upon the sea, and *his* left *foot* on the earth,

Rev 10:8 — And the voice which I heard from heaven spake unto me again, and said, Go *and* take the little book which is open in the hand of the angel which standeth upon the sea and upon the earth.

Rev 13:1 — And I stood upon the sand of the sea, and saw a beast rise up out of the sea, having seven heads and ten horns, and upon his horns ten crowns, and upon his heads the name of blasphemy.

Rev 15:2 — And I saw as it were a sea of glass mingled with fire: and them that had gotten the victory over the beast, and over his image, and over his mark, *and* over the number of his name, stand on the sea of glass, having the harps of God.

Rev 16:3 — And the second angel poured out his vial upon the sea; and it became as the blood of a dead *man:* and every living soul died in the sea.

Rev 21:1 — And I saw a new heaven and a new earth: for the first heaven and the first earth were passed away; and there was no more sea.

SEAL

• A stamp used for signifying documents.

• Given as a pledge.

Ge 38:18 — And he said, What pledge shall I give thee? And she said, Thy signet, and thy bracelets, and thy staff that *is* in thine hand. And he gave *it* her, and came in unto her, and she conceived by him.

• Engraved.

Ex 28:11 — With the work of an engraver in stone, *like* the engravings of a signet, shalt thou engrave the two stones with the names of the children of Israel: thou shalt make them to be set in ouches of gold.

Ex 28:21 — And the stones shall be with the names of the children of Israel, twelve, according to their names, *like* the engravings of a signet; every one with his name shall they be according to the twelve tribes.

Ex 28:36 — And thou shalt make a plate *of* pure gold, and grave upon it, *like* the engravings of a signet, HOLINESS TO THE LORD.

Ex 39:6 — And they wrought onyx stones inclosed in ouches of gold, graven, as signets are graven, with the names of the children of Israel.

Ex 39:14 — And the stones *were* according to the names of the children of Israel, twelve, according to their names, *like* the engravings of a signet, every one with his name, according to the twelve tribes.

Ex 39:30 — And they made the plate of the holy crown *of* pure gold, and wrote upon it a writing, *like to* the engravings of a signet, HOLINESS TO THE LORD.

2Ti 2:19 — Nevertheless the foundation of God standeth sure, having this seal, The Lord knoweth them that are his. And, Let every one that nameth the name of Christ depart from iniquity.

• Decrees signified by.

1Ki 21:8 — So she wrote letters in Ahab's name, and sealed *them* with his seal, and sent the letters unto the elders and to the nobles that *were* in his city, dwelling with Naboth.

Est 8:8 — Write ye also for the Jews, as it liketh you, in the king's name, and seal *it* with the king's ring: for the writing which is written in the king's name, and sealed with the king's ring, may no man reverse.

• Documents sealed with Ahab's letter.

1Ki 21:8 — So she wrote letters in Ahab's name, and sealed *them* with his seal, and sent the letters unto the elders and to the nobles that *were* in his city, dwelling with Naboth.

• Documents sealed with covenants.

Ne 9:38–10:1

Isa 8:16 — Bind up the testimony, seal the law among my disciples.

• Documents sealed with decrees.

Est 8:8 — Write ye also for the Jews, as it liketh you, in the king's name, and seal *it* with the king's ring: for the writing which is written in the king's name, and sealed with the king's ring, may no man reverse.

Da 6:9 — Wherefore king Darius signed the writing and the decree.

• Documents sealed with deeds.

Jer 32:10 — And I subscribed the evidence, and sealed *it,* and took witnesses, and weighed *him* the money in the balances.

• Treasures secured by.

Dt 32:34 — *Is* not this laid up in store with me, *and* sealed up among my treasures?

• Lion's den made sure by.

Da 6:17 — And a stone was brought and laid upon the mouth of the den; and the king sealed it with his own signet, and with the signet of his lords; that the purpose might not be changed concerning Daniel.

• Sepulchre of Jesus.

Mt 27:66 — So they went, and made the sepulchre sure, sealing the stone, and setting a watch.

• Circumcision a seal of righteousness.

Ro 4:11 — And he received the sign of circumcision, a seal of the righteousness of the faith which *he had yet* being uncircumcised: that he might be the father of all them that believe, though they be not circumcised; that righteousness might be imputed unto them also:

• Figurative.

• Of secrecy.

Da 12:9 — And he said, Go thy way, Daniel: for the words *are* closed up and sealed till the time of the end.

Rev 5:1 — And I saw in the right hand of him that sat on the throne a book written within and on the backside, sealed with seven seals.

• Of certainty of divine approval.

Rev 7:3–4

Jn 6:27 — Labour not for the meat which perisheth, but for that meat which endureth unto everlasting life, which the Son of man shall give unto you: for him hath God the Father sealed.

Ro 15:28 — When therefore I have performed this, and have sealed to them this fruit, I will come by you into Spain.

2Co 1:22 — Who hath also sealed us, and given the earnest of the Spirit in our hearts.

Eph 1:13 — In whom ye also *trusted,* after that ye heard the word of truth, the gospel of your salvation: in whom also after that ye believed, ye were sealed with that holy Spirit of promise,

Eph 4:30 — And grieve not the holy Spirit of God, whereby ye are sealed unto the day of redemption.

• An amphibious animal.

• Skins of, according to some versions [called badgers' skins in KJV], were used as covering of tabernacle.

Ex 25:5 — And rams' skins dyed red, and badgers' skins, and shittim wood,

Ex 26:14 — And thou shalt make a covering for the tent *of* rams' skins dyed red, and a covering above *of* badgers' skins.

Ex 35:7 — And rams' skins dyed red, and badgers' skins, and shittim wood,

Ex 35:23 — And every man, with whom was found blue, and purple, and scarlet, and fine linen, and goats' *hair,* and red skins of rams, and badgers' skins, brought *them.*

Ex 36:19 — And he made a covering for the tent *of* rams' skins dyed red, and a covering *of* badgers' skins above *that.*

Ex 39:34 — And the covering of rams' skins dyed red, and the covering of badgers' skins, and the vail of the covering,

Nu 4:25 — And they shall bear the curtains of the tabernacle, and the tabernacle of the congregation, his covering, and the covering of the badgers' skins that *is* above upon it, and the hanging for the door of the tabernacle of the congregation,

SEAMEN ✻See: Mariner

SEASONS

Ge 1:14 — And God said, Let there be lights in the firmament of the heaven to divide the day from the night; and let them be for signs, and for seasons, and for days, and years:

Ge 8:22 — While the earth remaineth, seedtime and harvest, and cold and heat, and summer and winter, and day and night shall not cease.

Ps 104:19 — He appointed the moon for seasons: the sun knoweth his going down.

Jer 33:20 — Thus saith the LORD; If ye can break my covenant of the day, and my covenant of the night, and that there should not be day and night in their season;

Da 2:21 — And he changeth the times and the seasons: he removeth kings, and setteth up kings: he giveth wisdom unto the wise, and knowledge to them that know understanding:

Mt 21:41 — They say unto him, He will miserably destroy those wicked men, and will let out *his* vineyard unto other husbandmen, which shall render him the fruits in their seasons.

Mt 24:32 — Now learn a parable of the fig tree; When his branch is yet tender, and putteth forth leaves, ye know that summer is nigh:

Mk 12:2 — And at the season he sent to the husbandmen a servant, that he might receive from the husbandmen of the fruit of the vineyard.

Ac 1:7 — And he said unto them, It is not for you to know the times or the seasons, which the Father hath put in his own power.

1Th 5:1 — But of the times and the seasons, brethren, ye have no need that I write unto you.

SEBA

• Son of Cush.

Ge 10:7 — And the sons of Cush; Seba, and Havilah, and Sabtah, and Raamah, and Sabtechah: and the sons of Raamah; Sheba, and Dedan.

1Ch 1:9 — And the sons of Cush; Seba, and Havilah, and Sabta, and Raamah, and Sabtecha. And the sons of Raamah; Sheba, and Dedan.

• A region in Ethiopia.

Ps 72:10 — The kings of Tarshish and of the isles shall bring presents: the kings of Sheba and Seba shall offer gifts.

Isa 43:3 — For I *am* the LORD thy God, the Holy One of Israel, thy Saviour: I gave Egypt *for* thy ransom, Ethiopia and Seba for thee.

SEBAT • The eleventh month, February.

Zec 1:7 — Upon the four and twentieth day of the eleventh month, which *is* the month Sebat, in the second year of Darius, came the word of the LORD unto Zechariah, the son of Berechiah, the son of Iddo the prophet, saying,

SECOND COMING

Mk 13:32–37; Php 3:20–21; 1Th 4:11–18; 2Th 3:10–12; Jude 1:14–15

Mt 16:27 — For the Son of man shall come in the glory of his Father with his angels; and then he shall reward every man according to his works.

Mt 24:36 — But of that day and hour knoweth no *man,* no, not the angels of heaven, but my Father only.

Mt 24:44 — Therefore be ye also ready: for in such an hour as ye think not the Son of man cometh.

Mt 25:32 — And before him shall be gathered all nations: and he shall separate them one from another, as a shepherd divideth *his* sheep from the goats:

Jn 14:3 — And if I go and prepare a place for you, I will come again, and receive you unto myself; that where I am, *there* ye may be also.

Ac 1:11 — Which also said, Ye men of Galilee, why stand ye gazing up into heaven? this same Jesus, which is taken up from you into heaven, shall so come in like manner as ye have seen him go into heaven.

Col 3:4 — When Christ, *who is* our life, shall appear, then shall ye also appear with him in glory.

1Th 5:2 — For yourselves know perfectly that the day of the Lord so cometh as a thief in the night.

1Th 5:23 — And the very God of peace sanctify you wholly; and *I pray God* your whole spirit and soul and body be preserved blameless unto the coming of our Lord Jesus Christ.

1Ti 6:14 — That thou keep *this* commandment without spot, unrebukeable, until the appearing of our Lord Jesus Christ:

2Ti 4:1 — I charge *thee* therefore before God, and the Lord Jesus Christ, who shall judge the quick and the dead at his appearing and his kingdom;

Tit 2:13 — Looking for that blessed hope, and the glorious appearing of the great God and our Saviour Jesus Christ;

Heb 9:28 — So Christ was once offered to bear the sins of many; and unto them that look for him shall he appear the second time without sin unto salvation.

Heb 10:37 — For yet a little while, and he that shall come will come, and will not tarry.

Jas 5:8 — Be ye also patient; stablish your hearts: for the coming of the Lord draweth nigh.

Rev 1:7 — Behold, he cometh with clouds; and every eye shall see him, and they *also* which pierced him: and all kindreds of the earth shall wail because of him. Even so, Amen.

Rev 22:20 — He which testifieth these things saith, Surely I come quickly. Amen. Even so, come, Lord Jesus.

SECOND DEATH

Rev 20:14 — And death and hell were cast into the lake of fire. This is the second death.

See: Wicked; punishment of

SECRET

• Alms to be given in.

Mt 6:4 — That thine alms may be in secret: and thy Father which seeth in secret himself shall reward thee openly.

• Prayer to be offered in.

Mt 6:6 — But thou, when thou prayest, enter into thy closet, and when thou hast shut thy door, pray to thy Father which is in secret; and thy Father which seeth in secret shall reward thee openly.

• Of others not to be divulged.

Pr 25:9 — Debate thy cause with thy neighbour *himself;* and discover not a secret to another:

Mt 18:15 — Moreover if thy brother shall trespass against thee, go and tell him his fault between thee and him alone: if he shall hear thee, thou hast gained thy brother.

• Unclassified scripture relating to.

Lk 8:16–17; Heb 4:12–13

Dt 29:29 — The secret *things belong* unto the LORD our God: but *those things which* are revealed *belong* unto us and to our children for ever, that *we* may do all the words of this law.

Dt 31:21 — And it shall come to pass, when many evils and troubles are befallen them, that this song shall testify against them as a witness; for it shall not be forgotten out of the mouths of their seed: for I know their imagination which they go about, even now, before I have brought them into the land which I sware.

1Sa 16:7 — But the LORD said unto Samuel, Look not on his countenance, or on the height of his stature; because I have refused him: for *the LORD seeth* not as man seeth; for man looketh on the outward appearance, but the LORD looketh on the heart.

2Sa 7:20 — And what can David say more unto thee? for thou, Lord GOD, knowest thy servant.

2Ki 19:27 — But I know thy abode, and thy going out, and thy coming in, and thy rage against me.

Ps 25:14 — The secret of the LORD *is* with them that fear him; and he will shew them his covenant.

Ps 44:21 — Shall not God search this out? for he knoweth the secrets of the heart.

Ps 90:8 — Thou hast set our iniquities before thee, our secret *sins* in the light of thy countenance.

Ecc 12:14 — For God shall bring every work into judgment, with every secret thing, whether *it be* good, or whether *it be* evil.

Da 2:28 — But there is a God in heaven that revealeth secrets, and maketh known to the king Nebuchadnezzar what shall be in the latter days. Thy dream, and the visions of thy head upon thy bed, are these;

Da 2:47 — The king answered unto Daniel, and said, Of a truth *it is,* that your God is a God of gods, and a Lord of kings, and a revealer of secrets, seeing thou couldst reveal this secret.

Am 3:7 — Surely the Lord GOD will do nothing, but he revealeth his secret unto his servants the prophets.

Mk 4:22 — For there is nothing hid, which shall not be manifested; neither was any thing kept secret, but that it should come abroad.

Ro 2:16 — In the day when God shall judge the secrets of men by Jesus Christ according to my gospel.

1Co 4:5 — Therefore judge nothing before the time, until the Lord come, who both will bring to light the hidden things of darkness, and will make manifest the counsels of the hearts: and then shall every man have praise of God.

See: Mysteries

SECRETARY

2Ki 12:10–12; 22:1–14

2Sa 8:17 — And Zadok the son of Ahitub, and Ahimelech the son of Abiathar, *were* the priests; and Seraiah *was* the scribe;

2Sa 20:24 — And Adoram *was* over the tribute: and Jehoshaphat the son of Ahilud *was* recorder:

1Ki 4:3 — Elihoreph and Ahiah, the sons of Shisha, scribes; Jehoshaphat the son of Ahilud, the recorder.

2Ki 18:18 — And when they had called to the king, there came out to them Eliakim the son of Hilkiah, which *was* over the household, and Shebna the scribe, and Joah the son of Asaph the recorder.

2Ki 18:37 — Then came Eliakim the son of Hilkiah, which *was* over the household, and Shebna the scribe, and Joah the son of Asaph the recorder, to Hezekiah with *their* clothes rent, and told him the words of Rab-shakeh.

1Ch 27:32 — Also Jonathan David's uncle was a counsellor, a wise man, and a scribe: and Jehiel the son of Hachmoni *was* with the king's sons:

Est 3:12 — Then were the king's scribes called on the thirteenth day of the first month, and there was written according to all that Haman had commanded unto the king's lieutenants, and to the governors that *were* over every province, and to the rulers of every people of every province according to the writing thereof, and *to* every people after their language; in the name of king Ahasuerus was it written, and sealed with the king's ring.

Est 8:9 — Then were the king's scribes called at that time in the third month, that *is,* the month Sivan, on the three and twentieth *day* thereof; and it was written according to all that Mordecai commanded unto the Jews, and to the lieutenants, and the deputies and rulers of the provinces which *are* from India unto Ethiopia, an hundred twenty and seven provinces, unto every province according to the writing thereof, and unto every people after their language, and to the Jews according to their writing, and according to their language.

- **Military.**

2Ki 25:19 — And out of the city he took an officer that was set over the men of war, and five men of them that were in the king's presence, which were found in the city, and the principal scribe of the host, which mustered the people of the land, and threescore men of the people of the land *that were* found in the city:

2Ch 26:11 — Moreover Uzziah had an host of fighting men, that went out to war by bands, according to the number of their account by the hand of Jeiel the scribe and Maaseiah the ruler, under the hand of Hananiah, *one* of the king's captains.

See: Amanuensis

See: Scribe

SECUNDUS

- **A Thessalonian Christian.**
- **Accompanies Paul from Corinth.**

Ac 20:4–6

SECURITY

- **For debt.**

See: Debt

See: Surety

- **False.**
  - **From the evils of sin; promises peace and long life.**

Job 29:18 — Then I said, I shall die in my nest, and I shall multiply *my* days as the sand.

  - **Is ignorant of God and truth.**

Ps 10:4 — The wicked, through the pride of his countenance, will not seek *after God:* God *is* not in all his thoughts.

Ps 50:21 — These *things* hast thou done, and I kept silence; thou thoughtest that I was altogether *such an one* as thyself: *but* I will reprove thee, and set *them* in order before thine eyes.

  - **Trusts in lies.**

Isa 28:15 — Because ye have said, We have made a covenant with death, and with hell are we at agreement; when the overflowing scourge shall pass through, it shall not come unto us: for we have made lies our refuge, and under falsehood have we hid ourselves:

Rev 3:17 — Because thou sayest, I am rich, and increased with goods, and have need of nothing; and knowest not that thou art wretched, and miserable, and poor, and blind, and naked:

  - **Is inconsiderate and forgetful.**

Isa 47:7 — And thou saidst, I shall be a lady for ever: *so* that thou didst not lay these *things* to thy heart, neither didst remember the latter end of it.

  - **Relies on earthly treasures.**

Jer 49:4 — Wherefore gloriest thou in the valleys, thy flowing valley, O backsliding daughter? that trusted in her treasures, *saying,* Who shall come unto me?

Jer 49:16 — Thy terribleness hath deceived thee, *and* the pride of thine heart, O thou that dwellest in the clefts of the rock, that holdest the height of the hill: though thou shouldest make thy nest as high as the eagle, I will bring thee down from thence, saith the LORD.

  - **Is deceived by pride.**

Ob 1:3 — The pride of thine heart hath deceived thee, thou that dwellest in the clefts of the rock, whose habitation *is* high; that saith in his heart, Who shall bring me down to the ground?

Rev 18:7 — How much she hath glorified herself, and lived deliciously, so much torment and sorrow give her: for she saith in her heart, I sit a queen, and am no widow, and shall see no sorrow.

  - **Puts off the evil day.**

Am 6:3 — Ye that put far away the evil day, and cause the seat of violence to come near;

  - **Leads to increased guilt.**

Ecc 8:11 — Because sentence against an evil work is not executed speedily, therefore the heart of the sons of men is fully set in them to do evil.

  - **Its refugees shall be scattered.**

Isa 28:17 — Judgment also will I lay to the line, and righteousness to the plummet: and the hail shall sweep away the refuge of lies, and the waters shall overflow the hiding place.

  - **Ruin shall overtake it.**

Isa 47:9 — But these two *things* shall come to thee in a moment in one day, the loss of children, and widowhood: they shall come upon thee in their perfection for the multitude of thy sorceries, *and* for the great abundance of thine enchantments.

Am 9:10 — All the sinners of my people shall die by the sword, which say, The evil shall not overtake nor prevent us.

  - **God is against it.**

Jer 21:13 — Behold, I *am* against thee, O inhabitant of the valley, *and* rock of the plain, saith the LORD; which say, Who shall come down against us? or who shall enter into our habitations?

Eze 39:6 — And I will send a fire on Magog, and among them that dwell carelessly in the isles: and they shall know that I *am* the LORD.

Am 6:1 — Woe to them *that are* at ease in Zion, and trust in the mountain of Samaria, *which are* named chief of the nations, to whom the house of Israel came!

→See: Confidence; false

→See: Self-Deception

→See: Self-Delusion

SECURITY IN SALVATION

Jn 10:27–29

Jn 1:12 — But as many as received him, to them gave he power to become the sons of God, *even* to them that believe on his name:

Jn 5:13 — And he that was healed wist not who it was: for Jesus had conveyed himself away, a multitude being in *that* place.

SEDITION

• Charged against Paul.

Ac 24:5 — For we have found this man *a* pestilent *fellow,* and a mover of sedition among all the Jews throughout the world, and a ringleader of the sect of the Nazarenes:

• How punished.

Ac 5:36–37

SEDUCTION

2Ti 3:6 — For of this sort are they which creep into houses, and lead captive silly women laden with sins, led away with divers lusts,

2Ti 3:13 — But evil men and seducers shall wax worse and worse, deceiving, and being deceived.

• Laws concerning.

Ex 22:16–17; Dt 22:23–29

→See: Rape

• Instances of.

• Of Dinah.

Ge 34:2

• Tamar.

2Sa 13:1–14

SEED

• Every herb, tree, and grass yields its own.

Ge 1:11–12

Ge 1:29 — And God said, Behold, I have given you every herb bearing seed, which *is* upon the face of all the earth, and every tree, in the which *is* the fruit of a tree yielding seed; to you it shall be for meat.

• Each kind has its own body.

1Co 15:38 — But God giveth it a body as it hath pleased him, and to every seed his own body.

• Not to be mingled in sowing.

Le 19:19 — Ye shall keep my statutes. Thou shalt not let thy cattle gender with a diverse kind: thou shalt not sow thy field with mingled seed: neither shall a garment mingled of linen and woollen come upon thee.

Dt 22:9 — Thou shalt not sow thy vineyard with divers seeds: lest the fruit of thy seed which thou hast sown, and the fruit of thy vineyard, be defiled.

• Parables concerning.

Mt 13:1–58; Lk 8:1–56

• Illustrative.

Gal 6:7–8

Ecc 11:6 — In the morning sow thy seed, and in the evening withhold not thine hand: for thou knowest not whether shall prosper, either this or that, or whether they both *shall be* alike good.

Hos 10:12 — Sow to yourselves in righteousness, reap in mercy; break up your fallow ground: for *it is* time to seek the LORD, till he come and rain righteousness upon you.

2Co 9:6 — But this *I say,* He which soweth sparingly shall reap also sparingly; and he which soweth bountifully shall reap also bountifully.

• Sowing of, type of burial of the body.

1Co 15:36–38

SEEKERS

2Ch 15:12–13; 30:18–19; Job 8:5–6; Ps 17:1–2; 24:3–6; 40:1–4; 42:1–4; 63:1–8; 70:4–5; 77:1–9; 130:5–6; 145:18–19; Pr 2:3–5; SS 3:1–4; Isa 26:8–9; 44:3–4; 49:9–12; 55:6–7; 61:1–3; La 3:25–26; Eze 18:21–23; Joel 2:12–13; Am 5:4–6; Zec 8:20–23; Mt 7:7–12; Lk 11:9–13; 14:26–33

Ge 49:18 — I have waited for thy salvation, O LORD.

Dt 4:29 — But if from thence thou shalt seek the LORD thy God, thou shalt find *him,* if thou seek him with all thy heart and with all thy soul.

1Ch 16:11 — Seek the LORD and his strength, seek his face continually.

1Ch 22:19 — Now set your heart and your soul to seek the LORD your God; arise therefore, and build ye the sanctuary of the LORD God, to bring the ark of the covenant of the LORD, and the holy vessels of God, into the house that is to be built to the name of the LORD.

1Ch 28:9 — And thou, Solomon my son, know thou the God of thy father, and serve him with a perfect heart and with a willing mind: for the LORD searcheth all hearts, and understandeth all the imaginations of the thoughts: if thou seek him, he will be found of thee; but if thou forsake him, he will cast thee off for ever.

2Ch 11:16 — And after them out of all the tribes of Israel such as set their hearts to seek the LORD God of Israel came to Jerusalem, to sacrifice unto the LORD God of their fathers.

2Ch 15:2 — And he went out to meet Asa, and said unto him, Hear ye me, Asa, and all Judah and Benjamin; The LORD *is* with you, while ye be with him; and if ye seek him, he will be found of you; but if ye forsake him, he will forsake you.

2Ch 26:5 — And he sought God in the days of Zechariah, who had understanding in the visions of God: and as long as he sought the LORD, God made him to prosper.

2Ch 31:21 — And in every work that he began in the service of the house of God, and in the law, and in the commandments, to seek his God, he did *it* with all his heart, and prospered.

Ezr 8:22 — For I was ashamed to require of the king a band of soldiers and horsemen to help us against the enemy in the way: because we had spoken unto the king, saying, The hand of our God *is* upon all them for good that seek him; but his power and his wrath *is* against all them that forsake him.

Job 5:8 — I would seek unto God, and unto God would I commit my cause:

Ps 9:10 — And they that know thy name will put their trust in thee: for thou, LORD, hast not forsaken them that seek thee.

Ps 14:2 — The LORD looked down from heaven upon the children of men, to see if there were any that did understand, *and* seek God.

Ps 22:26 — The meek shall eat and be satisfied: they shall praise the LORD that seek him: your heart shall live for ever.

Ps 25:5 — Lead me in thy truth, and teach me: for thou *art* the God of my salvation; on thee do I wait all the day.

Ps 25:15 — Mine eyes *are* ever toward the LORD; for he shall pluck my feet out of the net.

Ps 27:4 — One *thing* have I desired of the LORD, that will I seek after; that I may dwell in the house of the LORD all the days of my life, to behold the beauty of the LORD, and to enquire in his temple.

Ps 27:8 — *When thou saidst,* Seek ye my face; my heart said unto thee, Thy face, LORD, will I seek.

Ps 27:14 — Wait on the LORD: be of good courage, and he shall strengthen thine heart: wait, I say, on the LORD.

Ps 33:20 — Our soul waiteth for the LORD: he *is* our help and our shield.

Ps 34:4 — I sought the LORD, and he heard me, and delivered me from all my fears.

Ps 34:10 — The young lions do lack, and suffer hunger: but they that seek the LORD shall not want any good *thing.*

Ps 69:32 — The humble shall see *this, and* be glad: and your heart shall live that seek God.

Ps 78:34 — When he slew them, then they sought him: and they returned and enquired early after God.

Ps 81:10 — I *am* the LORD thy God, which brought thee out of the land of Egypt: open thy mouth wide, and I will fill it.

Ps 83:16 — Fill their faces with shame; that they may seek thy name, O LORD.

Ps 84:2 — My soul longeth, yea, even fainteth for the courts of the LORD: my heart and my flesh crieth out for the living God.

Ps 105:4 — Seek the LORD, and his strength: seek his face evermore.

Ps 119:2 — Blessed *are* they that keep his testimonies, *and that* seek him with the whole heart.

Ps 119:10 — With my whole heart have I sought thee: O let me not wander from thy commandments.

Ps 143:6 — I stretch forth my hands unto thee: my soul *thirsteth* after thee, as a thirsty land. Selah.

Pr 8:17 — I love them that love me; and those that seek me early shall find me.

Pr 8:34 — Blessed *is* the man that heareth me, watching daily at my gates, waiting at the posts of my doors.

Pr 28:5 — Evil men understand not judgment: but they that seek the LORD understand all *things.*

Isa 8:19 — And when they shall say unto you, Seek unto them that have familiar spirits, and unto wizards that peep, and that mutter: should not a people seek unto their God? for the living to the dead?

Isa 45:19 — I have not spoken in secret, in a dark place of the earth: I said not unto the seed of Jacob, Seek ye me in vain: I the LORD speak righteousness, I declare things that are right.

Isa 45:22 — Look unto me, and be ye saved, all the ends of the earth: for I *am* God, and *there is* none else.

Isa 49:23 — And kings shall be thy nursing fathers, and their queens thy nursing mothers: they shall bow down to thee with *their* face toward the earth, and lick up the dust of thy feet; and thou shalt know that I *am* the LORD: for they shall not be ashamed that wait for me.

Isa 51:1 — Hearken to me, ye that follow after righteousness, ye that seek the LORD: look unto the rock *whence* ye are hewn, and to the hole of the pit *whence* ye are digged.

Isa 59:20 — And the Redeemer shall come to Zion, and unto them that turn from transgression in Jacob, saith the LORD.

Jer 29:13 — And ye shall seek me, and find *me,* when ye shall search for me with all your heart.

Jer 42:3 — That the LORD thy God may shew us the way wherein we may walk, and the thing that we may do.

Jer 50:4 — In those days, and in that time, saith the LORD, the children of Israel shall come, they and the children of Judah together, going and weeping: they shall go, and seek the LORD their God.

La 3:41 — Let us lift up our heart with *our* hands unto God in the heavens.

Da 9:3 — And I set my face unto the Lord God, to seek by prayer and supplications, with fasting, and sackcloth, and ashes:

Hos 3:5 — Afterward shall the children of Israel return, and seek the LORD their God, and David their king; and shall fear the LORD and his goodness in the latter days.

Hos 5:15 — I will go *and* return to my place, till they acknowledge their offence, and seek my face: in their affliction they will seek me early.

Hos 10:12 — Sow to yourselves in righteousness, reap in mercy; break up your fallow ground: for *it is* time to seek the LORD, till he come and rain righteousness upon you.

Am 5:8 — *Seek him* that maketh the seven stars and Orion, and turneth the shadow of death into the morning, and maketh the day dark with night: that calleth for the waters of the sea, and poureth them out upon the face of the earth: The LORD *is* his name:

Am 5:14 — Seek good, and not evil, that ye may live: and so the LORD, the God of hosts, shall be with you, as ye have spoken.

Am 8:12 — And they shall wander from sea to sea, and from the north even to the east, they shall run to and fro to seek the word of the LORD, and shall not find *it.*

Zep 2:3 — Seek ye the LORD, all ye meek of the earth, which have wrought his judgment; seek righteousness, seek meekness: it may be ye shall be hid in the day of the LORD's anger.

Mt 5:6 — Blessed *are* they which do hunger and thirst after righteousness: for they shall be filled.

Mt 6:33 — But seek ye first the kingdom of God, and his righteousness; and all these things shall be added unto you.

Lk 6:21 — Blessed *are ye* that hunger now: for ye shall be filled. Blessed *are ye* that weep now: for ye shall laugh.

Lk 13:24 — Strive to enter in at the strait gate: for many, I say unto you, will seek to enter in, and shall not be able.

Lk 16:16 — The law and the prophets *were* until John: since that time the kingdom of God is preached, and every man presseth into it.

Jn 6:37 — All that the Father giveth me shall come to me; and him that cometh to me I will in no wise cast out.

Ac 2:21 — And it shall come to pass, *that* whosoever shall call on the name of the Lord shall be saved.

Ac 17:27 — That they should seek the Lord, if haply they might feel after him, and find him, though he be not far from every one of us:

Ro 3:11 — There is none that understandeth, there is none that seeketh after God.

Ro 10:13 — For whosoever shall call upon the name of the Lord shall be saved.

Heb 7:25 — Wherefore he is able also to save them to the uttermost that come unto God by him, seeing he ever liveth to make intercession for them.

Heb 9:28 — So Christ was once offered to bear the sins of many; and unto them that look for him shall he appear the second time without sin unto salvation.

Heb 11:6 — But without faith *it is* impossible to please *him:* for he that cometh to God must believe that he is, and *that* he is a rewarder of them that diligently seek him.

Jas 4:8 — Draw nigh to God, and he will draw nigh to you. Cleanse *your* hands, *ye* sinners; and purify *your* hearts, *ye* double minded.

Rev 3:20 — Behold, I stand at the door, and knock: if any man hear my voice, and open the door, I will come in to him, and will sup with him, and he with me.

Rev 21:6 — And he said unto me, It is done. I am Alpha and Omega, the beginning and the end. I will give unto him that is athirst of the fountain of the water of life freely.

Rev 22:17 — And the Spirit and the bride say, Come. And let him that heareth say, Come. And let him that is athirst come. And whosoever will, let him take the water of life freely.

See: Backsliders

See: Penitent

See: Sin; confession of

See: Sin; forgiveness of

- **Instances of.**
  - **Asa.**
    2Ch 14:7
  - **Jehoshaphat.**
    2Ch 17:3–4
  - **Uzziah.**
    2Ch 26:5
  - **Hezekiah.**
    2Ch 31:21
  - **Josiah.**
    2Ch 34:3
  - **Ezra.**
    Ezr 7:10
  - **David.**
    Ps 34:4
  - **Daniel.**
    Da 9:3–4
  - **The Magi.**
    Mt 2:1–2

See: Penitent

See: Zeal, Religious

SEER See: Prophets

SEGUB

- **Son of Hiel, the rebuilder of Jericho.**

1Ki 16:34 — In his days did Hiel the Bethelite build Jericho: he laid the foundation thereof in Abiram his firstborn, and set up the gates thereof in his youngest *son* Segub, according to the word of the LORD, which he spake by Joshua the son of Nun.

- **Grandson of Judah.**

1Ch 2:4–5, 21–22

SEIR

- **A range of hills trending southwest from the Dead Sea.**

Dt 1:2 — (*There are* eleven days' *journey* from Horeb by the way of mount Seir unto Kadesh-barnea.)

- **Along the route from Horeb to Kadesh-barnea.**

Dt 1:1–2

- **Children of Israel journey by.**

Dt 1:2 — (*There are* eleven days' *journey* from Horeb by the way of mount Seir unto Kadesh-barnea.)

Dt 2:1 — Then we turned, and took our journey into the wilderness by the way of the Red sea, as the LORD spake unto me: and we compassed mount Seir many days.

Dt 33:2 — And he said, The LORD came from Sinai, and rose up from Seir unto them; he shined forth from mount Paran, and he came with ten thousands of saints: from his right hand *went* a fiery law for them.

- **Originally inhabited by Horites.**

Ge 36:20–30

Ge 14:6 — And the Horites in their mount Seir, unto El-paran, which *is* by the wilderness.

Dt 2:12 — The Horims also dwelt in Seir beforetime; but the children of Esau succeeded them, when they had destroyed them from before them, and dwelt in their stead; as Israel did unto the land of his possession, which the LORD gave unto them.

- **Later inhabited by the children of Esau after they destroyed the Horim.**

Ge 36:8–9; Dt 2:4–5

Ge 32:3 — And Jacob sent messengers before him to Esau his brother unto the land of Seir, the country of Edom.

Ge 33:14 — Let my lord, I pray thee, pass over before his servant: and I will lead on softly, according as the cattle that goeth before me and the children be able to endure, until I come unto my lord unto Seir.

Ge 33:16 — So Esau returned that day on his way unto Seir.

Nu 24:18 — And Edom shall be a possession, Seir also shall be a possession for his enemies; and Israel shall do valiantly.

Dt 2:12 — The Horims also dwelt in Seir beforetime; but the children of Esau succeeded them, when they had destroyed them from before them, and dwelt in their stead; as Israel did unto the land of his possession, which the LORD gave unto them.

Dt 2:22 — As he did to the children of Esau, which dwelt in Seir, when he destroyed the Horims from before them; and they succeeded them, and dwelt in their stead even unto this day:

• The southern boundary of the conquests of Joshua.

Jos 11:15–18

• A Horite chief.

Ge 36:20–21

1Ch 1:38 — And the sons of Seir; Lotan, and Shobal, and Zibeon, and Anah, and Dishon, and Ezar, and Dishan.

SEIRATH • A city of unknown location.

Jgs 3:26 — And Ehud escaped while they tarried, and passed beyond the quarries, and escaped unto Seirath.

SEIZIN

• Of real property.

✦See: Land

SELA

• Called also Selah.

• A city in Edom.

2Ki 14:7 — He slew of Edom in the valley of salt ten thousand, and took Selah by war, and called the name of it Joktheel unto this day.

Isa 16:1 — Send ye the lamb to the ruler of the land from Sela to the wilderness, unto the mount of the daughter of Zion.

SELA-HAMMAHLEKOTH • A rock in the wilderness of Maon.

1Sa 23:28 — Wherefore Saul returned from pursuing after David, and went against the Philistines: therefore they called that place Sela-hammahlekoth.

SELED • A descendant of Jerahmeel.

1Ch 2:30 — And the sons of Nadab; Seled, and Appaim: but Seled died without children.

SELEUCIA

• A city of Syria, on the Mediterranean.

• Paul visits.

Ac 13:4 — So they, being sent forth by the Holy Ghost, departed unto Seleucia; and from thence they sailed to Cyprus.

SELF-CONDEMNATION

1Ki 8:31–32; Pr 5:12–13; Mt 21:33–41; 25:24–27; Mk 12:1–12; Lk 19:21–22

2Sa 24:17 — And David spake unto the LORD when he saw the angel that smote the people, and said, Lo, I have sinned, and I have done wickedly: but these sheep, what have they done? let thine hand, I pray thee, be against me, and against my father's house.

Job 9:20 — If I justify myself, mine own mouth shall condemn me: *if I say, I am* perfect, it shall also prove me perverse.

Mt 23:31 — Wherefore ye be witnesses unto yourselves, that ye are the children of them which killed the prophets.

Jn 8:9 — And they which heard *it,* being convicted by *their own* conscience, went out one by one, beginning at the eldest, *even* unto the last: and Jesus was left alone, and the woman standing in the midst.

Ac 22:24 — The chief captain commanded him to be brought into the castle, and bade that he should be examined by scourging; that he might know wherefore they cried so against him.

Ro 2:1 — Therefore thou art inexcusable, O man, whosoever thou art that judgest: for wherein thou judgest another, thou condemnest thyself; for thou that judgest doest the same things.

✦See: Self-Crimination

✦See: Remorse

✦See: Repentance

• Instances of.

• Achan.

Jos 7:19–25

• David.

2Sa 12:5–7

• Ahab.

1Ki 20:39–42

SELF-CONFIDENCE ✦See: Confidence; false

SELF-CONTROL

• Of Saul.

1Sa 10:27 — But the children of Belial said, How shall this man save us? And they despised him, and brought him no presents. But he held his peace.

• Of David.

1Sa 24:1–15; 26:1–20

• Of Jesus.

Mt 26:62–63; 27:12–14

✦See: Abstinence, Total

✦See: Graces; Christian

✦See: Patience

✦See: Rashness

✦See: Tact

SELF-CRIMINATION

Nu 5:11–27; 1Ki 8:31–32

Ac 22:24 — The chief captain commanded him to be brought into the castle, and bade that he should be examined by scourging; that he might know wherefore they cried so against him.

→See: Self-Condemnation

- **Instances of.**
  - **Achan.**
    Jos 7:19–25

SELF-DECEPTION

Jas 1:26 — If any man among you seem to be religious, and bridleth not his tongue, but deceiveth his own heart, this man's religion *is* vain.

→See: Confidence; false
→See: Security; false

SELF-DEFENSE

- **Accused heard in.**
  Mt 27:11–14; Mk 15:2–5; Ac 2:37–40; 22:1–23:35; 24:10–21; 26:1–32
  Lk 23:3 — And Pilate asked him, saying, Art thou the King of the Jews? And he answered him and said, Thou sayest *it.*
  Jn 7:51 — Doth our law judge *any* man, before it hear him, and know what he doeth?

SELF-DELUSION

- **A characteristic of the wicked.**
  Ps 49:18 — Though while he lived he blessed his soul: and *men* will praise thee, when thou doest well to thyself.
- **Prosperity frequently leads to.**
  Lk 12:17–19
  Ps 30:6 — And in my prosperity I said, I shall never be moved.
  Hos 12:8 — And Ephraim said, Yet I am become rich, I have found me out substance: *in* all my labours they shall find none iniquity in me that *were* sin.
- **Obstinate sinners often given up to.**
  Ps 81:11–12; 2Th 2:10–11
  Hos 4:17 — Ephraim *is* joined to idols: let him alone.
- **Exhibited in thinking that**
  - **Our own ways are right.**
    Pr 14:12 — There is a way which seemeth right unto a man, but the end thereof *are* the ways of death.
  - **We should adhere to established wicked practices.**
    Jer 44:17 — But we will certainly do whatsoever thing goeth forth out of our own mouth, to burn incense unto the queen of heaven, and to pour out drink offerings unto her, as we have done, we, and our fathers, our kings, and our princes, in the cities of Judah, and in the streets of Jerusalem: for *then* had we plenty of victuals, and were well, and saw no evil.
  - **We are pure.**
    Pr 30:12 — *There is* a generation *that are* pure in their own eyes, and *yet* is not washed from their filthiness.
  - **We are better than others.**
    Lk 18:11 — The Pharisee stood and prayed thus with himself, God, I thank thee, that I am not as other men *are*, extortioners, unjust, adulterers, or even as this publican.
  - **We are rich in spiritual things.**
    Rev 3:17 — Because thou sayest, I am rich, and increased with goods, and have need of nothing; and knowest not that thou art wretched, and miserable, and poor, and blind, and naked:
  - **We may have peace while in sin.**
    Dt 29:19 — And it come to pass, when he heareth the words of this curse, that he bless himself in his heart, saying, I shall have peace, though I walk in the imagination of mine heart, to add drunkenness to thirst:
  - **We are above adversity.**
    Ps 10:6 — He hath said in his heart, I shall not be moved: for *I shall* never *be* in adversity.
  - **Gifts entitle us to heaven.**
    Mt 7:21–22
  - **Privileges entitle us to heaven.**
    Lk 13:25–26
    Mt 3:9 — And think not to say within yourselves, We have Abraham to *our* father: for I say unto you, that God is able of these stones to raise up children unto Abraham.
  - **God will not come to judge.**
    2Pe 3:4 — And saying, Where is the promise of his coming? for since the fathers fell asleep, all things continue as *they were* from the beginning of the creation.
  - **Our lives will be prolonged.**
    Isa 56:12 — Come ye, *say they,* I will fetch wine, and we will fill ourselves with strong drink; and to morrow shall be as this day, *and* much more abundant.
    Lk 12:19 — And I will say to my soul, Soul, thou hast much goods laid up for many years; take thine ease, eat, drink, *and* be merry.
    Jas 4:13 — Go to now, ye that say, To day or to morrow we will go into such a city, and continue there a year, and buy and sell, and get gain:
- **Frequently persevered in to the last.**
  Mt 25:11–12; Lk 13:24–25
  Mt 7:22 — Many will say to me in that day, Lord, Lord, have we not prophesied in thy name? and in thy name have cast out devils? and in thy name done many wonderful works?
- **Fatal consequences of.**
  Mt 24:48–51
  Mt 7:23 — And then will I profess unto them, I never knew you: depart from me, ye that work iniquity.
  Lk 12:20 — But God said unto him, *Thou* fool, this night thy soul shall be required of thee: then whose shall those things be, which thou hast provided?
  1Th 5:3 — For when they shall say, Peace and safety; then sudden destruction cometh upon them, as travail upon a woman with child; and they shall not escape.

- **Exemplified.**
  - **Ahab.**

1Ki 20:27 — And the children of Israel were numbered, and were all present, and went against them: and the children of Israel pitched before them like two little flocks of kids; but the Syrians filled the country.

1Ki 20:34 — And *Ben-hadad* said unto him, The cities, which my father took from thy father, I will restore; and thou shalt make streets for thee in Damascus, as my father made in Samaria. Then *said Ahab,* I will send thee away with this covenant. So he made a covenant with him, and sent him away.

  - **Israelites.**

Hos 12:8 — And Ephraim said, Yet I am become rich, I have found me out substance: *in* all my labours they shall find none iniquity in me that *were* sin.

  - **Jews.**

Jn 8:33 — They answered him, We be Abraham's seed, and were never in bondage to any man: how sayest thou, Ye shall be made free?

Jn 8:41 — Ye do the deeds of your father. Then said they to him, We be not born of fornication; we have one Father, *even* God.

  - **Church of Laodicea.**

Rev 3:17 — Because thou sayest, I am rich, and increased with goods, and have need of nothing; and knowest not that thou art wretched, and miserable, and poor, and blind, and naked:

See: Confidence; false

See: Security; false

SELF-DENIAL

Ge 22:1–12; Ps 132:3–5; Mt 5:29–30; 8:19–22; 10:37–39; 13:44–46; 16:24–25; 18:8–9; Mk 8:34–35; 12:43–44; Lk 5:27–28; 9:23–24, 57–60; 14:26–33; 18:27–30; 21:2–4; Ac 20:22–24; Ro 8:12–13, 35–36; 13:14–14:22; 15:1–5; 1Co 8:10–13; 9:18–19, 25–27; 10:23–24; Gal 5:16–17; Php 2:4–8; 3:7–9; 1Pe 2:11–16; 4:1–2

2Sa 24:24 — And the king said unto Araunah, Nay; but I will surely buy *it* of thee at a price: neither will I offer burnt offerings unto the Lord my God of that which doth cost me nothing. So David bought the threshingfloor and the oxen for fifty shekels of silver.

Pr 16:32 — *He that is* slow to anger *is* better than the mighty; and he that ruleth his spirit than he that taketh a city.

Pr 23:2 — And put a knife to thy throat, if thou *be* a man given to appetite.

Da 10:3 — I ate no pleasant bread, neither came flesh nor wine in my mouth, neither did I anoint myself at all, till three whole weeks were fulfilled.

Mt 19:12 — For there are some eunuchs, which were so born from *their* mother's womb: and there are some eunuchs, which were made eunuchs of men: and there be eunuchs, which have made themselves eunuchs for the kingdom of heaven's sake. He that is able to receive *it,* let him receive *it.*

Mt 19:21 — Jesus said unto him, If thou wilt be perfect, go *and* sell that thou hast, and give to the poor, and thou shalt have treasure in heaven: and come *and* follow me.

Mk 2:14 — And as he passed by, he saw Levi the *son* of Alphaeus sitting at the receipt of custom, and said unto him, Follow me. And he arose and followed him.

Mk 9:43 — And if thy hand offend thee, cut it off: it is better for thee to enter into life maimed, than having two hands to go into hell, into the fire that never shall be quenched:

Mk 10:29 — And Jesus answered and said, Verily I say unto you, There is no man that hath left house, or brethren, or sisters, or father, or mother, or wife, or children, or lands, for my sake, and the gospel's,

Lk 5:11 — And when they had brought their ships to land, they forsook all, and followed him.

Lk 12:33 — Sell that ye have, and give alms; provide yourselves bags which wax not old, a treasure in the heavens that faileth not, where no thief approacheth, neither moth corrupteth.

Jn 12:25 — He that loveth his life shall lose it; and he that hateth his life in this world shall keep it unto life eternal.

Ac 21:13 — Then Paul answered, What mean ye to weep and to break mine heart? for I am ready not to be bound only, but also to die at Jerusalem for the name of the Lord Jesus.

Ro 6:6 — Knowing this, that our old man is crucified with *him,* that the body of sin might be destroyed, that henceforth we should not serve sin.

1Co 6:12 — All things are lawful unto me, but all things are not expedient: all things are lawful for me, but I will not be brought under the power of any.

1Co 9:12 — If others be partakers of *this* power over you, *are* not we rather? Nevertheless we have not used this power; but suffer all things, lest we should hinder the gospel of Christ.

1Co 9:15 — But I have used none of these things: neither have I written these things, that it should be so done unto me: for *it were* better for me to die, than that any man should make my glorying void.

1Co 9:23 — And this I do for the gospel's sake, that I might be partaker thereof with *you.*

2Co 6:3 — Giving no offence in any thing, that the ministry be not blamed:

Gal 2:20 — I am crucified with Christ: nevertheless I live; yet not I, but Christ liveth in me: and the life which I now live in the flesh I live by the faith of the Son of God, who loved me, and gave himself for me.

Gal 5:24 — And they that are Christ's have crucified the flesh with the affections and lusts.

Gal 6:14 — But God forbid that I should glory, save in the cross of our Lord Jesus Christ, by whom the world is crucified unto me, and I unto the world.

Col 3:5 — Mortify therefore your members which are upon the earth; fornication, uncleanness, inordinate affection, evil concupiscence, and covetousness, which is idolatry:

2Ti 2:4 — No man that warreth entangleth himself with the affairs of *this* life; that he may please him who hath chosen him to be a soldier.

Tit 2:12 — Teaching us that, denying ungodliness and worldly lusts, we should live soberly, righteously, and godly, in this present world;

Heb 13:13 — Let us go forth therefore unto him without the camp, bearing his reproach.

3Jn 1:7 — Because that for his name's sake they went forth, taking nothing of the Gentiles.

Rev 12:11 — And they overcame him by the blood of the Lamb, and by the word of their testimony; and they loved not their lives unto the death.

✣See: Cross

✣See: Humility

- **Instances of.**
  - **Abraham, when he accorded to Lot, his junior, his preference of the land of Canaan.**
    Ge 13:9; 17:8
  - **Moses, in choosing rather to suffer affliction with the people of God than enjoy the pleasures of sin.**
    Heb 11:25
  - **Moses, in taking no compensation from the Israelites for his services.**
    Nu 16:15
  - **Samuel, in his administration of justice.**
    1Sa 12:3–4
  - **The widow of Zarephath, in sharing with Elijah the last of her sustenance.**
    1Ki 17:12–15
  - **Daniel, in his abstemiousness.**
    Da 1:8
  - **Daniel, in refusing rewards from Belshazzar.**
    Da 5:16–17
  - **Esther, in risking her life for the deliverance of her people.**
    Est 4:16
  - **The Rechabites, in refusing to drink wine or strong drink, or even to plant vineyards.**
    Jer 35:6–7
  - **Peter and other apostles, in abandoning their vocations and following Jesus.**
    Mt 4:20; 9:9; Mk 1:16–20; 2:14; Lk 5:11, 27–28
  - **Peter and other apostles, in forsaking all and following Jesus.**
    Mt 19:27; Mk 10:28
  - **The widow, who cast her all into the treasury.**
    Lk 21:4
  - **The early Christians, in having everything in common.**
    Ac 2:44–45; 4:34
  - **Joses, in selling his possessions, and giving all that he received to the apostles.**
    Ac 4:36–37
  - **Paul, in not counting even his life dear to himself.**
    Ac 20:24; Php 3:7–8
  - **Paul, in not coveting any man's silver or gold or apparel.**
    Ac 20:33
  - **Paul, in laboring for his own support while he also taught.**
    Ac 20:34–35; 1Co 4:12; 10:33

SELF-EXALTATION

Eze 31:10–14; Ob 1:3–4; Lk 14:7–11; 2Co 10:17–18

Job 12:3 — But I have understanding as well as you; I *am* not inferior to you: yea, who knoweth not such things as these?

2Co 10:5 — Casting down imaginations, and every high thing that exalteth itself against the knowledge of God, and bringing into captivity every thought to the obedience of Christ;

Gal 6:3 — For if a man think himself to be something, when he is nothing, he deceiveth himself.

2Th 2:4 — Who opposeth and exalteth himself above all that is called God, or that is worshipped; so that he as God sitteth in the temple of God, shewing himself that he is God.

✣See: Pride

✣See: Selfishness

✣See: Self-Righteousness

- **Instances of.**
  - **Pharaoh.**
    Ex 9:17
  - **Korah, Dathan, and Abiram.**
    Nu 16:1–3
  - **Sennacherib.**
    2Ch 32:9–19
  - **Prince of Tyre, making himself God.**
    Eze 28:2, 9
  - **Nebuchadnezzar.**
    Da 4:30; 5:20
  - **Belshazzar.**
    Da 5:23
  - **Simon the sorcerer.**
    Ac 8:9
  - **Herod, when deified by the people.**
    Ac 12:20–23

SELF-EXAMINATION

Ps 139:23–24; 1Co 11:27–28; Gal 6:3–5

Job 13:23 — How many *are* mine iniquities and sins? make me to know my transgression and my sin.

Ps 4:4 — Stand in awe, and sin not: commune with your own heart upon your bed, and be still. Selah.

Ps 19:12 — Who can understand *his* errors? cleanse thou me from secret *faults*.

Ps 26:2 — Examine me, O Lord, and prove me; try my reins and my heart.

Ps 77:6 — I call to remembrance my song in the night: I commune with mine own heart: and my spirit made diligent search.

Ps 119:59 — I thought on my ways, and turned my feet unto thy testimonies.

Jer 17:9 — The heart *is* deceitful above all *things,* and desperately wicked: who can know it?

La 3:40 — Let us search and try our ways, and turn again to the LORD.

Hag 1:7 — Thus saith the LORD of hosts; Consider your ways.

Mt 26:22 — And they were exceeding sorrowful, and began every one of them to say unto him, Lord, is it I?

Mk 14:19 — And they began to be sorrowful, and to say unto him one by one, *Is* it I? and another *said, Is* it I?

1Co 11:31 — For if we would judge ourselves, we should not be judged.

2Co 13:5 — Examine yourselves, whether ye be in the faith; prove your own selves. Know ye not your own selves, how that Jesus Christ is in you, except ye be reprobates?

↞See: Meditation

↞See: Repentance

↞See: Sin; confession of

SELF-INDULGENCE

• Instances of.

• Solomon.
Ecc 2:10

• The rich fool.
Lk 12:16–20

• Dives.
Lk 16:19

↞See: Gluttony

↞See: Idleness

↞See: Self-Denial

↞See: Slothfulness

SELF-RIGHTEOUSNESS

Dt 9:4–6; Job 11:4–6; 13:18–19; 16:17–18; 18:2–4; 21:27–29; 22:2–3; 32:1–2; 33:8–9; 35:7–8; Ps 10:5–6; Pr 30:12–13; Isa 65:3–5; Jer 2:22–23, 34–35; Eze 33:24–26; Zep 3:1–20; Mt 7:22–23; 9:10–13; 19:16–22; 22:12–13; 23:29–31; Mk 10:17–22; Lk 7:36–50; 10:25–37; 15:25–32; 16:14–15; 18:9–14, 18–23; Jn 9:39–41; Ro 2:17–20; 11:19–21; 2Co 10:17–18; Rev 3:17–18

Nu 16:3 — And they gathered themselves together against Moses and against Aaron, and said unto them, *Ye take* too much upon you, seeing all the congregation *are* holy, every one of them, and the LORD *is* among them: wherefore then lift ye up yourselves above the congregation of the LORD?

1Sa 2:9 — He will keep the feet of his saints, and the wicked shall be silent in darkness; for by strength shall no man prevail.

Job 6:13 — *Is* not my help in me? and is wisdom driven quite from me?

Job 12:2 — No doubt but ye *are* the people, and wisdom shall die with you.

Job 13:3 — Surely I would speak to the Almighty, and I desire to reason with God.

Job 13:13 — Hold your peace, let me alone, that I may speak, and let come on me what *will.*

Job 13:15 — Though he slay me, yet will I trust in him: but I will maintain mine own ways before him.

Job 35:2 — Thinkest thou this to be right, *that* thou saidst, My righteousness *is* more than God's?

Pr 12:15 — The way of a fool *is* right in his own eyes: but he that hearkeneth unto counsel *is* wise.

Pr 14:12 — There is a way which seemeth right unto a man, but the end thereof *are* the ways of death.

Pr 16:2 — All the ways of a man *are* clean in his own eyes; but the LORD weigheth the spirits.

Pr 20:6 — Most men will proclaim every one his own goodness: but a faithful man who can find?

Pr 21:2 — Every way of a man *is* right in his own eyes: but the LORD pondereth the hearts.

Pr 25:14 — Whoso boasteth himself of a false gift *is like* clouds and wind without rain.

Pr 25:27 — *It is* not good to eat much honey: so *for men* to search their own glory *is not* glory.

Pr 26:12 — Seest thou a man wise in his own conceit? *there is* more hope of a fool than of him.

Pr 27:2 — Let another man praise thee, and not thine own mouth; a stranger, and not thine own lips.

Pr 27:21 — *As* the fining pot for silver, and the furnace for gold; so *is* a man to his praise.

Pr 28:13 — He that covereth his sins shall not prosper: but whoso confesseth and forsaketh *them* shall have mercy.

Pr 28:26 — He that trusteth in his own heart is a fool: but whoso walketh wisely, he shall be delivered.

Isa 5:21 — Woe unto *them that are* wise in their own eyes, and prudent in their own sight!

Isa 28:17 — Judgment also will I lay to the line, and righteousness to the plummet: and the hail shall sweep away the refuge of lies, and the waters shall overflow the hiding place.

Isa 28:20 — For the bed is shorter than that *a man* can stretch himself *on it:* and the covering narrower than that he can wrap himself *in it.*

Isa 47:7 — And thou saidst, I shall be a lady for ever: *so* that thou didst not lay these *things* to thy heart, neither didst remember the latter end of it.

Isa 50:11 — Behold, all ye that kindle a fire, that compass *yourselves* about with sparks: walk in the light of your fire, and in the sparks *that* ye have kindled. This shall ye have of mine hand; ye shall lie down in sorrow.

Isa 64:6 — But we are all as an unclean *thing,* and all our righteousnesses *are* as filthy rags; and we all do fade as a leaf; and our iniquities, like the wind, have taken us away.

Jer 2:13 — For my people have committed two evils; they have forsaken me the fountain of living waters, *and* hewed them out cisterns, broken cisterns, that can hold no water.

Jer 7:4 — Trust ye not in lying words, saying, The temple of the LORD, The temple of the LORD, The temple of the LORD, *are* these.

Jer 8:8 — How do ye say, We *are* wise, and the law of the LORD *is* with us? Lo, certainly in vain made he *it;* the pen of the scribes *is* in vain.

Jer 17:5 — Thus saith the LORD; Cursed be the man that trusteth in man, and maketh flesh his arm, and whose heart departeth from the LORD.

Jer 49:4 — Wherefore gloriest thou in the valleys, thy flowing valley, O backsliding daughter? that trusted in her treasures, *saying,* Who shall come unto me?

Jer 49:16 — Thy terribleness hath deceived thee, *and* the pride of thine heart, O thou that dwellest in the clefts of the rock, that holdest the height of the hill: though thou shouldest make thy nest as high as the eagle, I will bring thee down from thence, saith the LORD.

Hos 12:8 — And Ephraim said, Yet I am become rich, I have found me out substance: *in* all my labours they shall find none iniquity in me that *were* sin.

Am 6:13 — Ye which rejoice in a thing of nought, which say, Have we not taken to us horns by our own strength?

Hab 2:4 — Behold, his soul *which* is lifted up is not upright in him: but the just shall live by his faith.

Mt 16:6 — Then Jesus said unto them, Take heed and beware of the leaven of the Pharisees and of the Sadducees.

Mk 2:16 — And when the scribes and Pharisees saw him eat with publicans and sinners, they said unto his disciples, How is it that he eateth and drinketh with publicans and sinners?

Mk 8:15 — And he charged them, saying, Take heed, beware of the leaven of the Pharisees, and *of* the leaven of Herod.

Lk 5:30 — But their scribes and Pharisees murmured against his disciples, saying, Why do ye eat and drink with publicans and sinners?

Lk 15:2 — And the Pharisees and scribes murmured, saying, This man receiveth sinners, and eateth with them.

Jn 9:34 — They answered and said unto him, Thou wast altogether born in sins, and dost thou teach us? And they cast him out.

Ro 3:27 — Where *is* boasting then? It is excluded. By what law? of works? Nay: but by the law of faith.

Ro 10:3 — For they being ignorant of God's righteousness, and going about to establish their own righteousness, have not submitted themselves unto the righteousness of God.

2Co 1:9 — But we had the sentence of death in ourselves, that we should not trust in ourselves, but in God which raiseth the dead:

Gal 6:3 — For if a man think himself to be something, when he is nothing, he deceiveth himself.

- **See: Hypocrisy**
- **See: Self-Exaltation**

- **Instances of.**
  - **Saul.**
    1Sa 15:13–31
  - **Pharisees.**
    Lk 11:33–54; Jn 8:33–59; 9:28–34
  - **Israel.**
    Ro 10:3
  - **Church of Laodicea.**
    Rev 3:17

SELF-WILL

- **Stubbornness.**
- **Forbidden.**

2Ch 30:8 — Now be ye not stiffnecked, as your fathers *were, but* yield yourselves unto the LORD, and enter into his sanctuary, which he hath sanctified for ever: and serve the LORD your God, that the fierceness of his wrath may turn away from you.

Ps 75:5 — Lift not up your horn on high: speak *not with* a stiff neck.

- **Proceeds from unbelief.**

2Ki 17:14 — Notwithstanding they would not hear, but hardened their necks, like to the neck of their fathers, that did not believe in the LORD their God.

- **Proceeds from pride.**

Ne 9:16 — But they and our fathers dealt proudly, and hardened their necks, and hearkened not to thy commandments,

Ne 9:29 — And testifiedst against them, that thou mightest bring them again unto thy law: yet they dealt proudly, and hearkened not unto thy commandments, but sinned against thy judgments, (which if a man do, he shall live in them;) and withdrew the shoulder, and hardened their neck, and would not hear.

- **Proceeds from an evil heart.**

Jer 7:24 — But they hearkened not, nor inclined their ear, but walked in the counsels *and* in the imagination of their evil heart, and went backward, and not forward.

- **God knows.**

Isa 48:4 — Because I knew that thou *art* obstinate, and thy neck *is* an iron sinew, and thy brow brass;

- **Exhibited in.**
  - **Refusing to hearken to God.**

Pr 1:24 — Because I have called, and ye refused; I have stretched out my hand, and no man regarded;

  - **Refusing to hearken to the messengers of God.**

1Sa 8:19 — Nevertheless the people refused to obey the voice of Samuel; and they said, Nay; but we will have a king over us;

Jer 44:16 — *As for* the word that thou hast spoken unto us in the name of the LORD, we will not hearken unto thee.

Zec 7:11 — But they refused to hearken, and pulled away the shoulder, and stopped their ears, that they should not hear.

  - **Refusing to walk in the ways of God.**

Ne 9:17 — And refused to obey, neither were mindful of thy wonders that thou didst among them; but hardened their necks, and in their rebellion appointed a captain to return to their bondage: but thou *art* a God ready to pardon, gracious and merciful, slow to anger, and of great kindness, and forsookest them not.

Ps 78:10 — They kept not the covenant of God, and refused to walk in his law;

Isa 42:24 — Who gave Jacob for a spoil, and Israel to the robbers? did not the LORD, he against whom we have sinned? for they would not walk in his ways, neither were they obedient unto his law.

- **Hearkening to parents.**
  Dt 21:18–19
- **Refusing to receive correction.**
  Dt 21:18 — If a man have a stubborn and rebellious son, which will not obey the voice of his father, or the voice of his mother, and *that,* when they have chastened him, will not hearken unto them:
  Jer 5:3 — O LORD, *are* not thine eyes upon the truth? thou hast stricken them, but they have not grieved; thou hast consumed them, *but* they have refused to receive correction: they have made their faces harder than a rock; they have refused to return.
  Jer 7:28 — But thou shalt say unto them, This *is* a nation that obeyeth not the voice of the LORD their God, nor receiveth correction: truth is perished, and is cut off from their mouth.
- **Rebelling against God.**
  Dt 31:27 — For I know thy rebellion, and thy stiff neck: behold, while I am yet alive with you this day, ye have been rebellious against the LORD; and how much more after my death?
  Ps 78:8 — And might not be as their fathers, a stubborn and rebellious generation; a generation *that* set not their heart aright, and whose spirit was not stedfast with God.
- **Resisting the Holy Ghost.**
  Ac 7:51 — Ye stiffnecked and uncircumcised in heart and ears, ye do always resist the Holy Ghost: as your fathers *did,* so *do* ye.
- **Walking in the counsels of an evil heart.**
  Jer 7:24 — But they hearkened not, nor inclined their ear, but walked in the counsels *and* in the imagination of their evil heart, and went backward, and not forward.
  Jer 23:17 — They say still unto them that despise me, The LORD hath said, Ye shall have peace; and they say unto every one that walketh after the imagination of his own heart, No evil shall come upon you.
- **Hardening the neck.**
  Ne 9:16 — But they and our fathers dealt proudly, and hardened their necks, and hearkened not to thy commandments,
- **Hardening the heart.**
  2Ch 36:13 — And he also rebelled against king Nebuchadnezzar, who had made him swear by God: but he stiffened his neck, and hardened his heart from turning unto the LORD God of Israel.
- **Going backward and not forward.**
  Jer 7:24 — But they hearkened not, nor inclined their ear, but walked in the counsels *and* in the imagination of their evil heart, and went backward, and not forward.
- **Heinousness of.**
  1Sa 15:23 — For rebellion *is as* the sin of witchcraft, and stubbornness *is as* iniquity and idolatry. Because thou hast rejected the word of the LORD, he hath also rejected thee from *being* king.
- **Ministers should be without.**
  Tit 1:7 — For a bishop must be blameless, as the steward of God; not selfwilled, not soon angry, not given to wine, no striker, not given to filthy lucre;
- **Ministers warn their people against.**
  Heb 3:7–12
- **Ministers pray that their people may be forgiven for.**
  Ex 34:9 — And he said, If now I have found grace in thy sight, O Lord, let my Lord, I pray thee, go among us; for it *is* a stiffnecked people; and pardon our iniquity and our sin, and take us for thine inheritance.
  Dt 9:27 — Remember thy servants, Abraham, Isaac, and Jacob; look not unto the stubbornness of this people, nor to their wickedness, nor to their sin:
- **Characteristic of the wicked.**
  Pr 7:11 — (She *is* loud and stubborn; her feet abide not in her house:
  2Pe 2:10 — But chiefly them that walk after the flesh in the lust of uncleanness, and despise government. Presumptuous *are they,* selfwilled, they are not afraid to speak evil of dignities.
- **The wicked cease not from.**
  Jgs 2:19 — And it came to pass, when the judge was dead, *that* they returned, and corrupted *themselves* more than their fathers, in following other gods to serve them, and to bow down unto them; they ceased not from their own doings, nor from their stubborn way.
- **Punishment for.**
  Dt 21:21 — And all the men of his city shall stone him with stones, that he die: so shalt thou put evil away from among you; and all Israel shall hear, and fear.
  Pr 29:1 — He, that being often reproved hardeneth *his* neck, shall suddenly be destroyed, and that without remedy.
- **Illustrated.**
  Ps 32:9 — Be ye not as the horse, *or* as the mule, *which* have no understanding: whose mouth must be held in with bit and bridle, lest they come near unto thee.
  Jer 31:18 — I have surely heard Ephraim bemoaning himself *thus;* Thou hast chastised me, and I was chastised, as a bullock unaccustomed *to the yoke:* turn thou me, and I shall be turned; for thou *art* the LORD my God.
- **Exemplified.**
  - **Simeon and Levi.**
    Ge 49:6 — O my soul, come not thou into their secret; unto their assembly, mine honour, be not thou united: for in their anger they slew a man, and in their selfwill they digged down a wall.
  - **Israelites.**
    Ex 32:9 — And the LORD said unto Moses, I have seen this people, and, behold, it *is* a stiffnecked people:
    Dt 9:6 — Understand therefore, that the LORD thy God giveth thee not this good land to possess it

for thy righteousness; for thou *art* a stiffnecked people.

Dt 9:13 — Furthermore the LORD spake unto me, saying, I have seen this people, and, behold, it *is* a stiffnecked people:

- **Saul.**

1Sa 15:19–23

- **David.**

2Sa 24:4 — Notwithstanding the king's word prevailed against Joab, and against the captains of the host. And Joab and the captains of the host went out from the presence of the king, to number the people of Israel.

- **Josiah.**

2Ch 35:22 — Nevertheless Josiah would not turn his face from him, but disguised himself, that he might fight with him, and hearkened not unto the words of Necho from the mouth of God, and came to fight in the valley of Megiddo.

- **Zedekiah.**

2Ch 36:13 — And he also rebelled against king Nebuchadnezzar, who had made him swear by God: but he stiffened his neck, and hardened his heart from turning unto the LORD God of Israel.

See: Obduracy

SELFISHNESS

Pr 24:11–12; Hag 1:9–10; Mt 19:21–22; Lk 6:32–34; Ro 15:1–3; Php 2:20–21; 2Ti 3:2–4; Jas 2:15–16

Ge 4:9 — And the LORD said unto Cain, Where *is* Abel thy brother? And he said, I know not: *Am* I my brother's keeper?

Nu 32:6 — And Moses said unto the children of Gad and to the children of Reuben, Shall your brethren go to war, and shall ye sit here?

Ps 38:11 — My lovers and my friends stand aloof from my sore; and my kinsmen stand afar off.

Pr 11:26 — He that withholdeth corn, the people shall curse him: but blessing *shall be* upon the head of him that selleth *it*.

Pr 18:17 — *He that is* first in his own cause *seemeth* just; but his neighbour cometh and searcheth him.

Pr 28:27 — He that giveth unto the poor shall not lack: but he that hideth his eyes shall have many a curse.

Eze 34:18 — *Seemeth it* a small thing unto you to have eaten up the good pasture, but ye must tread down with your feet the residue of your pastures? and to have drunk of the deep waters, but ye must foul the residue with your feet?

Mic 3:11 — The heads thereof judge for reward, and the priests thereof teach for hire, and the prophets thereof divine for money: yet will they lean upon the LORD, and say, *Is* not the LORD among us? none evil can come upon us.

Hag 1:4 — *Is it* time for you, O ye, to dwell in your cieled houses, and this house *lie* waste?

Zec 7:6 — And when ye did eat, and when ye did drink, did not ye eat *for yourselves,* and drink *for yourselves?*

Mal 1:10 — Who *is there* even among you that would shut the doors *for nought?* neither do ye kindle *fire* on mine altar for nought. I have no pleasure in you, saith the LORD of hosts, neither will I accept an offering at your hand.

Ro 14:15 — But if thy brother be grieved with *thy* meat, now walkest thou not charitably. Destroy not him with thy meat, for whom Christ died.

1Co 10:24 — Let no man seek his own, but every man another's *wealth.*

2Co 5:15 — And *that* he died for all, that they which live should not henceforth live unto themselves, but unto him which died for them, and rose again.

Gal 6:2 — Bear ye one another's burdens, and so fulfil the law of Christ.

Php 2:4 — Look not every man on his own things, but every man also on the things of others.

1Jn 3:17 — But whoso hath this world's good, and seeth his brother have need, and shutteth up his bowels *of compassion* from him, how dwelleth the love of God in him?

See: Liberality

See: Poor

See: Unselfishness

SEMACHIAH • Son of Shemaiah.

1Ch 26:7 — The sons of Shemaiah; Othni, and Rephael, and Obed, Elzabad, whose brethren *were* strong men, Elihu, and Semachiah.

SEMEI • An ancestor of Jesus.

Lk 3:26 — Which was *the son* of Maath, which was *the son* of Mattathias, which was *the son* of Semei, which was *the son* of Joseph, which was *the son* of Juda,

SENAAH • A city of unknown location.

Ezr 2:35 — The children of Senaah, three thousand and six hundred and thirty.

Ne 7:38 — The children of Senaah, three thousand nine hundred and thirty.

SENATE

- **The Sanhedrin.**

Ac 5:21 — And when they heard *that,* they entered into the temple early in the morning, and taught. But the high priest came, and they that were with him, and called the council together, and all the senate of the children of Israel and sent to the prison to have them brought.

- **Senator, an elder.**

Ps 105:22 — To bind his princes at his pleasure; and teach his senators wisdom.

See: Elder

See: Government

SENEH • A rock protecting the garrison of the Philistines at Michmash.

1Sa 14:4 — And between the passages, by which Jonathan sought to go over unto the Philistines' garrison, *there was* a sharp rock on the one side and a sharp rock on the other side: and the name of the one *was* Bozez, and the name of the other Seneh.

SENIR **See: Shenir**

SENNACHERIB

• King of Assyria.

• Invades Judah; lays siege to Jerusalem, but abandons the country and returns to Assyria.

2Ki 18:17–37; 2Ch 32:1–23; Isa 36:1–37:38

2Ki 19:8 — So Rab-shakeh returned, and found the king of Assyria warring against Libnah: for he had heard that he was departed from Lachish.

• Death of.

2Ki 19:35–37; Isa 37:36–38

SENSUALITY

Lk 12:19–20; 1Co 15:32–33; Jude 1:18–19

Ecc 2:24 — *There is* nothing better for a man, *than* that he should eat and drink, and *that* he should make his soul enjoy good in his labour. This also I saw, that it *was* from the hand of God.

Ecc 8:15 — Then I commended mirth, because a man hath no better thing under the sun, than to eat, and to drink, and to be merry: for that shall abide with him of his labour the days of his life, which God giveth him under the sun.

Ecc 11:9 — Rejoice, O young man, in thy youth; and let thy heart cheer thee in the days of thy youth, and walk in the ways of thine heart, and in the sight of thine eyes: but know thou, that for all these *things* God will bring thee into judgment.

Isa 22:13 — And behold joy and gladness, slaying oxen, and killing sheep, eating flesh, and drinking wine: let us eat and drink; for to morrow we shall die.

Isa 56:12 — Come ye, *say they,* I will fetch wine, and we will fill ourselves with strong drink; and to morrow shall be as this day, *and* much more abundant.

Lk 16:25 — But Abraham said, Son, remember that thou in thy lifetime receivedst thy good things, and likewise Lazarus evil things: but now he is comforted, and thou art tormented.

Jas 5:5 — Ye have lived in pleasure on the earth, and been wanton; ye have nourished your hearts, as in a day of slaughter.

◆See: Abstinence, Total
◆See: Adultery
◆See: Continence
◆See: Drunkenness
◆See: Fornication
◆See: Gluttony
◆See: Lasciviousness
◆See: Self-Denial
◆See: Self-Indulgence
◆See: Sodomy
◆See: Temperance

SENTRY ◆See: Watchman

SENUAH

• Father of Judah, a governor of Jerusalem.

Ne 11:9 — And Joel the son of Zichri *was* their overseer: and Judah the son of Senuah *was* second over the city.

SEORIM • A governor of the temple.

1Ch 24:8 — The third to Harim, the fourth to Seorim,

SEPHAR • A mountain in Arabia.

Ge 10:30 — And their dwelling was from Mesha, as thou goest unto Sephar a mount of the east.

SEPHARAD • An unknown place, to which the inhabitants of Jerusalem were exiled.

Ob 1:20 — And the captivity of this host of the children of Israel *shall possess* that of the Canaanites, *even* unto Zarephath; and the captivity of Jerusalem, which *is* in Sepharad, shall possess the cities of the south.

SEPHARVAIM • An Assyrian city, from which the king of Assyria colonized Samaria.

2Ki 17:24 — And the king of Assyria brought *men* from Babylon, and from Cuthah, and from Ava, and from Hamath, and from Sepharvaim, and placed *them* in the cities of Samaria instead of the children of Israel: and they possessed Samaria, and dwelt in the cities thereof.

2Ki 17:31 — And the Avites made Nibhaz and Tartak, and the Sepharvites burnt their children in fire to Adrammelech and Anammelech, the gods of Sepharvaim.

2Ki 18:34 — Where *are* the gods of Hamath, and of Arpad? where *are* the gods of Sepharvaim, Hena, and Ivah? have they delivered Samaria out of mine hand?

2Ki 19:13 — Where *is* the king of Hamath, and the king of Arpad, and the king of the city of Sepharvaim, of Hena, and Ivah?

Isa 36:19 — Where *are* the gods of Hamath and Arphad? where *are* the gods of Sepharvaim? and have they delivered Samaria out of my hand?

Isa 37:13 — Where *is* the king of Hamath, and the king of Arphad, and the king of the city of Sepharvaim, Hena, and Ivah?

SEPHARVITES • The people of Sepharvaim.

2Ki 17:31 — And the Avites made Nibhaz and Tartak, and the Sepharvites burnt their children in fire to Adrammelech and Anammelech, the gods of Sepharvaim.

SEPULCHRE ◆See: Burial

SERAH

• Called also Sarah.

• Daughter of Asher.

Ge 46:17 — And the sons of Asher; Jimnah, and Ishuah, and Isui, and Beriah, and Serah their sister: and the sons of Beriah; Heber, and Malchiel.

Nu 26:46 — And the name of the daughter of Asher *was* Sarah.

1Ch 7:30 — The sons of Asher; Imnah, and Isuah, and Ishuai, and Beriah, and Serah their sister.

SERAIAH

• David's scribe.

2Sa 8:17 — And Zadok the son of Ahitub, and Ahimelech the son of Abiathar, *were* the priests; and Seraiah *was* the scribe;

• Called also Sheva.

2Sa 20:25 — And Sheva *was* scribe: and Zadok and Abiathar *were* the priests:

• Called also Shisha.

1Ki 4:3 — Elihoreph and Ahiah, the sons of Shisha, scribes; Jehoshaphat the son of Ahilud, the recorder.

• Called also Shavsha.

1Ch 18:16 — And Zadok the son of Ahitub, and Abimelech the son of Abiathar, *were* the priests; and Shavsha was scribe;

• Chief priest at time of taking of Jerusalem.

2Ki 25:18 — And the captain of the guard took Seraiah the chief priest, and Zephaniah the second priest, and the three keepers of the door:

• Father of Ezra.

Ezr 7:1 — Now after these things, in the reign of Artaxerxes king of Persia, Ezra the son of Seraiah, the son of Azariah, the son of Hilkiah,

• Slain by Nebuchadnezzar.

2Ki 25:18–21; Jer 52:24–27

• An Israelitish captain who surrendered to Gedaliah.

2Ki 25:23 — And when all the captains of the armies, they and their men, heard that the king of Babylon had made Gedaliah governor, there came to Gedaliah to Mizpah, even Ishmael the son of Nethaniah, and Johanan the son of Careah, and Seraiah the son of Tanhumeth the Netophathite, and Jaazaniah the son of a Maachathite, they and their men.

Jer 40:8 — Then they came to Gedaliah to Mizpah, even Ishmael the son of Nethaniah, and Johanan and Jonathan the sons of Kareah, and Seraiah the son of Tanhumeth, and the sons of Ephai the Netophathite, and Jezaniah the son of a Maachathite, they and their men.

• Son of Kenaz.

1Ch 4:13–14

• A Simeonite.

1Ch 4:35 — And Joel, and Jehu the son of Josibiah, the son of Seraiah, the son of Asiel,

• A priest who returned from the Babylonian captivity.

Ezr 2:2 — Which came with Zerubbabel: Jeshua, Nehemiah, Seraiah, Reelaiah, Mordecai, Bilshan, Mizpar, Bigvai, Rehum, Baanah. The number of the men of the people of Israel:

Ne 12:1 — Now these *are* the priests and the Levites that went up with Zerubbabel the son of Shealtiel, and Jeshua: Seraiah, Jeremiah, Ezra,

Ne 12:12 — And in the days of Joiakim were priests, the chief of the fathers: of Seraiah, Meraiah; of Jeremiah, Hananiah;

• Called Azariah.

Ne 7:7 — Who came with Zerubbabel, Jeshua, Nehemiah, Azariah, Raamiah, Nahamani, Mordecai, Bilshan, Mispereth, Bigvai, Nehum, Baanah. The number, *I say*, of the men of the people of Israel *was this;*

• One who sealed the covenant with Nehemiah.

Ne 10:2 — Seraiah, Azariah, Jeremiah,

• Possibly identical with a priest who returned from the Babylonian captivity.

• A ruler of the temple after the captivity.

Ne 11:11 — Seraiah the son of Hilkiah, the son of Meshullam, the son of Zadok, the son of Meraioth, the son of Ahitub, *was* the ruler of the house of God.

• Son of Azriel.

• Commanded by king Jehoiakim to seize Jeremiah.

Jer 36:26 — But the king commanded Jerahmeel the son of Hammelech, and Seraiah the son of Azriel, and Shelemiah the son of Abdeel, to take Baruch the scribe and Jeremiah the prophet: but the LORD hid them.

• A servant of Zedekiah.

Jer 51:59 — The word which Jeremiah the prophet commanded Seraiah the son of Neriah, the son of Maaseiah, when he went with Zedekiah the king of Judah into Babylon in the fourth year of his reign. And *this* Seraiah was a quiet prince.

Jer 51:61 — And Jeremiah said to Seraiah, When thou comest to Babylon, and shalt see, and shalt read all these words;

SERAPHIM

• Celestial beings.

Isa 6:2 — Above it stood the seraphims: each one had six wings; with twain he covered his face, and with twain he covered his feet, and with twain he did fly.

Isa 6:6 — Then flew one of the seraphims unto me, having a live coal in his hand, *which* he had taken with the tongs from off the altar:

→See: Cherubim

SERED • Son of Zebulun.

Ge 46:14 — And the sons of Zebulun; Sered, and Elon, and Jahleel.

Nu 26:26 — *Of* the sons of Zebulun after their families: of Sered, the family of the Sardites: of Elon, the family of the Elonites: of Jahleel, the family of the Jahleelites.

SERGEANT

Ac 16:35 — And when it was day, the magistrates sent the serjeants, saying, Let those men go.

Ac 16:38 — And the serjeants told these words unto the magistrates: and they feared, when they heard that they were Romans.

SERGIUS PAULUS • A Roman deputy and convert of Paul.

Ac 13:7–12

SERMON

• Of Jesus, "on the mount".

Mt 5:6–7

• Of Jesus, by the sea.

Mt 13:1–52; Mk 4:2–33

See: Minister, a sacred teacher

See: Preaching

SERPENT

• Satan appears in the form of, to Eve.

Ge 3:1–15

2Co 11:3 — But I fear, lest by any means, as the serpent beguiled Eve through his subtilty, so your minds should be corrupted from the simplicity that is in Christ.

• Subtlety of.

Ge 3:1 — Now the serpent was more subtil than any beast of the field which the LORD God had made. And he said unto the woman, Yea, hath God said, Ye shall not eat of every tree of the garden?

Ecc 10:8 — He that diggeth a pit shall fall into it; and whoso breaketh an hedge, a serpent shall bite him.

Mt 10:16 — Behold, I send you forth as sheep in the midst of wolves: be ye therefore wise as serpents, and harmless as doves.

• Curse upon.

Ge 3:14–15

Ge 49:17 — Dan shall be a serpent by the way, an adder in the path, that biteth the horse heels, so that his rider shall fall backward.

• Feeds upon the dust.

Ge 3:14 — And the LORD God said unto the serpent, Because thou hast done this, thou *art* cursed above all cattle, and above every beast of the field; upon thy belly shalt thou go, and dust shalt thou eat all the days of thy life:

Isa 65:25 — The wolf and the lamb shall feed together, and the lion shall eat straw like the bullock: and dust *shall be* the serpent's meat. They shall not hurt nor destroy in all my holy mountain, saith the LORD.

Mic 7:17 — They shall lick the dust like a serpent, they shall move out of their holes like worms of the earth: they shall be afraid of the LORD our God, and shall fear because of thee.

• Unfit for food.

Mt 7:10 — Or if he ask a fish, will he give him a serpent?

• Venom of.

Pr 23:31–32; Ac 28:5–6

Dt 32:24 — *They shall be* burnt with hunger, and devoured with burning heat, and with bitter destruction: I will also send the teeth of beasts upon them, with the poison of serpents of the dust.

Dt 32:33 — Their wine *is* the poison of dragons, and the cruel venom of asps.

Job 20:16 — He shall suck the poison of asps: the viper's tongue shall slay him.

Ps 58:4 — Their poison *is* like the poison of a serpent: *they are* like the deaf adder *that* stoppeth her ear;

Ps 140:3 — They have sharpened their tongues like a serpent; adders' poison *is* under their lips. Selah.

• The staff of Moses transformed into.

Ex 4:3 — And he said, Cast it on the ground. And he cast it on the ground, and it became a serpent; and Moses fled from before it.

Ex 7:15 — Get thee unto Pharaoh in the morning; lo, he goeth out unto the water; and thou shalt stand by the river's brink against he come; and the rod which was turned to a serpent shalt thou take in thine hand.

• Fiery, sent as a plague upon the Israelites.

Nu 21:6–7

Dt 8:15 — Who led thee through that great and terrible wilderness, *wherein were* fiery serpents, and scorpions, and drought, where *there was* no water; who brought thee forth water out of the rock of flint;

1Co 10:9 — Neither let us tempt Christ, as some of them also tempted, and were destroyed of serpents.

• The wound of, miraculously healed by looking upon the brazen, set up by Moses.

Nu 21:8–9

• Charming of.

Ps 58:4–5

Ecc 10:11 — Surely the serpent will bite without enchantment; and a babbler is no better.

Jer 8:17 — For, behold, I will send serpents, cockatrices, among you, which *will* not *be* charmed, and they shall bite you, saith the LORD.

• Mentioned in Solomon's riddle.

Pr 30:19 — The way of an eagle in the air; the way of a serpent upon a rock; the way of a ship in the midst of the sea; and the way of a man with a maid.

• Constriction of.

Rev 9:19 — For their power is in their mouth, and in their tails: for their tails *were* like unto serpents, and had heads, and with them they do hurt.

• Sea serpent.

Am 9:3 — And though they hide themselves in the top of Carmel, I will search and take them out thence; and though they be hid from my sight in the bottom of the sea, thence will I command the serpent, and he shall bite them:

- **The seventy endued with power over.**
  Lk 10:19 — Behold, I give unto you power to tread on serpents and scorpions, and over all the power of the enemy: and nothing shall by any means hurt you.
- **The apostles given power over.**
  Mk 16:18 — They shall take up serpents; and if they drink any deadly thing, it shall not hurt them; they shall lay hands on the sick, and they shall recover.
  Ac 28:5 — And he shook off the beast into the fire, and felt no harm.
- **Figurative.**
  Isa 14:29 — Rejoice not thou, whole Palestina, because the rod of him that smote thee is broken: for out of the serpent's root shall come forth a cockatrice, and his fruit *shall be* a fiery flying serpent.
  Isa 30:6 — The burden of the beasts of the south: into the land of trouble and anguish, from whence *come* the young and old lion, the viper and fiery flying serpent, they will carry their riches upon the shoulders of young asses, and their treasures upon the bunches of camels, to a people *that* shall not profit *them.*
  Isa 65:25 — The wolf and the lamb shall feed together, and the lion shall eat straw like the bullock: and dust *shall be* the serpent's meat. They shall not hurt nor destroy in all my holy mountain, saith the LORD.

SERUG

- **An ancestor of Abraham.**
  Ge 11:20–23
  1Ch 1:26 — Serug, Nahor, Terah,
- **Called Saruch.**
  Lk 3:35 — Which was *the son* of Saruch, which was *the son* of Ragau, which was *the son* of Phalec, which was *the son* of Heber, which was *the son* of Sala,

SERVANT

- **Distinguished as bond servant, who was a slave, and hired servant.**
- **Bond.**
  - **Laws of Moses concerning.**
    Ex 21:1–11, 20–21, 26–27; Le 19:20–22; 25:35–55
    Ex 21:32 — If the ox shall push a manservant or a maidservant; he shall give unto their master thirty shekels of silver, and the ox shall be stoned.
    Le 25:6 — And the sabbath of the land shall be meat for you; for thee, and for thy servant, and for thy maid, and for thy hired servant, and for thy stranger that sojourneth with thee,
    Le 25:10 — And ye shall hallow the fiftieth year, and proclaim liberty throughout *all* the land unto all the inhabitants thereof: it shall be a jubile unto you; and ye shall return every man unto his possession, and ye shall return every man unto his family.
    Dt 15:12 — *And* if thy brother, an Hebrew man, or an Hebrew woman, be sold unto thee, and serve thee six years; then in the seventh year thou shalt let him go free from thee.
    Dt 15:14 — Thou shalt furnish him liberally out of thy flock, and out of thy floor, and out of thy winepress: *of that* wherewith the LORD thy God hath blessed thee thou shalt give unto him.
    Dt 15:18 — It shall not seem hard unto thee, when thou sendest him away free from thee; for he hath been worth a double hired servant *to thee,* in serving thee six years: and the LORD thy God shall bless thee in all that thou doest.
    Dt 24:7 — If a man be found stealing any of his brethren of the children of Israel, and maketh merchandise of him, or selleth him; then that thief shall die; and thou shalt put evil away from among you.
- **Manstealing forbidden.**
  Dt 21:10–14
  Dt 24:7 — If a man be found stealing any of his brethren of the children of Israel, and maketh merchandise of him, or selleth him; then that thief shall die; and thou shalt put evil away from among you.
  1Ti 1:10 — For whoremongers, for them that defile themselves with mankind, for menstealers, for liars, for perjured persons, and if there be any other thing that is contrary to sound doctrine;
  Rev 18:13 — And cinnamon, and odours, and ointments, and frankincense, and wine, and oil, and fine flour, and wheat, and beasts, and sheep, and horses, and chariots, and slaves, and souls of men.
- **Fugitive, not to be returned to master.**
  Dt 23:15–16
- **David erroneously supposed to be a fugitive slave.**
  1Sa 25:10 — And Nabal answered David's servants, and said, Who *is* David? and who *is* the son of Jesse? there be many servants now a days that break away every man from his master.
- **Instances of fugitive.**
  - **Hagar, commanded by an angel to return to her mistress.**
    Ge 16:9 — And the angel of the LORD said unto her, Return to thy mistress, and submit thyself under her hands.
- **Sought by Shimei.**
  1Ki 2:39–41
- **Interceded for, by Paul.**
  Phm 1:10–21
- **Rights of those born to a master.**
  Ge 14:14 — And when Abram heard that his brother was taken captive, he armed his trained *servants,* born in his own house, three hundred and eighteen, and pursued *them* unto Dan.
  Ge 17:13 — He that is born in thy house, and he that is bought with thy money, must needs be circumcised: and my covenant shall be in your flesh for an everlasting covenant.
  Ge 17:27 — And all the men of his house, born in the house, and bought with money of the stranger, were circumcised with him.
  Ex 21:4 — If his master have given him a wife, and she have born him sons or daughters; the wife

and her children shall be her master's, and he shall go out by himself.

Pr 29:21 — He that delicately bringeth up his servant from a child shall have him become *his* son at the length.

Ecc 2:7 — I got *me* servants and maidens, and had servants born in my house; also I had great possessions of great and small cattle above all that were in Jerusalem before me:

Jer 2:14 — *Is* Israel a servant? *is* he a homeborn *slave?* why is he spoiled?

- **Bought and sold.**

Ge 17:13 — He that is born in thy house, and he that is bought with thy money, must needs be circumcised: and my covenant shall be in your flesh for an everlasting covenant.

Ge 17:27 — And all the men of his house, born in the house, and bought with money of the stranger, were circumcised with him.

Ge 37:28 — Then there passed by Midianites merchantmen; and they drew and lifted up Joseph out of the pit, and sold Joseph to the Ishmeelites for twenty *pieces* of silver: and they brought Joseph into Egypt.

Ge 37:36 — And the Midianites sold him into Egypt unto Potiphar, an officer of Pharaoh's, *and* captain of the guard.

Ge 39:17 — And she spake unto him according to these words, saying, The Hebrew servant, which thou hast brought unto us, came in unto me to mock me:

Dt 28:68 — And the LORD shall bring thee into Egypt again with ships, by the way whereof I spake unto thee, Thou shalt see it no more again: and there ye shall be sold unto your enemies for bondmen and bondwomen, and no man shall buy *you.*

Est 7:4 — For we are sold, I and my people, to be destroyed, to be slain, and to perish. But if we had been sold for bondmen and bondwomen, I had held my tongue, although the enemy could not countervail the king's damage.

Eze 27:13 — Javan, Tubal, and Meshech, they *were* thy merchants: they traded the persons of men and vessels of brass in thy market.

Joel 3:6 — The children also of Judah and the children of Jerusalem have ye sold unto the Grecians, that ye might remove them far from their border.

Am 8:6 — That we may buy the poor for silver, and the needy for a pair of shoes; *yea,* and sell the refuse of the wheat?

Rev 18:13 — And cinnamon, and odours, and ointments, and frankincense, and wine, and oil, and fine flour, and wheat, and beasts, and sheep, and horses, and chariots, and slaves, and souls of men.

- **Captives of war made.**

Dt 21:10–14

Dt 20:14 — But the women, and the little ones, and the cattle, and all that is in the city, *even* all the spoil thereof, shalt thou take unto thyself; and thou shalt eat the spoil of thine enemies, which the LORD thy God hath given thee.

2Ki 5:2 — And the Syrians had gone out by companies, and had brought away captive out of the land of Israel a little maid; and she waited on Naaman's wife.

2Ch 28:8 — And the children of Israel carried away captive of their brethren two hundred thousand, women, sons, and daughters, and took also away much spoil from them, and brought the spoil to Samaria.

2Ch 28:10 — And now ye purpose to keep under the children of Judah and Jerusalem for bondmen and bondwomen unto you: *but are there* not with you, even with you, sins against the LORD your God?

La 5:13 — They took the young men to grind, and the children fell under the wood.

- **Captive bond servants shared by priests and Levites.**

Nu 31:28–47

- **Thieves punished by being made.**

Ge 43:18 — And the men were afraid, because they were brought into Joseph's house; and they said, Because of the money that was returned in our sacks at the first time are we brought in; that he may seek occasion against us, and fall upon us, and take us for bondmen, and our asses.

Ex 22:3 — If the sun be risen upon him, *there shall be* blood *shed* for him; *for* he should make full restitution; if he have nothing, then he shall be sold for his theft.

- **Defaulting debtors made.**

Le 25:39 — And if thy brother *that dwelleth* by thee be waxen poor, and be sold unto thee; thou shalt not compel him to serve as a bondservant:

Mt 18:25 — But forasmuch as he had not to pay, his lord commanded him to be sold, and his wife, and children, and all that he had, and payment to be made.

- **Children of defaulting debtors sold for.**

2Ki 4:1–7

- **Voluntary servitude of.**

Dt 15:16–17; Jos 9:11–21

Le 25:47 — And if a sojourner or stranger wax rich by thee, and thy brother *that dwelleth* by him wax poor, and sell himself unto the stranger *or* sojourner by thee, or to the stock of the stranger's family:

- **Given as dowry.**

Ge 29:24 — And Laban gave unto his daughter Leah Zilpah his maid *for* an handmaid.

Ge 29:29 — And Laban gave to Rachel his daughter Bilhah his handmaid to be her maid.

- **Owned by priests.**

Le 22:11 — But if the priest buy *any* soul with his money, he shall eat of it, and he that is born in his house: they shall eat of his meat.

Mk 14:66 — And as Peter was beneath in the palace, there cometh one of the maids of the high priest:

• **Slaves owned slaves.**

2Sa 9:10 — Thou therefore, and thy sons, and thy servants, shall till the land for him, and thou shalt bring in *the fruits,* that thy master's son may have food to eat: but Mephibosheth thy master's son shall eat bread alway at my table. Now Ziba had fifteen sons and twenty servants.

• **The master might marry, or give in marriage.**

Ex 21:7–10; Dt 21:10–14; 1Ch 2:34–35

• **Taken in concubinage.**

Ge 16:1–2

Ge 16:6 — But Abram said unto Sarai, Behold, thy maid *is* in thy hand; do to her as it pleaseth thee. And when Sarai dealt hardly with her, she fled from her face.

Ge 30:3 — And she said, Behold my maid Bilhah, go in unto her; and she shall bear upon my knees that I may also have children by her.

Ge 30:9 — When Leah saw that she had left bearing, she took Zilpah her maid, and gave her Jacob to wife.

• **Used as soldiers by Abraham.**

Ge 14:14 — And when Abram heard that his brother was taken captive, he armed his trained *servants,* born in his own house, three hundred and eighteen, and pursued *them* unto Dan.

• **Must be circumcised.**

Ge 17:13 — He that is born in thy house, and he that is bought with thy money, must needs be circumcised: and my covenant shall be in your flesh for an everlasting covenant.

Ge 17:27 — And all the men of his house, born in the house, and bought with money of the stranger, were circumcised with him.

Ex 12:44 — But every man's servant that is bought for money, when thou hast circumcised him, then shall he eat thereof.

• **Must enjoy religious privileges with the master's household.**

Dt 29:10–11

Dt 12:12 — And ye shall rejoice before the LORD your God, ye, and your sons, and your daughters, and your menservants, and your maidservants, and the Levite that *is* within your gates; forasmuch as he hath no part nor inheritance with you.

Dt 12:18 — But thou must eat them before the LORD thy God in the place which the LORD thy God shall choose, thou, and thy son, and thy daughter, and thy manservant, and thy maidservant, and the Levite that *is* within thy gates: and thou shalt rejoice before the LORD thy God in all that thou puttest thine hands unto.

Dt 16:11 — And thou shalt rejoice before the LORD thy God, thou, and thy son, and thy daughter, and thy manservant, and thy maidservant, and the Levite that *is* within thy gates, and the stranger, and the fatherless, and the widow, that *are* among you, in the place which the LORD thy God hath chosen to place his name there.

Dt 16:14 — And thou shalt rejoice in thy feast, thou, and thy son, and thy daughter, and thy manservant, and thy maidservant, and the Levite, the stranger, and the fatherless, and the widow, that *are* within thy gates.

• **Must have rest on the Sabbath.**

Ex 20:10 — But the seventh day *is* the sabbath of the LORD thy God: *in it* thou shalt not do any work, thou, nor thy son, nor thy daughter, thy manservant, nor thy maidservant, nor thy cattle, nor thy stranger that *is* within thy gates:

Ex 23:12 — Six days thou shalt do thy work, and on the seventh day thou shalt rest: that thine ox and thine ass may rest, and the son of thy handmaid, and the stranger, may be refreshed.

Dt 5:14 — But the seventh day *is* the sabbath of the LORD thy God: *in it* thou shalt not do any work, thou, nor thy son, nor thy daughter, nor thy manservant, nor thy maidservant, nor thine ox, nor thine ass, nor any of thy cattle, nor thy stranger that *is* within thy gates; that thy manservant and thy maidservant may rest as well as thou.

• **Equal status of, with other disciples of Jesus.**

1Co 7:21–22

1Co 12:13 — For by one Spirit are we all baptized into one body, whether *we be* Jews or Gentiles, whether *we be* bond or free; and have been all made to drink into one Spirit.

Gal 3:28 — There is neither Jew nor Greek, there is neither bond nor free, there is neither male nor female: for ye are all one in Christ Jesus.

Eph 6:8 — Knowing that whatsoever good thing any man doeth, the same shall he receive of the Lord, whether *he be* bond or free.

• **Kindness to, enjoined.**

Le 25:43 — Thou shalt not rule over him with rigour; but shalt fear thy God.

Eph 6:9 — And, ye masters, do the same things unto them, forbearing threatening: knowing that your Master also is in heaven; neither is there respect of persons with him.

• **Bond service threatened, as a national punishment, for disobedience of Israel.**

Joel 3:7–8

Dt 28:68 — And the LORD shall bring thee into Egypt again with ships, by the way whereof I spake unto thee, Thou shalt see it no more again: and there ye shall be sold unto your enemies for bondmen and bondwomen, and no man shall buy *you.*

• **Degrading influences of bondage exemplified by cowardice.**

Ex 14:11–12; Jgs 5:16–18

Ex 16:3 — And the children of Israel said unto them, Would to God we had died by the hand of the LORD in the land of Egypt, when we sat by the flesh pots, *and* when we did eat bread to the full; for ye have brought us forth into this wilderness, to kill this whole assembly with hunger.

Jgs 5:23 — Curse ye Meroz, said the angel of the LORD, curse ye bitterly the inhabitants thereof; because they came not to the help of the LORD, to the help of the LORD against the mighty.

- **Emancipation of.**
  Ezr 1:1–4; Jer 34:8–22
  1Co 7:21 — Art thou called *being* a servant? care not for it: but if thou mayest be made free, use *it* rather.
- **Freedmen called libertines.**
  Ac 6:9 — Then there arose certain of *the synagogue,* which is called the synagogue of the Libertines, and Cyrenians, and Alexandrians, and of them of Cilicia and of Asia, disputing with Stephen.
- **Cruelty to.**
  - **Hagar.**
    Ge 16:1–16; Gal 4:22–31
  - **The Israelites.**
    Ex 1:8–2:4
    Ac 7:19 — The same dealt subtilly with our kindred, and evil entreated our fathers, so that they cast out their young children, to the end they might not live.
    Ac 7:34 — I have seen, I have seen the affliction of my people which is in Egypt, and I have heard their groaning, and am come down to deliver them. And now come, I will send thee into Egypt.
  - **Sick, abandoned.**
    1Sa 30:13 — And David said unto him, To whom *belongest* thou? and whence art thou? And he said, I *am* a young man of Egypt, servant to an Amalekite; and my master left me, because three days agone I fell sick.
- **Kindness to, by the centurion.**
  Mt 8:8–13; Lk 7:2–10
- **Kindness to, by Paul.**
  Phm 1:1–21
- **Instances of.**
  - **Joseph.**
    Ge 37:26–28
    Ge 37:36 — And the Midianites sold him into Egypt unto Potiphar, an officer of Pharaoh's, *and* captain of the guard.
  - **Israelites.**
    Ex 1:10–22; 5:7–14
    Dt 6:12 — *Then* beware lest thou forget the LORD, which brought thee forth out of the land of Egypt, from the house of bondage.
    Dt 6:21 — Then thou shalt say unto thy son, We were Pharaoh's bondmen in Egypt; and the LORD brought us out of Egypt with a mighty hand:
  - **Gibeonites.**
    Jos 9:22–27
  - **Canaanites.**
    1Ki 9:21 — Their children that were left after them in the land, whom the children of Israel also were not able utterly to destroy, upon those did Solomon levy a tribute of bondservice unto this day.
  - **Jews in Babylon.**
    Est 1:1–10:3
    2Ch 36:20 — And them that had escaped from the sword carried he away to Babylon; where they were servants to him and his sons until the reign of the kingdom of Persia:
  - **Emancipation of Jews.**
    Ezr 1:1–4
    2Ch 36:23 — Thus saith Cyrus king of Persia, All the kingdoms of the earth hath the LORD God of heaven given me; and he hath charged me to build him an house in Jerusalem, which *is* in Judah. Who *is there* among you of all his people? The LORD his God *be* with him, and let him go up.
- **Figurative.**
  Mt 24:45–51; Lk 12:35–48; 17:7–9; Jn 8:32–35; Ro 6:16–22; 1Co 7:21–23
  Le 25:42 — For they *are* my servants, which I brought forth out of the land of Egypt: they shall not be sold as bondmen.
  Le 25:55 — For unto me the children of Israel *are* servants; they *are* my servants whom I brought forth out of the land of Egypt: I *am* the LORD your God.
  Ps 116:16 — O LORD, truly I *am* thy servant; I *am* thy servant, *and* the son of thine handmaid: thou hast loosed my bonds.
  1Co 4:1 — Let a man so account of us, as of the ministers of Christ, and stewards of the mysteries of God.
  Gal 5:13 — For, brethren, ye have been called unto liberty; only *use* not liberty for an occasion to the flesh, but by love serve one another.
  1Pe 2:16 — As free, and not using *your* liberty for a cloke of maliciousness, but as the servants of God.
  2Pe 2:19 — While they promise them liberty, they themselves are the servants of corruption: for of whom a man is overcome, of the same is he brought in bondage.
  Rev 7:3 — Saying, Hurt not the earth, neither the sea, nor the trees, till we have sealed the servants of our God in their foreheads.

SERVANT, Good/Evil

- **Instances of Good.**
  - **Joseph.**
    Ge 39:2–20; 41:9–57; Ac 7:10
  - **Elisha.**
    2Ki 2:1–6
  - **Servants of Abraham.**
    Ge 24:1–67
  - **Servants of Boaz.**
    Ru 2:4
  - **Servants of Jonathan.**
    1Sa 14:7
  - **Servants of Abigail.**
    1Sa 25:14–17

• **Servants of David.**
2Sa 12:18; 15:15, 21

• **Servants of Ziba.**
2Sa 9:1–13

• **Servants of Naaman.**
2Ki 5:2–3, 13

• **Servants of Nehemiah.**
Ne 4:16, 23

• **Servants of centurion.**
Mt 8:9

• **Servants of Cornelius.**
Ac 10:7

• **Servants of Onesimus.**
Phm 1:11

• **Servants in the parable of the pounds and talents.**
Mt 25:14–23; Lk 19:12–19

• **Wicked and unfaithful.**

• **Jeroboam.**
1Ki 11:26 — And Jeroboam the son of Nebat, an Ephrathite of Zereda, Solomon's servant, whose mother's name *was* Zeruah, a widow woman, even he lifted up *his* hand against the king.

• **Gehazi.**
2Ki 5:20–27

• **Zimri.**
1Ki 16:9–10
2Ki 9:31 — And as Jehu entered in at the gate, she said, *Had* Zimri peace, who slew his master?

• **Onesimus.**
Phm 1:11 — Which in time past was to thee unprofitable, but now profitable to thee and to me:

• **Of Abraham and Lot.**
Ge 13:7 — And there was a strife between the herdmen of Abram's cattle and the herdmen of Lot's cattle: and the Canaanite and the Perizzite dwelled then in the land.

• **Of Abimelech.**
Ge 21:25 — And Abraham reproved Abimelech because of a well of water, which Abimelech's servants had violently taken away.

• **Of Ziba.**
2Sa 16:1–4; 19:26–27

• **Of Absalom.**
2Sa 13:28–29
2Sa 14:30 — Therefore he said unto his servants, See, Joab's field is near mine, and he hath barley there; go and set it on fire. And Absalom's servants set the field on fire.

• **Of Shimei.**
1Ki 2:39 — And it came to pass at the end of three years, that two of the servants of Shimei ran away unto Achish son of Maachah king of Gath. And they told Shimei, saying, Behold, thy servants *be* in Gath.

• **Of Joash.**
2Ki 12:19–21

• **Of Amon.**
2Ki 21:23 — And the servants of Amon conspired against him, and slew the king in his own house.

• **Of Job.**
Job 19:15–16

• **In the parable of the talents and pounds.**
Mt 25:24–30; Lk 19:20–26

• **In the parable of the vineyard.**
Mt 21:33–41; Mk 12:1–9

• **Conspiracy by.**
See: Conspiracy

• **Unclassified scripture relating to.**
Ge 16:6–9; Job 19:15–16; 31:13–14; Ps 123:1–4; Pr 30:1–33; Jer 34:8–17; Mt 10:24–25; 24:45–51; Lk 12:35–48; 16:1–13; 17:7–9; 1Co 7:21–24; Eph 6:5–9; Col 3:22–25; 1Ti 6:1–2; Tit 2:9–10; 1Pe 2:18–20

Ex 20:10 — But the seventh day *is* the sabbath of the LORD thy God: *in it* thou shalt not do any work, thou, nor thy son, nor thy daughter, thy manservant, nor thy maidservant, nor thy cattle, nor thy stranger that *is* within thy gates:

Dt 5:14 — But the seventh day *is* the sabbath of the LORD thy God: *in it* thou shalt not do any work, thou, nor thy son, nor thy daughter, nor thy manservant, nor thy maidservant, nor thine ox, nor thine ass, nor any of thy cattle, nor thy stranger that *is* within thy gates; that thy manservant and thy maidservant may rest as well as thou.

Ne 5:8 — And I said unto them, We after our ability have redeemed our brethren the Jews, which were sold unto the heathen; and will ye even sell your brethren? or shall they be sold unto us? Then held they their peace, and found nothing *to answer.*

Pr 12:9 — *He that is* despised, and hath a servant, *is* better than he that honoureth himself, and lacketh bread.

Pr 13:17 — A wicked messenger falleth into mischief: but a faithful ambassador *is* health.

Pr 17:2 — A wise servant shall have rule over a son that causeth shame, and shall have part of the inheritance among the brethren.

Pr 19:10 — Delight is not seemly for a fool; much less for a servant to have rule over princes.

Pr 25:13 — As the cold of snow in the time of harvest, *so is* a faithful messenger to them that send him: for he refresheth the soul of his masters.

Pr 26:6 — He that sendeth a message by the hand of a fool cutteth off the feet, *and* drinketh damage.

Pr 27:18 — Whoso keepeth the fig tree shall eat the fruit thereof: so he that waiteth on his master shall be honoured.

Pr 27:27 — And *thou shalt have* goats' milk enough for thy food, for the food of thy household, and *for* the maintenance for thy maidens.

Pr 29:19 — A servant will not be corrected by words: for though he understand he will not answer.

Pr 29:21 — He that delicately bringeth up his servant from a child shall have him become *his* son at the length.

Ecc 7:21 — Also take no heed unto all words that are spoken; lest thou hear thy servant curse thee:

Isa 52:3 — For thus saith the LORD, Ye have sold yourselves for nought; and ye shall be redeemed without money.

Jer 22:13 — Woe unto him that buildeth his house by unrighteousness, and his chambers by wrong; *that* useth his neighbour's service without wages, and giveth him not for his work;

La 5:8 — Servants have ruled over us: *there is* none that doth deliver *us* out of their hand.

Zep 1:9 — In the same day also will I punish all those that leap on the threshold, which fill their masters' houses with violence and deceit.

Mal 1:6 — A son honoureth *his* father, and a servant his master: if then I *be* a father, where *is* mine honour? and if I *be* a master, where *is* my fear? saith the LORD of hosts unto you, O priests, that despise my name. And ye say, Wherein have we despised thy name?

Mt 8:9 — For I am a man under authority, having soldiers under me: and I say to this *man,* Go, and he goeth; and to another, Come, and he cometh; and to my servant, Do this, and he doeth *it.*

Lk 22:27 — For whether *is* greater, he that sitteth at meat, or he that serveth? *is* not he that sitteth at meat? but I am among you as he that serveth.

Jn 13:16 — Verily, verily, I say unto you, The servant is not greater than his lord; neither he that is sent greater than he that sent him.

1Co 4:2 — Moreover it is required in stewards, that a man be found faithful.

→See: Employee

→See: Employer

→See: Master

SERVANT, Hired

• Jacob.

Ge 29:15 — And Laban said unto Jacob, Because thou *art* my brother, shouldest thou therefore serve me for nought? tell me, what *shall* thy wages *be?*

Ge 30:26 — Give *me* my wives and my children, for whom I have served thee, and let me go: for thou knowest my service which I have done thee.

• Jacob, reemployed.

Ge 30:27–34; 31:6–7

Ge 31:41 — Thus have I been twenty years in thy house; I served thee fourteen years for thy two daughters, and six years for thy cattle: and thou hast changed my wages ten times.

• Parable of laborers for a vineyard.

Mt 20:1–15

• Parable of the father of the prodigal son.

Lk 15:17 — And when he came to himself, he said, How many hired servants of my father's have bread enough and to spare, and I perish with hunger!

Lk 15:19 — And am no more worthy to be called thy son: make me as one of thy hired servants.

• The prodigal.

Lk 15:15–19

• Treatment of, more considerate than that accorded slaves.

Le 25:53 — *And* as a yearly hired servant shall he be with him: *and the other* shall not rule with rigour over him in thy sight.

• Await employment in marketplace.

Mt 20:1–3

• Wages paid in kind.

Ge 30:31–32

2Ch 2:10 — And, behold, I will give to thy servants, the hewers that cut timber, twenty thousand measures of beaten wheat, and twenty thousand measures of barley, and twenty thousand baths of wine, and twenty thousand baths of oil.

• Wages paid in money.

Mt 20:2 — And when he had agreed with the labourers for a penny a day, he sent them into his vineyard.

• Unclassified scripture relating to.

Le 25:39–41; Dt 24:14–15; Job 7:1–2; Mt 10:9–10

Le 19:13 — Thou shalt not defraud thy neighbour, neither rob *him:* the wages of him that is hired shall not abide with thee all night until the morning.

Job 14:6 — Turn from him, that he may rest, till he shall accomplish, as an hireling, his day.

Mal 3:5 — And I will come near to you to judgment; and I will be a swift witness against the sorcerers, and against the adulterers, and against false swearers, and against those that oppress the hireling in *his* wages, the widow, and the fatherless, and that turn aside the stranger *from his right,* and fear not me, saith the LORD of hosts.

Lk 10:7 — And in the same house remain, eating and drinking such things as they give: for the labourer is worthy of his hire. Go not from house to house.

Ro 4:4 — Now to him that worketh is the reward not reckoned of grace, but of debt.

Col 4:1 — Masters, give unto *your* servants that which is just and equal; knowing that ye also have a Master in heaven.

1Ti 5:18 — For the scripture saith, Thou shalt not muzzle the ox that treadeth out the corn. And, The labourer *is* worthy of his reward.

Jas 5:4 — Behold, the hire of the labourers who have reaped down your fields, which is of you kept back by fraud, crieth: and the cries of them which have reaped are entered into the ears of the Lord of sabaoth.

→See: Master

→See: Wages

SERVICE →See: Altruism

SETH

• Son of Adam.

Ge 4:25–26

Ge 5:3 — And Adam lived an hundred and thirty years, and begat *a son* in his own likeness, after his image; and called his name Seth:

Ge 5:8 — And all the days of Seth were nine hundred and twelve years: and he died.

1Ch 1:1 — Adam, Sheth, Enosh,

Lk 3:38 — Which was *the son* of Enos, which was *the son* of Seth, which was *the son* of Adam, which was *the son* of God.

• Called Sheth.

1Ch 1:1 — Adam, Sheth, Enosh,

SETHUR

• One of the twelve spies.

Nu 13:13 — Of the tribe of Asher, Sethur the son of Michael.

SEVEN

• Interesting facts concerning the number.

• Days.

• Week consists of.

Dt 5:13–14

Ge 2:3 — And God blessed the seventh day, and sanctified it: because that in it he had rested from all his work which God created and made.

Ex 20:11 — For *in* six days the LORD made heaven and earth, the sea, and all that in them *is*, and rested the seventh day: wherefore the LORD blessed the sabbath day, and hallowed it.

• Noah in the ark before the flood.

Ge 7:4 — For yet seven days, and I will cause it to rain upon the earth forty days and forty nights; and every living substance that I have made will I destroy from off the face of the earth.

Ge 7:10 — And it came to pass after seven days, that the waters of the flood were upon the earth.

• Noah remains in the ark after sending forth the dove.

Ge 8:10 — And he stayed yet other seven days; and again he sent forth the dove out of the ark;

Ge 8:12 — And he stayed yet other seven days; and sent forth the dove; which returned not again unto him any more.

• Mourning for Jacob lasted.

Ge 50:10 — And they came to the threshingfloor of Atad, which *is* beyond Jordan, and there they mourned with a great and very sore lamentation: and he made a mourning for his father seven days.

• Mourning of Job.

Job 2:13 — So they sat down with him upon the ground seven days and seven nights, and none spake a word unto him: for they saw that *his* grief was very great.

• The plague of bloody waters in Egypt lasted.

Ex 7:25 — And seven days were fulfilled, after that the LORD had smitten the river.

• The Israelites compassed Jericho.

Jos 6:4 — And seven priests shall bear before the ark seven trumpets of rams' horns: and the seventh day ye shall compass the city seven times, and the priests shall blow with the trumpets.

• The passover lasted.

Ex 12:15 — Seven days shall ye eat unleavened bread; even the first day ye shall put away leaven out of your houses: for whosoever eateth leavened bread from the first day until the seventh day, that soul shall be cut off from Israel.

• Saul directed by Samuel to tarry at Gilgal, awaiting the prophet's command.

1Sa 10:8 — And thou shalt go down before me to Gilgal; and, behold, I will come down unto thee, to offer burnt offerings, *and* to sacrifice sacrifices of peace offerings: seven days shalt thou tarry, till I come to thee, and shew thee what thou shalt do.

1Sa 13:8 — And he tarried seven days, according to the set time that Samuel *had appointed:* but Samuel came not to Gilgal; and the people were scattered from him.

• The elders of Jabesh-gilead ask for a truce of.

1Sa 11:3 — And the elders of Jabesh said unto him, Give us seven days' respite, that we may send messengers unto all the coasts of Israel: and then, if *there be* no man to save us, we will come out to thee.

• Dedication of the temple lasted double.

1Ki 8:65 — And at that time Solomon held a feast, and all Israel with him, a great congregation, from the entering in of Hamath unto the river of Egypt, before the LORD our God, seven days and seven days, *even* fourteen days.

• Ezekiel sits by the river Chebar in astonishment.

Eze 3:15 — Then I came to them of the captivity at Tel-abib, that dwelt by the river of Chebar, and I sat where they sat, and remained there astonished among them seven days.

• The feast of tabernacles lasted.

Le 23:34 — Speak unto the children of Israel, saying, The fifteenth day of this seventh month *shall be* the feast of tabernacles *for* seven days unto the LORD.

Le 23:42 — Ye shall dwell in booths seven days; all that are Israelites born shall dwell in booths:

• Consecration of priests and altars lasted.

Eze 43:25–26

Ex 29:30 — *And* that son that is priest in his stead shall put them on seven days, when he cometh into the tabernacle of the congregation to minister in the holy *place.*

Ex 29:35 — And thus shalt thou do unto Aaron, and to his sons, according to all *things* which I have commanded thee: seven days shalt thou consecrate them.

• Defilements lasted.

Le 12:2 — Speak unto the children of Israel, saying, If a woman have conceived seed, and born a man child: then she shall be unclean seven days; according to the days of the separation for her infirmity shall she be unclean.

Le 13:4 — If the bright spot *be* white in the skin of his flesh, and in sight *be* not deeper than the skin, and the hair thereof be not turned white; then the priest shall shut up *him that hath* the plague seven days:

- **Fasts of.**

1Sa 31:13 — And they took their bones, and buried *them* under a tree at Jabesh, and fasted seven days.

2Sa 12:16 — David therefore besought God for the child; and David fasted, and went in, and lay all night upon the earth.

2Sa 12:18 — And it came to pass on the seventh day, that the child died. And the servants of David feared to tell him that the child was dead: for they said, Behold, while the child was yet alive, we spake unto him, and he would not hearken unto our voice: how will he then vex himself, if we tell him that the child is dead?

2Sa 12:22 — And he said, While the child was yet alive, I fasted and wept: for I said, Who can tell *whether* GOD will be gracious to me, that the child may live?

- **The firstborn of flocks and sheep shall remain with mother, before being offered.**

Ex 22:30 — Likewise shalt thou do with thine oxen, *and* with thy sheep: seven days it shall be with his dam; on the eighth day thou shalt give it me.

- **The feast of Ahasuerus continued.**

Est 1:5 — And when these days were expired, the king made a feast unto all the people that were present in Shushan the palace, both unto great and small, seven days, in the court of the garden of the king's palace;

- **Paul tarries at Tyre.**

Ac 21:4 — And finding disciples, we tarried there seven days: who said to Paul through the Spirit, that he should not go up to Jerusalem.

- **Paul tarries at Puteoli.**

Ac 28:14 — Where we found brethren, and were desired to tarry with them seven days: and so we went toward Rome.

- **Weeks.**

- **In Daniel's vision concerning the coming of the Messiah.**

Da 9:25 — Know therefore and understand, *that* from the going forth of the commandment to restore and to build Jerusalem unto the Messiah the Prince *shall be* seven weeks, and threescore and two weeks: the street shall be built again, and the wall, even in troublous times.

- **Ten times.**

Da 9:24 — Seventy weeks are determined upon thy people and upon thy holy city, to finish the transgression, and to make an end of sins, and to make reconciliation for iniquity, and to bring in everlasting righteousness, and to seal up the vision and prophecy, and to anoint the most Holy.

- **The period between the Passover and the Pentecost.**

Le 23:15 — And ye shall count unto you from the morrow after the sabbath, from the day that ye brought the sheaf of the wave offering; seven sabbaths shall be complete:

- **Months.**

- **Holy convocations in the seventh month.**

Le 23:24–44; Nu 29:1–40

Eze 45:25 — In the seventh *month,* in the fifteenth day of the month, shall he do the like in the feast of the seven days, according to the sin offering, according to the burnt offering, and according to the meat offering, and according to the oil.

- **Years.**

- **Jacob serves for each of his wives.**

Ge 29:15–30

- **Of plenty.**

Ge 41:1–32

Ge 41:53 — And the seven years of plenteousness, that was in the land of Egypt, were ended.

- **Famine lasted in Egypt.**

Ge 41:1–32, 54–56

- **Famine lasted in Canaan.**

2Sa 24:13 — So Gad came to David, and told him, and said unto him, Shall seven years of famine come unto thee in thy land? or wilt thou flee three months before thine enemies, while they pursue thee? or that there be three days' pestilence in thy land? now advise, and see what answer I shall return to him that sent me.

2Ki 8:1 — Then spake Elisha unto the woman, whose son he had restored to life, saying, Arise, and go thou and thine household, and sojourn wheresoever thou canst sojourn: for the LORD hath called for a famine; and it shall also come upon the land seven years.

- **Insanity of Nebuchadnezzar.**

Da 4:32 — And they shall drive thee from men, and thy dwelling *shall be* with the beasts of the field: they shall make thee to eat grass as oxen, and seven times shall pass over thee, until thou know that the most High ruleth in the kingdom of men, and giveth it to whomsoever he will.

- **Seven times, the period between the jubilees.**

Le 25:8 — And thou shalt number seven sabbaths of years unto thee, seven times seven years; and the space of the seven sabbaths of years shall be unto thee forty and nine years.

- **Miscellany of sevens.**

- **Of clean beasts taken into the ark.**

Ge 7:2 — Of every clean beast thou shalt take to thee by sevens, the male and his female: and of beasts that *are* not clean by two, the male and his female.

• Abraham gives Abimelech seven lambs.

Ge 21:28 — And Abraham set seven ewe lambs of the flock by themselves.

• Rams and bullocks to the number of, required in sacrifices.

Le 23:18 — And ye shall offer with the bread seven lambs without blemish of the first year, and one young bullock, and two rams: they shall be *for* a burnt offering unto the LORD, with their meat offering, and their drink offerings, *even* an offering made by fire, of sweet savour unto the LORD.

Nu 23:1 — And Balaam said unto Balak, Build me here seven altars, and prepare me here seven oxen and seven rams.

Nu 29:32 — And on the seventh day seven bullocks, two rams, *and* fourteen lambs of the first year without blemish:

1Ch 15:26 — And it came to pass, when God helped the Levites that bare the ark of the covenant of the LORD, that they offered seven bullocks and seven rams.

Eze 45:23 — And seven days of the feast he shall prepare a burnt offering to the LORD, seven bullocks and seven rams without blemish daily the seven days; and a kid of the goats daily *for* a sin offering.

• Blood sprinkling seven times.

Le 4:6 — And the priest shall dip his finger in the blood, and sprinkle of the blood seven times before the LORD, before the vail of the sanctuary.

Le 14:7 — And he shall sprinkle upon him that is to be cleansed from the leprosy seven times, and shall pronounce him clean, and shall let the living bird loose into the open field.

• Oil sprinkling seven times.

Le 14:16 — And the priest shall dip his right finger in the oil that *is* in his left hand, and shall sprinkle of the oil with his finger seven times before the LORD:

• Seven kine and seven ears of corn in Pharaoh's vision.

Ge 41:2–7

• The Israelites compassed Jericho seven times, on the seventh day sounding seven trumpets.

Jos 6:4 — And seven priests shall bear before the ark seven trumpets of rams' horns: and the seventh day ye shall compass the city seven times, and the priests shall blow with the trumpets.

• Elisha's servant looked seven times for appearance of rain.

1Ki 18:43 — And said to his servant, Go up now, look toward the sea. And he went up, and looked, and said, *There is* nothing. And he said, Go again seven times.

• Naaman required to wash in Jordan seven times.

2Ki 5:10 — And Elisha sent a messenger unto him, saying, Go and wash in the Jordan seven times, and thy flesh shall come again to thee, and thou shalt be clean.

• Seven steps in the temple seen in Ezekiel's vision.

Eze 40:22 — And their windows, and their arches, and their palm trees, *were* after the measure of the gate that looketh toward the east; and they went up unto it by seven steps; and the arches thereof *were* before them.

Eze 40:26 — And *there were* seven steps to go up to it, and the arches thereof *were* before them: and it had palm trees, one on this side, and another on that side, upon the posts thereof.

• The heat of Nebuchadnezzar's furnace intensified sevenfold.

Da 3:19 — Then was Nebuchadnezzar full of fury, and the form of his visage was changed against Shadrach, Meshach, and Abed-nego: *therefore* he spake, and commanded that they should heat the furnace one seven times more than it was wont to be heated.

• The light of the sun intensified sevenfold.

Isa 30:26 — Moreover the light of the moon shall be as the light of the sun, and the light of the sun shall be sevenfold, as the light of seven days, in the day that the LORD bindeth up the breach of his people, and healeth the stroke of their wound.

• The threatened sevenfold punishment of Israel.

Le 26:18–21

• Silver purified seven times.

Ps 12:6 — The words of the LORD *are* pure words: *as* silver tried in a furnace of earth, purified seven times.

• Worshiping seven times a day.

Ps 119:164 — Seven times a day do I praise thee because of thy righteous judgments.

• Seven chamberlains at the court of Ahasuerus.

Est 1:10 — On the seventh day, when the heart of the king was merry with wine, he commanded Mehuman, Biztha, Harbona, Bigtha, and Abagtha, Zethar, and Carcas, the seven chamberlains that served in the presence of Ahasuerus the king,

• Seven princes at the court of Ahasuerus.

Est 1:14 — And the next unto him *was* Carshena, Shethar, Admatha, Tarshish, Meres, Marsena, *and* Memucan, the seven princes of Persia and Media, which saw the king's face, *and* which sat the first in the kingdom;)

• Seven counsellors at the court of Artaxerxes.

Ezr 7:14 — Forasmuch as thou art sent of the king, and of his seven counsellors, to enquire concerning Judah and Jerusalem, according to the law of thy God which *is* in thine hand;

- **Seven maidens given to Esther.**

Est 2:9 — And the maiden pleased him, and she obtained kindness of him; and he speedily gave her her things for purification, with such things as belonged to her, and seven maidens, *which were* meet to be given her, out of the king's house: and he preferred her and her maids unto the best *place* of the house of the women.

- **Symbolic of many sons.**

Ru 4:15 — And he shall be unto thee a restorer of *thy* life, and a nourisher of thine old age: for thy daughter in law, which loveth thee, which is better to thee than seven sons, hath born him.

1Sa 2:5 — *They that were* full have hired out themselves for bread; and *they that were* hungry ceased: so that the barren hath born seven; and she that hath many children is waxed feeble.

Jer 15:9 — She that hath borne seven languisheth: she hath given up the ghost; her sun is gone down while *it was* yet day: she hath been ashamed and confounded: and the residue of them will I deliver to the sword before their enemies, saith the LORD.

- **Symbolic of liberality.**

Ecc 11:1–2

- **Seven magi.**

Pr 26:16 — The sluggard *is* wiser in his own conceit than seven men that can render a reason.

- **Seven women shall seek polygamous marriage.**

Isa 4:1 — And in that day seven women shall take hold of one man, saying, We will eat our own bread, and wear our own apparel: only let us be called by thy name, to take away our reproach.

- **Seven shepherds to be sent forth against Assyria.**

Mic 5:5–6

- **Seven lamps and pipes.**

Zec 4:2 — And said unto me, What seest thou? And I said, I have looked, and behold a candlestick all *of* gold, with a bowl upon the top of it, and his seven lamps thereon, and seven pipes to the seven lamps, which *are* upon the top thereof:

- **Seven deacons in the apostolic church.**

Ac 6:3 — Wherefore, brethren, look ye out among you seven men of honest report, full of the Holy Ghost and wisdom, whom we may appoint over this business.

- **Seven churches in Asia.**

Rev 1:4 — John to the seven churches which are in Asia: Grace *be* unto you, and peace, from him which is, and which was, and which is to come; and from the seven Spirits which are before his throne;

Rev 1:20 — The mystery of the seven stars which thou sawest in my right hand, and the seven golden candlesticks. The seven stars are the angels of the seven churches: and the seven candlesticks which thou sawest are the seven churches.

- **Seven seals.**

Rev 5:1 — And I saw in the right hand of him that sat on the throne a book written within and on the backside, sealed with seven seals.

- **Seven thunders.**

Rev 10:3 — And cried with a loud voice, as *when* a lion roareth: and when he had cried, seven thunders uttered their voices.

- **Seven heads and seven crowns.**

Rev 12:3 — And there appeared another wonder in heaven; and behold a great red dragon, having seven heads and ten horns, and seven crowns upon his heads.

Rev 13:1 — And I stood upon the sand of the sea, and saw a beast rise up out of the sea, having seven heads and ten horns, and upon his horns ten crowns, and upon his heads the name of blasphemy.

Rev 17:9 — And here *is* the mind which hath wisdom. The seven heads are seven mountains, on which the woman sitteth.

- **Seven kings.**

Rev 17:10 — And there are seven kings: five are fallen, and one is, *and* the other is not yet come; and when he cometh, he must continue a short space.

- **Seven stars.**

Am 5:8 — *Seek him* that maketh the seven stars and Orion, and turneth the shadow of death into the morning, and maketh the day dark with night: that calleth for the waters of the sea, and poureth them out upon the face of the earth: The LORD *is* his name:

Rev 1:16 — And he had in his right hand seven stars: and out of his mouth went a sharp twoedged sword: and his countenance *was* as the sun shineth in his strength.

Rev 1:20 — The mystery of the seven stars which thou sawest in my right hand, and the seven golden candlesticks. The seven stars are the angels of the seven churches: and the seven candlesticks which thou sawest are the seven churches.

Rev 3:1 — And unto the angel of the church in Sardis write; These things saith he that hath the seven Spirits of God, and the seven stars; I know thy works, that thou hast a name that thou livest, and art dead.

- **Seven spirits.**

Rev 1:4 — John to the seven churches which are in Asia: Grace *be* unto you, and peace, from him which is, and which was, and which is to come; and from the seven Spirits which are before his throne;

Rev 3:4 — Thou hast a few names even in Sardis which have not defiled their garments;

and they shall walk with me in white: for they are worthy.

Rev 4:5 — And out of the throne proceeded lightnings and thunderings and voices: and *there were* seven lamps of fire burning before the throne, which are the seven Spirits of God.

Rev 5:6 — And I beheld, and, lo, in the midst of the throne and of the four beasts, and in the midst of the elders, stood a Lamb as it had been slain, having seven horns and seven eyes, which are the seven Spirits of God sent forth into all the earth.

- **Seven eyes of the Lord.**

Zec 3:9 — For behold the stone that I have laid before Joshua; upon one stone *shall be* seven eyes: behold, I will engrave the graving thereof, saith the LORD of hosts, and I will remove the iniquity of that land in one day.

Zec 4:10 — For who hath despised the day of small things? for they shall rejoice, and shall see the plummet in the hand of Zerubbabel *with* those seven; they *are* the eyes of the LORD, which run to and fro through the whole earth.

Rev 5:6 — And I beheld, and, lo, in the midst of the throne and of the four beasts, and in the midst of the elders, stood a Lamb as it had been slain, having seven horns and seven eyes, which are the seven Spirits of God sent forth into all the earth.

- **Seven golden candlesticks.**

Rev 1:12 — And I turned to see the voice that spake with me. And being turned, I saw seven golden candlesticks;

- **Seven angels with seven trumpets.**

Rev 8:2 — And I saw the seven angels which stood before God; and to them were given seven trumpets.

- **Seven plagues.**

Rev 15:1 — And I saw another sign in heaven, great and marvellous, seven angels having the seven last plagues; for in them is filled up the wrath of God.

- **Seven horns and seven eyes.**

Rev 5:6 — And I beheld, and, lo, in the midst of the throne and of the four beasts, and in the midst of the elders, stood a Lamb as it had been slain, having seven horns and seven eyes, which are the seven Spirits of God sent forth into all the earth.

- **Seven angels with seven plagues.**

Rev 15:6 — And the seven angels came out of the temple, having the seven plagues, clothed in pure and white linen, and having their breasts girded with golden girdles.

- **Seven golden vials.**

Rev 15:7 — And one of the four beasts gave unto the seven angels seven golden vials full of the wrath of God, who liveth for ever and ever.

- **Scarlet colored beast having seven heads.**

Rev 17:3 — So he carried me away in the spirit into the wilderness: and I saw a woman sit upon a scarlet coloured beast, full of names of blasphemy, having seven heads and ten horns.

Rev 17:7 — And the angel said unto me, Wherefore didst thou marvel? I will tell thee the mystery of the woman, and of the beast that carrieth her, which hath the seven heads and ten horns.

SEVENEH

- **A city in Egypt.**
- **Called also Syene.**

Eze 29:10 — Behold, therefore I *am* against thee, and against thy rivers, and I will make the land of Egypt utterly waste *and* desolate, from the tower of Syene even unto the border of Ethiopia.

Eze 30:6 — Thus saith the LORD; They also that uphold Egypt shall fall; and the pride of her power shall come down: from the tower of Syene shall they fall in it by the sword, saith the Lord GOD.

SEVENTY

- **The Senate of the Israelites composed of seventy elders.**

Nu 11:24–25

Ex 24:1 — And he said unto Moses, Come up unto the LORD, thou, and Aaron, Nadab, and Abihu, and seventy of the elders of Israel; and worship ye afar off.

Ex 24:9 — Then went up Moses, and Aaron, Nadab, and Abihu, and seventy of the elders of Israel:

Nu 11:16 — And the LORD said unto Moses, Gather unto me seventy men of the elders of Israel, whom thou knowest to be the elders of the people, and officers over them; and bring them unto the tabernacle of the congregation, that they may stand there with thee.

- **Seventy disciples sent forth by Jesus.**

Lk 10:1–17

- **The Jews in captivity in Babylon seventy years.**

Jer 25:11–12

Jer 29:10 — For thus saith the LORD, That after seventy years be accomplished at Babylon I will visit you, and perform my good word toward you, in causing you to return to this place.

Da 9:2 — In the first year of his reign I Daniel understood by books the number of the years, whereof the word of the LORD came to Jeremiah the prophet, that he would accomplish seventy years in the desolations of Jerusalem.

Zec 1:12 — Then the angel of the LORD answered and said, O LORD of hosts, how long wilt thou not have mercy on Jerusalem and on the cities of Judah, against which thou hast had indignation these threescore and ten years?

Zec 7:5 — Speak unto all the people of the land, and to the priests, saying, When ye fasted and mourned in the fifth and seventh *month,* even those seventy years, did ye at all fast unto me, *even* to me?

See: Israel

• Seventy weeks in the vision of Daniel.

Da 9:24 — Seventy weeks are determined upon thy people and upon thy holy city, to finish the transgression, and to make an end of sins, and to make reconciliation for iniquity, and to bring in everlasting righteousness, and to seal up the vision and prophecy, and to anoint the most Holy.

SEX

Ge 2:23–25; 39:7–12; Mt 15:19–20; 1Co 6:18–7:9; Col 3:5–6

Mt 19:6 — Wherefore they are no more twain, but one flesh. What therefore God hath joined together, let not man put asunder.

Mt 19:9 — And I say unto you, Whosoever shall put away his wife, except *it be* for fornication, and shall marry another, committeth adultery: and whoso marrieth her which is put away doth commit adultery.

1Co 6:11 — And such were some of you: but ye are washed, but ye are sanctified, but ye are justified in the name of the Lord Jesus, and by the Spirit of our God.

1Co 6:13 — Meats for the belly, and the belly for meats: but God shall destroy both it and them. Now the body *is* not for fornication, but for the Lord; and the Lord for the body.

1Co 6:15 — Know ye not that your bodies are the members of Christ? shall I then take the members of Christ, and make *them* the members of an harlot? God forbid.

Eph 5:25 — Husbands, love your wives, even as Christ also loved the church, and gave himself for it;

Eph 5:28 — So ought men to love their wives as their own bodies. He that loveth his wife loveth himself.

1Ti 3:12 — Let the deacons be the husbands of one wife, ruling their children and their own houses well.

2Ti 2:22 — Flee also youthful lusts: but follow righteousness, faith, charity, peace, with them that call on the Lord out of a pure heart.

Heb 13:4 — Marriage *is* honourable in all, and the bed undefiled: but whoremongers and adulterers God will judge.

SHAALABBIN ➜See: Shaalbim

SHAALBIM

• A city of Dan.

Jos 19:42 — And Shaalabbin, and Ajalon, and Jethlah,

Jgs 1:35 — But the Amorites would dwell in mount Heres in Aijalon, and in Shaalbim: yet the hand of the house of Joseph prevailed, so that they became tributaries.

• One of Solomon's commissary cities.

1Ki 4:9 — The son of Dekar, in Makaz, and in Shaalbim, and Beth-shemesh, and Elon-beth-hanan:

• Called Shaalabbin.

Jos 19:42 — And Shaalabbin, and Ajalon, and Jethlah,

SHAAPH

• Son of Jahdai.

1Ch 2:47 — And the sons of Jahdai; Regem, and Jotham, and Gesham, and Pelet, and Ephah, and Shaaph.

• Son of Caleb.

1Ch 2:49 — She bare also Shaaph the father of Madmannah, Sheva the father of Machbenah, and the father of Gibea: and the daughter of Caleb *was* Achsa.

SHAARAIM

• A city of Judah, called also Sharaim.

Jos 15:36 — And Sharaim, and Adithaim, and Gederah, and Gederothaim; fourteen cities with their villages:

1Sa 17:52 — And the men of Israel and of Judah arose, and shouted, and pursued the Philistines, until thou come to the valley, and to the gates of Ekron. And the wounded of the Philistines fell down by the way to Shaaraim, even unto Gath, and unto Ekron.

• A city of Simeon.

1Ch 4:31 — And at Beth-marcaboth, and Hazar-susim, and at Beth-birei, and at Shaaraim. These *were* their cities unto the reign of David.

SHAASHGAZ • A chamberlain of Ahasuerus.

Est 2:14 — In the evening she went, and on the morrow she returned into the second house of the women, to the custody of Shaashgaz, the king's chamberlain, which kept the concubines: she came in unto the king no more, except the king delighted in her, and that she were called by name.

SHABBETHAI

• A Levite.

• Assistant to Ezra.

Ezr 10:15 — Only Jonathan the son of Asahel and Jahaziah the son of Tikvah were employed about this *matter:* and Meshullam and Shabbethai the Levite helped them.

• An expounder of the law.

Ne 8:7 — Also Jeshua, and Bani, and Sherebiah, Jamin, Akkub, Shabbethai, Hodijah, Maaseiah, Kelita, Azariah, Jozabad, Hanan, Pelaiah, and the Levites, caused the people to understand the law: and the people *stood* in their place.

• A chief Levite.

• Attendant of the temple.

Ne 11:16 — And Shabbethai and Jozabad, of the chief of the Levites, *had* the oversight of the outward business of the house of God.

SHACHIA • Son of Shaharaim.

1Ch 8:10 — And Jeuz, and Shachia, and Mirma. These *were* his sons, heads of the fathers.

SHADRACH

• Called also Hananiah.

• A Hebrew captive in Babylon.

Da 1:1–21; 2:49–3:30

Da 2:17 — Then Daniel went to his house, and made the thing known to Hananiah, Mishael, and Azariah, his companions:

SHAGE • Father of Jonathan, one of David's guard.

1Ch 11:34 — The sons of Hashem the Gizonite, Jonathan the son of Shage the Hararite,

SHAHARAIM • A Benjamite.

1Ch 8:8 — And Shaharaim begat *children* in the country of Moab, after he had sent them away; Hushim and Baara *were* his wives.

SHAHAZIMAH • A city in Issachar.

Jos 19:22 — And the coast reacheth to Tabor, and Shahazimah, and Beth-shemesh; and the outgoings of their border were at Jordan: sixteen cities with their villages.

SHALEM

- **A city in Shechem.**
- **Translated "in peace".**

Ge 33:18 — And Jacob came to Shalem, a city of Shechem, which *is* in the land of Canaan, when he came from Padan-aram; and pitched his tent before the city.

SHALIM • A district of unknown location.

1Sa 9:4 — And he passed through mount Ephraim, and passed through the land of Shalisha, but they found *them* not: then they passed through the land of Shalim, and *there they were* not: and he passed through the land of the Benjamites, but they found *them* not.

SHALISHA • A district bordering on Mount Ephraim.

1Sa 9:4 — And he passed through mount Ephraim, and passed through the land of Shalisha, but they found *them* not: then they passed through the land of Shalim, and *there they were* not: and he passed through the land of the Benjamites, but they found *them* not.

SHALLECHETH • One of the gates of the temple.

1Ch 26:16 — To Shuppim and Hosah *the lot came forth* westward, with the gate Shallecheth, by the causeway of the going up, ward against ward.

SHALLUM

• King of Israel.

2Ki 15:13–15

2Ki 15:10 — And Shallum the son of Jabesh conspired against him, and smote him before the people, and slew him, and reigned in his stead.

• Husband of Huldah, the prophetess.

2Ki 22:14 — So Hilkiah the priest, and Ahikam, and Achbor, and Shaphan, and Asahiah, went unto Huldah the prophetess, the wife of Shallum the son of Tikvah, the son of Harhas, keeper of the wardrobe; (now she dwelt in Jerusalem in the college;) and they communed with her.

2Ch 34:22 — And Hilkiah, and *they* that the king *had appointed,* went to Huldah the prophetess, the wife of Shallum the son of Tikvath, the son of Hasrah, keeper of the wardrobe; (now she dwelt in Jerusalem in the college:) and they spake to her to that *effect.*

• Son of Sisamai.

1Ch 2:40–41

✦See: Jehoahaz; called also Shallum. King of Judah, and successor of Josiah

• Grandson of Simeon.

1Ch 4:25 — Shallum his son, Mibsam his son, Mishma his son.

• Son of Zadok.

1Ch 6:12–13

Ezr 7:2 — The son of Shallum, the son of Zadok, the son of Ahitub,

• Called Meshullam.

1Ch 9:11 — And Azariah the son of Hilkiah, the son of Meshullam, the son of Zadok, the son of Meraioth, the son of Ahitub, the ruler of the house of God;

Ne 11:11 — Seraiah the son of Hilkiah, the son of Meshullam, the son of Zadok, the son of Meraioth, the son of Ahitub, *was* the ruler of the house of God.

✦See: Shillem

• A chief porter of the temple.

1Ch 9:17 — And the porters *were,* Shallum, and Akkub, and Talmon, and Ahiman, and their brethren: Shallum *was* the chief;

1Ch 9:19 — And Shallum the son of Kore, the son of Ebiasaph, the son of Korah, and his brethren, of the house of his father, the Korahites, *were* over the work of the service, keepers of the gates of the tabernacle: and their fathers, *being* over the host of the LORD, *were* keepers of the entry.

1Ch 9:31 — And Mattithiah, *one* of the Levites, who *was* the firstborn of Shallum the Korahite, had the set office over the things that were made in the pans.

• Father of Jehizkiah.

2Ch 28:12 — Then certain of the heads of the children of Ephraim, Azariah the son of Johanan, Berechiah the son of Meshillemoth, and Jehizkiah the son of Shallum, and Amasa the son of Hadlai, stood up against them that came from the war,

• The ancestor of a family of returned exiles.

Ezr 2:42 — The children of the porters: the children of Shallum, the children of Ater, the children of Talmon, the children of Akkub, the children of Hatita, the children of Shobai, *in* all an hundred thirty and nine.

Ne 7:45 — The porters: the children of Shallum, the children of Ater, the children of Talmon, the children of Akkub, the children of Hatita, the children of Shobai, an hundred thirty and eight.

• A porter who put away his wife.

Ezr 10:24 — Of the singers also; Eliashib: and of the porters; Shallum, and Telem, and Uri.

• A son of Bani, who put away his wife.

Ezr 10:42 — Shallum, Amariah, *and* Joseph.

• A Jew who repaired a portion of the wall of Jerusalem.

Ne 3:12 — And next unto him repaired Shallum the son of Halohesh, the ruler of the half part of Jerusalem, he and his daughters.

• Uncle of Jeremiah.

Jer 32:7 — Behold, Hanameel the son of Shallum thine uncle shall come unto thee, saying, Buy thee my field that *is* in Anathoth: for the right of redemption *is* thine to buy *it.*

• Father of Maaseiah.

Jer 35:4 — And I brought them into the house of the LORD, into the chamber of the sons of Hanan, the son of Igdaliah, a man of God, which *was* by the chamber of the princes, which *was* above the chamber of Maaseiah the son of Shallum, the keeper of the door:

SHALLUN • A Jew who repaired a gate of Jerusalem.

Ne 3:15 — But the gate of the fountain repaired Shallun the son of Col-hozeh, the ruler of part of Mizpah; he built it, and covered it, and set up the doors thereof, the locks thereof, and the bars thereof, and the wall of the pool of Siloah by the king's garden, and unto the stairs that go down from the city of David.

SHALMAI • One of the Nethinim.

Ezr 2:46 — The children of Hagab, the children of Shalmai, the children of Hanan,

Ne 7:48 — The children of Lebana, the children of Hagaba, the children of Shalmai,

SHALMAN

• Identified by some authorities with Shahnaneser.

Hos 10:14 — Therefore shall a tumult arise among thy people, and all thy fortresses shall be spoiled, as Shalman spoiled Beth-arbel in the day of battle: the mother was dashed in pieces upon *her* children.

• Other authorities disagree, and leave his identity uncertain.

SHALMANESER

• King of Assyria.

• Overthrows the kingdom of Israel.

2Ki 17:3–6; 18:9–11

SHAMA • One of David's heroes.

1Ch 11:44 — Uzzia the Ashterathite, Shama and Jehiel the sons of Hothan the Aroerite,

SHAMARIAH • Son of Rehoboam.

2Ch 11:19 — Which bare him children; Jeush, and Shamariah, and Zaham.

SHAME

• Jesus ashamed of those who deny him.

Mk 8:38 — Whosoever therefore shall be ashamed of me and of my words in this adulterous and sinful generation; of him also shall the Son of man be ashamed, when he cometh in the glory of his Father with the holy angels.

Lk 9:26 — For whosoever shall be ashamed of me and of my words, of him shall the Son of man be ashamed, when he shall come in his own glory, and *in his* Father's, and of the holy angels.

• Of Adam and Eve.

Ge 3:10 — And he said, I heard thy voice in the garden, and I was afraid, because I *was* naked; and I hid myself.

• Destitute of, the Israelites when they worshiped the golden calf.

Ex 32:25 — And when Moses saw that the people *were* naked; (for Aaron had made them naked unto *their* shame among their enemies:)

• Destitute of, the unjust.

Zep 3:5 — The just LORD *is* in the midst thereof; he will not do iniquity: every morning doth he bring his judgment to light, he faileth not; but the unjust knoweth no shame.

• Of the cross.

Heb 12:2 — Looking unto Jesus the author and finisher of *our* faith; who for the joy that was set before him endured the cross, despising the shame, and is set down at the right hand of the throne of God.

SHAMER

• A Levite.

• Father of Bani.

1Ch 6:46 — The son of Amzi, the son of Bani, the son of Shamer,

• An Asherite.

1Ch 7:34 — And the sons of Shamer; Ahi, and Rohgah, Jehubbah, and Aram.

• Son of Heber. Called Shomer.

1Ch 7:32 — And Heber begat Japhlet, and Shomer, and Hotham, and Shua their sister.

SHAMGAR • A deliverer of Israel.

Jgs 3:31 — And after him was Shamgar the son of Anath, which slew of the Philistines six hundred men with an ox goad: and he also delivered Israel.

Jgs 5:6 — In the days of Shamgar the son of Anath, in the days of Jael, the highways were unoccupied, and the travelers walked through byways.

SHAMHUTH • One of David's captains.

1Ch 27:8 — The fifth captain for the fifth month *was* Shamhuth the Izrahite: and in his course *were* twenty and four thousand.

SHAMIR

• A city in the mountains of Judah.

Jos 15:48 — And in the mountains, Shamir, and Jattir, and Socoh,

• A city in Mount Ephraim. Home and burial place of Tola, the judge.

Jgs 10:1–2

• A Levite.

• Son of Michah.

1Ch 24:24 — *Of* the sons of Uzziel; Michah: of the sons of Michah; Shamir.

SHAMMA • Son of Zophah, an Asherite.

1Ch 7:37 — Bezer, and Hod, and Shamma and Shilshah, and Ithran, and Beera.

SHAMMAH

• Son of Reuel.

Ge 36:13 — And these *are* the sons of Reuel; Nahath, and Zerah, Shammah, and Mizzah: these were the sons of Bashemath Esau's wife.

Ge 36:17 — And these *are* the sons of Reuel Esau's son; duke Nahath, duke Zerah, duke Shammah, duke Mizzah: these *are* the dukes *that came* of Reuel in the land of Edom; these *are* the sons of Bashemath Esau's wife.

1Ch 1:37 — The sons of Reuel; Nahath, Zerah, Shammah, and Mizzah.

• David's brother.

1Sa 16:9 — Then Jesse made Shammah to pass by. And he said, Neither hath the LORD chosen this.

1Sa 17:13 — And the three eldest sons of Jesse went *and* followed Saul to the battle: and the names of his three sons that went to the battle *were* Eliab the first born, and next unto him Abinadab, and the third Shammah.

• Called Shimeah.

2Sa 13:3 — But Amnon had a friend, whose name *was* Jonadab, the son of Shimeah David's brother: and Jonadab *was* a very subtil man.

2Sa 13:32 — And Jonadab, the son of Shimeah David's brother, answered and said, Let not my lord suppose *that* they have slain all the young men the king's sons; for Amnon only is dead: for by the appointment of Absalom this hath been determined from the day that he forced his sister Tamar.

2Sa 21:21 — And when he defied Israel, Jonathan the son of Shimeah the brother of David slew him.

• Called Shimma.

1Ch 2:13 — And Jesse begat his firstborn Eliab, and Abinadab the second, and Shimma the third,

• Called Shimea.

1Ch 20:7 — But when he defied Israel, Jonathan the son of Shimea David's brother slew him.

• One of David's mighty men.

• Son of Agee.

2Sa 23:11–12

• One of David's mighty men.

2Sa 23:25 — Shammah the Harodite, Elika the Harodite,

• Called Shammoth.

1Ch 11:27 — Shammoth the Harorite, Helez the Pelonite,

• One of David's mighty men.

• A Hararite.

2Sa 23:33 — Shammah the Hararite, Ahiam the son of Sharar the Hararite,

SHAMMAI

• Son of Onam.

1Ch 2:28 — And the sons of Onam were, Shammai, and Jada. And the sons of Shammai; Nadab, and Abishur.

1Ch 2:32 — And the sons of Jada the brother of Shammai; Jether and Jonathan: and Jether died without children.

• Father of Maon.

1Ch 2:44–45

• Son of Ezra.

1Ch 4:17 — And the sons of Ezra *were*, Jether, and Mered, and Epher, and Jalon: and she bare Miriam, and Shammai, and Ishbah the father of Eshtemoa.

SHAMMOTH

• One of David's mighty men.

1Ch 11:27 — Shammoth the Harorite, Helez the Pelonite,

• Called Shammah.

2Sa 23:25 — Shammah the Harodite, Elika the Harodite,

SHAMMUA

• The representative of Reuben among the twelve spies sent into Canaan.

Nu 13:4 — And these *were* their names: of the tribe of Reuben, Shammua the son of Zaccur.

See: Shammuah

• A Levite.

• Father of Abda.

Ne 11:17 — And Mattaniah the son of Micha, the son of Zabdi, the son of Asaph, *was* the principal to begin the thanksgiving in prayer: and Bakbukiah the second among his brethren, and Abda the son of Shammua, the son of Galal, the son of Jeduthun.

• Called Shemaiah.

1Ch 9:16 — And Obadiah the son of Shemaiah, the son of Galal, the son of Jeduthun, and Berechiah the son of Asa, the son of Elkanah, that dwelt in the villages of the Netophathites.

• A priest.

Ne 12:18 — Of Bilgah, Shammua; of Shemaiah, Jehonathan;

SHAMMUAH

• Son of David.

2Sa 5:14 — And these *be* the names of those that were born unto him in Jerusalem; Shammuah, and Shobab, and Nathan, and Solomon,

• **Called Shimea.**

1Ch 3:5 — And these were born unto him in Jerusalem; Shimea, and Shobab, and Nathan, and Solomon, four, of Bath-shua the daughter of Ammiel:

• **Called Shammua.**

1Ch 14:4 — Now these *are* the names of *his* children which he had in Jerusalem; Shammua, and Shobab, Nathan, and Solomon,

SHAMSHERAI • Son of Jeroham.

1Ch 8:26 — And Shamsherai, and Shehariah, and Athaliah,

SHAPHAM • Chief of Gad.

1Ch 5:12 — Joel the chief, and Shapham the next, and Jaanai, and Shaphat in Bashan.

SHAPHAN

• **A scribe of king Josiah.**

2Ki 22:3–14; 2Ch 34:8–20

• **Father of Gemariah.**

Jer 36:10–12

• **Father of Ahikam and grandfather of Gedaliah.**

2Ki 22:12 — And the king commanded Hilkiah the priest, and Ahikam the son of Shaphan, and Achbor the son of Michaiah, and Shaphan the scribe, and Asahiah a servant of the king's, saying,

2Ki 25:22 — And *as for* the people that remained in the land of Judah, whom Nebuchadnezzar king of Babylon had left, even over them he made Gedaliah the son of Ahikam, the son of Shaphan, ruler.

2Ch 34:20 — And the king commanded Hilkiah, and Ahikam the son of Shaphan, and Abdon the son of Micah, and Shaphan the scribe, and Asaiah a servant of the king's, saying,

Jer 26:24 — Nevertheless the hand of Ahikam the son of Shaphan was with Jeremiah, that they should not give him into the hand of the people to put him to death.

Jer 39:14 — Even they sent, and took Jeremiah out of the court of the prison, and committed him unto Gedaliah the son of Ahikam the son of Shaphan, that he should carry him home: so he dwelt among the people.

Jer 40:5 — Now while he was not yet gone back, *he said,* Go back also to Gedaliah the son of Ahikam the son of Shaphan, whom the king of Babylon hath made governor over the cities of Judah, and dwell with him among the people: or go wheresoever it seemeth convenient unto thee to go. So the captain of the guard gave him victuals and a reward, and let him go.

Jer 40:9 — And Gedaliah the son of Ahikam the son of Shaphan sware unto them and to their men, saying, Fear not to serve the Chaldeans: dwell in the land, and serve the king of Babylon, and it shall be well with you.

Jer 40:11 — Likewise when all the Jews that *were* in Moab, and among the Ammonites, and in Edom, and that *were* in all the countries, heard that the king of Babylon had left a remnant of Judah, and that he had set over them Gedaliah the son of Ahikam the son of Shaphan;

Jer 41:2 — Then arose Ishmael the son of Nethaniah, and the ten men that were with him, and smote Gedaliah the son of Ahikam the son of Shaphan with the sword, and slew him, whom the king of Babylon had made governor over the land.

Jer 43:6 — *Even* men, and women, and children, and the king's daughters, and every person that Nebuzar-adan the captain of the guard had left with Gedaliah the son of Ahikam the son of Shaphan, and Jeremiah the prophet, and Baruch the son of Neriah.

• **Father of Elasah.**

Jer 29:3 — By the hand of Elasah the son of Shaphan, and Gemariah the son of Hilkiah, (whom Zedekiah king of Judah sent unto Babylon to Nebuchadnezzar king of Babylon) saying,

• **Father of Jaazaniah.**

Eze 8:11 — And there stood before them seventy men of the ancients of the house of Israel, and in the midst of them stood Jaazaniah the son of Shaphan, with every man his censer in his hand; and a thick cloud of incense went up.

SHAPHAT

• **The representative of Simeon among the spies sent into Canaan.**

Nu 13:5 — Of the tribe of Simeon, Shaphat the son of Hori.

• **Father of Elisha.**

1Ki 19:16 — And Jehu the son of Nimshi shalt thou anoint *to be* king over Israel: and Elisha the son of Shaphat of Abel-meholah shalt thou anoint *to be* prophet in thy room.

1Ki 19:19 — So he departed thence, and found Elisha the son of Shaphat, who *was* plowing *with* twelve yoke *of oxen* before him, and he with the twelfth: and Elijah passed by him, and cast his mantle upon him.

2Ki 3:11 — But Jehoshaphat said, *Is there* not here a prophet of the LORD, that we may enquire of the LORD by him? And one of the king of Israel's servants answered and said, Here *is* Elisha the son of Shaphat, which poured water on the hands of Elijah.

2Ki 6:31 — Then he said, God do so and more also to me, if the head of Elisha the son of Shaphat shall stand on him this day.

• **Son of Shemaiah.**

1Ch 3:22 — And the sons of Shechaniah; Shemaiah; and the sons of Shemaiah; Hattush, and Igeal, and Bariah, and Neariah, and Shaphat, six.

• **A Gadite.**

1Ch 5:12 — Joel the chief, and Shapham the next, and Jaanai, and Shaphat in Bashan.

• **Son of Adlai.**

1Ch 27:29 — And over the herds that fed in Sharon *was* Shitrai the Sharonite: and over the herds *that were* in the valleys *was* Shaphat the son of Adlai:

SHAPHER

• A mountain.

• Camping place of the Israelites in the desert.

Nu 33:23–24

SHARAI • A descendant of Bani, who put away his Gentile wife.

Ezr 10:40 — Machnadebai, Shashai, Sharai,

SHARAIM ✦See: Shaaraim

SHARAR

• Father of Ahiam.

2Sa 23:33 — Shammah the Hararite, Ahiam the son of Sharar the Hararite,

• Called Sacar.

1Ch 11:35 — Ahiam the son of Sacar the Hararite, Eliphal the son of Ur,

SHAREZER

• Son of Sennacherib.

2Ki 19:37 — And it came to pass, as he was worshipping in the house of Nisroch his god, that Adrammelech and Sharezer his sons smote him with the sword: and they escaped into the land of Armenia. And Esar-haddon his son reigned in his stead.

Isa 37:38 — And it came to pass, as he was worshipping in the house of Nisroch his god, that Adrammelech and Sharezer his sons smote him with the sword; and they escaped into the land of Armenia: and Esar-haddon his son reigned in his stead.

• A delegate to priests and prophets to consult as to a day of humiliation.

Zec 7:2 — When they had sent unto the house of God Sherezer and Regem-melech, and their men, to pray before the LORD,

SHARON

• The maritime slope of Palestine north of Joppa.

• David's herds in.

1Ch 27:29 — And over the herds that fed in Sharon *was* Shitrai the Sharonite: and over the herds *that were* in the valleys *was* Shaphat the son of Adlai:

• Roses and beauty of.

SS 2:1 — I *am* the rose of Sharon, *and* the lily of the valleys.

Isa 33:9 — The earth mourneth *and* languisheth: Lebanon is ashamed *and* hewn down: Sharon is like a wilderness; and Bashan and Carmel shake off *their fruits*.

Isa 35:2 — It shall blossom abundantly, and rejoice even with joy and singing: the glory of Lebanon shall be given unto it, the excellency of Carmel and Sharon, they shall see the glory of the LORD, *and* the excellency of our God.

Isa 65:10 — And Sharon shall be a fold of flocks, and the valley of Achor a place for the herds to lie down in, for my people that have sought me.

• Called Saron.

Ac 9:35 — And all that dwelt at Lydda and Saron saw him, and turned to the Lord.

• A place of unascertained location.

1Ch 5:16 — And they dwelt in Gilead in Bashan, and in her towns, and in all the suburbs of Sharon, upon their borders.

SHARUHEN • A city in Simeon.

Jos 19:6 — And Beth-lebaoth, and Sharuhen; thirteen cities and their villages:

SHASHAI • A descendant of Bani, who put away his Gentile wife.

Ezr 10:40 — Machnadebai, Shashai, Sharai,

SHASHAK • A Benjamite.

1Ch 8:14 — And Ahio, Shashak, and Jeremoth,

1Ch 8:25 — And Iphedeiah, and Penuel, the sons of Shashak;

SHAUL

• Son of Simeon.

Ge 46:10 — And the sons of Simeon; Jemuel, and Jamin, and Ohad, and Jachin, and Zohar, and Shaul the son of a Canaanitish woman.

Ex 6:15 — And the sons of Simeon; Jemuel, and Jamin, and Ohad, and Jachin, and Zohar, and Shaul the son of a Canaanitish woman: these *are* the families of Simeon.

Nu 26:13 — Of Zerah, the family of the Zarhites: of Shaul, the family of the Shaulites.

1Ch 4:24 — The sons of Simeon *were*, Nemuel, and Jamin, Jarib, Zerah, *and* Shaul:

• An ancient king of Edom.

1Ch 1:48–49

• Called Saul.

Ge 36:37 — And Samlah died, and Saul of Rehoboth *by* the river reigned in his stead.

• Son of Uzziah.

1Ch 6:24 — Tahath his son, Uriel his son, Uzziah his son, and Shaul his son.

SHAVEH

• A valley.

• Called also "the king's dale".

Ge 14:17 — And the king of Sodom went out to meet him after his return from the slaughter of Chedorlaomer, and of the kings that *were* with him, at the valley of Shaveh, which *is* the king's dale.

• Absalom's pillar in.

2Sa 18:18 — Now Absalom in his lifetime had taken and reared up for himself a pillar, which *is* in the king's dale: for he said, I have no son to keep my name in remembrance: and he called the pillar after his own name: and it is called unto this day, Absalom's place.

SHAVEH KIRIATHAIM • A valley in Moab.

Ge 14:5 — And in the fourteenth year came Chedorlaomer, and the kings that *were* with him, and smote the Rephaims in Ashteroth Karnaim, and the Zuzims in Ham, and the Emims in Shaveh Kiriathaim,

SHAVING

• Forbidden to Nazarites.

Nu 6:5 — All the days of the vow of his separation there shall no razor come upon his head: until the days be fulfilled, in the which he separateth *himself* unto the LORD, he shall be holy, *and* shall let the locks of the hair of his head grow.

Jgs 13:5 — For, lo, thou shalt conceive, and bear a son; and no razor shall come on his head: for the child shall be a Nazarite unto God from the womb: and he shall begin to deliver Israel out of the hand of the Philistines.

• Forbidden to priests.

Eze 44:20 — Neither shall they shave their heads, nor suffer their locks to grow long; they shall only poll their heads.

See: Beard

SHAVSHA

See: Seraiah; called also Sheva, Shisha, and Shavsha. David's scribe

SHEAL • A descendant of Bani, who put away his Gentile wife.

Ezr 10:29 — And of the sons of Bani; Meshullam, Malluch, and Adaiah, Jashub, and Sheal, and Ramoth.

SHEALTIEL

• Called also Salathiel.

• Father of Zerubbabel and ancestor of Jesus.

1Ch 3:17 — And the sons of Jeconiah; Assir, Salathiel his son,

Ezr 3:2 — Then stood up Jeshua the son of Jozadak, and his brethren the priests, and Zerubbabel the son of Shealtiel, and his brethren, and builded the altar of the God of Israel, to offer burnt offerings thereon, as *it is* written in the law of Moses the man of God.

Ezr 3:8 — Now in the second year of their coming unto the house of God at Jerusalem, in the second month, began Zerubbabel the son of Shealtiel, and Jeshua the son of Jozadak, and the remnant of their brethren the priests and the Levites, and all they that were come out of the captivity unto Jerusalem; and appointed the Levites, from twenty years old and upward, to set forward the work of the house of the LORD.

Ezr 5:2 — Then rose up Zerubbabel the son of Shealtiel, and Jeshua the son of Jozadak, and began to build the house of God which *is* at Jerusalem: and with them *were* the prophets of God helping them.

Ne 12:1 — Now these *are* the priests and the Levites that went up with Zerubbabel the son of Shealtiel, and Jeshua: Seraiah, Jeremiah, Ezra,

Hag 1:1 — In the second year of Darius the king, in the sixth month, in the first day of the month, came the word of the LORD by Haggai the prophet unto Zerubbabel the son of Shealtiel, governor of Judah, and to Joshua the son of Josedech, the high priest, saying,

Hag 1:12 — Then Zerubbabel the son of Shealtiel, and Joshua the son of Josedech, the high priest, with all the remnant of the people, obeyed the voice of the LORD their God, and the words of Haggai the prophet, as the LORD their God had sent him, and the people did fear before the LORD.

Hag 1:14 — And the LORD stirred up the spirit of Zerubbabel the son of Shealtiel, governor of Judah, and the spirit of Joshua the son of Josedech, the high priest, and the spirit of all the remnant of the people; and they came and did work in the house of the LORD of hosts, their God,

Hag 2:2 — Speak now to Zerubbabel the son of Shealtiel, governor of Judah, and to Joshua the son of Josedech, the high priest, and to the residue of the people, saying,

Hag 2:23 — In that day, saith the LORD of hosts, will I take thee, O Zerubbabel, my servant, the son of Shealtiel, saith the LORD, and will make thee as a signet: for I have chosen thee, saith the LORD of hosts.

Mt 1:12 — And after they were brought to Babylon, Jechonias begat Salathiel; and Salathiel begat Zorobabel;

Lk 3:27 — Which was *the son* of Joanna, which was *the son* of Rhesa, which was *the son* of Zorobabel, which was *the son* of Salathiel, which was *the son* of Neri,

SHEAR-JASHUB • A son of Isaiah.

Isa 7:3 — Then said the LORD unto Isaiah, Go forth now to meet Ahaz, thou, and Shear-jashub thy son, at the end of the conduit of the upper pool in the highway of the fuller's field;

SHEARIAH • Son of Azel.

1Ch 8:38 — And Azel had six sons, whose names *are* these, Azrikam, Bocheru, and Ishmael, and Sheariah, and Obadiah, and Hanan. All these *were* the sons of Azel.

1Ch 9:44 — And Azel had six sons, whose names *are* these, Azrikam, Bocheru, and Ishmael, and Sheariah, and Obadiah, and Hanan: these *were* the sons of Azel.

SHEBA

• Son of Raamah.

Ge 10:7 — And the sons of Cush; Seba, and Havilah, and Sabtah, and Raamah, and Sabtechah: and the sons of Raamah; Sheba, and Dedan.

1Ch 1:9 — And the sons of Cush; Seba, and Havilah, and Sabta, and Raamah, and Sabtecha. And the sons of Raamah; Sheba, and Dedan.

• Son of Joktan.

Ge 10:28 — And Obal, and Abimael, and Sheba,

1Ch 1:22 — And Ebal, and Abimael, and Sheba,

• Son of Jokshan.

Ge 25:3 — And Jokshan begat Sheba, and Dedan. And the sons of Dedan were Asshurim, and Letushim, and Leummim.

1Ch 1:32 — Now the sons of Keturah, Abraham's concubine: she bare Zimran, and Jokshan, and Medan, and Midian, and Ishbak, and Shuah. And the sons of Jokshan; Sheba, and Dedan.

• A Benjamite who led an insurrection against David.

2Sa 20:1–26

• A Gadite.

1Ch 5:13 — And their brethren of the house of their fathers *were,* Michael, and Meshullam, and Sheba, and Jorai, and Jachan, and Zia, and Heber, seven.

• A city of Simeon.

Jos 19:2 — And they had in their inheritance Beer-sheba, or Sheba, and Moladah,

• Queen of, visits Solomon.

1Ki 10:1–13; 2Ch 9:1–12

• Kings of, bring gifts to Solomon.

Ps 72:10 — The kings of Tarshish and of the isles shall bring presents: the kings of Sheba and Seba shall offer gifts.

• Rich in gold.

Ps 72:15 — And he shall live, and to him shall be given of the gold of Sheba: prayer also shall be made for him continually; *and* daily shall he be praised.

• Rich in incense.

Jer 6:20 — To what purpose cometh there to me incense from Sheba, and the sweet cane from a far country? your burnt offerings *are* not acceptable, nor your sacrifices sweet unto me.

• Merchandise of.

Eze 27:22–23

Eze 38:13 — Sheba, and Dedan, and the merchants of Tarshish, with all the young lions thereof, shall say unto thee, Art thou come to take a spoil? hast thou gathered thy company to take a prey? to carry away silver and gold, to take away cattle and goods, to take a great spoil?

• Prophecies concerning the people of, coming into the kingdom of Messiah.

Isa 60:6 — The multitude of camels shall cover thee, the dromedaries of Midian and Ephah; all they from Sheba shall come: they shall bring gold and incense; and they shall shew forth the praises of the LORD.

See: Sabeans

SHEBAH • A name given by Isaac to a well.

Ge 26:33 — And he called it Shebah: therefore the name of the city *is* Beer-sheba unto this day.

SHEBAM

• A city of Reuben.

Nu 32:3 — Ataroth, and Dibon, and Jazer, and Nimrah, and Heshbon, and Elealeh, and Shebam, and Nebo, and Beon,

• Apparently called also Shibmah and Sibmah.

See: Sibmah

SHEBANIAH

• A priest in the time of David.

1Ch 15:24 — And Shebaniah, and Jehoshaphat, and Nethaneel, and Amasai, and Zechariah, and Benaiah, and Eliezer, the priests, did blow with the trumpets before the ark of God: and Obed-edom and Jehiah *were* doorkeepers for the ark.

• A Levite who joined Nehemiah in covenant.

Ne 9:4–5

Ne 10:10 — And their brethren, Shebaniah, Hodijah, Kelita, Pelaiah, Hanan,

• A priest who joined Nehemiah in covenant.

Ne 10:4 — Hattush, Shebaniah, Malluch,

Ne 12:14 — Of Melicu, Jonathan; of Shebaniah, Joseph;

• A Levite who joined Nehemiah in covenant.

Ne 10:12 — Zaccur, Sherebiah, Shebaniah,

SHEBARIM • A place near Ai.

Jos 7:5 — And the men of Ai smote of them about thirty and six men: for they chased them *from* before the gate *even* unto Shebarim, and smote them in the going down: wherefore the hearts of the people melted, and became as water.

SHEBER • A son of Caleb.

1Ch 2:48 — Maachah, Caleb's concubine, bare Sheber, and Tirhanah.

SHEBNA

• A scribe of Hezekiah.

2Ki 18:18 — And when they had called to the king, there came out to them Eliakim the son of Hilkiah, which *was* over the household, and Shebna the scribe, and Joah the son of Asaph the recorder.

2Ki 18:26 — Then said Eliakim the son of Hilkiah, and Shebna, and Joah, unto Rab-shakeh, Speak, I pray thee, to thy servants in the Syrian language; for we understand *it:* and talk not with us in the Jews' language in the ears of the people that *are* on the wall.

2Ki 18:37 — Then came Eliakim the son of Hilkiah, which *was* over the household, and Shebna the scribe, and Joah the son of Asaph the recorder, to Hezekiah with *their* clothes rent, and told him the words of Rab-shakeh.

2Ki 19:2 — And he sent Eliakim, which *was* over the household, and Shebna the scribe, and the elders of the priests, covered with sackcloth, to Isaiah the prophet the son of Amoz.

Isa 36:3 — Then came forth unto him Eliakim, Hilkiah's son, which was over the house, and Shebna the scribe, and Joah, Asaph's son, the recorder.

Isa 36:11 — Then said Eliakim and Shebna and Joah unto Rabshakeh, Speak, I pray thee, unto thy servants in the Syrian language; for we understand *it:* and speak not to us in the Jews' language, in the ears of the people that *are* on the wall.

Isa 36:22 — Then came Eliakim, the son of Hilkiah, that *was* over the household, and Shebna the scribe, and Joah, the son of Asaph, the recorder, to Hezekiah with *their* clothes rent, and told him the words of Rabshakeh.

Isa 37:2 — And he sent Eliakim, who *was* over the household, and Shebna the scribe, and the elders of the priests covered with sackcloth, unto Isaiah the prophet the son of Amoz.

- **An official of the king.**

Isa 22:15–19

SHEBUEL

- **Son of Gershom.**

1Ch 23:16 — Of the sons of Gershom, Shebuel *was* the chief.

1Ch 26:24 — And Shebuel the son of Gershom, the son of Moses, *was* ruler of the treasures.

- **Called Shubael.**

1Ch 24:20 — And the rest of the sons of Levi *were these:* Of the sons of Amram; Shubael: of the sons of Shubael; Jehdeiah.

- **A singer.**
- **Son of Heman.**

1Ch 25:4 — Of Heman: the sons of Heman; Bukkiah, Mattaniah, Uzziel, Shebuel, and Jerimoth, Hananiah, Hanani, Eliathah, Giddalti, and Romamti-ezer, Joshbekashah, Mallothi, Hothir, *and* Mahazioth:

- **Called Shubael.**

1Ch 25:20 — The thirteenth to Shubael, *he,* his sons, and his brethren, *were* twelve:

SHECANIAH

- **A priest of the time of David.**

1Ch 24:11 — The ninth to Jeshua, the tenth to Shecaniah,

- **A priest of the time of Hezekiah.**

2Ch 31:15 — And next him *were* Eden, and Miniamin, and Jeshua, and Shemaiah, Amariah, and Shecaniah, in the cities of the priests, in *their* set office, to give to their brethren by courses, as well to the great as to the small:

SHECHANIAH

- **A descendant of David.**

1Ch 3:21–22

- **Father of Shemaiah and possibly identical with a descendant of David.**

Ne 3:29 — After them repaired Zadok the son of Immer over against his house. After him repaired also Shemaiah the son of Shechaniah, the keeper of the east gate.

- **Two men whose descendants returned with Ezra from captivity in Babylon.**

Ezr 8:3 — Of the sons of Shechaniah, of the sons of Pharosh; Zechariah: and with him were reckoned by genealogy of the males an hundred and fifty.

Ezr 8:5 — Of the sons of Shechaniah; the son of Jahaziel, and with him three hundred males.

- **A Jew who proposed to Ezra the putting away of Gentile wives.**

Ezr 10:2 — And Shechaniah the son of Jehiel, *one* of the sons of Elam, answered and said unto Ezra, We have trespassed against our God, and have taken strange wives of the people of the land: yet now there is hope in Israel concerning this thing.

- **Father-in-law of Tobiah.**

Ne 6:18 — For *there were* many in Judah sworn unto him, because he *was* the son in law of Shechaniah the son of Arah; and his son Johanan had taken the daughter of Meshullam the son of Berechiah.

- **A Levite who returned with Zerubbabel from captivity in Babylon.**

Ne 12:3 — Shechaniah, Rehum, Meremoth,

SHECHEM

- **A district in the central part of the land of Canaan; Abraham dwells in.**
- **Called also Sichem and Sychem.**

Ge 12:6 — And Abram passed through the land unto the place of Sichem, unto the plain of Moreh. And the Canaanite *was* then in the land.

- **Jacob buys a piece of ground in, and erects an altar.**

Ge 33:18–20

- **The flocks and herds of Jacob kept in.**

Ge 37:12–14

- **Joseph buried in.**

Jos 24:32 — And the bones of Joseph, which the children of Israel brought up out of Egypt, buried they in Shechem, in a parcel of ground which Jacob bought of the sons of Hamor the father of Shechem for an hundred pieces of silver: and it became the inheritance of the children of Joseph.

- **Jacob buried in.**

Ge 50:13 — For his sons carried him into the land of Canaan, and buried him in the cave of the field of Machpelah, which Abraham bought with the field for a possession of a buryingplace of Ephron the Hittite, before Mamre.

Ac 7:16 — And were carried over into Sychem, and laid in the sepulchre that Abraham bought for a sum of money of the sons of Emmor *the father* of Sychem.

- **A city of refuge in Mount Ephraim.**

Jos 20:7 — And they appointed Kedesh in Galilee in mount Naphtali, and Shechem in mount Ephraim, and Kirjath-arba, which *is* Hebron, in the mountain of Judah.

Jos 21:21 — For they gave them Shechem with her suburbs in mount Ephraim, *to be* a city of refuge for the slayer; and Gezer with her suburbs,

Jgs 21:19 — Then they said, Behold, *there is* a feast of the LORD in Shiloh yearly *in a place* which *is* on the north side of Bethel, on the east side of the highway that goeth up from Bethel to Shechem, and on the south of Lebonah.

• Called also Sychar.

John 4:5 — Then cometh he to a city of Samaria, which is called Sychar, near to the parcel of ground that Jacob gave to his son Joseph.

• Joshua assembled the tribes of Israel at, with all their elders, chiefs, and judges, and presented them before the Lord.

Jos 24:1–28

• Joshua buried at.

Jos 24:30–32

• Abimelech made king at.

Jgs 9:1–57

Jgs 8:31 — And his concubine that *was* in Shechem, she also bare him a son, whose name he called Abimelech.

• Rehoboam crowned at.

1Ki 12:1 — And Rehoboam went to Shechem: for all Israel were come to Shechem to make him king.

• Destroyed by Abimelech.

Jgs 9:45 — And Abimelech fought against the city all that day; and he took the city, and slew the people that *was* therein, and beat down the city, and sowed it with salt.

• Rebuilt by Jeroboam.

1Ki 12:25 — Then Jeroboam built Shechem in mount Ephraim, and dwelt therein; and went out from thence, and built Penuel.

• Men of, slain by Ishmael.

Jer 41:5 — That there came certain from Shechem, from Shiloh, and from Samaria, *even* fourscore men, having their beards shaven, and their clothes rent, and having cut themselves, with offerings and incense in their hand, to bring *them* to the house of the LORD.

• Jesus visits; disciples made in.

Jn 4:1–42

• Son of Hamor; seduces Jacob's daughter; slain by Jacob's sons.

Ge 34:1–31

Ge 33:19 — And he bought a parcel of a field, where he had spread his tent, at the hand of the children of Hamor, Shechem's father, for an hundred pieces of money.

Jos 24:32 — And the bones of Joseph, which the children of Israel brought up out of Egypt, buried they in Shechem, in a parcel of ground which Jacob bought of the sons of Hamor the father of Shechem for an hundred pieces of silver: and it became the inheritance of the children of Joseph.

Jgs 9:28 — And Gaal the son of Ebed said, Who *is* Abimelech, and who *is* Shechem, that we should serve him? *is* not *he* the son of Jerubbaal? and Zebul his officer? serve the men of Hamor the father of Shechem: for why should we serve him?

• Called Sychem.

Ac 7:16 — And were carried over into Sychem, and laid in the sepulchre that Abraham bought for a sum of money of the sons of Emmor *the father* of Sychem.

• Ancestor of the Shechemites.

Nu 26:31 — And *of* Asriel, the family of the Asrielites: and *of* Shechem, the family of the Shechemites:

Jos 17:2 — There was also *a lot* for the rest of the children of Manasseh by their families; for the children of Abiezer, and for the children of Helek, and for the children of Asriel, and for the children of Shechem, and for the children of Hepher, and for the children of Shemida: these *were* the male children of Manasseh the son of Joseph by their families.

• Son of Shemidah.

1Ch 7:19 — And the sons of Shemidah were, Ahian, and Shechem, and Likhi, and Aniam.

SHECHEMITES • Descendants of Shechem.

Nu 26:31 — And *of* Asriel, the family of the Asrielites: and *of* Shechem, the family of the Shechemites:

SHEDEUR • Father of Elizur.

Nu 1:5 — And these *are* the names of the men that shall stand with you: of *the tribe of* Reuben; Elizur the son of Shedeur.

Nu 2:10 — On the south side *shall be* the standard of the camp of Reuben according to their armies: and the captain of the children of Reuben *shall be* Elizur the son of Shedeur.

Nu 7:30 — On the fourth day Elizur the son of Shedeur, prince of the children of Reuben, *did offer:*

Nu 7:35 — And for a sacrifice of peace offerings, two oxen, five rams, five he goats, five lambs of the first year: this *was* the offering of Elizur the son of Shedeur.

Nu 10:18 — And the standard of the camp of Reuben set forward according to their armies: and over his host *was* Elizur the son of Shedeur.

SHEEP

• Offered in sacrifice

• By Abel.

Ge 4:4 — And Abel, he also brought of the firstlings of his flock and of the fat thereof. And the LORD had respect unto Abel and to his offering:

• By Noah.

Ge 8:20 — And Noah builded an altar unto the LORD; and took of every clean beast, and of every clean fowl, and offered burnt offerings on the altar.

• By Abraham.

Ge 22:13 — And Abraham lifted up his eyes, and looked, and behold behind *him* a ram caught in a thicket by his horns: and Abraham went and took the ram, and offered him up for a burnt offering in the stead of his son.

See: Offerings

• Required in the Mosaic offerings.

See: Offerings

• The land of Bashan adapted to the raising of.

Dt 32:14 — Butter of kine, and milk of sheep, with fat of lambs, and rams of the breed of Bashan, and goats, with the fat of kidneys of wheat; and thou didst drink the pure blood of the grape.

• The land of Bozrah adapted to the raising of.

Mic 2:12 — I will surely assemble, O Jacob, all of thee; I will surely gather the remnant of Israel; I will put them together as the sheep of Bozrah, as the flock in the midst of their fold: they shall make great noise by reason of *the multitude of* men.

• The land of Kedar adapted to the raising of.

Eze 27:21 — Arabia, and all the princes of Kedar, they occupied with thee in lambs, and rams, and goats: in these *were they* thy merchants.

• The land of Nebaioth adapted to the raising of.

Isa 60:7 — All the flocks of Kedar shall be gathered together unto thee, the rams of Nebaioth shall minister unto thee: they shall come up with acceptance on mine altar, and I will glorify the house of my glory.

• The land of Sharon adapted to the raising of.

Isa 65:10 — And Sharon shall be a fold of flocks, and the valley of Achor a place for the herds to lie down in, for my people that have sought me.

• Jacob's management of.

Ge 30:32–40

• Milk of, used for food.

Dt 32:14 — Butter of kine, and milk of sheep, with fat of lambs, and rams of the breed of Bashan, and goats, with the fat of kidneys of wheat; and thou didst drink the pure blood of the grape.

• Shearing of.

Ge 38:12–17

Ge 31:19 — And Laban went to shear his sheep: and Rachel had stolen the images that *were* her father's.

Isa 53:7 — He was oppressed, and he was afflicted, yet he opened not his mouth: he is brought as a lamb to the slaughter, and as a sheep before her shearers is dumb, so he openeth not his mouth.

• Feasting at the time of shearing.

1Sa 25:11 — Shall I then take my bread, and my water, and my flesh that I have killed for my shearers, and give *it* unto men, whom I know not whence they *be?*

1Sa 25:36 — And Abigail came to Nabal; and, behold, he held a feast in his house, like the feast of a king; and Nabal's heart *was* merry within him, for he *was* very drunken: wherefore she told him nothing, less or more, until the morning light.

2Sa 13:23 — And it came to pass after two full years, that Absalom had sheepshearers in Baal-hazor, which *is* beside Ephraim: and Absalom invited all the king's sons.

• First fleece of, belonged to priests and Levites.

Dt 18:4 — The firstfruit *also* of thy corn, of thy wine, and of thine oil, and the first of the fleece of thy sheep, shalt thou give him.

• Tribute paid in.

2Ki 3:4 — And Mesha king of Moab was a sheepmaster, and rendered unto the king of Israel an hundred thousand lambs, and an hundred thousand rams, with the wool.

1Ch 5:21 — And they took away their cattle; of their camels fifty thousand, and of sheep two hundred and fifty thousand, and of asses two thousand, and of men an hundred thousand.

2Ch 17:11 — Also *some* of the Philistines brought Jehoshaphat presents, and tribute silver; and the Arabians brought him flocks, seven thousand and seven hundred rams, and seven thousand and seven hundred he goats.

• Figurative.

1Ch 21:17 — And David said unto God, *Is it* not I *that* commanded the people to be numbered? even I it is that have sinned and done evil indeed; but *as for* these sheep, what have they done? let thine hand, I pray thee, O LORD my God, be on me, and on my father's house; but not on thy people, that they should be plagued.

Ps 74:1 — O God, why hast thou cast us off for ever? *why* doth thine anger smoke against the sheep of thy pasture?

Jer 13:20 — Lift up your eyes, and behold them that come from the north: where *is* the flock *that* was given thee, thy beautiful flock?

• Of backsliders.

Jer 50:6 — My people hath been lost sheep: their shepherds have caused them to go astray, they have turned them away *on* the mountains: they have gone from mountain to hill, they have forgotten their restingplace.

• Of lost sinners.

Mt 9:36 — But when he saw the multitudes, he was moved with compassion on them, because they fainted, and were scattered abroad, as sheep having no shepherd.

Mt 10:6 — <u>But go rather to the lost sheep of the house of Israel.</u>

• Of the righteous.

Eze 34:1–31; Jn 10:1–16

Jer 50:17 — Israel *is* a scattered sheep; the lions have driven *him* away: first the king of Assyria hath devoured him; and last this Nebuchadrezzar king of Babylon hath broken his bones.

Mt 26:31 — Then saith Jesus unto them, <u>All ye shall be offended because of me this night: for it is written, I will smite the shepherd, and the sheep of the flock shall be scattered abroad.</u>

Mk 14:27 — And Jesus saith unto them, <u>All ye shall be offended because of me this night: for it is written, I will smite the shepherd, and the sheep shall be scattered.</u>

• Of the defenselessness of ministers.

Mt 10:16 — <u>Behold, I send you forth as sheep in the midst of wolves: be ye therefore wise as serpents, and harmless as doves.</u>

• Parable of the lost.

Mt 18:11–13; Lk 15:4–7

SHEEP GATE • An ancient gate of Jerusalem.

Ne 3:1 — Then Eliashib the high priest rose up with his brethren the priests, and they builded the sheep gate; they sanctified it, and set up the doors of it; even unto the tower of Meah they sanctified it, unto the tower of Hananeel.

Ne 3:32 — And between the going up of the corner unto the sheep gate repaired the goldsmiths and the merchants.

Ne 12:39 — And from above the gate of Ephraim, and above the old gate, and above the fish gate, and the tower of Hananeel, and the tower of Meah, even unto the sheep gate: and they stood still in the prison gate.

Jn 5:2 — Now there is at Jerusalem by the sheep *market* a pool, which is called in the Hebrew tongue Bethesda, having five porches.

SHEEP MARKET

• Translated in some versions, "sheep gate".

• Of Jerusalem.

Jn 5:2 — Now there is at Jerusalem by the sheep *market* a pool, which is called in the Hebrew tongue Bethesda, having five porches.

SHEET

• Of Peter's vision.

Ac 10:11 — And saw heaven opened, and a certain vessel descending unto him, as it had been a great sheet knit at the four corners, and let down to the earth:

SHEHARIAH • A Benjamite.

1Ch 8:26 — And Shamsherai, and Shehariah, and Athaliah,

SHEKEL

• A weight, equal to twenty gerahs.

Ex 30:13 — This they shall give, every one that passeth among them that are numbered, half a shekel after the shekel of the sanctuary: (a shekel *is* twenty gerahs:) an half shekel *shall be* the offering of the LORD.

Nu 3:47 — Thou shalt even take five shekels apiece by the poll, after the shekel of the sanctuary shalt thou take *them:* (the shekel *is* twenty gerahs:)

Eze 45:12 — And the shekel *shall be* twenty gerahs: twenty shekels, five and twenty shekels, fifteen shekels, shall be your maneh.

• Used to weigh silver.

Jgs 17:2–3

Jos 7:21 — When I saw among the spoils a goodly Babylonish garment, and two hundred shekels of silver, and a wedge of gold of fifty shekels weight, then I coveted them, and took them; and, behold, they *are* hid in the earth in the midst of my tent, and the silver under it.

Jgs 8:26 — And the weight of the golden earrings that he requested was a thousand and seven hundred *shekels* of gold; beside ornaments, and collars, and purple raiment that *was* on the kings of Midian, and beside the chains that *were* about their camels' necks.

• Fractions of, used in currency.

Ex 30:13 — This they shall give, every one that passeth among them that are numbered, half a shekel after the shekel of the sanctuary: (a shekel *is* twenty gerahs:) an half shekel *shall be* the offering of the LORD.

1Sa 9:8 — And the servant answered Saul again, and said, Behold, I have here at hand the fourth part of a shekel of silver: *that* will I give to the man of God, to tell us our way.

Ne 10:32 — Also we made ordinances for us, to charge ourselves yearly with the third part of a shekel for the service of the house of our God;

• Used to weigh gold.

Nu 7:20–86

Ge 24:22 — And it came to pass, as the camels had done drinking, that the man took a golden earring of half a shekel weight, and two bracelets for her hands of ten *shekels* weight of gold;

Nu 7:14 — One spoon of ten *shekels* of gold, full of incense:

Jos 7:21 — When I saw among the spoils a goodly Babylonish garment, and two hundred shekels of silver, and a wedge of gold of fifty shekels weight, then I coveted them, and took them; and, behold, they *are* hid in the earth in the midst of my tent, and the silver under it.

1Ki 10:16 — And king Solomon made two hundred targets of beaten gold: six hundred *shekels* of gold went to one target.

• Used to weigh cinnamon.

Ex 30:23 — Take thou also unto thee principal spices, of pure myrrh five hundred *shekels,* and of sweet cinnamon half so much, *even* two hundred and fifty *shekels,* and of sweet calamus two hundred and fifty *shekels,*

• Used to weigh hair.

2Sa 14:26 — And when he polled his head, (for it was at every year's end that he polled *it:* because *the hair* was heavy on him, therefore he polled it:) he weighed the hair of his head at two hundred shekels after the king's weight.

• Used to weigh iron.

1Sa 17:7 — And the staff of his spear *was* like a weaver's beam; and his spear's head *weighed* six hundred shekels of iron: and one bearing a shield went before him.

• Used to weigh myrrh.

Ex 30:23 — Take thou also unto thee principal spices, of pure myrrh five hundred *shekels,* and of sweet cinnamon half so much, *even* two hundred and fifty *shekels,* and of sweet calamus two hundred and fifty *shekels,*

• Used to weigh rations.

Eze 4:10 — And thy meat which thou shalt eat *shall be* by weight, twenty shekels a day: from time to time shalt thou eat it.

- **Fines paid in.**

Dt 22:19 — And they shall amerce him in an hundred *shekels* of silver, and give *them* unto the father of the damsel, because he hath brought up an evil name upon a virgin of Israel: and she shall be his wife; he may not put her away all his days.

Dt 22:29 — Then the man that lay with her shall give unto the damsel's father fifty *shekels* of silver, and she shall be his wife; because he hath humbled her, he may not put her away all his days.

- **Fees paid in.**

1Sa 9:8 — And the servant answered Saul again, and said, Behold, I have here at hand the fourth part of a shekel of silver: *that* will I give to the man of God, to tell us our way.

- **Sanctuary revenues paid in.**

Ex 30:13 — This they shall give, every one that passeth among them that are numbered, half a shekel after the shekel of the sanctuary: (a shekel *is* twenty gerahs:) an half shekel *shall be* the offering of the LORD.

Ne 10:32 — Also we made ordinances for us, to charge ourselves yearly with the third part of a shekel for the service of the house of our God;

- **Of different standards.**
  - **Of the sanctuary.**

Ex 30:13 — This they shall give, every one that passeth among them that are numbered, half a shekel after the shekel of the sanctuary: (a shekel *is* twenty gerahs:) an half shekel *shall be* the offering of the LORD.

  - **Of the king's weight.**

2Sa 14:26 — And when he polled his head, (for it was at every year's end that he polled *it:* because *the hair* was heavy on him, therefore he polled it:) he weighed the hair of his head at two hundred shekels after the king's weight.

- **Corrupted.**

Am 8:5 — Saying, When will the new moon be gone, that we may sell corn? and the sabbath, that we may set forth wheat, making the ephah small, and the shekel great, and falsifying the balances by deceit?

SHEKINAH

- **The visible sign of God's presence on the ark of testimony in the Holy of Holies.**

2Ki 19:14–15

Ex 25:22 — And there I will meet with thee, and I will commune with thee from above the mercy seat, from between the two cherubims which *are* upon the ark of the testimony, of all *things* which I will give thee in commandment unto the children of Israel.

Le 16:2 — And the LORD said unto Moses, Speak unto Aaron thy brother, that he come not at all times into the holy *place* within the vail before the mercy seat, which *is* upon the ark; that he die not: for I will appear in the cloud upon the mercy seat.

2Sa 6:2 — And David arose, and went with all the people that *were* with him from Baale of Judah, to bring up from thence the ark of God, whose name is called by the name of the LORD of hosts that dwelleth *between* the cherubims.

Ps 80:1 — Give ear, O Shepherd of Israel, thou that leadest Joseph like a flock; thou that dwellest *between* the cherubims, shine forth.

Isa 37:16 — O LORD of hosts, God of Israel, that dwellest *between* the cherubims, thou *art* the God, *even* thou alone, of all the kingdoms of the earth: thou hast made heaven and earth.

Eze 9:3 — And the glory of the God of Israel was gone up from the cherub, whereupon he was, to the threshold of the house. And he called to the man clothed with linen, which *had* the writer's inkhorn by his side;

Eze 10:18 — Then the glory of the LORD departed from off the threshold of the house, and stood over the cherubims.

Heb 9:5 — And over it the cherubims of glory shadowing the mercyseat; of which we cannot now speak particularly.

SHELAH

- **Son of Judah.**

Ge 38:5 — And she yet again conceived, and bare a son; and called his name Shelah: and he was at Chezib, when she bare him.

Ge 38:11 — Then said Judah to Tamar his daughter in law, Remain a widow at thy father's house, till Shelah my son be grown: for he said, Lest peradventure he die also, as his brethren *did*. And Tamar went and dwelt in her father's house.

Ge 38:14 — And she put her widow's garments off from her, and covered her with a vail, and wrapped herself, and sat in an open place, which *is* by the way to Timnath; for she saw that Shelah was grown, and she was not given unto him to wife.

Ge 38:26 — And Judah acknowledged *them,* and said, She hath been more righteous than I; because that I gave her not to Shelah my son. And he knew her again no more.

Ge 46:12 — And the sons of Judah; Er, and Onan, and Shelah, and Pharez, and Zarah: but Er and Onan died in the land of Canaan. And the sons of Pharez were Hezron and Hamul.

Nu 26:20 — And the sons of Judah after their families were; of Shelah, the family of the Shelanites: of Pharez, the family of the Pharzites: of Zerah, the family of the Zarhites.

1Ch 2:3 — The sons of Judah; Er, and Onan, and Shelah: *which* three were born unto him of the daughter of Shua the Canaanitess. And Er, the firstborn of Judah, was evil in the sight of the LORD; and he slew him.

1Ch 4:21 — The sons of Shelah the son of Judah *were,* Er the father of Lecah, and Laadah the father of Mareshah, and the families of the house of them that wrought fine linen, of the house of Ashbea,

See: Salah

SHELANITES

- **Descendants of Shelah.**

Nu 26:20 — And the sons of Judah after their families were; of Shelah, the family of the Shelanites: of

Pharez, the family of the Pharzites: of Zerah, the family of the Zarhites.

• Apparently called Shilonites.

1Ch 9:5 — And of the Shilonites; Asaiah the firstborn, and his sons.

SHELEMIAH

• A porter of the tabernacle.

1Ch 26:14 — And the lot eastward fell to Shelemiah. Then for Zechariah his son, a wise counsellor, they cast lots; and his lot came out northward.

• Name of two descendants of Bani who put away Gentile wives.

Ezr 10:39 — And Shelemiah, and Nathan, and Adaiah,

Ezr 10:41 — Azareel, and Shelemiah, Shemariah,

• Father of Hananiah.

Ne 3:30 — After him repaired Hananiah the son of Shelemiah, and Hanun the sixth son of Zalaph, another piece. After him repaired Meshullam the son of Berechiah over against his chamber.

• A priest made treasurer by Nehemiah.

Ne 13:13 — And I made treasurers over the treasuries, Shelemiah the priest, and Zadok the scribe, and of the Levites, Pedaiah: and next to them *was* Hanan the son of Zaccur, the son of Mattaniah: for they were counted faithful, and their office *was* to distribute unto their brethren.

• Son of Cushi.

Jer 36:14 — Therefore all the princes sent Jehudi the son of Nethaniah, the son of Shelemiah, the son of Cushi, unto Baruch, saying, Take in thine hand the roll wherein thou hast read in the ears of the people, and come. So Baruch the son of Neriah took the roll in his hand, and came unto them.

• Son of Abdeel.

• Commanded to seize Jeremiah.

Jer 36:26 — But the king commanded Jerahmeel the son of Hammelech, and Seraiah the son of Azriel, and Shelemiah the son of Abdeel, to take Baruch the scribe and Jeremiah the prophet: but the LORD hid them.

• Father of Jehucal.

Jer 37:3 — And Zedekiah the king sent Jehucal the son of Shelemiah and Zephaniah the son of Maaseiah the priest to the prophet Jeremiah, saying, Pray now unto the LORD our God for us.

Jer 38:1 — Then Shephatiah the son of Mattan, and Gedaliah the son of Pashur, and Jucal the son of Shelemiah, and Pashur the son of Malchiah, heard the words that Jeremiah had spoken unto all the people, saying,

• Father of Irijah.

Jer 37:13 — And when he was in the gate of Benjamin, a captain of the ward *was* there, whose name *was* Irijah, the son of Shelemiah, the son of Hananiah; and he took Jeremiah the prophet, saying, Thou fallest away to the Chaldeans.

SHELEPH • Son of Joktan.

Ge 10:26 — And Joktan begat Almodad, and Sheleph, and Hazar-maveth, and Jerah,

1Ch 1:20 — And Joktan begat Almodad, and Sheleph, and Hazarmaveth, and Jerah,

SHELESH • Son of Helem.

1Ch 7:35 — And the sons of his brother Helem; Zophah, and Imna, and Shelesh, and Amal.

SHELOMI • Father of Ahihud.

Nu 34:27 — And the prince of the tribe of the children of Asher, Ahihud the son of Shelomi.

SHELOMITH

• Mother of a blasphemer.

Le 24:11 — And the Israelitish woman's son blasphemed the name *of the LORD*, and cursed. And they brought him unto Moses: (and his mother's name *was* Shelomith, the daughter of Dibri, of the tribe of Dan:)

• Daughter of Zerubbabel.

1Ch 3:19 — And the sons of Pedaiah *were*, Zerubbabel, and Shimei: and the sons of Zerubbabel; Meshullam, and Hananiah, and Shelomith their sister:

• Son of Shimei.

1Ch 23:9 — The sons of Shimei; Shelomith, and Haziel, and Haran, three. These *were* the chief of the fathers of Laadan.

• A son of Izhar.

1Ch 23:18 — Of the sons of Izhar; Shelomith the chief.

• Called Shelomoth.

1Ch 24:22 — Of the Izharites; Shelomoth: of the sons of Shelomoth; Jahath.

• A descendant of Eliezer.

1Ch 26:25–26

1Ch 26:28 — And all that Samuel the seer, and Saul the son of Kish, and Abner the son of Ner, and Joab the son of Zeruiah, had dedicated; *and* whosoever had dedicated *any thing, it was* under the hand of Shelomith, and of his brethren.

• A son or daughter of Rehoboam.

2Ch 11:20 — And after her he took Maachah the daughter of Absalom; which bare him Abijah, and Attai, and Ziza, and Shelomith.

• Ancestor of a family that returned with Ezra from captivity in Babylon.

Ezr 8:10 — And of the sons of Shelomith; the son of Josiphiah, and with him an hundred and threescore males.

SHELOMOTH ➻See: Shelomith; a son of Izhar

SHELUMIEL • Son of Zurishaddai, and leader of Simeon in time of Moses.

Nu 1:6 — Of Simeon; Shelumiel the son of Zurishaddai.

Nu 2:12 — And those which pitch by him *shall be* the tribe of Simeon: and the captain of the children of Simeon *shall be* Shelumiel the son of Zurishaddai.

Nu 7:36 — On the fifth day Shelumiel the son of Zurishaddai, prince of the children of Simeon, *did offer:*

Nu 7:41 — And for a sacrifice of peace offerings, two oxen, five rams, five he goats, five lambs of the first year: this *was* the offering of Shelumiel the son of Zurishaddai.

Nu 10:19 — And over the host of the tribe of the children of Simeon was Shelumiel the son of Zurishaddai.

SHEM

• Son of Noah.

• Preserved in the ark.

Ge 5:32 — And Noah was five hundred years old: and Noah begat Shem, Ham, and Japheth.

Ge 6:10 — And Noah begat three sons, Shem, Ham, and Japheth.

Ge 7:13 — In the selfsame day entered Noah, and Shem, and Ham, and Japheth, the sons of Noah, and Noah's wife, and the three wives of his sons with them, into the ark;

Ge 9:18 — And the sons of Noah, that went forth of the ark, were Shem, and Ham, and Japheth: and Ham is the father of Canaan.

1Ch 1:4 — Noah, Shem, Ham, and Japheth.

• His filial conduct.

Ge 9:23–27

• Descendants of.

Ge 10:21–31; 11:10–29; 1Ch 1:17–54

Ge 10:1 — Now these *are* the generations of the sons of Noah, Shem, Ham, and Japheth: and unto them were sons born after the flood.

• Called Sem.

Lk 3:36 — Which was *the son* of Cainan, which was *the son* of Arphaxad, which was *the son* of Sem, which was *the son* of Noe, which was *the son* of Lamech,

SHEMA

• A city of Judah.

Jos 15:26 — Amam, and Shema, and Moladah,

• A son of Hebron.

1Ch 2:43–44

• Son of Joel.

1Ch 5:8 — And Bela the son of Azaz, the son of Shema, the son of Joel, who dwelt in Aroer, even unto Nebo and Baal-meon:

• Called Shemaiah.

1Ch 5:4 — The sons of Joel; Shemaiah his son, Gog his son, Shimei his son,

• A Benjamite.

1Ch 8:13 — Beriah also, and Shema, who *were* heads of the fathers of the inhabitants of Aijalon, who drove away the inhabitants of Gath:

• A man who stood at the right hand of Ezra when he read the law of the people.

Ne 8:4 — And Ezra the scribe stood upon a pulpit of wood, which they had made for the purpose; and beside him stood Mattithiah, and Shema, and Anaiah, and Urijah, and Hilkiah, and Maaseiah, on his right hand; and on his left hand, Pedaiah, and Mishael, and Malchiah, and Hashum, and Hashbadana, Zechariah, *and* Meshullam.

SHEMAAH • Father of two of David's mighty men.

1Ch 12:3 — The chief *was* Ahiezer, then Joash, the sons of Shemaah the Gibeathite; and Jeziel, and Pelet, the sons of Azmaveth; and Berachah, and Jehu the Antothite,

SHEMAIAH

• A prophet in the time of Rehoboam.

• Prevents Rehoboam from war with Jeroboam.

1Ki 12:22–24; 2Ch 11:2–4

• Prophesies the punishment of Rehoboam by Shishak, king of Egypt.

2Ch 12:5 — Then came Shemaiah the prophet to Rehoboam, and *to* the princes of Judah, that were gathered together to Jerusalem because of Shishak, and said unto them, Thus saith the LORD, Ye have forsaken me, and therefore have I also left you in the hand of Shishak.

2Ch 12:7 — And when the LORD saw that they humbled themselves, the word of the LORD came to Shemaiah, saying, They have humbled themselves; *therefore* I will not destroy them, but I will grant them some deliverance; and my wrath shall not be poured out upon Jerusalem by the hand of Shishak.

• Writes chronicles.

2Ch 12:15 — Now the acts of Rehoboam, first and last, *are* they not written in the book of Shemaiah the prophet, and of Iddo the seer concerning genealogies? And *there were* wars between Rehoboam and Jeroboam continually.

• A descendant of David.

1Ch 3:22 — And the sons of Shechaniah; Shemaiah; and the sons of Shemaiah; Hattush, and Igeal, and Bariah, and Neariah, and Shaphat, six.

• A Simeonite.

1Ch 4:37 — And Ziza the son of Shiphi, the son of Allon, the son of Jedaiah, the son of Shimri, the son of Shemaiah;

• Son of Joel.

1Ch 5:4 — The sons of Joel; Shemaiah his son, Gog his son, Shimei his son,

• Called Shema.

1Ch 5:8 — And Bela the son of Azaz, the son of Shema, the son of Joel, who dwelt in Aroer, even unto Nebo and Baal-meon:

• **A Merarite.**

1Ch 9:14 — And of the Levites; Shemaiah the son of Hasshub, the son of Azrikam, the son of Hashabiah, of the sons of Merari;

• **In charge of the business of the temple in time of Nehemiah.**

Ne 11:15–16

• **Son of Galal.**

1Ch 9:16 — And Obadiah the son of Shemaiah, the son of Galal, the son of Jeduthun, and Berechiah the son of Asa, the son of Elkanah, that dwelt in the villages of the Netophathites.

• **Called Shammua.**

Ne 11:17 — And Mattaniah the son of Micha, the son of Zabdi, the son of Asaph, *was* the principal to begin the thanksgiving in prayer: and Bakbukiah the second among his brethren, and Abda the son of Shammua, the son of Galal, the son of Jeduthun.

• **A chief Levite in time of David; assisted in moving the ark from Obed-edom.**

1Ch 15:8 — Of the sons of Elizaphan; Shemaiah the chief, and his brethren two hundred:

1Ch 15:11 — And David called for Zadok and Abiathar the priests, and for the Levites, for Uriel, Asaiah, and Joel, Shemaiah, and Eliel, and Amminadab,

• **A Levite who assisted in the division of the priests.**

1Ch 24:6 — And Shemaiah the son of Nethaneel the scribe, *one* of the Levites, wrote them before the king, and the princes, and Zadok the priest, and Ahimelech the son of Abiathar, and *before* the chief of the fathers of the priests and Levites: one principal household being taken for Eleazar, and *one* taken for Ithamar.

• **A porter of the temple in time of David.**

1Ch 26:6–7

1Ch 26:4 — Moreover the sons of Obed-edom *were,* Shemaiah the firstborn, Jehozabad the second, Joah the third, and Sacar the fourth, and Nethaneel the fifth,

• **A Levite.**

• **Sent by Jehoshaphat to instruct the people in the law.**

2Ch 17:8 — And with them *he sent* Levites, *even* Shemaiah, and Nethaniah, and Zebadiah, and Asahel, and Shemiramoth, and Jehonathan, and Adonijah, and Tobijah, and Tob-adonijah, Levites; and with them Elishama and Jehoram, priests.

• **A Levite.**

• **Son of Jeduthun.**

2Ch 29:14 — And of the sons of Heman; Jehiel, and Shimei: and of the sons of Jeduthun; Shemaiah, and Uzziel.

• **A Levite.**

2Ch 31:15 — And next him *were* Eden, and Miniamin, and Jeshua, and Shemaiah, Amariah, and Shecaniah, in the cities of the priests, in *their* set office, to give to their brethren by courses, as well to the great as to the small:

• **A Levite who contributed largely for passover sacrifices.**

2Ch 35:9 — Conaniah also, and Shemaiah and Nethaneel, his brethren, and Hashabiah and Jeiel and Jozabad, chief of the Levites, gave unto the Levites for passover offerings five thousand *small cattle,* and five hundred oxen.

• **A Jew who returned from Babylon with Ezra.**

Ezr 8:13 — And of the last sons of Adonikam, whose names *are* these, Eliphelet, Jeiel, and Shemaiah, and with them threescore males.

• **A chief man with Ezra.**

Ezr 8:16 — Then sent I for Eliezer, for Ariel, for Shemaiah, and for Elnathan, and for Jarib, and for Elnathan, and for Nathan, and for Zechariah, and for Meshullam, chief men; also for Joiarib, and for Elnathan, men of understanding.

• **A priest who put away his Gentile wife.**

Ezr 10:21 — And of the sons of Harim; Maaseiah, and Elijah, and Shemaiah, and Jehiel, and Uzziah.

• **An Israelite who put away his Gentile wife.**

Ezr 10:31 — And *of* the sons of Harim; Eliezer, Ishijah, Malchiah, Shemaiah, Shimeon,

• **Keeper of the east gate of Jerusalem in the time of Nehemiah.**

Ne 3:29 — After them repaired Zadok the son of Immer over against his house. After him repaired also Shemaiah the son of Shechaniah, the keeper of the east gate.

• **A false prophet in the time of Nehemiah.**

Ne 6:10 — Afterward I came unto the house of Shemaiah the son of Delaiah the son of Mehetabeel, who *was* shut up; and he said, Let us meet together in the house of God, within the temple, and let us shut the doors of the temple: for they will come to slay thee; yea, in the night will they come to slay thee.

• **A priest who sealed the covenant with Nehemiah.**

Ne 10:8 — Maaziah, Bilgai, Shemaiah: these *were* the priests.

• **A priest with Zerubbabel.**

Ne 12:6 — Shemaiah, and Joiarib, Jedaiah,

Ne 12:18 — Of Bilgah, Shammua; of Shemaiah, Jehonathan;

• **A priest.**

Ne 12:35 — And *certain* of the priests' sons with trumpets; *namely,* Zechariah the son of Jonathan, the son of Shemaiah, the son of Mattaniah, the son of Michaiah, the son of Zaccur, the son of Asaph:

• **The name of three men who celebrated the dedication of the new wall of Jerusalem.**

Ne 12:34 — Judah, and Benjamin, and Shemaiah, and Jeremiah,

Ne 12:36 — And his brethren, Shemaiah, and Azarael, Milalai, Gilalai, Maai, Nethaneel, and Judah, Hanani, with the musical instruments of David the man of God, and Ezra the scribe before them.

Ne 12:42 — And Maaseiah, and Shemaiah, and Eleazar, and Uzzi, and Jehohanan, and Malchijah, and Elam, and Ezer. And the singers sang loud, with Jezrahiah *their* overseer.

• Father of the prophet Urijah.

Jer 26:20 — And there was also a man that prophesied in the name of the LORD, Urijah the son of Shemaiah of Kirjath-jearim, who prophesied against this city and against this land according to all the words of Jeremiah:

• A false prophet.

Jer 29:24–32

• Father of Delaiah.

Jer 36:12 — Then he went down into the king's house, into the scribe's chamber: and, lo, all the princes sat there, *even* Elishama the scribe, and Delaiah the son of Shemaiah, and Elnathan the son of Achbor, and Gemariah the son of Shaphan, and Zedekiah the son of Hananiah, and all the princes.

SHEMARIAH

• One of David's mighty men.

1Ch 12:5 — Eluzai, and Jerimoth, and Bealiah, and Shemariah, and Shephatiah the Haruphite,

• Name of two Israelites who put away Gentile wives.

Ezr 10:32 — Benjamin, Malluch, *and* Shemariah.

Ezr 10:41 — Azareel, and Shelemiah, Shemariah,

SHEMEBER • King of Zeboim.

Ge 14:2 — *That these* made war with Bera king of Sodom, and with Birsha king of Gomorrah, Shinab king of Admah, and Shemeber king of Zeboiim, and the king of Bela, which is Zoar.

SHEMER • Owner of the site on which Samaria was built.

1Ki 16:24 — And he bought the hill Samaria of Shemer for two talents of silver, and built on the hill, and called the name of the city which he built, after the name of Shemer, owner of the hill, Samaria.

SHEMIDA

• Called also Shemidah.

• Son of Gilead.

Nu 26:32 — And *of* Shemida, the family of the Shemidaites: and *of* Hepher, the family of the Hepherites.

Jos 17:2 — There was also *a lot* for the rest of the children of Manasseh by their families; for the children of Abiezer, and for the children of Helek, and for the children of Asriel, and for the children of Shechem, and for the children of Hepher, and for the children of Shemida: these *were* the male children of Manasseh the son of Joseph by their families.

1Ch 7:19 — And the sons of Shemidah were, Ahian, and Shechem, and Likhi, and Aniam.

SHEMINITH ✦See: Music

SHEMIRAMOTH

• A Levite musician.

1Ch 15:18 — And with them their brethren of the second *degree,* Zechariah, Ben, and Jaaziel, and Shemiramoth, and Jehiel, and Unni, Eliab, and Benaiah, and Maaseiah, and Mattithiah, and Elipheleh, and Mikneiah, and Obed-edom, and Jeiel, the porters.

1Ch 15:20 — And Zechariah, and Aziel, and Shemiramoth, and Jehiel, and Unni, and Eliab, and Maaseiah, and Benaiah, with psalteries on Alamoth;

1Ch 16:5 — Asaph the chief, and next to him Zechariah, Jeiel, and Shemiramoth, and Jehiel, and Mattithiah, and Eliab, and Benaiah, and Obed-edom: and Jeiel with psalteries and with harps; but Asaph made a sound with cymbals;

• A Levite sent by Jehoshaphat to instruct the people in the law.

2Ch 17:8 — And with them *he sent* Levites, *even* Shemaiah, and Nethaniah, and Zebadiah, and Asahel, and Shemiramoth, and Jehonathan, and Adonijah, and Tobijah, and Tob-adonijah, Levites; and with them Elishama and Jehoram, priests.

SHEMUEL

• A Simeonite appointed on the committee to divide the land of Canaan.

Nu 34:20 — And of the tribe of the children of Simeon, Shemuel the son of Ammihud.

✦See: Samuel

• Head of a family in Issachar.

1Ch 7:2 — And the sons of Tola; Uzzi, and Rephaiah, and Jeriel, and Jahmai, and Jibsam, and Shemuel, heads of their father's house, *to wit,* of Tola: *they were* valiant men of might in their generations; whose number *was* in the days of David two and twenty thousand and six hundred.

SHEN • A place of unknown location.

1Sa 7:12 — Then Samuel took a stone, and set *it* between Mizpeh and Shen, and called the name of it Eben-ezer, saying, Hitherto hath the LORD helped us.

SHENAZAR • Son of Jeconiah.

1Ch 3:18 — Malchiram also, and Pedaiah, and Shenazar, Jecamiah, Hoshama, and Nedabiah.

SHENIR

• Called also Senir.

• Amorite name of Mount Hermon.

Dt 3:9 — (*Which* Hermon the Sidonians call Sirion; and the Amorites call it Shenir;)

1Ch 5:23 — And the children of the half tribe of Manasseh dwelt in the land: they increased from Bashan unto Baal-hermon and Senir, and unto mount Hermon.

SS 4:8 — Come with me from Lebanon, *my* spouse, with me from Lebanon: look from the top of Amana, from the top of Shenir and Hermon, from the lions' dens, from the mountains of the leopards.

Eze 27:5 — They have made all thy *ship* boards of fir trees of Senir: they have taken cedars from Lebanon to make masts for thee.

SHEOL ⇨See: Hell

SHEPHAM • A place on the eastern boundary of the promised land.

Nu 34:10–11

SHEPHATIAH

• Son of David.

2Sa 3:4 — And the fourth, Adonijah the son of Haggith; and the fifth, Shephatiah the son of Abital;

1Ch 3:3 — The fifth, Shephatiah of Abital: the sixth, Ithream by Eglah his wife.

• A Benjamite, father of Meshullam.

1Ch 9:8 — And Ibneiah the son of Jeroham, and Elah the son of Uzzi, the son of Michri, and Meshullam the son of Shephatiah, the son of Reuel, the son of Ibnijah;

• A valiant man who joined David at Ziklag.

1Ch 12:5 — Eluzai, and Jerimoth, and Bealiah, and Shemariah, and Shephatiah the Haruphite,

• A ruler of Simeon.

1Ch 27:16 — Furthermore over the tribes of Israel: the ruler of the Reubenites *was* Eliezer the son of Zichri: of the Simeonites, Shephatiah the son of Maachah:

• Son of Jehoshaphat.

2Ch 21:2 — And he had brethren the sons of Jehoshaphat, Azariah, and Jehiel, and Zechariah, and Azariah, and Michael, and Shephatiah: all these *were* the sons of Jehoshaphat king of Israel.

• The name of two men, ancestors of families which returned to Jerusalem from captivity in Babylon.

Ezr 2:4 — The children of Shephatiah, three hundred seventy and two.

Ezr 2:57 — The children of Shephatiah, the children of Hattil, the children of Pochereth of Zebaim, the children of Ami.

Ezr 8:8 — And of the sons of Shephatiah; Zebadiah the son of Michael, and with him fourscore males.

Ne 7:9 — The children of Shephatiah, three hundred seventy and two.

Ne 7:59 — The children of Shephatiah, the children of Hattil, the children of Pochereth of Zebaim, the children of Amon.

• A descendant of Perez.

Ne 11:4 — And at Jerusalem dwelt *certain* of the children of Judah, and of the children of Benjamin. Of the children of Judah; Athaiah the son of Uzziah, the son of Zechariah, the son of Amariah, the son of Shephatiah, the son of Mahalaleel, of the children of Perez;

• An enemy of Jeremiah.

Jer 38:1 — Then Shephatiah the son of Mattan, and Gedaliah the son of Pashur, and Jucal the son of Shelemiah, and Pashur the son of Malchiah, heard the words that Jeremiah had spoken unto all the people, saying,

Jer 38:4 — Therefore the princes said unto the king, We beseech thee, let this man be put to death: for thus he weakeneth the hands of the men of war that remain in this city, and the hands of all the people, in speaking such words unto them: for this man seeketh not the welfare of this people, but the hurt.

SHEPHERD

• One who cares for flocks.

Ge 31:38–40; Ps 78:52–53

Jer 31:10 — Hear the word of the LORD, O ye nations, and declare *it* in the isles afar off, and say, He that scattered Israel will gather him, and keep him, as a shepherd *doth* his flock.

Am 3:12 — Thus saith the LORD; As the shepherd taketh out of the mouth of the lion two legs, or a piece of an ear; so shall the children of Israel be taken out that dwell in Samaria in the corner of a bed, and in Damascus *in* a couch.

Lk 2:8 — And there were in the same country shepherds abiding in the field, keeping watch over their flock by night.

• David the, defends his flock against a lion and a bear.

1Sa 17:34–35

• Causes the flock to rest.

Ps 23:2 — He maketh me to lie down in green pastures: he leadeth me beside the still waters.

SS 1:7 — Tell me, O thou whom my soul loveth, where thou feedest, where thou makest *thy flock* to rest at noon: for why should I be as one that turneth aside by the flocks of thy companions?

Jer 33:12 — Thus saith the LORD of hosts; Again in this place, which is desolate without man and without beast, and in all the cities thereof, shall be an habitation of shepherds causing *their* flocks to lie down.

• Numbering the flock.

Le 27:32 — And concerning the tithe of the herd, or of the flock, *even* of whatsoever passeth under the rod, the tenth shall be holy unto the LORD.

Jer 33:13 — In the cities of the mountains, in the cities of the vale, and in the cities of the south, and in the land of Benjamin, and in the places about Jerusalem, and in the cities of Judah, shall the flocks pass again under the hands of him that telleth *them*, saith the LORD.

• Knows his flock by name.

Jn 10:3–5

• Keeps the sheep and goats apart.

Mt 25:32 — And before him shall be gathered all nations: and he shall separate them one from another, as a shepherd divideth *his* sheep from the goats:

- **Waters the flocks.**
  Ge 29:2–10
- **Keeps the flocks in folds.**
  Nu 32:16 — And they came near unto him, and said, We will build sheepfolds here for our cattle, and cities for our little ones:
  1Sa 24:3 — And he came to the sheepcotes by the way, where *was* a cave; and Saul went in to cover his feet: and David and his men remained in the sides of the cave.
  2Sa 7:8 — Now therefore so shalt thou say unto my servant David, Thus saith the LORD of hosts, I took thee from the sheepcote, from following the sheep, to be ruler over my people, over Israel:
  Jn 10:1 — Verily, verily, I say unto you, He that entereth not by the door into the sheepfold, but climbeth up some other way, the same is a thief and a robber.
- **Watch towers of.**
  2Ch 26:10 — Also he built towers in the desert, and digged many wells: for he had much cattle, both in the low country, and in the plains: husbandmen *also,* and vine dressers in the mountains, and in Carmel: for he loved husbandry.
  Mic 4:8 — And thou, O tower of the flock, the strong hold of the daughter of Zion, unto thee shall it come, even the first dominion; the kingdom shall come to the daughter of Jerusalem.
- **Dogs of.**
  Job 30:1 — But now *they that are* younger than I have me in derision, whose fathers I would have disdained to have set with the dogs of my flock.
- **Was an abomination to the Egyptians.**
  Ge 46:34 — That ye shall say, Thy servants' trade hath been about cattle from our youth even until now, both we, *and* also our fathers: that ye may dwell in the land of Goshen; for every shepherd *is* an abomination unto the Egyptians.
- **Angels appeared to.**
  Lk 2:8–20
- **Instances of.**
  - **Abel.**
    Ge 4:2
  - **Rachel.**
    Ge 29:9
  - **Daughters of Jethro.**
    Ex 2:16
  - **Moses.**
    Ex 3:1
  - **David.**
    1Sa 16:11; 2Sa 7:8; Ps 78:70
- **Figurative.**
  Ge 49:24 — But his bow abode in strength, and the arms of his hands were made strong by the hands of the mighty *God* of Jacob; (from thence *is* the shepherd, the stone of Israel:)
  - **Of God's care.**
    Ps 23:1–6
    Ps 78:52 — But made his own people to go forth like sheep, and guided them in the wilderness like a flock.
    Ps 80:1 — Give ear, O Shepherd of Israel, thou that leadest Joseph like a flock; thou that dwellest *between* the cherubims, shine forth.
  - **Of prophets, priests, Levites, and civil authorities.**
    Eze 34:1–31
  - **Of Christ.**
    Jn 10:1–16
    Zec 13:7 — Awake, O sword, against my shepherd, and against the man *that is* my fellow, saith the LORD of hosts: smite the shepherd, and the sheep shall be scattered: and I will turn mine hand upon the little ones.
    Mt 26:31 — Then saith Jesus unto them, All ye shall be offended because of me this night: for it is written, I will smite the shepherd, and the sheep of the flock shall be scattered abroad.
    Heb 13:20 — Now the God of peace, that brought again from the dead our Lord Jesus, that great shepherd of the sheep, through the blood of the everlasting covenant,
    1Pe 2:25 — For ye were as sheep going astray; but are now returned unto the Shepherd and Bishop of your souls.
  - **Name given to Jesus.**
    Isa 40:11 — He shall feed his flock like a shepherd: he shall gather the lambs with his arm, and carry *them* in his bosom, *and* shall gently lead those that are with young.
    Mk 14:27 — And Jesus saith unto them, All ye shall be offended because of me this night: for it is written, I will smite the shepherd, and the sheep shall be scattered.
    Jn 10:11 — I am the good shepherd: the good shepherd giveth his life for the sheep.
    1Pe 2:25 — For ye were as sheep going astray; but are now returned unto the Shepherd and Bishop of your souls.
    1Pe 5:4 — And when the chief Shepherd shall appear, ye shall receive a crown of glory that fadeth not away.
- **Name given to Cyrus.**
  Isa 44:28 — That saith of Cyrus, *He is* my shepherd, and shall perform all my pleasure: even saying to Jerusalem, Thou shalt be built; and to the temple, Thy foundation shall be laid.

SHEPHI ✦See: Shepho

SHEPHO

- **Son of Shobal.**
  Ge 36:23 — And the children of Shobal *were* these; Alvan, and Manahath, and Ebal, Shepho, and Onam.
- **Called Shepi.**
  1Ch 1:40 — The sons of Shobal; Alian, and Manahath, and Ebal, Shephi, and Onam. And the sons of Zibeon; Aiah, and Anah.

SHEPHUPHAN • Son of Bela.

1Ch 8:5 — And Gera, and Shephuphan, and Huram.

SHERAH

• Daughter of Ephraim.

1Ch 7:24 — (And his daughter *was* Sherah, who built Beth-horon the nether, and the upper, and Uzzen-sherah.)

SHEREBIAH

• A Levite assistant to Ezra.

Ne 9:4–5

Ezr 8:18 — And by the good hand of our God upon us they brought us a man of understanding, of the sons of Mahli, the son of Levi, the son of Israel; and Sherebiah, with his sons and his brethren, eighteen;

Ezr 8:24 — Then I separated twelve of the chief of the priests, Sherebiah, Hashabiah, and ten of their brethren with them,

Ne 8:7 — Also Jeshua, and Bani, and Sherebiah, Jamin, Akkub, Shabbethai, Hodijah, Maaseiah, Kelita, Azariah, Jozabad, Hanan, Pelaiah, and the Levites, caused the people to understand the law: and the people *stood* in their place.

• A Levite who sealed the covenant with Nehemiah.

Ne 10:12 — Zaccur, Sherebiah, Shebaniah,

Ne 12:8 — Moreover the Levites: Jeshua, Binnui, Kadmiel, Sherebiah, Judah, *and* Mattaniah, *which was* over the thanksgiving, he and his brethren.

Ne 12:24 — And the chief of the Levites: Hashabiah, Sherebiah, and Jeshua the son of Kadmiel, with their brethren over against them, to praise *and* to give thanks, according to the commandment of David the man of God, ward over against ward.

SHERESH • Son of Machir.

1Ch 7:16 — And Maachah the wife of Machir bare a son, and she called his name Peresh; and the name of his brother *was* Sheresh; and his sons *were* Ulam and Rakem.

SHEREZER • A delegate to priests and prophets to consult as to a day of humiliation.

Zec 7:2 — When they had sent unto the house of God Sherezer and Regem-melech, and their men, to pray before the LORD,

SHERIFF

Da 3:2–3

SHESHACH • A symbolic name. Apparently applied to Babylon.

Jer 25:26 — And all the kings of the north, far and near, one with another, and all the kingdoms of the world, which *are* upon the face of the earth: and the king of Sheshach shall drink after them.

Jer 51:41 — How is Sheshach taken! and how is the praise of the whole earth surprised! how is Babylon become an astonishment among the nations!

SHESHAI • A son of Anak.

Nu 13:22 — And they ascended by the south, and came unto Hebron; where Ahiman, Sheshai, and Talmai, the children of Anak, *were.* (Now Hebron was built seven years before Zoan in Egypt.)

Jos 15:14 — And Caleb drove thence the three sons of Anak, Sheshai, and Ahiman, and Talmai, the children of Anak.

Jgs 1:10 — And Judah went against the Canaanites that dwelt in Hebron: (now the name of Hebron before *was* Kirjath-arba:) and they slew Sheshai, and Ahiman, and Talmai.

SHESHAN • A descendant of Jerahmeel.

1Ch 2:34–35

1Ch 2:31 — And the sons of Appaim; Ishi. And the sons of Ishi; Sheshan. And the children of Sheshan; Ahlai.

SHESHBAZZAR

• A name given, apparently, to Zerubbabel.

Ezr 1:8 — Even those did Cyrus king of Persia bring forth by the hand of Mithredath the treasurer, and numbered them unto Sheshbazzar, the prince of Judah.

Ezr 1:11 — All the vessels of gold and of silver *were* five thousand and four hundred. All *these* did Sheshbazzar bring up with *them of* the captivity that were brought up from Babylon unto Jerusalem.

Ezr 5:14 — And the vessels also of gold and silver of the house of God, which Nebuchadnezzar took out of the temple that *was* in Jerusalem, and brought them into the temple of Babylon, those did Cyrus the king take out of the temple of Babylon, and they were delivered unto *one,* whose name *was* Sheshbazzar, whom he had made governor;

Ezr 5:16 — Then came the same Sheshbazzar, *and* laid the foundation of the house of God which *is* in Jerusalem: and since that time even until now hath it been in building, and *yet* it is not finished.

See: Zerubbabel

SHETH

• Translated "tumult".

Nu 24:17 — I shall see him, but not now: I shall behold him, but not nigh: there shall come a Star out of Jacob, and a Sceptre shall rise out of Israel, and shall smite the corners of Moab, and destroy all the children of Sheth.

See: Seth

SHETHAR • A prince of Persia.

Est 1:14 — And the next unto him *was* Carshena, Shethar, Admatha, Tarshish, Meres, Marsena, *and* Memucan, the seven princes of Persia and Media, which saw the king's face, *and* which sat the first in the kingdom;)

SHETHAR-BOZNAI • An official of the king of Persia.

Ezr 5:3 — At the same time came to them Tatnai, governor on this side the river, and Shethar-boznai, and their companions, and said thus unto them, Who hath commanded you to build this house, and to make up this wall?

Ezr 5:6 — The copy of the letter that Tatnai, governor on this side the river, and Shethar-boznai, and his companions the Apharsachites, which *were* on this side the river, sent unto Darius the king:

Ezr 6:6 — Now *therefore,* Tatnai, governor beyond the river, Shethar-boznai, and your companions the Apharsachites, which *are* beyond the river, be ye far from thence:

Ezr 6:13 — Then Tatnai, governor on this side the river, Shethar-boznai, and their companions, according to that which Darius the king had sent, so they did speedily.

SHEVA

See: Seraiah; called also Sheva, Shisha, and Shavsha. David's scribe

• Son of Caleb.

1Ch 2:49 — She bare also Shaaph the father of Madmannah, Sheva the father of Machbenah, and the father of Gibea: and the daughter of Caleb *was* Achsa.

SHEWBREAD

Heb 9:2 — For there was a tabernacle made; the first, wherein *was* the candlestick, and the table, and the shewbread; which is called the sanctuary.

• Called Hallowed Bread.

1Sa 21:6 — So the priest gave him hallowed *bread:* for there was no bread there but the shewbread, that was taken from before the LORD, to put hot bread in the day when it was taken away.

• Ordinance concerning.

Le 24:5–9

• Required to be kept before the Lord continually.

Ex 25:30 — And thou shalt set upon the table shewbread before me alway.

2Ch 2:4 — Behold, I build an house to the name of the LORD my God, to dedicate *it* to him, *and* to burn before him sweet incense, and for the continual shewbread, and for the burnt offerings morning and evening, on the sabbaths, and on the new moons, and on the solemn feasts of the LORD our God. This *is an ordinance* for ever to Israel.

• Provided by a yearly per capita tax.

Ne 10:32–33

• Prepared by the Levites.

1Ch 9:32 — And *other* of their brethren, of the sons of the Kohathites, *were* over the shewbread, to prepare *it* every sabbath.

1Ch 23:29 — Both for the shewbread, and for the fine flour for meat offering, and for the unleavened cakes, and for *that which is baked in* the pan, and for that which is fried, and for all manner of measure and size;

• Unlawfully eaten by David.

Mt 12:3–4; Mk 2:25–26; Lk 6:3–4

1Sa 21:6 — So the priest gave him hallowed *bread:* for there was no bread there but the shewbread, that was taken from before the LORD, to put hot bread in the day when it was taken away.

• Placed on the table of shewbread.

Ex 40:22–23

See: Shewbread; table of

• Table of.

Heb 9:2 — For there was a tabernacle made; the first, wherein *was* the candlestick, and the table, and the shewbread; which is called the sanctuary.

• Ordinances concerning.

Ex 25:23–28; 37:10–15

• Its situation in the tabernacle.

Ex 26:35 — And thou shalt set the table without the vail, and the candlestick over against the table on the side of the tabernacle toward the south: and thou shalt put the table on the north side.

Ex 40:22 — And he put the table in the tent of the congregation, upon the side of the tabernacle northward, without the vail.

• Furniture of.

Ex 25:29–30

Ex 37:16 — And he made the vessels which *were* upon the table, his dishes, and his spoons, and his bowls, and his covers to cover withal, *of* pure gold.

Nu 4:7 — And upon the table of shewbread they shall spread a cloth of blue, and put thereon the dishes, and the spoons, and the bowls, and covers to cover withal: and the continual bread shall be thereon:

• Consecration of.

Ex 30:26–27

Ex 30:29 — And thou shalt sanctify them, that they may be most holy: whatsoever toucheth them shall be holy.

• How removed.

Nu 4:7 — And upon the table of shewbread they shall spread a cloth of blue, and put thereon the dishes, and the spoons, and the bowls, and covers to cover withal: and the continual bread shall be thereon:

Nu 4:15 — And when Aaron and his sons have made an end of covering the sanctuary, and all the vessels of the sanctuary, as the camp is to set forward; after that, the sons of Kohath shall come to bear *it:* but they shall not touch *any* holy thing, lest they die. These *things are* the burden of the sons of Kohath in the tabernacle of the congregation.

• For the temple.

1Ki 7:48 — And Solomon made all the vessels that *pertained* unto the house of the LORD: the altar of gold, and the table of gold, whereupon the shewbread *was,*

1Ki 7:50 — And the bowls, and the snuffers, and the basons, and the spoons, and the censers *of* pure gold; and the hinges *of* gold, *both* for the doors of the inner house, the most holy *place, and* for the doors of the house, *to wit,* of the temple.

2Ch 4:19 — And Solomon made all the vessels that *were for* the house of God, the golden altar also, and the tables whereon the shewbread *was set;*

2Ch 4:22 — And the snuffers, and the basons, and the spoons, and the censers, *of* pure gold: and the entry of the house, the inner doors thereof for the most holy *place,* and the doors of the house of the temple, *were of* gold.

SHIBBOLETH

Jgs 12:6 — Then said they unto him, Say now Shibboleth: and he said Sibboleth: for he could not frame to pronounce *it* right. Then they took him, and slew him at the passages of Jordan: and there fell at that time of the Ephraimites forty and two thousand.

SHIBMAH

• A city of Reuben.

Nu 32:38 — And Nebo, and Baal-meon, (their names being changed,) and Shibmah: and gave other names unto the cities which they builded.

• Apparently called also Shebam and Sibmah.

See: Sibmah

SHICRON • A city of Judah.

Jos 15:11 — And the border went out unto the side of Ekron northward: and the border was drawn to Shicron, and passed along to mount Baalah, and went out unto Jabneel; and the goings out of the border were at the sea.

SHIELD

• Defensive armor.

• Different kinds of, designated as buckler, shield, target.

Ps 35:2 — Take hold of shield and buckler, and stand up for mine help.

Eze 38:4 — And I will turn thee back, and put hooks into thy jaws, and I will bring thee forth, and all thine army, horses and horsemen, all of them clothed with all sorts *of armour, even* a great company *with* bucklers and shields, all of them handling swords:

• Used by Saul.

2Sa 1:21 — Ye mountains of Gilboa, *let there be* no dew, neither *let there be* rain, upon you, nor fields of offerings: for there the shield of the mighty is vilely cast away, the shield of Saul, *as though he had* not *been* anointed with oil.

• Used by the Benjamites.

2Ch 14:8 — And Asa had an army *of men* that bare targets and spears, out of Judah three hundred thousand; and out of Benjamin, that bare shields and drew bows, two hundred and fourscore thousand: all these *were* mighty men of valour.

2Ch 17:17 — And of Benjamin; Eliada a mighty man of valour, and with him armed men with bow and shield two hundred thousand.

• Uzziah equipped the children of Israel with.

2Ch 26:14 — And Uzziah prepared for them throughout all the host shields, and spears, and helmets, and habergeons, and bows, and slings *to cast* stones.

• Made of brass.

1Ki 14:27 — And king Rehoboam made in their stead brasen shields, and committed *them* unto the hands of the chief of the guard, which kept the door of the king's house.

• Made of gold.

1Ki 10:16–17; 2Ch 9:15–16

2Sa 8:7 — And David took the shields of gold that were on the servants of Hadadezer, and brought them to Jerusalem.

• Made of wood.

Eze 39:9–10

• Made with bosses.

Job 15:26 — He runneth upon him, *even* on *his* neck, upon the thick bosses of his bucklers:

• Stored in armories.

1Ki 10:17 — And he made three hundred shields of beaten gold; three pound of gold went to one shield: and the king put them in the house of the forest of Lebanon.

2Ch 11:12 — And in every several city *he put* shields and spears, and made them exceeding strong, having Judah and Benjamin on his side.

2Ch 32:5 — Also he strengthened himself, and built up all the wall that was broken, and raised *it* up to the towers, and another wall without, and repaired Millo *in* the city of David, and made darts and shields in abundance.

2Ch 32:27 — And Hezekiah had exceeding much riches and honour: and he made himself treasuries for silver, and for gold, and for precious stones, and for spices, and for shields, and for all manner of pleasant jewels;

• Stored in the tabernacle.

2Ki 11:10 — And to the captains over hundreds did the priest give king David's spears and shields, that *were* in the temple of the LORD.

2Ch 23:9 — Moreover Jehoiada the priest delivered to the captains of hundreds spears, and bucklers, and shields, that *had been* king David's, which *were* in the house of God.

• Covered when not in use.

Isa 22:6 — And Elam bare the quiver with chariots of men *and* horsemen, and Kir uncovered the shield.

• Painted red.

Na 2:3 — The shield of his mighty men is made red, the valiant men *are* in scarlet: the chariots *shall be* with flaming torches in the day of his preparation, and the fir trees shall be terribly shaken.

See: Arms

• Figurative.

• Of God's protection.

Ge 15:1 — After these things the word of the LORD came unto Abram in a vision, saying, Fear not, Abram: I *am* thy shield, *and* thy exceeding great reward.

Dt 33:29 — Happy *art* thou, O Israel: who *is* like unto thee, O people saved by the LORD, the shield of thy help, and who *is* the sword of thy excellency!

and thine enemies shall be found liars unto thee; and thou shalt tread upon their high places.

2Sa 22:3 — The God of my rock; in him will I trust: *he is* my shield, and the horn of my salvation, my high tower, and my refuge, my saviour; thou savest me from violence.

2Sa 22:36 — Thou hast also given me the shield of thy salvation: and thy gentleness hath made me great.

Ps 5:12 — For thou, LORD, wilt bless the righteous; with favour wilt thou compass him as *with* a shield.

Ps 18:2 — The LORD *is* my rock, and my fortress, and my deliverer; my God, my strength, in whom I will trust; my buckler, and the horn of my salvation, *and* my high tower.

Ps 18:35 — Thou hast also given me the shield of thy salvation: and thy right hand hath holden me up, and thy gentleness hath made me great.

Ps 33:20 — Our soul waiteth for the LORD: he *is* our help and our shield.

Ps 59:11 — Slay them not, lest my people forget: scatter them by thy power; and bring them down, O Lord our shield.

Ps 84:9 — Behold, O God our shield, and look upon the face of thine anointed.

Ps 84:11 — For the LORD God *is* a sun and shield: the LORD will give grace and glory: no good *thing* will he withhold from them that walk uprightly.

Ps 89:18 — For the LORD *is* our defence; and the Holy One of Israel *is* our king.

Pr 30:5 — Every word of God *is* pure: he *is* a shield unto them that put their trust in him.

- **Of God's truth.**

Ps 91:4 — He shall cover thee with his feathers, and under his wings shalt thou trust: his truth *shall be thy* shield and buckler.

- **Of an entire army.**

Jer 46:3 — Order ye the buckler and shield, and draw near to battle.

SHIGGAION

Ps 7:1–17

Hab 3:1 — A prayer of Habakkuk the prophet upon Shigionoth.

See: Music

SHIHON • A city in Issachar.

Jos 19:19 — And Haphraim, and Shihon, and Anaharath,

SHIHOR **See: Sihor**

SHIHOR-LIBNATH • A place on the border of Asher.

Jos 19:26 — And Alammelech, and Amad, and Misheal; and reacheth to Carmel westward, and to Shihor-libnath;

SHILHI • Grandfather of Jehoshaphat.

1Ki 22:42 — Jehoshaphat *was* thirty and five years old when he began to reign; and he reigned twenty and five years in Jerusalem. And his mother's name *was* Azubah the daughter of Shilhi.

2Ch 20:31 — And Jehoshaphat reigned over Judah: *he was* thirty and five years old when he began to reign, and he reigned twenty and five years in Jerusalem. And his mother's name *was* Azubah the daughter of Shilhi.

SHILHIM • A city of Judah.

Jos 15:32 — And Lebaoth, and Shilhim, and Ain, and Rimmon: all the cities *are* twenty and nine, with their villages:

SHILLEM

- **Called also Shallum.**
- **Son of Naphtali.**

Ge 46:24 — And the sons of Naphtali; Jahzeel, and Guni, and Jezer, and Shillem.

Nu 26:49 — Of Jezer, the family of the Jezerites: of Shillem, the family of the Shillemites.

1Ch 7:13 — The sons of Naphtali; Jahziel, and Guni, and Jezer, and Shallum, the sons of Bilhah.

SHILOAH

- **A stream or pool, probably identical with Siloah and Siloam.**

Isa 8:6 — Forasmuch as this people refuseth the waters of Shiloah that go softly, and rejoice in Rezin and Remaliah's son;

See: Siloah

See: Siloam

SHILOH

- **A name of Jesus.**

Ge 49:10 — The sceptre shall not depart from Judah, nor a lawgiver from between his feet, until Shiloh come; and unto him *shall* the gathering of the people *be.*

- **City of Ephraim.**
  - **North of Bethel, and on the highway from Bethel to Shechem.**

Jgs 21:19 — Then they said, Behold, *there is* a feast of the LORD in Shiloh yearly *in a place* which *is* on the north side of Bethel, on the east side of the highway that goeth up from Bethel to Shechem, and on the south of Lebonah.

  - **Tabernacle at.**

Jos 18:8–10

Jos 18:1 — And the whole congregation of the children of Israel assembled together at Shiloh, and set up the tabernacle of the congregation there. And the land was subdued before them.

Jgs 18:31 — And they set them up Micah's graven image, which he made, all the time that the house of God was in Shiloh.

Jgs 21:19 — Then they said, Behold, *there is* a feast of the LORD in Shiloh yearly *in a place* which *is* on the north side of Bethel, on the east side of the highway that goeth up from Bethel to Shechem, and on the south of Lebonah.

1Sa 1:3 — And this man went up out of his city yearly to worship and to sacrifice unto the LORD of hosts in Shiloh. And the two sons of Eli, Hophni and Phinehas, the priests of the LORD, *were* there.

1Sa 1:9 — So Hannah rose up after they had eaten in Shiloh, and after they had drunk. Now Eli the priest sat upon a seat by a post of the temple of the LORD.

1Sa 1:21 — And the man Elkanah, and all his house, went up to offer unto the LORD the yearly sacrifice, and his vow.

1Sa 1:24 — And when she had weaned him, she took him up with her, with three bullocks, and one ephah of flour, and a bottle of wine, and brought him unto the house of the LORD in Shiloh: and the child *was* young.

1Sa 2:14 — And he struck *it* into the pan, or kettle, or caldron, or pot; all that the fleshhook brought up the priest took for himself. So they did in Shiloh unto all the Israelites that came thither.

Ps 78:60 — So that he forsook the tabernacle of Shiloh, the tent *which* he placed among men;

Jer 7:12 — But go ye now unto my place which *was* in Shiloh, where I set my name at the first, and see what I did to it for the wickedness of my people Israel.

• Seat of government during the time of Joshua.

Jos 21:1–2

• The place of rendezvous for the tribes.

Jos 22:9 — And the children of Reuben and the children of Gad and the half tribe of Manasseh returned, and departed from the children of Israel out of Shiloh, which *is* in the land of Canaan, to go unto the country of Gilead, to the land of their possession, whereof they were possessed, according to the word of the LORD by the hand of Moses.

Jos 22:12 — And when the children of Israel heard *of it,* the whole congregation of the children of Israel gathered themselves together at Shiloh, to go up to war against them.

Jgs 21:12 — And they found among the inhabitants of Jabesh-gilead four hundred young virgins, that had known no man by lying with any male: and they brought them unto the camp to Shiloh, which is in the land of Canaan.

• Eli dwelt at.

1Sa 4:12–13

1Sa 1:9 — So Hannah rose up after they had eaten in Shiloh, and after they had drunk. Now Eli the priest sat upon a seat by a post of the temple of the LORD.

• Eli dies at.

1Sa 4:18 — And it came to pass, when he made mention of the ark of God, that he fell from off the seat backward by the side of the gate, and his neck brake, and he died: for he was an old man, and heavy. And he had judged Israel forty years.

• Ahijah the prophet dwells at.

1Ki 14:2 — And Jeroboam said to his wife, Arise, I pray thee, and disguise thyself, that thou be not known to be the wife of Jeroboam; and get thee to Shiloh: behold, there *is* Ahijah the prophet, which told me that *I should be* king over this people.

• Devoted men from, slain by Ishmael.

Jer 41:5–9

SHILONI • Father of Zechariah.

Ne 11:5 — And Maaseiah the son of Baruch, the son of Col-hozeh, the son of Hazaiah, the son of Adaiah, the son of Joiarib, the son of Zechariah, the son of Shiloni.

SHILONITE

• A man of Shiloh.

1Ki 11:29 — And it came to pass at that time when Jeroboam went out of Jerusalem, that the prophet Ahijah the Shilonite found him in the way; and he had clad himself with a new garment; and they two *were* alone in the field:

1Ki 12:15 — Wherefore the king hearkened not unto the people; for the cause was from the LORD, that he might perform his saying, which the LORD spake by Ahijah the Shilonite unto Jeroboam the son of Nebat.

1Ki 15:29 — And it came to pass, when he reigned, *that* he smote all the house of Jeroboam; he left not to Jeroboam any that breathed, until he had destroyed him, according unto the saying of the LORD, which he spake by his servant Ahijah the Shilonite:

2Ch 9:29 — Now the rest of the acts of Solomon, first and last, *are* they not written in the book of Nathan the prophet, and in the prophecy of Ahijah the Shilonite, and in the visions of Iddo the seer against Jeroboam the son of Nebat?

2Ch 10:15 — So the king hearkened not unto the people: for the cause was of God, that the LORD might perform his word, which he spake by the hand of Ahijah the Shilonite to Jeroboam the son of Nebat.

• Used, apparently, to denote a descendant of Shelah.

1Ch 9:5 — And of the Shilonites; Asaiah the firstborn, and his sons.

See: Shelanites

SHILSHAH

• Son of Zophah.

1Ch 7:37 — Bezer, and Hod, and Shamma and Shilshah, and Ithran, and Beera.

SHIMEA

See: Shammuah

See: Shammah; David's brother

• A Merarite Levite.

1Ch 6:30 — Shimea his son, Haggiah his son, Asaiah his son.

• **Grandfather of Asaph.**

1Ch 6:39 — And his brother Asaph, who stood on his right hand, *even* Asaph the son of Berachiah, the son of Shimea,

SHIMEAH

• **A Benjamite.**

• **Son of Mikloth.**

1Ch 8:32 — And Mikloth begat Shimeah. And these also dwelt with their brethren in Jerusalem, over against them.

• **Called Shimeam.**

1Ch 9:38 — And Mikloth begat Shimeam. And they also dwelt with their brethren at Jerusalem, over against their brethren.

↞See: Shammah; David's brother

SHIMEAM ↞See: Shimeah; a Benjamite. Son of Mikloth

SHIMEATH • Mother of an assassin of King Joash.

2Ki 12:21 — For Jozachar the son of Shimeath, and Jehozabad the son of Shomer, his servants, smote him, and he died; and they buried him with his fathers in the city of David: and Amaziah his son reigned in his stead.

2Ch 24:26 — And these are they that conspired against him; Zabad the son of Shimeath an Ammonitess, and Jehozabad the son of Shimrith a Moabitess.

SHIMEATHITES • A family of scribes.

1Ch 2:55 — And the families of the scribes which dwelt at Jabez; the Tirathites, the Shimeathites, *and* Suchathites. These *are* the Kenites that came of Hemath, the father of the house of Rechab.

SHIMEI

• **Called also Shimi.**

• **Son of Gershon.**

Ex 6:17 — The sons of Gershon; Libni, and Shimi, according to their families.

Nu 3:18 — And these *are* the names of the sons of Gershon by their families; Libni, and Shimei.

1Ch 6:17 — And these *be* the names of the sons of Gershom; Libni, and Shimei.

1Ch 23:7 — Of the Gershonites *were,* Laadan, and Shimei.

1Ch 23:10 — And the sons of Shimei *were,* Jahath, Zina, and Jeush, and Beriah. These four *were* the sons of Shimei.

• **A Benjamite.**

• **Curses David; David's magnanimity toward.**

2Sa 16:5–13; 19:16–23; 1Ki 2:36–46

• **An officer of David.**

1Ki 1:8 — But Zadok the priest, and Benaiah the son of Jehoiada, and Nathan the prophet, and Shimei, and Rei, and the mighty men which *belonged* to David, were not with Adonijah.

• **One of Solomon's commissary officers.**

1Ki 4:18 — Shimei the son of Elah, in Benjamin:

• **Grandson of Jeconiah.**

1Ch 3:19 — And the sons of Pedaiah *were,* Zerubbabel, and Shimei: and the sons of Zerubbabel; Meshullam, and Hananiah, and Shelomith their sister:

• **Son of Zacchur.**

1Ch 4:26–27

• **A Reubenite.**

• **Son of Gog.**

1Ch 5:4 — The sons of Joel; Shemaiah his son, Gog his son, Shimei his son,

• **A Merarite.**

• **Son of Libni.**

1Ch 6:29 — The sons of Merari; Mahli, Libni his son, Shimei his son, Uzza his son,

• **A Gershonite.**

• **Son of Jahath.**

1Ch 6:42 — The son of Ethan, the son of Zimmah, the son of Shimei,

• **Father of a family in Benjamin. In KJV, called Shimhi.**

1Ch 8:21 — And Adaiah, and Beraiah, and Shimrath, the sons of Shimhi;

• **A Levite.**

1Ch 23:9 — The sons of Shimei; Shelomith, and Haziel, and Haran, three. These *were* the chief of the fathers of Laadan.

• **A leader of singers in time of David.**

1Ch 25:17 — The tenth to Shimei, *he,* his sons, and his brethren, *were* twelve:

• **David's overseer of vineyards.**

1Ch 27:27 — And over the vineyards was Shimei the Ramathite: over the increase of the vineyards for the wine cellars *was* Zabdi the Shiphmite:

• **A son of Heman.**

2Ch 29:14 — And of the sons of Heman; Jehiel, and Shimei: and of the sons of Jeduthun; Shemaiah, and Uzziel.

• **A Levite.**

• **Treasurer of tithes and offerings in time of Hezekiah.**

2Ch 31:12–13

• **A Levite who put away his Gentile wife.**

Ezr 10:23 — Also of the Levites; Jozabad, and Shimei, and Kelaiah, (the same *is* Kelita,) Pethahiah, Judah, and Eliezer.

• **The name of two Israelites who put away Gentile wives.**

Ezr 10:33 — Of the sons of Hashum; Mattenai, Mattathah, Zabad, Eliphelet, Jeremai, Manasseh, *and* Shimei.

Ezr 10:38 — And Bani, and Binnui, Shimei,

• **A Benjamite.**

• **Grandfather of Mordecai.**

Est 2:5 — *Now* in Shushan the palace there was a certain Jew, whose name *was* Mordecai, the son of Jair, the son of Shimei, the son of Kish, a Benjamite;

• The ancestor of a family.

• Possibly identical with Shimi.

Zec 12:13 — The family of the house of Levi apart, and their wives apart; the family of Shimei apart, and their wives apart;

SHIMEON • An Israelite who put away his Gentile wife.

Ezr 10:31 — And *of* the sons of Harim; Eliezer, Ishijah, Malchiah, Shemaiah, Shimeon,

SHIMHI

• Father of a family in Benjamin.

• In some versions, called Shimei.

1Ch 8:21 — And Adaiah, and Beraiah, and Shimrath, the sons of Shimhi;

SHIMI ➔See: Shimei; called also Shimi. Son of Gershon

SHIMMA ➔See: Shammah; David's brother

SHIMON • A man of Judah.

1Ch 4:20 — And the sons of Shimon *were,* Amnon, and Rinnah, Ben-hanan, and Tilon. And the sons of Ishi *were,* Zoheth, and Ben-zoheth.

SHIMRATH • Son of Shimhi.

1Ch 8:21 — And Adaiah, and Beraiah, and Shimrath, the sons of Shimhi;

SHIMRI

• Head of a family in Simeon.

1Ch 4:37–38

• Father of one of David's mighty men.

1Ch 11:45 — Jediael the son of Shimri, and Joha his brother, the Tizite,

• A Merarite. In King James Version, called Simri.

1Ch 26:10 — Also Hosah, of the children of Merari, had sons; Simri the chief, (for *though* he was not the firstborn, yet his father made him the chief;)

• A Levite in the time of Hezekiah.

2Ch 29:13 — And of the sons of Elizaphan; Shimri, and Jeiel: and of the sons of Asaph; Zechariah, and Mattaniah:

SHIMRITH

• A Moabitess.

• Mother of Jehozabad, murderer of King Joash.

2Ch 24:26 — And these are they that conspired against him; Zabad the son of Shimeath an Ammonitess, and Jehozabad the son of Shimrith a Moabitess.

• Called Shomer.

2Ki 12:21 — For Jozachar the son of Shimeath, and Jehozabad the son of Shomer, his servants, smote him, and he died; and they buried him with his fathers in the city of David: and Amaziah his son reigned in his stead.

SHIMROM ➔See: Shimron

SHIMRON

• Son of Issachar.

Ge 46:13 — And the sons of Issachar; Tola, and Phuvah, and Job, and Shimron.

Nu 26:24 — Of Jashub, the family of the Jashubites: of Shimron, the family of the Shimronites.

• Called Shimrom.

1Ch 7:1 — Now the sons of Issachar *were,* Tola, and Puah, Jashub, and Shimrom, four.

• A city in Zebulun.

Jos 11:1 — And it came to pass, when Jabin king of Hazor had heard *those things,* that he sent to Jobab king of Madon, and to the king of Shimron, and to the king of Achshaph,

Jos 19:15 — And Kattath, and Nahallal, and Shimron, and Idalah, and Bethlehem: twelve cities with their villages.

➔See: Shimron-Meron

SHIMRON-MERON

• A city conquered by Joshua.

Jos 12:20 — The king of Shimron-meron, one; the king of Achshaph, one;

• Probably identical with Shimron, a city in Zebulon.

SHIMRONITES • The family of Shimron.

Nu 26:24 — Of Jashub, the family of the Jashubites: of Shimron, the family of the Shimronites.

SHIMSHAI

• A scribe.

Ezr 4:8–9

Ezr 4:17 — *Then* sent the king an answer unto Rehum the chancellor, and *to* Shimshai the scribe, and *to* the rest of their companions that dwell in Samaria, and *unto* the rest beyond the river, Peace, and at such a time.

Ezr 4:23 — Now when the copy of king Artaxerxes' letter *was* read before Rehum, and Shimshai the scribe, and their companions, they went up in haste to Jerusalem unto the Jews, and made them to cease by force and power.

SHINAB • King of Admah.

Ge 14:2 — *That these* made war with Bera king of Sodom, and with Birsha king of Gomorrah, Shinab king of Admah, and Shemeber king of Zeboiim, and the king of Bela, which is Zoar.

SHINAR

• Land of.

➔See: Babylon

SHIP

• Built by Noah.

Ge 6:13–22

• Built by Solomon.

1Ki 9:26 — And king Solomon made a navy of ships in Ezion-geber, which is beside Eloth, on the shore of the Red sea, in the land of Edom.

2Ch 8:17 — Then went Solomon to Ezion-geber, and to Eloth, at the sea side in the land of Edom.

• Built by Jehoshaphat.

2Ch 20:35–36

1Ki 22:48 — Jehoshaphat made ships of Tharshish to go to Ophir for gold: but they went not; for the ships were broken at Ezion-geber.

• Built of gopher wood.

Ge 6:14 — Make thee an ark of gopher wood; rooms shalt thou make in the ark, and shalt pitch it within and without with pitch.

• Built of fir wood.

Eze 27:5 — They have made all thy *ship* boards of fir trees of Senir: they have taken cedars from Lebanon to make masts for thee.

• Built of bulrushes.

Isa 18:2 — That sendeth ambassadors by the sea, even in vessels of bulrushes upon the waters, *saying,* Go, ye swift messengers, to a nation scattered and peeled, to a people terrible from their beginning hitherto; a nation meted out and trodden down, whose land the rivers have spoiled!

• Sealed with pitch.

Ge 6:14 — Make thee an ark of gopher wood; rooms shalt thou make in the ark, and shalt pitch it within and without with pitch.

• Equipped with helm.

Jas 3:4 — Behold also the ships, which though *they be* so great, and *are* driven of fierce winds, yet are they turned about with a very small helm, whithersoever the governor listeth.

• Equipped with rudder.

Ac 27:40 — And when they had taken up the anchors, they committed *themselves* unto the sea, and loosed the rudder bands, and hoisted up the mainsail to the wind, and made toward shore.

• Equipped with tackling.

Isa 33:23 — Thy tacklings are loosed; they could not well strengthen their mast, they could not spread the sail: then is the prey of a great spoil divided; the lame take the prey.

Ac 27:19 — And the third *day* we cast out with our own hands the tackling of the ship.

• Equipped with sails.

Isa 33:23 — Thy tacklings are loosed; they could not well strengthen their mast, they could not spread the sail: then is the prey of a great spoil divided; the lame take the prey.

Ac 27:1 — And when it was determined that we should sail into Italy, they delivered Paul and certain other prisoners unto *one* named Julius, a centurion of Augustus' band.

Ac 27:9 — Now when much time was spent, and when sailing was now dangerous, because the fast was now already past, Paul admonished *them,*

Ac 27:17 — Which when they had taken up, they used helps, undergirding the ship; and, fearing lest they should fall into the quicksands, strake sail, and so were driven.

Ac 27:40 — And when they had taken up the anchors, they committed *themselves* unto the sea, and loosed the rudder bands, and hoisted up the mainsail to the wind, and made toward shore.

• Sails embroidered.

Eze 27:7 — Fine linen with broidered work from Egypt was that which thou spreadest forth to be thy sail; blue and purple from the isles of Elishah was that which covered thee.

• Equipped with masts.

Isa 33:23 — Thy tacklings are loosed; they could not well strengthen their mast, they could not spread the sail: then is the prey of a great spoil divided; the lame take the prey.

Eze 27:5 — They have made all thy *ship* boards of fir trees of Senir: they have taken cedars from Lebanon to make masts for thee.

• Equipped with oars.

Jnh 1:13 — Nevertheless the men rowed hard to bring *it* to the land; but they could not: for the sea wrought, and was tempestuous against them.

Mk 6:48 — And he saw them toiling in rowing; for the wind was contrary unto them: and about the fourth watch of the night he cometh unto them, walking upon the sea, and would have passed by them.

• Equipped with figurehead.

Ac 28:11 — And after three months we departed in a ship of Alexandria, which had wintered in the isle, whose sign was Castor and Pollux.

• Equipped with anchor.

Ac 27:29–30

Ac 27:40 — And when they had taken up the anchors, they committed *themselves* unto the sea, and loosed the rudder bands, and hoisted up the mainsail to the wind, and made toward shore.

• Equipped with lifeboats.

Ac 27:30 — And as the shipmen were about to flee out of the ship, when they had let down the boat into the sea, under colour as though they would have cast anchors out of the foreship,

Ac 27:32 — Then the soldiers cut off the ropes of the boat, and let her fall off.

• Used in commerce.

Ac 21:3 — Now when we had discovered Cyprus, we left it on the left hand, and sailed into Syria, and landed at Tyre: for there the ship was to unlade her burden.

Ac 27:10 — And said unto them, Sirs, I perceive that this voyage will be with hurt and much damage, not only of the lading and ship, but also of our lives.

- **Used in commerce with Tarshish.**

1Ki 22:48 — Jehoshaphat made ships of Tharshish to go to Ophir for gold: but they went not; for the ships were broken at Ezion-geber.

Isa 60:9 — Surely the isles shall wait for me, and the ships of Tarshish first, to bring thy sons from far, their silver and their gold with them, unto the name of the LORD thy God, and to the Holy One of Israel, because he hath glorified thee.

Jnh 1:3 — But Jonah rose up to flee unto Tarshish from the presence of the LORD, and went down to Joppa; and he found a ship going to Tarshish: so he paid the fare thereof, and went down into it, to go with them unto Tarshish from the presence of the LORD.

- **Used with Ophir.**

1Ki 10:11 — And the navy also of Hiram, that brought gold from Ophir, brought in from Ophir great plenty of almug trees, and precious stones.

2Ch 8:18 — And Huram sent him by the hands of his servants ships, and servants that had knowledge of the sea; and they went with the servants of Solomon to Ophir, and took thence four hundred and fifty talents of gold, and brought *them* to king Solomon.

- **Used with Adramyttium.**

Ac 27:2 — And entering into a ship of Adramyttium, we launched, meaning to sail by the coasts of Asia; *one* Aristarchus, a Macedonian of Thessalonica, being with us.

- **Used for passenger traffic.**

Isa 60:9 — Surely the isles shall wait for me, and the ships of Tarshish first, to bring thy sons from far, their silver and their gold with them, unto the name of the LORD thy God, and to the Holy One of Israel, because he hath glorified thee.

Jnh 1:3 — But Jonah rose up to flee unto Tarshish from the presence of the LORD, and went down to Joppa; and he found a ship going to Tarshish: so he paid the fare thereof, and went down into it, to go with them unto Tarshish from the presence of the LORD.

Ac 20:13 — And we went before to ship, and sailed unto Assos, there intending to take in Paul: for so had he appointed, minding himself to go afoot.

Ac 27:2 — And entering into a ship of Adramyttium, we launched, meaning to sail by the coasts of Asia; *one* Aristarchus, a Macedonian of Thessalonica, being with us.

Ac 27:37 — And we were in all in the ship two hundred threescore and sixteen souls.

Ac 28:11 — And after three months we departed in a ship of Alexandria, which had wintered in the isle, whose sign was Castor and Pollux.

- **Used for ferriage.**

2Sa 19:18 — And there went over a ferry boat to carry over the king's household, and to do what he thought good. And Shimei the son of Gera fell down before the king, as he was come over Jordan;

- **Repaired by calking.**

Eze 27:9 — The ancients of Gebal and the wise *men* thereof were in thee thy calkers: all the ships of the sea with their mariners were in thee to occupy thy merchandise.

- **Wrecked at Ezion-geber.**

2Ch 20:35–37

1Ki 22:48 — Jehoshaphat made ships of Tharshish to go to Ophir for gold: but they went not; for the ships were broken at Ezion-geber.

- **Wrecked at Melita.**

Ac 27:14 — But not long after there arose against it a tempestuous wind, called Euroclydon.

Ac 27:44 — And the rest, some on boards, and some on *broken pieces* of the ship. And so it came to pass, that they escaped all safe to land.

- **Warships used by Chittim.**

Nu 24:24 — And ships *shall come* from the coast of Chittim, and shall afflict Asshur, and shall afflict Eber, and he also shall perish for ever.

Da 11:30 — For the ships of Chittim shall come against him: therefore he shall be grieved, and return, and have indignation against the holy covenant: so shall he do; he shall even return, and have intelligence with them that forsake the holy covenant.

See: Mariner

SHIPHI • Father of Ziza.

1Ch 4:37 — And Ziza the son of Shiphi, the son of Allon, the son of Jedaiah, the son of Shimri, the son of Shemaiah;

SHIPHRAH • A Hebrew midwife.

Ex 1:15 — And the king of Egypt spake to the Hebrew midwives, of which the name of the one *was* Shiphrah, and the name of the other Puah:

SHIPHTAN • Father of the representative of Ephraim on the committee which divided the promised land among the Israelites.

Nu 34:24 — And the prince of the tribe of the children of Ephraim, Kemuel the son of Shiphtan.

SHISHA See: Seraiah; called also Sheva, Shisha, and Shavsha. David's scribe

SHISHAK

- **King of Egypt.**
- **Gives asylum to Jeroboam.**

1Ki 11:40 — Solomon sought therefore to kill Jeroboam. And Jeroboam arose, and fled into Egypt, unto Shishak king of Egypt, and was in Egypt until the death of Solomon.

- **Spoils Jerusalem.**

1Ki 14:25–26; 2Ch 12:2–9

SHITRAI • A chief herder of David.

1Ch 27:29 — And over the herds that fed in Sharon *was* Shitrai the Sharonite: and over the herds *that were* in the valleys *was* Shaphat the son of Adlai:

SHITTIM

• Called also Abel-shittim.

Nu 33:49 — And they pitched by Jordan, from Beth-jesimoth *even* unto Abel-shittim in the plains of Moab.

• A camping place of Israel.

Nu 25:1 — And Israel abode in Shittim, and the people began to commit whoredom with the daughters of Moab.

Nu 33:49 — And they pitched by Jordan, from Beth-jesimoth *even* unto Abel-shittim in the plains of Moab.

• Joshua sends spies from.

Jos 2:1 — And Joshua the son of Nun sent out of Shittim two men to spy secretly, saying, Go view the land, even Jericho. And they went, and came into an harlot's house, named Rahab, and lodged there.

• Valley of.

Joel 3:18 — And it shall come to pass in that day, *that* the mountains shall drop down new wine, and the hills shall flow with milk, and all the rivers of Judah shall flow with waters, and a fountain shall come forth of the house of the LORD, and shall water the valley of Shittim.

• Balaam prophesies in.

Mic 6:5 — O my people, remember now what Balak king of Moab consulted, and what Balaam the son of Beor answered him from Shittim unto Gilgal; that ye may know the righteousness of the LORD.

• A tree, the wood of which is fragrant; planted and cultivated.

• Called also Shittah.

Isa 41:19 — I will plant in the wilderness the cedar, the shittah tree, and the myrtle, and the oil tree; I will set in the desert the fir tree, *and* the pine, and the box tree together:

• The ark of the covenant made of.

Ex 25:10 — And they shall make an ark *of* shittim wood: two cubits and a half *shall be* the length thereof, and a cubit and a half the breadth thereof, and a cubit and a half the height thereof.

• Staves of the ark made of.

Ex 25:13 — And thou shalt make staves *of* shittim wood, and overlay them with gold.

Ex 38:6 — And he made the staves *of* shittim wood, and overlaid them with brass.

• Boards in the tabernacle made of.

Ex 26:15–37

• The altar of burnt offerings made of.

Ex 38:1 — And he made the altar of burnt offering *of* shittim wood: five cubits *was* the length thereof, and five cubits the breadth thereof; *it was* foursquare; and three cubits the height thereof.

Ex 38:6 — And he made the staves *of* shittim wood, and overlaid them with brass.

SHIZA

• A Reubenite.

• Father of one of David's mighty men.

1Ch 11:42 — Adina the son of Shiza the Reubenite, a captain of the Reubenites, and thirty with him,

SHOA • An unknown country or city, or a symbolic term.

Eze 23:23 — The Babylonians, and all the Chaldeans, Pekod, and Shoa, and Koa, *and* all the Assyrians with them: all of them desirable young men, captains and rulers, great lords and renowned, all of them riding upon horses.

SHOBAB

• Son of David.

2Sa 5:14 — And these *be* the names of those that were born unto him in Jerusalem; Shammuah, and Shobab, and Nathan, and Solomon,

1Ch 3:5 — And these were born unto him in Jerusalem; Shimea, and Shobab, and Nathan, and Solomon, four, of Bath-shua the daughter of Ammiel:

1Ch 14:4 — Now these *are* the names of *his* children which he had in Jerusalem; Shammua, and Shobab, Nathan, and Solomon,

• Son of Caleb.

1Ch 2:18 — And Caleb the son of Hezron begat *children* of Azubah *his* wife, and of Jerioth: her sons *are* these; Jesher, and Shobab, and Ardon.

SHOBACH

• Captain of the host of Hadarezer.

2Sa 10:16 — And Hadarezer sent, and brought out the Syrians that *were* beyond the river: and they came to Helam; and Shobach the captain of the host of Hadarezer *went* before them.

• Slain by David's army.

2Sa 10:18 — And the Syrians fled before Israel; and David slew *the men of* seven hundred chariots of the Syrians, and forty thousand horsemen, and smote Shobach the captain of their host, who died there.

• Called Shophach.

1Ch 19:16 — And when the Syrians saw that they were put to the worse before Israel, they sent messengers, and drew forth the Syrians that *were* beyond the river: and Shophach the captain of the host of Hadarezer *went* before them.

1Ch 19:18 — But the Syrians fled before Israel; and David slew of the Syrians seven thousand *men which fought in* chariots, and forty thousand footmen, and killed Shophach the captain of the host.

SHOBAI • A porter, whose descendants returned to Jerusalem with Zerubbabel.

Ezr 2:42 — The children of the porters: the children of Shallum, the children of Ater, the children of Talmon, the children of Akkub, the children of Hatita, the children of Shobai, *in* all an hundred thirty and nine.

Ne 7:45 — The porters: the children of Shallum, the children of Ater, the children of Talmon, the children of Akkub, the children of Hatita, the children of Shobai, an hundred thirty and eight.

SHOBAL

• Son of Seir.

Ge 36:20 — These *are* the sons of Seir the Horite, who inhabited the land; Lotan, and Shobal, and Zibeon, and Anah,

Ge 36:23 — And the children of Shobal *were* these; Alvan, and Manahath, and Ebal, Shepho, and Onam.

Ge 36:29 — These *are* the dukes *that came* of the Horites; duke Lotan, duke Shobal, duke Zibeon, duke Anah,

1Ch 1:38 — And the sons of Seir; Lotan, and Shobal, and Zibeon, and Anah, and Dishon, and Ezar, and Dishan.

1Ch 1:40 — The sons of Shobal; Alian, and Manahath, and Ebal, Shephi, and Onam. And the sons of Zibeon; Aiah, and Anah.

• Son of Caleb.

1Ch 2:50 — These were the sons of Caleb the son of Hur, the firstborn of Ephratah; Shobal the father of Kirjath-jearim,

1Ch 2:52 — And Shobal the father of Kirjath-jearim had sons; Haroeh, *and* half of the Manahethites.

• Son of Judah.

1Ch 4:1–2

SHOBEK • A Jew who sealed the covenant with Nehemiah.

Ne 10:24 — Hallohesh, Pileha, Shobek,

SHOBI

• Son of Nahash.

• Brought supplies to David in his flight from Absalom.

2Sa 17:27 — And it came to pass, when David was come to Mahanaim, that Shobi the son of Nahash of Rabbah of the children of Ammon, and Machir the son of Ammiel of Lo-debar, and Barzillai the Gileadite of Rogelim,

SHOCHO

• A city of Judah

↞See: Socoh; called also Shocho, Shochoh, Shoco, Sochoh.

SHOCHOH

• A city of Judah

↞See: Socoh; called also Shocho, Shochoh, Shoco, Sochoh.

SHOCO

• A city of Judah

↞See: Socoh; called also Shocho, Shochoh, Shoco, Sochoh.

SHOE

• Taken off on holy ground.

Ex 3:5 — And he said, Draw not nigh hither: put off thy shoes from off thy feet, for the place whereon thou standest is holy ground.

Jos 5:15 — And the captain of the LORD's host said unto Joshua, Loose thy shoe from off thy foot; for the place whereon thou standest *is* holy. And Joshua did so.

Ac 7:33 — Then said the Lord to him, Put off thy shoes from thy feet: for the place where thou standest is holy ground.

• Put off in mourning.

Eze 24:17 — Forbear to cry, make no mourning for the dead, bind the tire of thine head upon thee, and put on thy shoes upon thy feet, and cover not *thy* lips, and eat not the bread of men.

• Of the children of Israel did not wax old.

Dt 29:5 — And I have led you forty years in the wilderness: your clothes are not waxen old upon you, and thy shoe is not waxen old upon thy foot.

• Loosed in token of refusal to observe the levirate marriage.

Ru 4:7–8

Dt 25:9 — Then shall his brother's wife come unto him in the presence of the elders, and loose his shoe from off his foot, and spit in his face, and shall answer and say, So shall it be done unto that man that will not build up his brother's house.

• Poor sold for a pair of.

Am 2:6 — Thus saith the LORD; For three transgressions of Israel, and for four, I will not turn away *the punishment* thereof; because they sold the righteous for silver, and the poor for a pair of shoes;

Am 8:6 — That we may buy the poor for silver, and the needy for a pair of shoes; *yea,* and sell the refuse of the wheat?

• Made of iron.

Dt 33:25 — Thy shoes *shall be* iron and brass; and as thy days, *so shall* thy strength *be.*

• Made of badgers' skins.

Eze 16:10 — I clothed thee also with broidered work, and shod thee with badgers' skin, and I girded thee about with fine linen, and I covered thee with silk.

• Latchet of.

Ge 14:23 — That I will not *take* from a thread even to a shoelatchet, and that I will not take any thing that *is* thine, lest thou shouldest say, I have made Abram rich:

Isa 5:27 — None shall be weary nor stumble among them; none shall slumber nor sleep; neither shall the girdle of their loins be loosed, nor the latchet of their shoes be broken:

Mk 1:7 — And preached, saying, There cometh one mightier than I after me, the latchet of whose shoes I am not worthy to stoop down and unloose.

• Loosing of, a humble service.

Lk 3:16 — John answered, saying unto *them* all, I indeed baptize you with water; but one mightier than I cometh, the latchet of whose shoes I am not worthy to unloose: he shall baptize you with the Holy Ghost and with fire:

SHOHAM

• A Merarite.

1Ch 24:27 — The sons of Merari by Jaaziah; Beno, and Shoham, and Zaccur, and Ibri.

SHOMER

✦See: Shamer; an Asherite; called Shomer

✦See: Shimrith

SHOPHACH ✦See: Shobach

SHOPHAN

• A city in Gad.

• Called Atroth-shophan in some versions.

Nu 32:35 — And Atroth, Shophan, and Jaazer, and Jogbehah,

SHOSHANNIM

• Called also Shushan, Shoshannim-Eduth.

• A wind instrument.

• Mentioned in the titles of Pss 45, 60, 69, 80.

Ps 45:1 — [To the chief Musician upon Shoshannim, for the sons of Korah, Maschil, A Song of loves.] My heart is inditing a good matter: I speak of the things which I have made touching the king: my tongue *is* the pen of a ready writer.

Ps 60:1 — [To the chief Musician upon Shushaneduth, Michtam of David, to teach; when he strove with Aramnaharaim and with Aramzobah, when Joab returned, and smote of Edom in the valley of salt twelve thousand.] O God, thou hast cast us off, thou hast scattered us, thou hast been displeased; O turn thyself to us again.

Ps 69:1 — [To the chief Musician upon Shoshannim, A Psalm of David.] Save me, O God; for the waters are come in unto *my* soul.

Ps 80:1 — [To the chief Musician upon Shoshannimeduth, A Psalm of Asaph.] Give ear, O Shepherd of Israel, thou that leadest Joseph like a flock; thou that dwellest *between* the cherubims, shine forth.

✦See: Music; instruments of

SHOUTING

• In joy and praise.

2Ch 15:12–14; Ezr 3:11–13; Lk 19:37–41; Ac 3:8–9; Rev 5:12–14

1Ch 15:28 — Thus all Israel brought up the ark of the covenant of the LORD with shouting, and with sound of the cornet, and with trumpets, and with cymbals, making a noise with psalteries and harps.

Ps 5:11 — But let all those that put their trust in thee rejoice: let them ever shout for joy, because thou defendest them: let them also that love thy name be joyful in thee.

Ps 47:1 — O clap your hands, all ye people; shout unto God with the voice of triumph.

Isa 12:6 — Cry out and shout, thou inhabitant of Zion: for great *is* the Holy One of Israel in the midst of thee.

Lk 17:15 — And one of them, when he saw that he was healed, turned back, and with a loud voice glorified God,

SHOVEL

• A utensil in the tabernacle.

Ex 27:3 — And thou shalt make his pans to receive his ashes, and his shovels, and his basons, and his fleshhooks, and his firepans: all the vessels thereof thou shalt make *of* brass.

Ex 38:3 — And he made all the vessels of the altar, the pots, and the shovels, and the basons, *and* the fleshhooks, and the firepans: all the vessels thereof made he *of* brass.

Nu 4:14 — And they shall put upon it all the vessels thereof, wherewith they minister about it, *even* the censers, the fleshhooks, and the shovels, and the basons, all the vessels of the altar; and they shall spread upon it a covering of badgers' skins, and put to the staves of it.

• A utensil in the temple.

1Ki 7:40 — And Hiram made the lavers, and the shovels, and the basons. So Hiram made an end of doing all the work that he made king Solomon for the house of the LORD:

Jer 52:18 — The caldrons also, and the shovels, and the snuffers, and the bowls, and the spoons, and all the vessels of brass wherewith they ministered, took they away.

SHRINE • An idolatrous symbol of the Temple of Diana.

Ac 19:24 — For a certain *man* named Demetrius, a silversmith, which made silver shrines for Diana, brought no small gain unto the craftsmen;

SHUA

• A Canaanite and father-in-law of Judah.

Ge 38:2 — And Judah saw there a daughter of a certain Canaanite, whose name *was* Shuah; and he took her, and went in unto her.

Ge 38:12 — And in process of time the daughter of Shuah Judah's wife died; and Judah was comforted, and went up unto his sheepshearers to Timnath, he and his friend Hirah the Adullamite.

1Ch 2:3 — The sons of Judah; Er, and Onan, and Shelah: *which* three were born unto him of the daughter of Shua the Canaanitess. And Er, the firstborn of Judah, was evil in the sight of the LORD; and he slew him.

• Daughter of Heber.

1Ch 7:32 — And Heber begat Japhlet, and Shomer, and Hotham, and Shua their sister.

SHUAH

• Son of Abraham by his wife, or concubine, Keturah.

Ge 25:2 — And she bare him Zimran, and Jokshan, and Medan, and Midian, and Ishbak, and Shuah.

1Ch 1:32 — Now the sons of Keturah, Abraham's concubine: she bare Zimran, and Jokshan, and Medan, and Midian, and Ishbak, and Shuah. And the sons of Jokshan; Sheba, and Dedan.

• Brother of Chelub.

1Ch 4:11 — And Chelub the brother of Shuah begat Mehir, which *was* the father of Eshton.

SHUAL

• Son of Zophah.

1Ch 7:36 — The sons of Zophah; Suah, and Harnepher, and Shual, and Beri, and Imrah,

• A country of unknown location.

1Sa 13:17 — And the spoilers came out of the camp of the Philistines in three companies: one company turned unto the way *that leadeth to* Ophrah, unto the land of Shual:

SHUBAEL

✦See: Shebuel; a singer. Son of Heman

✦See: Shebuel; son of Gershom

SHUHAM

• Son of Dan.

Nu 26:42 — These *are* the sons of Dan after their families: of Shuham, the family of the Shuhamites. These *are* the families of Dan after their families.

• Called Hushim.

Ge 46:23 — And the sons of Dan; Hushim.

SHUNAMMITE

• A person from Shunem.

• Abishag, the damsel who nourished David.

1Ki 1:3 — So they sought for a fair damsel throughout all the coasts of Israel, and found Abishag a Shunammite, and brought her to the king.

• Desired by Adonijah as wife.

1Ki 2:13–25

• A woman who gave hospitality to Elisha, and whose son he raised to life.

2Ki 4:8–37

SHUNEM

• A city allotted to the tribe of Issachar.

Jos 19:18 — And their border was toward Jezreel, and Chesulloth, and Shunem,

• Elisha dwells at, with the Shunammite.

2Ki 4:1–44

• A maid found in, to nourish David.

1Ki 1:3 — So they sought for a fair damsel throughout all the coasts of Israel, and found Abishag a Shunammite, and brought her to the king.

SHUNI • Son of Gad.

Ge 46:16 — And the sons of Gad; Ziphion, and Haggi, Shuni, and Ezbon, Eri, and Arodi, and Areli.

Nu 26:15 — The children of Gad after their families: of Zephon, the family of the Zephonites: of Haggi, the family of the Haggites: of Shuni, the family of the Shunites:

SHUPHAM • Son of Benjamin.

Nu 26:39 — Of Shupham, the family of the Shuphamites: of Hupham, the family of the Huphamites.

SHUPPIM

• Son of Ir.

1Ch 7:12 — Shuppim also, and Huppim, the children of Ir, *and* Hushim, the sons of Aher.

1Ch 7:15 — And Machir took to wife *the sister* of Huppim and Shuppim, whose sister's name *was* Maachah;) and the name of the second *was* Zelophehad: and Zelophehad had daughters.

• A Levite.

1Ch 26:16 — To Shuppim and Hosah *the lot came forth* westward, with the gate Shallecheth, by the causeway of the going up, ward against ward.

SHUR • A wilderness southwest of Palestine.

Ge 16:7 — And the angel of the LORD found her by a fountain of water in the wilderness, by the fountain in the way to Shur.

Ge 20:1 — And Abraham journeyed from thence toward the south country, and dwelled between Kadesh and Shur, and sojourned in Gerar.

Ge 25:18 — And they dwelt from Havilah unto Shur, that *is* before Egypt, as thou goest toward Assyria: *and* he died in the presence of all his brethren.

Ex 15:22 — So Moses brought Israel from the Red sea, and they went out into the wilderness of Shur; and they went three days in the wilderness, and found no water.

1Sa 15:7 — And Saul smote the Amalekites from Havilah *until* thou comest to Shur, that *is* over against Egypt.

1Sa 27:8 — And David and his men went up, and invaded the Geshurites, and the Gezrites, and the Amalekites: for those *nations were* of old the inhabitants of the land, as thou goest to Shur, even unto the land of Egypt.

SHUSHAN

• Capital of the Medo-Persian empire.

Est 1:2–3

Est 8:15 — And Mordecai went out from the presence of the king in royal apparel of blue and white, and with a great crown of gold, and with a garment of fine linen and purple: and the city of Shushan rejoiced and was glad.

• King's palace at.

Est 8:14–15

Ne 1:1 — The words of Nehemiah the son of Hachaliah. And it came to pass in the month Chisleu, in the twentieth year, as I was in Shushan the palace,

Est 1:2 — *That* in those days, when the king Ahasuerus sat on the throne of his kingdom, which *was* in Shushan the palace,

Est 1:5 — And when these days were expired, the king made a feast unto all the people that were present in Shushan the palace, both unto great and small, seven days, in the court of the garden of the king's palace;

Est 2:5 — *Now* in Shushan the palace there was a certain Jew, whose name *was* Mordecai, the son of Jair, the son of Shimei, the son of Kish, a Benjamite;

Est 2:8 — So it came to pass, when the king's commandment and his decree was heard, and when many maidens were gathered together unto Shushan the palace, to the custody of Hegai, that Esther was brought also unto the king's house, to the custody of Hegai, keeper of the women.

Est 4:8 — Also he gave him the copy of the writing of the decree that was given at Shushan to destroy them, to shew *it* unto Esther, and to declare *it* unto her, and to charge her that she should go in unto the king, to make supplication unto him, and to make request before him for her people.

Est 4:16 — Go, gather together all the Jews that are present in Shushan, and fast ye for me, and neither eat nor drink three days, night or day: I also and my maidens will fast likewise; and so will I go in unto the king, which *is* not according to the law: and if I perish, I perish.

Est 9:11 — On that day the number of those that were slain in Shushan the palace was brought before the king.

Est 9:15 — For the Jews that *were* in Shushan gathered themselves together on the fourteenth day also of the month Adar, and slew three hundred men at Shushan; but on the prey they laid not their hand.

SHUSHAN-EDUTH See: Music

SHUTHELAH

• Son of Ephraim.

Nu 26:35–36

1Ch 7:20 — And the sons of Ephraim; Shuthelah, and Bered his son, and Tahath his son, and Eladah his son, and Tahath his son,

• Son of Zabad.

1Ch 7:21 — And Zabad his son, and Shuthelah his son, and Ezer, and Elead, whom the men of Gath *that were* born in *that* land slew, because they came down to take away their cattle.

SHUTTLE

Job 7:6 — My days are swifter than a weaver's shuttle, and are spent without hope.

SIA See: Siaha

SIAHA

• Called also Sia.

• One of the Nethinim.

Ezr 2:44 — The children of Keros, the children of Siaha, the children of Padon,

Ne 7:47 — The children of Keros, the children of Sia, the children of Padon,

SIBBECAI See: Sibbechai

SIBBECHAI

• Called also Sibbecai.

• A captain in David's army.

2Sa 21:18 — And it came to pass after this, that there was again a battle with the Philistines at Gob: then Sibbechai the Hushathite slew Saph, which *was* of the sons of the giant.

1Ch 11:29 — Sibbecai the Hushathite, Ilai the Ahohite,

1Ch 20:4 — And it came to pass after this, that there arose war at Gezer with the Philistines; at which time Sibbechai the Hushathite slew Sippai, *that was* of the children of the giant: and they were subdued.

1Ch 27:11 — The eighth *captain* for the eighth month *was* Sibbecai the Hushathite, of the Zarhites: and in his course *were* twenty and four thousand.

SIBMAH

• A city of Reuben.

Isa 16:8–9

Jos 13:19 — And Kirjathaim, and Sibmah, and Zareth-shahar in the mount of the valley,

Jer 48:32 — O vine of Sibmah, I will weep for thee with the weeping of Jazer: thy plants are gone over the sea, they reach *even* to the sea of Jazer: the spoiler is fallen upon thy summer fruits and upon thy vintage.

• Apparently called also Shebam.

Nu 32:3 — Ataroth, and Dibon, and Jazer, and Nimrah, and Heshbon, and Elealeh, and Shebam, and Nebo, and Beon,

• Apparently called also Shibmah.

Nu 32:38 — And Nebo, and Baal-meon, (their names being changed,) and Shibmah: and gave other names unto the cities which they builded.

SIBRAIM • A city of Syria.

Eze 47:16 — Hamath, Berothah, Sibraim, which *is* between the border of Damascus and the border of Hamath; Hazar-hatticon, which is by the coast of Hauran.

SICHEM See: Shechem

SICK

• Visiting.

Ps 41:6 — And if he come to see *me,* he speaketh vanity: his heart gathereth iniquity to itself; *when* he goeth abroad, he telleth *it.*

• Visiting, a duty.

Mt 25:36 — Naked, and ye clothed me: I was sick, and ye visited me: I was in prison, and ye came unto me.

Mt 25:43 — I was a stranger, and ye took me not in: naked, and ye clothed me not: sick, and in prison, and ye visited me not.

Jas 1:27 — Pure religion and undefiled before God and the Father is this, To visit the fatherless and widows in their affliction, *and* to keep himself unspotted from the world.

• Figurative.

Isa 1:5–6

Hos 5:13 — When Ephraim saw his sickness, and Judah *saw* his wound, then went Ephraim to the Assyrian, and sent to king Jareb: yet could he not heal you, nor cure you of your wound.

See: Afflicted, Duty to the

See: Afflictions

SICKLE

• An agricultural implement used for cutting grain.

Dt 23:25 — When thou comest into the standing corn of thy neighbour, then thou mayest pluck the ears with thine hand; but thou shalt not move a sickle unto thy neighbour's standing corn.

Jer 50:16 — Cut off the sower from Babylon, and him that handleth the sickle in the time of harvest: for fear of the oppressing sword they shall turn every one to his people, and they shall flee every one to his own land.

Mk 4:29 — But when the fruit is brought forth, immediately he putteth in the sickle, because the harvest is come.

• Figurative.

• Of the judgments of God.

Rev 14:14–19

Joel 3:13 — Put ye in the sickle, for the harvest is ripe: come, get you down; for the press is full, the fats overflow; for their wickedness *is* great.

SICKNESS

See: Afflictions

See: Disease

SIDDIM

• Vale of, a valley of uncertain location.

• Scene of the defeat of the king of Sodom.

Ge 14:3 — All these were joined together in the vale of Siddim, which is the salt sea.

Ge 14:8 — And there went out the king of Sodom, and the king of Gomorrah, and the king of Admah, and the king of Zeboiim, and the king of Bela (the same *is* Zoar;) and they joined battle with them in the vale of Siddim;

Ge 14:10 — And the vale of Siddim *was full of* slimepits; and the kings of Sodom and Gomorrah fled, and fell there; and they that remained fled to the mountain.

SIDON

• Son of Canaan.

Ge 10:15 — And Canaan begat Sidon his firstborn, and Heth,

• Called also Zidon.

1Ch 1:13 — And Canaan begat Zidon his firstborn, and Heth,

• A city on the northern boundary of the Canaanites.

Ge 10:19 — And the border of the Canaanites was from Sidon, as thou comest to Gerar, unto Gaza; as thou goest, unto Sodom, and Gomorrah, and Admah, and Zeboim, even unto Lasha.

• Designated by Jacob as the border of Zebulun.

Ge 49:13 — Zebulun shall dwell at the haven of the sea; and he *shall be* for an haven of ships; and his border *shall be* unto Zidon.

• Was on the northern boundary of Asher.

Jos 19:28 — And Hebron, and Rehob, and Hammon, and Kanah, *even* unto great Zidon;

2Sa 24:6 — Then they came to Gilead, and to the land of Tahtim-hodshi; and they came to Danjaan, and about to Zidon,

• Belonged to the land of Israel according to promise.

Jos 13:6 — All the inhabitants of the hill country from Lebanon unto Misrephoth-maim, *and* all the Sidonians, them will I drive out from before the children of Israel: only divide thou it by lot unto the Israelites for an inheritance, as I have commanded thee.

• Inhabitants of, dwelt in security and carelessness.

Jgs 18:7 — Then the five men departed, and came to Laish, and saw the people that *were* therein, how they dwelt careless, after the manner of the Zidonians, quiet and secure; and *there was* no magistrate in the land, that might put *them* to shame in *any* thing; and they *were* far from the Zidonians, and had no business with *any* man.

• Israelites failed to make conquest of.

Jgs 1:31 — Neither did Asher drive out the inhabitants of Accho, nor the inhabitants of Zidon, nor of Ahlab, nor of Achzib, nor of Helbah, nor of Aphik, nor of Rehob:

Jgs 3:3 — *Namely,* five lords of the Philistines, and all the Canaanites, and the Sidonians, and the Hivites that dwelt in mount Lebanon, from mount Baal-hermon unto the entering in of Hamath.

• The inhabitants of, contributed cedar for the first and second temple.

1Ki 5:6 — Now therefore command thou that they hew me cedar trees out of Lebanon; and my servants shall be with thy servants: and unto thee will I give hire for thy servants according to all that thou shalt appoint: for thou knowest that *there is* not among us any that can skill to hew timber like unto the Sidonians.

1Ch 22:4 — Also cedar trees in abundance: for the Zidonians and they of Tyre brought much cedar wood to David.

Ezr 3:7 — They gave money also unto the masons, and to the carpenters; and meat, and drink, and oil, unto them of Zidon, and to them of Tyre, to bring cedar trees from Lebanon to the sea of Joppa, according to the grant that they had of Cyrus king of Persia.

• Solomon marries women of.

1Ki 11:1 — But king Solomon loved many strange women, together with the daughter of Pharaoh, women of the Moabites, Ammonites, Edomites, Zidonians, *and* Hittites;

- **Ahab marries a woman of.**

1Ki 16:31 — And it came to pass, as if it had been a light thing for him to walk in the sins of Jeroboam the son of Nebat, that he took to wife Jezebel the daughter of Ethbaal king of the Zidonians, and went and served Baal, and worshipped him.

- **People of, come to hear Jesus.**

Mk 3:8 — And from Jerusalem, and from Idumaea, and *from* beyond Jordan; and they about Tyre and Sidon, a great multitude, when they had heard what great things he did, came unto him.

Lk 6:17 — And he came down with them, and stood in the plain, and the company of his disciples, and a great multitude of people out of all Judaea and Jerusalem, and from the sea coast of Tyre and Sidon, which came to hear him, and to be healed of their diseases;

- **Inhabitants of, offend Herod.**

Ac 12:20–23

- **Commerce of.**

Isa 23:2 — Be still, ye inhabitants of the isle; thou whom the merchants of Zidon, that pass over the sea, have replenished.

Isa 23:4 — Be thou ashamed, O Zidon: for the sea hath spoken, *even* the strength of the sea, saying, I travail not, nor bring forth children, neither do I nourish up young men, *nor* bring up virgins.

Isa 23:12 — And he said, Thou shalt no more rejoice, O thou oppressed virgin, daughter of Zidon: arise, pass over to Chittim; there also shalt thou have no rest.

- **Seamen of.**

Eze 27:8 — The inhabitants of Zidon and Arvad were thy mariners: thy wise *men,* O Tyrus, *that* were in thee, were thy pilots.

- **Prophecies concerning.**

Jer 25:15–22; 27:3–11; Eze 28:21–23; Joel 3:4–8

Jer 47:4 — Because of the day that cometh to spoil all the Philistines, *and* to cut off from Tyrus and Zidon every helper that remaineth: for the LORD will spoil the Philistines, the remnant of the country of Caphtor.

Eze 32:30 — There *be* the princes of the north, all of them, and all the Zidonians, which are gone down with the slain; with their terror they are ashamed of their might; and they lie uncircumcised with *them that be* slain by the sword, and bear their shame with them that go down to the pit.

- **Jesus visits the region of, and heals the daughter of the Syrophenician woman.**

Mt 15:21–28; Mk 7:24–31

- **Visited by Paul.**

Ac 27:3 — And the next *day* we touched at Sidon. And Julius courteously entreated Paul, and gave *him* liberty to go unto his friends to refresh himself.

SIEGE

- **Offer of peace must be made to the city before beginning.**

Dt 20:10–12

- **Conducted by erecting embankments parallel to the walls of the besieged city.**

Dt 20:19–20

Isa 29:3 — And I will camp against thee round about, and will lay siege against thee with a mount, and I will raise forts against thee.

Isa 37:33 — Therefore thus saith the LORD concerning the king of Assyria, He shall not come into this city, nor shoot an arrow there nor come before it with shields, nor cast a bank against it.

- **Battering-rams used in.**

↞See: Battering-Ram

- **Distress of the inhabitants during.**

2Ki 6:24–29

2Ki 25:3 — And on the ninth *day* of the *fourth* month the famine prevailed in the city, and there was no bread for the people of the land.

Isa 9:20 — And he shall snatch on the right hand, and be hungry; and he shall eat on the left hand, and they shall not be satisfied: they shall eat every man the flesh of his own arm:

Isa 36:12 — But Rabshakeh said, Hath my master sent me to thy master and to thee to speak these words? *hath he* not *sent me* to the men that sit upon the wall, that they may eat their own dung, and drink their own piss with you?

Jer 19:9 — And I will cause them to eat the flesh of their sons and the flesh of their daughters, and they shall eat every one the flesh of his friend in the siege and straitness, wherewith their enemies, and they that seek their lives, shall straiten them.

- **Cannibalism in.**

2Ki 6:28–29

- **Instances of.**
  - **Jericho.**
    Jos 6:1–27
  - **Rabbah.**
    2Sa 11:1
  - **Abel.**
    2Sa 20:15
  - **Gibbethon.**
    1Ki 15:27
  - **Tirzah.**
    1Ki 16:17
  - **Jerusalem, by the children of Judah.**
    Jgs 1:8
  - **Jerusalem, by David.**
    2Sa 5:6, 9
  - **Jerusalem, by Rezin, king of Syria, and Pekah, son of Remaliah, king of Israel.**
    2Ki 16:5
  - **Jerusalem, by Nebuchadnezzar.**
    2Ki 24:10–11; 25:1–3; Jer 52:1–34; Da 1:1

• **Jerusalem, by Sennacherib.**

2Ch 32:1–23

• **Samaria.**

1Ki 20:1; 2Ki 6:24; 17:5; 18:9–11

SIEVE

• **Figurative.**

Isa 30:28 — And his breath, as an overflowing stream, shall reach to the midst of the neck, to sift the nations with the sieve of vanity: and *there shall be* a bridle in the jaws of the people, causing *them* to err.

Am 9:9 — For, lo, I will command, and I will sift the house of Israel among all nations, like as *corn* is sifted in a sieve, yet shall not the least grain fall upon the earth.

Lk 22:31 — And the Lord said, Simon, Simon, behold, Satan hath desired *to have* you, that he may sift *you* as wheat:

SIGHT

Lk 7:22 — Then Jesus answering said unto them, Go your way, and tell John what things ye have seen and heard; how that the blind see, the lame walk, the lepers are cleansed, the deaf hear, the dead are raised, to the poor the gospel is preached.

Jn 9:25 — He answered and said, Whether he be a sinner *or no,* I know not: one thing I know, that, whereas I was blind, now I see.

Ro 2:19 — And art confident that thou thyself art a guide of the blind, a light of them which are in darkness,

2Pe 1:9 — But he that lacketh these things is blind, and cannot see afar off, and hath forgotten that he was purged from his old sins.

Rev 3:17 — Because thou sayest, I am rich, and increased with goods, and have need of nothing; and knowest not that thou art wretched, and miserable, and poor, and blind, and naked:

SIGN

• **A miracle to confirm faith.**

Mk 8:11–12

Mt 12:38 — Then certain of the scribes and of the Pharisees answered, saying, Master, we would see a sign from thee.

Mt 16:4 — A wicked and adulterous generation seeketh after a sign; and there shall no sign be given unto it, but the sign of the prophet Jonas. And he left them, and departed.

Mt 24:3 — And as he sat upon the mount of Olives, the disciples came unto him privately, saying, Tell us, when shall these things be? and what *shall be* the sign of thy coming, and of the end of the world?

Mt 24:30 — And then shall appear the sign of the Son of man in heaven: and then shall all the tribes of the earth mourn, and they shall see the Son of man coming in the clouds of heaven with power and great glory.

Mk 13:4 — Tell us, when shall these things be? and what *shall be* the sign when all these things shall be fulfilled?

Jn 2:11 — This beginning of miracles did Jesus in Cana of Galilee, and manifested forth his glory; and his disciples believed on him.

Jn 3:2 — The same came to Jesus by night, and said unto him, Rabbi, we know that thou art a teacher come from God: for no man can do these miracles that thou doest, except God be with him.

Jn 4:48 — Then said Jesus unto him, Except ye see signs and wonders, ye will not believe.

• **Asked for by, and given to.**

• **Abraham.**

Ge 15:8–17

• **Moses.**

Ex 4:1–9

• **Gideon.**

Jgs 6:36–40

Jgs 6:17 — And he said unto him, If now I have found grace in thy sight, then shew me a sign that thou talkest with me.

• **Hezekiah.**

2Ki 20:8 — And Hezekiah said unto Isaiah, What *shall be* the sign that the LORD will heal me, and that I shall go up into the house of the LORD the third day?

• **Zacharias.**

Lk 1:18 — And Zacharias said unto the angel, Whereby shall I know this? for I am an old man, and my wife well stricken in years.

• **Given to Jeroboam.**

1Ki 13:3–5

• **A token of coming events.**

Mt 16:3–4

Mt 24:3 — And as he sat upon the mount of Olives, the disciples came unto him privately, saying, Tell us, when shall these things be? and what *shall be* the sign of thy coming, and of the end of the world?

See: Miracles, Other

SIGNAL

• **Used in war.**

Isa 18:3 — All ye inhabitants of the world, and dwellers on the earth, see ye, when he lifteth up an ensign on the mountains; and when he bloweth a trumpet, hear ye.

See: Armies

See: Ensign

See: Trumpets

SIHON

• **King of the Amorites.**

• **His seat of government at Heshbon.**

Nu 21:26 — For Heshbon *was* the city of Sihon the king of the Amorites, who had fought against the former king of Moab, and taken all his land out of his hand, even unto Arnon.

• **The proverbial chant celebrating the victory of Sihon over the Moabites.**

Nu 21:26–30

• Conquest of his kingdom by the Israelites.

Nu 21:21–25; Dt 2:24–37

Dt 3:2 — And the LORD said unto me, Fear him not: for I will deliver him, and all his people, and his land, into thy hand; and thou shalt do unto him as thou didst unto Sihon king of the Amorites, which dwelt at Heshbon.

Dt 3:6 — And we utterly destroyed them, as we did unto Sihon king of Heshbon, utterly destroying the men, women, and children, of every city.

Dt 3:8 — And we took at that time out of the hand of the two kings of the Amorites the land that *was* on this side Jordan, from the river of Arnon unto mount Hermon;

SIHOR

• Called also Shihor.

• A river of Egypt, given by some authorities as the Nile.

Jos 13:3 — From Sihor, which *is* before Egypt, even unto the borders of Ekron northward, *which* is counted to the Canaanite: five lords of the Philistines; the Gazathites, and the Ashdothites, the Eshkalonites, the Gittites, and the Ekronites; also the Avites:

1Ch 13:5 — So David gathered all Israel together, from Shihor of Egypt even unto the entering of Hemath, to bring the ark of God from Kirjath-jearim.

Isa 23:3 — And by great waters the seed of Sihor, the harvest of the river, *is* her revenue; and she is a mart of nations.

Jer 2:18 — And now what hast thou to do in the way of Egypt, to drink the waters of Sihor? or what hast thou to do in the way of Assyria, to drink the waters of the river?

SILAS

• Called also Silvanus.

• Sent to Paul, in Antioch, from Jerusalem.

Ac 15:22–34

• Becomes Paul's companion.

Ac 15:40–41

2Co 1:19 — For the Son of God, Jesus Christ, who was preached among you by us, *even* by me and Silvanus and Timotheus, was not yea and nay, but in him was yea.

1Th 1:1 — Paul, and Silvanus, and Timotheus, unto the church of the Thessalonians *which is* in God the Father and *in* the Lord Jesus Christ: Grace *be* unto you, and peace, from God our Father, and the Lord Jesus Christ.

2Th 1:1 — Paul, and Silvanus, and Timotheus, unto the church of the Thessalonians in God our Father and the Lord Jesus Christ:

• Imprisoned with Paul in Philippi.

Ac 16:19–40

• Driven, with Paul, from Thessalonica.

Ac 17:4–10

• Left by Paul at Berea.

Ac 17:14 — And then immediately the brethren sent away Paul to go as it were to the sea: but Silas and Timotheus abode there still.

• Rejoins Paul at Corinth.

Ac 17:15 — And they that conducted Paul brought him unto Athens: and receiving a commandment unto Silas and Timotheus for to come to him with all speed, they departed.

Ac 18:5 — And when Silas and Timotheus were come from Macedonia, Paul was pressed in the spirit, and testified to the Jews *that* Jesus *was* Christ.

• Carries Peter's epistle to Asia Minor.

1Pe 5:12 — By Silvanus, a faithful brother unto you, as I suppose, I have written briefly, exhorting, and testifying that this is the true grace of God wherein ye stand.

SILK

• Wearing apparel made of.

Pr 31:22 — She maketh herself coverings of tapestry; her clothing *is* silk and purple.

Eze 16:10 — I clothed thee also with broidered work, and shod thee with badgers' skin, and I girded thee about with fine linen, and I covered thee with silk.

Eze 16:13 — Thus wast thou decked with gold and silver; and thy raiment *was of* fine linen, and silk, and broidered work; thou didst eat fine flour, and honey, and oil: and thou wast exceeding beautiful, and thou didst prosper into a kingdom.

• Merchandise of.

Rev 18:12 — The merchandise of gold, and silver, and precious stones, and of pearls, and fine linen, and purple, and silk, and scarlet, and all thyine wood, and all manner vessels of ivory, and all manner vessels of most precious wood, and of brass, and iron, and marble,

See: Cotton

See: Linen

SILLA • A place of uncertain location.

2Ki 12:20 — And his servants arose, and made a conspiracy, and slew Joash in the house of Millo, which goeth down to Silla.

SILOAH See: Siloam

SILOAM

• Called also Shiloah and Siloah.

• A pool in Jerusalem.

Ne 3:15 — But the gate of the fountain repaired Shallun the son of Col-hozeh, the ruler of part of Mizpah; he built it, and covered it, and set up the doors thereof, the locks thereof, and the bars thereof, and the wall of the pool of Siloah by the king's garden, and unto the stairs that go down from the city of David.

Isa 8:6 — Forasmuch as this people refuseth the waters of Shiloah that go softly, and rejoice in Rezin and Remaliah's son;

• Jesus directs the blind man, whom he healed, to wash in.

Jn 9:1–11

• Tower of, in the wall of Jerusalem, falls and kills eighteen people.

Lk 13:4 — Or those eighteen, upon whom the tower in Siloam fell, and slew them, think ye that they were sinners above all men that dwelt in Jerusalem?

SILVANUS ↞See: Silas

SILVER

• From Tarshish.

Eze 27:12 — Tarshish *was* thy merchant by reason of the multitude of all *kind of* riches; with silver, iron, tin, and lead, they traded in thy fairs.

• Refining of.

Jer 6:29–30; Eze 22:18–22

Pr 17:3 — The fining pot *is* for silver, and the furnace for gold: but the LORD trieth the hearts.

Pr 25:4 — Take away the dross from the silver, and there shall come forth a vessel for the finer.

Pr 26:23 — Burning lips and a wicked heart *are like* a potsherd covered with silver dross.

Zec 13:9 — And I will bring the third part through the fire, and will refine them as silver is refined, and will try them as gold is tried: they shall call on my name, and I will hear them: I will say, It *is* my people: and they shall say, The LORD *is* my God.

Mal 3:3 — And he shall sit *as* a refiner and purifier of silver: and he shall purify the sons of Levi, and purge them as gold and silver, that they may offer unto the LORD an offering in righteousness.

↞See: Refining

• Used for money.

Ge 23:13–16

Ge 13:2 — And Abram *was* very rich in cattle, in silver, and in gold.

Ge 17:12 — And he that is eight days old shall be circumcised among you, every man child in your generations, he that is born in the house, or bought with money of any stranger, which *is* not of thy seed.

Ge 20:16 — And unto Sarah he said, Behold, I have given thy brother a thousand *pieces* of silver: behold, he *is* to thee a covering of the eyes, unto all that *are* with thee, and with all *other:* thus she was reproved.

Am 8:6 — That we may buy the poor for silver, and the needy for a pair of shoes; *yea,* and sell the refuse of the wheat?

Mt 10:9 — Provide neither gold, nor silver, nor brass in your purses,

Mt 26:15 — And said *unto them,* What will ye give me, and I will deliver him unto you? And they covenanted with him for thirty pieces of silver.

Mk 14:11 — And when they heard *it,* they were glad, and promised to give him money. And he sought how he might conveniently betray him.

Ac 19:19 — Many of them also which used curious arts brought their books together, and burned them before all *men:* and they counted the price of them, and found it fifty thousand *pieces* of silver.

↞See: Money

• For ornamentation of, and in the manufacture of, the utensils for the tabernacle.

Ex 26:19 — And thou shalt make forty sockets of silver under the twenty boards; two sockets under one board for his two tenons, and two sockets under another board for his two tenons.

Ex 27:17 — All the pillars round about the court *shall be* filleted with silver; their hooks *shall be of* silver, and their sockets of brass.

Ex 35:24 — Every one that did offer an offering of silver and brass brought the LORD's offering: and every man, with whom was found shittim wood for any work of the service, brought *it.*

Ex 36:24 — And forty sockets of silver he made under the twenty boards; two sockets under one board for his two tenons, and two sockets under another board for his two tenons.

Ex 38:25 — And the silver of them that were numbered of the congregation *was* an hundred talents, and a thousand seven hundred and threescore and fifteen shekels, after the shekel of the sanctuary:

Nu 7:13 — And his offering *was* one silver charger, the weight thereof *was* an hundred and thirty *shekels,* one silver bowl of seventy shekels, after the shekel of the sanctuary; both of them *were* full of fine flour mingled with oil for a meat offering:

Nu 7:19 — He offered *for* his offering one silver charger, the weight whereof *was* an hundred and thirty *shekels,* one silver bowl of seventy shekels, after the shekel of the sanctuary; both of them full of fine flour mingled with oil for a meat offering:

Nu 7:25 — His offering *was* one silver charger, the weight whereof *was* an hundred and thirty *shekels,* one silver bowl of seventy shekels, after the shekel of the sanctuary; both of them full of fine flour mingled with oil for a meat offering:

Nu 7:31 — His offering *was* one silver charger of the weight of an hundred and thirty *shekels,* one silver bowl of seventy shekels, after the shekel of the sanctuary; both of them full of fine flour mingled with oil for a meat offering:

Nu 7:37 — His offering *was* one silver charger, the weight whereof *was* an hundred and thirty *shekels,* one silver bowl of seventy shekels, after the shekel of the sanctuary; both of them full of fine flour mingled with oil for a meat offering:

Nu 7:43 — His offering *was* one silver charger of the weight of an hundred and thirty *shekels,* a silver bowl of seventy shekels, after the shekel of the sanctuary; both of them full of fine flour mingled with oil for a meat offering:

Nu 7:49 — His offering *was* one silver charger, the weight whereof *was* an hundred and thirty *shekels,* one silver bowl of seventy shekels, after the shekel of the sanctuary; both of them full of fine flour mingled with oil for a meat offering:

Nu 7:55 — His offering *was* one silver charger of the weight of an hundred and thirty *shekels,* one silver bowl of seventy shekels, after the shekel of the sanctuary; both of them full of fine flour mingled with oil for a meat offering:

Nu 7:61 — His offering *was* one silver charger, the weight whereof *was* an hundred and thirty *shekels,* one silver bowl of seventy shekels, after the shekel of the sanctuary; both of them full of fine flour mingled with oil for a meat offering:

Nu 7:67 — His offering *was* one silver charger, the weight whereof *was* an hundred and thirty *shekels,* one silver bowl of seventy shekels, after the shekel of the sanctuary; both of them full of fine flour mingled with oil for a meat offering:

Nu 7:73 — His offering *was* one silver charger, the weight whereof *was* an hundred and thirty *shekels,* one silver bowl of seventy shekels, after the shekel of the sanctuary; both of them full of fine flour mingled with oil for a meat offering:

Nu 7:79 — His offering *was* one silver charger, the weight whereof *was* an hundred and thirty *shekels,* one silver bowl of seventy shekels, after the shekel of the sanctuary; both of them full of fine flour mingled with oil for a meat offering:

Nu 7:85 — Each charger of silver *weighing* an hundred and thirty *shekels,* each bowl seventy: all the silver vessels *weighed* two thousand and four hundred *shekels,* after the shekel of the sanctuary:

• For ornamentation of the temple.

1Ch 29:2–5

1Ch 28:14 — *He gave* of gold by weight for *things* of gold, for all instruments of all manner of service; *silver also* for all instruments of silver by weight, for all instruments of every kind of service:

Ezr 5:14 — And the vessels also of gold and silver of the house of God, which Nebuchadnezzar took out of the temple that *was* in Jerusalem, and brought them into the temple of Babylon, those did Cyrus the king take out of the temple of Babylon, and they were delivered unto *one,* whose name *was* Sheshbazzar, whom he had made governor;

Ezr 6:5 — And also let the golden and silver vessels of the house of God, which Nebuchadnezzar took forth out of the temple which is at Jerusalem, and brought unto Babylon, be restored, and brought again unto the temple which is at Jerusalem, *every one* to his place, and place *them* in the house of God.

Ezr 8:26 — I even weighed unto their hand six hundred and fifty talents of silver, and silver vessels an hundred talents, *and* of gold an hundred talents;

Da 5:2 — Belshazzar, whiles he tasted the wine, commanded to bring the golden and silver vessels which his father Nebuchadnezzar had taken out of the temple which *was* in Jerusalem; that the king, and his princes, his wives, and his concubines, might drink therein.

• Cups made of.

Ge 44:2 — And put my cup, the silver cup, in the sack's mouth of the youngest, and his corn money. And he did according to the word that Joseph had spoken.

• Trumpets made of.

Nu 10:2 — Make thee two trumpets of silver; of a whole piece shalt thou make them: that thou mayest use them for the calling of the assembly, and for the journeying of the camps.

• Cords made of.

Ecc 12:6 — Or ever the silver cord be loosed, or the golden bowl be broken, or the pitcher be broken at the fountain, or the wheel broken at the cistern.

• Chains made of.

Isa 40:19 — The workman melteth a graven image, and the goldsmith spreadeth it over with gold, and casteth silver chains.

• Shrines made of.

Ac 19:24 — For a certain *man* named Demetrius, a silversmith, which made silver shrines for Diana, brought no small gain unto the craftsmen;

• Idols made of.

Ex 20:23 — Ye shall not make with me gods of silver, neither shall ye make unto you gods of gold.

Isa 30:22 — Ye shall defile also the covering of thy graven images of silver, and the ornament of thy molten images of gold: thou shalt cast them away as a menstruous cloth; thou shalt say unto it, Get thee hence.

Hos 13:2 — And now they sin more and more, and have made them molten images of their silver, *and* idols according to their own understanding, all of it the work of the craftsmen: they say of them, Let the men that sacrifice kiss the calves.

• Baskets, or filigree, made of.

Pr 25:11 — A word fitly spoken *is like* apples of gold in pictures of silver.

• Jewels made of.

SS 1:11 — We will make thee borders of gold with studs of silver.

See: Jewels

• Palace made of.

SS 8:9 — If she *be* a wall, we will build upon her a palace of silver: and if she *be* a door, we will inclose her with boards of cedar.

• Vessels of.

Nu 7:85 — Each charger of silver *weighing* an hundred and thirty *shekels,* each bowl seventy: all the silver vessels *weighed* two thousand and four hundred *shekels,* after the shekel of the sanctuary:

2Sa 8:10 — Then Toi sent Joram his son unto king David, to salute him, and to bless him, because he had fought against Hadadezer, and smitten him: for Hadadezer had wars with Toi. And *Joram* brought with him vessels of silver, and vessels of gold, and vessels of brass:

1Ki 10:25 — And they brought every man his present, vessels of silver, and vessels of gold, and garments, and armour, and spices, horses, and mules, a rate year by year.

2Ki 12:13 — Howbeit there were not made for the house of the LORD bowls of silver, snuffers, basons, trumpets, any vessels of gold, or vessels of silver, of the money *that was* brought into the house of the LORD:

1Ch 18:10 — He sent Hadoram his son to king David, to enquire of his welfare, and to congratulate him, because he had fought against Hadarezer, and smitten him; (for Hadarezer had war with Tou;) and *with him* all manner of vessels of gold and silver and brass.

2Ch 24:14 — And when they had finished *it,* they brought the rest of the money before the king and Jehoiada, whereof were made vessels for the house of the LORD, *even* vessels to minister, and to offer *withal,* and spoons, and vessels of gold and silver. And they offered burnt offerings in the house of the LORD continually all the days of Jehoiada.

Ezr 1:6 — And all they that *were* about them strengthened their hands with vessels of silver, with gold, with goods, and with beasts, and with precious things, beside all *that* was willingly offered.

Ezr 5:14 — And the vessels also of gold and silver of the house of God, which Nebuchadnezzar took out of the temple that *was* in Jerusalem, and brought them into the temple of Babylon, those did Cyrus the king take out of the temple of Babylon, and they were delivered unto *one,* whose name *was* Sheshbazzar, whom he had made governor;

Ezr 6:5 — And also let the golden and silver vessels of the house of God, which Nebuchadnezzar took forth out of the temple which is at Jerusalem, and brought unto Babylon, be restored, and brought again unto the temple which is at Jerusalem, *every one* to his place, and place *them* in the house of God.

Ezr 8:26 — I even weighed unto their hand six hundred and fifty talents of silver, and silver vessels an hundred talents, *and* of gold an hundred talents;

Da 5:2 — Belshazzar, whiles he tasted the wine, commanded to bring the golden and silver vessels which his father Nebuchadnezzar had taken out of the temple which *was* in Jerusalem; that the king, and his princes, his wives, and his concubines, might drink therein.

Da 11:8 — And shall also carry captives into Egypt their gods, with their princes, *and* with their precious vessels of silver and of gold; and he shall continue *more* years than the king of the north.

• Abundance of.

1Ch 29:2–7

1Ki 10:27 — And the king made silver *to be* in Jerusalem as stones, and cedars made he *to be* as the sycomore trees that *are* in the vale, for abundance.

1Ch 22:14 — Now, behold, in my trouble I have prepared for the house of the LORD an hundred thousand talents of gold, and a thousand thousand talents of silver; and of brass and iron without weight; for it is in abundance: timber also and stone have I prepared; and thou mayest add thereto.

2Ch 1:15 — And the king made silver and gold at Jerusalem *as plenteous* as stones, and cedar trees made he as the sycomore trees that *are* in the vale for abundance.

Ecc 2:8 — I gathered me also silver and gold, and the peculiar treasure of kings and of the provinces: I gat me men singers and women singers, and the delights of the sons of men, *as* musical instruments, and that of all sorts.

Isa 2:7 — Their land also is full of silver and gold, neither *is there any* end of their treasures; their land is also full of horses, neither *is there any* end of their chariots:

• Dross from.

Pr 25:4 — Take away the dross from the silver, and there shall come forth a vessel for the finer.

Pr 26:23 — Burning lips and a wicked heart *are like* a potsherd covered with silver dross.

• Reprobate.

Jer 6:30 — Reprobate silver shall *men* call them, because the LORD hath rejected them.

• Workers in.

2Ch 2:14 — The son of a woman of the daughters of Dan, and his father *was* a man of Tyre, skilful to work in gold, and in silver, in brass, in iron, in stone, and in timber, in purple, in blue, and in fine linen, and in crimson; also to grave any manner of graving, and to find out every device which shall be put to him, with thy cunning men, and with the cunning men of my lord David thy father.

Ac 19:24 — For a certain *man* named Demetrius, a silversmith, which made silver shrines for Diana, brought no small gain unto the craftsmen;

↞See: Smith

↞See: Money

• Symbolic.

Da 2:32 — This image's head *was* of fine gold, his breast and his arms of silver, his belly and his thighs of brass,

Da 2:35 — Then was the iron, the clay, the brass, the silver, and the gold, broken to pieces together, and became like the chaff of the summer threshingfloors; and the wind carried them away, that no place was found for them: and the stone that smote the image became a great mountain, and filled the whole earth.

SILVERSMITH

Ac 19:24 — For a certain *man* named Demetrius, a silversmith, which made silver shrines for Diana, brought no small gain unto the craftsmen;

↞See: Smith

SIMEON

• Son of Jacob.

Ex 1:1–2

Ge 29:33 — And she conceived again, and bare a son; and said, Because the LORD hath heard that I *was* hated, he hath therefore given me this *son* also: and she called his name Simeon.

Ge 35:23 — The sons of Leah; Reuben, Jacob's firstborn, and Simeon, and Levi, and Judah, and Issachar, and Zebulun:

1Ch 2:1 — These *are* the sons of Israel; Reuben, Simeon, Levi, and Judah, Issachar, and Zebulun,

• **With Levi avenges upon the Shechemites the seduction of Dinah.**

Ge 34:1–31; 49:5–7

• **Jacob's denunciation of.**

Ge 49:5–7

Ge 34:30 — And Jacob said to Simeon and Levi, Ye have troubled me to make me to stink among the inhabitants of the land, among the Canaanites and the Perizzites: and I *being* few in number, they shall gather themselves together against me, and slay me; and I shall be destroyed, I and my house.

• **Goes down into Egypt to buy corn; is bound by Joseph, and detained.**

Ge 42:24 — And he turned himself about from them, and wept; and returned to them again, and communed with them, and took from them Simeon, and bound him before their eyes.

Ge 42:36 — And Jacob their father said unto them, Me have ye bereaved *of my children:* Joseph *is* not, and Simeon *is* not, and ye will take Benjamin *away:* all these things are against me.

Ge 43:23 — And he said, Peace *be* to you, fear not: your God, and the God of your father, hath given you treasure in your sacks: I had your money. And he brought Simeon out unto them.

• **His sons.**

1Ch 4:24–37

Ge 46:10 — And the sons of Simeon; Jemuel, and Jamin, and Ohad, and Jachin, and Zohar, and Shaul the son of a Canaanitish woman.

Ex 6:15 — And the sons of Simeon; Jemuel, and Jamin, and Ohad, and Jachin, and Zohar, and Shaul the son of a Canaanitish woman: these *are* the families of Simeon.

• **Descendants of.**

Nu 26:12–14

See: Simeon; tribe of

• **Tribe of.**

• **Military enrollment of, at Sinai.**

Nu 1:22–23

Nu 2:13 — And his host, and those that were numbered of them, *were* fifty and nine thousand and three hundred.

• **Military enrollment of, in the plains of Moab.**

Nu 26:14 — These *are* the families of the Simeonites, twenty and two thousand and two hundred.

• **Place of, in camp and march.**

Nu 10:18–19

Nu 2:12 — And those which pitch by him *shall be* the tribe of Simeon: and the captain of the children of Simeon *shall be* Shelumiel the son of Zurishaddai.

• **Inheritance allotted to.**

Jos 19:1–9; Jgs 1:3–17; 1Ch 4:24–43

• **Stood on Mount Gerizim to bless at the time of the rehearsal of the law.**

Dt 27:12 — These shall stand upon mount Gerizim to bless the people, when ye are come over Jordan; Simeon, and Levi, and Judah, and Issachar, and Joseph, and Benjamin:

• **Joined with the people of Judah and Benjamin in the renewal of the passover.**

2Ch 15:1–15

• **Idolatry of.**

2Ch 34:1–7

See: Israel

• **A devout man in Jerusalem. Blesses Jesus in the temple.**

Lk 2:25–35

• **An ancestor of Jesus.**

Lk 3:30 — Which was *the son* of Simeon, which was *the son* of Juda, which was *the son* of Joseph, which was *the son* of Jonan, which was *the son* of Eliakim,

• **A disciple. Called also Niger.**

Ac 13:1 — Now there were in the church that was at Antioch certain prophets and teachers; as Barnabas, and Simeon that was called Niger, and Lucius of Cyrene, and Manaen, which had been brought up with Herod the tetrarch, and Saul.

• **Name given to Peter.**

Ac 15:14 — Simeon hath declared how God at the first did visit the Gentiles, to take out of them a people for his name.

See: Peter

SIMILITUDE

Hos 12:10 — I have also spoken by the prophets, and I have multiplied visions, and used similitudes, by the ministry of the prophets.

See: Figure
See: Parables
See: Symbols and Similitudes
See: Types

SIMON

See: Peter

• **One of the twelve apostles. Called the Canaanite.**

Mt 10:4 — Simon the Canaanite, and Judas Iscariot, who also betrayed him.

Mk 3:18 — And Andrew, and Philip, and Bartholomew, and Matthew, and Thomas, and James the *son* of Alphaeus, and Thaddaeus, and Simon the Canaanite,

• **Called Zelotes.**

Lk 6:15 — Matthew and Thomas, James the *son* of Alphaeus, and Simon called Zelotes,

Ac 1:13 — And when they were come in, they went up into an upper room, where abode both Peter, and James, and John, and Andrew, Philip, and Thomas, Bartholomew, and Matthew, James *the son* of Alphaeus, and Simon Zelotes, and Judas *the brother* of James.

• A brother of Jesus.

Mt 13:55 — Is not this the carpenter's son? is not his mother called Mary? and his brethren, James, and Joses, and Simon, and Judas?

Mk 6:3 — Is not this the carpenter, the son of Mary, the brother of James, and Joses, and of Juda, and Simon? and are not his sisters here with us? And they were offended at him.

• A leper. Jesus dines with.

Mt 26:6 — Now when Jesus was in Bethany, in the house of Simon the leper,

Mk 14:3 — And being in Bethany in the house of Simon the leper, as he sat at meat, there came a woman having an alabaster box of ointment of spikenard very precious; and she brake the box, and poured *it* on his head.

• A man of Cyrene. Compelled to carry Jesus' cross.

Mt 27:32 — And as they came out, they found a man of Cyrene, Simon by name: him they compelled to bear his cross.

Mk 15:21 — And they compel one Simon a Cyrenian, who passed by, coming out of the country, the father of Alexander and Rufus, to bear his cross.

Lk 23:26 — And as they led him away, they laid hold upon one Simon, a Cyrenian, coming out of the country, and on him they laid the cross, that he might bear *it* after Jesus.

• A Pharisee. Jesus dines with.

Lk 7:36–44

• The father of Judas Iscariot.

Jn 6:71 — He spake of Judas Iscariot *the son* of Simon: for he it was that should betray him, being one of the twelve.

Jn 12:4 — Then saith one of his disciples, Judas Iscariot, Simon's *son*, which should betray him,

Jn 13:2 — And supper being ended, the devil having now put into the heart of Judas Iscariot, Simon's *son*, to betray him;

Jn 13:26 — Jesus answered, He it is, to whom I shall give a sop, when I have dipped *it*. And when he had dipped the sop, he gave *it* to Judas Iscariot, *the son* of Simon.

• A sorcerer. Converted by Philip; rebuked by Peter.

Ac 8:9–13; 8:18–24

• A tanner. Peter lodges with.

Ac 9:43 — And it came to pass, that he tarried many days in Joppa with one Simon a tanner.

Ac 10:6 — He lodgeth with one Simon a tanner, whose house is by the sea side: he shall tell thee what thou oughtest to do.

Ac 10:17 — Now while Peter doubted in himself what this vision which he had seen should mean, behold, the men which were sent from Cornelius had made enquiry for Simon's house, and stood before the gate,

Ac 10:32 — Send therefore to Joppa, and call hither Simon, whose surname is Peter; he is lodged in the house of *one* Simon a tanner by the sea side: who, when he cometh, shall speak unto thee.

SIMONY • Ecclesiastical corruption.

Ac 8:18–19

SIMRI

• A Merarite.

1Ch 26:10 — Also Hosah, of the children of Merari, had sons; Simri the chief, (for *though* he was not the firstborn, yet his father made him the chief;)

• In some versions, called Shimri.

SIN

• Miscellany of minor sub-topics.

• Paul's dicussion of the responsibility for.

Ro 2:1–9:33

• Degrees in.

Lk 7:41–47; 12:47–48

• Progressive.

Jer 16:11–12

Dt 29:19 — And it come to pass, when he heareth the words of this curse, that he bless himself in his heart, saying, I shall have peace, though I walk in the imagination of mine heart, to add drunkenness to thirst:

1Ki 16:31 — And it came to pass, as if it had been a light thing for him to walk in the sins of Jeroboam the son of Nebat, that he took to wife Jezebel the daughter of Ethbaal king of the Zidonians, and went and served Baal, and worshipped him.

Ps 1:1 — Blessed *is* the man that walketh not in the counsel of the ungodly, nor standeth in the way of sinners, nor sitteth in the seat of the scornful.

Isa 5:18 — Woe unto them that draw iniquity with cords of vanity, and sin as it were with a cart rope:

Isa 30:1 — Woe to the rebellious children, saith the LORD, that take counsel, but not of me; and that cover with a covering, but not of my spirit, that they may add sin to sin:

Jer 9:3 — And they bend their tongues *like* their bow *for* lies: but they are not valiant for the truth upon the earth; for they proceed from evil to evil, and they know not me, saith the LORD.

Hos 13:2 — And now they sin more and more, and have made them molten images of their silver, *and* idols according to their own understanding, all of it the work of the craftsmen: they say of them, Let the men that sacrifice kiss the calves.

2Ti 3:13 — But evil men and seducers shall wax worse and worse, deceiving, and being deceived.

• Its progressiveness exemplified in Joseph's brethren.

• Jealousy.

Ge 37:4 — And when his brethren saw that their father loved him more than all his brethren, they hated him, and could not speak peaceably unto him.

• Conspiracy.

Ge 37:18 — And when they saw him afar off, even before he came near unto them, they conspired against him to slay him.

• **Murder.**

Ge 37:20 — Come now therefore, and let us slay him, and cast him into some pit, and we will say, Some evil beast hath devoured him: and we shall see what will become of his dreams.

• **Sinfulness of.**

Job 22:5 — *Is* not thy wickedness great? and thine iniquities infinite?

Ps 25:11 — For thy name's sake, O LORD, pardon mine iniquity; for it *is* great.

Isa 1:18 — Come now, and let us reason together, saith the LORD: though your sins be as scarlet, they shall be as white as snow; though they be red like crimson, they shall be as wool.

Ro 7:13 — Was then that which is good made death unto me? God forbid. But sin, that it might appear sin, working death in me by that which is good; that sin by the commandment might become exceeding sinful.

• **Defiles.**

Ps 51:2 — Wash me throughly from mine iniquity, and cleanse me from my sin.

Ps 51:7 — Purge me with hyssop, and I shall be clean: wash me, and I shall be whiter than snow.

Isa 1:18 — Come now, and let us reason together, saith the LORD: though your sins be as scarlet, they shall be as white as snow; though they be red like crimson, they shall be as wool.

1Jn 1:7 — But if we walk in the light, as he is in the light, we have fellowship one with another, and the blood of Jesus Christ his Son cleanseth us from all sin.

See: Defilement

• **To be hated.**

Dt 7:26 — Neither shalt thou bring an abomination into thine house, lest thou be a cursed thing like it: *but* thou shalt utterly detest it, and thou shalt utterly abhor it; for it *is* a cursed thing.

Ps 119:113 — I hate *vain* thoughts: but thy law do I love.

• **Against the body.**

Ecc 5:6 — Suffer not thy mouth to cause thy flesh to sin; neither say thou before the angel, that it *was* an error: wherefore should God be angry at thy voice, and destroy the work of thine hands?

• **The besetting.**

Heb 12:1 — Wherefore seeing we also are compassed about with so great a cloud of witnesses, let us lay aside every weight, and the sin which doth so easily beset us, and let us run with patience the race that is set before us,

• **Little sins.**

SS 2:15 — Take us the foxes, the little foxes, that spoil the vines: for our vines *have* tender grapes.

• **Unpardonable.**

1Jn 5:16–17

Mt 12:31 — Wherefore I say unto you, All manner of sin and blasphemy shall be forgiven unto men: but the blasphemy *against* the *Holy* Ghost shall not be forgiven unto men.

Mk 3:29 — But he that shall blaspheme against the Holy Ghost hath never forgiveness, but is in danger of eternal damnation:

Lk 12:10 — And whosoever shall speak a word against the Son of man, it shall be forgiven him: but unto him that blasphemeth against the Holy Ghost it shall not be forgiven.

• **Instances of unpardonable.**

• **Israel's.**

Nu 14:26–45

• **Eli's house.**

1Sa 3:14 — And therefore I have sworn unto the house of Eli, that the iniquity of Eli's house shall not be purged with sacrifice nor offering for ever.

See: Reprobacy

• **No escape from the consequences of.**

Ge 3:8–12; Isa 28:18–22; Am 9:1–4

Mt 23:33 — *Ye* serpents, *ye* generation of vipers, how can ye escape the damnation of hell?

Heb 2:3 — How shall we escape, if we neglect so great salvation; which at the first began to be spoken by the Lord, and was confirmed unto us by them that heard *him;*

See: Punishment; divine; no escape from

• **Attempt to cover, vain.**

Isa 29:15 — Woe unto them that seek deep to hide their counsel from the LORD, and their works are in the dark, and they say, Who seeth us? and who knoweth us?

Isa 59:6 — Their webs shall not become garments, neither shall they cover themselves with their works: their works *are* works of iniquity, and the act of violence *is* in their hands.

• **Secret sins.**

Lk 12:2–3

Ps 19:12 — Who can understand *his* errors? cleanse thou me from secret *faults.*

Ps 44:21 — Shall not God search this out? for he knoweth the secrets of the heart.

Ps 64:2 — Hide me from the secret counsel of the wicked; from the insurrection of the workers of iniquity:

Ps 90:8 — Thou hast set our iniquities before thee, our secret *sins* in the light of thy countenance.

Ecc 12:14 — For God shall bring every work into judgment, with every secret thing, whether *it be* good, or whether *it be* evil.

Eze 8:12 — Then said he unto me, Son of man, hast thou seen what the ancients of the house of Israel do in the dark, every man in the chambers of his imagery? for they say, The LORD seeth us not; the LORD hath forsaken the earth.

Eze 11:5 — And the Spirit of the LORD fell upon me, and said unto me, Speak; Thus saith the LORD; Thus have ye said, O house of Israel: for I know the things that come into your mind, *every one of* them.

Mt 10:26 — Fear them not therefore: for there is nothing covered, that shall not be revealed; and hid, that shall not be known.

Lk 8:17 — For nothing is secret, that shall not be made manifest; neither *any thing* hid, that shall not be known and come abroad.

Jn 3:20 — For every one that doeth evil hateth the light, neither cometh to the light, lest his deeds should be reproved.

Ro 2:16 — In the day when God shall judge the secrets of men by Jesus Christ according to my gospel.

Eph 5:12 — For it is a shame even to speak of those things which are done of them in secret.

• Fools mock at.

Pr 14:9 — Fools make a mock at sin: but among the righteous *there is* favour.

• Against knowledge.

Lk 12:47–48; Ro 2:17–23; 2Pe 2:21–22

Pr 26:11 — As a dog returneth to his vomit, *so* a fool returneth to his folly.

Jn 9:41 — Jesus said unto them, If ye were blind, ye should have no sin: but now ye say, We see; therefore your sin remaineth.

Jn 15:22 — If I had not come and spoken unto them, they had not had sin: but now they have no cloke for their sin.

Ro 1:21 — Because that, when they knew God, they glorified *him* not as God, neither were thankful; but became vain in their imaginations, and their foolish heart was darkened.

Ro 1:32 — Who knowing the judgment of God, that they which commit such things are worthy of death, not only do the same, but have pleasure in them that do them.

Heb 10:26 — For if we sin wilfully after that we have received the knowledge of the truth, there remaineth no more sacrifice for sins,

Jas 4:17 — Therefore to him that knoweth to do good, and doeth *it* not, to him it is sin.

See: Ignorance; sins of

• Not imputed to.

• The righteous.

Ps 32:2 — Blessed *is* the man unto whom the LORD imputeth not iniquity, and in whose spirit *there is* no guile.

• The ignorant.

Ro 5:13 — (For until the law sin was in the world: but sin is not imputed when there is no law.

• The redeemed.

2Co 5:19 — To wit, that God was in Christ, reconciling the world unto himself, not imputing their trespasses unto them; and hath committed unto us the word of reconciliation.

• Pleasures of.

Job 20:12–16; 21:12–13

Lk 8:14 — And that which fell among thorns are they, which, when they have heard, go forth, and are choked with cares and riches and pleasures of *this* life, and bring no fruit to perfection.

See: Pleasure; worldly

• In believers a reproach to the Lord.

2Sa 12:14 — Howbeit, because by this deed thou hast given great occasion to the enemies of the LORD to blaspheme, the child also *that is* born unto thee shall surely die.

• None in heaven.

Rev 22:3–4

• Unclassified scriptures relating to, defining and illustrating.

Pr 24:8–9; Mt 7:17–18; 12:33–35; 13:24–25, 38–39; 15:2–20; Ro 5:12–21; Eph 2:1–2; Jas 1:14–15; 2:10–11; 4:1–3; 1Jn 3:8–10; 5:16–17

Dt 29:18 — Lest there should be among you man, or woman, or family, or tribe, whose heart turneth away this day from the LORD our God, to go *and* serve the gods of these nations; lest there should be among you a root that beareth gall and wormwood;

2Ch 12:14 — And he did evil, because he prepared not his heart to seek the LORD.

Job 14:4 — Who can bring a clean *thing* out of an unclean? not one.

Job 22:5 — *Is* not thy wickedness great? and thine iniquities infinite?

Ps 25:11 — For thy name's sake, O LORD, pardon mine iniquity; for it *is* great.

Ps 95:10 — Forty years long was I grieved with *this* generation, and said, It *is* a people that do err in their heart, and they have not known my ways:

Pr 4:23 — Keep thy heart with all diligence; for out of it *are* the issues of life.

Ecc 5:6 — Suffer not thy mouth to cause thy flesh to sin; neither say thou before the angel, that it *was* an error: wherefore should God be angry at thy voice, and destroy the work of thine hands?

Isa 1:6 — From the sole of the foot even unto the head *there is* no soundness in it; *but* wounds, and bruises, and putrifying sores: they have not been closed, neither bound up, neither mollified with ointment.

Isa 1:18 — Come now, and let us reason together, saith the LORD: though your sins be as scarlet, they shall be as white as snow; though they be red like crimson, they shall be as wool.

Isa 44:20 — He feedeth on ashes: a deceived heart hath turned him aside, that he cannot deliver his soul, nor say, *Is there* not a lie in my right hand?

Jer 7:24 — But they hearkened not, nor inclined their ear, but walked in the counsels *and* in the imagination of their evil heart, and went backward, and not forward.

Jer 17:9 — The heart *is* deceitful above all *things,* and desperately wicked: who can know it?

Eze 20:16 — Because they despised my judgments, and walked not in my statutes, but polluted my sabbaths: for their heart went after their idols.

Mt 5:28 — But I say unto you, That whosoever looketh on a woman to lust after her hath committed adultery with her already in his heart.

Mt 12:31 — Wherefore I say unto you, All manner of sin and blasphemy shall be forgiven unto men: but the blasphemy *against* the *Holy* Ghost shall not be forgiven unto men.

Mk 3:29 — But he that shall blaspheme against the Holy Ghost hath never forgiveness, but is in danger of eternal damnation:

Lk 6:45 — A good man out of the good treasure of his heart bringeth forth that which is good; and an evil man out of the evil treasure of his heart bringeth forth that which is evil: for of the abundance of the heart his mouth speaketh.

Lk 12:10 — And whosoever shall speak a word against the Son of man, it shall be forgiven him: but unto him that blasphemeth against the Holy Ghost it shall not be forgiven.

Jn 8:34 — Jesus answered them, Verily, verily, I say unto you, Whosoever committeth sin is the servant of sin.

Jn 8:44 — Ye are of your father the devil, and the lusts of *your* father ye will do. He was a murderer from the beginning, and abode not in the truth, because there is no truth in him. When he speaketh a lie, he speaketh of his own: for he is a liar, and the father of it.

Ro 7:7 — What shall we say then? *Is* the law sin? God forbid. Nay, I had not known sin, but by the law: for I had not known lust, except the law had said, Thou shalt not covet.

Ro 7:13 — Was then that which is good made death unto me? God forbid. But sin, that it might appear sin, working death in me by that which is good; that sin by the commandment might become exceeding sinful.

Ro 14:23 — And he that doubteth is damned if he eat, because *he eateth* not of faith: for whatsoever *is* not of faith is sin.

1Co 5:6 — Your glorying *is* not good. Know ye not that a little leaven leaveneth the whole lump?

Heb 3:13 — But exhort one another daily, while it is called To day; lest any of you be hardened through the deceitfulness of sin.

Heb 12:15 — Looking diligently lest any man fail of the grace of God; lest any root of bitterness springing up trouble *you*, and thereby many be defiled;

Jas 4:17 — Therefore to him that knoweth to do good, and doeth *it* not, to him it is sin.

2Pe 1:4 — Whereby are given unto us exceeding great and precious promises: that by these ye might be partakers of the divine nature, having escaped the corruption that is in the world through lust.

1Jn 3:4 — Whosoever committeth sin transgresseth also the law: for sin is the transgression of the law.

1Jn 3:6 — Whosoever abideth in him sinneth not: whosoever sinneth hath not seen him, neither known him.

1Jn 3:15 — Whosoever hateth his brother is a murderer: and ye know that no murderer hath eternal life abiding in him.

✦See: Atonement

✦See: Conviction

✦See: Depravity of Man

✦See: Regeneration

✦See: Repentance

✦See: Reprobacy

✦See: Salvation

✦See: Sanctification

✦See: Wicked; punishment of

• Confession of.

Ezr 9:4–7, 10–15; Ne 1:6–9; 9:2–3, 5–38; Job 42:5–6; Ps 38:3–4; 40:11–12; 51:2–5; 73:21–22; 119:59–60; Isa 59:12–15; 64:5–7; Jer 3:21–22; 8:14–15; 31:18–19; La 3:40–42; Da 9:5–6, 8–11; Lk 15:17–21; 1Jn 1:8–10

Le 16:21 — And Aaron shall lay both his hands upon the head of the live goat, and confess over him all the iniquities of the children of Israel, and all their transgressions in all their sins, putting them upon the head of the goat, and shall send *him* away by the hand of a fit man into the wilderness:

Nu 14:40 — And they rose up early in the morning, and gat them up into the top of the mountain, saying, Lo, we *be here*, and will go up unto the place which the LORD hath promised: for we have sinned.

2Sa 24:10 — And David's heart smote him after that he had numbered the people. And David said unto the LORD, I have sinned greatly in that I have done: and now, I beseech thee, O LORD, take away the iniquity of thy servant; for I have done very foolishly.

2Sa 24:17 — And David spake unto the LORD when he saw the angel that smote the people, and said, Lo, I have sinned, and I have done wickedly: but these sheep, what have they done? let thine hand, I pray thee, be against me, and against my father's house.

1Ch 21:17 — And David said unto God, *Is it* not I *that* commanded the people to be numbered? even I it is that have sinned and done evil indeed; but *as for* these sheep, what have they done? let thine hand, I pray thee, O LORD my God, be on me, and on my father's house; but not on thy people, that they should be plagued.

2Ch 29:6 — For our fathers have trespassed, and done *that which was* evil in the eyes of the LORD our God, and have forsaken him, and have turned away their faces from the habitation of the LORD, and turned *their* backs.

Job 7:20 — I have sinned; what shall I do unto thee, O thou preserver of men? why hast thou set me as a mark against thee, so that I am a burden to myself?

Job 9:20 — If I justify myself, mine own mouth shall condemn me: *if I say, I am* perfect, it shall also prove me perverse.

Job 13:23 — How many *are* mine iniquities and sins? make me to know my transgression and my sin.

Job 40:4 — Behold, I am vile; what shall I answer thee? I will lay mine hand upon my mouth.

Ps 32:5 — I acknowledged my sin unto thee, and mine iniquity have I not hid. I said, I will confess my transgressions unto the LORD; and thou forgavest the iniquity of my sin. Selah.

Ps 38:18 — For I will declare mine iniquity; I will be sorry for my sin.

Ps 41:4 — I said, LORD, be merciful unto me: heal my soul; for I have sinned against thee.

Ps 69:5 — O God, thou knowest my foolishness; and my sins are not hid from thee.

Ps 106:6 — We have sinned with our fathers, we have committed iniquity, we have done wickedly.

Ps 119:176 — I have gone astray like a lost sheep; seek thy servant; for I do not forget thy commandments.

Ps 130:3 — If thou, LORD, shouldest mark iniquities, O Lord, who shall stand?

Isa 6:5 — Then said I, Woe *is* me! for I am undone; because I *am* a man of unclean lips, and I dwell in the midst of a people of unclean lips: for mine eyes have seen the King, the LORD of hosts.

Isa 26:13 — O LORD our God, *other* lords besides thee have had dominion over us: *but* by thee only will we make mention of thy name.

Jer 3:25 — We lie down in our shame, and our confusion covereth us: for we have sinned against the LORD our God, we and our fathers, from our youth even unto this day, and have not obeyed the voice of the LORD our God.

Jer 14:7 — O LORD, though our iniquities testify against us, do thou *it* for thy name's sake: for our backslidings are many; we have sinned against thee.

Jer 14:20 — We acknowledge, O LORD, our wickedness, *and* the iniquity of our fathers: for we have sinned against thee.

La 1:18 — The LORD is righteous; for I have rebelled against his commandment: hear, I pray you, all people, and behold my sorrow: my virgins and my young men are gone into captivity.

La 1:20 — Behold, O LORD; for I *am* in distress: my bowels are troubled; mine heart is turned within me; for I have grievously rebelled: abroad the sword bereaveth, at home *there is* as death.

Da 9:15 — And now, O Lord our God, that hast brought thy people forth out of the land of Egypt with a mighty hand, and hast gotten thee renown, as at this day; we have sinned, we have done wickedly.

1Co 15:9 — For I am the least of the apostles, that am not meet to be called an apostle, because I persecuted the church of God.

Jas 5:16 — Confess *your* faults one to another, and pray one for another, that ye may be healed. The effectual fervent prayer of a righteous man availeth much.

- **Consequences of, entailed upon children.**

Le 26:39–40; Ps 109:9–10; Isa 14:20–22; Jer 31:29–30; Ro 5:12–21

Ex 20:5 — Thou shalt not bow down thyself to them, nor serve them: for I the LORD thy God *am* a jealous God, visiting the iniquity of the fathers upon the children unto the third and fourth *generation* of them that hate me;

Ex 34:7 — Keeping mercy for thousands, forgiving iniquity and transgression and sin, and that will by no means clear *the guilty;* visiting the iniquity of the fathers upon the children, and upon the children's children, unto the third and to the fourth *generation.*

Nu 14:33 — And your children shall wander in the wilderness forty years, and bear your whoredoms, until your carcases be wasted in the wilderness.

Job 5:4 — His children are far from safety, and they are crushed in the gate, neither *is there* any to deliver *them.*

Job 18:19 — He shall neither have son nor nephew among his people, nor any remaining in his dwellings.

Job 21:19 — God layeth up his iniquity for his children: he rewardeth him, and he shall know *it.*

Ps 21:10 — Their fruit shalt thou destroy from the earth, and their seed from among the children of men.

Ps 37:28 — For the LORD loveth judgment, and forsaketh not his saints; they are preserved for ever: but the seed of the wicked shall be cut off.

Pr 14:11 — The house of the wicked shall be overthrown: but the tabernacle of the upright shall flourish.

Isa 65:7 — Your iniquities, and the iniquities of your fathers together, saith the LORD, which have burned incense upon the mountains, and blasphemed me upon the hills: therefore will I measure their former work into their bosom.

Jer 32:18 — Thou shewest lovingkindness unto thousands, and recompensest the iniquity of the fathers into the bosom of their children after them: the Great, the Mighty God, the LORD of hosts, *is* his name,

La 5:7 — Our fathers have sinned, *and are* not; and we have borne their iniquities.

See: Wicked

- **Conviction of.**

See: Conviction

See: Repentance; instances of

- **Forgiveness of.**

Ex 34:6–7; Le 5:4–13; 1Ki 8:22–50; Ps 32:1–2; 85:2–3; Isa 6:6–7; 43:25–26; 44:21–22; 55:6–7; Eze 18:21–22; 33:14–16; Mt 6:14–15; 12:31–32; 18:23–27; Ac 13:38–39; 26:16–18; Ro 4:7–8; Heb 10:17–18; 1Jn 2:1–2

Le 4:20 — And he shall do with the bullock as he did with the bullock for a sin offering, so shall he do with this: and the priest shall make an atonement for them, and it shall be forgiven them.

Le 4:26 — And he shall burn all his fat upon the altar, as the fat of the sacrifice of peace offerings: and the priest shall make an atonement for him as concerning his sin, and it shall be forgiven him.

Le 4:31 — And he shall take away all the fat thereof, as the fat is taken away from off the sacrifice of peace offerings; and the priest shall burn *it* upon the altar for a sweet savour unto the LORD; and the priest shall make an atonement for him, and it shall be forgiven him.

Le 4:35 — And he shall take away all the fat thereof, as the fat of the lamb is taken away from the sacrifice of the peace offerings; and the priest shall burn them upon the altar, according to the offerings made by fire unto the LORD: and the priest shall make an atonement for his sin that he hath committed, and it shall be forgiven him.

Nu 14:18 — The LORD *is* longsuffering, and of great mercy, forgiving iniquity and transgression, and by no means clearing *the guilty*, visiting the iniquity of the fathers upon the children unto the third and fourth *generation*.

Nu 14:20 — And the LORD said, I have pardoned according to thy word:

Nu 15:25 — And the priest shall make an atonement for all the congregation of the children of Israel, and it shall be forgiven them; for it is ignorance: and they shall bring their offering, a sacrifice made by fire unto the LORD, and their sin offering before the LORD, for their ignorance:

2Sa 12:13 — And David said unto Nathan, I have sinned against the LORD. And Nathan said unto David, The LORD also hath put away thy sin; thou shalt not die.

Job 10:14 — If I sin, then thou markest me, and thou wilt not acquit me from mine iniquity.

Ps 19:12 — Who can understand *his* errors? cleanse thou me from secret *faults*.

Ps 25:7 — Remember not the sins of my youth, nor my transgressions: according to thy mercy remember thou me for thy goodness' sake, O LORD.

Ps 25:11 — For thy name's sake, O LORD, pardon mine iniquity; for it *is* great.

Ps 25:18 — Look upon mine affliction and my pain; and forgive all my sins.

Ps 32:5 — I acknowledged my sin unto thee, and mine iniquity have I not hid. I said, I will confess my transgressions unto the LORD; and thou forgavest the iniquity of my sin. Selah.

Ps 51:9 — Hide thy face from my sins, and blot out all mine iniquities.

Ps 65:3 — Iniquities prevail against me: *as for* our transgressions, thou shalt purge them away.

Ps 79:9 — Help us, O God of our salvation, for the glory of thy name: and deliver us, and purge away our sins, for thy name's sake.

Ps 99:8 — Thou answeredst them, O LORD our God: thou wast a God that forgavest them, though thou tookest vengeance of their inventions.

Ps 103:12 — As far as the east is from the west, *so* far hath he removed our transgressions from us.

Ps 130:4 — But *there is* forgiveness with thee, that thou mayest be feared.

Isa 1:18 — Come now, and let us reason together, saith the LORD: though your sins be as scarlet, they shall be as white as snow; though they be red like crimson, they shall be as wool.

Jer 2:22 — For though thou wash thee with nitre, and take thee much sope, *yet* thine iniquity is marked before me, saith the Lord GOD.

Jer 5:1 — Run ye to and fro through the streets of Jerusalem, and see now, and know, and seek in the broad places thereof, if ye can find a man, if there be *any* that executeth judgment, that seeketh the truth; and I will pardon it.

Jer 5:7 — How shall I pardon thee for this? thy children have forsaken me, and sworn by *them that are* no gods: when I had fed them to the full, they then committed adultery, and assembled themselves by troops in the harlots' houses.

Jer 31:34 — And they shall teach no more every man his neighbour, and every man his brother, saying, Know the LORD: for they shall all know me, from the least of them unto the greatest of them, saith the LORD; for I will forgive their iniquity, and I will remember their sin no more.

Jer 33:8 — And I will cleanse them from all their iniquity, whereby they have sinned against me; and I will pardon all their iniquities, whereby they have sinned, and whereby they have transgressed against me.

Mt 1:21 — And she shall bring forth a son, and thou shalt call his name JESUS: for he shall save his people from their sins.

Mt 3:6 — And were baptized of him in Jordan, confessing their sins.

Mt 6:12 — And forgive us our debts, as we forgive our debtors.

Mt 9:2 — And, behold, they brought to him a man sick of the palsy, lying on a bed: and Jesus seeing their faith said unto the sick of the palsy; Son, be of good cheer; thy sins be forgiven thee.

Mt 9:6 — But that ye may know that the Son of man hath power on earth to forgive sins, (then saith he to the sick of the palsy,) Arise, take up thy bed, and go unto thine house.

Mt 18:35 — So likewise shall my heavenly Father do also unto you, if ye from your hearts forgive not every one his brother their trespasses.

Mt 26:28 — For this is my blood of the new testament, which is shed for many for the remission of sins.

Mk 2:5 — When Jesus saw their faith, he said unto the sick of the palsy, Son, thy sins be forgiven thee.

Mk 2:7 — Why doth this *man* thus speak blasphemies? who can forgive sins but God only?

Mk 3:28 — Verily I say unto you, All sins shall be forgiven unto the sons of men, and blasphemies wherewith soever they shall blaspheme:

Mk 11:26 — But if ye do not forgive, neither will your Father which is in heaven forgive your trespasses.

Lk 3:3 — And he came into all the country about Jordan, preaching the baptism of repentance for the remission of sins;

Lk 5:21 — And the scribes and the Pharisees began to reason, saying, Who is this which speaketh blasphemies? Who can forgive sins, but God alone?

Lk 5:24 — But that ye may know that the Son of man hath power upon earth to forgive sins, (he said unto the sick of the palsy,) I say unto thee, Arise, and take up thy couch, and go into thine house.

Lk 12:10 — And whosoever shall speak a word against the Son of man, it shall be forgiven him: but unto him that blasphemeth against the Holy Ghost it shall not be forgiven.

Lk 24:47 — And that repentance and remission of sins should be preached in his name among all nations, beginning at Jerusalem.

Jn 8:11 — She said, No man, Lord. And Jesus said unto her, Neither do I condemn thee: go, and sin no more.

Jn 20:23 — Whose soever sins ye remit, they are remitted unto them; *and* whose soever *sins* ye retain, they are retained.

Ac 2:38 — Then Peter said unto them, Repent, and be baptized every one of you in the name of Jesus Christ for the remission of sins, and ye shall receive the gift of the Holy Ghost.

Ac 10:36 — The word which *God* sent unto the children of Israel, preaching peace by Jesus Christ: (he is Lord of all:)

Ac 10:43 — To him give all the prophets witness, that through his name whosoever believeth in him shall receive remission of sins.

Eph 4:32 — And be ye kind one to another, tenderhearted, forgiving one another, even as God for Christ's sake hath forgiven you.

Col 2:13 — And you, being dead in your sins and the uncircumcision of your flesh, hath he quickened together with him, having forgiven you all trespasses;

Heb 8:12 — For I will be merciful to their unrighteousness, and their sins and their iniquities will I remember no more.

Heb 9:22 — And almost all things are by the law purged with blood; and without shedding of blood is no remission.

Heb 10:2 — For then would they not have ceased to be offered? because that the worshippers once purged should have had no more conscience of sins.

Jas 5:15 — And the prayer of faith shall save the sick, and the Lord shall raise him up; and if he have committed sins, they shall be forgiven him.

Jas 5:20 — Let him know, that he which converteth the sinner from the error of his way shall save a soul from death, and shall hide a multitude of sins.

1Jn 1:7 — But if we walk in the light, as he is in the light, we have fellowship one with another, and the blood of Jesus Christ his Son cleanseth us from all sin.

1Jn 1:9 — If we confess our sins, he is faithful and just to forgive us *our* sins, and to cleanse us from all unrighteousness.

1Jn 2:12 — I write unto you, little children, because your sins are forgiven you for his name's sake.

1Jn 5:16 — If any man see his brother sin a sin *which is* not unto death, he shall ask, and he shall give him life for them that sin not unto death. There is a sin unto death: I do not say that he shall pray for it.

Rev 1:5 — And from Jesus Christ, *who is* the faithful witness, *and* the first begotten of the dead, and the prince of the kings of the earth. Unto him that loved us, and washed us from our sins in his own blood,

See: Atonement

See: Conviction

See: Offerings

See: Repentance

• Fruits of.

Ge 3:7–24; 4:9–14; 6:5–7; 1Ki 13:33–34; Ps 9:15–16; Pr 5:22–23; 10:29–31; 11:5–7, 18–19; 12:13–14; 13:5–6; Isa 57:20–21; Eze 23:31–35; Mk 7:21–23; Ro 5:12–21; 1Co 6:9–11; Gal 5:19–21; 6:7–8

Dt 29:18 — Lest there should be among you man, or woman, or family, or tribe, whose heart turneth away this day from the LORD our God, to go *and* serve the gods of these nations; lest there should be among you a root that beareth gall and wormwood;

Job 4:8 — Even as I have seen, they that plow iniquity, and sow wickedness, reap the same.

Job 5:2 — For wrath killeth the foolish man, and envy slayeth the silly one.

Job 13:26 — For thou writest bitter things against me, and makest me to possess the iniquities of my youth.

Job 20:11 — His bones are full *of the sin* of his youth, which shall lie down with him in the dust.

Ps 5:10 — Destroy thou them, O God; let them fall by their own counsels; cast them out in the multitude of their transgressions; for they have rebelled against thee.

Ps 10:2 — The wicked in *his* pride doth persecute the poor: let them be taken in the devices that they have imagined.

Ps 94:23 — And he shall bring upon them their own iniquity, and shall cut them off in their own wickedness; *yea*, the LORD our God shall cut them off.

Ps 141:10 — Let the wicked fall into their own nets, whilst that I withal escape.

Pr 1:31 — Therefore shall they eat of the fruit of their own way, and be filled with their own devices.

Pr 3:35 — The wise shall inherit glory: but shame shall be the promotion of fools.

Pr 8:36 — But he that sinneth against me wrongeth his own soul: all they that hate me love death.

Pr 10:24 — The fear of the wicked, it shall come upon him: but the desire of the righteous shall be granted.

Pr 11:27 — He that diligently seeketh good procureth favour: but he that seeketh mischief, it shall come unto him.

Pr 11:29 — He that troubleth his own house shall inherit the wind: and the fool *shall be* servant to the wise of heart.

Pr 12:21 — There shall no evil happen to the just: but the wicked shall be filled with mischief.

Pr 12:26 — The righteous *is* more excellent than his neighbour: but the way of the wicked seduceth them.

Pr 13:15 — Good understanding giveth favour: but the way of transgressors *is* hard.

Pr 22:8 — He that soweth iniquity shall reap vanity: and the rod of his anger shall fail.

Pr 27:8 — As a bird that wandereth from her nest, so *is* a man that wandereth from his place.

Pr 28:1 — The wicked flee when no man pursueth: but the righteous are bold as a lion.

Pr 29:6 — In the transgression of an evil man *there is* a snare: but the righteous doth sing and rejoice.

Pr 30:20 — Such *is* the way of an adulterous woman; she eateth, and wipeth her mouth, and saith, I have done no wickedness.

Isa 3:9 — The shew of their countenance doth witness against them; and they declare their sin as Sodom, they hide *it* not. Woe unto their soul! for they have rewarded evil unto themselves.

Isa 3:11 — Woe unto the wicked! *it shall be* ill *with him:* for the reward of his hands shall be given him.

Isa 9:18 — For wickedness burneth as the fire: it shall devour the briers and thorns, and shall kindle in the thickets of the forest, and they shall mount up *like* the lifting up of smoke.

Isa 14:21 — Prepare slaughter for his children for the iniquity of their fathers; that they do not rise, nor possess the land, nor fill the face of the world with cities.

Isa 50:11 — Behold, all ye that kindle a fire, that compass *yourselves* about with sparks: walk in the light of your fire, and in the sparks *that* ye have kindled. This shall ye have of mine hand; ye shall lie down in sorrow.

Jer 2:17 — Hast thou not procured this unto thyself, in that thou hast forsaken the LORD thy God, when he led thee by the way?

Jer 2:19 — Thine own wickedness shall correct thee, and thy backslidings shall reprove thee: know therefore and see that *it is* an evil *thing* and bitter, that thou hast forsaken the LORD thy God, and that my fear *is* not in thee, saith the Lord GOD of hosts.

Jer 4:18 — Thy way and thy doings have procured these *things* unto thee; this *is* thy wickedness, because it is bitter, because it reacheth unto thine heart.

Jer 5:25 — Your iniquities have turned away these *things,* and your sins have withholden good *things* from you.

Jer 7:19 — Do they provoke me to anger? saith the LORD: *do they* not *provoke* themselves to the confusion of their own faces?

Jer 14:16 — And the people to whom they prophesy shall be cast out in the streets of Jerusalem because of the famine and the sword; and they shall have none to bury them, them, their wives, nor their sons, nor their daughters: for I will pour their wickedness upon them.

Jer 21:14 — But I will punish you according to the fruit of your doings, saith the LORD: and I will kindle a fire in the forest thereof, and it shall devour all things round about it.

Eze 11:21 — But *as for them* whose heart walketh after the heart of their detestable things and their abominations, I will recompense their way upon their own heads, saith the Lord GOD.

Eze 22:31 — Therefore have I poured out mine indignation upon them; I have consumed them with the fire of my wrath: their own way have I recompensed upon their heads, saith the Lord GOD.

Hos 8:7 — For they have sown the wind, and they shall reap the whirlwind: it hath no stalk: the bud shall yield no meal: if so be it yield, the strangers shall swallow it up.

Hos 10:13 — Ye have plowed wickedness, ye have reaped iniquity; ye have eaten the fruit of lies: because thou didst trust in thy way, in the multitude of thy mighty men.

Hos 12:14 — Ephraim provoked *him* to anger most bitterly: therefore shall he leave his blood upon him, and his reproach shall his Lord return unto him.

Hos 13:9 — O Israel, thou hast destroyed thyself; but in me *is* thine help.

Mic 7:13 — Notwithstanding the land shall be desolate because of them that dwell therein, for the fruit of their doings.

Ac 9:5 — And he said, Who art thou, Lord? And the Lord said, <u>I am Jesus whom thou persecutest: *it is* hard for thee to kick against the pricks.</u>

Ro 7:5 — For when we were in the flesh, the motions of sins, which were by the law, did work in our members to bring forth fruit unto death.

1Co 3:3 — For ye are yet carnal: for whereas *there is* among you envying, and strife, and divisions, are ye not carnal, and walk as men?

1Pe 4:3 — For the time past of *our* life may suffice us to have wrought the will of the Gentiles, when we walked in lasciviousness, lusts, excess of wine, revellings, banquetings, and abominable idolatries:

• Known to God.

Ex 16:8–9; Nu 14:26–27; Jos 7:10–15; Job 14:16–17; 34:21–22; Ps 44:20–21; Am 9:1–4; Jn 4:17–19

Ge 3:11 — And he said, Who told thee that thou *wast* naked? Hast thou eaten of the tree, whereof I commanded thee that thou shouldest not eat?

Ge 4:10 — And he said, What hast thou done? the voice of thy brother's blood crieth unto me from the ground.

Ge 18:13 — And the LORD said unto Abraham, Wherefore did Sarah laugh, saying, Shall I of a surety bear a child, which am old?

Ex 16:12 — I have heard the murmurings of the children of Israel: speak unto them, saying, At even ye shall eat flesh, and in the morning ye shall be filled with bread; and ye shall know that I *am* the LORD your God.

Nu 12:2 — And they said, Hath the LORD indeed spoken only by Moses? hath he not spoken also by us? And the LORD heard *it.*

Dt 1:34 — And the LORD heard the voice of your words, and was wroth, and sware, saying,

Dt 31:21 — And it shall come to pass, when many evils and troubles are befallen them, that this song shall testify against them as a witness; for it shall not be forgotten out of the mouths of their seed: for I know their imagination which they go about, even now, before I have brought them into the land which I sware.

Dt 32:34 — *Is* not this laid up in store with me, *and* sealed up among my treasures?

Job 10:14 — If I sin, then thou markest me, and thou wilt not acquit me from mine iniquity.

Job 11:11 — For he knoweth vain men: he seeth wickedness also; will he not then consider *it?*

Job 13:27 — Thou puttest my feet also in the stocks, and lookest narrowly unto all my paths; thou settest a print upon the heels of my feet.

Job 20:27 — The heaven shall reveal his iniquity; and the earth shall rise up against him.

Job 24:23 — *Though* it be given him *to be* in safety, whereon he resteth; yet his eyes *are* upon their ways.

Job 34:25 — Therefore he knoweth their works, and he overturneth *them* in the night, so that they are destroyed.

Ps 69:5 — O God, thou knowest my foolishness; and my sins are not hid from thee.

Ps 90:8 — Thou hast set our iniquities before thee, our secret *sins* in the light of thy countenance.

Ps 94:11 — The LORD knoweth the thoughts of man, that they *are* vanity.

Ecc 5:8 — If thou seest the oppression of the poor, and violent perverting of judgment and justice in a province, marvel not at the matter: for *he that is* higher than the highest regardeth; and *there be* higher than they.

Isa 29:15 — Woe unto them that seek deep to hide their counsel from the LORD, and their works are in the dark, and they say, Who seeth us? and who knoweth us?

Jer 2:22 — For though thou wash thee with nitre, and take thee much sope, *yet* thine iniquity is marked before me, saith the Lord GOD.

Jer 16:17 — For mine eyes *are* upon all their ways: they are not hid from my face, neither is their iniquity hid from mine eyes.

Jer 29:23 — Because they have committed villany in Israel, and have committed adultery with their neighbours' wives, and have spoken lying words in my name, which I have not commanded them; even I know, and *am* a witness, saith the LORD.

Eze 21:24 — Therefore thus saith the Lord GOD; Because ye have made your iniquity to be remembered, in that your transgressions are discovered, so that in all your doings your sins do appear; because, *I say,* that ye are come to remembrance, ye shall be taken with the hand.

Hos 5:3 — I know Ephraim, and Israel is not hid from me: for now, O Ephraim, thou committest whoredom, *and* Israel is defiled.

Hos 7:2 — And they consider not in their hearts *that* I remember all their wickedness: now their own doings have beset them about; they are before my face.

Am 5:12 — For I know your manifold transgressions and your mighty sins: they afflict the just, they take a bribe, and they turn aside the poor in the gate *from their right.*

Am 9:8 — Behold, the eyes of the Lord GOD *are* upon the sinful kingdom, and I will destroy it from off the face of the earth; saving that I will not utterly destroy the house of Jacob, saith the LORD.

Hab 2:11 — For the stone shall cry out of the wall, and the beam out of the timber shall answer it.

Mal 2:14 — Yet ye say, Wherefore? Because the LORD hath been witness between thee and the wife of thy youth, against whom thou hast dealt treacherously: yet *is* she thy companion, and the wife of thy covenant.

Mt 10:26 — Fear them not therefore: for there is nothing covered, that shall not be revealed; and hid, that shall not be known.

Mt 22:18 — But Jesus perceived their wickedness, and said, Why tempt ye me, *ye* hypocrites?

Mt 26:46 — Rise, let us be going: behold, he is at hand that doth betray me.

Lk 6:8 — But he knew their thoughts, and said to the man which had the withered hand, Rise up, and stand forth in the midst. And he arose and stood forth.

Jn 5:42 — But I know you, that ye have not the love of God in you.

Jn 6:64 — But there are some of you that believe not. For Jesus knew from the beginning who they were that believed not, and who should betray him.

Jn 13:11 — For he knew who should betray him; therefore said he, Ye are not all clean.

Rev 2:23 — And I will kill her children with death; and all the churches shall know that I am he which searcheth the reins and hearts: and I will give unto every one of you according to your works.

✣See: God, Omniscient

✣See: Jesus, Omniscience of

• Love of.

Job 20:12–13; Jn 3:19–20; 1Pe 3:19–20

Job 15:16 — How much more abominable and filthy *is* man, which drinketh iniquity like water?

Pr 2:14 — Who rejoice to do evil, *and* delight in the frowardness of the wicked;

Pr 4:17 — For they eat the bread of wickedness, and drink the wine of violence.

Pr 10:23 — *It is* as sport to a fool to do mischief: but a man of understanding hath wisdom.

Pr 16:30 — He shutteth his eyes to devise froward things: moving his lips he bringeth evil to pass.

Pr 26:11 — As a dog returneth to his vomit, *so* a fool returneth to his folly.

Jer 14:10 — Thus saith the LORD unto this people, Thus have they loved to wander, they have not refrained their feet, therefore the LORD doth not accept them; he will now remember their iniquity, and visit their sins.

Eze 20:16 — Because they despised my judgments, and walked not in my statutes, but polluted my sabbaths: for their heart went after their idols.

Hos 4:8 — They eat up the sin of my people, and they set their heart on their iniquity.

Hos 9:10 — I found Israel like grapes in the wilderness; I saw your fathers as the firstripe in the fig tree at her first time: *but* they went to Baal-peor, and separated themselves unto *that* shame; and *their* abominations were according as they loved.

Mic 7:3 — That they may do evil with both hands earnestly, the prince asketh, and the judge *asketh* for a reward; and the great *man,* he uttereth his mischievous desire: so they wrap it up.

Jn 12:43 — For they loved the praise of men more than the praise of God.

2Pe 2:22 — But it is happened unto them according to the true proverb, The dog *is* turned to his own vomit again; and the sow that was washed to her wallowing in the mire.

- See: Reprobacy
- See: Wicked; described

• National, punishment of.

Ge 6:5–7; 7:21–22; Le 26:14–38; Job 34:29–30; Jer 25:31–38; Eze 16:49–50

Dt 9:5 — Not for thy righteousness, or for the uprightness of thine heart, dost thou go to possess their land: but for the wickedness of these nations the LORD thy God doth drive them out from before thee, and that he may perform the word which the LORD sware unto thy fathers, Abraham, Isaac, and Jacob.

Isa 19:4 — And the Egyptians will I give over into the hand of a cruel lord; and a fierce king shall rule over them, saith the Lord, the LORD of hosts.

Jer 12:17 — But if they will not obey, I will utterly pluck up and destroy that nation, saith the LORD.

Jer 46:28 — Fear thou not, O Jacob my servant, saith the LORD: for I *am* with thee; for I will make a full end of all the nations whither I have driven thee: but I will not make a full end of thee, but correct thee in measure; yet will I not leave thee wholly unpunished.

Jnh 1:2 — Arise, go to Nineveh, that great city, and cry against it; for their wickedness is come up before me.

- See: Government
- See: Nation

• Instances of.

• The Sodomites.

Ge 18:20 — And the LORD said, Because the cry of Sodom and Gomorrah is great, and because their sin is very grievous;

• The Egyptians.

Ex 7:1–14:31

- See: Egypt

• The Israelites.

Le 26:14–39; 2Ki 24:3–4; Ezr 9:1–15; Ne 9:36–37; Isa 1:21–23; 5:1–30; 59:1–15; Jer 2:1–37; 5:1–6:30; 9:1–26; 23:1–40; 30:11–15; Eze 2:1–10; 7:1–27; 22:1–31; 24:6–14; 33:25–26; 36:16–20; 39:23–24; 44:4–14; Hos 4:1–11; 6:8–10; 7:1–7; 13:1–16; Am 2:1–16; 5:1–27; Mic 6:1–16; 7:2–6

Dt 32:30 — How should one chase a thousand, and two put ten thousand to flight, except their Rock had sold them, and the LORD had shut them up?

2Sa 21:1 — Then there was a famine in the days of David three years, year after year; and David enquired of the LORD. And the LORD answered, *It is* for Saul, and for *his* bloody house, because he slew the Gibeonites.

2Sa 24:1 — And again the anger of the LORD was kindled against Israel, and he moved David against them to say, Go, number Israel and Judah.

2Ki 24:20 — For through the anger of the LORD it came to pass in Jerusalem and Judah, until he had cast them out from his presence, that Zedekiah rebelled against the king of Babylon.

2Ch 36:21 — To fulfil the word of the LORD by the mouth of Jeremiah, until the land had enjoyed her sabbaths: *for* as long as she lay desolate she kept sabbath, to fulfil threescore and ten years.

Isa 3:4 — And I will give children *to be* their princes, and babes shall rule over them.

Isa 3:8 — For Jerusalem is ruined, and Judah is fallen: because their tongue and their doings *are* against the LORD, to provoke the eyes of his glory.

La 1:3 — Judah is gone into captivity because of affliction, and because of great servitude: she dwelleth among the heathen, she findeth no rest: all her persecutors overtook her between the straits.

La 1:8 — Jerusalem hath grievously sinned; therefore she is removed: all that honoured her despise her, because they have seen her nakedness: yea, she sigheth, and turneth backward.

La 1:14 — The yoke of my transgressions is bound by his hand: they are wreathed, *and* come up upon my neck: he hath made my strength to fall, the Lord hath delivered me into *their* hands, *from whom* I am not able to rise up.

La 4:6 — For the punishment of the iniquity of the daughter of my people is greater than the punishment of the sin of Sodom, that was overthrown as in a moment, and no hands stayed on her.

Eze 28:18 — Thou hast defiled thy sanctuaries by the multitude of thine iniquities, by the iniquity of thy traffick; therefore will I bring forth a fire from the midst of thee, it shall devour thee, and I will bring thee to ashes upon the earth in the sight of all them that behold thee.

• Babylon.

Jer 50:45–51:64

- See: Babylon; prophecies concerning
- See: Assyria; prophecies concerning
- See: Damascus; prophecies concerning
- See: Edom; prophecies concerning
- See: Elam; prophecies concerning
- See: Ethiopia; prophecies concerning the conversion of
- See: Philistines; prophecies against
- See: Syria; prophecies concerning

• Punishment of.

Ge 3:16–19; 6:5–7; Ex 32:33–34; Le 26:14–21; Nu 15:30–31; Ps 95:10–11; Jer 44:2–3, 5–6

Ge 2:17 — But of the tree of the knowledge of good and evil, thou shalt not eat of it: for in the day that thou eatest thereof thou shalt surely die.

Ge 4:7 — If thou doest well, shalt thou not be accepted? and if thou doest not well, sin lieth at the door. And unto thee *shall be* his desire, and thou shalt rule over him.

Ge 6:3 — And the LORD said, My spirit shall not always strive with man, for that he also *is* flesh: yet his days shall be an hundred and twenty years.

Ge 18:20 — And the LORD said, Because the cry of Sodom and Gomorrah is great, and because their sin is very grievous;

Ge 19:13 — For we will destroy this place, because the cry of them is waxen great before the face of the LORD; and the LORD hath sent us to destroy it.

Ex 34:7 — Keeping mercy for thousands, forgiving iniquity and transgression and sin, and that will by no means clear *the guilty;* visiting the iniquity of the fathers upon the children, and upon the children's children, unto the third and to the fourth *generation.*

Nu 32:23 — But if ye will not do so, behold, ye have sinned against the LORD: and be sure your sin will find you out.

Job 21:17 — How oft is the candle of the wicked put out! and *how oft* cometh their destruction upon them! *God* distributeth sorrows in his anger.

See: Punishment

See: Wicked; punishment of

• Repugnant to God.

Ge 6:6–7; Ps 5:4–6; Pr 6:16–19; 15:8–9; Jer 44:21–22

Nu 22:32 — And the angel of the LORD said unto him, Wherefore hast thou smitten thine ass these three times? behold, I went out to withstand thee, because *thy* way is perverse before me:

Dt 25:16 — For all that do such things, *and* all that do unrighteously, *are* an abomination unto the LORD thy God.

Dt 32:19 — And when the LORD saw *it,* he abhorred *them,* because of the provoking of his sons, and of his daughters.

2Sa 11:27 — And when the mourning was past, David sent and fetched her to his house, and she became his wife, and bare him a son. But the thing that David had done displeased the LORD.

1Ki 14:22 — And Judah did evil in the sight of the LORD, and they provoked him to jealousy with their sins which they had committed, above all that their fathers had done.

Ps 10:3 — For the wicked boasteth of his heart's desire, and blesseth the covetous, *whom* the LORD abhorreth.

Ps 11:5 — The LORD trieth the righteous: but the wicked and him that loveth violence his soul hateth.

Ps 78:59 — When God heard *this,* he was wroth, and greatly abhorred Israel:

Ps 95:10 — Forty years long was I grieved with *this* generation, and said, It *is* a people that do err in their heart, and they have not known my ways:

Ps 106:40 — Therefore was the wrath of the LORD kindled against his people, insomuch that he abhorred his own inheritance.

Pr 3:32 — For the froward *is* abomination to the LORD: but his secret *is* with the righteous.

Pr 11:20 — They that are of a froward heart *are* abomination to the LORD: but *such as are* upright in *their* way *are* his delight.

Pr 15:26 — The thoughts of the wicked *are* an abomination to the LORD: but *the words* of the pure *are* pleasant words.

Pr 21:27 — The sacrifice of the wicked *is* abomination: how much more, *when* he bringeth it with a wicked mind?

Isa 43:24 — Thou hast bought me no sweet cane with money, neither hast thou filled me with the fat of thy sacrifices: but thou hast made me to serve with thy sins, thou hast wearied me with thine iniquities.

Jer 25:7 — Yet ye have not hearkened unto me, saith the LORD; that ye might provoke me to anger with the works of your hands to your own hurt.

Jer 44:4 — Howbeit I sent unto you all my servants the prophets, rising early and sending *them,* saying, Oh, do not this abominable thing that I hate.

Hab 1:13 — *Thou art* of purer eyes than to behold evil, and canst not look on iniquity: wherefore lookest thou upon them that deal treacherously, *and* holdest thy tongue when the wicked devoureth *the man that is* more righteous than he?

Zec 8:17 — And let none of you imagine evil in your hearts against his neighbour; and love no false oath: for all these *are things* that I hate, saith the LORD.

Lk 16:15 — And he said unto them, Ye are they which justify yourselves before men; but God knoweth your hearts: for that which is highly esteemed among men is abomination in the sight of God.

Rev 2:6 — But this thou hast, that thou hatest the deeds of the Nicolaitanes, which I also hate.

Rev 2:15 — So hast thou also them that hold the doctrine of the Nicolaitanes, which thing I hate.

See: God, Holiness of

See: Holiness

• Repugnant to the righteous.

Ge 39:7–9; Ps 101:3–4; 120:5–7; 139:19–22; Ro 7:23–24; 2Pe 2:7–8

Dt 7:26 — Neither shalt thou bring an abomination into thine house, lest thou be a cursed thing like it: *but* thou shalt utterly detest it, and thou shalt utterly abhor it; for it *is* a cursed thing.

Job 1:1 — There was a man in the land of Uz, whose name *was* Job; and that man was perfect and upright, and one that feared God, and eschewed evil.

Job 21:16 — Lo, their good *is* not in their hand: the counsel of the wicked is far from me.

Job 22:18 — Yet he filled their houses with good *things:* but the counsel of the wicked is far from me.

Ps 26:5 — I have hated the congregation of evildoers; and will not sit with the wicked.

Ps 26:9 — Gather not my soul with sinners, nor my life with bloody men:

Ps 84:10 — For a day in thy courts *is* better than a thousand. I had rather be a doorkeeper in the house of my God, than to dwell in the tents of wickedness.

Ps 101:7 — He that worketh deceit shall not dwell within my house: he that telleth lies shall not tarry in my sight.

Ps 119:104 — Through thy precepts I get understanding: therefore I hate every false way.

Ps 119:113 — I hate *vain* thoughts: but thy law do I love.

Ps 119:128 — Therefore I esteem all *thy* precepts *concerning* all *things to be* right; *and* I hate every false way.

Ps 119:163 — I hate and abhor lying: *but* thy law do I love.

Ps 120:2 — Deliver my soul, O LORD, from lying lips, *and* from a deceitful tongue.

Pr 8:13 — The fear of the LORD *is* to hate evil: pride, and arrogancy, and the evil way, and the froward mouth, do I hate.

Pr 29:27 — An unjust man *is* an abomination to the just: and *he that is* upright in the way *is* abomination to the wicked.

Jer 9:2 — Oh that I had in the wilderness a lodging place of wayfaring men; that I might leave my people, and go from them! for they *be* all adulterers, an assembly of treacherous men.

Ro 7:15 — For that which I do I allow not: for what I would, that do I not; but what I hate, that do I.

Ro 7:19 — For the good that I would I do not: but the evil which I would not, that I do.

Jude 1:23 — And others save with fear, pulling *them* out of the fire; hating even the garment spotted by the flesh.

Rev 2:2 — I know thy works, and thy labour, and thy patience, and how thou canst not bear them which are evil: and thou hast tried them which say they are apostles, and are not, and hast found them liars:

See: Holiness

• Separates from God.

Dt 31:17–18; Job 23:8–9; Ps 78:59–61; Isa 59:1–2; Am 3:2–3

Jos 7:12 — Therefore the children of Israel could not stand before their enemies, *but* turned *their* backs before their enemies, because they were accursed: neither will I be with you any more, except ye destroy the accursed from among you.

2Ch 24:20 — And the Spirit of God came upon Zechariah the son of Jehoiada the priest, which stood above the people, and said unto them, Thus saith God, Why transgress ye the commandments of the LORD, that ye cannot prosper? because ye have forsaken the LORD, he hath also forsaken you.

Job 13:24 — Wherefore hidest thou thy face, and holdest me for thine enemy?

Job 23:3 — Oh that I knew where I might find him! *that* I might come *even* to his seat!

Isa 64:7 — And *there is* none that calleth upon thy name, that stirreth up himself to take hold of thee: for thou hast hid thy face from us, and hast consumed us, because of our iniquities.

Eze 23:18 — So she discovered her whoredoms, and discovered her nakedness: then my mind was alienated from her, like as my mind was alienated from her sister.

Hos 9:12 — Though they bring up their children, yet will I bereave them, *that there shall* not *be* a man *left:* yea, woe also to them when I depart from them!

Mic 3:4 — Then shall they cry unto the LORD, but he will not hear them: he will even hide his face from them at that time, as they have behaved themselves ill in their doings.

Mt 7:23 — And then will I profess unto them, I never knew you: depart from me, ye that work iniquity.

Mt 25:41 — Then shall he say also unto them on the left hand, Depart from me, ye cursed, into everlasting fire, prepared for the devil and his angels:

Lk 13:27 — But he shall say, I tell you, I know you not whence ye are; depart from me, all *ye* workers of iniquity.

Ro 8:7 — Because the carnal mind *is* enmity against God: for it is not subject to the law of God, neither indeed can be.

Heb 12:14 — Follow peace with all *men,* and holiness, without which no man shall see the Lord:

See: God, Holiness of

See: Wicked; punishment of

SIN MONEY

2Ki 12:16 — The trespass money and sin money was not brought into the house of the LORD: it was the priests'.

See: Conscience Money

SIN, a city of Egypt

Eze 30:15 — And I will pour my fury upon Sin, the strength of Egypt; and I will cut off the multitude of No.

SIN, Desert of

• A wilderness between Elim and Sinai.

• Children of Israel journey through.

Ex 16:1 — And they took their journey from Elim, and all the congregation of the children of Israel came unto the wilderness of Sin, which *is* between Elim and Sinai, on the fifteenth day of the second month after their departing out of the land of Egypt.

• Children of Israel murmur for bread in.

Ex 16:2 — And the whole congregation of the children of Israel murmured against Moses and Aaron in the wilderness:

• Manna and quails given in, to children of Israel.

Ex 16:4–36

• Children of Israel numbered in.

Nu 26:64 — But among these there was not a man of them whom Moses and Aaron the priest numbered, when they numbered the children of Israel in the wilderness of Sinai.

SINA See: Sinai

SINAI

• A mountain in the peninsula east of the Red Sea.

• Children of Israel arrive at, in their wanderings in the wilderness.

Ex 16:1 — And they took their journey from Elim, and all the congregation of the children of Israel came unto the wilderness of Sin, which *is* between

Elim and Sinai, on the fifteenth day of the second month after their departing out of the land of Egypt.

Ex 19:2 — For they were departed from Rephidim, and were come *to* the desert of Sinai, and had pitched in the wilderness; and there Israel camped before the mount.

Dt 1:2 — (*There are* eleven days' *journey* from Horeb by the way of mount Seir unto Kadesh-barnea.)

- **The law delivered to Moses upon.**

Ex 19:3–20:26; 23:2–4; 24:12–18; 32:15–16

Le 7:38 — Which the LORD commanded Moses in mount Sinai, in the day that he commanded the children of Israel to offer their oblations unto the LORD, in the wilderness of Sinai.

Le 25:1 — And the LORD spake unto Moses in mount Sinai, saying,

Le 26:46 — These *are* the statutes and judgments and laws, which the LORD made between him and the children of Israel in mount Sinai by the hand of Moses.

Le 27:34 — These *are* the commandments, which the LORD commanded Moses for the children of Israel in mount Sinai.

Nu 3:1 — These also *are* the generations of Aaron and Moses in the day *that* the LORD spake with Moses in mount Sinai.

Dt 4:15 — Take ye therefore good heed unto yourselves; for ye saw no manner of similitude on the day *that* the LORD spake unto you in Horeb out of the midst of the fire:

Dt 5:26 — For who *is there of* all flesh, that hath heard the voice of the living God speaking out of the midst of the fire, as we *have,* and lived?

Dt 29:1 — These *are* the words of the covenant, which the LORD commanded Moses to make with the children of Israel in the land of Moab, beside the covenant which he made with them in Horeb.

Dt 33:2 — And he said, The LORD came from Sinai, and rose up from Seir unto them; he shined forth from mount Paran, and he came with ten thousands of saints: from his right hand *went* a fiery law for them.

Ne 9:13 — Thou camest down also upon mount Sinai, and spakest with them from heaven, and gavest them right judgments, and true laws, good statutes and commandments:

Ps 68:8 — The earth shook, the heavens also dropped at the presence of God: *even* Sinai itself *was moved* at the presence of God, the God of Israel.

Ps 68:17 — The chariots of God *are* twenty thousand, *even* thousands of angels: the Lord *is* among them, *as in* Sinai, in the holy *place.*

Mal 4:4 — Remember ye the law of Moses my servant, which I commanded unto him in Horeb for all Israel, *with* the statutes and judgments.

Ac 7:30 — And when forty years were expired, there appeared to him in the wilderness of mount Sina an angel of the Lord in a flame of fire in a bush.

Ac 7:38 — This is he, that was in the church in the wilderness with the angel which spake to him in the mount Sina, and *with* our fathers: who received the lively oracles to give unto us:

- **Figurative.**

Gal 4:24–25

⇝See: Horeb

⇝See: Israelites

- **Wilderness of.**
  - **Children of Israel journeyed in.**

Nu 10:12 — And the children of Israel took their journeys out of the wilderness of Sinai; and the cloud rested in the wilderness of Paran.

  - **Children of Israel kept the passover in.**

Nu 9:1–5

  - **Children of Israel numbered in.**

Nu 26:64 — But among these there was not a man of them whom Moses and Aaron the priest numbered, when they numbered the children of Israel in the wilderness of Sinai.

SINCERITY

- **Does not exempt from guilt.**

Ge 20:1–18

⇝See: Ignorance; sins of

- **Forgiveness of enemies must be sincere.**

Mt 18:35 — So likewise shall my heavenly Father do also unto you, if ye from your hearts forgive not every one his brother their trespasses.

- **Servants must render honest service.**

Eph 6:5–7

- **Whatsoever is done must be in.**

1Co 10:31 — Whether therefore ye eat, or drink, or whatsoever ye do, do all to the glory of God.

- **Jesus was an example of.**

1Pe 2:22 — Who did no sin, neither was guile found in his mouth:

- **Ministers should be examples of.**

Tit 2:7 — In all things shewing thyself a pattern of good works: in doctrine *shewing* uncorruptness, gravity, sincerity,

- **Opposed to fleshly wisdom.**

2Co 1:12 — For our rejoicing is this, the testimony of our conscience, that in simplicity and godly sincerity, not with fleshly wisdom, but by the grace of God, we have had our conversation in the world, and more abundantly to you-ward.

- **Should characterize.**
  - **Our love to God.**

2Co 8:8 — I speak not by commandment, but by occasion of the forwardness of others, and to prove the sincerity of your love.

2Co 8:24 — Wherefore shew ye to them, and before the churches, the proof of your love, and of our boasting on your behalf.

  - **Our love to Jesus.**

Eph 6:24 — Grace *be* with all them that love our Lord Jesus Christ in sincerity. Amen.

• Our service to God.

Jos 24:14 — Now therefore fear the LORD, and serve him in sincerity and in truth: and put away the gods which your fathers served on the other side of the flood, and in Egypt; and serve ye the LORD.

• Our faith.

1Ti 1:5 — Now the end of the commandment is charity out of a pure heart, and *of* a good conscience, and *of* faith unfeigned:

• Our love to one another.

Ro 12:9 — *Let* love be without dissimulation. Abhor that which is evil; cleave to that which is good.

1Pe 1:22 — Seeing ye have purified your souls in obeying the truth through the Spirit unto unfeigned love of the brethren, *see that ye* love one another with a pure heart fervently:

1Jn 3:18 — My little children, let us not love in word, neither in tongue; but in deed and in truth.

• Our whole conduct.

2Co 1:12 — For our rejoicing is this, the testimony of our conscience, that in simplicity and godly sincerity, not with fleshly wisdom, but by the grace of God, we have had our conversation in the world, and more abundantly to you-ward.

• The preaching of the gospel.

1Th 2:3–5

2Co 2:17 — For we are not as many, which corrupt the word of God: but as of sincerity, but as of God, in the sight of God speak we in Christ.

• A characteristic of the doctrines of the gospel.

1Pe 2:2 — As newborn babes, desire the sincere milk of the word, that ye may grow thereby:

• The gospel sometimes preached without.

Php 1:16 — The one preach Christ of contention, not sincerely, supposing to add affliction to my bonds:

• The wicked devoid of.

Ps 5:9 — For *there is* no faithfulness in their mouth; their inward part *is* very wickedness; their throat *is* an open sepulchre; they flatter with their tongue.

Ps 55:21 — *The words* of his mouth were smoother than butter, but war *was* in his heart: his words were softer than oil, yet *were* they drawn swords.

• Exhortations to.

1Co 5:8 — Therefore let us keep the feast, not with old leaven, neither with the leaven of malice and wickedness; but with the unleavened *bread* of sincerity and truth.

1Pe 2:1 — Wherefore laying aside all malice, and all guile, and hypocrisies, and envies, and all evil speakings,

• Prayer for, on behalf of others.

Php 1:10 — That ye may approve things that are excellent; that ye may be sincere and without offence till the day of Christ;

• Blessedness of.

Ps 32:2 — Blessed *is* the man unto whom the LORD imputeth not iniquity, and in whose spirit *there is* no guile.

• Exemplified by.

• Men of Zebulun.

1Ch 12:33 — Of Zebulun, such as went forth to battle, expert in war, with all instruments of war, fifty thousand, which could keep rank: *they were* not of double heart.

• Hezekiah.

Isa 38:3 — And said, Remember now, O LORD, I beseech thee, how I have walked before thee in truth and with a perfect heart, and have done *that which is* good in thy sight. And Hezekiah wept sore.

• Nathanael.

Jn 1:47 — Jesus saw Nathanael coming to him, and saith of him, Behold an Israelite indeed, in whom is no guile!

• Paul.

2Co 1:12 — For our rejoicing is this, the testimony of our conscience, that in simplicity and godly sincerity, not with fleshly wisdom, but by the grace of God, we have had our conversation in the world, and more abundantly to you-ward.

• Timothy.

2Ti 1:5 — When I call to remembrance the unfeigned faith that is in thee, which dwelt first in thy grandmother Lois, and thy mother Eunice; and I am persuaded that in thee also.

• Lois and Eunice.

2Ti 1:5 — When I call to remembrance the unfeigned faith that is in thee, which dwelt first in thy grandmother Lois, and thy mother Eunice; and I am persuaded that in thee also.

SINEWS

Job 10:11 — Thou hast clothed me with skin and flesh, and hast fenced me with bones and sinews.

Job 30:17 — My bones are pierced in me in the night season: and my sinews take no rest.

Isa 48:4 — Because I knew that thou *art* obstinate, and thy neck *is* an iron sinew, and thy brow brass;

Eze 37:6 — And I will lay sinews upon you, and will bring up flesh upon you, and cover you with skin, and put breath in you, and ye shall live; and ye shall know that I *am* the LORD.

Eze 37:8 — And when I beheld, lo, the sinews and the flesh came up upon them, and the skin covered them above: but *there was* no breath in them.

SINGERS See: Music

SINGING See: Music

SINIM

• An unknown land.

• Conjectured by some authorities to be China.

Isa 49:12 — Behold, these shall come from far: and, lo, these from the north and from the west; and these from the land of Sinim.

SINITES • A tribe of Canaanites.

Ge 10:17 — And the Hivite, and the Arkite, and the Sinite,

1Ch 1:15 — And the Hivite, and the Arkite, and the Sinite,

SINLESSNESS

Php 1:9–11; 1Pe 4:1–2

Ps 119:3 — They also do no iniquity: they walk in his ways.

Ac 24:16 — And herein do I exercise myself, to have always a conscience void of offence toward God, and *toward* men.

1Th 3:13 — To the end he may stablish your hearts unblameable in holiness before God, even our Father, at the coming of our Lord Jesus Christ with all his saints.

1Th 5:23 — And the very God of peace sanctify you wholly; and *I pray God* your whole spirit and soul and body be preserved blameless unto the coming of our Lord Jesus Christ.

1Jn 1:8 — If we say that we have no sin, we deceive ourselves, and the truth is not in us.

1Jn 1:10 — If we say that we have not sinned, we make him a liar, and his word is not in us.

1Jn 3:6 — Whosoever abideth in him sinneth not: whosoever sinneth hath not seen him, neither known him.

1Jn 3:9 — Whosoever is born of God doth not commit sin; for his seed remaineth in him: and he cannot sin, because he is born of God.

SINNER See: Wicked

SION

• A name of Mount Hermon.

Dt 4:48 — From Aroer, which *is* by the bank of the river Arnon, even unto mount Sion, which *is* Hermon,

See: Zion

SIPHMOTH

• A city of Judah.

1Sa 30:28 — And to *them* which *were* in Aroer, and to *them* which *were* in Siphmoth, and to *them* which *were* in Eshtemoa,

SIPPAI

• A Philistine giant.

1Ch 20:4 — And it came to pass after this, that there arose war at Gezer with the Philistines; at which time Sibbechai the Hushathite slew Sippai, *that was* of the children of the giant: and they were subdued.

• Called Saph.

2Sa 21:18 — And it came to pass after this, that there was again a battle with the Philistines at Gob: then Sibbechai the Hushathite slew Saph, which *was* of the sons of the giant.

SIRAH • The name of a well.

2Sa 3:26 — And when Joab was come out from David, he sent messengers after Abner, which brought him again from the well of Sirah: but David knew *it* not.

SIRION • Sidonian name of Mount Hermon.

Dt 3:9 — (*Which* Hermon the Sidonians call Sirion; and the Amorites call it Shenir;)

Ps 29:6 — He maketh them also to skip like a calf; Lebanon and Sirion like a young unicorn.

SISAMAI • Son of Eleasah.

1Ch 2:40 — And Eleasah begat Sisamai, and Sisamai begat Shallum,

SISERA

• Captain of a Canaanitish army.

1Sa 12:9 — And when they forgat the LORD their God, he sold them into the hand of Sisera, captain of the host of Hazor, and into the hand of the Philistines, and into the hand of the king of Moab, and they fought against them.

• Defeated by Barak; slain by Jael.

Jgs 4:1–24; 5:20–31

Ps 83:9 — Do unto them as *unto* the Midianites; as *to* Sisera, as *to* Jabin, at the brook of Kison:

• One of the Nethinim.

Ezr 2:53 — The children of Barkos, the children of Sisera, the children of Thamah,

Ne 7:55 — The children of Barkos, the children of Sisera, the children of Tamah,

SITNAH • A name given by Isaac to a well.

Ge 26:21 — And they digged another well, and strove for that also: and he called the name of it Sitnah.

SIVAN • Third month, or June.

Est 8:9 — Then were the king's scribes called at that time in the third month, that *is,* the month Sivan, on the three and twentieth *day* thereof; and it was written according to all that Mordecai commanded unto the Jews, and to the lieutenants, and the deputies and rulers of the provinces which *are* from India unto Ethiopia, an hundred twenty and seven provinces, unto every province according to the writing thereof, and unto every people after their language, and to the Jews according to their writing, and according to their language.

SKEPTICISM

Job 21:15 — What *is* the Almighty, that we should serve him? and what profit should we have, if we pray unto him?

Job 22:17 — Which said unto God, Depart from us: and what can the Almighty do for them?

Ps 14:1 — The fool hath said in his heart, *There is* no God. They are corrupt, they have done abominable works, *there is* none that doeth good.

Ps 53:1 — The fool hath said in his heart, *There is* no God. Corrupt are they, and have done abominable iniquity: *there is* none that doeth good.

Zep 1:12 — And it shall come to pass at that time, *that* I will search Jerusalem with candles, and punish the men that are settled on their lees: that say in their heart, The LORD will not do good, neither will he do evil.

Mal 3:14 — Ye have said, It *is* vain to serve God: and what profit *is it* that we have kept his ordinance, and that we have walked mournfully before the LORD of hosts?

• Of Pharaoh.

Ex 5:2 — And Pharaoh said, Who *is* the LORD, that I should obey his voice to let Israel go? I know not the LORD, neither will I let Israel go.

• Of Thomas.

Jn 20:25–28

See: Unbelief

SKIN

• Clothes of.

Ge 3:21 — Unto Adam also and to his wife did the LORD God make coats of skins, and clothed them.

• For covering the tabernacle.

Nu 4:8–14

Ex 25:5 — And rams' skins dyed red, and badgers' skins, and shittim wood,

• Diseases of.

Le 13:38–39

Dt 28:27 — The LORD will smite thee with the botch of Egypt, and with the emerods, and with the scab, and with the itch, whereof thou canst not be healed.

Job 7:5 — My flesh is clothed with worms and clods of dust; my skin is broken, and become loathsome.

See: Boil

See: Leprosy

SKIRT See: Dress

SLANDER

• Comes from the evil heart.

Lk 6:45 — A good man out of the good treasure of his heart bringeth forth that which is good; and an evil man out of the evil treasure of his heart bringeth forth that which is evil: for of the abundance of the heart his mouth speaketh.

• Often arises from hatred.

Ps 109:3— They compassed me about also with words of hatred; and fought against me without a cause.

• Idleness leads to.

1Ti 5:13 — And withal they learn *to be* idle, wandering about from house to house; and not only idle, but tattlers also and busybodies, speaking things which they ought not.

• The wicked addicted to.

Ps 50:20 — Thou sittest *and* speakest against thy brother; thou slanderest thine own mother's son.

• Hypocrites addicted to.

Pr 11:9 — An hypocrite with *his* mouth destroyeth his neighbour: but through knowledge shall the just be delivered.

• A characteristic of the devil.

Rev 12:10 — And I heard a loud voice saying in heaven, Now is come salvation, and strength, and the kingdom of our God, and the power of his Christ: for the accuser of our brethren is cast down, which accused them before our God day and night.

• The wicked love.

Ps 52:4 — Thou lovest all devouring words, O *thou* deceitful tongue.

• They who indulge in, are fools.

Pr 10:18 — He that hideth hatred *with* lying lips, and he that uttereth a slander, *is* a fool.

• Women warned against.

Tit 2:3 — The aged women likewise, that *they be* in behaviour as becometh holiness, not false accusers, not given to much wine, teachers of good things;

• Ministers' wives should avoid.

1Ti 3:11 — Even so *must their* wives be grave, not slanderers, sober, faithful in all things.

• Christ was exposed to.

Ps 35:11 — False witnesses did rise up; they laid to my charge *things* that I knew not.

Mt 26:60 — But found none: yea, though many false witnesses came, *yet* found they none. At the last came two false witnesses,

• Rulers exposed to.

Jude 1:8 — Likewise also these *filthy* dreamers defile the flesh, despise dominion, and speak evil of dignities.

• Ministers exposed to.

Ro 3:8 — And not *rather,* (as we be slanderously reported, and as some affirm that we say,) Let us do evil, that good may come? whose damnation is just.

2Co 6:8 — By honour and dishonour, by evil report and good report: as deceivers, and *yet* true;

• The nearest relations exposed to.

Ps 50:20 — Thou sittest *and* speakest against thy brother; thou slanderest thine own mother's son.

• Saints exposed to.

Ps 38:12 — They also that seek after my life lay snares *for me:* and they that seek my hurt speak mischievous things, and imagine deceits all the day long.

Ps 109:2 — For the mouth of the wicked and the mouth of the deceitful are opened against me: they have spoken against me with a lying tongue.

1Pe 4:4 — Wherein they think it strange that ye run not with *them* to the same excess of riot, speaking evil of *you:*

• Saints should keep their tongues from.

Ps 34:13 — Keep thy tongue from evil, and thy lips from speaking guile.

1Pe 3:10 — For he that will love life, and see good days, let him refrain his tongue from evil, and his lips that they speak no guile:

• Saints should lay aside.

Eph 4:31 — Let all bitterness, and wrath, and anger, and clamour, and evil speaking, be put away from you, with all malice:

• Saints should be warned against.

Tit 3:1–2

• Saints should give no occasion for.

1Pe 2:12 — Having your conversation honest among the Gentiles: that, whereas they speak against you as evildoers, they may by *your* good works, which they shall behold, glorify God in the day of visitation.

1Pe 3:16 — Having a good conscience; that, whereas they speak evil of you, as of evildoers, they may be ashamed that falsely accuse your good conversation in Christ.

- **Saints should return good for.**

1Co 4:13 — Being defamed, we intreat: we are made as the filth of the world, *and are* the offscouring of all things unto this day.

- **Saints blessed in enduring.**

Mt 5:11 — Blessed are ye, when *men* shall revile you, and persecute *you*, and shall say all manner of evil against you falsely, for my sake.

- **Saints characterized as avoiding.**

Ps 15:1 — Lord, who shall abide in thy tabernacle? who shall dwell in thy holy hill?

Ps 15:3 — *He that* backbiteth not with his tongue, nor doeth evil to his neighbour, nor taketh up a reproach against his neighbour.

- **Should not be listened to.**

1Sa 24:9 — And David said to Saul, Wherefore hearest thou men's words, saying, Behold, David seeketh thy hurt?

- **Causes anger.**

Pr 25:23 — The north wind driveth away rain: so *doth* an angry countenance a backbiting tongue.

- **Effects of.**
  - **Separating friends.**

  Pr 16:28 — A froward man soweth strife: and a whisperer separateth chief friends.

  Pr 17:9 — He that covereth a transgression seeketh love; but he that repeateth a matter separateth *very* friends.

  - **Deadly wounds.**

  Pr 18:8 — The words of a talebearer *are* as wounds, and they go down into the innermost parts of the belly.

  Pr 26:22 — The words of a talebearer *are* as wounds, and they go down into the innermost parts of the belly.

  - **Strife.**

  Pr 26:20 — Where no wood is, *there* the fire goeth out: so where *there is* no talebearer, the strife ceaseth.

  - **Discord among brethren.**

  Pr 6:19 — A false witness *that* speaketh lies, and he that soweth discord among brethren.

  - **Murder.**

  Ps 31:13 — For I have heard the slander of many: fear *was* on every side: while they took counsel together against me, they devised to take away my life.

  Eze 22:9 — In thee are men that carry tales to shed blood: and in thee they eat upon the mountains: in the midst of thee they commit lewdness.

- **The tongue of, is a scourge.**

Job 5:21 — Thou shalt be hid from the scourge of the tongue: neither shalt thou be afraid of destruction when it cometh.

- **The tongue of, is venomous.**

Ps 140:3 — They have sharpened their tongues like a serpent; adders' poison *is* under their lips. Selah.

Ecc 10:11 — Surely the serpent will bite without enchantment; and a babbler is no better.

- **The tongue of, is destructive.**

Pr 11:9 — An hypocrite with *his* mouth destroyeth his neighbour: but through knowledge shall the just be delivered.

- **End of, is mischievous madness.**

Ecc 10:13 — The beginning of the words of his mouth *is* foolishness: and the end of his talk *is* mischievous madness.

- **Men shall give account for.**

Mt 12:36 — But I say unto you, That every idle word that men shall speak, they shall give account thereof in the day of judgment.

- **Punishment for.**

Dt 19:16–21

- **Unclassified scripture relating to.**

Dt 22:13–19; Ps 41:6–9; Ro 1:29–30

Ex 23:1 — Thou shalt not raise a false report: put not thine hand with the wicked to be an unrighteous witness.

Job 5:21 — Thou shalt be hid from the scourge of the tongue: neither shalt thou be afraid of destruction when it cometh.

Ps 50:20 — Thou sittest *and* speakest against thy brother; thou slanderest thine own mother's son.

Ps 101:5 — Whoso privily slandereth his neighbour, him will I cut off: him that hath an high look and a proud heart will not I suffer.

Pr 10:18 — He that hideth hatred *with* lying lips, and he that uttereth a slander, *is* a fool.

Pr 25:23 — The north wind driveth away rain: so *doth* an angry countenance a backbiting tongue.

Jer 6:28 — They *are* all grievous revolters, walking with slanders: *they are* brass and iron; they *are* all corrupters.

Jer 9:4 — Take ye heed every one of his neighbour, and trust ye not in any brother: for every brother will utterly supplant, and every neighbour will walk with slanders.

1Co 6:10 — Nor thieves, nor covetous, nor drunkards, nor revilers, nor extortioners, shall inherit the kingdom of God.

2Co 12:20 — For I fear, lest, when I come, I shall not find you such as I would, and *that* I shall be found unto you such as ye would not: lest *there be* debates, envyings, wraths, strifes, backbitings, whisperings, swellings, tumults:

Jas 4:11 — Speak not evil one of another, brethren. He that speaketh evil of *his* brother, and judgeth his brother, speaketh evil of the law, and judgeth the law: but if thou judge the law, thou art not a doer of the law, but a judge.

1Pe 2:1 — Wherefore laying aside all malice, and all guile, and hypocrisies, and envies, and all evil speakings,

2Pe 2:10 — But chiefly them that walk after the flesh in the lust of uncleanness, and despise government.

Presumptuous *are they,* selfwilled, they are not afraid to speak evil of dignities.

- **Instances of.**
  - **Joseph, by Potiphar's wife.**
    Ge 39:14–18
  - **Land of Canaan misrepresented by the spies.**
    Nu 14:36
  - **Mephibosheth, by Ziba.**
    2Sa 16:3; 19:24–30
  - **David, by his enemies.**
    Ps 31:13; 35:21; 41:5; 64:3; 140:3
  - **Naboth, by Jezebel.**
    1Ki 21:9–14
  - **Jeremiah, by the Jews.**
    Jer 18:18
  - **Jesus, by the Jews falsely charging that he was a winebibber.**
    Mt 11:19
  - **Jesus, by the Jews falsely charging that he blasphemed.**
    Mk 14:64; Jn 5:18
  - **Jesus, by the Jews falsely charging that he had a devil.**
    Jn 8:48; 8:52; 10:20
  - **Jesus, by the Jews falsely charging that he was seditious.**
    Lk 22:65; 23:5
  - **Jesus, by the Jews falsely charging that he was a king.**
    Lk 23:2; Jn 18:37; 19:1–5
  - **Paul.**
    - **See: Paul, Ministry, Ac 16–28**
    - **See: Paul, Ministry, Ac 9–15**
  - **See: Accusation, False**
  - **See: Falsehood, False Witness**
  - **See: Speaking; evil**

SLAVERY **See: Servant; bond**

SLEEP

- **From God.**
  Ps 127:2
- **Of the sluggard.**
  Pr 6:9–10
- **Of Jesus.**
  Mt 8:24 — And, behold, there arose a great tempest in the sea, insomuch that the ship was covered with the waves: but he was asleep.
  Mk 4:38 — And he was in the hinder part of the ship, asleep on a pillow: and they awake him, and say unto him, Master, carest thou not that we perish?
  Lk 8:23 — But as they sailed he fell asleep: and there came down a storm of wind on the lake; and they were filled *with water,* and were in jeopardy.
- **A symbol of death.**
  Jn 11:11–12
  Job 14:12 — So man lieth down, and riseth not: till the heavens *be* no more, they shall not awake, nor be raised out of their sleep.
  Mt 9:24 — He said unto them, Give place: for the maid is not dead, but sleepeth. And they laughed him to scorn.
  Mk 5:39 — And when he was come in, he saith unto them, Why make ye this ado, and weep? the damsel is not dead, but sleepeth.
  Lk 8:52 — And all wept, and bewailed her: but he said, Weep not; she is not dead, but sleepeth.
  1Th 4:14 — For if we believe that Jesus died and rose again, even so them also which sleep in Jesus will God bring with him.
  - **See: Death**

SLIME

- **A cement made of asphaltum.**
- **Valley of Siddim afforded.**
  Ge 14:10 — And the vale of Siddim *was full of* slimepits; and the kings of Sodom and Gomorrah fled, and fell there; and they that remained fled to the mountain.
- **Used at Babel.**
  Ge 11:3 — And they said one to another, Go to, let us make brick, and burn them throughly. And they had brick for stone, and slime had they for morter.
- **Used in Noah's ark.**
  Ge 6:14 — Make thee an ark of gopher wood; rooms shalt thou make in the ark, and shalt pitch it within and without with pitch.
- **Used in ark of Moses.**
  Ex 2:3 — And when she could not longer hide him, she took for him an ark of bulrushes, and daubed it with slime and with pitch, and put the child therein; and she laid *it* in the flags by the river's brink.
- **Inflammable.**
  Isa 34:9 — And the streams thereof shall be turned into pitch, and the dust thereof into brimstone, and the land thereof shall become burning pitch.

SLING

- **Used for throwing stones.**
  Pr 26:8 — As he that bindeth a stone in a sling, so *is* he that giveth honour to a fool.
- **David slays Goliath with.**
  1Sa 17:40–50
- **Dextrous use of.**
  Jgs 20:16 — Among all this people *there were* seven hundred chosen men lefthanded; every one could sling stones at an hair *breadth,* and not miss.
- **Used in war.**
  Jgs 20:16 — Among all this people *there were* seven hundred chosen men lefthanded; every one could sling stones at an hair *breadth,* and not miss.
  2Ki 3:25 — And they beat down the cities, and on every good piece of land cast every man his stone, and filled it; and they stopped all the wells of water, and felled all the good trees: only in Kir-haraseth left

they the stones thereof; howbeit the slingers went about *it,* and smote it.

2Ch 26:14 — And Uzziah prepared for them throughout all the host shields, and spears, and helmets, and habergeons, and bows, and slings *to cast* stones.

See: Armies

See: Arms

SLOTHFULNESS

Pr 6:6–11; 10:4–5; 24:30–34; 26:13–16; Mt 25:26–27; 2Th 3:10–12

Pr 10:26 — As vinegar to the teeth, and as smoke to the eyes, so *is* the sluggard to them that send him.

Pr 12:24 — The hand of the diligent shall bear rule: but the slothful shall be under tribute.

Pr 12:27 — The slothful *man* roasteth not that which he took in hunting: but the substance of a diligent man *is* precious.

Pr 13:4 — The soul of the sluggard desireth, and *hath* nothing: but the soul of the diligent shall be made fat.

Pr 15:19 — The way of the slothful *man is* as an hedge of thorns: but the way of the righteous *is* made plain.

Pr 18:9 — He also that is slothful in his work is brother to him that is a great waster.

Pr 19:15 — Slothfulness casteth into a deep sleep; and an idle soul shall suffer hunger.

Pr 19:24 — A slothful *man* hideth his hand in *his* bosom, and will not so much as bring it to his mouth again.

Pr 20:4 — The sluggard will not plow by reason of the cold; *therefore* shall he beg in harvest, and *have* nothing.

Pr 21:25 — The desire of the slothful killeth him; for his hands refuse to labour.

Pr 22:13 — The slothful *man* saith, *There is* a lion without, I shall be slain in the streets.

Pr 23:21 — For the drunkard and the glutton shall come to poverty: and drowsiness shall clothe *a man* with rags.

Ecc 10:18 — By much slothfulness the building decayeth; and through idleness of the hands the house droppeth through.

Isa 56:10 — His watchmen *are* blind: they are all ignorant, they *are* all dumb dogs, they cannot bark; sleeping, lying down, loving to slumber.

Ro 12:11 — Not slothful in business; fervent in spirit; serving the Lord;

Heb 6:12 — That ye be not slothful, but followers of them who through faith and patience inherit the promises.

See: Idleness

See: Industry

SLUGGARD **See: Idleness**

SMITH

- **A worker in metals.**
- **Tubal-cain.**

Ge 4:22 — And Zillah, she also bare Tubal-cain, an instructer of every artificer in brass and iron: and the sister of Tubal-cain *was* Naamah.

- **Bezaleel.**

Ex 31:1–11

- **The Philistines.**

1Sa 13:19 — Now there was no smith found throughout all the land of Israel: for the Philistines said, Lest the Hebrews make *them* swords or spears:

- **Jewish, carried captive to Babylon.**

2Ki 24:14 — And he carried away all Jerusalem, and all the princes, and all the mighty men of valour, *even* ten thousand captives, and all the craftsmen and smiths: none remained, save the poorest sort of the people of the land.

Jer 24:1 — The LORD shewed me, and, behold, two baskets of figs *were* set before the temple of the LORD, after that Nebuchadrezzar king of Babylon had carried away captive Jeconiah the son of Jehoiakim king of Judah, and the princes of Judah, with the carpenters and smiths, from Jerusalem, and had brought them to Babylon.

- **The manufacturers of idols.**

Isa 41:7 — So the carpenter encouraged the goldsmith, *and* he that smootheth *with* the hammer him that smote the anvil, saying, It is ready for the sodering: and he fastened it with nails, *that* it should not be moved.

Isa 44:12 — The smith with the tongs both worketh in the coals, and fashioneth it with hammers, and worketh it with the strength of his arms: yea, he is hungry, and his strength faileth: he drinketh no water, and is faint.

- **Genius of, from God.**

Ex 31:3–5; 35:30–35

Isa 54:16 — Behold, I have created the smith that bloweth the coals in the fire, and that bringeth forth an instrument for his work; and I have created the waster to destroy.

SMITING **See: Assault and Battery**

SMOKE

- **Figurative.**

Isa 6:4 — And the posts of the door moved at the voice of him that cried, and the house was filled with smoke.

Hos 13:3 — Therefore they shall be as the morning cloud, and as the early dew that passeth away, as the chaff *that* is driven with the whirlwind out of the floor, and as the smoke out of the chimney.

SMYRNA

- **A city of Ionia.**
- **One of the "seven churches" in.**

Rev 1:11 — Saying, I am Alpha and Omega, the first and the last: and, What thou seest, write in a book, and send *it* unto the seven churches which are in Asia; unto Ephesus, and unto Smyrna, and unto Pergamos, and unto Thyatira, and unto Sardis, and unto Philadelphia, and unto Laodicea.

Rev 2:8 — And unto the angel of the church in Smyrna write; These things saith the first and the last, which was dead, and is alive;

SNAIL

- **A crustacean.**
- **Forbidden as food.**

Le 11:30 — And the ferret, and the chameleon, and the lizard, and the snail, and the mole.

- **Perishable.**

Ps 58:8 — As a snail *which* melteth, let *every one of them* pass away: *like* the untimely birth of a woman, *that* they may not see the sun.

SNARE

Am 3:5 — Can a bird fall in a snare upon the earth, where no gin *is* for him? shall *one* take up a snare from the earth, and have taken nothing at all?

- **Figurative.**
  - **Of the evils in life of the wicked.**

Job 18:8–10

  - **Of the devices of the wicked to deceive the righteous.**

Ps 91:3 — Surely he shall deliver thee from the snare of the fowler, *and* from the noisome pestilence.

Jer 5:26 — For among my people are found wicked *men:* they lay wait, as he that setteth snares; they set a trap, they catch men.

See: Ambush

See: Conspiracy

See: Pit

SNOW

- **In Palestine.**

2Sa 23:20 — And Benaiah the son of Jehoiada, the son of a valiant man, of Kabzeel, who had done many acts, he slew two lionlike men of Moab: he went down also and slew a lion in the midst of a pit in time of snow:

- **In Uz.**

Job 6:16 — Which are blackish by reason of the ice, *and* wherein the snow is hid:

Job 9:30 — If I wash myself with snow water, and make my hands never so clean;

Job 37:6 — For he saith to the snow, Be thou *on* the earth; likewise to the small rain, and to the great rain of his strength.

- **On mount Lebanon.**

Jer 18:14 — Will *a man* leave the snow of Lebanon *which cometh* from the rock of the field? *or* shall the cold flowing waters that come from another place be forsaken?

- **Figurative.**
  - **Of purity.**

Ps 51:7 — Purge me with hyssop, and I shall be clean: wash me, and I shall be whiter than snow.

Isa 1:18 — Come now, and let us reason together, saith the LORD: though your sins be as scarlet, they shall be as white as snow; though they be red like crimson, they shall be as wool.

La 4:7 — Her Nazarites were purer than snow, they were whiter than milk, they were more ruddy in body than rubies, their polishing *was* of sapphire:

SNUFFDISHES

- **In the tabernacle.**

Ex 25:38 — And the tongs thereof, and the snuffdishes thereof, *shall be of* pure gold.

SNUFFERS

- **Provided for the lamps in the temple.**

1Ki 7:50 — And the bowls, and the snuffers, and the basons, and the spoons, and the censers *of* pure gold; and the hinges *of* gold, *both* for the doors of the inner house, the most holy *place, and* for the doors of the house, *to wit,* of the temple.

2Ki 12:13 — Howbeit there were not made for the house of the LORD bowls of silver, snuffers, basons, trumpets, any vessels of gold, or vessels of silver, of the money *that was* brought into the house of the LORD:

2Ki 25:14 — And the pots, and the shovels, and the snuffers, and the spoons, and all the vessels of brass wherewith they ministered, took they away.

Jer 52:18 — The caldrons also, and the shovels, and the snuffers, and the bowls, and the spoons, and all the vessels of brass wherewith they ministered, took they away.

SO • King of Egypt.

2Ki 17:4 — And the king of Assyria found conspiracy in Hoshea: for he had sent messengers to So king of Egypt, and brought no present to the king of Assyria, as *he had done* year by year: therefore the king of Assyria shut him up, and bound him in prison.

SOAP

- **A washing compound.**

Jer 2:22 — For though thou wash thee with nitre, and take thee much sope, *yet* thine iniquity is marked before me, saith the Lord GOD.

Mal 3:2 — But who may abide the day of his coming? and who shall stand when he appeareth? for he *is* like a refiner's fire, and like fullers' sope:

SOBRIETY

- **Commanded.**

1Pe 1:13 — Wherefore gird up the loins of your mind, be sober, and hope to the end for the grace that is to be brought unto you at the revelation of Jesus Christ;

1Pe 5:8 — Be sober, be vigilant; because your adversary the devil, as a roaring lion, walketh about, seeking whom he may devour:

- **The gospel designed to teach.**

Tit 2:12 — Teaching us that, denying ungodliness and worldly lusts, we should live soberly, righteously, and godly, in this present world;

- **With watchfulness.**

1Th 5:6 — Therefore let us not sleep, as *do* others; but let us watch and be sober.

• With prayer.

1Pe 4:7 — But the end of all things is at hand: be ye therefore sober, and watch unto prayer.

• Required in ministers.

1Ti 3:2–3

Tit 1:8 — But a lover of hospitality, a lover of good men, sober, just, holy, temperate;

• Required in wives of ministers.

1Ti 3:11 — Even so *must their* wives be grave, not slanderers, sober, faithful in all things.

• Required in aged men.

Tit 2:2 — That the aged men be sober, grave, temperate, sound in faith, in charity, in patience.

• Required in young men.

Tit 2:6 — Young men likewise exhort to be sober minded.

• Required in young women.

Tit 2:4 — That they may teach the young women to be sober, to love their husbands, to love their children,

• Required in all saints.

1Th 5:6 — Therefore let us not sleep, as *do* others; but let us watch and be sober.

1Th 5:8 — But let us, who are of the day, be sober, putting on the breastplate of faith and love; and for an helmet, the hope of salvation.

• Women should exhibit in dress.

1Ti 2:9 — In like manner also, that women adorn themselves in modest apparel, with shamefacedness and sobriety; not with broided hair, or gold, or pearls, or costly array;

• We should estimate our character and talents with.

Ro 12:3 — For I say, through the grace given unto me, to every man that is among you, not to think *of himself* more highly than he ought to think; but to think soberly, according as God hath dealt to every man the measure of faith.

• We should live in.

Tit 2:12 — Teaching us that, denying ungodliness and worldly lusts, we should live soberly, righteously, and godly, in this present world;

• Motive for.

1Pe 4:7 — But the end of all things is at hand: be ye therefore sober, and watch unto prayer.

1Pe 5:8 — Be sober, be vigilant; because your adversary the devil, as a roaring lion, walketh about, seeking whom he may devour:

⇷See: Temperance

⇷See: Drunkenness

SOCHO • Son of Heber.

1Ch 4:18 — And his wife Jehudijah bare Jered the father of Gedor, and Heber the father of Socho, and Jekuthiel the father of Zanoah. And these *are* the sons of Bithiah the daughter of Pharaoh, which Mered took.

SOCHOH ⇷See: Socoh

SOCOH

• A city of Judah.

Jos 15:35 — Jarmuth, and Adullam, Socoh, and Azekah,

• Called also Shocho, Shochoh, Shoco, Sochoh.

1Sa 17:1 — Now the Philistines gathered together their armies to battle, and were gathered together at Shochoh, which *belongeth* to Judah, and pitched between Shochoh and Azekah, in Ephes-dammim.

• One of Solomon's commissaries in.

1Ki 4:10 — The son of Hesed, in Aruboth; to him *pertained* Sochoh, and all the land of Hepher:

• Rebuilt and fortified by Rehoboam.

2Ch 11:7 — And Beth-zur, and Shoco, and Adullam,

• Taken by Philistines.

2Ch 28:18 — The Philistines also had invaded the cities of the low country, and of the south of Judah, and had taken Beth-shemesh, and Ajalon, and Gederoth, and Shocho with the villages thereof, and Timnah with the villages thereof, Gimzo also and the villages thereof: and they dwelt there.

• A city in the mountains of Judah.

Jos 15:48 — And in the mountains, Shamir, and Jattir, and Socoh,

SODI • A man of Zebulun.

Nu 13:10 — Of the tribe of Zebulun, Gaddiel the son of Sodi.

SODOM

• Called also Sodoma.

• Situated in the plain of the Jordan.

Ge 13:10 — And Lot lifted up his eyes, and beheld all the plain of Jordan, that it *was* well watered every where, before the LORD destroyed Sodom and Gomorrah, *even* as the garden of the LORD, like the land of Egypt, as thou comest unto Zoar.

• The southeastern limit of the Canaanites.

Ge 10:19 — And the border of the Canaanites was from Sidon, as thou comest to Gerar, unto Gaza; as thou goest, unto Sodom, and Gomorrah, and Admah, and Zeboim, even unto Lasha.

• Lot dwells at.

Ge 13:12 — Abram dwelled in the land of Canaan, and Lot dwelled in the cities of the plain, and pitched *his* tent toward Sodom.

• King of, joins other kings of the nations resisting the invasion of Chedorlaomer.

Ge 14:1–12

• Wickedness of the inhabitants of.

Ge 19:4–13; Eze 16:48–49

Ge 13:13 — But the men of Sodom *were* wicked and sinners before the LORD exceedingly.

Dt 32:32 — For their vine *is* of the vine of Sodom, and of the fields of Gomorrah: their grapes *are* grapes of gall, their clusters *are* bitter:

Isa 3:9 — The shew of their countenance doth witness against them; and they declare their sin as Sodom, they hide *it* not. Woe unto their soul! for they have rewarded evil unto themselves.

Jer 23:14 — I have seen also in the prophets of Jerusalem an horrible thing: they commit adultery, and walk in lies: they strengthen also the hands of evildoers, that none doth return from his wickedness: they are all of them unto me as Sodom, and the inhabitants thereof as Gomorrah.

La 4:6 — For the punishment of the iniquity of the daughter of my people is greater than the punishment of the sin of Sodom, that was overthrown as in a moment, and no hands stayed on her.

Eze 16:46 — And thine elder sister *is* Samaria, she and her daughters that dwell at thy left hand: and thy younger sister, that dwelleth at thy right hand, *is* Sodom and her daughters.

Jude 1:7 — Even as Sodom and Gomorrha, and the cities about them in like manner, giving themselves over to fornication, and going after strange flesh, are set forth for an example, suffering the vengeance of eternal fire.

• Abraham's intercession for.

Ge 18:16–33

• Destroyed on account of the wickedness of the people.

Ge 19:1–29

Dt 29:23 — *And that* the whole land thereof *is* brimstone, and salt, *and* burning, *that* it is not sown, nor beareth, nor any grass groweth therein, like the overthrow of Sodom, and Gomorrah, Admah, and Zeboim, which the LORD overthrew in his anger, and in his wrath:

Isa 13:19 — And Babylon, the glory of kingdoms, the beauty of the Chaldees' excellency, shall be as when God overthrew Sodom and Gomorrah.

Jer 49:18 — As in the overthrow of Sodom and Gomorrah and the neighbour *cities* thereof, saith the LORD, no man shall abide there, neither shall a son of man dwell in it.

Jer 50:40 — As God overthrew Sodom and Gomorrah and the neighbour *cities* thereof, saith the LORD; *so* shall no man abide there, neither shall any son of man dwell therein.

La 4:6 — For the punishment of the iniquity of the daughter of my people is greater than the punishment of the sin of Sodom, that was overthrown as in a moment, and no hands stayed on her.

Am 4:11 — I have overthrown *some* of you, as God overthrew Sodom and Gomorrah, and ye were as a firebrand plucked out of the burning: yet have ye not returned unto me, saith the LORD.

Zep 2:9 — Therefore *as* I live, saith the LORD of hosts, the God of Israel, Surely Moab shall be as Sodom, and the children of Ammon as Gomorrah, *even* the breeding of nettles, and saltpits, and a perpetual desolation: the residue of my people shall spoil them, and the remnant of my people shall possess them.

Mt 10:15 — Verily I say unto you, It shall be more tolerable for the land of Sodom and Gomorrha in the day of judgment, than for that city.

Lk 17:29 — But the same day that Lot went out of Sodom it rained fire and brimstone from heaven, and destroyed *them* all.

Ro 9:29 — And as Esaias said before, Except the Lord of Sabaoth had left us a seed, we had been as Sodoma, and been made like unto Gomorrha.

2Pe 2:6 — And turning the cities of Sodom and Gomorrah into ashes condemned *them* with an overthrow, making *them* an ensample unto those that after should live ungodly;

• Figurative.

• Of wickedness.

Eze 16:46–56

Dt 23:17 — There shall be no whore of the daughters of Israel, nor a sodomite of the sons of Israel.

Dt 32:32 — For their vine *is* of the vine of Sodom, and of the fields of Gomorrah: their grapes *are* grapes of gall, their clusters *are* bitter:

Isa 1:10 — Hear the word of the LORD, ye rulers of Sodom; give ear unto the law of our God, ye people of Gomorrah.

SODOMITES

• Inhabitants of Sodom.

• Wickedness of.

Ge 19:4–14

• Destroyed by fire as a judgment.

Ge 19:24–25

• To be judged according to opportunity.

Mt 11:24 — But I say unto you, That it shall be more tolerable for the land of Sodom in the day of judgment, than for thee.

Lk 10:12 — But I say unto you, that it shall be more tolerable in that day for Sodom, than for that city.

• A proverbial term of reproach applied to those who practice sodomy.

Dt 23:17 — There shall be no whore of the daughters of Israel, nor a sodomite of the sons of Israel.

1Ki 14:24 — And there were also sodomites in the land: *and* they did according to all the abominations of the nations which the LORD cast out before the children of Israel.

1Ki 15:12 — And he took away the sodomites out of the land, and removed all the idols that his fathers had made.

1Ki 22:46 — And the remnant of the sodomites, which remained in the days of his father Asa, he took out of the land.

2Ki 23:7 — And he brake down the houses of the sodomites, that *were* by the house of the LORD, where the women wove hangings for the grove.

Job 36:14 — They die in youth, and their life *is* among the unclean.

• "Harlot" is translation of a Hebrew feminine form translated elsewhere "sodomite".

Ge 38:21–22

Dt 23:17 — There shall be no whore [harlot] of the daughters of Israel, nor a sodomite of the sons of Israel.

Hos 4:14 — I will not punish your daughters when they commit whoredom, nor your spouses when they commit adultery: for themselves are separated with whores, and they sacrifice with harlots: therefore the people *that* doth not understand shall fall.

See: Sodomy

SODOMY

Ge 19:5–8; Le 18:22–23; 20:15–16; Ro 1:26–27; 1Ti 1:9–10

Ex 22:19 — Whosoever lieth with a beast shall surely be put to death.

Le 20:13 — If a man also lie with mankind, as he lieth with a woman, both of them have committed an abomination: they shall surely be put to death; their blood *shall be* upon them.

Dt 23:17 — There shall be no whore of the daughters of Israel, nor a sodomite of the sons of Israel.

Dt 27:21 — Cursed *be* he that lieth with any manner of beast. And all the people shall say, Amen.

Jgs 19:22 — *Now* as they were making their hearts merry, behold, the men of the city, certain sons of Belial, beset the house round about, *and* beat at the door, and spake to the master of the house, the old man, saying, Bring forth the man that came into thine house, that we may know him.

1Ki 14:24 — And there were also sodomites in the land: *and* they did according to all the abominations of the nations which the LORD cast out before the children of Israel.

1Ki 15:12 — And he took away the sodomites out of the land, and removed all the idols that his fathers had made.

1Ki 22:46 — And the remnant of the sodomites, which remained in the days of his father Asa, he took out of the land.

2Ki 23:7 — And he brake down the houses of the sodomites, that *were* by the house of the LORD, where the women wove hangings for the grove.

Ro 1:24 — Wherefore God also gave them up to uncleanness through the lusts of their own hearts, to dishonour their own bodies between themselves:

1Co 6:9 — Know ye not that the unrighteous shall not inherit the kingdom of God? Be not deceived: neither fornicators, nor idolaters, nor adulterers, nor effeminate, nor abusers of themselves with mankind,

See: Sodomites

SOLDERING

Isa 41:7 — So the carpenter encouraged the goldsmith, *and* he that smootheth *with* the hammer him that smote the anvil, saying, It is ready for the sodering: and he fastened it with nails, *that* it should not be moved.

SOLDIERS

• Military enrollment of Israel in the wilderness of Sinai.

Nu 1:1–2:34

• Military enrollment of Israel in the plains of Moab.

Nu 26:1–65

• Levies of, in the ratio of one man to ten subject to duty.

Jgs 20:10 — And we will take ten men of an hundred throughout all the tribes of Israel, and an hundred of a thousand, and a thousand out of ten thousand, to fetch victual for the people, that they may do, when they come to Gibeah of Benjamin, according to all the folly that they have wrought in Israel.

• Dress in scarlet.

Na 2:3 — The shield of his mighty men is made red, the valiant men *are* in scarlet: the chariots *shall be* with flaming torches in the day of his preparation, and the fir trees shall be terribly shaken.

• Cowards excused from duty as.

Dt 20:8 — And the officers shall speak further unto the people, and they shall say, What man *is there that is* fearful and fainthearted? let him go and return unto his house, lest his brethren's heart faint as well as his heart.

Jgs 7:3 — Now therefore go to, proclaim in the ears of the people, saying, Whosoever *is* fearful and afraid, let him return and depart early from mount Gilead. And there returned of the people twenty and two thousand; and there remained ten thousand.

• Others exempt from service.

Dt 20:5–9

Dt 24:5 — When a man hath taken a new wife, he shall not go out to war, neither shall he be charged with any business: *but* he shall be free at home one year, and shall cheer up his wife which he hath taken.

• Come to John.

Lk 3:14 — And the soldiers likewise demanded of him, saying, And what shall we do? And he said unto them, Do violence to no man, neither accuse *any* falsely; and be content with your wages.

• Mock Jesus.

Mt 27:27–31; Mk 15:16–20; Lk 23:36–37

Lk 23:11 — And Herod with his men of war set him at nought, and mocked *him,* and arrayed him in a gorgeous robe, and sent him again to Pilate.

• Officers concerned in the betrayal of Jesus.

Lk 22:4 — And he went his way, and communed with the chief priests and captains, how he might betray him unto them.

• Crucified Jesus.

Mt 27:31–37; Mk 15:16–24; Jn 19:23–24

Mt 27:27 — Then the soldiers of the governor took Jesus into the common hall, and gathered unto him the whole band *of soldiers.*

• Guard the sepulchre.

Mt 28:11–15

Mt 27:65 — Pilate said unto them, Ye have a watch: go your way, make *it* as sure as ye can.

• Guard prisoners.

Ac 12:4–6

Ac 28:16 — And when we came to Rome, the centurion delivered the prisoners to the captain of the guard: but Paul was suffered to dwell by himself with a soldier that kept him.

- **Maintain the peace.**

Ac 21:31–35

- **Their duty as sentinels.**

Ac 12:19 — And when Herod had sought for him, and found him not, he examined the keepers, and commanded that *they* should be put to death. And he went down from Judaea to Caesarea, and *there* abode.

- **Perform escort duty.**

Ac 21:31–33; 22:24–28; 23:31–33; 27:42–43

Ac 21:35 — And when he came upon the stairs, so it was, that he was borne of the soldiers for the violence of the people.

Ac 23:23 — And he called unto *him* two centurions, saying, Make ready two hundred soldiers to go to Caesarea, and horsemen threescore and ten, and spearmen two hundred, at the third hour of the night;

Ac 27:1 — And when it was determined that we should sail into Italy, they delivered Paul and certain other prisoners unto *one* named Julius, a centurion of Augustus' band.

Ac 27:31 — Paul said to the centurion and to the soldiers, Except these abide in the ship, ye cannot be saved.

Ac 28:16 — And when we came to Rome, the centurion delivered the prisoners to the captain of the guard: but Paul was suffered to dwell by himself with a soldier that kept him.

- **Figurative.**
  - **Of the divine protection.**

Isa 59:16–17

  - **Of the Christian.**

Eph 6:11–17

2Ti 2:3 — Thou therefore endure hardness, as a good soldier of Jesus Christ.

  - **Jesus called Captain of our Salvation.**

Heb 2:10 — For it became him, for whom *are* all things, and by whom *are* all things, in bringing many sons unto glory, to make the captain of their salvation perfect through sufferings.

➜See: Armies

SOLOMON

- **Son of David by Bath-sheba.**

2Sa 12:24 — And David comforted Bath-sheba his wife, and went in unto her, and lay with her: and she bare a son, and he called his name Solomon: and the LORD loved him.

1Ki 1:13 — Go and get thee in unto king David, and say unto him, Didst not thou, my lord, O king, swear unto thine handmaid, saying, Assuredly Solomon thy son shall reign after me, and he shall sit upon my throne? why then doth Adonijah reign?

1Ki 1:17 — And she said unto him, My lord, thou swarest by the LORD thy God unto thine handmaid, *saying,* Assuredly Solomon thy son shall reign after me, and he shall sit upon my throne.

1Ki 1:21 — Otherwise it shall come to pass, when my lord the king shall sleep with his fathers, that I and my son Solomon shall be counted offenders.

- **Named Jedidiah, by Nathan the prophet.**

2Sa 12:24–25

- **Ancestor of Joseph.**

Mt 1:6 — And Jesse begat David the king; and David the king begat Solomon of her *that had been the wife* of Urias;

- **Succeeds David to the throne of Israel.**

1Ki 1:11–48; 1Ch 28:1–21

1Ki 2:12 — Then sat Solomon upon the throne of David his father; and his kingdom was established greatly.

1Ch 23:1 — So when David was old and full of days, he made Solomon his son king over Israel.

Ecc 1:12 — I the Preacher was king over Israel in Jerusalem.

- **Anointed king a second time.**

1Ch 29:22 — And did eat and drink before the LORD on that day with great gladness. And they made Solomon the son of David king the second time, and anointed *him* unto the LORD *to be* the chief governor, and Zadok *to be* priest.

- **His prayer for wisdom, and his vision.**

1Ki 3:5–14; 2Ch 1:7–12

- **Covenant renewed in a vision after the dedication of the temple.**

1Ki 9:1–9; 2Ch 7:12–22

- **His rigorous reign.**

1Ki 2:1–46

- **Builds the temple.**

1Ki 5:1–6:38; 2Ch 2:1–4:22; Ac 7:45–47

1Ki 9:10 — And it came to pass at the end of twenty years, when Solomon had built the two houses, the house of the LORD, and the king's house,

1Ch 6:10 — And Johanan begat Azariah, (he *it is* that executed the priest's office in the temple that Solomon built in Jerusalem:)

2Ch 7:11 — Thus Solomon finished the house of the LORD, and the king's house: and all that came into Solomon's heart to make in the house of the LORD, and in his own house, he prosperously effected.

Jer 52:20 — The two pillars, one sea, and twelve brasen bulls that *were* under the bases, which king Solomon had made in the house of the LORD: the brass of all these vessels was without weight.

- **Dedicates the temple.**

1Ki 8:1–66; 2Ch 6:1–42

- **Renews courses of priests and Levites, and forms of service according to Moses and David.**

2Ch 8:12–16

2Ch 35:4 — And prepare *yourselves* by the houses of your fathers, after your courses, according to the writing of David king of Israel, and according to the writing of Solomon his son.

Ne 12:45 — And both the singers and the porters kept the ward of their God, and the ward of the purification, according to the commandment of David, *and* of Solomon his son.

- **Builds his palace.**

1Ki 3:1 — And Solomon made affinity with Pharaoh king of Egypt, and took Pharaoh's daughter, and brought her into the city of David, until he had made an end of building his own house, and the house of the LORD, and the wall of Jerusalem round about.

1Ki 7:1 — But Solomon was building his own house thirteen years, and he finished all his house.

1Ki 7:8 — And his house where he dwelt *had* another court within the porch, *which* was of the like work. Solomon made also an house for Pharaoh's daughter, whom he had taken *to wife,* like unto this porch.

1Ki 9:10 — And it came to pass at the end of twenty years, when Solomon had built the two houses, the house of the LORD, and the king's house,

2Ch 7:11 — Thus Solomon finished the house of the LORD, and the king's house: and all that came into Solomon's heart to make in the house of the LORD, and in his own house, he prosperously effected.

2Ch 8:1 — And it came to pass at the end of twenty years, wherein Solomon had built the house of the LORD, and his own house,

Ecc 2:4 — I made me great works; I builded me houses; I planted me vineyards:

- **Builds his house of the forest of Lebanon.**

1Ki 7:2–7

- **Builds his house for Pharaoh's daughter.**

1Ki 7:8–12

1Ki 9:24 — But Pharaoh's daughter came up out of the city of David unto her house which *Solomon* had built for her: then did he build Millo.

2Ch 8:11 — And Solomon brought up the daughter of Pharaoh out of the city of David unto the house that he had built for her: for he said, My wife shall not dwell in the house of David king of Israel, because *the places are* holy, whereunto the ark of the LORD hath come.

Ecc 2:4 — I made me great works; I builded me houses; I planted me vineyards:

- **Ivory throne of.**

1Ki 10:18–20

1Ki 7:7 — Then he made a porch for the throne where he might judge, *even* the porch of judgment: and *it was* covered with cedar from one side of the floor to the other.

- **Porches of judgment.**

1Ki 7:7 — Then he made a porch for the throne where he might judge, *even* the porch of judgment: and *it was* covered with cedar from one side of the floor to the other.

- **Builds Millo, the wall of Jerusalem.**

1Ki 9:15–19

2Ch 9:25 — And Solomon had four thousand stalls for horses and chariots, and twelve thousand horsemen; whom he bestowed in the chariot cities, and with the king at Jerusalem.

- **Provides an armory.**

1Ki 10:16–17

- **Plants vineyards and orchards of all kinds of fruit trees; makes pools.**

Ecc 2:4–6

- **Imports apes and peacocks.**

1Ki 10:22 — For the king had at sea a navy of Tharshish with the navy of Hiram: once in three years came the navy of Tharshish, bringing gold, and silver, ivory, and apes, and peacocks.

- **Drinking vessels of his houses.**

1Ki 10:21 — And all king Solomon's drinking vessels *were of* gold, and all the vessels of the house of the forest of Lebanon *were of* pure gold; none *were of* silver: it was nothing accounted of in the days of Solomon.

2Ch 9:20 — And all the drinking vessels of king Solomon *were of* gold, and all the vessels of the house of the forest of Lebanon *were of* pure gold: none *were of* silver; it was *not* any thing accounted of in the days of Solomon.

- **Musicians and musical instruments of his court.**

1Ki 10:12 — And the king made of the almug trees pillars for the house of the LORD, and for the king's house, harps also and psalteries for singers: there came no such almug trees, nor were seen unto this day.

2Ch 9:11 — And the king made *of* the algum trees terraces to the house of the LORD, and to the king's palace, and harps and psalteries for singers: and there were none such seen before in the land of Judah.

Ecc 2:8 — I gathered me also silver and gold, and the peculiar treasure of kings and of the provinces: I gat me men singers and women singers, and the delights of the sons of men, *as* musical instruments, and that of all sorts.

- **The splendor of his court.**

1Ki 10:5–9; 2Ch 9:3–8

1Ki 10:12 — And the king made of the almug trees pillars for the house of the LORD, and for the king's house, harps also and psalteries for singers: there came no such almug trees, nor were seen unto this day.

Ecc 2:9 — So I was great, and increased more than all that were before me in Jerusalem: also my wisdom remained with me.

Mt 6:29 — And yet I say unto you, That even Solomon in all his glory was not arrayed like one of these.

Lk 12:27 — Consider the lilies how they grow: they toil not, they spin not; and yet I say unto you, that Solomon in all his glory was not arrayed like one of these.

- **Commerce of.**

1Ki 10:11–12, 28–29; 2Ch 1:16–17; 8:17–18; 9:13–22

1Ki 9:28 — And they came to Ophir, and fetched from thence gold, four hundred and twenty talents, and brought *it* to king Solomon.

1Ki 10:22 — For the king had at sea a navy of Tharshish with the navy of Hiram: once in three years came the navy of Tharshish, bringing gold, and silver, ivory, and apes, and peacocks.

2Ch 9:28 — And they brought unto Solomon horses out of Egypt, and out of all lands.

• Presents received by.

2Ch 9:23–24

1Ki 10:10 — And she gave the king an hundred and twenty talents of gold, and of spices very great store, and precious stones: there came no more such abundance of spices as these which the queen of Sheba gave to king Solomon.

2Ch 9:9 — And she gave the king an hundred and twenty talents of gold, and of spices great abundance, and precious stones: neither was there any such spice as the queen of Sheba gave king Solomon.

• Is visited by the queen of Sheba.

1Ki 10:1–13; 2Ch 9:1–12

• Wealth of.

1Ki 9:1–28; 10:14–15

1Ki 10:10 — And she gave the king an hundred and twenty talents of gold, and of spices very great store, and precious stones: there came no more such abundance of spices as these which the queen of Sheba gave to king Solomon.

1Ki 10:23 — So king Solomon exceeded all the kings of the earth for riches and for wisdom.

1Ki 10:27 — And the king made silver *to be* in Jerusalem as stones, and cedars made he *to be* as the sycomore trees that *are* in the vale, for abundance.

2Ch 1:15 — And the king made silver and gold at Jerusalem *as plenteous* as stones, and cedar trees made he as the sycomore trees that *are* in the vale for abundance.

2Ch 9:1 — And when the queen of Sheba heard of the fame of Solomon, she came to prove Solomon with hard questions at Jerusalem, with a very great company, and camels that bare spices, and gold in abundance, and precious stones: and when she was come to Solomon, she communed with him of all that was in her heart.

2Ch 9:9 — And she gave the king an hundred and twenty talents of gold, and of spices great abundance, and precious stones: neither was there any such spice as the queen of Sheba gave king Solomon.

2Ch 9:13 — Now the weight of gold that came to Solomon in one year was six hundred and threescore and six talents of gold;

2Ch 9:24 — And they brought every man his present, vessels of silver, and vessels of gold, and raiment, harness, and spices, horses, and mules, a rate year by year.

2Ch 9:27 — And the king made silver in Jerusalem as stones, and cedar trees made he as the sycomore trees that *are* in the low plains in abundance.

Ecc 1:16 — I communed with mine own heart, saying, Lo, I am come to great estate, and have gotten more wisdom than all *they* that have been before me in Jerusalem: yea, my heart had great experience of wisdom and knowledge.

• Has seven hundred wives and three hundred concubines.

Dt 17:17 — Neither shall he multiply wives to himself, that his heart turn not away: neither shall he greatly multiply to himself silver and gold.

1Ki 11:3 — And he had seven hundred wives, princesses, and three hundred concubines: and his wives turned away his heart.

• His seven hundred wives' and three hundred concubines' influence over him.

1Ki 11:4 — For it came to pass, when Solomon was old, *that* his wives turned away his heart after other gods: and his heart was not perfect with the LORD his God, as *was* the heart of David his father.

Ne 13:26 — Did not Solomon king of Israel sin by these things? yet among many nations was there no king like him, who was beloved of his God, and God made him king over all Israel: nevertheless even him did outlandish women cause to sin.

• Marries one of Pharaoh's daughters.

1Ki 3:1 — And Solomon made affinity with Pharaoh king of Egypt, and took Pharaoh's daughter, and brought her into the city of David, until he had made an end of building his own house, and the house of the LORD, and the wall of Jerusalem round about.

• Builds idolatrous temples.

1Ki 11:1–8

2Ki 23:13 — And the high places that *were* before Jerusalem, which *were* on the right hand of the mount of corruption, which Solomon the king of Israel had builded for Ashtoreth the abomination of the Zidonians, and for Chemosh the abomination of the Moabites, and for Milcom the abomination of the children of Ammon, did the king defile.

• His idolatry.

1Ki 3:3–4

2Ki 23:13 — And the high places that *were* before Jerusalem, which *were* on the right hand of the mount of corruption, which Solomon the king of Israel had builded for Ashtoreth the abomination of the Zidonians, and for Chemosh the abomination of the Moabites, and for Milcom the abomination of the children of Ammon, did the king defile.

• Extent of his dominions.

1Ki 4:21 — And Solomon reigned over all kingdoms from the river unto the land of the Philistines, and unto the border of Egypt: they brought presents, and served Solomon all the days of his life.

1Ki 4:24 — For he had dominion over all *the region* on this side the river, from Tiphsah even to Azzah, over all the kings on this side the river: and he had peace on all sides round about him.

1Ki 8:65 — And at that time Solomon held a feast, and all Israel with him, a great congregation, from the entering in of Hamath unto the river of Egypt, before the LORD our God, seven days and seven days, *even* fourteen days.

2Ch 7:8 — Also at the same time Solomon kept the feast seven days, and all Israel with him, a very great congregation, from the entering in of Hamath unto the river of Egypt.

2Ch 9:26 — And he reigned over all the kings from the river even unto the land of the Philistines, and to the border of Egypt.

• Receives tribute.

1Ki 4:21 — And Solomon reigned over all kingdoms from the river unto the land of the Philistines, and unto the border of Egypt: they brought presents, and served Solomon all the days of his life.

1Ki 9:21 — Their children that were left after them in the land, whom the children of Israel also were not able utterly to destroy, upon those did Solomon levy a tribute of bondservice unto this day.

2Ch 8:8 — *But* of their children, who were left after them in the land, whom the children of Israel consumed not, them did Solomon make to pay tribute until this day.

• Officers of.

1Ki 4:1–19; 2Ch 8:9–10

1Ki 2:35 — And the king put Benaiah the son of Jehoiada in his room over the host: and Zadok the priest did the king put in the room of Abiathar.

• His purveyors.

1Ki 4:7–19

• Divides his kingdom into subsistence departments; the daily subsistence rate for his court.

1Ki 4:7–23, 27–28

• Military equipment of.

Dt 17:15–16; 1Ki 10:16–17

1Ki 4:26 — And Solomon had forty thousand stalls of horses for his chariots, and twelve thousand horsemen.

1Ki 4:28 — Barley also and straw for the horses and dromedaries brought they unto the place where *the officers* were, every man according to his charge.

1Ki 10:26 — And Solomon gathered together chariots and horsemen: and he had a thousand and four hundred chariots, and twelve thousand horsemen, whom he bestowed in the cities for chariots, and with the king at Jerusalem.

1Ki 10:28 — And Solomon had horses brought out of Egypt, and linen yarn: the king's merchants received the linen yarn at a price.

2Ch 1:14 — And Solomon gathered chariots and horsemen: and he had a thousand and four hundred chariots, and twelve thousand horsemen, which he placed in the chariot cities, and with the king at Jerusalem.

2Ch 9:25 — And Solomon had four thousand stalls for horses and chariots, and twelve thousand horsemen; whom he bestowed in the chariot cities, and with the king at Jerusalem.

• Cedes certain cities to Hiram.

1Ki 9:10–13

2Ch 8:2 — That the cities which Huram had restored to Solomon, Solomon built them, and caused the children of Israel to dwell there.

• Wisdom and fame of.

1Ki 4:29–34; 10:3–4, 23–24; 1Ch 29:24–25; 2Ch 9:2–7, 22–23

1Ki 10:8 — Happy *are* thy men, happy *are* these thy servants, which stand continually before thee, *and* that hear thy wisdom.

Ecc 1:16 — I communed with mine own heart, saying, Lo, I am come to great estate, and have gotten more wisdom than all *they* that have been before me in Jerusalem: yea, my heart had great experience of wisdom and knowledge.

Mt 12:42 — The queen of the south shall rise up in the judgment with this generation, and shall condemn it: for she came from the uttermost parts of the earth to hear the wisdom of Solomon; and, behold, a greater than Solomon *is* here.

• Piety of.

1Ki 3:5–15; 8:1–66

1Ki 4:29 — And God gave Solomon wisdom and understanding exceeding much, and largeness of heart, even as the sand that *is* on the sea shore.

• Beloved of God.

2Sa 12:24 — And David comforted Bath-sheba his wife, and went in unto her, and lay with her: and she bare a son, and he called his name Solomon: and the LORD loved him.

• Justice of, illustrated in his judgment of the two harlots.

1Ki 3:16–28

• Oppressions of.

1Ki 12:4 — Thy father made our yoke grievous: now therefore make thou the grievous service of thy father, and his heavy yoke which he put upon us, lighter, and we will serve thee.

2Ch 10:4 — Thy father made our yoke grievous: now therefore ease thou somewhat the grievous servitude of thy father, and his heavy yoke that he put upon us, and we will serve thee.

• Reigns forty years.

2Ch 9:30 — And Solomon reigned in Jerusalem over all Israel forty years.

• Death of.

2Ch 9:29–31

• Prophecies concerning.

2Sa 7:12–16; 1Ki 11:9–13; 1Ch 17:11–14; 28:6–7

Ps 132:11 — The LORD hath sworn *in* truth unto David; he will not turn from it; Of the fruit of thy body will I set upon thy throne.

• A type of Christ.

Ps 45:2–17; 72:1–20

SOLOMON'S PORCH • A part of the outer court of the temple.

Jn 10:23 — And Jesus walked in the temple in Solomon's porch.

Ac 3:11 — And as the lame man which was healed held Peter and John, all the people ran together unto them in the porch that is called Solomon's, greatly wondering.

Ac 5:12 — And by the hands of the apostles were many signs and wonders wrought among the people; (and they were all with one accord in Solomon's porch.

SON

• Figurative.

• Of man's relation to God.

Ex 4:22 — And thou shalt say unto Pharaoh, Thus saith the LORD, Israel *is* my son, *even* my firstborn:

✦See: Adoption

✦See: God, Fatherhood of

✦See: Jesus, Son of God

✦See: Jesus, Son of Man

SON-IN-LAW

• Unjust, Jacob.

Ge 30:37–42

• Faithful, Peter.

Mk 1:29–30

Lk 4:38 — And he arose out of the synagogue, and entered into Simon's house. And Simon's wife's mother was taken with a great fever; and they besought him for her.

SONG

• Sung at the passover.

Mt 26:30 — And when they had sung an hymn, they went out into the mount of Olives.

Mk 14:26 — And when they had sung an hymn, they went out into the mount of Olives.

• Didactic.

Dt 32:1–52

✦See: Psalms; didactic

• Impersonation of the church.

SS 1:1–8:14

• Of Moses and the Lamb.

Rev 15:3–4

• New.

Ps 33:3 — Sing unto him a new song; play skilfully with a loud noise.

Ps 40:3 — And he hath put a new song in my mouth, *even* praise unto our God: many shall see *it*, and fear, and shall trust in the LORD.

• Prophetic.

✦See: Psalms; prophetic

• Spiritual, singing of, enjoined.

Eph 5:19 — Speaking to yourselves in psalms and hymns and spiritual songs, singing and making melody in your heart to the Lord;

Col 3:16 — Let the word of Christ dwell in you richly in all wisdom; teaching and admonishing one another in psalms and hymns and spiritual songs, singing with grace in your hearts to the Lord.

• Of praise.

✦See: Praise

✦See: Psalms; praise

✦See: Psalms; thanksgiving

✦See: Thankfulness

• Of redemption.

Rev 5:9–10

• Of the redeemed.

Rev 14:2–5

• Of thanksgiving.

✦See: Psalms; thanksgiving

✦See: Thankfulness

• War.

Ex 15:1–21; Nu 21:27–30; Jgs 5:1–31; 2Sa 1:19–27; 22:1–51

• Solomon wrote one thousand and five.

1Ki 4:32 — And he spake three thousand proverbs: and his songs were a thousand and five.

✦See: Poetry

✦See: Praise

✦See: Psalms; thanksgiving

SOOTHSAYER ✦See: Sorcery

SOPATER • A Christian of Berea.

Ac 20:4 — And there accompanied him into Asia Sopater of Berea; and of the Thessalonians, Aristarchus and Secundus; and Gaius of Derbe, and Timotheus; and of Asia, Tychicus and Trophimus.

SOPHERETH • A servant of Solomon, whose descendants returned from captivity to Jerusalem.

Ezr 2:55 — The children of Solomon's servants: the children of Sotai, the children of Sophereth, the children of Peruda,

Ne 7:57 — The children of Solomon's servants: the children of Sotai, the children of Sophereth, the children of Perida,

SORCERY

• Divination by an alleged assistance of evil spirits.

• Forbidden.

Le 19:26–28; Dt 18:9–14

Le 19:31 — Regard not them that have familiar spirits, neither seek after wizards, to be defiled by them: I *am* the LORD your God.

Le 20:6 — And the soul that turneth after such as have familiar spirits, and after wizards, to go a whoring after them, I will even set my face against that soul, and will cut him off from among his people.

• Denounced.

Isa 8:19 — And when they shall say unto you, Seek unto them that have familiar spirits, and unto wizards that peep, and that mutter: should not a people seek unto their God? for the living to the dead?

Mal 3:5 — And I will come near to you to judgment; and I will be a swift witness against the sorcerers, and against the adulterers, and against false swearers, and against those that oppress the hireling in *his* wages, the widow, and the fatherless, and that turn aside the stranger *from his right,* and fear not me, saith the LORD of hosts.

• Practiced by.

• The Egyptians.

Isa 19:11–12

Isa 19:3 — And the spirit of Egypt shall fail in the midst thereof; and I will destroy the counsel thereof: and they shall seek to the idols, and to the charmers, and to them that have familiar spirits, and to the wizards.

• The magicians.

Ex 7:11 — Then Pharaoh also called the wise men and the sorcerers: now the magicians of Egypt, they also did in like manner with their enchantments.

Ex 7:22 — And the magicians of Egypt did so with their enchantments: and Pharaoh's heart was hardened, neither did he hearken unto them; as the LORD had said.

Ex 8:7 — And the magicians did so with their enchantments, and brought up frogs upon the land of Egypt.

Ex 8:18 — And the magicians did so with their enchantments to bring forth lice, but they could not: so there were lice upon man, and upon beast.

• Balaam.

Nu 22:1–23:30

• Jezebel.

2Ki 9:22 — And it came to pass, when Joram saw Jehu, that he said, *Is it* peace, Jehu? And he answered, What peace, so long as the whoredoms of thy mother Jezebel and her witchcrafts *are so* many?

• The Ninevites.

Na 3:4–5

• The Babylonians.

Isa 47:9–13; Eze 21:21–22

Da 2:2 — Then the king commanded to call the magicians, and the astrologers, and the sorcerers, and the Chaldeans, for to shew the king his dreams. So they came and stood before the king.

Da 2:10 — The Chaldeans answered before the king, and said, There is not a man upon the earth that can shew the king's matter: therefore *there is* no king, lord, nor ruler, *that* asked such things at any magician, or astrologer, or Chaldean.

Da 2:27 — Daniel answered in the presence of the king, and said, The secret which the king hath demanded cannot the wise *men,* the astrologers, the magicians, the soothsayers, shew unto the king;

• Belshazzar.

Da 5:7 — The king cried aloud to bring in the astrologers, the Chaldeans, and the soothsayers. *And* the king spake, and said to the wise *men* of Babylon, Whosoever shall read this writing, and shew me the interpretation thereof, shall be clothed with scarlet, and *have* a chain of gold about his neck, and shall be the third ruler in the kingdom.

Da 5:15 — And now the wise *men,* the astrologers, have been brought in before me, that they should read this writing, and make known unto me the interpretation thereof: but they could not shew the interpretation of the thing:

• Simon Magus.

Ac 8:9 — But there was a certain man, called Simon, which beforetime in the same city used sorcery, and bewitched the people of Samaria, giving out that himself was some great one:

Ac 8:11 — And to him they had regard, because that of long time he had bewitched them with sorceries.

• Elymas.

Ac 13:8 — But Elymas the sorcerer (for so is his name by interpretation) withstood them, seeking to turn away the deputy from the faith.

• The damsel at Philippi.

Ac 16:16 — And it came to pass, as we went to prayer, a certain damsel possessed with a spirit of divination met us, which brought her masters much gain by soothsaying:

• Vagabond Jews.

Ac 19:13 — Then certain of the vagabond Jews, exorcists, took upon them to call over them which had evil spirits the name of the Lord Jesus, saying, We adjure you by Jesus whom Paul preacheth.

• Sons of Sceva.

Ac 19:14–15

• Astrologers.

Mic 3:6–7

Jer 10:2 — Thus saith the LORD, Learn not the way of the heathen, and be not dismayed at the signs of heaven; for the heathen are dismayed at them.

• False prophets.

Jer 29:8–9; Eze 13:6–9

Jer 14:14 — Then the LORD said unto me, The prophets prophesy lies in my name: I sent them not, neither have I commanded them, neither spake unto them: they prophesy unto you a false vision and divination, and a thing of nought, and the deceit of their heart.

Jer 27:9 — Therefore hearken not ye to your prophets, nor to your diviners, nor to your dreamers, nor to your enchanters, nor to your sorcerers, which speak unto you, saying, Ye shall not serve the king of Babylon:

Eze 22:28 — And her prophets have daubed them with untempered *morter,* seeing vanity, and divining lies unto them, saying, Thus saith the Lord GOD, when the LORD hath not spoken.

Mt 24:24 — For there shall arise false Christs, and false prophets, and shall shew great signs and wonders; insomuch that, if *it were* possible, they shall deceive the very elect.

• To cease.

Eze 12:23–24

Eze 13:23 — Therefore ye shall see no more vanity, nor divine divinations: for I will deliver my people out of your hand: and ye shall know that I *am* the LORD.

Mic 5:12 — And I will cut off witchcrafts out of thine hand; and thou shalt have no *more* soothsayers:

• Messages of, false.

Eze 21:29 — Whiles they see vanity unto thee, whiles they divine a lie unto thee, to bring thee upon the necks of *them that are* slain, of the wicked, whose day is come, when their iniquity *shall have* an end.

Zec 10:2 — For the idols have spoken vanity, and the diviners have seen a lie, and have told false dreams; they comfort in vain: therefore they went their way as a flock, they were troubled, because *there was* no shepherd.

2Th 2:9 — *Even him,* whose coming is after the working of Satan with all power and signs and lying wonders,

• Diviners shall be confounded.

Mic 3:7 — Then shall the seers be ashamed, and the diviners confounded: yea, they shall all cover their lips; for *there is* no answer of God.

• Belongs to the works of the flesh.

Gal 5:20 — Idolatry, witchcraft, hatred, variance, emulations, wrath, strife, seditions, heresies,

• Wickedness of.

1Sa 15:23 — For rebellion *is as* the sin of witchcraft, and stubbornness *is as* iniquity and idolatry. Because thou hast rejected the word of the LORD, he hath also rejected thee from *being* king.

• Vainness of.

Isa 44:25 — That frustrateth the tokens of the liars, and maketh diviners mad; that turneth wise *men* backward, and maketh their knowledge foolish;

• Punishment for.

Ex 22:18 — Thou shalt not suffer a witch to live.

Le 20:27 — A man also or woman that hath a familiar spirit, or that is a wizard, shall surely be put to death: they shall stone them with stones: their blood *shall be* upon them.

Dt 13:5 — And that prophet, or that dreamer of dreams, shall be put to death; because he hath spoken to turn *you* away from the LORD your God, which brought you out of the land of Egypt, and redeemed you out of the house of bondage, to thrust thee out of the way which the LORD thy God commanded thee to walk in. So shalt thou put the evil away from the midst of thee.

• Divining by familiar spirits.

Le 20:27 — A man also or woman that hath a familiar spirit, or that is a wizard, shall surely be put to death: they shall stone them with stones: their blood *shall be* upon them.

1Ch 10:13 — So Saul died for his transgression which he committed against the LORD, *even* against the word of the LORD, which he kept not, and also for asking *counsel* of *one that had* a familiar spirit, to enquire *of it;*

2Ch 33:6 — And he caused his children to pass through the fire in the valley of the son of Hinnom: also he observed times, and used enchantments, and used witchcraft, and dealt with a familiar spirit, and with wizards: he wrought much evil in the sight of the LORD, to provoke him to anger.

Isa 8:19 — And when they shall say unto you, Seek unto them that have familiar spirits, and unto wizards that peep, and that mutter: should not a people seek unto their God? for the living to the dead?

Isa 19:3 — And the spirit of Egypt shall fail in the midst thereof; and I will destroy the counsel thereof: and they shall seek to the idols, and to the charmers, and to them that have familiar spirits, and to the wizards.

Isa 29:4 — And thou shalt be brought down, *and* shalt speak out of the ground, and thy speech shall be low out of the dust, and thy voice shall be, as of one that hath a familiar spirit, out of the ground, and thy speech shall whisper out of the dust.

• Divining by entrails.

Eze 21:21 — For the king of Babylon stood at the parting of the way, at the head of the two ways, to use divination: he made *his* arrows bright, he consulted with images, he looked in the liver.

• Divining by images.

2Ki 23:24 — Moreover the *workers with* familiar spirits, and the wizards, and the images, and the idols, and all the abominations that were spied in the land of Judah and in Jerusalem, did Josiah put away, that he might perform the words of the law which were written in the book that Hilkiah the priest found in the house of the LORD.

Eze 21:21 — For the king of Babylon stood at the parting of the way, at the head of the two ways, to use divination: he made *his* arrows bright, he consulted with images, he looked in the liver.

• Divining by rods.

Hos 4:12 — My people ask counsel at their stocks, and their staff declareth unto them: for the spirit of whoredoms hath caused *them* to err, and they have gone a whoring from under their God.

• Saul consulted the witch of Endor.

1Sa 28:7–25

• Books of, destroyed.

Ac 19:19 — Many of them also which used curious arts brought their books together, and burned them before all *men:* and they counted the price of them, and found it fifty thousand *pieces* of silver.

SOREK • Valley of.

Jgs 16:4 — And it came to pass afterward, that he loved a woman in the valley of Sorek, whose name *was* Delilah.

SORREL • A color.

Zec 1:8 — I saw by night, and behold a man riding upon a red horse, and he stood among the myrtle trees that *were* in the bottom; and behind him *were there* red horses, speckled, and white.

SORROW

- **God takes notice of Hagar's.**
  Ge 21:17–20
- **God takes notice of Israelites.**
  Ex 3:7–10
- **For sin.**
  2Co 7:10–11
  See: Repentance
  See: Sin; confession of
- **No sorrow in heaven.**
  Rev 21:4 — And God shall wipe away all tears from their eyes; and there shall be no more death, neither sorrow, nor crying, neither shall there be any more pain: for the former things are passed away.
- **"Sorrow and sighing shall flee away".**
  Isa 35:10 — And the ransomed of the LORD shall return, and come to Zion with songs and everlasting joy upon their heads: they shall obtain joy and gladness, and sorrow and sighing shall flee away.
- **Of Hannah.**
  1Sa 1:15 — And Hannah answered and said, No, my lord, I *am* a woman of a sorrowful spirit: I have drunken neither wine nor strong drink, but have poured out my soul before the LORD.
- **Of David for Absalom.**
  2Sa 18:33–19:8
- **Of Mary and Martha.**
  Jn 11:19–40
- **Jeremiah.**
  La 1:12 — *Is it* nothing to you, all ye that pass by? behold, and see if there be any sorrow like unto my sorrow, which is done unto me, wherewith the LORD hath afflicted *me* in the day of his fierce anger.
- **Jesus.**
  Mt 26:37–44; Mk 14:34–42; Lk 22:42–44
  Isa 53:11 — He shall see of the travail of his soul, *and* shall be satisfied: by his knowledge shall my righteous servant justify many; for he shall bear their iniquities.
- **From bereavement.**
  - **Of Jacob for Joseph.**
    Ge 37:34–35
  - **Of Jacob for Benjamin.**
    Ge 43:14 — And God Almighty give you mercy before the man, that he may send away your other brother, and Benjamin. If I be bereaved *of my children,* I am bereaved.
- **Of the lost.**
  Mt 8:12 — But the children of the kingdom shall be cast out into outer darkness: there shall be weeping and gnashing of teeth.
  Mt 13:42 — And shall cast them into a furnace of fire: there shall be wailing and gnashing of teeth.
  Mt 13:50 — And shall cast them into the furnace of fire: there shall be wailing and gnashing of teeth.
  Mt 22:13 — Then said the king to the servants, Bind him hand and foot, and take him away, and cast *him* into outer darkness; there shall be weeping and gnashing of teeth.
  Mt 24:51 — And shall cut him asunder, and appoint *him* his portion with the hypocrites: there shall be weeping and gnashing of teeth.
  Mt 25:30 — And cast ye the unprofitable servant into outer darkness: there shall be weeping and gnashing of teeth.
  Lk 13:28 — There shall be weeping and gnashing of teeth, when ye shall see Abraham, and Isaac, and Jacob, and all the prophets, in the kingdom of God, and you *yourselves* thrust out.
  Lk 16:23 — And in hell he lift up his eyes, being in torments, and seeth Abraham afar off, and Lazarus in his bosom.
  See: Wicked; punishment of

See: Afflictions, Benefits of
See: Afflictions; consolation in
See: Afflictions; design of
See: Afflictions; resignation in
See: Suffering

SOSIPATER • Kinsman of Paul.

Ro 16:21 — Timotheus my workfellow, and Lucius, and Jason, and Sosipater, my kinsmen, salute you.

SOSTHENES

- **Chief ruler of the synagogue in Corinth.**
  Ac 18:17 — Then all the Greeks took Sosthenes, the chief ruler of the synagogue, and beat *him* before the judgment seat. And Gallio cared for none of those things.
- **A Christian with whom Paul wrote the first letter to the Corinthians.**
  1Co 1:1 — Paul, called *to be* an apostle of Jesus Christ through the will of God, and Sosthenes *our* brother,

SOTAI • A servant of Solomon whose descendants returned from captivity to Jerusalem.

Ezr 2:55 — The children of Solomon's servants: the children of Sotai, the children of Sophereth, the children of Peruda,
Ne 7:57 — The children of Solomon's servants: the children of Sotai, the children of Sophereth, the children of Perida,

SOUL

See: Immortality
See: Man; spirit
See: Righteous
See: Spirit
See: Wicked; punishment of

SOUNDING

• In navigation.

Ac 27:28 — And sounded, and found *it* twenty fathoms: and when they had gone a little further, they sounded again, and found *it* fifteen fathoms.

SOVEREIGNTY

• Of God.

See: God, Sovereign

• Of Man.

See: Man; dominion of

SOWER

• Parable of the.

Mt 13:3–8; Mk 4:3–20; Lk 8:5–8

• Sowing.

Ecc 11:4 — He that observeth the wind shall not sow; and he that regardeth the clouds shall not reap.

Isa 28:25 — When he hath made plain the face thereof, doth he not cast abroad the fitches, and scatter the cummin, and cast in the principal wheat and the appointed barley and rie in their place?

• Figurative.

Gal 6:7–8

Ps 126:5 — They that sow in tears shall reap in joy.

Pr 11:18 — The wicked worketh a deceitful work: but to him that soweth righteousness *shall be* a sure reward.

Isa 32:20 — Blessed *are* ye that sow beside all waters, that send forth *thither* the feet of the ox and the ass.

Hos 8:7 — For they have sown the wind, and they shall reap the whirlwind: it hath no stalk: the bud shall yield no meal: if so be it yield, the strangers shall swallow it up.

Hos 10:12 — Sow to yourselves in righteousness, reap in mercy; break up your fallow ground: for *it is* time to seek the LORD, till he come and rain righteousness upon you.

SPAIN

• Paul purposes to visit.

Ro 15:24 — Whensoever I take my journey into Spain, I will come to you: for I trust to see you in my journey, and to be brought on my way thitherward by you, if first I be somewhat filled with your *company.*

Ro 15:28 — When therefore I have performed this, and have sealed to them this fruit, I will come by you into Spain.

SPAN • About nine or ten inches.

Ex 28:16 — Foursquare it shall be *being* doubled; a span *shall be* the length thereof, and a span *shall be* the breadth thereof.

Ex 39:9 — It was foursquare; they made the breastplate double: a span *was* the length thereof, and a span the breadth thereof, *being* doubled.

SPARROW

• Nests of.

Ps 84:3 — Yea, the sparrow hath found an house, and the swallow a nest for herself, where she may lay her young, *even* thine altars, O LORD of hosts, my King, and my God.

• Two, sold for a farthing.

Mt 10:29 — Are not two sparrows sold for a farthing? and one of them shall not fall on the ground without your Father.

Lk 12:6 — Are not five sparrows sold for two farthings, and not one of them is forgotten before God?

SPEAKING

• Evil.

Ps 10:7–8; 12:3–4; 41:5–9; 52:2–4; 64:2–5; 120:1–7; Pr 6:16–19; 10:31–32; 12:5–6, 17–19; 16:27–28; 26:20–23; Isa 32:6–7; Mt 12:34–37; Ro 1:29–30; 3:13–14; Tit 1:10–11; Jas 3:5–6, 8–10; 1Pe 3:9–10; 2Pe 2:7–8

Ex 22:28 — Thou shalt not revile the gods, nor curse the ruler of thy people.

Job 19:18 — Yea, young children despised me; I arose, and they spake against me.

Ps 34:13 — Keep thy tongue from evil, and thy lips from speaking guile.

Ps 35:21 — Yea, they opened their mouth wide against me, *and* said, Aha, aha, our eye hath seen *it.*

Ps 59:12 — *For* the sin of their mouth *and* the words of their lips let them even be taken in their pride: and for cursing and lying *which* they speak.

Ps 69:12 — They that sit in the gate speak against me; and I *was* the song of the drunkards.

Ps 69:26 — For they persecute *him* whom thou hast smitten; and they talk to the grief of those whom thou hast wounded.

Ps 70:3 — Let them be turned back for a reward of their shame that say, Aha, aha.

Ps 102:8 — Mine enemies reproach me all the day; *and* they that are mad against me are sworn against me.

Ps 106:33 — Because they provoked his spirit, so that he spake unadvisedly with his lips.

Ps 119:23 — Princes also did sit *and* speak against me: *but* thy servant did meditate in thy statutes.

Ps 140:3 — They have sharpened their tongues like a serpent; adders' poison *is* under their lips. Selah.

Ps 140:11 — Let not an evil speaker be established in the earth: evil shall hunt the violent man to overthrow *him.*

Pr 4:24 — Put away from thee a froward mouth, and perverse lips put far from thee.

Pr 8:13 — The fear of the LORD *is* to hate evil: pride, and arrogancy, and the evil way, and the froward mouth, do I hate.

Pr 10:11 — The mouth of a righteous *man is* a well of life: but violence covereth the mouth of the wicked.

Pr 10:19 — In the multitude of words there wanteth not sin: but he that refraineth his lips *is* wise.

Pr 11:11 — By the blessing of the upright the city is exalted: but it is overthrown by the mouth of the wicked.

Pr 12:13 — The wicked is snared by the transgression of *his* lips: but the just shall come out of trouble.

Pr 13:3 — He that keepeth his mouth keepeth his life: *but* he that openeth wide his lips shall have destruction.

Pr 14:25 — A true witness delivereth souls: but a deceitful *witness* speaketh lies.

Pr 15:1 — A soft answer turneth away wrath: but grievous words stir up anger.

Pr 15:4 — A wholesome tongue *is* a tree of life: but perverseness therein *is* a breach in the spirit.

Pr 15:28 — The heart of the righteous studieth to answer: but the mouth of the wicked poureth out evil things.

Pr 17:4 — A wicked doer giveth heed to false lips; *and* a liar giveth ear to a naughty tongue.

Pr 17:9 — He that covereth a transgression seeketh love; but he that repeateth a matter separateth *very* friends.

Pr 17:20 — He that hath a froward heart findeth no good: and he that hath a perverse tongue falleth into mischief.

Pr 18:8 — The words of a talebearer *are* as wounds, and they go down into the innermost parts of the belly.

Pr 18:21 — Death and life *are* in the power of the tongue: and they that love it shall eat the fruit thereof.

Pr 18:23 — The poor useth intreaties; but the rich answereth roughly.

Pr 19:1 — Better *is* the poor that walketh in his integrity, than *he that is* perverse in his lips, and is a fool.

Pr 19:22 — The desire of a man *is* his kindness: and a poor man *is* better than a liar.

Pr 19:28 — An ungodly witness scorneth judgment: and the mouth of the wicked devoureth iniquity.

Pr 24:2 — For their heart studieth destruction, and their lips talk of mischief.

Pr 25:23 — The north wind driveth away rain: so *doth* an angry countenance a backbiting tongue.

Pr 26:28 — A lying tongue hateth *those that are* afflicted by it; and a flattering mouth worketh ruin.

Ecc 7:22 — For oftentimes also thine own heart knoweth that thou thyself likewise hast cursed others.

Ecc 10:11 — Surely the serpent will bite without enchantment; and a babbler is no better.

Ecc 10:20 — Curse not the king, no not in thy thought; and curse not the rich in thy bedchamber: for a bird of the air shall carry the voice, and that which hath wings shall tell the matter.

Isa 6:5 — Then said I, Woe *is* me! for I am undone; because I *am* a man of unclean lips, and I dwell in the midst of a people of unclean lips: for mine eyes have seen the King, the LORD of hosts.

Jer 20:10 — For I heard the defaming of many, fear on every side. Report, *say they,* and we will report it. All my familiars watched for my halting, *saying,* Peradventure he will be enticed, and we shall prevail against him, and we shall take our revenge on him.

Mt 5:22 — <u>But I say unto you, That whosoever is angry with his brother without a cause shall be in danger of the judgment: and whosoever shall say to his brother, Raca, shall be in danger of the council: but whosoever shall say, Thou fool, shall be in danger of hell fire.</u>

Mt 5:37 — <u>But let your communication be, Yea, yea; Nay, nay: for whatsoever is more than these cometh of evil.</u>

Lk 6:45 — <u>A good man out of the good treasure of his heart bringeth forth that which is good; and an evil man out of the evil treasure of his heart bringeth forth that which is evil: for of the abundance of the heart his mouth speaketh.</u>

Ac 23:5 — Then said Paul, I wist not, brethren, that he was the high priest: for it is written, Thou shalt not speak evil of the ruler of thy people.

1Co 6:10 — Nor thieves, nor covetous, nor drunkards, nor revilers, nor extortioners, shall inherit the kingdom of God.

Eph 4:25 — Wherefore putting away lying, speak every man truth with his neighbour: for we are members one of another.

Eph 4:29 — Let no corrupt communication proceed out of your mouth, but that which is good to the use of edifying, that it may minister grace unto the hearers.

Eph 4:31 — Let all bitterness, and wrath, and anger, and clamour, and evil speaking, be put away from you, with all malice:

Eph 5:4 — Neither filthiness, nor foolish talking, nor jesting, which are not convenient: but rather giving of thanks.

Tit 3:2 — To speak evil of no man, to be no brawlers, *but* gentle, shewing all meekness unto all men.

Jas 1:19 — Wherefore, my beloved brethren, let every man be swift to hear, slow to speak, slow to wrath:

Jas 1:26 — If any man among you seem to be religious, and bridleth not his tongue, but deceiveth his own heart, this man's religion *is* vain.

Jas 4:11 — Speak not evil one of another, brethren. He that speaketh evil of *his* brother, and judgeth his brother, speaketh evil of the law, and judgeth the law: but if thou judge the law, thou art not a doer of the law, but a judge.

1Pe 2:1 — Wherefore laying aside all malice, and all guile, and hypocrisies, and envies, and all evil speakings,

2Pe 2:10 — But chiefly them that walk after the flesh in the lust of uncleanness, and despise government. Presumptuous *are they,* selfwilled, they are not afraid to speak evil of dignities.

Jude 1:8 — Likewise also these *filthy* dreamers defile the flesh, despise dominion, and speak evil of dignities.

Jude 1:10 — But these speak evil of those things which they know not: but what they know naturally, as brute beasts, in those things they corrupt themselves.

➜See: Accusation, False

➜See: Blasphemy

➜See: Busybody

➜See: Falsehood

✦**See: Flattery**

✦**See: Slander**

✦**See: Talebearer**

✦**See: Uncharitableness**

• **Folly in.**

Job 16:3–4; Pr 18:6–7; Ecc 10:13–14; Mt 12:36–37

Job 38:2 — Who *is* this that darkeneth counsel by words without knowledge?

Pr 10:14 — Wise *men* lay up knowledge: but the mouth of the foolish *is* near destruction.

Pr 12:23 — A prudent man concealeth knowledge: but the heart of fools proclaimeth foolishness.

Pr 13:3 — He that keepeth his mouth keepeth his life: *but* he that openeth wide his lips shall have destruction.

Pr 14:3 — In the mouth of the foolish is a rod of pride: but the lips of the wise shall preserve them.

Pr 15:2 — The tongue of the wise useth knowledge aright: but the mouth of fools poureth out foolishness.

Pr 15:7 — The lips of the wise disperse knowledge: but the heart of the foolish *doeth* not so.

Pr 15:14 — The heart of him that hath understanding seeketh knowledge: but the mouth of fools feedeth on foolishness.

Pr 18:13 — He that answereth a matter before he heareth *it,* it *is* folly and shame unto him.

Pr 26:4 — Answer not a fool according to his folly, lest thou also be like unto him.

Pr 26:7 — The legs of the lame are not equal: so *is* a parable in the mouth of fools.

Pr 26:9 — *As* a thorn goeth up into the hand of a drunkard, so *is* a parable in the mouth of fools.

Pr 29:11 — A fool uttereth all his mind: but a wise *man* keepeth it in till afterwards.

Pr 29:20 — Seest thou a man *that is* hasty in his words? *there is* more hope of a fool than of him.

Pr 30:10 — Accuse not a servant unto his master, lest he curse thee, and thou be found guilty.

Ecc 5:3 — For a dream cometh through the multitude of business; and a fool's voice *is known* by multitude of words.

Ecc 5:7 — For in the multitude of dreams and many words *there are* also *divers* vanities: but fear thou God.

Eph 5:4 — Neither filthiness, nor foolish talking, nor jesting, which are not convenient: but rather giving of thanks.

✦**See: Fool**

• **Wisdom in.**

Ps 15:1–3; 145:5–7, 11–12; Pr 10:19–21, 31–32; 11:12–14; 12:16–20; 13:2–3; 15:1–2; 16:23–24; 17:27–28; Ecc 12:9–11; 1Pe 3:15–16

Job 16:5 — *But* I would strengthen you with my mouth, and the moving of my lips should asswage *your grief.*

Job 27:4 — My lips shall not speak wickedness, nor my tongue utter deceit.

Ps 37:30 — The mouth of the righteous speaketh wisdom, and his tongue talketh of judgment.

Ps 39:1 — I said, I will take heed to my ways, that I sin not with my tongue: I will keep my mouth with a bridle, while the wicked is before me.

Ps 50:23 — Whoso offereth praise glorifieth me: and to him that ordereth *his* conversation *aright* will I shew the salvation of God.

Ps 77:12 — I will meditate also of all thy work, and talk of thy doings.

Ps 119:13 — With my lips have I declared all the judgments of thy mouth.

Ps 119:27 — Make me to understand the way of thy precepts: so shall I talk of thy wondrous works.

Ps 119:46 — I will speak of thy testimonies also before kings, and will not be ashamed.

Ps 119:54 — Thy statutes have been my songs in the house of my pilgrimage.

Ps 119:172 — My tongue shall speak of thy word: for all thy commandments *are* righteousness.

Ps 141:3 — Set a watch, O LORD, before my mouth; keep the door of my lips.

Pr 10:11 — The mouth of a righteous *man is* a well of life: but violence covereth the mouth of the wicked.

Pr 10:13 — In the lips of him that hath understanding wisdom is found: but a rod *is* for the back of him that is void of understanding.

Pr 12:6 — The words of the wicked *are* to lie in wait for blood: but the mouth of the upright shall deliver them.

Pr 12:14 — A man shall be satisfied with good by the fruit of *his* mouth: and the recompense of a man's hands shall be rendered unto him.

Pr 12:23 — A prudent man concealeth knowledge: but the heart of fools proclaimeth foolishness.

Pr 14:3 — In the mouth of the foolish is a rod of pride: but the lips of the wise shall preserve them.

Pr 15:4 — A wholesome tongue *is* a tree of life: but perverseness therein *is* a breach in the spirit.

Pr 15:7 — The lips of the wise disperse knowledge: but the heart of the foolish *doeth* not so.

Pr 15:23 — A man hath joy by the answer of his mouth: and a word *spoken* in due season, how good *is it!*

Pr 15:26 — The thoughts of the wicked *are* an abomination to the LORD: but *the words* of the pure *are* pleasant words.

Pr 15:28 — The heart of the righteous studieth to answer: but the mouth of the wicked poureth out evil things.

Pr 16:21 — The wise in heart shall be called prudent: and the sweetness of the lips increaseth learning.

Pr 17:7 — Excellent speech becometh not a fool: much less do lying lips a prince.

Pr 18:4 — The words of a man's mouth *are as* deep waters, *and* the wellspring of wisdom *as* a flowing brook.

Pr 18:20 — A man's belly shall be satisfied with the fruit of his mouth; *and* with the increase of his lips shall he be filled.

Pr 19:1 — Better *is* the poor that walketh in his integrity, than *he that is* perverse in his lips, and is a fool.

Pr 20:15 — There is gold, and a multitude of rubies: but the lips of knowledge *are* a precious jewel.

Pr 21:23 — Whoso keepeth his mouth and his tongue keepeth his soul from troubles.

Pr 22:11 — He that loveth pureness of heart, *for* the grace of his lips the king *shall be* his friend.

Pr 24:6 — For by wise counsel thou shalt make thy war: and in multitude of counsellors *there is* safety.

Pr 25:11 — A word fitly spoken *is like* apples of gold in pictures of silver.

Pr 25:15 — By long forbearing is a prince persuaded, and a soft tongue breaketh the bone.

Pr 26:5 — Answer a fool according to his folly, lest he be wise in his own conceit.

Pr 29:11 — A fool uttereth all his mind: but a wise *man* keepeth it in till afterwards.

Pr 31:26 — She openeth her mouth with wisdom; and in her tongue *is* the law of kindness.

Ecc 3:7 — A time to rend, and a time to sew; a time to keep silence, and a time to speak;

Ecc 9:17 — The words of wise *men are* heard in quiet more than the cry of him that ruleth among fools.

Ecc 10:12 — The words of a wise man's mouth *are* gracious; but the lips of a fool will swallow up himself.

Am 5:13 — Therefore the prudent shall keep silence in that time; for it *is* an evil time.

Zep 3:13 — The remnant of Israel shall not do iniquity, nor speak lies; neither shall a deceitful tongue be found in their mouth: for they shall feed and lie down, and none shall make *them* afraid.

Zec 8:16 — These *are* the things that ye shall do; Speak ye every man the truth to his neighbour; execute the judgment of truth and peace in your gates:

Mt 12:35 — A good man out of the good treasure of the heart bringeth forth good things: and an evil man out of the evil treasure bringeth forth evil things.

Mt 12:37 — For by thy words thou shalt be justified, and by thy words thou shalt be condemned.

Lk 6:45 — A good man out of the good treasure of his heart bringeth forth that which is good; and an evil man out of the evil treasure of his heart bringeth forth that which is evil: for of the abundance of the heart his mouth speaketh.

Eph 4:22 — That ye put off concerning the former conversation the old man, which is corrupt according to the deceitful lusts;

Eph 4:25 — Wherefore putting away lying, speak every man truth with his neighbour: for we are members one of another.

Eph 4:29 — Let no corrupt communication proceed out of your mouth, but that which is good to the use of edifying, that it may minister grace unto the hearers.

Php 1:27 — Only let your conversation be as it becometh the gospel of Christ: that whether I come and see you, or else be absent, I may hear of your affairs, that ye stand fast in one spirit, with one mind striving together for the faith of the gospel;

Col 4:6 — Let your speech *be* alway with grace, seasoned with salt, that ye may know how ye ought to answer every man.

Jas 1:19 — Wherefore, my beloved brethren, let every man be swift to hear, slow to speak, slow to wrath:

Jas 1:26 — If any man among you seem to be religious, and bridleth not his tongue, but deceiveth his own heart, this man's religion *is* vain.

Jas 3:2 — For in many things we offend all. If any man offend not in word, the same *is* a perfect man, *and* able also to bridle the whole body.

Jas 3:13 — Who *is* a wise man and endued with knowledge among you? let him shew out of a good conversation his works with meekness of wisdom.

1Pe 2:12 — Having your conversation honest among the Gentiles: that, whereas they speak against you as evildoers, they may by *your* good works, which they shall behold, glorify God in the day of visitation.

Rev 14:5 — And in their mouth was found no guile: for they are without fault before the throne of God.

See: Wisdom

SPEAR

• An implement of war.

• Spears and javelins differed in weight and size, but had similar uses.

• Goliath's.

1Sa 17:7 — And the staff of his spear *was* like a weaver's beam; and his spear's head *weighed* six hundred shekels of iron: and one bearing a shield went before him.

• Saul's.

1Sa 18:10–11

• Stored in the tabernacle.

2Ch 23:9 — Moreover Jehoiada the priest delivered to the captains of hundreds spears, and bucklers, and shields, that *had been* king David's, which *were* in the house of God.

• Changed into pruning-hooks.

Isa 2:4 — And he shall judge among the nations, and shall rebuke many people: and they shall beat their swords into plowshares, and their spears into pruninghooks: nation shall not lift up sword against nation, neither shall they learn war any more.

Mic 4:3 — And he shall judge among many people, and rebuke strong nations afar off; and they shall beat their swords into plowshares, and their spears into pruninghooks: nation shall not lift up a sword against nation, neither shall they learn war any more.

• Pruning-hooks beat into.

Joel 3:10 — Beat your plowshares into swords, and your pruninghooks into spears: let the weak say, I *am* strong.

• Plunged into Jesus' side.

Zec 12:10 — And I will pour upon the house of David, and upon the inhabitants of Jerusalem, the spirit of grace and of supplications: and they shall look upon me whom they have pierced, and they shall mourn for him, as one mourneth for *his* only *son,* and shall be in bitterness for him, as one that is in bitterness for *his* firstborn.

Jn 19:34 — But one of the soldiers with a spear pierced his side, and forthwith came there out blood and water.

Jn 20:27 — Then saith he to Thomas, reach hither thy finger, and behold my hands; and reach hither thy hand, and thrust *it* into my side: and be not faithless, but believing.

Rev 1:7 — Behold, he cometh with clouds; and every eye shall see him, and they *also* which pierced him: and all kindreds of the earth shall wail because of him. Even so, Amen.

SPEECH

Pr 6:2 — Thou art snared with the words of thy mouth, thou art taken with the words of thy mouth.

Pr 10:19 — In the multitude of words there wanteth not sin: but he that refraineth his lips *is* wise.

Mt 5:37 — But let your communication be, Yea, yea; Nay, nay: for whatsoever is more than these cometh of evil.

2Co 1:17 — When I therefore was thus minded, did I use lightness? or the things that I purpose, do I purpose according to the flesh, that with me there should be yea yea, and nay nay?

Eph 4:29 — Let no corrupt communication proceed out of your mouth, but that which is good to the use of edifying, that it may minister grace unto the hearers.

Php 1:7 — Even as it is meet for me to think this of you all, because I have you in my heart; inasmuch as both in my bonds, and in the defence and confirmation of the gospel, ye all are partakers of my grace.

Tit 2:8 — Sound speech, that cannot be condemned; that he that is of the contrary part may be ashamed, having no evil thing to say of you.

Jas 5:12 — But above all things, my brethren, swear not, neither by heaven, neither by the earth, neither by any other oath: but let your yea be yea; and *your* nay, nay; lest ye fall into condemnation.

SPELT →See: Rye

SPICES

• In the formula for the sacred oil.

Ex 25:6 — Oil for the light, spices for anointing oil, and for sweet incense,

Ex 35:8 — And oil for the light, and spices for anointing oil, and for the sweet incense,

• Stores of.

2Ki 20:13 — And Hezekiah hearkened unto them, and shewed them all the house of his precious things, the silver, and the gold, and the spices, and the precious ointment, and *all* the house of his armour, and all that was found in his treasures: there was nothing in his house, nor in all his dominion, that Hezekiah shewed them not.

• Used in the temple.

1Ch 9:29 — *Some* of them also *were* appointed to oversee the vessels, and all the instruments of the sanctuary, and the fine flour, and the wine, and the oil, and the frankincense, and the spices.

• Exported from Gilead.

Ge 37:25 — And they sat down to eat bread: and they lifted up their eyes and looked, and, behold, a company of Ishmeelites came from Gilead with their camels bearing spicery and balm and myrrh, going to carry *it* down to Egypt.

• Sent as a present by Jacob to Joseph.

Ge 43:11 — And their father Israel said unto them, If *it must be* so now, do this; take of the best fruits in the land in your vessels, and carry down the man a present, a little balm, and a little honey, spices, and myrrh, nuts, and almonds:

• Presented by the queen of Sheba to Solomon.

1Ki 10:2 — And she came to Jerusalem with a very great train, with camels that bare spices, and very much gold, and precious stones: and when she was come to Solomon, she communed with him of all that was in her heart.

1Ki 10:10 — And she gave the king an hundred and twenty talents of gold, and of spices very great store, and precious stones: there came no more such abundance of spices as these which the queen of Sheba gave to king Solomon.

• Sold in the markets of Tyre.

Eze 27:22 — The merchants of Sheba and Raamah, they *were* thy merchants: they occupied in thy fairs with chief of all spices, and with all precious stones, and gold.

• Used in the embalming of Asa.

2Ch 16:14 — And they buried him in his own sepulchres, which he had made for himself in the city of David, and laid him in the bed which was filled with sweet odours and divers kinds *of spices* prepared by the apothecaries' art: and they made a very great burning for him.

• Prepared for embalming the body of Jesus.

Lk 23:56–24:1; Jn 19:39–40

Mk 16:1 — And when the sabbath was past, Mary Magdalene, and Mary the *mother* of James, and Salome, had bought sweet spices, that they might come and anoint him.

SPIDER

• Mentioned in one of Agur's riddles.

Pr 30:28 — The spider taketh hold with her hands, and is in kings' palaces.

• Web of, figurative of the hope of the hypocrite.

Job 8:14 — Whose hope shall be cut off, and whose trust *shall be* a spider's web.

Isa 59:5 — They hatch cockatrice' eggs, and weave the spider's web: he that eateth of their eggs dieth, and that which is crushed breaketh out into a viper.

SPIES

Ge 42:9 — And Joseph remembered the dreams which he dreamed of them, and said unto them, Ye *are* spies; to see the nakedness of the land ye are come.

• **Sent to investigate Canaan.**
Nu 13:1–33

• **Sent to investigate Jaazer.**
Nu 21:32 — And Moses sent to spy out Jaazer, and they took the villages thereof, and drove out the Amorites that *were* there.

• **Sent to investigate Jericho.**
Jos 2:1 — And Joshua the son of Nun sent out of Shittim two men to spy secretly, saying, Go view the land, even Jericho. And they went, and came into an harlot's house, named Rahab, and lodged there.

• **Used by David.**
1Sa 26:4 — David therefore sent out spies, and understood that Saul was come in very deed.

• **Used at the court of Absalom.**
2Sa 17:1–17
2Sa 15:10 — But Absalom sent spies throughout all the tribes of Israel, saying, As soon as ye hear the sound of the trumpet, then ye shall say, Absalom reigneth in Hebron.

• **Pharisees acted as.**
Lk 20:20 — And they watched *him,* and sent forth spies, which should feign themselves just men, that they might take hold of his words, that so they might deliver him unto the power and authority of the governor.

• **In the church of Galatia.**
Gal 2:4 — And that because of false brethren unawares brought in, who came in privily to spy out our liberty which we have in Christ Jesus, that they might bring us into bondage:

SPIKENARD

• **An aromatic plant.**
SS 4:13–14

• **Perfume prepared from.**
SS 1:12 — While the king *sitteth* at his table, my spikenard sendeth forth the smell thereof.

• **A fragrant oil from, used in anointing.**
Mk 14:3 — And being in Bethany in the house of Simon the leper, as he sat at meat, there came a woman having an alabaster box of ointment of spikenard very precious; and she brake the box, and poured *it* on his head.
Jn 12:3 — Then took Mary a pound of ointment of spikenard, very costly, and anointed the feet of Jesus, and wiped his feet with her hair: and the house was filled with the odour of the ointment.

SPINDLE

• **Used in spinning.**
Pr 31:19 — She layeth her hands to the spindle, and her hands hold the distaff.

SPINNING

• **By hand.**
Ex 35:25 — And all the women that were wise hearted did spin with their hands, and brought that which they had spun, *both* of blue, and of purple, *and* of scarlet, and of fine linen.
Pr 31:19 — She layeth her hands to the spindle, and her hands hold the distaff.

SPIRIT

• **Called inner man.**
Ro 7:22 — For I delight in the law of God after the inward man:
Eph 3:16 — That he would grant you, according to the riches of his glory, to be strengthened with might by his Spirit in the inner man;

See: Angel
See: Demons
See: God, a Spirit
See: Holy Spirit
See: Man; spirit
See: Satan

SPIRITUAL BLESSINGS

See: Blessing; spiritual, from God
See: Holy Spirit
See: Sanctification

SPIRITUAL BLINDNESS **See: Blindness; spiritual**

SPIRITUAL DILIGENCE **See: Zeal, Religious**

SPIRITUAL PEACE

See: Joy
See: Peace

SPIRITUALISM

See: Necromancy
See: Sorcery

SPIRITUALITY

• **Described as the great and enduring good.**
Lk 10:42 — But one thing is needful: and Mary hath chosen that good part, which shall not be taken away from her.

• **Described as love and devotion to God.**
Dt 6:5 — And thou shalt love the LORD thy God with all thine heart, and with all thy soul, and with all thy might.
Jos 22:5 — But take diligent heed to do the commandment and the law, which Moses the servant of the LORD charged you, to love the LORD your God, and to walk in all his ways, and to keep his commandments, and to cleave unto him, and to serve him with all your heart and with all your soul.
1Ki 8:23 — And he said, LORD God of Israel, *there is* no God like thee, in heaven above, or on earth beneath, who keepest covenant and mercy with thy servants that walk before thee with all their heart:
Ps 1:2 — But his delight *is* in the law of the LORD; and in his law doth he meditate day and night.

Ps 51:6 — Behold, thou desirest truth in the inward parts: and in the hidden *part* thou shalt make me to know wisdom.

• Brings peace.

Isa 26:3 — Thou wilt keep *him* in perfect peace, *whose* mind *is* stayed *on thee:* because he trusteth in thee.

Jer 33:6 — Behold, I will bring it health and cure, and I will cure them, and will reveal unto them the abundance of peace and truth.

Ro 8:6 — For to be carnally minded *is* death; but to be spiritually minded *is* life and peace.

Ro 14:17 — For the kingdom of God is not meat and drink; but righteousness, and peace, and joy in the Holy Ghost.

• Indifference to worldly good.

1Co 7:29–31; Col 3:1–3

• Brings thirst for heavenly blessings.

Mt 5:6 — Blessed *are* they which do hunger and thirst after righteousness: for they shall be filled.

Jn 6:27 — Labour not for the meat which perisheth, but for that meat which endureth unto everlasting life, which the Son of man shall give unto you: for him hath God the Father sealed.

• Is produced by the indwelling of the Holy Spirit.

Jn 14:16–17

Ro 8:4 — That the righteousness of the law might be fulfilled in us, who walk not after the flesh, but after the Spirit.

SPITTING

• In the face, as an indignity.

Nu 12:14 — And the LORD said unto Moses, If her father had but spit in her face, should she not be ashamed seven days? let her be shut out from the camp seven days, and after that let her be received in *again.*

Dt 25:9 — Then shall his brother's wife come unto him in the presence of the elders, and loose his shoe from off his foot, and spit in his face, and shall answer and say, So shall it be done unto that man that will not build up his brother's house.

Job 30:10 — They abhor me, they flee far from me, and spare not to spit in my face.

Mt 26:67 — Then did they spit in his face, and buffeted him; and others smote *him* with the palms of their hands,

Mt 27:30 — And they spit upon him, and took the reed, and smote him on the head.

• Jesus used spittle in healing.

Mk 7:33 — And he took him aside from the multitude, and put his fingers into his ears, and he spit, and touched his tongue;

Mk 8:23 — And he took the blind man by the hand, and led him out of the town; and when he had spit on his eyes, and put his hands upon him, he asked him if he saw ought.

SPOILS

• Of war.

Ge 14:11–12; Nu 31:9–10

Dt 2:35 — Only the cattle we took for a prey unto ourselves, and the spoil of the cities which we took.

• Divided between the combatants and non-combatants of the Israelites, including priests and Levites.

Nu 31:25–54

1Sa 30:24 — For who will hearken unto you in this matter? but as his part *is* that goeth down to the battle, so *shall* his part *be* that tarrieth by the stuff: they shall part alike.

• Dedicated to the Lord.

1Sa 15:15 — And Saul said, They have brought them from the Amalekites: for the people spared the best of the sheep and of the oxen, to sacrifice unto the LORD thy God; and the rest we have utterly destroyed.

1Ch 26:27 — Out of the spoils won in battles did they dedicate to maintain the house of the LORD.

2Ch 15:11 — And they offered unto the LORD the same time, of the spoil *which* they had brought, seven hundred oxen and seven thousand sheep.

SPONGE

Mt 27:48 — And straightway one of them ran, and took a spunge, and filled *it* with vinegar, and put *it* on a reed, and gave him to drink.

Mk 15:36 — And one ran and filled a spunge full of vinegar, and put *it* on a reed, and gave him to drink, saying, Let alone; let us see whether Elias will come to take him down.

Jn 19:29 — Now there was set a vessel full of vinegar: and they filled a spunge with vinegar, and put *it* upon hyssop, and put *it* to his mouth.

SPOONS

• Of the tabernacle.

Nu 7:1–89

Ex 25:29 — And thou shalt make the dishes thereof, and spoons thereof, and covers thereof, and bowls thereof, to cover withal: *of* pure gold shalt thou make them.

Nu 4:7 — And upon the table of shewbread they shall spread a cloth of blue, and put thereon the dishes, and the spoons, and the bowls, and covers to cover withal: and the continual bread shall be thereon:

• Of the temple.

1Ki 7:50 — And the bowls, and the snuffers, and the basons, and the spoons, and the censers *of* pure gold; and the hinges *of* gold, *both* for the doors of the inner house, the most holy *place, and* for the doors of the house, *to wit,* of the temple.

2Ch 4:22 — And the snuffers, and the basons, and the spoons, and the censers, *of* pure gold: and the entry of the house, the inner doors thereof for the most holy *place,* and the doors of the house of the temple, *were of* gold.

SPRING

• Season of, promised annual return of.

Ge 8:22 — While the earth remaineth, seedtime and harvest, and cold and heat, and summer and winter, and day and night shall not cease.

• **Described.**

SS 2:11–13

Pr 27:25 — The hay appeareth, and the tender grass sheweth itself, and herbs of the mountains are gathered.

• **Figurative.**

• **Corrupt.**

Pr 25:26 — A righteous man falling down before the wicked *is as* a troubled fountain, and a corrupt spring.

Jas 3:11 — Doth a fountain send forth at the same place sweet *water* and bitter?

See: Wells

SPRINKLING

• **Of blood.**

Le 14:7 — And he shall sprinkle upon him that is to be cleansed from the leprosy seven times, and shall pronounce him clean, and shall let the living bird loose into the open field.

Le 14:51 — And he shall take the cedar wood, and the hyssop, and the scarlet, and the living bird, and dip them in the blood of the slain bird, and in the running water, and sprinkle the house seven times:

Le 16:14 — And he shall take of the blood of the bullock, and sprinkle *it* with his finger upon the mercy seat eastward; and before the mercy seat shall he sprinkle of the blood with his finger seven times.

Heb 9:13 — For if the blood of bulls and of goats, and the ashes of an heifer sprinkling the unclean, sanctifieth to the purifying of the flesh:

Heb 9:19 — For when Moses had spoken every precept to all the people according to the law, he took the blood of calves and of goats, with water, and scarlet wool, and hyssop, and sprinkled both the book, and all the people,

Heb 9:21 — Moreover he sprinkled with blood both the tabernacle, and all the vessels of the ministry.

Heb 11:28 — Through faith he kept the passover, and the sprinkling of blood, lest he that destroyed the firstborn should touch them.

Heb 12:24 — And to Jesus the mediator of the new covenant, and to the blood of sprinkling, that speaketh better things than *that of* Abel.

1Pe 1:2 — Elect according to the foreknowledge of God the Father, through sanctification of the Spirit, unto obedience and sprinkling of the blood of Jesus Christ: Grace unto you, and peace, be multiplied.

See: Blood

• **Of water.**

Nu 8:7 — And thus shalt thou do unto them, to cleanse them: Sprinkle water of purifying upon them, and let them shave all their flesh, and let them wash their clothes, and *so* make themselves clean.

Eze 36:25 — Then will I sprinkle clean water upon you, and ye shall be clean: from all your filthiness, and from all your idols, will I cleanse you.

Heb 9:19 — For when Moses had spoken every precept to all the people according to the law, he took the blood of calves and of goats, with water, and scarlet wool, and hyssop, and sprinkled both the book, and all the people,

Heb 10:22 — Let us draw near with a true heart in full assurance of faith, having our hearts sprinkled from an evil conscience, and our bodies washed with pure water.

STABILITY

• **Of character.**

Jas 1:23–25

Ps 57:7 — My heart is fixed, O God, my heart is fixed: I will sing and give praise.

Ps 108:1 — O God, my heart is fixed; I will sing and give praise, even with my glory.

Ps 112:7 — He shall not be afraid of evil tidings: his heart is fixed, trusting in the LORD.

Mt 10:22 — And ye shall be hated of all *men* for my name's sake: but he that endureth to the end shall be saved.

Mt 24:13 — But he that shall endure unto the end, the same shall be saved.

Mk 4:20 — And these are they which are sown on good ground; such as hear the word, and receive *it*, and bring forth fruit, some thirtyfold, some sixty, and some an hundred.

1Co 7:20 — Let every man abide in the same calling wherein he was called.

1Co 15:58 — Therefore, my beloved brethren, be ye stedfast, unmovable, always abounding in the work of the Lord, forasmuch as ye know that your labour is not in vain in the Lord.

2Th 2:15 — Therefore, brethren, stand fast, and hold the traditions which ye have been taught, whether by word, or our epistle.

2Th 3:3 — But the Lord is faithful, who shall stablish you, and keep *you* from evil.

Heb 10:23 — Let us hold fast the profession of *our* faith without wavering; (for he is faithful that promised;)

Heb 13:9 — Be not carried about with divers and strange doctrines. For *it is* a good thing that the heart be established with grace; not with meats, which have not profited them that have been occupied therein.

Rev 22:11 — He that is unjust, let him be unjust still: and he which is filthy, let him be filthy still: and he that is righteous, let him be righteous still: and he that is holy, let him be holy still.

See: Character of Saints

See: Decision

See: Perseverance

STACHYS • A Christian in Rome.

Ro 16:9 — Salute Urbane, our helper in Christ, and Stachys my beloved.

STACTE • An unknown spice used in compounding the sacred perfume.

Ex 30:34 — And the LORD said unto Moses, Take unto thee sweet spices, stacte, and onycha, and galbanum; *these* sweet spices with pure frankincense: of each shall there be a like *weight:*

STAIRS

• Of David.

Ne 3:15 — But the gate of the fountain repaired Shallun the son of Col-hozeh, the ruler of part of Mizpah; he built it, and covered it, and set up the doors thereof, the locks thereof, and the bars thereof, and the wall of the pool of Siloah by the king's garden, and unto the stairs that go down from the city of David.

Ne 12:37 — And at the fountain gate, which was over against them, they went up by the stairs of the city of David, at the going up of the wall, above the house of David, even unto the water gate eastward.

STALL

• For cattle.

Pr 15:17 — Better *is* a dinner of herbs where love is, than a stalled ox and hatred therewith.

STAMMERING

Isa 32:4 — The heart also of the rash shall understand knowledge, and the tongue of the stammerers shall be ready to speak plainly.

Isa 33:19 — Thou shalt not see a fierce people, a people of a deeper speech than thou canst perceive; of a stammering tongue, *that thou canst* not understand.

• Of Moses.

Ex 4:10 — And Moses said unto the LORD, O my Lord, I *am* not eloquent, neither heretofore, nor since thou hast spoken unto thy servant: but I *am* slow of speech, and of a slow tongue.

STANDARD

• An ensign used by each of the tribes of Israel in camp and march.

Nu 1:52 — And the children of Israel shall pitch their tents, every man by his own camp, and every man by his own standard, throughout their hosts.

Nu 2:2 — Every man of the children of Israel shall pitch by his own standard, with the ensign of their father's house: far off about the tabernacle of the congregation shall they pitch.

• Banners used as.

Ps 20:5 — We will rejoice in thy salvation, and in the name of our God we will set up *our* banners: the LORD fulfil all thy petitions.

SS 6:4 — Thou *art* beautiful, O my love, as Tirzah, comely as Jerusalem, terrible as *an army* with banners.

SS 6:10 — Who *is* she *that* looketh forth as the morning, fair as the moon, clear as the sun, *and* terrible as *an army* with banners?

• Used in war.

Jer 4:21 — How long shall I see the standard, *and* hear the sound of the trumpet?

• Used to direct the route to defensed cities.

Jer 4:6 — Set up the standard toward Zion: retire, stay not: for I will bring evil from the north, and a great destruction.

• Used to call attention to news.

Jer 50:2 — Declare ye among the nations, and publish, and set up a standard; publish, *and* conceal not: say, Babylon is taken, Bel is confounded, Merodach is broken in pieces; her idols are confounded, her images are broken in pieces.

Jer 51:12 — Set up the standard upon the walls of Babylon, make the watch strong, set up the watchmen, prepare the ambushes: for the LORD hath both devised and done that which he spake against the inhabitants of Babylon.

See: Armies

See: Banner

See: Ensign

• Figurative.

Isa 49:22 — Thus saith the Lord GOD, Behold, I will lift up mine hand to the Gentiles, and set up my standard to the people: and they shall bring thy sons in *their* arms, and thy daughters shall be carried upon *their* shoulders.

Isa 62:10 — Go through, go through the gates; prepare ye the way of the people; cast up, cast up the highways; gather out the stones; lift up a standard for the people.

Jer 4:6 — Set up the standard toward Zion: retire, stay not: for I will bring evil from the north, and a great destruction.

STARS

• Created by God.

Ge 1:16 — And God made two great lights; the greater light to rule the day, and the lesser light to rule the night: *he made* the stars also.

Job 26:13 — By his spirit he hath garnished the heavens; his hand hath formed the crooked serpent.

Ps 8:3 — When I consider thy heavens, the work of thy fingers, the moon and the stars, which thou hast ordained;

Ps 33:6 — By the word of the LORD were the heavens made; and all the host of them by the breath of his mouth.

Ps 136:7 — To him that made great lights: for his mercy *endureth* for ever:

Ps 136:9 — The moon and stars to rule by night: for his mercy *endureth* for ever.

Am 5:8 — *Seek him* that maketh the seven stars and Orion, and turneth the shadow of death into the morning, and maketh the day dark with night: that calleth for the waters of the sea, and poureth them out upon the face of the earth: The LORD *is* his name:

• Differ in splendor.

1Co 15:41 — *There is* one glory of the sun, and another glory of the moon, and another glory of the stars: for *one* star differeth from *another* star in glory.

• Worship of, forbidden.

Dt 4:19 — And lest thou lift up thine eyes unto heaven, and when thou seest the sun, and the moon, and the stars, *even* all the host of heaven, shouldest be driven to worship them, and serve them, which the

LORD thy God hath divided unto all nations under the whole heaven.

• Worshiped.

Ac 7:42–43

2Ki 17:16 — And they left all the commandments of the LORD their God, and made them molten images, *even* two calves, and made a grove, and worshipped all the host of heaven, and served Baal.

2Ki 21:3 — For he built up again the high places which Hezekiah his father had destroyed; and he reared up altars for Baal, and made a grove, as did Ahab king of Israel; and worshipped all the host of heaven, and served them.

2Ki 23:5 — And he put down the idolatrous priests, whom the kings of Judah had ordained to burn incense in the high places in the cities of Judah, and in the places round about Jerusalem; them also that burned incense unto Baal, to the sun, and to the moon, and to the planets, and to all the host of heaven.

Jer 19:13 — And the houses of Jerusalem, and the houses of the kings of Judah, shall be defiled as the place of Tophet, because of all the houses upon whose roofs they have burned incense unto all the host of heaven, and have poured out drink offerings unto other gods.

Am 5:26 — But ye have borne the tabernacle of your Moloch and Chiun your images, the star of your god, which ye made to yourselves.

Zep 1:5 — And them that worship the host of heaven upon the housetops; and them that worship *and* that swear by the LORD, and that swear by Malcham;

• Constellations of.

Isa 13:10 — For the stars of heaven and the constellations thereof shall not give their light: the sun shall be darkened in his going forth, and the moon shall not cause her light to shine.

• Orion.

Job 9:9 — Which maketh Arcturus, Orion, and Pleiades, and the chambers of the south.

Am 5:8 — *Seek him* that maketh the seven stars and Orion, and turneth the shadow of death into the morning, and maketh the day dark with night: that calleth for the waters of the sea, and poureth them out upon the face of the earth: The LORD *is* his name:

• Serpent.

Job 26:13 — By his spirit he hath garnished the heavens; his hand hath formed the crooked serpent.

• Planets.

2Ki 23:5 — And he put down the idolatrous priests, whom the kings of Judah had ordained to burn incense in the high places in the cities of Judah, and in the places round about Jerusalem; them also that burned incense unto Baal, to the sun, and to the moon, and to the planets, and to all the host of heaven.

• The morning star.

Job 38:7 — When the morning stars sang together, and all the sons of God shouted for joy?

Rev 2:28 — And I will give him the morning star.

Rev 22:16 — I Jesus have sent mine angel to testify unto you these things in the churches. I am the root and the offspring of David, *and* the bright and morning star.

• Darkening of.

Rev 8:11–12

Job 9:7 — Which commandeth the sun, and it riseth not; and sealeth up the stars.

Ecc 12:2 — While the sun, or the light, or the moon, or the stars, be not darkened, nor the clouds return after the rain:

Isa 13:10 — For the stars of heaven and the constellations thereof shall not give their light: the sun shall be darkened in his going forth, and the moon shall not cause her light to shine.

Isa 34:4 — And all the host of heaven shall be dissolved, and the heavens shall be rolled together as a scroll: and all their host shall fall down, as the leaf falleth off from the vine, and as a falling *fig* from the fig tree.

Joel 2:10 — The earth shall quake before them; the heavens shall tremble: the sun and the moon shall be dark, and the stars shall withdraw their shining:

Joel 3:15 — The sun and the moon shall be darkened, and the stars shall withdraw their shining.

• Comets.

Jude 1:13 — Raging waves of the sea, foaming out their own shame; wandering stars, to whom is reserved the blackness of darkness for ever.

• Falling of.

Da 8:10 — And it waxed great, *even* to the host of heaven; and it cast down *some* of the host and of the stars to the ground, and stamped upon them.

Mt 24:29 — Immediately after the tribulation of those days shall the sun be darkened, and the moon shall not give her light, and the stars shall fall from heaven, and the powers of the heavens shall be shaken:

Mk 13:25 — And the stars of heaven shall fall, and the powers that are in heaven shall be shaken.

Rev 6:13 — And the stars of heaven fell unto the earth, even as a fig tree casteth her untimely figs, when she is shaken of a mighty wind.

Rev 8:10 — And the third angel sounded, and there fell a great star from heaven, burning as it were a lamp, and it fell upon the third part of the rivers, and upon the fountains of waters;

Rev 9:1 — And the fifth angel sounded, and I saw a star fall from heaven unto the earth: and to him was given the key of the bottomless pit.

Rev 12:4 — And his tail drew the third part of the stars of heaven, and did cast them to the earth: and the dragon stood before the woman which was ready to be delivered, for to devour her child as soon as it was born.

• Guides the wise men.

Mt 2:9–10

Mt 2:2 — Saying, Where is he that is born King of the Jews? for we have seen his star in the east, and are come to worship him.

Mt 2:7 — Then Herod, when he had privily called the wise men, enquired of them diligently what time the star appeared.

- **Figurative.**
  - **Of the deliverer.**

Nu 24:17 — I shall see him, but not now: I shall behold him, but not nigh: there shall come a Star out of Jacob, and a Sceptre shall rise out of Israel, and shall smite the corners of Moab, and destroy all the children of Sheth.

  - **Seven stars of the seven churches.**

Rev 1:16 — And he had in his right hand seven stars: and out of his mouth went a sharp twoedged sword: and his countenance *was* as the sun shineth in his strength.

Rev 1:20 — The mystery of the seven stars which thou sawest in my right hand, and the seven golden candlesticks. The seven stars are the angels of the seven churches: and the seven candlesticks which thou sawest are the seven churches.

  - **Crown of twelve stars.**

Rev 12:1 — And there appeared a great wonder in heaven; a woman clothed with the sun, and the moon under her feet, and upon her head a crown of twelve stars:

  - **Of Jesus.**

Rev 22:16 — I Jesus have sent mine angel to testify unto you these things in the churches. I am the root and the offspring of David, *and* the bright and morning star.

STATE

✦See: **Church and State**

✦See: **Government**

STATECRAFT

- **Wisdom in.**

Pr 28:2 — For the transgression of a land many *are* the princes thereof: but by a man of understanding *and* knowledge the state *thereof* shall be prolonged.

- **School in.**

Da 1:3–5

- **Skilled in.**
  - **Instances of.**
    - **Joseph.**

Ge 47:15–26

    - **Samuel.**

1Sa 11:12–15

    - **Nathan.**

1Ki 1:11–14

    - **Jeroboam.**

1Ki 12:26–33

    - **Daniel.**

✦See: **Daniel**

✦See: **Government**

✦See: **King**

✦See: **Rulers**

STAVES

- **Used as weapons.**

Mt 26:47 — And while he yet spake, lo, Judas, one of the twelve, came, and with him a great multitude with swords and staves, from the chief priests and elders of the people.

Mk 14:43 — And immediately, while he yet spake, cometh Judas, one of the twelve, and with him a great multitude with swords and staves, from the chief priest and the scribes and the elders.

- **Symbolic.**

Zec 11:7–14

STEADFASTNESS

✦See: **Decision**

✦See: **Perseverance**

✦See: **Stability**

STEALING ✦See: **Theft and Thieves**

STEEL

- **In some versions, brass.**
- **Bows of.**

2Sa 22:35 — He teacheth my hands to war; so that a bow of steel is broken by mine arms.

Job 20:24 — He shall flee from the iron weapon, *and* the bow of steel shall strike him through.

Ps 18:34 — He teacheth my hands to war, so that a bow of steel is broken by mine arms.

- **Strength of.**

Jer 15:12 — Shall iron break the northern iron and the steel?

STEPHANAS • A Christian in Corinth, whose household Paul baptized.

1Co 1:16 — And I baptized also the household of Stephanas: besides, I know not whether I baptized any other.

1Co 16:15 — I beseech you, brethren, (ye know the house of Stephanas, that it is the firstfruits of Achaia, and *that* they have addicted themselves to the ministry of the saints,)

1Co 16:17 — I am glad of the coming of Stephanas and Fortunatus and Achaicus: for that which was lacking on your part they have supplied.

STEPHEN

- **A Christian martyr.**
- **Appointed one of the committee of seven to oversee the daily ministration.**

Ac 6:5–6

Ac 6:3 — Wherefore, brethren, look ye out among you seven men of honest report, full of the Holy Ghost and wisdom, whom we may appoint over this business.

- **Faith and power of.**

Ac 6:8–10

Ac 6:5 — And the saying pleased the whole multitude: and they chose Stephen, a man full of faith and of the Holy Ghost, and Philip, and Prochorus, and Nicanor, and Timon, and Parmenas, and Nicolas a proselyte of Antioch:

- **False charges against.**
  Ac 6:11–15
- **Defense of.**
  Ac 7:1–60
- **Stoned.**
  Ac 7:54–8:1
  Ac 22:20 — And when the blood of thy martyr Stephen was shed, I also was standing by, and consenting unto his death, and kept the raiment of them that slew him.
- **Burial of.**
  Ac 8:2 — And devout men carried Stephen *to his burial,* and made great lamentation over him.
- **Gentle and forgiving spirit of.**
  Ac 7:59–60

STERILITY

- **Of women.**
  ✦**See: Barrenness, sterility of women**

STEWARD

Ge 15:2 — And Abram said, Lord GOD, what wilt thou give me, seeing I go childless, and the steward of my house is this Eliezer of Damascus?

Ge 43:19 — And they came near to the steward of Joseph's house, and they communed with him at the door of the house,

1Ch 28:1 — And David assembled all the princes of Israel, the princes of the tribes, and the captains of the companies that ministered to the king by course, and the captains over the thousands, and captains over the hundreds, and the stewards over all the substance and possession of the king, and of his sons, with the officers, and with the mighty men, and with all the valiant men, unto Jerusalem.

Lk 8:3 — And Joanna the wife of Chuza Herod's steward, and Susanna, and many others, which ministered unto him of their substance.

- **Figurative.**
  - **The faithful steward described.**
    Lk 12:35–38
    Lk 12:42 — And the Lord said, Who then is that faithful and wise steward, whom *his* lord shall make ruler over his household, to give *them their* portion of meat in due season?
  - **The unfaithful, described.**
    Lk 16:1–8
  - **The parable of the pounds.**
    Lk 19:12–27
  - **The parable of the talents.**
    Mt 25:14–30
  - **Must be faithful.**
    1Co 4:1–2
    Tit 1:7 — For a bishop must be blameless, as the steward of God; not selfwilled, not soon angry, not given to wine, no striker, not given to filthy lucre;

1Pe 4:10 — As every man hath received the gift, *even so* minister the same one to another, as good stewards of the manifold grace of God.

STICKS

- **Used as cymbals.**
  Eze 37:16 — Moreover, thou son of man, take thee one stick, and write upon it, For Judah, and for the children of Israel his companions: then take another stick, and write upon it, For Joseph, the stick of Ephraim, and *for* all the house of Israel his companions:

STIFF-NECKED

✦**See: Impenitence**
✦**See: Obduracy**

STILL

- **Man.**
  Job 37:14 — Hearken unto this, O Job: stand still, and consider the wondrous works of God.
  Ps 4:4 — Stand in awe, and sin not: commune with your own heart upon your bed, and be still. Selah.
  Ps 46:10 — Be still, and know that I *am* God: I will be exalted among the heathen, I will be exalted in the earth.

STOCKS

- **Feet fastened in, as a punishment.**
  Job 13:27 — Thou puttest my feet also in the stocks, and lookest narrowly unto all my paths; thou settest a print upon the heels of my feet.
  Job 33:11 — He putteth my feet in the stocks, he marketh all my paths.
  Pr 7:22 — He goeth after her straightway, as an ox goeth to the slaughter, or as a fool to the correction of the stocks;
- **In prisons.**
  Jer 20:2 — Then Pashur smote Jeremiah the prophet, and put him in the stocks that *were* in the high gate of Benjamin, which *was* by the house of the LORD.
  Ac 16:24 — Who, having received such a charge, thrust them into the inner prison, and made their feet fast in the stocks.

STOICISM

- **A Grecian philosophy.**
- **Inculcating doctrines of severe morality, self-denials, and inconvenient services.**
- **Scripture analogies to.**
  - **John the Baptist wears camel's hair and subsists on locusts and wild honey.**
    Mt 3:4 — And the same John had his raiment of camel's hair, and a leathern girdle about his loins; and his meat was locusts and wild honey.
  - **John the Baptist comes "neither eating nor drinking".**
    Mt 11:18 — For John came neither eating nor drinking, and they say, He hath a devil.

Lk 7:33 — For John the Baptist came neither eating bread nor drinking wine; and ye say, He hath a devil.

• **Jesus requires self-denials and crosses.**

Mt 10:38–39; Mk 8:34–35; Lk 9:23–26

Mt 16:24 — Then said Jesus unto his disciples, If any *man* will come after me, let him deny himself, and take up his cross, and follow me.

Lk 14:27 — And whosoever doth not bear his cross, and come after me, cannot be my disciple.

• **Jesus requires the subordination of natural affection.**

Mt 10:37 — He that loveth father or mother more than me is not worthy of me: and he that loveth son or daughter more than me is not worthy of me.

Lk 14:26 — If any *man* come to me, and hate not his father, and mother, and wife, and children, and brethren, and sisters, yea, and his own life also, he cannot be my disciple.

• **Paul teaches that the "law of the mind" is at war with the "law of the members".**

Ro 7:14–24

• **Paul teaches that the body must be kept under.**

1Co 9:27 — But I keep under my body, and bring *it* into subjection: lest that by any means, when I have preached to others, I myself should be a castaway.

• **Paul advises celibacy.**

1Co 7:1–9; 7:25–26; 7:32–33; 7:39–40

• **School of, at Athens.**

Ac 17:18 — Then certain philosophers of the Epicureans, and of the Stoicks, encountered him. And some said, What will this babbler say? other some, He seemeth to be a setter forth of strange gods: because he preached unto them Jesus, and the resurrection.

See: Asceticism

STOICS

See: Asceticism

See: Stoicism

STOMACHER

• **An article of dress.**

Isa 3:24 — And it shall come to pass, *that* instead of sweet smell there shall be stink; and instead of a girdle a rent; and instead of well set hair baldness; and instead of a stomacher a girding of sackcloth; *and* burning instead of beauty.

STONES

• **Commandments engraved upon.**

Ex 34:1–4; Dt 9:9–11; 10:1–3

Ex 24:12 — And the LORD said unto Moses, Come up to me into the mount, and be there: and I will give thee tables of stone, and a law, and commandments which I have written; that thou mayest teach them.

Ex 31:18 — And he gave unto Moses, when he had made an end of communing with him upon mount Sinai, two tables of testimony, tables of stone, written with the finger of God.

Dt 4:13 — And he declared unto you his covenant, which he commanded you to perform, *even* ten commandments; and he wrote them upon two tables of stone.

Dt 5:22 — These words the LORD spake unto all your assembly in the mount out of the midst of the fire, of the cloud, and of the thick darkness, with a great voice: and he added no more. And he wrote them in two tables of stone, and delivered them unto me.

• **The law of Moses written upon.**

Jos 8:32 — And he wrote there upon the stones a copy of the law of Moses, which he wrote in the presence of the children of Israel.

• **Houses built of.**

Isa 9:10 — The bricks are fallen down, but we will build with hewn stones: the sycomores are cut down, but we will change *them into* cedars.

Am 5:11 — Forasmuch therefore as your treading *is* upon the poor, and ye take from him burdens of wheat: ye have built houses of hewn stone, but ye shall not dwell in them; ye have planted pleasant vineyards, but ye shall not drink wine of them.

• **Temple built of.**

1Ki 5:17–18; 7:9–12; Lk 21:5–6

Mt 24:2 — And Jesus said unto them, See ye not all these things? verily I say unto you, There shall not be left here one stone upon another, that shall not be thrown down.

Lk 19:44 — And shall lay thee even with the ground, and thy children within thee; and they shall not leave in thee one stone upon another; because thou knewest not the time of thy visitation.

• **Prepared in the quarries.**

1Ki 6:7 — And the house, when it was in building, was built of stone made ready before it was brought thither: so that there was neither hammer nor axe *nor* any tool of iron heard in the house, while it was in building.

• **Hewn.**

Ex 34:1 — And the LORD said unto Moses, Hew thee two tables of stone like unto the first: and I will write upon *these* tables the words that were in the first tables, which thou brakest.

Dt 10:1 — At that time the LORD said unto me, Hew thee two tables of stone like unto the first, and come up unto me into the mount, and make thee an ark of wood.

1Ki 5:17 — And the king commanded, and they brought great stones, costly stones, *and* hewed stones, to lay the foundation of the house.

1Ki 6:36 — And he built the inner court with three rows of hewed stone, and a row of cedar beams.

1Ki 7:9 — All these *were of* costly stones, according to the measures of hewed stones, sawed with saws, within and without, even from the foundation unto the coping, and so on the outside toward the great court.

2Ki 12:12 — And to masons, and hewers of stone, and to buy timber and hewed stone to repair the breaches of the house of the LORD, and for all that was laid out for the house to repair *it.*

2Ki 22:6 — Unto carpenters, and builders, and masons, and to buy timber and hewn stone to repair the house.

1Ch 22:2 — And David commanded to gather together the strangers that *were* in the land of Israel; and he set masons to hew wrought stones to build the house of God.

2Ch 34:11 — Even to the artificers and builders gave they *it,* to buy hewn stone, and timber for couplings, and to floor the houses which the kings of Judah had destroyed.

La 3:9 — He hath inclosed my ways with hewn stone, he hath made my paths crooked.

• Sawn.

1Ki 7:9 — All these *were of* costly stones, according to the measures of hewed stones, sawed with saws, within and without, even from the foundation unto the coping, and so on the outside toward the great court.

• Hewers of.

1Ki 5:18 — And Solomon's builders and Hiram's builders did hew *them,* and the stonesquarers: so they prepared timber and stones to build the house.

2Ki 12:12 — And to masons, and hewers of stone, and to buy timber and hewed stone to repair the breaches of the house of the LORD, and for all that was laid out for the house to repair *it.*

1Ch 22:15 — Moreover *there are* workmen with thee in abundance, hewers and workers of stone and timber, and all manner of cunning men for every manner of work.

• City walls built of.

Ne 4:3 — Now Tobiah the Ammonite *was* by him, and he said, Even that which they build, if a fox go up, he shall even break down their stone wall.

• Memorial pillars of.

Ge 28:18–22; 31:45–52; Jos 4:2–9, 20–24

Jos 24:25 — So Joshua made a covenant with the people that day, and set them a statute and an ordinance in Shechem.

1Sa 7:12 — Then Samuel took a stone, and set *it* between Mizpeh and Shen, and called the name of it Eben-ezer, saying, Hitherto hath the LORD helped us.

• Great, as landmarks, Abel.

1Sa 6:18 — And the golden mice, *according to* the number of all the cities of the Philistines *belonging* to the five lords, *both* of fenced cities, and of country villages, even unto the great *stone* of Abel, whereon they set down the ark of the LORD: *which stone remaineth* unto this day in the field of Joshua, the Beth-shemite.

• Great, as landmarks, Ezel.

1Sa 20:19 — And *when* thou hast stayed three days, *then* thou shalt go down quickly, and come to the place where thou didst hide thyself when the business was *in hand,* and shalt remain by the stone Ezel.

• Great, as landmarks, Zoheleth.

1Ki 1:9 — And Adonijah slew sheep and oxen and fat cattle by the stone of Zoheleth, which *is* by En-rogel, and called all his brethren the king's sons, and all the men of Judah the king's servants:

• Cast upon accursed ground.

2Ki 3:19 — And ye shall smite every fenced city, and every choice city, and shall fell every good tree, and stop all wells of water, and mar every good piece of land with stones.

2Ki 3:25 — And they beat down the cities, and on every good piece of land cast every man his stone, and filled it; and they stopped all the wells of water, and felled all the good trees: only in Kir-haraseth left they the stones thereof; howbeit the slingers went about *it,* and smote it.

• Used in building altars.

Jos 8:31 — As Moses the servant of the LORD commanded the children of Israel, as it is written in the book of the law of Moses, an altar of whole stones, over which no man hath lift up *any* iron: and they offered thereon burnt offerings unto the LORD, and sacrificed peace offerings.

• Used for weighing.

Le 19:36 — Just balances, just weights, a just ephah, and a just hin, shall ye have: I *am* the LORD your God, which brought you out of the land of Egypt.

• Used for closing sepulchres.

Mt 27:60 — And laid it in his own new tomb, which he had hewn out in the rock: and he rolled a great stone to the door of the sepulchre, and departed.

Mk 15:46 — And he bought fine linen, and took him down, and wrapped him in the linen, and laid him in a sepulchre which was hewn out of a rock, and rolled a stone unto the door of the sepulchre.

Mk 16:3 — And they said among themselves, Who shall roll us away the stone from the door of the sepulchre?

• Sepulchres hewn in.

Mt 27:60— And laid it in his own new tomb, which he had hewn out in the rock: and he rolled a great stone to the door of the sepulchre, and departed.

Mk 15:46 — And he bought fine linen, and took him down, and wrapped him in the linen, and laid him in a sepulchre which was hewn out of a rock, and rolled a stone unto the door of the sepulchre.

Mk 16:3 — And they said among themselves, Who shall roll us away the stone from the door of the sepulchre?

• Idols made of.

Dt 4:28 — And there ye shall serve gods, the work of men's hands, wood and stone, which neither see, nor hear, nor eat, nor smell.

Dt 28:36 — The LORD shall bring thee, and thy king which thou shalt set over thee, unto a nation which neither thou nor thy fathers have known; and there shalt thou serve other gods, wood and stone.

Dt 28:64 — And the LORD shall scatter thee among all people, from the one end of the earth even unto the other; and there thou shalt serve other gods, which neither thou nor thy fathers have known, *even* wood and stone.

Dt 29:17 — And ye have seen their abominations, and their idols, wood and stone, silver and gold, which *were* among them:)

2Ki 19:18 — And have cast their gods into the fire: for they *were* no gods, but the work of men's hands, wood and stone: therefore they have destroyed them.

Isa 37:19 — And have cast their gods into the fire: for they *were* no gods, but the work of men's hands, wood and stone: therefore they have destroyed them.

Eze 20:32 — And that which cometh into your mind shall not be at all, that ye say, We will be as the heathen, as the families of the countries, to serve wood and stone.

- **Great, in Solomon's temple.**

1Ki 5:17–18; 7:9–12

- **Magnificent, in Herod's.**

Mk 13:1 — And as he went out of the temple, one of his disciples saith unto him, Master, see what manner of stones and what buildings *are here!*

- **Skill in throwing.**

Jgs 20:16 — Among all this people *there were* seven hundred chosen men lefthanded; every one could sling stones at an hair *breadth,* and not miss.

1Ch 12:2 — *They were* armed with bows, and could use both the right hand and the left in *hurling* stones and *shooting* arrows out of a bow, *even* of Saul's brethren of Benjamin.

See: Sling

See: Adamant

See: Chalcedony

See: Marble

See: Onyx

See: Pillar

See: Stones; precious

- **Figurative.**

Ge 49:24 — But his bow abode in strength, and the arms of his hands were made strong by the hands of the mighty *God* of Jacob; (from thence *is* the shepherd, the stone of Israel:)

Zec 3:9 — For behold the stone that I have laid before Joshua; upon one stone *shall be* seven eyes: behold, I will engrave the graving thereof, saith the LORD of hosts, and I will remove the iniquity of that land in one day.

- **Of temptation, "stone of stumbling".**

Isa 8:14 — And he shall be for a sanctuary; but for a stone of stumbling and for a rock of offence to both the houses of Israel, for a gin and for a snare to the inhabitants of Jerusalem.

Ro 9:33 — As it is written, Behold, I lay in Sion a stumblingstone and rock of offence: and whosoever believeth on him shall not be ashamed.

1Pe 2:8 — And a stone of stumbling, and a rock of offence, *even to them* which stumble at the word, being disobedient: whereunto also they were appointed.

- **Of Christ, "a tried stone," "a precious stone," "a sure foundation".**

Isa 28:16 — Therefore thus saith the Lord GOD, Behold, I lay in Zion for a foundation a stone, a tried stone, a precious corner *stone,* a sure foundation: he that believeth shall not make haste.

- **Of Christ's rejection, the rejected corner stone.**

Mt 21:42–44; Lk 20:17–18

Ps 118:22 — The stone *which* the builders refused is become the head *stone* of the corner.

Mk 12:10 — And have ye not read this scripture; The stone which the builders rejected is become the head of the corner:

Ac 4:11 — This is the stone which was set at nought of you builders, which is become the head of the corner.

1Pe 2:4 — To whom coming, *as unto* a living stone, disallowed indeed of men, but chosen of God, *and* precious,

- **Of Christ, the true foundation.**

Isa 28:16 — Therefore thus saith the Lord GOD, Behold, I lay in Zion for a foundation a stone, a tried stone, a precious corner *stone,* a sure foundation: he that believeth shall not make haste.

Mt 16:18 — And I say also unto thee, That thou art Peter, and upon this rock I will build my church; and the gates of hell shall not prevail against it.

1Co 3:11 — For other foundation can no man lay than that is laid, which is Jesus Christ.

Eph 2:20 — And are built upon the foundation of the apostles and prophets, Jesus Christ himself being the chief corner *stone;*

Rev 21:14 — And the wall of the city had twelve foundations, and in them the names of the twelve apostles of the Lamb.

- **Of Christ, the water of life.**

1Co 10:4 — And did all drink the same spiritual drink: for they drank of that spiritual Rock that followed them: and that Rock was Christ.

- **Of the impenitent heart.**

Eze 36:26 — A new heart also will I give you, and a new spirit will I put within you: and I will take away the stony heart out of your flesh, and I will give you an heart of flesh.

- **Of the witness of the Spirit, the white stone.**

Rev 2:17 — He that hath an ear, let him hear what the Spirit saith unto the churches; To him that overcometh will I give to eat of the hidden manna, and will give him a white stone, and in the stone a new name written, which no man knoweth saving he that receiveth *it.*

- **Symbolic.**
  - **Of the kingdom of Christ.**

Da 2:34 — Thou sawest till that a stone was cut out without hands, which smote the image upon his feet *that were* of iron and clay, and brake them to pieces.

Da 2:45 — Forasmuch as thou sawest that the stone was cut out of the mountain without hands, and that it brake in pieces the iron, the brass, the clay, the silver, and the gold; the great God hath made known to the king what shall come to pass hereafter: and the dream is certain, and the interpretation thereof sure.

- **Precious.**
  - **In the breastplate and ephod.**
    Ex 28:9–21; 39:6–14
  - **Voluntary offerings of, by the Israelites for the breastplate and ephod.**
    Ex 35:27 — And the rulers brought onyx stones, and stones to be set, for the ephod, and for the breastplate;
  - **Exported from Sheba.**
    2Ch 9:9–10
    1Ki 10:2 — And she came to Jerusalem with a very great train, with camels that bare spices, and very much gold, and precious stones: and when she was come to Solomon, she communed with him of all that was in her heart.
    1Ki 10:10 — And she gave the king an hundred and twenty talents of gold, and of spices very great store, and precious stones: there came no more such abundance of spices as these which the queen of Sheba gave to king Solomon.
    Eze 27:22 — The merchants of Sheba and Raamah, they *were* thy merchants: they occupied in thy fairs with chief of all spices, and with all precious stones, and gold.
  - **Exported from Ophir.**
    1Ki 10:11 — And the navy also of Hiram, that brought gold from Ophir, brought in from Ophir great plenty of almug trees, and precious stones.
  - **Partial catalogue of.**
    Eze 28:13 — Thou hast been in Eden the garden of God; every precious stone *was* thy covering, the sardius, topaz, and the diamond, the beryl, the onyx, and the jasper, the sapphire, the emerald, and the carbuncle, and gold: the workmanship of thy tabrets and of thy pipes was prepared in thee in the day that thou wast created.
  - **Seen in the foundation of the New Jerusalem in John's apocalyptic vision.**
    Rev 21:19–20
  - **In kings' crowns.**
    2Sa 12:30 — And he took their king's crown from off his head, the weight whereof *was* a talent of gold with the precious stones: and it was *set* on David's head. And he brought forth the spoil of the city in great abundance.
    1Ch 20:2 — And David took the crown of their king from off his head, and found it to weigh a talent of gold, and *there were* precious stones in it; and it was set upon David's head: and he brought also exceeding much spoil out of the city.
  - **Figurative.**
    Isa 54:11–12

See: Agate
See: Amethyst
See: Beryl
See: Carbuncle
See: Chrysolyte
See: Chrysoprasus
See: Coral
See: Crystal
See: Diamond
See: Emerald
See: Jacinth
See: Jasper
See: Ligure
See: Ruby
See: Sapphire
See: Sardius
See: Sardonyx
See: Topaz

STONING

- **Capital punishment by.**
  Ex 19:13 — There shall not an hand touch it, but he shall surely be stoned, or shot through; whether *it be* beast or man, it shall not live: when the trumpet soundeth long, they shall come up to the mount.
  Dt 13:10 — And thou shalt stone him with stones, that he die; because he hath sought to thrust thee away from the LORD thy God, which brought thee out of the land of Egypt, from the house of bondage.
  Dt 17:5 — Then shalt thou bring forth that man or that woman, which have committed that wicked thing, unto thy gates, *even* that man or that woman, and shalt stone them with stones, till they die.
  Dt 22:21 — Then they shall bring out the damsel to the door of her father's house, and the men of her city shall stone her with stones that she die: because she hath wrought folly in Israel, to play the whore in her father's house: so shalt thou put evil away from among you.
  Heb 11:37 — They were stoned, they were sawn asunder, were tempted, were slain with the sword: they wandered about in sheepskins and goatskins; being destitute, afflicted, tormented;
- **Instances of.**
  - **Sabbath breaker.**
    Nu 15:36
  - **Achan.**
    Jos 7:25
  - **Naboth.**
    1Ki 21:13
  - **Stephen.**
    Ac 7:59
  - **Paul.**
    Ac 14:19; 2Co 11:25

See: Witness

STOOL

2Ki 4:10 — Let us make a little chamber, I pray thee, on the wall; and let us set for him there a bed, and a table, and a stool, and a candlestick: and it shall be, when he cometh to us, that he shall turn in thither.

- **Footstool.**
  - **Figurative.**
    - **Of the earth.**

Isa 66:1 — Thus saith the LORD, The heaven *is* my throne, and the earth *is* my footstool: where *is* the house that ye build unto me? and where *is* the place of my rest?

Mt 5:35 — Nor by the earth; for it is his footstool: neither by Jerusalem; for it is the city of the great King.

Ac 7:49 — Heaven *is* my throne, and earth *is* my footstool: what house will ye build me? saith the Lord: or what *is* the place of my rest?

- **Of the temple.**

1Ch 28:2 — Then David the king stood up upon his feet, and said, Hear me, my brethren, and my people: *As for me,* I *had* in mine heart to build an house of rest for the ark of the covenant of the LORD, and for the footstool of our God, and had made ready for the building:

La 2:1 — How hath the Lord covered the daughter of Zion with a cloud in his anger, *and* cast down from heaven unto the earth the beauty of Israel, and remembered not his footstool in the day of his anger!

- **Of the sanctuary.**

Ps 99:5 — Exalt ye the LORD our God, and worship at his footstool; *for* he *is* holy.

Ps 132:7 — We will go into his tabernacles: we will worship at his footstool.

- **Of the enemies of Jesus.**

Ps 110:1 — The LORD said unto my Lord, Sit thou at my right hand, until I make thine enemies thy footstool.

Mt 22:44 — The Lord said unto my Lord, Sit thou on my right hand, till I make thine enemies thy footstool?

Mk 12:36 — For David himself said by the Holy Ghost, The Lord said to my Lord, Sit thou on my right hand, till I make thine enemies thy footstool.

Lk 20:43 — Till I make thine enemies thy footstool.

Ac 2:35 — Until I make thy foes thy footstool.

Heb 1:13 — But to which of the angels said he at any times, Sit on my right hand, until I make thine enemies thy footstool?

STOREHOUSES ✦See: Treasure-Houses

STORK

- **Forbidden as food.**

Le 11:19 — And the stork, the heron after her kind, and the lapwing, and the bat.

- **Nest of, in fir trees.**

Ps 104:17 — Where the birds make their nests: *as for* the stork, the fir trees *are* her house.

- **Migratory.**

Jer 8:7 — Yea, the stork in the heaven knoweth her appointed times; and the turtle and the crane and the swallow observe the time of their coming; but my people know not the judgment of the LORD.

- **Figurative.**

Zec 5:9 — Then lifted I up mine eyes, and looked, and, behold, there came out two women, and the wind *was* in their wings; for they had wings like the wings of a stork: and they lifted up the ephah between the earth and the heaven.

STRAIGHT

- **Name of a street in Damascus.**

Ac 9:11 — And the Lord *said* unto him, Arise, and go into the street which is called Straight, and enquire in the house of Judas for *one* called Saul, of Tarsus: for, behold, he prayeth,

- **Figurative.**
  - **Of righteousness, "straight paths".**

Isa 40:3–4

Mt 3:3 — For this is he that was spoken of by the prophet Esaias, saying, The voice of one crying in the wilderness, Prepare ye the way of the Lord, make his paths straight.

Heb 12:13 — And make straight paths for your feet, lest that which is lame be turned out of the way; but let it rather be healed.

STRAIT GATE

Mt 7:13–14

Lk 13:24 — Strive to enter in at the strait gate: for many, I say unto you, will seek to enter in, and shall not be able.

STRANGERS

- **Mosaic law relating to.**
  - **Authorized bondservice of.**

Le 25:44–45

- **Usury of.**

Dt 15:3 — Of a foreigner thou mayest exact *it again:* but *that* which is thine with thy brother thine hand shall release;

Dt 23:20 — Unto a stranger thou mayest lend upon usury; but unto thy brother thou shalt not lend upon usury: that the LORD thy God may bless thee in all that thou settest thine hand to in the land whither thou goest to possess it.

- **Authorized sale to, of flesh of animals that had died.**

Dt 14:21 — Ye shall not eat *of* any thing that dieth of itself: thou shalt give it unto the stranger that *is* in thy gates, that he may eat it; or thou mayest sell it unto an alien: for thou *art* an holy people unto the LORD thy God. Thou shalt not seethe a kid in his mother's milk.

• Forbid their being made kings over Israel.

Dt 17:15 — Thou shalt in any wise set *him* king over thee, whom the LORD thy God shall choose: *one* from among thy brethren shalt thou set king over thee: thou mayest not set a stranger over thee, which *is* not thy brother.

• Forbid their eating the passover.

Ex 12:43 — And the LORD said unto Moses and Aaron, This *is* the ordinance of the passover: There shall no stranger eat thereof:

Ex 12:48 — And when a stranger shall sojourn with thee, and will keep the passover to the LORD, let all his males be circumcised, and then let him come near and keep it; and he shall be as one that is born in the land: for no uncircumcised person shall eat thereof.

• Forbid their eating things offered in sacrifice.

Ex 29:33 — And they shall eat those things wherewith the atonement was made, to consecrate *and* to sanctify them: but a stranger shall not eat *thereof,* because they *are* holy.

Le 22:10 — There shall no stranger eat *of* the holy thing: a sojourner of the priest, or an hired servant, shall not eat *of* the holy thing.

Le 22:12 — If the priest's daughter also be *married* unto a stranger, she may not eat of an offering of the holy things.

Le 22:25 — Neither from a stranger's hand shall ye offer the bread of your God of any of these; because their corruption *is* in them, *and* blemishes *be* in them: they shall not be accepted for you.

• Forbid their blaspheming.

Le 24:16 — And he that blasphemeth the name of the LORD, he shall surely be put to death, *and* all the congregation shall certainly stone him: as well the stranger, as he that is born in the land, when he blasphemeth the name *of the LORD,* shall be put to death.

• Forbid their approaching the tabernacle.

Nu 1:51 — And when the tabernacle setteth forward, the Levites shall take it down: and when the tabernacle is to be pitched, the Levites shall set it up: and the stranger that cometh nigh shall be put to death.

• Forbid their eating blood.

Le 17:10 — And whatsoever man *there be* of the house of Israel, or of the strangers that sojourn among you, that eateth any manner of blood; I will even set my face against that soul that eateth blood, and will cut him off from among his people.

• Forbid injustice to.

Ex 12:49 — One law shall be to him that is homeborn, and unto the stranger that sojourneth among you.

Le 24:22 — Ye shall have one manner of law, as well for the stranger, as for one of your own country: for I *am* the LORD your God.

Nu 9:14 — And if a stranger shall sojourn among you, and will keep the passover unto the LORD; according to the ordinance of the passover, and according to the manner thereof, so shall he do: ye shall have one ordinance, both for the stranger, and for him that was born in the land.

Dt 1:16 — And I charged your judges at that time, saying, Hear *the causes* between your brethren, and judge righteously between *every* man and his brother, and the stranger *that is* with him.

Jer 22:3 — Thus saith the LORD; Execute ye judgment and righteousness, and deliver the spoiled out of the hand of the oppressor: and do no wrong, do no violence to the stranger, the fatherless, nor the widow, neither shed innocent blood in this place.

• Forbid oppression of.

Ex 22:21 — Thou shalt neither vex a stranger, nor oppress him: for ye were strangers in the land of Egypt.

Le 23:9 — And the LORD spake unto Moses, saying,

Dt 24:14 — Thou shalt not oppress an hired servant *that is* poor and needy, *whether he be* of thy brethren, or of thy strangers that *are* in thy land within thy gates:

Dt 24:17 — Thou shalt not pervert the judgment of the stranger, *nor* of the fatherless; nor take a widow's raiment to pledge:

Dt 27:19 — Cursed *be* he that perverteth the judgment of the stranger, fatherless, and widow. And all the people shall say, Amen.

Jer 22:3 — Thus saith the LORD; Execute ye judgment and righteousness, and deliver the spoiled out of the hand of the oppressor: and do no wrong, do no violence to the stranger, the fatherless, nor the widow, neither shed innocent blood in this place.

• Instances of oppression.

Eze 22:29; Mal 3:5

• Required to observe the Sabbath.

Ex 20:10 — But the seventh day *is* the sabbath of the LORD thy God: *in it* thou shalt not do any work, thou, nor thy son, nor thy daughter, thy manservant, nor thy maidservant, nor thy cattle, nor thy stranger that *is* within thy gates:

Ex 23:12 — Six days thou shalt do thy work, and on the seventh day thou shalt rest: that thine ox and thine ass may rest, and the son of thy handmaid, and the stranger, may be refreshed.

• Might offer oblations.

Le 22:18–19

Le 17:8 — And thou shalt say unto them, Whatsoever man *there be* of the house of Israel, or of the strangers which sojourn among you, that offereth a burnt offering of sacrifice,

• Were buried in separate burial places.

Mt 27:7 — And they took counsel, and bought with them the potter's field, to bury strangers in.

• Kindness to, required.

Le 19:33–34

• Love of, enjoined.

Dt 10:18–19

• **Abhorrence of, forbidden.**

Dt 23:7 — Thou shalt not abhor an Edomite; for he *is* thy brother: thou shalt not abhor an Egyptian; because thou wast a stranger in his land.

• **Marriage with, forbidden.**

Dt 25:5 — If brethren dwell together, and one of them die, and have no child, the wife of the dead shall not marry without unto a stranger: her husband's brother shall go in unto her, and take her to him to wife, and perform the duty of an husband's brother unto her.

• **Hospitality to.**

See: Alms

See: Heathen

See: Hospitality

See: Proselyte

STRANGLED

• **Things dying by strangulation, forbidden as food.**

Ac 15:20 — But that we write unto them, that they abstain from pollutions of idols, and *from* fornication, and *from* things strangled, and *from* blood.

Ac 15:29 — That ye abstain from meats offered to idols, and from blood, and from things strangled, and from fornication: from which if ye keep yourselves, ye shall do well. Fare ye well.

Ac 21:25 — As touching the Gentiles which believe, we have written *and* concluded that they observe no such thing, save only that they keep themselves from *things* offered to idols, and from blood, and from strangled, and from fornication.

STRATEGY

• **In war.**

Ge 14:14–15; 32:7–8; Jos 8:3–25; Jgs 7:16–23; 20:29–43; 2Sa 15:32–34; 17:7–14; Ne 6:1–19

Isa 15:1 — The burden of Moab. Because in the night Ar of Moab is laid waste, *and* brought to silence; because in the night Kir of Moab is laid waste, *and* brought to silence;

Jer 6:5 — Arise, and let us go by night, and let us destroy her palaces.

See: Ambush

See: Armies

STRAW

• **Used for provender.**

Ge 24:32 — And the man came into the house: and he ungirded his camels, and gave straw and provender for the camels, and water to wash his feet, and the men's feet that *were* with him.

Isa 65:25 — The wolf and the lamb shall feed together, and the lion shall eat straw like the bullock: and dust *shall be* the serpent's meat. They shall not hurt nor destroy in all my holy mountain, saith the LORD.

• **Used for brick.**

Ex 5:7 — Ye shall no more give the people straw to make brick, as heretofore: let them go and gather straw for themselves.

STRAY

• **Animals straying to be returned.**

Dt 22:1–3

Ex 23:4 — If thou meet thine enemy's ox or his ass going astray, thou shalt surely bring it back to him again.

• **Instances of animals straying.**

• **Kish's.**

1Sa 9:1–27

STRENGTH

• **A title given Jehovah.**

1Sa 15:29 — And also the Strength of Israel will not lie nor repent: for he *is* not a man, that he should repent.

• **Spiritual.**

See: Power; spiritual

STRESS

2Co 4:6–18; 11:18–33; Php 4:6–7

Pr 29:25 — The fear of man bringeth a snare: but whoso putteth his trust in the LORD shall be safe.

STRIFE

Pr 6:12–14, 16–19; 23:29–30; 26:20–21; Isa 41:11–12; Mt 5:39–41; 10:34–36; 18:15–17; Mk 3:24–25; Lk 12:51–53, 58–59; Ro 16:17–18; 1Co 1:10–13; 3:3–4; 4:6–7; 6:1–7; 11:16–19; Gal 5:1–26; Php 1:15–16; 2:14–15; 1Ti 1:5–7; 3:2–3; 6:3–5, 20–21; 2Ti 2:23–25; Tit 3:1–3; Jas 3:14–16; 4:1–2

Ge 13:8 — And Abram said unto Lot, Let there be no strife, I pray thee, between me and thee, and between my herdmen and thy herdmen; for we *be* brethren.

Num. 27:14 — For ye rebelled against my commandment in the desert of Zin, in the strife of the congregation, to sanctify me at the water before their eyes: that is the water of Meribah in Kadesh in the wilderness of Zin.

Dt 1:12 — How can I myself alone bear your cumbrance, and your burden, and your strife?

Ps 31:20 — Thou shalt hide them in the secret of thy presence from the pride of man: thou shalt keep them secretly in a pavilion from the strife of tongues.

Ps 55:9 — Destroy, O Lord, *and* divide their tongues: for I have seen violence and strife in the city.

Ps 80:6 — Thou makest us a strife unto our neighbours: and our enemies laugh among themselves.

Pr 3:30 — Strive not with a man without cause, if he have done thee no harm.

Pr 10:12 — Hatred stirreth up strifes: but love covereth all sins.

Pr 13:10 — Only by pride cometh contention: but with the well advised *is* wisdom.

Pr 15:18 — A wrathful man stirreth up strife: but *he that is* slow to anger appeaseth strife.

Pr 16:28 — A froward man soweth strife: and a whisperer separateth chief friends.

Pr 17:1 — Better *is* a dry morsel, and quietness therewith, than an house full of sacrifices *with* strife.

Pr 17:14 — The beginning of strife *is as* when one letteth out water: therefore leave off contention, before it be meddled with.

Pr 17:19 — He loveth transgression that loveth strife: *and* he that exalteth his gate seeketh destruction.

Pr 18:6 — A fool's lips enter into contention, and his mouth calleth for strokes.

Pr 18:19 — A brother offended *is harder to be won* than a strong city: and *their* contentions *are* like the bars of a castle.

Pr 19:13 — A foolish son *is* the calamity of his father: and the contentions of a wife *are* a continual dropping.

Pr 20:3 — *It is* an honour for a man to cease from strife: but every fool will be meddling.

Pr 21:19 — *It is* better to dwell in the wilderness, than with a contentious and an angry woman.

Pr 22:10 — Cast out the scorner, and contention shall go out; yea, strife and reproach shall cease.

Pr 25:8 — Go not forth hastily to strive, lest *thou know not* what to do in the end thereof, when thy neighbour hath put thee to shame.

Pr 25:24 — *It is* better to dwell in the corner of the housetop, than with a brawling woman and in a wide house.

Pr 26:17 — He that passeth by, *and* meddleth with strife *belonging* not to him, *is like* one that taketh a dog by the ears.

Pr 27:15 — A continual dropping in a very rainy day and a contentious woman are alike.

Pr 28:25 — He that is of a proud heart stirreth up strife: but he that putteth his trust in the LORD shall be made fat.

Pr 29:22 — An angry man stirreth up strife, and a furious man aboundeth in transgression.

Pr 30:33 — Surely the churning of milk bringeth forth butter, and the wringing of the nose bringeth forth blood: so the forcing of wrath bringeth forth strife.

Isa 58:4 — Behold, ye fast for strife and debate, and to smite with the fist of wickedness: ye shall not fast as *ye do this* day, to make your voice to be heard on high.

Hab 1:3 — Why dost thou shew me iniquity, and cause *me* to behold grievance? for spoiling and violence *are* before me: and there are *that* raise up strife and contention.

Mt 5:25 — Agree with thine adversary quickly, whiles thou art in the way with him; lest at any time the adversary deliver thee to the judge, and the judge deliver thee to the officer, and thou be cast into prison.

Mt 12:25 — And Jesus knew their thoughts, and said unto them, Every kingdom divided against itself is brought to desolation; and every city or house divided against itself shall not stand:

Lk 11:17 — But he, knowing their thoughts, said unto them, Every kingdom divided against itself is brought to desolation; and a house *divided* against a house falleth.

Ro 2:8 — But unto them that are contentious, and do not obey the truth, but obey unrighteousness, indignation and wrath,

Ro 12:18 — If it be possible, as much as lieth in you, live peaceably with all men.

Ro 13:13 — Let us walk honestly, as in the day; not in rioting and drunkenness, not in chambering and wantonness, not in strife and envying.

Ro 14:1 — Him that is weak in the faith receive ye, *but* not to doubtful disputations.

Ro 14:19 — Let us therefore follow after the things which make for peace, and things wherewith one may edify another.

Ro 14:21 — *It is* good neither to eat flesh, nor to drink wine, nor *any thing* whereby thy brother stumbleth, or is offended, or is made weak.

1Co 3:1 — And I, brethren, could not speak unto you as unto spiritual, but as unto carnal, *even* as unto babes in Christ.

2Co 12:20 — For I fear, lest, when I come, I shall not find you such as I would, and *that* I shall be found unto you such as ye would not: lest *there be* debates, envyings, wraths, strifes, backbitings, whisperings, swellings, tumults:

Php 2:3 — *Let* nothing *be done* through strife or vainglory; but in lowliness of mind let each esteem other better than themselves.

1Ti 2:8 — I will therefore that men pray every where, lifting up holy hands, without wrath and doubting.

2Ti 2:14 — Of these things put *them* in remembrance, charging *them* before the Lord that they strive not about words to no profit, *but* to the subverting of the hearers.

Tit 3:9 — But avoid foolish questions, and genealogies, and contentions, and strivings about the law; for they are unprofitable and vain.

See: Anger

See: Envy

See: Jealousy

See: Malice

- **Instances of.**
  - **Between Abraham and Lot's herdmen.**
    Ge 13:6–7
  - **Abimelech's.**
    Ge 21:25
  - **Isaac's and those of Gerar.**
    Ge 26:20–22
  - **Laban and Jacob.**
    Ge 31:36 — And Jacob was wroth, and chode with Laban: and Jacob answered and said to Laban, What *is* my trespass? what *is* my sin, that thou hast so hotly pursued after me?
  - **Israelites.**
    Dt 1:12 — How can I myself alone bear your cumbrance, and your burden, and your strife?
  - **Jephthah and his brethren.**
    Jgs 11:2 — And Gilead's wife bare him sons; and his wife's sons grew up, and they thrust out Jephthah, and said unto him, Thou shalt not inherit in our father's house; for thou *art* the son of a strange woman.

• **Jephthah and Ephraimites.**
Jgs 12:1–6

• **Israel and Judah, about David.**
2Sa 19:41–43

• **Disciples, over who might be greatest.**
Mk 9:34 — But they held their peace: for by the way they had disputed among themselves, who *should be* the greatest.
Lk 22:24 — And there was also a strife among them, which of them should be accounted the greatest.

• **Jews, concerning Jesus.**
Jn 10:19 — There was a division therefore again among the Jews for these sayings.

• **Christians at Antioch, about circumcision.**
Ac 15:2 — When therefore Paul and Barnabas had no small dissension and disputation with them, they determined that Paul and Barnabas, and certain other of them, should go up to Jerusalem unto the apostles and elders about this question.

• **Paul and Barnabas, about Mark.**
Ac 15:38–39

• **Pharisees and Sadducees, concerning the resurrection.**
Ac 23:7–10

• **Corinthians.**
1Co 1:11–12
1Co 6:6 — But brother goeth to law with brother, and that before the unbelievers.

STRIPES

• **Inflicted on Paul.**
2Co 6:5 — In stripes, in imprisonments, in tumults, in labours, in watchings, in fastings;
2Co 11:23 — Are they ministers of Christ? (I speak as a fool) I *am* more; in labours more abundant, in stripes above measure, in prisons more frequent, in deaths oft.

See: Scourging

STUBBLE

• **Figurative.**

• **Of the wicked.**
Ex 15:7 — And in the greatness of thine excellency thou hast overthrown them that rose up against thee: thou sentest forth thy wrath, *which* consumed them as stubble.
Job 21:18 — They are as stubble before the wind, and as chaff that the storm carrieth away.
Ps 83:13 — O my God, make them like a wheel; as the stubble before the wind.
Isa 5:24 — Therefore as the fire devoureth the stubble, and the flame consumeth the chaff, *so* their root shall be as rottenness, and their blossom shall go up as dust: because they have cast away the law of the LORD of hosts, and despised the word of the Holy One of Israel.
Isa 40:24 — Yea, they shall not be planted; yea, they shall not be sown: yea, their stock shall not take root in the earth: and he shall also blow upon them, and they shall wither, and the whirlwind shall take them away as stubble.
Isa 41:2 — Who raised up the righteous *man* from the east, called him to his foot, gave the nations before him, and made *him* rule over kings? he gave *them* as the dust to his sword, *and* as driven stubble to his bow.
Isa 47:14 — Behold, they shall be as stubble; the fire shall burn them; they shall not deliver themselves from the power of the flame: *there shall* not *be* a coal to warm at, *nor* fire to sit before it.
Jer 13:24 — Therefore will I scatter them as the stubble that passeth away by the wind of the wilderness.
Joel 2:5 — Like the noise of chariots on the tops of mountains shall they leap, like the noise of a flame of fire that devoureth the stubble, as a strong people set in battle array.
Na 1:10 — For while *they be* folden together *as* thorns, and while they are drunken *as* drunkards, they shall be devoured as stubble fully dry.
Mal 4:1 — For, behold, the day cometh, that shall burn as an oven; and all the proud, yea, and all that do wickedly, shall be stubble: and the day that cometh shall burn them up, saith the LORD of hosts, that it shall leave them neither root nor branch.

STUBBORNNESS See: Obduracy

STUDENTS

• **Poverty of.**
2Ki 4:1 — Now there cried a certain woman of the wives of the sons of the prophets unto Elisha, saying, Thy servant my husband is dead; and thou knowest that thy servant did fear the LORD: and the creditor is come to take unto him my two sons to be bondmen.

• **In state school.**
Da 1:1–21

• **In schools of the prophets.**
2Ki 2:2–3
1Sa 19:20 — And Saul sent messengers to take David: and when they saw the company of the prophets prophesying, and Samuel standing *as* appointed over them, the Spirit of God was upon the messengers of Saul, and they also prophesied.
1Ki 20:35 — And a certain man of the sons of the prophets said unto his neighbour in the word of the LORD, Smite me, I pray thee. And the man refused to smite him.
2Ki 2:5 — And the sons of the prophets that *were* at Jericho came to Elisha, and said unto him, Knowest thou that the LORD will take away thy master from thy head to day? And he answered, Yea, I know *it;* hold ye your peace.
2Ki 2:7 — And fifty men of the sons of the prophets went, and stood to view afar off: and they two stood by Jordan.
2Ki 2:15 — And when the sons of the prophets which *were* to view at Jericho saw him, they said, The spir-

it of Elijah doth rest on Elisha. And they came to meet him, and bowed themselves to the ground before him.

2Ki 4:1 — Now there cried a certain woman of the wives of the sons of the prophets unto Elisha, saying, Thy servant my husband is dead; and thou knowest that thy servant did fear the LORD: and the creditor is come to take unto him my two sons to be bondmen.

See: Instruction

See: School

STUDY

Lk 2:40–52

Ne 8:8 — So they read in the book in the law of God distinctly, and gave the sense, and caused *them* to understand the reading.

2Ti 2:5 — And if a man also strive for masteries, *yet* is he not crowned, except he strive lawfully.

2Ti 4:13 — The cloke that I left at Troas with Carpus, when thou comest, bring *with thee,* and the books, *but* especially the parchments.

STUMBLING

- **Figurative.**
  - **Causes of.**

Ps 69:6 — Let not them that wait on thee, O Lord GOD of hosts, be ashamed for my sake: let not those that seek thee be confounded for my sake, O God of Israel.

- **Stone of.**

Ro 9:32–33

Isa 8:14 — And he shall be for a sanctuary; but for a stone of stumbling and for a rock of offence to both the houses of Israel, for a gin and for a snare to the inhabitants of Jerusalem.

1Pe 2:8 — And a stone of stumbling, and a rock of offence, *even to them* which stumble at the word, being disobedient: whereunto also they were appointed.

- **Stumbling-block.**

Eze 14:3–4; 1Co 8:9–13

Le 19:14 — Thou shalt not curse the deaf, nor put a stumblingblock before the blind, but shalt fear thy God: I *am* the LORD.

Ps 119:165 — Great peace have they which love thy law: and nothing shall offend them.

Isa 57:14 — And shall say, Cast ye up, cast ye up, prepare the way, take up the stumblingblock out of the way of my people.

Jer 6:21 — Therefore thus saith the LORD, Behold, I will lay stumblingblocks before this people, and the fathers and the sons together shall fall upon them; the neighbour and his friend shall perish.

Eze 3:20 — Again, When a righteous *man* doth turn from his righteousness, and commit iniquity, and I lay a stumblingblock before him, he shall die: because thou hast not given him warning, he shall die in his sin, and his righteousness which he hath done shall not be remembered; but his blood will I require at thine hand.

Eze 7:19 — They shall cast their silver in the streets, and their gold shall be removed: their silver and their gold shall not be able to deliver them in the day of the wrath of the LORD: they shall not satisfy their souls, neither fill their bowels: because it is the stumblingblock of their iniquity.

Eze 14:7 — For every one of the house of Israel, or of the stranger that sojourneth in Israel, which separateth himself from me, and setteth up his idols in his heart, and putteth the stumblingblock of his iniquity before his face, and cometh to a prophet to enquire of him concerning me; I the LORD will answer him by myself:

Zep 1:3 — I will consume man and beast; I will consume the fowls of the heaven, and the fishes of the sea, and the stumblingblocks with the wicked; and I will cut off man from off the land, saith the LORD.

Lk 11:52 — Woe unto you, lawyers! for ye have taken away the key of knowledge: ye entered not in yourselves, and them that were entering in ye hindered.

Ro 11:9 — And David saith, Let their table be made a snare, and a trap, and a stumblingblock, and a recompence unto them:

Ro 14:13 — Let us not therefore judge one another any more: but judge this rather, that no man put a stumblingblock or an occasion to fall in *his* brother's way.

1Co 1:23 — But we preach Christ crucified, unto the Jews a stumblingblock, and unto the Greeks foolishness;

Rev 2:14 — But I have a few things against thee, because thou hast there them that hold the doctrine of Balaam, who taught Balac to cast a stumblingblock before the children of Israel, to eat things sacrificed unto idols, and to commit fornication.

See: Temptation

SUAH

- **An Asherite.**
- **Son of Zophah.**

1Ch 7:36 — The sons of Zophah; Suah, and Harnepher, and Shual, and Beri, and Imrah,

SUBJECTS

See: Citizens

See: Government

See: Patriotism

See: Rulers

SUBMISSION

- **To authority.**
  - **Jesus an example of.**

Mt 26:39 — And he went a little farther, and fell on his face, and prayed, saying, O my Father, if it be possible, let this cup pass from me: nevertheless not as I will, but as thou *wilt.*

Mt 26:42 — He went away again the second time, and prayed, saying, O my Father, if this cup may not pass away from me, except I drink it, thy will be done.

Mk 14:36 — And he said, Abba, Father, all things *are* possible unto thee; take away this cup from me: nevertheless not what I will, but what thou wilt.

Lk 22:42 — Saying, Father, if thou be willing, remove this cup from me: nevertheless not my will, but thine, be done.

Heb 5:8 — Though he were a Son, yet learned he obedience by the things which he suffered;

- **Of Paul.**

1Co 16:7 — For I will not see you now by the way; but I trust to tarry a while with you, if the Lord permit.

See: Obedience

SUBSTITUTION

Ex 28:38 — And it shall be upon Aaron's forehead, that Aaron may bear the iniquity of the holy things, which the children of Israel shall hallow in all their holy gifts; and it shall be always upon his forehead, that they may be accepted before the LORD.

- **The offering for the offerer.**

Le 16:21–22

Le 1:4 — And he shall put his hand upon the head of the burnt offering; and it shall be accepted for him to make atonement for him.

- **The Levites for the firstborn of the Israelites.**

Nu 3:12 — And I, behold, I have taken the Levites from among the children of Israel instead of all the firstborn that openeth the matrix among the children of Israel: therefore the Levites shall be mine;

Nu 3:41 — And thou shalt take the Levites for me (I *am* the LORD) instead of all the firstborn among the children of Israel; and the cattle of the Levites instead of all the firstlings among the cattle of the children of Israel.

Nu 3:45 — Take the Levites instead of all the firstborn among the children of Israel, and the cattle of the Levites instead of their cattle; and the Levites shall be mine: I *am* the LORD.

Nu 8:18 — And I have taken the Levites for all the firstborn of the children of Israel.

- **The life of Ahab for that of Ben-hadad.**

1Ki 20:42 — And he said unto him, Thus saith the LORD, Because thou hast let go out of *thy* hand a man whom I appointed to utter destruction, therefore thy life shall go for his life, and thy people for his people.

See: Suffering; vicarious

SUBURBS

Nu 35:3–5

Jos 14:4 — For the children of Joseph were two tribes, Manasseh and Ephraim: therefore they gave no part unto the Levites in the land, save cities to dwell *in,* with their suburbs for their cattle and for their substance.

SUCCESSION

- **Of priests, irregularity in.**

Heb 7:1–28

See: Priest, Miscellaneous Facts Concerning

See: Priest, Mosaic

- **Of kings.**

See: King

SUCCOTH

- **A city probably east of the Jordan.**
  - **Jacob builds a house in.**

Ge 33:17 — And Jacob journeyed to Succoth, and built him an house, and made booths for his cattle: therefore the name of the place is called Succoth.

  - **Allotted to Gad.**

Jos 13:27 — And in the valley, Beth-aram, and Beth-nimrah, and Succoth, and Zaphon, the rest of the kingdom of Sihon king of Heshbon, Jordan and *his* border, *even* unto the edge of the sea of Chinnereth on the other side Jordan eastward.

  - **People of, punished by Gideon.**

Jgs 8:5–8, 14–16

  - **Located near the Jordan.**

1Ki 7:46 — In the plain of Jordan did the king cast them, in the clay ground between Succoth and Zarthan.

2Ch 4:17 — In the plain of Jordan did the king cast them, in the clay ground between Succoth and Zeredathah.

Ps 60:6 — God hath spoken in his holiness; I will rejoice, I will divide Shechem, and mete out the valley of Succoth.

Ps 108:7 — God hath spoken in his holiness; I will rejoice, I will divide Shechem, and mete out the valley of Succoth.

- **First camping place of the Israelites on leaving Rameses.**

Nu 33:5–6

Ex 12:37 — And the children of Israel journeyed from Rameses to Succoth, about six hundred thousand on foot *that were* men, beside children.

Ex 13:20 — And they took their journey from Succoth, and encamped in Etham, in the edge of the wilderness.

SUFFERING

- **For Christ.**

Ro 8:17–23; 1Co 4:12–13; 2Co 4:11–18; Php 2:27–30; 2Th 1:4–5; 1Pe 4:13–14

Ac 9:16 — For I will shew him how great things he must suffer for my name's sake.

Ro 8:26 — Likewise the Spirit also helpeth our infirmities: for we know not what we should pray for as we ought: but the Spirit itself maketh intercession for us with groanings which cannot be uttered.

2Co 1:7 — And our hope of you *is* stedfast, knowing, that as ye are partakers of the sufferings, so *shall ye be* also of the consolation.

Php 1:29 — For unto you it is given in the behalf of Christ, not only to believe on him, but also to suffer for his sake;

Php 3:10 — That I may know him, and the power of his resurrection, and the fellowship of his sufferings, being made conformable unto his death;

Col 1:24 — Who now rejoice in my sufferings for you, and fill up that which is behind of the afflictions of Christ in my flesh for his body's sake, which is the church:

2Ti 2:12 — If we suffer, we shall also reign with *him:* if we deny *him,* he also will deny us:

Jas 5:10 — Take, my brethren, the prophets, who have spoken in the name of the Lord, for an example of suffering affliction, and of patience.

1Pe 5:10 — But the God of all grace, who hath called us unto his eternal glory by Christ Jesus, after that ye have suffered a while, make you perfect, stablish, strengthen, settle *you.*

See: Afflictions

See: Persecution

• **Of Christ.**

Lk 24:46–47; Jn 11:50–52; Ro 5:6–8; 1Co 1:17–18, 23–24; 2Co 5:14–15; Gal 2:20–21; 1Th 5:9–10; Heb 2:9–10; 5:8–9; 9:15–16; 10:18–20

Lk 24:26 — Ought not Christ to have suffered these things, and to enter into his glory?

Jn 6:51 — I am the living bread which came down from heaven: if any man eat of this bread, he shall live for ever: and the bread that I will give is my flesh, which I will give for the life of the world.

Jn 10:11 — I am the good shepherd: the good shepherd giveth his life for the sheep.

Jn 10:15 — As the Father knoweth me, even so know I the Father: and I lay down my life for the sheep.

Ro 4:25 — Who was delivered for our offences, and was raised again for our justification.

Ro 14:15 — But if thy brother be grieved with *thy* meat, now walkest thou not charitably. Destroy not him with thy meat, for whom Christ died.

1Co 8:11 — And through thy knowledge shall the weak brother perish, for whom Christ died?

1Co 15:3 — For I delivered unto you first of all that which I also received, how that Christ died for our sins according to the scriptures;

Gal 1:4 — Who gave himself for our sins, that he might deliver us from this present evil world, according to the will of God and our Father:

Eph 5:2 — And walk in love, as Christ also hath loved us, and hath given himself for us an offering and a sacrifice to God for a sweetsmelling savour.

Eph 5:25 — Husbands, love your wives, even as Christ also loved the church, and gave himself for it;

Heb 2:14 — Forasmuch then as the children are partakers of flesh and blood, he also himself likewise took part of the same; that through death he might destroy him that had the power of death, that is, the devil;

Heb 2:18 — For in that he himself hath suffered being tempted, he is able to succour them that are tempted.

Heb 9:28 — So Christ was once offered to bear the sins of many; and unto them that look for him shall he appear the second time without sin unto salvation.

Heb 10:10 — By the which will we are sanctified through the offering of the body of Jesus Christ once *for all.*

1Pe 2:21 — For even hereunto were ye called: because Christ also suffered for us, leaving us an example, that ye should follow his steps:

1Pe 2:24 — Who his own self bare our sins in his own body on the tree, that we, being dead to sins, should live unto righteousness: by whose stripes ye were healed.

1Pe 3:18 — For Christ also hath once suffered for sins, the just for the unjust, that he might bring us to God, being put to death in the flesh, but quickened by the Spirit:

1Pe 4:1 — Forasmuch then as Christ hath suffered for us in the flesh, arm yourselves likewise with the same mind: for he that hath suffered in the flesh hath ceased from sin;

1Jn 3:16 — Hereby perceive we the love *of God,* because he laid down his life for us: and we ought to lay down *our* lives for the brethren.

See: Atonement

See: Jesus, Death of; design of his death

See: Jesus, Sufferings of

• **Vicarious.**

Ex 9:13–16

Jn 15:13 — Greater love hath no man than this, that a man lay down his life for his friends.

Ro 9:3 — For I could wish that myself were accursed from Christ for my brethren, my kinsmen according to the flesh:

1Pe 2:21 — For even hereunto were ye called: because Christ also suffered for us, leaving us an example, that ye should follow his steps:

1Jn 3:16 — Hereby perceive we the love *of God,* because he laid down his life for us: and we ought to lay down *our* lives for the brethren.

See: Suffering; of Christ

• **Instances of.**

• **Goliath for the Philistines.**

1Sa 17:1–58

SUICIDE

Am 9:2 — Though they dig into hell, thence shall mine hand take them; though they climb up to heaven, thence will I bring them down:

Rev 9:6 — And in those days shall men seek death, and shall not find it; and shall desire to die, and death shall flee from them.

• **Temptation to, of Jesus.**

Mt 4:5–6; Lk 4:9–11

• **Of the Philippian jailer.**

Ac 16:27 — And the keeper of the prison awaking out of his sleep, and seeing the prison doors open, he drew out his sword, and would have killed himself, supposing that the prisoners had been fled.

See: Death; desired

- **Instances of.**
  - **Samson.**
    Jgs 16:29–30
  - **Saul and his armor-bearer.**
    1Sa 31:4–5; 1Ch 10:4–5
  - **Ahithophel.**
    2Sa 17:23
  - **Zimri.**
    1Ki 16:18
  - **Judas.**
    Mt 27:5; Ac 1:18

SUING

Mt 5:40 — And if any man will sue thee at the law, and take away thy coat, let him have *thy* cloke also.

See: Creditor

See: Debtor

SUKKIIMS

- **An African race.**
- **Invaded Judah with Shishak.**

2Ch 12:3 — With twelve hundred chariots, and threescore thousand horsemen: and the people *were* without number that came with him out of Egypt; the Lubim, the Sukkiims, and the Ethiopians.

SUMMER

- **Season of, promised while the earth remains.**

Ge 8:22 — While the earth remaineth, seedtime and harvest, and cold and heat, and summer and winter, and day and night shall not cease.

- **Cool rooms for.**

Jgs 3:20 — And Ehud came unto him; and he was sitting in a summer parlour, which he had for himself alone. And Ehud said, I have a message from God unto thee. And he arose out of *his* seat.

Jgs 3:24 — When he was gone out, his servants came; and when they saw that, behold, the doors of the parlour *were* locked, they said, Surely he covereth his feet in his summer chamber.

Am 3:15 — And I will smite the winter house with the summer house; and the houses of ivory shall perish, and the great houses shall have an end, saith the Lord.

- **Fruits of.**

2Sa 16:1–2; Am 8:1–2

Isa 16:9 — Therefore I will bewail with the weeping of Jazer the vine of Sibmah: I will water thee with my tears, O Heshbon, and Elealeh: for the shouting for thy summer fruits and for thy harvest is fallen.

Isa 28:4 — And the glorious beauty, which is on the head of the fat valley, shall be a fading flower, *and* as the hasty fruit before the summer; which *when* he that looketh upon it seeth, while it is yet in his hand he eateth it up.

Jer 40:10 — As for me, behold, I will dwell at Mizpah to serve the Chaldeans, which will come unto us: but ye, gather ye wine, and summer fruits, and oil, and put *them* in your vessels, and dwell in your cities that ye have taken.

Jer 40:12 — Even all the Jews returned out of all places whither they were driven, and came to the land of Judah, to Gedaliah, unto Mizpah, and gathered wine and summer fruits very much.

Jer 48:32 — O vine of Sibmah, I will weep for thee with the weeping of Jazer: thy plants are gone over the sea, they reach *even* to the sea of Jazer: the spoiler is fallen upon thy summer fruits and upon thy vintage.

Mic 7:1 — Woe is me! for I am as when they have gathered the summer fruits, as the grapegleanings of the vintage: *there is* no cluster to eat: my soul desired the firstripe fruit.

- **Drought of.**

Ps 32:4 — For day and night thy hand was heavy upon me: my moisture is turned into the drought of summer. Selah.

- **Given by God.**

Ps 74:17 — Thou hast set all the borders of the earth: thou hast made summer and winter.

- **The time for labor and harvest.**

Pr 6:6–8

Pr 10:5 — He that gathereth in summer *is* a wise son: *but* he that sleepeth in harvest *is* a son that causeth shame.

Pr 30:25 — The ants *are* a people not strong, yet they prepare their meat in the summer;

Jer 8:20 — The harvest is past, the summer is ended, and we are not saved.

- **Snow in.**

Pr 26:1 — As snow in summer, and as rain in harvest, so honour is not seemly for a fool.

- **Threshing in.**

Da 2:35 — Then was the iron, the clay, the brass, the silver, and the gold, broken to pieces together, and became like the chaff of the summer threshingfloors; and the wind carried them away, that no place was found for them: and the stone that smote the image became a great mountain, and filled the whole earth.

- **Approach of.**

Mt 24:32 — Now learn a parable of the fig tree; When his branch is yet tender, and putteth forth leaves, ye know that summer is nigh:

Mk 13:28 — Now learn a parable of the fig tree; When her branch is yet tender, and putteth forth leaves, ye know that summer is near:

Lk 21:30 — When they now shoot forth, ye see and know of your own selves that summer is now nigh at hand.

- **Figurative.**

Jer 8:20 — The harvest is past, the summer is ended, and we are not saved.

SUN

• Created.

Ge 1:14–18

Ps 74:16 — The day *is* thine, the night also *is* thine: thou hast prepared the light and the sun.

Ps 136:7 — To him that made great lights: for his mercy *endureth* for ever:

Jer 31:35 — Thus saith the LORD, which giveth the sun for a light by day, *and* the ordinances of the moon and of the stars for a light by night, which divideth the sea when the waves thereof roar; The LORD of hosts *is* his name:

• Rising and setting of.

Ecc 1:5 — The sun also ariseth, and the sun goeth down, and hasteth to his place where he arose.

• Diurnal motion of.

Ps 19:4 — Their line is gone out through all the earth, and their words to the end of the world. In them hath he set a tabernacle for the sun,

Ps 19:6 — His going forth *is* from the end of the heaven, and his circuit unto the ends of it: and there is nothing hid from the heat thereof.

• Worship of, forbidden.

Dt 4:19 — And lest thou lift up thine eyes unto heaven, and when thou seest the sun, and the moon, and the stars, *even* all the host of heaven, shouldest be driven to worship them, and serve them, which the LORD thy God hath divided unto all nations under the whole heaven.

Dt 17:3 — And hath gone and served other gods, and worshipped them, either the sun, or moon, or any of the host of heaven, which I have not commanded;

• Worshiped.

Job 31:26–28

Jer 8:2 — And they shall spread them before the sun, and the moon, and all the host of heaven, whom they have loved, and whom they have served, and after whom they have walked, and whom they have sought, and whom they have worshipped: they shall not be gathered, nor be buried; they shall be for dung upon the face of the earth.

Eze 6:4 — And your altars shall be desolate, and your images shall be broken: and I will cast down your slain *men* before your idols.

Eze 6:6 — In all your dwellingplaces the cities shall be laid waste, and the high places shall be desolate; that your altars may be laid waste and made desolate, and your idols may be broken and cease, and your images may be cut down, and your works may be abolished.

Eze 8:16 — And he brought me into the inner court of the LORD's house, and, behold, at the door of the temple of the LORD, between the porch and the altar, *were* about five and twenty men, with their backs toward the temple of the LORD, and their faces toward the east; and they worshipped the sun toward the east.

• Kings of Judah dedicate horses to.

2Ki 23:11 — And he took away the horses that the kings of Judah had given to the sun, at the entering in of the house of the LORD, by the chamber of Nathan-melech the chamberlain, which *was* in the suburbs, and burned the chariots of the sun with fire.

• Miracles concerning.

• Darkening of.

Ex 10:21–23; Lk 23:44–45

Isa 5:30 — And in that day they shall roar against them like the roaring of the sea: and if *one* look unto the land, behold darkness *and* sorrow, and the light is darkened in the heavens thereof.

Isa 24:23 — Then the moon shall be confounded, and the sun ashamed, when the LORD of hosts shall reign in mount Zion, and in Jerusalem, and before his ancients gloriously.

Eze 32:7 — And when I shall put thee out, I will cover the heaven, and make the stars thereof dark; I will cover the sun with a cloud, and the moon shall not give her light.

Joel 2:10 — The earth shall quake before them; the heavens shall tremble: the sun and the moon shall be dark, and the stars shall withdraw their shining:

Joel 2:31 — The sun shall be turned into darkness, and the moon into blood, before the great and the terrible day of the LORD come.

Joel 3:15 — The sun and the moon shall be darkened, and the stars shall withdraw their shining.

Am 8:9 — And it shall come to pass in that day, saith the Lord GOD, that I will cause the sun to go down at noon, and I will darken the earth in the clear day:

Mic 3:6 — Therefore night *shall be* unto you, that ye shall not have a vision; and it shall be dark unto you, that ye shall not divine; and the sun shall go down over the prophets, and the day shall be dark over them.

Mt 24:29 — Immediately after the tribulation of those days shall the sun be darkened, and the moon shall not give her light, and the stars shall fall from heaven, and the powers of the heavens shall be shaken:

Mt 27:45 — Now from the sixth hour there was darkness over all the land unto the ninth hour.

Mk 13:24 — But in those days, after that tribulation, the sun shall be darkened, and the moon shall not give her light,

Mk 15:33 — And when the sixth hour was come, there was darkness over the whole land until the ninth hour.

Lk 21:25 — And there shall be signs in the sun, and in the moon, and in the stars; and upon the earth distress of nations, with perplexity; the sea and the waves roaring;

Ac 2:20 — The sun shall be turned into darkness, and the moon into blood, before that great and notable day of the Lord come:

Rev 6:12 — And I beheld when he had opened the sixth seal, and, lo, there was a great earthquake; and the sun became black as sackcloth of hair, and the moon became as blood;

Rev 8:12 — And the fourth angel sounded, and the third part of the sun was smitten, and the third part of the moon, and the third part of the stars; so as the third part of them was darkened, and the day shone not for a third part of it, and the night likewise.

Rev 9:2 — And he opened the bottomless pit; and there arose a smoke out of the pit, as the smoke of a great furnace; and the sun and the air were darkened by reason of the smoke of the pit.

Rev 16:8 — And the fourth angel poured out his vial upon the sun; and power was given unto him to scorch men with fire.

• Stands still.

Jos 10:12–13

Hab 3:11 — The sun *and* moon stood still in their habitation: at the light of thine arrows they went, *and* at the shining of thy glittering spear.

• Shadow of, goes back on Ahaz's dial.

2Ki 20:11 — And Isaiah the prophet cried unto the LORD: and he brought the shadow ten degrees backward, by which it had gone down in the dial of Ahaz.

Isa 38:8 — Behold, I will bring again the shadow of the degrees, which is gone down in the sun dial of Ahaz, ten degrees backward. So the sun returned ten degrees, by which degrees it was gone down.

• Does not shine in heaven.

Rev 21:23 — And the city had no need of the sun, neither of the moon, to shine in it: for the glory of God did lighten it, and the Lamb *is* the light thereof.

• Figurative.

Isa 60:19–20

Jgs 5:31 — So let all thine enemies perish, O LORD: but *let* them that love him *be* as the sun when he goeth forth in his might. And the land had rest forty years.

Ps 84:11 — For the LORD God *is* a sun and shield: the LORD will give grace and glory: no good *thing* will he withhold from them that walk uprightly.

Isa 30:26 — Moreover the light of the moon shall be as the light of the sun, and the light of the sun shall be sevenfold, as the light of seven days, in the day that the LORD bindeth up the breach of his people, and healeth the stroke of their wound.

Jer 15:9 — She that hath borne seven languisheth: she hath given up the ghost; her sun is gone down while *it was* yet day: she hath been ashamed and confounded: and the residue of them will I deliver to the sword before their enemies, saith the LORD.

Mal 4:2 — But unto you that fear my name shall the Sun of righteousness arise with healing in his wings; and ye shall go forth, and grow up as calves of the stall.

Rev 1:16 — And he had in his right hand seven stars: and out of his mouth went a sharp twoedged sword: and his countenance *was* as the sun shineth in his strength.

Rev 12:1 — And there appeared a great wonder in heaven; a woman clothed with the sun, and the moon under her feet, and upon her head a crown of twelve stars:

Rev 19:17 — And I saw an angel standing in the sun; and he cried with a loud voice, saying to all the fowls that fly in the midst of heaven, Come and gather yourselves together unto the supper of the great God;

SUN DIAL

2Ki 20:11 — And Isaiah the prophet cried unto the LORD: and he brought the shadow ten degrees backward, by which it had gone down in the dial of Ahaz.

Isa 38:8 — Behold, I will bring again the shadow of the degrees, which is gone down in the sun dial of Ahaz, ten degrees backward. So the sun returned ten degrees, by which degrees it was gone down.

SUNSTROKE

2Ki 4:19 — And he said unto his father, My head, my head. And he said to a lad, Carry him to his mother.

SUPEREROGATION • The doctrine of excessive and meritorious righteousness.

Eze 33:12–13

Lk 17:10 — So likewise ye, when ye shall have done all those things which are commanded you, say, We are unprofitable servants: we have done that which was our duty to do.

SUPERSCRIPTION

• On the cross.

Mt 27:37 — And set up over his head his accusation written, THIS IS JESUS THE KING OF THE JEWS.

Mk 15:26 — And the superscription of his accusation was written over, THE KING OF THE JEWS.

Lk 23:38 — And a superscription also was written over him in letters of Greek, and Latin, and Hebrew, THIS IS THE KING OF THE JEWS.

Jn 19:19 — And Pilate wrote a title, and put *it* on the cross. And the writing was, JESUS OF NAZARETH THE KING OF THE JEWS.

SUPERSTITION

Ac 25:19 — But had certain questions against him of their own superstition, and of one Jesus, which was dead, whom Paul affirmed to be alive.

• Instances of.

• Israelites, with the ark of the covenant.

1Sa 4:3, 10–11

• Philistines, refusing to tread the threshold of the temple of Dagon.

1Sa 5:5

• The belief of the Syrians concerning the help of the gods.

1Ki 20:23

• Jews, attributing their calamities to having ceased offering sacrifices to the queen of heaven.

Jer 44:17–19

• Nebuchadnezzar, supposing that the spirit of the gods was upon Daniel.

Da 4:8–9

• The sailors who cast Jonah into the sea.

Jnh 1:4–16

• The disciples, supposing they saw a spirit when Jesus came walking upon the sea.
Mt 14:26; Mk 6:49–50

• Herod, imagining that John the Baptist had risen from the dead.
Mk 6:14, 16

• The Gadarenes, on account of Jesus casting devils out of the Gadarene.
Mt 8:34

• The disciples who were frightened at the appearance of Peter.
Ac 12:14–15

• The Ephesians, in their sorceries.
Ac 19:13–19

• The people of the island of Melita, in imagining Paul to be a god.
Ac 28:6

✣See: Idolatry

✣See: Sorcery

SUPPER

✣See: Eucharist

✣See: Feasts

SUR • Gate of the temple.

2Ki 11:6 — And a third part *shall be* at the gate of Sur; and a third part at the gate behind the guard: so shall ye keep the watch of the house, that it be not broken down.

SURETY

Ex 22:26–27; Dt 24:10–13; Pr 6:1–5

Ge 44:32 — For thy servant became surety for the lad unto my father, saying, If I bring him not unto thee, then I shall bear the blame to my father for ever.

Pr 11:15 — He that is surety for a stranger shall smart *for it:* and he that hateth suretiship is sure.

Pr 17:18 — A man void of understanding striketh hands, *and* becometh surety in the presence of his friend.

Pr 20:16 — Take his garment that is surety *for* a stranger: and take a pledge of him for a strange woman.

Pr 22:26 — Be not thou *one* of them that strike hands, *or* of them that are sureties for debts.

Pr 27:13 — Take his garment that is surety for a stranger, and take a pledge of him for a strange woman.

Eze 18:7 — And hath not oppressed any, *but* hath restored to the debtor his pledge, hath spoiled none by violence, hath given his bread to the hungry, and hath covered the naked with a garment;

Eze 18:12 — Hath oppressed the poor and needy, hath spoiled by violence, hath not restored the pledge, and hath lifted up his eyes to the idols, hath committed abomination,

Eze 33:15 — *If* the wicked restore the pledge, give again that he had robbed, walk in the statutes of life, without committing iniquity; he shall surely live, he shall not die.

Am 2:8 — And they lay *themselves* down upon clothes laid to pledge by every altar, and they drink the wine of the condemned in the house of their god.

SURFEITING

✣See: Drunkenness

✣See: Gluttony

SUSANCHITES • Inhabitants of Samaria.

Ezr 4:9–10

SUSANNA • A woman who ministered to Jesus.

Lk 8:3 — And Joanna the wife of Chuza Herod's steward, and Susanna, and many others, which ministered unto him of their substance.

SUSI • A Manassite.

Nu 13:11 — Of the tribe of Joseph, namely, of the tribe of Manasseh, Gaddi the son of Susi.

SUSPICION ✣See: Accusation, False

SWADDLE

• Of children.

Job 38:9 — When I made the cloud the garment thereof, and thick darkness a swaddlingband for it,

La 2:22 — Thou hast called as in a solemn day my terrors round about, so that in the day of the LORD's anger none escaped nor remained: those that I have swaddled and brought up hath mine enemy consumed.

Eze 16:4 — And *as for* thy nativity, in the day thou wast born thy navel was not cut, neither wast thou washed in water to supple *thee;* thou wast not salted at all, nor swaddled at all.

Lk 2:7 — And she brought forth her firstborn son, and wrapped him in swaddling clothes, and laid him in a manger; because there was no room for them in the inn.

Lk 2:12 — And this *shall be* a sign unto you; Ye shall find the babe wrapped in swaddling clothes, lying in a manger.

SWALLOW

• Builds its nest in the sanctuary.

Ps 84:3 — Yea, the sparrow hath found an house, and the swallow a nest for herself, where she may lay her young, *even* thine altars, O LORD of hosts, my King, and my God.

• Chattering of, figurative the mourning of the afflicted.

Isa 38:14 — Like a crane *or* a swallow, so did I chatter: I did mourn as a dove: mine eyes fail *with looking* upward: O LORD, I am oppressed; undertake for me.

• Migration of.

Jer 8:7 — Yea, the stork in the heaven knoweth her appointed times; and the turtle and the crane and the swallow observe the time of their coming; but my people know not the judgment of the LORD.

SWAN

• Forbidden as food.

Le 11:18 — And the swan, and the pelican, and the gier eagle,

Dt 14:16 — The little owl, and the great owl, and the swan,

SWEARING

See: Blasphemy

See: God; name of; not to be profaned

See: Oath

SWEAT

Ge 3:19 — In the sweat of thy face shalt thou eat bread, till thou return unto the ground; for out of it wast thou taken: for dust thou *art,* and unto dust shalt thou return.

• An offense in the sanctuary.

Eze 44:18 — They shall have linen bonnets upon their heads, and shall have linen breeches upon their loins; they shall not gird *themselves* with any thing that causeth sweat.

• Of blood.

Lk 22:44 — And being in an agony he prayed more earnestly: and his sweat was as it were great drops of blood falling down to the ground.

SWEET INCENSE

• Made of spices.

Ex 25:6 — Oil for the light, spices for anointing oil, and for sweet incense,

See: Incense

SWINE

• Forbidden as food.

Le 11:7 — And the swine, though he divide the hoof, and be clovenfooted, yet he cheweth not the cud; he *is* unclean to you.

Dt 14:8 — And the swine, because it divideth the hoof, yet cheweth not the cud, it is unclean unto you: ye shall not eat of their flesh, nor touch their dead carcase.

• Used for food.

Isa 65:4 — Which remain among the graves, and lodge in the monuments, which eat swine's flesh, and broth of abominable *things is in* their vessels;

Isa 66:17 — They that sanctify themselves, and purify themselves in the gardens behind one *tree* in the midst, eating swine's flesh, and the abomination, and the mouse, shall be consumed together, saith the LORD.

• Used for sacrifice.

Isa 66:3 — He that killeth an ox *is as if* he slew a man; he that sacrificeth a lamb, *as if* he cut off a dog's neck; he that offereth an oblation, *as if he offered* swine's blood; he that burneth incense, *as if* he blessed an idol. Yea, they have chosen their own ways, and their soul delighteth in their abominations.

• Wild boar.

Ps 80:13 — The boar out of the wood doth waste it, and the wild beast of the field doth devour it.

• Jewels in the nose of.

Pr 11:22 — *As* a jewel of gold in a swine's snout, *so is* a fair woman which is without discretion.

• Viciousness of.

Mt 7:6 — Give not that which is holy unto the dogs, neither cast ye your pearls before swine, lest they trample them under their feet, and turn again and rend you.

• Jesus sends devils into.

Mt 8:28–32; Mk 5:11–14; Lk 8:32–33

• Feeding of.

Lk 15:15–16

• Sow returns to her wallow.

2Pe 2:22 — But it is happened unto them according to the true proverb, The dog *is* turned to his own vomit again; and the sow that was washed to her wallowing in the mire.

SWORD

• Used by Gideon.

Jgs 7:20 — And the three companies blew the trumpets, and brake the pitchers, and held the lamps in their left hands, and the trumpets in their right hands to blow *withal:* and they cried, The sword of the LORD, and of Gideon.

• Used by Goliath.

1Sa 21:9 — And the priest said, The sword of Goliath the Philistine, whom thou slewest in the valley of Elah, behold, it *is here* wrapped in a cloth behind the ephod: if thou wilt take that, take *it:* for *there is* no other save that here. And David said, *There is* none like that; give it me.

• Used by Peter.

Mt 26:51 — And, behold, one of them which were with Jesus stretched out *his* hand, and drew his sword, and struck a servant of the high priest's, and smote off his ear.

Jn 18:10 — Then Simon Peter having a sword drew it, and smote the high priest's servant, and cut off his right ear. The servant's name was Malchus.

• David's army equipped with.

1Ch 21:5 — And Joab gave the sum of the number of the people unto David. And all *they of* Israel were a thousand thousand and an hundred thousand men that drew sword: and Judah *was* four hundred threescore and ten thousand men that drew sword.

• To be beaten into plowshares.

Isa 2:4 — And he shall judge among the nations, and shall rebuke many people: and they shall beat their swords into plowshares, and their spears into pruninghooks: nation shall not lift up sword against nation, neither shall they learn war any more.

Mic 4:3 — And he shall judge among many people, and rebuke strong nations afar off; and they shall beat their swords into plowshares, and their spears into pruninghooks: nation shall not lift up a sword against nation, neither shall they learn war any more.

• **Made of plowshares.**

Joel 3:10 — Beat your plowshares into swords, and your pruninghooks into spears: let the weak say, I *am* strong.

• **Two-edged.**

Heb 4:12 — For the word of God *is* quick, and powerful, and sharper than any twoedged sword, piercing even to the dividing asunder of soul and spirit, and of the joints and marrow, and *is* a discerner of the thoughts and intents of the heart.

Rev 1:16 — And he had in his right hand seven stars: and out of his mouth went a sharp twoedged sword: and his countenance *was* as the sun shineth in his strength.

Rev 2:12 — And to the angel of the church in Pergamos write; These things saith he which hath the sharp sword with two edges;

• **Figurative.**

• **Of war.**

Ge 27:40 — And by thy sword shalt thou live, and shalt serve thy brother; and it shall come to pass when thou shalt have the dominion, that thou shalt break his yoke from off thy neck.

• **Of judgments.**

Dt 32:41 — If I whet my glittering sword, and mine hand take hold on judgment; I will render vengeance to mine enemies, and will reward them that hate me.

Ps 17:13 — Arise, O LORD, disappoint him, cast him down: deliver my soul from the wicked, *which is* thy sword:

Hos 11:6 — And the sword shall abide on his cities, and shall consume his branches, and devour *them,* because of their own counsels.

Zec 13:7 — Awake, O sword, against my shepherd, and against the man *that is* my fellow, saith the LORD of hosts: smite the shepherd, and the sheep shall be scattered: and I will turn mine hand upon the little ones.

• **Of the malicious tongue.**

Ps 57:4 — My soul *is* among lions: *and* I lie *even among* them that are set on fire, *even* the sons of men, whose teeth *are* spears and arrows, and their tongue a sharp sword.

Pr 25:18 — A man that beareth false witness against his neighbour *is* a maul, and a sword, and a sharp arrow.

• **Symbolic.**

Ge 3:24 — So he drove out the man; and he placed at the east of the garden of Eden Cherubim, and a flaming sword which turned every way, to keep the way of the tree of life.

Jos 5:13 — And it came to pass, when Joshua was by Jericho, that he lifted up his eyes and looked, and, behold, there stood a man over against him with his sword drawn in his hand: and Joshua went unto him, and said unto him, *Art* thou for us, or for our adversaries?

Rev 1:16 — And he had in his right hand seven stars: and out of his mouth went a sharp twoedged sword: and his countenance *was* as the sun shineth in his strength.

SYCAMINE • A tree.

Lk 17:6 — And the Lord said, If ye had faith as a grain of mustard seed, ye might say unto this sycamine tree, Be thou plucked up by the root, and be thou planted in the sea; and it should obey you.

SYCAMORE

• **A tree.**

• **Abundant in the land of Canaan.**

1Ki 10:27 — And the king made silver *to be* in Jerusalem as stones, and cedars made he *to be* as the sycomore trees that *are* in the vale, for abundance.

2Ch 1:15 — And the king made silver and gold at Jerusalem *as plenteous* as stones, and cedar trees made he as the sycomore trees that *are* in the vale for abundance.

2Ch 9:27 — And the king made silver in Jerusalem as stones, and cedar trees made he as the sycomore trees that *are* in the low plains in abundance.

Isa 9:10 — The bricks are fallen down, but we will build with hewn stones: the sycomores are cut down, but we will change *them into* cedars.

• **Groves of, cared for.**

1Ch 27:28 — And over the olive trees and the sycomore trees that *were* in the low plains *was* Baal-hanan the Gederite: and over the cellars of oil *was* Joash:

• **Destroyed by frost.**

Ps 78:47 — He destroyed their vines with hail, and their sycomore trees with frost.

• **Care of.**

Am 7:14 — Then answered Amos, and said to Amaziah, I *was* no prophet, neither *was* I a prophet's son; but I *was* an herdman, and a gatherer of sycomore fruit:

• **Zacchaeus climbs into.**

Lk 19:4 — And he ran before, and climbed up into a sycomore tree to see him: for he was to pass that *way.*

SYCHAR

• **A city of refuge in Mount Ephraim.**

See: Shechem; called also Sychar

SYCHEM

• **A district in the central part of the land of Canaan; Abraham dwells in.**

See: Shechem; called also Sichem and Sychem

SYENE • A city in Egypt.

Eze 29:10 — Behold, therefore I *am* against thee, and against thy rivers, and I will make the land of Egypt utterly waste *and* desolate, from the tower of Syene even unto the border of Ethiopia.

Eze 30:6 — Thus saith the LORD; They also that uphold Egypt shall fall; and the pride of her power shall come down: from the tower of Syene shall they fall in it by the sword, saith the Lord GOD.

SYMBOLS AND SIMILITUDES

• Of the Holy Spirit.

• Water.

Jn 7:38–39

Jn 3:5 — Jesus answered, Verily, verily, I say unto thee, Except a man be born of water and *of* the Spirit, he cannot enter into the kingdom of God.

• Cleansing by.

Eze 16:9 — Then washed I thee with water; yea, I throughly washed away thy blood from thee, and I anointed thee with oil.

Eze 36:25 — Then will I sprinkle clean water upon you, and ye shall be clean: from all your filthiness, and from all your idols, will I cleanse you.

Eph 5:26 — That he might sanctify and cleanse it with the washing of water by the word,

Heb 10:22 — Let us draw near with a true heart in full assurance of faith, having our hearts sprinkled from an evil conscience, and our bodies washed with pure water.

• Vivifying.

Isa 44:3–4

Ps 1:3 — And he shall be like a tree planted by the rivers of water, that bringeth forth his fruit in his season; his leaf also shall not wither; and whatsoever he doeth shall prosper.

Isa 27:3 — I the LORD do keep it; I will water it every moment: lest *any* hurt it, I will keep it night and day.

Isa 27:6 — He shall cause them that come of Jacob to take root: Israel shall blossom and bud, and fill the face of the world with fruit.

Isa 58:11 — And the LORD shall guide thee continually, and satisfy thy soul in drought, and make fat thy bones: and thou shalt be like a watered garden, and like a spring of water, whose waters fail not.

• Fire.

Mt 3:11 — I indeed baptize you with water unto repentance: but he that cometh after me is mightier than I, whose shoes I am not worthy to bear: he shall baptize you with the Holy Ghost, and *with* fire:

• Purifying.

Mal 3:2–3

Isa 4:4 — When the Lord shall have washed away the filth of the daughters of Zion, and shall have purged the blood of Jerusalem from the midst thereof by the spirit of judgment, and by the spirit of burning.

• Illuminating.

Ex 13:21 — And the LORD went before them by day in a pillar of a cloud, to lead them the way; and by night in a pillar of fire, to give them light; to go by day and night:

Ps 78:14 — In the daytime also he led them with a cloud, and all the night with a light of fire.

• Searching.

Zep 1:12 — And it shall come to pass at that time, *that* I will search Jerusalem with candles, and punish the men that are settled on their lees: that say in their heart, The LORD will not do good, neither will he do evil.

1Co 2:10 — But God hath revealed *them* unto us by his Spirit: for the Spirit searcheth all things, yea, the deep things of God.

• Wind.

SS 4:16 — Awake, O north wind; and come, thou south; blow upon my garden, *that* the spices thereof may flow out. Let my beloved come into his garden, and eat his pleasant fruits.

• Incomprehensible.

Jn 3:8 — The wind bloweth where it listeth, and thou hearest the sound thereof, but canst not tell whence it cometh, and whither it goeth: so is every one that is born of the Spirit.

1Co 12:11 — But all these worketh that one and the selfsame Spirit, dividing to every man severally as he will.

• Powerful.

1Ki 19:11 — And he said, Go forth, and stand upon the mount before the LORD. And, behold, the LORD passed by, and a great and strong wind rent the mountains, and brake in pieces the rocks before the LORD; *but* the LORD *was* not in the wind: and after the wind an earthquake; *but* the LORD *was* not in the earthquake:

Ac 2:2 — And suddenly there came a sound from heaven as of a rushing mighty wind, and it filled all the house where they were sitting.

• Sensible in its effects.

Jn 3:8 — The wind bloweth where it listeth, and thou hearest the sound thereof, but canst not tell whence it cometh, and whither it goeth: so is every one that is born of the Spirit.

• Reviving.

Eze 37:9–10

Eze 37:14 — And shall put my spirit in you, and ye shall live, and I shall place you in your own land: then shall ye know that I the LORD have spoken *it,* and performed *it,* saith the LORD.

• Oil.

Ps 45:7 — Thou lovest righteousness, and hatest wickedness: therefore God, thy God, hath anointed thee with the oil of gladness above thy fellows.

• Healing.

Isa 1:6 — From the sole of the foot even unto the head *there is* no soundness in it; *but* wounds, and bruises, and putrifying sores: they have not been closed, neither bound up, neither mollified with ointment.

Lk 10:34 — And went to *him,* and bound up his wounds, pouring in oil and wine, and set him on his own beast, and brought him to an inn, and took care of him.

Rev 18:13 — And cinnamon, and odours, and ointments, and frankincense, and wine, and oil, and fine flour, and wheat, and beasts, and sheep, and horses, and chariots, and slaves, and souls of men.

- **Comforting.**

Isa 61:3 — To appoint unto them that mourn in Zion, to give unto them beauty for ashes, the oil of joy for mourning, the garment of praise for the spirit of heaviness; that they might be called trees of righteousness, the planting of the LORD, that he might be glorified.

Heb 1:9 — Thou hast loved righteousness, and hated iniquity; therefore God, *even* thy God, hath anointed thee with the oil of gladness above thy fellows.

- **Illuminating.**

Zec 4:2–3, 11–13; Mt 25:3–4

1Jn 2:20 — But ye have an unction from the Holy One, and ye know all things.

1Jn 2:27 — But the anointing which ye have received of him abideth in you, and ye need not that any man teach you: but as the same anointing teacheth you of all things, and is truth, and is no lie, and even as it hath taught you, ye shall abide in him.

- **Consecrating.**

Ex 29:7 — Then shalt thou take the anointing oil, and pour *it* upon his head, and anoint him.

Ex 30:30 — And thou shalt anoint Aaron and his sons, and consecrate them, that *they* may minister unto me in the priest's office.

Isa 61:1 — The Spirit of the Lord GOD *is* upon me; because the LORD hath anointed me to preach good tidings unto the meek; he hath sent me to bind up the brokenhearted, to proclaim liberty to the captives, and the opening of the prison to *them that are* bound;

- **Rain and dew.**

Ps 72:6 — He shall come down like rain upon the mown grass: as showers *that* water the earth.

- **Fertilizing.**

Eze 34:26–27

Hos 6:3 — Then shall we know, *if* we follow on to know the LORD: his going forth is prepared as the morning; and he shall come unto us as the rain, as the latter *and* former rain unto the earth.

Hos 10:12 — Sow to yourselves in righteousness, reap in mercy; break up your fallow ground: for *it is* time to seek the LORD, till he come and rain righteousness upon you.

Hos 14:5 — I will be as the dew unto Israel: he shall grow as the lily, and cast forth his roots as Lebanon.

- **Refreshing.**

Ps 68:9 — Thou, O God, didst send a plentiful rain, whereby thou didst confirm thine inheritance, when it was weary.

Isa 18:4 — For so the LORD said unto me, I will take my rest, and I will consider in my dwelling place like a clear heat upon herbs, *and* like a cloud of dew in the heat of harvest.

- **Abundant.**

Ps 133:3 — As the dew of Hermon, *and as the dew* that descended upon the mountains of Zion: for there the LORD commanded the blessing, *even* life for evermore.

- **Imperceptible.**

Mk 4:26–28

2Sa 17:12 — So shall we come upon him in some place where he shall be found, and we will light upon him as the dew falleth on the ground: and of him and of all the men that *are* with him there shall not be left so much as one.

- **A dove.**

Mt 3:16 — And Jesus, when he was baptized, went up straightway out of the water: and, lo, the heavens were opened unto him, and he saw the Spirit of God descending like a dove, and lighting upon him:

- **A voice.**

Isa 6:8 — Also I heard the voice of the Lord, saying, Whom shall I send, and who will go for us? Then said I, Here *am* I; send me.

- **Speaking.**

Mt 10:20 — For it is not ye that speak, but the Spirit of your Father which speaketh in you.

- **Guiding.**

Isa 30:21 — And thine ears shall hear a word behind thee, saying, This *is* the way, walk ye in it, when ye turn to the right hand, and when ye turn to the left.

Jn 16:13 — Howbeit when he, the Spirit of truth, is come, he will guide you into all truth: for he shall not speak of himself; but whatsoever he shall hear, *that* shall he speak: and he will shew you things to come.

- **Warning.**

Heb 3:7–11

- **A seal.**

Rev 7:2 — And I saw another angel ascending from the east, having the seal of the living God: and he cried with a loud voice to the four angels, to whom it was given to hurt the earth and the sea,

- **Impressing.**

Job 38:14 — It is turned as clay *to* the seal; and they stand as a garment.

2Co 3:18 — But we all, with open face beholding as in a glass the glory of the Lord, are changed into the same image from glory to glory, *even* as by the Spirit of the Lord.

- **Earnest.**

Eph 1:13–14

2Co 1:22 — Who hath also sealed us, and given the earnest of the Spirit in our hearts.

Eph 4:30 — And grieve not the holy Spirit of God, whereby ye are sealed unto the day of redemption.

- **Cloven tongues.**

Ac 2:3 — And there appeared unto them cloven tongues like as of fire, and it sat upon each of them.

Ac 2:6 — Now when this was noised abroad, the multitude came together, and were confounded, because that every man heard them speak in his own language.

Ac 2:11 — Cretes and Arabians, we do hear them speak in our tongues the wonderful works of God.

• Trees of life and knowledge.

Ge 2:9 — And out of the ground made the LORD God to grow every tree that is pleasant to the sight, and good for food; the tree of life also in the midst of the garden, and the tree of knowledge of good and evil.

Ge 2:17 — But of the tree of the knowledge of good and evil, thou shalt not eat of it: for in the day that thou eatest thereof thou shalt surely die.

Ge 3:3 — But of the fruit of the tree which *is* in the midst of the garden, God hath said, Ye shall not eat of it, neither shall ye touch it, lest ye die.

Ge 3:24 — So he drove out the man; and he placed at the east of the garden of Eden Cherubim, and a flaming sword which turned every way, to keep the way of the tree of life.

Rev 22:2 — In the midst of the street of it, and on either side of the river, *was there* the tree of life, which bare twelve *manner* of fruits, *and* yielded her fruit every month: and the leaves of the tree *were* for the healing of the nations.

• Rainbow.

Ge 9:12–13

• Circumcision, of the covenant of Abraham.

Ge 17:11 — And ye shall circumcise the flesh of your foreskin; and it shall be a token of the covenant betwixt me and you.

Ro 4:11 — And he received the sign of circumcision, a seal of the righteousness of the faith which *he had yet* being uncircumcised: that he might be the father of all them that believe, though they be not circumcised; that righteousness might be imputed unto them also:

• Passover, of the sparing of the firstborn, and of the atonement made by Christ.

Ex 12:3–28

1Co 5:7 — Purge out therefore the old leaven, that ye may be a new lump, as ye are unleavened. For even Christ our passover is sacrificed for us:

• Of the divine presence, the pillar of cloud.

Ex 13:21–22; 14:19–20

Ex 19:9 — And the LORD said unto Moses, Lo, I come unto thee in a thick cloud, that the people may hear when I speak with thee, and believe thee for ever. And Moses told the words of the people unto the LORD.

Ex 19:16 — And it came to pass on the third day in the morning, that there were thunders and lightnings, and a thick cloud upon the mount, and the voice of the trumpet exceeding loud; so that all the people that *was* in the camp trembled.

• Of thunder on Mount Sinai.

Ex 19:9 — And the LORD said unto Moses, Lo, I come unto thee in a thick cloud, that the people may hear when I speak with thee, and believe thee for ever. And Moses told the words of the people unto the LORD.

Ex 19:16 — And it came to pass on the third day in the morning, that there were thunders and lightnings, and a thick cloud upon the mount, and the voice of the trumpet exceeding loud; so that all the people that *was* in the camp trembled.

• Darkness, of God's inscrutability.

Heb 12:18–19

Ex 20:21 — And the people stood afar off, and Moses drew near unto the thick darkness where God *was*.

Le 16:2 — And the LORD said unto Moses, Speak unto Aaron thy brother, that he come not at all times into the holy *place* within the vail before the mercy seat, which *is* upon the ark; that he die not: for I will appear in the cloud upon the mercy seat.

1Ki 8:12 — Then spake Solomon, The LORD said that he would dwell in thick darkness.

Ps 18:11 — He made darkness his secret place; his pavilion round about him *were* dark waters *and* thick clouds of the skies.

Ps 97:2 — Clouds and darkness *are* round about him: righteousness and judgment *are* the habitation of his throne.

• The smitten rock, of Christ.

Ex 17:6 — Behold, I will stand before thee there upon the rock in Horeb; and thou shalt smite the rock, and there shall come water out of it, that the people may drink. And Moses did so in the sight of the elders of Israel.

1Co 10:4 — And did all drink the same spiritual drink: for they drank of that spiritual Rock that followed them: and that Rock was Christ.

• The sprinkled blood, of the covenant.

Ex 24:8 — And Moses took the blood, and sprinkled *it* on the people, and said, Behold the blood of the covenant, which the LORD hath made with you concerning all these words.

• Wine, of the atoning blood.

Mt 26:27–29; Mk 14:23–25; Lk 22:17–18

Lk 22:20 — Likewise also the cup after supper, saying, This cup *is* the new testament in my blood, which is shed for you.

• The brazen serpent, of Christ.

Nu 21:8–9

Jn 3:14 — And as Moses lifted up the serpent in the wilderness, even so must the Son of man be lifted up:

• Sacrificial animals.

Ge 15:8–11

Jn 1:29 — The next day John seeth Jesus coming unto him, and saith, Behold the Lamb of God, which taketh away the sin of the world.

Jn 1:36 — And looking upon Jesus as he walked, he saith, Behold the Lamb of God!

• Waving the wave offering and heaving the heave offering.

Ex 29:24–28; Le 8:27–29

Le 9:21 — And the breasts and the right shoulder Aaron waved *for* a wave offering before the LORD; as Moses commanded.

- **The whole system of Mosaic rites.**

Heb 9:9–10, 18–23

- **Tabernacle.**

Heb 9:1–12, 23–24

Ps 15:1 — LORD, who shall abide in thy tabernacle? who shall dwell in thy holy hill?

Eze 37:27 — My tabernacle also shall be with them: yea, I will be their God, and they shall be my people.

Heb 8:2 — A minister of the sanctuary, and of the true tabernacle, which the Lord pitched, and not man.

Heb 8:5 — Who serve unto the example and shadow of heavenly things, as Moses was admonished of God when he was about to make the tabernacle: for, See, saith he, *that* thou make all things according to the pattern shewed to thee in the mount.

- **Sanctuary.**

Ps 20:2 — Send thee help from the sanctuary, and strengthen thee out of Zion;

- **Canaan, of the spiritual rest.**

Heb 3:11–12

Heb 4:5 — And in this *place* again, If they shall enter into my rest.

- **Salt.**

Nu 18:19 — All the heave offerings of the holy things, which the children of Israel offer unto the LORD, have I given thee, and thy sons and thy daughters with thee, by a statute for ever: it is a covenant of salt for ever before the LORD unto thee and to thy seed with thee.

- **Offering water to drink.**

Ge 24:13–15, 42–44

- **Lapping water.**

Jgs 7:4–8

- **Invitation to approach.**

1Sa 14:8–12

- **Bow-shot, by Jonathan.**

1Sa 20:21–37

- **Bow-shot, by Joash.**

2Ki 13:15–19

- **Men meeting Saul.**

1Sa 10:2–7

- **Rain and thunder.**

1Sa 12:16–18

- **Rent altar.**

1Ki 13:3 — And he gave a sign the same day, saying, This *is* the sign which the LORD hath spoken; Behold, the altar shall be rent, and the ashes that *are* upon it shall be poured out.

1Ki 13:5 — The altar also was rent, and the ashes poured out from the altar, according to the sign which the man of God had given by the word of the LORD.

- **Rending of the vail.**

Mt 27:51 — And, behold, the veil of the temple was rent in twain from the top to the bottom; and the earth did quake, and the rocks rent;

Mk 15:38 — And the veil of the temple was rent in twain from the top to the bottom.

Lk 23:45 — And the sun was darkened, and the veil of the temple was rent in the midst.

- **Wounding.**

1Ki 20:35–40

- **Praying toward the temple.**

1Ki 8:29 — That thine eyes may be open toward this house night and day, *even* toward the place of which thou hast said, My name shall be there: that thou mayest hearken unto the prayer which thy servant shall make toward this place.

Da 6:10 — Now when Daniel knew that the writing was signed, he went into his house; and his windows being open in his chamber toward Jerusalem, he kneeled upon his knees three times a day, and prayed, and gave thanks before his God, as he did aforetime.

- **Harvest.**

2Ki 19:29 — And this *shall be* a sign unto thee, Ye shall eat this year such things as grow of themselves, and in the second year that which springeth of the same; and in the third year sow ye, and reap, and plant vineyards, and eat the fruits thereof.

- **Isaiah's children.**

Isa 8:18 — Behold, I and the children whom the LORD hath given me *are* for signs and for wonders in Israel from the LORD of hosts, which dwelleth in mount Zion.

- **Nakedness.**

Isa 20:2–4

- **Almond rod.**

Jer 1:11 — Moreover the word of the LORD came unto me, saying, Jeremiah, what seest thou? And I said, I see a rod of an almond tree.

- **Sticks and staves.**

Eze 37:16–17; Zec 11:10–11

Zec 11:7 — And I will feed the flock of slaughter, *even* you, O poor of the flock. And I took unto me two staves; the one I called Beauty, and the other I called Bands; and I fed the flock.

Zec 11:14 — Then I cut asunder mine other staff, *even* Bands, that I might break the brotherhood between Judah and Israel.

- **Food.**

2Ki 19:29 — And this *shall be* a sign unto thee, Ye shall eat this year such things as grow of themselves, and in the second year that which springeth of the same; and in the third year sow ye, and reap, and plant vineyards, and eat the fruits thereof.

Isa 37:30 — And this *shall be* a sign unto thee, Ye shall eat *this* year such as groweth of itself; and the second year that which springeth of the same: and in the third year sow ye, and reap, and plant vineyards, and eat the fruit thereof.

- **Shadow on Ahaz's dial.**
  2Ki 20:8–11; Isa 38:7–8
- **Cooking.**
  Eze 4:9–15; 24:3–5
  Jer 1:13 — And the word of the LORD came unto me the second time, saying, What seest thou? And I said, I see a seething pot; and the face thereof *is* toward the north.
- **Girdle.**
  Jer 13:1–7
  Ac 21:11 — And when he was come unto us, he took Paul's girdle, and bound his own hands and feet, and said, Thus saith the Holy Ghost, So shall the Jews at Jerusalem bind the man that owneth this girdle, and shall deliver *him* into the hands of the Gentiles.
- **Bottles.**
  Jer 19:1–2
  Jer 13:12 — Therefore thou shalt speak unto them this word; Thus saith the LORD God of Israel, Every bottle shall be filled with wine: and they shall say unto thee, Do we not certainly know that every bottle shall be filled with wine?
  Jer 19:10 — Then shalt thou break the bottle in the sight of the men that go with thee,
- **Breaking of potter's vessel.**
  Jer 19:1–15
- **Good and bad figs.**
  Jer 24:1–10
- **Basket of fruit.**
  Jer 24:1–3; Am 8:1–2
- **Wine.**
  Jer 25:15–17
  Mt 26:27 — And he took the cup, and gave thanks, and gave *it* to them, saying, <u>Drink ye all of it;</u>
  Mk 14:23 — And he took the cup, and when he had given thanks, he gave *it* to them: and they all drank of it.
  Lk 22:17 — And he took the cup, and gave thanks, and said, <u>Take this, and divide *it* among yourselves:</u>
- **Yokes.**
  Jer 27:2–3
  Jer 28:10 — Then Hananiah the prophet took the yoke from off the prophet Jeremiah's neck, and brake it.
- **Jeremiah's deeds of land.**
  Jer 32:1–16
- **Book cast into Euphrates.**
  Jer 51:63 — And it shall be, when thou hast made an end of reading this book, *that* thou shalt bind a stone to it, and cast it into the midst of Euphrates:
- **Dumbness.**
  Eze 3:26–27; Lk 1:20–22, 62–64
  Eze 24:27 — In that day shall thy mouth be opened to him which is escaped, and thou shalt speak, and be no more dumb: and thou shalt be a sign unto them; and they shall know that I *am* the LORD.
  Eze 29:21 — In that day will I cause the horn of the house of Israel to bud forth, and I will give thee the opening of the mouth in the midst of them; and they shall know that I *am* the LORD.
  Eze 33:22 — Now the hand of the LORD was upon me in the evening, afore he that was escaped came; and had opened my mouth, until he came to me in the morning; and my mouth was opened, and I was no more dumb.
- **Siege.**
  Eze 4:1–3
- **Posture.**
  Eze 4:4–8
- **Unclean food.**
  Eze 4:9–17
- **Ezekiel's beard.**
  Eze 5:1–4
- **Change of domicile.**
  Eze 12:3–11
- **Eating bread with carefulness.**
  Eze 12:17–20
- **Eating and drinking in fear.**
  Eze 12:18 — Son of man, eat thy bread with quaking, and drink thy water with trembling and with carefulness;
- **Vine.**
  Eze 19:10–14
  Eze 15:2 — Son of man, What is the vine tree more than any tree, *or than* a branch which is among the trees of the forest?
- **Death.**
  Eze 24:16–19
- **Boiling pot.**
  Eze 24:1–5
- **Mourning forbidden.**
  Eze 24:15–18
- **Two sticks.**
  Eze 37:15–28
- **Handwriting on the wall.**
  Da 5:5–6; 5:16–28
- **Plumb line.**
  Am 7:7–8
- **Marrying a whore.**
  Hos 1:2–9; 3:1–4
- **Roll.**
  Zec 5:2–4
- **Ephah.**
  Zec 5:6–11
- **Jonas.**
  Lk 11:29–30
  Mt 16:4 — <u>A wicked and adulterous generation seeketh after a sign; and there shall no sign be given unto it, but the sign of the prophet Jonas.</u> And he left them, and departed.
- **Star in the east.**
  Mt 2:2 — Saying, Where is he that is born King of the Jews? for we have seen his star in the east, and are come to worship him.
- **Smitten rock.**
  Ex 17:6 — Behold, I will stand before thee there upon the rock in Horeb; and thou shalt smite the rock, and there shall come water out of it, that the people may

drink. And Moses did so in the sight of the elders of Israel.

1Co 10:4 — And did all drink the same spiritual drink: for they drank of that spiritual Rock that followed them: and that Rock was Christ.

• Salt.

Col 4:6 — Let your speech *be* alway with grace, seasoned with salt, that ye may know how ye ought to answer every man.

• Bread.

Mt 26:26 — And as they were eating, Jesus took bread, and blessed *it,* and brake *it,* and gave *it* to the disciples, and said, Take, eat; this is my body.

Mk 14:22 — And as they did eat, Jesus took bread, and blessed, and brake *it,* and gave to them, and said, Take, eat: this is my body.

Lk 22:19 — And he took bread, and gave thanks, and brake *it,* and gave unto them, saying, This is my body which is given for you: this do in remembrance of me.

• Childhood.

Mk 10:14–15; Lk 18:16–17

Mt 18:3 — And said, Verily I say unto you, Except ye be converted, and become as little children, ye shall not enter into the kingdom of heaven.

• Manna.

Jn 6:31–58

• Ablutions, a symbol of purity.

See: Ablution

See: Purification

• For symbolisms of color.

See: Colors

See: Allegory

See: Instruction; by symbols and parables

See: Instruction; of children

See: Instruction; in religion

SYMPATHY

Job 2:11–13; Php 2:1–2

Job 6:14 — To him that is afflicted pity *should be shewed* from his friend; but he forsaketh the fear of the Almighty.

Job 22:29 — When *men* are cast down, then thou shalt say, *There is* lifting up; and he shall save the humble person.

Ecc 7:2 — *It is* better to go to the house of mourning, than to go to the house of feasting: for that is the end of all men; and the living will lay *it* to his heart.

Jas 1:27 — Pure religion and undefiled before God and the Father is this, To visit the fatherless and widows in their affliction, *and* to keep himself unspotted from the world.

1Pe 3:8 — Finally, *be ye* all of one mind, having compassion one of another, love as brethren, *be* pitiful, *be* courteous:

See: Afflicted, Duty to the

See: Afflictions

See: Jesus, Compassion of

See: Pity

SYNAGOGUE

• Primarily an assembly.

Ac 13:43 — Now when the congregation was broken up, many of the Jews and religious proselytes followed Paul and Barnabas: who, speaking to them, persuaded them to continue in the grace of God.

Jas 2:2 — For if there come unto your assembly a man with a gold ring, in goodly apparel, and there come in also a poor man in vile raiment;

• Constitutes a court of justice.

Lk 12:11 — And when they bring you unto the synagogues, and *unto* magistrates, and powers, take ye no thought how or what thing ye shall answer, or what ye shall say:

Ac 9:2 — And desired of him letters to Damascus to the synagogues, that if he found any of this way, whether they were men or women, he might bring them bound unto Jerusalem.

• Had powers of criminal courts.

Mt 10:17 — But beware of men: for they will deliver you up to the councils, and they will scourge you in their synagogues;

Mt 23:34 — Wherefore, behold, I send unto you prophets, and wise men, and scribes: and *some* of them ye shall kill and crucify; and *some* of them shall ye scourge in your synagogues, and persecute *them* from city to city:

Ac 22:19 — And I said, Lord, they know that I imprisoned and beat in every synagogue them that believed on thee:

Ac 26:11 — And I punished them oft in every synagogue, and compelled *them* to blaspheme; and being exceedingly mad against them, I persecuted *them* even unto strange cities.

• Had powers of ecclesiastical courts.

Jn 9:22 — These *words* spake his parents, because they feared the Jews: for the Jews had agreed already, that if any man did confess that he was Christ, he should be put out of the synagogue.

Jn 9:34 — They answered and said unto him, Thou wast altogether born in sins, and dost thou teach us? And they cast him out.

Jn 12:42 — Nevertheless among the chief rulers also many believed on him; but because of the Pharisees they did not confess *him,* lest they should be put out of the synagogue:

Jn 16:2 — They shall put you out of the synagogues: yea, the time cometh, that whosoever killeth you will think that he doeth God service.

• Place of assembly where Scriptures were read and expounded upon.

Ne 8:1–8; Lk 4:15–33; Ac 13:5–44

Ne 9:3 — And they stood up in their place, and read in the book of the law of the LORD their God *one* fourth part of the day; and *another* fourth part they confessed, and worshipped the LORD their God.

Ne 9:5 — Then the Levites, Jeshua, and Kadmiel, Bani, Hashabniah, Sherebiah, Hodijah, Shebaniah, *and* Pethahiah, said, Stand up *and* bless the LORD your God for ever and ever: and blessed be thy glorious name, which is exalted above all blessing and praise.

Mt 4:23 — And Jesus went about all Galilee, teaching in their synagogues, and preaching the gospel of the kingdom, and healing all manner of sickness and all manner of disease among the people.

Mt 9:35 — And Jesus went about all the cities and villages, teaching in their synagogues, and preaching the gospel of the kingdom, and healing every sickness and every disease among the people.

Mt 13:54 — And when he was come into his own country, he taught them in their synagogue, insomuch that they were astonished, and said, Whence hath this *man* this wisdom, and *these* mighty works?

Mk 1:39 — And he preached in their synagogues throughout all Galilee, and cast out devils.

Lk 13:10 — And he was teaching in one of the synagogues on the sabbath.

Jn 18:20 — Jesus answered him, I spake openly to the world; I ever taught in the synagogue, and in the temple, whither the Jews always resort; and in secret have I said nothing.

Ac 9:20 — And straightway he preached Christ in the synagogues, that he is the Son of God.

Ac 14:1 — And it came to pass in Iconium, that they went both together into the synagogue of the Jews, and so spake, that a great multitude both of the Jews and also of the Greeks believed.

Ac 15:21 — For Moses of old time hath in every city them that preach him, being read in the synagogues every sabbath day.

Ac 17:2 — And Paul, as his manner was, went in unto them, and three sabbath days reasoned with them out of the scriptures,

Ac 17:10 — And the brethren immediately sent away Paul and Silas by night unto Berea: who coming *thither* went into the synagogue of the Jews.

Ac 18:4 — And he reasoned in the synagogue every sabbath, and persuaded the Jews and the Greeks.

Ac 18:19 — And he came to Ephesus, and left them there: but he himself entered into the synagogue, and reasoned with the Jews.

Ac 18:26 — And he began to speak boldly in the synagogue: whom when Aquila and Priscilla had heard, they took him unto *them,* and expounded unto him the way of God more perfectly.

- **In Jerusalem.**

Ac 6:9 — Then there arose certain of *the synagogue,* which is called the synagogue of the Libertines, and Cyrenians, and Alexandrians, and of them of Cilicia and of Asia, disputing with Stephen.

- **In Damascus.**

Ac 9:2 — And desired of him letters to Damascus to the synagogues, that if he found any of this way, whether they were men or women, he might bring them bound unto Jerusalem.

Ac 9:20 — And straightway he preached Christ in the synagogues, that he is the Son of God.

- **In other cities.**

Ac 14:1 — And it came to pass in Iconium, that they went both together into the synagogue of the Jews, and so spake, that a great multitude both of the Jews and also of the Greeks believed.

Ac 17:1 — Now when they had passed through Amphipolis and Apollonia, they came to Thessalonica, where was a synagogue of the Jews:

Ac 17:10 — And the brethren immediately sent away Paul and Silas by night unto Berea: who coming *thither* went into the synagogue of the Jews.

Ac 18:4 — And he reasoned in the synagogue every sabbath, and persuaded the Jews and the Greeks.

- **Built by Jairus.**

Lk 7:5 — For he loveth our nation, and he hath built us a synagogue.

- **Jesus performed healing in.**

Mt 12:9–13; Lk 13:11–14

- **Alms given in.**

Mt 6:2 — Therefore when thou doest *thine* alms, do not sound a trumpet before thee, as the hypocrites do in the synagogues and in the streets, that they may have glory of men. Verily I say unto you, They have their reward.

- **Of Satan.**

Rev 2:9 — I know thy works, and tribulation, and poverty, (but thou art rich) and I *know* the blasphemy of them which say they are Jews, and are not, but *are* the synagogue of Satan.

Rev 3:9 — Behold, I will make them of the synagogue of Satan, which say they are Jews, and are not, but do lie; behold, I will make them to come and worship before thy feet, and to know that I have loved thee.

See: Church

SYNTYCHE • A Christian woman in Philippi.

Php 4:2 — I beseech Euodias, and beseech Syntyche, that they be of the same mind in the Lord.

SYRACUSE

- **A city of Sicily.**
- **Paul visits.**

Ac 28:12 — And landing at Syracuse, we tarried *there* three days.

SYRIA

- **Highlands lying between the river Euphrates and the Mediterranean Sea.**
- **Called Aram, from the son of Shem.**

Ge 10:22–23

Nu 23:7 — And he took up his parable, and said, Balak the king of Moab hath brought me from Aram, out of the mountains of the east, *saying,* Come, curse me Jacob, and come, defy Israel.

1Ch 1:17 — The sons of Shem; Elam, and Asshur, and Arphaxad, and Lud, and Aram, and Uz, and Hul, and Gether, and Meshech.

1Ch 2:23 — And he took Geshur, and Aram, with the towns of Jair, from them, with Kenath, and the towns thereof, *even* threescore cities. All these *belonged to* the sons of Machir the father of Gilead.

• In the time of Abraham it seems to have embraced the region between the rivers Tigris and Euphrates.

Ge 24:10 — And the servant took ten camels of the camels of his master, and departed; for all the goods of his master *were* in his hand: and he arose, and went to Mesopotamia, unto the city of Nahor.

Ge 25:20 — And Isaac was forty years old when he took Rebekah to wife, the daughter of Bethuel the Syrian of Padan-aram, the sister to Laban the Syrian.

• Including Padan aram.

Ge 25:20 — And Isaac was forty years old when he took Rebekah to wife, the daughter of Bethuel the Syrian of Padan-aram, the sister to Laban the Syrian.

Ge 28:5 — And Isaac sent away Jacob: and he went to Padan-aram unto Laban, son of Bethuel the Syrian, the brother of Rebekah, Jacob's and Esau's mother.

• Minor kingdoms within the region.

• Aram-zobah, called also Zobah and Zoba.

1Sa 14:47 — So Saul took the kingdom over Israel, and fought against all his enemies on every side, against Moab, and against the children of Ammon, and against Edom, and against the kings of Zobah, and against the Philistines: and whithersoever he turned himself, he vexed *them.*

2Sa 8:3 — David smote also Hadadezer, the son of Rehob, king of Zobah, as he went to recover his border at the river Euphrates.

2Sa 10:6 — And when the children of Ammon saw that they stank before David, the children of Ammon sent and hired the Syrians of Beth-rehob, and the Syrians of Zoba, twenty thousand footmen, and of king Maacah a thousand men, and of Ish-tob twelve thousand men.

2Sa 10:8 — And the children of Ammon came out, and put the battle in array at the entering in of the gate: and the Syrians of Zoba, and of Rehob, and Ish-tob, and Maacah, *were* by themselves in the field.

1Ki 11:23 — And God stirred him up *another* adversary, Rezon the son of Eliadah, which fled from his lord Hadadezer king of Zobah:

1Ch 18:5 — And when the Syrians of Damascus came to help Hadarezer king of Zobah, David slew of the Syrians two and twenty thousand men.

1Ch 18:9 — Now when Tou king of Hamath heard how David had smitten all the host of Hadarezer king of Zobah;

1Ch 19:6 — And when the children of Ammon saw that they had made themselves odious to David, Hanun and the children of Ammon sent a thousand talents of silver to hire them chariots and horsemen out of Mesopotamia, and out of Syria-maachah, and out of Zobah.

Ps 60:1 — [To the chief Musician upon Shushan-eduth, Michtam of David, to teach; when he strove with Aram-naharaim and with Aram-zobah, when Joab returned, and smote of Edom in the valley of salt twelve thousand.] O God, thou hast cast us off, thou hast scattered us, thou hast been displeased; O turn thyself to us again.

• Geshur.

2Sa 15:8 — For thy servant vowed a vow while I abode at Geshur in Syria, saying, If the LORD shall bring me again indeed to Jerusalem, then I will serve the LORD.

• Aram-rehob, called also Beth-Rehob.

2Sa 10:6 — And when the children of Ammon saw that they stank before David, the children of Ammon sent and hired the Syrians of Beth-rehob, and the Syrians of Zoba, twenty thousand footmen, and of king Maacah a thousand men, and of Ish-tob twelve thousand men.

2Sa 10:8 — And the children of Ammon came out, and put the battle in array at the entering in of the gate: and the Syrians of Zoba, and of Rehob, and Ish-tob, and Maacah, *were* by themselves in the field.

• Damascus.

2Sa 8:5–6; 1Ch 18:5–6

• Hamath.

2Sa 8:9–10

• Conquest of.

• By David.

2Sa 8:3–13

• By Jeroboam.

2Ki 14:25 — He restored the coast of Israel from the entering of Hamath unto the sea of the plain, according to the word of the LORD God of Israel, which he spake by the hand of his servant Jonah, the son of Amittai, the prophet, which *was* of Gath-hepher.

2Ki 14:28 — Now the rest of the acts of Jeroboam, and all that he did, and his might, how he warred, and how he recovered Damascus, and Hamath, *which belonged* to Judah, for Israel, are they not written in the book of the chronicles of the kings of Israel?

• By Tiglath-pileser, king of Assyria.

2Ki 16:7–9; 18:33–34

• People of, colonized in Samaria by the king of Assyria.

2Ki 17:24 — And the king of Assyria brought *men* from Babylon, and from Cuthah, and from Ava, and from Hamath, and from Sepharvaim, and placed *them* in the cities of Samaria instead of the children of Israel: and they possessed Samaria, and dwelt in the cities thereof.

• Confederate with Nebuchadnezzar.

2Ki 24:2 — And the LORD sent against him bands of the Chaldees, and bands of the Syrians, and bands of the Moabites, and bands of the children of Ammon, and sent them against Judah to destroy it, according to the word of the LORD, which he spake by his servants the prophets.

Jer 39:5 — But the Chaldeans' army pursued after them, and overtook Zedekiah in the plains of Jericho: and when they had taken him, they brought him up to Nebuchadnezzar king of Babylon to Riblah in the land of Hamath, where he gave judgment upon him.

• The Roman province of, included the land of Canaan.

Lk 2:2–3

• The Roman province of, included the land of Phenicia.

Mk 7:26 — The woman was a Greek, a Syrophenician by nation; and she besought him that he would cast forth the devil out of her daughter.

Ac 21:3 — Now when we had discovered Cyprus, we left it on the left hand, and sailed into Syria, and landed at Tyre: for there the ship was to unlade her burden.

• The fame of Jesus extended over.

Mt 4:24 — And his fame went throughout all Syria: and they brought unto him all sick people that were taken with divers diseases and torments, and those which were possessed with devils, and those which were lunatick, and those that had the palsy; and he healed them.

• Paul goes to, with letters to apprehend the Christians; is converted and begins his evangelistic ministry.

Ac 9:1–31

⇜See: Paul, Ministry, Ac 16–28

⇜See: Paul, Ministry, Ac 9–15

• Paul preaches in.

Ac 15:41

Ac 18:18 — And Paul *after this* tarried *there* yet a good while, and then took his leave of the brethren, and sailed thence into Syria, and with him Priscilla and Aquila; having shorn *his* head in Cenchrea: for he had a vow.

Ac 21:3 — Now when we had discovered Cyprus, we left it on the left hand, and sailed into Syria, and landed at Tyre: for there the ship was to unlade her burden.

Gal 1:21 — Afterwards I came into the regions of Syria and Cilicia;

• Damascus, the capital of.

⇜See: Damascus

• Wars between, and the kingdoms of Judah and Israel.

⇜See: Israel

• Prophecies concerning.

Isa 7:8–16; 8:4–7; 17:1–3; Jer 49:23–27; Am 1:3–5

Jer 1:15 — For, lo, I will call all the families of the kingdoms of the north, saith the LORD; and they shall come, and they shall set every one his throne at the entering of the gates of Jerusalem, and against all the walls thereof round about, and against all the cities of Judah.

Zec 9:1 — The burden of the word of the LORD in the land of Hadrach, and Damascus *shall be* the rest thereof: when the eyes of man, as of all the tribes of Israel, *shall be* toward the LORD.

SYRIA-MAACHAH

• Called also Maachah.

• A small kingdom.

1Ch 19:6 — And when the children of Ammon saw that they had made themselves odious to David, Hanun and the children of Ammon sent a thousand talents of silver to hire them chariots and horsemen out of Mesopotamia, and out of Syria-maachah, and out of Zobah.

⇜See: Maachah; called also Maacah and Maachathi

SYROPHENICIAN • The nationality of a woman whose daughter was cured by Jesus.

Mt 15:21–28; Mk 7:24–30

T

TAANACH

• Called also Tanach .

• A city conquered by Joshua.

Jos 12:21 — The king of Taanach, one; the king of Megiddo, one;

• Allotted to Manasseh.

Jos 17:11 — And Manasseh had in Issachar and in Asher Beth-shean and her towns, and Ibleam and her towns, and the inhabitants of Dor and her towns, and the inhabitants of Endor and her towns, and the inhabitants of Taanach and her towns, and the inhabitants of Megiddo and her towns, *even* three countries.

1Ch 7:29 — And by the borders of the children of Manasseh, Beth-shean and her towns, Taanach and her towns, Megiddo and her towns, Dor and her towns. In these dwelt the children of Joseph the son of Israel.

• Canaanites not driven from.

Jos 17:12 — Yet the children of Manasseh could not drive out *the inhabitants of* those cities; but the Canaanites would dwell in that land.

Jgs 1:27 — Neither did Manasseh drive out *the inhabitants of* Beth-shean and her towns, nor Taanach and her towns, nor the inhabitants of Dor and her towns, nor the inhabitants of Ibleam and her towns, nor the inhabitants of Megiddo and her towns: but the Canaanites would dwell in that land.

• Assigned to the Levites.

Jos 21:25 — And out of the half tribe of Manasseh, Tanach with her suburbs, and Gath-rimmon with her suburbs; two cities.

• The scene of Barak's victory.

Jgs 5:19 — The kings came *and* fought, then fought the kings of Canaan in Taanach by the waters of Megiddo; they took no gain of money.

• One of Solomon's commissaries at.

1Ki 4:12 — Baana the son of Ahilud; *to him pertained* Taanach and Megiddo, and all Beth-shean, which is by Zartanah beneath Jezreel, from Beth-shean to Abel-meholah, *even* unto *the place that is* beyond Jokneam:

TAANATH-SHILOH • A city of Ephraim.

Jos 16:6 — And the border went out toward the sea to Michmethah on the north side; and the border went about eastward unto Taanath-shiloh, and passed by it on the east to Janohah;

TABBAOTH • One of the Nethinim.

Ezr 2:43 — The Nethinims: the children of Ziha, the children of Hasupha, the children of Tabbaoth,

Ne 7:46 — The Nethinims: the children of Ziha, the children of Hashupha, the children of Tabbaoth,

TABBATH • A place of uncertain location.

Jgs 7:22 — And the three hundred blew the trumpets, and the LORD set every man's sword against his fellow, even throughout all the host: and the host fled to Beth-shittah in Zererath, *and* to the border of Abel-meholah, unto Tabbath.

TABEAL • Father of one whom the kings of Syria and Israel sought to make king in Judah instead of Ahaz.

Isa 7:6 — Let us go up against Judah, and vex it, and let us make a breach therein for us, and set a king in the midst of it, *even* the son of Tabeal:

TABEEL

• A Persian official in Samaria.

Ezr 4:7 — And in the days of Artaxerxes wrote Bishlam, Mithredath, Tabeel, and the rest of their companions, unto Artaxerxes king of Persia; and the writing of the letter *was* written in the Syrian tongue, and interpreted in the Syrian tongue.

See: Tabeal

TABERAH • A place in the wilderness where the Israelites were punished for their murmuring.

Nu 11:3 — And he called the name of the place Taberah: because the fire of the LORD burnt among them.

Dt 9:22 — And at Taberah, and at Massah, and at Kibroth-hattaavah, ye provoked the LORD to wrath.

TABERNACLE

• One existed before Moses received the pattern authorized on Mount Sinai.

Ex 33:7–11

• The one instituted by Moses was called.

• Sanctuary.

Ex 25:8 — And let them make me a sanctuary; that I may dwell among them.

• Tent of Meeting.

Ex 27:21 — In the tabernacle of the congregation without the vail, which *is* before the testimony, Aaron and his sons shall order it from evening to morning before the LORD: *it shall be* a statute for ever unto their generations on the behalf of the children of Israel.

• Tent.

Ex 33:7 — And Moses took the tabernacle, and pitched it without the camp, afar off from the camp, and called it the Tabernacle of the congregation. And it came to pass, *that* every one which sought the LORD went out unto the tabernacle of the congregation, which *was* without the camp.

2Ch 5:5 — And they brought up the ark, and the tabernacle of the congregation, and all the holy vessels that *were* in the tabernacle, these did the priests and the Levites bring up.

- **Sanctuary of Testimony.**

Ex 38:21 — This is the sum of the tabernacle, *even* of the tabernacle of testimony, as it was counted, according to the commandment of Moses, *for* the service of the Levites, by the hand of Ithamar, son to Aaron the priest.

Nu 1:50 — But thou shalt appoint the Levites over the tabernacle of testimony, and over all the vessels thereof, and over all things that *belong* to it: they shall bear the tabernacle, and all the vessels thereof; and they shall minister unto it, and shall encamp round about the tabernacle.

- **Tent of Testimony.**

Nu 17:7–8

2Ch 24:6 — And the king called for Jehoiada the chief, and said unto him, Why hast thou not required of the Levites to bring in out of Judah and out of Jerusalem the collection, *according to the commandment* of Moses the servant of the LORD, and of the congregation of Israel, for the tabernacle of witness?

- **Temple of the Lord.**

1Sa 1:9 — So Hannah rose up after they had eaten in Shiloh, and after they had drunk. Now Eli the priest sat upon a seat by a post of the temple of the LORD.

1Sa 3:3 — And ere the lamp of God went out in the temple of the LORD, where the ark of God *was,* and Samuel was laid down *to sleep;*

- **House of the Lord.**

Jos 6:24 — And they burnt the city with fire, and all that *was* therein: only the silver, and the gold, and the vessels of brass and of iron, they put into the treasury of the house of the LORD.

- **Pattern of, revealed to Moses.**

Ex 39:42–43

Ex 25:9 — According to all that I shew thee, *after* the pattern of the tabernacle, and the pattern of all the instruments thereof, even so shall ye make *it.*

Ex 26:30 — And thou shalt rear up the tabernacle according to the fashion thereof which was shewed thee in the mount.

Ex 39:32 — Thus was all the work of the tabernacle of the tent of the congregation finished: and the children of Israel did according to all that the LORD commanded Moses, so did they.

Ac 7:44 — Our fathers had the tabernacle of witness in the wilderness, as he had appointed, speaking unto Moses, that he should make it according to the fashion that he had seen.

Heb 8:5 — Who serve unto the example and shadow of heavenly things, as Moses was admonished of God when he was about to make the tabernacle: for, See, saith he, *that* thou make all things according to the pattern shewed to thee in the mount.

- **Materials for, voluntarily offered.**

Ex 25:1–8; 35:4–29; 36:3–7

- **Value of the substance contributed for.**

Ex 38:24–31

- **Workmen who constructed it were inspired.**

Ex 31:1–11; 35:30–35

- **Description of.**
  - **Frame.**

Ex 26:15–37; 36:20–38

  - **Outer covering.**

Ex 26:7–14; 36:14–19

Ex 25:5 — And rams' skins dyed red, and badgers' skins, and shittim wood,

  - **Second covering.**

Ex 25:5 — And rams' skins dyed red, and badgers' skins, and shittim wood,

Ex 26:14 — And thou shalt make a covering for the tent *of* rams' skins dyed red, and a covering above *of* badgers' skins.

Ex 35:7 — And rams' skins dyed red, and badgers' skins, and shittim wood,

Ex 35:23 — And every man, with whom was found blue, and purple, and scarlet, and fine linen, and goats' *hair,* and red skins of rams, and badgers' skins, brought *them.*

Ex 36:19 — And he made a covering for the tent *of* rams' skins dyed red, and a covering *of* badgers' skins above *that.*

Ex 39:34 — And the covering of rams' skins dyed red, and the covering of badgers' skins, and the vail of the covering,

  - **Curtains of.**

Ex 26:1–14, 31–37; 27:9–16; 36:8–19

Ex 35:15 — And the incense altar, and his staves, and the anointing oil, and the sweet incense, and the hanging for the door at the entering in of the tabernacle,

Ex 35:17 — The hangings of the court, his pillars, and their sockets, and the hanging for the door of the court,

Ex 36:35 — And he made a vail *of* blue, and purple, and scarlet, and fine twined linen: *with* cherubims made he it of cunning work.

Ex 36:37 — And he made an hanging for the tabernacle door *of* blue, and purple, and scarlet, and fine twined linen, of needlework;

  - **Court of.**

Ex 27:9–17; 38:9–16

Ex 38:18 — And the hanging for the gate of the court *was* needlework, *of* blue, and purple, and scarlet, and fine twined linen: and twenty cubits *was* the length, and the height in the breadth *was* five cubits, answerable to the hangings of the court.

Ex 40:8 — And thou shalt set up the court round about, and hang up the hanging at the court gate.

Ex 40:33 — And he reared up the court round about the tabernacle and the altar, and set up the hanging of the court gate. So Moses finished the work.

- **Holy place of.**

Ex 26:31–37; 40:22–26; Heb 9:2–6

Heb 9:8 — The Holy Ghost this signifying, that the way into the holiest of all was not yet made manifest, while as the first tabernacle was yet standing:

- **The Most Holy Place.**

Ex 26:33–35; 40:20–21; Heb 9:3–5, 7–8

- **Furniture of.**

Ex 25:10–40; 27:1–8; 37:1–38:8

Ex 27:19 — All the vessels of the tabernacle in all the service thereof, and all the pins thereof, and all the pins of the court, *shall be of* brass.

See: Altar

See: Ark

See: Candlestick

See: Cherubim

See: Laver

See: Mercy Seat

See: Shewbread

- **Completed.**

Ex 39:32 — Thus was all the work of the tabernacle of the tent of the congregation finished: and the children of Israel did according to all that the LORD commanded Moses, so did they.

- **Dedicated.**

Nu 7:1–89

- **Sanctified.**

Ex 40:9–16

Ex 29:43 — And there I will meet with the children of Israel, and *the tabernacle* shall be sanctified by my glory.

Nu 7:1 — And it came to pass on the day that Moses had fully set up the tabernacle, and had anointed it, and sanctified it, and all the instruments thereof, both the altar and all the vessels thereof, and had anointed them, and sanctified them;

- **Anointed with holy oil.**

Ex 30:25–26

Le 8:10 — And Moses took the anointing oil, and anointed the tabernacle and all that *was* therein, and sanctified them.

Nu 7:1 — And it came to pass on the day that Moses had fully set up the tabernacle, and had anointed it, and sanctified it, and all the instruments thereof, both the altar and all the vessels thereof, and had anointed them, and sanctified them;

- **Sprinkled with blood.**

Le 16:15–20

Heb 9:21 — Moreover he sprinkled with blood both the tabernacle, and all the vessels of the ministry.

Heb 9:23 — *It was* therefore necessary that the patterns of things in the heavens should be purified with these; but the heavenly things themselves with better sacrifices than these.

- **Filled with the cloud of glory.**

Ex 40:34–38

- **How prepared for removal during the journeyings of the Israelites.**

Nu 4:5–15

Nu 1:51 — And when the tabernacle setteth forward, the Levites shall take it down: and when the tabernacle is to be pitched, the Levites shall set it up: and the stranger that cometh nigh shall be put to death.

- **How and by whom carried.**

Nu 4:5–33; 7:6–9

- **Strangers forbidden to enter.**

Nu 1:51 — And when the tabernacle setteth forward, the Levites shall take it down: and when the tabernacle is to be pitched, the Levites shall set it up: and the stranger that cometh nigh shall be put to death.

- **Duties of the Levites concerning.**

See: Levites

- **Defilement of, punished.**

Le 15:31 — Thus shall ye separate the children of Israel from their uncleanness; that they die not in their uncleanness, when they defile my tabernacle that *is* among them.

Nu 19:13 — Whosoever toucheth the dead body of any man that is dead, and purifieth not himself, defileth the tabernacle of the LORD; and that soul shall be cut off from Israel: because the water of separation was not sprinkled upon him, he shall be unclean; his uncleanness *is* yet upon him.

Nu 19:20 — But the man that shall be unclean, and shall not purify himself, that soul shall be cut off from among the congregation, because he hath defiled the sanctuary of the LORD: the water of separation hath not been sprinkled upon him; he *is* unclean.

Eze 5:11 — Wherefore, *as* I live, saith the Lord GOD; Surely, because thou hast defiled my sanctuary with all thy detestable things, and with all thine abominations, therefore will I also diminish *thee;* neither shall mine eye spare, neither will I have any pity.

Eze 23:38 — Moreover this they have done unto me: they have defiled my sanctuary in the same day, and have profaned my sabbaths.

- **Duties of the priests in relation to.**

See: Priest, Duties of

See: Priest, High

- **Israelites worship at.**

Nu 16:42–43

Nu 10:3 — And when they shall blow with them, all the assembly shall assemble themselves to thee at the door of the tabernacle of the congregation.

Nu 16:19 — And Korah gathered all the congregation against them unto the door of the tabernacle of the congregation: and the glory of the LORD appeared unto all the congregation.

Nu 20:6 — And Moses and Aaron went from the presence of the assembly unto the door of the tabernacle of the congregation, and they fell upon their faces: and the glory of the LORD appeared unto them.

Nu 25:6 — And, behold, one of the children of Israel came and brought unto his brethren a Midianitish woman in the sight of Moses, and in the sight of all the congregation of the children of Israel, who *were* weeping *before* the door of the tabernacle of the congregation.

1Sa 2:22 — Now Eli was very old, and heard all that his sons did unto all Israel; and how they lay with the women that assembled *at* the door of the tabernacle of the congregation.

Ps 27:4 — One *thing* have I desired of the LORD, that will I seek after; that I may dwell in the house of the LORD all the days of my life, to behold the beauty of the LORD, and to enquire in his temple.

• Offerings brought to.

Dt 12:5–6, 11–14

Le 17:4 — And bringeth it not unto the door of the tabernacle of the congregation, to offer an offering unto the LORD before the tabernacle of the LORD; blood shall be imputed unto that man; he hath shed blood; and that man shall be cut off from among his people:

Nu 31:54 — And Moses and Eleazar the priest took the gold of the captains of thousands and of hundreds, and brought it into the tabernacle of the congregation, *for* a memorial for the children of Israel before the LORD.

• Causes tried at.

Dt 12:5–6, 11–14

• Tribes encamped around, while in the wilderness.

Nu 2:1–34

• All males required to appear before, three times each year.

Ex 23:17 — Three times in the year all thy males shall appear before the Lord GOD.

• Tabernacle tax.

Ex 30:11–16

• Carried in front of the children of Israel in the line of march.

Nu 10:33–36; Jos 3:3–6

• The Lord reveals himself at.

Nu 12:4–10; Dt 31:14–15

Le 1:1 — And the LORD called unto Moses, and spake unto him out of the tabernacle of the congregation, saying,

Nu 1:1 — And the LORD spake unto Moses in the wilderness of Sinai, in the tabernacle of the congregation, on the first *day* of the second month, in the second year after they were come out of the land of Egypt, saying,

Nu 7:89 — And when Moses was gone into the tabernacle of the congregation to speak with him, then he heard the voice of one speaking unto him from off the mercy seat that *was* upon the ark of testimony, from between the two cherubims: and he spake unto him.

• Pitched at Gilgal.

Jos 4:18–19

• Pitched at Shiloh.

Jgs 20:26–27; 1Sa 4:3–4

Jos 18:1 — And the whole congregation of the children of Israel assembled together at Shiloh, and set up the tabernacle of the congregation there. And the land was subdued before them.

Jos 19:51 — These *are* the inheritances which Eleazar the priest, and Joshua the son of Nun, and the heads of the fathers of the tribes of the children of Israel, divided for an inheritance by lot in Shiloh before the LORD, at the door of the tabernacle of the congregation. So they made an end of dividing the country.

Jgs 18:31 — And they set them up Micah's graven image, which he made, all the time that the house of God was in Shiloh.

Jgs 20:18 — And the children of Israel arose, and went up to the house of God, and asked counsel of God, and said, Which of us shall go up first to the battle against the children of Benjamin? And the LORD said, Judah *shall go up* first.

Jgs 21:19 — Then they said, Behold, *there is* a feast of the LORD in Shiloh yearly *in a place* which *is* on the north side of Bethel, on the east side of the highway that goeth up from Bethel to Shechem, and on the south of Lebonah.

1Sa 2:14 — And he struck *it* into the pan, or kettle, or caldron, or pot; all that the fleshhook brought up the priest took for himself. So they did in Shiloh unto all the Israelites that came thither.

Jer 7:12 — But go ye now unto my place which *was* in Shiloh, where I set my name at the first, and see what I did to it for the wickedness of my people Israel.

Jer 7:14 — Therefore will I do unto *this* house, which is called by my name, wherein ye trust, and unto the place which I gave to you and to your fathers, as I have done to Shiloh.

• Pitched at Nob.

1Sa 21:1–6

• Pitched at Gibeon.

1Ch 21:29 — For the tabernacle of the LORD, which Moses made in the wilderness, and the altar of the burnt offering, *were* at that season in the high place at Gibeon.

• Renewed by David, and pitched on Mount Zion.

1Ch 16:1–2

1Ch 15:1 — And *David* made him houses in the city of David, and prepared a place for the ark of God, and pitched for it a tent.

2Ch 1:4 — But the ark of God had David brought up from Kirjath-jearim to *the place which* David had prepared for it: for he had pitched a tent for it at Jerusalem.

• Solomon offers sacrifice at.

2Ch 1:3–6

• Brought to the temple by Solomon.

1Ki 8:4–5

1Ki 8:1 — Then Solomon assembled the elders of Israel, and all the heads of the tribes, the chief of the fathers of the children of Israel, unto king Solomon in Jerusalem, that they might bring up the ark of the covenant of the LORD out of the city of David, which *is* Zion.

2Ch 5:5 — And they brought up the ark, and the tabernacle of the congregation, and all the holy vessels that *were* in the tabernacle, these did the priests and the Levites bring up.

• Symbol of spiritual things.

Heb 9:1–12

Ps 15:1 — LORD, who shall abide in thy tabernacle? who shall dwell in thy holy hill?

Heb 8:2 — A minister of the sanctuary, and of the true tabernacle, which the Lord pitched, and not man.

Heb 8:5 — Who serve unto the example and shadow of heavenly things, as Moses was admonished of God when he was about to make the tabernacle: for, See, saith he, *that* thou make all things according to the pattern shewed to thee in the mount.

Heb 9:24 — For Christ is not entered into the holy places made with hands, *which are* the figures of the true; but into heaven itself, now to appear in the presence of God for us:

See: Levites

See: Priest, Duties of

See: Priest, High

See: Temple

TABERNACLES, FEAST OF

• Called also Feast of Ingathering.

• Instituted.

Le 23:34–43; Nu 29:12–40; Dt 16:13–16

Ex 23:16 — And the feast of harvest, the firstfruits of thy labours, which thou hast sown in the field: and the feast of ingathering, *which is* in the end of the year, when thou hast gathered in thy labours out of the field.

Ex 34:22 — And thou shalt observe the feast of weeks, of the firstfruits of wheat harvest, and the feast of ingathering at the year's end.

• Design of.

Le 23:42–43

• The law read in connection with, every seventh year.

Dt 31:10–12

Ne 8:18 — Also day by day, from the first day unto the last day, he read in the book of the law of God. And they kept the feast seven days; and on the eighth day *was* a solemn assembly, according unto the manner.

• Observance of, after the captivity.

Ne 8:14–18

Ezr 3:4 — They kept also the feast of tabernacles, as *it is* written, and *offered* the daily burnt offerings by number, according to the custom, as the duty of every day required;

• Observance of, by Jesus.

Jn 7:2 — Now the Jews' feast of tabernacles was at hand.

Jn 7:14 — Now about the midst of the feast Jesus went up into the temple, and taught.

• Observance of, omitted.

Ne 8:17 — And all the congregation of them that were come again out of the captivity made booths, and sat under the booths: for since the days of Jeshua the son of Nun unto that day had not the children of Israel done so. And there was very great gladness.

• Penalty for not observing.

Zec 14:16–19

• Jeroboam institutes an idolatrous feast to correspond to, in the eighth month.

1Ki 12:32–33

1Ch 27:11 — The eighth *captain* for the eighth month *was* Sibbecai the Hushathite, of the Zarhites: and in his course *were* twenty and four thousand.

TABITHA

• A Christian woman in Joppa.

• Restored to life by Peter.

Ac 9:36–41

TABLE

• An article of furniture.

Jgs 1:7 — And Adoni-bezek said, Threescore and ten kings, having their thumbs and their great toes cut off, gathered *their meat* under my table: as I have done, so God hath requited me. And they brought him to Jerusalem, and there he died.

1Sa 20:29 — And he said, Let me go, I pray thee; for our family hath a sacrifice in the city; and my brother, he hath commanded me *to be there:* and now, if I have found favour in thine eyes, let me get away, I pray thee, and see my brethren. Therefore he cometh not unto the king's table.

1Sa 20:34 — So Jonathan arose from the table in fierce anger, and did eat no meat the second day of the month: for he was grieved for David, because his father had done him shame.

2Ki 4:10 — Let us make a little chamber, I pray thee, on the wall; and let us set for him there a bed, and a table, and a stool, and a candlestick: and it shall be, when he cometh to us, that he shall turn in thither.

Jn 2:15 — And when he had made a scourge of small cords, he drove them all out of the temple, and the sheep, and the oxen; and poured out the changers' money, and overthrew the tables;

• Made of silver.

1Ch 28:16 — And by weight *he gave* gold for the tables of shewbread, for every table; and *likewise* silver for the tables of silver:

• Figurative.

• Of the altar.

Mal 1:7 — Ye offer polluted bread upon mine altar; and ye say, Wherein have we polluted thee? In that ye say, The table of the LORD *is* contemptible.

Mal 1:12 — But ye have profaned it, in that ye say, The table of the LORD *is* polluted; and the fruit thereof, *even* his meat, *is* contemptible.

• Of the Lord's Supper.

1Co 10:21 — Ye cannot drink the cup of the Lord, and the cup of devils: ye cannot be partakers of the Lord's table, and of the table of devils.

- **Of idolatrous feasts.**

1Co 10:21 — Ye cannot drink the cup of the Lord, and the cup of devils: ye cannot be partakers of the Lord's table, and of the table of devils.

- **Of charities.**

Ac 6:2 — Then the twelve called the multitude of the disciples *unto them,* and said, It is not reason that we should leave the word of God, and serve tables.

- **Of shewbread.**

See: Shewbread; table of

- **Of testimony.**

Ex 31:18 — And he gave unto Moses, when he had made an end of communing with him upon mount Sinai, two tables of testimony, tables of stone, written with the finger of God.

Ex 32:15 — And Moses turned, and went down from the mount, and the two tables of the testimony *were* in his hand: the tables *were* written on both their sides; on the one side and on the other *were* they written.

Ex 34:29 — And it came to pass, when Moses came down from mount Sinai with the two tables of testimony in Moses' hand, when he came down from the mount, that Moses wist not that the skin of his face shone while he talked with him.

- **The commandments engraved upon.**

Ex 20:3–17; Dt 5:4–22

Ex 24:12 — And the LORD said unto Moses, Come up to me into the mount, and be there: and I will give thee tables of stone, and a law, and commandments which I have written; that thou mayest teach them.

Dt 4:13 — And he declared unto you his covenant, which he commanded you to perform, *even* ten commandments; and he wrote them upon two tables of stone.

Dt 9:10 — And the LORD delivered unto me two tables of stone written with the finger of God; and on them *was written* according to all the words, which the LORD spake with you in the mount out of the midst of the fire in the day of the assembly.

Hos 8:12 — I have written to him the great things of my law, *but* they were counted as a strange thing.

- **The commandments broken.**

Ex 32:15–19; Dt 9:9–11

Ex 24:12 — And the LORD said unto Moses, Come up to me into the mount, and be there: and I will give thee tables of stone, and a law, and commandments which I have written; that thou mayest teach them.

Ex 31:18 — And he gave unto Moses, when he had made an end of communing with him upon mount Sinai, two tables of testimony, tables of stone, written with the finger of God.

Dt 4:13 — And he declared unto you his covenant, which he commanded you to perform, *even* ten commandments; and he wrote them upon two tables of stone.

Dt 9:17 — And I took the two tables, and cast them out of my two hands, and brake them before your eyes.

- **A second set engraved.**

Dt 10:1–14

Ex 34:1 — And the LORD said unto Moses, Hew thee two tables of stone like unto the first: and I will write upon *these* tables the words that were in the first tables, which thou brakest.

- **Placed in the ark.**

Dt 10:5 — And I turned myself and came down from the mount, and put the tables in the ark which I had made; and there they be, as the LORD commanded me.

1Ki 8:9 — *There was* nothing in the ark save the two tables of stone, which Moses put there at Horeb, when the LORD made *a covenant* with the children of Israel, when they came out of the land of Egypt.

Heb 9:4 — Which had the golden censer, and the ark of the covenant overlaid round about with gold, wherein *was* the golden pot that had manna, and Aaron's rod that budded, and the tables of the covenant;

- **A slab on which inscriptions were made.**

Isa 30:8 — Now go, write it before them in a table, and note it in a book, that it may be for the time to come for ever and ever:

Hab 2:2 — And the LORD answered me, and said, Write the vision, and make *it* plain upon tables, that he may run that readeth it.

Lk 1:63 — And he asked for a writing table, and wrote, saying, His name is John. And they marvelled all.

- **Figurative.**

Pr 3:3 — Let not mercy and truth forsake thee: bind them about thy neck; write them upon the table of thine heart:

Jer 17:1 — The sin of Judah *is* written with a pen of iron, *and* with the point of a diamond: *it is* graven upon the table of their heart, and upon the horns of your altars;

2Co 3:3 — *Forasmuch as ye are* manifestly declared to be the epistle of Christ ministered by us, written not with ink, but with the Spirit of the living God; not in tables of stone, but in fleshy tables of the heart.

TABOR

- **A mountain on the border of Issachar.**

Jos 19:22 — And the coast reacheth to Tabor, and Shahazimah, and Beth-shemesh; and the outgoings of their border were at Jordan: sixteen cities with their villages.

Jgs 8:18 — Then said he unto Zebah and Zalmunna, What manner of men *were they* whom ye slew at Tabor? And they answered, As thou *art,* so *were* they; each one resembled the children of a king.

Ps 89:12 — The north and the south thou hast created them: Tabor and Hermon shall rejoice in thy name.

Jer 46:18 — *As* I live, saith the King, whose name *is* the LORD of hosts, Surely as Tabor *is* among the mountains, and as Carmel by the sea, *so* shall he come.

Hos 5:1 — Hear ye this, O priests; and hearken, ye house of Israel; and give ye ear, O house of the king; for judgment *is* toward you, because ye have been a snare on Mizpah, and a net spread upon Tabor.

- **Assembling place of Barak's army.**

Jgs 4:6 — And she sent and called Barak the son of Abinoam out of Kedesh-naphtali, and said unto him, Hath not the LORD God of Israel commanded, *saying,* Go and draw toward mount Tabor, and take with thee ten thousand men of the children of Naphtali and of the children of Zebulun?

Jgs 4:12 — And they shewed Sisera that Barak the son of Abinoam was gone up to mount Tabor.

Jgs 4:14 — And Deborah said unto Barak, Up; for this *is* the day in which the LORD hath delivered Sisera into thine hand: is not the LORD gone out before thee? So Barak went down from mount Tabor, and ten thousand men after him.

- **A plain of unknown location.**

1Sa 10:3 — Then shalt thou go on forward from thence, and thou shalt come to the plain of Tabor, and there shall meet thee three men going up to God to Bethel, one carrying three kids, and another carrying three loaves of bread, and another carrying a bottle of wine:

- **A Levitical city in Zebulun.**

1Ch 6:77 — Unto the rest of the children of Merari *were given* out of the tribe of Zebulun. Rimmon with her suburbs, Tabor with her suburbs:

See: Chisloth-Tabor

TABRET **See: Timbrel**

TABRIMON • Father of Ben-hadad.

1Ki 15:18 — Then Asa took all the silver and the gold *that were* left in the treasures of the house of the LORD, and the treasures of the king's house, and delivered them into the hand of his servants: and king Asa sent them to Ben-hadad, the son of Tabrimon, the son of Hezion, king of Syria, that dwelt at Damascus, saying,

TACT

Pr 15:1 — A soft answer turneth away wrath: but grievous words stir up anger.

Pr 25:15 — By long forbearing is a prince persuaded, and a soft tongue breaketh the bone.

- **In preaching.**

1Co 9:19–22

2Co 12:6 — For though I would desire to glory, I shall not be a fool; for I will say the truth: but *now* I forbear, lest any man should think of me above that which he seeth me *to be,* or *that* he heareth of me.

- **Of Gideon.**

Jgs 8:1–3

- **Of Saul, in managing malcontents.**

1Sa 11:12–15

1Sa 10:27 — But the children of Belial said, How shall this man save us? And they despised him, and brought him no presents. But he held his peace.

1Sa 11:7 — And he took a yoke of oxen, and hewed them in pieces, and sent *them* throughout all the coasts of Israel by the hands of messengers, saying, Whosoever cometh not forth after Saul and after Samuel, so shall it be done unto his oxen. And the fear of the LORD fell on the people, and they came out with one consent.

- **Nabal's wife.**

1Sa 25:18–37

- **In David's popular methods.**
  - **In mourning for Abner.**

    2Sa 3:28–37
  - **In organizing the temple music.**

    1Ch 15:16–24
  - **In securing popular consent to bringing the ark to Jerusalem.**

    1Ch 13:1–4

- **Joab's trick in obtaining David's consent to the return of Absalom.**

2Sa 14:1–22

- **The wise woman of Abel.**

2Sa 20:16–22

- **Solomon, in arbitrating between the harlots.**

1Ki 3:24–28

- **Mordecai, in concealing Esther's nationality.**

Est 2:10 — Esther had not shewed her people nor her kindred: for Mordecai had charged her that she should not shew *it.*

- **Esther, in placating the king.**

Est 5:1–7:10

- **Paul, in circumcising Timothy.**

Ac 16:3 — Him would Paul have to go forth with him; and took and circumcised him because of the Jews which were in those quarters: for they knew all that his father was a Greek.

- **Paul, in turning the preaching of adversaries to account.**

Php 1:10–22

- **Paul, in stimulating benevolent giving.**

2Co 8:1–8; 9:1–5

- **Paul, in arraying the two religious factions of the Jews against each other when he was in trouble.**

Ac 23:6–10

- **The town clerk of Ephesus.**

Ac 19:35–41

- **The church council at Jerusalem.**

Ac 21:20–25

TACTICS

See: Armies

See: Strategy

TADMOR

• A city built in the wilderness by Solomon.

1Ki 9:18 — and Baalath, and Tadmor in the wilderness, in the land,

2Ch 8:4 — And he built Tadmor in the wilderness, and all the store cities, which he built in Hamath.

TAHAN

• Son of Ephraim.

Nu 26:35 — These *are* the sons of Ephraim after their families: of Shuthelah, the family of the Shuthalhites: of Becher, the family of the Bachrites: of Tahan, the family of the Tahanites.

• A descendant of Ephraim.

1Ch 7:25 — And Rephah *was* his son, also Resheph, and Telah his son, and Tahan his son,

TAHAPANES ➔See: Tahpanhes

TAHATH

• A camping place of the Israelites.

Nu 33:26–27

• A Kohathite.

1Ch 6:24 — Tahath his son, Uriel his son, Uzziah his son, and Shaul his son.

1Ch 6:37 — The son of Tahath, the son of Assir, the son of Ebiasaph, the son of Korah,

• The name of two Ephraimites.

1Ch 7:20 — And the sons of Ephraim; Shuthelah, and Bered his son, and Tahath his son, and Eladah his son, and Tahath his son,

TAHPANHES

• Called also Tahapanes and Tehaphnehes.

• A city in Egypt.

Jer 43:7–9

Jer 2:16 — Also the children of Noph and Tahapanes have broken the crown of thy head.

Jer 44:1 — The word that came to Jeremiah concerning all the Jews which dwell in the land of Egypt, which dwell at Migdol, and at Tahpanhes, and at Noph, and in the country of Pathros, saying,

Jer 46:14 — Declare ye in Egypt, and publish in Migdol, and publish in Noph and in Tahpanhes: say ye, Stand fast, and prepare thee; for the sword shall devour round about thee.

Eze 30:18 — At Tehaphnehes also the day shall be darkened, when I shall break there the yokes of Egypt: and the pomp of her strength shall cease in her: as for her, a cloud shall cover her, and her daughters shall go into captivity.

TAHPENES • A queen of Egypt.

1Ki 11:19–20

TAHREA

• Son of Micah.

1Ch 9:41 — And the sons of Micah *were,* Pithon, and Melech, and Tahrea, *and Ahaz.*

• Called Tarea.

1Ch 8:35 — And the sons of Micah *were,* Pithon, and Melech, and Tarea, and Ahaz.

TAHTIM-HODSHI • An unknown place.

2Sa 24:6 — Then they came to Gilead, and to the land of Tahtim-hodshi; and they came to Dan-jaan, and about to Zidon,

TAILORING

Ex 31:2–3

Ex 31:6 — And I, behold, I have given with him Aholiab, the son of Ahisamach, of the tribe of Dan: and in the hearts of all that are wise hearted I have put wisdom, that they may make all that I have commanded thee;

Ex 31:10 — And the cloths of service, and the holy garments for Aaron the priest, and the garments of his sons, to minister in the priest's office,

Ex 39:1 — And of the blue, and purple, and scarlet, they made cloths of service, to do service in the holy *place,* and made the holy garments for Aaron; as the LORD commanded Moses.

TALEBEARER

Ps 15:1–3; Pr 26:20–22

Le 19:16 — Thou shalt not go up and down *as* a talebearer among thy people: neither shalt thou stand against the blood of thy neighbour: I *am* the LORD.

Pr 11:13 — A talebearer revealeth secrets: but he that is of a faithful spirit concealeth the matter.

Pr 16:28 — A froward man soweth strife: and a whisperer separateth chief friends.

Pr 17:9 — He that covereth a transgression seeketh love; but he that repeateth a matter separateth *very* friends.

Pr 18:8 — The words of a talebearer *are* as wounds, and they go down into the innermost parts of the belly.

Pr 20:19 — He that goeth about *as* a talebearer revealeth secrets: therefore meddle not with him that flattereth with his lips.

1Ti 5:11 — But the younger widows refuse: for when they have begun to wax wanton against Christ, they will marry;

1Ti 5:13 — And withal they learn *to be* idle, wandering about from house to house; and not only idle, but tattlers also and busybodies, speaking things which they ought not.

➔See: Busybody

➔See: Slander

➔See: Speaking; evil

• Instances of.

• Joseph.

Ge 37:2

• Israelites.

2Sa 3:23

• Tobiah.

Ne 6:1–19

TALENT

1Ki 9:14 — And Hiram sent to the king sixscore talents of gold.

1Ki 9:28 — And they came to Ophir, and fetched from thence gold, four hundred and twenty talents, and brought *it* to king Solomon.

1Ki 10:10 — And she gave the king an hundred and twenty talents of gold, and of spices very great store, and precious stones: there came no more such abundance of spices as these which the queen of Sheba gave to king Solomon.

1Ki 10:14 — Now the weight of gold that came to Solomon in one year was six hundred threescore and six talents of gold.

• A weight equal to three thousand shekels, about one hundred and twenty-five pounds.

Ex 38:25–26

• Value of.

• Gold, about 6000 pounds, or 29,100 dollars.

• Silver, 400 pounds, or 1940 dollars.

Mt 18:24 — And when he had begun to reckon, one was brought unto him, which owed him ten thousand talents.

Mt 25:15 — And unto one he gave five talents, to another two, and to another one; to every man according to his several ability; and straightway took his journey.

Mt 25:28 — Take therefore the talent from him, and give *it* unto him which hath ten talents.

TALKING

• With God.

See: Communion

TALMAI

• A son of Anak.

Nu 13:22 — And they ascended by the south, and came unto Hebron; where Ahiman, Sheshai, and Talmai, the children of Anak, *were.* (Now Hebron was built seven years before Zoan in Egypt.)

Jos 15:14 — And Caleb drove thence the three sons of Anak, Sheshai, and Ahiman, and Talmai, the children of Anak.

Jgs 1:10 — And Judah went against the Canaanites that dwelt in Hebron: (now the name of Hebron before *was* Kirjath-arba:) and they slew Sheshai, and Ahiman, and Talmai.

• King of Geshur.

2Sa 3:3 — And his second, Chileab, of Abigail the wife of Nabal the Carmelite; and the third, Absalom the son of Maacah the daughter of Talmai king of Geshur;

2Sa 13:37 — But Absalom fled, and went to Talmai, the son of Ammihud, king of Geshur. And *David* mourned for his son every day.

1Ch 3:2 — The third, Absalom the son of Maachah the daughter of Talmai king of Geshur: the fourth, Adonijah the son of Haggith:

TALMON

• A porter of the temple.

1Ch 9:17 — And the porters *were,* Shallum, and Akkub, and Talmon, and Ahiman, and their brethren: Shallum *was* the chief;

• Family of, return from captivity with Zerubbabel.

Ezr 2:42 — The children of the porters: the children of Shallum, the children of Ater, the children of Talmon, the children of Akkub, the children of Hatita, the children of Shobai, *in* all an hundred thirty and nine.

Ne 7:45 — The porters: the children of Shallum, the children of Ater, the children of Talmon, the children of Akkub, the children of Hatita, the children of Shobai, an hundred thirty and eight.

Ne 11:19 — Moreover the porters, Akkub, Talmon, and their brethren that kept the gates, *were* an hundred seventy and two.

Ne 12:25 — Mattaniah, and Bakbukiah, Obadiah, Meshullam, Talmon, Akkub, *were* porters keeping the ward at the thresholds of the gates.

TAMAH

• One of the Nethinim.

Ne 7:55 — The children of Barkos, the children of Sisera, the children of Tamah,

• Called Thamah.

Ezr 2:53 — The children of Barkos, the children of Sisera, the children of Thamah,

TAMAR

• Wife of the sons of Judah.

Ge 38:6–24

Ru 4:12 — And let thy house be like the house of Pharez, whom Tamar bare unto Judah, of the seed which the LORD shall give thee of this young woman.

1Ch 2:4 — And Tamar his daughter in law bare him Pharez and Zerah. All the sons of Judah *were* five.

• Called Thamar.

Mt 1:3 — And Judas begat Phares and Zara of Thamar; and Phares begat Esrom; and Esrom begat Aram;

• Daughter of David.

2Sa 13:1–32

1Ch 3:9 — *These were* all the sons of David, beside the sons of the concubines, and Tamar their sister.

• Daughter of Absalom.

2Sa 14:27 — And unto Absalom there were born three sons, and one daughter, whose name *was* Tamar: she was a woman of a fair countenance.

• A city of unknown location.

Eze 47:19 — And the south side southward, from Tamar *even* to the waters of strife *in* Kadesh, the river to the great sea. And *this is* the south side southward.

Eze 48:28 — And by the border of Gad, at the south side southward, the border shall be even from Tamar *unto* the waters of strife *in* Kadesh, *and* to the river toward the great sea.

TAMBOURINE ⇜See: Timbrel

TAMMUZ • A Syrian idol.

Eze 8:14 — Then he brought me to the door of the gate of the LORD's house which *was* toward the north; and, behold, there sat women weeping for Tammuz.

TANACH ⇜See: Taanach

TANHUMETH • Father of Seraiah.

2Ki 25:23 — And when all the captains of the armies, they and their men, heard that the king of Babylon had made Gedaliah governor, there came to Gedaliah to Mizpah, even Ishmael the son of Nethaniah, and Johanan the son of Careah, and Seraiah the son of Tanhumeth the Netophathite, and Jaazaniah the son of a Maachathite, they and their men.

Jer 40:8 — Then they came to Gedaliah to Mizpah, even Ishmael the son of Nethaniah, and Johanan and Jonathan the sons of Kareah, and Seraiah the son of Tanhumeth, and the sons of Ephai the Netophathite, and Jezaniah the son of a Maachathite, they and their men.

TANNING

Ac 10:5–6

Ac 9:43 — And it came to pass, that he tarried many days in Joppa with one Simon a tanner.

TANTALIZING

1Sa 1:6–7

1Ki 18:27 — And it came to pass at noon, that Elijah mocked them, and said, Cry aloud: for he *is* a god; either he is talking, or he is pursuing, or he is in a journey, *or* peradventure he sleepeth, and must be awaked.

TAPESTRY

Pr 7:16 — I have decked my bed with coverings of tapestry, with carved *works,* with fine linen of Egypt.

Pr 31:22 — She maketh herself coverings of tapestry; her clothing *is* silk and purple.

• Of the tabernacle.

Ex 26:1–14, 31–37; 27:9–17; 36:8–18

• Gold thread woven in.

Ex 39:3 — And they did beat the gold into thin plates, and cut *it into* wires, to work *it* in the blue, and in the purple, and in the scarlet, and in the fine linen, *with* cunning work.

• In palaces.

Est 1:6 — *Where were* white, green, and blue, *hangings,* fastened with cords of fine linen and purple to silver rings and pillars of marble: the beds *were of* gold and silver, upon a pavement of red, and blue, and white, and black, marble.

SS 1:5 — I *am* black, but comely, O ye daughters of Jerusalem, as the tents of Kedar, as the curtains of Solomon.

• In groves.

2Ki 23:7 — And he brake down the houses of the sodomites, that *were* by the house of the LORD, where the women wove hangings for the grove.

⇜See: Curtains

⇜See: Embroidery

TAPHATH • Daughter of Solomon.

1Ki 4:11 — The son of Abinadab, in all the region of Dor; which had Taphath the daughter of Solomon to wife:

TAPPUAH

• A city of Judah.

Jos 12:17 — The king of Tappuah, one; the king of Hepher, one;

Jos 15:34 — And Zanoah, and En-gannim, Tappuah, and Enam,

• A city in Ephraim.

Jos 16:8 — The border went out from Tappuah westward unto the river Kanah; and the goings out thereof were at the sea. This *is* the inheritance of the tribe of the children of Ephraim by their families.

Jos 17:8 — *Now* Manasseh had the land of Tappuah: but Tappuah on the border of Manasseh *belonged* to the children of Ephraim;

• Son of Hebron.

1Ch 2:43 — And the sons of Hebron; Korah, and Tappuah, and Rekem, and Shema.

TARAH • A camping place of the Israelites.

Nu 33:27–28

TARALAH • A city in Benjamin.

Jos 18:27 — And Rekem, and Irpeel, and Taralah,

TAREA

• A son of Micah.

1Ch 8:35 — And the sons of Micah *were,* Pithon, and Melech, and Tarea, and Ahaz.

• Called Tahrea.

1Ch 9:41 — And the sons of Micah *were,* Pithon, and Melech, and Tahrea, *and Ahaz.*

TARES

• Parable of.

Mt 13:24–30, 38–42

TARGET

• A defensive article of armor.

• Used by spearmen.

2Ch 14:8 — And Asa had an army *of men* that bare targets and spears, out of Judah three hundred thousand; and out of Benjamin, that bare shields and drew bows, two hundred and fourscore thousand: all these *were* mighty men of valour.

• Made of brass.

1Sa 17:6 — And *he had* greaves of brass upon his legs, and a target of brass between his shoulders.

• Made of gold.

1Ki 10:16 — And king Solomon made two hundred targets of beaten gold: six hundred *shekels* of gold went to one target.

2Ch 9:15 — And king Solomon made two hundred targets of beaten gold: six hundred *shekels* of beaten gold went to one target.

✦See: Shield

TARIFF ✦See: Duty

TARPELITES

- **An Assyrian tribe.**
- **Colonists in Samaria.**

Ezr 4:9 — Then *wrote* Rehum the chancellor, and Shimshai the scribe, and the rest of their companions; the Dinaites, the Apharsathchites, the Tarpelites, the Apharsites, the Archevites, the Babylonians, the Susanchites, the Dehavites, *and* the Elamites,

TARSHISH

- **Son of Javan.**

Ge 10:4 — And the sons of Javan; Elishah, and Tarshish, Kittim, and Dodanim.

1Ch 1:7 — And the sons of Javan; Elishah, and Tarshish, Kittim, and Dodanim.

- **Called also Tharshish [probably Spain].**

Ge 10:4–5

Ps 72:10 — The kings of Tarshish and of the isles shall bring presents: the kings of Sheba and Seba shall offer gifts.

Isa 66:19 — And I will set a sign among them, and I will send those that escape of them unto the nations, *to* Tarshish, Pul, and Lud, that draw the bow, *to* Tubal, and Javan, *to* the isles afar off, that have not heard my fame, neither have seen my glory; and they shall declare my glory among the Gentiles.

- **Solomon makes valuable imports from.**

1Ki 10:22 — For the king had at sea a navy of Tharshish with the navy of Hiram: once in three years came the navy of Tharshish, bringing gold, and silver, ivory, and apes, and peacocks.

2Ch 9:21 — For the king's ships went to Tarshish with the servants of Huram: every three years once came the ships of Tarshish bringing gold, and silver, ivory, and apes, and peacocks.

- **Commerce and wealth of.**

Isa 23:1–14

1Ki 10:22 — For the king had at sea a navy of Tharshish with the navy of Hiram: once in three years came the navy of Tharshish, bringing gold, and silver, ivory, and apes, and peacocks.

1Ki 22:48 — Jehoshaphat made ships of Tharshish to go to Ophir for gold: but they went not; for the ships were broken at Ezion-geber.

2Ch 9:21 — For the king's ships went to Tarshish with the servants of Huram: every three years once came the ships of Tarshish bringing gold, and silver, ivory, and apes, and peacocks.

2Ch 20:36 — And he joined himself with him to make ships to go to Tarshish: and they made the ships in Ezion-gaber.

Ps 48:7 — Thou breakest the ships of Tarshish with an east wind.

Isa 2:16 — And upon all the ships of Tarshish, and upon all pleasant pictures.

Isa 60:9 — Surely the isles shall wait for me, and the ships of Tarshish first, to bring thy sons from far, their silver and their gold with them, unto the name of the LORD thy God, and to the Holy One of Israel, because he hath glorified thee.

Jer 10:9 — Silver spread into plates is brought from Tarshish, and gold from Uphaz, the work of the workman, and of the hands of the founder: blue and purple is their clothing: they *are* all the work of cunning *men*.

Eze 27:12 — Tarshish *was* thy merchant by reason of the multitude of all *kind of* riches; with silver, iron, tin, and lead, they traded in thy fairs.

Eze 27:25 — The ships of Tarshish did sing of thee in thy market: and thou wast replenished, and made very glorious in the midst of the seas.

Eze 38:13 — Sheba, and Dedan, and the merchants of Tarshish, with all the young lions thereof, shall say unto thee, Art thou come to take a spoil? hast thou gathered thy company to take a prey? to carry away silver and gold, to take away cattle and goods, to take a great spoil?

- **Jonah would flee to.**

Jnh 1:3 — But Jonah rose up to flee unto Tarshish from the presence of the LORD, and went down to Joppa; and he found a ship going to Tarshish: so he paid the fare thereof, and went down into it, to go with them unto Tarshish from the presence of the LORD.

Jnh 4:2 — And he prayed unto the LORD, and said, I pray thee, O LORD, *was* not this my saying, when I was yet in my country? Therefore I fled before unto Tarshish: for I knew that thou *art* a gracious God, and merciful, slow to anger, and of great kindness, and repentest thee of the evil.

- **Prophecies concerning.**

Isa 23:1–14

Ps 72:10 — The kings of Tarshish and of the isles shall bring presents: the kings of Sheba and Seba shall offer gifts.

Isa 2:16 — And upon all the ships of Tarshish, and upon all pleasant pictures.

Isa 60:9 — Surely the isles shall wait for me, and the ships of Tarshish first, to bring thy sons from far, their silver and their gold with them, unto the name of the LORD thy God, and to the Holy One of Israel, because he hath glorified thee.

Isa 66:19 — And I will set a sign among them, and I will send those that escape of them unto the nations, *to* Tarshish, Pul, and Lud, that draw the bow, *to* Tubal, and Javan, *to* the isles afar off, that have not heard my fame, neither have seen my glory; and they shall declare my glory among the Gentiles.

- **Son of Bilhan.**

1Ch 7:10 — The sons also of Jediael; Bilhan: and the sons of Bilhan; Jeush, and Benjamin, and Ehud, and Chenaanah, and Zethan, and Tharshish, and Ahishahar.

• A Persian prince.

Est 1:14 — And the next unto him *was* Carshena, Shethar, Admatha, Tarshish, Meres, Marsena, *and* Memucan, the seven princes of Persia and Media, which saw the king's face, *and* which sat the first in the kingdom;)

TARSUS, capital of Cilicia, in Asia Minor

• Paul's birthplace.

Ac 9:11 — And the Lord *said* unto him, Arise, and go into the street which is called Straight, and enquire in the house of Judas for *one* called Saul, of Tarsus: for, behold, he prayeth,

Ac 21:39 — But Paul said, I am a man *which am* a Jew of Tarsus, *a city* in Cilicia, a citizen of no mean city: and, I beseech thee, suffer me to speak unto the people.

Ac 22:3 — I am verily a man *which am* a Jew, born in Tarsus, a city in Cilicia, yet brought up in this city at the feet of Gamaliel, *and* taught according to the perfect manner of the law of the fathers, and was zealous toward God, as ye all are this day.

• Paul sent to, from Jerusalem, to avoid assassination.

Ac 9:30 — *Which* when the brethren knew, they brought him down to Caesarea, and sent him forth to Tarsus.

• Paul brought from, by Barnabas.

Ac 11:25–26

TARTAK • An Assyrian idol.

2Ki 17:31 — And the Avites made Nibhaz and Tartak, and the Sepharvites burnt their children in fire to Adrammelech and Anammelech, the gods of Sepharvaim.

TARTAN • An Assyrian general.

2Ki 18:17 — And the king of Assyria sent Tartan and Rabsaris and Rab-shakeh from Lachish to king Hezekiah with a great host against Jerusalem. And they went up and came to Jerusalem. And when they were come up, they came and stood by the conduit of the upper pool, which is in the highway of the fuller's field.

Isa 20:1 — In the year that Tartan came unto Ashdod, (when Sargon the king of Assyria sent him,) and fought against Ashdod, and took it;

TASKMASTERS

Ex 5:13–14

See: Master

See: Oppression

See: Servant

TASTE

• The sense of, lost.

2Sa 19:35 — I *am* this day fourscore years old: *and* can I discern between good and evil? can thy servant taste what I eat or what I drink? can I hear any more the voice of singing men and singing women? wherefore then should thy servant be yet a burden unto my lord the king?

TATNAI • A Persian governor in Samaria.

Ezr 5:3 — At the same time came to them Tatnai, governor on this side the river, and Shethar-boznai, and their companions, and said thus unto them, Who hath commanded you to build this house, and to make up this wall?

Ezr 5:6 — The copy of the letter that Tatnai, governor on this side the river, and Shethar-boznai, and his companions the Apharsachites, which *were* on this side the river, sent unto Darius the king:

Ezr 6:6 — Now *therefore,* Tatnai, governor beyond the river, Shethar-boznai, and your companions the Apharsachites, which *are* beyond the river, be ye far from thence:

Ezr 6:13 — Then Tatnai, governor on this side the river, Shethar-boznai, and their companions, according to that which Darius the king had sent, so they did speedily.

TATTLER **See: Talebearer**

TATTOOING

• Forbidden.

Le 19:28 — Ye shall not make any cuttings in your flesh for the dead, nor print any marks upon you: I *am* the LORD.

TAVERNS **See: Three Taverns**

TAX

• Poll.

Ex 30:11–16

Ex 38:26 — A bekah for every man, *that is,* half a shekel, after the shekel of the sanctuary, for every one that went to be numbered, from twenty years old and upward, for six hundred thousand and three thousand and five hundred and fifty *men.*

Ne 10:32 — Also we made ordinances for us, to charge ourselves yearly with the third part of a shekel for the service of the house of our God;

Lk 2:1 — And it came to pass in those days, that there went out a decree from Caesar Augustus, that all the world should be taxed.

• Jesus pays.

Mt 17:24–27

• Land.

Ge 41:34 — Let Pharaoh do *this,* and let him appoint officers over the land, and take up the fifth part of the land of Egypt in the seven plenteous years.

Ge 41:48 — And he gathered up all the food of the seven years, which were in the land of Egypt, and laid up the food in the cities: the food of the field, which *was* round about every city, laid he up in the same.

2Ki 23:35 — And Jehoiakim gave the silver and the gold to Pharaoh; but he taxed the land to give the money according to the commandment of Pharaoh: he exacted the silver and the gold of the people of the land, of every one according to his taxation, to give *it* unto Pharaoh-nechoh.

• **Land mortgaged for.**

Ne 5:3–4

• **Priests exempted from.**

Ge 47:26 — And Joseph made it a law over the land of Egypt unto this day, *that* Pharaoh should have the fifth *part;* except the land of the priests only, *which* became not Pharaoh's.

Ezr 7:24 — Also we certify you, that touching any of the priests and Levites, singers, porters, Nethinims, or ministers of this house of God, it shall not be lawful to impose toll, tribute, or custom, upon them.

• **Paid in grain.**

Am 5:11 — Forasmuch therefore as your treading *is* upon the poor, and ye take from him burdens of wheat: ye have built houses of hewn stone, but ye shall not dwell in them; ye have planted pleasant vineyards, but ye shall not drink wine of them.

Am 7:1 — Thus hath the Lord GOD shewed unto me; and, behold, he formed grasshoppers in the beginning of the shooting up of the latter growth; and, lo, *it was* the latter growth after the king's mowings.

• **Paid in provisions.**

1Ki 4:7–28

• **Personal.**

2Ki 15:19–20

1Ki 9:15 — And this *is* the reason of the levy which king Solomon raised; for to build the house of the LORD, and his own house, and Millo, and the wall of Jerusalem, and Hazor, and Megiddo, and Gezer.

2Ki 23:35 — And Jehoiakim gave the silver and the gold to Pharaoh; but he taxed the land to give the money according to the commandment of Pharaoh: he exacted the silver and the gold of the people of the land, of every one according to his taxation, to give *it* unto Pharaoh-nechoh.

• **Resisted by Israelites.**

1Ki 12:18 — Then king Rehoboam sent Adoram, who *was* over the tribute; and all Israel stoned him with stones, that he died. Therefore king Rehoboam made speed to get him up to his chariot, to flee to Jerusalem.

2Ch 10:18 — Then king Rehoboam sent Hadoram that *was* over the tribute; and the children of Israel stoned him with stones, that he died. But king Rehoboam made speed to get him up to *his* chariot, to flee to Jerusalem.

• **World-wide, levied by Caesar.**

Lk 2:1–3

• **Collectors of.**

2Sa 20:24 — And Adoram *was* over the tribute: and Jehoshaphat the son of Ahilud *was* recorder:

1Ki 4:6 — And Ahishar *was* over the household: and Adoniram the son of Abda *was* over the tribute.

Isa 33:18 — Thine heart shall meditate terror. Where *is* the scribe? where *is* the receiver? where *is* he that counted the towers?

Da 11:20 — Then shall stand up in his estate a raiser of taxes *in* the glory of the kingdom: but within few days he shall be destroyed, neither in anger, nor in battle.

Mk 2:14 — And as he passed by, he saw Levi the *son* of Alphaeus sitting at the receipt of custom, and said unto him, Follow me. And he arose and followed him.

Lk 3:13 — And he said unto them, Exact no more than that which is appointed you.

Lk 5:27 — And after these things he went forth, and saw a publican, named Levi, sitting at the receipt of custom: and he said unto him, Follow me.

• **Collectors of, unpopular.**

Mt 5:46 — For if ye love them which love you, what reward have ye? do not even the publicans the same?

Mt 9:11 — And when the Pharisees saw *it,* they said unto his disciples, Why eateth your Master with publicans and sinners?

Mt 11:19 — The Son of man came eating and drinking, and they say, Behold a man gluttonous, and a winebibber, a friend of publicans and sinners. But wisdom is justified of her children.

Mt 18:17 — And if he shall neglect to hear them, tell *it* unto the church: but if he neglect to hear the church, let him be unto thee as an heathen man and a publican.

Mt 21:31 — Whether of them twain did the will of *his* father? They say unto him, The first. Jesus saith unto them, Verily I say unto you, That the publicans and the harlots go into the kingdom of God before you.

Lk 18:11 — The Pharisee stood and prayed thus with himself, God, I thank thee, that I am not as other men *are,* extortioners, unjust, adulterers, or even as this publican.

• **Collectors of, stoned.**

2Ch 10:18 — Then king Rehoboam sent Hadoram that *was* over the tribute; and the children of Israel stoned him with stones, that he died. But king Rehoboam made speed to get him up to *his* chariot, to flee to Jerusalem.

TAXES

Lk 2:3–5; Ro 13:1–7; 1Ti 2:1–3

Da 4:32 — And they shall drive thee from men, and thy dwelling *shall be* with the beasts of the field: they shall make thee to eat grass as oxen, and seven times shall pass over thee, until thou know that the most High ruleth in the kingdom of men, and giveth it to whomsoever he will.

Mt 22:21 — They say unto him, Caesar's. Then saith he unto them, Render therefore unto Caesar the things which are Caesar's; and unto God the things that are God's.

TEACHERS

• **Samuel, head of school of prophets.**

1Sa 19:20 — And Saul sent messengers to take David: and when they saw the company of the prophets prophesying, and Samuel standing *as* appointed over them, the Spirit of God was upon the messengers of Saul, and they also prophesied.

• **Elisha, head of, at Gilgal.**

2Ki 4:38 — And Elisha came again to Gilgal: and *there was* a dearth in the land; and the sons of the prophets *were* sitting before him: and he said unto his servant, Set on the great pot, and seethe pottage for the sons of the prophets.

See: Instruction

See: Jesus, Teacher

See: Minister, a sacred teacher; duties of

• False.

1Ti 1:7 — Desiring to be teachers of the law; understanding neither what they say, nor whereof they affirm.

2Ti 4:2 — Preach the word; be instant in season, out of season; reprove, rebuke, exhort with all longsuffering and doctrine.

2Pe 2:1 — But there were false prophets also among the people, even as there shall be false teachers among you, who privily shall bring in damnable heresies, even denying the Lord that bought them, and bring upon themselves swift destruction.

• Admonition against.

Dt 13:1–3; Mt 15:2–20; 23:2–33; Lk 11:38–52

Mt 5:19 — Whosoever therefore shall break one of these least commandments, and shall teach men so, he shall be called the least in the kingdom of heaven: but whosoever shall do and teach *them,* the same shall be called great in the kingdom of heaven.

Mt 7:15 — Beware of false prophets, which come to you in sheep's clothing, but inwardly they are ravening wolves.

See: Minister, False and Corrupt

TEACHING

See: Instruction

See: Minister, a sacred teacher; duties of

TEARS

Ps 6:6 — I am weary with my groaning; all the night make I my bed to swim; I water my couch with my tears.

Ps 39:12 — Hear my prayer, O LORD, and give ear unto my cry; hold not thy peace at my tears: for I *am* a stranger with thee, *and* a sojourner, as all my fathers *were.*

Ps 42:3 — My tears have been my meat day and night, while they continually say unto me, Where *is* thy God?

• Observed by God.

Isa 38:3–5

Ps 56:8 — Thou tellest my wanderings: put thou my tears into thy bottle: *are they* not in thy book?

• Wiped away.

Rev 7:17 — For the Lamb which is in the midst of the throne shall feed them, and shall lead them unto living fountains of waters: and God shall wipe away all tears from their eyes.

• None in heaven.

Rev 21:4 — And God shall wipe away all tears from their eyes; and there shall be no more death, neither sorrow, nor crying, neither shall there be any more pain: for the former things are passed away.

• Figurative.

Ps 80:5 — Thou feedest them with the bread of tears; and givest them tears to drink in great measure.

TEBAH • Son of Nahor.

Ge 22:24 — And his concubine, whose name *was* Reumah, she bare also Tebah, and Gaham, and Thahash, and Maachah.

TEBALIAH • Son of Hosah.

1Ch 26:11 — Hilkiah the second, Tebaliah the third, Zechariah the fourth: all the sons and brethren of Hosah *were* thirteen.

TEBETH • The tenth month, or January.

Est 2:16 — So Esther was taken unto king Ahasuerus into his house royal in the tenth month, which *is* the month Tebeth, in the seventh year of his reign.

Eze 29:1 — In the tenth year, in the tenth *month,* in the twelfth *day* of the month, the word of the LORD came unto me, saying,

TECHNICALITIES

• Legal.

Mt 12:2 — But when the Pharisees saw *it,* they said unto him, Behold, thy disciples do that which is not lawful to do upon the sabbath day.

Mt 12:10 — And, behold, there was a man which had *his* hand withered. And they asked him, saying, Is it lawful to heal on the sabbath days? that they might accuse him.

Lk 6:2 — And certain of the Pharisees said unto them, Why do ye that which is not lawful to do on the sabbath days?

Lk 6:7 — And the scribes and Pharisees watched him, whether he would heal on the sabbath day; that they might find an accusation against him.

TEETH

Pr 10:26 — As vinegar to the teeth, and as smoke to the eyes, so *is* the sluggard to them that send him.

• Gnashing of.

Ps 112:10 — The wicked shall see *it,* and be grieved; he shall gnash with his teeth, and melt away: the desire of the wicked shall perish.

La 2:16 — All thine enemies have opened their mouth against thee: they hiss and gnash the teeth: they say, We have swallowed *her* up: certainly this *is* the day that we looked for; we have found, we have seen *it.*

Mt 8:12 — But the children of the kingdom shall be cast out into outer darkness: there shall be weeping and gnashing of teeth.

Mt 13:42 — And shall cast them into a furnace of fire: there shall be wailing and gnashing of teeth.

Mt 13:50 — And shall cast them into the furnace of fire: there shall be wailing and gnashing of teeth.

Mt 22:13 — Then said the king to the servants, Bind him hand and foot, and take him away, and cast *him* into outer darkness; there shall be weeping and gnashing of teeth.

Mt 24:51 — And shall cut him asunder, and appoint *him* his portion with the hypocrites: there shall be weeping and gnashing of teeth.

Mt 25:30 — And cast ye the unprofitable servant into outer darkness: there shall be weeping and gnashing of teeth.

Mk 9:18 — And wheresoever he taketh him, he teareth him: and he foameth, and gnasheth with his teeth, and pineth away: and I spake to thy disciples that they should cast him out; and they could not.

Lk 13:28 — There shall be weeping and gnashing of teeth, when ye shall see Abraham, and Isaac, and Jacob, and all the prophets, in the kingdom of God, and you *yourselves* thrust out.

TEHAPHNEHES ⇽See: Tahpanhes

TEHINNAH • Son of Eshton.

1Ch 4:12 — And Eshton begat Beth-rapha, and Paseah, and Tehinnah the father of Ir-nahash. These *are* the men of Rechah.

TEIL TREE

Isa 6:13 — But yet in it *shall be* a tenth, and *it* shall return, and shall be eaten: as a teil tree, and as an oak, whose substance is in them, when they cast *their leaves: so* the holy seed *shall be* the substance thereof.

TEKEL

Da 5:25 — And this *is* the writing that was written, MENE, MENE, TEKEL, UPHARSIN.

Da 5:27 — TEKEL; Thou art weighed in the balances, and art found wanting.

TEKOA

• Son of Ashur.

1Ch 2:24 — And after that Hezron was dead in Caleb-ephratah, then Abiah Hezron's wife bare him Ashur the father of Tekoa.

1Ch 4:5 — And Ashur the father of Tekoa had two wives, Helah and Naarah.

• Some authorities interpret these passages to mean that Ashur colonized the town of Tekoah.

⇽See: Tekoah

TEKOAH

• Called also Tekoa.

• A city in Judah.

2Ch 11:6 — He built even Bethlehem, and Etam, and Tekoa,

• Home of the woman who interceded for Absalom.

2Sa 14:2 — And Joab sent to Tekoah, and fetched thence a wise woman, and said unto her, I pray thee, feign thyself to be a mourner, and put on now mourning apparel, and anoint not thyself with oil, but be as a woman that had a long time mourned for the dead:

2Sa 14:4 — And when the woman of Tekoah spake to the king, she fell on her face to the ground, and did obeisance, and said, Help, O king.

2Sa 14:9 — And the woman of Tekoah said unto the king, My lord, O king, the iniquity *be* on me, and on my father's house: and the king and his throne *be* guiltless.

• Rebuilt by Rehoboam.

2Ch 11:6 — He built even Bethlehem, and Etam, and Tekoa,

• Desert of.

2Ch 20:20 — And they rose early in the morning, and went forth into the wilderness of Tekoa: and as they went forth, Jehoshaphat stood and said, Hear me, O Judah, and ye inhabitants of Jerusalem; Believe in the LORD your God, so shall ye be established; believe his prophets, so shall ye prosper.

• People of, work on the new wall of Jerusalem.

Ne 3:5 — And next unto them the Tekoites repaired; but their nobles put not their necks to the work of their Lord.

Ne 3:27 — After them the Tekoites repaired another piece, over against the great tower that lieth out, even unto the wall of Ophel.

• Prophecy concerning.

Jer 6:1 — O ye children of Benjamin, gather yourselves to flee out of the midst of Jerusalem, and blow the trumpet in Tekoa, and set up a sign of fire in Beth-haccerem: for evil appeareth out of the north, and great destruction.

• Home of Amos.

Am 1:1 — The words of Amos, who was among the herdmen of Tekoa, which he saw concerning Israel in the days of Uzziah king of Judah, and in the days of Jeroboam the son of Joash king of Israel, two years before the earthquake.

⇽See: Tekoa

TEL-ABIB • Residence of Jewish captives in Babylonia.

Eze 3:15 — Then I came to them of the captivity at Tel-abib, that dwelt by the river of Chebar, and I sat where they sat, and remained there astonished among them seven days.

TEL-HARSA

• Called also Tel-Haresha.

• A place in Babylonia.

Ezr 2:59 — And these *were* they which went up from Tel-melah, Tel-harsa, Cherub, Addan, *and* Immer: but they could not shew their father's house, and their seed, whether they *were* of Israel:

Ne 7:61 — And these *were* they which went up *also* from Telmelah, Telharesha, Cherub, Addon, and Immer: but they could not shew their father's house, nor their seed, whether they *were* of Israel.

TEL-MELAH • A place in Babylonia.

Ezr 2:59 — And these *were* they which went up from Tel-melah, Tel-harsa, Cherub, Addan, *and* Immer: but they could not shew their father's house, and their seed, whether they *were* of Israel:

Ne 7:61 — And these *were* they which went up *also* from Telmelah, Telharesha, Cherub, Addon, and Immer: but they could not shew their father's house, nor their seed, whether they *were* of Israel.

TELAH • Son of Rephah.

1Ch 7:25 — And Rephah *was* his son, also Resheph, and Telah his son, and Tahan his son,

TELAIM • A place of unknown location.

1Sa 15:4 — And Saul gathered the people together, and numbered them in Telaim, two hundred thousand footmen, and ten thousand men of Judah.

TELASSAR

• Called also Thelasar.

• A city or district conquered by the Assyrians.

2Ki 19:12 — Have the gods of the nations delivered them which my fathers have destroyed; *as* Gozan, and Haran, and Rezeph, and the children of Eden which *were* in Thelasar?

Isa 37:12 — Have the gods of the nations delivered them which my fathers have destroyed, *as* Gozan, and Haran, and Rezeph, and the children of Eden which *were* in Telassar?

TELEM

• A city of Judah.

Jos 15:24 — Ziph, and Telem, and Bealoth,

• A porter who put away his Gentile wife.

Ezr 10:24 — Of the singers also; Eliashib: and of the porters; Shallum, and Telem, and Uri.

TEMA

• Son of Ishmael.

Ge 25:15 — Hadar, and Tema, Jetur, Naphish, and Kedemah:

1Ch 1:30 — Mishma and Dumah, Massa, Hadad, and Tema,

• A people of Arabia, probably descended from Tema, Ishmael's son.

Job 6:19 — The troops of Tema looked, the companies of Sheba waited for them.

Isa 21:14 — The inhabitants of the land of Tema brought water to him that was thirsty, they prevented with their bread him that fled.

Jer 25:23 — Dedan, and Tema, and Buz, and all *that are* in the utmost corners,

TEMAN

• Son of Eliphaz.

Ge 36:11 — And the sons of Eliphaz were Teman, Omar, Zepho, and Gatam, and Kenaz.

Ge 36:15 — These *were* dukes of the sons of Esau: the sons of Eliphaz the firstborn *son* of Esau; duke Teman, duke Omar, duke Zepho, duke Kenaz,

Ge 36:42 — Duke Kenaz, duke Teman, duke Mibzar,

1Ch 1:36 — The sons of Eliphaz; Teman, and Omar, Zephi, and Gatam, Kenaz, and Timna, and Amalek.

1Ch 1:53 — Duke Kenaz, duke Teman, duke Mibzar,

• A people supposed to be descended from Teman, son of Eliphaz.

• Called also Temani and Temanites.

Ge 36:34 — And Jobab died, and Husham of the land of Temani reigned in his stead.

Job 2:11 — Now when Job's three friends heard of all this evil that was come upon him, they came every one from his own place; Eliphaz the Temanite, and Bildad the Shuhite, and Zophar the Naamathite: for they had made an appointment together to come to mourn with him and to comfort him.

• Prophecies concerning.

Jer 49:7 — Concerning Edom, thus saith the LORD of hosts; *Is* wisdom no more in Teman? is counsel perished from the prudent? is their wisdom vanished?

Eze 25:13 — Therefore thus saith the Lord GOD; I will also stretch out mine hand upon Edom, and will cut off man and beast from it; and I will make it desolate from Teman; and they of Dedan shall fall by the sword.

Am 1:12 — But I will send a fire upon Teman, which shall devour the palaces of Bozrah.

Ob 1:9 — And thy mighty *men,* O Teman, shall be dismayed, to the end that every one of the mount of Esau may be cut off by slaughter.

Hab 3:3 — God came from Teman, and the Holy One from mount Paran. Selah. His glory covered the heavens, and the earth was full of his praise.

TEMANI ➜See: Teman

TEMANITE ➜See: Teman

TEMENI • Son of Ashur.

1Ch 4:6 — And Naarah bare him Ahuzam, and Hepher, and Temeni, and Haahashtari. These *were* the sons of Naarah.

TEMPER

➜See: Anger

➜See: Malice

➜See: Self-Control

TEMPERANCE

Est 1:7–8; Pr 23:1–3; Da 1:12–16; 1Th 5:6–8; 1Ti 3:2–3; Tit 1:7–8; 2:2–3; 2Pe 1:5–6

Pr 25:16 — Hast thou found honey? eat so much as is sufficient for thee, lest thou be filled therewith, and vomit it.

Da 1:8 — But Daniel purposed in his heart that he would not defile himself with the portion of the king's meat, nor with the wine which he drank: therefore he requested of the prince of the eunuchs that he might not defile himself.

Ro 13:14 — But put ye on the Lord Jesus Christ, and make not provision for the flesh, to *fulfil* the lusts *thereof.*

1Co 9:25 — And every man that striveth for the mastery is temperate in all things. Now they *do it* to obtain a corruptible crown; but we an incorruptible.

1Co 9:27 — But I keep under my body, and bring *it* into subjection: lest that by any means, when I have preached to others, I myself should be a castaway.

Php 4:5 — Let your moderation be known unto all men. The Lord *is* at hand.

1Ti 3:8 — Likewise *must* the deacons *be* grave, not doubletongued, not given to much wine, not greedy of filthy lucre;

Tit 2:12 — Teaching us that, denying ungodliness and worldly lusts, we should live soberly, righteously, and godly, in this present world;

See: Abstinence, Total

See: Drunkenness

See: Wine

TEMPLE

• Ezekiel's vision of.

Eze 40:1–48:35

Eze 37:26 — Moreover I will make a covenant of peace with them; it shall be an everlasting covenant with them: and I will place them, and multiply them, and will set my sanctuary in the midst of them for evermore.

Eze 37:28 — And the heathen shall know that I the LORD do sanctify Israel, when my sanctuary shall be in the midst of them for evermore.

• Herod's.

• Forty-six years in building.

Jn 2:20 — Then said the Jews, Forty and six years was this temple in building, and wilt thou rear it up in three days?

• Goodly stones of.

Mk 13:1 — And as he went out of the temple, one of his disciples saith unto him, Master, see what manner of stones and what buildings *are here!*

Lk 21:5 — And as some spake of the temple, how it was adorned with goodly stones and gifts, he said,

• Magnificence of.

Mt 24:1 — And Jesus went out, and departed from the temple: and his disciples came to *him* for to shew him the buildings of the temple.

• Beautiful gate of.

Ac 3:10 — And they knew that it was he which sat for alms at the Beautiful gate of the temple: and they were filled with wonder and amazement at that which had happened unto him.

• Solomon's porch.

Jn 10:23 — And Jesus walked in the temple in Solomon's porch.

Ac 3:11 — And as the lame man which was healed held Peter and John, all the people ran together unto them in the porch that is called Solomon's, greatly wondering.

Ac 5:12 — And by the hands of the apostles were many signs and wonders wrought among the people; (and they were all with one accord in Solomon's porch.

• Treasury of.

Mk 12:41–44

• Zacharias, officiating priest in, has a vision of an angel; receives promise of a son.

Lk 1:5–23, 57–64

• Jesus brought to, according to the law and custom.

Lk 2:21–39

• Simeon blesses Jesus in.

Lk 2:25–35

• Anna, the prophetess, dwells in.

Lk 2:36–37

• Jesus in, when a youth.

Lk 2:46 — And it came to pass, that after three days they found him in the temple, sitting in the midst of the doctors, both hearing them, and asking them questions.

• Jesus taken to the pinnacle of, in his temptation.

Mt 4:5–7; Lk 4:9–12

• Jesus teaches in.

Mk 11:27–33; 12:35–44; Jn 5:14–47; 7:14–28; 8:1–59; 10:23–38

Mk 14:49 — I was daily with you in the temple teaching, and ye took me not: but the scriptures must be fulfilled.

Jn 18:20 — Jesus answered him, I spake openly to the world; I ever taught in the synagogue, and in the temple, whither the Jews always resort; and in secret have I said nothing.

• Jesus performs miracles in.

Mt 21:14–15

• Jesus drives money changers from.

Mt 21:12–13; Mk 11:15–17; Lk 19:45–46; Jn 2:15–16

• Captains of.

Lk 22:52 — Then Jesus said unto the chief priests, and captains of the temple, and the elders, which were come to him, Be ye come out, as against a thief, with swords and staves?

Ac 4:1 — And as they spake unto the people, the priests, and the captain of the temple, and the Sadducees, came upon them,

Ac 5:24 — Now when the high priest and the captain of the temple and the chief priests heard these things, they doubted of them whereunto this would grow.

Ac 5:26 — Then went the captain with the officers, and brought them without violence: for they feared the people, lest they should have been stoned.

- **Judas casts down the pieces of silver in.**
  Mt 27:5 — And he cast down the pieces of silver in the temple, and departed, and went and hanged himself.
- **Vail of, rent at the time of the crucifixion.**
  Mt 27:51 — And, behold, the veil of the temple was rent in twain from the top to the bottom; and the earth did quake, and the rocks rent;
- **The disciples worship in, after the resurrection.**
  Lk 24:53 — And were continually in the temple, praising and blessing God. Amen.
  Ac 2:46 — And they, continuing daily with one accord in the temple, and breaking bread from house to house, did eat their meat with gladness and singleness of heart,
  Ac 3:1 — Now Peter and John went up together into the temple at the hour of prayer, *being* the ninth *hour.*
- **Peter heals the lame man at the gate of.**
  Ac 3:1–16
- **Disciples preach in.**
  Ac 5:20–21
  Ac 5:42 — And daily in the temple, and in every house, they ceased not to teach and preach Jesus Christ.
- **Paul's vision in.**
  Ac 22:17–21
- **Paul observes the rights of.**
  Ac 21:26–30
- **Paul is apprehended in.**
  Ac 21:33 — Then the chief captain came near, and took him, and commanded *him* to be bound with two chains; and demanded who he was, and what he had done.
- **Prophecies concerning its destruction, by Daniel.**
  Da 8:11–15; 11:30–31
- **Jesus foretells the destruction of.**
  Mt 24:1–51
  Mk 13:2 — And Jesus answering said unto him, Seest thou these great buildings? there shall not be left one stone upon another, that shall not be thrown down.
  Lk 21:6 — *As for* these things which ye behold, the days will come, in the which there shall not be left one stone upon another, that shall not be thrown down.

- **Figurative.**
  - **Of the body of Jesus.**
    Mt 26:61 — And said, This *fellow* said, I am able to destroy the temple of God, and to build it in three days.
    Mt 27:40 — And saying, Thou that destroyest the temple, and buildest *it* in three days, save thyself. If thou be the Son of God, come down from the cross.
    Jn 2:19 — Jesus answered and said unto them, Destroy this temple, and in three days I will raise it up.
  - **Of the indwelling of God.**
    1Co 3:16–17
    2Co 6:16 — And what agreement hath the temple of God with idols? for ye are the temple of the living God; as God hath said, I will dwell in them, and walk in *them;* and I will be their God, and they shall be my people.
  - **Of the church.**
    Eph 2:21 — In whom all the building fitly framed together groweth unto an holy temple in the Lord:
    2Th 2:4 — Who opposeth and exalteth himself above all that is called God, or that is worshipped; so that he as God sitteth in the temple of God, shewing himself that he is God.
    Rev 3:12 — Him that overcometh will I make a pillar in the temple of my God, and he shall go no more out: and I will write upon him the name of my God, and the name of the city of my God, *which is* new Jerusalem, which cometh down out of heaven from my God: and *I will write upon him* my new name.
  - **Of the kingdom of Christ.**
    Rev 11:1–19
    Rev 14:15 — And another angel came out of the temple, crying with a loud voice to him that sat on the cloud, Thrust in thy sickle, and reap: for the time is come for thee to reap; for the harvest of the earth is ripe.
    Rev 14:17 — And another angel came out of the temple which is in heaven, he also having a sharp sickle.
  - **Of Christ, the head of the church, sending forth the forces of righteousness against the powers of evil.**
    Rev 15:5–16:17

- **Idolatrous.**
  - **Of Dagon, at Ashdod.**
    1Sa 5:2 — When the Philistines took the ark of God, they brought it into the house of Dagon, and set it by Dagon.
  - **Of the calves, at Bethel.**
    1Ki 12:31 — And he made an house of high places, and made priests of the lowest of the people, which were not of the sons of Levi.
    1Ki 12:33 — So he offered upon the altar which he had made in Bethel the fifteenth day of the eighth month, *even* in the month which he had devised of his own heart; and ordained a feast unto the children of Israel: and he offered upon the altar, and burnt incense.
  - **Of Rimmon, at Damascus.**
    2Ki 5:18 — In this thing the LORD pardon thy servant, *that* when my master goeth into the house of Rimmon to worship there, and he leaneth on my hand, and I bow myself in the house of Rimmon: when I bow down myself in the house of Rimmon, the LORD pardon thy servant in this thing.
  - **Of Baal, at Samaria.**
    2Ki 10:21 — And Jehu sent through all Israel: and all the worshippers of Baal came, so that there

was not a man left that came not. And they came into the house of Baal; and the house of Baal was full from one end to another.

2Ki 10:27 — And they brake down the image of Baal, and brake down the house of Baal, and made it a draught house unto this day.

• Of Baal, at Babylon.

2Ch 36:7 — Nebuchadnezzar also carried of the vessels of the house of the LORD to Babylon, and put them in his temple at Babylon.

Da 1:2 — And the Lord gave Jehoiakim king of Judah into his hand, with part of the vessels of the house of God: which he carried into the land of Shinar to the house of his god; and he brought the vessels into the treasure house of his god.

• Of Diana, at Ephesus.

Ac 19:27 — So that not only this our craft is in danger to be set at nought; but also that the temple of the great goddess Diana should be despised, and her magnificence should be destroyed, whom all Asia and the world worshippeth.

• Trophies stored in.

1Ch 10:9–10

1Sa 31:10 — And they put his armour in the house of Ashtaroth: and they fastened his body to the wall of Beth-shan.

Da 1:2 — And the Lord gave Jehoiakim king of Judah into his hand, with part of the vessels of the house of God: which he carried into the land of Shinar to the house of his god; and he brought the vessels into the treasure house of his god.

✧See: Tabernacle

TEMPLE, Solomon's

• Called also.

• Temple of the Lord.

2Ki 11:10 — And to the captains over hundreds did the priest give king David's spears and shields, that *were* in the temple of the LORD.

• Holy Temple.

Ps 79:1 — O God, the heathen are come into thine inheritance; thy holy temple have they defiled; they have laid Jerusalem on heaps.

• Holy House.

1Ch 29:3 — Moreover, because I have set my affection to the house of my God, I have of mine own proper good, of gold and silver, *which* I have given to the house of my God, over and above all that I have prepared for the holy house,

• House of God.

1Ch 29:2 — Now I have prepared with all my might for the house of my God the gold for *things to be made* of gold, and the silver for *things* of silver, and the brass for *things* of brass, the iron for *things* of iron, and wood for *things* of wood; onyx stones, and *stones* to be set, glistering stones, and of divers colours, and all manner of precious stones, and marble stones in abundance.

2Ch 23:9 — Moreover Jehoiada the priest delivered to the captains of hundreds spears, and bucklers, and shields, that *had been* king David's, which *were* in the house of God.

• House of the Lord.

2Ch 23:5 — And a third part *shall be* at the king's house; and a third part at the gate of the foundation: and all the people *shall be* in the courts of the house of the LORD.

2Ch 23:12 — Now when Athaliah heard the noise of the people running and praising the king, she came to the people into the house of the LORD:

Jer 28:5 — Then the prophet Jeremiah said unto the prophet Hananiah in the presence of the priests, and in the presence of all the people that stood in the house of the LORD,

• Father's House.

Jn 2:16 — And said unto them that sold doves, Take these things hence; make not my Father's house an house of merchandise.

• House of the God of Jacob.

Isa 2:3 — And many people shall go and say, Come ye, and let us go up to the mountain of the LORD, to the house of the God of Jacob; and he will teach us of his ways, and we will walk in his paths: for out of Zion shall go forth the law, and the word of the LORD from Jerusalem.

• House of My Glory.

Isa 60:7 — All the flocks of Kedar shall be gathered together unto thee, the rams of Nebaioth shall minister unto thee: they shall come up with acceptance on mine altar, and I will glorify the house of my glory.

• House of Prayer.

Isa 56:7 — Even them will I bring to my holy mountain, and make them joyful in my house of prayer: their burnt offerings and their sacrifices *shall be* accepted upon mine altar; for mine house shall be called an house of prayer for all people.

Mt 21:13 — And said unto them, It is written, My house shall be called the house of prayer; but ye have made it a den of thieves.

• House of Sacrifice.

2Ch 7:12 — And the LORD appeared to Solomon by night, and said unto him, I have heard thy prayer, and have chosen this place to myself for an house of sacrifice.

• House of their Sanctuary.

2Ch 36:17 — Therefore he brought upon them the king of the Chaldees, who slew their young men with the sword in the house of their sanctuary, and had no compassion upon young man or maiden, old man, or him that stooped for age: he gave *them* all into his hand.

• Holy and Beautiful House.

Isa 64:11 — Our holy and our beautiful house, where our fathers praised thee, is burned up with fire: and all our pleasant things are laid waste.

• Holy Mount.

Isa 27:13 — And it shall come to pass in that day, *that* the great trumpet shall be blown, and they shall come which were ready to perish in the land of Assyria, and the outcasts in the land of Egypt, and shall worship the LORD in the holy mount at Jerusalem.

• Mountain of the Lord's House.

Isa 2:2 — And it shall come to pass in the last days, *that* the mountain of the LORD's house shall be established in the top of the mountains, and shall be exalted above the hills; and all nations shall flow unto it.

• Palace.

1Ch 29:1 — Furthermore David the king said unto all the congregation, Solomon my son, whom alone God hath chosen, *is yet* young and tender, and the work *is* great: for the palace *is* not for man, but for the LORD God.

1Ch 29:19 — And give unto Solomon my son a perfect heart, to keep thy commandments, thy testimonies, and thy statutes, and to do all *these things,* and to build the palace, for the which I have made provision.

• Sanctuary.

2Ch 20:8 — And they dwelt therein, and have built thee a sanctuary therein for thy name, saying,

• Tabernacle of Witness.

2Ch 24:6 — And the king called for Jehoiada the chief, and said unto him, Why hast thou not required of the Levites to bring in out of Judah and out of Jerusalem the collection, *according to the commandment* of Moses the servant of the LORD, and of the congregation of Israel, for the tabernacle of witness?

• Zion.

Ps 20:2 — Send thee help from the sanctuary, and strengthen thee out of Zion;

Ps 48:12 — Walk about Zion, and go round about her: tell the towers thereof.

Ps 74:2 — Remember thy congregation, *which* thou hast purchased of old; the rod of thine inheritance, *which* thou hast redeemed; this mount Zion, wherein thou hast dwelt.

Ps 87:2 — The LORD loveth the gates of Zion more than all the dwellings of Jacob.

Isa 2:3 — And many people shall go and say, Come ye, and let us go up to the mountain of the LORD, to the house of the God of Jacob; and he will teach us of his ways, and we will walk in his paths: for out of Zion shall go forth the law, and the word of the LORD from Jerusalem.

• Greatness of.

2Ch 2:5–6

• Beauty of.

Isa 64:11 — Our holy and our beautiful house, where our fathers praised thee, is burned up with fire: and all our pleasant things are laid waste.

• Holiness of.

Jn 2:14–16

1Ki 8:10 — And it came to pass, when the priests were come out of the holy *place,* that the cloud filled the house of the LORD,

1Ki 9:3 — And the LORD said unto him, I have heard thy prayer and thy supplication, that thou hast made before me: I have hallowed this house, which thou hast built, to put my name there for ever; and mine eyes and mine heart shall be there perpetually.

La 1:10 — The adversary hath spread out his hand upon all her pleasant things: for she hath seen *that* the heathen entered into her sanctuary, whom thou didst command *that* they should not enter into thy congregation.

Mt 23:17 — *Ye* fools and blind: for whether is greater, the gold, or the temple that sanctifieth the gold?

• David undertakes the building of.

2Sa 7:2–3; Ps 132:2–5

1Ch 22:7 — And David said to Solomon, My son, as for me, it was in my mind to build an house unto the name of the LORD my God:

1Ch 28:2 — Then David the king stood up upon his feet, and said, Hear me, my brethren, and my people: *As for me,* I *had* in mine heart to build an house of rest for the ark of the covenant of the LORD, and for the footstool of our God, and had made ready for the building:

Ac 7:46 — Who found favour before God, and desired to find a tabernacle for the God of Jacob.

• David undertakes the building of and is forbidden of God because he was a man of war.

2Sa 7:4–12

1Ki 5:3 — Thou knowest how that David my father could not build an house unto the name of the LORD his God for the wars which were about him on every side, until the LORD put them under the soles of his feet.

1Ch 22:8 — But the word of the LORD came to me, saying, Thou hast shed blood abundantly, and hast made great wars: thou shalt not build an house unto my name, because thou hast shed much blood upon the earth in my sight.

1Ch 28:3 — But God said unto me, Thou shalt not build an house for my name, because thou *hast been* a man of war, and hast shed blood.

• Not asked for by God.

2Sa 7:7 — In all *the places* wherein I have walked with all the children of Israel spake I a word with any of the tribes of Israel, whom I commanded to feed my people Israel, saying, Why build ye not me an house of cedar?

• The building of, committed to Solomon.

2Sa 7:13 — He shall build an house for my name, and I will stablish the throne of his kingdom for ever.

• David makes preparation for.

1Ch 22:1–19; 28:14–18; 29:1–5

2Ch 3:1 — Then Solomon began to build the house of the LORD at Jerusalem in mount Moriah, where *the LORD* appeared unto David his father, in the place that David had prepared in the threshingfloor of Ornan the Jebusite.

2Ch 5:1 — Thus all the work that Solomon made for the house of the LORD was finished: and Solomon brought in *all* the things that David his father had dedicated; and the silver, and the gold, and all the instruments, put he among the treasures of the house of God.

• Built by Solomon.

Ac 7:47 — But Solomon built him an house.

• Solomon makes levies of men for the building of.

1Ki 5:13–16; 2Ch 2:17–18

2Ch 2:2 — And Solomon told out threescore and ten thousand men to bear burdens, and fourscore thousand to hew in the mountain, and three thousand and six hundred to oversee them.

• Materials for, furnished by Hiram.

1Ki 5:8–18

• Pattern and building of.

1Ki 6:1–38; 7:13–51; 1Ch 28:11–19; 2Ch 3:1–4:22

Ac 7:47 — But Solomon built him an house.

• Time when begun.

1Ki 6:1 — And it came to pass in the four hundred and eightieth year after the children of Israel were come out of the land of Egypt, in the fourth year of Solomon's reign over Israel, in the month Zif, which *is* the second month, that he began to build the house of the LORD.

1Ki 6:37 — In the fourth year was the foundation of the house of the LORD laid, in the month Zif:

2Ch 3:2 — And he began to build in the second *day* of the second month, in the fourth year of his reign.

• Time finished.

1Ki 6:38 — And in the eleventh year, in the month Bul, which *is* the eighth month, was the house finished throughout all the parts thereof, and according to all the fashion of it. So was he seven years in building it.

• Site of.

1Ch 21:28–22:1

2Ch 3:1 — Then Solomon began to build the house of the LORD at Jerusalem in mount Moriah, where *the LORD* appeared unto David his father, in the place that David had prepared in the threshingfloor of Ornan the Jebusite.

• Site where Abraham offered Isaac.

Ge 22:2 — And he said, Take now thy son, thine only *son* Isaac, whom thou lovest, and get thee into the land of Moriah; and offer him there for a burnt offering upon one of the mountains which I will tell thee of.

Ge 22:4 — Then on the third day Abraham lifted up his eyes, and saw the place afar off.

• Materials prepared for.

1Ki 5:17–18

• No tools used in the erection of.

1Ki 6:7 — And the house, when it was in building, was built of stone made ready before it was brought thither: so that there was neither hammer nor axe *nor* any tool of iron heard in the house, while it was in building.

• Foundations of.

1Ki 5:17–18

Lk 21:5 — And as some spake of the temple, how it was adorned with goodly stones and gifts, he said,

• Apartments and furnishings of. Oracle, or Holy of Holies, in.

1Ki 6:19–20

1Ki 8:6 — And the priests brought in the ark of the covenant of the LORD unto his place, into the oracle of the house, to the most holy *place, even* under the wings of the cherubims.

• Called Most Holy House.

2Ch 3:8 — And he made the most holy house, the length whereof *was* according to the breadth of the house, twenty cubits, and the breadth thereof twenty cubits: and he overlaid it with fine gold, *amounting* to six hundred talents.

• Called Inner House.

1Ki 6:27 — And he set the cherubims within the inner house: and they stretched forth the wings of the cherubims, so that the wing of the one touched the *one* wall, and the wing of the other cherub touched the other wall; and their wings touched one another in the midst of the house.

• Called Holiest of All.

Heb 9:3 — And after the second veil, the tabernacle which is called the Holiest of all;

• Description of.

1Ki 6:19–35; 2Ch 3:8–14

1Ki 6:16 — And he built twenty cubits on the sides of the house, both the floor and the walls with boards of cedar: he even built *them* for it within, *even* for the oracle, *even* for the most holy *place.*

2Ch 4:22 — And the snuffers, and the basons, and the spoons, and the censers, *of* pure gold: and the entry of the house, the inner doors thereof for the most holy *place,* and the doors of the house of the temple, *were of* gold.

• Gold used in.

2Ch 3:8–10

• Contents of the Holy of Holies.

• Ark.

2Ch 5:2–10

1Ki 6:19 — And the oracle he prepared in the house within, to set there the ark of the covenant of the LORD.

1Ki 8:6 — And the priests brought in the ark of the covenant of the LORD unto his place, into the oracle of the house, to the most holy *place, even* under the wings of the cherubims.

See: Ark

• Cherubims.

1Ki 6:23–28; 2Ch 3:10–13; 5:7–8

See: Ark

See: Cherubim

See: Vail

See: Mercy Seat

• **Holy Place.**

1Ki 8:8 — And they drew out the staves, that the ends of the staves were seen out in the holy *place* before the oracle, and they were not seen without: and there they are unto this day.

1Ki 8:10 — And it came to pass, when the priests were come out of the holy *place,* that the cloud filled the house of the LORD,

• **Called the Greater House.**

2Ch 3:5 — And the greater house he cieled with fir tree, which he overlaid with fine gold, and set thereon palm trees and chains.

• **Called Temple.**

1Ki 6:17 — And the house, that *is,* the temple before it, was forty cubits *long.*

• **Description of.**

1Ki 6:15–18; 2Ch 3:5–7, 14–17

2Ch 3:3 — Now these *are the things wherein* Solomon was instructed for the building of the house of God. The length by cubits after the first measure *was* threescore cubits, and the breadth twenty cubits.

• **Contents of the Holy Place.**

• **The table of shewbread.**

1Ki 7:48 — And Solomon made all the vessels that *pertained* unto the house of the LORD: the altar of gold, and the table of gold, whereupon the shewbread *was,*

2Ch 29:18 — Then they went in to Hezekiah the king, and said, We have cleansed all the house of the LORD, and the altar of burnt offering, with all the vessels thereof, and the shewbread table, with all the vessels thereof.

See: Shewbread; table of

• **Other tables of gold and silver.**

2Ch 4:18–19

1Ch 28:16 — And by weight *he gave* gold for the tables of shewbread, for every table; and *likewise* silver for the tables of silver:

• **Candlesticks and their utensils.**

1Ki 7:49–50; 2Ch 4:20–22

1Ch 28:15 — Even the weight for the candlesticks of gold, and for their lamps of gold, by weight for every candlestick, and for the lamps thereof: and for the candlesticks of silver by weight, *both* for the candlestick, and *also* for the lamps thereof, according to the use of every candlestick.

2Ch 4:7 — And he made ten candlesticks of gold according to their form, and set *them* in the temple, five on the right hand, and five on the left.

See: Candlestick

• **Altar of incense and its furniture.**

1Ch 28:17–18

1Ki 6:20 — And the oracle in the forepart *was* twenty cubits in length, and twenty cubits in breadth, and twenty cubits in the height thereof: and he overlaid it with pure gold; and so covered the altar *which was of* cedar.

1Ki 7:48 — And Solomon made all the vessels that *pertained* unto the house of the LORD: the altar of gold, and the table of gold, whereupon the shewbread *was,*

1Ki 7:50 — And the bowls, and the snuffers, and the basons, and the spoons, and the censers *of* pure gold; and the hinges *of* gold, *both* for the doors of the inner house, the most holy *place, and* for the doors of the house, *to wit,* of the temple.

2Ch 4:19 — And Solomon made all the vessels that *were for* the house of God, the golden altar also, and the tables whereon the shewbread *was set;*

2Ch 4:22 — And the snuffers, and the basons, and the spoons, and the censers, *of* pure gold: and the entry of the house, the inner doors thereof for the most holy *place,* and the doors of the house of the temple, *were of* gold.

See: Altar; of incense

• **Porch of, called Porch of the Lord.**

2Ch 15:8 — And when Asa heard these words, and the prophecy of Oded the prophet, he took courage, and put away the abominable idols out of all the land of Judah and Benjamin, and out of the cities which he had taken from mount Ephraim, and renewed the altar of the LORD, that *was* before the porch of the LORD.

• **Dimensions of.**

1Ki 6:3 — And the porch before the temple of the house, twenty cubits *was* the length thereof, according to the breadth of the house; *and* ten cubits *was* the breadth thereof before the house.

2Ch 3:4 — And the porch that *was* in the front *of the house,* the length *of it was* according to the breadth of the house, twenty cubits, and the height *was* an hundred and twenty: and he overlaid it within with pure gold.

• **Doors of.**

2Ch 29:7 — Also they have shut up the doors of the porch, and put out the lamps, and have not burned incense nor offered burnt offerings in the holy *place* unto the God of Israel.

• **Overlaid with gold.**

2Ch 3:4 — And the porch that *was* in the front *of the house,* the length *of it was* according to the breadth of the house, twenty cubits, and the height *was* an hundred and twenty: and he overlaid it within with pure gold.

• **Pillars of.**

1Ki 7:15–22; 2Ch 3:15–17; 4:12–13

2Ki 11:14 — And when she looked, behold, the king stood by a pillar, as the manner *was,* and the princes and the trumpeters by the king, and all the people of the land rejoiced, and blew with trumpets: and Athaliah rent her clothes, and cried, Treason, Treason.

2Ki 23:3 — And the king stood by a pillar, and made a covenant before the LORD, to walk after the LORD, and to keep his commandments and his testimonies and his statutes with all *their* heart and all *their* soul, to perform the words of this covenant that were written in this book. And all the people stood to the covenant.

2Ki 25:17 — The height of the one pillar *was* eighteen cubits, and the chapiter upon it *was* brass: and the height of the chapiter three cubits; and the wreathen work, and pomegranates upon the chapiter round about, all of brass: and like unto these had the second pillar with wreathen work.

• Chambers of.

1Ki 6:5–10; 2Ki 11:2–3

• Offerings brought to.

Ne 10:37–39

• Treasuries in.

See: Treasure

• Courts of.

• Of the priests.

2Ch 4:9 — Furthermore he made the court of the priests, and the great court, and doors for the court, and overlaid the doors of them with brass.

• Inner.

1Ki 6:36 — And he built the inner court with three rows of hewed stone, and a row of cedar beams.

• Surrounded by rows of stones and cedar beams.

1Ki 6:36 — And he built the inner court with three rows of hewed stone, and a row of cedar beams.

1Ki 7:12 — And the great court round about *was* with three rows of hewed stones, and a row of cedar beams, both for the inner court of the house of the LORD, and for the porch of the house.

• Contents of the courts.

• Altar of burnt offering.

2Ch 15:8 — And when Asa heard these words, and the prophecy of Oded the prophet, he took courage, and put away the abominable idols out of all the land of Judah and Benjamin, and out of the cities which he had taken from mount Ephraim, and renewed the altar of the LORD, that *was* before the porch of the LORD.

See: Altar

• The brazen sea.

1Ki 7:23–37; 2Ch 4:2–5

1Ki 7:44 — And one sea, and twelve oxen under the sea;

1Ki 7:46 — In the plain of Jordan did the king cast them, in the clay ground between Succoth and Zarthan.

2Ch 4:10 — And he set the sea on the right side of the east end, over against the south.

• Ten lavers.

1Ki 7:38–46

2Ch 4:6 — He made also ten lavers, and put five on the right hand, and five on the left, to wash in them: such things as they offered for the burnt offering they washed in them; but the sea *was* for the priests to wash in.

• Great court of.

2Ch 4:9 — Furthermore he made the court of the priests, and the great court, and doors for the court, and overlaid the doors of them with brass.

Jer 19:14 — Then came Jeremiah from Tophet, whither the LORD had sent him to prophesy; and he stood in the court of the LORD'S house; and said to all the people,

Jer 26:2 — Thus saith the LORD; Stand in the court of the LORD'S house, and speak unto all the cities of Judah, which come to worship in the LORD'S house, all the words that I command thee to speak unto them; diminish not a word:

• Covered place for the Sabbath and king's entry.

2Ki 16:18 — And the covert for the sabbath that they had built in the house, and the king's entry without, turned he from the house of the LORD for the king of Assyria.

• Gates of.

• Higher gate.

2Ki 15:35 — Howbeit the high places were not removed: the people sacrificed and burned incense still in the high places. He built the higher gate of the house of the LORD.

• New gate.

Jer 26:10 — When the princes of Judah heard these things, then they came up from the king's house unto the house of the LORD, and sat down in the entry of the new gate of the LORD'S *house.*

Jer 36:10 — Then read Baruch in the book the words of Jeremiah in the house of the LORD, in the chamber of Gemariah the son of Shaphan the scribe, in the higher court, at the entry of the new gate of the LORD'S house, in the ears of all the people.

• Beautiful gate.

Ac 3:2 — And a certain man lame from his mother's womb was carried, whom they laid daily at the gate of the temple which is called Beautiful, to ask alms of them that entered into the temple;

• Eastern gate, closed on working days, open on the Sabbath.

Eze 46:1–2

• Gifts received at.

2Ch 24:8–11

• Uses of.

• A dwelling place of the Lord.

1Ki 8:10–11; 2Ch 5:13–14; 7:1–3; Eze 10:3–4

1Ki 8:13 — I have surely built thee an house to dwell in, a settled place for thee to abide in for ever.

1Ki 9:3 — And the LORD said unto him, I have heard thy prayer and thy supplication, that thou hast made before me: I have hallowed this house, which thou hast built, to put my name there for ever; and mine eyes and mine heart shall be there perpetually.

2Ki 21:7 — And he set a graven image of the grove that he had made in the house, of which the LORD said to David, and to Solomon his son, In this house, and in Jerusalem, which I have chosen out of all tribes of Israel, will I put my name for ever:

1Ch 29:1 — Furthermore David the king said unto all the congregation, Solomon my son, whom alone God hath chosen, *is yet* young and tender, and the work *is* great: for the palace *is* not for man, but for the LORD God.

2Ch 7:16 — For now have I chosen and sanctified this house, that my name may be there for ever: and mine eyes and mine heart shall be there perpetually.

Mic 1:2 — Hear, all ye people; hearken, O earth, and all that therein is: and let the Lord GOD be witness against you, the Lord from his holy temple.

• A dwelling place to contain the ark of the covenant.

1Ki 8:21 — And I have set there a place for the ark, wherein *is* the covenant of the LORD, which he made with our fathers, when he brought them out of the land of Egypt.

• A dwelling place for the offering of sweet incense.

2Ch 2:4 — Behold, I build an house to the name of the LORD my God, to dedicate *it* to him, *and* to burn before him sweet incense, and for the continual shewbread, and for the burnt offerings morning and evening, on the sabbaths, and on the new moons, and on the solemn feasts of the LORD our God. This *is an ordinance* for ever to Israel.

• A dwelling place for the continual shewbread and the burnt offerings.

2Ch 2:4 — Behold, I build an house to the name of the LORD my God, to dedicate *it* to him, *and* to burn before him sweet incense, and for the continual shewbread, and for the burnt offerings morning and evening, on the sabbaths, and on the new moons, and on the solemn feasts of the LORD our God. This *is an ordinance* for ever to Israel.

• A place for prayer and worship.

1Ki 8:1–66; 2Ki 19:14–15; Eze 46:2–3; Zec 7:2–3; 8:21–22

2Ch 30:27 — Then the priests the Levites arose and blessed the people: and their voice was heard, and their prayer came *up* to his holy dwelling place, *even* unto heaven.

Isa 27:13 — And it shall come to pass in that day, *that* the great trumpet shall be blown, and they shall come which were ready to perish in the land of Assyria, and the outcasts in the land of Egypt, and shall worship the LORD in the holy mount at Jerusalem.

Isa 56:7 — Even them will I bring to my holy mountain, and make them joyful in my house of prayer: their burnt offerings and their sacrifices *shall be* accepted upon mine altar; for mine house shall be called an house of prayer for all people.

Jer 7:2 — Stand in the gate of the LORD's house, and proclaim there this word, and say, Hear the word of the LORD, all *ye of* Judah, that enter in at these gates to worship the LORD.

Jer 26:2 — Thus saith the LORD; Stand in the court of the LORD's house, and speak unto all the cities of Judah, which come to worship in the LORD's house, all the words that I command thee to speak unto them; diminish not a word:

Eze 46:9 — But when the people of the land shall come before the LORD in the solemn feasts, he that entereth in by the way of the north gate to worship shall go out by the way of the south gate; and he that entereth by the way of the south gate shall go forth by the way of the north gate: he shall not return by the way of the gate whereby he came in, but shall go forth over against it.

Mk 11:17 — And he taught, saying unto them, Is it not written, My house shall be called of all nations the house of prayer? but ye have made it a den of thieves.

Lk 1:10 — And the whole multitude of the people were praying without at the time of incense.

Lk 2:37 — And she *was* a widow of about fourscore and four years, which departed not from the temple, but served *God* with fastings and prayers night and day.

Lk 18:10 — Two men went up into the temple to pray; the one a Pharisee, and the other a publican.

Ac 3:1 — Now Peter and John went up together into the temple at the hour of prayer, *being* the ninth *hour.*

Ac 22:17 — And it came to pass, that, when I was come again to Jerusalem, even while I prayed in the temple, I was in a trance;

• A place for prayer made toward.

1Ki 8:38 — What prayer and supplication soever be *made* by any man, *or* by all thy people Israel, which shall know every man the plague of his own heart, and spread forth his hands toward this house:

Da 6:10 — Now when Daniel knew that the writing was signed, he went into his house; and his windows being open in his chamber toward Jerusalem, he kneeled upon his knees three times a day, and prayed, and gave thanks before his God, as he did aforetime.

Jnh 2:4 — Then I said, I am cast out of thy sight; yet I will look again toward thy holy temple.

• A dwelling place for armory.

2Ch 23:9–10

2Ki 11:10 — And to the captains over hundreds did the priest give king David's spears and shields, that *were* in the temple of the LORD.

• A place for refuge.

Ne 6:10–11

2Ki 11:15 — But Jehoiada the priest commanded the captains of the hundreds, the officers of the host, and said unto them, Have her forth without the ranges: and him that followeth her kill with the sword. For the priest had said, Let her not be slain in the house of the LORD.

• **Facts about.**

• **Dedication of.**

1Ki 8:1–66; 2Ch 5:1–7:22

• **Services in, organized by David.**

1Ch 15:16 — And David spake to the chief of the Levites to appoint their brethren *to be* the singers with instruments of musick, psalteries and harps and cymbals, sounding, by lifting up the voice with joy.

1Ch 23:24 — These *were* the sons of Levi after the house of their fathers; *even* the chief of the fathers, as they were counted by number of names by their polls, that did the work for the service of the house of the LORD, from the age of twenty years and upward.

• **Pillaged by Shishak.**

1Ki 14:25–26

• **Pillaged by Jehoash, king of Israel.**

2Ki 14:14 — And he took all the gold and silver, and all the vessels that were found in the house of the LORD, and in the treasures of the king's house, and hostages, and returned to Samaria.

• **Repaired by Jehoash, king of Judah.**

2Ki 12:4–14; 2Ch 24:7–14

• **Repaired by Josiah.**

2Ki 22:3–7; 2Ch 34:8–13

• **Ahaz changes the pattern of the altar in.**

2Ki 16:10–17

• **Purified by Hezekiah.**

2Ch 29:15–19

• **Converted into an idolatrous shrine by Manasseh.**

2Ki 21:4–7; 2Ch 33:4–7

• **Treasures of, used in the purchase of peace.**

• **By Asa, from Ben-hadad.**

1Ki 15:18 — Then Asa took all the silver and the gold *that were* left in the treasures of the house of the LORD, and the treasures of the king's house, and delivered them into the hand of his servants: and king Asa sent them to Ben-hadad, the son of Tabrimon, the son of Hezion, king of Syria, that dwelt at Damascus, saying,

• **By Jehoash, king of Judah, from Hazael.**

2Ki 12:18 — And Jehoash king of Judah took all the hallowed things that Jehoshaphat, and Jehoram, and Ahaziah, his fathers, kings of Judah, had dedicated, and his own hallowed things, and all the gold *that was* found in the treasures of the house of the LORD, and in the king's house, and sent *it* to Hazael king of Syria: and he went away from Jerusalem.

• **By Hezekiah, from the king of Assyria.**

2Ki 18:15–16

• **Ezekiel's vision concerning.**

Eze 8:16 — And he brought me into the inner court of the LORD'S house, and, behold, at the door of the temple of the LORD, between the porch and the altar, *were* about five and twenty men, with their backs toward the temple of the LORD, and their faces toward the east; and they worshipped the sun toward the east.

• **Jews swore by.**

Mt 23:16–22

• **Destroyed by Nebuchadnezzar, and the valuable contents carried to Babylon.**

2Ki 25:9–17; Jer 27:19–22; 52:13–17

2Ki 24:13 — And he carried out thence all the treasures of the house of the LORD, and the treasures of the king's house, and cut in pieces all the vessels of gold which Solomon king of Israel had made in the temple of the LORD, as the LORD had said.

2Ch 36:7 — Nebuchadnezzar also carried of the vessels of the house of the LORD to Babylon, and put them in his temple at Babylon.

2Ch 36:19 — And they burnt the house of God, and brake down the wall of Jerusalem, and burnt all the palaces thereof with fire, and destroyed all the goodly vessels thereof.

Ezr 1:7 — Also Cyrus the king brought forth the vessels of the house of the LORD, which Nebuchadnezzar had brought forth out of Jerusalem, and had put them in the house of his gods;

Ps 79:1 — O God, the heathen are come into thine inheritance; thy holy temple have they defiled; they have laid Jerusalem on heaps.

Isa 64:11 — Our holy and our beautiful house, where our fathers praised thee, is burned up with fire: and all our pleasant things are laid waste.

Jer 27:16 — Also I spake to the priests and to all this people, saying, Thus saith the LORD; Hearken not to the words of your prophets that prophesy unto you, saying, Behold, the vessels of the LORD'S house shall now shortly be brought again from Babylon: for they prophesy a lie unto you.

Jer 28:3 — Within two full years will I bring again into this place all the vessels of the LORD'S house, that Nebuchadnezzar king of Babylon took away from this place, and carried them to Babylon:

La 2:7 — The Lord hath cast off his altar, he hath abhorred his sanctuary, he hath given up into the hand of the enemy the walls of her palaces; they have made a noise in the house of the LORD, as in the day of a solemn feast.

La 4:1 — How is the gold become dim! *how* is the most fine gold changed! the stones of the sanctuary are poured out in the top of every street.

• **Vessels of, used by Belshazzar.**

Da 5:2–3

• **Destruction of, foretold.**

Jer 27:18–22

Isa 66:6 — A voice of noise from the city, a voice from the temple, a voice of the LORD that rendereth recompence to his enemies.

Eze 7:22 — My face will I turn also from them, and they shall pollute my secret *place:* for the robbers shall enter into it, and defile it.

Eze 7:25 — Destruction cometh; and they shall seek peace, and *there shall be* none.

Mt 24:2 — And Jesus said unto them, See ye not all these things? verily I say unto you, There shall not be left here one stone upon another, that shall not be thrown down.

Mk 13:2 — And Jesus answering said unto him, Seest thou these great buildings? there shall not be left one stone upon another, that shall not be thrown down.

- **Restoration of, ordered by Cyrus.**
  Ezr 1:7–11
- **The second.**
  - **Restored by Zerubbabel.**
    Ezr 1:1–11; 2:68–69; 3:2–4:24; 5:2–17; 6:3–5; Ne 7:70–72
    Isa 44:28 — That saith of Cyrus, *He is* my shepherd, and shall perform all my pleasure: even saying to Jerusalem, Thou shalt be built; and to the temple, Thy foundation shall be laid.
    Hag 2:3 — Who *is* left among you that saw this house in her first glory? and how do ye see it now? *is it* not in your eyes in comparison of it as nothing?
  - **Building of, suspended.**
    Ezr 4:1–24
  - **Resumed.**
    Ezr 4:24–6:22; Hag 1:2–9
    Hag 2:15 — And now, I pray you, consider from this day and upward, from before a stone was laid upon a stone in the temple of the LORD:
    Zec 8:9 — Thus saith the LORD of hosts; Let your hands be strong, ye that hear in these days these words by the mouth of the prophets, which *were* in the day *that* the foundation of the house of the LORD of hosts was laid, that the temple might be built.
  - **Finished.**
    Ezr 6:14–15
  - **Dedicated.**
    Ezr 6:15–18
  - **Artaxerxes' favorable action toward.**
    Ezr 7:1–28; 8:25–34
- **Prophecies of its restoration.**
  Da 8:13–14; Hag 1:1–2:23; Zec 4:8–10; 6:12–15; 8:9–15
  Isa 44:28 — That saith of Cyrus, *He is* my shepherd, and shall perform all my pleasure: even saying to Jerusalem, Thou shalt be built; and to the temple, Thy foundation shall be laid.
  Zec 1:16 — Therefore thus saith the LORD; I am returned to Jerusalem with mercies: my house shall be built in it, saith the LORD of hosts, and a line shall be stretched forth upon Jerusalem.
  Mal 3:1 — Behold, I will send my messenger, and he shall prepare the way before me: and the Lord, whom ye seek, shall suddenly come to his temple, even the messenger of the covenant, whom ye delight in: behold, he shall come, saith the LORD of hosts.

TEMPORAL BLESSINGS ◈See: Blessing

TEMPTATION

Ge 3:1–13; Ex 34:12–16; Dt 8:11–14, 17–18; 2Ch 32:30–31; Pr 1:10–17; 2:10–12; 4:14–15; 5:6–21; 6:27–28; 7:7–23; 9:15–17; Isa 33:15–16; Jer 2:24–25; 35:5–7; Mt 4:1–11; 18:6–9; Mk 10:21–25; 13:21–22; Lk 4:1–13; 8:13–14; 22:31–32; Jn 16:1–2; Ro 6:12–14; 8:35–39; 1Co 8:9–13; 10:28–32; 2Co 11:14–15; Eph 6:13–17; 1Ti 6:9–10; Heb 12:3–4; Jas 1:2–4, 12–16; 1Pe 1:6–7; 5:8–9; Rev 12:10–11

Ge 20:6 — And God said unto him in a dream, Yea, I know that thou didst this in the integrity of thy heart; for I also withheld thee from sinning against me: therefore suffered I thee not to touch her.

Dt 7:25 — The graven images of their gods shall ye burn with fire: thou shalt not desire the silver or gold *that is* on them, nor take *it* unto thee, lest thou be snared therein: for it *is* an abomination to the LORD thy God.

Dt 13:3 — Thou shalt not hearken unto the words of that prophet, or that dreamer of dreams: for the LORD your God proveth you, to know whether ye love the LORD your God with all your heart and with all your soul.

1Ch 21:1 — And Satan stood up against Israel, and provoked David to number Israel.

Ps 119:165 — Great peace have they which love thy law: and nothing shall offend them.

Pr 2:16 — To deliver thee from the strange woman, *even* from the stranger *which* flattereth with her words;

Pr 12:26 — The righteous *is* more excellent than his neighbour: but the way of the wicked seduceth them.

Pr 13:14 — The law of the wise *is* a fountain of life, to depart from the snares of death.

Pr 14:27 — The fear of the LORD *is* a fountain of life, to depart from the snares of death.

Pr 16:29 — A violent man enticeth his neighbour, and leadeth him into the way *that is* not good.

Pr 19:27 — Cease, my son, to hear the instruction *that causeth* to err from the words of knowledge.

Pr 28:10 — Whoso causeth the righteous to go astray in an evil way, he shall fall himself into his own pit: but the upright shall have good *things* in possession.

Ecc 7:26 — And I find more bitter than death the woman, whose heart *is* snares and nets, *and* her hands *as* bands: whoso pleaseth God shall escape from her; but the sinner shall be taken by her.

Hos 7:5 — In the day of our king the princes have made *him* sick with bottles of wine; he stretched out his hand with scorners.

Am 2:12 — But ye gave the Nazarites wine to drink; and commanded the prophets, saying, Prophesy not.

Mt 5:19 — Whosoever therefore shall break one of these least commandments, and shall teach men so, he shall be called the least in the kingdom of heaven: but whosoever shall do and teach *them,* the same shall be called great in the kingdom of heaven.

Mt 12:45 — Then goeth he, and taketh with himself seven other spirits more wicked than himself, and they enter in and dwell there: and the last *state* of that man is worse than the first. Even so shall it be also unto this wicked generation.

Mt 13:22 — He also that received seed among the thorns is he that heareth the word; and the care of this world, and the deceitfulness of riches, choke the word, and he becometh unfruitful.

Mt 26:31 — Then saith Jesus unto them, All ye shall be offended because of me this night: for it is written, I will smite the shepherd, and the sheep of the flock shall be scattered abroad.

Mt 26:41 — Watch and pray, that ye enter not into temptation: the spirit indeed *is* willing, but the flesh *is* weak.

Mk 4:15 — And these are they by the way side, where the word is sown; but when they have heard, Satan cometh immediately, and taketh away the word that was sown in their hearts.

Mk 4:17 — And have no root in themselves, and so endure but for a time: afterward, when affliction or persecution ariseth for the word's sake, immediately they are offended.

Mk 14:38 — Watch ye and pray, lest ye enter into temptation. The spirit truly *is* ready, but the flesh *is* weak.

Lk 11:4 — And forgive us our sins; for we also forgive every one that is indebted to us. And lead us not into temptation; but deliver us from evil.

Lk 22:3 — Then entered Satan into Judas surnamed Iscariot, being of the number of the twelve.

Lk 22:40 — And when he was at the place, he said unto them, Pray that ye enter not into temptation.

Lk 22:46 — And said unto them, Why sleep ye? rise and pray, lest ye enter into temptation.

Ro 7:5 — For when we were in the flesh, the motions of sins, which were by the law, did work in our members to bring forth fruit unto death.

Ro 12:21 — Be not overcome of evil, but overcome evil with good.

Ro 14:13 — Let us not therefore judge one another any more: but judge this rather, that no man put a stumblingblock or an occasion to fall in *his* brother's way.

Ro 14:15 — But if thy brother be grieved with *thy* meat, now walkest thou not charitably. Destroy not him with thy meat, for whom Christ died.

Ro 14:21 — *It is* good neither to eat flesh, nor to drink wine, nor *any thing* whereby thy brother stumbleth, or is offended, or is made weak.

1Co 7:5 — Defraud ye not one the other, except *it be* with consent for a time, that ye may give yourselves to fasting and prayer; and come together again, that Satan tempt you not for your incontinency.

1Co 10:13 — There hath no temptation taken you but such as is common to man: but God *is* faithful, who will not suffer you to be tempted above that ye are able; but will with the temptation also make a way to escape, that ye may be able to bear *it*.

2Co 2:11 — Lest Satan should get an advantage of us: for we are not ignorant of his devices.

2Co 11:3 — But I fear, lest by any means, as the serpent beguiled Eve through his subtilty, so your minds should be corrupted from the simplicity that is in Christ.

2Co 12:7 — And lest I should be exalted above measure through the abundance of the revelations, there was given to me a thorn in the flesh, the messenger of Satan to buffet me, lest I should be exalted above measure.

Gal 4:14 — And my temptation which was in my flesh ye despised not, nor rejected; but received me as an angel of God, *even* as Christ Jesus.

Gal 5:17 — For the flesh lusteth against the Spirit, and the Spirit against the flesh: and these are contrary the one to the other: so that ye cannot do the things that ye would.

Eph 4:27 — Neither give place to the devil.

Eph 6:11 — Put on the whole armour of God, that ye may be able to stand against the wiles of the devil.

1Th 3:5 — For this cause, when I could no longer forbear, I sent to know your faith, lest by some means the tempter have tempted you, and our labour be in vain.

1Ti 5:15 — For some are already turned aside after Satan.

2Ti 3:13 — But evil men and seducers shall wax worse and worse, deceiving, and being deceived.

Heb 2:18 — For in that he himself hath suffered being tempted, he is able to succour them that are tempted.

Heb 4:15 — For we have not an high priest which cannot be touched with the feeling of our infirmities; but was in all points tempted like as *we are, yet* without sin.

Jas 4:7 — Submit yourselves therefore to God. Resist the devil, and he will flee from you.

1Pe 4:12 — Beloved, think it not strange concerning the fiery trial which is to try you, as though some strange thing happened unto you:

2Pe 2:9 — The Lord knoweth how to deliver the godly out of temptations, and to reserve the unjust unto the day of judgment to be punished:

2Pe 2:18 — For when they speak great swelling *words* of vanity, they allure through the lusts of the flesh, *through much* wantonness, those that were clean escaped from them who live in error.

2Pe 3:17 — Ye therefore, beloved, seeing ye know *these things* before, beware lest ye also, being led away with the error of the wicked, fall from your own stedfastness.

1Jn 2:16 — For all that *is* in the world, the lust of the flesh, and the lust of the eyes, and the pride of life, is not of the Father, but is of the world.

1Jn 2:26 — These *things* have I written unto you concerning them that seduce you.

1Jn 4:4 — Ye are of God, little children, and have overcome them: because greater is he that is in you, than he that is in the world.

Rev 3:10 — Because thou hast kept the word of my patience, I also will keep thee from the hour of temptation, which shall come upon all the world, to try them that dwell upon the earth.

Rev 12:17 — And the dragon was wroth with the woman, and went to make war with the remnant of her seed, which keep the commandments of God, and have the testimony of Jesus Christ.

See: Demons

See: Faith, Trial of

See: Satan

• A test.

Ge 22:1–14; Dt 13:1–3; Job 1:8–22; 2:3–10; Ps 66:10–13; Jas 1:2–3; 1Pe 1:6–7

Dt 8:2 — And thou shalt remember all the way which the LORD thy God led thee these forty years in the wilderness, to humble thee, *and* to prove thee, to know what *was* in thine heart, whether thou wouldest keep his commandments, or no.

Dt 8:5 — Thou shalt also consider in thine heart, that, as a man chasteneth his son, *so* the LORD thy God chasteneth thee.

2Ch 32:31 — Howbeit in *the business of* the ambassadors of the princes of Babylon, who sent unto him to enquire of the wonder that was *done* in the land, God left him, to try him, that he might know all *that was* in his heart.

Da 12:10 — Many shall be purified, and made white, and tried; but the wicked shall do wickedly: and none of the wicked shall understand; but the wise shall understand.

Zec 13:9 — And I will bring the third part through the fire, and will refine them as silver is refined, and will try them as gold is tried: they shall call on my name, and I will hear them: I will say, It *is* my people: and they shall say, The LORD *is* my God.

Heb 11:17 — By faith Abraham, when he was tried, offered up Isaac: and he that had received the promises offered up his only begotten *son,*

Jas 1:12 — Blessed *is* the man that endureth temptation: for when he is tried, he shall receive the crown of life, which the Lord hath promised to them that love him.

See: Afflictions; design of

See: Faith, Trial of

• Leading into.

• Prayer against being led into.

Mt 6:13 — And lead us not into temptation, but deliver us from evil: For thine is the kingdom, and the power, and the glory, for ever. Amen.

Lk 22:40 — And when he was at the place, he said unto them, Pray that ye enter not into temptation.

• Instances of.

• Abraham leads Pharaoh.

Ge 12:18–19

• Abimelech.

Ge 20:9 — Then Abimelech called Abraham, and said unto him, What hast thou done unto us? and what have I offended thee, that thou hast brought on me and on my kingdom a great sin? thou hast done deeds unto me that ought not to be done.

• Balak tempts Balaam.

Nu 22:1–24:25

• The old prophet of Bethel, the prophet of Judah.

1Ki 13:15–19

• Gideon leads Israel into sin.

Jgs 8:27 — And Gideon made an ephod thereof, and put it in his city, *even* in Ophrah: and all Israel went thither a whoring after it: which thing became a snare unto Gideon, and to his house.

• Jeroboam leads Israel into.

1Ki 15:30 — Because of the sins of Jeroboam which he sinned, and which he made Israel sin, by his provocation wherewith he provoked the LORD God of Israel to anger.

See: Temptation; resistance to

See: Temptation; yielding to

• Resistance to.

Ge 39:7–10; Job 31:5–17, 19–34, 38–40; Ps 73:2–26; Mt 4:1–11; 24:42–44; 26:38–42; Mk 13:33–37; 14:37–38; Lk 4:1–13; 12:35–38; 21:33–36; Rev 3:2–3

Ne 4:9 — Nevertheless we made our prayer unto our God, and set a watch against them day and night, because of them.

Job 31:1 — I made a covenant with mine eyes; why then should I think upon a maid?

Ps 17:4 — Concerning the words of men, by the word of thy lips I have kept *me from* the paths of the destroyer.

Ps 94:17 — Unless the LORD *had been* my help, my soul had almost dwelt in silence.

Ps 119:101 — I have refrained my feet from every evil way, that I might keep thy word.

Ps 119:110 — The wicked have laid a snare for me: yet I erred not from thy precepts.

Am 4:12 — Therefore thus will I do unto thee, O Israel: *and* because I will do this unto thee, prepare to meet thy God, O Israel.

Mt 25:13 — Watch therefore, for ye know neither the day nor the hour wherein the Son of man cometh.

1Co 16:13 — Watch ye, stand fast in the faith, quit you like men, be strong.

1Pe 4:7 — But the end of all things is at hand: be ye therefore sober, and watch unto prayer.

• Instances of.

• Joseph resists the temptation to commit adultery.

Ge 39:7–12

• Balaam, in refusing to curse the children of Israel.

Nu 22:7–18; 24:12–13

• The prophet of Judah.

1Ki 13:7–9

• Micaiah.

1Ki 22:13–28

• Job.

Job 1:6–21; 2:4–10

• Rechabites.

Jer 35:1–19

• David, to injure Saul.

1Sa 26:5–25

• The people of Jerusalem, not to trust Jehovah.

2Ki 18:30–36

• Jesus.

Mt 4:1–11

• Yielding to.

• Instances of.

• Adam and Even.

Ge 3:1–19

• Sarah, to lie.

Ge 18:13–15

Ge 12:13 — Say, I pray thee, thou *art* my sister: that it may be well with me for thy sake; and my soul shall live because of thee.

Ge 20:13 — And it came to pass, when God caused me to wander from my father's house, that I said unto her, This *is* thy kindness which thou shalt shew unto me; at every place whither we shall come, say of me, He *is* my brother.

- **Isaac, to lie.**

Ge 26:7 — And the men of the place asked *him* of his wife; and he said, She *is* my sister: for he feared to say, *She is* my wife; lest, *said he,* the men of the place should kill me for Rebekah; because she *was* fair to look upon.

- **Jacob, to defraud Esau.**

Ge 27:6–13

- **Balaam.**

Nu 22:15–22

2Pe 2:15 — Which have forsaken the right way, and are gone astray, following the way of Balaam *the son* of Bosor, who loved the wages of unrighteousness;

- **Achan.**

Jos 7:21 — When I saw among the spoils a goodly Babylonish garment, and two hundred shekels of silver, and a wedge of gold of fifty shekels weight, then I coveted them, and took them; and, behold, they *are* hid in the earth in the midst of my tent, and the silver under it.

- **David, to commit adultery.**

2Sa 11:2–5

- **David, to number Israel.**

1Ch 21:1–30

- **Solomon, to become an idolater through the influences of his wives.**

1Ki 11:4 — For it came to pass, when Solomon was old, *that* his wives turned away his heart after other gods: and his heart was not perfect with the LORD his God, as *was* the heart of David his father.

Ne 13:26 — Did not Solomon king of Israel sin by these things? yet among many nations was there no king like him, who was beloved of his God, and God made him king over all Israel: nevertheless even him did outlandish women cause to sin.

- **The prophet of Judah.**

1Ki 13:11–19

- **Hezekiah.**

2Ki 20:12–20; Isa 39:1–4, 6–7

- **Peter.**

Mt 26:69–74; Mk 14:67–71; Lk 22:55–60

TEN

- **Used for an indefinite number.**

Ge 31:7 — And your father hath deceived me, and changed my wages ten times; but God suffered him not to hurt me.

Le 26:26 — *And* when I have broken the staff of your bread, ten women shall bake your bread in one oven, and they shall deliver *you* your bread again by weight: and ye shall eat, and not be satisfied.

Nu 14:22 — Because all those men which have seen my glory, and my miracles, which I did in Egypt and in the wilderness, and have tempted me now these ten times, and have not hearkened to my voice;

Zec 8:23 — Thus saith the LORD of hosts; In those days *it shall come to pass,* that ten men shall take hold out of all languages of the nations, even shall take hold of the skirt of him that is a Jew, saying, We will go with you: for we have heard *that* God *is* with you.

TEN COMMANDMENTS ✦See: Commandments

TENANTS

- **Evicted.**

Mt 21:41 — They say unto him, He will miserably destroy those wicked men, and will let out *his* vineyard unto other husbandmen, which shall render him the fruits in their seasons.

Mk 12:9 — What shall therefore the lord of the vineyard do? he will come and destroy the husbandmen, and will give the vineyard unto others.

Lk 20:16 — He shall come and destroy these husbandmen, and shall give the vineyard to others. And when they heard *it,* they said, God forbid.

TENT

- **Used for dwelling.**

Ge 4:20 — And Adah bare Jabal: he was the father of such as dwell in tents, and *of such as have* cattle.

- **Used for dwelling by Noah.**

Ge 9:21 — And he drank of the wine, and was drunken; and he was uncovered within his tent.

- **Used for dwelling by Abraham.**

Ge 12:8 — And he removed from thence unto a mountain on the east of Bethel, and pitched his tent, *having* Bethel on the west, and Hai on the east: and there he builded an altar unto the LORD, and called upon the name of the LORD.

Ge 13:18 — Then Abram removed *his* tent, and came and dwelt in the plain of Mamre, which *is* in Hebron, and built there an altar unto the LORD.

Ge 18:1 — And the LORD appeared unto him in the plains of Mamre: and he sat in the tent door in the heat of the day;

- **Used for dwelling by Lot.**

Ge 13:5 — And Lot also, which went with Abram, had flocks, and herds, and tents.

- **Used for dwelling by Moses.**

Ex 18:7 — And Moses went out to meet his father in law, and did obeisance, and kissed him; and they asked each other of *their* welfare; and they came into the tent.

- **Used for dwelling by children of Israel.**

Nu 24:5–6

2Sa 20:1 — And there happened to be there a man of Belial, whose name *was* Sheba, the son of Bichri, a Benjamite: and he blew a trumpet, and said, We have no part in David, neither have we inheritance in the son of Jesse: every man to his tents, O Israel.

1Ki 12:16 — So when all Israel saw that the king hearkened not unto them, the people answered the king, saying, What portion have we in David? neither *have we* inheritance in the son of Jesse: to your tents, O Israel: now see to thine own house, David. So Israel departed unto their tents.

• Used for dwelling by the Midianites.

Jgs 6:5 — For they came up with their cattle and their tents, and they came as grasshoppers for multitude; *for* both they and their camels were without number: and they entered into the land to destroy it.

• Used for dwelling by Cushites.

Hab 3:7 — I saw the tents of Cushan in affliction: *and* the curtains of the land of Midian did tremble.

• Used for dwelling by Arabians.

Isa 13:20 — It shall never be inhabited, neither shall it be dwelt in from generation to generation: neither shall the Arabian pitch tent there; neither shall the shepherds make their fold there.

• Used for dwelling by shepherds.

Isa 38:12 — Mine age is departed, and is removed from me as a shepherd's tent: I have cut off like a weaver my life: he will cut me off with pining sickness: from day *even* to night wilt thou make an end of me.

Jer 6:3 — The shepherds with their flocks shall come unto her; they shall pitch *their* tents against her round about; they shall feed every one in his place.

• Women had tents apart from men.

Ge 24:67 — And Isaac brought her into his mother Sarah's tent, and took Rebekah, and she became his wife; and he loved her: and Isaac was comforted after his mother's *death.*

Ge 31:33 — And Laban went into Jacob's tent, and into Leah's tent, and into the two maidservants' tents; but he found *them* not. Then went he out of Leah's tent, and entered into Rachel's tent.

• Used for cattle.

2Ch 14:15 — They smote also the tents of cattle, and carried away sheep and camels in abundance, and returned to Jerusalem.

• Manufacture of.

Ac 18:3 — And because he was of the same craft, he abode with them, and wrought: for by their occupation they were tentmakers.

• Used as a place of worship.

✦See: Tabernacle

TERAH

• Father of Abraham.

Ge 11:24–32

• Was an idolater.

Jos 24:2 — And Joshua said unto all the people, Thus saith the LORD God of Israel, Your fathers dwelt on the other side of the flood in old time, *even* Terah, the father of Abraham, and the father of Nachor: and they served other gods.

• Called Thara.

Lk 3:34 — Which was *the son* of Jacob, which was *the son* of Isaac, which was *the son* of Abraham, which was *the son* of Thara, which was *the son* of Nachor,

TERAPHIM

• Household idols.

• Used by Laban; stolen by Rachael.

Ge 31:30–35

Ge 31:19 — And Laban went to shear his sheep: and Rachel had stolen the images that *were* her father's.

• Used by Micah; stolen by the Danites.

Jgs 18:17–20

Jgs 17:5 — And the man Micah had an house of gods, and made an ephod, and teraphim, and consecrated one of his sons, who became his priest.

Jgs 18:14 — Then answered the five men that went to spy out the country of Laish, and said unto their brethren, Do ye know that there is in these houses an ephod, and teraphim, and a graven image, and a molten image? now therefore consider what ye have to do.

• Condemned and disposed of by Jacob.

Ge 31:35–39; 35:2–4

• Destroyed by Josiah.

✦See: Idol

TERESH

• A Persian chamberlain.

• Plotted against Ahasuerus.

Est 2:21–23

Est 6:2 — And it was found written, that Mordecai had told of Bigthana and Teresh, two of the king's chamberlains, the keepers of the door, who sought to lay hand on the king Ahasuerus.

TERTIUS • Paul's amanuensis in writing the book of Romans.

Ro 16:22 — I Tertius, who wrote *this* epistle, salute you in the Lord.

TERTULLUS • Accuser of Paul before Felix.

Ac 24:1–2

TESTAMENT

• A will.

Heb 9:16–18

• The new.

Mt 26:28 — For this is my blood of the new testament, which is shed for many for the remission of sins.

Mk 14:24 — And he said unto them, This is my blood of the new testament, which is shed for many.

Lk 22:20 — Likewise also the cup after supper, saying, This cup *is* the new testament in my blood, which is shed for you.

1Co 11:25 — After the same manner also *he took* the cup, when he had supped, saying, This cup is the new testament in my blood: this do ye, as oft as ye drink *it,* in remembrance of me.

✦See: Covenant

TESTIMONY

- **Legal.**
  - **See: Evidence**
  - **See: Witness**
- **Ark of.**
  - **See: Ark**
- **Religious.**

1Ch 16:8–9; Ps 26:6–7; 145:11–12; Isa 12:4–6; Mk 5:19–20; Lk 8:38–39; 12:8–9; Jn 4:28–30, 41–42; Ro 10:9–10; 1Co 1:5–6; Php 3:7–14; 1Ti 6:12–13

Ps 9:11 — Sing praises to the LORD, which dwelleth in Zion: declare among the people his doings.

Ps 18:49 — Therefore will I give thanks unto thee, O LORD, among the heathen, and sing praises unto thy name.

Ps 119:27 — Make me to understand the way of thy precepts: so shall I talk of thy wondrous works.

Ps 119:172 — My tongue shall speak of thy word: for all thy commandments *are* righteousness.

Isa 32:4 — The heart also of the rash shall understand knowledge, and the tongue of the stammerers shall be ready to speak plainly.

Isa 43:10 — Ye *are* my witnesses, saith the LORD, and my servant whom I have chosen: that ye may know and believe me, and understand that I *am* he: before me there was no God formed, neither shall there be after me.

Isa 44:8 — Fear ye not, neither be afraid: have not I told thee from that time, and have declared *it?* ye *are* even my witnesses. Is there a God beside me? yea, *there is* no God; I know not *any.*

Isa 45:24 — Surely, shall *one* say, in the LORD have I righteousness and strength: *even* to him shall *men* come; and all that are incensed against him shall be ashamed.

Jer 51:10 — The LORD hath brought forth our righteousness: come, and let us declare in Zion the work of the LORD our God.

Mt 5:15 — Neither do men light a candle, and put it under a bushel, but on a candlestick; and it giveth light unto all that are in the house.

Mt 10:32 — Whosoever therefore shall confess me before men, him will I confess also before my Father which is in heaven.

Mk 4:21 — And he said unto them, Is a candle brought to be put under a bushel, or under a bed? and not to be set on a candlestick?

Mk 5:16 — And they that saw *it* told them how it befell to him that was possessed with the devil, and *also* concerning the swine.

Lk 8:16 — No man, when he hath lighted a candle, covereth it with a vessel, or putteth *it* under a bed; but setteth *it* on a candlestick, that they which enter in may see the light.

Lk 24:48 — And ye are witnesses of these things.

Jn 4:39 — And many of the Samaritans of that city believed on him for the saying of the woman, which testified, He told me all that ever I did.

Jn 15:27 — And ye also shall bear witness, because ye have been with me from the beginning.

Ac 1:8 — But ye shall receive power, after that the Holy Ghost is come upon you: and ye shall be witnesses unto me both in Jerusalem, and in all Judaea, and in Samaria, and unto the uttermost part of the earth.

Ac 1:22 — Beginning from the baptism of John, unto that same day that he was taken up from us, must one be ordained to be a witness with us of his resurrection.

1Co 12:3 — Wherefore I give you to understand, that no man speaking by the Spirit of God calleth Jesus accursed: and *that* no man can say that Jesus is the Lord, but by the Holy Ghost.

1Co 13:1 — Though I speak with the tongues of men and of angels, and have not charity, I am become *as* sounding brass, or a tinkling cymbal.

Eph 5:19 — Speaking to yourselves in psalms and hymns and spiritual songs, singing and making melody in your heart to the Lord;

2Ti 1:8 — Be not thou therefore ashamed of the testimony of our Lord, nor of me his prisoner: but be thou partaker of the afflictions of the gospel according to the power of God;

Heb 2:3 — How shall we escape, if we neglect so great salvation; which at the first began to be spoken by the Lord, and was confirmed unto us by them that heard *him;*

Heb 2:12 — Saying, I will declare thy name unto my brethren, in the midst of the church will I sing praise unto thee.

1Pe 3:15 — But sanctify the Lord God in your hearts: and *be* ready always to *give* an answer to every man that asketh you a reason of the hope that is in you with meekness and fear:

1Pe 5:1 — The elders which are among you I exhort, who am also an elder, and a witness of the sufferings of Christ, and also a partaker of the glory that shall be revealed:

Rev 12:11 — And they overcame him by the blood of the Lamb, and by the word of their testimony; and they loved not their lives unto the death.

- **See: Confession**
- **Religious, exemplified.**

Job 19:25–27; Ps 16:5–9; 18:2–3, 35–36; 23:1–6; 26:12–27:6; 28:6–8; 30:1–6; 34:1–4, 8–9; 40:1–3; 57:7–9; 62:1–2; 66:16–20; 71:15–18; 73:23–26; 91:2–13; 116:1–14; 119:26–27; 145:4–7, 10–12; Da 4:1–37; Jn 9:30–33; Ac 2:4–11; 4:18–20; 5:31–32; 22:1–30; 26:12–23; 2Co 4:13–14; Php 3:4–14; 2Ti 4:7–8; Tit 1:1–2; 3:3–7; 1Jn 1:1–4

Ps 22:22 — I will declare thy name unto my brethren: in the midst of the congregation will I praise thee.

Ps 27:13 — *I had fainted,* unless I had believed to see the goodness of the LORD in the land of the living.

Ps 35:28 — And my tongue shall speak of thy righteousness *and* of thy praise all the day long.

Ps 40:9 — I have preached righteousness in the great congregation: lo, I have not refrained my lips, O LORD, thou knowest.

Ps 54:7 — For he hath delivered me out of all trouble: and mine eye hath seen *his desire* upon mine enemies.

Ps 71:24 — My tongue also shall talk of thy righteousness all the day long: for they are confounded, for they are brought unto shame, that seek my hurt.

Ps 73:28 — But *it is* good for me to draw near to God: I have put my trust in the Lord GOD, that I may declare all thy works.

Ps 77:12 — I will meditate also of all thy work, and talk of thy doings.

Ps 89:1 — I will sing of the mercies of the LORD for ever: with my mouth will I make known thy faithfulness to all generations.

Ps 119:13 — With my lips have I declared all the judgments of thy mouth.

Ps 119:46 — I will speak of thy testimonies also before kings, and will not be ashamed.

Ps 119:67 — Before I was afflicted I went astray: but now have I kept thy word.

Ps 119:71 — *It is* good for me that I have been afflicted; that I might learn thy statutes.

Jn 9:17 — They say unto the blind man again, What sayest thou of him, that he hath opened thine eyes? He said, He is a prophet.

Ac 3:15 — And killed the Prince of life, whom God hath raised from the dead; whereof we are witnesses.

Ac 13:31 — And he was seen many days of them which came up with him from Galilee to Jerusalem, who are his witnesses unto the people.

1Co 15:15 — Yea, and we are found false witnesses of God; because we have testified of God that he raised up Christ: whom he raised not up, if so be that the dead rise not.

2Co 5:1 — For we know that if our earthly house of *this* tabernacle were dissolved, we have a building of God, an house not made with hands, eternal in the heavens.

Gal 2:20 — I am crucified with Christ: nevertheless I live; yet not I, but Christ liveth in me: and the life which I now live in the flesh I live by the faith of the Son of God, who loved me, and gave himself for me.

2Ti 1:12 — For the which cause I also suffer these things: nevertheless I am not ashamed: for I know whom I have believed, and am persuaded that he is able to keep that which I have committed unto him against that day.

1Pe 5:12 — By Silvanus, a faithful brother unto you, as I suppose, I have written briefly, exhorting, and testifying that this is the true grace of God wherein ye stand.

2Pe 1:16 — For we have not followed cunningly devised fables, when we made known unto you the power and coming of our Lord Jesus Christ, but were eyewitnesses of his majesty.

TETRARCH • A Roman ruler.

Mt 14:1 — At that time Herod the tetrarch heard of the fame of Jesus,

THADDAEUS • One of the twelve apostles.

Mt 10:3 — Philip, and Bartholomew; Thomas, and Matthew the publican; James *the son* of Alphaeus, and Lebbaeus, whose surname was Thaddaeus;

Mk 3:18 — And Andrew, and Philip, and Bartholomew, and Matthew, and Thomas, and James the *son* of Alphaeus, and Thaddaeus, and Simon the Canaanite,

THAHASH • Son of Nahor.

Ge 22:24 — And his concubine, whose name *was* Reumah, she bare also Tebah, and Gaham, and Thahash, and Maachah.

THAMAH

• Called also Tamah.

• One of the Nethinim.

Ezr 2:53 — The children of Barkos, the children of Sisera, the children of Thamah,

Ne 7:55 — The children of Barkos, the children of Sisera, the children of Tamah,

THAMAR ↞See: Tamar; wife of the sons of Judah

THANK OFFERINGS ↞See: Offerings

THANKFULNESS

• Jesus set an example of.

Mt 11:25 — At that time Jesus answered and said, I thank thee, O Father, Lord of heaven and earth, because thou hast hid these things from the wise and prudent, and hast revealed them unto babes.

Mt 26:27 — And he took the cup, and gave thanks, and gave *it* to them, saying, Drink ye all of it;

Jn 11:41 — Then they took away the stone *from the place* where the dead was laid. And Jesus lifted up *his* eyes, and said, Father, I thank thee that thou hast heard me.

• The heavenly host engage in.

Rev 7:11–12; 11:16–17

Rev 4:9 — And when those beasts give glory and honour and thanks to him that sat on the throne, who liveth for ever and ever,

• Commanded.

Ps 50:14 — Offer unto God thanksgiving; and pay thy vows unto the most High:

• Should be offered to God.

Ps 50:14 — Offer unto God thanksgiving; and pay thy vows unto the most High:

• Should be offered to Christ.

1Ti 1:12 — And I thank Christ Jesus our Lord, who hath enabled me, for that he counted me faithful, putting me into the ministry;

• Should be offered through Christ.

Ro 1:8 — First, I thank my God through Jesus Christ for you all, that your faith is spoken of throughout the whole world.

Col 3:17 — And whatsoever ye do in word or deed, *do* all in the name of the Lord Jesus, giving thanks to God and the Father by him.

Heb 13:15 — By him therefore let us offer the sacrifice of praise to God continually, that is, the fruit of *our* lips giving thanks to his name.

• Should be offered in the name of Christ.

Eph 5:20 — Giving thanks always for all things unto God and the Father in the name of our Lord Jesus Christ;

• Should be offered in behalf of ministers.

2Co 1:11 — Ye also helping together by prayer for us, that for the gift *bestowed* upon us by the means of many persons thanks may be given by many on our behalf.

• Should be offered in private worship.

Da 6:10 — Now when Daniel knew that the writing was signed, he went into his house; and his windows being open in his chamber toward Jerusalem, he kneeled upon his knees three times a day, and prayed, and gave thanks before his God, as he did aforetime.

• Should be offered in public worship.

Ps 35:18 — I will give thee thanks in the great congregation: I will praise thee among much people.

• Should be offered in everything.

1Th 5:18 — In every thing give thanks: for this is the will of God in Christ Jesus concerning you.

• Should be offered upon the completion of great undertakings.

Ne 12:31 — Then I brought up the princes of Judah upon the wall, and appointed two great *companies of them that gave* thanks, *whereof one* went on the right hand upon the wall toward the dung gate:

Ne 12:40 — So stood the two *companies of them that gave* thanks in the house of God, and I, and the half of the rulers with me:

• Should be offered before taking food.

Jn 6:11 — And Jesus took the loaves; and when he had given thanks, he distributed to the disciples, and the disciples to them that were set down; and likewise of the fishes as much as they would.

Ac 27:35 — And when he had thus spoken, he took bread, and gave thanks to God in presence of them all: and when he had broken *it,* he began to eat.

• Should be offered always.

Eph 1:16 — Cease not to give thanks for you, making mention of you in my prayers;

Eph 5:20 — Giving thanks always for all things unto God and the Father in the name of our Lord Jesus Christ;

1Th 1:2 — We give thanks to God always for you all, making mention of you in our prayers;

• Should be offered as the remembrance of God's holiness.

Ps 30:4 — Sing unto the LORD, O ye saints of his, and give thanks at the remembrance of his holiness.

Ps 97:12 — Rejoice in the LORD, ye righteous; and give thanks at the remembrance of his holiness.

• Should be offered for the goodness and mercy of God.

Ps 136:1–3

Ps 106:1 — Praise ye the LORD. O give thanks unto the LORD; for *he is* good: for his mercy *endureth* for ever.

Ps 107:1 — O give thanks unto the LORD, for *he is* good: for his mercy *endureth* for ever.

• Should be offered for the gift of Christ.

2Co 9:15 — Thanks *be* unto God for his unspeakable gift.

• Should be offered for Christ's power and reign.

Rev 11:17 — Saying, We give thee thanks, O Lord God Almighty, which art, and wast, and art to come; because thou hast taken to thee thy great power, and hast reigned.

• Should be offered for the reception and effectual working of the word of God in others.

1Th 2:13 — For this cause also thank we God without ceasing, because, when ye received the word of God which ye heard of us, ye received *it* not *as* the word of men, but as it is in truth, the word of God, which effectually worketh also in you that believe.

• Should be offered in deliverance through Christ, from indwelling sin.

Ro 7:23–25

• Should be offered for victory over death and the grave.

1Co 15:57 — But thanks *be* to God, which giveth us the victory through our Lord Jesus Christ.

• Should be offered for wisdom and might.

Da 2:23 — I thank thee, and praise thee, O thou God of my fathers, who hast given me wisdom and might, and hast made known unto me now what we desired of thee: for thou hast *now* made known unto us the king's matter.

• Should be offered for the triumph of the gospel.

2Co 2:14 — Now thanks *be* unto God, which always causeth us to triumph in Christ, and maketh manifest the savour of his knowledge by us in every place.

• Should be offered for the conversion of others.

Ro 6:17 — But God be thanked, that ye were the servants of sin, but ye have obeyed from the heart that form of doctrine which was delivered you.

• Should be offered for faith exhibited by others.

Ro 1:8 — First, I thank my God through Jesus Christ for you all, that your faith is spoken of throughout the whole world.

2Th 1:3 — We are bound to thank God always for you, brethren, as it is meet, because that your faith groweth exceedingly, and the charity of every one of you all toward each other aboundeth;

• Should be offered for love exhibited by others.

2Th 1:3 — We are bound to thank God always for you, brethren, as it is meet, because that your faith groweth exceedingly, and the charity of every one of you all toward each other aboundeth;

• Should be offered for the grace bestowed on others.

Php 1:3–5; Col 1:3–6

1Co 1:4 — I thank my God always on your behalf, for the grace of God which is given you by Jesus Christ;

• Should be offered for the zeal exhibited by others.

2Co 8:16 — But thanks *be* to God, which put the same earnest care into the heart of Titus for you.

• Should be offered for nearness of God's presence.

Ps 75:1 — Unto thee, O God, do we give thanks, *unto thee* do we give thanks: for *that* thy name is near thy wondrous works declare.

• Should be offered for appointment to the ministry.

1Ti 1:12 — And I thank Christ Jesus our Lord, who hath enabled me, for that he counted me faithful, putting me into the ministry;

• Should be offered for willingness to offer our property for God's service.

1Ch 29:6–14

• Should be offered for the supply of our bodily wants.

Ro 14:6–7; 1Ti 4:3–4

• Should be offered for all men.

1Ti 2:1 — I exhort therefore, that, first of all, supplications, prayers, intercessions, *and* giving of thanks, be made for all men;

• Should be offered for all things.

2Co 9:11 — Being enriched in every thing to all bountifulness, which causeth through us thanksgiving to God.

Eph 5:20 — Giving thanks always for all things unto God and the Father in the name of our Lord Jesus Christ;

• Should be accompanied by intercession for others.

1Ti 2:1 — I exhort therefore, that, first of all, supplications, prayers, intercessions, *and* giving of thanks, be made for all men;

2Ti 1:3 — I thank God, whom I serve from *my* forefathers with pure conscience, that without ceasing I have remembrance of thee in my prayers night and day;

Phm 1:4 — I thank my God, making mention of thee always in my prayers,

• Should always accompany prayer.

Ne 11:17 — And Mattaniah the son of Micha, the son of Zabdi, the son of Asaph, *was* the principal to begin the thanksgiving in prayer: and Bakbukiah the second among his brethren, and Abda the son of Shammua, the son of Galal, the son of Jeduthun.

Php 4:6 — Be careful for nothing; but in every thing by prayer and supplication with thanksgiving let your requests be made known unto God.

Col 4:2 — Continue in prayer, and watch in the same with thanksgiving;

• Should always accompany praise.

Ps 92:1 — *It is a* good *thing* to give thanks unto the LORD, and to sing praises unto thy name, O most High:

Heb 13:15 — By him therefore let us offer the sacrifice of praise to God continually, that is, the fruit of *our* lips giving thanks to his name.

• Expressed in psalms.

1Ch 16:7 — Then on that day David delivered first *this psalm* to thank the LORD into the hand of Asaph and his brethren.

• Ministers appointed to offer, in public.

1Ch 16:4 — And he appointed *certain* of the Levites to minister before the ark of the LORD, and to record, and to thank and praise the LORD God of Israel:

1Ch 16:7 — Then on that day David delivered first *this psalm* to thank the LORD into the hand of Asaph and his brethren.

1Ch 23:30 — And to stand every morning to thank and praise the LORD, and likewise at even;

2Ch 31:2 — And Hezekiah appointed the courses of the priests and the Levites after their courses, every man according to his service, the priests and Levites for burnt offerings and for peace offerings, to minister, and to give thanks, and to praise in the gates of the tents of the LORD.

• Saints exhorted to.

Ps 105:1 — O give thanks unto the LORD; call upon his name: make known his deeds among the people.

Col 3:15 — And let the peace of God rule in your hearts, to the which also ye are called in one body; and be ye thankful.

• Saints resolve to offer.

Ps 18:49 — Therefore will I give thanks unto thee, O LORD, among the heathen, and sing praises unto thy name.

Ps 30:12 — To the end that *my* glory may sing praise to thee, and not be silent. O LORD my God, I will give thanks unto thee for ever.

• Saints habitually offer.

Da 6:10 — Now when Daniel knew that the writing was signed, he went into his house; and his windows being open in his chamber toward Jerusalem, he kneeled upon his knees three times a day, and prayed, and gave thanks before his God, as he did aforetime.

• Saints offer sacrifices of.

Ps 116:17 — I will offer to thee the sacrifice of thanksgiving, and will call upon the name of the LORD.

• Saints abound in the faith with.

Col 2:7 — Rooted and built up in him, and stablished in the faith, as ye have been taught, abounding therein with thanksgiving.

• Saints magnify God by.

Ps 69:30 — I will praise the name of God with a song, and will magnify him with thanksgiving.

- **Saints come before God with.**

Ps 95:2 — Let us come before his presence with thanksgiving, and make a joyful noise unto him with psalms.

- **Saints should enter God's gates with.**

Ps 100:4 — Enter into his gates with thanksgiving, *and* into his courts with praise: be thankful unto him, *and* bless his name.

- **Of hypocrites, full of boasting.**

Lk 18:11 — The Pharisee stood and prayed thus with himself, God, I thank thee, that I am not as other men *are*, extortioners, unjust, adulterers, or even as this publican.

- **The wicked averse to.**

Ro 1:21 — Because that, when they knew God, they glorified *him* not as God, neither were thankful; but became vain in their imaginations, and their foolish heart was darkened.

- **Exemplified.**
  - **David.**

1Ch 29:13 — Now therefore, our God, we thank thee, and praise thy glorious name.

  - **Levites.**

2Ch 5:12–13

  - **Daniel.**

Da 2:23 — I thank thee, and praise thee, O thou God of my fathers, who hast given me wisdom and might, and hast made known unto me now what we desired of thee: for thou hast *now* made known unto us the king's matter.

  - **Jonah.**

Jnh 2:9 — But I will sacrifice unto thee with the voice of thanksgiving; I will pay *that* that I have vowed. Salvation *is* of the LORD.

  - **Simeon.**

Lk 2:28 — Then took he him up in his arms, and blessed God, and said,

  - **Anna.**

Lk 2:38 — And she coming in that instant gave thanks likewise unto the Lord, and spake of him to all them that looked for redemption in Jerusalem.

  - **Paul.**

Ac 28:15 — And from thence, when the brethren heard of us, they came to meet us as far as Appii Forum, and The three taverns: whom when Paul saw, he thanked God, and took courage.

THANKFULNESS, Miscellaneous

- **Enjoined.**

Ex 13:8–10, 14–16; Dt 16:9–15; Ps 50:14–15; 105:1–106:1; 107:1–2, 42–43; Pr 3:9–10; Eph 5:19–20; Col 3:15–17; 1Ti 4:3–5

Ge 35:1 — And God said unto Jacob, Arise, go up to Bethel, and dwell there: and make there an altar unto God, that appeared unto thee when thou fleddest from the face of Esau thy brother.

Ex 12:14 — And this day shall be unto you for a memorial; and ye shall keep it a feast to the LORD throughout your generations; ye shall keep it a feast by an ordinance for ever.

Ex 12:17 — And ye shall observe *the feast of* unleavened bread; for in this selfsame day have I brought your armies out of the land of Egypt: therefore shall ye observe this day in your generations by an ordinance for ever.

Ex 12:42 — It *is* a night to be much observed unto the LORD for bringing them out from the land of Egypt: this *is* that night of the LORD to be observed of all the children of Israel in their generations.

Ex 13:3 — And Moses said unto the people, Remember this day, in which ye came out from Egypt, out of the house of bondage; for by strength of hand the LORD brought you out from this *place:* there shall no leavened bread be eaten.

Ex 16:32 — And Moses said, This *is* the thing which the LORD commandeth, Fill an omer of it to be kept for your generations; that they may see the bread wherewith I have fed you in the wilderness, when I brought you forth from the land of Egypt.

Ex 34:26 — The first of the firstfruits of thy land thou shalt bring unto the house of the LORD thy God. Thou shalt not seethe a kid in his mother's milk.

Le 19:24 — But in the fourth year all the fruit thereof shall be holy to praise the LORD *withal.*

Le 23:14 — And ye shall eat neither bread, nor parched corn, nor green ears, until the selfsame day that ye have brought an offering unto your God: *it shall be* a statute for ever throughout your generations in all your dwellings.

Dt 12:18 — But thou must eat them before the LORD thy God in the place which the LORD thy God shall choose, thou, and thy son, and thy daughter, and thy manservant, and thy maidservant, and the Levite that *is* within thy gates: and thou shalt rejoice before the LORD thy God in all that thou puttest thine hands unto.

Dt 26:10 — And now, behold, I have brought the firstfruits of the land, which thou, O LORD, hast given me. And thou shalt set it before the LORD thy God, and worship before the LORD thy God:

Jgs 5:11 — *They that are delivered* from the noise of archers in the places of drawing water, there shall they rehearse the righteous acts of the LORD, *even* the righteous acts *toward the inhabitants* of his villages in Israel: then shall the people of the LORD go down to the gates.

Ps 48:11 — Let mount Zion rejoice, let the daughters of Judah be glad, because of thy judgments.

Ps 98:1 — O sing unto the LORD a new song; for he hath done marvellous things: his right hand, and his holy arm, hath gotten him the victory.

Ps 107:15 — Oh that *men* would praise the LORD *for* his goodness, and *for* his wonderful works to the children of men!

Ps 107:22 — And let them sacrifice the sacrifices of thanksgiving, and declare his works with rejoicing.

Ps 118:1 — O give thanks unto the LORD; for *he is* good: because his mercy *endureth* for ever.

Ps 118:4 — Let them now that fear the LORD say, that his mercy *endureth* for ever.

Ecc 7:14 — In the day of prosperity be joyful, but in the day of adversity consider: God also hath set the one over against the other, to the end that man should find nothing after him.

Isa 48:20 — Go ye forth of Babylon, flee ye from the Chaldeans, with a voice of singing declare ye, tell this, utter it *even* to the end of the earth; say ye, The LORD hath redeemed his servant Jacob.

Joel 2:26 — And ye shall eat in plenty, and be satisfied, and praise the name of the LORD your God, that hath dealt wondrously with you: and my people shall never be ashamed.

Ro 2:4 — Or despisest thou the riches of his goodness and forbearance and longsuffering; not knowing that the goodness of God leadeth thee to repentance?

Ro 15:27 — It hath pleased them verily; and their debtors they are. For if the Gentiles have been made partakers of their spiritual things, their duty is also to minister unto them in carnal things.

Eph 5:4 — Neither filthiness, nor foolish talking, nor jesting, which are not convenient: but rather giving of thanks.

Php 4:6 — Be careful for nothing; but in every thing by prayer and supplication with thanksgiving let your requests be made known unto God.

Col 1:12 — Giving thanks unto the Father, which hath made us meet to be partakers of the inheritance of the saints in light:

Col 2:7 — Rooted and built up in him, and stablished in the faith, as ye have been taught, abounding therein with thanksgiving.

Col 4:2 — Continue in prayer, and watch in the same with thanksgiving;

1Th 5:18 — In every thing give thanks: for this is the will of God in Christ Jesus concerning you.

1Ti 2:1 — I exhort therefore, that, first of all, supplications, prayers, intercessions, *and* giving of thanks, be made for all men;

Heb 13:15 — By him therefore let us offer the sacrifice of praise to God continually, that is, the fruit of *our* lips giving thanks to his name.

Jas 1:9 — Let the brother of low degree rejoice in that he is exalted:

See: Joy

See: Praise

See: Psalms

• Exemplified.

Ge 48:15–16; Ex 15:1–21; Nu 21:17–18; Ps 9:1–2; 22:23–25; 30:11–12; 35:9–10; 40:2–3; 41:11–12; 44:7–8; 54:6–7; 56:12–13; 59:16–17; 66:8–9, 12–16; 71:23–24; 92:1–2; 102:18–20; 116:12–14; 136:1–26; Ac 2:46–47

Ge 32:10 — I am not worthy of the least of all the mercies, and of all the truth, which thou hast shewed unto thy servant; for with my staff I passed over this Jordan; and now I am become two bands.

Ge 48:11 — And Israel said unto Joseph, I had not thought to see thy face: and, lo, God hath shewed me also thy seed.

1Ki 8:56 — Blessed *be* the LORD, that hath given rest unto his people Israel, according to all that he promised: there hath not failed one word of all his good promise, which he promised by the hand of Moses his servant.

1Ch 29:14 — But who *am* I, and what *is* my people, that we should be able to offer so willingly after this sort? for all things *come* of thee, and of thine own have we given thee.

Ezr 7:27 — Blessed *be* the LORD God of our fathers, which hath put *such a thing* as this in the king's heart, to beautify the house of the LORD which *is* in Jerusalem:

Ps 9:4 — For thou hast maintained my right and my cause; thou satest in the throne judging right.

Ps 13:6 — I will sing unto the LORD, because he hath dealt bountifully with me.

Ps 26:7 — That I may publish with the voice of thanksgiving, and tell of all thy wondrous works.

Ps 28:7 — The LORD *is* my strength and my shield; my heart trusted in him, and I am helped: therefore my heart greatly rejoiceth; and with my song will I praise him.

Ps 30:1 — I will extol thee, O LORD; for thou hast lifted me up, and hast not made my foes to rejoice over me.

Ps 30:3 — O LORD, thou hast brought up my soul from the grave: thou hast kept me alive, that I should not go down to the pit.

Ps 31:7 — I will be glad and rejoice in thy mercy: for thou hast considered my trouble; thou hast known my soul in adversities;

Ps 31:21 — Blessed *be* the LORD: for he hath shewed me his marvellous kindness in a strong city.

Ps 35:18 — I will give thee thanks in the great congregation: I will praise thee among much people.

Ps 40:5 — Many, O LORD my God, *are* thy wonderful works *which* thou hast done, and thy thoughts *which are* to us-ward: they cannot be reckoned up in order unto thee: *if* I would declare and speak *of them,* they are more than can be numbered.

Ps 66:20 — Blessed *be* God, which hath not turned away my prayer, nor his mercy from me.

Ps 68:19 — Blessed *be* the Lord, *who* daily loadeth us *with benefits, even* the God of our salvation. Selah.

Ps 71:15 My mouth shall shew forth thy righteousness *and* thy salvation all the day; for I know not the numbers *thereof.*

Ps 79:13 — So we thy people and sheep of thy pasture will give thee thanks for ever: we will shew forth thy praise to all generations.

Ps 89:1 — I will sing of the mercies of the LORD for ever: with my mouth will I make known thy faithfulness to all generations.

Ps 92:4 — For thou, LORD, hast made me glad through thy work: I will triumph in the works of thy hands.

Ps 98:1 — O sing unto the LORD a new song; for he hath done marvellous things: his right hand, and his holy arm, hath gotten him the victory.

Ps 100:4 — Enter into his gates with thanksgiving, *and* into his courts with praise: be thankful unto him, *and* bless his name.

Ps 104:1 — Bless the LORD, O my soul. O LORD my God, thou art very great; thou art clothed with honour and majesty.

Ps 116:17 — I will offer to thee the sacrifice of thanksgiving, and will call upon the name of the LORD.

Ps 119:65 — Thou hast dealt well with thy servant, O LORD, according unto thy word.

Ps 119:108 — Accept, I beseech thee, the freewill offerings of my mouth, O LORD, and teach me thy judgments.

Isa 63:7 — I will mention the lovingkindnesses of the LORD, *and* the praises of the LORD, according to all that the LORD hath bestowed on us, and the great goodness toward the house of Israel, which he hath bestowed on them according to his mercies, and according to the multitude of his lovingkindnesses.

Da 2:23 — I thank thee, and praise thee, O thou God of my fathers, who hast given me wisdom and might, and hast made known unto me now what we desired of thee: for thou hast *now* made known unto us the king's matter.

Da 4:2 — I thought it good to shew the signs and wonders that the high God hath wrought toward me.

Da 4:34 — And at the end of the days I Nebuchadnezzar lifted up mine eyes unto heaven, and mine understanding returned unto me, and I blessed the most High, and I praised and honoured him that liveth for ever, whose dominion *is* an everlasting dominion, and his kingdom *is* from generation to generation:

Da 6:22 — My God hath sent his angel, and hath shut the lions' mouths, that they have not hurt me: forasmuch as before him innocency was found in me; and also before thee, O king, have I done no hurt.

Ac 28:15 — And from thence, when the brethren heard of us, they came to meet us as far as Appii Forum, and The three taverns: whom when Paul saw, he thanked God, and took courage.

Ro 14:6 — He that regardeth the day, regardeth *it* unto the Lord; and he that regardeth not the day, to the Lord he doth not regard *it*. He that eateth, eateth to the Lord, for he giveth God thanks; and he that eateth not, to the Lord he eateth not, and giveth God thanks.

Col 1:3 — We give thanks to God and the Father of our Lord Jesus Christ, praying always for you,

1Ti 1:12 — And I thank Christ Jesus our Lord, who hath enabled me, for that he counted me faithful, putting me into the ministry;

See: Joy

See: Praise

See: Psalms

See: Worship

• Of man to man.

• The Israelites to Joshua.

Jos 19:49–50

• The spies, to Rahab.

Jos 6:22–25

• Saul, to the Kenites.

1Sa 15:6 — And Saul said unto the Kenites, Go, depart, get you down from among the Amalekites, lest I destroy you with them: for ye shewed kindness to all the children of Israel, when they came up out of Egypt. So the Kenites departed from among the Amalekites.

• Naomi, to Boaz.

Ru 2:19–20

• David, to the men of Jabesh-gilead.

2Sa 2:5–7

• David, to Hanun.

2Sa 10:2 — Then said David, I will shew kindness unto Hanun the son of Nahash, as his father shewed kindness unto me. And David sent to comfort him by the hand of his servants for his father. And David's servants came into the land of the children of Ammon.

• David, to Barzillai.

1Ki 2:7 — But shew kindness unto the sons of Barzillai the Gileadite, and let them be of those that eat at thy table: for so they came to me when I fled because of Absalom thy brother.

• Paul, to Phebe.

Ro 16:1–4

• Paul, to Onesiphorus.

2Ti 1:16–18

• The people of Melita, to Paul.

Ac 28:10 — Who also honoured us with many honours; and when we departed, they laded *us* with such things as were necessary.

THANKFULNESS, to God

• Instances of.

• Eve.

Ge 4:1, 25

• Noah.

Ge 8:20

• Melchizedek.

Ge 14:20

• Lot.

Ge 19:19

• Sarah.

Ge 21:6–7

• Abraham.

Ge 12:7; 13:4

• Abraham's servant.

Ge 24:27, 35

• Isaac.

Ge 26:22

• Leah.

Ge 29:32–35

• Rachel.

Ge 30:6

• Jacob.

Ge 31:42; 35:3, 7

• Joseph.

Ge 41:51–52

• Moses.

Ex 15:1–19

• Miriam.

Ex 15:20–22

• **Jethro.**
Ex 18:10

• **Israel.**
Ex 4:31; Nu 21:17; 31:49–54; 1Ch 29:22

• **Deborah.**
Jgs 5:1–31

• **Hannah.**
1Sa 1:27–28

• **Samuel.**
1Sa 7:12

• **David.**
2Sa 6:1–23

• **The Queen of Sheba.**
1Ki 10:9

• **Hiram.**
2Ch 2:12

• **Jehoshaphat's army.**
2Ch 20:27–28

• **The Levites.**
Ne 9:4–38

• **The Jews.**
Ne 12:43

• **The mariners.**
Jnh 1:16

• **The shepherds.**
Lk 2:20

• **Those whom Jesus healed.**

• **The man with palsy.**
Lk 5:25 — And immediately he rose up before them, and took up that whereon he lay, and departed to his own house, glorifying God.

• **The healed demoniac.**
Lk 8:39 — Return to thine own house, and shew how great things God hath done unto thee. And he went his way, and published throughout the whole city how great things Jesus had done unto him.

• **The woman bent with infirmity.**
Lk 13:13 — And he laid *his* hands on her: and immediately she was made straight, and glorified God.

• **One of the ten lepers whom Jesus healed.**
Lk 17:15–16

• **Blind Bartimaeus.**
Mk 10:46–52
Lk 18:43 — And immediately he received his sight, and followed him, glorifying God: and all the people, when they saw *it*, gave praise unto God.

• **The centurion for his son.**
Jn 4:53 — So the father knew that *it was* at the same hour, in the which Jesus said unto him, Thy son liveth: and himself believed, and his whole house.

• **The lame man healed by Peter.**
Ac 3:8 — And he leaping up stood, and walked, and entered with them into the temple, walking, and leaping, and praising God.

• **Before taking food, by Jesus.**
Mk 8:6–7
Mt 14:19 — And he commanded the multitude to sit down on the grass, and took the five loaves, and the two fishes, and looking up to heaven, he blessed, and brake, and gave the loaves to *his* disciples, and the disciples to the multitude.

• **Before taking food, by Paul.**
Ac 27:35 — And when he had thus spoken, he took bread, and gave thanks to God in presence of them all: and when he had broken *it*, he began to eat.

See: Praise

See: Prayer; thanksgiving and, before taking food

THANKSGIVING

See: Praise

See: Thankfulness

THARA **See: Tarah**

THARSHISH

• **Son of Bilhan.**
1Ch 7:10 — The sons also of Jediael; Bilhan: and the sons of Bilhan; Jeush, and Benjamin, and Ehud, and Chenaanah, and Zethan, and Tharshish, and Ahishahar.

See: Tarshish; called also Tharshish, probably Spain

THEATER

Ac 19:29 — And the whole city was filled with confusion: and having caught Gaius and Aristarchus, men of Macedonia, Paul's companions in travel, they rushed with one accord into the theatre.

Ac 19:31 — And certain of the chief of Asia, which were his friends, sent unto him, desiring *him* that he would not adventure himself into the theatre.

THEBEZ • A city, in besieging which Abimelech was slain.

Jgs 9:50–56
2Sa 11:21 — Who smote Abimelech the son of Jerubbesheth? did not a woman cast a piece of a millstone upon him from the wall, that he died in Thebez? why went ye nigh the wall? then say thou, Thy servant Uriah the Hittite is dead also.

THEFT AND THIEVES

Ex 22:1–4, 10–15; Le 6:2–7; Dt 23:24–25; Pr 6:30–31; Jer 7:9–10; Hos 4:1–2; Mt 6:19–20; Mk 7:21–22; Lk 19:45–46

Ex 20:15 — Thou shalt not steal.

Ex 21:16 — And he that stealeth a man, and selleth him, or if he be found in his hand, he shall surely be put to death.

Le 19:11 — Ye shall not steal, neither deal falsely, neither lie one to another.

Le 19:13 — Thou shalt not defraud thy neighbour, neither rob *him:* the wages of him that is hired shall not abide with thee all night until the morning.

Dt 5:19 — Neither shalt thou steal.

Ps 50:18 — When thou sawest a thief, then thou consentedst with him, and hast been partaker with adulterers.

Ps 62:10 — Trust not in oppression, and become not vain in robbery: if riches increase, set not your heart *upon them.*

Ps 119:61 — The bands of the wicked have robbed me: *but* I have not forgotten thy law.

Pr 21:7 — The robbery of the wicked shall destroy them; because they refuse to do judgment.

Isa 61:8 — For I the LORD love judgment, I hate robbery for burnt offering; and I will direct their work in truth, and I will make an everlasting covenant with them.

Jer 2:26 — As the thief is ashamed when he is found, so is the house of Israel ashamed; they, their kings, their princes, and their priests, and their prophets,

Eze 22:29 — The people of the land have used oppression, and exercised robbery, and have vexed the poor and needy: yea, they have oppressed the stranger wrongfully.

Na 3:1 — Woe to the bloody city! it is all full of lies *and* robbery; the prey departeth not;

Zec 5:3 — Then said he unto me, This *is* the curse that goeth forth over the face of the whole earth: for every one that stealeth shall be cut off *as* on this side according to it; and every one that sweareth shall be cut off *as* on that side according to it.

Mt 15:19 — For out of the heart proceed evil thoughts, murders, adulteries, fornications, thefts, false witness, blasphemies:

Mt 19:18 — He saith unto him, Which? Jesus said, Thou shalt do no murder, Thou shalt not commit adultery, Thou shalt not steal, Thou shalt not bear false witness,

Mt 21:13 — And said unto them, It is written, My house shall be called the house of prayer; but ye have made it a den of thieves.

Mt 27:38 — Then were there two thieves crucified with him, one on the right hand, and another on the left.

Mt 27:44 — The thieves also, which were crucified with him, cast the same in his teeth.

Mk 11:17 — And he taught, saying unto them, Is it not written, My house shall be called of all nations the house of prayer? but ye have made it a den of thieves.

Mk 15:27 — And with him they crucify two thieves; the one on his right hand, and the other on his left.

Lk 18:20 — Thou knowest the commandments, Do not commit adultery, Do not kill, Do not steal, Do not bear false witness, Honour thy father and thy mother.

Jn 10:1 — Verily, verily, I say unto you, He that entereth not by the door into the sheepfold, but climbeth up some other way, the same is a thief and a robber.

Ro 2:21 — Thou therefore which teachest another, teachest thou not thyself? thou that preachest a man should not steal, dost thou steal?

Ro 13:9 — For this, Thou shalt not commit adultery, Thou shalt not kill, Thou shalt not steal, Thou shalt not bear false witness, Thou shalt not covet; and if *there be* any other commandment, it is briefly comprehended in this saying, namely, Thou shalt love thy neighbour as thyself.

1Co 6:8 — Nay, ye do wrong, and defraud, and that *your* brethren.

1Co 6:10 — Nor thieves, nor covetous, nor drunkards, nor revilers, nor extortioners, shall inherit the kingdom of God.

Eph 4:28 — Let him that stole steal no more: but rather let him labour, working with *his* hands the thing which is good, that he may have to give to him that needeth.

Tit 2:10 — Not purloining, but shewing all good fidelity; that they may adorn the doctrine of God our Saviour in all things.

1Pe 4:15 — But let none of you suffer as a murderer, or *as* a thief, or *as* an evildoer, or as a busybody in other men's matters.

Rev 3:3 — Remember therefore how thou hast received and heard, and hold fast, and repent. If therefore thou shalt not watch, I will come on thee as a thief, and thou shalt not know what hour I will come upon thee.

Rev 9:21 — Neither repented they of their murders, nor of their sorceries, nor of their fornication, nor of their thefts.

See: Dishonesty

- **Figurative.**

Ob 1:5 — If thieves came to thee, if robbers by night, (how art thou cut off!) would they not have stolen till they had enough? if the grapegatherers came to thee, would they not leave *some* grapes?

- **Instances of.**
  - **By Rachel, of the household gods.**

    Ge 31:19, 34–35
  - **Achan.**

    Jos 7:11
  - **Micah.**

    Jgs 17:2
  - **The spies of Laish.**

    Jgs 18:14–27
  - **Judas.**

    Jn 12:6

THELASAR

- **A city or district.**
- **Conquered by the Assyrians.**

2Ki 19:12 — Have the gods of the nations delivered them which my fathers have destroyed; *as* Gozan, and Haran, and Rezeph, and the children of Eden which *were* in Thelasar?

- **Called also Telassar.**

Isa 37:12 — Have the gods of the nations delivered them which my fathers have destroyed, *as* Gozan, and Haran, and Rezeph, and the children of Eden which *were* in Telassar?

THEOCRACY

- **Established.**

Dt 5:25–29; 33:2–5

Ex 19:8 — And all the people answered together, and said, All that the LORD hath spoken we will do. And Moses returned the words of the people unto the LORD.

Ex 24:3 — And Moses came and told the people all the words of the LORD, and all the judgments: and all the people answered with one voice, and said, All the words which the LORD hath said will we do.

Ex 24:7 — And he took the book of the covenant, and read in the audience of the people: and they said, All that the LORD hath said will we do, and be obedient.

Jgs 8:23 — And Gideon said unto them, I will not rule over you, neither shall my son rule over you: the LORD shall rule over you.

1Sa 12:12 — And when ye saw that Nahash the king of the children of Ammon came against you, ye said unto me, Nay; but a king shall reign over us: when the LORD your God *was* your king.

• Rejected by Israel.

1Sa 8:7 — And the LORD said unto Samuel, Hearken unto the voice of the people in all that they say unto thee: for they have not rejected thee, but they have rejected me, that I should not reign over them.

1Sa 8:19 — Nevertheless the people refused to obey the voice of Samuel; and they said, Nay; but we will have a king over us;

1Sa 10:19 — And ye have this day rejected your God, who himself saved you out of all your adversities and your tribulations; and ye have said unto him, *Nay,* but set a king over us. Now therefore present yourselves before the LORD by your tribes, and by your thousands.

2Ch 13:8 — And now ye think to withstand the kingdom of the LORD in the hand of the sons of David; and ye *be* a great multitude, and *there are* with you golden calves, which Jeroboam made you for gods.

See: God, Sovereign

See: Government

THEOLOGY See: God

THEOPHILUS • A Christian to whom Luke addressed the books of Luke and Acts.

Lk 1:3 — It seemed good to me also, having had perfect understanding of all things from the very first, to write unto thee in order, most excellent Theophilus,

Ac 1:1 — The former treatise have I made, O Theophilus, of all that Jesus began both to do and teach,

THESSALONIANS See: Thessalonica

THESSALONICA

• A city of Macedonia.

• Paul visits.

Ac 17:1 — Now when they had passed through Amphipolis and Apollonia, they came to Thessalonica, where was a synagogue of the Jews:

Php 4:16 — For even in Thessalonica ye sent once and again unto my necessity.

• People of, persecute Paul.

Ac 17:5–8

Ac 17:11 — These were more noble than those in Thessalonica, in that they received the word with all readiness of mind, and searched the scriptures daily, whether those things were so.

Ac 17:13 — But when the Jews of Thessalonica had knowledge that the word of God was preached of Paul at Berea, they came thither also, and stirred up the people.

• Men of, accompany Paul.

Ac 20:4 — And there accompanied him into Asia Sopater of Berea; and of the Thessalonians, Aristarchus and Secundus; and Gaius of Derbe, and Timotheus; and of Asia, Tychicus and Trophimus.

Ac 27:2 — And entering into a ship of Adramyttium, we launched, meaning to sail by the coasts of Asia; *one* Aristarchus, a Macedonian of Thessalonica, being with us.

• Paul writes to Christians in.

1Th 1:1 — Paul, and Silvanus, and Timotheus, unto the church of the Thessalonians *which is* in God the Father and *in* the Lord Jesus Christ: Grace *be* unto you, and peace, from God our Father, and the Lord Jesus Christ.

2Th 1:1 — Paul, and Silvanus, and Timotheus, unto the church of the Thessalonians in God our Father and the Lord Jesus Christ:

• Demas goes to.

2Ti 4:10 — For Demas hath forsaken me, having loved this present world, and is departed unto Thessalonica; Crescens to Galatia, Titus unto Dalmatia.

THEUDAS • A Jewish insurrectionist.

Ac 5:36 — For before these days rose up Theudas, boasting himself to be somebody; to whom a number of men, about four hundred, joined themselves: who was slain; and all, as many as obeyed him, were scattered, and brought to nought.

THIMNATHAH • A city in Dan.

Jos 19:43 — And Elon, and Thimnathah, and Ekron,

THINKING

Eph 4:17–27

Php 4:8 — Finally, brethren, whatsoever things are true, whatsoever things *are* honest, whatsoever things *are* just, whatsoever things *are* pure, whatsoever things *are* lovely, whatsoever things *are* of good report; if *there be* any virtue, and if *there be* any praise, think on these things.

Jas 4:7 — Submit yourselves therefore to God. Resist the devil, and he will flee from you.

THIRST

• Figurative, the ardent desire of the devout mind.

Ps 42:1–4; Am 8:11–13; Jn 4:14–15

Ps 63:1 — O God, thou *art* my God; early will I seek thee: my soul thirsteth for thee, my flesh longeth for thee in a dry and thirsty land, where no water is;

Ps 143:6 — I stretch forth my hands unto thee: my soul *thirsteth* after thee, as a thirsty land. Selah.

Isa 55:1 — Ho, every one that thirsteth, come ye to the waters, and he that hath no money; come ye, buy, and eat; yea, come, buy wine and milk without money and without price.

Mt 5:6 — Blessed *are* they which do hunger and thirst after righteousness: for they shall be filled.

Jn 7:37 — In the last day, that great *day* of the feast, Jesus stood and cried, saying, If any man thirst, let him come unto me, and drink.

Rev 21:6 — And he said unto me, It is done. I am Alpha and Omega, the beginning and the end. I will give unto him that is athirst of the fountain of the water of life freely.

Rev 22:17 — And the Spirit and the bride say, Come. And let him that heareth say, Come. And let him that is athirst come. And whosoever will, let him take the water of life freely.

See: Desire; spiritual

See: Diligence

See: Hunger; spiritual

See: Zeal, Religious

THISTLE

• A noxious plant.

Ge 3:18 — Thorns also and thistles shall it bring forth to thee; and thou shalt eat the herb of the field;

Job 31:40 — Let thistles grow instead of wheat, and cockle instead of barley. The words of Job are ended.

Hos 10:8 — The high places also of Aven, the sin of Israel, shall be destroyed: the thorn and the thistle shall come up on their altars; and they shall say to the mountains, Cover us; and to the hills, Fall on us.

• Parables of.

2Ki 14:9 — And Jehoash the king of Israel sent to Amaziah king of Judah, saying, The thistle that *was* in Lebanon sent to the cedar that *was* in Lebanon, saying, Give thy daughter to my son to wife: and there passed by a wild beast that *was* in Lebanon, and trode down the thistle.

2Ch 25:18 — And Joash king of Israel sent to Amaziah king of Judah, saying, The thistle that *was* in Lebanon sent to the cedar that *was* in Lebanon, saying, Give thy daughter to my son to wife: and there passed by a wild beast that *was* in Lebanon, and trode down the thistle.

Mt 7:16 — Ye shall know them by their fruits. Do men gather grapes of thorns, or figs of thistles?

THOMAS

• Called Didymus.

• One of the twelve apostles.

Mt 10:3 — Philip, and Bartholomew; Thomas, and Matthew the publican; James *the son* of Alphaeus, and Lebbaeus, whose surname was Thaddaeus;

Mk 3:18 — And Andrew, and Philip, and Bartholomew, and Matthew, and Thomas, and James the *son* of Alphaeus, and Thaddaeus, and Simon the Canaanite,

Lk 6:15 — Matthew and Thomas, James the *son* of Alphaeus, and Simon called Zelotes,

• Present at the raising of Lazarus.

Jn 11:16 — Then said Thomas, which is called Didymus, unto his fellowdisciples, Let us also go, that we may die with him.

• Asks Jesus the way to the Father's house.

Jn 14:5 — Thomas saith unto him, Lord, we know not whither thou goest; and how can we know the way?

• Absent when Jesus first appeared to the disciples after the resurrection.

Jn 20:24 — But Thomas, one of the twelve, called Didymus, was not with them when Jesus came.

• Skepticism of.

Jn 20:25 — The other disciples therefore said unto him, We have seen the Lord. But he said unto them, Except I shall see in his hands the print of the nails, and put my finger into the print of the nails, and thrust my hand into his side, I will not believe.

• Sees Jesus after the resurrection.

Jn 20:26–29; 21:1–2

• Dwells with the other apostles in Jerusalem.

Ac 1:13–14

• Loyalty of, to Jesus.

Jn 11:16 — Then said Thomas, which is called Didymus, unto his fellowdisciples, Let us also go, that we may die with him.

Jn 20:28 — And Thomas answered and said unto him, My Lord and my God.

THORN

• The ground cursed with.

Ge 3:18 — Thorns also and thistles shall it bring forth to thee; and thou shalt eat the herb of the field;

• Used as an awl.

Job 41:2 — Canst thou put an hook into his nose? or bore his jaw through with a thorn?

• Used for fuel.

Ps 58:9 — Before your pots can feel the thorns, he shall take them away as with a whirlwind, both living, and in *his* wrath.

Ps 118:12 — They compassed me about like bees; they are quenched as the fire of thorns: for in the name of the LORD I will destroy them.

Ecc 7:6 — For as the crackling of thorns under a pot, so *is* the laughter of the fool: this also *is* vanity.

• Hedges formed of.

Hos 2:6 — Therefore, behold, I will hedge up thy way with thorns, and make a wall, that she shall not find her paths.

Mic 7:4 — The best of them *is* as a brier: the most upright *is sharper* than a thorn hedge: the day of thy watchmen *and* thy visitation cometh; now shall be their perplexity.

• Crown of, mockingly put on Jesus' head.

Mt 27:29 — And when they had platted a crown of thorns, they put *it* upon his head, and a reed in his right hand: and they bowed the knee before him, and mocked him, saying, Hail, King of the Jews!

Mk 15:17 — And they clothed him with purple, and platted a crown of thorns, and put it about his *head,*

Jn 19:2 — And the soldiers platted a crown of thorns, and put *it* on his head, and they put on him a purple robe,

Jn 19:5 — Then came Jesus forth, wearing the crown of thorns, and the purple robe. And *Pilate* saith unto them, Behold the man!

- **Figurative.**
  - **Of afflictions.**

Nu 33:55 — But if ye will not drive out the inhabitants of the land from before you; then it shall come to pass, that those which ye let remain of them *shall be* pricks in your eyes, and thorns in your sides, and shall vex you in the land wherein ye dwell.

2Co 12:7 — And lest I should be exalted above measure through the abundance of the revelations, there was given to me a thorn in the flesh, the messenger of Satan to buffet me, lest I should be exalted above measure.

- **Of the adversities of the wicked.**

Pr 22:5 — Thorns *and* snares *are* in the way of the froward: he that doth keep his soul shall be far from them.

- **Of the evils that spring from the heart to choke the truth.**

Mt 13:7 — And some fell among thorns; and the thorns sprung up, and choked them:

Mt 13:22 — He also that received seed among the thorns is he that heareth the word; and the care of this world, and the deceitfulness of riches, choke the word, and he becometh unfruitful.

THREE TAVERNS

- **A town in Italy.**
- **Roman Christians meet Paul in.**

Ac 28:15 — And from thence, when the brethren heard of us, they came to meet us as far as Appii Forum, and The three taverns: whom when Paul saw, he thanked God, and took courage.

THRESHING

- **By beating.**

Ru 2:17 — So she gleaned in the field until even, and beat out that she had gleaned: and it was about an ephah of barley.

- **By treading.**

Dt 25:4 — Thou shalt not muzzle the ox when he treadeth out *the corn.*

Isa 25:10 — For in this mountain shall the hand of the LORD rest, and Moab shall be trodden down under him, even as straw is trodden down for the dunghill.

Hos 10:11 — And Ephraim *is as* an heifer *that is* taught, *and* loveth to tread out *the corn;* but I passed over upon her fair neck: I will make Ephraim to ride; Judah shall plow, *and* Jacob shall break his clods.

1Co 9:9 — For it is written in the law of Moses, Thou shalt not muzzle the mouth of the ox that treadeth out the corn. Doth God take care for oxen?

1Ti 5:18 — For the scripture saith, Thou shalt not muzzle the ox that treadeth out the corn. And, The labourer *is* worthy of his reward.

- **With instruments of wood.**

2Sa 24:22 — And Araunah said unto David, Let my lord the king take and offer up what *seemeth* good unto him: behold, *here be* oxen for burnt sacrifice, and threshing instruments and *other* instruments of the oxen for wood.

- **With instruments of iron.**

Am 1:4 — But I will send a fire into the house of Hazael, which shall devour the palaces of Ben-hadad.

- **With a cart wheel.**

Isa 28:27–28

- **Floors for.**

Ge 50:10–11; Ru 3:2–14

Jgs 6:37 — Behold, I will put a fleece of wool in the floor; *and* if the dew be on the fleece only, and *it be* dry upon all the earth *beside,* then shall I know that thou wilt save Israel by mine hand, as thou hast said.

1Sa 23:1 — Then they told David, saying, Behold, the Philistines fight against Keilah, and they rob the threshingfloors.

2Sa 6:6 — And when they came to Nachon's threshingfloor, Uzzah put forth *his hand* to the ark of God, and took hold of it; for the oxen shook *it.*

Hos 9:2 — The floor and the winepress shall not feed them, and the new wine shall fail in her.

Joel 2:24 — And the floors shall be full of wheat, and the fats shall overflow with wine and oil.

- **Floor of Araunah bought by David for a place of sacrifice.**

2Sa 24:16–25

- **Floor for, in barns.**

2Ki 6:27 — And he said, If the LORD do not help thee, whence shall I help thee? out of the barnfloor, or out of the winepress?

THRONE

- **Of Pharaoh.**

Ge 41:40 — Thou shalt be over my house, and according unto thy word shall all my people be ruled: only in the throne will I be greater than thou.

Ex 11:5 — And all the firstborn in the land of Egypt shall die, from the firstborn of Pharaoh that sitteth upon his throne, even unto the firstborn of the maidservant that *is* behind the mill; and all the firstborn of beasts.

- **Of David.**

Ps 132:11–12

1Ki 2:12 — Then sat Solomon upon the throne of David his father; and his kingdom was established greatly.

1Ki 2:24 — Now therefore, *as* the LORD liveth, which hath established me, and set me on the throne of David my father, and who hath made me an house, as he promised, Adonijah shall be put to death this day.

Isa 9:7 — Of the increase of *his* government and peace *there shall be* no end, upon the throne of David, and upon his kingdom, to order it, and to establish it with judgment and with justice from henceforth even for ever. The zeal of the LORD of hosts will perform this.

Jer 13:13 — Then shalt thou say unto them, Thus saith the LORD, Behold, I will fill all the inhabitants of this land, even the kings that sit upon David's throne, and the priests, and the prophets, and all the inhabitants of Jerusalem, with drunkenness.

Jer 17:25 — Then shall there enter into the gates of this city kings and princes sitting upon the throne of David, riding in chariots and on horses, they, and their princes, the men of Judah, and the inhabitants of Jerusalem: and this city shall remain for ever.

Lk 1:32 — He shall be great, and shall be called the Son of the Highest: and the Lord God shall give unto him the throne of his father David:

• Of Solomon.

2Ch 9:17–19

1Ki 2:19 — Bath-sheba therefore went unto king Solomon, to speak unto him for Adonijah. And the king rose up to meet her, and bowed himself unto her, and sat down on his throne, and caused a seat to be set for the king's mother; and she sat on his right hand.

• Of ivory.

1Ki 10:18–20

• Of Solomon, called the Throne of the Lord.

1Ch 29:23 — Then Solomon sat on the throne of the LORD as king instead of David his father, and prospered; and all Israel obeyed him.

• Of Herod.

Ac 12:21 — And upon a set day Herod, arrayed in royal apparel, sat upon his throne, and made an oration unto them.

• Of Israel.

1Ki 8:20 — And the LORD hath performed his word that he spake, and I am risen up in the room of David my father, and sit on the throne of Israel, as the LORD promised, and have built an house for the name of the LORD God of Israel.

1Ki 10:9 — Blessed be the LORD thy God, which delighted in thee, to set thee on the throne of Israel: because the LORD loved Israel for ever, therefore made he thee king, to do judgment and justice.

2Ch 6:10 — The LORD therefore hath performed his word that he hath spoken: for I am risen up in the room of David my father, and am set on the throne of Israel, as the LORD promised, and have built the house for the name of the LORD God of Israel.

• Abdicated by David.

1Ki 1:32–40

• Figurative.

• Anthropomorphic use of.

• Of God.

2Ch 18:18 — Again he said, Therefore hear the word of the LORD; I saw the LORD sitting upon his throne, and all the host of heaven standing on his right hand and *on* his left.

Ps 9:4 — For thou hast maintained my right and my cause; thou satest in the throne judging right.

Ps 9:7 — But the LORD shall endure for ever: he hath prepared his throne for judgment.

Ps 11:4 — The LORD *is* in his holy temple, the LORD's throne *is* in heaven: his eyes behold, his eyelids try, the children of men.

Ps 47:8 — God reigneth over the heathen: God sitteth upon the throne of his holiness.

Ps 89:14 — Justice and judgment *are* the habitation of thy throne: mercy and truth shall go before thy face.

Ps 97:2 — Clouds and darkness *are* round about him: righteousness and judgment *are* the habitation of his throne.

Ps 103:19 — The LORD hath prepared his throne in the heavens; and his kingdom ruleth over all.

Isa 6:1 — In the year that king Uzziah died I saw also the Lord sitting upon a throne, high and lifted up, and his train filled the temple.

Isa 66:1 — Thus saith the LORD, The heaven *is* my throne, and the earth *is* my footstool: where *is* the house that ye build unto me? and where *is* the place of my rest?

Mt 5:34 — But I say unto you, Swear not at all; neither by heaven; for it is God's throne:

Mt 23:22 — And he that shall swear by heaven, sweareth by the throne of God, and by him that sitteth thereon.

Heb 8:1 — Now of the things which we have spoken *this is* the sum: We have such an high priest, who is set on the right hand of the throne of the Majesty in the heavens;

Heb 12:2 — Looking unto Jesus the author and finisher of *our* faith; who for the joy that was set before him endured the cross, despising the shame, and is set down at the right hand of the throne of God.

Rev 14:3 — And they sung as it were a new song before the throne, and before the four beasts, and the elders: and no man could learn that song but the hundred *and* forty *and* four thousand, which were redeemed from the earth.

Rev 14:5 — And in their mouth was found no guile: for they are without fault before the throne of God.

• Of Christ.

Rev 4:2–10; 7:9–17

Mt 19:28 — And Jesus said unto them, Verily I say unto you, That ye which have followed me, in the regeneration when the Son of man shall sit in the throne of his glory, ye also shall sit upon twelve thrones, judging the twelve tribes of Israel.

Mt 25:31 — When the Son of man shall come in his glory, and all the holy angels with him, then shall he sit upon the throne of his glory:

Ac 2:30 — Therefore being a prophet, and knowing that God had sworn with an oath to him, that of the fruit of his loins, according to the flesh, he would raise up Christ to sit on his throne;

Rev 1:4 — John to the seven churches which are in Asia: Grace *be* unto you, and peace, from him which is, and which was, and which is to come; and from the seven Spirits which are before his throne;

Rev 3:21 — To him that overcometh will I grant to sit with me in my throne, even as I also overcame, and am set down with my Father in his throne.

Rev 19:4 — And the four and twenty elders and the four beasts fell down and worshipped God that sat on the throne, saying, Amen; Alleluia.

Rev 21:5 — And he that sat upon the throne said, Behold, I make all things new. And he said unto me, Write: for these words are true and faithful.

Rev 22:3 — And there shall be no more curse: but the throne of God and of the Lamb shall be in it; and his servants shall serve him:

THUMB

• Blood put on, in consecration.

Ex 29:20 — Then shalt thou kill the ram, and take of his blood, and put *it* upon the tip of the right ear of Aaron, and upon the tip of the right ear of his sons, and upon the thumb of their right hand, and upon the great toe of their right foot, and sprinkle the blood upon the altar round about.

Le 8:23 — And he slew *it;* and Moses took of the blood of it, and put *it* upon the tip of Aaron's right ear, and upon the thumb of his right hand, and upon the great toe of his right foot.

• Blood put on in purification.

Le 14:14 — And the priest shall take *some* of the blood of the trespass offering, and the priest shall put *it* upon the tip of the right ear of him that is to be cleansed, and upon the thumb of his right hand, and upon the great toe of his right foot:

Le 14:25 — And he shall kill the lamb of the trespass offering, and the priest shall take *some* of the blood of the trespass offering, and put *it* upon the tip of the right ear of him that is to be cleansed, and upon the thumb of his right hand, and upon the great toe of his right foot:

• Oil put on.

Le 14:17 — And of the rest of the oil that *is* in his hand shall the priest put upon the tip of the right ear of him that is to be cleansed, and upon the thumb of his right hand, and upon the great toe of his right foot, upon the blood of the trespass offering:

Le 14:28 — And the priest shall put of the oil that *is* in his hand upon the tip of the right ear of him that is to be cleansed, and upon the thumb of his right hand, and upon the great toe of his right foot, upon the place of the blood of the trespass offering:

• Of prisoners cut off.

Jgs 1:6–7

See: Hand

THUMMIM See: Urim and Thummim

THUNDER

• Sent as a plague upon the Egyptians.

Ex 9:23–34

• Sent as a plague upon the Philistines, in battle with the children of Israel.

1Sa 7:10 — And as Samuel was offering up the burnt offering, the Philistines drew near to battle against Israel: but the LORD thundered with a great thunder on that day upon the Philistines, and discomfited them; and they were smitten before Israel.

• Sent as a judgment.

Isa 29:6 — Thou shalt be visited of the LORD of hosts with thunder, and with earthquake, and great noise, with storm and tempest, and the flame of devouring fire.

• On Sinai.

Heb 12:18–19

Ex 19:16 — And it came to pass on the third day in the morning, that there were thunders and lightnings, and a thick cloud upon the mount, and the voice of the trumpet exceeding loud; so that all the people that *was* in the camp trembled.

Ps 77:18 — The voice of thy thunder *was* in the heaven: the lightnings lightened the world: the earth trembled and shook.

• A token of divine anger.

1Sa 12:17–18

• A manifestation of divine power.

Job 26:14 — Lo, these *are* parts of his ways: but how little a portion is heard of him? but the thunder of his power who can understand?

Ps 77:18 — The voice of thy thunder *was* in the heaven: the lightnings lightened the world: the earth trembled and shook.

• Sons of Zebedee called sons of.

Mk 3:17 — And James the *son* of Zebedee, and John the brother of James; and he surnamed them Boanerges, which is, The sons of thunder:

THYATIRA

• Home of Lydia, a convert of Paul.

Ac 16:14 — And a certain woman named Lydia, a seller of purple, of the city of Thyatira, which worshipped God, heard *us:* whose heart the Lord opened, that she attended unto the things which were spoken of Paul.

• John given a message for.

Rev 1:11 — Saying, I am Alpha and Omega, the first and the last: and, What thou seest, write in a book, and send *it* unto the seven churches which are in Asia; unto Ephesus, and unto Smyrna, and unto Pergamos, and unto Thyatira, and unto Sardis, and unto Philadelphia, and unto Laodicea.

Rev 2:18 — And unto the angel of the church in Thyatira write; These things saith the Son of God, who hath his eyes like unto a flame of fire, and his feet *are* like fine brass;

Rev 2:24 — But unto you I say, and unto the rest in Thyatira, as many as have not this doctrine, and which have not known the depths of Satan, as they speak; I will put upon you none other burden.

THYINE • An aromatic wood.

Rev 18:12 — The merchandise of gold, and silver, and precious stones, and of pearls, and fine linen, and purple, and silk, and scarlet, and all thyine wood, and all manner vessels of ivory, and all manner vessels of most precious wood, and of brass, and iron, and marble,

TIBERIAS

• A city on the Sea of Galilee.

Jn 6:23 — (Howbeit there came other boats from Tiberias nigh unto the place where they did eat bread, after that the Lord had given thanks:)

• Sea of, a name given to the Sea of Galilee.

Jn 6:1 — After these things Jesus went over the sea of Galilee, which is *the sea* of Tiberias.

Jn 21:1 — After these things Jesus shewed himself again to the disciples at the sea of Tiberias; and on this wise shewed he *himself.*

See: Galilee; called Sea of Tiberias

TIBERIUS CAESAR • Emperor of Rome.

Lk 3:1 — Now in the fifteenth year of the reign of Tiberius Caesar, Pontius Pilate being governor of Judaea, and Herod being tetrarch of Galilee, and his brother Philip tetrarch of Ituraea and of the region of Trachonitis, and Lysanias the tetrarch of Abilene,

TIBHATH • A city conquered by David.

1Ch 18:8 — Likewise from Tibhath, and from Chun, cities of Hadarezer, brought David very much brass, wherewith Solomon made the brasen sea, and the pillars, and the vessels of brass.

TIBNI

• Chosen by half of Israel to be king.

• Death of.

1Ki 16:21–22

TIDAL

• King of nations.

Ge 14:1 — And it came to pass in the days of Amraphel king of Shinar, Arioch king of Ellasar, Chedorlaomer king of Elam, and Tidal king of nations;

Ge 14:9 — With Chedorlaomer the king of Elam, and with Tidal king of nations, and Amraphel king of Shinar, and Arioch king of Ellasar; four kings with five.

TIGLATH-PILESER

• Called also Tilgath-Pilneser, king of Assyria.

• Invades Israel; carries part of the people captive to Assyria.

2Ki 15:29 — In the days of Pekah king of Israel came Tiglath-pileser king of Assyria, and took Ijon, and Abel-beth-maachah, and Janoah, and Kedesh, and Hazor, and Gilead, and Galilee, all the land of Naphtali, and carried them captive to Assyria.

1Ch 5:6 — Beerah his son, whom Tilgath-pilneser king of Assyria carried away *captive:* he *was* prince of the Reubenites.

1Ch 5:26 — And the God of Israel stirred up the spirit of Pul king of Assyria, and the spirit of Tilgath-pilneser king of Assyria, and he carried them away, even the Reubenites, and the Gadites, and the half tribe of Manasseh, and brought them unto Halah, and Habor, and Hara, and to the river Gozan, unto this day.

• Forms an alliance with Ahaz; captures Damascus.

2Ki 16:7–10; 2Ch 28:19–21

TIKVAH

• Called also Tikvath, father of Shallum.

2Ki 22:14 — So Hilkiah the priest, and Ahikam, and Achbor, and Shaphan, and Asahiah, went unto Huldah the prophetess, the wife of Shallum the son of Tikvah, the son of Harhas, keeper of the wardrobe; (now she dwelt in Jerusalem in the college;) and they communed with her.

2Ch 34:22 — And Hilkiah, and *they* that the king *had appointed,* went to Huldah the prophetess, the wife of Shallum the son of Tikvath, the son of Hasrah, keeper of the wardrobe; (now she dwelt in Jerusalem in the college:) and they spake to her to that *effect.*

• Father of Jahaziah.

Ezr 10:15 — Only Jonathan the son of Asahel and Jahaziah the son of Tikvah were employed about this *matter:* and Meshullam and Shabbethai the Levite helped them.

TILE

• Brick.

Eze 4:1 — Thou also, son of man, take thee a tile, and lay it before thee, and pourtray upon it the city, *even* Jerusalem:

Lk 5:19 — And when they could not find by what *way* they might bring him in because of the multitude, they went upon the housetop, and let him down through the tiling with *his* couch into the midst before Jesus.

TILGATH-PILNESER **See: Tiglath-Pileser**

TILON • Son of Shimon.

1Ch 4:20 — And the sons of Shimon *were,* Amnon, and Rinnah, Ben-hanan, and Tilon. And the sons of Ishi *were,* Zoheth, and Ben-zoheth.

TIMAEUS • Father of a blind man cured by Jesus.

Mk 10:46 — And they came to Jericho: and as he went out of Jericho with his disciples and a great number of people, blind Bartimaeus, the son of Timaeus, sat by the highway side begging.

TIMBREL

• Called also Tabret an instrument of music of the tambourine sort.

• Used by Miriam.

Ex 15:20 — And Miriam the prophetess, the sister of Aaron, took a timbrel in her hand; and all the women went out after her with timbrels and with dances.

• Used by Jephthah's daughter.

Jgs 11:34 — And Jephthah came to Mizpeh unto his house, and, behold, his daughter came out to meet him with timbrels and with dances: and she *was his* only child; beside her he had neither son nor daughter.

• Used in religious service.

2Sa 6:5 — And David and all the house of Israel played before the LORD on all manner of *instruments made of* fir wood, even on harps, and on psalteries, and on timbrels, and on cornets, and on cymbals.

1Ch 13:8 — And David and all Israel played before God with all *their* might, and with singing, and with harps, and with psalteries, and with timbrels, and with cymbals, and with trumpets.

Ps 68:25 — The singers went before, the players on instruments *followed* after; among *them were* the damsels playing with timbrels.

Ps 81:2 — Take a Psalm, and bring hither the timbrel, the pleasant harp with the psaltery.

Ps 149:3 — Let them praise his name in the dance: let them sing praises unto him with the timbrel and harp.

Ps 150:4 — Praise him with the timbrel and dance: praise him with stringed instruments and organs.

• Used in dances.

Job 21:12 — They take the timbrel and harp, and rejoice at the sound of the organ.

See: Music; instruments of

TIME

• Beginning of.

Ge 1:1 — In the beginning God created the heaven and the earth.

Ge 1:14 — And God said, Let there be lights in the firmament of the heaven to divide the day from the night; and let them be for signs, and for seasons, and for days, and years:

• Epochs of.

• Before the flood.

Jos 24:2 — And Joshua said unto all the people, Thus saith the LORD God of Israel, Your fathers dwelt on the other side of the flood in old time, *even* Terah, the father of Abraham, and the father of Nachor: and they served other gods.

• The Exodus

Ex 19:1 — In the third month, when the children of Israel were gone forth out of the land of Egypt, the same day came they *into* the wilderness of Sinai.

Ex 40:17 — And it came to pass in the first month in the second year, on the first *day* of the month, *that* the tabernacle was reared up.

1Ki 6:1 — And it came to pass in the four hundred and eightieth year after the children of Israel were come out of the land of Egypt, in the fourth year of Solomon's reign over Israel, in the month Zif, which *is* the second month, that he began to build the house of the LORD.

• Daniel's reckoning of time, and times, and half times.

Da 7:25 — And he shall speak *great* words against the most High, and shall wear out the saints of the most High, and think to change times and laws: and they shall be given into his hand until a time and times and the dividing of time.

Da 12:7 — And I heard the man clothed in linen, which *was* upon the waters of the river, when he held up his right hand and his left hand unto heaven, and sware by him that liveth for ever that *it shall be* for a time, times, and an half; and when he shall have accomplished to scatter the power of the holy people, all these *things* shall be finished.

• Indicated by a sundial.

2Ki 20:9–11

Isa 38:8 — Behold, I will bring again the shadow of the degrees, which is gone down in the sun dial of Ahaz, ten degrees backward. So the sun returned ten degrees, by which degrees it was gone down.

• Division of, into watches.

Ex 14:24 — And it came to pass, that in the morning watch the LORD looked unto the host of the Egyptians through the pillar of fire and of the cloud, and troubled the host of the Egyptians,

1Sa 11:11 — And it was *so* on the morrow, that Saul put the people in three companies; and they came into the midst of the host in the morning watch, and slew the Ammonites until the heat of the day: and it came to pass, that they which remained were scattered, so that two of them were not left together.

Mt 14:25 — And in the fourth watch of the night Jesus went unto them, walking on the sea.

Mk 6:48 — And he saw them toiling in rowing; for the wind was contrary unto them: and about the fourth watch of the night he cometh unto them, walking upon the sea, and would have passed by them.

• One day as a thousand years.

2Pe 3:8 — But, beloved, be not ignorant of this one thing, that one day *is* with the Lord as a thousand years, and a thousand years as one day.

• Fullness of.

Gal 4:4 — But when the fulness of the time was come, God sent forth his Son, made of a woman, made under the law,

Eph 1:10 — That in the dispensation of the fulness of times he might gather together in one all things in Christ, both which are in heaven, and which are on earth; *even* in him:

• End of.

Job 26:10 — He hath compassed the waters with bounds, until the day and night come to an end.

Rev 10:6 — And sware by him that liveth for ever and ever, who created heaven, and the things that therein are, and the earth, and the things that therein are, and the sea, and the things which are therein, that there should be time no longer:

TIMNA

• Concubine of Eliphaz.

Ge 36:12 — And Timna was concubine to Eliphaz Esau's son; and she bare to Eliphaz Amalek: these *were* the sons of Adah Esau's wife.

• Daughter of Seir.

Ge 36:22 — And the children of Lotan were Hori and Hemam; and Lotan's sister *was* Timna.

1Ch 1:39 — And the sons of Lotan; Hori, and Homam: and Timna *was* Lotan's sister.

• Son of Eliphaz.

1Ch 1:36 — The sons of Eliphaz; Teman, and Omar, Zephi, and Gatam, Kenaz, and Timna, and Amalek.

TIMNAH

• A duke of Edom.

Ge 36:40 — And these *are* the names of the dukes *that came* of Esau, according to their families, after their places, by their names; duke Timnah, duke Alvah, duke Jetheth,

1Ch 1:51 — Hadad died also. And the dukes of Edom were; duke Timnah, duke Aliah, duke Jetheth,

• A city in Judah.

Jos 15:10 — And the border compassed from Baalah westward unto mount Seir, and passed along unto the side of mount Jearim, which *is* Chesalon, on the north side, and went down to Beth-shemesh, and passed on to Timnah:

2Ch 28:18 — The Philistines also had invaded the cities of the low country, and of the south of Judah, and had taken Beth-shemesh, and Ajalon, and Gederoth, and Shocho with the villages thereof, and Timnah with the villages thereof, Gimzo also and the villages thereof: and they dwelt there.

• A city in the mountains of Judah.

Jos 15:57 — Cain, Gibeah, and Timnah; ten cities with their villages:

TIMNATH

• A city.

Ge 38:12–14

• Given by some authorities as identical with Timnah, a city in Judah.

• Home of Samson's wife.

Jgs 14:1–2

Jgs 14:5 — Then went Samson down, and his father and his mother, to Timnath, and came to the vineyards of Timnath: and, behold, a young lion roared against him.

Jgs 15:6 — Then the Philistines said, Who hath done this? And they answered, Samson, the son in law of the Timnite, because he had taken his wife, and given her to his companion. And the Philistines came up, and burnt her and her father with fire.

• Believed by some authorities to be identical with the Timnah.

TIMNATH-HERES

See: Timnath-Serah

TIMNATH-SERAH

• A city.

• Called also Timnath-Heres.

• Given to Joshua.

Jos 19:50 — According to the word of the LORD they gave him the city which he asked, *even* Timnath-serah in mount Ephraim: and he built the city, and dwelt therein.

• Joshua buried in.

Jos 24:30 — And they buried him in the border of his inheritance in Timnath-serah, which *is* in mount Ephraim, on the north side of the hill of Gaash.

Jgs 2:9 — And they buried him in the border of his inheritance in Timnath-heres, in the mount of Ephraim, on the north side of the hill Gaash.

TIMON • A member of the committee of seven appointed to supervise the daily ministration.

Ac 6:5 — And the saying pleased the whole multitude: and they chose Stephen, a man full of faith and of the Holy Ghost, and Philip, and Prochorus, and Nicanor, and Timon, and Parmenas, and Nicolas a proselyte of Antioch:

TIMOTHY

• Called also Timotheus, the companion of Paul.

• Parentage of.

Ac 16:1 — Then came he to Derbe and Lystra: and, behold, a certain disciple was there, named Timotheus, the son of a certain woman, which was a Jewess, and believed; but his father *was* a Greek:

• Reputation and Christian faith of.

Ac 16:2 — Which was well reported of by the brethren that were at Lystra and Iconium.

1Co 4:17 — For this cause have I sent unto you Timotheus, who is my beloved son, and faithful in the Lord, who shall bring you into remembrance of my ways which be in Christ, as I teach every where in every church.

1Co 16:10 — Now if Timotheus come, see that he may be with you without fear: for he worketh the work of the Lord, as I also *do*.

2Ti 1:5 — When I call to remembrance the unfeigned faith that is in thee, which dwelt first in thy grandmother Lois, and thy mother Eunice; and I am persuaded that in thee also.

2Ti 3:15 — And that from a child thou hast known the holy scriptures, which are able to make thee wise unto salvation through faith which is in Christ Jesus.

- **Circumcised; becomes Paul's companion.**

Ac 16:3 — Him would Paul have to go forth with him; and took and circumcised him because of the Jews which were in those quarters: for they knew all that his father was a Greek.

1Th 3:2 — And sent Timotheus, our brother, and minister of God, and our fellowlabourer in the gospel of Christ, to establish you, and to comfort you concerning your faith:

- **Left by Paul at Berea.**

Ac 17:14 — And then immediately the brethren sent away Paul to go as it were to the sea: but Silas and Timotheus abode there still.

- **Rejoins Paul at Corinth.**

Ac 17:15 — And they that conducted Paul brought him unto Athens: and receiving a commandment unto Silas and Timotheus for to come to him with all speed, they departed.

Ac 18:5 — And when Silas and Timotheus were come from Macedonia, Paul was pressed in the spirit, and testified to the Jews *that* Jesus *was* Christ.

- **Sent into Macedonia.**

Ac 19:22 — So he sent into Macedonia two of them that ministered unto him, Timotheus and Erastus; but he himself stayed in Asia for a season.

- **Rejoined by Paul; accompanies Paul to Asia.**

Ac 20:1–4

- **Sends salutation to the Romans.**

Ro 16:21 — Timotheus my workfellow, and Lucius, and Jason, and Sosipater, my kinsmen, salute you.

- **Sent to the Corinthians.**

1Co 16:10–11, 19–21

1Co 4:17 — For this cause have I sent unto you Timotheus, who is my beloved son, and faithful in the Lord, who shall bring you into remembrance of my ways which be in Christ, as I teach every where in every church.

- **Preaches to the Corinthians.**

2Co 1:19 — For the Son of God, Jesus Christ, who was preached among you by us, *even* by me and Silvanus and Timotheus, was not yea and nay, but in him was yea.

- **Sent to the Philippians.**

Php 2:19 — But I trust in the Lord Jesus to send Timotheus shortly unto you, that I also may be of good comfort, when I know your state.

Php 2:23 — Him therefore I hope to send presently, so soon as I shall see how it will go with me.

- **Sent to the Thessalonians.**

1Th 3:2 — And sent Timotheus, our brother, and minister of God, and our fellowlabourer in the gospel of Christ, to establish you, and to comfort you concerning your faith:

1Th 3:6 — But now when Timotheus came from you unto us, and brought us good tidings of your faith and charity, and that ye have good remembrance of us always, desiring greatly to see us, as we also *to see* you:

- **Left by Paul in Ephesus.**

1Ti 1:3 — As I besought thee to abide still at Ephesus, when I went into Macedonia, that thou mightest charge some that they teach no other doctrine,

- **Confined with Paul in Rome.**

Php 2:19–23; 4:21–23; Phm 1:23–25; Heb 13:23–25

Phm 1:1 — Paul, a prisoner of Jesus Christ, and Timothy our brother, unto Philemon our dearly beloved, and fellowlabourer,

- **Ordained bishop of the Ephesians.**

2Ti 4:19–22

- **Joins Paul in the Epistle to the Philippians.**

Php 1:1 — Paul and Timotheus, the servants of Jesus Christ, to all the saints in Christ Jesus which are at Philippi, with the bishops and deacons:

- **Joins Paul in the Epistle to the Colossians.**

Col 1:1–2

- **Joins Paul in the Epistle to the Thessalonians.**

1Th 1:1 — Paul, and Silvanus, and Timotheus, unto the church of the Thessalonians *which is* in God the Father and *in* the Lord Jesus Christ: Grace *be* unto you, and peace, from God our Father, and the Lord Jesus Christ.

2Th 1:1 — Paul, and Silvanus, and Timotheus, unto the church of the Thessalonians in God our Father and the Lord Jesus Christ:

- **Joins Paul in the Epistle to Philemon.**

Phm 1:1 — Paul, a prisoner of Jesus Christ, and Timothy our brother, unto Philemon our dearly beloved, and fellowlabourer,

- **Acts as Paul's amanuensis in writing the first letter to the Corinthians.**

1Co 16:19–21

- **Acts as Paul's amanuensis in writing the letter to the Hebrews.**

Heb 13:23–25

- **Zeal of.**

Php 2:19–22

1Ti 6:12 — Fight the good fight of faith, lay hold on eternal life, whereunto thou art also called, and hast professed a good profession before many witnesses.

- **Power of.**

1Ti 4:14 — Neglect not the gift that is in thee, which was given thee by prophecy, with the laying on of the hands of the presbytery.

2Ti 1:6 — Wherefore I put thee in remembrance that thou stir up the gift of God, which is in thee by the putting on of my hands.

- **Paul's love for.**

2Ti 1:2–4

1Co 4:17 — For this cause have I sent unto you Timotheus, who is my beloved son, and faithful in the Lord, who shall bring you into remembrance of my ways which be in Christ, as I teach every where in every church.

Php 2:22 — But ye know the proof of him, that, as a son with the father, he hath served with me in the gospel.

1Ti 1:2 — Unto Timothy, *my* own son in the faith: Grace, mercy, *and* peace, from God our Father and Jesus Christ our Lord.

1Ti 1:18 — This charge I commit unto thee, son Timothy, according to the prophecies which went before on thee, that thou by them mightest war a good warfare;

• Paul writes to.

1Ti 1:1–2; 2Ti 1:1–2

TIN

Nu 31:22 — Only the gold, and the silver, the brass, the iron, the tin, and the lead,

Eze 22:18 — Son of man, the house of Israel is to me become dross: all they *are* brass, and tin, and iron, and lead, in the midst of the furnace; they are *even* the dross of silver.

Eze 22:20 — *As* they gather silver, and brass, and iron, and lead, and tin, into the midst of the furnace, to blow the fire upon it, to melt *it;* so will I gather *you* in mine anger and in my fury, and I will leave *you there,* and melt you.

Eze 27:12 — Tarshish *was* thy merchant by reason of the multitude of all *kind of* riches; with silver, iron, tin, and lead, they traded in thy fairs.

TIPHSAH

• A city on the Euphrates.

1Ki 4:24 — For he had dominion over all *the region* on this side the river, from Tiphsah even to Azzah, over all the kings on this side the river: and he had peace on all sides round about him.

• A city of unknown location.

2Ki 15:16 — Then Menahem smote Tiphsah, and all that *were* therein, and the coasts thereof from Tirzah: because they opened not *to him,* therefore he smote *it; and* all the women therein that were with child he ripped up.

TIRAS • Son of Japheth.

Ge 10:2 — The sons of Japheth; Gomer, and Magog, and Madai, and Javan, and Tubal, and Meshech, and Tiras.

1Ch 1:5 — The sons of Japheth; Gomer, and Magog, and Madai, and Javan, and Tubal, and Meshech, and Tiras.

TIRE • A headdress.

Isa 3:18 — In that day the Lord will take away the bravery of *their* tinkling ornaments *about their feet,* and *their* cauls, and *their* round tires like the moon,

Eze 24:17 — Forbear to cry, make no mourning for the dead, bind the tire of thine head upon thee, and put on thy shoes upon thy feet, and cover not *thy* lips, and eat not the bread of men.

TIRHAKAH • A king of Ethiopia.

2Ki 19:9 — And when he heard say of Tirhakah king of Ethiopia, Behold, he is come out to fight against thee: he sent messengers again unto Hezekiah, saying,

Isa 37:9 — And he heard say concerning Tirhakah king of Ethiopia, He is come forth to make war with thee. And when he heard *it,* he sent messengers to Hezekiah, saying,

TIRHANAH • Son of Caleb.

1Ch 2:48 — Maachah, Caleb's concubine, bare Sheber, and Tirhanah.

TIRIA • Son of Jehaleleel.

1Ch 4:16 — And the sons of Jehaleleel; Ziph, and Ziphah, Tiria, and Asareel.

TIRSHATHA • A title of Persian governors.

Ezr 2:63 — And the Tirshatha said unto them, that they should not eat of the most holy things, till there stood up a priest with Urim and with Thummim.

Ne 7:65 — And the Tirshatha said unto them, that they should not eat of the most holy things, till there stood *up* a priest with Urim and Thummim.

Ne 7:70 — And some of the chief of the fathers gave unto the work. The Tirshatha gave to the treasure a thousand drams of gold, fifty basons, five hundred and thirty priests' garments.

Ne 8:9 — And Nehemiah, which *is* the Tirshatha, and Ezra the priest the scribe, and the Levites that taught the people, said unto all the people, This day *is* holy unto the LORD your God; mourn not, nor weep. For all the people wept, when they heard the words of the law.

TIRZAH

• A daughter of Zelophehad.

Nu 26:33 — And Zelophehad the son of Hepher had no sons, but daughters: and the names of the daughters of Zelophehad *were* Mahlah, and Noah, Hoglah, Milcah, and Tirzah.

Nu 36:11 — For Mahlah, Tirzah, and Hoglah, and Milcah, and Noah, the daughters of Zelophehad, were married unto their father's brothers' sons:

Jos 17:3 — But Zelophehad, the son of Hepher, the son of Gilead, the son of Machir, the son of Manasseh, had no sons, but daughters: and these *are* the names of his daughters, Mahlah, and Noah, Hoglah, Milcah, and Tirzah.

• Special legislation in regard to the inheritance of.

Nu 27:1–11; 36:1–13; Jos 17:3–4

• A city of Canaan.

• Captured by Joshua.

Jos 12:24 — The king of Tirzah, one: all the kings thirty and one.

• Becomes the residence of the kings of Israel.

1Ki 16:8–9

1Ki 14:17 — And Jeroboam's wife arose, and departed, and came to Tirzah: *and* when she came to the threshold of the door, the child died;

1Ki 15:21 — And it came to pass, when Baasha heard *thereof,* that he left off building of Ramah, and dwelt in Tirzah.

1Ki 15:33 — In the third year of Asa king of Judah began Baasha the son of Ahijah to reign over all Israel in Tirzah, twenty and four years.

1Ki 16:6 — So Baasha slept with his fathers, and was buried in Tirzah: and Elah his son reigned in his stead.

1Ki 16:15 — In the twenty and seventh year of Asa king of Judah did Zimri reign seven days in Tirzah. And the people *were* encamped against Gibbethon, which *belonged* to the Philistines.

1Ki 16:17 — And Omri went up from Gibbethon, and all Israel with him, and they besieged Tirzah.

1Ki 16:23 — In the thirty and first year of Asa king of Judah began Omri to reign over Israel, twelve years: six years reigned he in Tirzah.

• Royal residence moved from.

1Ki 16:23–24

• Base of military operations of Menahem.

2Ki 15:14 — For Menahem the son of Gadi went up from Tirzah, and came to Samaria, and smote Shallum the son of Jabesh in Samaria, and slew him, and reigned in his stead.

2Ki 15:16 — Then Menahem smote Tiphsah, and all that *were* therein, and the coasts thereof from Tirzah: because they opened not *to him,* therefore he smote *it; and* all the women therein that were with child he ripped up.

• Beauty of.

SS 6:4 — Thou *art* beautiful, O my love, as Tirzah, comely as Jerusalem, terrible as *an army* with banners.

TITHES

• Paid by Abraham to Melchizedek.

Heb 7:2–6

Ge 14:20 — And blessed be the most high God, which hath delivered thine enemies into thy hand. And he gave him tithes of all.

• Jacob vows a tenth of all his property to God.

Ge 28:22 — And this stone, which I have set *for* a pillar, shall be God's house: and of all that thou shalt give me I will surely give the tenth unto thee.

• Mosaic laws instituting.

Le 27:30–33; Nu 18:21–24; Dt 12:6–7; 14:22–29; 26:12–15

Dt 12:17 — Thou mayest not eat within thy gates the tithe of thy corn, or of thy wine, or of thy oil, or the firstlings of thy herds or of thy flock, nor any of thy vows which thou vowest, nor thy freewill offerings, or heave offering of thine hand:

Dt 12:19 — Take heed to thyself that thou forsake not the Levite as long as thou livest upon the earth.

• Customs relating to.

Ne 10:37–38; Heb 7:5–9

Am 4:4 — Come to Bethel, and transgress; at Gilgal multiply transgression; and bring your sacrifices every morning, *and* your tithes after three years:

• Tithe of tithes for priests.

Nu 18:26 — Thus speak unto the Levites, and say unto them, When ye take of the children of Israel the tithes which I have given you from them for your inheritance, then ye shall offer up an heave offering of it for the LORD, *even* a tenth *part* of the tithe.

Ne 10:38 — And the priest the son of Aaron shall be with the Levites, when the Levites take tithes: and the Levites shall bring up the tithe of the tithes unto the house of our God, to the chambers, into the treasure house.

• Stored in the temple.

2Ch 31:11–12; Ne 10:38–39

Ne 12:44 — And at that time were some appointed over the chambers for the treasures, for the offerings, for the firstfruits, and for the tithes, to gather into them out of the fields of the cities the portions of the law for the priests and Levites: for Judah rejoiced for the priests and for the Levites that waited.

Ne 13:5 — And he had prepared for him a great chamber, where aforetime they laid the meat offerings, the frankincense, and the vessels, and the tithes of the corn, the new wine, and the oil, which was commanded *to be given* to the Levites, and the singers, and the porters; and the offerings of the priests.

Ne 13:12 — Then brought all Judah the tithe of the corn and the new wine and the oil unto the treasuries.

Mal 3:10 — Bring ye all the tithes into the storehouse, that there may be meat in mine house, and prove me now herewith, saith the LORD of hosts, if I will not open you the windows of heaven, and pour you out a blessing, that *there shall* not *be room* enough *to receive it.*

• Payment of, resumed in Hezekiah's reign.

2Ch 31:5–10

• Under Nehemiah.

Ne 13:12 — Then brought all Judah the tithe of the corn and the new wine and the oil unto the treasuries.

• Withheld.

Ne 13:10 — And I perceived that the portions of the Levites had not been given *them:* for the Levites and the singers, that did the work, were fled every one to his field.

Mal 3:8 — Will a man rob God? Yet ye have robbed me. But ye say, Wherein have we robbed thee? In tithes and offerings.

• Customary in later times.

Mt 23:23 — Woe unto you, scribes and Pharisees, hypocrites! for ye pay tithe of mint and anise and cummin, and have omitted the weightier *matters* of the law, judgment, mercy, and faith: these ought ye to have done, and not to leave the other undone.

Lk 11:42 — But woe unto you, Pharisees! for ye tithe mint and rue and all manner of herbs, and pass over judgment and the love of God: these ought ye to have done, and not to leave the other undone.

Lk 18:12 — I fast twice in the week, I give tithes of all that I possess.

• **Observed by idolaters.**

Am 4:4–5

↞**See: Alms**

↞**See: Beneficence**

↞**See: Giving**

↞**See: Liberality**

↞**See: Tax**

TITLE

• **To real estate.**

↞**See: Land**

TITUS

• **A Greek companion of Paul.**

• **Paul's love for.**

2Co 7:6–7, 13–14

2Co 2:13 — I had no rest in my spirit, because I found not Titus my brother: but taking my leave of them, I went from thence into Macedonia.

2Co 8:23 — Whether *any do enquire* of Titus, *he is* my partner and fellowhelper concerning you: or our brethren *be enquired of, they are* the messengers of the churches, *and* the glory of Christ.

Tit 1:4 — To Titus, *mine* own son after the common faith: Grace, mercy, *and* peace, from God the Father and the Lord Jesus Christ our Saviour.

• **With Paul in Macedonia.**

2Co 7:5–6; 13:11–14

• **Affection of, for the Corinthians.**

2Co 7:15 — And his inward affection is more abundant toward you, whilst he remembereth the obedience of you all, how with fear and trembling ye received him.

• **Sent to Corinth.**

2Co 8:16–22; 12:17–18

2Co 8:6 — Insomuch that we desired Titus, that as he had begun, so he would also finish in you the same grace also.

• **Character of.**

2Co 12:18 — I desired Titus, and with *him* I sent a brother. Did Titus make a gain of you? walked we not in the same spirit? *walked we* not in the same steps?

• **Paul's amanuensis in writing to the Corinthians.**

2Co 13:11–14

• **Accompanies Paul to Jerusalem.**

Gal 2:1–3

• **Compare.**

Ac 15:1–29

• **Left by Paul in Crete.**

Tit 1:5 — For this cause left I thee in Crete, that thou shouldest set in order the things that are wanting, and ordain elders in every city, as I had appointed thee:

• **Left by Paul to rejoin him in Nicopolis.**

Tit 3:12 — When I shall send Artemas unto thee, or Tychicus, be diligent to come unto me to Nicopolis: for I have determined there to winter.

• **Ordained bishop of the Cretians.**

Tit 3:12–15

• **Paul writes to.**

Tit 1:1–4

• **With Paul in Rome.**

2Ti 4:19–22

2Ti 4:10 — For Demas hath forsaken me, having loved this present world, and is departed unto Thessalonica; Crescens to Galatia, Titus unto Dalmatia.

• **Goes to Dalmatia.**

2Ti 4:10 — For Demas hath forsaken me, having loved this present world, and is departed unto Thessalonica; Crescens to Galatia, Titus unto Dalmatia.

TOAH

• **A Levite**

↞**See: Nahath; called also Toah and Tohu.**

TOB

• **A district in Syria.**

Jgs 11:3 — Then Jephthah fled from his brethren, and dwelt in the land of Tob: and there were gathered vain men to Jephthah, and went out with him.

Jgs 11:5 — And it was so, that when the children of Ammon made war against Israel, the elders of Gilead went to fetch Jephthah out of the land of Tob:

• **Called Ish-Tob.**

2Sa 10:6 — And when the children of Ammon saw that they stank before David, the children of Ammon sent and hired the Syrians of Beth-rehob, and the Syrians of Zoba, twenty thousand footmen, and of king Maacah a thousand men, and of Ish-tob twelve thousand men.

2Sa 10:8 — And the children of Ammon came out, and put the battle in array at the entering in of the gate: and the Syrians of Zoba, and of Rehob, and Ish-tob, and Maacah, *were* by themselves in the field.

TOB-ADONIJAH

• **A Levite.**

• **Sent by Jehoshaphat to instruct the people in the law.**

2Ch 17:8 — And with them *he sent* Levites, *even* Shemaiah, and Nethaniah, and Zebadiah, and Asahel, and Shemiramoth, and Jehonathan, and Adonijah, and Tobijah, and Tob-adonijah, Levites; and with them Elishama and Jehoram, priests.

TOBIAH

• **Ancestor of a family of Babylonian captives.**

Ezr 2:60 — The children of Delaiah, the children of Tobiah, the children of Nekoda, six hundred fifty and two.

Ne 7:62 — The children of Delaiah, the children of Tobiah, the children of Nekoda, six hundred forty and two.

• An enemy of the Jews in the time of Nehemiah.

• Opposes the rebuilding of the wall of Jerusalem.

Ne 4:7–8

Ne 2:10 — When Sanballat the Horonite, and Tobiah the servant, the Ammonite, heard *of it,* it grieved them exceedingly that there was come a man to seek the welfare of the children of Israel.

Ne 2:19 — But when Sanballat the Horonite, and Tobiah the servant, the Ammonite, and Geshem the Arabian, heard *it,* they laughed us to scorn, and despised us, and said, What *is* this thing that ye do? will ye rebel against the king?

Ne 4:3 — Now Tobiah the Ammonite *was* by him, and he said, Even that which they build, if a fox go up, he shall even break down their stone wall.

• Conspires to injure and intimidate Nehemiah.

Ne 6:1–14

Ne 6:19 — Also they reported his good deeds before me, and uttered my words to him. *And* Tobiah sent letters to put me in fear.

• Subverts nobles of Judah.

Ne 6:17–18

• Allies himself with Eliashib, the priest.

Ne 13:4–9

TOBIJAH

• A Levite sent by Jehoshaphat to instruct the people in the law.

2Ch 17:8 — And with them *he sent* Levites, *even* Shemaiah, and Nethaniah, and Zebadiah, and Asahel, and Shemiramoth, and Jehonathan, and Adonijah, and Tobijah, and Tob-adonijah, Levites; and with them Elishama and Jehoram, priests.

• A captive in Babylon.

Zec 6:10 — Take of *them of* the captivity, *even* of Heldai, of Tobijah, and of Jedaiah, which are come from Babylon, and come thou the same day, and go into the house of Josiah the son of Zephaniah;

Zec 6:14 — And the crowns shall be to Helem, and to Tobijah, and to Jedaiah, and to Hen the son of Zephaniah, for a memorial in the temple of the LORD.

TOCHEN • A city in Simeon.

1Ch 4:32 — And their villages *were,* Etam, and Ain, Rimmon, and Tochen, and Ashan, five cities:

TOE

• Anointed in consecration.

Le 8:23–24

Ex 29:20 — Then shalt thou kill the ram, and take of his blood, and put *it* upon the tip of the right ear of Aaron, and upon the tip of the right ear of his sons, and upon the thumb of their right hand, and upon the great toe of their right foot, and sprinkle the blood upon the altar round about.

• Anointed in purification.

Le 14:14 — And the priest shall take *some* of the blood of the trespass offering, and the priest shall put *it* upon the tip of the right ear of him that is to be cleansed, and upon the thumb of his right hand, and upon the great toe of his right foot:

Le 14:17 — And of the rest of the oil that *is* in his hand shall the priest put upon the tip of the right ear of him that is to be cleansed, and upon the thumb of his right hand, and upon the great toe of his right foot, upon the blood of the trespass offering:

Le 14:25 — And he shall kill the lamb of the trespass offering, and the priest shall take *some* of the blood of the trespass offering, and put *it* upon the tip of the right ear of him that is to be cleansed, and upon the thumb of his right hand, and upon the great toe of his right foot:

Le 14:28 — And the priest shall put of the oil that *is* in his hand upon the tip of the right ear of him that is to be cleansed, and upon the thumb of his right hand, and upon the great toe of his right foot, upon the place of the blood of the trespass offering:

• Of prisoners of war cut off.

Jgs 1:6–7

• Six, on each foot.

2Sa 21:20 — And there was yet a battle in Gath, where was a man of *great* stature, that had on every hand six fingers, and on every foot six toes, four and twenty in number; and he also was born to the giant.

1Ch 20:6 — And yet again there was war at Gath, where was a man of *great* stature, whose fingers and toes *were* four and twenty, six *on each hand,* and six *on each foot:* and he also was the son of the giant.

TOGARMAH

• Son of Gomer.

Ge 10:3 — And the sons of Gomer; Ashkenaz, and Riphath, and Togarmah.

1Ch 1:6 — And the sons of Gomer; Ashchenaz, and Riphath, and Togarmah.

• Descendants of.

Eze 27:14 — They of the house of Togarmah traded in thy fairs with horses and horsemen and mules.

Eze 38:6 — Gomer, and all his bands; the house of Togarmah of the north quarters, and all his bands: *and* many people with thee.

TOHU

• A Levite

→See: Nahath; called also Toah and Tohu.

TOI

• Called also Tou.

• King of Hamath.

2Sa 8:9–10; 1Ch 18:9–10

TOKEN

• A sign.

Ex 3:12 — And he said, Certainly I will be with thee; and this *shall be* a token unto thee, that I have sent thee: When thou hast brought forth the people out of Egypt, ye shall serve God upon this mountain.

• Sun and moon for time and seasons.

Ge 1:14 — And God said, Let there be lights in the firmament of the heaven to divide the day from the night; and let them be for signs, and for seasons, and for days, and years:

• The mark of Cain.

Ge 4:15 — And the LORD said unto him, Therefore whosoever slayeth Cain, vengeance shall be taken on him sevenfold. And the LORD set a mark upon Cain, lest any finding him should kill him.

• Rainbow, that the world might no more be destroyed by a flood.

Ge 9:12–17

• Circumcision, of the covenant of Abraham.

Ge 17:11 — And ye shall circumcise the flesh of your foreskin; and it shall be a token of the covenant betwixt me and you.

• Presents.

Ge 21:27 — And Abraham took sheep and oxen, and gave them unto Abimelech; and both of them made a covenant.

Ge 21:30 — And he said, For *these* seven ewe lambs shalt thou take of my hand, that they may be a witness unto me, that I have digged this well.

• Miracles of Moses, of the divine authority of his missions.

Ex 4:1–9

• Blood of the pascal lamb.

Ex 12:13 — And the blood shall be to you for a token upon the houses where ye *are:* and when I see the blood, I will pass over you, and the plague shall not be upon you to destroy *you,* when I smite the land of Egypt.

• The passover.

Ex 13:9 — And it shall be for a sign unto thee upon thine hand, and for a memorial between thine eyes, that the LORD'S law may be in thy mouth: for with a strong hand hath the LORD brought thee out of Egypt.

• Consecration of the firstborn.

Ex 13:14–16

• The Sabbath.

Ex 31:13 — Speak thou also unto the children of Israel, saying, Verily my sabbaths ye shall keep: for it is a sign between me and you throughout your generations; that ye may know that I *am* the LORD that doth sanctify you.

Ex 31:17 — It *is* a sign between me and the children of Israel for ever: for *in* six days the LORD made heaven and earth, and on the seventh day he rested, and was refreshed.

• A fringe.

Nu 15:38–40

• Scarlet thread.

Jos 2:18 — Behold, *when* we come into the land, thou shalt bind this line of scarlet thread in the window which thou didst let us down by: and thou shalt bring thy father, and thy mother, and thy brethren, and all thy father's household, home unto thee.

Jos 2:21 — And she said, According unto your words, so *be* it. And she sent them away, and they departed: and she bound the scarlet line in the window.

• Cover of the altar.

Nu 16:38–40

• Aaron's rod.

Nu 17:10 — And the LORD said unto Moses, Bring Aaron's rod again before the testimony, to be kept for a token against the rebels; and thou shalt quite take away their murmurings from me, that they die not.

• Memorial stones.

Jos 4:2–9

• Dew on Gideon's fleece.

Jgs 6:36–40

• Prayer for tokens of mercy.

Ps 86:17 — Shew me a token for good; that they which hate me may see *it,* and be ashamed: because thou, LORD, hast holpen me, and comforted me.

TOLA

• Son of Issachar.

1Ch 7:1–2

Ge 46:13 — And the sons of Issachar; Tola, and Phuvah, and Job, and Shimron.

Nu 26:23 — *Of* the sons of Issachar after their families: *of* Tola, the family of the Tolaites: of Pua, the family of the Punites:

• A judge of Israel.

Jgs 10:1–2

TOLAD ✦See: Eltolad

TOLERATION

• Religious.

Mic 4:4–5; Mk 9:38–40; Lk 9:49–50; Ro 14:1–23; 1Co 10:28–32

Ac 17:11 — These were more noble than those in Thessalonica, in that they received the word with all readiness of mind, and searched the scriptures daily, whether those things were so.

Ac 28:31 — Preaching the kingdom of God, and teaching those things which concern the Lord Jesus Christ, with all confidence, no man forbidding him.

✦See: **Intolerance, Religious**

TOLL

✦See: **Tax**

✦See: **Tribute**

TOMB ✦See: Burial

TOMBSTONE

• At Rachel's grave.

Ge 35:20 — And Jacob set a pillar upon her grave: that *is* the pillar of Rachel's grave unto this day.

⇜See: Pillar

TONGS

Ex 25:38 — And the tongs thereof, and the snuffdishes thereof, *shall be of* pure gold.

Nu 4:9 — And they shall take a cloth of blue, and cover the candlestick of the light, and his lamps, and his tongs, and his snuffdishes, and all the oil vessels thereof, wherewith they minister unto it:

1Ki 7:49 — And the candlesticks of pure gold, five on the right *side,* and five on the left, before the oracle, with the flowers, and the lamps, and the tongs *of* gold,

TONGUE

• Language.

Ge 10:5 — By these were the isles of the Gentiles divided in their lands; every one after his tongue, after their families, in their nations.

Ge 10:20 — These *are* the sons of Ham, after their families, after their tongues, in their countries, *and* in their nations.

Isa 66:18 — For I *know* their works and their thoughts: it shall come, that I will gather all nations and tongues; and they shall come, and see my glory.

Rev 7:9 — After this I beheld, and, lo, a great multitude, which no man could number, of all nations, and kindreds, and people, and tongues, stood before the throne, and before the Lamb, clothed with white robes, and palms in their hands;

• Confusion of.

Ge 11:1–9

• Gift of.

Ac 2:1–18; 1Co 14:1–40

Ac 2:33 — Therefore being by the right hand of God exalted, and having received of the Father the promise of the Holy Ghost, he hath shed forth this, which ye now see and hear.

Ac 10:46 — For they heard them speak with tongues, and magnify God. Then answered Peter,

Ac 19:6 — And when Paul had laid *his* hands upon them, the Holy Ghost came on them; and they spake with tongues, and prophesied.

1Co 12:10 — To another the working of miracles; to another prophecy; to another discerning of spirits; to another *divers* kinds of tongues; to another the interpretation of tongues:

1Co 12:28 — And God hath set some in the church, first apostles, secondarily prophets, thirdly teachers, after that miracles, then gifts of healings, helps, governments, diversities of tongues.

1Co 12:30 — Have all the gifts of healing? do all speak with tongues? do all interpret?

• Loquacious.

Pr 10:8 — The wise in heart will receive commandments: but a prating fool shall fall.

Pr 10:19 — In the multitude of words there wanteth not sin: but he that refraineth his lips *is* wise.

• Restrained by wisdom.

Pr 17:27 — He that hath knowledge spareth his words: *and* a man of understanding is of an excellent spirit.

Pr 21:23 — Whoso keepeth his mouth and his tongue keepeth his soul from troubles.

Ecc 3:7 — A time to rend, and a time to sew; a time to keep silence, and a time to speak;

• Hasty.

Pr 29:20 — Seest thou a man *that is* hasty in his words? *there is* more hope of a fool than of him.

• An evil.

⇜See: Slander

⇜See: Speaking; evil

TONGUES

• The miraculous gift of the early Christians.

1Co 14:2–19, 21–28

1Co 12:10 — To another the working of miracles; to another prophecy; to another discerning of spirits; to another *divers* kinds of tongues; to another the interpretation of tongues:

1Co 12:28 — And God hath set some in the church, first apostles, secondarily prophets, thirdly teachers, after that miracles, then gifts of healings, helps, governments, diversities of tongues.

1Co 12:30 — Have all the gifts of healing? do all speak with tongues? do all interpret?

1Co 13:8 — Charity never faileth: but whether *there be* prophecies, they shall fail; whether *there be* tongues, they shall cease; whether *there be* knowledge, it shall vanish away.

1Co 14:39 — Wherefore, brethren, covet to prophesy, and forbid not to speak with tongues.

TOOLS ⇜See: Agriculture; implements of

TOPAZ

• A precious stone.

Eze 28:13 — Thou hast been in Eden the garden of God; every precious stone *was* thy covering, the sardius, topaz, and the diamond, the beryl, the onyx, and the jasper, the sapphire, the emerald, and the carbuncle, and gold: the workmanship of thy tabrets and of thy pipes was prepared in thee in the day that thou wast created.

Rev 21:20 — The fifth, sardonyx; the sixth, sardius; the seventh, chrysolite; the eighth, beryl; the ninth, a topaz; the tenth, a chrysoprasus; the eleventh, a jacinth; the twelfth, an amethyst.

• In the breastplate.

Ex 28:17 — And thou shalt set in it settings of stones, *even* four rows of stones: *the first* row *shall be* a sardius, a topaz, and a carbuncle: *this shall be* the first row.

Ex 39:10 — And they set in it four rows of stones: *the first* row *was* a sardius, a topaz, and a carbuncle: this *was* the first row.

• Ethiopian, celebrated.

Job 28:19 — The topaz of Ethiopia shall not equal it, neither shall it be valued with pure gold.

TOPHEL • A place in the wilderness of Sinai.

Dt 1:1 — These *be* the words which Moses spake unto all Israel on this side Jordan in the wilderness, in the plain over against the Red *sea,* between Paran, and Tophel, and Laban, and Hazeroth, and Dizahab.

TOPHET

• Called also Topheth.

• A place in the valley of the sons of Hinnom.

2Ki 23:10 — And he defiled Topheth, which *is* in the valley of the children of Hinnom, that no man might make his son or his daughter to pass through the fire to Molech.

• Jewish children passed through the fire to Molech in.

Jer 7:31–32; 19:11–14

2Ki 23:10 — And he defiled Topheth, which *is* in the valley of the children of Hinnom, that no man might make his son or his daughter to pass through the fire to Molech.

2Ch 28:3 — Moreover he burnt incense in the valley of the son of Hinnom, and burnt his children in the fire, after the abominations of the heathen whom the LORD had cast out before the children of Israel.

2Ch 33:6 — And he caused his children to pass through the fire in the valley of the son of Hinnom: also he observed times, and used enchantments, and used witchcraft, and dealt with a familiar spirit, and with wizards: he wrought much evil in the sight of the LORD, to provoke him to anger.

Jer 19:6 — Therefore, behold, the days come, saith the LORD, that this place shall no more be called Tophet, nor The valley of the son of Hinnom, but The valley of slaughter.

Jer 32:35 — And they built the high places of Baal, which *are* in the valley of the son of Hinnom, to cause their sons and their daughters to pass through *the fire* unto Molech; which I commanded them not, neither came it into my mind, that they should do this abomination, to cause Judah to sin.

• Destroyed by Josiah.

2Ki 23:10 — And he defiled Topheth, which *is* in the valley of the children of Hinnom, that no man might make his son or his daughter to pass through the fire to Molech.

• Horror of.

Isa 30:33 — For Tophet *is* ordained of old; yea, for the king it is prepared; he hath made *it* deep *and* large: the pile thereof *is* fire and much wood; the breath of the LORD, like a stream of brimstone, doth kindle it.

TOPOGRAPHY

• Of Canaan.

Jos 13:15–33; 15:1–63

Jos 18:9 — And the men went and passed through the land, and described it by cities into seven parts in a book, and came *again* to Joshua to the host at Shiloh.

TORMENTS

• Of the wicked.

Lk 16:23–28; Rev 14:10–11

See: Wicked; punishment of

TORTOISE

Le 11:29 — These also *shall be* unclean unto you among the creeping things that creep upon the earth; the weasel, and the mouse, and the tortoise after his kind,

TOTAL ABSTINENCE See: Abstinence, Total

TOU See: Toi

TOUCH

1Co 7:1 — Now concerning the things whereof ye wrote unto me: *It is* good for a man not to touch a woman.

TOW

Jgs 16:9 — Now *there were* men lying in wait, abiding with her in the chamber. And she said unto him, The Philistines *be* upon thee, Samson. And he brake the withs, as a thread of tow is broken when it toucheth the fire. So his strength was not known.

Isa 1:31 — And the strong shall be as tow, and the maker of it as a spark, and they shall both burn together, and none shall quench *them.*

See: Flax

TOWEL

Jn 13:4–5

TOWER

• Of Babel.

Ge 11:1–9

• Of Edar.

Ge 35:21 — And Israel journeyed, and spread his tent beyond the tower of Edar.

• Of Penuel.

Jgs 8:8–9

Jgs 8:17 — And he beat down the tower of Penuel, and slew the men of the city.

• Of Shechem.

Jgs 9:46 — And when all the men of the tower of Shechem heard *that,* they entered into an hold of the house of the god Berith.

Jgs 9:49 — And all the people likewise cut down every man his bough, and followed Abimelech, and put *them* to the hold, and set the hold on fire upon them; so that all the men of the tower of Shechem died also, about a thousand men and women.

• **Of Meah.**

Ne 3:1 — Then Eliashib the high priest rose up with his brethren the priests, and they builded the sheep gate; they sanctified it, and set up the doors of it; even unto the tower of Meah they sanctified it, unto the tower of Hananeel.

Ne 12:39 — And from above the gate of Ephraim, and above the old gate, and above the fish gate, and the tower of Hananeel, and the tower of Meah, even unto the sheep gate: and they stood still in the prison gate.

• **Of Hananeel.**

Ne 3:1 — Then Eliashib the high priest rose up with his brethren the priests, and they builded the sheep gate; they sanctified it, and set up the doors of it; even unto the tower of Meah they sanctified it, unto the tower of Hananeel.

Ne 12:39 — And from above the gate of Ephraim, and above the old gate, and above the fish gate, and the tower of Hananeel, and the tower of Meah, even unto the sheep gate: and they stood still in the prison gate.

Jer 31:38 — Behold, the days come, saith the LORD, that the city shall be built to the LORD from the tower of Hananeel unto the gate of the corner.

Zec 14:10 — All the land shall be turned as a plain from Geba to Rimmon south of Jerusalem: and it shall be lifted up, and inhabited in her place, from Benjamin's gate unto the place of the first gate, unto the corner gate, and *from* the tower of Hananeel unto the king's winepresses.

• **Of David.**

SS 4:4 — Thy neck *is* like the tower of David builded for an armoury, whereon there hang a thousand bucklers, all shields of mighty men.

• **Of Syene.**

Eze 29:10 — Behold, therefore I *am* against thee, and against thy rivers, and I will make the land of Egypt utterly waste *and* desolate, from the tower of Syene even unto the border of Ethiopia.

• **Of Siloam.**

Lk 13:4 — Or those eighteen, upon whom the tower in Siloam fell, and slew them, think ye that they were sinners above all men that dwelt in Jerusalem?

• **In the walls of Jerusalem.**

Ne 12:38–39

2Ch 26:9 — Moreover Uzziah built towers in Jerusalem at the corner gate, and at the valley gate, and at the turning *of the wall,* and fortified them.

2Ch 32:5 — Also he strengthened himself, and built up all the wall that was broken, and raised *it* up to the towers, and another wall without, and repaired Millo *in* the city of David, and made darts and shields in abundance.

• **Of other cities.**

2Ch 14:7 — Therefore he said unto Judah, Let us build these cities, and make about *them* walls, and towers, gates, and bars, *while* the land *is* yet before us; because we have sought the LORD our God, we have sought *him,* and he hath given us rest on every side. So they built and prospered.

• **In the desert.**

2Ch 26:10 — Also he built towers in the desert, and digged many wells: for he had much cattle, both in the low country, and in the plains: husbandmen *also,* and vine dressers in the mountains, and in Carmel: for he loved husbandry.

• **For watchmen or sentinels.**

2Ki 9:17 — And there stood a watchman on the tower in Jezreel, and he spied the company of Jehu as he came, and said, I see a company. And Joram said, Take an horseman, and send to meet them, and let him say, *Is it* peace?

2Ki 18:8 — He smote the Philistines, *even* unto Gaza, and the borders thereof, from the tower of the watchmen to the fenced city.

• **As fortress.**

Mt 21:33 — Hear another parable: There was a certain householder, which planted a vineyard, and hedged it round about, and digged a winepress in it, and built a tower, and let it out to husbandmen, and went into a far country:

• **Parable of.**

Lk 14:28–29

See: Fort

• **Figurative.**

• **Of divine protection.**

2Sa 22:3 — The God of my rock; in him will I trust: *he is* my shield, and the horn of my salvation, my high tower, and my refuge, my saviour; thou savest me from violence.

2Sa 22:51 — *He is* the tower of salvation for his king: and sheweth mercy to his anointed, unto David, and to his seed for evermore.

Ps 18:2 — The LORD *is* my rock, and my fortress, and my deliverer; my God, my strength, in whom I will trust; my buckler, and the horn of my salvation, *and* my high tower.

Ps 61:3 — For thou hast been a shelter for me, *and* a strong tower from the enemy.

Ps 144:2 — My goodness, and my fortress; my high tower, and my deliverer; my shield, and *he* in whom I trust; who subdueth my people under me.

Pr 18:10 — The name of the LORD *is* a strong tower: the righteous runneth into it, and is safe.

TOWN See: Cities

TOWN CLERK

Ac 19:35 — And when the townclerk had appeased the people, he said, *Ye* men of Ephesus, what man is there that knoweth not how that the city of the Ephesians is a worshipper of the great goddess Diana, and of the *image* which fell down from Jupiter?

TRACHONITIS • A part of the tetrarchy of Philip.

Lk 3:1 — Now in the fifteenth year of the reign of Tiberius Caesar, Pontius Pilate being governor of Judaea, and Herod being tetrarch of Galilee, and his brother Philip tetrarch of Ituraea and of the region of Trachonitis, and Lysanias the tetrarch of Abilene,

TRADE

• Occupation.

Look under name of each trade.

• Commerce.

✦See: Commerce

TRADITION

• The decisions and minor precepts taught by Paul.

1Co 11:2 — Now I praise you, brethren, that ye remember me in all things, and keep the ordinances, as I delivered *them* to you.

2Th 2:15 — Therefore, brethren, stand fast, and hold the traditions which ye have been taught, whether by word, or our epistle.

2Th 3:6 — Now we command you, brethren, in the name of our Lord Jesus Christ, that ye withdraw yourselves from every brother that walketh disorderly, and not after the tradition which he received of us.

• Commandments of men.

Mt 12:1–8; 15:2–6; Mk 7:3–9; Lk 6:1–11

Col 2:8 — Beware lest any man spoil you through philosophy and vain deceit, after the tradition of men, after the rudiments of the world, and not after Christ.

1Pe 1:18 — Forasmuch as ye know that ye were not redeemed with corruptible things, *as* silver and gold, from your vain conversation *received* by tradition from your fathers;

• Not authoritative.

Mt 15:3–20

1Ti 1:4 — Neither give heed to fables and endless genealogies, which minister questions, rather than godly edifying which is in faith: *so do.*

1Ti 4:7 — But refuse profane and old wives' fables, and exercise thyself *rather* unto godliness.

TRAFFIC

• Suspended on the Sabbath.

Ne 13:15–22

TRAITOR

• Judas.

Mt 26:14–16, 46–50; Mk 14:10–11, 43–45; Lk 22:3–6; 22:21–23, 47–48; Jn 13:27–30; 18:2–8

Jn 13:2 — And supper being ended, the devil having now put into the heart of Judas Iscariot, Simon's *son,* to betray him;

Jn 18:13 — And led him away to Annas first; for he was father in law to Caiaphas, which was the high priest that same year.

✦See: Treason

TRAMP

Pr 6:11 — So shall thy poverty come as one that travelleth, and thy want as an armed man.

TRANCE

• Of Balaam.

Nu 24:4 — He hath said, which heard the words of God, which saw the vision of the Almighty, falling *into a trance,* but having his eyes open:

Nu 24:16 — He hath said, which heard the words of God, and knew the knowledge of the most High, *which* saw the vision of the Almighty, falling *into a trance,* but having his eyes open:

• Of Peter.

Ac 10:10 — And he became very hungry, and would have eaten: but while they made ready, he fell into a trance,

• Of Paul.

Ac 22:17 — And it came to pass, that, when I was come again to Jerusalem, even while I prayed in the temple, I was in a trance;

TRANSFIGURATION

• Of Moses.

Ex 34:29–35

• Of Jesus.

Mt 17:2–9; Mk 9:2–10; Lk 9:29–36; 2Pe 1:16–18

• Of Stephen.

Ac 6:15 — And all that sat in the council, looking stedfastly on him, saw his face as it had been the face of an angel.

TRANSLATION

• Of Enoch.

Ge 5:24 — And Enoch walked with God: and he *was* not; for God took him.

Heb 11:5 — By faith Enoch was translated that he should not see death; and was not found, because God had translated him: for before his translation he had this testimony, that he pleased God.

• Of Elijah.

2Ki 2:1–12

• Of Jesus.

Ac 1:9–11

Mk 16:19 — So then after the Lord had spoken unto them, he was received up into heaven, and sat on the right hand of God.

Lk 24:51 — And it came to pass, while he blessed them, he was parted from them, and carried up into heaven.

• Desired by Paul.

2Co 5:4 — For we that are in *this* tabernacle do groan, being burdened: not for that we would be unclothed, but clothed upon, that mortality might be swallowed up of life.

TRAP

Jos 23:13 — Know for a certainty that the LORD your God will no more drive out *any of* these nations from before you; but they shall be snares and traps unto you, and scourges in your sides, and thorns in your eyes, until ye perish from off this good land which the LORD your God hath given you.

Job 18:10 — The snare *is* laid for him in the ground, and a trap for him in the way.

Jer 5:26 — For among my people are found wicked *men:* they lay wait, as he that setteth snares; they set a trap, they catch men.

TREACHERY

Jer 9:8 — Their tongue *is as* an arrow shot out; it speaketh deceit: *one* speaketh peaceably to his neighbour with his mouth, but in heart he layeth his wait.

- **Of Rahab to her people.**
  Jos 2:1–24
- **Of the man of Bethel.**
  Jgs 1:24–25
- **Of Jael.**
  Jgs 4:18–21
- **Of Shechemites.**
  Jgs 9:23 — Then God sent an evil spirit between Abimelech and the men of Shechem; and the men of Shechem dealt treacherously with Abimelech:
- **Of Joab.**
  2Sa 3:26–27
- **Of Baanah and Rechab.**
  2Sa 4:6 — And they came thither into the midst of the house, *as though* they would have fetched wheat; and they smote him under the fifth *rib:* and Rechab and Baanah his brother escaped.
- **Of David to Uriah.**
  2Sa 11:1–27
- **Of Joab to Amasa.**
  2Sa 20:9–10
- **Of Jehu.**
  2Ki 10:18–28
- **Of the enemies of Nehemiah.**
  Ne 6:1–19

  See: Conspiracy

  See: Treason

TREASON

- **Instances of.**
  - **Aaron and Miriam against Moses.**
    Nu 12:1–11
  - **Korah, Dathan, and Abiram against Moses and Aaron.**
    Nu 16:1–33
  - **Rahab against Jericho.**
    Jos 2:1–24
  - **The betrayer of Bethel.**
    Jgs 1:24–25
  - **The Shechemites against Abimelech.**
    Jgs 9:22–25
  - **The Ephraimites against Jephthah.**
    Jgs 12:1–4
  - **The Israelites against Saul.**
    1Sa 10:27
  - **The Israelites against Rehoboam.**
    1Ki 12:16–19
  - **The Egyptian servant against the Amalekites.**
    1Sa 30:15–16
  - **Abner against Ish-bosheth.**
    2Sa 3:6–21
  - **Jehoiada against Athaliah.**
    2Ki 11:14–16
  - **Absalom against his father.**

    See: Absalom
- **Death penalty for.**
  Est 2:23 — And when inquisition was made of the matter, it was found out; therefore they were both hanged on a tree: and it was written in the book of the chronicles before the king.
- **Jesus falsely accused of.**
  Mt 27:29–30; Lk 23:2–3; Jn 19:14–15

  Mt 27:11 — And Jesus stood before the governor: and the governor asked him, saying, Art thou the King of the Jews? And Jesus said unto him, Thou sayest.

  Lk 23:38 — And a superscription also was written over him in letters of Greek, and Latin, and Hebrew, THIS IS THE KING OF THE JEWS.

  Jn 19:12 — And from thenceforth Pilate sought to release him: but the Jews cried out, saying, If thou let this man go, thou art not Caesar's friend: whosoever maketh himself a king speaketh against Caesar.

  Jn 19:19 — And Pilate wrote a title, and put *it* on the cross. And the writing was, JESUS OF NAZARETH THE KING OF THE JEWS.
- **Paul falsely accused of.**
  Ac 17:7 — Whom Jason hath received: and these all do contrary to the decrees of Caesar, saying that there is another king, *one* Jesus.
- **David's amnesty of the traitors.**
  2Sa 19:16–23
- **David's amnesty of the traitors to Amasa.**
  2Sa 19:13 — And say ye to Amasa, *Art* thou not of my bone, and of my flesh? God do so to me, and more also, if thou be not captain of the host before me continually in the room of Joab.

  See: Conspiracy

  See: Treachery

TREASURE

- **A thing of highly estimated value.**
- **Money.**
  Ge 42:27–28; 43:21–23

  Ge 42:25 — Then Joseph commanded to fill their sacks with corn, and to restore every man's money into his sack, and to give them provision for the way: and thus did he unto them.

  Ge 42:35 — And it came to pass as they emptied their sacks, that, behold, every man's bundle of money *was* in his sack: and when *both* they and their father saw the bundles of money, they were afraid.

  Ge 43:18 — And the men were afraid, because they were brought into Joseph's house; and they said, Because of the money that was returned in our sacks at the first time are we brought in; that he may seek occasion against us, and fall upon us, and take us for bondmen, and our asses.

- **Precious stones.**

1Ch 29:8 — And they with whom *precious* stones were found gave *them* to the treasure of the house of the LORD, by the hand of Jehiel the Gershonite.

- **Jesus forbids the hoarding of.**

Mt 6:19 — Lay not up for yourselves treasures upon earth, where moth and rust doth corrupt, and where thieves break through and steal:

Mt 19:21 — Jesus said unto him, If thou wilt be perfect, go *and* sell that thou hast, and give to the poor, and thou shalt have treasure in heaven: and come *and* follow me.

Lk 12:33 — Sell that ye have, and give alms; provide yourselves bags which wax not old, a treasure in the heavens that faileth not, where no thief approacheth, neither moth corrupteth.

- **Hidden.**

Mt 13:44 — Again, the kingdom of heaven is like unto treasure hid in a field; the which when a man hath found, he hideth, and for joy thereof goeth and selleth all that he hath, and buyeth that field.

- **Figurative.**
  - **Of the graces of the spirit.**

Pr 21:20 — *There is* treasure to be desired and oil in the dwelling of the wise; but a foolish man spendeth it up.

Isa 33:6 — And wisdom and knowledge shall be the stability of thy times, *and* strength of salvation: the fear of the LORD *is* his treasure.

  - **Of spiritual understanding.**

Mt 13:52 — Then said he unto them, Therefore every scribe *which is* instructed unto the kingdom of heaven is like unto a man *that is* an householder, which bringeth forth out of his treasure *things* new and old.

Col 2:3 — In whom are hid all the treasures of wisdom and knowledge.

  - **Of the object of the affections.**

Mt 6:21 — For where your treasure is, there will your heart be also.

Lk 12:34 — For where your treasure is, there will your heart be also.

  - **Of spiritual calling.**

2Co 4:6–7

- **Gospel called.**

2Co 4:7 — But we have this treasure in earthen vessels, that the excellency of the power may be of God, and not of us.

- **Parable of.**

Mt 13:44 — Again, the kingdom of heaven is like unto treasure hid in a field; the which when a man hath found, he hideth, and for joy thereof goeth and selleth all that he hath, and buyeth that field.

TREASURE CITIES

- **Built for the storage of the king's substance.**

Ex 1:11 — Therefore they did set over them taskmasters to afflict them with their burdens. And they built for Pharaoh treasure cities, Pithom and Raamses.

1Ki 9:19 — And all the cities of store that Solomon had, and cities for his chariots, and cities for his horsemen, and that which Solomon desired to build in Jerusalem, and in Lebanon, and in all the land of his dominion.

2Ch 8:4 — And he built Tadmor in the wilderness, and all the store cities, which he built in Hamath.

2Ch 8:6 — And Baalath, and all the store cities that Solomon had, and all the chariot cities, and the cities of the horsemen, and all that Solomon desired to build in Jerusalem, and in Lebanon, and throughout all the land of his dominion.

TREASURE-HOUSES

- **Of kings.**

2Ch 32:27–28; Ezr 1:7–8

2Ki 20:13 — And Hezekiah hearkened unto them, and shewed them all the house of his precious things, the silver, and the gold, and the spices, and the precious ointment, and *all* the house of his armour, and all that was found in his treasures: there was nothing in his house, nor in all his dominion, that Hezekiah shewed them not.

1Ch 27:25 — And over the king's treasures *was* Azmaveth the son of Adiel: and over the storehouses in the fields, in the cities, and in the villages, and in the castles, *was* Jehonathan the son of Uzziah:

Est 3:9 — If it please the king, let it be written that they may be destroyed: and I will pay ten thousand talents of silver to the hands of those that have the charge of the business, to bring *it* into the king's treasuries.

- **Records preserved in.**

Ezr 5:17–6:1

- **Treasurers in charge of.**

Ezr 7:20–21

- **Heathen temples used for.**

Da 1:2 — And the Lord gave Jehoiakim king of Judah into his hand, with part of the vessels of the house of God: which he carried into the land of Shinar to the house of his god; and he brought the vessels into the treasure house of his god.

- **Tabernacle used for.**

Nu 31:54 — And Moses and Eleazar the priest took the gold of the captains of thousands and of hundreds, and brought it into the tabernacle of the congregation, *for* a memorial for the children of Israel before the LORD.

Jos 6:19 — But all the silver, and gold, and vessels of brass and iron, *are* consecrated unto the LORD: they shall come into the treasury of the LORD.

Jos 6:24 — And they burnt the city with fire, and all that *was* therein: only the silver, and the gold, and the vessels of brass and of iron, they put into the treasury of the house of the LORD.

• Solomon's temple used for.

2Ki 12:4–14; 22:4–5; 1Ch 28:11–12; Mk 12:41–42

1Ki 7:51 — So was ended all the work that king Solomon made for the house of the LORD. And Solomon brought in the things which David his father had dedicated; *even* the silver, and the gold, and the vessels, did he put among the treasures of the house of the LORD.

2Ki 12:18 — And Jehoash king of Judah took all the hallowed things that Jehoshaphat, and Jehoram, and Ahaziah, his fathers, kings of Judah, had dedicated, and his own hallowed things, and all the gold *that was* found in the treasures of the house of the LORD, and in the king's house, and sent *it* to Hazael king of Syria: and he went away from Jerusalem.

Mt 27:6 — And the chief priests took the silver pieces, and said, It is not lawful for to put them into the treasury, because it is the price of blood.

Lk 21:1 — And he looked up, and saw the rich men casting their gifts into the treasury.

Jn 8:20 — These words spake Jesus in the treasury, as he taught in the temple: and no man laid hands on him; for his hour was not yet come.

• Under the charge of the Levites.

1Ch 26:20 — And of the Levites, Ahijah *was* over the treasures of the house of God, and over the treasures of the dedicated things.

• Chambers provided in the temple for various kinds of offerings.

Ne 10:38–39

Ne 13:5 — And he had prepared for him a great chamber, where aforetime they laid the meat offerings, the frankincense, and the vessels, and the tithes of the corn, the new wine, and the oil, which was commanded *to be given* to the Levites, and the singers, and the porters; and the offerings of the priests.

Ne 13:9 — Then I commanded, and they cleansed the chambers: and thither brought I again the vessels of the house of God, with the meat offering and the frankincense.

Ne 13:12 — Then brought all Judah the tithe of the corn and the new wine and the oil unto the treasuries.

Mal 3:10 — Bring ye all the tithes into the storehouse, that there may be meat in mine house, and prove me now herewith, saith the LORD of hosts, if I will not open you the windows of heaven, and pour you out a blessing, that *there shall* not *be room* enough *to receive it.*

• Priests and Levites in charge of.

1Ch 26:20–28

1Ch 9:26 — For these Levites, the four chief porters, were in *their* set office, and were over the chambers and treasuries of the house of God.

Ne 12:44 — And at that time were some appointed over the chambers for the treasures, for the offerings, for the firstfruits, and for the tithes, to gather into them out of the fields of the cities the portions of the law for the priests and Levites: for Judah rejoiced for the priests and for the Levites that waited.

Ne 13:13 — And I made treasurers over the treasuries, Shelemiah the priest, and Zadok the scribe, and of the Levites, Pedaiah: and next to them *was* Hanan the son of Zaccur, the son of Mattaniah: for they were counted faithful, and their office *was* to distribute unto their brethren.

TREATY

• Between nations of Israelites and Gibeonites.

Jos 9:3–15

• Between nations of Judah and Syria.

1Ki 15:19 — *There is* a league between me and thee, *and* between my father and thy father: behold, I have sent unto thee a present of silver and gold; come and break thy league with Baasha king of Israel, that he may depart from me.

• Cession of territory by.

1Ki 9:10–14

1Ki 20:34 — And *Ben-hadad* said unto him, The cities, which my father took from thy father, I will restore; and thou shalt make streets for thee in Damascus, as my father made in Samaria. Then *said Ahab,* I will send thee away with this covenant. So he made a covenant with him, and sent him away.

• Sacredness of.

Jos 2:8–21; 9:16–21

• Reciprocity.

1Ki 5:1–12

• With idolatrous nations forbidden.

Ex 34:12 — Take heed to thyself, lest thou make a covenant with the inhabitants of the land whither thou goest, lest it be for a snare in the midst of thee:

Ex 34:15 — Lest thou make a covenant with the inhabitants of the land, and they go a whoring after their gods, and do sacrifice unto their gods, and *one* call thee, and thou eat of his sacrifice;

TREE

• Of life.

Ge 2:9 — And out of the ground made the LORD God to grow every tree that is pleasant to the sight, and good for food; the tree of life also in the midst of the garden, and the tree of knowledge of good and evil.

Ge 3:22 — And the LORD God said, Behold, the man is become as one of us, to know good and evil: and now, lest he put forth his hand, and take also of the tree of life, and eat, and live for ever:

Ge 3:24 — So he drove out the man; and he placed at the east of the garden of Eden Cherubim, and a flaming sword which turned every way, to keep the way of the tree of life.

Rev 22:14 — Blessed *are* they that do his commandments, that they may have right to the tree of life, and may enter in through the gates into the city.

• Of knowledge.

Ge 3:3–6, 11–12

Ge 2:9 — And out of the ground made the LORD God to grow every tree that is pleasant to the sight, and good for food; the tree of life also in the midst of the garden, and the tree of knowledge of good and evil.

Ge 2:17 — But of the tree of the knowledge of good and evil, thou shalt not eat of it: for in the day that thou eatest thereof thou shalt surely die.

Ge 3:17 — And unto Adam he said, Because thou hast hearkened unto the voice of thy wife, and hast eaten of the tree, of which I commanded thee, saying, Thou shalt not eat of it: cursed *is* the ground for thy sake; in sorrow shalt thou eat *of* it all the days of thy life;

• Figurative.

Ps 1:3 — And he shall be like a tree planted by the rivers of water, that bringeth forth his fruit in his season; his leaf also shall not wither; and whatsoever he doeth shall prosper.

Jer 17:8 — For he shall be as a tree planted by the waters, and *that* spreadeth out her roots by the river, and shall not see when heat cometh, but her leaf shall be green; and shall not be careful in the year of drought, neither shall cease from yielding fruit.

• Symbolic.

Da 4:10–12

TRESPASS

Ex 22:9 — For all manner of trespass, *whether it be* for ox, for ass, for sheep, for raiment, *or* for any manner of lost thing, which *another* challengeth to be his, the cause of both parties shall come before the judges; *and* whom the judges shall condemn, he shall pay double unto his neighbour.

• Of an ox.

Ex 21:28–36

• Of a brother.

Mt 18:15–18; Lk 17:3–4

• Creditor shall not enter debtor's house to take a pledge.

Dt 24:10 — When thou dost lend thy brother any thing, thou shalt not go into his house to fetch his pledge.

• Trespass offering.

See: Offerings

TRIAL

• Before court.

Le 24:10–14

• Right of.

Ac 16:37–39; 22:25–30

Jn 7:51 — Doth our law judge *any* man, before it hear him, and know what he doeth?

See: Court

See: Justice

See: Prisoners

• Of Faith.

See: Faith

See: Temptation

TRIALS

Ps 55:16–23; 119:65–72

1Pe 1:7 — That the trial of your faith, being much more precious than of gold that perisheth, though it be tried with fire, might be found unto praise and honour and glory at the appearing of Jesus Christ:

1Pe 4:12 — Beloved, think it not strange concerning the fiery trial which is to try you, as though some strange thing happened unto you:

1Pe 5:7 — Casting all your care upon him; for he careth for you.

TRIBULATION

Jn 16:33 — These things I have spoken unto you, that in me ye might have peace. In the world ye shall have tribulation: but be of good cheer; I have overcome the world.

See: Afflictions

See: Suffering

TRIBUTE

• From conquered nations.

Jgs 1:30–33; Mt 17:24–27; 22:15–22; Lk 2:1–5

Jos 16:10 — And they drave not out the Canaanites that dwelt in Gezer: but the Canaanites dwell among the Ephraimites unto this day, and serve under tribute.

2Ki 15:19 — *And* Pul the king of Assyria came against the land: and Menahem gave Pul a thousand talents of silver, that his hand might be with him to confirm the kingdom in his hand.

2Ki 23:35 — And Jehoiakim gave the silver and the gold to Pharaoh; but he taxed the land to give the money according to the commandment of Pharaoh: he exacted the silver and the gold of the people of the land, of every one according to his taxation, to give *it* unto Pharaoh-nechoh.

• By Arabians to.

• Solomon.

2Ch 9:14 — Beside *that which* chapmen and merchants brought. And all the kings of Arabia and governors of the country brought gold and silver to Solomon.

• Jehoshaphat.

2Ch 17:11 — Also *some* of the Philistines brought Jehoshaphat presents, and tribute silver; and the Arabians brought him flocks, seven thousand and seven hundred rams, and seven thousand and seven hundred he goats.

See: Duty

See: Tax

TRINITY

• The Holy.

Isa 11:2–3; 61:1–3; 63:9–10; Jn 1:32–33; 3:34–35; 14:16–17; 16:13–15; Ac 1:4–5; 10:36–38; Ro 1:3–4; 8:9–11, 26–27; 1Co 2:10–11; 12:3–6; 2Co 1:21–22; 2Th 2:13–14; Tit 3:4–6; 1Jn 5:6–7

Ge 1:26 — And God said, Let us make man in our image, after our likeness: and let them have dominion over the fish of the sea, and over the fowl of the air, and over the cattle, and over all the earth, and over every creeping thing that creepeth upon the earth.

Ge 3:22 — And the LORD God said, Behold, the man is become as one of us, to know good and evil: and now, lest he put forth his hand, and take also of the tree of life, and eat, and live for ever:

Isa 6:3 — And one cried unto another, and said, Holy, holy, holy, *is* the LORD of hosts: the whole earth *is* full of his glory.

Isa 6:8 — Also I heard the voice of the Lord, saying, Whom shall I send, and who will go for us? Then said I, Here *am* I; send me.

Isa 42:1 — Behold my servant, whom I uphold; mine elect, *in whom* my soul delighteth; I have put my spirit upon him: he shall bring forth judgment to the Gentiles.

Isa 48:16 — Come ye near unto me, hear ye this; I have not spoken in secret from the beginning; from the time that it was, there *am* I: and now the Lord GOD, and his Spirit, hath sent me.

Mt 1:18 — Now the birth of Jesus Christ was on this wise: When as his mother Mary was espoused to Joseph, before they came together, she was found with child of the Holy Ghost.

Mt 1:20 — But while he thought on these things, behold, the angel of the Lord appeared unto him in a dream, saying, Joseph, thou son of David, fear not to take unto thee Mary thy wife: for that which is conceived in her is of the Holy Ghost.

Mt 3:11 — I indeed baptize you with water unto repentance: but he that cometh after me is mightier than I, whose shoes I am not worthy to bear: he shall baptize you with the Holy Ghost, and *with* fire:

Mt 3:16 — And Jesus, when he was baptized, went up straightway out of the water: and, lo, the heavens were opened unto him, and he saw the Spirit of God descending like a dove, and lighting upon him:

Mt 12:18 — Behold my servant, whom I have chosen; my beloved, in whom my soul is well pleased: I will put my spirit upon him, and he shall shew judgment to the Gentiles.

Mt 12:28 — But if I cast out devils by the Spirit of God, then the kingdom of God is come unto you.

Mt 28:19 — Go ye therefore, and teach all nations, baptizing them in the name of the Father, and of the Son, and of the Holy Ghost:

Mk 1:8 — I indeed have baptized you with water: but he shall baptize you with the Holy Ghost.

Lk 1:35 — And the angel answered and said unto her, The Holy Ghost shall come upon thee, and the power of the Highest shall overshadow thee: therefore also that holy thing which shall be born of thee shall be called the Son of God.

Lk 3:16 — John answered, saying unto *them* all, I indeed baptize you with water; but one mightier than I cometh, the latchet of whose shoes I am not worthy to unloose: he shall baptize you with the Holy Ghost and with fire:

Lk 3:22 — And the Holy Ghost descended in a bodily shape like a dove upon him, and a voice came from heaven, which said, Thou art my beloved Son; in thee I am well pleased.

Lk 4:1 — And Jesus being full of the Holy Ghost returned from Jordan, and was led by the Spirit into the wilderness,

Lk 4:14 — And Jesus returned in the power of the Spirit into Galilee: and there went out a fame of him through all the region round about.

Lk 4:18 — The Spirit of the Lord is upon me, because he hath anointed me to preach the gospel to the poor; he hath sent me to heal the brokenhearted, to preach deliverance to the captives, and recovering of sight to the blind, to set at liberty them that are bruised,

Jn 7:39 — (But this spake he of the Spirit, which they that believe on him should receive: for the Holy Ghost was not yet *given;* because that Jesus was not yet glorified.)

Jn 14:26 — But the Comforter, *which is* the Holy Ghost, whom the Father will send in my name, he shall teach you all things, and bring all things to your remembrance, whatsoever I have said unto you.

Jn 15:26 — But when the Comforter is come, whom I will send unto you from the Father, *even* the Spirit of truth, which proceedeth from the Father, he shall testify of me:

Jn 16:7 — Nevertheless I tell you the truth; It is expedient for you that I go away: for if I go not away, the Comforter will not come unto you; but if I depart, I will send him unto you.

Jn 20:22 — And when he had said this, he breathed on *them,* and saith unto them, Receive ye the Holy Ghost:

Ac 1:2 — Until the day in which he was taken up, after that he through the Holy Ghost had given commandments unto the apostles whom he had chosen:

Ac 2:33 — Therefore being by the right hand of God exalted, and having received of the Father the promise of the Holy Ghost, he hath shed forth this, which ye now see and hear.

1Co 6:19 — What? know ye not that your body is the temple of the Holy Ghost *which is* in you, which ye have of God, and ye are not your own?

1Co 8:6 — But to us *there is but* one God, the Father, of whom *are* all things, and we in him; and one Lord Jesus Christ, by whom *are* all things, and we by him.

2Co 3:17 — Now the Lord is that Spirit: and where the Spirit of the Lord *is,* there *is* liberty.

2Co 5:5 — Now he that hath wrought us for the selfsame thing *is* God, who also hath given unto us the earnest of the Spirit.

2Co 13:14 — The grace of the Lord Jesus Christ, and the love of God, and the communion of the Holy Ghost, *be* with you all. Amen.

Gal 4:4 — But when the fulness of the time was come, God sent forth his Son, made of a woman, made under the law,

Gal 4:6 — And because ye are sons, God hath sent forth the Spirit of his Son into your hearts, crying, Abba, Father.

Php 1:19 — For I know that this shall turn to my salvation through your prayer, and the supply of the Spirit of Jesus Christ,

Col 2:2 — That their hearts might be comforted, being knit together in love, and unto all riches of the full assurance of understanding, to the acknowledgement of the mystery of God, and of the Father, and of Christ;

2Th 2:16 — Now our Lord Jesus Christ himself, and God, even our Father, which hath loved us, and hath given *us* everlasting consolation and good hope through grace,

1Ti 3:16 — And without controversy great is the mystery of godliness: God was manifest in the flesh, justified in the Spirit, seen of angels, preached unto the Gentiles, believed on in the world, received up into glory.

Heb 9:14 — How much more shall the blood of Christ, who through the eternal Spirit offered himself without spot to God, purge your conscience from dead works to serve the living God?

1Pe 1:2 — Elect according to the foreknowledge of God the Father, through sanctification of the Spirit, unto obedience and sprinkling of the blood of Jesus Christ: Grace unto you, and peace, be multiplied.

1Pe 3:18 — For Christ also hath once suffered for sins, the just for the unjust, that he might bring us to God, being put to death in the flesh, but quickened by the Spirit:

Rev 4:8 — And the four beasts had each of them six wings about *him;* and *they were* full of eyes within: and they rest not day and night, saying, Holy, holy, holy, Lord God Almighty, which was, and is, and is to come.

See: God

See: Holy Spirit

See: Jesus, Divinity of

See: Jesus, Preexistence of

See: Jesus, Relation of, to the Father

TROAS

- **A seaport in Mysia, in Asia Minor.**
- **Paul visits.**

Ac 20:5–6

Ac 16:8 — And they passing by Mysia came down to Troas.

Ac 16:11 — Therefore loosing from Troas, we came with a straight course to Samothracia, and the next day to Neapolis;

2Co 2:12 — Furthermore, when I came to Troas to *preach* Christ's gospel, and a door was opened unto me of the Lord,

2Ti 4:13 — The cloke that I left at Troas with Carpus, when thou comest, bring *with thee,* and the books, *but* especially the parchments.

TROGYLLIUM

- **A town and promontory in Caria, of Asia Minor.**
- **Visited by Paul.**

Ac 20:15 — And we sailed thence, and came the next *day* over against Chios; and the next *day* we arrived at Samos, and tarried at Trogyllium; and the next *day* we came to Miletus.

TROPHIES

- **Goliath's head and armor.**

1Sa 17:54 — And David took the head of the Philistine, and brought it to Jerusalem; but he put his armour in his tent.

1Sa 21:9 — And the priest said, The sword of Goliath the Philistine, whom thou slewest in the valley of Elah, behold, it *is here* wrapped in a cloth behind the ephod: if thou wilt take that, take *it:* for *there is* no other save that here. And David said, *There is* none like that; give it me.

- **Saul's head and armor.**

1Sa 31:8–10

- **Placed in temples.**

See: Temple

TROPHIMUS

- **An Ephesian companion of Paul.**
- **Accompanies Paul from Greece to Asia.**

Ac 20:4 — And there accompanied him into Asia Sopater of Berea; and of the Thessalonians, Aristarchus and Secundus; and Gaius of Derbe, and Timotheus; and of Asia, Tychicus and Trophimus.

- **With Paul in Jerusalem, made the occasion of an attack on Paul.**

Ac 21:27–30

- **Left ill at Miletus.**

2Ti 4:20 — Erastus abode at Corinth: but Trophimus have I left at Miletum sick.

TROUBLE

- **Borrowing.**

Mt 6:25–34; Mk 5:35–36; Jn 16:6–7

Jn 14:1 — Let not your heart be troubled: ye believe in God, believe also in me.

Php 4:6 — Be careful for nothing; but in every thing by prayer and supplication with thanksgiving let your requests be made known unto God.

1Pe 5:7 — Casting all your care upon him; for he careth for you.

See: Afflictions

See: Suffering

- **Instances of.**
  - **Israelites at the Red Sea.**

    Ex 14:10–12
  - **About water.**

    Ex 15:23–25; 17:2–3; Nu 20:1–13
  - **About food.**

    Ex 16:2–3; Nu 11:4–33

- **When Moses tarried in the mount.**
  Ex 32:1
- **When the spies brought their adverse report.**
  Nu 13:28–29; 13:31–14:12
- **Elijah, under the juniper tree and in the cave.**
  1Ki 19:4–15
- **The disciples, as to how the multitude could be fed.**
  Mt 14:15; Mk 6:37
- **The disciples, in the tempest, when Jesus was asleep in the ship.**
  Mt 8:23–26; Mk 4:36–39; Lk 8:22–24
- **The disciples, when Jesus was crucified.**
  Lk 24:4–9, 24–31, 36–40
- **Mary at the sepulchre.**
  Jn 20:11–17
- **The people in the shipwreck.**
  Ac 27:22–25, 30–36

TRUCE

- **In battle.**
  2Sa 2:26–31

TRUMPET

- **Made of ram's horn.**
  Jos 6:4–6
  Jos 6:8 — And it came to pass, when Joshua had spoken unto the people, that the seven priests bearing the seven trumpets of rams' horns passed on before the LORD, and blew with the trumpets: and the ark of the covenant of the LORD followed them.
  Jos 6:13 — And seven priests bearing seven trumpets of rams' horns before the ark of the LORD went on continually, and blew with the trumpets: and the armed men went before them; but the rereward came after the ark of the LORD, *the priests* going on, and blowing with the trumpets.
- **Made of silver.**
  Nu 10:2 — Make thee two trumpets of silver; of a whole piece shalt thou make them: that thou mayest use them for the calling of the assembly, and for the journeying of the camps.
- **Uses of, prescribed by Moses.**
  Nu 10:1–10
- **Used in war.**
  Job 39:24–25
  Jer 4:19 — My bowels, my bowels! I am pained at my very heart; my heart maketh a noise in me; I cannot hold my peace, because thou hast heard, O my soul, the sound of the trump, the alarm of war.
  Jer 6:1 — O ye children of Benjamin, gather yourselves to flee out of the midst of Jerusalem, and blow the trumpet in Tekoa, and set up a sign of fire in Beth-haccerem: for evil appeareth out of the north, and great destruction.
  Jer 6:17 — Also I set watchmen over you, *saying,* Hearken to the sound of the trumpet. But they said, We will not hearken.
  Jer 42:14 — Saying, No; but we will go into the land of Egypt, where we shall see no war, nor hear the sound of the trumpet, nor have hunger of bread; and there will we dwell:
  Jer 51:27 — Set ye up a standard in the land, blow the trumpet among the nations, prepare the nations against her, call together against her the kingdoms of Ararat, Minni, and Ashchenaz; appoint a captain against her; cause the horses to come up as the rough caterpillers.
  Eze 7:14 — They have blown the trumpet, even to make all ready; but none goeth to the battle: for my wrath *is* upon all the multitude thereof.
  Am 2:2 — But I will send a fire upon Moab, and it shall devour the palaces of Kirioth: and Moab shall die with tumult, with shouting, *and* with the sound of the trumpet:
  Am 3:6 — Shall a trumpet be blown in the city, and the people not be afraid? shall there be evil in a city, and the LORD hath not done *it?*
  Zep 1:16 — A day of the trumpet and alarm against the fenced cities, and against the high towers.
  1Co 14:8 — For if the trumpet give an uncertain sound, who shall prepare himself to the battle?
- **To summon soldiers.**
  - **By Phinehas.**
    Nu 31:6 — And Moses sent them to the war, a thousand of *every* tribe, them and Phinehas the son of Eleazar the priest, to the war, with the holy instruments, and the trumpets to blow in his hand.
  - **By Ehud.**
    Jgs 3:27 — And it came to pass, when he was come, that he blew a trumpet in the mountain of Ephraim, and the children of Israel went down with him from the mount, and he before them.
  - **By Gideon.**
    Jgs 6:34 — But the Spirit of the LORD came upon Gideon, and he blew a trumpet; and Abi-ezer was gathered after him.
  - **By Saul.**
    1Sa 13:3 — And Jonathan smote the garrison of the Philistines that *was* in Geba, and the Philistines heard *of it.* And Saul blew the trumpet throughout all the land, saying, Let the Hebrews hear.
  - **By Joab.**
    2Sa 2:28 — So Joab blew a trumpet, and all the people stood still, and pursued after Israel no more, neither fought they any more.
    2Sa 18:16 — And Joab blew the trumpet, and the people returned from pursuing after Israel: for Joab held back the people.
    2Sa 20:22 — Then the woman went unto all the people in her wisdom. And they cut off the head of Sheba the son of Bichri, and cast *it* out to Joab. And he blew a trumpet, and they retired from the city, every man to his tent. And Joab returned to Jerusalem unto the king.
  - **By Absalom.**
    2Sa 15:10 — But Absalom sent spies throughout all the tribes of Israel, saying, As soon as ye hear

the sound of the trumpet, then ye shall say, Absalom reigneth in Hebron.

- **By Sheba.**

2Sa 20:1 — And there happened to be there a man of Belial, whose name *was* Sheba, the son of Bichri, a Benjamite: and he blew a trumpet, and said, We have no part in David, neither have we inheritance in the son of Jesse: every man to his tents, O Israel.

- **By Nehemiah.**

Ne 4:18 — For the builders, every one had his sword girded by his side, and *so* builded. And he that sounded the trumpet *was* by me.

Ne 4:20 — In what place *therefore* ye hear the sound of the trumpet, resort ye thither unto us: our God shall fight for us.

- **By Gideon's soldiers.**

Jgs 7:8–22

- **In war, of Abijah.**

2Ch 13:12 — And, behold, God himself is with us for *our* captain, and his priests with sounding trumpets to cry alarm against you. O children of Israel, fight ye not against the LORD God of your fathers; for ye shall not prosper.

2Ch 13:14 — And when Judah looked back, behold, the battle *was* before and behind: and they cried unto the LORD, and the priests sounded with the trumpets.

- **In the siege of Jericho.**

Jos 6:4–20

- **Sounded in time of danger.**

Eze 33:3–6

Joel 2:1 — Blow ye the trumpet in Zion, and sound an alarm in my holy mountain: let all the inhabitants of the land tremble: for the day of the LORD cometh, for *it is* nigh at hand;

- **Used at Sinai.**

Ex 19:13–19

Ex 20:18 — And all the people saw the thunderings, and the lightnings, and the noise of the trumpet, and the mountain smoking: and when the people saw *it,* they removed, and stood afar off.

Heb 12:19 — And the sound of a trumpet, and the voice of words; *which* voice they that heard intreated that the word should not be spoken to them any more:

- **Used on the great day of atonement.**

Isa 27:13 — And it shall come to pass in that day, *that* the great trumpet shall be blown, and they shall come which were ready to perish in the land of Assyria, and the outcasts in the land of Egypt, and shall worship the LORD in the holy mount at Jerusalem.

- **Used at the jubilee.**

Le 25:9 — Then shalt thou cause the trumpet of the jubile to sound on the tenth *day* of the seventh month, in the day of atonement shall ye make the trumpet sound throughout all your land.

- **Used at the bringing up of the ark.**

2Sa 6:5 — And David and all the house of Israel played before the LORD on all manner of *instruments made of* fir wood, even on harps, and on psalteries, and on timbrels, and on cornets, and on cymbals.

2Sa 6:15 — So David and all the house of Israel brought up the ark of the LORD with shouting, and with the sound of the trumpet.

1Ch 13:8 — And David and all Israel played before God with all *their* might, and with singing, and with harps, and with psalteries, and with timbrels, and with cymbals, and with trumpets.

1Ch 15:28 — Thus all Israel brought up the ark of the covenant of the LORD with shouting, and with sound of the cornet, and with trumpets, and with cymbals, making a noise with psalteries and harps.

- **Used at the anointing of kings.**

1Ki 1:34 — And let Zadok the priest and Nathan the prophet anoint him there king over Israel: and blow ye with the trumpet, and say, God save king Solomon.

1Ki 1:39 — And Zadok the priest took an horn of oil out of the tabernacle, and anointed Solomon. And they blew the trumpet; and all the people said, God save king Solomon.

2Ki 9:13 — Then they hasted, and took every man his garment, and put *it* under him on the top of the stairs, and blew with trumpets, saying, Jehu is king.

2Ki 11:14 — And when she looked, behold, the king stood by a pillar, as the manner *was,* and the princes and the trumpeters by the king, and all the people of the land rejoiced, and blew with trumpets: and Athaliah rent her clothes, and cried, Treason, Treason.

- **Used at the dedication of Solomon's temple.**

2Ch 5:12–13

2Ch 7:6 — And the priests waited on their offices: the Levites also with instruments of musick of the LORD, which David the king had made to praise the LORD, because his mercy *endureth* for ever, when David praised by their ministry; and the priests sounded trumpets before them, and all Israel stood.

- **Used in worship.**

Ps 81:3–4

1Ch 15:24 — And Shebaniah, and Jehoshaphat, and Nethaneel, and Amasai, and Zechariah, and Benaiah, and Eliezer, the priests, did blow with the trumpets before the ark of God: and Obed-edom and Jehiah *were* doorkeepers for the ark.

1Ch 16:42 — And with them Heman and Jeduthun with trumpets and cymbals for those that should make a sound, and with musical instruments of God. And the sons of Jeduthun *were* porters.

1Ch 25:5 — All these *were* the sons of Heman the king's seer in the words of God, to lift up the horn. And God gave to Heman fourteen sons and three daughters.

- **Used at Jehoshaphat's triumph.**

2Ch 20:28 — And they came to Jerusalem with psalteries and harps and trumpets unto the house of the LORD.

- **Used at the foundation of the second temple.**

Ezr 3:10–11

• **Used at the dedication of the wall.**

Ne 12:35 — And *certain* of the priests' sons with trumpets; *namely,* Zechariah the son of Jonathan, the son of Shemaiah, the son of Mattaniah, the son of Michaiah, the son of Zaccur, the son of Asaph:

Ne 12:41 — And the priests; Eliakim, Maaseiah, Miniamin, Michaiah, Elioenai, Zechariah, *and* Hananiah, with trumpets;

• **Figurative.**

Isa 27:13 — And it shall come to pass in that day, *that* the great trumpet shall be blown, and they shall come which were ready to perish in the land of Assyria, and the outcasts in the land of Egypt, and shall worship the LORD in the holy mount at Jerusalem.

Eze 33:3 — If when he seeth the sword come upon the land, he blow the trumpet, and warn the people;

Joel 2:1 — Blow ye the trumpet in Zion, and sound an alarm in my holy mountain: let all the inhabitants of the land tremble: for the day of the LORD cometh, for *it is* nigh at hand;

Zec 9:14 — And the LORD shall be seen over them, and his arrow shall go forth as the lightning: and the LORD GOD shall blow the trumpet, and shall go with whirlwinds of the south.

Mt 6:2 — Therefore when thou doest *thine* alms, do not sound a trumpet before thee, as the hypocrites do in the synagogues and in the streets, that they may have glory of men. Verily I say unto you, They have their reward.

• **Symbolic.**

Rev 8:1–9:14

Mt 24:31 — And he shall send his angels with a great sound of a trumpet, and they shall gather together his elect from the four winds, from one end of heaven to the other.

1Co 15:52 — In a moment, in the twinkling of an eye, at the last trump: for the trumpet shall sound, and the dead shall be raised incorruptible, and we shall be changed.

1Th 4:16 — For the Lord himself shall descend from heaven with a shout, with the voice of the archangel, and with the trump of God: and the dead in Christ shall rise first:

Rev 1:10 — I was in the Spirit on the Lord's day, and heard behind me a great voice, as of a trumpet,

Rev 4:1 — After this I looked, and, behold, a door *was* opened in heaven: and the first voice which I heard *was* as it were of a trumpet talking with me; which said, Come up hither, and I will shew thee things which must be hereafter.

Rev 10:7 — But in the days of the voice of the seventh angel, when he shall begin to sound, the mystery of God should be finished, as he hath declared to his servants the prophets.

Rev 11:15 — And the seventh angel sounded; and there were great voices in heaven, saying, The kingdoms of this world are become *the kingdoms* of our Lord, and of his Christ; and he shall reign for ever and ever.

⇜**See: Music; instruments of**

TRUMPETS

• **Feast of.**

• **When and how observed.**

Le 23:24–25; Nu 29:1–6

• **Celebrated after the captivity with joy.**

Ne 8:9–12

Ne 8:2 — And Ezra the priest brought the law before the congregation both of men and women, and all that could hear with understanding, upon the first day of the seventh month.

⇜**See: Feasts**

TRUST

⇜**See: Faith**

TRUSTEE

• **Mosaic law concerning.**

Ex 22:7–13; Le 6:2–7

• **The parable of the pounds.**

Mt 25:14–28; Lk 19:12–27

⇜**See: Steward**

TRUTH

• **Saints should worship God in.**

Ps 145:18 — The LORD *is* nigh unto all them that call upon him, to all that call upon him in truth.

Jn 4:24 — God *is* a Spirit: and they that worship him must worship *him* in spirit and in truth.

• **Saints serve God in.**

Jos 24:14 — Now therefore fear the LORD, and serve him in sincerity and in truth: and put away the gods which your fathers served on the other side of the flood, and in Egypt; and serve ye the LORD.

1Sa 12:24 — Only fear the LORD, and serve him in truth with all your heart: for consider how great *things* he hath done for you.

• **Saints walk before God in.**

1Ki 2:4 — That the LORD may continue his word which he spake concerning me, saying, If thy children take heed to their way, to walk before me in truth with all their heart and with all their soul, there shall not fail thee (said he) a man on the throne of Israel.

2Ki 20:3 — I beseech thee, O LORD, remember now how I have walked before thee in truth and with a perfect heart, and have done *that which is* good in thy sight. And Hezekiah wept sore.

• **Saints keep religious feasts with.**

1Co 5:8 — Therefore let us keep the feast, not with old leaven, neither with the leaven of malice and wickedness; but with the unleavened *bread* of sincerity and truth.

• **Saints esteem, as inestimable.**

Pr 23:23 — Buy the truth, and sell *it* not; *also* wisdom, and instruction, and understanding.

• **Saints love.**

Zec 8:19 — Thus saith the LORD of hosts; The fast of the fourth *month,* and the fast of the fifth, and the fast of the seventh, and the fast of the tenth, shall be to the house of Judah joy and gladness, and cheerful feasts; therefore love the truth and peace.

- **Saints rejoice in.**

1Co 13:6 — Rejoiceth not in iniquity, but rejoiceth in the truth;

- **Saints speak, to one another.**

Zec 8:16 — These *are* the things that ye shall do; Speak ye every man the truth to his neighbour; execute the judgment of truth and peace in your gates:

Eph 4:25 — Wherefore putting away lying, speak every man truth with his neighbour: for we are members one of another.

- **Saints execute judgment with.**

Zec 8:16 — These *are* the things that ye shall do; Speak ye every man the truth to his neighbour; execute the judgment of truth and peace in your gates:

- **Saints meditate upon.**

Php 4:8 — Finally, brethren, whatsoever things are true, whatsoever things *are* honest, whatsoever things *are* just, whatsoever things *are* pure, whatsoever things *are* lovely, whatsoever things *are* of good report; if *there be* any virtue, and if *there be* any praise, think on these things.

- **Saints bind, about the neck.**

Pr 3:3 — Let not mercy and truth forsake thee: bind them about thy neck; write them upon the table of thine heart:

- **Saints write, upon the tables of the heart.**

Pr 3:3 — Let not mercy and truth forsake thee: bind them about thy neck; write them upon the table of thine heart:

- **The fruit of the Spirit is in.**

Eph 5:9 — (For the fruit of the Spirit is in all goodness and righteousness and truth;)

- **Ministers should speak.**

2Co 12:6 — For though I would desire to glory, I shall not be a fool; for I will say the truth: but *now* I forbear, lest any man should think of me above that which he seeth me *to be,* or *that* he heareth of me.

Gal 4:16 — Am I therefore become your enemy, because I tell you the truth?

- **Ministers teach in.**

1Ti 2:7 — Whereunto I am ordained a preacher, and an apostle, (I speak the truth in Christ, *and* lie not;) a teacher of the Gentiles in faith and verity.

- **Ministers approve themselves by.**

2Co 6:7–8

- **Magistrates should be men of.**

Ex 18:21 — Moreover thou shalt provide out of all the people able men, such as fear God, men of truth, hating covetousness; and place *such* over them, *to be* rulers of thousands, *and* rulers of hundreds, rulers of fifties, and rulers of tens:

- **Kings are preserved by.**

Pr 20:28 — Mercy and truth preserve the king: and his throne is upholden by mercy.

- **They who speak, show forth righteousness.**

Pr 12:17 — *He that* speaketh truth sheweth forth righteousness: but a false witness deceit.

- **They who speak, are the delight of God.**

Pr 12:22 — Lying lips *are* abomination to the LORD: but they that deal truly *are* his delight.

- **The wicked destitute of.**

Hos 4:1 — Hear the word of the LORD, ye children of Israel: for the LORD hath a controversy with the inhabitants of the land, because *there is* no truth, nor mercy, nor knowledge of God in the land.

- **The wicked speak not.**

Jer 9:5 — And they will deceive every one his neighbour, and will not speak the truth: they have taught their tongue to speak lies, *and* weary themselves to commit iniquity.

- **The wicked uphold not.**

Isa 59:14–15

- **The wicked plead not for.**

Isa 59:4 — None calleth for justice, nor *any* pleadeth for truth: they trust in vanity, and speak lies; they conceive mischief, and bring forth iniquity.

- **The wicked are not valiant for.**

Jer 9:3 — And they bend their tongues *like* their bow *for* lies: but they are not valiant for the truth upon the earth; for they proceed from evil to evil, and they know not me, saith the LORD.

- **The wicked punished for want of.**

Jer 9:5 — And they will deceive every one his neighbour, and will not speak the truth: they have taught their tongue to speak lies, *and* weary themselves to commit iniquity.

Jer 9:9 — Shall I not visit them for these *things?* saith the LORD: shall not my soul be avenged on such a nation as this?

Hos 4:1 — Hear the word of the LORD, ye children of Israel: for the LORD hath a controversy with the inhabitants of the land, because *there is* no truth, nor mercy, nor knowledge of God in the land.

Hos 4:3 — Therefore shall the land mourn, and every one that dwelleth therein shall languish, with the beasts of the field, and with the fowls of heaven; yea, the fishes of the sea also shall be taken away.

- **The gospel as, came by Christ.**

Jn 1:17 — For the law was given by Moses, *but* grace and truth came by Jesus Christ.

- **The gospel as, is in Christ.**

1Ti 2:7 — Whereunto I am ordained a preacher, and an apostle, (I speak the truth in Christ, *and* lie not;) a teacher of the Gentiles in faith and verity.

- **John bare witness to.**

Jn 5:33 — Ye sent unto John, and he bare witness unto the truth.

- **Is according to godliness.**

Tit 1:1 — Paul, a servant of God, and an apostle of Jesus Christ, according to the faith of God's elect, and the acknowledging of the truth which is after godliness;

- **Is sanctifying.**

Jn 17:17 — Sanctify them through thy truth: thy word is truth.

Jn 17:19 — And for their sakes I sanctify myself, that they also might be sanctified through the truth.

• Is purifying.

1Pe 1:22 — Seeing ye have purified your souls in obeying the truth through the Spirit unto unfeigned love of the brethren, *see that ye* love one another with a pure heart fervently:

• Is part of the Christian armor.

Eph 6:14 — Stand therefore, having your loins girt about with truth, and having on the breastplate of righteousness;

• Revealed abundantly to saints.

Jer 33:6 — Behold, I will bring it health and cure, and I will cure them, and will reveal unto them the abundance of peace and truth.

• Abides continually with saints.

2Jn 1:2 — For the truth's sake, which dwelleth in us, and shall be with us for ever.

• Should be acknowledged.

2Ti 2:25 — In meekness instructing those that oppose themselves; if God peradventure will give them repentance to the acknowledging of the truth;

• Should be believed.

2Th 2:12–13

1Ti 4:3 — Forbidding to marry, *and commanding* to abstain from meats, which God hath created to be received with thanksgiving of them which believe and know the truth.

• Should be obeyed.

Ro 2:8 — But unto them that are contentious, and do not obey the truth, but obey unrighteousness, indignation and wrath,

Gal 3:1 — O foolish Galatians, who hath bewitched you, that ye should not obey the truth, before whose eyes Jesus Christ hath been evidently set forth, crucified among you?

• Should be loved.

2Th 2:10 — And with all deceivableness of unrighteousness in them that perish; because they received not the love of the truth, that they might be saved.

• Should be manifested.

2Co 4:2 — But have renounced the hidden things of dishonesty, not walking in craftiness, nor handling the word of God deceitfully; but by manifestation of the truth commending ourselves to every man's conscience in the sight of God.

• Should be rightly divided.

2Ti 2:15 — Study to shew thyself approved unto God, a workman that needeth not to be ashamed, rightly dividing the word of truth.

• The wicked turn away from.

2Ti 4:4 — And they shall turn away *their* ears from the truth, and shall be turned unto fables.

• The wicked resist.

2Ti 3:8 — Now as Jannes and Jambres withstood Moses, so do these also resist the truth: men of corrupt minds, reprobate concerning the faith.

• The wicked destitute of.

1Ti 6:5 — Perverse disputings of men of corrupt minds, and destitute of the truth, supposing that gain is godliness: from such withdraw thyself.

• The church is the pillar and ground of.

1Ti 3:15 — But if I tarry long, that thou mayest know how thou oughtest to behave thyself in the house of God, which is the church of the living God, the pillar and ground of the truth.

• The devil is devoid of.

Jn 8:44 — Ye are of your father the devil, and the lusts of *your* father ye will do. He was a murderer from the beginning, and abode not in the truth, because there is no truth in him. When he speaketh a lie, he speaketh of his own: for he is a liar, and the father of it.

TRUTH, of God

• Is one of his attributes.

Dt 32:4 — *He is* the Rock, his work *is* perfect: for all his ways *are* judgment: a God of truth and without iniquity, just and right *is* he.

Isa 65:16 — That he who blesseth himself in the earth shall bless himself in the God of truth; and he that sweareth in the earth shall swear by the God of truth; because the former troubles are forgotten, and because they are hid from mine eyes.

• He keeps, forever.

Ps 146:6 — Which made heaven, and earth, the sea, and all that therein *is:* which keepeth truth for ever:

• Abundant.

Ex 34:6 — And the LORD passed by before him, and proclaimed, The LORD, The LORD God, merciful and gracious, longsuffering, and abundant in goodness and truth,

• Inviolable.

Nu 23:19 — God *is* not a man, that he should lie; neither the son of man, that he should repent: hath he said, and shall he not do *it?* or hath he spoken, and shall he not make it good?

Tit 1:2 — In hope of eternal life, which God, that cannot lie, promised before the world began;

• Enduring to all generations.

Ps 100:5 — For the LORD *is* good; his mercy *is* everlasting; and his truth *endureth* to all generations.

• Exhibited in.

• His ways.

Rev 15:3 — And they sing the song of Moses the servant of God, and the song of the Lamb, saying, Great and marvellous *are* thy works, Lord God Almighty; just and true *are* thy ways, thou King of saints.

• His works.

Ps 33:4 — For the word of the LORD *is* right; and all his works *are done* in truth.

Ps 111:7 — The works of his hands *are* verity and judgment; all his commandments *are* sure.

Da 4:37 — Now I Nebuchadnezzar praise and extol and honour the King of heaven, all whose works *are* truth, and his ways judgment: and those that walk in pride he is able to abase.

• **His judicial statutes.**

Ps 19:9 — The fear of the LORD *is* clean, enduring for ever: the judgments of the LORD *are* true *and* righteous altogether.

• **His word.**

Ps 119:160 — Thy word *is* true *from* the beginning: and every one of thy righteous judgments *endureth* for ever.

Jn 17:17 — Sanctify them through thy truth: thy word is truth.

• **His fulfillment of promises in Christ.**

2Co 1:20 — For all the promises of God in him *are* yea, and in him Amen, unto the glory of God by us.

• **His fulfillment of his covenant.**

Mic 7:20 — Thou wilt perform the truth to Jacob, *and* the mercy to Abraham, which thou hast sworn unto our fathers from the days of old.

• **His dealings with saints.**

Ps 25:10 — All the paths of the LORD *are* mercy and truth unto such as keep his covenant and his testimonies.

• **His deliverance of saints.**

Ps 57:3 — He shall send from heaven, and save *from* the reproach of him that would swallow me up. Selah. God shall send forth his mercy and his truth.

• **His punishment of the wicked.**

Rev 16:7 — And I heard another out of the altar say, Even so, Lord God Almighty, true and righteous *are* thy judgments.

• **Is a shield and buckler to saints.**

Ps 91:4 — He shall cover thee with his feathers, and under his wings shalt thou trust: his truth *shall be thy* shield and buckler.

• **We should confide in.**

Ps 31:5 — Into thine hand I commit my spirit: thou hast redeemed me, O LORD God of truth.

Tit 1:2 — In hope of eternal life, which God, that cannot lie, promised before the world began;

• **Plead in prayer.**

Ps 89:49 — Lord, where *are* thy former lovingkindnesses, *which* thou swarest unto David in thy truth?

• **Pray for its manifestation to ourselves.**

2Ch 6:17 — Now then, O LORD God of Israel, let thy word be verified, which thou hast spoken unto thy servant David.

• **Pray for its exhibition to others.**

2Sa 2:6 — And now the LORD shew kindness and truth unto you: and I also will requite you this kindness, because ye have done this thing.

• **Make known, to others.**

Isa 38:19 — The living, the living, he shall praise thee, as I *do* this day: the father to the children shall make known thy truth.

• **Magnify.**

Ps 71:22 — I will also praise thee with the psaltery, *even* thy truth, O my God: unto thee will I sing with the harp, O thou Holy One of Israel.

Ps 138:2 — I will worship toward thy holy temple, and praise thy name for thy lovingkindness and for thy truth: for thou hast magnified thy word above all thy name.

• **Is denied by the devil.**

Ge 3:4–5

• **Is denied by the self-righteous.**

1Jn 1:10 — If we say that we have not sinned, we make him a liar, and his word is not in us.

• **Is denied by unbelievers.**

1Jn 5:10 — He that believeth on the Son of God hath the witness in himself: he that believeth not God hath made him a liar; because he believeth not the record that God gave of his Son.

• **Unclassified scripture relating to.**

Ps 85:10–11; Isa 59:14–15; Jn 8:31–32; 18:37–38

Ex 34:6 — And the LORD passed by before him, and proclaimed, The LORD, The LORD God, merciful and gracious, longsuffering, and abundant in goodness and truth,

Dt 32:4 — *He is* the Rock, his work *is* perfect: for all his ways *are* judgment: a God of truth and without iniquity, just and right *is* he.

Ps 31:5 — Into thine hand I commit my spirit: thou hast redeemed me, O LORD God of truth.

Ps 33:4 — For the word of the LORD *is* right; and all his works *are done* in truth.

Ps 40:10 — I have not hid thy righteousness within my heart; I have declared thy faithfulness and thy salvation: I have not concealed thy lovingkindness and thy truth from the great congregation.

Ps 51:6 — Behold, thou desirest truth in the inward parts: and in the hidden *part* thou shalt make me to know wisdom.

Ps 57:3 — He shall send from heaven, and save *from* the reproach of him that would swallow me up. Selah. God shall send forth his mercy and his truth.

Ps 57:10 — For thy mercy is great unto the heavens, and thy truth unto the clouds.

Ps 86:15 — But thou, O Lord, *art* a God full of compassion, and gracious, longsuffering, and plenteous in mercy and truth.

Ps 89:14 — Justice and judgment *are* the habitation of thy throne: mercy and truth shall go before thy face.

Ps 96:13 — Before the LORD: for he cometh, for he cometh to judge the earth: he shall judge the world with righteousness, and the people with his truth.

Ps 98:3 — He hath remembered his mercy and his truth toward the house of Israel: all the ends of the earth have seen the salvation of our God.

Ps 100:5 — For the LORD *is* good; his mercy *is* everlasting; and his truth *endureth* to all generations.

Ps 108:4 — For thy mercy *is* great above the heavens: and thy truth *reacheth* unto the clouds.

Pr 12:19 — The lip of truth shall be established for ever: but a lying tongue *is* but for a moment.

Pr 16:13 — Righteous lips *are* the delight of kings; and they love him that speaketh right.

Isa 25:1 — O LORD, thou *art* my God; I will exalt thee, I will praise thy name; for thou hast done wonderful *things; thy* counsels of old *are* faithfulness *and* truth.

Isa 65:16 — That he who blesseth himself in the earth shall bless himself in the God of truth; and he that sweareth in the earth shall swear by the God of truth; because the former troubles are forgotten, and because they are hid from mine eyes.

Jer 5:3 — O LORD, *are* not thine eyes upon the truth? thou hast stricken them, but they have not grieved; thou hast consumed them, *but* they have refused to receive correction: they have made their faces harder than a rock; they have refused to return.

Da 4:37 — Now I Nebuchadnezzar praise and extol and honour the King of heaven, all whose works *are* truth, and his ways judgment: and those that walk in pride he is able to abase.

Da 10:21 — But I will shew thee that which is noted in the scripture of truth: and *there is* none that holdeth with me in these things, but Michael your prince.

Mic 7:20 — Thou wilt perform the truth to Jacob, *and* the mercy to Abraham, which thou hast sworn unto our fathers from the days of old.

Jn 1:14 — And the Word was made flesh, and dwelt among us, (and we beheld his glory, the glory as of the only begotten of the Father,) full of grace and truth.

Jn 14:6 — Jesus saith unto him, I am the way, the truth, and the life: no man cometh unto the Father, but by me.

Jn 14:17 — *Even* the Spirit of truth; whom the world cannot receive, because it seeth him not, neither knoweth him: but ye know him; for he dwelleth with you, and shall be in you.

Jn 16:13 — Howbeit when he, the Spirit of truth, is come, he will guide you into all truth: for he shall not speak of himself; but whatsoever he shall hear, *that* shall he speak: and he will shew you things to come.

Jn 17:17 — Sanctify them through thy truth: thy word is truth.

Jn 17:19 — And for their sakes I sanctify myself, that they also might be sanctified through the truth.

Ro 2:2 — But we are sure that the judgment of God is according to truth against them which commit such things.

TRYPHENA • A Christian woman in Rome.

Ro 16:12 — Salute Tryphena and Tryphosa, who labour in the Lord. Salute the beloved Persis, which laboured much in the Lord.

TRYPHOSA • A Christian woman in Rome.

Ro 16:12 — Salute Tryphena and Tryphosa, who labour in the Lord. Salute the beloved Persis, which laboured much in the Lord.

TUBAL

• Son of Japheth.

Ge 10:2 — The sons of Japheth; Gomer, and Magog, and Madai, and Javan, and Tubal, and Meshech, and Tiras.

1Ch 1:5 — The sons of Japheth; Gomer, and Magog, and Madai, and Javan, and Tubal, and Meshech, and Tiras.

• Descendants of, become a nation.

Eze 38:2–3

Isa 66:19 — And I will set a sign among them, and I will send those that escape of them unto the nations, *to* Tarshish, Pul, and Lud, that draw the bow, *to* Tubal, and Javan, *to* the isles afar off, that have not heard my fame, neither have seen my glory; and they shall declare my glory among the Gentiles.

Eze 27:13 — Javan, Tubal, and Meshech, they *were* thy merchants: they traded the persons of men and vessels of brass in thy market.

Eze 32:26 — There *is* Meshech, Tubal, and all her multitude: her graves *are* round about him: all of them uncircumcised, slain by the sword, though they caused their terror in the land of the living.

Eze 39:1 — Therefore, thou son of man, prophesy against Gog, and say, Thus saith the Lord GOD; Behold, I *am* against thee, O Gog, the chief prince of Meshech and Tubal:

TUBAL-CAIN • The inventor of edge tools.

Ge 4:22 — And Zillah, she also bare Tubal-cain, an instructer of every artificer in brass and iron: and the sister of Tubal-cain *was* Naamah.

TUMOR

• A morbid swelling.

1Sa 6:4–5

1Sa 5:6 — But the hand of the LORD was heavy upon them of Ashdod, and he destroyed them, and smote them with emerods, *even* Ashdod and the coasts thereof.

1Sa 5:9 — And it was *so,* that, after they had carried it about, the hand of the LORD was against the city with a very great destruction: and he smote the men of the city, both small and great, and they had emerods in their secret parts.

1Sa 5:12 — And the men that died not were smitten with the emerods: and the cry of the city went up to heaven.

1Sa 6:11 — And they laid the ark of the LORD upon the cart, and the coffer with the mice of gold and the images of their emerods.

1Sa 6:17 — And these *are* the golden emerods which the Philistines returned *for* a trespass offering unto the LORD; for Ashdod one, for Gaza one, for Askelon one, for Gath one, for Ekron one;

See: Boil

TURTLEDOVE **See: Dove, Turtle**

TUTOR

Gal 4:1–2

2Ki 10:1 — And Ahab had seventy sons in Samaria. And Jehu wrote letters, and sent to Samaria, unto the rulers of Jezreel, to the elders, and to them that brought up Ahab's *children,* saying,

Ac 22:3 — I am verily a man *which am* a Jew, born in Tarsus, a city in Cilicia, yet brought up in this city at the feet of Gamaliel, *and* taught according to the perfect manner of the law of the fathers, and was zealous toward God, as ye all are this day.

TWINS

• Jacob and Esau.

Ge 25:24–26

• Pharez and Zarah.

Ge 38:27–30

TYCHICUS

• An Asian companion of Paul.

• Accompanies Paul from Greece to Asia.

Ac 20:4 — And there accompanied him into Asia Sopater of Berea; and of the Thessalonians, Aristarchus and Secundus; and Gaius of Derbe, and Timotheus; and of Asia, Tychicus and Trophimus.

• With Paul in Nicopolis.

Tit 3:12–15

• With Paul in Rome.

Eph 6:21–22; Col 4:7–8

• Paul's amanuensis in writing to the Ephesians and Colossians.

Eph 6:21–23; Col 4:7–18

• Sent to Ephesus.

Eph 6:21–22

2Ti 4:12 — And Tychicus have I sent to Ephesus.

• Sent to Colosse.

Col 4:7–8

TYPES

• Miscellaneous.

• Bride, a type of the church.

Rev 21:2 — And I John saw the holy city, new Jerusalem, coming down from God out of heaven, prepared as a bride adorned for her husband.

Rev 21:9 — And there came unto me one of the seven angels which had the seven vials full of the seven last plagues, and talked with me, saying, Come hither, I will shew thee the bride, the Lamb's wife.

Rev 22:17 — And the Spirit and the bride say, Come. And let him that heareth say, Come. And let him that is athirst come. And whosoever will, let him take the water of life freely.

• The sanctuary a type of the heavenly sanctuary.

Heb 9:1–12

Ex 40:2 — On the first day of the first month shalt thou set up the tabernacle of the tent of the congregation.

Ex 40:24 — And he put the candlestick in the tent of the congregation, over against the table, on the side of the tabernacle southward.

Heb 8:2 — A minister of the sanctuary, and of the true tabernacle, which the Lord pitched, and not man.

Heb 8:5 — Who serve unto the example and shadow of heavenly things, as Moses was admonished of God when he was about to make the tabernacle: for, See, saith he, *that* thou make all things according to the pattern shewed to thee in the mount.

• The saving of Noah and his family, of the salvation through the gospel.

1Pe 3:20–21

• Defilement a type of sin.

✦See: Defilement

✦See: Purification

• Leaven a type of sin.

✦See: Leaven

• Ablutions were.

✦See: Ablution

✦See: Allegory

✦See: Parables

✦See: Symbols and Similitudes

• Of the Saviour.

Heb 9:7–15; 9:18–10:10

Col 2:17 — Which are a shadow of things to come; but the body *is* of Christ.

• High priest, typical of the mediatorship.

Ex 28:29–30; Zec 6:12–13; Heb 5:1–14

Ex 28:1 — And take thou unto thee Aaron thy brother, and his sons with him, from among the children of Israel, that he may minister unto me in the priest's office, *even* Aaron, Nadab and Abihu, Eleazar and Ithamar, Aaron's sons.

Ex 28:12 — And thou shalt put the two stones upon the shoulders of the ephod *for* stones of memorial unto the children of Israel: and Aaron shall bear their names before the LORD upon his two shoulders for a memorial.

Ex 28:38 — And it shall be upon Aaron's forehead, that Aaron may bear the iniquity of the holy things, which the children of Israel shall hallow in all their holy gifts; and it shall be always upon his forehead, that they may be accepted before the LORD.

Le 16:15 — Then shall he kill the goat of the sin offering, that *is* for the people, and bring his blood within the vail, and do with that blood as he did with the blood of the bullock, and sprinkle it upon the mercy seat, and before the mercy seat:

Heb 8:2 — A minister of the sanctuary, and of the true tabernacle, which the Lord pitched, and not man.

Heb 10:21 — And *having* an high priest over the house of God;

• The institutions ordained by Moses.

Lk 24:25–27, 44–47; Col 2:14–17; Heb 10:1–14

Mt 26:54 — But how then shall the scriptures be fulfilled, that thus it must be?

• The sacrifices.

Le 4:2–3; Heb 9:7–15, 18–25; 10:1–22; 13:11–13

Le 4:12 — Even the whole bullock shall he carry forth without the camp unto a clean place, where the ashes are poured out, and burn him on the wood with fire: where the ashes are poured out shall he be burnt.

Heb 10:29 — Of how much sorer punishment, suppose ye, shall he be thought worthy, who hath trodden under foot the Son of God, and hath counted the blood of the covenant, wherewith he was sanctified, an unholy thing, and hath done despite unto the Spirit of grace?

1Pe 1:19 — But with the precious blood of Christ, as of a lamb without blemish and without spot:

Rev 5:6 — And I beheld, and, lo, in the midst of the throne and of the four beasts, and in the midst of the elders, stood a Lamb as it had been slain, having seven horns and seven eyes, which are the seven Spirits of God sent forth into all the earth.

- **The morning and evening sacrifice.**

Jn 1:29 — The next day John seeth Jesus coming unto him, and saith, Behold the Lamb of God, which taketh away the sin of the world.

Jn 1:36 — And looking upon Jesus as he walked, he saith, Behold the Lamb of God!

- **The red heifer.**

Nu 19:2–6; Heb 9:13–14

- **The paschal lamb.**

1Co 5:7 — Purge out therefore the old leaven, that ye may be a new lump, as ye are unleavened. For even Christ our passover is sacrificed for us:

- **The brazen altar.**

Ex 27:1–2

Heb 13:10 — We have an altar, whereof they have no right to eat which serve the tabernacle.

- **The laver of brass.**

Ex 30:18–20; Eph 5:26–27

Zec 13:1 — In that day there shall be a fountain opened to the house of David and to the inhabitants of Jerusalem for sin and for uncleanness.

- **Mercy seat.**

Ex 25:17–22

Heb 4:16 — Let us therefore come boldly unto the throne of grace, that we may obtain mercy, and find grace to help in time of need.

- **The veil.**

Ex 40:21 — And he brought the ark into the tabernacle, and set up the vail of the covering, and covered the ark of the testimony; as the LORD commanded Moses.

2Ch 3:14 — And he made the vail *of* blue, and purple, and crimson, and fine linen, and wrought cherubims thereon.

Heb 10:20 — By a new and living way, which he hath consecrated for us, through the veil, that is to say, his flesh;

- **Manna.**

Jn 6:32–35

1Co 10:3 — And did all eat the same spiritual meat;

- **Cities of refuge.**

Nu 35:6 — And among the cities which ye shall give unto the Levites *there shall be* six cities for refuge, which ye shall appoint for the manslayer, that he may flee thither: and to them ye shall add forty and two cities.

Heb 6:18 — That by two immutable things, in which *it was* impossible for God to lie, we might have a strong consolation, who have fled for refuge to lay hold upon the hope set before us:

- **Brazen serpent.**

Jn 3:14–15

Nu 21:9 — And Moses made a serpent of brass, and put it upon a pole, and it came to pass, that if a serpent had bitten any man, when he beheld the serpent of brass, he lived.

- **Tree of life.**

Ge 2:9 — And out of the ground made the LORD God to grow every tree that is pleasant to the sight, and good for food; the tree of life also in the midst of the garden, and the tree of knowledge of good and evil.

Jn 1:4 — In him was life; and the life was the light of men.

Rev 22:2 — In the midst of the street of it, and on either side of the river, *was there* the tree of life, which bare twelve *manner* of fruits, *and* yielded her fruit every month: and the leaves of the tree *were* for the healing of the nations.

- **Adam.**

Ro 5:14 — Nevertheless death reigned from Adam to Moses, even over them that had not sinned after the similitude of Adam's transgression, who is the figure of him that was to come.

1Co 15:45 — And so it is written, The first man Adam was made a living soul; the last Adam *was made* a quickening spirit.

- **Abel.**

Ge 4:8 — And Cain talked with Abel his brother: and it came to pass, when they were in the field, that Cain rose up against Abel his brother, and slew him.

Ge 4:10 — And he said, What hast thou done? the voice of thy brother's blood crieth unto me from the ground.

Heb 12:24 — And to Jesus the mediator of the new covenant, and to the blood of sprinkling, that speaketh better things than *that of* Abel.

- **Noah.**

Ge 5:29 — And he called his name Noah, saying, This *same* shall comfort us concerning our work and toil of our hands, because of the ground which the LORD hath cursed.

2Co 1:5 — For as the sufferings of Christ abound in us, so our consolation also aboundeth by Christ.

- **Melchizedek.**

Heb 7:1–17

- **Moses.**

Heb 3:2–6

Dt 18:15 — The LORD thy God will raise up unto thee a Prophet from the midst of thee, of thy brethren, like unto me; unto him ye shall hearken;

Dt 18:18 — I will raise them up a Prophet from among their brethren, like unto thee, and will put my words in his mouth; and he shall speak unto them all that I shall command him.

Ac 3:20— And he shall send Jesus Christ, which before was preached unto you:

Ac 3:22 — For Moses truly said unto the fathers, A prophet shall the Lord your God raise up unto you of your brethren, like unto me; him shall ye hear in all things whatsoever he shall say unto you.

Ac 7:37 — This is that Moses, which said unto the children of Israel, A prophet shall the Lord your God raise up unto you of your brethren, like unto me; him shall ye hear.

• David.

Ps 89:19–20

2Sa 8:15 — And David reigned over all Israel; and David executed judgment and justice unto all his people.

Eze 37:24 — And David my servant *shall be* king over them; and they all shall have one shepherd: they shall also walk in my judgments, and observe my statutes, and do them.

Php 2:9 — Wherefore God also hath highly exalted him, and given him a name which is above every name:

• Eliakim.

Isa 22:20–22

Rev 3:7 — And to the angel of the church in Philadelphia write; These things saith he that is holy, he that is true, he that hath the key of David, he that openeth, and no man shutteth; and shutteth, and no man openeth;

• Jonah.

Jnh 1:17 — Now the LORD had prepared a great fish to swallow up Jonah. And Jonah was in the belly of the fish three days and three nights.

Mt 12:40 — For as Jonas was three days and three nights in the whale's belly; so shall the Son of man be three days and three nights in the heart of the earth.

TYRANNUS

• An Ephesian.

• Paul taught in the school of, for two years.

Ac 19:9–10

TYRANNY

See: Government; monarchical; tyranny in

TYRE

• Kingdom of.

• Hiram, king of.

1Ki 5:1 — And Hiram king of Tyre sent his servants unto Solomon; for he had heard that they had anointed him king in the room of his father: for Hiram was ever a lover of David.

• Also called Huram.

2Ch 2:3 — And Solomon sent to Huram the king of Tyre, saying, As thou didst deal with David my father, and didst send him cedars to build him an house to dwell therein, *even so deal with me.*

• Sends material to David for his palace.

2Ch 2:3 — And Solomon sent to Huram the king of Tyre, saying, As thou didst deal with David my father, and didst send him cedars to build him an house to dwell therein, *even so deal with me.*

• Men and materials sent from, to Solomon, for the erection of the temple and his castles.

1Ki 5:1–11; 9:10–11; 2Ch 2:3–16

See: Hiram

• City of.

• Situated on the shore of the Mediterranean, on the northern boundary of Asher.

Jos 19:29 — And *then* the coast turneth to Ramah, and to the strong city Tyre; and the coast turneth to Hosah; and the outgoings thereof are at the sea from the coast to Achzib:

• Pleasant site of.

Hos 9:13 — Ephraim, as I saw Tyrus, *is* planted in a pleasant place: but Ephraim shall bring forth his children to the murderer.

• Fortified.

Jos 19:29 — And *then* the coast turneth to Ramah, and to the strong city Tyre; and the coast turneth to Hosah; and the outgoings thereof are at the sea from the coast to Achzib:

2Sa 24:7 — And came to the strong hold of Tyre, and to all the cities of the Hivites, and of the Canaanites: and they went out to the south of Judah, *even* to Beer-sheba.

• Commerce of.

1Ki 9:26–28; Isa 23:1–18; Eze 27:1–28:19

1Ki 10:11 — And the navy also of Hiram, that brought gold from Ophir, brought in from Ophir great plenty of almug trees, and precious stones.

Zec 9:2 — And Hamath also shall border thereby; Tyrus, and Zidon, though it be very wise.

Ac 21:3 — Now when we had discovered Cyprus, we left it on the left hand, and sailed into Syria, and landed at Tyre: for there the ship was to unlade her burden.

• Merchants of.

Isa 23:8 — Who hath taken this counsel against Tyre, the crowning *city,* whose merchants *are* princes, whose traffickers *are* the honourable of the earth?

• Antiquity of.

Isa 23:7 — *Is* this your joyous *city,* whose antiquity *is* of ancient days? her own feet shall carry her afar off to sojourn.

• Riches of.

Isa 23:8 — Who hath taken this counsel against Tyre, the crowning *city,* whose merchants *are* princes, whose traffickers *are* the honourable of the earth?

Zec 9:3 — And Tyrus did build herself a strong hold, and heaped up silver as the dust, and fine gold as the mire of the streets.

• Besieged by Nebuchadnezzar.

Eze 26:7 — For thus saith the Lord GOD; Behold, I will bring upon Tyrus Nebuchadrezzar king of Babylon, a king of kings, from the north, with horses, and with chariots, and with horsemen, and companies, and much people.

Eze 29:18 — Son of man, Nebuchadrezzar king of Babylon caused his army to serve a great service against Tyrus: every head *was* made bald, and every shoulder *was* peeled: yet had he no wages, nor his army, for Tyrus, for the service that he had served against it:

• Jesus goes to the coasts of.

Mt 15:21 — Then Jesus went thence, and departed into the coasts of Tyre and Sidon.

• Jesus heals the daughter of the Syrophenician woman near.

Mt 15:21–28; Mk 7:24–31

• Multitudes from, come to hear Jesus, and to be healed of their diseases.

Mk 3:8 — And from Jerusalem, and from Idumaea, and *from* beyond Jordan; and they about Tyre and Sidon, a great multitude, when they had heard what great things he did, came unto him.

Lk 6:17 — And he came down with them, and stood in the plain, and the company of his disciples, and a great multitude of people out of all Judaea and Jerusalem, and from the sea coast of Tyre and Sidon, which came to hear him, and to be healed of their diseases;

• Herod's hostility toward.

Ac 12:20–23

• Paul visits.

Ac 21:3–7

• To be judged according to its opportunity and privileges.

Mt 11:21–22; Lk 10:13–14

• Prophecies relating to.

Isa 23:1–18; Jer 27:1–11; Eze 26:1–28:26; Joel 3:4–8; Am 1:9–10; Zec 9:2–4

Ps 45:12 — And the daughter of Tyre *shall be there* with a gift; *even* the rich among the people shall intreat thy favour.

Ps 87:4 — I will make mention of Rahab and Babylon to them that know me: behold Philistia, and Tyre, with Ethiopia; this *man* was born there.

Jer 25:22 — And all the kings of Tyrus, and all the kings of Zidon, and the kings of the isles which are beyond the sea,

Jer 47:4 — Because of the day that cometh to spoil all the Philistines, *and* to cut off from Tyrus and Zidon every helper that remaineth: for the LORD will spoil the Philistines, the remnant of the country of Caphtor.

U

UCAL • A man mentioned only in Pr 30:1.

Pr 30:1 — The words of Agur the son of Jakeh, *even* the prophecy: the man spake unto Ithiel, even unto Ithiel and Ucal,

UEL • An Israelite who put away his Gentile wife.

Ezr 10:34 — Of the sons of Bani; Maadai, Amram, and Uel,

ULAI • A river of Chaldea.

Da 8:2 — And I saw in a vision; and it came to pass, when I saw, that I *was* at Shushan *in* the palace, which *is* in the province of Elam; and I saw in a vision, and I was by the river of Ulai.

Da 8:16 — And I heard a man's voice between *the banks of* Ulai, which called, and said, Gabriel, make this *man* to understand the vision.

ULAM

• Son of Sheresh.

1Ch 7:16–17

• Son of Eshek.

1Ch 8:39–40

ULLA • An Asherite.

1Ch 7:39 — And the sons of Ulla; Arah, and Haniel, and Rezia.

UMMAH • A city of Asher.

Jos 19:30 — Ummah also, and Aphek, and Rehob: twenty and two cities with their villages.

UNBELIEF

Nu 11:21–23; 20:12–13; Ps 78:21–22; 95:8–11; Isa 6:9–10; 53:1–3; Jer 5:12–14; Mt 10:14–15; 11:16–19; 13:13–15; 17:19–20; Mk 4:24–25; 6:2–6; Lk 7:31–35; 14:16–24; 19:41–42; 24:25–26, 36–45; Jn 1:10–11; 3:11–12; 5:43–44, 46–47; 6:60–62, 70–71; 8:45–47, 52–53; 10:25–26, 37–38; 12:39–40, 47–48; 16:8–9; Ac 13:40–41; Ro 9:31–32; 10:6–7; 11:30–32; 1Co 1:22–23; 2Co 6:14–16; 2Th 2:11–12; Heb 3:16–4:3; Jas 1:6–7; 1Pe 2:7–8; 1Jn 2:22–23

Ex 4:1 — And Moses answered and said, But, behold, they will not believe me, nor hearken unto my voice: for they will say, The LORD hath not appeared unto thee.

Ps 78:19 — Yea, they spake against God; they said, Can God furnish a table in the wilderness?

Ps 78:32 — For all this they sinned still, and believed not for his wondrous works.

Ps 106:7 — Our fathers understood not thy wonders in Egypt; they remembered not the multitude of thy mercies; but provoked *him* at the sea, *even* at the Red sea.

Ps 106:24 — Yea, they despised the pleasant land, they believed not his word:

Isa 7:9 — And the head of Ephraim *is* Samaria, and the head of Samaria *is* Remaliah's son. If ye will not believe, surely ye shall not be established.

Isa 58:3 — Wherefore have we fasted, *say they,* and thou seest not? *wherefore* have we afflicted our soul, and thou takest no knowledge? Behold, in the day of your fast ye find pleasure, and exact all your labours.

Mal 1:2 — I have loved you, saith the LORD. Yet ye say, Wherein hast thou loved us? *Was* not Esau Jacob's brother? saith the LORD: yet I loved Jacob,

Mal 1:7 — Ye offer polluted bread upon mine altar; and ye say, Wherein have we polluted thee? In that ye say, The table of the LORD *is* contemptible.

Mt 13:58 — And he did not many mighty works there because of their unbelief.

Mt 17:17 — Then Jesus answered and said, O faithless and perverse generation, how long shall I be with you? how long shall I suffer you? bring him hither to me.

Mt 21:32 — For John came unto you in the way of righteousness, and ye believed him not: but the publicans and the harlots believed him: and ye, when ye had seen *it,* repented not afterward, that ye might believe him.

Mk 9:24 — And straightway the father of the child cried out, and said with tears, Lord, I believe; help thou mine unbelief.

Mk 16:14 — Afterward he appeared unto the eleven as they sat at meat, and upbraided them with their unbelief and hardness of heart, because they believed not them which had seen him after he was risen.

Mk 16:16 — He that believeth and is baptized shall be saved; but he that believeth not shall be damned.

Lk 8:12 — Those by the way side are they that hear; then cometh the devil, and taketh away the word out of their hearts, lest they should believe and be saved.

Lk 8:18 — Take heed therefore how ye hear: for whosoever hath, to him shall be given; and whosoever hath not, from him shall be taken even that which he seemeth to have.

Lk 10:16 — He that heareth you heareth me; and he that despiseth you despiseth me; and he that despiseth me despiseth him that sent me.

Lk 12:46 — The lord of that servant will come in a day when he looketh not for *him,* and at an hour when he is not aware, and will cut him in sunder, and will appoint him his portion with the unbelievers.

Lk 13:34 — O Jerusalem, Jerusalem, which killest the prophets, and stonest them that are sent unto thee; how often would I have gathered thy children together, as a hen *doth gather* her brood under *her* wings, and ye would not!

Lk 16:31 — And he said unto him, If they hear not Moses and the prophets, neither will they be persuaded, though one rose from the dead.

Lk 18:8 — I tell you that he will avenge them speedily. Nevertheless when the Son of man cometh, shall he find faith on the earth?

Lk 22:67 — Art thou the Christ? tell us. And he said unto them, If I tell you, ye will not believe:

Lk 24:11 — And their words seemed to them as idle tales, and they believed them not.

Lk 24:21 — But we trusted that it had been he which should have redeemed Israel: and beside all this, to day is the third day since these things were done.

Jn 3:7 — Marvel not that I said unto thee, Ye must be born again.

Jn 3:18 — He that believeth on him is not condemned: but he that believeth not is condemned already, because he hath not believed in the name of the only begotten Son of God.

Jn 3:32 — And what he hath seen and heard, that he testifieth; and no man receiveth his testimony.

Jn 3:36 — He that believeth on the Son hath everlasting life: and he that believeth not the Son shall not see life; but the wrath of God abideth on him.

Jn 4:48 — Then said Jesus unto him, Except ye see signs and wonders, ye will not believe.

Jn 5:38 — And ye have not his word abiding in you: for whom he hath sent, him ye believe not.

Jn 5:40 — And ye will not come to me, that ye might have life.

Jn 6:36 — But I said unto you, That ye also have seen me, and believe not.

Jn 6:64 — But there are some of you that believe not. For Jesus knew from the beginning who they were that believed not, and who should betray him.

Jn 6:66 — From that *time* many of his disciples went back, and walked no more with him.

Jn 8:24 — I said therefore unto you, that ye shall die in your sins: for if ye believe not that I am *he*, ye shall die in your sins.

Jn 12:37 — But though he had done so many miracles before them, yet they believed not on him:

Jn 14:17 — *Even* the Spirit of truth; whom the world cannot receive, because it seeth him not, neither knoweth him: but ye know him; for he dwelleth with you, and shall be in you.

Jn 20:27 — Then saith he to Thomas, reach hither thy finger, and behold my hands; and reach hither thy hand, and thrust *it* into my side: and be not faithless, but believing.

Ac 19:9 — But when divers were hardened, and believed not, but spake evil of that way before the multitude, he departed from them, and separated the disciples, disputing daily in the school of one Tyrannus.

Ac 22:18 — And saw him saying unto me, Make haste, and get thee quickly out of Jerusalem: for they will not receive thy testimony concerning me.

Ac 28:24 — And some believed the things which were spoken, and some believed not.

Ro 1:18 — For the wrath of God is revealed from heaven against all ungodliness and unrighteousness of men, who hold the truth in unrighteousness;

Ro 3:3 — For what if some did not believe? shall their unbelief make the faith of God without effect?

Ro 4:20 — He staggered not at the promise of God through unbelief; but was strong in faith, giving glory to God;

Ro 10:14 — How then shall they call on him in whom they have not believed? and how shall they believe in him of whom they have not heard? and how shall they hear without a preacher?

Ro 10:16 — But they have not all obeyed the gospel. For Esaias saith, Lord, who hath believed our report?

Ro 10:21 — But to Israel he saith, All day long I have stretched forth my hands unto a disobedient and gainsaying people.

Ro 11:20 — Well; because of unbelief they were broken off, and thou standest by faith. Be not highminded, but fear:

Ro 14:23 — And he that doubteth is damned if he eat, because *he eateth* not of faith: for whatsoever *is* not of faith is sin.

1Co 1:18 — For the preaching of the cross is to them that perish foolishness; but unto us which are saved it is the power of God.

1Co 2:14 — But the natural man receiveth not the things of the Spirit of God: for they are foolishness unto him: neither can he know *them*, because they are spiritually discerned.

1Co 14:22 — Wherefore tongues are for a sign, not to them that believe, but to them that believe not: but prophesying *serveth* not for them that believe not, but for them which believe.

2Th 3:2 — And that we may be delivered from unreasonable and wicked men: for all *men* have not faith.

1Ti 1:13 — Who was before a blasphemer, and a persecutor, and injurious: but I obtained mercy, because I did *it* ignorantly in unbelief.

2Ti 2:13 — If we believe not, *yet* he abideth faithful: he cannot deny himself.

Tit 1:15 — Unto the pure all things *are* pure: but unto them that are defiled and unbelieving *is* nothing pure; but even their mind and conscience is defiled.

Heb 3:12 — Take heed, brethren, lest there be in any of you an evil heart of unbelief, in departing from the living God.

Heb 4:6 — Seeing therefore it remaineth that some must enter therein, and they to whom it was first preached entered not in because of unbelief:

Heb 4:11 — Let us labour therefore to enter into that rest, lest any man fall after the same example of unbelief.

Heb 11:6 — But without faith *it is* impossible to please *him:* for he that cometh to God must believe that he is, and *that* he is a rewarder of them that diligently seek him.

Heb 11:31 — By faith the harlot Rahab perished not with them that believed not, when she had received the spies with peace.

Heb 12:25 — See that ye refuse not him that speaketh. For if they escaped not who refused him that spake on earth, much more *shall not* we *escape,* if we turn away from him that *speaketh* from heaven:

2Pe 3:4 — And saying, Where is the promise of his coming? for since the fathers fell asleep, all things continue as *they were* from the beginning of the creation.

1Jn 4:3 — And every spirit that confesseth not that Jesus Christ is come in the flesh is not of God: and this is that *spirit* of antichrist, whereof ye have heard that it should come; and even now already is it in the world.

1Jn 5:10 — He that believeth on the Son of God hath the witness in himself: he that believeth not God hath made him a liar; because he believeth not the record that God gave of his Son.

1Jn 5:12 — He that hath the Son hath life; *and* he that hath not the Son of God hath not life.

Jude 1:5 — I will therefore put you in remembrance, though ye once knew this, how that the Lord, having saved the people out of the land of Egypt, afterward destroyed them that believed not.

Rev 21:8 — But the fearful, and unbelieving, and the abominable, and murderers, and whoremongers, and sorcerers, and idolaters, and all liars, shall have their part in the lake which burneth with fire and brimstone: which is the second death.

- **Instances of.**
  - **Eve.**
    Ge 3:4–6
  - **Moses and Aaron.**
    Nu 20:12
  - **Israelites.**
    Dt 9:23; 2Ki 17:14; Ps 78:1–72
  - **Naaman.**
    2Ki 5:12
  - **Samaritan lord.**
    2Ki 7:2
  - **Disciples.**
    Mt 17:17; Lk 24:11, 25
  - **Zacharias.**
    Lk 1:20
  - **Chief priests.**
    Lk 22:67
  - **The Jews.**
    Mk 1:45; 2:6–11; 8:11–12; 15:29–32; Jn 5:38, 40, 43, 46–47
  - **Disciples.**
    Mt 17:20; Mk 4:38, 40; Lk 24:41–45
  - **Brethren of Christ.**
    Jn 7:5
  - **Thomas.**
    Jn 20:25
  - **Jews of Iconium.**
    Ac 14:2
  - **Thessalonian Jews.**
    Ac 17:5
  - **Jews in Jerusalem.**
    Ro 15:31
  - **Ephesians.**
    Ac 19:9
  - **Saul.**
    1Ti 1:13
  - **People of Jericho.**
    Heb 11:31

UNCHARITABLENESS

Isa 29:20–21; Mt 7:1–5; Lk 6:37–42; Ro 14:1–15; 1Co 4:3–5; 13:1–6; Jas 4:11–12

Lk 12:57 — Yea, and why even of yourselves judge ye not what is right?

Jn 7:24 — Judge not according to the appearance, but judge righteous judgment.

Jn 8:7 — So when they continued asking him, he lifted up himself, and said unto them, He that is without sin among you, let him first cast a stone at her.

Ro 2:1 — Therefore thou art inexcusable, O man, whosoever thou art that judgest: for wherein thou judgest another, thou condemnest thyself; for thou that judgest doest the same things.

1Co 4:7 — For who maketh thee to differ *from another?* and what hast thou that thou didst not receive? now if thou didst receive *it,* why dost thou glory, as if thou hadst not received *it?*

- **See: Accusation, False**
- **See: Charitableness**
- **See: Slander**
- **See: Speaking; evil**
- **See: Talebearer**

- **Instances of.**
  - **The Israelites toward Moses, charging him with having made them abhorred by the Egyptians.**
    Ex 5:21
  - **The Israelites toward Moses, charging him with bringing them out of Egypt to die.**
    Ex 14:11–12
  - **The Israelites in murmuring against Moses.**
    See: Murmuring; instances of
  - **The tribes west of Jordan toward the two and one-half tribes.**
    Nu 32:1–33; Jos 22:11–31
  - **Of Eli toward Hannah.**
    1Sa 1:14–17
  - **Eliab toward David, charging him with presumption, when he offered to fight Goliath.**
    1Sa 17:28
  - **Princes of Ammon toward David, when he sent commissioners to convey his sympathy to Hanun.**
    2Sa 10:3
  - **Bildad toward Job.**
    Job 8:1–22
  - **Eliphaz toward Job.**
    Job 15:1–35; 22:1–30; 42:7–8
  - **Zophar toward Job.**
    Job 11:1–6; 20:1–29
  - **Nathanael, when he said, "Can any good thing come out of Nazareth?".**
    Jn 1:46
  - **The Jews, charging Paul with teaching contrary to the law and against the temple.**
    Ac 21:28

UNCIRCUMCISION

Eph 2:11 — Wherefore remember, that ye *being* in time past Gentiles in the flesh, who are called Uncircumcision by that which is called the Circumcision in the flesh made by hands;

• Uncircumcised heart.

Eze 28:10 — Thou shalt die the deaths of the uncircumcised by the hand of strangers: for I have spoken *it,* saith the Lord GOD.

Eze 44:7 — In that ye have brought *into my sanctuary* strangers, uncircumcised in heart, and uncircumcised in flesh, to be in my sanctuary, to pollute it, *even* my house, when ye offer my bread, the fat and the blood, and they have broken my covenant because of all your abominations.

Eze 44:9 — Thus saith the Lord GOD; No stranger, uncircumcised in heart, nor uncircumcised in flesh, shall enter into my sanctuary, of any stranger that *is* among the children of Israel.

UNCLEAN

• Creatures designated as such.

Le 11:1–47; Dt 14:1–29

See: Uncleanness

UNCLEANNESS

Le 5:2–3; 7:20–21; 21:1–15; 22:2–8; Nu 5:2–3; 9:6–11; 19:1–22; Dt 23:10–11

Le 17:15 — And every soul that eateth that which died *of itself,* or that which was torn *with beasts, whether it be* one of your own country, or a stranger, he shall both wash his clothes, and bathe *himself* in water, and be unclean until the even: then shall he be clean.

Nu 31:19 — And do ye abide without the camp seven days: whosoever hath killed any person, and whosoever hath touched any slain, purify *both* yourselves and your captives on the third day, and on the seventh day.

See: Ablution

See: Defilement

See: Purification

See: Sanitation

UNCTION

• Figurative.

1Jn 2:20 — But ye have an unction from the Holy One, and ye know all things.

1Jn 2:27 — But the anointing which ye have received of him abideth in you, and ye need not that any man teach you: but as the same anointing teacheth you of all things, and is truth, and is no lie, and even as it hath taught you, ye shall abide in him.

See: Anointing

UNFAITHFULNESS

Pr 24:11–12; Isa 5:1–7; Hos 10:1–2; Mt 21:19–20, 33–43; 25:1–46; Mk 11:13–14; 12:1–9; Lk 13:6–9; 19:12–27; 2Pe 1:8–9

Mt 3:10 — And now also the axe is laid unto the root of the trees: therefore every tree which bringeth not forth good fruit is hewn down, and cast into the fire.

Mt 13:12 — For whosoever hath, to him shall be given, and he shall have more abundance: but whosoever hath not, from him shall be taken away even that he hath.

Jn 15:2 — Every branch in me that beareth not fruit he taketh away: and every *branch* that beareth fruit, he purgeth it, that it may bring forth more fruit.

See: Sin; fruits of

See: Unfruitfulness

See: Righteousness; fruits of

• Of friends.

See: Friends; false friends

UNFRUITFULNESS

Mt 13:4–7; 21:19–20; Lk 13:6–9

Isa 5:2 — And he fenced it, and gathered out the stones thereof, and planted it with the choicest vine, and built a tower in the midst of it, and also made a winepress therein: and he looked that it should bring forth grapes, and it brought forth wild grapes.

Mt 3:10 — And now also the axe is laid unto the root of the trees: therefore every tree which bringeth not forth good fruit is hewn down, and cast into the fire.

Mt 7:19 — Every tree that bringeth not forth good fruit is hewn down, and cast into the fire.

Mk 11:13 — And seeing a fig tree afar off having leaves, he came, if haply he might find any thing thereon: and when he came to it, he found nothing but leaves; for the time of figs was not *yet.*

Lk 3:9 — And now also the axe is laid unto the root of the trees: every tree therefore which bringeth not forth good fruit is hewn down, and cast into the fire.

Jn 15:2 — Every branch in me that beareth not fruit he taketh away: and every *branch* that beareth fruit, he purgeth it, that it may bring forth more fruit.

Jn 15:4 — Abide in me, and I in you. As the branch cannot bear fruit of itself, except it abide in the vine; no more can ye, except ye abide in me.

Jn 15:6 — If a man abide not in me, he is cast forth as a branch, and is withered; and men gather them, and cast *them* into the fire, and they are burned.

See: Sin; fruits of

See: Unfaithfulness

See: Righteousness; fruits of

UNICORN

• Intractable.

Job 39:9–12

• Horned.

Dt 33:17 — His glory *is like* the firstling of his bullock, and his horns *are like* the horns of unicorns: with them he shall push the people together to the ends of the earth: and they *are* the ten thousands of Ephraim, and they *are* the thousands of Manasseh.

Ps 22:21 — Save me from the lion's mouth: for thou hast heard me from the horns of the unicorns.

Ps 92:10 — But my horn shalt thou exalt like *the horn of* an unicorn: I shall be anointed with fresh oil.

• Great strength of.

Job 39:9–12

Nu 23:22 — God brought them out of Egypt; he hath as it were the strength of an unicorn.

Nu 24:8 — God brought him forth out of Egypt; he hath as it were the strength of an unicorn: he shall eat up the nations his enemies, and shall break their bones, and pierce *them* through with his arrows.

- **Agile.**

Ps 29:6 — He maketh them also to skip like a calf; Lebanon and Sirion like a young unicorn.

- **Figurative.**
  - **Of the judgments of God.**

Isa 34:7 — And the unicorns shall come down with them, and the bullocks with the bulls; and their land shall be soaked with blood, and their dust made fat with fatness.

UNION

- **Advantages of.**

Ecc 4:9–12

Pr 15:22 — Without counsel purposes are disappointed: but in the multitude of counsellors they are established.

- **Of the righteous.**

See: Unity; of the righteous

- **Of the righteous with Christ.**

See: Righteous; promises to, expressed or implied; unity of, with Christ

UNITY

- **Of the Godhead.**

See: God, Unity of

- **Of the righteous.**

Ro 15:5–6; Php 3:16–17

Ps 133:1 — Behold, how good and how pleasant *it is* for brethren to dwell together in unity!

Isa 52:8 — Thy watchmen shall lift up the voice; with the voice together shall they sing: for they shall see eye to eye, when the LORD shall bring again Zion.

Mt 23:8 — But be not ye called Rabbi: for one is your Master, *even* Christ; and all ye are brethren.

Ac 4:32 — And the multitude of them that believed were of one heart and of one soul: neither said any *of them* that ought of the things which he possessed was his own; but they had all things common.

Ro 12:16 — *Be* of the same mind one toward another. Mind not high things, but condescend to men of low estate. Be not wise in your own conceits.

Ro 14:19 — Let us therefore follow after the things which make for peace, and things wherewith one may edify another.

1Co 1:10 — Now I beseech you, brethren, by the name of our Lord Jesus Christ, that ye all speak the same thing, and *that* there be no divisions among you; but *that* ye be perfectly joined together in the same mind and in the same judgment.

2Co 13:11 — Finally, brethren, farewell. Be perfect, be of good comfort, be of one mind, live in peace; and the God of love and peace shall be with you.

Eph 4:3 — Endeavouring to keep the unity of the Spirit in the bond of peace.

Php 1:27 — Only let your conversation be as it becometh the gospel of Christ: that whether I come and see you, or else be absent, I may hear of your affairs, that ye stand fast in one spirit, with one mind striving together for the faith of the gospel;

Php 2:2 — Fulfil ye my joy, that ye be likeminded, having the same love, *being* of one accord, of one mind.

1Pe 3:8 — Finally, *be ye* all of one mind, having compassion one of another, love as brethren, *be* pitiful, *be* courteous:

See: Communion

See: Fellowship

UNLEAVENED BREAD

See: Bread

See: Passover

UNNI

- **A musician in the time of David.**

1Ch 15:18 — And with them their brethren of the second *degree,* Zechariah, Ben, and Jaaziel, and Shemiramoth, and Jehiel, and Unni, Eliab, and Benaiah, and Maaseiah, and Mattithiah, and Elipheleh, and Mikneiah, and Obed-edom, and Jeiel, the porters.

1Ch 15:20 — And Zechariah, and Aziel, and Shemiramoth, and Jehiel, and Unni, and Eliab, and Maaseiah, and Benaiah, with psalteries on Alamoth;

- **A Levite in the time of Nehemiah.**

Ne 12:9 — Also Bakbukiah and Unni, their brethren, *were* over against them in the watches.

UNNO **See: Unni; a Levite in the time of Nehemiah**

UNPARDONABLE SIN

Mt 12:31–32; Heb 6:4–6

2Ki 24:4 — And also for the innocent blood that he shed: for he filled Jerusalem with innocent blood; which the LORD would not pardon.

Lk 12:10 — And whosoever shall speak a word against the Son of man, it shall be forgiven him: but unto him that blasphemeth against the Holy Ghost it shall not be forgiven.

1Jn 5:16 — If any man see his brother sin a sin *which is* not unto death, he shall ask, and he shall give him life for them that sin not unto death. There is a sin unto death: I do not say that he shall pray for it.

See: Obduracy

See: Reprobacy

- **Instances of.**
  - **Israel.**

Nu 14:26–45

  - **Eli's house.**

1Sa 3:14

UNSELFISHNESS

Ro 15:1–3; 1Co 9:19–23; 13:4–5; 2Co 5:14–15; Php 2:3–4

Ro 12:10 — *Be* kindly affectioned one to another with brotherly love; in honour preferring one another;

1Co 10:24 — Let no man seek his own, but every man another's *wealth.*

1Co 10:33 — Even as I please all *men* in all *things,* not seeking mine own profit, but the *profit* of many, that they may be saved.

2Co 8:9 — For ye know the grace of our Lord Jesus Christ, that, though he was rich, yet for your sakes he became poor, that ye through his poverty might be rich.

Jas 2:8 — If ye fulfil the royal law according to the scripture, Thou shalt love thy neighbour as thyself, ye do well:

- **Instances of.**
  - **Abraham.**
    Ge 13:9; 14:23–24
  - **King of Sodom.**
    Ge 14:21
  - **Children of Heth.**
    Ge 23:6, 11
  - **Judah.**
    Ge 44:33–34
  - **Moses.**
    Nu 11:29; 14:12–19
  - **Gideon.**
    Jgs 8:22–23
  - **Saul.**
    1Sa 11:12–13
  - **Jonathan.**
    1Sa 23:17–18
  - **David.**
    1Sa 24:17; 2Sa 15:19–20; 23:16–17; 1Ch 21:17; Ps 69:6
  - **Araunah.**
    2Sa 24:22–24
  - **Nehemiah.**
    Ne 5:14–18
  - **Jews.**
    Est 9:15
  - **Daniel.**
    Da 5:17
  - **Jonah.**
    Jnh 1:12–13
  - **Joseph.**
    Mt 1:19
  - **The disciples.**
    Ac 4:34–35
  - **Priscilla and Aquila.**
    Ro 16:3–4
  - **Paul.**
    1Co 10:33; Php 1:18; 4:17; 2Th 3:8
  - **Philemon.**
    Phm 1:13–14

See: Charitableness
See: Fellowship
See: Fraternity
See: Selfishness

UPHARSIN • Divided.

Da 5:25 — And this *is* the writing that was written, MENE, MENE, TEKEL, UPHARSIN.

Da 5:28 — PERES; Thy kingdom is divided, and given to the Medes and Persians.

UPHAZ

- **A country famous for gold.**

Jer 10:9 — Silver spread into plates is brought from Tarshish, and gold from Uphaz, the work of the workman, and of the hands of the founder: blue and purple is their clothing: they *are* all the work of cunning *men.*

Da 10:5 — Then I lifted up mine eyes, and looked, and behold a certain man clothed in linen, whose loins *were* girded with fine gold of Uphaz:

See: Ophir

UPRIGHTNESS See: Righteousness

UR

- **Abraham's native place.**
  Ge 11:27–28
  - **Abraham leaves.**

Ge 11:31 — And Terah took Abram his son, and Lot the son of Haran his son's son, and Sarai his daughter in law, his son Abram's wife; and they went forth with them from Ur of the Chaldees, to go into the land of Canaan; and they came unto Haran, and dwelt there.

Ge 15:7 — And he said unto him, I *am* the LORD that brought thee out of Ur of the Chaldees, to give thee this land to inherit it.

Ne 9:7 — Thou *art* the LORD the God, who didst choose Abram, and broughtest him forth out of Ur of the Chaldees, and gavest him the name of Abraham;

- **Father of one of David's mighty men.**

1Ch 11:35 — Ahiam the son of Sacar the Hararite, Eliphal the son of Ur,

URBANE • A Christian in Rome.

Ro 16:9 — Salute Urbane, our helper in Christ, and Stachys my beloved.

URIAH

- **One of David's mighty men.**

2Sa 23:39 — Uriah the Hittite: thirty and seven in all.

1Ch 11:41 — Uriah the Hittite, Zabad the son of Ahlai,

  - **David's adultery with the wife of.**
    2Sa 11:2–5

1Ki 15:5 — Because David did *that which was* right in the eyes of the LORD, and turned not aside from any *thing* that he commanded him all the days of his life, save only in the matter of Uriah the Hittite.

  - **Summoned from seat of war by David.**
    2Sa 11:6–13

- **Noble spirit of.**
  2Sa 11:11 — And Uriah said unto David, The ark, and Israel, and Judah, abide in tents; and my lord Joab, and the servants of my lord, are encamped in the open fields; shall I then go into mine house, to eat and to drink, and to lie with my wife? *as* thou livest, and *as* thy soul liveth, I will not do this thing.
- **David compasses the death of.**
  2Sa 11:14–25
- **David marries the widow of.**
  2Sa 11:26–27
- **Called Urias.**
  Mt 1:6 — And Jesse begat David the king; and David the king begat Solomon of her *that had been the wife* of Urias;

• A priest.

- **The father of Meremoth.**
  Ezr 8:33 — Now on the fourth day was the silver and the gold and the vessels weighed in the house of our God by the hand of Meremoth the son of Uriah the priest; and with him *was* Eleazar the son of Phinehas; and with them *was* Jozabad the son of Jeshua, and Noadiah the son of Binnui, Levites;
- **Called Urijah (Uriah in some versions).**
  Ne 3:4 — And next unto them repaired Meremoth the son of Urijah, the son of Koz. And next unto them repaired Meshullam the son of Berechiah, the son of Meshezabeel. And next unto them repaired Zadok the son of Baana.
  Ne 3:21 — After him repaired Meremoth the son of Urijah the son of Koz another piece, from the door of the house of Eliashib even to the end of the house of Eliashib.

See: Urijah; A Priest. Assistant to Ezra

• A priest.

- **Witness to one of Isaiah's prophecies.**
  Isa 8:2 — And I took unto me faithful witnesses to record, Uriah the priest, and Zechariah the son of Jeberechiah.
- **Probably identical with Urijah.**
  2Ki 16:10 — And king Ahaz went to Damascus to meet Tiglath-pileser king of Assyria, and saw an altar that *was* at Damascus: and king Ahaz sent to Urijah the priest the fashion of the altar, and the pattern of it, according to all the workmanship thereof.

See: Urijah; a priest in the time of Ahaz

URIAS See: Uriah; one of David's mighty men

URIEL

• A Levite. Son of Tahath.
1Ch 6:24 — Tahath his son, Uriel his son, Uzziah his son, and Shaul his son.

• A Levite. Assisted in moving the ark.
1Ch 15:11–12
1Ch 15:5 — Of the sons of Kohath; Uriel the chief, and his brethren an hundred and twenty:

• Grandfather of King Abijah.
2Ch 13:2 — He reigned three years in Jerusalem. His mother's name also *was* Michaiah the daughter of Uriel of Gibeah. And there was war between Abijah and Jeroboam.

URIJAH

• A priest in the time of Ahaz.

- **Builds a new altar for Ahaz.**
  2Ki 16:10–16
- **Probably identical with Uriah, witness to a prophecy of Isaiah.**
  Isa 8:2 — And I took unto me faithful witnesses to record, Uriah the priest, and Zechariah the son of Jeberechiah.

See: Uriah; A priest. The father of Meremoth

• A priest.

- **Assistant to Ezra.**
  Ne 8:4 — And Ezra the scribe stood upon a pulpit of wood, which they had made for the purpose; and beside him stood Mattithiah, and Shema, and Anaiah, and Urijah, and Hilkiah, and Maaseiah, on his right hand; and on his left hand, Pedaiah, and Mishael, and Malchiah, and Hashum, and Hashbadana, Zechariah, *and* Meshullam.

• A prophet in the time of Jehoiakim.

- **Prophesies against Judah.**
  Jer 26:20 — And there was also a man that prophesied in the name of the LORD, Urijah the son of Shemaiah of Kirjath-jearim, who prophesied against this city and against this land according to all the words of Jeremiah:
- **Fled to Egypt; taken; slain by Jehoiakim.**
  Jer 26:21–23

URIM AND THUMMIM

• Signifying light and perfection.

• In the breastplate.
Ex 28:30 — And thou shalt put in the breastplate of judgment the Urim and the Thummim; and they shall be upon Aaron's heart, when he goeth in before the LORD: and Aaron shall bear the judgment of the children of Israel upon his heart before the LORD continually.
Le 8:8 — And he put the breastplate upon him: also he put in the breastplate the Urim and the Thummim.

• Eleazar to ask counsel for Joshua, after the judgment of.
Nu 27:21 — And he shall stand before Eleazar the priest, who shall ask *counsel* for him after the judgment of Urim before the LORD: at his word shall they go out, and at his word they shall come in, *both* he, and all the children of Israel with him, even all the congregation.

• **Priests only might interpret.**

Dt 33:8 — And of Levi he said, *Let* thy Thummim and thy Urim *be* with thy holy one, whom thou didst prove at Massah, *and with* whom thou didst strive at the waters of Meribah;

Ezr 2:63 — And the Tirshatha said unto them, that they should not eat of the most holy things, till there stood up a priest with Urim and with Thummim.

Ne 7:65 — And the Tirshatha said unto them, that they should not eat of the most holy things, till there stood *up* a priest with Urim and Thummim.

• **Israelites consult.**

Jgs 1:1 — Now after the death of Joshua it came to pass, that the children of Israel asked the LORD, saying, Who shall go up for us against the Canaanites first, to fight against them?

Jgs 20:18 — And the children of Israel arose, and went up to the house of God, and asked counsel of God, and said, Which of us shall go up first to the battle against the children of Benjamin? And the LORD said, Judah *shall go up* first.

Jgs 20:23 — (And the children of Israel went up and wept before the LORD until even, and asked counsel of the LORD, saying, Shall I go up again to battle against the children of Benjamin my brother? And the LORD said, Go up against him.)

• **Withheld answer from King Saul.**

1Sa 28:6 — And when Saul enquired of the LORD, the LORD answered him not, neither by dreams nor by Urim, nor by prophets.

USURPATION

• **Of political functions.**

• **By Absalom.**

2Sa 15:1–12

• **By Adonijah.**

1Ki 1:5–9

• **By Baasha.**

1Ki 15:27–28

• **By Zimri.**

1Ki 16:9–10

• **By Jehu.**

2Ki 9:11–37

• **By Athaliah.**

2Ki 11:1–16

• **By Shallum.**

2Ki 15:10 — And Shallum the son of Jabesh conspired against him, and smote him before the people, and slew him, and reigned in his stead.

• **In ecclesiastical affairs.**

• **By Saul, in assuming priestly functions.**

1Sa 13:8–14

• **By Solomon, in thrusting Abiathar out of the priesthood.**

1Ki 2:26–27

• **By Uzziah, in assuming priestly offices.**

2Ch 26:16–21

• **By Ahaz.**

2Ki 16:12–13

See: Church and State; state superior to the church

See: Government; ecclesiastical

• **Of executive power.**

• **In ordering Naboth's death and confiscation of his vineyard.**

1Ki 21:7–19

• **In the scheme of Joseph to dispossess the Egyptians of their real and personal property.**

Ge 47:13–26

• **Of Pharaoh, making bondservants of the Israelites.**

Ex 1:9–22

• **Moses accused of.**

Nu 16:3 — And they gathered themselves together against Moses and against Aaron, and said unto them, *Ye take* too much upon you, seeing all the congregation *are* holy, every one of them, and the LORD *is* among them: wherefore then lift ye up yourselves above the congregation of the LORD?

USURY

• **Interest, not necessarily unreasonable exaction, but all income from loans.**

• **Forbidden.**

Le 25:35–37

Ex 22:25 — If thou lend money to *any of* my people *that is* poor by thee, thou shalt not be to him as an usurer, neither shalt thou lay upon him usury.

Dt 23:19 — Thou shalt not lend upon usury to thy brother; usury of money, usury of victuals, usury of any thing that is lent upon usury:

Ps 15:5 — *He that* putteth not out his money to usury, nor taketh reward against the innocent. He that doeth these *things* shall never be moved.

Pr 28:8 — He that by usury and unjust gain increaseth his substance, he shall gather it for him that will pity the poor.

Jer 15:10 — Woe is me, my mother, that thou hast borne me a man of strife and a man of contention to the whole earth! I have neither lent on usury, nor men have lent to me on usury; *yet* every one of them doth curse me.

Eze 18:8 — He *that* hath not given forth upon usury, neither hath taken any increase, *that* hath withdrawn his hand from iniquity, hath executed true judgment between man and man,

Eze 18:13 — Hath given forth upon usury, and hath taken increase: shall he then live? he shall not live: he hath done all these abominations; he shall surely die; his blood shall be upon him.

Eze 18:17 — *That* hath taken off his hand from the poor, *that* hath not received usury nor increase, hath executed my judgments, hath walked in my statutes; he shall not die for the iniquity of his father, he shall surely live.

Eze 22:12 — In thee have they taken gifts to shed blood; thou hast taken usury and increase, and thou hast greedily gained of thy neighbours by extortion, and hast forgotten me, saith the Lord GOD.

- **Exaction of, rebuked.**

Ne 5:1–13

- **Authorized, of strangers.**

Dt 23:20 — Unto a stranger thou mayest lend upon usury; but unto thy brother thou shalt not lend upon usury: that the LORD thy God may bless thee in all that thou settest thine hand to in the land whither thou goest to possess it.

- **Exacted by Jews.**

Eze 22:12 — In thee have they taken gifts to shed blood; thou hast taken usury and increase, and thou hast greedily gained of thy neighbours by extortion, and hast forgotten me, saith the Lord GOD.

- **Just men innocent of the vice of requiring.**

Eze 18:8 — He *that* hath not given forth upon usury, neither hath taken any increase, *that* hath withdrawn his hand from iniquity, hath executed true judgment between man and man,

See: Interest

See: Money

UTHAI

- **Son of Ammihud.**

1Ch 9:4 — Uthai the son of Ammihud, the son of Omri, the son of Imri, the son of Bani, of the children of Pharez the son of Judah.

- **Son of Bigvai.**
  - **Returned from Babylon with Ezra.**

Ezr 8:14 — Of the sons also of Bigvai; Uthai, and Zabbud, and with them seventy males.

UZ

- **Son of Aram.**

Ge 10:23 — And the children of Aram; Uz, and Hul, and Gether, and Mash.

1Ch 1:17 — The sons of Shem; Elam, and Asshur, and Arphaxad, and Lud, and Aram, and Uz, and Hul, and Gether, and Meshech.

- **Son of Nahor (Huz in KJV).**

Ge 2:21 — And the LORD God caused a deep sleep to fall upon Adam and he slept: and he took one of his ribs, and closed up the flesh instead thereof;

  - **In King James Version called Huz.**

Ge 2:21 — And the LORD God caused a deep sleep to fall upon Adam and he slept: and he took one of his ribs, and closed up the flesh instead thereof;

- **Son of Dishan.**

Ge 36:28 — The children of Dishan *are* these: Uz, and Aran.

1Ch 1:42 — The sons of Ezer; Bilhan, and Zavan, *and* Jakan. The sons of Dishan; Uz, and Aran.

- **A country of unknown location.**
  - **Home of Job.**

Job 1:1 — There was a man in the land of Uz, whose name *was* Job; and that man was perfect and upright, and one that feared God, and eschewed evil.

  - **Prophecies concerning.**

Jer 25:20 — And all the mingled people, and all the kings of the land of Uz, and all the kings of the land of the Philistines, and Ashkelon, and Azzah, and Ekron, and the remnant of Ashdod,

La 4:21 — Rejoice and be glad, O daughter of Edom, that dwellest in the land of Uz; the cup also shall pass through unto thee: thou shalt be drunken, and shalt make thyself naked.

UZAI • Father of Palal.

Ne 3:25 — Palal the son of Uzai, over against the turning *of the wall,* and the tower which lieth out from the king's high house, that *was* by the court of the prison. After him Pedaiah the son of Parosh.

UZAL • Son of Joktan.

Ge 10:27 — And Hadoram, and Uzal, and Diklah,

1Ch 1:21 — Hadoram also, and Uzal, and Diklah,

UZZA

See: Uzzah; called also Uzza. Son of Abinadab, driver of the cart in moving the ark

- **Proprietor of the burial place of kings Manasseh and Amon.**

2Ki 21:18 — And Manasseh slept with his fathers, and was buried in the garden of his own house, in the garden of Uzza: and Amon his son reigned in his stead.

2Ki 21:26 — And he was buried in his sepulchre in the garden of Uzza: and Josiah his son reigned in his stead.

- **Son of Shimei (Uzzah in some versions).**

1Ch 6:29 — The sons of Merari; Mahli, Libni his son, Shimei his son, Uzza his son,

- **Son of Ehud.**

1Ch 8:7 — And Naaman, and Ahiah, and Gera, he removed them, and begat Uzza, and Ahihud.

- **One of the Nethinim.**

Ezr 2:49 — The children of Uzza, the children of Paseah, the children of Besai,

Ne 7:51 — The children of Gazzam, the children of Uzza, the children of Phaseah,

UZZAH

- **Called also Uzza.**
  - **Son of Abinadab and a driver of the cart in moving the ark.**

2Sa 6:3 — And they set the ark of God upon a new cart, and brought it out of the house of Abinadab that *was* in Gibeah: and Uzzah and Ahio, the sons of Abinadab, drave the new cart.

1Ch 13:7 — And they carried the ark of God in a new cart out of the house of Abinadab: and Uzza and Ahio drave the cart.

• Stricken dead for touching the ark.

2Sa 6:6–8; 1Ch 13:9–11

See: Uzza; son of Shimei

UZZEN-SHERAH • A city of unknown location.

1Ch 7:24 — (And his daughter *was* Sherah, who built Beth-horon the nether, and the upper, and Uzzen-sherah.)

UZZI

• A priest.

• Son of Bukki.

1Ch 6:5–6

1Ch 6:51 — Bukki his son, Uzzi his son, Zerahiah his son,

Ezr 7:4 — The son of Zerahiah, the son of Uzzi, the son of Bukki,

• Grandson of Issachar.

1Ch 7:2–3

• Grandson of Benjamin.

1Ch 7:7 — And the sons of Bela; Ezbon, and Uzzi, and Uzziel, and Jerimoth, and Iri, five; heads of the house of *their* fathers, mighty men of valour; and were reckoned by their genealogies twenty and two thousand and thirty and four.

• Son of Michri.

1Ch 9:8 — And Ibneiah the son of Jeroham, and Elah the son of Uzzi, the son of Michri, and Meshullam the son of Shephatiah, the son of Reuel, the son of Ibnijah;

• An overseer of the Levites.

Ne 11:22 — The overseer also of the Levites at Jerusalem *was* Uzzi the son of Bani, the son of Hashabiah, the son of Mattaniah, the son of Micha. Of the sons of Asaph, the singers *were* over the business of the house of God.

• A priest in the time of Nehemiah.

Ne 12:19 — And of Joiarib, Mattenai; of Jedaiah, Uzzi;

Ne 12:42 — And Maaseiah, and Shemaiah, and Eleazar, and Uzzi, and Jehohanan, and Malchijah, and Elam, and Ezer. And the singers sang loud, with Jezrahiah *their* overseer.

UZZIA • One of David's mighty men.

1Ch 11:44 — Uzzia the Ashterathite, Shama and Jehiel the sons of Hothan the Aroerite,

UZZIAH

• King of Judah.

2Ki 15:1–2

2Ch 26:1 — Then all the people of Judah took Uzziah, who *was* sixteen years old, and made him king in the room of his father Amaziah.

2Ch 26:3 — Sixteen years old *was* Uzziah when he began to reign, and he reigned fifty and two years in Jerusalem. His mother's name also was Jecoliah of Jerusalem.

• Called Azariah.

2Ki 14:21 — And all the people of Judah took Azariah, which *was* sixteen years old, and made him king instead of his father Amaziah.

• Rebuilds Elath.

2Ki 14:22 — He built Elath, and restored it to Judah, after that the king slept with his fathers.

2Ch 26:2 — He built Eloth, and restored it to Judah, after that the king slept with his fathers.

• Reigns righteously.

2Ch 26:4–5

2Ki 15:3 — And he did *that which was* right in the sight of the LORD, according to all that his father Amaziah had done;

• Defeats the Philistines.

2Ch 26:6–7

• Takes tribute from the Ammonites; strengthens the kingdom.

2Ch 26:8 — And the Ammonites gave gifts to Uzziah: and his name spread abroad *even* to the entering in of Egypt; for he strengthened *himself* exceedingly.

• Strengthens the fortifications of Jerusalem.

2Ch 26:9 — Moreover Uzziah built towers in Jerusalem at the corner gate, and at the valley gate, and at the turning *of the wall,* and fortified them.

• Promotes cattle raising and agriculture.

2Ch 26:10 — Also he built towers in the desert, and digged many wells: for he had much cattle, both in the low country, and in the plains: husbandmen *also,* and vine dressers in the mountains, and in Carmel: for he loved husbandry.

• Military establishment of.

2Ch 26:11–15

• Is presumptuous in burning incense; stricken with leprosy; quarantined.

2Ch 26:16–21

2Ki 15:5 — And the LORD smote the king, so that he was a leper unto the day of his death, and dwelt in a several house. And Jotham the king's son *was* over the house, judging the people of the land.

• Jotham regent during quarantine of.

2Ki 15:5 — And the LORD smote the king, so that he was a leper unto the day of his death, and dwelt in a several house. And Jotham the king's son *was* over the house, judging the people of the land.

2Ch 26:21 — And Uzziah the king was a leper unto the day of his death, and dwelt in a several house, *being* a leper; for he was cut off from the house of the LORD: and Jotham his son *was* over the king's house, judging the people of the land.

• Death of.

2Ki 15:7 — So Azariah slept with his fathers; and they buried him with his fathers in the city of David: and Jotham his son reigned in his stead.

2Ch 26:23 — So Uzziah slept with his fathers, and they buried him with his fathers in the field of the burial which *belonged* to the kings; for they said, He *is* a leper: and Jotham his son reigned in his stead.

• **History of, written by Isaiah.**

2Ch 26:22 — Now the rest of the acts of Uzziah, first and last, did Isaiah the prophet, the son of Amoz, write.

Isa 1:1 — The vision of Isaiah the son of Amoz, which he saw concerning Judah and Jerusalem in the days of Uzziah, Jotham, Ahaz, *and* Hezekiah, kings of Judah.

• **Earthquake in the reign of.**

Am 1:1 — The words of Amos, who was among the herdmen of Tekoa, which he saw concerning Israel in the days of Uzziah king of Judah, and in the days of Jeroboam the son of Joash king of Israel, two years before the earthquake.

Zec 14:5 — And ye shall flee *to* the valley of the mountains; for the valley of the mountains shall reach unto Azal: yea, ye shall flee, like as ye fled from before the earthquake in the days of Uzziah king of Judah: and the LORD my God shall come, *and* all the saints with thee.

• **Son of Uriel.**

1Ch 6:24 — Tahath his son, Uriel his son, Uzziah his son, and Shaul his son.

• **Father of Jehonathan.**

1Ch 27:25 — And over the king's treasures *was* Azmaveth the son of Adiel: and over the storehouses in the fields, in the cities, and in the villages, and in the castles, *was* Jehonathan the son of Uzziah:

• **A priest.**

• **Puts away his Gentile wife.**

Ezr 10:21 — And of the sons of Harim; Maaseiah, and Elijah, and Shemaiah, and Jehiel, and Uzziah.

• **Father of Athaiah.**

Ne 11:4 — And at Jerusalem dwelt *certain* of the children of Judah, and of the children of Benjamin. Of the children of Judah; Athaiah the son of Uzziah, the son of Zechariah, the son of Amariah, the son of Shephatiah, the son of Mahalaleel, of the children of Perez;

UZZIEL • A son of Kohath.

Ex 6:18 — And the sons of Kohath; Amram, and Izhar, and Hebron, and Uzziel: and the years of the life of Kohath *were* an hundred thirty and three years.

Ex 6:22 — And the sons of Uzziel; Mishael, and Elzaphan, and Zithri.

Le 10:4 — And Moses called Mishael and Elzaphan, the sons of Uzziel the uncle of Aaron, and said unto them, Come near, carry your brethren from before the sanctuary out of the camp.

• **A Simeonite captain.**

1Ch 4:42 — And *some* of them, *even* of the sons of Simeon, five hundred men, went to mount Seir, having for their captains Pelatiah, and Neariah, and Rephaiah, and Uzziel, the sons of Ishi.

• **Son of Bela.**

1Ch 7:7 — And the sons of Bela; Ezbon, and Uzzi, and Uzziel, and Jerimoth, and Iri, five; heads of the house of *their* fathers, mighty men of valour; and were reckoned by their genealogies twenty and two thousand and thirty and four.

• **One of David's musicians.**

1Ch 25:4 — Of Heman: the sons of Heman; Bukkiah, Mattaniah, Uzziel, Shebuel, and Jerimoth, Hananiah, Hanani, Eliathah, Giddalti, and Romamti-ezer, Joshbekashah, Mallothi, Hothir, *and* Mahazioth:

• **A Levite.**

• **Son of Jeduthun.**

2Ch 29:14 — And of the sons of Heman; Jehiel, and Shimei: and of the sons of Jeduthun; Shemaiah, and Uzziel.

• **A goldsmith.**

• **Aided in repairing the walls of Jerusalem.**

Ne 3:8 — Next unto him repaired Uzziel the son of Harhaiah, of the goldsmiths. Next unto him also repaired Hananiah the son of *one of* the apothecaries, and they fortified Jerusalem unto the broad wall.

V

VAIL

• Hangings.

• Used in the tabernacle to divide the Holy of Holies from the Holy Place; called the second veil.

Heb 3:1–19; 9:1–28

Heb 6:19 — Which *hope* we have as an anchor of the soul, both sure and stedfast, and which entereth into that within the veil;

• Ordinances prescribing.

Ex 26:31–33

• Made by Bezaleel and Aholiab.

Ex 36:35–36

→See: Veil

• A covering for the ark.

Ex 35:12 — The ark, and the staves thereof, *with* the mercy seat, and the vail of the covering,

Ex 39:34 — And the covering of rams' skins dyed red, and the covering of badgers' skins, and the vail of the covering,

Ex 40:21 — And he brought the ark into the tabernacle, and set up the vail of the covering, and covered the ark of the testimony; as the LORD commanded Moses.

Nu 4:5 — And when the camp setteth forward, Aaron shall come, and his sons, and they shall take down the covering vail, and cover the ark of testimony with it:

• Of the temple.

2Ch 3:14 — And he made the vail *of* blue, and purple, and crimson, and fine linen, and wrought cherubims thereon.

• Rent at the time of the crucifixion of Jesus.

Mt 27:51 — And, behold, the veil of the temple was rent in twain from the top to the bottom; and the earth did quake, and the rocks rent;

Mk 15:38 — And the veil of the temple was rent in twain from the top to the bottom.

Lk 23:45 — And the sun was darkened, and the veil of the temple was rent in the midst.

• Figurative.

Heb 10:20 — By a new and living way, which he hath consecrated for us, through the veil, that is to say, his flesh;

VAJEZATHA • Son of Haman.

Est 9:9 — And Parmashta, and Arisai, and Aridai, and Vajezatha,

VALOR →See: Courage

VALUES

Ps 119:9 — Wherewithal shall a young man cleanse his way? by taking heed *thereto* according to thy word.

Mt 10:31 — Fear ye not therefore, ye are of more value than many sparrows.

2Ti 3:15 — And that from a child thou hast known the holy scriptures, which are able to make thee wise unto salvation through faith which is in Christ Jesus.

VANIAH

• An Israelite.

• Puts away his Gentile wife.

Ezr 10:36 — Vaniah, Meremoth, Eliashib,

VANITY

• A consequence of the fall.

Ro 8:20 — For the creature was made subject to vanity, not willingly, but by reason of him who hath subjected *the same* in hope,

• Every man is.

Ps 39:11 — When thou with rebukes dost correct man for iniquity, thou makest his beauty to consume away like a moth: surely every man *is* vanity. Selah.

• Every state of man is.

Ps 62:9 — Surely men of low degree *are* vanity, *and* men of high degree *are* a lie: to be laid in the balance, they *are* altogether *lighter* than vanity.

• Man at his best estate is.

Ps 39:5 — Behold, thou hast made my days *as* an handbreadth; and mine age *is* as nothing before thee: verily every man at his best state *is* altogether vanity. Selah.

• Man is like to.

Ps 144:4 — Man is like to vanity: his days *are* as a shadow that passeth away.

• The thoughts of man are.

Ps 94:11 — The LORD knoweth the thoughts of man, that they *are* vanity.

• The days of man are.

Job 7:16 — I loathe *it;* I would not live alway: let me alone; for my days *are* vanity.

Ecc 6:12 — For who knoweth what *is* good for man in *this* life, all the days of his vain life which he spendeth as a shadow? for who can tell a man what shall be after him under the sun?

• Childhood and youth are.

Ecc 11:10 — Therefore remove sorrow from thy heart, and put away evil from thy flesh: for childhood and youth *are* vanity.

• The beauty of man is.

Ps 39:11 — When thou with rebukes dost correct man for iniquity, thou makest his beauty to consume away like a moth: surely every man *is* vanity. Selah.

Pr 31:30 — Favour *is* deceitful, and beauty *is* vain: *but* a woman *that* feareth the LORD, she shall be praised.

- **The help of man is.**

Ps 60:11 — Give us help from trouble: for vain *is* the help of man.

La 4:17 — As for us, our eyes as yet failed for our vain help: in our watching we have watched for a nation *that* could not save *us*.

- **Man's own righteousness is.**

Isa 57:12 — I will declare thy righteousness, and thy works; for they shall not profit thee.

- **Worldly wisdom is.**

Ecc 2:15 — Then said I in my heart, As it happeneth to the fool, so it happeneth even to me; and why was I then more wise? Then I said in my heart, that this also *is* vanity.

Ecc 2:21 — For there is a man whose labour *is* in wisdom, and in knowledge, and in equity; yet to a man that hath not laboured therein shall he leave it *for* his portion. This also *is* vanity and a great evil.

1Co 3:20 — And again, The Lord knoweth the thoughts of the wise, that they are vain.

- **Worldly pleasure is.**

Ecc 2:1 — I said in mine heart, Go to now, I will prove thee with mirth, therefore enjoy pleasure: and, behold, this also *is* vanity.

- **Worldly anxiety is.**

Ps 39:6 — Surely every man walketh in a vain shew: surely they are disquieted in vain: he heapeth up *riches,* and knoweth not who shall gather them.

Ps 127:2 — *It is* vain for you to rise up early, to sit up late, to eat the bread of sorrows: *for* so he giveth his beloved sleep.

- **Worldly labor is.**

Ecc 2:11 — Then I looked on all the works that my hands had wrought, and on the labour that I had laboured to do: and, behold, all *was* vanity and vexation of spirit, and *there was* no profit under the sun.

Ecc 4:4 — Again, I considered all travail, and every right work, that for this a man is envied of his neighbour. This *is* also vanity and vexation of spirit.

- **Worldly enjoyment is.**

Ecc 2:10–11

Ecc 2:3 — I sought in mine heart to give myself unto wine, yet acquainting mine heart with wisdom; and to lay hold on folly, till I might see what *was* that good for the sons of men, which they should do under the heaven all the days of their life.

- **Worldly possessions are.**

Ecc 2:4–11

- **Treasures of wickedness are.**

Pr 10:2 — Treasures of wickedness profit nothing: but righteousness delivereth from death.

- **Heaping up riches is.**

Ecc 2:26 — For *God* giveth to a man that *is* good in his sight wisdom, and knowledge, and joy: but to the sinner he giveth travail, to gather and to heap up, that he may give to *him that is* good before God. This also *is* vanity and vexation of spirit.

Ecc 4:8 — There is one *alone,* and *there is* not a second; yea, he hath neither child nor brother: yet *is there* no end of all his labour; neither is his eye satisfied with riches; neither *saith he,* For whom do I labour, and bereave my soul of good? This *is* also vanity, yea, it *is* a sore travail.

- **Love of riches is.**

Ecc 5:10 — He that loveth silver shall not be satisfied with silver; nor he that loveth abundance with increase: this *is* also vanity.

- **Unblessed riches are.**

Ecc 6:2 — A man to whom God hath given riches, wealth, and honour, so that he wanteth nothing for his soul of all that he desireth, yet God giveth him not power to eat thereof, but a stranger eateth it: this *is* vanity, and it *is* an evil disease.

- **Riches gotten by falsehood are.**

Pr 21:6 — The getting of treasures by a lying tongue *is* a vanity tossed to and fro of them that seek death.

- **All earthly things are.**

Ecc 1:2 — Vanity of vanities, saith the Preacher, vanity of vanities; all *is* vanity.

- **Foolish questions are.**

1Ti 1:6–7

1Ti 6:20 — O Timothy, keep that which is committed to thy trust, avoiding profane *and* vain babblings, and oppositions of science falsely so called:

2Ti 2:14 — Of these things put *them* in remembrance, charging *them* before the Lord that they strive not about words to no profit, *but* to the subverting of the hearers.

2Ti 2:16 — But shun profane *and* vain babblings: for they will increase unto more ungodliness.

Tit 3:9 — But avoid foolish questions, and genealogies, and contentions, and strivings about the law; for they are unprofitable and vain.

- **The conduct of the ungodly is.**

1Pe 1:18 — Forasmuch as ye know that ye were not redeemed with corruptible things, *as* silver and gold, from your vain conversation *received* by tradition from your fathers;

- **The religion of hypocrites is.**

Jas 1:26 — If any man among you seem to be religious, and bridleth not his tongue, but deceiveth his own heart, this man's religion *is* vain.

- **The worship of the wicked is.**

Isa 1:13 — Bring no more vain oblations; incense is an abomination unto me; the new moons and sabbaths, the calling of assemblies, I cannot away with; *it is* iniquity, even the solemn meeting.

Mt 6:7 — But when ye pray, use not vain repetitions, as the heathen *do:* for they think that they shall be heard for their much speaking.

- **Lying words are.**

Jer 7:8 — Behold, ye trust in lying words, that cannot profit.

- **False teaching is but.**

Jer 23:32 — Behold, I *am* against them that prophesy false dreams, saith the LORD, and do tell them, and cause my people to err by their lies, and by their lightness; yet I sent them not, nor commanded them: therefore they shall not profit this people at all, saith the LORD.

• Mere external religion is.

1Ti 4:8 — For bodily exercise profiteth little: but godliness is profitable unto all things, having promise of the life that now is, and of that which is to come.

Heb 13:9 — Be not carried about with divers and strange doctrines. For *it is* a good thing that the heart be established with grace; not with meats, which have not profited them that have been occupied therein.

• Almsgiving without charity is.

1Co 13:3 — And though I bestow all my goods to feed *the poor,* and though I give my body to be burned, and have not charity, it profiteth me nothing.

• Faith without works is.

Jas 2:14 — What *doth it* profit, my brethren, though a man say he hath faith, and have not works? can faith save him?

• Idolatry is.

Isa 44:9–10

2Ki 17:15 — And they rejected his statutes, and his covenant that he made with their fathers, and his testimonies which he testified against them; and they followed vanity, and became vain, and went after the heathen that *were* round about them, *concerning* whom the LORD had charged them, that they should not do like them.

Ps 31:6 — I have hated them that regard lying vanities: but I trust in the LORD.

Jer 10:8 — But they are altogether brutish and foolish: the stock *is* a doctrine of vanities.

Jer 18:15 — Because my people hath forgotten me, they have burned incense to vanity, and they have caused them to stumble in their ways *from* the ancient paths, to walk in paths, *in* a way not cast up;

• Wealth gotten by, diminishes.

Pr 13:11 — Wealth *gotten* by vanity shall be diminished: but he that gathereth by labour shall increase.

• Saints hate the thoughts of.

Ps 119:113 — I hate *vain* thoughts: but thy law do I love.

• Saints pray to be kept from.

Ps 119:37 — Turn away mine eyes from beholding vanity; *and* quicken thou me in thy way.

Pr 30:8 — Remove far from me vanity and lies: give me neither poverty nor riches; feed me with food convenient for me:

• Saints avoid.

Ps 24:4 — He that hath clean hands, and a pure heart; who hath not lifted up his soul unto vanity, nor sworn deceitfully.

• Saints avoid those given to.

Ps 26:4 — I have not sat with vain persons, neither will I go in with dissemblers.

• The wicked especially characterized by.

Job 11:11 — For he knoweth vain men: he seeth wickedness also; will he not then consider *it?*

• The wicked though full of, affect to be wise.

Job 11:12 — For vain man would be wise, though man be born *like* a wild ass's colt.

• The wicked love.

Ps 4:2 — O ye sons of men, how long *will ye turn* my glory into shame? *how long* will ye love vanity, *and* seek after leasing? Selah.

• The wicked imagine.

Ps 2:1 — Why do the heathen rage, and the people imagine a vain thing?

Ac 4:25 — Who by the mouth of thy servant David hast said, Why did the heathen rage, and the people imagine vain things?

Ro 1:21 — Because that, when they knew God, they glorified *him* not as God, neither were thankful; but became vain in their imaginations, and their foolish heart was darkened.

• The wicked devise.

Ps 36:4 — He deviseth mischief upon his bed; he setteth himself in a way *that is* not good; he abhorreth not evil.

• The wicked speak.

Ps 10:7 — His mouth is full of cursing and deceit and fraud: under his tongue *is* mischief and vanity.

Ps 12:2 — They speak vanity every one with his neighbour: *with* flattering lips *and* with a double heart do they speak.

Ps 41:6 — And if he come to see *me,* he speaketh vanity: his heart gathereth iniquity to itself; *when* he goeth abroad, he telleth *it.*

• The wicked count God's service as.

Job 21:15 — What *is* the Almighty, that we should serve him? and what profit should we have, if we pray unto him?

Mal 3:14 — Ye have said, It *is* vain to serve God: and what profit *is it* that we have kept his ordinance, and that we have walked mournfully before the LORD of hosts?

• The wicked allure others by words of.

2Pe 2:18 — For when they speak great swelling *words* of vanity, they allure through the lusts of the flesh, *through much* wantonness, those that were clean escaped from them who live in error.

• The wicked walk after.

Jer 2:5 — Thus saith the LORD, What iniquity have your fathers found in me, that they are gone far from me, and have walked after vanity, and are become vain?

• The wicked walk in.

Ps 39:6 — Surely every man walketh in a vain shew: surely they are disquieted in vain: he heapeth up *riches,* and knoweth not who shall gather them.

Eph 4:17 — This I say therefore, and testify in the Lord, that ye henceforth walk not as other Gentiles walk, in the vanity of their mind,

• The wicked inherit.

Jer 16:19 — O LORD, my strength, and my fortress, and my refuge in the day of affliction, the Gentiles shall come unto thee from the ends of the earth, and shall say, Surely our fathers have inherited lies, vanity, and *things* wherein *there is* no profit.

- **The wicked reap.**

Pr 22:8 — He that soweth iniquity shall reap vanity: and the rod of his anger shall fail.

Jer 12:13 — They have sown wheat, but shall reap thorns: they have put themselves to pain, *but* shall not profit: and they shall be ashamed of your revenues because of the fierce anger of the LORD.

- **The wicked judicially given up to.**

Ps 78:33 — Therefore their days did he consume in vanity, and their years in trouble.

Isa 57:13 — When thou criest, let thy companies deliver thee; but the wind shall carry them all away; vanity shall take *them:* but he that putteth his trust in me shall possess the land, and shall inherit my holy mountain;

- **Fools follow those given to.**

Pr 12:11 — He that tilleth his land shall be satisfied with bread: but he that followeth vain *persons is* void of understanding.

- **Following those given to, leads to poverty.**

Pr 28:19 — He that tilleth his land shall have plenty of bread: but he that followeth after vain *persons* shall have poverty enough.

- **All should know and acknowledge.**

Dt 4:35 — Unto thee it was shewed, that thou mightest know that the LORD he *is* God; *there is* none else beside him.

See: Pride

VASHNI **See: Joel**

VASHTI

- **Wife of king Ahasuerus.**
- **Put away for refusing to exhibit herself at a royal banquet.**

Est 1:9–2:1

Est 2:4 — And let the maiden which pleaseth the king be queen instead of Vashti. And the thing pleased the king; and he did so.

Est 2:17 — And the king loved Esther above all the women, and she obtained grace and favour in his sight more than all the virgins; so that he set the royal crown upon her head, and made her queen instead of Vashti.

VEDAN

- **Called Dan in King James Version.**
- **A place whose merchants traded with Tyre.**

Eze 27:19 — Dan also and Javan going to and fro occupied in thy fairs: bright iron, cassia, and calamus, were in thy market.

VEGETARIANS

- **Persons who eat no flesh.**

Ro 14:2 — For one believeth that he may eat all things: another, who is weak, eateth herbs.

VEGETATION

- **Created the third day.**

Ge 1:11 — And God said, Let the earth bring forth grass, the herb yielding seed, *and* the fruit tree yielding fruit after his kind, whose seed *is* in itself, upon the earth: and it was so.

Ge 2:5 — And every plant of the field before it was in the earth, and every herb of the field before it grew: for the LORD God had not caused it to rain upon the earth, and *there was* not a man to till the ground.

- **For food.**

Ge 1:29–30

VEIL

- **Worn by Rebekah.**

Ge 24:65 — For she *had* said unto the servant, What man *is* this that walketh in the field to meet us? And the servant *had* said, It *is* my master: therefore she took a vail, and covered herself.

- **Worn by Tamar.**

Ge 38:14 — And she put her widow's garments off from her, and covered her with a vail, and wrapped herself, and sat in an open place, which *is* by the way to Timnath; for she saw that Shelah was grown, and she was not given unto him to wife.

Ge 38:19 — And she arose, and went away, and laid by her vail from her, and put on the garments of her widowhood.

- **Worn by Moses, to screen his face when he descended from Mount Sinai.**

2Co 3:13–16

Ex 34:33 — And *till* Moses had done speaking with them, he put a vail on his face.

Ex 34:35 — And the children of Israel saw the face of Moses, that the skin of Moses' face shone: and Moses put the vail upon his face again, until he went in to speak with him.

See: Dress

See: Vail

See: Wimple

VENERATION

- **For parents.**

Ge 48:15–16

See: Old Age

See: Parents

See: Reverence

VENGEANCE

- **Belongs to God.**

Ps 94:1 — O LORD God, to whom vengeance belongeth; O God, to whom vengeance belongeth, shew thyself.

Ro 12:19 — Dearly beloved, avenge not yourselves, but *rather* give place unto wrath: for it is written, Vengeance *is* mine; I will repay, saith the Lord.

- **Instances of.**
  - **Sons of Jacob on Hamor and Shechem.**

Ge 34:20–31

✦See: **Judgments**

✦See: **Revenge**

✦See: **Retaliation**

VERDICT

• Against Jesus.

Mt 27:24–26

Mt 26:66 — What think ye? They answered and said, He is guilty of death.

Mk 15:15 — And *so* Pilate, willing to content the people, released Barabbas unto them, and delivered Jesus, when he had scourged *him,* to be crucified.

Lk 23:24 — And Pilate gave sentence that it should be as they required.

Jn 19:16 — Then delivered he him therefore unto them to be crucified. And they took Jesus, and led *him* away.

✦See: **Court**

VERMILION

• A color.

Jer 22:14 — That saith, I will build me a wide house and large chambers, and cutteth him out windows; and *it is* cieled with cedar, and painted with vermilion.

Eze 23:14 — And *that* she increased her whoredoms: for when she saw men pourtrayed upon the wall, the images of the Chaldeans pourtrayed with vermilion,

✦See: **Colors**

VESTMENTS

• Of priests.

✦See: **Priest, High**

✦See: **Priest, Mosaic**

VICARIOUS

• Death.

• The ram for Isaac.

Ge 22:13 — And Abraham lifted up his eyes, and looked, and behold behind *him* a ram caught in a thicket by his horns: and Abraham went and took the ram, and offered him up for a burnt offering in the stead of his son.

• Jesus for sinners.

✦See: **Jesus, Death of**

✦See: **Jesus, Mission of**

✦See: **Jesus, Sufferings of**

✦See: **Atonement**

✦See: **Jesus, Saviour**

✦See: **Suffering; vicarious**

VICEGERENCY

• Of Elisha, in miraculously rewarding the Shunammite.

2Ki 4:16–17

• Of Elisha, in cursing Gehazi.

2Ki 5:27 — The leprosy therefore of Naaman shall cleave unto thee, and unto thy seed for ever. And he went out from his presence a leper *as white* as snow.

• Of the apostles.

Mt 16:19 — And I will give unto thee the keys of the kingdom of heaven: and whatsoever thou shalt bind on earth shall be bound in heaven: and whatsoever thou shalt loose on earth shall be loosed in heaven.

Mt 18:18 — Verily I say unto you, Whatsoever ye shall bind on earth shall be bound in heaven: and whatsoever ye shall loose on earth shall be loosed in heaven.

Jn 20:23 — Whose soever sins ye remit, they are remitted unto them; *and* whose soever *sins* ye retain, they are retained.

VICTORIES

• In battle, from God.

Ps 76:5–6

Ps 55:18 — He hath delivered my soul in peace from the battle *that was* against me: for there were many with me.

• Celebrated in song.

Jgs 5:1–31; 2Sa 22:1–51

• Celebrated by women.

1Sa 18:6–7

2Sa 1:20 — Tell *it* not in Gath, publish *it* not in the streets of Askelon; lest the daughters of the Philistines rejoice, lest the daughters of the uncircumcised triumph.

✦See: **Armies**

✦See: **War; God in**

VICTORY

1Sa 30:1–31

Jn 16:33 — These things I have spoken unto you, that in me ye might have peace. In the world ye shall have tribulation: but be of good cheer; I have overcome the world.

Ro 8:37 — Nay, in all these things we are more than conquerors through him that loved us.

2Co 2:14 — Now thanks *be* unto God, which always causeth us to triumph in Christ, and maketh manifest the savour of his knowledge by us in every place.

1Jn 4:4 — Ye are of God, little children, and have overcome them: because greater is he that is in you, than he that is in the world.

VIGILANCE

• Instances of.

• King of Jericho.

Jos 2:1–3

✦See: **Watchman**

VINE

• Degeneracy of.

Jer 2:21 — Yet I had planted thee a noble vine, wholly a right seed: how then art thou turned into the degenerate plant of a strange vine unto me?

• **Fable of.**

Jgs 9:12–13

• **Pruned.**

Jn 15:1–5

Isa 5:6 — And I will lay it waste: it shall not be pruned, nor digged; but there shall come up briers and thorns: I will also command the clouds that they rain no rain upon it.

• **Parables of.**

Ps 80:8–14; Eze 17:6–10; 19:10–14

• **Symbolic.**

Jn 15:1–5

See: Vineyard

VINEGAR

• **A sour wine.**

• **Forbidden to Nazarites.**

Nu 6:3 — He shall separate *himself* from wine and strong drink, and shall drink no vinegar of wine, or vinegar of strong drink, neither shall he drink any liquor of grapes, nor eat moist grapes, or dried.

• **Used with food.**

Ru 2:14 — And Boaz said unto her, At mealtime come thou hither, and eat of the bread, and dip thy morsel in the vinegar. And she sat beside the reapers: and he reached her parched *corn,* and she did eat, and was sufficed, and left.

Ps 69:21 — They gave me also gall for my meat; and in my thirst they gave me vinegar to drink.

Pr 10:26 — As vinegar to the teeth, and as smoke to the eyes, so *is* the sluggard to them that send him.

Pr 25:20 — *As* he that taketh away a garment in cold weather, *and as* vinegar upon nitre, so *is* he that singeth songs to an heavy heart.

• **Offered to Christ on the cross.**

Mt 27:34 — They gave him vinegar to drink mingled with gall: and when he had tasted *thereof,* he would not drink.

Mt 27:48 — And straightway one of them ran, and took a spunge, and filled *it* with vinegar, and put *it* on a reed, and gave him to drink.

Mk 15:23 — And they gave him to drink wine mingled with myrrh: but he received *it* not.

Jn 19:29 — Now there was set a vessel full of vinegar: and they filled a spunge with vinegar, and put *it* upon hyssop, and put *it* to his mouth.

VINEYARD

• **Cottages in.**

Isa 1:8 — And the daughter of Zion is left as a cottage in a vineyard, as a lodge in a garden of cucumbers, as a besieged city.

• **Towers in.**

Isa 5:2 — And he fenced it, and gathered out the stones thereof, and planted it with the choicest vine, and built a tower in the midst of it, and also made a winepress therein: and he looked that it should bring forth grapes, and it brought forth wild grapes.

Mt 21:33 — Hear another parable: There was a certain householder, which planted a vineyard, and hedged it round about, and digged a winepress in it, and built a tower, and let it out to husbandmen, and went into a far country:

Mk 12:1 — And he began to speak unto them by parables. A certain *man* planted a vineyard, and set an hedge about *it,* and digged *a place for* the winefat, and built a tower, and let it out to husbandmen, and went into a far country.

• **Winepress in.**

Isa 5:2 — And he fenced it, and gathered out the stones thereof, and planted it with the choicest vine, and built a tower in the midst of it, and also made a winepress therein: and he looked that it should bring forth grapes, and it brought forth wild grapes.

• **Pools in.**

Ecc 2:4 — I made me great works; I builded me houses; I planted me vineyards:

Ecc 2:6 — I made me pools of water, to water therewith the wood that bringeth forth trees:

• **Leased.**

SS 8:11–12; Mt 21:33–39

Isa 7:23 — And it shall come to pass in that day, *that* every place shall be, where there were a thousand vines at a thousand silverlings, it shall *even* be for briers and thorns.

• **Of kings.**

1Ch 27:26–28

• **Neglected.**

Pr 24:30–31

• **Plain of the.**

Jgs 11:33 — And he smote them from Aroer, even till thou come to Minnith, *even* twenty cities, and unto the plain of the vineyards, with a very great slaughter. Thus the children of Ammon were subdued before the children of Israel.

• **Parables of.**

Isa 5:1–7; 27:2–3; Mt 20:1–16; 21:28–31, 33–41; Lk 13:6–9

Jer 12:10 — Many pastors have destroyed my vineyard, they have trodden my portion under foot, they have made my pleasant portion a desolate wilderness.

See: Vine

See: Wine

See: Abstinence, Total

VIOL

• **An instrument of music.**

Isa 5:12 — And the harp, and the viol, the tabret, and pipe, and wine, are in their feasts: but they regard not the work of the LORD, neither consider the operation of his hands.

See: Music; instruments of

See: Psaltery

VIOLENCE

Ge 6:11 — The earth also was corrupt before God, and the earth was filled with violence.

Isa 53:9 — And he made his grave with the wicked, and with the rich in his death; because he had done no violence, neither *was any* deceit in his mouth.

Eze 45:9 — Thus saith the Lord GOD; Let it suffice you, O princes of Israel: remove violence and spoil, and execute judgment and justice, take away your exactions from my people, saith the Lord GOD.

Jn 3:8 — The wind bloweth where it listeth, and thou hearest the sound thereof, but canst not tell whence it cometh, and whither it goeth: so is every one that is born of the Spirit.

VIPER

• A serpent.

Job 20:16 — He shall suck the poison of asps: the viper's tongue shall slay him.

Isa 30:6 — The burden of the beasts of the south: into the land of trouble and anguish, from whence *come* the young and old lion, the viper and fiery flying serpent, they will carry their riches upon the shoulders of young asses, and their treasures upon the bunches of camels, to a people *that* shall not profit *them*.

Isa 59:5 — They hatch cockatrice' eggs, and weave the spider's web: he that eateth of their eggs dieth, and that which is crushed breaketh out into a viper.

• Fastens on Paul's hand.

Ac 28:3 — And when Paul had gathered a bundle of sticks, and laid *them* on the fire, there came a viper out of the heat, and fastened on his hand.

➜See: Serpent

• Figurative.

Mt 3:7 — But when he saw many of the Pharisees and Sadducees come to his baptism, he said unto them, O generation of vipers, who hath warned you to flee from the wrath to come?

Mt 23:33 — *Ye* serpents, *ye* generation of vipers, how can ye escape the damnation of hell?

Lk 3:7 — Then said he to the multitude that came forth to be baptized of him, O generation of vipers, who hath warned you to flee from the wrath to come?

VIRGIN

• Proofs of.

Dt 22:13–21

• Dowry of.

Ex 2:17 — And the shepherds came and drove them away: but Moses stood up and helped them, and watered their flock.

• Character of, to be protected.

Dt 22:17–21, 23–24

• Betrothal of, a quasi-marriage.

Dt 22:23–24

• Distinguishing apparel of.

2Sa 13:18 — And *she had* a garment of divers colours upon her: for with such robes were the king's daughters *that were* virgins apparelled. Then his servant brought her out, and bolted the door after her.

• Priests might marry none but.

Le 21:14 — A widow, or a divorced woman, or profane, *or* an harlot, these shall he not take: but he shall take a virgin of his own people to wife.

• Mourn in the temple.

La 1:4 — The ways of Zion do mourn, because none come to the solemn feasts: all her gates are desolate: her priests sigh, her virgins are afflicted, and she *is* in bitterness.

La 2:10 — The elders of the daughter of Zion sit upon the ground, *and* keep silence: they have cast up dust upon their heads; they have girded themselves with sackcloth: the virgins of Jerusalem hang down their heads to the ground.

• Virginity of, bewailed.

Jgs 11:37–39

• Parable of the wise and foolish.

Mt 25:1–13

• Mother of Jesus a.

Isa 7:14 — Therefore the Lord himself shall give you a sign; Behold, a virgin shall conceive, and bear a son, and shall call his name Immanuel.

Mt 1:23 — Behold, a virgin shall be with child, and shall bring forth a son, and they shall call his name Emmanuel, which being interpreted is, God with us.

Lk 1:27 — To a virgin espoused to a man whose name was Joseph, of the house of David; and the virgin's name *was* Mary.

• Advised by Paul not to marry.

1Co 7:1–40

• Figurative.

• Of the church.

Isa 62:5 — For *as* a young man marrieth a virgin, *so* shall thy sons marry thee: and *as* the bridegroom rejoiceth over the bride, *so* shall thy God rejoice over thee.

Jer 14:17 — Therefore thou shalt say this word unto them; Let mine eyes run down with tears night and day, and let them not cease: for the virgin daughter of my people is broken with a great breach, with a very grievous blow.

Jer 31:4 — Again I will build thee, and thou shalt be built, O virgin of Israel: thou shalt again be adorned with thy tabrets, and shalt go forth in the dances of them that make merry.

Jer 31:13 — Then shall the virgin rejoice in the dance, both young men and old together: for I will turn their mourning into joy, and will comfort them, and make them rejoice from their sorrow.

2Co 11:2 — For I am jealous over you with godly jealousy: for I have espoused you to one husband, that I may present *you as* a chaste virgin to Christ.

• Of personal purity.

1Co 7:25 — Now concerning virgins I have no commandment of the Lord: yet I give my judgment, as one that hath obtained mercy of the Lord to be faithful.

1Co 7:37 — Nevertheless he that standeth stedfast in his heart, having no necessity, but hath power over his own will, and hath so decreed in his heart that he will keep his virgin, doeth well.

Rev 14:4 — These are they which were not defiled with women; for they are virgins. These are they which follow the Lamb whithersoever he goeth. These were redeemed from among men, *being* the firstfruits unto God and to the Lamb.

VIRGINITY ↞See: Virgin

VIRTUE

• Power.

Lk 6:19 — And the whole multitude sought to touch him: for there went virtue out of him, and healed *them* all.

Lk 8:46 — And Jesus said, Somebody hath touched me: for I perceive that virtue is gone out of me.

• Excellence.

Php 4:8 — Finally, brethren, whatsoever things are true, whatsoever things *are* honest, whatsoever things *are* just, whatsoever things *are* pure, whatsoever things *are* lovely, whatsoever things *are* of good report; if *there be* any virtue, and if *there be* any praise, think on these things.

2Pe 1:5 — And beside this, giving all diligence, add to your faith virtue; and to virtue knowledge;

↞See: Chastity

↞See: Continence

↞See: Courage

VISION, New Testament

• Of Zacharias, in the temple.

Lk 1:13–22

• Of Joseph, take Mary as your wife.

Mt 1:20 — But while he thought on these things, behold, the angel of the Lord appeared unto him in a dream, saying, Joseph, thou son of David, fear not to take unto thee Mary thy wife: for that which is conceived in her is of the Holy Ghost.

• Of Joseph, God's direction.

Mt 2:13 — And when they were departed, behold, the angel of the Lord appeareth to Joseph in a dream, saying, Arise, and take the young child and his mother, and flee into Egypt, and be thou there until I bring thee word: for Herod will seek the young child to destroy him.

• Of John the Baptist, at the baptism of Jesus.

Jn 1:32–34

Mt 3:16 — And Jesus, when he was baptized, went up straightway out of the water: and, lo, the heavens were opened unto him, and he saw the Spirit of God descending like a dove, and lighting upon him:

Mk 1:10 — And straightway coming up out of the water, he saw the heavens opened, and the Spirit like a dove descending upon him:

Lk 3:22 — And the Holy Ghost descended in a bodily shape like a dove upon him, and a voice came from heaven, which said, Thou art my beloved Son; in thee I am well pleased.

• Peter, James, and John, of the transfiguration of Jesus and the appearance of Moses and Elijah.

Mt 17:1–9; Lk 9:28–36

• Of the people, of the tongues of fire at Pentecost.

Ac 2:2–3

• Of Stephen, of Christ.

Ac 7:55–56

• Dreams as outpouring of the Holy Spirit.

Ac 2:17 — And it shall come to pass in the last days, saith God, I will pour out of my Spirit upon all flesh: and your sons and your daughters shall prophesy, and your young men shall see visions, and your old men shall dream dreams:

• Of Paul, of Christ, on the way to Damascus.

Ac 9:3–6

1Co 9:1 — Am I not an apostle? am I not free? have I not seen Jesus Christ our Lord? are not ye my work in the Lord?

• Of Paul, of Ananias.

Ac 9:12 — And hath seen in a vision a man named Ananias coming in, and putting *his* hand on him, that he might receive his sight.

• Of Paul, of a man of Macedonia, saying, "Come over into Macedonia, and help us".

Ac 16:9 — And a vision appeared to Paul in the night; There stood a man of Macedonia, and prayed him, saying, Come over into Macedonia, and help us.

• Of Paul, in Corinth.

Ac 18:9–10

• Of Paul, in a trance.

Ac 22:17–21

• Of Paul, of paradise.

2Co 12:1–4

• Of Ananias, of Christ.

Ac 9:10–12

• Of Cornelius, the centurion, of an angel.

Ac 10:3 — He saw in a vision evidently about the ninth hour of the day an angel of God coming in to him, and saying unto him, Cornelius.

• Of Peter, of the sheet let down from heaven.

Ac 10:9–18

VISION, Old Testament

• A mode of revelation.

Ob 1:1–21

Nu 12:6 — And he said, Hear now my words: If there be a prophet among you, *I* the LORD will make myself known unto him in a vision, *and* will speak unto him in a dream.

1Sa 3:1 — And the child Samuel ministered unto the LORD before Eli. And the word of the LORD was precious in those days; *there was* no open vision.

2Ch 26:5 — And he sought God in the days of Zechariah, who had understanding in the visions of

God: and as long as he sought the LORD, God made him to prosper.

Ps 89:19 — Then thou spakest in vision to thy holy one, and saidst, I have laid help upon *one that is* mighty; I have exalted *one* chosen out of the people.

Pr 29:18 — Where *there is* no vision, the people perish: but he that keepeth the law, happy *is* he.

Jer 14:14 — Then the LORD said unto me, The prophets prophesy lies in my name: I sent them not, neither have I commanded them, neither spake unto them: they prophesy unto you a false vision and divination, and a thing of nought, and the deceit of their heart.

Jer 23:16 — Thus saith the LORD of hosts, Hearken not unto the words of the prophets that prophesy unto you: they make you vain: they speak a vision of their own heart, *and* not out of the mouth of the LORD.

Da 1:17 — As for these four children, God gave them knowledge and skill in all learning and wisdom: and Daniel had understanding in all visions and dreams.

Hos 12:10 — I have also spoken by the prophets, and I have multiplied visions, and used similitudes, by the ministry of the prophets.

Joel 2:28 — And it shall come to pass afterward, *that* I will pour out my spirit upon all flesh; and your sons and your daughters shall prophesy, your old men shall dream dreams, your young men shall see visions:

Hab 2:2 — And the LORD answered me, and said, Write the vision, and make *it* plain upon tables, that he may run that readeth it.

Ac 2:17 — And it shall come to pass in the last days, saith God, I will pour out of my Spirit upon all flesh: and your sons and your daughters shall prophesy, and your young men shall see visions, and your old men shall dream dreams:

• Of Abraham, concerning his descendants.

Ge 15:1–17

• Of Abimelech, concerning Sarah.

Ge 20:3 — But God came to Abimelech in a dream by night, and said to him, Behold, thou *art but* a dead man, for the woman which thou hast taken; for she *is* a man's wife.

Ge 20:6 — And God said unto him in a dream, Yea, I know that thou didst this in the integrity of thy heart; for I also withheld thee from sinning against me: therefore suffered I thee not to touch her.

• Of Jacob, of the ladder with ascending and descending angels.

Ge 28:12 — And he dreamed, and behold a ladder set up on the earth, and the top of it reached to heaven: and behold the angels of God ascending and descending on it.

• Of Jacob, concerning his flock.

Ge 31:10–11

• Of Laban, concerning speech to Jacob.

Ge 31:24 — And God came to Laban the Syrian in a dream by night, and said unto him, Take heed that thou speak not to Jacob either good or bad.

• Of Jacob, at Beer-sheba.

Ge 46:2 — And God spake unto Israel in the visions of the night, and said, Jacob, Jacob. And he said, Here *am* I.

• Dream of the cupbearer.

Ge 40:9 — And the chief butler told his dream to Joseph, and said to him, In my dream, behold, a vine *was* before me;

• Dream of the baker.

Ge 40:16 — When the chief baker saw that the interpretation was good, he said unto Joseph, I also *was* in my dream, and, behold, *I had* three white baskets on my head:

• Of Joshua, of the captain of the Lord's host.

Jos 5:13–15

• Of Moses, of the burning bush.

Ex 3:2 — And the angel of the LORD appeared unto him in a flame of fire out of the midst of a bush: and he looked, and, behold, the bush burned with fire, and the bush *was* not consumed.

• Of Moses, of the glory of God.

Ex 24:9–11; 33:18–23

• Of the Israelites, of the manifestation of the glory of God.

Heb 12:18–21

Ex 24:10 — And they saw the God of Israel: and *there was* under his feet as it were a paved work of a sapphire stone, and as it were the body of heaven in *his* clearness.

Ex 24:17 — And the sight of the glory of the LORD *was* like devouring fire on the top of the mount in the eyes of the children of Israel.

• Of Balaam, in a trance.

→See: Balaam

• Of Solomon, request of the Lord for wisdom.

1Ki 3:15 — And Solomon awoke; and, behold, *it was* a dream. And he came to Jerusalem, and stood before the ark of the covenant of the LORD, and offered up burnt offerings, and offered peace offerings, and made a feast to all his servants.

• Of Elisha, at the translation of Elijah.

2Ki 2:11 — And it came to pass, as they still went on, and talked, that, behold, *there appeared* a chariot of fire, and horses of fire, and parted them both asunder; and Elijah went up by a whirlwind into heaven.

• Of Elisha's servant, of the chariots of the Lord.

2Ki 6:17 — And Elisha prayed, and said, LORD, I pray thee, open his eyes, that he may see. And the LORD opened the eyes of the young man; and he saw: and, behold, the mountain *was* full of horses and chariots of fire round about Elisha.

• Of Micaiah, of the defeat of the Israelites; of the Lord on his throne; and of a lying spirit.

1Ki 22:17–23; 2Ch 18:16–22

• Of David, of the angel of the Lord by the threshing floor of Ornan.
1Ch 21:15–18

• Of Job, of a spirit.
Job 4:12–16

• God speaks to man through dreams.
Job 33:15 — In a dream, in a vision of the night, when deep sleep falleth upon men, in slumberings upon the bed;

• Of Isaiah, of the Lord and his glory in the temple.
Isa 6:1–13

• Of Isaiah, of the valley of vision.
Isa 22:1–25

• Of Jeremiah, of an almond rod.
Jer 1:11 — Moreover the word of the LORD came unto me, saying, Jeremiah, what seest thou? And I said, I see a rod of an almond tree.

• Of Jeremiah, of the seething pot.
Jer 1:13 — And the word of the LORD came unto me the second time, saying, What seest thou? And I said, I see a seething pot; and the face thereof *is* toward the north.

• Of Ezekiel, of the glory of God.
Eze 1:12–14; 23:1–49
Eze 1:3 — The word of the LORD came expressly unto Ezekiel the priest, the son of Buzi, in the land of the Chaldeans by the river Chebar; and the hand of the LORD was there upon him.

• Of Ezekiel, of the roll.
Eze 2:9 — And when I looked, behold, an hand *was* sent unto me; and, lo, a roll of a book *was* therein;

• Of Ezekiel, of the man of fire.
Eze 8:1–9:11

• Of Ezekiel, of the coals of fire.
Eze 10:1–7

• Of Ezekiel, of the dry bones.
Eze 37:1–14

• Of Ezekiel, of the city and temple.
Eze 40:1–48:35

• Of Ezekiel, of the waters.
Eze 47:1–12

• Of Nebuchadnezzar.
Da 4:5 — I saw a dream which made me afraid, and the thoughts upon my bed and the visions of my head troubled me.

• Of Daniel, of the four beasts.
Da 7:1–28

• Of Daniel, of the Ancient of days.
Da 7:9–27

• Of Daniel, of the ram and the he goat.
Da 8:1–27

• Of Daniel, of the angel.
Da 10:1–21

• Of Amos, of grasshoppers.
Am 7:1–2

• Of Amos, of fire.
Am 7:4 — Thus hath the Lord GOD shewed unto me: and, behold, the Lord GOD called to contend by fire, and it devoured the great deep, and did eat up a part.

• Of Amos, of a plumb line.
Am 7:7–8

• Of Amos, of summer fruit.
Am 8:1–2

• Of Amos, of the temple.
Am 9:1 — I saw the LORD standing upon the altar: and he said, Smite the lintel of the door, that the posts may shake: and cut them in the head, all of them; and I will slay the last of them with the sword: he that fleeth of them shall not flee away, and he that escapeth of them shall not be delivered.

• Of Zechariah, of horses.
Zec 1:8–11

• Of Zechariah, of horns and carpenters.
Zec 1:18–21

• Of Zechariah, of the high priest.
Zec 3:1–5

• Of Zechariah, of the golden candlestick.
Zec 4:1–14

• Of Zechariah, of the flying roll.
Zec 5:1–4

• Of Zechariah, of the mountains and chariots.
Zec 6:1–8

VISION, Revelation

• Of John, on the Isle of Patmos.
Rev 1:1–22:21

• Of Christ and the golden candlesticks.
Rev 1:10–20

• Of Christ and the open door.
Rev 4:1 — After this I looked, and, behold, a door *was* opened in heaven: and the first voice which I heard *was* as it were of a trumpet talking with me; which said, Come up hither, and I will shew thee things which must be hereafter.

• Of Christ and a rainbow and throne.
Rev 4:2–3

• Of Christ and the twenty-four elders.
Rev 4:4 — And round about the throne *were* four and twenty seats: and upon the seats I saw four and twenty elders sitting, clothed in white raiment; and they had on their heads crowns of gold.

• Of Christ and the seven lamps.
Rev 4:5 — And out of the throne proceeded lightnings and thunderings and voices: and *there were* seven lamps of fire burning before the throne, which are the seven Spirits of God.

• Of Christ and the sea of glass.
Rev 4:6 — And before the throne *there was* a sea of glass like unto crystal: and in the midst of the throne, and round about the throne, *were* four beasts full of eyes before and behind.

• Of Christ and the four living creatures.
Rev 4:6–8

• Of Christ and the book with seven seals.
Rev 5:1–5

• Of Christ and the golden vials.
Rev 5:8 — And when he had taken the book, the four beasts and four *and* twenty elders fell down before the Lamb, having every one of them harps, and golden vials full of odours, which are the prayers of saints.

• Of Christ of the six seals.
Rev 6:1–17

• Of Christ and the four horses.
Rev 6:2–8

• Of Christ and the earthquake and celestial phenomena.
Rev 6:12–14

• Of Christ and the four angels.
Rev 7:1 — And after these things I saw four angels standing on the four corners of the earth, holding the four winds of the earth, that the wind should not blow on the earth, nor on the sea, nor on any tree.

• Of Christ and the sealing of the one hundred and forty-four thousand.
Rev 7:2–8

• Of Christ of the seventh seal and seven angels.
Rev 8:1–11:19

• Of Christ of the censer.
Rev 8:5 — And the angel took the censer, and filled it with fire of the altar, and cast *it* into the earth: and there were voices, and thunderings, and lightnings, and an earthquake.

• Of Christ and the hail and fire.
Rev 8:7 — The first angel sounded, and there followed hail and fire mingled with blood, and they were cast upon the earth: and the third part of trees was burnt up, and all green grass was burnt up.

• Of Christ and the mountain cast into the sea.
Rev 8:8–9

• Of Christ and the falling star.
Rev 8:10–11
Rev 9:1 — And the fifth angel sounded, and I saw a star fall from heaven unto the earth: and to him was given the key of the bottomless pit.

• Of Christ and the third part of sun and moon and stars darkened.
Rev 8:12 — And the fourth angel sounded, and the third part of the sun was smitten, and the third part of the moon, and the third part of the stars; so as the third part of them was darkened, and the day shone not for a third part of it, and the night likewise.

• Of Christ and the bottomless pit.
Rev 9:2 — And he opened the bottomless pit; and there arose a smoke out of the pit, as the smoke of a great furnace; and the sun and the air were darkened by reason of the smoke of the pit.

• Of Christ and the locusts.
Rev 9:3–11

• Of Christ and the four angels loosed from the Euphrates.
Rev 9:14 — Saying to the sixth angel which had the trumpet, Loose the four angels which are bound in the great river Euphrates.

• Of Christ and the army of horsemen.
Rev 9:16–19

• Of Christ and the angel having a book.
Rev 10:1–10

• Of Christ and the seven thunders.
Rev 10:3–4

• Of Christ and the measurement of the temple.
Rev 11:1–2

• Of Christ and the two witnesses.
Rev 11:3–12

• Of Christ and the court of the Gentiles.
Rev 11:2 — But the court which is without the temple leave out, and measure it not; for it is given unto the Gentiles: and the holy city shall they tread under foot forty *and* two months.

• Of Christ and the two olive trees and two candlesticks.
Rev 11:4 — These are the two olive trees, and the two candlesticks standing before the God of the earth.

• Of Christ and the beast out of the bottomless pit.
Rev 11:7 — And when they shall have finished their testimony, the beast that ascendeth out of the bottomless pit shall make war against them, and shall overcome them, and kill them.

• Of Christ and the fall of the city.
Rev 11:13 — And the same hour was there a great earthquake, and the tenth part of the city fell, and in the earthquake were slain of men seven thousand: and the remnant were affrighted, and gave glory to the God of heaven.

• Of Christ and the second and third woes.
Rev 11:14 — The second woe is past; *and,* behold, the third woe cometh quickly.

• Of Christ and a woman clothed with the sun; birth of the man child.
Rev 12:1–17

• Of Christ and a red dragon.
Rev 12:3–17

• Of Christ and the war in heaven.
Rev 12:7–9

• Of Christ and the beast rising out of the sea.
Rev 13:1–10

• Of Christ and the beast coming out of the earth.
Rev 13:11–18

• Of Christ and the Lamb on Mount Zion.
Rev 14:1–5

• Of Christ and the angel having the everlasting gospel.
Rev 14:6–7

• Of Christ and the angel proclaiming the fall of Babylon.
Rev 14:8–13

• Of Christ and the Son of man with a sickle.
Rev 14:14–16

• Of Christ and the angel reaping the harvest.
Rev 14:14–20

• Of Christ and the angel coming out of the temple.
Rev 14:17–19

• Of Christ and an angel having power over fire.
Rev 14:18 — And another angel came out from the altar, which had power over fire; and cried with a loud cry to him that had the sharp sickle, saying, Thrust in thy sharp sickle, and gather the clusters of the vine of the earth; for her grapes are fully ripe.

• Of Christ and the vine and the winepress.
Rev 14:18–20

• Of Christ and the angels with the seven last plagues.
Rev 15:1–8

• Of Christ and the sea of glass.
Rev 15:2 — And I saw as it were a sea of glass mingled with fire: and them that had gotten the victory over the beast, and over his image, and over his mark, *and* over the number of his name, stand on the sea of glass, having the harps of God.

• Of Christ and the temple opened.
Rev 15:5 — And after that I looked, and, behold, the temple of the tabernacle of the testimony in heaven was opened:

• Of Christ and the plague upon the men who had the mark of the beast.
Rev 16:2 — And the first went, and poured out his vial upon the earth; and there fell a noisome and grievous sore upon the men which had the mark of the beast, and *upon* them which worshipped his image.

• Of Christ and the sea turned into blood.
Rev 16:3 — And the second angel poured out his vial upon the sea; and it became as the blood of a dead *man:* and every living soul died in the sea.

• Of Christ and the seven angels with the seven vials of the wrath of God.
Rev 16:1–17:18

• Of Christ and the destruction of Babylon.
Rev 18:1–24

• Of Christ of the multitude praising.
Rev 19:1–9

• Of Christ of him who is faithful and true riding a white horse.
Rev 19:11–16

• Of Christ and the angel in the sun.
Rev 19:17–21

• Of Christ and Satan bound a thousand years.
Rev 20:1–3

• Of Christ and the thrones of judgment, and the resurrection, and the loosing of Satan.
Rev 20:1–10

• Of Christ and the great white throne.
Rev 20:11 — And I saw a great white throne, and him that sat on it, from whose face the earth and the heaven fled away; and there was found no place for them.

• Of Christ opening of the book of life.
Rev 20:12 — And I saw the dead, small and great, stand before God; and the books were opened: and another book was opened, which is *the book* of life: and the dead were judged out of those things which were written in the books, according to their works.

• Of Christ and death and hell.
Rev 20:14 — And death and hell were cast into the lake of fire. This is the second death.

• Of Christ and the New Jerusalem.
Rev 21:1–27

• Of Christ and the river of life.
Rev 22:1 — And he shewed me a pure river of water of life, clear as crystal, proceeding out of the throne of God and of the Lamb.

• Of Christ and the tree of life.
Rev 22:2 — In the midst of the street of it, and on either side of the river, *was there* the tree of life, which bare twelve *manner* of fruits, *and* yielded her fruit every month: and the leaves of the tree *were* for the healing of the nations.

See: Dream

VISITORS See: Guest

VOICE

• Of God.
Jn 12:28–30; Ac 26:14–15
Eze 1:24 — And when they went, I heard the noise of their wings, like the noise of great waters, as the voice of the Almighty, the voice of speech, as the noise of an host: when they stood, they let down their wings.
Eze 1:28 — As the appearance of the bow that is in the cloud in the day of rain, so *was* the appearance of the brightness round about. This *was* the appearance of the likeness of the glory of the LORD. And when I saw *it,* I fell upon my face, and I heard a voice of one that spake.
Eze 10:5 — And the sound of the cherubims' wings was heard *even* to the outer court, as the voice of the Almighty God when he speaketh.

Jn 5:37 — And the Father himself, which hath sent me, hath borne witness of me. Ye have neither heard his voice at any time, nor seen his shape.

Ac 7:31 — When Moses saw *it,* he wondered at the sight: and as he drew near to behold *it,* the voice of the Lord came unto him,

Ac 9:4 — And he fell to the earth, and heard a voice saying unto him, Saul, Saul, why persecutest thou me?

Ac 9:7 — And the men which journeyed with him stood speechless, hearing a voice, but seeing no man.

See: Anthropomorphisms

VOLCANOES

Isa 34:9–10; 64:1–3; Na 1:5–6

Dt 4:11 — And ye came near and stood under the mountain; and the mountain burned with fire unto the midst of heaven, with darkness, clouds, and thick darkness.

Dt 5:23 — And it came to pass, when ye heard the voice out of the midst of the darkness, (for the mountain did burn with fire,) that ye came near unto me, *even* all the heads of your tribes, and your elders;

Jgs 5:5 — The mountains melted from before the LORD, *even* that Sinai from before the LORD God of Israel.

Ps 97:5 — The hills melted like wax at the presence of the LORD, at the presence of the Lord of the whole earth.

Ps 104:32 — He looketh on the earth, and it trembleth: he toucheth the hills, and they smoke.

Ps 144:5 — Bow thy heavens, O LORD, and come down: touch the mountains, and they shall smoke.

Jer 51:25 — Behold, I *am* against thee, O destroying mountain, saith the LORD, which destroyest all the earth: and I will stretch out mine hand upon thee, and roll thee down from the rocks, and will make thee a burnt mountain.

Mic 1:4 — And the mountains shall be molten under him, and the valleys shall be cleft, as wax before the fire, *and* as the waters *that are* poured down a steep place.

See: Earthquakes

See: Mountain

VOLUPTUOUSNESS

See: Lasciviousness

See: Sensuality

VOPHSI • Father of Nahbi.

Nu 13:14 — Of the tribe of Naphtali, Nahbi the son of Vophsi.

VOWS

• Mosaic laws concerning.

Le 23:37–38

Nu 29:39 — These *things* ye shall do unto the LORD in your set feasts, beside your vows, and your freewill offerings, for your burnt offerings, and for your meat offerings, and for your drink offerings, and for your peace offerings.

• Estimation of the redemption price of things offered in vows to be made by the priest.

Le 27:1–13

• The redemption price of the offering of real estate, to be valued by the priest.

Le 27:14–15

• The redemption price of the offering of a field.

Le 27:16–25

• Edible things offered in, to be eaten the same day they were offered.

Le 7:16–18

• Things offered in, to be brought to the tabernacle or temple.

Dt 12:17–18

Dt 12:6 — And thither ye shall bring your burnt offerings, and your sacrifices, and your tithes, and heave offerings of your hand, and your vows, and your freewill offerings, and the firstlings of your herds and of your flocks:

Dt 12:11 — Then there shall be a place which the LORD your God shall choose to cause his name to dwell there; thither shall ye bring all that I command you; your burnt offerings, and your sacrifices, your tithes, and the heave offering of your hand, and all your choice vows which ye vow unto the LORD:

Dt 12:26 — Only thy holy things which thou hast, and thy vows, thou shalt take, and go unto the place which the LORD shall choose:

• Things offered in, belonged to the priests.

Nu 18:14 — Every thing devoted in Israel shall be thine.

• Rash.

• By Jephthah, in consecration of daughter as sacrifice if campaign against Ammonites successful.

Jgs 11:29–40

• By the Israelites, to destroy the Benjamites.

Jgs 20:1–21:25

• Things forbidden to be offered.

• Receipts of the whore and price of a dog.

Dt 23:18 — Thou shalt not bring the hire of a whore, or the price of a dog, into the house of the LORD thy God for any vow: for even both these *are* abomination unto the LORD thy God.

• A minor, of himself.

Mk 7:11–13

• Unclassified scripture relating to.

Ge 28:20–21; Le 5:4–13; 22:18–25; Nu 15:2–16; 30:1–16; Dt 23:21–23; Ps 50:14–15; 66:13–14; 116:14–19; Ecc 5:4–6

Ge 31:13 — I *am* the God of Bethel, where thou anointedst the pillar, *and* where thou vowedst a vow unto me: now arise, get thee out from this land, and return unto the land of thy kindred.

Dt 23:18 — Thou shalt not bring the hire of a whore, or the price of a dog, into the house of the LORD thy God for any vow: for even both these *are* abomination unto the LORD thy God.

Job 22:27 — Thou shalt make thy prayer unto him, and he shall hear thee, and thou shalt pay thy vows.

Ps 22:25 — My praise *shall be* of thee in the great congregation: I will pay my vows before them that fear him.

Ps 56:12 — Thy vows *are* upon me, O God: I will render praises unto thee.

Ps 61:5 — For thou, O God, hast heard my vows: thou hast given *me* the heritage of those that fear thy name.

Ps 61:8 — So will I sing praise unto thy name for ever, that I may daily perform my vows.

Ps 65:1 — Praise waiteth for thee, O God, in Sion: and unto thee shall the vow be performed.

Ps 76:11 — Vow, and pay unto the LORD your God: let all that be round about him bring presents unto him that ought to be feared.

Pr 20:25 — *It is* a snare to the man *who* devoureth *that which is* holy, and after vows to make enquiry.

Jnh 2:9 — But I will sacrifice unto thee with the voice of thanksgiving; I will pay *that* that I have vowed. Salvation *is* of the LORD.

Na 1:15 — Behold upon the mountains the feet of him that bringeth good tidings, that publisheth peace! O Judah, keep thy solemn feasts, perform thy vows: for the wicked shall no more pass through thee; he is utterly cut off.

➔See: Contracts

➔See: Covenant

• Instances of.

• Jacob.

Ge 28:20–22

• The mother of Micah, in the dedication of silver for the making of an idol.

Jgs 17:2–3

• Hannah, to consecrate unto the Lord the child for which she prayed.

1Sa 1:11, 27–28

• Elkanah.

1Sa 1:21

• Absalom.

2Sa 15:7–8

• Job, not to entertain thoughts of fornication.

Job 31:1

• David.

Ps 132:2

• Ananias and Sapphira, in the dedication of the proceeds of the sale of their land.

Ac 5:1–11

• The Jews, to slay Paul.

Ac 23:12–15

• Jephthah, and of the Israelites.

➔See: Vows; rash

➔See: Nazarite

VULTURE • A carnivorous bird.

Le 11:14 — And the vulture, and the kite after his kind;

Dt 14:13 — And the glede, and the kite, and the vulture after his kind,

Job 28:7 — *There is* a path which no fowl knoweth, and which the vulture's eye hath not seen:

Isa 34:15 — There shall the great owl make her nest, and lay, and hatch, and gather under her shadow: there shall the vultures also be gathered, every one with her mate.

WAFER

Ex 29:23 — And one loaf of bread, and one cake of oiled bread, and one wafer out of the basket of the unleavened bread that *is* before the LORD:

Nu 6:19 — And the priest shall take the sodden shoulder of the ram, and one unleavened cake out of the basket, and one unleavened wafer, and shall put *them* upon the hands of the Nazarite, after *the hair of* his separation is shaven:

WAGES

- **Of Jacob.**

  Ge 29:15–30; 30:28–34

  Ge 31:7 — And your father hath deceived me, and changed my wages ten times; but God suffered him not to hurt me.

  Ge 31:41 — Thus have I been twenty years in thy house; I served thee fourteen years for thy two daughters, and six years for thy cattle: and thou hast changed my wages ten times.

- **Parable concerning.**

  Mt 20:1–15

  See: Master

  See: Servant

- **Unclassified scripture relating to.**

  Dt 24:14–15

  Le 19:13 — Thou shalt not defraud thy neighbour, neither rob *him:* the wages of him that is hired shall not abide with thee all night until the morning.

  Dt 25:4 — Thou shalt not muzzle the ox when he treadeth out *the corn.*

  Jer 22:13 — Woe unto him that buildeth his house by unrighteousness, and his chambers by wrong; *that* useth his neighbour's service without wages, and giveth him not for his work;

  Hag 1:6 — Ye have sown much, and bring in little; ye eat, but ye have not enough; ye drink, but ye are not filled with drink; ye clothe you, but there is none warm; and he that earneth wages earneth wages *to put it* into a bag with holes.

  Mal 3:5 — And I will come near to you to judgment; and I will be a swift witness against the sorcerers, and against the adulterers, and against false swearers, and against those that oppress the hireling in *his* wages, the widow, and the fatherless, and that turn aside the stranger *from his right,* and fear not me, saith the LORD of hosts.

  Mt 10:10 — Nor scrip for *your* journey, neither two coats, neither shoes, nor yet staves: for the workman is worthy of his meat.

  Lk 3:14 — And the soldiers likewise demanded of him, saying, And what shall we do? And he said unto them, Do violence to no man, neither accuse *any* falsely; and be content with your wages.

  Lk 10:7 — And in the same house remain, eating and drinking such things as they give: for the labourer is worthy of his hire. Go not from house to house.

  Ro 4:4 — Now to him that worketh is the reward not reckoned of grace, but of debt.

  Ro 6:23 — For the wages of sin *is* death; but the gift of God *is* eternal life through Jesus Christ our Lord.

  Col 4:1 — Masters, give unto *your* servants that which is just and equal; knowing that ye also have a Master in heaven.

  Jas 5:4 — Behold, the hire of the labourers who have reaped down your fields, which is of you kept back by fraud, crieth: and the cries of them which have reaped are entered into the ears of the Lord of sabaoth.

WAGON

Nu 7:3–9

Ge 45:19 — Now thou art commanded, this do ye; take you wagons out of the land of Egypt for your little ones, and for your wives, and bring your father, and come.

Ge 45:27 — And they told him all the words of Joseph, which he had said unto them: and when he saw the wagons which Joseph had sent to carry him, the spirit of Jacob their father revived:

See: Cart

WAILING

- **Of the wicked.**

  Mt 13:42 — And shall cast them into a furnace of fire: there shall be wailing and gnashing of teeth.

WAITING

- **Upon God.**
  - **As the God of providence.**

    Jer 14:22 — Are there *any* among the vanities of the Gentiles that can cause rain? or can the heavens give showers? *art* not thou he, O LORD our God? therefore we will wait upon thee: for thou hast made all these *things.*

  - **As the God of salvation.**

    Ps 25:5 — Lead me in thy truth, and teach me: for thou *art* the God of my salvation; on thee do I wait all the day.

  - **As the giver of all temporal blessings.**

    Ps 104:27–28; 145:15–16

- **For mercy.**

  Ps 123:2 — Behold, as the eyes of servants *look* unto the hand of their masters, *and* as the eyes of a maiden unto the hand of her mistress; so our eyes *wait* upon the LORD our God, until that he have mercy upon us.

- **For pardon.**

  Ps 39:7–8

• For the consolation of Israel.

Lk 2:25 — And, behold, there was a man in Jerusalem, whose name *was* Simeon; and the same man *was* just and devout, waiting for the consolation of Israel: and the Holy Ghost was upon him.

• For salvation.

Ps 62:1–2

Ge 49:18 — I have waited for thy salvation, O LORD.

• For guidance and teaching.

Ps 25:5 — Lead me in thy truth, and teach me: for thou *art* the God of my salvation; on thee do I wait all the day.

• For protection.

Ps 59:9–10

Ps 33:20 — Our soul waiteth for the LORD: he *is* our help and our shield.

• For the fulfillment of his word.

Hab 2:3 — For the vision *is* yet for an appointed time, but at the end it shall speak, and not lie: though it tarry, wait for it; because it will surely come, it will not tarry.

• For the fulfillment of his promises.

Ac 1:4 — And, being assembled together with *them,* commanded them that they should not depart from Jerusalem, but wait for the promise of the Father, which, *saith he,* ye have heard of me.

• For the hope of righteousness by faith.

Gal 5:5 — For we through the Spirit wait for the hope of righteousness by faith.

• For the coming of Christ.

1Co 1:7 — So that ye come behind in no gift; waiting for the coming of our Lord Jesus Christ:

1Th 1:10 — And to wait for his Son from heaven, whom he raised from the dead, *even* Jesus, which delivered us from the wrath to come.

• Is good.

Ps 52:9 — I will praise thee for ever, because thou hast done *it:* and I will wait on thy name; for *it is* good before thy saints.

• God calls us to.

Zep 3:8 — Therefore wait ye upon me, saith the LORD, until the day that I rise up to the prey: for my determination *is* to gather the nations, that I may assemble the kingdoms, to pour upon them mine indignation, *even* all my fierce anger: for all the earth shall be devoured with the fire of my jealousy.

• Exhortations and encouragements to.

Ps 27:14 — Wait on the LORD: be of good courage, and he shall strengthen thine heart: wait, I say, on the LORD.

Ps 37:7 — Rest in the LORD, and wait patiently for him: fret not thyself because of him who prospereth in his way, because of the man who bringeth wicked devices to pass.

Hos 12:6 — Therefore turn thou to thy God: keep mercy and judgment, and wait on thy God continually.

• Should be with the soul.

Ps 62:1 — Truly my soul waiteth upon God: from him *cometh* my salvation.

Ps 62:5 — My soul, wait thou only upon God; for my expectation *is* from him.

• Should be with earnest desire.

Ps 130:6 — My soul *waiteth* for the Lord more than they that watch for the morning: *I say, more than* they that watch for the morning.

• Should be with patience.

Ps 37:7 — Rest in the LORD, and wait patiently for him: fret not thyself because of him who prospereth in his way, because of the man who bringeth wicked devices to pass.

Ps 40:1 — I waited patiently for the LORD; and he inclined unto me, and heard my cry.

• Should be with resignation.

La 3:26 — *It is* good that *a man* should both hope and quietly wait for the salvation of the LORD.

• Should be with hope in his word.

Ps 130:5 — I wait for the LORD, my soul doth wait, and in his word do I hope.

• Should be with full confidence.

Mic 7:7 — Therefore I will look unto the LORD; I will wait for the God of my salvation: my God will hear me.

• Should be continually.

Hos 12:6 — Therefore turn thou to thy God: keep mercy and judgment, and wait on thy God continually.

• Should be all the day.

Ps 25:5 — Lead me in thy truth, and teach me: for thou *art* the God of my salvation; on thee do I wait all the day.

• Should be specially in adversity.

Ps 59:1–9

Isa 8:17 — And I will wait upon the LORD, that hideth his face from the house of Jacob, and I will look for him.

• Should be in the way of his judgments.

Isa 26:8 — Yea, in the way of thy judgments, O LORD, have we waited for thee; the desire of *our* soul *is* to thy name, and to the remembrance of thee.

• Saints resolve on.

Ps 52:9 — I will praise thee for ever, because thou hast done *it:* and I will wait on thy name; for *it is* good before thy saints.

Ps 59:9 — *Because of* his strength will I wait upon thee: for God *is* my defence.

• Saints have expectation from.

Ps 62:5 — My soul, wait thou only upon God; for my expectation *is* from him.

• Saints plead, in prayer.

Ps 25:21 — Let integrity and uprightness preserve me; for I wait on thee.

Isa 33:2 — O LORD, be gracious unto us; we have waited for thee: be thou their arm every morning, our salvation also in the time of trouble.

• The patience of saints often tried in.

Ps 69:3 — I am weary of my crying: my throat is dried: mine eyes fail while I wait for my God.

- **They who engage in.**
  - **Wait upon him only.**

    Ps 62:5 — My soul, wait thou only upon God; for my expectation *is* from him.
  - **Are heard.**

    Ps 40:1 — I waited patiently for the LORD; and he inclined unto me, and heard my cry.
  - **Are blessed.**

    Isa 30:18 — And therefore will the LORD wait, that he may be gracious unto you, and therefore will he be exalted, that he may have mercy upon you: for the LORD *is* a God of judgment: blessed *are* all they that wait for him.

    Da 12:12 — Blessed *is* he that waiteth, and cometh to the thousand three hundred and five and thirty days.
  - **Experience his goodness.**

    La 3:25 — The LORD *is* good unto them that wait for him, to the soul *that* seeketh him.
  - **Shall not be ashamed.**

    Ps 25:3 — Yea, let none that wait on thee be ashamed: let them be ashamed which transgress without cause.

    Isa 49:23 — And kings shall be thy nursing fathers, and their queens thy nursing mothers: they shall bow down to thee with *their* face toward the earth, and lick up the dust of thy feet; and thou shalt know that I *am* the LORD: for they shall not be ashamed that wait for me.
  - **Shall renew their strength.**

    Isa 40:31 — But they that wait upon the LORD shall renew *their* strength; they shall mount up with wings as eagles; they shall run, and not be weary; *and* they shall walk, and not faint.
  - **Shall inherit the earth.**

    Ps 37:9 — For evildoers shall be cut off: but those that wait upon the LORD, they shall inherit the earth.
  - **Shall be saved.**

    Pr 20:22 — Say not thou, I will recompense evil; *but* wait on the LORD, and he shall save thee.

    Isa 25:9 — And it shall be said in that day, Lo, this *is* our God; we have waited for him, and he will save us: this *is* the LORD; we have waited for him, we will be glad and rejoice in his salvation.
  - **Shall rejoice in salvation.**

    Isa 25:9 — And it shall be said in that day, Lo, this *is* our God; we have waited for him, and he will save us: this *is* the LORD; we have waited for him, we will be glad and rejoice in his salvation.
  - **Shall receive the glorious things prepared by God for them.**

    Isa 64:4 — For since the beginning of the world *men* have not heard, nor perceived by the ear, neither hath the eye seen, O God, beside thee, *what* he hath prepared for him that waiteth for him.
- **Predicted of the Gentiles.**

  Isa 42:4 — He shall not fail nor be discouraged, till he have set judgment in the earth: and the isles shall wait for his law.

  Isa 60:9 — Surely the isles shall wait for me, and the ships of Tarshish first, to bring thy sons from far, their silver and their gold with them, unto the name of the LORD thy God, and to the Holy One of Israel, because he hath glorified thee.
- **Illustrated.**

  Ps 123:2 — Behold, as the eyes of servants *look* unto the hand of their masters, *and* as the eyes of a maiden unto the hand of her mistress; so our eyes *wait* upon the LORD our God, until that he have mercy upon us.

  Lk 12:36 — And ye yourselves like unto men that wait for their lord, when he will return from the wedding; that when he cometh and knocketh, they may open unto him immediately.

  Jas 5:7 — Be patient therefore, brethren, unto the coming of the Lord. Behold, the husbandman waiteth for the precious fruit of the earth, and hath long patience for it, until he receive the early and latter rain.
- **Exemplified.**
  - **Jacob.**

    Ge 49:18 — I have waited for thy salvation, O LORD.
  - **David.**

    Ps 39:7 — And now, Lord, what wait I for? my hope *is* in thee.
  - **Isaiah.**

    Isa 8:17 — And I will wait upon the LORD, that hideth his face from the house of Jacob, and I will look for him.
  - **Micah.**

    Mic 7:7 — Therefore I will look unto the LORD; I will wait for the God of my salvation: my God will hear me.
  - **Joseph.**

    Mk 15:43 — Joseph of Arimathaea, an honourable counsellor, which also waited for the kingdom of God, came, and went in boldly unto Pilate, and craved the body of Jesus.

WALKING

- **With God.**
  - **According to his commands.**

    Ps 1:1–6

    Dt 5:33 — Ye shall walk in all the ways which the LORD your God hath commanded you, that ye may live, and *that it may be* well with you, and *that* ye may prolong *your* days in the land which ye shall possess.

    Jer 7:23 — But this thing commanded I them, saying, Obey my voice, and I will be your God, and ye shall be my people: and walk ye in all the ways that I have commanded you, that it may be well unto you.
  - **In his ways.**

    Dt 28:9 — The LORD shall establish thee an holy people unto himself, as he hath sworn unto thee, if thou shalt keep the commandments of the LORD thy God, and walk in his ways.

Jos 22:5 — But take diligent heed to do the commandment and the law, which Moses the servant of the LORD charged you, to love the LORD your God, and to walk in all his ways, and to keep his commandments, and to cleave unto him, and to serve him with all your heart and with all your soul.

• In the old paths.

Jer 6:16 — Thus saith the LORD, Stand ye in the ways, and see, and ask for the old paths, where is the good way, and walk therein, and ye shall find rest for your souls. But they said, We will not walk *therein.*

• As taught by him.

1Ki 8:36 — Then hear thou in heaven, and forgive the sin of thy servants, and of thy people Israel, that thou teach them the good way wherein they should walk, and give rain upon thy land, which thou hast given to thy people for an inheritance.

Isa 2:3 — And many people shall go and say, Come ye, and let us go up to the mountain of the LORD, to the house of the God of Jacob; and he will teach us of his ways, and we will walk in his paths: for out of Zion shall go forth the law, and the word of the LORD from Jerusalem.

Isa 30:21 — And thine ears shall hear a word behind thee, saying, This *is* the way, walk ye in it, when ye turn to the right hand, and when ye turn to the left.

• Uprightly.

Pr 2:7 — He layeth up sound wisdom for the righteous: *he is* a buckler to them that walk uprightly.

• In his statutes and judgments.

Eze 37:24 — And David my servant *shall be* king over them; and they all shall have one shepherd: they shall also walk in my judgments, and observe my statutes, and do them.

• In newness of life.

Ro 6:4 — Therefore we are buried with him by baptism into death: that like as Christ was raised up from the dead by the glory of the Father, even so we also should walk in newness of life.

• Not after the flesh, but after the Spirit.

Ro 8:1 — *There is* therefore now no condemnation to them which are in Christ Jesus, who walk not after the flesh, but after the Spirit.

Gal 5:16 — *This* I say then, Walk in the Spirit, and ye shall not fulfil the lust of the flesh.

• Honestly, as in the day.

Ro 13:13 — Let us walk honestly, as in the day; not in rioting and drunkenness, not in chambering and wantonness, not in strife and envying.

• By faith, not by sight.

2Co 5:7 — (For we walk by faith, not by sight:)

• In love, following Christ.

Eph 5:2 — And walk in love, as Christ also hath loved us, and hath given himself for us an offering and a sacrifice to God for a sweetsmelling savour.

• Worthy of the Lord.

Col 1:10 — That ye might walk worthy of the Lord unto all pleasing, being fruitful in every good work, and increasing in the knowledge of God;

• In Christ.

Col 2:6 As ye have therefore received Christ Jesus the Lord, *so* walk ye in him:

• By the gospel rule.

Php 3:16 — Nevertheless, whereto we have already attained, let us walk by the same rule, let us mind the same thing.

• In the light, as God is.

1Jn 1:7 — But if we walk in the light, as he is in the light, we have fellowship one with another, and the blood of Jesus Christ his Son cleanseth us from all sin.

• In white raiment.

Rev 3:4 — Thou hast a few names even in Sardis which have not defiled their garments; and they shall walk with me in white: for they are worthy.

• In the light of heaven.

Rev 21:24 — And the nations of them which are saved shall walk in the light of it: and the kings of the earth do bring their glory and honour into it.

• Instances of.

• Enoch.

Ge 5:24

• Noah.

Ge 6:9

WALLS, of the cities

• Of Bashan, destroyed by the Israelites.

Dt 3:5–6

• Of Jericho.

Jos 6:1–27

Jos 2:15 — Then she let them down by a cord through the window: for her house *was* upon the town wall, and she dwelt upon the wall.

• Of Jerusalem.

See: Jerusalem

• Of Babylon.

Jer 51:44 — And I will punish Bel in Babylon, and I will bring forth out of his mouth that which he hath swallowed up: and the nations shall not flow together any more unto him: yea, the wall of Babylon shall fall.

• Broad.

Jer 51:58 — Thus saith the LORD of hosts; The broad walls of Babylon shall be utterly broken, and her high gates shall be burned with fire; and the people shall labour in vain, and the folk in the fire, and they shall be weary.

• Of Beth-shan.

1Sa 31:10 — And they put his armour in the house of Ashtaroth: and they fastened his body to the wall of Beth-shan.

• Of Rabbah.

2Sa 11:20 — And if so be that the king's wrath arise, and he say unto thee, Wherefore approached ye so nigh unto the city when ye did fight? knew ye not that they would shoot from the wall?

- **Of Abel.**

2Sa 20:15 — And they came and besieged him in Abel of Beth-maachah, and they cast up a bank against the city, and it stood in the trench: and all the people that *were* with Joab battered the wall, to throw it down.

2Sa 20:21 — The matter *is* not so: but a man of mount Ephraim, Sheba the son of Bichri by name, hath lifted up his hand against the king, *even* against David: deliver him only, and I will depart from the city. And the woman said unto Joab, Behold, his head shall be thrown to thee over the wall.

- **Houses built upon.**

Jos 2:15 — Then she let them down by a cord through the window: for her house *was* upon the town wall, and she dwelt upon the wall.

- **Double.**

2Ki 25:4 — And the city was broken up, and all the men of war *fled* by night by the way of the gate between two walls, which *is* by the king's garden: (now the Chaldees *were* against the city round about:) and *the king* went the way toward the plain.

Isa 22:11 — Ye made also a ditch between the two walls for the water of the old pool: but ye have not looked unto the maker thereof, neither had respect unto him that fashioned it long ago.

- **Sentinels on.**

  See: Watchman

- **Figurative.**
  - **Of the new Jerusalem.**

Rev 21:17–21

Rev 21:12 — And had a wall great and high, *and* had twelve gates, and at the gates twelve angels, and names written thereon, which are *the names* of the twelve tribes of the children of Israel:

Rev 21:14 — And the wall of the city had twelve foundations, and in them the names of the twelve apostles of the Lamb.

WAR

- **Divine approval of.**

2Sa 22:35 — He teacheth my hands to war; so that a bow of steel is broken by mine arms.

- **Civil.**

Jgs 12:1–6; 20:1–48; 2Sa 2:12–31; 20:1–26

2Sa 3:1 — Now there was long war between the house of Saul and the house of David: but David waxed stronger and stronger, and the house of Saul waxed weaker and weaker.

1Ki 14:30 — And there was war between Rehoboam and Jeroboam all *their* days.

1Ki 16:21 — Then were the people of Israel divided into two parts: half of the people followed Tibni the son of Ginath, to make him king; and half followed Omri.

Isa 19:2 — And I will set the Egyptians against the Egyptians: and they shall fight every one against his brother, and every one against his neighbour; city against city, *and* kingdom against kingdom.

- **Forbidden.**

2Ch 11:4 — Thus saith the LORD, Ye shall not go up, nor fight against your brethren: return every man to his house: for this thing is done of me. And they obeyed the words of the LORD, and returned from going against Jeroboam.

- **Averted.**

Jos 22:11–34

- **Enemy harangued by general of opposing side.**

2Ki 18:19–36; 2Ch 13:4–12

- **Of extermination.**

Nu 31:7–17; Dt 2:33–34; 20:13–18; Jos 8:24–25; 10:2–40; 11:11–23; 1Sa 15:3–9; 27:8–11

Dt 3:6 — And we utterly destroyed them, as we did unto Sihon king of Heshbon, utterly destroying the men, women, and children, of every city.

Jos 6:21 — And they utterly destroyed all that *was* in the city, both man and woman, young and old, and ox, and sheep, and ass, with the edge of the sword.

Jos 6:24 — And they burnt the city with fire, and all that *was* therein: only the silver, and the gold, and the vessels of brass and of iron, they put into the treasury of the house of the LORD.

- **God in.**

Ex 14:13–14; Dt 3:21–22; 7:17–24; 31:6–8; 32:29–30; Jos 1:5–7; 1Sa 17:45–47; 30:7–8; 2Sa 5:22–24; Am 5:8–9

Dt 1:30 — The LORD your God which goeth before you, he shall fight for you, according to all that he did for you in Egypt before your eyes;

Dt 20:1 — When thou goest out to battle against thine enemies, and seest horses, and chariots, *and* a people more than thou, be not afraid of them: for the LORD thy God *is* with thee, which brought thee up out of the land of Egypt.

Dt 20:4 — For the LORD your God *is* he that goeth with you, to fight for you against your enemies, to save you.

Dt 31:23 — And he gave Joshua the son of Nun a charge, and said, Be strong and of a good courage: for thou shalt bring the children of Israel into the land which I sware unto them: and I will be with thee.

Jos 1:1 — Now after the death of Moses the servant of the LORD it came to pass, that the LORD spake unto Joshua the son of Nun, Moses' minister, saying,

Jos 1:9 — Have not I commanded thee? Be strong and of a good courage; be not afraid, neither be thou dismayed: for the LORD thy God *is* with thee whithersoever thou goest.

Jgs 1:2 — And the LORD said, Judah shall go up: behold, I have delivered the land into his hand.

Jgs 6:16 — And the LORD said unto him, Surely I will be with thee, and thou shalt smite the Midianites as one man.

Jgs 7:9 — And it came to pass the same night, that the LORD said unto him, Arise, get thee down unto the host; for I have delivered it into thine hand.

Jgs 11:29 — Then the Spirit of the LORD came upon Jephthah, and he passed over Gilead, and Manasseh, and passed over Mizpeh of Gilead, and from Mizpeh of Gilead he passed over *unto* the children of Ammon.

1Sa 19:5 — For he did put his life in his hand, and slew the Philistine, and the LORD wrought a great salvation for all Israel: thou sawest *it,* and didst rejoice: wherefore then wilt thou sin against innocent blood, to slay David without a cause?

2Sa 22:18 — He delivered me from my strong enemy, *and* from them that hated me: for they were too strong for me.

1Ki 20:28 — And there came a man of God, and spake unto the king of Israel, and said, Thus saith the LORD, Because the Syrians have said, The LORD *is* God of the hills, but he *is* not God of the valleys, therefore will I deliver all this great multitude into thine hand, and ye shall know that I *am* the LORD.

Ps 18:34 — He teacheth my hands to war, so that a bow of steel is broken by mine arms.

Ps 76:3 — There brake he the arrows of the bow, the shield, and the sword, and the battle. Selah.

Jer 46:15 — Why are thy valiant *men* swept away? they stood not, because the LORD did drive them.

Zec 10:5 — And they shall be as mighty *men,* which tread down *their enemies* in the mire of the streets in the battle: and they shall fight, because the LORD *is* with them, and the riders on horses shall be confounded.

• God uses, as a judgment.

Le 26:31–39; Dt 28:25–68; 2Ch 12:1–12; 24:23–24; 36:1–23; Ps 44:9–16; 60:1–3; Isa 5:1–8, 25–30; 9:8–12; 13:3–4; 34:2–6; Jer 46:15–17; 47:6–7; Eze 23:22–25; Zep 1:7–18

Ex 23:24 — Thou shalt not bow down to their gods, nor serve them, nor do after their works: but thou shalt utterly overthrow them, and quite break down their images.

Le 26:17 — And I will set my face against you, and ye shall be slain before your enemies: they that hate you shall reign over you; and ye shall flee when none pursueth you.

Dt 32:30 — How should one chase a thousand, and two put ten thousand to flight, except their Rock had sold them, and the LORD had shut them up?

Jgs 2:14 — And the anger of the LORD was hot against Israel, and he delivered them into the hands of spoilers that spoiled them, and he sold them into the hands of their enemies round about, so that they could not any longer stand before their enemies.

2Ki 15:37 — In those days the LORD began to send against Judah Rezin the king of Syria, and Pekah the son of Remaliah.

1Ch 5:22 — For there fell down many slain, because the war *was* of God. And they dwelt in their steads until the captivity.

1Ch 5:26 — And the God of Israel stirred up the spirit of Pul king of Assyria, and the spirit of Tilgath-pilneser king of Assyria, and he carried them away, even the Reubenites, and the Gadites, and the half tribe of Manasseh, and brought them unto Halah, and Habor, and Hara, and to the river Gozan, unto this day.

1Ch 21:12 — Either three years' famine; or three months to be destroyed before thy foes, while that the sword of thine enemies overtaketh *thee;* or else three days the sword of the LORD, even the pestilence, in the land, and the angel of the LORD destroying throughout all the coasts of Israel. Now therefore advise thyself what word I shall bring again to him that sent me.

2Ch 15:6 — And nation was destroyed of nation, and city of city: for God did vex them with all adversity.

2Ch 33:11 — Wherefore the LORD brought upon them the captains of the host of the king of Assyria, which took Manasseh among the thorns, and bound him with fetters, and carried him to Babylon.

Job 19:29 — Be ye afraid of the sword: for wrath *bringeth* the punishments of the sword, that ye may know *there is* a judgment.

Ps 105:25 — He turned their heart to hate his people, to deal subtilly with his servants.

Isa 13:9 — Behold, the day of the LORD cometh, cruel both with wrath and fierce anger, to lay the land desolate: and he shall destroy the sinners thereof out of it.

Isa 19:2 — And I will set the Egyptians against the Egyptians: and they shall fight every one against his brother, and every one against his neighbour; city against city, *and* kingdom against kingdom.

Isa 43:28 — Therefore I have profaned the princes of the sanctuary, and have given Jacob to the curse, and Israel to reproaches.

Isa 45:7 — I form the light, and create darkness: I make peace, and create evil: I the LORD do all these *things.*

Jer 12:7 — I have forsaken mine house, I have left mine heritage; I have given the dearly beloved of my soul into the hand of her enemies.

Jer 12:12 — The spoilers are come upon all high places through the wilderness: for the sword of the LORD shall devour from the *one* end of the land even to the *other* end of the land: no flesh shall have peace.

Jer 46:21 — Also her hired men *are* in the midst of her like fatted bullocks; for they also are turned back, *and* are fled away together: they did not stand, because the day of their calamity was come upon them, *and* the time of their visitation.

Jer 48:10 — Cursed *be* he that doeth the work of the LORD deceitfully, and cursed *be* he that keepeth back his sword from blood.

Jer 49:5 — Behold, I will bring a fear upon thee, saith the Lord GOD of hosts, from all those that be about thee; and ye shall be driven out every man right forth; and none shall gather up him that wandereth.

Jer 50:25 — The LORD hath opened his armoury, and hath brought forth the weapons of his indignation: for this *is* the work of the Lord GOD of hosts in the land of the Chaldeans.

Am 3:6 — Shall a trumpet be blown in the city, and the people not be afraid? shall there be evil in a city, and the LORD hath not done *it?*

Am 4:11 — I have overthrown *some* of you, as God overthrew Sodom and Gomorrah, and ye were as a firebrand plucked out of the burning: yet have ye not returned unto me, saith the LORD.

Zec 8:10 — For before these days there was no hire for man, nor any hire for beast; neither *was there any* peace to him that went out or came in because of the affliction: for I set all men every one against his neighbour.

Zec 14:2 — For I will gather all nations against Jerusalem to battle; and the city shall be taken, and the houses rifled, and the women ravished; and half of the city shall go forth into captivity, and the residue of the people shall not be cut off from the city.

• Repugnant to God.

1Ch 22:8–9; Ps 120:6–7

Ps 68:30 — Rebuke the company of spearmen, the multitude of the bulls, with the calves of the people, *till every one* submit himself with pieces of silver: scatter thou the people *that* delight in war.

Rev 13:10 — He that leadeth into captivity shall go into captivity: he that killeth with the sword must be killed with the sword. Here is the patience and the faith of the saints.

• God sends panic in.

Ex 15:14–16

• God threatens defeat in.

2Ch 18:12–16; Isa 30:15–17; Eze 15:6–8; 21:9–17

Dt 32:25 — The sword without, and terror within, shall destroy both the young man and the virgin, the suckling *also* with the man of gray hairs.

1Sa 2:10 — The adversaries of the LORD shall be broken to pieces; out of heaven shall he thunder upon them: the LORD shall judge the ends of the earth; and he shall give strength unto his king, and exalt the horn of his anointed.

• God inflicts defeat in.

Jos 7:12–13; 2Ch 12:5–8; 24:23–24; Jer 46:15–16

Ps 76:3 — There brake he the arrows of the bow, the shield, and the sword, and the battle. Selah.

Ps 78:66 — And he smote his enemies in the hinder parts: he put them to a perpetual reproach.

Ps 79:10 — Wherefore should the heathen say, Where *is* their God? let him be known among the heathen in our sight *by* the revenging of the blood of thy servants *which is* shed.

Isa 5:25 — Therefore is the anger of the LORD kindled against his people, and he hath stretched forth his hand against them, and hath smitten them: and the hills did tremble, and their carcases *were* torn in the midst of the streets. For all this his anger is not turned away, but his hand *is* stretched out still.

• Counsels of.

Jos 22:10–34; Jgs 7:10–11; 2Sa 17:1–15; Ps 48:4–7

2Sa 16:20 — Then said Absalom to Ahithophel, Give counsel among you what we shall do.

Pr 11:14 — Where no counsel *is*, the people fall: but in the multitude of counsellors *there is* safety.

Pr 20:18 — *Every* purpose is established by counsel: and with good advice make war.

• Wisdom required in.

Ecc 9:14–18; Lk 14:31–32

Pr 21:22 — A wise *man* scaleth the city of the mighty, and casteth down the strength of the confidence thereof.

Pr 24:6 — For by wise counsel thou shalt make thy war: and in multitude of counsellors *there is* safety.

• Tumult of.

Am 2:2 — But I will send a fire upon Moab, and it shall devour the palaces of Kirioth: and Moab shall die with tumult, with shouting, *and* with the sound of the trumpet:

• Slain in, neglected.

Isa 14:19 — But thou art cast out of thy grave like an abominable branch, *and as* the raiment of those that are slain, thrust through with a sword, that go down to the stones of the pit; as a carcase trodden under feet.

Isa 18:6 — They shall be left together unto the fowls of the mountains, and to the beasts of the earth: and the fowls shall summer upon them, and all the beasts of the earth shall winter upon them.

• Evils of.

Ps 79:1–3; Isa 3:25–26; 5:29–30; 6:11–12; 9:19–21; 13:15–16; 15:1–9; 16:9–10; 19:2–16; 32:13–14; 33:8–9; 34:7–15; Jer 4:19–31; 5:16–17; 6:24–26; 7:33–34; 8:16–17; 9:10–21; 15:8–9; 19:7–9; 46:3–12; 51:30–58; La 1:1–5:22; Eze 39:17–19; Joel 2:2–10; Am 6:9–10; Lk 21:20–26; Rev 19:17–18

2Sa 2:26 — Then Abner called to Joab, and said, Shall the sword devour for ever? knowest thou not that it will be bitterness in the latter end? how long shall it be then, ere thou bid the people return from following their brethren?

Ps 46:8 — Come, behold the works of the LORD, what desolations he hath made in the earth.

Ps 137:9 — Happy *shall he be,* that taketh and dasheth thy little ones against the stones.

Isa 3:5 — And the people shall be oppressed, every one by another, and every one by his neighbour: the child shall behave himself proudly against the ancient, and the base against the honourable.

Isa 9:5 — For every battle of the warrior *is* with confused noise, and garments rolled in blood; but *this* shall be with burning *and* fuel of fire.

Isa 18:6 — They shall be left together unto the fowls of the mountains, and to the beasts of the earth: and the fowls shall summer upon them, and all the beasts of the earth shall winter upon them.

Jer 10:20 — My tabernacle is spoiled, and all my cords are broken: my children are gone forth of me, and they *are* not: *there is* none to stretch forth my tent any more, and to set up my curtains.

Jer 13:14 — And I will dash them one against another, even the fathers and the sons together, saith the LORD: I will not pity, nor spare, nor have mercy, but destroy them.

Jer 14:18 — If I go forth into the field, then behold the slain with the sword! and if I enter into the city, then behold them that are sick with famine! yea, both the prophet and the priest go about into a land that they know not.

Jer 25:33 — And the slain of the LORD shall be at that day from *one* end of the earth even unto the *other* end of the earth: they shall not be lamented, neither gathered, nor buried; they shall be dung upon the ground.

Jer 47:3 — At the noise of the stamping of the hoofs of his strong *horses,* at the rushing of his chariots, *and at* the rumbling of his wheels, the fathers shall not look back to *their* children for feebleness of hands;

Jer 48:28 — O ye that dwell in Moab, leave the cities, and dwell in the rock, and be like the dove *that* maketh her nest in the sides of the hole's mouth.

Jer 48:33 — And joy and gladness is taken from the plentiful field, and from the land of Moab; and I have caused wine to fail from the winepresses: none shall tread with shouting; *their* shouting *shall be* no shouting.

Eze 33:27 — Say thou thus unto them, Thus saith the Lord GOD; *As* I live, surely they that *are* in the wastes shall fall by the sword, and him that *is* in the open field will I give to the beasts to be devoured, and they that be in the forts and in the caves shall die of the pestilence.

Hos 10:14 — Therefore shall a tumult arise among thy people, and all thy fortresses shall be spoiled, as Shalman spoiled Beth-arbel in the day of battle: the mother was dashed in pieces upon *her* children.

Hos 13:16 — Samaria shall become desolate; for she hath rebelled against her God: they shall fall by the sword: their infants shall be dashed in pieces, and their women with child shall be ripped up.

Am 1:13 — Thus saith the LORD; For three transgressions of the children of Ammon, and for four, I will not turn away *the punishment* thereof; because they have ripped up the women with child of Gilead, that they might enlarge their border:

Am 8:3 — And the songs of the temple shall be howlings in that day, saith the Lord GOD: *there shall be* many dead bodies in every place; they shall cast *them* forth with silence.

Na 2:10 — She is empty, and void, and waste: and the heart melteth, and the knees smite together, and much pain *is* in all loins, and the faces of them all gather blackness.

Na 3:3 — The horseman lifteth up both the bright sword and the glittering spear: and *there is* a multitude of slain, and a great number of carcases; and *there is* none end of *their* corpses; they stumble upon their corpses:

Na 3:10 — Yet *was* she carried away, she went into captivity: her young children also were dashed in pieces at the top of all the streets: and they cast lots for her honourable men, and all her great men were bound in chains.

Zec 14:2 — For I will gather all nations against Jerusalem to battle; and the city shall be taken, and the houses rifled, and the women ravished; and half of the city shall go forth into captivity, and the residue of the people shall not be cut off from the city.

• To cease.

Ps 46:9 — He maketh wars to cease unto the end of the earth; he breaketh the bow, and cutteth the spear in sunder; he burneth the chariot in the fire.

Isa 2:4 — And he shall judge among the nations, and shall rebuke many people: and they shall beat their swords into plowshares, and their spears into pruninghooks: nation shall not lift up sword against nation, neither shall they learn war any more.

Mic 4:3 — And he shall judge among many people, and rebuke strong nations afar off; and they shall beat their swords into plowshares, and their spears into pruninghooks: nation shall not lift up a sword against nation, neither shall they learn war any more.

• Wars and rumors of.

Mt 24:6 — And ye shall hear of wars and rumours of wars: see that ye be not troubled: for all *these things* must come to pass, but the end is not yet.

Mk 13:7 — And when ye shall hear of wars and rumours of wars, be ye not troubled: for *such things* must needs be; but the end *shall* not *be* yet.

Lk 21:9 — But when ye shall hear of wars and commotions, be not terrified: for these things must first come to pass; but the end *is* not by and by.

See: Armies

See: Arms

See: Fort

See: Soldiers

See: Strategy

See: Tower

See: Watchman

WAR, Armor for, figurative

• A girdle of truth.

Eph 6:14 — Stand therefore, having your loins girt about with truth, and having on the breastplate of righteousness;

• The breastplate of righteousness.

Eph 6:14 — Stand therefore, having your loins girt about with truth, and having on the breastplate of righteousness;

• Preparation of the gospel.

Eph 6:15 — And your feet shod with the preparation of the gospel of peace;

• Shield of faith.

Eph 6:16 — Above all, taking the shield of faith, wherewith ye shall be able to quench all the fiery darts of the wicked.

• Helmet of salvation.

Eph 6:17 — And take the helmet of salvation, and the sword of the Spirit, which is the word of God:

1Th 5:8 — But let us, who are of the day, be sober, putting on the breastplate of faith and love; and for an helmet, the hope of salvation.

• Sword of the Spirit.

Eph 6:17 — And take the helmet of salvation, and the sword of the Spirit, which is the word of God:

• Called armor of God.

Eph 6:11 — Put on the whole armour of God, that ye may be able to stand against the wiles of the devil.

• Called armor of righteousness.

2Co 6:7 — By the word of truth, by the power of God, by the armour of righteousness on the right hand and on the left,

• Called armor of light.

Ro 13:12 — The night is far spent, the day is at hand: let us therefore cast off the works of darkness, and let us put on the armour of light.

• Not carnal.

2Co 10:4 — (For the weapons of our warfare *are* not carnal, but mighty through God to the pulling down of strong holds;)

• Mighty through God.

2Co 10:4–5

• The whole, is required.

Eph 6:13 — Wherefore take unto you the whole armour of God, that ye may be able to withstand in the evil day, and having done all, to stand.

• Must be put on.

Ro 13:12 — The night is far spent, the day is at hand: let us therefore cast off the works of darkness, and let us put on the armour of light.

Eph 6:11 — Put on the whole armour of God, that ye may be able to stand against the wiles of the devil.

• To be on right hand and left.

2Co 6:7 — By the word of truth, by the power of God, by the armour of righteousness on the right hand and on the left,

WAR, figurative

• Warfare of saints.

• Is not after the flesh.

2Co 10:3 — For though we walk in the flesh, we do not war after the flesh:

• Is a good warfare.

1Ti 1:18–19

• Called the good fight of faith.

1Ti 6:12 — Fight the good fight of faith, lay hold on eternal life, whereunto thou art also called, and hast professed a good profession before many witnesses.

• Is against the devil.

Ge 3:15 — And I will put enmity between thee and the woman, and between thy seed and her seed; it shall bruise thy head, and thou shalt bruise his heel.

2Co 2:11 — Lest Satan should get an advantage of us: for we are not ignorant of his devices.

Eph 6:12 — For we wrestle not against flesh and blood, but against principalities, against powers, against the rulers of the darkness of this world, against spiritual wickedness in high *places.*

Jas 4:7 — Submit yourselves therefore to God. Resist the devil, and he will flee from you.

1Pe 5:8 — Be sober, be vigilant; because your adversary the devil, as a roaring lion, walketh about, seeking whom he may devour:

Rev 12:17 — And the dragon was wroth with the woman, and went to make war with the remnant of her seed, which keep the commandments of God, and have the testimony of Jesus Christ.

• Is against the flesh.

1Co 9:25–27

Ro 7:23 — But I see another law in my members, warring against the law of my mind, and bringing me into captivity to the law of sin which is in my members.

2Co 12:7 — And lest I should be exalted above measure through the abundance of the revelations, there was given to me a thorn in the flesh, the messenger of Satan to buffet me, lest I should be exalted above measure.

Gal 5:17 — For the flesh lusteth against the Spirit, and the Spirit against the flesh: and these are contrary the one to the other: so that ye cannot do the things that ye would.

1Pe 2:11 — Dearly beloved, I beseech *you* as strangers and pilgrims, abstain from fleshly lusts, which war against the soul;

• Is against enemies.

Ps 38:19 — But mine enemies *are* lively, *and* they are strong: and they that hate me wrongfully are multiplied.

Ps 56:2 — Mine enemies would daily swallow *me* up: for *they be* many that fight against me, O thou most High.

Ps 59:3 — For, lo, they lie in wait for my soul: the mighty are gathered against me; not *for* my transgression, nor *for* my sin, O LORD.

• Is against the world.

1Jn 5:4–5

Jn 16:33 — These things I have spoken unto you, that in me ye might have peace. In the world ye shall have tribulation: but be of good cheer; I have overcome the world.

• Is against death.

Heb 2:14–15

1Co 15:26 — The last enemy *that* shall be destroyed *is* death.

• Often arises from the opposition of friends or relatives.

Mt 10:35–36

Mic 7:6 — For the son dishonoureth the father, the daughter riseth up against her mother, the daughter in law against her mother in law; a man's enemies *are* the men of his own house.

• To be carried on under Christ, as our Captain.

Heb 2:10 — For it became him, for whom *are* all things, and by whom *are* all things, in bringing many sons unto glory, to make the captain of their salvation perfect through sufferings.

• To be carried under the Lord's banner.

Ps 60:4 — Thou hast given a banner to them that fear thee, that it may be displayed because of the truth. Selah.

• To be carried with faith.

1Ti 1:18–19

• To be carried with a good conscience.

1Ti 1:18–19

• To be carried with steadfastness in the faith.

1Co 16:13 — Watch ye, stand fast in the faith, quit you like men, be strong.

Heb 10:23 — Let us hold fast the profession of *our* faith without wavering; (for he is faithful that promised;)

1Pe 5:9 — Whom resist stedfast in the faith, knowing that the same afflictions are accomplished in your brethren that are in the world.

• To be carried with earnestness.

Jude 1:3 — Beloved, when I gave all diligence to write unto you of the common salvation, it was needful for me to write unto you, and exhort *you* that ye should earnestly contend for the faith which was once delivered unto the saints.

• To be carried with watchfulness.

1Co 16:13 — Watch ye, stand fast in the faith, quit you like men, be strong.

1Pe 5:8 — Be sober, be vigilant; because your adversary the devil, as a roaring lion, walketh about, seeking whom he may devour:

• To be carried with sobriety.

1Th 5:6 — Therefore let us not sleep, as *do* others; but let us watch and be sober.

1Pe 5:8 — Be sober, be vigilant; because your adversary the devil, as a roaring lion, walketh about, seeking whom he may devour:

• To be carried with endurance of hardness.

2Ti 2:3 — Thou therefore endure hardness, as a good soldier of Jesus Christ.

2Ti 2:10 — Therefore I endure all things for the elect's sakes, that they may also obtain the salvation which is in Christ Jesus with eternal glory.

• To be carried with self-denial.

1Co 9:25–27

• To be carried with confidence in God.

Ps 27:1–3

• To be carried with prayer.

Ps 35:1–3

Eph 6:18 — Praying always with all prayer and supplication in the Spirit, and watching thereunto with all perseverance and supplication for all saints;

• To be carried without earthly entanglements.

2Ti 2:4 — No man that warreth entangleth himself with the affairs of *this* life; that he may please him who hath chosen him to be a soldier.

• Mere professors do not maintain.

Jer 9:3 — And they bend their tongues *like* their bow *for* lies: but they are not valiant for the truth upon the earth; for they proceed from evil to evil, and they know not me, saith the LORD.

• Saints are all engaged in.

Php 1:30 — Having the same conflict which ye saw in me, and now hear *to be* in me.

• Saints must stand firm in.

Eph 6:13–14

• Saints exhorted to diligence in.

1Ti 6:12 — Fight the good fight of faith, lay hold on eternal life, whereunto thou art also called, and hast professed a good profession before many witnesses.

Jude 1:3 — Beloved, when I gave all diligence to write unto you of the common salvation, it was needful for me to write unto you, and exhort *you* that ye should earnestly contend for the faith which was once delivered unto the saints.

• Saints encouraged in.

Isa 41:11–12

Isa 51:12 — I, *even* I, *am* he that comforteth you: who *art* thou, that thou shouldest be afraid of a man *that* shall die, and of the son of man *which* shall be made as grass;

Mic 7:8 — Rejoice not against me, O mine enemy: when I fall, I shall arise; when I sit in darkness, the LORD *shall be* a light unto me.

1Jn 4:4 — Ye are of God, little children, and have overcome them: because greater is he that is in you, than he that is in the world.

• Saints helped by God in.

Isa 41:13–14

Ps 118:13 — Thou hast thrust sore at me that I might fall: but the LORD helped me.

• Saints protected by God in.

Ps 140:7 — O GOD the Lord, the strength of my salvation, thou hast covered my head in the day of battle.

• Saints comforted by God in.

2Co 7:5–6

• Saints strengthened by God in.

Ps 20:2 — Send thee help from the sanctuary, and strengthen thee out of Zion;

Ps 27:14 — Wait on the LORD: be of good courage, and he shall strengthen thine heart: wait, I say, on the LORD.

Isa 41:10 — Fear thou not; for I *am* with thee: be not dismayed; for I *am* thy God: I will strengthen thee; yea, I will help thee; yea, I will uphold thee with the right hand of my righteousness.

• Saints strengthened by Christ in.

2Co 12:9 — And he said unto me, My grace is sufficient for thee: for my strength is made perfect in weakness. Most gladly therefore will I rather glory in my infirmities, that the power of Christ may rest upon me.

2Ti 4:17 — Notwithstanding the Lord stood with me, and strengthened me; that by me the preaching might be fully known, and *that* all the Gentiles might hear: and I was delivered out of the mouth of the lion.

• Saints delivered by Christ in.

2Ti 4:18 — And the Lord shall deliver me from every evil work, and will preserve *me* unto his heavenly kingdom: to whom *be* glory for ever and ever. Amen.

• Saints thank God for victory in.

Ro 7:25 — I thank God through Jesus Christ our Lord. So then with the mind I myself serve the law of God; but with the flesh the law of sin.

1Co 15:57 — But thanks *be* to God, which giveth us the victory through our Lord Jesus Christ.

WAR, Spiritual, Victory in, is from God

1Co 15:57 — But thanks *be* to God, which giveth us the victory through our Lord Jesus Christ.

2Co 2:14 — Now thanks *be* unto God, which always causeth us to triumph in Christ, and maketh manifest the savour of his knowledge by us in every place.

• Victory in.

• Through Christ.

Ro 7:25 — I thank God through Jesus Christ our Lord. So then with the mind I myself serve the law of God; but with the flesh the law of sin.

1Co 15:57 — But thanks *be* to God, which giveth us the victory through our Lord Jesus Christ.

2Co 12:9 — And he said unto me, My grace is sufficient for thee: for my strength is made perfect in weakness. Most gladly therefore will I rather glory in my infirmities, that the power of Christ may rest upon me.

Rev 12:11 — And they overcame him by the blood of the Lamb, and by the word of their testimony; and they loved not their lives unto the death.

• By faith.

Heb 11:33–37; 1Jn 5:4–5

• Over the devil.

Ro 16:20 — And the God of peace shall bruise Satan under your feet shortly. The grace of our Lord Jesus Christ *be* with you. Amen.

1Jn 2:14 — I have written unto you, fathers, because ye have known him *that is* from the beginning. I have written unto you, young men, because ye are strong, and the word of God abideth in you, and ye have overcome the wicked one.

• Over the flesh.

Ro 7:24–25

Gal 5:24 — And they that are Christ's have crucified the flesh with the affections and lusts.

• Over the world.

1Jn 5:4–5

• Over all that exalts itself.

2Co 10:5 — Casting down imaginations, and every high thing that exalteth itself against the knowledge of God, and bringing into captivity every thought to the obedience of Christ;

• Over death and the grave.

1Co 15:54–55

Isa 25:8 — He will swallow up death in victory; and the Lord GOD will wipe away tears from off all faces; and the rebuke of his people shall he take away from off all the earth: for the LORD hath spoken *it.*

Isa 26:19 — Thy dead *men* shall live, *together with* my dead body shall they arise. Awake and sing, ye that dwell in dust: for thy dew *is as* the dew of herbs, and the earth shall cast out the dead.

Hos 13:14 — I will ransom them from the power of the grave; I will redeem them from death: O death, I will be thy plagues; O grave, I will be thy destruction: repentance shall be hid from mine eyes.

• Triumphant.

Ro 8:37 — Nay, in all these things we are more than conquerors through him that loved us.

2Co 10:5 — Casting down imaginations, and every high thing that exalteth itself against the knowledge of God, and bringing into captivity every thought to the obedience of Christ;

• They who overcome in.

• Shall eat of the hidden manna.

Rev 2:17 — He that hath an ear, let him hear what the Spirit saith unto the churches; To him that overcometh will I give to eat of the hidden manna, and will give him a white stone, and in the stone a new name written, which no man knoweth saving he that receiveth *it.*

• Shall eat of the tree of life.

Rev 2:7 — He that hath an ear, let him hear what the Spirit saith unto the churches; To him that overcometh will I give to eat of the tree of life, which is in the midst of the paradise of God.

• Shall be clothed in white raiment.

Rev 3:5 — He that overcometh, the same shall be clothed in white raiment; and I will not blot out his name out of the book of life, but I will confess his name before my Father, and before his angels.

• Shall be pillars in the temple of God.

Rev 3:12 — Him that overcometh will I make a pillar in the temple of my God, and he shall go no more out: and I will write upon him the name of my God, and the name of the city of my God, *which is* new Jerusalem, which cometh down out of heaven from my God: and *I will write upon him* my new name.

• Shall sit with Christ in his throne.

Rev 3:21 — To him that overcometh will I grant to sit with me in my throne, even as I also overcame, and am set down with my Father in his throne.

• Shall have a white stone, and in it a new name written.

Rev 2:17 — He that hath an ear, let him hear what the Spirit saith unto the churches; To him that overcometh will I give to eat of the hidden manna, and will give him a white stone, and in the stone a new name written, which no man knoweth saving he that receiveth *it.*

• Shall have power over the nations.

Rev 2:26 — And he that overcometh, and keepeth my works unto the end, to him will I give power over the nations:

• Shall have the name of God written upon them by Christ.

Rev 3:12 — Him that overcometh will I make a pillar in the temple of my God, and he shall go no more out: and I will write upon him the name of my God, and the name of the city of my God, *which is* new Jerusalem, which cometh down out of heaven from my God: and *I will write upon him* my new name.

• Shall have God as their God.

Rev 21:7 — He that overcometh shall inherit all things; and I will be his God, and he shall be my son.

• Shall have the morning star.

Rev 2:28 — And I will give him the morning star.

• Shall shall inherit all things.

Rev 21:7 — He that overcometh shall inherit all things; and I will be his God, and he shall be my son.

• Shall be confessed by Christ before God the Father.

Rev 3:5 — He that overcometh, the same shall be clothed in white raiment; and I will not blot out his name out of the book of life, but I will confess his name before my Father, and before his angels.

• Shall be sons of God.

Rev 21:7 — He that overcometh shall inherit all things; and I will be his God, and he shall be my son.

• Shall not be hurt by the second death.

Rev 2:11 — He that hath an ear, let him hear what the Spirit saith unto the churches; He that overcometh shall not be hurt of the second death.

• Shall not have their names blotted out of the book of life.

Rev 3:5 — He that overcometh, the same shall be clothed in white raiment; and I will not blot out his name out of the book of life, but I will confess his name before my Father, and before his angels.

• Symbolized by a red horse.

Rev 6:4 — And there went out another horse *that was* red: and *power* was given to him that sat thereon to take peace from the earth, and that they should kill one another: and there was given unto him a great sword.

• In heaven.

• Symbolic.

Rev 12:7 — And there was war in heaven: Michael and his angels fought against the dragon; and the dragon fought and his angels,

WARFARE

⇜See: War

• Spiritual.

⇜See: War, figurative

WARNING ⇜See: Wicked; warned

WASHING

• Of hands, a token of innocency.

Dt 21:6 — And all the elders of that city, *that are* next unto the slain *man,* shall wash their hands over the heifer that is beheaded in the valley:

Ps 26:6 — I will wash mine hands in innocency: so will I compass thine altar, O LORD:

Ps 73:13 — Verily I have cleansed my heart *in* vain, and washed my hands in innocency.

Mt 27:24 — When Pilate saw that he could prevail nothing, but *that* rather a tumult was made, he took water, and washed *his* hands before the multitude, saying, I am innocent of the blood of this just person: see ye *to it.*

⇜See: Ablution

⇜See: Purification

• Figurative.

• Of regeneration.

Ps 51:7 — Purge me with hyssop, and I shall be clean: wash me, and I shall be whiter than snow.

Pr 30:12 — *There is* a generation *that are* pure in their own eyes, and *yet* is not washed from their filthiness.

Isa 1:16 — Wash you, make you clean; put away the evil of your doings from before mine eyes; cease to do evil;

Isa 4:4 — When the Lord shall have washed away the filth of the daughters of Zion, and shall have purged the blood of Jerusalem from the midst thereof by the spirit of judgment, and by the spirit of burning.

Zec 13:1 — In that day there shall be a fountain opened to the house of David and to the inhabitants of Jerusalem for sin and for uncleanness.

1Co 6:11 — And such were some of you: but ye are washed, but ye are sanctified, but ye are justified in the name of the Lord Jesus, and by the Spirit of our God.

Eph 5:26 — That he might sanctify and cleanse it with the washing of water by the word,

Tit 3:5 — Not by works of righteousness which we have done, but according to his mercy he saved us, by the washing of regeneration, and renewing of the Holy Ghost;

WATCH

• A division of time.

⇜See: Night; divided into watches

WATCHFULNESS

1Ki 2:3–4; Job 36:18–21; Pr 4:25–26; Mt 24:42–51; 26:40–41; Mk 13:9–23, 32–37; Lk 12:35–40; 21:8–36; Ac 20:28–31; 1Co 7:29–31; Jude 1:20–21; Rev 3:2–3

Ex 23:13 — And in all *things* that I have said unto you be circumspect: and make no mention of the name of other gods, neither let it be heard out of thy mouth.

Ex 34:12 — Take heed to thyself, lest thou make a covenant with the inhabitants of the land whither thou goest, lest it be for a snare in the midst of thee:

Dt 4:9 — Only take heed to thyself, and keep thy soul diligently, lest thou forget the things which thine eyes have seen, and lest they depart from thy heart all the days of thy life: but teach them thy sons, and thy sons' sons;

Dt 4:23 — Take heed unto yourselves, lest ye forget the covenant of the LORD your God, which he made with you, and make you a graven image, *or* the likeness of any *thing,* which the LORD thy God hath forbidden thee.

Dt 6:17 — Ye shall diligently keep the commandments of the LORD your God, and his testimonies, and his statutes, which he hath commanded thee.

Dt 11:16 — Take heed to yourselves, that your heart be not deceived, and ye turn aside, and serve other gods, and worship them;

Dt 12:13 — Take heed to thyself that thou offer not thy burnt offerings in every place that thou seest:

Dt 27:9 — And Moses and the priests the Levites spake unto all Israel, saying, Take heed, and hearken, O Israel; this day thou art become the people of the LORD thy God.

Jos 22:5 — But take diligent heed to do the commandment and the law, which Moses the servant of the LORD charged you, to love the LORD your God, and to walk in all his ways, and to keep his commandments, and to cleave unto him, and to serve him with all your heart and with all your soul.

Jos 23:11 — Take good heed therefore unto yourselves, that ye love the LORD your God.

1Ki 8:25 — Therefore now, LORD God of Israel, keep with thy servant David my father that thou promisedst him, saying, There shall not fail thee a man in my sight to sit on the throne of Israel; so that thy children take heed to their way, that they walk before me as thou hast walked before me.

2Ch 19:7 — Wherefore now let the fear of the LORD be upon you; take heed and do *it:* for *there is* no iniquity with the LORD our God, nor respect of persons, nor taking of gifts.

Ne 4:9 — Nevertheless we made our prayer unto our God, and set a watch against them day and night, because of them.

Ps 39:1 — I said, I will take heed to my ways, that I sin not with my tongue: I will keep my mouth with a bridle, while the wicked is before me.

Ps 102:7 — I watch, and am as a sparrow alone upon the house top.

Ps 119:9 — Wherewithal shall a young man cleanse his way? by taking heed *thereto* according to thy word.

Ps 141:3 — Set a watch, O LORD, before my mouth; keep the door of my lips.

Pr 4:23 — Keep thy heart with all diligence; for out of it *are* the issues of life.

Pr 8:34 — Blessed *is* the man that heareth me, watching daily at my gates, waiting at the posts of my doors.

Pr 16:17 — The highway of the upright *is* to depart from evil: he that keepeth his way preserveth his soul.

Pr 28:26 — He that trusteth in his own heart is a fool: but whoso walketh wisely, he shall be delivered.

Na 2:1 — He that dasheth in pieces is come up before thy face: keep the munition, watch the way, make *thy* loins strong, fortify *thy* power mightily.

Hab 2:1 — I will stand upon my watch, and set me upon the tower, and will watch to see what he will say unto me, and what I shall answer when I am reproved.

Mal 2:15 — And did not he make one? Yet had he the residue of the spirit. And wherefore one? That he might seek a godly seed. Therefore take heed to your spirit, and let none deal treacherously against the wife of his youth.

Mt 6:1 — Take heed that ye do not your alms before men, to be seen of them: otherwise ye have no reward of your Father which is in heaven.

Mt 16:6 — Then Jesus said unto them, Take heed and beware of the leaven of the Pharisees and of the Sadducees.

Mt 18:10 — Take heed that ye despise not one of these little ones; for I say unto you, That in heaven their angels do always behold the face of my Father which is in heaven.

Mt 24:4 — And Jesus answered and said unto them, Take heed that no man deceive you.

Mt 25:13 — Watch therefore, for ye know neither the day nor the hour wherein the Son of man cometh.

Mk 4:24 — And he said unto them, Take heed what ye hear: with what measure ye mete, it shall be measured to you: and unto you that hear shall more be given.

Lk 8:18 — Take heed therefore how ye hear: for whosoever hath, to him shall be given; and whosoever hath not, from him shall be taken even that which he seemeth to have.

Lk 11:35 — Take heed therefore that the light which is in thee be not darkness.

Lk 12:15 — And he said unto them, Take heed, and beware of covetousness: for a man's life consisteth not in the abundance of the things which he possesseth.

Ro 11:21 — For if God spared not the natural branches, *take heed* lest he also spare not thee.

Ro 13:11 — And that, knowing the time, that now *it is* high time to awake out of sleep: for now *is* our salvation nearer than when we believed.

1Co 9:27 — But I keep under my body, and bring *it* into subjection: lest that by any means, when I have preached to others, I myself should be a castaway.

1Co 10:12 — Wherefore let him that thinketh he standeth take heed lest he fall.

1Co 11:28 — But let a man examine himself, and so let him eat of *that* bread, and drink of *that* cup.

1Co 16:13 — Watch ye, stand fast in the faith, quit you like men, be strong.

Gal 6:1 — Brethren, if a man be overtaken in a fault, ye which are spiritual, restore such an one in the spirit of meekness; considering thyself, lest thou also be tempted.

Eph 5:15 — See then that ye walk circumspectly, not as fools, but as wise,

Eph 6:18 — Praying always with all prayer and supplication in the Spirit, and watching thereunto with all perseverance and supplication for all saints;

Php 3:2 — Beware of dogs, beware of evil workers, beware of the concision.

Php 4:5 — Let your moderation be known unto all men. The Lord *is* at hand.

Col 4:2 — Continue in prayer, and watch in the same with thanksgiving;

Col 4:17 — And say to Archippus, Take heed to the ministry which thou hast received in the Lord, that thou fulfil it.

1Th 5:4 — But ye, brethren, are not in darkness, that that day should overtake you as a thief.

1Th 5:6 — Therefore let us not sleep, as *do* others; but let us watch and be sober.

1Th 5:21 — Prove all things; hold fast that which is good.

1Ti 4:16 — Take heed unto thyself, and unto the doctrine; continue in them: for in doing this thou shalt both save thyself, and them that hear thee.

2Ti 4:5 — But watch thou in all things, endure afflictions, do the work of an evangelist, make full proof of thy ministry.

Heb 2:1 — Therefore we ought to give the more earnest heed to the things which we have heard, lest at any time we should let *them* slip.

Heb 3:12 — Take heed, brethren, lest there be in any of you an evil heart of unbelief, in departing from the living God.

Heb 12:15 — Looking diligently lest any man fail of the grace of God; lest any root of bitterness springing up trouble *you,* and thereby many be defiled;

1Pe 1:13 — Wherefore gird up the loins of your mind, be sober, and hope to the end for the grace that is to be brought unto you at the revelation of Jesus Christ;

1Pe 1:17 — And if ye call on the Father, who without respect of persons judgeth according to every man's work, pass the time of your sojourning *here* in fear:

1Pe 4:7 — But the end of all things is at hand: be ye therefore sober, and watch unto prayer.

1Pe 5:8 — Be sober, be vigilant; because your adversary the devil, as a roaring lion, walketh about, seeking whom he may devour:

2Pe 1:19 — We have also a more sure word of prophecy; whereunto ye do well that ye take heed, as unto a light that shineth in a dark place, until the day dawn, and the day star arise in your hearts:

2Pe 3:17 — Ye therefore, beloved, seeing ye know *these things* before, beware lest ye also, being led away with the error of the wicked, fall from your own stedfastness.

1Jn 5:18 — We know that whosoever is born of God sinneth not; but he that is begotten of God keepeth himself, and that wicked one toucheth him not.

2Jn 1:8 — Look to yourselves, that we lose not those things which we have wrought, but that we receive a full reward.

Rev 3:11 — Behold, I come quickly: hold that fast which thou hast, that no man take thy crown.

Rev 16:15 — Behold, I come as a thief. Blessed *is* he that watcheth, and keepeth his garments, lest he walk naked, and they see his shame.

See: Temptation

WATCHMAN

• A sentinel.

• On the walls of cities.

SS 3:3 — The watchmen that go about the city found me: *to whom I said,* Saw ye him whom my soul loveth?

SS 5:7 — The watchmen that went about the city found me, they smote me, they wounded me; the keepers of the walls took away my veil from me.

• On the walls of Jerusalem.

2Sa 18:24–25

2Sa 13:34 — But Absalom fled. And the young man that kept the watch lifted up his eyes, and looked, and, behold, there came much people by the way of the hill side behind him.

Ne 4:9 — Nevertheless we made our prayer unto our God, and set a watch against them day and night, because of them.

Ne 7:3 — And I said unto them, Let not the gates of Jerusalem be opened until the sun be hot; and while they stand by, let them shut the doors, and bar *them:* and appoint watches of the inhabitants of Jerusalem, every one in his watch, and every one *to be* over against his house.

Isa 52:8 — Thy watchmen shall lift up the voice; with the voice together shall they sing: for they shall see eye to eye, when the LORD shall bring again Zion.

Isa 62:6 — I have set watchmen upon thy walls, O Jerusalem, *which* shall never hold their peace day nor night: ye that make mention of the LORD, keep not silence,

• On the walls of Babylon.

Jer 51:12 — Set up the standard upon the walls of Babylon, make the watch strong, set up the watchmen, prepare the ambushes: for the LORD hath both devised and done that which he spake against the inhabitants of Babylon.

• On towers.

Isa 21:5–12

2Ki 9:17 — And there stood a watchman on the tower in Jezreel, and he spied the company of Jehu as he came, and said, I see a company. And Joram said, Take an horseman, and send to meet them, and let him say, *Is it* peace?

2Ch 20:24 — And when Judah came toward the watch tower in the wilderness, they looked unto the multitude, and, behold, they *were* dead bodies fallen to the earth, and none escaped.

Jer 31:6 — For there shall be a day, *that* the watchmen upon the mount Ephraim shall cry, Arise ye, and let us go up to Zion unto the LORD our God.

• At the gates of the temple.

2Ki 11:6–7

• Alarm of, given by trumpets.

Eze 33:3–6

• Unfaithfulness in the discharge of duty of, punished by death.

Eze 33:6 — But if the watchman see the sword come, and blow not the trumpet, and the people be not warned; if the sword come, and take *any* person from among them, he is taken away in his iniquity; but his blood will I require at the watchman's hand.

Mt 28:14 — And if this come to the governor's ears, we will persuade him, and secure you.

Ac 12:19 — And when Herod had sought for him, and found him not, he examined the keepers, and commanded that *they* should be put to death. And he went down from Judaea to Caesarea, and *there* abode.

WATER

• Creation of.

Ps 148:4–5

• **Covered the whole earth.**

Ge 1:9 — And God said, Let the waters under the heaven be gathered together unto one place, and let the dry *land* appear: and it was so.

• **Daily allowance of.**

Eze 4:11 — Thou shalt drink also water by measure, the sixth part of an hin: from time to time shalt thou drink.

• **City waterworks.**

2Ki 20:20 — And the rest of the acts of Hezekiah, and all his might, and how he made a pool, and a conduit, and brought water into the city, *are* they not written in the book of the chronicles of the kings of Judah?

• **Vision of, by Ezekiel.**

Eze 47:1–5

• **Of separation.**

Nu 19:2–22

• **Libation of.**

1Sa 7:6 — And they gathered together to Mizpeh, and drew water, and poured *it* out before the LORD, and fasted on that day, and said there, We have sinned against the LORD. And Samuel judged the children of Israel in Mizpeh.

• **Irrigation with.**

See: Irrigation

• **Miraculously supplied to.**

• **The Israelites.**

Ex 17:1 — And all the congregation of the children of Israel journeyed from the wilderness of Sin, after their journeys, according to the commandment of the LORD, and pitched in Rephidim: and *there was* no water for the people to drink.

Ex 17:6 — Behold, I will stand before thee there upon the rock in Horeb; and thou shalt smite the rock, and there shall come water out of it, that the people may drink. And Moses did so in the sight of the elders of Israel.

Nu 20:11 — And Moses lifted up his hand, and with his rod he smote the rock twice: and the water came out abundantly, and the congregation drank, and their beasts *also.*

• **Samson.**

Jgs 15:19 — But God clave an hollow place that *was* in the jaw, and there came water thereout; and when he had drunk, his spirit came again, and he revived: wherefore he called the name thereof Enhakkore, which *is* in Lehi unto this day.

• **Jehoshaphat's army.**

2Ki 3:16–20

• **Purified by Elisha.**

2Ki 2:19–22

• **Red Sea divided.**

Ex 14:21–22

• **The river Jordan divided.**

Jos 3:14–17; 2Ki 2:6–8

2Ki 2:14 — And he took the mantle of Elijah that fell from him, and smote the waters, and said, Where *is* the LORD God of Elijah? and when he also had smitten the waters, they parted hither and thither: and Elisha went over.

• **Jesus walks on.**

Mt 14:25 — And in the fourth watch of the night Jesus went unto them, walking on the sea.

• **Changed to wine.**

Jn 2:1–11

• **Changed to blood.**

Rev 16:3–5

• **Figurative.**

• **Water of life.**

Jn 7:37–39

Jn 4:14 — But whosoever drinketh of the water that I shall give him shall never thirst; but the water that I shall give him shall be in him a well of water springing up into everlasting life.

Rev 21:6 — And he said unto me, It is done. I am Alpha and Omega, the beginning and the end. I will give unto him that is athirst of the fountain of the water of life freely.

Rev 22:17 — And the Spirit and the bride say, Come. And let him that heareth say, Come. And let him that is athirst come. And whosoever will, let him take the water of life freely.

• **Of affliction.**

2Sa 22:17 — He sent from above, he took me; he drew me out of many waters;

Ps 69:1 — Save me, O God; for the waters are come in unto *my* soul.

Isa 30:20 — And *though* the Lord give you the bread of adversity, and the water of affliction, yet shall not thy teachers be removed into a corner any more, but thine eyes shall see thy teachers:

Isa 43:2 — When thou passest through the waters, I *will be* with thee; and through the rivers, they shall not overflow thee: when thou walkest through the fire, thou shalt not be burned; neither shall the flame kindle upon thee.

• **Of salvation.**

Isa 12:3 — Therefore with joy shall ye draw water out of the wells of salvation.

Isa 49:10 — They shall not hunger nor thirst; neither shall the heat nor sun smite them: for he that hath mercy on them shall lead them, even by the springs of water shall he guide them.

Isa 55:1 — Ho, every one that thirsteth, come ye to the waters, and he that hath no money; come ye, buy, and eat; yea, come, buy wine and milk without money and without price.

Eze 36:25 — Then will I sprinkle clean water upon you, and ye shall be clean: from all your filthiness, and from all your idols, will I cleanse you.

Jn 4:10 — Jesus answered and said unto her, If thou knewest the gift of God, and who it is that saith to thee, Give me to drink; thou wouldest have asked of him, and he would have given thee living water.

Jn 7:38 — He that believeth on me, as the scripture hath said, out of his belly shall flow rivers of living water.

• **Domestic love.**

Pr 5:15 — Drink waters out of thine own cistern, and running waters out of thine own well.

• **Symbolic.**

Isa 8:7 — Now therefore, behold, the Lord bringeth up upon them the waters of the river, strong and many, *even* the king of Assyria, and all his glory: and he shall come up over all his channels, and go over all his banks:

Rev 8:11 — And the name of the star is called Wormwood: and the third part of the waters became wormwood; and many men died of the waters, because they were made bitter.

Rev 12:15 — And the serpent cast out of his mouth water as a flood after the woman, that he might cause her to be carried away of the flood.

Rev 16:4 — And the third angel poured out his vial upon the rivers and fountains of waters; and they became blood.

Rev 17:1 — And there came one of the seven angels which had the seven vials, and talked with me, saying unto me, Come hither; I will shew unto thee the judgment of the great whore that sitteth upon many waters:

Rev 17:15 — And he saith unto me, The waters which thou sawest, where the whore sitteth, are peoples, and multitudes, and nations, and tongues.

WAX

Ps 22:14 — I am poured out like water, and all my bones are out of joint: my heart is like wax; it is melted in the midst of my bowels.

Ps 68:2 — As smoke is driven away, *so* drive *them* away: as wax melteth before the fire, *so* let the wicked perish at the presence of God.

Ps 97:5 — The hills melted like wax at the presence of the LORD, at the presence of the Lord of the whole earth.

Mic 1:4 — And the mountains shall be molten under him, and the valleys shall be cleft, as wax before the fire, *and* as the waters *that are* poured down a steep place.

WAY

• **Figurative.**

• **Of holiness.**

Isa 35:8–9

Ps 16:11 — Thou wilt shew me the path of life: in thy presence *is* fulness of joy; at thy right hand *there are* pleasures for evermore.

Jer 6:16 — Thus saith the LORD, Stand ye in the ways, and see, and ask for the old paths, where is the good way, and walk therein, and ye shall find rest for your souls. But they said, We will not walk *therein*.

Hos 14:9 — Who *is* wise, and he shall understand these *things?* prudent, and he shall know them? for the ways of the LORD *are* right, and the just shall walk in them: but the transgressors shall fall therein.

• **Of righteousness, narrow.**

Mt 7:14 — Because strait *is* the gate, and narrow *is* the way, which leadeth unto life, and few there be that find it.

• **Of sin, broad.**

Mt 7:13 — Enter ye in at the strait gate: for wide *is* the gate, and broad *is* the way, that leadeth to destruction, and many there be which go in thereat:

• **Jesus the.**

Jn 14:6 — Jesus saith unto him, I am the way, the truth, and the life: no man cometh unto the Father, but by me.

Heb 9:8 — The Holy Ghost this signifying, that the way into the holiest of all was not yet made manifest, while as the first tabernacle was yet standing:

• **Doctrines taught by Christ.**

Ac 9:2 — And desired of him letters to Damascus to the synagogues, that if he found any of this way, whether they were men or women, he might bring them bound unto Jerusalem.

Ac 19:23 — And the same time there arose no small stir about that way.

Ac 22:4 — And I persecuted this way unto the death, binding and delivering into prisons both men and women.

Ac 24:14 — But this I confess unto thee, that after the way which they call heresy, so worship I the God of my fathers, believing all things which are written in the law and in the prophets:

Ac 24:22 — And when Felix heard these things, having more perfect knowledge of *that* way, he deferred them, and said, When Lysias the chief captain shall come down, I will know the uttermost of your matter.

WEALTH ✦See: Riches

WEAPONS

✦See: Armor

✦See: Arms

WEARINESS

Heb 12:12 — Wherefore lift up the hands which hang down, and the feeble knees;

WEASEL

Le 11:29 — These also *shall be* unclean unto you among the creeping things that creep upon the earth; the weasel, and the mouse, and the tortoise after his kind,

WEATHER

• **Signs of.**

Mt 16:2–3

• **Sayings concerning.**

Job 37:9 — Out of the south cometh the whirlwind: and cold out of the north.

Job 37:17 — How thy garments *are* warm, when he quieteth the earth by the south *wind?*

Job 37:22 — Fair weather cometh out of the north: with God is terrible majesty.

➜**See: Meteorology and Celestial Phenomena**

WEAVING

Isa 19:9 — Moreover they that work in fine flax, and they that weave networks, shall be confounded.

Isa 38:12 — Mine age is departed, and is removed from me as a shepherd's tent: I have cut off like a weaver my life: he will cut me off with pining sickness: from day *even* to night wilt thou make an end of me.

• Bezaleel skilled in.

Ex 35:35 — Them hath he filled with wisdom of heart, to work all manner of work, of the engraver, and of the cunning workman, and of the embroiderer, in blue, and in purple, in scarlet, and in fine linen, and of the weaver, *even* of them that do any work, and of those that devise cunning work.

• Wrought by women.

2Ki 23:7 — And he brake down the houses of the sodomites, that *were* by the house of the LORD, where the women wove hangings for the grove.

• Of the ephod.

Ex 28:32 — And there shall be an hole in the top of it, in the midst thereof: it shall have a binding of woven work round about the hole of it, as it were the hole of an habergeon, that it be not rent.

Ex 39:22 — And he made the robe of the ephod *of* woven work, all *of* blue.

• Of coats.

Ex 39:27 — And they made coats *of* fine linen *of* woven work for Aaron, and for his sons,

• Weaver's shuttle.

Job 7:6 — My days are swifter than a weaver's shuttle, and are spent without hope.

• Weaver's beam.

Jgs 16:14 — And she fastened *it* with the pin, and said unto him, The Philistines *be* upon thee, Samson. And he awaked out of his sleep, and went away with the pin of the beam, and with the web.

2Sa 21:19 — And there was again a battle in Gob with the Philistines, where Elhanan the son of Jaare-oregim, a Bethlehemite, slew *the brother of* Goliath the Gittite, the staff of whose spear *was* like a weaver's beam.

1Ch 11:23 — And he slew an Egyptian, a man of *great* stature, five cubits high; and in the Egyptian's hand *was* a spear like a weaver's beam; and he went down to him with a staff, and plucked the spear out of the Egyptian's hand, and slew him with his own spear.

WEDDING ➜See: Marriage

WEEDING

Mt 13:28 — He said unto them, An enemy hath done this. The servants said unto him, Wilt thou then that we go and gather them up?

WEEPING

Ro 12:15 — Rejoice with them that do rejoice, and weep with them that weep.

1Co 7:30 — And they that weep, as though they wept not; and they that rejoice, as though they rejoiced not; and they that buy, as though they possessed not;

• In perdition.

Mt 8:12 — But the children of the kingdom shall be cast out into outer darkness: there shall be weeping and gnashing of teeth.

Mt 22:13 — Then said the king to the servants, Bind him hand and foot, and take him away, and cast *him* into outer darkness; there shall be weeping and gnashing of teeth.

Mt 24:51 — And shall cut him asunder, and appoint *him* his portion with the hypocrites: there shall be weeping and gnashing of teeth.

Mt 25:30 — And cast ye the unprofitable servant into outer darkness: there shall be weeping and gnashing of teeth.

• None in heaven.

Rev 7:17 — For the Lamb which is in the midst of the throne shall feed them, and shall lead them unto living fountains of waters: and God shall wipe away all tears from their eyes.

• Penitential.

Jer 50:4 — In those days, and in that time, saith the LORD, the children of Israel shall come, they and the children of Judah together, going and weeping: they shall go, and seek the LORD their God.

Joel 2:12 — Therefore also now, saith the LORD, turn ye *even* to me with all your heart, and with fasting, and with weeping, and with mourning:

• Instances of.

• The Israelites.

Jgs 2:4–5

• Peter.

Mt 26:75 — And Peter remembered the word of Jesus, which said unto him, Before the cock crow, thou shalt deny me thrice. And he went out, and wept bitterly.

Mk 14:72 — And the second time the cock crew. And Peter called to mind the word that Jesus said unto him, Before the cock crow twice, thou shalt deny me thrice. And when he thought thereon, he wept.

Lk 22:62 — And Peter went out, and wept bitterly.

• While doing good.

Ps 126:5–6

• For others.

Jer 9:1 — Oh that my head were waters, and mine eyes a fountain of tears, that I might weep day and night for the slain of the daughter of my people!

• On account of tribulation.

Am 5:16–17

Jer 22:10 — Weep ye not for the dead, neither bemoan him: *but* weep sore for him that goeth away: for he shall return no more, nor see his native country.

- **Instances of.**
  - **Abraham for Sarah.**
    Ge 23:2
  - **Esau.**
    Ge 27:38
  - **Jacob and Esau.**
    Ge 33:4
  - **Jacob.**
    Ge 37:35
  - **Joseph.**
    Ge 42:24; 43:30; 45:2, 14; 46:29; 50:1, 17
  - **Hannah.**
    1Sa 1:7
  - **Jonathan and David.**
    1Sa 20:41
  - **David.**
    2Sa 1:17; 3:32; 13:36; 15:23, 30; 18:33
  - **Hezekiah.**
    2Ki 20:3; Isa 38:3
  - **Jesus, over Jerusalem.**
    Lk 19:41
  - **Jesus, at the grave of Lazarus.**
    Jn 11:35
  - **Mary, when she washed the feet of Jesus.**
    Lk 7:38; Jn 11:2, 33
  - **Mary Magdalene.**
    Jn 20:11
  - **Paul.**
    Ac 20:19; Php 3:18

WEIGHTS

- **Must be just.**
  Le 19:35–36; Dt 25:13–15; Mic 6:10–11
  Pr 11:1 — A false balance *is* abomination to the LORD: but a just weight *is* his delight.
  Pr 16:11 — A just weight and balance *are* the LORD'S: all the weights of the bag *are* his work.
  Pr 20:10 — Divers weights, *and* divers measures, both of them *are* alike abomination to the LORD.
  Pr 20:23 — Divers weights *are* an abomination unto the LORD; and a false balance *is* not good.
  See: Measure

WELLS

- **The occasion of feuds.**
  - **Between Abraham and Abimelech.**
    Ge 21:25–30
  - **Between Isaac and Abimelech.**
    Ge 26:15–22, 32–33
  - **Of Jacob.**
    Jn 4:6 — Now Jacob's well was there. Jesus therefore, being wearied with *his* journey, sat thus on the well: *and* it was about the sixth hour.
  - **Of Solomon.**
    Ecc 2:6 — I made me pools of water, to water therewith the wood that bringeth forth trees:
  - **Of Uzziah.**
    2Ch 26:10 — Also he built towers in the desert, and digged many wells: for he had much cattle, both in the low country, and in the plains: husbandmen *also,* and vine dressers in the mountains, and in Carmel: for he loved husbandry.
  - **Of Hezekiah.**
    See: Gihon
- **At Haran.**
  Ge 24:16 — And the damsel *was* very fair to look upon, a virgin, neither had any man known her: and she went down to the well, and filled her pitcher, and came up.
- **Figurative.**
  - **Of salvation.**
    Isa 12:3 — Therefore with joy shall ye draw water out of the wells of salvation.
    Jn 4:14 — But whosoever drinketh of the water that I shall give him shall never thirst; but the water that I shall give him shall be in him a well of water springing up into everlasting life.
  - **Without water.**
    Jer 15:18 — Why is my pain perpetual, and my wound incurable, *which* refuseth to be healed? wilt thou be altogether unto me as a liar, *and as* waters *that* fail?
    2Pe 2:17 — These are wells without water, clouds that are carried with a tempest; to whom the mist of darkness is reserved for ever.
  See: Spring

WEN • A tumor.

Le 22:22 — Blind, or broken, or maimed, or having a wen, or scurvy, or scabbed, ye shall not offer these unto the LORD, nor make an offering by fire of them upon the altar unto the LORD.

WHALE

- **Created.**
  Ge 1:21 — And God created great whales, and every living creature that moveth, which the waters brought forth abundantly, after their kind, and every winged fowl after his kind: and God saw that *it was* good.
- **Called sea monster, in some versions.**
  Job 7:12 — *Am* I a sea, or a whale, that thou settest a watch over me?
  See: Dragon

WHEAT

Rev 6:6 — And I heard a voice in the midst of the four beasts say, A measure of wheat for a penny, and three measures of barley for a penny; and *see* thou hurt not the oil and the wine.

- **Grown in Palestine.**
  1Ki 5:11 — And Solomon gave Hiram twenty thousand measures of wheat *for* food to his household, and twenty measures of pure oil: thus gave Solomon to Hiram year by year.
  Ps 81:16 — He should have fed them also with the finest of the wheat: and with honey out of the rock should I have satisfied thee.
  Ps 147:14 — He maketh peace *in* thy borders, *and* filleth thee with the finest of the wheat.

• Offerings of.

Nu 18:12 — All the best of the oil, and all the best of the wine, and of the wheat, the firstfruits of them which they shall offer unto the LORD, them have I given thee.

• Prophecy of the sale of a measure of, for a penny.

Rev 6:6 — And I heard a voice in the midst of the four beasts say, A measure of wheat for a penny, and three measures of barley for a penny; and *see* thou hurt not the oil and the wine.

• Parables of.

Mt 13:25 — But while men slept, his enemy came and sowed tares among the wheat, and went his way.

Lk 16:7 — Then said he to another, And how much owest thou? And he said, An hundred measures of wheat. And he said unto him, Take thy bill, and write fourscore.

• Winnowing of.

Mt 3:12 — Whose fan *is* in his hand, and he will throughly purge his floor, and gather his wheat into the garner; but he will burn up the chaff with unquenchable fire.

Lk 3:17 — Whose fan *is* in his hand, and he will throughly purge his floor, and will gather the wheat into his garner; but the chaff he will burn with fire unquenchable.

• Ground in a mortar.

Pr 27:22 — Though thou shouldest bray a fool in a mortar among wheat with a pestle, *yet* will not his foolishness depart from him.

• Chaff of.

Jer 23:28 — The prophet that hath a dream, let him tell a dream; and he that hath my word, let him speak my word faithfully. What *is* the chaff to the wheat? saith the LORD.

Mt 3:12 — Whose fan *is* in his hand, and he will throughly purge his floor, and gather his wheat into the garner; but he will burn up the chaff with unquenchable fire.

Lk 3:17 — Whose fan *is* in his hand, and he will throughly purge his floor, and will gather the wheat into his garner; but the chaff he will burn with fire unquenchable.

• Growth of, figurative vicarious death.

Jn 12:24 — Verily, verily, I say unto you, Except a corn of wheat fall into the ground and die, it abideth alone: but if it die, it bringeth forth much fruit.

• Figurative.

• Of God's mercy.

Ps 81:16 — He should have fed them also with the finest of the wheat: and with honey out of the rock should I have satisfied thee.

Ps 147:14 — He maketh peace *in* thy borders, *and* filleth thee with the finest of the wheat.

• Of self-righteousness.

Jer 12:13 — They have sown wheat, but shall reap thorns: they have put themselves to pain, *but* shall not profit: and they shall be ashamed of your revenues because of the fierce anger of the LORD.

WHEEL

• Potter's.

Jer 18:3 — Then I went down to the potter's house, and, behold, he wrought a work on the wheels.

• Figurative.

Pr 20:26 — A wise king scattereth the wicked, and bringeth the wheel over them.

Ecc 12:6 — Or ever the silver cord be loosed, or the golden bowl be broken, or the pitcher be broken at the fountain, or the wheel broken at the cistern.

• Symbolic.

Eze 1:15–21; 10:9–19

Eze 3:13 — *I heard* also the noise of the wings of the living creatures that touched one another, and the noise of the wheels over against them, and a noise of a great rushing.

Eze 11:22 — Then did the cherubims lift up their wings, and the wheels beside them; and the glory of the God of Israel *was* over them above.

WHIP

1Ki 12:11 — And now whereas my father did lade you with a heavy yoke, I will add to your yoke: my father hath chastised you with whips, but I will chastise you with scorpions.

Pr 26:3 — A whip for the horse, a bridle for the ass, and a rod for the fool's back.

Na 3:2 — The noise of a whip, and the noise of the rattling of the wheels, and of the pransing horses, and of the jumping chariots.

WHIRLWIND

• Destructive.

Pr 1:27 — When your fear cometh as desolation, and your destruction cometh as a whirlwind; when distress and anguish cometh upon you.

• From the south in the land of Uz.

Job 37:9 — Out of the south cometh the whirlwind: and cold out of the north.

• From the south in the valley of the Euphrates.

Isa 21:1 — The burden of the desert of the sea. As whirlwinds in the south pass through; *so* it cometh from the desert, from a terrible land.

• From the south in the land of Canaan.

Zec 9:14 — And the LORD shall be seen over them, and his arrow shall go forth as the lightning: and the LORD GOD shall blow the trumpet, and shall go with whirlwinds of the south.

• From the north.

Eze 1:4 — And I looked, and, behold, a whirlwind came out of the north, a great cloud, and a fire infolding itself, and a brightness *was* about it, and out of the midst thereof as the colour of amber, out of the midst of the fire.

• Elijah translated in.

2Ki 2:1 — And it came to pass, when the LORD would take up Elijah into heaven by a whirlwind, that Elijah went with Elisha from Gilgal.

2Ki 2:11 — And it came to pass, as they still went on, and talked, that, behold, *there appeared* a chariot of fire, and horses of fire, and parted them both asunder; and Elijah went up by a whirlwind into heaven.

- **God answered Job in.**

Job 38:1 — Then the LORD answered Job out of the whirlwind, and said,

See: Meteorology and Celestial Phenomena

- **Figurative.**
  - **Of the judgment of God.**

Jer 23:19 — Behold, a whirlwind of the LORD is gone forth in fury, even a grievous whirlwind: it shall fall grievously upon the head of the wicked.

Jer 30:23 — Behold, the whirlwind of the LORD goeth forth with fury, a continuing whirlwind: it shall fall with pain upon the head of the wicked.

  - **Of the fruits of unrighteousness.**

Hos 8:7 — For they have sown the wind, and they shall reap the whirlwind: it hath no stalk: the bud shall yield no meal: if so be it yield, the strangers shall swallow it up.

  - **Of divine judgments.**

Eze 1:4 — And I looked, and, behold, a whirlwind came out of the north, a great cloud, and a fire infolding itself, and a brightness *was* about it, and out of the midst thereof as the colour of amber, out of the midst of the fire.

WHISPER

See: Busybody

See: Slander

See: Talebearer

WHISPERER

- **A slanderer.**

Ro 1:29 — Being filled with all unrighteousness, fornication, wickedness, covetousness, maliciousness; full of envy, murder, debate, deceit, malignity; whisperers,

2Co 12:20 — For I fear, lest, when I come, I shall not find you such as I would, and *that* I shall be found unto you such as ye would not: lest *there be* debates, envyings, wraths, strifes, backbitings, whisperings, swellings, tumults:

See: Slander

See: Speaking; evil

WHITE See: Colors

WHORE

- **Revenues of, not to be brought to the sanctuary.**

Dt 23:18 — Thou shalt not bring the hire of a whore, or the price of a dog, into the house of the LORD thy God for any vow: for even both these *are* abomination unto the LORD thy God.

See: Harlot

WHOREDOM

- **Licentious rites of, in idolatrous worship.**

Le 19:29 — Do not prostitute thy daughter, to cause her to be a whore; lest the land fall to whoredom, and the land become full of wickedness.

Dt 31:16 — And the LORD said unto Moses, Behold, thou shalt sleep with thy fathers; and this people will rise up, and go a whoring after the gods of the strangers of the land, whither they go *to be* among them, and will forsake me, and break my covenant which I have made with them.

Jgs 2:17 — And yet they would not hearken unto their judges, but they went a whoring after other gods, and bowed themselves unto them: they turned quickly out of the way which their fathers walked in, obeying the commandments of the LORD; *but* they did not so.

2Ki 9:22 — And it came to pass, when Joram saw Jehu, that he said, *Is it* peace, Jehu? And he answered, What peace, so long as the whoredoms of thy mother Jezebel and her witchcrafts *are so* many?

See: Idolatry

- **Figurative.**

Eze 16:1–63; 23:1–49; Rev 17:1–6

WHOREMONGER

Rev 21:8 — But the fearful, and unbelieving, and the abominable, and murderers, and whoremongers, and sorcerers, and idolaters, and all liars, shall have their part in the lake which burneth with fire and brimstone: which is the second death.

Rev 22:15 — For without *are* dogs, and sorcerers, and whoremongers, and murderers, and idolaters, and whosoever loveth and maketh a lie.

See: Adultery

See: Sensuality

WICKED

- **God is angry with.**

Ps 5:5–6

Ps 7:11 — God judgeth the righteous, and God is angry *with the wicked* every day.

Ro 9:13 — As it is written, Jacob have I loved, but Esau have I hated.

1Co 10:5 — But with many of them God was not well pleased: for they were overthrown in the wilderness.

- **Spirit of God withdrawn from.**

Hos 4:17–19

Ge 6:3 — And the LORD said, My spirit shall not always strive with man, for that he also *is* flesh: yet his days shall be an hundred and twenty years.

Ro 1:24 — Wherefore God also gave them up to uncleanness through the lusts of their own hearts, to dishonour their own bodies between themselves:

Ro 1:26 — For this cause God gave them up unto vile affections: for even their women did change the natural use into that which is against nature:

Ro 1:28 — And even as they did not like to retain God in *their* knowledge, God gave them over to a reprobate mind, to do those things which are not convenient;

• **Hate the righteous.**
Mt 5:11–12; Lk 6:22–23

• **Worship of, offensive to God.**
Ps 50:16–17; Isa 1:10–15

• **Present and future state of the wicked and righteous contrasted.**
Job 8:1–22; Ps 49:1–20

• **Prosperity of.**
Job 5:3–5; 21:7–13; Ps 37:35–36; 49:10–15; 73:3–22; 92:6–7; Ecc 8:12–13; Jer 12:1–2; Hab 1:3–4, 13–17

Job 12:6 — The tabernacles of robbers prosper, and they that provoke God are secure; into whose hand God bringeth *abundantly.*

Job 15:21 — A dreadful sound *is* in his ears: in prosperity the destroyer shall come upon him.

Job 15:23 — He wandereth abroad for bread, *saying,* Where *is it?* he knoweth that the day of darkness is ready at his hand.

Job 15:27 — Because he covereth his face with his fatness, and maketh collops of fat on *his* flanks.

Job 15:29 — He shall not be rich, neither shall his substance continue, neither shall he prolong the perfection thereof upon the earth.

Job 20:5 — That the triumphing of the wicked *is* short, and the joy of the hypocrite *but* for a moment?

Job 20:22 — In the fulness of his sufficiency he shall be in straits: every hand of the wicked shall come upon him.

Ps 37:1 — Fret not thyself because of evildoers, neither be thou envious against the workers of iniquity.

Mal 3:15 — And now we call the proud happy; yea, they that work wickedness are set up; yea, *they that* tempt God are even delivered.

• **Hate reproof.**
1Ki 22:8 — And the king of Israel said unto Jehoshaphat, *There is* yet one man, Micaiah the son of Imlah, by whom we may enquire of the LORD: but I hate him; for he doth not prophesy good concerning me, but evil. And Jehoshaphat said, Let not the king say so.

2Ch 18:7 — And the king of Israel said unto Jehoshaphat, *There is* yet one man, by whom we may enquire of the LORD: but I hate him; for he never prophesied good unto me, but always evil: the same is Micaiah the son of Imla. And Jehoshaphat said, Let not the king say so.

• **God's mercy to.**
Job 33:14–30

• **God's love for.**
Mt 18:11–14; Jn 3:16–17; 1Jn 4:9–10

Dt 5:29 — O that there were such an heart in them, that they would fear me, and keep all my commandments always, that it might be well with them, and with their children for ever!

Dt 32:29 — O that they were wise, *that* they understood this, *that* they would consider their latter end!

Ro 5:8 — But God commendeth his love toward us, in that, while we were yet sinners, Christ died for us.

1Jn 3:16 — Hereby perceive we the love *of God,* because he laid down his life for us: and we ought to lay down *our* lives for the brethren.

• **Dread God.**
Job 18:11 — Terrors shall make him afraid on every side, and shall drive him to his feet.

• **Eliphaz's exhortation to.**
Job 22:21–30

• **Temporal punishment of.**
Job 15:20–35; 18:5–21; 20:5–29; 21:7–33; 24:2–24; 27:13–23; Eze 12:19–20; Zec 14:7–19

Jer 5:25 — Your iniquities have turned away these *things,* and your sins have withholden good *things* from you.

Eze 11:10 — Ye shall fall by the sword; I will judge you in the border of Israel; and ye shall know that I *am* the LORD.

• **False hope of.**
Job 8:13–18

• **Gospel invitation to, illustrated by the parables of the householder.**
Mt 20:1–16

• **Gospel invitation to, and marriage supper.**
Mt 22:1–14

• **Warned.**
Jer 7:13–15, 23–25; 25:4–6; 26:2–7, 12–13; 29:17–19; Da 4:4–27; 5:4–29; Zep 2:1–2; Lk 3:7–9; Jude 1:4–7; Rev 3:1–3, 16–19

Eze 33:8 — When I say unto the wicked, O wicked *man,* thou shalt surely die; if thou dost not speak to warn the wicked from his way, that wicked *man* shall die in his iniquity; but his blood will I require at thine hand.

1Co 10:11 — Now all these things happened unto them for ensamples: and they are written for our admonition, upon whom the ends of the world are come.

• **Terrors of, at the judgment.**
Rev 1:7 — Behold, he cometh with clouds; and every eye shall see him, and they *also* which pierced him: and all kindreds of the earth shall wail because of him. Even so, Amen.

• **Death of.**
Ps 49:14 — Like sheep they are laid in the grave; death shall feed on them; and the upright shall have dominion over them in the morning; and their beauty shall consume in the grave from their dwelling.

Ps 73:4 — For *there are* no bands in their death: but their strength *is* firm.

See: Impenitence
See: Obduracy
See: Penitence
See: Reprobacy
See: Seekers
See: Sin; confession of

• **Contrasted with the righteous.**
Ps 1:1–6; 17:14–15; 37:17–22, 37–38; 73:1–28; 91:7–8; 107:33–38; Pr 10:23–25, 28–30; 11:5–6, 10–11, 18–21; 12:5–7; 28:4–5, 13–14; Isa 32:1–8; 65:13–14; Ro 2:7–10; Eph 2:12–14; 1Th 5:5–8; 1Pe 4:17–18; 1Jn 1:6–7; 3:3–17

Ps 11:5 — The LORD trieth the righteous: but the wicked and him that loveth violence his soul hateth.

Ps 32:10 — Many sorrows *shall be* to the wicked: but he that trusteth in the LORD, mercy shall compass him about.

Ps 68:6 — God setteth the solitary in families: he bringeth out those which are bound with chains: but the rebellious dwell in a dry *land.*

Ps 75:10 — All the horns of the wicked also will I cut off; *but* the horns of the righteous shall be exalted.

Ps 125:5 — As for such as turn aside unto their crooked ways, the LORD shall lead them forth with the workers of iniquity: *but* peace *shall be* upon Israel.

Pr 10:6 — Blessings *are* upon the head of the just: but violence covereth the mouth of the wicked.

Pr 10:9 — He that walketh uprightly walketh surely: but he that perverteth his ways shall be known.

Pr 10:21 — The lips of the righteous feed many: but fools die for want of wisdom.

Pr 10:32 — The lips of the righteous know what is acceptable: but the mouth of the wicked *speaketh* frowardness.

Pr 11:3 — The integrity of the upright shall guide them: but the perverseness of transgressors shall destroy them.

Pr 11:8 — The righteous is delivered out of trouble, and the wicked cometh in his stead.

Pr 11:23 — The desire of the righteous *is* only good: *but* the expectation of the wicked *is* wrath.

Pr 11:31 — Behold, the righteous shall be recompensed in the earth: much more the wicked and the sinner.

Pr 12:3 — A man shall not be established by wickedness: but the root of the righteous shall not be moved.

Pr 12:13 — The wicked is snared by the transgression of *his* lips: but the just shall come out of trouble.

Pr 12:21 — There shall no evil happen to the just: but the wicked shall be filled with mischief.

Pr 12:26 — The righteous *is* more excellent than his neighbour: but the way of the wicked seduceth them.

Pr 13:6 — Righteousness keepeth *him that is* upright in the way: but wickedness overthroweth the sinner.

Pr 13:13 — Whoso despiseth the word shall be destroyed: but he that feareth the commandment shall be rewarded.

Pr 13:17 — A wicked messenger falleth into mischief: but a faithful ambassador *is* health.

Pr 13:21 — Evil pursueth sinners: but to the righteous good shall be repaid.

Pr 14:19 — The evil bow before the good; and the wicked at the gates of the righteous.

Pr 14:22 — Do they not err that devise evil? but mercy and truth *shall be* to them that devise good.

Pr 14:32 — The wicked is driven away in his wickedness: but the righteous hath hope in his death.

Pr 15:6 — In the house of the righteous *is* much treasure: but in the revenues of the wicked is trouble.

Pr 21:18 — The wicked *shall be* a ransom for the righteous, and the transgressor for the upright.

Pr 21:26 — He coveteth greedily all the day long: but the righteous giveth and spareth not.

Pr 22:5 — Thorns *and* snares *are* in the way of the froward: he that doth keep his soul shall be far from them.

Pr 28:1 — The wicked flee when no man pursueth: but the righteous are bold as a lion.

Pr 28:18 — Whoso walketh uprightly shall be saved: but *he that is* perverse *in his* ways shall fall at once.

Mal 3:18 — Then shall ye return, and discern between the righteous and the wicked, between him that serveth God and him that serveth him not.

Php 2:15 — That ye may be blameless and harmless, the sons of God, without rebuke, in the midst of a crooked and perverse nation, among whom ye shine as lights in the world;

Tit 1:15 — Unto the pure all things *are* pure: but unto them that are defiled and unbelieving *is* nothing pure; but even their mind and conscience is defiled.

• Described.

Dt 32:32–33; Job 15:20–35; 20:12–13; 24:2–24; Ps 7:14–16; 10:4–11; 36:1–4; 50:17–20; 52:1–4; 53:1–5; 58:3–5; 59:6–7; 64:3–6; 73:4–12; 94:3–8; Pr 1:29–30; 2:12–19; 6:12–15; 15:9–10; Isa 1:4–6; 5:11–12, 18–25; 26:10–11; 30:9–11; 32:6–7; 57:20–21; 59:2–8; Jer 2:22–25; 5:4–5, 26–28; 9:3–6; 30:12–15; Mic 3:1–2; 7:2–4; Jn 3:18–20; Ro 1:20–32; 3:10–18; 8:7–8; Eph 2:1–3; 4:17–19; 5:11–12; 1Ti 1:9–10; 2Ti 3:2–13; Tit 1:15–16; 2Pe 2:12–19; 1Jn 3:14–15; Jude 1:12–13; Rev 3:17–18

Ge 13:13 — But the men of Sodom *were* wicked and sinners before the LORD exceedingly.

Ge 18:20 — And the LORD said, Because the cry of Sodom and Gomorrah is great, and because their sin is very grievous;

Le 18:25 — And the land is defiled: therefore I do visit the iniquity thereof upon it, and the land itself vomiteth out her inhabitants.

Dt 9:13 — Furthermore the LORD spake unto me, saying, I have seen this people, and, behold, it *is* a stiffnecked people:

Dt 9:24 — Ye have been rebellious against the LORD from the day that I knew you.

Dt 32:10 — He found him in a desert land, and in the waste howling wilderness; he led him about, he instructed him, he kept him as the apple of his eye.

1Sa 24:13 — As saith the proverb of the ancients, Wickedness proceedeth from the wicked: but mine hand shall not be upon thee.

1Ki 21:20 — And Ahab said to Elijah, Hast thou found me, O mine enemy? And he answered, I have found *thee:* because thou hast sold thyself to work evil in the sight of the LORD.

2Ch 28:10 — And now ye purpose to keep under the children of Judah and Jerusalem for bondmen and bondwomen unto you: *but are there* not with you, even with you, sins against the LORD your God?

2Ch 28:22 — And in the time of his distress did he trespass yet more against the LORD: this *is that* king Ahaz.

Ezr 9:11 — Which thou hast commanded by thy servants the prophets, saying, The land, unto which ye go to possess it, is an unclean land with the filthiness of the people of the lands, with their abominations, which have filled it from one end to another with their uncleanness.

Job 14:4 — Who can bring a clean *thing* out of an unclean? not one.

Job 15:16 — How much more abominable and filthy *is* man, which drinketh iniquity like water?

Job 22:5 — *Is* not thy wickedness great? and thine iniquities infinite?

Ps 5:9 — For *there is* no faithfulness in their mouth; their inward part *is* very wickedness; their throat *is* an open sepulchre; they flatter with their tongue.

Ps 37:12 — The wicked plotteth against the just, and gnasheth upon him with his teeth.

Ps 49:20 — Man *that is* in honour, and understandeth not, is like the beasts *that* perish.

Ps 119:155 — Salvation *is* far from the wicked: for they seek not thy statutes.

Pr 4:16 — For they sleep not, except they have done mischief; and their sleep is taken away, unless they cause *some* to fall.

Pr 10:23 — *It is* as sport to a fool to do mischief: but a man of understanding hath wisdom.

Pr 13:19 — The desire accomplished is sweet to the soul: but *it is* abomination to fools to depart from evil.

Pr 14:9 — Fools make a mock at sin: but among the righteous *there is* favour.

Pr 27:22 — Though thou shouldest bray a fool in a mortar among wheat with a pestle, *yet* will not his foolishness depart from him.

Pr 28:4 — They that forsake the law praise the wicked: but such as keep the law contend with them.

Ecc 3:18 — I said in mine heart concerning the estate of the sons of men, that God might manifest them, and that they might see that they themselves are beasts.

Ecc 8:11 — Because sentence against an evil work is not executed speedily, therefore the heart of the sons of men is fully set in them to do evil.

Isa 3:9 — The shew of their countenance doth witness against them; and they declare their sin as Sodom, they hide *it* not. Woe unto their soul! for they have rewarded evil unto themselves.

Isa 30:1 — Woe to the rebellious children, saith the LORD, that take counsel, but not of me; and that cover with a covering, but not of my spirit, that they may add sin to sin:

Isa 63:19 — We are *thine:* thou never barest rule over them; they were not called by thy name.

Jer 3:5 — Will he reserve *his anger* for ever? will he keep *it* to the end? Behold, thou hast spoken and done evil things as thou couldest.

Jer 4:22 — For my people *is* foolish, they have not known me; they *are* sottish children, and they have none understanding: they *are* wise to do evil, but to do good they have no knowledge.

Jer 6:7 — As a fountain casteth out her waters, so she casteth out her wickedness: violence and spoil is heard in her; before me continually is grief and wounds.

Jer 6:15 — Were they ashamed when they had committed abomination? nay, they were not at all ashamed, neither could they blush: therefore they shall fall among them that fall: at the time *that* I visit them they shall be cast down, saith the LORD.

Jer 8:6 — I hearkened and heard, *but* they spake not aright: no man repented him of his wickedness, saying, What have I done? every one turned to his course, as the horse rusheth into the battle.

Jer 8:12 — Were they ashamed when they had committed abomination? nay, they were not at all ashamed, neither could they blush: therefore shall they fall among them that fall: in the time of their visitation they shall be cast down, saith the LORD.

Jer 11:8 — Yet they obeyed not, nor inclined their ear, but walked every one in the imagination of their evil heart: therefore I will bring upon them all the words of this covenant, which I commanded *them* to do; but they did *them* not.

Jer 11:15 — What hath my beloved to do in mine house, *seeing* she hath wrought lewdness with many, and the holy flesh is passed from thee? when thou doest evil, then thou rejoicest.

Jer 13:10 — This evil people, which refuse to hear my words, which walk in the imagination of their heart, and walk after other gods, to serve them, and to worship them, shall even be as this girdle, which is good for nothing.

Jer 14:10 — Thus saith the LORD unto this people, Thus have they loved to wander, they have not refrained their feet, therefore the LORD doth not accept them; he will now remember their iniquity, and visit their sins.

Jer 17:1 — The sin of Judah *is* written with a pen of iron, *and* with the point of a diamond: *it is* graven upon the table of their heart, and upon the horns of your altars;

Eze 3:7 — But the house of Israel will not hearken unto thee; for they will not hearken unto me: for all the house of Israel *are* impudent and hardhearted.

Eze 11:12 — And ye shall know that I *am* the LORD: for ye have not walked in my statutes, neither executed my judgments, but have done after the manners of the heathen that *are* round about you.

Eze 16:47 — Yet hast thou not walked after their ways, nor done after their abominations: but, as *if that were* a very little *thing,* thou wast corrupted more than they in all thy ways.

Eze 20:16 — Because they despised my judgments, and walked not in my statutes, but polluted my sabbaths: for their heart went after their idols.

Hos 4:8 — They eat up the sin of my people, and they set their heart on their iniquity.

Hos 7:3 — They make the king glad with their wickedness, and the princes with their lies.

Hos 7:9 — Strangers have devoured his strength, and he knoweth *it* not: yea, gray hairs are here and there upon him, yet he knoweth not.

Hos 9:10 — I found Israel like grapes in the wilderness; I saw your fathers as the firstripe in the fig tree at her first time: *but* they went to Baal-peor, and separated themselves unto *that* shame; and *their* abominations were according as they loved.

Hos 13:12 — The iniquity of Ephraim *is* bound up; his sin *is* hid.

Am 5:10 — They hate him that rebuketh in the gate, and they abhor him that speaketh uprightly.

Zep 3:5 — The just LORD *is* in the midst thereof; he will not do iniquity: every morning doth he bring his judgment to light, he faileth not; but the unjust knoweth no shame.

Zep 3:7 — I said, Surely thou wilt fear me, thou wilt receive instruction; so their dwelling should not be cut off, howsoever I punished them: but they rose early, *and* corrupted all their doings.

Hag 2:14 — Then answered Haggai, and said, So *is* this people, and so *is* this nation before me, saith the LORD; and so *is* every work of their hands; and that which they offer there *is* unclean.

Mt 4:16 — The people which sat in darkness saw great light; and to them which sat in the region and shadow of death light is sprung up.

Mt 6:23 — <u>But if thine eye be evil, thy whole body shall be full of darkness. If therefore the light that is in thee be darkness, how great *is* that darkness!</u>

Mt 18:11 — <u>For the Son of man is come to save that which was lost.</u>

Mk 4:11 — And he said unto them, <u>Unto you it is given to know the mystery of the kingdom of God: but unto them that are without, all these *things* are done in parables:</u>

Lk 1:79 — To give light to them that sit in darkness and *in* the shadow of death, to guide our feet into the way of peace.

Lk 19:10 — <u>For the Son of man is come to seek and to save that which was lost.</u>

Jn 5:42 — <u>But I know you, that ye have not the love of God in you.</u>

Jn 8:34 — Jesus answered them, <u>Verily, verily, I say unto you, Whosoever committeth sin is the servant of sin.</u>

Jn 8:44 — <u>Ye are of your father the devil, and the lusts of *your* father ye will do. He was a murderer from the beginning, and abode not in the truth, because there is no truth in him. When he speaketh a lie, he speaketh of his own: for he is a liar, and the father of it.</u>

Ac 8:21 — Thou hast neither part nor lot in this matter: for thy heart is not right in the sight of God.

Ac 8:23 — For I perceive that thou art in the gall of bitterness, and *in* the bond of iniquity.

Ac 13:10 — And said, O full of all subtilty and all mischief, *thou* child of the devil, *thou* enemy of all righteousness, wilt thou not cease to pervert the right ways of the Lord?

Ro 2:8 — But unto them that are contentious, and do not obey the truth, but obey unrighteousness, indignation and wrath,

Ro 8:5 — For they that are after the flesh do mind the things of the flesh; but they that are after the Spirit the things of the Spirit.

Ro 9:8 — That is, They which are the children of the flesh, these *are* not the children of God: but the children of the promise are counted for the seed.

Eph 2:12 — That at that time ye were without Christ, being aliens from the commonwealth of Israel, and strangers from the covenants of promise, having no hope, and without God in the world:

Php 2:15 — That ye may be blameless and harmless, the sons of God, without rebuke, in the midst of a crooked and perverse nation, among whom ye shine as lights in the world;

Col 1:21 — And you, that were sometime alienated and enemies in *your* mind by wicked works, yet now hath he reconciled:

1Th 5:7 — For they that sleep sleep in the night; and they that be drunken are drunken in the night.

2Th 1:8 — In flaming fire taking vengeance on them that know not God, and that obey not the gospel of our Lord Jesus Christ:

Tit 3:3 — For we ourselves also were sometimes foolish, disobedient, deceived, serving divers lusts and pleasures, living in malice and envy, hateful, *and* hating one another.

2Pe 2:10 — But chiefly them that walk after the flesh in the lust of uncleanness, and despise government. Presumptuous *are they,* selfwilled, they are not afraid to speak evil of dignities.

1Jn 3:8 — He that committeth sin is of the devil; for the devil sinneth from the beginning. For this purpose the Son of God was manifested, that he might destroy the works of the devil.

1Jn 3:10 — In this the children of God are manifest, and the children of the devil: whosoever doeth not righteousness is not of God, neither he that loveth not his brother.

• Prayer of.

Job 35:12–13; Pr 1:24–28; Zec 7:12–13; Mal 2:11–13; Jas 1:6–7

Dt 1:45 — And ye returned and wept before the LORD; but the LORD would not hearken to your voice, nor give ear unto you.

Dt 3:26 — But the LORD was wroth with me for your sakes, and would not hear me: and the LORD said unto me, Let it suffice thee; speak no more unto me of this matter.

2Sa 22:42 — They looked, but *there was* none to save; *even* unto the LORD, but he answered them not.

Job 27:9 — Will God hear his cry when trouble cometh upon him?

Ps 18:41 — They cried, but *there was* none to save *them: even* unto the LORD, but he answered them not.

Ps 66:18 — If I regard iniquity in my heart, the Lord will not hear *me:*

Pr 15:8 — The sacrifice of the wicked *is* an abomination to the LORD: but the prayer of the upright *is* his delight.

Pr 15:29 — The LORD *is* far from the wicked: but he heareth the prayer of the righteous.

Pr 21:13 — Whoso stoppeth his ears at the cry of the poor, he also shall cry himself, but shall not be heard.

Pr 21:27 — The sacrifice of the wicked *is* abomination: how much more, *when* he bringeth it with a wicked mind?

Pr 28:9 — He that turneth away his ear from hearing the law, even his prayer *shall be* abomination.

Isa 1:15 — And when ye spread forth your hands, I will hide mine eyes from you: yea, when ye make many prayers, I will not hear: your hands are full of blood.

Isa 45:19 — I have not spoken in secret, in a dark place of the earth: I said not unto the seed of Jacob, Seek ye me in vain: I the LORD speak righteousness, I declare things that are right.

Isa 59:2 — But your iniquities have separated between you and your God, and your sins have hid *his* face from you, that he will not hear.

Jer 11:11 — Therefore thus saith the LORD, Behold, I will bring evil upon them, which they shall not be able to escape; and though they shall cry unto me, I will not hearken unto them.

Jer 14:12 — When they fast, I will not hear their cry; and when they offer burnt offering and an oblation, I will not accept them: but I will consume them by the sword, and by the famine, and by the pestilence.

Jer 15:1 — Then said the LORD unto me, Though Moses and Samuel stood before me, *yet* my mind *could* not *be* toward this people: cast *them* out of my sight, and let them go forth.

Jer 18:17 — I will scatter them as with an east wind before the enemy; I will shew them the back, and not the face, in the day of their calamity.

La 3:8 — Also when I cry and shout, he shutteth out my prayer.

La 3:44 — Thou hast covered thyself with a cloud, that *our* prayer should not pass through.

Eze 8:18 — Therefore will I also deal in fury: mine eye shall not spare, neither will I have pity: and though they cry in mine ears with a loud voice, *yet* will I not hear them.

Eze 20:3 — Son of man, speak unto the elders of Israel, and say unto them, Thus saith the Lord GOD; Are ye come to enquire of me? *As* I live, saith the Lord GOD, I will not be enquired of by you.

Eze 20:31 — For when ye offer your gifts, when ye make your sons to pass through the fire, ye pollute yourselves with all your idols, even unto this day: and shall I be enquired of by you, O house of Israel? *As* I live, saith the Lord GOD, I will not be enquired of by you.

Hos 5:6 — They shall go with their flocks and with their herds to seek the LORD; but they shall not find *him;* he hath withdrawn himself from them.

Mic 3:4 — Then shall they cry unto the LORD, but he will not hear them: he will even hide his face from them at that time, as they have behaved themselves ill in their doings.

Mal 1:9 — And now, I pray you, beseech God that he will be gracious unto us: this hath been by your means: will he regard your persons? saith the LORD of hosts.

Jn 9:31 — Now we know that God heareth not sinners: but if any man be a worshipper of God, and doeth his will, him he heareth.

Jas 4:3 — Ye ask, and receive not, because ye ask amiss, that ye may consume *it* upon your lusts.

1Pe 3:7 — Likewise, ye husbands, dwell with *them* according to knowledge, giving honour unto the wife, as unto the weaker vessel, and as being heirs together of the grace of life; that your prayers be not hindered.

• Punishment of.

Ge 3:16–19; 6:12–13; Ex 32:33–35; Le 26:16–39; Dt 7:9–10; 28:15–68; 1Sa 3:11–14; 2Sa 22:27–28; 23:6–7; 1Ki 21:20–21; 1Ch 10:13–14; Job 4:8–9; 10:14–15; 15:20–24, 28–30; 18:5–21; 20:5–29; 21:7–33; 27:8–23; Ps 1:4–6; 2:4–5; 7:11–13; 18:26–27; 21:9–10; 28:4–5; 36:12–37:2; 37:9–10, 13–22, 34–38; 58:6–9; 64:7–8; 68:1–2; 73:2–21; 78:1–67; 89:31–32; 107:33–34; 109:6–19; 119:118–119; Pr 6:12–15; 10:6–8; 10:24–25, 27–31; 11:5–8; 12:2–3; 13:5–6; 16:4–5; 21:15–16; Ecc 8:12–13; Isa 5:11–14; 13:8–9; 24:17–18; 28:18–22; 33:11–12; 57:20–21; 64:5–7; 65:12–14; Jer 8:12–14, 20–9:1; La 5:16–17; Eze 3:18–20; 5:8–17; 7:4–6; 9:5–7; 18:1–32; 22:20–21; 24:13–14; 33:7–20; Hos 2:9–13; 5:4–6; 7:12–13; 12:14–13:1; Joel 2:1–2; 3:13–16; Am 5:18–20; 8:14–9:5; Na 1:8–10; Zep 1:12–18; Zec 5:2–4; Mal 3:17–4:1; Mt 5:19–30; 7:26–27; 13:12–15, 38–42, 49–50; 18:7–9, 34–35; 24:50–51; 25:32–33; Mk 12:1–9; Lk 9:24–26; 12:4–5, 46–47; 13:5–7, 27–28; 16:22–28; 17:1–2; 19:26–27; 23:30–31; Jn 3:15–16; Ro 2:8–9; 8:6–7; 1Co 6:9–10; 10:5–11; 15:21–22; Gal 5:19–21; Eph 5:5–6; Php 3:18–19; 2Th 1:5–9; 2:8–10; 2Ti 2:12–13; Heb 2:2–3; 10:27–31; Jas 1:14–15; 5:1–3; 1Pe 4:17–18; 2Pe 2:3–9, 12–17; 1Jn 3:14–15; Jude 1:5–7, 11–15; Rev 2:22–23; 6:15–17; 9:4–6; 14:9–11; 16:2–21; 19:17–21

Ge 2:17 — But of the tree of the knowledge of good and evil, thou shalt not eat of it: for in the day that thou eatest thereof thou shalt surely die.

Ge 4:7 — If thou doest well, shalt thou not be accepted? and if thou doest not well, sin lieth at the door. And unto thee *shall be* his desire, and thou shalt rule over him.

Ge 6:3 — And the LORD said, My spirit shall not always strive with man, for that he also *is* flesh: yet his days shall be an hundred and twenty years.

Ge 6:7 — And the LORD said, I will destroy man whom I have created from the face of the earth; both man, and beast, and the creeping thing, and the fowls of the air; for it repenteth me that I have made them.

Ex 20:5 — Thou shalt not bow down thyself to them, nor serve them: for I the LORD thy God *am* a jealous God, visiting the iniquity of the fathers upon the children unto the third and fourth *generation* of them that hate me;

Ex 34:7 — Keeping mercy for thousands, forgiving iniquity and transgression and sin, and that will by no means clear *the guilty;* visiting the iniquity of the fathers upon the children, and upon the children's children, unto the third and to the fourth *generation.*

Le 26:14 — But if ye will not hearken unto me, and will not do all these commandments;

Nu 15:31 — Because he hath despised the word of the LORD, and hath broken his commandment, that soul shall utterly be cut off; his iniquity *shall be* upon him.

Nu 32:23 — But if ye will not do so, behold, ye have sinned against the LORD: and be sure your sin will find you out.

Dt 11:26 — Behold, I set before you this day a blessing and a curse;

Dt 11:28 — And a curse, if ye will not obey the commandments of the LORD your God, but turn aside out of the way which I command you this day, to go after other gods, which ye have not known.

Dt 30:15 — See, I have set before thee this day life and good, and death and evil;

Dt 30:19 — I call heaven and earth to record this day against you, *that* I have set before you life and death, blessing and cursing: therefore choose life, that both thou and thy seed may live:

Dt 31:29 — For I know that after my death ye will utterly corrupt *yourselves,* and turn aside from the way which I have commanded you; and evil will befall you in the latter days; because ye will do evil in the sight of the LORD, to provoke him to anger through the work of your hands.

1Sa 12:25 — But if ye shall still do wickedly, ye shall be consumed, both ye and your king.

2Sa 3:39 — And I *am* this day weak, though anointed king; and these men the sons of Zeruiah *be* too hard for me: the LORD shall reward the doer of evil according to his wickedness.

2Sa 7:14 — I will be his father, and he shall be my son. If he commit iniquity, I will chasten him with the rod of men, and with the stripes of the children of men:

1Ch 15:13 — For because ye *did it* not at the first, the LORD our God made a breach upon us, for that we sought him not after the due order.

1Ch 28:9 — And thou, Solomon my son, know thou the God of thy father, and serve him with a perfect heart and with a willing mind: for the LORD searcheth all hearts, and understandeth all the imaginations of the thoughts: if thou seek him, he will be found of thee; but if thou forsake him, he will cast thee off for ever.

2Ch 15:2 — And he went out to meet Asa, and said unto him, Hear ye me, Asa, and all Judah and Benjamin; The LORD *is* with you, while ye be with him; and if ye seek him, he will be found of you; but if ye forsake him, he will forsake you.

Job 5:3 — I have seen the foolish taking root: but suddenly I cursed his habitation.

Job 5:14 — They meet with darkness in the daytime, and grope in the noonday as in the night.

Job 8:20 — Behold, God will not cast away a perfect *man,* neither will he help the evil doers:

Job 8:22 — They that hate thee shall be clothed with shame; and the dwelling place of the wicked shall come to nought.

Job 11:20 — But the eyes of the wicked shall fail, and they shall not escape, and their hope *shall be as* the giving up of the ghost.

Job 19:29 — Be ye afraid of the sword: for wrath *bringeth* the punishments of the sword, that ye may know *there is* a judgment.

Job 31:3 — *Is* not destruction to the wicked? and a strange *punishment* to the workers of iniquity?

Job 34:22 — *There is* no darkness, nor shadow of death, where the workers of iniquity may hide themselves.

Job 36:12 — But if they obey not, they shall perish by the sword, and they shall die without knowledge.

Job 36:17 — But thou hast fulfilled the judgment of the wicked: judgment and justice take hold *on thee.*

Ps 2:9 — Thou shalt break them with a rod of iron; thou shalt dash them in pieces like a potter's vessel.

Ps 3:7 — Arise, O LORD; save me, O my God: for thou hast smitten all mine enemies *upon* the cheek bone; thou hast broken the teeth of the ungodly.

Ps 5:5 — The foolish shall not stand in thy sight: thou hatest all workers of iniquity.

Ps 9:5 — Thou hast rebuked the heathen, thou hast destroyed the wicked, thou hast put out their name for ever and ever.

Ps 9:17 — The wicked shall be turned into hell, *and* all the nations that forget God.

Ps 10:15 — Break thou the arm of the wicked and the evil *man:* seek out his wickedness *till* thou find none.

Ps 11:6 — Upon the wicked he shall rain snares, fire and brimstone, and an horrible tempest: *this shall be* the portion of their cup.

Ps 18:14 — Yea, he sent out his arrows, and scattered them; and he shot out lightnings, and discomfited them.

Ps 32:10 — Many sorrows *shall be* to the wicked: but he that trusteth in the LORD, mercy shall compass him about.

Ps 34:16 — The face of the LORD *is* against them that do evil, to cut off the remembrance of them from the earth.

Ps 34:21 — Evil shall slay the wicked: and they that hate the righteous shall be desolate.

Ps 39:11 — When thou with rebukes dost correct man for iniquity, thou makest his beauty to consume away like a moth: surely every man *is* vanity. Selah.

Ps 50:22 — Now consider this, ye that forget God, lest I tear *you* in pieces, and *there be* none to deliver.

Ps 52:5 — God shall likewise destroy thee for ever, he shall take thee away, and pluck thee out of *thy* dwelling place, and root thee out of the land of the living. Selah.

Ps 55:19 — God shall hear, and afflict them, even he that abideth of old. Selah. Because they have no changes, therefore they fear not God.

Ps 55:23 — But thou, O God, shalt bring them down into the pit of destruction: bloody and deceitful men shall not live out half their days; but I will trust in thee.

Ps 56:7 — Shall they escape by iniquity? in *thine* anger cast down the people, O God.

Ps 59:5 — Thou therefore, O LORD God of hosts, the God of Israel, awake to visit all the heathen: be not merciful to any wicked transgressors. Selah.

Ps 59:8 — But thou, O LORD, shalt laugh at them; thou shalt have all the heathen in derision.

Ps 62:3 — How long will ye imagine mischief against a man? ye shall be slain all of you: as a bowing wall *shall ye be, and as* a tottering fence.

Ps 68:6 — God setteth the solitary in families: he bringeth out those which are bound with chains: but the rebellious dwell in a dry *land.*

Ps 68:21 — But God shall wound the head of his enemies, *and* the hairy scalp of such an one as goeth on still in his trespasses.

Ps 73:27 — For, lo, they that are far from thee shall perish: thou hast destroyed all them that go a whoring from thee.

Ps 75:8 — For in the hand of the LORD *there is* a cup, and the wine is red; it is full of mixture; and he poureth out of the same: but the dregs thereof, all the wicked of the earth shall wring *them* out, *and* drink *them.*

Ps 75:10 — All the horns of the wicked also will I cut off; *but* the horns of the righteous shall be exalted.

Ps 89:10 — Thou hast broken Rahab in pieces, as one that is slain; thou hast scattered thine enemies with thy strong arm.

Ps 91:8 — Only with thine eyes shalt thou behold and see the reward of the wicked.

Ps 92:7 — When the wicked spring as the grass, and when all the workers of iniquity do flourish; *it is* that they shall be destroyed for ever:

Ps 92:9 — For, lo, thine enemies, O LORD, for, lo, thine enemies shall perish; all the workers of iniquity shall be scattered.

Ps 94:13 — That thou mayest give him rest from the days of adversity, until the pit be digged for the wicked.

Ps 94:23 — And he shall bring upon them their own iniquity, and shall cut them off in their own wickedness; *yea,* the LORD our God shall cut them off.

Ps 97:3 — A fire goeth before him, and burneth up his enemies round about.

Ps 101:8 — I will early destroy all the wicked of the land; that I may cut off all wicked doers from the city of the LORD.

Ps 104:35 — Let the sinners be consumed out of the earth, and let the wicked be no more. Bless thou the LORD, O my soul. Praise ye the LORD.

Ps 106:18 — And a fire was kindled in their company; the flame burned up the wicked.

Ps 106:43 — Many times did he deliver them; but they provoked *him* with their counsel, and were brought low for their iniquity.

Ps 107:17 — Fools because of their transgression, and because of their iniquities, are afflicted.

Ps 119:21 — Thou hast rebuked the proud *that are* cursed, which do err from thy commandments.

Ps 119:155 — Salvation *is* far from the wicked: for they seek not thy statutes.

Ps 129:4 — The LORD *is* righteous: he hath cut asunder the cords of the wicked.

Ps 139:19 — Surely thou wilt slay the wicked, O God: depart from me therefore, ye bloody men.

Ps 145:20 — The LORD preserveth all them that love him: but all the wicked will he destroy.

Ps 146:9 — The LORD preserveth the strangers; he relieveth the fatherless and widow: but the way of the wicked he turneth upside down.

Ps 147:6 — The LORD lifteth up the meek: he casteth the wicked down to the ground.

Pr 2:22 — But the wicked shall be cut off from the earth, and the transgressors shall be rooted out of it.

Pr 3:33 — The curse of the LORD *is* in the house of the wicked: but he blesseth the habitation of the just.

Pr 10:3 — The LORD will not suffer the soul of the righteous to famish: but he casteth away the substance of the wicked.

Pr 10:14 — Wise *men* lay up knowledge: but the mouth of the foolish *is* near destruction.

Pr 11:3 — The integrity of the upright shall guide them: but the perverseness of transgressors shall destroy them.

Pr 11:19 — As righteousness *tendeth* to life: so he that pursueth evil *pursueth it* to his own death.

Pr 11:21 — *Though* hand *join* in hand, the wicked shall not be unpunished: but the seed of the righteous shall be delivered.

Pr 11:23 — The desire of the righteous *is* only good: *but* the expectation of the wicked *is* wrath.

Pr 11:31 — Behold, the righteous shall be recompensed in the earth: much more the wicked and the sinner.

Pr 12:7 — The wicked are overthrown, and *are* not: but the house of the righteous shall stand.

Pr 13:2 — A man shall eat good by the fruit of *his* mouth: but the soul of the transgressors *shall eat* violence.

Pr 13:9 — The light of the righteous rejoiceth: but the lamp of the wicked shall be put out.

Pr 13:21 — Evil pursueth sinners: but to the righteous good shall be repaid.

Pr 13:25 — The righteous eateth to the satisfying of his soul: but the belly of the wicked shall want.

Pr 14:12 — There is a way which seemeth right unto a man, but the end thereof *are* the ways of death.

Pr 14:19 — The evil bow before the good; and the wicked at the gates of the righteous.

Pr 14:32 — The wicked is driven away in his wickedness: but the righteous hath hope in his death.

Pr 16:25 — There is a way that seemeth right unto a man, but the end thereof *are* the ways of death.

Pr 18:3 — When the wicked cometh, *then* cometh also contempt, and with ignominy reproach.

Pr 19:16 — He that keepeth the commandment keepeth his own soul; *but* he that despiseth his ways shall die.

Pr 21:12 — The righteous *man* wisely considereth the house of the wicked: *but God* overthroweth the wicked for *their* wickedness.

Pr 22:5 — Thorns *and* snares *are* in the way of the froward: he that doth keep his soul shall be far from them.

Pr 22:23 — For the LORD will plead their cause, and spoil the soul of those that spoiled them.

Pr 24:20 — For there shall be no reward to the evil *man;* the candle of the wicked shall be put out.

Pr 24:22 — For their calamity shall rise suddenly; and who knoweth the ruin of them both?

Pr 26:10 — The great *God* that formed all *things* both rewardeth the fool, and rewardeth transgressors.

Pr 28:14 — Happy *is* the man that feareth alway: but he that hardeneth his heart shall fall into mischief.

Pr 28:18 — Whoso walketh uprightly shall be saved: but *he that is* perverse *in his* ways shall fall at once.

Pr 29:1 — He, that being often reproved hardeneth *his* neck, shall suddenly be destroyed, and that without remedy.

Pr 29:16 — When the wicked are multiplied, transgression increaseth: but the righteous shall see their fall.

Ecc 2:26 — For *God* giveth to a man that *is* good in his sight wisdom, and knowledge, and joy: but to the sinner he giveth travail, to gather and to heap up, that he may give to *him that is* good before God. This also *is* vanity and vexation of spirit.

Ecc 7:17 — Be not over much wicked, neither be thou foolish: why shouldest thou die before thy time?

Isa 2:19 — And they shall go into the holes of the rocks, and into the caves of the earth, for fear of the LORD, and for the glory of his majesty, when he ariseth to shake terribly the earth.

Isa 3:11 — Woe unto the wicked! *it shall be* ill *with him:* for the reward of his hands shall be given him.

Isa 5:24 — Therefore as the fire devoureth the stubble, and the flame consumeth the chaff, *so* their root shall be as rottenness, and their blossom shall go up as dust: because they have cast away the law of the LORD of hosts, and despised the word of the Holy One of Israel.

Isa 9:18 — For wickedness burneth as the fire: it shall devour the briers and thorns, and shall kindle in the thickets of the forest, and they shall mount up *like* the lifting up of smoke.

Isa 10:3 — And what will ye do in the day of visitation, and in the desolation *which* shall come from far? to whom will ye flee for help? and where will ye leave your glory?

Isa 11:4 — But with righteousness shall he judge the poor, and reprove with equity for the meek of the earth: and he shall smite the earth with the rod of his mouth, and with the breath of his lips shall he slay the wicked.

Isa 13:11 — And I will punish the world for *their* evil, and the wicked for their iniquity; and I will cause the arrogancy of the proud to cease, and will lay low the haughtiness of the terrible.

Isa 26:21 — For, behold, the LORD cometh out of his place to punish the inhabitants of the earth for their iniquity: the earth also shall disclose her blood, and shall no more cover her slain.

Isa 33:14 — The sinners in Zion are afraid; fearfulness hath surprised the hypocrites. Who among us shall dwell with the devouring fire? who among us shall dwell with everlasting burnings?

Isa 40:2 — Speak ye comfortably to Jerusalem, and cry unto her, that her warfare is accomplished, that her iniquity is pardoned: for she hath received of the LORD'S hand double for all her sins.

Isa 48:22 — *There is* no peace, saith the LORD, unto the wicked.

Isa 50:11 — Behold, all ye that kindle a fire, that compass *yourselves* about with sparks: walk in the light of your fire, and in the sparks *that* ye have kindled. This shall ye have of mine hand; ye shall lie down in sorrow.

Jer 13:14 — And I will dash them one against another, even the fathers and the sons together, saith the LORD: I will not pity, nor spare, nor have mercy, but destroy them.

Jer 13:16 — Give glory to the LORD your God, before he cause darkness, and before your feet stumble upon the dark mountains, and, while ye look for light, he turn it into the shadow of death, *and* make *it* gross darkness.

Jer 13:22 — And if thou say in thine heart, Wherefore come these things upon me? For the greatness of thine iniquity are thy skirts discovered, *and* thy heels made bare.

Jer 14:10 — Thus saith the LORD unto this people, Thus have they loved to wander, they have not refrained their feet, therefore the LORD doth not accept them; he will now remember their iniquity, and visit their sins.

Jer 14:12 — When they fast, I will not hear their cry; and when they offer burnt offering and an oblation, I will not accept them: but I will consume them by the sword, and by the famine, and by the pestilence.

Jer 16:18 — And first I will recompense their iniquity and their sin double; because they have defiled my land, they have filled mine inheritance with the carcases of their detestable and abominable things.

Jer 21:14 — But I will punish you according to the fruit of your doings, saith the LORD: and I will kindle a fire in the forest thereof, and it shall devour all things round about it.

Jer 25:31 — A noise shall come *even* to the ends of the earth; for the LORD hath a controversy with the nations, he will plead with all flesh; he will give them *that are* wicked to the sword, saith the LORD.

Jer 36:31 — And I will punish him and his seed and his servants for their iniquity; and I will bring upon them, and upon the inhabitants of Jerusalem, and upon the men of Judah, all the evil that I have pronounced against them; but they hearkened not.

Jer 44:23 — Because ye have burned incense, and because ye have sinned against the LORD, and have not obeyed the voice of the LORD, nor walked in his law, nor in his statutes, nor in his testimonies; therefore this evil is happened unto you, as at this day.

Jer 49:12 — For thus saith the LORD; Behold, they whose judgment *was* not to drink of the cup have assuredly drunken; and *art* thou he *that* shall altogether go unpunished? thou shalt not go unpunished, but thou shalt surely drink *of it.*

La 3:39 — Wherefore doth a living man complain, a man for the punishment of his sins?

La 4:22 — The punishment of thine iniquity is accomplished, O daughter of Zion; he will no more carry thee away into captivity: he will visit thine iniquity, O daughter of Edom; he will discover thy sins.

Eze 5:4 — Then take of them again, and cast them into the midst of the fire, and burn them in the fire; *for* thereof shall a fire come forth into all the house of Israel.

Eze 9:10 — And as for me also, mine eye shall not spare, neither will I have pity, *but* I will recompense their way upon their head.

Eze 11:21 — But *as for them* whose heart walketh after the heart of their detestable things and their abominations, I will recompense their way upon their own heads, saith the Lord GOD.

Eze 20:8 — But they rebelled against me, and would not hearken unto me: they did not every man cast away the abominations of their eyes, neither did they forsake the idols of Egypt: then I said, I will pour out my fury upon them to accomplish my anger against them in the midst of the land of Egypt.

Eze 22:14 — Can thine heart endure, or can thine hands be strong, in the days that I shall deal with thee? I the LORD have spoken *it,* and will do *it.*

Eze 22:31 — Therefore have I poured out mine indignation upon them; I have consumed them with the fire of my wrath: their own way have I recompensed upon their heads, saith the Lord GOD.

Eze 25:7 — Behold, therefore I will stretch out mine hand upon thee, and will deliver thee for a spoil to the heathen; and I will cut thee off from the people, and I will cause thee to perish out of the countries: I will destroy thee; and thou shalt know that I *am* the LORD.

Da 12:2 — And many of them that sleep in the dust of the earth shall awake, some to everlasting life, and some to shame *and* everlasting contempt.

Hos 5:9 — Ephraim shall be desolate in the day of rebuke: among the tribes of Israel have I made known that which shall surely be.

Hos 9:7 — The days of visitation are come, the days of recompence are come; Israel shall know *it:* the prophet *is* a fool, the spiritual man *is* mad, for the multitude of thine iniquity, and the great hatred.

Hos 9:9 — They have deeply corrupted *themselves,* as in the days of Gibeah: *therefore* he will remember their iniquity, he will visit their sins.

Hos 9:15 — All their wickedness *is* in Gilgal: for there I hated them: for the wickedness of their doings I will drive them out of mine house, I will love them no more: all their princes *are* revolters.

Hos 10:8 — The high places also of Aven, the sin of Israel, shall be destroyed: the thorn and the thistle shall come up on their altars; and they shall say to the mountains, Cover us; and to the hills, Fall on us.

Hos 12:2 — The LORD hath also a controversy with Judah, and will punish Jacob according to his ways; according to his doings will he recompense him.

Hos 13:3 — Therefore they shall be as the morning cloud, and as the early dew that passeth away, as the chaff *that* is driven with the whirlwind out of the floor, and as the smoke out of the chimney.

Hos 14:9 — Who *is* wise, and he shall understand these *things?* prudent, and he shall know them? for the ways of the LORD *are* right, and the just shall walk in them: but the transgressors shall fall therein.

Am 3:2 — You only have I known of all the families of the earth: therefore I will punish you for all your iniquities.

Am 9:10 — All the sinners of my people shall die by the sword, which say, The evil shall not overtake nor prevent us.

Jnh 3:9 — Who can tell *if* God will turn and repent, and turn away from his fierce anger, that we perish not?

Mic 2:3 — Therefore thus saith the LORD; Behold, against this family do I devise an evil, from which ye shall not remove your necks; neither shall ye go haughtily: for this time *is* evil.

Mic 6:13 — Therefore also will I make *thee* sick in smiting thee, in making *thee* desolate because of thy sins.

Na 1:2 — God *is* jealous, and the LORD revengeth; the LORD revengeth, and *is* furious; the LORD will take vengeance on his adversaries, and he reserveth *wrath* for his enemies.

Mt 3:7 — But when he saw many of the Pharisees and Sadducees come to his baptism, he said unto them, O generation of vipers, who hath warned you to flee from the wrath to come?

Mt 3:10 — And now also the axe is laid unto the root of the trees: therefore every tree which bringeth not forth good fruit is hewn down, and cast into the fire.

Mt 3:12 — Whose fan *is* in his hand, and he will throughly purge his floor, and gather his wheat into the garner; but he will burn up the chaff with unquenchable fire.

Mt 7:13 — Enter ye in at the strait gate: for wide *is* the gate, and broad *is* the way, that leadeth to destruction, and many there be which go in thereat:

Mt 7:19 — Every tree that bringeth not forth good fruit is hewn down, and cast into the fire.

Mt 7:23 — And then will I profess unto them, I never knew you: depart from me, ye that work iniquity.

Mt 8:12 — But the children of the kingdom shall be cast out into outer darkness: there shall be weeping and gnashing of teeth.

Mt 10:28 — And fear not them which kill the body, but are not able to kill the soul: but rather fear him which is able to destroy both soul and body in hell.

Mt 10:33 — But whosoever shall deny me before men, him will I also deny before my Father which is in heaven.

Mt 11:23 — And thou, Capernaum, which art exalted unto heaven, shalt be brought down to hell: for if the mighty works, which have been done in thee, had been done in Sodom, it would have remained until this day.

Mt 12:34 — O generation of vipers, how can ye, being evil, speak good things? for out of the abundance of the heart the mouth speaketh.

Mt 13:30 — Let both grow together until the harvest: and in the time of harvest I will say to the reapers, Gather ye together first the tares, and bind them in bundles to burn them: but gather the wheat into my barn.

Mt 15:13 — But he answered and said, Every plant, which my heavenly Father hath not planted, shall be rooted up.

Mt 16:26 — For what is a man profited, if he shall gain the whole world, and lose his own soul? or what shall a man give in exchange for his soul?

Mt 21:19 — And when he saw a fig tree in the way, he came to it, and found nothing thereon, but leaves only, and said unto it, Let no fruit grow on thee henceforward for ever. And presently the fig tree withered away.

Mt 21:41 — They say unto him, He will miserably destroy those wicked men, and will let out *his* vineyard unto other husbandmen, which shall render him the fruits in their seasons.

Mt 21:44 — And whosoever shall fall on this stone shall be broken: but on whomsoever it shall fall, it will grind him to powder.

Mt 22:13 — Then said the king to the servants, Bind him hand and foot, and take him away, and cast *him* into outer darkness; there shall be weeping and gnashing of teeth.

Mt 23:33 — *Ye* serpents, *ye* generation of vipers, how can ye escape the damnation of hell?

Mt 25:30 — And cast ye the unprofitable servant into outer darkness: there shall be weeping and gnashing of teeth.

Mt 25:41 — Then shall he say also unto them on the left hand, Depart from me, ye cursed, into everlasting fire, prepared for the devil and his angels:

Mt 25:46 — And these shall go away into everlasting punishment: but the righteous into life eternal.

Mt 26:24 — The Son of man goeth as it is written of him: but woe unto that man by whom the Son of man is betrayed! it had been good for that man if he had not been born.

Mk 4:12 — That seeing they may see, and not perceive; and hearing they may hear, and not understand; lest at any time they should be converted, and *their* sins should be forgiven them.

Mk 4:25 — For he that hath, to him shall be given: and he that hath not, from him shall be taken even that which he hath.

Mk 8:36 — For what shall it profit a man, if he shall gain the whole world, and lose his own soul?

Mk 8:38 — Whosoever therefore shall be ashamed of me and of my words in this adulterous and sinful generation; of him also shall the Son of man be ashamed, when he cometh in the glory of his Father with the holy angels.

Mk 9:43 — And if thy hand offend thee, cut it off: it is better for thee to enter into life maimed, than having two hands to go into hell, into the fire that never shall be quenched:

Mk 12:40 — Which devour widows' houses, and for a pretence make long prayers: these shall receive greater damnation.

Mk 14:21 — The Son of man indeed goeth, as it is written of him: but woe to that man by whom the Son of man is betrayed! good were it for that man if he had never been born.

Mk 16:16 — He that believeth and is baptized shall be saved; but he that believeth not shall be damned.

Lk 3:7 — Then said he to the multitude that came forth to be baptized of him, O generation of vipers, who hath warned you to flee from the wrath to come?

Lk 3:17 — Whose fan *is* in his hand, and he will throughly purge his floor, and will gather the wheat into his garner; but the chaff he will burn with fire unquenchable.

Lk 6:49 — But he that heareth, and doeth not, is like a man that without a foundation built an house upon the earth; against which the stream did beat vehemently, and immediately it fell; and the ruin of that house was great.

Lk 8:18 — Take heed therefore how ye hear: for whosoever hath, to him shall be given; and whosoever hath not, from him shall be taken even that which he seemeth to have.

Lk 13:3 — I tell you, Nay: but, except ye repent, ye shall all likewise perish.

Lk 13:9 — And if it bear fruit, *well:* and if not, *then* after that thou shalt cut it down.

Lk 13:24 — Strive to enter in at the strait gate: for many, I say unto you, will seek to enter in, and shall not be able.

Lk 20:18 — Whosoever shall fall upon that stone shall be broken; but on whomsoever it shall fall, it will grind him to powder.

Lk 22:22 — And truly the Son of man goeth, as it was determined: but woe unto that man by whom he is betrayed!

Jn 3:18 — He that believeth on him is not condemned: but he that believeth not is condemned already, because he hath not believed in the name of the only begotten Son of God.

Jn 3:36 — He that believeth on the Son hath everlasting life: and he that believeth not the Son shall not see life; but the wrath of God abideth on him.

Jn 5:14 — Afterward Jesus findeth him in the temple, and said unto him, Behold, thou art made whole: sin no more, lest a worse thing come unto thee.

Jn 5:29 — And shall come forth; they that have done good, unto the resurrection of life; and they that have done evil, unto the resurrection of damnation.

Jn 7:34 — Ye shall seek me, and shall not find *me:* and where I am, *thither* ye cannot come.

Jn 8:21 — Then said Jesus again unto them, I go my way, and ye shall seek me, and shall die in your sins: whither I go, ye cannot come.

Jn 12:40 — He hath blinded their eyes, and hardened their heart; that they should not see with *their* eyes, nor understand with *their* heart, and be converted, and I should heal them.

Jn 15:2 — Every branch in me that beareth not fruit he taketh away: and every *branch* that beareth fruit, he purgeth it, that it may bring forth more fruit.

Jn 17:12 — While I was with them in the world, I kept them in thy name: those that thou gavest me I have kept, and none of them is lost, but the son of perdition; that the scripture might be fulfilled.

Ac 1:18 — Now this man purchased a field with the reward of iniquity; and falling headlong, he burst asunder in the midst, and all his bowels gushed out.

Ac 1:25 — That he may take part of this ministry and apostleship, from which Judas by transgression fell, that he might go to his own place.

Ac 3:23 — And it shall come to pass, *that* every soul, which will not hear that prophet, shall be destroyed from among the people.

Ro 1:18 — For the wrath of God is revealed from heaven against all ungodliness and unrighteousness of men, who hold the truth in unrighteousness;

Ro 2:5 — But after thy hardness and impenitent heart treasurest up unto thyself wrath against the day of wrath and revelation of the righteous judgment of God;

Ro 2:12 — For as many as have sinned without law shall also perish without law: and as many as have sinned in the law shall be judged by the law;

Ro 5:12 — Wherefore, as by one man sin entered into the world, and death by sin; and so death passed upon all men, for that all have sinned:

Ro 5:21 — That as sin hath reigned unto death, even so might grace reign through righteousness unto eternal life by Jesus Christ our Lord.

Ro 6:16 — Know ye not, that to whom ye yield yourselves servants to obey, his servants ye are to whom ye obey; whether of sin unto death, or of obedience unto righteousness?

Ro 6:21 — What fruit had ye then in those things whereof ye are now ashamed? for the end of those things *is* death.

Ro 8:2 — For the law of the Spirit of life in Christ Jesus hath made me free from the law of sin and death.

Ro 8:13 — For if ye live after the flesh, ye shall die: but if ye through the Spirit do mortify the deeds of the body, ye shall live.

Ro 9:22 — *What* if God, willing to shew *his* wrath, and to make his power known, endured with much longsuffering the vessels of wrath fitted to destruction:

Ro 11:22 — Behold therefore the goodness and severity of God: on them which fell, severity; but toward thee, goodness, if thou continue in *his* goodness: otherwise thou also shalt be cut off.

Ro 14:23 — And he that doubteth is damned if he eat, because *he eateth* not of faith: for whatsoever *is* not of faith is sin.

1Co 3:17 — If any man defile the temple of God, him shall God destroy; for the temple of God is holy, which *temple* ye are.

1Co 5:5 — To deliver such an one unto Satan for the destruction of the flesh, that the spirit may be saved in the day of the Lord Jesus.

1Co 5:13 — But them that are without God judgeth. Therefore put away from among yourselves that wicked person.

1Co 9:27 — But I keep under my body, and bring *it* into subjection: lest that by any means, when I have preached to others, I myself should be a castaway.

2Co 7:10 — For godly sorrow worketh repentance to salvation not to be repented of: but the sorrow of the world worketh death.

Gal 3:10 — For as many as are of the works of the law are under the curse: for it is written, Cursed *is* every one that continueth not in all things which are written in the book of the law to do them.

Gal 6:8 — For he that soweth to his flesh shall of the flesh reap corruption; but he that soweth to the Spirit shall of the Spirit reap life everlasting.

Col 3:25 — But he that doeth wrong shall receive for the wrong which he hath done: and there is no respect of persons.

1Th 1:10 — And to wait for his Son from heaven, whom he raised from the dead, *even* Jesus, which delivered us from the wrath to come.

1Th 5:3 — For when they shall say, Peace and safety; then sudden destruction cometh upon them, as travail upon a woman with child; and they shall not escape.

1Ti 1:20 — Of whom is Hymenaeus and Alexander; whom I have delivered unto Satan, that they may learn not to blaspheme.

1Ti 5:24 — Some men's sins are open beforehand, going before to judgment; and some *men* they follow after.

Heb 6:8 — But that which beareth thorns and briers *is* rejected, and *is* nigh unto cursing; whose end *is* to be burned.

Jas 5:20 — Let him know, that he which converteth the sinner from the error of his way shall save a soul from death, and shall hide a multitude of sins.

1Pe 3:12 — For the eyes of the Lord *are* over the righteous, and his ears *are open* unto their prayers: but the face of the Lord *is* against them that do evil.

Rev 3:3 — Remember therefore how thou hast received and heard, and hold fast, and repent. If therefore thou shalt not watch, I will come on thee as a thief, and thou shalt not know what hour I will come upon thee.

Rev 9:15 — And the four angels were loosed, which were prepared for an hour, and a day, and a month, and a year, for to slay the third part of men.

Rev 9:18 — By these three was the third part of men killed, by the fire, and by the smoke, and by the brimstone, which issued out of their mouths.

Rev 11:18 — And the nations were angry, and thy wrath is come, and the time of the dead, that they should be judged, and that thou shouldest give reward unto thy servants the prophets, and to the saints, and them that fear thy name, small and great; and shouldest destroy them which destroy the earth.

Rev 18:5 — For her sins have reached unto heaven, and God hath remembered her iniquities.

Rev 19:15 — And out of his mouth goeth a sharp sword, that with it he should smite the nations: and he shall rule them with a rod of iron: and he treadeth the winepress of the fierceness and wrath of Almighty God.

Rev 20:10 — And the devil that deceived them was cast into the lake of fire and brimstone, where the beast and the false prophet *are,* and shall be tormented day and night for ever and ever.

Rev 20:15 — And whosoever was not found written in the book of life was cast into the lake of fire.

Rev 21:8 — But the fearful, and unbelieving, and the abominable, and murderers, and whoremongers, and sorcerers, and idolaters, and all liars, shall have their part in the lake which burneth with fire and brimstone: which is the second death.

Rev 21:27 — And there shall in no wise enter into it any thing that defileth, neither *whatsoever* worketh abomination, or *maketh* a lie: but they which are written in the Lamb's book of life.

Rev 22:19 — And if any man shall take away from the words of the book of this prophecy, God shall take away his part out of the book of life, and out of the holy city, and *from* the things which are written in this book.

See: Hell

See: Judgments

See: Punishment

WICKED, Compared with

• Abominable branches.

Isa 14:19 — But thou art cast out of thy grave like an abominable branch, *and as* the raiment of those that are slain, thrust through with a sword, that go down to the stones of the pit; as a carcase trodden under feet.

• Ashes under the feet.

Mal 4:3 — And ye shall tread down the wicked; for they shall be ashes under the soles of your feet in the day that I shall do *this,* saith the LORD of hosts.

• Bad fishes.

Mt 13:48 — Which, when it was full, they drew to shore, and sat down, and gathered the good into vessels, but cast the bad away.

• Beasts.

Ps 49:12 — Nevertheless man *being* in honour abideth not: he is like the beasts *that* perish.

2Pe 2:12 — But these, as natural brute beasts, made to be taken and destroyed, speak evil of the things that they understand not; and shall utterly perish in their own corruption;

• The blind.

Zep 1:17 — And I will bring distress upon men, that they shall walk like blind men, because they have sinned against the LORD: and their blood shall be poured out as dust, and their flesh as the dung.

Mt 15:14 — Let them alone: they be blind leaders of the blind. And if the blind lead the blind, both shall fall into the ditch.

• Brass and iron.

Jer 6:28 — They *are* all grievous revolters, walking with slanders: *they are* brass and iron; they *are* all corrupters.

Eze 22:18 — Son of man, the house of Israel is to me become dross: all they *are* brass, and tin, and iron, and lead, in the midst of the furnace; they are *even* the dross of silver.

• Briers and thorns.

Isa 55:13 — Instead of the thorn shall come up the fir tree, and instead of the brier shall come up the myrtle tree: and it shall be to the LORD for a name, for an everlasting sign *that* shall not be cut off.

Eze 2:6 — And thou, son of man, be not afraid of them, neither be afraid of their words, though briers and thorns *be* with thee, and thou dost dwell among scorpions: be not afraid of their words, nor be dismayed at their looks, though they *be* a rebellious house.

• Bulls of Bashan.

Ps 22:12 — Many bulls have compassed me: strong *bulls* of Bashan have beset me round.

• Carcases trodden under feet.

Isa 14:19 — But thou art cast out of thy grave like an abominable branch, *and as* the raiment of those that are slain, thrust through with a sword, that go down to the stones of the pit; as a carcase trodden under feet.

• Chaff.

Job 21:18 — They are as stubble before the wind, and as chaff that the storm carrieth away.

Ps 1:4 — The ungodly *are* not so: but *are* like the chaff which the wind driveth away.

Mt 3:12 — Whose fan *is* in his hand, and he will throughly purge his floor, and gather his wheat into the garner; but he will burn up the chaff with unquenchable fire.

• Clouds without water.

Jude 1:12 — These are spots in your feasts of charity, when they feast with you, feeding themselves without fear: clouds *they are* without water, carried about of winds; trees whose fruit withereth, without fruit, twice dead, plucked up by the roots;

• Corn blasted.

2Ki 19:26 — Therefore their inhabitants were of small power, they were dismayed and confounded; they were *as* the grass of the field, and *as* the green herb, *as* the grass on the house tops, and *as corn* blasted before it be grown up.

• Corrupt trees.

Lk 6:43 — For a good tree bringeth not forth corrupt fruit; neither doth a corrupt tree bring forth good fruit.

• Deaf adders.

Ps 58:4 — Their poison *is* like the poison of a serpent: *they are* like the deaf adder *that* stoppeth her ear;

• Dogs.

Pr 26:11 — As a dog returneth to his vomit, *so* a fool returneth to his folly.

Mt 7:6 — Give not that which is holy unto the dogs, neither cast ye your pearls before swine, lest they trample them under their feet, and turn again and rend you.

2Pe 2:22 — But it is happened unto them according to the true proverb, The dog *is* turned to his own vomit again; and the sow that was washed to her wallowing in the mire.

• **Dross.**

Eze 22:18–19

Ps 119:119 — Thou puttest away all the wicked of the earth *like* dross: therefore I love thy testimonies.

• **Early dew that passeth away.**

Jos 13:3 — From Sihor, which *is* before Egypt, even unto the borders of Ekron northward, *which* is counted to the Canaanite: five lords of the Philistines; the Gazathites, and the Ashdothites, the Eshkalonites, the Gittites, and the Ekronites; also the Avites:

• **Evil figs.**

Jer 24:8 — And as the evil figs, which cannot be eaten, they are so evil; surely thus saith the LORD, So will I give Zedekiah the king of Judah, and his princes, and the residue of Jerusalem, that remain in this land, and them that dwell in the land of Egypt:

• **Fading oaks.**

Isa 1:30 — For ye shall be as an oak whose leaf fadeth, and as a garden that hath no water.

• **Fiery oven.**

Ps 21:9 — Thou shalt make them as a fiery oven in the time of thine anger: the LORD shall swallow them up in his wrath, and the fire shall devour them.

Hos 7:4 — They *are* all adulterers, as an oven heated by the baker, *who* ceaseth from raising after he hath kneaded the dough, until it be leavened.

• **Fire of thorns.**

Ps 118:12 — They compassed me about like bees; they are quenched as the fire of thorns: for in the name of the LORD I will destroy them.

• **Fools building upon sand.**

Mt 7:26 — And every one that heareth these sayings of mine, and doeth them not, shall be likened unto a foolish man, which built his house upon the sand:

• **Fuel of fire.**

Isa 9:19 — Through the wrath of the LORD of hosts is the land darkened, and the people shall be as the fuel of the fire: no man shall spare his brother.

• **Garden without water.**

Isa 1:30 — For ye shall be as an oak whose leaf fadeth, and as a garden that hath no water.

• **Goats.**

Mt 25:32 — And before him shall be gathered all nations: and he shall separate them one from another, as a shepherd divideth *his* sheep from the goats:

• **Grass.**

Ps 37:2 — For they shall soon be cut down like the grass, and wither as the green herb.

Ps 92:7 — When the wicked spring as the grass, and when all the workers of iniquity do flourish; *it is* that they shall be destroyed for ever:

• **Grass on the housetop.**

2Ki 19:26 — Therefore their inhabitants were of small power, they were dismayed and confounded; they were *as* the grass of the field, and *as* the green herb, *as* the grass on the house tops, and *as corn* blasted before it be grown up.

• **Green bay tree.**

Ps 37:35 — I have seen the wicked in great power, and spreading himself like a green bay tree.

• **Green herbs.**

Ps 37:2 — For they shall soon be cut down like the grass, and wither as the green herb.

• **Heath in the desert.**

Jer 17:6 — For he shall be like the heath in the desert, and shall not see when good cometh; but shall inhabit the parched places in the wilderness, *in* a salt land and not inhabited.

• **Horses rushing into the battle.**

Jer 8:6 — I hearkened and heard, *but* they spake not aright: no man repented him of his wickedness, saying, What have I done? every one turned to his course, as the horse rusheth into the battle.

• **Idols.**

Ps 115:8 — They that make them are like unto them; *so is* every one that trusteth in them.

• **Lions greedy of prey.**

Ps 17:12 — Like as a lion *that* is greedy of his prey, and as it were a young lion lurking in secret places.

• **Melting wax.**

Ps 68:2 — As smoke is driven away, *so* drive *them* away: as wax melteth before the fire, *so* let the wicked perish at the presence of God.

• **Morning clouds.**

Hos 13:3 — Therefore they shall be as the morning cloud, and as the early dew that passeth away, as the chaff *that* is driven with the whirlwind out of the floor, and as the smoke out of the chimney.

• **Motheaten garments.**

Isa 50:9 — Behold, the Lord GOD will help me; who *is* he *that* shall condemn me? lo, they all shall wax old as a garment; the moth shall eat them up.

Isa 51:8 — For the moth shall eat them up like a garment, and the worm shall eat them like wool: but my righteousness shall be for ever, and my salvation from generation to generation.

• **Passing whirlwinds.**

Pr 10:25 — As the whirlwind passeth, so *is* the wicked no *more:* but the righteous *is* an everlasting foundation.

• **Potsherds.**

Pr 26:23 — Burning lips and a wicked heart *are like* a potsherd covered with silver dross.

• **Raging waves of the sea.**

Jude 1:13 — Raging waves of the sea, foaming out their own shame; wandering stars, to whom is reserved the blackness of darkness for ever.

• **Reprobate silver.**

Jer 6:30 — Reprobate silver shall *men* call them, because the LORD hath rejected them.

• **Scorpions.**

Eze 2:6 — And thou, son of man, be not afraid of them, neither be afraid of their words, though briers and thorns *be* with thee, and thou dost dwell among scorpions: be not afraid of their words, nor be dismayed at their looks, though they *be* a rebellious house.

• **Serpents.**

Ps 58:4 — Their poison *is* like the poison of a serpent: *they are* like the deaf adder *that* stoppeth her ear;

Mt 23:33 — Ye serpents, *ye* generation of vipers, how can ye escape the damnation of hell?

• **Smoke.**

Hos 13:3 — Therefore they shall be as the morning cloud, and as the early dew that passeth away, as the chaff *that* is driven with the whirlwind out of the floor, and as the smoke out of the chimney.

• **Stony ground.**

Mt 13:5 — Some fell upon stony places, where they had not much earth: and forthwith they sprung up, because they had no deepness of earth:

• **Stubble.**

Job 21:18 — They are as stubble before the wind, and as chaff that the storm carrieth away.

Mal 4:1 — For, behold, the day cometh, that shall burn as an oven; and all the proud, yea, and all that do wickedly, shall be stubble: and the day that cometh shall burn them up, saith the LORD of hosts, that it shall leave them neither root nor branch.

• **Swine.**

Mt 7:6 — Give not that which is holy unto the dogs, neither cast ye your pearls before swine, lest they trample them under their feet, and turn again and rend you.

2Pe 2:22 — But it is happened unto them according to the true proverb, The dog *is* turned to his own vomit again; and the sow that was washed to her wallowing in the mire.

• **Tares.**

Mt 13:38 — The field is the world; the good seed are the children of the kingdom; but the tares are the children of the wicked *one;*

• **Troubled sea.**

Isa 57:20 — But the wicked *are* like the troubled sea, when it cannot rest, whose waters cast up mire and dirt.

• **Visions of the night.**

Job 20:8 — He shall fly away as a dream, and shall not be found: yea, he shall be chased away as a vision of the night.

• **Wandering stars.**

Jude 1:13 — Raging waves of the sea, foaming out their own shame; wandering stars, to whom is reserved the blackness of darkness for ever.

• **Wayward children.**

Mt 11:16 — But whereunto shall I liken this generation? It is like unto children sitting in the markets, and calling unto their fellows,

• **Wells without water.**

2Pe 2:17 — These are wells without water, clouds that are carried with a tempest; to whom the mist of darkness is reserved for ever.

• **Wheels.**

Ps 83:13 — O my God, make them like a wheel; as the stubble before the wind.

• **Whited sepulchres.**

Mt 23:27 — Woe unto you, scribes and Pharisees, hypocrites! for ye are like unto whited sepulchres, which indeed appear beautiful outward, but are within full of dead *men's* bones, and of all uncleanness.

• **Wild ass's colts.**

Job 11:12 — For vain man would be wise, though man be born *like* a wild ass's colt.

WIDOW

• **Vows of, binding.**

Nu 30:9 — But every vow of a widow, and of her that is divorced, wherewith they have bound their souls, shall stand against her.

• **When daughters of priests, to be supported by their fathers.**

Le 22:13 — But if the priest's daughter be a widow, or divorced, and have no child, and is returned unto her father's house, as in her youth, she shall eat of her father's meat: but there shall no stranger eat thereof.

• **Priests forbidden to marry.**

Le 21:14 — A widow, or a divorced woman, or profane, *or* an harlot, these shall he not take: but he shall take a virgin of his own people to wife.

• **Marriage of, authorized.**

Ro 7:3 — So then if, while *her* husband liveth, she be married to another man, she shall be called an adulteress: but if her husband be dead, she is free from that law; so that she is no adulteress, though she be married to another man.

1Co 7:39 — The wife is bound by the law as long as her husband liveth; but if her husband be dead, she is at liberty to be married to whom she will; only in the Lord.

• **Widows' dower.**

➜**See: Dowry**

• **Unclassified scripture relating to.**

Ex 22:22–24; Dt 14:28–29; 16:11–14; 24:19–21; 25:5–10; Isa 10:1–2; Jer 7:6–7; 1Ti 5:3–6, 9–12

Dt 10:18 — He doth execute the judgment of the fatherless and widow, and loveth the stranger, in giving him food and raiment.

Dt 24:17 — Thou shalt not pervert the judgment of the stranger, *nor* of the fatherless; nor take a widow's raiment to pledge:

Dt 27:19 — Cursed *be* he that perverteth the judgment of the stranger, fatherless, and widow. And all the people shall say, Amen.

Job 22:5 — *Is* not thy wickedness great? and thine iniquities infinite?

Job 22:9 — Thou hast sent widows away empty, and the arms of the fatherless have been broken.

Job 24:3 — They drive away the ass of the fatherless, they take the widow's ox for a pledge.

Job 24:21 — He evil entreateth the barren that *beareth* not: and doeth not good to the widow.

Job 29:13 — The blessing of him that was ready to perish came upon me: and I caused the widow's heart to sing for joy.

Job 31:16 — If I have withheld the poor from *their* desire, or have caused the eyes of the widow to fail;

Job 31:22 — *Then* let mine arm fall from my shoulder blade, and mine arm be broken from the bone.

Ps 68:5 — A father of the fatherless, and a judge of the widows, *is* God in his holy habitation.

Ps 94:6 — They slay the widow and the stranger, and murder the fatherless.

Ps 146:9 — The LORD preserveth the strangers; he relieveth the fatherless and widow: but the way of the wicked he turneth upside down.

Pr 15:25 — The LORD will destroy the house of the proud: but he will establish the border of the widow.

Isa 1:17 — Learn to do well; seek judgment, relieve the oppressed, judge the fatherless, plead for the widow.

Isa 1:23 — Thy princes *are* rebellious, and companions of thieves: every one loveth gifts, and followeth after rewards: they judge not the fatherless, neither doth the cause of the widow come unto them.

Jer 22:3 — Thus saith the LORD; Execute ye judgment and righteousness, and deliver the spoiled out of the hand of the oppressor: and do no wrong, do no violence to the stranger, the fatherless, nor the widow, neither shed innocent blood in this place.

Jer 49:11 — Leave thy fatherless children, I will preserve *them* alive; and let thy widows trust in me.

Eze 22:7 — In thee have they set light by father and mother: in the midst of thee have they dealt by oppression with the stranger: in thee have they vexed the fatherless and the widow.

Zec 7:10 — And oppress not the widow, nor the fatherless, the stranger, nor the poor; and let none of you imagine evil against his brother in your heart.

Mal 3:5 — And I will come near to you to judgment; and I will be a swift witness against the sorcerers, and against the adulterers, and against false swearers, and against those that oppress the hireling in *his* wages, the widow, and the fatherless, and that turn aside the stranger *from his right,* and fear not me, saith the LORD of hosts.

Mt 23:14 — Woe unto you, scribes and Pharisees, hypocrites! for ye devour widows' houses, and for a pretence make long prayer: therefore ye shall receive the greater damnation.

Mk 12:40 — Which devour widows' houses, and for a pretence make long prayers: these shall receive greater damnation.

Lk 20:47 — Which devour widows' houses, and for a shew make long prayers: the same shall receive greater damnation.

Ac 6:1 — And in those days, when the number of the disciples was multiplied, there arose a murmuring of the Grecians against the Hebrews, because their widows were neglected in the daily ministration.

1Ti 5:16 — If any man or woman that believeth have widows, let them relieve them, and let not the church be charged; that it may relieve them that are widows indeed.

Jas 1:27 — Pure religion and undefiled before God and the Father is this, To visit the fatherless and widows in their affliction, *and* to keep himself unspotted from the world.

• Instances of.

• Naomi.

Ru 1:3

• Ruth.

Ru 1:1–4:22

• The widow of Zarephath, who sustained Elijah during a famine.

1Ki 17:1–24

• The woman whose sons Elisha saved from being sold for debt.

2Ki 4:1–7

• Anna.

Lk 2:36–37

• The woman who gave two mites in the temple.

Mk 12:41–44; Lk 21:2

• Nain, whose only son Jesus raised from the dead.

Lk 7:11–15

See: Women

See: Marriage; Levirate, the brother required to marry a brother's widow

WIFE

• Called Desire of the Eyes.

Eze 24:16 — Son of man, behold, I take away from thee the desire of thine eyes with a stroke: yet neither shalt thou mourn nor weep, neither shall thy tears run down.

• Called Help.

Ge 2:18 — And the LORD God said, *It is* not good that the man should be alone; I will make him an help meet for him.

Ge 2:20 — And Adam gave names to all cattle, and to the fowl of the air, and to every beast of the field; but for Adam there was not found an help meet for him.

• Called Fruitful Vine.

Ps 128:3 — Thy wife *shall be* as a fruitful vine by the sides of thine house: thy children like olive plants round about thy table.

• The judgment denounced against Eve.

Ge 3:16 — Unto the woman he said, I will greatly multiply thy sorrow and thy conception; in sorrow thou shalt bring forth children; and thy desire *shall be* to thy husband, and he shall rule over thee.

• Relation of, to husband.

Ge 2:23–24; 1Co 11:3–12

Ge 2:18 — And the LORD God said, *It is* not good that the man should be alone; I will make him an help meet for him.

• Domestic duties of.

Pr 31:13–27

Ge 18:6 — And Abraham hastened into the tent unto Sarah, and said, Make ready quickly three measures of fine meal, knead *it,* and make cakes upon the hearth.

- **Beloved, by Isaac.**
  Ge 24:67 — And Isaac brought her into his mother Sarah's tent, and took Rebekah, and she became his wife; and he loved her: and Isaac was comforted after his mother's *death*.
- **Beloved, by Jacob.**
  Ge 29:30 — And he went in also unto Rachel, and he loved also Rachel more than Leah, and served with him yet seven other years.
- **Hated.**
  Ge 29:31–33
- **Loyal.**
  Ge 31:14–16
- **Unfaithful.**
  Nu 5:14–31
- **Potiphar's.**
  Ge 39:7 — And it came to pass after these things, that his master's wife cast her eyes upon Joseph; and she said, Lie with me.
- **Bath-sheba.**
  2Sa 11:2–5
- **Contentious, Zipporah.**
  Ex 4:25 — Then Zipporah took a sharp stone, and cut off the foreskin of her son, and cast *it* at his feet, and said, Surely a bloody husband *art* thou to me.
  See: Wife; unclassified scripture relating to
- **Idolatrous, Solomon's wives.**
  1Ki 11:4–8
  Ne 13:26 — Did not Solomon king of Israel sin by these things? yet among many nations was there no king like him, who was beloved of his God, and God made him king over all Israel: nevertheless even him did outlandish women cause to sin.
- **Jezebel.**
  1Ki 21:1–29; 2Ki 9:30–37
- **Incorruptible, Vashti.**
  Est 1:10–22
- **Tactful, Abigail.**
  1Sa 25:14–42
  1Sa 25:3 — Now the name of the man *was* Nabal; and the name of his wife Abigail: and *she was* a woman of good understanding, and of a beautiful countenance: but the man *was* churlish and evil in his doings; and he *was* of the house of Caleb.
- **Bought.**
  Ge 29:1–35; Ex 21:7–11
  Ru 4:10 — Moreover Ruth the Moabitess, the wife of Mahlon, have I purchased to be my wife, to raise up the name of the dead upon his inheritance, that the name of the dead be not cut off from among his brethren, and from the gate of his place: ye *are* witnesses this day.
- **Gotten by violence.**
  Jgs 21:1–25
- **Procured.**
  Ge 24:1–67; 34:4–10
  Ge 38:6 — And Judah took a wife for Er his firstborn, whose name *was* Tamar.
- **Vows of.**
  Nu 30:6–16
  See: Divorce
  See: Marriage
  See: Virgin
- **Unclassified scripture relating to.**
  Ge 2:23–24; Est 1:20–22; Ps 128:3–4; Pr 19:13–14; 30:21–23; 31:10–31; 1Co 7:2–6, 10–14, 27–29, 32–34, 38–40; 11:7–9, 11–12; 14:34–35; Eph 5:22–25; Col 3:18–19; 1Ti 5:9–10; Tit 2:3–5; 1Pe 3:1–7
  Ge 2:18 — And the LORD God said, *It is* not good that the man should be alone; I will make him an help meet for him.
  Ge 3:16 — Unto the woman he said, I will greatly multiply thy sorrow and thy conception; in sorrow thou shalt bring forth children; and thy desire *shall be* to thy husband, and he shall rule over thee.
  Pr 12:4 — A virtuous woman *is* a crown to her husband: but she that maketh ashamed *is* as rottenness in his bones.
  Pr 14:1 — Every wise woman buildeth her house: but the foolish plucketh it down with her hands.
  Pr 18:22 — *Whoso* findeth a wife findeth a good *thing*, and obtaineth favour of the LORD.
  Pr 21:9 — *It is* better to dwell in a corner of the housetop, than with a brawling woman in a wide house.
  Pr 21:19 — *It is* better to dwell in the wilderness, than with a contentious and an angry woman.
  Pr 25:24 — *It is* better to dwell in the corner of the housetop, than with a brawling woman and in a wide house.
  1Co 7:16 — For what knowest thou, O wife, whether thou shalt save *thy* husband? or how knowest thou, O man, whether thou shalt save *thy* wife?
  1Co 11:3 — But I would have you know, that the head of every man is Christ; and the head of the woman *is* the man; and the head of Christ *is* God.
  Eph 5:28 — So ought men to love their wives as their own bodies. He that loveth his wife loveth himself.
  Eph 5:31 — For this cause shall a man leave his father and mother, and shall be joined unto his wife, and they two shall be one flesh.
  Eph 5:33 — Nevertheless let every one of you in particular so love his wife even as himself; and the wife *see* that she reverence *her* husband.
  1Ti 3:11 — Even so *must their* wives be grave, not slanderers, sober, faithful in all things.
  1Ti 5:14 — I will therefore that the younger women marry, bear children, guide the house, give none occasion to the adversary to speak reproachfully.
  See: Husband
  See: Parents
  See: Widow
  See: Women

WILDERNESS

- **Wandering of the Israelites in.**
  See: Israel

• Typical of the sinner's state.

Dt 32:10 — He found him in a desert land, and in the waste howling wilderness; he led him about, he instructed him, he kept him as the apple of his eye.

• Jesus' temptation in.

Mk 1:12–13

Mt 4:1 — Then was Jesus led up of the Spirit into the wilderness to be tempted of the devil.

Lk 4:1 — And Jesus being full of the Holy Ghost returned from Jordan, and was led by the Spirit into the wilderness,

↞See: Desert

WILL

• The mental faculty.

• Freedom of, recognized by God.

Ge 4:6–10; Isa 1:18–20

Dt 5:29 — O that there were such an heart in them, that they would fear me, and keep all my commandments always, that it might be well with them, and with their children for ever!

1Ki 20:42 — And he said unto him, Thus saith the LORD, Because thou hast let go out of *thy* hand a man whom I appointed to utter destruction, therefore thy life shall go for his life, and thy people for his people.

Isa 43:26 — Put me in remembrance: let us plead together: declare thou, that thou mayest be justified.

Jer 36:3 — It may be that the house of Judah will hear all the evil which I purpose to do unto them; that they may return every man from his evil way; that I may forgive their iniquity and their sin.

Jer 36:7 — It may be they will present their supplication before the LORD, and will return every one from his evil way: for great *is* the anger and the fury that the LORD hath pronounced against this people.

Jn 7:17 — If any man will do his will, he shall know of the doctrine, whether it be of God, or *whether* I speak of myself.

↞See: Blessing; divine, contingent upon obedience

↞See: Choice

↞See: Contingencies

• Of God, the supreme rule of duty.

Jn 6:38–40

Mt 6:10 — Thy kingdom come. Thy will be done in earth, as *it is* in heaven.

Mt 12:50 — For whosoever shall do the will of my Father which is in heaven, the same is my brother, and sister, and mother.

Mt 26:39 — And he went a little farther, and fell on his face, and prayed, saying, O my Father, if it be possible, let this cup pass from me: nevertheless not as I will, but as thou *wilt.*

Mt 26:42 — He went away again the second time, and prayed, saying, O my Father, if this cup may not pass away from me, except I drink it, thy will be done.

Mk 3:35 — For whosoever shall do the will of God, the same is my brother, and my sister, and mother.

Mk 14:36 — And he said, Abba, Father, all things *are* possible unto thee; take away this cup from me: nevertheless not what I will, but what thou wilt.

Lk 11:2 — And he said unto them, When ye pray, say, Our Father which art in heaven, Hallowed be thy name. Thy kingdom come. Thy will be done, as in heaven, so in earth.

Lk 22:42 — Saying, Father, if thou be willing, remove this cup from me: nevertheless not my will, but thine, be done.

Jn 4:34 — Jesus saith unto them, My meat is to do the will of him that sent me, and to finish his work.

Jn 5:30 — I can of mine own self do nothing: as I hear, I judge: and my judgment is just; because I seek not mine own will, but the will of the Father which hath sent me.

Ac 18:21 — But bade them farewell, saying, I must by all means keep this feast that cometh in Jerusalem: but I will return again unto you, if God will. And he sailed from Ephesus.

Ro 12:2 — And be not conformed to this world: but be ye transformed by the renewing of your mind, that ye may prove what is that good, and acceptable, and perfect, will of God.

Ro 15:32 — That I may come unto you with joy by the will of God, and may with you be refreshed.

1Co 4:19 — But I will come to you shortly, if the Lord will, and will know, not the speech of them which are puffed up, but the power.

1Co 16:7 — For I will not see you now by the way; but I trust to tarry a while with you, if the Lord permit.

Heb 6:3 — And this will we do, if God permit.

↞See: Agency

• A testament.

• Of Abraham.

Ge 25:5–6

• Jacob.

Ge 48:1–49:33

• David.

1Ki 2:1–9

• Jehoshaphat.

2Ch 21:3 — And their father gave them great gifts of silver, and of gold, and of precious things, with fenced cities in Judah: but the kingdom gave he to Jehoram; because he *was* the firstborn.

• May not be annulled.

Gal 3:15 — Brethren, I speak after the manner of men; Though *it be* but a man's covenant, yet *if it be* confirmed, no man disannulleth, or addeth thereto.

• In force after death only.

Heb 9:16–17

↞See: Testament

WILLFULNESS

↞See: Obduracy

↞See: Self-Will

WILLOW

Le 23:40 — And ye shall take you on the first day the boughs of goodly trees, branches of palm trees, and the boughs of thick trees, and willows of the brook; and ye shall rejoice before the LORD your God seven days.

Ps 137:2 — We hanged our harps upon the willows in the midst thereof.

Eze 17:5 — He took also of the seed of the land, and planted it in a fruitful field; he placed *it* by great waters, *and* set it *as* a willow tree.

• Figurative.

Isa 44:4 — And they shall spring up as among the grass, as willows by the water courses.

WIMPLE

Isa 3:22 — The changeable suits of apparel, and the mantles, and the wimples, and the crisping pins,

WIND

• Blasting.

2Ki 19:7 — Behold, I will send a blast upon him, and he shall hear a rumour, and shall return to his own land; and I will cause him to fall by the sword in his own land.

2Ki 19:35 — And it came to pass that night, that the angel of the LORD went out, and smote in the camp of the Assyrians an hundred fourscore and five thousand: and when they arose early in the morning, behold, they *were* all dead corpses.

• East.

• Hot and blasting in Egypt.

Ge 41:6 — And, behold, seven thin ears and blasted with the east wind sprung up after them.

• In the valley of the Euphrates.

Eze 19:12 — But she was plucked up in fury, she was cast down to the ground, and the east wind dried up her fruit: her strong rods were broken and withered; the fire consumed them.

• In Canaan.

Hos 13:15 — Though he be fruitful among *his* brethren, an east wind shall come, the wind of the LORD shall come up from the wilderness, and his spring shall become dry, and his fountain shall be dried up: he shall spoil the treasure of all pleasant vessels.

Lk 12:55 — And when *ye see* the south wind blow, ye say, There will be heat; and it cometh to pass.

• At Nineveh.

Jnh 4:8 — And it came to pass, when the sun did arise, that God prepared a vehement east wind; and the sun beat upon the head of Jonah, that he fainted, and wished in himself to die, and said, *It is* better for me to die than to live.

• Tempestuous in Uz.

Job 27:21 — The east wind carrieth him away, and he departeth: and as a storm hurleth him out of his place.

• West.

• Took away the plague of locusts from the land of Egypt.

Ex 10:19 — And the LORD turned a mighty strong west wind, which took away the locusts, and cast them into the Red sea; there remained not one locust in all the coasts of Egypt.

• North.

• Free from humidity in Canaan.

Pr 25:23 — The north wind driveth away rain: so *doth* an angry countenance a backbiting tongue.

• South.

• Soothing.

Job 37:17 — How thy garments *are* warm, when he quieteth the earth by the south *wind?*

• Tempestuous.

Job 37:9 — Out of the south cometh the whirlwind: and cold out of the north.

• Purifying.

Job 37:21 — And now *men* see not the bright light which is in the clouds: but the wind passeth, and cleanseth them.

• Figurative.

Hos 4:19 — The wind hath bound her up in her wings, and they shall be ashamed because of their sacrifices.

• Of the judgments of God.

Jer 22:22 — The wind shall eat up all thy pastors, and thy lovers shall go into captivity: surely then shalt thou be ashamed and confounded for all thy wickedness.

Hos 13:15 — Though he be fruitful among *his* brethren, an east wind shall come, the wind of the LORD shall come up from the wilderness, and his spring shall become dry, and his fountain shall be dried up: he shall spoil the treasure of all pleasant vessels.

Mt 7:25 — And the rain descended, and the floods came, and the winds blew, and beat upon that house; and it fell not: for it was founded upon a rock.

• Of the Spirit.

Jn 3:8 — The wind bloweth where it listeth, and thou hearest the sound thereof, but canst not tell whence it cometh, and whither it goeth: so is every one that is born of the Spirit.

• Of heresy.

Eph 4:14 — That we *henceforth* be no more children, tossed to and fro, and carried about with every wind of doctrine, by the sleight of men, *and* cunning craftiness, whereby they lie in wait to deceive;

WINDOW

Eze 40:16–36

Ge 6:16 — A window shalt thou make to the ark, and in a cubit shalt thou finish it above; and the door of the ark shalt thou set in the side thereof; *with* lower, second, and third *stories* shalt thou make it.

Ge 26:8 — And it came to pass, when he had been there a long time, that Abimelech king of the Philistines looked out at a window, and saw, and, behold, Isaac *was* sporting with Rebekah his wife.

Jos 2:15 — Then she let them down by a cord through the window: for her house *was* upon the town wall, and she dwelt upon the wall.

Jos 2:21 — And she said, According unto your words, so *be* it. And she sent them away, and they departed: and she bound the scarlet line in the window.

1Ki 6:4 — And for the house he made windows of narrow lights.

Ac 20:9 — And there sat in a window a certain young man named Eutychus, being fallen into a deep sleep: and as Paul was long preaching, he sunk down with sleep, and fell down from the third loft, and was taken up dead.

WINE

• Made from grapes.

Ge 40:11 — And Pharaoh's cup *was* in my hand: and I took the grapes, and pressed them into Pharaoh's cup, and I gave the cup into Pharaoh's hand.

Ge 49:11 — Binding his foal unto the vine, and his ass's colt unto the choice vine; he washed his garments in wine, and his clothes in the blood of grapes:

Isa 25:6 — And in this mountain shall the LORD of hosts make unto all people a feast of fat things, a feast of wines on the lees, of fat things full of marrow, of wines on the lees well refined.

Jer 40:10 — As for me, behold, I will dwell at Mizpah to serve the Chaldeans, which will come unto us: but ye, gather ye wine, and summer fruits, and oil, and put *them* in your vessels, and dwell in your cities that ye have taken.

Jer 40:12 — Even all the Jews returned out of all places whither they were driven, and came to the land of Judah, to Gedaliah, unto Mizpah, and gathered wine and summer fruits very much.

• Made from pomegranates.

SS 8:2 — I would lead thee, *and* bring thee into my mother's house, *who* would instruct me: I would cause thee to drink of spiced wine of the juice of my pomegranate.

• Kept in jars.

Jer 13:12 — Therefore thou shalt speak unto them this word; Thus saith the LORD God of Israel, Every bottle shall be filled with wine: and they shall say unto thee, Do we not certainly know that every bottle shall be filled with wine?

Jer 48:12 — Therefore, behold, the days come, saith the LORD, that I will send unto him wanderers, that shall cause him to wander, and shall empty his vessels, and break their bottles.

• Kept in skins.

Lk 5:37–38

Jos 9:4 — They did work wilily, and went and made as if they had been ambassadors, and took old sacks upon their asses, and wine bottles, old, and rent, and bound up;

Jos 9:13 — And these bottles of wine, which we filled, *were* new; and, behold, they be rent: and these our garments and our shoes are become old by reason of the very long journey.

Job 32:19 — Behold, my belly *is* as wine *which* hath no vent; it is ready to burst like new bottles.

Mt 9:17 — Neither do men put new wine into old bottles: else the bottles break, and the wine runneth out, and the bottles perish: but they put new wine into new bottles, and both are preserved.

• Kept in bottles.

Lk 5:37–38

Jos 9:4 — They did work wilily, and went and made as if they had been ambassadors, and took old sacks upon their asses, and wine bottles, old, and rent, and bound up;

Jos 9:13 — And these bottles of wine, which we filled, *were* new; and, behold, they be rent: and these our garments and our shoes are become old by reason of the very long journey.

Job 32:19 — Behold, my belly *is* as wine *which* hath no vent; it is ready to burst like new bottles.

Jer 13:12 — Therefore thou shalt speak unto them this word; Thus saith the LORD God of Israel, Every bottle shall be filled with wine: and they shall say unto thee, Do we not certainly know that every bottle shall be filled with wine?

Jer 48:12 — Therefore, behold, the days come, saith the LORD, that I will send unto him wanderers, that shall cause him to wander, and shall empty his vessels, and break their bottles.

Mt 9:17 — Neither do men put new wine into old bottles: else the bottles break, and the wine runneth out, and the bottles perish: but they put new wine into new bottles, and both are preserved.

• Cellars for.

1Ch 27:27 — And over the vineyards was Shimei the Ramathite: over the increase of the vineyards for the wine cellars *was* Zabdi the Shiphmite:

• New.

Hag 1:11 — And I called for a drought upon the land, and upon the mountains, and upon the corn, and upon the new wine, and upon the oil, and upon *that* which the ground bringeth forth, and upon men, and upon cattle, and upon all the labour of the hands.

• Old.

Lk 5:39 — No man also having drunk old *wine* straightway desireth new: for he saith, The old is better.

• Medicinal use of.

Pr 31:6–7

• Recommended by Paul to Timothy.

1Ti 5:23 — Drink no longer water, but use a little wine for thy stomach's sake and thine often infirmities.

• Used at meals.

Mt 26:27–29

Mk 14:23 — And he took the cup, and when he had given thanks, he gave *it* to them: and they all drank of it.

• Made by Jesus at the marriage feast in Cana.

Jn 2:9–10

• Sacramental use of.

Mt 26:27–29; Lk 22:17–20

• Forbidden to priests while on duty.

Le 10:9 — Do not drink wine nor strong drink, thou, nor thy sons with thee, when ye go into the tabernacle of the congregation, lest ye die: *it shall be* a statute for ever throughout your generations:

Eze 44:21 — Neither shall any priest drink wine, when they enter into the inner court.

• Forbidden to Nazarites.

Nu 6:2–3

See: Nazarite

• Abstinence from, of Daniel.

Da 1:5 — And the king appointed them a daily provision of the king's meat, and of the wine which he drank: so nourishing them three years, that at the end thereof they might stand before the king.

Da 1:8 — But Daniel purposed in his heart that he would not defile himself with the portion of the king's meat, nor with the wine which he drank: therefore he requested of the prince of the eunuchs that he might not defile himself.

Da 1:16 — Thus Melzar took away the portion of their meat, and the wine that they should drink; and gave them pulse.

Da 10:3 — I ate no pleasant bread, neither came flesh nor wine in my mouth, neither did I anoint myself at all, till three whole weeks were fulfilled.

• Abstinence from, of courtiers of Ahasuerus.

Est 1:8 — And the drinking *was* according to the law; none did compel: for so the king had appointed to all the officers of his house, that they should do according to every man's pleasure.

• Abstinence from, of Timothy.

1Ti 5:23 — Drink no longer water, but use a little wine for thy stomach's sake and thine often infirmities.

• Samson's mother forbidden to drink.

Jgs 13:4–5

• Forbidden to kings.

Pr 31:4 — *It is* not for kings, O Lemuel, *it is* not for kings to drink wine; nor for princes strong drink:

• Denied to the Israelites in the wilderness, that they might know that the Lord was their God.

Dt 29:6 — Ye have not eaten bread, neither have ye drunk wine or strong drink: that ye might know that I *am* the LORD your God.

• Offered with sacrifices.

Ex 29:40 — And with the one lamb a tenth deal of flour mingled with the fourth part of an hin of beaten oil; and the fourth part of an hin of wine *for* a drink offering.

Le 23:13 — And the meat offering thereof *shall be* two tenth deals of fine flour mingled with oil, an offering made by fire unto the LORD *for* a sweet savour: and the drink offering thereof *shall be* of wine, the fourth *part* of an hin.

Nu 15:5 — And the fourth *part* of an hin of wine for a drink offering shalt thou prepare with the burnt offering or sacrifice, for one lamb.

Nu 15:10 — And thou shalt bring for a drink offering half an hin of wine, for an offering made by fire, of a sweet savour unto the LORD.

Nu 28:7 — And the drink offering thereof *shall be* the fourth *part* of an hin for the one lamb: in the holy *place* shalt thou cause the strong wine to be poured unto the LORD *for* a drink offering.

Nu 28:14 — And their drink offerings shall be half an hin of wine unto a bullock, and the third *part* of an hin unto a ram, and a fourth *part* of an hin unto a lamb: this *is* the burnt offering of every month throughout the months of the year.

• Given by Melchizedek to Abraham.

Ge 14:18 — And Melchizedek king of Salem brought forth bread and wine: and he *was* the priest of the most high God.

• Fermented.

Pr 23:31–32

Le 10:9 — Do not drink wine nor strong drink, thou, nor thy sons with thee, when ye go into the tabernacle of the congregation, lest ye die: *it shall be* a statute for ever throughout your generations:

Nu 6:3 — He shall separate *himself* from wine and strong drink, and shall drink no vinegar of wine, or vinegar of strong drink, neither shall he drink any liquor of grapes, nor eat moist grapes, or dried.

Nu 28:7 — And the drink offering thereof *shall be* the fourth *part* of an hin for the one lamb: in the holy *place* shalt thou cause the strong wine to be poured unto the LORD *for* a drink offering.

Dt 14:26 — And thou shalt bestow that money for whatsoever thy soul lusteth after, for oxen, or for sheep, or for wine, or for strong drink, or for whatsoever thy soul desireth: and thou shalt eat there before the LORD thy God, and thou shalt rejoice, thou, and thine household,

Dt 29:6 — Ye have not eaten bread, neither have ye drunk wine or strong drink: that ye might know that I *am* the LORD your God.

Mk 2:22 — And no man putteth new wine into old bottles: else the new wine doth burst the bottles, and the wine is spilled, and the bottles will be marred: but new wine must be put into new bottles.

• Refined.

Isa 25:6 — And in this mountain shall the LORD of hosts make unto all people a feast of fat things, a feast of wines on the lees, of fat things full of marrow, of wines on the lees well refined.

Jer 48:11 — Moab hath been at ease from his youth, and he hath settled on his lees, and hath not been emptied from vessel to vessel, neither hath he gone into captivity: therefore his taste remained in him, and his scent is not changed.

• Of staggering.

Ps 60:3 — Thou hast shewed thy people hard things: thou hast made us to drink the wine of astonishment.

• Inflames the eyes.

Ge 49:12 — His eyes *shall be* red with wine, and his teeth white with milk.

• Commerce in.

Rev 18:13 — And cinnamon, and odours, and ointments, and frankincense, and wine, and oil, and fine flour, and wheat, and beasts, and sheep, and horses, and chariots, and slaves, and souls of men.

• Banquets of.

Est 5:6 — And the king said unto Esther at the banquet of wine, What *is* thy petition? and it shall be granted thee: and what *is* thy request? even to the half of the kingdom it shall be performed.

• Given to Jesus at the crucifixion.

Mt 27:48 — And straightway one of them ran, and took a spunge, and filled *it* with vinegar, and put *it* on a reed, and gave him to drink.

Mk 15:23 — And they gave him to drink wine mingled with myrrh: but he received *it* not.

Lk 23:36 — And the soldiers also mocked him, coming to him, and offering him vinegar,

Jn 19:29 — Now there was set a vessel full of vinegar: and they filled a spunge with vinegar, and put *it* upon hyssop, and put *it* to his mouth.

• Intoxication from the use of.

Ps 104:15 — And wine *that* maketh glad the heart of man, *and* oil to make *his* face to shine, and bread *which* strengtheneth man's heart.

Pr 4:17 — For they eat the bread of wickedness, and drink the wine of violence.

• Instances of intoxication from.

• Noah.

Ge 9:21

• Lot.

Ge 19:32

• Joseph and his brethren.

Ge 43:34

• Nabal.

1Sa 25:36

• Amnon.

2Sa 13:28–29

• Ahasuerus.

Est 1:10

• Kings of Israel.

Hos 7:5

• Falsely charged against the disciples.

Ac 2:13

• Figurative.

• Of the divine judgments.

Ps 60:3 — Thou hast shewed thy people hard things: thou hast made us to drink the wine of astonishment.

Ps 75:8 — For in the hand of the LORD *there is* a cup, and the wine is red; it is full of mixture; and he poureth out of the same: but the dregs thereof, all the wicked of the earth shall wring *them* out, *and* drink *them*.

Jer 51:7 — Babylon *hath been* a golden cup in the LORD'S hand, that made all the earth drunken: the nations have drunken of her wine; therefore the nations are mad.

• Of the joy of wisdom.

Pr 9:2 — She hath killed her beasts; she hath mingled her wine; she hath also furnished her table.

Pr 9:5 — Come, eat of my bread, and drink of the wine *which* I have mingled.

• Of the joys of religion.

Isa 25:6 — And in this mountain shall the LORD of hosts make unto all people a feast of fat things, a feast of wines on the lees, of fat things full of marrow, of wines on the lees well refined.

Isa 55:1 — Ho, every one that thirsteth, come ye to the waters, and he that hath no money; come ye, buy, and eat; yea, come, buy wine and milk without money and without price.

Joel 2:19 — Yea, the LORD will answer and say unto his people, Behold, I will send you corn, and wine, and oil, and ye shall be satisfied therewith: and I will no more make you a reproach among the heathen:

• Of abominations.

Rev 14:8 — And there followed another angel, saying, Babylon is fallen, is fallen, that great city, because she made all nations drink of the wine of the wrath of her fornication.

Rev 16:19 — And the great city was divided into three parts, and the cities of the nations fell: and great Babylon came in remembrance before God, to give unto her the cup of the wine of the fierceness of his wrath.

• Symbolic.

• Of the blood of Jesus.

Mk 14:23–24; Jn 6:53–56

Mt 26:28 — <u>For this is my blood of the new testament, which is shed for many for the remission of sins.</u>

Lk 22:20 — Likewise also the cup after supper, saying, <u>This cup *is* the new testament in my blood, which is shed for you.</u>

• Unclassified scripture relating to.

Ps 104:14–15; Pr 31:6–7

Dt 14:26 — And thou shalt bestow that money for whatsoever thy soul lusteth after, for oxen, or for sheep, or for wine, or for strong drink, or for whatsoever thy soul desireth: and thou shalt eat there before the LORD thy God, and thou shalt rejoice, thou, and thine household,

Dt 33:28 — Israel then shall dwell in safety alone: the fountain of Jacob *shall be* upon a land of corn and wine; also his heavens shall drop down dew.

2Ki 18:32 — Until I come and take you away to a land like your own land, a land of corn and wine, a land of bread and vineyards, a land of oil olive and of honey, that ye may live, and not die: and hearken not unto Hezekiah, when he persuadeth you, saying, The LORD will deliver us.

2Ch 32:28 — Storehouses also for the increase of corn, and wine, and oil; and stalls for all manner of beasts, and cotes for flocks.

Ne 10:39 — For the children of Israel and the children of Levi shall bring the offering of the corn, of the new wine, and the oil, unto the chambers, where *are* the vessels of the sanctuary, and the priests that minister, and the porters, and the singers: and we will not forsake the house of our God.

Ps 4:7 — Thou hast put gladness in my heart, more than in the time *that* their corn and their wine increased.

Ecc 2:3 — I sought in mine heart to give myself unto wine, yet acquainting mine heart with wisdom; and to lay hold on folly, till I might see what *was* that good for the sons of men, which they should do under the heaven all the days of their life.

Ecc 2:11 — Then I looked on all the works that my hands had wrought, and on the labour that I had laboured to do: and, behold, all *was* vanity and vexation of spirit, and *there was* no profit under the sun.

Isa 56:12 — Come ye, *say they,* I will fetch wine, and we will fill ourselves with strong drink; and to morrow shall be as this day, *and* much more abundant.

Hos 2:8 — For she did not know that I gave her corn, and wine, and oil, and multiplied her silver and gold, *which* they prepared for Baal.

Hos 2:22 — And the earth shall hear the corn, and the wine, and the oil; and they shall hear Jezreel.

Hos 7:14 — And they have not cried unto me with their heart, when they howled upon their beds: they assemble themselves for corn and wine, *and* they rebel against me.

Joel 1:5 — Awake, ye drunkards, and weep; and howl, all ye drinkers of wine, because of the new wine; for it is cut off from your mouth.

Joel 2:24 — And the floors shall be full of wheat, and the fats shall overflow with wine and oil.

Joel 3:3 — And they have cast lots for my people; and have given a boy for an harlot, and sold a girl for wine, that they might drink.

Am 6:6 — That drink wine in bowls, and anoint themselves with the chief ointments: but they are not grieved for the affliction of Joseph.

Hab 2:5 — Yea also, because he transgresseth by wine, *he is* a proud man, neither keepeth at home, who enlargeth his desire as hell, and *is* as death, and cannot be satisfied, but gathereth unto him all nations, and heapeth unto him all people:

Hag 1:11 — And I called for a drought upon the land, and upon the mountains, and upon the corn, and upon the new wine, and upon the oil, and upon *that* which the ground bringeth forth, and upon men, and upon cattle, and upon all the labour of the hands.

Zec 9:17 — For how great *is* his goodness, and how great *is* his beauty! corn shall make the young men cheerful, and new wine the maids.

Zec 10:7 — And *they of* Ephraim shall be like a mighty *man,* and their heart shall rejoice as through wine: yea, their children shall see *it,* and be glad; their heart shall rejoice in the LORD.

1Ti 5:23 — Drink no longer water, but use a little wine for thy stomach's sake and thine often infirmities.

See: Vine

See: Vineyard

• Admonitions against the use of.

Pr 23:29–32; 31:4–5; Jer 35:2–10, 18–19

Le 10:9 — Do not drink wine nor strong drink, thou, nor thy sons with thee, when ye go into the tabernacle of the congregation, lest ye die: *it shall be* a statute for ever throughout your generations:

Nu 6:3 — He shall separate *himself* from wine and strong drink, and shall drink no vinegar of wine, or vinegar of strong drink, neither shall he drink any liquor of grapes, nor eat moist grapes, or dried.

Jgs 13:4 — Now therefore beware, I pray thee, and drink not wine nor strong drink, and eat not any unclean *thing:*

Pr 20:1 — Wine *is* a mocker, strong drink *is* raging: and whosoever is deceived thereby is not wise.

Pr 21:17 — He that loveth pleasure *shall be* a poor man: he that loveth wine and oil shall not be rich.

Isa 5:11 — Woe unto them that rise up early in the morning, *that* they may follow strong drink; that continue until night, *till* wine inflame them!

Isa 5:22 — Woe unto *them that are* mighty to drink wine, and men of strength to mingle strong drink:

Isa 24:9 — They shall not drink wine with a song; strong drink shall be bitter to them that drink it.

Isa 28:1 — Woe to the crown of pride, to the drunkards of Ephraim, whose glorious beauty is a fading flower, which *are* on the head of the fat valleys of them that are overcome with wine!

Isa 28:3 — The crown of pride, the drunkards of Ephraim, shall be trodden under feet:

Isa 28:7 — But they also have erred through wine, and through strong drink are out of the way; the priest and the prophet have erred through strong drink, they are swallowed up of wine, they are out of the way through strong drink; they err in vision, they stumble *in* judgment.

Jer 23:9 — Mine heart within me is broken because of the prophets; all my bones shake; I am like a drunken man, and like a man whom wine hath overcome, because of the LORD, and because of the words of his holiness.

Jer 35:14 — The words of Jonadab the son of Rechab, that he commanded his sons not to drink wine, are performed; for unto this day they drink none, but obey their father's commandment: notwithstanding I have spoken unto you, rising early and speaking; but ye hearkened not unto me.

Eze 44:21 — Neither shall any priest drink wine, when they enter into the inner court.

Hos 4:11 — Whoredom and wine and new wine take away the heart.

Lk 1:15 — For he shall be great in the sight of the Lord, and shall drink neither wine nor strong drink; and he shall be filled with the Holy Ghost, even from his mother's womb.

Ro 14:21 — *It is* good neither to eat flesh, nor to drink wine, nor *any thing* whereby thy brother stumbleth, or is offended, or is made weak.

Eph 5:18 — And be not drunk with wine, wherein is excess; but be filled with the Spirit;

Tit 2:3 — The aged women likewise, that *they be* in behaviour as becometh holiness, not false accusers, not given to much wine, teachers of good things;

➜See: Abstinence, Total

➜See: Drunkenness

WINE PRESS

Nu 18:27 — And *this* your heave offering shall be reckoned unto you, as though *it were* the corn of the threshingfloor, and as the fulness of the winepress.

Nu 18:30 — Therefore thou shalt say unto them, When ye have heaved the best thereof from it, then it shall be counted unto the Levites as the increase of the threshingfloor, and as the increase of the winepress.

Dt 15:14 — Thou shalt furnish him liberally out of thy flock, and out of thy floor, and out of thy winepress: *of that* wherewith the LORD thy God hath blessed thee thou shalt give unto him.

Jgs 6:11 — And there came an angel of the LORD, and sat under an oak which *was* in Ophrah, that *pertained* unto Joash the Abi-ezrite: and his son Gideon threshed wheat by the winepress, to hide *it* from the Midianites.

• In vineyards.

Isa 5:2 — And he fenced it, and gathered out the stones thereof, and planted it with the choicest vine, and built a tower in the midst of it, and also made a winepress therein: and he looked that it should bring forth grapes, and it brought forth wild grapes.

Mt 21:33 — Hear another parable: There was a certain householder, which planted a vineyard, and hedged it round about, and digged a winepress in it, and built a tower, and let it out to husbandmen, and went into a far country:

Mk 12:1 — And he began to speak unto them by parables. A *certain* man planted a vineyard, and set an hedge about *it*, and digged *a place for* the winefat, and built a tower, and let it out to husbandmen, and went into a far country.

• Trodden with joy and shouting.

Jer 48:33 — And joy and gladness is taken from the plentiful field, and from the land of Moab; and I have caused wine to fail from the winepresses: none shall tread with shouting; *their* shouting *shall be* no shouting.

• Figurative.

• Treading the, of the sufferings of Christ.

Isa 63:2–3

• Treading the, of the judgments of God.

Rev 14:19–20

La 1:15 — The Lord hath trodden under foot all my mighty *men* in the midst of me: he hath called an assembly against me to crush my young men: the Lord hath trodden the virgin, the daughter of Judah, *as* in a winepress.

WINEBIBBER

• Jesus falsely accused of being a.

Mt 11:19 — The Son of man came eating and drinking, and they say, Behold a man gluttonous, and a winebibber, a friend of publicans and sinners. But wisdom is justified of her children.

Lk 7:34 — The Son of man is come eating and drinking; and ye say, Behold a gluttonous man, and a winebibber, a friend of publicans and sinners!

WINNOWING

• Of grain.

Ru 3:2 — And now *is* not Boaz of our kindred, with whose maidens thou wast? Behold, he winnoweth barley to night in the threshingfloor.

Isa 30:24 — The oxen likewise and the young asses that ear the ground shall eat clean provender, which hath been winnowed with the shovel and with the fan.

Mt 3:12 — Whose fan *is* in his hand, and he will throughly purge his floor, and gather his wheat into the garner; but he will burn up the chaff with unquenchable fire.

WINTER

• Annual return of, shall never cease.

Ge 8:22 — While the earth remaineth, seedtime and harvest, and cold and heat, and summer and winter, and day and night shall not cease.

• Plowing in, in Canaan.

Pr 20:4 — The sluggard will not plow by reason of the cold; *therefore* shall he beg in harvest, and *have* nothing.

• Rainy season in, in Canaan.

SS 2:11 — For, lo, the winter is past, the rain is over *and* gone;

• Shipping suspended in, on the Mediterranean Sea.

Ac 27:12 — And because the haven was not commodious to winter in, the more part advised to depart thence also, if by any means they might attain to Phenice, *and there* to winter; *which is* an haven of Crete, and lieth toward the south west and north west.

Ac 28:11 — And after three months we departed in a ship of Alexandria, which had wintered in the isle, whose sign was Castor and Pollux.

• Paul remains one, at Nicopolis.

Tit 3:12 — When I shall send Artemas unto thee, or Tychicus, be diligent to come unto me to Nicopolis: for I have determined there to winter.

• Summer and winter houses.

Jer 36:22 — Now the king sat in the winterhouse in the ninth month: and *there was a fire* on the hearth burning before him.

Am 3:15 — And I will smite the winter house with the summer house; and the houses of ivory shall perish, and the great houses shall have an end, saith the LORD.

➜See: Meteorology and Celestial Phenomena

WISDOM

• Of Joseph.

Ge 41:25–39

Ge 41:16 — And Joseph answered Pharaoh, saying, *It is* not in me: God shall give Pharaoh an answer of peace.

Ac 7:10 — And delivered him out of all his afflictions, and gave him favour and wisdom in the sight of Pharaoh king of Egypt; and he made him governor over Egypt and all his house.

• Of Moses.

Ac 7:22 — And Moses was learned in all the wisdom of the Egyptians, and was mighty in words and in deeds.

• Of Bezaleel.

Ex 31:3–5; 35:31–36:1

• Of Aholiab.

Ex 35:34–36:1

Ex 31:6 — And I, behold, I have given with him Aholiab, the son of Ahisamach, of the tribe of Dan: and in the hearts of all that are wise hearted I have put wisdom, that they may make all that I have commanded thee;

• Of other skilled artisans.

Ex 36:2 — And Moses called Bezaleel and Aholiab, and every wise hearted man, in whose heart the LORD had put wisdom, *even* every one whose heart stirred him up to come unto the work to do it:

• Of women.

Ex 35:26 — And all the women whose heart stirred them up in wisdom spun goats' *hair.*

• Of Hiram.

1Ki 7:14 — He *was* a widow's son of the tribe of Naphtali, and his father *was* a man of Tyre, a worker in brass: and he was filled with wisdom, and understanding, and cunning to work all works in brass. And he came to king Solomon, and wrought all his work.

2Ch 2:14 — The son of a woman of the daughters of Dan, and his father *was* a man of Tyre, skilful to work in gold, and in silver, in brass, in iron, in stone, and in timber, in purple, in blue, and in fine linen, and in crimson; also to grave any manner of graving, and to find out every device which shall be put to him, with thy cunning men, and with the cunning men of my lord David thy father.

• Of Solomon.

1Ki 3:16–28; 4:29–34

1Ki 3:12 — Behold, I have done according to thy words: lo, I have given thee a wise and an understanding heart; so that there was none like thee before thee, neither after thee shall any arise like unto thee.

1Ki 5:12 — And the LORD gave Solomon wisdom, as he promised him: and there was peace between Hiram and Solomon; and they two made a league together.

1Ki 10:24 — And all the earth sought to Solomon, to hear his wisdom, which God had put in his heart.

• Of Ethan, Heman, Chalcol, and Darda.

1Ki 4:31 — For he was wiser than all men; than Ethan the Ezrahite, and Heman, and Chalcol, and Darda, the sons of Mahol: and his fame was in all nations round about.

• Of the princess of Issachar.

1Ch 12:32 — And of the children of Issachar, *which were men* that had understanding of the times, to know what Israel ought to do; the heads of them *were* two hundred; and all their brethren *were* at their commandment.

• Of Ezra.

Ezr 7:25 — And thou, Ezra, after the wisdom of thy God, that *is* in thine hand, set magistrates and judges, which may judge all the people that *are* beyond the river, all such as know the laws of thy God; and teach ye them that know *them* not.

• Of Daniel.

Da 1:17 — As for these four children, God gave them knowledge and skill in all learning and wisdom: and Daniel had understanding in all visions and dreams.

Da 5:14 — I have even heard of thee, that the spirit of the gods *is* in thee, and *that* light and understanding and excellent wisdom is found in thee.

• Of Paul.

2Pe 3:15 — And account *that* the longsuffering of our Lord *is* salvation; even as our beloved brother Paul also according to the wisdom given unto him hath written unto you;

• Of the Magi.

Mt 2:1–12

• Spiritual.

• Unclassified scripture relating to.

Job 12:2–3, 7–13, 16–17; 28:12–28; Pr 1:20–2:20; 3:13–26, 34–35; 4:4–13, 18–22; 7:2–4; 8:1–9:6; 9:9–12; 10:13–14; 13:14–16; 14:6–8; 16:20–24; 22:17–21; 24:13–14; Ecc 9:13–18; Jer 9:23–24; Da 11:32–33; 12:3–4; Mt 6:22–23; 7:24–25; 25:1–13; Mk 12:32–34; Lk 11:34–36; Jn 17:7–8; 1Co 2:6–16; Eph 4:11–13; 5:15–17; Php 3:7–8; 1Th 5:4–5

Dt 32:29 — O that they were wise, *that* they understood this, *that* they would consider their latter end!

Job 5:27 — Lo this, we have searched it, so it *is;* hear it, and know thou *it* for thy good.

Job 8:8 — For enquire, I pray thee, of the former age, and prepare thyself to the search of their fathers:

Job 8:10 — Shall not they teach thee, *and* tell thee, and utter words out of their heart?

Job 12:22 — He discovereth deep things out of darkness, and bringeth out to light the shadow of death.

Job 32:9 — Great men are not *always* wise: neither do the aged understand judgment.

Job 42:5 — I have heard of thee by the hearing of the ear: but now mine eye seeth thee.

Ps 2:10 — Be wise now therefore, O ye kings: be instructed, ye judges of the earth.

Ps 9:10 — And they that know thy name will put their trust in thee: for thou, LORD, hast not forsaken them that seek thee.

Ps 76:1 — In Judah *is* God known: his name *is* great in Israel.

Ps 107:43 — Whoso *is* wise, and will observe these *things,* even they shall understand the lovingkindness of the LORD.

Ps 111:10 — The fear of the LORD *is* the beginning of wisdom: a good understanding have all they that do *his commandments:* his praise endureth for ever.

Pr 1:5 — A wise *man* will hear, and will increase learning; and a man of understanding shall attain unto wise counsels:

Pr 1:7 — The fear of the LORD *is* the beginning of knowledge: *but* fools despise wisdom and instruction.

Pr 5:12 — And say, How have I hated instruction, and my heart despised reproof;

Pr 10:8 — The wise in heart will receive commandments: but a prating fool shall fall.

Pr 10:21 — The lips of the righteous feed many: but fools die for want of wisdom.

Pr 10:23 — *It is* as sport to a fool to do mischief: but a man of understanding hath wisdom.

Pr 11:9 — An hypocrite with *his* mouth destroyeth his neighbour: but through knowledge shall the just be delivered.

Pr 11:12 — He that is void of wisdom despiseth his neighbour: but a man of understanding holdeth his peace.

Pr 12:1 — Whoso loveth instruction loveth knowledge: but he that hateth reproof *is* brutish.

Pr 12:8 — A man shall be commended according to his wisdom: but he that is of a perverse heart shall be despised.

Pr 12:15 — The way of a fool *is* right in his own eyes: but he that hearkeneth unto counsel *is* wise.

Pr 14:16 — A wise *man* feareth, and departeth from evil: but the fool rageth, and is confident.

Pr 14:18 — The simple inherit folly: but the prudent are crowned with knowledge.

Pr 14:33 — Wisdom resteth in the heart of him that hath understanding: but *that which is* in the midst of fools is made known.

Pr 15:2 — The tongue of the wise useth knowledge aright: but the mouth of fools poureth out foolishness.

Pr 15:7 — The lips of the wise disperse knowledge: but the heart of the foolish *doeth* not so.

Pr 15:14 — The heart of him that hath understanding seeketh knowledge: but the mouth of fools feedeth on foolishness.

Pr 15:33 — The fear of the LORD *is* the instruction of wisdom; and before honour *is* humility.

Pr 16:16 — How much better *is it* to get wisdom than gold! and to get understanding rather to be chosen than silver!

Pr 17:10 — A reproof entereth more into a wise man than an hundred stripes into a fool.

Pr 17:24 — Wisdom *is* before him that hath understanding; but the eyes of a fool *are* in the ends of the earth.

Pr 18:15 — The heart of the prudent getteth knowledge; and the ear of the wise seeketh knowledge.

Pr 19:8 — He that getteth wisdom loveth his own soul: *he that* keepeth understanding shall find good.

Pr 19:20 — Hear counsel, and receive instruction, that thou mayest be wise in thy latter end.

Pr 21:11 — When the scorner is punished, the simple is made wise: and when the wise is instructed, he receiveth knowledge.

Pr 23:12 — Apply thine heart unto instruction, and thine ears to the words of knowledge.

Pr 23:19 — Hear thou, my son, and be wise, and guide thine heart in the way.

Pr 23:23 — Buy the truth, and sell *it* not; *also* wisdom, and instruction, and understanding.

Pr 28:5 — Evil men understand not judgment: but they that seek the LORD understand all *things.*

Pr 28:7 — Whoso keepeth the law *is* a wise son: but he that is a companion of riotous *men* shameth his father.

Pr 29:3 — Whoso loveth wisdom rejoiceth his father: but he that keepeth company with harlots spendeth *his* substance.

Ecc 8:1 — Who *is* as the wise *man?* and who knoweth the interpretation of a thing? a man's wisdom maketh his face to shine, and the boldness of his face shall be changed.

Ecc 8:5 — Whoso keepeth the commandment shall feel no evil thing: and a wise man's heart discerneth both time and judgment.

Ecc 10:12 — The words of a wise man's mouth *are* gracious; but the lips of a fool will swallow up himself.

Ecc 12:11 — The words of the wise *are* as goads, and as nails fastened by the masters of assemblies, *which* are given from one shepherd.

Isa 2:3 — And many people shall go and say, Come ye, and let us go up to the mountain of the LORD, to the house of the God of Jacob; and he will teach us of his ways, and we will walk in his paths: for out of Zion shall go forth the law, and the word of the LORD from Jerusalem.

Isa 11:9 — They shall not hurt nor destroy in all my holy mountain: for the earth shall be full of the knowledge of the LORD, as the waters cover the sea.

Isa 29:24 — They also that erred in spirit shall come to understanding, and they that murmured shall learn doctrine.

Isa 33:6 — And wisdom and knowledge shall be the stability of thy times, *and* strength of salvation: the fear of the LORD *is* his treasure.

Jer 31:34 — And they shall teach no more every man his neighbour, and every man his brother, saying, Know the LORD: for they shall all know me, from the least of them unto the greatest of them, saith the LORD; for I will forgive their iniquity, and I will remember their sin no more.

Da 12:10 — Many shall be purified, and made white, and tried; but the wicked shall do wickedly: and none of the wicked shall understand; but the wise shall understand.

Hos 6:3 — Then shall we know, *if* we follow on to know the LORD: his going forth is prepared as the morning; and he shall come unto us as the rain, as the latter *and* former rain unto the earth.

Hos 6:6 — For I desired mercy, and not sacrifice; and the knowledge of God more than burnt offerings.

Hos 14:9 — Who *is* wise, and he shall understand these *things?* prudent, and he shall know them? for the ways of the LORD *are* right, and the just shall walk in them: but the transgressors shall fall therein.

Mt 11:19 — The Son of man came eating and drinking, and they say, Behold a man gluttonous, and a winebibber, a friend of publicans and sinners. But wisdom is justified of her children.

Lk 1:17 — And he shall go before him in the spirit and power of Elias, to turn the hearts of the fathers to the children, and the disobedient to the wisdom of the just; to make ready a people prepared for the Lord.

Lk 7:35 — But wisdom is justified of all her children.

Jn 7:17 — If any man will do his will, he shall know of the doctrine, *whether* it be of God, or whether I speak of myself.

Jn 8:32 — And ye shall know the truth, and the truth shall make you free.

Jn 10:4 — And when he putteth forth his own sheep, he goeth before them, and the sheep follow him: for they know his voice.

Jn 10:14 — I am the good shepherd, and know my *sheep*, and am known of mine.

Jn 17:3 — And this is life eternal, that they might know thee the only true God, and Jesus Christ, whom thou hast sent.

Jn 17:25 — O righteous Father, the world hath not known thee: but I have known thee, and these have known that thou hast sent me.

Ac 6:10 — And they were not able to resist the wisdom and the spirit by which he spake.

Ro 15:14 — And I myself also am persuaded of you, my brethren, that ye also are full of goodness, filled with all knowledge, able also to admonish one another.

Ro 16:19 — For your obedience is come abroad unto all *men*. I am glad therefore on your behalf: but yet I would have you wise unto that which is good, and simple concerning evil.

1Co 3:18 — Let no man deceive himself. If any man among you seemeth to be wise in this world, let him become a fool, that he may be wise.

1Co 8:3 — But if any man love God, the same is known of him.

1Co 13:11 — When I was a child, I spake as a child, I understood as a child, I thought as a child: but when I became a man, I put away childish things.

1Co 14:20 — Brethren, be not children in understanding: howbeit in malice be ye children, but in understanding be men.

2Co 2:11 — Lest Satan should get an advantage of us: for we are not ignorant of his devices.

2Co 8:7 — Therefore, as ye abound in every *thing, in* faith, and utterance, and knowledge, and *in* all diligence, and *in* your love to us, *see* that ye abound in this grace also.

Gal 4:9 — But now, after that ye have known God, or rather are known of God, how turn ye again to the weak and beggarly elements, whereunto ye desire again to be in bondage?

Php 3:10 — That I may know him, and the power of his resurrection, and the fellowship of his sufferings, being made conformable unto his death;

Col 3:10 — And have put on the new *man*, which is renewed in knowledge after the image of him that created him:

Col 3:16 — Let the word of Christ dwell in you richly in all wisdom; teaching and admonishing one another in psalms and hymns and spiritual songs, singing with grace in your hearts to the Lord.

1Ti 2:4 — Who will have all men to be saved, and to come unto the knowledge of the truth.

2Ti 3:15 — And that from a child thou hast known the holy scriptures, which are able to make thee wise unto salvation through faith which is in Christ Jesus.

Jas 3:13 — Who *is* a wise man and endued with knowledge among you? let him shew out of a good conversation his works with meekness of wisdom.

1Jn 4:6 — We are of God: he that knoweth God heareth us; he that is not of God heareth not us. Hereby know we the spirit of truth, and the spirit of error.

See: Knowledge

See: Speaking; wisdom in

• Spiritual, from God.

Ex 4:11–12; 8:9–10; Dt 4:5–6, 35–36; Job 11:5–6; 22:21–22; 32:7–8; 35:10–11; 38:36–37; Ps 19:1–2; 25:8–9; Pr 2:6–7; 3:5–6; Isa 11:1–3; 42:6–7; Da 2:20–23; Mt 11:25–27; 16:16–17; Lk 1:76–79; 12:11–12; Jn 1:4–5, 7–9; 8:31–32; 16:13–14; Ro 1:19–20; 1Co 2:9–14; Col 1:26–28; 2Pe 1:2–5

Dt 29:4 — Yet the LORD hath not given you an heart to perceive, and eyes to see, and ears to hear, unto this day.

1Ch 22:12 — Only the LORD give thee wisdom and understanding, and give thee charge concerning Israel, that thou mayest keep the law of the LORD thy God.

Ne 9:20 — Thou gavest also thy good spirit to instruct them, and withheldest not thy manna from their mouth, and gavest them water for their thirst.

Job 4:3 — Behold, thou hast instructed many, and thou hast strengthened the weak hands.

Job 33:16 — Then he openeth the ears of men, and sealeth their instruction,

Job 36:22 — Behold, God exalteth by his power: who teacheth like him?

Ps 16:7 — I will bless the LORD, who hath given me counsel: my reins also instruct me in the night seasons.

Ps 25:12 — What man *is* he that feareth the LORD? him shall he teach in the way *that* he shall choose.

Ps 25:14 — The secret of the LORD *is* with them that fear him; and he will shew them his covenant.

Ps 32:8 — I will instruct thee and teach thee in the way which thou shalt go: I will guide thee with mine eye.

Ps 36:9 — For with thee *is* the fountain of life: in thy light shall we see light.

Ps 51:6 — Behold, thou desirest truth in the inward parts: and in the hidden *part* thou shalt make me to know wisdom.

Ps 71:17 — O God, thou hast taught me from my youth: and hitherto have I declared thy wondrous works.

Ps 94:12 — Blessed *is* the man whom thou chastenest, O LORD, and teachest him out of thy law;

Ps 112:4 — Unto the upright there ariseth light in the darkness: *he is* gracious, and full of compassion, and righteous.

Ps 119:130 — The entrance of thy words giveth light; it giveth understanding unto the simple.

Pr 1:23 — Turn you at my reproof: behold, I will pour out my spirit unto you, I will make known my words unto you.

Ecc 2:26 — For *God* giveth to a man that *is* good in his sight wisdom, and knowledge, and joy: but to the sinner he giveth travail, to gather and to heap up, that he may give to *him that is* good before God. This also *is* vanity and vexation of spirit.

Isa 30:21 — And thine ears shall hear a word behind thee, saying, This *is* the way, walk ye in it, when ye turn to the right hand, and when ye turn to the left.

Isa 42:16 — And I will bring the blind by a way *that* they knew not; I will lead them in paths *that* they have not known: I will make darkness light before them, and crooked things straight. These things will I do unto them, and not forsake them.

Isa 48:17 — Thus saith the LORD, thy Redeemer, the Holy One of Israel; I *am* the LORD thy God which teacheth thee to profit, which leadeth thee by the way *that* thou shouldest go.

Isa 54:13 — And all thy children *shall be* taught of the LORD; and great *shall be* the peace of thy children.

Jer 24:7 — And I will give them an heart to know me, that I *am* the LORD: and they shall be my people, and I will be their God: for they shall return unto me with their whole heart.

Da 1:17 — As for these four children, God gave them knowledge and skill in all learning and wisdom: and Daniel had understanding in all visions and dreams.

Mt 13:11 — He answered and said unto them, Because it is given unto you to know the mysteries of the kingdom of heaven, but to them it is not given.

Lk 21:15 — For I will give you a mouth and wisdom, which all your adversaries shall not be able to gainsay nor resist.

Lk 24:32 — And they said one to another, Did not our heart burn within us, while he talked with us by the way, and while he opened to us the scriptures?

Lk 24:45 — Then opened he their understanding, that they might understand the scriptures,

Jn 1:1 — In the beginning was the Word, and the Word was with God, and the Word was God.

Jn 1:17 — For the law was given by Moses, *but* grace and truth came by Jesus Christ.

Jn 6:45 — It is written in the prophets, And they shall be all taught of God. Every man therefore that hath heard, and hath learned of the Father, cometh unto me.

Jn 8:12 — Then spake Jesus again unto them, saying, I am the light of the world: he that followeth me shall not walk in darkness, but shall have the light of life.

Jn 9:5 — As long as I am in the world, I am the light of the world.

Jn 9:39 — And Jesus said, For judgment I am come into this world, that they which see not might see; and that they which see might be made blind.

Jn 12:46 — I am come a light into the world, that whosoever believeth on me should not abide in darkness.

Jn 14:7 — If ye had known me, ye should have known my Father also: and from henceforth ye know him, and have seen him.

Jn 17:6 — I have manifested thy name unto the men which thou gavest me out of the world: thine they were, and thou gavest them me; and they have kept thy word.

Jn 17:26 — And I have declared unto them thy name, and will declare *it:* that the love wherewith thou hast loved me may be in them, and I in them.

Jn 18:37 — Pilate therefore said unto him, Art thou a king then? Jesus answered, Thou sayest that I am a king. To this end was I born, and for this cause came I into the world, that I should bear witness unto the truth. Every one that is of the truth heareth my voice.

1Co 1:30 — But of him are ye in Christ Jesus, who of God is made unto us wisdom, and righteousness, and sanctification, and redemption:

1Co 12:8 — For to one is given by the Spirit the word of wisdom; to another the word of knowledge by the same Spirit;

2Co 4:6 — For God, who commanded the light to shine out of darkness, hath shined in our hearts, to *give* the light of the knowledge of the glory of God in the face of Jesus Christ.

Php 3:15 — Let us therefore, as many as be perfect, be thus minded: and if in any thing ye be otherwise minded, God shall reveal even this unto you.

2Ti 1:7 — For God hath not given us the spirit of fear; but of power, and of love, and of a sound mind.

Jas 3:17 — But the wisdom that is from above is first pure, then peaceable, gentle, *and* easy to be intreated, full of mercy and good fruits, without partiality, and without hypocrisy.

2Pe 1:8 — For if these things be in you, and abound, they make *you that ye shall* neither *be* barren nor unfruitful in the knowledge of our Lord Jesus Christ.

2Pe 1:12 — Wherefore I will not be negligent to put you always in remembrance of these things, though ye know *them,* and be established in the present truth.

2Pe 3:18 — But grow in grace, and *in* the knowledge of our Lord and Saviour Jesus Christ. To him *be* glory both now and for ever. Amen.

1Jn 2:20 — But ye have an unction from the Holy One, and ye know all things.

1Jn 2:27 — But the anointing which ye have received of him abideth in you, and ye need not that any man teach you: but as the same anointing teacheth you of all things, and is truth, and is no lie, and even as it hath taught you, ye shall abide in him.

1Jn 5:20 — *And* we know that the Son of God is come, and hath given us an understanding, that we may know him that is true, and we are in him that is true, *even* in his Son Jesus Christ. This is the true God, and eternal life.

See: God, Wisdom of

• Prayer for spiritual.

Ps 25:4–5; 119:18–19, 26–27, 33–34, 124–125; Eph 1:16–19; 3:14–19; 6:18–20; Php 1:9–10; Col 1:9–10; 2:1–3; 4:2–4

Nu 27:21 — And he shall stand before Eleazar the priest, who shall ask *counsel* for him after the judgment of Urim before the LORD: at his word shall they go out, and at his word they shall come in, *both* he, and all the children of Israel with him, even all the congregation.

Jgs 20:18 — And the children of Israel arose, and went up to the house of God, and asked counsel of God, and said, Which of us shall go up first to the battle against the children of Benjamin? And the LORD said, Judah *shall go up* first.

1Ki 3:7 — And now, O LORD my God, thou hast made thy servant king instead of David my father: and I *am but* a little child: I know not *how* to go out or come in.

1Ki 3:9 — Give therefore thy servant an understanding heart to judge thy people, that I may discern between good and bad: for who is able to judge this thy so great a people?

1Ki 8:36 — Then hear thou in heaven, and forgive the sin of thy servants, and of thy people Israel, that thou teach them the good way wherein they should walk, and give rain upon thy land, which thou hast given to thy people for an inheritance.

2Ch 1:10 — Give me now wisdom and knowledge, that I may go out and come in before this people: for who can judge this thy people, *that is so* great?

Job 34:32 — *That which* I see not teach thou me: if I have done iniquity, I will do no more.

Ps 5:8 — Lead me, O LORD, in thy righteousness because of mine enemies; make thy way straight before my face.

Ps 27:11 — Teach me thy way, O LORD, and lead me in a plain path, because of mine enemies.

Ps 31:3 — For thou *art* my rock and my fortress; therefore for thy name's sake lead me, and guide me.

Ps 39:4 — LORD, make me to know mine end, and the measure of my days, what it *is; that* I may know how frail I *am.*

Ps 43:3 — O send out thy light and thy truth: let them lead me; let them bring me unto thy holy hill, and to thy tabernacles.

Ps 86:11 — Teach me thy way, O LORD; I will walk in thy truth: unite my heart to fear thy name.

Ps 90:12 — So teach *us* to number our days, that we may apply *our* hearts unto wisdom.

Ps 119:12 — Blessed *art* thou, O LORD: teach me thy statutes.

Ps 119:66 — Teach me good judgment and knowledge: for I have believed thy commandments.

Ps 119:68 — Thou *art* good, and doest good; teach me thy statutes.

Ps 119:73 — Thy hands have made me and fashioned me: give me understanding, that I may learn thy commandments.

Ps 119:80 — Let my heart be sound in thy statutes; that I be not ashamed.

Ps 119:135 — Make thy face to shine upon thy servant; and teach me thy statutes.

Ps 119:144 — The righteousness of thy testimonies *is* everlasting: give me understanding, and I shall live.

Ps 119:169 — Let my cry come near before thee, O LORD: give me understanding according to thy word.

Ps 119:171 — My lips shall utter praise, when thou hast taught me thy statutes.

Ps 139:24 — And see if *there be any* wicked way in me, and lead me in the way everlasting.

2Ti 2:7 — Consider what I say; and the Lord give thee understanding in all things.

Jas 1:5 — If any of you lack wisdom, let him ask of God, that giveth to all *men* liberally, and upbraideth not; and it shall be given him.

See: Desire; spiritual

• Worldly.

Ge 3:6–7; Job 4:18–21; Pr 15:21–22; 24:3–7; Ecc 1:18–2:26; 7:11–13, 16–25; 8:16–17; 10:2–3; Isa 28:24–29; 29:14–16; 47:10–11; Jer 8:7–9; 9:23–24; Mt 7:24–27; Ro 1:21–23; 1Co 1:17–26; 2:1–14; 3:18–20; 8:1–2; 1Ti 6:20–21

Job 5:13 — He taketh the wise in their own craftiness: and the counsel of the froward is carried headlong.

Job 11:2 — Should not the multitude of words be answered? and should a man full of talk be justified?

Job 11:12 — For vain man would be wise, though man be born *like* a wild ass's colt.

Job 37:24 — Men do therefore fear him: he respecteth not any *that are* wise of heart.

Pr 3:7 — Be not wise in thine own eyes: fear the LORD, and depart from evil.

Pr 16:25 — There is a way that seemeth right unto a man, but the end thereof *are* the ways of death.

Pr 17:2 — A wise servant shall have rule over a son that causeth shame, and shall have part of the inheritance among the brethren.

Pr 17:10 — A reproof entereth more into a wise man than an hundred stripes into a fool.

Pr 18:1 — Through desire a man, having separated himself, seeketh *and* intermeddleth with all wisdom.

Pr 20:18 — *Every* purpose is established by counsel: and with good advice make war.

Pr 21:20 — *There is* treasure to be desired and oil in the dwelling of the wise; but a foolish man spendeth it up.

Pr 21:22 — A wise *man* scaleth the city of the mighty, and casteth down the strength of the confidence thereof.

Pr 21:30 — *There is* no wisdom nor understanding nor counsel against the LORD.

Pr 28:11 — The rich man *is* wise in his own conceit; but the poor that hath understanding searcheth him out.

Ecc 8:1 — Who *is* as the wise *man?* and who knoweth the interpretation of a thing? a man's wisdom maketh his face to shine, and the boldness of his face shall be changed.

Ecc 10:10 — If the iron be blunt, and he do not whet the edge, then must he put to more strength: but wisdom *is* profitable to direct.

Isa 5:21 — Woe unto *them that are* wise in their own eyes, and prudent in their own sight!

Jer 49:7 — Concerning Edom, thus saith the LORD of hosts; *Is* wisdom no more in Teman? is counsel perished from the prudent? is their wisdom vanished?

Mt 6:23 — But if thine eye be evil, thy whole body shall be full of darkness. If therefore the light that is in thee be darkness, how great *is* that darkness!

Mt 11:25 — At that time Jesus answered and said, I thank thee, O Father, Lord of heaven and earth, because thou hast hid these things from the wise and prudent, and hast revealed them unto babes.

Lk 10:21 — In that hour Jesus rejoiced in spirit, and said, I thank thee, O Father, Lord of heaven and earth, that thou hast hid these things from the wise and prudent, and hast revealed them unto babes: even so, Father; for so it seemed good in thy sight.

Lk 16:8 — And the lord commended the unjust steward, because he had done wisely: for the children of this world are in their generation wiser than the children of light.

2Co 1:12 — For our rejoicing is this, the testimony of our conscience, that in simplicity and godly sincerity, not with fleshly wisdom, but by the grace of God, we have had our conversation in the world, and more abundantly to you-ward.

Col 2:8 — Beware lest any man spoil you through philosophy and vain deceit, after the tradition of men, after the rudiments of the world, and not after Christ.

See: Knowledge

WISE MEN

• Of Egypt.

Ge 41:8 — And it came to pass in the morning that his spirit was troubled; and he sent and called for all the magicians of Egypt, and all the wise men thereof: and Pharaoh told them his dream; but *there was* none that could interpret them unto Pharaoh.

Ge 41:24 — And the thin ears devoured the seven good ears: and I told *this* unto the magicians; but *there was* none that could declare *it* to me.

Ex 7:11 — Then Pharaoh also called the wise men and the sorcerers: now the magicians of Egypt, they also did in like manner with their enchantments.

• Solomon.

1Ki 4:29–34

• Of Babylon.

Da 4:18 — This dream I king Nebuchadnezzar have seen. Now thou, O Belteshazzar, declare the interpretation thereof, forasmuch as all the wise *men* of my kingdom are not able to make known unto me the interpretation: but thou *art* able; for the spirit of the holy gods *is* in thee.

Da 5:8 — Then came in all the king's wise *men:* but they could not read the writing, nor make known to the king the interpretation thereof.

• Of the East.

Mt 2:1–12

See: Wisdom

WITCHCRAFT

• Law concerning.

Ex 2:18 — And when they came to Reuel their father, he said, How *is it that* ye are come so soon to day?

Le 19:31 — Regard not them that have familiar spirits, neither seek after wizards, to be defiled by them: I *am* the LORD your God.

Le 20:6 — And the soul that turneth after such as have familiar spirits, and after wizards, to go a whoring after them, I will even set my face against that soul, and will cut him off from among his people.

Le 20:27 — A man also or woman that hath a familiar spirit, or that is a wizard, shall surely be put to death: they shall stone them with stones: their blood *shall be* upon them.

• Witch of Endor.

1Sa 28:7–25

• Witches destroyed.

1Sa 28:3 — Now Samuel was dead, and all Israel had lamented him, and buried him in Ramah, even in his own city. And Saul had put away those that had familiar spirits, and the wizards, out of the land.

1Sa 28:9 — And the woman said unto him, Behold, thou knowest what Saul hath done, how he hath cut off those that have familiar spirits, and the wizards, out of the land: wherefore then layest thou a snare for my life, to cause me to die?

See: Sorcery

WITNESS

Le 5:1 — And if a soul sin, and hear the voice of swearing, and *is* a witness, whether he hath seen or known *of it;* if he do not utter *it,* then he shall bear his iniquity.

Pr 18:17 — *He that is* first in his own cause *seemeth* just; but his neighbour cometh and searcheth him.

- **Qualified by oath.**

1Ki 8:31–32

Ex 22:11 — *Then* shall an oath of the LORD be between them both, that he hath not put his hand unto his neighbour's goods; and the owner of it shall accept *thereof,* and he shall not make *it* good.

Nu 5:19 — And the priest shall charge her by an oath, and say unto the woman, If no man have lain with thee, and if thou hast not gone aside to uncleanness *with another* instead of thy husband, be thou free from this bitter water that causeth the curse:

Nu 5:21 — Then the priest shall charge the woman with an oath of cursing, and the priest shall say unto the woman, The LORD make thee a curse and an oath among thy people, when the LORD doth make thy thigh to rot, and thy belly to swell;

- **Qualified by laying hands on the accused.**

Le 24:14 — Bring forth him that hath cursed without the camp; and let all that heard *him* lay their hands upon his head, and let all the congregation stone him.

- **Two necessary to establish a fact.**

Nu 35:30 — Whoso killeth any person, the murderer shall be put to death by the mouth of witnesses: but one witness shall not testify against any person *to cause him* to die.

Dt 17:6 — At the mouth of two witnesses, or three witnesses, shall he that is worthy of death be put to death; *but* at the mouth of one witness he shall not be put to death.

Dt 19:15 — One witness shall not rise up against a man for any iniquity, or for any sin, in any sin that he sinneth: at the mouth of two witnesses, or at the mouth of three witnesses, shall the matter be established.

Mt 18:16 — But if he will not hear *thee, then* take with thee one or two more, that in the mouth of two or three witnesses every word may be established.

Jn 8:17 — It is also written in your law, that the testimony of two men is true.

2Co 13:1 — This *is* the third *time* I am coming to you. In the mouth of two or three witnesses shall every word be established.

1Ti 5:19 — Against an elder receive not an accusation, but before two or three witnesses.

Heb 10:28 — He that despised Moses' law died without mercy under two or three witnesses:

- **Required to cast the first stone in executing sentence.**

Dt 17:5–7

Dt 13:9 — But thou shalt surely kill him; thine hand shall be first upon him to put him to death, and afterwards the hand of all the people.

Ac 7:58 — And cast *him* out of the city, and stoned *him:* and the witnesses laid down their clothes at a young man's feet, whose name was Saul.

- **To the transfer of land.**

Ge 21:25–30; 23:16–18; Ru 4:1–9; Jer 32:9–12

Ge 23:11 — Nay, my lord, hear me: the field give I thee, and the cave that *is* therein, I give it thee; in the presence of the sons of my people give I it thee: bury thy dead.

Jer 32:25 — And thou hast said unto me, O Lord GOD, Buy thee the field for money, and take witnesses; for the city is given into the hand of the Chaldeans.

Jer 32:44 — Men shall buy fields for money, and subscribe evidences, and seal *them,* and take witnesses in the land of Benjamin, and in the places about Jerusalem, and in the cities of Judah, and in the cities of the mountains, and in the cities of the valley, and in the cities of the south: for I will cause their captivity to return, saith the LORD.

- **To marriage.**

Ru 4:10–11; Isa 8:2–3

- **Incorruptible.**

Ps 15:4 — In whose eyes a vile person is contemned; but he honoureth them that fear the LORD. *He that* sweareth to *his own* hurt, and changeth not.

- **Corrupted by money.**

Mt 28:11–15

Ac 6:11 — Then they suborned men, which said, We have heard him speak blasphemous words against Moses, and *against* God.

Ac 6:13 — And set up false witnesses, which said, This man ceaseth not to speak blasphemous words against this holy place, and the law:

- **Figurative.**
  - **Of instruction in righteousness.**

Rev 11:3 — And I will give *power* unto my two witnesses, and they shall prophesy a thousand two hundred *and* threescore days, clothed in sackcloth.

See: Court

See: Evidence

See: Falsehood

See: Falsehood, False Witness

See: Holy Spirit

See: Testimony

See: Testimony; religious

WIZARD **See: Sorcery**

WOLF

• **Ravenous.**

Ge 49:27 — Benjamin shall ravin *as* a wolf: in the morning he shall devour the prey, and at night he shall divide the spoil.

Jer 5:6 — Wherefore a lion out of the forest shall slay them, *and* a wolf of the evenings shall spoil them, a leopard shall watch over their cities: every one that goeth out thence shall be torn in pieces: because their transgressions are many, *and* their backslidings are increased.

Eze 22:27 — Her princes in the midst thereof *are* like wolves ravening the prey, to shed blood, *and* to destroy souls, to get dishonest gain.

Zep 3:3 — Her princes within her *are* roaring lions; her judges *are* evening wolves; they gnaw not the bones till the morrow.

Jn 10:12 — But he that is an hireling, and not the shepherd, whose own the sheep are not, seeth the wolf coming, and leaveth the sheep, and fleeth: and the wolf catcheth them, and scattereth the sheep.

• **Figurative.**

• **Of the enemies of the righteous.**

Mt 7:15 — Beware of false prophets, which come to you in sheep's clothing, but inwardly they are ravening wolves.

Mt 10:16 — Behold, I send you forth as sheep in the midst of wolves: be ye therefore wise as serpents, and harmless as doves.

Jn 10:12 — But he that is an hireling, and not the shepherd, whose own the sheep are not, seeth the wolf coming, and leaveth the sheep, and fleeth: and the wolf catcheth them, and scattereth the sheep.

Ac 20:29 — For I know this, that after my departing shall grievous wolves enter in among you, not sparing the flock.

• **Of the reconciling power of the gospel.**

Isa 11:6 — The wolf also shall dwell with the lamb, and the leopard shall lie down with the kid; and the calf and the young lion and the fatling together; and a little child shall lead them.

WOMEN

• **Creation of.**

Ge 2:21–22

Ge 1:27 — So God created man in his *own* image, in the image of God created he him; male and female created he them.

• **Named.**

Ge 2:23 — And Adam said, This *is* now bone of my bones, and flesh of my flesh: she shall be called Woman, because she was taken out of Man.

• **Fall of, and curse upon.**

Ge 3:1–16

2Co 11:3 — But I fear, lest by any means, as the serpent beguiled Eve through his subtilty, so your minds should be corrupted from the simplicity that is in Christ.

1Ti 2:14 — And Adam was not deceived, but the woman being deceived was in the transgression.

• **Promise to.**

Ge 3:15 — And I will put enmity between thee and the woman, and between thy seed and her seed; it shall bruise thy head, and thou shalt bruise his heel.

• **Had separate apartments in dwellings.**

Ge 24:67 — And Isaac brought her into his mother Sarah's tent, and took Rebekah, and she became his wife; and he loved her: and Isaac was comforted after his mother's *death*.

Ge 31:33 — And Laban went into Jacob's tent, and into Leah's tent, and into the two maidservants' tents; but he found *them* not. Then went he out of Leah's tent, and entered into Rachel's tent.

Est 2:9 — And the maiden pleased him, and she obtained kindness of him; and he speedily gave her her things for purification, with such things as belonged to her, and seven maidens, *which were* meet to be given her, out of the king's house: and he preferred her and her maids unto the best *place* of the house of the women.

Est 2:11 — And Mordecai walked every day before the court of the women's house, to know how Esther did, and what should become of her.

• **Veiled the face.**

Ge 24:65 — For she *had* said unto the servant, What man *is* this that walketh in the field to meet us? And the servant *had* said, It *is* my master: therefore she took a vail, and covered herself.

See: Vail

• **Vows of.**

Nu 30:3–16

• **When jealously charged with infidelity, guilt or innocence to be determined by trial.**

Nu 5:12–31

• **Took part in ancient worship.**

Ex 15:20–21

Ex 38:8 — And he made the laver *of* brass, and the foot of it *of* brass, of the lookingglasses of *the women* assembling, which assembled *at* the door of the tabernacle of the congregation.

1Sa 2:22 — Now Eli was very old, and heard all that his sons did unto all Israel; and how they lay with the women that assembled *at* the door of the tabernacle of the congregation.

• **Took part in choir.**

1Ch 25:5–6

Ezr 2:65 — Beside their servants and their maids, of whom *there were* seven thousand three hundred thirty and seven: and *there were* among them two hundred singing men and singing women.

Ne 7:67 — Beside their manservants and their maidservants, of whom *there were* seven thousand three hundred thirty and seven: and they had two hundred forty and five singing men and singing women.

• **Worshiped in separate compartments.**

Ex 38:8 — And he made the laver *of* brass, and the foot of it *of* brass, of the lookingglasses of *the women* assembling, which assembled *at* the door of the tabernacle of the congregation.

1Sa 2:2 — *There is* none holy as the LORD: for *there is* none beside thee: neither *is there* any rock like our God.

• **Consecrated jewels to tabernacle.**

Ex 35:22 — And they came, both men and women, as many as were willing hearted, *and* brought bracelets, and earrings, and rings, and tablets, all jewels of gold: and every man that offered *offered* an offering of gold unto the LORD.

• **Consecrated mirrors to tabernacle.**

Ex 38:8 — And he made the laver *of* brass, and the foot of it *of* brass, of the lookingglasses of *the women* assembling, which assembled *at* the door of the tabernacle of the congregation.

• **Required to attend reading of the law.**

Dt 31:12 — Gather the people together, men, and women, and children, and thy stranger that *is* within thy gates, that they may hear, and that they may learn, and fear the LORD your God, and observe to do all the words of this law:

Jos 8:35 — There was not a word of all that Moses commanded, which Joshua read not before all the congregation of Israel, with the women, and the little ones, and the strangers that were conversant among them.

• **Purifications of.**

• **After menstruation.**

Le 19:19–33

2Sa 11:4 — And David sent messengers, and took her; and she came in unto him, and he lay with her; for she was purified from her uncleanness: and she returned unto her house.

• **After childbirth.**

Le 12:1–8

Lk 2:22 — And when the days of her purification according to the law of Moses were accomplished, they brought him to Jerusalem, to present *him* to the Lord;

• **Difference in ceremonies made between male and female children.**

Le 12:1–8

• **Religious privileges of, among early Christians.**

Ac 12:12–13

Ac 1:14 — These all continued with one accord in prayer and supplication, with the women, and Mary the mother of Jesus, and with his brethren.

1Co 11:5 — But every woman that prayeth or prophesieth with *her* head uncovered dishonoureth her head: for that is even all one as if she were shaven.

1Co 14:34 — Let your women keep silence in the churches: for it is not permitted unto them to speak; but *they are commanded* to be under obedience, as also saith the law.

1Ti 2:11 — Let the woman learn in silence with all subjection.

• **Domestic duties of.**

Pr 31:15–19

Ge 18:6 — And Abraham hastened into the tent unto Sarah, and said, Make ready quickly three measures of fine meal, knead *it,* and make cakes upon the hearth.

Mt 24:41 — Two *women shall be* grinding at the mill; the one shall be taken, and the other left.

• **Cooked.**

Ge 18:6 — And Abraham hastened into the tent unto Sarah, and said, Make ready quickly three measures of fine meal, knead *it,* and make cakes upon the hearth.

• **Spun.**

Ex 35:25–26; Pr 31:19–24

1Sa 2:19 — Moreover his mother made him a little coat, and brought *it* to him from year to year, when she came up with her husband to offer the yearly sacrifice.

• **Embroidered.**

Pr 31:22 — She maketh herself coverings of tapestry; her clothing *is* silk and purple.

• **Made garments.**

Ac 9:39 — Then Peter arose and went with them. When he was come, they brought him into the upper chamber: and all the widows stood by him weeping, and shewing the coats and garments which Dorcas made, while she was with them.

• **Gleaned.**

Ru 2:8 — Then said Boaz unto Ruth, Hearest thou not, my daughter? Go not to glean in another field, neither go from hence, but abide here fast by my maidens:

• **Kept vineyards.**

SS 1:6 — Look not upon me, because I *am* black, because the sun hath looked upon me: my mother's children were angry with me; they made me the keeper of the vineyards; *but* mine own vineyard have I not kept.

• **Tended flocks and herds.**

Ge 24:13–14, 19–20

Ge 24:11 — And he made his camels to kneel down without the city by a well of water at the time of the evening, *even* the time that women go out to draw *water.*

Ge 29:9 — And while he yet spake with them, Rachel came with her father's sheep: for she kept them.

Ex 2:16 — Now the priest of Midian had seven daughters: and they came and drew *water,* and filled the troughs to water their father's flock.

• **Worked in fields.**

Isa 27:11 — When the boughs thereof are withered, they shall be broken off: the women come, *and* set them on fire: for it *is* a people of no understanding: therefore he that made them will not have mercy on them, and he that formed them will shew them no favour.

Eze 26:6 — And her daughters which *are* in the field shall be slain by the sword; and they shall know that I *am* the LORD.

Eze 26:8 — He shall slay with the sword thy daughters in the field: and he shall make a fort against thee, and cast a mount against thee, and lift up the buckler against thee.

- **Was doorkeeper.**

Jn 18:16–17; Ac 12:13–14

Mt 26:69 — Now Peter sat without in the palace: and a damsel came unto him, saying, Thou also wast with Jesus of Galilee.

- **Forbidden to wear men's costume.**

Dt 22:5 — The woman shall not wear that which pertaineth unto a man, neither shall a man put on a woman's garment: for all that do so *are* abomination unto the LORD thy God.

- **Wore hair long.**

1Co 11:5–15

- **Rules for dress of Christian.**

1Ti 2:9–10; 1Pe 3:3–4

- **Ornaments of.**

Isa 3:16–23

- **Weaker than men.**

1Pe 3:7 — Likewise, ye husbands, dwell with *them* according to knowledge, giving honour unto the wife, as unto the weaker vessel, and as being heirs together of the grace of life; that your prayers be not hindered.

- **Are timid.**

Isa 19:16 — In that day shall Egypt be like unto women: and it shall be afraid and fear because of the shaking of the hand of the LORD of hosts, which he shaketh over it.

Jer 50:37 — A sword *is* upon their horses, and upon their chariots, and upon all the mingled people that *are* in the midst of her; and they shall become as women: a sword *is* upon her treasures; and they shall be robbed.

Jer 51:30 — The mighty men of Babylon have forborn to fight, they have remained in *their* holds: their might hath failed; they became as women: they have burned her dwellingplaces; her bars are broken.

Na 3:13 — Behold, thy people in the midst of thee *are* women: the gates of thy land shall be set wide open unto thine enemies: the fire shall devour thy bars.

- **Are affectionate.**

2Sa 1:26 — I am distressed for thee, my brother Jonathan: very pleasant hast thou been unto me: thy love to me was wonderful, passing the love of women.

- **Are tender to her offspring.**

Isa 49:15 — Can a woman forget her sucking child, that she should not have compassion on the son of her womb? yea, they may forget, yet will I not forget thee.

La 4:10 — The hands of the pitiful women have sodden their own children: they were their meat in the destruction of the daughter of my people.

- **Are mirthsome.**

Jgs 11:34 — And Jephthah came to Mizpeh unto his house, and, behold, his daughter came out to meet him with timbrels and with dances: and she *was his* only child; beside her he had neither son nor daughter.

Jgs 21:21 — And see, and, behold, if the daughters of Shiloh come out to dance in dances, then come ye out of the vineyards, and catch you every man his wife of the daughters of Shiloh, and go to the land of Benjamin.

Jer 31:13 — Then shall the virgin rejoice in the dance, both young men and old together: for I will turn their mourning into joy, and will comfort them, and make them rejoice from their sorrow.

Zec 9:17 — For how great *is* his goodness, and how great *is* his beauty! corn shall make the young men cheerful, and new wine the maids.

- **Are courteous to strangers.**

Ge 24:17 — And the servant ran to meet her, and said, Let me, I pray thee, drink a little water of thy pitcher.

- **Could not marry without consent of parents.**

Ge 24:3–4

Ge 34:6 — And Hamor the father of Shechem went out unto Jacob to commune with him.

Ex 22:17 — If her father utterly refuse to give her unto him, he shall pay money according to the dowry of virgins.

- **Not to be given in marriage considered a calamity.**

Jgs 11:37 — And she said unto her father, Let this thing be done for me: let me alone two months, that I may go up and down upon the mountains, and bewail my virginity, I and my fellows.

Ps 78:63 — The fire consumed their young men; and their maidens were not given to marriage.

Isa 4:1 — And in that day seven women shall take hold of one man, saying, We will eat our own bread, and wear our own apparel: only let us be called by thy name, to take away our reproach.

- **Taken captive.**

Nu 31:17–18; Eze 30:17–18

Nu 31:9 — And the children of Israel took *all* the women of Midian captives, and their little ones, and took the spoil of all their cattle, and all their flocks, and all their goods.

Nu 31:15 — And Moses said unto them, Have ye saved all the women alive?

Nu 31:35 — And thirty and two thousand persons in all, of women that had not known man by lying with him.

La 1:18 — The LORD is righteous; for I have rebelled against his commandment: hear, I pray you, all people, and behold my sorrow: my virgins and my young men are gone into captivity.

- **Shrewd.**

2Sa 20:16–22

- **Punishment to be inflicted on men for seducing, when betrothed.**

Dt 22:23–27

- **Punishment for seducing, when not betrothed.**

Ex 22:16–17; Dt 22:28–29

• Treated with cruelty in war.

Dt 32:25 — The sword without, and terror within, shall destroy both the young man and the virgin, the suckling *also* with the man of gray hairs.

La 2:21 — The young and the old lie on the ground in the streets: my virgins and my young men are fallen by the sword; thou hast slain *them* in the day of thine anger; thou hast killed, *and* not pitied.

La 5:11 — They ravished the women in Zion, *and* the maids in the cities of Judah.

• Virtuous, held in high estimation.

Pr 31:10–30

Ru 3:11 — And now, my daughter, fear not; I will do to thee all that thou requirest: for all the city of my people doth know that thou *art* a virtuous woman.

• Fond of self-indulgence.

Isa 32:9–11

• Fond of ornaments.

Jer 2:32 — Can a maid forget her ornaments, *or* a bride her attire? yet my people have forgotten me days without number.

• Subtle and deceitful.

Pr 6:24–29, 32–35; 7:6–27

Ecc 7:26 — And I find more bitter than death the woman, whose heart *is* snares and nets, *and* her hands *as* bands: whoso pleaseth God shall escape from her; but the sinner shall be taken by her.

• Silly, and easily led into error.

2Ti 3:6 — For of this sort are they which creep into houses, and lead captive silly women laden with sins, led away with divers lusts,

• Zealous in promoting superstition and idolatry.

Jer 7:18 — The children gather wood, and the fathers kindle the fire, and the women knead *their* dough, to make cakes to the queen of heaven, and to pour out drink offerings unto other gods, that they may provoke me to anger.

Eze 13:17 — Likewise, thou son of man, set thy face against the daughters of thy people, which prophesy out of their own heart; and prophesy thou against them,

Eze 13:23 — Therefore ye shall see no more vanity, nor divine divinations: for I will deliver my people out of your hand: and ye shall know that I *am* the LORD.

• Active in instigating iniquity.

Nu 31:15–16

1Ki 21:25 — But there was none like unto Ahab, which did sell himself to work wickedness in the sight of the LORD, whom Jezebel his wife stirred up.

Ne 13:26 — Did not Solomon king of Israel sin by these things? yet among many nations was there no king like him, who was beloved of his God, and God made him king over all Israel: nevertheless even him did outlandish women cause to sin.

• Guilty of sodomy.

2Ki 23:7 — And he brake down the houses of the sodomites, that *were* by the house of the LORD, where the women wove hangings for the grove.

Ro 1:26 — For this cause God gave them up unto vile affections: for even their women did change the natural use into that which is against nature:

WOMEN, Good

• Instances of.

• Deborah, a judge, prophetess, and military leader.

Jgs 4:1–5:31

• Mother of Samson.

Jgs 13:23

• Naomi.

Ru 1:1–3:1

• Ruth.

Ru 1:4; 1:14–4:22

• Hannah, the mother of Samuel.

1Sa 1:9–18, 24–28

• Widow of Zarephath, who fed Elijah during the famine.

1Ki 17:8–24

• The Shunammite, who gave hospitality to Elisha.

2Ki 4:8–38

• Vashti.

Est 1:11–12

• Esther.

Est 4:15–17

• Mary.

Lk 1:26–38

• Elisabeth.

Lk 1:6, 41–45

• Anna.

Lk 2:37

• The widow who cast her mite into the treasury.

Mk 12:41–44; Lk 21:2–4

• Mary and Martha.

Mk 14:3–9; Lk 10:42; Jn 11:5

• Mary Magdalene.

Mk 16:1; Lk 8:2; Jn 20:1–2, 11–16

• Pilate's wife.

Mt 27:19

• Dorcas.

Ac 9:36

• Lydia.

Ac 16:14

• Priscilla.

Ac 18:26

• Phebe.

Ro 16:1–2

• Julia.

Ro 16:15

• Mary.

Ro 16:6

• Lois and Eunice.

2Ti 1:5

• Philippians.

Php 4:3

- **Figurative.**
  - **Of the church of Christ.**

    Ps 45:2–15

    Gal 4:26 — But Jerusalem which is above is free, which is the mother of us all.

    Rev 12:1 — And there appeared a great wonder in heaven; a woman clothed with the sun, and the moon under her feet, and upon her head a crown of twelve stars:
  - **Of saints.**

    Mt 25:1–4

    2Co 11:2 — For I am jealous over you with godly jealousy: for I have espoused you to one husband, that I may present *you as* a chaste virgin to Christ.

    Rev 14:4 — These are they which were not defiled with women; for they are virgins. These are they which follow the Lamb whithersoever he goeth. These were redeemed from among men, *being* the firstfruits unto God and to the Lamb.

WOMEN, Roles of

- **As rulers and patriotic.**

  Isa 3:12 — *As for* my people, children *are* their oppressors, and women rule over them. O my people, they which lead thee cause *thee* to err, and destroy the way of thy paths.
  - **Deborah.**

    Jgs 4:4 — And Deborah, a prophetess, the wife of Lapidoth, she judged Israel at that time.
  - **Athaliah.**

    2Ki 11:1–16; 2Ch 22:2–3, 10–12
  - **Queen of Sheba.**

    1Ki 10:1–13
  - **Candace.**

    Ac 8:27 — And he arose and went: and, behold, a man of Ethiopia, an eunuch of great authority under Candace queen of the Ethiopians, who had the charge of all her treasure, and had come to Jerusalem for to worship,
  - **Persian queen sat on throne with the king.**

    Ne 2:6 — And the king said unto me, (the queen also sitting by him,) For how long shall thy journey be? and when wilt thou return? So it pleased the king to send me; and I set him a time.
- **Patriotic.**
  - **Miriam.**

    Ex 15:20 — And Miriam the prophetess, the sister of Aaron, took a timbrel in her hand; and all the women went out after her with timbrels and with dances.
  - **Deborah.**

    Jgs 5:1–31
  - **Women of Israel.**

    1Sa 18:6 — And it came to pass as they came, when David was returned from the slaughter of the Philistine, that the women came out of all cities of Israel, singing and dancing, to meet king Saul, with tabrets, with joy, and with instruments of musick.
  - **Women of the Philistines.**

    2Sa 1:20 — Tell *it* not in Gath, publish *it* not in the streets of Askelon; lest the daughters of the Philistines rejoice, lest the daughters of the uncircumcised triumph.
- **Aid in defensive operations.**

  Jgs 9:53 — And a certain woman cast a piece of a millstone upon Abimelech's head, and all to brake his skull.
- **As poets.**
  - **Miriam.**

    Ex 15:21 — And Miriam answered them, Sing ye to the LORD, for he hath triumphed gloriously; the horse and his rider hath he thrown into the sea.
  - **Deborah.**

    Jgs 5:1–31
  - **Hannah.**

    1Sa 2:1–10
  - **Elisabeth.**

    Lk 1:42–45
  - **Mary.**

    Lk 1:46–55
- **As prophets.**
  - **Miriam.**

    Ex 15:20–21

    Mic 6:4 — For I brought thee up out of the land of Egypt, and redeemed thee out of the house of servants; and I sent before thee Moses, Aaron, and Miriam.
  - **Deborah.**

    Jgs 4:4–5
  - **Huldah.**

    2Ki 22:14–20; 2Ch 34:22–28
  - **Noadiah.**

    Ne 6:14 — My God, think thou upon Tobiah and Sanballat according to these their works, and on the prophetess Noadiah, and the rest of the prophets, that would have put me in fear.
  - **Anna.**

    Lk 2:36–38
  - **Philip's daughters.**

    Ac 21:9 — And the same man had four daughters, virgins, which did prophesy.
  - **False prophets.**

    Eze 13:17–23
- **In business.**

  Pr 31:14–18

  Pr 31:24 — She maketh fine linen, and selleth *it;* and delivereth girdles unto the merchant.
- **Property rights of.**
  - **In inheritance.**

    Nu 27:1–11; 36:1–13; Jos 17:3–6

    Job 42:15 — And in all the land were no women found *so* fair as the daughters of Job: and their father gave them inheritance among their brethren.
  - **To sell real estate.**

    Ru 4:3–9

- **Sold for husband's debts.**
  Mt 18:25 — But forasmuch as he had not to pay, his lord commanded him to be sold, and his wife, and children, and all that he had, and payment to be made.
- **First to sin.**
  Ge 3:6 — And when the woman saw that the tree *was* good for food, and that it *was* pleasant to the eyes, and a tree to be desired to make *one* wise, she took of the fruit thereof, and did eat, and gave also unto her husband with her; and he did eat.
- **Last at the cross.**
  Mt 27:55–56; Mk 15:40–41
- **First at the sepulchre.**
  Mk 15:46–16:6; Lk 23:27–28, 55–24:10
  Lk 23:49 — And all his acquaintance, and the women that followed him from Galilee, stood afar off, beholding these things.
- **First to whom the risen Lord appeared.**
  Jn 20:14–18
  Mk 16:9 — Now when *Jesus* was risen early the first *day* of the week, he appeared first to Mary Magdalene, out of whom he had cast seven devils.
- **Converted by preaching of Paul.**
  Ac 16:14–15
  Ac 17:4 — And some of them believed, and consorted with Paul and Silas; and of the devout Greeks a great multitude, and of the chief women not a few.
  Ac 17:12 — Therefore many of them believed; also of honourable women which were Greeks, and of men, not a few.
  Ac 17:34 — Howbeit certain men clave unto him, and believed: among the which *was* Dionysius the Areopagite, and a woman named Damaris, and others with them.
- **Social status of.**
  - **In Persia.**
    Est 1:10–22; Da 5:1–12
  - **In Roman customs.**
    Ac 24:24 — And after certain days, when Felix came with his wife Drusilla, which was a Jewess, he sent for Paul, and heard him concerning the faith in Christ.
    Ac 25:13 — And after certain days king Agrippa and Bernice came unto Caesarea to salute Festus.
    Ac 25:23 — And on the morrow, when Agrippa was come, and Bernice, with great pomp, and was entered into the place of hearing, with the chief captains, and principal men of the city, at Festus' commandment Paul was brought forth.
    Ac 26:30 — And when he had thus spoken, the king rose up, and the governor, and Bernice, and they that sat with them:
- **Unclassified scripture relating to.**
  Ge 2:21–24; Est 1:20–22; Pr 19:13–14; 27:15–16; 30:21–23; 31:10–31; Ecc 7:26–28; Isa 3:16–24; 32:9–12; Eze 13:17–23; 1Co 11:3–15; 14:34–35; 1Ti 2:9–15; 5:1–16; 2Ti 3:6–7; Tit 2:3–5
  Ge 2:18 — And the LORD God said, *It is* not good that the man should be alone; I will make him an help meet for him.
  Ge 3:16 — Unto the woman he said, I will greatly multiply thy sorrow and thy conception; in sorrow thou shalt bring forth children; and thy desire *shall be* to thy husband, and he shall rule over thee.
  Ps 68:11 — The Lord gave the word: great *was* the company of those that published *it*.
  Pr 11:16 — A gracious woman retaineth honour: and strong *men* retain riches.
  Pr 11:22 — *As* a jewel of gold in a swine's snout, *so is* a fair woman which is without discretion.
  Pr 12:4 — A virtuous woman *is* a crown to her husband: but she that maketh ashamed *is* as rottenness in his bones.
  Pr 14:1 — Every wise woman buildeth her house: but the foolish plucketh it down with her hands.
  Pr 18:22 — *Whoso* findeth a wife findeth a good *thing*, and obtaineth favour of the LORD.
  Pr 21:9 — *It is* better to dwell in a corner of the housetop, than with a brawling woman in a wide house.
  Pr 21:19 — *It is* better to dwell in the wilderness, than with a contentious and an angry woman.
  Pr 25:24 — *It is* better to dwell in the corner of the housetop, than with a brawling woman and in a wide house.
  1Ti 3:11 — Even so *must their* wives be grave, not slanderers, sober, faithful in all things.
  See: Widow
  See: Wife

See: Husband
See: Parents

WOMEN, Wicked

2Ki 9:30–37; Jer 44:15–19
2Ki 23:7 And he brake down the houses of the sodomites, that *were* by the house of the LORD, where the women wove hangings for the grove.
Jer 44:25 — Thus saith the LORD of hosts, the God of Israel, saying; Ye and your wives have both spoken with your mouths, and fulfilled with your hand, saying, We will surely perform our vows that we have vowed, to burn incense to the queen of heaven, and to pour out drink offerings unto her: ye will surely accomplish your vows, and surely perform your vows.
Eze 8:14 — Then he brought me to the door of the gate of the LORD'S house which *was* toward the north; and, behold, there sat women weeping for Tammuz.
Ro 1:26 — For this cause God gave them up unto vile affections: for even their women did change the natural use into that which is against nature:

- **Zeal of, in licentious practices of idolatry.**
  Hos 4:13–14
  2Ki 23:7 — And he brake down the houses of the sodomites, that *were* by the house of the LORD, where the women wove hangings for the grove.
- **Guileful and licentious.**
  Pr 2:16–19; 5:3–20; 6:24–29, 32–35; 7:6–27

Ecc 7:26 — And I find more bitter than death the woman, whose heart *is* snares and nets, *and* her hands *as* bands: whoso pleaseth God shall escape from her; but the sinner shall be taken by her.

Eze 16:32 — *But as* a wife that committeth adultery, *which* taketh strangers instead of her husband!

- **Commits forgery.**

1Ki 21:8 — So she wrote letters in Ahab's name, and sealed *them* with his seal, and sent the letters unto the elders and to the nobles that *were* in his city, dwelling with Naboth.

- **Silly and wayward.**

2Ti 3:6 — For of this sort are they which creep into houses, and lead captive silly women laden with sins, led away with divers lusts,

- **Instances of.**

  - **Eve, in yielding to temptation and seducing her husband.**
    Ge 3:6; 1Ti 2:14
  - **Sarah, in her jealousy and malice toward Hagar.**
    Ge 21:9–11, 21
  - **Lot's wife, in her rebellion against her situation, and against the destruction of Sodom.**
    Ge 19:26; Lk 17:32
  - **The daughters of Lot, in their incestuous lust.**
    Ge 19:31–38
  - **Rebekah, in her partiality for Jacob, and her sharp practice to secure for him Isaac's blessing.**
    Ge 27:11–17
  - **Rachel, in her jealousy of Leah.**
    Ge 30:1
  - **Rachel, in stealing images.**
    Ge 31:19, 34
  - **Leah, in her imitation of Rachel in the matter of children.**
    Ge 30:9–18
  - **Dinah, in her fornication.**
    Ge 34:1–2
  - **Tamar, in her adultery.**
    Ge 38:14–24
  - **Potiphar's wife, in her lascivious lust and slander against Joseph.**
    Ge 39:7–20
  - **Zipporah, in her persecution of Moses on account of his religious obligations.**
    Ex 4:25–26
  - **Miriam, in her sedition with Aaron against Moses.**
    Nu 12:1–16
  - **Rahab, in her harlotry.**
    Jos 2:1
  - **Delilah, in her conspiracy against Samson.**
    Jgs 16:4–20
  - **Peninnah, the wife of Elkanah, in her jealous taunting of Hannah.**
    1Sa 1:4–8
  - **The Midianitish woman in the camp of Israel, taken in adultery.**
    Nu 25:6–8
  - **Michal, in her derision of David's religious zeal.**
    2Sa 6:16, 20–23
  - **Bath-sheba, in her adultery, in becoming the wife of her husband's murderer.**
    2Sa 11:4–5, 27; 12:9–10
  - **Solomon's wives, in their idolatrous and wicked influence over Solomon.**
    1Ki 11:1–11; Ne 13:26
  - **Jezebel, in her persecution and destruction of the prophets of the Lord.**
    1Ki 18:4, 13
  - **Jezebel, in her persecution of Elijah.**
    1Ki 19:2
  - **Jezebel, in her conspiracy against Naboth, to despoil him of his vineyard.**
    1Ki 21:1–16
  - **Jezebel, in her evil counsels to, and influence over, Ahab.**
    1Ki 21:17–27; 2Ki 9:30–37
  - **The cannibal mothers of Samaria.**
    2Ki 6:28–29
  - **Athaliah, in destroying the royal household and usurping the throne.**
    2Ki 11:1–16; 2Ch 22:10, 12; 23:12–15
  - **The sodomites of Judah.**
    2Ki 23:7
  - **Noadiah, a false prophetess, in troubling the Jews when they were restoring Jerusalem.**
    Ne 6:14
  - **Haman's wife, in counseling him to hang Mordecai.**
    Est 5:14; 6:13
  - **Job's wife, in counseling him to curse God.**
    Job 2:9; 19:17
  - **The idolatrous wives of Hosea.**
    Hos 1:2–3; 3:1
  - **Herodias, in her incestuous marriage with Herod.**
    Mt 14:3–4; Mk 6:17–19; Lk 3:19
  - **Herodias, compassing the death of John the Baptist.**
    Mt 14:6–11; Mk 6:24–28
  - **The daughter of Herodias, in her complicity with her mother in securing the death of John the Baptist.**
    Mt 14:8; Mk 6:18–28
  - **Sapphira, in her blasphemous falsehood.**
    Ac 5:2–10

• **The woman taken in adultery and brought to Jesus in the temple.**

Jn 8:1–11

• **Figurative.**

• **Of backsliding.**

Jer 6:2 — I have likened the daughter of Zion to a comely and delicate *woman.*

Rev 17:4 — And the woman was arrayed in purple and scarlet colour, and decked with gold and precious stones and pearls, having a golden cup in her hand full of abominations and filthiness of her fornication:

Rev 17:18 — And the woman which thou sawest is that great city, which reigneth over the kings of the earth.

• **Of the wicked.**

Mt 25:1–13

Isa 32:9 — Rise up, ye women that are at ease; hear my voice, ye careless daughters; give ear unto my speech.

Isa 32:11 — Tremble, ye women that are at ease; be troubled, ye careless ones: strip you, and make you bare, and gird *sackcloth* upon *your* loins.

• **Symbolic.**

• **Of wickedness.**

Zec 5:7–8; Rev 17:1–18

Rev 19:2 — For true and righteous *are* his judgments: for he hath judged the great whore, which did corrupt the earth with her fornication, and hath avenged the blood of his servants at her hand.

See: Wife

WONDERFUL

• **A name of the Messiah.**

Jgs 13:18 — And the angel of the LORD said unto him, Why askest thou thus after my name, seeing it is secret?

Isa 9:6 — For unto us a child is born, unto us a son is given: and the government shall be upon his shoulder: and his name shall be called Wonderful, Counsellor, The mighty God, The everlasting Father, The Prince of Peace.

See: Jesus, Names, Appellations, and Titles of

WOOL

• **Used for clothing.**

Le 13:47–52

Le 13:59 — This *is* the law of the plague of leprosy in a garment of woollen or linen, either in the warp, or woof, or any thing of skins, to pronounce it clean, or to pronounce it unclean.

Pr 31:13 — She seeketh wool, and flax, and worketh willingly with her hands.

Eze 34:3 — Ye eat the fat, and ye clothe you with the wool, ye kill them that are fed: *but* ye feed not the flock.

Eze 44:17 — And it shall come to pass, *that* when they enter in at the gates of the inner court, they shall be clothed with linen garments; and no wool shall come upon them, whiles they minister in the gates of the inner court, and within.

• **Prohibited in the priest's temple dress.**

Eze 44:17 — And it shall come to pass, *that* when they enter in at the gates of the inner court, they shall be clothed with linen garments; and no wool shall come upon them, whiles they minister in the gates of the inner court, and within.

• **Mixing of, with other fabrics forbidden.**

Le 19:19 — Ye shall keep my statutes. Thou shalt not let thy cattle gender with a diverse kind: thou shalt not sow thy field with mingled seed: neither shall a garment mingled of linen and woollen come upon thee.

Dt 22:11 — Thou shalt not wear a garment of divers sorts, *as* of woollen and linen together.

• **Fleece of.**

Jgs 6:37 — Behold, I will put a fleece of wool in the floor; *and* if the dew be on the fleece only, and *it be* dry upon all the earth *beside,* then shall I know that thou wilt save Israel by mine hand, as thou hast said.

• **First fleece of, belonged to the priests.**

Dt 18:4 — The firstfruit *also* of thy corn, of thy wine, and of thine oil, and the first of the fleece of thy sheep, shalt thou give him.

WORD

• **A title of Jesus.**

Jn 1:1 — In the beginning was the Word, and the Word was with God, and the Word was God.

Jn 1:14 — And the Word was made flesh, and dwelt among us, (and we beheld his glory, the glory as of the only begotten of the Father,) full of grace and truth.

1 Jn 5:7 — For there are three that bear record in heaven, the Father, the Word, and the Holy Ghost: and these three are one.

Rev 19:13 — And he *was* clothed with a vesture dipped in blood: and his name is called The Word of God.

See: Jesus, Names, Appellations, and Titles of

WORD OF GOD

• **Called Book.**

Ps 40:7 — Then said I, Lo, I come: in the volume of the book *it is* written of me,

Rev 22:19 — And if any man shall take away from the words of the book of this prophecy, God shall take away his part out of the book of life, and out of the holy city, and *from* the things which are written in this book.

• **Called Book of the Lord.**

Isa 34:16 — Seek ye out of the book of the LORD, and read: no one of these shall fail, none shall want her mate: for my mouth it hath commanded, and his spirit it hath gathered them.

• Called Book of the Law.

Ne 8:3 — And he read therein before the street that *was* before the water gate from the morning until midday, before the men and the women, and those that could understand; and the ears of all the people *were attentive* unto the book of the law.

Gal 3:10 — For as many as are of the works of the law are under the curse: for it is written, Cursed *is* every one that continueth not in all things which are written in the book of the law to do them.

• Called Good Word of God.

Heb 6:5 — And have tasted the good word of God, and the powers of the world to come,

• Called Holy Scriptures.

Ro 1:2 — (Which he had promised afore by his prophets in the holy scriptures,)

2Ti 3:15 — And that from a child thou hast known the holy scriptures, which are able to make thee wise unto salvation through faith which is in Christ Jesus.

• Called Law of the Lord.

Ps 1:2 — But his delight *is* in the law of the LORD; and in his law doth he meditate day and night.

Isa 30:9 — That this *is* a rebellious people, lying children, children *that* will not hear the law of the LORD:

• Called Oracles of God.

Ro 3:2 — Much every way: chiefly, because that unto them were committed the oracles of God.

1Pe 4:11 — If any man speak, *let him speak* as the oracles of God; if any man minister, *let him do it* as of the ability which God giveth: that God in all things may be glorified through Jesus Christ, to whom be praise and dominion for ever and ever. Amen.

• Called Scriptures.

1Co 15:3 — For I delivered unto you first of all that which I also received, how that Christ died for our sins according to the scriptures;

• Called Scriptures of Truth.

Da 10:21 — But I will shew thee that which is noted in the scripture of truth: and *there is* none that holdeth with me in these things, but Michael your prince.

• Called Sword of the Spirit.

Eph 6:17 — And take the helmet of salvation, and the sword of the Spirit, which is the word of God:

• Called the Word.

Jas 1:21–23

1Pe 2:2 — As newborn babes, desire the sincere milk of the word, that ye may grow thereby:

• Called Word of God.

Lk 11:28 — But he said, <u>Yea rather, blessed *are* they that hear the word of God, and keep it.</u>

Heb 4:12 — For the word of God *is* quick, and powerful, and sharper than any twoedged sword, piercing even to the dividing asunder of soul and spirit, and of the joints and marrow, and *is* a discerner of the thoughts and intents of the heart.

• Called Word of Christ.

Col 3:16 — Let the word of Christ dwell in you richly in all wisdom; teaching and admonishing one another in psalms and hymns and spiritual songs, singing with grace in your hearts to the Lord.

• Called Word of Life.

Php 2:16 — Holding forth the word of life; that I may rejoice in the day of Christ, that I have not run in vain, neither laboured in vain.

• Called Word of Truth.

2Ti 2:15 — Study to shew thyself approved unto God, a workman that needeth not to be ashamed, rightly dividing the word of truth.

Jas 1:18 — Of his own will begat he us with the word of truth, that we should be a kind of firstfruits of his creatures.

• Likened to seed.

Mt 13:3–8, 18–23, 37–38; Mk 4:3–20, 26–32; Lk 8:5–15

• Likened to a two-edged sword.

Heb 4:12 — For the word of God *is* quick, and powerful, and sharper than any twoedged sword, piercing even to the dividing asunder of soul and spirit, and of the joints and marrow, and *is* a discerner of the thoughts and intents of the heart.

• To be read publicly.

Dt 31:11–13; Jos 8:33–35; 2Ch 17:7–9; Ne 8:1–8

2Ki 23:2 — And the king went up into the house of the LORD, and all the men of Judah and all the inhabitants of Jerusalem with him, and the priests, and the prophets, and all the people, both small and great: and he read in their ears all the words of the book of the covenant which was found in the house of the LORD.

Ne 8:13 — And on the second day were gathered together the chief of the fathers of all the people, the priests, and the Levites, unto Ezra the scribe, even to understand the words of the law.

Ne 8:18 — Also day by day, from the first day unto the last day, he read in the book of the law of God. And they kept the feast seven days; and on the eighth day *was* a solemn assembly, according unto the manner.

Jer 36:6 — Therefore go thou, and read in the roll, which thou hast written from my mouth, the words of the LORD in the ears of the people in the LORD'S house upon the fasting day: and also thou shalt read them in the ears of all Judah that come out of their cities.

Ac 13:15 — And after the reading of the law and the prophets the rulers of the synagogue sent unto them, saying, *Ye* men *and* brethren, if ye have any word of exhortation for the people, say on.

Ac 13:27 — For they that dwell at Jerusalem, and their rulers, because they knew him not, nor yet the voices of the prophets which are read every sabbath day, they have fulfilled *them* in condemning *him.*

Col 4:16 — And when this epistle is read among you, cause that it be read also in the church of the Laodiceans; and that ye likewise read the *epistle* from Laodicea.

1Th 5:27 — I charge you by the Lord that this epistle be read unto all the holy brethren.

• The people stood and responded by saying, "Amen".

Dt 27:12–26; Ne 8:5–6

Ex 24:7 — And he took the book of the covenant, and read in the audience of the people: and they said, All that the LORD hath said will we do, and be obedient.

• Expounded.

Ne 8:8 — So they read in the book in the law of God distinctly, and gave the sense, and caused *them* to understand the reading.

• Expounded by Jesus.

Lk 4:16–27

Lk 24:27 — And beginning at Moses and all the prophets, he expounded unto them in all the scriptures the things concerning himself.

Lk 24:45 — Then opened he their understanding, that they might understand the scriptures,

• Searched.

Ac 17:11 — These were more noble than those in Thessalonica, in that they received the word with all readiness of mind, and searched the scriptures daily, whether those things were so.

• Searching of, enjoined.

Jn 5:39 — Search the scriptures; for in them ye think ye have eternal life: and they are they which testify of me.

Jn 7:52 — They answered and said unto him, Art thou also of Galilee? Search, and look: for out of Galilee ariseth no prophet.

• Texts of, to be written on doorposts.

Dt 6:9 — And thou shalt write them upon the posts of thy house, and on thy gates.

Dt 11:20 — And thou shalt write them upon the door posts of thine house, and upon thy gates:

• Not to be added to, or taken from.

Rev 22:18–19

Dt 4:2 — Ye shall not add unto the word which I command you, neither shall ye diminish *ought* from it, that ye may keep the commandments of the LORD your God which I command you.

Dt 12:32 — What thing soever I command you, observe to do it: thou shalt not add thereto, nor diminish from it.

• Conviction of sin from reading.

2Ki 22:9–13; 2Ch 17:7–10; 34:1–33

• Fulfilled by Jesus.

Mt 5:17 — Think not that I am come to destroy the law, or the prophets: I am not come to destroy, but to fulfil.

Lk 24:27 — And beginning at Moses and all the prophets, he expounded unto them in all the scriptures the things concerning himself.

Jn 19:24 — They said therefore among themselves, Let us not rend it, but cast lots for it, whose it shall be: that the scripture might be fulfilled, which saith, They parted my raiment among them, and for my vesture they did cast lots. These things therefore the soldiers did.

• Testify of Jesus.

Jn 5:39 — Search the scriptures; for in them ye think ye have eternal life: and they are they which testify of me.

Ac 10:43 — To him give all the prophets witness, that through his name whosoever believeth in him shall receive remission of sins.

Ac 18:28 — For he mightily convinced the Jews, *and that* publickly, shewing by the scriptures that Jesus was Christ.

1Co 15:3 — For I delivered unto you first of all that which I also received, how that Christ died for our sins according to the scriptures;

See: Jesus, Prophecies Concerning

• Taught by the apostles.

Ac 2:1–3:26

Ac 8:32 — The place of the scripture which he read was this, He was led as a sheep to the slaughter; and like a lamb dumb before his shearer, so opened he not his mouth:

Ac 8:35 — Then Philip opened his mouth, and began at the same scripture, and preached unto him Jesus.

Ac 13:27 — For they that dwell at Jerusalem, and their rulers, because they knew him not, nor yet the voices of the prophets which are read every sabbath day, they have fulfilled *them* in condemning *him.*

Ac 17:2 — And Paul, as his manner was, went in unto them, and three sabbath days reasoned with them out of the scriptures,

Ac 18:24 — And a certain Jew named Apollos, born at Alexandria, an eloquent man, *and* mighty in the scriptures, came to Ephesus.

Ac 28:23 — And when they had appointed him a day, there came many to him into *his* lodging; to whom he expounded and testified the kingdom of God, persuading them concerning Jesus, both out of the law of Moses, and *out of* the prophets, from morning till evening.

• The standard of the judgment.

Jn 12:48 — He that rejecteth me, and receiveth not my words, hath one that judgeth him: the word that I have spoken, the same shall judge him in the last day.

Ro 2:16 — In the day when God shall judge the secrets of men by Jesus Christ according to my gospel.

• Not to be handled deceitfully.

2Co 4:2 — But have renounced the hidden things of dishonesty, not walking in craftiness, nor handling the word of God deceitfully; but by manifestation of the truth commending ourselves to every man's conscience in the sight of God.

• Unclassified scripture relating to.

Ex 24:3–4; Dt 4:5–6; 6:6–9; 11:18–21; 17:18–19; 27:2–3; 30:11–14; 31:9–13; Jos 8:32–35; Ps 19:7–11; 78:7–8; 107:19–20; 111:7–8; 119:11–12, 14–16, 18–20, 23–25, 30–31, 40–41, 45–52, 66–67, 76–78, 81–83, 92–93, 96–100, 103–105, 127–131, 140–144, 147–148, 151–153, 157– 163, 172–174; 147:19–20; Pr 6:20–23; 30:5–6; Ecc 12:10–11; Isa 55:10–11; Jer 23:28–29; Am 8:11–13; Mt 7:24–25; Lk 6:47–48; 8:11–15; Jn 8:31–32; 17:19–20; Ro 3:1–2; 4:23–24; Gal 1:8–9, 11–12; Eph 1:12–13; 3:3–5; 1Th 4:1–2; 2Th 2:14–15; 1Ti 4:5–6; 6:3–4; 2Ti 2:8–9; 3:15–17; Heb 1:1–2; 2:1–3; Jas 1:18–19, 21–25; 1Pe 1:23–25;

2Pe 1:19–21; 3:1–2, 15–16; 1Jn 1:4–5; 2:7–8; Rev 1:2–3; 22:18–19

Ex 13:9 — And it shall be for a sign unto thee upon thine hand, and for a memorial between thine eyes, that the LORD'S law may be in thy mouth: for with a strong hand hath the LORD brought thee out of Egypt.

Ex 19:9 — And the LORD said unto Moses, Lo, I come unto thee in a thick cloud, that the people may hear when I speak with thee, and believe thee for ever. And Moses told the words of the people unto the LORD.

Dt 4:2 — Ye shall not add unto the word which I command you, neither shall ye diminish *ought* from it, that ye may keep the commandments of the LORD your God which I command you.

Dt 4:8 — And what nation *is there so* great, that hath statutes and judgments *so* righteous as all this law, which I set before you this day?

Dt 4:10 — *Specially* the day that thou stoodest before the LORD thy God in Horeb, when the LORD said unto me, Gather me the people together, and I will make them hear my words, that they may learn to fear me all the days that they shall live upon the earth, and *that* they may teach their children.

Dt 4:14 — And the LORD commanded me at that time to teach you statutes and judgments, that ye might do them in the land whither ye go over to possess it.

Dt 8:3 — And he humbled thee, and suffered thee to hunger, and fed thee with manna, which thou knewest not, neither did thy fathers know; that he might make thee know that man doth not live by bread only, but by every *word* that proceedeth out of the mouth of the LORD doth man live.

Dt 12:32 — What thing soever I command you, observe to do it: thou shalt not add thereto, nor diminish from it.

Dt 27:8 — And thou shalt write upon the stones all the words of this law very plainly.

Dt 29:29 — The secret *things belong* unto the LORD our God: but *those things which* are revealed *belong* unto us and to our children for ever, that *we* may do all the words of this law.

Dt 31:19 — Now therefore write ye this song for you, and teach it the children of Israel: put it in their mouths, that this song may be a witness for me against the children of Israel.

Dt 31:21 — And it shall come to pass, when many evils and troubles are befallen them, that this song shall testify against them as a witness; for it shall not be forgotten out of the mouths of their seed: for I know their imagination which they go about; even now, before I have brought them into the land which I sware.

Dt 31:26 — Take this book of the law, and put it in the side of the ark of the covenant of the LORD your God, that it may be there for a witness against thee.

Jos 1:8 — This book of the law shall not depart out of thy mouth; but thou shalt meditate therein day and night, that thou mayest observe to do according to all that is written therein: for then thou shalt make thy way prosperous, and then thou shalt have good success.

Jos 3:9 — And Joshua said unto the children of Israel, Come hither, and hear the words of the LORD your God.

2Sa 22:31 — *As for* God, his way *is* perfect; the word of the LORD *is* tried: he *is* a buckler to all them that trust in him.

1Ch 16:15 — Be ye mindful always of his covenant; the word *which* he commanded to a thousand generations;

2Ch 15:3 — Now for a long season Israel *hath been* without the true God, and without a teaching priest, and without law.

Job 22:22 — Receive, I pray thee, the law from his mouth, and lay up his words in thine heart.

Job 23:12 — Neither have I gone back from the commandment of his lips; I have esteemed the words of his mouth more than my necessary *food.*

Ps 1:2 — But his delight *is* in the law of the LORD; and in his law doth he meditate day and night.

Ps 12:6 — The words of the LORD *are* pure words: *as* silver tried in a furnace of earth, purified seven times.

Ps 17:4 — Concerning the words of men, by the word of thy lips I have kept *me from* the paths of the destroyer.

Ps 18:30 — *As for* God, his way *is* perfect: the word of the LORD is tried: he *is* a buckler to all those that trust in him.

Ps 33:4 — For the word of the LORD *is* right; and all his works *are done* in truth.

Ps 33:6 — By the word of the LORD were the heavens made; and all the host of them by the breath of his mouth.

Ps 37:31 — The law of his God *is* in his heart; none of his steps shall slide.

Ps 40:8 — I delight to do thy will, O my God: yea, thy law *is* within my heart.

Ps 43:3 — O send out thy light and thy truth: let them lead me; let them bring me unto thy holy hill, and to thy tabernacles.

Ps 56:4 — In God I will praise his word, in God I have put my trust; I will not fear what flesh can do unto me.

Ps 78:1 — Give ear, O my people, *to* my law: incline your ears to the words of my mouth.

Ps 85:8 — I will hear what God the LORD will speak: for he will speak peace unto his people, and to his saints: but let them not turn again to folly.

Ps 93:5 — Thy testimonies are very sure: holiness becometh thine house, O LORD, for ever.

Ps 94:12 — Blessed *is* the man whom thou chastenest, O LORD, and teachest him out of thy law;

Ps 102:18 — This shall be written for the generation to come: and the people which shall be created shall praise the LORD.

Ps 119:9 — Wherewithal shall a young man cleanse his way? by taking heed *thereto* according to thy word.

Ps 119:28 — My soul melteth for heaviness: strengthen thou me according unto thy word.

Ps 119:33 — Teach me, O LORD, the way of thy statutes; and I shall keep it *unto* the end.

Ps 119:35 — Make me to go in the path of thy commandments; for therein do I delight.

Ps 119:54 — Thy statutes have been my songs in the house of my pilgrimage.

Ps 119:61 — The bands of the wicked have robbed me: *but* I have not forgotten thy law.

Ps 119:70 — Their heart is as fat as grease; *but* I delight in thy law.

Ps 119:72 — The law of thy mouth *is* better unto me than thousands of gold and silver.

Ps 119:74 — They that fear thee will be glad when they see me; because I have hoped in thy word.

Ps 119:86 — All thy commandments *are* faithful: they persecute me wrongfully; help thou me.

Ps 119:89 — For ever, O LORD, thy word is settled in heaven.

Ps 119:109 — My soul *is* continually in my hand: yet do I not forget thy law.

Ps 119:111 — Thy testimonies have I taken as an heritage for ever: for they *are* the rejoicing of my heart.

Ps 119:113 — I hate *vain* thoughts: but thy law do I love.

Ps 119:115 — Depart from me, ye evildoers: for I will keep the commandments of my God.

Ps 119:119 — Thou puttest away all the wicked of the earth *like* dross: therefore I love thy testimonies.

Ps 119:133 — Order my steps in thy word: and let not any iniquity have dominion over me.

Ps 119:138 — Thy testimonies *that* thou hast commanded *are* righteous and very faithful.

Ps 119:165 — Great peace have they which love thy law: and nothing shall offend them.

Ps 119:167 — My soul hath kept thy testimonies; and I love them exceedingly.

Ps 138:2 — I will worship toward thy holy temple, and praise thy name for thy lovingkindness and for thy truth: for thou hast magnified thy word above all thy name.

Ps 147:15 — He sendeth forth his commandment *upon* earth: his word runneth very swiftly.

Pr 22:21 — That I might make thee know the certainty of the words of truth; that thou mightest answer the words of truth to them that send unto thee?

Ecc 5:1 — Keep thy foot when thou goest to the house of God, and be more ready to hear, than to give the sacrifice of fools: for they consider not that they do evil.

Isa 2:3 — And many people shall go and say, Come ye, and let us go up to the mountain of the LORD, to the house of the God of Jacob; and he will teach us of his ways, and we will walk in his paths: for out of Zion shall go forth the law, and the word of the LORD from Jerusalem.

Isa 8:16 — Bind up the testimony, seal the law among my disciples.

Isa 8:20 — To the law and to the testimony: if they speak not according to this word, *it is* because *there is* no light in them.

Isa 28:13 — But the word of the LORD was unto them precept upon precept, precept upon precept; line upon line, line upon line; here a little, *and* there a little; that they might go, and fall backward, and be broken, and snared, and taken.

Isa 30:21 — And thine ears shall hear a word behind thee, saying, This *is* the way, walk ye in it, when ye turn to the right hand, and when ye turn to the left.

Isa 34:16 — Seek ye out of the book of the LORD, and read: no one of these shall fail, none shall want her mate: for my mouth it hath commanded, and his spirit it hath gathered them.

Isa 40:8 — The grass withereth, the flower fadeth: but the word of our God shall stand for ever.

Isa 51:7 — Hearken unto me, ye that know righteousness, the people in whose heart *is* my law; fear ye not the reproach of men, neither be ye afraid of their revilings.

Jer 8:9 — The wise *men* are ashamed, they are dismayed and taken: lo, they have rejected the word of the LORD; and what wisdom *is* in them?

Jer 13:15 — Hear ye, and give ear; be not proud: for the LORD hath spoken.

Jer 15:16 — Thy words were found, and I did eat them; and thy word was unto me the joy and rejoicing of mine heart: for I am called by thy name, O LORD God of hosts.

Jer 22:29 — O earth, earth, earth, hear the word of the LORD.

Jer 23:36 — And the burden of the LORD shall ye mention no more: for every man's word shall be his burden; for ye have perverted the words of the living God, of the LORD of hosts our God.

Eze 3:3 — And he said unto me, Son of man, cause thy belly to eat, and fill thy bowels with this roll that I give thee. Then did I eat *it;* and it was in my mouth as honey for sweetness.

Eze 3:10 — Moreover he said unto me, Son of man, all my words that I shall speak unto thee receive in thine heart, and hear with thine ears.

Eze 44:5 — And the LORD said unto me, Son of man, mark well, and behold with thine eyes, and hear with thine ears all that I say unto thee concerning all the ordinances of the house of the LORD, and all the laws thereof; and mark well the entering in of the house, with every going forth of the sanctuary.

Da 8:26 — And the vision of the evening and the morning which was told *is* true: wherefore shut thou up the vision; for it *shall be* for many days.

Da 10:21 — But I will shew thee that which is noted in the scripture of truth: and *there is* none that holdeth with me in these things, but Michael your prince.

Da 12:4 — But thou, O Daniel, shut up the words, and seal the book, *even* to the time of the end: many shall run to and fro, and knowledge shall be increased.

Da 12:9 — And he said, Go thy way, Daniel: for the words *are* closed up and sealed till the time of the end.

Hos 6:5 — Therefore have I hewed *them* by the prophets; I have slain them by the words of my mouth: and thy judgments *are as* the light *that* goeth forth.

Mic 2:7 — O *thou that art* named the house of Jacob, is the spirit of the LORD straitened? *are* these his doings? do not my words do good to him that walketh uprightly?

Hab 2:2 — And the LORD answered me, and said, Write the vision, and make *it* plain upon tables, that he may run that readeth it.

Zec 7:7 — *Should ye* not *hear* the words which the LORD hath cried by the former prophets, when Jerusalem was inhabited and in prosperity, and the cities thereof round about her, when *men* inhabited the south and the plain?

Mt 4:4 — But he answered and said, It is written, Man shall not live by bread alone, but by every word that proceedeth out of the mouth of God.

Mt 5:17 — Think not that I am come to destroy the law, or the prophets: I am not come to destroy, but to fulfil.

Mt 11:13 — For all the prophets and the law prophesied until John.

Mt 11:15 — He that hath ears to hear, let him hear.

Mt 13:23 — But he that received seed into the good ground is he that heareth the word, and understandeth *it;* which also beareth fruit, and bringeth forth, some an hundredfold, some sixty, some thirty.

Mt 13:33 — Another parable spake he unto them; The kingdom of heaven is like unto leaven, which a woman took, and hid in three measures of meal, till the whole was leavened.

Mt 15:3 — But he answered and said unto them, Why do ye also transgress the commandment of God by your tradition?

Mt 15:9 — But in vain they do worship me, teaching *for* doctrines the commandments of men.

Mt 22:29 — Jesus answered and said unto them, Ye do err, not knowing the scriptures, nor the power of God.

Mk 1:15 — And saying, The time is fulfilled, and the kingdom of God is at hand: repent ye, and believe the gospel.

Mk 4:20 — And these are they which are sown on good ground; such as hear the word, and receive *it,* and bring forth fruit, some thirtyfold, some sixty, and some an hundred.

Mk 7:9 — And he said unto them, Full well ye reject the commandment of God, that ye may keep your own tradition.

Mk 7:13 — Making the word of God of none effect through your tradition, which ye have delivered: and many such like things do ye.

Mk 12:24 — And Jesus answering said unto them, Do ye not therefore err, because ye know not the scriptures, neither the power of God?

Mk 13:31 — Heaven and earth shall pass away: but my words shall not pass away.

Lk 1:37 — For with God nothing shall be impossible.

Lk 4:22 — And all bare him witness, and wondered at the gracious words which proceeded out of his mouth. And they said, Is not this Joseph's son?

Lk 11:28 — But he said, Yea rather, blessed *are* they that hear the word of God, and keep it.

Lk 13:21 — It is like leaven, which a woman took and hid in three measures of meal, till the whole was leavened.

Lk 16:17 — And it is easier for heaven and earth to pass, than one tittle of the law to fail.

Lk 16:29 — Abraham saith unto him, They have Moses and the prophets; let them hear them.

Lk 16:31 — And he said unto him, If they hear not Moses and the prophets, neither will they be persuaded, though one rose from the dead.

Lk 24:32 — And they said one to another, Did not our heart burn within us, while he talked with us by the way, and while he opened to us the scriptures?

Lk 24:45 — Then opened he their understanding, that they might understand the scriptures,

Jn 2:22 — When therefore he was risen from the dead, his disciples remembered that he had said this unto them; and they believed the scripture, and the word which Jesus had said.

Jn 5:24 — Verily, verily, I say unto you, He that heareth my word, and believeth on him that sent me, hath everlasting life, and shall not come into condemnation; but is passed from death unto life.

Jn 5:39 — Search the scriptures; for in them ye think ye have eternal life: and they are they which testify of me.

Jn 6:63 — It is the spirit that quickeneth; the flesh profiteth nothing: the words that I speak unto you, *they* are spirit, and *they* are life.

Jn 10:35 — If he called them gods, unto whom the word of God came, and the scripture cannot be broken;

Jn 15:3 — Now ye are clean through the word which I have spoken unto you.

Jn 17:8 — For I have given unto them the words which thou gavest me; and they have received *them,* and have known surely that I came out from thee, and they have believed that thou didst send me.

Jn 17:14 — I have given them thy word; and the world hath hated them, because they are not of the world, even as I am not of the world.

Jn 17:17 — Sanctify them through thy truth: thy word is truth.

Jn 20:31 — But these are written, that ye might believe that Jesus is the Christ, the Son of God; and that believing ye might have life through his name.

Ac 10:15 — And the voice *spake* unto him again the second time, What God hath cleansed, *that* call not thou common.

Ac 17:11 — These were more noble than those in Thessalonica, in that they received the word with all readiness of mind, and searched the scriptures daily, whether those things were so.

Ac 20:32 — And now, brethren, I commend you to God, and to the word of his grace, which is able to build you up, and to give you an inheritance among all them which are sanctified.

Ac 26:18 — To open their eyes, *and* to turn *them* from darkness to light, and *from* the power of Satan unto God, that they may receive forgiveness of sins, and inheritance among them which are sanctified by faith that is in me.

Ac 26:22 — Having therefore obtained help of God, I continue unto this day, witnessing both to small and great, saying none other things than those which the prophets and Moses did say should come:

Ro 6:17 — But God be thanked, that ye were the servants of sin, but ye have obeyed from the heart that form of doctrine which was delivered you.

Ro 9:4 — Who are Israelites; to whom *pertaineth* the adoption, and the glory, and the covenants, and the giving of the law, and the service *of God,* and the promises;

Ro 9:6 — Not as though the word of God hath taken none effect. For they *are* not all Israel, which are of Israel:

Ro 10:17 — So then faith *cometh* by hearing, and hearing by the word of God.

Ro 12:2 — And be not conformed to this world: but be ye transformed by the renewing of your mind, that ye may prove what is that good, and acceptable, and perfect, will of God.

Ro 15:4 — For whatsoever things were written aforetime were written for our learning, that we through patience and comfort of the scriptures might have hope.

Ro 16:26 — But now is made manifest, and by the scriptures of the prophets, according to the commandment of the everlasting God, made known to all nations for the obedience of faith:

1Co 2:13 — Which things also we speak, not in the words which man's wisdom teacheth, but which the Holy Ghost teacheth; comparing spiritual things with spiritual.

1Co 7:6 — But I speak this by permission, *and* not of commandment.

1Co 7:10 — And unto the married I command, *yet* not I, but the Lord, Let not the wife depart from *her* husband:

1Co 7:12 — But to the rest speak I, not the Lord: If any brother hath a wife that believeth not, and she be pleased to dwell with him, let him not put her away.

1Co 9:10 — Or saith he *it* altogether for our sakes? For our sakes, no doubt, *this* is written: that he that ploweth should plow in hope; and that he that thresheth in hope should be partaker of his hope.

1Co 10:11 — Now all these things happened unto them for ensamples: and they are written for our admonition, upon whom the ends of the world are come.

1Co 11:2 — Now I praise you, brethren, that ye remember me in all things, and keep the ordinances, as I delivered *them* to you.

1Co 15:3 — For I delivered unto you first of all that which I also received, how that Christ died for our sins according to the scriptures;

2Co 2:17 — For we are not as many, which corrupt the word of God: but as of sincerity, but as of God, in the sight of God speak we in Christ.

2Co 3:6 — Who also hath made us able ministers of the new testament; not of the letter, but of the spirit: for the letter killeth, but the spirit giveth life.

2Co 8:10 — And herein I give *my* advice: for this is expedient for you, who have begun before, not only to do, but also to be forward a year ago.

Eph 5:26 — That he might sanctify and cleanse it with the washing of water by the word,

Eph 6:17 — And take the helmet of salvation, and the sword of the Spirit, which is the word of God:

Php 2:16 — Holding forth the word of life; that I may rejoice in the day of Christ, that I have not run in vain, neither laboured in vain.

Col 1:5 — For the hope which is laid up for you in heaven, whereof ye heard before in the word of the truth of the gospel;

Col 3:16 — Let the word of Christ dwell in you richly in all wisdom; teaching and admonishing one another in psalms and hymns and spiritual songs, singing with grace in your hearts to the Lord.

1Th 1:5 — For our gospel came not unto you in word only, but also in power, and in the Holy Ghost, and in much assurance; as ye know what manner of men we were among you for your sake.

1Th 1:8 — For from you sounded out the word of the Lord not only in Macedonia and Achaia, but also in every place your faith to God-ward is spread abroad; so that we need not to speak any thing.

1Th 2:13 — For this cause also thank we God without ceasing, because, when ye received the word of God which ye heard of us, ye received *it* not *as* the word of men, but as it is in truth, the word of God, which effectually worketh also in you that believe.

1Th 5:20 — Despise not prophesyings.

2Ti 1:13 — Hold fast the form of sound words, which thou hast heard of me, in faith and love which is in Christ Jesus.

2Ti 2:15 — Study to shew thyself approved unto God, a workman that needeth not to be ashamed, rightly dividing the word of truth.

Heb 4:2 — For unto us was the gospel preached, as well as unto them: but the word preached did not profit them, not being mixed with faith in them that heard *it.*

Heb 4:12 — For the word of God *is* quick, and powerful, and sharper than any twoedged sword, piercing even to the dividing asunder of soul and spirit, and of the joints and marrow, and *is* a discerner of the thoughts and intents of the heart.

Heb 6:5 — And have tasted the good word of God, and the powers of the world to come,

Heb 10:7 — Then said I, Lo, I come (in the volume of the book it is written of me,) to do thy will, O God.

Heb 10:28 — He that despised Moses' law died without mercy under two or three witnesses:

Heb 11:3 — Through faith we understand that the worlds were framed by the word of God, so that things which are seen were not made of things which do appear.

1Pe 2:2 — As newborn babes, desire the sincere milk of the word, that ye may grow thereby:

2Pe 1:4 — Whereby are given unto us exceeding great and precious promises: that by these ye might be partakers of the divine nature, having escaped the corruption that is in the world through lust.

1Jn 2:12 — I write unto you, little children, because your sins are forgiven you for his name's sake.

1Jn 2:14 — I have written unto you, fathers, because ye have known him *that is* from the beginning. I have written unto you, young men, because ye are strong, and the word of God abideth in you, and ye have overcome the wicked one.

1Jn 2:21 — I have not written unto you because ye know not the truth, but because ye know it, and that no lie is of the truth.

1Jn 5:11 — And this is the record, that God hath given to us eternal life, and this life is in his Son.

1Jn 5:13 — These things have I written unto you that believe on the name of the Son of God; that ye may know that ye have eternal life, and that ye may believe on the name of the Son of God.

Jude 1:3 — Beloved, when I gave all diligence to write unto you of the common salvation, it was needful for me to write unto you, and exhort *you* that ye should earnestly contend for the faith which was once delivered unto the saints.

Jude 1:17 — But, beloved, remember ye the words which were spoken before of the apostles of our Lord Jesus Christ;

→See: Commandments

• Inspiration of.

Isa 30:12–13; Jer 36:1–2, 27–28; 51:59–64; Mt 22:31–32; Lk 1:1–4, 68–73; Ro 3:1–2; 1Co 2:12–13; 1Th 4:1–3; 1Ti 6:3–5; 2Ti 3:16–17; Heb 1:1–2; 3:7–8; 1Pe 1:11–12; 1Jn 1:1–5; Rev 1:1–2, 17–19; 22:6–8

Ex 19:7 — And Moses came and called for the elders of the people, and laid before their faces all these words which the LORD commanded him.

Ex 20:1 — And God spake all these words, saying,

Ex 24:4 — And Moses wrote all the words of the LORD, and rose up early in the morning, and builded an altar under the hill, and twelve pillars, according to the twelve tribes of Israel.

Ex 24:12 — And the LORD said unto Moses, Come up to me into the mount, and be there: and I will give thee tables of stone, and a law, and commandments which I have written; that thou mayest teach them.

Ex 25:21 — And thou shalt put the mercy seat above upon the ark; and in the ark thou shalt put the testimony that I shall give thee.

Ex 31:18 — And he gave unto Moses, when he had made an end of communing with him upon mount Sinai, two tables of testimony, tables of stone, written with the finger of God.

Ex 32:16 — And the tables *were* the work of God, and the writing *was* the writing of God, graven upon the tables.

Ex 34:27 — And the LORD said unto Moses, Write thou these words: for after the tenor of these words I have made a covenant with thee and with Israel.

Ex 34:32 — And afterward all the children of Israel came nigh: and he gave them in commandment all that the LORD had spoken with him in mount Sinai.

Le 26:46 — These *are* the statutes and judgments and laws, which the LORD made between him and the children of Israel in mount Sinai by the hand of Moses.

Dt 4:5 — Behold, I have taught you statutes and judgments, even as the LORD my God commanded me, that ye should do so in the land whither ye go to possess it.

Dt 4:14 — And the LORD commanded me at that time to teach you statutes and judgments, that ye might do them in the land whither ye go over to possess it.

Dt 11:18 — Therefore shall ye lay up these my words in your heart and in your soul, and bind them for a sign upon your hand, that they may be as frontlets between your eyes.

Dt 31:19 — Now therefore write ye this song for you, and teach it the children of Israel: put it in their mouths, that this song may be a witness for me against the children of Israel.

Dt 31:22 — Moses therefore wrote this song the same day, and taught it the children of Israel.

2Ki 17:13 — Yet the LORD testified against Israel, and against Judah, by all the prophets, *and by* all the seers, saying, Turn ye from your evil ways, and keep my commandments *and* my statutes, according to all the law which I commanded your fathers, and which I sent to you by my servants the prophets.

2Ch 33:18 — Now the rest of the acts of Manasseh, and his prayer unto his God, and the words of the seers that spake to him in the name of the LORD God of Israel, behold, they *are written* in the book of the kings of Israel.

Job 23:12 — Neither have I gone back from the commandment of his lips; I have esteemed the words of his mouth more than my necessary *food.*

Ps 78:5 — For he established a testimony in Jacob, and appointed a law in Israel, which he commanded our fathers, that they should make them known to their children:

Ps 99:7 — He spake unto them in the cloudy pillar: they kept his testimonies, and the ordinance *that* he gave them.

Ps 147:19 — He sheweth his word unto Jacob, his statutes and his judgments unto Israel.

Ecc 12:11 — The words of the wise *are* as goads, and as nails fastened by the masters of assemblies, *which* are given from one shepherd.

Isa 34:16 — Seek ye out of the book of the LORD, and read: no one of these shall fail, none shall want her mate: for my mouth it hath commanded, and his spirit it hath gathered them.

Isa 59:21 — As for me, this *is* my covenant with them, saith the LORD; My spirit that *is* upon thee, and my words which I have put in thy mouth, shall not depart out of thy mouth, nor out of the mouth of thy seed, nor out of the mouth of thy seed's seed, saith the LORD, from henceforth and for ever.

Jer 30:2 — Thus speaketh the LORD God of Israel, saying, Write thee all the words that I have spoken unto thee in a book.

Jer 36:32 — Then took Jeremiah another roll, and gave it to Baruch the scribe, the son of Neriah; who wrote therein from the mouth of Jeremiah all the words of the book which Jehoiakim king of Judah had burned in the fire: and there were added besides unto them many like words.

Eze 11:25 — Then I spake unto them of the captivity all the things that the LORD had shewed me.

Da 10:21 — But I will shew thee that which is noted in the scripture of truth: and *there is* none that holdeth with me in these things, but Michael your prince.

Hos 8:12 — I have written to him the great things of my law, *but* they were counted as a strange thing.

Zec 7:12 — Yea, they made their hearts *as* an adamant stone, lest they should hear the law, and the words which the LORD of hosts hath sent in his spirit by the former prophets: therefore came a great wrath from the LORD of hosts.

Ac 1:16 — Men *and* brethren, this scripture must needs have been fulfilled, which the Holy Ghost by the mouth of David spake before concerning Judas, which was guide to them that took Jesus.

Ac 28:25 — And when they agreed not among themselves, they departed, after that Paul had spoken one word, Well spake the Holy Ghost by Esaias the prophet unto our fathers,

1Co 7:10 — And unto the married I command, *yet* not I, but the Lord, Let not the wife depart from *her* husband:

1Co 14:37 — If any man think himself to be a prophet, or spiritual, let him acknowledge that the things that I write unto you are the commandments of the Lord.

Eph 6:17 — And take the helmet of salvation, and the sword of the Spirit, which is the word of God:

Col 3:16 — Let the word of Christ dwell in you richly in all wisdom; teaching and admonishing one another in psalms and hymns and spiritual songs, singing with grace in your hearts to the Lord.

1Th 2:13 — For this cause also thank we God without ceasing, because, when ye received the word of God which ye heard of us, ye received *it* not *as* the word of men, but as it is in truth, the word of God, which effectually worketh also in you that believe.

Heb 4:12 — For the word of God *is* quick, and powerful, and sharper than any twoedged sword, piercing even to the dividing asunder of soul and spirit, and of the joints and marrow, and *is* a discerner of the thoughts and intents of the heart.

Heb 5:12 — For when for the time ye ought to be teachers, ye have need that one teach you again which *be* the first principles of the oracles of God; and are become such as have need of milk, and not of strong meat.

2Pe 1:21 — For the prophecy came not in old time by the will of man: but holy men of God spake *as they were* moved by the Holy Ghost.

2Pe 3:2 — That ye may be mindful of the words which were spoken before by the holy prophets, and of the commandment of us the apostles of the Lord and Saviour:

2Pe 3:15 — And account *that* the longsuffering of our Lord *is* salvation; even as our beloved brother Paul also according to the wisdom given unto him hath written unto you;

Rev 1:11 — Saying, I am Alpha and Omega, the first and the last: and, What thou seest, write in a book, and send *it* unto the seven churches which are in Asia; unto Ephesus, and unto Smyrna, and unto Pergamos, and unto Thyatira, and unto Sardis, and unto Philadelphia, and unto Laodicea.

Rev 2:7 — He that hath an ear, let him hear what the Spirit saith unto the churches; To him that overcometh will I give to eat of the tree of life, which is in the midst of the paradise of God.

Rev 19:10 — And I fell at his feet to worship him. And he said unto me, See *thou do it* not: I am thy fellowservant, and of thy brethren that have the testimony of Jesus: worship God: for the testimony of Jesus is the spirit of prophecy.

• Unbelief in.

Ps 50:16–17; Pr 1:29–30; Isa 28:9–14; 30:9–11; Jn 5:46–47; 1Co 1:22–23; 2Ti 4:3–4; 2Pe 3:15–16

Pr 13:13 — Whoso despiseth the word shall be destroyed: but he that feareth the commandment shall be rewarded.

Isa 5:24 — Therefore as the fire devoureth the stubble, and the flame consumeth the chaff, *so* their root shall be as rottenness, and their blossom shall go up as dust: because they have cast away the law of the LORD of hosts, and despised the word of the Holy One of Israel.

Isa 53:1 — Who hath believed our report? and to whom is the arm of the LORD revealed?

Jer 6:10 — To whom shall I speak, and give warning, that they may hear? behold, their ear *is* uncircumcised, and they cannot hearken: behold, the word of the LORD is unto them a reproach; they have no delight in it.

Jer 8:9 — The wise *men* are ashamed, they are dismayed and taken: lo, they have rejected the word of the LORD; and what wisdom *is* in them?

Hos 8:12 — I have written to him the great things of my law, *but* they were counted as a strange thing.

Am 2:12 — But ye gave the Nazarites wine to drink; and commanded the prophets, saying, Prophesy not.

Mic 2:6 — Prophesy ye not, *say they to them that* prophesy: they shall not prophesy to them, *that* they shall not take shame.

Lk 16:31 — And he said unto him, If they hear not Moses and the prophets, neither will they be persuaded, though one rose from the dead.

Lk 24:25 — Then he said unto them, O fools, and slow of heart to believe all that the prophets have spoken:

Jn 3:20 — For every one that doeth evil hateth the light, neither cometh to the light, lest his deeds should be reproved.

Jn 8:37 — I know that ye are Abraham's seed; but ye seek to kill me, because my word hath no place in you.

Jn 8:45 — And because I tell *you* the truth, ye believe me not.

1Co 1:18 — For the preaching of the cross is to them that perish foolishness; but unto us which are saved it is the power of God.

2Ti 3:8 — Now as Jannes and Jambres withstood Moses, so do these also resist the truth: men of corrupt minds, reprobate concerning the faith.

1Pe 2:8 — And a stone of stumbling, and a rock of offence, *even to them* which stumble at the word, being disobedient: whereunto also they were appointed.

Rev 22:19 — And if any man shall take away from the words of the book of this prophecy, God shall take away his part out of the book of life, and out of the holy city, and *from* the things which are written in this book.

WORDS

• Of Jesus.

• Gracious.

Lk 4:22 — And all bare him witness, and wondered at the gracious words which proceeded out of his mouth. And they said, Is not this Joseph's son?

• Spirit and life.

Jn 6:63 — It is the spirit that quickeneth; the flesh profiteth nothing: the words that I speak unto you, *they* are spirit, and *they* are life.

• Eternal life.

Jn 6:68 — Then Simon Peter answered him, Lord, to whom shall we go? thou hast the words of eternal life.

• Shall judge.

Jn 12:47–48

• Of the wise.

• As goads, and as nails well fastened.

Ecc 12:11 — The words of the wise *are* as goads, and as nails fastened by the masters of assemblies, *which* are given from one shepherd.

• Gracious.

Ecc 10:12 — The words of a wise man's mouth *are* gracious; but the lips of a fool will swallow up himself.

• Spoken in season.

Pr 15:23 — A man hath joy by the answer of his mouth: and a word *spoken* in due season, how good *is it!*

Isa 50:4 — The Lord God hath given me the tongue of the learned, that I should know how to speak a word in season to *him that is* weary: he wakeneth morning by morning, he wakeneth mine ear to hear as the learned.

• Fitly spoken, like apples of gold in filigree of silver.

Pr 25:11 — A word fitly spoken *is like* apples of gold in pictures of silver.

• Of the perfect man, gentle.

Jas 3:2 — For in many things we offend all. If any man offend not in word, the same *is* a perfect man, *and* able also to bridle the whole body.

• Should be acceptable to God.

Ps 19:14 — Let the words of my mouth, and the meditation of my heart, be acceptable in thy sight, O Lord, my strength, and my redeemer.

• Of the teacher, should be plain.

1Co 14:9 — So likewise ye, except ye utter by the tongue words easy to be understood, how shall it be known what is spoken? for ye shall speak into the air.

1Co 14:19 — Yet in the church I had rather speak five words with my understanding, that *by my voice* I might teach others also, than ten thousand words in an *unknown* tongue.

• Unprofitable, to be avoided.

2Ti 2:14 — Of these things put *them* in remembrance, charging *them* before the Lord that they strive not about words to no profit, *but* to the subverting of the hearers.

• Unspeakable, heard by Paul in paradise.

2Co 12:4 — How that he was caught up into paradise, and heard unspeakable words, which it is not lawful for a man to utter.

• Vain, not to be regarded.

Ex 5:9 — Let there more work be laid upon the men, that they may labour therein; and let them not regard vain words.

Eph 5:6 — Let no man deceive you with vain words: for because of these things cometh the wrath of God upon the children of disobedience.

• Vain, like a tempest.

Job 8:2 — How long wilt thou speak these *things?* and *how long shall* the words of thy mouth be like a strong wind?

• Without knowledge, darken counsel.

Job 38:2 — Who *is* this that darkeneth counsel by words without knowledge?

• Idle, account must be given for in the day of judgment.

Mt 12:36–37

• Hasty, folly of.

Pr 29:20 — Seest thou a man *that is* hasty in his words? *there is* more hope of a fool than of him.

• In a multitude of, is sin.

Pr 10:19 — In the multitude of words there wanteth not sin: but he that refraineth his lips *is* wise.

• Fool known by the multitude of.

Ecc 5:3 — For a dream cometh through the multitude of business; and a fool's voice *is known* by multitude of words.

• Fool will swallow himself.

Ecc 10:12–14

• Seditious, deceive the simple.

Ro 16:18 — For they that are such serve not our Lord Jesus Christ, but their own belly; and by good words and fair speeches deceive the hearts of the simple.

• Deceitful, are a snare to him who utters them.

Pr 6:2 — Thou art snared with the words of thy mouth, thou art taken with the words of thy mouth.

• Of the hypocrite, softer than oil.

Ps 55:21 — *The words* of his mouth were smoother than butter, but war *was* in his heart: his words were softer than oil, yet *were* they drawn swords.

• Of the talebearer, wounds to the soul.

Pr 18:8 — The words of a talebearer *are* as wounds, and they go down into the innermost parts of the belly.

↞See: **Busybody**

↞See: **Slander**

↞See: **Speaking; evil**

↞See: **Talebearer**

WORK

↞See: **Industry**

↞See: **Labor**

WORKS

• Good.

• Jesus an example of.

Jn 10:32 — Jesus answered them, Many good works have I shewed you from my Father; for which of those works do ye stone me?

Ac 10:38 — How God anointed Jesus of Nazareth with the Holy Ghost and with power: who went about doing good, and healing all that were oppressed of the devil; for God was with him.

• Holy women should manifest.

1Ti 2:10 — But (which becometh women professing godliness) with good works.

1Ti 5:10 — Well reported of for good works; if she have brought up children, if she have lodged strangers, if she have washed the saints' feet, if she have relieved the afflicted, if she have diligently followed every good work.

• God remembers.

Heb 6:9–10

Ne 13:14 — Remember me, O my God, concerning this, and wipe not out my good deeds that I have done for the house of my God, and for the offices thereof.

• Shall be brought into judgment.

Ecc 12:14 — For God shall bring every work into judgment, with every secret thing, whether *it be* good, or whether *it be* evil.

2Co 5:10 — For we must all appear before the judgment seat of Christ; that every one may receive the things *done* in *his* body, according to that he hath done, whether *it be* good or bad.

• In the judgment, will be an evidence of faith.

Mt 25:34–40; Jas 2:14–20

• Ministers should be patterns of.

Tit 2:7 — In all things shewing thyself a pattern of good works: in doctrine *shewing* uncorruptness, gravity, sincerity,

• Ministers should exhort to.

1Ti 6:17–18

Tit 3:1 — Put them in mind to be subject to principalities and powers, to obey magistrates, to be ready to every good work,

Tit 3:8 — *This is* a faithful saying, and these things I will that thou affirm constantly, that they which have believed in God might be careful to maintain good works. These things are good and profitable unto men.

Tit 3:14 — And let ours also learn to maintain good works for necessary uses, that they be not unfruitful.

• God is glorified by.

Jn 15:8 — Herein is my Father glorified, that ye bear much fruit; so shall ye be my disciples.

• Designed to lead others to glorify God.

Mt 5:16 — Let your light so shine before men, that they may see your good works, and glorify your Father which is in heaven.

1Pe 2:12 — Having your conversation honest among the Gentiles: that, whereas they speak against you as evildoers, they may by *your* good works, which they shall behold, glorify God in the day of visitation.

• A blessing attends.

Jas 1:25 — But whoso looketh into the perfect law of liberty, and continueth *therein,* he being not a forgetful hearer, but a doer of the work, this man shall be blessed in his deed.

• Of the righteous, are manifest.

1Ti 5:25 — Likewise also the good works *of some* are manifest beforehand; and they that are otherwise cannot be hid.

• Parables relating to.

• The talents and pounds.

Mt 25:14–29; Lk 19:12–27

• Of the laborers in the vineyard.

Mt 20:11–15

• The two sons.

Mt 21:28–31

• Of the barren fig tree.

Lk 13:6–9

• Unclassified scripture relating to.

Ps 106:30–31; Jer 22:15–16; Eze 18:5–9; Mt 6:1–4; 19:16–21; 25:34–46; Jn 15:2–8; 1Co 3:6–9; Col 3:12–14; 1Th 1:7–8; 1Ti 5:9–10; 6:18–19; 2Ti 3:16–17; Tit 3:1–2; Jas 1:22–27; 3:17–18

Dt 6:25 — And it shall be our righteousness, if we observe to do all these commandments before the LORD our God, as he hath commanded us.

Dt 24:13 — In any case thou shalt deliver him the pledge again when the sun goeth down, that he may sleep in his own raiment, and bless thee: and it shall be righteousness unto thee before the LORD thy God.

Ne 5:19 — Think upon me, my God, for good, *according* to all that I have done for this people.

Ne 13:14 — Remember me, O my God, concerning this, and wipe not out my good deeds that I have done for the house of my God, and for the offices thereof.

Job 30:25 — Did not I weep for him that was in trouble? was *not* my soul grieved for the poor?

Ps 37:3 — Trust in the LORD, and do good; *so* shalt thou dwell in the land, and verily thou shalt be fed.

Ps 90:17 — And let the beauty of the LORD our God be upon us: and establish thou the work of our hands upon us; yea, the work of our hands establish thou it.

Eze 14:14 — Though these three men, Noah, Daniel, and Job, were in it, they should deliver *but* their own souls by their righteousness, saith the Lord GOD.

Eze 14:20 — Though Noah, Daniel, and Job, *were* in it, *as* I live, saith the Lord GOD, they shall deliver neither son nor daughter; they shall *but* deliver their own souls by their righteousness.

Mt 3:8 — Bring forth therefore fruits meet for repentance:

Mt 10:42 — And whosoever shall give to drink unto one of these little ones a cup of cold *water* only in the name of a disciple, verily I say unto you, he shall in no wise lose his reward.

Mt 18:5 — And whoso shall receive one such little child in my name receiveth me.

Mk 10:17 — And when he was gone forth into the way, there came one running, and kneeled to him, and asked him, Good Master, what shall I do that I may inherit eternal life?

Lk 10:25 — And, behold, a certain lawyer stood up, and tempted him, saying, Master, what shall I do to inherit eternal life?

Jn 3:21 — But he that doeth truth cometh to the light, that his deeds may be made manifest, that they are wrought in God.

Jn 15:14 — Ye are my friends, if ye do whatsoever I command you.

Ac 10:4 — And when he looked on him, he was afraid, and said, What is it, Lord? And he said unto him, Thy prayers and thine alms are come up for a memorial before God.

Ac 10:38 — How God anointed Jesus of Nazareth with the Holy Ghost and with power: who went about doing good, and healing all that were oppressed of the devil; for God was with him.

Ro 2:13 — (For not the hearers of the law *are* just before God, but the doers of the law shall be justified.

2Co 9:8 — And God *is* able to make all grace abound toward you; that ye, always having all sufficiency in all *things,* may abound to every good work:

Gal 6:4 — But let every man prove his own work, and then shall he have rejoicing in himself alone, and not in another.

Eph 2:10 — For we are his workmanship, created in Christ Jesus unto good works, which God hath before ordained that we should walk in them.

Php 1:11 — Being filled with the fruits of righteousness, which are by Jesus Christ, unto the glory and praise of God.

Php 2:13 — For it is God which worketh in you both to will and to do of *his* good pleasure.

Col 1:10 — That ye might walk worthy of the Lord unto all pleasing, being fruitful in every good work, and increasing in the knowledge of God;

Col 3:17 — And whatsoever ye do in word or deed, *do* all in the name of the Lord Jesus, giving thanks to God and the Father by him.

1Th 1:3 — Remembering without ceasing your work of faith, and labour of love, and patience of hope in our Lord Jesus Christ, in the sight of God and our Father;

2Th 2:17 — Comfort your hearts, and stablish you in every good word and work.

1Ti 2:10 — But (which becometh women professing godliness) with good works.

2Ti 2:21 — If a man therefore purge himself from these, he shall be a vessel unto honour, sanctified, and meet for the master's use, *and* prepared unto every good work.

Tit 2:14 — Who gave himself for us, that he might redeem us from all iniquity, and purify unto himself a peculiar people, zealous of good works.

Tit 3:8 — *This is* a faithful saying, and these things I will that thou affirm constantly, that they which have believed in God might be careful to maintain good works. These things are good and profitable unto men.

Tit 3:14 — And let ours also learn to maintain good works for necessary uses, that they be not unfruitful.

Heb 6:10 — For God *is* not unrighteous to forget your work and labour of love, which ye have shewed toward his name, in that ye have ministered to the saints, and do minister.

Heb 10:24 — And let us consider one another to provoke unto love and to good works:

Heb 13:21 — Make you perfect in every good work to do his will, working in you that which is wellpleasing in his sight, through Jesus Christ; to whom *be* glory for ever and ever. Amen.

Jas 3:13 — Who *is* a wise man and endued with knowledge among you? let him shew out of a good conversation his works with meekness of wisdom.

Rev 14:13 — And I heard a voice from heaven saying unto me, Write, Blessed *are* the dead which die in the Lord from henceforth: Yea, saith the Spirit, that they may rest from their labours; and their works do follow them.

Rev 22:14 — Blessed *are* they that do his commandments, that they may have right to the tree of life, and may enter in through the gates into the city.

• Insufficiency of, for salvation.

Ps 49:7–8; 127:1–2; Eze 33:12–19; Lk 17:7–10; 18:9–14; Ro 3:20–4:22; 9:31–32; 1Co 13:1–3; Gal 2:21–3:29; 4:9–11; Eph 2:8–9; Php 3:3–9; Col 2:20–23; Tit 3:4–5; Heb 4:3–10; 6:1–2; 9:1–14; Jas 2:10–11

Ecc 1:14 — I have seen all the works that are done under the sun; and, behold, all *is* vanity and vexation of spirit.

Isa 43:26 — Put me in remembrance: let us plead together: declare thou, that thou mayest be justified.

Isa 57:12 — I will declare thy righteousness, and thy works; for they shall not profit thee.

Isa 64:6 — But we are all as an unclean *thing,* and all our righteousnesses *are* as filthy rags; and we all do fade as a leaf; and our iniquities, like the wind, have taken us away.

Eze 7:19 — They shall cast their silver in the streets, and their gold shall be removed: their silver and their gold shall not be able to deliver them in the day of the wrath of the LORD: they shall not satisfy their souls, neither fill their bowels: because it is the stumblingblock of their iniquity.

Da 9:18 — O my God, incline thine ear, and hear; open thine eyes, and behold our desolations, and the city which is called by thy name: for we do not present our supplications before thee for our righteousnesses, but for thy great mercies.

Mt 5:20 — For I say unto you, That except your righteousness shall exceed *the righteousness* of the scribes and Pharisees, ye shall in no case enter into the kingdom of heaven.

Ac 13:39 — And by him all that believe are justified from all things, from which ye could not be justified by the law of Moses.

Ro 8:3 — For what the law could not do, in that it was weak through the flesh, God sending his own Son in the likeness of sinful flesh, and for sin, condemned sin in the flesh:

Ro 9:16 — So then *it is* not of him that willeth, nor of him that runneth, but of God that sheweth mercy.

Ro 11:6 — And if by grace, then *is it* no more of works: otherwise grace is no more grace. But if *it be* of works, then is it no more grace: otherwise work is no more work.

Gal 2:16 — Knowing that a man is not justified by the works of the law, but by the faith of Jesus Christ, even we have believed in Jesus Christ, that we might be justified by the faith of Christ, and not by the works of the law: for by the works of the law shall no flesh be justified.

Gal 2:19 — For I through the law am dead to the law, that I might live unto God.

Gal 5:2 — Behold, I Paul say unto you, that if ye be circumcised, Christ shall profit you nothing.

Gal 5:4 — Christ is become of no effect unto you, whosoever of you are justified by the law; ye are fallen from grace.

Gal 5:6 — For in Jesus Christ neither circumcision availeth any thing, nor uncircumcision; but faith which worketh by love.

Gal 5:18 — But if ye be led of the Spirit, ye are not under the law.

Gal 6:15 — For in Christ Jesus neither circumcision availeth any thing, nor uncircumcision, but a new creature.

2Ti 1:9 — Who hath saved us, and called *us* with an holy calling, not according to our works, but according to his own purpose and grace, which was given us in Christ Jesus before the world began,

• Of God.

⇜See: God, Works of

WORLD ⇜See: Earth

WORLDLINESS

1Sa 8:19–20; Job 20:4–29; 21:11–15; Ps 49:16–18; 73:2–22; Pr 14:12–13; 23:20–21; Ecc 2:1–12; 6:11–12; 8:15–17; 11:9–10; Isa 22:12–13; 24:7–11; 32:9–11; 47:7–9; Am 6:3–7; Mt 6:25–34; 16:25–26; 18:1–4; 22:2–6; 24:38–39; Mk 8:35–37; 9:33–36; Lk 9:46–48; 14:17–24; 16:1–13, 19–25; 17:26–29; 1Co 7:29–31; Php 3:18–19; 2Ti 3:2–7; Heb 11:24–26; Jas 2:1–4; 1Pe 4:3–4; 2Pe 2:12–15; 1Jn 2:15–17; Jude 1:11–13

Pr 15:21 — Folly *is* joy to *him that is* destitute of wisdom: but a man of understanding walketh uprightly.

Pr 21:17 — He that loveth pleasure *shall be* a poor man: he that loveth wine and oil shall not be rich.

Pr 27:1 — Boast not thyself of to morrow; for thou knowest not what a day may bring forth.

Pr 27:7 — The full soul loatheth an honeycomb; but to the hungry soul every bitter thing is sweet.

Ecc 1:8 — All things *are* full of labour; man cannot utter *it:* the eye is not satisfied with seeing, nor the ear filled with hearing.

Ecc 10:19 — A feast is made for laughter, and wine maketh merry: but money answereth all *things.*

Isa 28:4 — And the glorious beauty, which is on the head of the fat valley, shall be a fading flower, *and* as the hasty fruit before the summer; which *when* he that looketh upon it seeth, while it is yet in his hand he eateth it up.

Hos 9:1 — Rejoice not, O Israel, for joy, as *other* people: for thou hast gone a whoring from thy God, thou hast loved a reward upon every cornfloor.

Hos 9:11 — *As for* Ephraim, their glory shall fly away like a bird, from the birth, and from the womb, and from the conception.

Hos 9:13 — Ephraim, as I saw Tyrus, *is* planted in a pleasant place: but Ephraim shall bring forth his children to the murderer.

Am 8:10 — And I will turn your feasts into mourning, and all your songs into lamentation; and I will bring up sackcloth upon all loins, and baldness upon every head; and I will make it as the mourning of an only *son,* and the end thereof as a bitter day.

Mic 2:10 — Arise ye, and depart; for this *is* not *your* rest: because it is polluted, it shall destroy *you,* even with a sore destruction.

Mic 6:14 — Thou shalt eat, but not be satisfied; and thy casting down *shall be* in the midst of thee; and thou shalt take hold, but shalt not deliver; and *that* which thou deliverest will I give up to the sword.

Hag 1:6 — Ye have sown much, and bring in little; ye eat, but ye have not enough; ye drink, but ye are not filled with drink; ye clothe you, but there is none warm; and he that earneth wages earneth wages *to put it* into a bag with holes.

Mt 10:39 — He that findeth his life shall lose it: and he that loseth his life for my sake shall find it.

Mt 13:22 — He also that received seed among the thorns is he that heareth the word; and the care of this world, and the deceitfulness of riches, choke the word, and he becometh unfruitful.

Mk 4:19 — And the cares of this world, and the deceitfulness of riches, and the lusts of other things entering in, choke the word, and it becometh unfruitful.

Lk 8:14 — And that which fell among thorns are they, which, when they have heard, go forth, and are choked with cares and riches and pleasures of *this* life, and bring no fruit to perfection.

Lk 12:19 — And I will say to my soul, Soul, thou hast much goods laid up for many years; take thine ease, eat, drink, *and* be merry.

Lk 17:33 — Whosoever shall seek to save his life shall lose it; and whosoever shall lose his life shall preserve it.

Lk 21:34 — And take heed to yourselves, lest at any time your hearts be overcharged with surfeiting, and drunkenness, and cares of this life, and so that day come upon you unawares.

Jn 5:44 — How can ye believe, which receive honour one of another, and seek not the honour that *cometh* from God only?

Jn 12:25 — He that loveth his life shall lose it; and he that hateth his life in this world shall keep it unto life eternal.

Jn 12:43 — For they loved the praise of men more than the praise of God.

Jn 15:19 — If ye were of the world, the world would love his own: but because ye are not of the world, but I have chosen you out of the world, therefore the world hateth you.

Ro 12:2 — And be not conformed to this world: but be ye transformed by the renewing of your mind, that ye may prove what is that good, and acceptable, and perfect, will of God.

1Co 10:6 — Now these things were our examples, to the intent we should not lust after evil things, as they also lusted.

1Co 15:32 — If after the manner of men I have fought with beasts at Ephesus, what advantageth it me, if the dead rise not? let us eat and drink; for to morrow we die.

Col 3:2 — Set your affection on things above, not on things on the earth.

Col 3:5 — Mortify therefore your members which are upon the earth; fornication, uncleanness, inordinate affection, evil concupiscence, and covetousness, which is idolatry:

1Ti 5:6 — But she that liveth in pleasure is dead while she liveth.

2Ti 2:4 — No man that warreth entangleth himself with the affairs of *this* life; that he may please him who hath chosen him to be a soldier.

2Ti 2:22 — Flee also youthful lusts: but follow righteousness, faith, charity, peace, with them that call on the Lord out of a pure heart.

Tit 2:12 — Teaching us that, denying ungodliness and worldly lusts, we should live soberly, righteously, and godly, in this present world;

Tit 3:3 — For we ourselves also were sometimes foolish, disobedient, deceived, serving divers lusts and pleasures, living in malice and envy, hateful, *and* hating one another.

Jas 4:4 — Ye adulterers and adulteresses, know ye not that the friendship of the world is enmity with God? whosoever therefore will be a friend of the world is the enemy of God.

Jas 4:9 — Be afflicted, and mourn, and weep: let your laughter be turned to mourning, and *your* joy to heaviness.

Jas 5:5 — Ye have lived in pleasure on the earth, and been wanton; ye have nourished your hearts, as in a day of slaughter.

1Pe 1:14 — As obedient children, not fashioning yourselves according to the former lusts in your ignorance:

1Pe 1:24 — For all flesh *is* as grass, and all the glory of man as the flower of grass. The grass withereth, and the flower thereof falleth away:

1Pe 2:11 — Dearly beloved, I beseech *you* as strangers and pilgrims, abstain from fleshly lusts, which war against the soul;

2Pe 2:18 — For when they speak great swelling *words* of vanity, they allure through the lusts of the flesh, *through much* wantonness, those that were clean escaped from them who live in error.

Jude 1:16 — These are murmurers, complainers, walking after their own lusts; and their mouth speaketh great swelling *words,* having men's persons in admiration because of advantage.

Jude 1:19 — These be they who separate themselves, sensual, having not the Spirit.

See: Covetousness

See: Pleasure

See: Riches

- **Instances of.**
  - **Esau.**
    Ge 25:30–34; Heb 12:16
  - **Jacob.**
    Ge 25:31–34; 27:36; 30:37–43
  - **Judah.**
    Ge 37:26–27
  - **Israelites.**
    Nu 11:33–34; Ps 78:18, 29–31
  - **Balaam.**
    Nu 22:1–24:25; 2Pe 2:15; Jude 1:11
  - **Eli's sons.**
    1Sa 2:12–17
  - **Gehazi.**
    2Ki 5:21–27
  - **Herod.**
    Mt 14:6–7
  - **Cretians.**
    Tit 1:12

WORM

Ex 16:20 — Notwithstanding they hearkened not unto Moses; but some of them left of it until the morning, and it bred worms, and stank: and Moses was wroth with them.

Ex 16:24 — And they laid it up till the morning, as Moses bade: and it did not stink, neither was there any worm therein.

Jnh 4:7 — But God prepared a worm when the morning rose the next day, and it smote the gourd that it withered.

- **Herod eaten of.**

  Ac 12:23 — And immediately the angel of the Lord smote him, because he gave not God the glory: and he was eaten of worms, and gave up the ghost.

- **Figurative.**

  Job 25:6 — How much less man, *that is* a worm? and the son of man, *which is* a worm?

Isa 41:14 — Fear not, thou worm Jacob, *and* ye men of Israel; I will help thee, saith the LORD, and thy redeemer, the Holy One of Israel.

Isa 66:24 — And they shall go forth, and look upon the carcases of the men that have transgressed against me: for their worm shall not die, neither shall their fire be quenched; and they shall be an abhorring unto all flesh.

• Of remorse.

Mk 9:44 — Where their worm dieth not, and the fire is not quenched.

Mk 9:46 — Where their worm dieth not, and the fire is not quenched.

Mk 9:48 — Where their worm dieth not, and the fire is not quenched.

WORMWOOD

• A bitter plant.

Dt 29:18 — Lest there should be among you man, or woman, or family, or tribe, whose heart turneth away this day from the LORD our God, to go *and* serve the gods of these nations; lest there should be among you a root that beareth gall and wormwood;

• Figurative.

Dt 29:18 — Lest there should be among you man, or woman, or family, or tribe, whose heart turneth away this day from the LORD our God, to go *and* serve the gods of these nations; lest there should be among you a root that beareth gall and wormwood;

Pr 5:4 — But her end is bitter as wormwood, sharp as a twoedged sword.

Jer 9:15 — Therefore thus saith the LORD of hosts, the God of Israel; Behold, I will feed them, *even* this people, with wormwood, and give them water of gall to drink.

Jer 23:15 — Therefore thus saith the LORD of hosts concerning the prophets; Behold, I will feed them with wormwood, and make them drink the water of gall: for from the prophets of Jerusalem is profaneness gone forth into all the land.

La 3:19 — Remembering mine affliction and my misery, the wormwood and the gall.

• Symbolic.

Rev 8:11 — And the name of the star is called Wormwood: and the third part of the waters became wormwood; and many men died of the waters, because they were made bitter.

WORRY

Mt 6:25–34; 10:16–42

Ps 127:2 — *It is* vain for you to rise up early, to sit up late, to eat the bread of sorrows: *for* so he giveth his beloved sleep.

Php 4:6 — Be careful for nothing; but in every thing by prayer and supplication with thanksgiving let your requests be made known unto God.

1Pe 5:7 — Casting all your care upon him; for he careth for you.

WORSHIP

• To be rendered to God only.

Ex 20:3 — Thou shalt have no other gods before me.

Dt 5:7 — Thou shalt have none other gods before me.

Dt 6:13 — Thou shalt fear the LORD thy God, and serve him, and shalt swear by his name.

Mt 4:10 — Then saith Jesus unto him, Get thee hence, Satan: for it is written, Thou shalt worship the Lord thy God, and him only shalt thou serve.

Lk 4:8 — And Jesus answered and said unto him, Get thee behind me, Satan: for it is written, Thou shalt worship the Lord thy God, and him only shalt thou serve.

Ac 10:26 — But Peter took him up, saying, Stand up; I myself also am a man.

Ac 14:15 — And saying, Sirs, why do ye these things? We also are men of like passions with you, and preach unto you that ye should turn from these vanities unto the living God, which made heaven, and earth, and the sea, and all things that are therein:

Col 2:18 — Let no man beguile you of your reward in a voluntary humility and worshipping of angels, intruding into those things which he hath not seen, vainly puffed up by his fleshly mind,

Rev 19:10 — And I fell at his feet to worship him. And he said unto me, See *thou do it* not: I am thy fellowservant, and of thy brethren that have the testimony of Jesus: worship God: for the testimony of Jesus is the spirit of prophecy.

Rev 22:8 — And I John saw these things, and heard *them*. And when I had heard and seen, I fell down to worship before the feet of the angel which shewed me these things.

• Of Jesus.

See: Jesus, Worship of

• Acceptable to God.

Ge 4:4 — And Abel, he also brought of the firstlings of his flock and of the fat thereof. And the LORD had respect unto Abel and to his offering:

Ge 8:21 — And the LORD smelled a sweet savour; and the LORD said in his heart, I will not again curse the ground any more for man's sake; for the imagination of man's heart *is* evil from his youth; neither will I again smite any more every thing living, as I have done.

• Of the wicked rejected.

Ge 4:5 — But unto Cain and to his offering he had not respect. And Cain was very wroth, and his countenance fell.

Ge 4:7 — If thou doest well, shalt thou not be accepted? and if thou doest not well, sin lieth at the door. And unto thee *shall be* his desire, and thou shalt rule over him.

See: Prayer; of the wicked not heard

• "Iniquity of the holy things".

Ex 28:38 — And it shall be upon Aaron's forehead, that Aaron may bear the iniquity of the holy things, which the children of Israel shall hallow in all their holy gifts; and it shall be always upon his forehead, that they may be accepted before the LORD.

• Public, in the temple.

Jer 26:2 — Thus saith the LORD; Stand in the court of the LORD'S house, and speak unto all the cities of Judah, which come to worship in the LORD'S house, all the words that I command thee to speak unto them; diminish not a word:

Lk 18:10 — Two men went up into the temple to pray; the one a Pharisee, and the other a publican.

Lk 24:53 — And were continually in the temple, praising and blessing God. Amen.

• David's ordinances for.

1Ch 23:1–26:32

• Family.

Dt 16:11 — And thou shalt rejoice before the LORD thy God, thou, and thy son, and thy daughter, and thy manservant, and thy maidservant, and the Levite that *is* within thy gates, and the stranger, and the fatherless, and the widow, that *are* among you, in the place which the LORD thy God hath chosen to place his name there.

Dt 16:14 — And thou shalt rejoice in thy feast, thou, and thy son, and thy daughter, and thy manservant, and thy maidservant, and the Levite, the stranger, and the fatherless, and the widow, that *are* within thy gates.

• Family of Abraham.

Ge 12:7–8

Ge 13:4 — Unto the place of the altar, which he had made there at the first: and there Abram called on the name of the LORD.

Ge 13:18 — Then Abram removed *his* tent, and came and dwelt in the plain of Mamre, which *is* in Hebron, and built there an altar unto the LORD.

• Family of Jacob.

Ge 35:2–3

• Family of Job.

Job 1:5 — And it was so, when the days of *their* feasting were gone about, that Job sent and sanctified them, and rose up early in the morning, and offered burnt offerings *according* to the number of them all: for Job said, It may be that my sons have sinned, and cursed God in their hearts. Thus did Job continually.

• Family of the Philippian jailer.

Ac 16:34 — And when he had brought them into his house, he set meat before them, and rejoiced, believing in God with all his house.

• In private homes.

Ac 1:13–14; 20:7–9

Ac 5:42 — And daily in the temple, and in every house, they ceased not to teach and preach Jesus Christ.

Ac 12:12 — And when he had considered *the thing,* he came to the house of Mary the mother of John, whose surname was Mark; where many were gathered together praying.

Ro 16:5 — Likewise *greet* the church that is in their house. Salute my wellbeloved Epaenetus, who is the firstfruits of Achaia unto Christ.

1Co 16:19 — The churches of Asia salute you. Aquila and Priscilla salute you much in the Lord, with the church that is in their house.

Col 4:15 — Salute the brethren which are in Laodicea, and Nymphas, and the church which is in his house.

Phm 1:2 — And to *our* beloved Apphia, and Archippus our fellowsoldier, and to the church in thy house:

• In the night.

Isa 30:29 — Ye shall have a song, as in the night *when* a holy solemnity is kept; and gladness of heart, as when one goeth with a pipe to come into the mountain of the LORD, to the mighty One of Israel.

Ac 16:25 — And at midnight Paul and Silas prayed, and sang praises unto God: and the prisoners heard them.

• Jesus prays a whole night.

Lk 6:12 — And it came to pass in those days, that he went out into a mountain to pray, and continued all night in prayer to God.

• Attitudes in.

• Bowing.

Ex 34:8 — And Moses made haste, and bowed his head toward the earth, and worshipped.

2Ch 20:18 — And Jehoshaphat bowed his head with *his* face to the ground: and all Judah and the inhabitants of Jerusalem fell before the LORD, worshipping the LORD.

• Prostration.

Ge 17:3 — And Abram fell on his face: and God talked with him, saying,

Mk 3:11 — And unclean spirits, when they saw him, fell down before him, and cried, saying, Thou art the Son of God.

• Prayer in.

See: Prayer

• God's presence in.

Le 19:30 — Ye shall keep my sabbaths, and reverence my sanctuary: I *am* the LORD.

Ps 77:13 — Thy way, O God, *is* in the sanctuary: who *is so* great a God as *our* God?

Ps 84:4 — Blessed *are* they that dwell in thy house: they will be still praising thee. Selah.

Isa 56:7 — Even them will I bring to my holy mountain, and make them joyful in my house of prayer: their burnt offerings and their sacrifices *shall be* accepted upon mine altar; for mine house shall be called an house of prayer for all people.

Heb 10:25 — Not forsaking the assembling of ourselves together, as the manner of some *is;* but exhorting *one another:* and so much the more, as ye see the day approaching.

• Loved by his people.

Ps 84:1–3

Ps 27:4 — One *thing* have I desired of the LORD, that will I seek after; that I may dwell in the house of the LORD all the days of my life, to behold the beauty of the LORD, and to enquire in his temple.

Ps 84:10 — For a day in thy courts *is* better than a thousand. I had rather be a doorkeeper in the house of my God, than to dwell in the tents of wickedness.

Zec 8:21 — And the inhabitants of one *city* shall go to another, saying, Let us go speedily to pray before the LORD, and to seek the LORD of hosts: I will go also.

• Benedictions pronounced.

→See: Benedictions

• The whole nation required to assemble for, including men, women, children, servants, and strangers.

Dt 31:11–13

Dt 16:11 — And thou shalt rejoice before the LORD thy God, thou, and thy son, and thy daughter, and thy manservant, and thy maidservant, and the Levite that *is* within thy gates, and the stranger, and the fatherless, and the widow, that *are* among you, in the place which the LORD thy God hath chosen to place his name there.

• The whole nation required to assemble for in Mount Gerizim and Mount Ebal.

Jos 8:32–35

• The word of God read in public assemblies.

Dt 27:12–26; 31:11–13; Jos 8:33–35; 2Ki 23:1–3; Ne 8:1–8, 13–18; Lk 4:16–17

Ex 24:7 — And he took the book of the covenant, and read in the audience of the people: and they said, All that the LORD hath said will we do, and be obedient.

Mt 21:23 — And when he was come into the temple, the chief priests and the elders of the people came unto him as he was teaching, and said, By what authority doest thou these things? and who gave thee this authority?

• Of angels, forbidden.

Rev 22:8–9

Rev 19:10 — And I fell at his feet to worship him. And he said unto me, See *thou do it* not: I am thy fellowservant, and of thy brethren that have the testimony of Jesus: worship God: for the testimony of Jesus is the spirit of prophecy.

→See: Afflictions; prayer in
→See: Blasphemy
→See: Children
→See: Church
→See: Consecration
→See: Dedication
→See: Idolatry
→See: Instruction; in religion
→See: Levites
→See: Minister, a sacred teacher
→See: Minister, Miscellany of Minor Sub-Topics
→See: Music
→See: Offerings
→See: Praise
→See: Prayer
→See: Preaching
→See: Priest, Duties of
→See: Priest, High
→See: Psalms
→See: Religion
→See: Sacrilege
→See: Servant
→See: Strangers
→See: Tabernacle
→See: Temple
→See: Thanksgiving
→See: Women
→See: Word of God
→See: Young Men

• Unclassified scripture relating to.

Ge 35:2–3; Ex 3:5–6; 19:10–13, 21–24; 20:24–26; 24:1–2; 28:34–35; 30:19–21; 40:34–35; 1Ki 8:3–11; 2Ch 5:13–14; Ezr 3:10–13; Ps 24:3–6; 26:6–8; 63:1–2; 66:13–14; 84:1–4; 92:13–14; 98:2–3; 100:1–4; 103:1–4; 107:6–8; 116:12–14; 118:18–19; 126:1–3; 132:13–14; Ecc 5:1–2; Isa 1:11–15; 12:5–6; 29:13–16; 43:22–24; 56:6–7; 66:1–2; Jer 31:11–12; Am 5:21–24; Zec 8:21–22; Mal 3:3–4; Mt 18:19–20; Jn 4:23–24; Ac 2:1–4; 17:24–25; 1Co 11:20–22; 14:15–17; Rev 14:6–7

Ex 5:1 — And afterward Moses and Aaron went in, and told Pharaoh, Thus saith the LORD God of Israel, Let my people go, that they may hold a feast unto me in the wilderness.

Ex 15:2 — The LORD *is* my strength and song, and he is become my salvation: he *is* my God, and I will prepare him an habitation; my father's God, and I will exalt him.

Ex 17:4 — And Moses cried unto the LORD, saying, What shall I do unto this people? they be almost ready to stone me.

Ex 25:8 — And let them make me a sanctuary; that I may dwell among them.

Ex 25:22 — And there I will meet with thee, and I will commune with thee from above the mercy seat, from between the two cherubims which *are* upon the ark of the testimony, of all *things* which I will give thee in commandment unto the children of Israel.

Ex 29:43 — And there I will meet with the children of Israel, and *the tabernacle* shall be sanctified by my glory.

Ex 34:8 — And Moses made haste, and bowed his head toward the earth, and worshipped.

Le 10:3 — Then Moses said unto Aaron, This *is it* that the LORD spake, saying, I will be sanctified in them that come nigh me, and before all the people I will be glorified. And Aaron held his peace.

Le 16:2 — And the LORD said unto Moses, Speak unto Aaron thy brother, that he come not at all times into the holy *place* within the vail before the mercy seat, which *is* upon the ark; that he die not: for I will appear in the cloud upon the mercy seat.

Jos 5:15 — And the captain of the LORD's host said unto Joshua, Loose thy shoe from off thy foot; for the place whereon thou standest *is* holy. And Joshua did so.

2Ki 17:36 — But the LORD, who brought you up out of the land of Egypt with great power and a stretched out arm, him shall ye fear, and him shall ye worship, and to him shall ye do sacrifice.

1Ch 16:29 — Give unto the LORD the glory *due* unto his name: bring an offering, and come before him: worship the LORD in the beauty of holiness.

2Ch 7:1 — Now when Solomon had made an end of praying, the fire came down from heaven, and consumed the burnt offering and the sacrifices; and the glory of the LORD filled the house.

2Ch 30:27 — Then the priests the Levites arose and blessed the people: and their voice was heard, and their prayer came *up* to his holy dwelling place, *even* unto heaven.

Ne 10:39 — For the children of Israel and the children of Levi shall bring the offering of the corn, of the new wine, and the oil, unto the chambers, where *are* the vessels of the sanctuary, and the priests that minister, and the porters, and the singers: and we will not forsake the house of our God.

Ps 5:7 — But as for me, I will come *into* thy house in the multitude of thy mercy: *and* in thy fear will I worship toward thy holy temple.

Ps 22:22 — I will declare thy name unto my brethren: in the midst of the congregation will I praise thee.

Ps 27:4 — One *thing* have I desired of the LORD, that will I seek after; that I may dwell in the house of the LORD all the days of my life, to behold the beauty of the LORD, and to enquire in his temple.

Ps 29:2 — Give unto the LORD the glory due unto his name; worship the LORD in the beauty of holiness.

Ps 35:18 — I will give thee thanks in the great congregation: I will praise thee among much people.

Ps 36:8 — They shall be abundantly satisfied with the fatness of thy house; and thou shalt make them drink of the river of thy pleasures.

Ps 42:4 — When I remember these *things,* I pour out my soul in me: for I had gone with the multitude, I went with them to the house of God, with the voice of joy and praise, with a multitude that kept holyday.

Ps 48:9 — We have thought of thy lovingkindness, O God, in the midst of thy temple.

Ps 51:19 — Then shalt thou be pleased with the sacrifices of righteousness, with burnt offering and whole burnt offering: then shall they offer bullocks upon thine altar.

Ps 55:14 — We took sweet counsel together, *and* walked unto the house of God in company.

Ps 65:4 — Blessed *is the man whom* thou choosest, and causest to approach *unto thee, that* he may dwell in thy courts: we shall be satisfied with the goodness of thy house, *even* of thy holy temple.

Ps 66:4 — All the earth shall worship thee, and shall sing unto thee; they shall sing *to* thy name. Selah.

Ps 77:13 — Thy way, O God, *is* in the sanctuary: who *is so* great a God as *our* God?

Ps 84:10 — For a day in thy courts *is* better than a thousand. I had rather be a doorkeeper in the house of my God, than to dwell in the tents of wickedness.

Ps 89:7 — God is greatly to be feared in the assembly of the saints, and to be had in reverence of all *them that are* about him.

Ps 93:5 — Thy testimonies are very sure: holiness becometh thine house, O LORD, for ever.

Ps 95:6 — O come, let us worship and bow down: let us kneel before the LORD our maker.

Ps 107:32 — Let them exalt him also in the congregation of the people, and praise him in the assembly of the elders.

Ps 116:17 — I will offer to thee the sacrifice of thanksgiving, and will call upon the name of the LORD.

Ps 119:108 — Accept, I beseech thee, the freewill offerings of my mouth, O LORD, and teach me thy judgments.

Ps 122:1 — I was glad when they said unto me, Let us go into the house of the LORD.

Ps 132:7 — We will go into his tabernacles: we will worship at his footstool.

Ps 138:2 — I will worship toward thy holy temple, and praise thy name for thy lovingkindness and for thy truth: for thou hast magnified thy word above all thy name.

Ps 149:1 — Praise ye the LORD. Sing unto the LORD a new song, *and* his praise in the congregation of saints.

Isa 2:3 — And many people shall go and say, Come ye, and let us go up to the mountain of the LORD, to the house of the God of Jacob; and he will teach us of his ways, and we will walk in his paths: for out of Zion shall go forth the law, and the word of the LORD from Jerusalem.

Isa 4:5 — And the LORD will create upon every dwelling place of mount Zion, and upon her assemblies, a cloud and smoke by day, and the shining of a flaming fire by night: for upon all the glory *shall be* a defence.

Isa 25:9 — And it shall be said in that day, Lo, this *is* our God; we have waited for him, and he will save us: this *is* the LORD; we have waited for him, we will be glad and rejoice in his salvation.

Isa 30:29 — Ye shall have a song, as in the night *when* a holy solemnity is kept; and gladness of heart, as when one goeth with a pipe to come into the mountain of the LORD, to the mighty One of Israel.

Isa 38:20 — The LORD *was ready* to save me: therefore we will sing my songs to the stringed instruments all the days of our life in the house of the LORD.

Isa 40:31 — But they that wait upon the LORD shall renew *their* strength; they shall mount up with wings as eagles; they shall run, and not be weary; *and* they shall walk, and not faint.

Isa 49:13 — Sing, O heavens; and be joyful, O earth; and break forth into singing, O mountains: for the LORD hath comforted his people, and will have mercy upon his afflicted.

Isa 52:9 — Break forth into joy, sing together, ye waste places of Jerusalem: for the LORD hath comforted his people, he hath redeemed Jerusalem.

Eze 22:8 — Thou hast despised mine holy things, and hast profaned my sabbaths.

Hos 6:6 — For I desired mercy, and not sacrifice; and the knowledge of God more than burnt offerings.

Mic 4:2 — And many nations shall come, and say, Come, and let us go up to the mountain of the LORD, and to the house of the God of Jacob; and he will teach us of his ways, and we will walk in his paths: for the law shall go forth of Zion, and the word of the LORD from Jerusalem.

Hab 2:20 — But the LORD *is* in his holy temple: let all the earth keep silence before him.

Zep 3:18 — I will gather *them that are* sorrowful for the solemn assembly, *who* are of thee, *to whom* the reproach of it *was* a burden.

Lk 4:8 — And Jesus answered and said unto him, Get thee behind me, Satan: for it is written, Thou shalt worship the Lord thy God, and him only shalt thou serve.

1Co 11:13 — Judge in yourselves: is it comely that a woman pray unto God uncovered?

Php 3:3 — For we are the circumcision, which worship God in the spirit, and rejoice in Christ Jesus, and have no confidence in the flesh.

1Ti 2:8 — I will therefore that men pray every where, lifting up holy hands, without wrath and doubting.

Heb 10:25 — Not forsaking the assembling of ourselves together, as the manner of some *is;* but exhorting *one another:* and so much the more, as ye see the day approaching.

Heb 12:28 — Wherefore we receiving a kingdom which cannot be moved, let us have grace, whereby we may serve God acceptably with reverence and godly fear:

1Pe 2:5 — Ye also, as lively stones, are built up a spiritual house, an holy priesthood, to offer up spiritual sacrifices, acceptable to God by Jesus Christ.

Rev 11:1 — And there was given me a reed like unto a rod: and the angel stood, saying, Rise, and measure the temple of God, and the altar, and them that worship therein.

Rev 15:4 — Who shall not fear thee, O Lord, and glorify thy name? for *thou* only *art* holy: for all nations shall come and worship before thee; for thy judgments are made manifest.

See: Praise

See: Prayer

See: Thankfulness

• Enjoined.

Ex 23:17–18; Dt 12:5–7, 11–12; 16:6–8; 31:11–13; Ps 96:8–9; Joel 1:14–15; 2:15–17; Zec 14:16–18

Ge 35:1 — And God said unto Jacob, Arise, go up to Bethel, and dwell there: and make there an altar unto God, that appeared unto thee when thou fleddest from the face of Esau thy brother.

Ex 34:23 — Thrice in the year shall all your men children appear before the Lord GOD, the God of Israel.

Dt 33:19 — They shall call the people unto the mountain; there they shall offer sacrifices of righteousness: for they shall suck *of* the abundance of the seas, and *of* treasures hid in the sand.

2Ki 17:36 — But the LORD, who brought you up out of the land of Egypt with great power and a stretched out arm, him shall ye fear, and him shall ye worship, and to him shall ye do sacrifice.

Ps 45:11 — So shall the king greatly desire thy beauty: for he *is* thy Lord; and worship thou him.

Ps 76:11 — Vow, and pay unto the LORD your God: let all that be round about him bring presents unto him that ought to be feared.

Ps 97:7 — Confounded be all they that serve graven images, that boast themselves of idols: worship him, all *ye* gods.

Ps 99:5 — Exalt ye the LORD our God, and worship at his footstool; *for* he *is* holy.

Na 1:15 — Behold upon the mountains the feet of him that bringeth good tidings, that publisheth peace! O Judah, keep thy solemn feasts, perform thy vows: for the wicked shall no more pass through thee; he is utterly cut off.

Hag 1:8 — Go up to the mountain, and bring wood, and build the house; and I will take pleasure in it, and I will be glorified, saith the LORD.

Mt 8:4 — And Jesus saith unto him, See thou tell no man; but go thy way, shew thyself to the priest, and offer the gift that Moses commanded, for a testimony unto them.

Mk 1:44 — And saith unto him, See thou say nothing to any man: but go thy way, shew thyself to the priest, and offer for thy cleansing those things which Moses commanded, for a testimony unto them.

Lk 5:14 — And he charged him to tell no man: but go, and shew thyself to the priest, and offer for thy cleansing, according as Moses commanded, for a testimony unto them.

Heb 10:25 — Not forsaking the assembling of ourselves together, as the manner of some *is;* but exhorting *one another:* and so much the more, as ye see the day approaching.

Rev 14:7 — Saying with a loud voice, Fear God, and give glory to him; for the hour of his judgment is come: and worship him that made heaven, and earth, and the sea, and the fountains of waters.

Rev 19:10 — And I fell at his feet to worship him. And he said unto me, See *thou do it* not: I am thy fellowservant, and of thy brethren that have the testimony of Jesus: worship God: for the testimony of Jesus is the spirit of prophecy.

WOUNDS

• Treatment of.

Pr 20:30 — The blueness of a wound cleanseth away evil: so *do* stripes the inward parts of the belly.

Isa 1:6 — From the sole of the foot even unto the head *there is* no soundness in it; *but* wounds, and bruises, and putrifying sores: they have not been closed, neither bound up, neither mollified with ointment.

Lk 10:34 — And went to *him,* and bound up his wounds, pouring in oil and wine, and set him on his own beast, and brought him to an inn, and took care of him.

WRATH

See: Anger

See: God; Anger of

WRESTLING

• Figurative.

Ge 32:24–25

Ge 30:8 — And Rachel said, With great wrestlings have I wrestled with my sister, and I have prevailed: and she called his name Naphtali.

Eph 6:12 — For we wrestle not against flesh and blood, but against principalities, against powers, against the rulers of the darkness of this world, against spiritual wickedness in high *places.*

WRITING

• Copyists were called scribes.

See: Scribe

See: Book

See: Engraving

See: Ink

See: Inkhorn

See: Letters

See: Pen

See: Table; a slab on which inscriptions were made

Y

YARN

1Ki 10:28 — And Solomon had horses brought out of Egypt, and linen yarn: the king's merchants received the linen yarn at a price.

2Ch 1:16 — And Solomon had horses brought out of Egypt, and linen yarn: the king's merchants received the linen yarn at a price.

See: Weaving

YEAR

Ge 1:14 — And God said, Let there be lights in the firmament of the heaven to divide the day from the night; and let them be for signs, and for seasons, and for days, and years:

• Divided into months.

Ex 12:2 — This month *shall be* unto you the beginning of months: it *shall be* the first month of the year to you.

Nu 10:10 — Also in the day of your gladness, and in your solemn days, and in the beginnings of your months, ye shall blow with the trumpets over your burnt offerings, and over the sacrifices of your peace offerings; that they may be to you for a memorial before your God: I *am* the LORD your God.

Nu 28:11 — And in the beginnings of your months ye shall offer a burnt offering unto the LORD; two young bullocks, and one ram, seven lambs of the first year without spot;

See: Month

• Annual feasts.

Le 25:5 — That which groweth of its own accord of thy harvest thou shalt not reap, neither gather the grapes of thy vine undressed: *for* it is a year of rest unto the land.

See: Feasts

• Redemption of houses sold, limited to one.

Le 25:29–30

• Land to rest one, in seven.

Le 25:5 — That which groweth of its own accord of thy harvest thou shalt not reap, neither gather the grapes of thy vine undressed: *for* it is a year of rest unto the land.

• Of release.

Dt 15:9 — Beware that there be not a thought in thy wicked heart, saying, The seventh year, the year of release, is at hand; and thine eye be evil against thy poor brother, and thou givest him nought; and he cry unto the LORD against thee, and it be sin unto thee.

• Age computed by.

• Of Abraham.

Ge 25:7 — And these *are* the days of the years of Abraham's life which he lived, an hundred threescore and fifteen years.

• Of Jacob.

Ge 47:9 — And Jacob said unto Pharaoh, The days of the years of my pilgrimage *are* an hundred and thirty years: few and evil have the days of the years of my life been, and have not attained unto the days of the years of the life of my fathers in the days of their pilgrimage.

See: Longevity

• A thousand, with the Lord as one day.

Ps 90:4 — For a thousand years in thy sight *are but* as yesterday when it is past, and *as* a watch in the night.

2Pe 3:8 — But, beloved, be not ignorant of this one thing, that one day *is* with the Lord as a thousand years, and a thousand years as one day.

• Satan to be bound a thousand.

Rev 20:2–4

Rev 20:7 — And when the thousand years are expired, Satan shall be loosed out of his prison,

See: Jubilee

See: Millennium

See: Time

YOKE

• Figurative.

Mt 11:29–30

Le 26:13 — I *am* the LORD your God, which brought you forth out of the land of Egypt, that ye should not be their bondmen; and I have broken the bands of your yoke, and made you go upright.

Isa 9:4 — For thou hast broken the yoke of his burden, and the staff of his shoulder, the rod of his oppressor, as in the day of Midian.

Isa 10:27 — And it shall come to pass in that day, *that* his burden shall be taken away from off thy shoulder, and his yoke from off thy neck, and the yoke shall be destroyed because of the anointing.

Jer 2:20 — For of old time I have broken thy yoke, *and* burst thy bands; and thou saidst, I will not transgress; when upon every high hill and under every green tree thou wanderest, playing the harlot.

Jer 5:5 — I will get me unto the great men, and will speak unto them; for they have known the way of the LORD, *and* the judgment of their God: but these have altogether broken the yoke, *and* burst the bonds.

Jer 28:2 — Thus speaketh the LORD of hosts, the God of Israel, saying, I have broken the yoke of the king of Babylon.

Jer 28:4 — And I will bring again to this place Jeconiah the son of Jehoiakim king of Judah, with all the captives of Judah, that went into Babylon, saith the LORD: for I will break the yoke of the king of Babylon.

Jer 28:10 — Then Hananiah the prophet took the yoke from off the prophet Jeremiah's neck, and brake it.

Jer 30:8 — For it shall come to pass in that day, saith the LORD of hosts, *that* I will break his yoke from off thy neck, and will burst thy bonds, and strangers shall no more serve themselves of him:

La 1:14 — The yoke of my transgressions is bound by his hand: they are wreathed, *and* come up upon my neck: he hath made my strength to fall, the Lord hath delivered me into *their* hands, *from whom* I am not able to rise up.

La 3:27 — *It is* good for a man that he bear the yoke in his youth.

Ac 15:10 — Now therefore why tempt ye God, to put a yoke upon the neck of the disciples, which neither our fathers nor we were able to bear?

YOUNG MEN

Ex 24:3–5; 1Ki 12:6–15; Ps 148:12–13; Pr 1:1–7:27; 19:26–27; 23:15–24:34; 31:1–3; Jer 22:18–21; Mt 19:16–22; Mk 10:17–22; Lk 15:11–32; 18:18–23; 2Ti 2:22–23; Heb 11:24–26; 1Jn 2:13–17

2Ch 10:8 — But he forsook the counsel which the old men gave him, and took counsel with the young men that were brought up with him, that stood before him.

Ps 119:9 — Wherewithal shall a young man cleanse his way? by taking heed *thereto* according to thy word.

Pr 10:1 — The proverbs of Solomon. A wise son maketh a glad father: but a foolish son *is* the heaviness of his mother.

Pr 13:1 — A wise son *heareth* his father's instruction: but a scorner heareth not rebuke.

Pr 15:5 — A fool despiseth his father's instruction: but he that regardeth reproof is prudent.

Pr 15:20 — A wise son maketh a glad father: but a foolish man despiseth his mother.

Pr 17:2 — A wise servant shall have rule over a son that causeth shame, and shall have part of the inheritance among the brethren.

Pr 17:25 — A foolish son *is* a grief to his father, and bitterness to her that bare him.

Pr 19:13 — A foolish son *is* the calamity of his father: and the contentions of a wife *are* a continual dropping.

Pr 20:29 — The glory of young men *is* their strength: and the beauty of old men *is* the grey head.

Pr 27:11 — My son, be wise, and make my heart glad, that I may answer him that reproacheth me.

Pr 28:7 — Whoso keepeth the law *is* a wise son: but he that is a companion of riotous *men* shameth his father.

Pr 29:3 — Whoso loveth wisdom rejoiceth his father: but he that keepeth company with harlots spendeth *his* substance.

1Ti 4:12 — Let no man despise thy youth; but be thou an example of the believers, in word, in conversation, in charity, in spirit, in faith, in purity.

Tit 2:6 — Young men likewise exhort to be sober minded.

• Instances of religious.

✦See: David

✦See: Joseph, Son of Jacob

✦See: Joshua

✦See: Samuel

✦See: Solomon

✦See: Uriah

• The rich young man.

Mt 19:16–22; Mk 10:17–22; Lk 18:18–23

✦See: Children

✦See: Parents

Z

ZAANAIM

• Called also Zaanannim.

• A plain near Kedesh.

Jos 19:33 — And their coast was from Heleph, from Allon to Zaanannim, and Adami, Nekeb, and Jabneel, unto Lakum; and the outgoings thereof were at Jordan:

Jgs 4:11 — Now Heber the Kenite, *which was* of the children of Hobab the father in law of Moses, had severed himself from the Kenites, and pitched his tent unto the plain of Zaanaim, which *is* by Kedesh.

ZAANAN

• Called also Zenan.

• A place of uncertain location.

Jos 15:37 — Zenan, and Hadashah, and Migdal-gad,

Mic 1:11 — Pass ye away, thou inhabitant of Saphir, having thy shame naked: the inhabitant of Zaanan came not forth in the mourning of Beth-ezel; he shall receive of you his standing.

ZAANANNIM ✧See: Zaanaim

ZAAVAN

• Called also Zavan.

• A son of Ezer.

Ge 36:27 — The children of Ezer *are* these; Bilhan, and Zaavan, and Akan.

1Ch 1:42 — The sons of Ezer; Bilhan, and Zavan, *and* Jakan. The sons of Dishan; Uz, and Aran.

ZABAAI

• Son of Bebai.

Ezr 10:28 — Of the sons also of Bebai; Jehohanan, Hananiah, Zabbai, *and* Athlai.

• Father of Baruch.

Ne 3:20 — After him Baruch the son of Zabbai earnestly repaired the other piece, from the turning *of the wall* unto the door of the house of Eliashib the high priest.

ZABAD

• Son of Nathan.

1Ch 2:36–37

• An Ephraimite.

1Ch 7:21 — And Zabad his son, and Shuthelah his son, and Ezer, and Elead, whom the men of Gath *that were* born in *that* land slew, because they came down to take away their cattle.

• One of David's valiant men.

1Ch 11:41 — Uriah the Hittite, Zabad the son of Ahlai,

• An assassin of King Joash.

2Ch 25:3–4

2Ch 24:26 — And these are they that conspired against him; Zabad the son of Shimeath an Ammonitess, and Jehozabad the son of Shimrith a Moabitess.

• Called Jozachar.

2Ki 12:21 — For Jozachar the son of Shimeath, and Jehozabad the son of Shomer, his servants, smote him, and he died; and they buried him with his fathers in the city of David: and Amaziah his son reigned in his stead.

• Three Israelites who divorced their Gentile wives.

Ezr 10:27 — And of the sons of Zattu; Elioenai, Eliashib, Mattaniah, and Jeremoth, and Zabad, and Aziza.

Ezr 10:33 — Of the sons of Hashum; Mattenai, Mattathah, Zabad, Eliphelet, Jeremai, Manasseh, *and* Shimei.

Ezr 10:43 — Of the sons of Nebo; Jeiel, Mattithiah, Zabad, Zebina, Jadau, and Joel, Benaiah.

ZABBUD • A returned exile.

Ezr 8:14 — Of the sons also of Bigvai; Uthai, and Zabbud, and with them seventy males.

ZABDI

• Father of Carmi.

Jos 7:17–18

Jos 7:1 — But the children of Israel committed a trespass in the accursed thing: for Achan, the son of Carmi, the son of Zabdi, the son of Zerah, of the tribe of Judah, took of the accursed thing: and the anger of the LORD was kindled against the children of Israel.

• A Benjamite.

1Ch 8:19 — And Jakim, and Zichri, and Zabdi,

• David's storekeeper.

1Ch 27:27 — And over the vineyards was Shimei the Ramathite: over the increase of the vineyards for the wine cellars *was* Zabdi the Shiphmite:

• Son of Asaph.

Ne 11:17 — And Mattaniah the son of Micha, the son of Zabdi, the son of Asaph, *was* the principal to begin the thanksgiving in prayer: and Bakbukiah the second among his brethren, and Abda the son of Shammua, the son of Galal, the son of Jeduthun.

ZABDIEL

• Father of Jashobeam.

1Ch 27:2 — Over the first course for the first month *was* Jashobeam the son of Zabdiel: and in his course *were* twenty and four thousand.

• An overseer of one hundred and twenty-eight mighty men of valor, who dwelt in Jerusalem.

Ne 11:14 — And their brethren, mighty men of valour, an hundred twenty and eight: and their overseer *was* Zabdiel, the son of *one of* the great men.

ZABUD • A chief officer of Solomon.

1Ki 4:5 — And Azariah the son of Nathan *was* over the officers: and Zabud the son of Nathan *was* principal officer, *and* the king's friend:

ZABULON ↞See: Zebulun

ZACCAI • A Jew whose descendants returned from exile.

Ezr 2:9 — The children of Zaccai, seven hundred and threescore.

Ne 7:14 — The children of Zaccai, seven hundred and threescore.

ZACCHAEUS

• A collector of tribute in Jericho.

• Entertains Jesus.

Lk 19:1–10

ZACCHUR

• A Simeonite.

1Ch 4:26 — And the sons of Mishma; Hamuel his son, Zacchur his son, Shimei his son.

↞See: Zaccur

ZACCUR

• A Reubenite.

Nu 13:4 — And these *were* their names: of the tribe of Reuben, Shammua the son of Zaccur.

• Called also Zacchur.

↞See: Zacchur

• A Merarite.

1Ch 24:27 — The sons of Merari by Jaaziah; Beno, and Shoham, and Zaccur, and Ibri.

• Son of Asaph.

1Ch 25:2 — Of the sons of Asaph; Zaccur, and Joseph, and Nethaniah, and Asarelah, the sons of Asaph under the hands of Asaph, which prophesied according to the order of the king.

1Ch 25:10 — The third to Zaccur, *he,* his sons, and his brethren, *were* twelve:

Ne 12:35 — And *certain* of the priests' sons with trumpets; *namely,* Zechariah the son of Jonathan, the son of Shemaiah, the son of Mattaniah, the son of Michaiah, the son of Zaccur, the son of Asaph:

• Son of Imri.

Ne 3:2 — And next unto him builded the men of Jericho. And next to them builded Zaccur the son of Imri.

ZACHARIAH

• Son of Jeroboam, and last of the house of Jehu.

2Ki 15:8–12

2Ki 10:30 — And the LORD said unto Jehu, Because thou hast done well in executing *that which is* right in mine eyes, *and* hast done unto the house of Ahab according to all that *was* in mine heart, thy children of the fourth *generation* shall sit on the throne of Israel.

2Ki 14:29 — And Jeroboam slept with his fathers, *even* with the kings of Israel; and Zachariah his son reigned in his stead.

• Grandfather of Hezekiah.

2Ki 18:2 — Twenty and five years old was he when he began to reign; and he reigned twenty and nine years in Jerusalem. His mother's name also *was* Abi, the daughter of Zachariah.

2Ch 29:1 — Hezekiah began to reign *when he was* five and twenty years old, and he reigned nine and twenty years in Jerusalem. And his mother's name *was* Abijah, the daughter of Zechariah.

ZACHARIAS

• A man slain by the Jews.

• Referred to by Jesus.

Mt 23:35 — That upon you may come all the righteous blood shed upon the earth, from the blood of righteous Abel unto the blood of Zacharias son of Barachias, whom ye slew between the temple and the altar.

Lk 11:51 — From the blood of Abel unto the blood of Zacharias, which perished between the altar and the temple: verily I say unto you, It shall be required of this generation.

• Father of John the Baptist.

Lk 1:5–80

Lk 3:2 — Annas and Caiaphas being the high priests, the word of God came unto John the son of Zacharias in the wilderness.

↞See: Elisabeth

↞See: John, the Baptist

ZACHER

• A Benjamite.

1Ch 8:31 — And Gedor, and Ahio, and Zacher.

• Called Zechariah.

1Ch 9:37 — And Gedor, and Ahio, and Zechariah, and Mikloth.

ZADOK

• High priest in time of David's reign.

2Sa 19:11 — And king David sent to Zadok and to Abiathar the priests, saying, Speak unto the elders of Judah, saying, Why are ye the last to bring the king back to his house? seeing the speech of all Israel is come to the king, *even* to his house.

2Sa 20:25 — And Sheva *was* scribe: and Zadok and Abiathar *were* the priests:

1Ch 15:11 — And David called for Zadok and Abiathar the priests, and for the Levites, for Uriel, Asaiah, and Joel, Shemaiah, and Eliel, and Amminadab,

1Ch 16:39 — And Zadok the priest, and his brethren the priests, before the tabernacle of the LORD in the high place that *was* at Gibeon,

• Removes the ark from Jerusalem at the time of Absalom's usurpation; returns with it at David's command.

2Sa 15:24–36; 17:17–21

2Sa 17:15 — Then said Hushai unto Zadok and to Abiathar the priests, Thus and thus did Ahithophel counsel Absalom and the elders of Israel; and thus and thus have I counselled.

• Stands aloof from Adonijah at the time of his attempted usurpation.

1Ki 1:8 — But Zadok the priest, and Benaiah the son of Jehoiada, and Nathan the prophet, and Shimei, and Rei, and the mighty men which *belonged* to David, were not with Adonijah.

1Ki 1:26 — But me, *even* me thy servant, and Zadok the priest, and Benaiah the son of Jehoiada, and thy servant Solomon, hath he not called.

• Summoned by David to anoint Solomon.

1Ki 1:32–40, 44–45

• Performs the function of high priest after Abiathar was deposed by Solomon.

1Ki 2:35 — And the king put Benaiah the son of Jehoiada in his room over the host: and Zadok the priest did the king put in the room of Abiathar.

1Ch 29:22 — And did eat and drink before the LORD on that day with great gladness. And they made Solomon the son of David king the second time, and anointed *him* unto the LORD *to be* the chief governor, and Zadok *to be* priest.

• Father of Jerusha.

2Ki 15:33 — Five and twenty years old was he when he began to reign, and he reigned sixteen years in Jerusalem. And his mother's name *was* Jerusha, the daughter of Zadok.

2Ch 27:1 — Jotham *was* twenty and five years old when he began to reign, and he reigned sixteen years in Jerusalem. His mother's name also *was* Jerushah, the daughter of Zadok.

• Son of Ahitub.

1Ch 6:12 — And Ahitub begat Zadok, and Zadok begat Shallum,

• A man of valor.

1Ch 12:28 — And Zadok, a young man mighty of valour, and of his father's house twenty and two captains.

• Son of Baana.

Ne 3:4 — And next unto them repaired Meremoth the son of Urijah, the son of Koz. And next unto them repaired Meshullam the son of Berechiah, the son of Meshezabeel. And next unto them repaired Zadok the son of Baana.

• A priest.

Ne 3:29 — After them repaired Zadok the son of Immer over against his house. After him repaired also Shemaiah the son of Shechaniah, the keeper of the east gate.

• A returned exile.

Ne 10:21 — Meshezabeel, Zadok, Jaddua,

• Son of Meraioth.

Ne 11:11 — Seraiah the son of Hilkiah, the son of Meshullam, the son of Zadok, the son of Meraioth, the son of Ahitub, *was* the ruler of the house of God.

• A treasurer of the temple.

Ne 13:13 — And I made treasurers over the treasuries, Shelemiah the priest, and Zadok the scribe, and of the Levites, Pedaiah: and next to them *was* Hanan the son of Zaccur, the son of Mattaniah: for they were counted faithful, and their office *was* to distribute unto their brethren.

ZAHAM • Grandson of Solomon.

2Ch 11:19 — Which bare him children; Jeush, and Shamariah, and Zaham.

ZAIR • A city in Edom.

2Ki 8:21 — So Joram went over to Zair, and all the chariots with him: and he rose by night, and smote the Edomites which compassed him about, and the captains of the chariots: and the people fled into their tents.

ZALAPH • Father of Hanun.

Ne 3:30 — After him repaired Hananiah the son of Shelemiah, and Hanun the sixth son of Zalaph, another piece. After him repaired Meshullam the son of Berechiah over against his chamber.

ZALMON

• A hill in Samaria.

Jgs 9:48 — And Abimelech gat him up to mount Zalmon, he and all the people that *were* with him; and Abimelech took an axe in his hand, and cut down a bough from the trees, and took it, and laid *it* on his shoulder, and said unto the people that *were* with him, What ye have seen me do, make haste, *and* do as I *have done.*

• Called also Salmon, probably.

Ps 68:14 — When the Almighty scattered kings in it, it was *white* as snow in Salmon.

• One of David's warriors.

2Sa 23:28 — Zalmon the Ahohite, Maharai the Netophathite,

ZALMONAH • One of the camping places of Israel.

Nu 33:41–42

ZALMUNNA • King of Midian.

Jgs 8:5–21

Ps 83:11 — Make their nobles like Oreb, and like Zeeb: yea, all their princes as Zebah, and as Zalmunna:

ZAMZUMMIMS

• Called also Zuzims.

• A race of giants.

Dt 2:20–21

Ge 14:5 — And in the fourteenth year came Chedorlaomer, and the kings that *were* with him, and smote the Rephaims in Ashteroth Karnaim, and the Zuzims in Ham, and the Emims in Shaveh Kiriathaim,

ZANOAH

• A city of western Judah.

Jos 15:34 — And Zanoah, and En-gannim, Tappuah, and Enam,

Ne 3:13 — The valley gate repaired Hanun, and the inhabitants of Zanoah; they built it, and set up the doors thereof, the locks thereof, and the bars thereof, and a thousand cubits on the wall unto the dung gate.

Ne 11:30 — Zanoah, Adullam, and *in* their villages, at Lachish, and the fields thereof, at Azekah, and *in* the villages thereof. And they dwelt from Beer-sheba unto the valley of Hinnom.

• A city of eastern Judah.

Jos 15:56 — And Jezreel, and Jokdeam, and Zanoah,

• A descendant of Caleb.

1Ch 4:18 — And his wife Jehudijah bare Jered the father of Gedor, and Heber the father of Socho, and Jekuthiel the father of Zanoah. And these *are* the sons of Bithiah the daughter of Pharaoh, which Mered took.

ZAPHNATH-PAANEAH • A name given to Joseph by Pharaoh.

Ge 41:45 — And Pharaoh called Joseph's name Zaphnath-paaneah; and he gave him to wife Asenath the daughter of Poti-pherah priest of On. And Joseph went out over *all* the land of Egypt.

ZAPHON • A city in Gad.

Jos 13:27 — And in the valley, Beth-aram, and Beth-nimrah, and Succoth, and Zaphon, the rest of the kingdom of Sihon king of Heshbon, Jordan and *his* border, *even* unto the edge of the sea of Chinnereth on the other side Jordan eastward.

ZARA

• Called also Zarah.

• Son of Judah.

Mt 1:3 — And Judas begat Phares and Zara of Thamar; and Phares begat Esrom; and Esrom begat Aram;

ZARAH

• Called also Zerah and Zara.

• Son of Judah and Tamar.

Ge 38:30 — And afterward came out his brother, that had the scarlet thread upon his hand: and his name was called Zarah.

Ge 46:12 — And the sons of Judah; Er, and Onan, and Shelah, and Pharez, and Zarah: but Er and Onan died in the land of Canaan. And the sons of Pharez were Hezron and Hamul.

Nu 26:20 — And the sons of Judah after their families were; of Shelah, the family of the Shelanites: of Pharez, the family of the Pharzites: of Zerah, the family of the Zarhites.

1Ch 2:4 — And Tamar his daughter in law bare him Pharez and Zerah. All the sons of Judah *were* five.

1Ch 2:6 — And the sons of Zerah; Zimri, and Ethan, and Heman, and Calcol, and Dara: five of them in all.

Ne 11:24 — And Pethahiah the son of Meshezabeel, of the children of Zerah the son of Judah, *was* at the king's hand in all matters concerning the people.

ZAREAH

• A city of Judah.

Ne 11:29 — And at En-rimmon, and at Zareah, and at Jarmuth,

See: Zorah

ZARED

• Called also Zered.

• A brook.

Dt 2:13–14

Nu 21:12 — From thence they removed, and pitched in the valley of Zared.

ZAREPHATH

• A city between Tyre and Sidon.

• Elijah performs two miracles in.

1Ki 17:8–24

• Called Sarepta.

Lk 4:26 — But unto none of them was Elias sent, save unto Sarepta, *a city* of Sidon, unto a woman *that was* a widow.

ZARETAN

• Probably identical with Zartanah and Zarthan.

• A city of uncertain location.

Jos 3:16 — That the waters which came down from above stood *and* rose up upon an heap very far from the city Adam, that *is* beside Zaretan: and those that came down toward the sea of the plain, *even* the salt sea, failed, *and* were cut off: and the people passed over right against Jericho.

1Ki 4:12 — Baana the son of Ahilud; *to him pertained* Taanach and Megiddo, and all Beth-shean, which is by Zartanah beneath Jezreel, from Beth-shean to Abel-meholah, *even* unto *the place that is* beyond Jokneam:

1Ki 7:46 — In the plain of Jordan did the king cast them, in the clay ground between Succoth and Zarthan.

ZARETH-SHAHAR • A city in Reuben.

Jos 13:19 — And Kirjathaim, and Sibmah, and Zareth-shahar in the mount of the valley,

ZATTHU See: Zattu

ZATTU

• One whose descendants returned with Zerubbabel.

Ezr 2:8 — The children of Zattu, nine hundred forty and five.

Ezr 10:27 — And of the sons of Zattu; Elioenai, Eliashib, Mattaniah, and Jeremoth, and Zabad, and Aziza.

Ne 7:13 — The children of Zattu, eight hundred forty and five.

• Probably identical with Zatthu.

• One who sealed the covenant with Nehemiah.

Ne 10:14 — The chief of the people; Parosh, Pahath-moab, Elam, Zatthu, Bani,

ZAVAN ✦See: Zaavan

ZAZA • Son of Jonathan.

1Ch 2:33 — And the sons of Jonathan; Peleth, and Zaza. These were the sons of Jerahmeel.

ZEAL, Religious

Jos 24:15–16; 2Sa 24:24–25; Ps 42:1–2; 96:2–3; Isa 62:6–7; Hag 2:4–5; Zec 14:20–21; Mt 5:13–16; Mk 4:21–22; Lk 8:16–17; 22:32–33; Ro 1:8–9; 1Co 7:29–34; 2Co 4:8–10, 16–18; Eph 5:15–16; 6:14–20; Php 1:27–28; 3:4–14; Heb 11:15–16, 24–27; 13:13–15; Jas 5:19–20; 2Pe 1:10–11; Jude 1:22–23; Rev 5:4–5

1Ki 9:4 — And if thou wilt walk before me, as David thy father walked, in integrity of heart, and in uprightness, to do according to all that I have commanded thee, *and* wilt keep my statutes and my judgments:

1Ki 15:14 — But the high places were not removed: nevertheless Asa's heart was perfect with the LORD all his days.

1Ch 29:17 — I know also, my God, that thou triest the heart, and hast pleasure in uprightness. As for me, in the uprightness of mine heart I have willingly offered all these things: and now have I seen with joy thy people, which are present here, to offer willingly unto thee.

2Ch 15:15 — And all Judah rejoiced at the oath: for they had sworn with all their heart, and sought him with their whole desire; and he was found of them: and the LORD gave them rest round about.

2Ch 19:3 — Nevertheless there are good things found in thee, in that thou hast taken away the groves out of the land, and hast prepared thine heart to seek God.

Ezr 7:23 — Whatsoever is commanded by the God of heaven, let it be diligently done for the house of the God of heaven: for why should there be wrath against the realm of the king and his sons?

Job 16:19 — Also now, behold, my witness *is* in heaven, and my record *is* on high.

Ps 60:4 — Thou hast given a banner to them that fear thee, that it may be displayed because of the truth. Selah.

Ps 96:10 — Say among the heathen *that* the LORD reigneth: the world also shall be established that it shall not be moved: he shall judge the people righteously.

Ps 119:139 — My zeal hath consumed me, because mine enemies have forgotten thy words.

Pr 11:30 — The fruit of the righteous *is* a tree of life; and he that winneth souls *is* wise.

Ecc 9:10 — Whatsoever thy hand findeth to do, do *it* with thy might; for *there is* no work, nor device, nor knowledge, nor wisdom, in the grave, whither thou goest.

Isa 58:12 — And *they that shall be* of thee shall build the old waste places: thou shalt raise up the foundations of many generations; and thou shalt be called, The repairer of the breach, The restorer of paths to dwell in.

Isa 60:1 — Arise, shine; for thy light is come, and the glory of the LORD is risen upon thee.

Da 12:3 — And they that be wise shall shine as the brightness of the firmament; and they that turn many to righteousness as the stars for ever and ever.

Mic 5:7 — And the remnant of Jacob shall be in the midst of many people as a dew from the LORD, as the showers upon the grass, that tarrieth not for man, nor waiteth for the sons of men.

Hab 2:2 — And the LORD answered me, and said, Write the vision, and make *it* plain upon tables, that he may run that readeth it.

Jn 6:27 — Labour not for the meat which perisheth, but for that meat which endureth unto everlasting life, which the Son of man shall give unto you: for him hath God the Father sealed.

Jn 9:4 — I must work the works of him that sent me, while it is day: the night cometh, when no man can work.

Ac 10:42 — And he commanded us to preach unto the people, and to testify that it is he which was ordained of God *to be* the Judge of quick and dead.

Ac 26:29 — And Paul said, I would to God, that not only thou, but also all that hear me this day, were both almost, and altogether such as I am, except these bonds.

Ro 7:22 — For I delight in the law of God after the inward man:

Ro 12:11 — Not slothful in business; fervent in spirit; serving the Lord;

1Co 5:8 — Therefore let us keep the feast, not with old leaven, neither with the leaven of malice and wickedness; but with the unleavened *bread* of sincerity and truth.

1Co 13:3 — And though I bestow all my goods to feed *the poor,* and though I give my body to be burned, and have not charity, it profiteth me nothing.

1Co 14:12 — Even so ye, forasmuch as ye are zealous of spiritual *gifts,* seek that ye may excel to the edifying of the church.

1Co 15:58 — Therefore, my beloved brethren, be ye stedfast, unmovable, always abounding in the work of the Lord, forasmuch as ye know that your labour is not in vain in the Lord.

2Co 4:13 — We having the same spirit of faith, according as it is written, I believed, and therefore have I spoken; we also believe, and therefore speak;

2Co 7:11 — For behold this selfsame thing, that ye sorrowed after a godly sort, what carefulness it wrought in you, yea, *what* clearing of yourselves, yea, *what* indignation, yea, *what* fear, yea, *what* vehement desire, yea, *what* zeal, yea, *what* revenge! In all *things* ye have approved yourselves to be clear in this matter.

2Co 9:2 — For I know the forwardness of your mind, for which I boast of you to them of Macedonia, that Achaia was ready a year ago; and your zeal hath provoked very many.

Gal 4:18 — But *it is* good to be zealously affected always in *a* good *thing*, and not only when I am present with you.

Gal 6:9 — And let us not be weary in well doing: for in due season we shall reap, if we faint not.

Php 2:15 — That ye may be blameless and harmless, the sons of God, without rebuke, in the midst of a crooked and perverse nation, among whom ye shine as lights in the world;

Php 3:20 — For our conversation is in heaven; from whence also we look for the Saviour, the Lord Jesus Christ:

Col 4:5 — Walk in wisdom toward them that are without, redeeming the time.

2Th 3:13 — But ye, brethren, be not weary in well doing.

Tit 2:14 — Who gave himself for us, that he might redeem us from all iniquity, and purify unto himself a peculiar people, zealous of good works.

Tit 3:1 — Put them in mind to be subject to principalities and powers, to obey magistrates, to be ready to every good work,

Heb 10:34 — For ye had compassion of me in my bonds, and took joyfully the spoiling of your goods, knowing in yourselves that ye have in heaven a better and an enduring substance.

1Pe 2:2 — As newborn babes, desire the sincere milk of the word, that ye may grow thereby:

2Pe 3:14 — Wherefore, beloved, seeing that ye look for such things, be diligent that ye may be found of him in peace, without spot, and blameless.

Jude 1:3 — Beloved, when I gave all diligence to write unto you of the common salvation, it was needful for me to write unto you, and exhort *you* that ye should earnestly contend for the faith which was once delivered unto the saints.

Rev 3:19 — As many as I love, I rebuke and chasten: be zealous therefore, and repent.

Rev 22:17 — And the Spirit and the bride say, Come. And let him that heareth say, Come. And let him that is athirst come. And whosoever will, let him take the water of life freely.

• Exemplified.

Ex 32:31–32; Dt 9:18–19; Jos 24:14–16; 1Ki 8:42–43; Ps 9:19–20; 40:7–10; 69:7–9; 71:17–18; 74:18–23; 115:1–2; Ecc 12:9–10; Jer 9:1–3; 26:12–15; Da 3:17–18; Mic 7:1–2; Hab 1:2–4; Mk 5:19–20; 14:29–31; Lk 1:15–17; 19:41–42; Jn 1:40–42, 45–46; 4:34–35; Ac 4:8–13, 18–20; 5:29–32; 11:19–20; 18:24–28; Ro 9:1–3; 15:18–21; 2Co 8:1–5, 16–18; 12:20–21; Eph 4:25–26; Php 1:12–18; Col 4:7–11; 1Th 1:2–8; 3:1–2; 2Pe 1:12–13; 2:4–5; 2Jn 1:4–7

Nu 10:29 — And Moses said unto Hobab, the son of Raguel the Midianite, Moses' father in law, We are journeying unto the place of which the LORD said, I will give it you: come thou with us, and we will do thee good: for the LORD hath spoken good concerning Israel.

Nu 11:29 — And Moses said unto him, Enviest thou for my sake? would God that all the LORD's people were prophets, *and* that the LORD would put his spirit upon them!

1Sa 17:26 — And David spake to the men that stood by him, saying, What shall be done to the man that killeth this Philistine, and taketh away the reproach from Israel? for who *is* this uncircumcised Philistine, that he should defy the armies of the living God?

1Ki 22:14 — And Micaiah said, *As* the LORD liveth, what the LORD saith unto me, that will I speak.

2Ch 6:33 — Then hear thou from the heavens, *even* from thy dwelling place, and do according to all that the stranger calleth to thee for; that all people of the earth may know thy name, and fear thee, as *doth* thy people Israel, and may know that this house which I have built is called by thy name.

Job 6:10 — Then should I yet have comfort; yea, I would harden myself in sorrow: let him not spare; for I have not concealed the words of the Holy One.

Ps 51:13 — *Then* will I teach transgressors thy ways; and sinners shall be converted unto thee.

Ps 74:10 — O God, how long shall the adversary reproach? shall the enemy blaspheme thy name for ever?

Ps 94:16 — Who will rise up for me against the evildoers? *or* who will stand up for me against the workers of iniquity?

Ps 101:8 — I will early destroy all the wicked of the land; that I may cut off all wicked doers from the city of the LORD.

Ps 119:53 — Horror hath taken hold upon me because of the wicked that forsake thy law.

Ps 119:126 — *It is* time for *thee*, LORD, to work: *for* they have made void thy law.

Ps 119:136 — Rivers of waters run down mine eyes, because they keep not thy law.

Ps 119:139 — My zeal hath consumed me, because mine enemies have forgotten thy words.

Ps 119:158 — I beheld the transgressors, and was grieved; because they kept not thy word.

Pr 28:4 — They that forsake the law praise the wicked: but such as keep the law contend with them.

Isa 2:3 — And many people shall go and say, Come ye, and let us go up to the mountain of the LORD, to the house of the God of Jacob; and he will teach us of his ways, and we will walk in his paths: for out of Zion shall go forth the law, and the word of the LORD from Jerusalem.

Isa 2:5 — O house of Jacob, come ye, and let us walk in the light of the LORD.

Isa 6:8 — Also I heard the voice of the Lord, saying, Whom shall I send, and who will go for us? Then said I, Here *am* I; send me.

Isa 59:17 — For he put on righteousness as a breastplate, and an helmet of salvation upon his head; and he put on the garments of vengeance *for* clothing, and was clad with zeal as a cloke.

Isa 62:1 — For Zion's sake will I not hold my peace, and for Jerusalem's sake I will not rest, until the righteousness thereof go forth as brightness, and the salvation thereof as a lamp *that* burneth.

Jer 13:17 — But if ye will not hear it, my soul shall weep in secret places for *your* pride; and mine eye shall weep sore, and run down with tears, because the LORD's flock is carried away captive.

Jer 17:16 — As for me, I have not hastened from *being* a pastor to follow thee: neither have I desired the woeful day; thou knowest: that which came out of my lips was *right* before thee.

Jer 18:20 — Shall evil be recompensed for good? for they have digged a pit for my soul. Remember that I stood before thee to speak good for them, *and* to turn away thy wrath from them.

Jer 20:9 — Then I said, I will not make mention of him, nor speak any more in his name. But *his word* was in mine heart as a burning fire shut up in my bones, and I was weary with forbearing, and I could not *stay*.

Eze 9:4 — And the LORD said unto him, Go through the midst of the city, through the midst of Jerusalem, and set a mark upon the foreheads of the men that sigh and that cry for all the abominations that be done in the midst thereof.

Eze 44:15 — But the priests the Levites, the sons of Zadok, that kept the charge of my sanctuary when the children of Israel went astray from me, they shall come near to me to minister unto me, and they shall stand before me to offer unto me the fat and the blood, saith the Lord GOD:

Mic 3:8 — But truly I am full of power by the spirit of the LORD, and of judgment, and of might, to declare unto Jacob his transgression, and to Israel his sin.

Mt 23:37 — O Jerusalem, Jerusalem, *thou* that killest the prophets, and stonest them which are sent unto thee, how often would I have gathered thy children together, even as a hen gathereth her chickens under *her* wings, and ye would not!

Mk 6:6 — And he marvelled because of their unbelief. And he went round about the villages, teaching.

Mk 16:20 — And they went forth, and preached every where, the Lord working with *them,* and confirming the word with signs following. Amen.

Ac 4:2 — Being grieved that they taught the people, and preached through Jesus the resurrection from the dead.

Ac 4:31 — And when they had prayed, the place was shaken where they were assembled together; and they were all filled with the Holy Ghost, and they spake the word of God with boldness.

Ac 4:33 — And with great power gave the apostles witness of the resurrection of the Lord Jesus: and great grace was upon them all.

Ac 5:21 — And when they heard *that,* they entered into the temple early in the morning, and taught. But the high priest came, and they that were with him, and called the council together, and all the senate of the children of Israel and sent to the prison to have them brought.

Ac 5:25 — Then came one and told them, saying, Behold, the men whom ye put in prison are standing in the temple, and teaching the people.

Ac 5:42 — And daily in the temple, and in every house, they ceased not to teach and preach Jesus Christ.

Ac 6:4 — But we will give ourselves continually to prayer, and to the ministry of the word.

Ac 6:10 — And they were not able to resist the wisdom and the spirit by which he spake.

Ac 8:4 — Therefore they that were scattered abroad went every where preaching the word.

Ac 8:12 — But when they believed Philip preaching the things concerning the kingdom of God, and the name of Jesus Christ, they were baptized, both men and women.

Ac 8:25 — And they, when they had testified and preached the word of the Lord, returned to Jerusalem, and preached the gospel in many villages of the Samaritans.

Ac 8:30 — And Philip ran thither to *him,* and heard him read the prophet Esaias, and said, Understandest thou what thou readest?

Ac 8:35 — Then Philip opened his mouth, and began at the same scripture, and preached unto him Jesus.

Ac 8:40 — But Philip was found at Azotus: and passing through he preached in all the cities, till he came to Caesarea.

Ac 11:24 — For he was a good man, and full of the Holy Ghost and of faith: and much people was added unto the Lord.

Ac 11:26 — And when he had found him, he brought him unto Antioch. And it came to pass, that a whole year they assembled themselves with the church, and taught much people. And the disciples were called Christians first in Antioch.

Ro 1:11 — For I long to see you, that I may impart unto you some spiritual gift, to the end ye may be established;

Ro 10:1 — Brethren, my heart's desire and prayer to God for Israel is, that they might be saved.

1Co 16:10 — Now if Timotheus come, see that he may be with you without fear: for he worketh the work of the Lord, as I also *do.*

2Co 5:9 — Wherefore we labour, that, whether present or absent, we may be accepted of him.

2Co 6:11 — O *ye* Corinthians, our mouth is open unto you, our heart is enlarged.

Eph 4:32 — And be ye kind one to another, tenderhearted, forgiving one another, even as God for Christ's sake hath forgiven you.

Eph 6:21 — But that ye also may know my affairs, *and* how I do, Tychicus, a beloved brother and faithful minister in the Lord, shall make known to you all things:

Php 2:22 — But ye know the proof of him, that, as a son with the father, he hath served with me in the gospel.

Php 2:26 — For he longed after you all, and was full of heaviness, because that ye had heard that he had been sick.

Php 2:30 — Because for the work of Christ he was nigh unto death, not regarding his life, to supply your lack of service toward me.

Php 4:3 — And I intreat thee also, true yokefellow, help those women which laboured with me in the gospel, with Clement also, and *with* other my fellowlabourers, whose names *are* in the book of life.

Col 1:7 — As ye also learned of Epaphras our dear fellowservant, who is for you a faithful minister of Christ;

2Pe 1:15 — Moreover I will endeavour that ye may be able after my decease to have these things always in remembrance.

Jude 1:3 — Beloved, when I gave all diligence to write unto you of the common salvation, it was needful for me to write unto you, and exhort *you* that ye should earnestly contend for the faith which was once delivered unto the saints.

Rev 3:19 — As many as I love, I rebuke and chasten: be zealous therefore, and repent.

- **Instances of.**
  - **Moses.**
    Ex 2:12; 11:8; 32:19–20
  - **Phinehas.**
    Nu 25:7–13; Ps 106:30
  - **Joshua.**
    Nu 11:27–29; Jos 7:6; 8:2, 28
  - **Gideon.**
    Jgs 6:11–32
  - **Jephthah.**
    Jgs 11:30–31, 34–39
  - **Samuel.**
    1Sa 12:23; 15:11, 35–16:1
  - **Saul.**
    1Sa 14:38–44
  - **David.**
    2Sa 6:1–23; 7:2; 8:11–12
  - **Elijah.**
    1Ki 19:10
  - **Obadiah.**
    1Ki 18:3–4
  - **Jehoash.**
    2Ki 12:2–16
  - **Jehu.**
    2Ki 9:1–10:36
  - **Jehoiada.**
    2Ki 11:4–17; 2Ch 23:1–17
  - **Asa.**
    1Ki 15:11–15; 2Ch 14:1–5, 15
  - **Jehoshaphat.**
    2Ch 17:3–10; 19:1–11
  - **Hezekiah.**
    2Ch 30:1–31:21; Isa 37:1
  - **Josiah.**
    2Ki 22:1–23:37; 2Ch 34:3–7, 29–33
  - **Priests.**
    1Ch 9:13; Ezr 8:17–18
  - **Ezra.**
    Ezr 7:10; 9:1–10:44
  - **Nehemiah.**
    Ne 4:1–5:19; 8:1–18; 13:7–9, 15–28
  - **Jeremiah.**
    Jer 25:3–4
  - **Shepherds.**
    Lk 2:17–18
  - **Anna.**
    Lk 2:38
  - **Andrew and Philip.**
    Jn 1:41–46
  - **Two blind men proclaiming the miracle of healing, contrary to the injunction of Jesus.**
    Mt 9:30–31
  - **The restored leper.**
    Mk 1:44–45
  - **The healed deaf mute.**
    Mk 7:36
  - **Peter rebuking Jesus.**
    Mt 16:22
  - **Samaritan woman.**
    Jn 4:28–30, 39
  - **Peter.**
    Ac 2:14–40; 3:12–26
  - **John.**
    ➾See: John, the Baptist
  - **Paul and Barnabas.**
    Ac 11:22–26; 14:14–15
  - **Phebe.**
    Ro 16:1–2
  - **Ephesians.**
    Rev 2:2–3, 6

➾See: Jesus, Zeal of

➾See: Zeal, Religious; exemplified by Paul

- **Exemplified by Paul.**

Ac 9:20–29; 13:16–14:28; 15:30–36; 16:31–32; 17:2–3, 16–17, 22–31; 18:4–6; 19:8–10; 20:18–27, 33–34; 24:14–25; 26:1–29; 28:23–28; Ro 1:9–15; 9:1–3; 11:13–14; 15:15–32; 1Co 2:1–4, 6–7; 3:1–2, 5–7; 4:1–21; 9:15–23; 10:33–11:1; 15:1–32; 2Co 1:15–19; 2:12–17; 4:1–2, 8–15; 5:13–14; 6:3–10; 10:14–16; 11:22–33; 12:14–15, 17–19; 13:6–9; Gal 1:15–16; Php 1:17–18, 22–25; 2:16–17; 3:4–17; 4:11–12; Col 1:28–2:1; 1Th 1:5–6; 2:2–6, 8–11; 2Th 3:7–9; 2Ti 1:11–13; 2:9–10; 3:10–11

Ac 15:26 — Men that have hazarded their lives for the name of our Lord Jesus Christ.

Ac 15:41 — And he went through Syria and Cilicia, confirming the churches.

Ac 16:10 — And after he had seen the vision, immediately we endeavoured to go into Macedonia, assuredly gathering that the Lord had called us for to preach the gospel unto them.

Ac 16:13 — And on the sabbath we went out of the city by a river side, where prayer was wont to be made; and we sat down, and spake unto the women which resorted *thither.*

Ac 16:17 — The same followed Paul and us, and cried, saying, These men are the servants of the most high God, which shew unto us the way of salvation.

Ac 18:19 — And he came to Ephesus, and left them there: but he himself entered into the synagogue, and reasoned with the Jews.

Ac 18:23 — And after he had spent some time *there,* he departed, and went over *all* the country of Galatia and Phrygia in order, strengthening all the disciples.

Ac 19:21 — After these things were ended, Paul purposed in the spirit, when he had passed through Macedonia and Achaia, to go to Jerusalem, saying, After I have been there, I must also see Rome.

Ac 20:7 — And upon the first *day* of the week, when the disciples came together to break bread, Paul preached unto them, ready to depart on the morrow; and continued his speech until midnight.

Ac 20:31 — Therefore watch, and remember, that by the space of three years I ceased not to warn every one night and day with tears.

Ac 21:13 — Then Paul answered, What mean ye to weep and to break mine heart? for I am ready not to be bound only, but also to die at Jerusalem for the name of the Lord Jesus.

Ac 28:30 — And Paul dwelt two whole years in his own hired house, and received all that came in unto him,

Ro 1:1 — Paul, a servant of Jesus Christ, called *to be* an apostle, separated unto the gospel of God,

Ro 10:1 — Brethren, my heart's desire and prayer to God for Israel is, that they might be saved.

1Co 1:17 — For Christ sent me not to baptize, but to preach the gospel: not with wisdom of words, lest the cross of Christ should be made of none effect.

1Co 1:23 — But we preach Christ crucified, unto the Jews a stumblingblock, and unto the Greeks foolishness;

1Co 2:13 — Which things also we speak, not in the words which man's wisdom teacheth, but which the Holy Ghost teacheth; comparing spiritual things with spiritual.

1Co 9:12 — If others be partakers of *this* power over you, *are* not we rather? Nevertheless we have not used this power; but suffer all things, lest we should hinder the gospel of Christ.

1Co 9:27 — But I keep under my body, and bring *it* into subjection: lest that by any means, when I have preached to others, I myself should be a castaway.

1Co 13:1 — Though I speak with the tongues of men and of angels, and have not charity, I am become *as* sounding brass, or a tinkling cymbal.

2Co 1:12 — For our rejoicing is this, the testimony of our conscience, that in simplicity and godly sincerity, not with fleshly wisdom, but by the grace of God, we have had our conversation in the world, and more abundantly to you-ward.

2Co 1:24 — Not for that we have dominion over your faith, but are helpers of your joy: for by faith ye stand.

2Co 3:6 — Who also hath made us able ministers of the new testament; not of the letter, but of the spirit: for the letter killeth, but the spirit giveth life.

2Co 3:12 — Seeing then that we have such hope, we use great plainness of speech:

2Co 5:11 — Knowing therefore the terror of the Lord, we persuade men; but we are made manifest unto God; and I trust also are made manifest in your consciences.

2Co 5:18 — And all things *are* of God, who hath reconciled us to himself by Jesus Christ, and hath given to us the ministry of reconciliation;

2Co 5:20 — Now then we are ambassadors for Christ, as though God did beseech *you* by us: we pray *you* in Christ's stead, be ye reconciled to God.

2Co 7:2 — Receive us; we have wronged no man, we have corrupted no man, we have defrauded no man.

2Co 10:3 — For though we walk in the flesh, we do not war after the flesh:

2Co 11:7 — Have I committed an offence in abasing myself that ye might be exalted, because I have preached to you the gospel of God freely?

2Co 11:9 — And when I was present with you, and wanted, I was chargeable to no man: for that which was lacking to me the brethren which came from Macedonia supplied: and in all *things* I have kept myself from being burdensome unto you, and so will I keep *myself.*

2Co 11:12 — But what I do, that I will do, that I may cut off occasion from them which desire occasion; that wherein they glory, they may be found even as we.

2Co 12:10 — Therefore I take pleasure in infirmities, in reproaches, in necessities, in persecutions, in distresses for Christ's sake: for when I am weak, then am I strong.

2Co 12:21 — *And* lest, when I come again, my God will humble me among you, and *that* I shall bewail many which have sinned already, and have not repented of the uncleanness and fornication and lasciviousness which they have committed.

Gal 1:10 — For do I now persuade men, or God? or do I seek to please men? for if I yet pleased men, I should not be the servant of Christ.

Gal 2:2 — And I went up by revelation, and communicated unto them that gospel which I preach among the Gentiles, but privately to them which were of reputation, lest by any means I should run, or had run, in vain.

Gal 3:1 — O foolish Galatians, who hath bewitched you, that ye should not obey the truth, before whose eyes Jesus Christ hath been evidently set forth, crucified among you?

Gal 4:11 — I am afraid of you, lest I have bestowed upon you labour in vain.

Gal 4:19 — My little children, of whom I travail in birth again until Christ be formed in you,

Gal 5:11 — And I, brethren, if I yet preach circumcision, why do I yet suffer persecution? then is the offence of the cross ceased.

Eph 6:17 — And take the helmet of salvation, and the sword of the Spirit, which is the word of God:

Eph 6:20 — For which I am an ambassador in bonds: that therein I may speak boldly, as I ought to speak.

Php 1:20 — According to my earnest expectation and *my* hope, that in nothing I shall be ashamed, but *that* with all boldness, as always, *so* now also Christ shall be magnified in my body, whether *it be* by life, or by death.

Php 1:27 — Only let your conversation be as it becometh the gospel of Christ: that whether I come and see you, or else be absent, I may hear of your affairs, that ye stand fast in one spirit, with one mind striving together for the faith of the gospel;

Php 4:17 — Not because I desire a gift: but I desire fruit that may abound to your account.

Col 1:24 — Who now rejoice in my sufferings for you, and fill up that which is behind of the afflictions of Christ in my flesh for his body's sake, which is the church:

1Ti 4:10 — For therefore we both labour and suffer reproach, because we trust in the living God, who is the Saviour of all men, specially of those that believe.

2Ti 1:3 — I thank God, whom I serve from *my* forefathers with pure conscience, that without ceasing I have remembrance of thee in my prayers night and day;

2Ti 1:7 — For God hath not given us the spirit of fear; but of power, and of love, and of a sound mind.

Heb 13:18 — Pray for us: for we trust we have a good conscience, in all things willing to live honestly.

• Without knowledge.

Mt 8:19–20; Lk 9:57–58; Ro 10:2–3; Gal 1:13–14; Php 1:15–18

Ecc 7:16 — Be not righteous over much; neither make thyself over wise: why shouldest thou destroy thyself?

Jn 16:2 — They shall put you out of the synagogues: yea, the time cometh, that whosoever killeth you will think that he doeth God service.

Ac 21:20 — And when they heard *it,* they glorified the Lord, and said unto him, Thou seest, brother, how many thousands of Jews there are which believe; and they are all zealous of the law:

Gal 4:17 — They zealously affect you, *but* not well; yea, they would exclude you, that ye might affect them.

• In punishing the wicked.

• Moses and Levites.

Ex 32:26–29

Ex 32:20 — And he took the calf which they had made, and burnt *it* in the fire, and ground *it* to powder, and strawed *it* upon the water, and made the children of Israel drink *of it.*

• Phinehas.

Nu 25:11–13; Ps 106:30–31

• Israelites.

Jos 22:11–20; Jgs 20:1–48

• Samuel.

1Sa 15:33 — And Samuel said, As thy sword hath made women childless, so shall thy mother be childless among women. And Samuel hewed Agag in pieces before the LORD in Gilgal.

• David.

2Sa 4:9–12

2Sa 1:14 — And David said unto him, How wast thou not afraid to stretch forth thine hand to destroy the LORD'S anointed?

• Elijah.

1Ki 18:40 — And Elijah said unto them, Take the prophets of Baal; let not one of them escape. And they took them: and Elijah brought them down to the brook Kishon, and slew them there.

• Jehu.

2Ki 10:15–28

• Jehoiada.

2Ki 11:18 — And all the people of the land went into the house of Baal, and brake it down; his altars and his images brake they in pieces thoroughly, and slew Mattan the priest of Baal before the altars. And the priest appointed officers over the house of the LORD.

• Josiah.

2Ki 23:20 — And he slew all the priests of the high places that *were* there upon the altars, and burned men's bones upon them, and returned to Jerusalem.

• In reproving iniquity.

See: Reproof; faithfulness in

ZEBADIAH

• Two Benjamites.

1Ch 8:15 — And Zebadiah, and Arad, and Ader,

1Ch 8:17 — And Zebadiah, and Meshullam, and Hezeki, and Heber,

• An Israelite who joined David at Ziklag.

1Ch 12:7 — And Joelah, and Zebadiah, the sons of Jeroham of Gedor.

• A Korhite porter in the temple.

1Ch 26:2 — And the sons of Meshelemiah *were,* Zechariah the firstborn, Jediael the second, Zebadiah the third, Jathniel the fourth,

• Son of Asahel.

1Ch 27:7 — The fourth *captain* for the fourth month *was* Asahel the brother of Joab, and Zebadiah his son after him: and in his course *were* twenty and four thousand.

• An itinerant Levite teacher.

2Ch 17:8 — And with them *he sent* Levites, *even* Shemaiah, and Nethaniah, and Zebadiah, and Asahel, and Shemiramoth, and Jehonathan, and Adonijah, and Tobijah, and Tob-adonijah, Levites; and with them Elishama and Jehoram, priests.

• Son of Ishmael and counselor of the king.

2Ch 19:11 — And, behold, Amariah the chief priest is over you in all matters of the LORD; and Zebadiah the son of Ishmael, the ruler of the house of Judah, for all the king's matters: also the Levites *shall be* officers before you. Deal courageously, and the LORD shall be with the good.

• Son of Shephaniah.

Ezr 8:8 — And of the sons of Shephatiah; Zebadiah the son of Michael, and with him fourscore males.

• A priest who defiled himself by marrying an idolatrous woman.

Ezr 10:20 — And of the sons of Immer; Hanani, and Zebadiah.

ZEBAH

• King of Midian.

Jgs 8:5–21

Ps 83:11 — Make their nobles like Oreb, and like Zeeb: yea, all their princes as Zebah, and as Zalmunna:

ZEBAIM • A place the exact location of which is unknown.

Ezr 2:57 — The children of Shephatiah, the children of Hattil, the children of Pochereth of Zebaim, the children of Ami.

Ne 7:59 — The children of Shephatiah, the children of Hattil, the children of Pochereth of Zebaim, the children of Amon.

ZEBEDEE • Father of James and John.

Mt 4:21 — And going on from thence, he saw other two brethren, James *the son* of Zebedee, and John his brother, in a ship with Zebedee their father, mending their nets; and he called them.

Mt 20:20 — Then came to him the mother of Zebedee's children with her sons, worshipping *him,* and desiring a certain thing of him.

Mt 27:56 — Among which was Mary Magdalene, and Mary the mother of James and Joses, and the mother of Zebedee's children.

Mk 1:20 — And straightway he called them: and they left their father Zebedee in the ship with the hired servants, and went after him.

ZEBINA • Son of Nebo.

Ezr 10:43 — Of the sons of Nebo; Jeiel, Mattithiah, Zabad, Zebina, Jadau, and Joel, Benaiah.

ZEBOIM

• One of the cities in the valley of Siddim.

Ge 10:19 — And the border of the Canaanites was from Sidon, as thou comest to Gerar, unto Gaza; as thou goest, unto Sodom, and Gomorrah, and Admah, and Zeboim, even unto Lasha.

Dt 29:23 — *And that* the whole land thereof *is* brimstone, and salt, *and* burning, *that* it is not sown, nor beareth, nor any grass groweth therein, like the overthrow of Sodom, and Gomorrah, Admah, and Zeboim, which the LORD overthrew in his anger, and in his wrath:

Hos 11:8 — How shall I give thee up, Ephraim? *how* shall I deliver thee, Israel? how shall I make thee as Admah? *how* shall I set thee as Zeboim? mine heart is turned within me, my repentings are kindled together.

• Called also Zeboiim.

Ge 14:2 — *That these* made war with Bera king of Sodom, and with Birsha king of Gomorrah, Shinab king of Admah, and Shemeber king of Zeboiim, and the king of Bela, which is Zoar.

Ge 14:8 — And there went out the king of Sodom, and the king of Gomorrah, and the king of Admah, and the king of Zeboiim, and the king of Bela (the same *is* Zoar;) and they joined battle with them in the vale of Siddim;

• A city and valley in Benjamin.

1Sa 13:18 — And another company turned the way *to* Beth-horon: and another company turned *to* the way of the border that looketh to the valley of Zeboim toward the wilderness.

Ne 11:34 — Hadid, Zeboim, Neballat,

ZEBUDAH • Wife of Josiah, king of Judah.

2Ki 23:36 — Jehoiakim *was* twenty and five years old when he began to reign; and he reigned eleven years in Jerusalem. And his mother's name *was* Zebudah, the daughter of Pedaiah of Rumah.

ZEBUL • An officer of Abimelech.

Jgs 9:28–41

ZEBULUN

• Son of Jacob and Leah.

Ge 30:20 — And Leah said, God hath endued me *with* a good dowry; now will my husband dwell with me, because I have born him six sons: and she called his name Zebulun.

Ge 35:23 — The sons of Leah; Reuben, Jacob's firstborn, and Simeon, and Levi, and Judah, and Issachar, and Zebulun:

Ge 46:14 — And the sons of Zebulun; Sered, and Elon, and Jahleel.

Ge 49:13 — Zebulun shall dwell at the haven of the sea; and he *shall be* for an haven of ships; and his border *shall be* unto Zidon.

Ex 1:3 — Issachar, Zebulun, and Benjamin,

1Ch 2:1 — These *are* the sons of Israel; Reuben, Simeon, Levi, and Judah, Issachar, and Zebulun,

• Descendants of.

Nu 26:26–27

Ge 46:14 — And the sons of Zebulun; Sered, and Elon, and Jahleel.

• Called also Zabulun.

• Tribe of.

• Place of, in march and camp.

Nu 2:3 — And on the east side toward the rising of the sun shall they of the standard of the camp of Judah pitch throughout their armies: and Nahshon the son of Amminadab *shall be* captain of the children of Judah.

Nu 2:7 — *Then* the tribe of Zebulun: and Eliab the son of Helon *shall be* captain of the children of Zebulun.

Nu 10:14 — In the first *place* went the standard of the camp of the children of Judah according to their armies: and over his host *was* Nahshon the son of Amminadab.

Nu 10:16 — And over the host of the tribe of the children of Zebulun *was* Eliab the son of Helon.

• Territory awarded to.

Jos 19:10–16

Ge 49:13 — Zebulun shall dwell at the haven of the sea; and he *shall be* for an haven of ships; and his border *shall be* unto Zidon.

Mt 4:13 — And leaving Nazareth, he came and dwelt in Capernaum, which is upon the sea coast, in the borders of Zabulon and Nephthalim:

- **Aboriginal inhabitants of the territory of, not expelled.**

Jgs 1:30 — Neither did Zebulun drive out the inhabitants of Kitron, nor the inhabitants of Nahalol; but the Canaanites dwelt among them, and became tributaries.

- **Levitical cities of.**

Jos 21:34–35

1Ch 6:77 — Unto the rest of the children of Merari *were given* out of the tribe of Zebulun. Rimmon with her suburbs, Tabor with her suburbs:

- **Moses' benediction upon.**

Dt 33:18–19

- **Loyalty of, in resisting the enemies of Israel.**
  - **With Barak against Sisera.**

Jgs 4:6 — And she sent and called Barak the son of Abinoam out of Kedesh-naphtali, and said unto him, Hath not the LORD God of Israel commanded, *saying,* Go and draw toward mount Tabor, and take with thee ten thousand men of the children of Naphtali and of the children of Zebulun?

Jgs 4:10 — And Barak called Zebulun and Naphtali to Kedesh; and he went up with ten thousand men at his feet: and Deborah went up with him.

Jgs 5:14 — Out of Ephraim *was there* a root of them against Amalek; after thee, Benjamin, among thy people; out of Machir came down governors, and out of Zebulun they that handle the pen of the writer.

Jgs 5:18 — Zebulun and Naphtali *were* a people *that* jeoparded their lives unto the death in the high places of the field.

  - **With Gideon against the Midianites.**

Jgs 6:35 — And he sent messengers throughout all Manasseh; who also was gathered after him: and he sent messengers unto Asher, and unto Zebulun, and unto Naphtali; and they came up to meet them.

  - **With David when made king over Israel.**

1Ch 12:38–40

1Ch 12:33 — Of Zebulun, such as went forth to battle, expert in war, with all instruments of war, fifty thousand, which could keep rank: *they were* not of double heart.

- **Joins with Hezekiah in renewing the passover.**

2Ch 30:11 — Nevertheless divers of Asher and Manasseh and of Zebulun humbled themselves, and came to Jerusalem.

2Ch 30:18 — For a multitude of the people, *even* many of Ephraim, and Manasseh, Issachar, and Zebulun, had not cleansed themselves, yet did they eat the passover otherwise than it was written. But Hezekiah prayed for them, saying, The good LORD pardon every one

- **Conquest of, by Tiglath-pileser; carried to Assyria into captivity.**

2Ki 15:29 — In the days of Pekah king of Israel came Tiglath-pileser king of Assyria, and took Ijon, and Abel-beth-maachah, and Janoah, and Kedesh, and Hazor, and Gilead, and Galilee, all the land of Naphtali, and carried them captive to Assyria.

Isa 9:1 — Nevertheless the dimness *shall* not *be* such as *was* in her vexation, when at the first he lightly afflicted the land of Zebulun and the land of Naphtali, and afterward did more grievously afflict *her by* the way of the sea, beyond Jordan, in Galilee of the nations.

- **Jesus dwelt in the land of.**

Mt 4:15 — The land of Zabulon, and the land of Nephthalim, *by* the way of the sea, beyond Jordan, Galilee of the Gentiles;

- **Twelve thousand sealed.**

Rev 7:8 — Of the tribe of Zabulon *were* sealed twelve thousand. Of the tribe of Joseph *were* sealed twelve thousand. Of the tribe of Benjamin *were* sealed twelve thousand.

See: Israel

ZECHARIAH

- **A Reubenite.**

1Ch 5:7 — And his brethren by their families, when the genealogy of their generations was reckoned, *were* the chief, Jeiel, and Zechariah,

- **Three Levites in the days of David.**

1Ch 9:21 — *And* Zechariah the son of Meshelemiah *was* porter of the door of the tabernacle of the congregation.

1Ch 15:18 — And with them their brethren of the second *degree,* Zechariah, Ben, and Jaaziel, and Shemiramoth, and Jehiel, and Unni, Eliab, and Benaiah, and Maaseiah, and Mattithiah, and Elipheleh, and Mikneiah, and Obed-edom, and Jeiel, the porters.

1Ch 15:20 — And Zechariah, and Aziel, and Shemiramoth, and Jehiel, and Unni, and Eliab, and Maaseiah, and Benaiah, with psalteries on Alamoth;

1Ch 15:24 — And Shebaniah, and Jehoshaphat, and Nethaneel, and Amasai, and Zechariah, and Benaiah, and Eliezer, the priests, did blow with the trumpets before the ark of God: and Obed-edom and Jehiah *were* doorkeepers for the ark.

1Ch 16:5 — Asaph the chief, and next to him Zechariah, Jeiel, and Shemiramoth, and Jehiel, and Mattithiah, and Eliab, and Benaiah, and Obed-edom: and Jeiel with psalteries and with harps; but Asaph made a sound with cymbals;

1Ch 26:2 — And the sons of Meshelemiah *were,* Zechariah the firstborn, Jediael the second, Zebadiah the third, Jathniel the fourth,

1Ch 26:14 — And the lot eastward fell to Shelemiah. Then for Zechariah his son, a wise counsellor, they cast lots; and his lot came out northward.

• A Benjamite.

1Ch 9:37 — And Gedor, and Ahio, and Zechariah, and Mikloth.

• Called Zacher.

1Ch 8:31 — And Gedor, and Ahio, and Zacher.

• Two Kohathites.

1Ch 24:25 — The brother of Michah *was* Isshiah: of the sons of Isshiah; Zechariah.

2Ch 34:12 — And the men did the work faithfully: and the overseers of them *were* Jahath and Obadiah, the Levites, of the sons of Merari; and Zechariah and Meshullam, of the sons of the Kohathites, to set *it* forward; and *other of* the Levites, all that could skill of instruments of musick.

• A Merarite porter in the temple.

1Ch 26:11 — Hilkiah the second, Tebaliah the third, Zechariah the fourth: all the sons and brethren of Hosah *were* thirteen.

• Father of Iddo.

1Ch 27:21 — Of the half *tribe* of Manasseh in Gilead, Iddo the son of Zechariah: of Benjamin, Jaasiel the son of Abner:

• A prince sent by Jehoshaphat along with priests and Levites to teach in the cities.

2Ch 17:7 — Also in the third year of his reign he sent to his princes, *even* to Ben-hail, and to Obadiah, and to Zechariah, and to Nethaneel, and to Michaiah, to teach in the cities of Judah.

• A Levite, and father of Jahaziel.

2Ch 20:14 — Then upon Jahaziel the son of Zechariah, the son of Benaiah, the son of Jeiel, the son of Mattaniah, a Levite of the sons of Asaph, came the Spirit of the LORD in the midst of the congregation;

• Son of Jehoshaphat.

2Ch 21:2 — And he had brethren the sons of Jehoshaphat, Azariah, and Jehiel, and Zechariah, and Azariah, and Michael, and Shephatiah: all these *were* the sons of Jehoshaphat king of Israel.

• High priest, and son or grandson of Jehoiada. Put to death for prophesying against Jerusalem.

2Ch 24:20–22

2Ch 24:25 — And when they were departed from him, (for they left him in great diseases,) his own servants conspired against him for the blood of the sons of Jehoiada the priest, and slew him on his bed, and he died: and they buried him in the city of David, but they buried him not in the sepulchres of the kings.

Mt 23:35 — That upon you may come all the righteous blood shed upon the earth, from the blood of righteous Abel unto the blood of Zacharias son of Barachias, whom ye slew between the temple and the altar.

Lk 11:51 — From the blood of Abel unto the blood of Zacharias, which perished between the altar and the temple: verily I say unto you, It shall be required of this generation.

• A prophet in the reign of Uzziah.

2Ch 26:5 — And he sought God in the days of Zechariah, who had understanding in the visions of God: and as long as he sought the LORD, God made him to prosper.

• A ruler of the temple.

2Ch 35:8 — And his princes gave willingly unto the people, to the priests, and to the Levites: Hilkiah and Zechariah and Jehiel, rulers of the house of God, gave unto the priests for the passover offerings two thousand and six hundred *small cattle,* and three hundred oxen.

• The prophet.

Zec 2:4 — And said unto him, Run, speak to this young man, saying, Jerusalem shall be inhabited *as* towns without walls for the multitude of men and cattle therein:

• Son of Berechiah.

Zec 1:1 — In the eighth month, in the second year of Darius, came the word of the LORD unto Zechariah, the son of Berechiah, the son of Iddo the prophet, saying,

• Prophesied in the reign of Darius.

Ezr 4:24–5:1

Ezr 6:14 — And the elders of the Jews builded, and they prospered through the prophesying of Haggai the prophet and Zechariah the son of Iddo. And they builded, and finished *it,* according to the commandment of the God of Israel, and according to the commandment of Cyrus, and Darius, and Artaxerxes king of Persia.

Zec 1:1 — In the eighth month, in the second year of Darius, came the word of the LORD unto Zechariah, the son of Berechiah, the son of Iddo the prophet, saying,

Zec 1:7 — Upon the four and twentieth day of the eleventh month, which *is* the month Sebat, in the second year of Darius, came the word of the LORD unto Zechariah, the son of Berechiah, the son of Iddo the prophet, saying,

Zec 7:1 — And it came to pass in the fourth year of king Darius, *that* the word of the LORD came unto Zechariah in the fourth *day* of the ninth month, *even* in Chisleu;

• Probably the priest mentioned in Ne 12:16.

Ne 12:16 — Of Iddo, Zechariah; of Ginnethon, Meshullam;

• Two chiefs who returned with Ezra.

Ezr 8:3 — Of the sons of Shechaniah, of the sons of Pharosh; Zechariah: and with him were reckoned by genealogy of the males an hundred and fifty.

Ezr 8:11 — And of the sons of Bebai; Zechariah the son of Bebai, and with him twenty and eight males.

Ezr 8:16 — Then sent I for Eliezer, for Ariel, for Shemaiah, and for Elnathan, and for Jarib, and for Elnathan, and for Nathan, and for Zechariah, and for Meshullam, chief men; also for Joiarib, and for Elnathan, men of understanding.

• Name of various Jews after the captivity.

Ne 11:4–5

Ezr 10:26 — And of the sons of Elam; Mattaniah, Zechariah, and Jehiel, and Abdi, and Jeremoth, and Eliah.

Ne 8:4 — And Ezra the scribe stood upon a pulpit of wood, which they had made for the purpose; and beside him stood Mattithiah, and Shema, and Anaiah, and Urijah, and Hilkiah, and Maaseiah, on his right hand; and on his left hand, Pedaiah, and Mishael, and Malchiah, and Hashum, and Hashbadana, Zechariah, *and* Meshullam.

Ne 11:12 — And their brethren that did the work of the house *were* eight hundred twenty and two: and Adaiah the son of Jeroham, the son of Pelaliah, the son of Amzi, the son of Zechariah, the son of Pashur, the son of Malchiah,

Ne 12:16 — Of Iddo, Zechariah; of Ginnethon, Meshullam;

• A priest and temple musician.

Ne 12:35 — And *certain* of the priests' sons with trumpets; *namely,* Zechariah the son of Jonathan, the son of Shemaiah, the son of Mattaniah, the son of Michaiah, the son of Zaccur, the son of Asaph:

Ne 12:41 — And the priests; Eliakim, Maaseiah, Miniamin, Michaiah, Elioenai, Zechariah, *and* Hananiah, with trumpets;

• Perhaps identical with a prophet in the region of Uzziah.

Isa 8:2 — And I took unto me faithful witnesses to record, Uriah the priest, and Zechariah the son of Jeberechiah.

• A Levite in the reign of Hezekiah.

2Ch 29:13 — And of the sons of Elizaphan; Shimri, and Jeiel: and of the sons of Asaph; Zechariah, and Mattaniah:

✢See: Zachariah

ZEDAD • A place near Hamath.

Nu 34:8 — From mount Hor ye shall point out *your border* unto the entrance of Hamath; and the goings forth of the border shall be to Zedad:

Eze 47:15 — And this *shall be* the border of the land toward the north side, from the great sea, the way of Hethlon, as men go to Zedad;

ZEDEKIAH

• Made king of Judah by Nebuchadnezzar.

2Ki 24:17–18

1Ch 3:15 — And the sons of Josiah *were,* the firstborn Johanan, the second Jehoiakim, the third Zedekiah, the fourth Shallum.

2Ch 36:10 — And when the year was expired, king Nebuchadnezzar sent, and brought him to Babylon, with the goodly vessels of the house of the LORD, and made Zedekiah his brother king over Judah and Jerusalem.

Jer 37:1 — And king Zedekiah the son of Josiah reigned instead of Coniah the son of Jehoiakim, whom Nebuchadrezzar king of Babylon made king in the land of Judah.

• Throws off allegiance to Nebuchadnezzar.

Eze 17:12–21

2Ki 24:20 — For through the anger of the LORD it came to pass in Jerusalem and Judah, until he had cast them out from his presence, that Zedekiah rebelled against the king of Babylon.

2Ch 36:13 — And he also rebelled against king Nebuchadnezzar, who had made him swear by God: but he stiffened his neck, and hardened his heart from turning unto the LORD God of Israel.

Jer 52:3 — For through the anger of the LORD it came to pass in Jerusalem and Judah, till he had cast them out from his presence, that Zedekiah rebelled against the king of Babylon.

• Forms an alliance with the king of Egypt.

Eze 17:11–18

• The allegiance denounced by Jeremiah.

Jer 21:1–14; 24:8–10; 27:12–22; 32:3–5; 34:1–22; 37:7–10; 38:14–28

2Ch 36:12 — And he did *that which was* evil in the sight of the LORD his God, *and* humbled not himself before Jeremiah the prophet *speaking* from the mouth of the LORD.

Jer 37:17 — Then Zedekiah the king sent, and took him out: and the king asked him secretly in his house, and said, Is there *any* word from the LORD? And Jeremiah said, There is: for, said he, thou shalt be delivered into the hand of the king of Babylon.

• The allegiance denounced by Ezekiel.

Eze 12:10–16; 17:12–21

• Imprisons Jeremiah on account of his denunciations.

Jer 32:2–3; 37:15–21; 38:5–28

• Seeks the intercession of Jeremiah with God in his behalf.

Jer 21:1–3; 38:14–27

Jer 37:3 — And Zedekiah the king sent Jehucal the son of Shelemiah and Zephaniah the son of Maaseiah the priest to the prophet Jeremiah, saying, Pray now unto the LORD our God for us.

• Wicked reign of.

2Ki 24:19–20; 2Ch 36:12–13; Jer 38:24–26

Jer 37:2 — But neither he, nor his servants, nor the people of the land, did hearken unto the words of the LORD, which he spake by the prophet Jeremiah.

Jer 38:5 — Then Zedekiah the king said, Behold, he is in your hand: for the king *is* not *he that* can do *any* thing against you.

Jer 38:19 — And Zedekiah the king said unto Jeremiah, I am afraid of the Jews that are fallen to the Chaldeans, lest they deliver me into their hand, and they mock me.

Jer 52:2 — And he did *that which was* evil in the eyes of the LORD, according to all that Jehoiakim had done.

• Nebuchadnezzar destroys the city and temple; takes him captive to Babylon; blinds his eyes; slays his sons.

2Ki 25:1–10; 2Ch 36:17–20; Jer 32:1–2; 39:1–10; 52:4–30

Jer 1:3 — It came also in the days of Jehoiakim the son of Josiah king of Judah, unto the end of the eleventh year of Zedekiah the son of Josiah king of Judah, unto the carrying away of Jerusalem captive in the fifth month.

Jer 51:59 — The word which Jeremiah the prophet commanded Seraiah the son of Neriah, the son of Maaseiah, when he went with Zedekiah the king of Judah into Babylon in the fourth year of his reign. And *this* Seraiah was a quiet prince.

• Grandson of Jehoiakim.

1Ch 3:16 — And the sons of Jehoiakim: Jeconiah his son, Zedekiah his son.

• A false prophet.

Jer 29:21–23

• A prince of Judah.

Jer 36:12 — Then he went down into the king's house, into the scribe's chamber: and, lo, all the princes sat there, *even* Elishama the scribe, and Delaiah the son of Shemaiah, and Elnathan the son of Achbor, and Gemariah the son of Shaphan, and Zedekiah the son of Hananiah, and all the princes.

• A false prophet. Prophesies to Ahab victory over the Syrians, instead of defeat.

1Ki 22:11 — And Zedekiah the son of Chenaanah made him horns of iron: and he said, Thus saith the LORD, With these shalt thou push the Syrians, until thou have consumed them.

2Ch 18:10 — And Zedekiah the son of Chenaanah had made him horns of iron, and said, Thus saith the LORD, With these thou shalt push Syria until they be consumed.

• Smites Micaiah, the true prophet.

1Ki 22:24 — But Zedekiah the son of Chenaanah went near, and smote Micaiah on the cheek, and said, Which way went the Spirit of the LORD from me to speak unto thee?

2Ch 18:23 — Then Zedekiah the son of Chenaanah came near, and smote Micaiah upon the cheek, and said, Which way went the Spirit of the LORD from me to speak unto thee?

ZEEB • A prince of Midian.

Jgs 7:25 — And they took two princes of the Midianites, Oreb and Zeeb; and they slew Oreb upon the rock Oreb, and Zeeb they slew at the winepress of Zeeb, and pursued Midian, and brought the heads of Oreb and Zeeb to Gideon on the other side Jordan.

Jgs 8:3 — God hath delivered into your hands the princes of Midian, Oreb and Zeeb: and what was I able to do in comparison of you? Then their anger was abated toward him, when he had said that.

Ps 83:11 — Make their nobles like Oreb, and like Zeeb: yea, all their princes as Zebah, and as Zalmunna:

ZELAH

• A city in Benjamin.

• Saul buried in.

Jos 18:28 — And Zelah, Eleph, and Jebusi, which *is* Jerusalem, Gibeath, *and* Kirjath; fourteen cities with their villages. This *is* the inheritance of the children of Benjamin according to their families.

2Sa 21:14 — And the bones of Saul and Jonathan his son buried they in the country of Benjamin in Zelah, in the sepulchre of Kish his father: and they performed all that the king commanded. And after that God was intreated for the land.

ZELEK • An Ammonite.

2Sa 23:37 — Zelek the Ammonite, Nahari the Beerothite, armourbearer to Joab the son of Zeruiah,

1Ch 11:39 — Zelek the Ammonite, Naharai the Berothite, the armourbearer of Joab the son of Zeruiah,

ZELOPHEHAD

• Grandson of Gilead.

• His daughters petition for his inheritance.

Nu 27:1–11; 36:1–13; Jos 17:3–6

1Ch 7:15 — And Machir took to wife *the sister* of Huppim and Shuppim, whose sister's name *was* Maachah;) and the name of the second *was* Zelophehad: and Zelophehad had daughters.

ZELOTES ✧See: Simon

ZELZAH • A city of Benjamin.

1Sa 10:2 — When thou art departed from me to day, then thou shalt find two men by Rachel's sepulchre in the border of Benjamin at Zelzah; and they will say unto thee, The asses which thou wentest to seek are found: and, lo, thy father hath left the care of the asses, and sorroweth for you, saying, What shall I do for my son?

ZEMARAIM

• A city of Benjamin.

Jos 18:22 — And Beth-arabah, and Zemaraim, and Bethel,

• A part of Mount Ephraim.

2Ch 13:4 — And Abijah stood up upon mount Zemaraim, which *is* in mount Ephraim, and said, Hear me, thou Jeroboam, and all Israel;

ZEMARITES • A tribe descended from Canaan.

Ge 10:18 — And the Arvadite, and the Zemarite, and the Hamathite: and afterward were the families of the Canaanites spread abroad.

1Ch 1:16 — And the Arvadite, and the Zemarite, and the Hamathite.

ZEMIRA • A son of Becher.

1Ch 7:8 — And the sons of Becher; Zemira, and Joash, and Eliezer, and Elioenai, and Omri, and Jerimoth, and Abiah, and Anathoth, and Alameth. All these *are* the sons of Becher.

ZENAN • A city of Judah.

Jos 15:37 — Zenan, and Hadashah, and Migdal-gad,

ZENAS • A Christian believer and lawyer.

Tit 3:13 — Bring Zenas the lawyer and Apollos on their journey diligently, that nothing be wanting unto them.

ZEPHANIAH

• A priest sent with message soliciting the prophet's intercession and prayers.

Jer 21:1–2

• Shows Jeremiah the false prophet's letter.

Jer 29:25–29

• Taken to Riblah and slain.

2Ki 25:18–21; Jer 52:24–27

• A Kohathite.

1Ch 6:36 — The son of Elkanah, the son of Joel, the son of Azariah, the son of Zephaniah,

• A prophet in the days of Josiah.

Zep 1:1 — The word of the LORD which came unto Zephaniah the son of Cushi, the son of Gedaliah, the son of Amariah, the son of Hizkiah, in the days of Josiah the son of Amon, king of Judah.

• Father of Josiah.

Zec 6:10 — Take of *them of* the captivity, *even* of Heldai, of Tobijah, and of Jedaiah, which are come from Babylon, and come thou the same day, and go into the house of Josiah the son of Zephaniah;

Zec 6:14 — And the crowns shall be to Helem, and to Tobijah, and to Jedaiah, and to Hen the son of Zephaniah, for a memorial in the temple of the LORD.

ZEPHATH • A Canaanitish city.

Jgs 1:17 — And Judah went with Simeon his brother, and they slew the Canaanites that inhabited Zephath, and utterly destroyed it. And the name of the city was called Hormah.

See: Hormah

ZEPHATHAH • A valley west of Judah.

2Ch 14:10 — Then Asa went out against him, and they set the battle in array in the valley of Zephathah at Mareshah.

ZEPHI See: Zepho

ZEPHO

• Called also Zephi.

• Son of Eliphaz.

Ge 36:11 — And the sons of Eliphaz were Teman, Omar, Zepho, and Gatam, and Kenaz.

Ge 36:15 — These *were* dukes of the sons of Esau: the sons of Eliphaz the firstborn *son* of Esau; duke Teman, duke Omar, duke Zepho, duke Kenaz,

1Ch 1:36 — The sons of Eliphaz; Teman, and Omar, Zephi, and Gatam, Kenaz, and Timna, and Amalek.

ZEPHON • Son of Gad.

Nu 26:15 — The children of Gad after their families: of Zephon, the family of the Zephonites: of Haggi, the family of the Haggites: of Shuni, the family of the Shunites:

ZER • A city in Naphtali.

Jos 19:35 — And the fenced cities *are* Ziddim, Zer, and Hammath, Rakkath, and Chinnereth,

ZERAH

• Son of Reuel.

Ge 36:13 — And these *are* the sons of Reuel; Nahath, and Zerah, Shammah, and Mizzah: these were the sons of Bashemath Esau's wife.

Ge 36:17 — And these *are* the sons of Reuel Esau's son; duke Nahath, duke Zerah, duke Shammah, duke Mizzah: these *are* the dukes *that came* of Reuel in the land of Edom; these *are* the sons of Bashemath Esau's wife.

1Ch 1:37 — The sons of Reuel; Nahath, Zerah, Shammah, and Mizzah.

• Father of Jobab.

Ge 36:33 — And Bela died, and Jobab the son of Zerah of Bozrah reigned in his stead.

1Ch 1:44 — And when Bela was dead, Jobab the son of Zerah of Bozrah reigned in his stead.

See: Zarah

• Son of Simeon.

Nu 26:13 — Of Zerah, the family of the Zarhites: of Shaul, the family of the Shaulites.

1Ch 4:24 — The sons of Simeon *were,* Nemuel, and Jamin, Jarib, Zerah, *and* Shaul:

• A Gershonite.

1Ch 6:21 — Joah his son, Iddo his son, Zerah his son, Jeaterai his son.

• A Levite.

1Ch 6:41 — The son of Ethni, the son of Zerah, the son of Adaiah,

• King of Ethiopia.

2Ch 14:9–15

ZERAHIAH

• An ancestor of Ezra.

1Ch 6:6 — And Uzzi begat Zerahiah, and Zerahiah begat Meraioth,

1Ch 6:51 — Bukki his son, Uzzi his son, Zerahiah his son,

Ezr 7:4 — The son of Zerahiah, the son of Uzzi, the son of Bukki,

• Father of Elihoenai.

Ezr 8:4 — Of the sons of Pahath-moab; Elihoenai the son of Zerahiah, and with him two hundred males.

ZERED See: Zared

ZEREDA • A city or district of Ephraim.

1Ki 11:26 — And Jeroboam the son of Nebat, an Ephrathite of Zereda, Solomon's servant, whose mother's name *was* Zeruah, a widow woman, even he lifted up *his* hand against the king.

ZEREDATHAH • In Manasseh.

2Ch 4:17 — In the plain of Jordan did the king cast them, in the clay ground between Succoth and Zeredathah.

ZERERATH • A district of uncertain location.

Jgs 7:22 — And the three hundred blew the trumpets, and the LORD set every man's sword against his fellow, even throughout all the host: and the host fled to Beth-shittah in Zererath, *and* to the border of Abel-meholah, unto Tabbath.

ZERESH • Wife of Haman.

Est 5:10–14

Est 6:13 — And Haman told Zeresh his wife and all his friends every *thing* that had befallen him. Then said his wise men and Zeresh his wife unto him, If Mordecai *be* of the seed of the Jews, before whom thou hast begun to fall, thou shalt not prevail against him, but shalt surely fall before him.

ZERETH • Son of Ashur.

1Ch 4:7 — And the sons of Helah *were,* Zereth, and Jezoar, and Ethnan.

ZERI • Son of Jeduthun.

1Ch 25:3 — Of Jeduthun: the sons of Jeduthun; Gedaliah, and Zeri, and Jeshaiah, Hashabiah, and Mattithiah, six, under the hands of their father Jeduthun, who prophesied with a harp, to give thanks and to praise the LORD.

ZEROR • Father of Abiel.

1Sa 9:1 — Now there was a man of Benjamin, whose name *was* Kish, the son of Abiel, the son of Zeror, the son of Bechorath, the son of Aphiah, a Benjamite, a mighty man of power.

ZERUAH • Mother of Jeroboam.

1Ki 11:26 — And Jeroboam the son of Nebat, an Ephrathite of Zereda, Solomon's servant, whose mother's name *was* Zeruah, a widow woman, even he lifted up *his* hand against the king.

ZERUBBABEL

• Called also Sheshbazzar.

• Directs the rebuilding of the altar and temple after his return from captivity in Babylon.

Ezr 3:2–8; 4:2–3; 5:14–16; Hag 1:12–14

Ezr 5:2 — Then rose up Zerubbabel the son of Shealtiel, and Jeshua the son of Jozadak, and began to build the house of God which *is* at Jerusalem: and with them *were* the prophets of God helping them.

• Leads the emancipated Jews back from Babylon.

Ezr 1:8–2:70; Ne 12:1–47

• Appoints the Levites to inaugurate the rebuilding of the temple.

Ezr 3:2–8

• Prophecies relating to.

Zec 4:6–10

Hag 2:2 — Speak now to Zerubbabel the son of Shealtiel, governor of Judah, and to Joshua the son of Josedech, the high priest, and to the residue of the people, saying,

• Called Zorobabel in the genealogy of Joseph.

Mt 1:12 — And after they were brought to Babylon, Jechonias begat Salathiel; and Salathiel begat Zorobabel;

Lk 3:27 — Which was *the son* of Joanna, which was *the son* of Rhesa, which was *the son* of Zorobabel, which was *the son* of Salathiel, which was *the son* of Neri,

ZERUIAH

• Sister of David.

1Ch 2:16 — Whose sisters *were* Zeruiah, and Abigail. And the sons of Zeruiah; Abishai, and Joab, and Asahel, three.

• Mother of three of David's great soldiers.

2Sa 16:9–11

2Sa 2:18 — And there were three sons of Zeruiah there, Joab, and Abishai, and Asahel: and Asahel *was as* light of foot as a wild roe.

2Sa 3:39 — And I *am* this day weak, though anointed king; and these men the sons of Zeruiah *be* too hard for me: the LORD shall reward the doer of evil according to his wickedness.

2Sa 17:25 — And Absalom made Amasa captain of the host instead of Joab: which Amasa was a man's son, whose name *was* Ithra an Israelite, that went in to Abigail the daughter of Nahash, sister to Zeruiah Joab's mother.

1Ch 2:16 — Whose sisters *were* Zeruiah, and Abigail. And the sons of Zeruiah; Abishai, and Joab, and Asahel, three.

ZETHAM • A son of Laadan.

1Ch 23:8 — The sons of Laadan; the chief *was* Jehiel, and Zetham, and Joel, three.

1Ch 26:22 — The sons of Jehieli; Zetham, and Joel his brother, *which were* over the treasures of the house of the LORD.

ZETHAN • Son of Bilhan.

1Ch 7:10 — The sons also of Jediael; Bilhan: and the sons of Bilhan; Jeush, and Benjamin, and Ehud, and Chenaanah, and Zethan, and Tharshish, and Ahishahar.

ZETHAR • One of the seven chamberlains of the king of Persia.

Est 1:10 — On the seventh day, when the heart of the king was merry with wine, he commanded Mehuman, Biztha, Harbona, Bigtha, and Abagtha, Zethar, and Carcas, the seven chamberlains that served in the presence of Ahasuerus the king,

ZIA • A Gadite.

1Ch 5:13 — And their brethren of the house of their fathers *were,* Michael, and Meshullam, and Sheba, and Jorai, and Jachan, and Zia, and Heber, seven.

ZIBA

• Paul's servant.

• His fidelity to Mephibosheth.

2Sa 9:1–13

• His fidelity to David.

2Sa 16:1–4; 19:26–29

2Sa 19:17 — And *there were* a thousand men of Benjamin with him, and Ziba the servant of the house of Saul, and his fifteen sons and his twenty servants with him; and they went over Jordan before the king.

ZIBEON

• A Hivite.

Ge 36:2 — Esau took his wives of the daughters of Canaan; Adah the daughter of Elon the Hittite, and Aholibamah the daughter of Anah the daughter of Zibeon the Hivite;

Ge 36:14 — And these were the sons of Aholibamah, the daughter of Anah the daughter of Zibeon, Esau's wife: and she bare to Esau Jeush, and Jaalam, and Korah.

• Son of Seir.

Ge 36:20 — These *are* the sons of Seir the Horite, who inhabited the land; Lotan, and Shobal, and Zibeon, and Anah,

Ge 36:24 — And these *are* the children of Zibeon; both Ajah, and Anah: this *was that* Anah that found the mules in the wilderness, as he fed the asses of Zibeon his father.

Ge 36:29 — These *are* the dukes *that came* of the Horites; duke Lotan, duke Shobal, duke Zibeon, duke Anah,

1Ch 1:38 — And the sons of Seir; Lotan, and Shobal, and Zibeon, and Anah, and Dishon, and Ezar, and Dishan.

1Ch 1:40 — The sons of Shobal; Alian, and Manahath, and Ebal, Shephi, and Onam. And the sons of Zibeon; Aiah, and Anah.

ZIBIA • A Benjamite.

1Ch 8:9 — And he begat of Hodesh his wife, Jobab, and Zibia, and Mesha, and Malcham,

ZIBIAH • Wife of Ahaziah.

2Ki 12:1 — In the seventh year of Jehu Jehoash began to reign; and forty years reigned he in Jerusalem. And his mother's name *was* Zibiah of Beer-sheba.

2Ch 24:1 — Joash *was* seven years old when he began to reign, and he reigned forty years in Jerusalem. His mother's name also *was* Zibiah of Beer-sheba.

ZICHRI

• Son of Izhar.

Ex 6:21 — And the sons of Izhar; Korah, and Nepheg, and Zichri.

• Three Benjamites.

1Ch 8:19 — And Jakim, and Zichri, and Zabdi,

1Ch 8:23 — And Abdon, and Zichri, and Hanan,

1Ch 8:27 — And Jaresiah, and Eliah, and Zichri, the sons of Jeroham.

• A Levite.

1Ch 9:15 — And Bakbakkar, Heresh, and Galal, and Mattaniah the son of Micah, the son of Zichri, the son of Asaph;

• Two chiefs in the days of David.

1Ch 26:25 — And his brethren by Eliezer; Rehabiah his son, and Jeshaiah his son, and Joram his son, and Zichri his son, and Shelomith his son.

1Ch 27:16 — Furthermore over the tribes of Israel: the ruler of the Reubenites *was* Eliezer the son of Zichri: of the Simeonites, Shephatiah the son of Maachah:

• Father of Amasiah.

2Ch 17:16 — And next him *was* Amasiah the son of Zichri, who willingly offered himself unto the LORD; and with him two hundred thousand mighty men of valour.

• Father of Elishaphat.

2Ch 23:1 — And in the seventh year Jehoiada strengthened himself, and took the captains of hundreds, Azariah the son of Jeroham, and Ishmael the son of Jehohanan, and Azariah the son of Obed, and Maaseiah the son of Adaiah, and Elishaphat the son of Zichri, into covenant with him.

• An Ephraimite.

2Ch 28:7 — And Zichri, a mighty man of Ephraim, slew Maaseiah the king's son, and Azrikam the governor of the house, and Elkanah *that was* next to the king.

• Father of Joel.

Ne 11:9 — And Joel the son of Zichri *was* their overseer: and Judah the son of Senuah *was* second over the city.

• A priest.

Ne 12:17 — Of Abijah, Zichri; of Miniamin, of Moadiah, Piltai;

ZIDDIM • A city in Naphtali.

Jos 19:35 — And the fenced cities *are* Ziddim, Zer, and Hammath, Rakkath, and Chinnereth,

ZIDKIJAH • A chief prince of the exiles who returned to Jerusalem.

Ne 10:1 — Now those that sealed *were*, Nehemiah, the Tirshatha, the son of Hachaliah, and Zidkijah,

ZIDON • See: Sidon

ZIF • Second month, or May.

1Ki 6:1 — And it came to pass in the four hundred and eightieth year after the children of Israel were come out of the land of Egypt, in the fourth year of Solomon's reign over Israel, in the month Zif, which *is* the second month, that he began to build the house of the LORD.

1Ki 6:37 — In the fourth year was the foundation of the house of the LORD laid, in the month Zif:

ZIHA

• One of the Nethinim.

Ezr 2:43 — The Nethinims: the children of Ziha, the children of Hasupha, the children of Tabbaoth,

Ne 7:46 — The Nethinims: the children of Ziha, the children of Hashupha, the children of Tabbaoth,

• A ruler of the Nethinim.

Ne 11:21 — But the Nethinims dwelt in Ophel: and Ziha and Gispa *were* over the Nethinims.

ZIKLAG

• A city within the territory allotted to the tribe of Judah.

Jos 15:31 — And Ziklag, and Madmannah, and Sansannah,

• Reallotted to the tribe of Simeon.

Jos 19:5 — And Ziklag, and Beth-marcaboth, and Hazar-susah,

• David dwells at.

1Sa 27:5–6

2Sa 1:1 — Now it came to pass after the death of Saul, when David was returned from the slaughter of the Amalekites, and David had abode two days in Ziklag;

1Ch 12:1 — Now these *are* they that came to David to Ziklag, while he yet kept himself close because of Saul the son of Kish: and they *were* among the mighty men, helpers of the war.

• Amalekites destroy.

1Sa 30:1–31

• Inhabited by the returned exiles of Judah.

Ne 11:28 — And at Ziklag, and at Mekonah, and in the villages thereof,

ZILLAH • Wife of Lamech.

Ge 4:22–23

Ge 4:19 — And Lamech took unto him two wives: the name of the one *was* Adah, and the name of the other Zillah.

ZILPAH

• Leah's handmaid.

Ge 29:24 — And Laban gave unto his daughter Leah Zilpah his maid *for* an handmaid.

• Mother of Gad and Asher by Jacob.

Ge 30:9–13

Ge 35:26 — And the sons of Zilpah, Leah's handmaid; Gad, and Asher: these *are* the sons of Jacob, which were born to him in Padan-aram.

Ge 37:2 — These *are* the generations of Jacob. Joseph, *being* seventeen years old, was feeding the flock with his brethren; and the lad *was* with the sons of Bilhah, and with the sons of Zilpah, his father's wives: and Joseph brought unto his father their evil report.

Ge 46:18 — These *are* the sons of Zilpah, whom Laban gave to Leah his daughter, and these she bare unto Jacob, *even* sixteen souls.

ZILTHAI

• A Benjamite.

1Ch 8:20 — And Elienai, and Zilthai, and Eliel,

• A captain of Manasseh.

1Ch 12:20 — As he went to Ziklag, there fell to him of Manasseh, Adnah, and Jozabad, and Jediael, and Michael, and Jozabad, and Elihu, and Zilthai, captains of the thousands that *were* of Manasseh.

ZIMMAH

• A son of Jahath.

1Ch 6:20 — Of Gershom; Libni his son, Jahath his son, Zimmah his son,

• Two Gershonites.

1Ch 6:42 — The son of Ethan, the son of Zimmah, the son of Shimei,

2Ch 29:12 — Then the Levites arose, Mahath the son of Amasai, and Joel the son of Azariah, of the sons of the Kohathites: and of the sons of Merari, Kish the son of Abdi, and Azariah the son of Jehalelel: and of the Gershonites; Joah the son of Zimmah, and Eden the son of Joah:

ZIMRAN • Son of Abraham.

Ge 25:2 — And she bare him Zimran, and Jokshan, and Medan, and Midian, and Ishbak, and Shuah.

1Ch 1:32 — Now the sons of Keturah, Abraham's concubine: she bare Zimran, and Jokshan, and Medan, and Midian, and Ishbak, and Shuah. And the sons of Jokshan; Sheba, and Dedan.

ZIMRI

• A chief of Simeon.

Nu 25:6–8

Nu 25:14 — Now the name of the Israelite that was slain, *even* that was slain with the Midianitish woman, *was* Zimri, the son of Salu, a prince of a chief house among the Simeonites.

• King of Israel.

1Ki 16:9–20

2Ki 9:31 — And as Jehu entered in at the gate, she said, *Had* Zimri peace, who slew his master?

• Son of Zerah.

1Ch 2:6 — And the sons of Zerah; Zimri, and Ethan, and Heman, and Calcol, and Dara: five of them in all.

• A Benjamite.

1Ch 8:36 — And Ahaz begat Jehoadah; and Jehoadah begat Alemeth, and Azmaveth, and Zimri; and Zimri begat Moza,

1Ch 9:42 — And Ahaz begat Jarah; and Jarah begat Alemeth, and Azmaveth, and Zimri; and Zimri begat Moza;

• An unknown place.

Jer 25:25 — And all the kings of Zimri, and all the kings of Elam, and all the kings of the Medes,

ZIN

• A desert south of Judah.

Nu 34:3–4

Nu 13:21 — So they went up, and searched the land from the wilderness of Zin unto Rehob, as men come to Hamath.

Nu 20:1 — Then came the children of Israel, *even* the whole congregation, into the desert of Zin in the first month: and the people abode in Kadesh; and Miriam died there, and was buried there.

Nu 27:14 — For ye rebelled against my commandment in the desert of Zin, in the strife of the congregation, to sanctify me at the water before their eyes: that *is* the water of Meribah in Kadesh in the wilderness of Zin.

Nu 33:36 — And they removed from Ezion-gaber, and pitched in the wilderness of Zin, which *is* Kadesh.

Dt 32:51 — Because ye trespassed against me among the children of Israel at the waters of Meribah-Kadesh, in the wilderness of Zin; because ye sanctified me not in the midst of the children of Israel.

Jos 15:1 — *This* then was the lot of the tribe of the children of Judah by their families; *even* to the border of Edom the wilderness of Zin southward *was* the uttermost part of the south coast.

Jos 15:3 — And it went out to the south side to Maaleh-acrabbim, and passed along to Zin, and ascended up on the south side unto Kadesh-barnea, and passed along to Hezron, and went up to Adar, and fetched a compass to Karkaa:

ZINA

• A son of Shimei.

1Ch 23:10 — And the sons of Shimei *were*, Jahath, Zina, and Jeush, and Beriah. These four *were* the sons of Shimei.

• Called Zizah.

1Ch 23:11 — And Jahath was the chief, and Zizah the second: but Jeush and Beriah had not many sons; therefore they were in one reckoning, according to *their* father's house.

ZION

• Called also Sion, stronghold of Jerusalem.

• Taken from the Jebusites by David.

2Sa 5:6–9; 1Ch 11:5–7

• Called thereafter "the city of David".

2Sa 5:7 — Nevertheless David took the strong hold of Zion: the same *is* the city of David.

2Sa 5:9 — So David dwelt in the fort, and called it the city of David. And David built round about from Millo and inward.

2Sa 6:12 — And it was told king David, saying, The LORD hath blessed the house of Obed-edom, and all that *pertaineth* unto him, because of the ark of God. So David went and brought up the ark of God from the house of Obed-edom into the city of David with gladness.

2Sa 6:16 — And as the ark of the LORD came into the city of David, Michal Saul's daughter looked through a window, and saw king David leaping and dancing before the LORD; and she despised him in her heart.

1Ki 8:1 — Then Solomon assembled the elders of Israel, and all the heads of the tribes, the chief of the fathers of the children of Israel, unto king Solomon in Jerusalem, that they might bring up the ark of the covenant of the LORD out of the city of David, which *is* Zion.

1Ch 11:5 — And the inhabitants of Jebus said to David, Thou shalt not come hither. Nevertheless David took the castle of Zion, which *is* the city of David.

1Ch 11:7 — And David dwelt in the castle; therefore they called it the city of David.

1Ch 15:1 — And *David* made him houses in the city of David, and prepared a place for the ark of God, and pitched for it a tent.

1Ch 15:29 — And it came to pass, *as* the ark of the covenant of the LORD came to the city of David, that Michal the daughter of Saul looking out at a window saw king David dancing and playing: and she despised him in her heart.

2Ch 5:2 — Then Solomon assembled the elders of Israel, and all the heads of the tribes, the chief of the fathers of the children of Israel, unto Jerusalem, to bring up the ark of the covenant of the LORD out of the city of David, which *is* Zion.

• Ark of the covenant placed in.

2Sa 6:12 — And it was told king David, saying, The LORD hath blessed the house of Obed-edom, and all that *pertaineth* unto him, because of the ark of God. So David went and brought up the ark of God from the house of Obed-edom into the city of David with gladness.

2Sa 6:16 — And as the ark of the LORD came into the city of David, Michal Saul's daughter looked through a window, and saw king David leaping and dancing before the LORD; and she despised him in her heart.

1Ki 8:1 — Then Solomon assembled the elders of Israel, and all the heads of the tribes, the chief of the fathers of the children of Israel, unto king Solomon in Jerusalem, that they might bring up the ark of the covenant of the LORD out of the city of David, which *is* Zion.

1Ch 15:1 — And *David* made him houses in the city of David, and prepared a place for the ark of God, and pitched for it a tent.

1Ch 15:29 — And it came to pass, *as* the ark of the covenant of the LORD came to the city of David, that Michal the daughter of Saul looking out at a window saw king David dancing and playing: and she despised him in her heart.

2Ch 5:2 — Then Solomon assembled the elders of Israel, and all the heads of the tribes, the chief of the fathers of the children of Israel, unto Jerusalem, to bring up the ark of the covenant of the LORD out of the city of David, which *is* Zion.

• Ark of the covenant removed from, to Solomon's temple on Mount Moriah.

1Ki 8:1 — Then Solomon assembled the elders of Israel, and all the heads of the tribes, the chief of the fathers of the children of Israel, unto king Solomon in Jerusalem, that they might bring up the ark of the covenant of the LORD out of the city of David, which *is* Zion.

2Ch 3:1 — Then Solomon began to build the house of the LORD at Jerusalem in mount Moriah, where *the LORD* appeared unto David his father, in the place that David had prepared in the threshingfloor of Ornan the Jebusite.

2Ch 5:2 — Then Solomon assembled the elders of Israel, and all the heads of the tribes, the chief of the fathers of the children of Israel, unto Jerusalem, to bring up the ark of the covenant of the LORD out of the city of David, which *is* Zion.

• Collectively, the place, the forms, and the assemblies of the Israelitish worship.

Ps 48:11–12; Isa 52:1–2, 7–8

2Ki 19:21 — This *is* the word that the LORD hath spoken concerning him; The virgin the daughter of Zion hath despised thee, *and* laughed thee to scorn; the daughter of Jerusalem hath shaken her head at thee.

2Ki 19:31 — For out of Jerusalem shall go forth a remnant, and they that escape out of mount Zion: the zeal of the LORD *of hosts* shall do this.

Ps 9:11 — Sing praises to the LORD, which dwelleth in Zion: declare among the people his doings.

Ps 48:2 — Beautiful for situation, the joy of the whole earth, *is* mount Zion, *on* the sides of the north, the city of the great King.

Ps 74:2 — Remember thy congregation, *which* thou hast purchased of old; the rod of thine inheritance, *which* thou hast redeemed; this mount Zion, wherein thou hast dwelt.

Ps 132:13 — For the LORD hath chosen Zion; he hath desired *it* for his habitation.

Ps 137:1 — By the rivers of Babylon, there we sat down, yea, we wept, when we remembered Zion.

Isa 35:10 — And the ransomed of the LORD shall return, and come to Zion with songs and everlasting joy upon their heads: they shall obtain joy and gladness, and sorrow and sighing shall flee away.

Isa 40:9 — O Zion, that bringest good tidings, get thee up into the high mountain; O Jerusalem, that bringest good tidings, lift up thy voice with strength; lift *it* up, be not afraid; say unto the cities of Judah, Behold your God!

Isa 49:14 — But Zion said, The LORD hath forsaken me, and my Lord hath forgotten me.

Isa 51:16 — And I have put my words in thy mouth, and I have covered thee in the shadow of mine hand, that I may plant the heavens, and lay the foundations of the earth, and say unto Zion, Thou *art* my people.

Isa 60:14 — The sons also of them that afflicted thee shall come bending unto thee; and all they that despised thee shall bow themselves down at the soles of thy feet; and they shall call thee, The city of the LORD, The Zion of the Holy One of Israel.

Isa 62:1 — For Zion's sake will I not hold my peace, and for Jerusalem's sake I will not rest, until the righteousness thereof go forth as brightness, and the salvation thereof as a lamp *that* burneth.

Isa 62:11 — Behold, the LORD hath proclaimed unto the end of the world, Say ye to the daughter of Zion, Behold, thy salvation cometh; behold, his reward *is* with him, and his work before him.

Jer 31:6 — For there shall be a day, *that* the watchmen upon the mount Ephraim shall cry, Arise ye, and let us go up to Zion unto the LORD our God.

Jer 50:5 — They shall ask the way to Zion with their faces thitherward, *saying,* Come, and let us join ourselves to the LORD in a perpetual covenant *that* shall not be forgotten.

La 1:4 — The ways of Zion do mourn, because none come to the solemn feasts: all her gates are desolate: her priests sigh, her virgins are afflicted, and she *is* in bitterness.

Joel 2:1 — Blow ye the trumpet in Zion, and sound an alarm in my holy mountain: let all the inhabitants of the land tremble: for the day of the LORD cometh, for *it is* nigh at hand;

Joel 2:15 — Blow the trumpet in Zion, sanctify a fast, call a solemn assembly:

Mt 21:5 — Tell ye the daughter of Sion, Behold, thy King cometh unto thee, meek, and sitting upon an ass, and a colt the foal of an ass.

Jn 12:15 — Fear not, daughter of Sion: behold, thy King cometh, sitting on an ass's colt.

Ro 9:33 — As it is written, Behold, I lay in Sion a stumblingstone and rock of offence: and whosoever believeth on him shall not be ashamed.

Ro 11:26 — And so all Israel shall be saved: as it is written, There shall come out of Sion the Deliverer, and shall turn away ungodliness from Jacob:

1Pe 2:6 — Wherefore also it is contained in the scripture, Behold, I lay in Sion a chief corner stone, elect, precious: and he that believeth on him shall not be confounded.

• Name of, applied to Jerusalem.

Ps 87:2 — The LORD loveth the gates of Zion more than all the dwellings of Jacob.

Ps 87:5 — And of Zion it shall be said, This and *that man* was born in her: and the highest himself shall establish her.

Ps 149:2 — Let Israel rejoice in him that made him: let the children of Zion be joyful in their King.

SS 3:11 — Go forth, O ye daughters of Zion, and behold king Solomon with the crown wherewith his mother crowned him in the day of his espousals, and in the day of the gladness of his heart.

Isa 33:14 — The sinners in Zion are afraid; fearfulness hath surprised the hypocrites. Who among us shall dwell with the devouring fire? who among us shall dwell with everlasting burnings?

Isa 33:20 — Look upon Zion, the city of our solemnities: thine eyes shall see Jerusalem a quiet habitation, a tabernacle *that* shall not be taken down; not one of the stakes thereof shall ever be removed, neither shall any of the cords thereof be broken.

Jer 9:19 — For a voice of wailing is heard out of Zion, How are we spoiled! we are greatly confounded, because we have forsaken the land, because our dwellings have cast *us* out.

Jer 30:17 — For I will restore health unto thee, and I will heal thee of thy wounds, saith the LORD; because they called thee an Outcast, *saying,* This *is* Zion, whom no man seeketh after.

Zec 9:13 — When I have bent Judah for me, filled the bow with Ephraim, and raised up thy sons, O Zion, against thy sons, O Greece, and made thee as the sword of a mighty man.

• **Called the city of God.**

87:2–3

Isa 60:14 — The sons also of them that afflicted thee shall come bending unto thee; and all they that despised thee shall bow themselves down at the soles of thy feet; and they shall call thee, The city of the LORD, The Zion of the Holy One of Israel.

• **Restoration of, promised.**

Isa 52:1–2, 7–8; Zec 8:2–3

Isa 51:3 — For the LORD shall comfort Zion: he will comfort all her waste places; and he will make her wilderness like Eden, and her desert like the garden of the LORD; joy and gladness shall be found therein, thanksgiving, and the voice of melody.

Isa 51:11 — Therefore the redeemed of the LORD shall return, and come with singing unto Zion; and everlasting joy *shall be* upon their head: they shall obtain gladness and joy; *and* sorrow and mourning shall flee away.

Isa 51:16 — And I have put my words in thy mouth, and I have covered thee in the shadow of mine hand, that I may plant the heavens, and lay the foundations of the earth, and say unto Zion, Thou *art* my people.

Isa 59:20 — And the Redeemer shall come to Zion, and unto them that turn from transgression in Jacob, saith the LORD.

Isa 60:14 — The sons also of them that afflicted thee shall come bending unto thee; and all they that despised thee shall bow themselves down at the soles of thy feet; and they shall call thee, The city of the LORD, The Zion of the Holy One of Israel.

Ob 1:17 — But upon mount Zion shall be deliverance, and there shall be holiness; and the house of Jacob shall possess their possessions.

Ob 1:21 — And saviours shall come up on mount Zion to judge the mount of Esau; and the kingdom shall be the LORD'S.

Zep 3:14 — Sing, O daughter of Zion; shout, O Israel; be glad and rejoice with all the heart, O daughter of Jerusalem.

Zep 3:16 — In that day it shall be said to Jerusalem, Fear thou not: *and to* Zion, Let not thine hands be slack.

Zec 1:14 — So the angel that communed with me said unto me, Cry thou, saying, Thus saith the LORD of hosts; I am jealous for Jerusalem and for Zion with a great jealousy.

Zec 1:17 — Cry yet, saying, Thus saith the LORD of hosts; My cities through prosperity shall yet be spread abroad; and the LORD shall yet comfort Zion, and shall yet choose Jerusalem.

Zec 2:7 — Deliver thyself, O Zion, that dwellest *with* the daughter of Babylon.

Zec 2:10 — Sing and rejoice, O daughter of Zion: for, lo, I come, and I will dwell in the midst of thee, saith the LORD.

Zec 9:9 — Rejoice greatly, O daughter of Zion; shout, O daughter of Jerusalem: behold, thy King cometh unto thee: he *is* just, and having salvation; lowly, and riding upon an ass, and upon a colt the foal of an ass.

Zec 9:13 — When I have bent Judah for me, filled the bow with Ephraim, and raised up thy sons, O Zion, against thy sons, O Greece, and made thee as the sword of a mighty man.

• **Name of, applied to the city of the redeemed.**

Heb 12:22 — But ye are come unto mount Sion, and unto the city of the living God, the heavenly Jerusalem, and to an innumerable company of angels,

Rev 14:1 — And I looked, and, lo, a Lamb stood on the mount Sion, and with him an hundred forty *and* four thousand, having his Father's name written in their foreheads.

See: Church

See: Jerusalem

ZIOR • A city in Judah.

Jos 15:54 — And Humtah, and Kirjath-arba, which *is* Hebron, and Zior; nine cities with their villages:

ZIPH

• **Two cities of Judah.**

1Sa 23:14–15

Jos 15:24 — Ziph, and Telem, and Bealoth,

Jos 15:55 — Maon, Carmel, and Ziph, and Juttah,

1Sa 23:24 — And they arose, and went to Ziph before Saul: but David and his men *were* in the wilderness of Maon, in the plain on the south of Jeshimon.

1Sa 26:2 — Then Saul arose, and went down to the wilderness of Ziph, having three thousand chosen men of Israel with him, to seek David in the wilderness of Ziph.

2Ch 11:8 — And Gath, and Mareshah, and Ziph,

• **Grandson of Caleb.**

1Ch 2:42 — Now the sons of Caleb the brother of Jerahmeel *were,* Mesha his firstborn, which was the father of Ziph; and the sons of Mareshah the father of Hebron.

• **Son of Jehaleleel.**

1Ch 4:16 — And the sons of Jehaleleel; Ziph, and Ziphah, Tiria, and Asareel.

ZIPHAH • A son of Jehaleleel.

1Ch 4:16 — And the sons of Jehaleleel; Ziph, and Ziphah, Tiria, and Asareel.

ZIPHION

• **A son of Gad.**

Ge 46:16 — And the sons of Gad; Ziphion, and Haggi, Shuni, and Ezbon, Eri, and Arodi, and Areli.

• **Called Zephon.**

Nu 26:15 — The children of Gad after their families: of Zephon, the family of the Zephonites: of Haggi, the family of the Haggites: of Shuni, the family of the Shunites:

ZIPHRON • A place in the north of Palestine.

Nu 34:9 — And the border shall go on to Ziphron, and the goings out of it shall be at Hazar-enan: this shall be your north border.

ZIPPOR • Father of Balak.

Nu 22:2 — And Balak the son of Zippor saw all that Israel had done to the Amorites.

Nu 22:4 — And Moab said unto the elders of Midian, Now shall this company lick up all *that are* round about us, as the ox licketh up the grass of the field. And Balak the son of Zippor *was* king of the Moabites at that time.

Nu 22:10 — And Balaam said unto God, Balak the son of Zippor, king of Moab, hath sent unto me, *saying,*

Nu 22:16 — And they came to Balaam, and said to him, Thus saith Balak the son of Zippor, Let nothing, I pray thee, hinder thee from coming unto me:

Nu 23:18 — And he took up his parable, and said, Rise up, Balak, and hear; hearken unto me, thou son of Zippor:

Jos 24:9 — Then Balak the son of Zippor, king of Moab, arose and warred against Israel, and sent and called Balaam the son of Beor to curse you:

ZIPPORAH

• Wife of Moses.

Ex 2:16–22

• Reproaches Moses.

Ex 4:25–26

• Separates from Moses, is brought again to him by her father.

Ex 18:2–6

• Miriam and Aaron upbraid Moses concerning.

Nu 12:1 — And Miriam and Aaron spake against Moses because of the Ethiopian woman whom he had married: for he had married an Ethiopian woman.

ZITHRI • A son of Uzziel.

Ex 6:22 — And the sons of Uzziel; Mishael, and Elzaphan, and Zithri.

ZIZ • A pass in Judah.

2Ch 20:16 — To morrow go ye down against them: behold, they come up by the cliff of Ziz; and ye shall find them at the end of the brook, before the wilderness of Jeruel.

ZIZA

• A Simeonite.

1Ch 4:37 — And Ziza the son of Shiphi, the son of Allon, the son of Jedaiah, the son of Shimri, the son of Shemaiah;

• Son of Rehoboam.

2Ch 11:20 — And after her he took Maachah the daughter of Absalom; which bare him Abijah, and Attai, and Ziza, and Shelomith.

ZIZAH

• A Gershonite.

1Ch 23:11 — And Jahath was the chief, and Zizah the second: but Jeush and Beriah had not many sons; therefore they were in one reckoning, according to *their* father's house.

• Called Zina.

1Ch 23:10 — And the sons of Shimei *were,* Jahath, Zina, and Jeush, and Beriah. These four *were* the sons of Shimei.

ZOAN

• A city in Egypt.

• Built seven years after Hebron in the land of Canaan.

Nu 13:22 — And they ascended by the south, and came unto Hebron; where Ahiman, Sheshai, and Talmai, the children of Anak, *were.* (Now Hebron was built seven years before Zoan in Egypt.)

• Prophecies concerning.

Eze 30:14 — And I will make Pathros desolate, and will set fire in Zoan, and will execute judgments in No.

• Wise men from, were counselors of Pharaoh.

Isa 19:11 — Surely the princes of Zoan *are* fools, the counsel of the wise counsellors of Pharaoh is become brutish: how say ye unto Pharaoh, I *am* the son of the wise, the son of ancient kings?

Isa 19:13 — The princes of Zoan are become fools, the princes of Noph are deceived; they have also seduced Egypt, *even they that are* the stay of the tribes thereof.

• Princes of.

Isa 30:4 — For his princes were at Zoan, and his ambassadors came to Hanes.

ZOAR

• A city of the Moabites, near the Jordan.

Ge 13:10 — And Lot lifted up his eyes, and beheld all the plain of Jordan, that it *was* well watered every where, before the LORD destroyed Sodom and Gomorrah, *even* as the garden of the LORD, like the land of Egypt, as thou comest unto Zoar.

• Territory of.

Dt 34:3 — And the south, and the plain of the valley of Jericho, the city of palm trees, unto Zoar.

Isa 15:5 — My heart shall cry out for Moab; his fugitives *shall flee* unto Zoar, an heifer of three years old: for by the mounting up of Luhith with weeping shall they go it up; for in the way of Horonaim they shall raise up a cry of destruction.

Jer 48:34 — From the cry of Heshbon *even* unto Elealeh, *and even* unto Jahaz, have they uttered their voice, from Zoar *even* unto Horonaim, *as* an heifer of three years old: for the waters also of Nimrim shall be desolate.

• King of, fought against Chedorlaomer.

Ge 14:2 — *That these* made war with Bera king of Sodom, and with Birsha king of Gomorrah, Shinab king of Admah, and Shemeber king of Zeboiim, and the king of Bela, which is Zoar.

Ge 14:8 — And there went out the king of Sodom, and the king of Gomorrah, and the king of Admah, and the king of Zeboiim, and the king of Bela (the same *is* Zoar;) and they joined battle with them in the vale of Siddim;

• Not destroyed with Sodom and Gomorrah.

Ge 19:20–23

Ge 19:30 — And Lot went up out of Zoar, and dwelt in the mountain, and his two daughters with him; for he feared to dwell in Zoar: and he dwelt in a cave, he and his two daughters.

ZOBA *See: Zobah

ZOBAH

• Called also Zoba, Aram-Zobah, Hamath-Zobah.

• A kingdom in the north of Palestine.

1Sa 14:47 — So Saul took the kingdom over Israel, and fought against all his enemies on every side, against Moab, and against the children of Ammon, and against Edom, and against the kings of Zobah, and against the Philistines: and whithersoever he turned himself, he vexed *them.*

• Conquest of, by David.

2Sa 8:3–8; 1Ki 11:23–24; 1Ch 18:2–9

2Sa 8:12 — Of Syria, and of Moab, and of the children of Ammon, and of the Philistines, and of Amalek, and of the spoil of Hadadezer, son of Rehob, king of Zobah.

• Its inhabitants mercenaries of the Ammonites against David.

2Sa 10:6-19; 1Ch 19:6–19

• David writes a psalm after the conquest of.

Ps 60:1 — [To the chief Musician upon Shushan-eduth, Michtam of David, to teach; when he strove with Aram-naharaim and with Aram-zobah, when Joab returned, and smote of Edom in the valley of salt twelve thousand.] O God, thou hast cast us off, thou hast scattered us, thou hast been displeased; O turn thyself to us again.

• Invaded by Solomon.

2Ch 8:3 — And Solomon went to Hamath-zobah, and prevailed against it.

ZOBEBAH • Daughter of Coz.

1Ch 4:8 — And Coz begat Anub, and Zobebah, and the families of Aharhel the son of Harum.

ZODIAC

• Signs of.

Job 38:32 — Canst thou bring forth Mazzaroth in his season? or canst thou guide Arcturus with his sons?

ZOHAR

• Father of Ephron.

Ge 23:8 — And he communed with them, saying, If it be your mind that I should bury my dead out of my sight; hear me, and intreat for me to Ephron the son of Zohar,

Ge 25:9 — And his sons Isaac and Ishmael buried him in the cave of Machpelah, in the field of Ephron the son of Zohar the Hittite, which *is* before Mamre;

• Son of Simeon.

Ge 46:10 — And the sons of Simeon; Jemuel, and Jamin, and Ohad, and Jachin, and Zohar, and Shaul the son of a Canaanitish woman.

Exodus 6:15 — And the sons of Simeon; Jemuel, and Jamin, and Ohad, and Jachin, and Zohar, and Shaul the son of a Canaanitish woman: these *are* the families of Simeon.

ZOHELETH • A stone near En-rogel.

1Ki 1:9 — And Adonijah slew sheep and oxen and fat cattle by the stone of Zoheleth, which *is* by En-rogel, and called all his brethren the king's sons, and all the men of Judah the king's servants:

ZOHETH • Son of Ishi.

1Ch 4:20 — And the sons of Shimon *were,* Amnon, and Rinnah, Ben-hanan, and Tilon. And the sons of Ishi *were,* Zoheth, and Ben-zoheth.

ZOPHAH • Son of Helem.

1Ch 7:35–36

ZOPHAI • Son of Elkanah.

1Ch 6:26 — *As for* Elkanah: the sons of Elkanah; Zophai his son, and Nahath his son,

ZOPHAR • One of Job's three friends.

Job 11:1–20; 20:1–29; 42:7–9

Job 2:11 — Now when Job's three friends heard of all this evil that was come upon him, they came every one from his own place; Eliphaz the Temanite, and Bildad the Shuhite, and Zophar the Naamathite: for they had made an appointment together to come to mourn with him and to comfort him.

ZOPHIM

• A place on the top of Pisgah.

Nu 23:14 — And he brought him into the field of Zophim, to the top of Pisgah, and built seven altars, and offered a bullock and a ram on *every* altar.

• A city on Mount Ephraim.

1Sa 1:1 — Now there was a certain man of Ramathaim-zophim, of mount Ephraim, and his name was Elkanah, the son of Jeroham, the son of Elihu, the son of Tohu, the son of Zuph, an Ephrathite:

ZORAH

• Called also Zareah and Zoreah.

• A city of Dan or Judah.

Jos 15:33 — *And* in the valley, Eshtaol, and Zoreah, and Ashnah,

Jos 19:41 — And the coast of their inheritance was Zorah, and Eshtaol, and Ir-shemesh,

• The city of Samson.

Jgs 13:24–25

Jgs 13:2 — And there was a certain man of Zorah, of the family of the Danites, whose name *was* Manoah; and his wife *was* barren, and bare not.

Jgs 16:31 — Then his brethren and all the house of his father came down, and took him, and brought *him* up, and buried him between Zorah and Eshtaol in the buryingplace of Manoah his father. And he judged Israel twenty years.

• Representatives of the tribe of Dan sent from, to spy out the land with a view to its conquest.

Jgs 18:1–31

• Fortified by Rehoboam.

2Ch 11:10 — And Zorah, and Aijalon, and Hebron, which *are* in Judah and in Benjamin fenced cities.

• Repeopled after the captivity.

Ne 11:29 — And at En-rimmon, and at Zareah, and at Jarmuth,

ZOROBABEL

• Called also Zerubbabel and Sheshbazzar.

• An ancestor of Joseph.

Mt 1:12–13

Lk 3:27 — Which was *the son* of Joanna, which was *the son* of Rhesa, which was *the son* of Zorobabel, which was *the son* of Salathiel, which was *the son* of Neri,

See: Zerubbabel

ZUAR • Father of Nethaneel.

Nu 1:8 — Of Issachar; Nethaneel the son of Zuar.

Nu 2:5 — And those that do pitch next unto him *shall be* the tribe of Issachar: and Nethaneel the son of Zuar *shall be* captain of the children of Issachar.

Nu 7:18 — On the second day Nethaneel the son of Zuar, prince of Issachar, did offer:

Nu 7:23 — And for a sacrifice of peace offerings, two oxen, five rams, five he goats, five lambs of the first year: this *was* the offering of Nethaneel the son of Zuar.

Nu 10:15 — And over the host of the tribe of the children of Issachar *was* Nethaneel the son of Zuar.

ZUPH

• A Kohathite.

1Sa 1:1 — Now there was a certain man of Ramathaim-zophim, of mount Ephraim, and his name was Elkanah, the son of Jeroham, the son of Elihu, the son of Tohu, the son of Zuph, an Ephrathite:

1Ch 6:35 — The son of Zuph, the son of Elkanah, the son of Mahath, the son of Amasai,

• A district northwest of Jerusalem.

1Sa 9:5 — *And* when they were come to the land of Zuph, Saul said to his servant that *was* with him, Come, and let us return; lest my father leave *caring* for the asses, and take thought for us.

ZUR

• A prince of Midian.

Nu 25:15 — And the name of the Midianitish woman that was slain *was* Cozbi, the daughter of Zur; he *was* head over a people, *and* of a chief house in Midian.

Nu 25:18 — For they vex you with their wiles, wherewith they have beguiled you in the matter of Peor, and in the matter of Cozbi, the daughter of a prince of Midian, their sister, which was slain in the day of the plague for Peor's sake.

Nu 31:8 — And they slew the kings of Midian, beside the rest of them that were slain; *namely,* Evi, and Rekem, and Zur, and Hur, and Reba, five kings of Midian: Balaam also the son of Beor they slew with the sword.

Jos 13:21 — And all the cities of the plain, and all the kingdom of Sihon king of the Amorites, which reigned in Heshbon, whom Moses smote with the princes of Midian, Evi, and Rekem, and Zur, and Hur, and Reba, *which were* dukes of Sihon, dwelling in the country.

• A Benjamite.

1Ch 8:30 — And his firstborn son Abdon, and Zur, and Kish, and Baal, and Nadab,

1Ch 9:36 — And his firstborn son Abdon, then Zur, and Kish, and Baal, and Ner, and Nadab,

ZURIEL • A Merarite.

Nu 3:35 — And the chief of the house of the father of the families of Merari *was* Zuriel the son of Abihail: *these* shall pitch on the side of the tabernacle northward.

ZURISHADDAI • Father of Shelumiel.

Nu 1:6 — Of Simeon; Shelumiel the son of Zurishaddai.

Nu 2:12 — And those which pitch by him *shall be* the tribe of Simeon: and the captain of the children of Simeon *shall be* Shelumiel the son of Zurishaddai.

Nu 7:36 — On the fifth day Shelumiel the son of Zurishaddai, prince of the children of Simeon, *did offer:*

Nu 7:41 — And for a sacrifice of peace offerings, two oxen, five rams, five he goats, five lambs of the first year: this *was* the offering of Shelumiel the son of Zurishaddai.

Nu 10:19 — And over the host of the tribe of the children of Simeon was Shelumiel the son of Zurishaddai.

ZUZIMS See: Zamzummims

Translation Index

A

1908, 2723, 2920, 4811: Ezr 4:6; Pr 30:10; 2Pe 2:11; Rev 12:10
accustomed (see **custom**) — 3928: *Jer 13:23*
Aceldama — ***184***: *Ac 1:19*
Achaia (see **Grecia, Greece**) — ***882***: Ac 18:12; 1Co 16:15
Achan — 5912: *Jos 7:1, 18-20, 24; 22:20*
Achar — 5917: 1Ch 2:7
Achaz, Ahaz — 271 ➳ ***881***: 2Ki 15:38; Mt 1:9
Achbor — 5907: Ge 36:38; 2Ki 22:12
Achim — ***885***: *Mt 1:14*
Achish — 397: 1Sa 21:10; 1Ki 2:39
Achmetha — 307: *Ezr 6:2*
Achor — 5911: Jos 7:24; Hos 2:15
Achsa, Achsah — 5915: Jgs 1:12; 1Ch 2:49
Achshaph — 407: *Jos 11:1; 12:20; 19:25*
Achzib — 392: Jos 15:44; Mic 1:14

ACKNOWLEDGE, d, ing, ment, th — 3045, 5324 ➳ ***1921, 1922***: Dt 21:17; Hos 5:15; 2Co 1:14
man is to acknowledge:
God: Pr 3:6; 1Jn 2:23
sin: Ps 32:5; 51:3; Jer 3:13
the truth; 2Ti 2:25; Tit 1:1

acquaint, ance, ed, ing — 3045, 4378, 5090, 5532 ➳ ***1110, 2398***: Job 22:21; Ps 55:13; Lk 2:44
acquit (see **quit**) — 5352: *Job 10:14; Na 1:3*
acre, s — 4618, 6776: *1Sa 14:14; Isa 5:10*
act, s — 1697, 4639, 4640, 5656, 5949, 6467 ➳ ***1888***: Dt 11:3; 1Ki 10:6; Jn 8:4
actions — 5949: *1Sa 2:3*
activity — 2428: *Ge 47:6*
Adadah — 5735: *Jos 15:22*
Adah — 5711: Ge 4:19; ; 36:2
Adaiah — 5718: 2Ki 22:1; Ne 11:5
Adalia — 118: *Est 9:8*
Adam — 120, 121 ➳ ***76***: Ge 2:19; Lk 3:38
Adamah — 128: *Jos 19:36*
Adami — 129: *Jos 19:33*
Adar, Addar — (see **Hazar-addar**) — 143, 144, 146: Jos 15:3; Ezr 6:15
Adbeel — 110: *Ge 25:13; 1Ch 1:29*
add, ed, eth; addition, s — 3254, 3255, 3914, 4514, 5595 ➳ ***1928, 2007, 2018, 2023, 4323, 4369***: 1Ki 7:29; Isa 29:1; Mt 6:27
Addan — 135: *Ezr 2:59*
adder, s — 5919, 6620, 6848, 8207: Ge 49:17; Ps 140:3; Pr 23:32
Addi — ***78***: *Lk 3:28*
addicted — ***5201***: *1Co 16:15*
Addon — 114: *Ne 7:61*
Ader — 5738: *1Ch 8:15*
Adiel — 5717: *1Ch 4:36; 9:12; ; 27:25*
Adin — 5720: Ezr 2:15; Ne 7:20
Adina — 5721: *1Ch 11:42*
Adino — 5722: *2Sa 23:8*
Adithaim — 5723: *Jos 15:36*
adjure, d — 422, 7650 ➳ ***1844, 3726***: Jos 6:26; 1Ki 22:16; Mt 26:63
Adlai — 5724: *1Ch 27:29*
Admah — 126: Ge 10:19; Hos 11:8
Admatha — 133: *Est 1:14*
administered; administration, s — ***1247, 1248***: *1Co 8:19, 20; 12:5; 2Co 9:12*
admired; admiration — ***2295, 2296***: *2Th 1:10; Jude 16; Rev 17:6*
admonish, ed, ing; admonition — 2094, 5749 ➳ ***3559, 3560, 3867, 5537***: Ecc 4:13; Ro 15:14; 2Th 3:15
Adna — 5733: *Ezr 10:30; Ne 12:15*
Adnah — 5734: *1Ch 12:20; 2Ch 17:14*
ado — ***2350***: *Mk 5:39*
Adoni-bezek — 137: *Jgs 1:5-7*
Adonijah — 138: 1Ki 1:5; Ne 10:16
Adonikam — 140: *Ezr 2:13; 8:13; Ne 7:18*
Adoniram — 141: *1Ki 4:6; 5:14*
Adoni-zedek — 139: *Jos 10:1, 3*

ADOPTION — ***5206***: Ro 8:23; Gal 4:5
means of adoption by God:
through Christ: Jn 1:12; Gal 3:26; Eph 1:3-5
through the Holy Spirit: Ro 8:15
results of adoption by God:
becoming sons of God: Gal 4:7
becoming heirs of God: Ro 8:16, 17; 1Pe 1:3, 4

Adoraim — 115: *2Ch 11:9*
Adoram (see **Hadoram**) — 151: *2Sa 20:24; 1Ki 12:18*
adorn, ed, ing — 5710 ➳ ***2885, 2889***: Isa 61:10; 1Ti 2:9; Rev 21:2
Adrammelech — 152: 2Ki 17:31; 19:37
Adramyttium — ***98***: *Ac 27:2*
Adria — ***99***: *Ac 27:27*
Adriel — 5741: *1Sa 18:19; 2Sa 21:8*
Adullam — 5725: 1Sa 22:1; Mic 1:15
Adullamite — 5726: *Ge 38:1, 12, 20*
adultery; adulterer; adulteress; adulterous (see **chaste**; **fornication**) — 802/376, 3432, 5003, 5004, 5005 ➳ ***3428, 3429, 3430, 3431***: Pr 6:26; Eze 23:43; Ro 7:3
Adummim — 131: *Jos 15:7; 18:17*
advanced — 1431, 5375, 6213: *1Sa 12:6; Est 3:1; 5:11; 10:2*

Antothijah — 6070: *1Ch 8:24*
Anub — 6036: *1Ch 4:8*
anvil — 6471: *Isa 41:7*
any — 259, 376, 1697, 1991, 3254, 3605, 3972, 4310, 5315, 5750, 5769 ≈ ***1520, 1536, 2089, 3361, 3364, 3367, 3379, 3387, 3588, 3762, 3763, 3765, 3956, 4218, 4455, 4458, 5100***: Ge 3:1; Eze 7:11; Ac 4:12
apart — 905, 5079, 5674, 6395 ≈ ***659, 2596/2398*** Ex 13:12; Ps 4:3; Mt 14:13; Jas 1:21
Apelles — ***559***: *Ro 16:10*
apes — 6971: *1Ki 10:22; 2Ch 9:21*
Apharsachites, Apharsathchites (see **Apharsites**) — 671: *Ezr 4:9; 5:6; 6:6*
Apharsites (see **Apharsachites**) — 670: *Ezr 4:9*
Aphek, Aphik — 663: Jos 12:18; Jgs 1:31
Aphekah — 664: *Jos 15:53*
Aphiah — 647: *1Sa 9:1*
Aphrah — 1036: *Mic 1:10*
Aphses — 6483: *1Ch 24:15*
apiece — 5982/259 ≈ ***303***: 1Ki 7:15; Lk 9:3
Appolonia — ***624***: *Ac 17:1*
Apollos — ***625***: Ac 18:24; 1Co 1:12
Apollyon — ***623***: *Rev 9:11*

APOSTLE, s, ship — ***651, 652, 5570***: Mt 10:2; 2Ti 1:11
 called and ordained by Christ: Mk 3:14; Jn 15:16; Gal 1:15, 16
 characteristics of:
  witnesses of the resurrected, ascended Christ: Ac 1:2-9, 21, 22; 1Co 15:7, 8
  directly commissioned by God: Mt 16:19; 2Co 13:10
  performed miracles: Ac 3:6-8; 19:11, 12

apothecary, ies — 4842, 7543: Ex 30:25; 2Ch 16:14
apparel, led — 899, 1264, 3830, 3847, 4254, 4403, 8071 ≈ ***2066, 2440, 2441, 2689***: Jgs 17:10; Isa 3:22; Lk 7:25
apparently — 4758: *Nu 12:8*
appeal, ed — ***1941***: *Ac 25:11, 12, 21, 25; 26:32; 28:19*
appear, ance, ed, eth, ing — 1540, 1570, 3318, 4286, 6437, 6524, 7200 ≈ ***82, 398, 602, 1718, 2014, 2015, 2064, 3700, 5316, 5318, 5319***: Nu 9:15; Mal 3:2; Mt 6:16
appease, d, eth — 3722, 6440, 7918, 8252 ≈ ***2687***: *Ge 32:20; Est 2:1; Pr 15:18; Ac 19:35*
appertain, ed, eth — 2969: 2Ch 26:18; Jer 10:7
appetite — 2416, 5315, 8264: Pr 23:2; Isa 29:8
Apphia — ***682***: *Phm 2*
Appii — ***675***: *Ac 28:15*
apple, s — 380, 380/1323, 892, 1323, 8598: Dt 32:10; SS 2:3; Joel 1:12
apply, ed — 935, 5186, 5414, 5437, 7896: Ps 90:12; Pr 2:2; Ecc 8:9
appoint, ed, eth — 559, 561, 977, 1121, 169 6, 2163, 2296, 2706, 2708, 2710, 2764, 3045, 3198, 3245, 3259, 3677, 3983, 4150, 4151, 4487, 4662, 5324, 5344, 5414, 5567, 5975, 6213, 6310, 6485, 6635, 6680, 6942, 6966, 7136, 7760, 7896, 7971 ≈ ***322, 606, 1299, 1303, 1935, 2476, 2525, 2749, 4160, 4287, 4384, 4929, 5021, 5087***: Job 2:11; Mt 26:19; Ac 20:13
apprehend, ed — ***2638, 4084***: *Ac 12:4; 2Co 11:32; Php 3:12, 13*
approach, ed, eth, ing — 5066, 7126, 7132, 7138 ≈ ***676, 1448***: Le 18:6; Eze 42:13; Lk 12:33
approve, ed, est — 7200, 7521 ≈ ***584, 1381, 1384, 4921***: Ps 49:13; Php 1:10; 2Ti 2:15
apron, s — 2290 ≈ ***4612***: *Ge 3:7; Ac 19:12*
apt — 6213 ≈ ***1317***: *2Ki 24:16; 1Ch 7:40; 1Ti 3:2; 2Ti 2:24*
Aquila — ***207***: Ac 18:2; Ro 16:3
Ar — 6144: Dt 2:9; Isa 15:1
Ara — 690: *1Ch 7:38*
Arab — 694: *Jos 15:52*
Arabah — 6160: *Jos 18:18*
Arabia — 6152 ≈ ***688***: 1Ki 10:15; Gal 1:17
Arabian, s — 6163 ≈ ***690***: Ne 2:19; Ac 2:11
Arad — 6166: Nu 21:1; Jgs 1:16
Arah — 733: 1Ch 7:39; Ezr 2:5
Aram (see **Aram-naharaim; Mesopotamia**) — 758 ≈ ***689***: Nu 23:7; Lk 3:33
Aramitess — 761: *1Ch 7:14*
Aram-naharaim — 763: *Ps 60:title*
Aram-zobah — 760: *Ps 60:title*
Aran — 765: *Ge 36:28; 1Ch 1:42*
Ararat — 780: *Ge 8:4; Jer 51:27*
Araunah (see **Ornan**) — 771: 2Sa 24:16, 18
Arba, Arbah — 704: Ge 35:27; Jos 14:15
Arbathite — 6164: *2Sa 23:31; 1Ch 11:32*
Arbite — 701: *2Sa 23:35*
archangel (see **angel**) — ***743***:*1Th 4:16; Jude 9*
Archelaus — ***745***: *Mt 2:22*
archer, s — 1167/2671, 1869/7198, 2686, 3384, 3384/376/7198, 3384/7198, 7228: Ge 21:20; 1Ch 10:3; Jer 50:29
arches — 361: Eze 40:16, 21
Archevites — 756: *Ezr 4:9*
Archi, Archite — 757: Jos 16:2; 2Sa 17:5
Archippus — ***751***: *Col 4:17; Phm 2*
Arcturus — 5906: *Job 9:9; 38:32*
Ard, ites — 714, 716: *Ge 46:21; Nu 26:40*

Azarael, Azreel — 5832: 1Ch 12:6; Ne 12:36
Azariah — 5838: 1Ki 4:2, 5; Da 1:6, 7
Azaz — 5811: *1Ch 5:8*
Azaziah — 5812: 1Ch 15:21; 2Ch 31:13
Azbuk — 5802: *Ne 3:16*
Azekah — 5825: Jos 10:10; Jer 34:7
Azel — 682: *1Ch 8:37, 38; 9:43, 44*
Azem — 6107: *Jos 15:29; 19:3*
Azgad — 5803: Ezr 2:12; Ne 7:17
Aziel — (see **Jaaziel**): 5815: *1Ch 15:20*
Aziza — 5819: *Ezr 10:27*
Azmaveth — 5820: 2Sa 23:31; Ezr 2:24
Azmon — 6111: *Nu 34:4, 5; Jos 15:4*
Aznoth-tabor — 243: *Jos 19:34*
Azor — ***107***: *Mt 1:13, 14*
Azotus (see **Ashdod**) — ***108***: *Ac 8:40*
Azriel — 5837: *1Ch 5:24; 27:19; Jer 36:26*
Azrikam — 5839: 1Ch 3:23; Ne 11:15
Azubah — 5806: 1Ki 22:42; 2Ch 20:31
Azur, Azzur — 5809: Ne 10:17; Jer 28:1
Azzah — 5804: *Dt 2:23; 1Ki 4:24; Jer 25:20*
Azzan — 5821: *Nu 34:26*

B

BAAL, im — 1168 ≈ ***896***: Nu 22:41; Ro 11:4
Baal-worship practiced by:
Israel's kings: 1Ki 16:31, 32
false prophets: 1Ki 18:25; Jer 2:8; 23:13
the majority of Israel: Jgs 2:13; Jer 7:9

Baalah — 1173: Jos 15:9; 1Ch 13:6
Baalath — 1191: Jos 19:44; 1Ki 9:18
Baalath-beer — 1192: *Jos 19:8*
Baal-berith — 1170: *Jgs 8:33; 9:4*
Baale — 1184: *2Sa 6:2*
Baal-gad — 1171: *Jos 11:17; 12:7; 13:5*
Baal-hamon — 1174: *SS 8:11*
Baal-hanan — 1177: Ge 36:38; 1Ch 27:28
Baal-hazor — 1178: *2Sa 13:23*
Baal-hermon — 1179: *Jgs 3:3; 1Ch 5:23*
Baali — 1180: *Hos 2:16*
Baalis — 1185: *Jer 40:14*
Baal-meon — 1186: Nu 32:38; 1Ch 5:8
Baal-peor — 1187: Dt 4:3; Hos 9:10
Baal-perazim (see **Perazim**) — 1188: *2Sa 5:20; 1Ch 14:11*
Baal-shalisha — 1190: *2Ki 4:42*
Baal-tamar — 1193: *Jgs 20:33*
Baal-zebub (see **Beelzebub**) — 1176: *2Ki 1:2, 3, 6, 16*
Baal-zephon — 1189: *Ex 14:2, 9; Nu 33:7*
Baana, Baanah — 1195: 2Sa 4:2; Ne 3:4
Baara — 1199: *1Ch 8:8*
Baaseiah — 1202: *1Ch 6:40*
Baasha — 1201: 1Ki 15:16; Jer 41:9
babbler; babblings — 1167/3956, 7879 ≈ ***2757, 4691***: Pr 23:29; Ecc 10:11; 1Ti 6:20
babe, s (see **infant**) — 5288, 5768, 8586 ≈ ***1025, 3516***: Ex 2:6; Ps 8:2; Lk 1:41
Babel — 894: *Ge 10:10; 11:9*
Babylon, ians, 's (see **Chaldea**) — 896, 1121/894 ≈ ***897***: Ezr 2:6; Jer 20:4; Mt 1:11
Babylonish — 8152: *Jos 7:21*
Baca — 1056: *Ps 84:6*
Bachrites — 1076: *Nu 26:35*
back — 268, 310, 322, 1354, 1355, 1458, 1639, 1973, 2015, 2820, 3437, 3607, 3693, 4185, 4513, 5253, 5437, 5472, 5493, 6203, 6437, 6544, 7725, 7926 ≈ ***617, 650, 3557, 3694, 4762, 5288, 5289, 5290***: Ex 23:27; Na 2:8; Jn 18:6; Rev 5:1
backbite, eth, ing, r, s — 5643, 7270 ≈ ***2636, 2637***: *Ps 15:3; Pr 25:23; Ro 1:30; 2Co 12:20*

BACKSLIDING, s; backslider — 4878, 5472, 5637, 7726, 7728: Pr 14:14; Jer 49:4; Hos 4:16
causes of backsliding:
absence of spiritual leadership: Ex 32:1
love of the world: 2Ti 4:10
results of backsliding:
correction and reproof: Jer 2:19
judgment: Jer 15:6
mercy for turning from backsliding: Jer 3:12-15; Hos 14:4

badgers — 8476: Ex 25:5; Eze 16:10
badness — 7455: *Ge 41:19*
bag, s — 2754, 3599, 3627, 6696, 6872 ≈ ***905, 1101***: Dt 25:13; Pr 7:20; Lk 12:33
Baharumite — 978: *1Ch 11:33*
Bahurim — 980: 2Sa 3:16; 1Ki 2:8
Bajith — 1006: *Isa 15:2*
Bakbakkar — 1230: *1Ch 9:15*
Bakbuk — 1227: *Ezr 2:51; Ne 7:53*
Bakbukiah — 1229: *Ne 11:17; 12:9, 25*
bake, d, n, r, s, th — 644, 1310, 5746, 7246, 8601: Ge 40:1; Isa 44:15; Eze 4:12
bakemeats — 3978/4640/644: *Ge 40:17*
Balaam — 1109 ≈ ***903***: Nu 22:5; Jude 11
Balak — 1111 ≈ ***904***: Nu 22:2; Mic 6:5; Rev 2:14
balance, ing, s — 3976, 3977, 4657, 7070: Job 6:2; Am 8:5; Rev 6:5
bald, ness — 1371, 1372, 1754, 5556, 7139, 7142, 7144, 7146: Le 11:22; Mic 1:16
ball — 1754: *Isa 22:18*

C

D

enough — 1767, 1952, 3027, 3605, 4672, 7227, 7644, 7654 ❧ ***566, 713, 714, 2425, 2880, 4052:*** Ge 24:25; Pr 30:15; Mt 10:25
enrich, ed, est (see **rich**) — 6238 ❧ ***4148:*** 1Sa 17:25; Ps 65:9; 1Co 1:5
En-rimmon — 5884: *Ne 11:29*
En-rogel — 5883: 2Sa 17:17; 1Ki 1:9
ensample, s (see **example**) — ***5179, 5262:*** 1Co 10:11; Php 3:17; 1Pe 5:3
En-shemesh — 5885: *Jos 15:7; 18:17*
ensign, s — 226, 5251, 5264: Nu 2:2; Isa 5:26; Zec 9:16
ensnared (see **snare**) — 4170: *Job 34:30*
ensue (see **follow; pursue**) — **1377**: *1Pe 3:11*
entangle, d — 943 ❧ ***1707, 1758:*** Ex 14:3; Mt 22:15; 2Ti 2:4
En-tappuah — 5887: *Jos 17:7*
enter, ed, eth, ing; entrance, s — 872, 935, 1980, 2978, 3996, 5181, 5674, 6310, 6607, 6608 ❧ ***305, 1524, 1525, 1529, 1531, 1684, 1910, 2064, 3922:*** Ge 12:11; Nu 34:8; Mt 8:5; Mk 8:13
enterprise — 8454: *Job 5:12*
entertain, ed — ***3579, 5381***: *Heb 13:2*
entice, d, ing — 5496, 6601 ❧ ***1185, 3981, 4086:*** Ex 22:16; Pr 1:10; Jas 1:14
entire — ***3648***: *Jas 1:4*
entreat, ed, ies, y (see **exhort**) — 2470, 2589, 2603, 6279, 6293 ❧ ***818, 2138, 2559, 3868, 3870, 3874, 5195, 5530:*** Ge 23:8; Job 24:21; Lk 18:32; 2Co 8:4
entry, ies — 872, 3996, 6310, 6607: 1Ch 9:19; Pr 8:3; Eze 40:38
environ — 5437: *Jos 7:9*

ENVY, ied, ies, iest, ieth, ing, ings — 7065, 7068 ❧ ***2205, 2206, 5354, 5355:*** Nu 11:29; Ps 73:3; 1Co 3:3
 warnings against envy: Ps 37:1; Pr 3:31; Gal 5:26
 consequences of envy:
  evil works: Jas 3:16
  ill health: Pr 14:30
  death: Job 5:2

Epaenetus — ***1866***: *Ro 16:5*
Epaphras — ***1889***: *Col 1:7; 4:12; Phm 23*
Epaphroditus — ***1891***: *Php 2:25; 4:18; subscript*
ephah — 374: Ex 16:36; Isa 5:10; Zec 5:6
Ephah — 5891: Ge 25:4; Isa 60:6
Ephai — 5778: *Jer 40:8*
Epher — 6081: Ge 25:4; 1Ch 1:33;
Ephes-dammim — 658: *1Sa 17:1*
Ephesian, s — ***2180***: Ac 19:28; 21:29
Ephesus — ***2181***: 1Co 15:32; Rev 1:11
Ephlal — 654: *1Ch 2:37*
ephod — 642, 646: Ex 25:7; Jgs 8:27; Hos 3:4
Ephod — 641: *Nu 34:23*
ephphata — ***2188***: *Mk 7:34*
Ephraim, 's; Ephrain — 669, 6085 ❧ ***2187:*** Ge 41:52; 2Ch 13:19; Jn 11:54
Ephraimite, s — 669, 673: *Jos 16:10; Jgs 12:4-6*
Ephratah, Ephrath — 672: Ru 4:11; Mic 5:2
Ephrathite, s — 673: 1Sa 1:1; 1Ki 11:26
Ephron — 6085: Ge 23:8; 50:13; Jos 15:9
Epicureans — ***1946***: *Ac 17:18*
epistle, s — ***1992:*** Ac 15:30; 2Co 3:1-3
equal, ity, ly, s — 1809, 4339, 6186, 6187, 7737, 7947, 8505 ❧ ***2465, 2470, 2471, 4915:*** Ex 36:22; Job 28:17; 2Co 8:14
equity — 3476, 3477, 3788, 4334, 4339, 5229: Ps 98:9; Isa 59:14; Mic 3:9
Er — 6147 ❧ ***2262:*** Ge 38:3; Lk 3:28
Eran — 6197: *Nu 26:36*
Eranites — 6198: *Nu 26:36*
Erastus — ***2037:*** Ac 19:22; Ro 16:23
ere (see **afore; before**): 2962, 3806, 3808 ❧ ***4250:*** Ex 1:19; Jer 47:6; Jn 4:49
Erech — 751: *Ge 10:10*
erected — 5324: *Ge 33:20*
Eri — 6179: *Ge 46:16; Nu 26:16*
Erites — 6180: *Nu 26:16*
errand — 1697: *Ge 24:33; Jgs 3:19; 2Ki 9:5*
err, ed, eth; error, s — 4869, 7683, 7684, 7686, 7691, 7944, 7960, 8432, 8582, 8595 ❧ ***51, 635, 795, 4105, 4106:*** Le 5:18; Da 6:4; Mk 12:24; Heb 9:7
Esar — haddon — 634: 2Ki 19:37; Ezr 4:2
Esau — 6215 ❧ ***2269:*** Ge 25:25; Mal 1:2; Heb 12:16
escape, d, eth, ing — 3318, 4422, 4498, 4655, 5337, 5674, 6403, 6405, 6412, 6413, 7611 ❧ ***575, 668, 1295, 1309, 1545, 1628, 1831, 5343:*** Ge 19:17; Am 9:1; Ro 2:3
eschew, ed, eth — 5493 ❧ ***1578:*** *Job 1:1, 8; 2:3; 1Pe 3:11*
Esek — 6320: *Ge 26:20*
Esh-baal (see **Ish-bosheth**) — 792:*1Ch 8:33; 9:39*
Esh-ban — 790: *Ge 36:26; 1Ch 1:41*
Eshcol — 812: Ge 14:13; Nu 13:23
Eshean — 824: *Jos 15:52*
Eshek — 6232: *1Ch 8:39*
Eshkalonites — 832: *Jos 13:3*
Eshtaol — 847: Jos 15:33; Jgs 13:25
Eshtaulites — 848: *1Ch 2:53*

Eshtemoa, Eshtemoh — 851: Jos 21:14; 1Sa 30:28; 1Ch 4:17

Eshton — 850: *1Ch 4:11, 12*

Esli — ***2069***: *Lk 3:25*

especially (see **special**) — 3966 ✒ ***3122:*** Ps 31:11; Ac 26:3; 2Ti 4:13

espousals; espoused — 781, 2861, 3623 ✒ ***718, 3423:*** SS 3:11; Jer 2:2; Mt 1:18; 2Co 11:2

espy, ied (see **spy**) — 6822, 7200, 7270, 8446: *Ge 42:27; Jos 14:7; Jer 48:19*

Esrom; Hezron — 2696 ✒ ***2074:*** Ge 46:9; Ru 4:18; Mt 1:3

ESTABLISH, ed, eth, ment (see **stablish**) — 553, 571, 15:39, 2388, 3245, 3322, 3427, 3559, 5324, 5564, 5582, 5975, 6965, 6966, 8627 ✒ ***950, 2476, 3549, 4732, 4741:*** 2Ch 32:1; Ps 7:9; Ro 3:31; Heb 10:9

God establishes:

covenants: Ge 9:9; Ex 6:4; Eze 16:62

kingdoms: 2Sa 7:12; 1Ki 2:12

saints: Ac 16:5; 1Th 3:2; 2Pe 1:12

estate, s (see **state**) — 1700, 3027, 3651, 3653, 4612, 4971, 5324, 6440, 8448 ✒ ***3588, 4012:*** Est 1:19; Eze 36:11; Col 4:8; Jude 6

esteem, ed, eth, ing — 2803, 5034, 6186, 6845, 7043 ✒ ***1848, 2233, 2919, 3049:*** Job 36:19; Isa 29:16; Ro 14:5; Heb 11:26

Esther (see **Hadassah**) — 635: Est 2:7; 8:1

estimate, ion, ions — 6186, 6187: Le 5:15; 27:25; Nu 18:16

estranged — 2144, 5234: Job 19:13; Jer 19:4; Eze 14:5

Etam — 5862: Jgs 15:8; 1Ch 4:3

ETERNAL; eternity (see **ever**) — 5703, 5769, 6924 ✒ ***126, 165, 166:*** Isa 57:15; Mt 19:16; Eph 3:11

that which is eternal:

eternal God: Dt 33:27; 1Ti 1:17; Heb 9:14

eternal glory: 2Co 4:17; 2Ti 2:10; 1Pe 5:10

eternal life: Mt 19:16; Jn 17:3; Ro 6:23

eternal damnation: Mk 3:29; Jude 7

Etham — 864: *Ex 13:20; Nu 33:6-8*

Ethan — 387: 1Ki 4:31; 1Ch 2:6

Ethanim — 388: *1Ki 8:2*

Ethbaal — 856: *1Ki 16:31*

Ether — 6281: *Jos 15:42; 19:7*

Ethiopia — 3568 ✒ ***128:*** Na 3:9; Ac 8:27

Ethiopian, s — 3569 ✒ ***128:*** Nu 12:1; Ac 8:27

Ethnan — 869: *1Ch 4:7*

Ethni — 867: *1Ch 6:41*

Eubulus — ***2108***: *2Ti 4:21*

Eunice — ***2131***: *2Ti 1:5*

eunuch, s — 5631 ✒ ***2134, 2135:*** Isa 39:7; Jer 38:7; Mt 19:12

Euodias — ***2136***: *Php 4:2*

Euphrates — 6578 ✒ ***2166:*** Ge 2:14; Rev 9:14

Euroclydon — ***2148***: *Ac 27:14*

Eutychus — ***2161***: *Ac 20:9*

evangelist, s — ***2099***: *Ac 21:8; Eph 4:11; 2Ti 4:5*

Eve — 2332 ✒ ***2096:*** *Ge 3:20; 4:1; 2Co 11:3; 1Ti 2:13*

even — 227, 389, 518, 637, 853, 1571, 1887, 3588, 3602, 3651, 4334, 5704, 5705, 6664, 7535 ✒ ***737, 891, 1063, 1096, 1161, 2073, 2089, 2193, 2504, 2505, 2522, 2531, 2532, 2536, 2548, 3303, 3483, 3676, 3739/5158, 3761, 3779, 5037, 5613, 5615, 5618***: Ezr 1:8; Zep 2:5; Phm 19

even, ing, ings, tide; eveningtide — 6150, 6153, 6256/6153 ✒ ***3796, 3798, 3798/5610***: 1Ki 22:35; Jer 5:6; Ac 28:23

event — 4745: *Ecc 2:14; 9:2, 3*

ever, lasting, more (see **eternal**) — 1755, 3605/3117, 3808, 3809, 5331, 5703, 5704, 5750, 5760, 5769, 5865, 5957, 6783, 6924, 8548 ✒ ***104, 126, 166, 1336, 3588/165, 3745, 3842, 4218, 4253:*** Ge 3:22; Dt 28:29; Mt 6:13; Jn 4:29

every — 259, 376, 802, 3605, 3632, 5437, 7218 ✒ ***303, 376, 537, 1330, 1520, 1538, 2596, 3650, 3837, 3840, 3956, 5100, 5101:*** Ge 1:21; Jgs 8:34; Mt 3:10; Rev 1:7

Evi — 189: *Nu 31:8; Jos 13:21*

evidence, s; evident, ly — 5612, 5921/6440 ✒ ***1212, 1650, 1732, 2612, 4270, 4271, 5320:*** Job 6:28; Jer 32:10; Heb 7:14

EVIL, s; evil — doer — 205, 1100, 1681, 7451, 7455, 7489 ✒ ***92, 987, 988, 2549, 2551, 2554, 2555, 2556, 2557, 2559, 2560, 2635, 2636, 4190, 4487, 5337:*** Ge 2:9; Ps 37:1; Lk 3:19

the wicked man:

is evil: 2Ki 21:2; Mt 7:11

knows evil: Ge 3:22; 2Sa 19:35; Heb 5:14

speaks evil: Mt 5:11; Eph 4:31; Jas 4:11

plans evil: Ge 6:5; Ps 21:11

runs to evil: Pr 1:16

does evil: Jgs 2:11; 1Ki 14:9; Mk 3:4

the righteous man:

foresees evil: Pr 22:3

hates evil: Ro 12:9

shuns evil: Pr 4:14; 1Th 5:22

departs from evil: Pr 14:16; 1Pe 3:11

evilfavouredness — 1697/7451: *Dt 17:1*

Evil — merodach — 192: *2Ki 25:27; Jer 52:31*

F

fat, fleshed, ling, ness, s, ted, ter, test — 75, 1254, 1277, 1878, 1879, 1880, 2459, 2502, 2954, 3342, 3368, 4770, 4806, 4924, 4932, 4945, 6309, 6335, 6371, 8080, 8081, 8082 ✎ ***4096, 4618, 4619:*** Ps 66:15; Da 1:15; Ro 11:17

FATHER, less, s — 1, 25, 369/1, 1121/376, 1730, 1733, 2524, 2859, 3490 ✎ ***540, 3737, 3962, 3964, 3967, 3970, 3971, 3995:*** Ge 2:24; Ex 22:22; Mt 2:22; Heb 7:3
 the Fatherhood of God in relation to:
  Jesus Christ: Mt 11:25-27; Jn 5:18
  the saint: Mt 6:9; 1Co 8:6
  Israel: Jer 3:19; Mal 1:6

fathoms — ***3712***: *Ac 27:28*

fault, less, s, t y — 2397, 2398, 2399, 3972, 5771, 7564, 7844 ✎ ***156, 158, 264, 273, 299, 816, 818, 1651, 2275, 3201, 3900:*** Ex 5:16; Hos 10:2; Heb 8:7

favour, able, ed, edst, est, eth — 2580, 2594, 2603, 2617, 2654, 2655, 2896, 3190, 4758, 6440, 7520, 7522, 7965, 8389, 8467 ✎ ***5485, 5487:*** Ge 18:3; Ps 77:7; La 4:16; Lk 1:28

FEAR, ed, ful, fully, fulness, ing — 367, 1481, 1674, 1763, 2342, 2731, 2844, 2849, 3025, 3372, 3373, 3374, 4032, 4034, 4035, 4116, 4172, 6206, 6342, 6343, 6345, 6427, 6440, 7267, 7374, 7461, 8175 ✎ ***870, 1167, 1169, 1630/1510, 2124, 2125, 2192, 5398, 5399, 5400, 5401:*** Ge 9:2; Ps 139:14; Mt 8:26; Ac 10:22
 the fear of God:
  encouraged: Jos 24:14; Ecc 12:13; Mt 10:28; 1Pe 2:17
  promises connected with:
   God's mercy: Lk 1:50
   God's instruction: Ps 25:12
   length of life: Pr 10:27
 the fear of man:
  to be avoided: Isa 51:12; Lk 12:4
  consequences of:
   a snare: Pr 29:25
   cowardice: Jn 9:22, 23
   compromise: Gal 2:11-13

feast, ed, ing, s — 2282, 2287, 3899, 3900, 4150, 4580, 4960, 6213 ✎ ***755, 1173, 1408, 1456, 1858, 1859, 4910:*** Ge 19:3; Job 1:4; Jude 12

feather, ed, s — 84, 2624, 3671, 5133: Le 1:16; Ps 78:27; Eze 17:3

feeble, minded, ness, r — 535, 537, 2826, 3524, 3766, 3782, 5848, 6099, 6313, 7503, 7510 ✎ ***772, 3642, 3886:*** Ge 30:42; 1Sa 2:5; 1Th 5:14; Heb 12:12

feed, est, eth, ing; feedingplace; fed — 398, 1197, 1277, 2109, 2110, 2939, 2963, 3557, 3938, 4806, 4829, 5095, 7462 ✎ ***1006, 4165, 4222, 5142, 5526, 5595:*** Ps 80:5; Na 2:11; Mt 25:37; Jn 21:15

feel, ing; felt — 995, 3045, 4184, 4959 ✎ ***524, 1097, 3958, 4834, 5584:*** Ge 27:22; Ps 58:9; Eph 4:19

feign, ed, edly, est — 908, 4820, 5234, 8267 ✎ ***4112, 5271:*** 1Sa 21:13; Ps 17:1; Lk 20:20

Felix — ***5344***: Ac 23:24, 24:3

feller — 3772: *Isa 14:8*

fellow, citizens, disciples, heirs, helpers, labourer, prisoner, servant, soldier, worker — ***4789, 4847, 4869, 4889, 4904, 4961***: Jn 11:16; Ro 16:7; Eph 2:19; Phm 1

fellow, s — 376, 582, 2266, 2269, 2270, 2273, 5997, 7453, 7464 ✎ ***435, 2083, 3353:*** Ex 2:13; Ps 45:7; Ac 18:13

fellowship — 2266, 8667/3027 ✎ ***2842, 2844, 3852, 4790***: Le 6:2; 2Co 6:14; Eph 5:11

female — 802, 5347 ✎ ***2338:*** Ge 7:2; Dt 4:16; Mt 19:4

fence, d (see **defence**) — 1219, 1443, 1447, 4013, 4390, 4692, 4694, 5823, 7753: Nu 32:17; Ps 62:3; Hos 8:14

fens — 1207: *Job 40:21*

ferret — 604: *Le 11:30*

ferry — 5679: *2Sa 19:18*

FERVENT, ly — ***1618, 1619, 2204, 2205:*** Col 4:12; 1Pe 4:8; 2Pe 3:10
 fervency should be shown in:
  spirit: Ac 18:25; Ro 12:11
  mind: 2Co 7:7
  love: 1Pe 1:22; 4:8
  prayer: Col 4:12; Jas 5:16

Festus — ***5347***: Ac 24:27; 26:24

fetch, ed, eth — 635, 935, 1806, 3318, 3947, 5080, 5375, 5437, 5670, 5927, 7725 ✎ ***1806:*** Ge 18:7; Dt 19:5; Ac 16:37

fetters — 2131, 3525, 5178 ✎ ***3976:*** Jgs 16:21; Job 36:8; Mk 5:4

fever — 6920 ✎ ***4445, 4446:*** Dt 28:22; Mt 8:14; Ac 28:8

few, er, est, ness — 259, 4213, 4557, 4591, 4592, 4962, 7116 ✎ ***1024, 3641, 4935:*** Le 25:16; Ecc 5:2; Mt 7:14

fidelity — ***4102***: *Tit 2:10*

field, s — 776, 1251, 2351, 2513, 3010, 7704, 7709, 8309 ✎ ***68, 5561, 5564:*** Ge 2:5; Job 5:10; Mt 6:28; Ac 1:18

furrow, s — 1417, 4618, 5869, 6170, 8525: Job 39:10; Eze 17:7; Hos 10:4

further, ance, ed, more — 637, 3148, 3254, 5375, 5750, 6329 ✑ ***1161, 1339, 1534, 2089, 3063, 4118, 4206, 4297:*** Ex 4:6; Ezr 8:36; Ac 4:17; Php 1:12

fury (see **furious**) — 2528, 2534, 2740: Job 20:23; Isa 27:4; Da 3:13

G

Gaal — 1603: Jgs 9:26, 35

Gaash — 1608: Jos 24:30; 2Sa 23:30

Gaba, Geba (see **Gibeah**) — 1387: Ezr 2:26; Isa 10:29

Gabbai — 1373: *Ne 11:8*

Gabbatha — ***1042***: *Jn 19:13*

Gabriel — 1403 ✑ ***1043:*** Da 8:16; Lk 1:19

Gad — 1410 ✑ ***1045:*** Ge 30:11; Rev 7:5

Gadarenes — ***1046:*** *Mk 5:1; Lk 8:26, 37*

gaddest — 235: *Jer 2:36*

Gaddi — 1426: *Nu 13:11*

Gaddiel — 1427: *Nu 13:10*

Gadi — 1424: *2Ki 15:14, 17*

Gadite, s — 1425: Jos 1:12; 2Sa 23:36

Gaham — 1514: *Ge 22:24*

Gahar — 1515: *Ezr 2:47; Ne 7:49*

gain, ed, s — 1214, 2084, 4242, 8393, 8636 ✑ ***1281, 2039, 2770, 2771, 4122, 4160, 4200, 4333***: Job 22:3; Eze 22:12; Ac 16:19

gainsay, ers, ing — ***369, 471, 483, 485***: Lk 21:15; Ro 10:21; Tit 1:9

Gaius — ***1050***: Ro 16:23; 3Jn 1

Galal — 1559: *1Ch 9:15, 16; Ne 11:17*

Galatia — ***1053, 1054***: Ac 16:6; 2Ti 4:10

Galatians — ***1052:*** *Gal 3:1; subscript*

galbanum — 2464: *Ex 30:34*

Galeed — 1567: *Ge 31:47, 48*

Galilean, s — ***1057***: Mk 14:70; Ac 2:7

Galilee — 1551 ✑ ***1056:*** Jos 20:7; Mt 2:22

gall — 4845, 4846, 7219 ✑ ***5521:*** Dt 29:18; Job 16:13; Mt 27:34

gallant — 117: *Isa 33:21*

gallery, ies — 862, 7298: *SS 4:5; Eze 41:15, 16; 42:3, 5*

galley — 590: *Isa 33:21*

Gallim — 1554: *1Sa 25:44; Isa 10:30*

Gallio — ***1058***: *Ac 18:12, 14, 17*

gallows — 6086: Est 5:14; 7:9; 9:13

Gamaliel — 1583 ✑ ***1059:*** Nu 1:10; Ac 5:34

Gammadims — 1575: *Eze 27:11*

Gamul — 1577: *1Ch 24:17*

gap, ed, s — 6473, 6475, 6556: *Job 16:10; Ps 22:13; Eze 13:5; 22:30*

garden, er, s — 1588, 1593, 1594 ✑ ***2779, 2780:*** Ge 2:8; Am 4:9; Jn 20:15

Gareb — 1619: 2Sa 23:38; Jer 31:39

garlands — ***4725:*** *Ac 14:13*

garlic — 7762: *Nu 11:5*

garment, s — 155, 899, 3801, 3830, 3831, 4055, 4060, 4063, 4594, 7897, 8008, 8071, 8162, 8509 ✑ ***1742, 2067, 2440, 4158, 4749, 5509:*** Ex 28:2; Job 38:9; Mt 9:16

Garmite — 1636: *1Ch 4:19*

garner, s — 214, 4200 ✑ ***596:*** *Ps 144:13; Joel 1:17; Mt 3:12; Lk 3:17*

garnish, ed — 6823, 8235 ✑ ***2885***: Job 26:13; Mt 23:29; Rev 21:19

garrison, s — 4673, 4675, 4676, 5333 ✑ ***5432:*** 1Sa 10:5; Eze 26:11; 2Co 11:32

Gashmu, Geshem — 1654: *Ne 2:19; 6:1, 2, 6*

Gatam — 1609: *Ge 36:11, 16; 1Ch 1:36*

gate, s — 1817, 5592, 6607, 8179, 8651 ✑ ***2374, 4439, 4440, 4489:*** Ge 19:1; Dt 3:5; Mt 16:18; Ac 3:2

Gath — 1661: Jos 11:22; 1Sa 17:4

gather, ed, er, erest, eth, ing — 103, 622, 625, 626, 717, 962, 1103, 1219, 1413, 1481, 1716, 2199, 2490, 3254, 3259, 3349, 3664, 3673, 3950, 3953, 4390, 4723, 5413, 5596, 5619, 5756, 6192, 6213, 6651, 6817, 6908, 6910, 6950, 6960, 7035, 7197, 7408, 8085 ✑ ***346, 1865, 1996, 1997, 3048, 3792, 4816, 4822, 4863, 4867, 4896, 4962, 5166:*** Ge 6:21; Am 7:14; Mk 13:27; Eph 1:10

Gath-hepher, Gittah-hepher — 1662: *2Ki 14:25*

Gath-rimmon — 1667: Jos 19:45; 1Ch 6:69

gay — ***2986***: *Jas 2:3*

Gaza — 5804 ✑ Ge 10:19; Ac 8:26

Gazathites, Gazites — 5841: *Jos 13:3; Jgs 16:2*

gaze; gazing, stock — 7200, 7210 ✑ ***1689, 2301:*** Ex 19:21; Ac 1:11; Heb 10:33

Gazer, Gezer — 1507: 2Sa 5:25; 1Ch 6:67

Gazez — 1495: *1Ch 2:46*

Gazzam — 1502: *Ezr 2:48; Ne 7:51*

Geba — 1387: *Jos.21:17; 2Ki 23:8; Isa 10:29*

Gebal — 1381: *Ps 83:7; Eze 27:9*

Geber — 1398: *1Ki 4:13, 19*

Gebim — 1374: *Isa 10:31*

Gedaliah — 1436: 2Ki 25:22; Zep 1:1

Geder — 1445: *Jos 12:13*

Gederah — 1449: *Jos 15:36*

Gederathite — 1452: *1Ch 12:4*

Gederite — 1451: *1Ch 27:28*
Gederoth — 1450: *Jos 15:41; 2Ch 28:18*
Gederothaim — 1453: *Jos 15:36*
Gedor — 1446: Jos 15:58; 1Ch 4:
Gehazi — 1522: 2Ki 4:12; 5:20
Geliloth — 1553: *Jos 18:17*
Gemalli — 1582: *Nu 13:12*
Gemariah — 1587: Jer 29:3; 36:10
gender, ed, eth — 3205, 7250 ➾ ***1080:*** Le 19:19; Job 38:29; Gal 4:24
genealogy, ies — 3187 ➾ ***1076:*** 1Ch 5:17; Ezr 8:1; Tit 3:9
general, ly — 3605, 8269 ➾ ***3831:*** 1Ch 27:34; Jer 48:38; Heb 12:23
generation, s — 1755, 8435 ➾ ***1074, 1078, 1081, 1085:*** Ge 5:1; Da 4:3; Mt 1:1, 17
Gennesaret (see **Chinnereth**) — ***1082***: *Mt 14:34; Mk 6:53; Lk 5:1*
GENTILE, s — 1471 ➾ ***1484, 1672***: Jer 4:7; Ro 2:9
God's outreach to the Gentiles:
extended through Christ: Isa 42:1; 49:6
extended through Paul: Ac 9:15
the saint's witness to the Gentiles:
instruct them: 1Ti 2:7
live honesty among them: 1Pe 2:12

gentle, ness, y — 3814, 6031, 6038 ➾ ***1932, 1933, 2261, 5544:*** 2Sa 18:5; 1Th 2:7; Tit 3:2
Genubath — 1592: *1Ki 11:20*
Gera — 1617: Ge 46:21; Jgs 3:15; 1Ch 8:3
gerahs — 1626: Ex 30:13; Eze 45:12
Gerar — 1642: Ge 10:19; 26:1; 2Ch 14:13
Gergesenes — ***1086***: *Mt 8:28*
Gerizim — 1630: Dt 11:29; Jgs 9:7
Gershom, Gershon: 1647, 1648: Ex 2:22; Ezr 8:2
Gershonite, s — 1649: Nu 3:21; 1Ch 26:21
Gesham — 1529: *1Ch 2:47*
Geshur — 1650: 2Sa 3:3; 13:37
Geshuri, Geshurites — 1651: Dt 3:14; 1Sa 27:8
get, teth, ting; gat; got, ten — 622, 776, 935, 1214, 1245, 1980, 3212, 3254, 3318, 3381, 3423, 3513, 3947, 4422, 4672, 5060, 5110, 5111, 5265, 5381, 5414, 5674, 5927, 6213, 6329, 6467, 6965, 7069, 7075, 7121, 7392, 7408, 7426, 7725 ➾ ***645, 1684, 1826, 1831, 2147, 2597, 4122, 5217:*** Ge 12:1; Ecc 2:7; La 5:9; Mt 4:10; Ac 21:1
Gether — 1666: *Ge 10:23; 1Ch 1:17*
Gethsemane — ***1068***: *Mt 26:36; Mk 14:32*
Geuel — 1345: *Nu 13:15*
Gezer — 1507: *Jos 10:33; 1Ch 6:67*
Gezrites — 1511: *1Sa 27:8*
ghost, Ghost — 1478, 5315 ➾ ***1606, 1634, 4151:*** Ge 25:8; Job 11:20; Ro 5:5
Giah — 1520: *2Sa 2:24*
giant, s — 1368, 5303, 5497, 7497: Ge 6:4; Nu 13:33; Job 16:14
Gibbar — 1402: *Ezr 2:20*
Gibbethon — 1405: Jos 19:44; 1Ki 15:27
Gibea — 1388: *1Ch 2:49*
Gibeah — 1390: Jgs 19:12; Hos 10:9
Gibeath — 1394: *Jos 18:28*
Gibeathite — 1395: *1Ch 12:3*
Gibeon — 1391: Jos 9:3; 1Ki 3:4
Gibeonite, s: 1393: 2Sa 21:1; Ne 3:7
Giblites — 1382: *Jos 13:5*
Giddalti — 1437: *1Ch 25:4, 29*
Giddel — 1435: *Ezr 2:47, 56; Ne 7:49, 58*
Gideon — 1439 ➾ ***1066***: Jgs 6:11; Heb 11:32
Gideoni — 1441: Nu 1:11; 10:24
Gidom — 1440: *Jgs 20:45*
GIFT, s (see **give**) — 814, 4503, 4864, 4976, 4978, 4979, 4991, 5078, 5083, 5379, 7810, 8641 ➾ ***334, 1390, 1394, 1431, 1434, 1445, 3311, 5485, 5486:*** Ge 25:6; Da 2:6; Mt 2:11
gifts given by God:
the Holy Spirit: Ac 2:38
the grace of God: Ro 5:15
eternal life: Jn 4:10

Gihon — 1521: Ge 2:13; 1Ki 1:33
Gilalai — 1562: *Ne 12:36*
Gilboa — 1533: 1Sa 31:1; 2Sa 1:6
Gilead — 1568: Jgs 11:2; Jer 8:22
Gileadite, s — 1568, 1569: Jgs 11:1; 2Ki 15:25
Gilgal — 1537: Jos 4:19; Hos 4:15; Am 4:4
Giloh — 1542: *Jos 15:51; 2Sa 15:12*
Gilonite — 1526: *2Sa 15:12; 23:34*
Gimzo — 1579: *2Ch 28:18*
gin, s — 4170: *Ps 140:5; 141:6*
gird, ed, edst, eth, ing, le, les; girt — 73, 232, 247, 631, 640, 2280, 2289, 2290, 2296, 4206, 4228, 8151 ➾ ***328, 1241, 2223, 2224, 4024:*** Ex 12:11; Isa 3:24; Lk 12:35; Jn 21:7
Girgashite, s; Girgasite — 1622: 1Ch 1:14; Ne 9:8
girl, s — 3207: *Joel 3:3; Zec 8:5*
Gispa — 1658: *Ne 11:21*
Gittaim — 1664: *2Sa 4:3; Ne 11:33*
Gittite, s — 1663: 2Sa 6:10; 1Ch 13:13
Gittith — 1665: *Ps 8:title; 81:title; 84:title*

GIVE, n, r, s, th; gave, est (see **gift; grant**) — 4113, 935, 1167, 1262, 1478, 1576, 1696, 1961, 2505, 2603, 3051, 3052, 3190, 3254, 3289, 4646, 4900, 4991, 5066, 5221, 5301, 5375, 5414, 5415, 5462, 5534, 6213, 7311, 7725, 7760, 7761, 7971, 7999 ✑ ***402, 437, 591, 632, 1096, 1239, 1291, 1325, 1377, 1394, 1395, 1402, 1433, 1502, 1547, 1781, 1788, 1825, 1907, 1929, 2010, 2014, 2227, 2468, 2702, 2753, 3004, 3140, 3330, 3548, 3844, 3860, 3923, 3930, 3936, 3943, 4160, 4222, 4272, 4337, 4342, 4369, 4823, 4980, 5087, 5461, 5483, 5524:*** Ge 1:15; Ezr 4:21; 2Co 9:7; 1Pe 3:7
- exhortations to give: Ex 25:2; Lk 12:33
- rules for giving:
  - according to ability: Dt 16:17
  - cheerfully: 2Co 9:7
  - with simplicity: Ro 12:8

Gizonite — 1493: *1Ch 11:34*

glad, ly, ness — 1523, 1524, 2302, 2304, 2868, 2896, 3190, 7440, 7796, 7797, 8056, 8057, 8342 ✑ ***20, 21, 780, 2097, 2165, 2167, 2234, 2236, 5463, 5479:*** Nu 10:10; Ps 31:7; Mk 6:20

glass, es — 1549, 7209 ✑ ***2072, 27334, 5193, 5194:*** Job 37:18; Isa 3:23; Jas 1:23

glean, ed, ing, ings — 3950, 3951, 5953, 5955: Le 19:10; Ru 2:3; Jer 49:9

glede — 7201: *Dt 14:13*

glistering; glitter, ing — 1300, 3851, 6320 ✑ ***1823:*** Dt 32:41; Eze 21:10; Lk 9:29

gloominess — 653: *Joel 2:2; Zep 1:5*

glorify, ing, ed, eth (see **glory**) — 1922, 1984, 3513, 6286 ✑ ***1392, 1740, 2744, 4888:*** Le 10:3; Ps 50:23; Lk 2:20

GLORY, est, eth; glorious, ly (see **glorify**) — 117, 142, 155, 215, 1921, 1925, 1926, 1935, 1984, 2892, 3367, 3513, 3519, 3520, 6286, 6643, 7623, 8597 ✑ ***1223/1391, 1391, 1392, 1722/1391, 1741, 2620, 2744, 2745, 2746, 2755, 2811:*** Ex 15:6; Isa 24:23; Mt 4:8; 1Co 5:6
- God's glory:
  - declared by His creation: Ps 19:1
  - like devouring fire: Ex 24:17
  - effects changes in the saints: 2Co 3:18
- man's glory:
  - temporal: Ps 49:16, 17
  - transitory: Hos 9:11; 1Pe 1:24

glutton, ous — 2151 ✑ ***5314:*** Dt 21:20; Pr 23:21; Mt 11:19

gnash, ed, eth, ing — 2786 ✑ ***1030, 1031, 5149:*** Job 16:9; La 2:6; Mt 8:12

gnat — ***2971***: *Mt 23:2*

gnaw, ed — 1633 ✑ ***3145:*** *Zep 3:3; Rev 16:10*

go, est, eth, ing, ings; gone; went, est — 230, 235, 236, 258, 369, 656, 782, 833, 838, 935, 1540, 1718, 1869, 1946, 1961, 1979, 1980, 2114, 2498, 2559, 3051, 3212, 3318, 3381, 3996, 4059, 4161, 4163, 4174, 4185, 4570, 4609, 4703, 4994, 5066, 5075, 5128, 5181, 5186, 5221, 5265, 5312, 5362, 5375, 5437, 5472, 5493, 5503, 5648, 5674, 5927, 5930, 5944, 5954, 6213, 6310, 6471, 6485, 6544, 6585, 6805, 6806, 6807, 6923, 7121, 7126, 7272, 7311, 7368, 7503, 7683, 7686, 7725, 7751, 7845, 7847, 7971, 8444, 8582, 8637 ✑ ***33, 71, 305, 402, 424, 549, 565, 576, 589, 630, 863, 1136, 1276, 1279, 1330, 1339, 1353, 1524, 1525, 1578, 1607, 1681, 1684, 1821, 1826, 1831, 1910, 1994, 2021, 2064, 2212, 2597, 2718, 3327, 3596, 3597, 3854, 3899, 3928, 3985, 3987, 4013, 4043, 4105, 4108, 4160, 4198, 4254, 4260, 4281, 4313, 4320, 4334, 4344, 4570, 4782, 4848, 4897, 4905, 5055, 5217, 5221, 5233, 5298, 5342, 5562:*** Jos 1:7; Hab 3:13; Ac 18:22; 3Jn 7

goad, s — 1861, 4451: *Jgs 3:31; 1Sa 13:21; Ecc 12:11*

goat, s, skins — 689, 3277, 5795, 6260, 6842, 8163, 8495 ✑ ***122/1192, 2055, 2056, 5131:*** Ge 15:9; Ezr 6:17; Heb 11:37

Goath — 1601: *Jer 31:39*

Gob — 1359: *2Sa 21:18, 19*

goblet — 101: *SS 7:2*

GOD, s, ward (see **Jah**; **Jehovah**; **Jesus**; **spirit**) — 410, 426, 430, 433, 1008, 3068, 3069, 4136/430, 6697 ✑ ***2316, 2962, 4314/2316***: Ex 6:3; Mt 1:23; Ac 19:20
- God's attributes:
  - holiness: Le 20:7; Isa 5:16
  - eternal existence: Ps 90:2; Isa 40:28
  - truthfulness: Ps 31:5; Jn 14:6
  - righteousness: Ps 116:5; Da 9:14
  - mercifulness: Ps 138:8; Eph 2:4
  - goodness: 2Ch 5:13; Mt 19:16, 17
  - omniscience: Ps 139:1-4
  - omnipresence: Ps 139:7-10
- God's incomparability: Dt 32:29; Isa 43:10-13

goddess — 430 ✑ ***2299: 1Ki*** *11:5, 33; Ac 19:27, 35, 37*

GODHEAD — ***2304, 2305, 2320:*** *Ac 17:29; Ro 1:20; Col 2:9*
- the Godhead contains:
  - unity of essence: Dt 6:4; Jn 10:30; 14:8-10; 1Jn 5:7

plurality of Persons: Ge 1:26; Mt 28:19; Eph 4:4-6

GODLY, iness — ***516/2316, 2150, 2152, 2153, 2316, 2317, 2596/2316:*** Ps 4:3; Mal 2:15; 1Th 1:8; 1Ti 2:2
things which are godly:
godly living: 2Ti 3:12; Tit 2:12
godly edifying: 1Ti 1:4
godly fear: Heb 12:28
godly sorrow: 2Co 7:10, 11
godly jealousy: 2Co 11:2

Gog — 1463 ✑ ***1136***: Eze 38:2; Rev 20:8
Golan — 1474: Dt 4:43; 1Ch 6:71
gold, en, smith — 1220, 1222, 1722, 2091, 2742, 3800, 4062, 5458, 6337, 6884 ✑ ***5552, 5553, 5554, 5557:*** Ge 2:11; Isa 40:19; Heb 9:4
Golgotha — ***1115***: *Mt 27:33; Mk 15:22; Jn 19:17*
Goliath — 1555: 1Sa 17:4; 2Sa 21:19
Gomer — 1586: Ge 10:2; Hos 1:3
Gomorrah, Gomorrha — 6017 ✑ ***1116:*** Ge 19:24; Am 4:11; Jude 7

GOOD, lier, liest, liness, ly, ness — 117, 145, 155, 410, 1319, 1580, 1926, 1935, 2492, 2522, 2530, 2532, 2617, 2623, 2895, 2896, 2898, 3190, 3191, 3276, 3303/8389, 3474, 3788, 3966, 4261, 4758, 5750, 6287, 6643, 6743, 6965, 7368, 7443, 7965, 7999, 8231, 8232, 8233 ✑ ***14, 15, 18, 515, 865, 979, 2095, 2097, 2106, 2107, 2133, 2108, 2109, 2140, 2162, 2163, 2425, 2480, 2565, 2567, 2570, 2573, 2750, 2986, 3112, 4851, 5358, 5542, 5543, 5544:*** Ge 1:4; 1Sa 9:2; Mk 3:4; Jas 2:2
good things to be practiced by saints:
good will: Eph 6:7; Php 1:15
good courage: Jos 1:6; Ps 27:14; Isa 41:16
good words: 1Ki 12:7; 2Th 2:17
good works: Mt 5:16; Col 1:10; Heb 10:24

goodman — 376 ✑ ***3611***: Pr 7:19; Mt 20:11; Mk 14:14
goods — 202, 2428, 2896, 2898, 4399, 5232, 7075, 7399 ✑ ***18, 3776, 4147, 4632, 4647, 5223, 5224:*** Ge 14:11; Ne 9:25; Mt 12:29
gopher — 1613: *Ge 6:14*
gore, d — 5055: *Ex 21:28, 31*
gorgeous, ly — 4358 ✑ ***1741, 2986***: *Eze 23:12; Lk 7:25; 23:11*
Goshen — 1657: Ge 45:10; Ex 8:22

GOSPEL — ***2097, 2098, 4283:*** Mt 4:23; 1Co 9:23; Gal 3:8
Biblical titles ascribed to the gospel:
gospel of God: Ro 1:1; 1Th 2:8, 9; 1Pe 4:17
gospel of Christ: Ro 1:16; 1Co 9:12; Php 1:27; 1Th 3:2
gospel of peace: Ro 10:15; Eph 6:15

gourd, s — 6498, 7021: *2Ki 4:39; Jnh 4:6, 7, 9, 10*
govern, ment, ments, or, ors — 441, 2280, 2710, 4475, 4910, 4951, 5057, 5148, 5387, 5461, 5921, 6213, 6346, 6347, 6485, 7989, 8269 ✑ ***755, 1481, 2116, 2230, 2232, 2233, 2941, 2963, 3623:*** Job 34:17; Isa 9:6; Mt 2:6; 2Pe 2:10
Gozan — 1470: 2Ki 17:6; 1Ch 5:26

GRACE, ious, iously — 2580, 2587, 2589, 2603, 8467 ✑ ***2143, 5485, 5543:*** Ge 6:8; Pr 11:16; Hos 14:2; Lk 2:40
God is the source of grace: Ps 84:11; Jn 1:16, 17; 1Pe 5:5
salvation comes by grace: Ac 15:11; Eph 2:8; Tit 2:11
benefits derived from grace:
God's power: 2Co 12:9; 2Ti 2:1
God's mercy: 1Ti 1:14
redemption: Eph 1:7

graff, ed (see **engrafted**) — ***1461:*** *Ro 11:17, 19, 23, 24*
grain — 6872 ✑ ***2848:*** Am 9:9; Mt 13:31; 1Co 15:37
grandmother — ***3125***: *2Ti 1:5*
grant, ed (see **give**) — 935, 5414, 6213, 7558 ✑ ***1325, 2036, 5483:*** Ru 1:9; Job 10:12; Mt 20:21
grape, gleanings, s; grapegatherer, s — 891, 1154, 1155, 1219, 5563, 5955, 6025, 6528 ✑ ***4713:*** Le 19:10; Jer 49:9; Mic 7:1; Mt 7:16
grass — 1758, 1877, 1883, 2682, 3418, 6211, 6212 ✑ ***5528:*** Ge 1:11; Le 11:22; Mt 6:30
grasshopper, s — 697, 1462, 2284: Jgs 6:5; Job 39:20; Na 3:17
grate — 4345: Ex 27:4; 35:16; 39:39
grave, clothes, s — 1164, 6900, 6913, 7585, 7845 ✑ ***86, 2750, 3419, 4586:*** 1Sa 2:6; Jer 8:1; Jn 11:44
grave, d, en, eth, ing (see **engrave**) — 2672, 2710, 2747, 2790, 2801, 4734, 6456, 6458, 6459, 6603, 6605 ✑ ***5480:*** Isa 22:16; Zec 3:9; Ac 17:29
gravity — ***4587***: *1Ti 3:4; Tit 2:7*
gray, headed; grey — 7867, 7872: Job 15:10; Pr 20:29; Hos 7:9
grease — 2459: *Ps 119:70*
great, er, est, ly, ness — 410, 417, 430, 679, 1004, 1167, 1241, 1396, 1419, 1420, 1431, 1432, 1433, 1462, 1560, 1980, 2030, 2342, 2750, 3029, 3244, 3514, 3515, 3833, 3966, 4166, 4306, 4459,

4768, 5006, 6099, 6105, 6343, 7091, 7227, 7229, 7230, 7235, 7236, 7238, 7239, 7260, 7350, 7390, 7451, 7689, 7690, 7991, 8514 ✑ ***1419, 1420, 1431, 1433, 1568, 1569, 1971, 1974, 1980, 2245, 2425, 3029, 3112, 3123, 3166, 3167, 3170, 3171, 3173, 3174, 3175, 3176, 3179, 3186, 3187, 3745, 3816, 3817, 3819, 3827, 4055, 4080, 4118, 4119, 4183, 4185, 4186, 4214, 4768, 4970, 5082, 5118, 5246, 5479:*** Ge 1:16; Job 1:3; Jn 3:29; Eph 1:19

greaves — 4697: *1Sa 17:6*

Grecia, Greece (see **Achaia**) — 3120 ✑ ***1671:*** Da 8:21; Zec 9:13; Ac 20:2

Grecians (see **Greek**) — 3125 ✑ ***1675:*** *Joel 3:6; Ac 6:1; 9:29; 11:20*

greedy, ly, ness — 1214, 3700, 5794/5315, 8378 ✑ ***146, 866, 1632, 4124:*** Ps 17:12; Pr 21:26; Eph 4:19

Greek, s (see **Grecians**) — ***1672, 1673, 1674, 1676:*** Mk 7:26; Ro 1:14; Rev 9:11

green, ish, ness: — 3, 1877, 3387, 3418, 3419, 3422, 3768, 3892, 6291, 7373, 7488 ✑ ***5200, 5515:*** Ge 1:30; Le 13:49; Job 8:12; Mk 6:39

greet, eth, ing, s — 7592/7965 ✑ ***782, 783, 5463:*** 1Sa 25:5; Mt 23:7; Jas 1:1

grief, s; grieve, ance, ed, eth, ing, ous, ously, ousness — 109, 2342, 2399, 2470, 2483, 2556, 2734, 3013, 3015, 3415, 3510, 3511, 3512, 3513, 3514, 3515, 3707, 3708, 3735, 3811, 4341, 4604, 4784, 4786, 4834, 4843, 5493, 5701, 5999, 6087, 6089, 6277, 6330, 6962, 6973, 7114, 7185, 7186, 7451, 7489, 8463 ✑ ***926, 1171, 1278, 1418, 2560, 3076, 3077, 3636, 4190, 4360, 4818:*** Ge 6:6; Ru 1:13; Isa 53:3; Mt 8:6; 2Co 2:5

grind, ers, ing — 2911, 2912, 2913 ✑ ***229, 3030:*** Ecc 12:3; Isa 3:15; Mt 21:44

grizzled — 1261; *Ge 31:10, 12; Zec 6:3, 6*

groan, ed, eth, ing, ings — 584, 585, 602, 603, 5008, 5009 ✑ ***1690, 4726, 4727, 4959:*** Ex 6:5; Jgs 2:18; Ro 8:26

grope, th — 1659, 4959: Dt 28:29; Job 5:14; Isa 59:10

gross — 6205 ✑ ***3975:*** Isa 60:2; Jer 13:16; Mt 13:15

ground, ed — 127, 776, 2513, 2758, 2912, 4145, 6083, 7383, 7704 ✑ ***68, 1093, 1474, 1475, 2311, 5476, 5561, 5564:*** Ge 1:5; Isa 30:32; Eph 3:17

grove, s — 815, 842: Ge 21:33; Dt 16:21; Isa 17:8

grow, eth, n, th; grew — 648, 1342, 1431, 1711, 2498, 2583, 3212, 3318, 3332, 3954, 5599, 5927, 6335, 6509, 6524, 6779, 6965, 7235, 7236, 7680, 7685, 7971, 8025 ✑ ***305, 837, 1096, 3373, 4886, 5232:*** Ezr 9:6; Am 7:1; Mt 13:32; 2Th 1:3

grudge, ing, ingly — 3885, 5201 ✑ ***1112, 1537/3077, 4727:*** Le 19:18; Jas 5:9; 1Pe 4:9

guard — 2876, 4928, 4929, 7323 ✑ ***4759:*** Ge 41:10; Jer 39:9-11; Ac 28:16

guest, chamber, s — 7121 ✑ ***345, 2646, 2647:*** Pr 9:18; Mk 14:14; Lk 19:7

guide, ed, es — 441, 833, 1869, 3289, 5090, 5095, 5148, 7101 ✑ ***2720, 3594, 3595, 3616:*** Ex 15:13; Ps 25:9; Mt 23:16

guile (see **beguile**) — 4820, 6195, 7423 ✑ ***1388:*** Ex 21:14; Ps 32:2; Jn 1:47; 1Pe 2:1

GUILT, less, y, iness — 816, 817, 5352, 5355, 7563 ✑ ***338, 1777, 3784, 5267:*** Ge 26:10; Dt 19:13; Mt 12:7

subjects of guilt:

the whole world: Ro 3:19

lawbreakers: Jas 2:10

consequences of guilt:

an uneasy conscience: Ps 32:3; Jn 8:7-9; Ac 2:36, 37

judgment: Nu 32:23; Ezr 9:13, 14; Ro 2:1, 3

gulf — ***5490***: *Lk 16:26*

Guni — 1476: Ge 46:24; 1Ch 5:15

Gunites — 1477: *Nu 26:48*

Gur — 1483: *2Ki 9:27*

Gur-baal — 1485: *2Ch 26:7*

gush, ed — 2100, 5140, 8210 ✑ ***1632***: Ps 78:20; Jer 9:18; Ac 1:18

gutter, s — 6794, 7298: *Ge 30:38, 41; 2Sa 5:8*

H

ha (see **ah; aha**) — 1889: *Job 39:25*

Haahashtari — 326: *1Ch 4:6*

Habiah — 2252: *Ezr 2:61; Ne 7:63*

Habakkuk — 2265: *Hab: title; 1:1; 3:1*

Habaziniah — 2262: *Jer 35:3*

habergeon, s — 8302, 8473: Ex 28:32; 2Ch 26:14; Job 41:26

habitable; habitation, s — 1628, 2073, 2918, 3427, 4186, 4349, 4351, 4380, 4583, 4585, 4907, 4908, 4999, 5115, 5116, 7931, 7932, 7933, 8398 ✑ ***1886, 2732, 2733, 3613, 4638:*** Ex 15:2; Pr 8:31; Ac 1:20; Jude 6

Habor — 2249: 1Ki 17:6; 1Ch 5:26

Hachaliah — 2440: *Ne 1:1; 10:1*

Hachilah — 2444: *1Sa 23:19: 26:1, 3*

Hachmoni, Hachmonite (see **Tachmonite**) — 2453: *1Ch 11:11; 27:32*

as sovereign over authorities: 1Pe 3:22
as High Priest on behalf of the saints: Heb 4:14
where the saint's citizenship is: Php 3:20

heavy, er, ly, ness — 1674, 3513, 3514, 3515, 3517, 3544, 4133, 4751, 5136, 5620, 6440, 7186, 7451, 8386, 8424, 8589 ⚭ ***85, 916, 926, 2726, 3076, 3077:*** Ex 14:25; Ezr 9:5; Mt 11:28; 1Pe 1:6
Heber (see **Eber**) — 2268, 5677 ⚭ ***1443:*** Jgs 4:11; Lk 3:35
Heberites — 2277: *Nu 26:45*
Hebrew, ess, s — 5680 ⚭ ***1145, 1444, 1446, 1447:*** Ge 14:13; Jer 34:9; Ac 6:1
Hebron (see **Kirjath-arba**) — 2275: Ge 13:18; 1Ki 2:11
Hebronites — 2276: Nu 3:27; 1Ch 26:23
hedge, d, s — 1443, 1447, 1448, 4534, 4881, 5526, 7753 ⚭ ***5418/4060***: Job 1:10; Na 3:17; Mt 21:33
heed (see **hear; hearken; listen**) — 238, 2095, 3820, 5438, 5535, 7181, 7182, 7200, 8104 ⚭ ***433, 991, 1907, 3708, 4337, 4648:*** Ge 31:24; Ezr 4:22; Mt 6:1
heel, s — 6117, 6119, 6120, 8328 ⚭ ***4418:*** Ge 3:15; Job 13:27; Jn 13:18
Hegai, Hege — 1896: *Est 2:3, 8, 15*
heifer, s — 5697, 6510, 7311 ⚭ ***1151:*** Dt 21:4; Hos 4:16; Heb 9:13
height, s — 1116, 1361, 1363, 1364, 4791, 6967, 7218, 7312, 7314, 7419 ⚭ ***5311, 5313:*** Ge 6:15; Isa 14:14; Ro 8:39
heinous — 2154: *Job 31:11*
heir, s — 3423 ⚭ ***2816, 2818, 4789:*** Ge 15:3; Mt 21:38; Heb 11:9
Helah — 2458: *1Ch 4:5, 7*
Helam — 2431: *2Sa 10:16, 17*
Helbah — 2462: *Jgs 1:31*
Helbon — 2463: *Eze 27:18*
Heldai (see **Helem**) — 2469: *1Ch 27:15; Zec 6:10*
Heleb (see **Heled**) — 2466: *2Sa 23:29*
Heled (see **Heleb**) — 2460: *1Ch 11:30*
Helek — 2507: *Nu 26:30; Jos 17:2*
Helekites — 2516: *Nu 26:30*
Helem (see **Heldai**) — 2494: *1Ch 7:35; Zec 6:14*
Heleph — 2501: *Jos 19:33*
Helez — 2503: 2Sa 23:26; 1Ch 11:27
Helkai — 2517: *Ne 12:15*
Helkath — 2520: *Jos 19:25; 21:31*

HELL — 7585 ⚭ ***86, 1067, 5020:*** Dt 32:22; Mt 5:22; Lk 10:15
hell is:
a place under God's dominion: Lk 12:5; Rev 1:8
a place of damnation: Mt 23:33
a place of torment: Mk 9:43-48; Lk 16:23
hell will be cast into the lake of fire: Rev 20:14

helm — ***4079***: *Jas 3:4*
helmet, s — 3553, 6959 ⚭ ***4030:*** 2Ch 26:14; Jer 46:4; Eph 6:17
Helon — 2497: Nu 1:9; 10:16
help, ed, er, ers, eth, ing — 2388, 3444, 3447, 3467, 5375, 5583, 5800, 5826, 5828, 5833, 6965, 7125, 8668 ⚭ ***482, 484, 996, 997, 998, 1947, 4815, 4820, 4878, 4903, 4904, 4943:*** Ge 2:18; Ps 22:1; Lk 1:54; Ac 18:27
helve — 6086: *Dt 19:5*
hem, s — 7757 ⚭ ***2899:*** Ex 28:33; 39:24; Mt 9:20
Hemam (see **Homam**) — 1967: *Ge 36:22*
Heman — 1968: 1Ki 4:31; 25:4
Hemdan — 2533: *Ge 36:26*
hemlock — 3939, 7219: *Hos 10:4; Am 6:12*
hen — ***3733***: *Mt 23:37; Lk 13:34*
Hen — 2581: *Zec 6:14*
Hena — 2012: *2Ki 18:34; 19:13; Isa 37:13*
Henadad — 2582: *Ezr 3:9; Ne 3:18, 24; 10:9*
hence, forth, forward — 731, 1973, 2088, 3588, 3226, 731, 3370, 3212, 3226, 3254, 3318, 3370, 3588, 5750, 6258 ⚭ ***534, 575/3588/3568, 737, 1782, 1821, 2089, 3063, 3371, 3568, 3765, 5025, 5217:*** Ge 37:17; Nu 15:23; Lk 1:48; Ac 1:5
Hepher — 2660: Nu 26:32; 1Ki 4:10
Hepherites — 2662: *Nu 26:32*
Hephzibah — 2657: *2Ki 21:1; Isa 62:4*
her, s, self (see **he**) — 5315 ⚭ ***844, 846, 1438:*** Ge 2:22; Mt 9:21; 2Jn 1
herald — 3744: *Da 3:4*
herb, s — 216, 219, 1877, 2682, 3419, 6212 ⚭ ***3001:*** Ge 1:11; Dt 11:10; Mt 13:32
herd, man, men, s — 951, 1241, 4635, 4735, 5349, 5739, 7462, 7473 ⚭ ***34:*** Ge 13:5; Pr 27:23; Am 1:1; Mt 8:30
here, after, by, in, of, tofore, unto, with — 268, 310, 311/1836, 543/8032, 645, 865/8032, 1988, 2005, 2008, 2009, 2063, 2088, 2236, 3541, 4672, 5921, 6311, 8033, 8543, 8552 ⚭ ***575/737, 575/3568, 848, 1519, 1537, 1722/5129, 1759, 2089, 3195, 3326/5023, 3370, 3568, 3778, 3918, 3936, 4258, 4840, 5026, 5028, 5124, 5602:*** Nu 32:6; Isa 41:23; Mt 9:26; 2Co 13:2; 1Jn 2:3
Heres — 2776: *Jgs 1:35*
Heresh — 2792: *1Ch 9:15*

1949, 2192, 2270, 2476, 2722, 2902, 2983, 4160, 4601, 4623, 4912, 5083, 5084, 5392, 5438: Ge 19:16; La 2:2; Ro 14:4; Rev 2:1

hole, s — 2356, 4526, 4631, 4718, 5344, 5357, 6310, 6354 ✒ ***5454:*** Ex 28:32; Jer 48:28; Lk 9:58

hollow — 3709, 4388, 5014, 8168, 8258: Ge 32:25; Jgs 15:19; Jer 52:21

Holon (see **Hilen**) — 2473: Jos 15:51; Jer 48:21

HOLY, NESS, day, er, est, ly — 2287, 2623, 4720, 6918, 6942, 6944 ✒ ***39, 40, 1859, 2413, 3741, 3743:*** Ex 3:5; Ps 42:4; Isa 65:5; Lk 1:75; Heb 9:3

holiness is:
an attribute of God: Le 11:44; Job 6:10; Mk 1:24
beautiful: 1Ch 16:29; Ps 29:2; 110:3
God's desired state for His people: Ro 6:19; 1Pe 1:15

Homam (see **Hemam**) — 1950: *1Ch 1:39*

home, born — 168, 249, 1004, 4725, 5115, 7725, 8432 ✒ ***1438, 1736, 2398, 3614, 3624, 3626:*** Ex 12:49; Ps 68:12; Mt 8:6

homer, s — 2563, 3963: Nu 11:32; Hos 3:2

honest, ly, y — ***2156, 2570, 2573, 4586, 4587:*** Lk 8:15; Ro 13:13; 1Ti 2:2

honey, comb — 1706, 3293, 3295/1706, 5317/6688, 6688/1706 ✒ ***3192, 3193/2781:*** 3295, Ex 3:8; Ps 19:10; Mt 3:4

HONOUR, able, ed, est, eth, s — 142, 1921, 1922, 1923, 1926, 1927, 1935, 3366, 3367, 3513, 3519, 5375/6440, 8597 ✒ ***820, 1391, 1392, 1741, 1784, 2158, 5091, 5092, 5093:*** Nu 22:17; Isa 3:3; Ac 28:10

honor should be rendered to:
God: Ps 66:1, 2; Mal 1:6; Jn 5:22, 23
parents: Ex 20:12; Mk 7:10; Eph 6:2
rulers: 1Th 5:12, 13; Heb 13:17; 1Pe 2:17
one's wife: 1Pe 3:7
widows: 1Ti 5:3
elderly people: Le 19:32; 1Ti 5:1

hoods — 6797: *Isa 3:23*

hoof, s — 6536, 6541: Le 11:3; Ps 69:31; Mic 4:13

hook, s — 100, 2053, 2397, 2443, 6793, 8240 ✒ ***44:*** 2Ki 19:28; Am 4:2; Mt 17:27

HOPE, d, ing, s — 982, 983, 986, 2342, 2620, 2976, 3176, 3689, 4009, 4268, 4723, 7663, 7664, 8431, 8615 ✒ ***560, 1679, 1680:*** Est 9:1; Jer 2:25; 1Co 13:7

the hope of the righteous:
centered in God: Ps 39:7; Joel 3:16; 1Ti 1:1
obtained through:
The Father and the Son: 2Th 2:16
access to grace through Jesus Christ: Ro 5:1, 2
results of:
a desire to purify oneself: 1Jn 3:3
continual bearing of fruit: Jer 17:7, 8
the hope of the wicked:
has no basis: Job 27:8
shall come to nothing: Job 8:13; Pr 10:28

Hophni — 2652: *1Sa 1:3; 2:34; 4:4, 11, 17*

Hor — 2023: Num 33:37; Dt 32:50

Horam — 2036: *Jos 10:33*

Horeb (see **Sinai**) — 2722: Ex 3:1; Ps 106:19

Horah-gidgad — 2735: *Nu 33:32, 33*

Hori — 2753: Ge 36:22, 30; 1Ch 1:39

Horim; Horite, s — 2752: Ge 36:20; Dt 2:12

Hormah (see **Zephath**) — 2767: Nu 14:45; 1Sa 30:30

horn, s — 3104, 7161, 7162 ✒ ***2768:*** Ge 22:13; Jos 6:4; Lk 1:69

hornet, s — 6880: *Ex 23:28; Dt 7:20; Jos 24:12*

Horonaim — 2773: *Isa 15:5; Jer 48:3, 5, 34*

Horonite — 2772: *Ne 2:10, 19; 13:28*

horrible, ly — 367, 2152, 6427, 7588, 8175, 8178, 8186: Ps 11:6; Jer 2:12; Hos 6:10

horse, man, men, s — 5483, 5484, 6571, 7395 ✒ ***2460, 2461, 2462***: Jer 4:29; Jas 3:3; Rev 9:7

horseback — 5483, 7392/5483: *2Ki 9:18, 19; Est 6:9, 11; 8:10*

horsehoofs — 6119/5483: *Jgs 5:22*

horseleach — 5936: *Pr 30:15*

Hosah — 2621: Jos 19:29; 1Ch 16:38

hosanna — ***5614***: *Mt 21:9, 15; Mk 11:9, 10; Jn 12:13*

hose — 6361: *Da 3:21*

Hosea — 1954 ✒ ***5617***: Hos 1:1; Ro 9:25

Hoshaiah — 1955: *Ne 13:22; Jer 42:1; 43:2*

Hoshama — 1953: *1Ch 3:18*

Hoshea (see **Joshua**) — 1954: Dt 32:44; 2Ki 15:30; Ne 10:23

hospitality — ***5381, 5382:*** Ro 12:13; Tit 1:8; 1Pe 4:9

host, s — 2428, 4264, 6635 ✒ ***3581, 3830, 4756***: Nu 1:52; Mal 1:4; Ro 16:23

hot, ly, test — 228, 784, 1814, 2369, 2525, 2527, 2534, 2734, 3179, 7565 ✒ ***2200, 2743***: Ge 31:36; 2Sa 11:15; Rev 3:15

Hotham, Hothan — 2369: *1Ch 7:32; 11:44*

Hothir — 1956: *1Ch 25:4, 28*

hough, ed — 6131: Jos 11:6, 9; 2Sa 8:4; 1Ch 18:4

hour, s — 8160 ➾ ***734, 2256, 5610***: Da 3:6; Jn 11:9; 1Co 8:7

house, s; household, er, ers; housetop, s — 1004, 1005, 1406, 5657, 5854 ➾ *2322, 3609, 3610, 3613, 3614, 3615, 3616, 3617, 3624, 3832:* Ge 7:1; Job 1:3; Mt 13:27; Lk 12:3; Ac 4:34

how, beit, soever — 199, 349, 389, 578, 637, 657, 834, 854, 854/834, 1571, 1963, 3588, 3605, 3651, 4069, 4100, 4101, 5704, 7535 ➾ ***235, 1161, 2193, 2245, 2531, 3305, 3704, 3745, 3754, 4012, 4080, 4212, 4214, 4459, 5101, 5613:*** Ge 27:20; 1Ki 11:13; Zep 3:7; Mt 6:23

howl, ed, ing, ings — 3213, 3214 ➾ ***3649:*** Isa 13:6; Am 8:3; Jas 5:1

huge — 7230: *2Ch 16:8*

Hukkok, Hukok-2712: *Jos 19:34; 1Ch 6:75*

Hul — 2343: *Ge 10:23; 1Ch 1:17*

Huldah — 2468: *2Ki 22:14; 2Ch 34:22*

humble, d, dst, ness, th, ly (see **humility**) — 1792, 3665, 5869, 6031, 6041, 6800, 7511, 7743, 7812, 7817, 8213, 8214, 8217 ➾ ***5011, 5012, 5013:*** 2Ch 7:14; Mic 6:8; 2Co 12:21

HUMILITY; humiliation (see **humble**) — 5014, 6038 ➾ ***5012, 5014:*** Pr 15:33; Ac 8:33; Col 2:18

humility is:
- esteemed by God: Pr 16:19; 29:23; Isa 57:15; Jas 4:6
- demonstrated by godly men: Mt 8:8; Lk 18:13
- followed by honor: Mt 18:4; Jas 4:10; 1Pe 5:6

Humtah — 2547: *Jos 15:54*

hundred, s, fold, eth — 520, 3967, 3969, 6471, 8180 ➾ ***1250, 1540, 1541, 1542, 1812, 3461, 4001, 5071, 5145, 5516:*** Ge 26:12; Ne 5:11; Mk 6:40; Ro 4:19

hunger, bitten, ed; hungry — 7456, 7457, 7458 ➾ ***3042, 3983, 4361:*** Ex 16:3; Job 18:12; Lk 1:53

hunt, ed, er, ers, est, eth, ing — 4686, 6658, 6679, 6718, 6719, 7291: Ge 10:9; Eze 13:18; Mic 7:2

Hupham, ites — 2349, 2350: *Nu 26:39*

Huppah — 2647: *1Ch 24:13*

Huppim — 2650: *Ge 46:21; 1Ch 7:12, 15*

Hur — 2354: Ex 17:10; Ne 3:9

Hurai (see **Hiddai**) — 2360: *1Ch 11:32*

Huram (see **Hiram**) — 2361, 2438: 1Ch 8:5; 2Ch 2:3

Huri — 2359: *1Ch 5:14*

hurl, eth, ing — 7993, 8175: *Nu 35:20; 1Ch 12:2; Job 27:21*

hurt, ful, ing — 1697, 2248, 2250, 2255, 2257, 3637, 5062, 5142, 6031, 6087, 6485, 7451, 7489, 7665, 7667 ➾ ***91, 983, 984, 2559, 5196:*** 1Sa 25:34; Ezr 4:15; Mk 16:18

husband, s — 376, 582, 1167, 2860, 2992, 2993, 7464 ➾ ***435, 5220, 5362:*** Ge 3:6; Ex 4:25; Jn 4:18

husbandman; husbandmen; husbandry — 127, 376/127, 376/5467/127, 406, 1461, 3009, 5647 ➾ ***1091, 1092:*** Ge 9:20; Joel 1:11; 1Co 3:9; Jas 5:7

Hushah — 2364: *1Ch 4:4*

Hushai — 2365: 2Sa 15:32; 1Ki 4:16

Husham — 2367: *Ge 36:34, 35; 1Ch 1:45, 46*

Hushathite — 2843: 2Sa 21:18; 1Ch 27:11

Hushim (see **Shuham**) — 2366: *Ge 46:23; 1Ch 7:12; 8:8, 11*

husk, s — 2085, 6861 ➾ ***2769:*** *Nu 6:4; 2Ki 4:42; Lk 15:16*

Huz — 5780: *Ge 22:21*

Huzzab — 5324: *Na 2:7*

Hymenaeus — ***5211***: *1Ti 1:20; 2Ti 2:17*

hymn, s — ***5214, 5215***: *Mt 26:30; Mk 14:26; Eph 5:19; Col 3:16*

HYPOCRISY, ies; hypocrite, s; hypocritical — 120, 2611, 2612 ➾ ***505, 5272, 5273:*** Isa 10:6; Mt 7:5; Jas 3:17

descriptions of hypocrisy:
- hiding hatred: Pr 26:24
- speaking villany: Isa 32:6
- making merchandise of those who hear: 2Pe 2:3

warnings against hypocrisy: Job 15:31; Lk 12:1

punishment of hypocrisy:
- heaping up wrath: Job 36:13
- judgment: Isa 33:14; Mt 24:51

hyssop — 231 ➾ ***5301:*** Ex 12:22; Ps 51:7; Jn 19:29

I

I; me; my, self — 589, 1473, 1691, 1700, 3165, 3450: Ge 2:23; Jnh 1:2; Mt 3:17; Heb 1:5

Ibhar — 2984: *2Sa 5:15; 1Ch 3:6; 14:5*

Ibleam — 2991: Jos 17:11; 2Ki 9:27

Ibneiah — 2997: *1Ch 9:8*

Ibnijah — 2998: *1Ch 9:8*

Ibri — 5681: *1Ch 24:27*

Ibzan — 78: *Jgs 12:8, 10*

ice — 7140: *Job 6:16; 38:29; Ps 147:17*

Ichabod — 350: *1Sa 4:21; 14:3*

Iconium — ***2430***: Ac 13:51; 2Ti 3:11

incontinency; incontinent — **192, 193**: *1Co 7:5; 2Ti 3:3*
incorruptible; incorruption (see **uncorruptible**) — ***861, 862:*** 1Co 9:25; 15:42; 1Pe 1:4
increase, d, ing, st, th — 553, 1342, 1431, 2981, 3254, 4768, 5107, 5927, 6105, 6509, 6555, 7227, 7230, 7231, 7235, 7239, 7685, 7698, 7679, 8317, 8393, 8570, 8635 ➺ ***837, 838, 1743, 4052, 4121, 4147, 4298, 4369***: Ge 7:17; Job 10:16; Jn 3:30; Col 1:10
incredible — ***571***: *Ac 26:8*
incurable — 369/4832, 605: 2Ch 21:18; Job 34:6; Mic 1:9
indebted — ***3784***: *Lk 11:4*
indeed — 61, 389, 546, 551, 552, 1571 ➺ ***230, 235, 1063, 2532, 3303, 3689***: Ge 17:19; Nu *21:2*; Mt 3:11; Jn *1:47*
India — 1912: *Est 1:1; 8:9*
indigation — 2194, 2195, 2197, 2534, 3707, 3708, 7110 ➺ ***23, 24, 2205, 2372, 3709***: Dt 29:28; Ps 78:49; Heb 10:27
inditing — 7370: *Ps 45:1*
industrious — 4399, 6213: *1Ki 11:28*
inexcusable — ***379***: *Ro 2:1*
infallible — *: *Ac 1:3*
infamy; infamous — 1681, 2931/8034: *Pr 25:10; Eze 22:5; 36:3*
infant, s (see **babe**) — 5764, 5768 ➺ ***1025***: Isa 65:20; Hos 13:16; Lk 18:15
inferior — 772, 5307 ➺ ***2274***: Job 12:3; Da 2:39; 2Co 12:13
infidel — ***571***: *2Co 6:15; 1Ti 5:8*
infinite — 369/7093, 369/4557, 369/7097: *Job 22:5; Ps 147:5; Na 3:9*
infirmity, ies — 1738, 2470, 4245 ➺ ***769, 771, 3554***: Pr 18:14; Lk 7:21; Heb 4:15
inflame, ation (see **enflaming**) — 1814, 1816, 6867: *Le 13:28; Dt 28:22; Isa 5:11*
inflicted — *: *2Co 2:6*
influences — 4575: *Job 38:31*
infolding — 3947: *Eze 1:4*
inform, ed — 995, 3384 ➺ ***1718, 2727***: Dt 17:10; Da 9:22; Ac 21:21
ingathering — 614: *Ex 23:16; 34:22*
inhabit, ant, ants, ed, ers, est, eth, ing — 1481, 1509, 1753, 3427, 4186, 6728, 7931, 7934, 8453 ➺ ***2730***: 1Ch 5:9; Job 28:4; Pr 10:30; Rev 8:13
inherit, ance, ances, ed, eth, or — 2490, 2506, 3423, 3425, 4181, 5157, 5159 ➺ ***2816, 2817, 2819, 2820***: Ge 15:7; Isa 65:9; Mt 5:5; Eph 1:11
iniquity, ies (see **sin**) — 205, 1697/5771, 1942, 5753, 5758, 5766, 5771, 5775, 5999, 5932 ➺ ***92, 93, 458, 3892***: Le 16:21; Ps 51:2; Lk 13:27; Ro 4:7
injured; injurious — ***91, 5197***: *Gal 4:12; 1Ti 1:13*
injustice — 2555: *Job 16:17*
ink, horn — 1773, 7083 ➺ ***3188***: Jer 36:18; Eze 9:2; 2Co 3:3
inn — 4411 ➺ ***2646, 3829***: Ge 42:27; Ex 4:24; Lk 2:7
inner, most — 2315, 6441, 6442 ➺ ***2080, 2082***: Pr 18:8; Eze 8:3; Ac 16:24
innocent, s; innocency — 2136, 2600, 2643, 5352, 5355, 5356 ➺ ***121***: Ge 20:5; Joel 3:19; Mt 27:4
innumerable — 369/4557 ➺ ***382, 3461***: Job 21:33; Lk 12:1; Heb 11:12
inordinate — 5691 ➺ ***3806***: *Eze 23:11; Col 3:5*
inquire, d, st; inquiry; inquisition — 1158, 1239, 1240, 1245, 1875, 7592, 7836 ➺ ***198, 1231, 1331, 1567, 1833, 1934, 2212, 4441, 4802***: Dt 19:18; Job 10:6; Ac 10:17; 1Pe 1:10
inscription — ***1924***: *Ac 17:23*
inside — 1004: *1Ki 6:15*
insomuch (see **forasmuch**; **forsomuch**) — ***1519, 5620***: Mal 2:13; Mt 8:24; 2Co 8:6

INSPIRATION — 5397 ➺ ***2315***: *Job 32:8; 2Ti 3:16*
given to the OT prophets: Ne 9:30; Heb 1:1
given through dreams and visions: Nu 12:6; Ac 8:29
given in order that:
man might have understanding: Job 32:8
man might have instruction: 2Ti 3:17
man might be forewarned: 1Ti 4:1

instant, ly — 6621, 7281 ➺ ***1616, 1722, 1945, 2186, 4342, 4705, 5610***: Isa 29:5; Lk 7:4; Ro 12:12
instead — 8478: Ge 2:21; 2Ki 14:21; Jer 22:11

INSTRUCTION; instruct, ed, ers, ers, or — 995, 3045, 3245, 3250, 3256, 3384, 3806, 3810, 3913, 3925, 4148, 4561, 7919 ➺ ***2727, 3100, 3453, 3807, 3809, 3810, 3811, 4264, 4822***: Dt 4:36; Pr 1:2; 1Co 4:15; 2Ti 2:25
instruction is necessary: Dt 6:6, 7; Eze 44:23; Col 3:16
instruction is valuable: Pr 1:8, 9; Ecc 12:11
punishment to the despisers of instruction:
the wrath of God: Jer 32:31-33
judgment: Zep 3:7
poverty and shame: Pr 13:18

instrument, s — 1761, 3627, 4482, 7991 ➺ ***3696***: Nu 35:16; Ps 33:2; Ro 6:13

J

K

kernels — 2785: *Nu 6:4*

Keros — 7026: *Ezr 2:44; Ne 7:47*

kettle — 1731: *1Sa 2:14*

Keturah — 6989: *Ge 25:1, 4; 1Ch 1:32, 33*

key, s — 4668 ➤ ***2807***: Jgs 3:25; Mt 16:19; Rev 3:7

Kezia — 7103: *Job 42:14*

Keziz — 7104: *Jos 18:21*

Kibroth-hattaavah — 6914: Nu 11:34; 33:16

Kibzaim — 6911: *Jos 21:22*

kick, ed — 1163 ➤ ***2979***: *Dt 32:15; 1Sa 2:29; Ac 9:5; 26:14*

kid, s — 1423, 1423/5975, 8163, 8166 ➤ ***2056***: Ge 37:31; 1Sa 10:3; Lk 15:29

kidneys — 3629: Le 3:4; Dt 32:14; Isa 34:6

kill, ed, edst, est, eth, ing — 2026, 2076, 2491, 2873, 4191, 5221, 5362, 6991, 7523, 7819, 7821 ➤ ***337, 615, 1315, 2289, 2380, 4969, 5407***: Ex 12:6; Mt 5:21; Ac 10:13

kin, sfolk, sman, smen, swoman, swomen (see **kindred**) — 1320, 1350, 3045, 4129, 7138, 7607, 7608 ➤ ***4773***: Nu 5:8; Pr 7:4; Lk 14:12; Mk 6:4

Kinah — 7016: *Jos 15:22*

KINDNESS; kind, ly, s — 2177, 2617, 2896, 4327, 4940, 5921/3820 ➤ ***1085, 5100, 5360, 5363, 5387, 5449, 5541, 5543, 5544***: Ge 1:11; Jos 2:14; Ro 12:10; 1Co 12:10

God's kindness:

motivates Him to turn from executing judgment: Joel 2:12, 13; Jnh 4:2

is manifested by making salvation available: Eph 2:4-7; Tit 3:4-7

kindle, d, th — 215, 11197, 1814, 2734, 2787, 3341, 3344, 3648, 3857, 5400, 6919, 6999, 8313 ➤ ***381, 681***: Ex 35:3; Isa 44:15; Ac 28:2

kindred, s (see **kin**) — 251, 1353, 4138, 4940 ➤ ***1085, 3965, 4772, 5443***: Ge 12:1; Ps 22:27; Ac 4:6

kine (see **cow**) — 504, 1241, 6510: Ge 41:2; 1Sa 6:7; Am 4:1

KING, dom, **ly, s** — 4410, 4427, 4437, 4428, 4430, 4437, 4438, 4467, 4468 ➤ ***932, 933, 935, 936, 937***: Ge 10:10; Da 5:20; Mt 10:18

duties of kings:

rule in the fear of God: 2Sa 23:3

deter evil works: Ro 13:3

execute judgment: Pr 29:4

warnings to Israelite kings:

do not amass horses: Dt 17:16

do not practice polygamy: Dt 17:17

do not greatly accumulate wealth: Dt 17:17

Kir — 7024: 2Ki 16:9; Isa 15:1; Am 1:5

Kir-haraseth, Kir-hareseth, Kir-haresh, Kir-heres — 7025: *2Ki 3:25; Isa 16:7, 11; Jer 48:31, 36*

Kiriathaim, Kirjathaim — 7156, 7741: Ge 14:5; Jer 48:1

Kirjath-arba (see **Hebron**) — 7153: Jos 14:15; Ne 11:25

Kirjath-arim, Kirjath-jearim — 7157: Jgs 18:12; Ezr 2:25

Kirjath-baal — 7154: *Jos 15:60; 18:14*

Kirjath-huzoth — 7155: *Nu 22:39*

Kirjath-sannah — 7158: *Jos 15:49*

Kirjath-sepher (see **Debir**) — 7158: *Jos 15:15, 16; Jgs 1:11, 12*

Kishi (see **Kushaiah**) — 7029: *1Ch 6:44*

Kishion, Kishon, Kison — 7028, 7191: Jos 19:20; Jgs 4:7; Ps 83:9

kiss, ed, es — 5390, 5401 ➤ ***2705, 5368, 5370:*** Ge 27:26; Pr 27:6; Lk 7:38

kite — 344: *Le 11:14; Dt 14:13*

Kithlish — 3798: *Jos 15:40*

Kitron — 7003: *Jgs 1:30*

knead, ed, ingtroughs — 3888, 4863: Ex 8:3; Jer 7:18; Hos 7:4

knee, s — 755, 1290, 1291 ➤ ***1119***: Jgs 7:5; Na 2:10; Php 2:10

kneel, ed, ing — 1288, 1289, 3766 ➤ ***1120, 5087/1119:*** Ps 95:6; Da 6:10; Mk 1:40

knife, ves (see **penknife**) — 2719, 3979, 4252, 7915: Ge 22:6; Jos 5:2; Ezr 1:9

knit — 2270, 3162, 7194 ➤ ***1210, 4822***: Jgs 20:11; Ac 10:11; Col 2:2

knock, ed, eth, ing — 1849 ➤ ***2925***: SS 5:2; Mt 7:7, 8; Ac 12:16

knop, s — 3730, 6497: Ex 25:33; 37:19; 1Ki 6:18

KNOWLEDGE; know, est, eth, ing, n; knew, est (see **wist**) — 854, 995, 998, 1843, 1844, 1847, 3045, 3046, 4093, 5234, 5869, 7922 ➤ ***50, 56, 319, 1097, 1107, 1108, 1110, 1231, 1232, 1492, 1921, 1987, 1990, 2467, 2589, 4135, 4267, 4892, 4907, 5318***: Ge 2:9; Isa 58:2; Mt 9:4; Jude 10

God's knowledge is:

comprehensive: Ps 69:5; Isa 40:28; Jer 23:24

used to search hearts and weigh actions: 1Sa 2:3; Ps 44:21; Jer 17:10

a source of assurance to the saints: Na 1:7; Jn 10:14; 2Ti 2:19

knowledge of God:

is to be sought: Pr 2:3-5; Col 1:9; 2Pe 3:18

results in blessings: Pr 2:6-9; Isa 33:6

Koa — 6970: *Eze 23:23*
Kohath — 6955: Ge 46:11; Nu 3:17
Kohathites — 6956: Nu 3:27; Jos 21:4
Kolaiah — 6964: *Ne 11:7; Jer 29:21*
Korah — 7141 ***2879***: Ge 36:5; Jude 11
Korahite, s; Korathites; Korhites (see **Kore**) — 7145: Nu 26:58; 1Ch 9:19
Korah — 7141 ≈ ***2879***: Ex 6:21; Jude 11
Kore (see **Korahite**) — 6981, 7145: 1Ch 26:19; 2Ch 31:14
Koz — 6976: Ezr 2:61; Ne 3:4
Kushaiah (see **Kishi**) — 6984: *1Ch 15:17*

L

Laadah — 3935: *1Ch 4:21*
Laadan (see **Libni**) — 3936: 1Ch 7:26; 23:7
Laban, 's — 3837: Ge 24:29; Dt 1:1
labour, ed, er, ers, eth, ing, s (see **work**) — 213, 1518, 3018, 3021, 3022, 3027, 3205, 4399, 4639, 5445, 5647, 5656, 5998, 5999, 6001, 6089, 6092, 6213, 6468, 7712 ≈ ***75, 2038, 2040, 2041, 2872, 2873, 4704, 4866, 4904, 5389***: Ge 31:42; Ne 4:21; Lk 10:7; 1Th 2:9
lace — 6616: *Ex 28:28, 37; 39:21, 31*
Lachish — 3923: Jos 10:3; Isa 36:2
lack, ed, est, eth, ing — 1097, 2637, 2638, 4270, 5737, 6485, 7038, 7673 ≈ ***170, 1641, 1729, 3007, 3361/2192, 3361/3918, 5302, 5303, 5332***: Dt 2:7; Ecc 9:8; 1Co 16:17
lad, s — 5288 ≈ ***3808***: 1Sa 20:21; 2Ki 4:19; Jn 6:9
ladder — 5551: *Ge 28:12*
lady, ies — 1404, 8282 ≈ ***2959***: Jgs 5:29; Est 1:18; Isa 47:5; 2Jn 1
Lael — 3815: *Nu 3:24*
Lahad — 3854: *1Ch 4:2*
Lahai-roi — 883: Ge 24:62; 25:11
Lahmam — 3903: *Jos 15:40*
Lahmi — 3902: 1Ch 20:5
Laish (see **Leshem**) — 3919: Jgs 18:7; 2Sa 3:15; Isa 10:30
lake — ***3041***: Lk 5:1; 8:22; Rev 20:10
Lakum — 3946: *Jos 19:33*
lama — ***2982***: *Mt 27:46; Mk 15:34*
lamb, s (see **sheep**) — 563, 1121/6629, 2922, 2924, 3532, 3535, 3733, 3775, 3776, 7716 ≈ ***286, 704, 721***: Ge 22:7; Ps 114:4; Jn 1:29; 1Pe 1:19
lame — 5223, 6452, 6455 ≈ ***5560***: Le 21:18; 2Sa 9:3; Mt 11:5
Lamech — 3929 ≈ ***2984***: Ge 4:18; Lk 3:36
lament, able, ation, ed — 56, 421, 578, 592, 1058, 4553, 5091, 5092, 5594, 6088, 6969, 7015, 7017, 8567 ≈ ***2354, 2355, 2870, 2875***: Jgs 11:40; La 2:5; Lk 23:27
lamp, s — 3940, 5216 ≈ ***2985***: Ex 25:37; Job 12:5; Rev 8:10
lance — 3591: *Jer 50:42*
lancets — 7420: *1Ki 18:28*
land, ed, ing, s — 127, 249, 776, 3004, 7004 ≈ ***68, 1093, 2609, 2718, 3584, 5561, 5564***: Ge 2:11; Job 28:13; Ac 28:12
landmark, s — 1366, 1367: Dt 19:14; Job 24:2; Pr 23:10
lanes — ***4505***: *Lk 14:21*
language, s — 1697, 3937, 3956, 3961, 8193 ≈ ***1258***: Ge 11:1; Da 3:4; Ac 2:6
languish, ed, eth, ing — 535, 1741: Isa 16:8; Joel 1:10; Na 1:4
lanterns — ***5322***: *Jn 18:3*
Laodicea — ***2993***: Col 2:1; Rev 1:11
Laodiceans — ***2994***: *Col 4:16; Rev 3:14*
lap, ped, peth — 899, 2436, 2684, 3952: Jgs 7:5; Ne 5:13; Pr 16:33
Lapidoth — 3941: *Jgs 4:4*
lapwing — 1744: *Le 11:19; Dt 14:18*
large, ness (see **enlarge**) — 4800, 7304, 7337, 7341, 7342, 7342/3027, 7842 ≈ ***2425, 3173, 4080, 5118***: 1Ki 4:29; Isa 22:18; Mk 14:15
lasciviousness — ***766***: Mk 7:22; Gal 5:19; Jude 4
Lasea — ***2996***: *Ac 27:8*
Lasha — 3962: *Ge 10:19*
Lasharon — 8289: *Jos 12:18*
last, ed, ing (see **late**) — 314, 318, 319, 1961, 5769, 6119 ≈ ***2078, 4218, 5305***: Dt 33:15; Jgs 14:17; Jn 6:39
latchet (see **shoe**) — 8288 ≈ ***2438***: *Isa 5:27; Mk 1:7; Lk 3:16; Jn 1:27*
late, ly; latter (see **last**) — 309, 314, 319, 320, 865, 3954, 4456 ≈ ***2078, 3568, 3797, 4373, 5305***: Ex 4:8; Mic 2:8; Jn 11:8; Ac 18:2
Latin — ***4513***: *Lk 23:38; Jn 19:20*
lattice — 822, 2762, 7639: *Jgs 5:28; 2Ki 1:2; SS 2:9*
laud — ***1867***: *Ro 15:11*
laugh, ed, eth, ing, ter — 3932, 6711, 6712, 7814, 7832 ≈ ***1070, 1071, 2606***: Ge 17:17; Ps 2:4; Lk 6:21; Jas 4:9
launch, ed — ***321, 1877***: *Lk 8:22; Ac 21:1; 27:2, 4*
laver, s — 3595: Ex 30:18; 1Ki 7:38; 2Ki 16:17
lavish — 2107: *Isa 46:6*

LAW, ful, fully, giver, less, s, yer — 1881, 1882, 2524, 2545, 2706, 2710, 2859, 2860, 2994, 3544,

M

male, s — 376, 2138, 2142, 2145 ⇒ ***730***: Ge 1:27; Nu 3:22; Mt 19:4

malefactor, s — ***2555, 2557***: *Lk 23:32, 33, 39; Jn 18:30*

malice; malicious, ness — ***2549, 4190***: Eph 4:31; 1Pe 2:1; 3Jn 10

malignity — ***2550***: *Ro 1:29*

Mallothi — 4413: *1Ch 25:4, 26*

mallows — 4408: *Job 30:4*

Malluch, Melicu — 4409: Ezr 10:29; Ne 12:14

mammon — 3126: *Mt 6:24; Lk 16:9, 11, 13*

Mamre — 4471: Ge 13:18; 23:17

MAN, KIND; men, children — 120, 312, 376, 582, 582/1121, 606, 1121, 1167, 1320, 1368, 1396, 1397, 1400, 1538, 2138, 2145, 4962, 4974, 5315, 5958 ⇒ ***245, 407, 435, 441, 442, 444, 730, 733, 1538, 2478, 3367, 3494, 3495, 3762, 3956, 4753, 5046, 5100, 5449***: Ex 34:23; Ru 2:1; Eph 6:7; 1Ti 2:1

mankind:

created by God: Ge 1:26; Isa 45:12; 64:8

created in God's image: Ge 1:27; 1Co 11:7

in relation to God:

taught knowledge by God: Ps 94:10

set over the works of God's hands: Ps 8:6-8; Heb 2:8

preparations of his heart are from God: Pr 16:1

his steps are subject to God: Pr 20:24

his wrath praises God: Ps 76:10

Manaen — ***3127***: *Ac 13:1*

Manahath — 4506: *Ge 36:23; 1Ch 1:40; 8:6*

Manahethites — 2679, 2680: *1Ch 2:52, 54*

Manasseh; Manasses, Manassites — 4519, 4520 ⇒ ***3128***: Ge 41:51; Jos 17:6; Mt 1:10

mandrakes — 1736: *Ge 30:14-16; SS 7:13*

maneh — 4488: *Eze 45:12*

manger — 5336: *Lk 2:7, 12, 16*

manifest, ation, ed, ly — 1305 ⇒ ***602, 852, 1212, 1552, 1717, 1718, 4271, 5318, 5319, 5321:*** Ecc 3:18 Mk 4:22; Ro 8:19; 2Co 3:3

manna — 4478 ⇒ ***3131***: Ex 16:15; Ps 78:24; Heb 9:4

manner, s — 734, 1571, 1697, 1699, 1870, 1881, 2177, 2708, 3541, 3605, 3651, 3654, 4941, 8452 ⇒ ***72, 195, 442, 686, 981, 1483, 1485, 1486, 2239, 3592, 3634, 3697, 3779, 4012, 4169, 4187, 4217, 4458, 5158, 5159, 5179, 5615***: Ge 19:31; Est 1:13; Ac 13:18

Manoah — 4495: Jgs 13:2; 16:31

manservant, s; menservants (see **man**) — 5650 ⇒ ***3816***: Ne 7:67; Jer 34:9; Lk 12:45

mansions — ***3438***: *Jn 14:2*

manslayer, s (see **man**) — 7523 ⇒ ***409***: *Nu 35:6, 12; 1Ti 1:9*

mantle, s — 155, 4595, 4598, 8063: Jgs 4:18; Isa 3:22; Ezr 9:3

many; manifold — 1995, 3513, 3605, 7227, 7230, 7231, 7233, 7235, 7690 ⇒ ***2425, 3745, 4119, 4164, 4179, 4182, 4183, 4214, 5118***: Ge 17:4; Mt 3:7; 1Pe 1:6

Maoch — 4582: *1Sa 27:2*

Maon, ites — 4584: Jgs 10:12; 1Ch 2:45

mar, red — 3510, 4893, 5420, 7843 ⇒ ***622***: Ru 4:6; Isa 52:14; Jer 13:7; Mk 2:22

Mara — 4755: *Ru 1:20*

Marah — 4785: *Ex 15:23; Nu 33:8, 9*

Maralah — 4831: *Jos 19:11*

Maranatha — ***3134***: *1Co 16:22*

marble — 8336, 7893, ⇒ ***3139***: 1Ch 29:2; Est 1:6; Rev 18:12

march, ed, edst — 1980, 3212, 5265, 6805: Ex 14:10; Jgs 5:4; Jer 46:22

Marcus, Mark — ***3138***: Ac 12:12; Col 4:10

Mareshah — 4762: Jos 15:44; Mic 1:15

mariners — 4419, 7751: *Eze 27:8, 9, 27, 29; Jnh 1:5*

mark, ed, est, eth, s — 226, 995, 2856, 3045, 3799, 4307, 4645, 6437, 7085, 7181, 7200, 7760, 7896, 8104, 8388, 8420 ⇒ ***1907, 3138, 4648, 4649, 4742, 5480***: Ge 4:15; Job 7:20; Lk 14:7

market, s; marketplace, s (see **shambles**) — 4627 ⇒ ***58:*** Eze 27:13; Mt 20:3; Lk 11:43

Maroth — 4796: *Mic 1:12*

marrow — 2459, 4221, 4229, 8250 ⇒ ***3452***: Job 21:24; Pr 3:8; Heb 4:12

MARRIAGE; marry, ed, eth, ing — 376, 802, 1166, 1984, 2859, 2992, 3427, 3947, 5375, 5772 ⇒ ***1060, 1061, 1062, 1096, 1447, 1448, 1547, 1548***: Ge 38:8; Ne 13:27; 1Ti 4:3

instituted by God: Ge 2:21, 22, Mt 19:6

purposes of:

avoid fornication: 1Co 7:2

replenish the earth: Ge 1:28

raise up a godly seed: Mal 2:15

duties inherent in:

living harmoniously with the spouse: 1Pe 3:7

not defrauding the spouse: 1Co 7:3-5

husbands are to love wives: Eph 5:25

wives are to submit to husbands: Eph 5:22

blessings received from:

God's favor: Pr 18:22

satisfaction: Pr 5:18, 19

Mars' — ***697***: *Ac 17:22*

mint — ***2238***: *Mt 23:23; Lk 11:42*

Miphkad — 4663: *Ne 3:31*

MIRACLE, s — 226, 4159, 6381 ✎ ***1411, 4592***: Ex 7:9; Jn 2:11; Ac 2:22
 purposes of miracles:
  to demonstrate God's power: Ex 7:5; 14:18; 1Ki 18:36-38
  to glorify God: 2Ki 5:14, 15; Lk 13:10-13; Ac 12:9-12
  to witness to Christ's Deity: Mt 9:2-7; Jn 2:7-11; 9:1-7; 11:38-45
  to strengthen faith: Jgs 6:36-40; Mt 8:24-27; Ac 12:6-11

mire; miry — 1206, 1207, 2563, 2916, 2917, 3121, 7516 ✎ ***1004***: 2Sa 22:43 ; Eze 47:11; 2Pe 2:22

Miriam — 4813: Ex 15:20; Nu 12:1; Mic 6:4

Mirma — 4821: *1Ch 8:10*

mirth — 4885, 7797, 8057, 8342: Ge 31:27; Isa 24:8; Jer 7:34

miscarrying — 7921: *Hos 9:14*

mischief, s; mischievous — 205, 611, 1942, 1943, 2154, 4209, 4827, 5771, 5999, 7451, 7489 ✎ ***4468***: Ge 42:4; Ps 21:11; Mic 7:3; Ac 13:10

miserable, ly; misery, ies — 4788, 5999, 6001, 7451 ✎ ***1652, 2560, 5004***: Job 3:20; La 1:7; Mt 21:41

Misgab — 4869: *Jer 48:1*

Mishael — 4332: Ex 6:22; Ne 8:4; Da 1:6

Mishal, Misheal — 4861: *Jos 19:26; 21:30*

Misham — 4936: *1Ch 8:12*

Mishma — 4927: *Ge 25:14; 1Ch 1:30; 4:25, 26*

Mishmannah — 4925: *1Ch 12:10*

Mishraites — 4954: *1Ch 2:53*

Mispereth — 4559: *Ne 7:7*

miss, ed, ing — 2398, 6485: Jgs 20:16; 1Sa 20:18; 1Ki 20:39

mist — 108 ✎ ***887, 2217***: *Ge 2:6; Ac 13:11; 2Pe 2:17*

mistress — 1172, 1404: 1Ki 17:17; Ps 123:2; Na 3:4

misused — 8591: *2Ch 36:16*

mite, s — ***3016***: *Mk 12:42; Lk 12:59; 21:2*

Mithcah — 4989: *Nu 33:28, 29*

Mithnite — 4981: *1Ch 11:43*

Mithredath — 4990: *Ezr 1:8; 4:7*

mitre — 4701, 6797: Ex 28:4; Le 8:9; Zec 3:5

Mitylene — ***3412***: *Ac 20:14*

mixed; mixture — 1101, 4107, 4469, 4538, 6151, 6154 ✎ ***194, 3395, 4786***: Ex 12:38; Isa 1:22; Jn 19:39

Mizar — 4706: *Ps 42:6*

Mizpah, Mizpeh — 4708, 4709: Ge 31:49; 1Sa 7:5; Jer 40:6

Mizpar — 4558: *Ezr 2:2*

Mizraim — 4714: *Ge 10:6, 13; 1Ch 1:8, 11*

Mizzah — 4199: *Ge 36:13, 17; 1Ch 1:37*

Mnason — ***3416***: *Ac 21:16*

Moab; Moabite, ess, ish, s — 4124, 4125: Ru 2:6; Ne 13:1; Am 2:1

Moadiah — 4153: *Ne 12:17*

mock, ed, er, ers, est, ing, ings — 2048, 2049, 3887, 3931, 3932, 3934, 5953, 6711, 7046, 7048, 7832 ✎ ***1701, 1702, 1703, 3456, 5512***: Ge 19:14; Pr 20:1; Ac 2:13; Gal 6:7

moderately; moderation — 6666 ✎ ***1933***: *Joel 2:23; Php 4:5*

modest — ***2887***: *1Ti 2:9*

moist, ened, ure — 3892, 3955, 8248 ✎ ***2429***: Nu 6:3; Job 21:24; Lk 8:6

Moladah — 4137: Jos 15:26; Ne 11:26

mole, s — 2661, 8580: *Le 11:30; Isa 2:20*

Molech, Moloch — 4432 ✎ ***3434***: 1Ki 11:7; Am 5:26; Ac 7:43

Molid — 4140: *1Ch 2:29*

mollified — 7401: *Isa 1:6*

moment — 7281 ✎ ***823, 3901, 4743***: Ex 33:5; Ps 30:5; 1Co 15:52

MONEY, changers — 3701, 3702, 7192 ✎ ***694, 2772, 2773, 2855, 3546, 4715, 5365, 5475, 5536***: Ge 17:12; Ezr 3:7; Mt 21:12
 love of money leads to:
  spiritual error: 1Ti 6:9, 10
  perversion of judgment: Ex 23:8; Isa 1:23
  trouble: Pr 15:27

monsters — 8577: *La 4:3*

month, ly, s; moon, s — 2320, 3391, 3393, 3394, 3842 ✎ ***3376, 3561, 4582, 5072, 5150***: Ezr 3:5; Isa 47:13; Lk 1:24

monuments — 5341: *Isa 65:4*

Morasthite — 4183: *Jer 26:18; Mic 1:1*

Mordecai — 4782: Ne 7:7; Est 2:22

more (see **most**) — 1490, 1980, 2351, 3254, 3254/5750, 3499, 3513, 3588, 3651, 4480, 4481, 5674, 5736, 5922, 5973, 6105, 6440, 7138, 7227, 7231, 7235, 7608, 7725, 8145 ✎ ***197, 243, 316, 414, 1065, 1308, 1508, 1617, 1833, 2001, 2115, 3122, 3123, 3185, 3187, 3370, 3745, 3761, 3765, 3844, 4053, 4054, 4055, 4056, 4057, 4119, 4179, 4325, 4369, 4707, 5112, 5228, 5236, 5245***: Ge 3:1; Pr 31:7; Mt 5:37; Jas 4:6

moreover — 518, 637, 1571, 3148, 5750 ✎ ***235/2532, 1161/2532, 2089, 3739/1161/3063***: Ru 4:10; Ro 5:20; 2Pe 1:15

N

navel — 8270, 8306, 8326: *Job 40:16; Pr 3:8; SS 7:2; Eze 16:4*

naves — 1354: *1Ki 7:33*

navy — 590: *1Ki 9:26, 27; 10:11, 22*

Nazarene, s — ***3480***: *Mt 2:23; Ac 24:5*

Nazareth — ***3478***: Lk 1:26; Ac 2:22

Nazarite, s — 5139: Nu 6:2; La 4:7

Neah — 5269: *Jos 19:13*

Neapolis — ***3496***: *Ac 16:11*

near, er; nigh — 413, 681, 3027, 4952, 5060, 5921, 5973, 7126, 7132, 7138, 7607, 7608, 7934 ✒ ***316, 1448, 1451, 1452, 3844, 3897, 4139, 4314, 4317, 4334***: Ex 3:5; Isa 29:13; Ro 13:11

Neariah — 5294: *1Ch 3:22, 23; 4:42*

Nebai — 5109: *Ne 10:19*

Nebaioth, Nebajoth — 5032: Ge 25:13; 1Ch 1:29

Neballat — 5041: *Ne 11:34*

Nebat — 5028: 1Ki 11:26; 2Ki 3:3

Nebo (see **Pisgah**) — 5015: Dt 32:49; Isa 15:2

Nebuchadnezzar, Nebuchadrezzar — 5019, 5020: Jer 25:1; Da 3:1

Nebushasban — 5021: *Jer 39:13*

Nebuzaradan — 5018: 2Ki 25:8; Jer 39:9-11

necessary; necessity, ies (see **need; ought**) — 2706 ✒ ***316, 318, 1876, 2192, 4314/3588/5532, 5532:*** Job 23:12; Ro 12:13; 2Co 6:4; Heb 7:12

Necho (see **Pharoah-Necho**) — 5224: *2Ch 35:20, 22; 36:4*

neck, s — 1621, 1627, 4665, 6203, 6677 ✒ ***5137***: Jos 10:24; Isa 48:4; Mt 18:6

necromancer — 1875/4191: *Dt 18:11*

Nedabiah — 5072: *1Ch 3:18*

need, ed, est, eth, ful, s, y (see **necessary**) — 34, 1800, 2637, 2638, 2818, 2819, 4270, 6878, 7326 ✒ ***316, 422, 1163, 2006, 2121, 2192/318, 2192/5532, 3784, 3843, 4326, 5532, 5535***: Dt 15:8; Ezr 6:9; Lk 10:42; Php 4:12

needle, s, work — 4639/7551, 7553 ✒ ***4476***: Ex 26:36; Ps 45:14; Mt 19:24

Neginah, Neginoth — 5058: Ps 4:title; 61:title

neglect, ed, ing; negligent — 7952 ✒ ***272, 857, 3865, 3878***: 2Ch 29:11; Mt 18:17; Ac 6:1; Col 2:23

Nehelamite — 5161: *Jer 29:24, 31, 32*

Nehemiah — 5166: Ezr 2:2; Ne 1:1

Nehiloth — 5155: *Ps 5:title*

Nehum (see **Rehum**) — 5149: *Ne 7:7*

Nehushta — 5179: *2Ki 24:8*

Nehushtan — 5180: *2Ki 18:4*

Neiel — 5272: *Jos 19:27*

neighbour, s — 5997, 7138, 7453, 7468, 7934 ✒ ***1069, 4040, 4139***: Jos 9:16; Jer 29:23; Lk 10:27

neigh, ed, ing, ings — 4684, 6670: *Jer 5:8; 8:16; 13:27*

neither — 408, 518, 1077, 1115, 1571/369, 1571/3808, 3808 ✒ ***2228, 2532/3762, 3364, 3366, 3383, 3761, 3777***: Ge 9:11; 1Ki 5:4; Mt 13:13

Nekeb — 5346: *Jos 19:33*

Nekoda — 5353: *Ezr 2:48, 60: Ne 7:50, 62*

Nemuel — 5241: *Nu 26:9, 12; 1Ch 4:24*

Nemuelites — 5242: *Nu 26:12*

Nepheg — 5298: Ex 6:21; 2Sa 5:15

nephew, s — 1121, 5220 ✒ ***1549:*** Jgs 12:14; Job 18:19; 1Ti 5:4

Nepishesim (see **Nephusim**) — 5300: *Ne 7:52*

Nephtoah — 5318: *Jos 15:9; 18:15*

Nephusim (see **Nepishesim**) — 5304: *Ezr 2:50*

Ner — 5369: 1Sa 14:50; 1Ch 8:33

Nereus — ***3517***: *Ro 16:15*

Nergal — 5370: *2Ki 17:30*

Nergal-sharezer — 5371: *Jer 39:3, 13*

Neri — ***3518***: *Lk 3:27*

Neriah — 5374: Jer 36:4; 51:59

Nero — ***3505***: *2Ti subscript*

nest, s — 7064, 7077 ✒ ***2682***: Nu 24:21; Ps 104:17; Mt 8:20

net, s, work, works — 2355, 2764, 4364, 4365, 4639, 4685, 4686, 7568, 7638, 7639 ✒ ***293, 1350, 4522***: Ex 27:4; Jer 52:22; Lk 5:5

Nethaneel — 5417: Nu 1:8; Ezr 10:22

Nethaniah — 5418: 2Ki 25:23; Jer 40:8

nether, most (see **low**) — 7347, 8481, 8482: Ex 19:17; Dt 24:6; 1Ki 6:6

Nethinims — 5411, 5412: Ezr 7:24; Ne 3:26

Netophah — 5199: *Ezr 2:22; Ne 7:26*

Netophati; Netophathite, s — 5200: 2Sa 23:28; Jer 40:8

nettles — 2738, 7057: Job 30:7; Isa 34:13; Zep 2:9

never — 369, 408/3808, 518/5331, 1074/5331, , 1077, 1253, 1755, 3588, 3808, 3808/5331, 3808/5704/5769, 3808/5769, 5957/3809, 5704/5769, 5769/1077, 5769/3808, 7535 ✒ ***3361, 3364/1519/3588/165, 3364/4219, 3364/4455, 3368, 3756, 3756/1519/3588/165, 3761/1520, 3762, 3762/4455, 3763, 3764***: Jgs 2:1; Ps 31:1; Mt 7:23

nevertheless — 61, 389, 403, 657, 1297, 1571, 3588/518, 7535 ✒ ***235, 1161, 2544, 3305, 3676/3305, 4133***: Est 5:10; Jnh 1:13; 2Ti 1:12

O

oppress, ed, eth, ing, ion, ions, or, ors — 376/2555, 1790, 1792, 2541, 3238, 3905, 3906, 4642, 4939, 5065, 6115, 6125, 6184, 6206, 6216, 6217, 6231, 6233, 6234, 6693, 6887, 7429, 7533, 7701, 7703 ✒ ***2616, 2669***: Ecc 4:1; Zec 9:8; Ac 7:24; Jas 2:6

or — 176, 854, 2006, 5704 ✒ ***1161, 1535, 2228, 2532, 3383, 5037***: Nu 5:6; Jer 23:33; Col 1:16

oracle, s — 1687, 1697 ✒ ***3051***: 1Ki 6:5; Ps 28:2; Ro 3:2

oration; orator — 3908 ✒ ***1215, 4489***: *Isa 3:3; Ac 12:21; 24:1*

orchard, s — 6508: *Ecc 2:5; SS 4:13*

ORDAIN, ed, eth; (see **ordinance**) — 3245, 3559, 4483, 4931, 5414, 5975, 6186, 6213, 6466, 6965, 7760, 8239 ✒ ***1299, 2525, 2680, 2919, 3724, 4160, 4270, 4282, 4309, 5021, 5087, 5500***: Nu 28:6; Isa 26:12; Mk 3:14

God has ordained:
- Christ to be:
  - High Priest: Heb 6:20; 9:11
  - Judge: Ac 10:42; 17:31
- civil authorities to govern: Ro 13:1
- priests to offer sacrifices: Heb 5:1; 8:3
- prophets to proclaim His messages: Jer 1:5

order, ed, eth, ings, ly — 1700, 3027, 3559, 4634, 4941, 5468, 6186, 6187, 6471, 6680, 7947, 8626 ✒ ***1299, 1930, 2517, 4748, 5001, 5010***: Le 1:7; 1Ch 24:19; Lk 1:8; Ac 21:24

ordinance, s; ordinary (see **ordain**) — 2706, 2708, 3027, 4687, 4931, 4941 ✒ ***1296, 1345, 1378, 1379, 3862***: Ex 12:14; Eze 16:27; Ro 13:2; Col 2:14

Oreb — 6157: Jgs 7:25; Ps 83:11; Isa 10:26

Oren — 767: *1Ch 2:25*

organ, s — 5748: *Ge 4:21; Job 21:12; 30:31; Ps 150:4*

Orion — 3685: *Job 9:9; 38:31; Am 5:8*

ornament, s — 642, 2481, 3880, 5716, 5914, 6287, 6807, 7720: Ex 33:4; Pr 1:9; 1Pe 3:4

Ornan (see **Araunah**) — 771: 1Ch 21:15; 2Ch 3:1

Orpah — 6204: *Ru 1:4, 14*

orphans — 3490: *La 5:3*

ospray — 5822: *Le 11:13; Dt 14:12*

ossifrage — 6538: *Le 11:13; Dt 14:12*

ostrich, es — 3283, 5133: *Job 39:13; La 4:3*

other, s (see **another**) — 251, 259, 312, 317, 428, 2063, 2088, 3541, 3671, 5048, 5676, 6311, 7453, 7605, 8145 ✒ ***237, 240, 243, 244, 245, 492, 846, 1520, 1565, 1622, 2084, 2087, 2548, 3062, 3588, 3739, 4008***: Le 5:7; Ps 38:16; Mt 6:1

otherwise — 176, 3808 ✒ ***243, 247, 1490, 1893, 2085, 2088***: 2Sa 18:13; Ro 11:6; 1Ti 5:25

Othni — 6273: *1Ch 26:7*

Othniel — 6274: Jos 15:17; Jgs 3:9

ouches — 4865: Ex 28:11; 39:6

ought, est (see **necessary**) — 1697, 3972, 4465 ✒ ***1163, 3762, 3784, 5100, 5534***: Jos 21:45; Ac 10:6; Jas 3:10

our, s, selves (see **us**; **we**) — 587 ✒ ***846, 1438, 2249, 2251, 2257***: Ge 1:26; Ps 100:3; Mk 12:7

out, er, goings, most, side, ward, wardly — 2351, 2435, 4161, 5869, 7020, 7097, 8444 ✒ ***1623, 1722/3588/5318, 1722/5318, 1854, 1855, 1857, 4383***: Ps 65:8; Eze 40:5; Lk 11:39; Ro 2:28

outcast, s — 1760, 5080: Ps 147:2; Isa 11:12; Jer 30:17

outlandish — 5237: *Ne 13:26*

outlived; overlived — 748/3117/310: *Jos 24:31; Jgs 2:7*

outrageous — 7858: *Pr 27:4*

outrun — ***4370/5032***: *Jn 20:4*

outstretched — 5186: *Dt 26:8; Jer 21:5; 27:5*

outwent — ***4281***: *Mk 6:33*

oven, s — 8574 ✒ ***2823***: Ex 8:3; Mal 4:1; Lk 12:28

over — 413, 413/4136, 1157, 1591, 1869, 2498, 3148, 4136, 4480, 4605, 5048, 5226, 5227, 5414, 5674, 5676, 5736, 5921, 5921/5676, 5921/6440, 5922/6440, 5975, 5980, 6440, 6743, 6903, 7235 ✒ ***481, 495, 561, 1224, 1276, 1277, 1330, 1537/1727, 1608, 1722, 1883, 1909, 1924, 2596, 2634, 2713, 3346, 3860, 3928, 4008, 4012, 4121, 4291, 5055, 5228, 5231, 5240***: 1Sa 2:1; Hab 1:11; Eph 1:22; 1Pe 3:12

overcharge, d — ***925, 1912***: *Lk 21:34; 2Co 2:5*

OVERCOME, th; overcame — 1464, 1986, 2476, 3201, 3898, 5674, 7292 ✒ ***2274, 2634, 3528***: Ge 49:19; Jer 23:9; Ac 19:16

overcoming evil is:
- given to saints through Christ: Lk 10:19; Ro 8:37; 1Jn 5:5
- guaranteed to saints: 1Jn 2:13; 4:4; 5:4, 5
- rewarded by God: Rev 2:7; 3:5; 21:7

overdrive — 1849: *Ge 33:13*

overflow, ed, eth, ing, n — 1065, 2230, 3332, 4390, 6687, 7783, 7857, 7858 ✒ ***2626***: Da 11:22; Joel 2:24; 2Pe 3:6

overlay, ing; overlaid — 2645, 5968, 6823, 6826, 7901 ✒ ***4028***: Ex 25:11; 1Ch 29:4; Heb 9:4

overmuch — ***4055***: *2Co 2:7*

overpass; overpast; overran; overrunning — 5674: 2Sa 18:23; Isa 26:20; Jer 5:28

overplus — 5736: *Le 25:27*

oversee, r, rs; oversight — 4870, 5329, 5414, 5921, 6485, 6486, 6496, 7860 ➡ ***1983, 1985***: Pr 6:7; Ac 20:28; 1Pe 5:2

overshadow, ed — ***1982***: Mt 17:5; Lk 1:35; Ac 5:15

overspread, ing — 3671, 5310: *Ge 9:19; Da 9:27*

overtake, n, th; overtook — 1692, 5066, 5381 ➡ ***2638, 4301***: Ex 15:9; La 1:3; Gal 6:1

overthrow, eth, n; overthrew — 1760, 2015, 2018, 2040, 3782, 4073, 4114, 5186, 5286, 5287, 5307, 5422, 5557, 5791, 8045, 8058 ➡ ***390, 396, 2647, 2690, 2692, 2693***: Pr 13:6; Jon 3:4; Ac 5:39; 2Ti 2:18

overturn, ed, eth — 2015, 5754: Jgs 7:13; Job 9:5; Eze 21:27

overwhelm, ed — 3680, 5307, 5848, 7857: Job 6:27; Ps 55:5; 61:2

owe, d, st, th — ***3781, 3784, 4359***: Mt 18:24; Lk 16:5; Phm 18

owl, s — 1323/3284, 3244, 3563, 3917, 7091: Ps 102:6; Isa 13:21; Mic 1:8

own — 249, 3027, 3548, 5315, 7522 ➡ ***830, 848, 849, 1103, 1438, 1683, 1699, 2398, 2596, 4572***: Dt 3:14; Joel 3:4; Jas 1:14

own, er, ers, eth — 113, 249, 1167, 3548, 7069, 7522 ➡ ***830, 846, 848, 1103, 1438, 1683, 1699, 2076, 2398, 2596, 2962, 3490, 4572***: Le 16:29; Ecc 5:11; Ac 21:11

ox, en — 441, 504, 1241, 5091, 6499, 7794, 8377, 8450 ➡ ***1016, 5022***: Ge 12:16; Ex 20:17; Lk 13:15

Ozem — 684: *1Ch 2:15, 25*

Ozias, Uzziah — 5818 ➡ ***3604***: 2Ki 15:13; Ezr 10:21; Mt 1:8

Ozni; Oznites — 244: *Nu 26:16*

P

Paarai — 6474: *2Sa 23:35*

Pacatiana — ***3818***: *1Ti subscript*

paces — 6806: *2Sa 6:13*

pacify, ed, eth — 3240, 3711, 3722, 7918: Est 7:10; Pr 16:14; Ecc 10:4

Padan, Padan-aram — 6307: Ge 25:20; 48:7

paddle — 3489: *Dt 23:13*

Padon — 6303: *Ezr 2:44; Ne 7:47*

Pagiel — 6295: Nu 1:13; 7:72; 10:26

Pahath-moab — 6355: Ezr 2:6; Ne 3:11

Pai, Pau — 6464: *Ge 36:39; 1Ch 1:50*

pain, ed, ful, fulness, s — 2256, 2342, 2427, 2470, 2479, 3176, 3510, 3511, 4341, 4712, 5999, 6735 ➡ ***928, 3449, 4192, 5604***: Job 14:22; Ps 73:16; 2Co 11:27; Rev 16:10

paint, ed, edst, ing — 3583, 4886, 6320, 7760: 2Ki 9:30; Jer 4:30; Eze 23:40

pair — ***2201, 2218***: *Am 2:6; 8:6; Lk 2:24; Rev 6:5*

palace, s — 643, 759, 1002, 1004, 1055, 1964, 1965, 2038, 2918 ➡ ***833, 4232***: 1Ki 16:18; Ps 45:8; Mt 26:3

Palal — 6420: *Ne 3:25*

pale, ness — 2357, 3420 ➡ ***5515***: *Isa 29:22; Jer 30:6; Rev 6:8*

Palestina, Palestine, Philistia (see **Philistia**) — 6429: Ex 15:14; Ps 60:8; Joel 3:4

Pallu, Phallu — 6396: Ge 46:9; Nu 26:5

Palluites — 6384: *Nu 26:5*

palm, s — 3709, 8558, 8560, 8561 ➡ ***4474, 4475, 5404***: Ex 15:27; SS 7:7; Jn 18:22

palmerworm — 1501; *Joel 1:4; 2:25; Am 4:9*

palsy, ies — ***3885, 3886***: Mt 4:24; Lk 5:18; Ac 8:7

Palti — 6408: *Nu 13:9*

Paltiel, Phaltiel (see **Phalti**) — 6409: 2Sa 3:15

Paltite (see **Pelonite**) — 6407: *2Sa 23:26*

Pamphylia — ***3828***: Ac 2:10; 14:24; 27:5

pan, s — 2281, 3595, 4227, 4958, 5518, 6517, 6745: Le 2:5; 2Sa 13:9; 2Ch 35:13

pangs — 2256, 2427, 6735, 6887: Isa 13:8; Jer 22:23; Mic 4:9

Pannag — 6346: *Eze 27:17*

pant, ed, eth — 5503, 6165, 7602, 8582: Ps 38:10; Isa 21:4; Am 2:7

paper — 6169 ➡ ***5489***: *Isa 19:7; 2Jn 12*

Paphos — ***3974***: *Ac 13:6, 13*

paps — 7699 ➡ ***3149***: *Eze 23:21; Lk 11:27; 23:29; Rev 1:13*

PARABLE, s — 4912 ➡ ***3850, 3942***: Job 27:1; Ps 78:2; Mt 13:34

- purposes of parables:
  - hide truth from the unreceptive: Mt 13:13, 14
  - reveal truth to the receptive: Mt 13:10-12
- sample Old Testament parables:
  - the king of the trees: Jgs 9:8-15
  - the great eagles and the vine: Eze 17:3-8
- sample New Testament parables:
  - the seed and the sower: Mt 13:3-9; Mk 4:3-9; Lk 8:5-8
  - the wheat and the tares: Mt 13:24-30
  - the mustard seed: Mt 13:31, 32; Mk 4:30-32; Lk 13:18, 19

paradise — ***3857***: *Lk 23:43; 2Co 12:4; Rev 2:7*
Parah — 6511: *Jos 18:23*
paramours — 6370: *Eze 23:20*
Paran — 6290: Ge 21:21; Nu 10:12; Hab 3:3
Parbar — 6503: *1Ch 26:18*
parcel — 2513 ❧ ***5564***: Ge 33:19; Ru 4:3; Jn 4:5
parched: — 2788, 7039, 8273: Le 23:14; Isa 35:7; Jer 17:6
parchments — ***3200***: *2Ti 4:13*
pardon, ed, eth (see **forgive**) — 3722, 5375, 5545, 5547, 7521: Ex 23:21; La 3:42; Mic 7:18
pare — 6213: *Dt 21:12*

PARENTS — ***1118, 3962, 4269***: Mt 10:21; Jn 9:2; 1Ti 5:4
- parental duties to children:
  - providing for them: 2Co 12:14
  - loving them: Tit 2:4
  - training them: Pr 22:6
  - chastening them: Pr 13:24
  - governing them: 1Ti 3:12

parlour, s — 2315, 3957, 5944: Jgs 3:20; 1Sa 9:22; 1Ch 28:11
Parmashta — 6534: *Est 9:9*
Parmenas — ***3937***: *Ac 6:5*
Parnach — 6535: *Nu 34:25*
Parosh, Pharosh — 6551: Ezr 8:3; Ne 3:25
Parshandatha — 6577: *Est 9:7*
part, ed, eth, ing, ly, s — 517, 905, 1335, 1697, 2505, 2506, 2673, 2677, 3027, 3411, 4481, 4490, 4940, 5337, 5409, 6316, 6418, 6447, 6504, 6536, 7098, 7117, 7118 ❧ ***1161, 1266, 1339, 2819, 2825, 3307, 3310, 3313/5100, 3348, 4119, 5124/3303***: Le 11:3; Eze 21:21; Lk 10:42; 1Co 11:18
partake, r, st — 2506 ❧ ***482, 1096/4791, 2841, 2844, 3310, 3335, 3348, 3353, 4777, 4790, 4791, 4829, 4830***: Ps 50:18; Ro 11:17; 2Pe 1:4
Parthians — ***3934***: *Ac 2:9*
partial, ity — 5375/6440 ❧ ***87, 1252, 4346***: *Mal 2:9; 1Ti 5:21; Jas 2:4; 3:17*
particular, ly — ***1520/1538/2596, 2596/3313, 3588/1520***: Ac 21:19; 1Co 12:27; Heb 9:5
parties — *: *Ex 22:9*
partition — 5674 ❧ ***5418***: *1Ki 6:21; Eph 2:14*
partner, s — 2505 ❧ ***2844, 3353***: Pr 29:24; Lk 5:7; 2Co 8:23
partridge — 7124: *1Sa 26:20; Jer 17:11*
Paruah — 6515: *1Ki 4:17*
Parvaim — 6516: *2Ch 3:6*
Pasach — 6457: *1Ch 7:33*
Pas-dammim — 6450: *1Ch 11:13*
Paseah, Phaseah — 6454: Ezr 2:49; Ne 7:51
Pashur — 6583: 1Ch 9:12; Jer 20:1
pass, ed, edst, eth, ing; past (see **passengers**) — 369, 935, 1431, 1980, 2498, 2499, 3615, 4569, 5493, 5674, 5709, 5710, 6213, 6437, 6452, 6924, 7223, 7291, 7725, 8032 ❧ ***390, 421, 492, 524, 565, 1096, 1224, 1230, 1276, 1279, 1330, 1353, 2064, 3327, 3819, 3844, 3855, 3881, 3899, 3928, 3944, 4266, 4281, 4302, 5230, 5235, 5242***: Ge 8:1; Job 14:20; 2Ti 2:18; 1Jn 2:17
passage, s — 1552, 4569, 5674, 5676: Nu 20:21; Jgs 12:5; Jer 22:20
passengers (see **pass**) — 5674/1870: *Pr 9:15; Eze 39:11, 14, 15*
passion, s — ***3663, 3958***: *Ac 1:3; 14:15; Jas 5:17*
passover, s — 6453 ❧ ***3957***: Ex 12:11; 2Ch 30:17; 1Co 5:7
pastor, s — 7462 ❧ ***4166***: Jer 2:8; 17:16; Eph 4:11
pasture, s — 3733, 4829, 4830, 4945, 4999, 7471 ❧ ***3542***: Ge 47:4; 1Ki 4:23; Jn 10:9
Patara — ***3959***: *Ac 21:1*
pate (see **head**) — 6936: *Ps 7:16*
path, s, way — 734, 1870, 4546, 4570, 4934, 5410, 7635 ❧ ***5147, 5163***: Ps 16:11; Pr 12:28; Mt 3:3

PATIENCE; patient, ly — 750, 2342, 6960 ❧ ***420, 1933, 3114, 3115, 3116, 5278, 5281***: Ecc 7:8; Lk 8:15; Heb 6:15
- exhortations to patience: 1Th 5:14; Heb 12:1
- when to practice patience:
  - when under persecution: Lk 21:16-19
  - when undergoing tribulation: Ro 12:12
- products of patience:
  - experience: Ro 5:4
  - hope: Ro 15:4
  - completeness: Jas 1:4

Patmos — ***3963***: *Rev 1:9*
patriarch, s — ***3966***: *Ac 2:29; 7:8, 9; Heb 7:4*
patrimony — 5921: *Dt 18:8*
Patrobas — ***3969***: *Ro 16:14*
pattern, s — 4758, 8403, 8508 ❧ ***5179, 5262, 5296***: Ex 25:9; Jos 22:28; Tit 2:7

PAUL; Paulus (see **Saul**) — ***3972***: Ac 13:7; 2Pe 3:15
- his character:
  - before conversion:
    - blasphemer: 1Ti 1:13
    - persecutor of the church: Ac 9:1, 2; Gal 1:13
    - blameless under the Mosaic law: Php 3:6
  - after conversion:
    - proclaimer of the gospel: Ac 9:28, 29

philosophers; philosophy — ***5385, 5386***: *Ac 17:18; Col 2:8*

Phinehas — 6372: Nu 25:7; 1Sa 1:3

Phlegon — ***5393***: *Ro 16:14*

Phrygia — ***5435***: Ac 2:10; 16:6; 18:23

Phurah — 6513: *Jgs 7:10, 11*

Phut, Put — 6316: Eze 27:10; Na 3:9

Phuvah, Pua, Puah (see **Punites**) — 6312, 6326: Ge 46:13; Ex 1:15; Nu 26:23

Phygellus — ***5436***: *2Ti 1:15*

phylacteries — ***5440***: *Mt 23:5*

physician, s — 7495 ❧ ***2395***: Jer 8:22; Mt 9:12; Lk 8:43

Pi-beseth — 6364: *Eze 30:17*

pick — 5365: *Pr 30:17*

pictures — 4906, 7914: *Nu 33:52; Pr 25:11; Isa 2:16*

piece, s — 95, 829, 915, 1335, 1506, 1917, 2513, 3603, 4060, 4749, 5409, 6400, 6595, 7168, 7518 ❧ ***1288, 1406, 1915, 3313, 4138***: Ge 15:17; Ne 3:11; Lk 15:8

pierce, d, ing, ings, th — 738, 1281, 1856, 4094, 4272, 5344, 5365 ❧ ***1330, 1338, 1574, 3572, 4044***: Nu 24:8; Zec 12:10; Heb 4:12

piety — ***2151***: *1Ti 5:4*

pigeon, s — 1469, 3123 ❧ ***4058***: Ge 15:9; Le 1:14; Lk 2:24

Pi-hahiroth — 6367: *Ex 14:2, 9; Nu 33:7, 8*

Pilate — ***4091***: Mk 15:1; 1Ti 6:13

Pildash — 6394: *Ge 22:22*

pile — 4071: *Isa 30:33; Eze 24:9*

Pileha — 6401: *Ne 10:24*

pilgrims ; pilgrimage — 4033 ❧ ***3927***: Ge 47:9; Ps 119:54; Heb 11:13

pillar, s — 547, 4552, 4676, 4678, 4690, 5324, 5333, 5982, 8490 ❧ ***4769***: Ex 13:21; 1Sa 2:8; Gal 2:9

pillow, s — 3523, 3704, 4763 ❧ ***4344***: Ge 28:11; 1Sa 19:13; Mk 4:38

pilots — 2259: *Eze 27:8, 27-29*

Piltai — 6408: *Ne 12:17*

pin, s — 3489: Ex 27:19; Jgs 16:14; Isa 3:22

pine, ing, th — 1803, 2100, 4743, 6086, 8081, 8410 ❧ ***3583***: Ne 8:15; Isa 38:12; Mk 9:18

pinnacle — ***4419***: *Mt 4:5; Lk 4:9*

Pinon — 6373: *Ge 36:41; 1Ch 1:52*

pipe, d, ers, s — 2485, 2490, 4166, 5345, 6804 ❧ ***832, 834, 836:*** 1Ki 1:40; Zec 4:2; Rev 18:22

Piram — 6502: *Jos 10:3*

Pirathon — 6552: *Jgs 12:15*

Pirathonite — 6553: Jgs 12:13; 2Sa 23:30

Pisgah (see **Nebo**) — 6449: Dt 3:27; 34:1

Pisidia — ***4099***: *Ac 13:14; 14:24*

Pison — 6376: *Ge 2:11*

Pispah — 6462: *1Ch 7:38*

piss, eth — 7890, 8366: 1Ki 14:10; 2Ki 9:8; Isa 36:12

pit, s — 875, 953, 1356, 1360, 1475, 6354, 7585, 7743/7882, 7745, 7816, 7825, 7845, 7882 ❧ ***999, 5421***: Nu 16:30; Ps 119:85; Lk 14:5

pitch, ed — 167, 2203, 2583, 3722, 3724, 5186, 6965, 8628 ❧ ***4078***: Ge 6:14; Jer 52:4; Heb 8:2

pitcher, s — 3537, 5035 ❧ ***2765***: Jgs 7:16; La 4:2; Mk 14:13

Pithom — 6619: *Ex 1:11*

Pithon — 6377: *1Ch 8:35; 9:41*

pity, ed, eth, ful — 2347, 2550, 2551, 2603, 2617, 5110, 7355, 7356, 7362 ❧ ***1653, 2155, 4184***: Pr 19:17; Am 1:11; Jas 5:11

place, d, s (see **plat**) — 168, 776, 870, 1004, 1367, 2723, 3027, 3240, 3241, 3427, 3653, 3947, 4349, 4585, 4612, 4634, 4724, 4725, 4800, 5414, 5975, 5977, 6607, 7675, 7760, 7931, 8414, 8478 ❧ ***201, 402, 1502, 1564, 1786, 3692, 3699, 3837, 4042, 5117, 5562, 5564, 5602***: Ge 1:9; Isa 5:8; Mk 1:45; Rev 2:5

plague, d, s — 1698, 4046, 4347, 5060, 5061, 5062, 5063 ❧ ***3148, 4127***: Ex 11:1; Ps 73:5; Rev 9:20

plain, ly, ness — 559, 874, 1237, 1540, 4334, 5046, 5228, 5549, 6568, 6703, 7737, 8535 ❧ ***1718, 3123, 3954***: Ge 25:27; Hab 2:2; 2Co 3:12

plain, s — 58, 436, 1236, 1237, 3603, 4334, 6160, 8219 ❧ ***5117/3977***: Dt 1:1; Ob 19; Lk 6:17

plaiting; platted — ***1708, 4120***: Mt 27:29; Jn 19:2; 1Pe 3:3

planes — 4741: *Isa 44:13*

planets — 4208: *2Ki 23:5*

planks — 5646, 6086, 6763: *1Ki 6:15; Eze 41:25, 26*

plant, ation, ed, edst, ers, eth, ing, ings — 4302, 5189, 5192, 5193, 5194, 5195, 7880, 7973, 8291, 8362, 8363 ❧ ***4854, 5451, 5452***: Ge 2:5; Jer 31:5; Eze 17:7; 1Co 3:7

plaster, ed — 1528, 2902, 4799, 7874, 7875: Le 14:43; Isa 38:21; Da 5:5

plat (see **place**) — 2513: *2Ki 9:26*

plate, s; platter — 3871, 5633, 6341, 6731 ❧ ***3953, 4094***: Ex 28:36; Jer 10:9; Mt 23:25

play, ed, edst, er, ers, eth, ing — 2490, 5059, 6711, 7832, 8173 ❧ ***3815***: 2Ki 3:15; Ps 68:25; Zec 8:5; 1Co 10:7

plea; plead, ed, eth, ings (see **implead**) — 1777, 1779, 3198, 7378, 8199: Dt 17:8; Jgs 6:31; Isa 59:4; Mic 6:2

pleasant, ness — 2530, 2531, 2532, 2580, 3303, 4022, 4261, 4262, 4999, 5116, 5273, 5276, 5278, 6027, 6148, 6643, 8191, 8378, 8588: Ge 2:9; Pr 3:17; Mal 3:4

PLEASE, d, ing, th; pleasure, s — 2654, 2655, 2656, 2837, 2895, 2896/5869, 2896/6440, 2974, 3190/5869, 3477/5869, 5273, 5315, 5606, 5719, 5730, 6148, 7451/5869, 7470, 7521, 7522, 8057, 8232, ≈ ***699, 700, 701, 2100, 2101/1511, 2106, 2107, 2237, 2307, 2309, 3588/1380, 4684, 4909, 5171, 5485, 5569*****:** Dt 1:23; Est 8:5; Lk 12:32; 2Pe 1:17

how to please God:

- come to Him by faith: Heb 11:5, 6
- grow in wisdom: Lk 2:52
- walk uprightly: 1Th 4:1
- do good: Heb 13:16
- praise Him: Ps 69:30, 31

pledge, s — 2254, 2258, 5667, 6148, 6161, 6162: Ex 22:26; Isa 36:8; Am 2:8

Pleiades — 3598: *Job 9:9; 38:31*

plenty, ful, fully; plenteous, ness — 398, 1277, 3498, 3499, 3759, 4195, 4723, 5071, 7227, 7230, 7235, 7646, 7647, 8082, 8443 ≈ ***2164, 4183***: Ge 27:28; Pr 21:5; Mt 9:37; Lk 12:16

plotteth — 2161: *Ps 37:12*

plow, ed, ers, eth, ing, man, men, shares; plough (see **shares**) — 406, 855, 2790, 5215 ≈ ***722, 723***: Dt 22:10; Isa 2:4; Lk 17:7

pluck, ed, eth — 717, 1497, 2040, 2965, 3318, 3615, 4803, 4804, 5255, 5337, 5375, 5423, 5428, 5493, 6131, 6132, 7993, 8025, 8045 ≈ ***726, 1288, 1544, 1610, 1807, 1808, 1846, 5089*****:** Ge 8:11; Le 1:16; Jude 12

plumbline — 594: *Am 7:7, 8*

plummet — 68, 913, 4949: *2Ki 21:13; Isa 28:17; Zec 4:10*

plunge — 2881: *Job 9:31*

Pochereth — 6380: *Ezr 2:57; Ne 7:59*

poets — ***4163***: *Ac 17:28*

point, ed, s — 19, 184, 1980, 2742, 5980, 6856, 8376 ≈ ***2079, 3195***: Job 41:30; Jer 17:1; Jn 4:47

poison — 2534, 7219 ≈ ***2447***: Dt 32:24; Job 20:16; Ro 3:13

pole — 5251: *Nu 21:8, 9*

policy — 7922: *Da 8:25*

polish, ed, ing — 1305, 1508, 2404, 7044: Isa 49:2; La 4:7; Da 10:6

poll, ed, s — 1494, 1538, 1548, 3697: Nu 3:47; 2Sa 14:26; Mic 1:16

pollute, d, ng, ion, ions — 947, 1351, 2490, 2610, 2930, 2931, 6121 ≈ ***234, 2840, 3393***: Ex 20:25; Eze 22:10; Ac 21:28; 2Pe 2:20

Pollux — ***1359***: *Ac 28:11*

pomegranate, s — 7416: Ex 28:33; SS 4:3; Hag 2:19

pommels — 1543: *2Ch 4:12, 13*

pomp — 1347, 7588 ≈ ***5325***: Isa 5:14; Eze 7:24; Ac 25:23

ponder, ed, eth — 6424, 8505 ≈ ***4820****:* Pr 4:26; 21:2; Lk 2:19

ponds — 98, 99: *Ex 7:19; 8:5; Isa 19:10*

Pontius — ***4194***: Mt 27:2; Ac 4:27

Pontus — ***4195***: *Ac 2:9; 18:2; 1Pe 1:1*

pool, s — 98, 1293, 1295, 4723 ≈ ***2861***: Ex 7:19; Ne 2:14; Jn 5:2

poor, er, est (see **poverty**) — 34, 1800, 1803, 2489, 3423, 4134, 4270, 4542, 6033, 6035/6041, 6041, 7326 ≈ ***3993, 3998, 4433, 4434*****:** Le 27:8; Ru 3:10; 2Ki 24:14; Mt 5:3

poplar, s — 3839: *Ge 30:37; Hos 4:13*

populous — 527, 7227: *Dt 26:5; Na 3:8*

Poratha — 6334: *Est 9:8*

porch, es — 197, 4528 ≈ ***4259, 4440, 4745***: Jgs 3:23; Eze 41:15; Ac 3:11

Porcius — ***4201***: *Ac 24:27*

port, er, ers — 7778, 8179, 8652 ≈ ***2377***: 2Ki 7:11; Ne 2:13; Jn 10:3

portion, s — 270, 1697, 2256, 2505, 2506, 2508, 2513, 2706, 4490, 4521, 6310, 6598, 7926 ≈ ***3313, 4620***: Ge 14:24; 1Sa 1:4; Lk 12:42

portray, ed — 2707, 2710: *Eze 4:1; 8:10; 23:14*

possess, ed, est, eth, ing, ion, ions, or, ors — 270, 272, 423, 2631, 3423, 3424, 3425, 4180, 4181, 4639, 4735, 4736, 5157, 5159, 7069, 7272 ≈ ***1139, 2192, 2697, 2722, 2932, 2933, 2935, 4047, 5224, 5564*****:** Dt 26:1; Da 7:22; Lk 12:15; 2Co 6:10

possible — ***102, 1410, 1415***: Mt 19:26; Ro 12:18; Heb 10:4

post, s — 520, 1755, 4201, 4947, 5592, 7323: Ex 12:7; Job 9:25; Am 9:1

posterity — 310, 319, 1755, 7611: Nu 9:10; Ps 49:13; Da 11:4

pot, s; potsherd, s; potter, s (see **sherds**) — 610, 1375, 1731, 2789, 3335, 3627, 4715, 5518, 6353, 6517, 6803, 8240 ≈ ***2763, 2764, 3582, 4713*****:** Job 2:8; Zec 11:13; Mk 7:4; Heb 9:4

potentate — ***1413***: *1Ti 6:15*

Potiphar — 6318: *Ge 37:36; 39:1*

Poti-pherah — 6319: *Ge 41:45, 50; 46:20*

presidents — 5632: *Da 6:2-4, 6, 7*

press, ed, es, eth — 1660, 1765, 4600, 5181, 5781, 6333, 6484, 6555, 6693, 7818 ✑ ***598, 916, 971, 1377, 1945, 1968, 3793, 4085, 4912***: Jgs 16:16; Joel 3:13; Lk 8:19

pressfat — 3342: *Hag 2:16*

presume, d; presumptuous, ly — 2086, 2087, 2102, 3027, 4390, 6075 ✑ ***5113***: Ex 21:14; Est 7:5; 2Pe 2:10

pretense — ***4392***: *Mt 23:14; Mk 12:40; Php 1:18*

prevail, ed, est — 553, 1396, 2388, 3201, 3202, 3513, 3898, 5810, 6113, 6206, 7186, 7287, 8630 ✑ ***2480, 2729, 3528, 5623***: Ge 7:18; Ob 7; Rev 5:5

prevent, ed, est — 6923 ✑ ***4399, 5348***: Job 3:12; Mt 17:25; 1Th 4:15

prey — 400, 957, 961, 962, 2863, 2963, 2964, 4455, 5706, 7997, 7998: Ge 49:9; Jer 21:9; Zep 3:8

price, s (see **prize**) — 3365, 3701, 4242, 4377, 4736, 4901, 6187, 7939 ✑ ***4185, 4186, 5092***: Le 25:16; Ac 4:34; 1Co 6:20

prick, ed, ing, s — 3992, 7899, 8150 ✑ ***2669, 2759***: Ps 73:21; Eze 28:24; Ac 9:5

PRIEST, HOOD, s (see **Levite**) — 3547, 3548, 3549, 3550, 3649 ✑ ***748, 749, 2405, 2406, 2407, 2409, 2420***: Ex 2:16; Hos 4:4; Rev 1:6
- the priesthood under the Mosaic law:
  - the high priest:
    - functions of:
      - represent the nation of Israel before God: Ex 28:29
      - offer atonement for Israel: Ex 30:10; Heb 9:7
    - special laws pertaining to: Le 21:10-15
  - other priests:
    - functions of:
      - offer sacrifices to God: Le 1:7-9
      - handle cases of leprosy: Le 14:2-32
      - officiate over domestic disputes: Nu 5:13-27
    - special laws pertaining to: Le 10:8, 9; 21:1-7; 22:2-9

prince, s, ss — 324, 2831, 3548, 5057, 5081, 5257, 5387, 5461, 6579, 7101, 7227, 7261, 7333, 7336, 7991, 8269, 8282, 8323 ✑ ***747, 758, 2232***: Nu 7:11; La 1:1; Ac 3:15

principal; principality, ies — 1, 117, 3548, 4761, 5257, 7218, 7225, 7795, 8269, 8291 ✑ ***746, 3588/2596/1851/5607***: Le 5:6; Pr 4:7; Ac 25:23; Tit 3:1

principles — ***746, 4747***: *Heb 5:12; 6:1*

print, ed — 2707, 2710, 5414 ✑ ***5179***: *Le 19:28; Job 13: 27; 19:23; Jn 20:25*

Prisca — ***4251***: *2Ti 4:19*

Priscilla — ***4252***: Ac 18:2; Ro 16:3

prison, er, ers, s — 615, 616, 631, 1004/612, 1004/3608, 1004/5470, 1004/6486, 4115, 4307, 4525, 4929, 6115, 6495, 7615, 7628 ✑ ***1198, 1201, 1202, 3612, 3860, 5084, 5438***: Ge 39:20; Lk 21:12

private, ly — ***2596/2398***: Mt 24:3; Gal 2:2; 2Pe 1:20

privy, ily — 652, 2314, 2934, 3045, 3909, 5643, 6845, 8212, 8649 ✑ ***2977, 3918, 3922, 4894***: Dt 23:1; 1Sa 24:4; Eze 21:14; Ac 5:2

prize, d — 3365 ✑ ***1017***: *Zec 11:13; 1Co 9:24; Php 3:14*

proceed, ed, eth, ing — 3254, 3318, 4161 ✑ ***1607, 1831, 4298, 4369***: Ex 25:35; Hab 1:4; Rev 22:1

process — 7093, 7227, 7235: Ge 4:3; Jgs 11:4; 2Ch 21:19

Prochorus — ***4402***: *Ac 6:5*

proclaim, ation, ed, eth, ing — 2199, 3745, 5674/6963, 6942, 7121, 7440, 8085 ✑ ***2784***: Ex 34:5; Da 5:29; Lk 12:3

procure, d, th — 1245, 6213: *Pr 11:27; Jer 2:17; 4:18; 26:19; 33:9*

produce — 7126: *Isa 41:21*

profane, d, ing, ness, th — 2455, 2490, 2491, 2610, 2613 ✑ ***952, 953***: Jer 23:15; Mal 2:10; Mt 12:5; 2Ti 2:16

profess, ed, ing, ion — 5046 ✑ ***1861, 3670, 3671, 5335***: Dt 26:3; Tit 1:16; Heb 3:1

profit, able, ed, eth, ing — 1215, 3148, 3276, 3504, 4195, 5532, 6743, 7737 ✑ ***2076, 2173, 4297, 4298, 4851, 5539, 5622, 5623, 5624***: Job 22:2; Hab 2:18; Mt 16:26; 1Ti 4:15

profound — 6009: *Hos 5:2*

progenitors — 2029: *Ge 49:26*

prognosticators — 3045: *Isa 47:13*

prolong, ed, eth — 748, 754, 3254, 4900, 5186: Dt 4:26; Ecc 7:15; Isa 13:22

promise, d, dst, s, ing — 559, 562, 1696, 1697, 2421 ✑ ***1843, 1860, 1861, 1862, 3670, 4279***: Ne 9:15; Eze 13:22; Ro 9:4; 2Pe 2:19

promote, d, ion — 1431, 3513, 5128, 6744, 7311: Est 3:1; Pr 3:35; Da 3:30

pronounce, d, ing — 981, 1696, 7126: Le 5:4; Ne 6:12; Jer 36:18

proof, s — ***1382, 1732, 4135, 5039***: Ac 1:3; Php 2:22; 2Ti 4:5

proper — 5459 ✑ ***791, 2398***: 1Ch 29:3; 1Co 7:7; Heb 11:23

prophesy, ed, eth, ing, ings; prophecy, ies (see **prophet**) — 2372, 4853, 5012, 5013, 5016, 5017, 5030, 5197 ≈ ***4394, 4395, 4397***: Pr 30:1; Isa 30:10; Mk 7:6; 1Co 11:5

PROPHET, ess, s (see **prophesy**) — 2374, 5012, 5029, 5030, 5031, 5197 ≈ ***4396, 4397, 4398, 5578***: Ge 20:7; 1Ch 17:1; Lk 2:36; Ac 13:6
- true prophets:
  - requirements of:
    - possessors of God's spirit: Nu 11:25
    - empowered by God: 1Sa 3:19, 20
  - ministry of: Eze 3:17-21; Hos 12:10
- false prophets:
  - how to discern:
    - enticement to idolatry: Dt 13:1-3
    - unfulfilled prophecy: Dt 18:21, 22
  - will be judged: Jer 28:15-17; Eze 13:8-16

propitiation — ***2434, 2435:*** *Ro 3:25; 1Jn 2:2; 4:10*

proportion — 4626, 6187 ≈ ***356***: *1Ki 7:36; Job 41:12; Ro 12:6*

proselyte, s — ***4339***: *Mt 23:15; Ac 2:10; 6:5; 13:43*

prospect — 6440: *Eze 40:44-46; 42:15; 43:4*

PROSPER, ITY, ed, eth, ous, ously — 1980, 3787, 6743, 6744, 7919, 7951, 7965, 7999 ≈ ***2137***: Ge 39:3; Pr 17:8; Zec 1:17; Ro 1:10
- the prosperity of the righteous results from:
  - seeking the Lord: 2Ch 26:5
  - meditating on God's word: Jos 1:8; Ps 1:3
  - laboring whole-heartedly: 2Ch 31:21
- the prosperity of the wicked will:
  - be transitory: Ps 37:35, 36
  - end in destruction: Job 15:21

prostitute — 2490: *Le 19:29*

protection — 5643: *Dt 32:38*

protest, ed, ing — 5749 ≈ ***3513***: Ge 43:3; Jer 11:7; Zec 3:6

proud, ly; pride — 1341, 1343, 1344, 1346, 1347, 1348, 1349, 1362, 1363, 1364, 1419, 1431, 1466, 2086, 2087, 2102, 2103, 2121, 3093, 7292, 7293, 7295, 7311, 7342, 7407, 7830 ≈ ***212, 5187, 5243, 5244***: Job 9:13; Ob 3; Lk 1:51

prove, d, ing, th — 974, 5254 ≈ ***584, 1381, 3936, 3985, 4256, 4822:*** Ex 16:4; Da 1:14; Jn 6:6

provender — 1098, 1101, 4554: Ge 24:25; Jgs 19:19; Isa 30:24

proverb, s — 2420, 4911, 4912 ≈ ***3850, 3942***: Dt 28:37; Pr 1:1; Jn 16:29

provide, d, ing, th; provision; providence — 1697, 2372, 3557, 3559, 3740, 3899, 6213, 6679, 6718, 6720, 7200 ≈ ***2090, 2932, 3936, 4160, 4265, 4306, 4307***: Ge 22:8; Da 1:5; Ac 24:2; 2Co 8:21

province, s — 4082, 4083 ≈ ***1885***: Ezr 2:1; Est 1:1; Ac 25:1

provoke, d, dst, ing, th; provocation — 3707, 3708, 4784, 4808, 4843, 5006, 5496, 5674, 7264, 7265 ≈ ***653, 2042, 3863, 3893, 3894, 3947, 3948, 3949, 4292***: Ex 23:21; Pr 20:2; Gal 5:26; Heb 3:8

prudent, ly; prudence — 995, 6175, 6191, 6195, 7080, 7919, 7922 ≈ ***4908, 5428***: 1Sa 16:18; Mt 11:25; Eph 1:8

prune, d, ing; pruninghooks — 2167, 2168, 4211: Le 25:3; Isa 5:6; Joel 3:10

psalm, ist, s — 2158, 2167, 2172, 4210 ≈ ***5567, 5568***: 2Sa 23:1; Eph 5:19

psaltery, ies — 3627, 5035, 6460: 1Sa 10:5; Ne 12:27; Ps 81:2; Da 3:5

Ptolemais — ***4424:*** *Ac 21:7*

public, ly — ***1219, 3856***: *Mt 1:19; Ac 18:28; 20:20*

publican, s — ***754, 5057***: Mt 10:3; Mk 2:15; Lk 7:29

publish, ed, eth — 559, 1319, 1540, 1696, 7121, 8085 ≈ ***1096, 1308, 2784***: Est 1:20; Na 1:15; Mk 1:45

Publius — ***4196***: *Ac 28:7, 8*

Pudens — ***4227***: *2Ti 4:21*

puff, ed, eth — 6315 ≈ ***5448***: Ps 10:5; 1Co 4:6; Col 2:18

Puhites — 6336: *1Ch 2:53*

Pul (see **Tiglath-pileser**) — 6322: *2Ki 15:19; 1Ch 5:26; Isa 66:19*

pull, ed, ing — 935, 2040, 3318, 4026, 5256, 5414, 5422, 5423, 5428, 6582, 6584, 7725 ≈ ***385, 726, 1288, 1544, 2506, 2507***: Ge 8:9; Jer 1:10; Lk 6:42; Jude 23

pulpit — 4026: *Ne 8:4*

pulse — 2235: *2Sa 17:28; Da 1:12, 16*

punish, ed, ment, ments — 2399, 2403, 2820, 3256, 5221, 5358, 5771, 6064, 6066, 6485, 7489 ≈ ***1349, 1557, 2009, 2849, 2851, 5097, 5098, 5099***: Ge 4:13; Isa 10:12; Mt 25:46; Ac 22:5

Punites (see **Phuvah**) — 6324: *Nu 26:23*

Punon — 6325: *Nu 33:42, 43*

Pur, Purim — 6332: *Est 3:7; 9:24, 26, 28, 29, 31, 32*

purchase, d — 1350, 4735, 4736, 7069 ≈ ***2932, 4046, 4047***: Ge 25:10; Jer 32:11; Ac 1:18

purge, d, ing, th — 1305, 1740, 2212, 2398, 2891, 3722, 6884 ≈ ***1245, 1571, 2508, 2511, 2512, 4160/2512:*** Ps 51:7; Isa 6:7; Jn 15:2

Q

R

Raamah — 7484: *Ge 10:7; 1Ch 1:9; Eze 27:22*
Raamiah — 7485: *Ne 7:7*
Raamses, Rameses — 7486: Ge 47:11; Ex 1:11
Rabbah, Rabbath — 7237: 2Sa 11:1; Eze 21:20
Rabbi (see **Rabboni**) — ***4461***: Mt 23:7; Jn 3:2
Rabbith — 7245: *Jos 19:20*
Rabboni (see **Rabbi**) — ***4462***: *Jn 20:16*
Rab-mag — 7248: *Jer 39:3, 13*
Rab-saris — 7249: *2Ki 18:17; Jer 39:3, 13*
Rab-shakeh — 7262: 2Ki 18:17; Isa 36:11
Raca — ***4469***: *Mt 5:22*
race — 734, 4793 ~ ***73, 4712***: *Ps 19:5; Ecc 9:11; 1Co 9:24; Heb 12:1*
Rachab, Rahab — 7294, 7343 ~ ***4460, 4477***: Jos 2:1; Mt 1:5
Rachal — 7403: *1Sa 30:29*
Rachel — 7354 ~ ***4478***: Jer 31:15; Mt 2:18
Raddai — 7288: *1Ch 2:14*
rafters — 7351: *SS 1:17*
Ragau, Reu — 7466 ~ ***4466***: 1Ch 1:25; Lk 3:35
rag, ged, s — ***899***, 4418, 7168: Pr 23:21; Isa 2:21; Jer 38:11
rage, d, ing, th — 1348, 1984, 1993, 2195, 2197, 2534, 5674, 5678, 7264, 7266, 7267, 7283 ~ ***66, 2830, 5433***: Ps 46:6; Pr 14:16; Ac 4:25
Raguel — 7467: *Nu 10:29*
Raham — 7357: *1Ch 2:44*
rail, ed, er, ing, ings — 2778, 5860 ~ ***987, 988, 989, 3059, 3060***: 1Sa 25:14; Mk 15:29; 1Co 5:11; 1Ti 6:4
raiment (see **clothe**) — 899, 3682, 3830, 4055, 4254, 4403, 7553, 8008, 8071 ~ ***1742, 2066, 2440, 2441, 4629***: Ge 24:53; Dt 8:4; Jn 19:24
rain, ed, y — 1653, 1656, 3138, 3384, 4175, 4305, 4306, 4456, 5464, 8164 ~ ***1026, 1026/5025, 1028, 5205***: Pr 27:15; Am 4:7; Rev 11:6
rainbow — ***2463***: *Rev 4:3; 10:1*
raise, d, ing, r, th — 1361, 2210, 5375, 5549, 5674, 5782, 5872, 5927, 5975, 6209, 6965, 6966, 7613 ~ ***386, 450, 1326, 1453, 1817, 1825, 1892, 160/1999, 4891***: Dt 18:15; Zec 2:13; Jn 5:21; Ac 24:12
raisins — 6778: 1Sa 25:18; 2Sa 16:1; 1Ch 12:40
Rakem — 7552: *1Ch 7:16*
Rakkath — 7557: *Jos 19:35*
Rakkon — 7542: *Jos 19:46*
ram, s — 352, 1798, 3104, 3733: Ex 25:5; Jos 6:4; Ezr 6:9
rang — 1949: *1Sa 4:5; 1Ki 1:45*
range, ing, s — 3491, 3600, 7713, 8264: Le 11:35; Job 39:8; Pr 28:15
rank, s — 734, 1277, 6471 ~ ***4237***: Ge 41:5; 1Ch 12:33; Mk 6:40
ransom, ed — 1350, 3724, 6299, 6306 ~ ***487, 3083***: Ex 30:12; Isa 35:10; Mt 20:28
Rapha — 7498: *1Ch 8:2, 37*
Raphu — 7505: *Nu 13:9*
rare — 3358: *Da 2:11*
rase — 6168: *Ps 137:7*
rash, ly — 926, 4116 ~ ***4312***: *Ecc 5:2; Isa 32:4; Ac 19:36*
rate — 1697: Ex 16:4; 2Ki 25:30; 2Ch 8:13
rather — 408, 977 ~ ***2228, 2309, 3123, 3304, 4056, 4133***: Ps 84:10; Pr 8:10; Mt 10:6; Heb 13:19
rattleth; rattling — ***7439, 7494***: *Job 39:23; Na 3:2*
raven, ing, ous — 2963, 2966, 5861, 6530 ~ ***724, 727***: Ps 22:13; Eze 39:4; Mt 7:15
raven, s — 6158 **2876**: Ge 49:27; 1Ki 17:4; Lk 12:24
ravished — 3823, 6031, 7686, 7693: SS 4:9; La 5:11; Zec 14:2
raw — 2416, 4995: Ex 12:9; Le 13:10; 1Sa 2:15
razor — 4177, 8593: Jgs 13:5; Isa 7:20; Eze 5:1
reach, ed, eth, ing — 1272, 1961, 4229, 4291, 5060, 5381, 6293, 6643, 7971 ~ ***190, 1901, 2185, 5342***: Da 4:22; Php 3:13; Rev 18:5
read, est, eth, ing — 4744, 7121, 7123 ~ ***314, 320, 6642:*** Ex 24:7; Ne 8:8; Lk 10:26
ready, ness — 631, 1951, 2363, 2896, 3559, 4106, 4116, 4131, 4672, 5750, 6263, 6264, 7126, 7138, 8003 ~ ***1451, 2090, 2092, 2093, 2130, 3195, 4288, 4289, 4689***: Ecc 5:1; Mt 22:4; Ac 17:11
Reaia, Reaiah (see **Haroeh**) — 7211: *1Ch 4:2; 5:5; Ezr 2:47; Ne 7:50*
realm — 4437, 4438: 2Ch 20:30; Ezr 7:13; Da 1:20

REAP, ed, er, ers, est, eth, ing — 7114 ~ ***270, 2325, 2327***: 1Sa 6:13; Mt 13:30; Lk 19:22
- one can reap:
  - what is sown: Job 4:8; Hos 10:13; Gal 6:7, 8
  - what is not sown: Mt 25:24; Jn 4:38
  - how much is sown: 2Co 9:6

rear, ed — 5324, 6965 ~ ***1453***: Le 26:1; 2Sa 18:18; Jn 2:20
rearward (see **hinder**) — 314, 622: Nu 10:25; 1Sa 29:2; Isa 52:12
reason, able, ed, ing, s — 413, 1697, 2808, 2940, 3198, 4480, 4486, 5921, 5973, 6440, 6903, 8199,

REGENERATION — ***3824***: *Mt 19:28; Tit 3:5*
initiated by God: Jn 1:12, 13; Jas 1:18; 1Pe 1:3
accomplished through:
the cross of Christ: Jn 3:14, 15
the blood of Christ: Rev 1:5, 6
the word of God: 1Pe 1:23
the gospel: 1Co 4:15
evidences of:
obedience to God: 1Jn 3:24
a righteous life: Eph 4:22-24; 1Jn 2:29
love of the brethren: 1Jn 3:14; 4:7

region, s — 2256, 5299 ≫ ***2825, 4066, 5561***: Dt 3:4; 1Ki 4:11; Lk 3:1
register — 3791, 5612: *Ezr 2:62; Ne 7:5, 64*
Rehabiah — 7345: *1Ch 23:17; 24:21; 26:25*
rehearse, d — 1696, 5046, 7760, 8567 ≫ ***312, 756***: Jgs 5:11; 1Sa 8:21; Ac 11:4
Rehob — 7340: Nu 13:21; 2Sa 8:3; Ne 10:11
Rehoboam, Roboam — 7346 ≫ ***4497***: 1Ki 11:43; Mt 1:7
Rehoboth — 7344: *Ge 10:11; 26:22; 36:37; 1Ch 1:48*
Rehum (see **Nehum**) — 7348: Ezr 2:2; Ne 3:17
Rei — 7472: *1Ki 1:8*
reign, ed, eth, ing — 4427, 4437, 4438, 4467, 4910, 6113, 7287, 7786 ≫ ***757, 936, 2192/932, 2231, 4821***: Ge 37:8; 1Sa 9:17; Ro 5:14
reins — 2504, 3629 ≫ ***3510***: Job 16:13; Isa 11:5; Rev 2:23
reject, ed, eth — 2310, 3988 ≫ ***96, 114, 593, 1609, 3868***: Hos 4:6; Mt 21:42; Jn 12:48
rejoice, d, ing, st, th — 1523, 1524, 1525, 2302, 4885, 5937, 5947, 5951, 5965, 5970, 6670, 7440, 7442, 7797, 7832, 8055, 8056, 8057, 8643 ≫ ***21, 2165, 2620, 2744, 2745, 2746, 4796, 5463***: Le 23:40; Jer 11:15; Jn 3:29
Rekem — 7552: Nu 31:8; Jos 13:21; 1Ch 2:43
release, d — 2010, 8058, 8059 ≫ ***630***: Dt 15:1; Est 2:18; Mt 27:26
relieve, d, th; relief — 833, 2388, 7725 ≫ ***1248, 1884***: Ps 146:9; Ac 11:29; 1Ti 5:10
RELIGION; religious — ***2356, 2357, 2454, 4576***: Ac 13:43; Gal 1:13; Jas 1:26
true religion:
its character:
fearing and loving God: Dt 10:12
not being corrupted by the world: Jas 1:27
doing good works: Isa 1:16, 17
its commendation: Ecc 12:13, 14; Mk 12:32-34
false religion:
its character:
rebellion against God: Isa 65:2-5
evil works: Tit 1:16
its condemnation: Isa 1:11-15; 44:18-20; Mt 23:27, 28

rely, ed — 8172: *2Ch 13:18; 16:7, 8*
remain, der, ed, est, eth, ing — 1481, 1961, 3117, 3241, 3320, 3427, 3462, 3498, 3885, 5117, 5736, 5975, 6965, 7604, 7611, 7931, 8245, 8277, 8300 ≫ ***620, 1265, 3062, 3063, 3306, 3588, 4035, 4052***: Ge 7:23; Ob 14; Jn 1:33
Remaliah — ***7425***: 2Ki 15:25; Isa 8:6
remedy — 4832: *2Ch 36:16; Pr 6:15; 29:1*

REMEMBER, ed, est, eth, ing; remembrance — 2142, 2143, 2146, 6485 ≫ ***363, 364, 3403, 3415, 3417, 3418, 3421, 5179, 5279, 5280, 5294***: Ge 9:15; La 3:19; Mt 5:23; Php 1:3
God remembers:
his covenants: Ge 9:15, 16; Le 26:42
the frailty of man: Ps 78:39; 103:14
his mercy and truth toward Israel: Ps 98:3
the sins of Babylon: Rev 18:5
God does not remember forgiven sin: Isa 43:25

Remeth — 7432: *Jos 19:21*
remit, ted; remission — **859, 863, 3929**: Mt 26:28; Jn 20:23; Heb 9:22
Remmon, Remmon-methoar — 7417: *Jos 19:7, 13*
remnant — 310, 319, 3498, 3499, 5629, 6413, 7604, 7605, 7611, 8293, 8300 ≫ ***2640, 3005, 3062***: Ex 26:12; Isa 1:9; Ro 9:27
remove, d, ing, th — 167, 1473, 1540, 1556, 2186, 2189, 3014, 3670, 4131, 4171, 4185, 5074, 5079, 5110, 5128, 5206, 5253, 5265, 5437, 5472, 5493, 5496, 5674, 6275, 7368, 7493 ≫ ***142, 2795, 3179, 3327, 3331, 3346, 3351, 3911***: Ge 8:13; Jer 4:1; Heb 12:27
Remphan — ***4481***: *Ac 7:43*
rend, ing; rent, est — 1234, 2963, 5364, 6533, 6561, 7167 ≫ ***1284, 4048, 4486, 4682, 4977, 4978***: Ps 7:2; Eze 13:11; Mt 7:6
render, ed, est, eth, ing (see **repay**) — 5415, 7725, 7999 ≫ ***467, 591***: Nu 18:9; Pr 12:14; 1Pe 3:9
renew, ed, est, ing — 2318, 2498 ≫ ***340, 341, 342, 365***: Job 29:20; Ps 51:10; Ro 12:2
renounced — ***550***: *2Co 4:2*
renown, ed — 1984, 7121, 8034: Ge 6:4; Eze 26:17; Da 9:15
repair, ed, er, ing — 918, 1129, 1448, 2318, 2388, 2393, 2421, 3247, 5462, 5975, 7495: Jgs 21:23; Ezr 9:9; Isa 58:12

repay, ed, eth (see **render**) — 7999 ✒ ***467, 591, 661***: Dt 7:10; Pr 13:21; Lk 10:35

repeateth; repititions — 8138 ✒ ***945***: *Pr 17:9; Mt 6:7*

REPENT, ANCE, ed, est, eth, ing, ings — 5150, 5162, 5164, 7725 ✒ ***278, 3338, 3340, 3341***: Ex 13:17; Lk 15:7; Heb 6:1

with respect to God, repentance:
- indicates a change in proposed action: 2Sa 24:16; Am 7:3, 6; Jnh 3:10
- does not mean a change of character: Nu 23:19; 1Sa 15:29; Jer 4:28

with respect to man, repentance:
- is required by God: Eze 18:30, 31; Ac 3:19; 2Pe 3:9
- should be accompanied by:
  - self-abasement: 1Ki 21:27; Job 42:5, 6
  - sorrow over sin: Mk 14:72; Jas 4:9
  - confession of sin: Lk 18:13

Rephael — 7501: *1Ch 26:7*

Rephah — 7506: *1Ch 7:25*

Rephaiah — 7509: 1Ch 3:21; Ne 3:9

Rephaim, s — 7497: Ge 14:5; 2Sa 5:18; Isa 17:5

Rephidim — 7508: Ex 17:1; Nu 33:14

replenish, ed — 4390: Ge 1:28; Isa 2:6; Eze 26:2

repliest — ***470***: *Ro 9:20*

report, ed — 559, 1681, 1697, 5046, 7725, 8034, 8052, 8085, 8088 ✒ ***189, 191, 312, 518, 987, 1310, 1426, 2162, 2163, 3140, 3141***: Ne 6:6; Jer 20:10; 3Jn 12

reproach, ed, es, est, eth, fully — 1421, 1442, 2617, 2659, 2778, 2781, 3637, 3639, 7036 ✒ ***819, 3059, 3679, 3680, 3681, 5195, 5196, 5484***: Job 16:10; Ps 15:3; Ro 15:3

reprobate, s — 3988 ✒ ***96***: Jer 6:30; 2Co 13:5; Tit 1:16

REPROOF, s; reprove, d, r, eth — 1605, 1606, 3198, 3256, 8433 ✒ ***1650, 1651***: Pr 17:10; Eze 3:26; 2Ti 3:16

reproof should lead to:
- avoidance of evil: Pr 6:23, 24
- getting understanding: Pr 15:32
- acquiring wisdom: Pr 29:15
- soundness in doctrine: Tit 1:13

reputed; reputation — 2804, 3368 ✒ ***1380, 1784, 2758, 5093***: Ecc 10:1; Da 4:35; Gal 2:2

request, ed, s (see **ask**) — 782, 1156, 1245, 1246, 1697, 7592, 7596 ✒ ***155, 1162, 1189***: Jgs 8:26; Ezr 7:6; Php 1:4

require, d, ing, st, th — 977, 1245, 1875, 1961, 3117, 7592, 7593 ✒ ***154, 155, 523, 1096, 1567, 2212, 4238***: Ge 9:5; Ru 3:11; Lk 23:24

requite, d, ing — 1580, 5414, 6213, 7725, 7999 ✒ ***287, 591***: 2Ch 6:23; Jer 51:56; 1Ti 5:4

rescue, d, th — 3467, 5337, 5338, 6299, 7725 ✒ ***287, 591, 1807***: Dt 28:31; Da 6:27; Ac 23:27

resemble, ance, d — 5869, 8389 ✒ ***3666***: *Jgs 8:18; Zec 5:6; Lk 13:18*

Resen — 7449: *Ge 10:12*

reserve, d, th (see **residue**) — 680, 2820, 3498, 3947, 5201, 7604, 8104 ✒ ***2641, 5083***: Ru 2:18; Na 1:2; 1Pe 1:4

Resheph — 7566: *1Ch 7:25*

residue (see **reserve**) — 319, 3498, 3499, 7605, 7606, 7611 ✒ ***2645, 3062***: Ex 10:5; Zep 2:9; Mk 16:13

resist, ed, eth — 7853 ✒ ***436, 478, 496, 498***: Zec 3:1; Mt 5:39; Ro 13:2

resolved — ***1097***: *Lk 16:4*

resort, ed — 935, 3320, 6908 ✒ ***2064, 4848, 4863, 4905***: Ne 4:20; Mk 2:13; Jn 18:20

respect, ed, er, eth — 3045, 4856, 5027, 5234, 5375, 6437, 7200, 8159 ✒ ***578, 678, 1914, 2596, 3313, 3382, 4380, 4381, 4382***: Ge 4:4; Ps 40:4; Ac 10:34

respite — 7309, 7503: *Ex 8:15; 1Sa 11:3*

rest, ed, eth, ing, place, s — 270, 1824, 1826, 2308, 2342, 2583, 2790, 3498, 3499, 4494, 4496, 4771, 5117, 5118, 5183, 5564, 7257, 7258, 7280, 7599, 7604, 7605, 7606, 7611, 7673, 7677, 7901, 7931, 7954, 7965, 8058, 8172, 8252, 8300 ✒ ***372, 373, 425, 1515, 1879, 1954, 1981, 2192/372, 2270, 2663, 2664, 2681, 2838, 3062, 4520:*** Pr 14:33; Jer 50:6; Mt 11:28; Ro 2:17

restitution (see **restore**) — 7999, 8545 ✒ ***605***: *Ex 22:3, 5, 6, 12; Job 20:18; Ac 3:21*

restore, d, th (see **restitution**) — 2421, 5414, 5927, 7725, 7999, 8421 ✒ ***591, 600, 2675***: Ge 20:7; Ezr 6:5; Mk 9:12

restrain, ed, est — 662, 1639, 2296, 3543, 3607, 4513, 4622, 6113 ✒ ***2664***: Job 15:4; Isa 63:15; Ac 14:18

RESURRECTION — ***386, 1454, 1815***: Mt 27:53; Php 3:11; Rev 20:5

the resurrection of Christ was:
- prophesied in the Old Testament: Ps 16:10; Isa 53:8-10
- accomplished by God's power: Ac 2:22-24; 1Pe 3:18
- an evidence of His Deity: Jn 2:18, 19; Ac 2:32-36

the resurrection of the saved:

Sheminith — 8067: *1Ch 15:21; Ps 6:title; 12:title*

Shemiramoth — 8070: *1Ch 15:18, 20; 16:5; 2Ch 17:8*

Shen — 8129: *1Sa 7:12*

Shenazar — 8137: *1Ch 3:18*

Shepham (see **Shiphmite**) — 8221: *Nu 34:10, 11*

Shephatiah — 8203: 2Sa 3:4; Ezr 2:4; Jer 38:1

shepherd, s (see **sheep**) — 7462, 7462/6629, 7473 ➳ ***4166***: Nu 27:17; Na 3:18; 1Pe 5:4

Shephi, Shepho — 8195: *Ge 36:23; 1Ch 1:40*

Shephuphan, Shupham — 8197: *Nu 26:39; 1Ch 8:5*

Sherah — 7609: *1Ch 7:24*

sherd, s (see **pot**) — 2789: *Isa 30:14; Eze 23:34*

Sherebiah — 8274: Ezr 8:18; Ne 8:7

Sheresh — 8329: *1Ch 7:16*

sheriffs — 8614: *Da 3:2, 3*

Sheshach — 8347: *Jer 25:26; 51:41*

Sheshai — 8344: *Nu 13:22; Jos 15:14; Jgs 1:10*

Sheshan — 8348: *1Ch 2:31, 34, 35*

Sheshbazzar (see **Zerubbabel**) — 8339: *Ezr 1:8, 11; 5:14, 16*

Shethar — 8369: *Est 1:14*

Shethar-boznai — 8370: *Ezr 5:3, 6; 6:6, 13*

Sheva (see **Seraiah**; **Shavsha**) — 7724: *2Sa 20:25: 1Ch 2:49*

Shibboleth (see **Sibboleth**) — 7641: *Jgs 12:6*

Shibmah, Sibmah — 7643: Nu 32:38; Isa 16:8

Shicron — 7942: *Jos 15:11*

shield, s — 3591, 4043, 6793, 7982 ➳ ***2375***: Ge 15:1; 2Sa 8:7; Eph 6:16

Shiggaion, Shigionoth — 7692: *Ps 7:title; Hab 3:1*

Shihon — 7866: *Jos 19:19*

Shihor, Sihor — 7883: Jos 13:3; 1Ch 13:5

Shihor-libnath — 7884: *Jos 19:26*

Shilhi — 7977: *1Ki 22:42; 2Ch 20:31*

Shilhim — 7978: *Jos 15:32*

Shillem — 8006: *Ge 46:24; Nu 26:49*

Shillemites — 8016: *Nu 26:49*

Shiloah, Siloah — 7975: *Ne 3:15; Isa 8:6*

Shiloh — 7886, 7887: Ge 49:10; 1Sa 1:3

Shiloni — 8023: *Ne 11:5*

Shilonite, s — 7888: 1Ki 11:29; 15:29; 1Ch 9:5

Shilshah — 8030: *1Ch 7:37*

Shimea — 8092: *1Ch 3:5; 6:30, 39; 20:7*

Shimeah, Shimma — 8039, 8092, 8093, 8096: 2Sa 13:3; 1Ch 2:13

Shimeam — 8043: *1Ch 9:38*

Shimeath — 8100: *2Ki 12:21; 2Ch 24:26*

Shimeathites — 8101: *1Ch 2:55*

Shimei, Shimhi, Shimi — 8096, 8097: Ex 6:17; 2Sa 16:5; 1Ch 8:21

Shimeon, Simeon (see **Simon; Simeonites**) — 8095, 8099 ➳ ***4826***: Ge 29:33; Ezr 10:31; Lk 2:25

Shimites — 8097: *Nu 3:21*

Shimon — 7889: *1Ch 4:20*

Shimrath — 8119: *1Ch 8:21*

Shimri, Simri — 8113: 1Ch 26:10; 2Ch 29:13

Shimrith (see **Shomer**) — 8116: *2Ch 24:26*

Shimrom, Shimron — 8110: Ge 46:13; 1Ch 7:1

Shimronites — 8117: *Nu 26:24*

Shimron-meron — 8112: *Jos 12:20*

Shimshai — 8124: *Ezr 4:8, 9, 17, 23*

Shinab — 8134: *Ge 14:2*

Shinar — 8152: Isa 11:11; Zec 5:11

shine, d, ing, th; shone — 166, 215, 1984, 2094, 3313, 5050, 5051, 5774, 6245, 6670, 7160, 7227 ➳ ***796, 797, 826, 1584, 2989, 4015, 4034, 4744, 5316***: Ex 34:29; Dt 33:2; Jn 1:5

ship, master, men, ing, s, wreck — 582/591, 5600, 6716, 7227/2259 ➳ ***2942, 3489, 3490, 3491, 3492, 4142, 4143***: Isa 33:21; Jnh 1:6; Ac 27:27; 2Co 11:25

Shiphi — 8230: *1Ch 4:37*

Shiphmite — 8225: *1Ch 27:27*

Shiphrah — 8236: *Ex 1:15*

Shiphtan — 8204: *Nu 34:24*

Shisha — 7894: *1Ki 4:3*

Shishak — 7895: 1Ki 11:40; 2Ch 12:2

Shitrai — 7861: *1Ch 27:29*

shittah, shittim — 7848: Ex 25:5; Isa 41:19

Shittim — 7848, 7851, 7848: Jos 2:1; Mic 6:5,

shivers — ***4937***: *Rev 2:27*

Shiza — 7877: *1Ch 11:42*

Shoa — 7772: *Eze 23:23*

Shobab — 7727: *2Sa 5:14; 1Ch 2:18; 3:5; 14:4*

Shobach (see **Shophach**) — 7731: *2Sa 10:16, 18*

Shobai — 7630: *Ezr 2:42; Ne 7:45*

Shobal — 7732: Ge 36:20; 1Ch 1:38

Shobek — 7733: *Ne 10:24*

Shobi — 7629: *2Sa 17:27*

Shocho, Shochoh, Shoco, Socho, Sochoh, Socoh — 7755: 1Sa 17:1; 1Ki 4:10; 1Ch 4:18

shock, s — 1430: *Jgs 15:5; Job 5:26*

shoe, latchet, s; shod (see **latchet**) — 4515, 5274, 5275, 8288/5275 ➳ ***2438, 5265, 5266:*** Ge 14:23; Ex 3:5; Mk 6:9

Shoham — 7719: *1Ch 24:27*

step, ped, peth, s — 838, 1978, 4609, 4703, 6119, 6471, 6587, 6806 ✒ ***1684, 2487, 2597***: 1Sa 20:3; Pr 4:12; Jn 5:4

stern — ***4403***: *Ac 27:29*

STEWARD, SHIP, s — 376/834/5921, 1121/4943, 8269 ✒ ***2012, 3621, 3622, 3623***: Ge 15:2; 1Ch 28:1; Lk 16:2

stewardship requires:
- accountability: Lk 12:42-48; Ro 14:11, 12
- faithfulness: 1Co 4:2
- blamelessness: Tit 1:7

stick, eth; stuck — 1692, 1695, 3920, 4600, 5181, 8205: Job 33:21; Ps 119:31; Eze 29:4

stick, s — 6086 ✒ ***5434***: Nu 15:32; 2Ki 6:6; Ac 28:3

stiff, ened, hearted, necked — 2389, 3820, 6277, 7185/6203, 7186/6203 ✒ ***4644***: Jer 17:23; Eze 2:4; Ac 7:51

still, ed, est, eth — 1826, 1827, 2013, 2790, 2814, 4496, 5265, 5750, 5975, 7503, 7623, 7673, 8252 ✒ ***2089, 2476, 4357, 5392***: Nu 13:30; Ps 65:7; Mk 4:39

sting, eth, s — 6567 ✒ ***2759***: *Pr 23:32; 1Co 15:55, 56; Rev 9:10*

stink, eth, ing; stank — 887, 889, 4716 ✒ ***3605***: Ge 34:30; 2Sa 10:6; Jn 11:39

stir, red, reth, s — 1624, 5375, 5496, 5782, 5916, 5927, 6965, 8663 ✒ ***329, 383, 1326, 1892, 3947, 3951, 4531, 4787, 4797, 5017***: Job 17:8; Hag 1:14; Lk 23:5

stock, s — 944, 1503, 4115, 5465, 5914, 6086, 6133, 6729 ✒ ***1085, 3586***: Pr 7:22; Jer 2:27; Ac 16:24

Stoics — ***4770***: *Ac 17:18*

stomacher — 6614: *Isa 3:24*

stomach's — ***4751***: *1Ti 5:23*

stone, d, s, est, ing, y — 68, 69, 810, 1496, 2106, 2687, 2789, 5553, 5619, 6344, 6697, 6872, 7275, 8068 ✒ ***2642, 2991, 3034, 3035, 3036, 3037, 4074, 4075, 5586***: Ex 19:13; 1Sa 30:6; Mt 13:5

stonesquarers — 1382: ***1Ki*** *5:18*

stool, s (see **footstool**) — 70, 3678: *Ex 1:16; 2Ki 4:10*

stoop, ed, eth, ing — 3486, 3766, 6915, 7164, 7812, 7817 ✒ ***2955, 3879***: Ge 49:9; Isa 46:1; Mk 1:7

stop, ped, peth — 331, 2629, 2856, 3513, 5462, 5534, 5640, 6113, 7092, 8610 ✒ ***1993, 4912, 5420***: Job 5:16; Zec 7:11; 2Co 11:10

store; storehouse, s — 214, 618, 686, 834, 1995, 3462, 3965, 4543, 4863, 6487, 7235, 8498 ✒ ***597, 2343, 5009***: 2Ch 8:4; Mal 3:10; 1Co 16:2

stork — 2624: Le 11:19; Jer 8:7; Zec 5:9

storm, y — 2230, 5492, 5584, 5591, 7722, 8178, 8183 ✒ ***2978***: Isa 4:6; Na 1:3; Lk 8:23

story, ies — 4097, 4609: 2Ch 13:22; Eze 42:3; Am 9:6

stout, hearted, ness — 47, 1433, 2388, 3820, 7229: Ps 76:5; Isa 9:9; Da 7:20

straight — 3474, 4334, 5676, 8626 ✒ ***461, 2113, 2116, 2117, 3717***: Jos 6:5; Ecc 1:15; Heb 12:13

straightway — 3651, 4116, 6258, 6597, 6693, 7114 ✒ ***1824, 2112, 2117, 3916***: 1Sa 28:20; Ac 5:10; Jas 1:24

strait, en, ened, eneth, est, ly, ness, s — 680, 3334, 4164, 4689, 4712, 5148, 6693, 6862, 6887, 7114 ✒ ***196, 547, 4183, 4728, 4729, 4730, 4912***: Job 12:23; Mk 1:43; 2Co 6:12

strain — ***1368***: *Mt 23:24*

strange, ly, r, rs — 312, 376/1616, 276/2114, 376/5237, 582, 1121/5235, 1121/5236, 1481, 1616, 1970, 2114, 3937, 4033, 5234, 5235, 5236, 5237, 6012, 8453 ✒ ***241, 245, 1722/3940, 1854, 1937, 2087, 3579, 3580, 3581, 3927, 3937, 3939, 3940, 3941, 5381***: Ge 35:2; Ps 144:11; Mt 25:35

strangle, d, ing — 2614, 4267 ✒ ***4156***: *Job 7:15; Na 2:12; Ac 15:20, 29; 21:25*

straw, ed; strewed — 2219, 2236, 4963, 8401 ✒ ***1287, 4766***: Ge 24:25; 2Ch 34:4; Mt 21:8

streaks — 6479, 8258: *Ge 30:37; Le 14:37*

stream, s — 650, 793, 2975, 2988, 5103, 5104, 5140, 5158, 6388 ✒ ***4215***: Nu 21:15; Isa 11:15; Lk 6:48

street, s — 2351, 6440, 7339, 7784 ✒ ***58, 4113, 4505***: 2Ch 29:4; Jer 5:1; Ac 9:11

STRENGTH, en, ed, edst, eth, ing (see **strong**) — 193, 202, 353, 360, 386, 553, 556, 905, 1082, 1369, 1396, 1679, 2220, 2388, 2391, 2392, 2428, 2633, 3027, 3581, 4206, 4581, 5326, 5331, 5332, 5582, 5797, 5807, 5810, 6106, 6109, 6697, 6965, 7292, 7293, 7296, 8443, 8510, 8632, 8633 ✒ ***772, 1411, 1412, 1743, 1765, 1849, 1991, 2479, 2480, 2901, 2904, 4599, 4732, 4741***: Dt 3:28; Ps 8:2; Ac 9:19

God's strength is:
- mighty in dominion: Ps 89:9, 10; Isa 40:10
- mighty in judgment: Lk 1:51; Rev 18:8
- mighty in deliverance: Ex 13:3; Ps 140:7
- mighty in battle: Ps 24:8; 89:10

stretch, ed, est, eth, ing — 1457, 4058, 4298, 4900, 5186, 5203, 5628, 6504, 6566, 7323, 7554,

4310, 4330, 4722, 4778, 4841, 5159, 5254, 5278, 5302: Est 3:8; Php 3:8; 1Pe 1:11
- Christ's sufferings:
  - characteristics of:
    - extensive: Ps 22:14, 15
    - accompanied by ridicule: Mt 27:27-31
    - undergone voluntarily: Isa 50:6
  - purposes of:
    - to bring men to God: 1Pe 3:18
    - to bring salvation to men: Heb 2:9, 10
- suffering for Christ:
  - is required of saints: Ac 9:15, 16; 2Co 11:23; Php 1:29
  - will be rewarded: Mt 5:11, 12; Ro 8:17; 1Pe 3:14

suffice, d, eth; sufficiency; sufficient, ly — 1767, 4078, 4672, 5606, 5607, 7227, 7648, 7654 ✒ ***713, 714, 841, 2425, 2426***: Job 20:22; Isa 23:18; Jn 14:8; 2Co 2:6

suit, s — 2470, 6187, 7379: *Jgs 17:10; 2Sa 15:4; Job 11:19; Isa 3:22*

Sukkiims — 5525: *2Ch 12:3*

sum — 3724, 4557, 6485, 6575, 7217, 7218, 8508, 8552 ✒ ***2774, 5092***: Ex 21:30; Ps 139:17; Ac 22:28

summer — 4747, 6972, 7007, 7019 ✒ ***2330***: Ge 8:22; Jer 8:20; Lk 21:30

sumptuously — ***2983***: *Lk 16:19*

sun, rising — 216, 2535, 2775, 4217/8121, 8121, 8122 ✒ ***2246***: Nu 21:11; Jos 10:12; Mt 5:45

sunder, ed — 6504: Job 41:17; Na 1:13; Lk 12:46

sundry — ***4181***: *Heb 1:1*

sup, ped; supper — 4041 ✒ ***1172, 1173***: Hab 1:9; 1Co 11:25; Rev 19:9

superfluity; superfluous — 8311 ✒ ***4050, 4053***: *Le 21:18; 22:23; 2Co 9:1; Jas 1:21*

superscription — ***1923***: Mt 22:20; Mk 12:16; Lk 20:24

superstition; superstitious — ***1174, 1175***: *Ac 17:22; 25:19*

supplant, ed — 6117: *Ge 27:36; Jer 9:4*

supple — 4935: *Eze 16:4*

suppliants — 6282: *Zep 3:10*

supplication, s (see **pray**) — 2470, 2603, 2604, 6419, 8467, 8469 ✒ ***1162, 2428***: 1Sa 13:12; Job 41:3; Ac 1:14

supply, ed, eth — ***378, 2024, 4137, 4322***: 2Co 11:9; Eph 4:16; Php 4:19

support — ***472, 482***: *Ac 20:35; 1Th 5:14*

suppose, d, ing — 559 ✒ ***1380, 2233, 3049, 3543, 3633, 5274, 5282***: 2Sa 13:32; Jn 20:15; Ac 7:25

supreme — ***5242***: *1Pe 2:13*

Sur — 5495: *2Ki 11:6*

SURE — 539, 546, 548, 571, 982, 983, 2388, 3045, 3245, 4009, 6965, 7011, 7292, 8104 ✒ ***804, 805, 949, 1097, 1492, 4103, 4731***: Ge 23:17; Isa 22:23; Jn 6:69
- Christians have:
  - a sure foundation: Isa 28:16; 2Ti 2:19
  - a sure hope: Heb 6:19
  - a sure word: 2Pe 1:19
  - sure mercies: Isa 55:3; Ac 13:24

surely — 199, 389, 403, 518, 518/3808, 551, 3588, 3588/518, 3651, 3808, 7535 ✒ ***230, 2229, 3483, 3843, 4135***: Ge 9:5; Jer 3:20; Jn 17:8

surety, ies — 389, 552, 3045, 6148, 6161 ✒ ***230, 1450***: Job 17:3; Pr 11:15; Heb 7:22

surfeiting — ***2897***: *Lk 21:34*

surmisings — ***5283***: *1Ti 6:4*

surname, d — 3655 ✒ ***1941, 2007/3686, 2564***: Isa 44:5; Mk 3:16; Ac 15:37

surprised — 270, 8610: *Isa 33:14; Jer 48:41; 51:41*

Susanchites — 7801: *Ezr 4:9*

Susanna — ***4677***: *Lk 8:3*

Susi — 5485: *Nu 13:11*

sustain, ed; sustenance — 3557, 4241, 5564 ✒ ***5527***: Jgs 6:4; Ne 9:21; Ac 7:11

swaddled; swaddling, band — 2853, 2854, 2946 ✒ ***4683***: Job 38:9; Eze 16:4; Lk 2:7

swallow, ed, eth — 1104, 1105, 1572, 1866, 3886, 5693, 7602 ✒ ***2666***: Nu 16:30; Job 5:5; 2Co 2:7

swan — 8580: *Le 11:18; Dt 14:16*

sware, st; swear, ers, eth, ing; sworn — 422, 423, 1167/7621, 3027/5920/3676, 5375, 7650 ✒ ***3660***: Le 6:5; Mal 3:5; Mt 5:34

swarm, s — 5712, 6157: *Ex 8:21, 22, 24, 29, 31; Jgs 14:8*

sweat — 2188, 3154 ✒ ***2402***: *Ge 3:19; Eze 44:18; Lk 22:44*

sweep, ing; swept — 1640, 2894, 3261, 5502 ✒ ***4563***: Pr 28:3; Isa 14:23; Lk 11:25

sweet, er, ly, ness — 1314, 2896, 3190, 4339, 4452, 4477, 4575, 4966, 4985, 4986, 4987, 4988, 5207, 5208, 5273, 5276, 5561, 5674, 6070, 6148, 6149, 8492 ✒ ***1099***: Jgs 14:18; 2Sa 23:1; Php 4:18

sweetsmelling — ***2175***: *Eph 5:2*

Satan: 1Ch 21:1; Mt 4:1; 2Co 11:3
evil companions: 2Sa 13:3-5; Pr 7:6
sinful desires: Pr 28:20; Jas 1:14
exhortations to resist temptation: Pr 1:10; Ro 6:13
encouragement while under temptation: 1Co 10:13; Heb 2:8; 2Pe 2:9

ten, s, th — 4643, 6218, 6224, 6235, 6236, 6237, 6241, 7231, 7233, 7239, 7240 ➳ ***1176, 1181, 1182, 3461, 3463***: Nu 14:22; Dt 1:15; Rev 11:13
tend, eth — *: Pr 10:16; 14:23; 21:5
tender, hearted, ness — 3126, 3127, 7390/3824, 7391, 7401 ➳ ***527, 2155, 3629, 4698***: Ge 18:7; Dt 28:56; Eph 4:32
tenons — 3027: *Ex 26:17, 19; 36:22, 24*
tenor — 6310: *Ge 43:7; Ex 34:27*
tent, makers, s — 167, 168, 2583, 4908, 4264, 5521, 6898 ➳ ***4635***: 1Sa 4:10; Isa 13:20; Ac 18:3
Terah — 8646 ➳ ***2291***: Ge 11:24-28; Lk 3:34
teraphim — 8655: Jgs 17:5; 18:14; Hos 3:4
Teresh — 8657: *Est 2:21; 6:2*
termed — 559: *Isa 62:4*
terraces — 4546: *2Ch 9:11*
terrestrial — ***1919***: *1Co 15:40*
terrible, ly, ness — 366, 367, 574, 1763, 2152, 3372, 4172, 6184, 6206, 8606 ➳ ***5398***: Dt 26:8; Na 2:3; Heb 12:21
terrify, ed, est; terror, s — 367, 928, 1091, 1161, 1204, 2283, 2847, 2851, 2865, 4032, 4048, 4172, 4288, 4637, 6206, 6343 ➳ ***1629, 4422, 4426, 5401***: Job 7:14; Eze 32:23; Lk 21:9
Tertius — ***5060***: *Ro 16:22*
Tertullus — ***5061***: *Ac 24:1, 2*
testament — ***1242***: Lk 22:20; 2Co 3:6; Rev 11:19
testator — ***1303***: *Heb 9:16, 17*
testify, ed, eth, ing — 5749, 6030 ➳ ***1263, 1957, 3140, 3142, 3143, 4303, 4828***: Ru 1:21; Hos 7:10; 1Pe 5:12
testimony, ies — 5713, 5715, 8584 ➳ ***3140, 3141, 3142***: Nu 1:50; Ne 9:34; 2Th 1:10
tetrarch — ***5075, 5076***: Mt 14:1; Lk 3:1; Ac 13:1
Thaddaeus (see **Lebbaeus**) — ***2280***: *Mt 10:3; Mk 3:18*
Thahash — 8477: *Ge 22:24*
than — 518, 1768, 3588, 4480, 4481, 5921, 5973, 6440 ➳ ***1508, 1883, 2228, 2260, 3844, 4133, 5228, 5245***: Job 9:25; Da 1:20; Ro 1:25; Heb 4:12
THANK, S, ed, ful, fulness, giving, ing, worthy — 1288, 1960, 3029, 3034, 8426 ➳ ***437, 1843, 2168, 2169, 2170, 2192/5485, 3670, 5485***: Le 7:12; 1Ch 16:4; Ac 24:3; 1Pe 2:19
giving thanks unto God:
exhorted: Dt 8:10; Ps 105:1; Col 3:15
reasons for:
His holiness: Ps 30:4
His goodness: Ps 106:1
victory over death: 1Co 15:57

that — 834, 2088, 3588 ➳ ***1565, 3754***: Ge 1:4; Jer 9:26; 2Jn 1
theatre — ***2302***: *Ac 19:29, 31*
Thebez — 8405: *Jgs 9:50; 2Sa 11:21*
thee, ward; thou; thy, self; thine; ye; you, ward (see **your**) — 859, 5315 ➳ ***846, 1438, 1519/5209, 2398, 4314/5209, 4571, 4572, 4671, 4674, 4675, 4771, 5209, 5210***: 1Sa 19:4; Ob 4; Eph 3:2; Phm 4
theft, s (see **thief**) — 1591 ➳ ***2809, 2829***: *Ex 22:3, 4; Mt 15:19; Mk 7:22; Rev 9:21*
them, selves; their, s; they — 853, 905, 1992, 2007, 3027, 5315, 6440 —**240, 846, 848, 1438, 1565, 3441, 3588**: Jos 4:3; Ob 5; Mt 5:3
then — 116, 176, 227, 233, 1571, 3117, 3588 ➳ ***686, 1161, 1534, 1899, 2532, 3063, 3303, 3766, 3767, 5037, 5119, 5119/1161/2532***: Ge 4:26; Jer 8:22; 2Co 12:10
thence, forth — 310/3651, 1973, 2007, 8033, 8536 ➳ ***1537/5127, 1564, 2089, 3606***: Le 22:27; 2Ch 32:23; Mk 1:19
Theophilus — ***2321***: *Lk 1:3; Ac 1:1*
there (see **thither; yonder**) — 8033 ➳ ***847, 1563, 1722/846, 1759, 1927, 5602***: Nu 1:4; Zec 1:8; 1Jn 2:10
thereabout — ***4012/5127***: *Lk 24:4*
thereat; thereby — 2004, 5921 ➳ ***1223/846, 1223/5026, 1722/846***: Pr 20:1; Jer 18:16; Mt 7:13
therefore — 1571, 2006, 2063, 3588, 3606/6903/1768, 3606/6903/1836, 3651, 5921/3651, 5921/3652 ➳ ***235, 473/5607, 686/3767, 1063, 1160, 1211, 1223/5124, 1352, 1360, 1519/5124, 5106, 5620***: 2Ch 19:2; Ac 2:26; Rev 2:5
therefrom — *: *Jos 23:6; 2Ki 3:3; 13:2*
therein; thereinto — 413, 1459, 2004, 4393, 5921, 7130, 8033, 8432 ➳ ***1519/846, 1722/846, 1722/3739, 1722/5129, 5125***: Dt 2:10; Am 6:8; Lk 21:21
thereof — ***846, 1538/846, 4012/846***: Job 3:9; Na 1:8; 2Ti 3:5
thereon; thereupon — 5921 ➳ ***1722/846, 1883/846, 1909/846, 1911, 1913, 1924, 1945, 2026***: Est 5:14; Zep 2:7; 1Co 3:10

THOUGHT, S, est (see **think**; **trow**) — 559, 1672, 1696, 1697, 1819, 2031, 2154, 2161, 2711, 2803, 4093, 4180, 4209, 4284, 5587, 5588, 5869, 6246, 6248, 6250, 6419, 6925, 7454, 7476, 7807, 8312 ✎ ***1260, 1261, 1270, 1380, 1760, 1761, 1911, 1963, 2106, 2233, 2919, 3049, 3053, 3309, 3540, 3543, 4305***: Ge 20:11; Ecc 10:20; Heb 4:12

- thoughts to encourage:
  - wise thoughts: Ps 48:9; Mal 3:16; Php 4:8
  - repentant thoughts: Ps 119:59; Mk 14:72
- thoughts to avoid:
  - evil thoughts: Ge 6:5; Mt 15:19; Ac 8:20
  - foolish thoughts: Est 6:6; Pr 24:9
  - anxious thoughts: Da 5:6; Mt 6:34

THOUSAND, s — 505, 506, 7232, 7233, 7239, 7240 ✎ ***1367, 2035, 3461, 3463, 4000, 5070, 5153, 5505***: Le 26:8; Am 5:3; Jude 14

- the thousand year reign of Christ:
  - with regard to Christ:
    - He will reign over all the earth: Ps 72:8-11
    - He will reign from Jerusalem: Isa 2:2, 3; Mic 4:2
    - He will judge righteously: Ps 72:2; Isa 11:4, 5; Jer 33:15
  - with regard to the saints:
    - the apostles will judge the tribes of Israel: Mt 19:28
    - the saints will execute judgment: Ps 149:6-9
    - the saints will reign with Christ: Rev 5:9, 10; 20:4
  - with regard to Israel:

U

up, on, side, ward (see **on; upper**) — 4605, 4791, 5921/6440 ✑ ***507, 1909***: Ps 146:9; Hag 1:11; Ac 1:2; Rev 1:17

upbraid, ed, eth — 2778 ✑ ***3679***: *Jgs 8:15; Mt 11:20; Mk 16:14; Jas 1:5*

Upharsin (see **Peres**) — 6537: *Da 5:25*

Uphaz — 210: *Jer 10:9; Da 10:5*

uphold, en, est, ing; upheld — 5564, 5582, 5965, 8551 ✑ ***5342***: Ps 63:8; Pr 29:23; Isa 63:5; Heb 1:3

upper, most (see **up**) — 3730, 4947, 5942, 5944, 5945, 7393, 8222 ✑ ***508, 510, 4410, 4411, 5250, 5253***: Ex 12:7; Dt 24:6; Mt 23:6; Ac 19:1

UPRIGHT, LY, ness — 3474, 3476, 3477, 3483, 4334, 4339, 4749, 5228, 5229, 5977, 6968, 8535, 8537, 8549, 8552 ✑ ***3716, 3717***: Ecc 7:29; Mic 2:7; Gal 2:14

characteristics of one who walks uprightly:

he fears God: Pr 14:2

he is guided by his integrity: Pr 11:3

he is maintained by his righteousness: Pr 13:6

he will experience peace: Ps 37:37

uprising — 6965: *Ps 139:2*

uproar — 1993 ✑ ***387, 2350, 2351, 4714, 4797***: 1Ki 1:41; Mk 14:2; Ac 20:1

Ur — 218: Ge 11:28; 1Ch 11:35

Urbane — ***3773:*** *Ro 16:9*

urge, d; urgent — 509, 2388, 2685, 6484, 6555 ✑ ***1758***: Ex 12:33; 2Ki 2:17; Lk 11:53

Uri — 221: Ex 38:22; 1Ch 2:20; Ezr 10:24

Uriah; Urias; Urijah — 223 ✑ ***3774***: 2Sa 12:15; Ne 3:4; Mt 1:6

Uriel — 222: *1Ch 6:24; 15:5, 11; 2Ch 13:2*

Urim — 224: 1Sa 28:6; Ezr 2:63

us, ward (see **our; we**) — 413 ✑ ***1519, 2248***: Ps 2:3; Mk 1:24; Eph 1:19

use, d, ing, s, st — 559, 671, 1696, 3231, 3947, 4399, 4912, 4941, 5172, 5656, 6213, 7080 ✑ ***390, 831, 1096/1722, 1247, 1838, 1908, 2192, 3348, 5195, 5382, 5383, 5530, 5532, 5540***: Le 7:24; Jer 31:23; Tit 3:14; 1Pe 2:16

usurer; usury — 5378, 5383, 5391, 5392 ✑ ***5110***: Ex 22:25; Ne 5:7; Mt 25:27

Uthai — 5793: *1Ch 9:4; Ezr 8:14*

utmost; outmost; uttermost — 314, 319, 657, 3671, 7020, 7093, 7097, 7098, 7112 ✑ ***206, 1231, 2075, 2078, 2556, 2596, 3833, 3838, 4009, 5056***: Nu 22:36; Ps 2:8; Lk 11:31; Heb 7:25

utter, ance, ed, eth, ing (see **say; speak**) — 502, 559, 1696, 1897, 2435, 2531, 3318, 3617, 4008, 4448, 4475, 4911, 5042, 5046, 5414, 6030, 6315 ✑ ***215, 669, 1325, 2044, 2075, 2556, 2980, 3004, 3056***: Le 5:1; Hab 3:10; Ac 2:4

utterly — 3605, 3615, 3632, 3966 ✑ ***2618, 2704, 3654***: Le 26:44; Isa 2:18; Rev 18:8

Uz — 5780: Job 1:1; La 4:21

Uzai — 186: *Ne 3:25*

Uzal — 187: *Ge 10:27; 1Ch 1:21*

Uzza, Uzzah — 5798: 2Sa 6:3; 2Ki 21:18

Uzzen-sherah — 242: *1Ch 7:24*

Uzzi — 5813: Ezr 7:4; Ne 11:22

Uzzia — 5814: *1Ch 11:44*

Uzziel — 5816: Ex 6:18; Ne 3:8

Uzzielites — 5817: *Nu 3:27; 1Ch 26:23*

V

vagabond, s — 5110, 5128 ✑ ***4022***: *Ge 4:12, 14; Ps 109:10; Ac 19:13*

Vajezatha — 2055: *Est 9:9*

vale; valley, s — 1237, 1516, 5158, 6010, 8219 ✑ ***5327***: Dt 8:7; Eze 6:3; Lk 3:5

valiant, est, ly; valour — 47, 691, 1121/2428, 1368, 1396, 2388, 2428 ✑ ***2478***: Jos 1:14; Ps 60:12; Heb 11:34

value, d, st — 457, 5541, 6186, 6187 ✑ ***1308, 5091***: Le 27:12; Job 13:4; Mt 27:9

Vaniah — 2057: *Ezr 10:36*

vanish, ed, eth — 853, 3212, 4414, 5628, 6789 ✑ ***854, 1096/855, 2673***: Isa 51:6; Jer 49:7; Jas 4:14

VANITY, ies; vain, glory, ly — 205, 1891, 1892, 2600, 3576, 5014, 7307, 7385, 7386, 7387, 7723, 8193, 8267, 8414 ✑ ***1432, 1500, 2754, 2755, 2756, 2757, 2758, 2761, 2788, 3150, 3151, 3152, 3154, 3155***: Ecc 1:2; La 2:14; Php 2:3

vanity is a characteristic of:

man's life: Ecc 2:1; Isa 57:12; 1Co 13:3

man's character: Ps 39:11; 62:9; 94:11

man's wisdom: Ecc 2:15, 21; 1Co 3:19, 20

false religion: Isa 1:13; Jer 23:32; Mt 6:7; Jas 1:26

vapour, s — 108, 5387, 5927, 7008 ✑ ***822***: Job 36:27; Ps 148:8; Jer 10:13

variableness — ***3883***: *Jas 1:17*

variance — ***1369, 2054***: *Mt 10:35; Gal 5:20*

Vashni — 2059: *1Ch 6:28*

Vashti — 2060: Est 1:9; 2:1

vaunt, eth — 6286 ✑ ***4068***: *Jgs 7:2; 1Co 13:4*

vehement, ly — 2759, 3050 ✑ ***1171, 1722/4053, 1972, 2159, 2759, 4366***: Jnh 4:8; Lk 6:48; 2Co 7:11

veil, s — 4304, 4533, 6532, 6809, 7289 ✒ ***2571, 2665***: Ru 3:15; Isa 3:23; Heb 6:19

vein — 4161: *Job 28:1*

VENGEANCE (see **avenge; revenge**) — 5358, 5359, 5360 ✒ ***1349, 1557, 3709***: Jgs 11:36; Lk 21:22; Jude 7

God's vengeance is:

His to perform: Dt 32:35; Ro 12:19; Heb 10:30

rendered to His enemies: Dt 32:41; Eze 25:14; Na 1:2

a cause for the righteous to rejoice: Ps 58:10

venison — 6718, 6720: Ge 25:28; 27:3

venom, ous — 7219: *Dt 32:33; Ac 28:4*

vent — 6605: *Job 32:19*

venture — 8537: *1Ki 22:34; 2Ch 18:33*

verified — 539: *Ge 42:20; 1Ki 8:26; 2Ch 6:17*

verily (see **amen; truly**) — 61, 389, 403, 518, 518/3808, 530, 559, 7069 ✒ ***230, 281, 1063, 1222, 2532, 3303, 3304, 3483, 3689, 3767***: Ps 37:3; Lk 12:37; Ro 15:27

verity (see **true**) — 571 ✒ ***225***: *Ps 111:7; 1Ti 2:7*

vermilion — 8350: *Jer 22:14; Eze 23:14*

very — 199, 430, 552, 651, 898, 899, 1419, 1767, 1851, 1854, 1942, 2088, 3190, 3304, 3453, 3559, 3966, 4213, 4295, 4592, 4605, 4801, 5464, 5690, 5704/3966, 6106, 6621, 6985, 7023, 7230, 7260, 7690 ✒ ***85, 230, 662, 846, 927, 957, 1565, 1582, 1646, 1888, 2236, 2532, 2566, 2735, 3029, 3827, 4036, 4118, 4119, 4184, 4185, 4186, 4708, 4970, 5228***: Ge 1:31; Da 2:12; Mt 10:30; Php 1:6

vessel, s — 3627, 3984, 5035 ✒ ***30, 4632***: Le 6:28; Ezr 5:14; Mt 13:48; 1Pe 3:7

vestments; vesture, s — 899, 3682, 3830, 4403 ✒ ***2440, 2441, 4018:*** 2Ki 10:22; Ps 22:18; Jn 19:24

vestry — 4458: *2Ki 10:22*

VEXATION, s; vex, ed — 926, 1766, 2000, 2111, 2113, 3013, 3238, 3334, 3707, 4103, 4164, 4843, 6087, 6213/7451, 6687, 6973, 7114, 7469, 7475, 7489, 7492, 7561, 7667 ✒ ***928, 1139, 2559, 2669, 3791, 3958***: Ex 22:21; 2Ch 15:5; Ac 12:1

types of vexation:

vexation of body: Nu 20:5; Ne 9:27; Mt 15:22

vexation of soul: Jgs 16:16; Ps 6:3; 2Pe 2:8

vexation of spirit: Ecc 1:14; Isa 65:14

vial, s — 6378 ✒ ***5357***: 1Sa 10:1; Rev 5:8; 15:7

VICTORY — 3467, 5331, 8668 ✒ ***3528, 3529, 3534***: 2Sa 19:2; 1Ch 29:11; Mt 12:20

God provides victory over:

enemies: 2Sa 23:10; Ps 98:1

the world: 1Jn 5:4

death: Isa 25:8; 1Co 15:57

victual, s — 400, 737, 3557, 3899, 3978, 4202, 4241, 6718, 6720, 7668 ✒ ***1033, 1979***: Ex 12:39; Dt 23:19; Lk 9:12

view, ed (see **see**) — 995, 5048, 7200, 7270, 7663: Jos 2:1; 2Ki 2:7; Ezr 8:15

vigilant — ***1127, 3524***: *1Ti 3:2; 1Pe 5:8*

vile, ly, r — 959, 1602, 2149, 2151, 2933, 5034, 5036, 5039, 5217, 5240, 7034, 8182 ✒ ***819, 4508, 5014***: 2Sa 1:21; Job 30:8; Ro 1:26

village, s — 1323, 2691, 3715, 3723, 3724, 6518, 6519, 6520, 6521 ✒ ***2864, 2968***: Ex 8:13; 2Ch 28:18; Mk 11:2

villainy — 5039: *Isa 32:6; Jer 29:23*

vine, dressers, s, yards; vintage — 1208, 1210, 1612, 2156, 3196, 3657, 3754, 3755, 5139, 8321 ✒ ***288, 289, 290***: 2Ki 25:12; Zec 11:2; Mt 20:1; Jn 15:1

vinegar — 2558 ✒ ***3690***: Nu 6:3; Pr 10:26; Lk 23:36

viol, s — 5035: *Isa 5:12; 14:11; Am 5:23; 6:5*

violated; violence; violent, ly — 1497, 1498, 1499, 1500, 2554, 2555, 4835, 6184, 6231 ✒ ***970, 971, 973, 1286, 1411, 3731***: Ge 6:11; Eze 22:26; Mk 5:13

viper, s — 660 ✒ ***2191***: Job 20:16; Isa 30:6; Mt 3:7

virgin, ity, s — 1330, 1331, 3933, 5959 ✒ ***3932, 3933***: Le 21:13; Isa 7:14; Lk 2:36

virtue; virtuous, ly — 2428 ✒ ***703, 1411***: Ru 3:11; Pr 31:29; Php 4:8

visage (see **countenance; face**): — 600, 4758, 8389: *Isa 52:14; La 4:8; Da 3:19*

VISION, S; visible — 2376, 2377, 2378, 2380, 2384, 4236, 4758, 4759, 7200, 7203 ✒ ***3701, 3705, 3706, 3707***: 1Ch 17:15; Hos 12:10; Col 1:16

visions were communicated by means of:

trances: Nu 24:16; Ac 10:10-12

bodily translation: Eze 8:3; Rev 4:1, 2

audible voices: Ac 16:9

visions were communicated to:

OT saints: Ge 15:1; Ex 3:2, 3; Da 2:19; Hab 2:2, 3

NT saints: Ac 9:10-16; 18:9; Rev 1:12-16

Gentiles: Da 4:5; Ac 10:3

west, ern, ward — 3220, 3996/8121, 46281 ➳ ***1424, 3047, 5566***: Nu 34:6; Jos 23:4; Mt 8:11

wet — 6647, 7372: *Job 24:8; Da 4:15, 23, 25, 33; 5:21*

whale, s — 8565, 8577 ➳ ***2785***: *Ge 1:21; Job 7:12; Eze 32:2; Mt 12:40*

what, soever — 335/2088, 349, 375, 376/834, 834, 853, 853/834, 853/3605/834, 1401, 1571, 1697/4100, 3605/834, 3627, 3964/1768, 4310, 4479 ➳ ***510, 686, 1063, 1221, 2228, 2245, 3588/3739, 3634, 3697/4219, 3699, 3739, 3739/302, 3739/1437, 3739/1437/5100, 3745, 3745/302, 3745/1437, 3748, 3748/302, 3956/1437/5100, 3956/3754/1437, 3956/3754/5100, 4169, 4214, 4217, 4459, 5101***: 2Ch 1:7; Hos 6:4; Lk 1:29; Col 3:17

wheat, en — 1250, 1715, 2406, 2591, 7383 ➳ ***4621***: Ex 29:2; Dt 8:8; Mt 13:25

wheel, s — 70, 212, 1534, 1535, 1536, 6471: 1Ki 7:30; Eze 1:15; Da 7:9

whelp, s — 1121, 1482, 1484: 2Sa 17:8; Jer 51:38; Na 2:11

when, soever — 310, 518, 1767, 1768, 1961, 3117, 3588, 3644, 4481, 4970, 5704, 5750, 5921, 6256, 6310 ➳ ***1437, 1722/3588, 1722/3739, 1875, 1893, 2259, 2531, 3326, 3698, 3704, 3752, 3753/3588, 4218, 5613/1437, 5753:*** Joel 3:1; Mt 25:37; Ro 15:24

whence (see **where**) — 335/2088, 370, 834/2088, 834/8033, 1992 ➳ ***3606, 3739, 4158***: Ecc 1:7; Na 3:7; Heb 11:15

where, soever (see **whence**) — 335, 335/2088, 346, 346/645, 351, 370, 375, 413, 413/834/8033, 413/3605, 575, 645, 657, 834, 834/8033, 1768, 3605, 3605/834, 3606/1768, 5921, 8033, 8536 ➳ ***296, 1330, 1337, 1722/3739, 1722/3956, 1722/5117, 2596, 3606, 3699, 3699/302, 3699/1487, 3757, 3837, 4226***: Le 13:12; La 2:12; Col 3:1

whereabout — 834: *1Sa 21:2*

whereas — 518, 834, 3282/834, 1768, 3588, 6258, 8478, 8478/834 ➳ ***1722/3759, 3699, 3748***: Dt 19:6; Da 2:41; 1Co 3:3

whereby — 834, 4100, 4482 ➳ ***1223/3739, 1722/3739, 2596/5101, 4012/3757, 4314/3739***: Jer 3:8; Zep 2:8; Php 3:21

wherefore — 199, 3588/389, 3605/6903/1836, 3651, 3861, 4069, 4100, 4100/2063, 4100/2088, 5921/3651, 5921/4100, 8478/4100 ➳ ***686, 686/1065, 1161, 1223/3739, 1223/5124, 1302, 1352, 1355, 1519/3739, 1519/5101, 1909/3739, 2443/5101, 3606, 3739/5484, 3767, 5101, 5101/1752, 5105, 5484/5101, 5620***: Ru 1:7; Mal 2:14; Phm 8

wherein, soever, to — 834, 834/413/8432, 834/2004, 834/8033, 834/8432, 1459, 2098, 4100, 8033 ➳ ***1223/3757, 1519/3739, 1519/3757, 1722/3739, 1722/3739/302, 1722/3757, 1909/3739, 1909/3757, 3757, 4012/3739***: Nu 14:24; Zec 9:11; 2Co 11:21

whereof — 834 ➳ ***1537/3739, 1909/3739, 3739, 4012/3739, 4012/5101***: Job 6:4; Hos 2:12; 1Ti 1:7

whereon; whereupon — 413, 834, 834/5921, 5921, 5921/4100 ➳ ***1722/3739, 1909/3739, 3606***: Jos 5:15; Am 4:7; Jn 4:38

whereto; whereunto — 834, 834/8033, 4100 ➳ ***1519/3739, 3739, 5101***: Ps 71:3; Isa 55:11; 2Pe 1:19

wherewith, al — 834, 1697, 4100 ➳ ***1722/5101, 3739, 3745, 5101***: 1Ki 8:59; Mic 6:6; Mt 6:31

whet — 3913, 7043, 8150: *Dt 32:41; Ps 7:12; 64:3; Ecc 10:10*

whether — 176, 335, 518, 996, 2006, 3588, 3808, 4100, 4480, 5704, 5750 ➳ ***1487, 1535, 3379, 3739, 4220, 5037, 5101***: Ge 43:6; Nu 9:21; Lk 5:23; Ro 14:8

which — 227, 428, 589, 595, 834, 1768, 1836, 1931, 1958, 1992, 2004, 2088, 2098, 3426, 3651, 4100, 4310, 4480 ➳ ***302, 846, 1352, 1520, 2076, 2532, 3588, 3739, 3748, 4169, 5101:*** Dt 28:1; 1Ki 8:1; 2Pe 3:10

while, s, st — 518, 834, 3117, 3588, 4705, 5704, 5750, 5751, 7350 ➳ ***1722, 2193, 2250, 2540, 3153, 3397, 3588, 3641, 3739, 3752, 3755, 3819, 4340, 5099, 5550, 5613***: 1Sa 7:2; Job 27:3; Ac 5:4; Heb 10:33

whip, s — 7752: 1Ki 12:11; Pr 26:3; Na 3:2

whirleth; whirlwind, s — 1980, 3907, 5492, 5590, 5591, 7307, 8175: 2Ki 2:1; Ecc 1:6; Zec 9:14

whisper, ed, er, ers, ings — 3907, 5372, 6850 ➳ ***5587, 5588***: 2Sa 12:19; Ps 41:7; Ro 1:29

whit — 1697, 3632 ➳ ***3367, 3650***: Dt 13:16; Jn 7:23; 2Co 11:5

white, d, r — 1858, 2353, 2751, 3835, 3836, 6703, 6705, 6713, 6715, 7388 ➳ ***2867, 2896, 3021, 3022***: Ge 30:35; Ps 51:7; Ac 23:3

who; whom, soever; whose; whoso, ever — 376/834, 413/4310, 428, 589, 834, 834/413, 834/1931, 834/1992, 834/6440, 853/834, 853/4310, 2098, 3588, 3605/834, 4310, 4310/834, 4479, 4479/1768 5973, ➳ ***1437, 1437/5100, 1536, 2532/846, 3588, 3739, 3739/302, 3739/1437, 3745/302, 3746, 3748,***

3748/302, 3778, 3956/3588, 3956/3739, 3956/3739/302, 5100, 5101: 2Ki 19:22; Da 3:1; Mk 3:35; 1Jn 2:5

whole, ly, some — 854/3605, 1295, 2421, 3117, 3605, 3606, 3615, 3632, 4390, 4749, 4832, 5352, 6942, 7495, 7760, 7965, 8003, 8549, 8552 ➤ ***537, 1510/1722, 2480, 3390, 3648, 3650, 3651, 3956, 4982, 5198, 5199***: Le 6:22; Isa 1:5; 1Ti 6:3

whore, dom, doms, ing, ish, monger, mongers, s — 2181, 2183, 2184, 6948, 8457 ➤ ***4204, 4205***: Eze 16:33; Hos 1:2; Eph 5:5; Rev 17:1

why — 3282/4100, 4069, 4100, 5921/4100, 5922/4101 ➤ ***1063, 1302, 1519/5101, 2444, 3754***: Ge 4:6; SS 1:7; Col 2:20

WICKED, ly, ness — 205, 605, 1100, 1942, 2154, 2162, 2617, 4209, 4849, 5753, 5763, 5766, 5767, 5999, 6001, 6090, 7451, 7455, 7489, 7561, 7562, 7563, 7564 ➤ ***113, 459, 824, 2549, 2556, 4189, 4190, 4191, 5129***: Dt 25:1; Ps 5:4; Mal 4:1; Mt 12:45

wicked things:

wicked men: Ge 13:13; Job 20:29; Pr 17:23

wicked hearts: Dt 15:9

wicked works: Ne 9:35; Ps 37:7; Col 1:21

wicked practices: Le 20:17; 2Ki 17:11

wide, ness — 2267, 3027, 4060, 6605, 7337, 7341, 7342 ➤ ***4116***: Dt 15:8; Eze 41:10; Mt 7:13

widow, hood, s — 489, 490, 491 ➤ ***5503***: Ge 38:11; Isa 47:9; Ac 6:1

wife, s; wives — 802, 1166, 1753, 2994, 5389, 7695 ➤ ***1126, 1134, 1135, 3994***: Pr 18:22; Da 6:24; Mk 1:30; 1Ti 4:7

wild — 338, 689, 891, 2123, 2416, 3277, 6167, 6171, 6501, 6728, 7704, 8377 ➤ ***66, 2342***: Le 26:22; Jer 2:24; Mt 3:4

wilderness — 3452, 4057, 6160, 6723, 6728, 8414 ➤ ***2047, 2048***: Dt 32:10; Am 6:14; Ac 7:30

wiles; wilily — 5231, 6195 ➤ ***3180***: *Nu 25:18; Jos 9:4; Eph 6:11*

WILL, eth, fully, ing; wilt; would, est — 14, 305, 2654, 2655, 2656, 2974, 3045, 3426, 3820, 3863, 4310, 5068, 5071, 5081, 5314, 5315, 5414, 6195, 6634, 7470, 7522 ➤ ***210, 830, 1012, 1013, 1014, 1096, 1106, 1497, 1595, 1596, 1635, 2106, 2107, 2133, 2172, 2307, 2309, 2596, 2843, 3106, 3195, 3785, 4288, 4289***: Ge 24:5; Ezr 1:6; Ro 9:16; Heb 10:26

God's will:

cannot be withstood: Job 9:12; Da 4:35; Ro 9:20

is to be submitted to: Ps 143:1; Eph 6:5, 6; Jas 4:15

is connected with:

the new birth: Jn 1:12, 13; Jas 1:18

spiritual growth: Col 4:12; 1Th 4:3

man's will:

is in bondage due to sin: Jn 8:34; Ro 6:16; 2Pe 2:19

can accept or reject God: Ex 32:26; Mt 27:17; Jn 6:67

willow, s — 6155, 6851: Le 23:40; Ps 137:2; Eze 17:5

wimples — 4304: *Isa 3:22*

win, neth; won — 1234, 3947 ➤ ***2770***: Pr 11:30; Php 3:8; 1Pe 3:1

wind, s, y — 7307, 7308 ➤ ***416, 417, 4151, 4154***: Ge 8:1; Ps 55:8; Mt 7:25

winding — 3583, 4141, 5437: *1Ki 6:8; Eze 41:7*

window, s — 699, 2474, 3551, 6672, 8121, 8260, 8261 ➤ ***2376***: Jos 2:15; 2Ki 7:2; Ac 20:9

WINE, bibber, fat, press, s — 1660, 2561, 2562, 3342, 4469, 5433/3196, 5435, 6025, 6071, 6333, 7941, 8105, 8492 ➤ ***1098, 3025, 3630, 3631, 3632, 3943, 5276, 5776***: Job 24:11; Isa 63:2; Mt 11:19; 1Ti 3:3

uses of wine:

beverage: Ge 27:25; Est 1:7

part of an offering: Ex 29:40

medicinal agent: 1Ti 5:23

characteristics of wine:

cheers the heart: Ps 104:15

is deceptive: Pr 20:1; 23:31, 32

can lead men astray: Pr 23:33; Isa 28:7; Hos 4:11

warnings against the abuse of wine: Isa 5:11; Hab 2:15; Eph 5:18

wing, ed, s — 83, 84, 1611, 3671, 6731 ➤ ***4420***: Dt 4:17; 1Ki 6:24; Lk 13:34

wink, ed, eth — 7169, 7335 ➤ ***5237***: Ps 35:19; Pr 10:10; Ac 17:30

winnow, ed, eth — 2219: *Ru 3:2; Isa 30:24*

winter, ed, house — 2778, 2779, 5638 ➤ ***3914, 3915, 3916, 5494***: Jer 36:22; Mt 24:20; Ac 28:11

wipe, d, ing, th — 4229 ➤ ***631, 1591, 1813***: 2Ki 21:13; Lk 10:11; Rev 7:17

wires — 6616: *Ex 39:3*

WISDOM; wise, ly, r — 995, 998, 2449, 2450, 2451, 2452, 2454, 2942, 3198, 3820, 3823, 6031, 6195, 6493, 7919, 7922, 8394, 8454 ➤ ***3097, 3588, 3779, 3838, 3843, 4678, 4679, 4680, 4920, 5428, 5429, 5430***: Ecc 10:3; Da 12:3; Lk 2:40; 1Co 1:25

God's wisdom:

described as:

required of saints: Mk 10:42-44; Jn 4:34; 1Co 15:58
done in God's power: Mk 16:20; Ac 1:8, 9; 1Co 3:8, 9
rewarded: Mt 10:42; Jn 4:35, 36

workfellow — ***4904***: *Ro 16:21*
world, ly, s — 776, 2309, 2465, 5769, 8398 ✒ ***165, 166, 1093, 2886, 2889, 3625***: Job 18:18; Isa 64:4; Tit 2:12; Heb 1:2
worm, s, wood — 2119, 3939, 5580, 7415, 8438 ✒ ***894, 4662, 4663***: Ex 16:24; Pr 5:4; Ac 12:23
worse; worst (see **bad**) — 2196, 5062, 7451, 7489 ✒ ***1640, 2276, 5302, 5501***: Ge 19:9; Eze 7:24; Mk 2:21

WORSHIP, PED, per, pers, peth, ping — 5457, 5647, 7812 ✒ ***1391, 1479, 1799, 2151, 2318, 2323, 2356, 3000, 3511, 4352, 4353, 4573, 4574, 4576***: Ex 34:14; Da 2:46; Jn 9:31
God is to be worshipped:
as Creator: Ps 95:6
in the beauty of holiness: 1Ch 16:29
in spirit and in truth: Jn 4:24
with one accord: Mt 18:19; Ac 1:14; 4:24-30
with praise: Ps 9:11; Isa 42:12; Heb 13:15

worth, ies, ily — 117, 376, 639, 1121, 2428, 3644, 4242, 4373, 4392, 6994, 7939: Ru 4:11; Na 2:5; Mt 3:11
wound, ed, edst, eth, ing, s — 1214, 1795, 1856, 2342, 2392, 2470, 2490, 2491, 2671, 3859, 4204, 4205, 4272, 4347, 5061, 5218, 5221, 6094, 6481, 6482 ✒ ***1210, 2007, 4127, 4958, 4969, 5134, 5135, 5180***: Ex 21:25; Job 5:18; La 2:12; Lk 10:34
wrap, ped — 1563, 2280, 3664, 3874, 4593, 5440, 5686, 5968, 8276 ✒ ***1750, 1794, 4683***: 1Sa 21:9; Mic 7:3; Mt 27:59
wrath, ful, s; wroth — 639, 2196, 2197, 2534, 2734, 2740, 3707, 3708, 5674, 5678, 7107, 7109, 7110, 7264, 7265, 7267 ✒ ***2372, 2373, 3709, 3710, 3949, 3950***: 2Ki 5:11; Ps 69:24; Ro 1:18; 2Co 12:20
wreath, ed, en, s — 1434, 5688, 7639, 8276: Ex 28:14; 2Ch 4:13; La 1:14
wrest — 5186, 6087 ✒ ***4761***: Dt 16:19; Ps 56:5; 2Pe 3:16
wrestle, d, ings — 79, 5319, 6617 ✒ ***2076, 3823***: *Ge 30:8; 32:24, 25; Eph 6:12*
wretched, ness — 7451 ✒ ***5005***: *Nu 11:15; Ro 7:24; Rev 3:17*
wring, ed, ing; wrung — 4330, 4454, 4680: Le 1:15; Pr 30:33; Isa 51:17
wrinkle, s — 7059 ✒ ***4512***: *Job 16:8; Eph 5:27*
write, er, est, eth, ing, ings; written; wrote — 3789, 3790, 3791, 3792, 4385, 5608, 7560 ✒ ***583, 975, 1123, 1125, 1449, 1722/1121, 1924, 1989, 4093, 4270***: Da 5:24; Mk 10:5; Jn 5:47
wrong, ed, eth, fully — 2554, 2555, 3238, 3808/4941, 5627, 5753, 5792, 6127, 6231, 7451, 7563, 8267 ✒ ***91, 92, 93, 95***: Est 1:6; Pr 8:36; 2Co 7:2; 1Pe 2:19
wrought, est (see **make**) — 1496, 1980, 2790, 4639, 4865, 5647, 5648, 5656, 5927, 5953, 6213, 6466, 7194, 7551, 7760 ✒ ***1096, 1754, 2038, 2716, 4160, 4903***: Nu 23:23; Ru 2:19; Mt 26:10; 2Th 3:8

Y

yarn — 4723: *1Ki 10:28; 2Ch 1:16*
yea; yes — 432, 637, 637/3588, 834, 1571, 3588 ✒ ***235, 1161, 2228, 2532, 3304, 3483***: 1Sa 15:20; Jer 27:21; Phm 20
year, ly, s — 3117, 8027, 8140, 8141 ✒ ***1096/3173, 1332, 1333, 1541, 1763, 2094, 2250, 4070, 5063, 5148***: Le 25:29; Ne 10:32; Gal 4:10; Jas 4:13
yearn, ed — 3648: *Ge 43:30; 1Ki 3:26*
yell, ed — 5286, 5414/6963: *Jer 2:15; 51:38*
yellow — 3422, 6669: *Le 13:30, 32, 36; Ps 68:13*
yesterday; yesternight — 570, 865, 8543 ✒ ***5504***: Ge 19:34; 2Ki 9:26; Jn 4:52
yet — 227, 389, 518, 559, 637, 1297, 1571, 2962, 3588/518, 3651, 5704/2008, 5704/6258, 5728, 5750 ✒ ***188, 235, 1063, 1065, 1161, 2089, 2532, 2236, 2579, 2596, 3195, 3305, 3364, 3369, 3380, 3764, 3765, 3768***: Jos 3:4; 1Ch 12:1; 1Co 12:20
yield, ed, eth, ing — 1478, 1580, 3052, 3254, 5186, 5375, 5414, 5414/3027, 6213, 7235 ✒ ***591, 863, 1325, 1634, 3936, 3982, 4160***: Ne 9:37; Jer 17:8; Ac 5:10
yoke, d, s — 4132, 4133, 5923, 6776 ✒ ***2086, 2201, 2218***: La 1:14; 2Co 6:14; Gal 5:1
yokefellow — ***4805***: *Php 4:3*
yonder (see **there**; **thither**) — 1973, 3541, 5676, 5704/3541 ✒ ***1563***: Nu 16:37; 2Ki 4:25; Mt 17:20
your, s, selves (see **thee**) — 853, 859, 3027, 5315, 5869 ✒ ***240, 1438, 2398, 2596/5209, 3588, 3844/1438, 4314, 5209, 5210/846, 5212, 5213, 5213/846, 5216, 5216/846***: Le 11:43; Zep 3:20; Lk 6:20; 1Th 5:11

YOUTH, ful; young, er, est — 667, 970, 979, 1121, 1121/1241, 1123, 1469, 1482, 3127, 3206, 3242, 3715, 5288, 5288/970, 5291, 5763, 5958,

Z